# The Europa World Year Book 1995

# The Europa World Year Book 1995

VOLUME II

KAZAKHSTAN – ZIMBABWE

EUROPA PUBLICATIONS LIMITED

**First published 1926**

© **Europa Publications Limited 1995**
18 Bedford Square, London, WC1B 3JN, England

All rights reserved. No part of this
publication may be photocopied, recorded,
or otherwise reproduced, stored in a retrieval
system or transmitted in any form or by any
electronic or mechanical means without the
prior permission of the copyright owner.

**Australia and New Zealand**
James Bennett (Collaroy) Pty Ltd, 4 Collaroy Street,
Collaroy, NSW 2097, Australia

**Japan**
Maruzen Co Ltd, POB 5050, Tokyo International 100-31

ISBN 0-946653-96-8 (The Set)
1-85743-015-8 (Vol. II)
ISSN 0956-2273

Library of Congress Catalog Card Number 59-2942

Printed in England by
Staples Printers Rochester Limited
Rochester, Kent

Bound by
Hartnolls Ltd
Bodmin, Cornwall

# FOREWORD

THE EUROPA WORLD YEAR BOOK (formerly THE EUROPA YEAR BOOK: A WORLD SURVEY) was first published in 1926. Since 1960 it has appeared in annual two-volume editions, and has become established as an authoritative reference work, providing a wealth of detailed information on the political, economic and commercial institutions of the world.

Volume I contains international organizations and the first part of the alphabetical survey of countries of the world, from Afghanistan to Jordan. Volume II contains countries from Kazakhstan to Zimbabwe. All sections have been extensively revised and updated, and the process of expanding chapters devoted to the former Soviet republics and to Yugoslavia and its successor states has continued for this edition.

Readers are referred to our seven regional books, AFRICA SOUTH OF THE SAHARA, EASTERN EUROPE AND THE COMMONWEALTH OF INDEPENDENT STATES, THE FAR EAST AND AUSTRALASIA, THE MIDDLE EAST AND NORTH AFRICA, SOUTH AMERICA, CENTRAL AMERICA AND THE CARIBBEAN, THE USA AND CANADA and WESTERN EUROPE, for additional information on the geography, history and economy of these areas.

The information is revised annually by a variety of methods, including direct mailing to all the institutions listed. Many other sources are used, such as national statistical offices, government departments and diplomatic missions. The editors thank the innumerable individuals and organizations throughout the world whose generous co-operation in providing current information for this edition is invaluable in presenting the most accurate and up-to-date material available, and acknowledge particular indebtedness for material from the following publications: the United Nations' *Demographic Yearbook, Statistical Yearbook* and *Industrial Statistics Yearbook* (published from 1994 as *Industrial Commodity Statistics Yearbook*); the Food and Agriculture Organization of the United Nations' *Production Yearbook, Yearbook of Fishery Statistics* and *Yearbook of Forest Products*; the International Monetary Fund's *International Financial Statistics*; and *The Military Balance 1994–95*, a publication of the International Institute for Strategic Studies, 23 Tavistock Street, London, WC2E 7NQ.

July 1995.

# CONTENTS

| | | | | |
|---|---|---|---|---|
| Abbreviations | Page ix | Niger | Page | 2285 |
| Late Information | xiii | Nigeria | | 2300 |
| Kazakhstan | 1731 | Norway | | 2325 |
| Kenya | 1744 | Norwegian External Territories: | | |
| Kiribati | 1760 |     Svalbard | | 2344 |
| The Democratic People's Republic of | |     Jan Mayen | | 2345 |
|     Korea (North Korea) | 1766 |     Norwegian Dependencies | | 2346 |
| The Republic of Korea (South Korea) | 1780 | Oman | | 2347 |
| Kuwait | 1802 | Pakistan | | 2358 |
| Kyrgyzstan | 1819 | Palau | | 2386 |
| Laos | 1830 | Panama | | 2390 |
| Latvia | 1841 | Papua New Guinea | | 2407 |
| Lebanon | 1855 | Paraguay | | 2421 |
| Lesotho | 1875 | Peru | | 2435 |
| Liberia | 1886 | The Philippines | | 2454 |
| Libya | 1900 | Poland | | 2480 |
| Liechtenstein | 1914 | Portugal | | 2502 |
| Lithuania | 1918 | Portuguese Overseas Territory: | | |
| Luxembourg | 1932 |     Macau | | 2525 |
| The former Yugoslav republic of Macedonia | 1941 | Qatar | | 2533 |
| Madagascar | 1951 | Romania | | 2540 |
| Malawi | 1966 | The Russian Federation | | 2562 |
| Malaysia | 1977 | Rwanda | | 2591 |
| Maldives | 2003 | Saint Christopher and Nevis | | 2604 |
| Mali | 2010 | Saint Lucia | | 2611 |
| Malta | 2023 | Saint Vincent and the Grenadines | | 2618 |
| The Marshall Islands | 2032 | San Marino | | 2624 |
| Mauritania | 2037 | São Tomé and Príncipe | | 2628 |
| Mauritius | 2049 | Saudi Arabia | | 2634 |
| Mexico | 2062 | Senegal | | 2651 |
| The Federated States of Micronesia | 2089 | Seychelles | | 2669 |
| Moldova | 2093 | Sierra Leone | | 2676 |
| Monaco | 2105 | Singapore | | 2690 |
| Mongolia | 2109 | Slovakia | | 2709 |
| Morocco | 2123 | Slovenia | | 2722 |
| Mozambique | 2141 | Solomon Islands | | 2737 |
| Myanmar | 2158 | Somalia | | 2745 |
| Namibia | 2174 | South Africa | | 2760 |
| Nauru | 2187 | Spain | | 2791 |
| Nepal | 2191 | Spanish External Territories: | | |
| The Netherlands | 2205 |     Spanish North Africa | | 2825 |
|     Netherlands Dependencies: | | Sri Lanka | | 2831 |
|         Aruba | 2225 | Sudan | | 2851 |
|         The Netherlands Antilles | 2230 | Suriname | | 2867 |
| New Zealand | 2239 | Swaziland | | 2877 |
|     New Zealand's Dependent and Associated Territories: | | Sweden | | 2886 |
|         Ross Dependency | 2257 | Switzerland | | 2908 |
|         Tokelau | 2257 | Syria | | 2929 |
|         Cook Islands | 2260 | Taiwan (see China, Vol. I) | | |
|         Niue | 2265 | Tajikistan | | 2945 |
| Nicaragua | 2268 | Tanzania | | 2957 |

# CONTENTS

| | | | | |
|---|---|---|---|---|
| Thailand | Page 2972 | Pitcairn Islands | Page 3248 |
| Togo | 2993 | St Helena and Dependencies | 3250 |
| Tonga | 3008 | South Georgia and the South Sandwich Islands | 3253 |
| Trinidad and Tobago | 3014 | | |
| Tunisia | 3027 | The Turks and Caicos Islands | 3254 |
| Turkey | 3043 | The United States of America | 3258 |
| Turkmenistan | 3066 | United States Commonwealth Territories: | |
| Tuvalu | 3076 | The Northern Mariana Islands | 3319 |
| Uganda | 3081 | Puerto Rico | 3323 |
| Ukraine | 3094 | United States External Territories: | |
| The United Arab Emirates | 3110 | American Samoa | 3333 |
| The United Kingdom: | | Guam | 3337 |
| Great Britain | 3125 | The United States Virgin Islands | 3341 |
| Northern Ireland | 3176 | Other Territories | 3344 |
| United Kingdom Crown Dependencies: | | Uruguay | 3345 |
| The Isle of Man | 3188 | Uzbekistan | 3360 |
| The Channel Islands | 3192 | Vanuatu | 3370 |
| British Dependent Territories: | | The Vatican City | 3377 |
| Anguilla | 3198 | Venezuela | 3384 |
| Bermuda | 3202 | Viet Nam | 3405 |
| The British Antarctic Territory | 3207 | Western Samoa | 3423 |
| The British Indian Ocean Territory | 3207 | Yemen | 3429 |
| The British Virgin Islands | 3208 | Yugoslavia | 3447 |
| The Cayman Islands | 3212 | Zaire | 3468 |
| The Falkland Islands | 3217 | Zambia | 3484 |
| Gibraltar | 3221 | Zimbabwe | 3497 |
| Hong Kong | 3227 | | |
| Montserrat | 3244 | Index of Territories | 3514 |

# ABBREVIATIONS

| | | | |
|---|---|---|---|
| AB | Aktiebolag (Joint-Stock Company) | C-in-C | Commander-in-Chief |
| Abog. | Abogado (Lawyer) | circ. | circulation |
| Acad. | Academician; Academy | CIS | Commonwealth of Independent States |
| ACT | Australian Capital Territory | cm | centimetre(s) |
| AD | anno Domini | Cnr | Corner |
| ADB | African Development Bank; Asian Development Bank | Co | Company; County |
| | | CO | Colorado |
| ADC | aide-de-camp | Col | Colonel |
| Adm. | Admiral | Col. | Colonia |
| admin. | administration | Comm. | Commission; Commendatore |
| AfDB | African Development Bank | Commdr | Commander |
| AG | Aktiengesellschaft (Joint-Stock Company) | Commdt | Commandant |
| a.i. | ad interim | Commr | Commissioner |
| AID | (US) Agency for International Development | Cond. | Condominio |
| AIDS | Acquired Immunodeficiency Syndrome | Confed. | Confederation |
| AK | Alaska | Cont. | Contador (Accountant) |
| Al. | Aleja (Alley, Avenue) | Corp. | Corporate |
| AL | Alabama | Corpn | Corporation |
| ALADI | Asociación Latino-Americana de Integración | CP | Case Postale; Caixa Postal; Casella Postale (Post Box); Communist Party |
| Alt. | Alternate | CPSU | Communist Party of the Soviet Union |
| AM | Amplitude Modulation | Cres. | Crescent |
| a.m. | ante meridiem (before noon) | CSCE | Conference on Security and Co-operation in Europe |
| amalg. | amalgamated | | |
| AP | Andhra Pradesh | CSTAL | Confederación Sindical de los Trabajadores de América Latina |
| Apdo | Apartado (Post Box) | | |
| approx. | approximately | CT | Connecticut |
| Apt | Apartment | CTCA | Confederación de Trabajadores Centro-americanos |
| AR | Arkansas | | |
| AŞ | Anonim Şirketi (Joint-Stock Company) | Cttee | Committee |
| A/S | Aktieselskab (Joint-Stock Company) | cu | cubic |
| ASEAN | Association of South East Asian Nations | cwt | hundredweight |
| asscn | association | | |
| assoc. | associate | DC | District of Columbia; Distrito Central |
| asst | assistant | d.d. | dioničko društvo, delniška družba (Joint-Stock Company) |
| Aug. | August | | |
| auth. | authorized | DDR | Deutsche Democratische Republik (German Democratic Republic) |
| Ave | Avenue | | |
| Avda | Avenida (Avenue) | DE | Departamento Estatal; Delaware |
| Avv. | Avvocato (Lawyer) | Dec. | December |
| AZ | Arizona | Del. | Delegación |
| | | Dem. | Democratic; Democrat |
| BC | British Columbia | Dep. | Deputy |
| BC | before Christ | dep. | deposits |
| Bd | Board | Dept | Department |
| Bd, Bld, Blv., Blvd | Boulevard | devt | development |
| | | DF | Distrito Federal |
| b/d | barrels per day | Diag. | Diagonal |
| Bhd | Berhad (Public Limited Company) | Dir | Director |
| Bldg | Building | Div. | Division(al) |
| BP | Boîte postale (Post Box) | DM | Deutsche Mark |
| br.(s) | branch(es) | DN | Distrito Nacional |
| Brig. | Brigadier | Doc. | Docent |
| bte | boîte (box) | Dott. | Dottore |
| BTN | Brussels Tariff Nomenclature | Dr | Doctor |
| bul. | bulvar (boulevard) | Dr. | Drive |
| | | Dra | Doctora |
| C | Centigrade | Dr Hab. | Doktor Habilitowany (Assistant Professor) |
| c. | circa; cuadra(s) (block(s)) | dr.(e) | drachma(e) |
| CA | California | Drs | Doctorandus |
| CACM | Central American Common Market | dwt | dead weight tons |
| Cad. | Caddesi (Street) | | |
| cap. | capital | E | East; Eastern |
| Capt. | Captain | EBRD | European Bank for Reconstruction and Development |
| CARICOM | Caribbean Community | | |
| CCL | Caribbean Congress of Labour | EC | European Community |
| Cdre | Commodore | ECA | (United Nations) Economic Commission for Africa |
| Cen. | Central | | |
| CEO | Chief Executive Officer | ECE | (United Nations) Economic Commission for Europe |
| CFA | Communauté Financière Africaine; Co-opération Financière en Afrique centrale | | |
| | | ECLAC | (United Nations) Economic Commission for Latin America and the Caribbean |
| CFP | Communauté française du Pacifique; Comptoirs français du Pacifique | | |
| | | Econ. | Economist; Economics |
| Chair. | Chairman/woman | ECOSOC | (United Nations) Economic and Social Council |
| CI | Channel Islands | ECOWAS | Economic Community of West African States |
| Cia | Companhia | ECU | European Currency Unit |
| Cía | Compañía | ECWA | (United Nations) Economic Commission for Western Asia |
| Cie | Compagnie | | |
| c.i.f. | cost, insurance and freight | | |

# ABBREVIATIONS

| | | | |
|---|---|---|---|
| Edif. | Edificio (building) | Iur. | Lawyer |
| edn | edition | | |
| EEA | European Economic Area | Jan. | January |
| EFTA | European Free Trade Association | Jnr | Junior |
| e.g. | exempli gratia (for example) | Jr | Jonkheer (Netherlands); Junior |
| eKv | electron kilovolt | Jt | Joint |
| eMv | electron megavolt | | |
| Eng. | Engineer; Engineering | kg | kilogram(s) |
| Esc. | Escuela; Escudos; Escritorio | KG | Kommandit Gesellschaft (Limited Partnership) |
| ESCAP | (United Nations) Economic and Social Commission for Asia and the Pacific | kHz | kilohertz |
| | | KK | Kaien Kaisha (Limited Company) |
| esq. | esquina (corner) | km | kilometre(s) |
| est. | established; estimate; estimated | KS | Kansas |
| etc. | et cetera | kv. | kvartal (apartment block) |
| EU | European Union | kW | kilowatt(s) |
| excl. | excluding | kWh | kilowatt hours |
| exec. | executive | KY | Kentucky |
| Ext. | Extension | | |
| | | LA | Louisiana |
| F | Fahrenheit | lauk | laukums (square) |
| f. | founded | lb | pound(s) |
| FAO | Food and Agriculture Organization | LIBOR | London Inter-Bank Offered Rate |
| Feb. | February | Lic. | Licenciado |
| Fed. | Federation; Federal | Licda | Licenciada |
| FL | Florida | LNG | liquefied natural gas |
| FM | frequency modulation | LPG | liquefied petroleum gas |
| fmr(ly) | former(ly) | Lt, Lieut | Lieutenant |
| f.o.b. | free on board | Ltd | Limited |
| Fr | Father | | |
| Fr. | Franc | m | metre(s) |
| Fri. | Friday | m. | million |
| FRY | Federal Republic of Yugoslavia | MA | Massachusetts |
| ft | foot (feet) | Maj. | Major |
| | | Man. | Manager; managing |
| g | gram(s) | mbH | mit beschränkter Haftung (with limited liability) |
| GA | Georgia | | |
| GATT | General Agreement on Tariffs and Trade | Mc/s | megacycles per second |
| GDP | gross domestic product | MD | Maryland |
| Gen. | General | ME | Maine |
| GeV | giga electron volts | Me | Maître |
| GmbH | Gesellschaft mit beschränkter Haftung (Limited Liability Company) | Mercosul | Mercado Comum do Sul (Southern Cone Common Market) |
| GNP | gross national product | Mercosur | Mercado Común del Sur (Southern Cone Common Market) |
| Gov. | Governor | | |
| Govt | Government | mem.(s) | member(s) |
| grt | gross registered tons | MEP | Member of the European Parliament |
| GWh | gigawatt hours | MEV | mega electron volts |
| | | mfrs | manufacturers |
| ha | hectares | Mgr | Monseigneur; Monsignor |
| HE | His/Her Eminence; His/Her Excellency | MHz | megahertz |
| hf | hlutafelag (Limited Company) | MI | Michigan |
| HI | Hawaii | Mil. | Military |
| hl | hectolitre(s) | Mlle | Mademoiselle |
| HM | His/Her Majesty | mm | millimetre(s) |
| Hon. | Honorary, Honourable | Mme | Madame |
| hp | horsepower | MN | Minnesota |
| HQ | Headquarters | MO | Missouri |
| HRH | His/Her Royal Highness | Mon. | Monday |
| | | MP | Member of Parliament; Madhya Pradesh |
| IA | Iowa | MS | Mississippi |
| IBRD | International Bank for Reconstruction and Development (World Bank) | MSS | Manuscripts |
| | | MT | Montana |
| ICC | International Chamber of Commerce | MW | megawatt(s); medium wave |
| ICFTU | International Confederation of Free Trade Unions | MWh | megawatt hour(s) |
| ID | Idaho | N | North; Northern |
| IDA | International Development Association | n.a. | not available |
| IDB | Inter-American Development Bank | nab. | naberezhnaya (embankment, quai) |
| i.e. | id est (that is to say) | NAFTA | North American Free Trade Agreement |
| IL | Illinois | nám. | náměstí (square) |
| ILO | International Labour Organisation/Office | Nat. | National |
| IMF | International Monetary Fund | NATO | North Atlantic Treaty Organisation |
| in (ins) | inch (inches) | NB | New Brunswick |
| IN | Indiana | NC | North Carolina |
| Inc, Incorp., Incd | Incorporated | NCO | Non-Commissioned Officer |
| | | ND | North Dakota |
| incl. | including | NE | Nebraska |
| Ind. | Independent | NH | New Hampshire |
| Ing. | Engineer | NJ | New Jersey |
| Insp. | Inspector | NM | New Mexico |
| Int. | International | NMP | net material product |
| Inž. | Engineer | no | numéro, número (number) |
| Ir | Engineer | no. | number |
| IRF | International Road Federation | Nov. | November |
| irreg. | irregular | nr | near |
| Is | Islands | nrt | net registered tons |
| ISIC | International Standard Industrial Classification | NS | Nova Scotia |

x

# ABBREVIATIONS

| | |
|---|---|
| NSW | New South Wales |
| NV | Naamloze Vennootschap (Limited Company); Nevada |
| NY | New York |
| NZ | New Zealand |
| OAPEC | Organization of Arab Petroleum Exporting Countries |
| OAS | Organization of American States |
| OAU | Organization of African Unity |
| Oct. | October |
| OECD | Organisation for Economic Co-operation and Development |
| OECS | Organization of Eastern Caribbean States |
| Of. | Oficina (Office) |
| OH | Ohio |
| OIC | Organization of the Islamic Conference |
| OK | Oklahoma |
| OPEC | Organization of the Petroleum Exporting Countries |
| opp. | opposite |
| OR | Oregon |
| Org. | Organization |
| ORIT | Organización Regional Interamericana de Trabajadores |
| OSCE | Organization for Security and Co-operation in Europe |
| p. | page |
| p.a. | per annum |
| PA | Pennsylvania |
| Parl. | Parliament(ary) |
| per. | pereulok (lane, alley) |
| Perm. Rep. | Permanent Representative |
| PK | Post Box (Turkish) |
| pl. | platz; place; ploshchad (square) |
| PLC | Public Limited Company |
| PLO | Palestine Liberation Organization |
| p.m. | post meridiem (after noon) |
| PMB | Private Mail Bag |
| POB | Post Office Box |
| PR | Puerto Rico |
| Pr. | prospekt (avenue) |
| Pres. | President |
| Prin. | Principal |
| Prof. | Professor |
| Propr | Proprietor |
| Prov. | Province; Provincial; Provinciale (Dutch) |
| prov. | provulok (lane) |
| PT | Perseroan Terbatas (Limited Company) |
| Pte | Private; Puente (Bridge) |
| Pty | Proprietary |
| p.u. | paid up |
| publ. | publication; published |
| Publr | Publisher |
| Pvt. | Private |
| Qld | Queensland |
| q.v. | quod vide (to which refer) |
| Rag. | Ragioniere (Accountant) |
| Rd | Road |
| R(s) | rand, rupee(s) |
| reg., regd | register; registered |
| reorg. | reorganized |
| Rep. | Republic; Republican; Representative |
| Repub. | Republic |
| res | reserve(s) |
| retd | retired |
| Rev. | Reverend |
| RI | Rhode Island |
| RJ | Rio de Janeiro |
| Rm | Room |
| ro-ro | roll-on roll-off |
| Rp.(s) | rupiah(s) |
| RSFSR | Russian Soviet Federative Socialist Republic |
| Rt | Right |
| S | South; Southern; San |
| SA | Société Anonyme, Sociedad Anónima (limited company); South Australia |
| SADC | Southern African Development Community |
| SARL | Sociedade Anônima de Responsabilidade Limitada (Joint-Stock Company of Limited Liability) |
| SC | South Carolina |
| SD | South Dakota |
| Sdn Bhd | Sendirian Berhad (Private Limited Company) |
| SDR | Special Drawing Right(s) |
| Sec. | Secretary |
| Secr. | Secretariat |
| Sen. | Senior; Senator |
| Sept. | September |
| SER | Sua Eccellenza Reverendissima (His Eminence) |
| SFRY | Socialist Federal Republic of Yugoslavia |
| SITC | Standard International Trade Classification |
| SJ | Society of Jesus |
| s/n | sin número (without number) |
| Soc. | Society |
| Sok. | Sokak (Street) |
| SP | São Paulo |
| SpA | Società per Azioni (Joint-Stock Company) |
| Sq. | Square |
| sq | square (in measurements) |
| Sr | Senior; Señor |
| Sra | Señora |
| Srl | Società a Responsabilità Limitata (Limited Company) |
| SSR | Soviet Socialist Republic |
| St | Saint, Sint; Street |
| Sta | Santa |
| Ste | Sainte |
| str. | strada (Street) |
| subs. | subscriptions; subscribed |
| Sun. | Sunday |
| Supt | Superintendent |
| sv. | Saint |
| Tas. | Tasmania |
| TAŞ | Turkiye Anonim Şirketi (Turkish Joint-Stock Company) |
| TD | Teachta Dála (Member of Parliament) |
| tech., techn. | technical |
| tel. | telephone |
| TEU | 20-ft equivalent unit |
| Thurs. | Thursday |
| TN | Tennessee |
| Treas. | Treasurer |
| Tues. | Tuesday |
| TV | television |
| TX | Texas |
| u. | utca (street) |
| u/a | unit of account |
| UAE | United Arab Emirates |
| UEE | Unidade Econômica Estatal |
| UK | United Kingdom |
| ul. | ulitsa (street) |
| UM | ouguiya |
| UN | United Nations |
| UNCTAD | United Nations Conference on Trade and Development |
| UNDP | United Nations Development Programme |
| UNESCO | United Nations Educational, Scientific and Cultural Organization |
| UNHCR | United Nations High Commissioner for Refugees |
| Univ. | University |
| UNRWA | United Nations Relief and Works Agency for Palestine Refugees in the Near East |
| UP | Uttar Pradesh |
| USA | United States of America |
| USAID | United States Agency for International Development |
| USSR | Union of Soviet Socialist Republics |
| UT | Utah |
| VA | Virginia |
| VAT | Value Added Tax |
| VEB | Volkseigener Betrieb (Public Company) |
| Ven. | Venerable |
| VHF | Very High Frequency |
| VI | (US) Virgin Islands |
| Vic. | Victoria |
| viz. | videlicet (namely) |
| Vn | Veien (Street) |
| vol.(s) | volume(s) |
| VT | Vermont |
| W | West; Western |
| WA | Western Australia; Washington (State) |
| WCL | World Confederation of Labour |
| Wed. | Wednesday |
| WEU | Western European Union |

## ABBREVIATIONS

| | | | |
|---|---|---|---|
| WFTU | World Federation of Trade Unions | WV | West Virginia |
| WHO | World Health Organization | WY | Wyoming |
| WI | Wisconsin | | |
| WTO | World Trade Organization | yr | year |

# LATE INFORMATION

## KAZAKHSTAN (p. 1739)
### Government Change
(July 1995)

In early July the Minister of Justice, NAGASHYBAY AMANGALY-ULY SHAYKENOV, was appointed concurrently to the post of Deputy Prime Minister.

## LATVIA (p. 1850)
### Government Change
(July 1995)

The Ministry of State Reform was disbanded on 1 July, and its duties transferred to other institutions.

## LEBANON (p. 1865)
### Government Change
(June 1995)

**Minister of the Environment:** PIERRE PHARAON (Greek Catholic).

## LESOTHO (p. 1882)
### Government Changes
(July 1995)

**Deputy Prime Minister and Minister of Home Affairs and Local Government:** BETHUEL PAKALITHA MOSISILI.
**Minister of Education and Manpower Development:** TSELISO MAKHAKHE.
**Minister of Natural Resources:** Dr KHAUHELO DEBORAH RADITAPOLE.
**Minister of Health and Social Welfare:** SEKOALA TOLOANE.
**Minister of Agriculture, Co-operatives and Youth Affairs:** MOPSHATLA MABITLE.
**Minister of Foreign Affairs:** KELEBONE ALBERT MAOPE.
**Minister of Justice and Human Rights, Law and Constitutional Affairs:** MOLAPO QHOBELA.
**Minister of Works:** NTSUKUNYANE MPHANYA.
**Minister of Tourism, Sports and Culture:** PASHO MOCHESANE.
**Minister of Transport and Communications:** LESAO LEHOHLA.

## LIBYA (p. 1909)
### Government Changes
(July 1995)

#### GENERAL SECRETARIAT OF THE GENERAL PEOPLE'S CONGRESS
**Assistant Secretary-General:** MAHMOUD AL-HITKI.
**Secretary for Women's Affairs:** THURIYAH RAMADAN ABU TABRIKA.
**Secretary for Affairs of the People's Congresses:** AHMAD IBRAHIM MANSUR.
**Secretary for Affairs of the People's Committees:** ALI MURSI ASH-SHAIRI.

#### GENERAL PEOPLE'S COMMITTEE
**Secretary for Industry and Mining:** Dr MUFTAH AL-KHUZAH.
**Secretary for Information and Culture:** FAWZIYAH BASHIR SHALABI.
**Secretary for Tourism:** Eng. BUKHARI HAWDAH.
**Secretary for Animal Resources:** Dr MASOUD ABU SUWWAH.

## LITHUANIA (p. 1927)
### Government Change
(July 1995)

In early July ALEKSANDRAS VASILIAUSKAS tendered his resignation as Minister of the Economy. It was also reported that the Ministry of the Economy would be abolished later in the year.

## MALAWI (p. 1973)
### Government Changes
(July 1995)

**First Vice-President and Minister of Defence:** JUSTIN MALEWEZI.
**Minister without Portfolio:** HARRY I. THOMSON.
**Minister of Physical Planning and Surveys:** PETER FACHI.
**Minister of Education:** Dr CASSIM CHILUMPHA.
**Minister of Health and Population:** SAM MPASU.
**Minister of Transport and Civil Aviation:** Dr GEORGE NTAFU.
**Minister of Tourism:** PATRICK B. MBEWE.
**Minister of Relief and Rehabilitation Affairs:** ROLPH PATEL.
**Minister of Natural Resources:** ZILILO CHIBAMBO.
**Attorney-General and Minister of Justice:** COLLINS CHIZUMIRA.
**Minister of Local Government and Rural Development:** Dr MATEBO MZUNDA.
**Minister of Works and Supplies:** Dr J. B. MPONDA MKANDAWIRE.
**Minister of Youth, Sports and Culture:** KAMANGADADZI CHAMBALO.
**Minister of Research and Environmental Affairs:** BITWELL KAWONGA.
**Minister of Commerce and Industry:** PETER KALILOMBE.
**Minister of Energy and Mining:** Rev. Dr JOMBO LEMANI.
**Minister of Labour and Manpower Development:** RICHARD SEMBENUKA.

## MEXICO (p. 2074)
### Government Change
(June 1995)

**Secretary of the Interior:** EMILIO CHAUYFFET CHEMOR.

## THE PHILIPPINES (p. 2468)
### Government Changes
(July 1995)

**Secretary of Health:** HILARIOM RAMIRO.
**Secretary of Tourism:** EDUARDO BILABIL.
**Secretary of the Environment and Natural Resources:** VICTOR RAMOS.
**Secretary of Social Welfare and Development:** LINE LAIGO.

## SAINT CHRISTOPHER AND NEVIS (p. 2609)
### National Assembly

A general election, conducted on 3 July 1995, was won by the Labour Party, which secured seven of the 11 elective seats in the National Assembly. The Concerned Citizens' Movement won two seats, while the People's Action Movement and the Nevis Reformation Party each won one seat.

## TURKEY (p. 3054)
### Government Change
(July 1995)

**Minister of Public Works and Housing:** HALİL CULHAOĞLU.

# LATE INFORMATION

**UGANDA** (p. 3089)
**Government Changes**
(July 1995)

**Second Deputy Prime Minister and Minister of Public Service:** Dr Eric T. Adriko.

**Third Deputy Prime Minister and Minister of Tourism, Wildlife and Antiquities:** Brig. Moses Ali.

**Minister of Agriculture, Animal Industry and Fisheries:** John Nasasira.

**Minister of Lands and Urban Development:** Maj. Tom Butime.

**Minister of Women's Affairs and Community Development:** Albina Opio.

# KAZAKHSTAN

## Introductory Survey

**Location, Climate, Language, Religion, Flag, Capital**

The Republic of Kazakhstan (until December 1991 the Kazakh Soviet Socialist Republic) is the second largest of the former Soviet republics, extending some 1,900 km (1,200 miles) from the Volga river in the west to the Altai mountains in the east, and about 1,300 km (800 miles) from the Siberian plain in the north to the Central Asian deserts in the south. To the south it borders Turkmenistan, Uzbekistan and Kyrgyzstan. To the east the border is with the People's Republic of China. There is a long border in the north with the Russian Federation and a coastline of 2,320 km (1,440 miles) on the Caspian Sea in the south-west. The climate is of a strongly continental type, but there are wide variations throughout the territory. Average temperatures in January range from −18°C (0°F) in the north to −3°C (27°F) in the south. In July average temperatures are 19°C (66°F) in the north and 28°C–30°C (82°F–86°F) in the south. Levels of precipitation are equally varied: average annual rainfall in mountainous regions reaches 1,600 mm, whereas in the central desert areas it is less than 100 mm. Kazakh, a member of the Central Turkic group of languages, replaced Russian as the official language in September 1989; since 1940 it has been written in the Cyrillic script. The predominant religion is Islam, most ethnic Kazakhs being Sunni Muslims of the Hanafi school. Other ethnic groups have their own religious communities, notably the (Christian) Eastern Orthodox Church, which is attended mainly by Slavs. The national flag (proportions 2 by 1) consists of a light blue field, at the centre of which is a yellow sun (a disk surrounded by 32 rays), framed by the wings of a flying eagle, also in yellow, with a vertical stripe of national ornamentation in yellow near the hoist. The capital is Almaty (Alma-Ata), but it is due to be transferred to Akmola (formerly Tselinograd) in approximately 2000.

**Recent History**

The Kazakhs are descended from Mongol and Turkic tribes that settled in the area in about the first century BC. They emerged as a distinct ethnic group from a tribal confederation known as Kazakh Orda, which was formed in the late 15th century AD. Following the dissolution of the Kazakh Orda in the early 17th century, the Kazakhs split into smaller nomadic groups, which were united in three large federations, or Hordes. In the first half of the 18th century, as a result of invasions from the east by the Oirot Mongols, the three Hordes sought protection from the Russian Tsar. Although the threat from the Oirots was ended, after they were conquered by the Manzhous (Manchus) in 1758, the Russians retained control over the Kazakhs, and deposed the Khans (leaders) of the Hordes. Following the abolition of serfdom in Russia in 1861, many Russian and Ukrainian peasants moved to Kazakhstan and were granted Kazakh lands. Resentment against immigration led to disaffection with Russian rule, and in 1916 a major rebellion against Russian control was brutally repressed, with some 150,000 people killed.

After the February Revolution and the Bolshevik *coup d'état* in 1917, there was civil war throughout Kazakhstan. Bolshevik forces finally overcame those of the anti-Bolshevik White Army, foreign interventionists and local nationalists. On 26 August 1920 the Kyrgyz Autonomous Soviet Socialist Republic (ASSR—until the mid-1920s the Kazakhs were known to the Russians as Kyrgyz, to distinguish them from the unrelated Cossacks) was created within the Russian Soviet Federative Socialist Republic (RSFSR—the Russian Federation). As a result of the National Delimitation of Central Asia in 1924–25, the Kyrgyz ASSR was enlarged by the inclusion of certain Kazakh-populated territories originally belonging to the Turkestan ASSR (which had been established within the RSFSR in 1918, and covered much of the area now occupied by the four other Central Asian republics of the former USSR). In 1925 the Kyrgyz ASSR was renamed the Kazakh ASSR. The Karakalpak region was detached from the Kazakh ASSR in 1932; it became an autonomous republic within the Uzbek Soviet Socialist Republic (SSR) in 1936. On 5 December 1936 the Kazakh ASSR became a full Union Republic of the USSR, the Kazakh SSR.

Under Soviet rule parts of Kazakhstan were heavily industrialized, while communications and infrastructure were greatly improved. However, Kazakhstan was one of the worst-affected regions during the campaign in the early 1930s to collectivize agriculture and settle nomadic peoples: more than 1m. people are estimated to have died as a result of starvation. There was also severe repression from the 1930s onwards, and Russian immigration was greatly increased. Those deported from parts of the USSR during the Second World War (including Germans, Crimean Tatars and Caucasian peoples) were often sent to Kazakhstan, causing resentment among the local inhabitants.

During Nikita Khrushchev's period in office as Soviet leader (1953–64) large areas of previously uncultivated land in Kazakhstan were transformed into arable land under the 'Virgin Lands' scheme. This and other schemes, which included the nuclear testing sites in eastern Kazakhstan, the Baikonur space centre at Leninsk and the huge industrial sites in the north and east of Kazakhstan, all attracted large numbers of ethnic Russians to the republic; the ethnic Russian proportion of the population rose from 19.7% in 1926 to 42.7% in 1959.

Mikhail Gorbachev's accession to power, in 1985, and his subsequent campaign against corruption (which involved replacing prominent allies of the late Soviet leader, Leonid Brezhnev, with a new generation of officials) had important consequences in Kazakhstan. In mid-December 1986 some 3,000 people took part in protests in the capital, Almaty (Alma-Ata), after Gennadi Kolbin, an ethnic Russian, was appointed First Secretary of the Communist Party of Kazakhstan (CPK), replacing the prominent, although corrupt, Dinmukhamed Kunayev, an ethnic Kazakh. Four people died, and 200 were injured, when the protesters were dispersed by police. Despite the protests, Kolbin remained in office and dismissed many of Kunayev's former associates, some of whom were accused of nepotism and bribe-taking.

As in other Soviet republics, linguistic and environmental issues were the main subjects of public debate after the introduction of Gorbachev's policy of *glasnost* (openness). Complaints about the lack of school instruction in the Kazakh language led to a decree, issued in March 1987, advocating improvements in the teaching of both Kazakh and Russian. In September 1989 the Kazakh Supreme Soviet (parliament) adopted legislation establishing Kazakh as the official language of the republic, while Russian remained a language of inter-ethnic communication. However, all officials communicating with the general public would be required to know both languages.

As a result of the intensive development of Kazakhstan's economy, the republic suffered from serious environmental problems. Many of the unofficial, quasi-political groups which were established in Kazakhstan in the late 1980s were concerned with such issues as the effects of nuclear testing near Semipalatinsk (in the east of the republic), industrial pollution and the degradation of arable land as a result of over-intensive farming. The effects of nuclear tests at Semipalatinsk caused particular anxiety; local residents complained of medical conditions normally caused by exposure to excessive radiation. The campaign to end nuclear testing was led by one of Kazakhstan's largest unofficial groups, Nevada-Semipalatinsk, which regularly organized large demonstrations in Almaty. In 1991 it was announced that nuclear testing would not continue in Semipalatinsk after the end of the year. In September 1990 an explosion in a factory producing nuclear fuel in Ulba, in eastern Kazakhstan, led to the contamination of a large area, including the nearby city of Ust-Kamenogorsk, by toxic gases: official reports estimated that as many as 120,000 people might have been affected by the incident. Demonstrators demanded the closure of the plant and the imposition of stricter controls on the city's many non-ferrous metallurgical works.

The introduction of Kazakh as the official language was opposed by many non-Kazakh residents. A local branch of the Russian nationalist organization, Yedinstvo (Unity), was established, and some members campaigned for annexation of Kazakhstan's northern regions by the RSFSR. The publication, in September 1990, of the Russian author and ex-dissident Aleksandr Solzhenitsyn's proposal for the transfer of territory to Russia led to demonstrations by ethnic Kazakhs demanding the preservation of Kazakhstan's boundaries. Further instances of inter-ethnic conflict arose between Kazakhs and other national groups, apparently as a result of high unemployment and economic hardship. In June 1989 a gang of Kazakh youths rioted in Novy Uzen, in south-western Kazakhstan, demanding that immigrant Lezghins and other Caucasian settlers in the area be expelled, and their jobs given to locals. Five people were reported killed, and 118 injured, during several days of rioting, and some 3,500 people fled the region. There were reports of further inter-ethnic violence in the region later in the year.

In June 1989 Kolbin was transferred to Moscow, and Nursultan Nazarbayev, an ethnic Kazakh who had been Chairman of the republic's Council of Ministers since March 1984, was appointed First Secretary of the CPK. Nazarbayev, a prominent politician in republican and Soviet affairs, strongly supported economic reform while emphasizing the need for political stability. In September 1989 the political and administrative system in Kazakhstan was reformed: a permanent Supreme Soviet was to be established, and elections were to be conducted on a multi-candidate basis. In addition, the state duties that had hitherto been the responsibility of the First Secretary of the CPK were transferred to the office of Chairman of the Supreme Soviet, to which post Nazarbayev was elected in February 1990. Elections to the new Supreme Soviet took place on 25 March. Many candidates stood unopposed, and the system of reserved seats for CPK-affiliated organizations was retained, resulting in an overwhelming communist majority when the Supreme Soviet first convened in April. In the same month the new body elected Nazarbayev to the newly-established post of President of Kazakhstan.

On 25 October 1990 a declaration of sovereignty was adopted by the Kazakh Supreme Soviet, asserting republican control over natural resources and the economy, while emphasizing the equality of all nationalities living in the republic. Nevertheless, there were protests against the legislation in the predominantly Slav-populated city of Ust-Kamenogorsk; Kazakh nationalist groups, considering the declaration too weak, also expressed their disapproval. Nazarbayev strongly supported the concept of a treaty to redefine the respective all-Union (Soviet) and republican powers, and the Kazakh Government participated in discussions on the new Union Treaty in early 1991. However, Nazarbayev was also a strong advocate of economic sovereignty for Kazakhstan, where some 90% of enterprises were under all-Union control. When miners staged a strike in the north-eastern city of Karaganda in March 1991, demanding improved living conditions and greater control over profits from their mines, Nazarbayev persuaded the Soviet authorities to transfer control of enterprises in Kazakhstan to the jurisdiction of the Kazakh Government.

Kazakhstan took part in the referendum on the future of the USSR, which took place in nine Soviet republics in March 1991. Of the 88.2% of the electorate who voted in Kazakhstan, 94.1% endorsed the proposal to preserve the USSR as a 'union of sovereign states with equal rights'. In June the Kazakh Supreme Soviet voted to adopt a draft Union Treaty in principle, although Nazarbayev expressed reservations about certain aspects of the proposed federation.

Kazakhstan was to sign the new Union Treaty on 20 August 1991, but the event was forestalled by the attempted *coup d'état* in Moscow, beginning on 19 August. Nazarbayev was initially cautious, advocating calm, without openly condemning the coup. On 20 August, however, he issued a statement which denounced the group leading the putsch, the State Committee for the State of Emergency (SCSE), as illegal and harmful to economic and political progress. As the coup attempt collapsed, Nazarbayev resigned from the Politburo and Central Committee of the Communist Party of the Soviet Union (CPSU), in protest at the open support granted to the SCSE leaders by the CPSU leadership. At the same time the CPK was ordered to cease activities in state and government organs. In September the CPK withdrew from the CPSU; it was replaced by the independent Socialist Party of Kazakhstan (SPK).

In October 1991 Kazakhstan signed, with eight other republics, a treaty to establish an economic community, and in the following month Nazarbayev agreed to the draft treaty of the new Union of Sovereign States. When these accords were largely nullified by the proposed Commonwealth of Independent States (CIS, see p. 126), agreed by the leaders of the three Slavic republics (Russia, Ukraine and Belarus) in December, Nazarbayev expressed an initial reluctance to participate in a new political formation that he had not been invited to negotiate. Nevertheless, on 13 December, together with the other Central Asian republics, Kazakhstan agreed to join the new Commonwealth. The country was formally recognized as a co-founder of the CIS at the Almaty meeting on 21 December.

On 16 December 1991 Kazakhstan became the last of the republics to declare its independence from the USSR. The country's name was changed to the Republic of Kazakhstan. This tardiness in issuing a declaration of independence was attributed to Nazarbayev's concern to preserve the delicate inter-ethnic balance between Russians and Kazakhs in the republic and also to prevent further discussion of the cession of Kazakhstan's northern territories to the Russian Federation. Above all, it was seen as evidence, together with his determination to retain many of the personnel and structures of the CPK (although reformed as the SPK) as the channel for economic policy in the republic, of his view that the need for, and consequences of, economic reform would be considerably more important than those of political change. There was little political opposition to Nazarbayev's policies, however, and he had also gained popularity by banning nuclear tests at the Semipalatinsk site in August. On 1 December Nazarbayev was the only candidate in elections to the presidency, at which he won 98.8% of the votes cast. (Some 87.4% of the electorate took part in the poll.)

Despite the country's multiplicity of ethnic groups (more than 100), Kazakhstan did not experience the inter-ethnic violence affecting some other former Soviet republics. Nevertheless, some racial unrest was reported during 1992, particularly among Kazakhstan's Russian community (which now constituted an estimated 38% of the total population, while ethnic Kazakhs comprised 40%). There were increasing demands, both by Russian citizens and legislators, that the Russian language be guaranteed equal status with Kazakh in a new constitution, the content of which was debated nationwide during 1992. In the event, the new Constitution, adopted in January 1993, invoked the law of 1989 (which denoted Kazakh as the state language, with Russian as a language of inter-ethnic communication). It also required that the President of the Republic be a fluent speaker of Kazakh. Despite the low occurrence of racial tension in Kazakhstan, a significant increase in emigration from the country was reported, particularly by ethnic Germans (more than 300,000 of whom left Kazakhstan in the early 1990s) and Russians, but also by other minorities. However, this was, to some extent, counter-balanced by the return of ethnic Kazakhs from Mongolia, Tajikistan, Turkmenistan, Kyrgyzstan and other countries in the region. Kazakhstan was also unaffected by religious conflict (unlike its close neighbour, Tajikistan). The 1993 Constitution defined Kazakhstan as a secular State, and the Government consistently disavowed any tendency towards Islamic fundamentalism.

Kazakhstan's political structures remained largely unaltered during 1992, with the Government and the Supreme Kenges (as the legislature was now known) still dominated by former communists. In June some 5,000 opposition supporters demonstrated in Almaty against continued communist predominance, demanding the Government's resignation and the formation of a new, coalition Council of Ministers. In October, in order to present a stronger opposition front, the three most prominent nationalist opposition parties (the Azat movement, the Republican Party and the Zheltoksan National Democratic Party) united to form the Republican Party—Azat (RP—A). In mid-1992 attempts to revive the CPK were thwarted by the Supreme Court's refusal to register the party. In February 1993 a new public movement, the Union of National Unity of Kazakhstan, was established, with a declared aim of promoting social harmony and countering radical nationalism. Nazarbayev, who had held no party affiliation since August 1991, agreed to chair the Union, whose membership represented most of the ethnic groups and regions of Kazakhstan.

Later in 1993 the Union was reorganized as a political party, the People's Unity Party (PUP).

In December 1993 the Supreme Kenges voted to dissolve itself and to grant Nazarbayev the power to rule by decree until elections (in early 1994) to a new, standing legislature (reduced in size from 360 to 177 seats). The first free multi-party elections in Kazakhstan's history were duly held on 7 March 1994, with the participation of 74% of the electorate. A number of irregularities were reported by international observers monitoring the election, with many prospective candidates allegedly being prevented from registering. Of the 754 candidates who successfully registered, the overwhelming majority (75%) were ethnic Kazakhs, a fact that prompted allegations of discrimination against the Russian community. In the event, the final composition of the new Kenges was 59% Kazakh, 28% Russian and 13% other nationalities. Of the political parties and organizations, the PUP obtained the greatest number of seats (33), which, when combined with the 42 seats won by candidates from the so-called 'President's List' (candidates nominated by Nazarbayev), ensured that Nazarbayev's supporters emerged as the strongest force in the assembly. Other parties and groups achieved a significantly lower representation: the Confederation of Kazakh Trade Unions (CKTU) won 11 seats, the People's Congress Party of Kazakhstan (PCPK) nine and the SPK eight. The Kazakhstan Peasants' Union and the Slavic Movement—Lad (Concord) each obtained four seats, with six smaller, specialized groups taking one seat each. The remaining 59 seats went to independent candidates, the majority of whom were reported to be pro-Nazarbayev. The final seat in the Kenges was filled later in the year, following a legal judgment on the outcome of the poll.

In late March 1994 the CPK (which claimed a membership of some 50,000) was finally granted legal status. In May the CPK and other opposition parties, including the SPK, the PCPK and the RP—A, together with CKTU, formed a 'constructive opposition bloc' within the Supreme Kenges with the stated aim of acting as a guarantor against 'dictatorship by executive bodies' in Kazakhstan.

Divisions between the Government and the Supreme Kenges over economic and other issues became increasingly apparent during 1994. In May 96 members of the Kenges passed a vote of 'no confidence' in the Government's economic, social and legal policies, which, they claimed, were impeding Kazakhstan's economic reforms. In June Nazarbayev announced a major government reorganization, in an attempt to stimulate the economic reform process. In subsequent months the President implemented further measures intended to streamline the state administration and to eradicate senior-level corruption. The Government tendered its resignation in October, having admitted its failure to implement successful economic reforms. Akezhan Kazhegeldin, an economist and First Deputy Prime Minister in the outgoing Council of Ministers, was appointed by Nazarbayev as the Prime Minister of a new Government.

Meanwhile, in July 1994 the Supreme Kenges approved proposals to transfer the capital from the south to the northern city of Akmola (formerly Tselinograd) in approximately 2000. The proposals, which had originally been made by Nazarbayev, cited Almaty's overcrowded conditions and its situation in an area vulnerable to earthquakes; however, unofficial sources suggested that the move was designed to strengthen the Government's control over the largely Russian-populated nothern regions.

There was renewed tension between Kazakhstan's state bodies in early 1995, as the Supreme Kenges refused to adopt the new Government's draft budget, which, it claimed, would exacerbate social hardships. The Government countered that its budgetary proposals were necessary to ensure increased IMF assistance and foreign investment; Nazarbayev also expressed his support for the Government's proposals. A constitutional crisis evolved in late February, when the Constitutional Court declared the result of the 1994 general election to be null and void owing to 'procedural infringements'. An attempt by the Kenges to amend the Constitution in order to overrule the Court's decision was unsuccessful, and in March 1995 the legislature was forced to tender its resignation. This was followed by the resignation of the Government (necessitated by the fact that it had been approved by an unconstitutional parliament). Nazarbayev accepted the resignation of the Kenges and the Government, although later in the month the Government was reinstated, virtually unchanged. As a result of the crisis, Nazarbayev was effectively empowered to rule by decree until the holding of fresh elections. Opposition parties claimed that the crisis had been orchestrated by Nazarbayev in order to assume absolute power and to remove an obstructionist parliament. In late March Nazarbayev ordered the holding of a referendum on the extension of his term of office until 1 December 2000 (which, he claimed, was necessary to ensure stability in the republic). Some 91% of the electorate participated in the referendum, which was held on 29 April; of these, more than 95% were reported to have voted in favour of the extension of the President's term (thus exempting him from the need to seek re-election in late 1996). A further referendum, on amendments to the Constitution, was reportedly due to be held in August, following which elections to a new legislature (a bicameral body) were to take place.

Nazarbayev strongly defended the preservation of the CIS, and in January 1993 Kazakhstan signed, with six other CIS members, a charter pledging closer political and economic integration. Since then, however, Nazarbayev has promoted his personal vision of a 'Eurasian Union', as an alternative body to the CIS, which would be based on an even closer integration of CIS member states. In the mean time, Kazakhstan has partially realized an integration of this type with the neighbouring CIS states of Kyrgyzstan and Uzbekistan. In early 1994 the three countries formed a trilateral economic area, and in February 1995 an Interstate Council was established to supervise its implementation.

Relations with the neighbouring Russian Federation, the most influential CIS member state, have been intermittently strained by the issue of Kazakhstan's large Russian minority. However, in May 1992 the two countries signed a treaty of friendship, co-operation and mutual assistance, which was to be valid for a period of 25 years, and which provided, *inter alia*, for Russian assistance in the establishment of Kazakhstan's armed forces. This treaty was strengthened by further Russian-Kazakh agreements, concluded in January 1995, which provided for a customs union and currency convertibility between the two countries, as well as closer military ties. The long-standing debate over the issue of dual citizenship (as demanded by Kazakhstan's Russian population but rejected by the Government as potentially destabilizing) was brought to an end by an agreement on reciprocal citizenship, also signed in January 1995, which granted ethnic minorities of either country the 'patronage' of both states. Nevertheless, there was sporadic unrest within Kazakhstan's Russian community during 1994, particularly in response to the arrest and conviction of Boris Suprunyuk, the editor of a Russian-language newspaper, on charges of 'inciting inter-ethnic strife'. In a further attempt to preserve social stability and ethnic harmony, in March 1995 Nazarbayev established a new forum on inter-ethnic issues—the Association of Peoples of Kazakhstan—which was to have the status of a 'consultative presidential body'.

Relations with Germany have been largely concerned with the issue of the nearly 700,000 ethnic Germans remaining in Kazakhstan. (During the early 1940s, at Stalin's order, large numbers of ethnic Germans were deported to Kazakhstan from their homes in the Volga region.) In September 1992 Nazarbayev visited Germany, where, during talks with President von Weizsäcker, he pledged the full observance of the Kazakh Germans' civil rights.

As the largest and most influential of the five Central Asian republics of the former USSR, Kazakhstan has been regarded as a potential guarantor of peace in the region. However, the issue of the formerly Soviet, now Russian-controlled, nuclear warheads still deployed in Kazakhstan (effectively making the country the fourth-largest nuclear power in the world) has been the focus of international concern. Following the dissolution of the USSR in late 1991, Kazakhstan stated its commitment to becoming a non-nuclear state, either by destroying its nuclear weapons or transferring them to the Russian Federation. In September 1992 Kazakhstan's Supreme Kenges ratified the first Strategic Arms Reduction Treaty, which had been signed by the USA and the USSR in July 1991 and the provisions of which affected Kazakhstan as a (nuclear) successor state to the USSR. In December 1993 the Kenges ratified the Treaty on the Non-Proliferation of Nuclear Weapons (see p. 68). The republic was to have eliminated or removed all nuclear weapons by the end of the 1990s. The

USA has provided Kazakhstan with substantial technical and financial aid for the dismantling of the remainder of the republic's nuclear arsenal. In November 1994 it was confirmed that some 600 kg of enriched uranium had been airlifted, in a secret operation, from Kazakhstan to the USA for safe storage.

## Government

Under the terms of the 1993 Constitution, supreme legislative power is vested in the 177-member Supreme Kenges, which is elected by universal adult suffrage for a five-year term. The President of the Republic, who is directly elected every five years, is the Head of State and holds supreme executive power, in conjunction with the Council of Ministers. The President appoints the Prime Minister and Deputy Prime Ministers, as well as the Ministers of Foreign Affairs, Defence, Finance and Internal Affairs. The remaining ministers are nominated by the Prime Minister. Government appointments are subject to approval by parliament.

In February 1995 the Constitutional Court declared the result of the 1994 legislative elections to be invalid, and the Supreme Kenges and the Government approved by it were subsequently obliged to resign (see Recent History).

For administrative purposes, Kazakhstan is divided into 21 local governments (19 regions and two cities).

## Defence

In May 1992 President Nazarbayev issued a decree on the establishment of Kazakhstan's armed forces (until independence, Kazakhstan had no armed forces separate from those of the USSR). By June 1994 the estimated strength of the national armed forces was 40,000 (army 25,000 and air force 15,000). In 1993 it was announced that a navy was to be established; in the mean time, Kazakhstan was to continue to participate, with Russia and Turkmenistan, in the operation of the Caspian Sea Flotilla, a former Soviet force based, under Russian command, at Astrakhan (Russia). In mid-1992 Kazakhstan signed a collective security treaty with five other members of the Commonwealth of Independent States. A nuclear successor state to the USSR, Kazakhstan has pledged to dismantle its nuclear capabilities, having ratified the first Strategic Arms Reduction Treaty in 1992 and the Treaty on the Non-Proliferation of Nuclear Weapons in 1993. In the mean time, Kazakhstan's nuclear arsenal remains under Russian control. In May 1994 Kazakhstan joined NATO's 'partnership for peace' programme of military co-operation (see p. 192). Defence expenditure for 1993 was forecast at 140,800m. roubles (some 11% of total budgetary spending).

## Economic Affairs

In 1993, according to estimates by the World Bank, Kazakhstan's gross national product (GNP), measured at average 1991–93 prices, was US $26,490m., equivalent to $1,540 per head. During 1985–93, it was estimated, GNP per head declined, in real terms, by an average annual rate of 4.6%. During the same period the population increased by an annual average of 1.0%. Kazakhstan's gross domestic product (GDP) increased, in real terms, by an annual average of 1.1% in 1980–92. However, it declined by 13.0% in 1992 and by 12.9% in the following year; in 1994 GDP was estimated to have declined by 25.4%.

Agriculture (including forestry) contributed 47.7% of net material product (NMP) in 1992. In that year the sector provided 24.0% of total employment. There are large areas of land suitable for agriculture, and Kazakhstan is a major producer and exporter of agricultural products. The principal crops include fruits, sugar beet, vegetables, potatoes, cotton and, most importantly, cereals. Livestock-breeding is also important. Kazakhstan is a significant producer of karakul and astrakhan wools. During 1985–93 agricultural GDP increased, in real terms, at an average rate of 1.1% per year. In 1994 agricultural production declined by 21.2%, compared with the previous year.

Industry, excluding construction, contributed 40.6% of NMP in 1992. In the same year industry provided 20.4% of total employment. Industrial GDP (including construction) was estimated to have declined by 0.3% per year during 1985–93, and by 28.5% in 1994.

Mining and quarrying provided 3.5% of employment in 1992. Kazakhstan possesses immense mineral wealth, and large-scale mining and processing industries have been developed. There are major coalfields (in the Karaganda, Turgay, Ekibastuz and Maykuben basins), as well as substantial deposits of iron ore, lead, titanium, magnesium, chromium, tungsten, molybdenum, gold, silver, copper and manganese. Petroleum is extracted, and Kazakhstan possesses what are believed to be among the world's largest unexploited oilfields (in the Caspian depression) and substantial reserves of natural gas. In early 1995 total reserves (onshore and offshore) of petroleum and natural gas were estimated to be 4,500m. metric tons and 5,900,000m. cu m, respectively.

Manufacturing provided 15.8% of employment in 1992, and an estimated 30.6% of GDP in 1991. Parts of Kazakhstan are highly industrialized, and the most important sectors are associated with the transformation of raw materials, including metal-processing, fuel, power, chemicals, machine-building, textiles and food-processing. The GDP of the manufacturing sector declined at an average annual rate of 3.2% in 1985–93.

In 1991 some 54.4% of Kazakhstan's total energy consumption was derived from coal, followed by petroleum (27.5%) and natural gas (13.8%). Although domestic output of electricity increased considerably during the 1980s, Kazakhstan is still obliged to import some 14% of its annual requirements. In the early 1990s thermal power stations (mainly coal-fired) provided about 87% of annual domestic electricity production, while hydroelectric and nuclear power stations accounted for the remainder (12% and 1%, respectively).

In 1992 Kazakhstan recorded a visible trade deficit of US $1,670m., and there was a deficit of $2,080m. on the current account of the balance of payments. In 1994 Kazakhstan's principal trading partners were other republics of the former USSR, accounting collectively for 61% of its total trade turnover (Russian Federation 40%, other republics 21%). Outside the former USSR, the most important trading partners in that year were Germany, the Netherlands, Switzerland, the Czech Republic and Italy (together accounting for 24% of Kazakhstan's total trade turnover), and Asian countries (11%). The principal exports in 1994 included ferrous and non-ferrous metals (40% of total exports), followed by mineral products, including petroleum and petroleum products (33%), and chemicals (10%). Major imports included energy products and electricity (31%), machinery and transport equipment (29%) and chemicals.

The 1993 budget proposals projected a deficit of 198,400m. roubles. Kazakhstan's total external debt was US $1,639.6m. at the end of 1993, of which $1,552.2m. was long-term public debt. It was estimated to have risen to some $2,500m. by the end of 1994. Consumer prices increased by an annual average of 1,381% in 1992, by 2,165% in 1993 and by 1,900% in 1994. In January 1995 more than 150,000 people were registered as unemployed.

Kazakhstan was admitted to the IMF and the World Bank in 1992. In addition to its membership of the economic bodies of the Commonwealth of Independent States (CIS, see p. 126), Kazakhstan has joined the Asian Development Bank (ADB, see p. 107), is a 'Country of Operations' of the European Bank for Reconstruction and Development (EBRD, see p. 140), and is a member of the Economic Co-operation Organization (ECO, see p. 238). In early 1995 Kazakhstan signed an agreement of partnership and co-operation with the European Union (see p. 143).

Even before the dissolution of the USSR in December 1991, Kazakhstan's Government had announced plans for tentative economic reforms, including (in October 1990) proposals for the transfer to private ownership of state enterprises. By late-1994 some 60% of all formerly state-owned enterprises had been transferred to private control. Since independence, Kazakhstan has been beset by extensive economic difficulties similar to those prevalent in other former republics of the USSR, largely resulting from the collapse of the Soviet central planning and internal trading systems. Consequently, there was an annual contraction in all sectors of the Kazakh economy in 1991–94, with output severely hampered by widespread payment arrears between enterprises. Furthermore, as a result of Kazakhstan's traditional dependence on the Russian Federation, as well as its initial decision to remain within the rouble zone, the country's economy was considerably influenced by developments in Russia—in particular, a dramatic rise in the annual rate of inflation. However, when the Central Bank of the Russian Federation announced in July 1993 that pre-1993 banknotes would no longer be legal tender, the Kazakh Government saw no option but to introduce its own currency: this (the tenge) came into circulation in November 1993.

# KAZAKHSTAN

Despite the difficulties experienced in the early 1990s, Kazakhstan's prospects for eventual economic recovery and prosperity are considered to be highly favourable, owing to the country's immense, and as yet largely unexploited, hydrocarbon and other mineral reserves. In the early 1990s Kazakhstan signed joint-venture agreements with several foreign companies to develop, in particular, the country's deposits of petroleum and natural gas. It was hoped that the problem of the inefficient transportation of raw materials, both inside and outside the republic, would be alleviated following an agreement, concluded in January 1995, by the Governments of Kazakhstan, Russia and Oman to proceed with the construction of a new pipeline for the export of Kazakh (and Russian) petroleum.

## Social Welfare

Reforms were introduced in the early 1990s with the aim of making Kazakhstan's social welfare system self-financing (during the Soviet period it had been dependent on transfers from the all-Union budget). Three new funds were introduced, of which the Pension and Social Insurance Funds were to be financed entirely by the employer and employee contributions. To counter the increase in unemployment that was expected as a result of the market economic reforms taking place in Kazakhstan, the Government established a State Employment Fund in 1991. The Fund's operations were subsequently extended to include the relief and support of ethnic Kazakh immigrants. In 1990 there were 136 hospital beds per 10,000 inhabitants. In 1984–89, according to UN estimates, there was one physician per 242 persons. The state budget for 1993 forecast expenditure of 180,500m. roubles for health and social security (14.7% of total spending).

## Education

Education is fully funded by the state at primary and secondary level. Most pupils are taught in Russian, although since the adoption of Kazakh as the state language there have been attempts to extend the provision of Kazakh-language education. In 1988 64.2% of all pupils at general day schools were taught in Russian, 33.0% in Kazakh, 1.9% in Uzbek, 0.4% in Uighur and 0.1% in Tajik. Higher education is conducted in 55 institutions of higher education, including three universities. In the 1990/91 academic year there were 287,400 students in higher education. In 1991 plans were announced for the establishment of a new university of Turkestan. Ethnic Kazakhs form a greater proportion of students in higher education than in primary and secondary education, since many ethnic Russians choose to study at universities outside the republic. In 1984/85 Kazakhs formed 46% of students in specialized secondary education, but 54% of students in higher education. In 1989, according to census results, the rate of adult illiteracy was only 2.5% (males 0.9%; females 3.9%).

## Public Holidays

**1995:** 1 January (New Year), 28 January (Constitution Day), 8 March (International Women's Day), 22 March (Nauryz, Kazakh New Year), 1 May (Solidarity Day), 9 May (Victory Day, Day of Remembrance), 25 October (State Sovereignty Day), 31 December (New Year).

**1996:** 1 January (New Year), 28 January (Constitution Day), 8 March (International Women's Day), 22 March (Nauryz, Kazakh New Year), 1 May (Solidarity Day), 9 May (Victory Day, Day of Remembrance), 25 October (State Sovereignty Day), 31 December (New Year).

## Weights and Measures

The metric system is in force.

# Statistical Survey

Principal sources: IMF, *Kazakhstan, Economic Review*, and *International Financial Statistics: Supplement on Countries of the Former Soviet Union*; World Bank, *Kazakhstan: The Transition to a Market Economy* and *Statistical Handbook: States of the Former USSR*.

## Area and Population

### AREA, POPULATION AND DENSITY

| | |
|---|---:|
| Area (sq km) | 2,717,300* |
| Population (census results)† | |
| 17 January 1979 | 14,684,283 |
| 12 January 1989 | |
| Males | 7,974,004 |
| Females | 8,490,460 |
| Total | 16,464,464 |
| Population (official estimates at mid-year) | |
| 1992 | 16,903,000 |
| 1993 | 16,972,600 |
| 1994 | 16,763,000 |
| Density (per sq km) at mid-1994 | 6.2 |

* 1,049,150 sq miles.
† Figures refer to *de jure* population. The *de facto* total was at the 1989 census 16,536,511.

### PRINCIPAL ETHNIC GROUPS (permanent inhabitants, 1 January 1994)

| | Number | % |
|---|---:|---:|
| Kazakh | 7,474,478 | 44.3 |
| Russian | 6,041,586 | 35.8 |
| Ukrainian | 856,665 | 5.1 |
| German | 613,820 | 3.6 |
| Uzbek | 371,662 | 2.2 |
| Tatar | 330,584 | 2.0 |
| Belarusian | 177,584 | 1.1 |
| Azerbaijani | 101,950 | 0.6 |
| Others | 902,002 | 5.3 |
| **Total** | **16,870,362** | **100.0** |

### PRINCIPAL TOWNS (estimated population at 1 January 1990)

| | | | | |
|---|---:|---|---|---:|
| Almaty (Alma-Ata) (capital) | 1,147,000 | | Kustanai | 228,000 |
| Karaganda | 613,000 | | Temirtau | 213,000 |
| Chimkent | 401,000 | | Uralsk | 207,000 |
| Semipalatinsk | 339,000 | | Aktau† | 165,000 |
| Pavlodar | 337,000 | | Kzyl-Orda | 156,000 |
| Ust-Kamenogorsk | 330,000 | | Atyrau‡ | 151,000 |
| Jambul | 311,000 | | Kokshetau | 139,000 |
| Akmola* | 281,000 | | Ekibastuz | 137,000 |
| Aktyubinsk | 260,000 | | Rudniy | 126,000 |
| Petropavlovsk | 245,000 | | Taldi-Kurgan | 122,000 |
| | | | Jezkazgan | 110,000 |

* Formerly Tselinograd.   † Formerly Shevchenko.
‡ Formerly Guriyev.

Source: UN, *Demographic Yearbook*.

### BIRTHS, MARRIAGES AND DEATHS

| | Registered live births | | Registered marriages | | Registered deaths | |
|---|---:|---:|---:|---:|---:|---:|
| | Number | Rate (per 1,000) | Number | Rate (per 1,000) | Number | Rate (per 1,000) |
| 1987 | 417,139 | 25.8 | 160,909 | 9.8 | 122,835 | 7.6 |
| 1988 | 407,116 | 24.9 | 162,962 | 10.0 | 126,898 | 7.8 |
| 1989 | 382,269 | 23.1 | 165,380 | 10.0 | 126,378 | 7.6 |

Source: UN, *Demographic Yearbook*.

**1991:** Registered live births 354,101, Rate (per 1,000) 21.1; Registered deaths 134,572, Rate (per 1,000) 8.0.
**1992:** Registered live births 338,475, Rate (per 1,000) 20.0; Registered deaths 137,705, Rate (per 1,000) 8.1.

Source: UN, *Population and Vital Statistics Report*.

**Expectation of life** (years at birth, 1989): 68.7 (males 63.9; females 73.1) (Source: Goskomstat USSR).

# KAZAKHSTAN

*Statistical Survey*

**EMPLOYMENT** (ISIC Major Divisions, annual averages, '000 persons)*

|  | 1990 | 1991 | 1992 |
|---|---|---|---|
| Agriculture, hunting, forestry and fishing | 1,686 | 1,715 | 1,762 |
| Mining and quarrying | 235 | 251 | 257 |
| Manufacturing | 1,247 | 1,218 | 1,160 |
| Electricity, gas and water | 66 | 73 | 83 |
| Construction | 833 | 690 | 681 |
| Trade, restaurants and hotels | 470 | 461 | 437 |
| Transport, storage and communications | 704 | 700 | 665 |
| Financing, insurance, real estate and business services | 40 | 42 | 46 |
| Community, social and personal services | 1,867 | 1,901 | 1,906 |
| Activities not adequately defined | 415 | 443 | 359 |
| **Total** | **7,563** | **7,494** | **7,356** |

* Figures refer to employees (including members of producers' co-operatives).

Source: International Labour Office, *Year Book of Labour Statistics*.

## Agriculture

**PRINCIPAL CROPS** ('000 metric tons)

|  | 1991 | 1992 | 1993 |
|---|---|---|---|
| Wheat | 6,889 | 18,285* | 12,500* |
| Rice (paddy) | 521 | 468* | 400* |
| Barley | 3,085 | 8,511* | 6,850* |
| Maize | 330 | 368* | 300* |
| Rye | 480 | 533* | 400* |
| Oats | 231 | 727* | 600* |
| Millet | 235 | 448* | 200* |
| Sorghum | 27† | 78* | 50* |
| Other cereals | 136 | 230* | 200* |
| Potatoes | 2,143 | 2,570 | 2,300 |
| Peas (dry) | n.a. | 104* | 100* |
| Soybeans | 16 | 13* | 18† |
| Sunflower seed | 109 | 98 | 192* |
| Rapeseed | 20* | 23† | 25† |
| Cottonseed | 177* | 150* | 165† |
| Cabbages |  | 225* | 172* |
| Tomatoes |  | 380* | 320* |
| Cucumbers and gherkins | 955 | 120* | 113* |
| Onions (dry) |  | 80* | 85* |
| Carrots |  | 48* | 40* |
| Other vegetables |  | 95 | 70 |
| Watermelons | 120 | 250 | 202 |
| Grapes | 66 | 63 | 85† |
| Sugar beets | 726 | 1,160 | 900 |
| Apples | n.a. | 95* | 95* |
| Pears | n.a. | 14* | 7† |
| Peaches and nectarines | n.a. | 19* | 22† |
| Plums | n.a. | 26† | 16† |
| Tobacco (leaves) | 4 | 2* | 3† |
| Cotton (lint) | 94 | 79* | 86* |

* Unofficial figure.
† FAO estimate(s). Data for watermelons include melons, pumpkins and squash.

Source: mainly FAO, *Production Yearbook*.

**LIVESTOCK** ('000 head at 1 January)

|  | 1991 | 1992 | 1993 |
|---|---|---|---|
| Horses | 1,626 | 1,510* | 1,500* |
| Asses | n.a. | 45* | 45* |
| Cattle | 9,756 | 9,084 | 8,313 |
| Buffaloes | n.a. | 120* | 110* |
| Camels | 143 | 60* | 60* |
| Pigs | 3,224 | 2,794 | 2,459 |
| Sheep and goats† | 35,657 | 34,600 | 33,650 |
| Poultry | 59,899 | 58,000† | 57,000* |

* FAO estimate.
† Of which sheep comprise an estimated 98%.
‡ Unofficial figure.

Source: mainly FAO, *Production Yearbook*.

**LIVESTOCK PRODUCTS** ('000 metric tons)

|  | 1991 | 1992 | 1993 |
|---|---|---|---|
| Beef and veal | 724 | 580* | 551* |
| Mutton and lamb | 260 | 239† | 230† |
| Goat meat | 16* | 7† | 7† |
| Pig meat | 274 | 260* | 235* |
| Poultry meat | 185 | 190* | 180† |
| Other meat | 65 | 68 | 65 |
| Cows' milk | 5,496 | 4,948* | 4,500* |
| Sheep's milk† | 20 | 20 | 20 |
| Goats' milk† | 39 | 32 | 34 |
| Cheese | n.a. | 50.0† | 53.0† |
| Butter | 75.8 | 70.0* | 65.0* |
| Hen eggs | 225.7* | 190.8† | 185.0† |
| Honey | n.a. | 30.0† | 28.0† |
| Wool: |  |  |  |
| greasy | 104.4 | 105.0† | 100.0† |
| clean | 62.6 | 63.0† | 60.0† |

* Unofficial figure.  † FAO estimates.

Source: FAO, *Production Yearbook*.

## Fishing

(metric tons, live weight)

|  | 1991 | 1992* |
|---|---|---|
| Freshwater bream | 22,152 | 21,430 |
| Common carp | 1,553 | 1,503 |
| Crucian carp | 5,995 | 5,800 |
| Roach | 2,461 | 2,380 |
| Silver carp | 1,892 | 1,830 |
| Hoven's carp | 9,835 | 9,520 |
| Northern pike | 1,227 | 1,187 |
| Wels (Som) catfish | 2,025 | 1,958 |
| European perch | 1,167 | 1,130 |
| Pike-perch | 4,213 | 4,080 |
| Sturgeon | 1,766 | 1,708 |
| Azov tyulka | 27,200 | 26,310 |
| **Total catch** (incl. others) | **82,690** | **80,000** |

* FAO estimates.

Source: FAO, *Yearbook of Fishery Statistics*.

## Mining

('000 metric tons, unless otherwise indicated)

|  | 1991 | 1992 | 1993 |
|---|---|---|---|
| Hard coal | 130,382 | 126,543 | 111,874 |
| Brown coal | 3,919 | 4,490 | 4,673 |
| Crude petroleum* | 26,580 | 25,794 | 19,287 |
| Natural gas (million cu m) | 7,885 | 8,112 | 5,416 |
| Iron ore | 21,993 | 17,671 | n.a. |

* Including gas condensate.

**Crude petroleum** (estimated production, '000 metric tons): 16,800 in 1994.

**Gold** (estimated production, metric tons): 12 in 1992; 13 in 1993.

# KAZAKHSTAN

## Industry

**SELECTED PRODUCTS**
('000 metric tons, unless otherwise indicated)

|  | 1989 | 1990 | 1991 |
|---|---|---|---|
| Margarine | 86.1 | 71.4 | 47.6 |
| Cotton yarn | 41.7 | 39.9 | 36.9 |
| Fabrics ('000 sq metres) | 329,811 | 325,461 | 248,708 |
| Footwear ('000 pairs) | 35,189 | 36,464 | 35,410 |
| Sulphuric acid | 1,896 | 3,151 | 2,815 |
| Synthetic rubber | 33.4 | 32.0 | 25.6 |
| Rubber tyres ('000) | 2,450 | 2,633 | 3,029 |
| Coke (6% humidity) | 4,137 | 3,711 | 3,404 |
| Building bricks (million) | 2,468 | 2,285 | 2,126 |
| Pig-iron | 5,279 | 5,226 | 4,952 |
| Crude steel | 6,831 | 6,754 | 6,377 |
| Electric energy (million kWh) | 89,657 | 87,379 | 86,128 |

**1992:** Cotton yarn 38,600 metric tons; Rubber tyres 2,904,000; Pig-iron 4,666,000 metric tons; Electric energy 84,300 million kWh.
**1993:** Electric energy 76,112 million kWh.

## Finance

**CURRENCY AND EXCHANGE RATES**
**Monetary Units**
100 tein = 1 tenge.

**Sterling and Dollar Equivalents** (30 November 1994)
£1 sterling = 68.87 tenge;
US $1 = 44.00 tenge;
1,000 tenge = £14.52 = $22.73.

Note: The tenge was introduced on 15 November 1993, replacing the Russian (formerly Soviet) rouble at an exchange rate of 1 tenge = 500 roubles. On 18 November the rate was adjusted to 250 roubles per tenge. Based on the official rate of exchange, the average value of the Soviet currency (roubles per US dollar) was: 0.6274 in 1989; 0.5856 in 1990; 0.5819 in 1991. However, a multiple exchange rate system was in operation, with separate non-commercial and tourist rates. A commercial exchange rate was introduced on 1 November 1990, replacing the official rate for most transactions. The commercial rate (roubles per US dollar) was: 1.692 at 31 December 1990; 1.671 at 31 December 1991. Between November 1989 and April 1991 the tourist exchange rate valued the rouble at one-tenth of the official rate. In April 1991 this rate, renamed the 'special rate', was set at $1 = 27.6 roubles. It was subsequently adjusted. The average market exchange rate in 1991 was $1 = 31.2 roubles. Following the dissolution of the USSR in December 1991, Russia and several other former Soviet republics retained the rouble as their monetary unit. The average interbank market rate in 1992 was $1 = 222.1 Russian roubles. Some of the figures in this Survey are still in terms of roubles.

**BUDGET** ('000 million roubles)*

| Revenue | 1991 | 1992 | 1993† |
|---|---|---|---|
| Current revenue | 19.3 | 278.6 | 999.0 |
| Taxation | 17.7 | 261.0 | 944.9 |
| Income taxes | 9.9 | 91.6 | 276.0 |
| Individual | 3.1 | 29.9 | 77.2 |
| Corporate | 6.8 | 61.7 | 198.8 |
| Taxes on property | — | 2.7 | 2.1 |
| Taxes on goods and services | 6.6 | 88.1 | 301.6 |
| Turnover tax/value added tax | 4.4 | 72.5 | 218.4 |
| Excises | 1.5 | 8.7 | 83.2 |
| Taxes on international trade | — | 28.5 | 96.1 |
| Taxes on natural resources | 0.7 | 9.1 | 76.1 |
| Tax for Investment Fund | — | 39.8 | 190.8 |
| Non-tax revenue | 1.6 | 15.8 | 54.2 |
| of which Foreign economic activities | — | 1.4 | 21.6 |
| Capital revenue | — | 0.6 | 2.2 |
| Grants | 4.2 | 20.7 | 30.0 |
| Net transfers from USSR budget | 4.2 | — | — |
| **Total** | 23.5 | 298.2 | 1,031.3 |

| Expenditure | 1991 | 1992 | 1993† |
|---|---|---|---|
| Financing of the economy | 12.9 | 78.6 | 207.4 |
| Investment Fund | — | 34.6 | 190.8 |
| Fund for Natural Resources | — | 5.6 | 24.1 |
| Foreign economic activities | — | 68.7 | 135.0 |
| Financing of social and cultural programmes | 14.2 | 96.9 | 406.2 |
| Education | 6.3 | 47.1 | 198.7 |
| Health care | 3.0 | 26.0 | 101.6 |
| Social security | 4.3 | 16.6 | 78.9 |
| Other | 0.6 | 7.2 | 27.0 |
| Defence, public order and safety | — | 23.7 | 140.8 |
| State authorities and administration | 1.0 | 9.3 | 44.6 |
| Other purposes | 2.9 | 27.4 | 80.7 |
| Adjustments | — | 43.1 | — |
| Strategic defence | — | 10.8 | — |
| External interest payments due | — | 32.3 | — |
| **Total** | 30.9 | 387.4 | 1,229.7 |

\* Figures represent a consolidation of the operations of the central Government and local governments, excluding extrabudgetary units and social-security schemes.
† Forecasts.

**INTERNATIONAL RESERVES** (US $ million at 31 December)

|  | 1992 |
|---|---|
| Foreign exchange | 120.4 |

**MONEY SUPPLY** (million roubles at 31 December)

|  | 1991 | 1992 |
|---|---|---|
| Currency outside banks | 13,959 | 154,271 |

**COST OF LIVING** (Consumer price index; base: 1992 = 100)

|  | 1991 | 1993 |
|---|---|---|
| Food | 4.7 | 2,297 |
| Clothing | 4.7 | 1,606 |
| Rent | n.a. | 16,258 |
| **All items** (incl. others) | 3.3 | 2,265 |

Source: International Labour Office, *Year Book of Labour Statistics*.

**NATIONAL ACCOUNTS**
**Net Material Product** (million roubles at current prices)

|  | 1990 | 1991 | 1992 |
|---|---|---|---|
| Agriculture and forestry | 13,962 | 22,862 | 505,487 |
| Industry* | 7,003 | 24,764 | 430,360 |
| Construction | 5,338 | 9,022 | 62,402 |
| Transport and communications | 3,257 | 5,666 | 14,150 |
| Trade and catering | 1,602 | 2,682 | 15,165 |
| Other material services | 2,196 | 1,837 | 32,041 |
| **Total** | 33,358 | 66,833 | 1,059,605 |

\* Principally mining, manufacturing, electricity, gas and water.

# KAZAKHSTAN

## BALANCE OF PAYMENTS (US $ million)*

| | 1990 | 1991 | 1992 |
|---|---|---|---|
| Merchandise exports | 14,270 | 10,210 | 7,370 |
| Merchandise imports | −24,550 | −13,370 | −9,040 |
| **Trade balance** | −10,280 | −3,160 | −1,670 |
| Services and transfers (net) | 7,290 | 1,860 | −410 |
| **Current balance** | −2,990 | −1,300 | −2,080 |
| Foreign direct investment (net) | — | — | 100 |
| Other capital (net) | −260 | 30 | −160 |
| Net errors and omissions | n.a. | n.a. | −50 |
| **Overall balance** | n.a. | n.a. | −2,200 |

* Figures are rounded to the nearest $10 million.

# External Trade

## PRINCIPAL COMMODITIES (million roubles at domestic prices)

| Imports f.o.b. | 1989 | 1990 |
|---|---|---|
| Petroleum and gas | 1,447 | 1,181 |
| Electric energy | 371 | 420 |
| Iron and steel | 1,040 | 986 |
| Non-ferrous metals | 272 | 275 |
| Chemicals and chemical products | 1,703 | 1,727 |
| Products of machine-building industry | 5,359 | 5,510 |
| Wood and paper products | 988 | 832 |
| Construction materials | 313 | 331 |
| Products of light industry | 3,113 | 3,374 |
| Products of food industry | 1,871 | 1,880 |
| Agricultural products (unprocessed) | 457 | 392 |
| **Total** (incl. others) | 17,569 | 17,830 |
| USSR (former) | 14,571 | 14,314 |
| Other countries | 2,998 | 3,516 |

| Exports f.o.b. | 1989 | 1990 |
|---|---|---|
| Petroleum and gas | 875 | 795 |
| Electric energy | 224 | 233 |
| Coal | 312 | 306 |
| Iron and steel | 1,077 | 1,036 |
| Non-ferrous metals | 791 | 777 |
| Chemicals and chemical products | 1,121 | 1,082 |
| Products of machine-building industry | 836 | 786 |
| Products of light industry | 1,625 | 1,536 |
| Products of food industry | 617 | 612 |
| Agricultural products (unprocessed) | 1,146 | 1,764 |
| **Total** (incl. others) | 9,094 | 9,350 |
| USSR (former) | 8,201 | 8,443 |
| Other countries | 893 | 906 |

**1994** (US $ million): Imports 3,488.1 (former USSR 2,202.1); Exports 3,075.6 (former USSR 1,809.7).

## PRINCIPAL TRADING PARTNERS
(million roubles at domestic prices)
### Trade with the former USSR

| Imports f.o.b. | 1991 | 1992 |
|---|---|---|
| Azerbaijan | 291 | 3,424 |
| Belarus | 340 | 14,238 |
| Kyrgyzstan | 544 | 9,313 |
| Russia | 8,720 | 257,722 |
| Tajikistan | 175 | 1,445 |
| Turkmenistan | 265 | 9,830 |
| Ukraine | 1,669 | 37,931 |
| Uzbekistan | 866 | 12,705 |
| **Total** (incl. others) | 13,220 | 346,942 |

| Exports f.o.b. | 1991 | 1992 |
|---|---|---|
| Azerbaijan | 141 | 5,876 |
| Belarus | 622 | 8,958 |
| Kyrgyzstan | 477 | 8,073 |
| Latvia | 232 | 900 |
| Lithuania | 179 | 1,950 |
| Moldova | 147 | 1,112 |
| Russia | 8,515 | 246,703 |
| Tajikistan | 342 | 3,700 |
| Turkmenistan | 208 | 9,519 |
| Ukraine | 1,339 | 33,638 |
| Uzbekistan | 1,266 | 20,544 |
| **Total** (incl. others) | 13,745 | 342,021 |

**Trade with all other countries** (US $ million): *Imports:* 1,912 in 1991; 1,523 in 1992. *Exports:* 776 in 1991; 1,489 in 1992.

# Transport

## RAILWAYS (traffic)

| | 1989 | 1990 | 1991 |
|---|---|---|---|
| Passenger-km (million) | 18,921 | 19,734 | 19,365 |
| Freight net ton-km (million) | 409,573 | 406,963 | 374,230 |

Source: UN, *Statistical Yearbook*.

# Communications Media

| | 1989 | 1990 | 1991 |
|---|---|---|---|
| Telephones ('000 main lines in use) | 1,620* | 1,740* | 1,876 |

* Estimate.

Source: UN, *Statistical Yearbook*.

**Book production** (1992): 1,226 titles; 30,512,000 copies (Source: UNESCO, *Statistical Yearbook*).

# Education
(1989/90)

| | Institutions | Students |
|---|---|---|
| Secondary schools | 8,064 | 3,021,070 |
| Secondary specialized schools | 244 | 255,400 |
| Higher schools (incl. universities) | 55 | 285,600 |

**1990/91:** 287,400 students in higher schools.
**1993/94:** 1,227,130 students in primary schools; 1,782,471 students in general secondary schools.

(Source: UNESCO, *Statistical Yearbook*).

# Directory

## The Constitution

The new Constitution of the Republic of Kazakhstan was adopted on 28 January 1993 and included among its principal provisions the following:

All nationalities in Kazakhstan are guaranteed equal status; Kazakh is the state language, although Russian is used as a language of inter-ethnic communication. The President of the Republic (who must be a fluent speaker of Kazakh) is elected by universal adult suffrage for a five-year term. The President is Head of State and holds supreme executive power in conjunction with the Council of Ministers. The Prime Minister, Deputy Prime Ministers and Ministers of Foreign Affairs, Defence, Finance and Internal Affairs, together with the Chairman of the State Committee for National Security and all ambassadors, are appointed by the President; other ministers are appointed by the Prime Minister. Ministerial appointments are subject to parliamentary approval. The highest legislative body is the Supreme Kenges, which is directly elected by universal suffrage for a period of five years. A Constitutional Court has supreme jurisdiction in constitutional matters.

## The Government

### HEAD OF STATE

**President of the Republic of Kazakhstan:** NURSULTAN A. NAZARBAYEV (elected 1 December 1991; a referendum on 29 April 1995 extended his term of office until 1 December 2000).

**Vice-President:** YERIK M. ASANBAYEV.

### COUNCIL OF MINISTERS
(May 1995)

**Prime Minister:** AKEZHAN MAGZHAN-ULY KAZHEGELDIN.
**First Deputy Prime Ministers:** VITALY LEONIDOVICH METTE, NIGMETZHAN KABATAY-ULY ISINGARIN.
**Deputy Prime Ministers:** AKMETZHAN SMAGUL-ULY YESIMOV, VIKTOR VASILYEVICH SOBOLEV, IMANGALY TASMAGAMBETOV.
**Chief of Staff of the Council of Ministers:** BERDIBEK SAPARBAYEV.
**Minister of Foreign Affairs:** KASYMZHOMART KEMEL-ULY TOKAYEV.
**Minister of Defence:** SAGADAT KOZHAKHMET-ULY NURMAGAMBETOV.
**Minister of Finance:** ALEKSANDR SERGEYEVICH PAVLOV.
**Minister of Internal Affairs:** BOLAT ABDRAKHMAN-ULY BAYEKENOV.
**Minister of Geology and Protection of Natural Resources:** SERIKBEK ZHUSUPBEK-ULY DAUKEYEV.
**Minister of Youth, Sport and Tourism:** BYRGANYM SARYK-KYZY AITIMOVA.
**Minister of Health:** VASILY NIKOLAYEVICH DEVYATKO.
**Minister of Culture:** TALGAT ASYL-ULY MAMASHEV.
**Minister of Science and New Technologies:** VLADIMIR SERGEYEVICH SHKOLNIK.
**Minister of the Petroleum and Gas Industry:** NURLAN UTEP-ULY BALGYNBAYEV.
**Minister of Education:** YEREZHEP ABULKHAIR-ULY NAMBETKAZIYEV.
**Minister of the Press and the Media:** ALTYNBEK SARSENBAY-ULY SARSENBAYEV.
**Minister of Trade and Industry:** GARRY GVIDOVICH SHTOLK.
**Minister of Agriculture:** ZHANIBEK SALIM-ULY KARIBZHANOV.
**Minister of Social Welfare:** BAYKARIM WILLIAM-ULY TOTENOV.
**Minister of Regional Construction:** AMALBEK KAZYSAT-ULY TSHANOV.
**Minister of Transport and Communications:** SERIK KARABATYR-ULY ALIGOZGANOV.
**Minister of Labour:** PETR IVANOVICH SHKREPA.
**Minister of Ecology and Bioresources:** SVYATOSLAV ALEKSANDROVICH MEDVEDEV.
**Minister of the Economy:** ALTAY ABLAY-ULY TLEUBERDIN.
**Minister of Energy and Coal:** VIKTOR KHRAPUNOV.
**Minister of Justice:** NAGASHYBAY AMANGALY-ULY SHAYKENOV.

### Chairmen of Principal State Committees

**Chairman of the State Committee for the Defence Industry:** KADYR KARKABAT-ULY BAYKENOV.
**Chairman of the State Committee for Emergency Situations:** NIKOLAY MIKHAILOVICH MAKIYEVSKY.
**Chairman of the State Committee for Financial Control:** SEYT-SULTAN SULEYMEN-ULY AIMBETOV.
**Chairman of the State Committee for Land Use and Land Relations:** BAKYT SAGYNDYK-ULY OSPANOV.
**Chairman of the State Comittee for the Management of State Property:** SARYBAY SULTAN-ULY KALMURZAYEV.
**Chairman of the State Committee for Price and Anti-Monopoly Policy:** PETR VLADIMIROVICH SVOIK.
**Chairman of the State Committee for Privatization:** (vacant).
**Chairman of the State Committee for Statistics and Analysis:** VLADIMIR IVANOVICH GORYACHKOVSKY.

### MINISTRIES

**Ministry of Agriculture:** Almaty, pl. Respubliki 15; tel. (3272) 63-44-44.
**Ministry of Culture:** Almaty.
**Ministry of Defence:** Almaty; tel. (3272) 69-35-28.
**Ministry of Ecology and Bioresources:** 480091 Almaty, Panfilova 106; tel. (3272) 63-12-73; telex 251232; fax (3272) 63-52-44.
**Ministry of the Economy:** Almaty, pr. Ablaikhana 97.
**Ministry of Education:** Almaty, Jambula 25; tel. (3272) 61-03-09.
**Ministry of Energy and Coal:** Almaty, Bogenbay Batyr 142; tel. (3272) 62-64-10.
**Ministry of Finance:** Almaty, pr. Ablaikhana 97; tel. (3272) 62-40-75; fax (3272) 62-27-70.
**Ministry of Foreign Affairs:** Almaty, Zheltoksan 167; tel. (3272) 63-25-38; fax (3272) 61-02-12.
**Ministry of Geology and Protection of Natural Resources:** Almaty.
**Ministry of Health:** Almaty, pr. Ablaikhana 63; tel. (3272) 33-46-11; fax (3272) 33-17-19.
**Ministry of Internal Affairs:** Almaty, Kalinina 95; tel. (3272) 62-84-57.
**Ministry of Justice:** Almaty, Aiteke bi 67; tel. (3272) 62-64-01; fax (3272) 63-84-31.
**Ministry of Labour:** Almaty.
**Ministry of the Petroleum and Gas Industry:** Almaty.
**Ministry of the Press and the Media:** 480013 Almaty, pl. Respubliky 13; tel. (3272) 67-93-97; fax (3272) 63-66-34.
**Ministry of Regional Construction:** Almaty.
**Ministry of Science and New Technologies:** Almaty.
**Ministry of Social Welfare:** Almaty, Karla Marksa 122; tel. (3272) 63-67-78.
**Ministry of Trade and Industry:** Almaty, pr. Ablaikhana 93–95; tel. (3272) 62-38-12.
**Ministry of Transport and Communications:** 480083 Almaty, pr. Seyfullina 458; tel. (3272) 39-28-87; fax (3272) 39-32-55.
**Ministry of Youth, Sport and Tourism:** Almaty, pr. Abaya 48; tel. (3272) 67-39-86.

### Principal State Committees

**State Committee for the Defence Industry:** Almaty.
**State Committee for Emergency Situations:** Almaty.
**State Committee for Financial Control:** Almaty.
**State Committee for Land Use and Land Relations:** Almaty.
**State Committee for the Management of State Property:** Almaty, pr. Ablaikhana 93–95; tel. (3272) 62-85-62.
**State Committee for Price and Anti-Monopoly Policy:** Almaty; tel. (3272) 69-50-62.
**State Committee for Privatization:** Almaty, pr. Ablaikhana 93–95; tel. (3272) 62-85-62.
**State Committee for Statistics and Analysis:** Almaty, pr. Abaya 125; tel. (3272) 62-14-61.

## Legislature

### SUPREME KENGES

**Chairman:** ABISH KEKILBAYEV; 480091 Almaty, Government House; tel. (3272) 62-78-30.

# KAZAKHSTAN

## General Election, 7 March 1994

| | Seats |
|---|---|
| People's Unity Party | 33 |
| Confederation of Kazakh Trade Unions | 11 |
| People's Congress Party of Kazakhstan | 9 |
| Socialist Party of Kazakhstan | 8 |
| Kazakhstan Peasants' Union | 4 |
| Slavic Movement—Lad | 4 |
| Other parties and groups | 6 |
| Independent candidates | 59 |
| Candidates from the 'President's List' | 42 |
| **Total** | **176*** |

* The 177th seat was filled at a later date, following a judicial ruling.

The Supreme Kenges resigned in March 1995 (see Recent History).

## Political Organizations

**Communist Party of Kazakhstan (CPK):** Almaty; suspended Aug. 1991, re-registered March 1994.

**Kazakhstan Peasants' Union:** Almaty; agrarian party.

**People's Congress Party of Kazakhstan:** Almaty; f. 1991; advocates civil peace; represents all ethnic groups in Kazakhstan; Chair. OLZHAS SULEYMENOV.

**People's Unity Party (PUP):** 480013 Almaty, pl. Respubliky 13, Rm 501; tel. (3272) 63-77-89; f. 1993, originally as a socio-political movement, before becoming a political party; centrist; opposes radical nationalism, promotes social and ethnic harmony; Leader NURSULTAN NAZARBAYEV; Chair. KUANYSH SULTANOV; Chair. of Political Bd SERIK ABDRAKHMANOV.

**Republican Party—Azat:** Almaty; f. 1992 by merger of three nationalist opposition parties: the Azat (Freedom) movement, the Republican Party and the Zheltoksan (December) National-Democratic Party; Chair. KAMAL ORMANTAYEV.

**Slavic Movement—Lad:** 480012 Almaty, Vinogradova 85, kv. 408; tel. (3272) 63-38-20; f. 1992; socio-cultural organization representing the rights of the Slavic communities; Chair. ALEKSANDRA V. DOKUCHAYEVA; 30,000 mems.

**Socialist Party of Kazakhstan (SPK):** Almaty; f. 1991 to replace Communist Party of Kazakhstan; Co-Chair. YERMUKHAN YERTYSBAYEV; 50,000 mems.

Smaller parties include the radical nationalist Kazakh movement, Alash, and the Russian nationalist group, Yedinstvo (Unity).

## Diplomatic Representation

### EMBASSIES IN KAZAKHSTAN

**Afghanistan:** Almaty, pr. Abaya 16, kv. 30; tel. (3272) 62-95-19; Chargé d'affaires a.i.: ABDUL AZIZ ILYASSI.

**Armenia:** 480075 Almaty, pr. Seyfullina 579, 7th Floor; tel. and fax (3272) 69-29-08; Chargé d'affaires a.i.: ARMEN MELIKIAN.

**Bulgaria:** Almaty, pr. Ablaikhana 74, kv. 165; tel. (3272) 33-80-17; Chargé d'affaires a.i.: YORDAN TRENCHEV.

**Canada:** Almaty, pr. Abaya 157, kv. 21/22; tel. (3272) 50-93-81; fax (3272) 50-93-80; Chargé d'affaires a.i.: MICHAEL VAINOVICH.

**China, People's Republic:** Almaty, Furmanova 137; tel. (3272) 63-49-66; fax (3272) 63-92-91; Ambassador: CHEN DI.

**Cuba:** Almaty, Zenkova 70, kv. 23; tel. and fax (3272) 61-59-25; Chargé d'affaires a.i.: ROBERTO CRUZ GALINDO.

**Egypt:** Almaty, Zenkova 59; tel. (3272) 60-16-22; Chargé d'affaires a.i.: FAROUK MUHAMMAD.

**France:** 480110 Almaty, Furmanova 173; tel. (3272) 50-62-36; fax (3272) 50-61-59; Ambassador: BERTRAND PESSARD DE FOUCAULT.

**Georgia:** Almaty, Gornaya 246; tel. (3272) 64-86-53; Ambassador: TEIMURAZ GOGOLADZE.

**Germany:** 480110 Almaty, Furmanova 173; tel. (3272) 50-61-55; telex 251409; fax (3272) 50-62-76; Ambassador: Dr EIKE BRACKLO.

**Hungary:** Almaty, Tulebayeva 162, kv. 29; tel. (3272) 63-64-37; fax (3272) 50-70-99; Ambassador: JÓZSEF TORMA.

**India:** Almaty, Internatsionalnaya 71; tel. (3272) 67-14-11; fax (3272) 67-67-69; Ambassador: RAJIV SEKRI.

**Iran:** Almaty, Kabanbay Batyr 119; tel. (3272) 67-78-46; fax (3272) 54-27-54; Ambassador: RASUL ESLAMI.

**Israel:** Almaty, Zheltoksan 87; tel. (3272) 62-48-17; fax (3272) 62-23-36; Ambassador: BENZ CARMEL.

**Italy:** Almaty, Samal 2-69, 6th Floor; tel. (3272) 54-17-99; telex 251567; fax (3272) 54-19-98; Ambassador: MAURIZIO TEUCCI.

**Japan:** Almaty, Samal 1, d. 36; tel. (3272) 53-32-04; Ambassador: AKIRA MATSUI.

**Korea, Democratic People's Republic:** Almaty, 'Ainabulak-3', Voronyezhskaya 58; tel. (3272) 35-08-53; fax (3272) 25-27-66; Ambassador: NAM LI GIL.

**Korea, Republic:** Almaty, Jarkentskaya 2/77; tel. (3272) 53-26-60; fax (3272) 50-70-59; Ambassador: KIM CHANG-KEON.

**Kyrgyzstan:** Almaty, Hotel Kazakhstan, Rm 1310; tel. (3272) 61-92-03; Ambassador: TILEKTESH ISHEMKULOV.

**Lebanon:** Almaty, Lenina 52, Hotel Kazakhstan, Rm 1318; tel. (3272) 61-92-11; Ambassador: ASSIF NASSER.

**Libya:** Almaty, Satpayeva 10-2; tel. (3272) 62-67-17; fax (3272) 62-22-23; Chargé d'affaires a.i.: OMAR ALI GEIT.

**Lithuania:** Almaty, pr. Abaya 68/74; tel. (3272) 42-75-55; fax (3272) 42-68-90; Chargé d'affaires a.i.: JUOZAS AŠEMBERGAS.

**Mongolia:** Almaty, Kazybek bi, d. 18 (ug. 8 Marta); tel. (3272) 60-17-23; Ambassador: ERDENIYN BYAMBAJAV.

**Pakistan:** 480004 Almaty, Tulebaeva 25; tel. (3272) 33-35-48; fax (3272) 33-13-00; Ambassador: RIAZ MOHAMMAD KHAN.

**Poland:** Almaty, Lenina 44, kv. 99; tel. (3272) 61-49-24; fax (3272) 61-43-47; Chargé d'affaires a.i.: PIOTR BORAWSKI.

**Romania:** 480100 Almaty, Pushkina 97; tel. (3272) 61-36-83; fax (3272) 63-69-73; Ambassador: MIHAI ENESCU.

**Russia:** Almaty, Jandosova 4; tel. (3272) 44-64-91; fax (3272) 44-83-23; Ambassador: VYACHESLAV I. DOLGOV.

**Tajikistan:** Almaty, Emelyeva 70; tel. (3272) 61-17-60; fax (3272) 61-02-25; Ambassador: SAID SHARIPOV.

**Turkey:** 480100 Almaty, Tole bi 29; tel. (3272) 61-81-53; telex 251226; fax (3272) 50-62-08; Ambassador: MUSTAFA AŞULLA.

**Ukraine:** Almaty, Lenina 52, Hotel Kazakhstan, Rm 611; tel. (3272) 61-90-33; fax (3272) 61-90-34; Ambassador: VIKTOR V. BOGATYR.

**United Kingdom:** 480110 Almaty, Furmanova 173; tel. (3272) 50-61-91; telex 613398; fax (3272) 50-62-60; Ambassador: NOEL JONES.

**USA:** 480012 Almaty, Furmanova 97–99; tel. (3272) 63-39-05; fax (3272) 63-38-83; Ambassador: WILLIAM H. COURTNEY.

**Uzbekistan:** Almaty, Baribayeva 36; tel. (3272) 61-83-16; Ambassador: NASIRJAN N. YAKUBOV.

## Judicial System

**Chairman of the Supreme Court:** MIKHAIL MALAKHOV.
**Procurator-General:** Gen. ZHARMAKHAN A. TUYAKBAYEV.
**Chairman of the Constitutional Court:** MURAT BAYMAKHANOV.

## Religion

The major religion of the Kazakhs is Islam. They are almost exclusively Sunni Muslims of the Hanafi school. The Russian Orthodox Church is the dominant Christian denomination; it is attended mainly by Slavs. There are also Protestant Churches (mainly Baptists), as well as a Roman Catholic presence (with adherents totalling an estimated 314,781 at 31 December 1993).

### ISLAM

The Kazakhs were converted to Islam only in the early 19th century, and for many years there remained elements of animist practices among them. Over the period 1985–90 the number of mosques in Kazakhstan increased from 25 to 60, 12 of which were newly-built. By 1991 there were an estimated 230 Muslim religious communities functioning in Kazakhstan and an Islamic institute had been opened in Almaty. The Islamic revival intensified following Kazakhstan's independence from the USSR, and during 1991–94 some 4,000 mosques were reported to have been opened. Until 1990 the Muslims of Kazakhstan were under the spiritual jurisdiction of the muftiate of Central Asia and Kazakhstan, which was based in Tashkent (Uzbekistan). In 1990 the Muslim authorities in Kazakhstan established an independent muftiate.

**Mufti of Kazakhstan:** RATBEK Haji RATBEK NYSANBAY-ULY, Almaty.

### CHRISTIANITY

#### The Roman Catholic Church

**Apostolic Administrator:** Rt Rev. JAN PAWEŁ LENGA, (Titular Bishop of Arba), 470077 Karaganda, Oktyabrskaya 25; tel. and fax (3212) 22-14-72.

# KAZAKHSTAN

## The Press

In 1989 there were 453 officially-registered newspaper titles published in Kazakhstan, of which 160 were in Kazakh. Newspapers were also published in Russian, Uighur, German and Korean. There were 94 periodicals, including 31 in Kazakh.

### PRINCIPAL DAILY NEWSPAPERS

**Express:** 480044 Almaty, pr. Zhibek zholy 50; tel. (3272) 33-92-11; f. 1922; 5 a week; in Russian; Editor-in-Chief S. LESKOVSKY.

**Kazakhstanskaya Pravda** (Pravda of Kazakhstan): 480044 Almaty, Gogolya 39; tel. (3272) 63-05-86; f. 1920; 5 a week; publ. by the Council of Ministers; in Russian; Editor-in-Chief G. DILDYAYEV. (Suspended in 1994.)

**Khalyk Kenesi** (Councils of the People): 480002 Almaty, pr. Zhibek zholy 64; tel. (3272) 33-10-85; f. 1990; 5 a week; publ. by the Supreme Kenges; in Kazakh; Editor-in-Chief ZH. KENZHALIN.

**Yegemen Kazakhstan** Almaty, Gogolya 39; tel. (3272) 63-25-46; f. 1919; 6 a week; organ of the Council of Ministers; in Kazakh; Editor-in-Chief N. ORAZALIN.

### OTHER PUBLICATIONS

**Ana Tili:** 480091 Almaty, Zheltoksan 112; tel. (3272) 62-66-35; f. 1990; weekly; publ. by the Kazakh Tili society; in Kazakh; Editor-in-Chief ZH. BEISENBAYULY; circ. 30,000.

**Ara-Shmel** (Bumble-bee): Almaty, Gogolya 39; tel. (3272) 63-59-46; f. 1956; monthly; satirical; in Kazakh and Russian; Editor-in-Chief S. ZHUMABEKOV; circ. 53,799.

**Arai-Zaria** (Dawn): Almaty, Furmanova 53; tel. (3272) 32-29-45; f. 1987; monthly; publ. by the Ministry of Youth, Sport and Tourism; socio-political; Editor-in-Chief S. KUTTYKADAMOV.

**Aziya Kino** (Asian Cinema): 480100 Almaty, Tole bi 23A; tel. (3272) 61-86-55; f. 1994; monthly; in Russian and Kazakh; Editor-in-Chief G. ABIKEYEVA.

**Baldyrgan** (Sprout): 480044 Almaty, pr. Zhibek zholy 50; tel. (3272) 33-16-73; f. 1958; monthly; illustrated; for pre-school and first grades of school; in Kazakh; Editor-in-Chief T. MOLDAGALIYEV; circ. 150,000.

**Densaulik** (Health): Almaty, pr. Ablaikhana 63; f. 1990; monthly; organ of the Ministry of Health; in Kazakh; Editor-in-Chief L. IOFFE.

**Deutsche Allgemeine:** 480044 Almaty, pr. Zhibek zholy 50; tel. (3272) 33-42-69; in German; Editor-in-Chief KONSTANTIN EHRLICH; circ. 10,000.

**Dyelovaya Nedyelya** (Working Week): 480044 Almaty, pr. Zhibek zholy 50; tel. (3272) 33-59-48; f. 1992; weekly; in Russian; Editor-in-Chief O. CHERVINSKY.

**Ekonomika i Zhizn** (Economics and Life): 480091 Almaty, Zheltoksan 118; tel. (3272) 63-96-86; f. 1926; monthly; publ. by the Council of Ministers; in Russian; Editor-in-Chief M. T. SARSENOV; circ. 12,000.

**Karavan:** 480004 Almaty, Chaikovskogo 11; tel. (3272) 32-83-40; f. 1991; weekly; in Russian; Editor-in-Chief I. MELTSER.

**Kazakh Adebieti:** 480091 Almaty, pr. Ablaikhana 105; tel. (3272) 69-54-62; f. 1934; weekly; organ of the Union of Writers of Kazakhstan; in Kazakh; Editor-in-Chief A. ZHAKSYBAYEV.

**Kazakhstan:** Almaty, pl. Respubliky; tel. (3272) 62-37-27; f. 1992; weekly; publ. by the Ministry of the Press and the Media; economic reform; in English; Editor-in-Chief N. ORAZBEKOV.

**Kazakhstan Aielderi** (Women of Kazakhstan): 480044 Almaty, pr. Zhibek zholy 50; tel. (3272) 33-29-52; f. 1929; monthly; in Kazakh; Editor-in-Chief ZH. SOLTIYEVA; circ. 332,952.

**Kazakhstan Mektebi** (Kazakh School): 480004 Almaty, pr. Ablaikhana 34; tel. (3272) 39-76-65; f. 1925; monthly; journal of the Ministry of Education; in Kazakh; Editor-in-Chief S. ABISHEVA; circ. 10,000.

**Kazakhstan Mugalimi:** 480091 Almaty, pr. Ablaikhana 34; tel. (3272) 39-76-81; f. 1952; weekly; publ. by the Ministry of Education; in Kazakh; Editor-in-Chief ZH. TEMIRBEKOV; circ. 71,602.

**Khalyk Kongresi** (People's Congress): 480012 Almaty, Vinogradova 85; tel. (3272) 63-49-67; f. 1992; weekly; publ. by the People's Congress Party of Kazakhstan and the 'Nevada-Semipalatinsk' anti-nuclear movement; in Kazakh (also appears in Russian, as *Narodny Kongress*); Editor-in-Chief S. MURATBEKOV.

**Korye Ilbo:** 480044 Almaty, pr. Zhibek zholy 50; tel. (3272) 33-90-17; f. 1923; weekly; in Korean and Russian; Editor-in-Chief YAN WON SIK.

**Novoye Pokoleniye** (New Generation): 480091 Almaty, Zheltoksan 79; tel. (3272) 63-26-86; f. 1994; weekly; Editor-in-Chief V. TABDULLIN.

**Panorama:** 480091 Almaty, Mira 111; tel. (3272) 62-12-08; f. 1991; weekly; in Russian; Editor-in-Chief LERA TSOY.

**Parasat** (Intellect): 480044 Almaty, pr. Zhibek zholy 50; tel. (3272) 33-49-29; f. 1958; socio-political, literary, illustrated; in Kazakh; Editor-in-Chief S. ELUBAYEV; circ. 135,000.

**Prostor** (Wide Horizons): 480091 Almaty, pr. Ablaikhana 105; tel. (3272) 69-63-19; f. 1933; monthly; journal of the Union of Writers of Kazakhstan; fiction; in Russian; Editor-in-Chief R. V. PETROV; circ. 15,000.

**Russky Yazyk i Literatura** (Russian Language and Literature): 480091 Almaty, pr. Ablaikhana 34; tel. (3272) 39-76-68; f. 1962; monthly; journal of the Ministry of Education; in Russian; Editor-in-Chief B. S. MUKANOV; circ. 17,465.

**Shalkar:** 480044 Almaty, pr. Zhibek zholy 50; tel. (3272) 33-86-85; f. 1976; weekly; in Kazakh (in the Arabic script); Editor-in-Chief U. KADYRKHANOV; circ. 10,500.

**Soviety Kazakhstana** (Councils of Kazakhstan): 480002 Almaty, pr. Zhibek zholy 15; tel. (3272) 34-92-19; f. 1990; weekly; publ. by the Supreme Kenges; in Russian; Editor-in-Chief YU. GURSKY; circ. 30,000.

**Sport:** 480044 Almaty, pr. Zhibek zholy 50; tel. (3272) 33-92-90; f. 1959; weekly; publ. by the Ministry of Youth, Sport and Tourism; in Kazakh and Russian; Editor-in-Chief NESIP ZHUNUSPAYEV; circ. 20,000.

**Uighur Avazi:** 480044 Almaty, pr. Zhibek zholy 50; tel. (3272) 33-84-59; f. 1957; 2 a week; in Uighur; Editor-in-Chief I. AZAMATOV.

**Ukrainskiye Novini** (Ukrainian News): 480044 Almaty, pr. Zhibek zholy 50; tel. (3272) 33-17-11; f. 1994; weekly; in Ukrainian; Editor-in-Chief A. GARKAVETS.

**Ulan:** 480044 Almaty, pr. Zhibek zholy 50; tel. (3272) 33-80-03; f. 1930; weekly; in Kazakh; Editor-in-Chief S. KALIYEV; circ. 183,014.

**Zerde** (Intellect): 480044 Almaty, pr. Zhibek zholy 50; tel. (3272) 33-83-81; f. 1960; monthly; popular, scientific, technical; in Kazakh; Editor-in-Chief E. RAUSHANULY; circ. 68,629.

**Zhalyn:** 480002 Almaty, Lenina 7; tel. (3272) 33-22-21; f. 1969; monthly; in Kazakh; Editor-in-Chief M. KULKENOV.

**Zhuldyz** (Star): 480091 Almaty, pr. Ablaikhana 105; tel. (3272) 62-51-37; f. 1928; monthly; journal of the Union of Writers of Kazakhstan; literary, artistic, socio-political; in Kazakh; Editor-in-Chief MUKHTAR MAGAUIN; circ. 134,206.

### NEWS AGENCY

**KazTAG** (Kazakh Telegraph Agency): Almaty, pr. Ablaikhana 75; tel. (3272) 62-50-37; Dir AMANGELDY AKHMETALITOV.

## Publishers

**Gylym** (Science): 480100 Almaty, Pushkina 111–113; tel. (3272) 61-18-77; f. 1946; books on natural sciences, humanities and scientific research journals; Dir S. G. BAIMENOV; Editor-in-Chief M. A. AIMBETOV.

**Kainar** (Spring): 480124 Almaty, pr. Abaya 143; tel. (3272) 42-66-67; f. 1962; agriculture; Dir KH. A. TLEMISOV; Chief Editor I. I. ISKUZHIN.

**Kazakhskaya Entsiklopediya** (Kazakh Encyclopaedia): Almaty, pr. Ablaikhana 93–95; tel. (3272) 62-55-66; f. 1968; Chief Editor R. N. NURGALIYEV.

**Kazakhstan Publishing House:** 480124 Almaty, pr. Abaya 143; tel. (3272) 42-29-29; political and popular edns; Dir E. KH. SYZDYKOV; Chief Editor N. D. SITKO.

**Oner** (Art): 480124 Almaty, pr. Abaya 143; tel. (3272) 42-08-88; f. 1980; Dir S. S. ORAZALINOV; Chief Editor A. A. ASKAROV.

**Rauan** (Science): 480124 Almaty, pr. Abaya 143; tel. (3272) 42-25-37; f. 1947; fiction by young writers; Dir ZH. H. NUSKABAYEV; Editor-in-Chief K. KURMANOV.

**Zhazushy** (Writer): 480124 Almaty, pr. Abaya 143; tel. (3272) 42-28-49; fiction; Dir KALDARBEK NAIMANBAYEV.

## Radio and Television

**Kazakh State Television and Radio Broadcasting Corporation:** 480013 Almaty, Zheltoksan 175A; tel. (3272) 63-37-16; Pres. ASHIRBEK KOPESHEV.

**Kazakh Radio:** 480013 Almaty, Zheltoksan 175A; tel. (3272) 63-56-29; telex 251114; fax (3272) 63-12-07; f. 1923; broadcasts in Kazakh, Russian, Uighur, German and other minority languages; Gen. Dir A. N. MIDIKE.

**Kazakh Television:** 480013 Almaty, Zheltoksan 175A; tel. (3272) 69-51-88; fax (3272) 63-12-07; f. 1959; broadcasts in Kazakh, Uighur, Russian and German.

KAZAKHSTAN                                                                                                                    *Directory*

## Finance

(cap. = capital; dep. = deposits; res = reserves; brs = branches; amounts in roubles, unless otherwise indicated)

### BANKING

In 1990–91 the Almaty branch of the Soviet State Bank (Gosbank) was transformed into an independent Kazakh central bank (National Bank of Kazakhstan—NBK) and the establishment of private and public financial institutions was legalized. By the end of 1992 the banking system comprised the NBK, the Kazakhstan Savings Bank (renamed the People's Bank in January 1994, with 4,477 of the 5,035 bank branches in the country) and 157 other banks, 11 being co-operative banks and 48 privately owned.

#### Central Bank

**National Bank of Kazakhstan (NBK):** 480070 Almaty, Koktem-3 21; tel. (3272) 47-37-97; telex 251216; fax (3272) 50-60-90; Chair. Daulet Kh. Sembayev.

#### Other Banks

**Agroprombank:** Almaty; deals mainly with the agricultural sector; 231 brs.

**Center Bank—Kazakh Central Joint-Stock Bank:** 480096 Almaty, Bogenbay Batyr 248; tel. (3272) 50-99-66; telex 613856; fax (3272) 50-94-96; f. 1988 as Co-op Bank of the Almaty Union of Co-operatives; name changed 1991; cap. 4.5m. tenge, dep. 131.3m. tenge (Jan. 1995), res 12.4m. tenge (Jan. 1994); Chair. of Council Bakytbek R. Baiseytov; Chair. of Bd Jumangeldy R. Amankulov; 22 brs.

**Chimkent Co-op Bank—Soyuzbank:** 486018 Chimkent, pl. Lenina 2A; tel. (3252) 3-56-91; f. 1988; cap. 1m. (1988); commercial bank; Chair. B. Bektayev.

**Eximbank:** 480100 Almaty, Lenina 39; tel. (3272) 61-83-82; telex 251206; fax (3272) 61-57-04; fmrly br. of Vneshekonombank USSR, then Kazakh Republican Foreign Trade Bank, then Alem Bank Kazakhstan; cap. US $16.3m, dep. US $907.2m, res US $8.6m. (Jan. 1994); Chair. of Bd Berlin K. Irshiyev; more than 20 brs.

**Igilik-Bank:** 480091 Almaty, Tole bi 57; tel. (3272) 63-42-82; telex 251486; fax (3272) 50-62-90; f. 1991; Pres. and Chair. T. A. Abjarkenov.

**Kazdorbank:** 480091 Almaty, Gogolya 84; tel. (3272) 32-58-00; telex 251318; fax (3272) 32-24-95; f. 1989; commercial bank; cap. 689.4m., dep. 13,465.4m., res 298.0m. (Dec. 1992); Pres. Shamil H. Bekbulatov; Chair. Razia R. Achibayeva.

**KRAMDS Bank—Innovation Commercial Bank:** 480046 Almaty, Rozybakieva 101; tel. (3272) 46-29-18; telex 251309; fax (3272) 46-09-58; f. 1989; private commercial bank, financial subsidiary of KRAMDS Corpn; cap. US $7.5m. (Dec. 1994); Chair. of Bd Leonid Ablozhey; 40 brs.

**Kredsotsbank:** Almaty; commercial bank; deals mainly with housing management and municipal facilities.

**Neftechimbank—Commercial Bank for Oil and Chemical Industry Development:** 486024 Chimkent, Nekrasova; tel. (3252) 23-53-00; fax (3252) 24-69-78.

**People's Bank of Kazakhstan:** Almaty; f. 1991 as successor to republican br. of the all-Union Sberbank (Savings Bank of Kazakhstan), renamed Jan. 1994; 4,477 brs.

**Technopolice Bank:** 480013 Almaty, pl. Respubliki 13; tel. (3272) 63-26-74; telex 251265; fax (3272) 63-23-49; f. 1991; private commercial bank; 98% Russian ownership; cap. 174.8m., res 49.4m., dep. 5,091.7m. (Jan. 1993); Chair. Eduard O. Akopian; Man. Dir. Sergey F. Ustinov.

**Turanbank—Kazakh Corporation Bank:** 480091 Almaty, Aiteke bi 55; tel. (3272) 62-17-74; telex 251393; fax (3272) 62-29-31; f. 1922; cap. 63.9m. tenge, dep. 1,989.0m. tenge, res 90.3m. tenge (Jan. 1994); Chair. Oraz M. Beysenov; First Dep. Chair. Orynbasar Tokayev; 84 brs.

Foreign banks with branches in Almaty include the Bank of China (People's Republic of China), the Industrial and Commercial Bank of China (People's Republic of China), Dresdner Bank (Germany), Stolichny Bank (Russia) and Neftechimbank (Russia).

#### Bankers' Organizations

**Commercial Banks' Association of Kazakhstan:** Almaty.

### COMMODITY EXCHANGE

**Karaganda Regional Commodity Exchange:** 470074 Karaganda, pr. Stroiteley 28; tel. (3212) 74-04-82; telex 251338; fax (3212) 74-43-25; f. 1991; auth. cap. 15m.; Gen. Man. Georgy Revazov.

Kazakhstan also has a Metal Exchange.

## Trade and Industry

### STATE PROPERTY AGENCY

**State Committee for State Property:** Almaty, pr. Ablaikhana 93–95; tel. (3272) 62-85-62; f. 1991; responsible for the management of all, and the divestment of most, state-owned enterprises; Chair. (vacant).

### CHAMBER OF COMMERCE

**Chamber of Commerce and Industry of Kazakhstan:** 480091 Almaty, pr. Ablaikhana 93–95; tel. (3272) 62-14-46; telex 251228; fax (3272) 62-05-94; Chair. H. Rakishev.

### EMPLOYERS' ORGANIZATION

**Union of Small Businesses:** Almaty; f. 1991; Pres. Chingiz Rysebekov.

### FOREIGN TRADE ORGANIZATION

**Kazakhintorg:** 480091 Almaty, Gogolya 11; tel. (3272) 32-83-81; telex 251238; import and export; subsidiary of Ministry of Trade and Industry; Gen. Dir Saken Seydualiyev.

### MAJOR STATE INDUSTRIAL ENTERPRISES

**Altynalmas:** Almaty; incorporates Kazakhstan's gold-producing cos; Pres. Abdrakhman Begalinov.

**Chimkent Industrial Amalgamation:** 486008 Chimkent, Orjonikidze 28; tel. (3252) 12-29-43; telex 184112; specializes in the production of press-forging equipment; Dir-Gen. Eduard Davijan; 4,110 employees.

**Jambul Industrial Corporation** (Khimprom): 484026 Jambul; tel. (3262) 23-25-69; telex 251282; fax (3262) 23-28-73; production of phosphorus and its derivatives; Gen. Dir Mukhan D. Atabayev; 6,000 employees.

**Kazakhstanenergo** (Kazakhstan Energy Co): Almaty, Bogenbay Batyr 142; state-owned electricity co; Pres. Gennady Shchukin.

**Kazakhstankaspiyshelf** (Kazakhstan Caspian Shelf): Almaty; Pres. Batalbek Kuandykov.

**Kaznefteprodukt:** Almaty, Bogenbay Batyr 142; state petroleum and natural gas co.

**Mangyshlakneft Production Association:** 466200 Aktau; tel. 24-557; petroleum and natural gas co.

**Tengizneftegas Production Association:** Almaty, Bogenbay Batyr 142; state hydrocarbons production co for Tengiz field.

  **Tengiz Chevroil:** Almaty, pr. Ablaikhana 77; f. 1993; joint venture with Chevron Corpn (USA).

### CO-OPERATIVE ORGANIZATION

**Kazakhtrebsoyuz:** Almaty, Komsomolskaya 57; tel. (3272) 62-34-94; union of co-operative entrepreneurs; Chair. Umirzak Sarsenov.

### TRADE UNIONS

**Confederation of Kazakh Trade Unions:** Almaty; Chair. Siyazbek Mukashev.

## Transport

### RAILWAYS

In 1993 the total length of rail track in use was 14,148 km (3,050 km of which were electrified). The rail network is most concentrated in the north of the country, where it joins the rail lines of the Russian Federation. From the capital, Almaty, lines run north-eastward, to join the Trans-Siberian Railway, and west, to Chimkent, and then north-west along the Syr-Dar'ya river, to Orenburg in European Russia. From Chu lines run to central and northern regions of Kazakhstan, while a main line runs from Chimkent south to Uzbekistan. In June 1991 an international line was opened between Druzhba, on the eastern border of Kazakhstan, and Alataw Shankou, in the Xinjiang Uygur (Sinkiand Uighur) Autonomous Republic of the the People's Republic of China. A passenger service was inaugurated on this line in mid-1992. In January 1994 a new express passenger service from Almaty to Nukus (Uzbekistan) opened, going via Tashkent and other cities of Uzbekistan and Turkmenistan. The country's rail services are operated by three organizations: Almaty Railways, Tselinnaya Railways and Western Kazakhstan Railways. These are ultimately responsible to the Department of Railways at the Ministry of Transport and Communications.

**Department of Railways (Ministry of Transport and Communications):** 480091 Almaty, Vinogradova 56; tel. (3272) 60-49-06; fax (3272) 39-32-55; Dir I. P. Segal.

# KAZAKHSTAN

**Almaty Railways:** 480091 Almaty, Furmanova 127; tel. (3272) 60-40-00; fax (3272) 62-71-06; 4,581 km; Dir AMANGELDY J. OMAROV.

**Tselinaya Railways:** 473000 Akmola, Lenina 47; tel. (31722) 14-44-00; fax (31722) 2-50-95; 5,750 km; Dir ALEKSANDR V. STARODUB.

**Western Kazakhstan Railways:** 463000 Aktyubinsk, A. Moldagulovoy 49; tel. (31322) 55-16-07; fax (31322) 55-39-52; 3,817 km; Dir MARAT S. KHAMZIN.

## ROADS

At 1 January 1994 there was a total of 87,873 km of public roads (of which 82,568 km were hard-surfaced). Kazakhstan is linked by road with the Russian Federation (46 border crossings), Kyrgyzstan (7), Uzbekistan (7), and, via Uzbekistan and Turkmenistan, with Iran. There are six road connections with the People's Republic of China (including two international crossings, at Korgas and Bakhty). Kazakhstan's road network is under the control of the Department of Roads at the Ministry of Transport and Communications.

**Department of Roads (Ministry of Transport and Communications):** Almaty, Gogolya 86; tel. (3272) 32-47-69; Dir S. LARICHEV.

## INLAND WATERWAYS

Kazakhstan's 4,002-km network of inland waterways is operated by the Department of Water Transport at the Ministry of Transport and Communications. The Department unites 12 joint-stock river transport companies and seven state enterprises.

**Department of Water Transport (Ministry of Transport and Communications):** 480083 Almaty, pr. Seyfullina 458; tel. (3272) 32-04-85; Dir PETR D. KOVALENKO.

## CIVIL AVIATION

There are 18 domestic airports and three airports with international services (at Almaty, Aktau and Atyrau). All are under the supervision of the national joint-stock airline company, Kazakhstan eue zholy. There are also six private airline companies in operation. Almaty airport has scheduled links with cities in the Russian Federation and other former Soviet republics, as well as with destinations in Europe (Frankfurt am Main, Hannover, Vienna, Zürich and Istanbul), other parts of Asia (Delhi, Karachi, Beijing) and the Middle East (Tel-Aviv, Sharjah, Teheran). The Department of Aviation at the Ministry of Transport and Communications is the state co-ordinating body of airlines in Kazakhstan.

**Department of Aviation (Ministry of Transport and Communications):** 480083 Almaty, pr. Seyfullina 458; tel. (3272) 39-28-87; fax (3272) 39-32-55; Dir S. BURANBAYEV.

**Kazakhstan eue zholy** (Kazakhstan Airlines): Almaty, Zheltoksan 59; tel. (3272) 33-63-49; fax (3272) 33-55-06; Pres. AMANTAY B. ZHOLDYBAYEV.

# KENYA

## Introductory Survey

**Location, Climate, Language, Religion, Flag, Capital**

The Republic of Kenya lies astride the equator on the east coast of Africa, with Somalia to the north-east, Ethiopia and Sudan to the north, Uganda to the west and Tanzania to the south. The climate varies with altitude: the coastal region is hot and humid, with temperatures averaging between 20°C and 32°C (69°–90°F), while inland, at more than 1,500 m (5,000 ft) above sea-level, temperatures average 7°–27°C (45°–80°F). The highlands and western areas receive ample rainfall (an annual average of 1,000 mm–1,250 mm) but most of northern Kenya is very dry (about 250 mm). Kiswahili is the official language, while English, Kikuyu and Luo are also widely spoken. Most of the country's inhabitants follow traditional beliefs. There is a significant Christian community, while Muslims form a smaller proportion of the population. The national flag (proportions 3 by 2) has three broad horizontal stripes, of black, red and green, separated by two narrow white stripes. Superimposed in the centre is a red shield, with black and white markings, upon crossed white spears. The capital is Nairobi.

**Recent History**

Kenya was formerly a British colony (inland) and protectorate (along the coast). The first significant African nationalist organization was the Kenya African Union (KAU), founded in 1944, which was supported mainly by the Kikuyu, the largest ethnic group in Kenya. In 1947 Jomo Kenyatta, a Kikuyu, became President of the KAU. During 1952 a campaign of terrorism was launched by Mau Mau, a predominantly Kikuyu secret society which aimed to expel European (mainly British) settlers from Kenya. The British authorities declared a state of emergency in October 1952 and banned the KAU in 1953, when Kenyatta was imprisoned for alleged involvement with Mau Mau activities. The terrorist campaign ceased in 1956, and the state of emergency was revoked in January 1960.

Kenyatta was released from prison in 1961 and elected to the Legislative Council in 1962. Following general elections in May 1963, Kenya was granted internal self-government in June. The country became independent, within the Commonwealth, on 12 December 1963, and a republic exactly one year later. Kenyatta, then leader of the Kenya African National Union (KANU), was appointed Prime Minister in June 1963 and became the country's first President in December 1964. In December 1966 Kenya's two parliamentary chambers, the Senate and the House of Representatives, were merged to form a unicameral National Assembly.

Through the dominance of KANU (the only party contesting elections to the National Assembly in 1969 and 1974), Kenyatta established some stability in Kenya. However, the assassination in 1969 of Tom Mboya, a cabinet minister and the Secretary-General of KANU, led to civil unrest and the banning of the opposition Kenya People's Union. Political discontent was heightened by the assassination, in March 1975, of an outspoken and popular politician, J. M. Kariuki.

Following the death of President Kenyatta in August 1978, the Vice-President, Daniel arap Moi, was proclaimed President in October, and was the only candidate at a presidential election held in November 1979. In June 1982 the National Assembly officially declared Kenya a one-party state. A series of political detentions and increasing press censorship were followed by an attempted coup in August, in which several hundred people were killed. At legislative elections in September 1983, several cabinet ministers lost their seats. Nevertheless, at a simultaneous presidential election President Moi was returned unopposed for a second term.

During 1984 President Moi attempted to reduce corruption and to increase discipline within both KANU and the civil service; in September he directed that all civil servants must in future be members of KANU. In August 1986 KANU approved an open 'queue-voting' system to replace the secret ballot in the preliminary stage of a general election. This new system was opposed by church leaders, on the grounds that it would discourage voting by church ministers, civil servants and others whose political impartiality was necessary for their work. In December the National Assembly adopted constitutional amendments which increased the power of the President by transferring control of the civil service to the President's office, and reduced the independence of the judiciary by giving the President the power to dismiss the Attorney-General and the Auditor-General without endorsement by a legal tribunal. In June 1987 it was announced that only members of KANU were to be entitled to vote during the preliminary stages of a general election.

During 1986 and 1987 the Government acted to suppress an unofficial left-wing opposition group known as Mwakenya (the Union of Nationalists to Liberate Kenya). By early 1987 more than 100 people (mainly university teachers, students and journalists) had been arrested in connection with the activities of Mwakenya. In July of that year the human rights organization, Amnesty International, published allegations that Kenyan political detainees had been tortured and that two had died in custody.

In February 1988 Moi was nominated unopposed to serve a third term as President. In the same month preliminary elections under the 'queue-voting' system produced a KANU-approved list to contest 123 of the 188 elective seats in the National Assembly at a general election that was held in March (54 candidates received more than 70% of votes cast, and were therefore deemed to have been elected at the preliminary stage, while 11 were elected unopposed). Allegations of electoral malpractice were made against the authorities. In an extensive cabinet reshuffle following the election, the Vice-President, Mwai Kibaki, was replaced by Josephat Karanja, hitherto an assistant minister and a former High Commissioner to the United Kingdom. In July the National Assembly adopted constitutional amendments that allowed the President to dismiss senior judges at will, and which increased from 24 hours to 14 days the legally permissible period of detention without trial for people suspected of capital offences. These measures led to an intensification of criticism of the Government's record on human rights. Elections to the leadership of KANU were held in September; in December Kenneth Matiba, the Minister of Transport and Communications, resigned and was expelled from KANU, after criticizing the conduct of the party elections.

In April 1989 Josephat Karanja was the subject of a unanimous parliamentary vote of 'no confidence', following allegations that he had used his position as Vice-President to further his own personal and tribal interests. Karanja, while denying the charges against him, resigned shortly afterwards; President Moi immediately appointed Prof. George Saitoti, the Minister of Finance, as the new Vice-President. In June President Moi released all political prisoners who were being held without trial, and offered an amnesty to dissidents living in exile abroad; while this action was applauded by Amnesty International, that organization repeated allegations that many convicted Kenyan political prisoners had been given unfair trials.

In February 1990 the Minister of Foreign Affairs and International Co-operation, Dr Robert Ouko, died; it was suspected that he had been murdered. Later in that month accusations that the Government was implicated in Dr Ouko's death led to anti-Government riots in Nairobi and the western town of Kisumu. The Government responded by banning all demonstrations from the beginning of March, and requested an investigation by British police into Dr Ouko's death (the results of this were presented to the Kenyan authorities in September 1990, and in October President Moi ordered a judicial inquiry into the affair). In May 1990 a broad alliance of intellectuals, lawyers and clergy, under the leadership of Kenneth Matiba, began to exert pressure on the Government to legalize political opposition to KANU. In July President Moi ordered the arrests of several prominent members of the alliance, including Matiba. Shortly afterwards serious rioting erupted in Nairobi and its environs: more than 20 people were killed, and more than 1,000 rioters were reportedly arrested. In August a prominent Anglican bishop, who had publicly criticized the Government, died in a car crash, following threats to his life from members of the Cabinet; the most senior of these, Peter Okondo, the Minister of Labour, subsequently resigned his post. The Government ordered a public inquest into the bishop's death. In November Amnesty International reported that several hundred persons who had been detained at the time of the July riots remained in prison, and accused the Kenyan authorities of torturing some prisoners.

In December 1990, having considered the findings of a political review committee that had recently tested public opinion, KANU abolished the system of 'queue-voting' which had been approved by the party in 1986, and resolved to cease expelling party members. In January 1991 KANU agreed to readmit to the party 31 people who had previously been expelled. In June Kenneth Matiba was released from prison, apparently on grounds of ill health. In the following month four of the persons who had been arrested during the unrest of July 1990 were found guilty of sedition, and each was sentenced to seven years' imprisonment. During July 1991 the human rights organization, Africa Watch, published allegations that the Government was permitting the torture of detainees and exerting undue influence on the judiciary. In August six opposition leaders, including Oginga Odinga (Kenya's Vice-President in 1964–66), formed a new political movement, the Forum for the Restoration of Democracy (FORD); the Government immediately outlawed the grouping, but it continued to operate.

In September 1991 the judicial inquiry into the death (in February 1990) of Dr Robert Ouko was presented with evidence that Dr Ouko had been murdered. In November 1991 President Moi dismissed the Minister of Industry, Nicholas Biwott, in response to widespread suspicion that the latter was implicated in the alleged assassination of Dr Ouko. Shortly afterwards President Moi ordered the dissolution of the judicial inquiry. A suspect was eventually charged with the murder of the former Minister of Foreign Affairs and International Co-operation; however, he was acquitted in July 1994.

In November 1991 several members of FORD were arrested prior to a planned pro-democracy rally in Nairobi; protesters at the rally (which took place despite having been banned by the Government) were dispersed by the security forces. The Kenyan authorities were condemned internationally for suppressing the demonstration, and most of the opposition figures who had been detained were subsequently released. Bilateral and multilateral creditors suspended aid to Kenya indefinitely, pending the acceleration of both economic and political reforms; the donors emphasized, in particular, the desirability of an improvement in Kenya's human rights record. In early December a special conference of KANU delegates, chaired by President Moi, acceded to the domestic and international pressure for reform, and resolved to permit the introduction of a multi-party political system. Soon afterwards the National Assembly approved appropriate amendments to the Constitution.

In mid-December 1991 President Moi dismissed the Minister of Manpower Development and Employment, Peter Oloo Aringo, who had publicly criticized the Government; Aringo subsequently resigned as Chairman of KANU. Later in December Mwai Kibaki, the Minister of Health and a former Vice-President, resigned from the Government, in protest against alleged electoral malpractice by KANU and against the unsatisfactory outcome of the judicial inquiry into the death of Dr Ouko. Kibaki immediately founded the Democratic Party (DP). Five other ministers and deputy ministers resigned their posts in December 1991 and January 1992.

Several new political parties were registered during 1992, as the opposition prepared to contest the next presidential and legislative elections, which were scheduled to take place by March 1993. During the first half of 1992 some 2,000 people were reportedly killed in tribal clashes in western Kenya. In March the Government banned all political rallies, purportedly in order to suppress the unrest, and restrictions were placed on the activities of the press. Following a two-day general strike in early April, organized by FORD, the Government ended the ban on political rallies.

In June 1992, during the period of voter-registration for the forthcoming elections, opposition parties protested that administrative and legal obstacles were effectively disenfranchising some sectors of the electorate. From mid-1992 FORD was weakened by mounting internal divisions; in August the organization split into two opposing factions, and in October these were registered as separate political parties, FORD—Asili and FORD—Kenya, respectively led by Kenneth Matiba and Oginga Odinga.

In November 1992 President Moi announced that the elections would take place in early December; soon afterwards, however, they were rescheduled to 29 December, owing to a ruling by the High Court that the opposition parties required more time to nominate candidates. At the presidential election Moi was re-elected, winning 36.35% of the votes, ahead of Kenneth Matiba (26.00%), Mwai Kibaki (19.45%) and Oginga Odinga (17.48%); Moi was sworn in for a further five-year term as President in early January 1993. Of the 188 elective seats in the National Assembly, KANU won 100 (including 16 that were not contested), FORD—Asili and FORD—Kenya secured 31 each, the DP took 23, and the remaining seats were divided between the Kenya Social Congress, the Kenya National Congress and an independent candidate. (In November 1994 one FORD—Kenya representative and the independent member of the National Assembly were found guilty of electoral malpractice and retrospectively disqualified from the elections.) Some 15 former cabinet ministers lost their seats. Votes were cast predominantly in accordance with ethnic affiliations, with the two largest tribes, the Kikuyu and Luo, overwhelmingly rejecting KANU. The leaders of FORD—Asili, FORD—Kenya and the DP initially launched a campaign to have the results declared invalid, alleging that gross electoral irregularities had taken place. In January 1993, however, a Commonwealth monitoring group stated that the outcome of the elections reflected 'the will of the people', despite accusing the Government of corruption, intimidation and incompetence. An extensive reshuffle of cabinet posts was implemented that month.

In February 1993 copies of three anti-Government publications were impounded, on the alleged grounds that they contained seditious material, and in April, four opposition members were arrested and charged with participating in an illegal demonstration. At the beginning of May a general strike was co-ordinated by the Central Organization of Trade Unions (COTU), in support of demands by its members for wage increases and for the dismissal of Prof. George Saitoti, the Vice-President and Minister of Planning and National Development; although the former demand was partially acceded to, the Secretary-General of COTU was arrested and charged with inciting industrial unrest. In late May and early June a leader of the banned radically fundamentalist Islamic Party of Kenya (IPK) was detained on three separate occasions and charged with sedition. In mid-June a parliamentary representative of FORD—Asili defected to KANU, as a result of which FORD—Kenya became the largest opposition party in the National Assembly. In early September several hundred supporters of the IPK rioted in Mombasa. In November the international donor community agreed to resume the provision of aid to Kenya, in response to the Government's progress in implementing political and economic reforms.

Tribal clashes in western regions continued during 1993 and escalated significantly in mid-October. In November the human rights organization, Africa Watch, reiterated persistent accusations by the opposition that the Government was covertly inciting the ethnic violence in order to discredit the newly-introduced political pluralism. During that month, however, several people were arrested and charged with co-ordinating the unrest.

In January 1994 Oginga Odinga died; he was succeeded as the Chairman of FORD—Kenya by Michael Wamalwa Kijana, hitherto the party's Vice-President. In February a petition by Kenneth Matiba to challenge the validity of Moi's election as President in December 1992 was rejected by the Court of Appeal; a book by Matiba which was reported to be critical of Moi had been banned in January 1994. In early June the main opposition groups, excluding FORD—Asili, formed a loose coalition, the United National Democratic Front (UNDA), in an attempt to gain a tactical advantage over the Government at further elections; however, UNDA was subsequently divided by disagreements. During mid-1994 university staff and employees of the public health sector organized strike action in protest at the Government's refusal to recognize their respective trade unions and to grant improved conditions of employment: many of the striking workers were dismissed. In early November members of FORD—Asili who were opposed

# KENYA

*Introductory Survey*

to Kenneth Matiba formed a rival party executive, under the leadership of Salim Ndamwe.

During 1994 and early 1995 the Government continued to suppress opposition activity: anti-Government political meetings were repeatedly dispersed by the security forces, and adverse criticism of the Government in the national media was not tolerated. Inter-ethnic violence continued to disrupt national unity.

Kenya's relations with Tanzania were strained during the late 1970s. However, the Kenya–Tanzania border, which had been closed prior to the dissolution of the East African Community (EAC) in 1977, was reopened in November 1983, following an agreement on the distribution of EAC assets and liabilities between the three former members (Kenya, Tanzania and Uganda), and in December Kenya and Tanzania agreed to establish full diplomatic relations. Following the seizure of power by the National Resistance Army in Uganda in January 1986, President Moi offered full co-operation to the new Ugandan President, Yoweri Museveni. After visits to Kenya by President Museveni and President Mwinyi of Tanzania in June, it was announced that joint commissions were to be formed to enhance co-operation between the three countries. However, a dispute developed between Kenya and Uganda over the alleged ill-treatment of Ugandans resident in Kenya, following the arrest of some 500 Ugandan 'illegal aliens' in March 1987 and the death in police custody of a Ugandan national. In September Uganda claimed that Kenya was harbouring anti-Museveni rebels, and stationed troops at its border with Kenya. These claims were denied, and in December, when Ugandan troops allegedly entered Kenya in pursuit of rebels, Ugandan and Kenyan armed forces exchanged fire across the border for several days. At least 15 people were reported to have been killed. Later in December President Moi and President Museveni agreed to withdraw troops from either side of the border. In July 1988, however, the Ugandan Government accused Kenya of complicity in smuggling weapons to rebels in Uganda, and the Kenyan authorities accused Ugandan troops of making incursions across the Kenya–Uganda border. In March 1989 the Ugandan authorities strongly denied Kenyan allegations that Ugandan troops had been involved in an attack by Ugandan cattle-rustlers on Kenyan security forces earlier in that month, and that a Ugandan military aircraft had been responsible for the bombing of a town in north-western Kenya shortly afterwards. In August 1990 President Moi visited President Museveni, indicating a renewed *détente* between Kenya and Uganda. In November 1991 the Presidents of Kenya, Uganda and Tanzania declared their commitment to developing mutual co-operation. In November 1993 the three leaders met in Arusha, Tanzania, and established a permanent tripartite commission for co-operation.

During 1987 the Kenyan Government expressed suspicion of Libyan activities in the country: in December it ordered the closure of the Libyan diplomatic mission, alleging that Libya had encouraged unrest among students. In June 1988 relations between Kenya and Sudan deteriorated, as the two countries exchanged mutual accusations of aiding rebel factions. In early 1989 Sudan renewed a long-standing dispute with Kenya over the sovereignty of territory on the Kenyan side of the two countries' common border. At that time tension also developed between the Kenyan authorities and ethnic Somalis from both sides of the Kenya–Somalia border, when Somalis were alleged to be largely responsible for wildlife-poaching and banditry in north-eastern Kenya. In September President Moi protested strongly to the Somali Government, following an incursion into Kenya by Somali troops (reportedly pursuing Somali rebels), which resulted in the deaths of four Kenyan citizens.

In October 1990 Kenya severed diplomatic relations with Norway, following protests by the Norwegian Government to Kenya about the arrest on treason charges during that month of a Kenyan dissident who had been exiled in Norway; diplomatic relations were eventually restored in March 1994.

In late 1994 Kenya was reportedly sheltering about 280,000 refugees, including more than 200,000 from Somalia. The Moi Government, which claims that the refugees place an intolerable burden on the country's resources, has repeatedly requested the UN to repatriate the total refugee population. During early 1995 the Government protested strongly to the UN, following the granting of refugee status in Uganda to an alleged Kenyan guerrilla leader.

## Government

Legislative power is vested in the unicameral National Assembly, with 202 members (188 elected by universal adult suffrage, the Attorney-General, the Speaker and 12 members nominated by the President), who serve a term of five years, subject to dissolution. Executive power is held by the President, also directly elected for five years. He is assisted by an appointed Vice-President and Cabinet.

## Defence

In June 1994 Kenya's armed forces numbered 24,200, comprising an army of 20,500, an air force of 2,500 and a navy of 1,200. Military service is voluntary. There is a paramilitary force of 5,000 police. Defence was provisionally allocated K£324.6m. in the budget for 1993/94, representing 4.7% of total current expenditure and 0.9% of development expenditure. Military assistance is received from the United Kingdom, and from the USA, whose Rapid Deployment Force uses port and onshore facilities in Kenya.

## Economic Affairs

In 1993, according to estimates by the World Bank, Kenya's gross national product (GNP), measured at average 1991–93 prices, was US $6,743m., equivalent to $270 per head. During 1985–93, it was estimated, GNP per head increased, in real terms, at an average annual rate of 0.3%. Over the same period the population increased by an annual average of 3.0%. Kenya's gross domestic product (GDP) increased, in real terms, by an annual average of 4.0% during 1980–92.

Agriculture (including forestry and fishing) contributed an estimated 29% of GDP in 1993, and employed about 76% of the total labour force in that year. The principal cash crops are coffee (which contributed 18.0% of export earnings in 1990) and tea (accounting for 17.7% of export earnings in 1990). Horticultural produce, pyrethrum, sisal, sugar cane and cotton are also important. Maize is the principal subsistence crop. There is a significant dairy industry for domestic consumption and export. During 1980–92 agricultural GDP increased by an annual average of 2.9%.

Industry (including mining, manufacturing, construction and power) contributed an estimated 19% of GDP in 1992, and employed about 20% of the modern-sector labour force in that year. During 1980–92 industrial GDP increased by an annual average of 3.9%.

Mining contributed an estimated 0.3% of GDP in 1991, and employed only 0.3% of the modern-sector labour force in 1992. Soda ash is the principal mineral export. Fluorspar, salt, limestone, rubies, gold and vermiculite are also mined.

Manufacturing contributed an estimated 12% of GDP in 1992, and engaged some 13.0% of the modern-sector labour force in that year. The most important industries are food-processing, the manufacture of petroleum products (using imported crude petroleum), chemicals, cement, paper and paper products, beverages and tobacco, textiles and clothing, leather products, rubber products, metal products, ceramics, electrical equipment and transport equipment. During 1980–92 manufacturing GDP increased by an annual average of 4.8%.

Of total electricity generated in 1988, hydroelectric power accounted for about 82%. Geothermal energy supplies about 15% of Kenya's energy requirements. In 1992 imports of fuel and energy comprised 16% of the value of total imports. Energy for domestic use is derived principally from fuel wood and charcoal.

Tourism makes an important contribution to Kenya's economy, and has been the country's principal source of foreign exchange since 1987.

In 1993 Kenya recorded a visible trade deficit of US $307.2m., but there was a surplus of $152.5m. on the current account of the balance of payments. In the first nine months of 1991 the principal source of imports (an estimated 18%) was the United Kingdom, which was also the main market for exports (an estimated 17.5%). Other major trading partners in that year were Germany, Japan and the United Arab Emirates. The principal exports in 1990 were coffee, tea and petroleum products. The principal imports in that year were crude petroleum, vehicles, industrial machinery and iron and steel.

In the financial year ending 30 June 1994 the estimated budgetary deficit was equivalent to 6.5% of GDP. Kenya's external debt was US $6,994m. at the end of 1993, of which

$5,121m. was long-term public debt. In that year the cost of debt-servicing was equivalent to 28.0% of the value of exports of goods and services. The annual rate of inflation averaged 17.8% in 1985–93. Consumer prices increased by 45.8% in 1993; however, the inflation rate fell to 12.2% in the year to October 1994. Some 16% of the urban labour force were estimated to be unemployed in early 1992.

Kenya is a member of the Preferential Trade Area for Eastern and Southern African States (see p. 240); in November 1993 Kenya was among the PTA countries to sign a treaty providing for the establishment of a Common Market for Eastern and Southern Africa. The International Tea Promotion Association is based in Kenya (see p. 236).

Kenya's agricultural development has been intermittently hindered by low rainfall and by rural ethnic unrest, while the high rate of population growth has exacerbated unemployment, and a deterioration in the terms of trade, beginning in the 1980s, has led to persistent balance-of-payments deficits. In November 1991 Kenya's bilateral and multilateral creditors announced that they would withhold allocations of aid, pending evidence of economic and political reforms; international donor assistance was eventually resumed in November 1993. Substantial arrears were amassed on the external debt over the period when Kenya was denied international funding. The seventh Development Plan (1994–96), introduced in December 1993, aimed to reduce the number of public-sector employees, decrease the high level of state subsidies to certain public enterprises, accelerate the transfer of more than 100 non-profitable and non-strategic parastatal companies to private-sector ownership, and to eliminate all currency controls. In January 1995 the Nairobi Stock Exchange was opened to foreign investors.

## Social Welfare

There are state schemes for the provision of pensions and welfare benefits, and a National Social Security Fund. The Government administers hospitals and medical services, and missions, private charities and commercial firms provide further facilities. A National Council of Social Services co-ordinates the work of voluntary agencies. In 1989 there were 268 hospitals, with 32,534 beds. There were 3,266 physicians working in the country (15.3 per 100,000 of the population) in that year. According to the budget for 1993/94 (provisional), 4.3% of total government expenditure was allocated to health and 1.6% to housing, community and social welfare.

## Education

Education is not compulsory. The Government provides, or assists in the provision of, schools. Primary education is provided free of charge. The education system involves eight years of primary education (beginning at six years of age), four years at secondary school and four years of university education. The total enrolment at primary schools increased from about 900,000 in 1963 to 5,392,319 in 1990. The number of pupils in secondary schools increased from 31,923 in 1963 to 614,161 in 1990. In the latter year the total enrolment at primary and secondary schools was equivalent to 77% of the school-age population (boys 79%; girls 74%). According to estimates by UNESCO, the adult literacy rate in 1990 was 69% (males 79.8%; females 58.5%). There are four state universities, with total enrolment of 35,421 students in 1990. The education sector was provisionally allocated 13.9% of total expenditure by the central Government in the budget for 1993/94.

## Public Holidays

**1995:** 1 January (New Year's Day), 3 March* (Id al-Fitr, end of Ramadan), 14–17 April (Easter), 1 May (Labour Day), 10 May* (Id al-Adha, Feast of the Sacrifice), 1 June (Madaraka Day, anniversary of self-government), 20 October (Kenyatta Day), 12 December (Independence Day), 25–26 December (Christmas).

**1996:** 1 January (New Year's Day), 21 February* (Id al-Fitr, end of Ramadan), 5–8 April (Easter), 29 April* (Id al-Adha, Feast of the Sacrifice), 1 May (Labour Day), 1 June (Madaraka Day, anniversary of self-government), 20 October (Kenyatta Day), 12 December (Independence Day), 25–26 December (Christmas).

* These holidays are determined by the Islamic lunar calendar and may vary by one or two days from the dates given.

## Weights and Measures

The metric system is in use.

# Statistical Survey

Source (unless otherwise stated): Central Bureau of Statistics, POB 30256, Nairobi; tel (2) 33970.

## Area and Population

### AREA, POPULATION AND DENSITY

| | |
|---|---:|
| Area (sq km) | 580,367* |
| Population (census results)† | |
| 24 August 1989 | |
|   Males | 10,628,368 |
|   Females | 10,815,268 |
|   Total | 21,443,636 |
| Density (per sq km) at August 1989 | 36.7 |

* 224,081 sq miles. Total includes 11,230 sq km (4,336 sq miles) of inland water.
† Provisional.

### PRINCIPAL ETHNIC GROUPS (at census of August 1989)

| | | | |
|---|---:|---|---:|
| African | 21,163,076 | European | 34,560 |
| Arab | 41,595 | Other | 115,220* |
| Asian | 89,185 | **Total** | 21,443,636 |

* Includes persons who did not state 'tribe' or 'race'.

### PRINCIPAL TOWNS (population at census of August 1989)

| | | | |
|---|---:|---|---:|
| Nairobi (capital) | 1,346,000 | Meru | 78,100 |
| Mombasa | 465,000 | Thika | 57,100 |
| Kisumu* | 185,100 | Kitale | 53,000 |
| Nakuru | 162,800 | Kisii | 44,000 |
| Eldoret* | 104,900 | Kericho | 40,000 |
| Nyeri* | 88,600 | Malindi* | 35,200 |

* Boundaries extended between 1979 and 1989.

### BIRTHS AND DEATHS (UN estimates, annual averages)

| | 1975–80 | 1980–85 | 1985–90 |
|---|---:|---:|---:|
| Birth rate (per 1,000) | 53.6 | 48.8 | 45.6 |
| Death rate (per 1,000) | 15.5 | 13.2 | 11.4 |

**Expectation of life** (UN estimates, years at birth, 1985–90): 57.9 (males 55.9; females 59.9).

Source: UN, *World Population Prospects: The 1992 Revision*.

KENYA                                                                                           Statistical Survey

**ECONOMICALLY ACTIVE POPULATION**
(ILO estimates, '000 persons at mid-1980)

|  | Males | Females | Total |
|---|---|---|---|
| Agriculture, etc. | 3,174 | 2,555 | 5,729 |
| Industry | 403 | 81 | 484 |
| Services | 534 | 324 | 859 |
| **Total** | 4,111 | 2,961 | 7,072 |

Source: ILO, *Economically Active Population Estimates and Projections, 1950–2025*.

**Mid-1993** (estimates in '000): Agriculture, etc. 8,252; Total labour force 10,908. (Source: FAO, *Production Yearbook*.)

**EMPLOYMENT*** ('000 registered employees at June each year)

|  | 1990 | 1991 | 1992 |
|---|---|---|---|
| Agriculture and forestry | 269.7 | 272.0 | 272.3 |
| Mining and quarrying | 4.2 | 4.3 | 4.4 |
| Manufacturing | 187.7 | 188.9 | 189.6 |
| Electricity and water | 22.4 | 22.4 | 22.3 |
| Construction | 71.4 | 72.4 | 73.4 |
| Trade, restaurants and hotels | 114.0 | 116.7 | 118.4 |
| Transport, storage and communications | 74.2 | 76.2 | 76.9 |
| Financing, insurance, real estate and business services | 65.2 | 66.3 | 66.9 |
| Community, social and personal services | 600.2 | 622.4 | 638.4 |
| **Total** | 1,409.0 | 1,441.8 | 1,462.6 |
| Males | 1,100.5 | 1,117.1 | 1,133.5 |
| Females | 308.5 | 324.6 | 329.1 |

* This table refers only to employment in the modern sector. There were an estimated 347,892 self-employed and unpaid family workers and employees at small-scale establishments registered at June 1991.

**LIVESTOCK** (FAO estimates, '000 head, year ending September)

|  | 1991 | 1992 | 1993 |
|---|---|---|---|
| Cattle | 13,000 | 12,000 | 11,000 |
| Sheep | 6,500 | 6,000 | 5,500 |
| Goats | 8,000 | 7,500 | 7,300 |
| Pigs | 105 | 105 | 105 |
| Camels | 820 | 810 | 810 |

Poultry (FAO estimates, million): 25 in 1991; 25 in 1992; 25 in 1993.
Source: FAO, *Production Yearbook*.

**LIVESTOCK PRODUCTS** ('000 metric tons)

|  | 1991 | 1992 | 1993 |
|---|---|---|---|
| Beef and veal* | 245 | 230 | 210 |
| Mutton and lamb* | 26 | 24 | 22 |
| Goats' meat* | 31 | 30 | 29 |
| Pig meat* | 5 | 5 | 5 |
| Poultry meat* | 48 | 48 | 48 |
| Other meat* | 29 | 29 | 29 |
| Edible offals* | 57 | 53 | 53 |
| Cows' milk* | 2,166 | 2,000 | 1,830 |
| Sheep's milk* | 29 | 26 | 24 |
| Goats' milk* | 100 | 94 | 91 |
| Butter and ghee | 3.5† | 3.1† | 3.5 |
| Cheese | 0.3 | 0.2 | 0.2 |
| Poultry eggs* | 42.0 | 42.0 | 42.0 |
| Honey* | 18.0 | 19.0 | 19.5 |
| Wool: |  |  |  |
| greasy* | 2.2 | 2.0 | 1.9 |
| clean* | 1.1 | 1.0 | 0.9 |
| Cattle hides* | 38.1 | 36.8 | 33.6 |

* FAO estimates.   † Unofficial figure.
Source: FAO, mainly *Production Yearbook*.

## Agriculture

**PRINCIPAL CROPS** ('000 metric tons)

|  | 1991 | 1992 | 1993 |
|---|---|---|---|
| Wheat | 195 | 126 | 150* |
| Rice (paddy) | 47 | 41 | 25† |
| Barley† | 37 | 34 | 37 |
| Maize | 2,340 | 2,522* | 1,748* |
| Millet | 49 | 70 | 58 |
| Sorghum | 98 | 129 | 90 |
| Potatoes† | 230 | 240 | 250 |
| Sweet potatoes† | 550 | 600 | 630 |
| Cassava (Manioc) | 761 | 780† | 790† |
| Pulses | 189 | 215 | 200† |
| Cottonseed* | 20 | 11 | 11 |
| Cotton lint* | 10 | 6 | 5 |
| Coconuts | 42 | 43† | 43† |
| Vegetables† | 643 | 655 | 655† |
| Sugar cane† | 4,580 | 4,167 | 4,210 |
| Pineapples | 245* | 270* | 270 |
| Bananas† | 210 | 220 | 220 |
| Plantains† | 350 | 360 | 360 |
| Cashew nuts† | 15 | 15 | 15 |
| Coffee (green) | 86 | 85 | 76* |
| Tea (made) | 204 | 188 | 211* |
| Sisal | 39 | 34 | 34† |

* Unofficial figure(s).   † FAO estimate(s).
Source: FAO, *Production Yearbook*.

## Forestry

**ROUNDWOOD REMOVALS**
(FAO estimates, '000 cubic metres, excluding bark)

|  | 1990 | 1991 | 1992 |
|---|---|---|---|
| Sawlogs, veneer logs and logs for sleepers | 460 | 460 | 460 |
| Pulpwood | 357 | 357 | 357 |
| Other industrial wood | 930 | 961 | 993 |
| Fuel wood | 33,190 | 34,328 | 35,501 |
| **Total** | 34,937 | 36,106 | 36,897 |

Source: FAO, *Yearbook of Forest Products*.

**SAWNWOOD PRODUCTION** (FAO estimates, '000 cubic metres)

|  | 1990 | 1991 | 1992 |
|---|---|---|---|
| **Total** | 185 | 185 | 185 |

Source: FAO, *Yearbook of Forest Products*.

KENYA

## Fishing

('000 metric tons, live weight)

|  | 1990 | 1991 | 1992 |
|---|---|---|---|
| Silver cyprinid | 46.7 | 58.1 | 57.5 |
| Nile tilapia | 38.3 | 27.5 | 29.3 |
| Nile perch | 71.9 | 57.3 | 56.9 |
| Other fishes (incl. unspecified) | 43.8 | 54.7 | 53.8 |
| Other aquatic animals | 1.0 | 1.1 | 1.0 |
| **Total catch** | 201.8 | 198.6 | 198.5 |
| Inland waters | 191.9 | 191.2 | 191.3 |
| Indian Ocean | 9.9 | 7.4 | 7.2 |

Source: FAO, *Yearbook of Fishery Statistics*.

## Mining

(metric tons)

|  | 1990 | 1991 | 1992 |
|---|---|---|---|
| Soda ash | 231,900 | 219,500 | 181,330 |
| Fluorspar | 80,529 | 77,402 | 80,630 |
| Salt | 70,318 | 72,441 | 72,494 |
| Limestone products† | 35,733 | 32,017 | 30,656 |

† Excluding limestone used for production of cement.

## Industry

**SELECTED PRODUCTS** ('000 metric tons, unless otherwise indicated)

|  | 1990 | 1991 | 1992 |
|---|---|---|---|
| Wheat flour | 172 | 186 | 222 |
| Raw sugar | 414 | 427 | 397 |
| Beer ('000 hectolitres) | 3,311 | 3,140 | 3,686 |
| Cigarettes (million) | 6,648 | 6,473 | 7,031 |
| Cement | 1,512 | 1,423 | 1,507 |
| Motor spirit (petrol) | 335 | 328 | 348 |
| Kerosene and jet fuel | 492 | 421 | 455 |
| Distillate fuel oils | 563 | 542 | 580 |
| Residual fuel oil | 670 | 648 | 670 |
| Electric energy (million kWh) | 3,044 | 3,237 | 3,215 |

## Finance

**CURRENCY AND EXCHANGE RATES**

**Monetary Units**
100 cents = 1 Kenya shilling (Ks.);
Ks. 20 = 1 Kenya pound (K£).

**Sterling and Dollar Equivalents** (31 December 1994)
£1 sterling = Ks. 70.15;
US $1 = Ks. 44.84;
Ks. 1,000 = £14.255 = $22.302.

**Average Exchange Rate** (Ks. per US $)
1992  32.217
1993  58.001
1994  56.051

Note: The foregoing information refers to the Central Bank's mid-point exchange rate. However, with the introduction of a foreign exchange bearer certificate (FEBC) scheme in October 1991, a dual exchange rate system is in effect. In May 1994 foreign exchange transactions were liberalized and the Kenya shilling became fully convertible against other currencies.

**BUDGET** (K£ million, year ending 30 June)

| Revenue | 1991/92 | 1992/93* | 1993/94* |
|---|---|---|---|
| Current: |  |  |  |
| Direct taxes | 851.39 | 997.94 | 1,243.76 |
| Import duties | 255.93 | 459.15 | 733.39 |
| Excise duties | 340.46 | 418.35 | 550.90 |
| Sales tax | 927.77 | 1,107.14 | 1,418.29 |
| Other indirect taxes | 100.90 | 87.37 | 98.15 |
| Interest, profits and dividends (incl. rent) | 186.24 | 244.33 | 253.09 |
| Current transfers | 10.76 | 8.74 | 6.84 |
| Sales of goods and services | 74.37 | 83.06 | 104.15 |
| Loan repayments | 12.41 | 9.46 | 9.85 |
| Compulsory fees, fines and penalties | 32.96 | 40.59 | 56.72 |
| Other | 7.27 | 32.88 | 85.85 |
| **Total current** | 2,800.46 | 3,489.01 | 4,560.99 |
| Capital: |  |  |  |
| Long-term borrowing | 11.50 | 318.00 | 329.05 |
| Internal borrowing | 344.50 | 2,006.85 | 4,323.71 |
| Loan repayments | 12.41 | 9.46 | 9.85 |
| Capital transfers | 62.20 | 38.67 | 36.97 |
| **Total capital** | 431.01 | 2,372.98 | 4,699.58 |
| **Total** | 3,231.47 | 5,861.99 | 9,260.57 |

| Expenditure | 1991/92 | 1992/93* | 1993/94* |
|---|---|---|---|
| Current: |  |  |  |
| General public services | 421.62 | 524.32 | 742.82 |
| Defence | 206.52 | 243.70 | 310.61 |
| Education | 663.16 | 783.72 | 1,029.52 |
| Health | 152.44 | 175.30 | 235.34 |
| Housing, community and social welfare | 51.54 | 56.33 | 69.63 |
| Economic services | 328.12 | 407.70 | 466.51 |
| Other services | 1,971.58 | 3,123.21 | 3,733.97 |
| **Total current** | 3,794.98 | 5,314.28 | 6,588.40 |
| Development: |  |  |  |
| General public services | 164.65 | 236.89 | 402.17 |
| Mining, manufacturing and construction | 8.82 | 17.04 | 61.59 |
| Housing, social and community welfare | 40.90 | 49.99 | 60.84 |
| Roads | 84.16 | 116.14 | 121.48 |
| Education | 59.09 | 71.20 | 99.21 |
| Health | 37.58 | 56.96 | 118.46 |
| Agriculture and forestry | 110.77 | 199.94 | 440.89 |
| Defence | 25.86 | 26.61 | 14.00 |
| Electricity, gas and water | 41.01 | 41.34 | 63.75 |
| **Total development** (incl. others) | 649.88 | 878.06 | 1,554.88 |
| **Total** | 4,444.86 | 6,192.34 | 8,143.28 |

* Provisional.

**INTERNATIONAL RESERVES** (US $ million at 31 December)

|  | 1991 | 1992 | 1993 |
|---|---|---|---|
| Gold* | 15.0 | 12.2 | 14.3 |
| IMF special drawing rights | 1.4 | 0.8 | 1.1 |
| Reserve position in IMF | 17.5 | 16.8 | 16.8 |
| Foreign exchange | 98.1 | 35.4 | 387.7 |
| **Total** | 132.0 | 65.2 | 419.9 |

* National valuation of gold reserves (80,000 troy oz in each year).

Source: IMF, *International Financial Statistics*.

**MONEY SUPPLY** (Ks. million at 31 December)

|  | 1991 | 1992 | 1993 |
|---|---|---|---|
| Currency outside banks | 12,761 | 17,205 | 21,355 |
| Demand deposits at commercial banks | 19,155 | 26,621 | 33,664 |

Source: IMF, *International Financial Statistics*.

# KENYA

*Statistical Survey*

**COST OF LIVING** (Consumer Price Index for low-income group in Nairobi; annual averages; base: 1990 = 100.)

|  | 1991 | 1992 |
|---|---|---|
| Food | 123.5 | 166.9 |
| Fuel and light | 114.7 | 122.6 |
| Clothing | 114.5 | 134.9 |
| Rent | 119.3 | 154.5 |
| **All items** (incl. others) | 119.3 | 154.5 |

**1993:** Food 242.4; All items 225.2.

Source: ILO, *Year Book of Labour Statistics*.

## NATIONAL ACCOUNTS (K£ million at current prices)

### Composition of the Gross National Product

|  | 1990 | 1991* | 1992* |
|---|---|---|---|
| Compensation of employees | 3,643.2 | 4,026.3 | 4,812.2 |
| Operating surplus | } 4,897.4 | 5,773.6 | 6,792.9 |
| Consumption of fixed capital | | | |
| **Gross domestic product (GDP) at factor cost†** | 8,540.6 | 9,799.9 | 11,605.1 |
| Indirect taxes | 1,399.0 | 1,562.4 | 1,815.7 |
| *Less* Subsidies | 0.1 | 0.1 | 0.1 |
| **GDP in purchasers' values** | 9,939.3 | 11,362.1 | 13,420.8 |
| Factor income received from abroad | 5.5 | 8.2 | 2.8 |
| *Less* Factor income paid abroad | 461.5 | 597.9 | 731.6 |
| **Gross national product (GNP)** | 9,483.2 | 10,772.4 | 12,691.9 |

* Figures are provisional.
† Includes non-monetary economy.

Source: Central Bureau of Statistics.

### Expenditure on the Gross Domestic Product

|  | 1991 | 1992 | 1993 |
|---|---|---|---|
| Government final consumption expenditure | 1,880.3 | 2,073.8 | 2,108.9 |
| Private final consumption expenditure | 6,971.9 | 8,467.3 | 10,649.0 |
| Increase in stocks | 217.6 | 44.9 | 112.3 |
| Gross fixed capital formation | 2,133.6 | 2,189.0 | 2,473.7 |
| **Total domestic expenditure** | 11,203.4 | 12,775.0 | 15,343.9 |
| Exports of goods and services | 3,025.6 | 3,464.4 | 6,745.9 |
| *Less* Imports of goods and services | 3,166.3 | 3,452.1 | 5,939.2 |
| **GDP in purchasers' values** | 11,062.6 | 12,787.3 | 16,150.6 |

Source: Central Bureau of Statistics.

### Gross Domestic Product by Economic Activity (at factor cost)

|  | 1989 | 1990 | 1991 |
|---|---|---|---|
| Agriculture, hunting, forestry and fishing | 2,271 | 2,375 | 2,797 |
| Mining and quarrying | 19 | 23 | 28 |
| Manufacturing | 855 | 987 | 1,167 |
| Electricity, gas and water | 109 | 79 | 100 |
| Construction | 477 | 539 | 749 |
| Trade, restaurants and hotels | 829 | 948 | 1,133 |
| Transport, storage and communication | 486 | 598 | 682 |
| Finance, insurance, real estate and business services | 1,170 | 1,589 | 1,518 |
| Government services | 1,167 | 1,299 | 1,459 |
| Other community, social and personal services | 228 | 251 | 331 |
| Other producers | 97 | 114 | 132 |
| **Sub-total** | 7,708 | 8,803 | 10,096 |
| *Less* Imputed bank service charge | 282 | 263 | 296 |
| **Total** | 7,426 | 8,541 | 9,800 |

Source: UN, *National Accounts Statistics*.

## BALANCE OF PAYMENTS (US $ million)

|  | 1991 | 1992 | 1993 |
|---|---|---|---|
| Merchandise exports f.o.b. | 1,053.7 | 1,004.0 | 1,185.6 |
| Merchandise imports f.o.b. | −1,697.3 | −1,594.3 | −1,492.8 |
| **Trade balance** | −643.5 | −590.3 | −307.2 |
| Exports of services | 1,134.9 | 1,139.7 | 1,134.1 |
| Imports of services | −628.9 | −574.8 | −582.8 |
| Other income received | 17.0 | 8.6 | 9.8 |
| Other income paid | −438.5 | −362.9 | −342.4 |
| Private unrequited transfers (net) | 144.4 | 68.3 | 147.1 |
| Official unrequited transfers (net) | 204.5 | 214.2 | 93.9 |
| **Current balance** | −210.1 | −97.1 | −152.5 |
| Direct investment (net) | 18.8 | 6.4 | 1.5 |
| Other capital (net) | 77.7 | −276.5 | 0.3 |
| Net errors and omissions | 69.6 | 110.3 | 257.5 |
| **Overall balance** | −43.9 | −256.9 | 411.8 |

Source: IMF, *International Financial Statistics*.

# External Trade

**PRINCIPAL COMMODITIES** (distribution by SITC, US $'000)*

| Imports c.i.f. | 1987 | 1988 | 1990 |
|---|---|---|---|
| **Food and live animals** | 69,371 | 46,650 | 139,462 |
| **Crude materials (inedible) except fuels** | 47,841 | 56,509 | 79,321 |
| **Mineral fuels, lubricants, etc** | 348,735 | 290,566 | 424,471 |
| Petroleum and petroleum products | 344,373 | 284,369 | 412,188 |
| **Animal and vegetable oils and fats** | 50,512 | 71,458 | 45,549 |
| **Chemicals and related products** | 310,174 | 355,147 | 234,798 |
| Plastic materials, etc | 68,447 | 91,074 | 62,617 |
| **Basic manufactures** | 245,711 | 320,538 | 272,080 |
| Iron and steel | 102,613 | 135,780 | 119,213 |
| **Machinery and transport equipment** | 596,459 | 763,908 | 856,476 |
| Machinery specialized for particular industries | 130,719 | 147,638 | 124,041 |
| General industrial machinery, equipment and parts | 83,925 | 99,002 | 99,286 |
| Telecommunications and sound equipment | 61,507 | 96,346 | 104,809 |
| Other electrical machinery, apparatus, etc | 59,007 | 81,665 | 95,378 |
| Road vehicles and parts | 164,207 | 201,425 | 236,513 |
| Passenger motor cars (excl. buses) | 42,034 | 48,670 | 76,805 |
| Motor vehicles for goods transport and special purposes | 77,298 | 88,046 | 95,881 |
| Aircraft and aircraft parts | 17,631 | 47,539 | 132,729 |
| **Miscellaneous manufactured articles** | 63,520 | 75,152 | 64,580 |
| **Total** (incl. others) | 1,737,805 | 1,986,741 | 2,135,583 |

KENYA

| Exports f.o.b. | 1987 | 1988 | 1990 |
|---|---|---|---|
| **Food and live animals** | 589,893 | 655,243 | 480,114 |
| Cereals and cereal preparations | 26,546 | 25,838 | 23,243 |
| Vegetables and fruit | 93,892 | 106,807 | 79,042 |
| Coffee (green and roasted) | 236,743 | 275,964 | 143,551 |
| Tea | 216,215 | 227,179 | 195,761 |
| **Crude materials (inedible) except fuels** | 97,010 | 121,820 | 184,742 |
| Textile fibres and waste | 15,322 | 15,963 | 23,140 |
| **Mineral fuels, lubricants, etc** | 125,571 | 136,634 | 134,821 |
| Petroleum and petroleum products | 125,225 | 136,230 | 134,644 |
| **Chemicals and related products** | 38,950 | 31,531 | 42,697 |
| **Basic manufactures** | 57,896 | 78,726 | 118,227 |
| **Machinery and transport equipment** | 24,278 | 20,599 | 108,978 |
| Road vehicles and parts | 10,432 | 9,946 | 59,620 |
| Motor vehicles for goods transport and special purposes | 3,362 | 2,692 | 24,080 |
| **Miscellaneous manufactured goods** | 17,172 | 18,916 | 37,828 |
| **Total** (incl. others) | 961,042 | 1,072,524 | 1,028,393 |

* Figures for 1989 are not available. Not all data for 1990 are comparable with those for previous years.

Source: UN, *International Trade Statistics Yearbook*.

**PRINCIPAL TRADING PARTNERS** (US $'000)

| Imports c.i.f. | 1989 | 1990 | 1991 |
|---|---|---|---|
| Belgium-Luxembourg | n.a. | 51,086 | n.a. |
| Finland | n.a. | 29,977 | n.a. |
| France* | 190,902 | 116,617 | 112,791 |
| Germany, Federal Republic | 192,950 | 152,010 | 171,376 |
| India | 40,537 | 33,192 | 37,682 |
| Italy | 97,198 | 96,397 | 68,793 |
| Japan | 238,341 | 243,285 | 227,177 |
| Malaysia | n.a. | 40,269 | n.a. |
| Netherlands | 62,883 | 70,082 | 45,226 |
| Saudi Arabia | 41,207 | 58,836 | 99,560 |
| Sweden | n.a. | 27,842 | n.a. |
| United Arab Emirates | 245,912 | 154,537 | 246,104 |
| United Kingdom | 340,762 | 310,536 | 322,059 |
| USA | 159,402 | 172,599 | 98,834 |
| **Total** (incl. others) | 2,173,423 | 2,135,853 | 1,980,199 |

| Exports f.o.b. | 1988 | 1989 | 1990 |
|---|---|---|---|
| Belgium-Luxembourg | 29,017 | n.a. | 17,155 |
| Burundi | 13,111 | 6,180 | 20,313 |
| Djibouti | 1,234 | 998 | 22,798 |
| Egypt | 11,318 | 10,563 | 15,165 |
| France* | 19,763 | 20,807 | 17,301 |
| Germany, Federal Republic | 128,355 | 86,451 | 79,111 |
| Italy | 36,913 | 26,369 | 16,377 |
| Netherlands | 54,993 | 48,452 | 40,606 |
| Pakistan | 30,305 | n.a. | 59,754 |
| Rwanda | 26,425 | 16,428 | 75,207 |
| Somalia | 7,891 | 7,789 | 16,190 |
| Spain | 12,583 | n.a. | 8,559 |
| Sudan | 24,532 | 20,427 | 14,926 |
| Sweden | 23,946 | n.a. | 12,356 |
| Tanzania | 27,433 | 26,764 | 22,295 |
| Uganda | 94,226 | 64,212 | 190,322 |
| United Kingdom | 210,585 | 193,563 | 136,320 |
| USA | 52,036 | 48,101 | 28,341 |
| Zaire | 12,093 | 6,567 | 24,636 |
| **Total** (incl. others) | 1,072,498 | 993,338 | 1,028,393 |

* Including Monaco.

Source: UN, *International Trade Statistics Yearbook*.

# Transport

**RAILWAYS** (traffic)

| | 1990 | 1991 | 1992* |
|---|---|---|---|
| Passengers carried ('000) | 3,109 | 2,635 | 2,563 |
| Passenger-km (million) | 677 | 658 | 557 |
| Freight carried ('000 metric tons) | 3,317 | 3,581 | 2,821 |
| Freight ton-km (million) | 1,865 | 1,627 | 1,755 |

* Provisional.

**ROAD TRAFFIC** (motor vehicles in use at 31 December)

| | 1990 | 1991 | 1992* |
|---|---|---|---|
| Motor cars | 156,851 | 164,234 | 171,813 |
| Buses and coaches | 13,445 | 14,740 | 16,323 |
| Goods vehicles | 32,183 | 32,794 | 35,344 |
| Vans | 88,396 | 92,585 | 95,967 |
| Tractors, trailers and semi-trailers | 37,908 | 39,264 | 40,699 |
| Motor cycles and mopeds | 23,536 | 24,895 | 25,912 |

* Provisional.

**INTERNATIONAL SEA-BORNE SHIPPING**
(estimated freight traffic, '000 metric tons)

| | 1990 | 1991 | 1992* |
|---|---|---|---|
| Goods loaded | 2,297 | 1,791 | 2,083 |
| Goods unloaded | 5,192 | 5,310 | 5,810 |

* Provisional.

**CIVIL AVIATION** (traffic on scheduled services)

| | 1990 | 1991 | 1992 |
|---|---|---|---|
| Kilometres flown (million) | 16 | 13 | 14 |
| Passengers carried ('000) | 794 | 760 | 721 |
| Passenger-km (million) | 1,652 | 1,479 | 1,333 |
| Total ton-km (million) | 204 | 175 | 174 |

Source: UN, *Statistical Yearbook*.

# Tourism

| | 1990 | 1991 | 1992 |
|---|---|---|---|
| Tourist arrivals ('000) | 814 | 818 | 699 |
| Tourist receipts (million US dollars) | 466 | 432 | 442 |

Source: UN, *Statistical Yearbook*.

KENYA

## Communications Media

|  | 1990 | 1991 | 1992 |
|---|---|---|---|
| Radio receivers ('000 in use) | 3,000 | 2,100 | 2,200 |
| Television receivers ('000 in use) | 225 | 234 | 245 |
| Telephones ('000 main lines in use)* | 183 | 200† | n.a. |
| Book production (titles) | 348 | 239‡ | n.a. |
| Daily newspapers: | | | |
| Titles | 5 | n.a. | 5 |
| Average circulation ('000 copies) | 350† | n.a. | 354† |

* Year ending 30 June.
† Estimate.
‡ Excluding pamphlets.

Sources: UNESCO, *Statistical Yearbook*; UN, *Statistical Yearbook*.

## Education

(1990)

|  | Institutions | Teachers | Pupils |
|---|---|---|---|
| Primary | 14,691 | 172,117 | 5,392,319 |
| General secondary | 2,758 | 35,097 | 614,161 |
| Technical* | 36 | 1,147 | 11,700 |
| Teacher Training | 24 | n.a. | 17,914 |
| Universities | 4 | 4,392 | 35,421 |

* 1988 figures.

Sources: Ministry of Education, Nairobi; UNESCO, *Statistical Yearbook*.

# Directory

## The Constitution

The Constitution was introduced at independence on 12 December 1963. Subsequent amendments, including the adoption of republican status on 12 December 1964, were consolidated in 1969. A further amendment in December 1991 permitted the establishment of a multi-party system. The Constitution can be amended by the affirmative vote on Second and Third Reading of 65% of the membership of the National Assembly (excluding the Speaker and Attorney-General).

The central legislative authority is the unicameral National Assembly, in which there are 188 directly elected Representatives, 12 members nominated by the President and two ex-officio members, the Attorney-General and the Speaker. The maximum term of the National Assembly is five years from its first meeting (except in wartime). It can be dissolved by the President at any time, and the National Assembly may force its own dissolution by a vote of 'no confidence', whereupon Presidential and Assembly elections have to be held within 90 days.

Executive power is vested in the President, Vice-President and Cabinet. Both the Vice-President and the Cabinet are appointed by the President, who must be a member of the Assembly and at least 35 years of age. Election of the President, for a five-year term, is by direct popular vote; the winning candidate at a presidential election must receive no less than 25% of the votes in at least five of Kenya's eight provinces. If a President dies, or a vacancy otherwise occurs during a President's period of office, the Vice-President becomes interim President for up to 90 days while a successor is elected.

## The Government

### HEAD OF STATE

**President:** DANIEL ARAP MOI (took office 14 October 1978; elected August 1983, commenced further term of office February 1988, re-elected December 1992).

### CABINET
(May 1995)

**President and Commander-in-Chief of the Armed Forces:** DANIEL ARAP MOI.
**Vice-President and Minister of Planning and National Development:** Prof. GEORGE SAITOTI.
**Minister of Agriculture, Livestock and Marketing:** SIMEON NYACHAE.
**Minister of Finance:** WYCLIFF MUDAVADI.
**Minister of Foreign Affairs and International Co-operation:** STEPHEN MUSYOKA.
**Minister of Education:** JOSEPH KAMOTHO.
**Minister of Land Reclamation, Regional and Water Development:** DARIUS MBELA.
**Minister of Energy:** (vacant).
**Minister of Environment and Natural Resources:** JOHN SAMBU.
**Minister of Transport and Communication:** DALMAS OTIENO.
**Minister of Commerce and Industry:** KIRUGI M'MUKINDIA.
**Minister of Tourism:** NOAH NGALA.
**Minister of Health:** JOSHUA ANGATIA.
**Minister of Local Government:** WILLIAM OLE NTIMAMA.
**Minister of Home Affairs and National Heritage:** FRANCIS LOTODO.
**Minister of Lands and Urban Development:** JACKSON MULINGE.
**Minister of Labour and Manpower Development:** PHILIP MASINDE.
**Minister of Information and Broadcasting:** JOHNSTONE MAKAU.
**Minister of Culture and Social Services:** JACKSON KALWEO.
**Minister of Co-operative Development:** KAMWITHI MUNYI.
**Minister of Public Works and Housing:** Prof. JONATHAN NG'ENO.
**Minister of Research, Technical Training and Technology:** ZACHARY ONYONKA.
**Minister of State in the President's Office:** HUSSEIN MOHAMED, KIPKALIA KONES.
**Attorney-General:** AMOS WAKO.

### MINISTRIES

**Office of the President:** Harambee House, Harambee Ave, POB 30510, Nairobi; tel. (2) 27411.
**Office of the Vice-President and Ministry of Planning and National Development:** Treasury Bldg, Harambee Ave, POB 30007, Nairobi; tel. (2) 338111; telex 22696.
**Ministry of Agriculture, Livestock and Marketing:** Kilimo House, Cathedral Rd, POB 30028, Nairobi; tel. (2) 728370; telex 33042.
**Ministry of Commerce and Industry:** Co-operative House, Haile Selassie Ave, POB 47024, Nairobi; tel. (2) 340010.
**Ministry of Co-operative Development:** Kencom House, Moi Ave, Nairobi; tel. (2) 340081.
**Ministry of Culture and Social Services:** Reinsurance Plaza, Taifa Rd, POB 45958, Nairobi; tel. (2) 339650.
**Ministry of Education:** Jogoo House 'B', Harambee Ave, POB 30040, Nairobi; tel. (2) 28411.
**Ministry of Energy:** Nyayo House, Kenyatta Ave, POB 30582, Nairobi; tel. (2) 331242; telex 23094.
**Ministry of Environment and Natural Resources:** Kencom House, POB 30126, Nairobi; tel. (2) 29261.
**Ministry of Finance:** Treasury Bldg, Harambee Ave, POB 30007, Nairobi; tel. (2) 338111; telex 22696.
**Ministry of Foreign Affairs:** Harambee House, POB 30551, Nairobi; tel. (2) 334433; telex 22003.
**Ministry of Health:** Medical HQ, Afya House, Cathedral Rd, POB 30016, Nairobi; tel. (2) 717077; fax (2) 725902.
**Ministry of Home Affairs and National Heritage:** Nairobi.
**Ministry of Information and Broadcasting:** Jogoo House, POB 30025, Nairobi; tel. (2) 28411; telex 22244.
**Ministry of Labour and Manpower Development:** National Social Security House, POB 40326, Nairobi; tel. (2) 729800.
**Ministry of Land Reclamation, Regional and Water Development:** Maji House, Ngong Rd, POB 49720 Nairobi; tel. (2) 723103.

KENYA

Ministry of Lands and Settlement: POB 30450, Nairobi; tel. (2) 718050.
Ministry of Local Government: Jogoo House 'A', POB 30004, Nairobi; tel. (2) 28411.
Ministry of Public Works and Housing: POB 30260, Nairobi; tel. (2) 723101.
Ministry of Research, Technical Training and Technology: Utalii House, Uhuru Highway, POB 30623, Nairobi; tel. (2) 336173.
Ministry of Tourism and Wildlife: Utalii House, 5th Floor, Uhuru Highway, POB 54666, Nairobi; tel. (2) 331030; telex 25016.
Ministry of Transport and Communication: Transcom House, Ngong Rd, POB 52692, Nairobi; tel. (2) 729200; telex 22272; fax (2) 726326.

## President and Legislature

### PRESIDENT

Election, 29 December 1992

| Candidates | Votes | % |
| --- | --- | --- |
| DANIEL ARAP MOI | 1,962,866 | 36.35 |
| KENNETH MATIBA | 1,404,266 | 26.00 |
| MWAI KIBAKI | 1,050,617 | 19.45 |
| OGINGA ODINGA | 944,197 | 17.48 |
| GEORGE MOSETI ANYONA | 14,273 | 0.26 |
| CHIBULE WA TSUMA | 10,221 | 0.19 |
| JOHN HARUN MWAU | 8,118 | 0.15 |
| MUKARU NG'ANG'A | 5,776 | 0.11 |
| Total | 5,400,334 | 100.00 |

### NATIONAL ASSEMBLY

Speaker: FRANCIS OLE KAPARO.

General Election, 29 December 1992

| Party | Seats |
| --- | --- |
| KANU | 100* |
| FORD—Asili | 31* |
| FORD—Kenya | 31† |
| DP | 23 |
| KSC | 1 |
| KNC | 1 |
| Independent | 1† |
| Total | 188 |

* In June 1993 a representative of FORD—Asili defected to KANU.
† In November 1994 the election to the National Assembly of one FORD—Kenya representative and of the independent member was nullified.

In addition to the 188 directly elected seats, 12 are held by nominees of the President. The Attorney-General and the Speaker are, ex officio, members of the National Assembly.

## Political Organizations

Kenya was a *de facto* one-party state between 1969 and June 1982, when it became a *de jure* one-party state. In December 1991 the Constitution was amended to legalize a multi-party political system.

**Democratic Party (DP):** Nairobi; f. 1991; Pres. MWAI KIBAKI.
**Forum for the Restoration of Democracy—Asili (FORD—Asili)\*:** Nairobi; f. 1992; Chair. KENNETH MATIBA; Sec.-Gen. MARTIN J. SHIKUKU.
**Forum for the Restoration of Democracy—Kenya (FORD—Kenya):** Nairobi; f. 1992; Chair. MICHAEL KIJANA WAMALWA; Sec.-Gen. MUNYUA WAIYAKI.
**Islamic Party of Kenya (IPK):** Mombasa; f. 1992; Islamic fundamentalist; banned; Chair. OMAR MWINYI; Sec.-Gen. ABDULRAHMAN WANDATI.
**Kenya African National Union (KANU):** POB 72394, Nairobi; f. 1960; sole legal party 1982–91; Pres. DANIEL ARAP MOI; Chair. WILSON NDOLO AYAH; Sec.-Gen. JOSEPH KAMOTHO.
**Kenya National Congress (KNC):** f. 1992.
**Kenya National Democratic Alliance Party (KENDA):** f. 1991; Chair. MUKARU NG'ANG'A.
**Kenya Social Congress (KSC):** f. 1992; Chair. GEORGE MOSETI ANYONA.
**Labour Party Democracy:** Chair. MOHAMED IBRAHIM NOOR.

*Directory*

**National Development Party (NDP):** f. 1994; Chair. STEPHEN OMONDI OLUDHE.
**Party for Independent Candidates of Kenya (PICK):** Leader: HARUN MWAU.
**People's Union of Justice and New Order:** Kisumu; Islamic support; Leader WILSON OWILI.
**Rural National Democratic Party:** f. 1992; supports farmers' interests; Chair. SEBASTIAN MUNENE.
**Social Democratic Party:** Nairobi; f. 1992.
**United Muslims of Africa (UMA):** f. 1993; Leader EMMANUEL MAITHA.
**United National Democratic Alliance (UNDA):** f. 1994; an informal coalition of main opposition parties (excl. FORD–Asili) formed to present an agreed list of candidates at elections.
**Youth Associated with the Restoration of Democracy (YARD):** Chair. ELIUD AMBANI MULAMA.

* A breakaway faction of FORD—Asili, led by SALIM NDAMWE, was formed in November 1994.

## Diplomatic Representation

### EMBASSIES AND HIGH COMMISSIONS IN KENYA

**Argentina:** POB 30283, Nairobi; tel. (2) 335242; telex 22544; Ambassador: JOSÉ MARÍA CANTILO.
**Australia:** POB 30360, Nairobi; tel. (2) 445034; telex 22203; fax (2) 444617; High Commissioner: L. W. HERRON.
**Austria:** City House, Wabera St, POB 30560, Nairobi; tel. (2) 228281; telex 22076; fax (2) 331792; Ambassador: Dr PAUL HARTIG.
**Bangladesh:** POB 41645, Nairobi; tel. (2) 562815; telex 25077; High Commissioner: SHARIFUL HAQ.
**Belgium:** Limuru Rd, POB 30461, Nairobi; tel. (2) 741564; telex 22269; fax (2) 741568; Ambassador: RENIER NIJSKENS.
**Brazil:** Jeevan Bharati Bldg, Harambee Ave, POB 30751, Nairobi; tel. (2) 337722; telex 22498; fax (2) 336245; Ambassador: LUÍS FELIPE TEIXEIRA SOARES.
**Burundi:** Development House, Moi Ave, POB 44439, Nairobi; tel. (2) 218458; telex 22425; Ambassador: VANANT BAATAKANWA.
**Canada:** Comcraft House, Haile Selassie Ave, POB 30481, Nairobi; tel. (2) 214804; fax (2) 226987; High Commissioner: LUCIE GENEVIEVE EDWARDS.
**Chile:** International House, Mama Ngina St, POB 45554, Nairobi; tel. (2) 331320; telex 22348; fax (2) 215648; Ambassador: Dr VICENTE SÁNCHEZ.
**China, People's Republic:** Woodlands Rd, POB 30508, Nairobi; tel. (2) 722559; telex 22235; Ambassador: WU MINGLIAN.
**Colombia:** Muthaiga Rd, POB 48494, Nairobi; tel. (2) 765927; fax (2) 765911; Ambassador: Dr GERMÁN GARCÍA-DURÁN.
**Costa Rica:** POB 76639, Nairobi; tel. and fax (2) 569078.
**Cyprus:** Eagle House, Kimathi St, POB 30739, Nairobi; tel. (2) 220881; telex 22436; High Commissioner: MICHAEL SPANOS.
**Czech Republic:** Harambee Ave, POB 48785; tel. (2) 210494; telex 25115; fax (2) 223447.
**Denmark:** HFCK Bldg, Koinange St, POB 40412, Nairobi; tel. (2) 331088; telex 22216; fax (2) 331492; Ambassador: HENNING KJELDGAARD.
**Djibouti:** POB 59528, Nairobi; tel. (2) 229633; Ambassador: SALEH HAJI FARAH.
**Egypt:** Harambee Plaza, 7th Floor, POB 30285, Nairobi; tel. (2) 225991; telex 22335; Ambassador: MARAWAN ZAKI BADR.
**Ethiopia:** State House Ave, POB 45198, Nairobi; tel. (2) 723027; telex 22864; fax (2) 723401; Ambassador: OFATO ALEW.
**Finland:** International House, City Hall Way, POB 30379, Nairobi; tel. (2) 334777; telex 22010; Ambassador: DAVID JOHANSSON.
**France:** Barclays Plaza, 9th Floor, POB 41784, Nairobi; tel. (2) 339783; telex 22279; fax (2) 339421; Ambassador: MICHEL ROUGAGNOU.
**Germany:** Williamson House, 4th Ngong Ave, POB 30180, Nairobi; tel. (2) 712527; telex 22221; fax (2) 714886; Ambassador: BERND MÜTZELBURG.
**Greece:** Nation Centre, Kimathi St, POB 30543, Nairobi; tel. (2) 340722; telex 22008; Ambassador: GEORGES VANDALIS.
**Holy See:** Apostolic Nunciature, Manyani Rd West, POB 14326, Nairobi; tel. (2) 442975; fax (2) 446789; Apostolic Pro-Nuncio: Most Rev. CLEMENTE FACCANI, Titular Archbishop of Serra.
**Hungary:** Agip House, 2nd Floor, POB 30523, Nairobi; tel. (2) 226914; telex 22364; fax (2) 569433; Chargé d'affaires: ZSIGMOND D. PATAY.

# KENYA

**India:** Jeevan Bharati Bldg, Harambee Ave, POB 30074, Nairobi; tel. (2) 222361; telex 22079; fax (2) 334167; High Commissioner: KIRAN DOSHI.
**Indonesia:** Utalii House, Uhuru Highway, POB 48868, Nairobi; tel. (2) 215873; telex 23171; Ambassador: DALINDRA AMAN.
**Iran:** POB 49170, Nairobi; tel. (2) 720343; telex 22563; Ambassador: HAMID MOAYYER.
**Iraq:** Loresho Ridge, POB 49213, Nairobi; tel. (2) 581143; telex 22176; Chargé d'affaires: HIKMAT A. SATTAR HUSSEIN.
**Israel:** POB 30354, Nairobi; tel. (2) 722182; telex 22412; fax (2) 715966; Ambassador: MENASHE ZIPORI.
**Italy:** International Life House, Mama Ngina St, POB 30107, Nairobi; tel. (2) 337356; telex 22251; fax (2) 337056; Ambassador: Dr ROBERTO DI LEO.
**Japan:** Kenyatta Ave, POB 60202, Nairobi; tel. (2) 332955; fax (2) 216530; Ambassador: SHINSUKE HORIUCHI.
**Korea, Republic:** Anniversary Towers, University Way, POB 30455, Nairobi; tel. (2) 333581; telex 22300; Ambassador: KWON SOON TAE.
**Kuwait:** Muthaiga Rd, POB 42353, Nairobi; tel. (2) 767144; telex 22467; Chargé d'affaires: JABER SALEM HUSSAIN EBRAHEEM.
**Lesotho:** International House, Mama Ngina St, POB 44096, Nairobi; tel. (2) 337493; telex 22489; High Commissioner: (vacant).
**Malawi:** Waiyaki Way (between Mvuli and Church Rds), POB 30453, Nairobi; tel. (2) 440569; telex 22749; fax 440568; High Commissioner: M. V. L. PHIRI (acting).
**Mexico:** POB 14145, Nairobi; tel. (2) 582850; telex 23065; fax (2) 581500; Ambassador: A. GONZÁLEZ.
**Morocco:** POB 61098, Nairobi; tel. (2) 222264; telex 22531; Ambassador: MEHDI BENNANI.
**Mozambique:** POB 66923, Nairobi; tel. (2) 581857; Chargé d'affaires: EDWARDO ADRIANO.
**Netherlands:** Uchumi House, Nkrumah Ave, POB 41537, Nairobi; tel. (2) 227111; telex 22285; fax (2) 339155; Ambassador: RUUD J. TREFFERS.
**Nigeria:** Hurlingham, POB 30516, Nairobi; tel. (2) 564116; telex 22194; fax (2) 562776; High Commissioner: CLARKSON N. UMELO.
**Norway:** Nairobi; Ambassador: ARMAN AARDAL.
**Pakistan:** St Michel Rd, Westlands, POB 30045, Nairobi; tel. (2) 443911; telex 25907; fax (2) 446507; High Commissioner: AMIR M. KHAN.
**Poland:** Kabarnet Rd, POB 30086, Nairobi; tel. (2) 566288; telex 22266; fax (2) 562588; Ambassador: ADAM T. KOWALEWSKI.
**Portugal:** POB 34020, Nairobi; tel. (2) 338990; telex 22634; Ambassador: Dr PAULO COUTO BARBOSA.
**Romania:** POB 48412, Nairobi; tel. (2) 227515; Chargé d'affaires: GHEORGHE DRAGOS.
**Russia:** Lenana Rd, POB 30049, Nairobi; tel. (2) 722559; telex 25261; fax (2) 721888; Ambassador: VLADIMIR S. KITAYEV.
**Rwanda:** International Life House, Mama Ngina St, POB 48579, Nairobi; tel. (2) 334341; telex 22463; Ambassador: CYPRIEN HABIMANA.
**Saudi Arabia:** POB 58297, Nairobi; tel. (2) 762781; telex 22990; Chargé d'affaires: GHORM SAID MAWHAN.
**Slovakia:** Milimani Rd, POB 30204, Nairobi; tel. (2) 721896; telex 25371; fax (2) 721898.
**Spain:** Bruce House, Standard St, POB 45503, Nairobi; tel. (2) 336330; telex 22157; Ambassador: LUIS G. MERINO.
**Sri Lanka:** International Life House, Mama Ngina St, POB 48145, Nairobi; tel. (2) 227577; telex 25081; High Commissioner: Dr G. G. M. SIKURAJAPATHY.
**Sudan:** Minet ICDC House, 7th Floor, POB 48784, Nairobi; tel. (2) 720853; Ambassador: Dr ABDEL LATIF ABDEL HAMID IBRAHIM.
**Swaziland:** Silopark House, POB 41887, Nairobi; tel. (2) 339231; telex 22085; High Commissioner: Prince CHURCHILL B. H. DLAMINI.
**Sweden:** International House, Mama Ngina St, POB 30600, Nairobi; tel. (2) 229042; telex 22264; fax (2) 218908; Ambassador: NILS GUNNAR REVELIUS.
**Switzerland:** International Life House, Mama Ngina St, POB 30752, Nairobi; tel. (2) 228735; telex 22181; Ambassador: Dr ARMIN KAMER.
**Tanzania:** Continental House, POB 47790, Nairobi; tel. (2) 331056; High Commissioner: MIRISHO SAM HAGGAI SARAKIKYA.
**Thailand:** POB 58349, Nairobi; tel. (2) 715800; telex 22836; Ambassador: APIPHONG JAYANAMA.
**Turkey:** Gigiri Rd, off Limuru Rd, POB 30785, Nairobi; tel. (2) 520404; telex 22346; fax (2) 521237; Chargé d'affaires: CUNEYT YAVUZCAN.
**Uganda:** POB 60855, Nairobi; tel. (2) 330801; telex 22732; High Commissioner: J. TOMUSANGE.
**United Kingdom:** Bruce House, Standard St, POB 30465, Nairobi; tel. (2) 335944; telex 22219; fax (2) 333196; High Commissioner: SIMON NICHOLAS PETER HEMANS.
**USA:** cnr Moi and Haile Selassie Aves, POB 30137, Nairobi; tel. (2) 334141; telex 22964; fax (2) 340838; Ambassador: AURELIA BRAZEAL.
**Venezuela:** International House, Mama Ngina St, POB 34477, Nairobi; tel. (2) 341078; telex 22671; fax (2) 337487; Ambassador: ALBERTO LIZARRALDE MARADEY.
**Yemen:** Ngong Rd, POB 44642, Nairobi; tel. (2) 564379; Ambassador: Dr HUSSEIN AL-GALAL.
**Yugoslavia:** State House Ave, POB 30504, Nairobi; tel. (2) 720671; telex 22515; Ambassador: LJUBE ZAFIROV.
**Zaire:** Electricity House, Harambee Ave, POB 48106, Nairobi; tel. (2) 229771; telex 22057; Ambassador: ATENDA MONGEBE OMWANGO.
**Zambia:** Nyerere Rd, POB 48741, Nairobi; tel. (2) 724850; telex 22193; fax (2) 718494; High Commissioner: ENESS CHISHALA CHIYENGE.
**Zimbabwe:** Minet ICDC House, Mamlaka Rd, POB 30806, Nairobi; tel. (2) 711071; telex 25033; High Commissioner: ANGELINA MAKWAVARARA.

## Judicial System

**The Kenya Court of Appeal:** POB 30187, Nairobi; the final court of appeal for Kenya in civil and criminal process; sits at Nairobi, Mombasa, Kisumu, Nakuru and Nyeri.

   **Chief Justice:** FRED KWASI APALOO.

   **Justices of Appeal:** MATHEW MULI, J. M. GACHUHI, J. R. O. MASIME, J. E. GICHERU, R. O. KWACH, A. M. COCKAR.

**The High Court of Kenya:** Harambee Ave, POB 40112, Nairobi; tel. (2) 21221; has unlimited criminal and civil jurisdiction at first instance, and sits as a court of appeal from subordinate courts in both criminal and civil cases. The High Court is also a court of admiralty. There are two resident puisne judges at Mombasa, and a resident puisne judge at Nakuru, Eldoret, Kakamega, Kisumu and Nyeri. Regular sessions are held in Kisii and Meru.

**Resident Magistrates' Courts:** have country-wide jurisdiction, with powers of punishment by imprisonment up to five years or by fine up to K£500. If presided over by a chief magistrate or senior resident magistrate the court is empowered to pass any sentence authorized by law. For certain offences, a resident magistrate may pass minimum sentences authorized by law.

**District Magistrates' Courts:** of first, second and third class; have jurisdiction within districts and powers of punishment by imprisonment for up to five years, or by fines of up to K£500.

**Kadhi's Courts:** have jurisdiction within districts, to determine questions of Islamic law.

## Religion

Most of the population hold traditional African beliefs, although there are significant numbers of African Christians. The Arab inhabitants are Muslims, and the Indian population is partly Muslim and partly Hindu. The Europeans and Goans are predominantly Christian. Muslims are found mainly along the coastline; however, the Islamic faith has also established itself among Africans around Nairobi and among some ethnic groups in the northern districts. East Africa is also an important centre for the Bahá'í faith.

### CHRISTIANITY

**National Council of Churches of Kenya:** Church House, Moi Ave, POB 45009, Nairobi; tel. (2) 338211; f. 1943 as Christian Council of Kenya; 35 full mems and eight assoc. mems; Chair. Rev. Dr GEORGE WANJAU; Sec.-Gen. Rev. SAMUEL KOBIA.

#### The Anglican Communion

Anglicans are adherents of the Church of the Province of Kenya, comprising 20 dioceses. It became a separate church in 1970, and had some 2m. members in 1994.

**Archbishop of Kenya and Bishop of Nairobi:** (vacant), POB 40502, Nairobi; tel. (2) 714755; fax (2) 718442; Acting Primate: Rt Rev. DAVID M. GITARI (Bishop of Kirinyaga).

#### Greek Orthodox Church

**Archbishop of East Africa:** NICADEMUS of IRINOUPOULIS, Nairobi; jurisdiction covers Kenya, Tanzania and Uganda.

KENYA

### The Roman Catholic Church

Kenya comprises four archdioceses and 15 dioceses. At 31 December 1993 there were an estimated 5,834,082. adherents in the country.

**Kenya Episcopal Conference:** National Catholic Secretariat, POB 48062, Nairobi; tel. (2) 443133; fax (2) 442910; f. 1976; Pres. Most Rev. Zacchaeus Okoth, Archbishop of Kisumu.

**Archbishop of Kisumu:** Most Rev. Zacchaeus Okoth, POB 1728, Kisumu; tel. (35) 43950; fax (35) 42425.

**Archbishop of Mombasa:** Most Rev. John Njenga, Catholic Secretariat, Nyerere Ave, POB 83131, Mombasa; tel. (11) 476673; fax (11) 473166.

**Archbishop of Nairobi:** Cardinal Maurice Otunga, Archbishop's House, POB 14231, Nairobi; tel. (2) 441919.

**Archbishop of Nyeri:** Most Rev. Nicodemus Kirima, POB 288, Nyeri; tel. (171) 2366.

### Other Christian Churches

**African Christian Church and Schools:** POB 1365, Thika; tel. (151) 47; f. 1948; 50,000 mems; Moderator Rt Rev. John Njunguna; Gen. Sec. Rev. Samuel Mwangi.

**African Church of the Holy Spirit:** POB 183, Kakamega; f. 1927; 20,000 mems; Exec. Sec. Rev. Peter Ihaji.

**African Israel Nineveh Church:** Nineveh HQ, POB 701, Kisumu; f. 1942; 350,000 mems; High Priest Rt Rev. John Kivuli, II; Gen. Sec. Rev. John arap Tonui.

**Baptist Convention of Kenya:** Pres. Rev. Eliud Mungai, POB 14907, Nairobi.

**Evangelical Lutheran Church in Kenya:** Pres. Pastor John Kururia, POB 874, Kisii; tel. (381) 20237; 28,000 mems.

**Methodist Church in Kenya:** POB 47633, Nairobi; tel. (2) 724841; f. 1862 (autonomous since 1967); 300,000 mems (1994); Presiding Bishop Prof. Zablon Nthamburi.

**Presbyterian Church of East Africa:** POB 48268, Nairobi; tel. (2) 504417; fax (2) 504442; Moderator Rt Rev. Bernard Muindi; Sec.-Gen. Rev. Dr Samuel Mwaniki.

Other denominations active in Kenya include the Africa Gospel Church, the Africa Inland Church, the African Brotherhood Church, the African Independent Pentecostal Church, the African Interior Church, the Church of God in East Africa, the Episcopal Church of Kenya, the Free Pentecostal Fellowship of Kenya, the Full Gospel Churches of Kenya, the Lutheran Church in Kenya, the National Independent Church of Africa, the Pentecostal Assemblies of God, the Pentecostal Evangelistic Fellowship of God and the Reformed Church of East Africa.

### BAHÁ'Í FAITH

**National Spiritual Assembly:** POB 47562, Nairobi; tel. (2) 725447; mems resident in 9,654 localities.

### ISLAM

**Supreme Council of Kenyan Muslims:** Nat. Chair. A. H. S. Al-Busaidy; Sec.-Gen. Alhaji Shaban Bakari.

## The Press

### PRINCIPAL DAILIES

**Daily Nation:** POB 49010, Nairobi; tel. (2) 337710; English; f. 1960; banned by Govt in June 1989 from reporting parliamentary proceedings; Editor-in-Chief Wangethi Mwangi; Man. Editor Tom Mshindi; circ. 170,000.

**Kenya Leo:** POB 30958, Nairobi; tel. (2) 337798; f. 1983; Kiswahili; KANU party newspaper; Man. Editor Job Mutungi.

**Kenya Times:** POB 30958, Nairobi; tel. (2) 24251; telex 25008; f. 1983; English; KANU party newspaper; Editor-in-Chief John Khakhudu Agunda; circ. 52,000.

**The Standard:** POB 30080, Nairobi; tel. (2) 540280; telex 24032; fax (2) 553939; English; f. 1902; Editor-in-Chief Paul Okwany Odondo; Man. Editor Kamau Kanyanga; circ. 70,000.

**Taifa Leo:** POB 49010, Nairobi; tel. (2) 337691; Kiswahili; f. 1960; daily and weekly edns; Editor Robert Mwangi; circ. 57,000.

### SELECTED PERIODICALS

#### Weeklies and Fortnightlies

**Coast Week:** weekly; Editor Adrian Grimwood; circ. 40,000.

**Kenrail:** POB 30121, Nairobi; tel. (2) 221211; telex 22254; English and Kiswahili; publ. by Kenya Railways Corpn; Editor J. N. Luseno; circ. 20,000.

**Kenya Gazette:** POB 30746, Nairobi; tel. (2) 334075; f. 1898; official notices; weekly; circ. 8,000.

**The People:** Nairobi; Editor-in-Chief Bedan Mbugua.

**Society:** Changamwe Rd, Industrial Area, Nairobi; weekly; Editor-in-Chief Pius Nyamora.

**The Standard on Sunday:** POB 30080, Nairobi; tel. (2) 540280; telex 24032; fax (2) 553939; English; Man. Editor Esther Kamweru; circ. 90,000.

**Sunday Nation:** POB 49010, Nairobi; f. 1960; English; Man. Editor Bernard Nderitu; circ. 170,000.

**Sunday Times:** POB 30958, Nairobi; tel. (2) 337798; telex 25008; Robert Otani.

**Taifa Jumapili:** POB 49010, Nairobi; tel. (2) 1987; Kiswahili; Editor Robert K. Mwangi; circ. 56,000.

**Taifa Weekly:** POB 49010, Nairobi; tel. (2) 337691; f. 1960; Kiswahili; Editor Robert K. Mwangi; circ. 68,000.

**The Weekly Review:** POB 42271, Nairobi; f. 1975; English; Editor Amboka Andere; circ. 32,000.

**What's On:** Rehema House, POB 49010, Nairobi; tel. (2) 27651; telex 25092; Editor Nancy Kairo; circ. 10,000.

#### Monthlies

**East African Medical Journal:** POB 41632, Nairobi; tel. (2) 724617; fax (2) 724617; English; f. 1923; Editor-in-Chief Dr P. H. Rees; circ. 4,000.

**East African Report on Trade and Industry:** POB 30339, Nairobi; journal of Kenya Asscn of Mfrs; Editor Gordon Boy; circ. 3,000.

**Executive:** POB 47186, Nairobi; tel. (2) 555811; telex 24095; fax (2) 557815; f. 1980; business; Editor Ali Zaidi; circ. 16,000.

**Kenya Export News:** POB 30339, Nairobi; tel. (2) 25502; English; publ. for Kenya External Trade Authority, Ministry of Commerce and Industry; Editor Prof. Samuel Njoroge; circ. 5,000.

**Kenya Farmer (Journal of the Agricultural Society of Kenya):** c/o English Press, POB 30127, Nairobi; tel. (2) 20377; f. 1954; English and Kiswahili; Editor Robert Irungu; circ. 20,000.

**Kenya Yetu:** POB 8053, Nairobi; tel. (2) 223201; telex 22244; f. 1965; Kiswahili; publ. by Ministry of Information and Broadcasting; Editor M. Ndavi; circ. 10,000.

**Nairobi Handbook:** POB 30127, Accra Rd, Nairobi; Editor Mrs R. Ouma; circ. 20,000.

**The Nairobi Law Monthly:** Tumaini House, 4th Floor, Nkrumah Ave, POB 53234, Nairobi; tel. (2) 330480; f. 1987; banned by Govt March–July 1991; English; Editor-in-Chief Gitobu Imanyara.

**News from Kenya:** POB 8053, Nairobi; tel. (2) 28411; telex 22244; publ. by Ministry of Information and Broadcasting.

**Today in Africa:** PO Kijabe; English; Editors Mwaura Njoroge, Njuguna Ngunjiri; circ. 13,000.

#### Other Periodicals

**African Ecclesial Review:** POB 4002, Eldoret; scripture, religion and development; 6 a year; Editor Agatha Radoli; circ. 2,500.

**Afya:** POB 30125, Nairobi; tel. (2) 501301; telex 23254; fax (2) 506112; journal for medical and health workers; quarterly.

**Busara:** POB 30022, Nairobi; literary; 2 a year; Editor Kimani Gecau; circ. 3,000.

**East African Agricultural and Forestry Journal:** POB 30148, Nairobi; f. 1935; English; quarterly; Editor J. O. Mugah; circ. 1,000.

**Eastern African Economic Review:** POB 30022, Nairobi; f. 1954; 2 a year; Editor J. K. Maitha.

**Economic Review of Agriculture:** POB 30028, Nairobi; tel. (2) 728370; telex 33042; f. 1968; publ. by Ministry of Agriculture, Livestock and Marketing; quarterly; Editor Okiya Okoiti.

**Education in Eastern Africa:** POB 5869, Nairobi; f. 1970; 2 a year; Editor John C. B. Bigala; circ. 2,000.

**Finance:** Nairobi; monthly; Editor-in-Chief Njehu Gatabaki.

**Inside Kenya Today:** POB 8053, Nairobi; tel. (2) 223201; telex 22244; English; publ. by Ministry of Information and Broadcasting; quarterly; Editor M. Ndavi; circ. 10,000.

**Journal of the Language Association of Eastern Africa:** POB 30571, Nairobi; tel. (2) 28411; telex 22244; publ. by Ministry of Information and Broadcasting; 2 a year; Editor T. P. Gorman; circ. 2,000.

**Kenya Education Journal:** POB 2768, Nairobi; f. 1958; English; 3 a year; Editor W. G. Bowman; circ. 5,500.

**Kenya Statistical Digest:** POB 30007, Nairobi; tel. (2) 338111; telex 22696; publ. by Ministry of Finance; quarterly.

**Target:** POB 72839, Nairobi; f. 1964; English; 6 a year; religious; Editor Rebeka Njau (acting); circ. 17,000.

KENYA

*Directory*

## NEWS AGENCIES

**Kenya News Agency (KNA):** Information House, POB 8053, Nairobi; tel. (2) 223201; telex 22244; f. 1963; Dir S. Musandu.

### Foreign Bureaux

**Agence France-Presse (AFP):** International Life House, Mama Ngina St, POB 30671, Nairobi; tel. (2) 332043; telex 22243; Bureau Chief Didier Lapeyronie.

**Agenzia Nazionale Stampa Associata (ANSA)** (Italy): Agip House, POB 20444, Nairobi; tel. (2) 711338; telex 23251; fax (2) 229383; Representative Adolfo D'Amico.

**Associated Press (AP)** (USA): Chester House, Koinange St, POB 47590, Nairobi; tel. (2) 340663; telex 25101; Bureau Chief Reid G. Miller.

**Deutsche Presse-Agentur (dpa)** (Germany): Chester House, 1st Floor, Koinange St, POB 48546, Nairobi; tel. (2) 330274; telex 22330; fax (2) 221902; Bureau Chief Dr Hubert Kahl.

**Informatsionnoye Telegrafnoye Agentstvo Rossii—Telegrafnoye Agentstvo Suverennykh Stran (ITAR—TASS)** (Russia): Likoni Lane, POB 49602, Nairobi; tel. (2) 721978; telex 22192; fax (2) 721978; Correspondent Grigory N. Potapov.

**Inter Press Service (IPS)** (Italy): Press Centre, Chester House, Koinange St, POB 54386, Nairobi; tel. (2) 335418; Correspondent Horace Awori.

**Kyodo Tsushin** (Japan): Mbaaz Ave, POB 58281, Nairobi; tel. (2) 339504; telex 22915; Bureau Chief Junji Miura.

**Reuters** (UK): Finance House, 12th Floor, Loita St, Nairobi; Bureau Chief Nick Kotch.

**United Press International (UPI)** (USA): POB 76282, Nairobi; tel. (2) 337349; fax (2) 213625; Correspondent Joe Khamisi.

**Xinhua (New China) News Agency** (People's Republic of China): Ngong Rd at Rose Ave, POB 30728, Nairobi; tel. (2) 722494; telex 23241; Dir and Chief Correspondent Ye Zhixiong.

## Publishers

**Camerapix:** POB 45048, Nairobi; tel. (2) 223511; telex 22576; fax (2) 217244; f. 1960; architecture and design, travel, topography, natural history; CEO Mohamed Amin.

**East African Educational Publishers Ltd:** cnr Mpaka Rd and Woodvale Grove, Westlands, POB 45314, Nairobi; tel. (2) 444700; f. 1965; academic, educational, creative writing in Kenyan languages; Man. Dir Henry Chakava.

**East African Publishing House Ltd:** POB 30571, Nairobi; tel. (2) 557417; f. 1965; educational, academic and general; also publs periodicals; Man. Dir Edward N. Wainaina.

**Evangel:** POB 28963, Nairobi; tel. (2) 802033; f. 1952; Gen. Man. Richard Ondeng.

**Foundation Books:** Kencom House, Moi Ave, POB 73435, Nairobi; tel. (2) 761520; f. 1974; Man. Dir F. O. Okwanya.

**Gaba Publications:** Amecea Pastoral Institute, POB 4002, Eldoret; tel. (321) 33286; religious; Dir Sister Agatha Radoli.

**Kenya Literature Bureau:** Belle Vewarea, off Mombasa Rd, POB 30022, Nairobi; tel. (2) 506142; f. 1977; parastatal body under Ministry of Education; literary, educational, cultural and scientific books and journals; Chair. Jane Kiano; Man. Dir S. C. Lang'at.

**Jomo Kenyatta Foundation:** POB 30533, Nairobi; tel. (2) 557222; f. 1966; primary, secondary, university textbooks; Man. Dir Herbert Chabala.

**Longman Kenya Ltd:** POB 18033, Nairobi; tel. (2) 541345; telex 24101; fax (2) 540037; f. 1965; textbooks and educational materials; Man. Dir Dr E. M. Mugiri.

**Macmillan Kenya (Publishers) Ltd:** POB 30797, Nairobi; tel. (2) 224485; fax (2) 212179; Man. Dir David Muita.

**Newspread International:** POB 46854, Nairobi; tel. (2) 331402; telex 22143; fax (2) 714435; reference, economic development; Exec. Editor Kul Bhushan.

**Oxford University Press (Eastern Africa):** Waiyaki Way, ABC Place, POB 72532, Nairobi; tel. (2) 440555; fax (2) 443972; f. 1954; educational and general; Regional Man. Abdullah Ismaily.

**Paulines Publications-Africa:** POB 49026, Nairobi; tel. (2) 442319; fax (2) 442144; religious.

**Transafrica Press:** Kenwood House, Kimathi St, POB 48239, Nairobi; tel. (2) 331762; f. 1976; general, educational and children's; CEO John Nottingham.

### Government Publishing House

**Government Printing Press:** POB 30128, Nairobi.

## PUBLISHERS' ORGANIZATION

**Kenya Publishers' Association:** POB 72532, Nairobi; tel. (2) 336377; Sec. Abdullah Ismaily (acting).

## Radio and Television

In 1992, according to UNESCO, there were an estimated 2.2m. radio receivers and 245,000 television receivers in use.

**Kenya Broadcasting Corporation (KBC):** Broadcasting House, POB 30456, Nairobi; tel. (2) 334567; telex 25361; f. 1989 as a state corpn to succeed Voice of Kenya (f. 1959); responsible for radio and television broadcasting; Chair. Dr Julius Kiano; Man. Dir Philip Okundi; Dir of Broadcasting David ole Nasieku.

**Radio:** three services: National (Kiswahili); General (English); Vernacular (Hindustani, Kikuyu, Kikamba, Kimeru, Kimasai, Somali, Borana, Luhya, Kalenjin, Kisii, Kuria, Rendile, Burji, Teso, Turkana and Luo).

**Television:** broadcasting financed by licence fees, commercial advertisements and a state subsidy; services in Kiswahili and English; operates on four channels for approximately 50 hours per week. In June 1994 it was announced that a private television station, Cable Television Network (CTN), would begin broadcasting later in the year.

## Finance

(cap. = capital; res = reserves; dep. = deposits; brs = branches; amounts in Kenya shillings)

### BANKING

#### Central Bank

**Central Bank of Kenya:** Haile Selassie Ave, POB 60000, Nairobi; tel. (2) 226431; telex 22324; fax (2) 340192; f. 1966; bank of issue; cap. and res 2,057.6m., dep. 21,900.4m. (June 1992); Gov. Micah Cheserem; Dep. Gov. Eliphaz Riungu.

#### Commercial Banks

**Barclays Bank of Kenya Ltd:** Bank House, Moi Ave, POB 30120, Nairobi; tel. (2) 332230; telex 22210; fax (2) 335219; f. 1978; cap. 572m. (Dec. 1990); Chair. Samuel Njoroge Waruhiu; Man. Dir R. A. Bird; 54 brs.

**Biashara Bank of Kenya Ltd:** Investment House, Muindi Mbingu St, POB 30831, Nairobi; tel. (2) 221064; telex 25161; fax 221679; f. 1984; cap. and res 135.6m., dep. 1,186.6m. (Sept. 1993); Chair. Simeon Nyachee.

**Commercial Bank of Africa Ltd:** Commercial Bank Bldg, cnr Wabera and Standard Sts, POB 30437, Nairobi; tel. (2) 228881; telex 23205; fax (2) 335827; f. 1967; 100% owned by Kenyan shareholders; cap. and res 593m., dep. 3,321m. (Dec. 1994); Chair. M. H. Da Gama Rose; Man. Dir J. A. M. Docherty; 6 brs.

**Consolidated Bank of Kenya Ltd:** POB 51133, Nairobi; tel. (2) 220175; telex 22482; fax (2) 340213; f. 1989; state-owned; cap. and res 400.2m., dep. 953.8m. (March 1993); Man. Dir E. K. Mathiu.

**Delphis Bank Ltd:** Koinange St, POB 44080, Nairobi; tel. (2) 228461; telex 22493; fax (2) 219469; f. 1991; CEO F. H. J. Barnes.

**Kenya Commercial Bank Ltd:** Kencom House, Moi Ave, POB 48400, Nairobi; tel. (2) 339441; telex 23085; fax (2) 338006; f. 1970; 70% state-owned; cap. and res 2,183m., dep. 31,367m. (Dec. 1993); Exec. Chair. A. T. Kaminchia; Gen. Man. E. K. Arab Bii; 264 brs and sub-brs.

**Meridien BIAO Bank Kenya Ltd:** Windsor House, Muindi Mbingu St, POB 30132, Nairobi; tel. (2) 219411; telex 22116; fax (2) 219392; f. 1991; placed under statutory management of Central Bank of Kenya in 1995; Man. Francis Kirembu.

**Middle East Bank Kenya Ltd:** Kenyatta Ave, POB 47387, Nairobi; tel. (2) 335168; telex 23132; fax (2) 336182; f. 1981; 75% owned by Kenyan shareholders; cap. 75m., dep. 1,223.4m. (Dec. 1993); Chair. A. K. Esmail; Man. Dir S. S. Dinamani; 2 brs.

**National Bank of Kenya Ltd (Banki ya Taifa La Kenya Ltd):** National Bank Bldg, Harambee Ave, POB 72866, Nairobi; tel. (2) 226471; telex 22619; fax (2) 330784; f. 1968; 80% state-owned; cap. and res 1,922m., dep. 12,687m. (Sept. 1994); Exec. Chair. John Simba; Gen. Man. Ahmed H. Ahmed; 33 brs.

**Pan African Bank Ltd:** ICEA Bldg, 14th Floor, Kenyatta Ave, POB 45334, Nairobi; tel. (2) 225325; telex 23058; fax (2) 218490; f. 1982; cap. 100m. (Dec. 1990); Chair. and Man. Dir Mohammad Aslam; 8 brs.

**Stanbic Bank Kenya Ltd:** Kenyatta Ave, POB 30550, Nairobi; tel. (2) 335888; telex 22397; fax (2) 330227; f. 1970 as Grindlays Bank

# KENYA

International (Kenya); 40% state-owned; cap. 15m. (Sept. 1992), dep. 366.7m. (Sept. 1986); Chair. A. D. B. WRIGHT; 2 brs.

**Standard Chartered Bank Kenya Ltd:** Stanbank House, Moi Ave, POB 30003, Nairobi; tel. (2) 330200; telex 22209; fax (2) 330506; 74.5% owned by Standard Chartered Bank Africa; cap. and res 1,747m., dep. 21,426.6m. (Dec. 1993); Chair. JULIUS GECAU; Man. Dir and CEO ALAN CLEARY; 43 brs.

**Trust Bank Ltd:** Trustforte Bldg, Moi Ave, POB 46342, Nairobi; tel. (2) 226413; telex 25143; fax (2) 334995; f. 1988; cap. and res 627m., dep. 6,273m. (Sept. 1994); Chair. AJAY I. SHAH; Gen. Man. H. V. BHATT; 13 brs.

### Merchant Banks

**Diamond Trust of Kenya Ltd:** Nation Centre, 8th Floor, Kimathi St, POB 61711, Nairobi; tel. (2) 210988; fax (2) 336836; f. 1945; cap. 56.5m. (Dec. 1990); Chair. ZAHER AHAMED; Man. Dir and CEO NIZAR S. MERUANI.

**Kenya Commercial Finance Co Ltd:** POB 21984, Nairobi; tel. (2) 339074; telex 23085; f. 1971; cap. 100m. (1991), dep. 2,666m. (1990); Chair. A. T. KAMINCHA; Chief Man. M. S. FAZAL.

**Kenya National Capital Corporation Ltd:** POB 73469, Nairobi; tel. (2) 336077; telex 22159; f. 1977; 60% owned by National Bank of Kenya, 40% by Kenya National Assurance Co; cap. 80m., dep. 940m. (1991); Chair. WANJOHI MURIITHI; Gen. Man. J. P. OKORA.

**Pan African Credit and Finance Ltd:** ICEA Bldg, 5th Floor, Kenyatta Ave, POB 47529, Nairobi; tel. (2) 25325; telex 23058; fax (2) 722410; 98.65% owned by Pan African Bank; cap. 40m. (Dec. 1990); Chair. and Man. Dir MOHAMMAD ASLAM.

**Standard Chartered Financial Services Ltd:** International House, 1st Floor, Mama Ngina St, POB 40310, Nairobi; tel. (2) 336333; telex 22089; fax (2) 334934; 100% owned by Standard Chartered Bank Kenya; cap. and res 161.7m. (Dec. 1992), dep. 1,700m. (Dec. 1992); Chair. A. CLEARY; Man. Dir W. VON ISENBURG.

### Foreign Banks

**ABN AMRO Bank NV** (Netherlands): Nyerere Rd, POB 30262, Nairobi; tel. (2) 710455; telex 22262; fax (2) 713391; Gen. Man. W. A. E. J. LEMSTRA; 2 brs.

**Bank of Baroda** (India): Bank of Baroda Bldg, cnr Mondlane St and Tom Mboya St, POB 30033, Nairobi; tel. (2) 337611; telex 22250; fax (2) 333089; Exec. Chair. AFUL DESAI; 6 brs.

**Bank of India:** Kenyatta Ave, POB 30246, Nairobi; tel. (2) 221414; telex 22725; fax (2) 334545; Chief Man. P. V. PALSOKAR.

**MashreqBank PSC** (UAE): ICEA Bldg, Kenyatta Ave, POB 11129, Nairobi; tel. (2) 330562; telex 22596; fax (2) 330792; Man. MUHAMMAD RAFIQUE.

**Banque Indosuez** (France): Reinsurance Plaza, Taifa Rd, POB 69562, Nairobi; tel. (2) 215859; telex 23091; fax (2) 214166; Regional Man. JEAN-MICHEL BROCATO.

**Citibank NA** (USA): Fehda Towers, 6th Floor, Muindi Mbingu St, POB 30711, Nairobi; tel. (2) 334286; telex 22051; fax (2) 337340; Gen. Man. PAUL FLETCHER.

**First American Bank of Kenya Ltd** (USA): ICEA Bldg, 6th/7th Floors, Kenyatta Ave, POB 30691, Nairobi; tel. (2) 333960; telex 222398; fax (2) 230969; f. 1987; cap. and res 167m., dep. 1,557m. (1992); Chair. N. N. MERALI; Man. Dir MANLIO BLASETTI; 1 br.

**Habib Bank AG Zurich** (Switzerland): National House, Koinange St, POB 30584, Nairobi; tel. (2) 334984; telex 22982; fax (2) 218699; Gen. Man. BAKIRALI NASIR.

### Co-operative Bank

**Co-operative Bank of Kenya Ltd:** Co-operative House, Haile Selassie Ave, POB 48231, Nairobi; tel. (2) 228453; telex 22938; fax (2) 227747; f. 1968; cap. and res 294.2m., dep. 3,009.5m. (June 1993); Chair. HOSEA KIPLAGAT; Gen. Man. ERASTUS K. MUREITHI; 11 brs.

### Development Banks

**East African Development Bank:** Bruce House, 4th Floor, Standard St, POB 47685, Nairobi; tel. (2) 340642; telex 22689; fax (2) 216651; loan finance to, and promotion of regional projects; Man. J. F. OWITI.

**Industrial Development Bank Ltd:** National Bank Bldg, Harambee Ave, POB 44036, Nairobi; tel. (2) 337079; telex 22339; fax (2) 334594; f. 1973; 49% state-owned; finances industrial projects; cap. 258m. (June 1991); Chair. J. K. NDOTO; Man. Dir Dr YUSUF NZIBO.

### STOCK EXCHANGE

**Nairobi Stock Exchange:** Nation Centre, Kimathi St, POB 43633, Nairobi; tel. (2) 230692; fax (2) 224200; f. 1954; 21 mems; Chair. J. M. MBARU; CEO JOB K. KIHUMBA.

## INSURANCE

**American Life Insurance Co:** American Life House, POB 49460, Nairobi; tel. (2) 721124; telex 22621; fax 723140; general.

**Blue Shield Insurance Co Ltd:** POB 49610; Nairobi; tel. (2) 227932; fax (2) 337808; f. 1983; life and general.

**Cannon Assurance (Kenya) Ltd:** Haile Selassie Ave, POB 30216, Nairobi; tel. (2) 335478; telex 25482; f. 1974; life and general; cap. 20m.; CEO I. J. TALWAR.

**Corporate Insurance Co Ltd:** Postbank House, Koinange and Banda Sts, POB 34172, Nairobi; tel. (2) 25302; telex 25134; f. 1983; life and general; cap. 10m.; CEO WILLIAM MURUNGU.

**Heritage Insurance Co Ltd:** Norwich Union Bldg, Mama Ngina St, POB 30390, Nairobi; tel. (2) 725303; telex 22476; fax (2) 722835; f. 1975; general; CEO T. C. GOSS.

**Insurance Co of East Africa Ltd (ICEA):** ICEA Bldg, Kenyatta Ave, POB 46143, Nairobi; tel. (2) 21652; life and general; CEO R. C. WOOTTON.

**Intra Africa Assurance Co Ltd:** Williamson House, 4th Ngong Ave, POB 43241, Nairobi; tel. (2) 712607; f. 1977; CEO H. G. MKANGI.

**Jubilee Insurance Co Ltd:** POB 30376, Nairobi; tel. (2) 340343; telex 22199; fax (2) 216882; f. 1937; life and general; Chair. ABDUL JAFFER.

**Kenindia Assurance Co Ltd:** Kenindia House, Loita St, POB 44372, Nairobi; tel. (2) 333100; telex 23173; fax (2) 218380; f. 1979; life and general; CEO D. SWAMINATHAN.

**Kenya National Assurance Co Ltd:** Bima House, Harambee Ave, POB 20425, Nairobi; tel. (2) 338660; telex 23057; fax (2) 210617; f. 1964; state-owned; all classes of insurance and reinsurance; cap. 10m.; Exec. Chair. HENRY KOSGEY; Gen. Man. E. G. BUNYASSI.

**Kenya Reinsurance Corporation:** Reinsurance Plaza, Taifa Rd, POB 30271, Nairobi; tel. (2) 332690; telex 22046; fax (2) 339161; f. 1970; CEO WILLIAM MBOTE.

**Lion of Kenya Insurance Co Ltd:** POB 30190, Nairobi; tel. (2) 338800; telex 22717; f. 1978; general; CEO I. A. GALLOWAY.

**Monarch Insurance Co Ltd:** Chester House, 2nd Floor, Koinange St, POB 44003, Nairobi; tel. (2) 330042; f. 1979; general; Gen. Man. J. K. KARIUKI.

**Pan African Insurance Co Ltd:** Pan Africa House, Kenyatta Ave, POB 62551, Nairobi; tel. (2) 339544; telex 22750; f. 1946; life and general; cap. 10m.; CEO D. K. NGINI.

**Phoenix of East Africa Assurance Co Ltd:** Ambank House, University Way, POB 30129, Nairobi; tel. (2) 338784; fax (2) 211848; general; Gen. Man. M. J. ADAMS; Exec. Dir MOYEZ ALIBHAI.

**Provincial Insurance Co of East Africa Ltd:** Old Mutual Bldg, Kimathi St, POB 43013, Nairobi; tel. (2) 330173; telex 22852; f. 1980; general; cap. 5m.; CEO E. C. BATES.

**Prudential Assurance Co of Kenya Ltd:** Yaya Centre, Argwings Kodhek Rd, POB 76190, Nairobi; tel. (2) 567374; telex 22280; f. 1979; general; cap. 8m.; CEO E. THOMAS.

**Royal Insurance Co of East Africa Ltd:** Mama Ngina St, POB 40001, Nairobi; tel. (2) 330171; telex 23249; fax (2) 727396; f. 1979; general; CEO S. K. KAMAU.

# Trade and Industry

**Kenya National Trading Corporation Ltd:** Uchumi House, Nkrumah Ave, POB 30587, Nairobi; tel. (2) 29141; telex 22298; f. 1965; promotes national control of trade in both locally produced and imported items; exports coffee and sugar; CEO S. W. O. OGESSA.

## CHAMBER OF COMMERCE

**Kenya National Chamber of Commerce and Industry:** Ufanisi House, Haile Selassie Ave, POB 47024, Nairobi; tel. (2) 334413; f. 1965; 46 brs; Nat. Chair. DAVID GITAU; CEO C. K. GATHIRIMU.

## TRADE ASSOCIATIONS

**East African Tea Trade Association:** Tea Trade Centre, Nyerere Ave, POB 85174, Mombasa; tel. (11) 315687; fax (11) 225823; f. 1957; organizes Mombasa weekly tea auctions; CEO MARK RADOLI; 167 mems.

**Export Processing Zones Authority:** POB 50563, Nairobi; tel. (2) 712800; fax (2) 713704; established by the govt. to promote investment in Export Processing Zones; CEO SILAS ITA.

**Export Promotion Council:** POB 43137, Nairobi; tel. (2) 333555; telex 22468; fax (2) 226036; promotes exports; Chair. SAM MUUMBI.

**Kenya Association of Manufacturers:** POB 30225, Nairobi; tel. (2) 746005; fax (2) 746028; Chair. A. C. JUMA; CEO JOHN W. KURIA; 560 mems.

# KENYA

## STATUTORY BOARDS

**Central Province Marketing Board:** POB 189, Nyeri.

**Coffee Board of Kenya:** POB 30566, Nairobi; tel. (2) 332896; telex 25706; fax (2) 330546; f. 1947; Chair. Pithon Mwangi; Gen. Man. Aggrey Murunga.

**Kenya Dairy Board:** POB 30406, Nairobi.

**Kenya Meat Corporation:** POB 30414, Nairobi; tel. (2) 340750; telex 22150; f. 1953; purchasing, processing and marketing of beef livestock; Chair. H. P. Barclay.

**Kenya Sisal Board:** Mutual Bldg, Kimathi St, POB 41179, Nairobi; tel. (2) 223457; f. 1946; CEO J. H. Wairagu; Man. Dir Kenneth Mukuma.

**Kenya Sugar Authority:** Hill Plaza Bldg, Ngong Rd, POB 51500, Nairobi; tel. (2) 710600; telex 25105; fax (2) 723903; Chair. R. O. Otutu; CEO J. A. Mudavadi.

**National Cereals and Produce Board:** POB 30586, Nairobi; tel. (2) 555288; telex 22769; f. 1966; Chair. James Matua; Dir Maj. W. K. Koitaba.

**Pyrethrum Board of Kenya:** POB 420, Nakuru; tel. (37) 211567; telex 33080; fax (37) 45274; f. 1935; 18 mems; Chair. T. O. Omato; CEO J. M. G. Wainaina.

**Tea Board of Kenya:** POB 20064, Nairobi; tel. (2) 569102; fax (2) 562120; f. 1950; regulates tea industry on all matters of policy, licenses tea planting and processing, combats pests and diseases, controls the export of tea, finances research on tea, promotes Kenyan tea internationally; 17 mems; Chair. Johnstone O. Moronge; CEO George M. Kimani.

## DEVELOPMENT ORGANIZATIONS

**Agricultural Development Corporation:** POB 47101, Nairobi; tel. (2) 338530; telex 22856; fax (2) 336524; f. 1965 to promote agricultural development and reconstruction; CEO Dr Walter Kilele.

**Agricultural Finance Corporation:** POB 30367, Nairobi; tel. (2) 333733; telex 22649; a statutory organization providing agricultural loans; Gen. Man. G. K. Toroitich.

**Development Finance Company of Kenya Ltd:** Finance House, 16th Floor, Loita St, POB 30483, Nairobi; tel. (2) 340401; telex 22662; fax (2) 338426; f. 1963; private co with govt participation; paid-up cap. Ks. 139m. (1991); Chair. H. N. K. arap Mengech; Gen. Man. J. V. Bosse.

**Horticultural Crops Development Authority:** POB 42601, Nairobi; tel. (2) 337381; telex 22687; fax (2) 228386; f. 1968; invests in production, dehydration, processing and freezing of fruit and vegetables; exports of fresh fruit and vegetables; Chair. Kasanga Mulwa; Man. Dir M. A. S. Mulandi.

**Housing Finance Co of Kenya Ltd:** Rehani House, Kenyatta Ave, POB 30088; Nairobi; tel. (2) 333910; f. 1965; cap. Ks 20m., dep. 2,300m. (1989); Man. Dir Walter Mukuria.

**Industrial and Commercial Development Corporation:** Uchumi House, Aga Khan Walk, POB 45519, Nairobi; tel. (2) 229213; telex 22429; fax (2) 333880; f. 1954; govt-financed; assists industrial and commercial development; Chair. Reuben Chesire; Exec. Dir Mohammed Kaittany.

**Investment Promotion Centre:** National Bank Bldg, 8th Floor, Harambee Ave, POB 55704, Nairobi; tel. (2) 221401; telex 25460; fax (2) 336663; promotes and facilitates local and foreign investment; Exec. Chair. Martin P. Kunguru.

**Kenya Fishing Industries Ltd:** Nairobi; cap. Ks. 5m.; Man. Dir Abdalla Mbwana.

**Kenya Industrial Estates Ltd:** Nairobi Industrial Estate, Likoni Rd, POB 78029, Nairobi; tel. (2) 542300; telex 24191; fax (2) 553124; f. 1967 to finance and develop small-scale industries.

**Kenya Industrial Research and Development Institute:** POB 30650, Nairobi; tel. (2) 557762; f. 1942, reorg. 1979; research and advisory services in scientific, technical and industrial development; Dir Dr R. O. Arunga.

**Kenya Planters' Co-operative Union:** Nairobi; coffee cultivation and processing; Chair. A. Mwangi; Man. Dir James Nyaga.

**Kenya Tea Development Authority:** POB 30213, Nairobi; tel. (2) 21441; telex 22645; f. 1960 to develop tea growing, manufacturing and marketing among African smallholders; in 1987 it supervised an area of 56,500 ha, cultivated by 150,414 registered growers, and operated 39 factories; Chair. Eric Kotut; Man. Dir Cyrus Irungu.

**Settlement Fund Trustees:** POB 30449, Nairobi; administers a land purchase programme involving over 1.2m. ha for resettlement of African farmers.

## EMPLOYERS' ASSOCIATIONS

**Federation of Kenya Employers:** Waajiri House, Argwings Kodhek Rd, POB 48311, Nairobi; tel. (2) 721929; telex 22642; Chair. J. P. N. Simba; Exec. Dir Tom D. Owuor; the following are affiliates:

**Association of Local Government Employers:** POB 52, Muranga; Chair. S. K. Itongu.

**Distributive and Allied Industries Employers' Association:** POB 30587, Nairobi; Chair. P. J. Mwaura.

**Engineering and Allied Industries Employers' Association:** POB 48311, Nairobi; tel. (2) 721929; Chair. D. M. Njoroge.

**Kenya Association of Building and Civil Engineering Contractors:** POB 43598, Nairobi; Chair. G. S. Hirani.

**Kenya Association of Hotelkeepers and Caterers:** POB 46406, Nairobi; tel. (2) 726640; fax (2) 721505; f. 1944; Chair. J. Mwendwa.

**Kenya Bankers' (Employers') Association:** POB 30003, Nairobi; tel. (2) 330200; Chair. J. A. M. Docherty.

**Kenya Sugar Employers' Union:** POB 262, Kisumu; Chair. L. Okech.

**Kenya Tea Growers' Association:** POB 320, Kericho; tel. (2) 21010; telex 22070; fax (2) 339559; Chair. M. K. A. Sang.

**Kenya Vehicle Manufacturers' Association:** POB 1436, Thika; Chair. G. J. Pulfer.

**Motor Trade and Allied Industries Employers' Association:** POB 48311, Nairobi; tel. (2) 721929; fax (2) 721990; Exec. Sec. G. N. Konditi.

**Sisal Growers' and Employers' Association:** POB 47523, Nairobi; tel. (2) 720170; telex 22642; fax (2) 721990; Chair. A. G. Combos.

**Timber Industries Employers' Association:** POB 18070, Nairobi; Chair. H. S. Bambrah.

## TRADE UNIONS

**Central Organization of Trade Unions (Kenya) (COTU):** Solidarity Bldg, Digo Rd, POB 13000, Nairobi; tel. (2) 761375; fax (2) 762695; f. 1965 as the sole trade union fed.; Chair. Benjamin K. Nzioka; Sec.-Gen. Joseph J. Mugalla; the following unions are affiliates:

**Amalgamated Union of Kenya Metalworkers:** POB 73651, Nairobi; Gen. Sec. F. E. Omido.

**Dockworkers' Union:** POB 98207, Mombasa; tel. (11) 491427; f. 1954; Gen. Sec. J. Khamis.

**Kenya Airline Pilots' Association.**

**Kenya Building, Construction, Civil Engineering and Allied Trades Workers' Union:** POB 49628, Nairobi; Gen. Sec. John Murugu.

**Kenya Chemical and Allied Workers' Union:** POB 73820, Nairobi; Gen. Sec. Were Dibi Oguto.

**Kenya Electrical Trades Allied Workers' Union.**

**Kenya Engineering Workers' Union:** POB 90443, Mombasa; Gen. Sec. Justus Mulei.

**Kenya Game Hunting and Safari Workers' Union:** POB 47509, Nairobi; Gen. Sec. J. M. Ndolo.

**Kenya Local Government Workers' Union:** POB 55827, Nairobi; Gen. Sec. Wasike Ndombi.

**Kenya Petroleum and Oil Workers' Union:** POB 10376, Nairobi; Gen. Sec. Jacob Ochino.

**Kenya Plantation and Agricultural Workers' Union:** POB 1161, Nakuru; Gen. Sec. Stanley Muiruri Karanja.

**Kenya Quarry and Mine Workers' Union:** POB 48125, Nairobi; tel. (2) 332120; f. 1961; Gen. Sec. Wafula Wa Musamia.

**Kenya Railways and Harbours Union:** POB 72029, Nairobi; Gen. Sec. Raphael Okango.

**Kenya Scientific Research, International Technical and Allied Institutions Workers' Union:** Ngumba House, Tom Mboya St, POB 55094, Nairobi; tel. (2) 339964; Sec.-Gen. Samson Owen Kubai.

**Kenya Shipping Clearing and Warehouse Workers' Union.**

**Kenya Shoe and Leather Workers' Union:** POB 49629, Nairobi; Gen. Sec. James Awich.

**Kenya Union of Commercial, Food and Allied Workers.**

**Kenya Union of Domestic, Hotel, Educational Institution, Hospitals and Allied Workers.**

**Kenya Union of Journalists:** POB 47035, Nairobi; Gen. Sec. George Odiko.

**Kenya Union of Printing, Publishing, Paper Manufacturers and Allied Workers:** POB 12144, Nairobi; Gen. Sec. John Bosco.

**Kenya Union of Sugar Plantation Workers:** POB 174, Muhoroni; Gen. Sec. Onyango Midika.

KENYA                                                                                                                           *Directory*

**National Seamen's Union of Kenya:** POB 81123, Mombasa; Gen. Sec. I. S. ABDALLAH MWARUA.
**Railway Workers' Union.**
**Tailors' and Textile Workers' Union.**
**Transport and Allied Workers' Union:** POB 74108, Nairobi; tel. (2) 23618; Gen. Sec. JULIAS MALII.
**Union of Posts and Telecommunications Employees:** POB 48155, Nairobi.

### Independent Unions

**Kenya Medical Practitioners' and Dentists' Union:** not officially recognized; Nat. Chair. GIBBON ATEKA.
**Kenya National Union of Teachers:** POB 30407, Nairobi; f. 1957; Sec.-Gen. A. A. ADONGO.
**University Academic Staff Union:** Nairobi; not officially registered; Interim Chair. Dr KORWA ABAR.

## Transport

### RAILWAYS

In 1993 there were 2,740 km of track open for traffic including sidings.
**Kenya Railways Corporation:** POB 30121, Nairobi; tel. (2) 221211; telex 22254; fax (2) 340049; f. 1977; Exec. Chair. Prof. J. K. MUSUVA; Gen. Man. E. Y. HARIZ (acting).

### ROADS

At the end of 1993 there were 63,120 km of classified roads, of which 6,438 km were main roads and 18,982 km were secondary roads. Only 13.7% of road surfaces were paved. An all-weather road links Nairobi to Addis Ababa, in Ethiopia, and there is a 590-km road link between Kitale (Kenya) and Juba (Sudan). In early 1995 the Government was negotiating with the World Bank for a loan to finance the urgent rehabilitation of the important internal road link between Nairobi and Mombasa.
**Abamba Public Road Services:** POB 40322, Nairobi; tel. (2) 556062; fax (2) 559884; operates bus services from Nairobi to all major towns in Kenya and to Kampala in Uganda.
**East African Road Services Ltd:** POB 30475, Nairobi; tel. (2) 764622; telex 23285; f. 1947; operates bus services from Nairobi to all major towns in Kenya; Chair. S. H. NATHOO; Gen. Man. E. H. MALIK.
**Nyayo Bus Service Corp.:** POB 47174, Nairobi; tel. (2) 803588; f. 1986; operates bus services within and between major towns in Kenya.
**Speedways Trans-Africa Freighters:** POB 75755, Nairobi; tel. (2) 544267; telex 23000; largest private road haulier in East Africa, with over 200 trucks; CEO HASSAN KANYARE.

### SHIPPING

Major shipping operations in Kenya are handled at the international seaport of Mombasa, which has 16 deep-water births with a total length of 3,044 m and facilities for the off-loading of bulk carriers, tankers and container vessels. An inland container depot with a potential full capacity of 120,000 20-ft (6-m) equivalent units was opened in Nairobi in 1984. Two further inland depots were scheduled to begin operating in early 1994 at Eldoret and Kisumu.
**Kenya Ports Authority:** POB 95009, Mombasa; tel. (11) 565222; telex 21243; fax (11) 311867; f. 1977; sole operator of coastal port facilities and inland container depots; Chair. SAJJAD RASHID; Man. Dir ALBERT C. MUMBA.
**Kenya Cargo Handling Services Ltd:** POB 95187, Mombasa; tel. (11) 25955; telex 20047; division of Kenya Ports Authority; Man. Dir JOSHUA KEGODE.
**Inchcape Shipping Services Kenya Ltd:** POB 90194, Mombasa; tel. (11) 314245; telex 21278; fax (11) 314224.
**Kenya Shipping Agency Ltd:** Southern House, Moi Ave, POB 84831, Mombasa; tel. (11) 20501; telex 21013; fax (11) 314494; subsidiary of Kenya National Trading Corpn Ltd; dry cargo, container, bulk carrier and tanker agents.
**Lykes Lines:** POB 30182, Nairobi; tel. (2) 332320; telex 22317; fax (2) 723861; services to USA ports.
**Mackenzie Maritime Ltd:** POB 90120, Mombasa; tel. (11) 221273; telex 21205; fax (11) 316260; agents for Amada Shipping, Ellerman Lines PLC, Deutsche Ost-Afrika Linie, Thos and Jas Harison, P & O Containers Ltd, Mitsui OSK Lines.
**Marship Ltd:** Jubilee Bldg, Moi Ave, POB 80443, Mombasa; tel. (11) 314705; telex 21442; fax (11) 316654; f. 1986; shipbrokers, ship management and chartering agents.
**Mitchell Cotts Kenya Ltd:** Cotts House, Wabera St, POB 30182, Nairobi; tel. (2) 221273; telex 22317; fax (2) 214228; agents for DOAL, Cie Maritime Belge SA, Nippon Yusen Kaisha.
**Southern Line Ltd:** POB 90102, Mombasa; tel. (11) 20507; telex 21288; operating dry cargo and tanker vessels between East African ports, Red Sea ports, the Persian (Arabian) Gulf and Indian Ocean islands.
**Spanfreight Shipping Ltd:** Kimathi House, Kimathi St, POB 52612, Nairobi; tel. (2) 715400; telex 25262; fax (2) 722196.
**Specialized Shipping Agencies:** Mombasa.
**Star East Africa Co:** POB 86725, Mombasa; tel. (11) 314060; telex 21251; fax (11) 312818; shipping agents and brokers.
**Wigglesworth and Co Ltd:** POB 90501, Mombasa; tel. (11) 25241; telex 21246.

### CIVIL AVIATION

Jomo Kenyatta International Airport, at Nairobi, was inaugurated in 1978. Moi International Airport, at Mombasa, also handles international traffic. Wilson Airport in Nairobi services domestic flights as do airports at Malindi and Kisumu. Kenya has about 400 airstrips. During the mid-1990s a US$10.9m. programme to rehabilitate and expand Jomo Kenyatta International and Moi International Airports was underway. A third international airport, at Eldoret, was due to be constructed by 1997.
**Kenya Airports Authority:** Jomo Kenyatta International Airport, POB 19001, Nairobi; tel. (2) 822950; telex 25552; fax (2) 822078; f. 1991; responsible for the provision and management of aerodromes and services and facilities thereof, approves and controls private airstrips; Man. Dir B. S. OMUSE.
**Air Kenya Aviation:** Wilson Airport, POB 30357, Nairobi; tel. (2) 501601; telex 22939; fax (2) 500845; f. 1985; operates internal scheduled and charter passenger services; Man. Dir JOHN BUCKLEY.
**Kenya Airways Ltd:** Jomo Kenyatta International Airport, POB 19002, Nairobi; tel. (2) 822171; telex 22771; fax (2) 822480; f. 1977 following the dissolution of East African Airways; passenger services to Africa, Asia and Europe; freight service to the United Kingdom and the Netherlands; internal services from Nairobi to Kisumu, Mombasa and Malindi; has a freight subsidiary (Kenya Airfreight Handling Ltd) and a charter subsidiary (Kenya Flamingo Airways); Chair. PHILIP NDEGWA; Man. Dir BRIAN DAVIES.

### CIVIL AVIATION AUTHORITY

**Kenya Directorate of Civil Aviation:** Jomo Kenyatta International Airport, POB 30163, Nairobi; tel. (2) 822950; telex 25239; f. 1948; under Kenya govt control since 1977; responsible for the conduct of civil aviation; advises the Govt on civil aviation policy; Dir J. P. AYUGA.

## Tourism

Kenya's main attractions as a tourist centre are its wildlife, with 25 National Parks and 23 game reserves, the Indian Ocean coast and a good year-round climate.
Tourist arrivals numbered 814,400 in 1990, but declined to 817,550 in 1991 and to 698,540 in 1992, when earnings from the sector totalled US $442m. (compared with $432m. in 1991).
**Kenya Tourist Development Corporation:** Utalii House, Uhuru Highway, POB 42013, Nairobi; tel. (2) 330820; telex 23009; fax (2) 227815; f. 1965; Chair. PAUL KITOLOLO; Man. Dir ELIAS MUSYOKA.

# KIRIBATI

## Introductory Survey

### Location, Climate, Language, Religion, Flag, Capital

The Republic of Kiribati (pronounced 'Kir-a-bas') comprises 33 atolls, in three principal groups, scattered within an area of about 5m. sq km (2m. sq miles) in the mid-Pacific Ocean. The country extends about 3,870 km (2,400 miles) from east to west and about 2,050 km (1,275 miles) from north to south. Its nearest neighbours are Nauru, to the west, and Tuvalu and Tokelau, to the south. The climate is equatorial or tropical, with daytime temperatures varying between 26°C (79°F) and 32°C (90°F). There is a season of north-westerly trade winds from March to October and a season of rains and gales from October to March. Average annual rainfall, however, varies greatly, from 3,000 mm (118 ins) in the northern islands to 1,500 mm (59 ins) in Tarawa and 700 mm (28 ins) in the Line Islands. Droughts occur in the central and southern islands. The principal languages are I-Kiribati (Gilbertese) and English, and the islands' inhabitants are mostly Christians. The national flag (proportions 2 by 1) depicts a golden frigate bird in flight, on a red background, above a rising sun and alternating wavy horizontal lines of blue and white, representing the sea. The capital is the island of Bairiki, in Tarawa Atoll.

### Recent History

In 1892 the United Kingdom established a protectorate over the 16 atolls of the Gilbert Islands and the nine Ellice Islands (now Tuvalu). The two groups were administered together by the Western Pacific High Commission (WPHC), which was based in Fiji until its removal to the British Solomon Islands (now Solomon Islands) in 1953. The phosphate-rich Ocean Island (now Banaba), west of the Gilberts, was annexed by the United Kingdom in 1900. The Gilbert and Ellice Islands were annexed in 1915, effective from January 1916, when the protectorate became a colony. The local representative of the WPHC was the Resident Commissioner, based on Tarawa Atoll in the Gilbert group. Later in 1916 the new Gilbert and Ellice Islands Colony (GEIC) was extended to include Ocean Island and two of the Line Islands, far to the east. Christmas Island (now Kiritimati), another of the Line Islands, was added in 1919, and the eight Phoenix Islands (then uninhabited) in 1937. The Line and Phoenix Islands, south of Hawaii, were also claimed by the USA. A joint British-US administration for two of the Phoenix group, Canton (now Kanton) and Enderbury, was agreed in April 1939.

During the Second World War the GEIC was invaded by Japanese forces, who occupied the Gilbert Islands in 1942–43. Tarawa Atoll was the scene of some of the fiercest fighting in the Pacific between Japan and the USA.

As part of the British Government's programme of developing its own nuclear weapons, the first test of a British hydrogen bomb was conducted near Christmas Island in May 1957, when a device was exploded in the atmosphere. Two further tests took place in the same vicinity later that year.

In 1963, to prepare the GEIC for self-government, the first of a series of legislative and executive bodies were established. In January 1972 a Governor of the GEIC was appointed to assume almost all the functions previously exercised in the colony by the High Commissioner. At the same time, the five uninhabited Central and Southern Line Islands, previously administered directly by the High Commissioner, became part of the GEIC. In May 1974 the Legislative Council was replaced by a new body, the House of Assembly, with 28 elected members and three official members. A Chief Minister, Naboua Ratieta, was elected by the House and chose between four and six other ministers.

In October 1975 the Ellice Islands were allowed to secede from the GEIC to form a separate territory, Tuvalu. The remainder of the GEIC was renamed the Gilbert Islands, and the House of Assembly's membership was reduced.

In 1975 the British Government refused to recognize as legitimate a demand for independence by the people of Ocean Island (Banaba), who had been in litigation with the British Government since 1971 over revenues derived from exports of phosphate. Open-cast mining had so adversely affected the island's environment that most of the Banabans had been resettled on Rabi Island, 2,600 km (1,600 miles) away in the Fiji group. The Banabans rejected the British Government's argument that phosphate revenues should be distributed over the whole territory of the Gilbert Islands. In 1976 the British High Court dismissed the Banabans' claim for unpaid royalties but upheld that for damages. In May 1977 the British Government offered an *ex gratia* payment of $A10m., without admitting liability for damages and on condition that no further appeal would be made to the courts. The offer was rejected.

The Gilbert Islands obtained internal self-government on 1 January 1977. Later in that year the number of elected members in the House of Assembly was increased to 36, and provision was subsequently made for a member appointed by the Rabi Council of Leaders. Following a general election in February 1978, Ieremia Tabai, Leader of the Opposition in the previous House, was elected Chief Minister. On 12 July 1979 the Gilbert Islands became an independent republic within the Commonwealth, under the name of Kiribati. The House of Assembly was renamed the Maneaba ni Maungatabu, and Ieremia Tabai became the country's first President (Beretitenti). In September Kiribati signed a treaty of friendship with the USA, which relinquished its claim to the Line and Phoenix Islands, including Kanton and Enderbury. Kiribati did not become a member of the UN (owing to financial considerations), although it has joined some UN agencies.

In April 1981 the Banaban community on Rabi accepted the British Government's earlier *ex gratia* offer of compensation, but they continued to seek self-government. The 1979 Constitution provided for an independent commission of inquiry, which was to review the political status of the Banabans three years after Kiribati had achieved independence. However, the inquiry was not commissioned until August 1985.

The first general election since independence took place in March and April 1982. The members of the new Maneaba all sat as independents. In accordance with the 1979 Constitution, the legislature nominated (from among its members) candidates for the country's first presidential election, to be held on the basis of direct popular vote. President Tabai was confirmed in office at the election in May. However, the Government resigned in December, following the Maneaba's second rejection of proposals to increase salaries for civil servants. As a result, the Maneaba was dissolved, and another general election took place in January 1983, at which two members of the outgoing Cabinet lost their seats. The formation of the new Maneaba necessitated a further presidential election in February, at which Tabai was re-elected for his third term of office. At a general election in March 1987 two cabinet ministers and 14 other members of the Maneaba lost their seats. Tabai was re-elected to the presidency in May.

At a general election in May 1991 eight incumbent members of the Maneaba lost their seats and 16 new members were chosen. A presidential election took place in July of the same year, when the former Vice-President, Teatao Teannaki, narrowly defeated Roniti Teiwaki to replace Tabai, who had served the maximum presidential mandate permitted by the Constitution.

In January 1992 the Maneaba approved a motion (proposed by opposition delegates) urging the Government to seek compensation from Japan for damage caused during the Second World War. The motion, which had been presented to previous sessions of the legislature, was thought to have been prompted by the success of a similar claim by the Marshall Islands. In late 1994 the intention to pursue a compensation claim with the Japanese was reiterated by the newly-elected President, Teburoro Tito (see below).

In late 1993 Roniti Teiwaki, then leader of the opposition Maneaban Te Mauri, expressed concern that Kiribati had become too reliant on foreign aid, which was frequently invested in projects initiated and managed by the donor countries. He was particularly critical of the use of Australian aid for infrastructural works, and of a project to extend the

Bairiki airport runway, financed by the People's Republic of China and carried out with Chinese labour.

In late May 1994 the Government was defeated on a motion of confidence, following opposition allegations that government ministers had misused travel allowances. The Maneaba was dissolved and, in accordance with the Constitution, was replaced by an interim Council of State, composed of the Chairman of the Public Service Commission, the Speaker of the Maneaba and the Chief Justice.

At legislative elections held on 22 and 29 July 1994 five cabinet ministers lost their seats. Thirteen of the newly-elected members were supporters of the Maneaban Te Mauri, while only eight were known to support the previously dominant National Progressive Party grouping. At the presidential election on 30 September 1994 Teburoro Tito, of the Maneaban Te Mauri, was elected, receiving 51.1% of the total votes. Upon his appointment, the new President declared that reducing Kiribati's dependence on foreign aid would be a major objective for his Government. He also announced his intention to pursue civil and criminal action against members of the previous Government for alleged misuse of public funds while in office. In the following month a defamation case brought against Tito by Teannaki (which had been initiated during the latter's tenure as President) was resolved by the Magistrate's Court in Tito's favour. However, the Chief Justice, Faqir Muhammad, subsequently overturned the decision, provoking widespread controversy. In mid-November a motion of 'no confidence' in the Chief Justice was approved by more than two-thirds of the members of the Maneaba, and Muhammad was consequently suspended from office. Tito also announced the establishment of a tribunal to investigate the events surrounding the affair. However, doubts about the constitutionality of the Government's actions led to a decision by the High Court to suspend the tribunal and revoke the suspension of the Chief Justice. The matter was to be referred to the Court of Appeal.

Owing to the high rate of population growth within the territory (about 2% per year), it was announced in 1988 that nearly 5,000 inhabitants were to be resettled on outlying atolls, mainly in the Line Islands. By September 1989 about 200 people had been resettled. A new scheme, aimed at further alleviating pressure on the Gilbert Islands by encouraging resettlement in the Line Islands, was announced by the new Government in late 1994.

In 1989 a UN report on the 'greenhouse effect' (the heating of the earth's atmosphere, and a resultant rise in sea-level) listed Kiribati as one of the countries that would completely disappear beneath the sea in the 21st century, unless drastic action were taken. None of the land on the islands is more than two metres above sea-level, making the country extremely vulnerable to the effects of climate change. A rise in sea-level would not only cause flooding, but would also upset the balance between sea and fresh water (below the coral sands), rendering water supplies undrinkable.

### Government

Legislative power is vested in the unicameral Maneaba ni Maungatabu. It has 39 members elected by universal adult suffrage for four years (subject to dissolution), one nominated representative of the Banaban community and, if he is not an elected member, the Attorney-General as an *ex-officio* member. The Head of State is the Beretitenti (President), who is also Head of Government. The President is elected by direct popular vote. The President governs with the assistance of the Vice-President and Cabinet, whom he appoints from among members of the Maneaba. Executive authority is vested in the Cabinet, which is responsible to the Maneaba.

### Economic Affairs

In 1993, according to estimates by the World Bank, Kiribati's gross national product (GNP), measured at average 1991–93 prices, was US $54m., equivalent to US $710 per head. During 1985–93, it was estimated, GNP per head decreased, in real terms, at an average annual rate of 1.3%. Over the same period the population increased by an annual average of 2.0%. Kiribati's gross domestic product (GDP) increased, in real terms, by an annual average of 1.1% in 1982–92.

Agriculture (including fishing), which employs the majority of the working population, contributed 25.1% of GDP in 1992. The principal cash crop is coconuts, yielding copra, which accounted for 77.1% of domestic export earnings in 1992. Bananas, screw-pine (*Pandanus*), breadfruit and papaya are cultivated as food crops. The cultivation of seaweed began in the mid-1980s: production increased from 70 metric tons in 1988 to 798 tons in 1990, when seaweed provided 24% of domestic export earnings. However, the proportion declined to 5.1% in 1992. Pigs and chickens are kept. Kiribati depends on imports of rice, wheat flour and meat. The closure of the state fishing company was announced in 1991, as a result of a dramatic decline in the fish catch: fish provided only 6.4% of export earnings in 1992 (compared with 32% in 1990). However, the sale of fishing licences to foreign fleets provides an important source of income. South Korean, Japanese, Taiwanese and US fleets are the principal applicants. In 1991 important fishing projects were initiated, with Japanese funding, in outer islands, and in the following year more than 100 I-Kiribati fishermen gained employment on Japanese fishing vessels. In 1992 Kiribati received US $5.7m. in income from the Regional Fisheries Treaty with the USA. The payment represented some 57% of the total amount paid to South Pacific countries in that year under the Treaty. Agricultural GDP increased by an annual average of 1.9% in 1982–92.

Industry (including manufacturing, construction and power) contributed 9.2% of GDP in 1992. Mining of phosphate rock on the island of Banaba, which ceased in 1979, formerly provided some 80% of export earnings. Interest from a phosphate reserve fund, established in 1956, continues to be an important source of budgetary income. Solar-evaporated salt is produced.

Manufacturing, which contributed 2.1% of GDP in 1992, is confined to the small-scale production of coconut-based products, soap, foods, handicrafts, furniture, leather goods and garments. Manufacturing GDP declined by an annual average of 0.4% in 1982–92. Mineral fuels accounted for 7.8% of total import costs in 1992.

Tourism makes a significant contribution to the economy (providing 14.9% of GDP in 1992), and there is considerable optimism regarding the further development of this sector.

In 1992 Kiribati recorded a trade deficit of $A44.0m., and in 1988 there was a surplus of $A7.6m. on the current account of the balance of payments. In 1992 the principal sources of imports were Australia (38.4%), Japan (22.7%) and Fiji (11.3%). The major imports in that year were foodstuffs, machinery and transport equipment, mineral fuels and basic manufactures. The principal recipient of exports in 1992 was Bangladesh (accounting for 77.1% of total domestic exports), which since 1991 has purchased Kiribati's entire shipments of copra. The major exports were copra, fish and seaweed. In 1993 the value of exports was equivalent to 14% of the value of imports.

In 1990 there was an estimated recurrent budgetary surplus of $A3.0m. A development budget of more than US $26m. was approved in early 1992. Kiribati's total external debt for 1987 was estimated at $A3.6m. The annual rate of inflation averaged 4.7% in 1985–92; consumer prices increased by an annual average of 3.3% in 1992. About 2.8% of the labour force were unemployed in 1990.

Kiribati is a member of the South Pacific Commission (see p. 215) and the South Pacific Forum (p. 217), and is a signatory to the South Pacific Regional Trade and Economic Co-operation Agreement (SPARTECA—see p. 218).

According to United Nations criteria, Kiribati is one of the world's least-developed nations. The ending of phosphate mining in 1979 deprived the country of its principal source of export earnings. During the 1980s Kiribati was vulnerable to fluctuations in the price of copra on the international market, and its dependence on imports of almost all essential commodities resulted in a permanent visible trade deficit; the country also remained reliant on foreign assistance for its development budget. A project linking North and South Tarawa, as well as several outer islands, by a series of causeways and bridges was due to be completed by the mid-1990s. The introduction of a privatization programme in 1989 envisaged the sale of many of the country's 37 government-owned enterprises by the mid-1990s. In late 1994 the new Government announced an economic development programme that particularly emphasized the improvement of transport and communications in the islands. The Government recommended more frequent international flights to the country and the construction of airfields on all inhabited islands, as well as work to upgrade roads and ports. It was hoped that these measures would not only encourage foreign business concerns to invest

# KIRIBATI

*Introductory Survey, Statistical Survey*

in the islands, but would also enhance Kiribati's potential for tourism.

### Social Welfare

The Government maintains a free medical service. Each atoll has a dispensary, with a medical assistant in charge. In 1982 Kiribati had 34 government-controlled hospital establishments, and in 1985 there were 33 physicians working in the country and, there was a total of 308 hospital beds. In late 1994 the Government recommended the increased study and exploitation of traditional medicines.

### Education

Education is compulsory for nine years between the ages of six and 14 years. This generally involves seven years at a primary school and at least five years at a secondary school. Every atoll is provided with at least one primary school. An estimated 92% of children aged six to 12 receive primary education. The Government administers a technical college and training colleges for teachers, nurses and seamen (the last, the Marine Training Centre, trains about 200 seamen each year for employment by overseas shipping companies). An extra-mural centre of the University of the South Pacific (based in Fiji) is located on SouthTarawa. Government expenditure on education in 1991 was $A4.4m.

### Public Holidays

**1995:** 1 January (New Year), 14–17 April (Easter), 12 July (Independence Day), 4 August (Youth Day), 25–26 December (Christmas).

**1996:** 1 January (New Year), 5–8 April (Easter), 12 July (Independence Day), 4 August (Youth Day), 25–26 December (Christmas).

# Statistical Survey

Source (unless otherwise stated): Statistics Office, Ministry of Finance and Economic Planning, POB 67, Bairiki, Tarawa; tel. 21820; fax 21307.

## AREA AND POPULATION

**Area:** 810.5 sq km (312.9 sq miles). *Principal atolls* (sq km): Banaba (island) 6.29; Tarawa 31.02 (North 15.26, South 15.76); Abemama 27.37; Tabiteuea (North 25.78, South 11.85); Total Gilbert group (incl. others) 285.52; Kanton (Phoenix Is) 9.15; Teraina (Fanning) 33.73; Kiritimati (Christmas—Line Is) 388.39.

**Population:** 72,335 (males 35,770, females 36,565) at census of 7 November 1990; 77,000 (official estimate) at mid-1993. *Principal atolls* (1990): Banaba (island) 284; Abaiang 5,233; Tarawa 29,028 (North 3,648, South—including Bairiki, the capital—25,380); Tabiteuea 4,532 (North 3,201, South 1,331); Total Gilbert group (incl. others) 67,508; Kanton (Phoenix Is) 45; Kiritimati 2,537; Total Line and Phoenix Is (incl. others) 4,827.

**Density** (mid-1993): 95.0 per sq km.

**Ethnic Groups** (census of 1990): Micronesians 71,558; Polynesians 361; Europeans 155; Others 261; Total 72,335.

**Births, Marriages and Deaths** (registrations, 1988): Live births 1,479 (birth rate 21.7 per 1,000); Marriages 352 (marriage rate 5.2 per 1,000); Deaths 332 (death rate 4.9 per 1,000).

**Expectation of Life** (World Bank estimates, years at birth, 1992): 56.

**Economically Active Population** (1990 census): Total employed 31,713 (males 16,929, females 14,784), incl. 11,167 in paid employment; Total unemployed 914 (males 539, females 375).

## AGRICULTURE, ETC.

**Principal Crops** (FAO estimates, '000 metric tons, 1993): Roots and tubers 8; Coconuts 65; Vegetables and melons 5; Bananas 4; Other fruits 1. Source: FAO, *Production Yearbook*.

**Livestock** (FAO estimates, year ending September): Pigs 9,000 (1993); Chickens 177,000 (1982). Source: FAO, *Production Yearbook*.

**Livestock Products** (FAO estimates, metric tons, 1993): Total meat 1,000; Hen eggs 130. Source: FAO, *Production Yearbook*.

**Fishing** (FAO estimates, metric tons, live weight): Total catch 29,417 in 1990; 29,639 in 1991; 30,535 in 1992. Figures exclude aquatic plants (metric tons): 350 in 1990; 400 in 1991; 400 in 1992. Source: FAO, *Yearbook of Fishery Statistics*.

## INDUSTRY

**Copra Production** (metric tons): 5,911 in 1986; 6,026 in 1987; 14,406 in 1988.

**Electric Energy** (million kWh): 7 per year in 1988–91. Source: UN, *Industrial Statistics Yearbook*.

## FINANCE

**Currency and Exchange Rates:** Australian currency: 100 cents = 1 Australian dollar ($A). *Sterling and US Dollar Equivalents* (31 December 1994): £1 sterling = $A2.017; US $1 = $A1.289; $A100 = £49.58 = US $77.57. *Average Exchange Rate* (US $ per Australian dollar): 0.7353 in 1992; 0.6801 in 1993; 0.7317 in 1994.

**Budget** ($A'000): *1988: Revenue:* Recurrent 18,560; Development 6,387; Total 24,947. *Expenditure:* Recurrent 18,029; Development 3,405; Total 21,434. *1989: Revenue:* Recurrent 18,112. *Expenditure:* Recurrent 20,021; Development 3,469; Total 23,490. *1990: Revenue:* Recurrent 25,084. *Expenditure:* Recurrent 22,130; Development 7,114; Total 29,244.

**Cost of Living** (Consumer Price Index for Tarawa; base: 1980 = 100): 165.8 in 1990; 174.9 in 1991; 180.6 in 1992. Source: ILO, *Year Book of Labour Statistics*.

**Gross Domestic Product by Economic Activity** ($A '000 at current prices, 1992): Agriculture and fishing 11,022; Manufacturing 920; Electricity and water 800; Construction 2,300; Trade and hotels 6,530; Transport and communications 7,130; Finance and insurance, real estate and business services 3,210; Community, social and personal services 11,935; *Sub-total* 43,847; Indirect taxes *less* subsidies 2,413; *Total* (in purchasers' values) 46,260.

**Balance of Payments** ($A million, 1988): Merchandise exports f.o.b. 6.6; Merchandise imports f.o.b. –27.5; *Trade balance* –20.9; Exports of services 23.7; Imports of services –19.6; *Balance on goods and services* –16.8; Private unrequited transfers (net) 3.4; Government unrequited transfers (net) 21.1; *Current balance* 7.6; Capital account (net) –5.5; Net errors and omissions –2.7; *Total* (net monetary movements) –0.6.

## EXTERNAL TRADE

**Principal Commodities** ($A '000, 1992): *Imports f.o.b.:* Food and live animals 10,654; Beverages and tobacco 2,534; Crude materials (inedible) except fuels 626; Mineral fuels, lubricants, etc. 3,951; Animal and vegetable oils and fats 95; Chemicals 1,746; Basic manufactures 4,051; Machinery and transport equipment 23,885; Miscellaneous manufactured articles 2,788; Total (incl. others) 50,530. *Exports f.o.b.:* Copra 4,350; Shark fins 118; Fish 363; Seaweed 286; Pet fish 258; Total (incl. others) 5,645 (excl. re-exports 868).

**Principal Trading Partners** ($A '000, 1992): *Imports:* Australia 19,399; People's Republic of China 1,666; Fiji 5,720; France 4,773; Japan 11,451; New Zealand 2,734; USA 1,447; Total (incl. others) 50,530. *Exports* (excl. re-exports): Bangladesh 4,350; Denmark 296; Fiji 176; USA 608; Total (incl. others) 5,645.

## TRANSPORT

**Road Traffic** (motor vehicles registered on South Tarawa, 1988): Motor cycles 571; Passenger cars 222; Buses 80; Trucks 35; Others 9. *Outer islands* (registered motor vehicles, 1985): Motor cycles 805; Others 111.

**Shipping** (international freight traffic, '000 metric tons, 1990): Goods loaded 15; Goods unloaded 26. Source: UN, *Monthly Bulletin of Statistics*.

**Civil Aviation** (1988): Aircraft movements 8,706; Passenger arrivals 6,645; Passenger departures (1986) 6,688; Freight (metric tons) 188.1.

KIRIBATI

## TOURISM

**Visitor Arrivals** (1987): 8,000.

## COMMUNICATIONS MEDIA

**Radio Receivers** (1992): 15,000 in use*.

**Telephones** (exchange lines, 1988): 911 in use.

**Non-Daily Newspapers** (provisional, 1988): 2; estimated circulation 4,000*.

* Source: UNESCO, *Statistical Yearbook*.

## EDUCATION

**Primary** (1992): 95 govt schools; 16,020 students; 545 teachers.
**Secondary** (1992): 9 schools (1990); 3,357 students; 237 teachers.
**Tertiary** (1988): 6 institutions; 568 students; 52 teachers.
Source: mainly UNESCO, *Statistical Yearbook*.

# Directory

## The Constitution

A new Constitution was promulgated at independence on 12 July 1979. The main provisions are as follows:

The Constitution states that Kiribati is a sovereign democratic Republic and that the Constitution is the supreme law. It guarantees protection of all fundamental rights and freedoms of the individual and provides for the determination of citizenship.

The President, known as the Beretitenti, is Head of State and Head of the Government and presides over the Cabinet which consists of the Beretitenti, the Kauoman-ni-Beretitenti (Vice-President), the Attorney-General and not more than eight other ministers appointed by the Beretitenti from an elected parliament known as the Maneaba ni Maungatabu. The Constitution provided that the pre-independence Chief Minister became the first Beretitenti, but that in future the Beretitenti would be elected. After each general election for the Maneaba, the chamber nominates, from among its members, three or four candidates from whom the Beretitenti is elected by universal adult suffrage. Executive authority is vested in the Cabinet, which is directly responsible to the Maneaba ni Maungatabu. The Constitution also provides for a Council of State consisting of the Chairman of the Public Services Commission, the Chief Justice and the Speaker of the Maneaba.

Legislative power resides with the single-chamber Maneaba ni Maungatabu, composed of 39 members elected by universal adult suffrage for four years (subject to dissolution), one nominated member (see below) and the Attorney-General as an *ex-officio* member if he is not elected. The Maneaba is presided over by the Speaker, who is elected by the Maneaba from among persons who are not members of the Maneaba.

One chapter makes special provision for Banaba and the Banabans, stating that one seat in the Maneaba is reserved for a nominated member of the Banaban community. The Banabans' inalienable right to enter and reside in Banaba is guaranteed and, where any right over or interest in land there has been acquired by the Republic of Kiribati or by the Crown before independence, the Republic is required to hand back the land on completion of phosphate extraction. A Banaba Island Council is provided for, as is an independent commission of inquiry to review the provisions relating to Banaba.

The Constitution also makes provision for finance, for a Public Service and for an independent judiciary (see Judicial System).

## The Government

### HEAD OF STATE

**President (Beretitenti):** TEBURORO TITO (elected 30 September 1994).
**Vice-President (Kauoman-ni-Beretitenti):** TEWAREKA TENTOA.

### THE CABINET
(May 1995)

**President and Minister of Foreign Affairs and International Trade:** TEBURORO TITO.
**Vice-President and Minister of Home Affairs and Rural Development:** TEWAREKA TENTOA.
**Minister of Finance and Economic Planning:** BENIAMINA TINGA.
**Minister of Education, Science and Technology:** WILLIE TOKATAAKIE.
**Minister of Transport, Communications and Tourism:** MANRAOI KAIEA.
**Minister of Commerce, Industry and Employment:** TANIERU AWERIKA.
**Minister of Works and Energy:** EMILE SCHUTZ.
**Minister of the Environment and Natural Resource Development:** ANOTE TONG.
**Minister of Health, Family Planning and Social Welfare:** KATAOTIKA TEKEE.
**Minister of the Line and Phoenix Groups:** TEIRAOI TETABEA.
**Attorney-General:** MICHAEL TAKABWEBWE.

### MINISTRIES

**Ministry of Commerce, Industry and Employment:** POB 69, Bairiki, Tarawa; tel. 21097; telex 77051; fax 21452.
**Ministry of Education, Science and Technology:** POB 263, Bikenibeu, Tarawa; tel. 28091; fax 28222.
**Ministry of the Environment and Natural Resource Development:** POB 64, Bairiki, Tarawa; tel. 21099; telex 77039.
**Ministry of Finance and Economic Planning:** POB 67, Bairiki, Tarawa; tel. 21820; fax 21307.
**Ministry of Foreign Affairs and International Trade:** POB 68, Bairiki, Tarawa; tel. 21342; fax 21466.
**Ministry of Health, Family Planning and Social Welfare:** POB 268, Bikenibeu, Tarawa; tel. 28100; fax 28152.
**Ministry of Home Affairs and Rural Development:** POB 75, Bairiki, Tarawa; tel. 21092; fax 21133.
**Ministry of the Line and Phoenix Groups:** Kiritimati Island; tel. 81316; fax 81278.
**Ministry of Tourism:** Tarawa.
**Ministry of Transport and Communications:** POB 487, Betio, Tarawa; tel. 26003; telex 77022; fax 26193.
**Ministry of Works and Energy:** POB 498, Betio, Tarawa; tel. 26192; telex 77045.

## President and Legislature

### PRESIDENT

**Election, 30 September 1994**

| Candidate | Votes | % |
|---|---|---|
| TEBURORO TITO | 10,834 | 51.1 |
| TEWAREKA TENTOA | 3,886 | 18.3 |
| RONITI TEIWAKI | 3,383 | 16.0 |
| PETER TABERANNANG TIMEON | 3,080 | 14.5 |
| **Total** | 21,183 | 100.0 |

### MANEABA NI MAUNGATABU
(House of Assembly)

This is a unicameral body comprising 39 elected members (most of whom formally present themselves for election as independent candidates), and one nominated representative of the Banaban community. A general election was held on 22 and 29 July 1994.

**Speaker:** TEKIREE TAMUERA.

## Political Organizations

There are no organized political parties in Kiribati. However, loose groupings of individuals supporting similar policies do exist, the most prominent being the Maneaban Te Mauri, led by TEBURORO TITO, and the National Progressive Party, led by TEATAO TEANNAKI.

## Diplomatic Representation

### EMBASSY AND HIGH COMMISSIONS IN KIRIBATI

**Australia:** POB 77, Bairiki, Tarawa; tel. 21184; fax 21440; High Commissioner: STEWART D. BROOKS.

# KIRIBATI

**China, People's Republic:** Bairiki, Tarawa; Ambassador: Wang Shaohua.

**New Zealand:** POB 53, Bairiki, Tarawa; tel. 21400; fax 21402; High Commissioner: Brian Marshall.

## Judicial System

There are 26 Magistrates' Courts (each consisting of one presiding magistrate and eight other magistrates) hearing civil, criminal and land cases. When hearing civil or criminal cases, the presiding magistrate sits with two other magistrates, and when hearing land cases with four other magistrates. A single magistrate has national jurisdiction in civil and criminal matters. Appeal from the Magistrates' Courts lies, in civil and criminal matters, to a single judge of the High Court, and, in matters concerning land, divorce and inheritance, to the High Court's Land Division, which consists of a judge and two Land Appeal Magistrates.

The High Court of Kiribati is a superior court of record and has unlimited jurisdiction. It consists of the Chief Justice and a Puisne Judge. Appeal from a single judge of the High Court, both as a Court of the First Instance and in its appellate capacity, lies to the Kiribati Court of Appeal, which is also a court of record and consists of a panel of five judges.

All judicial appointments are made by the Beretitenti (President).

**High Court:** POB 501, Betio, Tarawa; tel. 26007; fax 26149.
**Chief Justice:** Faqir Muhammad.
**Puisne Judge:** (vacant).
**Chief Registrar:** Teaiaki Koae.
**Judges of the Kiribati Court of Appeal:** Faqir Muhammad (President), Sir Harry Gibbs (Vice-President), Sir Gaven John Donne, Peter David Connolly, Raymond George Reynolds, John Douglas Dillon.

## Religion

### CHRISTIANITY

Most of the population are Christians: 53.4% Roman Catholic and 39.2% members of the Kiribati Protestant Church, according to the 1990 census.

#### The Roman Catholic Church

Kiribati forms part of the diocese of Tarawa and Nauru, suffragan to the archdiocese of Suva (Fiji). At 31 December 1992 the diocese contained an estimated 40,800 adherents. The Bishop participates in the Catholic Bishops' Conference of the Pacific, based in Suva (Fiji).

**Bishop of Tarawa and Nauru:** Most Rev. Paul Eusebius Mea Kaiuea, Bishop's House, POB 79, Bairiki, Tarawa; tel. 21159; fax 21401.

#### The Anglican Communion

Kiribati is within the diocese of Polynesia, part of the Anglican Church in Aotearoa, New Zealand and Polynesia. The Bishop in Polynesia is resident in Fiji.

#### Protestant Church

**Kiribati Protestant Church:** POB 80, Bairiki, Tarawa; tel. 21195; fax 21453; f. 1988; Moderator Rev. Teeta Ioran.

#### Other Churches

Seventh-day Adventist, Church of God and Assembly of God communities are also represented, as is the Church of Jesus Christ of Latter-day Saints (Mormon).

### BAHÁ'Í FAITH

**National Spiritual Assembly:** POB 269, Bikenibeu, Tarawa; tel. 28074; fax 28196; 2,146 mems resident in 98 localities in 1994.

## The Press

**Atoll Pioneer:** Information Department, POB 76, Bairiki, Tarawa; weekly.

**Te Itoi ni Kiribati:** POB 231, Bikenibeu, Tarawa; tel. 28138; fax 21341; f. 1914; Roman Catholic Church newsletter; monthly; circ. 2,300.

**Te Kaotan te Ota:** POB 80, Bairiki, Tarawa; tel. 21195; f. 1913; Protestant Church newspaper; monthly; Editor Ihaingateiti Maerere; circ. 1,700.

**Te Uekera:** Broadcasting and Publications Authority, POB 78, Bairiki, Tarawa; tel. 21162; fax 21096; f. 1945; fortnightly; English and I-Kiribati; Editor Ngauea Uatioa; circ. 2,000.

*Directory*

## Radio

In 1992, according to UNESCO, there were an estimated 15,000 radio receivers in use.

**Radio Kiribati:** Broadcasting and Publications Authority, POB 78, Bairiki, Tarawa; tel. 21161; telex 77024; fax 21096; f. 1954; statutory body; station Radio Kiribati broadcasting on SW and MW transmitters; programmes in I-Kiribati and English; some advertising; Man. (vacant).

## Finance

(cap. = capital; dep. = deposits; res = reserves)

### BANKING

**The Bank of Kiribati Ltd:** POB 66, Bairiki, Tarawa; tel. 21095; telex 77052; fax 21200; f. 1984; 51% owned by Westpac Banking Corpn (Australia), 49% by Govt of Kiribati; cap. $A0.6m., dep. $A30.0m., res $A0.5m. (Sept. 1993); total assets $A33.7m. (Sept. 1994); Chair. Paul Friend; Gen. Man. David Olley; br. on Kiritimati.

**Development Bank of Kiribati:** POB 33, Bairiki, Tarawa; tel. 21345; telex 77024; fax 21297; f. 1987; took over the assets of the National Loans Board; auth. cap. $A2m.; Gen. Man. Rose Sinclair (acting); Deputy Gen. Man. Itaea Riteri (acting); 3 brs.

### INSURANCE

**Kiribati Insurance Corpn:** POB 38, Bairiki, Tarawa; tel. 21260; fax 21426; f. 1981; only insurance co; reinsures overseas; CEOs Teairo Tooma, Teibaba Abera.

## Trade and Industry

### DEVELOPMENT ORGANIZATION

**Development Finance Institution (DFI):** POB 33, Bairiki, Tarawa; tel. 21345; fax 21297; f. 1987; identifies, promotes and finances small-scale projects; Gen. Man. Rose Sinclair (acting).

### CO-OPERATIVE SOCIETIES

Co-operative societies dominate trading in Tarawa and enjoy a virtual monopoly outside the capital, except for Banaba and Kiritimati. In 1982 there were 29 co-operative societies.

**The Kiribati Copra Co-operative Society Ltd:** POB 489, Betio, Tarawa; tel. 26534; telex 77020; f. 1976; the sole exporter of copra; seven cttee mems; 25 mem. socs; Chair. Koraubara Tetabea; Man. Biromina Awiu.

### TRADE UNIONS

**Kiribati Trades Union Congress (KTUC):** POB 418, Betio, Tarawa; tel. 26319; f. 1982; unions and asscns affiliated to the KTUC include the Fishermen's Union, the Co-operative Workers' Union, the Seamen's Union, the Teachers' Union, the Nurses' Asscn, the Public Employees' Asscn, the Bankers' Union, Butaritari Rural Workers' Union, Christmas Island Union of Federated Workers, the Pre-School Teachers' Asscn, Makim Island Rural Workers' Org., Nanolelei Retailers' Union and the Plantation Workers' Union of Fanning Island; 2,100 mems; Pres. Irata Teeta; Gen. Sec. Valo Valo.

## Transport

### ROADS

Wherever practicable, roads are built on all atolls, and connecting causeways between islets are also being built as funds and labour permit. A programme to construct causeways between North and South Tarawa, which was initiated in late 1988, was due to be completed by the mid-1990s. Kiribati has about 640 km of roads that are suitable for motor vehicles.

### SHIPPING

The Chief Container Service (CCS) operates a monthly container service from Australia to Kiribati, via Papua New Guinea, Vanuatu and Solomon Islands. Pacific Forum Line offers a monthly container service from Auckland (New Zealand) to Fiji, Tuvalu, Kiribati and Marshall Islands. Oil tankers, chartered by Mobil Oil Australia, deliver fuel to Kiribati, mainly from Fiji. Bali Hai Service runs a container service once every two months from Pusan (Republic of Korea), Kobe, Nagoya and Yokohama (Japan) to Tarawa and to Lautoka and Suva (Fiji), Apia (Western Samoa), Pago Pago (American Samoa), Papeete (French Polynesia), Nouméa (New Caledonia), Port Vila and Santo (Vanuatu) and Honiara (Solomon Islands). Bank Line and Columbus Line vessels call at Tarawa to

KIRIBATI

load copra once every two or three months. Local ships, owned by the Shipping Corpn of Kiribati, call at Kiritimati (Christmas Island), Tabuaeran (Fanning Island) and Teraina (Washington Island) three or four times each year for cargo/passenger traffic and also load copra for shipment to Majuro (Marshall Islands).

**Shipping Corporation of Kiribati:** POB 495, Betio, Tarawa; tel. 26195; telex 77030; fax 26204; operates five passenger/freight vessels on inter-island services; govt-owned; Man. Capt. TABEA RIWATA.

### CIVIL AVIATION

There are two international airports (Bonriki on South Tarawa, Cassidy on Kiritimati) and 16 other airfields in Kiribati. The airport at Bairiki was enlarged in the early 1990s, using a loan from the Bank of China. Air Nauru and Air Marshall Islands also operate international services to Tarawa.

**Air Tungaru Corporation:** POB 274, Bikenibeu, Tarawa; tel. 28232; telex 77023; fax 28277; f. 1977; national airline; operates scheduled passenger and cargo services between Tarawa's Bonriki Airport and 15 outer islands; also flies to Honolulu (Hawaii) and Fiji; Chair. TEKEN TOKATAAKE; Chief Exec. MATE T. MOANIBA.

## Tourism

Previous attempts to establish tourism have been largely unsuccessful, owing mainly to the remoteness of the islands. There were an estimated 8,000 visitors in 1987. In 1988 there were about 40 hotel rooms in Bairiki. In 1989 the Government adopted a plan to develop hotels in the Line Islands and to exploit sites of Second World War battles. The promotion of game-fishing and 'ecotourism', particularly bird-watching, was expected to increase tourist arrivals to Kiritimati in the mid-1990s.

**Kiribati Visitors Bureau:** POB 261, Bikenibeu, Tarawa; tel. 28288; telex 77022; fax 26193; Govt Tourist Officer TEEM URIAM.

# THE DEMOCRATIC PEOPLE'S REPUBLIC OF KOREA

## Introductory Survey

### Location, Climate, Language, Religion, Flag, Capital

The Democratic People's Republic of Korea (North Korea) occupies the northern part of the Korean peninsula, bordered to the north by the People's Republic of China and, for a very short section to the north-east, by the Russian Federation, and to the south by the Republic of Korea. The climate is continental, with cold, dry winters and hot, humid summers; temperatures range from −6° to 25°C (21° to 77°F). The language is Korean. Buddhism, Christianity and Chundo Kyo are officially cited as the principal religions. The national flag (proportions 65 by 33) is red, with blue stripes on the upper and lower edges, each separated from the red by a narrow white stripe. Left of centre is a white disc containing a five-pointed red star. The capital is Pyongyang.

### Recent History

Korea was formerly an independent monarchy. It was occupied by Japanese forces in 1905 and annexed by Japan in 1910, when the Emperor was deposed. Following Japan's surrender in August 1945, ending the Second World War, Korea was divided at latitude 38°N into military occupation zones, with Soviet forces in the North and US forces in the South. In the North a Provisional People's Committee, led by Kim Il Sung of the Korean Communist Party (KCP), was established in February 1946 and given government status by the Soviet occupation forces. In July 1946 the KCP merged with another group to form the North Korean Workers' Party. In 1947 a legislative body, the Choe Ko In Min Hoe Ui (Supreme People's Assembly—SPA), was established, and Kim Il Sung became Premier. A new assembly was elected in August 1948, and the Democratic People's Republic of Korea (DPRK) was proclaimed on 9 September. In the same year the Republic of Korea (q.v.) was proclaimed in the South. Initially, the DPRK was recognized only by the USSR and other communist countries. Soviet forces withdrew from North Korea in December 1948. By a merger between communists in the North and South, the Korean Workers' Party (KWP) was formed in June 1949. The KWP, led by Kim Il Sung until his death in 1994, has held power in North Korea ever since. Through the intensive promotion of the 'personality cult' of Kim Il Sung (the 'Great Leader') and, more recently, of his son Kim Jong Il (the 'Dear Leader') and a policy of strict surveillance of the entire population, internal opposition to the KWP has effectively been eliminated. The only organized opposition to the regime (albeit in exile) appears to be the Salvation Front for the Democratic Unification of Chosun, which was established by former military and other officials of the DPRK in the early 1990s, and which has branches in Moscow, Tokyo and Beijing.

The two republics each claimed to have legitimate jurisdiction over the whole Korean peninsula. North Korean forces crossed the 38th parallel in June 1950, precipitating a three-year war between North and South. The UN mounted a collective defence action in support of South Korea, and the invasion was repelled. North Korean forces were supported by the People's Republic of China from October 1950. Peace talks began in July 1951 and an armistice agreement was concluded in July 1953. The cease-fire line, roughly following the 38th parallel, remains the frontier between North and South Korea. A demilitarized zone (DMZ), supervised by UN forces, separates the two countries.

A new Constitution, adopted in December 1972, created the office of President, and Kim Il Sung was duly elected to the post. The appointment of Kim Jong Il to several key positions within the KWP in 1980 appeared to confirm him as his father's choice of successor. Kim Jong Il's visit to Beijing in June 1983 was interpreted as signifying Chinese approval of this proposed first communist dynasty. In July 1984 Radio Pyongyang referred to Kim Jong Il, for the first time, as the 'sole successor' to his father, but there were reports of domestic opposition to the President's heir, particularly among older members of the KWP.

In November 1986 false reports that Kim Il Sung had been assassinated prompted speculation that there had been an attempted coup. However, stability was apparently quickly restored, and, after an election to the eighth SPA, in the same month (when the 655 members were elected unopposed), Kim Il Sung was re-elected President, and a new Administration Council (cabinet) was formed. Li Gun Mo, a member of the Central People's Committee, was elected Premier, a post which he retained until December 1988, when he was replaced by Yon Hyong Muk, a former Vice-Premier and a member of the Politburo of the KWP. In March 1990 it was rumoured that Kim Il Sung would transfer presidential power to Kim Jong Il, immediately prior to forthcoming elections to the SPA. In the event, however, Kim Il Sung was re-elected President, although Kim Jong Il was appointed to his first state (as distinct from party) post as First Vice-Chairman of the National Defence Committee.

In February 1991 it was rumoured that there had been an unsuccessful coup against Kim Jong Il, planned by army officers opposed to his succession. In December Kim Jong Il was appointed Supreme Commander of the Korean People's Army, in place of his father (who had held the post since the DPRK's foundation), and in January 1992 he was reported to have been given control of foreign policy, thereby confirming the likelihood of his succession. In April Kim Jong Il was appointed to the rank of Marshal, while his father assumed the title of Grand Marshal.

In what was interpreted as a partial attempt to adapt to new international conditions, following the collapse of communist regimes worldwide, the SPA (according to South Korean reports) made several amendments to the DPRK's Constitution in April 1992. Principal among these were the deletion of all references to Marxist-Leninist ideology, and the promotion of 'economic openness' to allow (limited) foreign investment in North Korea (although, at the same time, the KWP's guiding principle of *Juche*, or self-reliance, was strongly emphasized). The Constitution also legalized the accession (in December 1991) of Kim Jong Il to the post of Supreme Commander of the Korean People's Army (hitherto the post had been constitutionally reserved for the President).

There were reports of further popular unrest during 1992, in response to the deteriorating economic situation and the resulting decline in living standards. Economic measures introduced by the Government in mid-1992, including a drastic devaluation of the won, reportedly led to violent protests in several towns in September. These reports were, however, denied by the DPRK leadership.

In December 1992 there was a minor reshuffle of the Administration Council, which included the replacement of Yon Hyong Muk as Premier by Kang Song San, an economist who had previously held the post in 1984–86. His appointment was interpreted by foreign observers as an attempt to provide fresh stimulus for economic reform, in order to prevent further decline. There was also a reshuffle of the hierarchy of the KWP in the same month.

The extent of the DPRK's economic difficulties was indicated by the budget proposals for 1993, which envisaged substantial reductions in expenditure as compared with 1992, and by the persistent reports of serious food riots, which circulated during the year. It was noted that both Kim Il Sung's birthday and that of his son were much less lavishly celebrated in 1993 than in previous years. Kim Jong Il's absence from public view for some three months in 1993 prompted speculation as to his physical and mental state of health. By the end of the year, although there were again rumours that the junior Kim might finally succeed his father as President, the unexpected return to political life of Kim Il Sung's younger brother, Kim Yong Ju, in December, after a

17-year absence, and his elevation to the position of Vice President and to membership of the Central Committee of the KWP's Politburo appeared to be to the detriment of Kim Jong Il. The junior Kim was again noticeably absent from public life in early 1994.

In July 1994, shortly before he was due to host a summit meeting with the South Korean President (see below), Kim Il Sung died, reportedly of a heart attack. One hundred days of national mourning were observed throughout the country, and, contrary to expectations, Kim Jong Il was not appointed to the three leading posts of President of the DPRK, General Secretary of the KWP and Chairman of the party's Central Military Commission. Indeed, Kim did not appear in public during this period, giving rise to speculation that he was either in poor health or that a struggle for power was taking place. The official media, however, continually referred to Kim Jong Il as the 'Great Leader' (the title hitherto reserved for his father). The death of Marshal O Jin U (the most prominent of the older generation of political leaders), in February 1995, was regarded as an opportunity for Kim Jong Il to take full control of the political and military apparatus, and, although Kim Il Sung's former posts still remained vacant in March, it appeared that the younger Kim would assume them when an appropriate period of mourning had elapsed.

In late January 1992 the US Department of State issued a condemnatory report detailing alleged violations of human rights in the DPRK. On the basis of statements made by the few people who have defected from the DPRK, the report estimated that there were 12 concentration camps in the DPRK, in which between 105,000 and 150,000 political prisoners and their family members were being detained. In 1994 the human rights organization, Amnesty International, announced that it had located a further camp, while the International Human Rights League estimated the number of political detainees to be more than 200,000. The DPRK Government has consistently denied the existence of such camps.

In 1971 talks took place for the first time between the Red Cross Societies of both North and South Korea. In 1972 both parties affirmed that reunification should be achieved through peaceful means. Reunification talks were, however, suspended in 1973, and hopes for better relations were undermined by a series of clashes between North and South Korean vessels in disputed waters during 1974. Propaganda campaigns, suspended by agreement in 1972, were resumed by both sides, and minor border incidents continued. In October 1978 the UN command accused North Korea of threatening the 1953 truce, after the discovery of an underground tunnel (the third since 1974) beneath the DMZ. During the 1980s the increasing prominence of Kim Il Sung's son, Kim Jong Il, who advocated an uncompromising policy towards the South, appeared to aggravate the situation.

In January 1984 the DPRK suggested tripartite talks on reunification, involving North and South Korea and the USA. This offer marked a significant change in position, since South Korea was to be directly included for the first time, but the proposal was rejected by President Chun of South Korea, who favoured direct bilateral talks between the two Koreas. During 1984 the DPRK's propaganda campaign was moderated, and in September the DPRK provided emergency relief to flood-stricken areas of the South. In November the first talks, on possible economic co-operation, were held, and negotiations continued in 1985.

However, in February 1986, during the annual South Korean-US 'Team Spirit' military manoeuvres (which were first conducted in 1976), North Korea suspended all negotiations with the South. In November South Korea denounced the DPRK's proposed construction of a dam at Mount Kumgang, near the DMZ, as a potential military threat, since the accumulated water could be suddenly released to flood Seoul and isolate South Korean troops deployed along the frontier. (South Korea eventually decided to neutralize the perceived threat by building a counter-dam further down the Han river.)

By late 1987 the DPRK appeared to have adopted a more conciliatory approach to relations with the South, particularly with regard to the issues of reunification and proposed reductions in armed forces. In November, however, a South Korean airliner exploded during a flight over South-East Asia, with the loss of 115 lives. South Korea accused the North of having ordered the destruction of the aircraft, and pledged to inflict 'severe punishment'. Despite the confession, in January 1988, of an alleged North Korean agent (who implicated Kim Jong Il in the planning of the attack), North Korea denied the accusation, and hinted that, unless the North and South resolved their differences, a military confrontation was likely; however, it repeated Kim Il Sung's proposal, in his 1988 New Year message, for the convening of a joint conference. In August three sessions of talks were held at the 'peace village' of Panmunjom (in the DMZ) between delegates of the legislatures of North and South Korea, although the discussions (the first formal contact between the two countries since 1986) produced no conclusive results. Further negotiations in February and October 1989 were suspended by the DPRK, and a planned exchange visit of some 600 members of families who had been separated by the Korean War was also postponed.

In January 1990 Kim Il Sung proposed that senior-level negotiations be initiated between North and South to deliberate an eventual relaxation of travel restrictions between the two countries. The proposal was welcomed by President Roh of South Korea, who subsequently announced that the annual US-South Korean military exercises would be reduced in size and duration. In February the DPRK denied reports in the Japanese and Western press that it was seeking to manufacture nuclear weapons at its Yongbyon nuclear installation, which was believed to comprise two reactors and a reprocessing facility. In March US and South Korean military engineers discovered a fourth underground tunnel beneath the DMZ.

Following an agreement reached during inter-Korean talks (which had been resumed in mid-1990), in early September the DPRK Premier, Yon Hyong Muk, visited Seoul for two days of discussions with his South Korean counterpart, Kang Young-Hoon. The meeting represented the highest-level contact between the two countries since the end of the Korean War, although no significant agreements on political or military matters were reached. Yon Hyong Muk also met President Roh, who expressed his wish to meet Kim Il Sung to discuss means of realizing reunification before the end of the century. Further, inconclusive talks between the two Premiers were held in October, in Pyongyang, and in December, in Seoul. A fourth round of negotiations, which was planned for February 1991, was aborted by the DPRK, again in protest at the annual US-South Korean military exercises.

The DPRK's unilateral application for UN membership, first announced in May 1991, represented a radical departure from its earlier insistence that the two Koreas should occupy a single UN seat. This development was welcomed by South Korea, and both countries were admitted separately to the UN in mid-September. Hitherto both had held observer status at the UN General Assembly and were members of certain UN specialized agencies.

Following a further postponement in mid-1991, the fourth round of prime-ministerial talks took place in Pyongyang in October of that year. Both parties agreed on the title and the envisaged provisions of an accord governing future inter-Korean relations. The 'Agreement on Reconciliation, Non-aggression and Exchanges and Co-operation between the South and the North' was signed at the conclusion of the fifth round of prime-ministerial talks, held in Seoul in early December. The accord was widely regarded as the most important development in inter-Korean relations since the end of the Korean War. Under the Agreement, both states pledged, *inter alia*, to desist from mutual slander, vilification and sabotage, to promote economic and other co-operation and the reunion of separated family members, and to work towards a full peace treaty to replace the 1953 armistice agreement. The accord was declared effective in mid-February 1992, during the sixth round of negotiations, held in Pyongyang. By late 1992, however, very few of the accord's provisions had been implemented. Further rounds of prime-ministerial talks, held during 1992, produced no significant progress, and in November the DPRK threatened to suspend contacts with the South altogether, in protest at the latter's decision to resume the 'Team Spirit' military exercises in March 1993. (The 1992 exercises had been cancelled, owing to the temporary improvement in relations between the two states.) Relations had also been seriously impaired by the South's announcement, in October 1992, that an extensive North Korean espionage network had been discovered to be in operation in South Korea, and by the North's repeated refusals to agree to simultaneous nuclear inspections in both Korean states (see below). In

December the planned ninth meeting of Premiers was cancelled.

The controversy surrounding the DPRK's suspected nuclear programme (see below) prevented any improvement occurring in inter-Korean relations during 1993 and the first half of 1994, and two meetings held at Panmunjom (in October 1993 and March 1994) proved to be abortive. Relations were also strained by the DPRK's withdrawal, in May 1994, of its mission to the Military Armistice Commission (the body, based at Panmunjom, that oversees the maintenance of the truce that ended the Korean War). However, following talks between Kim Il Sung and the former US President, Jimmy Carter, who visited the DPRK in a private capacity in June, it was announced that the first summit meeting at presidential level between the two Korean states would be held in Pyongyang on 25–27 July. Two highly successful preparatory meetings were held at Panmunjom, but the death of Kim Il Sung on 8 July led to the indefinite postponement of the summit meeting. Following the signature of the US-DPRK nuclear accord in October (see below), inter-Korean relations were expected to improve significantly, and in November South Korea announced that it was to permit direct trade with, and investment in, the DPRK.

A further cause of tension in inter-Korean relations has been the issue of the DPRK's suspected nuclear ambitions, and in the early 1990s there was growing international concern that the DPRK had intensified its clandestine nuclear programme at Yongbyon, and would soon be capable of manufacturing a nuclear weapon. During 1991 pressure was increasingly applied, by the USA and Japan in particular, for the DPRK to sign the Nuclear Safeguards Agreement (NSA) with the International Atomic Energy Agency (IAEA, see p. 66). This was required by the DPRK's signature, in 1985, of the Treaty on the Non-Proliferation of Nuclear Weapons (the Non-Proliferation Treaty—NPT), in order that IAEA representatives be permitted to inspect the country's nuclear facilities. However, the DPRK consistently refused to allow such inspections to take place unless there were to be a simultaneous inspection (or withdrawal) of US nuclear weapons sited in South Korea. Tension was eased considerably by the USA's decision, in October 1991, to remove all its tactical nuclear weapons from South Korea, and by President Roh's declaration, in the following month, that South Korea would not manufacture, deploy or use nuclear, chemical or biological weapons. In early December the South Korean Government stated that all US nuclear weapons had been withdrawn, and proposed that simultaneous inspections of military bases in the South and nuclear facilities in the North be conducted. Later in the month the two Korean states concluded an agreement 'to create a non-nuclear Korean peninsula'. In early January 1992 the USA and South Korea announced the cancellation of that year's joint military manoeuvres. The DPRK welcomed this decision and, in late January, signed the NSA (which was ratified by the SPA in April). In mid-March delegates of North and South, meeting at Panmunjom, agreed to form a Joint Nuclear Control Commission (JNCC) to permit inter-Korean nuclear inspections to take place.

In May 1992 North Korea submitted to the IAEA an unexpectedly detailed report on its nuclear facilities, describing, *inter alia*, the Yongbyon installation as a research laboratory. In the same month IAEA inspectors were permitted to visit North Korean nuclear facilities (the first in a series of official visits during that year). Despite the findings of the IAEA inspectors (who concluded that the Yongbyon plant was 'primitive' and far from completion, although potentially capable of producing plutonium), suspicions persisted regarding the DPRK's nuclear ambitions. Moreover, North Korea repeatedly failed to agree to separate nuclear inspections by the JNCC, finally announcing, in January 1993, its intention to boycott all future inter-Korean nuclear talks (in protest at the imminent resumption of the 'Team Spirit' manoeuvres). The situation became critical in February, when the DPRK refused to allow IAEA inspections of two 'undeclared' sites near Yongbyon, claiming that these were military sites unrelated to nuclear activities. In response, the IAEA adopted a resolution insisting that the DPRK permit a special inspection of the sites (which, it suspected, housed quantities of enriched plutonium) by 25 March. In an unprecedented move, the DPRK announced in early March that it was to withdraw from the NPT. (The IAEA stipulates that, for such a withdrawal to become effective, a period of 90 days from the date of the announcement must elapse.) The DPRK was also reported to have declared a 'semi-state of war' throughout the country, stating that the 'Team Spirit' exercises, currently under way, presented a threat to its national security, although this was revoked later in the month, following the conclusion of the South Korean-US manoeuvres.

Meanwhile, in mid-March 1993 the IAEA extended to the end of the month the deadline for the admission of inspectors; however, no agreement was reached, and on 1 April the IAEA voted to inform the UN Security Council that the DPRK was in 'non-compliance' with the NPT. An attempt by the Security Council in early April to prepare a resolution demanding that the DPRK rescind its decision to withdraw from the NPT and submit to IAEA inspections was abandoned, following indications by the People's Republic of China that it would veto any such motion. In mid-May the Security Council adopted a more circumspect resolution, urging the DPRK to reconsider its decision to withdraw from the NPT and calling on the country to allow an inspection by the IAEA of its nuclear facilities. South Korea, welcoming the resolution, indicated its willingness to participate in efforts to dissuade the DPRK from withdrawing from the NPT, and suggested a resumption of direct contacts between North and South.

Negotiations between representatives of the DPRK and the USA began in May 1993, and on 11 June, following bilateral talks at the UN headquarters in New York, USA, the two countries issued a joint statement in which North Korea agreed to the resumption of discussions with the IAEA regarding access to the Yongbyon facilities, as well as to reopen contacts with South Korea, with the eventual aim of organizing a meeting between Kim Il Sung and Kim Young-Sam. At the same time the USA agreed to assist the DPRK in the development of its non-military nuclear programme. International concern about the DPRK's arms programme was, meanwhile, heightened by the successful testing of a medium-range missile, the Rodong-1, in May. In response to US pressure, the DPRK subsequently agreed to further negotiations with the IAEA. Talks at the organization's headquarters in Vienna, Austria, in early September were, however, inconclusive, and further meetings were cancelled.

Negotiations with South Korea resumed in Panmunjom in early October 1993, but disagreement over the question of nuclear inspections impeded progress in preparations for a meeting of the two countries' presidential envoys. At the same time the DPRK's representative at the UN General Assembly declared that North Korea would henceforth discuss the nuclear issue only with the USA. (By such a dialogue, it was widely suggested, the DPRK might hope to extract diplomatic and economic concessions from the USA.) Accordingly, a representative of the US Congress visited the DPRK in mid-October, and, following negotiations described as 'productive' with Kim Il Sung, was permitted to cross the border into South Korea (the first US citizen to do so since the end of the Korean War). Two further rounds of inter-Korean talks took place at Panmunjom in the same month.

In early November 1993 the UN General Assembly adopted a resolution urging the DPRK to comply with IAEA inspection demands; the DPRK subsequently cancelled a planned meeting with South Korean officials. In mid-November, as joint US-South Korean military exercises proceeded, the DPRK stated that it would allow inspections of its nuclear facilities (notably excluding the disputed sites) if the 1994 larger-scale 'Team Spirit' exercises were cancelled. In late November 1993 discreet negotiations between the DPRK and the USA took place in New York, at which it was believed that the USA had displayed a more conciliatory attitude than hitherto. None the less, the DPRK's renewed threat to withdraw from the NPT unless further high-level negotiations took place was followed, at the beginning of December, by a reiterated refusal to submit to IAEA inspections, and shortly afterwards the IAEA stated that soon it would no longer be able to continue 'meaningful' surveillance of the DPRK's nuclear programme.

Following further DPRK-US discussions in New York, in early December 1993, the DPRK offered to allow greater access to its nuclear sites—a proposal that was not accepted by the USA, principally since inspectors' access to the two most sensitive sites at Yongbyon would be restricted. However, negotiations continued, and towards the end of December it was reported that the DPRK had accepted in principle the opening of all nuclear sites (albeit to apparently limited inspections). Further optimism was afforded by a visit to the DPRK by the UN Secretary-General, Dr Boutros Boutros-Ghali, during which he held discussions with Kim Il Sung and Kim Jong Il. By the second half of January 1994, however, difficulties were encountered in establishing the extent of IAEA inspections. Tensions were further exacerbated by the announcement that the USA was to deploy *Patriot* air-defence missiles in South Korea. In late February, shortly before the expiry of a new IAEA deadline for the DPRK to submit to inspections, representatives of the USA and the DPRK, meeting in New York, reached an agreement whereby IAEA inspectors would be allowed to visit all the DPRK's declared nuclear facilities, while negotiations with South Korea regarding the eventual exchange of presidential envoys would resume.

Accordingly, IAEA inspectors travelled to the DPRK at the beginning of March 1994. They were however, impeded in their efforts to remove samples from nuclear installations, and it was also discovered that seals that had been placed by IAEA representatives on nuclear materials during previous visits had been broken, leading the IAEA to conclude that the DPRK had, in all probability, produced more plutonium than had been admitted. While uncertainty remained as to whether the DPRK had already produced a nuclear weapon, North Korea's obstruction of the IAEA's investigations, together with a lack of progress in the inter-Korean talks, led the USA to cancel the bilateral negotiations that had been envisaged in the previous month's agreement.

In June 1994 the DPRK again threatened to withdraw from the NPT and also declare war against South Korea, if economic sanctions were imposed by the UN. Renewed negotiations between the USA and the DPRK were interrupted by the death of Kim Il Sung in early July, but resumed in the following month. The two countries reached an agreement on the replacement of the DPRK's existing nuclear reactors by light-water reactors, which were considered to be less easily adapted to the production of nuclear weaponry. The agreement also recommended that a restricted form of diplomatic representation between the two countries be established. The DPRK discounted, however, the possibility of an inspection by the IAEA of the two contentious sites at Yongbyon. Further negotiations in October led to the signing of an agreement under which the USA undertook to establish an international consortium to finance and supply the light-water reactors while North Korea agreed to suspend operation of its existing reactors and halt construction at two further sites. To compensate for the DPRK's consequent shortfall in energy production, the USA further undertook to deliver at no cost 500,000 metric tons of heavy fuel oil per year to North Korea, until the light-water reactors were fully operational.

In November 1994 a team of IAEA inspectors travelled to Pyongyang to oversee the DPRK's alleged suspension of its nuclear programme. However, in early 1995 the nuclear accord of October 1994 appeared jeopardized by disagreement over the provenance of the light-water reactors to be supplied to the DPRK. In March a number of countries, led by the USA, South Korea and Japan, created the Korean Peninsula Energy Development Organization, which insisted that the DPRK accept a South Korean-designed reactor. This demand was opposed by North Korea, however, which favoured a Russian model. Negotiations between the USA and the DPRK recommenced in April 1995, but were subsequently abandoned; in May it was announced that talks would resume at an unspecified date.

The DPRK's international standing was severely damaged in October 1983, when 17 South Koreans, including four visiting government ministers, were killed in a bomb explosion in Rangoon, Burma (now Yangon, Myanmar). North Korea was held responsible for the attack, and Burma severed relations with Pyongyang, while Japan imposed sanctions. The destruction of a South Korean aircraft in November 1987, allegedly by North Korean agents (see above), caused the USA to place the DPRK on its list of countries which support terrorism, and to reimpose restrictions on contacts between US and North Korean diplomats. Japan responded to the attack by reimposing sanctions during 1988. North Korea, in response, severed diplomatic contacts with Japan, although mutual trade continued. In late 1990 there was a significant *rapprochement* between North Korea and Japan, and in January 1991 a Japanese government delegation visited Pyongyang for discussions concerning the possible normalization of diplomatic relations. The Japanese delegation offered apologies, on behalf of its Government, for Japanese colonial aggression on the Korean peninsula between 1910 and 1945. Moreover, the Japanese Government expressed its willingness to make reparations for Japanese abuses of human rights in Korea during the colonial period. Subsequent negotiations in 1991 foundered, however, owing to the DPRK's demand for reparations for damage inflicted after 1945 (which the Japanese Government denied) and to Japan's insistence that the DPRK's nuclear installations be opened to outside inspection. In November 1992 the eighth round of Japanese-DPRK normalization talks collapsed, as the North Korean delegation abandoned the proceedings. Relations with Japan were further strained after the DPRK's successful testing of the Rodong-1 intermediate-range missile in the Sea of Japan in May 1993. The missile, according to US intelligence reports, would be capable of reaching most of Japan's major cities (and possibly of carrying either a conventional or a nuclear warhead). None the less, Japan, like South Korea, opposed the possible imposition of international economic sanctions on the DPRK, in response to North Korea's failure to submit to inspections of its nuclear facilities. Attempts to resume normalization talks in 1994 proved to be unsuccessful. In March 1995, however, a Japanese parliamentary group visited the DPRK, and reached an agreement for the resumption of talks later in 1995.

Relations with the USA in the early 1990s were similarly affected by the DPRK's suspected nuclear ambitions. Direct talks between the two countries on resolving the nuclear issue were commenced in mid-1993 and continued throughout 1994 (see above). In late 1994 it was announced that agreement had been reached to establish liaison offices in Washington and Pyongyang in 1995, in preparation for an eventual resumption of full diplomatic relations. Restrictions on trade and investment were to be eased. The USA insisted, however, that normal relations would only be restored when North Korea ceased to export ballistic missiles and withdrew its troops from the border with South Korea; North Korea, in turn, stated that liaison offices could only be opened when light-water nuclear reactors, pledged in the October 1994 agreement between the DPRK and the USA, had been supplied. The gradual improvement in US-DPRK relations was briefly threatened in mid-December, following the shooting-down of a US army helicopter which had apparently entered North Korean airspace. The DPRK initially refused to negotiate the surviving pilot's release; however, following direct bilateral talks in late December, the pilot was repatriated. In January 1995 the DPRK pledged to open its ports to US commercial shipping and to remove restrictions on the import of goods from the USA.

During the years of the so-called Sino–Soviet dispute the DPRK fluctuated in its allegiance to each of its powerful northern neighbours, the People's Republic of China and the USSR. However, in the mid-1980s the DPRK placed increased emphasis on its links with the USSR, culminating in a new arrangement for the supply of Soviet aircraft to North Korea, and an exchange visit by senior officials from each Government. In May 1987, however, Kim Il Sung made an official visit to China, where he was believed to have sought to establish closer relations and to enlist Chinese support for (unsuccessful) North Korean efforts to co-host the 1988 Olympic Games. Another visit by Kim Il Sung to Beijing, in November 1989, was interpreted by some Western observers as an attempt to establish closer relations, in the light of the erosion of communist power in many Eastern European countries.

The DPRK's diplomatic isolation became more pronounced in the early 1990s, as formerly communist countries, in Eastern Europe and elsewhere, moved to foster relations with South Korea. This process culminated in the establishment of full diplomatic relations between the USSR and South Korea in September 1990. A further humiliation to the North Korean regime was the USSR's stipulation that, from January 1991, the barter trading system between the two countries would be abolished in favour of trade in convertible currencies at world market prices. In February 1993 the Russian Federation (which, following the dissolution of the USSR, assumed responsibility for many of the USSR's international undertakings) announced that the treaty of friendship, co-operation and mutual assistance, which the USSR and the DPRK had signed in 1961, was no longer valid. In May 1993, however, an agreement was reported to have been signed on technological and scientific co-operation between the DPRK and the

# DEMOCRATIC PEOPLE'S REPUBLIC OF KOREA (NORTH KOREA)

Russian Federation, and in September 1994 discussions were held to re-establish former trade agreements and to reschedule North Korea's debt repayments to the Russian Federation.

Following the establishment of full diplomatic relations between South Korea and the People's Republic of China, in August 1992, Sino-North Korean relations deteriorated considerably. However, since the USSR effectively ceased petroleum supplies in 1991, China has become the DPRK's major source, supplying as much as two-thirds of its petroleum requirements. On the question of North Korea's nuclear programme, China has appeared largely conciliatory, and during 1993 and the first months of 1994 indicated that it would veto any attempt by the UN Security Council to impose economic sanctions on the DPRK.

## Government

The highest organ of state power is the unicameral Supreme People's Assembly (SPA), with 687 members, elected (unopposed) for five years by universal adult suffrage. The SPA elects, for its duration, the President of the Republic and, on the latter's recommendation, other members of the Central People's Committee to direct the Government. The SPA appoints the Premier while the Committee appoints other Ministers to form the Administration Council. The Administration Council is composed of Commissions and Ministries, of which Commissions have the higher status.

Political power is held by the communist Korean Workers' Party (KWP), which dominates the Democratic Front for the Reunification of the Fatherland (including two other minor parties). The Front presents an approved list of candidates for elections to representative bodies. The KWP's highest authority is the Party Congress, which elects a Central Committee to supervise Party work. The Committee elects a Political Bureau (Politburo) to direct policy. The Presidium of the Politburo is the KWP's most powerful policy-making body.

North Korea comprises nine provinces and two cities, each with an elected People's Assembly.

## Defence

Military service is selective: army five to eight years, navy five to 10 years, and air force three to four years. According to Western estimates, the total strength of the armed forces in June 1994 was 1,128,000: army 1,000,000, air force 82,000, and navy 46,000. Security and border troops numbered 115,000, and there was a workers' and peasants' militia ('Red Guards') numbering about 3.8m. The ratio of North Korea's armed forces to total population is believed to be the highest in the world. Government expenditure on defence in 1994 was officially budgeted at 4,816.9m. won, or 11.6% of planned budgetary spending, although South Korean sources estimate the actual proportion of total budget allocation to be nearer to 30%.

## Economic Affairs

In 1993, according to South Korean estimates, the DPRK's gross national product (GNP) was about US $20,500m., equivalent to $904 per head. The same sources estimated that in 1993 the North Korean economy declined for a fourth successive year, contracting by 4.3%, in real terms—compared with the average annual growth rate of 7.9% that was envisaged during the third (1987–93) Seven-Year Plan. Provisional South Korean estimates suggest that the North Korean economy contracted by some 4% in 1994. During 1985–93, according to estimates by the World Bank, the population increased by an annual average of 1.9%.

At mid-1993, according to FAO estimates, 30.9% of the labour force were employed in agriculture (including forestry and fishing). The principal crops are rice, maize, potatoes, sweet potatoes and soybeans. The DPRK is not self-sufficient in food, and imports substantial amounts of wheat, rice and maize annually. The raising of livestock (principally cattle and pigs), forestry and fishing are important. During 1983–89, according to the FAO, agricultural production increased by an annual average of 2.3%; during 1989–93, however, output declined by an average of 6.2% per year, although production increased by an estimated 1.6% in 1994.

At mid-1980 the industrial sector employed about 30% of the labour force. In recent years industrial development has concentrated on heavy industry (metallurgy, electricity, machine-building, cement and chemicals), and expansion has been particularly evident in the steel and mining industries. In the early 1980s the machine-building industry contributed about one-third of total industrial output. The textile industry has provided significant exports. According to Soviet estimates, industrial production in the DPRK in 1993 declined by 5%, compared with 1992. South Korean sources estimated that in 1993 the manufacturing sector suffered a decline in output of some 2%, compared with 1992.

The DPRK possesses considerable mineral wealth, with large deposits of coal, iron, lead, copper, zinc, tin, silver and gold. An estimated 40%–50% of the world's deposits of magnesite are located in the DPRK. In 1992, South Korean sources estimate, production of iron ore amounted to 5.7m. tons and that of non-ferrous metals to 0.2m. tons. There are no known deposits of petroleum, and hence the country relies on imports from the People's Republic of China and Iran; in 1993 total petroleum imports stood at 1.4m. tons. South Korean sources estimated that in 1993 the DPRK's mining production declined by 7.2%, compared with the previous year.

In the early 1980s almost three-quarters of the DPRK's energy supply was derived from coal, followed in importance by petroleum, hydroelectricity and wood-burning. Under the 1987–93 Plan, production of coal-fired and nuclear power was to be expanded. A 30-MW nuclear reactor was believed to have been inaugurated in 1987. In 1992, according to South Korean sources, about 60% of the DPRK's electricity was generated by hydroelectric power stations, with most of the country's remaining requirements being provided by thermal power stations. According to North Korean sources, electricity production in 1994 increased by some 30%, compared with 1986. The DPRK's total power production decreased by 8.7% in 1993, according to South Korean estimates.

In 1994 total exports were estimated, by South Korean sources, to be US $810m., which represented a decrease of 21%, compared with 1993. In the same year imports were estimated to amount to US $1,020m., a decrease of 37%, compared with the previous year. Following the dissolution of the USSR in late 1991, China emerged as the DPRK's major trading partner (accounting for 34% of total trade turnover in 1993), followed by Japan (18%) and Russia. Trade with South Korea accounted for some 9% of total trade turnover in 1994. The principal exports in the late 1980s were non-ferrous metals, coal, rice, marine products, silk and cement. The principal imports were petroleum, chemicals, cereals, coking coal, machinery and capital equipment.

The 1994 budget envisaged revenue and expenditure balancing at 41,525.2m. won. The DPRK's total external debt was estimated to be US $10,320m. in 1993, by far the greatest proportion of which was owed to the states of the former USSR. The average annual rate of inflation in 1993 was estimated to be 5%.

It is almost impossible to present an accurate economic profile of the DPRK, owing to the lack of reliable statistical data relating to the country. It would appear that North Korea's economic situation declined sharply in the early 1990s, following, first, the abandonment (from 1 January 1991) of the barter trading system between the DPRK and the USSR (then its major trading partner) in favour of trade conducted exclusively in convertible currencies, a substantial reduction in deliveries of crude petroleum and grain from the USSR, and, finally, the dissolution of the USSR in late 1991. A further set-back was the imposition, in late 1992, of similar trading regulations by the People's Republic of China, which had become the DPRK's principal trading partner. The continuing shortages of fuel supplies reportedly led to a serious decline in the productivity of industrial enterprises, with resulting widespread shortages of basic consumer goods. According to South Korean sources, the economy contracted for four successive years during 1990–93. In late 1993 the Government announced that the 1987–93 economic plan was to be extended by three years, conceding that certain targets had not been achieved. The new plan emphasized a need for improved productivity in the agricultural, light industry and energy sectors, and sought a 50% increase in annual exports by 1996. It also envisaged the extension of free economic and trade zones to attract foreign investment: transport, communications and tourism infrastructure was to be greatly developed, including the construction of an airport at Sonbong.

## Social Welfare

The state provides rest homes, sanatoria and free medical services. In 1982 there were 1,531 general hospitals, 979 specialized hospitals and 5,414 clinics. In 1989 there were 27 physicians and 136 hospital beds per 10,000 of the population.

# DEMOCRATIC PEOPLE'S REPUBLIC OF KOREA (NORTH KOREA)

The 1994 state budget allocated 8,218.3m. won (19.8% of total expenditure) to social welfare.

### Education
Universal compulsory primary and secondary education were introduced in 1956 and 1958, respectively, and are provided at state expense. Free and compulsory 11-year education in state schools was introduced in 1975. Children enter kindergarten at five years of age, and primary school at the age of six. After four years, they advance to senior middle school for six years. In 1986 there were 519 university-level institutions and colleges; in the following year 325,000 students were enrolled in such institutions. English is compulsory as a second language at the age of 14. The adult literacy rate was estimated to be 99% in 1984.

### Public Holidays
**1995:** 1 January (New Year), 16–17 February (Kim Jong Il's Birthday), 8 March (International Women's Day), 15 April (Kim Il Sung's birthday), 1 May (May Day), 15 August (Anniversary of Liberation), 9 September (Independence Day), 10 October (Anniversary of the foundation of the Korean Workers' Party), 27 December (Anniversary of the Constitution).
**1996:** 1 January (New Year), 16–17 February (Kim Jong Il's Birthday), 8 March (International Women's Day), 15 April (Kim Il Sung's birthday), 1 May (May Day), 15 August (Anniversary of Liberation), 9 September (Independence Day), 10 October (Anniversary of the foundation of the Korean Workers' Party), 27 December (Anniversary of the Constitution).

### Weights and Measures
The metric system is in force.

# Statistical Survey

## Area and Population

**AREA, POPULATION AND DENSITY***

| | |
|---|---|
| Area (sq km) | 120,538† |
| Population (official estimates)‡ | |
| 31 December 1960 | 10,789,000 |
| 1 October 1963 | 11,568,000 |
| Population (UN estimates at mid-year)§ | |
| 1991 | 22,189,000 |
| 1992 | 22,618,000 |
| 1993 | 23,054,000 |
| Density (per sq km) at mid-1993 | 191.3 |

* Excluding the demilitarized zone between North and South Korea, with an area of 1,262 sq km (487 sq miles).
† 46,540 sq miles.
‡ Source: Institute of Economics of the World Socialist System, Moscow.
§ Source: UN, *World Population Prospects: The 1992 Revision.*

**PRINCIPAL TOWNS** (estimated population, 1986)

| | | | |
|---|---|---|---|
| Pyongyang (capital) | 2,000,000 | Sinuiju | 330,000 |
| Hamhung | 670,000 | Kaesong | 310,000 |
| Chongjin | 530,000 | Anju | 205,000 |

Source: Korean Central News Agency.

**BIRTHS AND DEATHS** (UN estimates, annual averages)

| | 1975–80 | 1980–85 | 1985–90 |
|---|---|---|---|
| Birth rate (per 1,000) | 23.0 | 22.0 | 23.5 |
| Death rate (per 1,000) | 6.1 | 5.6 | 5.4 |

**Expectation of life** (UN estimates, years at birth, 1985–90): 69.8 (males 66.2; females 72.7).
Source: UN, *World Population Prospects: The 1992 Revision.*

**ECONOMICALLY ACTIVE POPULATION**
(ILO estimates, '000 persons at mid-1980)

| | Males | Females | Total |
|---|---|---|---|
| Agriculture, etc. | 1,484 | 1,870 | 3,355 |
| Industry | 1,654 | 719 | 2,373 |
| Services | 1,103 | 1,007 | 2,110 |
| **Total** | **4,241** | **3,597** | **7,838** |

Source: ILO, *Economically Active Population Estimates and Projections, 1950–2025.*
**Mid-1993** (estimates in '000): Agriculture, etc. 3,782; Total 12,223 (Source: FAO, *Production Yearbook*).

## Agriculture

**PRINCIPAL CROPS**
(FAO estimates unless otherwise indicated, '000 metric tons)

| | 1991 | 1992 | 1993 |
|---|---|---|---|
| Wheat | 135 | 123 | 100 |
| Rice (paddy) | 4,420 | 4,260 | 2,940 |
| Barley | 145 | 130 | 120 |
| Maize | 2,480 | 2,100* | 1,960* |
| Oats | 62 | 50 | 40 |
| Millet | 60 | 50 | 40 |
| Sorghum | 14 | 10 | 10 |
| Potatoes | 1,975 | 1,800 | 1,750 |
| Sweet potatoes | 500 | 500 | 500 |
| Pulses | 330 | 310 | 290 |
| Soybeans | 440* | 400* | 380 |
| Cottonseed | 29 | 31 | 32 |
| Cotton (lint) | 10 | 10 | 11 |
| Tobacco (leaves) | 66 | 64 | 64 |
| Hemp fibre | 10 | 11 | 12 |

* Unofficial figure.
Source: FAO, *Production Yearbook.*

**LIVESTOCK** (FAO estimates, '000 head, year ending September)

| | 1991 | 1992 | 1993 |
|---|---|---|---|
| Horses | 45 | 46 | 46 |
| Asses | 3 | 3 | 3 |
| Cattle | 1,300 | 1,300 | 1,300 |
| Pigs | 3,300 | 3,300 | 3,200 |
| Sheep | 390 | 390 | 390 |
| Goats | 300 | 300 | 300 |

Poultry (FAO estimates, million): 21 in 1991; 22 in 1992; 22 in 1993.
Source: FAO, *Production Yearbook.*

**LIVESTOCK PRODUCTS** (FAO estimates, '000 metric tons)

| | 1991 | 1992 | 1993 |
|---|---|---|---|
| Beef and veal | 45 | 45 | 30 |
| Mutton and lamb | 2 | 2 | 2 |
| Goat meat | 2 | 2 | 2 |
| Pig meat | 161 | 157 | 150 |
| Poultry meat | 48 | 48 | 44 |
| Cows' milk | 90 | 93 | 88 |
| Poultry eggs | 148 | 148 | 148 |
| Cattle hides | 6.3 | 6.3 | 4.2 |

Source: FAO, *Production Yearbook.*

DEMOCRATIC PEOPLE'S REPUBLIC OF KOREA (NORTH KOREA)  *Statistical Survey*

## Forestry

**ROUNDWOOD REMOVALS**
(FAO estimates, '000 cu m, excluding bark)

|  | 1990 | 1991 | 1992 |
|---|---|---|---|
| Industrial wood* | 600 | 600 | 600 |
| Fuel wood | 4,092 | 4,137 | 4,183 |
| **Total** | 4,692 | 4,737 | 4,783 |

* Assumed to be unchanged since 1970.

**Sawnwood production** ('000 cu m, incl. railway sleepers): 280 (coniferous 185, broadleaved 95) per year in 1970–92 (FAO estimates).

Source: FAO, *Yearbook of Forest Products*.

## Fishing

(FAO estimates, '000 metric tons, live weight)

|  | 1990 | 1991 | 1992 |
|---|---|---|---|
| Inland waters | 110 | 100 | 110 |
| Pacific Ocean | 1,640 | 1,600 | 1,640 |
| **Total catch** | 1,750 | 1,700 | 1,750 |

Source: FAO, *Yearbook of Fishery Statistics*.

## Mining

(estimated production, '000 metric tons, unless otherwise indicated)

|  | 1989 | 1990 | 1991 |
|---|---|---|---|
| Hard coal | 65,000 | 66,000 | 67,000 |
| Brown coal and lignite | 20,000 | 21,000 | 22,000 |
| Iron ore* | 4,400 | 4,400 | 4,700 |
| Copper ore* | 15 | 15 | n.a. |
| Lead ore* | 120 | 120 | 120 |
| Magnesite | 1,500 | 1,500 | n.a. |
| Tungsten concentrates (metric tons)* | 500 | 1,000 | 1,000 |
| Zinc ore* | 230 | 230 | 200 |
| Salt (unrefined) | 572 | 572 | 580 |
| Phosphate rock | 500 | 500 | 500 |
| Sulphur† | 200 | 200 | 210 |
| Fluorspar‡ | 40 | 40 | 41 |
| Graphite | 35 | 35 | n.a. |
| Silver (metric tons)* | 50 | 50 | 50 |
| Gold (kg)* | 5,000 | 5,000 | 5,000 |

Note: Except for coal, figures are from the US Bureau of Mines. No recent data are available for the production of molybdenum ore and asbestos.

* Figures relate to the metal content of ores and concentrates.
† Figures refer to the sulphur content of iron and copper pyrites, including pyrite concentrates obtained from copper, lead and zinc ores.
‡ Metallurgical grade.

Source: UN, *Industrial Statistics Yearbook*.

## Industry

**SELECTED PRODUCTS**
(estimated production, '000 metric tons, unless otherwise indicated)

|  | 1989 | 1990 | 1991 |
|---|---|---|---|
| Nitrogenous fertilizers (a)* | 583 | 660 | n.a. |
| Phosphate fertilizers (b)* | 137 | 137 | n.a. |
| Motor spirit (petrol) | 975 | 1,000 | 1,000 |
| Kerosene | 230 | 235 | 235 |
| Distillate fuel oils | 1,065 | 1,070 | 1,070 |
| Residual fuel oils | 635 | 640 | 640 |
| Coke-oven coke (excl. breeze)† | 3,600 | 3,600 | 3,600 |
| Cement† | 16,300 | 16,300 | 16,329 |
| Pig-iron† | 6,500 | 6,500 | 6,500 |
| Crude steel† | 8,000 | 8,000 | n.a. |
| Refined copper (unwrought)† | 22 | 22 | 24 |
| Lead (primary metal)† | 95 | 95 | n.a. |
| Zinc (primary metal)† | 210 | 210 | n.a. |
| Electric energy (million kWh) | 53,500 | 53,500 | 53,500 |

* Output is measured in terms of (a) nitrogen or (b) phosphoric acid.
† Data from the US Bureau of Mines.

Source: UN, *Industrial Statistics Yearbook*.

## Finance

**CURRENCY AND EXCHANGE RATES**

**Monetary Units**
100 chon (jun) = 1 won.

**Sterling and Dollar Equivalents** (31 December 1994)
£1 sterling = 3.364 won;
US $1 = 2.150 won;
100 won = £29.73 = $46.51.

**BUDGET** (projected, million won)

|  | 1992 | 1993 | 1994 |
|---|---|---|---|
| Revenue | 39,500.9 | 40,449.9 | 41,525.2 |
| Expenditure | 39,500.9 | 40,449.9 | 41,525.2 |
| Economic development | 26,675.1 | 27,423.8 | 28,164.0 |
| Socio-cultural sector | 7,730.6 | 7,751.5 | 8,218.3 |
| Defence | 4,582.1 | 4,692.2 | 4,816.9 |
| Administration and management | 513.1 | 582.4 | 326.0 |

## External Trade

**SELECTED COMMODITIES** (FAO estimates, US $ million)

| Imports | 1989 | 1990 | 1991 |
|---|---|---|---|
| Wheat and meslin (unmilled) | 25.0 | 45.0 | 114.0 |
| Raw sugar | 85.0 | 104.0 | 100.0 |
| Natural rubber | 9.0 | 6.5 | 6.0 |
| Cotton lint | 40.0 | 32.0 | 22.0 |
| Soybean oil | 7.7 | 6.0 | 5.5 |

| Exports | 1989 | 1990 | 1991 |
|---|---|---|---|
| Rice | 18.0 | 8.0 | 2.0 |
| Apples | 1.5 | 1.5 | 1.5 |
| Tobacco (unmanufactured) | 0.2 | 0.1 | 0.8 |
| Silk | 18.0 | 15.0 | 15.0 |

Source: UN, *Statistical Yearbook for Asia and the Pacific*.

**1994** (estimates, US $ million): Total imports 1,020; Total exports 810.

# DEMOCRATIC PEOPLE'S REPUBLIC OF KOREA (NORTH KOREA)

**SELECTED TRADING PARTNERS, 1991** (US $ million)

| | Imports | Exports |
|---|---|---|
| Australia | 20 | — |
| Canada | 50 | — |
| China, People's Republic | 524 | 85 |
| France | 8 | 12 |
| Germany | 48 | 72 |
| Hong Kong | 124 | 40 |
| India | 47 | 14 |
| Indonesia | 16 | 25 |
| Japan | 223 | 284 |
| Russia | 858 | 563 |
| Singapore | 37 | 11 |
| United Kingdom | 10 | 6 |
| **Total** (incl. others) | 2,280 | 1,240 |

Source: Ministry of Foreign Affairs of the Republic of Korea.

**1993** (US $ million): China (Imports 602, Exports 298); Japan (Imports 220, Exports 252).

## Transport

**SHIPPING**

**Merchant Fleet** ('000 gross registered tons at 30 June)

| | 1990 | 1991 | 1992 |
|---|---|---|---|
| Oil tankers | 13 | 13 | 112 |
| Total | 442 | 511 | 602 |

Source: UN, *Statistical Yearbook*.

**International Sea-Borne Freight Traffic** (estimates, '000 metric tons)

| | 1988 | 1989 | 1990 |
|---|---|---|---|
| Goods loaded | 630 | 640 | 635 |
| Goods unloaded | 5,386 | 5,500 | 5,520 |

Source: UN, *Monthly Bulletin of Statistics*.

## Communications Media

| | 1990 | 1991 | 1992 |
|---|---|---|---|
| Telephones ('000 main lines in use) | 780 | 800 | n.a. |
| Radio receivers ('000 in use) | 2,600 | 2,650 | 2,750 |
| Television receivers ('000 in use) | 330 | n.a. | 400 |

**Daily newspapers:** 11 (estimated circulation 5 million) in 1992.

Sources: UNESCO, *Statistical Yearbook*; UN, *Statistical Yearbook*.

## Education

(1987)

| | Institutions | Teachers | Students |
|---|---|---|---|
| Pre-primary | 16,964 | 35,000 | 728,000 |
| Primary | 4,813 | 59,000 | 1,543,000 |
| Secondary | n.a. | 111,000 | 2,468,000 |
| Universities and colleges | 519* | 23,000 | 325,000 |
| Others | n.a. | 4,000 | 65,000 |

* Of which 46 were university-level institutions and 473 were colleges (1986).

Source: mainly UNESCO, *Statistical Yearbook*.

# Directory

## The Constitution

A new Constitution was adopted on 27 December 1972. According to South Korean sources, several amendments were made in April 1992, including the deletion of references to Marxism-Leninism, the extension of the term of the Supreme People's Assembly from four to five years. and the promotion of limited 'economic openness'. Its main provisions are summarized below:

The Democratic People's Republic of Korea is an independent socialist state; the revolutionary traditions of the State are stressed (its ideological basis being the *Juche* idea of the Korean Workers' Party) as is the desire to achieve national reunification by peaceful means on the basis of national independence.

National sovereignty rests with the working people, who exercise power through the Supreme People's Assembly and People's Assemblies at lower levels, which are elected by universal, secret and direct suffrage.

Defence is emphasized as well as the rights of overseas nationals, the principles of friendly relations between nations based on equality, mutual respect and non-interference, proletarian internationalism, support for national liberation struggles and due observance of law.

Culture and education provide the working people with knowledge to advance a socialist way of life. Education is free and there are universal and compulsory one-year pre-school and 10-year senior middle school programmes.

The basic rights and duties of citizens are laid down and guaranteed. These include the right to vote (for citizens who are more than 17 years of age), to work (the working day being eight hours), to free medical care and material assistance for the old, infirm or disabled, and to political asylum. National defence is the supreme duty of citizens.

### THE GOVERNMENT

**The President**

The President, as Head of State, is elected for a four-year term of office by the Supreme People's Assembly. He convenes and presides over Administration Council meetings and is the Chairman of the National Defence Commission. The President promulgates laws of the Supreme People's Assembly and decisions of the Central People's Committee and of the Standing Committee. He has the right to issue orders, to grant pardons, to ratify or abrogate treaties and to receive foreign envoys. The President is responsible to the Supreme People's Assembly.

**The Supreme People's Assembly**

The Supreme People's Assembly is the highest organ of state power, exercises exclusive legislative authority and is elected by direct, equal, universal and secret ballot for a term of five years. Its chief functions are: (i) to adopt or amend legal or constitutional enactments; (ii) to determine state policy; (iii) to elect the President, Vice-Presidents, Secretary and members of the Central People's Committee (on the President's recommendation); (iv) to elect members of the Standing Committee of the Supreme People's Assembly, the Premier of the Administration Council (on the President's recommendation), the President of the Central Court and other legal officials; (v) to approve the State Plan and Budget; (vi) to decide on matters of war and peace. It holds regular and extraordinary sessions, the former being twice a year, the latter as necessary at the request of at least one-third of the deputies.

# DEMOCRATIC PEOPLE'S REPUBLIC OF KOREA (NORTH KOREA)

Legislative enactments are adopted when approved by more than half of those deputies present. The Standing Committee is the permanent body of the Supreme People's Assembly. It examines and decides on bills; amends legislation in force when the Supreme People's Assembly is not in session; interprets the law; organizes and conducts the election of deputies and judicial personnel.

### The Central People's Committee

The Central People's Committee comprises the President, Vice-Presidents, Secretary and Members. The Committee exercises the following chief functions: (a) to direct the work of the Administration Council as well as organs at local level; (b) to implement the Constitution and legislative enactments; (c) to establish and abolish Ministries, appoint Vice-Premiers and other members of the Administration Council; (d) to appoint and recall ambassadors and defence personnel; (e) to confer titles, decorations, diplomatic appointments; (f) to grant general amnesties, make administrative changes; (g) to declare a state of war. It is assisted by a number of Commissions dealing with internal policy, foreign policy, national defence, justice and security and other matters as may be established. The Central People's Committee is responsible to the Supreme People's Assembly's Standing Committee.

### The Administration Council

The Administration Council is the administrative and executive body of the Supreme People's Assembly. It comprises the Premier, Vice-Premiers and such other Ministers as may be appointed. Its major functions are the following: (i) to direct the work of Ministries and other organs responsible to it; (ii) to work out the State Plan and take measures to make it effective; (iii) to compile the State Budget and to give effect to it; (iv) to organize and execute the work of all sectors of the economy as well as transport, education and social welfare; (v) to conclude treaties; (vi) to develop the armed forces and maintain public security; and (vii) to annul decisions and directives of state administrative departments which run counter to those of the Administration Council. The Administration Council is responsible to the President, Central People's Committee and the Supreme People's Assembly.

### People's Assemblies

The People's Assemblies of the province (or municipality directly under central authority), city (or district) and county are local organs of power. The People's Assemblies or Committees exercise local budgetary functions, elect local administrative and judicial personnel and carry out the decisions at local level of higher executive and administrative organs.

## THE JUDICIARY

Justice is administered by the Central Court (the highest judicial organ of the State), the local Court, the People's Court and the Special Court. Judges and other legal officials are elected by the Supreme People's Assembly. The Central Court protects State property, Constitutional rights, guarantees that all State bodies and citizens observe state laws and executes judgments. Justice is administered by the court comprising one judge and two people's assessors. The court is independent and judicially impartial. Judicial affairs are conducted by the Central Procurator's Office which exposes and institutes criminal proceedings against accused persons. The Office of the Central Procurator is responsible to the Supreme People's Assembly, the President, and the Central People's Committee.

# The Government

## HEAD OF STATE

**President:** (vacant, following the death of Kim Il Sung on 8 July 1994).

**Vice-Presidents:** Pak Song Chol, Li Jong Ok, Kim Yong Ju, Kim Pyong Sik.

### CENTRAL PEOPLE'S COMMITTEE
(May 1995)

**Members:**

| | |
|---|---|
| Pak Song Chol | Pak Sung Il |
| Li Jong Ok | Rim Hyong Gu |
| Kim Yong Ju | Paek Bom Su |
| Kim Pyong Sik | Hyon Chol Gyu |
| So Yun Sok | Li Gil Song |
| Choe Mun Son | Yon Hyong Muk |
| Kim Hak Bong | Li Gun Mo |
| Kang Hyon Su | Rim Su Man |

**Secretary:** Chi Chang Ik

### ADMINISTRATION COUNCIL
(May 1995)

**Premier:** Kang Song San.

**Vice-Premiers:**

| | |
|---|---|
| Kim Yong Nam | Kim Chang Ju |
| Choe Yong Rim | Kim Yun Hyok |
| Hong Song Nam | Chang Chol |
| Kim Hwan | Kong Jin Tae |
| Kim Bok Sin | |

**Minister of Foreign Affairs:** Kim Yong Nam.
**Minister of Public Security:** Paek Hak Rim.
**Chairman of the State Planning Commission:** Hong Sok Hyong.
**Chairman of the Light Industry Commission:** Kim Bok Sin.
**Minister of the Chemical Industry:** Kim Hwan.
**Chairman of the External Economic Affairs Commission:** Li Song Dae.
**Chairman of the Transport Commission:** Li Yong Mu.
**Minister of the Power Industry:** Li Ji Chan.
**Chairman of the Agricultural Commission:** Kim Won Jin.
**Chairman of the Fisheries Commission:** (vacant).
**Chairman of the State Construction Commission:** Kim Ung Sang.
**Chairman of the Public Welfare Commission:** Kong Jin Tae.
**Chairman of the State Scientific and Technological Commission:** Choe Hui Jong.
**Chairman of the Electronics and Automation Industry Commission:** Kim Chang Ho.
**Minister of the Metal Industry:** Choe Yong Rim.
**Minister of the Machinery Industry:** Kwak Bom Gi.
**Minister of Mining:** Kim Pyong Gil.
**Minister of the Coal Industry:** Kim Ri Ryong.
**Minister of Natural Resources Development:** Kim Se Yong.
**Minister of the Shipping Industry:** Li Sok.
**Minister of Construction:** Cho Yun Hui.
**Minister of the Building Materials Industry:** Li Dong Chun.
**Minister of Forestry:** Li Chun Sok.
**Minister of Local Industry:** Kim Song Gu.
**Minister of the Atomic Energy Industry:** Choe Hak Gun.
**Minister of City Management:** Li Chol Bong.
**Minister of Communications:** Kim Hak Sop.
**Minister of Labour Administration:** Li Jae Yun.
**Minister of Finance:** Yun Gi Jong.
**Chairman of the Education Commission and Minister of Higher Education:** Choe Gi Ryong.
**Minister of Culture and Arts:** Chang Chol.
**Minister of Public Health:** Kim Su Hak.
**Minister of Railways:** Pak Yong Sok.
**Minister of Marine Transport:** O Song Ryol.
**Minister of Commerce:** Lim Jong Sang.
**President of the Academy of Sciences:** Kim Gil Yon.
**Chairman of the State Physical Culture and Sports Commission:** Pak Myong Chol.
**Governor of the Central Bank:** Chong Song Taek.
**Director of the Central Statistics Bureau:** Sin Gyong Sik.
**Chairman of the Materials Supply Commission:** Kim Jae Guk.
**Director of the Secretariat of the Administration Council:** Chae Gyu Bin.

### MINISTRIES

All Ministries and Commissions are in Pyongyang.

### POLITBURO OF THE CENTRAL COMMITTEE OF THE KOREAN WORKERS' PARTY

**Presidium:** Marshal Kim Jong Il.

**Full members:** Kang Song San, Li Jong Ok, Pak Song Chol, Kim Yong Ju, Kim Yong Nam, Gen. Choe Gwang, Kye Ung Tae, Chon Byong Ho, Han Song Ryong, So Yun Sok.

There are also 8 candidate members and 11 secretaries.

# Legislature

### CHOE KO IN MIN HOE UI
(Supreme People's Assembly)

The 687 members of the Ninth Supreme People's Assembly (SPA) were elected unopposed for a four-year term on 22 April 1990.

An amendment to the Constitution, in 1992, however, extended the term to five years. Its permanent body is the Standing Committee. The Chairman and Vice-Chairmen of the SPA hold concurrently the equivalent positions on the Standing Committee.
**Chairman:** YANG HYONG SOP.
**Vice-Chairmen:** RYO YON GU, PAEK IN JUN.

## Political Organizations

**Democratic Front for the Reunification of the Fatherland:** Pyongyang; f. 1946; a vanguard organization comprising political parties and mass working people's organizations seeking the unification of North and South Korea; Chair. CHONG DU HWAN; Mems of Presidium PAK SONG CHOL, RYOM TAE JUN, HAN DOK SU, KIM PYONG SIK, RYU MI YONG, RYO YON GU.

The component parties are:

**Chondoist Chongu Party:** Pyongyang; tel. 34241; f. 1946; supports policies of Korean Workers' Party; follows the guiding principle of *Innaechon* (the realization of 'heaven on earth'); Chair. RYU MI YONG.

**Korean Workers' Party (KWP):** Pyongyang; f. 1945; merged with the South Korean Workers' Party in 1949; the guiding principle is the *Juche* idea, based on the concept that man is the master and arbiter of all things; 3m. mems; Gen. Sec. of Cen. Cttee (vacant); Sec. Marshal KIM JONG IL.

**Social Democratic Party (SDP)** (Choson Sahoeminjudang): Pyongyang; tel. 42924; f. 1945; advocates national independence and a democratic socialist society; supports policies of Korean Workers' Party; Chair. KIM PYONG SIK; First Vice-Chair. KANG PYONG HAK.

The component mass working people's organizations are:
**General Federation of Trade Unions of Korea (GFTUK).**
**Korean Democratic Women's Union (KDWU).**
**League of Socialist Working Youth of Korea (LSWYK).**
**Union of Agricultural Working People of Korea.**
(See under Trade Unions.)

There is one opposition organization in exile, with branches in Tokyo, Moscow and Beijing:

**Salvation Front for the Democratic Unification of Chosun:** f. early 1990s; seeks the overthrow of the Kim dynasty, the establishment of democracy in the DPRK and Korean reunification; Chair. PAK KAP DONG.

## Diplomatic Representation

### EMBASSIES IN THE DEMOCRATIC PEOPLE'S REPUBLIC OF KOREA

**Albania:** Pyongyang; Ambassador: ISMAIL NEZIR DJALOSHI.
**Algeria:** Taedongkang District, Munsudong, Pyongyang; tel. 90372; Ambassador: MOKHTAR REGUIEG.
**Benin:** Pyongyang; Ambassador: A. OGIST.
**Bulgaria:** Taedongkang District, Munsudong, POB 15, Pyongyang; tel. 817341; telex 35015; Ambassador: YORDAN MUTAFCHIYEV.
**China, People's Republic:** Pyongyang; tel. 390274; Ambassador: QIAO ZONGHUAI.
**Cuba:** POB 5, Pyongyang; tel. 817370; telex 35013; Ambassador: JOSÉ RAMÓN RODRÍGUEZ VARONA.
**Egypt:** Pyongyang; tel. 817406; telex 35020; fax 817611; Ambassador: ALI HEGAZI.
**Ethiopia:** Pyongyang; Ambassador: FANTAHUN HAILE MIKAEL.
**Hungary:** Haebangsandong, POB 22, Pyongyang; tel. 813114; fax 813421; Ambassador: LÁSZALÓ IVÁN.
**India:** 6 Munsudong, Taedongkang District, Pyongyang; tel. 817277; Ambassador: SHEHKHOLEN KIPGEN.
**Indonesia:** 5 Foreigners' Bldg, Munsudong, Taedongkang District, POB 178, Pyongyang; tel. 817387; telex 35030; fax 817620; Ambassador: MUHARAM SOEMADIPRADJA.
**Iran:** Pyongyang; Ambassador: H. P. LIYAN.
**Libya:** Pyongyang; Secretary of People's Bureau: ASHARIF G. AL-KABASH.
**Mali:** Pyongyang; Ambassador: NAKOUNTE DIAKITÉ.
**Mongolia:** Pyongyang; Ambassador: SH. GUNGAADORJ.
**Nigeria:** POB 535, Pyongyang; tel. 817286; telex 5225; fax 817613; Ambassador: OLUGBENGA A. ASHIRU.
**Pakistan:** Munsudong, Taedongkang District, Pyongyang; tel. 817479; telex 5502; fax 817622; Ambassador: Lt-Gen. R. D. BHATTI.
**Poland:** Munsudong, Taedongkang District, Pyongyang; tel. 817327; Ambassador: RYSZARD BATURO.
**Portugal:** Pyongyang; Ambassador: JOSÉ MANUEL VILLAS-BOAS.
**Romania:** Pyongyang; telex 5481; Ambassador: NICOLAE GIRBA.
**Russia:** Sinyangdong, Chung Kuyuck, Pyongyang; tel. 813101; telex 35001; Ambassador: YURI FADEYEV.
**Syria:** Munsudong, Taedongkang District, Pyongyang; tel. 349323; telex 35018; Ambassador: YASSER AL-FARRA.
**Viet Nam:** Pyongyang; Ambassador: DUONG CHINH THUC.
**Yugoslavia:** Pyongyang; Ambassador: MILAN SESLIJA.

## Judicial System

The judicial organs include the Central Court, the Court of the Province (or city under central authority) and the People's Court. Each court is composed of judges and people's assessors.

Procurators supervise the ordinances and regulations of all ministries and the decisions and directives of local organs of state power to see that they conform to the Constitution, laws and decrees, as well as to the decisions and other measures of the Administration Council (Cabinet). Procurators bring suits against criminals in the name of the state, and participate in civil cases to protect the interests of the state and citizens.

**Central Court:** Pyongyang; the highest judicial organ; supervises the work of all courts.
**President:** CHOE WON IK.
**First Vice-President:** KIM YONG HWAN.
**Central Procurator's Office:** supervises work of procurator's offices in provinces, cities and counties.
**Procurator-General:** LI RYONG SOP.

## Religion

The religions which are officially reported to be practised in the DPRK are Buddhism, Christianity and Chundo Kyo, a religion peculiar to Korea combining elements of Buddhism and Christianity. Religious co-ordinating bodies are believed to be under strict state control.

**Council of Korean Religionists:** Pyongyang; f. 1989; brings together members of religious organizations in North Korea; Pres. CHANG JAE CHOL; Vice-Pres. PAK TAE HO.

### BUDDHISM

In 1989, according to official estimates, there were 10,000 Buddhists in the DPRK.

**Korean Buddhists Federation:** POB 77, Pyongyang; tel. 43698; f. 1945; Chair. of Cen. Cttee PAK TAE HO; Sec.-Gen. SIM SANG RYON.

### CHRISTIANITY

In 1989, according to North Korean sources, there were approximately 25,000 Christians (including 15,000 Roman Catholics) in the country, many of whom worshipped in one of about 500 house churches.

**Korean Christians Federation:** Pyongyang; f. 1946; Chair. of Cen. Cttee KANG YONG SOP.

#### The Roman Catholic Church

For ecclesiastical purposes, North and South Korea are nominally under a unified jurisdiction. North Korea contains two dioceses (Hamhung and Pyongyang), both suffragan to the archdiocese of Seoul (in South Korea), and the territorial abbacy of Tokwon (Tokugen), directly responsible to the Holy See.

**Korean Roman Catholic Association:** Changchung 1-dong, Songyo District, Pyongyang; tel. 23492; f. 1988; Chair. of Cen. Cttee CHANG JAE CHOL; Sec.-Gen. PAK KYONG SU.

**Diocese of Hamhung:** Catholic Mission, Hamhung; Bishop (vacant); Apostolic Administrator of Hamhung and of the Abbacy of Tokwon: Fr PLACIDUS DONG-HO RI, 134-1 Wae Gwan Dong, Gwan Eub, Chil kok kun, Kyeong Buk 718-800, Republic of Korea; tel. (545) 971-0621.

**Diocese of Pyongyang:** Catholic Mission, Pyongyang; Bishop Rt Rev. FRANCIS TAKEOKA HONG (absent); Apostolic Administrator HE Cardinal STEPHEN SOU-HWAN KIM, Archbishop of Seoul.

### CHUNDO KYO

**Korean Chundoists Association:** Pyongyang; tel. 34241; f. 1946; Chair. of Central Guidance Cttee RYU MI YONG; Sec.-Gen. KIM JONG HO.

# The Press

In 1992 there were 11 daily newspapers in the DPRK, with an estimated combined circulation of 5m. copies per issue.

## PRINCIPAL NEWSPAPERS

**Choldo Sinmun:** Pyongyang; f. 1947; every two days.

**Joson Inmingun** (Korean People's Army): Pyongyang; f. 1948; daily; Editor-in-Chief YUN CHI HO.

**Kyowon Sinmun:** Pyongyang; f. 1948; publ. by the Education Commission; weekly.

**Minju Choson** (Democratic Korea): Pyongyang; f. 1946; govt organ; 6 a week; Editor-in-Chief KIM JONG SUK; circ. 200,000.

**Nongup Keunroja:** Pyongyang; publ. of Cen. Cttee of the Union of Agricultural Working People of Korea.

**Pyongyang Sinmun:** Pyongyang; f. 1957; general news; 6 a week; Editor-in-Chief KIM JONG HWAN.

**Rodong Chongnyon** (Working Youth): Pyongyang; f. 1946; organ of the Cen. Cttee of the League of Socialist Working Youth of Korea; 6 a week; Editor-in-Chief LI JONG GI.

**Rodong Sinmun** (Labour Daily): Pyongyang; f. 1946; organ of the Cen. Cttee of the Korean Workers' Party; daily; Editor-in-Chief HYON JUN GUK; circ. 1.5m.

**Rodongja Sinmun** (Workers' Newspaper): Pyongyang; f. 1945; organ of the Gen. Fed. of Trade Unions of Korea; Editor-in-Chief LEE SONG JU.

**Saenal** (New Day): Pyongyang; f. 1971; League of Socialist Working Youth of Korea; 2 a week.

**Sonyon Sinmun:** Pyongyang; f. 1946; League of Socialist Working Youth of Korea; 2 a week; circ. 120,000.

**Tongil Sinbo:** Kangan 1-dong, Youth Ave, Sonkyo District, Pyongyang; f. 1972; non-affiliated; weekly; Chief Editor JO HYON YONG; circ. 300,000.

## PRINCIPAL PERIODICALS

**Chollima:** Pyongyang; popular magazine; monthly.

**Choson** (Korea): Pyongyang; social, economic, political and cultural; monthly.

**Chosonminjujuuiinmingonghwaguk Palmyonggongbo** (Official Report of Inventions in the DPRK): Pyongyang; 6 a year.

**Choson Munhak** (Korean Literature): Pyongyang; organ of the Cen. Cttee of the Korean Writers' Union; monthly.

**Choson Yesul** (Korean Arts): Pyongyang; organ of the Cen. Cttee of the Gen. Fed. of Literature and Arts of Korea; monthly.

**Hwahakgwa Hwahakgoneop:** Pyongyang; organ of the Hamhung br. of the Korean Acad. of Sciences; chemistry and chemical engineering; 6 a year.

**Jokook Tongil:** Kangan 1-dong, Youth Ave, Sonkyo District, Pyongyang; organ of the Cttee for the Peaceful Unification of Korea; f. 1961; Chief Editor LI MYONG GYU; monthly; circ. 70,000.

**Kulloja** (Workers): 1 Munshindong, Tongdaewon, Pyongyang; f. 1946; organ of the Cen. Cttee of the Korean Workers' Party; Assoc. Editor LI JONG NAM; monthly; circ. 300,000.

**Kwahakwon Tongbo** (Bulletins of the Academy of Science): Pyongyang; organ of the Standing Cttee of the Korean Acad. of Sciences; 6 a year.

**Munhwao Haksup** (Study of Korean Language): Pyongyang; publ. by the Publishing House of the Acad. of Social Sciences; quarterly.

**Punsok Hwahak:** Pyongyang; organ of the Cen. Analytical Inst. of the Korean Acad. of Sciences; quarterly.

**Ryoksagwahak** (Historical Science): Pyongyang; publ. by the Acad. of Social Sciences; quarterly.

**Saengmulhak** (Biology): Pyongyang; publ. by the Science and Encyclopaedia Publishing House; quarterly.

**Sahoekwahak** (Social Science): Pyongyang; publ. by the Acad. of Social Sciences; 6 a year.

**Suhakkwa Mulli:** Pyongyang; organ of the Physics and Mathematics Cttee of the Korean Acad. of Sciences; quarterly.

## FOREIGN LANGUAGE PUBLICATIONS

**The Democratic People's Republic of Korea:** Korea Pictorial, Pyongyang; f. 1956; illustrated news; Korean, Russian, Chinese, English, French, Arabic and Spanish edns; monthly.

**Foreign Trade of the DPRK:** Foreign Trade Publishing House, Potonggang District, Pyongyang; economic developments and export promotion; English, French and Russian edns; monthly.

**Korea:** Pyongyang; f. 1956; illustrated; Korean, Arabic, Chinese, English, French, Spanish and Russian edns; monthly.

**Korea Today:** Foreign Languages Publishing House, Pyongyang; current affairs; Chinese, English, French, Russian and Spanish edns; monthly.

**Korean Women:** Pyongyang; English and French edns; quarterly.

**Korean Youth and Students:** Pyongyang; English and French edns; monthly.

**The Pyongyang Times:** Sochondong, Sosong District, Pyongyang; tel. 51951; English, Spanish and French edns; weekly.

## NEWS AGENCIES

**Korean Central News Agency (KCNA):** Potonggangdong 1, Potonggang District, Pyongyang; f. 1946; sole distributing agency for news in the DPRK; publs daily bulletins in English, Russian, French and Spanish; Pres. KIM GI RYONG; Vice-Pres. PAK HYON GYU.

### Foreign Bureaux

**Informatsionnoye Telegrafnoye Agentstvo Rossii—Telegrafnoye Agentstvo Suverennykh Stran (ITAR—TASS)** (Russia): Taedonggang Kuyuck, Munsudong, Bldg 4, Flat 30, Pyongyang; tel. 817318; telex 35003; Correspondent ALEKSANDR VALIYEV.

The **Xinhua (New China) News Agency** (People's Republic of China) is also represented in the DPRK.

### Press Association

**Union of Korean Journalists:** Pyongyang; tel. 36897; f. 1946; assists in the ideological work of the Korean Workers' Party; Chair. of Cen. Cttee HYON JUN GUK.

# Publishers

**Academy of Sciences Publishing House:** Central District, Nammundong, Pyongyang; f. 1953; publs *Kwahakwon Tongbo* (Journal of the Acad. of Sciences of the DPRK) bi-monthly; *Kwahakgwa Kwahakgoneop* (Journal of Chemistry and the Chemical Industry) bi-monthly; also quarterly journals of geology and geography, metals, biology, analytical chemistry, mathematics and physics, and electricity.

**Academy of Social Sciences Publishing House:** Pyongyang.

**Agricultural Press:** Pyongyang; Pres. HO GYONG PIL.

**Central Science and Technology Information Agency:** Pyongyang; f. 1963; Pres. LI SANG SOL.

**Educational Books Publishing House:** Pyongyang; f. 1945.

**Foreign Language Press Group:** Pyongyang; f. 1949; Pres. HWANG SUN MYONG.

**Foreign Trade Publishing House:** Oesong District, Pyongyang.

**Higher Educational Books Publishing House:** Pyongyang; f. 1960; Acting Pres. KIM WON GIL.

**Industry Publishing House:** Pyongyang; f. 1948; technical and economic.

**Kim Il Sung University Publishing House:** Pyongyang; f. 1965.

**Korean Social Democratic Party Publishing House:** Pyongyang; tel. 43684; Pres. KIM SOK JUN.

**Korean Workers' Party Publishing House:** Pyongyang; f. 1945; fiction, politics; Dir KIM YONG HAK.

**Kumsong Youth Publishing House:** Pyongyang; f. 1946; Pres. KANG CHOL BU.

**Literature and Art Publishing House:** Pyongyang; f. by merger of Mass Culture Publishing House and Publishing House of the Gen. Fed. of Literary and Art Unions; Pres. CHONG SO CHON.

**Photo Service:** Pyongyang.

**Science and Encyclopaedia Publishing House:** Pyongyang; f. 1952; Dir RIM GWANG SON.

**Transportation Publishing House:** f. 1952; Editor PAEK JONG HAN (acting).

**Working People's Organizations Publishing House:** Pyongyang; f. 1946; Pres. CHAE JUN BYONG.

### WRITERS' UNION

**Korean Writers' Union:** Pyongyang; Chair. Cen. Cttee KIM BYONG HUN.

# Radio and Television

In 1992, according to UNESCO estimates, there were 2.8m. radio receivers and 400,000 television receivers in use. A television network covers most of the country. Colour transmissions are available in Pyongyang. Radio Pyongyang broadcasts programmes for overseas listeners.

**DPRK Radio and Television Broadcasting Committee:** Jonsungdong, Moranbong District, Pyongyang; tel. 816035; telex 5508; fax 812100; programmes relayed nationally with local programmes supplied by local radio cttees; loudspeakers are installed in factories and in open spaces in all towns; home broadcasting 22 hours daily; foreign broadcasts in Russian, Chinese, English, French, German, Japanese, Spanish and Arabic; Chair. CHONG HA CHOL.

**Kaesong Television:** Kaesong; broadcasts five hours on weekdays, 11 hours at weekends.

**Korean Central Television Station:** Ministry of Post and Communications, Pyongyang; broadcasts five hours daily.

**Mansudae Television Station:** Mansudae, Pyongyang; telex 5612; f. 1983; broadcasts nine hours of cultural programmes, music and dance, foreign films and news reports at weekends.

## Finance

(cap. = capital; res = reserves; dep. = deposits; m. = million; brs = branches; amounts in won, unless otherwise stated)

### BANKING

#### Central Bank

**Central Bank of the DPRK:** Munsudong, Central District, Pyongyang; tel. 35982; telex 5965; f. 1946; bank of issue; supervisory and control bank; Gov. CHONG SONG TAEK; 227 brs.

#### State Banks

**Credit Bank of Korea:** Chongryu 1-dong, Munsudong, Taedongkang District, Pyongyang; tel. 814285; telex 5939; fax 817806; f. 1986; Pres. PAK GI JU; Gen. Man. CHOE GYONG IL.

**Foreign Trade Bank of the DPRK:** Jungsongdong, Seungri St, Central District, Pyongyang; tel. 34531; telex 5460; fax 814467; f. 1959; deals mostly in international settlements; Gov. KIM UNG CHOL.

**Korea Changgwang Credit Bank Corpn:** Daedongmundong, Seungri St, Central District, Pyongyang; tel. 31674; telex 36015; fax 814414; f. 1983; commercial, joint-stock and state bank; cap. 442.0m., res 884.8m., dep. 6,914.8m. (Dec. 1991); Chair. SIN HO; Pres. MAENG BOK SIK; 172 brs.

**Korea Daesong Bank:** Segoridong, Potonggang District, Pyongyang; tel. 43002; telex 5479; fax 814576; f. 1978; Pres. KIM YUN SIK; Vice-Pres. CHANG GON IL.

**Kumgang Bank:** Central District, Pyongyang; telex 5355.

#### Joint-Venture Banks

In March 1995 it was announced that Korea Daesong Bank and Peregrine Co (Hong Kong) were to establish a joint-venture development bank in North Korea, providing financial services for foreign transactions. Peregrine Co was to be the majority shareholder.

**ING-North East Asia Bank:** Najin-Sonbong Free Economic Zone; f. 1995; 70% owned by Internationale Nederlanden Groep (Netherlands), 30% owned by Korea Foreign Insurance Co; cap. US $15m.; br. in Pyongyang.

**Korea Joint Venture Bank:** Pyongyang; tel. 814151; telex 36001; fax 814497; f. 1989 with co-operation of the Federation of Korean Traders and Industrialists in Japan; cap. US $1,932.5m. (1994); Pres. CHON YON SIK; Vice-Pres. PAK IL RAK; 6 brs.

**Korean Unification Development Bank:** Pyongyang; f. 1991; 51% owned by Zhongce Investment Corpn (Hong Kong), 49% owned by Osandok General Bureau; cap. US $30m.; Pres LI IL MAN, OEI HONGLEONG.

### INSURANCE

**State Insurance Bureau:** Central District, Pyongyang; tel. 38196; handles all life, fire, accident, marine, hull insurance and reinsurance.

**Korea Foreign Insurance Co** (Chosunbohom): Pyongchon District, Pyongyang; tel. 45477; telex 36014; fax 814464; f. 1947; conducts marine, automobile, aviation and fire insurance, reinsurance of all classes, and all foreign insurance; brs in Chongjin, Hungnam and Nampo, and agencies in foreign ports; Pres. CHON MYONG HUI.

**Korea Mannyon Insurance Co:** Pyongyang; Pres. PAK IL HYONG.

## Trade and Industry

**DPRK Committee for the Promotion of External Economic Co-operation:** Jungsongdong, Central District, Pyongyang; tel. 33974; telex 5229; fax 814498; Chair. KIM JONG U.

**Korean Association for the Promotion of Asian Trade:** Pyongyang; Pres. LI SONG ROK.

**Korean Committee for the Promotion of International Trade:** Central District, Pyongyang; Chair. LI SONG ROK.

**Korean Council of the Central Federation of Consumption Co-operative Trade Union:** Pyongyang.

**Korean General International Joint Venture Co:** Pyongyang; f. 1986; promotes joint economic ventures with foreign countries; Chair. KIM DAL HYON.

**Korean International Joint Venture Promotion Committee:** Pyongyang; Chair. CHAE HUI JONG.

**Korean General Merchandise Export and Import Corpn:** Pyongyang.

### TRADING CORPORATIONS

**Korea Building Materials Export and Import Corpn:** Central District, Pyongyang; telex 5467; chemical building materials, woods, timbers, cement, sheet glass, etc; Dir SIN DONG BOM.

**Korea Cement Export Corpn:** Central District, Pyongyang; telex 5467; f. 1982; cement and building materials.

**Korea Cereals Export and Import Corpn:** Central District, Pyongyang; telex 5618; high-quality vegetable starches, etc.

**Korea Chemicals Export and Import Corpn:** Central District, Pyongyang; telex 5358; petroleum and petroleum products, raw materials for the chemical industry, rubber and rubber products, fertilizers, etc.

**Korea Daesong Jeil Trading Corpn:** Potonggang District, Pyongyang; telex 5473; machinery and equipment, chemical products, textiles, agricultural products, etc.

**Korea Daesong Jesam Trading Corpn:** Potonggang District, Pyongyang; telex 5474; remedies for diabetes, tonics, etc.

**Korea Ferrous Metals Export and Import Corpn:** Potonggang District, Pyongyang; telex 5509; steel products.

**Korea Film Export and Import Corpn:** Daidongmundong, Central District, POB 113, Pyongyang; tel. 34263; telex 5986; fax 814410; f. 1956; feature films, cartoons, scientific and documentary films; Dir-Gen. PAK CHAN JONG.

**Korea First Equipment Export and Import Co:** Central District, Pyongyang; tel. 34825; telex 5466; f. 1960; export and import of ferrous and non-ferrous metallurgical plants, geological exploration and mining equipment, communication equipment, machine-building plant, etc.; construction of public facilities such as airports, hotels, tourist facilities, etc.; joint-venture business in similar projects; Pres. CHAE WON CHOL.

**Korea Foodstuffs Export and Import Corpn:** Tongdaewon District, Pyongyang; telex 5353; cereals, wines, meat, canned foods, fruits, cigarettes, etc.

**Korea Fruit and Vegetables Export Corpn:** Central District, Pyongyang; tel. 35117; telex 5506; vegetables, fruit and their products.

**Korea General Company for Economic Co-operation:** Central District, Pyongyang; telex 5466; overseas construction, equipment for hydroelectric power plants, equipment for rice-cleaning mills.

**Korea General Export and Import Corpn:** Central District, Pyongyang; telex 5359; plate glass, tiles, granite, locks, medicinal herbs, foodstuffs and light industrial products.

**Korea Hyopdong Trading Corpn:** Central District, Pyongyang; telex 5614; fabrics, glass products, ceramics, chemical goods, building materials, foodstuffs, machinery, etc.

**Korea Jangsu Trading Co:** Potonggang District, Pyongyang; medicinal products and clinical equipment.

**Korea Jeil Equipment Export and Import Corpn:** Chungsongdong, Central District, Pyongyang; tel. 34825; telex 5466; f. 1960; ferrous and non-ferrous metallurgical plant, geological exploration and mining equipment, power plant, communications and broadcasting equipment machine-building equipment, railway equipment, construction of public facilities; Pres. CHO ZANG DOK.

**Korea Jesam Equipment Export and Import Corpn:** Central District, Pyongyang; chemical, textile, pharmaceutical and light industry plant.

**Korea Kwangmyong Trading Corpn:** Central District, Pyongyang; telex 5613; dried herbs, dried and pickled vegetables; Dir CHOE KWAN SU.

**Korea Light Industry Products Export and Import Corpn:** Juchetab St, Tongdaewon District, Pyongyang; tel. 37661; telex 5353; exports silk, cigarettes, canned goods, drinking glasses, ceramics, handbags, pens, plastic flowers, musical instruments, etc.; imports chemicals, dyestuffs, machinery, etc.; Dir CHOE PYONG HYON.

**Korea Machinery and Equipment Export and Import Corpn:** Potonggang District, Pyongyang; tel. 33449; telex 5936; f. 1948;

metallurgical machinery and equipment, electric machines, building machinery, farm machinery, diesel engines, etc.

**Korea Maibong Trading Corpn:** Central District, Pyongyang; non-ferrous metal ingots and allied products, non-metallic minerals, agricultural and marine products.

**Korea Manpung Trading Corpn:** Central District, Pyongyang; chemical and agricultural products, machinery and equipment.

**Korea Mansu Trading Corpn:** Chollima St, Central District, POB 250, Pyongyang; tel. 43075; telex 36027; fax 812100; f. 1974; antibiotics, pharmaceuticals, vitamin compounds, drugs, medicinal herbs; Dir KIM CHANG HUN.

**Korea Marine Products Export and Import Corpn:** Central District, Pyongyang; telex 5463; canned, frozen, dried, salted and smoked fish, fishing equipment and supplies.

**Korea Minerals Export and Import Corpn:** Central District, Pyongyang; telex 5469; minerals, solid fuel, graphite, precious stones, etc.

**Korea Namheung Trading Co:** Tongdaewon District, Pyongyang; telex 5491; high-purity reagents, synthetic resins, vinyl films, essential oils, menthol and peppermint oil.

**Korea Non-ferrous Metals Export and Import Corpn:** Potonggang District, Pyongyang; telex 5352.

**Korea Okyru Trading Corpn:** Central District, Pyongyang; agricultural and marine products, household goods, clothing, chemical and light industrial products.

**Korea Ponghwa General Trading Corpn:** Central District, Pyongyang; telex 5462; machinery, metal products, minerals and chemicals.

**Korea Publications Export and Import Corpn:** Yokjondong, Yonggwang St, Central District, Pyongyang; tel. 33251; telex 36062; export of books, periodicals, postcards, paintings, cassettes, postage stamps and records; import of books; Pres. KIM GI JUN.

**Korea Pyongchon Trading Co:** Central District, Pyongyang; telex 5354; axles, springs, spikes, bolts and bicycles.

**Korea Pyongyang Trading Co Ltd:** Central District, POB 550, Pyongyang; telex 5354; pig iron, steel, magnesia clinker, textiles, etc.

**Korea Rungrado Trading Corpn:** Potonggang District, Pyongyang; telex 5497; food and animal products; Gen. Dir PAK GYU HONG.

**Korea Senbong Trading Corpn:** Central District, Pyongyang; ferrous and non-ferrous metals, rolled steels, mineral ores, chemicals, etc.

**Korea Somyu Hyopdong Trading Corpn:** Oesong District, Pyongyang; telex 5496; clothing and textiles.

**Korea Songhwa Trading Corpn:** Oesong District, Pyongyang; ceramics, glass, hardware, leaf tobaccos, fruit and wines.

**Korea Technical Corpn:** Central District, Pyongyang; telex 5466; scientific and technical co-operation.

**Korea Unha Trading Corpn:** Tongdaewon District, Pyongyang; telex 5492; clothing and fibres.

### TRADE FAIR

**Korea International Exhibition Corpn:** Sosong District, Pyongyang; organizes commodity exhbns of the DPRK abroad and of foreign producers in the DPRK; Dir KIM DONG MYONG.

### TRADE UNIONS

**General Federation of Trade Unions of Korea (GFTUK):** POB 333, Pyongyang; telex 38022; fax 812100; f. 1945; 1.6m. mems (1986); nine affiliated unions; Chair. JU SONG IL; Vice-Chair. LI JIN SU.

**Metals and Machine Workers' Union:** Pyongyang; Chair. KIM HUI SU.

**Mining and Power Industry Workers' Union:** Pyongyang; Chair. KIM KUK SAM.

**Union of Civil Servants:** Pyongyang.

**Union of Construction and Forestry Workers:** Pyongyang; Chair. CHOE TOK SUN.

**Union of Educational and Cultural Workers:** Pyongyang; Chair. NAM SUN HUI.

**Union of Transport Workers and Fishermen:** Pyongyang; Chair. PAEK JONG HUNG.

**General Federation of Agricultural and Forestry Technique of Korea:** Chung Kuyuck Nammundong, Pyongyang; f. 1946; 523,000 mems.

**General Federation of Literature and Arts of Korea:** Pyongyang; f. 1946; seven br. unions; Chair. of Cen. Cttee PAEK IN JUN.

**Korean Architects' Union:** Pyongyang; f. 1954; 500 mems; Chair. KIM JUNG HI.

**Korean Democratic Lawyers' Association:** Pyongyang; f. 1954; Chair. CHOE CHANG HON.

**Korean Democratic Scientists' Association:** Pyongyang; f. 1956.

**Korean Democratic Women's Union:** Pyongyang; Chair. Cen. Cttee KIM SONG AE.

**Korean General Federation of Science and Technology:** Jungsongdong, Sungri St, Central District, Pyongyang; tel. 3338536; telex 38022; fax 81446; f. 1946; 550,000 mems.

**Korean Medical Association:** Pyongyang; f. 1970.

**League of Socialist Working Youth of Korea:** Pyongyang; Chair. Cen. Cttee CHOE RYONG HAE; Vice-Chair. CHOE HYON DOK, KIM SONG CHOL.

**Union of Agricultural Working People of Korea:** Pyongyang; f. 1965 to replace fmr Korean Peasants' Union; 2.4m. mems; Chair. Cen. Cttee CHOE SONG SUK.

**Union of Korean Journalists:** Pyongyang; tel. 36897; f. 1946; Chair. Cen. Cttee HYON JUN GUK.

## Transport

### RAILWAYS

Railways are responsible for some 60% of passenger journeys and for some 90% of the volume of freight transported. In 1991 the total length of track was 8,533 km (of which 3,194 km, or 37%, had been electrified by 1990). In late 1994 it was estimated that some 74% of the railway system had been electrified. There are international train services to Moscow (Russia) and Beijing (People's Republic of China).

There is an underground railway system in Pyongyang, comprising two lines with a combined length of 32 km.

### ROADS

In 1991, according to South Korean estimates, the road network totalled 23,000 km (of which 1,861 km were paved), including 524 km of multi-lane highways. The road network totalled an estimated 23,219 km in 1993.

### INLAND WATERWAYS

The Yalu (Amnok-gang) and Taedong, Tumen and Ryesong are the most important commercial rivers. Regular passenger and freight services: Nampo–Chosan–Supung; Chungsu–Sinuiju–Dasado; Nampo–Jeudo; Pyongyang–Nampo.

### SHIPPING

The principal ports are Nampo, Wonsan, Chongjin, Rajin, Hungnam, Songnim and Haeju. In 1990 North Korean ports had a combined capacity for handling 34.9m. tons of cargo. In 1989 North Korea's merchant fleet comprised 82 vessels, amounting to a total displacement of 396,249 grt.

**Korea Chartering Corpn:** Central District, Pyongyang; telex 5357; arranges cargo transportation and chartering.

**Korea Foreign Transportation Corpn:** Central District, Pyongyang; telex 5498; arranges transportation of export and import cargoes (transit goods and charters).

**Korean-Polish Shipping Co Ltd:** Moranbong District, Pyongyang; tel. 814384; telex 35037; maritime trade mainly with Polish, Far East and DPRK ports.

**Korea Tonghae Shipping Co:** Oesong District, Pyongyang; telex 5461; arranges transportation by Korean vessels.

**Ocean Shipping Agency of the DPRK:** Moranbong District, Pyongyang; telex 5470; Pres. PAEK IK BOM.

### CIVIL AVIATION

The international airport is at Sunan, 24 km from Pyongyang.

**Chosonminhang/General Civil Aviation Bureau of the DPRK:** Sunan Airport, Sunan District, Pyongyang; tel. 37917; telex 5471; fax 814625; f. 1954; internal services and external flights by Air Koryo to Beijing (People's Republic of China), Bangkok (Thailand), Moscow and Khabarovsk (Russia), Sofia (Bulgaria) and Berlin (Germany); charter services are operated to Asia, Africa and Europe; Pres. KIM YO UNG.

## Tourism

The DPRK was formally admitted to the World Tourism Organization in 1987. Tourism is permitted only in officially accompanied parties. In 1989 there were more than 30 tourist hotels (including nine in Pyongyang) with 12,000 beds. There were about 100,000 visitors in 1991. A feasibility study was undertaken in 1992 regarding the development of Mount Kumgang as a tourist attraction. The study proposed the construction of an international airport at Kumnan and of a number of hotels and leisure facilities in the Wonsan area. Local ports were also to be upgraded. It was hoped that the development, due to cost some US $20,000m. and to be completed by 2004, would attract 3m. tourists to the area each year. According to official estimates, some 15,000 tourists attended an international sports and cultural festival in Pyongyang in April 1995.

**Korean International Youth Tourist Company:** Mankyongdae District, Pyongyang; tel. 73406; telex 5476; f. 1985; Dir HWANG CHUN YONG.

**Kumgangsan International Tourist Company:** Central District, Pyongyang; tel. 31562; telex 5474; fax 812100; f. 1988; Dir KIM KWAN DU.

**National Directorate of Tourism of the DPRK:** Central District, Pyongyang; tel. 817201; telex 5998; fax 817607; f. 1986; state-run tourism promotion organization.

**Ryohaengsa** (Korea International Travel Company): Central District, Pyongyang; tel. 817201; telex 5998; fax 817607; f. 1953; has relations with more than 200 tourist companies throughout the world; Pres. CHO SONG HUN.

# THE REPUBLIC OF KOREA

## Introductory Survey

### Location, Climate, Language, Religion, Flag, Capital

The Republic of Korea (South Korea) forms the southern part of the Korean peninsula, in eastern Asia. To the north, separated by a frontier which roughly follows the 38th parallel, is the country's only neighbour, the Democratic People's Republic of Korea (North Korea). To the west is the Yellow Sea, to the south is the East China Sea, and to the east is the Sea of Japan. The climate is marked by cold, dry winters, with an average temperature of −6°C (21°F), and hot, humid summers, with an average temperature of 25°C (77°F). The language is Korean. Mahayana Buddhism is the principal religion, with almost 9m. adherents. Christians number some 17.5m., of whom about 83% are Protestants. Other religions include Confucianism and Chundo Kyo, a religion peculiar to Korea, combining elements of Shaman, Buddhist and Christian doctrines. The national flag (proportions 3 by 2) consists of a disc divided horizontally by an S-shaped line, red above and blue below, in the centre of a white field, with parallel black bars (broken and unbroken) in each corner. The capital is Seoul.

### Recent History

(For more details of the history of Korea up to 1953, including the Korean War, see the chapter on the Democratic People's Republic of Korea—DPRK—p. 1766.)

UN-supervised elections to a new legislature, the National Assembly (Kuk Hoe), took place in May 1948. The Assembly adopted a democratic Constitution, and South Korea became the independent Republic of Korea on 15 August 1948, with Dr Syngman Rhee, leader of the Liberal Party, as the country's first President. He remained in the post until his resignation in April 1960. Elections in July were won by the Democratic Party, led by Chang Myon, but his Government was deposed in May 1961 by a military coup, led by Gen. Park Chung-Hee. Power was assumed by the Supreme Council for National Reconstruction, which dissolved the National Assembly, suspended the Constitution and disbanded all existing political parties. In January 1963 the military leadership formed the Democratic Republican Party (DRP). Under a new Constitution, Gen. Park became President of the Third Republic in December.

Opposition to Park's regime led to the imposition of martial law in October 1972. A Constitution for the Fourth Republic, giving the President greatly increased powers, was approved by national referendum in November. A new body, the National Conference for Unification (NCU), was elected in December. The NCU re-elected President Park for a six-year term, and the DRP obtained a decisive majority in elections to the new National Assembly. In May 1975 opposition to the Government was effectively banned, and political trials followed. Elections to the NCU were held in May 1978, and the President was re-elected for a further six-year term in July. In October 1979 serious rioting erupted when Kim Young-Sam, the leader of the opposition New Democratic Party (NDP), was accused of subversive activities and expelled from the National Assembly. On 26 October Park was assassinated in an alleged coup attempt, led by the head of the Korean Central Intelligence Agency. On the following day martial law was reintroduced (except on the island of Cheju), and the Prime Minister, Choi Kyu-Hah, became acting President. He was elected President by the NCU on 6 December. Instability in the DRP and the army resulted in a military coup on 12–13 December, led by the head of the Defence Security Command, Lt-Gen. Chun Doo-Hwan, who arrested the Army Chief of Staff (the martial law administrator) and effectively took power. Nevertheless, President Choi was inaugurated on 21 December to complete his predecessor's term of office (1978–84).

President Choi promised liberalizing reforms, but in May 1980 demonstrations by students and confrontation with the army led to the arrest of about 30 political leaders, including Kim Dae-Jung, former head of the NDP. Martial law was extended throughout the country, the National Assembly was suspended, and all political activity was banned. Almost 200 people were killed when troops stormed the southern city of Kwangju, which had been taken over by students and dissidents. In August President Choi resigned, and Gen. Chun was elected President. Acting Prime Minister Nam Duck-Woo formed a new State Council (cabinet) in September, and in the same month Kim Dae-Jung was sentenced to death for plotting rebellion, which provoked strong international protest. (This sentence was subsequently suspended.) In October a new Constitution was approved overwhelmingly by referendum. In the following month, none the less, some 835 people were banned from participation in the political process (although the list of those excluded had been reduced to 567 by the end of the month).

Martial law was ended in January 1981, and new political parties were formed. In February President Chun was re-elected: the start of his new term, in March, inaugurated the Fifth Republic. President Chun's Democratic Justice Party (DJP) became the majority party in the new National Assembly, which was elected shortly afterwards. Amid opposition demands for liberalization, President Chun pledged that he would retire at the end of his term in 1988, thus becoming the country's first Head of State to transfer power constitutionally.

During 1984 there was an escalation of student unrest on campuses throughout South Korea. The Government subsequently adopted a more flexible attitude towards dissidents. Several thousand prisoners were released, and by November of that year only 15 of the original 835 names remained on the political 'blacklist' (which was finally abolished in March 1985). In January 1985 a new opposition movement, the New Korea Democratic Party (NKDP), was established by followers of Kim Young-Sam and Kim Dae-Jung. At the general election to the National Assembly, held in February, the DJP retained its majority, but the NKDP emerged as the major opposition force, boosted by the return from exile of Kim Dae-Jung immediately before the election. The new party secured 67 of the Assembly's 276 seats, while the DJP, which suffered losses in urban areas, won 148 seats. President Chun appointed a new State Council, with Lho Shin-Yong, a former Minister of Foreign Affairs, as Prime Minister. Shortly afterwards Roh Tae-Woo, a former Minister of Home Affairs and a retired army general, was appointed chairman of the DJP. The election thus signalled the emergence for the first time of a relatively powerful parliamentary opposition. Before the opening session of the new National Assembly many opposition members defected to join the NKDP, increasing the party's strength to 102 seats.

In April 1987 internal divisions within the NKDP led to the formation of a new opposition group, the Reunification Democratic Party (RDP); Kim Young-Sam was elected to the presidency of the new party in early May. The RDP identified the reunification of North and South Korea as 'the foremost historic task'. In April President Chun unexpectedly announced the suspension of the process of reform until after the Olympic Games (due to be held in Seoul in September 1988). While confirming that he would leave office in February 1988, Chun indicated that his successor would be elected by the existing electoral college system. President Chun's announcement precipitated violent clashes between anti-Government demonstrators and riot police in Seoul and other major cities.

In June 1987 the nomination of Roh Tae-Woo, the Chairman of the DJP, as the ruling party's presidential candidate provoked further violent demonstrations. However, at the end of June Roh Tae-Woo unexpectedly informed Chun that he would relinquish both the DJP chairmanship and his presidential candidature if the principal demands of the opposition for constitutional and electoral reform were not satisfied, and submitted a programme of reform for the President's approval. Under pressure from the DJP leadership and international opinion, Chun acceded, and negotiations on constitutional amendments, which had been the subject of continued discussions in 1986, were announced. On 31 August the DJP and the RDP announced that a bipartisan committee had agreed a draft constitution. Among its provisions were the reintroduction of direct presidential elections by universal suffrage, and the restriction of the presidential mandate to a single five-year term; the President's emergency powers were also to be reduced, and serving military officers were to be prohibited from taking government office. The constitutional amendments were approved by the National Assembly in mid-October. The changes were endorsed by 93.1% of the votes cast in a national referendum which took place on 27 October, and the amended Constitution was promulgated two days later.

At the invitation of Kim Young-Sam, Kim Dae-Jung joined the RDP in August 1987; in November, however, he became President of a new political organization, the Peace and Democracy Party (PDP), and declared himself a rival Presidential candidate. The presidential election took place on 16 December: Roh Tae-Woo received about 36% of the votes, while Kim Dae-Jung and Kim Young-Sam received about 27% each. Roh Tae-Woo was inaugurated as President on 25 February 1988, whereupon the Sixth Republic was established. A general election took place on 26 April. The DJP failed to achieve an overall majority in the National Assembly, winning only 87 of the 224 directly elective seats; however, as the largest single party, it was awarded 38 of the 75 additional seats. The PDP won 54 seats by direct election and 16 additional seats, thus becoming the main opposition party. Of the remaining 83 directly elective seats, the RDP won 46, and the New Democratic Republican Party (NDRP, the recently revived and renamed DRP), led by Kim Jong-Pil, secured 27. In May Kim Dae-Jung and Kim Young-Sam were re-elected to the respective presidencies of the PDP and the RDP.

Beginning in late May 1988 thousands of students joined demonstrations and marches throughout the country, demanding, in particular, a full inquiry into the army's suppression of the 1980 Kwangju uprising. In subsequent weeks there were many instances of violent confrontations with the police, prompting fears that civil unrest would disrupt the forthcoming Olympic Games in Seoul. However, the Games were concluded successfully, with only minor student disturbances, and a panel of members of the National Assembly began public hearings on various aspects of alleged official corruption and violations of human rights during the period of the Fifth Republic.

During 1988 the Government granted an increased measure of autonomy to national and private universities, permitted the formation of student associations, and eased restrictions on press freedom. The number of trade unions increased, and greater freedom to undertake foreign travel was granted to South Korean citizens. Several thousand prisoners, including political dissidents, were reported to have been released during the year. In 1989, however, the human rights organization, Amnesty International, stated that political arrests continued. Other sources estimated the number of political detainees in 1990 to be about 1,400.

In February 1990 the political situation altered dramatically when the DJP merged with the RDP and the NDRP to form a new party, the Democratic Liberal Party (DLP). Roh was subsequently elected President of the DLP, while Kim Young-Sam and Kim Jong-Pil were elected as two of the party's three Chairmen. The DLP thus gained control of more than two-thirds of the seats in the National Assembly. The PDP, which was effectively isolated as the sole opposition party in the National Assembly, condemned the merger as a 'betrayal of the Korean people', and demanded new elections. Students in Seoul and Kwangju staged demonstrations in protest against the merger. In March a new opposition group, the Democratic Party (DP), was formed, largely comprising members of the RDP who had opposed the merger.

In mid-1990 renewed industrial unrest coincided with further student demonstrations. In late July some 200,000 people participated in a rally in Seoul to protest against the adoption by the National Assembly of several items of controversial legislation, including plans to restructure the military leadership and to reorganize the broadcasting media. Shortly afterwards all the opposition members of the National Assembly tendered their resignation, in protest at the contentious legislation. Although the Assembly's Speaker refused to accept the resignations, the PDP deputies returned to the National Assembly only in mid-November, following an agreement with the DLP that local council elections would take place in the first half of 1991, to be followed by gubernatorial and mayoral elections in 1992 (although the elections for provincial governors and mayors were later postponed). The DLP also agreed to abandon plans for the transfer, by constitutional amendment, of executive powers to the State Council.

The agreed local elections, the first to be held in South Korea for 30 years, took place in March and June 1991, and resulted in a decisive victory for the DLP. Nevertheless, the Government was confronted by escalating domestic unrest during the first half of the year. Despite the appointment, in late April, of a new Minister of Home Affairs, demonstrations intensified, and in mid-May the 11th anniversary of the Kwangju uprising occasioned widespread unrest. In early June the newly-appointed Prime Minister, Ro Jai-Bong, was violently assaulted by students while he visited Hankuk University in Seoul.

Meanwhile, in April 1991 the PDP merged with the smaller, dissident Party for New Democratic Alliance to form the New Democratic Party (NDP). In September Kim Dae-Jung and Lee Ki-Taek, the respective leaders of the NDP and the DP, agreed to a merger of their parties (under the latter's name) to form a stronger opposition front. A relaxation of the ruling party's hitherto uncompromising attitude towards the political left was suggested by President Roh's meeting with leaders of the recently-established Minjung (People's) Party in late 1991. A further opposition party, the Unification National Party (UNP), was established in January 1992 by Chung Ju-Yung, the founder and honorary chairman of the powerful Hyundai industrial conglomerate.

At elections to the National Assembly, which took place in late March 1992, the DLP suffered an unexpected and humiliating reversal: although it obtained the largest overall share of the seats (149 of a total 299), it lost the two-thirds' majority that it had enjoyed in the previous Assembly, and failed by one seat to secure an absolute majority. The DLP's loss of popular support was attributed largely to the country's economic difficulties, including high rates of both interest and inflation and an increasingly large trade deficit. The DP secured a majority of the votes cast not only in its traditional south-western strongholds but also in Seoul, and, as a result, increased its total share of seats in the Assembly appreciably (to 97). The UNP took 31 seats (more than had been expected), thus exceeding the 20 seats required to obtain the status of an official negotiating faction in the Assembly. Independent candidates secured a total of 21 seats.

The latter half of 1992 was dominated by the campaign for the presidential election, which was to take place in December, with the state of the economy the most prominent issue. In May Kim Young-Sam was chosen as the DLP's candidate for the election, and in August he replaced Roh as the party's President. In the following month Roh resigned from the DLP altogether, also instructing members of the State Council to do so, in order to create a neutral government in anticipation of the December election. This development was welcomed by opposition legislators, who ended a boycott of the National Assembly (begun in mid-1992 to protest against the postponement of the gubernatorial and mayoral elections). However, there were serious divisions within the DLP, leading to defections from the party by opponents of Kim Young-Sam. In October some of these defectors established, with other opposition figures, the New Korea Party (NKP). In November the NKP formed an electoral alliance with the United People's Party (UPP, as the UNP had been renamed); this decision, however, was reversed in early 1993.

The presidential election, which took place on 18 December 1992, was won by Kim Young-Sam, who received some 42% of the votes. Kim thus became (at his inauguration on 25 February 1993) the first South Korean President since 1960 not to have military connections. Of the six other candidates, his nearest rivals were Kim Dae-Jung, who received 34% of the votes, and Chung Ju-Yung, with 16%. Following the election, Kim Dae-Jung announced his decision to retire from political life, resigning as joint President of the DP and as a member of the National Assembly. In February 1993 Chung Ju-Yung resigned as President of the UPP, following allegations that he had embezzled Hyundai finances to fund his election campaign. Subsequent defections by UPP members caused the party to lose its status as a parliamentary negotiating group.

In late February 1993 Kim Young-Sam appointed Hwang In-Sung, a former army officer, business executive and the Chairman of the DLP's Policy Committee, as Prime Minister. The formation of the new State Council followed later in the month. In early March President Kim announced an amnesty for almost 42,000 people, including more than 2,000 prisoners.

Following his inauguration, Kim Young-Sam acted swiftly to honour his campaign pledge to eliminate corruption in business and political life. Within weeks of their appointment three members of the State Council were forced to resign, following revelations of financial improbity. In all during 1993, Kim's anti-corruption measures were reported to have resulted in the dismissal of, or disciplinary action against, some 3,000 business, government and military figures. Investigations began into the circumstances surrounding the 1979 coup and into the involvement of ex-Presidents Chun Doo-Hwan and Roh Tae-Woo in the allocation of military contracts, although in September 1993 the Board of Audit and Inspection (BAI—the body effectively responsible for investigations of bureaucratic corruption) announced that it had found no evidence of wrongdoing in Roh's role in the allocation of a contract, during 1991, for the supply of military aircraft. Also indicted were two of Roh's former Ministers of National Defence, and in November Lee Jong-Koo (who had held the defence portfolio in 1990–91) was sentenced to three years' imprisonment, after having been convicted of accepting bribes from defence contractors.

The announcement of measures to restrict the activities of the country's industrial conglomerates (chaebol) was accompanied by legal proceedings, related to allegations of corruption, against several prominent business executives. In November 1993 Chung Ju-Yung was sentenced to three years' imprisonment, although the sentence was suspended on account of his age (78) and past contribution to South Korea's economic development. A presidential decree, issued in August (and subsequently endorsed by parliament), outlawed the opening of bank accounts under false names—a practice which, it was believed, had been used to conceal large-scale financial irregularities in public life. Under the decree, it was stipulated that all account-holders would have to reveal their true identity by mid-October. Meanwhile, the disclosure, in early September, of the assets of some 1,500 public officials, including politicians and members of the judiciary and military, and the submission of these accounts for scrutiny by a government ethics committee, prompted the resignation of several senior public figures, including the Chief Justice and the Prosecutor-General.

In May 1993, shortly before the anniversary of the Kwangju uprising, President Kim announced a series of measures that were intended to appease continuing resentment at the armed forces' brutal suppression of the rebellion: among his proposals were the declaration of 18 May (the day of the beginning of the uprising) as a national holiday, and the instigation of a true assessment of the number of persons killed, injured or missing as a result of the rebellion and its suppression. As in previous years, however, there were student protests to commemorate the event in Kwangju and Seoul, where riot police intervened to prevent students from marching to the homes of ex-Presidents Chun and Roh to demand a full investigation of the armed forces' actions in 1980.

Hwang In-Sung resigned as Prime Minister in mid-December 1993, following mass demonstrations in protest against the ending of South Korea's long-standing ban on imports of rice subsequently implemented a major reorganization of the State Council: Lee Hoi-Chang, hitherto Chairman of the BAI, was appointed Prime Minister, the two Deputy Prime Ministers (with responsibility for economic planning and for national unification) were replaced, and new appointments were made to, among others, the defence, agriculture and home affairs portfolios. However, Lee himself resigned in April 1994, reportedly following disagreement with Kim regarding the extent of his authority, as well as conflicts within the State Council. He was replaced as Prime Minister by Lee Yung-Duk, latterly the Deputy Prime Minister responsible for national unification.

Several radical students were arrested in July 1994, after contravening a government edict prohibiting public mourning, following the death, earlier in the month, of the North Korean President, Kim Il Sung. The Government's decision not to send a representative to Kim's state funeral provoked an angry response from the North Korean leadership. Also in July the UPP and a smaller opposition party, the New Political Reform Party, merged to form the New People's Party (NPP). In October the Government announced that its inquiry (begun in July 1993) into the role played by former Presidents Chun Doo-Hwan and Roh Tae-Woo in the 1979 coup had found that Chun and Roh had participated in a 'premeditated military rebellion'. The Government decided, however, not to prosecute the former Presidents, asserting that the two men had also made positive contributions to the development of South Korea. In the following month Lee Ki-Taek, the leader of the DP, resigned from the National Assembly in protest at the Government's decision not to prosecute.

The death of more than 30 people in the collapse of a motorway bridge in Seoul, in October 1994, led to the arrest of five city council officials, who were accused of negligence regarding statutory maintenance inspections. (The officials were released in April 1995.) President Kim viewed the disaster as another example of corruption, this time in the construction industry, and pledged to bring those responsible to justice. Earlier in the month Kim announced a reshuffle of three cabinet portfolios connected with the economy and finance. This was followed, in December, by a further, major restructuring of the State Council: Lee Hong-Ku (hitherto the Deputy Prime Minister responsible for national unification) replaced Lee Yung-Duk as Prime Minister, and a new enlarged Finance and Economics Board was created by the amalgamation of the Ministry of Finance and the Economic Planning Board. Kim Deok, the new Deputy Prime Minister responsible for national unification, was obliged to resign, however, in February 1995, following accusations of impropriety in his former position as Director of the Agency for National Security Planning.

In January 1995 Kim Jong-Pil resigned as Co-Chairman of the DLP, following criticism of his unenthusiastic attitude to President Kim's reform programme. A new political party, the United Liberal Democratic Party, was subsequently formed under the leadership of Kim Jong-Pil.

The South Korean Constitution (as amended in 1987) stipulates that the Republic of Korea shall seek peaceful unification of the Korean peninsula, 'based on the principles of freedom and democracy'. During the 1980s relations with the DPRK were characterized by mutual suspicion, aggravated by various incidents, including the discovery of several pro-North Korean spy rings, and the death in October 1983 of four South Korean government ministers in a bomb explosion in Rangoon, Burma (now Yangon, Myanmar), for which President Chun held the DPRK responsible. During 1985 representatives of the two states conferred on economic and humanitarian issues, but discussions were suspended in early 1986, when the North Korean leader, Kim Il Sung, denounced the annual 'Team Spirit' military manoeuvres, held jointly with US troops in South Korea. Future inter-Korean negotiations were likewise regularly suspended, owing to North Korean objections to the 'Team Spirit' exercises. In November 1987 the destruction of a South Korean airliner in mid-air over South-East Asia by a bomb that had allegedly been concealed aboard the aircraft by North Korean agents caused a new outbreak of verbal hostility between the two countries.

However, with the appointment of Roh Tae-Woo as South Korea's new President in 1988, there appeared to be a greater willingness by the South to foster closer relations with the DPRK. Roh's announcement, in early 1990, that the forthcoming 'Team Spirit' manoeuvres would be reduced in size and duration also contributed to an improvement in inter-Korean relations. In September of that year the DPRK Premier, Yon Hyong Muk, travelled to Seoul for discussions with his South Korean counterpart, Kang Young-Hoon. The meeting represented the most senior-level contact between the two countries since the end of the Korean War in 1953. Further talks between the two premiers took place in October and December 1990. The DPRK's abandonment, announced in May 1991, of its long-standing position that the two Koreas should occupy a single seat at the UN was widely regarded as a significant concession. Accordingly, North and South were admitted separately to the UN in mid-September.

Prime-ministerial negotiations resumed in October 1991, in Pyongyang, and in December, in Seoul, and resulted in the signature of an 'Agreement on Reconciliation, Non-aggression and Exchanges and Co-operation between the South and the North', which was widely considered to be the most important development in inter-Korean relations since 1953. In late

# REPUBLIC OF KOREA (SOUTH KOREA)

December both states pledged to ban nuclear weapons from the Korean peninsula, and in early 1992 they agreed to form a joint commission to facilitate the simultaneous inspection of nuclear installations in the North and US military bases in the South. In recognition of the recent inter-Korean *rapprochement*, South Korea cancelled the 1992 'Team Spirit' exercises, and in the latter half of the year the DPRK permitted the inspection of its nuclear facilities by the International Atomic Energy Agency (IAEA, see p. 66). This apparent progress on military and nuclear issues was, however, reversed by the North's decision, in January 1993, to boycott all future inter-Korean nuclear talks, followed by its threatened withdrawal from the Treaty on the Non-Proliferation of Nuclear Weapons in March 1993.

Inter-Korean relations deteriorated further in the first half of 1994; when the UN announced that it was considering the imposition of economic sanctions on North Korea, the DPRK, in turn, threatened to declare war on South Korea. The North Korean leadership was also incensed by South Korea's decision not to send a representative to the funeral, in July, of Kim Il Sung, and by its refusal to permit public mourning ceremonies within South Korea. The nuclear accord between the USA and the DPRK, signed in October, was criticized by right-wing politicians in South Korea for making too many concessions on the nuclear issue to the DPRK. The Government, however, agreed to finance, in part, the construction and supply to the DPRK of nuclear reactors less easily adapted to the production of a nuclear bomb (which had been a key element of the agreement), provided that reactors of a South Korean design were used. North Korea, however, refused to accept a South Korean model. (For further details, see chapter on the DPRK.)

Following President Roh's inauguration in 1988, relations with several communist countries showed signs of improvement. Trade with the USSR and the People's Republic of China expanded from 1988 onwards, and in 1989 and 1990 South Korea established full diplomatic relations with many eastern European countries. This process culminated in the establishment of diplomatic relations with the USSR in September 1990, followed by several meetings between Roh and President Gorbachev of the USSR. These developments were fiercely denounced by the DPRK, whose diplomatic isolation was furthered with South Korea's establishment of full diplomatic relations with the People's Republic of China (hitherto the North's principal ally) in August 1992. With effect from April 1993 South Koreans were no longer required to seek government approval before visiting China.

In August 1993 the Russian authorities published a new report into the shooting down, by Soviet forces, of a South Korean passenger aircraft in 1983. The report, which largely concurred with the findings of a recent investigation of the incident by the International Civil Aviation Organization, concluded that the airliner, which had been following an incorrect course, had been mistaken for a US aircraft engaged in espionage: previously, the Soviet authorities had maintained that the Korean aircraft was itself on a spying mission. In September 1993 it was announced that South Korea and Russia were to participate in joint naval exercises, and in 1994 it was reported that Russia was to supply South Korea with 'defensive missiles' in order to repay a part of its debt to South Korea.

Relations between South Korea and the USA were frequently strained during the Carter administration (1977–81), in particular by the proposal to withdraw US ground troops from South Korea (which was abandoned in 1979) and by the trial of Kim Dae-Jung (see above). The US commitment to South Korea was confirmed, however, during a visit by President Ronald Reagan of the USA in November 1983. Nevertheless, the USA continued to exert pressure on Chun to introduce further democratic reforms. In October 1989, during a visit to the USA, President Roh gave assurance of his Government's commitment to creating greater democracy in South Korea. Disputes between the USA and South Korea in the late 1980s over trade issues had subsided by mid-1991. President George Bush of the USA visited South Korea in January 1992, and the two leaders agreed to cancel the forthcoming 'Team Spirit' exercises. In the previous month it had been announced that all US nuclear weapons had been withdrawn from South Korean territory; however, the 'Team Spirit' exercises were resumed in 1993.

In July 1993, during a visit to Seoul, President Bill Clinton of the USA affirmed his country's continuing commitment to the defence of South Korea. In subsequent months, although the DPRK refused to discuss the issue of its nuclear programme with South Korea, the USA was reported to have formulated its own negotiating position in consultation with Kim Young-Sam's administration. In November, moreover, Clinton stated that an attack by the DPRK on South Korea would be tantamount to an act of aggression against the USA. Later in the month South Korean and US forces co-operated in joint logistics and communications exercises in South Korea, and in January 1994 it was announced that the USA was to deploy *Patriot* air-defence missiles on South Korean territory. The 1994 'Team Spirit' exercises were cancelled, as part of the agreement for the admission of IAEA representatives to the DPRK's nuclear installations, and the 1995 exercises were initially cancelled in late 1994, following the conclusion of the USA-DPRK agreement (see above), although it was indicated that the manoeuvres could take place later in 1995 if the agreement was not fully implemented.

Relations between South Korea and Japan, which had long been strained, were eased by President Chun's official visit to Japan in September 1984, the first such visit undertaken by a South Korean head of state. During the visit, Emperor Hirohito and Prime Minister Nakasone formally expressed their regret for Japanese aggression in Korea in the past. On the occasion of President Roh's visit to Japan in May 1990 Emperor Akihito offered official apologies for the cruelties of Japanese colonial rule in Korea. In January 1992 the Japanese Prime Minister, Kiichi Miyazawa, visited South Korea, where he publicly expressed regret at the enslavement during the Second World War of an estimated 100,000 Korean women, who were used by the Japanese military for sexual purposes ('comfort women'), but declined to state whether the Japanese Government would consider financial compensation. In late 1994 the Japanese Government announced that it would not make compensation payments directly to individuals, but would finance a US $1,000m. programme to construct vocational training centres for the women concerned.

### Government

Under the Constitution of the Sixth Republic (adopted in October 1987), executive power is held by the President, who is directly elected for one term of five years by universal suffrage. The President appoints and governs with the assistance of the State Council (Cabinet), led by the Prime Minister. Legislative power is vested in the unicameral National Assembly (Kuk Hoe), popularly elected for a four-year term. The Assembly has 299 members.

### Defence

Protection of the frontier separating North and South Korea is a responsibility of the UN. Military service lasts for 26 months in the army and for 30 months in the navy and in the air force. In June 1994 the strength of the armed forces was 633,000: army 520,000, navy 60,000, air force 53,000. Paramilitary forces included a 3.5m.-strong civilian defence corps. In June 1994 36,250 US troops were stationed in South Korea. Budget estimates for 1995 allocated 11,570,000m. won to defence, an increase of 9.9% from the previous year.

### Economic Affairs

In 1993, according to estimates by the World Bank, South Korea's gross national product (GNP), measured at average 1991–93 prices, was US $338,062m., equivalent to $7,670 per head. Provisional figures for 1994, according to South Korean sources, estimated GNP per head, measured in current prices, to be $8,483. During 1985–93, it was estimated, GNP per head increased, in real terms, at an average annual rate of 8.1%: among the highest growth rates in the world. Over the same period the population increased by an annual average of 1.0%. South Korea's gross domestic product (GDP) increased, in real terms, by an annual average of 9.4% in 1980–92. GDP increased by 5.8% in 1993 and by 8.4% in 1994.

According to provisional figures, agriculture (including forestry and fishing) contributed 7.0% of GDP in 1993. In 1994 13.6% of the employed labour force were engaged in the sector. The principal crop is rice, but maize, barley, potatoes, sweet potatoes and fruit are also important, as is the raising of livestock (principally pigs and cattle). Fishing provides food for domestic consumption, as well as a surplus for export. In the early 1990s South Korea was one of the world's leading ocean-fishing nations. During 1980–92 agricultural GDP increased by an annual average of 1.9%.

# REPUBLIC OF KOREA (SOUTH KOREA)

Industry (including mining and quarrying, manufacturing, power and construction) contributed 43.0% of GDP in 1993, and engaged 33.2% of the employed labour force in 1994. Industry is dominated by large conglomerate companies (chaebol), with greatly diversified interests, ranging from ship-building to electronics. During 1980–92 industrial GDP increased by an annual average of 11.6%.

South Korea is not richly endowed with natural resources, and mining and quarrying contributed only 0.3% of GDP in 1993. In 1994 0.2% of the employed labour force were engaged in the sector. There are deposits of coal (mainly anthracite), and in 1990 coal-mining accounted for 52% of the total value of mining output. Other minerals include iron ore, tungsten, gold, graphite and fluorite, and sizeable offshore reserves of natural gas have been discovered.

Manufacturing contributed 26.8% of GDP in 1993. In 1994 23.7% of the employed labour force were engaged in the sector. Measured by the value of output, the most important branches of manufacturing in 1990 were electrical machinery (accounting for 14.6% of the total), transport equipment (mainly road motor vehicles and ship-building—11.2%), chemical products (8.8%), textiles, iron and steel and food products. During 1980–92 manufacturing GDP increased by an annual average of 11.9%.

Energy is derived principally from nuclear power, coal and petroleum. In 1994 40.3% of total electricity output was generated by nuclear power (making South Korea the eighth largest producer, in percentage terms, of nuclear power-generated electricity in the world). South Korea also produces liquefied natural gas for domestic and industrial consumption. Imports of fuels comprised 15.1% of the value of merchandise imports in 1994.

An important source of 'invisible' export earnings is overseas construction work, mostly in the Middle East. The value of South Korean overseas construction contracts was US $7,441m. in 1994, an increase of 145% compared with 1993. Receipts from tourism are also significant (totalling $3,200m. in 1992). During 1980–92 the GDP of the services sector increased by an annual average of 9.3%

In 1993 South Korea recorded a visible trade surplus of US $1,860m., and there was a surplus of $384m. on the current account of the balance of payments. In 1994, according to provisional figures, a visible trade surplus of US $500m. and a current account deficit of $4,780m. were registered. Japan and the USA were the principal sources of imports in 1994 (accounting for, respectively, 24.8% and 21.1% of imports in that year); other important suppliers were Germany, Saudi Arabia and Australia. Similarly, the USA (21.4%) and Japan (14.1%) were the principal markets for exports in 1994; other significant purchasers included Hong Kong, Germany and Singapore. Following the restoration of diplomatic relations in 1992, the importance of the People's Republic of China as a trading partner increased significantly. The principal exports in 1994 were electrical machinery, textiles, clothing, telecommunications and sound equipment and chemical products. The principal imports were machinery and transport equipment (especially electrical machinery), petroleum and petroleum products, mineral fuels and other crude materials, basic manufactures, chemical products and miscellaneous manufactured goods.

The 1995 draft budget forecast an overall budgetary surplus of 700,000m. won. At the end of 1993 South Korea's total external debt was US $47,203m., of which $24,567m. was long-term public debt. In that year the cost of debt-servicing was equivalent to 9.2% of the value of exports of goods and services. The average annual rate of inflation was 5.9% in 1985–93; consumer prices increased by an average of 4.8% in 1993, and by 6.3% in 1994. Some 2.8% of the labour force were unemployed in 1993, and 2.4% in 1994.

South Korea is a member of the Asian Development Bank (see p. 107) and the Colombo Plan (see p. 238), and has applied to join the Organisation for Economic Co-operation and Development (OECD, see p. 194) from 1996.

After 1963 South Korea experienced rapid economic growth, which was attributed, in large part, to a sustained programme of export-orientated policies. By the mid-1980s South Korea was among the world's largest trading nations, and annual GNP growth exceeded 12% in 1986–88. However, this unprecedented economic growth was not sustained: in 1990–92 South Korea recorded annual deficits on external trade and on the current account of the balance of payments, and by 1992 the overall rate of GNP growth had declined to 4.7%, although growth rates of 5.8% and 8.4% respectively, were achieved in 1993 and 1994. Since his inauguration, in early 1993, President Kim Young-Sam has undertaken major economic reforms, with the stated aim of eliminating corruption (the value of the 'underground' economy is estimated to be equal to about 20% of GNP) and of restricting the scope of operations of the chaebol. (In January 1995 the Government announced measures to widen the ownership of the chaebol.) The further liberalization of the financial sector has been initiated (including the deregulation of interest rates), as have measures to promote greater efficiency in industry, to encourage the development of small and medium-sized enterprises, to foster foreign investment and to stimulate exports. Under a five-year economic plan, announced in mid-1993, it is aimed to achieve real average GNP growth of 6.9% per year, while exports are to increase by 10.4% annually. The deregulation of the financial markets, a condition for South Korea's planned membership of the OECD, is to be continued.

## Social Welfare

The Government provides social relief services for handicapped people, for wounded ex-servicemen and for war widows. Special grants or subsidies are also given by numerous official and voluntary bodies to aged people, to victims of disasters and to orphans. Under the national insurance scheme, medical and industrial accident insurance covers 24% of the total population and 26% of the economically active population. There is no system of unemployment benefit. In 1981 the country had 63,804 hospital beds, and in 1986 there were 35,657 practising physicians. Budget estimates for 1992 allocated 469,000m. won to health and 3,958,000m. won to social security and welfare (representing, respectively, 1.2% and 9.8% of total expenditure by the central Government).

## Education

Primary education, available free of charge, is compulsory for children between six and 12 years of age. Secondary education begins at 12 years of age and lasts for up to six years, comprising two cycles of three years each. Enrolment at secondary schools in 1992 included 85% of children in the appropriate age-group (males 84%; females 86%). In 1994 there were 127 university-level institutions and 368 graduate schools, with a combined student enrolment of 1,242,420. In 1990, according to UNESCO estimates, the rate of adult illiteracy averaged 3.7% (males 0.9%; females 6.5%). Budget estimates for 1992 allocated 6,538,000m. won to education (representing 16.2% of total spending by the central Government).

## Public Holidays

**1995:** 1–2 January (New Year), 30 January–1 February (Lunar New Year), 1 March (Sam Il Chul, Independence Movement Day), 5 April (Arbor Day), 5 May (Children's Day), 8 May (Buddha's Birthday), 18 May (Anniversary of the Kwangju uprising), 6 June (Memorial Day), 17 July (Constitution Day), 15 August (Liberation Day), 9–11 September (Choo-Suk, Korean Thanksgiving Day), 3 October (National Foundation Day), 25 December (Christmas Day).

**1996:** 1–2 January (New Year), 18–20 February (Lunar New Year), 1 March (Sam Il Chul, Independence Movement Day), 5 April (Arbor Day), 5 May (Children's Day), 18 May (Anniversary of the Kwangju uprising), 24 May (Buddha's Birthday), 6 June (Memorial Day), 17 July (Constitution Day), 15 August (Liberation Day), 26–28 September (Choo-Suk, Korean Thanksgiving Day), 3 October (National Foundation Day), 25 December (Christmas Day).

## Weights and Measures

The metric system is in force, although a number of traditional measures are also used.

REPUBLIC OF KOREA (SOUTH KOREA)

# Statistical Survey

Source (unless otherwise stated): National Statistical Office, Hanta Bldg, 647-15, Yoksam-dong, Kangnam-ku, Seoul 135-080; tel. (2) 222-1857; fax (2) 538-6974.

## Area and Population

### AREA, POPULATION AND DENSITY*

| | |
|---|---:|
| Area (sq km) | 99,391.8† |
| Population (census results)‡ | |
| 1 November 1985 | 40,448,486 |
| 1 November 1990 | |
| Males | 21,782,154 |
| Females | 21,628,745 |
| Total | 43,410,899 |
| Population (official estimates at mid-year) | |
| 1992 | 43,663,405 |
| 1993 | 44,056,087 |
| 1994 | 44,453,179 |
| Density (per sq km) at mid-1994 | 447.3 |

* Excluding the demilitarized zone between North and South Korea, with an area of 1,262 sq km (487 sq miles).
† 38,375 sq miles. The figure indicates territory under the jurisdiction of the Republic of Korea, surveyed on the basis of land register.
‡ Excluding adjustment for underenumeration, estimated at 480,000 in 1985.

### PRINCIPAL TOWNS (population at 1990 census)

| | | | |
|---|---:|---|---:|
| Seoul (capital) | 10,612,577 | Chonju | 517,059 |
| Pusan | 3,798,113 | Masan | 493,731 |
| Taegu | 2,229,040 | Chongju | 477,783 |
| Inchon | 1,817,919 | Chinju | 255,695 |
| Kwangju | 1,139,003 | Mokpo | 243,064 |
| Taejon | 1,049,578 | Cheju | 232,643 |
| Ulsan | 682,411 | Kunsan | 218,205 |
| Suwon | 644,805 | Chunchon | 174,224 |
| Songnam | 540,754 | Yosu | 173,169 |

Mid-1994 (official estimates): Seoul 10,726,900; Pusan 3,795,700.

### BIRTHS, MARRIAGES AND DEATHS*

| | Registered live births | | Registered marriages | | Registered deaths | |
|---|---:|---:|---:|---:|---:|---:|
| | Number | Rate (per 1,000) | Number | Rate (per 1,000) | Number | Rate (per 1,000) |
| 1986 | 636,296 | 15.4 | 376,312 | 9.1 | 238,923 | 5.8 |
| 1987 | 622,102 | 14.9 | 373,919 | 9.0 | 242,654 | 5.8 |
| 1988 | 630,347 | 15.0 | 383,874 | 9.1 | 234,970 | 5.6 |
| 1989 | 635,437 | 15.0 | 390,731 | 9.2 | 235,501 | 5.5 |
| 1990 | 643,918 | 15.0 | 393,010 | 9.2 | 239,624 | 5.6 |
| 1991 | 700,821 | 16.2 | 391,007 | 9.0 | 240,240 | 5.6 |
| 1992 | 712,287 | 16.3 | 326,415 | 7.5 | 231,519 | 5.3 |
| 1993 | 702,546 | 15.9 | 308,492 | 7.0 | 230,772 | 5.2 |

* Owing to late registration, figures are subject to continuous revision. The data for 1986–91 refer to events registered by the end of 1992, tabulated by year of occurrence. The data for 1992 and 1993 cover only events registered in each year.

**Expectation of life** (official estimates, years at birth, 1989): males 66.9; females 75.0 (Source: UN, *Demographic Yearbook*).

### ECONOMICALLY ACTIVE POPULATION*
(annual averages, '000 persons aged 15 years and over)

| | 1992 | 1993 | 1994 |
|---|---:|---:|---:|
| Agriculture, forestry and fishing | 2,991 | 2,828 | 2,699 |
| Mining and quarrying | 63 | 52 | 40 |
| Manufacturing | 4,828 | 4,652 | 4,695 |
| Electricity, gas and water | 66 | 65 | 71 |
| Construction | 1,658 | 1,685 | 1,777 |
| Trade, restaurants and hotels | 4,419 | 4,837 | 5,198 |
| Transport, storage and communications | 1,004 | 1,005 | 1,006 |
| Financing, insurance, real estate and business services | 1,228 | 1,360 | 1,494 |
| Community, social and personal services | 2,704 | 2,769 | 2,857 |
| **Total employed** | 18,961 | 19,253 | 19,837 |
| Unemployed | 465 | 550 | 489 |
| **Total labour force** | 19,426 | 19,803 | 20,326 |
| Males | 11,627 | 11,890 | 12,167 |
| Females | 7,779 | 7,913 | 8,159 |

* Excluding armed forces.

## Agriculture

### PRINCIPAL CROPS ('000 metric tons)

| | 1991 | 1992 | 1993 |
|---|---:|---:|---:|
| Wheat and rye | 0.6 | 0.6 | 1.5 |
| Barley | 198.5 | 182.8 | 191.1 |
| Naked barley | 141.1 | 131.9 | 128.1 |
| Maize | 74.6 | 92.2 | 82.2 |
| Foxtail (Italian) millet | 2.3 | 1.7 | 2.2 |
| Rice (brown) | 5,791.7 | 5,734.8 | 5,110.5 |
| Potatoes | 415.5 | 726.1 | 622.5 |
| Sweet potatoes and yams | 376.2 | 314.8 | 282.2 |
| Onions | 530.0 | 809.8 | 556.0 |
| Tomatoes | 90.4 | 117.4 | 143.3 |
| Cabbages | 198.7 | 176.4 | 146.3 |
| Cucumbers and gherkins | 267.1 | 273.0 | 348.5 |
| Melons | 203.5 | 209.8 | 231.5 |
| Water melons | 724.0 | 841.6 | 865.1 |
| Apples | 542.0 | 694.8 | 616.0 |
| Pears | 165.3 | 173.5 | 162.1 |
| Peaches | 121.7 | 115.8 | 123.5 |
| Grapes | 148.0 | 146.3 | 163.8 |
| Soybeans | 183.2 | 175.9 | 170.2 |

### LIVESTOCK (recorded numbers at December)

| | 1991 | 1992 | 1993 |
|---|---:|---:|---:|
| Cattle | 2,268,729 | 2,527,195 | 2,813,815 |
| Pigs | 5,046,029 | 5,462,683 | 5,927,504 |
| Goats | 346,358 | 501,203 | 557,617 |
| Sheep | 3,368 | 3,970 | 1,956 |
| Horses | 5,498 | 5,474 | 5,103 |
| Rabbits | 157,764 | 180,304 | 157,611 |
| Chickens | 74,855,074 | 73,323,537 | 72,945,362 |
| Ducks | 1,188,655 | 1,045,003 | 1,031,927 |
| Geese | 3,642 | 4,009 | 4,733 |
| Turkeys | 9,998 | 11,053 | 9,477 |
| Beehives | 532,826 | 596,512 | 640,311 |

REPUBLIC OF KOREA (SOUTH KOREA)

**LIVESTOCK PRODUCTS** ('000 metric tons)

|  | 1991 | 1992 | 1993 |
|---|---|---|---|
| Beef and veal | 132 | 137* | 175* |
| Pig meat | 530 | 752* | 796* |
| Poultry meat | 314 | 350 | 364† |
| Other meat | 5 | 5 | 5 |
| Cows' milk | 1,741 | 1,816* | 1,860* |
| Butter† | 44.7 | 47.0† | 47.3† |
| Hen eggs | 421.9 | 451.0* | 484.0* |
| Honey | 9.7 | 9.4 | 10.0† |
| Raw silk | 0.8 | 0.9 | 0.7 |
| Cattle hides (fresh)† | 13.1 | 13.4 | 17.1 |

* Unofficial figure.   † FAO estimate(s).
Source: FAO, *Production Yearbook*.

## Forestry

**ROUNDWOOD REMOVALS** ('000 cu m, excluding bark)*

|  | 1990 | 1991 | 1992 |
|---|---|---|---|
| Sawlogs, veneer logs and logs for sleepers | 1,066 | 1,066 | 1,066 |
| Pulpwood | 410 | 463 | 463 |
| Other industrial wood | 512 | 465 | 465 |
| Fuel wood | 4,491 | 4,491 | 4,491 |
| **Total** | 6,479 | 6,485 | 6,485 |

* FAO estimates.
Source: FAO, *Yearbook of Forest Products*.

**SAWNWOOD PRODUCTION** ('000 cu m, including sleepers)

|  | 1990 | 1991 | 1992 |
|---|---|---|---|
| Coniferous | 2,884 | 3,152 | 2,810 |
| Broadleaved | 1,013 | 889 | 703 |
| **Total** | 3,897 | 4,041 | 3,513 |

Source: FAO, *Yearbook of Forest Products*.

## Fishing

('000 metric tons)

|  | 1991 | 1992 | 1993 |
|---|---|---|---|
| Fish | 1,550.2 | 1,631.2 | 1,565.4 |
| Crustaceans | 109.4 | 115.0 | 122.2 |
| Molluscs | 828.7 | 920.0 | 931.8 |
| Other aquatic animals | 25.9 | 18.6 | 29.7 |
| Aquatic plants | 468.9 | 604.2 | 686.5 |
| **Total catch** | 2,983.2 | 3,289.0 | 3,335.5 |

## Mining

|  | 1991 | 1992 | 1993 |
|---|---|---|---|
| Anthracite ('000 metric tons) | 15,058 | 11,970 | 9,443 |
| Iron ore ('000 metric tons) | 222 | 222 | 219 |
| Lead ore (metric tons)* | 25,265 | 27,255 | 14,818 |
| Zinc ore (metric tons)* | 44,077 | 43,766 | 27,616 |
| Tungsten ore (metric tons)* | 1,405 | 445 | 0 |

* Figures refer to gross weight. The estimated metal content of ores was: Lead and zinc 50%; Tungsten 70%.

Source: mainly Ministry of Trade, Industry and Energy, *1993 Yearbook of Energy Statistics*.

**Silver ore** (metal content, metric tons): 265 in 1991 (Source: UN, *Industrial Statistics Yearbook*).

## Industry

**SELECTED PRODUCTS** ('000 metric tons, unless otherwise indicated)

|  | 1992 | 1993 | 1994 |
|---|---|---|---|
| Wheat flour | 1,553 | 1,554 | 1,591 |
| Refined sugar | 1,077 | 1,038 | 1,140 |
| Beer (million litres) | 1,567 | 1,525 | 1,718 |
| Cigarettes (million) | 96,648 | 96,887 | 90,774 |
| Cotton yarn—pure and mixed (metric tons) | 301,590 | 295,455 | 310,750 |
| Woven cotton fabrics—pure and mixed ('000 sq m)[1] | 483,306 | 479,506 | 479,522 |
| Woven silk fabrics—pure ('000 sq m) | 13,380,584 | 13,625,566 | 13,697,863 |
| Yarn of synthetic fibres (metric tons) | 482,715 | 408,219 | 378,339 |
| Synthetic fabrics ('000 sq m) | 3,093,687 | 2,459,299 | 2,540,315 |
| Plywood ('000 cu m) | 991 | 820 | 836 |
| Newsprint (metric tons) | 602,196 | 742,327 | 867,171 |
| Rubber tyres ('000)[2] | 38,120 | 42,285 | 47,105 |
| Caustic soda (metric tons) | 523,866 | 506,794 | 496,045 |
| Soda ash (metric tons) | 330,810 | 330,911 | 356,600 |
| Urea fertilizer (metric tons) | 889,456 | 831,066 | 905,746 |
| Liquefied petroleum gas (million litres) | 3,639 | 3,057 | 2,565 |
| Naphtha (million litres) | 11,422 | 12,368 | 11,645 |
| Kerosene (million litres) | 4,124 | 5,008 | 5,508 |
| Distillate fuel oil (million litres) | 24,289 | 26,681 | 26,784 |
| Bunker C oil (million litres) | 27,918 | 29,174 | 30,196 |
| Residual fuel oil (million litres) | 816 | 818 | 782 |
| Cement | 44,444 | 47,313 | 52,088 |
| Pig-iron | 19,238 | 21,870 | 21,169 |
| Crude steel | 28,050 | 33,026 | n.a. |
| Radio receivers ('000) | 619 | 550 | 276 |
| Television receivers ('000) | 16,311 | 15,956 | 17,102 |
| Passenger cars—assembled (number) | 1,259,484 | 1,527,753 | 1,755,367 |
| Lorries and trucks—assembled (number) | 286,313 | 300,544 | 317,402 |
| Merchant ships—launched ('000 grt) | 5,464 | 4,026 | n.a. |
| Electric energy (million kWh) | 130,963 | 144,437 | 165,030 |

[1] After undergoing finishing processes.
[2] Tyres for passenger cars and commercial vehicles.

## Finance

**CURRENCY AND EXCHANGE RATES**

**Monetary Units**
100 chun (jeon) = 10 hwan = 1 won.

**Sterling and Dollar Equivalents** (31 December 1994)
£1 sterling = 1,233.6 won;
US $1 = 788.5 won;
10,000 won = £8.106 = $12.682.

**Average Exchange Rate** (won per US $)
1992   780.65
1993   802.67
1994   803.44

# REPUBLIC OF KOREA (SOUTH KOREA)

## BUDGET ('000 million won)*

| Revenue | 1990 | 1991 | 1992† |
|---|---|---|---|
| Taxation | 28,363 | 32,196 | 37,652 |
| Taxes on income, profits and capital gains | 10,643 | 11,235 | 14,178 |
| Income tax | 4,723 | 6,459 | 8,250 |
| Corporation tax | 3,226 | 4,586 | 5,728 |
| Social security contributions | 1,450 | 1,799 | 2,202 |
| Employees | 441 | 517 | 629 |
| Employers | 1,009 | 1,282 | 1,573 |
| Taxes on property | 674 | 521 | 564 |
| Domestic taxes on goods and services | 10,880 | 11,956 | 14,920 |
| Value-added tax | 6,964 | 8,253 | 10,384 |
| Excises | 3,602 | 3,392 | 4,184 |
| Import duties | 3,685 | 3,294 | 3,503 |
| Other current revenue | 2,969 | 3,752 | 4,159 |
| Entrepreneurial and property income | 1,709 | 2,346 | 2,611 |
| Administrative fees and charges, non-industrial and incidental sales | 532 | 601 | 664 |
| Fines and forfeits | 568 | 571 | 734 |
| Capital revenue | 757 | 870 | 945 |
| **Total** | 32,089 | 36,818 | 42,756 |

| Expenditure‡ | 1990 | 1991 | 1992† |
|---|---|---|---|
| General public services | 2,823 | 3,471 | 4,271 |
| Defence | 6,665 | 7,892 | 8,924 |
| Education | 5,647 | 5,614 | 6,538 |
| Health | 566 | 716 | 469 |
| Social security and welfare | 2,615 | 3,381 | 3,958 |
| Housing and community amenities | 433 | 649 | 1,102 |
| Recreational, cultural and religious affairs and services | 165 | 210 | 264 |
| Economic affairs and services | 5,532 | 6,851 | 6,675 |
| Agriculture, forestry, fishing and hunting | 2,746 | 2,839 | 3,099 |
| Mining and mineral resources, manufacturing and construction | 213 | 294 | 293 |
| Transport and communications | 266 | 287 | 400 |
| Other purposes | 4,558 | 6,834 | 8,162 |
| **Total** | 29,004 | 35,619 | 40,364 |
| Current§ | 24,648 | 29,968 | 34,670 |
| Capital | 4,356 | 5,651 | 5,693 |

* Figures refer to the consolidated operations of the central Government, including extrabudgetary accounts.
† Estimates.
‡ Excluding lending minus repayments ('000 million won): 4,292 in 1990; 4,693 in 1991; 4,400 (estimate) in 1992.
§ Including interest payments ('000 million won): 1,262 in 1990; 1,245 in 1991; 1,319 (estimate) in 1992.

Source: IMF, *Government Finance Statistics Yearbook*.

## INTERNATIONAL RESERVES (US $ million at 31 December)

|  | 1992 | 1993 | 1994 |
|---|---|---|---|
| Gold* | 32.6 | 33.3 | 33.6 |
| IMF special drawing rights | 42.0 | 58.1 | 76.3 |
| Reserve position in IMF | 438.7 | 465.9 | 530.8 |
| Foreign exchange | 16,639.9 | 20,803.9 | 23,088.0 |
| **Total** | 17,153.2 | 21,361.2 | 23,728.8 |

* National valuation.
Source: IMF, *International Financial Statistics*.

## MONEY SUPPLY ('000 million won at 31 December)

|  | 1991 | 1992 | 1993 |
|---|---|---|---|
| Currency outside banks | 7,913.1 | 8,580.6 | 12,109.1 |
| Demand deposits at deposit money banks | 37,619.0 | 36,519.2 | 33,239.8 |

## COST OF LIVING (Consumer Price Index; base: 1990 = 100)

|  | 1992 | 1993 | 1994 |
|---|---|---|---|
| Food | 119.3 | 123.8 | 135.4 |
| Housing | 119.8 | 126.8 | 132.3 |
| Fuel, light and water | 114.7 | 119.4 | 123.3 |
| Furniture and utensils | 109.7 | 113.2 | 117.0 |
| Clothing and footwear | 111.4 | 115.2 | 117.9 |
| Medical treatment | 111.2 | 114.3 | 118.0 |
| Education, reading matter and recreation | 115.4 | 124.3 | 132.5 |
| Transport and communication | 116.2 | 123.9 | 131.0 |
| **All items** (incl. others) | 116.1 | 121.7 | 129.3 |

## NATIONAL ACCOUNTS ('000 million won at current prices)

### National Income and Product

|  | 1991 | 1992 | 1993* |
|---|---|---|---|
| Compensation of employees | 101,360.3 | 113,876.0 | 124,703.5 |
| Operating surplus | 69,177.6 | 75,247.7 | 83,619.5 |
| **Domestic factor incomes** | 170,537.9 | 189,123.7 | 208,323.0 |
| Consumption of fixed capital | 21,589.8 | 23,925.9 | 26,697.9 |
| **Gross domestic product (GDP) at factor cost** | 192,127.7 | 213,049.6 | 235,020.9 |
| Indirect taxes | 24,857.2 | 28,915.8 | 32,581.3 |
| *Less* Subsidies | 1,250.5 | 1,573.2 | 2,054.1 |
| **GDP in purchasers' values** | 215,734.4 | 240,392.2 | 265,548.1 |
| Factor income from abroad *Less* Factor income paid abroad | −1,494.5 | −1,687.6 | −1,687.2 |
| **Gross national product** | 214,239.9 | 238,704.6 | 263,860.9 |
| *Less* Consumption of fixed capital | 21,589.8 | 23,925.9 | 26,697.9 |
| **National income in market prices** | 192,650.1 | 214,778.7 | 237,163.1 |
| Other current transfers from abroad (net) | 400.6 | 589.1 | 966.1 |
| **National disposable income** | 193,050.7 | 215,367.8 | 238,129.2 |

### Expenditure on the Gross Domestic Product

|  | 1991 | 1992 | 1993* |
|---|---|---|---|
| Government final consumption expenditure | 22,169.5 | 26,110.3 | 28,563.2 |
| Private final consumption expenditure | 115,042.8 | 129,735.2 | 143,743.3 |
| Increase in stocks | 973.0 | 35.2 | −3,115.2 |
| Gross fixed capital formation | 82,946.5 | 87,907.0 | 94,322.3 |
| Statistical discrepancy | −82.6 | −988.2 | 976.4 |
| **Total domestic expenditure** | 221,049.2 | 242,799.5 | 264,490.0 |
| Exports of goods and services | 60,735.0 | 69,432.7 | 78,007.1 |
| *Less* Imports of goods and services | 66,049.7 | 71,840.0 | 76,948.9 |
| **GDP in purchasers' values** | 215,734.4 | 240,392.2 | 265,548.1 |
| **GDP at constant 1990 prices** | 195,935.6 | 205,860.3 | 217,239.2 |

# REPUBLIC OF KOREA (SOUTH KOREA)

## Gross Domestic Product by Economic Activity

|  | 1991 | 1992 | 1993* |
|---|---|---|---|
| Agriculture, forestry and fishing | 16,549.8 | 17,805.8 | 18,785.0 |
| Mining and quarrying | 1,142.4 | 928.5 | 923.3 |
| Manufacturing | 61,527.3 | 66,710.1 | 71,960.0 |
| Electricity, gas and water | 4,506.7 | 5,285.2 | 6,080.4 |
| Construction | 30,035.3 | 32,870.6 | 36,228.2 |
| Trade, restaurants and hotels | 26,419.5 | 28,802.6 | 31,487.2 |
| Transport, storage and communications | 14,356.7 | 16,390.1 | 18,626.0 |
| Finance, insurance, real estate and business services | 33,052.3 | 39,923.0 | 45,303.4 |
| Government services | 15,898.0 | 18,824.3 | 21,119.5 |
| Other community, social and personal services | 7,714.1 | 9,385.7 | 10,647.7 |
| Private non-profit services to households | 4,984.0 | 6,142.4 | 7,005.9 |
| **Sub-total** | 216,186.1 | 243,068.5 | 268,166.6 |
| Import duties | 7,148.7 | 7,212.0 | 7,246.2 |
| Less Imputed bank service charge | 7,600.4 | 9,888.3 | 9,864.6 |
| **GDP in purchasers' values** | 215,734.4 | 240,392.2 | 265,548.1 |

* Provisional.

## BALANCE OF PAYMENTS (US $ million)

|  | 1991 | 1992 | 1993 |
|---|---|---|---|
| Merchandise exports f.o.b. | 69,581 | 75,169 | 80,950 |
| Merchandise imports f.o.b. | −76,561 | −77,315 | −79,090 |
| **Trade balance** | −6,980 | −2,146 | 1,860 |
| Exports of services | 12,161 | 12,645 | 15,416 |
| Imports of services | −13,324 | −14,695 | −16,643 |
| Other income received | 3,370 | 3,365 | 2,837 |
| Other income paid | −3,800 | −3,930 | −3,577 |
| Private unrequited transfers (net) | 20 | 257 | 633 |
| Official unrequited transfers (net) | −173 | −25 | −142 |
| **Current balance** | −8,726 | −4,529 | 384 |
| Direct investment (net) | −241 | −497 | −540 |
| Portfolio investment (net) | 3,116 | 5,742 | 10,725 |
| Other capital (net) | 3,950 | 1,909 | −6,845 |
| Net errors and omissions | 753 | 1,099 | −715 |
| **Overall balance** | −1,148 | 3,724 | 3,009 |

Source: IMF, *International Financial Statistics*.

## External Trade

Note: Figures exclude trade with the Democratic People's Republic of Korea.

### PRINCIPAL COMMODITIES (distribution by SITC, US $ million)

| Imports c.i.f. | 1992 | 1993 | 1994 |
|---|---|---|---|
| **Food and live animals** | 4,096.8 | 4,001.5 | 4,761.3 |
| **Crude materials (inedible) except fuels** | 8,321.3 | 8,875.9 | 9,404.5 |
| Metalliferous ores and metal scrap | 2,166.9 | 2,572.4 | 2,585.8 |
| **Mineral fuels, lubricants, etc.** | 14,636.1 | 15,052.6 | 15,414.5 |
| Coal, coke and briquettes | 1,616.0 | 1,732.8 | 1,776.6 |
| Coal, lignite and peat | 1,596.5 | n.a. | n.a. |
| Petroleum, petroleum products, etc. | 11,862.0 | 11,937.2 | 12,076.4 |
| Crude petroleum oils, etc. | 9,548.4 | 9,150.9 | 8,878.3 |
| Refined petroleum products | 2,283.7 | n.a. | n.a. |
| **Chemicals and related products** | 7,660.9 | 8,228.1 | 9,762.8 |
| Organic chemicals | 2,811.9 | 2,916.2 | 3,488.3 |
| **Basic manufactures** | 11,898.6 | 12,069.9 | 15,936.4 |
| Textile yarn, fabrics, etc. | 2,556.0 | 2,593.0 | 3,338.0 |
| Iron and steel | 3,262.9 | 3,124.8 | 4,486.2 |
| Non-ferrous metals | 2,025.4 | 2,226.4 | 3,066.3 |
| **Machinery and transport equipment** | 28,966.2 | 28,417.1 | 37,408.2 |
| Power-generating machinery and equipment | 2,782.3 | 2,492.8 | 2,767.8 |
| Machinery specialized for particular industries | 4,262.3 | 4,445.6 | 6,005.1 |

| Imports c.i.f. — *continued* | 1992 | 1993 | 1994 |
|---|---|---|---|
| General industrial machinery, equipment and parts | 4,619.6 | 4,187.0 | 5,674.1 |
| Office machines and automatic data-processing equipment | 1,735.4 | 2,000.6 | 2,615.0 |
| Telecommunications and sound equipment | 1,611.1 | 1,872.2 | 2,518.8 |
| Other electrical machinery, apparatus, etc | 8,487.9 | 8,599.8 | 10,724.1 |
| Thermionic valves, tubes, etc. | 6,011.6 | 5,649.7 | 6,982.5 |
| Electronic microcircuits | 4,049.6 | 3,344.2 | 4,231.0 |
| Transport equipment* | 3,884.3 | 3,675.2 | n.a. |
| Aircraft, associated equipment and parts* | 1,965.1 | 1,846.4 | 2,207.5 |
| **Miscellaneous manufactured articles** | 5,210.3 | 6,147.6 | 8,164.6 |
| Professional, scientific and controlling instruments, etc. | 2,113.8 | 2,450.0 | 3,241.9 |
| **Total** (incl. others) | 81,775.3 | 83,800.1 | 102,348.2 |

* Excluding tyres, engines and electrical parts.

| Exports f.o.b. | 1992 | 1993 | 1994 |
|---|---|---|---|
| **Food and live animals** | 2,118.5 | 2,060.3 | 2,294.6 |
| **Mineral fuels, lubricants, etc.** | 1,748.0 | n.a. | n.a. |
| Petroleum, petroleum products, etc. | 1,736.2 | n.a. | n.a. |
| Refined petroleum products | 1,629.5 | n.a. | n.a. |
| **Chemicals and related products** | 4,454.3 | 4,921.3 | 6,339.2 |
| Artificial resins, plastic materials, etc. | 2,022.1 | n.a. | n.a. |
| Products of polymerization, etc. | 1,567.7 | n.a. | n.a. |
| **Basic manufactures** | 18,491.0 | 20,685.8 | 22,949.2 |
| Textile yarn, fabrics, etc. | 8,207.7 | 8,954.2 | 10,693.4 |
| Woven fabrics of man-made fibres (excl. narrow or special fabrics) | 4,187.2 | 4,724.7 | 5,781.6 |
| Fabrics of continuous synthetic textile materials | 3,144.0 | 3,531.7 | 4,341.1 |
| Iron and steel | 4,549.4 | 4,930.2 | 4,680.2 |
| Universals, plates and sheets | 2,078.9 | n.a. | n.a. |
| **Machinery and transport equipment** | 32,556.4 | 36,951.0 | 47,067.4 |
| Office machines and automatic data-processing equipment | 3,091.0 | 3,474.3 | 3,607.2 |
| Automatic data-processing machines and units, etc. | 2,131.0 | 2,584.7 | 2,800.0 |
| Peripheral (incl. control) units | 1,603.6 | n.a. | n.a. |
| Telecommunications and sound equipment | 6,536.5 | 7,092.9 | 8,234.3 |
| Other electrical machinery, apparatus, etc. | 10,713.8 | 12,347.9 | 18,121.7 |
| Thermionic valves, tubes, etc. | 7,762.9 | 8,078.3 | 11,848.0 |
| Electronic microcircuits | 6,233.8 | 6,425.7 | 9,917.9 |
| Road vehicles and parts* | 4,376.0 | 5,725.1 | 6,631.7 |
| Passenger motor cars (excl. buses) | 2,537.4 | 3,892.3 | 4,471.8 |
| Other transport equipment* | 4,467.8 | 4,359.3 | 5,189.3 |
| Ships, boats and floating structures | 4,112.8 | 4,060.6 | 4,944.8 |
| Tankers of all kinds | 2,018.0 | n.a. | n.a. |
| Other vessels for the transport of goods | 2,071.1 | n.a. | n.a. |
| **Miscellaneous manufactured articles** | 15,874.7 | 14,233.3 | 13,504.0 |
| Clothing and accessories (excl. footwear) | 6,769.0 | 6,165.9 | 5,652.5 |
| Non-textile clothing and accessories, and headgear of all materials | 1,589.3 | 1,168.7 | 764.2 |
| Footwear | 3,183.8 | 2,309.1 | 1,780.2 |
| **Total** (incl. others) | 76,631.5 | 82,235.9 | 96,013.2 |

* Excluding tyres, engines and electrical parts.

# REPUBLIC OF KOREA (SOUTH KOREA)

## PRINCIPAL TRADING PARTNERS (US $ '000)

| Imports c.i.f. | 1992 | 1993 | 1994 |
|---|---|---|---|
| Australia | 3,085,796 | 3,346,685 | 3,782,481 |
| Brazil | 796,881 | n.a. | n.a. |
| Canada | 1,573,779 | 1,695,065 | 2,004,836 |
| China, People's Republic | 3,724,941 | n.a. | n.a. |
| France | 1,380,419 | 1,484,736 | 1,818,404 |
| Germany | 3,742,542 | 3,954,711 | 5,159,380 |
| Hong Kong | 793,969 | 934,766 | 659,958 |
| Indonesia | 2,291,969 | 2,588,386 | 2,842,867 |
| Iran | 1,062,012 | n.a. | n.a. |
| Italy | 1,348,398 | 1,397,604 | 1,954,264 |
| Japan | 19,457,651 | 20,015,519 | 25,389,988 |
| Malaysia | 1,758,214 | 1,946,508 | 1,875,974 |
| Oman | 1,329,362 | 1,117,103 | 787,899 |
| Saudi Arabia | 3,797,383 | 3,734,746 | 3,815,521 |
| Singapore | 1,788,369 | 1,540,013 | 1,659,875 |
| Taiwan | 1,315,239 | 1,407,114 | 1,799,544 |
| United Arab Emirates | 1,282,853 | 1,233,146 | 1,080,834 |
| United Kingdom | 1,355,249 | 1,400,962 | 1,662,054 |
| USA | 18,287,269 | 17,928,188 | 21,578,787 |
| **Total** (incl. others) | 81,775,257 | 83,800,145 | 102,348,175 |

| Exports f.o.b. | 1992 | 1993 | 1994 |
|---|---|---|---|
| Australia | 1,094,517 | 1,184,732 | 1,231,895 |
| Canada | 1,608,321 | 1,374,041 | 1,389,709 |
| China, People's Republic | 2,653,625 | n.a. | n.a. |
| France | 980,921 | 890,093 | 1,001,831 |
| Germany | 2,876,981 | 3,592,794 | 4,313,496 |
| Hong Kong | 5,909,029 | 6,430,766 | 8,014,974 |
| Indonesia | 1,934,667 | n.a. | n.a. |
| Italy | 869,214 | 605,132 | 756,116 |
| Japan | 11,599,453 | 11,564,418 | 13,522,860 |
| Liberia | 1,340,593 | n.a. | n.a. |
| Malaysia | 1,135,884 | n.a. | n.a. |
| Mexico | 905,362 | n.a. | n.a. |
| Netherlands | 1,014,286 | 950,022 | 1,121,421 |
| Panama | 1,841,799 | n.a. | n.a. |
| Saudi Arabia | 940,768 | 943,976 | 878,023 |
| Singapore | 3,221,771 | 3,109,474 | 4,151,772 |
| Thailand | 1,532,159 | n.a. | n.a. |
| United Kingdom | 1,829,720 | 1,661,128 | 1,782,590 |
| USA | 18,090,047 | 18,137,640 | 20,552,796 |
| **Total** (incl. others) | 76,631,515 | 82,235,866 | 96,013,237 |

## Transport

### RAILWAYS (traffic)

| | 1991 | 1992 | 1993 |
|---|---|---|---|
| Passengers carried ('000) | 679,281 | 716,364 | 723,057 |
| Freight ('000 metric tons) | 61,215 | 58,768 | 60,167 |

### ROAD TRAFFIC (motor vehicles in use at 31 December)

| | 1991 | 1992 | 1993 |
|---|---|---|---|
| Passenger cars | 2,727,852 | 3,461,057 | 4,271,253 |
| Goods vehicles | 1,077,467 | 1,261,522 | 1,448,634 |
| Buses and coaches | 427,650 | 483,575 | 527,958 |
| Motorcycles and mopeds | 1,576,404 | 1,763,045 | 1,936,345 |

### SHIPPING
**Merchant Fleet** (at 30 June)

| | 1991 | 1992 | 1993 |
|---|---|---|---|
| Number of vessels | 2,136 | 2,116 | 2,085 |
| Displacement ('000 grt) | 7,821 | 7,407 | 7,047 |

Source: Lloyd's Register of Shipping.

### Sea-borne Freight Traffic ('000 metric tons)*

| | 1991 | 1992 | 1993 |
|---|---|---|---|
| Goods loaded | 127,531 | 147,445 | 166,475 |
| Goods unloaded | 285,652 | 307,316 | 340,858 |

* Including coastwise traffic loaded and unloaded.

### CIVIL AVIATION

| | 1991 | 1992 | 1993 |
|---|---|---|---|
| Domestic services | | | |
| Passengers ('000) | 12,253 | 14,555 | 15,550 |
| Freight ('000 metric tons) | 200 | 242 | 273 |
| Mail ('000 items) | 351 | 365 | n.a. |
| International services | | | |
| Passengers ('000) | 10,271 | 11,257 | 11,651 |
| Freight ('000 metric tons) | 787 | 837 | 951 |
| Mail ('000 items) | 33,948 | 34,125 | n.a. |

## Tourism

### VISITORS BY COUNTRY OF RESIDENCE*

| | 1991 | 1992 | 1993 |
|---|---|---|---|
| Hong Kong | 72,675 | 94,241 | 151,745 |
| Japan | 1,455,090 | 1,398,604 | 1,492,069 |
| Taiwan | 281,349 | 295,986 | 145,344 |
| USA | 315,828 | 333,850 | 325,366 |
| **Total** (incl. others) | 3,196,340 | 3,231,081 | 3,331,226 |

* Including Koreans residing abroad.

Source: *Annual Statistical Report on Tourism*, Ministry of Transportation and Korea National Tourism Corporation.

## Communications Media

| | 1990 | 1991 | 1992 |
|---|---|---|---|
| Radio receivers ('000 in use) | 43,060 | 43,850 | 44,250 |
| Television receivers ('000 in use) | 9,000 | 9,100 | 9,300 |
| Telephones ('000 main lines in use) | 13,276 | 14,573 | n.a. |
| Book production*: | | | |
| Titles | 39,330 | 29,432 | 27,889 |
| Copies ('000) | 247,962 | 160,551 | 136,392 |
| Daily newspapers | 39 | n.a. | 63 |

* Including pamphlets: 3,363 titles and 20,889,000 copies in 1990; 2,652 titles and 22,859,000 copies in 1991; 2,872 titles and 14,386,000 copies in 1992.

Sources: UNESCO, *Statistical Yearbook*; UN, *Statistical Yearbook*.

## Education

(1994)

| | Institutions | Teachers | Pupils |
|---|---|---|---|
| Kindergarten | 8,910 | 24,288 | 510,100 |
| Primary schools | 5,900 | 139,096 | 4,099,395 |
| Middle schools | 2,645 | 99,775 | 2,508,657 |
| High schools | 1,784 | 97,064 | 2,060,825 |
| Junior vocational colleges | 135 | 9,375 | 506,806 |
| Junior teachers' colleges | 11 | 736 | 18,291 |
| Universities and colleges | 127 | 41,576 | 1,132,437 |
| Graduate schools | 368 | n.a. | 109,983 |

Source: Ministry of Education, *Statistical Yearbook of Education*.

# Directory

## The Constitution

The Constitution of the Sixth Republic (Ninth Amendment) was approved by national referendum on 29 October 1987. It came into effect on 25 February 1988. The main provisions are summarized below:

### THE EXECUTIVE

**The President**

The President is to be elected by universal, equal, direct and secret ballot of the people for one term of five years. Re-election of the President is prohibited. In times of national emergency and under certain conditions the President may issue emergency orders and take emergency action with regard to budgetary and economic matters. The President shall notify the National Assembly of these measures and obtain its concurrence, or they shall lose effect. He may, in times of war, armed conflict or similar national emergency, declare martial law in accordance with the provisions of law. He shall lift the emergency measures and martial law when the National Assembly so requests with the concurrence of a majority of the members. The President may not dissolve the National Assembly. He is authorized to take directly to the people important issues through national referendums. The President shall appoint the Prime Minister (with the consent of the National Assembly) and other public officials.

**The State Council**

The State Council shall be composed of the President, the Prime Minister and no more than 30 and no fewer than 15 others appointed by the President (on the recommendation of the Prime Minister), and shall deliberate on policies that fall within the power of the executive. No member of the armed forces shall be a member of the Council, unless retired from active duty.

**The Board of Audit and Inspection**

The Board of Audit and Inspection shall be established under the President to inspect the closing of accounts of revenue and expenditures, the accounts of the State and other organizations as prescribed by law, and to inspect the administrative functions of the executive agencies and public officials. It shall be composed of no fewer than five and no more than 11 members, including the Chairman. The Chairman shall be appointed by the President with the consent of the National Assembly, and the members by the President on the recommendation of the Chairman. Appointments shall be for four years and members may be reappointed only once.

### THE NATIONAL ASSEMBLY

The National Assembly shall be composed of not fewer than 200 members, a number determined by law, elected for four years by universal, equal, direct and secret ballot. The constituencies of members of the National Assembly, proportional representation and other matters pertaining to the National Assembly elections shall be determined by law. A regular session shall be held once a year and extraordinary sessions shall be convened upon requests of the President or one-quarter of the Assembly's members. The period of regular sessions shall not exceed 100 days and of extraordinary sessions 30 days. The legislative power shall be vested in the National Assembly. It has the power to recommend to the President the removal of the Prime Minister or any other Minister. The National Assembly shall have the authority to pass a motion for the impeachment of the President or any other public official, and may inspect or investigate state affairs, under procedures to be established by law.

### THE CONSTITUTION COURT

The Constitution Court shall be composed of nine members appointed by the President, three of whom shall be appointed from persons selected by the National Assembly and three from persons nominated by the Chief Justice. The term of office shall be six years. It shall pass judgment upon the constitutionality of laws upon the request of the courts, matters of impeachment and the dissolution of political parties. In these judgments the concurrence of six members or more shall be required.

### THE JUDICIARY

The courts shall be composed of the Supreme Court, which is the highest court of the State, and other courts at specified levels (for further details, see section on Judicial System). The Chief Justice and justices of the Supreme Court are appointed by the President, subject to the consent of the National Assembly. When the constitutionality of a law is a prerequisite to a trial, the Court shall request a decision of the Constitution Court. The Supreme Court shall have the power to pass judgment upon the constitutionality or legality of administrative decrees, and shall have final appellate jurisdiction over military tribunals. No judge shall be removed from office except following impeachment or a sentence of imprisonment.

### ELECTION MANAGEMENT

Election Management Committees shall be established for the purpose of fair management of elections and national referendums. The Central Election Management Committee shall be composed of three members appointed by the President, three appointed by the National Assembly and three appointed by the Chief Justice of the Supreme Court. Their term of office is six years, and they may not be expelled from office except following impeachment or a sentence of imprisonment.

### POLITICAL PARTIES

The establishment of political parties shall be free and the plural party system guaranteed. However, a political party whose aims or activities are contrary to the basic democratic order may be dissolved by the Constitution Court.

### AMENDMENTS

A motion to amend the Constitution shall be proposed by the President or by a majority of the total number of members of the National Assembly. Amendments extending the President's term of office or permitting the re-election of the President shall not be effective for the President in office at the time of the proposal. Proposed amendments to the Constitution shall be put before the public by the President for 20 days or more. Within 60 days of the public announcement, the National Assembly shall decide upon the proposed amendments, which require a two-thirds majority of the National Assembly. They shall then be submitted to a national referendum not later than 30 days after passage by the National Assembly and shall be determined by more than one-half of votes cast by more than one-half of voters eligible to vote in elections for members of the National Assembly. If these conditions are fulfilled, the proposed amendments shall be finalized and the President shall promulgate them without delay.

### FUNDAMENTAL RIGHTS

Under the Constitution all citizens are equal before the law. The right of habeas corpus is guaranteed. Freedom of speech, press, assembly and association are guaranteed, as are freedom of choice of residence and occupation. No state religion is to be recognized and freedom of conscience and religion is guaranteed. Citizens are protected against retrospective legislation, and may not be punished without due process of law.

Rights and freedoms may be restricted by law when this is deemed necessary for the maintenance of national security, order or public welfare. When such restrictions are imposed, no essential aspect of the right or freedom in question may be violated.

### GENERAL PROVISIONS

Peaceful unification of the Korean peninsula, on the principles of liberal democracy, is the prime national aspiration. The Constitution mandates the State to establish and implement a policy of unification. The Constitution expressly stipulates that the armed forces must maintain political neutrality at all times.

## The Government

**President:** KIM YOUNG-SAM (took office 25 February 1993).

### STATE COUNCIL
(May 1995)

**Prime Minister:** LEE HONG-KU.
**Deputy Prime Minister and Minister of the Finance and Economics Board:** HONG JAE-HYUNG.
**Deputy Prime Minister and Minister of the National Unification Board:** NA UNG-PAE.
**Minister of Foreign Affairs:** GONG RO-MYUNG.
**Minister of Home Affairs:** KIM YONG-TAE.
**Minister of Justice:** AHN WOO-MAHN.

REPUBLIC OF KOREA (SOUTH KOREA)

**Minister of National Defence:** LEE YANG-HO.
**Minister of Education:** KIM SOOK-HEE.
**Minister of Culture and Sports:** CHOO DON-SHIK.
**Minister of Agriculture, Forestry and Fisheries:** CHOI IN-KEE.
**Minister of International Trade and Industry:** PARK JAE-YOON.
**Minister of Construction and Transportation:** OH MYUNG.
**Minister of Health and Welfare:** SUH SANG-MOK.
**Minister of Labour:** LEE HYUNG-KOO.
**Minister of Data and Communications:** KONG SANG-HYON.
**Minister of Information:** OH IN-WHAN.
**Minister of Government Administration:** SEO SEOK-JAI.
**Minister of Science and Technology:** CHUNG KUN-MO.
**Minister of the Environment:** KIM CHUNG-WIE.
**Minister of Political Affairs (I):** KIM YOON-WHAN.
**Minister of Political Affairs (II):** KIM JANG-SOOK.
**Minister of Legislation:** KIM KI-SUK.
**Minister of Patriots and Veterans Affairs:** HWANG CHANG-PYUNG.

### MINISTRIES

**Office of the President:** Chong Wa Dae (The Blue House), 1 Sejong-no, Chongno-ku, Seoul.
**Office of the Prime Minister:** 77 Sejong-no, Chongno-ku, Seoul; tel. (2) 720-2006.
**Finance and Economics Board:** 1 Jungang-dong, Gwachon City, Kyonggi Province; tel. (2) 503-9020; fax (2) 503-9033.
**Ministry of Agriculture, Forestry and Fisheries:** 1 Jungang-dong, Gwachon City, Kyonggi Province; tel. (2) 503-7209; fax (2) 503-7249.
**Ministry of Construction and Transportation:** 1 Jungang-dong, Gwachon City, Kyonggi Province; tel. (2) 503-7312; telex 24755; fax (2) 503-7409.
**Ministry of Culture and Sports:** 82-1 Sejong-no, Chongno-ku, Seoul 110-050; tel. (2) 734-5833; telex 23203; fax (2) 736-8513.
**Ministry of Data and Communications:** 100 Sejong-no, Chongno-ku, Seoul 110-777; tel. (2) 750-2811; telex 24262.
**Ministry of Education:** 77 Sejong-no, Chongno-ku, Seoul 110-760; tel. (2) 720-3053; telex 24758; fax (2) 736-3402.
**Ministry of the Environment:** 7–16 Sincheon-dong, Songpa-ku, Seoul; tel. (2) 421-0220; fax (2) 421-0280.
**Ministry of Foreign Affairs:** 77 Sejong-no, Chongno-ku, Seoul; tel. (2) 720-2687; telex 24651; fax (2) 738-9047.
**Ministry of Government Administration:** 77 Sejong-no, Chongno-ku, Seoul; tel. (2) 720-4351; fax (2) 720-8681.
**Ministry of Health and Welfare:** 1 Jungang-dong, Gwachon City, Kyonggi Province; tel. (2) 503-7524; telex 23230; fax (2) 503-7568.
**Ministry of Home Affairs:** 77 Sejong-no, Chongno-ku, Seoul; tel. (2) 731-2121; telex 24756.
**Ministry of Information:** 77 Sejong-no, Chongno-ku, Seoul 110-050; tel. (2) 720-1456; fax (2) 734-6900.
**Ministry of International Trade and Industry:** 1 Jungang-dong, Gwachon City, Kyonggi Province; tel. (2) 503-9405; telex 24478; fax (2) 503-9496.
**Ministry of Justice:** 1 Jungang-dong, Gwachon City, Kyonggi Province; tel. (2) 503-7012; fax (2) 504-3337.
**Ministry of Labour:** 1 Jungang-dong, Gwachon City, Kyonggi Province; tel. (2) 503-9713; telex 24718; fax (2) 503-9771.
**Ministry of Legislation:** 77 Sejong-no, Chongno-ku, Seoul; tel. (2) 720-3373; fax (2) 738-3319.
**Ministry of National Defence:** 3-1 Yong San-dong, Yongsan-ku, Seoul; tel. (2) 795-0071; fax (2) 796-0369.
**Ministry of Patriots and Veterans Affairs:** 17-23 Yoido-dong, Yongdeungpo-ku, Seoul; tel. (2) 780-9607; fax (2) 784-1087.
**Ministry of Political Affairs (I):** 77 Sejong-no, Chongno-ku, Seoul; tel. (2) 720-2275.
**Ministry of Political Affairs (II):** 77 Sejong-no, Chongno-ku, Seoul; tel. (2) 720-2464; fax (2) 737-4648.
**Ministry of Science and Technology:** 1 Jungang-dong, Gwachon City, Kyonggi Province; tel. (2) 503-7609; telex 24230; fax (2) 503-7673.
**National Unification Board:** 77-6 Sejong-no, Chongno-ku, Seoul 110-760; tel. (2) 720-2104.

## President and Legislature

### PRESIDENT

Election, 18 December 1992

| Candidate | Votes | % of total |
|---|---|---|
| KIM YOUNG-SAM | 9,977,332 | 41.96 |
| KIM DAE-JUNG | 8,041,284 | 33.82 |
| CHUNG JU-YUNG | 3,880,067 | 16.32 |
| PARK CHAN-JONG | 1,516,047 | 6.38 |
| Others | 360,679 | 1.52 |
| **Total** | 23,775,409 | 100.00 |

### KUK HOE
(National Assembly)

**Speaker:** HWANG NAK-JOO.

General Election, 24 March 1992*

| Party | Votes (%) | Elected Representatives | Proportional Representatives | Total Seats |
|---|---|---|---|---|
| Democratic Liberal Party | 38.5 | 116 | 33 | 149 |
| Democratic Party | 29.2 | 75 | 22 | 97 |
| Unification National Party | 17.4 | 24 | 7 | 31 |
| New Political Reform Party | 1.8 | 1 | 0 | 1 |
| Minjung Party | 1.5 | 0 | 0 | 0 |
| Korean Justice Party | 0.1 | 0 | 0 | 0 |
| Independents | 11.5 | 21 | 0 | 21 |
| **Total** | 100.0 | 237 | 62 | 299 |

* Amendments to South Korean electoral law, introduced in March 1988, restored single-member constituencies, which had been abolished in 1971, and increased the number of seats in the National Assembly from 276 to 299. At the election of March 1992, 237 of the Assembly's seats were filled by direct election, while the remaining 62 seats were distributed among parties according to the share of votes secured.

## Political Organizations

**Democratic Liberal Party (DLP)** (Minjujayu Dang): 14-8 Yoido-dong, Yongdeungpo-ku, Seoul 150-010; tel. (2) 783-9811; fax (2) 780-5920; f. 1990 as a merger of the Democratic Justice Party (f. 1981), the New Democratic Republican Party (f. 1987) and the Reunification Democratic Party (f. 1987); Pres. KIM YOUNG-SAM.
**Democratic Party (DP)** (Minju Dang): 51-5 Yonggang-dong, Mapo-ku, Seoul 121-070; tel. (2) 711-2070; fax (2) 711-3328; f. 1990, merged with New Democratic Party (itself a merger of the Peace and Democracy Party and the Party for New Democratic Alliance) in 1991; scheduled to merge with the NPP in 1995; Pres. LEE KI-TAEK.
**Korean Justice Party** (Dai Han Jung Eui Dang): Korea Reinsurance Bldg, 2nd Floor, 80 Susong-dong, Chongno-ku, Seoul 110-040; tel. (2) 722-1078; fax (2) 722-1079; f. 1992; Pres. LEE BYANG-HO.
**Minjung (People's) Party:** f. 1990; left-wing; 7,000 mems; Permanent Rep. LEE WOO-JAE; Sec.-Gen. CHANG KI-PYO.
**New Korea Party (NKP):** Seoul; f. 1992 by defectors from the DLP and the DP; Pres. CHAE MUN-SHIK.
**New People's Party (NPP)** (Sin Min Dang): Keumyoung Bldg, 15-11 Yoido-dong, Yongdeungpo-ku, Seoul 150-010; tel. (2) 780-3400; fax (2) 784-8475; f. 1994 as a merger of the New Political Reform Party (f. 1992) and the United People's Party (f. 1992 as the Unification National Party); scheduled to merge with the DP in 1995; Pres. KIM POK-TONG.
**United Liberal Democratic Party:** Seoul; f. 1995 by defectors from the DLP; Pres. KIM JONG-PIL.

## Diplomatic Representation

### EMBASSIES IN THE REPUBLIC OF KOREA

**Argentina:** 135–53 Itaewon-dong, Yongsan-ku, Seoul; tel. (2) 793-4062; telex 24329; fax (2) 792-5820; Ambassador: RUBÉN A. VELA.
**Australia:** Kyobo Bldg, 11th Floor, Chongno 1-ka, Chongno-ku, Seoul; tel. (2) 730-6490; fax (2) 722-9264; Ambassador: MACK WILLIAMS.

# REPUBLIC OF KOREA (SOUTH KOREA)

**Austria:** Kyobo Bldg, Room 1913, 1-1, 1-ka, Chongno, Chongno-ku, Seoul 110-714; tel. (2) 732-9071; telex 32447; fax (2) 732-9486; Ambassador: FELIX MIKL.
**Bangladesh:** 33-5 Hannam 1-dong, Yongsan-ku, Seoul; tel. (2) 796-4056; fax (2) 790-5313; Ambassador: FAZLUR RAHMAN.
**Belgium:** 1-65 Dongbinggo-dong, Yongsan-ku, Seoul 140-230; tel. (2) 749-0381; telex 27551; fax (2) 797-1688; Ambassador: JACQUES VERMEULEN.
**Bolivia:** Garden Tower Bldg 1501, 98–78 Wooni-dong, Chongno-ku, Seoul 110-350; tel. (2) 742-7170; fax (2) 742-9667; Ambassador: FERNANDO MESSMER T.
**Brazil:** 192-11, Kum Jung Bldg, 305, 1-ka, Ulchiro, Chung-ku, Seoul; tel. (2) 756-3170; fax (2) 752-2180; Ambassador: LUIZ MATTOSO MAIA AMADO.
**Brunei:** 1-94 Dongbinggo-dong, Yongsan-ku, Seoul 140-230; tel. (2) 798-5565; fax (2) 798-5564; Ambassador: Pengiran Haji OMAR.
**Bulgaria:** Byuck San Bldg, 125, 4th Floor, 12-5, Tongja-dong, Yongsan-ku, Seoul 140-170; tel. (2) 727-5810; telex 28911; fax (2) 727-5812; Ambassador: BOIKO MIRCHEV.
**Canada:** Kolon Bldg, 10th Floor, 45 Mugyo-dong, Chung-ku, Seoul 100-170; tel. (2) 753-2605; telex 27425; fax (2) 755-0686; Chargé d'affaires a.i.: MAURICE HLADIK.
**Chile:** Youngpoong Bldg, 9th Floor, 142 Nonhyun-dong, Kangnam-ku, Seoul; tel. (2) 549-1654; telex 28495; fax (2) 549-1656; Ambassador: JULIO LAGARINI.
**China, People's Republic:** 83 Myong-dong, 2-ka, Chung-ku, Seoul; tel. (2) 779-7387; fax (2) 755-1589; Ambassador: ZHANG TINGYAN.
**Colombia:** House 125, Namsan Village, Itaewon-dong, Yongsan-ku, Seoul; tel. (2) 793-1369; telex 34447; fax (2) 796-6959; Ambassador: Dr MIGUEL DURÁN ORDÓÑEZ.
**Costa Rica:** 133, Namsan Village, Itaewon-dong, Yongsan-ku, Seoul; tel. (2) 793-1301; Ambassador: JORGE VILLAFRANCA NÚÑEZ.
**Czech Republic:** 657-42, Hannam-dong, Yongsan-ku, Seoul 140-210; tel. (2) 796-6453; fax (2) 796-6452.
**Denmark:** Namsong Bldg, 7th Floor, Suite 701, 260-199, Itaewon-dong, Yongsan-ku, Seoul; tel. (2) 795-4187; telex 23497; fax (2) 796-0986; Ambassador: JAN MARCUSSEN.
**Dominican Republic:** Garden Tower Bldg, Room 1601, 98-78 Wooni-dong, Chongno-ku, Seoul; tel. (2) 742-6867; fax (2) 744-1803; Ambassador: Dr JUAN ESTEBAN OLIVERO FELIZ.
**Ecuador:** Seoul; tel. (2) 563-0620; fax (2) 569-6044; Ambassador: LUIS ORTIZ-TERÁN.
**El Salvador:** Rm 1002, Garden Tower Bldg, 98-78, Wooni-dong, Chongno-ku, Seoul 110-350; tel. (2) 741-7527; fax (2) 741-7528; Chargé d'affaires a.i.: WALTER A. ANAYA.
**Finland:** Kyobo Bldg, Suite 1602, 1-1, 1-ka, Chongno, Chongno-ku, Seoul 110-714; tel. (2) 732-6737; telex 24343; fax (2) 723-4969; Ambassador: JORMA JULIN.
**France:** 30 Hap-dong, Seodaemun-ku, CPOB 1808, Seoul; tel. (2) 312-3272; telex 27368; fax (2) 393-6108; Ambassador: DOMINIQUE PERREAU.
**Gabon:** Yoosung Bldg, 4th Floor, 738-20, Hannam-dong, Yongsan-ku, Seoul; tel. (2) 793-9575; telex 23211; fax (2) 793-9574; Ambassador: JOSEPH MAMBOUNGOU.
**Germany:** Daehan Fire and Marine Insurance Bldg, 4th Floor, 51-1 Namchang-dong, Chung-ku, CPOB 1289, Seoul 100-060; tel. (2) 726-7114; telex 23620; fax (2) 726-7141; Ambassador: Dr DIETER SIEMES.
**Greece:** Hyunam Bldg, 27th Floor, 1, Janggyo-dong, Chung-ku, Seoul 100-797; tel. (2) 729-1401; fax (2) 729-1402; Ambassador: DIMITRIOS MANOLOPOULOS.
**Guatemala:** 602, Garden Tower Bldg, 98-78, Wooni-dong, Chongno-ku, Seoul 110-350; tel. (2) 790-3265; fax (2) 797-6019; Ambassador: MAYNOR JACOBO CUYUN SALGUERO.
**Haiti:** Seoul; tel. (2) 796-0570; Ambassador: (vacant).
**Holy See:** Kwang Hwa-Moon, POB 393, Seoul (Apostolic Nunciature); tel. (2) 736-5725; telex 29533; fax (2) 736-5738; Apostolic Pro-Nuncio: Most Rev. GIOVANNI BULAITIS, Titular Archbishop of Narona.
**Honduras:** Seoul; tel. (2) 582-4725; fax (2) 582-4726; Ambassador: RODOLFO ALVAREZ BACA.
**Hungary:** 1–103 Dongbinggo-dong, Yongsan-ku, Seoul 140-230; tel. (2) 792-2105; telex 24968; fax (2) 792-2109; Ambassador: SÁNDOR ETRE.
**India:** 37–3 Hannam-dong, Yongsan-ku, Seoul 140-210; tel. (2) 798-4257; telex 24641; fax (2) 796-9534; Ambassador: BUPHATRAY SHASHANK.
**Indonesia:** 55 Yoido-dong, Yongdeungpo-ku, Seoul 150-010; tel. (2) 783-5372; telex 23374; fax (2) 780-4280; Ambassador: SINGGIH HADIPRANOWO.

**Iran:** 726–126 Hannam-dong, Yongsan-ku, Seoul; tel. (2) 793-7751; fax (2) 792-7052; Ambassador: ZABIHOLLAH NOWFARASTI.
**Iraq:** Seoul; tel. (2) 792-6671; telex 22854; fax (2) 792-6674; Chargé d'affaires: BURHAN K. GHAZAL.
**Ireland:** 51-1, Namchang-dong, Chung-ku, Seoul; tel. (2) 774-6455; telex 32611; fax (2) 774-6458; Ambassador: RICHARD RYAN.
**Israel:** 732-21, Yoksam-dong, Kangnam-ku, Seoul; tel. (2) 563-8234; fax (2) 564-3449; Ambassador: ASHER NAIM.
**Italy:** 1–398 Hannam-dong, Yongsan-ku, Seoul 140-210; tel. (2) 796-0491; telex 24619; fax (2) 797-5560; Ambassador: DINO VOLPI-CELLI.
**Japan:** 18–11 Chunghak-dong, Chongno-ku, Seoul; tel. (2) 733-5626; telex 23687; Ambassador: TOSHIO GOTO.
**Libya:** 4–5 Hannam-dong, Yongsan-ku, Seoul; tel. (2) 797-6001; fax (2) 797-6007; Secretary of People's Bureau: F. M. FARHAT.
**Malaysia:** 4–1 Hannam-dong, Yongsan-ku, Seoul 140-210; tel. (2) 795-9203; telex 27382; fax (2) 794-5488; Ambassador: SYED ARIFF FADZILLAH.
**Mexico:** 33-6 Hannam-dong, Yongsan-ku, Seoul 140-210; tel. (2) 798-1694; fax (2) 790-0939; Ambassador: MANUEL URIBE CASTAÑEDA.
**Mongolia:** A-302, Namsan Village, San 1-139, Itaewon-dong, Yongsan-ku, Seoul; tel. (2) 793-5611; fax (2) 794-7605; Ambassador: PERENLIYN URJIYNHUNDEV.
**Morocco:** S–15, UN Village, 270–3, Hannam-dong, Yongsan-ku, Seoul; tel. (2) 793-6249; telex 22948; fax (2) 792-8178; Ambassador: NOUREDDINE SEFIANI.
**Myanmar:** 723-1 Hannam-dong, Yongsan-ku, Seoul 140-210; tel. (2) 792-3341; telex 28921; fax (2) 796-5570; Ambassador: U PHONE MYIINT.
**Netherlands:** Kyobo Bldg, 14th Floor, Chongno 1-ka, Chongno-ku, Seoul 110-714; tel. (2) 737-9514; telex 23624; fax (2) 735-1321; Ambassador: PAUL LAGENDIJK.
**New Zealand:** Rooms 1802-1805, Kyobo Building, 1 Chongno 1-ka, Chongno-ku, Seoul; tel. (2) 730-7794; fax (2) 737-4861; Ambassador: PETER D. KENNEDY.
**Nigeria:** 724-5 Hannam-dong, Yongsan-ku, CPOB 3754, Seoul; tel. (2) 797-2370; fax (2) 796-1848; Ambassador: EINEJE EGBADEKWU ONOBU.
**Norway:** 124–12 Itaewon-dong, Yongsan-ku, CPOB 355, Seoul; tel. (2) 795-6850; telex 25155; fax (2) 798-6072; Ambassador: GUNNAR H. LINDEMAN.
**Oman:** 309-3, Dongbinggo-dong, Yongsan-ku, Seoul; tel. (2) 790-2431; fax (2) 790-2430; Ambassador: HUSSAIN ALI ABD AL-LATIF.
**Pakistan:** 58–1 Shinmun-no, 1-ka, Chongno-ku, Seoul 110-061; tel. (2) 739-4422; telex 29346; fax (2) 739-0428; Ambassador: S. IFTIKHAR MURSHED.
**Panama:** 1101 Garden Tower Bldg, 98–78 Wooni-dong, Chongno-ku, Seoul; tel. (2) 765-0363; fax (2) 742-5874; Ambassador: ALFREDO ZEBEDE M.
**Papua New Guinea:** 36-1, Hannam 1-dong, Yongsan-ku, Seoul; tel. (2) 798-9854; fax (2) 798-9856; Ambassador: LUCY BOGARI.
**Paraguay:** 603, Garden Tower Bldg, 98-78, Wooni-dong, Chongno-ku, Seoul 110-350; tel. (2) 742-2190; fax (2) 742-2191; Chargé d'affaires: RAÚL MONTIEL GASTO.
**Peru:** House 129, Namsan Village, Itaewon-dong, Yongsan-ku, Seoul 140-202; tel. (2) 795-2235; telex 28612; fax (2) 797-3737; Ambassador: ALFREDO PELLA.
**Philippines:** 559–510 Yeoksam-dong, Kangnam-ku, Seoul; tel. (2) 568-9131; fax (2) 554-0576; Ambassador: (vacant).
**Poland:** 448-144 Huam-dong, Yongsan-ku, Seoul; tel. (2) 779-0163; fax (2) 779-0162; Ambassador: JEDRZEJ KRAKOWSKI.
**Portugal:** 8th Floor, Citicorp Center Bldg, 89–29, Shinmun-no 2-ka, Chongno-ku, Seoul 110-062; tel. (2) 738-2078; telex 23874; fax (2) 738-2077; Ambassador: MANUEL GERVÁSIO DE ALMEIDA LEITE.
**Qatar:** 1-17, Dongbinggodong, Yongsan-ku, Seoul; Ambassador: NASSER BIN HAMAD MUBARAK AL-KHALIFA.
**Romania:** 1-42 Hannam-dong, Yongsan-ku, UN Village, Seoul 140-211; tel. (2) 797-4924; telex 32321; fax (2) 794-3114; Ambassador: NICOLAE ROPOTEAN.
**Russia:** 1001-15, Daechi-dong, Kangnam-ku, Seoul; tel. (2) 552-7094; fax (2) 563-3589; Ambassador: GEORGY KUNADZE.
**Saudi Arabia:** 1–112, 2-ka, Shinmun-no, Chongno-ku, Seoul; tel. (2) 739-0631; telex 26216; fax (2) 732-3110.
**Singapore:** Citicorp Center Bldg, 89-29, Shinmun-no 2-ka, Chongno-ku, Seoul 110-062; tel. (2) 722-0442; fax (2) 722-5930; Ambassador: RAYMOND WONG.
**Slovakia:** 389-1, Hannam-dong, Yongsan-ku, Seoul 140-210; tel. (2) 794-5420; telex 33331; fax (2) 794-3982; Ambassador: ŠTEFAN MORÁVEK.

REPUBLIC OF KOREA (SOUTH KOREA)  *Directory*

**South Africa:** 1-37, Hannam-dong, Yongsan-ku, Seoul 140-210; tel. (2) 792-4855; fax (2) 792-4856; Ambassador: Alexander van Zyl.
**Spain:** 726-52 Hannam-dong, Yongsan-ku, Seoul 140-212; tel. (2) 794-3581; telex 25067; fax (2) 796-8207; Ambassador: Carlos A. Zaldivar.
**Sri Lanka:** Kyobo Bldg, Rm 2002, 1-1, Chongno, 1-ka, Chongno-ku, Seoul; tel. (2) 735-2966; fax (2) 737-9577; Ambassador: G. D. I. G. Seneviratne.
**Sudan:** 653-24, Hannam-dong, Yongsan-ku, Seoul; tel. (2) 793-8692; telex 25936; fax (2) 793-8693; Ambassador: Dr Hammad Bashir Attalla.
**Swaziland:** 98-78 Wooni-dong, Chongno-ku, Seoul; tel. (2) 744-0263; fax (2) 744-0265; Ambassador: Prince David Dlamini.
**Sweden:** 8th Floor, Boyung Bldg, 108–2, Pyung-dong, Chongno-ku, Seoul; tel. (2) 738-0846; telex 27231; fax (2) 733-1317; Ambassador: Hans Gronwall.
**Switzerland:** 32–10 Songwol-dong, Chongno-ku, Seoul 110-629; tel. (2) 739-9511; telex 27201; fax (2) 737-9392; Ambassador: Dr Walter Fetscherin.
**Thailand:** 653–7 Hannam-dong, Yongsan-ku, Seoul; tel. (2) 795-3098; telex 27906; fax (2) 798-3448; Ambassador: Chuchai Kasemsarn.
**Tunisia:** 7-13, Dongbinggo-dong, Yongsan-ku, Seoul 140-230; tel. (2) 790-4334; telex 25997; fax (2) 790-4333; Ambassador: Brahim Khelil.
**Turkey:** 726–116 Hannam-dong, Yongsan-ku, Seoul; tel. (2) 794-0255; telex 26538; fax (2) 797-8546; Ambassador: Kaya G. Toperi.
**United Arab Emirates:** 5-5, Hannam-dong, Yongsan-ku, Seoul; tel. (2) 540-4032; Ambassador: Abd al-Karim Muhammad.
**United Kingdom:** 4 Chung-dong, Chung-ku, Seoul; tel. (2) 735-7341; telex 27320; fax (2) 733-8368; Ambassador: Thomas Harris.
**USA:** 82 Sejong-no, Chongno-ku, Seoul; tel. (2) 397-4114; fax (2) 738-8845; Ambassador: Donald P. Gregg.
**Uruguay:** Daewoo Center Bldg 1802, Namdaemun 5-ka, Chung-ku, Seoul; tel. (2) 753-7893; telex 28242; fax (2) 777-4129; Ambassador: Osvaldo C. Pittaluga.
**Venezuela:** Garden Tower Bldg, 18th Floor, 98–78 Wooni-dong, Chongno-ku, Seoul; tel. (2) 741-0036; telex 28889; fax (2) 741-0046; Chargé d'affaires a.i.: Francisco A. Torres G.
**Viet Nam:** 33-1, Hannam-dong, Yongsan-ku, Seoul 140-210; tel. (2) 794-3570; fax (2) 793-1009; Ambassador: Nguyuen Phu Vinh.
**Yemen:** 657-40, Hannam-dong, Yongsan-ku, Seoul 140-210; tel. (2) 792-9883; telex 27801; fax (2) 792-9885; Chargé d'affaires: Abd al-Aziz Ahmed Baeisa.
**Yugoslavia:** 258-13, Itaewon-dong, Yongsan-ku, Seoul; tel. (2) 790-0803; telex 26980; fax (2) 790-0802; Chargé d'affaires a.i.: Miroslav Šestović.
**Zaire:** Seoul; tel. (2) 792-2347; telex 25929; fax (2) 790-7361; Ambassador: Lobe Kitambo.

# Judicial System

### SUPREME COURT

The Supreme Court is the highest court, consisting of no more than 14 Justices, including the Chief Justice. The Chief Justice is appointed by the President, with the consent of the National Assembly, for a term of six years. Other Justices of the Supreme Court are appointed for six years by the President on the recommendation of the Chief Justice. The appointment of the Justices of the Supreme Court, however, requires the consent of the National Assembly. The Chief Justice may not be reappointed. The court is empowered to receive and decide on appeals against decisions of the Appellate courts in civil and criminal cases. It is also authorized to act as the final tribunal to review decisions of courts-martial and to consider cases arising from presidential and parliamentary elections.

**Chief Justice:** Yun Kwan.
**Justices:** Kim Suk-Su, Choi Jong-Young, Park Man-Ho, Chon Kyung-Song, Chung Gwi-Ho, Ahn Yong-Deuk, Pak Joon-Seo, Lee Don-Hui, Kim Hyung-Sun, Chi Chang-Kwon, Shin Sung-Taik, Lee Yong-Hoon, Lee Im-Soo.

### CONSTITUTION COURT

The Constitution Court is composed of nine adjudicators appointed by the President, of whom three are chosen from among persons selected by the National Assembly and three from persons nominated by the Chief Justice. The Court adjudicates the following matters: constitutionality of a law (when requested by the other courts); impeachment; dissolution of a political party; disputes between state agencies, or between state agencies and local governments; and petitions relating to the Constitution.

### APPELLATE COURTS

There are five courts, situated in Seoul, Taegu, Pusan, Kwangju and Taejon, with five chief, 80 senior and 225 other judges. The courts have appellate jurisdiction in civil and criminal cases and can also pass judgment on administrative litigation against government decisions.

### DISTRICT COURTS

District Courts are established in all major cities; there are 13 chief, 207 senior and 721 other judges. They exercise jurisdiction over all civil and criminal cases in the first instance.

### FAMILY COURT

There is one family court, in Seoul, with a chief judge, six senior judges and 16 other judges. The court has jurisdiction in domestic matters and juvenile delinquency.

### COURTS-MARTIAL

These exercise jurisdiction over all offences committed by armed forces personnel and civilian employees. They are also authorized to try civilians accused of military espionage or interference with the execution of military duties.

# Religion

The traditional religions are Mahayana Buddhism, Confucianism and Chundo Kyo, a religion peculiar to Korea and combining elements of Shaman, Buddhist and Christian doctrines.

**RELIGIONS** (1992)

|  | Temples or Churches | Priests | Believers |
|---|---|---|---|
| Mahayana Buddhism | 10,634 | 30,811 | 8,985,223 |
| Chundo Kyo | 151 | 5,106 | 1,120,623 |
| Confucianism | 233 | 18,240 | 10,263,946 |
| Christianity (Protestant) | 42,589 | 84,554 | 14,463,301 |
| Christianity (Roman Catholic) | 918 | 8,561 | 3,057,822 |
| Taejong Kyo | 91 | 232 | 468,780 |
| Won Buddhism | 404 | 8,338 | 1,195,331 |
| Others | 1,869 | 23,409 | 6,737,383 |

### BUDDHISM

Korean Mahayana Buddhism has about 50 denominations. The Chogye-jong is the largest Buddhist order in Korea, having been introduced from China in AD 372. The Chogye Order accounts for almost one-half of all Korean Buddhists. In 1992 it had 1,800 out of 10,630 Buddhist temples and there were 15,000 monks.

**Korean United Buddhist Association (KUBA):** 46-18 Soosong-dong, Chongno-ku, Seoul 110-140; tel. (2) 737-7873; 28 mem. Buddhist orders; Pres. (vacant).

### CHRISTIANITY

**National Council of Churches in Korea:** Christian Bldg, Room 706, 136–46 Yonchi-dong, Chongro-ku, POB 134, Seoul 110; tel. (2) 763-8427; telex 26840; f. 1924 as National Christian Council; present name adopted 1946; six mem. churches; Moderator Rev. Choi Hee-Sup.

#### The Anglican Communion

South Korea has three Anglican dioceses, collectively forming the Anglican Church of Korea (founded as a separate province in April 1993), under its own Primate, the Most Rev. Simon Kim Soung-Soo.

**Bishop of Pusan:** Rt Rev. Bundo Chae-Hon Kim, POB 103, Tongnae-ku, Pusan 607–061; tel. (51) 554-5742; fax (51) 553-9643.
**Bishop of Seoul:** Most Rev. Simon Kim Soung-Soo, 3 Chong-dong, Chung-ku, Seoul 100-120; tel. (2) 735-6157; fax (2) 723-2640.
**Bishop of Taejon:** Rt Rev. Paul Yoon Hwan, POB 22, Taejon 300-600; tel. (42) 256-9987; fax (42) 255-8918.

#### The Roman Catholic Church

For ecclesiastical purposes, North and South Korea are nominally under a unified jurisdiction. South Korea comprises three archdioceses and 11 dioceses. The Catholic Conference of Korea was founded as the comprehensive authority of the Catholic Church in Korea.

# REPUBLIC OF KOREA (SOUTH KOREA)

**Bishops' Conference:** Catholic Conference of Korea, POB 16, Seoul 100-600; tel. (2) 466-0123; fax (2) 465-7978; f. 1949; Pres. Most Rev. PAUL MOON-HI RI, Archbishop of Taegu.

**Archbishop of Kwangju:** Most Rev. VICTORINUS KONG-HI YOUN, Archbishop's House, POB 28, Pukkwangju 500-600; tel. (62) 525-9004; fax (62) 521-3573.

**Archbishop of Seoul:** Cardinal STEPHEN SOU-HWAN KIM, Archbishop's House, 2-ka 1, Myong-dong, Chung-ku, Seoul 100-022; tel. (2) 771-7600; fax (2) 773-1947.

**Archbishop of Taegu:** Most Rev. PAUL MOON-HI RI, Archbishop's House, 225-1 Namsan 3-dong, Chung-ku, Taegu-shi 700-443; tel. (53) 253-9440; fax (53) 253-8840.

### Protestant Churches

**Korean Methodist Church:** 64-8, Taepyong-no, 1-ka, Chung-ku, Seoul 100-101; tel. (2) 399-2000; fax (2) 399-2005; f. 1930; 1,280,181 mems (1993); Bishop YONG EUN-PYO.

**Presbyterian Church in the Republic of Korea (PROK):** 810, Christian Bldg, 136-46 Yunchi–dong, Chongno-ku, Seoul 110-701; tel. (2) 763-7934; fax (2) 744-2742; f. 1953; 285,350 mems (1988); Gen. Sec. Rev. LEE KWAE-JAE.

**Presbyterian Church of Korea (PCK):** 135 Yunchi-dong, Chongno-ku, CPO Box 1125, Seoul 110; tel. (2) 741-4350; fax (2) 766-2427; 1,867,891 mems (1990); Moderator Rev. HAN YOUNG-JE; Gen. Sec. Rev. CHU KE-MYUNG.

There are some 112 other Protestant denominations in the country, including the Korea Baptist Convention and the Korea Evangelical Church.

# The Press

## NATIONAL DAILIES

**Chosun Ilbo:** 61, 1-ka, Taepyong-no, Chung-ku, Seoul 100-756; tel. (2) 724-5114; telex 23292; fax (2) 724-5278; f. 1920; morning, weekly and children's edns; independent; Pres. BANG SANG-HOON; Editor-in-Chief IHN BO-KIL; circ. 1,960,000.

**Daily Sports Seoul:** 25, 1-ka, Taepyong-no, Chung-ku, Seoul; tel. (2) 735-7711; fax (2) 720-2909; f. 1985; morning; sports and leisure; Pres. LEE HAN-SOO; Man. Editor LEE DONG-HWA.

**Daily Trade News:** 159-1, Samsong-dong, Kangnam-ku, Seoul; tel. (2) 551-0114; f. 1949; morning and evening; Publr PARK YONG-HAK; Man. Editor CHUNG HOY-WON.

**Dong-A Ilbo:** 139 Sejong-no, Chongno-ku, Seoul; tel. (2) 7217-114; telex 23627; fax (2) 734-7742; f. 1920; evening; independent; Pres. KWON O-KIE; Editor-in-Chief HONG IN-KEUN; circ. 1,095,000.

**First Economic Daily:** 40-1, 3-ka, Hangangno, Yongsan-ku, Seoul 140-013; tel. (2) 790-5811; fax (2) 792-7823; f. 1988; morning; Pres. HWANG MYUNG-SOON; Editor LEE SOO-SAM.

**Han-Joong Daily News:** 91-1, 2-ka, Myong-dong, Chung-ku, Seoul; tel. (2) 776-2801; fax (2) 779-7179; f. 1953; morning; Publr CHEOK MYUNG-SEON; Pres. LEE PYONG-CHU; Exec. Man. Dir LEE YONG-PAE.

**Hankook Ilbo:** 14 Chunghak-dong, Chongno-ku, Seoul; tel. (2) 724-2114; telex 23644; fax (2) 739-0266; f. 1954; morning; independent; Pres. CHANG CHAE-KUK; Editor-in-Chief YOON KOOK-BYUNG; circ. 2,000,000.

**Hankyoreh Shinmun** (One Nation): 116-25, Kongduck-dong, Mapo-ku, Seoul 121-020; tel. (2) 710-0114; fax (2) 710-1310; f. 1988; Chair. KIM MYONG-KOL; Editor-in-Chief SUNG HAN-PYO; circ. 500,000.

**Ilgan Sports** (The Daily Sports): 14 Chunghak-dong, Chongno-ku, Seoul 110-792; tel. (2) 724-2114; telex 23644; fax (2) 739-0266; morning; f. 1969; Publr CHO DOO-HUM; Editor KIM JIN-DONG; circ. 600,000.

**Joong-ang Ilbo** (Joong-ang Daily News): 7 Soonhwa-dong, Chung-ku, Seoul; tel. (2) 751-5114; telex 23224; fax (2) 757-5388; f. 1965; evening; Publr RHEE PIL-GON; Man. Editor LEE CHE-HUN; circ. 1,850,000.

**Korea Economic Daily:** 441, Chungnim-dong, Chung-ku, Seoul 100-791; tel. (2) 360-4114; fax (2) 312-6610; f. 1964; morning; Pres. PARK YONG-JUNG; Man. Dir and Editor-in-Chief CHOI KYU-YOUNG.

**The Korea Herald:** 1–12, 3-ka, Hoehyon-dong, Chung-ku, Seoul; tel. (2) 756-7711; telex 26543; fax (2) 773-7532; f. 1953; morning; English; independent; Publr PARK CHUNG-WOONG; Man. Editor MIN BYUNG-IL; circ. 150,000.

**The Korea Times:** 17–11 Chunghak-dong, Chongno-ku, Seoul 110-792; tel. (2) 724-2114; telex 23644; fax (2) 732-4125; f. 1950; morning; English; independent; Pres. CHO BYUNG-PIL; Man. Editor KIM MYONG-SIK; circ. 140,000.

**Kyung-hyang Shinmun:** 22 Chong-dong, Chung-ku, Seoul; tel. (2) 730-5151; fax (2) 739-2408; f. 1946; evening; independent; Pres. CHOI JONG-YUL; Editor HONG SUNG-MAN; circ. 733,000.

**Maeil Kyungje Shinmun:** 51-9, 1-ka, Pil-dong, Chung-ku, Seoul 100-728; tel. (2) 276-0201; fax (2) 274-8640; f. 1966; evening; economics and business; Pres. CHANG DAE-HWAN; Editor JANG BYUNG-CHANG; circ. 235,000.

**Munhwa Ilbo:** 92 Moogyo-dong, Chung-ku, Seoul 110-170; tel. (2) 310-8114; fax (2) 775-9281; f. 1991; evening; Pres. LEE GYU-HAENG; Editor CHOI SUNG-DOO.

**Naeway Economic Daily:** 1-12, 3-ka, Hoehyon-dong, Chung-ku, Seoul 100; tel. (2) 756-7711; telex 26543; fax (2) 756-4850; f. 1973; morning; Chair. PARK YONG-HAK; Pres. PARK CHUNG-WOONG; Man.Editor HAN DONG-HEE; circ. 300,000.

**Segye Times:** 63-1, 3-ka, Hangangno, Yongsan-ku, Seoul; tel. (2) 799-4114; f. 1989; morning; Pres. PARK BO-HEE; Editor MOK JUNG-GYUM.

**Seoul Kyungje Shinmun:** 19, Chunghak-dong, Chongno-ku, Seoul 100; tel. (2) 730-9092; telex 23644; fax (2) 732-2140; f. 1960; morning; Chair. CHANG KANG-CHAE; Man. Editor KIM SEO-WOONG; circ. 500,000.

**Seoul Shinmun:** 25, 1-ka, Taepyong-no, Chung-ku, Seoul; tel. (2) 721-5114; telex 24221; fax (2) 721-5019; f. 1945; morning; independent; Publr and Pres. SON CHU-HWAN; Man. Editor LEE DONG-HWA; circ. 700,000.

**Sonyon Chosun:** 61, 1-ka, Taepyong-no, Chung-ku, Seoul; tel. (2) 724-5114; fax (2) 724-5599; f. 1964; children's; Publr BANG SANG-HOON; circ. 400,000.

**Sonyon Dong-A:** 139 Sejong-no, Chongno-ku, Seoul; tel. (2) 721-7114; fax (2) 721-7383; f. 1964; children's; Publr KWON O-KI; Editor HONG IN-KEUN; circ. 415,000.

**Sonyon Hankook:** 14, Chunghak-dong, Chongno-ku, Seoul 110-792; tel. (2) 724-2401; fax (2) 732-3814; f. 1960; morning; Pres. CHANG CHAE-KUK; Editor BAE JAE-GYUN.

## LOCAL DAILIES

**Cheju Shinmun:** 2036 Yon-dong, Cheju; tel. (64) 40-6114; fax (64) 42-2004; f. 1945; evening; Chair. KIM DAE-SUNG; Man. Editor KANG BYUNG-HEE.

**Cholla Ilbo:** 748-3, 3-ka, Ua-dong, Tokjin-ku, Chonju, Chollabuk-do; tel. (652) 253-7111; f. 1988; morning; Pres. HWANG ON-SONG; Man. Editor SO CHAE-CHOL.

**Chonbuk Domin Shinmun:** 340-1, 1-ka, Kosa-dong, Chonju, Chollabuk-do; tel. (652) 86-3003; fax (652) 86-2849; f. 1988; morning; Pres. BAE YOUNG-SIK; Man. Editor YANG CHAE-SUK.

**Chungchong Ilbo:** 304 Sachang-dong, Cheongju, Chungchongbuk-do; tel. (431) 62-5551; fax (431) 62-2000; f. 1946; morning; Chair. MIN KON-SHIK; Editor LEE JAE-JOON.

**Chunnam Ilbo:** 700-5, Chunghung-dong, Puk-ku, Kwangju; tel. (62) 527-0015; fax (62) 527-0114; f. 1989; evening; Chair. LEE JUNG-IL; Editor-in-Chief HUH KWANG-OK.

**Halla Ilbo:** 568-1, Samdo 1-dong, Cheju; tel. (64) 50-2114; fax (64) 52-9790; f. 1989; evening; Pres. KANG YONG-SOK; Man. Editor HONG SONG-MOK.

**Inchon Shinmun:** 2, 4-ka, Hang-dong, Chung-ku, Inchon; tel. (32) 763-8811; fax (32) 763-8834; f. 1988; evening; Pres. MUN PYONG-HA; Man. Editor LEE JAE-HO.

**Jeonbuk Ilbo:** 710–5 Kumam-dong, Chonchu, Chollabuk-do; tel. (652) 74-1001; f. 1973; evening; Pres. SUH JUNG-SANG; Man. Editor LEE KON-WOONG.

**Jungdo Ilbo:** 274-7, Kalma-dong, Suh-ku, Taejon; tel. (42) 530-4114; f. 1951; evening; Chair. LEE UNG-YOL; Man. Editor SUNG KI-HOON.

**Kangweon Ilbo:** 53, 1-ka, Chungangno, Chunchon, Kangwon-do; tel. (361) 52-4881; fax (361) 52-5884; f. 1945; evening; Chair. SIM YOUNG-SOON; Man. Editor KIM KEUN-TAE.

**Kiho Shinmun:** 1, 1-ka, Chung-dong, Chung-ku, Inchon; tel. (32) 761-0001; fax (32) 761-0011; f. 1988; evening; Pres. SO KANG-HUN; Editor-in-Chief and Man. Editor KIM NAK-CHUN.

**Kookje Shinmun:** 252-127, Pomil-dong, Dong-ku, Pusan 601-062; tel. (51) 647-0051; fax (2) 647-0280; f. 1947; evening; Pres. NAM JUNG-SIK; Editor-in-Chief KANG CHONG-WON.

**Kwangju Ilbo:** 1-ka, Kumnam-no, Tong-ku, Kwangju; tel. (62) 222-8111; fax (62) 222-4918; f. 1952; evening; Pres. KIM CHONG-TAE; Man. Editor CHO DONG-SU.

**Kyeonggi Ilbo:** 203-2, Songjuk-dong, Changan-ku, Suwon, Kyonggi-do; tel. (331) 47-3333; fax (331) 47-3349; f. 1988; evening; Pres. SHIN SON-CHOL; Man. Editor LEE CHIN-YONG.

**Kyeongin Ilbo:** 1122-11, Ingye-dong, Kwonson-ku, Suwon, Kyonggi-do; tel. (331) 315-114; fax (331) 32-1231; f. 1960; evening; Pres. IM SANG-KYU; Man. Editor KIM HWA-YANG.

**Kyungnam Shinmun:** 100-5 Shinwol-dong, Changwon, Kyong-sangnam-do; tel. (551) 83-2211; fax (551) 83-2227; f. 1946; evening; Pres. KIM DONG-KYU; Editor PARK SUNG-KWAN.

REPUBLIC OF KOREA (SOUTH KOREA)	*Directory*

**Maeil Shinmun:** 71, 2-ka, Kyesan-dong, Chung-ku, Taegu; tel. (53) 255-5001; fax (53) 255-8902; f. 1946; evening; Chair. KIM BOO-KI; Editor LEE YONG-KEUN; circ. 300,000.

**Pusan Ilbo:** 1-10 Sujong-dong, Dong-ku, Pusan 601-738; tel. (51) 461-4114; fax (51) 463-8880; f. 1946; Publr SONG JUNG-JAE; Man. Editor JUNG YOUNG-HYUN; circ. 427,000.

**Taegu Ilbo:** 271-31, 3-ka, Tongin-dong, Chung-ku, Taegu 700-423; tel. (53) 421-8001; fax (53) 421-5040; f. 1989; morning; Pres. PARK GWON-HEUM; Editor KIM KYUNG-PAL.

**Taejeon Daily News:** 1-135 Munhwa-dong, Chung-ku, Taejeon-shi; tel. (42) 251-3311; fax (42) 254-3323; f. 1950; evening; Chair. SUH CHOON-WON; Editor KWAK DAE-YEON.

**Yungnam Ilbo:** 1124-3, 3-ka, Wondae, Suh-ku, Taegu; tel. (53) 756-8001; f. 1945; morning; Pres. JANG MYONG-SEOK; Man. Editor KIM SANG-TAE.

### SELECTED PERIODICALS

**Academy News:** 50 Unjung-dong, Pundang-ku, Seongnam-shi, Kyonggi-do 463-791; tel. (2) 234-8111; fax (342) 46-1531; organ of the Acad. of Korean Studies; Pres. LEE HYUN-JAE.

**Business Korea:** 26-3 Yoido-dong, Yongdeungpo-ku, Seoul 150-010; tel. (2) 784-4010; telex 32487; fax (2) 784-1915; f. 1983; monthly; Pres. KIM KYUNG-HAE; circ. 35,000.

**Dae Woo Securities Monthly:** 34-3 Yoido-dong, Yongdeungpo-ku, Seoul; tel. (2) 768-3731; telex 26332; fax (2) 784-0826; monthly; Pres. KIM CHANG-HEE.

**Donghwa News Graphic:** 43-1, 1-ka, Pil-dong, Chung-ku, Seoul; f. 1960; Publr CHUNG JAE-HO.

**Eumak Dong-A:** 139 Sejong-no, Chongno-ku, Seoul 110-715; tel. (2) 781-0640; telex 23627; fax (2) 705-4547; f. 1984; monthly; music; Publr KIM BYUNG-KWAN; Editor KWON O-KIE; circ. 85,000.

**Han Kuk No Chong** (FKTU News): Federation of Korean Trade Unions, FKTU Bldg, 35 Yoido-dong, Yongdeungpo-ku, Seoul; tel. (2) 782-3884; telex 29682; f. 1961; labour news; Publr PARK CHONG-KUN; circ. 20,000.

**Hyundae Munhak:** Mokjung Bldg, First Floor, 1361-5 Seocho-dong, Seocho-ku, Seoul; tel. (2) 563-8141; fax (2) 563-9319; f. 1955; literature; Publr KIM SUNG-SIK; circ. 200,000.

**Korea Business World:** Yoido, POB 720, Seoul 150-607; tel. (2) 532-1364; fax (2) 594-7663; f. 1985; monthly; English; Publr and Pres. LEE KIE-HONG; circ. 40,200.

**Korea Buyers Guide:** Korea World Trade Center, 159-1 Samsung-dong, Kangnam-ku, Seoul; tel. (2) 551-2376; fax (2) 551-2377; f. 1973; Pres. PARK SUNG-HWAN; circ. 30,000.

**Korea Journal:** CPOB 54, Seoul 100-022; tel. (2) 776-2804; telex 23231-2; organ of the UNESCO Korean Commission; Gen. Dir CHUNG HEE-CHAE.

**Korea Newsreview:** 1-12, 3-ka, Hoehyon-dong, Chung-ku, Seoul 100-771; tel. (2) 756-7711; telex 27738; weekly; English; Publr and Editor PARK CHUNG-WOONG.

**Korean Business Review:** 28-1, FKI Bldg, Yoido-dong, Yong-deungpo-ku, Seoul 150-756; tel. (2) 782-0821; telex 25544; fax (2) 782-6425; monthly; organ of the Fed. of Korean Industries; Publr YOO CHANG-SOON; Editor CHOI CHANG-NAK.

**KCCI Quarterly Review:** 45, 4-ka, Namdaemun-no, Chung-ku, CPOB 25, Seoul 100-743; tel. (2) 316-3114; fax (2) 757-9475; organ of the Korea Chamber of Commerce and Industry; Pres. KIM SANG-HA.

**Korea and World Affairs:** Seoul; tel. (2) 777-2628; fax (2) 319-9591; organ of the Research Center for Peace and Unification of Korea; Pres. CHANG DONG-HOON.

**Literature and Thought:** Seoul; tel. (2) 738-0542; fax (2) 738-2997; f. 1972; monthly; Pres. LIM HONG-BIN; circ. 10,000.

**News Maker:** 22, Jung-dong, Chung-ku, Seoul 110-702; tel. (2) 730-5151; fax (2) 720-7776; f. 1992; Pres. CHOI JONG-YUL; Editor CHO JANG-HEE.

**Reader's Digest:** 295-15, Doksan 1-dong, Kumchun-ku, Seoul 152-010; tel. (2) 866-8800; fax (2) 839-4545; f. 1978; Pres. KWON TAE-MYUNG; Editor HWANG WEE-BANG.

**Shin Dong-A** (New East Asia): 139 Sejong-no, Chongno-ku, Seoul 110-050; tel. (2) 721-0611; telex 23627; fax (2) 734-7742; f. 1931; monthly; general; Publr KIM BYUNG-KWAN; Editor KWON O-KIE; circ. 308,000.

**Taekwondo:** 635 Yuksam-dong, Kangnam-ku, Seoul 135-081; tel. (2) 566-2505; fax (2) 553-4728; f. 1973; organ of the World Taek-wondo Fed.; Pres. Dr KIM UN-YONG.

**This Month in Korea:** 37-2, 2-ka, Namsan-dong, Chung-ku, Seoul; tel. (2) 752-6310; fax (2) 752-2999; monthly travel magazine; Pres. SUH MYUNG-SUK; circ. 30,000.

**Weekly Chosun:** 61 Taepyong-no 1, Chung-ku, Seoul; tel. (2) 724-5114; fax (2) 724-6199; weekly; Publr BANG SANG-HOON; Editor CHOI JOON-MYONG; circ. 350,000.

**The Weekly Hankook:** 14 Chunghak-dong, Chongno-ku, Seoul; tel. (2) 732-4151; fax (2) 724-2444; f. 1964; Publr CHANG CHAE-KUK; circ. 400,000.

**Wolgan Mot:** 139 Sejong-no, Chongno-ku, Seoul 110; tel. (2) 733-5221; telex 23627; f. 1984; monthly; fashion; Publr KIM SEUNG-YUL; Editor KWON O-KIE; circ. 120,000.

**Women's Weekly:** 14 Chunghak-dong, Chongno-ku, Seoul; tel. (2) 735-9216; fax (2) 732-4125.

**Yosong Dong-A** (Women's Far East): 139 Sejong-no, Chongno-ku, Seoul 110-715; tel. (2) 721-7621; fax (2) 721-7676; f. 1933; monthly; women's magazine; Publr KIM BYUNG-KWAN; Editor KWON O-KIE; circ. 237,000.

### NEWS AGENCIES

**Naewoe Press:** 42-2 Chuja-dong, Chung-ku, Seoul 100-240; tel. (2) 279-7871; fax (2) 278-9176; f. 1974; Pres. LEE CHANG-HA.

**Yonhap (United) News Agency:** 85-1 Susong-dong, Chongno-ku, Seoul; tel. (2) 398-3114; telex 23618; fax (2) 738-0820; f. 1980; Pres. HYON SO-WHAN.

#### Foreign Bureaux

**Agence France-Presse (AFP):** Yonhap News Agency Bldg, 9th Floor, 85-1 Susong-dong, Chongno-ku, Seoul; tel. (2) 737-7354; fax (2) 737-6598; Bureau Chief KATE WEBB.

**Associated Press (AP)** (USA): Yonhap News Agency Bldg, 85-1 Susong-dong, Chongno-ku, Seoul; tel. (2) 736-4418; Bureau Chief KELLY SMITH TUNNEY.

**Central News Agency** (Taiwan): Seoul; tel. (2) 734-5432; Bureau Chief TSAI HANG-LI.

**Deutsche Press-Agentur** (Germany): Seoul; tel. (2) 738-3808; fax (2) 738-6040; Correspondent PETER LESSMANN.

**Informatsionnoye Telegrafnoye Agentstvo Rossii—Telegrafnoye Agentstvo Suverennych Stran (ITAR–TASS)** (Russia): 1–302, Chung Wha Art, 22-2, Itaewon-dong, Yongsan-ku, Seoul; tel. (2) 796-9193; fax (2) 796-9194; Correspondent NIKOLAY A. GERONIN.

**Jiji Tsushin-Sha (Jiji Press)** (Japan): Joong-ang Ilbo Bldg, 7, Seosomun-dong, Chung-ku, Seoul; tel. (2) 753-4525; fax (2) 753-8067; Chief Correspondent MORITA OSAMU.

**Kyodo Tsushin** (Japan): Yonhap News Agency Bldg, 85-1 Susong-dong, Chongno-ku, Seoul; tel. (2) 739-2791; telex 25001; Bureau Chief FUMIO GOTO.

**Reuters** (UK): Byuck San Bldg, 7th Floor, 12-5, Tongja-dong, Yongsan-ku, Seoul 140-170; tel. (2) 727-5151; telex 26900; fax (2) 727-5666; Country Man. TOM KIRKUP; Bureau Chief ANDREW STEELE.

**United Press International (UPI)** (USA): Room 901, Yonhap News Agency Bldg, 85-1 Susong-dong, Chongno-ku, Seoul; tel. (2) 737-9054; fax (2) 738-8206; Correspondent KIM JOON-HWAN.

### PRESS ASSOCIATIONS

**The Korean Newspaper Editors Association:** Korea Press Center, 13th Floor, 25, 1-ka, Taepyong-no, Chung-ku, Seoul; tel. (2) 732-1726; fax (2) 739-1985; f. 1957; 416 mems; Pres. AN PYONG-HUN.

**The Korean Newspapers Association:** Korea Press Center, 13th Floor, 25, 1-ka, Taepyong-no, Chung-ku, Seoul 100-745; tel. (2) 733-2251; fax (2) 720-3291; f. 1962; 44 mems; Pres. KIM PYONG-KWAN.

**Seoul Foreign Correspondents' Club:** Korea Press Center, 18th Floor, 25, 1-ka, Taepyong-no, Chung-ku, Seoul; tel. (2) 734-3272; fax (2) 734-7712; f. 1956; Pres. JOHN BURTON.

## Publishers

**Ahn Graphics:** Duson Bldg, 3rd Floor, 1-34 Tongsung-dong, Chongno-ku, Seoul 110-510; tel. (2) 763-2320; fax (2) 743-3352; f. 1985; literature, fine arts, history; Pres. KIM OK-CHUL.

**Bak-Young Publishing Co:** 219 Pyong-dong, Chongno-ku, Seoul 110-102; tel. (2) 733-6771; fax (2) 736-4818; f. 1952; sociology, philosophy, literature, linguistics, social science; Pres. AHN JONG-MAN.

**Bobmun Sa Publishing Co:** Hanchung Bldg, 4th Floor, 167-7, Yomni-dong, Mapo-ku, Seoul 121-090; tel. (2) 703-6541; fax (2) 703-6594; f. 1954; law, politics, philosophy, history; Pres. BAE HYO-SEON.

**Bumwoo Publishing Co:** 21-1, Kusu-dong, Mapo-ku, Seoul 121-130; tel. (2) 717-2121; fax (2) 717-0429; f. 1966; philosophy, religion, social science, technology, art, literature, history; Pres. YOON HYUNG-DOO.

REPUBLIC OF KOREA (SOUTH KOREA)  *Directory*

**Cheong Moon Gak Publishing Co Ltd:** 486-9 Kirum 3-dong, Seongbuk-ku, Seoul 136-113; tel. (2) 985-1451; fax (2) 982-8679; f. 1975; science, technology; Pres. KIM HONG-SEOK.

**Chongno Book Publication Co Ltd:** 84-9, Chongno 2-ka, Chongno-ku, Seoul 110-122; tel. (2) 733-2331; fax (2) 732-6202; f. 1983; philosophy, religion, social science, literature, history, children's; Pres. CHANG HA-KOO.

**Dong-A Publishing Co Ltd:** Seoul; tel. (2) 866-8800; telex 24687; fax (2) 862-0410; f. 1945; philosophy, religion, social science, literature; Pres. KIM HYUN-SHIK.

**Dong-Hwa Publishing Co:** 130-4 Wonhyoro 1-ka, Yongsan-ku, Seoul 140-111; tel. (2) 713-5411; fax (2) 701-7041; f. 1968; language, literature, fine arts, history, religion, philosophy; Pres. LIM IN-KYU.

**Eulyoo Publishing Co Ltd:** 46-1 Susong-dong, Chongno-ku, Seoul 110-140; tel. (2) 733-8151; fax (2) 732-9154; f. 1945; linguistics, literature, social science, history, philosophy; Pres. CHUNG CHIN-SOOK.

**Hangil Publishing Co:** 101-21, Anam-dong, 5-ka, Songbuk-ku, Seoul 136-075; tel. (2) 515-4811; fax (2) 515-4816; f. 1976; social science, history, literature; Pres. KIM EOUN-HO.

**Hollym Corporation Publishers:** 14-5 Kwanchol-dong, Chongno-ku, Seoul 110-111; tel. (2) 735-7554; fax (2) 730-5149; f. 1963; academic and general books on Korea in English; Pres. CHU SHIN-WON.

**Hyang Mun Sa Publishing Co:** 39-16 Kyonji-dong, Chongno-ku, Seoul 110-170; tel. (2) 538-5672; fax (2) 538-5673; f. 1950; science, agriculture, history, engineering, home economics; Pres. NAH JOONG-RYOL.

**Il Cho Kak:** 9 Gongpyung-dong, Chongno-ku, Seoul 110-160; tel. (2) 732-3333; fax (2) 738-5857; f. 1953; history, literature, sociology, linguistics, medicine, law, engineering; Pres. HAN MAN-NYUN.

**Il Ji Sa Publishing Co:** 46-1 Chunghak-dong, Chongno-ku, Seoul 110-150; tel. (2) 732-3980; fax (2) 722-2807; f. 1956; literature, social sciences, juvenile, fine arts, philosophy, linguistics, history; Pres. KIM SUNG-JAE.

**Jihak Publishing Co Ltd:** 180-20 Dongkyo-dong, Mapo-ku, Seoul 121-200; tel. (2) 325-8000; fax (2) 616-9549; f. 1965; philosophy, language, literature; Pres. KWON BYONG-ILL.

**Jip Moon Dang:** Seoul; tel. (2) 234-2227; fax (2) 234-2136; philosophy, social science, technology, history; Pres. LIM KYUNG-HWAN.

**Jisik Sanup Publications Co Ltd:** 301 Yangji Bldg, 102 Tongui-dong, Chongno-ku, Seoul 110-040; tel. (2) 734-1978; fax (2) 720-7900; f. 1969; religion, social science, art, literature, history, children's; Pres. KIM KYUNG-HEE.

**Jung-Ang Munwha Sa:** 172-11 Yomni-dong, Mapo-ku, Seoul 121-080; tel. (2) 717-2111; fax (2) 716-1369; f. 1972; study books, children's; Pres. KIM DUCK-KI.

**Jung Eum Sa Publishing and Magazine House:** 22-5, Chungmuro 5-ka, Chung-ku, Seoul 110-015; tel. (2) 272-5364; fax (2) 277-7241; f. 1928; philosophy, religion, social science, technology, art, history; Pres. SHIN SOO-KYUN.

**Kemongsa Publishing Co Ltd:** 772 Yoksam-dong, Kangnam-ku, Seoul 135-080; tel. (2) 531-5500; telex 22642; fax (2) 531-5590; f. 1946; picture books, juvenile, encyclopaedias, history, fiction; Pres. KIM JOON-SIK.

**Ki Moon Dang:** 286-20 Haengdang-dong, Songdong-ku, Seoul 133-070; tel. (2) 295-6171; fax (2) 295-8188; f. 1976; engineering, fine arts, dictionaries; Pres. KANG HAE-JAK.

**Korea Britannica Corpn:** 162-1 Changchung-dong 2-ka, Chung-ku, Seoul 100-392; tel. (2) 275-2151; fax (2) 273-2641; f. 1968; encyclopaedias, dictionaries; Pres. POLLY A. SAUER.

**Korea University Press:** 1-2, 5-ka, Anam-dong, Songbuk-ku, Seoul 136-701; tel. (2) 923-6311; fax (2) 923-6311; f. 1956; philosophy, history, language, literature, Korean studies, education, psychology, social science, natural science, engineering, agriculture, medicine; Pres. HONG IL-SICK.

**Kum Sung Publishing Co:** 242-63 Kongdok-dong, Mapo-ku, Seoul 121-022; tel. (2) 713-9651; fax (2) 717-9544; f. 1965; literature, juvenile, social sciences, history, fine arts; Pres. KIM NAK-JOON.

**Kyohak-sa Publishing Co Ltd:** 105-67 Kongdok-dong, Mapo-ku, Seoul 121-020; tel. (2) 717-4561; fax (2) 718-3976; f. 1952; dictionaries, educational, children's; Pres. YANG CHEOL-WOO.

**Kyung Hee University Press:** 1 Hoeki-dong, Dongdaemun-ku, Seoul 130-701; tel. (2) 961-0106; fax (2) 966-6954; f. 1960; general, social science, technology, language, literature; Pres. CHOE YOUNG-SEEK; Dir LEE KYU-JONG.

**Kyungnam University Press:** 28-42 Samchung-dong, Chongno-ku, Seoul 110-230; tel. (2) 735-3202; fax (2) 735-4359; Pres. PARK JAE-KYU.

**Mineum Publishing Co:** 506 Shinsa-dong, Kangnam-ku, Seoul 135-120; tel. (2) 515-2000; fax (2) 515-2007; f. 1966; literature, philosophy, linguistics, pure science; Pres. PARK MAENG-HO.

**Panmun Book Co Ltd:** 40 Chongno 1-ka, Chongno-ku, Seoul 110-121; tel. (2) 953-2451; telex 27546; fax (2) 953-2456; f. 1955; social science, pure science, technology, linguistics; Pres. LIU IK-HYUNG.

**Sam Joong Dang Publishing Co:** 261-23 Soke-dong, Yongsan-ku, Seoul 140-140; tel. (2) 704-6816; fax (2) 704-6819; f. 1931; literature, history, philosophy, social sciences, dictionaries; Pres. LEE MIN-CHUL.

**Sam Seong Dang Publishing Co:** 238-108 Yongdu-dong, Tongdaemun-ku, Seoul 130-070; tel. (2) 922-7781; fax (2) 922-2667; f. 1968; literature, fine arts, history, philosophy; Pres. KANG MYUNG-CHAE.

**Sam Seong Publishing Co Ltd:** 340-2 Tangsan-dong 6-ka, Yongdeungpo-ku, Seoul 150-046; tel. (2) 857-1331; telex 33142; fax (2) 869-4458; f. 1951; literature, history, juvenile, philosophy, arts, religion, science, encyclopaedias; Pres. KIM BONG-KYU.

**Se-Kwang Music Publishing Co:** 232-32 Seogye-dong, Yongsan-ku, Seoul 140-140; tel. (2) 719-2652; fax (2) 719-2191; f. 1953; music, art; Pres. PARK SEI-WON; Chair. PARK SHIN-JOON.

**Seoul International Publishing House:** 121, Karak Bon-dong, Songpa-ku, Seoul 138-160; tel. (2) 430-8321; fax (2) 448-0052; f. 1977; history, art; Pres. SHIM CHUNG-GIL.

**Seoul National University Press:** 56-1 Shinrim-dong, Kwanak-ku, Seoul 151-742; tel. (2) 889-0434; fax (2) 888-4148; f. 1961; philosophy, engineering, social science, art, literature; Pres. KIM CHONG-UN.

**Si-sa-young-o-sa, Inc:** 55-1, Chongno 2-ka, Chongno-ku, Seoul 110-122; tel. (2) 274-0509; telex 34193; fax (2) 277-2610; f. 1959; language, literature; Chair. and CEO MIN YOUNG-BIN.

**Sogang University Press:** 1 Shinsu-dong, Mapo-ku, Seoul 121-742; tel. (2) 705-8212; fax (2) 701-8962; f. 1978; philosophy, religion, science, art, history; Pres. PARK HONG.

**Sookmyung Women's University Press:** 53-12, Chongpa-dong 2-ka, Yongsan-ku, Seoul 140-742; tel. (2) 710-9162; fax (2) 718-2337; f. 1968; general; Pres. CHUNG KYU-SUN.

**Tamgu-Dang Publishing Co:** 101-1 Kyungwoon-dong, Chongno-ku, Seoul 110-310; tel. (2) 730-8961; fax (2) 738-4408; f. 1950; linguistics, literature, social sciences, history, fine arts; Pres. HONG SUK-WOO.

**Tong Moon Gwan:** 147 Gwanhoon-dong, Chongno-ku, Seoul 110-300; tel. (2) 732-4355; f. 1954; literature, art, philosophy, religion, history; Pres. LEE KYUM-NO.

**Yonsei University Press:** 134 Shinchon-dong, Sodaemun-ku, Seoul 120-749; tel. (2) 361-3378; fax (2) 393-1421; f. 1955; philosophy, religion, literature, history, art, social science, pure science; Pres. PARK SONG-JAE.

### PUBLISHERS' ASSOCIATION

**Korean Publishers Association:** 105-2 Sagan-dong, Chongno-ku, Seoul 110-190; tel. (2) 735-2701; fax (2) 738-5414; f. 1947; Pres. KIM NARK-JOON; Sec.-Gen. JUNG JONG-JIN.

## Radio and Television

In 1992, according to UNESCO, there were an estimated 44.3m. radio receivers and 9.3m. television receivers in use. South Korea's first cable television service (CATV) was scheduled to commence broadcasts in March 1995.

### RADIO

**Korean Broadcasting System (KBS):** 18 Yoido-dong, Yongdeungpo-ku, Seoul 150-010; tel. (2) 781-1000; telex 24599; f. 1926; publicly-owned corpn with 26 local broadcasting and 855 relay stations; overseas service in Korean, English, German, Indonesian, Chinese, Japanese, French, Spanish, Russian and Arabic; Pres. HONG DOO-PYO.

**Buddhist Broadcasting System (BBS):** 140 Mapo-dong, Mapo-ku, Seoul 121-059; tel. (2) 705-5114; fax (2) 705-5229; f. 1990; Pres. CHANG SANG-MOON.

**Christian Broadcasting System (CBS):** 917-1 Mok-dong, Yangchon-ku, Seoul 158-701; tel. (2) 650-7000; fax (2) 654-2456; f. 1954; independent religious network with six network stations in Seoul, Taegu, Pusan, Kwangju, Iri and Chongju; programmes in Korean; Pres. Rev. KWON HO-KYUNG.

**Educational Broadcasting System (EBS):** 92-6 Woomyun-dong, Seocho-ku, Seoul 137-791; tel. (2) 521-3431; fax (2) 521-0241; f. 1990; Pres. CHUNG YUN-CHOON.

# REPUBLIC OF KOREA (SOUTH KOREA)

**Munhwa Broadcasting Corporation (MBC):** 31 Yoido-dong, Yongdeungpo-ku, Seoul 150-728; tel. (2) 784-2000; telex 22203; fax (2) 782-3094; f. 1961; commercially-operated public corpn; 19 local affiliated stations; Pres. KANG SUNG-KOO; Vice-Pres. KIM MIN-SHIK.

**Pyong Hwa Broadcasting Corporation (PBC):** 2-3 Cho-dong, Chung-ku, Seoul 100-031; tel. (2) 270-2114; fax (2) 270-2210; f. 1990; religious and educational programmes; Pres. Rev. PARK SHIN-EON.

**Radio Station HLAZ:** MPOB 88, Seoul 121-707; tel. (2) 337-1460; fax (2) 333-2627; f. 1973; religious, educational service operated by Far East Broadcasting Co; programmes in Korean, Chinese, Russian and English; Dir Rev. BILLY KIM.

**Radio Station HLKX:** MPOB 88, Seoul 121-707; tel. (2) 337-1460; fax (2) 333-2627; f. 1956; religious, educational service operated by Far East Broadcasting Co; programmes in Korean, Chinese and English; Dir Rev. BILLY KIM.

**Seoul Broadcasting System (SBS):** 10-2 Yoido-dong, Yongdeungpo-ku, Seoul 150-010; tel. (2) 369-1114; fax (2) 780-2530; f. 1991; Pres. YOON SEI-YOUNG.

**US Forces Korea Network (AFKN):** Seoul; tel. (2) 791-6495; telex 22943; fax (2) 7914-5870; f. 1950; eight originating stations and 19 relay stations; 24 hours a day.

## TELEVISION

**Korean Broadcasting System (KBS):** 18 Yoido-dong, Yongdeungpo-ku, Seoul 150-010; tel. (2) 781-1000; telex 24599; f. 1961; publicly-owned corpn with 25 local broadcasting and 770 relay stations; Pres. HONG DOO-PYO.

**Munhwa Broadcasting Corporation (MBC-R/TV):** 31 Yoido-dong, Yongdeungpo-ku, Seoul 150-728; tel. (2) 784-2000; telex 22203; fax (2) 782-3094; f. 1961; public; 19 TV networks; Pres. KANG SUNG-GU.

**Seoul Broadcasting System (SBS):** 10-2 Yoido-dong, Yongdeungpo-ku, Seoul 150-010; tel. (2) 369-1114; fax (2) 780-2530; f. 1991; Pres. YOON SEI-YOUNG.

**US Forces Korea Network (AFKN):** Seoul; tel. (2) 7914-6495; telex 22943; fax (2) 7914-5870; f. 1957; main transmitting station in Seoul; 18 rebroadcast transmitters and translators; 140 hours weekly (see Radio).

# Finance

(cap. = capital; res = reserves; dep. = deposits; m. = million; brs = branches; amounts in won)

## BANKING

The modern financial system in South Korea was established in 1950 with the foundation of the central bank, the Bank of Korea. Under financial liberalization legislation, adopted in the late 1980s, banks were accorded greater freedom to engage in securities or insurance operations. In December 1993 there were 98 commercial banks in South Korea, comprising 14 nationwide banks, 10 provincial banks and 74 branches of foreign banks. The Office of Bank Supervision of the Bank of Korea oversees the operations of commercial banks.

Specialized banks were created in the 1960s to provide funds for sectors of the economy not covered by commercial banks. There are also three development banks: the Korea Development Bank, the Export-Import Bank of Korea and the Korea Long Term Credit Bank.

### Central Bank

**Bank of Korea:** 110, 3-ka, Namdaemun-no, Chung-ku, Seoul 100-794; tel. (2) 759-4114; telex 24711; fax (2) 759-5826; f. 1950; bank of issue; res 1,104,400m., dep. 18,234.9m. (Dec. 1993); Gov. KIM MYUNG-HO; Dep. Gov. SHIN BOK-YOUNG; 16 domestic brs, 9 overseas offices.

### Commercial Banks

**Bank of Seoul:** 10-1, 2-ka, Namdaemun-no, Chung-ku, Seoul 100-746; tel. (2) 771-6000; telex 23311; fax (2) 752-7389; f. 1959; cap. 650,000m., dep. 15,335,772m. (Dec. 1993); Pres. KIM YOUNG-SUK; 296 domestic brs, 6 overseas brs.

**Boram Bank:** 9-10, 2-ka, Ulchi-no, Chung-ku, Seoul 100-192; tel. (2) 771-5300; telex 33555; fax (2) 775-7472; f. 1991; cap. 110,400m., dep. 5,599,545m. (Dec. 1993); Chair. and Pres. KIM DONG-JAE; 50 brs.

**Cho Hung Bank:** 14, 1-ka, Namdaemun-no, Chung-ku, Seoul 100-757; tel. (2) 733-2000; telex 23321; fax (2) 720-2885; f. 1897; cap. 820,000m., dep. 22,154,352m. (Dec. 1994); Chair. and Pres. CHAN MOK-WOO; 358 domestic brs, 7 overseas brs.

**Commercial Bank of Korea Ltd:** 111-1, 2-ka, Namdaemun-no, Chung-ku, POB 126, Seoul 100-792; tel. (2) 775-0050; telex 24611; fax (2) 754-9203; f. 1899; cap. 650,000m., dep. 15,743,053m. (Dec. 1992); Pres. CHUNG JEE-TAE; 299 domestic brs, 7 overseas brs.

**Hana Bank:** 101-1, 1-ka, Ulchi-no, Chung-ku, Seoul 100-191; tel. (2) 754-2121; telex 25914; fax (2) 756-6358; f. 1991; cap. 81,562.5m., dep. 5,312,780.4m. (Dec. 1993); Pres. YOON BYUNG-CHUL; 48 domestic brs.

**Hanil Bank:** 130, 2-ka, Namdaemun-no, Chung-ku, CPOB 1033, Seoul; tel. (2) 771-2000; telex 28776; fax (2) 754-0479; f. 1932; cap. 660,000m., dep. 15,769,152m. (Dec. 1993); Pres. YOON SOUN-JUNG; Vice-Pres. LEE KWAN-WOO; 302 domestic brs, 9 overseas brs.

**KorAm Bank:** Hanmi Bldg, 1, Gongpyung-dong, Chongno-ku, KPOB 1084, Seoul 110-160; tel. (2) 731-8114; telex 27814; fax (2) 731-8115; f. 1983; jt venture with Bank of America; cap. 120,000m., dep. 1,810,247m. (Dec. 1993); Pres. HONG SE-PYO; Vice-Chair. ZAREH M. MISSERLIAN; 91 domestic brs.

**Korea Exchange Bank:** 181, 2-ka, Ulchi-no, Chung-ku, Seoul 100-192; tel. (2) 729-0114; telex 23141; fax (2) 757-7452; f. 1967; cap. 605,000m., dep. 12,278,898m. (Dec. 1993); Pres. CHANG MYUNG-SUN; Dep. Pres HUH JOON, LEE CHANG-WOO; 189 domestic brs, 19 overseas.

**Korea First Bank:** 100 Kongpyung-dong, Chongno-ku, CPOB 2242, Seoul 100-160; tel. (2) 733-0070; telex 23685; fax (2) 725-1466; f. 1929; cap. 650,000m., dep. 18,996,658m. (Dec. 1993); Chair. and Pres. RHEE CHUL-SOO; 276 domestic brs, 4 overseas brs.

**Shinhan Bank:** 120, 2-ka, Taepyong-no, Chung-ku, Seoul 100; tel. (2) 756-0505; telex 25583; fax (2) 774-7013; f. 1982; cap. 516,000m., dep. 5,726,573m. (Dec. 1993); Pres. RA EUNG-CHAN; Chair. LEE HUI-KEON; 156 domestic brs, 4 overseas.

**Taedong Bank:** 13-7, Pomo-dong, Susong-ku, Taegu 706-010; tel. (53) 742-6000; telex 54264; fax (53) 742-1540; f. 1989; cap. 200,000m., res 31,500m., dep. 2,242,700m. (Dec. 1993); Pres. CHO SONG-CHUN; 51 domestic brs.

### Development Banks

**Export-Import Bank of Korea:** 16-1 Yoido-dong, Yongdeungpo-ku, Seoul 150-010; tel. (2) 784-1021; telex 26595; fax (2) 784-1030; f. 1976; cap. 685,855m. (Dec. 1993); Chair. and Pres. KIM YOUNG-BIN; Vice-Pres. LEE HAK-SUNG; 3 domestic brs, 12 overseas brs.

**Korea Development Bank:** 10-2 Kwanchul-dong, Chongno-ku, CPOB 28, Seoul 110-111; tel. (2) 398-6114; telex 27463; fax (2) 733-4768; f. 1954; cap. 1,382,000m., dep. 6,115,016m. (Dec. 1993); Gov. LEE HYUNG-KOO; Chair. LEE KWANG-SU; 32 brs.

**Korea Long Term Credit Bank:** 15–22 Yoido-dong, Yongdeungpo-ku, Seoul 150-717; tel. (2) 782-0111; telex 26342; fax (2) 784-7310; f. 1967; assists in the development of private enterprises by medium- and long-term financing (incl. loans, guarantees and purchases of equities); cap. 410,800m., res 308,169.7m., dep. 8,311,312m. (Dec. 1993); Chair. HAM TAE-YONG; Pres. BONG CHONG-HYUN; 25 brs.

### Specialized Banks

**Citizen's National Bank:** 9-1, 2-ka, Namdaemun-no, Chung-ku, POB 815, Seoul 100; tel. (2) 317-2460; telex 26109; fax (2) 757-3679; f. 1963; cap. 96,001m., dep. 10,888,382m. (Dec. 1991); Pres. LEE KYU-CHEUNG; 290 brs.

**Industrial Bank of Korea:** 50, 2-ka, Ulchi-no, Chung-ku, POB 4153, Seoul; tel. (2) 729-7114; telex 23932; fax (2) 729-7095; f. 1961; cap. 307.7m., dep. 11,975.0m. (Dec. 1993); Pres. LEE WOO-YOUNG; Chair. LEE SANG-CHUL; 321 brs.

**Korea Housing Bank:** 36-3 Yoido-dong, Yongdeungpo-ku, POB 1187, Seoul 150-010; tel. (2) 769-7114; telex 32933; fax (2) 784-8324; f. 1967; cap. 69,000m., res 207,705m., dep. 14,261,410m. (Dec. 1993); Pres. PARK JONG-SUK; Chair. CHUNG YOUNG-MOH; 359 brs.

**Korea International Merchant Bank:** Young Poong Bldg, 4, 33 Seorin-dong, Chongno-ku, Seoul; tel. (2) 399-6500; telex 26370; fax (2) 399-6555; f. 1979; cap. 21,500m., res 90,920.3m., dep. 1,472,856m. (March 1994); Chair. CHO SUNG-JIN; Pres. CHA SUNG-CHUL.

**Korean-French Banking Corporation (SOGEKO):** Marine Center, 118, 2-ka, Namdaemun-no, Chung-ku, POB 8572, Seoul; tel. (2) 777-7711; telex 24188; f. 1977; cap. 18,500m., dep. 453,291m. (Mar. 1989); Pres. KIM DOO-BAE; Exec. Vice-Pres. JEAN VIDEAU.

**National Agricultural Co-operatives Federation:** 75 Chungjong-no 1-ka, Chung-ku, Seoul 100-707; tel. (2) 397-5114; telex 27235; fax (2) 397-5380; f. 1961; cap. 281,520m., dep. 14,079,700m. (1993); Chair. and Pres. WON CHURL-HEE; 673 brs.

**National Federation of Fisheries Co-operatives:** 88 Kyongun-dong, Chongno-ku, Seoul 110-310; tel. (2) 730-6211; telex 24359; fax (2) 730-8025; f. 1962; cap. 12,977m., dep. 588,889m. (1989); Chair. and Pres. LEE BANG-HO; 112 brs.

# REPUBLIC OF KOREA (SOUTH KOREA)

**National Livestock Co-operatives Federation:** 451, Songnae-dong, Kangdong-ku, Seoul 134-710; tel. (2) 485-3141; telex 25243; fax (2) 475-8129; f. 1981; cap. 57,102m., dep. 328,341m. (1989); Chair. and Pres. MYUNG UI-SIK; 35 brs.

## Provincial Banks

**Bank of Cheju Ltd:** 1349, 2-do, 1-dong, Cheju City, Cheju-Do; tel. (64) 52-4151; telex 66722; fax (64) 53-4131; f. 1969; cap. 26,350m., dep. 316,312m. (1989); Chair. and Pres. PARK BYUNG-SIK; Dep. Pres. and Dir KIM YOUNG-JAI; 27 brs.

**Chungbuk Bank Ltd:** 86-3 Young-dong, Chongju 360-020; tel. (431) 53-2131; telex 23507; fax (431) 55-6487; f. 1971; cap. 100,540m., res 78,698m., dep. 917,084m. (Dec. 1992); Pres. MIN HYOUNG-KEUN; Vice-Pres. PARK DONG-SOON; 43 brs.

**Chungchong Bank Ltd:** 48-1 Eunhaeng-dong, Chung-ku, Taejon; tel. (42) 253-7411; telex 45542; fax (42) 253-7411; f. 1968; cap. 93,000m., dep. 2,153,000m. (1992); Chair. and Pres. SUNG UK-KI; Dir and Dep. Pres. YOON EUN-JUNG; 82 brs.

**Jeonbuk Bank Ltd:** 1 Mukyo-dong, Chung-ku, Seoul 100-170; tel. (2) 777-9861; telex 24625; fax (2) 755-3698; f. 1969; cap. 102,300m., dep. 1,187,720m. (1994); Chair. and Pres. PARK CHAN-MOON; Vice-Pres. CHAE SOO-HWAN; 73 brs.

**Kangwon Bank Ltd:** 72-3 Wunkyo-dong, Chuncheon, Kangwon 200-080; tel. (361) 54-4351; telex 24556; fax (361) 50-9229; f. 1970; cap. 68,200m., dep. 1,086,426m. (Dec. 1993); Pres. CHOI JONG-MOON; Vice-Pres. HWANG HWAN-HAK; 41 brs.

**Kwangju Bank Ltd:** 1-11, 3-ka, Kumnam-no, Dong-ku, Kwangju 501-023; tel. (62) 223-4000; telex 66760; fax (62) 232-4678; f. 1968; cap. 143,000m., dep. 1,343,528m. (Dec. 1991); Chair. and Pres. SONG BYUNG-SOON; 55 brs.

**Kyungki Bank Ltd:** 1127, Kuwol-dong, Namdong-ku, Inchon 405-220; tel. (32) 420-5000; telex 26315; fax (32) 420-5456; f. 1969; cap. 150,150m., dep. 4,802,020m. (Dec. 1993); Chair. and Pres. CHOO BUM-KOOK; Dir and Dep. Pres. SUH EI-SUK; 118 brs.

**Kyungnam Bank:** 975-5, Yangduck-dong, Hoewon-ku, Masan; tel. (551) 90-8000; telex 27691; fax (551) 90-8999; f. 1970; cap. 115,000m., dep. 1,445,570m. (1989); Chair. and Pres. LEE JAI-JIN; Vice-Pres. KIM HYUNG-YUNG; 80 brs.

**Pusan Bank:** 830-38, Pomil-dong, Dong-ku, Pusan; tel. (51) 645-3700; telex 53392; fax (51) 642-3300; f. 1967; cap. 121,000m., dep. 4,145,496m. (Dec. 1993); Chair. and Pres. LEE CHANG-HEE; Dir and Dep. Pres. LEE YON-HYONG; 143 brs.

**Taegu Bank Ltd:** 118 2-ka, Susong-dong, Susong-ku, Taegu 706-032; tel. (53) 756-2001; telex 54334; fax (53) 756-2095; f. 1967; cap. 165,000m., dep. 3,468,454m. (Dec. 1993); Pres. HONG HWI-HUM; Dep. Pres. and Dir LEE SANG-KYUNG; 150 brs.

## Foreign Banks

**ABN-AMRO Bank** (Netherlands): Young Poong Bldg, 15th Floor, 33, Seorin-dong, Chongno-ku, CPOB 3035, Seoul; tel. (2) 399-6600; telex 24624; fax (2) 399-6647; f. 1979; Man. HERMAN ERBÉ.

**American Express Bank Ltd** (USA): Kwang Hwa Moon Bldg, 17th Floor, 64-8, 1-ka, Taepyung-no, Chung-ku, Seoul 100-101; tel. (2) 399-2929; telex 24484; fax (2) 399-2967; f. 1977; Gen. Man. JAMES VAUGHN.

**Arab Bank PLC:** Daewoo Center Bldg, 17th Floor, 541, 5-ka, Namdaemun-no, Chung-ku, Seoul 100-714; tel. (2) 757-0024; telex 34180; fax (2) 757-0124; Man. KIM EUN-YOUNG.

**Australia and New Zealand Banking Group Ltd** (Australia): Kyobo Bldg, 18th Floor, 1, 1-ka, Chongno, Chongno-ku, Seoul 110-714; tel. (2) 730-3151; telex 27338; fax (2) 737-6325; f. 1978; Gen. Man. M. G. WALSH.

**Bank of America National Trust & Savings Association** (USA): Hyonam Bldg, 9th Floor, 1 Changkyo-dong, Chung-ku, Seoul; tel. (2) 729-4500; telex 23294; fax (2) 729-4400; Country Man. CHANG YEONG-HO.

**Bank of Boston** (USA): Kyobo Bldg, 15th Floor, 1 Chongno-ku, Seoul 110-714; tel. (2) 733-6981; telex 23750; fax (2) 733-6989; f. 1982; Gen. Man. BARRY LAMONT.

**Bank of California N.A.** (USA): Kyobo Bldg, 12th Floor, 1, Chongno 1-ka, Chongno-ku, Seoul 110; tel. (2) 736-5431; telex 22815; fax (2) 732-9526; Gen. Man. MALCOLM A. MOSLEY.

**Bank of Hawaii:** Daeyungak Bldg, 14th Floor, 2-ka, Chungmu-no, Chung-ku, Seoul 100-011; tel. (2) 770-0831; telex 23589; fax (2) 757-3516; Man. KIM SON-YOUNG.

**Bank of Montreal** (Canada): Suhrin Bldg, 14th Floor, 88 Suhrin-dong, Chongno-ku, CPOB 8485, Seoul 110-110; tel. (2) 732-9206; telex 23198; fax (2) 732-9200; f. 1978; Man. ROBERT THOMAS MARTIN.

**Bank of New York** (USA): Samsung Main Bldg, 14th Floor, 250, 2-ka, Taepyung-no, Chung-ku, Seoul 100-742; tel. (2) 774-1441; telex 33211; fax (2) 774-1888; Gen. Man. HO YANG.

**Bank of Nova Scotia** (Canada): KCCI Bldg, 9th Floor, 45 Namdaemun-no, 4-ka, Chung-ku, Seoul 100-094; tel. (2) 757-7171; telex 29245; fax (2) 752-7189; Vice-Pres. and Man. C. D. MORIN.

**Bank of Tokyo Ltd** (Japan): Doosan Bldg, 12th Floor, 101, 1-ka, Ulchi-no, Chung-ku, Seoul; tel. (2) 310-6000; telex 23286; fax (2) 752-5040; f. 1967; Gen. Man. MAKAKI MAEDA.

**Bankers Trust Co** (USA): Seoul Center Bldg, 9–10th Floors, 91–1 Sokong-dong, Chung-ku, Seoul 100-070; tel. (2) 311-2600; telex 26390; fax (2) 756-2648; f. 1978; Man. Dir LEE KEUN-SAM.

**Banque Indosuez** (France): Kyobo Bldg, 22nd Floor, 1, 1-ka, Chong-no, Chongno-ku, CPOB 158, Seoul 110-714; tel. (2) 397-3200; telex 27198; fax (2) 738-0325; f. 1974; Regional Man. PIETER FANGMAN.

**Banque Nationale de Paris** (France): OCI Bldg, 8th Floor, 50 Sokong-dong, Chung-ku, Seoul 100-070; tel. (2) 753-2594; telex 26539; fax (2) 757-2530; cap. 4,000m.; f. 1976; Gen. Man. P. GRANDAMY.

**Banque Paribas** (France): Kyobo Bldg, 21st Floor, 1, 1-ka, Chongno, Chongno-ku, Seoul 100-714; tel. (2) 739-5151; telex 24144; fax (2) 739-5378; f. 1977; cap. 3,300m.; Man. MICHEL D. DUBOIS.

**Barclays Bank PLC** (UK): Kyobo Bldg, 13th Floor, 1, Chongno 1-ka, Chongno-ku, Seoul 110-601; tel. (2) 730-2541; telex 24480; fax (2) 730-5465; f. 1977; Chief Man. ALAN J. TIMBLICK.

**Chase Manhattan Bank, NA** (USA): 50, 1-ka, Ulchi-no, Chung-ku, Seoul 100; tel. (2) 758-5114; telex 23249; fax (2) 758-5421; f. 1967; cap. 9,000m.; Gen. Man. DOUGLAS ASPER.

**Chemical Bank** (USA): Daewoo Center Bldg, 11th Floor, 541, 5-ka, Namdaemun-no, Chung-ku, Seoul 100-612; tel. (2) 778-5411; telex 23736; fax (2) 755-1849; f. 1978; Man. Dir KEVIN KEHOE.

**Citibank N.A.** (USA): Citicorp Center Bldg, 89-29, Shinmun-no 2-ka, Chongno-ku, Seoul 110-062; tel. (2) 731-1114; telex 23293; fax (2) 733-8473; f. 1967; Vice-Pres. and Gen. Man. JOHN M. BEEMAN; br. in Pusan.

**Crédit Lyonnais Korea Group** (France): Yoowon Bldg, 8–10th Floors, 75-95, Seosomun-no, Chung-ku, Seoul 100-110; tel. (2) 772-8000; telex 23484; fax (2) 755-5379; f. 1978; cap. 30,000m.; Gen. Man. DOMINIQUE TISSIER.

**Dai-Ichi Kangyo Bank Ltd** (Japan): Nae Wei Bldg, 12th Floor, 6, 2-ka, Ulchi-no, Chung-ku, Seoul 100-192; tel. (2) 756-8181; telex 27387; fax (2) 754-6844; f. 1972; cap. 9,000m., dep. 19,225m. (Dec. 1992); Gen. Man. TATSUYA TORIKOE.

**Deutsche Bank AG** (Germany): 51–1 Namchang-dong, Chung-ku, CPOB 8904, Seoul 100-689; tel. (2) 754-3071; telex 26353; fax (2) 755-2364; f. 1978; Gen. Man. AXEL-PETER OHSE.

**Development Bank of Singapore:** Kyobo Bldg, 14th Floor, 1 Chongno 1-ka, Chongno-ku, CPOB 9896, Seoul 110-714; tel. (2) 732-9311; telex 22764; fax (2) 732-7953; f. 1981; Gen. Man. CHARLES C. K. ONG.

**First National Bank of Boston:** Kyobo Bldg, 15th Floor, 1, 1-ka, Chongno, Chongno-ku, Seoul 110-714; tel. (2) 733-6981; Gen. Man. WILLIAM A. GEMMEL.

**First National Bank of Chicago** (USA): Oriental Chemical Bldg, 15th Floor, 50, Sokong-dong, Chung-ku, Seoul 100-070; tel. (2) 316-9700; telex 27534; fax (2) 753-7917; f. 1976; Vice-Pres. and Gen. Man. MICHAEL S. BROWN.

**Fuji Bank Ltd** (Japan): Doosan Bldg, 15th Floor, 101-1, 1-ka, Ulchi-no, Chung-ku, Seoul 100-191; tel. (2) 311-2000; telex 27216; fax (2) 754-8177; f. 1972; Gen. Man. NAOMASA NOMURA.

**Hongkong and Shanghai Banking Corpn Ltd** (Hong Kong): Kyobo Bldg, 6th Floor, 1, 1-ka, Chongno, Chongno-ku, Seoul 110-714; tel. (2) 739-4211; telex 22022; fax (2) 739-1387; Man. M. HALE.

**Indian Overseas Bank:** Daeyungak Bldg, 3rd Floor, 25–5, 1-ka, Chungmu-no, Chung-ku, Seoul 100-011; tel. (2) 753-0741; telex 24150; fax (2) 756-0279; f. 1977; cap. 2,300m.; Country Head S. S. SHARMA.

**International Bank of Singapore Ltd:** Kyobo Bldg, 8th Floor, Suite 806, 1, 1-ka, Chongno, Chongno-ku, Seoul 110-714; tel. (2) 739-3441; telex 26485; fax (2) 732-9004; Gen. Man. KUIN SAM LAU.

**Internationale Nederlanden Bank (ING Bank)** (Netherlands): POB 81, Seoul 110-600; tel. (2) 399-3300; telex 22073; fax (2) 339-3313; cap. 3,000m.; Gen. Man. J. BOSMA.

**Long-Term Credit Bank of Japan Ltd:** Kwanghwamun Bldg, 14th Floor, 64-8, 1-ka, Taepyung-no, Chung-ku, Seoul; tel. (2) 399-2450; telex 24313; fax (2) 399-2480; Gen. Man. TSUTOMU WAKIYA.

**Mitsubishi Bank Ltd** (Japan): Press Center Bldg, 11th Floor, 25, 1-ka, Taepyung-no, Chung-ku, Seoul 100-745; tel. (2) 734-9561; telex 27240; fax (2) 734-2028; f. 1967; Gen. Man. YOSHIHARU ISHIKAWA.

**Morgan Guaranty Trust Co of New York** (USA): Kyobo Bldg, 22nd Floor, 1, 1-ka, Chong-no, Chongno-ku, Seoul; tel. (2) 732-2300; telex 24911; fax (2) 734-0148; Vice-Pres. DAVID S. HICKMAN.

REPUBLIC OF KOREA (SOUTH KOREA) — Directory

**National Australia Bank Ltd:** Kyobo Bldg, Suite 1401, 1, 1-ka, Chongno, Chongno-ku, Seoul 110-714; tel. (2) 739-4600; telex 28844; fax (2) 733-0738; Man. KERRY PETER JELBART.

**National Bank of Canada:** Leema Bldg, 6th Floor, 146-1, Soosong-dong, Chongno-ku, Seoul 110-140; tel. (2) 733-5012; telex 25043; fax (2) 736-1508; Vice-Pres. and Country Man. C. N. KIM.

**National Bank of Pakistan:** Kyobo Bldg, 12th Floor, 1, 1-ka, Chongno, Chongno-ku, Seoul 110-714; tel. (2) 732-0277; telex 32149; fax (2) 734-5817; f. 1987; Gen. Man. RAZEEUDDIN SHEIKH.

**Royal Bank of Canada:** Kyobo Bldg, 7th Floor, 1–1, 1–ka, Chongno, Chongno-ku, Seoul 110-714; tel. (2) 730-7791; telex 24834; fax (2) 736-2995; f. 1982; Gen. Man. DAVID POHL.

**Société Générale** (France): Kwanghwamun Bldg, 12th Floor, Sejong-no, Chung-ku, Seoul; tel. (2) 399-2129; telex 22266; fax (2) 399-2151; f. 1984; Gen. Man. ALAIN BELLISSARD.

**Standard Chartered PLC** (UK): Kwangwhamun POB 259, Nae Wei Bldg, 13th Floor, 9–1, 2-ka, Ulchi-no, Chung-ku, Seoul 100-192; tel. (2) 750-6114; telex 24242; fax (2) 757-7444; Man. D. N. HAWKINS.

**Swiss Bank Corpn:** Young Poong Bldg, 8th Floor, 33 Seorin-dong, Chongno-ku, Seoul; tel. (2) 399-6240; telex 32290; fax (2) 399-6243; Rep. P. FLURY.

**Tokai Bank Ltd:** Kyobo Bldg, 17th Floor, 1, 1-ka, Chongno, Chongno-ku, Seoul 110-714; tel. (2) 739-9810; telex 25716; fax (2) 739-9814; Gen. Man. SOICHIRO ICHIKAWA.

**Union de Banques Arabes et Françaises** (France): Samsung Main Bldg, 18th Floor, 250, 2-ka, Taepyung-no, Chung-ku, Seoul 100-742; tel. (2) 778-8081; telex 26400; fax (2) 754-6848; f. 1979; Gen. Man. JACQUES C. PSALTIS.

**Yamaguchi Bank Ltd:** Kukje Bldg, 3rd Floor, 69, 6-ka, Chungang-dong, Chung-ku, Pusan 600-011; tel. (51) 462-3281; telex 52561; Gen. Man. YAMAKI TOSHIAKI.

### Banking Association

**Korea Federation of Banks:** 33, Seorin-dong, Chongno-ku, Seoul 110-110; tel. (2) 399-5811; fax (2) 399-5810; f. 1928; Pres. CHONG CHUN-TAEK; Chair. LEE SANG-CHUL; Vice-Chair. LEE CHUNG-NYUNG.

### STOCK EXCHANGE

**Korea Stock Exchange:** 33 Yoido-dong, Yongdeungpo-ku, Seoul 150-010; tel. (2) 780-2271; fax (2) 786-0263.

### INSURANCE

In 1994 there were 33 life insurance companies and 14 non-life insurance companies.

#### Principal Life Companies

**Chun Buk Life Insurance Co Ltd:** 700-3, 2-ka, Chongnosong-dong, Chung-ku, Chun Buk 560-102; tel. (652) 87-8949; fax (652) 81-0444; f. 1990; cap. 10,000m.; Pres. YIM CHANG-YEL.

**Daehan Kyoyuk Insurance Co Ltd:** 1, 1-ka, Chongno, Chongno-ku, Seoul 110-714; tel. (2) 721-2121; fax (2) 737-9970; f. 1958; cap. 3,000m.; Pres. KIM YOUNG-SUK; 84 main brs.

**Daehan Life Insurance Co Ltd:** 60 Yoido-dong, Yongdeungpo-ku, Seoul 150-763; tel. (2) 789-5114; telex 26837; f. 1946; cap. 2,000m.; Pres. CHOI PYONG-EOGG; 1,071 brs.

**Daishin Life Insurance Co Ltd:** 943, Dogok-dong, Kangnam-ku, Seoul 135-270; tel. (2) 560-7000; fax (2) 563-2781; f. 1989; Pres. KIM HYE-MOON.

**Dongah Life Insurance Co Ltd:** 238, 1-ka, Shinmun-no, Chongno-ku, Seoul 110-061; tel. (2) 721-6000; fax (2) 720-2385; f. 1973; cap. 10,000m.; Pres. LEE HO-HYUNG; 900 brs.

**Dong Bu Aetna Life Insurance Co Ltd:** Hyun Am Bldg, 12th Floor, 1, Chonggyo-dong, Chung-ku, Seoul 100-200; tel. (2) 729-4991; fax (2) 729-4989; f. 1989; cap. 20,000m.; Pres. WOO JAE-KU.

**First Life Insurance Co Ltd:** 1303-35 Seocho-dong, Seochu-ku, Seoul 137-074; tel. (2) 568-0101; fax (2) 552-8669; f. 1954; Pres. LEE TAE-SIK.

**Han Duk Life Insurance Co Ltd:** Kookje Insurance Bldg, 7th Floor, 3-ka, Dongkwang-dong, Chung-ku, Pusan 600-023; tel. (51) 247-3211; fax (51) 247-3220; f. 1989; cap. 10,000m.; Pres. SUH WOO-SHICK.

**Han Kuk Life Insurance Co Ltd:** Daehan Fire Bldg, 51-1, Nam-chang-dong, Chung-ku, Seoul 110-060; tel. (2) 773-3355; fax (2) 773-1778; f. 1989; cap. 10,000m.; Pres. MO YOUNG-WOO.

**Hansung Life Insurance Co Ltd:** 3 Su Jeong-dong, Tong-ku, Pusan 601-030; tel. (51) 461-7700; fax (51) 465-0581; f. 1988; Pres. CHO YONG-KEUN.

**Hungkuk Life Insurance Co Ltd:** 17-12, 4-ka, Namdaemun-no, Chung-ku, Seoul 100-094; tel. (2) 772-7000; fax (2) 757-0664; f. 1958; cap. 8,000m. (1994); Pres. BAN SUNG-WOO.

**Korea Life Insurance Co Ltd:** 60 Yoido-dong, Yongdeungpo-ku, Seoul 150-783; tel. (2) 789-5114; telex 26837; fax (2) 784-7217; f. 1946; cap. 8,000m.; Pres. KIM KWANG-PYUNG.

**Kyung Nam Life Insurance Co Ltd:** 427-17, Pongam-dong, Hoewon-ku, Masan 630-500; tel. (551) 52-3110; fax (551) 52-3119; f. 1990; cap. 10,000m.; Pres. KANG SE-JUNG.

**New York Life Insurance of Korea Ltd:** 223, Naeja-dong, Chongno-ku, Seoul 110-053; tel. (2) 737-4455; fax (2) 737-9091; cap. 10,000m.; Pres. WILLIAM H. MOWAT.

**Pacific Life Insurance Co Ltd:** 820–9, Yoksam-dong, Kangnam-ku, Seoul 135-080; tel. (2) 561-0303; fax (2) 561-0321; f. 1989; cap. 10,000m.; Pres. LEE SUK-LYONG.

**Prudential Life Insurance Company of Korea Ltd:** Ilsong Bldg, 15th Floor, 157-37, Samsung-dong, Kangnam-ku, Seoul 135-090; tel. (2) 528-3800; fax (2) 528-3801; cap. 10,000m.; Pres. JAMES CHOI SPACKMAN.

**Pusan Life Insurance Co Ltd:** 1205-1, Choryang-dong, Dong-ku, Pusan 601-010; tel. (51) 464-9277; fax (51) 465-0581; f. 1988; cap. 40,000m.; Pres. AN SUK-SOON.

**Samsung Life Insurance Co Ltd:** 150, 2-ka, Taepyong-no, Chung-ku, Seoul 100-716; tel. (2) 751-8000; telex 25204; fax (2) 772-6108; f. 1957; Pres. HWANG HAK-SOO; 1,300 brs.

**Taegu Life Insurance Co Ltd:** Dooryu Bldg, 148-3, Dooryu 2-dong, Dalseo-ku, Taegu 704-062; tel. (53) 628-2300; fax (53) 628-9268; f. 1988; cap. 12,000m.; Pres. LEE YOUNG-TAEK.

#### Non-Life Companies

**Daehan Fire and Marine Insurance Co Ltd:** 51-1 Namchang-dong, Chung-ku, Seoul; tel. (2) 754-6234; telex 28230; fax (2) 774-7059; f. 1946; cap. 7,700m.; Vice-Chair. BAEK IL-HWAN.

**First Fire and Marine Insurance Co Ltd:** 12–1 Seosomun-dong, Chung-ku, CPOB 530, Seoul 100-110; tel. (2) 316-8114; telex 24365; fax (2) 756-6602; f. 1949; cap. 4,600m.; Chair. LEE TONG-HOON; Vice-Chair. KIM KI-TAEK.

**Haedong Fire and Marine Insurance Co Ltd:** 185–10, 2-ka, Chungjeong-no, Seodaemun-ku, CPOB 1821, Seoul 120; tel. (2) 363-2611; telex 27475; fax (2) 392-2933; f. 1953; cap. 3,500m.; Chair. KIM DONG-MAN; Pres. KIM HYO-IL.

**Hankuk Fidelity and Surety Co:** Dongho Bldg, 3rd Floor, 1422-10, Kwanyang-dong, Dongan-ku, Anyang, Kyungki-do 430-010; tel. (343) 24-0031; fax (343) 24-0036; f. 1989; cap. 60,000m.; Pres. KIM CHANG-RAK.

**Hyundai Marine and Fire Insurance Co Ltd:** 178, Sejong-no, Chongno-ku, Seoul; tel. (2) 732-1212; telex 27270; fax (2) 732-5687; f. 1955; cap. 30,000m.; Pres. CHUNG MONG-YUN.

**International Fire and Marine Insurance Co Ltd:** International Insurance Bldg, 120, 5-ka, Namdaemun-no, Chung-ku, Seoul 100-704; tel. (2) 753-1101; telex 27567; fax (2) 753-0745; f. 1947; cap. 10,784m.; Pres. KIM YOUNG-MAN; Vice-Chair. LEE KYUNG-SUH.

**Korea Automobile, Fire and Marine Insurance Co Ltd:** 21-9 Cho-dong, Chung-ku, Seoul; tel. (2) 262-3114; telex 24588; fax (2) 266-7357; f. 1962; cap. 20,000m.; Chair. BAEK NAM-UK; Pres. KIM TAEK-KEE.

**Korea Fidelity and Surety Co:** Sungwon Bldg, 141, Samsung-dong, Kangnam-ku, Seoul 135-090; tel. (2) 744-0021; telex 28485; fax (2) 743-0016; f. 1969; cap. 5,000m.; Pres. KOH SOON-BOK.

**Korean Reinsurance Company:** 80 Susong-dong, Chongno-ku, Seoul 110-140; tel. (2) 739-7141; telex 24241; fax (2) 739-3753; f. 1963; cap. 34,030m.; Chair. and Pres. SHIM HYUNG-SUP.

**Lucky Insurance Co Ltd:** Lucky Insurance Bldg, 85 Ta-dong, Chung-ku, Seoul 100-180; tel. (2) 310-2114; telex 28566; fax (2) 753-1002; f. 1959; cap. 21,712m.; Pres. LEE WHEE-YOUNG.

**Oriental Fire and Marine Insurance Co Ltd:** 25–1 Yoido-dong, Yongdeungpo-ku, Seoul 150-010; tel. (2) 785-7711; telex 27479; fax (2) 784-9264; f. 1922; cap. 16,500m.; Pres. CHU INN-KI.

**Samsung Fire and Marine Insurance Co Ltd:** Samsung Bldg, 87, 1-ka, Ulchiro 1-ka, Chung-ku, Seoul 100-191; tel. (2) 758-7000; telex 23160; fax (2) 752-4875; f. 1952, present name since 1994; cap. 12,081m.; Vice-Chair. and CEO LEE CHONG-KI.

**Shindongah Fire and Marine Insurance Co Ltd:** 63 Bldg, Yoido-dong, Yongdeungpo-ku, Seoul; tel. (2) 789-7300; telex 28323; fax (2) 755-8006; f. 1946; cap. 33,306m.; Pres. KIM CHUNG-HWAN.

**Ssang Yong Fire and Marine Insurance Co Ltd:** 60 Doryum-dong, Chongno-ku, Seoul 110-051; tel. (2) 724-9000; telex 28320; fax (2) 735-4218; f. 1948; cap. 13,440m.; Pres. HA JIN-O.

#### Insurance Associations

**Korea Life Insurance Association:** Kukdong Bldg, 16th Floor, 60–1, 3-ka, Chungmu-no, Chung-ku, Seoul 100-705; tel. (2) 275-0121; fax (2) 275-7696; f. 1950; 33 corporate mems; Chair. LEE KANG-HWAN.

# REPUBLIC OF KOREA (SOUTH KOREA)

**Korea Non-Life Insurance Association:** KRIC Bldg, 6th Floor, 80 Susong-dong, Chongno-ku, Seoul; tel. (2) 739-4161; telex 27947; fax (2) 739-3769; f. 1946; 16 corporate mems; Chair. Park Bong-Hwan.

## Trade and Industry

### CHAMBER OF TRADE AND INDUSTRY

**Korea Chamber of Commerce and Industry:** 45, 4-ka, Namdaemun-no, Chung-ku, CPOB 25, Seoul 100-743; tel. (2) 316-3114; telex 25728; fax (2) 757-9475; f. 1884; over 1m. mems; 56 local chambers; promotes development of the economy and of international economic co-operation; Pres. Kim Sang-Ha.

### FOREIGN TRADE ORGANIZATIONS

**Association of Foreign Trading Agents of Korea:** Dongjin Bldg, 218 Hangang-no, 2-ka, Yongsan-ku, Seoul 140-012; tel. (2) 792-1581; telex 23540; fax (2) 780-4337; f. 1970; 8,500 mems; Chair. Heung Yeol-Moon.

**Korea Consumer Goods Exporters Association:** KWTC Bldg, Room 1802, 159 Samsung-dong, Kangnam-ku, Seoul; tel. (2) 551-1862; fax (2) 551-1870; f. 1986; 230 corporate mems; Pres. Yo Young-Dong.

**Korea Export Association of Textiles:** Room 1803-4, 18th Floor, KWTC Bldg, 159, Samsong-dong, Kangnam-ku, Seoul; tel. (2) 551-1876; telex 23697; fax (2) 551-1896; f. 1981; 455 corporate mems; overseas br. in Brussels; Pres. Baek Young-Ki.

**Korea Export Industrial Corpn:** 188-5 Kuro-dong, Kuro-ku, Seoul; tel. (2) 853-1171; f. 1964; encourages industrial exports, provides assistance and operating capital, conducts market surveys; Pres. Kim Ki-Bae.

**Korea Foreign Trade Association:** KWTC Bldg, 159 Samsung-dong, Kangnam-ku, Seoul; tel. (2) 551-5114; telex 24265; fax (2) 551-5100; f. 1946; private, non-profitmaking business org. representing all licensed traders in South Korea; provides foreign businessmen with information, contacts and advice; 19,284 corporate mems; Chair. Nam Duck-Woo; Vice-Chair. Noh Chin-Shik.

**Korea Trade Promotion Corpn (KOTRA):** KWTC Bldg, 159 Samsung-dong, Kangnam-ku, CPOB 123, Seoul; tel. (2) 551-4181; telex 23659; fax (2) 551-4447; f. 1962; 78 overseas brs; Pres. Lee Sun-Ki.

**Korean Apparel Industry Association:** KWTC Bldg, Room 801, 159 Samsung-dong, Kangnam-ku, Seoul 135-729; tel. (2) 551-1456; fax (2) 551-1519; f. 1993; 741 corporate mems; Pres. Park Sei-Young.

### INDUSTRIAL ORGANIZATIONS

**Agricultural and Fishery Marketing Corporation:** 191 Hangang-no, 2-ka, Yongsan-ku, CPOB 3212, Seoul 140; tel. (2) 795-8201; telex 23297; fax (2) 790-5265; f. 1967; integrated development for secondary processing and marketing distribution for agricultural products and fisheries products; Pres. Ahn Kyo-Duck; Exec. Vice-Pres. Kim Jin-Kyu.

**Construction Association of Korea:** Construction Bldg, 8th Floor, 71-2, Nonhyon-dong, Kangnam-ku, Seoul 135-701; tel. (2) 547-6101; telex 28972; fax (2) 542-6264; f. 1947; national licensed contractors' asscn; 910 corporate mems (1992); Pres. Cho Nam-Wook; Vice-Pres. Sung Byung-Moon.

**Electronic Industries Association of Korea:** 648 Yoksam-dong, Kangnam-ku, CPOB 5650, Seoul 135-080; tel. (2) 553-0941; telex 28999; fax (2) 555-6195; f. 1976; 861 corporate mems; Chair. Ku Ja-Hak.

**Federation of Korean Industries:** FKI Bldg, 2nd Floor, 28-1 Yoido-dong, Yongdeungpo-ku, Seoul; tel. (2) 780-0821; telex 25544; fax (2) 784-1640; f. 1961; conducts research and survey work on domestic and overseas economic conditions and trends; advises the govt and other interested parties on economic matters; exchanges economic and trade missions with other countries; sponsors business conferences; 456 corporate mems and 68 business asscns; Chair. Yoo Chang-Soon.

**Korea Automobile Manufacturers Association:** 63 Bldg, 8th Floor, Yoido-dong, Yongdeungpo-ku, Seoul 150-763; tel. (2) 782-1360; fax (2) 782-0464; f. 1988; Chair. Kim Tae-Gon.

**Korea Coal Association:** 80-6 Susong-dong, Chongno-ku, Seoul; tel. (2) 734-8891; fax (2) 734-7959; f. 1949; 49 corporate mems; Pres. Lee Yun.

**Korea Federation of Textile Industries:** 944-31 Daechi-dong, Kangnam-ku, Seoul; tel. (2) 528-4001; telex 22677; fax (2) 528-4069; f. 1980; 47 corporate mems; Pres. Kim Kak-Choong.

**Korea Foods Industry Association:** 1002-6, Pangbae-dong, Seocho-ku, Seoul; tel. (2) 585-5052; fax (2) 586-4906; f. 1969; 104 corporate mems; Pres. Chun Myung-Ke.

**Korea Industrial Research Institutes:** FKI Bldg, 28-1 Yoido-dong, Yongdeungpo-ku, Seoul; tel. (2) 780-7601; fax (2) 785-5771; f. 1979; analyses industrial and technological information from abroad; Pres. Kim Chae-Kyum.

**Korea Iron and Steel Association:** 51-8 Susong-dong, Chongno-ku, Seoul; tel. (2) 732-9231; telex 26689; fax (2) 739-1090; f. 1975; 43 corporate mems; Chair. Kim Mahn-Je.

**Korea Oil Association:** Woojin Bldg, 1338-20 Seocho-dong, Kangnam-ku, Seoul; tel. (2) 566-3116; fax (2) 555-7825; f. 1980; 98 corporate mems; Pres. Ham Seong-Yong.

**Korea Productivity Center:** 122-1, Chuckson-dong, Chongno-ku, Seoul 110-052; tel. (2) 739-5868; telex 27672; fax (2) 739-6246; f. 1957; direction of enterprise management; 712 corporate mems; Chair. and CEO Moon Hi-Whoa.

**Korea Sericultural Association:** 17-9 Yoido-dong, Yongdeungpo-ku, Seoul; tel. (2) 783-6071; fax (2) 780-0706; f. 1946; improvement and promotion of silk production; 50,227 corporate mems; Pres. Kwon Young-Ha.

**Korea Shipbuilders' Association:** 65-1, Unni-dong, Chongno-ku, Seoul; tel. (2) 766-4631; fax (2) 766-4307; f. 1977; Pres. Choi Kwan-Sik.

**Korean Development Associates:** Seoul; tel. (2) 392-3854; fax (2) 312-3856; f. 1965; economic research; 25 corporate mems; Pres. Kim Dong-Kyu.

**Mining Association of Korea:** 35-24 Tongui-dong, Chongno-ku, Seoul 110; tel. (2) 736-2501; fax (2) 720-5592; f. 1918; 128 corporate mems; Pres. Lee Sang-Man.

**Spinners' and Weavers' Association of Korea:** 43-8 Kwanchul-dong, Chongno-ku, Seoul 110; tel. (2) 735-5741; telex 25986; fax (2) 735-5749; f. 1947; 24 corporate mems; Pres. Oh Ja-Bok.

### CO-OPERATIVES

**Central Federation of Fisheries Co-operatives:** 88 Kyeongun-dong, Chongno-ku, Seoul; tel. (2) 730-6211; fax (2) 732-4486; f. 1962; Pres. Hong Jong-Moon.

**Korea Coal Mining Industry Co-operative:** Seoul; tel. (2) 784-7821; fax (2) 784-7825; f. 1964; 117 corporate mems; Pres. Kim Sang-Bong.

**Korea Computers Co-operative:** Seoul; tel. (2) 780-0511; fax (2) 780-7509; f. 1981; Pres. Park Boung-Kyu.

**Korea Federation of Knitting Industry Co-operatives:** 48, 1-ka, Shinmun-no, Chongno-ku, Seoul 110; tel. (2) 735-5951; fax (2) 735-1447; f. 1962; mems: 10 regional co-operatives comprising 1,444 mfrs; Chair. Kim Kyung-O.

**Korea Federation of Non-ferrous Metal Industry Co-operatives:** Backsang Bldg, Room 715, 35-2, Yoido-dong, Yongdeungpo-ku, Seoul; tel. (2) 780-8551; fax (2) 784-9473; f. 1962; 470 corporate mems; Pres. Park Sang-Kyu.

**Korea Mining Industry Co-operative:** 35-24 Tongui-dong, Chongno-ku, Seoul; tel. (2) 735-3490; fax (2) 735-4658; f. 1966; 63 corporate mems; Pres. Bang Hae-Ju.

**Korea Steel Industry Co-operative:** 16-2, Yoido-dong, Yongdeungpo-ku, Seoul; tel. (2) 785-4127; fax (2) 785-4129; f. 1962; 75 corporate mems; Pres. Won Ha-Nam.

**Korea Woollen Spinners and Weavers Industry Co-operatives:** Room 1018/2, Chinyang Apt 120-3, 4-ka, Chungmu-no, Chung-ku, Seoul; tel. (2) 273-0677; fax (2) 277-9789; f. 1964; 50 corporate mems; Pres. Kim Yong-Shik.

**Korean Federation of Small Business (KFSB):** 16-2 Yoido-dong, Yongdeungpo-ku, Seoul 150-010; tel. (2) 785-0010; telex 26500; fax (2) 782-0247; f. 1962; 300 corporate mems; Pres. Park Sang-Kyu.

**National Agricultural Co-operative Federation (NACF):** 1, 1-ka, Uiju-no, Chung-ku, Seoul; tel. (2) 737-0021; fax (2) 737-7815; f. 1961; international banking, marketing, co-operative trade, utilization and processing, supply, co-operative insurance, banking and credit services, education and research; Pres. Han Ho-Sun.

### EMPLOYERS' ASSOCIATION

**Korea Employers' Federation:** Sungjee Bldg, 16th Floor, 538 Dohwa-dong, Mapo-ku, Seoul 121-743; tel. (2) 706-0618; fax (2) 706-1059; f. 1970; mems 1,503 companies, 10 regional employers' asscns; Pres. Lee Dong-Chan.

### TRADE UNIONS

**Federation of Korean Trade Unions (FKTU):** FKTU Bldg, 35 Yoido-dong, Yongdeungpo-ku, Seoul; tel. (2) 782-3884; telex 29682; fax (2) 784-6396; f. 1961; Pres. Park Chong-Kun; affiliated to ICFTU; 20 unions are affiliated with a membership of 1,803,408:

    **Federation of Foreign Organization Employees' Unions:** 175-9, Huam-dong, Yongsan-ku, Seoul; tel. (2) 757-2355; f. 1961; Pres. Kim Kyu-Ho; 31,552 mems.

REPUBLIC OF KOREA (SOUTH KOREA) — Directory

**Federation of Insurance Workers' Unions:** 69-32, Chungchong-no, 2-ka, Sodaemun-ku, Seoul; tel. (2) 312-3933; f. 1988; Pres. Kwon Se-Won; 18,789 mems.
**Federation of Korean Automobile Workers' Unions:** 678-27 Yuksam-dong, Kangnam-ku, Seoul; tel. (2) 554-0890; f. 1963; Pres. Han Hyo-Chae; 101,533 mems.
**Federation of Korean Chemical Workers' Unions:** Seoul; tel. (2) 738-2441; f. 1961; Pres. Kim Yoo-Kon; 192,365 mems.
**Federation of Korean Metalworkers' Unions:** 1570-2 Shinrim-dong, Kwanak-ku, Seoul; tel. (2) 864-2901; fax (2) 864-0457; f. 1961; Pres. Park In-Sang; 394,254 mems.
**Federation of Korean Mine Workers' Unions:** 78 Changsin-dong, Chongno-ku, Seoul; tel. (2) 763-3157; f. 1961; Pres. Kim Dong-Chul; 27,160 mems.
**Federation of Korean Printing Workers' Unions:** Seoul; tel. (2) 780-7969; f. 1961; Pres. Hwang Tae-Soo; 25,075 mems.
**Federation of Korean Seafarers' Unions:** Room 203, Koryo Bldg, 44-16, Dowha-dong, Mapo-ku, Seoul 121-040; tel. (2) 718-4541; telex 23362; fax (2) 701-7991; f. 1961; Pres. Cho Chun-Bok; 85,321 mems.
**Federation of Korean Telecommunications Workers' Unions:** 10th Floor, Central Telephone Office Bldg, 21, 1-ka, Chungmu-no, Chung-ku, Seoul; tel. (2) 756-1502; f. 1961; Pres. Kang Suk-Joo; 54,330 mems.
**Federation of Korean Textile Workers' Unions:** 382-31 Hapjung-dong, Mapo-ku, Seoul; tel. (2) 337-3111; fax (2) 335-1810; f. 1961; Pres. Song Soo-Il; 119,591 mems.
**Federation of Rubber Industry Workers' Unions:** Seoul; tel. (2) 780-2194; f. 1988; Pres. Kim Man-Ho; 61,639 mems.
**Federation of Taxi Drivers' Unions:** 217 Sokchon-dong, Songpa-ku, Seoul; tel. (2) 416-8325; f. 1988; Pres. Lee Kwang-Nam; 117,567 mems.
**Korea Communications Workers' Union:** 18, 1-ka, Chungmu-no, Chung-ku, Seoul 100-011; tel. (2) 771-6201; fax (2) 771-6203; f. 1958; Pres. Lee Jong-Sik; 24,961 mems.
**Korean Federation of Bank & Financial Workers' Unions:** 88 Da-dong, Chung-ku, Seoul; tel. (2) 756-2389; f. 1961; Pres. Lee Nam-Soon; 142,799 mems.
**Korean Federation of Port & Transport Workers' Unions:** Bauksan Bldg, 19, Dongga-dong, Yongsan-ku, Seoul; tel. (2) 727-4741; f. 1980; Pres. Kim Joon-Sang; 39,721 mems.
**Korean Monopoly Workers' Union:** 17-22, Namdaemun-no, 4-ka, Chung-ku, Seoul; tel. (2) 779-3341; f. 1960; Pres. Chong Jong-Ku; 12,405 mems.
**Korean National Electrical Workers' Union:** 167 Samsung-dong, Kangnam-ku, Seoul; tel. (2) 757-1567; f. 1961; Pres. Choi Tae-Il; 28,543 mems.
**Korean National United Workers' Federation:** 39-1 Dongja-dong, Yongsan-ku, Seoul; tel. (2) 757-1567; f. 1961; Pres. Kim Rak-Ki; 231,171 mems.
**Korean Railway Workers' Union:** 40, 3-ka, Hangang-no, Yongsan-ku, Seoul; tel. (2) 795-6174; f. 1947; Pres. Kim Jong-Wook; 31,041 mems.
**Korean Tourist Industry Workers' Federation:** 749, 5-ka, Namdaemun-no, Chung-ku, Seoul; tel. (2) 779-1297; f. 1970; Pres. Chong Yoong-Ki; 27,273 mems.

### Trade Fair

**Korea Exhibition Center:** 159 Samsung-dong, Kangnam-ku, Seoul 135-731; tel. (2) 551-0114; telex 24594; fax (2) 555-7414; f. 1986; Pres. Rim Kwang-Won.

## Transport

### RAILWAYS

**Korean National Railroad:** 122, 2-ka, Pongnae-dong, Chung-ku, Seoul; tel. (2) 392-1322; fax (2) 313-7105; f. 1963; operates all railways under the supervision of the Ministry of Construction and Transportation; total track length of 6,559 km (1994); Admin. Kin In-Ho.
**Seoul Metropolitan Subway Corpn:** 447-7 Bangbae-dong, Socho-ku, Seoul; tel. (2) 582-8923; telex 25172; fax (2) 583-9522; f. 1981; length of 116.5 km (102 stations, 4 lines); Pres. Han Jin-Hee.

### ROADS

In 1993 there were 61,96 km of roads, of which 84.7% were paved. A network of motorways (1,602 km in 1993) links all the principal towns, the most important being the 428-km Seoul–Pusan motorway.
**Korea Highway Corporation:** 293-1 Geumto-dong, Seongnam-shi, Gyeonggido; tel. 234-8141; telex 32212; f. 1969; responsible for construction, maintenance and management of toll roads; Pres. Yun Tae-Kyun.

### SHIPPING

In 1993 South Korea's merchant fleet (2,085 vessels) had a total displacement of 7.0m. grt. Major ports include Pusan, Inchon, Donghae, Masan, Yeosu, Gunsan, Mokpo, Pohang, Ulsan, Cheju and Kwangyang.
**Korea Maritime and Port Authority:** 112-2 Inui-dong, Chongno-ku, Seoul 110; tel. (2) 744-4030; telex 26528; f. 1976; operates under the Ministry of Construction and Transportation; supervises all aspects of shipping and port-related affairs; Admin. Ahn Kong-Hyuk.
**Korea Shipowners' Association:** 10th Floor, Sejong Bldg, 100 Dangju-dong, Chongno-ku, Seoul 110-017; tel. (2) 739-1551; telex 24187; fax (2) 739-1558; f. 1960; 33 shipping co mems; Chair. Cho Sang-Wook.
**Korea Shipping Association:** 3 Yangpyong 2-dong, 6-ka, Yongdeungpo-ku, Seoul; tel. (2) 675-2711; fax (2) 675-2714.

### Principal Companies

**Cho Yang Shipping Co Ltd:** Chongam Bldg, 85-3, Seosomun-dong, Chung-ku, CPOB 1163, Seoul; tel. (2) 771-4300; telex 24281; fax (2) 756-8245; f. 1961; Korea–Japan, Korea–Australia, Far East–Europe and Mediterranean liner services and world-wide tramping; Pres. Park Jae-Ik.
**Doo Yang Line Co Ltd:** Doo Yang Bldg, 170-7, Samsong-dong, Kangnam-ku, Seoul 100; tel. (2) 550-1700; telex 24691; fax (2) 564-9301; f. 1984; world-wide tramping; Pres. Cho Sang-Wook.
**Han Jin Shipping:** Marine Center Bldg, 7th Floor, 51 Sogong-dong, Chung-ku, Seoul; tel. (2) 728-5114; telex 23360; fax (2) 753-2442; f. 1977; Far East–North America and Asia feeder services; Pres. Lee Keun-Soo.
**Hyundai Merchant Marine Co Ltd:** Mukyo Hyundai Bldg, 92 Mukyo-dong, Chung-ku, Seoul 100; tel. (2) 311-5114; telex 24402; fax (2) 775-8788; f. 1976; Pres. Kim Joo-Yong.
**Korea Line Corporation:** Daeil Bldg, 43 Insa-dong, Chongno-ku, Seoul 100-290; tel. (2) 735-0371; telex 27296; fax (2) 739-1610; f. 1968; world-wide transportation service and shipping agency service in Korea; Pres. Song Ki-Won.
**Pan Ocean Shipping Co Ltd:** 51-1 Namchang-dong, Chung-ku, CPOB 3051, Seoul; tel. (2) 316-5530; telex 23511; fax (2) 754-8492; f. 1966; transportation of passenger cars and trucks, chemical and petroleum products, dry bulk cargo; Pres. Kim Kwang-Tae.

### CIVIL AVIATION

There are international airports at Kimpo (Seoul), Pusan and Cheju, and another is planned for the Seoul area.
**Asiana Airlines Inc:** Suite 194-15, 1-ka, Hoehyun-dong, Chung-ku, Seoul; tel. (2) 758-8114; telex 27321; fax (2) 757-9745; f. 1988; serves five major domestic cities and operates flights to four destinations in Japan (Tokyo, Nagoya, Fukuoka and Sendai); Pres. and Chair. (vacant).
**Korean Air:** 41-3 Seosomun-dong, Chung-ku, CPOB 864, Seoul; tel. (2) 755-2221; telex 27526; fax (2) 751-7799; f. 1962 by the Govt, privately owned since 1969; until 1989 the sole scheduled airline in the Republic of Korea; serves 11 major domestic cities and operates regional services and routes to the Americas, Europe, China and the Middle East; Pres. Cho Yang-Ho.

## Tourism

South Korea's mountain scenery and historic sites are the principal attractions for tourists. Cheju Island, about 100 km off the southern coast, is a popular resort. In 1993 there were 3,331,226 visitors to South Korea, of whom about 45% came from Japan. Receipts from tourism in 1992 amounted to US $3,200m.
**Korea National Tourism Corporation:** KNTC Bldg, 10 Ta-dong, Chung-ku, CPOB 903, Seoul 100; tel. (2) 757-6030; telex 28555; fax (2) 757-5997; f. 1962 as Korea Tourist Service; Pres. Cho Young-Kil.
**Korea Tourist Association:** Saman Bldg, 945, Taechi-dong, Kangnam-ku, Seoul; tel. (2) 556-2356; telex 25151; fax (2) 556-3818; f. 1963; Pres. Chang Chul-Hi.

# KUWAIT

## Introductory Survey

### Location, Climate, Language, Religion, Flag, Capital

The State of Kuwait lies at the north-west extreme of the Persian (Arabian) Gulf, bordered to the north-west by Iraq and to the south by Saudi Arabia. The State comprises a mainland region and nine small islands. The largest Kuwaiti island is Bubiyan, although the most populous is Failaka. Immediately to the south of Kuwait, along the Gulf, lies a Neutral (Partitioned) Zone of 5,700 sq km, which is shared between Kuwait and Saudi Arabia. Much of the country is arid desert, and the climate is generally hot and humid. Temperatures in July and August often exceed 45°C (113°F), and in the winter months temperatures frequently exceed 20°C (68°F)—although there is often frost at night. Average annual rainfall is only 111 mm (4.3 ins). The official language is Arabic, which is spoken by virtually all Kuwaiti nationals (estimated, on the basis of a later definition, to have comprised 28.6% of Kuwait's population at mid-1990) and by many of the non-Kuwaiti residents of the country. English is also used in commercial circles. Apart from other Arabs, the non-Kuwaitis are mainly Iranians, Indians and Pakistanis. At the 1975 census 95.0% of the population were Muslims (of whom about 70% are now thought to belong to the Sunni sect), while 4.5% were Christians, Hindus or adherents of other faiths. The national flag (proportions 2 by 1) has three equal horizontal stripes, of green, white and red, with a superimposed black trapezoid at the hoist. The capital is Kuwait City.

### Recent History

Kuwait became part of Turkey's Ottoman Empire in the 16th century. During the later years of Ottoman rule, Kuwait became a semi-autonomous Arab monarchy, with local administration controlled by a Sheikh of the Sabah family, which is still the ruling dynasty. In 1899, fearing an extension of Turkish control, the ruler of Kuwait made a treaty with the United Kingdom, accepting British protection while surrendering control over external relations. In 1918, at the end of the First World War, the Ottoman Empire was dissolved, and nominal Turkish suzerainty over Kuwait ended. The sheikhdom remained a self-governing British protectorate until 1961.

During the reign of Sheikh Ahmad (1921–50), work began on the development of Kuwait's petroleum industry, the basis of the country's modern prosperity. Petroleum was first discovered in Kuwait in 1938, but exploration was interrupted by the Second World War. After 1945 drilling resumed on a large scale, and extensive deposits of petroleum were found. Supported by revenues from petroleum exploitation, Kuwait City developed from a small dhow port into a thriving modern commercial centre. Sheikh Ahmad was succeeded in 1950 by his cousin, Sheikh Abdullah as-Salim as-Sabah, who used petroleum revenues substantially for the welfare of the nation. A programme of public works and educational development, inaugurated in 1951, transformed Kuwait into a well-equipped country, with a comprehensive system of welfare services.

Kuwait became fully independent on 19 June 1961, when the United Kingdom and Kuwait terminated the 1899 treaty by mutual agreement. The ruler took the title of Amir and assumed full executive power. Kuwait was admitted to the League of Arab States (Arab League—see p. 182) in July 1961, despite opposition from Iraq, which claimed that Kuwait was historically part of Iraqi territory. Kuwait's first election took place in December 1961, when voters chose 20 members of a Constituent Assembly (the other members being appointed cabinet ministers). The Assembly drafted a new Constitution, which was adopted in December 1962. In accordance with the provisions of the new document, a 50-member National Assembly, the Majlis al-Umma, was elected, under a limited franchise (see Government, below), in January 1963. In the absence of formal political parties (which remain illegal), candidates contested the poll as independents, although some known opponents of the Government were elected. In the same month the Amir appointed his brother, Sheikh Sabah as-Salem as-Sabah (the heir apparent), to be Prime Minister.

Iraq renounced its claim to Kuwait in October, and the two countries established diplomatic relations.

In January 1965, as a result of conflict between the paternalistic ruling family and the democratically-inclined Majlis, the powers of the Council of Ministers were strengthened. The Amir died in November 1965, and Sheikh Sabah succeeded to the throne. He was replaced as Prime Minister by his cousin, Sheikh Jaber al-Ahmad as-Sabah, who was named heir apparent in May 1966. The Neutral Zone (also known as the Partitioned Zone) between Kuwait and Saudi Arabia was formally divided between the two countries in 1969: revenues from petroleum production in the area are shared equally.

During the 1960s, as Kuwait's output of petroleum expanded, the country became increasingly wealthy. The Kuwaiti leadership's policies resulted in extensive redistribution of income, through public expenditure and a land compensation scheme, but there was some popular discontent concerning corruption and official manipulation of the media and the Majlis. In response, a more representative legislature was elected in January 1971 (again under a free, but limited, franchise), and an extensive ministerial reshuffle took place. A further general election took place in January 1975, but in August of the following year the Amir dissolved the Majlis, on the grounds that it was acting against the best interests of the State. The Amir died on 31 December 1977 and was succeeded by Crown Prince Jaber. In January 1978 the new Amir appointed Sheikh Saad al-Abdullah as-Salim as-Sabah to be his heir apparent. The new Crown Prince, hitherto Minister of Defence and the Interior, became Prime Minister in the following month. In accordance with an Amiri decree of August 1980, a new Majlis was elected in February 1981, although only about 3% of the population, out of the 6% who were eligible, registered to vote.

The collapse of the Souk al-Manakh, Kuwait's unofficial stock exchange, in September 1982 caused a prolonged financial crisis, and led to the resignations of the Ministers of Finance (in 1983) and of Justice (in 1985). The Majlis subsequently opposed several government measures, including proposed price increases for public services, educational reforms, and legislation to restrict the press, and in June 1986 the legislature questioned the competence of certain ministers. In July the Council of Ministers submitted its resignation to the Amir, who then dissolved the Majlis and suspended some articles of the Constitution, declaring his intention to rule by decree. The Crown Prince was immediately reappointed to the post of Prime Minister. An Amiri decree accorded the new Council of Ministers greater powers of censorship, including the right to suspend the publication of newspapers for a maximum period of two years.

During 1989 three Kuwaiti business executives circulated a petition asking the Government to restore the Majlis, and a committee of 45 prominent Kuwaiti citizens was formed to co-ordinate the campaign for democracy. In late November the Amir refused to accept the petition, which had been signed by more than 20,000 Kuwaiti citizens. In December the Government warned against the increasing politicization of the *diwaniyat* (traditional, private weekly meetings held by Kuwaiti citizens). In January 1990 police dispersed two pro-democracy demonstrations. Later in the month, however, the Government agreed to relax press censorship. In February 28 leading pro-democracy campaigners, all former members of the Majlis, met the Prime Minister to discuss the restoration of the legislature, and in March the Prime Minister declared that he would welcome the restoration of an elected assembly. On 10 June 62% of those who were eligible to vote participated in a general election for 50 members of a new 'provisional' National Council; a further 25 members were appointed by the Amir. The election was boycotted by pro-democracy activists, who demanded the full restoration of the Majlis.

Of all the Gulf states, Kuwait has been most vulnerable to regional disruption. Immediately after independence, British troops (soon replaced by an Arab League force) were dispatched to support the country against the territorial claim by

Iraq. The force remained until 1963, and relations between Kuwait and Iraq remained stable until 1973, when Iraqi troops occupied a Kuwaiti outpost on their joint border. Substantial donations to Iraq subsequently ensured Kuwait's territorial security. Kuwait was active in its support of the Arab cause after the Arab–Israeli war of June 1967, giving financial assistance to 'front-line' Arab countries and major Palestinian organizations. In the Arab–Israeli war of October 1973 Kuwaiti troops, stationed along the Suez Canal, were involved in military engagements. During 1973 and 1974 Kuwait played a leading role in controlling petroleum supplies as an economic weapon against pro-Israeli Western countries. Kuwait condemned the 1978 Camp David agreements between Egypt and Israel, and diplomatic relations between Kuwait and Egypt were severed between April 1979 and November 1987.

In May 1981 Kuwait joined five other Gulf states in establishing the Co-operation Council for the Arab States of the Gulf, generally known as the Gulf Co-operation Council (GCC, see p. 130).

After the outbreak of war between Iran and Iraq in September 1980, the Kuwaiti Government gave substantial aid to Iraq. Iran bombed Kuwaiti oil installations in September 1981, and in May 1984 Iran was blamed for attacks on Kuwaiti shipping in the Persian (Arabian) Gulf. Between 1983 and 1987 militant pro-Iranian groups claimed responsibility for a number of bomb attacks within Kuwait, including explosions at the main petroleum refinery. In June 1987 six Kuwaiti Shi'a Muslims, supporters of Iran, were sentenced to death for their part in sabotaging oil installations and plotting against the Government. In 1985–86 almost 27,000 expatriates, many of whom were Iranian, were deported. (In August 1987 the Government initiated a five-year plan to reduce the number of expatriates in the Kuwaiti work-force.)

In 1986 and 1987 a number of merchant ships sailing to or from Kuwait were attacked in the Gulf by Iranian forces. During 1987, in an attempt to deter Iranian attacks in the Gulf, Kuwait re-registered most of its fleet of oil tankers under foreign flags. The USA and the United Kingdom provided naval escorts for the ships registered under their respective flags, and Kuwait received assistance from Saudi Arabia, the USA and several European countries in clearing mines. Following the August 1988 cease-fire in the Iran–Iraq War, Kuwait resumed diplomatic relations with Iran in October of that year.

In September 1989 16 Kuwaiti Shi'ites, accused of planning terrorist acts during the Muslim pilgrimage to Mecca in July, were executed in Saudi Arabia. Ten of those executed were of Iranian origin. In Kuwait fears of Iranian influence over the Shi'ite minority (which then constituted about 30% of the Kuwaiti population) led to the introduction of stringent measures aimed at curbing subversion. (However, it was recognized that the established Shi'ite families that formed part of the merchant aristocracy in Kuwait had a financial commitment to the country that was likely to ensure their loyalty.) In June 1989 22 people who had been accused of plotting to overthrow the ruling family were sentenced to prison terms of up to 15 years.

In July 1990 President Saddam Hussain of Iraq implicitly criticized Kuwait (among other states) for disregarding the petroleum production quotas that had been stipulated by OPEC. He further accused Kuwait of having 'stolen' Iraqi petroleum reserves from a well in disputed territory. The Iraqi Minister of Foreign Affairs, Tareq Aziz, declared to the Secretary-General of the Arab League that Kuwait should not only cancel Iraq's war debt, but also compensate it for losses of revenue incurred during the war with Iran, and as a result of Kuwait's overproduction of petroleum—to which he attributed a decline in international prices for that commodity. In addition, Iraq alleged that Kuwait had violated its borders by establishing military posts and drilling oil wells on Iraqi territory. Later in the same month, despite regional mediation efforts, Iraq began to deploy armed forces on the Kuwait–Iraq border, immediately before a scheduled OPEC conference in Geneva, Switzerland. At the meeting the minimum reference price for sales of crude petroleum by OPEC countries was increased, as Iraq had demanded. On 31 July representatives of Kuwait and Iraq conferred in Jeddah, Saudi Arabia, in an attempt to resolve the dispute over Iraq's territorial claims and demands for financial compensation. Kuwait was reportedly prepared to contribute one-half of the compensation demanded, but would not concede any territory, and the negotiations collapsed.

On 2 August 1990 some 100,000 Iraqi troops invaded Kuwait (Kuwait's total military strength was about 20,000), in response to an invitation, the Iraqi Government claimed, by insurgents who had overthrown the Kuwaiti Government. The Amir and other members of the Government escaped to Saudi Arabia, where they established a 'Government-in-exile', and many other Kuwaiti citizens also fled the country. The UN Security Council immediately adopted a series of resolutions, of which the first (Resolution 660) condemned the invasion, demanded the immediate and unconditional withdrawal of Iraqi forces from Kuwait, and appealed for a negotiated settlement of the conflict. Resolution 661 then imposed a trade embargo on Iraq and Kuwait. Immediately after the invasion, the USA and the members of the European Community (EC, now European Union—EU—see p. 143) 'froze' all Kuwait's overseas assets to prevent an Iraqi-imposed regime from transferring them back to Kuwait.

On 4 August 1990 Iraq declared that a provisional, nine-member Kuwaiti Government had been formed, allegedly composed of Iraqi-sponsored Kuwaiti dissidents. Three days later, at the request of the Saudi Arabian Government, President Bush of the USA ordered the deployment of US troops and aircraft in Saudi Arabia, with the stated aim of securing that country's borders with Kuwait in the event of an Iraqi attack. The British and other European Governments, together with some members of the Arab League, agreed to provide military support for the US forces. On 8 August the Iraqi Government announced the formal annexation of Kuwait, and ordered the closure of foreign diplomatic missions there. On 28 August most of Kuwait was officially declared to be the 19th Governorate of Iraq, while a northern strip was incorporated into the Basra Governorate. During August many thousands of Arab and Asian expatriates had fled from Iraq and Kuwait into Jordan. Most European and American expatriates, however, were detained as hostages in Kuwait and Iraq, although foreign women and children were permitted to leave those countries at the end of August; by early December it was stated that all hostages had been released. Meanwhile, diplomatic efforts to achieve a peaceful solution to the crisis, undertaken by the UN and by numerous individual Governments, were unsuccessful.

Following the Iraqi invasion, there were reports that Iraqi forces were plundering Kuwait City and searching for Kuwaiti resistance fighters and Westerners in hiding. Iraqi troops reportedly burned houses and tortured or summarily executed persons suspected of opposing the occupation forces. Many installations were dismantled and transported to Iraq. By early October an estimated 430,000 Iraqi troops had been deployed in southern Iraq and Kuwait. There was evidence of attempts to alter the demographic character of Kuwait, by settling Iraqis and Palestinians in the country and by forcing Kuwaiti citizens to assume Iraqi citizenship. By October the population was estimated to have decreased from approximately 2m. (prior to the invasion by Iraq) to about 700,000, of whom Kuwaitis constituted an estimated 300,000 and Palestinians 200,000, while the remainder comprised other Arab expatriate workers and Asians.

In early October 1990 a conference took place in Jeddah, Saudi Arabia, at which the exiled Crown Prince Saad addressed approximately 1,000 distinguished Kuwaiti officials and citizens, including 'opposition' members of the dissolved Majlis. He agreed to establish committees to advise the Government on political, social and financial matters, and pledged to restore the country's Constitution and legislature and to organize free elections after the liberation of Kuwait.

In late November 1990 the UN Security Council adopted a resolution (678) which authorized the multinational force stationed in Saudi Arabia and the Gulf region to use 'all necessary means' to liberate Kuwait. It was implied that if, by 15 January 1991, Iraq had not begun to implement the terms of 10 resolutions that had so far been adopted relating to the invasion of Kuwait, military force would be employed to effect an Iraqi withdrawal. In the intervening period various unsuccessful diplomatic attempts were made, by the UN Secretary-General and the Governments of the USA, the USSR, EC members and Arab states, to avert a military confrontation. On 17 January the US-led multinational force launched its military campaign to liberate Kuwait with an intensive aerial bombardment of Iraq, and on 24 February (following the failure of a Soviet peace plan, deemed unacceptable by the USA and its allies, since it stipulated that a cease-fire should be declared before Iraq began to withdraw from Kuwait) US-led ground forces entered Kuwait, encountering relatively little effective Iraqi opposition. Within three days the Iraqi Government had agreed to accept all the resolutions of the UN Security Council concerning Kuwait, and on 28 February the US Government announced a suspension of military operations. In March the UN Security Council adopted a resolution that dictated the terms to Iraq for a permanent cease-fire, including the release of all allied prisoners of war and of Kuwaitis who had been detained as potential hostages. A further resolution required Iraq to repeal all laws and decrees concerning the annexation of Kuwait. Iraq promptly announced its compliance with both resolutions. Another resolution, adopted in April, provided for the establishment of a demilitarized zone, supervised by the UN Iraq-Kuwait Observer Mission (UNIKOM, see p. 49), between the two countries.

In mid-January 1991 members of the Kuwaiti Government-in-exile and opposition delegates attended a conference in Jeddah. Some Islamic and Arab nationalist groups demanded an immediate restoration of parliamentary and press freedom, while more radical opposition members demanded the resignation of the as-Sabah family from all key positions in the Government and the establishment of a constitutional monarchy. In February, however, the Government-in-exile excluded the possibility of early elections upon the liberation of Kuwait, maintaining that the need to rebuild and repopulate the country took precedence over that for political reform. The opposition was further frustrated by the stated aim of the UN resolutions to reinstate Kuwait's 'legitimate' Government that had been in office prior to the invasion by Iraq.

Immediately after the liberation of Kuwait the Amir decreed that martial law would be enforced in Kuwait for a period of three months (martial law did, in fact, remain in force until the end of June). In March 1991 the Amir announced the formation of a committee to administer martial law and to supervise the state's security. The committee's domestic objectives were to identify people who had collaborated with Iraq, to prevent the formation of 'vigilante' groups, and to identify civilians brought by the Iraqi authorities to settle in the emirate. On 4 March the Prime Minister and other members of the exiled Government returned to Kuwait; they were followed by the Amir 10 days later. The country was unstable, both because of the severe structural and environmental damage caused by the war, and of the resentment felt by the Kuwaiti people against many members of the Palestinian community who were suspected of having collaborated with Iraq (it was alleged by international human rights groups that Palestinians suspected of collaboration were being tortured by the Kuwaiti security forces). The Government also declared its intention to reduce the number of foreign workers in Kuwait. On 20 March the Council of Ministers resigned, apparently in response to public discontent at the Government's failure to restore supplies of electricity, water and food. The Crown Prince formed a new administration one month later. Although several specialists were appointed to strategic posts within the Government (most notably to the finance, planning and oil portfolios), other important positions (including the foreign affairs, interior and defence ministries) were allocated to members of the as-Sabah family.

In April 1991 the Amir announced that elections to restore the Majlis al-Umma would take place in 1992. (The elections were subsequently scheduled for October of that year.) Meanwhile, unauthorized opposition groups continued to demand an end to the nepotism of the ruling family, together with the legalization of political parties, the restoration of the freedom of the press and the establishment of an independent judiciary.

In May 1991 it was revealed that some 900 people were under investigation in connection with crimes committed during the Iraqi occupation; of these, about 200 had been accused of collaboration with the Iraqis. Those in detention included eight Kuwaiti army officers who were said to have been members of the short-lived provisional Government that had been formed in Kuwait following the Iraqi invasion. Shortly afterwards the human rights organization, Amnesty International, expressed concern that trials were being conducted in Kuwait without the provision of adequate defence counsel, and alleged that, in some cases, torture had been used to extract confessions from defendants. Crown Prince Saad admitted that the abduction and torture of non-Kuwaiti nationals was taking place, and promised that such abuses would be investigated. In June, at the time of the ending of martial law, the 29 death sentences that had hitherto been imposed on convicted collaborators were commuted to custodial terms. It was stated that outstanding trials in connection with the occupation were to be referred to civilian courts, and in August a tribunal was established to replace the martial law courts. The tribunal guaranteed defendants the right to greater legal protection as well as a right of appeal, and it was announced that persons being held in detention had to be brought to trial within a period of six months.

In August 1991 it was reported that Kuwaiti coastguards had repelled an attempt by Iraqi troops to land on Bubiyan Island, described as Iraq's most serious breach of the cease-fire agreement with Kuwait. However, a subsequent UNIKOM report on the incident implied that the Kuwaiti authorities had exaggerated certain details of the attempted landing in order to demonstrate to the USA and the United Kingdom that Iraq presented a continuing threat to Kuwait's security. It was revealed that the Iraqi Government had offered financial incentives for its forces to be allowed to land on the island to retrieve ammunition and other military equipment, left behind earlier in the year by retreating Iraqi troops.

In May 1991 it was announced that a US military presence would remain in Kuwait until September, by which time, it was envisaged, regional defence arrangements would have been completed. However, attempts to establish a force comprising troops from the six GCC states, in co-operation with contingents from Egypt and Syria, made little progress, and in August the US Government announced that it would maintain 1,500 troops in Kuwait for several more months (while reiterating that it would not agree to Kuwaiti suggestions that a permanent US force be stationed in Kuwait). In September the Kuwaiti and US Governments signed a 10-year agreement on military co-operation. The agreement permitted the storage of US supplies and equipment in Kuwait, and provided for the conduct of joint military training and exercises. In November the ministers responsible for foreign affairs in the six GCC states met their Egyptian and Syrian counterparts in Cairo, Egypt, to discuss the proposed formation of a joint peace-keeping force. At the meeting the Gulf representatives were hesitant about forming such an alliance with Egypt and Syria, and proposed, instead, the eventual formation of a Gulf-Arab force that would deploy troops only in cases of extreme necessity. In February 1992 Kuwait signed a defence accord with the United Kingdom, encompassing training, joint military exercises and the supply of military equipment. In August a similar agreement was concluded with the Government of France.

In December 1991 the leaders of the GCC states meeting in Kuwait (for the first time since the country's liberation), discussed regional security issues. In addition, proposals for increased economic co-operation, and for the establishment of a US $10,000m. development fund to assist those Arab states that had supported Kuwait at the time of the Gulf crisis and whose economies had been most severely affected by the disruption in the region, were provisionally approved.

In July 1991 it was estimated that the number of Kuwaiti nationals residing in the country had been reduced from more than 800,000 to about 600,000 since August 1990. The Palestinian population of Kuwait, which had totalled an estimated 400,000 prior to the Iraqi invasion, was estimated to have declined to 150,000. (By early 1992 the number of Palestinians remaining in Kuwait was said to be less than 50,000.) Many Palestinians leaving Kuwait had been subject to reprisals by Kuwaitis who suspected them of having collaborated during the occupation. International criticism of its failure to protect human rights prompted the Kuwaiti Government, in the second half of 1991, to take measures to prevent clandestine deportations of alleged collaborators and to permit international supervision of the expulsion of foreign nationals. It was widely believed that Kuwait had made efforts to curb its abuses of human rights in an attempt to obtain international support for its efforts to secure the release of Kuwaiti nationals (estimated at more than 600 in late 1994) who were being detained in Iraq. In late 1992 a government estimate suggested that, of a total population of more than 1.35m., some 45% were Kuwaiti nationals, while the number of non-Kuwaiti workers in the emirate had decreased by about 30%. By mid-1994, however, it was estimated that Kuwaiti nationals comprised only 38% of the 1.62m. inhabitants.

In January 1992 the Government ended its policy of censorship of the local press, following the adoption by journalists of a voluntary code of practice. However, censorship continued to be enforced on the state-controlled broadcasting media, and it was believed that the Government would continue to exercise some control over the output of the press.

Elections to the new Majlis, on 5 October 1992, were contested by some 280 candidates, many of whom (although nominally independent) were affiliated to one of several quasi-political organizations. As at previous elections, the franchise was restricted, with only about 81,400 men being eligible to vote, and small groups of women staged well-ordered protests against their exclusion from the political process. (Prior to the election, Crown Prince Saad had indicated that he would not be opposed to an eventual extension of the franchise.) Anti-Government candidates, notably those representing Islamic groups, were unexpectedly successful, securing 31 of the Assembly's 50 seats, and several of those elected had been members of the legislature dissolved in 1986. The Prime Minister submitted his Government's resignation, and in mid-October named a new administration which included six members of the Majlis. Prominent among these was Ali Ahmad al-Baghli, the new Minister of Oil, who was a known critic of the previous Government's economic policies; members of the Majlis were also accorded responsibility for, *inter alia*, education, Islamic affairs and justice. None the less, the ruling family retained control of the strategic foreign affairs, interior and defence portfolios.

The new Majlis quickly demonstrated a tendency to challenge the Government, voting, in December 1992, to establish a commission of inquiry into the circumstances surrounding the 1990 invasion. In January 1993 legislation was enacted whereby parliament would have automatic access to the financial accounts of all state-owned companies and investment organizations, and that sought to impose stricter penalties on persons convicted of the abuse of public funds. Demands for greater parliamentary scrutiny of the State's investments were, in large part, linked to recent revelations of the mismanagement of funds by the London-based Kuwait Investment Office (KIO), responsible for much of Kuwait's overseas investment portfolio, and also to emerging evidence of financial misconduct at the state-owned Kuwait Oil Tanker Co (KOTC). In March the Majlis abolished a stringent secrecy law, asserting that it could have been used to conceal official malpractice. Parliament also challenged the Government's defence programme during 1993, questioning the policy of investing petroleum revenues in arms procurement. A report into the KIO's business dealings, published in July by the finance and economy committee of the Majlis, was severely critical of the Government's management of overseas investments and of its failure to ensure the accountability of officials. (In all, the Kuwaiti authorities were known to be seeking to bring to justice 22 former executives of the KIO, including Sheikh Fahd Muhammad as-Sabah, who had been Chairman of the organization at the time of the Iraqi invasion, in connection with the alleged misappropriation of state funds.) In January 1994 the Majlis abrogated an earlier decree demanding that, in case of legal proceedings, government ministers be tried by a special court. Later in the month Sheikh Ali al-Khalifah as-Sabah, a former Minister of Finance and of Oil, and Abd al-Fatr al-Bader, a former Chairman of the company, were among five people who were brought to trial in connection with alleged embezzlement from the KOTC; hearings were subsequently adjourned, and legal proceedings continued into 1995.

In April 1995 the report of a Majlis inquiry into state purchases of weapons alleged widespread waste and corruption in defence expenditure, and urged the Government to instigate judicial proceedings against those said to be involved. In the following month the report of the parliamentary commission of inquiry into the circumstances surrounding the 1990 invasion revealed profound negligence on the part of government and military officials, who had apparently ignored warnings of an imminent invasion. The report was critical of the flight of members of the royal family and the Council of Ministers immediately after the invasion, effectively depriving the country of political leadership and military organization.

In April 1994 a reorganization of the Council of Ministers was announced. The ruling family retained control of the foreign affairs, interior and defence portfolios, although new ministers responsible for oil, health and for commerce and industry were appointed. In June the Majlis approved legislation that aimed to extend the franchise of naturalized Kuwaitis to vote.

Friction between Kuwait and Iraq in the aftermath of the Gulf War was exacerbated by the demarcation of the two countries' joint border. The UN commission that was given responsibility for delineating the frontier formalized the land border as it had been defined by British administrators in 1932 (which was officially agreed by Kuwait and Iraq in 1963). The boundary, the validity of which was now rejected by Iraq, was set about 570 m north of its pre-war position and divided the Iraqi port of Umm Qasr, with the effect that Iraq retained the town and much of the harbour while Kuwait was awarded hinterland which included an abandoned Iraqi naval base. In addition, the new border placed several Iraqi oil wells in the Rumaila field under Kuwaiti control. In August 1992, as tension in the Gulf region increased (owing to Iraq's refusal to submit to inspections of weapons facilities by the UN, as required by the 1991 cease-fire agreement), the USA deployed missiles on Kuwaiti territory, and some 7,500 US armed forces personnel participated in military exercises, which were conducted earlier than had originally been planned, in Kuwait. In late August 1992 the UN Security Council adopted a resolution guaranteeing the newly-delineated frontier. In the days immediately preceding the designated entry into force of the new border (15 January 1993) Iraqi forces made a series of incursions into Kuwaiti territory, from where they notably recovered armaments which had been left behind by retreating troops at the conclusion of the Gulf War (and which had been intended for destruction by, or under the supervision of, UNIKOM). In response, the USA led air attacks on Iraq, and more than 1,000 US troops were dispatched to Kuwait. Two days after the frontier entered into force, Iraq began to dismantle its police posts on what was now adjudged to be Kuwaiti territory. None the less, the USA proceeded with the deployment of further missiles in Kuwait, and in early February the Security Council approved, in principle, the dispatch to Kuwait of an armed force to patrol the border.

The formal delineation of the Kuwait–Iraq border was completed in March 1993, when the UN commission defined the maritime border between the two countries (along the median line of the Khawr Abd Allah waterway). In May Kuwait announced that construction was to begin of a trench, to be protected by mines and a wall of sand, along the entire length of the land border. Allegations made by Kuwait of Iraqi violations of the border, and of attempts to obstruct work on the trench, intensified during the second half of 1993, and there were sporadic reports of exchanges of fire in the border region. In November it was reported that between 250 and 350 Iraqi civilians had crossed the border in the Umm Qasr region, protesting against the digging of the trench on land hitherto farmed by Iraqis, while Iraqi troops were said to have attacked a border post. The incursions coincided with the commencement of the evacuation, under UN supervision, of Iraqi nationals and property from the Kuwaiti side of the border in the region of Umm Qasr and Abdali, and at the end of the month a 775-strong armed UNIKOM reinforcement was deployed in northern Kuwait, with authorization (under specific circumstances) to use its weapons to assist the unarmed force already in the demilitarized zone.

In April 1993 the Kuwaiti authorities announced the arrest of 14 people (11 Iraqis and three Kuwaitis) who were accused of complicity in an Iraqi plot to assassinate former US President George Bush while he was visiting Kuwait earlier in the month. Hearings by the State Security Court began in June, but were subsequently adjourned on several occasions. In June 1994 six defendants (five Iraqis and one Kuwaiti) were sentenced to death for their part in the conspiracy; seven others received custodial sentences of between six months and 12 years, and one was acquitted. Following an appeal, in March 1995 four of the death sentences were commuted, the lengthiest of the prison sentences was reduced, and one conviction was overturned. Kuwait refuted reports that the detainees had been subjected to torture, and rejected assertions made by Amnesty International that the accused had been denied adequate access to defence counsel. In June 1993 the State Security Court was reported to have issued death sentences against 17 people who had been found guilty of collaborating with Iraq in 1990–91; convicted *in absentia* was the leader of the provisional Government installed by Iraq in August 1990. In February 1994 Amnesty International again alleged serious violations of human rights in Kuwait, asserting that at least 120 alleged collaborators had been convicted following trials that failed to satisfy international minimum standards.

Although there was no apparent progress in attempts to create a wider Gulf-Arab defence force, ministers responsible for defence in the GCC countries, meeting in Abu Dhabi, United Arab Emirates, in November 1993, agreed on the need to strengthen and extend the capabilities of the Peninsula Shield Force (the GCC's Saudi-based rapid deployment force). Later in the month Kuwait signed a defence co-operation agreement with Russia, and in late December the two countries participated in joint naval exercises in the Gulf.

In early October 1994 (as the UN programme of monitoring Iraq's weapons capabilities was due to commence) Iraq deployed some 70,000 troops and 700 tanks in the south of the country, near the border with Kuwait, in what was widely interpreted as an attempt to bring about the easing of UN economic sanctions. In response, Kuwait immediately mobilized its army reserves, and dispatched some 20,000 troops to the border region. The USA committed land, naval and air forces (numbering almost 40,000 by mid-October) to the region; France and the United Kingdom deployed naval vessels, and some 1,200 British troops were dispatched to support the US military presence. On 10 October Iraq announced its intention to withdraw its troops northwards. Shortly afterwards an emergency meeting of the GCC Ministerial Council issued a communiqué demanding the withdrawal of Iraqi forces from the border area, the implementation by Iraq of all relevant resolutions of the UN Security Council, and the release of all Kuwaiti nationals detained in Iraq. In mid-October, following a diplomatic initiative by Russia, Iraq announced its willingness to recognize Kuwait's sovereignty and borders, on condition that the UN ease sanctions against Iraq after a period of six months. However, the UN Security Council adopted a resolution (949) requiring Iraq's unconditional recognition of Kuwait's sovereignty and borders and restricting the movement of Iraqi troops in the border area. Later in the month the USA (in a statement also signed by the United Kingdom and several GCC states) indicated that 'appropriate action' would be taken if Iraq deployed its forces south of latitude 32°N (the boundary of the southern air-exclusion zone in force since August 1992), and in late October 1994, during a visit to Kuwait, the US President, Bill Clinton, reiterated his country's commitment to the defence of Kuwait. On 10 November Iraq officially recognized Kuwait's sovereignty, territorial integrity and political independence, as well as its UN-defined borders. Although the declaration was welcomed by the Kuwaiti authorities, they continued to demand the release of all Kuwaiti citizens detained in Iraq and appealed for international sanctions against Iraq to be maintained until that country had complied with all pertinent UN resolutions.

During 1994 Kuwait continued to pursue defence co-operation agreements, and to participate in joint manoeuvres, with its allies. In late 1994, as part of a series of bilateral agreements on technological and military matters, Kuwait contracted to purchase military equipment valued at some US $750m. from Russia. By the end of the year most of the US and British troops that had been stationed in the Gulf region in October had been withdrawn. Pre-positioned heavy equipment and aircraft remained in the region, together with the multinational forces present prior to the October incident (see Defence, below).

In late May 1994 the governing body of the UN commission responsible for considering claims for compensation arising from the 1990–91 Gulf crisis approved the first disbursements (to 670 families or individuals in 16 countries), totalling US $2.7m.; further claims, the total value of which was estimated at some $150m., were under consideration.

### Government

Under the 1962 Constitution, executive power is vested in the Amir, the Head of State (who is chosen by and from members of the ruling family), and is exercised through the Council of Ministers. The Amir appoints the Prime Minister and, on the latter's recommendation, other ministers. Legislative power is vested in the unicameral Majlis al-Umma (National Assembly), with 50 elected members who serve for four years (subject to dissolution). Only literate adult male Kuwaiti citizens, excluding members of the armed forces, may vote. Those eligible to vote comprised only 15% of the adult population in 1992; however, legislation was approved by the Majlis in 1994 to enfranchise sons of naturalized Kuwaitis. The country is divided administratively into five governorates.

### Defence

In June 1994 Kuwait's active armed forces numbered an estimated 16,600: an army of 10,000, an air force of 2,500, a navy of 2,500, 1,000 central staff and 600 Amiri Guard. There was also a 5,000-strong paramilitary national guard. There is a two-year period of compulsory military service, although for university students it lasts one year. Excluding expenditure on arms procurement, the 1993/94 budget allocated KD 478.8m. to the Ministry of Defence (representing 12.4% of total estimated expenditure in the general budget). UNIKOM members (unarmed troops and observers) in Kuwait numbered 1,147 at June 1994.

### Economic Affairs

In 1993, according to estimates by the World Bank, Kuwait's gross national product (GNP), measured at average 1991–93 prices, was US $34,120m., equivalent to $23,350 per head. During 1985–93, it was estimated, GNP per head increased, in real terms, at an average annual rate of 0.8%. Over the same period the population decreased by an annual average of 2.9%, with the decline in population after 1990 more than offsetting population growth in previous years. At mid-1994, according to official estimates, Kuwaiti nationals accounted for about 38% of the total population. Kuwait's gross domestic product (GDP) increased, in real terms, by an annual average of 0.7% in 1980–89.

Agriculture (including hunting, forestry and fishing) contributed less than 1% of GDP in 1993. About 1.3% of the labour force were employed in the sector in 1988. The principal crops are melons, tomatoes, cucumbers and onions. Livestock, poultry and fishing are also important. During 1980–89 agricultural GDP increased by an estimated annual average of 18.8%.

Industry (including mining, manufacturing, construction and power) provided 57.1% of GDP in 1992, and employed 25.5% of the labour force in 1988. During 1980–89 industrial GDP increased by an annual average of 1.0%.

Mining and quarrying contributed 42.2% of GDP in 1992, although the sector engaged less than 1% of the labour force in 1988. The production of petroleum and its derivatives is the most important industry in Kuwait, providing 94.9% of export revenue in 1993. At the beginning of 1994 the country's proven recoverable reserves of petroleum were 96,500m. barrels, representing about 9.6% of world reserves. By mid-1994 Kuwait's petroleum production capacity was officially said to be 2.4m. barrels per day (b/d), considerably in excess of production levels before the 1990–91 crisis (1.5m. b/d) and of its OPEC production quota, agreed in late September 1993, of 2m. b/d. Refined petroleum products accounted for an estimated 71% of total petroleum exports in 1988. There are significant reserves of natural gas (1,500,000m. cu m at the beginning of 1992) in association with the petroleum deposits.

Manufacturing provided 14.4% of GDP in 1992, and employed 7.6% of the labour force in 1988. Petroleum refineries accounted for 70.7% of manufacturing activity, measured by gross value of output, in 1988. Of the other branches of manufacturing, the most important are non-metallic mineral products and food products. During 1980–89 manufacturing GDP declined by an annual average of 0.2%.

Services employed 73.2% of the labour force in 1988 and provided 42.6% of GDP in 1992. Kuwait's second most important source of revenue is investment abroad (the total value of which was estimated to be between US $35,000m. and $40,000m. in 1993), both in petroleum-related ventures and in other industries, chiefly in the USA, western Europe and Japan; many such investments are held by the Reserve Fund for Future Generations (RFFG), to which 10% of petroleum revenues must, by law, be added each year, and which is intended to provide an income in the future, after hydrocarbon resources have been exhausted. Prior to the Iraqi invasion the value of the RFFG was believed to have been some $65,000m.

Electrical energy is generated by using Kuwait's own petroleum and natural gas resources, and imports of gas.

In 1993 Kuwait recorded a trade surplus of US $4,373m., and there was a surplus of $6,344m. on the current account of the balance of payments. In 1993 the principal source of imports (14.9%) was the USA; other important suppliers in that year were Japan, France, Germany, the United Kingdom and Italy. The principal market for exports in 1987 was Japan (16.8%); other important purchasers in that year were Italy and the Netherlands. The principal exports are petroleum and petroleum products. The principal imports are machinery and transport equipment (42.5% of the total in 1993), basic manufactures (especially iron and steel and textiles) and other manufactured goods, and food and live animals.

A budget deficit of KD 1,400m. (not including spending on defence procurement, debt repayments or investment income) was recorded for the financial year ending 30 June 1994. Budget proposals for 1995/96 projected a deficit of some KD 1,088m., compared with an anticipated deficit of KD 1,490m. in 1994/95. The average annual rate of inflation was 1.6% in 1985–89, but by mid-1993 the rate had reached 8%. About 1.5% of the labour force were unemployed at the time of the 1985 census. Prior to the Iraqi invasion of Kuwait, the country had a high proportion of immigrant workers (85.7% of employed persons at the 1985 census are classified as non-Kuwaitis).

Kuwait is a member of the Gulf Co-operation Council (GCC, see p. 130) and the Council of Arab Economic Unity (see p. 133), both of which attempt to encourage regional economic co-operation and development; it also belongs to the Organization of Arab Petroleum Exporting Countries (OAPEC, see p. 207) and the Organization of the Petroleum Exporting Countries (OPEC, see p. 210). Kuwait is a major aid donor, disbursing loans to developing countries through the Kuwait Fund for Arab Economic Development (KFAED) and the Arab Fund for Economic and Social Development (AFESD, see p. 237).

The immediate costs of the military operation to liberate Kuwait (about US $22,000m.) and of rebuilding the country's infrastructure (some $20,000m.) were, in large part, met by liquidating about one-half of Kuwait's overseas investment portfolio (including about one-half of the RFFG) and by external borrowing totalling $5,500m. By late 1993, none the less, estimates of Kuwait's accumulated losses arising from the Iraqi annexation had reached some $170,000m. In 1994 the Government announced that it intended to eliminate the budget deficit by 2000, through the introduction of ambitious measures to reduce expenditure and augment revenue. Proposals included an increase in customs fees, the imposition of a direct tax on commercial and industrial profits, the reform of the welfare system, and the gradual withdrawal of subsidies on public services. The Government indicated that opportunities for foreign participation in Kuwaiti industry would be permitted, and in that year foreign equity interests of up to 40% were allowed in the banking sector. The privatization programme, due for completion by 1998, was also expanded; sectors scheduled for privatization in 1995 included telecommunications, power and water. In addition, proposals were anticipated to ease the burden of expenditure on public-sector wages—more than 95% of employed workers are in public service, while there is a shortage of labour in industries previously dominated by foreign workers expelled after the 1990 Iraqi invasion. Efforts during 1992–93 to rationalize the banking sector and finally to offset the effects of the 1982 failure of the Souk al-Manakh unofficial stock exchange were undermined by revelations of the mismanagement of Kuwait's overseas investments, together with allegations of fraud in the state-owned Kuwaiti Oil Tanker Co. Economic growth in 1994 was primarily attributable to a recovery in the non-petroleum sector. However, Kuwait's contribution to the cost of the international military response to Iraq's troop movements in October 1994 increased spending obligations for 1994/95 by an estimated $500m., increasing demands on government finances in the same financial year in which repayments of post-war debt principal were due to commence. Earlier in 1994 the Government had embarked on a wide-ranging programme of weapons procurement and military training, the cost of which was estimated at $11,700m. over a 10-year period.

**Social Welfare**

With the help of large government revenues from petroleum, Kuwait has developed a comprehensive system of social benefits and welfare. A Public Assistance Law covers all Kuwaiti nationals. Medical treatment was provided free of charge until 1984, when it was announced that 40% of the cost of medical treatment was to be borne by the patient. In 1983 Kuwait had 69 hospital establishments, and in 1988 there were 6,139 hospital beds and 3,256 physicians (17.1 per 10,000 inhabitants) working in the country. Of total planned expenditure by the central Government in the financial year 1993/94, an estimated KD 273.6m. (7.1%) was for public health, and KD 48.0m. (1.2%) was for social affairs and labour.

**Education**

Education is compulsory for eight years between the ages of six and 14. Although private schools exist, state education is free, and is graded into pre-primary (for children between four and six years of age), primary (for children aged six to 10), intermediate (10 to 14) and secondary (14 to 18). In 1989 enrolment at primary schools was equivalent to 93% of children in the relevant age-group, while secondary enrolment was equivalent to 85% of the appropriate age-group. In 1992/93 there were 122,930 pupils enrolled at primary schools, and 177,675 at intermediate and secondary schools. There is a teacher-training college, a technical college, and a university (which had some 20,000 enrolled students in the early 1990s). In addition, more than 2,000 Kuwaiti students receive education abroad. Education was allocated an estimated KD 320.6m. in the 1993/94 budget proposals, representing 8.3% of total expenditure.

In 1990, according to estimates by UNESCO, the average rate of adult illiteracy was 27.0% (males 22.9%; females 33.3%).

**Public Holidays**

**1995:** 1 January (New Year's Day), 1 February* (Ramadan begins), 25 February (Kuwaiti National Day), 3 March* (Id al-Fitr, end of Ramadan), 10 May* (Id al-Adha, Feast of the Sacrifice), 31 May* (Islamic New Year), 9 August* (Birth of the Prophet), 20 December* (Leilat al-Meiraj, Ascension of the Prophet).

**1996:** 1 January (New Year's Day), 22 January* (Ramadan begins), 21 February* (Id al-Fitr, end of Ramadan), 25 February (Kuwaiti National Day), 29 April* (Id al-Adha, Feast of the Sacrifice), 19 May* (Islamic New Year), 28 July* (Birth of the Prophet), 8 December* (Leilat al-Meiraj, Ascension of the Prophet).

* These holidays are dependent on the Islamic lunar calendar and may vary by one or two days from the dates given.

**Weights and Measures**

The metric system is in force.

KUWAIT

# Statistical Survey

Source (unless otherwise stated): Central Statistical Office, Ministry of Planning, POB 26188, 13122 Safat, Kuwait City; tel. 2454968; telex 22468; fax 2430464.

Note: Unless otherwise indicated, data refer to the State of Kuwait as constituted at 1 August 1990, prior to the Iraqi invasion and annexation of the territory and its subsequent liberation. Furthermore, no account has been taken of the increase in the area of Kuwait as a result of the adjustment to the border with Iraq that came into force on 15 January 1993.

## Area and Population

### AREA, POPULATION AND DENSITY

| | |
|---|---:|
| Area (sq km) | 17,818* |
| Population (census results)† | |
| 21 April 1980 | 1,357,952 |
| 20–21 April 1985 | |
| Males | 965,297 |
| Females | 732,004 |
| Total | 1,697,301 |
| Population (official estimates at mid-year)† | |
| 1992 | 1,422,199 |
| 1993 | 1,460,853 |
| 1994 | 1,620,086‡ |
| Density (per sq km) at mid-1994 | 90.9 |

* 6,880 sq miles.
† Figures include Kuwaiti nationals abroad. Based on the definition of citizenship in use in 1992, the total population at the 1985 census included 474,200 Kuwaiti nationals (240,068 males; 234,132 females). On the same basis, the estimated population at mid-1990 comprised 589,221 Kuwaitis (295,039 males; 294,182 females) and 1,473,054 non-Kuwaitis (839,675 males; 633,379 females). At mid-1993 an estimated 66.7% of the population were non-Kuwaitis.
‡ According to a report on population and labour by the Ministry of Planning, the estimated population at mid-1994 was 1,752,622 (males 1,083,126; females 669,496). Of the total, 669,630 (38.2%) were Kuwaiti nationals, and 1,082,992 (61.8%) were non-Kuwaitis.

### GOVERNORATES (population at 1985 census)

| Governorate | Area (sq km)* | Population | Capital |
|---|---:|---:|---|
| Capital | 199.8 | 241,356 | Kuwait City |
| Hawalli | } 368.4 { | 493,127 | Hawalli |
| Farwaniya | | 420,020 | Farwaniya |
| Al-Jahra | 11,230.2 | 241,285 | Jahra |
| Al-Ahmadi | 5,119.6 | 301,513 | Ahmadi City |

* Excluding the islands of Bubiyan and Warba (combined area 900 sq km).

### PRINCIPAL TOWNS (population at 1985 census)

| | | | | |
|---|---:|---|---:|---|
| Kuwait City (capital) | 44,335 | South Kheetan | 69,256 |
| Salmiya | 153,369 | Farwaniya | 68,701 |
| Hawalli | 145,126 | Sabahiya | 60,787 |
| Jaleeb al-Shuyukh | 114,771 | Fahaheel | 50,081 |
| Jahra | 111,222 | Abraq Kheetan | 45,120 |

### BIRTHS, MARRIAGES AND DEATHS

| | Registered live births | | Registered marriages | | Registered deaths | |
|---|---:|---:|---:|---:|---:|---:|
| | Number | Rate (per 1,000) | Number | Rate (per 1,000) | Number | Rate (per 1,000) |
| 1986* | 53,845 | 30.1 | 9,426 | 5.3 | 4,390 | 2.5 |
| 1987* | 51,983 | 27.7 | 9,591 | 5.1 | 4,287 | 2.3 |
| 1988 | 53,080 | 27.9 | 10,005 | 5.3 | 4,581 | 2.4 |
| 1989 | 52,858 | 26.7 | 10,108 | 5.1 | 4,628 | 2.3 |
| 1990† | 12,358 | n.a. | n.a. | n.a. | 1,177 | n.a. |
| 1991 | 17,207 | n.a. | 7,244‡ | n.a. | 3,372 | n.a. |
| 1992 | 34,817 | 24.5 | 10,803 | 7.6 | 3,369 | 2.4 |
| 1993 | 37,379 | 25.6 | n.a. | n.a. | n.a. | n.a. |

* Rates are based on unrevised estimates of mid-year population.
† Figures relate only to the first quarter of year.
‡ Provisional.

**Expectation of life** (UN estimates, years at birth, 1985–90): 74.5 (males 72.6; females 76.3) (Source: UN, *World Population Prospects: The 1992 Revision*).

### ECONOMICALLY ACTIVE POPULATION
(sample survey, persons aged 15 years and over, March 1988)*

| | Males | Females | Total |
|---|---:|---:|---:|
| Agriculture, hunting and fishing | 9,122 | 132 | 9,254 |
| Mining and quarrying | 6,329 | 201 | 6,530 |
| Manufacturing | 53,231 | 1,433 | 54,664 |
| Electricity, gas and water | 7,527 | 86 | 7,613 |
| Construction | 112,926 | 1,608 | 114,534 |
| Trade and restaurants | 79,278 | 4,057 | 83,335 |
| Transport, storage and communications | 35,119 | 2,653 | 37,772 |
| Finance, insurance, real estate and business services | 17,780 | 3,782 | 21,562 |
| Other services (including defence) | 224,328 | 159,256 | 383,584 |
| **Total** | 545,640 | 173,208 | 718,848 |
| Kuwaitis | 81,270 | 31,689 | 112,959 |
| Non-Kuwaitis | 464,370 | 141,519 | 605,889 |

* Figures exclude persons seeking work for the first time, totalling 11,067 (males 6,930; females 4,137), but include other unemployed persons.

## Agriculture

### PRINCIPAL CROPS (FAO estimates, '000 metric tons)

| | 1991 | 1992 | 1993 |
|---|---:|---:|---:|
| Tomatoes | 16 | 30 | 35 |
| Cucumbers and gherkins | 5 | 15 | 17 |
| Onions (dry) | 5 | 15 | 16 |
| Other vegetables | 7 | 14 | 17 |
| Melons | 2 | 4 | 4 |
| Dates | 1 | 1 | 1 |

Source: FAO, *Production Yearbook*.

# KUWAIT

**LIVESTOCK** (FAO estimates, '000 head, year ending September)

|  | 1991 | 1992 | 1993 |
|---|---|---|---|
| Cattle | 1 | 5 | 12 |
| Camels | n.a. | 1 | 1 |
| Sheep | 50 | 100 | 150 |
| Goats | 3 | 10 | 15 |

Poultry (FAO estimates, million): 1 in 1991; 3 in 1992; 10 in 1993.
Source: FAO, *Production Yearbook*.

**LIVESTOCK PRODUCTS** (FAO estimates, '000 metric tons)

|  | 1991 | 1992 | 1993 |
|---|---|---|---|
| Beef and veal | n.a. | n.a. | 1 |
| Mutton and lamb | 9 | 17 | 25 |
| Poultry meat | 10 | 21 | 37 |
| Cows' milk | 1 | 12 | 14 |
| Goats' milk | n.a. | 1 | 1 |
| Poultry eggs | 0.6 | 2.4 | 4.0 |
| Sheepskins | 3.0 | 6.0 | 8.8 |

Source: FAO, *Production Yearbook*.

## Fishing

('000 metric tons, live weight)

|  | 1991 | 1992 | 1993 |
|---|---|---|---|
| Fishes | 1.2 | 4.2 | 4.8 |
| Shrimps and prawns | 0.8 | 3.5 | 2.3 |
| **Total catch** | 2.0 | 7.7 | 7.1 |

## Mining*

('000 metric tons, unless otherwise indicated)

|  | 1989 | 1990 | 1991 |
|---|---|---|---|
| Crude petroleum | 74,051 | 59,550 | 9,766 |
| Natural gas (petajoules) | 212 | 204 | 19 |
| Salt (refined) | 38 | 30 | n.a. |

* Including an equal share of production with Saudi Arabia from the Neutral/Partitioned Zone.

Source: UN, *Industrial Statistics Yearbook*.

**1992:** Crude petroleum 53.65 million metric tons (Source: UN, *Monthly Bulletin of Statistics*).

## Industry

**SELECTED PRODUCTS** ('000 metric tons, unless otherwise stated)

|  | 1989 | 1990 | 1991 |
|---|---|---|---|
| Wheat flour | 153 | n.a. | n.a. |
| Sulphur (by-product)* | 475 | 300 | 300 |
| Chlorine | 16 | n.a. | n.a. |
| Caustic soda (Sodium hydroxide) | 18 | n.a. | n.a. |
| Nitrogenous fertilizers‡ | 386 | 204 | n.a. |
| Jet fuels§ | 1,510 | 1,110 | 600 |
| Motor spirit (petrol)§ | 2,510 | 1,880 | 900 |
| Naphthas§ | 3,800 | 3,200 | 126 |
| Kerosene§ | 1,890 | 1,700 | 600 |
| Distillate fuel oils§ | 9,900 | 7,300 | 900 |
| Residual fuel oils§ | 14,100 | 12,000 | 2,000 |
| Petroleum bitumen (asphalt)§ | 160 | 110 | 70 |
| Liquefied petroleum gas†§ | 2,710 | 2,410 | 100 |
| Quicklime* | 65 | 50 | 60 |
| Cement | 1,108 | 800 | 299† |
| Electric energy (million kWh)§ | 21,084 | 18,477 | 10,780 |

\* Data from the US Bureau of Mines.
† Provisional or estimated figure(s).
‡ Production in terms of nitrogen.
§ Including an equal share of production with Saudi Arabia from the Neutral/Partitioned Zone.

Source: mainly UN, *Industrial Statistics Yearbook*.

**1992** ('000 metric tons, unless otherwise indicated): Wheat flour 105; Chlorine 11; Caustic soda 12.2; Motor spirit 1,107*; Kerosene and jet fuels 1,545*; Distillate fuel oils 2,835*; Residual fuel oils 9,342*; Electric energy (million kWh) 16,885.
**1993** ('000 metric tons, unless otherwise indicated): Wheat flour 127; Chlorine 9.2; Caustic soda 15.5; Electric energy (million kWh) 20,178.
\* Source: UN, *Monthly Bulletin of Statistics*.

## Finance

**CURRENCY AND EXCHANGE RATES**

**Monetary Units**
1,000 fils = 10 dirhams = 1 Kuwaiti dinar (KD).

**Sterling and Dollar Equivalents** (31 December 1994)
£1 sterling = 469.5 fils;
US $1 = 300.1 fils;
100 Kuwaiti dinars = £212.98 = $333.20.

**Average Exchange Rate** (US $ per KD)
1989   3.4049
1992*  3.4087
1993   3.3147

* Figures for 1990 and 1991 are not available (see below).

Note: During the Iraqi occupation of Kuwait, between August 1990 and February 1991, the Kuwaiti dinar was replaced (at par) by the Iraqi dinar. As a result, Kuwaiti coins and notes were withdrawn from circulation. In March 1991, following the liberation of Kuwait, the Kuwaiti dinar was reintroduced, with the exchange rate set at the same level as on 1 August 1990, namely US $1 = 287.5 fils (KD1 = $3.4782).

**GENERAL BUDGET** (estimates, KD million, year ending 30 June)*

| Revenue | 1991/92 | 1992/93 | 1993/94 |
|---|---|---|---|
| Oil revenues | 495.9 | 2,000.3 | 2,419.8 |
| Taxes on non-oil companies | 2.8 | 5.0 | 8.0 |
| Custom duties and fees | 0.1 | 45.6 | 50.1 |
| Service charges | 134.0 | 146.6 | 202.7 |
|     Electricity and water | 12.6 | 46.9 | 52.3 |
|     Transport and communications | 32.9 | 49.7 | 77.5 |
| **Total revenue** (incl. others) | 647.4 | 2,218.0 | 2,713.0 |

# KUWAIT

*Statistical Survey*

| Expenditure | 1991/92 | 1992/93 | 1993/94 |
|---|---|---|---|
| Ministries and departments | | | |
|   Foreign affairs | 31.0 | 41.8 | 33.9 |
|   Finance | 3,985.8 | 1,632.8 | 1,265.3 |
|   Oil | 3.4 | 9.1 | 35.1 |
|   Defence | 476.3 | 493.0 | 478.8 |
|   Interior | 214.5 | 282.3 | 266.9 |
|   Education | 279.2 | 301.2 | 320.6 |
|   Information | 59.3 | 61.2 | 58.9 |
|   Public health | 207.5 | 241.7 | 273.6 |
|   Social affairs and labour | 78.2 | 87.2 | 48.0 |
|   Electricity and water | 207.1 | 302.5 | 252.7 |
|   Communications | 72.9 | 86.7 | 86.4 |
|   Public works | 56.0 | 130.7 | 107.0 |
| National Guards | 43.8 | 51.8 | 55.8 |
| Complementary credit | n.a. | n.a. | 371.5 |
| **Total expenditure** (incl. others) | 6,115.0 | 3,936.3 | 3,867.8 |

\* Figures exclude investment income.

**1994/95** (estimates, KD million, year ending 30 June): Total revenue 2,537; (of which oil revenues 2,234); Total expenditure 4,303.

### INTERNATIONAL RESERVES (US $ million at 31 December)

| | 1991 | 1992 | 1993 |
|---|---|---|---|
| Gold* | 111.5 | 104.7 | 106.2 |
| IMF special drawing rights | 183.5 | 179.2 | 67.4 |
| Reserve position in IMF | 158.9 | 132.9 | 230.5 |
| Foreign exchange | 3,066.6 | 4,834.8 | 3,916.3 |
| **Total** | 3,520.5 | 5,251.6 | 4,320.3 |

\* National valuation of gold reserves (2,539,000 troy ounces in each year).

Source: IMF, *International Financial Statistics*.

### MONEY SUPPLY (KD million at 31 December)

| | 1991 | 1992 | 1993 |
|---|---|---|---|
| Currency outside banks | 446.0 | 389.7 | 365.7 |
| Demand deposits at commercial banks | 784.0 | 652.6 | 731.6 |
| **Total money** | 1,230.0 | 1,042.3 | 1,097.3 |

Source: IMF, *International Financial Statistics*.

### COST OF LIVING
(Consumer Price Index, Kuwait City; base: 1978 = 100)

| | 1989 | 1990* | 1991† |
|---|---|---|---|
| Food | 128.4 | 144.2 | 158.9 |
| Beverages and tobacco | 177.8 | 201.9 | 226.7 |
| Housing | 169.6 | 172.4 | 175.4 |
| Clothing and footwear | 158.9 | 180.7 | 198.3 |
| Education and medical care | 193.9 | 205.3 | 222.9 |
| **All items** (incl. others) | 151.8 | 166.7 | 181.8 |

\* January to June.    † July to December.

### NATIONAL ACCOUNTS (KD million at current prices)
**Expenditure on the Gross Domestic Product**

| | 1990 | 1991 | 1992 |
|---|---|---|---|
| Government final consumption expenditure | 2,074 | 5,209 | 2,408 |
| Private final consumption expenditure | 2,834 | 2,132 | 2,517 |
| Increase in stocks | −21 | 156 | 130 |
| Gross fixed capital formation | 957 | 1,616 | 2,141 |
| **Total domestic expenditure** | 5,844 | 9,113 | 7,196 |
| Exports of goods and services | 2,382 | 489 | 2,280 |
| *Less* Imports of goods and services | 2,978 | 6,418 | 3,109 |
| **GDP in purchasers' values** | 5,247 | 3,184 | 6,367 |

### Gross Domestic Product by Economic Activity

| | 1990 | 1991 | 1992 |
|---|---|---|---|
| Agriculture, hunting, forestry and fishing | 32 | 8 | 22 |
| Mining and quarrying | 1,978 | 448 | 2,720 |
| Manufacturing | 628 | 226 | 932 |
| Electricity, gas and water* | −38 | −100 | −95 |
| Construction | 109 | 192 | 127 |
| Trade, restaurants and hotels | 402 | 528 | 489 |
| Transport, storage and communications | 198 | 87 | 128 |
| Finance, insurance, real estate and business services | 728 | 628 | 707 |
| Community, social and personal services | 1,251 | 1,245 | 1,422 |
| **Sub-total** | 5,288 | 3,262 | 6,452 |
| Import duties | 35 | 19 | 38 |
| *Less* Imputed bank service charges | 76 | 97 | 123 |
| **Total** | 5,247 | 3,184 | 6,367 |

\* Value added is negative because of the inclusion of expenditure on fuel in the cost of production.

### BALANCE OF PAYMENTS (US $ million)

| | 1991 | 1992 | 1993 |
|---|---|---|---|
| Merchandise exports f.o.b. | 869 | 6,548 | 10,413 |
| Merchandise imports f.o.b. | −4,053 | −6,292 | −6,040 |
| **Trade balance** | −3,184 | 256 | 4,373 |
| Exports of services | 992 | 1,494 | 1,345 |
| Imports of services | −5,090 | −4,590 | −2,157 |
| Other income received | 6,086 | 5,910 | 4,917 |
| Other income paid | −654 | −825 | −775 |
| Private unrequited transfers (net) | −426 | −829 | −1,229 |
| Official unrequited transfers (net) | −23,372 | −1,098 | −129 |
| **Current balance** | −25,648 | 317 | 6,344 |
| Direct investment (net) | −243 | −1,067 | −775 |
| Portfolio investment (net) | −612 | 263 | −46 |
| Other capital (net) | 39,628 | 12,063 | −2,329 |
| Net errors and omissions | −11,849 | −9,723 | −4,679 |
| **Overall balance** | 1,276 | 1,851 | −1,485 |

Source: IMF, *International Financial Statistics*.

# External Trade

**PRINCIPAL COMMODITIES** (distribution by SITC, KD '000)

| Imports c.i.f. | 1991* | 1992 | 1993 |
|---|---|---|---|
| **Food and live animals** | 89,427 | 253,485 | 282,258 |
| Live animals | 13,780 | 35,922 | 40,544 |
| Cereals and cereal preparations | 8,400 | 32,774 | 37,133 |
| Fruit and vegetables | 17,852 | 64,714 | 66,240 |
| **Chemicals** | 35,868 | 107,040 | 132,202 |
| **Basic manufactures** | 108,281 | 364,027 | 396,982 |
| Paper, paperboard and manufactures | 11,974 | 28,765 | 36,513 |
| Textile yarn, fabrics, etc. | 31,238 | 88,580 | 76,775 |
| Non-metallic mineral manufactures | 11,477 | 39,167 | 64,260 |
| Iron and steel | 15,876 | 102,531 | 95,458 |
| **Machinery and transport equipment** | 578,123 | 933,148 | 902,492 |
| Transport equipment | 326,030 | 473,345 | 461,006 |
| **Miscellaneous manufactured articles** | 144,803 | 395,675 | 320,273 |
| Clothing (excl. footwear) | 33,765 | 90,497 | 86,793 |
| Scientific instruments, watches, etc. | 29,066 | 54,607 | 47,731 |
| **Total** (incl. others) | 992,346 | 2,129,238 | 2,123,840 |

\* Figures are for July–December only. Total imports in 1991 were KD 1,353.3 million (Source: IMF, *International Financial Statistics*).

# KUWAIT

*Statistical Survey*

| Exports f.o.b. | 1983 | 1984 | 1985 |
|---|---|---|---|
| **Mineral fuels, lubricants, etc.** | 2,938,207 | 3,256,939 | 2,845,178 |
| Petroleum and petroleum products | 2,837,440 | 3,179,648 | 2,767,692 |
| Crude petroleum | 1,578,171 | 1,920,958 | n.a. |
| Refined petroleum products | 1,259,269 | 1,258,690 | n.a. |
| Gas (natural and manufactured) | 100,752 | 77,287 | 77,486 |
| **Chemicals** | 50,385 | 68,409 | 53,219 |
| **Basic manufactures** | 122,136 | 86,757 | 76,036 |
| **Machinery and transport equipment** | 144,547 | 125,487 | 130,895 |
| Transport equipment | 95,580 | 80,108 | 78,024 |
| **Total** (incl. others) | 3,363,757 | 3,631,470 | 3,185,068 |

**1986** (KD million): Petroleum and petroleum products 1,853.4; Chemicals 47.8; Basic manufactures 56.2; Machinery and transport equipment 90.9; Total (incl. others) 2,105.0.
**1987** (KD million): Petroleum and petroleum products 2,096.7; Chemicals 51.0; Basic manufactures 39.1; Machinery and transport equipment 56.7; Total (incl. others) 2,304.4.
**1988** (KD million): Petroleum and petroleum products 1,908.4; Chemicals 64.7; Basic manufactures 55.7; Machinery and transport equipment 71.5; Total (incl. others) 2,166.2.
**1989** (KD million): Petroleum and petroleum products 3,064.9; Chemicals 83.5; Basic manufactures 63.0; Machinery and transport equipment 84.6; Total (incl. others) 3,378.0.
**1990** (KD million): Petroleum and petroleum products 1,842.0; Chemicals 37.5; Basic manufactures 29.7; Machinery and transport equipment 46.3; Total (incl. others) 2,031.4.
**1991** (KD million): Petroleum and petroleum products 248.6; Machinery and transport equipment 43.8; Total (incl. others) 309.4.
**1992** (KD million): Petroleum and petroleum products 1,824.9; Chemicals 16.6; Basic manufactures 16.7; Machinery and transport equipment 50.6; Total (incl. others) 1,967.5.
**1993** (KD million): Petroleum and petroleum products 3,017.9; Total (incl. others) 3,179.4.

## PRINCIPAL TRADING PARTNERS (KD '000)

| Imports c.i.f. | 1991* | 1992 | 1993 |
|---|---|---|---|
| Australia | 10,537 | 30,376 | 28,826 |
| China, People's Republic | 10,153 | 36,467 | 40,527 |
| France | 25,183 | 108,624 | 234,005 |
| Germany | 90,566 | 196,247 | 167,765 |
| India | 12,945 | 49,293 | 49,026 |
| Italy | 43,423 | 122,940 | 126,673 |
| Japan | 161,183 | 269,494 | 269,128 |
| Korea, Republic | 20,209 | 39,576 | 40,093 |
| Netherlands | 15,839 | 31,892 | 37,791 |
| Saudi Arabia | 53,938 | 93,573 | 104,678 |
| Switzerland | 9,650 | 37,592 | 36,419 |
| Taiwan | 13,026 | 41,440 | 38,027 |
| Turkey | 3,495 | 26,057 | 34,418 |
| United Kingdom | 69,278 | 130,660 | 142,395 |
| USA | 291,383 | 433,486 | 316,288 |
| **Total** (incl. others) | 992,346 | 2,129,238 | 2,123,840 |

* Figures are for July–December only. Total imports in 1991 were KD 1,353.3 million (Source: IMF, *International Financial Statistics*).

| Exports f.o.b. | 1983 | 1984 | 1985 |
|---|---|---|---|
| Australia | 103,390 | 108,027 | 69,294 |
| Brazil | 65,748 | 43,878 | 10 |
| Egypt | 23,997 | 39,607 | 48,376 |
| France | 50,430 | 59,409 | 92,518 |
| Germany, Federal Republic | 74,161 | 45,531 | 22,115 |
| India | 79,007 | 103,983 | 66,892 |
| Iran | 56,502 | 19,629 | 10,320 |
| Iraq | 106,106 | 90,066 | 76,726 |
| Italy | 284,735 | 313,175 | 360,555 |
| Japan | 610,722 | 598,996 | 586,959 |
| Korea, Republic | 192,594 | 135,980 | 138,966 |
| Netherlands | 327,560 | 377,001 | 409,077 |
| Pakistan | 138,472 | 151,368 | 168,119 |
| Philippines | 79,225 | 117,822 | 69,141 |
| Saudi Arabia | 114,814 | 99,754 | 88,395 |
| Singapore | 201,378 | 288,608 | 78,811 |
| Taiwan | 296,908 | 231,331 | 233,893 |
| Turkey | 47,061 | 24,872 | 28,884 |
| United Arab Emirates | 56,833 | 31,347 | 28,543 |
| United Kingdom | 35,207 | 40,309 | 60,737 |
| USA | 58,496 | 92,812 | 60,084 |
| **Total** (incl. others) | 3,363,757 | 3,631,470 | 3,185,068 |

# Transport

**ROAD TRAFFIC** (motor vehicles in use at 31 December)

| | 1989 | 1992*† | 1993† |
|---|---|---|---|
| Passenger cars | 498,388 | 591,565 | 610,163 |
| Buses and coaches | 10,775 | 13,508 | 12,513 |
| Goods vehicles | 99,814 | 113,246 | 112,417 |

* Data for 1990 and 1991 are not available.
† Provisional figures.

## SHIPPING

**Merchant Fleet** (at 30 June)

| | 1991 | 1992 | 1993 |
|---|---|---|---|
| Number of vessels | 197 | 197 | 207 |
| Displacement ('000 grt) | 1,373 | 2,258 | 2,218 |

Source: Lloyd's Register of Shipping.

**International Sea-borne Freight Traffic*** ('000 metric tons)

| | 1988 | 1989 | 1990 |
|---|---|---|---|
| Goods loaded | 61,778 | 69,097 | 51,400 |
| Goods unloaded | 7,123 | 7,015 | 4,522 |

* Including Kuwait's share of traffic in the Neutral/Partitioned Zone.
Source: UN, *Monthly Bulletin of Statistics*.

**Goods unloaded** ('000 metric tons): 746 in 1991 (July–December only); 2,537 in 1992; 4,228 in 1993.

**CIVIL AVIATION** (traffic on scheduled services)

| | 1990 | 1991 | 1992 |
|---|---|---|---|
| Kilometres flown (million) | 18 | 11 | 29 |
| Passengers carried ('000) | 966 | 604 | 1,409 |
| Passenger-km (million) | 2,300 | 1,477 | 3,529 |
| Total ton-km (million) | 360 | 236 | 538 |

Source: UN, *Statistical Yearbook*.

KUWAIT                                                                                    Statistical Survey, Directory

## Communications Media

|  | 1990 | 1991 | 1992 |
|---|---|---|---|
| Radio receivers ('000 in use) | 700 | 715 | 720 |
| Television receivers ('000 in use) | 580 | 590 | 610 |
| Telephones ('000 main lines in use) | 331 | 335 | n.a. |
| Daily newspapers |  |  |  |
| Number | 9 | n.a. | 9 |
| Estimated average circulation ('000 copies) | 450 | n.a. | 480 |

Book production (titles published): 793 in 1988.
Sources: UNESCO, *Statistical Yearbook*; UN, *Statistical Yearbook*.

## Education

(state-controlled schools, 1994/95)

|  | Schools | Teachers | Students |
|---|---|---|---|
| Kindergarten | 138 | 2,461 | 37,264 |
| Primary | 174 | 6,678 | 91,376 |
| Intermediate | 155 | 7,139 | 86,387 |
| Secondary | 107 | 7,620 | 64,077 |
| Religious institutes | 5 | 215 | 1,381 |
| Special training institutes | 29 | 468 | 1,555 |

Private education (1990/91): 35 kindergarten schools (165 teachers, 3,509 students); 51 primary schools (1,204 teachers, 31,222 students); 53 intermediate schools (818 teachers, 19,168 students); 33 secondary schools (606 teachers, 11,508 students).

# Directory

## The Constitution

The principal provisions of the Constitution, promulgated on 16 November 1962, are set out below. On 29 August 1976 the Amir suspended four articles of the Constitution dealing with the National Assembly, the Majlis al-Umma. On 24 August 1980 the Amir issued a decree ordering the establishment of an elected legislature before the end of February 1981. The new Majlis was elected on 23 February 1981, and fresh legislative elections followed on 20 February 1985. The Majlis was dissolved by Amiri decree in July 1986, and some sections of the Constitution, including the stipulation that new elections should be held within two months of dissolving the legislature (see below), were suspended. A new Majlis was elected on 5 October and convened on 20 October 1992.

### SOVEREIGNTY

Kuwait is an independent sovereign Arab State; its sovereignty may not be surrendered, and no part of its territory may be relinquished. Offensive war is prohibited by the Constitution.

Succession as Amir is restricted to heirs of the late MUBARAK AS-SABAH, and an Heir Apparent must be appointed within one year of the accession of a new Amir.

### EXECUTIVE AUTHORITY

Executive power is vested in the Amir, who exercises it through the Council of Ministers. The Amir will appoint the Prime Minister 'after the traditional consultations', and will appoint and dismiss ministers on the recommendation of the Prime Minister. Ministers need not be members of the Majlis al-Umma, although all ministers who are not members of parliament assume membership ex officio in the legislature for the duration of office. The Amir also formulates laws, which shall not be effective unless published in the *Official Gazette*. The Amir establishes public institutions. All decrees issued in these respects shall be conveyed to the Majlis. No law is issued unless it is approved by the Majlis.

### LEGISLATURE

A National Assembly, the Majlis al-Umma, of 50 members will be elected for a four-year term by all natural-born Kuwaiti males over the age of 21 years, except servicemen and police, who may not vote. Candidates for election must possess the franchise, be over 30 years of age and literate. The Majlis will convene for at least eight months in any year, and new elections shall be held within two months of the last dissolution of the outgoing legislature.

Restrictions on the commercial activities of ministers include an injunction forbidding them to sell property to the Government.

The Amir may ask for reconsideration of a bill that has been approved by the Majlis and sent to him for ratification, but the bill would automatically become law if it were subsequently adopted by a two-thirds majority at the next sitting, or by a simple majority at a subsequent sitting. The Amir may declare martial law, but only with the approval of the legislature.

The Majlis may adopt a vote of 'no confidence' in a minister, in which case the minister must resign. Such a vote is not permissible in the case of the Prime Minister, but the legislature may approach the Amir on the matter, and the Amir shall then either dismiss the Prime Minister or dissolve the Majlis.

### CIVIL SERVICE
Entry to the civil service is confined to Kuwaiti citizens.

### PUBLIC LIBERTIES

Kuwaitis are equal before the law in prestige, rights and duties. Individual freedom is guaranteed. No one shall be seized, arrested or exiled except within the rules of law.

No punishment shall be administered except for an act or abstaining from an act considered a crime in accordance with a law applicable at the time of committing it, and no penalty shall be imposed more severe than that which could have been imposed at the time of committing the crime.

Freedom of opinion is guaranteed to everyone, and each has the right to express himself through speech, writing or other means within the limits of the law.

The press is free within the limits of the law, and it should not be suppressed except in accordance with the dictates of law.

Freedom of performing religious rites is protected by the State according to prevailing customs, provided it does not violate the public order and morality.

Trade unions will be permitted and property must be respected. An owner is not banned from managing his property except within the boundaries of law. No property should be taken from anyone, except within the prerogatives of law, unless a just compensation be given.

Houses may not be entered, except in cases provided by law. Every Kuwaiti has freedom of movement and choice of place of residence within the state. This right shall not be controlled except in cases stipulated by law.

Every person has the right to education and freedom to choose his type of work. Freedom to form peaceful societies is guaranteed within the limits of law.

## The Government

### HEAD OF STATE

**Amir of Kuwait:** His Highness Sheikh JABER AL-AHMAD AS-SABAH (acceded 31 December 1977).

### COUNCIL OF MINISTERS
(May 1995)

**Crown Prince and Prime Minister:** Sheikh SAAD AL-ABDULLAH AS-SALIM AS-SABAH.

**First Deputy Prime Minister and Minister of Foreign Affairs:** Sheikh SABAH AL-AHMAD AL-JABER AS-SABAH.

**Second Deputy Prime Minister and Minister of Finance:** NASSER ABDULLAH AR-RODHAN.

**Minister of Defence:** Sheikh AHMAD AL-HAMOUD AL-JABER AS-SABAH.

**Minister of Oil:** Dr ABD AL-MOHSIN MUDAEJ AL- MUDAEJ.

**Minister of the Interior:** Sheikh ALI AS-SABAH AS-SALEM AS-SABAH.

**Minister of Labour and Social Affairs:** AHMAD KHALED AL-KOLAIB.

**Minister of Education and Higher Education:** Dr AHMAD ABDULLAH AR-RAB'I.

**Minister of Public Works and Minister of State for Housing:** HABIB JAWHAR HAYAT.

**Minister of Communications, Electricity and Water:** JASEM MUHAMMAD AL-AOUN.

# KUWAIT

**Minister of Information:** Sheikh SA'UD NASIR SA'UD AS-SABAH.
**Minister of State for Cabinet Affairs and Minister of Planning:** ABD AL-AZIZ AD-DAKHIL.
**Minister of Health:** Dr ABD AR-RAHMAN SALEH AL-MEHILAN.
**Minister of Awqaf (Religious Endowments) and Islamic Affairs:** Dr ALI FAHAD AZ-ZUMAI'.
**Minister of Justice and Administrative Affairs:** MISHARI JASEM AL-ANJARI.
**Minister of Commerce and Industry:** HELAL MISHARI AL-MUTAIRI.

## PROVINCIAL GOVERNORS

**Ahmadi:** MUHAMMAD KHALED AL-HAMAD AS-SABAH.
**Farwaniya:** IBRAHIM JASSEM AL-MUDHAF.
**Hawalli:** DAUD MUSAED AS-SALIH.
**Jahra:** IBRAHIM DUAIJ AL-IBRAHIM AS-SABAH.
**Kuwait:** Sheikh ALI ABDULLAH AS-SALIM AS-SABAH.

## MINISTRIES

**Ministry of Awqaf and Islamic Affairs:** POB 13, 13001 Safat, al-Morkab St, Ministries Complex, Kuwait City; tel. 2466300; telex 44735; fax 2449943.
**Ministry of Commerce and Industry:** POB 2944, 13030 Safat, Kuwait City; tel. 2463600; telex 22682; fax 2424411.
**Ministry of Communications, Electricity and Water:** POB 12, 13001 Safat, Kuwait City; tel. 4896000; telex 22197; fax 4897484.
**Ministry of Defence:** POB 1170, 13012 Safat, Kuwait City; tel. 4848300; telex 22784.
**Ministry of Education:** POB 7, 13001 Safat, Hilali St, Kuwait City; tel. 4836800; telex 23166; fax 2445946.
**Ministry of Finance:** POB 9, 13001 Safat, al-Morkab St, Ministries Complex, Kuwait City; tel. 2468200; telex 22527; fax 2404025.
**Ministry of Foreign Affairs:** POB 3, 13001 Safat, Gulf St, Kuwait City; tel. 2425141; telex 22042.
**Ministry of Health:** POB 5, 13001 Safat, Arabian Gulf St, Kuwait City; tel. 2462900; telex 22729; fax 2458584.
**Ministry of Higher Education:** POB 27130, 13132 Safat, Kuwait City; tel. 2401300; fax 2407335.
**Ministry of State for Housing:** POB 2935, 13030 Safat, Kuwait City; fax 2428801.
**Ministry of Information:** POB 193, 13002 Safat, as-Sour St, Kuwait City; tel. 2415300; telex 46151; fax 2421926.
**Ministry of the Interior:** POB 11, 13001 Safat, Kuwait City; tel. 4818000; telex 22507.
**Ministry of Justice and Administrative Affairs:** POB 6, 13001 Safat, al-Morkab St, Ministries Complex, Kuwait City; tel. 2465600; telex 44660; fax 2466957.
**Ministry of Labour and Social Affairs:** POB 563, 13006 Safat, al-Morkab St, Ministries Complex, Kuwait City; tel. 2464500; telex 30329; fax 2419877.
**Ministry of Oil:** POB 5077, 13051 Safat, Fahd as-Salem St, Kuwait City; tel. 2415201; telex 22363; fax 2417088.
**Ministry of Planning:** POB 21688, 13122 Safat, Kuwait City; tel. 2454968; telex 22468; fax 2430464.
**Ministry of Public Works:** POB 8, 13001 Safat, Kuwait City; tel. 2455777.

## Legislature

**MAJLIS AL-UMMA**
(National Assembly)

**Speaker:** AHMAD ABD AL-AZIZ AS-SAADUN.

Elections to the restored Majlis took place on 5 October 1992, at which candidates who were known to oppose the outgoing Government secured 31 of the legislature's 50 seats.

## Political Organizations

Political parties are not permitted in Kuwait. However, several quasi-political organizations are in existence. Among those that secured representation in the Majlis at the October 1992 elections were:

**Islamic Constitutional Movement:** Sunni Muslim; moderate.
**Kuwait Democratic Forum:** secular; liberal.
**Salafeen:** Sunni Muslim; fundamentalist.
**National Islamic Coalition:** Shi'a Muslim.
**Constitutional Group:** supported by merchants.

## Diplomatic Representation

### EMBASSIES IN KUWAIT

**Afghanistan:** POB 33186, 73452 Rawdah, Block 1, 7 Mishref St, House 17, Kuwait City; tel. 5396916; Chargé d'affaires: TAZAKHAN WIAL.
**Algeria:** POB 578, 13006 Safat, Istiqlal St, Kuwait City; tel. 2519987; telex 44750; Ambassador: MUHAMMAD QADRI.
**Austria:** POB 33259, 73453 Rawdah, Kuwait City; tel. 2552532; telex 23866; Ambassador: Dr FERDINAND MAULTASCHL.
**Bahrain:** POB 196, 13002 Safat, Surra, Block 1, St 1, Villa 24, Kuwait City; tel. 5317351; fax 5330882; Ambassador: ABDUL RAHMAN M. AL-FADHEL.
**Bangladesh:** POB 22344, 13084 Safat, Khaldya, Block 1, St 14, House 3, Kuwait City; tel. 4834078; telex 22484; fax 4831603; Chargé d'affaires: MOHSIN ALI KHAN.
**Belgium:** POB 3280, 13033 Safat, Salmiya, Baghdad St, House 15, Kuwait City; tel. 5722014; telex 22535; fax 5748389; Ambassador: GUIDO SONCK.
**Bhutan:** POB 1510, 13016 Safat, Mishref St, Block 15, St 14, Villa 19, Rd 55, Kuwait City; tel. 5382873; telex 30185; Ambassador: TOBGYE S. DORJI.
**Bolivia:** POB 3115, 13032 Safat, Yarmouk, Area 3, Block 170, Ave 16, House 7, Kuwait City; tel. 5339964; telex 44016; fax 5320046; Ambassador: MIGUEL A. DUERI.
**Brazil:** POB 39761, 73058 Safat, Nuzha, Plot 2, Damascus St, House 12, Kuwait City; tel. 2561029; telex 22398; fax 2562153; Ambassador: ADERBAL COSTA.
**Bulgaria:** POB 12090, 71651 Shamiya, Salwa, Block 10, St 312, Kuwait City; tel. 5643877; telex 22122; fax 5654576; Ambassador: DIMITAR A. DIMITROV.
**Canada:** POB 25281, 13113 Safat, Daiya, Block 4, Al-Motawakell St, Villa 4, Kuwait City; tel. 2563025; telex 23549; fax 2564167; Ambassador: J. CHRISTOPHER POOLE.
**China, People's Republic:** POB 2346, 13024 Safat, Jabriya, Block 12, St 101, Villa 24, Kuwait City; tel. 5333340; fax 5333341; Ambassador: WANG JINGQI.
**Cuba:** POB 26385, 13124 Safat, Bayan, Block 5, St 5, House 16, Kuwait City; tel. 5382024; telex 44703; Ambassador: JORGE L. MANFUGAS LAVIGNE.
**Czech Republic:** POB 1151, 13012 Safat, Nuzha, Block 3, Kassima No. 56, St 34, House 13, Kuwait City; tel. 2548206; telex 22243.
**Egypt:** POB 11252, 35153 Ad-Desmah, Istiqlal St, Kuwait City; tel. 2519955; telex 22610; Ambassador: AMIN NAMMAR.
**Finland:** POB 26699, 13127 Safat, Surra, Block 4, St 1, Villa 8, Kuwait City; tel. 5312890; fax 5324198; Ambassador: PERTTI KAUKONEN.
**France:** POB 1037, 13011 Safat, Mansouriah, Block 1, St 13, Villa 24, Kuwait City; tel. 5312000; telex 22195; Ambassador: CHARLES DE BANCALIS DE MOREL D'ARAGON.
**Gabon:** POB 23956, 13100 Safat, Khaldiya, Block 2, Kuwait City; tel. 4830975; telex 22735.
**Germany:** Plot 1, St 14, Villa 13, Kuwait City; tel. 2520857; fax 2520763; Ambassador: GÜNTER MULACK.
**Greece:** POB 23812, 13099 Safat, Khaldiya, Block 4, St 44, House 4, Kuwait City; tel. 4817101; fax 4817103; Ambassador: STELIOS MALLIKOURTIS.
**Hungary:** POB 23955, 13100 Safat, Shamiya, Block 8, St 84, Villa 6, Kuwait City; tel. 4814080; telex 22662; Ambassador: BALINT GAL.
**India:** POB 1450, 13015 Safat, 34 Istiqlal St, Kuwait City; tel. 2530600; telex 22273; Ambassador: PREM SINGH.
**Indonesia:** POB 21560, 13076 Safat, Keifan, Block 5, ash-Shebani St, Building 21, Kuwait City; tel. 4839927; telex 22752; fax 4819250; Ambassador: ACHMAD HIDAYAT KUSUMANEGARA.
**Iran:** POB 4686, 13047 Safat, 24 Istiqlal St, Kuwait City; tel. 2533220; telex 22223; Ambassador: GHOLAMALI SANATI.
**Italy:** POB 4453, 13045 Safat, Sharq, F. Omar Bin al-Khattab St, al-Mulla Bldgs, Villa 6, Kuwait City; tel. 2445120; telex 22356; Ambassador: Dr LUCIO FORATTINI.
**Japan:** POB 2304, 13024 Safat, Jabriya, Block 9, Plot 496, Kuwait City; tel. 5312870; telex 22196; Ambassador: TSUYOSHI KUROKAWA.
**Jordan:** POB 15314, 35305 Diiyah, Istiqlal St, Embassies Area, Kuwait City; tel. 2533500; telex 30412; Ambassador: NABIL TAWFIQ AT-TAHOUNI.
**Korea, Republic:** POB 4272, 13043 Safat, Nuzha, Block 2, Div. 42, Damascus St, Villa 12, Kuwait City; tel. 2531816; telex 22353; Ambassador: SAE HOON AHN.
**Lebanon:** POB 253, 13003 Safat, 31 Istiqlal St, Kuwait City; tel. 2619765; telex 22330; Ambassador: MUHAMMAD ISA.

# KUWAIT

*Directory*

**Libya:** POB 21460, 13075 Safat, Diiyah, Block 1, Plot 2, ar-Roumy St, Kuwait City; tel. 2520814; telex 22256; Ambassador: (vacant).

**Malaysia:** POB 4105, 13042 Safat, Faiha, Block 7, St 70, Villa 1, Kuwait City; tel. 2546022; telex 22540; Ambassador: ZAINAL ABIDIN BIN ALIAS.

**Morocco:** Kuwait City; tel. 4813912; telex 22074; Ambassador: ABD AL-WAHED BEN MASOUD.

**Netherlands:** POB 21822, 13079 Safat, Jabriya, Block 9, Parcel 40A, Kuwait City; tel. 5312650; telex 22459; Ambassador: JOSEPHUS F. R. M. VELING.

**Niger:** POB 44451, 32059 Hawalli, Salwa, Area 10, Plot 447, Kuwait City; tel. 5652639; telex 23365; Ambassador: ADAMOU ZADA.

**Nigeria:** POB 6432, 32039 Hawalli, Surra, Area 1, St 14, House 25, Kuwait City; tel. 5320794; telex 22864; Ambassador: MUSTAFA SHEIKH SALEH.

**Oman:** POB 21975, 13080 Safat, Udailia, Block 3, Parcel 123, House 25, Kuwait City; tel. 2561962; telex 22057; Ambassador: SALIM BIN ABDULLAH BA'OMAR.

**Pakistan:** POB 988, 13010 Safat, Diiyah, Hamza St, Villa 29, Kuwait City; tel. 2532101; telex 44117; Ambassador: ZAHID SAID KHAN.

**Paraguay:** POB 886, 13009 Safat, Shuwaikh, Kuwait City; tel. 4814462; telex 22071.

**Philippines:** POB 26288, 13123 Safat, Rawdah, Area 3, St 34, Villa 24, Kuwait City; tel. 2524398; telex 22434; Ambassador: MAUYAG TAMANO.

**Poland:** POB 5066, 13051 Safat, Rawdah, Block 4, 3rd Ring Rd, Villa 13, Kuwait City; tel. 2510355; telex 50080; fax 2524760; Ambassador: JAN NATKANSKI.

**Qatar:** POB 1825, 13019 Safat, Diiyah, Istiqlal St, Kuwait City; tel. 2513599; telex 22038; Ambassador: AHMAD G. AR-RUMAIHI.

**Romania:** POB 11149, Dasmah, 35152 Kifan, Zone 4, Mouna St, House 34, Kuwait City; tel. 843419; telex 22148; Ambassador: GHEORGHE SERBANESCU.

**Russia:** POB 1765, 13018 Safat, Ad-Da'yia, Embassies Campus, Block 17, Kuwait City; tel. 2560427; Ambassador: PYOTR STEGNY.

**Saudi Arabia:** POB 20498, 13065 Safat, Arabian Gulf St, Kuwait City; tel. 2531155; telex 23458; Ambassador: Sheikh ABDULLAH ABDU-AZIZ AS-SUDAIRY.

**Senegal:** POB 23892, 13099 Safat, Rawdah, Parcel 3, St 35, House 9, Kuwait City; tel. 2542044; telex 22580; Ambassador: ABDOU LAHAD MBACKE.

**Somalia:** POB 22766, 13088 Safat, Diiyah, Block 1, ar-Roumi St, Bldg 41, Kuwait City; tel. 2555567; telex 23280; Ambassador: MUHAMMAD S. M. MALINGUR.

**Spain:** POB 22207, 13083 Safat, Surra, Block 3, St 14, Villa 19, Kuwait City; tel. 5325827; telex 22341; fax 5325826; Ambassador: CÉSAR ALBA Y FUSTER.

**Sri Lanka:** POB 16296, 35853 Qadisiah, Keifan, Plot 6, Al-Andalus St, House 31, Kuwait City; tel. 4844862; telex 46564; Ambassador: LATIF SHARIFDIN.

**Sudan:** POB 1076, 13011 Safat, Rawdah, Block 3, Abu Hayan St 26, Kuwait City; tel. 2519299; telex 22528; Ambassador: MUHAMMAD EL-AMIN ABDULLAH.

**Sweden:** POB 21448, 13075 Safat, Kuwait City; tel. 2523588; fax 2572157; Ambassador: TOMMY ARWITZ.

**Switzerland:** POB 23954, 13100 Safat, Qortuba, Area 2, St 1, House 122, Kuwait City; tel. 5340175; telex 22672; fax 5340176; Ambassador: DANIEL VON MURALT.

**Syria:** POB 25600, 13115 Safat, Rawdah, Plot 4, St 43, Villa 5, Kuwait City; tel. 2531164; telex 22270; Ambassador: Dr ISA DARWISH.

**Thailand:** POB 66647, 43757 Bayan, Surra, Area 3, Block 49, Ali bin Abi-Taleb St, Kuwait City; tel. 5317530; telex 44339; fax 5317532; Ambassador: MAITRI CHULADUL.

**Tunisia:** POB 5976, 13060 Safat, Faiha, Plot 9, St 91, Villa 10F, Kuwait City; tel. 2542144; telex 22518; Ambassador: MUHAMMAD AL-HABIB KAABASHI.

**Turkey:** POB 20627, 13067 Safat, Block 16, Plot 10, Istiqlal St, Kuwait City; tel. 2531785; telex 44806; fax 2560653; Ambassador: MEHMET NURI EZEN.

**United Arab Emirates:** POB 1828, 13019 Safat, Plot 70, Istiqlal St, Kuwait City; tel. 2518381; telex 22529; Ambassador: YOUSUF A. AS-SIRKAL.

**United Kingdom:** POB 2, 13001 Safat, Arabian Gulf St, Kuwait City; tel. 2403334; telex 44614; fax 2407395; Ambassador: WILLIAM H. FULLERTON.

**USA:** POB 77, 13001 Safat, Arabian Gulf St, Kuwait City; tel. 2424151; Ambassador: RYAN C. CROCKER.

**Venezuela:** POB 24440, 13105 Safat, Surra, Parcel 2, 11 Ali bin Abi-Taleb St, Kuwait City; tel. 5334578; telex 22782; Ambassador: RAFAEL OSUNA LOZADA.

**Yemen:** Abdullah as-Salam area, near school help, Ar-Riyad St, Kuwait City.

**Yugoslavia:** POB 20511, 13066 Safat, Shuwaikh 'B', al-Mansour St, Villa 15, Kuwait City; tel. 4813140; telex 46107; Ambassador: Dr HASAN DERVISBEGOVIĆ.

**Zaire:** POB 3998, 13040 Safat, Rawdah, Parcel 3, St 34, Villa 24, Kuwait City; tel. 2543688; telex 22460.

## Judicial System

### SPECIAL JUDICIARY

**Constitutional Court:** Comprises five judges. Interprets the provisions of the Constitution; considers disputes regarding the constitutionality of legislation, decrees and rules; has jurisdiction in challenges relating to the election of members, or eligibility for election, to the Majlis al-Umma.

### ORDINARY JUDICIARY

**Court of Cassation:** Comprises five judges. Is competent to consider the legality of verdicts of the Court of Appeal and State Security Court. Chief Justice: MUHAMMAD YOUSUF AR-RIFA'I.

**Court of Appeal:** Comprises three judges. Considers verdicts of the Court of First Instance. Chief Justice: RASHED AL-HAMMAD.

**Court of First Instance:** Comprises the following divisions: Civil and Commercial (one judge), Personal Status Affairs (one judge), Lease (three judges), Labour (one judge), Crime (three judges), Administrative Disputes (three judges), Appeal (three judges), Challenged Misdemeanours (three judges). Chief Justice: MUHAMMAD AS-SAKHOBY.

**State Security Court:** Comprises three judges and one or more divisions. Considers specified crimes against the State. Pres. SALAH AL-FAHD.

**Summary Courts:** Each governorate has a Summary Court, comprising one or more divisions. The courts have jurisdiction in the following areas: Civil and Commercial, Urgent Cases, Lease, Misdemeanours. The verdict in each case is delivered by one judge.

There is also a **Traffic Court**, with one presiding judge.

**Attorney-General:** MUHAMMAD ABD AL-HAIH AL-BANNAIY.

**Advocate-General:** HAMED AL-UTHMAN.

## Religion

### ISLAM

The Kuwaiti inhabitants are mainly Muslims of the Sunni and Shi'a sects. The Shi'ites comprise about 30% of the total.

### CHRISTIANITY

#### The Roman Catholic Church

*Latin Rite*

For ecclesiastical purposes, Kuwait forms an Apostolic Vicariate. At 31 December 1992 there were an estimated 80,000 adherents in the country.

**Vicar Apostolic:** Mgr FRANCIS ADEODATUS MICALLEF (Titular Bishop of Tinisa in Proconsulari), Bishop's House, POB 266, 13003 Safat, Kuwait City; tel. 2434637; fax 2409981.

*Melkite Rite*

The Greek-Melkite Patriarch of Antioch is resident in Damascus, Syria. The Patriarchal Vicariate (now Exarchate) of Kuwait had an estimated 4,500 adherents at 31 December 1984.

**Exarch Patriarchal:** Archimandrite BASILIOS KANAKRY, Vicariat Patrircal Melkite, POB 1205, Salmiya; tel. 615721.

*Syrian Rite*

The Syrian Catholic Patriarch of Antioch is resident in Beirut, Lebanon. The Patriarchal Exarchate of Iraq and Kuwait, with an estimated 1,250 adherents at 31 December 1992, is based in Basra, Iraq.

#### The Anglican Communion

Within the Episcopal Church in Jerusalem and the Middle East, Kuwait forms part of the diocese of Cyprus and the Gulf. The Anglican congregation in Kuwait is entirely expatriate. The Bishop in Cyprus and the Gulf is resident in Cyprus, while the Archdeacon in the Gulf is resident in the United Arab Emirates.

## Other Christian Churches

**National Evangelical Church in Kuwait:** Rev. NABIL ATTALLAH, pastor of the Arabic-language congregation; Rev. JERRY A. ZANDSTRA, pastor of the English-speaking congregation; POB 80, 13001 Safat, Kuwait City; tel. 2407195; fax 2431087; an independent Protestant Church founded by the Reformed Church in America; services in Arabic, English, Korean, Malayalam and other Indian languages; combined weekly congregation of some 7,500.

The Armenian, Greek, Coptic and Syrian Orthodox Churches are also represented in Kuwait.

# The Press

Freedom of the press and publishing is guaranteed in the Constitution, although press censorship was in force between mid-1986 and early 1992 (when journalists adopted a voluntary code of practice). The Government provides financial support to newspapers and magazines.

## DAILIES

**Al-Anbaa** (The News): POB 23915, Safat, Kuwait City; tel. 4830322; telex 22622; f. 1976; Arabic; general; Editor-in-Chief FAISAL YOUSUF AL-MARZOOQ; circ. 80,000.

**Arab Times:** POB 2270, 13023 Safat, Kuwait City; tel. 4813566; telex 22332; fax 4833628; f. 1977; English; Editor-in-Chief AHMAD ABD AL-AZIZ AL-JARALLAH; Man. Editor MISHAL AL-JARALLAH; circ. 31,134.

**Kuwait Times:** POB 1301, Safat, Kuwait City; tel. 4833199; telex 23843; f. 1963; (weekend edition also published); English; political; Owner and Editor-in-Chief YOUSUF ALYYAN; Man. Editor CLEMENT MESENAS; circ. 30,000.

**Al-Qabas** (Firebrand): POB 21800, 13078 Safat, Kuwait City; tel. 4812822; telex 23370; fax 4834320; f. 1972; Arabic; independent; Gen. Man. FOUZAN AL-FARES; circ. 90,000.

**Ar-Ra'i al-'Aam** (Public Opinion): POB 695, International Airport Rd, Shuwaikh Industrial Area, Kuwait City; tel. 4813134; telex 22636; fax 4849298; f. 1961; Arabic; political, social and cultural; Editor-in-Chief FAHAD A. AL-MUSSAEED; circ. 86,900.

**As-Seyassa** (Policy): POB 2270, Shuwaikh, Kuwait City; tel. 4816326; telex 22332; fax 4833628; f. 1965; Arabic; political; Editor-in-Chief AHMAD ABD AL-AZIZ AL-JARALLAH; circ. 126,616.

**Al-Watan** (The Homeland): Dar al-Watan KSC, POB 1142, Safat, Kuwait City; tel. 4840950; telex 22565; f. 1962; Arabic; political; Editor-in-Chief FATIMA HUSSEIN; Deputy Gen. Man. ABDULLAH ALI HINDI; circ. 56,758.

## WEEKLIES AND PERIODICALS

**'Alam al-Fann** (World of Art): POB 13341, 71953 Keifan; tel. 4810526; Editor-in-Chief MUHAMMAD A. NASHMI DAWASH.

**Arab Business Report:** POB 6000, Safat, Kuwait City; telex 3511; fortnightly; English; business management.

**Al-'Arabi** (The Arab): POB 748, 13008 Safat, Kuwait City; telex 44041; f. 1958; monthly; Arabic; cultural; publ. by the Ministry of Information for distribution throughout the Arab world; Editor-in-Chief Dr MUHAMMAD AR-RUMAIHI; circ. 350,000.

**Al-Balagh** (Communiqué): POB 4558, 13046 Safat, Kuwait City; tel. 4818606; telex 44389; fax 4819008; f. 1969; weekly; Arabic; general, political and Islamic; Editor-in-Chief ABD AR-RAHMAN RASHID AL-WALAYATI; circ. 29,000.

**Ad-Dakhiliya** (The Interior): POB 12500, 71655 Shamiah, Kuwait City; monthly; Arabic; official reports, transactions and proceedings; publ. by Public Relations Dept, Ministry of the Interior; Editor-in-Chief Lt-Col Dr ADEL AL-IBRAHIM.

**Al-Hadaf** (The Objective): POB 2270, 13023 Safat, Kuwait City; tel. 4813566; telex 22332; fax 4833628; f. 1961; weekly; Arabic; literary, political and cultural; Editor-in-Chief AHMAD ABD AL-AZIZ AL-JARALLAH; Chair. M. M. AS-SALEH; circ. 210,123.

**Hayatuna** (Our Life): POB 1708, Safat, Kuwait City; f. 1968; fortnightly; Arabic; medicine and hygiene; publ. by Al-Awadi Press Corporation; Editor-in-Chief YOUSUF ABD AL-AZIZ AL-MUZINI; circ. 6,000.

**Iftah Ya Simsim** (Open Sesame): POB 44247, Safat, Kuwait City; telex 44090; monthly; Arabic; children.

**Al-Iqtisadi al-Kuwaiti** (Kuwaiti Economist): POB 775, 13008 Safat, Kuwait City; tel. 2438087; fax 2404110; f. 1960; monthly; Arabic; commerce, trade and economics; publ. by Kuwait Chamber of Commerce and Industry; Editor MAJED JAMAL UD-DIN.

**Journal of the Gulf and Arab Peninsula Studies:** POB 17073, Khaldiya, Kuwait University, Kuwait City; quarterly; English.

**Journal of the Kuwait Medical Association:** POB 1202, 13013 Safat, Kuwait City; tel. 5333278; fax 5333276; f. 1967; quarterly; English; case reports, articles; Editor-in-chief Dr A. A. AR-RASHID; circ. 6,000.

**Al-Kuwait:** POB 193, Safat, Kuwait City; tel. 2415300; telex 46151; f. 1961; monthly; Arabic; Islamic culture; publ. by Ministry of Information; Editor HAMED Y. AL-GHARABALLY; circ. 50,400.

**Kuwait al-Youm** (Official Gazette): POB 193, 13002 Safat, Kuwait City; tel. 2415300; telex 46151; fax 2421926; f. 1954; weekly; Arabic; statistics, Amiri decrees, laws, govt announcements, decisions, invitations for tenders, etc.; publ. by the Ministry of Information; circ. 5,000.

**Al-Kuwaiti** (The Kuwaiti): Information Dept, POB 9758, 61008 Ahmadi, Kuwait City; tel. 3982747; telex 44211; fax 3981602; f. 1961; monthly journal of the Kuwait Oil Co; Arabic; Editor-in-Chief SALEM R. AR-ROOMI; circ. 6,000.

**The Kuwaiti Digest:** Information Dept, POB 9758, 61008 Ahmadi, Kuwait City; tel. 3982747; telex 44211; fax 3981602; f. 1972; quarterly journal of Kuwait Oil Co; English; Editor-in-Chief SALEM R. AR-ROOMI; circ. 8,000.

**Al-Majaless** (Meetings): POB 5605, Safat, Kuwait City; tel. 814429; telex 44728; weekly; Arabic; current affairs; circ. 60,206.

**Mejallat al-Kuwait** (Kuwait Magazine): POB 193, 13002 Safat, Kuwait City; tel. 2415300; telex 46151; f. 1961; fortnightly; Arabic; illustrated magazine; science, arts and literature; publ. by Ministry of Information.

**Mirat al-Umma** (Mirror of the Nation): POB 2270, Shuwaikh, Kuwait City; telex 22332; weekly; Arabic; Editor-in-Chief ALI BIN YOUSUF AR-ROUMI; circ. 79,500.

**An-Nahdha** (The Renaissance): POB 695, Shuwaikh, Kuwait City; telex 22636; f. 1967; weekly; Arabic; social and political; Editor YOUSUF AL-MASSAID; circ. 148,500.

**Osrati** (My Family): POB 2995, Safat, Kuwait City; tel. 816928; telex 44438; f. 1978; weekly; Arabic; women's magazine; publ. by Fahad al-Marzouk Establishment; Editor GHANIMA F. AL-MARZOUK; circ. 76,450.

**Ar-Ressaleh** (The Message): POB 2490, Shuwaikh, Kuwait City; f. 1961; weekly; Arabic; political, social and cultural; Editor JASSIM MUBARAK.

**Ar-Riyadhi al-'Arabi** (The Arab Sportsman): POB 1693, 13017 Safat, Kuwait City; tel. 4845307; telex 44728; weekly; Arabic; sports; circ. 101,822.

**Sa'd** (Good Luck): POB 695, Ismail Wasi, ar-Racalam, Kuwait City; tel. 813133; telex 22636; weekly; Arabic; children's magazine; Editor MANAL AL-MOSAFED; circ. 60,000.

**Sawt al-Khaleej** (Voice of the Gulf): POB 659, Safat, Kuwait City; telex 2636; f. 1962; politics and literature; Arabic; Editor-in-Chief SALAH BAKER KHRIEBET; Owner BAKER ALI KHRIEBET; circ. 20,000.

**At-Tali'** (The Ascendant): POB 1082, Mubarak al-Kabir St, Kuwait City; tel. 2439376; f. 1962; weekly; Arabic; politics and literature; Editor SAMI AHMAD AL-MUNAIS; circ. 10,000.

**Al-Yaqza** (The Awakening): POB 6000, Safat, Kuwait City; tel. 6831318; telex 44513; fax 2414102; f. 1966; weekly; Arabic; political, economic, social and general; Editor-in-Chief AHMAD YOUSUF BEHBEHANI; circ. 91,340.

## NEWS AGENCIES

**Kuwait News Agency (KUNA):** POB 24063, 13101 Safat, Kuwait City; tel. 2412044; telex 22758; fax 2414102; f. 1976; public corporate body; independent; also publishes research digests on topics of common and special interest; Chair. and Dir-Gen. YOUSUF AS-SUMAIT.

### Foreign Bureaux

**Informatsionnoye Telegrafnoye Agentstvo Rossii—Telegrafnoye Agentstvo Suverennykh Stran (ITAR—TASS)** (Russia): POB 1765, 13018 Safat, Kuwait City; Correspondent VIKTOR D. LEBEDEV.

**Middle East News Agency (MENA)** (Egypt): POB 1927, Safat, Fahd as-Salem St, Kuwait City; Dir REDA SOLIMAN.

**Reuters Middle East Ltd** (UK): 13083 Safat, Mubarak al-Kabir St, Kuwait Stock Exchange Bldg, 4th Floor, Kuwait City; tel. 2431920; telex 22428; fax 22420617; Bureau Man. MARC BOSMAN.

**Xinhua (New China) News Agency** (People's Republic of China): POB 22168, Safat, Sheikh Ahmad al-Jaber Bldg, 10 Dasman St, Kuwait City; Correspondent HUANG JIANMING.

Agence Arabe Syrienne d'Information, Anatolian News Agency (Turkey), JANA (Libya), QNA (Qatar) and RIA—Novosti (Russia) are also represented in Kuwait.

## PRESS ASSOCIATION

**Kuwait Journalist Association:** POB 5454, Safat, Kuwait City; tel. 4843351; fax 4842874; Chair. YOUSUF ALYYAN.

## Publishers

**Gulf Centre Publishing and Publicity:** POB 2722, 13028 Safat, Kuwait City; telex 46174; Propr HAMZA ISMAIL ESSLAH.

**Al-Jeel Publishing Co:** POB 44247, 32057 Hawalli, Kuwait City; tel. 4843183; telex 46443; children's education; Chair. and Gen. Man. OSSAMA EL-KAOUKJI.

**Kuwait Publishing House:** POB 5209, 13053 Safat, Kuwait City; tel. 2414697; telex 22771; Dir AMIN HAMADEH.

**At-Talia Printing and Publishing Co:** POB 1082, Airport Rd, Shuwaikh, 13011 Safat, Kuwait City; tel. 4840470; Man. AHMAD YUSEF AN-NAFISI.

### Government Publishing House

**Ministry of Information:** POB 193, 13002 Safat, as-Sour St, Kuwait City; tel. 2415300; telex 46151; fax 2421926.

## Radio and Television

In 1992, according to UNESCO, there were an estimated 720,000 radio receivers and 610,000 television receivers in use.

### RADIO

**Kuwait Broadcasting SCE:** POB 397, 13004 Safat, Kuwait City; tel. 2423774; telex 46285; fax 2415946; f. 1951; broadcasts for 70 hours daily in Arabic, Farsi, English and Urdu, some in stereo; Dir of Radio Dr ABD AL-AZIZ ALI MANSOUR; Dir of Radio Programmes ABD AR-RAHMAN HADI.

### TELEVISION

**Kuwait Television:** c/o POB 621, 13007 Safat, Kuwait City; tel. 2423774; telex 22169; fax 2419659; f. 1961 (transmission began privately in Kuwait in 1957); transmits in Arabic; colour television service began in 1973; has a total of five channels; Dir-Gen. of TV BADR AL-MODAF.

## Finance

(cap. = capital; res = reserves; dep. = deposits; m. = million; brs = branches; amounts in Kuwaiti dinars unless otherwise stated)

### BANKING
#### Central Bank

**Central Bank of Kuwait:** POB 526, 13006 Safat, Abdullah as-Salem St, Kuwait City; tel. 2449200; telex 22101; fax 2433461; f. 1969; cap. 5.0m., res 179.0m., total assets 1,435.3m. (Feb. 1994); Governor Sheikh SALEM ABD AL-AZIZ SA'UD AS-SABAH.

#### National Banks

**Al-Ahli Bank of Kuwait KSC:** POB 1387, 13014 Safat, Mubarak al-Kabir St, Safat Sq., Kuwait City; tel. 2400900; telex 22067; fax 2424557; f. 1967; wholly owned by private Kuwaiti interests; cap. 50.4m., res 36.5m., dep. 871.2m., total assets 1,010.8m (June 1994); Chair. MORAD YOUSUF BEHBEHANI; Dep. Chair. ABD SALAM ABDULLAH AL-AWADI; 10 brs in Kuwait.

**Bank of Bahrain and Kuwait:** POB 24396, 13104 Safat, Kuwait City; tel. 2417140; fax 2440937; f. 1977; owned equally by the Governments of Bahrain and Kuwait; cap. 56.9m., res 11.5m., dep. 568.6m., total assets 646.4m. (Dec. 1993); Chair. RASHED AZ-ZAYANI; Gen. Man. MURAD ALI MURAD.

**Bank of Kuwait and the Middle East KSC:** POB 71, 13001 Safat, Darwazat Abd ar-Razzak, Kuwait City; tel. 2459771; telex 22045; fax 2461430; began operations in Dec. 1971; 49.4% state-owned; cap. 49.5m., res 18.0m., dep. 713.1m., total assets 781.4m. (Dec. 1993); Chair. SALIH MUBARAK AL-FALAH; Gen. Man. SAUD AL-GHARABALLY; 10 brs.

**Burgan Bank SAK:** POB 5389, 13054 Safat, Ahmad al-Jaber St, Kuwait City; tel. 2439000; telex 22730; fax 2461148; f. 1975; 51% state-owned, 49% owned by private Kuwaiti interests; cap. 68.8m. res 71.7m., dep. 720.3m, total assets 860.8m. (Dec. 1994); Chair. and Man. Dir Sheikh AHMAD ABDULLAH AL-AHMAD AS-SABAH; Gen. Man. MUHAMMAD AQEEL TAWFIQI; 10 brs.

**Commercial Bank of Kuwait SAK:** POB 2861, 13029 Safat, Mubarak al-Kabir St, Kuwait City; tel. 2411001; telex 22004; fax 2450150; f. 1960 by Amiri decree; cap. 70.0m., res 27.1m., dep. 794.9m., total assets 953.6m. (June 1994); Chair. HAMAD AHMAD ABD AL-LATIF AL-HAMAD; Chief Gen. Man. MUHAMMAD ABD AR-RAHMAN AL-YAHYA; 17 brs.

**Gulf Bank KSC:** POB 3200, 13032 Safat, Mubarak al-Kabir St, Kuwait City; tel. 2449501; telex 22001; fax 2445212; f. 1960; cap. 78.2m., res 75.8m., dep. 825.3m, total assets 1,390.4m. (Dec. 1994); Chair. Dr ALI AL-HILAL AL-MUTAIRI; Chief Gen. Man. JOHN D. HARRIS; 15 brs.

**Industrial Bank of Kuwait KSC:** POB 3146, 13032 Safat, Joint Banking Centre, Commercial Area 9, Kuwait City; tel. 2457661; telex 22469; fax 2462057; 31.4% state-owned; f. 1973; cap. 20m., res 37.2m., dep. 73.3m., total assets 367.4m. (Dec. 1993); Chair. and Man. Dir SALEH MUHAMMAD AL-YOUSUF.

**Kuwait Finance House KSC (KFH):** POB 24989, 13110 Safat, Abdullah al-Mubarak St, Kuwait City; tel. 2445050; telex 23331; fax 2455135; f. 1977; Islamic banking and investment company; 49% state-owned; cap. 42.4m., res 16.1m., dep. 1,031.9m., total assets 1,226.6m. (June 1994); Chair. and Man. Dir BADER AL-MUKHAISEEM; Gen. Man. WALEED AR-RUWAIH; 16 brs.

**Kuwait Real Estate Bank KSC:** POB 22822, 13089 Safat, West Tower—Joint Banking Centre, Darwazat Abd ar-Razzak, Kuwait City; tel. 2458177; telex 22321; fax 2462516; f. 1973; wholly owned by private Kuwaiti interests; cap. 31.2m., res 37.6m., dep. 230.0m., total assets 340.8m. (June 1994); Chair. and Man. Dir SAAD ALI AN-NAHEDH; 3 brs.

**National Bank of Kuwait SAK (NBK):** POB 95, 13001 Safat, Abdullah as-Salem St, Kuwait City; tel. 2422011; telex 22451; fax 4310089; f. 1952; cap. 133.7m., res 191.6m., dep. 3,093.3m., total assets 3,535.6m. (June 1994); Chair. MUHAMMAD ABD AR-RAHMAN AL-BAHAR; Chief Gen. Man. IBRAHIM S. DABDOUB; 29 brs.

**Savings and Credit Bank:** POB 1454, 13015 Safat, al-Hilali St, Kuwait City; tel. 2411301; telex 22211; f. 1965; nominal cap. 1,000m.; Chair. and Gen. Man. YOUSUF ALI AL-HOUTI.

### INSURANCE

**Al-Ahleia Insurance Co SAK:** POB 1602, as-Sour St, Safat, Kuwait City; tel. 2448870; telex 23585; fax 2430308; f. 1962; all forms of insurance; cap. 9.7m.; Chair. YOUSUF IBRAHIM AL-GHANIM; Man. Dir OSAMAH MUHAMMAD AN-NISF; Gen. Man. Dr RAOUF H. MAKAR.

**Al-Ittihad al-Watani Insurance Co for the Near East SAL:** POB 781, 13008 Safat; tel. 2441830; telex 22442; fax 2432424.

**Arab Commercial Enterprises (Kuwait):** POB 2474, 13025 Safat; tel. 2413854; telex 22076; fax 2409450.

**Gulf Insurance Co KSC:** POB 1040, 13011 Safat, Kuwait City; tel. 2423384; telex 22203, fax 2422320; f. 1962; cap. 11.3m.; 75% state-owned; all forms of insurance; Chair. SULAIMAN HAMAD AD-DALALI.

**Kuwait Insurance Co SAK (KIC):** POB 769, Safat, Abdullah al-Salem St, Kuwait City; tel. 2420135; telex 22104; fax 2428530; f. 1960; cap. 17.6m.; all life and non-life insurance; Chair. MUHAMMAD SALEH BEHBEHANI; Gen. Man. ALI HAMAD AL-BAHAR.

**Kuwait Reinsurance Co KSC:** POB 21929, 13080 Safat, Al-Khaleejia Complex, 13th Floor, Al-Chark, Kuwait City; tel. 2432011; telex 22058; fax 2427823; Gen. Man. FATHI HAMAM.

**Kuwait Technical Insurance Office:** POB 25349, 13114 Safat; tel. 2413986; telex 23583; fax 2413986.

**Mohd Saleh Behbehani & Co:** POB 370, 13004 Safat; tel. 2412085; telex 22194; fax 2412089.

**New India Assurance Co:** POB 370, 13004 Safat; tel. 2412085; telex 22194; fax 2412089.

**The Northern Insurance Co Ltd:** POB 579, 13006 Safat; tel. 2427930; telex 22367; fax 2462739.

**Oriental Insurance Co Ltd (Al Mulla Group):** POB 22431, 13085 Safat; tel. 2424016; telex 22012; fax 2424017.

**Sumitomo Marine & Fire Insurance Co (Kuwait Agency):** POB 3458, 13055 Safat; tel. 2433087; telex 23754; fax 2430853.

**Warba Insurance Company SAK:** POB 24282, 13103 Safat; tel. 2445140; telex 22779; fax 2466131; f. 1976; Chair. and Man. Dir TEWFIK A. AL-GHARABALLY; 1 br.

Some 20 Arab and other foreign insurance companies are active in Kuwait.

### STOCK EXCHANGE

**Kuwait Stock Exchange:** POB 22235, 13083 Safat, Mubarak al-Kabir St, Kuwait City; tel. 2423130; telex 44015; fax 2420779; f. 1984; 47 companies listed in 1993; Pres. HISHAM AL-OTAIBI; Vice-Pres. ABDULLAH AS-SDAIRAWI.

## Trade and Industry

### PETROLEUM

**Kuwait Petroleum Corporation (KPC):** POB 26565, 13126 Safat, Salhia Complex, Fahed as-Salem St, Kuwait City; tel. 2455455;

telex 44875; fax 2423371; f. 1980; co-ordinating organization to manage the petroleum industry; controls companies listed below; Chair. Minister of Oil; Deputy Chair. NADER SULTAN.

**Kuwait Aviation Fuelling Co KSC:** POB 1654, 13017 Safat, Kuwait City; tel. 4330482; telex 23056; fax 4330475; Gen. Man. ABD AL-AZIZ AS-SERRI.

**Kuwait Foreign Petroleum Exploration Co KSC (KUFPEC):** POB 26565, 13126 Safat, Kuwait City; tel. 2455455; telex 44875; fax 2423371; f. 1981; state-owned; overseas oil exploration and development; Chair. and Man. Dir MAHMOUD A. AR-RAHMANI.

**Kuwait National Petroleum Co KSC (KNPC):** POB 70, 13001 Safat, Ali as-Salem St, Kuwait City; tel. 2420121; telex 22006; fax 2433839; f. 1960; oil refining, production of liquefied petroleum gas, and domestic marketing and distribution of petroleum by-products; output of 189,000 b/d of refined petroleum in 1991/92; Chair. and Man. Dir AHMAD ABD AL-MOHSIN AL-MUTAIR.

**Kuwait Oil Co KSC (KOC):** POB 9758, 61008 Ahmadi; tel. 3989111; telex 44211; fax 3983661; f. 1934; state-owned; Chair. and Man. Dir KHALID AL-FULAIJ.

**Kuwait Oil Tanker Co SAK** (see Transport—Shipping).

**Kuwait Petroleum International Ltd (KPI):** 80 New Bond St, London, W1, England; tel. (0171) 491-4000; marketing division of KPC; controls 6,500 petrol retail stations in Europe, under the trade name 'Q8' (adopted in 1986), and European refineries with capacity of 235,000 b/d; Pres. KAMEL HARAMI.

**Petrochemical Industries Co KSC (PIC)** (see Development Organizations).

**Arabian Oil Co:** Head Office: Tokyo; Kuwait Office: POB 1641, 13017 Safat, Kuwait City; tel. 2439201; telex 22095; fax 2421936; Field Office Ras al-Khafji, Partitioned Zone, Saudi Arabia; f. 1950; a Japanese company which holds concessions granted by Govts of Saudi Arabia and Kuwait in 1957 and 1958 respectively.

### CHAMBER OF COMMERCE

**Kuwait Chamber of Commerce and Industry:** POB 775, 13008 Safat, Chamber's Bldg, Ali as-Salem St, Kuwait City; tel. 2433864; fax 2404110; f. 1959; 46,000 mems; Pres. ABD AL-AZIZ HAMAD AS-SAQR; Dir-Gen. AHMAD R. AL-HAROUN.

### DEVELOPMENT ORGANIZATIONS

**Arab Planning Institute (API):** POB 5834, 13059 Safat, Kuwait City; tel. 4843130; telex 22996; fax 4842935; f. 1966; 50 mems; publishes annual directory and proceedings of seminars and discussion group meetings, offers research, training programmes and advisory services; Dir EBRAHIM ASH-SHAREEDAH.

**General Board for the South and Arabian Gulf:** POB 5994, Safat, Kuwait City; tel. 2424461; wholly state-owned; provides assistance to developing countries in the Arab world; Del. Mem. AHMAD AS-SAKKAF.

**Industrial Investments Company (IIC):** POB 26019, 13121 Safat, Kuwait City; tel. 2429073; telex 23132; fax 2448850; invests directly in industry; partly owned by the Kuwait Investment Authority.

**Kuwait Foreign Trading, Contracting and Investment Co SAK (KFTCIC):** POB 5665, 13057 Safat, Omar Bin al-Khattab St, Sharq, Kuwait City; tel. 2449031; telex 22021; fax 2446173; f. 1965 by Amiri decree; private banking, investments and real estate; 99.2% state-owned; Chair. and Man. Dir ABDULLAH AHMAD AL-GABANDI.

**Kuwait Fund for Arab Economic Development (KFAED):** POB 2921, 13030 Safat, cnr Mubarak al-Kabir St and al-Hilali St, Kuwait City; tel. 2468800; telex 22613; fax 2419091; f. 1961; cap. KD 2,000m.; state-owned; provides and administers financial and technical assistance to the countries of the developing world; Chair. Minister of Finance; Dir-Gen. BADER M. AL-HUMAIDHI.

**Kuwait Investment Authority (KIA):** POB 64, 13001 Safat, Kuwait City; tel. 2439595; telex 46089; fax 2454059; oversees the Kuwait Investment Office (London); responsible for the Kuwaiti General Reserve; Chair. Minister of Finance; Man. Dir ALI RASHID AL-BADR.

**Kuwait International Investment Co SAK (KIIC):** POB 22782, 13088 Safat, as-Salhia Commercial Complex, Kuwait City; tel. 2420762; fax 2454931; 30% state-owned; cap. p.u. 31.9m., total assets KD 146.9m. (1988); domestic real estate and share markets; Chair. and Man. Dir JASSIM MUHAMMAD AL-BAHAR.

**Kuwait Investment Co SAK (KIC):** POB 1005, 13011 Safat, Kuwait City; tel. 2438111; telex 22115; fax 2444896; f. 1961; 74% state-owned, 26% owned by private Kuwaiti interests; total resources KD 201.1m. (1993); international banking and investment; Chair. and Man. Dir BADER A. AR-RUSHAID AL-BADER.

**Kuwait Planning Board:** c/o Ministry of Planning, POB 15, 13001 Safat, Kuwait City; tel. 2428200; telex 22468; fax 2407326; f. 1962; supervises long-term development plans; through its Central Statistical Office publishes information on Kuwait's economic activity; Dir-Gen. AHMAD ALI AD-DUAIJ.

**National Industries Co SAK:** POB 417, 13005 Safat, Kuwait City; tel. 4849466; telex 22165; fax 4839582; f. 1960; 59.2% state-owned; cap. p.u. KD 24.3m.; has controlling interest in various construction enterprises; Chair. and Man. Dir MUFARREJ I. AL-MUFARREJ.

**Petrochemical Industries Co KSC (PIC):** POB 1084, 13011 Safat, Khalid Bin al-Walid St, Kuwait City; tel. 2422141; telex 22042; fax 2447159; f. 1963; state-owned; produced 851,700 metric tons of urea and 569,800 tons of ammonia in 1987/88; Chair. and Man. HANI HUSSAIN.

**Fertilizer Plants:** POB 1084, 13011 Safat, Kuwait City; tel. 2422141; telex 44212; fax 2447159; production of ammonia, urea, sulphuric acid and ammonium sulphate; four ammonia plants, three urea plants and one ammonium sulphate plant.

**Salt and Chlorine Plants:** POB 10277, 65453 Shuaiba, Kuwait; tel. 3263310; telex 46925; fax 3261587; f. 1963; production of salt, chlorine, caustic soda, hydrochloric acid, sodium hypochlorite, compressed hydrogen and distilled water; Operations Man. HAMAD AL-MISHWAT.

**Shuaiba Area Authority SAA:** POB 4690, 13047 Safat, Kuwait City; POB 10033, Shuaiba; tel. 3260903; telex 44205; f. 1964; an independent governmental authority to supervise and run the industrial area and Port of Shuaiba; has powers and duties to develop the area and its industries which include an oil refinery, cement factory, fishing plant, power stations and distillation plants, chemical fertilizer and petrochemical industries, sanitary ware factory, asbestos plant and sand lime bricks plant; Dir-Gen. SULEIMAN K. AL-HAMAD.

### TRADE UNIONS

**General Confederation of Kuwaiti Workers:** Kuwait City; f. 1968; central authority to which all trade unions are affiliated.

**KOC Workers Union:** Kuwait City; f. 1964; Chair. JASSIM ABD AL-WAHAB AT-TOURA.

**Federation of Petroleum and Petrochemical Workers:** Kuwait City; f. 1965; Chair. JASSIM ABD AL-WAHAB AT-TOURA.

## Transport

### ROADS

Roads in the towns are metalled, and the most important are motorways or dual carriageways. There are metalled roads linking Kuwait City to Ahmadi, Mina al-Ahmadi and other centres of population in Kuwait, and to the Iraqi and Saudi Arabian borders, giving a total road network of 4,273 km in 1989 (280 km of motorways, 1,232 km of other major roads and 2,761 km of secondary roads).

**Kuwait Public Transport Co SAK (KPTC):** POB 375, 13004 Safat, Hilali St, Kuwait City; tel. 2469420; telex 22246; fax 2401265; f. 1962; state-owned; provides internal bus service; regular service to Mecca, Saudi Arabia; Chair. of Board BARRAK K. AL-MARZOUK; Man. Dir ABD AL-WAHAB AL-HAROUN.

### SHIPPING

Kuwait has three commercial seaports. The largest, Shuwaikh, situated about 3 km from Kuwait City, was built in 1960. By 1987 it comprised 21 deep-water berths, with a total length of 4 km, three shallow-water berths and three basins for small craft, each with a depth of 3.35m. In 1988 3.6m. metric tons of cargo were imported and 133,185 tons were exported through the port. A total of 1,189 vessels passed through Shuwaikh in 1988.

Shuaiba Commercial Port, 56 km south of Kuwait City, was built in 1967 to facilitate the import of primary materials and heavy equipment, necessary for the construction of the Shuaiba Industrial Area. By 1987 the port comprised a total of 20 berths, plus two docks for small wooden boats. Four of the berths constitute a station for unloading containers. Shuaiba handled a total of 3,457,871 metric tons of dry cargo, barge cargo and containers in 1988.

Doha, the smallest port, was equipped in 1981 to receive small coastal ships carrying light goods between the Gulf states. It has 20 small berths, each 100 m long. Doha handled a total of 20,283 metric tons of dry cargo, barge cargo and containers in 1988.

The oil port at Mina al-Ahmadi, 40 km south of Kuwait City, is capable of handling the largest oil tankers afloat, and the loading of over 2m. barrels of oil per day. By 1987 the port comprised 12 tanker berths, one bitumen-carrier berth, two LPG export berths and bunkering facilities.

**Arab Maritime Petroleum Transport Co (AMPTC):** POB 22525, 13086 Safat, Gulf Bank Bldg, Mubarak al-Kabir St, Kuwait City;

tel. 2411815; telex 22180; fax 2437468; f. 1973; 3 tankers and 4 LPG carriers; sponsored by OAPEC and financed by Algeria, Bahrain, Iraq, Kuwait, Libya, Qatar, Saudi Arabia and the UAE; Chair. Sheikh RASHID AWAIDA ATH-THANI (Qatar); Vice-Chair. and Gen. Man. ABD AR-RAHMAN AHMAD AS-SULTAN.

**Kuwait Maritime Transport Co KSC:** POB 22595, 13086 Safat, Nafisi and Khatrash Bldg, Jaber al-Mubarak St, Kuwait City; tel. 2420519; telex 30967; fax 2420513; f. 1981.

**Kuwait Oil Tanker Co SAK (KOTC):** POB 810, 13009 Safat, as-Salhia Commercial Complex, Blocks 3, 5, 7 and 9, Kuwait City; tel. 2406805; telex 44766; fax 2445907; f. 1957; state-owned; operates 8 crude oil tankers, 26 other tankers and 4 LPG vessels; sole tanker agents for Mina al-Ahmadi, Shuaiba and Mina Abdullah and agents for other ports; LPG filling and distribution; Chair. and Man. Dir ABDULLAH AR-ROUMI.

**Kuwait Shipbuilding and Repairyard Co SAK (KSRC):** POB 21998, 13080 Safat, Kuwait City; tel. 4835488; telex 22438; fax 4830291; ship repairs and engineering services, underwater services, maintenance of refineries, power stations and storage tanks; maintains floating dock for vessels up to 35,000 dwt; synchrolift for vessels up to 5,000 dwt with transfer yard; five repair jetties up to 550 m in length and floating workshop for vessels lying at anchor; Chair. and Man. Dir MUSA J. MARAFI.

**Ports Public Authority:** POB 3874, 13039 Safat, Kuwait City; tel. 4812774; telex 22740; fax 4819714; there are plans to expand the ports to handle the increased cargo traffic projected for the 1990s; Chair. JASSEM AL'OUN; Dir-Gen. ABDUL RAHMAN AN-NAIBARI.

**United Arab Shipping Co SAG (UASC):** POB 3636, 13037 Safat, Shuwaikh, Airport Rd, Kuwait City; tel. 4843150; telex 22176; fax 4845388; f. 1976; national shipping company of six Arabian Gulf countries; services between Europe, Far East, Mediterranean ports, Japan and east coast of USA and South America, and ports of participant states on Persian (Arabian) Gulf and Red Sea; 47 vessels; subsidiary cos: Kuwait Shipping Agencies, Arab Transport Company (Aratrans), United Arab Chartering Company (London), Middle East Container Repair Company (Dubai), and United Arab Shipping Agencies Company; Chair. M. H. AR-RAYYES.

## CIVIL AVIATION

Kuwait International Airport opened in 1980, and was designed to receive up to 4.5m. passengers per year; in 1994 3.12m. arrivals and departures were recorded. In 1991 Kuwait Airways carried a total of 840,000 passengers.

**Directorate-General of Civil Aviation:** POB 17, 13001 Safat, tel. 735599; telex 23038; Dir-Gen. Sheikh JABER AL-ATHBY AS-SABAH.

**Kuwait Airways Corporation (KAC):** POB 394, Kuwait International Airport, 13004 Safat; tel. 4740166; telex 23036; fax 4314726; f. 1954; services to the Arabian peninsula, Asia, Africa and Europe; Chair. AHMAD AL-MISHARI; Dir-Gen. AHMAD AZ-ZABIN.

# Tourism

**Department of Tourism:** Ministry of Information, POB 193, 13002 Safat, as-Sour St, Kuwait City; tel. 2436644; telex 44041; fax 2429758.

**Touristic Enterprises Co (TEC):** POB 23310, 13094 Safat, Kuwait City; tel. 5652775; telex 22801; fax 5657594; f. 1976; 92% state-owned; manages 23 tourist facilities; Chair. BADER AL-BAHAR; Vice-Chair. YACOUB AR-RUSHAID.

# KYRGYZSTAN

## Introductory Survey

**Location, Climate, Language, Religion, Flag, Capital**

The Kyrgyz Republic (formerly the Kyrgyz Soviet Socialist Republic and, between December 1990 and May 1993, the Republic of Kyrgyzstan) is a small, land-locked state situated in eastern Central Asia. The country has also been known as Kyrgyzia (or Kirghizia). It borders Kazakhstan to the north, Uzbekistan to the west, Tajikistan to the south and west, and the People's Republic of China to the east. There are distinct variations in climate between low-lying and high-altitude areas. In the valleys the mean July temperature is 28°C (82°F), whereas in January it falls to an average of −18°C (−0.5°F). Annual precipitation ranges from 180 mm in the eastern Tian-Shan mountains to 750 mm–1,000 mm in the Fergana mountains. In the settled valleys the annual average varies between 100 mm and 500 mm. Kyrgyz replaced Russian as the official language in September 1989. It is a member of the south Turkic group of languages and is written in the Cyrillic script. (The Arabic script was in use until 1928, when it was replaced by the Latin script; this was replaced by Cyrillic in 1940.) In 1993 it was agreed to reintroduce the use of the Latin script. The major religion is Islam. The majority of ethnic Kyrgyz are Sunni Muslims of the Hanafi school, as are some other groups living in Kyrgyzstan, including Uzbeks and Tajiks. The national flag (proportions 5 by 3) consists of a red field, at the centre of which is a yellow sun, with 40 counter-clockwise rays surrounding a red-bordered yellow disc on which are superimposed two intersecting sets of three red, curved, narrow bands. The capital is Bishkek (known as Frunze between 1926 and 1991).

**Recent History**

The ancestors of the Kyrgyz (or Kirghiz) were probably settled on the upper reaches of the Yenisei until about the 10th century. From there they migrated south to the Tian-Shan region, a movement hastened by the rise of the Mongol Empire, in the 13th century. The Kyrgyz were ruled by various Turkic peoples until 1685, when they came under the control of the Mongol Oirots. The defeat of the Oirots by the Manzhous (Manchus), in 1758, left the Kyrgyz as nominal Chinese subjects, but the Chinese did not interfere with their independent nomadic life-styles. Kyrgyzia (or Kirghizia) came under the suzerainty of the Khanate of Kokand in the early 19th century, and was formally incorporated into the Russian Empire, as part of the Khanate, in 1876. The suppression of the 1916 rebellion in Central Asia caused a large-scale migration of the Kyrgyz to China.

Following the October Revolution of 1917 in Russia, there was a period of civil war, with anti-Bolshevik forces, including the Russian 'White' Army, and local armed groups (*basmachi*), fighting against the Bolshevik Red Army. Soviet power was established in the region by 1919. In 1918 the Turkestan Autonomous Soviet Socialist Republic (ASSR) was established within the Russian Soviet Federative Socialist Republic (RSFSR, or Russian Federation) and included Kyrgyzia until 1924, when the Kara-Kyrgyz Autonomous Oblast (Region) was created, also within the RSFSR. (The Russians used the term Kara-Kyrgyz for the Kyrgyz until the mid-1920s to distinguish them from the Kazakhs, who at that time were also known as Kyrgyz by the Russians.) In 1925 the region was renamed the Kyrgyz Autonomous Oblast, and it became the Kyrgyz ASSR in February 1926. On 5 December 1936 the Kyrgyz Soviet Socialist Republic (SSR) was established as a full union republic of the USSR.

During the 1920s Kyrgyzia developed considerably in cultural and educational terms. Literacy was greatly improved and a standard literary language was introduced. Economic and social development was also notable. Land reforms were implemented in 1920–21 and 1927–28, resulting in the settlement of many of the nomadic Kyrgyz. These were followed by the agricultural collectivization programme of the early 1930s, which was strongly opposed by many Kyrgyz, and prompted a partial revival of the *basmachi* movement, which had been largely suppressed by the mid-1920s.

Leading members of the Kyrgyz Communist Party (KCP) attempted to increase the role of ethnic Kyrgyz in the government of the republic, but these so-called 'national communists' were expelled from the KCP and often exiled or imprisoned, particularly during the late 1930s. Despite the suppression of nationalism while the USSR was led by Iosif Stalin, many aspects of Kyrgyz national culture were retained, and tensions with the all-Union (Soviet) authorities were evident in the post-1945 period. There were allegations that the murder of Sultan Ibraimov, the Chairman of the Kyrgyz Council of Ministers, in December 1980 was a result of his support for greater republican autonomy.

The election of Mikhail Gorbachev as Soviet leader in March 1985, and his introduction of reformist policies, led to the resignation of Turdakan Usubaliyev, the First Secretary of the KCP, in November of that year. His successor, Absamat Masaliyev, accused Usubaliyev of corruption and nepotism and dismissed many of his closest allies from office. However, Masaliyev's commitment to *perestroika* (denoting principally a policy of economic restructuring) did not extend beyond correcting the excesses of his predecessor, and he was frequently critical of Gorbachev's policy of *glasnost* (openness). The conservative Kyrgyz leadership also opposed the development of unofficial political groups. Nevertheless, several groups were established in 1989, with the intention of alleviating the acute housing crisis in the republic by seizing vacant land and building houses on it. One of these groups, Ashar, was partially tolerated by the authorities and soon developed a wider political role. Osh Aymaghi, a similar organization to Ashar based in Osh Oblast (region), where the majority of the population are ethnic Uzbeks, attempted to obtain land and homes for the ethnic Kyrgyz in the region.

Disputes over land and housing provision in the crowded Fergana valley region of Osh Oblast precipitated violent confrontation between Kyrgyz and Uzbeks in 1990. Osh had been incorporated into Kyrgyzia in 1924, although Uzbeks formed the majority of the population, and these had, of late, begun to demand the establishment of an Uzbek autonomous region in Osh. In early June 1990 at least 11 people died, and more than 200 were injured, as a result of conflict between Uzbeks and Kyrgyz. A state of emergency and a curfew were introduced, and the border between Uzbekistan and the Kyrgyz SSR was closed. However, the violence escalated, and order was not restored until August. According to official reports, more than 300 people died in the violence, but unofficial sources claimed that more than 1,000 people had been killed. The state of emergency remained in force until November.

Despite an increase in the influence of the nascent democratic movement, elections to the 350-member Kyrgyz Supreme Soviet (legislature) in February 1990 were conducted in traditional Soviet style, with KCP candidates winning most seats unopposed. In April the Supreme Soviet elected Masaliyev to the newly-instituted office of Chairman of the Supreme Soviet. He favoured the introduction of an executive presidency, as had been effected in other republics of the USSR. Election to the post was to be by the Supreme Soviet, and the overwhelming KCP majority in the legislature appeared to guarantee the election of Masaliyev. However, by October, when an extraordinary Supreme Soviet session was convened to elect the President, Masaliyev had been seriously discredited by the violence in Osh; moreover, the opposition, which had united as the Democratic Movement of Kyrgyzstan (DMK), had developed into a significant political force. In the first round of voting Masaliyev failed to achieve the necessary percentage of votes to be elected President, and he was refused permission to be renominated. In a further round of voting Askar Akayev, the liberal President of the Kyrgyz Academy of Sciences, was elected to the executive presidency. Akayev quickly allied himself with reformist politicians and economists, including leaders of the DMK (which had been influential in turning public opinion against Masaliyev following the events in Osh). Economic reformists were appointed to the newly-created State Committee for Economic Reform, and plans were announced for a programme to transfer state-controlled assets to private ownership. In December Masaliyev resigned as Chairman of the Supreme Soviet, and was replaced by Medetkan Sherimkulov.

In January 1991 Akayev introduced new government structures, replacing the unwieldy Council of Ministers by a smaller Cabinet of Ministers, comprising mainly younger, reformist politicians. In December 1990, despite opposition from the KCP (and Masaliyev in particular), the Kyrgyz Supreme Soviet had voted to change the name of the republic from the Kyrgyz SSR to the Republic of Kyrgyzstan, and in February 1991 the capital, Frunze (named after the Red Army commander who had conquered much of Central Asia in the Civil War), reverted to its pre-1926 name of Bishkek.

Although Kyrgyzstan was one of the more democratic of the five Soviet Central Asian republics, economic realities seemed to prevail against secession from the USSR. In the referendum on the preservation of the USSR, which was held in nine republics in March 1991, an overwhelming majority (87.7%) of eligible voters in Kyrgyzstan approved the proposal to retain the USSR as a 'renewed federation'.

Akayev's programme of political and economic reform had many opponents within the KCP and the security forces. In April 1991, apparently as a result of differences with President Akayev, Masaliyev resigned as First Secretary of the KCP. He was replaced by Jumgalbek Amanbayev. Although Amanbayev appeared more sympathetic to Akayev's reform programme, there was much opposition in the KCP leadership to controversial plans which would lead to the 'departyization' (removal of KCP cells from workplaces) of government and the security forces.

On 19 August 1991, when the State Committee for the State of Emergency (SCSE) announced that it had assumed power in Moscow, there was an attempt to depose Akayev in Kyrgyzstan. The KCP declared its support for the coup leaders, and the commander of the Turkestan Military District (which comprised the five Central Asian republics) threatened to dispatch troops and tanks to the republic. To pre-empt military action against him, Akayev dismissed Gen. Asasankulov, the Chairman of the republican KGB (state security service), and ordered troops of the Ministry of Internal Affairs to guard strategic buildings in Bishkek. Despite warnings from Vladimir Kryuchkov, the Chairman of the all-Union KGB and a member of the SCSE, Akayev established contact with Boris Yeltsin, President of the Russian Federation, and broadcast Yeltsin's opposition to the SCSE on republican television. On 20 August Akayev publicly denounced the coup and issued a decree prohibiting activity by any political party in government or state bodies. On the following day Akayev ordered all military units in Kyrgyzstan to remain in their barracks. On 26 August, after the coup had collapsed in Moscow, Akayev and Vice-President German Kuznetsov announced their resignation from the Communist Party of the Soviet Union (CPSU), and the entire politburo and secretariat of the KCP resigned. Following the coup attempt, Akayev continued with his policies of seeking fuller independence for Kyrgyzstan and the implementation of ambitious economic reforms. On 31 August the Kyrgyz Supreme Soviet voted to declare independence from the USSR. With the dissolution of the KCP and the CPSU, there was little remaining opposition to Akayev and his policies. On 12 October Akayev was re-elected President by direct popular vote, receiving 95% of the votes cast; no other candidate was nominated.

On 18 October 1991 Akayev signed, with representatives of seven other republics, a treaty to establish a new economic community, and in the following month the Kyrgyz Government approved the draft treaty of the proposed successor to the USSR, the Union of Sovereign States. When Russia, Belarus and Ukraine proposed the creation of the Commonwealth of Independent States (CIS, see p. 126), Akayev was quick to announce his approval. On 13 December all five Central Asian republics formally agreed to join the new Commonwealth, and on 21 December Kyrgyzstan was among the 11 signatories to the Alma-Ata Declaration (see p. 127).

As in other former Soviet republics following independence, a serious issue confronting Kyrgyzstan's Government was a rapid increase in criminal activity, in particular the cultivation of and trade in illegal drugs. President Akayev repeatedly declared his commitment to combating both organized crime and official corruption, which, he indicated, were impeding the country's economic reform process. Despite the deteriorating economic situation, Akayev's programme of economic and political reforms (considered to be the most radical of those taking place in the Central Asian republics of the former USSR) continued to enjoy widespread popular support. However, his policies were increasingly opposed by elements within the Uluk Kenesh (as the parliament was now known), notably by nationalists and former communists. In mid-1992 the KCP was revived as the Party of Communists of Kyrgyzstan (PCK), with Amanbayev as its Chairman. The party's membership was said to be some 10,000 (although this had risen to 25,000 by the time of the PCK's first congress in February 1993, when it was described as the largest party in Kyrgyzstan). During discussions to draft Kyrgyzstan's new Constitution, which were held throughout 1992, opposition forces demanded the restriction of the President's powers and a stronger role for the legislature. The Constitution, which was finally adopted on 5 May 1993, provided for a parliamentary system of government, with the Prime Minister as head of the executive (hitherto the Government had been subordinate to the President). Legislative power was to be vested in a smaller body, the 105-member Zhogorku Kenesh, following general elections (due to be held by 1995); in the mean time, the existing assembly, renamed the Zhogorku Kenesh, was to continue to act as the republic's parliament.

The new Constitution also to some degree mitigated the growing concern among Kyrgyzstan's large Slav and other ethnic groups that their civil rights were not sufficiently protected. During 1992 ethnic Russians (who then constituted some 20% of Kyrgyzstan's population) demanded that they be granted dual citizenship and that their language be accorded equal status with Kyrgyz. However, when the draft Constitution was adopted in December 1992, nationalist deputies succeeded in having Kyrgyz reconfirmed as the state language, with no reference to Russian even as a means of inter-ethnic communication (as it was in neighbouring Kazakhstan). The draft also required that the President have a fluent command of Kyrgyz. Akayev sought repeatedly to persuade the legislature to reverse its decision, in an effort to preserve social harmony and also to stem the increasing rate of emigration of non-Kyrgyz from the republic. (In mid-1993 it was estimated that some 145,000 Russians had left the country since 1989, while the population of ethnic Germans had decreased by more than one-half, owing to emigration.) Finally, in May 1993 the legislature voted to accord Russian the status of a language of inter-ethnic communication in the Constitution, although Akayev was unable to prevent the official name of the country being changed from the Republic of Kyrgyzstan to the less ethnically neutral Kyrgyz Republic. Akayev's efforts to encourage non-Kyrgyz to remain in the republic suffered a serious reverse in July, when the most prominent Slav in government, German Kuznetsov (now the First Deputy Prime Minister and one of Akayev's closest allies), announced his decision to return to Russia, prompted by a feeling of 'isolation' within the Kyrgyz administration. A further effort to restore the confidence of the Slav community in the Government was the opening of a Slavonic university in Bishkek in September.

Akayev's administration was further destabilized during 1993 by a series of corruption scandals, which his supporters claimed were orchestrated by communist and nationalist forces in an attempt to discredit the reformists. In March a special commission of inquiry was established to investigate the business dealings of the Vice-President, Feliks Kulov. A second commission was established by the legislature later in the year to investigate allegations that senior politicians—including the Prime Minister, Tursunbek Chyngyshev—had been involved in unauthorized gold exports. In early December Kulov resigned as Vice-President 'for ethical reasons', urging the Government to resign also. Several days later the legislature held a vote of confidence in Chyngyshev and his Government. When the motion failed to achieve the required two-thirds majority, Akayev dismissed the entire cabinet, in the interests of political stability. In mid-December the legislature approved the new Government, which was headed by Apas Jumagulov (who had been the last premier of Soviet Kyrgyzstan). The Government's composition was largely ethnic Kyrgyz, although it included one representative each of the Russian, German, Uzbek and Jewish communities. Amanbayev, the Chairman of the PCK, was appointed one of the six deputy Prime Ministers, although, following a parliamentary decree that ministers could not remain members of the legislature, he resigned his seat in the Kenesh, and also the party leadership. Despite the various obstacles to his reform process encountered during 1993, Akayev nevertheless received overwhelming support in a referendum of confidence in his presidency, held (on Akayev's initiative) on 30 January 1994. Of the 95.9% of the electorate that participated, 96.2% endorsed Akayev's leadership.

There appeared to be no decrease in the rate of emigration from Kyrgyzstan in 1994; more than 100,000 people were reported to have left the republic during the year (some 70% from the Russian minority). In June, in an attempt to curb the Russian exodus, Akayev announced that Russian was henceforth to have the status of official language in regions predominantly populated by Russian-speakers, as well as in 'vital areas of the national economy'. The procedure of application for dual citizenship was to be simplified, and the equitable representation of ethnic Russians in the state administration was to be guaranteed. Akayev also requested the Government to delay the final date for the full implementation of Kyrgyz as the official state language from 1995 to 2000. (In September Akayev extended this deadline until 2005.)

The longstanding division between conservatives and reformists within the legislature evolved into a parliamentary crisis in early September 1994, when more than 180 pro-reform deputies announced their intention to boycott the next session of the Zhogorku Kenesh in protest at the continuing obstruction of the economic reform process by former communists. The rebel deputies also demanded the dissolution of the Kenesh and the holding of fresh elections. On 5 September the entire Government tendered its resignation in response to the stalemate in the legislature, and Akayev announced that parliamentary elections would be held imminently. Opponents of the President suggested that the Government's resignation had been orchestrated in order to precipitate the removal of an obstructionist legislature. The Government was in fact promptly reinstated by Akayev, who announced the holding of a referendum on 22 October on two proposed constitutional amendments, including the replacement of the future unicameral Zhogorku Kenesh (as stipulated by the Constitution) by a bicameral legislature. Of the 87% of the electorate which participated in the referendum, more than 70% endorsed the institution of a new-style Zhogorku Kenesh comprising a 70-member People's Assembly (upper chamber) to represent regional interests at twice-yearly sessions, and a permanent 35-member Legislative Assembly (lower chamber) representing the population as a whole. The existing 350-member legislature was thus automatically dissolved, and a general election was scheduled for February 1995.

More than 1,000 candidates representing 15 ethnic groups contested the election to the two chambers of the new Zhogorku Kenesh, held on 5 February 1995 with the participation of some 62% of the electorate. However, only 16 of the 105 seats were filled, owing to the fact that in many constituencies the large number of candidates prevented any single one from receiving the required minimum share of the votes. Thus, a second round was held on 19 February (again with a 62% turnout), with voters in the respective constituencies deciding between the two leading candidates from the first round. However, as voting did not take place in some constituencies, only 73 of the remaining 89 seats were filled. A third round was to take place at a later date to decide the 16 vacant seats. However, as the Zhogorku Kenesh was already quorate, its two chambers held their inaugural sessions on 28 March; Mukar Cholponbayev, the former Minister of Justice, was elected Speaker of the Legislative Assembly, while Almambet Matubraimov, the former First Deputy Prime Minister, was elected Speaker of the People's Assembly. In early April Apas Jumagulov was reappointed Prime Minister. The remaining members of the Government were appointed (or reappointed) later in the month. The Government's composition, like that of its predecessor, was largely ethnic Kyrgyz.

In foreign policy, Kyrgyzstan has sought to establish good relations with Arab and other Muslim states, in particular Turkey, with which it shares close ethnic, cultural and linguistic ties. President Akayev has also stressed that, although Islam remains the dominant religion, Kyrgyzstan will continue to be a secular state, opposed to any manifestations of Islamic extremism. During the second half of 1992 the Kyrgyz Government participated in negotiations aimed at ending the civil conflict in neighbouring Tajikistan between forces of the Tajik Government and rebel Islamic groups. Kyrgyzstan did not initially send peace-keeping forces to Tajikistan, concerned that the conflict might consequently spread into Kyrgyzstan. In January 1993, however, it was reported that groups of armed Tajiks had crossed into Kyrgyzstan, seeking to incite an Islamic insurrection among the local population. In response, the Kyrgyz Government intensified controls along the border with Tajikistan, in an attempt to prevent further infiltration by Tajik groups. Kyrgyzstan subsequently contributed troops to a CIS peace-keeping mission on the Tajik–Afghan border. In January 1995 Kyrgyz peace-keepers came under attack for the first time; in the following month the Government dispatched a further 200 troops to reinforce the Kyrgyz contingent.

Kyrgyzstan has strongly defended the preservation of the CIS, recognizing its dependence on the Commonwealth for economic survival. Among other agreements, Kyrgyzstan signed (in mid-1992) a collective security treaty with five CIS members, and in early 1993 a charter on closer co-operation in all spheres was signed by six of the 10 (at the time) remaining member states, including Kyrgyzstan. Akayev has also endeavoured to maintain close relations with the most influential CIS member, the Russian Federation, and the issue of the almost 1m. Russians in Kyrgyzstan (see above) has been at the centre of discussions between the two states. In June 1992 Akayev and the Russian President, Boris Yeltsin, signed a treaty of friendship, co-operation and mutual assistance. Military agreements, including a treaty of non-aggression, have also been concluded. CIS (mainly Russian) troops were to remain in Kyrgyzstan for the immediate future to protect the country's border with the People's Republic of China.

Relations with the neighbouring Central Asian republics of Uzbekistan and Kazakhstan deteriorated sharply in May 1993, following Kyrgyzstan's sudden introduction of its own currency, the som. The Uzbek Government, fearing a massive influx of roubles into the republic, closed its border with Kyrgyzstan, suspending all trade and telecommunications links for several days. However, relations between the two states improved following talks, held in mid-June, during which Akayev apologized for the unexpected manner in which the new currency had been introduced. In January 1994 Kyrgyzstan joined the economic zone established by Kazakhstan and Uzbekistan earlier in the month, and in February 1995 an Interstate Council was established to co-ordinate economic activity in the zone.

### Government

Supreme legislative power in the Kyrgyz Republic is vested in the bicameral 105-member Zhogorku Kenesh (Supreme Council), which comprises a permanent 35-member Legislative Assembly (lower chamber) and a 70-member People's Assembly (upper chamber), the latter of which meets twice yearly to debate regional issues. The Zhogorku Kenesh is elected by universal suffrage for a term of five years. The President of the Republic, who is directly elected for a five-year term, is Head of State and Commander-in-Chief of the Armed Forces. The Prime Minister heads the Government (the supreme executive organ), the members of which are appointed by the President (subject to the approval of the Zhogorku Kenesh). For administrative purposes, Kyrgyzstan is divided into six regions (oblasts or dubans) and the municipality of Bishkek (the capital).

### Defence

Kyrgyzstan began to raise a national army in mid-1992; until independence the country's military structures and personnel had been wholly integrated into the USSR's armed forces. However, Kyrgyzstan joined the defence structures of the Commonwealth of Independent States (CIS), which succeeded the USSR, signing, with five other member states, a collective security treaty in May 1992. In June 1994 Kyrgyzstan's national army numbered an estimated 12,000. There was also a small air force. CIS forces were to remain in Kyrgyzstan for the immediate future to monitor the Kyrgyz-Chinese border. Military service is compulsory and lasts for 18 months. However, the rate of desertion is high. In June 1994 Kyrgyzstan joined NATO's 'partnership for peace' programme of military co-operation (see p. 192). Projected government expenditure on defence for 1994 was US $57.3m.

## Economic Affairs

In 1993, according to estimates by the World Bank, Kyrgyzstan's gross national product (GNP), measured at average 1991–93 prices, was US $3,752m., equivalent to $830 per head. During 1985–93, it was estimated GNP per head decreased, in real terms, at an average annual rate of 2.1%. Over the same period the population increased by an annual average of 1.6%. In real terms, Kyrgyzstan's gross domestic product (GDP) declined by 5% in 1991, by 19% in 1992, by some 17% in 1993 and by a reported 26% in 1994.

Agriculture (including forestry) contributed about 28% of GDP in 1991, when the sector provided 36% of employment. By tradition, the Kyrgyz are a pastoral nomadic people, and the majority of the population (62% in the early 1990s) reside in rural areas. Livestock-raising is the mainstay of agricultural activity; sheep constitute some 60% of the livestock numbers, followed in importance by cattle, goats and horses. Only about 7% of the country's terrain is arable; of this, some 70% depends on irrigation. The principal crops are grain, potatoes and other vegetables, fruit, cotton and tobacco; apiculture is also of considerable significance. In November 1994 it was reported that some 78% of the agricultural sector had been 'privatized'. In 1994 agricultural production was estimated to have declined by 17%, compared with the previous year.

Industry, including mining, manufacturing, power and construction, contributed some 45% of GDP, and provided 27% of employment, in 1991. The most important sectors are metallurgy, agricultural and other machinery, electronics and instruments, textiles, and food-processing (in particular, sugar-refining). Some 40% of the industrial sector was estimated to have been transferred to private ownership by early 1994. It was estimated that industrial production decreased by 25% in 1994, compared with 1993.

Kyrgyzstan has considerable mineral deposits, including coal, gold, tin, mercury, antimony, zinc, tungsten and uranium. In 1991 the mining sector employed between 3% and 7% of the industrial work-force. The Kumtor gold mines are believed to be the seventh largest deposits of gold in the world. However, unlike some of its Central Asian neighbours, Kyrgyzstan has insignificant reserves of petroleum and natural gas and relies heavily on imports from other former Soviet republics.

Kyrgyzstan's principal source of domestic energy production (and also a major export) is hydroelectricity (generated by the country's mountain rivers). In 1991 hydroelectricity provided 26.4% of total domestic energy requirements, while petroleum and natural gas provided 31.3% and 21.2%, respectively. The remainder was provided by hard coal (11.9%) and lignite (9.2%). In 1992 77% of domestic electricity generation came from hydroelectric power stations and the remaining 23% from thermal plants.

In 1992 Kyrgyzstan recorded a visible trade deficit of US $110.9m., while there was a deficit of $100.8m. on the current account of the balance of payments. Following independence, the overwhelming majority of Kyrgyzstan's foreign trade continued to be conducted with former republics of the USSR (some 92% in 1992); in 1994 the three leading trading partners were Uzbekistan, Kazakhstan and Russia. In the early 1990s the principal exports were machinery, non-ferrous metals and minerals, woollen and other textile goods, agricultural and food products, electric power, and electronic and engineering products. The principal imports were petroleum and natural gas, iron and steel, chemicals and pharmaceuticals, engineering products, construction materials and food products.

In 1992 there was a budgetary deficit of 14,720m. roubles. In 1994 the budgetary deficit was estimated to be 862m. soms, equivalent to some 8% of GDP. Kyrgyzstan's total external debt was US $308.3m. at the end of 1993, of which $248.1m. was long-term public debt. In 1991 the average annual rate of inflation was 85.0%, increasing rapidly, to 854.6% in 1992 and to a reported 1,465.9% in 1993, but declining to 86.2% in 1994. At the end of 1994 some 42,000 people were officially registered as unemployed (although the level of 'hidden unemployment' was reported to be substantially higher).

Kyrgyzstan became a member of the IMF and the World Bank in 1992. Kyrgyzstan participates in the economic bodies of the Commonwealth of Independent States (CIS, see p. 126), and has also joined the European Bank for Reconstruction and Development (see p. 140) as a 'Country of Operations', and the Economic Co-operation Organization (see p. 238). In 1993 Kyrgyzstan became a member of the Asian Development Bank (see p. 107). In early 1994 Kyrgyzstan established, with Kazakhstan and Uzbekistan, a trilateral economic area. In February 1995 Kyrgyzstan signed a 10-year 'partnership and co-operation' agreement with the European Union.

The overall economic decline that Kyrgyzstan experienced in 1991 was aggravated by the disintegration of the USSR. The resultant disruptions in economic links between the former Soviet republics particularly affected Kyrgyzstan's economy, which was highly integrated into the Soviet central planning system, with almost all its trade conducted with other Soviet republics. Reflecting the general economic decline, widespread shortages of basic commodities were reported throughout the country, with an estimated 70% of the population said to be living in poverty. In 1992 Kyrgyzstan's economic performance was estimated to be the lowest among the CIS member states (with the exception of Armenia). Economic development was further impeded by reductions in deliveries of petroleum and other fuels by traditional suppliers (principally the Russian Federation). Moreover, Kyrgyzstan's initial decision to retain the rouble as its national currency meant that the country's economy was inevitably linked to developments in the Russian Federation and other republics remaining in the rouble area. The introduction of price liberalization measures in Kyrgyzstan in 1991 and 1992, in common with policies implemented in the Russian Federation and other republics, led to a serious escalation in the rate of inflation (although this had been successfully reduced by early 1995).

In spite of the economic difficulties experienced following independence, Kyrgyzstan has a well-educated population, a relatively strong industrial base and a good infrastructure, as well as considerable mineral, agricultural and energy resources, on which future economic development might be based. It is recognized, however, that the exploitation of these resources will require substantial external assistance, and the Government has thus given priority to attracting foreign investment in Kyrgyzstan. With its economic reform programme attracting international approbation, including financial support from the IMF and other agencies, and its domestic political situation remaining relatively stable, foreign interest in Kyrgyzstan is likely to increase in the near future.

## Social Welfare

In order to counteract the decline in living standards and increase in unemployment that was expected to result from the implementation of free-market economic reforms in the early 1990s, the Government strengthened Kyrgyzstan's social security and welfare system, introducing subsidies on many basic consumer goods and services and 'freezing' housing rents and maintenance charges. In addition, two extrabudgetary funds—the Pension Fund and the Employment Fund—became operative in 1991, and were intended to assist the most seriously affected social groups. The Pension Fund supported some 600,000 pensioners in the early 1990s; the normal retirement age in Kyrgyzstan is 60 years for men and 55 years for women. In 1991 some 34,000 people applied for unemployment compensation. In January 1994 it was officially reported that, in the previous year, the birth rate had fallen by 10.6%, while an increase of 6% was recorded in the rate of infant mortality. These figures were directly linked with the general decline in the standard of living in the republic.

Of total projected budgetary expenditure in 1992, 2,283m. roubles (13.4%) was for health, and 2,697m. roubles (15.8%) for social security. In 1991 there were 34 physicians and 119 hospital beds per 10,000 inhabitants.

## Education

Education is officially compulsory for nine years, comprising four years of primary school (between the ages of six and nine), followed by five years of lower secondary school (ages 10 to 14). Pupils may then continue their studies in upper secondary schools (two years' duration), specialized secondary schools (two to four years) or technical and vocational schools (from 15 years of age upwards). In 1991/92 there were 42,000 students in specialized secondary schools and 49,000 students in technical and vocational schools. Higher education, lasting between four and six years, is provided in 17 establishments in Kyrgyzstan (including the Kyrgyz State University and the Kyrgyz-Russian University, the latter

# KYRGYZSTAN

having opened in Bishkek in 1993 for the Slavonic population). In 1993/94 there were some 48,000 students enrolled at institutes of higher education (including evening and correspondence schools). In 1993 some 600 Kyrgyz were studying at secondary and higher schools in Turkey.

In 1993/94 63.6% of pupils in primary and secondary schools were taught in Kyrgyz, 23.4% were taught in Russian, 12.7% in Uzbek and 0.3% in Tajik. However, Russian was the principal language of instruction in higher educational establishments: in 1993/94 64.6% of students were taught in Russian, 34.7% in Kyrgyz and 0.7% in Uzbek. According to census results, the rate of adult illiteracy in Kyrgyzstan in 1989 was only 3.0% (males 1.4%; females 4.5%). In 1992 18.4% of total budgetary expenditure (7,410m. roubles) was allocated to education.

## Public Holidays

**1995:** 1 January (New Year's Day), 7 January (Christmas), 8 March (International Women's Day), 21 March (Nooruz, Kyrgyz New Year), 1 May (International Labour Day), 9 May (Victory Day), 31 August (Independence Day).

**1996:** 1 January (New Year's Day), 7 January (Christmas), 8 March (International Women's Day), 21 March (Nooruz, Kyrgyz New Year), 1 May (International Labour Day), 9 May (Victory Day), 31 August (Independence Day).

In addition, the religious festivals of Orozo Ait and Kurban Ait are celebrated as public holidays.

## Weights and Measures

The metric system is in force.

# Statistical Survey

Principal source: IMF, *Kyrgyzstan, Economic Review* and *Supplement on Countries of the Former Soviet Union*; World Bank, *Kyrgyztan: The Transition to a Market Economy* and *Statistical Handbook: States of the Former USSR*.

## Area and Population

### AREA, POPULATION AND DENSITY

| | |
|---|---:|
| Area (sq km) | 198,500* |
| Population (census result) 12 January 1989† | |
| Males | 2,077,623 |
| Females | 2,180,132 |
| Total | 4,257,755 |
| Population (official estimates at 1 January) | |
| 1994 | 4,474,000 |
| 1995 | 4,476,400 |
| Density (per sq km) at 1 January 1995 | 22.6 |

* 76,600 sq miles.
† The figures refer to *de jure* population. The *de facto* total was 4,290,442.

### PRINCIPAL ETHNIC GROUPS (permanent inhabitants, 1989 census)

| | % |
|---|---:|
| Kyrgyz | 52.4 |
| Russian | 21.5 |
| Uzbek | 12.9 |
| Ukrainian | 2.5 |
| German | 2.4 |
| Tatar | 1.6 |
| Others | 6.7 |
| **Total** | **100.0** |

**1993 (%):** Kyrgyz 56.5; Russian 18.8; Ukrainian 2.1; German 1.0; Others 21.6.

**PRINCIPAL TOWNS** (estimated population at 1 July 1991): Bishkek (capital, formerly Frunze) 627,800; Osh 219,100.

Source: UN, *Demographic Yearbook*.

### BIRTHS, MARRIAGES AND DEATHS

| | Registered live births | | Registered marriages | | Registered deaths | |
|---|---:|---:|---:|---:|---:|---:|
| | Number | Rate (per 1,000) | Number | Rate (per 1,000) | Number | Rate (per 1,000) |
| 1987 | 136,588 | 32.6 | 40,161 | 9.6 | 30,597 | 7.3 |
| 1988 | 133,710 | 31.4 | 40,490 | 9.5 | 31,879 | 7.5 |
| 1989 | 131,508 | 30.4 | 41,790 | 9.7 | 31,156 | 7.2 |

**1992:** Registered live births 128,352 (birth rate 28.6 per 1,000); Registered deaths 32,163 (death rate 7.2 per 1,000).

**Expectation of life** (years at birth, 1991): 68.5 (males 64.3; females 72.4).

Source: UN, *Demographic Yearbook*.

### EMPLOYMENT (annual averages, '000 persons)

| | 1989 | 1990 | 1991 |
|---|---:|---:|---:|
| Agriculture and forestry | 577.2 | 572.0 | 622.7 |
| Industry* | 334.9 | 334.4 | 318.7 |
| Construction | 151.5 | 152.8 | 143.0 |
| Transport and communications | 95.2 | 94.0 | 93.5 |
| Trade and catering | 85.4 | 87.4 | 87.9 |
| Other services | 494.7 | 507.3 | 484.3 |
| **Total** | **1,738.9** | **1,747.9** | **1,754.1** |

* Principally mining, manufacturing, electricity, gas and water.

# KYRGYZSTAN

## Agriculture

**PRINCIPAL CROPS** ('000 metric tons)

|  | 1991 | 1992 | 1993 |
|---|---|---|---|
| Wheat | 434 | 634* | 800* |
| Barley | 556 | 582* | 550* |
| Maize | 365 | 281* | 238* |
| Potatoes | 326 | 362 | 300* |
| Seed cotton | 63 | 52 | 58† |
| Cabbages | n.a. | 61* | 32* |
| Tomatoes | n.a. | 201* | 150* |
| Cucumbers and gherkins | n.a. | 16* | 7* |
| Onions (dry) | n.a. | 40* | 40* |
| Carrots | n.a. | 40* | 35* |
| Other vegetables | n.a. | 46* | 41* |
| Grapes | 29 | 31 | 30† |
| Sugar beet | 13 | 130* | 200* |
| Apples | n.a. | 75* | 69† |
| Peaches and nectarines | n.a. | 15* | 12† |
| Plums | n.a. | 17* | 13* |
| Apricots | n.a. | 16* | 12† |
| Tobacco (leaves) | 43* | 56* | 60† |
| Cotton (lint) | 19 | 16* | 18* |

\* Unofficial figure.  † FAO estimate.

Source: mainly FAO, *Production Yearbook*.

**LIVESTOCK** ('000 head, at 1 January)

|  | 1991 | 1992 | 1993 |
|---|---|---|---|
| Horses | 313 | 315* | 310* |
| Cattle | 1,205 | 1,095 | 1,002† |
| Camels | n.a. | 50* | 50* |
| Pigs | 393 | 299 | 264† |
| Sheep | 9,545 | 9,200 | 9,000* |
| Goats | 428 | 300 | 300* |
| Poultry | 13,906 | 13,000† | 13,000* |

\* FAO estimate.   † Unofficial figure.

Source: mainly FAO, *Production Yearbook*.

**LIVESTOCK PRODUCTS** ('000 metric tons)

|  | 1991 | 1992 | 1993 |
|---|---|---|---|
| Beef and veal | 87 | 80* | 76* |
| Mutton and lamb | 64 | 60† | 55† |
| Goat meat | 7† | 5† | 4† |
| Pig meat | 33 | 34* | 33* |
| Poultry meat | 29 | 27† | 26† |
| Cows' milk | 1,132 | 900* | 800* |
| Cheese | n.a. | 12.0† | 12.0† |
| Butter* | 10.0 | 9.0 | 8.0 |
| Hen eggs | 36.0* | 31.0* | 30.0† |
| Wool: |  |  |  |
| greasy | 36.6 | 37.0† | 35.0† |
| scoured | 22.0 | 22.2† | 21.0† |

\* Unofficial figure(s).   † FAO estimate.

Source: FAO, *Production Yearbook*.

## Fishing

(metric tons, live weight)

|  | 1991 | 1992* |
|---|---|---|
| Hoven's carp | 746 | 747 |
| Other fishes | 453 | 453 |
| **Total catch** | 1,199 | 1,200 |

\* FAO estimates.

Source: FAO, *Yearbook of Fishery Statistics*.

## Mining

|  | 1990 | 1991 | 1992 |
|---|---|---|---|
| Coal ('000 metric tons) | 3,742 | 3,473 | 2,151 |
| Crude petroleum ('000 metric tons) | 155.0 | 142.7 | 113.0 |
| Natural gas (million cu metres) | 96.0 | 83.2 | 72.4 |

**1994** (estimates): Crude petroleum 90,000 metric tons; Natural gas 38.4m. cu metres.

## Industry

**SELECTED PRODUCTS**

|  | 1990 | 1991 | 1992 |
|---|---|---|---|
| Textile fabrics ('000 sq metres) | 134,251 | 142,778 | 121,284 |
| Carpets ('000 sq metres) | 2,004 | 1,661 | 1,701 |
| Footwear ('000 pairs) | 11,125 | 9,504 | 5,751 |
| Cement ('000 metric tons) | 1,387.3 | 1,320.3 | 1,095.7 |
| Trucks ('000) | 25.1 | 23.6 | 14.8 |
| Washing machines ('000) | 233.7 | 209.4 | 94.0 |
| Electric energy (million kWh) | 13,370 | 14,170 | 11,890 |

## Finance

**CURRENCY AND EXCHANGE RATES**

**Monetary Units**
100 tyiyns = 1 som.

**Sterling and Dollar Equivalents** (30 November 1994)
£1 sterling = 16.435 soms;
US $1 = 10.500 soms;
1,000 soms = £60.85 = $95.24.

Note: In May 1993 Kyrgyzstan introduced its own currency, the som, replacing the Russian (former Soviet) rouble. Based on the official rate of exchange, the average value of the Soviet currency (roubles per US dollar) was: 0.6274 in 1989; 0.5856 in 1990; 0.5819 in 1991. However, a multiple exchange rate system was in operation, with separate non-commercial and tourist rates. A commercial exchange rate was introduced on 1 November 1990, replacing the official rate for most transactions. The commercial rate (roubles per US dollar) was: 1.692 at 31 December 1990; 1.671 at 31 December 1991. Between November 1989 and April 1991 the tourist exchange rate valued the rouble at one-tenth of the official rate. In April 1991 this rate, renamed the 'special rate', was set at $1 = 27.6 roubles. It was subsequently adjusted. The average market exchange rate in 1991 was $1 = 31.2 roubles. Following the dissolution of the USSR in December 1991, Russia and several other former Soviet republics retained the rouble as their monetary unit. The average interbank market rate in 1992 was $1 = 222.1 roubles.

From 15 May 1993 (having been introduced on 10 May), the som became Kyrgyzstan's sole legal currency. The initial exchange rate was $1 = 4 soms, while Russian currency was exchanged at a rate of 1 som = 200 roubles. Some of the figures in this Survey are still expressed in terms of roubles.

**BUDGET** (million roubles)*

| Revenue | 1990 | 1991 | 1992† |
|---|---|---|---|
| Taxation | 2,185 | 2,660 | 22,360 |
| Turnover tax | 1,172 | 1,168 | — |
| Sales tax | — | 305 | — |
| Value-added tax | — | — | 7,650 |
| Excise duties | — | — | 2,790 |
| Profits taxes | 421 | 756 | 7,780 |
| Personal income taxes‡ | 196 | 383 | 2,690 |
| Social security contributions§ | 364 | — | — |
| Other revenue | 115 | 837 | 3,140 |
| Grants from USSR (net) | 905 | 1,928 | — |
| **Total** | 3,205 | 5,425 | 25,510 |

# KYRGYZSTAN

| Expenditure | 1990 | 1991 | 1992¶ |
|---|---|---|---|
| National economy | 1,553 | 1,573 | 3,276 |
| Education | 604 | 1,096 | 4,231 |
| Health | 318 | 565 | 2,283 |
| Culture and mass media | 79 | 96 | 328 |
| Social security | 416 | 1,025 | 2,697 |
| Law enforcement | n.a. | 68 | 616 |
| Contributions to Commonwealth of Independent States | — | — | 773 |
| Debt interest | — | — | 2,196 |
| **Total** (incl. others) | 3,184 | 4,727 | 17,053 |

* Figures represent a consolidation of the operations of the central Government and local governments.
† Figures are rounded to the nearest 10 million roubles.
‡ Revenue was split between the USSR and Kyrgyzstan in 1990. In later years all funds accrued to Kyrgyzstan.
§ Collection of social security contributions was treated as extra-budgetary from 1991, when a separate pension fund was established.
¶ Forecasts. The actual total (in million roubles) was 40,230 (Education 7,410; Health 4,130), excluding net lending (12,140).

**MONEY SUPPLY** (million roubles at 31 December)

| | 1990 | 1991 | 1992 |
|---|---|---|---|
| Currency outside banks | 1,766 | 2,883 | 17,904 |

**30 June 1993:** 158 million soms.

**COST OF LIVING** (Retail price index; previous year = 100)

| | 1991 | 1992 |
|---|---|---|
| All items | 185.0 | 954.6 |

**NATIONAL ACCOUNTS** (million roubles at current prices)

**Expenditure on the Gross Domestic Product**

| | 1989 | 1990 | 1991 |
|---|---|---|---|
| Government final consumption expenditure | 1,250 | 1,370 | 2,510 |
| Private final consumption expenditure | 5,036 | 5,572 | 7,971 |
| Increase in stocks | 625 | 448 | 1,092 |
| Gross fixed capital formation | 2,390 | 2,337 | 4,353 |
| **Total domestic expenditure** | 9,301 | 9,727 | 15,926 |
| Exports of goods and services / Less Imports of goods and services | −1,681 | −1,407 | −87 |
| **GDP in purchasers' values** | 7,620 | 8,320 | 15,839 |

**Gross Domestic Product by Economic Activity**

| | 1989 | 1990 | 1991 |
|---|---|---|---|
| Agriculture and forestry | 2,510 | 2,805 | 4,505 |
| Industry* | 2,250 | 2,348 | 5,985 |
| Construction | 785 | 840 | 1,100 |
| Transport and communications | 357 | 397 | 672 |
| Other material services | 562 | 617 | 1,011 |
| Non-material services | 1,157 | 1,313 | 2,566 |
| **GDP in purchasers' values** | 7,620 | 8,320 | 15,839 |

* Principally mining, manufacturing, electricity, gas and water.

**BALANCE OF PAYMENTS** (US $ million)

| | 1991 | 1992* |
|---|---|---|
| Merchandise exports f.o.b. | 3,719.0 | 284.8 |
| Merchandise imports c.i.f. | −3,855.0 | −395.7 |
| **Trade balance** | −136.0 | −110.9 |
| Services (net) | n.a. | −4.5 |
| Private unrequited transfers (net) | — | −7.4 |
| Official unrequited transfers (net) | 1,102.0 | 22.0 |
| **Current balance** | 966.0 | −100.8 |
| Capital (net) | 15.0 | −1.7 |
| Net errors and omissions | −981.0 | −44.9 |
| **Overall balance** | n.a. | −147.5 |

* Revised estimates.

# External Trade

**PRINCIPAL COMMODITIES** (million roubles)

| Imports | 1990 | 1991 | 1992 |
|---|---|---|---|
| Industrial products | 3,894.9 | 6,427.0 | 66,139.4 |
| Petroleum and gas | 269.0 | 693.9 | 19,654.3 |
| Coal | 38.1 | 84.6 | 2,137.1 |
| Iron and steel | 171.0 | 302.8 | 4,285.4 |
| Non-ferrous metallurgy | 98.0 | 283.2 | 2,509.0 |
| Chemical and petroleum products | 374.0 | 609.9 | 7,746.7 |
| Machinery and metalworking | 985.0 | 1,273.5 | 17,035.3 |
| Timber, wood and paper | 130.0 | 200.5 | 2,060.8 |
| Light industry | 966.0 | 1,513.6 | 5,170.7 |
| Food and beverages | 663.0 | 1,080.0 | 4,246.8 |
| Other commodities | 87.0 | 265.3 | 553.9 |
| Agricultural products (unprocessed) | 247.0 | 439.4 | 4,343.1 |
| Other commodities | 102.0 | 49.6 | 103.7 |
| **Total** (incl. others) | 4,243.9 | 6,916.0 | 70,586.2 |
| USSR (former) | 3,122.9 | 5,492.7 | 67,257.0 |
| Other countries | 1,121.0 | 1,423.3 | 3,329.2 |

| Exports | 1990 | 1991 | 1992 |
|---|---|---|---|
| Industrial products | 2,390.0 | 6,338.2 | 51,854.8 |
| Electricity | 67.1 | 188.4 | 3,046.9 |
| Non-ferrous metallurgy | 164.0 | 499.3 | 5,662.5 |
| Chemical and petroleum products | 24.0 | 217.7 | 940.0 |
| Machinery and metalworking | 893.0 | 2,017.6 | 21,507.1 |
| Construction materials | 13.0 | 67.0 | 1,455.2 |
| Light industry | 648.0 | 1,901.2 | 12,730.5 |
| Food and beverages | 516.0 | 1,317.0 | 3,721.4 |
| Agricultural products (unprocessed) | 92.0 | 185.1 | 824.7 |
| **Total** (incl. others) | 2,501.0 | 6,546.3 | 52,785.7 |
| USSR (former) | 2,448.0 | 6,481.7 | 46,303.4 |
| Other countries | 53.0 | 64.6 | 6,482.3 |

# KYRGYZSTAN

*Statistical Survey, Directory*

**PRINCIPAL TRADING PARTNERS** (million roubles)
**Trade with the former USSR**

| Imports | 1991 | 1992 |
|---|---|---|
| Armenia | 45.3 | 95.1 |
| Azerbaijan | 80.0 | 327.1 |
| Belarus | 223.0 | 1,033.4 |
| Georgia | 82.6 | 300.5 |
| Kazakhstan | 779.6 | 15,583.1 |
| Latvia | 43.6 | 153.2 |
| Lithuania | 56.1 | 215.6 |
| Moldova | 62.8 | 349.0 |
| Russia | 2,702.2 | 32,987.7 |
| Tajikistan | 81.5 | 461.7 |
| Turkmenistan | 109.3 | 4,105.4 |
| Ukraine | 389.3 | 5,478.1 |
| Uzbekistan | 817.1 | 6,136.3 |
| **Total** (incl. others) | 5,492.7 | 67,257.0 |

| Exports | 1991 | 1992 |
|---|---|---|
| Armenia | 98.2 | 109.9 |
| Azerbaijan | 119.1 | 397.0 |
| Belarus | 205.0 | 1,385.8 |
| Georgia | 80.8 | 191.4 |
| Kazakhstan | 848.8 | 10,358.4 |
| Latvia | 118.8 | 125.8 |
| Lithuania | 260.4 | 692.1 |
| Russia | 2,792.7 | 18,096.7 |
| Tajikistan | 274.7 | 647.9 |
| Turkmenistan | 278.1 | 1,126.6 |
| Ukraine | 600.3 | 8,008.2 |
| Uzbekistan | 718.7 | 4,794.3 |
| **Total** (incl. others) | 6,481.7 | 46,303.4 |

## Communications Media

| | 1989 | 1990 | 1991 |
|---|---|---|---|
| Telephones ('000 main lines in use) | 280* | 300* | 325 |

\* Provisional.

Source: UN, *Statistical Yearbook*.

## Education

(1993/94)

| | Institutions | Students |
|---|---|---|
| General schools | 1,832* | 933,700 |
| Primary | 111 | 6,300 |
| Lower secondary | 247 | 52,000 |
| Other secondary | 1,474 | 875,400 |
| Higher schools (incl. university-level) | 17 | 47,915† |

\* Of which 1,171 used Kyrgyz as the language of instruction, 128 Uzbek, 126 Russian, 2 Tajik and 405 used two or more languages of instruction.
† Including students enrolled on evening and correspondence classes.

Teachers: 5,140 in higher schools in 1991/92; 65,073 in general schools in 1992/93.

Source: mainly Ministry of Education and Science, Bishkek.

# Directory

## The Constitution

A new Constitution was proclaimed on 5 May 1993. The following is a summary of its main provisions (including amendments endorsed in a referendum held on 22 October 1994):

### GENERAL PROVISIONS

The Kyrgyz Republic (Kyrgyzstan) is a sovereign, unitary, democratic republic founded on the principle of lawful, secular government. All state power belongs to the people, who exercise this power through the state bodies on the basis of the Constitution and laws of the republic. Matters of legislation and other issues pertaining to the state may be decided by the people by referendum. The President of the Republic, the deputies of the Zhogorku Kenesh (Supreme Council), and representatives of local administrative bodies are all elected directly by the people. Elections are held on the basis of universal, equal and direct suffrage by secret ballot. All citizens of 18 years and over are eligible to vote.

The territory of the Kyrgyz Republic is integral and inviolable. The state language is Kyrgyz. The equality and free use of Russian and other languages are guaranteed. The rights and freedoms of citizens may not be restricted on account of ignorance of the state language.

### THE PRESIDENT

The President of the Kyrgyz Republic is Head of State and Commander-in-Chief of the Armed Forces, and represents Kyrgyzstan both within the country and internationally. Any citizen of the republic between the ages of 35 and 65, who has a fluent command of the state language, may stand for election. The President's term of office is five years; he/she may not serve more than two consecutive terms. The President is directly elected by the people.

The President appoints and dismisses (subject to approval by the legislature) the members of the Government as well as heads of administrative offices and other leading state posts; presents draft legislation to the Zhogorku Kenesh on his/her own intitiative; signs legislation approved by the Zhogorku Kenesh or returns it for further scrutiny; signs international agreements; may call referendums on issues of state; may dissolve the legislature (should a referendum demand this) and call fresh elections; announces a general or partial mobilization; and declares a state of war in the event of an invasion by a foreign power.

### ZHOGORKU KENESH (SUPREME COUNCIL)

Supreme legislative power is vested in the 105-member Zhogorku Kenesh, which comprises two chambers: the 35-member Legislative Assembly (lower chamber), which is a permanent chamber, and the 70-member People's Assembly (upper chamber), which sits twice yearly and represents regional interests. Members of both chambers are elected for a term of five years on the basis of universal, equal and direct suffrage by secret ballot.

The Zhogorku Kenesh approves amendments and additions to the Constitution; enacts legislation; determines key areas of domestic and foreign policy; confirms the republican budget and supervises its execution; determines questions pertaining to the administrative and territorial structure of the republic; designates presidential elections; approves the composition of the Government; approves the appointment of the Procurator-General and the Chairman of the National Bank; ratifies or abrogates international agreements, and decides questions of war and peace; and organizes referendums on issues of state.

### THE GOVERNMENT

The Government of the Kyrgyz Republic is the highest organ of executive power in Kyrgyzstan. The Prime Minister heads the Government, which also comprises the Deputy Prime Ministers, Ministers and Chairmen of State Committees. The members of the Government are appointed by the President on the recommendation of the Prime Minister; their appointment is approved by the Zhogorku Kenesh. The President supervises the work of the Government and has the right to chair its sessions. The Prime Minister must deliver an annual report to the Zhogorku Kenesh on the work of the Government.

The Government determines all questions of state administration, other than those ascribed to the Constitution or to the competence of the President and the Zhogorku Kenesh; drafts the republican budget and submits it to the Zhogorku Kenesh for approval; co-ordinates budgetary, financial, fiscal and monetary

# KYRGYZSTAN

policy; administers state property; takes measures to defend the country and state security; executes foreign policy; and strives to guarantee the rights and freedoms of the citizens and to protect property and social order.

### JUDICIAL SYSTEM

The judicial system comprises the Constitutional Court, the Supreme Court, the Higher Court of Arbitration and regional courts. Judges of the Constitutional Court are appointed by the Zhogorku Kenesh, on the recommendation of the President, for a term of 15 years, while those of the Supreme Court and the Higher Court of Arbitration are appointed by the Zhogorku Kenesh, on the recommendation of the President, for ten years. The Constitutional Court is the supreme judicial body protecting constitutionality. It comprises the Chairman/woman, his/her deputies and seven judges. The Supreme Court is the highest organ of judicial power in the sphere of civil, criminal and administrative justice.

## The Government

### HEAD OF STATE

**President of the Republic of Kyrgyzstan:** ASKAR AKAYEV (elected 28 October 1990; re-elected, by direct popular vote, 12 October 1991).

### GOVERNMENT
(May 1995)

**Prime Minister:** APAS JUMAGULOV.
**First Deputy Prime Minister:** ABDYJAPAR TAGAYEV
**Deputy Prime Minister (responsible for economics and industry):** ALEKSANDR MOISEYEV.
**Deputy Prime Minister (responsible for social policy):** OSMONAKUN IBRAIMOV.
**Deputy Prime Minister (responsible for agriculture):** JUMGALBEK AMANBAYEV.
**Minister of Industry and Trade:** ANDREY IORDAN.
**Minister of Foreign Affairs:** ROZA OTUNBAYEVA.
**Minister of Education and Science:** ASKAR KAKEYEV.
**Minister of Health:** NAKEN KASIYEV.
**Minister of Finance:** KEMELBEK NANAYEV (acting).
**Minister of Agriculture:** BEKBOLOT TALGARBEKOV (acting).
**Minister of Water Resources:** MEYRAJIN ZULPUYEV.
**Minister of Communications:** EMIL BEKTENOV.
**Minister of Justice:** LARISA GUTCHENKO.
**Minister of Labour and Social Welfare:** ZAFAR KHAKIMOV.
**Minister of Transport:** SYDYKBEK ABLESOV.
**Minister of Culture:** CHOLPONBEK BAZARBAYEV.
**Minister of Internal Affairs:** Col MADALBEK MOLDASHEV.
**Minister of Defence:** MYRZAKAN SUBANOV.

### Chairmen of State Committees

**Chairman of the State Committee for Architecture and Construction:** ISHEMBAY KADYRBEKOV.
**Chairman of the State Committee for the Economy:** TALAYBEK KOICHUMANOV.
**Chairman of the State Committee for the Environment:** ISKENDER MURATALIN (acting).
**Chairman of the State Committee for Foreign Investment:** ASKAR SARYGULOV.
**Chairman of the State Committee for Geology and the Use and Protection of Minerals:** SHAMSHI TEKENOV.
**Chairman of the State Committee for National Security:** ANARBEK K. BAKAYEV.
**Chairman of the State Committee for Tourism and Sport:** MURZA KAPAROV.

### MINISTRIES

**Office of the President:** 720000 Bishkek, Government House; tel. (3312) 21-24-66; fax (3312) 21-86-27.
**Office of the Prime Minister:** 720000 Bishkek, Government House; tel. (3312) 22-56-56; fax (3312) 21-86-27.
**Office of the Deputy Prime Ministers:** 720000 Bishkek, Government House; tel. (3312) 21-89-35 (Economic Policy Dept), 21-16-52 (Social Policy Dept); fax (3312) 21-86-27 (Agriculture Dept).
**Ministry of Agriculture:** 720300 Bishkek, Kievskaya 96; tel. (3312) 22-14-35; telex 251283; fax (3312) 22-59-50.
**Ministry of Communications:** 720000 Bishkek, pr. Chui 95; tel. (3312) 22-20-34; telex 351334; fax (3312) 28-83-02.
**Ministry of Culture:** 720301 Bishkek, Abdumomunova 205; tel. (3312) 22-25-32; fax (3312) 22-50-79.
**Ministry of Defence:** 720001 Bishkek, Logvinenko 25; tel. (3312) 22-78-79.
**Ministry of Education and Science:** 720040 Bishkek, Tynystanova 257; tel. (3312) 25-31-52; fax (3312) 22-85-94.
**Ministry of Finance:** 720874 Bishkek, pr. Erkindik 58; tel. (3312) 22-70-39; telex 227292; fax (3312) 22-59-90.
**Ministry of Foreign Affairs:** 720003 Bishkek, Abdumomunova 205; tel. (3312) 22-05-45; telex 251384; fax (3312) 22-57-35.
**Ministry of Health:** 720005 Bishkek, Moskovskaya 148; tel. (3312) 22-86-97; fax (3312) 22-84-24.
**Ministry of Industry and Trade:** 720000 Bishkek, pr. Chui; tel. (3312) 21-89-35; fax (3312) 22-97-03.
**Ministry of Internal Affairs:** 720011 Bishkek, Frunze 469; tel. (3312) 22-54-90; telex 288788; fax (3312) 22-32-78.
**Ministry of Justice:** 720040 Bishkek, Orozbekova 37; tel. (3312) 26-47-92; fax (3312) 25-11-15.
**Ministry of Labour and Social Welfare:** 720031 Bishkek, Mederova 46; tel. (3312) 22-27-26.
**Ministry of Transport:** 720017 Bishkek, Isanova 42; tel. (3312) 21-66-72; fax (3312) 26-75-97.
**Ministry of Water Resources:** 720020 Bishkek, Sovetskaya 4A; tel. (3312) 47-96-01; fax (3312) 47-49-07.

### Principal State Committees

**State Committee for Architecture and Construction:** 720017 Bishkek, pr. Engelsa 185; tel. (3312) 21-74-32; fax (3312) 21-75-35.
**State Committee for the Economy:** 720001 Bishkek, pr. Erkindik 58; tel. (3312) 22-89-22; fax (3312) 22-74-04.
**State Committee for the Environment:** 720300 Bishkek, Isanova 131; tel. (3312) 26-42-44; telex 251329; fax (3312) 26-23-21.
**State Committee for Foreign Investment:** 720002 Bishkek, Kievskaya 96; tel. (3312) 22-32-92; telex 251239; fax (3312) 22-63-91.
**State Committee for Geology and the Use and Protection of Minerals:** 720739 Bishkek, pr. Erkindik 2; tel. (3312) 26-46-26.
**State Committee for National Security:** 720000 Bishkek, pr. Erkindik 70; tel. (3312) 22-39-29.
**State Committee for Tourism and Sport:** 720033 Bishkek, Togolok Moldo 17; tel. (3312) 22-06-57; telex 251247; fax (3312) 21-28-45.

## Legislature

### ZHOGORKU KENESH (SUPREME COUNCIL)

The Zhogorku Kenesh is a bicameral legislative body, comprising the 70-member People's Assembly (upper chamber), which meets twice yearly to debate issues of regional interest, and the 35-member Legislative Assembly (lower chamber), which is a standing body representing the population as a whole.

#### People's Assembly

At elections to the People's Assembly, held on 5 February 1995, only 14 of the 70 seats were filled. This necessitated a second round of voting ('run-off' elections) on 19 February, at which a further 46 deputies were elected. A third round was to be held at a later date to decide the 10 remaining vacant seats.

**Speaker:** ALMAMBET MATUBRAIMOV.

#### Legislative Assembly

With only two of the 35 seats of the Legislative Assembly filled at elections on 5 February 1995, a second round of voting was held on 19 February, when a further 27 seats were filled. The remaining six seats were to be decided at a later date.

**Speaker:** MUKAR CHOLPONBAYEV.

## Political Organizations

**Agrarian Party of Kyrgyzstan:** Bishkek; tel. (3312) 22-68-52; f. 1993; represents farmers' interests; Chair. E. ALIYEV.
**Asaba Party of National Revival:** Bishkek; tel. (3312) 43-04-45; f. 1991; nationalist party; Chair. CH. BAZARBAYEV.
**Ashar:** Bishkek; tel. (3312) 25-71-88; f. 1989; sociopolitical movement concerned with provision of land and homes for ethnic Kyrgyz; Chair. ZHUMAGAZY USUP-CHONAIU.
**Ata-Meken (Motherland) Party:** Bishkek; tel. (3312) 26-22-49; f. 1992; centrist; Chair. OMURBEK TEKEBAYEV.
**Democratic Movement of Kyrgyzstan:** Bishkek; tel. (3312) 22-50-97; f. 1990; registered as a political party in 1993; campaigns for civil liberties; Pres. ZH. ZHEKSHEYEV.

# KYRGYZSTAN

**Ecological Movement of Kyrgyzstan:** Bishkek; tel. (3312) 26-55-28; f. 1994; Chair. T. CHODURAYEV.

**Erkin (Free) Kyrgyzstan Democratic Party:** Bishkek; tel. (3312) 25-50-94; f. 1991; nationalist party; Chair. TOPCHUBEK TURGANALIYEV.

**Kok-Zhar Sociopolitical Organization:** Bishkek; f. 1992; seeks to provide housing for the underprivileged; Chair. ZH. ISAYEV.

**Lop Nor—Kyrgyz Anti-Nuclear Movement:** Bishkek; f. 1994; seeks the total banning of nuclear testing at Lop Nor (People's Republic of China) and other sites; Chair. A.K. KARIMOV.

**National Unity Democratic Movement:** Bishkek; tel. (3312) 22-50-84; f. 1991; seeks to unite different ethnic groups; Chair. YU. RAZGULYAYEV.

**Party of Communists of Kyrgyzstan:** Bishkek; tel. (3312) 22-59-63; f. 1992 as successor to Kyrgyz Communist Party (disbanded in Aug. 1991); 25,000 mems; Leader SHERALY SYDYKOV.

**People's Assembly of Kyrgyzstan:** Bishkek; tel. (3312) 21-83-77; f. 1994; strives to promote social integration; Chair. S. BEGALIYEV.

**Republican Popular Party of Kyrgyzstan:** Bishkek; tel. (3312) 22-33-34; f. 1993 by prominent scientists and academics; centrist; Chair. ZH. SHARSHENALIYEV.

**Slavic Association Soglasiye (Accord):** Bishkek; represents Slavic minority in Kyrgyzstan; Vice-Pres. ANATOLY BULGAKOV.

**Social Democratic Party of Kyrgyzstan:** Bishkek; tel. (3312) 22-08-95; f. 1993; Co-Chair. ZH. IBRAMOV, A. ATAMBAYEV, A. MARYSHEV.

**Unity Party of Kyrgyzstan:** Bishkek; tel. (3312) 42-42-26; f. 1994; Leader A. MURALIYEV.

## Diplomatic Representation

### EMBASSIES IN KYRGYZSTAN

**Belarus:** Bishkek, Moskovskaya 210; tel. (3312) 24-29-43; Chargé d'affaires a.i.: SERGEI RUTSKY.

**China, People's Republic:** Bishkek, Toktogula 196; tel. (3312) 22-24-23; Ambassdor: PAN ZHANLIN.

**Germany:** Bishkek, Razzakova 28; tel. (3312) 22-48-11; fax (3312) 62-00-07; Chargé d'affaires a.i.: Dr JÜRGEN SCHELLER.

**India:** Bishkek, pr. Chui 164; tel. (3312) 21-08-62; Ambassador: RAM SWARUP MUKHERJEE.

**Iran:** Bishkek, Razzakova 36; tel. (3312) 22-69-64; Ambassador: MORTEZA TAVASSOLI.

**Kazakhstan:** Bishkek, Togolok Moldo 10; tel. (3312) 22-54-63; Ambassador: MUKHTAR SHAKHANOV.

**Russia:** Bishkek, Razzakova 17; tel. (3312) 22-16-91; fax (3312) 22-18-23; Ambassador: MIKHAIL A. ROMANOV.

**Turkey:** 720001 Bishkek, Moskovskaya 89; tel. (3312) 22-78-82; telex 245125; fax (3312) 26-88-35; Ambassador: METIN GÖKER.

**USA:** 720002 Bishkek, pr. Erkindik 66; tel. (3312) 22-29-20; telex 245133; fax (3312) 22-35-51; Ambassador: EILEEN A. MALLOY.

## Judicial System

(see under Constitution, p. 1827)

**Chairwoman of the Constitutional Court:** CHOLPON BAYEKOVA.
**Chairman of the Supreme Court:** K. D. BOOBEKOV.
**Procurator-General:** ASANBEK SHARSHENALIYEV.

## Religion

### ISLAM

The majority of Kyrgyz are Sunni Muslims (Hanafi school), as are some other groups living in the republic, such as Uzbeks and Tajiks. Muslims in Kyrgyzstan are officially under the jurisdiction of the Muslim Board of Central Asia, based in Uzbekistan. The Board is represented in the republic by a kazi.

**Kazi of Muslims of Kyrgyzstan:** KIMSANBAY Haji ABDRAKHMANOV.
**Islamic Centre of Kyrgyzstan:** Bishkek; Pres. SADYKZHAN Haji KAMALOV.

## The Press

In 1993 there were 128 newspapers published in Kyrgyzstan, including 73 published in Kyrgyz. The average circulation per issue was 1,129,000 copies. There were 15 periodicals, including 8 in Kyrgyz, with a total circulation of 87,000 copies (43,000 in Kyrgyz).

### PRINCIPAL NEWSPAPERS

**Bishkek Shamy** (Bishkek Evening Newspaper): Bishkek; tel. (3312) 42-57-86; f. 1989; weekly; official organ of the Bishkek City Council; in Kyrgyz; Editor B. ZHUMABAYEV; circ. 10,000.

**Char Tarap** (Echo of Events): Bishkek; tel. (3312) 28-94-63; f. 1994; weekly; in Kyrgyz; Editor KALEN SYDYKOVA; circ. 5,000. (Parallel edition in Russian, *Ekho Sobytii*, Editor MURSURKUL KABYLBEKOV.)

**Kyrgyz Madaniyaty** (Kyrgyz Culture): 720301 Bishkek, Bokonbayeva 99; tel. (3312) 26-14-58; f. 1967; weekly; organ of the Union of Writers; Editor NURALY KAPAROV; circ. 15,940.

**Kyrgyz Tuusu:** Bishkek; tel. (3312) 22-45-09; f. 1924; 5 a week; organ of the Government; in Kyrgyz; Editor A. MATISANOV.

**Kyrgyzstan Chronicle:** Bishkek; tel. (3312) 22-48-32; f. 1993; weekly; independent; in English; Editor BAYAN SARYGULOV; circ. 5,000.

**Slovo Kyrgyzstana** (Word of Kyrgyzstan): Bishkek; tel. (3312) 26-92-77; f. 1925; 5 a week; organ of the Government; in Russian; Editor A. I. MALEVANY.

**Vecherny Bishkek** (Bishkek Evening Newspaper): 720026 Bishkek, Abdumomunova 193; tel. (3312) 26-34-10; fax (3312) 26-34-85; f. 1974; 5 a week; official organ of the Bishkek City Council; in Russian; Editor KH. YA. MUSTAFAYEV; circ. 51,500.

**Yuzhniy Kurier** (Southern Courier): Bishkek; tel. (3312) 26-10-53; f. 1993; weekly; independent; in Russian; Editor ALEKSANDR KNYAZYEV; circ. 10,000.

**Zaman Kyrgyzstan** (Kyrgyzstan Herald): Bishkek; tel. (3312) 26-37-39; f. 1992; weekly; independent; in Kyrgyz (Latin script); Editor MURZA GAPAR; circ. 13,000.

### PRINCIPAL PERIODICALS

Monthly, unless otherwise indicated.

**Ala Too** (Ala Too Mountains): 720300 Bishkek, Abdumomunova 205; tel. (3312) 26-55-12; f. 1931; organ of the Union of Writers; politics, novels, short stories, plays, poems of Kyrgyz authors and translations into Kyrgyz; in Kyrgyz; Editor KENESH JUSUPOV; circ. 3,000.

**Chalkan** (Stinging-nettle): Bishkek; tel. (3312) 42-16-38; f. 1955; satirical; in Kyrgyz; Editor K. ALYMBAYEV; circ. 7,600.

**Den-sooluk** (Health): Bishkek; tel. (3312) 22-46-37; f. 1960; weekly; journal of the Ministry of Health; popular science; in Kyrgyz; Editor MAR ALIYEV; circ. 20,000.

**Kyrgyzstan Ayaldary** (Women of Kyrgyzstan): Bishkek; tel. (3312) 42-12-26; f. 1951; popular; in Kyrgyz; Editor S. AKMATBEKOVA; circ. 500.

**Literaturny Kyrgyzstan** (Literary Kyrgyzstan): 720301 Bishkek, Pushkina 70; tel. (3312) 26-14-63; f. 1955; journal of the Union of Writers; fiction, literary criticism, journalism; in Russian; Editor-in-Chief A. I. IVANOV; circ. 3,000.

**Zdravookhraneniye Kyrgyzstana** (Public Health System of Kyrgyzstan): 720005 Bishkek, Sovetskaya 34; tel. (3312) 44-41-39; f. 1938; 4 a year; publ. by the Ministry of Health; medical experimental work; in Russian; Editor-in-Chief N. K. KASIYEV; circ. 3,000.

### NEWS AGENCY

**Kyrgyzkabar** (Kyrgyz News Agency): Bishkek; formerly KyrgyzTag—Kyrgyz Telegraph Agency.

#### Foreign Bureaux

**Informatsionnoye Telegrafnoye Agentstvo Rossii—Telegrafnoye Agentstvo Suverennykh Stran (ITAR—TASS)** (Russia): Bishkek, Sovetskaya 175; tel. (3312) 26-59-20; Correspondent BORIS M. MAINAYEV.

**Interfax** (Russia): Bishkek, Toktogula 97, Rm 6; tel. and fax (3312) 26-72-87; Bureau Chief BERMET MALIKOVA.

**Rossiyskoye Informatsionnoye Agentstvo—Novosti (RIA—Novosti)** (Russia): Bishkek, Abdumomunova 207; tel. (3312) 26-40-95; fax (3312) 22-85-12; Bureau Chief TOLKUN NAMATBAYEVA.

## Publishers

**Akyl:** 720000 Bishkek, Sovetskaya 170; tel. (3312) 22-47-57; f. 1994; science, politics, economics, culture, literature; Chair. AMANBEK KARYPKULOV.

**Ilim** (Science): 720071 Bishkek, pr. Chui 265A; tel. (3312) 25-53-60; scientific and science fiction; Dir L. V. TARASOVA.

**Kyrgyzskaya Entsiklopediya** (Kyrgyz Encyclopaedia): 720040 Bishkek, pr. Erkindik 56; tel. (3312) 22-77-57; dictionaries and encyclopaedias; Editor-in-Chief AMANBEK KARYPKULOV.

# KYRGYZSTAN

**Kyrgyzstan** (Kyrgyzstan Publishing House): 720000 Bishkek, Sovetskaya 170; tel. (3312) 26-48-54; politics, science, economics, literature; Dir Berik N. Chalagyzov.

## Radio

**Kyrgyzstan State Radio and Television Broadcasting Co:** 720300 Bishkek, pr. Molodoy Gvardii 63.

**Kyrgyz Radio:** 720300 Bishkek, pr. Molodoy Gvardii 63; tel. (3312) 25-34-04; telex 245173; fax (3312) 25-79-30; broadcasts in Kyrgyz, German, English, Dungan and Russian; Gen. Dir Tugelbay Kazakov.

**Kyrgyz Television:** 720300 Bishkek, pr. Molodoy Gvardii 63; tel. (3312) 25-34-04; fax (3312) 25-79-30.

## Finance

(cap. = capital; res = reserves; m. = million; brs = branches; amounts in soms, unless otherwise indicated)

### BANKING

#### Central Bank

**National Bank of the Kyrgyz Republic:** 720040 Bishkek, Umetaliyeva 101; tel. (3312) 22-35-56; telex 245127; fax (3312) 62-07-30; f. 1992; cap. 50m. (March 1995); Chair. M. Sultanov.

#### Commercial Banks

In March 1994 there were 21 commercial banks in operation in Kyrgyzstan, some of the most important of which are listed below:

**Adil Bank** (International Kyrgyz-Swiss Joint-Stock Commercial Bank): 720001 Bishkek, pr. Chui 114; tel. (3312) 22-33-41; telex 245132; fax (3312) 22-15-57; f. 1992; cap. 1.5m., res 95,900 (March 1994); Pres. Yuruslan Zh. Toichbekov.

**Kyrgyzagro-prombank:** 720001 Bishkek, pr. Chui 168; tel. (3312) 25-34-37; fax (3312) 21-79-44; f. 1991; deals mainly with the agricultural sector; cap. 8.9m., res 2.1m. (March 1994); Pres. Umar O. Toigonbayev; 51 brs.

**Kyrgyzdyikanbank:** 720033 Bishkek, Togolok Moldo; tel. (3312) 21-38-53; fax (3312) 21-39-83; f. 1992; cap. 1.9m., res 167,900 (March 1994); Pres. Bakytnur A. Dosaliyev; 8 brs.

**Kyrgyzenergobank:** 720070 Bishkek, pr. Zhibek Zholu 326; tel. (3312) 27-39-33; fax (3312) 27-25-81; f. 1992; cap. 2.3m. (March 1994); Pres. Melis B. Bekmambetov

**Kyrgyzpromstroibank:** 720040 Bishkek, pr. Chui 168; tel. (3312) 21-76-72; fax (3312) 21-65-37; f. 1991; cap. 8.5m., res 2.6m. (March 1994); Pres. Muratbek O. Mukashev; 27 brs.

**Kyrgyzsberbank** (Savings Bank): Bishkek; f. 1991; cap. 925,000, res 371,100 (March 1994); 54 brs.

**Kyrgyzstan Bank:** 720010 Bishkek, pr. Molodoy Gvardii 27; tel. (3312) 25-52-98; fax (3312) 25-20-41; f. 1991; deals with the social sector and housing; cap. 23.8m., res 6.2m. (March 1994); Pres. Sharipa S. Sadybakasova; 25 brs.

**Kyrgyzvneshbank** (Bank for Foreign Economic Relations): 720040 Bishkek, pr. Erkendik 39; tel. (3312) 26-11-21; telex 245139; fax (3312) 26-10-37; f. 1992; cap. 15.4m., res 426,200 (March 1994); Pres. Semira Sh. Junushaliyeva; 2 brs.

**Maksat Bank:** 720300 Bishkek, Toktogula 187; tel. (3312) 24-33-67; fax (3312) 21-89-55; f. 1991; cap. 2.4m., res 1.1m. (March 1994); Pres. Vladimir I. Romanenko; 2 brs.

**Orient Bank:** 720000 Bishkek, Sovetskaya 176; tel. (3312) 22-07-20; fax (3312) 22-07-49; f. 1994; cap. 4.0m. (March 1994); Pres. Gamal K. Soodanbekov.

### COMMODITY EXCHANGE

**Kyrgyzstan Commodity and Raw Materials Exchange:** 720001 Bishkek, Belinskaya 40; tel. (3312) 22-13-75; fax (3312) 22-27-44; f. 1990; auth. cap. 175m. roubles; Gen. Dir Temir Sariyev.

## Trade and Industry

### STATE PROPERTY AGENCY

**State Property Fund:** 720040 Bishkek, pr. Erkindik 57; tel. (3312) 22-77-06; fax (3312) 26-40-04; responsible for the privatization of state-owned enterprises; Dir Esengul Omaruliyev.

### CHAMBER OF COMMERCE

**Chamber of Commerce and Industry of the Kyrgyz Republic:** 720001 Bishkek, Kievskaya 107; tel. (3312) 21-05-74; telex 251334; fax (3312) 21-05-75; Chair. Boris Perfiliyev.

### FOREIGN TRADE ORGANIZATION

**Kyrgyzvneshtorg Ltd:** 720033 Bishkek, Abdumomunova 276; tel. (3312) 22-53-61; telex 245100; fax (3312) 22-53-48; f. 1992; export-import org.; Gen. Dir Mr Kaliyev.

### STATE INDUSTRIAL COMPANIES

**Kumtor Operating Company:** Issyk-Kul Oblast, Kumtor; f. 1992; joint venture with Cameco Corpn (Canada); exploitation of seventh-largest gold deposit in the world.

**Kyrgyzaltyn:** Bishkek; state gold company.

**Kyrgyzneft Production Association:** 715622 Kochkor-Ata, Lenina 44; tel. 91396; state-owned petroleum and natural gas co.

### TRADE UNIONS

**Kyrgyzstan Federation of Trade Unions:** Bishkek.

## Transport

### RAILWAYS

Owing to the country's mountainous terrain, the railway network consists of only one main line (340 km) in northern Kyrgyzstan, which connects the republic, via Kazakhstan, with the railway system of the Russian Federation. Osh, Jalal-Abad and four other towns in regions of Kyrgyzstan bordering Uzbekistan are linked to that country by short lengths of railway track. Plans were under way in 1995 for the construction of a railway line to run from the north to the south of Kyrgyzstan. The new line, it was envisaged, would facilitate the direct delivery of raw materials extracted in southern regions to industrial enterprises in the north.

**Bishkek Railway Department:** Bishkek.

### ROADS

In the Soviet era Kyrgyzstan acquired a good network of roads. In the early 1990s the total length of roads in the republic was 28,400 km (of which some 22,400 km were hard-surfaced). Many of the best road links, however, are with neighbouring countries—mainly with Kazakhstan in the north and with Uzbekistan in the west. The administration of the road network, most passenger transport services by road, as well as about one-third of all road freight transport services, is undertaken by the Ministry of Transport.

### CIVIL AVIATION

There are two international airports: at Bishkek (Manas Airport), which provides links with cities in the Russian Federation and neighbouring Central Asian states, and at Osh. There are also airports at other regional centres.

**Kyrgyzstan Airways** (Kyrgyzstan Aba Zholdoru): 720062 Bishkek, Manas Airport; tel. (3312) 69-66-00; f. 1992; Gen. Dir. V. M. Alimov.

## Tourism

There was little tourism in Kyrgyzstan during the Soviet period. In the first years of independence tourist facilities remained very limited, and foreign visitors tended to be mountaineers. However, the Government hoped that the country's spectacular and largely unspoilt mountain scenery might attract foreign tourists and investment. The great crater lake of Issyk-Kul and some historical and cultural sites were also likely to be of interest if the industry was able to develop.

**State Committee for Tourism and Sport:** 720033 Bishkek, Togolok Moldo 17; tel. (3312) 22-06-57; telex 251247; fax (3312) 21-28-45; Chair. Murza Kaparov.

# LAOS

## Introductory Survey

### Location, Climate, Language, Religion, Flag, Capital

The Lao People's Democratic Republic is a land-locked country in South-East Asia, bordered by the People's Republic of China to the north, by Viet Nam to the east, by Cambodia to the south, by Thailand to the west and by Myanmar (formerly Burma) to the north-west. The climate is tropical, with a rainy monsoon season lasting from May to October. The official language, Lao or Laotian, is spoken by about two-thirds of the population. French is also spoken, and there are numerous tribal languages, including Meo. The principal religion is Buddhism. There are also some Christians and followers of animist beliefs. The national flag (proportions 3 by 2) has three horizontal stripes, of red, blue (half the total depth) and red, with a white disc in the centre. The capital is Vientiane.

### Recent History

Laos was formerly a part of French Indo-China and comprised the three principalities of Luang Prabang, Vientiane and Champassak. These were merged in 1946, when France recognized Sisavang Vong, ruler of Luang Prabang since 1904, as King of Laos. In May 1947 the King promulgated a democratic Constitution (although women were not allowed to vote until 1957). The Kingdom of Laos became independent, within the French Union, in July 1949, and full sovereignty was recognized by France in October 1953. The leading royalist politician was Prince Souvanna Phouma, who was Prime Minister in 1951–54, 1956–58, 1960 and in 1962–75. King Sisavang Vong died in October 1959, and was succeeded by his son, Savang Vatthana.

From 1950 the Royal Government was opposed by the Neo Lao Haksat (Lao Patriotic Front—LPF), an insurgent movement formed by a group of former anti-French activists. The LPF's Chairman was Prince Souphanouvong, a half-brother of Prince Souvanna Phouma, but its dominant element was the communist People's Party of Laos (PPL), led by Kaysone Phomvihane. During the 1950s the LPF's armed forces, the Pathet Lao, gradually secured control of the north-east of the country with the assistance of the Vietnamese communists, the Viet-Minh, who were engaged in war with the French (until 1954). Several agreements between the Royal Government and the LPF, attempting to end the guerrilla war and reunite the country, failed during the 1950s and early 1960s. By 1965 the *de facto* partition of Laos was established, with the LPF refusing to participate in national elections and consolidating its power over the north-eastern provinces.

During the 1960s, as the 'Ho Chi Minh Trail' (the communist supply route to South Viet Nam) ran through Pathet Lao-controlled areas, Laos remained closely involved with the war between communist forces and anti-communist troops (supported by the USA) in Viet Nam. In 1973 the Viet Nam peace negotiations included provisions for a cease-fire in Laos. A new Government was formed in April 1974 with royalist, neutralist and LPF participation. Prince Souvanna Phouma retained the post of Prime Minister, while Prince Souphanouvong was appointed Chairman of the Joint National Political Council. However, the LPF increased its power and eventually gained effective control of the country. This was confirmed by election victories in October and November 1975. In November King Savang Vatthana abdicated, and Prince Souvanna Phouma resigned.

In December 1975 the National Congress of People's Representatives (264 delegates elected by local authorities) abolished the monarchy and elected a 45-member legislative body, the Supreme People's Council (now known as the Supreme People's Assembly). Souphanouvong was appointed President of the newly-named Lao People's Democratic Republic and President of the Supreme People's Council. Kaysone Phomvihane, who had become Secretary-General of the Phak Pasason Pativat Lao (Lao People's Revolutionary Party—LPRP, a successor to the PPL), was appointed Prime Minister. The former King Savang Vatthana was named Supreme Counsellor to the President, but he refused to co-operate with the new regime and was arrested in March 1977. (He was subsequently stated to have died in a 're-education camp'.) The LPF was replaced in February 1979 by the Lao Front for National Construction (LFNC), under the leadership of the LPRP.

In October 1986 the ailing Souphanouvong announced his resignation from his duties as President of the Republic (while retaining the title) and of the Supreme People's Assembly. Phoumi Vongvichit, formerly a Vice-Chairman in the Council of Ministers, became acting President of the Republic, while Sisomphon Lovansai, a Vice-President of the Supreme People's Assembly and a member of the Politburo of the LPRP, became acting President of the Assembly. In November Kaysone Phomvihane was re-elected Secretary-General of the LPRP. In September 1987 it was announced that Phoumi Vongvichit had also replaced Souphanouvong as Chairman of the LFNC.

In June 1988 elections (the first since the formation of the Lao People's Democratic Republic in 1975) took place to determine the members of 113 district-level People's Councils. The LFNC approved 4,462 candidates to contest 2,410 seats. Provincial prefectural elections took place in November, when 898 candidates contested 651 seats. At a general election in March 1989, 121 candidates contested 79 seats in the enlarged Supreme People's Assembly. At its inaugural session in May, Nouhak Phoumsavanh (a Vice-Chairman of the Council of Ministers) was elected President of the Assembly.

Armed opposition to the Government persisted during the 1980s, particularly among hill tribes. In October 1982 Gen. Phoumi Nosavan, a 'conservative' who had been living in exile since 1965, formed the anti-communist Royal Lao Democratic Government, led by former Laotian military officers. However, many prominent exiles and resistance fighters in the United Front for the National Liberation of the Lao People (UFNLLP—formed in September 1980, and reportedly led by Gen. Phoumi since mid-1981) dissociated themselves from the Royal Government, which had established itself in southern Laos. In October 1988 the Government announced the capture of the Chief of Staff of the UFNLLP.

In December 1989 a right-wing organization, the United Lao National Liberation Front (ULNLF), proclaimed the 'Revolutionary Provisional Government' of Laos. The self-styled Government, which was headed by Outhong Souvannavong (the former President of the Royal Council of King Savang Vatthana), claimed to have used military force to 'liberate' one-third of Laotian territory. Although there were reports of attacks by insurgent guerrillas in northern Laos at this time, it was widely assumed that the ULNLF's claims were exaggerated and that its proclamation was an attempt to elicit popular support. Gen. Vang Pao, a leader of the Hmong tribe, who in the 1970s had been a commander of the Royalist army (allegedly trained by the US Central Intelligence Agency), was reported to have been allocated responsibility for defence in the 'Revolutionary Provisional Government', and Somphorn Wang (also formerly a prominent Royalist) was described as Secretary of State. In late 1992 Gen. Vang Pao reportedly travelled from the USA (where he had lived in exile since 1975) to Singapore to direct an unsuccessful military operation from Thailand. In October Gen. Vang Pao's brother, Vang Fung, and another Hmong rebel, Moua Yee Julan (who were allegedly preparing an incursion into Laos under Gen. Vang Pao's command), were arrested in Thailand. In September 1993 Thai troops launched a reportedly successful operation against Gen. Vang Pao's forces, expelling 320 rebels from Thai territory.

In June 1990 a draft Constitution, enshrining free-market principles, was published in the LPRP newspaper, *Pasason*. Later in June the Supreme People's Assembly approved legislation which included provision for the ownership of property, inheritance rights and contractual obligations.

In October 1990 three former government officials were arrested, in connection with 'activities aimed at overthrowing the regime'. It was reported in Thailand that they had formed part of a 'Social Democrat Group', which was actively seeking the introduction of multi-party democracy. In November 1992 all three were sentenced to 14 years' imprisonment.

In March 1991, at the Fifth Congress of the LPRP, Souphanouvong retired from all his previously-held party posts. Phoumi Vongvichit and Sisomphon Lovansai also retired, and the three were appointed to a newly-created advisory board to the party Central Committee. Kaysone Phomvihane's title was altered from General Secretary to President of the LPRP, and his power was slightly enhanced following the abolition of the party Secretariat. A new Politburo and a rejuvenated Party Central Committee were elected. Gen. Sisavat Keobounphan, the military Chief of the General Staff, was not re-elected to the Politburo (probably owing to allegations of corruption in his capacity as mayor of Vientiane). The leadership pledged a continuance of reforms aimed at replacing the centrally-planned economy with free-market principles, but denied the need for political pluralism. However, the national motto was changed, substituting the words 'democracy and prosperity' for 'socialism'.

On 14 August 1991 the Supreme People's Assembly adopted a new Constitution, which provided for a National Assembly, confirmed the leading role of the LPRP, enshrined the right to private ownership, and endowed the presidency with executive powers; new electoral legislation was also promulgated. Kaysone Phomvihane was appointed President of Laos, replacing Souphanouvong and Phoumi Vongvichit as President and Acting President respectively. Gen. Khamtay Siphandone, a Vice-Chairman of the Council of Ministers, Minister of National Defence and Supreme Commander of the Lao People's Army, replaced Kaysone Phomvihane as Chairman of the Council of Ministers, restyled Prime Minister under the new Constitution. (Phoumi Vongvichit died in January 1994, and Souphanouvong in January 1995.)

On 21 November 1992 Kaysone Phomvihane died. Gen. Khamtay Siphandone was elected to replace him as President of the LPRP, and on 25 November, at a specially convened meeting of the Supreme People's Assembly, Nouhak Phoumsavanh was elected President of State. On 20 December elections to the new National Assembly took place, in accordance with the Constitution; 99.33% of eligible voters participated in the election, in which 154 LFNC-approved candidates contested 85 seats. On 22 February 1993 the new National Assembly re-elected Nouhak Phoumsavanh as President, confirmed Khamtay Siphandone as Prime Minister, and implemented the most extensive reorganization of the Council of Ministers since the LPRP's accession to power in 1975. Gen. Phoune Sipraseuth, joint deputy Prime Minister and a member of the LPRP Politburo, died in December 1994.

From 1975 onwards Laos was dependent on Vietnamese economic and military assistance, permitting the stationing of Vietnamese troops (estimated in 1987 to number between 30,000 and 50,000) on its territory. In 1977 a 25-year treaty of friendship between the two countries was signed, and Laos supported the Vietnamese-led overthrow of the Khmer Rouge regime in Kampuchea (Cambodia) in January 1979. Following the outbreak of hostilities between Viet Nam and the People's Republic of China in that year, Laos allied itself with the former. Viet Nam withdrew its military presence from Laos during 1988. Laos and Viet Nam signed a protocol governing military co-operation in March 1994.

In July 1992 Laos (and Viet Nam) strengthened ties with members of the Association of South East Asian Nations (ASEAN—see p. 109) by signing the ASEAN Treaty of Amity and Co-operation, which provided for wider regional co-operation, and was regarded as a preliminary step to full membership of the Association. In July 1994 Laos attended an ASEAN summit meeting in Bangkok, Thailand, as an observer. In February 1993 Laos, Thailand, Viet Nam and Cambodia signed a joint communiqué providing for the resumption of co-operation in the development of the Mekong river. (Thailand's earlier demand that the Committee for Co-ordination of Investigations of the Lower Mekong Basin be reorganized had delayed the readmission of Cambodia to the Committee after an absence of 18 years.) In April 1995, meeting in Chiang Rai, Thailand, representatives of the four countries signed an agreement on the joint exploitation and development of the lower Mekong. The accord provided for the establishment of a Mekong Commission, membership of which would (it was envisaged) eventually be extended to the People's Republic of China and Myanmar.

Relations with the People's Republic of China improved in December 1986, when a Chinese delegation, led by the Deputy Minister of Foreign Affairs, made the first official Chinese visit to Laos since 1978. In December 1987, after an assurance from the People's Republic of China that support would be withdrawn from Laotian resistance groups operating from within China, the two countries agreed to restore full diplomatic relations and to encourage bilateral trade. Relations between the LPRP and the Chinese Communist Party were fully restored in August 1989. In October 1991 the Laotian and Chinese Prime Ministers signed a border treaty, which established a framework for meetings of a Laotian-Chinese joint border committee. In January 1992 the committee adopted a resolution providing for the demarcation of the common border. In June of that year, following the third meeting of the Joint Border Committee, an agreement on the delineation of boundaries was signed. In November 1994 Laos and China signed a reciprocal agreement on the transport of passengers and goods on each other's sections of the Mekong river. Under an agreement reached in July 1991, some 2,800 of the estimated 4,200 Laotian refugees in China had been voluntarily repatriated (with assistance from the office of the UN High Commissioner for Refugees—UNHCR) by late 1994.

From 1975 onwards relations with Thailand were characterized by mutual suspicion. Thailand intermittently closed its border to Lao imports and exports, causing considerable hardship. In 1984 a dispute concerning three villages on the Laotian–Thai border, over which both countries claimed sovereignty, led to clashes between Laotian and Thai troops. Attempts to resolve the matter by negotiation failed. In May 1987 a disagreement arose over the sovereignty of another area, and in December 1987 and early 1988 fighting took place there, each side claiming that the other had invaded its territory; hundreds of casualties were reported. In February 1988 the two sides agreed to declare a cease-fire, to withdraw their troops from the zone of battle, and to attempt to negotiate a peaceful solution. In March 1991, following the recent military coup in Thailand, representatives of the two countries signed an agreement providing for the immediate withdrawal of troops from the disputed border areas. The Thai Government also agreed to suppress the activities of Laotian insurgents operating from Thai territory. In December Thailand and Laos signed a border co-operation agreement. In January 1992 the Thai Government temporarily closed the border, following clashes between Laotian government troops and resistance forces, which caused about 400 Laotian civilians to seek refuge in Thailand.

Cultural links between Thailand and Laos were improved, and in June 1992 the Thai Crown Prince, Maha Vajiralongkorn, visited Vientiane for the first time. On the following day, however, about 300 guerrillas from a rebel group, the Free Democratic Lao National Salvation Force (based in Thailand), attacked three Laotian government posts, killing two people and causing significant damage. In late June a senior Thai military officer claimed that a Laotian government unit was receiving training in chemical warfare from Cuban and Vietnamese experts. The Laotian Government rejected the claim and dismissed previous accusations by Laotian resistance fighters and Western aid agencies of government use of chemical warfare to suppress the activities of rebel groups. Relations between the two countries improved again in July 1992, when the Thai authorities announced the arrest of 11 Laotian citizens who were accused of planning subversive activities against the Government in Vientiane. Further arrests were made in October. The first bridge (over the Mekong river) linking Laos and Thailand was opened in April 1994.

During the 1970s and 1980s thousands of Laotian refugees fled to Thailand to escape from civil war and food shortages. In January 1989 an estimated 90,000 Laotian refugees remained in border camps in Thailand. UNHCR began a programme of voluntary repatriation in 1980. By late 1990 fewer than 6,000 refugees had been repatriated under UNHCR supervision, while some 15,000 had returned independently, and others had been resettled abroad. In June 1991 UNHCR, Laos and Thailand signed an agreement guaranteeing the repatriation or resettlement in a third country of the remaining 60,000 Laotian refugees in Thailand by the end of 1994. By September 1994 some 18,000 Laotian refugees remained in Thailand. In July UNHCR, Laos and Thailand had agreed that the repatriation programme would be completed by early 1995, although refugees were still crossing into Laos in March of that year.

From 1989 the Laotian Government sought to improve relations with non-communist countries, in order to reduce its dependence on the USSR and Viet Nam (mainly for economic reasons). In November, following a visit to Japan by Kaysone Phomvihane (his first official visit to a non-communist country), the Japanese Government agreed to increase grant aid to Laos—direct loans having been halted in 1968. In early 1995 it was reported that Japan was considering the resumption of loans in yen to Laos. A treaty of friendship and co-operation was signed with Russia in March 1994.

In 1985 Laos agreed to co-operate with the USA in recovering the remains of US soldiers 'missing-in-action' in Laos since the war in Viet Nam. In August 1987 a US delegation visited Vientiane to discuss 'humanitarian co-operation' by Laos in tracing missing US soldiers, and agreed to provide Laos with aid. The first remains of US soldiers were passed to the US Government in February 1988. Laos postponed further searching for a short period in 1989, when the USA, alleging that Laos was failing to assist in the suppression of drugs-trafficking, suspended aid and preferential treatment. Laos was reported to have resumed co-operation in May. The USA restored aid to Laos in early 1990, following a visit to Vientiane by the Chairman of the US House of Representatives Committee on Narcotics and Drug Control. (In March 1992 Laos, Myanmar and Thailand signed a draft co-operation treaty on narcotics suppression.) In November 1991, in response to continued Laotian co-operation and the implementation of limited political and economic reforms, the US Government announced that diplomatic relations with Laos were to be upgraded to ambassadorial level. Further progress was achieved in tracing the remains of US soldiers during 1992, and in January 1993 a joint recovery operation was undertaken. In the same month, following 17 months of hearings, a special US Senate panel concluded (despite considerable public speculation to the contrary) that there was 'no compelling evidence' of the survival of US servicemen in the region. During 1993–94 Laos and the USA co-operated in several further operations to locate the remains of US soldiers, and it was envisaged that more searches would be conducted in 1995.

### Government

Under the terms of the 1991 Constitution, executive power is vested in the President of State, while legislative power resides with a National Assembly. The President is elected for five years by the National Assembly. Members of the National Assembly are elected for a period of five years by universal adult suffrage. The Lao People's Revolutionary Party remains the sole legal political party. With the approval of the National Assembly, the President appoints the Prime Minister and members of the Council of Ministers, who conduct the government of the country. The President also appoints provincial governors and mayors of municipalities, who are responsible for local administration.

### Defence

In June 1994, according to Western estimates, the strength of the armed forces was 37,000 (Lao People's Army 33,000, navy 500, air force 3,500). Military service is compulsory for a minimum of 18 months. There is a paramilitary self-defence force numbering more than 100,000. In 1993 defence expenditure was budgeted at 75,500m. kips.

### Economic Affairs

In 1993, according to estimates by the World Bank, Laos's gross national product (GNP), measured at average 1991–93 prices, was US $1,295m., equivalent to $290 per head. During 1985–93, it was estimated, GNP per head increased, in real terms, at an average annual rate of 2.1%. Over the same period the population increased by an annual average of 2.9%. Gross domestic product (GDP) increased, in real terms, by an annual average of 5.0% in 1985–93. Real GDP rose by 6.1% in 1993 and by an estimated 8.4% in 1994.

Agriculture (including forestry and fishing) contributed 51% of GDP in 1993. An estimated 70.3% of the working population were employed in the sector in that year. Rice is the staple crop, occupying an estimated 85% of cultivated land in the mid-1990s. Other crops include maize, cassava, potatoes and sweet potatoes; coffee is grown for export. The keeping of pigs, poultry and cattle and fish-farming are important. In 1992 forest covered about 12.5m. ha in Laos (54% of total land area), and logs and wood products were the principal export commodity in that year, accounting for 36% of total export revenue. During the early 1990s the Government initiated policies aimed at conserving the country's forest resources. The cultivation and illicit export of narcotic drugs is believed to be widespread. During 1983–93 agricultural production increased by an annual average of 3.9%; output declined by 6.7% in 1994.

Industry (including mining, manufacturing, construction and power) contributed 19.1% of GDP in 1991, and employed about 7% of the working population in 1980. During 1985–92 industrial GDP increased by an annual average of 9.7%.

Mining contributed only 0.1% of GDP in 1991. Laos has, however, considerable mineral resources: tin and gypsum are the major minerals that are exploited and exported, and coal is also mined. Other known mineral deposits include lead, zinc, nickel, potash, iron ore and small quantities of gold, silver and precious stones.

Manufacturing contributed 13.5% of GDP in 1991, although the sector employed less than 1% of the working population in the mid-1980s. It is mainly confined to the processing of raw materials (chiefly sawmilling) and agricultural produce, the production of textiles and garments, and the manufacture of handicrafts and basic consumer goods for the domestic market. Manufacturing GDP increased by an annual average of 12.5% in 1985–92.

Electrical energy is principally derived from hydroelectric power. Electricity is exported to Thailand, and is one of Laos's principal sources of foreign exchange (earning 30% of total export revenue in 1990). In the financial year 1993/94 electricity exports earned US $17.1m. By 1994 Laos had exploited only 300 MW of a total hydroelectric power potential estimated to be 18,000 MW, although several new projects were planned, with participation by foreign investors. Laos is totally dependent on imports, mainly from Thailand, for supplies of mineral fuels.

In 1992 Laos recorded an estimated visible trade deficit of US $111.7m., and there was a deficit of $40.9m. on the current account of the balance of payments. In 1993, according to official figures, there was a trade deficit of $194m. In 1990 Thailand was the principal trading partner, supplying 51.9% of imports and purchasing 34.1% of exports; other significant trading partners were Western Europe, Japan and the People's Republic of China. The main exports in 1992 were textile products (particularly garments), logs and wood products, electricity, coffee, tin and gypsum. The principal imports include food, mineral fuels, machinery and transport equipment.

In 1993 Laos recorded an overall budget deficit, excluding grants, equivalent to 7.8% of GDP. The country's external debt totalled US $1,986m. at the end of 1993, of which $1,948m. was long-term public debt. In that year the cost of debt-servicing was equivalent to 9.6% of revenue from exports of goods and services. Consumer prices increased by an annual average of 9.8% in 1992, by 6.3% in 1993, and by an estimated 6.7% in 1994. Unemployment was estimated at 17% of the labour force in 1987.

Laos is a member of the Asian Development Bank (see p. 107), and of the Colombo Plan (see p. 238), which promotes economic and social development in Asia and the Pacific.

From late 1986 the Government undertook a radical programme of economic liberalization, with the aim of transforming the hitherto centrally-planned economy into a market-orientated system. Supported by the international financial community, considerable success has been achieved in establishing sustained GDP growth and in reducing the rate of inflation (which was as high as 60% in 1989); fiscal reforms have been introduced, while government expenditure has been restricted; the ending of a ban on foreign investment and the implementation of a privatization programme have encouraged revenue from external sources (Thailand, the USA, Taiwan and Australia being among the most important investors), thus offsetting the loss of aid and concessionary trade arising from the disintegration of the communist bloc. The banking sector and public administration have been restructured; the reform of the legal system is in progress; price controls have been ended, and policies undertaken to expand the agricultural and manufacturing sectors. With assistance from the IMF, the Government aimed to achieve annual GDP growth of 7% in 1995 and 1996, to reduce inflation to 4.5% by 1996, and to reduce the budget deficit to 9.1% of GDP in that year. However, Laos remains highly dependent on external assistance (although its debt-servicing commitments remain manageable); a lack of modernization in the agricultural sector has impeded diversification, and the manufacturing base,

LAOS

while output is expanding rapidly, remains narrow. Moreover, the Government's ambitious plans for the development of hydroelectric potential have provoked considerable environmental concerns, as have the effects of the over-exploitation of forest resources.

### Social Welfare

Since 1975 the public health service has developed steadily; in 1985 Laos had 1,123 hospitals and clinics, with a total of 9,815 beds. In 1985 there were 558 doctors, 2,346 medical workers and 6,600 first-aid workers in the country. In 1989 there was one doctor for every 1,400 inhabitants in Vientiane, and one for every 12,600 citizens in other regions.

### Education

Education, which is officially compulsory for eight years between the ages of seven and 15, was greatly disrupted by the civil war, causing a high illiteracy rate, but educational facilities have since improved significantly. Lao is the medium of instruction, and in 1989 the illiteracy rate among the adult population was officially estimated to be 50% (males 35%; females 65%). A comprehensive education system is in force. In 1990 the Government issued a decree permitting the establishment of private schools, to help to accommodate the increasing number of students.

Primary education begins at six years of age and lasts for five years. Secondary education, beginning at the age of 11, lasts for six years, comprising two three-year cycles. In 1991 enrolment at primary schools included 59% of children in the primary age-group (males 66%; females 53%). In that year secondary enrolment included 15% of the relevant age-group (males 17%; females 13%). The total enrolment at primary and secondary schools was equivalent to 60% of the school-age population (males 70%; females 51%) in 1991, compared with 68% in 1987. Government expenditure on education in 1988 was 2,782m. kips.

### Public Holidays

**1995:** 24 January (Army Day), 13–15 April (Lao New Year), 1 May (Labour Day), 2 December (National Day).

**1996:** 24 January (Army Day), 13–15 April (Lao New Year), 1 May (Labour Day), 2 December (National Day).

### Weights and Measures

The metric system is in force.

# Statistical Survey

Source (unless otherwise stated): Service National de la Statistique, Vientiane.

## Area and Population

### AREA, POPULATION AND DENSITY

| | |
|---|---:|
| Area (sq km) | 236,800* |
| Population (census results) 1 March 1985 | |
| Males | 1,757,115 |
| Females | 1,827,688 |
| Total | 3,584,803 |
| Population (UN estimates at mid-year)† | |
| 1991 | 4,335,000 |
| 1992 | 4,469,000 |
| 1993 | 4,605,000 |
| Density (per sq km) at mid-1993 | 19.4 |

* 91,400 sq miles.

† Source: UN, *World Population Prospects: The 1992 Revision*.

### PROVINCES (population in 1990, official estimates)

| | |
|---|---:|
| Savannakhet | 640,000 |
| Champasak | 469,000 |
| Vientiane (municipality) | 442,000 |
| Luang Prabang | 339,000 |
| Vientiane | 312,000 |
| Oudomxay | 291,000 |
| Khammouane | 249,000 |
| Houaphanh | 243,000 |
| Saravan | 211,000 |
| Xiangkhouang | 189,000 |
| Sayabouri | 182,000 |
| Bolikhamsai | 145,000 |
| Phongsali | 142,000 |
| Luang Namtha | 114,000 |
| Attopu | 80,000 |
| Bokeo | 64,000 |
| Sekong | 58,000 |
| **Total** | **4,170,000** |

Source: State Planning Committee.

### PRINCIPAL TOWNS (population in 1985)

| | | | |
|---|---:|---|---:|
| Vientiane (capital)* | 377,000 | Luang Prabang | 68,000 |
| Savannakhet | 97,000 | Paksé | 47,000 |

* The population of the Vientiane municipality, according to official estimates, was 442,000 in 1990.

Source: Statistisches Bundesamt, Wiesbaden, Germany.

**1973:** Sayabouri 13,775; Khammouane 12,676.

### BIRTHS AND DEATHS (UN estimates, annual averages)

| | 1975–80 | 1980–85 | 1985–90 |
|---|---:|---:|---:|
| Birth rate (per 1,000) | 45.1 | 45.1 | 45.1 |
| Death rate (per 1,000) | 20.7 | 18.7 | 16.9 |

Source: UN, *World Population Prospects: The 1992 Revision*.

**Birth rate** (1992): 44.2 per 1,000.

**Death rate** (1992): 15.3 per 1,000.

**Expectation of life** (years at birth, 1992): Males 49.3; Females 52.3.

Source: UN, *Statistical Yearbook for Asia and the Pacific*.

### LABOUR FORCE (ILO estimates, '000 persons at mid-1980)

| | Males | Females | Total |
|---|---:|---:|---:|
| Agriculture, etc. | 717 | 675 | 1,393 |
| Industry | 79 | 51 | 130 |
| Services | 193 | 123 | 316 |
| **Total** | **990** | **849** | **1,839** |

Source: ILO, *Economically Active Population Estimates and Projections, 1950–2025*.

**Mid-1993** (estimates in '000): Agriculture, etc. 1,460; Total 2,077 (Source: FAO, *Production Yearbook*).

LAOS

## Agriculture

**PRINCIPAL CROPS** ('000 metric tons)

|  | 1991 | 1992 | 1993 |
|---|---|---|---|
| Rice (paddy) | 1,223 | 1,502 | 1,251 |
| Maize | 69 | 59 | 48 |
| Potatoes* | 33 | 35 | 34 |
| Sweet potatoes | 132 | 105 | 113 |
| Cassava (Manioc)* | 66 | 67 | 68 |
| Pulses | 37 | 42 | 41 |
| Soybeans | 6 | 6 | 6 |
| Groundnuts (in shell) | 6 | 8 | 6 |
| Cottonseed† | 9 | 11 | 12 |
| Cotton (lint) | 5 | 5 | 6 |
| Vegetables and melons* | 230 | 235 | 237 |
| Fruit (excl. melons)* | 137 | 144 | 149 |
| Sugar cane | 80 | 94 | 90 |
| Coffee (green) | 7 | 7 | 8 |
| Tobacco (leaves) | 5 | 5 | 3† |

* FAO estimates.  † Unofficial figure(s).

Source: FAO, *Production Yearbook*.

**LIVESTOCK** ('000 head, year ending September)

|  | 1991 | 1992 | 1993 |
|---|---|---|---|
| Horses | 36 | 29 | 29* |
| Cattle | 899 | 993 | 1,010 |
| Buffaloes | 1,099 | 1,131 | 1,167 |
| Pigs | 1,469 | 1,561 | 1,559 |
| Goats | 117 | 104 | 144 |

* FAO estimate.

Chickens (million): 8 in 1991; 9 in 1992; 9 in 1993.

Source: FAO, *Production Yearbook*.

**LIVESTOCK PRODUCTS** (FAO estimates, '000 metric tons)

|  | 1991 | 1992 | 1993 |
|---|---|---|---|
| Beef and veal | 9 | 10 | 9 |
| Buffalo meat | 24 | 25 | 25 |
| Pig meat | 54 | 58 | 59 |
| Poultry meat | 25 | 26 | 27 |
| Cows' milk | 10 | 11 | 11 |
| Hen eggs | 34.0 | 35.0 | 36.0 |
| Cattle and buffalo hides | 5.5 | 5.9 | 5.7 |

Source: FAO, *Production Yearbook*.

## Forestry

**ROUNDWOOD REMOVALS** ('000 cubic metres, excluding bark)

|  | 1990 | 1991 | 1992 |
|---|---|---|---|
| Sawlogs, veneer logs and logs for sleepers | 312 | 408 | 154 |
| Other industrial wood* | 105 | 108 | 111 |
| Fuel wood* | 3,883 | 4,008 | 4,133 |
| **Total** | 4,300 | 4,524 | 4,398 |

* FAO estimates.

Source: FAO, *Yearbook of Forest Products*.

**SAWNWOOD PRODUCTION**
('000 cubic metres, including railway sleepers)

|  | 1990 | 1991 | 1992 |
|---|---|---|---|
| **Total** | 78 | 71 | 110* |

* FAO estimate.

Source: FAO, *Yearbook of Forest Products*.

## Fishing

('000 metric tons, live weight)

|  | 1990* | 1991* | 1992 |
|---|---|---|---|
| Carps, barbels, etc | 10.0 | 12.0 | 14.0 |
| Other freshwater fishes | 18.0 | 17.0 | 16.0 |
| **Total catch** | 28.0 | 29.0 | 30.0 |

* FAO estimates.

Source: FAO, *Yearbook of Fishery Statistics*.

## Mining

|  | 1980 | 1990 | 1991 |
|---|---|---|---|
| Tin concentrates—metal content (metric tons)* | 276 | 500 | 500 |
| Gypsum ('000 metric tons)† | 104 | 113 | 100 |

* Source: UNCTAD, *International Tin Statistics*.
† Data from the US Bureau of Mines.

Source: UN, *Industrial Statistics Yearbook*.

**Salt** (metric tons): 10,300 in 1989.

**Coal** (metric tons): 1,750 in 1989; 3,532 in 1990; 1,250 in 1991.

Source: Statistisches Bundesamt, Wiesbaden, Germany.

## Industry

**SELECTED PRODUCTS**

|  | 1981 | 1982 | 1983 |
|---|---|---|---|
| Beer (hectolitres) | 12,019 | 13,103 | 13,000 |
| Soft drinks (hectolitres) | 15,365 | 12,643 | 12,370 |
| Textiles ('000 metres) | 954.7 | 1,214.0 | 1,451.4 |
| Clothing ('000 pieces) | 376.7 | 384.0 | 474.9 |
| Rubber tyres and tubes for motor cars ('000) | 728 | 638 | 1,000 |
| Plastic products (metric tons) | 69.0 | 207.0 | 185.1 |
| Washing powder (metric tons) | 444 | 987 | 970 |
| Domestic animal feed (metric tons) | 3,500 | 6,006 | 3,000 |
| Bricks (million) | 4.1 | 5.6 | 10.9 |

Source: State Planning Committee.

**Cigarettes** (million units): 1,100 per year in 1981–84; 1,125 in 1985; 1,200 per year in 1986–91 (estimates by US Department of Agriculture).

**Electric energy** (million kWh): 1,150 in 1981; 1,200 in 1982; 1,075 in 1983; 990 in 1984; 906 in 1985; 867 in 1986; 576 in 1987; 532 in 1988; 708 in 1989; 870 in 1990; 972 in 1991. Source: UN, *Industrial Statistics Yearbook*.

## Finance

**CURRENCY AND EXCHANGE RATES**

**Monetary Units**
100 at (cents) = 1 new kip.

**Sterling and Dollar Equivalents** (30 September 1994)
£1 sterling = 1,129.1 new kips;
US $1 = 716.0 new kips;
10,000 new kips = £8.856 = $13.966.

**Average Exchange Rate** (kips per US $)
1991    702.5
1992    720.0
1993    716.0

## LAOS

### BUDGET (million new kips)

| Revenue | 1988 | 1989 | 1990 |
|---|---|---|---|
| Tax receipts | 21,474 | 27,421 | 37,644 |
| Non-tax receipts | 7,057 | 8,135 | 23,316 |
| **Total** (excluding subsidies) | 28,531 | 35,556 | 60,960 |

**1991** (million new kips): Tax receipts 54,356; Non-tax receipts 24,611; **Total** 78,967.

**1992** (million new kips): Tax receipts 69,663; Non-tax receipts 28,776; **Total** 98,439.

| Expenditure | 1988 | 1989 | 1990* |
|---|---|---|---|
| General public services | 1,527 | 74 | — |
| Education | 2,169 | 2,885 | 3,146 |
| Health | 1,435 | 258 | 851 |
| Economic affairs and services | 36,962 | 52,784 | 56,357 |
|   Agriculture, forestry, fishing and hunting | 7,669 | 5,689 | 8,969 |
|   Mining, mineral resources, manufacturing and construction Fuel and energy | 10,122 | 22,472 | 18,535 |
|   Transport and communication | 17,495 | 24,540 | 29,126 |
| Other expenditure | 4,915 | 10,454 | 5,726 |
| **Total** | 47,008 | 66,455 | 66,080 |

Source: UN, *Statistical Yearbook for Asia and the Pacific*.

### INTERNATIONAL RESERVES
(US $ million, excluding gold, at 31 December)

| | 1988 | 1989 | 1990 |
|---|---|---|---|
| **Total** | 16.1 | 16.1 | 61.0 |

Source: World Bank, *World Tables*.

### MONEY SUPPLY (million new kips at 31 December)

| | 1990 | 1991 | 1992 |
|---|---|---|---|
| **Total money** | 25,090 | 28,226 | 35,145 |

Source: UN, *Statistical Yearbook for Asia and the Pacific*.

### COST OF LIVING (Consumer price index; base: 1987 = 100)

| | 1989 | 1990 | 1991 |
|---|---|---|---|
| Food | 198.9 | 227.8 | 256.6 |
| Clothing | 196.7 | 282.8 | 315.7 |
| Goods and services | 217.6 | 255.8 | 309.0 |
| **All items** (incl. others) | 201.9 | 242.3 | 267.4 |

Source: Statistisches Bundesamt, Wiesbaden.

### NATIONAL ACCOUNTS (million new kips at current prices)
**Expenditure on the Gross Domestic Product**

| | 1989 | 1990 | 1991 |
|---|---|---|---|
| Government final consumption expenditure | 34,929 | 61,754 | 69,499 |
| Private final consumption expenditure | 414,639 | 558,437 | 647,826 |
| Increase in stocks / Gross fixed capital formation | 55,560 | 75,572 | 91,435 |
| **Total domestic expenditure** | 505,128 | 695,763 | 808,760 |
| Exports of goods and services | 49,421 | 69,411 | 73,359 |
| *Less* Imports of goods and services | 128,613 | 150,154 | 156,550 |
| **GDP in purchasers' values** | 425,936 | 615,020 | 725,569 |
| **GDP at constant 1987 prices** | 213,769 | 228,105 | 237,098 |

Source: World Bank, *Historically Planned Economies: A Guide to the Data*.

### Gross Domestic Product by Economic Activity

| | 1989 | 1990 | 1991 |
|---|---|---|---|
| Agriculture, hunting, forestry and fishing | 258,246 | 374,456 | 386,503 |
| Mining and quarrying | 1,049 | 896 | 995 |
| Manufacturing | 37,575 | 59,662 | 97,723 |
| Electricity, gas and water | 3,745 | 8,839 | 12,451 |
| Construction | 12,499 | 17,908 | 27,029 |
| Wholesale and retail trade, restaurants and hotels | 33,878 | 44,516 | 56,838 |
| Transport, storage and communications | 29,902 | 31,687 | 40,521 |
| Finance, insurance, real estate and business services | 34,839 | 39,084 | 57,206 |
| Community, social and personal services | 19,590 | 35,800 | 45,709 |
| **GDP in purchasers' values** | 431,322 | 612,848 | 724,975 |

Source: UN, *Statistical Yearbook for Asia and the Pacific*.

### BALANCE OF PAYMENTS (US $ million)

| | 1990 | 1991 | 1992* |
|---|---|---|---|
| Merchandise exports f.o.b. | 78.7 | 96.6 | 132.7 |
| Merchandise imports f.o.b. | −185.4 | −209.7 | −244.4 |
| **Trade balance** | −106.7 | −113.1 | −111.7 |
| Exports of services | 23.7 | 36.6 | 58.8 |
| Imports of services | −28.1 | −45.6 | −57.8 |
| Other income received | 2.2 | 3.3 | 4.5 |
| Other income paid | −3.2 | −4.4 | −4.4 |
| Private unrequited transfers (net) | 10.9 | 10.4 | 8.6 |
| Official unrequited transfers (net) | 23.1 | 66.3 | 61.6 |
| **Current balance** | −78.1 | −46.5 | −40.9 |
| Long-term capital (net) | 51.1 | 44.6 | 72.1 |
| Short-term capital (net) / Net errors and omissions | 27.6 | 17.1 | −26.8 |
| **Overall balance** | 0.6 | 15.2 | 4.4 |

* Estimates.
Source: World Bank, *World Tables*.

## External Trade

### PRINCIPAL COMMODITIES (US $'000; data from partner countries)
**Trade with the USSR**

| Imports | 1983 | 1984 | 1985 |
|---|---|---|---|
| Petroleum and petroleum products | 9,197 | 10,521 | 12,545 |
| Woven cotton fabrics | 2,734 | 3,949 | 2,072 |
| Machinery and transport equipment | 50,586 | 38,172 | 42,910 |
| Lorries | 4,798 | 6,550 | 9,530 |
| Aircraft and parts | 6,673 | 5,166 | 1,632 |
| **Total** (incl. others) | 101,581 | 80,087 | 102,699 |

| Exports | 1983 | 1984 | 1985 |
|---|---|---|---|
| **Total** | 3,104 | 2,592 | 2,754 |

Source: Statistisches Bundesamt, Wiesbaden, Germany.

LAOS

*Statistical Survey*

**Trade with OECD countries**

| Imports | 1983 | 1984 | 1985 |
|---|---|---|---|
| Chemicals and related products | 1,672 | 1,346 | 1,525 |
| Basic manufactures | 4,272 | 2,989 | 4,762 |
| Iron and steel | 2,486 | 1,641 | 2,738 |
| Machinery and transport equipment | 21,836 | 5,663 | 9,253 |
| Power generating machinery and equipment | 5,469 | 637 | 405 |
| Machinery specialized for particular industries | 1,315 | 674 | 2,698 |
| General industrial machinery, equipment and parts | 1,960 | 1,339 | 1,236 |
| Electrical machinery, apparatus, etc. | 1,505 | 1,444 | 1,382 |
| Road vehicles and parts | 11,223 | 1,342 | 3,380 |
| Miscellaneous manufactured articles | 1,015 | 407 | 700 |

| Exports | 1983 | 1984 | 1985 |
|---|---|---|---|
| Food and live animals | 3,041 | 1,202 | 2,879 |
| Coffee, tea, cocoa, spices etc. | 3,015 | 1,202 | 2,792 |
| Crude materials (inedible) except fuels | 2,430 | 866 | 1,440 |
| Cork and wood | 2,356 | 581 | 1,386 |
| Chemicals and related products | 1,097 | 2 | 8 |
| Basic manufactures | 198 | 1,571 | 230 |
| Iron and steel | 9 | 1,383 | 79 |

Source: Statistisches Bundesamt, Wiesbaden, Germany.

**1994:** Imports 449,900; Exports 317,800.

**PRINCIPAL TRADING PARTNERS** (US $'000)*

| Imports | 1989 | 1990 | 1991 |
|---|---|---|---|
| Australia | 433 | 1,264 | 320 |
| Belgium/Luxembourg | 779 | 598 | 436 |
| China, People's Republic | 4,900 | 9,973 | 11,154 |
| France | 1,656 | 2,885 | 3,041 |
| Germany | 1,819 | 858 | 807 |
| Hong Kong | 600 | 1,196 | 3,292 |
| Italy | 415 | 710 | 6,093 |
| Japan | 24,525 | 19,604 | 21,360 |
| Netherlands | 1,200 | 1,280 | 147 |
| Sweden | 1,197 | 8,317 | 339 |
| Switzerland | 310 | 71 | 40 |
| Thailand | 70,200 | 65,643 | 76,622 |
| Turkey | — | 875 | 484 |
| United Kingdom | 1,458 | 2,173 | 2,070 |
| USA | 341 | 769 | 893 |

| Exports | 1989 | 1990 | 1991 |
|---|---|---|---|
| Canada | 218 | 933 | 643 |
| China, People's Republic | 11,400 | 6,221 | 2,222 |
| Denmark | 309 | 316 | 1,341 |
| France | 381 | 2,701 | 9,082 |
| Germany | 1,005 | 1,911 | 9,484 |
| Hong Kong | 600 | — | 121 |
| Italy | 361 | 346 | 943 |
| Japan | 8,079 | 4,577 | 4,463 |
| Netherlands | 721 | — | 1,850 |
| Norway | 15 | 802 | 481 |
| Thailand | 39,700 | 44,440 | 47,039 |
| United Kingdom | 2,244 | 97 | 70 |
| USA | 862 | 397 | 2,080 |

* Figures are based on data reported by partner countries, excluding Viet Nam, the former USSR and other former socialist countries.

Source: Statistisches Bundesamt, Wiesbaden, Germany.

# Transport

**ROAD TRAFFIC** (motor vehicles in use at 31 December)

| | 1990 | 1991 | 1992 |
|---|---|---|---|
| Passenger cars | 25,340 | 21,269 | 20,233 |
| Buses and coaches | 370 | 1,936 | 1,436 |
| Lorries and vans | 10,291 | 13,396 | 11,551 |
| Motorcycles and mopeds | n.a. | 74,823 | 105,921 |

Source: International Road Federation, *World Road Statistics*.

**SHIPPING**

**Inland Waterways** (traffic, '000)

| | 1981 | 1982 | 1983 |
|---|---|---|---|
| Freight (metric tons) | 12.8 | 45.2 | 42.6 |
| Freight ton-kilometres | 3,200 | 12,700 | 14,100 |
| Passengers | 137.8 | 139.6 | 263.8 |
| Passenger-kilometres | 4,700 | 3,500 | 10,000 |

Source: State Planning Committee.

**CIVIL AVIATION**
(traffic on scheduled services of Lao Aviation—International)

| | 1989 | 1990 | 1991 |
|---|---|---|---|
| Passengers carried ('000) | 50 | 115 | 115 |
| Passenger-kilometres (million) | 21 | 44 | 44 |
| Total ton-kilometres (million) | 2 | 4 | 4 |

Source: Statistisches Bundesamt, Wiesbaden, Germany.

# Communications Media

| | 1990 | 1991 | 1992 |
|---|---|---|---|
| Radio receivers ('000 in use) | 520 | 540 | 560 |
| Television receivers ('000 in use) | n.a. | 25 | 28 |
| Daily newspapers: | | | |
| Number | 3 | n.a. | 3 |
| Average circulation ('000 copies) | 14 | n.a. | 14 |

Non-daily newspapers (1988, estimates): 4 (circulation 20,000 copies).

Source: UNESCO, *Statistical Yearbook*.

Telephones in use: 6,600 in 1991 (Source: Statistisches Bundesamt, Wiesbaden, Germany).

# Education

(1991/92)

| | Institutions | Teachers | Students Males | Females | Total |
|---|---|---|---|---|---|
| Pre-primary | 608 | 1,618 | 12,048 | 13,627 | 25,675 |
| Primary | 7,140 | 21,036 | 327,531 | 253,261 | 580,792 |
| Secondary: | | | | | |
| General | n.a. | 8,936 | 71,755 | 45,749 | 117,504 |
| Vocational | n.a. | 544 | 2,461 | 1,242 | 3,703 |
| Teacher training | n.a. | 718 | 2,522 | 1,973 | 4,495 |
| University level* | n.a. | 476 | 1,977 | 1,448 | 3,425 |
| Other higher* | n.a. | 222 | 1,222 | 83 | 1,305 |

* 1989/90 figures.

Source: UNESCO, *Statistical Yearbook*.

# Directory

## The Constitution

The new Constitution was unanimously endorsed by the Supreme People's Assembly on 14 August 1991. Its main provisions are summarized below:

### POLITICAL SYSTEM

The Lao People's Democratic Republic (Lao PDR) is an independent, sovereign and united country and is indivisible.

The Lao PDR is a people's democratic state. The people's rights are exercised and ensured through the functioning of the political system, with the Lao People's Revolutionary Party as its leading organ. The people exercise power through the National Assembly, which functions in accordance with the principle of democratic centralism.

The State respects and protects all lawful activities of Buddhism and the followers of other religious faiths.

The Lao PDR pursues a foreign policy of peace, independence, friendship and co-operation. It adheres to the principles of peaceful co-existence with other countries, based on mutual respect for independence, sovereignty and territorial integrity.

### SOCIO-ECONOMIC SYSTEM

The economy is market-orientated, with intervention by the State. The State encourages all economic sectors to compete and co-operate in the expansion of production and trade.

Private ownership of property and rights of inheritance are protected by the State.

The State authorizes the operation of private schools and medical services, while promoting the expansion of public education and health services.

### FUNDAMENTAL RIGHTS AND OBLIGATIONS OF CITIZENS

Lao citizens, irrespective of their sex, social status, education, faith and ethnic group, are equal before the law.

Lao citizens aged 18 years and above have the right to vote, and those over 21 years to be candidates, in elections.

Lao citizens have freedom of religion, speech, press and assembly, and freedom to establish associations and to participate in demonstrations which do not contradict the law.

### THE NATIONAL ASSEMBLY

The National Assembly is the legislative organ, which also oversees the activities of the administration and the judiciary. Members of the National Assembly are elected for a period of five years by universal adult suffrage. The National Assembly elects its own Standing Committee, which consists of the Chairman and Vice-Chairman of the National Assembly (and thus also of the National Assembly Standing Committee) and a number of other members. The National Assembly convenes its ordinary session twice annually. The National Assembly Standing Committee may convene an extraordinary session of the National Assembly if it deems this necessary. The National Assembly is empowered to amend the Constitution; to endorse, amend or abrogate laws; to elect or remove the President of State and Vice-Presidents of State, as proposed by the Standing Committee of the National Assembly; to adopt motions expressing 'no confidence' in the Government; to elect or remove the President of the People's Supreme Court, on the recommendation of the National Assembly Standing Committee.

### THE PRESIDENT OF STATE

The President of State, who is also Head of the Armed Forces, is elected by the National Assembly for a five-year tenure. Laws adopted by the National Assembly must be promulgated by the President of State not later than 30 days after their enactment. The President is empowered to appoint or dismiss the Prime Minister and members of the Government, with the approval of the National Assembly; to appoint government officials at provincial and municipal levels; and to promote military personnel, on the recommendation of the Prime Minister.

### THE GOVERNMENT

The Government is the administrative organ of the State. It is composed of the Prime Minister, Deputy Prime Ministers and Ministers or Chairmen of Committees (which are equivalent to Ministries), who are appointed by the President, with the approval of the National Assembly, for a term of five years. The Government implements the Constitution, laws and resolutions adopted by the National Assembly and state decrees and acts of the President of State. The Prime Minister is empowered to appoint Deputy Ministers and Vice-Chairmen of Committees, and lower-level government officials.

### LOCAL ADMINISTRATION

The Lao PDR is divided into provinces, municipalities, districts and villages. Provincial governors and mayors of municipalities are appointed by the President of State. Deputy provincial governors, deputy mayors and district chiefs are appointed by the Prime Minister. Administration at village level is conducted by village heads.

### THE JUDICIARY

The people's courts comprise the People's Supreme Court, the people's provincial and municipal courts, the people's district courts and military courts. The President of the People's Supreme Court and the Public Prosecutor-General are elected by the National Assembly, on the recommendation of the National Assembly Standing Committee. The Vice-President of the People's Supreme Court and the judges of the people's courts at all levels are appointed by the National Assembly Standing Committee.

## The Government

### HEAD OF STATE

**President of State:** NOUHAK PHOUMSAVANH (took office November 1992; re-elected 22 February 1993).

### COUNCIL OF MINISTERS
(May 1995)

**Prime Minister and Supreme Commander of the Lao People's Army:** Gen. KHAMTAY SIPHANDONE.
**Deputy Prime Minister and Chairman of the Planning and Co-operation Committee:** KHAMPHOUI KEOBOUALAPHA.
**Minister of Foreign Affairs:** SOMSAVAT LENGSAVAT.
**Minister of Finance:** SAISOMPHON PHOMVIHAN.
**Minister of National Defence:** Lt-Gen. CHOUMMALI SAIGNASON.
**Minister to the Office of the Central Committee and to the Office of the Prime Minister:** KHAMSAI SOUPHANOUVONG.
**Minister of the Interior:** ASANG LAOLI.
**Minister of Trade and Tourism:** SOMPADITH VORASANE.
**Minister of Justice:** KHAMOUANE BOUPHA.
**Minister of Public Health:** VANNARETH RASAPHO (acting).
**Minister of Agriculture and Forestry:** Gen. SISAVAT KEOBOUNPHANH.
**Minister of Industry and Handicrafts:** SOULIVONG DALAVONG.
**Minister of Communications, Transport, Post and Construction:** PHAO BOUNNAPHON.
**Minister of Education, Sports and Fine Arts:** PHIMMASONE.
**Minister of Information and Culture:** OSAKAN THAMMATHEVA.
**Minister of Science and Technology:** SOULI NANTHAVONG.
**Minister of Labour and Social Welfare:** THONGLOUN SISOULIT.
**Minister to the Office of the President:** THONGDAM CHANTHAPHON.
**Chairman of the Party and State Inspection Committee:** MAYCHANTAN SENGMANI.
**Chairman of the Central Bank:** BUTSABONG SOUVANNAVONG.

The Council of Ministers also includes some 60 Deputy Ministers and Vice-Chairmen of Committees, and the Chairmen of the National Federations.

### MINISTRIES

All Ministries are in Vientiane.

**Ministry of Finance:** rue Luang Prabang, Vientiane; tel. (21) 314270.

**Ministry of Foreign Affairs:** rue That Luang, Vientiane; tel. (21) 414010.

**Ministry of Trade and Tourism:** rue Nongbone, Vientiane; tel. (21) 212380.

## Legislature

Under the terms of the 1991 Constitution (adopted by the Supreme People's Assembly), on 20 December 1992 154 candidates, approved by the Lao Front for National Construction, contested the 85 seats in the newly-created National Assembly.

**Chairman of the National Assembly:** Lt-Gen. SAMAN VIGNAKET.
**Deputy Chairmen:** KHAMBOU SOUNISAI, VONGPHET SAIKEU-YACHONGTOUA.

## Political Organizations

**Lao Front for National Construction—LFNC:** Vientiane; f. 1979 to replace the Lao Patriotic Front; comprises representatives of various political and social groups, of which the LPRP (see below) is the dominant force; fosters national solidarity and socialist economic development; Chair. MAISOUK SAISOMPHENG; Vice-Chair. VONGPHET SAIKEU-YACHONGTOUA; Sec. of Cen. Cttee Lt-Gen. SAMANE VIGNAKET.

**Phak Pasason Pativat Lao** (Lao People's Revolutionary Party—LPRP): Vientiane; f. 1955 as the People's Party of Laos; reorg. under present name in 1972; Cen. Cttee of 54 full mems; Pres. Gen. KHAMTAY SIPHANDONE.

### Political Bureau
Full members:
NOUHAK PHOUMSAVANH
Gen. KHAMTAY SIPHANDONE
MAYCHANTAN SENGMANI
Lt-Gen. SAMANE VIGNAKET
OUDOM KHATTIGNA
Lt-Gen. CHOUMMALI SAIGNASON
KHAMPHOUI KEOBOUALAPHA
THONGSING THAMMAVONG

Numerous factions are in armed opposition to the Government. The principal groups are:

**Ethnics' Liberation Organization of Laos:** Leader PA KAO HER.
**Free Democratic Lao National Salvation Force:** based in Thailand.
**United Front for the Liberation of Laos:** Leader PHOUNGPHET PHANARETH.
**United Front for the National Liberation of the Lao People:** f. 1980; led by Gen. PHOUMI NOSAVAN until his death in 1985.
**United Lao National Liberation Front:** Sayabouri Province; comprises an estimated 8,000 members, mostly Hmong (Meo) tribesmen; Sec.-Gen. VANG SHUR.

## Diplomatic Representation

### EMBASSIES IN LAOS

**Australia:** rue Pandit J. Nehru, quartier Phone Xay, BP 292, Vientiane; tel. (21) 413602; telex 4319; fax (21) 413601; Ambassador: ROLAND Y. RICH.
**Bulgaria:** rue Honkae, Vientiane; tel. (21) 412110; Ambassador: GEORGI DAMIANOV.
**Cambodia:** rue Thadeua, KM 2, BP 34, Vientiane; tel. (21) 314950; fax (21) 314951; Ambassador: KHEK LERANG.
**China, People's Republic:** ruelle Uat Nak, Muang Sisattanak, BP 898, Vientiane; tel. (21) 315103; Ambassador: LI JIAZHONG.
**Cuba:** Ban Sophanethong Neua, BP 1017, Vientiane; tel. (21) 315009; telex 4316; Ambassador: RICARDO A. DANZA SIGAS.
**France:** rue Sethathirath, Vientiane; tel. (21) 215258; telex 4308; Ambassador: GÉRARD CHESNEL.
**Germany:** rue Sok Paluang 26, BP 314, Vientiane; tel. (21) 312110; telex 4309; Ambassador: CLAUS SÖNKSEN.
**India:** rue That Luang, BP 225, Vientiane; tel. (21) 413802; telex 4326; Ambassador: Dr GAURI SHANKAR RAJHANS.
**Indonesia:** ave Phone Keng, BP 277, Vientiane; Ambassador: KASMAN SIAHAAN.
**Japan:** rue Sisangvone, Vientiane; tel. (21) 414401; fax (21) 414406; Ambassador: MASAO WADA.
**Korea, Democratic People's Republic:** quartier Wat Nak, Vientiane; tel (21) 315261; Ambassador: KIM UNG-JO.
**Malaysia:** place That Luang, quartier Nongbone, POB 789, Vientiane; tel. (21) 414205; telex 4316; Chargé d'affaires: NG BAK HAI.
**Mongolia:** rue Thadeua, BP 370, Vientiane; tel. (21) 312293; Ambassador: YUMBUUGIYN SANDAG.
**Myanmar:** Vientiane; Ambassador: U MAUNG MAUNG LAY.
**Poland:** route Thadeua, quartier Wat Nak, BP 1106, Vientiane; tel. (21) 312940; telex 4358; Ambassador: MARIAN EJMA-MULTANSKI.
**Russia:** rue Thadeua, BP 490, Vientiane; tel. (21) 312219; telex 804305; Ambassador: VLADIMIR FEDOTOV.
**Sweden:** rue Sok Paluang, BP 800, Vientiane; tel. (21) 313772; fax (21) 315001; Chargé d'affaires: OLOF MILTON.
**Thailand:** ave Phone Keng, Vientiane; tel. (21) 214581; fax (21) 4110017; Ambassador: SOMPHAND KOKILANON.
**USA:** rue Bartholonie, BP 114, Vientiane; tel. (21) 212581; fax (21) 212584; Ambassador: VICTOR L. TOMSETH.
**Viet Nam:** 1 rue That Luang, Vientiane; Ambassador: BUI BAN BAANH.

## Judicial System

**President of the People's Supreme Court:** KET KIETTISSAK.
**Vice-President:** DAVON VANGVICHIT.
**People's Supreme Court Judges:** NOUANTHONG VONGSA, SE SAISANADET, LESONG THONGVEUN, KHAMMOUN LATTANALASI.

## Religion

The 1991 Constitution guaranteed freedom of religious belief. The principal religion of Laos is Buddhism.

### BUDDHISM

**Lao Unified Buddhists' Association:** Maha Kudy, Wat That Luang, Vientiane; f. 1964; Pres. (vacant); Sec.-Gen. Rev. SIHO SIHAVONG.

### CHRISTIANITY
#### The Roman Catholic Church

For ecclesiastical purposes, Laos comprises four Apostolic Vicariates. At 31 December 1993 an estimated 1.2% of the population were adherents.

**Episcopal Conference of Laos and Cambodia:** Centre Catholique, Thakhek, Khammouane: f. 1971; Pres. Mgr JEAN-BAPTISTE OUTHAY THEPMANY, Vicar Apostolic of Savannakhet.
**Vicar Apostolic of Luang Prabang:** (vacant), Evêché, BP 74, Luang Prabang. (See below for Apostolic Administrator.)
**Vicar Apostolic of Paksé:** Mgr THOMAS KHAMPHAN (Titular Bishop of Semina), Centre Catholique, BP 77, Paksé, Champassak.
**Vicar Apostolic of Savannakhet:** Mgr JEAN-BAPTISTE OUTHAY THEPMANY (Titular Bishop of Sfasferia), Centre Catholique, Thakhek, Khammouane.
**Vicar Apostolic of Vientiane:** Mgr JEAN KHAMSÉ VITHAVONG (Titular Bishop of Moglaena), Centre Catholique, BP 113, Vientiane; also Apostolic Administrator of Luang Prabang.

#### The Anglican Communion

Laos is within the jurisdiction of the Anglican Bishop of Singapore.

### BAHÁ'Í FAITH

**National Spiritual Assembly:** BP 189, Vientiane; tel. 5673.

## The Press

**Aloun Mai** (New Dawn): Vientiane; f. 1985; theoretical and political organ of the LPRP.
**Heng Ngan:** 87 ave Lane Xang, BP 780, Vientiane; tel. (21) 212750; fortnightly; organ of the Federation of Lao Trade Unions; Editor BOUAPHENG BOUNSOULINH.
**Lao Dong** (Labour): Vientiane; f. 1986; fortnightly; organ of the Federation of Lao Trade Unions; circ. 46,000.
**Laos:** 80 rue Sethathirath, BP 310, Vientiane; telex 4328; quarterly; published in Lao and English; illustrated; Editor V. PHOMCHANHEUANG; English Editor O. PHRAKHAMSAY.
**Meying Lao:** Vientiane; f. 1980; monthly; women's magazine; Editor-in-Chief KHAMPHON PHIMMASENG; circ. 4,000.
**Noum Lao** (Lao Youth): Vientiane; f. 1979; fortnightly; organ of the Lao People's Revolutionary Youth Union; Editor DOUANGDY INTHAVONG; circ. 6,000.
**Pasason** (The People): 80 rue Sethathirath, BP 110, Vientiane; f. 1940; organ of the Cen. Cttee of the LPRP; Editor BOUABAN VOLAKHOUN; circ. 28,000.
**Siang Khong Gnaovason Song Thanva** (Voice of the 2nd December Youths): Vientiane; monthly; youth journal.
**Suksa May:** Vientiane; monthly; organ of the Ministry of Education, Sports and Fine Arts.
**Technical Science Magazine:** Vientiane; f. 1991; quarterly; organ of the Ministry of Science and Technology; scientific research and development.
**Valasan Khosana** (Propaganda Journal): Vientiane; f. 1987; organ of the Cen. Cttee of the LPRP.
**Valasan Pathet Lao:** 80 rue Sethathirath, BP 310, Vientiane; telex 4328; quarterly; illustrated; circ. 2,000.

**Vientiane May** (New Vientiane): BP 989, Vientiane; f. 1975; morning daily; organ of the LPRP Cttee of Vientiane province and city; Editor SICHANE (acting); circ. 2,500.

**Vientiane Times:** Vientiane; f. 1994; English; emphasis on investment opportunities; Editor SOMSANOUX MIXAY; circ. 1,000.

There is also a newspaper published by the Lao People's Army, and several provinces have their own newsletters.

### NEWS AGENCIES

**Khao San Pathet Lao (KPL):** BP 310, Vientiane; tel. (21) 215780; telex 4328; f. 1968; organ of the Cttee of Information, Press, Radio and Television Broadcasting; news service; daily bulletins in Lao, English and French; teletype transmission in English; Dir-Gen. BOUNTENG VONGSAY.

#### Foreign Bureaux

**Rossiyskoye Informatsionnoye Agentstvo—Novosti (RIA—Novosti)** (Russia): BP 626, Vientiane; tel. (21) 213510; telex 4340; f. 1963.

**Viet Nam News Agency (VNA):** Vientiane; Chief DO VAN PHUONG.

**Reuters** (UK) is also represented in Laos.

### PRESS ASSOCIATION

**Association of Lao Journalists:** BP 310, Vientiane; Vice-Pres. BOUABANE VORAKHOUN; Sec.-Gen. VILAYVIENG PHIMMASONE; Head of International Relations SOMSANOUK MIXAY.

## Publishers

**Khoualuang Kanphim:** 2–6 Khoualuang Market, Vientiane.

**Lao Printing Office:** rue Samsenthai, Vientiane.

**Lao-phanit:** Ministry of Education, Sports and Fine Arts, Bureau des Manuels Scolaires, Vientiane; educational, cookery, art, music, fiction.

**Pakpassak Kanphin:** 9–11 quai Fa-Hguun, Vientiane.

## Radio and Television

In 1992, according to UNESCO estimates, there were 560,000 radio receivers and 28,000 television receivers in use. In addition to the national service, there are several local radio stations. A domestic television service began in December 1983. In May 1988 a second national television station commenced transmissions from Savannakhet. In December 1993 the Ministry of Information and Culture signed a 15-year joint-venture contract with a Thai firm on the development of broadcasting services in Laos. Under the resultant International Broadcasting Corporation Lao Co Ltd, IBC Channel 3 was inaugurated in 1994 (see below). An agreement with Viet Nam Television, in late 1994, envisaged technical co-operation and the further exchange of television programmes via satellite.

**Lao National Radio:** BP 310, Vientiane; tel. and fax (21) 212430; f. 1951; state-owned; programmes in Lao, French, English, Thai, Khmer and Vietnamese; domestic and international services; Dir-Gen. BOUNTHANH INTHAXAY.

**Lao National Television:** BP 310, Vientiane; tel. (21) 212438; f. 1983; colour television service; Dir-Gen. BOUABANE VORAKHOUN.

**Laos Television 3:** Vientiane; operated by the International Broadcasting Corpn Lao Co Ltd; f. 1994 as IBC Channel 3; 30% govt-owned, 70% owned by the International Broadcasting Corpn Co Ltd of Thailand; restructuring reportedly in progress in 1995; programmes in Lao.

In 1990 resistance forces in Laos established an illegal radio station, broadcasting anti-Government propaganda: **Satthani Vithayou Kachai Siang Latthaban Potpoi Sat Lao** (Radio Station of the Government for the Liberation of the Lao Nation): f. 1990; programmes in Lao and Hmong languages; broadcasts four hours daily.

## Finance

(cap. = capital; dep. = deposits; br.(s) = branch(es); m. = million; amounts in old kips, unless otherwise stated)

### BANKING

The banking system was reorganized in 1988–89, ending the state monopoly of banking. Some commercial banking functions were transferred from the central bank and the state commercial bank to a new network of autonomous banks. The establishment of joint ventures with foreign financial institutions was permitted. In 1994 there were six private commercial banks in Laos, most of them Thai.

In August 1993 an agricultural promotion bank opened to encourage the production of foodstuffs in rural areas.

#### Central Bank

**Banque de la RDP Lao:** rue Yonnet, BP 19, Vientiane; tel. (21) 213109; telex 4304; fax (21) 213108; f. 1968 as Banque Pathetlao, took over the operations of Banque Nationale du Laos 1975; known as Banque d'Etat de la RDP Lao from 1982 until adoption of present name; Gov. BUTXABONG SOUVANNAVONG; 115 brs.

#### Commercial Banks

**Banque pour le Commerce Extérieur Lao (BCEL):** 1 rue Pangkham, BP 2925, Vientiane; tel. (21) 213200; telex 4301; fax (21) 213202; f. 1975; Man. Dir PHIANE PHILAKONE.

**Joint Development Bank:** ave Lane Xang, Vientiane; f. 1989; the first joint-venture bank between Laos and a foreign partner; 30% owned by Banque de la RDP Lao, 70% owned by a Thai company; cap. US $40m.

**Nakhonelouang Bank:** Vientiane; f. 1988; created by the Government as an autonomous bank.

**Sethathirath Bank:** Vientiane; f. 1988; created by the Government as an autonomous bank.

**Vientiane Commercial Bank Ltd:** 31 rue Dong Palan, BP 5001, Vientiane; tel. (21) 213510; fax (21) 213513; f. 1993; privately-owned joint venture by Laotian, Thai, Taiwanese and Australian investors; Pres. SILP REUNTHIRASAK.

#### Foreign Banks

**Bangkok Bank** (Thailand): Vientiane; f. 1993.

**Thai Military Bank:** 69 rue Khoun Boulom, Chanthabouli, BP 2423, Vientiane; tel. (21) 413111; the first foreign bank to be represented in Laos; Man. BUNCHONGSAK SKULKOO.

### INSURANCE

**Assurances Générales du Laos (AGL):** Vientiane Commercial Bank bldg, ave Lane Xang, BP 4223, Vientiane; tel. (21) 215903; telex 4355; fax (21) 215904; Dir-Gen. YVES GAUTHIER.

## Trade and Industry

**Lao National Chamber of Commerce and Industry:** rue Phonsay, BP 4596, Vientiane; tel. (21) 412392; fax (21) 414383; f. 1990; executive board comprising 11 mems and five advisers; Pres. KHAMMA PHOMKONG; Exec. Sec. CHITTACHONE VOLASAY.

**Société Lao Import-Export (SOLIMPEX):** 43–47 ave Lane Xang, BP 278, Vientiane; tel. (21) 213818; telex 4318; fax (21) 217054; Dir KANHKÈO SAYCOCIE; Dep. Dir KHEMMANI PHOLSENA.

### DEVELOPMENT ORGANIZATIONS

**National Office for Agriculture and Livestock:** Vientiane; public enterprise; imports and markets agricultural commodities; produces and distributes feed and animals.

**State Committee for Planning and Co-operation:** Vientiane; Chair. KHAMPHOUI KEOBOUALAPHA.

### STATE ENTERPRISES

**Electricité du Laos:** Vientiane; telex 4311; responsible for production and export of hydroelectricity.

**Entreprise d'Etat des Postes et Telecommunications Lao:** ave Lane Xang, 0100 Vientiane; tel. (21) 216974; telex 4400; fax (21) 216273; responsible for the postal service and telecommunications.

**Luen Fat Hong Lao Plywood Industry Co:** BP 83, Vientiane; tel. (21) 314990; fax (21) 314992; development and management of forests, logging and timber production.

### CO-OPERATIVES

**Central Leading Committee to Guide Agricultural Cooperatives:** Vientiane; f. 1978 to help organize and plan regulations and policies for co-operatives; by the end of 1986 there were some 4,000 co-operatives, employing about 74% of the agricultural labour force; Chair. (vacant); Chief KHAMSEN VONONOKEO.

### TRADE UNION ORGANIZATION

**Federation of Lao Trade Unions:** 87 ave Lane Xang, BP 780, Vientiane; tel. (21) 313682; f. 1956; 21-mem. Cen. Cttee and five-mem. Control Cttee; Chair. KHAMPAN PHILAVONG; Vice-Chair. BOUNPHON SANGSOMSAK; 70,000 mems.

## Transport

### RAILWAYS

The development of a railway network, the first phase of which would link Vientiane with Nong Kai, in Thailand, is under consideration. Plans were announced in November 1994 for the establishment of the National Railway Co Ltd of Laos, a joint venture between the Laotian Government (25%) and a Thai company, the Pacific Transportation Co Ltd (75%).

### ROADS

The road network provides the country's main method of transport, accounting for about 90% of freight traffic and 95% of passenger traffic in 1993 (according to the Asian Development Bank—ADB). In 1992 there were 14,130 km of roads, including 4,065 km of main roads and 5,990 km of secondary roads; 16% of the network was paved. The main routes link Vientiane and Luang Prabang with Ho Chi Minh City in southern Viet Nam and with northern Viet Nam and the Cambodian border, Vientiane with Savannakhet, Phong Saly to the Chinese border, Vientiane with Luang Prabang and the port of Ha Tinh (northern Viet Nam), and Savannakhet with the port of Da Nang (Viet Nam).

The first bridge across the Mekong river, linking Laos and Thailand between Tha Naleng (near Vientiane) and Nong Kai, was opened in April 1994.

### INLAND WATERWAYS

Laos is a land-locked country, and the Mekong river, which forms the western frontier of Laos for much of its length, is the country's greatest traffic artery. However, the size of river vessels is limited by rapids, and traffic is seasonal. In April 1995 Laos, Cambodia, Thailand and Viet Nam signed an agreement regarding the joint development of the lower Mekong. There are about 4,600 km of navigable waterways.

### CIVIL AVIATION

Wattai airport, Vientiane, is the principal airport. The development of Luang Prabang airport by Thailand, at a cost of 50m. baht, began in May 1994 and was scheduled for completion in November 1996. The airports at Paksé and Savannakhet were also to be upgraded to enable them to accommodate wide-bodied civilian aircraft.

**Lao Civil Aviation Department:** Vientiane; telex 4310; Dir PHOUN KHAMMOUNHUANG.

**Lao Aviation (International):** National Air Transport Co, 2 rue Pangkham, BP 119, Vientiane; tel. (21) 212050; telex 4336; fax (21) 212056; f. 1976; state airline, fmrly Lao Aviation; 30% state-owned; operated by China Travel Air Service; operates internal services; international services within South-East Asia; Gen. Man. Dir HU CHANG.

**Lao Aviation Development Venture Co Ltd:** Vientiane; f. 1995; joint venture between Lao Aviation (40%) and Yunnan Airlines of the People's Republic of China (60%); scheduled to operate domestic routes and international services within South-East Asia and to China.

## Tourism

Western tourists were first permitted to enter Laos in 1988. The number of visitors increased from 600 in 1988 to 12,000 in 1992. Tourist revenue in foreign currency in the latter year increased by 140%. In 1994, in order to stimulate the tourist industry, Vientiane ended restrictions on the movement of foreigners in Laos. In January–August of that year some 19,000 tourist arrivals were recorded. Also in 1994 Laos, Viet Nam and Thailand agreed measures for the joint development of tourism.

**National Tourism Authority of Lao PDR:** BP 3556, Vientiane; tel. (21) 212248; telex 4343; fax (21) 212769; Dir-Gen. PHONESOUK KHOUNSOMBAT.

# LATVIA

## Introductory Survey

### Location, Climate, Language, Religion, Flag, Capital

The Republic of Latvia (formerly the Latvian Soviet Socialist Republic) is situated in north-eastern Europe, on the east coast of the Baltic Sea. The country is bounded by Estonia to the north and by Lithuania to the south and south-west. To the east it borders the Russian Federation, and to the south-east Belarus. Owing to the influence of maritime factors, the climate is relatively temperate but changeable. Average temperatures in January range from −2.8°C (26.6°F) in the western coastal town of Liepāja to −6.6°C (20.1°F) in the inland town of Daugavpils. Mean temperatures for July range from 16.7°C (62.1°F) in Liepāja to 17.6°C (63.7°F) in Daugavpils. Average annual precipitation in Rīga is 617 mm. Latvian replaced Russian as the official language of the republic in 1988. It is an Indo-European language, a member of the Baltic group, and is written in the Latin script. At the census of 1989 22.3% of ethnic Russians living in the republic claimed fluency in Latvian. The major religion is Christianity: most ethnic Latvians are traditionally Lutherans or Roman Catholics, while ethnic Russians are largely adherents of the Russian Orthodox Church or Old Believers. The national flag (proportions 2 by 1) has a maroon background, with a narrow white horizontal stripe superimposed across the central part. The capital is Rīga (Riga).

### Recent History

After centuries during which Latvia had been partitioned and under the suzerainty of Poland, Sweden or Russia, a Latvian nationalist movement developed in the 1860s. By the early 1900s national-cultural groups had developed into a political movement advocating territorial autonomy for Latvia within the Russian Empire, a stance which continued until after the February Revolution of 1917 in Russia, when other national groups within the Empire were demanding complete independence. In November 1917, however, representatives of Latvian nationalist groups elected a provisional national council, which informed the Russian Government of its intention to establish a sovereign, independent Latvian state. On 18 November 1918 the Latvian National Council, which had been constituted on the previous day, proclaimed the independent Republic of Latvia, with Jānis Čakste as President.

Independence, under the nationalist Government of Kārlis Ulmanis, was fully achieved only after the expulsion of the Bolsheviks from Rīga, the capital (in May 1919), with the aid of German troops, and from the eastern province of Latgale, with Polish and Estonian assistance, in January 1920. A Latvian-Soviet peace treaty was finally signed in August 1920. Latvia's first Constitution was adopted in 1922. It introduced a democratic system of government, which, owing to an electoral system based on proportional representation, permitted a large number of small parties to be represented in the 100-member Saeima (legislature). As a result, there was little administrative stability, and in the period 1922–34 there were no fewer than 18 changes of government. However, under the dominant party, the Latvian Farmers' Union (LFU, led by Ulmanis), agrarian reforms were successfully introduced, making Latvia an important exporter of agricultural products. The world-wide economic decline of the early 1930s, together with the politically fragmented Saeima, prompted a (bloodless) *coup d'état*, in May 1934, led by Ulmanis. He introduced martial law throughout the country, dissolving the Saeima and banning all political parties, including the LFU. A Government of National Unity, with Ulmanis as Prime Minister and Minister of Foreign Affairs, assumed the legislative functions of the Saeima, pending the adoption of a new constitution by referendum (which was, in fact, never held). Ulmanis became President in 1936.

Under the Treaty of Non-Aggression (the 'Molotov-Ribbentrop Pact'), signed by Germany and the USSR on 23 August 1939, the incorporation of Latvia into the USSR was agreed by the two powers. A Treaty of Mutual Aid between the USSR and Latvia forced the Ulmanis Government to allow the establishment of Soviet military bases in Latvia, and on 17 June 1940 Soviet forces occupied Latvia, one day after their occupation of the neighbouring Baltic states of Estonia and Lithuania. The governments of the three Baltic states decided not to offer military resistance, being greatly outnumbered by the Soviet forces. In Latvia a new 'puppet' administration, under Augusts Kirchenšteins, replaced Ulmanis's Government, and elections to the Saeima took place in July, with only the nominations of candidates approved by Soviet officials permitted. On 21 July 1940 the legislature proclaimed the Latvian Soviet Socialist Republic (SSR), and on 5 August the Latvian SSR was formally incorporated into the USSR as a constituent union republic.

Immediately following the Soviet occupation, Latvians were subjected to arrests, 'disappearances' and executions, while their language, traditions and culture were suppressed. In the first year of Soviet rule almost 33,000 Latvians were deported to Siberia and other areas of the Russian Federation, while a further 1,350 were killed. In July 1941 Soviet rule in Latvia was interrupted by German occupation. Most German troops had withdrawn by 1944, although the Kurzeme region, in south-western Latvia, was retained by Germany until the end of the Second World War. Soviet Latvia was re-established in 1944–45, and the process of 'sovietization' was resumed. There were further mass deportations of Latvians to Russia and Central Asia. Independent political activities were prohibited, and exclusive political power was exercised by the Communist Party of Latvia (CPL), which, under the leadership of Jānis Kalnērziņš, was dominated by the so-called *latovichi* (russified Latvians who had spent the 1920s and 1930s in the USSR). A process of industrialization was initiated, which encouraged Russian and other Soviet immigration into the republic. Continued immigration led to Latvia's becoming the most 'russified' of the three Baltic states (at the time of the 1989 census Russians and other Slavs represented, respectively, 34% and 10% of the total population, while Latvians barely formed the majority ethnic group, representing 52%, compared with 75% in 1940). The only real opposition to the Soviet occupation was provided by Latvian partisans, whose armed resistance movement continued until the late 1950s.

By the early 1950s almost all of Latvia's privately-owned farms had been merged into collective farms. The problem of agricultural stagnation, which had accompanied Latvia's industrialization, was not addressed until the mid-1950s, when the Latvian authorities were accorded greater powers as a result of the policy of economic decentralization introduced in the USSR. Increased economic independence coincided with a movement within the CPL for greater cultural autonomy, which focused on the need to retain the Latvian language as the predominant language in the republic. In the late 1950s some 2,500 alleged members of this so-called 'nationalist group' were dismissed from positions of influence within the Government and the CPL. Among these was Kalnērziņš, who was replaced as First Secretary of the CPL by the pro-Soviet Arvīds Pelše in 1959. Under Pelše and his successor, Augusts Voss (First Secretary 1966–84), the limited autonomy that Latvia gained in the 1950s was reversed, and repression of Latvian cultural and literary life was increased.

In the late 1970s and early 1980s, however, there was a significant revival in traditional Latvian cultural activities. Political groups began to be established, including the Environmental Protection Club, founded in 1984, and Helsinki-86, established to monitor Soviet observance of the accords on East-West relations that were incorporated into the Final Act adopted in 1975 by the Conference on Security and Co-operation in Europe (CSCE, subsequently renamed the OSCE, see p. 198) at Helsinki, Finland. In June and August 1986 Helsinki-86 organized anti-Soviet demonstrations, which were suppressed by the police. In 1987 there were further demonstrations on the anniversaries of significant events in Latvian history. These nascent opposition movements, engendered by the greater freedom of expression permitted under the new Soviet policy of *glasnost* (openness), were strongly opposed by the CPL, headed since 1984 by Boris Pugo.

In 1988 the opposition movements began to unite into a significant political force in Latvia. Prominent intellectuals, led by Jānis Peters (the Chairman of the Latvian Writers' Union), criticized the CPL for its attitude to *perestroika* (restructuring) and advocated the introduction of more radical political and economic change. In June Latvia's cultural unions issued a joint resolution demanding that Latvian be made the state language, that the 'Secret Protocols' of the 1939 Treaty be published, and that measures be taken to address the problems of ecological degradation resulting from forced industrialization. Similar demands were made in the republic's press. In October 1988 representatives of the leading opposition movements, together with radicals from the CPL, organized the inaugural congress of the Popular Front of Latvia (PFL). Delegates adopted a policy of seeking sovereignty for Latvia within a renewed Soviet federation, and elected Dainis Ivāns as the party's first Chairman. The PFL quickly became the largest and most influential political force in Latvia, with an estimated 250,000 members by the end of 1988.

In September 1988 Boris Pugo was transferred to Moscow, and replaced as First Secretary of the CPL by Jan Vigris. The new CPL leadership came increasingly under the influence of members of the PFL (in October 1988 some 40,000 PFL members were also members of the CPL). On 29 September Latvian was designated the state language. During 1989 the nationalist movement began to adopt more radical policies. The Latvian National Independence Movement (LNIM), which had been formed in 1988, held its first congress in February 1989. The LNIM advocated full economic and political independence for Latvia, and its influence within the opposition movement (many of its members were also members of the PFL) led to the proposal, in May, by the leadership of the PFL to conduct a referendum on full independence for Latvia.

On 26 March 1989 candidates supported by the PFL won 26 of 34 seats in the elections to the USSR's Congress of People's Deputies. On 28 July, following similar moves by Lithuania and Estonia, the Latvian Supreme Soviet (legislature) adopted a declaration of sovereignty and economic independence. Growing support for full independence outside the USSR was demonstrated in October at the second congress of the PFL, at which delegates supported demands for total political and economic independence and for the introduction of a multi-party political system and a market-based economy. In December, despite the establishment of political groups opposed to the PFL (principally Interfront, a russophone-dominated group opposed to independence), candidates supported by the PFL won some 75% of seats contested in local elections.

In January 1990 the Latvian Supreme Soviet voted to abolish the constitutional provisions that guaranteed the CPL its monopoly of political power. On 15 February the Supreme Soviet adopted a declaration condemning the decision in 1940 to request admission to the USSR, and in the same month the flag, state emblems and anthem of pre-1940 Latvia were restored to official use. At elections to the Supreme Soviet, held in March and April, the PFL won a convincing victory: candidates endorsed by the PFL (who were members of various pro-independence political parties) won 131 of the 201 seats. The CPL and Interfront together won 59 seats, and there were 11 independents. In April, at an extraordinary congress, the CPL split into two parties. The majority of delegates rejected a motion to leave the Communist Party of the Soviet Union (CPSU), voting instead to remain an integral part of the CPSU and electing Alfreds Rubiks, an uncompromising opponent of independence, as First Secretary. Meanwhile, the pro-independence faction established the Independent Communist Party of Latvia, under the chairmanship of Ivars Kezbers.

The new Supreme Council (as the Supreme Soviet was now known) was convened in early May 1990, and elected Anatolijs Gorbunovs, a member of the CPSU-affiliated CPL, as its Chairman (*de facto* President of the Republic). On 4 May the Supreme Council adopted a resolution that declared the incorporation of Latvia into the USSR in 1940 as unlawful, and announced the beginning of a transitional period that was to lead to full political and economic independence. Four articles of the Constitution of 15 February 1922, which describe Latvia as an independent democratic state and assert the sovereignty of the Latvian people, were restored, and were to form the basis of the newly-declared Republic of Latvia's legitimacy. Ivars Godmanis, the Deputy Chairman of the PFL, was elected Prime Minister in a new, PFL-dominated Government.

On 30 April–1 May 1990 a rival body to the Supreme Soviet, the Congress of Latvia, had been convened. The Congress had been elected in an unofficial poll, in which some 700,000 people were reported to have participated: only citizens of the pre-1940 republic and their descendants had been permitted to vote. The Congress, in which members of the radical LNIM predominated, declared Latvia to be an occupied country and adopted resolutions on independence and the withdrawal of Soviet troops.

The Supreme Council's resolutions, although more cautious than independence declarations adopted in Lithuania and Estonia, severely strained relations with the Soviet authorities. On 14 May 1990 the Soviet President, Mikhail Gorbachev, issued a decree which annulled the Latvian declaration of independence, condemning it as a violation of the USSR Constitution. The declaration was also opposed within Latvia by some non-Latvians, who organized strikes and demonstrations to protest against the resolutions. Opposition to the pro-independence Government continued throughout 1990, with the Soviet authorities attempting to persuade Latvia to sign a new union treaty, and local anti-Government movements (allied with Soviet troops stationed in Latvia) conducting a campaign of propaganda and harassment against the Government. In December the Latvian Government claimed that special units of the Soviet Ministry of Internal Affairs (OMON units) had been responsible for a series of explosions in Rīga. In early January 1991 OMON troops seized the Rīga Press House, previously the property of the CPL. Two weeks later OMON units attempted to occupy a police station and to remove barricades that had been erected by Latvians in anticipation of military intervention. On 20 January a 'Committee of Public Salvation', headed by Rubiks, declared itself as a rival Government to that led by Godmanis. On the same day five people died when OMON troops attacked the Ministry of the Interior in Rīga.

The attempted seizure of power by the Committee of Public Salvation reinforced opposition in Latvia to inclusion in the new union treaty being prepared by nine Soviet republics. Latvia refused to conduct the all-Union referendum on the future of the USSR, which was scheduled for 17 March 1991 (although some 680,000 people, mostly Russians and Ukrainians, did participate on an unofficial basis). Instead of the official referendum, a referendum on Latvian independence took place on 3 March. Of those eligible to vote, 87.6% participated, of whom, according to official results, 73.7% endorsed proposals for 'a democratic and independent Latvian republic'.

When it was announced in August 1991 that President Gorbachev had been overthrown, immediate Soviet military intervention was anticipated in Latvia. Preparations were made for the establishment of a government-in-exile, and, despite the presence of Soviet troops in Rīga, an emergency session of the Supreme Council was convened on 21 August. The Supreme Council proclaimed the full independence of Latvia, also declaring the State Committee for the State of Emergency (the body which had assumed power in Moscow) to be unconstitutional. When the coup collapsed, the Godmanis Government quickly began to assert its control over events in Latvia. On 23 August the CPL was banned, and Rubiks was arrested and imprisoned.

Latvia's declaration of independence was quickly recognized by many countries (several states had in fact continued to recognize Latvia's *de jure* independent status throughout the period of Soviet occupation). In early September 1991 the USSR State Council formally recognized the independent Republic of Latvia. The country was admitted to the UN on 17 September. However, difficult internal political issues remained unresolved. Among the most controversial matters was that of citizenship of the new republic. In late 1991 the Supreme Council adopted legislation guaranteeing the citizenship of those people (including non-ethnic Latvians) who had been citizens of the pre-1940 republic, and their descendants. Other residents of Latvia (mainly Russians and other Slavs) would be required to apply for naturalization after the necessary legislation had been finalized. There were protests, both by non-ethnic Latvians and by international human rights observers, against the proposed requirements for naturalization, which, they claimed, were excessively harsh. During 1992 the Government proceeded with a programme to register, as well as to define the citizenship status of, all inhabitants of Latvia. The register was to be used in preparation for elections to the restored Saeima that were scheduled for June 1993. Final legislation governing citizenship was to be determined by the Saeima, following its election.

The general economic decline in Latvia in 1992 was accompanied, as in other former Soviet republics, by a considerable increase in criminal activity. In October the *Satversme* (Constitution) faction in the legislature proposed a vote of no confidence in the PFL-dominated Government, which, it claimed, was responsible for the country's economic and moral decline. However, Godmanis and all his ministers (with the exception of the Minister of Economic Reform) survived the vote. In the following week, none the less, the Minister of Foreign Affairs was forced to resign (allegedly owing to disagreement with the Government over the issue of citizenship), and further government resignations followed in early 1993. Moreover, the PFL, although still the ruling party, appeared increasingly unstable, as internal divisions led to the formation of separate 'splinter' groups (as occurred in many other Latvian political parties). A new political movement, Latvian Way, was established in February 1993: it represented a wide range of political views, and included, among other prominent figures, Gorbunovs, as well as members of the *Satversme* faction.

The first legislative elections since the restoration of independence took place on 5 and 6 June 1993, with the participation of 89.9% of the electorate. Only citizens of pre-1940 Latvia, and their descendants, were entitled to vote; consequently, some 27% of the population (mainly ethnic Russians) were excluded from the election. A total of 23 parties, movements and alliances contested the poll, of which eight secured representation in the newly-restored, 100-seat Saeima. Only 11 of the deputies elected were non-ethnic Latvians (six of whom were ethnic Russians). The results of the election (which was declared free and fair by international observers) demonstrated strong popular support for the more moderate nationalist parties, led by Latvian Way, while socialist-orientated parties failed entirely to gain representation. Latvian Way emerged as the strongest party, winning more than 32% of the votes and 36 seats in the assembly. The radical nationalist LNIM won 15 seats; the electoral coalition Harmony for Latvia—Revival of the Economy, which campaigned for the adoption of a liberal citizenship law, gained 13 seats, while the centrist, rural LFU took 12 seats. The Equal Rights Movement won seven seats, one of which was taken by its leader, Alfreds Rubiks, who was still in prison awaiting trial, following his arrest in August 1991. (In June 1994 the Saeima confirmed Rubiks's mandate, although the Supreme Court subsequently rejected an appeal for his release; in March 1995 Rubiks's trial was suspended, on account of his ill health.) The remainder of the seats were distributed between the right-wing Fatherland and Freedom Union (six), the Christian Democratic Union of Latvia (CDUL, six) and the Democratic Centre Party (five). Reflecting a massive loss of popular support following independence, the PFL failed to secure the 4% of the vote necessary for representation in the Saeima.

The first plenary session of the Saeima began on 6 July 1993 with the election of Anatolijs Gorbunovs as its Chairman (speaker). The Saeima also voted overwhelmingly to restore the Constitution of 1922. During the same sitting the parliament undertook to elect the President of the Republic from among three of its deputies: Gunars Meierovičs of Latvian Way, Aivars Jerumanis of the CDUL and Guntis Ulmanis (the great-nephew of Kārlis Ulmanis) of the LFU. When none of the candidates succeeded in gaining the majority vote necessary for election, Meierovičs withdrew from the contest and announced his support for Ulmanis. Following a second inconclusive round, Jerumanis withdrew his candidacy, and on 7 July a further round was held, in which Ulmanis succeeded in winning a majority of 53 votes. Ulmanis was inaugurated as President on the following day, whereupon he appointed Valdis Birkavs (formerly a Deputy Chairman of the Supreme Council and a leading member of Latvian Way) as Prime Minister, charging him with the formation of the new Government. The newly-styled Cabinet of Ministers was endorsed by the Saeima in late July; it represented a coalition agreement between Latvian Way and the LFU, although the former predominated in its composition.

Legislation on citizenship continued to be discussed by the Saeima during the latter half of 1993. Various parties and factions within the assembly submitted five separate draft citizenship laws for examination. However, the issue remained the focus of considerable concern outside the republic. In October the international human rights organization, Helsinki Watch, stated that Latvia's Department of Citizenship and Immigration had 'repeatedly committed unlawful acts by refusing without reason to register many residents'. As a consequence of these allegations, the head of the Department was dismissed in November. In the same month the Saeima approved the first reading of the draft citizenship law submitted by the governing coalition. The requirements for naturalization that it proposed included a minimum of 10 years' permanent residence, a knowledge of Latvian to conversational level, and an oath of loyalty to the republic. It also proposed an annual quota for naturalization. In late November a delegation of the CSCE arrived in Latvia to conduct a six-month examination of the citizenship issue. In March 1994 the Saeima approved the establishment of the new post of State Minister for Human Rights, in an attempt to counter accusations of violations of minority rights in Latvia.

Final legislation on citizenship and naturalization was adopted, at its third reading, by the Saeima in June 1994. It was criticized by the Council of Europe and the CSCE, among other international bodies, on account of its strict annual quota (from 2000) for the naturalization of non-ethnic Latvian residents born outside Latvia. Concerned that the new law would jeopardize Latvia's application for membership of the Council of Europe and potentially lead to international isolation, the Cabinet of Ministers persuaded President Ulmanis to reject the legislation and return it to the Saeima for reconsideration. Finally, in late July, the Saeima adopted an amended citizenship law: applicants were still required to prove knowledge of the Latvian language, but the annual quota was removed. The law barred application for citizenship only to residents suspected of crimes against the state. In February 1995 Latvia was admitted to the Council of Europe.

Meanwhile, in mid-July 1994 the LFU announced its withdrawal from the governing coalition, following disagreements with Latvian Way over economic and agricultural policy. Shortly thereafter the remaining members of the Cabinet of Ministers tendered their resignation, indicating that the Government was no longer able to fulfil its functions. However, all the ministers remained in office, in an interim capacity, until September, when a new Cabinet was appointed. It too was dominated by Latvian Way members, including the Prime Minister, Māris Gailis (hitherto Deputy Prime Minister and Minister of State Reform). Birkavs became Deputy Prime Minister and Minister of Foreign Affairs in the new Government. Four opposition factions within the Saeima—including those of the Latvian National Conservative Party (as the LNIM had been renamed) and the LFU—announced their union as a 'national bloc' to co-ordinate opposition activities in the legislature.

Latvia's relations with its eastern neighbour, the Russian Federation, were troubled by two issues during the early 1990s. The first concerned the rights of Latvia's large Russian community and the question of their citizenship (see above). Of comparable importance was the issue of former Soviet troops still stationed in Latvia (jurisdiction over whom had been transferred, following the dissolution of the USSR, to the Russian Federation). Negotiations between the two states in 1992 and early 1993 produced no definite date for the eventual withdrawal of all the troops, owing primarily to the Russian Government's difficulties in providing housing for them. Although the withdrawal of troops from Latvia did begin in early 1992, it appeared that the Russian Government was increasingly prepared to link continued withdrawals with the issue of human rights in Latvia. In October 1992 it was reported that the Russian President, Boris Yeltsin, had ordered the suspension of troop withdrawals from the Baltic states, owing to 'violations of the rights of the Russian-speaking populations' there. In early November, however, apparently in response to international pressure, the Russian Government denied that any such order had been implemented, also claiming that Yeltsin's statement had been intended for 'internal use only'. Troop withdrawals, it was stated, would continue as before.

Withdrawals of Russian troops proceeded throughout 1993; by October of that year it was reported that 17,784 officers and servicemen (of an estimated total of 100,000 prior to Latvian independence) remained in Latvia. However, the process was hampered, as before, by a series of disagreements and suspended withdrawals. Negotiations repeatedly foundered over the issue of the Russian military radar station at Skrunda, in western Latvia (the Russian Government wished to retain the base for a further six years, as a condition of which it undertook to withdraw all its remaining troops by the end of August 1994; however, the Latvian Government found this proposal unacceptable and demanded the complete withdrawal of Russia's military presence). The Russian-Latvian dialogue was jeopardized in January 1994 by an incident in which Latvian armed units, dispatched by the head of the local administration, took control of a Russian army base near Rīga, arresting two generals and taking them to the border with Russia. The Latvian Government acted quickly to control the situation and apologized to the Russian authorities for this action, which it described as an attempt to disrupt the bilateral negotiations. Although Russian troops in Latvia and the Baltic region were put on alert, the negotiations promptly resumed.

In February 1994 success was apparently achieved after two years of talks, when Latvia and Russia accepted a US-sponsored compromise and agreed in principle to the conditions and timetable for a final troop withdrawal. The draft agreement, which was initialled in March, permitted Russian use of the Skrunda base for a further four years (following which the base would be dismantled over an 18-month period). Troops not connected with the base (now numbering approximately 13,000) were to have left Latvia by 31 August 1994. The agreement was strongly condemned by radical Latvian nationalists, who were believed to have been responsible for sabotaging power supplies to Skrunda on two occasions. There were also reports of renewed attacks on Russian servicemen in Latvia. The accord was due to be officially signed at a meeting in late April between Presidents Ulmanis and Yeltsin. However, the progress of the agreement was threatened by the publication, in early April, of a decree by Yeltsin, which referred to the need to establish 30 new Russian military bases 'in the countries of the CIS and Latvia' for the purposes of 'military testing' and the 'security of Russia and the countries concerned'. Despite subsequent apologies by the Russian Government (which alluded to a 'technical error' in the decree's wording), the Latvian authorities remained deeply concerned, and suspended all negotiations with Russia. The urgency of the situation prompted deputies of Latvian Way in the Saeima to demand a vote of confidence in the Government, which it won by a margin of only one vote. The tension in relations with Russia was, however, resolved in late April, when Ulmanis visited Moscow and agreements were concluded on the complete withdrawal of the remaining 10,000 Russian troops by 31 August, as well as on social guarantees for the estimated 22,000 Russian military pensioners residing in Latvia. The withdrawal of all Russian troops was completed one day ahead of the scheduled deadline. In May 1995 a partially-constructed radar tower at Skrunda was demolished (with US financial assistance); however, the Russian Government retained the right to operate the radar station itself until 1998, under the terms of the agreement of April 1994.

During 1992 Latvia initiated measures to establish relations with members of the Commonwealth of Independent States (CIS, see p. 126), which had been formed by 11 republics upon the disintegration of the USSR in December 1991. In 1993 more than one-third of Latvia's foreign trade continued to be conducted with CIS member states. Latvia enjoys close political, economic and cultural relations with its Baltic neighbours, Estonia and Lithuania, with which it formed a consultative interparliamentary body, the Baltic Assembly, in late 1991. In the following year Latvia became a founder member, with Estonia, Lithuania and seven other countries of the region, of the Council of Baltic Sea States (see p. 238), which aimed to assist the political and economic development of its three former communist member states.

### Government

Under the terms of the 1922 Constitution (which was restored in July 1993), Latvia is an independent democratic parliamentary republic, in which the supreme legislative body is the Saeima (Parliament), whose 100 members are elected by universal adult suffrage for a three-year term. The President of the Republic, who is Head of State, is elected by a secret ballot of the Saeima for a period of three years. The President, who is also Head of the Armed Forces, may not serve for more than two consecutive terms. Executive power is held by the Cabinet of Ministers, which is headed by the Prime Minister. The Prime Minister is appointed by the President; the remaining members of the Cabinet are nominated by the Prime Minister. For administrative purposes, Latvia is divided into 26 districts and seven towns (including the capital, Rīga).

### Defence

Until independence (in August 1991), Latvia had no armed forces separate from those of the USSR. A Ministry of Defence was established in November 1991, and by June 1994 Latvia's defence forces totalled 6,850, of whom 4,300 were engaged in the border guard, 1,500 in the army, 900 in the navy and 150 in the air force. There are also a home guard (of an estimated 18,000) and security forces. Military service is compulsory from 19 years of age and lasts for 18 months. (Men and women of 18 years and older may join the national armed forces voluntarily.) The 1994 budget allocated an estimated 17.0m. lati (or 2.8% of total expenditure) to defence.

In August 1994 the withdrawal from Latvia of all former Soviet forces was completed. In February 1994 Latvia joined NATO's 'partnership for peace' programme (see p. 192).

### Economic Affairs

In 1993, according to estimates by the World Bank, Latvia's gross national product (GNP), measured at average 1991–93 prices, was US $5,257m., equivalent to $2,030 per head. During 1985–93, it was estimated, GNP per head declined, in real terms, at an average annual rate of 4.5%. Over the same period, the population decreased by an annual average of 0.1%. Latvia's gross domestic product (GDP) was estimated to have increased, in real terms, by an average of 0.6% per year during 1980–92. However, real GDP decreased by 34% in 1992, compared with the previous year. Following a less severe decrease (of 20%) in 1993, real GDP was reported to have achieved a modest increase in 1994.

Agriculture (including hunting, forestry and fishing) contributed 11.8% of GDP and provided 19.5% of employment in 1993. The principal sectors are dairy farming and pig-breeding. Cereals, sugar beet, potatoes and fodder crops are the main crops grown. As part of the process of land reform and 'privatization', the liquidation of collective and state farms was under way in the early 1990s. Agricultural production declined by 16% in 1992, compared with the previous year, and it decreased by a further 22% and 30% in 1993 and 1994, respectively.

Industry (including mining, manufacturing, construction and power) contributed 35.0% of GDP in 1993. In that year the sector provided 28.5% of employment. In early 1994 some 60% of industrial activity was performed by state-controlled enterprises. During 1980–92 industrial GDP increased by an annual average of 1.3%. However, industrial production decreased by 35% in 1992, by 36% in 1993 and by an estimated 9.5% in 1994.

In 1993 the mining sector contributed only 0.2% of GDP and employed only 0.2% of workers. Latvia has limited mineral resources (peat, dolomite, limestone, gypsum, amber, gravel and sand), and is consequently highly dependent on imported fuels to provide energy. In 1993 imports of mineral products represented 45.6% of the total value of Latvia's imports. Electric energy is supplied primarily by Estonia and Lithuania, while petroleum products are supplied by the Russian Federation and Lithuania.

Manufacturing accounted for 23.1% of GDP and provided 21.6% of employment in 1993. In that year the principal manufacturing branches were food products (accounting for 30.6% of total industrial output), machinery and equipment (17.9%), chemicals and chemical products (9.9%) and electricity, heating and water (9.6%).

The services sector has increased in importance in recent years: its contribution to GDP rose from 32% in 1990 to 53% in 1993. Latvia has emerged as an important regional banking centre. In 1993 output in the services sector was estimated to have declined by 10%, compared with 1992.

In 1993 Latvia recorded a visible trade surplus of 12.6m. lati, and there was a surplus of 289.0m. lati on the current account of the balance of payments. In 1994 Latvia's principal trading partner was the Russian Federation, which accounted for 26% of total trade (imports plus exports); other important trading partners were former republics of the USSR (particularly the neighbouring Baltic states of Estonia and Lithuania), Germany and Nordic countries. Member states of the European Union (EU) accounted collectively for about 25% of total Latvian trade in the same year. The principal exports in

1993 were machinery and equipment, food and agricultural products, and fuel. The principal imports in that year were mineral products, machinery and equipment and chemicals.

The 1994 state budget envisaged a deficit of 37.9m. lati. Latvia's total external debt at the end of 1993 was US $231.0m., of which $118.8m. was long-term public debt. By November 1994 Latvia's total external debt was reported to have increased to $324.4m. Consumer prices increased by 951.2% in 1992; however, under Latvia's stabilization programme, the rate of inflation was reduced to 109.2% during 1993 and to 35.9% in the following year. In February 1995 some 87,000 people were registered as unemployed (6.8% of the economically active population), of whom 37,700 were categorized as 'long-term unemployed'.

Latvia joined the IMF and the World Bank in 1992. It is also a member (as a 'country of operations') of the European Bank for Reconstruction and Development (EBRD, see p. 140). An agreement on a free-trade area between Latvia, Lithuania and Estonia entered into effect in April 1994. In July 1994 Latvia signed an agreement on free trade with the EU.

During the early 1990s the Latvian Government initiated economic reforms, with the aim of achieving a market economy and encouraging foreign investment in the country. The principal economic problem confronting Latvia was a severe shortage of fuels and raw materials, arising from the disruption of trading relations with republics of the former USSR and the transition to trade conducted between them in convertible currencies at world market prices. As a result, many Latvian enterprises were obliged to reduce, or cease, activity, and there was a significant decrease in industrial output. Widespread shortages of basic commodities were reported, and in early 1994, according to official sources, some 90% of the population were living 'below the minimum subsistence level'. However, the Government's programme of stabilization, initiated in 1992, achieved considerable success during the following year, when there was a dramatic fall in the monthly rate of inflation and a less serious decline in overall GDP than had been recorded in 1992. This trend continued into 1994, when a modest increase in GDP was recorded. A major priority for the immediate future is the escalation of the 'privatization' programme, which has been comparatively slow to take effect. The Government aimed to have transferred some 75% of state-owned enterprises to private ownership by the end of 1996.

In May 1992 Latvia introduced a parallel currency to the Russian rouble, the Latvian rouble (which, in July, became the sole legal tender). A new national currency, the lats (the currency which had operated until the Soviet annexation in 1940), was introduced in March 1993. The introduction of the lats had been completed by June, and in October it became the sole legal tender. The lats had become fully convertible by late 1994.

### Social Welfare

In 1994 expenditure from the state budget on health-care and social security totalled 284.7m. lati, equivalent to 47.5% of total budgetary expenditure. In 1992 there were 176 hospitals, with a total of 33,831 beds (equivalent to 130 beds per 10,000 persons). There were 372 other medical establishments, and 10,701 physicians (equivalent to one physician per 244 persons). In the same year there were 654,000 people in receipt of pensions, of which 496,700 were on account of old age.

### Education

Since the adoption of Latvian as the state language (replacing Russian) in 1988, the study of Latvian has become compulsory for all pupils. In the 1994/95 academic year some 72% of primary school pupils were taught in Latvian-language schools, while some 14% were taught in Russian-language schools; 13% were taught in schools offering instruction in both Latvian and Russian. In the same year 44.2% of secondary students attended Latvian-language schools, 44.1% attended Russian-language schools, and 11.6% attended schools offering instruction in both languages. In 1990/91 the first schools catering for the less numerous ethnic minorities were opened, and in 1994/95 there were six Polish schools (with a total of 601 pupils) and one Ukrainian school (126 pupils). In 1994/95 higher education was offered at 19 institutions, including universities, with a total enrolment of 37,600 students. The 1994 budget allocated 13.7% of state expenditure to education (82.1m. lati).

### Public Holidays

**1995:** 1 January (New Year's Day), 14 April (Good Friday), 1 May (Labour Day), 23–24 June (Midsummer Festival), 18 November (National Day, proclamation of the Republic), 25–26 December (Christmas), 31 December (New Year's Eve).

**1996:** 1 January (New Year's Day), 5 April (Good Friday), 1 May (Labour Day), 23–24 June (Midsummer Festival), 18 November (National Day, proclamation of the Republic), 25–26 December (Christmas), 31 December (New Year's Eve).

### Weights and Measures

The metric system is in force.

# Statistical Survey

Source (unless otherwise stated): State Committee for Statistics of Latvia, Rīga.

## Area and Population

**AREA, POPULATION AND DENSITY**

| | |
|---|---:|
| Area (sq km) | 64,589* |
| Population (census results)† | |
| 17 January 1979 | 2,502,816 |
| 12 January 1989 | |
| Males | 1,238,806 |
| Females | 1,427,761 |
| Total | 2,666,567 |
| Population (official estimates at 1 January) | |
| 1992 | 2,656,958 |
| 1993 | 2,606,176 |
| 1994 | 2,565,854 |
| Density (per sq km) at 1 January 1994 | 39.7 |

* 24,938 sq miles.
† Figures refer to the *de jure* population. The *de facto* total at the 1989 census was 2,680,029.

**POPULATION BY NATIONALITY** (permanent inhabitants)

| | 1989 census '000 | 1989 census % | 1994 estimates '000 | 1994 estimates % |
|---|---:|---:|---:|---:|
| Latvian | 1,388 | 52.0 | 1,391 | 54.2 |
| Russian | 906 | 34.0 | 849 | 33.1 |
| Belarusian | 120 | 4.5 | 105 | 4.1 |
| Ukrainian | 92 | 3.5 | 78 | 3.1 |
| Polish | 60 | 2.3 | 57 | 2.2 |
| Lithuanian | 34 | 1.3 | 33 | 1.3 |
| Jewish | 23 | 0.9 | 13 | 0.5 |
| **Total** (incl. others) | 2,667 | 100.0 | 2,566 | 100.0 |

**PRINCIPAL TOWNS** (estimated population at 1 January 1994)

| | | | |
|---|---:|---|---:|
| Rīga (Riga, the capital) | 856,281 | Jelgava | 71,332 |
| | | Jūrmala | 59,581 |
| Daugavpils | 121,974 | Ventspils | 47,484 |
| Liepāja | 104,628 | Rēzekne | 42,331 |

# LATVIA

*Statistical Survey*

## BIRTHS, MARRIAGES AND DEATHS

|  | Registered live births |  | Registered marriages |  | Registered deaths |  |
|---|---|---|---|---|---|---|
|  | Number | Rate (per 1,000) | Number | Rate (per 1,000) | Number | Rate (per 1,000) |
| 1986 | 41,960 | 16.1 | n.a. | n.a. | 31,328 | 12.0 |
| 1987 | 42,135 | 16.0 | 25,477 | 9.6 | 32,150 | 12.2 |
| 1988 | 41,275 | 15.5 | 25,296 | 9.5 | 32,241 | 12.2 |
| 1989 | 38,922 | 14.5 | 24,496 | 9.1 | 32,584 | 12.1 |
| 1990 | 37,918 | 14.2 | 23,619 | 8.8 | 34,812 | 13.0 |
| 1991 | 34,633 | 13.0 | 22,337 | 8.4 | 34,749 | 13.1 |
| 1992 | 31,569 | 12.0 | 18,906 | 7.2 | 35,420 | 13.5 |
| 1993 | 26,759 | 10.3 | 14,595 | 5.6 | 39,197 | 15.2 |

**Expectation of life** (years at birth, 1993): 67.2 (males 61.6; females 73.8).

## IMMIGRATION AND EMIGRATION ('000 persons)

|  | 1991 | 1992 | 1993 |
|---|---|---|---|
| Immigrants | 12.6 | 4.6 | 3.1 |
| Emigrants | 23.8 | 51.8 | 31.3 |

## EMPLOYMENT (annual averages, '000 persons)

|  | 1991 | 1992 | 1993 |
|---|---|---|---|
| Agriculture, hunting, forestry and fishing | 248 | 269 | 243 |
| Mining and quarrying | 4 | 3 | 2 |
| Manufacturing | 356 | 321 | 269 |
| Electricity and water | 11 | 16 | 16 |
| Construction | 130 | 89 | 68 |
| Trade, restaurants and hotels | 178 | 187 | 187 |
| Transport and communications | 107 | 105 | 108 |
| Finance and business services | 85 | 75 | 70 |
| Community, social and personal services | 254 | 243 | 238 |
| Public administration and defence, compulsory social security | 24 | 37 | 44 |
| **Total** | **1,397** | **1,345** | **1,245** |
| Males | 807 | 703 | 634 |
| Females | 590 | 642 | 611 |

## Agriculture

### PRINCIPAL CROPS ('000 metric tons)

|  | 1991 | 1992 | 1993 |
|---|---|---|---|
| Wheat | 186 | 324 | 305 |
| Barley | 762 | 426 | 446 |
| Rye | 146 | 295 | 341 |
| Oats | 177 | 60 | 74 |
| Other cereals | 37 | 22 | 33 |
| Potatoes | 944 | 1,167 | 1,272 |
| Pulses | 20.7 | 8.6 | 4.3 |
| Cabbages | n.a. | 150* | 134† |
| Tomatoes | n.a. | 5* | 5† |
| Cucumbers and gherkins | n.a. | 15* | 12* |
| Onions (dry) | n.a. | 26† | 24† |
| Carrots | n.a. | 35† | 30† |
| Sugar beets | 378 | 463 | 298 |
| Apples | n.a. | 43* | 55† |
| Plums | n.a. | 24* | 30† |

* Unofficial figures.   † FAO estimate.
Source: partly FAO, *Production Yearbook*.

## LIVESTOCK ('000 head at 1 January)

|  | 1992 | 1993 | 1994 |
|---|---|---|---|
| Cattle | 1,144 | 678 | 551 |
| Pigs | 867 | 482 | 501 |
| Sheep | 165 | 114 | 86 |
| Goats | 6 | 6 | n.a. |
| Horses | 28 | 26 | 27 |
| Poultry | 5,438 | 4,124 | 3,700 |

### LIVESTOCK PRODUCTS ('000 metric tons, unless otherwise indicated)

|  | 1991 | 1992 | 1993 |
|---|---|---|---|
| Beef and veal | 132 | 120 | 107 |
| Mutton and lamb | 4 | 4 | 4 |
| Pig meat | 126 | 101 | 68 |
| Poultry meat | 33 | 21 | 13 |
| Cows' milk | 1,739 | 1,479 | 1,157 |
| Cheese | n.a. | 15.1 | 10.2 |
| Butter | 38.3 | 31.8 | 33.0* |
| Hen eggs (million) | n.a. | 596 | 389 |
| Honey | 2.7 | 1.9 | 2.0† |
| Wool (metric tons): |  |  |  |
| greasy | 361 | 348 | 309 |
| scoured | 217 | 209 | 181 |

* Unofficial figure.   † FAO estimate.
Source: partly FAO, *Production Yearbook*.

## Forestry

### ROUNDWOOD REMOVALS ('000 cubic metres)

|  | 1989 | 1990 | 1991 |
|---|---|---|---|
| **Total** | 4,167 | 3,760 | 3,419 |

### SAWNWOOD PRODUCTION ('000 cubic metres)

|  | 1990 | 1991 | 1992 |
|---|---|---|---|
| **Total** (incl. railway sleepers) | 795.4 | 673.2 | 470.3 |

## Fishing

('000 metric tons, live weight)

|  | 1991 | 1992 | 1993 |
|---|---|---|---|
| Freshwater fishes | 1.3 | 0.7 | 0.9 |
| Marine fishes | 353.3 | 150.6 | 144.4 |
| Crustaceans and molluscs | 21.1 | 11.5 | 4.7 |
| **Total catch** | **375.7** | **162.8** | **150.0** |

## Mining

('000 metric tons, unless otherwise indicated)

|  | 1991 | 1992 | 1993 |
|---|---|---|---|
| Peat | 1,663 | 785 | 428 |
| for fuel | 298 | 408 | 334 |
| for agriculture | 1,365 | 377 | 94 |
| Non-ore building materials ('000 cu m) | 9,117 | 2,821 | 993 |

# Industry

**SELECTED PRODUCTS** ('000 metric tons, unless otherwise indicated)

|  | 1991 | 1992 | 1993 |
|---|---|---|---|
| Refined sugar | 128 | 118 | 47.8 |
| Beer ('000 hectolitres) | 1,295.3 | 858.9 | 457.0 |
| Cigarettes (million) | 4,765 | 3,435 | 2,589 |
| Woven cotton fabrics (million sq metres) | 45.0 | 19.6 | 5.6 |
| Linen fabrics (million sq metres) | 9.6 | 3.5 | 1.1 |
| Woollen fabrics (million sq metres) | 15.4 | 11.5 | 2.7 |
| Leather footwear ('000 pairs) | 7,778 | 8,885 | 2,653 |
| Rubber footwear ('000 pairs) | 7,571 | 3,599 | 1,536 |
| Plywood ('000 cu metres) | 43.8 | 47.9 | 57.7 |
| Pulp | 44.7 | n.a. | n.a. |
| Paper | 108.1 | 45.7 | 8.9 |
| Synthetic resins and plastics | 30.7 | 16.0 | 11.1 |
| Phosphate fertilizers* | 103.4 | n.a. | n.a. |
| Building bricks (million) | 455.7 | 237.0 | 70.6 |
| Cement | 720.0 | 340.0 | 114.0 |
| Crude steel | 373.1 | 247.8 | 300.4 |
| Washing machines ('000) | 427 | 18 | 18.2 |
| Radio receivers ('000) | 1,230 | 630.0 | 132.1 |
| Buses (number) | 15,849 | 15,139 | 10,579 |
| Electric energy (million kWh) | 5,644 | 3,834 | 3,923 |

* In terms of phosphoric acid.

# Finance

**CURRENCY AND EXCHANGE RATES**

**Monetary Units**
100 santimi = 1 lats (plural: lati).

**Sterling and Dollar Equivalents** (31 December 1994)
£1 sterling = 85.9 santimi;
US $1 = 54.9 santimi;
100 lati = £116.43 = $182.15.

Note: Between March and June 1993 Latvia reintroduced its national currency, the lats, replacing the Latvian rouble (Latvijas rublis), at a conversion rate of 1 lats = 200 Latvian roubles. The Latvian rouble had been introduced in May 1992, replacing (and initially at par with) the Russian (formerly Soviet) rouble. For details of exchange rates for the rouble, see the chapter on the Russian Federation.

**STATE BUDGET** ('000 lati)

| Revenue | 1994 |
|---|---|
| Turnover tax | 174,248* |
| Excise duties | 29,192* |
| Profit tax | 76,295* |
| Customs duties | 23,412* |
| Natural resources tax | 427 |
| Revenue from forestries | 2,638 |
| State duties | 2,230 |
| Social tax | 215,610* |
| Revenues from state property lease | 694 |
| Payments for state capital use | 7,654* |
| Duties and other non-tax payments | 10,473 |
| Receipts for interest payments on World Bank loan | 1,219* |
| Receipts from Bank of Latvia's balance of profit | 7,913 |
| Receipts for interest payments on EBRD | 499 |
| Others | 8,768 |
| **Total** | **561,272** |

* Including convertible currencies.

| Expenditure | 1994 |
|---|---|
| National economy | 33,596 |
| Agriculture | 10,955 |
| Forestry | 3,394 |
| Environmental protection | 1,573 |
| Traffic | 9,636 |
| Others | 8,038 |
| Social and cultural activities | 381,010 |
| Education | 82,080 |
| Cultural activities, radio and television | 13,172 |
| Health care | 34,183 |
| Physical training | 1,055 |
| Benefits and allowances | 33,571 |
| Pension payments | 198,072 |
| Compensation of employees | 8,663 |
| Social security | 5,206 |
| Social fund | 5,008 |
| Research and development | 5,426 |
| Maintenance of judicial and defence institutions | 62,297 |
| Maintenance of state governing bodies | 2,993 |
| Maintenance of state administration bodies | 24,252 |
| Interest payments on foreign loans | 8,720 |
| Contributions to international corporations | 1,436 |
| Repayments of domestic debt | 18,464 |
| Settlement of accounts with local budgets | 54 |
| Deductions for the Local Government Equalization Fund | 53,369 |
| Others | 7,585 |
| **Total** | **599,202** |

**INTERNATIONAL RESERVES**
(US $ million at 31 December, excluding gold)

|  | 1991 | 1992 |
|---|---|---|
| IMF special drawing rights | — | 26.58 |
| Reserve position in IMF | — | 0.01 |
| Foreign exchange | 24.36 | 44.56 |
| **Total** | **24.36** | **71.15** |

Source: IMF, *International Financial Statistics: Supplement on Countries of the Former Soviet Union.*

**MONEY SUPPLY** ('000 lati at 31 December)

|  | 1993 | 1994 |
|---|---|---|
| Currency in circulation | 179,131 | 232,100 |

**COST OF LIVING**
(Consumer price index; base: previous year = 100)

|  | 1992 | 1993 | 1994 |
|---|---|---|---|
| Food | 848.0 | 193.4 | 133.2 |
| Non-food commodities | 751.7 | 188.3 | 137.1 |
| Services | 2,823.6 | 340.2 | 141.1 |
| **All items** | **1,051.2** | **209.2** | **135.9** |

**NATIONAL ACCOUNTS**

**Gross Domestic Product by Economic Activity**
('000 lati at current prices)

|  | 1991 | 1992 | 1993 |
|---|---|---|---|
| Agriculture, hunting, forestry and fishing | 32,215 | 165,290 | 156,827 |
| Mining and quarrying | 270 | 1,425 | 2,414 |
| Manufacturing | 49,690 | 264,785 | 307,089 |
| Electricity, gas and water | 3,190 | 13,795 | 100,205 |
| Construction | 8,020 | 47,310 | 56,603 |
| Services | 45,800 | 445,965 | 708,685 |
| **GDP at factor cost** | **139,185** | **938,570** | **1,331,823** |
| Indirect taxes, *less* subsidies | 4,140 | 65,985 | 135,189 |
| **GDP in purchasers' values** | **143,325** | **1,004,555** | **1,467,012** |

## LATVIA

### BALANCE OF PAYMENTS (million lati)

| | 1992 | 1993 |
|---|---|---|
| Merchandise exports | 589.1 | 710.6 |
| Merchandise imports | −618.8 | −698.0 |
| **Trade balance** | **−29.7** | **−12.6** |
| Exports of services | 214.0 | 355.3 |
| Imports of services | −115.2 | −135.6 |
| Other income received | 1.9 | 11.5 |
| Other income paid | −0.8 | −6.6 |
| Unrequited transfers (net) | 70.8 | 51.8 |
| **Current balance** | **141.0** | **289.0** |
| Direct investment (net) | 20.1 | 33.0 |
| Other capital (net) | −73.9 | 62.9 |
| Net errors and omissions | −33.0 | −142.0 |
| **Overall balance** | **54.2** | **243.0** |

## External Trade

### PRINCIPAL COMMODITIES ('000 lati)

| Imports f.o.b.* | 1993 |
|---|---|
| Vegetable products | 11,698 |
| Prepared foodstuffs (incl. alcoholic and non-alcoholic beverages and tobacco products) | 21,090 |
| Mineral products | 291,732 |
| Products of chemical and allied industries | 45,184 |
| Plastic and rubber products | 11,354 |
| Textiles | 29,374 |
| Base metals | 28,365 |
| Machinery and equipment | 63,119 |
| Transport vehicles | 59,569 |
| **Total** (incl. others) | **639,247** |

* Excluding re-imports ('000 lati): 8,222 in 1993.

| Exports f.o.b.* | 1993 |
|---|---|
| Live animals and animal products | 42,383 |
| Prepared foodstuffs (incl. alcoholic and non-alcoholic beverages and tobacco products) | 45,287 |
| Mineral products | 96,360 |
| Products of chemical and allied industries | 46,372 |
| Forestry products | 59,392 |
| Textiles | 85,698 |
| Base metals | 56,862 |
| Machinery and equipment | 48,114 |
| Transport vehicles | 84,830 |
| **Total** (incl. others) | **675,611** |

* Excluding re-exports ('000 lati): 25,990 in 1993.

### PRINCIPAL TRADING PARTNERS (million lati)

| Imports f.o.b. | 1991 | 1992 | 1993 |
|---|---|---|---|
| Belarus | 1.87 | 19.85 | 26.48 |
| Estonia | 1.64 | 34.67 | 25.25 |
| Finland | 0.26 | 14.03 | 26.93 |
| Germany | 0.40 | 81.18 | 63.68 |
| Lithuania | 3.18 | 17.03 | 61.23 |
| Netherlands | — | 18.95 | 6.56 |
| Russia | 13.26 | 150.83 | 181.94 |
| Sweden | 0.13 | 20.55 | 33.61 |
| Ukraine | 2.75 | 19.42 | 19.10 |
| USA | 0.12 | 14.08 | 7.65 |
| **Total** (incl. others) | **31.55** | **543.34** | **647.47** |

| Exports f.o.b. | 1991 | 1992 | 1993 |
|---|---|---|---|
| Belarus | 2.66 | 26.94 | 34.39 |
| Belgium | — | 32.54 | 10.69 |
| Finland | 0.08 | 21.27 | 13.60 |
| Germany | 0.33 | 45.49 | 44.55 |
| Lithuania | 2.08 | 20.71 | 28.87 |
| Netherlands | — | 42.83 | 55.07 |
| Poland | — | 12.92 | 19.96 |
| Russia | 20.97 | 148.74 | 200.11 |
| Sweden | 0.25 | 43.06 | 43.78 |
| Ukraine | 4.63 | 47.09 | 40.09 |
| United Kingdom | — | 20.06 | 31.65 |
| **Total** (incl. others) | **38.53** | **576.88** | **701.60** |

## Transport

### RAILWAYS (traffic)

| | 1992 | 1993 | 1994 |
|---|---|---|---|
| Passenger journeys (million) | 83.1 | 59.6 | 55.7 |
| Passenger-kilometres (million) | 3,656 | 2,359 | 1,794 |
| Freight transported (million metric tons) | 31.8 | 30.6 | 27.8 |
| Freight ton-kilometres (million) | 10,115 | 9,852 | 9,520 |

### ROAD TRAFFIC (motor vehicles in use at 31 December)

| | 1991 | 1992 | 1993 |
|---|---|---|---|
| Passenger cars | 328,450 | 350,000 | 367,475 |
| Buses and coaches | 12,660 | 12,700 | 11,604 |
| Lorries and vans | 70,597 | 70,600 | 60,454 |
| Motorcycles and mopeds | 200,859 | 223,190 | n.a. |

Source: partly International Road Federation, *World Road Statistics*.

### SHIPPING

**Number of ships**

| | 1991 | 1992 | 1993 |
|---|---|---|---|
| Merchant vessels | 111 | 107 | 129 |

**Sea-borne freight traffic**

| | 1991 | 1992 | 1993 |
|---|---|---|---|
| Goods transported ('000 metric tons) | 23,813 | 15,173 | 13,106 |
| Goods turnover (million ton-kilometres) | 47,335 | 30,569 | 36,577 |

### CIVIL AVIATION (traffic)

| | 1991 | 1992 | 1993 |
|---|---|---|---|
| Passengers carried ('000) | 1,939.6 | 382.1 | 163.2 |
| Passenger-kilometres (million) | 2,999.3 | 450.5 | 210.6 |
| Cargo ton-kilometres ('000) | 17,975 | 3,069 | 7,135 |

## Communications Media

| | 1991 | 1992 | 1993 |
|---|---|---|---|
| Radio receivers ('000 in use)* | 1,396 | 1,378 | 1,400 |
| Television receivers ('000 in use)* | 1,126 | 1,105 | 1,100 |
| Telephones ('000 in use)* | 676 | 686 | 689 |
| Book production†: | | | |
| Titles | 1,387 | 1,509 | n.a. |
| Copies ('000) | 28,500 | 21,980 | n.a. |
| Daily newspapers: | | | |
| Number | n.a. | 17 | n.a. |
| Average circulation ('000) | n.a. | 517 | n.a. |
| Non-daily newspapers: | | | |
| Number | n.a. | 186 | n.a. |
| Other periodicals: | | | |
| Number | n.a. | 170 | n.a. |
| Average circulation ('000) | n.a. | 1,912 | n.a. |

* At 31 December.
† Including pamphlets (354 titles and 4,529,000 copies in 1992).
Source: partly UNESCO, *Statistical Yearbook*.

## Education

(1994/95)

| | Institutions | Students |
|---|---|---|
| Primary schools | 594* | 82,455 |
| Latvian | 451 | 59,589 |
| Russian | 63 | 11,481 |
| Latvian-Russian† | 75 | 10,941 |
| Polish | 5 | 444 |
| Secondary schools | 371 | 239,227 |
| Latvian | 186‡ | 105,693 |
| Russian | 126§ | 105,418 |
| Latvian-Russian† | 57 | 27,833 |
| Polish | 1 | 157 |
| Ukrainian | 1 | 126 |
| Vocational schools | 77 | 26,900 |
| Special secondary institutions | 53 | 18,200 |
| Higher education institutions (incl. universities) | 19 | 37,600 |
| Special schools (for the physically and mentally handicapped) | 52 | 7,436 |

* Including 106 junior schools (Grades 1–4).
† Mixed schools with two languages of instruction.
‡ Including one school with instruction in Estonian.
§ Including one school with instruction in Hebrew.

**Teachers** (1992): Pre-primary 9,530; Primary 12,758; Secondary 25,035 (general education 18,344, teacher training 323, vocational 6,368); Universities, etc. 4,478 (Source: UNESCO, *Statistical Yearbook*).

# Directory

## The Constitution

The Constitution of the Republic of Latvia, which had been adopted on 15 February 1922, was annulled at the time of the Soviet annexation in 1940. Latvia became a Union Republic of the USSR and a new Soviet-style Constitution became the legal basis for the governmental system of the republic. The constitutional authority for Latvian membership of the USSR, the Resolution on Latvian Entry into the USSR of 21 July 1940, was declared null and void on 4 May 1990. In the same declaration the Latvian Supreme Council announced the restoration of Articles 1, 2 and 3 of the 1922 Constitution, which describe Latvia as an independent and sovereign state, and Article 6, which states that the legislature (the Saeima) is elected by universal, equal, direct and secret vote, on the basis of proportional representation. On 6 July 1993 the 1922 Constitution was fully restored by the Saeima, following its election on 5 and 6 June. A summary of the Constitution's main provisions (including amendments adopted since its restoration) is given below.

### BASIC PROVISIONS

Latvia is an independent, democratic republic, in which the sovereign power of the State belongs to the people. The territory of the Republic of Latvia comprises the provinces of Vidzeme, Latgale, Kurzeme and Zemgale, within the boundaries stipulated by international treaties.

### THE SAEIMA

The Saeima (Parliament) comprises 100 representatives of the people, and is elected by universal, equal, direct and secret vote, on the basis of proportional representation, for a period of three years. All Latvian citizens who have attained 18 years of age are entitled to vote and are eligible for election to the Saeima.

The Saeima elects a Board, which consists of the Chairperson, two Deputies, and Secretaries. The Board convenes the sessions of the Saeima and decrees regular and extraordinary sittings. The sessions of the Saeima are public (sittings in camera are held only be special request).

The right of legislation belongs to both the Saeima and the people. Draft laws may be presented to the Saeima by the President of the Republic, the Cabinet of Ministers, the Committees of the Saeima, no fewer than five members of the Saeima, or, in special cases, by one-tenth of the electorate. Before the commencement of each financial year, the Saeima approves the state budget, the draft of which is submitted by the Cabinet of Ministers. The Saeima decides on the strength of the armed forces during peacetime. The ratification of the Saeima is indispensable to all international agreements dealing with issues resolved by legislation.

### THE PRESIDENT OF THE REPUBLIC

The President of the Republic is elected by a secret ballot of the Saeima for a period of three years. A majority of no fewer than 51 votes is required for his/her election. No person of less than 40 years of age may be elected President of the Republic. The office of President is not compatible with any other office, and the President may serve for no longer than two consecutive terms.

The President represents the State in an international capacity; he/she appoints Latvian representatives abroad, and receives representatives of foreign states accredited to Latvia; implements the decisions of the Saeima concerning the ratification of international treaties; is Head of the Armed Forces; appoints a Commander-in-Chief in time of war; has the power to declare war on the basis of a decision of the Saeima.

The President has the right to pardon criminals serving penal sentences; to convene extraordinary meetings of the Cabinet of Ministers for the discussion of an agenda prepared by him/her, and to preside over such meetings; to propose the dissolution of the Saeima. The President may be held criminally accountable if the Saeima sanctions thus with a majority vote of no fewer than two-thirds of its members.

### THE CABINET OF MINISTERS

The Cabinet comprises the Prime Minister and the ministers nominated by him/her. This task is entrusted to the Prime Minister by the President of the Republic. All state administrative institutions are subordinate to the Cabinet, which, in turn, is accountable to the Saeima. If the Saeima adopts a vote expressing 'no confidence' in the Prime Minister, the entire Cabinet must resign. The Cabinet discusses all draft laws presented by the ministries as well as issues concerning the activities of the ministries. If the State is threatened by foreign invasion or if events endangering the existing order of the State arise, the Cabinet has the right to proclaim a state of emergency.

### THE JUDICIARY

All citizens are equal before the law and the courts. Judges are independent and bound only by law. The appointment of judges is confirmed by the Saeima. Judges may be dismissed from office against their will only by a decision of the Supreme Court. The retiring age for judges is stipulated by law. Judgment may be passed solely by institutions which have been so empowered by law and in such a manner as specified by law.

LATVIA

## The Government

### HEAD OF STATE

**President:** GUNTIS ULMANIS (inaugurated 8 July 1993).

### CABINET OF MINISTERS
(May 1995)

**Prime Minister:** MĀRIS GAILIS.
**Deputy Prime Minister and Minister of Foreign Affairs:** VALDIS BIRKAVS.
**Minister of Finance:** INDRA SĀMĪTE.
**Minister of Defence:** (vacant).
**Minister of the Economy:** JĀNIS ZVANĪTĀJS.
**Minister of the Interior:** JĀNIS ĀDAMSONS.
**Minister of Education and Science:** JĀNIS GAIGALS.
**Minister of Culture:** JĀNIS DRIPE.
**Minister of Welfare:** ANDRIS BĒRZIŅŠ.
**Minister of Transport:** ANDRIS GŪTMANIS.
**Minister of Justice:** ROMĀNS APSĪTIS.
**Minister of State Reform:** VITA ANDA TĒRAUDA.
**Minister of the Environment and Regional Development:** JURIS IESALNIEKS.
**Minister of Agriculture:** ĀRIJS ŪDRIS.

### STATE MINISTERS*

**State Minister for Baltic and Nordic States:** GUNĀRS MEIEROVICS.
**State Ministers at the Ministry of Foreign Affairs:** OĻGERTS PAVLOVSKIS, JĀNIS RITENIS.
**State Minister for State Income:** AIJA POČA.
**State Minister for Energy:** JURIS OZOLIŅŠ.
**State Minister for Health Care:** PĒTERIS APINIS.
**State Minister for Human Rights:** JĀNIS ĀRVALDIS TUPESIS.
**State Minister for Environmental Protection:** INDULIS EMSIS.
**State Minister for Co-operation at the Ministry of Agriculture:** VILNIS EDVĪNS BRESIS.
**State Minister for Forestry:** ARVĪDS OZOLS.
**State Minister for Social Affairs:** VLADIMIRS MAKAROVS.
**State Minister for State Property:** DANIS TUNSTS.
**State Minister for Industrial Policy and Privatization:** RAIMONDS JONĪTIS.

* State Ministers, who are not full members of the Cabinet of Ministers, hold voting rights only in those issues concerning their departments.

### MINISTRIES

**Office of the Cabinet of Ministers:** Brīvības bulv. 36, Rīga 1520; tel. (2) 332-232; fax (2) 286-598.
**Ministry of Agriculture:** Republikas lauk. 2, Rīga 1981; tel. (2) 327-010; fax (2) 324-512.
**Ministry of Culture:** K. Valdemāra iela 11A, Rīga 1364; tel. (2) 224-772; fax (2) 227-916.
**Ministry of Defence:** K. Valdemāra iela 10/12, Rīga 1050; tel. (2) 210-124; fax 7830236.
**Ministry of the Economy:** Brīvības bulv. 36, Rīga 1519; tel. (2) 288-444; fax (2) 280-882.
**Ministry of Education and Science:** Vaļņu iela 2, Rīga 1098; tel. (2) 222-415; fax (2) 213-992.
**Ministry of the Environment and Regional Development:** Peldu iela 25, Rīga 1494; tel. (2) 223-612; fax (2) 228-159.
**Ministry of Finance:** Smilšu iela 1, Rīga 1919; tel. (2) 226-672; fax 7820010.
**Ministry of Foreign Affairs:** Brīvības bulv. 36, Rīga 1395; tel. (2) 223-307; fax (2) 227-755.
**Ministry of the Interior:** Raiņa bulv. 6, Rīga 1533; tel. (2) 287-260; fax (2) 223-853.
**Ministry of Justice:** Brīvības bulv. 34, Rīga 1536; tel. (2) 282-607; fax (2) 331-920.
**Ministry of State Reform:** Brīvības bulv. 36, Rīga 1170; tel. (2) 285-223; fax (2) 283-722.
**Ministry of Transport:** Brīvības bulv. 58, Rīga 1743; tel. (2) 226-992; fax (2) 217-180.
**Ministry of Welfare:** Skolas iela 28, Rīga 1331; tel. (2) 271-713; fax (2) 276-445.

## Legislature

### SAEIMA
(Parliament)

**Chairman:** ANATOLIJS GORBUNOVS.
**Deputy Chairmen:** AIVARS BERĶIS, ANDREJS KRASTIŅŠ.
**Office of the Saeima:** Jēkaba iela 11, Rīga 1811; tel. (2) 322-938; fax (2) 211-611.

**General Election, 5 and 6 June 1993**

| Parties, coalitions, etc. | % of votes | Seats |
|---|---|---|
| Latvian Way | 32.38 | 36 |
| Latvian National Independence Movement* | 13.35 | 15 |
| Harmony for Latvia—Revival of the Economy | 11.98 | 13 |
| Latvian Farmers' Union | 10.64 | 12 |
| Equal Rights Movement | 5.77 | 7 |
| Fatherland and Freedom Union† | 5.36 | 6 |
| Christian Democratic Union of Latvia | 5.01 | 6 |
| Democratic Centre Party‡ | 4.76 | 5 |
| Others | 10.75 | 0 |
| **Total** | **100.00** | **100** |

* Subsequently renamed the Latvian National Conservative Party.
† An electoral coalition of the Union of 18 November and the Latvian Fatherland National Union.
‡ Subsequently renamed the Democratic Party.

## Political Organizations

**Association for Fatherland and Freedom** (Apvienība Tēvzemei un brīvībai): Jēkaba iela 16, Rīga 1811; tel. (2) 325-041; fax (2) 211-077; f. 1995; Chair. MĀRIS GRĪNBLATS; 460 mems.

**Christian Democratic Union of Latvia** (Latvijas Kristīgo Demokrātu savienība): Lāčplēša iela 24, Rīga 1050; tel. and fax (2) 323-534; f. 1991; Chair. PAULIS KĻAVIŅŠ; 530 mems.

**Democratic Labour Party of Latvia** (Latvijas Demokrātiskā darba partija): Kungu iela 8, Rīga 1581; tel. (2) 225-911; fax (2) 225-039; f. 1990, following a split in the Communist Party of Latvia; Chair. JURIS BOJĀRS; 2,000 mems.

**Democratic Party Saimnieks (The Master)** (Demokrātiskā partija Saimnieks): Vaļņu iela 9, Rīga 1050; tel. (2) 216-754; f. 1995; Co-Chair. JURIS ČELMIŅŠ, ZIEDONIS ČEVERS.

**Latvian Farmers' Union** (Latvijas Zemnieku savienība): Republikas lauk. 2, Rīga 1010; tel. (2) 327-163; f. 1917, re-est. 1990; rural, centrist; Chair. ANDRIS ROZENTĀLS; 2,850 mems.

**Latvian National Conservative Party** (Latvijas Nacionālā Konservativā partija): Elizabetes iela 23, Rīga 1050; tel. (2) 320-436; fax (2) 320-451; f. 1988; Chair. of Bd ARISTIDS LAMBERGS; 1,500 mems.

**Latvian Social Democratic Workers' Party** (Latvijas Sociāldemokrātiskā strādnieku partija): Bruņinieku iela 29–31, Rīga 1112; tel. (2) 272-112; fax (2) 277-319; f. 1904; re-est. 1989; Chair. JĀNIS DINEVIČS; 400 mems.

**Latvian Way** (Latvijas ceļš): Tērbatas iela 4-9, Rīga 1011; tel. (2) 224-162; fax 7821121; f. 1993; unites prominent political figures from Latvia and abroad; advocates a democratic state based on the principles of legality and justice, the equality and rights of all citizens, a free market economy, private ownership of land, and closer ties between Latvia, Estonia and Lithuania; Chair. VALDIS BIRKAVS; 270 mems.

**National Harmony Party** (Tautas saskaņas partija): Lāčplēša iela 60, Rīga 101; tel. (2) 289-913; fax (2) 281-619; f. 1993; advocates the rapid integration of non-citizens into Latvian society; Chair. JĀNIS JURKĀNS.

**Political Association of Economists:** Jauniela 13, Rīga 1970; tel. (2) 213-859; f. 1994; Chair. EDVĪNS KIDE; 120 mems.

**Popular Front of Latvia** (Latvijas Tautas fronte): Vecpilsētas iela 13-15, Rīga 1050; tel. (2) 212-286; telex 161177; fax (2) 210-793; f. 1988; Chair. ULDIS AUGSTKALNS; 1,900 mems.

## Diplomatic Representation

### EMBASSIES IN LATVIA

**Belarus:** Elizabetes iela 29, Rīga 1010; tel. (2) 325-361; fax (2) 322-891; Ambassador: VALYANTSIN VYALICHKA.
**Canada:** Doma lauk. 4, Rīga 1977; tel. (2) 226-315; fax 7830141.

# LATVIA

**China, People's Republic:** Citadeles iela 2, Rīga 1010; tel. (2) 321-530; Chargé d'affaires a.i.: WANG KAIWEN.

**Cuba:** Vairogu iela 14, Rīga 1039; tel. and fax (2) 565-525; Ambassador: JORGE MARTÍ MARTÍNEZ.

**Denmark:** Pils iela 11, Rīga 1863; tel. (2) 226-210; fax (2) 229-218; Ambassador: MICHAEL METZ MØRCH.

**Estonia:** Skolas iela 13, Rīga 1010; tel. (2) 334-861; fax 7820461; Ambassador: TOOMAS TIIVEL.

**Finland:** Teātra iela 9, Rīga 1605; tel. (2) 216-040; telex 161125; fax (2) 229-549; Ambassador: ANTTI JUHANI LÁSSILA.

**France:** Raiņa bulv. 9, Rīga 1065; tel. (2) 213-972; Ambassador: JANE DEBENEST.

**Germany:** Basteja bulv. 14, Rīga 1050; tel. (2) 229-096; telex 161210; Ambassador: Dr REINHARD HOLUBEK.

**Israel:** Elizabetes iela 2, Rīga 1340; tel. (2) 320-739; fax 7830170; Ambassador: TOVA HERZL.

**Italy:** Teātra iela 9, Rīga 1605; tel. (2) 216-069; telex 161235; fax (2) 348-645; Ambassador: UBERTO PESTALOZZA.

**Lithuania:** Elizabetes iela 2, Rīga 1340; tel. (2) 321-519; fax (2) 321-589; Ambassador: ALGIRDAS ŽVIRĖNAS.

**Norway:** Zirgu iela 14, Rīga 1969; tel. (2) 216-744; fax 7820195; Ambassador: KNUT TØRAASEN.

**Poland:** Elizabetes iela 2, Rīga 1340; tel. (2) 321-617; telex 161212; fax (2) 321-233; Ambassador: JAROSŁAW LINDENBERG.

**Russia:** Antonijas iela 2, Rīga 1397; tel. (2) 220-693; fax 7830209; Ambassador: ALEKSANDR RANNIKH.

**Sweden:** Lāčplēša iela 13, Rīga 1050; tel. (2) 286-276; telex 161114; fax (2) 288-501; Ambassador: ANDREAS ÅDAHL.

**Switzerland:** Elizabetes iela 2, Rīga 1340; tel. (2) 323-188; fax 7810310; Ambassador: Dr GAUDENZ RUF.

**Ukraine:** Kalpaka bulv. 3, Rīga 1010; tel. and fax (2) 325-583; Chargé d'affaires a.i.: VOLODYMYR CHORNY.

**United Kingdom:** Alunana iela 5, Rīga 1010; tel. 7830113; fax 7830112; Ambassador: RICHARD RALPH.

**USA:** Raiņa bulv. 7, Rīga 1050; tel. (2) 210-005; fax (2) 226-530; Ambassador: INTS SILINS.

## Judicial System

**Supreme Court:** Brīvības bulv. 34, Rīga 1511; tel. (2) 289-434; following recognition of Latvian independence, the Soviet legal system ceased to be effective on Latvian territory and a complete reorganization of the judicial system was initiated. The Supreme Court is the final arbiter in criminal and civil cases.

**Chairman:** ANDRIS GUĻĀNS.

**Office of the Procurator-General:** Kalpaka bulv. 6, Rīga 1801; tel. (2) 320-085; fax (2) 212-231.

**Procurator-General:** JĀNIS SKRASTIŅŠ.

## Religion

From the 16th century the traditional religion of the Latvians was Lutheran Christian. Russian Orthodoxy was the religion of most of the Slav immigrants. After 1940, when Latvia was annexed by the USSR, many places of religious worship were closed and clergymen were imprisoned or exiled. In the late 1980s there was some improvement in the official attitude to religious affairs. Following the restoration of independence in 1991, religious organizations regained their legal rights, as well as property that had been confiscated during the Soviet occupation. Since 1988 more than 200 new religious organizations have been officially registered in Latvia, and at 1 January 1994 the statutes of 870 religious organizations were registered. The total number of congregations was 819, of which 291 were Lutheran, 192 Roman Catholic, 100 Orthodox, 56 Old Believers (Orthodox), 70 Baptists, 49 Pentecostal, 33 Adventist, three Methodist, two Reformed and five Hebrew congregations.

**Department of Religious Affairs:** Pils lauk. 4, Rīga 1050; tel. (2) 223-982; govt agency, attached to the Ministry of Justice; Dir JURIS ZĀLĪTE (acting).

### CHRISTIANITY

#### Protestant Churches

**Consistory of the Evangelical Lutheran Church of Latvia:** M. Pils iela 4, Rīga 1050; tel. (2) 226-057; fax 7820041; f. 1920; Archbishop JĀNIS VANAGS.

**Union of Latvian Pentecostal Congregations:** Jāņa iela 1, Jelgava 3000; tel. (30) 25-011; f. 1989; Bishop JĀNIS OZOLINKEVIČS.

**Union of the Latvian Baptist Congregations:** Lāčplēša iela 37, Rīga 1011; tel. (2) 223-379; fax (2) 279-523; f. 1861; Bishop JĀNIS EISĀNS.

**Union of the Seventh-day Adventists in Latvia:** Baznīcas iela 12A, Rīga 1050; tel. (2) 321-050; f. 1920; Pres. of Council VIKTORS GEIDE.

**United Methodist Church of Latvia:** Klaipēdas iela 56, Liepāja 3400; tel. (34) 32-161; re-established 1991; Superintendent ĀRIJS VĪKSNA.

#### The Roman Catholic Church

Latvia comprises the Archdiocese of Rīga and the Diocese of Liepāja. At 31 December 1993 there were an estimated 500,000 adherents in the country.

**Bishops' Conference** (Conferentia Episcopalis Lettoniae): M. Pils iela 2A, Rīga 1050; tel. (2) 227-266; f. 1992.

**Archbishop of Rīga:** Most Rev. JĀNIS PUJĀTS, Metropolijas Kurija, M. Pils iela 2A, Rīga 1050; tel. (2) 227-266; fax (2) 220-775.

#### The Orthodox Church

Although the Orthodox Church of Latvia has close ties with the Moscow Patriarchate, it has administrative independence. The spiritual head of the Orthodox Church is elected by its Saeima (or assembly).

**Synod of the Orthodox Church of Latvia:** M. Pils iela 14, Rīga 1050; tel. (2) 224-345; f. 1850; mems are mostly ethnic Slavs; Bishop ALEKSANDRS KUDRJAŠOVS.

**Latvian Old Believers Pomor Church:** Krasta iela 73, Rīga 1003; tel. (2) 222-981; f. 1760; Head of Central Council IVANS MIROĻUBOVS (Fr IOAN).

### JUDAISM

**Hebrew Religious Community of Rīga:** Peitavas iela 6/8, Rīga 1050; tel. (2) 224-549; f. 1764; Chair. of Bd MIHAILS ARONS.

### OTHER RELIGIOUS GROUPS

**Dievturu sadraudze:** Merķeļa iela 13, Rīga 1050; community celebrating the ancient Latvian animist religion; Leader JĀNIS SILIŅŠ.

**International Society for Krishna Consciousness:** K. Barona iela 56, Rīga 1011; tel. (2) 274-134; Co-ordinator HARIJS SAUŠS.

## The Press

Since the late 1980s, when the first independent newspapers appeared (free of the censorship of the Central Committee of the Communist Party of Latvia), both the circulation and content of newspapers and magazines have undergone considerable changes. At the end of 1994 1,546 publications were registered, although only 382 of these appeared regularly. A marked rise in production costs and, consequently, increased prices of newspapers and magazines, have led to a steady decline in sales. In 1992 187 magazines were published, with a total circulation of 15.7m., of which 12.3m. were in Latvian. In that year the number of newspapers published was 203, with an annual circulation of 234m. (of which 155m. were in Latvian). The 17 daily newspapers had a combined average circulation of 517,000 copies per issue in 1992. The joint-stock company Preses nams (Press House) is the leading publisher of newspapers and magazines in Latvia.

The publications listed below are in Latvian, unless otherwise indicated.

### DAILIES

**Diena** (Day): M. Pils iela 12, Rīga 1963; tel. (2) 220-019; fax 7820166; f. 1990; Latvian and Russian; social and political issues; Editor-in-Chief SARMĪTE ĒLERTE; circ. 110,000.

**Labrīt** (Good Morning): Balasta dambis 3, Rīga 1081; tel. (2) 465-700; fax 7860059; f. 1993; Latvian and Russian; Editor-in-Chief IVARS BUŠMANIS; circ. 36,000.

**Neatkarīgā Cīņa** (Independent Struggle): Balasta dambis 3, Rīga 1081; tel. (2) 461-200; fax (2) 462-291; f. 1990; Editor-in-Chief ANDRIS JAKUBĀNS; circ. 62,892.

**Rīgas Balss** (Voice of Riga): Balasta dambis 3, Rīga 1081; tel. (2) 463-842; fax 7860070; f. 1957; city evening newspaper; Latvian and Russian; Editor-in-Chief VALDA KRŪMIŅA; circ. 56,800 (Mon.–Thurs.), 69,570 (Fri.).

**SM-Segodņa** (SM-Today): Balasta dambis 3, Rīga 1081; tel. (2) 468-383; fax (2) 468-287; f. 1945; Russian; Editor-in-Chief ALEKSANDR BLINOV; circ. 65,000.

**Sports:** Balasta dambis 3, Rīga 1081; tel. (2) 464-117; fax 7860000; f. 1955; Editor DACE MILLERE; circ. 7,800.

# LATVIA

**Vakara Ziņas** (Evening News): Bezdelīgu iela 12, Rīga 1007; tel. (2) 617-595; fax (2) 612-383; f. 1993; Editor-in-Chief AINIS SAULĪTIS; circ. 53,000.

## WEEKLIES

**Atmoda Atpūtai** (Awakening for Leisure): K. Valdemāra iela 20, Rīga 1378; tel. (2) 281-416; f. 1988; family paper; Editor-in-Chief ELITA VEIDEMANE; circ. 9,500.

**The Baltic Observer:** Balasta dambis 3, Rīga 1081; tel. (2) 462-119; fax (2) 463-387; f. 1992; news from Estonia, Latvia and Lithuania; English; Editor-in-Chief KĀRLIS FREIBERGS; circ. 9,900.

**Dienas Bizness** (Daily Business): Balasta dambis 3, Rīga 1081; tel. (2) 464-690; fax (2) 464-719; f. 1992; Editor-in-Chief JURIS PAIDERS; circ. 17,000.

**Elpa** (Breath): Jāņa sēta 5, Rīga 1050; tel. (2) 211-776; fax (2) 223-280; f. 1990; environmental issues; Editor-in-Chief MAIRITA SOLIMA; circ. 3,900.

**Izglītība un Kultūra** (Education and Culture): Balasta dambis 3, Rīga 1081; tel. (2) 467-828; f. 1948; Editor ANDRA MANGALE; circ. 5,400.

**Latvijas Vēstnesis** (Latvian Herald): Bruņinieku iela 36-2, Rīga 1001; tel. (2) 298-833; fax (2) 299-410; f. 1993; official newspaper of the Republic of Latvia; Editor-in-Chief OSKARS GERTS; circ. 5,200.

**Lauku Avīze** (Country Newspaper): Balasta dambis 3, Rīga 1081; tel. (2) 460-339; f. 1988; popular agriculture; Editor-in-Chief VOLDEMĀRS KRUSTIŅŠ; circ. 120,000.

**Nakts** (Night): K. Barona iela 5–6, Rīga 1011; tel. (2) 224-100; f. 1992; art, music, politics; Editor-in-Chief ILMĀRS LATKOVSKIS; circ. 15,350.

## PRINCIPAL PERIODICALS

**Daugava:** Balasta dambis 3, Rīga 1081; tel. (2) 465-993; f. 1977; 6 a year; literary journal; Russian; Editor-in-Chief ROALDS DOBROVENSKIS; circ. 1,200.

**Karogs** (Banner): K. Barona iela 12, Rīga 1426; tel. (2) 287-626; f. 1940; literary monthly; Editor-in-Chief MĀRA ZĀLĪTE; circ. 2,500.

**Liesma** (Flame): Balasta dambis 3, Rīga 1081; tel. (2) 466-480; f. 1958; monthly; for young people; Editor-in-Chief DAINIS CAUNE; circ. 20,000.

**Mūsmājas** (Our Home): Balasta dambis 3, Rīga 1081; tel. (2) 467-954; fax 7860002; f. 1993; monthly; illustrated magazine for housewives; Latvian and Russian; Editor-in-Chief ILZE STRAUTIŅA; circ. 77,000.

**Rīgas Laiks** (Riga Times): Brīvības iela 40-33, Rīga 1050; tel. (2) 287-922; fax 7828541; f. 1993; Editor-in-Chief ULDIS TĪRONS.

**Santa:** Balasta dambis 3, Rīga 1081; tel. (2) 464-420; fax (2) 463-154; f. 1991; monthly; illustrated journal for young women; Latvian and Russian; Editor-in-Chief SANTA DANSBERGA-ANČA; circ. 70,000.

**Skola un Ģimene** (School and Family): Balasta dambis 3, Rīga 1081; tel. (2) 469-476; f. 1964; monthly; social and educational; Editor-in-Chief JĀNIS GULBIS; circ. 7,300.

## NEWS AGENCIES

**Baltic News Service:** Baznīcas iela 8, Rīga 1050; tel. 7288777; fax 7860025; f. 1990; news from Latvia, Lithuania, Estonia and the CIS; in English, Russian and the Baltic languages; Dir RAITIS BIKŠE.

**LETA** (Latvian Telegraph Agency): Palasta iela 10, Rīga 1502; tel. (2) 223-462; telex 161139; fax 7820438; f. 1920; govt information agency; Dir ZIGURDS URBULIS (acting).

### Foreign Bureau

**Reuters** (UK): Kaļķu iela, Rīga 1050; Country Man. ERIK HAMMAR.

### PRESS ASSOCIATIONS

**Latvian Association of Magazine Publishers:** Balasta dambis 3, Rīga 1081; tel. (2) 465-735; f. 1994; 20 mems; Pres. IVARS ZARIŅŠ.

**Latvian Journalists' Union** (Latvijas Žurnālistu savienība): Marstaļu 2, Rīga 1050; tel. (2) 211-433; fax 7820233; f. 1991; 1,200 mems; Pres. LIGITA AZOVSKA.

## Publishers

In 1993 1,614 book titles were published. The total number of copies was 14.4m. Books are published regularly by some 70 publishers (including four under state control), some of the most prominent of which are listed below.

**Avots** (Spring): Aspazijas bulv. 24, Rīga 1050; tel. (2) 225-824; f. 1980; fiction, children's, crafts, hobbies, art, agriculture, law, reference books, etc.; Dir JĀNIS LEJA.

**Jāņa sēta:** Elizabetes iela 83-85, Rīga 1011; tel. (2) 217-384; fax 7828039; f. 1991; maps, art catalogues, books; Dir AIVARS ZVIRBULIS.

**Jumava:** Balasta dambis 3, Rīga 1081; tel. (2) 465-969; f. 1994; translations, dictionaries, popular literature; Pres. JURIS VISOCKIS.

**Latvijas Enciklopēdija** (Latvian Encyclopaedia Publishers): Maskavas iela 68, Rīga 1003; tel. (2) 220-150; fax 7820113; f. 1963; encyclopaedias, dictionaries, reference books; Dir VIKTORS TĒRAUDS.

**Liesma** (Flame): Aspazijas bulv. 24, Rīga 1468; tel. (2) 223-063; f. 1965; fiction, poetry, literary criticism, fine arts; Dir VILIS JANSONS.

**Preses nams** (Press House): Balasta dambis 3, Rīga 1081; tel. (2) 465-732; f. 1990; Latvian fiction, translations of foreign literature, guidebooks; Dir MĀRA CAUNE.

**Sprīdītis:** R. Blaumaņa iela 32, Rīga 1011; tel. (2) 286-516; fax (2) 286-818; f. 1989; books for children and young people; Dir JĀZEPS OSMANIS.

**Vaga:** Lazaretes iela 3, Rīga 1010; tel. (2) 336-332; fax 7821488; f. 1990; fiction, children's and English textbooks; Dir MĀRIS OZOLIŅŠ.

**Zinātne** (Science): Turgeņeva iela 19, Rīga 1003; tel. (2) 212-797; fax (2) 227-825; f. 1951; scientific and scholarly books; Dir IVARS RIEKSTIŅŠ.

**Zvaigzne** (Star): K. Valdemāra iela 105, Rīga 1013; tel. (2) 372-396; fax 7828431; f. 1966; textbooks, children's books, fiction, medical, books for the blind; Pres. VIJA KILBLOKA.

### PUBLISHERS' ASSOCIATIONS

**Latvian Book Publishers' Association** (Latvijas Grāmatizdevēju asociācija): Aspazijas bulv. 24, Rīga 1050; tel. (2) 225-843; fax (2) 228-482; f. 1993; 38 mems; Pres. MĀRIS OZOLIŅŠ.

**Latvian Publishers' and Editors' Association:** Balasta dambis 3, Rīga 1081; tel. (2) 465-735; f. 1991; 44 mems; Pres. JURIS PAIDERS.

### WRITERS' UNION

**Latvian Writers' Union** (Latvijas Rakstnieku savienība): K. Barona iela 12, Rīga 1426; tel. (2) 287-629; fax (2) 287-605; 280 mems; Chair. VIKTORS AVOTIŅŠ.

## Radio and Television

Commercial broadcasting began in Latvia in 1991. There were more than 25 radio stations and 30 television broadcasting companies in Latvia at the beginning of 1995. In December 1992 there were 1.4m. radio receivers and 1.1m. television receivers in use.

**Latvian Radio and Television Council:** Smilšu iela 1–3, Rīga 1939; tel. (2) 206-509; fax (2) 206-562; f. 1992; defends social interests and maintains free accessibility to information; Chair. ZIGMUNDS SKUJIŅŠ.

**Latvijas Radio** (Latvian Radio): Doma lauk. 8, Rīga 1505; tel. (2) 206-722; fax 7820216; f. 1925; state-operated service; broadcasts in Latvian, Russian, Swedish, English and German; Dir-Gen. ARNOLDS KLOTIŅŠ.

**Latvijas Televīzija** (Latvian Television): Zaķusalas krastmala 3, Rīga 1509; tel. (2) 200-830; fax (2) 200-025; f. 1954; state-operated service; two channels in Latvian (Channel II also includes programmes in Russian, Polish, Ukrainian, German, English and French); Dir-Gen. IMANTS RĀKINS.

**NTV-5** (Independent Television-5): Maskavas iela 40–42, Rīga 1003; tel. (2) 225-758; fax (2) 214-802; f. 1991; entertainment programming; news reports in Latvian and English; Dir-Gen. DANS BĒRTULIS.

## Finance

(cap. = capital; dep. = deposits; res = reserves; m. = million; brs = branches)

### BANKING

#### Central Bank

**Bank of Latvia** (Latvijas banka): K. Valdemāra iela 2A, Rīga 1050; tel. (2) 323-863; telex 161146; fax (2) 220-543; f. 1922; cap. 366m. Latvian roubles, dep. 7,953m. Latvian roubles, res 58m. Latvian roubles; Pres. EINĀRS REPŠE; Chair of Board and Vice-Pres. ILMĀRS RIMŠĒVIČS.

#### Commercial Banks

**Baltic Transit Bank** (Baltijas Tranzītu banka): 13. janvāra iela 3, Rīga 1050; tel. (2) 229-145; telex 161353; fax 7820305; f. 1992; joint stock commercial bank; cap. US $10.2m.; Pres. GAĻINA ALIJEVA; 31 brs.

# LATVIA

**Banka Baltija:** Ģertrūdes iela 33-35, Rīga 1578; tel. (2) 292-910; telex 614426; fax 7828066; f. 1988; Chair. of Bd TĀLIS FREIMANIS; 37 brs.

**Centra banka:** Tirgoņu iela 8, Rīga 1610; tel. (2) 211-353; fax 7820159; f. 1992; Pres. PĒTERIS STRAZDIŅŠ.

**Communications Bank** (Sakaru banka): Elizabetes iela 41–43, Rīga 1010; tel. (2) 331-157; fax (2) 333-210; f. 1990; Pres. MĀRIS OZOLS.

**Credit Bank of Latvia** (Latvijas Kredītbanka): Smilšu iela 1/4, Rīga 1020; tel. (2) 226-631; telex 161303; fax 7821094; f. 1992; cap. 3.5m. lati; Pres. VILNIS BURTNIEKS; 4 brs.

**Industrial Bank of Latvia** (Latvijas Industriālā banka): Grēcinieku iela 6, Rīga 1587; tel. (2) 216-528; telex 161267; fax 7828103; f. 1991; Pres. VILIS DAMBIŅŠ.

**Investment Bank of Latvia** (Latvijas Investīciju banka): Kaļķu iela 15, Rīga 1050; tel. 7820323; telex 161337; fax 7820325; f. 1992; cap. DM 15.4m.; state-owned; Pres. AIVARS JURCĀNS.

**Land Bank of Latvia** (Latvijas Zemes banka): Republikas lauk. 2, Rīga 1924; tel. (2) 321-713; telex 161204; fax 7830130; f. 1992; cap. 3.5m. lati; Chair. of Bd ANDRIS RUSELIS; 10 brs.

**Latgale Commercial Bank** (Latgales komercbanka): 18 novembra iela 359A, Daugavpils 5400; tel. (54) 59-646; fax (54) 31-074; f. 1991; Pres. ANATOLY SUSHKO.

**Latvian Deposit Bank** (Latvijas Depozītu banka): Vaļņu iela 28, Rīga 1579; tel. (2) 203-041; fax 7820353; f. 1992; Pres. MIERVALDIS GULBIS.

**Olimpija Commercial Bank** (Olimpija komercbanka): Lāčplēša iela 70A, Rīga 1011; tel. (2) 289-861; telex 161100; fax 7821267; f. 1991; Chair. of Bd ERVĪNS CEIHNERS.

**Parex banka:** Smilšu iela 3, Rīga 1522; tel. 7820011; telex 161371; fax 7820012; f. 1992; Pres. VALERY KARGIN.

**Rīga Commercial Bank** (Rīgas komercbanka): Smilšu iela 6, Rīga 1803; tel. (2) 323-647; telex 161112; fax 7820080; f. 1991; cap. 6.0m. lati, dep. 48.8m. lati (Dec. 1994); Pres. VLADIMIR KULIK; 11 brs.

**Universal Bank of Latvia** (Latvijas Universālā banka): L. Pils iela 23, Rīga 1050; tel. (2) 212-808; telex 161361; fax 7820331; f. 1993; state-owned; Pres. ANDRIS BĒRZIŅŠ.

### Savings Bank

**Latvian Savings Bank** (Latvijas Republikas krājbanka): Palasta iela 1, Rīga 1954; tel. (2) 222-871; fax (2) 212-083; f. 1987; cap. 48m. Latvian roubles, dep. 175m. Latvian roubles; Pres. VALDIS ZEIKATS; 37 brs.

### Banking Association

**Association of Commercial Banks of Latvia:** Stabu iela 18, Rīga 1001; tel. (2) 271-650; fax (2) 272-500; f. 1992; 40 mems; Pres. TEODORS TVERIJONS.

### INSURANCE

**Alterna:** Elizabetes iela 23, Rīga 1209; tel. (2) 320-568; fax (2) 323-441; accident, freight, building insurance; Pres. ANDRIS TORGĀNS.

**Balta Ltd:** Antonijas iela 7, Rīga 1010; tel. and fax (2) 334-990; telex 161178; automobile, property, freight, travel insurance; Pres. VIKTORS GUSTSONS.

**Balva:** K. Valdemāra iela 36, Rīga 1365 tel. (2) 278-346; telex 161116; fax 7828441; f. 1991; personal transport, freight, accident, property insurance; Pres. VASILY RAGOZIN.

**Dukats:** Smilšu iela 18, Rīga 1981; tel. (2) 228-007; accident, credit, property, cargo insurance; brs throughout Latvia; Chair. of Bd JĀNIS VAITS.

**Estora:** Elizabetes iela 14, Rīga 1010; tel. (2) 227-048; fax (9) 345-356; accident, life, property, credit, contract insurance; Dir-Gen. ĒRIKS TEILĀNS.

**Ezerzeme:** Raiņa iela 28, Daugavpils 5403; tel. (54) 22-555; fax (54) 22-177; f. 1992; state, private firm, personal property, long- and short-term life, life, domestic animals, accident, freight, travel, funeral insurance; Chair. of Bd PĒTERIS SAVOSTJANOVS.

**Helga Joint Stock Insurance Company:** Zvaijžņāju gatve 3–22, Rīga 1080; tel. (2) 378-549; fax (2) 574-687.

**Latva:** Vaļņu iela 1, Rīga 1912; tel. (2) 212-341; fax (2) 210-134; f. 1940; state insurance co; accident, passenger, child and adult life insurance; Chair. JĀNIS MEDENS.

**Rīga Insurance Company:** Grēcinieku iela 22–24, Rm 314, Rīga 1050; tel. (2) 211-764; fax (2) 211-463; credit, contract, natural disasters, fire, freight insurance; Pres. MĀRIS KAIJAKS.

**Union Unlimited:** Laipu iela 2–4, Rīga 1050; tel. (2) 213-150; fax (2) 225-397; travel, property, athletes', freight, state, co-operative, joint-stock, credit, medical, accident insurance; Chair. of Bd AIVARS SALIŅŠ.

### COMMODITY AND STOCK EXCHANGES

**Latgale Exchange** (Latgales birža): Sakņu iela 29, Daugavpils 5403; tel. (54) 26-044; fax (54) 26-351; f. 1992; Gen. Dir ANATOLY BOTUSHANSKI.

**Latvian Stock Exchange** (Latvijas birža): Doma lauk. 6, Rīga 1050; tel. (2) 226-220; f. 1992; Dir-Gen. ALLA MAREJEVA.

**Latvian Universal Exchange** (Latvijas Universālā birža): Doma lauk. 6, Rīga 1050; tel. (2) 212-559; fax (2) 224-515; f. 1991; Pres. JĀNIS VALTERS.

**Rīga Exchange** (Rīgas birža): Doma lauk. 6, Rīga 1050; tel. and fax (2) 220-789; f. 1991; Dir AVIARS SILIŅŠ.

**Rīga Stock Exchange** (Rīgas Fondu birža): Doma lauk. 6, Rīga 1885; tel. (2) 212-431; fax (2) 229-411; f. 1993; Chair. of Bd. M. BENDIKS.

## Trade and Industry

### STATE PROPERTY AGENCIES

**Latvian Privatization Agency:** K. Valdemāra iela 31, Rīga 1887; tel. (2) 332-082; fax 7830363; Dir-Gen. JĀNIS NAGLIS.

**State Property Fund:** Smilša iela 1, Rīga 1980; tel. (2) 227-344; fax (2) 229-368; f. 1993; established to manage up to 80% of state enterprises and real estate.

### CHAMBER OF COMMERCE

**Latvian Chamber of Commerce and Industry** (Latvijas Tirdzniecības un Rūpniecības Kamera): Brīvības bulv. 21, Rīga 1849; tel. (2) 225-595; fax 7820092; f. 1934; re-established 1990; mem. of International Chamber of Commerce, Baltic Chambers of Commerce Association, Eurochamber; Pres. VIKTORS KULBERGS.

### DEVELOPMENT AGENCY

**Latvian Development Agency:** Pērses iela 2, Rīga 1442; tel. (2) 283-425; fax (2) 282-524; Dir ULDIS VĪTOLIŅŠ.

### BUSINESS AND TRADE ORGANIZATIONS

**Confederation of Small and Medium Business Enterprises of Latvia:** Ropazu iela 41, Rm 11, Rīga; tel. (2) 552-222; fax (2) 551-933; Pres. ERIKS ROZENCVEIGS.

**Interlatvija:** Kalpaka bulv. 1, Rīga 1010; tel. (2) 333-602; telex 161149; f. 1987; seeks to promote exports, imports and the establishment of joint ventures; Dir-Gen. MĀRIS FORSTS.

**Latvia International Commerce Centre:** Tirgoņu iela 8, Rīga; tel. (2) 211-602; telex 161176; fax (2) 331-920.

**Latvian Small Business Association:** Elizabetes iela 45–47, Rīga 1010; tel. (2) 332-647; fax (2) 334-807; Chair. MĀRIS BAIDEKALNS.

**PLUS (World Latvian Businessmen's Association):** Aldaru iela 83, Rīga 1050; tel. (2) 211-122; fax (2) 769-225; Dir GVIDO VOLBRUGS.

**World Trade Centre 'Rīga':** Elizabetes iela 2, Rīga 1340; tel. (2) 321-278; telex 161224; fax 7830035; f. 1992; Gen. Dir NORMUNDS BERGS.

### MAJOR STATE INDUSTRIAL COMPANIES

**Dauer State Enterprise:** Valkas 2, Daugavpils 5400; tel. (54) 35-943; fax (54) 320-03; construction; 1,745 employees.

**Kompresors State Enterprise:** Starta 1, Rīga 1026; tel. (2) 518-123; produces refrigeration equipment for domestic and industrial use; Dir-Gen. ALDIS ZICMANIS; 962 employees.

**Latvijas Balzams State Enterprise:** A. Čaka 160, Rīga 1010; tel. (2) 272-693; produces beverages, incl. *Rīga Black Balsam* vodka; Dir-Gen. LEONS DUKULIS; 530 employees.

**Latvijas Dzelzceļš State Enterprise:** Gogoļa iela 3, Rīga 1547; tel. (2) 234-400; fax 7820231; transports cargo and passengers; 30,000 employees.

**Liepājas Metalurgs State Plant:** Brīvības iela 93, Liepāja 3400; tel. (34) 23-750; telex 161114; steel, rolled ferrous metals; Dir VALERIJS TERENTJEVS; 2,787 employees.

**Liepāja State Machine-Building Plant:** Flotes 6, Liepāja 3401; tel. (34) 24-519; fax (34) 26-615; f. 1903; produces agricultural machinery, hydrocylinders; 1,512 employees.

**Lokomotīve State Enterprise:** Marijas 1, Daugavpils 5400; tel. (54) 33-146; fax (54) 36-051; carries out repairs of engines; 3,200 employees.

**Ogre State Enterprise:** Rīgas 98, Ogre 5000; tel. (50) 22-628; fax (50) 73-100; produces wool yarn, knitted products and fabrics; 3,713 employees.

**REMR State Enterprise:** K. Barona iela 130, Rīga 1012; tel. (2) 271-681; telex 161261; fax (2) 274-893; f. 1893; produces radioelectronics; Pres. ZIGURDS KRAGIS; 1,909 employees.

**RER Rīga State Electric Engineering Plant:** Ganības dambis 31, Rīga 1045; tel. (2) 382-077; fax (2) 383-417; produces electrical equipment, metal powder articles; 4,328 employees.

**Riga State Trawler Refrigerator Base:** Atlantijas iela 7, Rīga 1020; tel. (2) 342-010; fish processing; 5,900 employees.

**Rinar State Chemical Engineering Plant:** Biķernieku 18, Rīga 1039; tel. (2) 553-290; fax (2) 563-170; produces pumps, industrial piping armature; 951 employees.

**Rita State Enterprise:** Valentīnas 3–5, Rīga 1046; tel. (2) 611-540; telex 161218; fax (2) 619-146; knitted products and fabrics; 1,339 employees.

**RTR State Plant:** Šampētera 2, Rīga 1041; (2) 613-438; manufactures metal processing equipment; 1,144 employees.

**Sarma State Enterprise:** Bruņinieku iela 93, Rīga 1011; tel. (2) 292-602; fax (2) 292-603; production of textiles and knitted fabrics, clothing; 200 employees.

**Second Rīga State Construction Group:** Katlakalna 11, Rīga 1073; tel. (2) 242-203; construction; 700 employees.

**Sloka State Paper and Cellulose Factory:** Fabrikas 2, Jūrmala 2000; tel. (2) 732-222; fax (2) 732-401; produces paper for specialized uses, including book covers, ice-cream holders, etc.; Dir Mihails Piskuns; 1,326 employees.

**VEF State Enterprise:** Brīvības bulv. 214, Rīga 1039; tel. (2) 363-200; telex 16113; fax (2) 567-208; produces portable radios, telephones, cassette recorders; Dir-Gen. Ivars Bražis; 13,233 employees.

### TRADE UNIONS

**Latvian Free Trade Union Federation:** Bruņinieku iela 29–31, Rīga 1103; tel. (2) 270-351; telex 161105; fax (2) 276-649; f. 1990; Chair. Andris Siliņš.

## Transport

### RAILWAYS

In 1992 there were 2,406 km of railways on the territory of Latvia, of which 271 km were electrified. In the same year Latvian railways carried 31.8m. metric tons of freight and 83.1m. passengers.

**Latvian Railways** (Latvijas Dzelzceļš): Gogoļa iela 3, Rīga 1547; tel. (2) 234-400; fax 7820231; f. 1991; Dir-Gen. Andris Zorgevics.

### ROADS

At 31 December 1993 Latvia's total road network was 64,693 km, of which 7,036 km were highways, main or national roads and 13,502 km were secondary or regional roads. At the same date there were 367,475 passenger cars, 60,454 goods vehicles and 11,604 buses in use.

### SHIPPING

The major Latvian ports are at Rīga, Ventspils and Liepāja (which was used as a Russian naval port until its conversion into a trade port in the early 1990s). Ventspils is particularly important for the shipping of Russian petroleum exports (16.3m. metric tons in 1993). In 1993 some 27.2m. metric tons of freight were transported through Latvian ports.

**Maritime Department:** K. Valdemāra iela 63, Rīga 1142; tel. (2) 322-498; telex 161132; fax (2) 334-892; Dir Irmants Sarmulis.

### Port Authorities

**Liepāja Seaport:** Rožu iela 6, Liepāja 3400; tel. (34) 25-887; telex 161818; fax 7893418; Dir Aivars Boja.

**Rīga Fishing Seaport:** Atlantijas iela 27, Rīga 1020; tel. (2) 341-477; fax (2) 341-168; Dir G. Shevchuk.

**Riga Seaport:** Eksporta iela 6, Rīga 1242; tel. (2) 329-781; fax 7830051; Dir Gunārs Ross.

**Rīga Trade Port:** Eksporta iela 6, Rīga 1227; tel. (2) 329-224; fax (2) 324-967; Dir Juris Krivojs.

**Ventspils Seaport:** Užavas iela 8, Ventspils 3601; tel. (36) 22-586; telex 161863; fax (36) 21-297; Dir Alfrēds Mačtams.

### Shipping Companies

**Hanza Ltd.:** Smilšu iela 14, Rīga 1050; tel. (2) 226-834; fax (2) 220-662; cargo transportation.

**Janants and Co Ltd:** K. Barona iela 99, Rīga 1012; tel. (2) 278-343; telex 161152; cargo transportation.

**Latvian Shipping Company:** Basteja bulv. 2, Rīga 1807; tel. (2) 323-406; telex 161121; fax (2) 325-414; f. 1991; sea transportation of wide variety of goods; Pres. Pēteris Avotiņš.

**Rīga Shipping Company:** Balasta dambis 9, Rīga 1048; tel. (2) 601-133; telex 161159; fax 7820095; f. 1991; cargo transportation in the Baltic Sea and North Sea; Dir Antons Ikaunieks.

### CIVIL AVIATION

There are two international airports, at Rīga and at Jelgava (south-west of Rīga). The Department of Aviation of the Ministry of Transport co-ordinates the financing of air transport in Latvia, while the Administration of Civil Aviation supervises the operation and safety of flights. In 1993 the first private airline, Rīga Airlines, opened in Latvia.

**Administration of Civil Aviation:** Rīga Airport, Rīga 1053; tel. (2) 207-607; Dir-Gen. Andris Zalmanis.

**Department of Aviation:** Brīvības bulv. 58, Rīga 1743; tel. (2) 281-247; fax (2) 217-180; Dir Arnis Muižnieks.

**Rīga International Airport:** Rīga 1053; tel. (2) 207-135; fax (9) 348-654; Dir Dzintars Pomers.

**Baltic Express Lines:** Ģertrūdes iela 5A, Rīga 1010; tel. (2) 291-889; fax (2) 294-419; charter flights; Dir-Gen. Valerijs Litavars.

**Baltic International Airlines:** Pils lauk. 4, Rīga 1050; tel. (2) 229-545; fax (2) 327-269; joint Latvian–US co; former Latvian division of Aeroflot; operates flights from Rīga to Frankfurt (Germany) and London (United Kingdom); Pres. Oleg Korshe.

**Inversija:** Rīga Airport, Rīga 1053; tel. (2) 207-095; telex 614482; fax (2) 397-171; cargo service; operates routes to destinations in the CIS and in Asia, Africa and Western Europe; Dir-Gen. Jefim Bruk.

**Latvian Airlines** (Latvijas aviolīnijas—LATAVIO): Brīvības bulv. 54, Rīga 1050; tel. (2) 225-560; fax 7828137; national carrier, operating services to Russia, Western Europe and the Middle East; Pres. Jānis Dinevičs.

**RAF'AVIO:** Duntes iela 34, Rīga 1005; tel. (2) 392-092; fax (2) 391-779; charter flights; Dir Jurij Hmelevskij.

**Rīga Airlines** (Rīgas gaisas līnijas): Mellužu iela 1, Rīga 1067; tel. (2) 424-283; fax 7860189; f. 1992; operates services to Moscow and London; Pres. Māris Kārkliņš.

## Tourism

Since 1990 the Government of Latvia has given priority to the development of tourism, and has encouraged private and foreign investment in the sector. Many new or refurbished hotels were operating successfully in the early 1990s. Among Latvia's principal tourist attractions are the historic centre of Rīga, with its medieval and art nouveau buildings, the extensive beaches of the Baltic coastline, and Gauja National Park, which stretches east of the historic town of Sigulda for nearly 100 km along the Gauja river. Sigulda also offers winter sports facilities. Revenue from tourism during the first 10 months of 1994 was estimated to be about US $120m.

**Latvian Tourist Board:** Pils lauk. 4, Rīga 1050; tel. and fax (2) 229-945; f. 1993; Dir Olga Slaugotne.

**Latvia Tours:** Grēcinieku iela 22–24, Rīga 1050; tel. (2) 213-652; telex 161195; fax 7820020; Dir Gundega Zeltiņa.

# LEBANON

## Introductory Survey

**Location, Climate, Language, Religion, Flag, Capital**

The Republic of Lebanon lies in western Asia, bordered by Syria to the north and east, and by Israel and the emerging Palestinian Autonomous Areas to the south. The country has a coastline of about 220 km (135 miles) on the eastern shore of the Mediterranean Sea. The climate varies widely with altitude. The coastal lowlands are hot and humid in summer, becoming mild (cool and damp) in winter. In the mountains, which occupy much of Lebanon, the weather is cool in summer, with heavy snowfalls in winter. Rainfall is generally abundant. The official language is Arabic, which is spoken by almost all of the inhabitants. French is widely used as a second language, while Kurdish and Armenian are spoken by small ethnic minorities. About 10% of the population are Arab refugees from Palestine. The major religions are Islam and Christianity, and there is a very small Jewish community. In the early 1980s it was estimated that 57% of Lebanon's inhabitants were Muslims, with about 43% Christians. The principal Muslim sects are the Sunni and Shi'a, while there is also a significant Druze (Druse) community. Most of the Christians adhere to the Roman Catholic Church, principally the Maronite rite. There are also Armenian, Greek and Syrian sects (both Catholic and Eastern Orthodox), and small groups of Protestants. By the 1980s it was widely believed that the Shi'a Muslims, totalling an estimated 1.2m., constituted Lebanon's largest single community. The national flag (proportions 3 by 2) has three horizontal stripes, of red, white (half the depth) and red, with a representation of a cedar tree (in green and brown) in the centre of the white stripe. The capital is Beirut.

**Recent History**

Lebanon, the homeland of the ancient Phoenicians, became part of Turkey's Ottoman Empire in the 16th century. At the end of the First World War (1914–18), when the Ottoman Empire was dissolved, a Greater Lebanese state was created by the Allied powers. The new state was a response to the nationalist aspirations of the predominant Christian population in the area, but it included territories traditionally considered to be part of Syria, with largely Muslim populations. Lebanon was administered by France, under a League of Nations mandate, from 1920 until independence was declared on 26 November 1941. A republic was established in 1943, and full autonomy was granted to the new state in January 1944.

Unlike most other Arab countries, Lebanon is characterized by great religious and cultural diversity. At the time of independence, Christians formed a slight majority of the population, the largest single community (nearly 30% of the total) being the Maronite Christians, who mostly inhabited the north of the country and Beirut. Other Christian groups included Greek Orthodox communities, Greek Catholics and Armenians. The Muslim groups were the Sunnis (living mainly in the coastal towns of Tyre, Sidon and Beirut), and the Shi'as (a predominantly rural community in southern Lebanon and the northern Beka'a valley) and the much smaller Druzes, an ancient community in central Lebanon, with unorthodox Islamic beliefs. The relative size of the various communities provided the basis for the unwritten 'national pact' of 1943, which attempted to ensure a delicate balance of power between Christian and Muslim groups. Executive and legislative posts were to be shared in the ratio of six Christians to five Muslims, and seats in the Chamber of Deputies (renamed the National Assembly in 1979) were distributed on a religious, rather than an ideological, basis. By convention the President was a Maronite Christian, the Prime Minister a Sunni Muslim and the President of the National Assembly a Shi'a Muslim. This arrangement enabled Lebanon's various Christian and Muslim groups to coexist in a relatively tolerant and peaceful way for more than 30 years.

Lebanon's first President, from 1943 until 1952, was Sheikh Bishara el-Khoury. His successor was Camille Chamoun, who granted votes to women and adopted a pro-Western foreign policy. Following elections to the Chamber of Deputies in 1957, there was considerable unrest, mainly among Muslims who advocated Lebanon's closer alignment with Syria and Egypt. In July 1958 President Chamoun appealed to the USA for military assistance, and US forces remained in Beirut until October, by which time peace had been restored. Meanwhile, Chamoun was persuaded not to seek re-election, and the Chamber chose Gen. Fouad Chehab to be his successor. Chehab adopted a more neutralist foreign policy, and introduced state provision of health, education and other services. In 1964 he was succeeded by Charles Hélou, who continued many of Chehab's policies, but was faced by increasing controversy over the status of Palestinians in Lebanon.

After the establishment of Israel in 1948, and during the subsequent Arab–Israeli wars, thousands of Palestinians fled to Lebanon, where most of them were housed in refugee camps in the south of the country. Following the establishment of the Palestine Liberation Organization (PLO) in 1964, military training centres for Palestinian guerrilla fighters were established in the camps. From 1968 the *fedayeen* ('martyrs'), as the guerrillas were known, began making raids into Israel, provoking retaliatory attacks by Israeli forces against targets in southern Lebanon. In 1969 there were clashes between Lebanese security forces and the *fedayeen*, and many Christians, particularly the Maronites, advocated strict government control over the Palestinians' activities. The majority of Muslims, however, were strong supporters of the Palestinians' operations against Israel.

In 1970 Hélou was succeeded as President by Sulaiman Franjiya, who held office until 1976. The new President had to contend with an escalation of the Palestinian problem, which was exacerbated by an influx of Palestinian fighters who had been expelled from Jordan in July 1971. Conflict between Israeli forces and Palestinians based in Lebanon intensified, while Christian groups began their own armed campaign to control the *fedayeen*. In July 1974 there were clashes between Palestinian forces and armed members of the Phalangist Party (the Phalanges Libanaises, also known as al-Kata'eb, a militant right-wing Maronite Christian group).

In April 1975 there was further conflict between Phalangists and Palestinians. Unable to control the growing violence, the Government resigned in May, and the conflict quickly developed into full-scale civil war between the religious communities, with the Lebanese National Movement (LNM) of left-wing Muslims (including Palestinians), led by Kamal Joumblatt of the Parti Socialiste Progressiste (PSP, a mainly Druze-supported group), in conflict with conservative Christian groups, mainly the Phalangist militia. Although the initial cause of the violence was the status of Palestinians (who were strongly supported by the LNM), the constitutional order of the state soon became the main divisive issue. The LNM advocated an end to the confessional political system, which, it claimed, favoured Christians (by the 1970s it was generally accepted that Christians no longer formed a majority of the population, owing to Muslim immigration and the higher natural rate of increase of the indigenous Muslim population).

Numerous attempts to mediate in the civil war were made by Arab and Western states, and more than 50 cease-fire agreements failed before Arab summit meetings in Riyadh and Cairo secured a more durable cease-fire in October 1976. The achievement of a cease-fire was largely the result of intervention in the conflict by Syrian forces in mid-1976, in order to prevent an outright LNM victory. As a result of the October 1976 cease-fire, a 30,000-strong Arab Deterrent Force (ADF), composed mainly of Syrian troops, entered Lebanon and prevented the renewal of hostilities for a short time.

In September 1976 President Sulaiman Franjiya was succeeded by Elias Sarkis. In December Rashid Karami, who had been Prime Minister throughout the 1975–76 civil war, was succeeded by Selim al-Hoss. Legislative elections, due in April 1976, were postponed for an initial period of 26 months, and the term of the Chamber of Deputies was subsequently extended further. Although the constitutional forms of the

1855

State remained intact, the civil war, in which more than 30,000 people had died, had left the militias of the various warring factions in control of most of the country. In September 1976 Maronite militias united to form the Lebanese Forces (LF), which gradually took control of east Beirut and much of northern Lebanon. West Beirut was controlled by Muslim groups, while Palestinians dominated much of south-western Lebanon.

There was renewed fighting in March 1978, when a raid by forces of the Palestine National Liberation Movement (Al-Fatah), the main guerrilla group within the PLO, provoked Israeli retaliation. Israeli forces advanced into southern Lebanon, but the UN Security Council effected an Israeli withdrawal, and, by means of Resolution 425, established a UN Interim Force in Lebanon (UNIFIL, q.v.), initially of 4,000 troops, to maintain peace. The withdrawing Israeli forces, however, transferred control of a border strip to the pro-Israeli Christian militias of Major Saad Haddad.

In late 1978, following renewed fighting in Beirut between Syrian troops of the ADF and right-wing Christian militias, the ADF states agreed on a peace plan (the Beiteddin Declaration), which aimed to restore the authority of the Lebanese Government and army. Attempts to implement the plan enjoyed little success, however, and the fragmentation of the country, in accordance with religious and ethnic affiliations, continued.

The lack of progress towards political accord led to the resignation of Selim al-Hoss in June 1980; he was succeeded in October by Chafic al-Wazzan. In August 1982 the renamed National Assembly elected Bachir Gemayel to succeed President Sarkis, whose term expired in September. The election was boycotted by most of the Assembly's Muslim members. On 14 September the President-elect was assassinated; his brother, Amin, was elected to succeed him. Chafic al-Wazzan continued as Prime Minister. On 16 September, apparently in retaliation for the assassination of Bachir Gemayel, Phalangist forces entered the Palestinian refugee camps of Sabra and Shatila, in west Beirut, and massacred many of the inhabitants, allegedly with the consent of occupying Israeli forces.

In June 1982 Israeli forces had entered Lebanon, with the declared objective of finally eliminating the PLO's military threat to Israel's northern border. Israeli troops quickly defeated Palestinian forces in south-west Lebanon and surrounded the western sector of Beirut, trapping more than 6,000 Palestinian fighters there. In late August US diplomacy achieved an agreement that allowed the dispersal of the PLO fighters from Beirut to various Arab countries, and the arrival of a multinational peace-keeping force. Negotiations between Israel and Lebanon, begun in December 1982, culminated in an agreement, signed in May 1983, declaring an end to all hostilities (including an end to the theoretical state of war which had existed between the two countries since 1948) and the withdrawal of all foreign troops from the country. However, Syria failed to recognize the agreement, leaving 40,000 of its own troops and 7,000 PLO forces in the Beka'a valley and northern Lebanon. Israel also refused to withdraw its troops, although it redeployed its forces (reduced from 30,000 to 10,000 by the end of the year) south of Beirut, along the Awali river. Members of Major Saad Haddad's militia, the so-called South Lebanon Army (SLA), were employed to police the southern, Israeli-controlled area of Lebanon. Meanwhile, the 5,800-strong multinational force (2,000 French, 2,000 Italians, 1,600 Americans and about 100 British), which had been left to keep the peace in Beirut, was drawn increasingly into the fighting, coming under frequent attack from Muslim militiamen, who were suspicious of its role in supporting the Christian-led Government. In the two most devastating incidents, 241 US and 58 French marines were killed in almost simultaneous 'suicide bombings', perpetrated by Muslim groups in October 1983.

From September 1983 there was fierce inter-factional conflict between the forces of Yasser Arafat (Chairman of the PLO) and those of Syrian-backed rebels. After months of bitter fighting, a truce allowed Arafat, together with 24,000 of his troops, to leave Beirut, bound for Algeria, Tunisia and the Yemen Arab Republic. The conflict in Beirut was punctuated by numerous short-lived cease-fires, but attempts in late 1983 and early 1984 to achieve a comprehensive peace settlement failed, and in early February 1984 fighting erupted even more intensely than before. Attempts to reimpose state authority through a reconstituted army enjoyed little success: to the Muslim community, the Lebanese armed forces appeared to be no more than an instrument for use against them by the Christian President, in support of the Phalangist militia. Muslim soldiers, unwilling to fight members of their own communities, defected to the militias, while the Druze and Shi'ite sects co-operated with forces opposing the Government. On 5 February the Sunni Muslim Prime Minister, al-Wazzan, resigned, and shortly afterwards the USA, Italy and the United Kingdom decided to withdraw their peace-keeping troops from the multinational force (the French troops left in March).

By March 1984 successive defeats had left President Gemayel's forces with effective control only in eastern (mainly Christian-populated) Beirut. On 5 March Gemayel abrogated the agreement with Israel of May 1983, and on 30 April, with Syrian support, formed a government of national unity, headed by the former Prime Minister, Rashid Karami. A Syrian-sponsored security plan was implemented in July, but with limited success. Sporadic fighting continued between rival Christian and Muslim militias and, occasionally, between Sunni and Shi'ite Muslims, belonging, respectively, to the Murabitoun and Amal militias. The Lebanese army failed to gain control of Beirut, and President Gemayel's efforts to obtain approval for constitutional reform, already constrained by his fear of alienating his Christian supporters, were further handicapped by disagreements within the Cabinet.

The new Israeli Government, formed in September 1984, pledged to withdraw Israeli forces from Lebanon. The Lebanese Government demanded that UNIFIL be permitted to police the Israeli–Lebanese border, but when the last phase of the Israeli withdrawal was completed, in June 1985, Israel ensured that a buffer zone, between 10 km and 20 km wide, was in place along the border, policed by the pro-Israeli SLA. With Israeli presence in Lebanon reduced to a token force, Syria withdrew 10,000–12,000 troops from the Beka'a valley in July, leaving some 25,000 in position.

Sporadic conflict continued throughout 1985, but in December the leaders of the three main Lebanese militias (the Druze forces, Amal and the military arm of the Christian Phalangist Party, the LF) signed an accord in Damascus, providing for an immediate cease-fire and for the cessation of the civil war within one year. The militias were to be disarmed and disbanded, and a new constitutional regime was to be introduced within three years. However, the militias of the Shi'ite Hezbollah (Party of God) and the Sunni Murabitoun were not parties to the agreement, and influential elements within the Christian community were opposed to it. In late December there were clashes between members of the LF who supported the agreement and those who resented the concessions that had been made on their behalf by the LF leader, Elie Hobeika. In January 1986 Hobeika was forced into exile, and replaced as leader of the LF by Samir Geagea, who urged renegotiation of the Damascus accord, effectively ending any hope that it could be implemented.

During 1986 Palestinian guerrillas resumed rocket attacks on settlements in northern Israel, and Israel responded with air attacks on Palestinian targets in the Syrian-occupied Beka'a valley and in southern Lebanon. Meanwhile, Hezbollah, the fundamentalist Islamic movement supported by Iran, was gaining strength in the south, with an escalation of attacks on SLA positions within the Israeli buffer zone. There were also clashes between Hezbollah and UNIFIL, which was viewed by Hezbollah as an obstacle to the conflict with Israel.

Fighting between Palestinian guerrillas and Shi'ite Amal militiamen for control of the refugee camps in the south of Beirut developed into major clashes in May 1986. In June a cease-fire was imposed around the Beirut camps, as part of a Syrian-sponsored peace plan for Muslim west Beirut. The deployment of Lebanese and Syrian troops in west Beirut succeeded temporarily in curbing the activities of the Amal, Druze and Sunni militias in the area, but it failed to prevent fighting across the 'Green Line' dividing the city. In October there was further conflict between Amal and the Palestinians, around refugee camps in Tyre, Sidon and Beirut. A Syrian-supervised cease-fire at the camps began in April 1987, but conflict soon resumed. In September Amal and the PLO announced an agreement, designed to end the 'war of the camps', in which more than 2,500 people had died. However, the agreement was not implemented, and in October differences over the withdrawal of some 5,000–8,000 Palestinian guerrillas led to renewed fighting around disputed positions to the east of Sidon. In January 1988, avowedly as a gesture of support for protests by Palestinians residing in Israeli-occupied territories, Nabih Berri, the leader of Amal, announced the ending of the siege of the Palestinian refugee camps in Beirut and southern Lebanon.

In May 1987 the Prime Minister, Rashid Karami, resigned, following the failure of the Cabinet (in its first meeting for seven months) to agree on a policy to alleviate Lebanon's acute economic problems. President Gemayel refused to accept his resignation, but Karami was killed in a bomb explosion in June. Gemayel appointed Selim al-Hoss (Prime Minister in 1976–80) as acting Prime Minister.

In 1988 the need to elect a successor to President Gemayel (whose term of office was due to expire on 22 September of that year) produced a political crisis, when it proved impossible to find a candidate acceptable to all of the various warring factions. By mid-August, Gen. Michel Awn (the Commander-in-Chief of the Lebanese army), Raymond Eddé (the leader of the Maronite Bloc National) and Sulaiman Franjiya (who had been President in 1970–76) had emerged as the three leading contenders for the post. However, when the National Assembly met to elect a President on 18 August, it failed to achieve the required quorum. Earlier discussions between the Syrian and US Governments had failed to produce an acceptable compromise candidate, but, after renewed negotiations in September, they agreed to support the candidature of Mikhail ad-Daher, a Christian member of the National Assembly. However, Christian army and LF leaders remained opposed to the imposition of any candidate by foreign powers. A further attempt by the National Assembly to hold an election, on 22 September, again failed to achieve a quorum. When President Gemayel's term of office expired on that day, he appointed a six-member interim military government, comprising three Christians and three Muslims, and headed by Gen. Awn. However, the three Muslim officers whom the retiring President appointed immediately refused to serve in the new administration, while the two Christian members of the Muslim-dominated civilian Government of Selim al-Hoss resigned, in recognition of the interim military administration.

Lebanon was thus confronted by a constitutional crisis, with two Governments claiming legitimacy: the Christian military administration, based in east Beirut, and the predominantly Muslim civilian government, in west Beirut. It was feared that a continuation of this dual authority would formalize the *de facto* partition of the State into Christian and Muslim cantons. Concern over the stability of Lebanon's central institutions increased in October 1988, when the National Assembly failed to elect a successor to Hussain al-Hussaini, its President, or to renew his one-year mandate. In November Gen. Awn was dismissed as Commander-in-Chief of the army by Adel Osseiran, the Minister of Defence in Selim al-Hoss's Government. However, since Awn retained the loyalty of large sections of the army, he remained its *de facto* leader. Of Lebanon's central institutions, only the Central Bank remained intact, and it continued to make funds available to both Governments.

In February 1989 the Lebanese army achieved some success in a major confrontation with the LF, and there were hopes that the restored authority of government forces could result in the reunification of Beirut. In March, however, the most violent clashes for two years erupted in Beirut, between Awn's Lebanese army and its allies, on the one hand, and Syrian troops and their local militias, on the other. The hostilities were provoked initially by Awn's attempt to seize control of ports in Beirut held by Muslim forces. Awn, who was receiving considerable support from Iraq, declared his intention to expel all Syrian forces from Lebanon.

The renewed violence prompted more intensive diplomatic efforts to implement a permanent cease-fire. In May 1989, at an emergency summit meeting of Arab leaders in Casablanca, Morocco, a Tripartite Arab Committee, consisting of King Hassan of Morocco, King Fahd of Saudi Arabia and President Chadli of Algeria, was formed. Its aims were to implement a cease-fire agreement within six months, monitored by an Arab observer force, and to act as an intermediary between the conflicting forces in Lebanon, in order to facilitate an agreement on political reform and the election of a new President. A peace plan, announced in June 1989, was immediately rejected by Gen. Awn. By August it was estimated that more than 600 people had been killed in the fighting since March, and that some 500,000 had fled the city.

In September 1989 the Tripartite Arab Committee on Lebanon anounced a new peace plan, the most important feature of which was a proposal that the Lebanese National Assembly should meet to discuss a 'charter of national reconciliation', drafted by the Tripartite Arab Committee. The charter was approved by the Syrian Government and the leaders of Lebanon's Muslim militias, but was rejected by Gen. Awn because it did not provide for the withdrawal of Syrian forces. However, owing to his diplomatic isolation (the charter was supported by the USA, the USSR, the United Kingdom, France and almost every Arab nation), Awn relented. A cease-fire accordingly took effect on 23 September. The National Assembly subsequently met in Taif, Saudi Arabia, to discuss the charter, and it was finally approved, with some amendments, on 22 October, with the support of 58 of the 62 deputies attending the session (of the 99 deputies who had been elected in May 1972, only 73 survived). The charter provided for the transfer of executive power from the presidency to a cabinet, with portfolios divided equally among Christian and Muslim ministers, while the number of seats in the National Assembly was to be increased from 99 to 108, to be divided equally among Christian and Muslim deputies. Furthermore, following the election of a president and the formation of a new government, all Lebanese and non-Lebanese militias were to be disbanded within six months, while the internal security forces were to be strengthened. For a maximum period of two years the Syrian armed forces would assist the new Government in implementing the security plan. However, the endorsement of the charter of national reconciliation (the Taif agreement) was immediately denounced by Gen. Awn as a betrayal of Lebanese sovereignty.

Despite Awn's opposition to the Taif agreement, the National Assembly met in November 1989, in the northern town of Qlaiaat, to ratify the charter and to elect a new president. René Mouawad, a Maronite Christian deputy and a former Minister of Education and Arts, was elected President. The deputies also unanimously endorsed the Taif agreement and re-elected Hussain al-Hussaini as President of the National Assembly. Gen. Awn, however, declared the presidential election unconstitutional and the result null and void. On 7 November he declared himself President.

On 22 November 1989, only 17 days after his election, President Mouawad was assassinated in a bomb explosion. Two days later, the National Assembly convened and elected Elias Hrawi as the new President. At the same session, the deputies voted to extend the term of the National Assembly until 1994. A new government was formed by Selim al-Hoss on 25 November, and received a unanimous vote of confidence from the National Assembly. Shortly afterwards, the new Government announced that Gen. Awn had again been dismissed as Commander-in-Chief of the Lebanese army, and that Gen. Emile Lahud had been appointed in his place. In December, in an attempt to isolate Gen. Awn still further, the Central Bank halted all transfers of funds to areas of Beirut under his control.

The Christian communities were divided in their attitudes to the Taif agreement. Maronite leaders had sought to avoid open conflict with Gen. Awn by minimizing their approval of the accord, but the refusal of Samir Geagea, the leader of the LF, to reject the agreement precipitated violent clashes between the LF and Awn's forces in late January 1990. By early March more than 800 people had been killed, and more than 2,500 wounded, in inter-Christian fighting. In March Gen. Awn declared a halt to the conflict between Christian factions, implying a willingness to accept the Taif agreement in a modified form, but fighting resumed later in the month.

In April 1990 Samir Geagea announced the LF's recognition of the al-Hoss Government, formally accepting the Taif agreement, and in June Georges Saadé (who had initially refused to serve in the new Government) resumed his duties as Minister of Posts and Telecommunications. At the end of July 1990 the al-Hoss administration began an attempt to force Gen. Awn to relinquish his power base in east Beirut by seeking to prevent essential supplies from reaching his forces.

In August 1990 the National Assembly approved amendments to the Constitution, in accordance with the Taif agreement, granting a larger share of political power to Lebanon's Muslim community by increasing the number of seats in the National Assembly to 108, to be divided equally between Muslim and Christian deputies. On 21 September the Second Lebanese Republic was officially inaugurated, when President Hrawi formally approved the constitutional amendments. Gen. Awn continued to reject the reforms, but on 13 October he and his forces were expelled from east Beirut by Syrian forces and units of the Lebanese army loyal to President Hrawi. Awn took refuge in the French embassy, remaining there until August 1991, when he departed for France, having been granted political asylum by the French Government.

Later in October 1990 President Hrawi began to implement the initial security measures envisaged in the Taif agreement, ordering all militias to relinquish their positions to the Lebanese army, and to leave Beirut. The so-called Greater Beirut Security Plan (the assertion of state authority over the capital and adjacent areas) proceeded smoothly, for the most part, and in December the Lebanese army began to deploy in Beirut, all militia forces having withdrawn from the city. Most of the militias were transferred to southern Lebanon, where Israel regarded them as a security threat and responded by attacking positions held by the PLO and Hezbollah.

In December 1990 Selim al-Hoss submitted the resignation of his Government, and President Hrawi invited Omar Karami (Minister of Education and Arts in the outgoing administration) to form a government of national unity, as stipulated by the Taif agreement. Karami's new Cabinet, which included representatives of the principal Lebanese militias, was initially criticized for its alleged pro-Syrian bias, but was approved by the National Assembly in January 1991.

In early February 1991 seven battalions of the Lebanese army were deployed in southern Lebanon, in an attempt to control the activities of Palestinian forces around the refugee camps of Tyre and Sidon. In the week prior to the army's deployment, the Israeli army and the SLA had responded to PLO rocket attacks on the border strip by shelling Palestinian positions and launching a major offensive near the town of Jezzine, thus ending a two-year truce between the 7,000 Al-Fatah guerrillas in southern Lebanon and the combined forces of the Israeli army and the SLA. By mid-February the Lebanese army was established in most major southern Lebanese towns, but Israel remained unconvinced that it could guarantee the security of its border with Lebanon.

On 28 March 1991 the Government approved a plan to disband Lebanese and non-Lebanese militias in the country, which stipulated that the Lebanese army was to be responsible for security in the whole of Lebanon by 20 September. By mid-May the first of the two security plans that were embodied in the Taif agreement (the disbandment of the militias and the extension of the Government's authority through the use of the Lebanese army) appeared, for the most part, to have been successfully completed. However, the Iranian Revolutionary Guards in Lebanon insisted that they did not constitute a militia, and that their withdrawal depended on a decision of the Iranian Government, made in consultation with Syria. Hezbollah, meanwhile, insisted on maintaining armaments in the Beka'a valley and in southern Lebanon, in order to continue the struggle against Israel's occupation.

In early May 1991 the National Assembly approved amendments to the electoral law, as required by the 1989 Taif agreement (see above), and in early June 40 deputies were appointed to fill the 31 seats that had become vacant since the last general election (in 1972) and the nine new seats created under the Taif agreement. The term of office of the new assembly was to be four years.

In late May 1991 Lebanon and Syria signed a bilateral treaty, which established formal structures for the creation of links between the two countries in political, military and economic affairs, and confirmed the role of the Syrian army as guarantor of the two security plans contained in the Taif agreement. The treaty was immediately denounced by Israel as a further step towards the formal transformation of Lebanon into a Syrian protectorate, and Lebanese opponents of the treaty denounced it as a threat to Lebanon's independence. In September, as envisaged in the May agreement, Lebanon and Syria signed a security agreement permitting them to seek mutual military assistance in the event of a challenge to the stability of either country. In late March 1992 Syrian forces began to withdraw from Beirut, in preparation for their withdrawal to eastern Lebanon by September 1992, as stipulated by the Taif agreement.

Israel mounted fierce attacks on Palestinian bases in southern Lebanon in early June 1991, reinforcing statements by Israeli officials that Israel had no intention of withdrawing from the buffer zone along Lebanon's southern border, nor of reducing support for the SLA. On 1 July the Lebanese army began to deploy in and around Sidon, encountering some armed resistance from pro-Arafat Palestinian guerrillas. However, following the conclusion, on 4 July, of an accord between the Government and the PLO, whereby the PLO agreed to allow the Lebanese army peacefully to assume control of the area, the deployment of government forces was reported to have proceeded according to plan. Lebanese jurisdiction did not, however, extend to the village of Jezzine, where units of the SLA were in control, although the locality was technically outside Israel's buffer zone. In late November 1991 Israeli military activity in the region intensified, in response to alleged attacks by Hezbollah fighters. A further, more serious escalation of the conflict in southern Lebanon was precipitated in February 1992 by the assassination, by the Israeli air force, of Sheikh Abbas Moussawi, the Secretary-General of Hezbollah. Retaliation by Hezbollah fighters prompted an Israeli incursion beyond the buffer zone to attack Hezbollah positions. Although the Lebanese army had begun to occupy positions in southern Lebanon that had been vacated by UNIFIL, Hezbollah retained its freedom to conduct military operations, in an apparent reflection of Syria's belief that only by continued coercion would Israel withdraw from occupied Arab territories.

During the early months of 1992 Lebanon's economic situation worsened dramatically, and general strikes took place in April and May. There were widespread allegations of corruption and incompetence within the Government, and on 6 May the Prime Minister, Omar Karami, and his Cabinet were forced to resign. Following discussions in Damascus between President Hrawi and Syrian leaders, Rashid Solh was appointed Prime Minister (a position that he had previously held in 1974–75). A new cabinet, announced on 16 May, included 15 members of its predecessor and was regarded as insufficiently different in character from Karami's Government to modify the widespread perception of Lebanon as a Syrian protectorate, which many, including Karami, had blamed for the reluctance of western countries to invest in Lebanon's economic reconstruction.

In order to comply with the terms of the Taif agreement, Lebanon's first legislative elections since 1972 had to be held before November 1992. In early April the Government had indicated that the elections would be held in the summer of 1992, although it was not certain that Syrian forces would have withdrawn to the eastern area of the Beka'a valley by that time, as the Taif agreement stipulated that they should. Lebanese Christian groups accordingly threatened to boycott the elections, on the grounds that the continued Syrian presence would prejudice their outcome. The USA, too, urged the withdrawal of Syrian armed forces. The Lebanese Government, for its part, argued that the Lebanese army was still unable to guarantee the country's security in the absence of Syrian troops.

On 16 July 1992 the National Assembly approved a new electoral law whereby the number of seats in the Assembly was raised from 108 (the number fixed under the Taif agreement) to 128, to be divided equally between Christian and Muslim deputies. Voting in the elections to the National Assembly was held in three rounds, on 23 August, 30 August and 6 September 1992. The electoral turn-out was reported to be low in all three phases, especially in Maronite districts where the communities had been urged by their leaders to boycott the poll, and allegations of electoral malpractice prompted the resignation of the incumbent President of the National Assembly, Hussain al-Hussaini. Many candidates of the Iranian-supported Hezbollah, which contested the elections as a political party, were successful, especially in southern constituencies.

Following the elections to the National Assembly, the USA again urged Syria to withdraw its armed forces to the Beka'a. After a meeting between President Hrawi and President Assad of Syria, it was announced that a timetable for the withdrawal of Syrian armed forces would be compiled in October 1992. It subsequently became clear, however, that there would be no withdrawal until a comprehensive peace treaty had been concluded between Syria and Israel.

On 22 October 1992 Rafik Hariri was invited by President Hrawi to form a government. A new, 30-member cabinet was appointed on 31 October. Hariri, a Lebanese-born Saudi Arabian entrepreneur, included many technocrats in his new Cabinet, and offices were not, as previously, distributed on an entirely confessional basis. His appointment was viewed as likely to restore some confidence in the country's economy and to facilitate its reconstruction. On 12 November the new Government gained a vote of confidence in the National Assembly.

On 16 December 1992, in response to the deaths in the Occupied Territories of five members of the Israeli security forces, and to the abduction and murder by the Islamic Resistance Movement (Hamas) of an Israeli border policeman, the Israeli Cabinet ordered the deportation to Lebanon of 415 alleged Palestinian supporters of Hamas. Owing to the Lebanese Government's refusal to co-operate in this action, the deportees were stranded in the territory between Israel's self-declared southern Lebanese security zone and Lebanon proper. The deportations jeopardized the Middle East peace talks, in which Lebanese delegations had participated since the opening session of the peace conference in Madrid, Spain, in October 1991. Lebanon reacted cautiously to the Declaration of Principles on Palestinian Self-Rule in the Occupied Territories, signed by Israel and the PLO on 13 September 1993. Fears were expressed, for instance, that, if the Declaration of Principles were to provoke violent confrontations between rival Palestinian factions, most of the violence would be likely to occur in Lebanon, endangering the country's reconstruction. There was also concern about the ultimate fate of the estimated 350,000 Palestinian refugees residing in Lebanon. In late February 1994 Lebanon, together with the other Arab parties, withdrew from the Middle East peace process, following the murder, by a right-wing Jewish extremist, of some 50 Muslim worshippers in a mosque in Hebron on the West Bank. In August the Cabinet reaffirmed its opposition to the granting of permanent settlement and civic rights to Palestinian refugees in Lebanon. In late October President Hrawi expressed Lebanon's willingness to establish a joint commission with Israel in order to negotiate the withdrawal of Israeli armed forces from the south of the country.

Serious escalations of the conflict in southern Lebanon between Hezbollah fighters, the SLA and Israeli armed forces occurred in October and November 1992, and less intense fighting continued during the early months of 1993. In July the Government was reported to be attempting to curtail the activities of the Damascus-based Popular Front for the Liberation of Palestine-General Command (PFLP-GC), which had begun to mount guerrilla attacks on the positions of Israeli armed forces and Israeli-backed militias from southern Lebanon. On 25 July Israeli armed forces launched their heaviest artillery and air attacks on targets in southern Lebanon since 1982, with the declared aim of eradicating the threat posed by Hezbollah and Palestinian guerrillas. The positions of Syrian troops in Lebanon were also reported to have come under fire, and the Israeli operation displaced as many as 300,000 civilians towards the north and caused many civilian casualties. In August Hezbollah fighters were reported to have mounted further attacks on the positions of the pro-Israeli SLA in southern Lebanon. The violence remained at a high level during October and November. A sudden cessation of attacks by Hezbollah units on Israeli targets in January 1994, during the approach to a meeting between US President Clinton and President Assad of Syria, was cited as evidence, by Israeli observers, of Syrian control of Hezbollah. Hezbollah resumed attacks on Israeli targets in February, provoking the usual pattern of Israeli reprisals against Hezbollah targets. In June Israeli forces mounted an air attack on an alleged Hezbollah training camp in the Beka'a valley, close to the Syrian border. In early August further attacks by Israeli forces against Hezbollah targets in southern Lebanon caused the death of eight civilians, for which Israel subsequently made a formal apology. Israel claimed that Hezbollah had been involved in the planning of bomb attacks against Jewish targets in the United Kingdom and Argentina in July. An Israeli attack on the southern village of Nabatiyeh on 19 October, in which seven civilians were killed, deviated from the norm in that it was not a response to guerrilla activity in and around the southern Lebanese security zone, but, rather, appeared to have been made in retaliation for operations by the Islamic Resistance Movement (Hamas) in Israel itself. Hezbollah responded with rocket attacks on targets in northern and western Israel. There was a further escalation of the southern conflict in December, during which some six Israeli soldiers and eight members of the SLA were reported to have been killed. Israeli attacks on targets south of Beirut in January 1995 caused a brief closure of the city's international airport, for the first time since 1987. In February Israel imposed a blockade on southern Lebanese fishing ports, in retaliation for the imposition, by the Lebanese army, of stricter security controls between the southern Lebanese security zone and sovereign Lebanese territory. These were enforced owing to the alleged involvement of Israeli agents in the planning of a car-bomb explosion in Beirut in December 1994. The blockade remained in place at the end of March 1995, when the assassination of a Hezbollah leader by Israeli forces in southern Lebanon gave rise to fierce fighting between Hezbollah and Israeli forces in the area east of Sidon, and to rocket attacks by Hezbollah on Israeli targets in Galilee.

In March 1994, following terrorist attacks on Christian targets in Beirut, the Government proscribed the LF—the military wing of the Phalangist Party—for allegedly having promoted the establishment of a Christian enclave and, hence, the country's partition. In early May Hariri withdrew from all of his official duties, owing to a dispute with the President and with the President of the National Assembly, who both reportedly opposed his proposals to give the Government a measure of credibility with Lebanon's Maronite community by incorporating more of its representatives into the Cabinet. The dispute appeared to be resolved by President Assad of Syria's reported assurance to Hariri that pro-Syrian ministers within the Lebanese Cabinet would not seek to undermine the efficiency of the Government. Hariri resumed his duties later in May. At the beginning of September there was a minor reorganization of the Cabinet in which Michel Murr, the Deputy Prime Minister, replaced Beshara Merhej as Minister of the Interior. It was reported that this change was an attempt to increase the unity of the Government. In November the trial commenced in Beirut of Samir Geagea, the leader of the LF, who was charged with organizing a terrorist attack on a Maronite church in Beirut in late February 1994, and with the murder of the Maronite leader, Dany Chamoun, and his family in October 1990. It was feared that the trial would provoke further disaffection among Lebanon's Maronite community, which was far from reconciled to the post-Taif, Syrian-dominated Lebanese order. In September the LF had withdrawn its recognition of the Government and declared Syrian forces in Lebanon to be occupation forces. To many Maronites Geagea had been singled out to answer for atrocities committed during the civil war, while other, equally culpable parties, who accepted Syria's formal presence in Lebanon, were treated with indifference. The political ramifications of Geagea's trial seemed likely to complicate the choice of a successor to President Elias Hrawi, since any candidate would more than ever be bound to be dismissed as a Syrian foil. In early December Hariri abruptly announced his resignation as Prime Minister, a decision which was apparently due to his frustration at perceived attempts within the National Assembly to obstruct Lebanon's economic reconstruction. Hariri withdrew his resignation on 6 December, but not before it had caused a dramatic decline in the value of the Lebanese pound and emphasized the fragility of the recovery process.

**Government**

Under the 1926 Constitution (as subsequently amended), legislative power is held by the National Assembly (called the Chamber of Deputies until March 1979), with 128 members elected by universal adult suffrage for four years (subject to dissolution), on the basis of proportional representation. (The most recent general election to the legislature took place in August and September 1992.) Seats are allocated on a religious basis (equally divided between Christians and Muslims). The President of the Republic is elected for six years by the National Assembly. The President, in consultation with the deputies and the President of the National Assembly, appoints the Prime Minister and other ministers to form the Cabinet, in which executive power is vested.

**Defence**

In June 1994 the Lebanese armed forces numbered an estimated 44,300 (army 43,000, air force 800, navy 500). Paramilitary forces included an estimated 13,000 members of the Internal Security Force, which was being reorganized. In 1994 there were also 30,000 Syrian troops, the forces of the Israeli-backed 'South Lebanon Army' (numbering some 2,500) and possibly several thousand Palestinian guerrillas in Lebanon. UNIFIL forces numbered some 5,200 in June 1994.

All of the country's militia groups have been disbanded, with the exception of Hezbollah, whose active members numbered an estimated 3,000 in mid-1994. In early 1995 Amal was also reported to have resumed operations against the

SLA. Government expenditure on defence was budgeted at £L520,000m. in 1994.

**Economic Affairs**

According to an unofficial study by the Director of Statistics and Economic Studies at the Bank of Lebanon, the country's gross domestic product (GDP) in 1987, measured at current prices, was US $3,296m. (£L740,743m.). On the basis of this figure, Lebanon's GDP increased, in terms of constant prices, at an average annual rate of 22.7% between 1982 and 1987. Despite this recovery, real GDP in 1987 was only 5% higher than in 1974. In 1991, according to estimates by the Beirut Chamber of Commerce and Industry, Lebanon's GDP, measured at current prices, rose by 37% (to $3,700m.), compared with 1990. In 1992, according to Banque Audi SAL, Lebanon's GDP, measured at current prices, amounted to $6,460m. Banque Audi estimated that GDP increased by 7% in 1993, compared with 1992, and that GDP per head, measured in constant prices, rose by approximately 4.5%. GDP was estimated to have grown by a further 8.5% in 1994.

Agriculture (including forestry and fishing) contributed 8.5% of GDP in 1982 and an estimated 8.7% in 1987. Some 7.4% of the labour force were employed in the sector in 1993. The principal crops are citrus fruits, potatoes and tomatoes. Viticulture is also important. Food products and beverages accounted for an estimated 13.2% of industrial export earnings in 1994.

Industry (including manufacturing, construction and power) contributed 21.9% of GDP in 1982 and an estimated 20.3% in 1987. Lebanon's only mineral resources consist of small reserves of lignite and iron ore, and their contribution to GDP is insignificant.

Manufacturing contributed 13% of GDP in 1982 and an estimated 14.7% in 1987. The sector employed about 10% of the labour force in 1985. The most important branches have traditionally been food-processing, petroleum refining, textiles and furniture and woodworking. In 1986, in terms of output, petroleum-refining and food-processing continued to dominate the manufacturing sector. In 1987 the gross value of output in the manufacturing sector was estimated at US $5,188m. In 1994, according to Banque Audi, some 396 new manufacturing enterprises, employing 3,400 workers, commenced production. Of their total output, 26.3% consisted of metal products, 19.4% of food products and beverages and 12.1% of wooden furniture. In 1994, according to the Ministry of Industry and Oil, the industrial sector consisted of 23,518 manufacturing companies, which employed some 140,000 persons.

Energy is derived principally from thermal power stations, using imported petroleum.

Services contributed almost 70% of GDP in 1982 and an estimated 66% in 1987. It was estimated that almost 60% of the working population were employed in the provision of services in 1985. Trade and finance have traditionally dominated the sector. Financial services, in particular, withstood many of the disruptions inflicted on the economy by the civil conflict, not least due to the role of the Central Bank, one of the few Lebanese institutions that remained intact.

In 1994, according to estimates by Banque Audi, Lebanon's trade deficit rose by 23%, compared with 1993, to approaching US $5,000m. (imports $5,800m., exports $379m., based on customs receipts; it is thought that the value of exports is underestimated and might have actually amounted to about 20% of that of imports). The main destinations for Lebanese exports were Saudi Arabia (34.5%), Syria (21.5%), the UAE, France, Jordan and Kuwait. The principal industrial exports in 1994 were garments, food products and beverages and industrial machines and mixers.

The draft budget for 1995 projected expenditure of £L5,500,000m., and it initially forecast a deficit of £L2,350,000m. At the end of December 1993 Lebanon's total external debt was US $1,356m., of which $375m. was long-term public debt. In that year the cost of debt-servicing was equivalent to 6.5% of revenue from exports of goods and services. The rate of inflation was estimated to be 10% at the end of 1994. In 1985 28% of the labour force were unemployed, and by 1990 it was estimated that the rate of unemployment had risen as high as 50%.

Lebanon is a member of the Arab Fund for Economic and Social Development (see p. 237), the Arab Monetary Fund (p. 237) and the Islamic Development Bank (p. 180).

Lebanon's economic recovery proceeded satisfactorily in 1994, particularly with regard to the restoration of the country's infrastructure. Lebanon has been successful in attracting foreign interest in its new projects, not least as a result of the perceived efficiency of the Council for Development and Reconstruction, which oversees the process of reconstruction. There is optimism, too, that Lebanon may be able to regain some of its former role as an important Middle Eastern centre for financial services. Foreign banks have begun to return to Beirut, and it is planned to reactivate the Beirut Stock Exchange in 1995. Political disputes may delay the recovery. The Prime Minister's (swiftly revoked) decision to resign in December 1994 was attributed to difficulties the Government faced in gaining approval for a draft 10-year investment plan to which there is considerable, allegedly politically-motivated opposition within the National Assembly. It caused a significant fall in the value of the Lebanese pound and emphasized the vulnerability of a recovery programme that is so closely associated with Hariri's administration. It is feared, too, that the process of settling political scores which date back to the years of civil conflict may further jeopardize economic progress; and as long as there is no formal peace agreement with Israel the south of the country will remain unstable. Labour unrest erupted in November 1994 when the Confédération Générale des Travailleurs du Liban organized a general strike in support of an 88% increase in the basic wage.

**Social Welfare**

A scale of compensation for loss of employment was introduced by the Government in 1963. Medical services are provided mainly by private agencies, but there is a Social Security Fund which covers the medical expenses of workers. In 1973 Lebanon had 130 hospital establishments, with a total of 10,750 beds, and in 1983 there were 3,953 physicians working in the country (compared with 5,030 in 1979). In 1986 3.2% of budgetary expenditure was allocated to health.

**Education**

There are state-run primary and secondary schools, but private institutions provide the main facilities for secondary and higher education. Education is not compulsory, but state education is provided free of charge. Primary education begins at six years of age and lasts for five years. Secondary education, beginning at the age of 11, lasts for a further seven years, comprising a first cycle of four years and a second of three years. In 1991 the total enrolment at primary and secondary schools was equivalent to 87% of all school-age children (87% of boys; 87% of girls). Lebanon has the highest literacy rate in the Arab world. In 1970 the rate of illiteracy among people aged 10 years and over was 21.5% for males and 42.1% for females. In 1990, according to estimates by UNESCO, the average rate of adult illiteracy was 19.9% (males 12.2%; females 26.9%). In 1990 about 11% of budgetary expenditure was allocated to education.

**Public Holidays**

**1995:** 1 January (New Year's Day), 9 February (Feast of St Maron), 3 March* (Id al-Fitr, end of Ramadan), 22 March (Arab League Anniversary), 17 April (Easter, Western Church), 21–24 April (Easter, Eastern Church), 10 May* (Id al-Adha, Feast of the Sacrifice), 25 May (Ascension Day, Western Church), 31 May* (Islamic New Year), 9 June* (Ashoura), 9 August* (Mouloud, birth of Muhammad), 15 August (Assumption), 1 November (All Saints' Day), 22 November (Independence Day), 20 December* (Leilat al-Meiraj, ascension of Muhammad), 25 December (Christmas Day).

**1996:** 1 January (New Year's Day), 9 February (Feast of St Maron), 21 February* (Id al-Fitr, end of Ramadan), 22 March (Arab League Anniversay), 8 April (Easter, Western Church), 12–15 April (Easter, Eastern Church), 29 April* (Id al-Adha, Feast of the Sacrifice), 16 May (Ascension Day, Western Church), 19 May* (Islamic New Year), 28 May* (Ashoura), 28 July* (Mouloud, birth of Muhammad), 15 August (Assumption), 1 November (All Saints' Day), 22 November (Independence Day), 8 December* (Leilat al-Meiraj, ascension of Muhammad), 25 December (Christmas Day).

* These holidays are determined by the Islamic lunar calendar and may vary by one or two days from the dates given.
† This festival will occur twice (in the Islamic years A.H. 1414 and 1415) within the same Gregorian year.

**Weights and Measures**

The metric system is in force.

LEBANON

# Statistical Survey

Source (unless otherwise stated): Direction Centrale de la Statistique, Ministère du Plan, and Direction Générale des Douanes, Beirut.

## Area and Population

**AREA, POPULATION AND DENSITY**

| | |
|---|---:|
| Area (sq km) | 10,452* |
| Population (official estimate) 15 November 1970† | |
| Males | 1,080,015 |
| Females | 1,046,310 |
| Total | 2,126,325 |
| Population (UN estimates at mid-year)‡ | |
| 1990 | 2,740,000 |
| 1991 | 2,784,000 |
| 1992 | 2,838,000 |
| Density (per sq km) at mid-1992 | 271.5 |

* 4,036 sq miles.
† Figures are based on the results of a sample survey, excluding Palestinian refugees in camps. The total of registered Palestinian refugees was 497,958 at April 1994.
‡ Source: UN, *World Population Prospects: The 1992 Revision*.

**PRINCIPAL TOWNS** (estimated population in 1975)

Beirut (capital) 1,500,000; Tarabulus (Tripoli) 160,000; Zahleh 45,000; Saida (Sidon) 38,000; Sur (Tyre) 14,000.

**BIRTHS AND DEATHS** (UN estimates, annual averages)

| | 1975–80 | 1980–85 | 1985–90 |
|---|---:|---:|---:|
| Birth rate (per 1,000) | 30.1 | 29.3 | 27.9 |
| Death rate (per 1,000) | 8.7 | 8.8 | 7.8 |

Expectation of life (UN estimates, years at birth, 1985–90): 67.0 (males 65.1; females 69.0).

Source: UN, *World Population Prospects: The 1992 Revision*.

**EMPLOYMENT** (ISIC Major Divisions)

| | 1975 | 1985* |
|---|---:|---:|
| Agriculture, hunting, forestry and fishing | 147,724 | 103,400 |
| Manufacturing | 139,471 | 45,000 |
| Electricity, gas and water | 6,381 | 10,000 |
| Construction | 47,356 | 25,000 |
| Trade, restaurants and hotels | 129,716 | 78,000 |
| Transport, storage and communications | 45,529 | 20,500 |
| Other services | 227,921 | 171,000 |
| **Total** | **744,098** | **452,900** |

* Estimates.
Source: National Employment Office.

## Agriculture

**PRINCIPAL CROPS** ('000 metric tons)

| | 1991 | 1992 | 1993 |
|---|---:|---:|---:|
| Wheat | 59 | 62 | 55* |
| Barley | 19 | 21 | 20† |
| Sugar beet | 6 | 206 | 190* |
| Potatoes | 268 | 278 | 280* |
| Onions (dry) | 65 | 67 | 68* |
| Tobacco | 1 | 2† | 2* |
| Oranges | 261 | 263 | 270* |
| Tangerines, mandarins, clementines and satsumas | 58 | 21 | 35* |
| Lemons and limes | 90 | 93 | 94* |
| Grapefruit and pomelo | 55 | 54 | 53 |
| Apples | 214 | 145 | 160* |
| Grapes | 358 | 362 | 365* |
| Olives | 44 | 103 | 50* |
| Tomatoes | 213 | 230 | 235* |

* FAO estimate(s). † Unofficial figure.
Source: FAO, *Production Yearbook*.

**LIVESTOCK** ('000 head, year ending September)

| | 1991 | 1992* | 1993* |
|---|---:|---:|---:|
| Goats | 472 | 465 | 450 |
| Sheep | 238 | 240 | 250 |
| Cattle | 70 | 73 | 77 |
| Asses | 21 | 22 | 23 |
| Pigs | 44 | 42 | 40 |

Poultry (FAO estimates, million): 17 in 1991; 20 in 1992; 24 in 1993.
* FAO estimates. † Unofficial figure.
Source: FAO, *Production Yearbook*.

**LIVESTOCK PRODUCTS** ('000 metric tons)

| | 1991 | 1992* | 1993* |
|---|---:|---:|---:|
| Beef and veal* | 15 | 15 | 16 |
| Mutton and lamb* | 6 | 6 | 6 |
| Goat meat* | 3 | 3 | 3 |
| Poultry meat* | 53 | 55 | 55 |
| Cows' milk | 123 | 125 | 130 |
| Sheep's milk | 17 | 18 | 19 |
| Goats' milk | 32 | 34 | 34 |
| Cheese* | 13.2 | 13.5 | 14.0 |
| Poultry eggs* | 57.5 | 60.0 | 61.0 |

* FAO estimates. † Unofficial figures.
Source: FAO, *Production Yearbook*.

## Forestry

**ROUNDWOOD REMOVALS**
(FAO estimates, '000 cubic metres, excluding bark)

| | 1990 | 1991 | 1992 |
|---|---:|---:|---:|
| Industrial wood* | 7 | 9 | 7 |
| Fuel wood | 463 | 468 | 481 |
| **Total** | **470** | **477** | **488** |

* Official estimates.
Source: FAO, *Yearbook of Forest Products*.

# LEBANON

## SAWNWOOD PRODUCTION
('000 cubic metres, including railway sleepers)

|  | 1990 | 1991 | 1992 |
|---|---|---|---|
| Total | 13 | 11 | 9 |

Source: FAO, *Yearbook of Forest Products*.

## Fishing
(metric tons, live weight)

|  | 1990 | 1991 | 1992* |
|---|---|---|---|
| Inland waters | 80* | 100 | 100 |
| Mediterranean Sea | 1,420 | 1,700 | 1,700 |
| Total catch | 1,500 | 1,800 | 1,800 |

* FAO estimate(s).
Source FAO, *Yearbook of Fishery Statistics*.

## Mining
('000 metric tons)

|  | 1989 | 1990 | 1991 |
|---|---|---|---|
| Salt (unrefined) | 3 | 3 | 3 |

Source: US Bureau of Mines.

## Industry

### SELECTED PRODUCTS
(estimates, '000 metric tons, unless otherwise indicated)

|  | 1989 | 1990 | 1991 |
|---|---|---|---|
| Olive oil | 3 | 5* | 6 |
| Wine ('000 hectolitres)* | 110 | 100 | 110 |
| Cigarettes (million)† | 4,000 | 4,000 | 4,000 |
| Plywood ('000 cubic metres)* | 34 | 34 | 34 |
| Paper and paperboard | 37* | 37* | 42 |
| Jet fuels | 90 | 0 | 0 |
| Kerosene | 12 | 1 | 6 |
| Motor spirit (petrol) | 75 | 87 | 93 |
| Distillate fuel oils | 72 | 102 | 133 |
| Residual fuel oils | 229 | 226 | 283 |
| Liquefied petroleum gas‡ | 3 | 4 | 4 |
| Quicklime§ | 10 | 10 | 10 |
| Cement§ | 900 | 907 | 907 |
| Electric energy (million kWh) | 4,585 | 4,735 | 4,750 |

* Estimate(s) by the FAO.
† Estimates by the US Department of Agriculture.
‡ Estimates.
§ Estimates by the US Bureau of Mines.
Source: UN, *Industrial Statistics Yearbook*.

**1993** (FAO estimates): Olive oil 8,000 metric tons; Wine 90,000 hectolitres (Source: FAO, *Production Yearbook*).
**1994:** Electric energy (million kWh) 4,591.

## Finance

### CURRENCY AND EXCHANGE RATES
**Monetary Units**
100 piastres = 1 Lebanese pound (£L).

**Sterling and Dollar Equivalents** (31 December 1994)
£1 sterling = £L2,576.7;
US $1 = £L1,647.0;
£L10,000 = £3.881 sterling = $6.072.

**Average Exchange Rate** (£L per US $)
1992  1,712.8
1993  1,741.4
1994  1,680.1

### ORDINARY BUDGET ESTIMATES (£L million)

| Revenue | 1985 | 1986 |
|---|---|---|
| Direct taxation | 1,375 | 1,375 |
|   Income tax | 1,000 | 1,000 |
|   Property tax | 300 | 300 |
| Indirect taxation | 3,721 | 4,737 |
|   Customs and excise duties | 3,000 | 4,000 |
|   Car tax | 300 | 300 |
|   Fuel tax | 300 | 300 |
| National insurance | 150 | 175 |
| Other income* | 3,927 | 5,299 |
| Total | 9,567 | 12,712 |

* Including income from public enterprises and land revenues.
Source: Ministry of Finance.

| Expenditure | 1985 | 1986 |
|---|---|---|
| President's office | 17.5 |  |
| Chamber of deputies | 54.4 | 322.7 |
| Prime Minister's office | 240.5 |  |
| Ministry of justice | 77.1 | 95.3 |
| Ministry of foreign affairs | 187.5 | 361.6 |
| Ministry of interior | 739.9 | 900.4 |
| Ministry of finance | 147.0 | 184.8 |
| Ministry of national defence | 2,447.8 | 3,740.1 |
| Ministry of national education | 1,639.5 | 2,162.9 |
| Ministry of health | 360.3 | 578.1 |
| Ministry of labour and social affairs | 175.9 | 175.7 |
| Ministry of information | 63.0 | 81.9 |
| Ministry of public works and transport | 729.0 | 1,630.7 |
| Ministry of agriculture | 123.0 | 153.0 |
| Ministry of national economy | 160.5 | 760.5 |
| Ministry of posts and telecommunications | 60.1 | 80.3 |
| Ministry of hydroelectric resources | 559.9 | 754.7 |
| Ministry of tourism | 38.8 | 60.7 |
| Ministry of industry and oil | 6.0 | 6.4 |
| Ministry of housing and co-operatives | 53.0 | 60.6 |
| Payments on debt | 2,812.0 | 5,364.0 |
| Reserves | 684.4 | 462.4 |
| Total | 11,377.0 | 17,937.0 |

**1987** (estimates, £L million): Revenue 15,750; Expenditure 27,250.
**1988** (estimates, £L million): Revenue 31,700; Expenditure 70,000.
**1989** (estimates, £L million): Revenue 130,000; Expenditure 219,500.
**1990** (estimates, £L million): Revenue 210,000 (direct taxes and duties 66,600; indirect taxes 40,598; Expenditure 597,000 (debt service 183,557; defence 97,486; education 66,454; internal security 36,960).
**1991** (estimates, £L million): Total expenditure 1,150,000.
**1992** (estimates, £L million, net of supplementary items): Total expenditure 1,470,000.
**1993** (estimates, £L million): Revenue 1,700,000; Expenditure 3,800,000.
**1994** (estimates, £L million): Total expenditure 4,700,000.
**1995** (estimates, £L million): Revenue 3,150,000; Expenditure 5,500,000.

# LEBANON

## Statistical Survey

### CENTRAL BANK RESERVES (US $ million at 31 December)

| | 1991 | 1992 | 1993 |
|---|---|---|---|
| Gold* | 3,260.1 | 3,066.4 | 3,603.6 |
| IMF special drawing rights | 11.8 | 13.0 | 14.4 |
| Reserve position in IMF | 26.9 | 25.9 | 25.9 |
| Foreign exchange | 1,236.7 | 1,457.5 | 2,220.0 |
| **Total** | 4,535.6 | 4,562.8 | 5,863.9 |

* Valued at $353.50 per troy ounce in 1991, at $332.50 per ounce in 1992 and at $390.75 per ounce in 1993.

Source: IMF, *International Financial Statistics*.

### MONEY SUPPLY (£L '000 million at 31 December)

| | 1991 | 1992 | 1993 |
|---|---|---|---|
| Currency outside banks | 484.6 | 798.0 | 714.7 |
| Demand deposits at commercial banks | 202.0 | 393.5 | 422.4 |
| **Total money*** | 689.4 | 1,199.4 | 1,143.2 |

* Including private-sector demand deposits at Bank of Lebanon.

Source: IMF, *International Financial Statistics*.

### NATIONAL ACCOUNTS

**Expenditure on the Gross Domestic Product**
(official estimates, £L million at current prices)

| | 1980 | 1981 | 1982 |
|---|---|---|---|
| Government final consumption expenditure | 3,515 | 4,219 | 4,850 |
| Private final consumption expenditure | 12,905 | 15,488 | 15,840 |
| Increase in stocks | 2,196 | 3,459 | 1,179 |
| Gross fixed capital formation | | | |
| **Total domestic expenditure** | 18,616 | 23,166 | 21,869 |
| Exports of goods and services | 5,460 | 5,724 | 5,255 |
| *Less* Imports of goods and services | 10,076 | 12,090 | 14,525 |
| **GDP in purchasers' values** | 14,000 | 16,800 | 12,599 |
| **GDP at constant 1974 prices** | 4,900 | 4,923 | 3,082 |

**Gross Domestic Product by Economic Activity**
(official estimates, £L million at current prices)

| | 1980 | 1981 | 1982 |
|---|---|---|---|
| Agriculture, hunting, forestry and fishing | 1,288 | 1,435 | 1,076 |
| Manufacturing | 1,702 | 2,192 | 1,644 |
| Electricity, gas and water | 708 | 911 | 683 |
| Construction | 447 | 575 | 431 |
| Trade, restaurants and hotels | 4,008 | 4,753 | 3,565 |
| Transport, storage and communications | 530 | 628 | 471 |
| Finance, insurance, real estate and business services | 2,349 | 2,785 | 2,089 |
| Government services | 1,443 | 1,712 | 1,284 |
| Other community, social and personal services | 1,526 | 1,809 | 1,357 |
| **GDP in purchasers' values** | 14,000 | 16,800 | 12,600 |

(Unofficial estimates, US $ million at current prices*)

| | 1987 |
|---|---|
| Agriculture | 287 |
| Manufacturing | 483 |
| Energy and water | 28 |
| Construction | 158 |
| Commerce | 1,127 |
| Financial services | 286 |
| Non-financial services | 756 |
| Public administration | 171 |
| **GDP in purchasers' values** | 3,296† |

* Source: Gaspard, Toufic. *The Gross Domestic Product of Lebanon in 1987* in Bank of Lebanon Quarterly Bulletin, July–December 1988–December 1989.
† £L740,743 million.

## External Trade

### PRINCIPAL COMMODITIES (£L'000)

| Exports | 1984 | 1985 | 1986 |
|---|---|---|---|
| Food products | 51,767 | 113,103 | 321,300 |
| Beverages | 58,714 | 65,781 | 80,742 |
| Clothing | 121,346 | 257,946 | 660,542 |
| Textiles | 9,571 | 17,046 | 84,594 |
| Carpets | 23,221 | 4,714 | 14,193 |
| Tanned hides and leather | 12,881 | 35,727 | 129,734 |
| Footwear | 3,546 | 9,465 | 55,571 |
| Wooden products | 15,884 | 32,839 | 68,096 |
| Paints | 33,045 | 77,042 | 62,073 |
| Chemical products | 49,643 | 71,974 | 85,907 |
| Pharmaceutical products | 51,737 | 244,132 | 355,119 |
| Paper and paper and cardboard products | 62,371 | 155,538 | 312,362 |
| Ceramics and sanitary ware | — | 49,799 | 120,734 |
| Glassware | — | 33,732 | 27,378 |
| Cement | 12,471 | 28,606 | 6,815 |
| Non-metal mineral products | 49,370 | — | — |
| Metal products | 115,681 | 241,068 | 558,829 |
| Aluminium products | 44,744 | 138,244 | 362,344 |
| Machinery and electrical apparatus | 86,521 | 219,065 | 447,398 |
| Plastic products | 32,074 | 55,289 | 110,515 |
| Jewellery | — | 507,238 | 1,160,263 |
| **Total** (incl. others) | 2,462,000 | 4,973,000 | n.a. |

Source: the former Ministry of Economy.

**Total imports** (£L million): 5,100 in 1978; 7,500 in 1979; 10,000 in 1980; 12,500 in 1981; 13,100 in 1982; 15,500 in 1983; 14,800 in 1984; 23,000 in 1985.

### PRINCIPAL TRADING PARTNERS (£L'000)

| Imports | 1980 | 1981 | 1982 |
|---|---|---|---|
| Belgium | 401,100 | 456,600 | 478,900 |
| France | 1,315,900 | 1,571,300 | 1,660,700 |
| Germany, Fed. Rep. | 907,000 | 1,025,500 | 1,222,200 |
| Greece | 232,500 | 252,100 | 332,100 |
| Iraq | 296,400 | 369,000 | 340,200 |
| Italy | 1,729,800 | 2,041,800 | 2,446,000 |
| Japan | 711,600 | 728,800 | 793,300 |
| Netherlands | 265,700 | 355,100 | 374,100 |
| Romania | 748,600 | 973,200 | 894,900 |
| Saudi Arabia | 1,444,900 | 1,752,700 | 919,100 |
| Spain | 279,800 | 329,000 | 383,700 |
| Switzerland | 521,200 | 777,900 | 904,500 |
| Turkey | 269,600 | 364,400 | 627,200 |
| United Kingdom | 605,500 | 596,500 | 586,900 |
| USA | 1,117,800 | 1,359,100 | 1,460,800 |
| **Total** (incl. others) | 12,775,400 | 15,374,700 | 16,123,800 |

Source: Chamber of Commerce and Industry, Beirut.

## LEBANON

| Exports | 1981 | 1982 | 1983 |
|---|---|---|---|
| CMEA | 61,000 | 43,000 | 19,300 |
| EEC | 230,000 | 160,000 | 44,600 |
| Iraq | 1,440,000 | 1,163,000 | 190,500 |
| Jordan | 284,000 | 568,000 | 193,500 |
| Kuwait | 245,000 | 272,000 | 220,600 |
| Saudi Arabia | 1,478,000 | 1,559,000 | 1,293,500 |
| Syria | 610,000 | 390,000 | 305,800 |
| United Arab Emirates | 162,000 | 170,000 | 155,100 |
| **Total** (incl. others) | 5,444,000 | 5,256,000 | 2,694,200 |

Source: Chamber of Commerce and Industry, Beirut.

## Transport

**ROAD TRAFFIC** (motor vehicles in use)

|  | 1980 | 1981 | 1982 |
|---|---|---|---|
| Passenger cars (incl. taxis) | 362,013 | 403,532 | 473,372 |
| Buses | 2,980 | 3,161 | 3,348 |
| Lorries | 37,696 | 41,570 | 46,212 |
| Motor cycles | 15,903 | 16,253 | 16,797 |

**SHIPPING** (international sea-borne freight traffic, '000 metric tons)

|  | 1988 | 1989 | 1990 |
|---|---|---|---|
| Goods loaded | 148 | 150 | 152 |
| Goods unloaded | 1,120 | 1,140 | 1,150 |

Source: UN, *Monthly Bulletin of Statistics*.

**CIVIL AVIATION** (revenue traffic on scheduled services)

|  | 1989 | 1990 | 1991 |
|---|---|---|---|
| Kilometres flown (million) | 15 | 16 | 18 |
| Passengers carried ('000) | 183 | 572 | 536 |
| Passenger-km (million) | 324 | 941 | 1,150 |
| Freight ton-km (million) | 284 | 167 | 170 |
| Mail ton-km (million) | 1 | 1 | 2 |
| Total ton-km (million) | 314 | 254 | 276 |

Source: UN, *Statistical Yearbook*.

## Communications Media

|  | 1990 | 1991 | 1992 |
|---|---|---|---|
| Radio receivers ('000 in use) | 2,270 | 2,320 | 2,370 |
| Television receivers ('000 in use) | 890 | 905 | 920 |
| Daily newspapers (number) | 14 | n.a. | 16 |

Source: UNESCO, *Statistical Yearbook*.

## Education

|  | Teachers 1986 | Teachers 1988 | Teachers 1991† | Pupils 1986 | Pupils 1988 | Pupils 1991† |
|---|---|---|---|---|---|---|
| Pre-primary | 5,257 | n.a. | n.a. | 129,590 | 131,217 | 131,074 |
| Primary* | n.a. | n.a. | n.a. | 399,029 | 346,534 | 345,662 |
| Secondary: |  |  |  |  |  |  |
|   General* | n.a. | n.a. | n.a. | 279,849 | 241,964 | 248,097 |
|   Vocational | 4,400 | n.a. | 4,240 | 31,045 | n.a. | 37,403 |
| Higher | n.a. | n.a. | 5,400 | 83,891 | n.a. | 85,495 |

* Including schools operated by the UN Relief and Works Agency for Palestine Refugees in the Near East (UNRWA). The number of pupils at UNRWA primary schools in Lebanon was: 23,481 in 1986; 22,700 in 1988. The number of pupils enrolled in general education at UNRWA secondary schools was: 10,521 in 1986; 10,126 in 1988.
† Figures for 1989 and 1990 are not available.

Source: UNESCO, *Statistical Yearbook*.

# Directory

## The Constitution

The Constitution was promulgated on 23 May 1926 and amended by the Constitutional Laws of 1927, 1929, 1943, 1947 and 1990.

According to the Constitution, the Republic of Lebanon is an independent and sovereign state, and no part of the territory may be alienated or ceded. Lebanon has no state religion. Arabic is the official language. Beirut is the capital.

All Lebanese are equal in the eyes of the law. Personal freedom and freedom of the press are guaranteed and protected. The religious communities are entitled to maintain their own schools, on condition that they conform to the general requirements relating to public instruction, as defined by the state. Dwellings are inviolable; rights of ownership are protected by law. Every Lebanese citizen who has completed his twenty-first year is an elector and qualifies for the franchise.

### LEGISLATIVE POWER

Legislative power is exercised by one house, the National Assembly, with 108 seats (raised, without amendment of the Constitution, to 128 in 1992), which are divided equally between Christians and Muslims. Members of the National Assembly must be over 25 years of age, in possession of their full political and civil rights, and literate. They are considered representative of the whole nation, and are not bound to follow directives from their constituencies. They can be suspended only by a two-thirds majority of their fellow-members. Secret ballot was introduced in a new election law of April 1960.

In normal times the National Assembly holds two sessions yearly, from the first Tuesday after 15 March to the end of May, and from the first Tuesday after 15 October to the end of the year. The normal term of the National Assembly is four years; general elections take place within 60 days before the end of this period. If the Assembly is dissolved before the end of its term, elections are held within three months of dissolution.

Voting in the Assembly is public—by acclamation, or by standing and sitting. A quorum of two-thirds and a majority vote is required for constitutional issues. The only exceptions to this occur when the Assembly becomes an electoral college, and chooses the President of the Republic, or Secretaries to the National Assembly, or when the President is accused of treason or of violating the Constitution. In such cases voting is secret, and a two-thirds majority is needed for a proposal to be adopted.

### EXECUTIVE POWER

With the incorporation of the Taif agreement into the Lebanese Constitution in August 1990, executive power was effectively transferred from the presidency to the Cabinet. The President is elected for a term of six years and is not immediately re-eligible. He is responsible for the promulgation and execution of laws enacted by the National Assembly, but all presidential decisions (with the exception of those to appoint a Prime Minister or to accept the resignation of a government) require the co-signature of the Prime Minister, who is head of the Government, implementing its policies and speaking in its name. The President must receive the approval of the Cabinet before dismissing a minister or ratifying an international treaty. The ministers and the Prime Minister are chosen by the President of the Republic in consultation with the members and President of the National Assembly. They are not necessarily members of the National Assembly, although they are responsible to it and have access to its debates. The President of the Republic must be a Maronite Christian, and the Prime Minister a Sunni Muslim; the choice of the other ministers must reflect the level of representation of the communities in the Assembly.

## The Government

### HEAD OF STATE

**President:** ELIAS HRAWI (elected 24 November 1989).

### CABINET
(May 1995)

**Prime Minister and Minister of Finance:** RAFIK HARIRI (Sunni).

**Deputy Prime Minister and Minister of the Interior:** MICHEL MURR (Greek Orthodox).

**Minister of Foreign Affairs:** FARIS BOUEZ (Maronite).

**Minister of Defence:** MUHSIN DALLOUL (Shi'ite).

**Minister of Agriculture:** CHAWKI FAKHOURY (Greek Orthodox).

**Minister of Information:** FARID MKARI (Greek Orthodox).

**Minister of Education, Youth and Sports:** ROBERT GHANEM (Maronite).

**Minister of Labour:** ALI HRAJLI (Shi'ite).

**Minister of Public Health:** MARWAN HAMADEH (Druze).

**Minister of Public Works:** ASAAD HARDAN (Greek Orthodox).

**Minister of Industry and Oil:** CHAHE BARSOUMIAN (Armenian Orthodox).

**Minister of Economy and Trade:** YASSINE JABER (Shi'ite).

**Minister of Housing and Co-operatives:** MAHMOUD ABU HAMDAN (Shi'ite).

**Minister of Justice:** BAHIJ TABBARA (Sunni).

**Minister of Tourism:** NICHOLAS FATOUSH (Greek Catholic).

**Minister of Posts and Telecommunications:** EL-FADL CHALAK (Sunni).

**Minister for the Affairs of Displaced Persons:** WALID JOUMBLATT (Druze).

**Minister of Electricity and Water Resources:** ELIE HOBEIKA (Maronite).

**Minister of Municipal and Rural Affairs:** HAGOP DEMERJIAN (Armenian Orthodox).

**Minister of Culture and Higher Education:** MICHEL EDDÉ (Maronite).

**Minister of Transport:** OMAR MISKAWI (Sunni).

**Minister of Vocational and Technical Education:** ABDEL-RAHIM MRAD (Sunni).

**Minister of the Environment:** JOSEPH MOGHAIZEL (Greek Catholic).

**Minister of Emigrant Affairs:** ABD EL-KHALIL (Shi'ite).

**Minister of Social Affairs:** ESTEPHAN DOUEVHI (Maronite).

**Minister of State for Financial Affairs:** FUAD SINIORA (Sunni).

**Minister of State for Parliamentary Affairs and Administrative Reform:** ANWAR AL-KHALIL (Druze)

**Ministers of State without portfolio:** NADIM SALEM (Greek Catholic), KABALAN ISSA EL-KHOURY (Maronite), FAYEZ CHOKOR (Shi'ite).

### MINISTRIES

**Office of the President:** Baabda, Beirut; tel. (1) 220000; telex 21000.

**Office of the Prime Minister:** Grand Sérail, rue des Arts et Métiers, Sanayeh, Beirut; tel. (1) 221000.

**Ministry of Agriculture:** rue Sami Solh, Beirut; tel. (1) 380460.

**Ministry of Economy, Trade, Industry and Oil:** rue Artois, Beirut; tel. (1) 345051.

**Ministry of Education and Fine Arts:** rue Unesco, Beirut; tel. (1) 30511.

**Ministry of Finance:** rue de l'Etoile, Beirut; tel. (1) 251600.

**Ministry of Foreign and Emigrant Affairs:** rue Sursock, Achrafiyé, Beirut; tel. (1) 333100; telex 20726.

**Ministry of Housing and Co-operatives:** Grand Sérail, rue des Arts et Métiers, Sanayeh, Beirut; tel. (1) 336002.

**Ministry of Information:** rue Hamra, Beirut; tel. (1) 345800; telex 20786.

**Ministry of the Interior:** Grand Sérail, rue des Arts et Métiers, Sanayeh, Beirut; tel. (1) 369135.

**Ministry of Justice:** rue Sami Solh, Beirut; tel. (1) 384243.

**Ministry of Labour:** Shiah, Beirut; tel. (1) 274140.

**Ministry of Defence:** Yarze, Beirut; tel. (1) 452400; telex 20901.

**Ministry of Posts and Telecommunications:** rue Sami Solh, Beirut; tel. (1) 240100; telex 20900.

**Ministry of Health and Social Affairs:** rue du Musée, Beirut; tel. (1) 309843.

**Ministry of Public Works and Transport:** Shiah, Beirut; tel. (1) 270225.

**Ministry of State for Affairs of the South and Reconstruction:** Beirut.

**Ministry of Tourism:** rue Banque du Liban, Beirut; tel. (1) 340904; telex 20898.

**Ministry of Water and Electrical Resources:** Shiah, Beirut; tel. (1) 270256.

## Legislature

### MAJLIS ALNWAB
(National Assembly)

The first election to the National Assembly since 1972 was held in three rounds in August and September 1992, and in October there was a by-election to choose deputies for one district in which voting had earlier been postponed. Constitutional amendments, introduced in 1990, had raised the number of seats in the Assembly from 99 to 108. Prior to the election in 1992, the Government adopted legislation that further increased the number of seats, to 128. The equal distribution of seats among Christians and Muslims is determined by law, and the Cabinet must reflect the level of representation achieved by the various religious denominations within that, principal division. Deputies of the same religious denomination do not necessarily share the same political, or party allegiances. Many Christian, especially Maronite, voters refused to participate in the general election of 1992. The term of office of the National Assembly is four years.

**President:** NABIH BERRI.

**Vice-President:** ELIE FERZLI.

**Religious Groups in the National Assembly** (General election, 23 August, 30 August, 6 September and 11 October 1992)

| | |
|---|---|
| Maronite Catholics | 34 |
| Sunni Muslims | 27 |
| Shi'a Muslims | 27 |
| Greek Orthodox | 14 |
| Druzes | 8 |
| Greek-Melkite Catholics | 6 |
| Armenian Orthodox | 5 |
| Alawites | 2 |
| Armenian Catholics | 1 |
| Protestants | 1 |
| Others | 3 |
| **Total** | **128** |

## Political Organizations

**Armenian Revolutionary Federation (ARF):** POB 11–587, rue Spears, Beirut; f. 1890; principal Armenian party; also known as Tashnag Party, which was the dominant nationalist party in the independent Armenian Republic of Yerevan of 1917–21, prior to its becoming part of the USSR; socialist ideology; collective leadership.

**Al-Baath:** f. in Syria, 1940, by MICHEL AFLAK; secular pro-Syrian party with policy of Arab union, branches in several Middle Eastern countries; Sec.-Gen. ABDULLAH AL-AMIN, Beirut.

**Al-Baath:** pro-Iraqi wing of Al-Baath party; Sec.-Gen. ABD AL-MAJID RAFEI.

**Bloc National Libanais:** rue Pasteur, Gemmayze, Beirut; tel. (1) 584585; fax (1) 584591; f. 1943; right-wing Lebanese party with policy of power-sharing between Christians and Muslims and the

# LEBANON

*Directory*

exclusion of the military from politics; Leader RAYMOND EDDÉ; Pres. SÉLIM SALHAB; Sec.-Gen. JEAN HAWAT.

**Ad-Dustur** (Constitutional Party): rue Michel Chiha, Kantari, Beirut; f. 1943; led struggle against French mandate, established 1943 National Covenant; party of the political and business élite; Leader MICHEL BECHARA AL-KHOURY.

**Al-Harakiyines al-Arab:** Beirut; f. 1948 by GEORGES HABASH; Arab nationalist party, with Marxist tendencies.

**Al-Hayat al-Wataniya:** Beirut; f. 1964 by AMINE ARAYSSI.

**Al-Hizb ad-Damuqratiya al-Ishtiraqi al-masihi** (Christian Social Democratic Party): Beirut; f. 1988; formerly Christian Social Democratic Union; Sec.-Gen. WALID FARIS.

**Al-Jabha al-Damuqratiya al-Barlamaniya** (Parliamentary Democratic Front): Beirut; advocates maintenance of traditional power-sharing between Christians and Muslims; mainly Sunni Muslim support; Leader (vacant).

**Al-Kata'eb** (Phalanges Libanaises, Phalangist Party): POB 992, place Charles Hélou, Beirut; tel. (1) 338230; telex 42245; f. 1936 by the late PIERRE GEMAYEL; nationalist, reformist, democratic social party; largest Maronite party; 100,000 mems; announced merger with Parti National Libéral, May 1979; Leader GEORGES SAADÉ; Vice-Pres. GEORGES UMAYRAH; Sec.-Gen. KARIM PAQRADUNI.

**Mouvement de l'Action Nationale:** POB 5890, Centre Starco, Bloc Sud, Beirut; f. 1965; Founder and Leader OSMAN MOSBAH AD-DANA.

**An-Najjadé** (The Helpers): c/o Sawt al-Uruba, POB 3537, Beirut; f. 1936; Arab socialist unionist party; 3,000 mems; Founder and Pres. ADNANE MUSTAFA AL-HAKIM.

**An-Nida' al-Kawmi** (National Struggle): Immeuble Chammat, Ramlet el-Beida, Beirut; f. 1945; Founder and Leader KAZEM AS-SOLH.

**Parti Communiste Libanais** (Lebanese Communist Party): POB 633, Immeuble du Parti Communiste Libanais, rue al-Hout, Beirut; f. 1924; officially dissolved 1948–71; Marxist, much support among intellectuals; Leader and Sec.-Gen. FARUQ DAHRUJ (acting).

**Parti Démocrate:** Immeuble Labban, rue Kantari, Beirut; f. 1969; supports a secular, democratic policy, private enterprise and social justice; Sec.-Gen. JOSEPH MUGHAIZEL; Co-founder ÉMILE BITAR.

**Parti National Libéral** (Al-Wataniyin al-Ahrar): rue du Liban, Beirut; f. 1958; liberal reformist party; announced merger with Phalanges Libanaises, May 1979; Pres. DORY CHAMOUN; Deputy Leader KAZEM KHALIL.

**Parti Socialiste Nationaliste Syrien:** f. 1932, banned 1962–69; advocates a 'Greater Syria', composed of Lebanon, Syria, Iraq, Jordan, Palestine and Cyprus; Leader DAWOUD BAZ; Chair. HAFIZ AS-SAYEH; Sec.-Gen. ANWAR AL-FATAYRI.

**Parti Socialiste Progressiste** (At-Takadumi al-Ishteraki): POB 2893, Zkak el-Blat, Beirut; f. 1949; progressive party, advocates constitutional road to socialism and democracy; over 25,000 mems; mainly Druze support; Pres. WALID JOUMBLATT; Sec.-Gen. SHARIF FAYAD.

**Wa'ad Party:** Beirut; Leader ELIE HOBEIKA.

The **Lebanese Front** (f. 1976; Sec. DORY CHAMOUN) is a grouping of right-wing parties (mainly Christian). The **National Front** (f. 1969; Sec.-Gen. KAMAL SHATILA) is a grouping of left-wing parties (mainly Muslim). Other parties include the **Independent Nasserite Movement** (Murabitoun; Sunni Muslim Militia; Leader IBRAHIM QULAYAT) and the **Union of Working People's Forces** (Sec.-Gen. KAMAL SHATILA). The **Nasserite Popular Organization** and the **Arab Socialist Union** merged in January 1987, retaining the name of the former (Sec.-Gen. MUSTAFA SAAD). **Amal** (Hope) is a Shi'ite politico-military organization (Principal Controller of Command Council Sheikh MUHAMMAD MANDI SHAMS AD-DIN, Chair. SADR AD-DIN AS-SADR, Leader NABIH BERRI). The **Islamic Amal** is a breakaway group from Amal, based in Baalbek (Leader HUSSEIN MOUSSAVI). **Islamic Jihad** (Islamic Holy War) is a pro-Iranian fundamentalist guerrilla group (Leader IMAAD MOUGNIEH). **Hezbollah** (the Party of God) is a militant Shi'ite faction which was founded by Iranian Revolutionary Guards who were sent to Lebanon (Spiritual Leader Sheikh MUHAMMAD HUSSEIN FADLALLAH). The **Popular Liberation Army** is a Sunni Muslim faction, active in the south of Lebanon (Leader MUSTAFA SAAD). **Tawheed Islami** (the Islamic Unification Movement; f. 1982; Sunni Muslim; Leader Sheikh SAYED SHABAN) and the **Arab Democratic Party** (or the Red Knights; Alawites; pro-Syrian; Leader ALI EID) are based in Tripoli.

## Diplomatic Representation

### EMBASSIES IN LEBANON

**Algeria:** POB 4794, Hôtel Summerland, Jnah, Beirut; tel. (1) 868433; telex 27382; Ambassador: IBRAHIM ISSA.

**Argentina:** POB 11-5245, 5th Floor, Immeuble Antoun Saad, rue de l'Eglise Mar-Takla, Hazmieh, Beirut; tel. and fax (1) 428960; telex 40687; Ambassador: GUSTAVO ALBERTO URRUTIA.

**Armenia:** Beirut.

**Australia:** Hôtel Mayflower, Hamra, Beirut; telex 21754; Ambassador: PAUL ROBILLIARD.

**Austria:** 9th Floor, Tour Sadat, rue Sadat, Ras Beirut, Beirut; tel. (1) 801574; telex 23255; Ambassador: ANTON PROHASKA.

**Bahrain:** Sheikh Ahmed ath-Thani Bldg, Raoucheh, Beirut; tel. (1) 805495; telex 21686; Ambassador: MUHAMMAD BAHLOUL.

**Belgium:** Immeuble Hélou, Baabda, Beirut; tel. (1) 420585; telex 44040; Ambassador: PAUL PONJAERT.

**Brazil:** POB 166175, rue des Antonins, Baabda, Beirut; tel. (1) 455158; telex 41330; fax (1) 456308; Ambassador: BRIAN MICHAEL FRASER NEELE.

**Bulgaria:** Immeuble Hibri, rue de l'Australie, Beirut; Ambassador: KRASTIO KRASTEV.

**Chad:** Immeuble Kalot Frères, Pine Forest, ave Sami Solh, Beirut; Ambassador: (vacant).

**Chile:** 5th Floor, Immeuble Edouard Abou Jaoudé, Beirut; tel. (1) 404745; telex 41421; Chargé d'affaires a.i.: ALEX GEIGER.

**China, People's Republic:** rue Nicolas Ibrahim Sursock 72, Mar Elias, Beirut; tel. (1) 830314; telex 21344; Ambassador: ZHU PEIQING.

**Colombia:** POB 1496, Corniche Chouran, Immeuble Jaber al-Ahmad as-Sabbah, Beirut; tel. (1) 810416; telex 44260; Ambassador: ROBERTO DELGADO SAÑUDO.

**Cuba:** Immeuble Ghazzal, rue Abd as-Sabbah between rue Sakiet el-Janzir and rue de Vienne, Beirut; tel. (1) 866641; Ambassador: SEVERINO MANSUR JORGE.

**Czech Republic:** POB 40195, Baabda, Beirut.

**Egypt:** POB 690, rue Thomas Eddison, Beirut; tel. (1) 801769; Ambassador: SAYED ABUZEID OMAR.

**Finland:** POB 113-5966, 11th Floor, Sadat, rue Sadat, Ras Beirut, Beirut; tel. (1) 802276; telex 20568; fax (1) 803136; Ambassador: ARTO KURITTU.

**France:** Mar-Takla, Beirut; tel. (1) 429629; telex 41530; fax (1) 424426; Ambassador: JEAN-PIERRE LAFON.

**Germany:** POB 2820, Hôpital Notre Dame du Liban, Jounieh, Beirut; tel. (1) 830021; telex 45445; Ambassador: WOLFGANG ERCK.

**Greece:** 11th Floor, Immeuble Sarras, ave Elias Sarkis, Achrafiyé, Beirut; tel. (1) 219217; telex 40131; fax (1) 201324; Ambassador: ATHANASSIOS KANILLOS.

**Haiti:** Immeuble Sarkis, rue du Fleuve, Beirut; Ambassador: (vacant).

**Holy See:** POB 1882, rue Georges Picot, Beirut (Apostolic Nunciature); tel. (1) 903102; fax (1) 903763; Apostolic Nuncio: Most Rev. PABLO PUENTE, Titular Archbishop of Macri.

**Hungary:** POB 90618, Immeuble Ahmavani, Cornet Chahnian, Montana, Beirut; tel. (1) 922490; telex 41503; Ambassador: BALAIZS BOKOR.

**India:** POB 113-5240, Immeuble Sahmarani, rue Kantari 31, Hamra, Beirut; tel. (1) 353892; telex 20229; Ambassador: S. SIVASWAMI.

**Iran:** Immeuble Sakina Mattar, Jnah, Beirut; tel. (1) 300007; Ambassador: HOMAYOUN ALIZADEH.

**Italy:** POB 211, Immeuble Cosmidis, rue de Rome, Beirut; tel. (1) 868301; telex 48347; Ambassador: GIUSEPPE DE MICHELIS.

**Japan:** POB 3360, Immeuble Olfat Nagib Salha, Corniche Chouran, Beirut; tel. (1) 810408; telex 20864; Ambassador: MATSUME TAKAO.

**Jordan:** Immeuble Sodeco, rue Vienna, Beirut; tel. (1) 864950; telex 22228; Ambassador: FAKHRI ABU TALEB.

**Korea, Democratic People's Republic:** rue Selim Salaam, Moussaitbé, Beirut; tel. (1) 311490; Ambassador: LI YONG SOP.

**Kuwait:** The Stadium Roundabout, Bir Hassan, Beirut; tel. (1) 345631; telex 22105; Ambassador: AHMAD GHAITH ABDALLAH.

**Libya:** Hôtel Beau Rivage, Ramlet el-Baida, Beirut; tel. (1) 866240; telex 22181; Chair. of People's Bureau: ASHOUR ABD AL-HAMID AL-FOURTAS.

**Morocco:** Bir Hassan, Beirut; tel. (1) 832503; telex 20867; Ambassador: MUHAMMAD FREDJ DOUKKALI.

**Norway:** Immeuble Taher et Fakhry, rue Bliss, Ras Beirut, Beirut; tel. (1) 353730; telex 22690; Ambassador: PER HANGESTAD.

**Oman:** Bir Hassan, Beirut; Ambassador: (vacant).

**Pakistan:** 11th Floor, Immeuble Shell, Raoucheh, Beirut; tel. (1) 869706; Ambassador: MUHAMMAD QURBAN.

**Poland:** POB 3667, Immeuble Nassif, rue Souraty, Hamra, Beirut; tel. (1) 860618; Chargé d'affaires a.i.: PIOTR KOWALSKI.

**Qatar:** POB 6717, Beirut; tel. (1) 865271; telex 23727; Ambassador: MOHAMED ALI SAEED AN-NUAIMI.

**Romania:** Manara, Beirut; tel. (1) 867895; telex 21661; Ambassador: ION BESTELIU.

# LEBANON

**Russia:** rue Mar Elias et-Tina, Wata, Beirut; tel. (1) 867560; telex 40728; Ambassador: GENNADY ILITCHEV.
**Saudi Arabia:** rue Bliss, Manara, Beirut; tel. (1) 804272; telex 20830; Ambassador: AHMAD IBN MAHMOUD MAHMOUD AL-KAHEIMI.
**Spain:** Palais Chehab, Hadath Antounie, 3039 Beirut; tel. (1) 464120; telex 44346; Ambassador: CARLOS BARCENA PORTOLES.
**Switzerland:** POB 2008, 9th Floor, Centre Debs, Kaflik, Beirut; tel. (1) 916279; telex 45585; Ambassador: GIANFREDERICO PEDOTTI.
**Tunisia:** Hazmieh, Mar-Takla, Beirut; tel. (1) 453481; telex 44429; Ambassador: MOHAMED HADI BELKHODJA.
**Turkey:** Beirut; tel. (1) 412080; telex 43331; Ambassador: AYDAN KARDAHAN.
**United Arab Emirates:** Immeuble Wafic Tanbara, Jnah, Beirut; tel. (1) 646117; Ambassador: MUHAMMAD ABDULLAH AMER EL-FILACI.
**United Kingdom:** POB 60180, Immeuble Coolrite, Tripoli Autostrade, Jal ed-Dib, Beirut; tel. (1) 417007; telex 44104; fax (1) 402032; Ambassador: MAEVE GERALDINE FORT.
**USA:** Aoucar, Beirut; tel. (1) 417774; Ambassador: MARK HAMBLEY.
**Uruguay:** Immeuble Mohamad Hussein Ben Moutahar, rue Verdun, Ain et-Tine, Beirut; tel. (1) 803620; telex 45280; Ambassador: MANUEL SOLSONA-FLORES.
**Venezuela:** POB 603, Immeuble Sahmarani, rue Kantari, Beirut; tel. (1) 372394; telex 44599; Ambassador: NELCEN VALERA.
**Yemen:** Bir Hassan, Beirut; tel. (1) 832688; Ambassador: ABDALLAH NASSER MOUTHANA.
**Yugoslavia:** Beirut; tel. 866552; Chargé d'affaires: ZORAN VEJNOVIĆ.
Note: Lebanon and Syria have very close relations but do not exchange formal ambassadors.

# Judicial System

Law and justice in Lebanon are administered in accordance with the following codes, which are based upon modern theories of civil and criminal legislation:

(1) Code de la Propriété (1930).
(2) Code des Obligations et des Contrats (1932).
(3) Code de Procédure Civile (1933).
(4) Code Maritime (1947).
(6) Code de Procédure Pénale (Code Ottoman Modifié).
(7) Code Pénal (1943).
(8) Code Pénal Militaire (1946).
(9) Code d'Instruction Criminelle.

The following courts are now established:

(a) Fifty-six **'Single-Judge Courts'**, each consisting of a single judge, and dealing in the first instance with both civil and criminal cases; there are seventeen such courts at Beirut and seven at Tripoli.

(b) Eleven **Courts of Appeal**, each consisting of three judges, including a President and a Public Prosecutor, and dealing with civil and criminal cases; there are five such courts at Beirut.

(c) Four **Courts of Cassation**, three dealing with civil and commercial cases and the fourth with criminal cases. A Court of Cassation, to be properly constituted, must have at least three judges, one being the President and the other two Councillors. The First Court consists of the First President of the Court of Cassation, a President and two Councillors. The other two civil courts each consist of a President and three Councillors. If the Court of Cassation reverses the judgment of a lower court, it does not refer the case back but retries it itself.

**First President of the Court of Cassation:** AMIN NASSAR.

(d) **The Council of State**, which deals with administrative cases. It consists of a President, Vice-President and four Councillors. A Commissioner represents the Government.

**President of the Court of the Council of State:** YOUSUF SAAVOLLAH EL-KHOURY.

(e) **The Court of Justice**, which is a special court consisting of a President and four judges, deals with matters affecting the security of the state.

In addition to the above, Islamic, Christian and Jewish religious courts deal with affairs of personal status (marriage, death, inheritance, etc.).

# Religion

The largest single religious community in Lebanon was formerly the Maronite Christians, a Uniate sect of the Roman Catholic Church. Estimates for 1983 assessed the sizes of communities as: Shi'a Muslims 1.2m., Maronites 900,000, Sunni Muslims 750,000, Greek Orthodox 250,000, Druzes 250,000, Armenians 175,000. The Maronites inhabited the old territory of Mount Lebanon, i.e. immediately east of Beirut. In the south, towards the Israeli frontier, Shi'a villages are most common, while between the Shi'a and the Maronites live the Druzes (divided between the Yazbakis and the Joumblatis). The Beka'a valley has many Greek Christians (both Roman Catholic and Orthodox), while the Tripoli area is mainly Sunni Muslim. Altogether, of all the regions of the Middle East, Lebanon probably presents the closest juxtaposition of sects and peoples within a small territory. As Lebanese political life has traditionally been organized on a sectarian basis, the Maronites have also enjoyed considerable political influence (disproportionate to their actual numbers, according to the other religious communities), including a predominant voice in the nomination of the President of the Republic.

## CHRISTIANITY
### The Roman Catholic Church

*Armenian Rite*

**Patriarchate of Cilicia:** Patriarcat Arménien Catholique, rue de l'Hôpital Libanais, Jeitawi, 2400 Beirut; tel. (1) 583520; f. 1742; established in Beirut since 1932; includes patriarchal diocese of Beirut, with an estimated 12,000 adherents (31 December 1993); Patriarch JEAN-PIERRE XVIII KASPARIAN; Vicar-Gen. Mgr ANDRÉ BEDOGLOUYAN, Titular Bishop of Comana.

*Chaldean Rite*

**Diocese of Beirut:** Evêché Chaldéen-Catholique, POB 373, Hazmieh, Beirut; tel. (1) 429088; 10,000 adherents (31 December 1993); Bishop of Beirut (vacant); Patriarchal Administrator Mgr LOUIS AD-DAIRANY.

*Latin Rite*

**Apostolic Vicariate of Beirut:** Vicariat Apostolique, POB 11–4224, Beirut; tel. (9) 909420; 20,000 adherents (31 December 1993); Vicar Apostolic PAUL BASSIM, Titular Bishop of Laodicea in Lebanon.

*Maronite Rite*

**Patriarchate of Antioch and all the East:** Patriarcat Maronite, Bkerké; tel. (9) 915441; telex 45140; fax (9) 938844; includes patriarchal diocese of Batrun, Jobbé and Sarba; Patriarch: Cardinal NASRALLAH PIERRE SFEIR. The Maronite Church in Lebanon comprises four archdioceses and six dioceses. In December 1993 there were an estimated 1,864,805 adherents in the country.

**Archbishop of Antélias:** Mgr JOSEPH MOHSEN BÉCHARA, Archevêché Maronite, Cornet-Chahouane (summer); POB 40700, Antélias, Beirut (winter); tel. (2) 925005 (summer), 410020 (winter).

**Archbishop of Beirut:** KHALIL ABINADER, Archevêché Maronite, rue Collège de la Sagesse, Beirut; tel. (1) 200234; fax (1) 424727; also representative of the Holy See for Roman Catholics of the Coptic Rite in Lebanon.

**Archbishop of Tripoli:** GABRIEL TOUBIA, Archevêché Maronite, rue al-Moutran, Karm Saddé, Tripoli; tel. (6) 624324.

**Archbishop of Tyre:** MAROUN SADER, Archevêché Maronite, Tyre; tel. (7) 740059.

In addition, the Bishop of Sidon, IBRAHIM EL-HÉLOU, has the personal title of Archbishop.

*Melkite Rite*

**Patriarchate of Antioch:** Patriarcat Grec-Melkite-Catholique, POB 50076, Beirut, or BP 22249, Damascus, Syria; tel. (Beirut) (1) 413111; jurisdiction over an estimated 1.5m. Melkites throughout the world; Patriarch of Antioch and all the East, of Alexandria and of Jerusalem MAXIMOS V HAKIM. The Melkite Church in Lebanon comprises seven archdioceses. At 31 December 1993 there were an estimated 339,225 adherents in the country.

**Archbishop of Baalbek:** CYRILLE SALIM BUSTROS, Archevêché Grec-Catholique, Baalbek; tel. 870200.

**Archbishop of Baniyas:** ANTOINE HAYEK, Archevêché de Panéas, Jdeidet Marjeyoun; tel. 770016.

**Archbishop of Beirut and Gibail:** HABIB BACHA, Archevêché Grec-Melkite-Catholique, Sabdeh-Firdaous, Beirut; tel. 880866.

**Archbishop of Sidon:** GEORGES KWAÏTER, Archevêché Grec-Melkite-Catholique, POB 247, rue el-Moutran, Sidon; tel. (7) 720100; fax (7) 722055.

**Archbishop of Tripoli:** ELIAS NIJMÉ, Archevêché Grec-Catholique, POB 72, Tripoli; tel. (6) 431602.

**Archbishop of Tyre:** JEAN ASSAAD HADDAD, Archevêché Grec-Melkite-Catholique, Tyre; tel. (7) 740015.

**Archbishop of Zahleh and Furzol:** ANDRÉ HADDAD, Archevêché Grec-Melkite-Catholique, Saidat en-Najat, Zahleh; tel. (8) 820540; fax (8) 806496.

# LEBANON

*Syrian Rite*

**Patriarchate of Antioch:** Patriarcat Syrien-Catholique, rue de Damas, POB 116–5087, Beirut; tel. (1) 381532; jurisdiction over about 150,000 Syrian Catholics in the Middle East; Patriarch IGNACE ANTOINE II HAYEK.

**Patriarchal Exarchate of Lebanon:** Vicariat Patriarcal Syrien, rue de Syrie, Beirut; tel. (1) 226725; 23,000 adherents (31 December 1993); Exarch Patriarchal (vacant).

### The Anglican Communion

Within the Episcopal Church in Jerusalem and the Middle East, Lebanon forms part of the diocese of Jerusalem (see the chapter on Israel).

### Other Christian Groups

**Armenian Apostolic Orthodox:** Armenian Catholicosate of Cilicia, Antélias, POB 70317, Beirut, Lebanon; tel. (1) 410001; f. 1441 in Cilicia (now in Turkey), transferred to Antélias, Lebanon, 1930; Leader His Holiness KAREKIN II (SARKISSIAN), Catholicos of Cilicia; jurisdiction over an estimated 1m. adherents in Lebanon, Syria, Cyprus, Kuwait, Greece, Iran, the United Arab Emirates, the USA and Canada.

**Greek Orthodox:** Leader His Beatitude IGNATIUS IV, Patriarch of Antioch and all the East, Patriarcat Grec-Orthodoxe, POB 9, Damascus, Syria.

**National Evangelical Synod of Syria and Lebanon:** POB 70890, Antélias, Beirut; tel. (1) 411100; 70,000 adherents (1987); Gen. Sec. Rev. Dr SALIM SAHIOUNY.

**Protestants:** Leader Rev. Habib Badr, Pres. of Nat. Evangelical Union of the Lebanon, POB 5224, rue Maurice Barrès, Beirut; tel. (1) 341285.

**Syrian Orthodox:** Leader IGNATIUS ZAKKA I IWAS, Patriarch of Antioch and all the East, Patriarcat Syrien Orthodoxe, Bab Toma, POB 22260, Damascus, Syria; tel. 432401; telex 411876; fax 432400.

**Union of the Armenian Evangelical Churches in the Near East:** POB 11-377, Beirut; tel. (1) 443547; fax (1) 582191; f. 1846 in Turkey; comprises about 30 Armenian Evangelical Churches in Syria, Lebanon, Egypt, Cyprus, Greece, Iran and Turkey; 7,500 mems (1990); Pres. Rev. HOVHANNES KARJIAN; Gen. Sec. Rev. KRIKOR YOUMSHAJEKIAN.

### ISLAM

**Shi'a Muslims:** Leader Imam SAYED MOUSSA AS-SADR (went missing in August 1978, while visiting Libya), President of the Supreme Islamic Council of the Shi'a Community of Lebanon, Dar al-Iftaa al-Jaafari, Beirut; Deputy Pres. Sheikh ABD AL-AMIR QABALAN.

**Sunni Muslims:** Leader SG Sheikh Dr MUHAMMAD RASHID QABBANI (acting), Grand Mufti of Lebanon, Dar el-Fatwa, Ilewi Rushed St, Beirut.

**Druzes:** Leader SG Sheikh MUHAMMAD ABOUCHACRA, Supreme Spiritual Leader of the Druze Community, rue Abou Chacra, Beirut.

**Alawites:** a schism of Shi'ite Islam; there are an estimated 50,000 Alawites in northern Lebanon, in and around Tripoli.

### JUDAISM

**Jews:** Leader CHAHOUD CHREIM, Beirut.

# The Press

The most important dailies are *Al-Anwar* and *An-Nahar*, which have the highest circulations, *Al-Jarida* and *L'Orient-Le Jour*, the foremost French paper. The latter two are owned by Georges Naccashe, former Lebanese Ambassador to France, and tend to take a pro-Government line. In a country where most of the élite speak French, the other French daily, *Le Soir*, is also influential, and, for the same reason, the twice-weekly publication *Le Commerce du Levant* occupies an important place in the periodical press.

Political upheavals hindered the operation of the press, but even at the height of the civil conflict about two dozen newspapers and magazines appeared, reflecting every shade of political opinion. In January 1977, however, censorship was imposed on all publications. Some papers ceased publication, if only temporarily. Before this, Lebanon enjoyed the reputation of having one of the freest presses in the Middle East and was an important base for foreign correspondents. Some Lebanese papers subsequently introduced London and Paris editions.

### DAILIES

**Al-Amal** (Hope): POB 959, rue Libérateur, Beirut; tel. (1) 382992; telex 22072; f. 1939; Arabic; organ of the Phalangist Party; Chief Editor ELIAS RABABI; circ. 35,000.

**Al-Anwar** (Lights): POB 1038, Beirut; tel. (1) 450933; telex 44224; f. 1959; Arabic; independent; supplement, Sunday, cultural and social; published by Dar Assayad SAL; Propr SAID FREIHA; Editor ISSAM FREIHA; circ. 75,200.

**Ararat:** POB 756, Nor Hagin, Beirut; f. 1937; Armenian; Communist; Editor KRIKOR HAJENIAN; circ. 5,000.

**Aztag:** POB 11–587, rue Selim Boustani, Beirut; tel. (1) 366607; f. 1927; Armenian; circ. 6,500.

**Al-Bairaq** (The Standard): POB 1800, rue Monot, Beirut; f. 1911; Arabic; published by Soc. Libanaise de Presse; Editor RAYMOND KAWASS; circ. 3,000.

**Bairut:** POB 7944, Beirut; f. 1952; Arabic.

**Ach-Chaab** (The People): POB 5140, Beirut; f. 1961; Arabic; Nationalist; Propr and Editor MUHAMMAD AMIN DUGHAN; circ. 7,000.

**Ach-Chams** (The Sun): POB 7047, Beirut; f. 1925; Arabic.

**Ach-Charq** (The East): POB 838, rue Verdun, Beirut; f. 1945; Arabic; Editor AOUNI AL-KAAKI.

**Ad-Diyar** (The Homeland): Immeuble Shawki Dagher, Hazmieh, Beirut; tel. (1) 427440; Arabic.

**Ad-Dunya** (The World): POB 4599, Beirut; f. 1943; Arabic; political; Chief Editor SULIMAN ABOU ZAID; circ. 25,000.

**Al-Hakika** (The Truth): Beirut; Arabic; published by Amal.

**Al-Hayat** (Life): POB 11–987, Immeuble Gargarian, rue Emil Eddé, Hamra, Beirut; tel. (1) 352674; telex 43415; fax (1) 866177; f. 1946; Arabic; independent; circ. 31,034.

**Al-Jarida** (The (News) Paper): POB 220, place Tabaris, Beirut; f. 1953; Arabic; independent; Editor ABDULLA SKAFF; circ. 22,600.

**Al-Jumhuriya** (The Republic): POB 7111, Beirut; f. 1924; Arabic.

**Journal al-Haddis:** POB 300, Jounieh; f. 1927; Arabic; political; Owner GEORGES ARÈGE-SAADÉ.

**Al-Khatib** (The Speaker): POB 365, rue Georges Picot, Beirut; Arabic.

**Al-Kifah al-Arabi** (The Arab Struggle): POB 5158–14, Immeuble Rouche-Shams, Beirut; f. 1974; Arabic; political, socialist, Pan-Arab; Publr and Chief Editor WALID HUSSEINI.

**Lisan ul-Hal** (The Organ): POB 4619, rue Châteaubriand, Beirut; f. 1877; Arabic; Editor GEBRAN HAYEK; circ. 33,000.

**Al-Liwa'** (The Standard): POB 2402, Beirut; tel. 865080; telex 43409; f. 1963; Arabic; Propr ABD AL-GHANI SALAM; Editor SALAH SALAM; circ. 79,000.

**An-Nahar** (The Day): POB 11–226, rue Banque du Liban, Hamra, Beirut; tel. (1) 340960; telex 22322; fax (1) 348448; f. 1933; Arabic; independent; Publr, Pres. GHASSAN TUENI; circ. 100,000.

**An-Nas** (The People): POB 4886, ave Fouad Chehab, Beirut; tel. (1) 308695; f. 1959; Arabic; Editor-in-Chief HASSAN YAGHI; circ. 22,000.

**An-Nida** (The Appeal): POB 4744, Beirut; f. 1959; Arabic; published by the Lebanese Communist Party; Editor KARIM MROUÉ; circ. 10,000.

**Nida' al-Watan** (Call of the Homeland): POB 6324, Beirut; f. 1937; Arabic.

**An-Nidal** (The Struggle): POB 1354, Beirut; f. 1939; Arabic.

**L'Orient-Le Jour:** POB 166495, rue Banque du Liban, Beirut; tel. (1) 340560; telex 42590; f. 1942; French; independent; Chair. MICHEL EDDÉ; Dir CAMILLE MENASSA; Editorial Dir AMINE ABOU-KHALED; Editor ISSA GORAÏEB; circ. 23,000.

**Raqib al-Ahwal** (The Observer): POB 467, rue Patriarche Hoyek, Beirut; f. 1937; Arabic; Editor SIMA'N FARAH SEIF.

**Rayah** (Banner): POB 4101, Beirut; Arabic.

**Le Réveil:** POB 8383, blvd Sinn el-Fil, Beirut; f. 1977; French; Editor-in-Chief JEAN SHAMI; Dir RAYMOND DAOU; circ. 10,000.

**Ar-Ruwwad:** POB 2696, rue Mokhalsieh, Beirut; f. 1940; Arabic; Editor BESHARA MAROUN.

**Sada Lubnan** (Echo of Lebanon): POB 7884, Beirut; f. 1951; Arabic; Lebanese Pan-Arab; Editor MUHAMMAD BAALBAKI; circ. 25,000.

**As-Safeer** (The Ambassador): POB 113-5015, rue Mnaimneh, Beirut; tel. (1) 802520; telex 21484; Arabic; Editor-in-Chief TALAL SALMAN.

**Sawt al-Uruba** (The Voice of Europe): POB 3537, Beirut; f. 1959; Arabic; organ of the An-Najjadé Party; Editor ADNANE AL-HAKIM.

**Le Soir:** POB 1470, rue de Syrie, Beirut; f. 1947; French; independent; Dir DIKRAN TOSBATH; Editor ANDRÉ KECATI; circ. 16,500.

**At-Tayyar** (The Current): POB 1038, Beirut; Arabic; independent; circ. 75,000.

**Telegraf—Bairut:** POB 1061, rue Béchara el-Khoury, Beirut; f. 1930; Arabic; political, economic and social; Editor TOUFIC ASSAD MATNI; circ. 15,500 (5,000 outside Lebanon).

# LEBANON

**Al-Yaum** (Today): POB 1908, Beirut; f. 1937; Arabic; Editor WAFIC MUHAMMAD CHAKER AT-TIBY.

**Az-Zamane:** POB 6060, rue Boutros Karameh, Beirut; f. 1947; Arabic.

**Zartonk:** POB 617, rue Nahr Ibrahim, Beirut; tel. (1) 226611; fax (1) 448982; f. 1937; Armenian; official organ of Armenian Liberal Democratic Party; Man. Editor BAROUYR H. AGHBASHIAN.

## WEEKLIES

**Al-Alam al-Lubnani** (The Lebanese World): POB 462, Ministry of Foreign Affairs, Beirut; f. 1964; Arabic, English, Spanish, French; politics, literature and social economy; Editor-in-Chief FAYEK KHOURY; Gen. Editor CHEIKH FADI GEMAYEL; circ. 45,000.

**Achabaka** (Network): POB 1038, Dar Assayad, Beirut; f. 1956; Arabic; society and features; Founder SAID FREIHA; Editor GEORGE IBRAHIM EL-KHOURY; circ. 126,500.

**Al-Ahad** (Sunday): POB 1462, rue Andalouss, Chourah, Beirut; Arabic; political; organ of Hezbollah (the Party of God); Editor RIAD TAHA; circ. 32,000.

**Al-Akhbar** (The News): Beirut; f. 1954; Arabic; published by the Lebanese Communist Party; circ. 21,000.

**Al-Anwar Supplement:** POB 1038, Beirut; cultural-social; every Sunday; supplement to daily *Al-Anwar*; Editor ISSAM FREIHA; circ. 90,000.

**Argus:** Bureau of Lebanese and Arab Documentation, POB 16–5403, Beirut; tel. (1) 219113; Arabic, French and English; economic bulletin; circ. 1,000.

**Assayad** (The Hunter): POB 1038, Dar Assayad, Beirut; f. 1943; news magazine; Propr SAID FREIHA; Editor RAFIQUE KHOURY; circ. 94,700.

**Le Commerce du Levant:** POB 687, Immeuble de Commerce et Financement, rue Kantari, Beirut; tel. (1) 297770; f. 1929; weekly and special issue quarterly; French; commercial and financial; Editor: Société de la Presse Economique; Pres. MAROUN AKL; circ. 15,000.

**Dabbour:** POB 5723, place du Musée, Beirut; f. 1922; Arabic; Editors MICHEL RICHARD and FUAD MUKARZEL; circ. 12,000.

**Ad-Dyar:** POB 959, Immeuble Bellevue, rue Verdun, Beirut; f. 1941; Arabic; political; circ. 46,000.

**Al-Hadaf** (The Target): POB 212, Immeuble Esseilé, rue Béchir, Beirut; f. 1969; tel. (1) 420554; organ of Popular Front for the Liberation of Palestine (PFLP); Arabic; Editor-in-Chief SABER MOHI ED-DIN; circ. 40,000.

**Al-Hawadess** (Events): POB 1281, rue Clémenceau, Beirut; published from London (183–185 Askew Rd, W12 9AX; tel. 081-740 4500; telex 261601; fax 081-749 9781); f. 1911; Arabic; news; Editor-in-Chief MELHIM KAVAM; circ. 120,000.

**Al-Hurriya** (Freedom): POB 857, Beirut; f. 1960; Arabic; voice of the Democratic Front for the Liberation of Palestine (DFLP) and the Organization for Communist Action in Lebanon (OCAL) 1969–81, of DFLP 1981–; Editor DAOUD TALHAME; circ. 30,000.

**Al-Iza'a** (Broadcasting): POB 462, rue Selim Jazaerly, Beirut; f. 1938; Arabic; politics, art, literature and broadcasting; Editor FAYEK KHOURY; circ. 11,000.

**Al-Jumhur** (The Public): POB 1834, Moussaitbé, Beirut; telex 21541; f. 1936; Arabic; illustrated weekly news magazine; Editor FARID ABU SHAHLA; circ. 45,000, of which over 20,000 outside Lebanon.

**Kul Shay'** (Everything): POB 3250, rue Béchara el-Khoury, Beirut; Arabic.

**Al-Liwa'** (The Standard): POB 11-2402, Immeuble Saradar, ave de l'Indépendence, Beirut; tel. (1) 865050; telex 43409; fax (1) 644761; Arabic; Editor-in-Chief SALAH SALAM; Propr ABD AL-GHANI SALAAM.

**Magazine:** POB 1404, rue Sursock, Beirut; tel. (1) 202070; telex 41362; fax (1) 202070; f. 1956; French; political and social; published by Les Editions Orientales SAL; Pres. and Editor-in-Chief CHARLES ABOU ADAL; circ. 18,000.

**Massis:** c/o Patriarcat Arménien Catholique, rue de l'Hôpital Grec Orthodoxe, Jeitawi, 2400 Beirut; Armenian; Catholic; Editor Father ANTRANIK GRANIAN; circ. 2,500.

**Middle East Economic Survey:** Middle East Petroleum and Economic Publications (Cyprus), POB 4940, Nicosia, Cyprus; tel. (2) 445431; telex 2198; fax (2) 474988; f. 1957 (in Beirut); review and analysis of petroleum, finance and banking sectors, and of political developments; Publr BASIM W. ITAYIM; Editor IAN SEYMOUR.

**Al-Moharrir** (The Liberator): POB 5366, Beirut; f. 1962; Arabic; circ. 87,000; Gen. Man. WALID ABOU ZAHR.

**Al-Ousbou' al-Arabi** (Arab Week): POB 1404, rue Sursock, Beirut; f. 1959; tel. (1) 202070; telex 41362; fax (1) 202070; Arabic; political and social; Publrs Les Editions Orientales, SAL; Gen. Man. CHARLES ABOU ADAL; circ. 88,407 (circulates throughout the Arab World).

**Ar-Rassed:** POB 11–2808, Beirut; Arabic; Editor GEORGE RAJJI.

**Revue du Liban:** POB 165612, rue Issa Maalouf, Beirut; tel. (1) 339960; telex 20303; f. 1928; French; political, social, cultural; Publr MELHEM KARAM; Gen. Man. MICHEL MISK; circ. 22,000.

**Sabah al-Khair** (Good Morning): Beirut; Arabic; published by the Syrian Nationalist Party.

**Sahar:** POB 1038, Beirut; telex 22632; Arabic.

**Samar** (Conversation): POB 1038, Beirut; Arabic; photorama magazine; circ. 50,000.

**Ash-Shira'** (The Sail): POB 13-5250, Beirut; tel. (1) 862556; telex 42073; fax (1) 866050; Arabic; Editor HASSAN SABRA; circ. 40,000.

## OTHER SELECTED PERIODICALS

**Alam at-Tijarat** (Business World): Immeuble Strand, rue Hamra, Beirut; f. 1965 in association with Johnston International Publishing Corpn, New York; monthly; commercial; Editor NADIM MAKDISI; international circ. 17,500.

**Arab Construction World:** POB 13–5121, Chouran, Beirut; tel. (1) 352413; fax (1) 352419; f. 1985; every two months; published by Chatila Publishing House; Editor-in-Chief FAITH CHATICA; circ. 10,104.

**Arab Defense Journal:** POB 1038, Beirut; tel. (1) 452700; monthly; published by Dar Assayad SAL.

**Arab Economist:** POB 11–6068, Beirut; telex 21071; monthly; published by Centre for Economic, Financial and Social Research and Documentation SAL; Chair. Dr CHAFIC AKHRAS.

**Arab Health:** POB 13–5121, Chouran, Beirut; tel. (1) 352413; fax (1) 352419; f. 1985; quarterly; published by Chatila Publishing House; Editor-in-Chief FAITH CHATICA; circ. 12,959.

**The Arab World:** POB 567, Jounieh; tel. (09) 935096; f. 1985; 24 a year; published by Dar Naaman lith Thaqafa; Editor NAJI NAAMAN.

**Fairuz:** POB 1038, Hazmieh, Beirut; tel. (1) 452700; telex 444224; fax (1) 429884; f. 1982; monthly; Arabic; for women; published by Dar Assayad SAL; international circ. 84,000.

**Fikr** (Idea): monthly; Arabic; published by the Syrian Nationalist Party.

**Al-Idari** (The Manager): POB 918-1038, Beirut; tel. (1) 452700; telex 44224; fax (1) 452957; f. 1975; monthly; Arabic; business management and public administration; published by Dar Assayad International; Pres. and Gen. Man. BASSAM FREIHA; Chief Editor HASSAN EL-KHOURY; circ. 25,819.

**International Crude Oil and Product Prices:** Middle East Petroleum and Economic Publications (Cyprus), POB 4940, Nicosia, Cyprus; tel. (2) 445431; telex 2198; fax (2) 474988; f. 1971 (in Beirut); 2 a year; review and analysis of oil price trends in world markets; Publisher BASIM W. ITAYIM.

**Al-Intilak** (Outbreak): c/o Michel Nehme, Al-Intilak Printing and Publishing House, POB 4958, Beirut; f. 1960; monthly; Arabic; literary; Chief Editor MICHEL NEHME.

**Al-Khalij Business Magazine:** POB 11-8440, Beirut; tel. (1) 811149; telex 20680; fmrly based in Kuwait; every two months; Arabic; Editor-in-Chief ZULFICAR KOBFISSI; circ. 16,325.

**Lebanese and Arab Economy:** POB 11–1801, Sanayeh, Beirut; tel. (1) 349530; telex 42241; fax (1) 865802; f. 1951; monthly; Arabic, English and French; Publr Beirut Chamber of Commerce and Industry.

**Majallat al-Iza'at al-Lubnaniat** (Lebanese Broadcasting Magazine): Radio Lebanon, Ministry of Information, Sanayeh, Beirut; tel. (1) 863016; telex 20786; f. 1959; monthly; Arabic; broadcasting affairs.

**Al-Mouktataf** (The Selection): POB 11–1462, rue Andalous, Chouran, Beirut; monthly; Arabic; general.

**Qitâboul A'lamil A'rabi** (The Arab World Book): POB 567, Jounieh; tel. (9) 935096; f. 1991; 6 a year; Arabic; published by Dar Naaman lith Thaqafa; Editor NAJI NAAMAN.

**Rijal al-Amal** (Businessmen): POB 6065, Beirut; f. 1966; monthly; Arabic; business; Publr and Editor-in-Chief MAHIBA AL-MALKI; circ. 16,250.

**As-Sahafa wal I'lam** (Press and Information): POB 567, Jounieh; tel. (9) 935096; f. 1987; 12 a year; Arabic; published by Dar Naaman lith Thaqafa; Editor NAJI NAAMAN.

**Siyassa was Strategia** (Politics and Strategy): POB 567, Jounieh; tel. (9) 935096; f. 1981; 36 a year; Arabic; published by Dar Naaman lith Thaqafa; Editor NAJI NAAMAN.

**Tabibok** (Your Doctor): POB 90434, Beirut; tel. (11) 2212980; fax (11) 3711316; f. 1956; monthly; Arabic; medical, social, scientific; Editor Dr SAMI KABBANI; circ. 90,000.

# LEBANON

**At-Tarik** (The Road): Beirut; monthly; Arabic; cultural and theoretical; published by the Lebanese Communist Party; circ. 5,000.

**Welcome to Lebanon and the Middle East:** POB 4204, Centre Starco, Beirut; f. 1959; monthly; English; on entertainment, touring and travel; Editor SOUHAIL TOUFIK ABOU-JAMRA; circ. 6,000.

## NEWS AGENCIES

### Foreign Bureaux

**Agence France-Presse (AFP):** POB 4868, Immeuble Najjar, rue de Rome, Beirut; tel. (1) 347460; telex 20819; fax (1) 350318; Dir M. GAY-PARA; POB 166827, Immeuble Georges Massoud, rue d'Athènes, Achrafiye, east Beirut; tel. (1) 422445; telex 44279.

**Agenzia Nazionale Stampa Associata (ANSA)** (Italy): POB 1525, 2nd Floor, Immeuble Safieddine, rue Rashid Karame, Beirut; tel. (1) 810155; telex 20539; fax (1) 810201; cellular tel. 001212-4783734; Correspondent VITTORIO FRENQUELLUCCI.

**Allgemeiner Deutscher Nachrichtendienst (ADN)** (Germany): POB 114–5100, Immeuble Bitar-Rawas, Ramat el-Beida, Beirut; Correspondent HARALD DITTMAR.

**Associated Press (AP)** (USA): POB 3780, Immeuble Commodore, rue Ne' Meh Yafet, Beirut; tel. (1) 352310; telex 20636; Chief Middle East Correspondent (vacant).

**Informatsionnoye Telegrafnoye Agentstvo Rossii—Telegrafnoye Agentstvo Suverennykh Stran (ITAR—TASS)** (Russia): c/o Russian Embassy, Beirut; tel. (1) 813428; Chief ANATOLY M. GOLOVASTOV.

**Kyodo Tsushin** (Japan): POB 13-5060, Immeuble Makarem, rue Makdessi, Ras Beirut; tel. (1) 863861; telex 21203; Correspondent IBRAHIM KHOURY.

**Middle East News Agency (MENA)** (Egypt): POB 2268, 72 rue al-Geish, Beirut.

**Reuters** (United Kingdom): 5th Floor, Immeuble Union Nationale, Sanayeh, Beirut; Bureau Chief SAMIR SALAMEH.

**United Press International (UPI)** (USA): Immeuble An-Nahar, Hamra, Beirut; telex 20724; Bureau Man. RIAD KAJ.

**Xinhua (New China) News Agency** (People's Republic of China): POB 114-5075, Beirut; tel. (1) 830359; telex 21313.

BTA (Bulgaria), INA (Iraq), JANA (Libya) and Prensa Latina (Cuba) are also represented in Lebanon.

### PRESS ASSOCIATION

**Lebanese Press Syndicate:** POB 3084, Immeuble Press Order, ave Saeb Salam, Beirut; tel. (1) 865519; f. 1911; 18 mems; Pres. MUHAMMAD AL-BAALBAKI; Vice-Pres. FADEL SAID AKL; Sec. BASSEM AS-SABEH.

## Publishers

**Chatila Publishing House:** POB 13–5121, Chouran, Beirut; tel. (1) 352413; fax (1) 352419; publishes *Arab Health* (quarterly), *Arab Construction World* (every two months).

**Dar al-Adab:** POB 11-4123, Beirut; tel. and fax (1) 861633; f. 1953; literary and general; Man. RANA IDRISS.

**Dar Assayad SAL:** POB 1038, Hazmieh, Beirut; tel. (1) 450933; telex 44224; fax (1) 452957; f. 1943; publishes in Arabic *Al-Anwar* (daily, plus weekly supplement), *Assayad* (weekly), *Achabaka* (weekly), *Background Reports* (three a month), *Arab Defense Journal* (monthly), *Al-Idari* (monthly), *Fairuz* (monthly), *Computers* (monthly), *Al-Fares* (monthly), *Middle East Observer* (quarterly); has offices and correspondents in Arab countries and most parts of the world; Chair. ISSAM FREIHA; Pres. and Man. Dir BASSAM FREIHA.

**Arab Institute for Research and Publishing** (Al-Mouasasah al-Arabiyah Lildirasat Walnashr): POB 11–5460, Tour Carlton, Saqiat el-Janzeer, Beirut; tel. (1) 807900; telex 40067; fax (1) 685501; f. 1969; Dir. MAHER KAYYALI; works in Arabic and English.

**Editions Orientales SAL:** POB 1404, Immeuble Sayegh, rue Sursock, Beirut; tel. and fax (1) 202070; telex 41362; political and social newspapers and magazines; Pres. GEORGES ABOU ADAL; Gen. Man. and Editor-in-Chief CHARLES ABOU ADAL.

**Dar al-I'lam Lilmalayin:** POB 1085, rue Bitar, Mar Elias, Beirut; tel. (1) 863474; telex 23166; fax (1) 825272; f. 1945; dictionaries, encyclopaedias, reference books, textbooks, Islamic cultural books; Editorial Dir Dr ROHI BAALBAKI.

**Institute for Palestine Studies, Publishing and Research Organization:** POB 11–7164, rue Nsouli-Verdun, Beirut; tel. and fax (1) 868387; telex 23317; f. 1963; independent non-profit Arab research organization; to promote better understanding of the Palestine problem and the Arab–Israeli conflict; publishes books, reprints research papers, etc.; Chair. Dr HISHAM NASHABE; Exec. Sec. Prof. WALID KHALIDI.

**The International Documentary Center of Arab Manuscripts:** POB 2668, Immeuble Hanna, Ras Beirut, Beirut; f. 1965; publishes and reproduces ancient and rare Arabic texts; Propr ZOUHAIR BAALBAKI.

**Dar al-Kashaf:** POB 112091, rue A. Malhamee, Beirut; tel. (1) 815527; f. 1930; publishers of *Al-Kashaf* (Arab Youth Magazine), maps and atlases; printers and distributors; Propr M. A. FATHALLAH.

**Khayat Book and Publishing Co SAL:** 90–94 rue Bliss, Beirut; Middle East, Islam, oil, Arab publications and reprints; Man. Dir PAUL KHAYAT.

**Librairie du Liban:** POB 945, place Riad Solh, Beirut; tel. (9) 900805; telex 21037; fax (via New York, USA) 001-212-4782860; f. 1944; fiction, children's books, dictionaries, Middle East, travel, Islam; Proprs KHALIL and GEORGE SAYEGH.

**Dar al-Maaref Liban SAL:** POB 2320, Immeuble Esseilé, place Riad Solh, Beirut; f. 1959; children's books and textbooks in Arabic; Gen. Man. JOSEPH NASHOU.

**Dar al-Machreq SARL:** c/o Librairie orientale, POB 946, Beirut; tel. (1) 202423; telex 42733; fax (1) 200297; f. 1848; religion, art, Arabic and Islamic literature, history, languages, science, philosophy, school books, dictionaries and periodicals; Man. Dir CAMILLE HÉCHAIMÉ.

**Dar Naaman lith-Thaqafa:** POB 567, Jounieh; tel. (09) 935096; f. 1979; publishes *Encyclopedia of Contemporary Arab World,Qitāboul A'lamil A'rabi, Siyassa was Strategia, As-Sahafa wal I'lam* in Arabic and *The Arab World* in English; Propr NAJI NAAMAN; Exec. Man. MARCELLE AL-ASHKAR.

**Dar an-Nahar SAL:** POB 55-454, rue Zahret el-Ihsan, Achrafiyé, Beirut; f. 1967; tel. (1) 335530; telex 22322; a Pan-Arab publishing house; Pres. GHASSAN TUENI.

**Naufal Group:** POB 11-2161, Immeuble Naufal, rue Mamari, Beirut; tel. (1) 354394; telex 22210; f. 1970; subsidiary cos Macdonald Middle East Sarl, Les Editions Arabes; encyclopaedias, fiction, children's books, history, law and literature; Man. Dir. SAMI NAUFAL.

**Rihani Printing and Publishing House:** rue Jibb en-Nakhl, Beirut; f. 1963; Propr ALBERT RIHANI; Man. DAOUD STEPHAN.

**Dar as-Safir:** POB 113-5015, Immeuble As-Safir, rue Monimina, Hamra, Beirut; tel. (1) 802444; telex 21484; fax (1) 861806; f. 1974.

## Radio and Television

In 1992, according to UNESCO, there were an estimated 2,370,000 radio receivers and 920,000 television receivers in use.

### RADIO

**Radio Lebanon:** rue Arts et Métiers, Beirut; part of the Ministry of Information; tel. (1) 346880; telex 29786; f. 1937; Dir-Gen. QASSEM HAGE ALI; Technical Dir LOUIS RIZK; Dir of Programmes NIZAR MIKATI; Head of Administration A. AOUN.

The Home Service broadcasts in Arabic on short wave, and the Foreign Service broadcasts in Portuguese, Armenian, Arabic, Spanish, French and English.

### TELEVISION

**Lebanese Broadcasting Corporation International:** POB 111, Jounieh; tel. (9) 938938; telex 45949; fax (1) 937916; f. Aug. 1985 by the 'Lebanese Forces' Christian militia; programmes in Arabic, French and English on two channels; Chair. and CEO PIERRE EDDAHER.

**Télé-Liban (TL) SAL:** POB 11-5054, Beirut; tel. (1) 450100; telex 20923; f. 1959; commercial service; programmes in Arabic, French and English on three channels, and relays on three channels; Chair. and Dir-Gen. GEORGES SKAFF; Deputy Dir-Gen MUHAMMAD S. KARIMEH.

**Télé-Management SARL:** POB 113–5310, Beirut; tel. (1) 353510; telex 40529; f. 1972; exclusive airtime sales and programmes sales contractor to Télé-Liban SAL (channels 5, 7 and 9); Gen. Man. CLAUDE SAWAYA.

There are 50 'private' television and more than 100 'private' radio stations, usually of a sectarian nature.

## Finance

(cap. = capital; auth. = authorized; dep. = deposits; m. = million; £L = Lebanese £; res = reserves; brs = branches)

### BANKING

Beirut was, for many years, the leading financial and commercial centre in the Middle East, but this role was destroyed by the civil

# LEBANON

conflict. The technological revolution which has taken place in the banking sector worldwide in recent years means that the Government's ambition to regain this role is unlikely to be realized. At the end of 1994 there were 52 Lebanese banks, 14 subsidiaries and 12 foreign banks operating through a network of more than 590 branches. New banking and investment legislation required all Lebanese banks to meet the Bank for International Settlements' capital-asset ratio of 8% by February 1995.

## Central Bank

**Banque du Liban:** POB 11-5544, rue Masraf Loubnane, Beirut; tel. (1) 341230; telex 20744; fax (1) 782740; f. 1964 to take over the banking activities of the Banque de Syrie et du Liban in Lebanon; cap £L15m., total assets £L355,957m. (Dec. 1991); Gov. RIAD SALAMEH.

## Principal Commercial Banks

**Adcom Bank SAL:** POB 11-2431, Immeuble Ammar, rue Verdun, Beirut; tel. (1) 860160; telex 20884; f. 1960 as Advances and Commerce Bank; cap. £L50m., dep. £L19,600.9m. (Dec. 1990); Chair. and Gen. Man. HENRI R. SFEIR.

**Allied Business Bank:** POB 113, Immeuble Diab, rue Makdissi, 7165 Beirut; tel. (1) 864551; telex 21708; fax (1) 372711; f. 1982; cap. £L1,000m., dep. £L99,911.5m., res £L1,007.2m., total assets £L119,710.8m. (Dec. 1992); Chair. ABDULLAH S. ZAKHEM.

**Al Moughtareb Bank SAL:** POB 11-5508, Immeuble Sehnaoui, rue Banque du Liban, Beirut; tel. (1) 350060; telex 22106; fax (1) 602009; f. 1974; cap. £L4,000m., dep. £L36,166.8m., total assets £L42,176.8m. (Dec. 1993); Chair. HANI SAFI ED-DINE.

**Bank of Beirut and the Arab Countries SAL:** POB 11-1536, Immeuble de la Banque, 250 rue Clémenceau, Beirut; tel. (1) 867142; telex 20761; f. 1956; cap. £L15,000m. (Dec. 1993); Chair. and Gen. Man. TOUFIC S. ASSAF.

**Bank of Kuwait and the Arab World SAL:** Immeuble Intra Investment Co, rue Omar Ben Abd al-Aziz, Hamra, Beirut; tel. (1) 293890; telex 21524; f. 1959; cap. £L95m., res £L13.2m., dep. £L11,307.1m. (Dec. 1989); Chair. and Gen. Man. Dr AHMAD HAGE.

**Bank of Lebanon and Kuwait SAL:** POB 11-5556, Immeuble al-Hoss, rue Emile Eddé, Hamra, Beirut; tel. (1) 340270; telex 23013; fax (1) 340270; f. 1964; cap. £L150m., res £L10.5m., dep. £L8,093.8m. (Dec. 1989); Chair. Sheikh ALI SABAH-AS SALEM AS-SABAH; Gen. Man. T. SHWAYRI.

**Bank al-Madina SAL:** POB 113-7221, Immeuble Banque al-Madina, rue Commodore, Beirut; tel. (1) 351296; telex 23105; fax (1) 348305; f. 1982; cap. £L60m., res £L22.7m., dep. £L65,877m. (Dec. 1992); Chair. and Gen. Man. IBRAHIM ABOU AYASH.

**Banque Audi SAL:** POB 11-2560, ave Charles Malek, St Nicolas, Beirut; tel. (1) 331600; telex 43012; fax (1) 200955; f. 1962; cap. £L25,454m. (Dec. 1993); Chair. and Gen. Man. GEORGES W. AUDI; 22 brs.

**Banque de la Beka'a SAL:** POB 117, Centre Fakhoury, Zahleh; tel. (8) 803099; telex 21214; fax (8) 803217; f. 1965; cap. £L1,400m., dep. £L287,926m. (April 1992); Pres. and Gen. Man. CHAOUKI W. FAKHOURY.

**Banque Beyrouth pour le Commerce SAL:** POB 11-0216, Immeuble de la Banque Arabe, rue des Banques, Place Riad Solh, Beirut; tel. (1) 867459; telex 21457; fax (1) 865073; f. 1961; cap. £L6,000m., dep. £L316,746m., total assets £L324,407m. (Dec. 1993); Chair. and Gen. Man. RIFAAT EN-NIMR.

**Banque de Crédit National SAL:** Centre Moucarri, Autostrade Dora, Beirut; tel. (1) 582345; telex 42093; fax (1) 4782387; f. 1920 as Banque Jacob E. Safra, name changed 1959; cap. £L100m., dep. £L7,151.7m., res £L291.9m., total assets £L7,543.6m. (Dec. 1993); Chair. and Gen. Man. EDMOND J. SAFRA.

**Banque du Crédit Populaire SAL:** POB 11-5292, Immeuble Al-Ittihadia, ave Charles Malek, St Nicolas, Beirut; tel. (1) 200352; telex 40123; fax (1) 334102; f. 1963; cap. £L100m., res £L305.2m., dep. £L19,846.5m. (Dec. 1992); Chair. and Gen. Man. NEDIM B. DEMESHKIEH; 7 brs.

**Banque de l'Essor Economique Libanais SAL:** POB 80938, Centre Moucarri, Autostrade Dora, Beirut; tel. and fax (1) 582420; telex 42887; cap. £L2,000m., dep. £L5,075m. (Dec. 1992); Chair. and Gen. Man. IMAD M. JAFFAL; 7 brs.

**Banque de l'Industrie et du Travail SAL:** POB 11-3948, Immeuble BIT, rue Riad Solh, Beirut; tel. (1) 646894; telex 20698; fax (1) 602806; f. 1960; cap. £L500m., dep. £L72,000m., total assets £L107,808m. (Dec. 1992); Chair. and Gen. Man. Sheikh FOUAD JAMIL EL-KHAZEN; Man. Dir NABIL N. KHAIRALLAH; 11 brs in Lebanon.

**Banque Joseph Lati et Fils SAL:** Immeuble Dr Elie Karam, ave de l'Indépendance, Achrafiyé, Beirut; tel. (1) 336316; telex 21702; f. 1924; cap. £L30m., dep. £L3,129.1m. (Dec. 1989); Chair. and Gen. Man. ISAAC LATI.

**Banque du Liban et d'Outre-Mer SAL:** POB 11-1912, Centre Daher, rue Omar Ben Abd al-Aziz, Hamra, Beirut; tel. (1) 346290; telex 22483; fax (1) 602247; f. 1951; cap. £L36,000m. (Dec. 1994); Chair. and Gen. Man. Dr NAAMAN AZHARI; 30 brs in Lebanon.

**Banque Libanaise pour le Commerce SAL:** POB 11-1126, rue Riad Solh, Beirut; tel. (1) 445450; telex 42650; fax (1) 581927; f. 1950; cap. £L80m., dep. £L129,671.8m., res £L13,098.8m., total assets £L160,863.8m. (Dec. 1991); Chair. and Gen. Man. JEAN F. S. ABOUJAOUDE; 32 brs.

**Banque Libano-Française SAL:** POB 11-808, Immeuble Sehnaoui, rue Riad Solh, Beirut; tel. (1) 200420; telex 42317; fax (1) 337262; f. 1968; cap. £L20,000m. (Dec. 1993); Chair. FARID RAPHAEL.

**Banque de la Méditerranée SAL:** POB 11-348, rue Verdun, Ain et-Tine, Beirut; tel. (1) 866925; telex 20826; fax (1) 4782462; f. 1944; cap. £L23,434m. (Dec. 1993); Chair. and Gen. Man. Dr MUSTAPHA H. RAZIAN.

**Banque Misr-Liban SAL:** POB 11-7, rue Riad Solh, Beirut; tel. (1) 301575; telex 20537; fax (1) 868490; f. 1929; cap. £L6,000m., dep. £L112,262.2m., res £L11,971.5m. (Dec. 1993); Chair. ESSAM ED-DINE EL-AHMADI; 14 brs.

**Banque Saradar SAL:** POB 11-1121, Immeuble Saradar, Rabyé, Beirut; tel. (1) 416804; telex 41806; fax (1) 404490; f. 1948 as Banque Marius Saradar, name changed 1956; cap. £L5,000m., dep. £L355,115.8m. (Dec. 1993); Chair. and Gen. Man. MARIO JOE SARADAR; 6 brs.

**Beirut-Riyad Bank SAL:** POB 11-4668, Immeuble de la Banque Beirut-Riyad, rue Riad Solh, Beirut; tel. (1) 867360; telex 20610; f. 1959; cap. £L14,400m. (Dec. 1993); Pres. and Gen. Man. HUSSEIN MANSOUR; Dep. Chair. and Man. Dir ANWAR M. EL-KHALIL; 11 brs.

**Byblos Bank SAL:** POB 11-5605, Centre Commercial Aya, Beirut; tel. (1) 898200; telex 41601; fax (1) 898209; f. 1959; cap. £L51,759m., dep. £L1,055,668m., total assets £L1,228,551m. (Dec. 1994); Chair. and Gen. Man. Dr FRANÇOIS SEMAAN BASSIL; 27 brs.

**Crédit Commercial du Moyen-Orient SAL:** POB 11-8271, Centre Bahri, Place Sassine, Beirut; tel. (1) 216640; fax (1) 601957; cap. £L1,000m., res £L3,356.2m., dep. £L160,539.2m. (Dec. 1993); Chair. Dr GEORGES ACHI.

**Crédit Libanais SAL:** POB 166729, Centre Sofil, ave Charles Malek, Beirut; tel. (1) 200028; telex 40706; fax (1) 602615; f. 1961; cap. £L80,000m. (Dec. 1993); Chair. and Gen. Man. Dr JOSEPH M. TORBEY; 43 brs.

**Federal Bank of Lebanon SAL:** POB 11-2209, Immeuble Antoine Gebara, Dora, Beirut; tel. (1) 896183; telex 42307; fax (1) 268711; f. 1952; cap. £L10m., dep. £L29,995m. (Dec. 1993); Pres. and Chair. MICHEL A. SAAB; 7 brs.

**First Phoenician Bank SAL:** POB 90-1160, Centre Montelibano, New Jdeideh, Beirut; tel. (1) 887779; telex 43571; fax (1) 897078; f. 1958; fmrly First National Bank of Chicago (Lebanon) SAL, wholly-owned subsidiary of First National Bank of Chicago, USA, sold Dec. 1982; cap. £L5m., dep. £L3,019.2m. (Dec. 1991); Pres. and Chair. GEORGES M. HATEM.

**Fransabank SAL:** POB 11-0393, Centre Sabbag, rue Hamra, Hamra, Beirut; tel. (1) 340180; telex 20631; fax (1) 354572; f. 1978 as merger of Banque Sabbag and Banque Française pour le Moyen Orient SAL; cap £L8,800m., res £L6,077.4m., dep. £L650,205.5m. (Dec. 1992); Chair. ADNAN KASSAR; Dep. Chair. ADEL KASSAR; 33 brs.

**Housing Bank:** Beirut; f. 1995; cap. US $50m.

**Intercontinental Bank of Lebanon SAL:** POB 90263, Immeuble Ghantous, Beirut; tel. (1) 883464; telex 43467; fax (1) 483119; f. 1961; cap. £L8m., res £L567.2m. (Dec. 1993); Chair. and Gen. Man. FADY GEORGES AMATOURY.

**Jammal Trust Bank SAL:** POB 11-5640, Immeuble Jammal, rue Verdun, Beirut; tel. (1) 800360; telex 20959; fax (1) 864171; f. 1963 as Investment Bank, SAL; cap. £L200m., dep. £L20,705.3m. (Dec. 1989); Chair. and Gen. Man. ALI A. JAMMAL; 17 brs.

**Lebanese Swiss Bank SAL:** POB 11-9552, 57 rue Riad Solh, Beirut; tel. (1) 221720; telex 21072; fax (1) 893497; f. 1973; cap. £L3,000m., res £L1,633m. (Dec. 1993); Chair. and Gen. Man. Dr TANAL SABBAH; 3 brs.

**MEBCO Bank—Middle East Banking Co SAL:** POB 11-3540, Centre Continental, ave Charles de Gaulle, Beirut; tel. (1) 810600; telex 20729; f. 1959; cap. £L60m., dep. £L64,408.4m., res £L6,027m., total assets £L83,999.2m. (Dec. 1989); Chair. and Gen. Man. JAWAD CHALABI; 10 brs.

**Metropolitan Bank SAL:** POB 70216, Immeuble Nihaco, Autostrade Antelias, Beirut; tel. (1) 415824; telex 42130; fax (1) 406861; f. 1979; cap. £L3,000m., dep. £L49,389m. (Dec. 1994); Chair. and Gen. Man. MERSHED BAAKLINI.

**Near East Commercial Bank SAL:** POB 16-5766, Centre Sofil, ave Charles Malek, Beirut; tel. (1) 200331; telex 44664; fax (1) 422234; f. 1978; cap. £L7,000m., res £L27.1m., dep. £L44,607.8m. (Dec. 1994); Chair. and Gen. Man. HABIB J. HAKIM; 3 brs.

# LEBANON

**North Africa Commercial Bank SAL:** POB 11-9575, Centre Piccadilly, rue Hamra, Hamra, Beirut; tel. (1) 370425; telex 21582; fax (1) 346322; f. 1973 as Arab Libyan Tunisian Bank; adopted present name 1989; subsidiary of Libyan Arab Foreign Bank; cap. £L25m., dep. £L75,723.6m., res £L542.5m., total assets £L88,473.4m. (Dec. 1993); Chair. REJEB MISELLATI.

**Prosperity Bank of Lebanon SAL:** Immeuble Accra, Place des Canons, Beirut; tel. (1) 402211; telex 43355; f. 1963; cap. £L150m., total assets £L16,104.3m. (Dec. 1988); Pres. and Gen. Man. NAJIB ELIAS CHOUFANI; 7 brs.

**Rifbank SAL:** POB 11-5727, rue Kantari, Beirut; tel. (1) 362495; telex 22083; fax (1) 4781644; f. 1965; in association with The National Bank of Kuwait SAK, Kuwait Foreign Trading Contracting and Investment Co SAK, The Commercial Bank of Kuwait SAK, Kuwait Investment Co SAK; cap. £L2,160m., dep. £L124,233m., total assets £L137,417m. (Dec. 1993); Chair. IBRAHIM DABDOUB; Gen. Man. RIAD TAKY; 5 brs..

**Société Bancaire du Liban SAL:** POB 165192, place Sassine, Achrafiyé, Beirut; tel. (1) 215660; telex 48265; fax (1) 200455; f. 1899; cap. £L2,200m., dep. £L56,787m., res £L1,347m., total assets £L66,902m. (Dec. 1994); Chair. SELIM LEVY.

**Société Générale Libano-Européenne de Banque SAL:** POB 11-2955, Rond Point Salomé, Sin el-Fil, Beirut; tel. (1) 499813; telex 44453; fax (1) 512872; f. 1953; cap. £L16,649m. (Dec. 1993); Pres. MAURICE SEHNAOUI; Gen. Man. GÉRARD HANNOTIN; 16 brs.

**Société Nouvelle de la Banque de Syrie et du Liban SAL (SNBSL):** POB 11-957, rue Riad Solh, Beirut; tel. (1) 405563; telex 44060; fax (1) 405564; f. 1963; cap. £L350m., res £L2,910.2m., dep. £L125,938.7m. (Dec. 1992); Chair. NADIA EL-KHOURY; Gen. Man. ANTOINE ADM; 22 brs.

**Syrian Lebanese Commercial Bank SAL:** POB 11-8701, Immeuble Fakhros Darwiche, rue Hamra, Hamra, Beirut; tel. (1) 341261; telex 20853; f. 1974; cap. £L2,500m., res. £L4,276.5m., dep. £L37,518.6m. (Dec. 1992); Pres. and Gen. Man. MOHAMMED RIAD EL-HAKIM.

**Transorient Bank SAL:** POB 11-6260, Bauchrieh, rue Sérail, Beirut; tel. (1) 897706; telex 44925; fax (1) 897705; f. 1966; cap. £L6,095m., dep. £L135,404.5m., res £L17m., total assets £L157,209.3m. (Dec. 1993); joint venture with Lebanese private investors; Chair. ADIB S. MILLET; Gen. Man. GABRIEL M. ATALLAH; 8 brs.

**United Bank of Lebanon & Pakistan SAL:** POB 55544, Centre TAYAR, Sin el-Fil, Beirut; tel. (1) 499776; telex 20823; f. 1964; cap. £L600m., dep. £L16,485m. (Dec. 1989); Chair. SAEB JAROUDI; Vice-Chair. ANIS YASSINE.

**Universal Bank SAL:** POB 217, Immeuble Unigroup, Place Sayyad, Hazmieh, Beirut; tel. (1) 802500; telex 21798; fax (1) 412181; f. 1978; cap. £L1,000m., dep. £L102,000m. (Dec. 1993); Chair. and Gen. Man. GEORGE H. HADDAD.

**Wedge Bank Middle East SAL:** POB 16-5852, Centre Sofil, ave Charles Malek, Achrafiyé, Beirut; tel. (1) 201182; telex 43570; fax (1) 201184; f. 1983; cap. £L215m., dep. £L213,000m. (Dec. 1994); Pres. and Chair. MICHEL I. FARES.

### Development Banks

**Banque Nationale pour le Développement Industriel et Touristique SAL:** POB 11-8412, Immeuble Concorde, rue Rashid Karame, Beirut; tel. (1) 861990; telex 23086; f. 1973; cap. £L1,518m., res £L467m. (Dec. 1993); Chair. and Gen. Man. Dr OMAR HALABLAB.

**INFIBANK SAL:** POB 16-5110, ave Charles Malek, Achrafiyé, Beirut; tel. (1) 200951; telex 42297; f. 1974 as Investment and Finance Bank; medium- and long-term loans, 100% from Lebanese sources; owned by Banque Audi SAL (99.5%); cap. £L300m., res £L594,679m., dep. £L193,538.1m., total assets £L201,993.6m. (Dec. 1993); Chair. and Gen. Man. RAYMOND WADIH AUDI.

### Principal Foreign Banks

**Algemene Bank Nederland NV** (Netherlands): POB 113-5162, Beirut; tel. (1) 362821; telex 43984; cap. £L5m., res £L76.9m., dep. £L21,255m. (Dec. 1989); Man. Dir. E. NAHAS.

**American Express Bank** (USA): POB 90-688, Centre Mirna Chalouhi, rue Sin el-Fil, Beirut; tel. (1) 491470; telex 44481; fax (1) 4448301; cap. £L15m., res £L2.8m., dep. £L14,380.6m. (Dec. 1989); Gen. Man. GABY KASSIS.

**Arab African International Bank** (Egypt): POB 11-6066, Centre Ivoire, rue Commodore, Beirut; tel. (1) 350360; telex 22758; cap. £L25m., res £L2.1m., dep. £L3,205.7m. (Dec. 1989); Chief. Gen. Man. HUSSAIN B. ALDARWICHE.

**Arab Bank plc** (Jordan): POB 11-1015, rue Riad Solh, Beirut; tel. (1) 643412; telex 22893; fax (1) 868130; f. 1930; cap. £L550m. (Dec. 1993); Regional Man. Dr HISHAM BSAT.

**Banco di Roma SpA** (Italy): POB 11-968, Immeuble Borj el-Ghazal, place Tabaris, ave Fouad Chehab, Beirut; tel. (1) 332293; telex 49005; fax (1) 332932; cap. £L3,296.3m., dep. £L115,351m. (Dec. 1993); brs in Saida and Tripoli; Gen. Man. MICHEL CHERENTI.

**Bank Saderat Iran** (Iran): POB 113-6717, Immeuble Sabbagh et Daaboul, rue Hamra, Hamra, Beirut; tel. (1) 866860; telex 20738; fax (1) 866860; cap. £L32.5m., res £L20.8m., dep. £L1,365.5m. (Dec. 1989); Gen. Man. ALI AKBAR KAZEMI.

**Banque Nationale de Paris Intercontinentale SA** (France): POB 11-1608, rue de l'Archevêché Orthodoxe, Sursock, Beirut; tel. (1) 444389; telex 41401; fax (1) 200604; f. 1944; cap. £L7,027m. (Dec. 1993); 4 brs in Lebanon; Gen. Man. HENRI TYAN.

**British Bank of the Middle East** (Hong Kong): POB 90408, Immeuble Ghantous, Autostrade Dora, Beirut; tel. (1) 894300; telex 40462; f. 1946; cap. £L50m. (Dec. 1993); brs at Ras Beirut, Dora, Jounieh and Tripoli; Lebanon Area Man. C. CHONEIRY.

**Chase Manhattan Bank NA** (USA): POB 11-3684, rue Riad Solh, Beirut; tel. (1) 368460; telex 20357; cap. £L5m., dep. £L30.4m., total assets £L742.2m.; Vice-Pres. and Gen. Man. ELIE WAKIM.

**Citibank NA** (USA): POB 11-3648, Immeuble Zard Zard, rue Jounieh, Beirut; tel. (1) 413222; telex 22029; cap. £L5m., dep. £L5m., res £L1.5m., total assets £L774.4m.; Resident Vice-Pres. ANTOINE BOUSTANY.

**Habib Bank (Overseas) Ltd** (Pakistan): POB 5616, Centre Sabbag, rue Hamra, Hamra, Beirut; tel. (1) 340215; telex 20873; cap. £L5m., dep. £L1,002m. (Dec. 1989); Sr Vice-Pres. and Man. MASOOD ALAM.

**Jordan National Bank SA:** POB 5186, Immeuble Sehnaoui, rue Banque du Liban, Hamra, Beirut; tel. (1) 340451; telex 20512; fax (1) 353185; cap. £L2,171m., res £L46,586m. (Dec. 1993); Tripoli and Saida; Regional Gen. Man. Dr ABED H. BARBIR.

**Moscow Narodny Bank Ltd** (UK): rue de Rome, Hamra, Beirut; cap. £L5m., res £L8.1m., total assets £L32.7m. (Dec. 1985); Asst. Gen. Man. S. MAKKOUK.

**Saudi National Commercial Bank** (Saudi Arabia): POB 11-2355, Al-Kaaki Bldg, Sakiet al-Janzir, Beirut; tel. (1) 809353; telex 43619; fax (1) 867728; cap. £L6,625m., total assets £L66,224m. (Dec. 1992); Man. ABDULLAH HASSAN ABDAT.

Numerous foreign banks have representative offices in Beirut.

### Banking Association

**Association des Banques du Liban:** POB 80536, Centre Moucarri, Autostrade Dora, Beirut; tel. (1) 582346; telex 43069; f. 1959; serves and promotes the interests of the banking community in Lebanon; mems: 78 banks and 12 banking rep. offices; Pres. Dr FRANÇOIS BASSIL; Gen. Sec. Dr MAKRAM SADER.

## STOCK EXCHANGE

It is planned to reactivate trading on the Beirut Stock Exchange in 1995, after an independent regulatory organization has been established and legislation to protect investors enacted.

**Beirut Stock Exchange:** Hamra; Beirut; f. 1920; has not traded since 1983; 10 mems; Cttee Chair. GABRIEL SEHNAOUI.

## INSURANCE

In 1985 110 insurance companies (58 national, 52 foreign) were registered in Lebanon, but a large number were not operating. The total number of companies that conducted operations in 1984 was 67 (46 Lebanese, 21 foreign).

**Arabia Insurance Co Ltd SAL:** POB 11-2172, rue de Phénicie, Beirut; tel. (1) 363610; telex 40060; fax (1) 365139; f. 1944; Chair. and Gen. Man. BADR S. FAHOUM.

**Commercial Insurance Co SAL:** POB 84, Centre Starco Jounieh; tel. (1) 643873; telex 45994; fax (1) 869084; f. 1962; Chair. MAX R. ZACCAR.

**Compagnie Libanaise d'Assurances SAL:** POB 3685, rue Riad Solh, Beirut; tel. (1) 868988; telex 20379; f. 1951; cap. £L3,000m. (1991); Chair. JEAN F. S. ABOUJAOUDÉ; Gen. Man. MAMDOUH RAHMOUN.

**Al-Ittihad al-Watani:** POB 1270, Immeuble Al-Ittihadia, ave Fouad Chehab, St Nicolas, Beirut; tel. (1) 330840; telex 20839; f. 1947; cap. £L30m.; Chair. JOE I. KAIROUZ; Exec. Dir TANNOUS FEGHALI.

**Al-Mashrek Insurance and Reinsurance SAL:** POB 16-6154, Immeuble Amir, 65 rue Aabrine, Beirut; tel. (1) 200541; telex 43244; fax (1) 888078; f. 1962; cap. (auth. and p.u.) £L500m., (1992); Chair. and Gen. Man. ABRAHAM MATOSSIAN.

**Libano-Suisse Insurance Co SAL:** Immeuble Cité Dora, Dora, Beirut; tel. (1) 890439; telex 43766; f. 1959; cap. £L405m. (1991); Pres. and Gen. Man. MICHEL PIERRE PHARAON; Man. Lebanon Branch NAJI HABIS.

**'La Phénicienne' SAL:** POB 11-5652, Immeuble Hanna Haddad, rue Amine Gemayel, Sioufi, Beirut; tel. (1) 425484; telex 42357; fax (1) 424532; f. 1964; Chair. and Gen. Man. TANNOUS C. FEGHALI.

# LEBANON

## Trade and Industry

### DEVELOPMENT ORGANIZATION

**Council for Development and Reconstruction:** POB 116-5351, Tallet es-Serail, Beirut; tel. (1) 643982; fax (1) 4781622; f. 1976; aimed to achieve reconstruction after 1975–76 civil war, subsequently engaged in repairs to damage caused by inter-communal fighting; central tendering committee for the world's largest construction programme in any one city; acts on behalf of the Cabinet, reporting directly to the Prime Minister; Chair. FADL ALI SHALAQ.

### CHAMBERS OF COMMERCE AND INDUSTRY

**Beirut Chamber of Commerce and Industry:** POB 11-1801, Sanayeh, Beirut; tel. (1) 349530; telex 22269; fax (1) 865802; f. 1898; 32,000 mems; Pres. ADNAN KASSAR; Dir-Gen. Dr MOHI ED-DIN KAISSI.

**Tripoli Chamber of Commerce and Industry:** POB 27, blvd Tripoli, Tripoli; tel. 622790; telex 46024; Pres. HASSAN EL-MOUNLA.

**Chamber of Commerce and Industry in Sidon and South Lebanon:** POB 41, rue Maarouf Saad, Sidon; tel. 720123; telex 20402; fax 722986; f. 1933; Pres. MOHAMAD ZAATARI.

**Zahleh Chamber of Commerce and Industry:** POB 100, Zahleh; tel. (8) 802602; telex 48042; fax (8) 800050; f. 1939; 2,500 mems; Pres. EDMOND JREISSATI.

### EMPLOYERS' ASSOCIATION

**Association of Lebanese Industrialists:** POB 1520, Chamber of Commerce and Industry, rue Justinian, Beirut; Pres. JACQUES SARRAF.

### TRADE UNION FEDERATION

**Confédération Générale des Travailleurs du Liban (CGTL):** POB 4381, Beirut; f. 1958; 300,000 mems; only national labour centre in Lebanon and sole rep. of working classes; comprises 18 affiliated federations including all 150 unions in Lebanon; Chair. ELIAS ABU RIZQ.

## Transport

### RAILWAYS

**Office des Chemins de Fer de l'Etat Libanais et du Transport en Commun de Beyrouth et de sa Banlieue:** POB 109, Souk el-Arwam, Beirut; tel. (1) 443619; telex 43088; since 1961 all railways in Lebanon have been state-owned. Of the original network of some 412 km, only the lines from Beirut and Rayak to the Syrian border (222 km of standard gauge) were known to be working in mid-1994; Pres. RABIH AMMASH.

### ROADS

Lebanon has 7,100 km of roads, of which 1,990 km are main roads. Most are generally good by Middle Eastern standards. The two international motorways are the north–south coastal road and the road connecting Beirut with Damascus in Syria. Among the major roads are that crossing the Beka'a and continuing south to Bent-Jbail and the Shtaura–Baalbek road. Hard-surfaced roads connect Jezzine with Moukhtara, Bzebdine with Metn, Meyroub with Afka and Tannourine.

### SHIPPING

A two-phase programme to rehabilitate the port of Beirut is currently under way. In the first phase a new breakwater and a fourth basin are to be constructed, damaged and stolen equipment replaced and a new container area constructed, at an estimated cost of US $126m. In the second phase, due to commence in 1996, the construction of an industrial free zone, a fifth basin and a major container terminal are envisaged, at an estimated cost of $1,000m. The port of Beirut is currently administered by a 12-member committee appointed by the Cabinet, but its future status remains to be decided. Tripoli, the northern Mediterranean terminus of the oil pipeline from Iraq (the other is Haifa, Israel—not in use since 1948), is also a busy port, with good equipment and facilities. Jounieh, north of Beirut, is Lebanon's third most important port. Saida is still relatively unimportant as a port. The reconstructed port of an-Naqoura, in the South Lebanon Army-occupied security zone along the border with Israel, was inaugurated in June 1987.

**Siège Provisoire de la Commission Portuaire:** Immeuble de l'Electricité du Liban, rue du Fleuve, Beirut.

There are many shipping companies and agents in Beirut. The following are some of the largest:

**'Adriatica' di Nav. SpAN:** POB 11-1472, rue du Port, Immeuble Ras, Beirut; tel. (1) 580181; telex 44875; Gen. Man. J. WEHBE.

**Ameaster Tanker Services:** a division of American Lebanese Shipping Co SAL, POB 113–5388, Beirut; tel. (1) 354827; telex 20863; Pres. PAUL PARATORE; Man. N. BALTAGI.

**American Levant Shipping & Distributing Co:** POB 11-2736, Immeuble Andalusia, Gourand St, Gemmayze, Beirut; agents for: Holland America Line, Lykes Bros Steamship Co; correspondents throughout Middle East: Man. Dir SAMIR ISHAK.

**Arab Shipping and Chartering Co:** POB 1084, Beirut; tel. (1) 866386; telex 20768; agents for China National Chartering Corpn, China Ocean Shipping Co.

**Barrad Shipping Co SAL:** POB 181, Beirut; refrigerated tramp services; 3 cargo reefer vessels; Chair. P. H. HÉLOU.

**O. D. Debbas & Sons:** Head Office: POB 166678, Immeuble Debbas, 530 Corniche du Fleuve Blvd, Beirut; tel. (1) 585253; telex 44651; fax (1) 602515; f. 1892; Man. Dir OIDIH ELIE DEBBAS.

**Ets Derviche Y. Haddad:** POB 11-42, rue Derviche Haddad, Beirut; tel. (1) 447879; telex 44987; fax (1) 447875; agents for Armement Deppe, Antwerp, and Compagnie Maritime Belge, Antwerp.

**Fauzi Jemil Ghandour:** POB 1084, Beirut; tel. (1) 866386; telex 20711; agents for Denizçlik Bankasi TAO (Denizyollari), DB Deniz Nakliyati TAŞ (Dbcargo), Iraqi Maritime Transport Co, United Arab Shipping Co.

**T. Gargour & Fils:** POB 110-371, Garage Mercedes, Dora, Beirut; tel. (1) 899775; telex 43994; f. 1928; agents for Assoc. Levant Lines SAL; Dirs NICOLAS T. GARGOUR, HABIB T. GARGOUR.

**General United Trading and Shipping Co SARL:** POB 36, Tripoli; tel. (6) 600530; telex 23889; 6 cargo vessels.

**Henry Heald & Co SAL:** POB 64, Beirut; tel. (1) 893184; telex 42364; temporary address: c/o Orphanides and Murat, POB 24, Larnaca, Cyprus; f. 1837; agents for Nippon Yusen Kaisha, P. & O. Group, Swedish Orient Line, Finncarriers, Niver Lines, Greek South America Lines, Nordana, Shipping Corpn of India, Vanderzee Shipping Agency; Chair. J. L. JOLY; Dir H. JOLY.

**Hitti Frères:** POB 511, rue de Phénicie, Beirut; airlines and shipping agents.

**Mediterranean Maritime Co SAL:** POB 165658, Immeuble de la Bourse, rue Hoyek, Beirut; tel. (1) 249655; telex 42403; 1 tanker, 1 cargo vessel; managers for National Maritime Agencies Co W.LL., Kuwait.

**Mena Shipping and Tourist Agency:** POB 11-884, rue el Arz, Beirut; telex 20670; 5 cargo vessels; Man. Dir W. LEHETA.

**Rassem Trading:** POB 11-8460, Immeuble Agha, Raoucheh, Beirut; tel. (1) 866372; telex 21719; fax (1) 866372; 5 livestock transportation vessels, 4 general cargo vessels; Dirs F. R. W. MOUKAHAL, A. H. ZEIDO.

**Rodolphe Saadé & Co SAL:** POB 16–6526, Immeuble BUROTEC, rue Pasteur, Beirut; tel. (1) 583313; telex 41120; fax (1) 583319; agents for CMA, R. Farrell Lines; f. 1964; Travel Office: POB 11–2279, Immeuble Union, rue Spears, Beirut; tel. (1) 342047; telex 48396; fax (1) 346985; Pres. JACQUES R. SAADÉ.

**G. Sahyouni & Co SARL:** POB 175452, Immeuble Hafiz el-Hashem, Pont Karantina, Corniche en-Nahr, Beirut; tel. (1) 582601; telex 41236; fax (1) 582601; f. 1989; agents for Lloyd's, Pand OCL and Baltic Control; Financial Man. HENRY CHIDIAC; Man. Dir. GEORGE SAHYOUNI.

**Union Shipping and Chartering Agency:** POB 1084, Beirut; tel. (1) 866386; telex 20768; agents for Jugolinija (Rijeka), Jadroslobodna, Jugo Oceania, Atlanska Plovidba, Jadrolinija, Mediteranska Plovidba, Slobodna Plovidba.

### CIVIL AVIATION

Services from the country's principal airport, in Beirut, were subject to frequent disruptions after 1975; its location in predominantly Muslim west Beirut made it virtually inaccessible to non-Muslims. In 1986 a new airport, based on an existing military airfield, was opened at Halat, north of Beirut, by Christian concerns, but commercial operations from the airport were not authorized by the Government. Services to and from Beirut by Middle East Airlines (MEA) were suspended, and the airport closed, at the end of January 1987, after the Christian LF militia shelled the airport and threatened to attack MEA aircraft if services from their own airport, at Halat, did not receive official authorization. Beirut airport was reopened in May, after the LF accepted government assurances that Halat would receive the necessary authorization for civil use. However, the commission concluded that Halat did not possess the facilities to cater for international air traffic. More than 1m. passengers used Beirut International Airport in 1994.

**MEA (Middle East Airlines, Air Liban SAL):** POB 206, Immeuble MEA, blvd de l'Aéroport, Beirut; tel. (1) 316316; telex 20820;

# LEBANON

f. 1945; took over Lebanese International Airways in 1969; regular services throughout Europe, the Middle East, North and West Africa and the Far East; Chair. ABD AL-HAMID FAKHOURI; Man. Dir YOUSUF LAHOUD.

**Trans-Mediterranean Airways SAL (TMA):** Beirut International Airport, POB 11–3018, Beirut; tel. (1) 820550; telex 20637; f. 1953; worldwide cargo services between Europe, the Middle East, South-East Asia, the Far East and the USA; Chair. CHAFIC MOHARRAM.

## Tourism

Before the civil war, Lebanon was a major tourist centre, and its scenic beauty, sunny climate and historic sites attracted some 2m. visitors annually. In 1974 tourism contributed about 20% of the country's income. Since the end of the civil conflict tourist facilities, in particular hotels, have begun to be reconstructed, and the Arab Tourist Organization designated 1994 as the International Year of Tourism in Lebanon.

**Ministry of Tourism:** Beirut; f. 1966; official organization; Head of International Relations and Conventions Dept ANTOINE ACCAOUI; Head of Speleological Service SAMI KARKABI.

**National Council of Tourism in Lebanon (CNTL):** POB 11–5344, rue Banque du Liban, Beirut; tel. (1) 864532; telex 20898; taken over by Board of Foreign Economic Relations in 1983; re-established as a separate body 1985; government-sponsored autonomous organization responsible for the promotion of tourism; overseas offices in London, Paris, Brussels, Rome, Iraq and Cairo; Pres. SAMY MAROUN; Dir-Gen. NASSER SAFIEDDINE.

# LESOTHO

## Introductory Survey

### Location, Climate, Language, Religion, Flag, Capital

The Kingdom of Lesotho is a land-locked country, entirely surrounded by South Africa. The climate is generally mild, although cooler in the highlands: lowland temperatures range from a maximum of 32°C (90°F) in summer (October to April) to a minimum of −7°C (20°F) in winter. Rainfall averages about 725 mm (29 ins) per year, mostly falling in summer. The official languages are English and Sesotho. About 90% of the population are Christians. The largest denominations are the Roman Catholic, Lesotho Evangelical and Anglican Churches. The national flag (official proportions 3 by 2) is divided diagonally from lower hoist to upper fly, with the hoist triangle of white bearing, in brown silhouette, a traditional Basotho shield with crossed knobkerrie (club), barbed assegai (spear) and a thyrsus of ostrich feathers, and the fly triangle comprising a blue diagonal stripe and a green triangle. The capital is Maseru.

### Recent History

Lesotho was formerly Basutoland, a dependency of the United Kingdom. In 1868, at the request of the Basotho people's chief, the territory became a British protectorate. Basutoland was annexed to Cape Colony (now part of South Africa) in 1871 but detached in 1884. It became a separate British colony, and was administered as one of the High Commission Territories in southern Africa (the others being the protectorates of Bechuanaland, now Botswana, and Swaziland). The British Act of Parliament that established the Union of South Africa in 1910 also provided for the possible inclusion in South Africa of the three High Commission Territories, subject to local consent. Until 1960 successive South African Governments asked for the transfer of the three territories, but the native chiefs always objected to such a scheme.

Within Basutoland a revised Constitution, which established the colony's first Legislative Council, was introduced in 1956. A new document, granting limited powers of self-government, was adopted in September 1959. Basutoland's first general election, on the basis of universal adult suffrage, took place on 29 April 1965, and full internal self-government was achieved on the following day. Moshoeshoe II, Paramount Chief since 1960, was recognized as King. Of the 60 seats in the new Legislative Assembly, 31 were won by the Basutoland National Party (BNP), a conservative group supporting limited co-operation with South Africa. The BNP's leader, Chief Leabua Jonathan, failed to win a seat but won a by-election in July 1965, whereupon he became Prime Minister. Basutoland became independent, as Lesotho, on 4 October 1966. The new Constitution, which took effect at independence, provided for a bicameral legislature, comprising the 60-seat National Assembly and the 33-member Senate; executive power was vested in the Cabinet, which was presided over by the Prime Minister. The King was designated Head of State.

The BNP, restyled the Basotho National Party, remained in power at independence, with Chief Jonathan as Prime Minister. A constitutional crisis arose in December 1966, when King Moshoeshoe II attempted to obtain wider personal powers. In January 1967, however, the King signed an undertaking, on pain of compulsory abdication, to abide by the Constitution. A general election was held in January 1970, when the opposition Basotho Congress Party (BCP), a pan-Africanist group led by Dr Ntsu Mokhehle, appeared to have won a majority of seats in the National Assembly. However, Chief Jonathan declared a state of emergency, suspended the Constitution and arrested several BCP organizers. The election was annulled, and the Parliament prorogued. King Moshoeshoe was placed under house arrest and later exiled, although he returned in December 1970, after accepting a government order banning him from participating in politics. From January 1970 the country was effectively under the Prime Minister's personal control. An interim National Assembly of 93 members, comprising the former Senate (mainly Chiefs) and 60 members nominated by the Cabinet, was inaugurated in April 1973. The state of emergency was revoked in July. However, following a failed coup attempt in January 1974 by alleged supporters of the BCP, Chief Jonathan introduced strict new security laws. Mokhehle and other prominent members of the BCP went into exile abroad. The BCP subsequently split into two factions, internal and external; the latter, led by Mokhehle, was supported by the Lesotho Liberation Army (LLA), which was responsible for several terrorist attacks in Lesotho during the late 1970s and the 1980s. The South African Government consistently denied allegations that it supported the LLA.

Although Lesotho was economically dependent on South Africa, and the Government's official policy during the 1970s was one of 'dialogue' with its neighbour, Chief Jonathan repeatedly expressed criticism of the South African Government's policy of apartheid, and supported the African National Congress of South Africa (ANC), the South African opposition group which was banned in that country during 1960–90. In December 1982 South African forces launched a major assault on the homes of ANC members in Lesotho's capital, Maseru, killing more than 40 people. In August 1983 South Africa delivered an ultimatum to Lesotho, either to expel (or repatriate) 3,000 South African refugees or be subjected to economic sanctions. As a result, two groups of refugees left Lesotho, reportedly voluntarily.

In March 1983 Chief Jonathan announced that elections would be held, and in May of that year the Parliament Act was introduced to repeal the emergency order of 1970 that had suspended the Constitution. In January 1985 the National Assembly was dissolved, and in July the Government announced that legislative elections would take place in September. However, the elections were cancelled in August, when no candidates from the five opposition parties were nominated to contest them: the opposition parties maintained that their candidates had been denied access to the voters' rolls, thus preventing them from securing sufficient signatures to qualify for nomination. It was announced that Chief Jonathan and the BNP candidates in all 60 constituencies had been returned to office unopposed.

Lesotho's persistent refusal to sign a joint non-aggression pact led South Africa to impound consignments of armaments destined for Lesotho, and again to threaten to impose economic sanctions in August 1984. In December 1985 commando troops (alleged by the Lesotho Government to be South African) conducted a raid in Maseru, killing nine people (including several ANC members). On 1 January 1986 South Africa imposed a blockade on the border with Lesotho, impeding access to vital supplies of food and fuel. Five leading Lesotho politicians opposed to the Government were arrested on their return from talks in South Africa, and there were reports of fighting between factions of the armed forces, some members of which apparently resented the Lesotho Government's contacts with socialist states and the radical policies of the BNP's influential Youth League. On 20 January Chief Jonathan's Government was overthrown in a coup, led by Maj.-Gen. Justin Lekhanya, the head of the armed forces. A Military Council, chaired by Lekhanya, was established; the 1983 Parliament Act was revoked, and it was announced that executive and legislative powers were to be vested in King Moshoeshoe, assisted by the Military Council and by a (mainly civilian) Council of Ministers. One week after the coup about 60 ANC members were deported from Lesotho, and the South African blockade was ended on the same day. In March the Military Council suspended all formal political activity. In August Chief Jonathan and six of his former ministers were placed under house arrest; however, the High Court subsequently declared the detention order to be invalid. (Chief Jonathan died in 1987.) In September 1986 the Council of Ministers was restructured, giving increased responsibility to Lekhanya, and the Military Council held discussions with the leaders of the five main opposition parties.

Although the South African Government denied having any part in the coup, Lesotho's new rulers proved to be more amenable to South Africa's policy on regional security. In

March 1986 it was announced that the two Governments had reached an informal agreement whereby neither country would allow its territory to be used for attacks against the other. Throughout that year the Lesotho Government refrained from participating in attempts by other African states to press for the imposition of international economic sanctions against South Africa. By August more than 200 South African refugees, believed to be ANC members, were reported to have been expelled from Lesotho (although the Lesotho Government did not permit their extradition directly to South Africa). In March 1988 Lesotho and South Africa reached a final agreement on the Highlands Water Project (to supply water to South Africa: see Economic Affairs).

In June 1987 Charles Mofeli, leader of the United Democratic Party, was detained for a week after he had petitioned King Moshoeshoe and Lekhanya for a return to parliamentary democracy. In April 1988 the five main opposition parties appealed to the Organization of African Unity (OAU, see p. 200), the Commonwealth (see p. 119) and the South African Government to exert diplomatic pressure on the Lesotho Government to restore civilian rule. In the following month Ntsu Mokhehle was allowed to return to Lesotho after 14 years of exile. In 1989 the LLA was said to have disbanded, and by 1990 the two factions of the BCP had apparently reunited under the leadership of Mokhehle.

In mid-1989 some elements within the Government reportedly sought the resignation of Lekhanya from the chairmanship of the Military Council, following widespread reports that implicated him in the fatal shooting of a civilian at Maseru in December 1988: it was claimed that Lekhanya had falsely attributed responsibility for the incident to a subordinate. In September 1989, at an inquest into the civilian's death (which was reportedly instigated at the request of other members of the Military Council), Lekhanya admitted the truth of the allegations. Nevertheless, in October a verdict of justifiable homicide was announced.

In early 1990 a power struggle developed between Lekhanya and King Moshoeshoe. In February Lekhanya dismissed three members of the Military Council and one member of the Council of Ministers, accusing them of 'insubordination'. In response to the refusal of King Moshoeshoe to approve new appointments to the Military Council, Lekhanya suspended the monarch's executive and legislative powers. Shortly afterwards Lekhanya announced that a general election would take place during 1992; however, party political activity remained outlawed. In March 1990 the Military Council assumed the executive and legislative powers previously vested in King Moshoeshoe, and the King (who remained Head of State) was exiled in the United Kingdom. In June a National Constituent Assembly was inaugurated to draft a new constitution; the Assembly comprised 109 members, including Lekhanya, members of the Council of Ministers, representatives of banned political parties, traditional chiefs and business executives.

In October 1990 Lekhanya reportedly invited King Moshoeshoe to return to Lesotho from exile. However, the King announced that his return would be conditional upon the ending of military rule and the establishment of an interim government, pending the re-adoption of the 1966 Constitution. On 6 November 1990 Maj.-Gen. Lekhanya responded by promulgating an order that dethroned the King with immediate effect. Two days later Lesotho's 22 principal chiefs elected Moshoeshoe's eldest son, Prince Bereng Seeisa, as the new King; on 12 November he succeeded to the throne, as King Letsie III, having undertaken to remain detached from politics.

On 30 April 1991 Lekhanya was deposed as Chairman of the Military Council, in a coup organized by army officers who were reportedly dissatisfied with the level of their salaries. Col (later Maj.-Gen.) Elias Phitsoane Ramaema, a member of the Military Council, succeeded Lekhanya as the Chairman of a reorganized Military Council, and also joined a reshuffled Council of Ministers. Shortly afterwards Ramaema affirmed that elections would take place during 1992, as previously planned, and announced the repeal of the law that had banned party political activity since 1986. There was further unrest later in May 1991, when resentment against foreign-owned businesses precipitated riots in Maseru and other principal towns, resulting in some 34 deaths and 425 arrests. In June 20 officers were dismissed from the armed forces, following an unsuccessful attempt to overthrow Ramaema and to reinstate Lekhanya; the latter was placed under house arrest during August–September, owing to allegations that a further counter-coup was being plotted. By July the National Constituent Assembly had drafted a new Constitution. In September structural changes to the composition of the Council of Ministers were implemented.

In May 1992 Lesotho and South Africa agreed to establish diplomatic relations at ambassadorial level. In June it was announced that the general election would take place in November. Also in June the human rights organization, Amnesty International, demanded that the Lesotho authorities establish a commission of inquiry into alleged abuses of human rights by the country's security forces. The Council of Ministers was reshuffled in late June. Following talks in the United Kingdom between Ramaema and former King Moshoeshoe (held under the auspices of the Secretary-General of the Commonwealth), Moshoeshoe returned to Lesotho from exile in July. In August two members of the Military Council were dismissed, following allegations against them of corruption.

The transition from military rule to democratic government, which was scheduled to take place in November, was postponed at short notice; the general election was eventually held on 27 March 1993. The BCP secured all of the 65 seats in the new legislative National Assembly, winning 54% of the votes cast. Although international observers pronounced the election to have been generally 'free and fair', the BNP—which took 16% of the votes—rejected the result, alleging that there had been widespread irregularities. (In May the BNP declined the new administration's offer of two seats in the restored Senate.) On 2 April Ntsu Mokhehle was inaugurated as Prime Minister, and King Letsie swore allegiance to the new Constitution, under the terms of which he remained Head of State with no executive or legislative powers (executive authority being vested in the Cabinet, the composition of which was announced shortly afterwards).

In July 1993 two people were injured when security forces acted to disperse an unauthorized march by striking members of the Construction and Allied Workers Union of Lesotho (CAWULE), who were intending to present a petition, demanding increased pay and improved benefits, to Mokhehle. Although the BCP had hitherto encouraged the formation of independent trade unions, doubts in some quarters as to the Government's commitment to freedom of association were intensified after the incident by the detention of several CAWULE leaders under the provisions of the Internal Security Act (introduced by Chief Jonathan in 1984), which the BCP had previously undertaken to repeal.

Reports emerged in late 1993 of discontent within the armed forces. A mutiny in November by about 50 junior officers in the national army, the Royal Lesotho Defence Force (RLDF), was apparently precipitated by a proposal to place the military under the command of a senior member of the LLA—as part of government efforts to integrate its former armed wing (many members of which were still in South Africa) with the RLDF. Four senior army officers, all of whom were believed to be BCP supporters, were subsequently reported to have resigned their posts. Tensions increased in the first weeks of 1994, after members of the armed forces wrote to Mokhehle to demand that their salaries be doubled: Mokhehle responded that any increase in remuneration for the army would only be considered as part of a wider review of public sector pay that was currently in progress. Skirmishes followed near Maseru on two days in mid-January, involving rebellious troops and forces loyal to the Government. Although the rebels' leaders maintained that their actions were linked to the demand for increased pay, it was widely speculated that the mutiny reflected broader political differences (principally, it was suggested, between supporters of the new regime and of the BNP) within the military. Mediation efforts involving representatives of Botswana, South Africa, Zimbabwe, the Commonwealth, the OAU and the UN failed to prevent a day of more serious fighting (between about 600 rebels and a 150-strong loyalist contingent) before a truce entered force. At the beginning of February the rival factions surrendered their weapons and returned to barracks, in accordance with a Commonwealth-mediated peace accord that envisaged negotiations between the Mokhehle Government and the parties involved in the fighting. In all, at least five soldiers and three civilians were reported to have been killed in the conflict.

There was renewed army unrest in mid-April 1994, when the Deputy Prime Minister, Selometsi Baholo (who also held the finance portfolio), was shot dead during an abduction attempt by disaffected troops, who also briefly detained four other ministers. In May police officers (who, with prison guards, were staging a strike in support of demands for increased pay and allowances) briefly held the Minister of Information and Broadcasting and acting finance minister, Mpho Malie, hostage. Agreement was subsequently reached on increased allowances (although the demand for 60% salary increases was not met), and the Government announced the formation of an independent commission to review the salary structures of civil servants; the three-week strike ended at the end of the month. Meanwhile, the minister responsible for natural resources, Monyane Moleleki, fled to South Africa and subsequently resigned from the Government. A commission to investigate the armed forces unrest of January and April began work in mid-July.

In late July 1994 Mokhehle appointed a commission of inquiry into the circumstances surrounding the dethronement of former King Moshoeshoe II. In early August, however, King Letsie petitioned the High Court to abolish the commission on the grounds of bias on the part of its members.

In mid-August 1994 supporters of the BNP, led by Lekhanya, staged a demonstration in Maseru to demand the resignation of the Mokhehle Government and the restoration of Moshoeshoe II to the throne. On 17 August King Letsie made a radio broadcast announcing that he had dissolved parliament, dismissed the Mokhehle Government and suspended sections of the Constitution, citing 'popular dissatisfaction' with the BCP administration. (The King also denounced as treason Mokhehle's appeal for external assistance in quelling army unrest earlier in the year.) A provisional body would be established to govern, pending fresh elections, which were to be organized by an independent commission. Following the King's broadcast, several thousand people gathered outside the royal palace in Maseru to demonstrate their support for the deposed Government. However, army and police support for Letsie's 'royal coup' was evident, and clashes between demonstrators and the security forces resulted in four deaths (a further death was reported in disturbances two days later). A night-time curfew was imposed on the day of the broadcast. A prominent human rights lawyer, Hae Phoofolo, was appointed Chairman of the Transitional Council of Ministers; among the other members of the provisional Government was the Secretary-General of the BNP, Evaristus Retselisitsoe Sekhonyana, who was appointed Minister of Foreign Affairs. Phoofolo identified as a priority for his administration the amendment of the Constitution to facilitate the restoration of Moshoeshoe. In the mean time, King Letsie was to act as executive and legislative Head of State. A two-day general strike, co-ordinated by the BCP and the Lesotho Council of Non-governmental Organizations, in support of the ousted Government effectively paralysed economic activity in Maseru in late August.

The suspension of constitutional government was widely condemned outside Lesotho. Presidents Ketumile Masire of Botswana, Nelson Mandela of South Africa and Robert Mugabe of Zimbabwe led diplomatic efforts to restore the elected Government, supported by the OAU and the Commonwealth. Several countries threatened economic sanctions against Lesotho, and the USA withdrew financial assistance. King Letsie and Mokhehle attended negotiations in Pretoria, South Africa, in late August, at which Masire, Mandela and Mugabe urged Letsie to reinstate all elected institutions. Although there was agreement in principle on the restoration of Moshoeshoe II to the throne, subsequent deadlines for a resolution to the crisis failed to be met, owing to disputes regarding a programme for the return of the Mokhehle Government to office. A further two-day strike was widely observed in early September, and South African armed forces conducted manoeuvres near Lesotho territory.

On 14 September 1994 King Letsie and Mokhehle signed an agreement, guaranteed by Botswana, South Africa and Zimbabwe, providing for the restoration of Moshoeshoe as reigning monarch, and for the immediate restitution of the elected organs of government; the commision of inquiry into Moshoeshoe's dethronement was to be abandoned; persons involved in the 'royal coup' were to be immune from prosecution; the political neutrality of the armed forces and public service was to be guaranteed, and consultations were to be undertaken with the expressed aim of broadening the democratic process.

In mid-October 1994 Sekhonyana was ordered to pay a substantial fine (or be sentenced to two years' imprisonment) after being convicted of sedition and the incitement to violence of army and police troops against former LLA members earlier in the year.

In mid-November 1994 legislation providing for the reinstatement of Moshoeshoe was presented to the National Assembly; the bill was unanimously approved on 2 December, and was subsequently endorsed by the Senate. Accordingly, on 25 January 1995 Moshoeshoe II, who undertook not to intervene in politics, was restored to the throne, following the voluntary abdication of Letsie III, who took the title of Crown Prince (the new legislation provided for Letsie to succeed as monarch upon the death of his father).

Government changes in early February 1995 included the promotion of the Minister of Education and Training, Pakalitha Mosisili, to the post of Deputy Prime Minister (which had remained vacant since Baholo's assassination). In a further government reshuffle later in the month Malie was appointed Minister of Foreign Affairs.

The director and another senior officer of the National Security Service were held hostage by junior officers (who were demanding improved terms and conditions of service) for three weeks in March 1995, and were released only after intervention by the Commonwealth Secretary-General. Former government minister Monyane Moleleki was briefly detained by security forces in late March, following his return from exile in South Africa.

### Government

Lesotho is an hereditary monarchy. Under the terms of the Constitution, which came into effect following the March 1993 election, the King, who is Head of State, has no executive or legislative powers. The College of Chiefs is theoretically empowered, under traditional law, to elect and depose the King by a majority vote. Executive power is vested in the Cabinet, which is headed by the Prime Minister. Legislative power is exercised by a 65-member National Assembly, which is elected, at intervals of no more than five years, by universal adult suffrage in the context of a multi-party political system. The upper house, the Senate, comprises traditional chiefs and eight nominated members. Lesotho comprises 10 administrative districts, each with an appointed district co-ordinator.

### Defence

Military service is voluntary. The Royal Lesotho Defence Force comprised 2,000 men in June 1994. The 1995/96 budget allocated M102.5m. to defence (representing 6.4% of total estimated expenditure).

### Economic Affairs

In 1993, according to estimates by the World Bank, Lesotho's gross national product (GNP), measured at average 1991–93 prices, was US $1,254m., equivalent to $660 per head. During 1985–93, it was estimated, GNP per head increased, in real terms, at an average annual rate of 0.8%. Over the same period the population increased by an annual average of 2.6%. Lesotho's gross domestic product (GDP) increased, in real terms, by an annual average of 5.4% in 1980–92; GDP increased by 7.5% in the financial year ending 31 March 1994.

Agriculture, forestry and fishing contributed 11.5% of GDP in 1993, but was the largest source of employment, involving 77.2% of the labour force in that year. The principal agricultural exports are live animals, wool, cereals and mohair. Maize flour, wheat, asparagus and animal feed are also exported. The main subsistence crops are maize, sorghum and wheat. Lesotho remains a net importer of staple foodstuffs, since domestic production satisfies about 60% of requirements. During 1980–92 agricultural GDP increased by an annual average of 0.5%.

Industry (including mining, manufacturing, construction and power) provided 41.8% of GDP in 1993. During 1980–92 industrial GDP increased by an annual average of 8.5%.

Mining contributed an estimated 0.1% of GDP in 1993, and employed 0.9% of the labour force in 1985/86. Lesotho has reserves of diamonds, which during the late 1970s provided more than 50% of visible export earnings, but large-scale exploitation of these ceased in 1982; however, plans to reopen the Letseng-la Terai mine have been under consideration in recent years. Lesotho is also believed to possess uranium and petroleum deposits.

Manufacturing has enjoyed sustained growth, contributing 16.3% of GDP in 1993, although the sector employed only 2.7% of the labour force in 1985/86. The most important branches of the manufacturing sector, measured in terms of value added, in 1992 were food products and beverages (providing 53.9% of the total) and textiles and clothing (30.6%). During 1980–92 manufacturing GDP increased by an annual average of 12.3%.

More than 90% of Lesotho's energy requirements are imported from South Africa. The Highlands Water Project, on which a final agreement was reached with South Africa in March 1988, is to divert water from Lesotho's rivers for export to South Africa, and, in addition, to provide hydroelectricity sufficient for all Lesotho's needs: excavation work began in 1991, and the scheme is due to be completed by 2017.

In 1992 about 38% of Lesotho's adult male labour force were employed in South Africa. Basotho workers in South Africa are mainly employed in the gold mines, and in the education and health sectors. The remittances of migrant workers represent the most significant contribution to national income, exceeding the combined value-added of the primary and secondary sectors. Tourism is another important source of foreign exchange.

In 1993 Lesotho recorded a visible trade deficit of US $777.6m., but there was a surplus of $21.6m. on the current account of the balance of payments. In 1993 the principal source of imports (83%) was the Southern African Customs Union (SACU—i.e. chiefly South Africa: see below), which was also the principal market for exports (39%). A further 22% of exports went to countries of the European Union. The principal exports in 1993 were clothing (accounting for 57% of the total), footwear and furniture. The principal imports in 1981 were food and live animals, machinery and transport equipment and petroleum products.

In the financial year ending 31 March 1992 there was a budgetary deficit of M9.9m. (equivalent to 0.6% of GDP in that year). Lesotho's external debt totalled US $512.1m. at the end of 1993, of which $471.9m. was long-term public debt. In that year the cost of debt-servicing was equivalent to 5.5% of revenue from exports of goods and services. The annual rate of inflation averaged 14.5% in 1985–93; consumer prices increased by an average of 13.9% in 1993. It was estimated that more than 35% of the labour force were unemployed in late 1989.

Lesotho is a member of the Common Monetary Area (with Namibia, South Africa and Swaziland), and a member of SACU (with Botswana, Namibia, South Africa and Swaziland). Receipts from SACU were expected to provide some 60% of recurrent government revenue in the 1994/95 budget. Lesotho also belongs to the Southern African Development Community (SADC, see p. 219) and to the Preferential Trade Area for Eastern and Southern African States (PTA, see p. 240). In November 1993 Lesotho was among PTA members to sign a treaty establishing a Common Market for Eastern and Southern Africa.

Impediments to economic development in Lesotho include the lack of natural resources, vulnerability to drought, a relatively high rate of population growth and the country's dependence on South Africa (the Lesotho currency, the loti, is fixed at par with the South African rand, exposing Lesotho to fluctuations within the South African economy). From 1988 Lesotho undertook major economic reforms, supported by the IMF and other donors, and by the mid-1990s was enjoying strong GDP growth and had succeeded in attaining an overall budgetary surplus (equivalent to 3.5% of GNP in 1993/94), in lowering the rate of inflation and the external current-account deficit, while strengthening reserves of foreign exchange. Economic priorities for the second half of the decade include a programme of privatization and rationalization of the parastatal sector, together with the continued reform of the civil service; in the agricultural sector, high-value crops for export are to be developed, while infrastructural expansion, environmental protection and employment creation are emphasized. The Highlands Water Project offers considerable prospects for new revenues (sales of water to South Africa were due to commence in 1995–96), although the significant customs receipts derived from materials imported during the construction period will inevitably decline upon the completion of work. Moreover, concerns remain regarding political stability in Lesotho, and a recurrence of the instability of 1994 could lead to a loss of external assistance and deter foreign investors.

### Social Welfare

The Government administers 11 hospitals, including a mental hospital and a leper settlement, and 51 of the 153 rural clinics; it also operates a 'flying doctor' service. In addition, there are nine mission hospitals and a military hospital. In 1992 the country had 2,400 hospital beds (excluding the military hospital) and 139 practising physicians. Of projected expenditure by the central Government in the financial year 1992/93, M65.5m. (13.1%) was allocated to health, social security and welfare. Budget estimates for 1995/96 allocated M108.3m. (6.7% of total projected expenditure) to the health sector.

### Education

All primary education is available free of charge, and is provided mainly by the three main Christian missions (Lesotho Evangelical, Roman Catholic and Anglican), under the direction of the Ministry of Education. Lesotho has one of the highest levels of literacy among African countries: according to the population census of 1986, the average rate of adult illiteracy was 30% for males and 11% for females. Education at primary schools is officially compulsory for seven years between six and 13 years of age. Secondary education, beginning at the age of 13, lasts for up to five years, comprising a first cycle of three years and a second of two years. Of children in the relevant age-groups in 1993, 63.8% of males and 77.7% of females were enrolled at primary schools, while in 1991 49.5% of males and 60.8% of females were enrolled at secondary schools. The National University of Lesotho had 1,612 enrolled students in 1992. The 1995/96 budget envisaged expenditure of M335.6m. on education (20.9% of total estimated expenditure), the highest allocation to any sector.

### Public Holidays

**1995:** 1 January (New Year's Day), 28 January (anniversary of overthrow of Chief Jonathan's Government), 12 March (Moshoeshoe's Day), 14–17 April (Easter), 2 May (King's Birthday), 25 May (Ascension Day), 1 July (Family Day), 4 October (National Independence Day), 7 October (National Sports Day), 25, 26 December (Christmas and Boxing Day).

**1996:** 1 January (New Year's Day), 28 January (anniversary of overthrow of Chief Jonathan's Government), 12 March (Moshoeshoe's Day), 5–8 April (Easter), 2 May (King's Birthday), 16 May (Ascension Day), 1 July (Family Day), 4 October (National Independence Day), 7 October (National Sports Day), 25, 26 December (Christmas and Boxing Day).

### Weights and Measures

The metric system of weights and measures is in force.

# Statistical Survey

Source (unless otherwise stated): Bureau of Statistics, POB 455, Maseru 100; tel. 3852.

## Area and Population

### AREA, POPULATION AND DENSITY

| | |
|---|---:|
| Area (sq km) | 30,355* |
| Population (census results)† | |
| 12 April 1976 | |
| Males | 458,260 |
| Females | 605,928 |
| Total | 1,064,188 |
| 12 April 1986 (provisional) | 1,447,000 |
| Population (official estimates at mid-year)‡ | |
| 1985 | 1,528,000 |
| 1987 | 1,619,000 |
| 1989 | 1,700,000 |
| Density (per sq km) at mid-1989 | 56.0 |

* 11,720 sq miles.
† Excluding absentee workers in South Africa, numbering 152,627 (males 129,088; females 23,539) in 1976.
‡ Including absentee workers in South Arica. Mid-year estimates for 1986 and 1988 are not available.

**1992:** Estimated population 1,932,879, including 126,647 absentee workers in South Africa.

### DISTRICT POPULATIONS
(Each district* has the same name as its chief town)

| | 1976† | 1979‡ | 1981§ |
|---|---:|---:|---:|
| Berea | 146,124 | 155,616 | 162,400 |
| Butha-Buthe | 77,178 | 81,926 | 84,800 |
| Leribe | 206,558 | 222,180 | 234,400 |
| Mafeteng | 154,339 | 166,644 | 175,900 |
| Maseru | 257,809 | 277,307 | 292,200 |
| Mohale's Hoek | 136,311 | 144,013 | 152,300 |
| Mokhotlong | 73,508 | 78,237 | 80,900 |
| Qacha's Nek | 76,497 | 81,060 | 84,700 |
| Quthing | 88,491 | 93,769 | 98,300 |
| **Total** | 1,216,815 | 1,301,575 | 1,365,900 |

* A new district, Thaba-Tseka, was created in 1981, for which no population figures were available.
† Census of 12 April, including absentee workers in South Africa.
‡ Mid-year estimate.
§ Mid-year estimate, projected from the 1976 census.

**Capital:** Maseru, population 45,000 in 1976.

### BIRTHS AND DEATHS (UN estimates, annual averages)

| | 1975–80 | 1980–85 | 1985–90 |
|---|---:|---:|---:|
| Birth rate (per 1,000) | 41.9 | 40.4 | 36.3 |
| Death rate (per 1,000) | 16.5 | 12.6 | 11.0 |

**Expectation of life** (UN estimates, years at birth, 1985–90): 58.0 (males 55.5; females 60.5).

Source: UN, *World Population Prospects: The 1992 Revision*.

### ECONOMICALLY ACTIVE POPULATION
(ILO estimates, '000 persons at mid-1980)

| | Males | Females | Total |
|---|---:|---:|---:|
| Agriculture, etc. | 300 | 271 | 571 |
| Industry | 21 | 6 | 27 |
| Services | 38 | 26 | 64 |
| **Total labour force** | 359 | 303 | 662 |

Source: ILO, *Economically Active Population Estimates and Projections, 1950–2025*.

**Mid-1993** (estimates in '000): Agriculture, etc. 682; Total 884 (Source: FAO, *Production Yearbook*).

In 1992 about 38% of the total adult male labour force were in employment in South Africa.

## Agriculture

### PRINCIPAL CROPS ('000 metric tons)

| | 1991 | 1992 | 1993 |
|---|---:|---:|---:|
| Wheat | 11 | 9 | 13 |
| Maize | 108 | 55 | 92 |
| Sorghum | 13 | 14 | 52 |
| Roots and tubers* | 8 | 8 | 8 |
| Pulses | 6 | 3 | 3* |
| Vegetables* | 27 | 26 | 26 |
| Fruit* | 19 | 18 | 18 |

* FAO estimate(s).
Source: FAO, *Production Yearbook*.

### LIVESTOCK ('000 head, year ending September)

| | 1991 | 1992* | 1993* |
|---|---:|---:|---:|
| Cattle* | 660 | 600 | 650 |
| Sheep | 1,676 | 1,600 | 1,665 |
| Goats | 850 | 1,000 | 1,010 |
| Pigs* | 75 | 75 | 76 |
| Horses* | 122 | 122 | 123 |
| Asses* | 158 | 160 | 162 |

Poultry (million)*: 1 in 1991; 1 in 1992; 1 in 1993.
* FAO estimates.
Source: FAO, *Production Yearbook*.

### LIVESTOCK PRODUCTS ('000 metric tons)

| | 1991 | 1992* | 1993* |
|---|---:|---:|---:|
| Cows' milk* | 24 | 24 | 24 |
| Beef and veal* | 14 | 13 | 13 |
| Mutton and lamb* | 4 | 4 | 4 |
| Goat meat* | 3 | 3 | 3 |
| Pig meat* | 3 | 3 | 3 |
| Hen eggs* | 0.8 | 0.8 | 0.8 |
| Wool: | | | |
| greasy | 3.0† | 2.9 | 2.9 |
| clean* | 1.5 | 1.5 | 1.5 |

* FAO estimates.  † Unofficial figure.
Source: FAO, *Production Yearbook*.

LESOTHO

## Forestry

**ROUNDWOOD REMOVALS**
(FAO estimates, '000 cubic metres, excluding bark)

|  | 1990 | 1991 | 1992 |
|---|---|---|---|
| **Total** (all fuel wood) | 604 | 619 | 635 |

Source: FAO, *Yearbook of Forest Products*.

## Fishing

(FAO estimates, metric tons, live weight)

|  | 1990 | 1991 | 1992 |
|---|---|---|---|
| **Total catch** | 30 | 25 | 30 |

Source: FAO, *Yearbook of Fishery Statistics*.

## Mining

|  | 1979 | 1980 | 1981 |
|---|---|---|---|
| Diamonds (carats) | 64,886 | 105,245 | 52,291 |

**1982:** 48,000 carats (estimate) (Source: UN, *Industrial Statistics Yearbook*).

## Finance

**CURRENCY AND EXCHANGE RATES**

**Monetary Units**
100 lisente (singular: sente) = 1 loti (plural: maloti).

**Sterling, Dollar and Rand Equivalents** (31 December 1994)
£1 sterling = 5.545 maloti;
US $1 = 3.544 maloti;
R1 = 1 loti;
100 maloti = £18.03 = $28.21.

**Average Exchange Rate** (US $ per loti)
1992  0.35092
1993  0.30641
1994  0.28177

Note: The loti is fixed at par with the South African rand.

**BUDGET** ('000 maloti, year ending 31 March)

| Revenue* | 1989/90 | 1990/91 | 1991/92 |
|---|---|---|---|
| Taxation | 444,347 | 558,033 | 700,721 |
| Taxes on income, profits, etc. | 59,366 | 70,802 | 138,300 |
| Taxes on property | 201 | 352 | 585 |
| Domestic taxes on goods and services | 119,331 | 130,344 | 137,198 |
| Sales tax | 102,510 | 112,300 | 112,700 |
| Excises | 12,300 | 13,120 | 16,300 |
| Taxes on international trade | 264,764 | 355,985 | 424,336 |
| Import duties† | 263,770 | 355,000 | 424,000 |
| Other taxes | 685 | 550 | 302 |
| Other current revenue | 80,761 | 69,531 | 118,934 |
| Property income | 42,578 | 40,694 | 70,494 |
| Administrative fees, charges, etc. | 16,602 | 15,154 | 17,941 |
| Capital revenue | 85 | 115 | 300 |
| **Total** | 525,193 | 627,679 | 819,955 |

| Expenditure‡ | 1989/90 | 1990/91 | 1991/92 |
|---|---|---|---|
| General public services | 63,400 | 63,097 | 91,400 |
| Defence | 66,235 | 61,262 | 62,770 |
| Public order and safety | 32,805 | 35,409 | 44,950 |
| Education | 113,257 | 144,168 | 212,671 |
| Health | 67,587 | 88,266 | 111,173 |
| Social security and welfare | 13,502 | 13,411 | 14,965 |
| Housing and community amenities | 36,288 | 39,856 | 37,916 |
| Other community and social services | 4,940 | 4,906 | 6,528 |
| Economic services | 271,099 | 278,846 | 306,620 |
| Fuel and energy | 14,485 | 13,686 | 18,900 |
| Agriculture, forestry, fishing and hunting | 77,758 | 80,599 | 106,341 |
| Mining, manufacturing and construction | 74,473 | 67,180 | 47,695 |
| Transportation and communication | 77,825 | 82,759 | 96,134 |
| Other economic services | 26,558 | 34,622 | 37,550 |
| Other purposes | 101,060 | 94,305 | 80,965 |
| **Total** | 770,173 | 823,526 | 969,958 |
| Current | 435,184 | 456,155 | 622,340 |
| Capital | 334,989 | 367,371 | 347,618 |

* Excluding grants received from abroad ('000 maloti): 151,925 in 1989/90; 188,000 in 1990/91; 149,200 in 1991/92.
† Including Lesotho's allocated share of the Southern African Customs Union's collections of customs duties, excise duties and sales taxes not separately identifiable.
‡ Excluding net lending ('000 maloti): 10,313 in 1989/90; 8,950 in 1990/91; 9,050 in 1991/92.

Source: IMF, *Government Finance Statistics Yearbook*.

**1992/93** (million maloti): Revenue 1,019.6; Grants 141.8; Expenditure and net lending 1,085.2.
**1993/4** (million maloti, preliminary figures): Revenue 1,262.9; Grants 132.4; Expenditure and net lending 1,250.7.

Source: IMF, *Lesotho—Recent Economic Developments*.

**INTERNATIONAL RESERVES** (US $ million at 31 December)

|  | 1991 | 1992 | 1993 |
|---|---|---|---|
| IMF special drawing rights | 0.29 | 0.66 | 0.56 |
| Reserve position in IMF | 1.87 | 4.83 | 4.82 |
| Foreign exchange | 112.88 | 152.00 | 247.30 |
| **Total** | 115.04 | 157.49 | 252.69 |

Source: IMF, *International Financial Statistics*.

**MONEY SUPPLY** (million maloti at 31 December)

|  | 1991 | 1992 | 1993 |
|---|---|---|---|
| Currency outside banks | 37.01 | 39.86 | 43.75 |
| Demand deposits at commercial banks | 275.77 | 311.29 | 389.43 |
| **Total money** | 312.78 | 351.15 | 433.18 |

Source: IMF, *International Financial Statistics*.

**COST OF LIVING**
(Consumer Price Index for low-income households; base: 1980 = 100)

|  | 1990 | 1991 | 1992 |
|---|---|---|---|
| Food | 342.2 | 404.8 | 500.3 |
| **All items** | 350.9 | 413.6 | 484.0 |

Source: ILO: *Year Book of Labour Statistics*.

# LESOTHO

## Statistical Survey

### NATIONAL ACCOUNTS (million maloti at current prices)

**Expenditure on the Gross Domestic Product** (year ending 31 March)

|  | 1990/91 | 1991/92 | 1992/93 |
|---|---|---|---|
| Government final consumption expenditure | 234.6 | 314.2 | 380.5 |
| Private final consumption expenditure | 1,756.7 | 2,304.3 | 2,660.3 |
| Increase in stocks | −10.3 | −6.9 | −7.7 |
| Gross fixed capital formation | 1,162.4 | 1,248.8 | 1,424.0 |
| **Total domestic expenditure** | 3,143.4 | 3,860.4 | 4,457.1 |
| Exports of goods and services | 216.0 | 250.1 | 378.3 |
| *Less* Imports of goods and services | 1,850.2 | 2,371.8 | 2,809.5 |
| **GDP in purchasers' values** | 1,509.2 | 1,738.7 | 2,025.9 |

Source: IMF, *International Financial Statistics*.

**Gross Domestic Product by Economic Activity**

|  | 1991 | 1992 | 1993 |
|---|---|---|---|
| Agriculture, forestry and fishing | 173.6 | 159.9 | 244.1 |
| Mining and quarrying | 3.7 | 2.0 | 2.4 |
| Manufacturing | 208.0 | 291.3 | 347.1 |
| Electricity, gas and water | 18.1 | 34.5 | 52.5 |
| Construction | 386.4 | 460.8 | 485.3 |
| Trade, restaurants, and hotels | 148.4 | 179.0 | 217.1 |
| Transport and communications | 46.6 | 56.6 | 68.6 |
| Finance, insurance, real estate and business services | 242.3 | 278.4 | 316.4 |
| Government services | 245.3 | 285.7 | 323.2 |
| Other services | 48.2 | 59.3 | 68.2 |
| **Sub-total** | 1,520.6 | 1,807.5 | 2,125.0 |
| *Less* Imputed bank service charge | 85.6 | 91.0 | 93.5 |
| **GDP at factor cost** | 1,435.0 | 1,716.5 | 2,031.5 |
| Indirect taxes, *less* subsidies | 364.6 | 414.7 | 444.2 |
| **GDP in purchasers' values** | 1,799.7 | 2,131.2 | 2,475.7 |
| **GDP at constant 1980 prices** | 444.2 | 455.6 | 481.0 |

Sources: IMF, *Lesotho—Recent Economic Developments*.

### BALANCE OF PAYMENTS (US $ million)

|  | 1991 | 1992 | 1993 |
|---|---|---|---|
| Merchandise exports f.o.b. | 67.2 | 109.2 | 134.0 |
| Merchandise imports f.o.b. | −803.5 | −932.6 | −911.6 |
| **Trade balance** | −736.4 | −823.4 | −777.6 |
| Export of services | 40.9 | 41.3 | 36.7 |
| Imports of services | −83.5 | −81.7 | −72.3 |
| Other income received | 476.8 | 496.3 | 457.0 |
| Other income paid | −20.9 | −33.7 | −22.8 |
| Private unrequited transfers (net) | 2.7 | 3.9 | 2.6 |
| Official unrequited transfers (net) | 403.5 | 434.9 | 398.0 |
| **Current balance** | 83.1 | 37.6 | 21.6 |
| Direct investment (net) | 7.5 | 2.7 | 15.0 |
| Other capital (net) | −68.2 | −65.2 | 49.8 |
| Net errors and omissions | 20.1 | 74.8 | 16.1 |
| **Overall balance** | 42.4 | 49.9 | 102.4 |

Source: IMF, *International Financial Statistics*.

# External Trade

### PRINCIPAL COMMODITIES

| Imports c.i.f. ('000 maloti) | 1979 | 1980 | 1981 |
|---|---|---|---|
| Food and live animals | 68,559 | 76,918 | 82,902 |
| Beverages and tobacco | 13,725 | 16,233 | 21,761 |
| Clothing | 31,652 | 34,452 | 36,733 |
| Machinery and transport equipment | 44,084 | 58,397 | 74,647 |
| Petroleum products | 22,848 | 31,633 | 37,766 |
| Chemicals | 16,372 | 18,853 | 28,229 |
| Footwear | 10,556 | 12,423 | 14,338 |
| **Total** (incl. others) | 303,612 | 360,757 | 439,375 |

**Total imports** (million maloti): 567.2 in 1982; 539.7 in 1983; 634.5 in 1984; 751.0 in 1985; 803.3 in 1986; 954.8 in 1987; 1,327.5 in 1988; 1,406.5 in 1989; 1,801.3 in 1990; 2,255.7 in 1991; 3,013.9 in 1992 (Sources: Central Bank of Lesotho; IMF, *International Financial Statistics*).

| Exports f.o.b. (million maloti) | 1991 | 1992 | 1993* |
|---|---|---|---|
| Food and live animals | 21.6 | 22.9 | 25.7 |
| Live animals | 1.7 | 0.4 | 8.9 |
| Cereals | 9.7 | 4.8 | 6.9 |
| Crude materials (inedible) except fuels | 16.9 | 19.5 | n.a. |
| Wool | 3.6 | 15.3 | 16.9 |
| Mohair | 6.1 | 3.8 | 5.1 |
| Basic manufactures | 10.2 | 9.6 | 13.4 |
| Machinery and transport equipment | 5.2 | 35.0 | 25.5 |
| Miscellaneous manufactured articles | 129.3 | 220.1 | 348.2 |
| Furniture and parts | 0.8 | 2.7 | 27.5 |
| Clothing and accesssories (excl. footwear) | 112.5 | 216.9 | 250.8 |
| Footwear | 8.1 | 20.8 | 50.9 |
| **Total** (incl. others) | 186.2 | 310.9 | 438.9 |

* Estimated figures.

Source: Ministry of Trade, Industry, Tourism, Sports and Culture, Maseru, and IMF, *Lesotho—Recent Economic Developments*.

### PRINCIPAL TRADING PARTNERS (million maloti)

| Imports | 1991 | 1992 | 1993* |
|---|---|---|---|
| Africa | 2,114.5 | 2,596.9 | 2,572.0 |
| SACU† | 2,096.3 | 2,593.3 | 2,565.4 |
| Asia | 74.9 | 249.8 | 354.8 |
| Hong Kong | 40.1 | 93.6 | 90.0 |
| Japan | 0.6 | 43.8 | 53.0 |
| Taiwan | 33.5 | 54.4 | 108.3 |
| European Union | 29.8 | 117.6 | 85.9 |
| Italy | 14.7 | 30.3 | 9.1 |
| North America | 6.4 | 17.1 | 57.5 |
| USA | 6.1 | 16.0 | 33.5 |
| **Total** (incl. others) | 2,227.6 | 3,025.3 | 3,094.8 |

| Exports | 1991 | 1992 | 1993* |
|---|---|---|---|
| Africa | 78.9 | 154.4 | 150.9 |
| SACU† | 76.0 | 152.7 | 142.1 |
| Asia | 1.0 | 0.8 | 4.1 |
| European Union | 50.6 | 70.5 | 79.5 |
| North America | 52.1 | 83.3 | 120.1 |
| **Total** (incl. others) | 186.2 | 310.9 | 360.3 |

* Estimated figures.
† Southern African Customs Union, of which Lesotho is a member; also including Botswana, Namibia, South Africa and Swaziland.

Source: IMF, *Lesotho—Recent Economic Developments*.

## Transport

**ROAD TRAFFIC** (motor vehicles in use at 31 December)

|  | 1993 |
|---|---|
| Passenger cars | 5,944 |
| Buses and motorcoaches | 2,949 |
| Lorries and vans | 14,836 |

Source: IRF, *World Road Statistics*.

**CIVIL AVIATION** (traffic on scheduled services)

|  | 1990 | 1991 | 1992 |
|---|---|---|---|
| Kilometres flown (million) | 1 | 1 | 1 |
| Passengers carried ('000) | 53 | 56 | 21 |
| Passenger-km (million) | 13 | 14 | 8 |
| Total ton-km (million) | 1 | 1 | 1 |

Source: UN, *Statistical Yearbook*.

## Tourism

|  | 1990 | 1991 | 1992 |
|---|---|---|---|
| Tourist arrivals ('000) | 171 | 182 | 155 |
| Tourist receipts (US $ million) | 17 | 18 | 19 |

Source: UN, *Statistical Yearbook*.

## Communications Media

|  | 1990 | 1991 | 1992 |
|---|---|---|---|
| Radio receivers ('000 in use) | 48 | n.a. | 66 |
| Television receivers ('000 in use) | 10 | 11 | 11 |
| Telephones ('000 in use)* | 12 | 12 | n.a. |
| Daily newspapers |  |  |  |
| Number | 4 | n.a. | 2 |
| Average circulation ('000 copies) | 20 | n.a. | 14 |

* Estimates.

Sources: UNESCO, *Statistical Yearbook*; UN Economic Commission for Africa, *African Statistical Yearbook*.

## Education

(1992)

|  | Institutions | Teachers | Students |
|---|---|---|---|
| Primary | 1,201 | 7,051 | 362,657 |
| General secondary | 186 | 2,443 | 51,895 |
| Teachers' training college | 1 | 94 | 723 |
| Technical and vocational schools | 8 | 141 | 1,590 |
| University | 1 | 190 | 1,612 |

Source: Ministry of Information and Broadcasting, Maseru.

# Directory

## The Constitution

The Constitution of the Kingdom of Lesotho, which took effect at independence in October 1966, was suspended in January 1970. A new Constitution was promulgated following the March 1993 general election. Its main provisions are summarized below:

Lesotho is an hereditary monarchy. The King, who is Head of State, has no executive or legislative powers. Executive authority is vested in the Cabinet, which is headed by the Prime Minister, while legislative power is exercised by the 65-member National Assembly, which is elected, at intervals of no more than five years, by universal adult suffrage in the context of a multi-party political system. There is also a Senate, comprising traditional chiefs and 11 nominated members.

## The Government

### HEAD OF STATE

HM King MOSHOESHOE II (restored to the throne 25 January 1995).

### CABINET
(May 1995)

**Prime Minister and Minister of Defence and Public Service:** Dr NTSU MOKHEHLE.
**Deputy Prime Minister and Minister of Education and Manpower Development:** PAKALITHA MOSISILI.
**Minister of Finance and Economic Planning:** MOEKETSI SENAOANA.
**Minister of Foreign Affairs:** MPHO MALIE.
**Minister of Trade, Industry, Tourism, Sports and Culture:** SHAKHANE ROBONG MOKHEHLE.
**Minister of Agriculture, Co-operatives, Marketing and Youth Affairs:** NTSUKUNYANE MPHANYA.
**Minister of Home Affairs, Local Government, Rural and Urban Development:** LESAO LEHOHLA.
**Minister of Health and Social Welfare:** Dr KHAUHELO DEBORAH RADITAPOLE.
**Minister of Natural Resources, Water, Highlands Water Project, Energy, Mining, Technology and the Environment:** TSELISO MAKHAKHE.
**Minister of Transport and Telecommunications:** DAVID MOCHOCHOKO.
**Minister of Works:** MOLAPO QHOBELA.
**Minister of Information and Broadcasting:** LIRA MOTETE.
**Minister of Justice and Human Rights, Law and Constitutional Affairs:** KELEBONE MAOPE.
**Minister of Labour and Employment:** NOT'SI VICTOR MOLOPO.
**Minister without Portfolio:** SEPHIRI MONTANYANE.

### MINISTRIES

**Office of the Prime Minister:** POB 527, Maseru; tel. 311000.
**Ministry of Agriculture, Co-operatives, Marketing and Youth Affairs:** POB 24, Maseru 100; tel. 322741; telex 4330.
**Ministry of Defence and Public Service:** POB 527, Maseru 100; tel. 323861; telex 4330.
**Ministry of Education and Manpower Development:** POB 47, Maseru 100; tel. 313628; telex 4330.
**Ministry of Finance and Economic Planning:** POB 395, Maseru 100; tel. 311101; telex 4330; fax 310157.
**Ministry of Foreign Affairs:** POB 1387, Maseru 100; tel. 311150; telex 4330.
**Ministry of Health and Social Welfare:** POB 514, Maseru 100; tel. 324404; telex 433010.
**Ministry of Home Affairs, Local Government, Rural and Urban Development:** POB 174, Maseru; tel. 323771.
**Ministry of Information and Broadcasting:** POB 36, Maseru 100; tel. 323561; telex 4450; fax 310003.
**Ministry of Justice and Human Rights, Law and Constitutional Affairs:** POB 402, Maseru 100; tel. 311160; telex 4330.
**Ministry of Labour and Employment:** Private Bag A116, Maseru 100; tel. 322565.
**Ministry of Natural Resources, Water, Highlands Water Project, Energy, Mining, Technology and the Environment:** POB 426, Maseru 100; tel. 311741; telex 4253.
**Ministry of Trade, Industry, Tourism, Sports and Culture:** POB 747, Maseru 100; tel. 322138; telex 4384; fax 310121.

LESOTHO

*Directory*

**Ministry of Transport and Telecommunications:** POB 413, Maseru 100; tel. 323691; telex 4258; fax 310125.
**Ministry of Works:** POB 20, Maseru 100; tel. 323761.

## Legislature

### NATIONAL ASSEMBLY

**Speaker:** Dr J. G. KOLANE.
Elections to the 65-member National Assembly took place in March 1993. The Basotho Congress Party won all of the seats.

## Political Organizations

Party political activity was banned during the period March 1986–May 1991.
**Basotho Congress Party (BCP):** POB 111, Maseru; f. 1952; Leader Dr NTSU MOKHEHLE; 75,000 mems.
**Basotho Democratic Alliance (BDA):** Maseru; f. 1984; Pres. S. C. NCOJANE.
**Basotho National Party (BNP):** POB 124, Maseru 100; f. 1958; Sec.-Gen. EVARISTUS RETSELISITSOE SEKHONYANA; 280,000 mems.
**Communist Party of Lesotho (CPL):** Maseru; f. 1962 (banned 1970–91); supported mainly by migrant workers employed in South Africa; Sec.-Gen. MOKHAFISI JACOB KENA.
**Ha Reeng (Let's Go) Basotho Party:** Maseru; Leader KHAUTA KHASU.
**Kopanang Basotho Party (KBP):** Maseru; f. 1992; campaigns for women's rights; Leader LIMAKATSO NTAKATSANE.
**Lesotho Labour Party (LLP):** Maseru; f. 1991; Leader MAMOLEFI RANTHIMO.
**Marematlou Freedom Party (MFP):** POB 0443, Maseru 105; tel. 315804; f. 1962; Leader VINCENT MOEKETSE MALEBO; Deputy Leader THABO LEANYA; 300,000 mems.
**National Independence Party:** Maseru; f. 1984; Pres. ANTHONY C. MANYELI.
**Popular Front for Democracy:** Maseru; f. 1991.
**United Democratic Party (UDP):** POB 776, Maseru 100; f. 1967; Chair. BEN L. SHEA; Leader CHARLES D. MOFELI; Sec.-Gen. MOLOMO NKUEBE; 26,000 mems.

## Diplomatic Representation

### EMBASSIES AND HIGH COMMISSIONS IN LESOTHO

**Germany:** Maseru; telex 4379; Ambassador: HANS GUENTER GNOSTKE.
**South Africa:** Lesotho Bank Centre, Private Bag A266, Maseru 100; tel. 315758; fax 310128; Ambassador: P. GERHARD VISSER.
**United Kingdom:** POB 521, Maseru 100; tel. 313961; telex 4343; fax 310120; High Commissioner: JAMES ROY COWLING.
**USA:** POB 333, Maseru 100; tel. 312666; fax 310116; Ambassador: LEONARD H. O. SPEARMAN.

## Judicial System

### HIGH COURT

The High Court is a superior court of record, and in addition to any other jurisdiction conferred by statute it is vested with unlimited original jurisdiction to determine any civil or criminal matter. It also has appellate jurisdiction to hear appeals and reviews from the subordinate courts. Appeals may be made to the court of appeal.
**Chief Justice:** BRENDAN PETER CULLINAN.
**Judges:** M. L. LEHOHLA, J. L. KHEOLA, B. K. MOLAI.

### COURT OF APPEAL

**Judges:** ISMAIL MAHOMED (President), J. BROWNE, G. P. KOTZE, R. N. LEON, J. H. STEYN.

### SUBORDINATE COURTS

Each of the 10 districts possesses subordinate courts, presided over by magistrates.

### JUDICIAL COMMISSIONERS' COURTS

These courts hear civil and criminal appeals from central and local courts. Further appeal may be made to the high court and finally to the court of appeal.

### CENTRAL AND LOCAL COURTS

There are 71 such courts, of which 58 are local courts and 13 are central courts which also serve as courts of appeal from the local courts. They have limited civil and criminal jurisdiction.

## Religion

About 90% of the population profess Christianity.

### CHRISTIANITY

**African Federal Church Council:** POB 70, Peka 340; f.1927; links 48 African independent churches; Co-ordinator Rev. S. MOHONO.
**Christian Council of Lesotho:** POB 457, Maseru 100; tel. 323639; telex 4512; fax 310310; f. 1973; six mem. and four assoc. mem. churches; Chair. Rev. LEBOHANG KHEEKHE; Sec. R. M. TAOLE.

#### The Anglican Communion

Anglicans in Lesotho are adherents of the Church of the Province of Southern Africa, comprising 22 dioceses. The Metropolitan of the Province is the Archbishop of Cape Town, South Africa. Lesotho forms a single diocese, with an estimated 100,000 members.
**Bishop of Lesotho:** Rt Rev. PHILIP STANLEY MOKUKU, Bishop's House, POB 87, Maseru 100; tel. 311974; fax 31016.

#### The Roman Catholic Church

Lesotho comprises one archdiocese and three dioceses. At 31 December 1993 there were an estimated 701,337 adherents in the country.
**Lesotho Catholic Bishops' Conference:** Catholic Secretariat, POB 200, Maseru 100; tel. 312525; telex 4540; fax 310294; f. 1972 (statutes approved 1980); Pres. Rt Rev. EVARISTUS THATHO BITSOANE, Bishop of Qacha's Nek; Sec.-Gen. Fr GEORGE MAHLATSI.
**Archbishop of Maseru:** Most Rev. BERNARD MOHLALISI, Archbishop's House, 19 Orpen Rd, POB 267, Maseru 100; tel. 312565.

#### Other Christian Churches

**African Methodist Episcopal Church:** POB 223, Maseru; tel. 322616; f. 1903; 11,295 mems.
**Dutch Reformed Church in Africa:** POB 454, Maseru; tel. 314669; the Lesotho branch (f. 1957) had 7,396 mems in 1991.
**Lesotho Evangelical Church:** POB 260, Maseru; tel. 323942; f. 1833; independent since 1964; Moderator Rev. G. L. SIBOLLA; Exec. Sec. Rev. A. M. THEBE; 211,000 mems (1990).
**Methodist Church of Southern Africa:** POB 81, Maseru; tel. 322412; f. 1927; Supt Rev. D. SENKHANE; c. 10,000 mems and adherents (1989).

Other denominations active in Lesotho include the Apostolic Faith Mission (2,000 mems in 1991), the Assemblies of God (2,300 mems in 1992), the Full Gospel Church of God (3,500 mems in 1991) and the Seventh-day Adventists (4,000 mems in 1991). In addition, there are numerous African independent churches, with a combined membership estimated at 100,000.

### BAHÁ'Í FAITH

**National Spiritual Assembly:** POB 508, Maseru 100; tel. 312346; mems resident in 420 localities.

## The Press

**Lentsoe la Basotho:** POB 36, Maseru 100; tel. 323561; telex 4450; fax 310003; f. 1986; Sesotho; publ. by Ministry of Information and Broadcasting; Editor K. LESENYA; circ. 5,000.
**Leselinyana la Lesotho** (Light of Lesotho): POB 7, Morija 190; tel. 360244; f. 1863; fortnightly; Sesotho, with occasional articles in English; publ. by Lesotho Evangelical Church; Editor A. B. THOALANE; circ. 15,000.
**Lesotho Today:** POB 36, Maseru 100; tel. 323586; telex 4450; fax 310003; f. 1986; weekly; English; publ. by Ministry of Information and Broadcasting; Editor S. K. MAKHAKHE; circ. 2,500.
**Lesotho Weekly:** POB 353, Maseru.
**The Mirror:** POB 903, Maseru 100; tel. 315602; telex 4416; fax 310015.
**Moeletsi oa Basotho:** Mazenod Institute, POB 18, Mazenod 160; tel. 350254; telex 4271; f. 1933; weekly; Roman Catholic; Sesotho; Editor WILLIAM LESENYA; circ. 12,000.
**Molepe:** Maseru; bi-monthly; circ. 5,000.
**Mphatlatsane:** Maseru; daily; independent newspaper.

**Shoeshoe:** POB 36, Maseru 100; tel. 323561; telex 4340; fax 310003; quarterly; women's magazine.

### NEWS AGENCIES

**Lesotho News Agency (LENA):** POB 36, Maseru 100; tel. 315317; telex 4598; fax 310003; f. 1986; Dir LEBOHANG LEJAKANE; Editor KHOELI PHOLOSI.

#### Foreign Bureau

**Inter Press Service (IPS)** (Italy): c/o Lesotho News Agency, POB 36, Maseru; Correspondent LEBOHANG LEJAKANE.

## Publishers

**Macmillan Boleswa Publishers Lesotho (Pty) Ltd:** POB 7545, Maseru 100; tel. 317340; fax 310047.
**Mazenod Institute:** POB MZ 18, Mazenod 160; tel. 62224; telex 4271; f. 1931; Roman Catholic; Man. Fr B. MOHLALISI.
**Morija Sesuto Book Depot:** POB 4, Morija 190; f. 1861; owned by the Lesotho Evangelical Church; religious, educational and Sesotho language and literature.
**St Michael's Mission:** The Social Centre, POB 25, Roma; f. 1968; religious and educational; Man. Dir Fr M. FERRANGE.

#### Government Publishing House

**Government Printer:** Maseru.

## Radio and Television

In 1992 there were an estimated 66,000 radio receivers and 11,000 television receivers in use.

**Lesotho National Broadcasting Service:** POB 552, Maseru 100; tel. 323561; telex 4340; fax 310003; programmes in Sesotho and English; television transmissions began in 1988; CEO F. N. LETELE; Dir of Broadcasting T. NTSANE.

## Finance

(cap. = capital; res = reserves; dep. = deposits; m. = million; brs = branches; amounts in maloti)

### BANKING
#### Central Bank

**Central Bank of Lesotho:** POB 1184, Maseru 100; tel. 314281; telex 4367; fax 310051; f. 1980; bank of issue; cap. and res 90.3m., dep. 922.3m. (Dec. 1993); Gov. and Chair. Dr ANTHONY M. MARUPING; Gen. Man. ALEMU ABERRA.

#### Commercial Banks

**Barclays Bank PLC:** POB 115, Kingsway, Maseru 100; tel. 312423; telex 4346; fax 310068; Gen. Man. W. G. PRICE; 4 brs and 3 agencies.
**Lesotho Bank:** POB 1053, Maseru 100; tel. 315737; telex 4206; fax 310268; f. 1972; state-owned; commercial bank, also carries out development banking functions; cap. and res 81m., dep. 604m. (Dec. 1993); Chair. Dr M. MOKETE; Gen. Man. N. MONYANE; 8 brs and 15 agencies.
**Standard Chartered Bank Lesotho Ltd:** Standard Bank Bldg, 1st Floor, Kingsway, POB 1001, Maseru 100; tel. 312696; telex 4332; fax 310025; Chief Man. W. C. IRWIN; 3 brs and 7 agencies.

#### Development Banks

**Lesotho Agricultural Development Bank (LADB):** 58 Kingsway Rd, POB 845, Maseru 100; tel. 313277; telex 4269; fax 310139; f. 1980; state-owned; cap. 5m. (Dec. 1991); Chair. L. T. TYOANE; Man. Dir C. S. MOLELLE; 7 brs and 12 agencies.
**Lesotho Building Finance Corporation (LBFC):** Private Bag A59, Maseru 100; tel. 313514; telex 4326; state-owned; Man. Dir N. MONYANE; 3 brs.

### INSURANCE

**Lesotho National Insurance Co (Pty) Ltd:** Private Bag A65, Lesotho Insurance House, Kingsway, Maseru; tel. 323032; telex 4220.

## Trade and Industry

### DEVELOPMENT ORGANIZATIONS

**Lesotho Highlands Development Authority:** POB 7332, Maseru 100; tel. 311280; telex 4523; fax 310060; f. 1986 to supervise the Highlands Water Project, being undertaken jtly with South Africa; CEO MASUPHA SOLE.
**Lesotho National Development Corporation (LNDC):** Development House, 1st Floor, Kingsway Rd, Private Bag A96, Maseru 100; tel. 312012; telex 4341; fax 311038; f. 1967; 90% govt-owned; candle, carpet, tyre-retreading, explosives and furniture factories, potteries, two diamond prospecting operations, a fertilizer factory, an abattoir, a clothing factory, a diamond-cutting and polishing works, a jewellery factory, a housing co, a brewery, an international hotel with a gambling casino, Lesotho Airways Corpn and a training centre for motor mechanics; cap. p.u. M20m. (March 1993); Chair. Minister of Trade, Industry, Tourism, Sports and Culture; Man. Dir (vacant).
**Basotho Enterprises Development Corporation (BEDCO):** POB 1216, Maseru 100; tel. 312094; telex 4370; f. 1980; promotes and assists with the establishment and development of small-scale Basotho-owned enterprises; Man. Dir S. K. PHAFANE.
**Lesotho Co-operatives Handicrafts:** Maseru; f. 1978; marketing and distribution of handicrafts; Gen. Man. KHOTSO MATLA.

### CHAMBER OF COMMERCE

**Lesotho Chamber of Commerce and Industry:** POB 79, Maseru; tel. 323482.

### MARKETING ORGANIZATIONS

**Livestock Products Marketing Service:** POB 800, Maseru; telex 4344; f. 1973; sole organization for marketing livestock and livestock products; liaises closely with marketing boards in South Africa; projects include an abattoir, tannery, poultry and wool and mohair scouring plants; Gen. Man. S. R. MATLANYANE.
**Produce Marketing Corporation:** Maseru; telex 4365; f. 1974; Gen. Man. M. PHOOFOLO.

### EMPLOYERS' ORGANIZATION

**Association of Lesotho Employers:** POB 1509, Maseru; tel. 315736; telex 4368; f. 1961; represents mems in industrial relations and on govt bodies, and advises the Govt about employers' concerns; Pres. S. J. KAO; Exec. Dir T. MAKEKA.

### TRADE UNIONS

**Construction and Allied Workers Union of Lesotho (CAWULE):** Maseru.
**Lesotho General Workers' Union:** POB 322, Maseru; f. 1954; Chair. J. M. RAMAROTHOLE; Sec. T. MOTLOHI.
**Lesotho Transport and Telecommunication Workers' Union:** POB 266, Maseru; f. 1959; Pres. M. BERENG; Sec. P. MOTRAMAI.
**National Union of Construction and Allied Workers:** POB 327, Maseru; f. 1967; Pres. L. PUTSOANE; Sec. T. TLALE.
**National Union of Printing, Bookbinding and Allied Workers:** PO Mazenod 160; f. 1963; Pres. G. MOTEBANG; Gen. Sec. CLEMENT RATSIU.
**Union of Shop Distributive and Allied Workers:** POB 327, Maseru; f. 1966; Pres. P. BERENG; Sec. J. MOLAPO.

### CO-OPERATIVE SOCIETIES

**Co-op Lesotho Pty Ltd:** Ministry of Agriculture, Co-operatives, Marketing and Youth Affairs, POB 24, Maseru 100; tel. 322741; telex 4330.
**Registry of Co-operatives:** POB 89, Maseru; Registrar P. MOEKETSI.

## Transport

### RAILWAYS

Lesotho is linked with the South African railway system by a short line (2.6 km in length) from Maseru to Marseilles, on the Bloemfontein/Natal main line.

### ROADS

At 31 December 1993 Lesotho's road network totalled 5,324 km, of which 1,293 km were main roads and 787 km were secondary roads. About 798.6 km were paved. Construction of 300 km of new roads, under the Highlands Water Project, began in 1987. In the 1993/94 budget M80m. (5.7% of total expenditure) was allocated for the improvement of the road network.

## CIVIL AVIATION

The international airport is at Thota-Moli, about 20 km from Maseru. There are 40 airstrips in Lesotho, of which 14 receive charter and regular scheduled air services.

**Lesotho Airways Corporation:** Mejametalana Airport, POB 861, Maseru 100; tel. 312453; telex 4347; fax 310126; f. 1970; govt-owned; internal and regional flights and scheduled international services via South Africa and Swaziland; Chair. T. MAKHAKE; Man. Dir MICHAEL MACDONAGH.

# Tourism

In 1992 there were some 155,000 tourist arrivals, compared with 182,000 in 1991. Receipts from tourism in 1992 totalled about US $19m. in the latter year. Spectacular mountain scenery is the principal tourist attraction. The majority of visitors come from South Africa.

**Lesotho Tourist Board:** POB 1378, Maseru 100; tel. 313760; telex 4280; fax 310108; f. 1983; Man. Dir Mrs K. TLEBERE.

# LIBERIA

## Introductory Survey

**Location, Climate, Language, Religion, Flag, Capital**

The Republic of Liberia lies on the west coast of Africa, with Sierra Leone and Guinea to the north, and Côte d'Ivoire to the east. The climate is tropical, with temperatures ranging from 18°C (65°F) to 49°C (120°F). English is the official language but the 16 major ethnic groups speak their own languages and dialects. Liberia is officially a Christian state, though some Liberians hold traditional beliefs. There are about 670,000 Muslims. The national flag (proportions 19 by 10) has 11 horizontal stripes, alternately of red and white, with a dark blue square canton, containing a five-pointed white star, in the upper hoist. The capital is Monrovia.

**Recent History**

Founded by liberated black slaves from the southern USA, Liberia became an independent republic in 1847. The leader of the True Whig Party, William Tubman, who had been President of Liberia since 1944, died in July 1971 and was succeeded by his Vice-President, William R. Tolbert, who was re-elected in October 1975. The True Whig Party's monopoly of power was increasingly criticized, and in 1978 a major opposition group, the Progressive Alliance of Liberia, was formed. In April 1979 violent riots and looting (precipitated by government plans to increase the retail price of rice) prompted President Tolbert to assume emergency powers.

In April 1980 Tolbert was assassinated in a military coup, led by Master Sergeant (later Commander-in-Chief) Samuel Doe, who assumed power as Chairman of the newly-established People's Redemption Council (PRC), suspending the Constitution and proscribing all political parties. The new regime attracted international criticism for its summary execution of 13 former senior government officials who had been accused of corruption and mismanagement. Foreign relations improved, following the appointment in mid-1981, of a commission to draft a new constitution. It was announced that Liberia would return to civilian rule by January 1986. In July 1981, however, all civilian ministers received commissions, thus installing total military rule.

During the early 1980s there were frequent dismissals and resignations from the PRC and the Cabinet, as Doe demonstrated his avowed determination to eliminate corruption and abuse of public office. In August 1981 five members of the PRC were executed for plotting against the Government, and in 1982 several prominent public officials were replaced, following accusations of malpractices. There were further dismissals in 1983.

The draft Constitution was approved by 78.3% of registered voters in a national referendum in July 1984. In the same month Doe dissolved the PRC and appointed a 58-member Interim National Assembly, comprising 36 civilians and all the members of the former PRC. The ban on political organizations was repealed in the same month, to enable parties to secure registration prior to the presidential and legislative elections, which were due to take place in October 1985. In August 1984 Doe founded the National Democratic Party of Liberia (NDPL), and formally announced his candidacy for the presidency. By early 1985 a total of 11 political parties had been formed, but the opposition parties experienced considerable legal difficulties (including a prohibitive financial qualification) in attempting to complete the registration process. During the election campaign period several prominent opposition politicians were detained. Two influential parties, the Liberian People's Party (LPP) and the United People's Party (UPP), were proscribed, and only three parties besides the NDPL—the Liberian Action Party (LAP), the Liberia Unification Party (LUP) and the Unity Party (UP)—were eventually permitted to participate in the elections. Doe won the presidential election, receiving 50.9% of the votes. At the concurrent elections to the bicameral National Assembly the NDPL won 22 of the 26 seats in the Senate and 51 of the 64 seats in the House of Representatives. The three registered opposition parties complained of electoral malpractice, and urged a boycott of the National Assembly.

In November 1985 an attempted military coup, led by Brig.-Gen. Thomas Quiwonkpa (who had been dismissed as Commanding General of the Armed Forces in October 1983), was rapidly suppressed by troops loyal to the Government. Quiwonkpa and several of his supporters were killed, and subsequent fighting between rebels and government forces resulted in at least 600 deaths. Opposition leaders were detained, and meetings of students and others likely to be critical of the Government were banned.

On 6 January 1986 Doe was inaugurated as elected President. He appointed a new Cabinet, although most of its members had served in the previous administration. Several members of the opposition parties continued to boycott the National Assembly, and in March the LAP, the LUP and the UP formed a 'Grand Coalition', with the stated aim of restoring social, political and economic stability in Liberia. In May, however, opposition leaders proposed a 'power-sharing' agreement with the NDPL. In June the Government pardoned 30 political prisoners who had been accused of involvement in the November 1985 coup attempt. (It was reported that the USA had made the provision of economic aid for 1986 conditional upon an increase in political freedom in Liberia.) In August, none the less, the restoration of political harmony was undermined when the leaders of the LAP, the LUP and the UP were briefly detained. In September the Government revoked the ban on the UPP. Elections in December, to replace six opposition members of the National Assembly who had refused to take their seats, were boycotted by the three Grand Coalition parties, and the UPP withdrew shortly before the polls, alleging that the correct electoral procedures were not being followed; the NDPL thus took all six seats.

Several government members were dismissed during 1987, in connection with allegations of financial malpractice. In June Doe demanded the resignation of the Chief Justice and of three associate judges, in an attempt to restore credibility to the legal system, although criticism was attracted by the appointment as Chief Justice of Chea Cheapoo (a former Minister of Justice who had been dismissed in 1981, following allegations of dishonesty). In December 1987 Cheapoo was impeached before the Senate on charges of acting unconstitutionally, and was dismissed and banned from holding public office. He was later arrested on charges of criminal libel, following his allegations that Doe and the Minister of Justice had accepted bribes during negotiations with foreign petroleum companies. In February 1988 the Minister of Finance was dismissed, together with other senior financial officials.

In March 1988 Gabriel Kpolleh, the leader of the LUP, was among several people who were arrested on charges of planning to overthrow the Government. In October Kpolleh and nine others were sentenced to 10 years' imprisonment for treason. Meanwhile, in July the Government announced that an attempted coup had been suppressed, and that its leader, Gen. Nicholas Podier (the Vice-President in 1982–85), had been killed. In the same month the Constitution was amended (following a referendum) to allow the President to hold office for more than two terms. In August the Government banned political activity by students, in response to disturbances, and proscribed the national students' union.

In June 1989 the Minister of Finance was again replaced. In July the Minister of Defence, Maj-Gen. Gray Allison, was dismissed for his alleged involvement in a ritual murder, which had, it was said, been intended through witchcraft to bring about the downfall of President Doe. Allison was later sentenced to death for his complicity in the murder, although the human rights organization, Amnesty International, disputed the impartiality of his trial.

On 24 December 1989 an armed insurrection by rebel forces began in the north-eastern border region of Nimba County. In early 1990 several hundred deaths ensued in fighting between the Liberian army (the Armed Forces of Liberia—AFL) and the rebels, who claimed to be members of a hitherto unknown opposition group, the National Patriotic Front of Liberia (NPFL), led by a former government official, Charles Taylor.

The fighting swiftly degenerated into a war between Doe's ethnic group, the Krahn, and the local Gio and Mano tribes, and many thousands of people took refuge in neighbouring Guinea and Côte d'Ivoire.

By April 1990 the NPFL had overcome government resistance in Nimba County, gaining control of a large part of the area. Following the advance of rebels on the capital, Monrovia, in May, most foreign residents, including embassy staff, were evacuated. By late July NPFL forces had entered Monrovia; Taylor's authority as self-proclaimed President of his own interim administration, known as the National Patriotic Reconstruction Assembly, was, however, challenged by a faction of the NPFL, led by Prince Yormie Johnson, whose troops rapidly gained control of parts of Monrovia. In the subsequent conflict both government and rebel forces were responsible for numerous atrocities against civilians. The Economic Community of West African States (ECOWAS, see p. 138) repeatedly failed to negotiate a cease-fire, and in late August it dispatched a sea-borne force to enforce peace in the region. Doe and Johnson agreed to accept this ECOWAS Monitoring Group (ECOMOG, see p. 139), but its initial occupation of the port area of Monrovia encountered armed opposition by Taylor's forces.

On 30 August 1990 exiled representatives of Liberia's principal political parties, churches and other influential groups (although the NPFL boycotted the talks) met at a conference convened by ECOWAS in the Gambian capital, Banjul, where they elected Dr Amos Sawyer, the leader of the LPP, as President of an Interim Government of National Unity (IGNU). Doe was taken prisoner by Johnson's rebel Independent National Patriotic Front of Liberia (INPFL) on 9 September, and was killed the following day. In mid-September Sawyer proposed a peace settlement, which envisaged the creation of an interim legislature, in which the NPFL and INPFL would be represented. The proposal was rejected by Taylor, who continued to assert his claim to the presidency. In early October ECOMOG began an offensive, with the stated aim of establishing a neutral zone in Monrovia separating the three warring factions. By mid-October ECOMOG had gained control of central Monrovia, forcing NPFL units to retreat to the eastern outskirts of the capital. On 22 November Sawyer was inaugurated as interim President, under the auspices of ECOWAS, in Monrovia (having until then been based in Sierra Leone). Later that month, following ECOWAS-sponsored negotiations in the Malian capital, Bamako, the AFL, the NPFL and the INPFL signed a cease-fire agreement; however, renewed clashes, suppressed by ECOMOG forces, occurred between the INPFL and the AFL at the end of November. By January 1991 all rebel forces had withdrawn from Monrovia, and in that month Sawyer nominated ministers to the IGNU. Legislative power was vested in a 28-member Interim National Assembly, which represented the principal political factions, including the INPFL; however, the NPFL still refused to participate.

In February 1991, following a meeting of the ECOWAS mediation committee in the Togolese capital, Lomé, the AFL, the NPFL and the INPFL signed an agreement whereby a national conference was to facilitate the appointment of a new interim government. In early March it was announced that presidential and legislative elections would take place in October 1991. The national conference, convened in mid-March, was repeatedly adjourned as a result of procedural disputes. On 19 April the conference re-elected Amos Sawyer as Interim President, and appointed a member of the INPFL, Peter Naigow (a former minister in Doe's administration), as Vice-President.

In June 1991 Sawyer nominated a new Council of Ministers, which was subsequently approved by the Interim National Assembly. Later in the same month a resistance movement created by former supporters of the late President Doe, the United Liberation Movement of Liberia for Democracy (ULIMO), threatened to attack the NPFL if Taylor did not surrender to ECOMOG within 15 days. Meeting in Yamoussoukro, Côte d'Ivoire, at the end of June, Sawyer and Taylor pledged to co-operate to resolve the conflict. ECOWAS subsequently established a five-member committee (comprising representatives of Côte d'Ivoire, The Gambia, Guinea-Bissau, Senegal and Togo) to co-ordinate the peace negotiations. However, Sawyer announced that, owing to the impediments to the peace process, it was unlikely that elections would take place in October as originally planned. In August Sawyer denounced the execution, apparently at Johnson's instigation, of four members of the INPFL, including a senior officer who had reportedly complied with arrangements to relinquish weapons to ECOMOG. Members of the INPFL, including Naigow, subsequently resigned from the IGNU.

During March 1991 members of the NPFL perpetrated several border incursions into Sierra Leone. In April Sierra Leonean forces entered Liberian territory, and launched retaliatory attacks against NPFL bases, while the NPFL reportedly advanced within Sierra Leone. The Sierra Leonean Government alleged that the rebel offensive had been instigated by Taylor, in an attempt to force Sierra Leone to withdraw from ECOMOG. The NPFL denied involvement; it was reported, however, that NPFL forces were supporting a Sierra Leonean resistance movement, the Revolutionary United Front, in attacks against government forces (see chapter on Sierra Leone). In early September members of ULIMO initiated attacks from Sierra Leone against NPFL forces in north-western Liberia.

In mid-September 1991 Sawyer and Taylor, meeting in Yamoussoukro under the aegis of the five-nation committee, accepted conditions for a resolution to the conflict. The NPFL agreed to disarm and to restrict its troops to designated camps, under the supervision of ECOMOG, while an electoral commission, comprising representatives of the IGNU and the NPFL, was to be established to supervise the elections, and a joint Supreme Court was to be appointed to resolve electoral disputes. ECOMOG was to be reinforced by troops from Senegal, apparently in response to pressure from Taylor for an increase in the proportion of francophone troops in the force, thereby reducing the influence of the Nigerian contingent, which he believed to be opposed to his interests. However, Taylor subsequently refused to relinquish NPFL armaments to ECOMOG, and fighting between ULIMO and the NPFL continued near Mano River Bridge, on the border with Sierra Leone. At the end of October a further summit meeting in Yamoussoukro resulted in a peace agreement whereby the troops of all warring factions were to be disarmed and restricted to camps, while the NPFL was to relinquish the territory under its control to ECOMOG. It was also agreed that all Liberian forces would be withdrawn from Sierra Leone, and that a demilitarized zone, under the control of ECOMOG, would be created along Liberia's border with Sierra Leone. The conditions of the agreement were to be implemented within 60 days, and elections were to take place within six months. The INPFL initially refused to accept the terms of the agreement, and protested that it had been excluded from the summit meeting. Following a meeting with Sawyer, however, Johnson announced that the INPFL would be willing to rejoin the IGNU.

In November 1991 ULIMO began attacks in Grand Cape Mount County (in western Liberia), in contravention of the Yamoussoukro agreement, and in December the Sierra Leonean Government claimed that the NPFL had continued its offensive in Sierra Leone. Also in December the IGNU implemented sanctions that deprived the NPFL of basic commodities, in response to Taylor's continuing failure to comply with the terms of the Yamoussoukro agreement. In January 1992 the NPFL agreed to open several principal roads linking Monrovia with territory controlled by the NPFL, while ECOMOG established units in the port of Buchanan and on the border with Sierra Leone. None the less, the NPFL failed to disarm and restrict its forces to camps within the time limit that had been stipulated in the peace agreement. In the same month the Interim Election Commission and Supreme Court were established, in accordance with the Yamoussoukro peace agreement. In March the electoral commission announced that presidential and legislative elections were to take place in August. Later that month negotiations between ECOMOG and the NPFL were suspended, following continued demands by Taylor that NPFL troops be jointly deployed with the peace-keeping forces, and that all members of ULIMO be withdrawn from Liberia prior to the disarmament of the NPFL.

In early April 1992 the conditions of the Yamoussoukro agreement were reaffirmed at a summit meeting in Geneva, Switzerland, under the aegis of the five-nation committee; the demilitarized zone along the border with Sierra Leone was to be established by the end of April, and all factions were to be disarmed by the end of June. In mid-April the IGNU revoked the economic sanctions that had been imposed on the NPFL. Later that month, however, Taylor refused to allow the disarmament of the NPFL to proceed, on the grounds that it remained under attack by ULIMO forces (which initiated further offensives against the NPFL during April). At the end of April, however, in response to pressure from within the NPFL, Taylor announced that NPFL troops were to withdraw to a distance of 3 km from the border with Sierra Leone; ULIMO also agreed to co-operate in the implementation of the Yamoussoukro accord. In May ECOMOG began to disarm the rebel factions and to deploy troops in territory controlled by the NPFL, and, despite continued fighting between ULIMO and NPFL forces, established a demilitarized zone along the border with Sierra Leone. Later that month clashes occurred between NPFL troops and the Senegalese contingent of ECOMOG that was deployed at the demilitarized zone; six Senegalese soldiers were captured and killed by the NPFL. ECOMOG subsequently accused the NPFL of impeding the deployment of peace-keeping troops, while Taylor claimed that the Senegalese forces had colluded with ULIMO. In June Senegalese troops were withdrawn from NPFL-controlled territory to Monrovia. In July the NPFL accused the IGNU and factions within ECOMOG of planning to assassinate Taylor. Later that month the NPFL claimed that it had regained control of territory in western Liberia that had been captured by ULIMO earlier in the month.

In August 1992 a renewed offensive by ULIMO in western Liberia resulted in intense fighting. Although the ULIMO leader, Raleigh Seekie, claimed to support the peace initiative, at a meeting of his organization and ECOWAS officials in Freetown, Sierra Leone, later that month, he refused to sign an agreement whereby ULIMO armaments would be immediately relinquished to ECOMOG. By the end of August it was reported that ULIMO had gained control of Bomi and Grand Cape Mount Counties in western Liberia; more than 1,500 people had been killed in the offensive, while some 30,000 civilians had taken refuge in Monrovia. Taylor claimed that ULIMO had received military assistance from several countries that contributed troops to ECOMOG, and demanded that the peace-keeping force be replaced by UN military observers. In early September ECOMOG threatened to impose the terms of the Yamoussoukro accord by military force. In an apparent attempt to deter an ECOMOG attack, Taylor captured and held hostage 500 ECOMOG troops who had been deployed in territory controlled by the NPFL; the troops were released following mediation by the former US President, Jimmy Carter. In early October ECOMOG withdrew all its troops from territory under the control of the NPFL. In the same month Johnson announced that the NPFL and INPFL had signed a reconciliation agreement, but reiterated his support for the Yamoussoukro accord.

In mid-October 1992 the NPFL claimed that Nigerian aircraft under ECOMOG command had bombed NPFL bases at Kakata and Harbel (the site of the Roberts Field International Airport and the country's principal rubber plantation), near Monrovia, and at Buchanan, following an NPFL attack on ECOMOG forces stationed in the Monrovia region. In mid-October the NPFL launched a major offensive against ECOMOG bases on the outskirts of Monrovia, and captured a number of strategic areas; more than 100,000 civilians subsequently took refuge from the conflict in central Monrovia. Later that month an ECOWAS summit meeting in Cotonou, Benin, demanded that ULIMO and the NPFL observe an immediate cease-fire, and announced that economic sanctions (comprising a total land, sea and air blockade) would be imposed if either faction failed to comply with the terms of the Yamoussoukro agreement within 15 days of the declaration of the cease-fire; the implementation of sanctions was referred to the UN Security Council for endorsement. Hostilities continued, however, and ECOMOG forces began retaliatory attacks against NPFL positions around Monrovia. In late October it was reported that ECOMOG units had captured the INPFL base at Caldwell, near Monrovia, and that Johnson had surrendered. (It was subsequently stated that the INPFL had been disbanded.) In early November ECOMOG increased the aerial bombardment of NPFL-controlled territory, including Taylor's base at Gbarnga (in the central Bong County), while the NPFL repeatedly attacked the James Spriggs Payne Airport in Monrovia, in an attempt to impede supplies to ECOMOG.

Following the Cotonou meeting, division emerged between the countries (principally Nigeria and Senegal) that supported the use of military force in Liberia and those (Burkina Faso and Côte d'Ivoire) that advocated the exercise of restraint and were perceived to be sympathetic to the NPFL. At a further meeting, which took place in the Nigerian capital, Abuja, in November 1992, the participants declared a cease-fire, which, it was agreed, ECOMOG would impose by military force, if necessary; this decision was reportedly influenced by the USA's withdrawal of its Ambassador from Burkina, in protest at the Burkinabè Government's alleged support for the NPFL. It was further announced that the imposition of economic sanctions that had been threatened at the summit meeting in October was officially in force (although the UN Security Council had voted against the endorsement of the embargo). As a result of pressure from the countries represented in ECOMOG, Côte d'Ivoire subsequently sent 500 troops to reinforce the existing Ivorian contingent deployed at the border with Liberia to prevent the supply of armaments to the NPFL, while Burkina provisionally agreed to contribute troops to ECOMOG. Shortly before the date stipulated by ECOWAS for the cessation of hostilities, Taylor announced a unilateral cease-fire. However, ECOMOG claimed that the declaration was a diversionary tactic, and intense fighting continued between the NPFL and ECOMOG (which was supported by members of the AFL and militia loyal to the IGNU), while ULIMO maintained a second front in western Liberia. Later in November the UN Security Council adopted a resolution imposing a mandatory embargo on the supply of armaments to Liberia, and authorized the UN Secretary-General to send a special representative to the country. At the end of November it was reported that disagreements between Seekie and the challenger for the leadership of ULIMO, Alhaji G. V. Kromah, had resulted in the division of the organization into two factions.

In December 1992, following discussions with the UN Secretary-General's special representative, Trevor Gordon-Somers, Taylor announced that he was prepared to disarm and restrict his troops to camp, but insisted that the UN monitor the proceedings. In late December ECOMOG claimed that it had regained control of the strategic positions on the outskirts of Monrovia that had been seized by the NPFL in October, and January 1993 it was reported that ULIMO had gained control of Kakata, north-east of Monrovia, and the region of the Bong iron mines. Also in January Senegal announced that it was to withdraw its contingent (which comprised some 1,500 troops) from ECOMOG, citing the need for an increased security presence within Senegal. In February the Organization of African Unity (OAU, see p. 200) announced that it was prepared to intervene in Liberia, in apparent recognition of ECOMOG's failure to maintain neutrality. Later that month ECOMOG began to advance in south-eastern Liberia, recapturing Harbel, while ULIMO was reported to have gained control of Lofa County in western Liberia. At the end of February the Government of Côte d'Ivoire formally protested to ECOWAS, and threatened reprisals, following a bomb attack by Nigerian aircraft belonging to ECOMOG in the Ivorian border region of Danané. ECOMOG subsequently maintained that the area had been mistakenly believed to be Liberian territory, while the IGNU reiterated allegations that Ivorian forces were supporting the NPFL. In early March the NPFL protested to the UN, following ULIMO attacks that were allegedly launched from Guinean territory. Later in March ULIMO accepted an invitation from Sawyer to join the IGNU; ULIMO forces in Monrovia were subsequently disarmed, in accordance with the Yamoussoukro agreement.

In early April 1993, following a major offensive, ECOMOG announced that it had gained control of Buchanan (which was reopened to shipping later that year). In the same month the UN Security Council adopted a resolution that condemned attacks on ECOMOG and implied that the UN was prepared to undertake further measures against any faction that failed to comply with the Yamoussoukro accord. In May ECOMOG occupied the port of Greenville in south-eastern Liberia, thus depriving the NPFL (which remained in control of only one port, Harper) of a further means to import supplies. In the same month ECOMOG announced that consignments of humanitarian assistance to territory under the control of the NPFL would be diverted via Buchanan, under the supervision of ECOMOG, to prevent the NPFL from receiving clandestine imports of fuel and armaments from Côte d'Ivoire. The ensuing controversy over this decision resulted in increased tension between ECOMOG and humanitarian organizations, which objected to the restriction of their operations. (Taylor had previously accused ECOMOG forces of bombing humanitarian relief vehicles on several occasions.) Later in May ECOMOG repulsed an offensive by NPFL forces to the north of Monrovia; a further 50,000 civilians were reported to have fled to the capital, in response to renewed fighting in the area. In June some 600 refugees were found to be have been killed at the Harbel rubber plantation. Taylor denied accusations by the IGNU (which had conducted preliminary investigations into the incident) of NPFL involvement, maintaining that AFL troops stationed in the region of Harbel had perpetrated the massacre.

In July 1993 a conference, attended by the factions involved in the hostilities, was convened (under the auspices of the UN, the OAU and ECOWAS) in Geneva. Following several days of negotiations, the IGNU, the NPFL and ULIMO agreed to a cease-fire (which was to be monitored by a joint committee of the three factions, pending the deployment of UN observers and a reconstituted peace-keeping force), and to the establishment of a transitional government. Under the terms of the peace accord, which was formally signed in Cotonou on 25 July, the IGNU was to be replaced by a five-member transitional Council of State, and the existing legislature by a 35-member Transitional Legislative Assembly (comprising 13 representatives of the IGNU, 13 of the NPFL and nine of ULIMO), pending presidential and general elections, which were scheduled for February 1994. In response to demands by Taylor, the dominance of the Nigerian contingent in ECOMOG was to be considerably reduced, and the peace-keeping force was to be supplemented with additional troops from elsewhere in Africa. The agreement also included provisions for the delivery of humanitarian assistance to civilians and for the repatriation of refugees.

At the end of July 1993 the cease-fire came into effect; in early August, however, ECOMOG accused the NPFL of violating the Cotonou accord by repeatedly entering territory under the control of the peace-keeping force. In the same month a UN mission was dispatched to Liberia to investigate the massacre of refugees at Harbel in June. In August the IGNU, the NPFL and ULIMO each appointed a representative to the Council of State, while a list of nine candidates, nominated by the three factions, elected the two remaining members (who were representatives of the IGNU and ULIMO respectively) from among their number. Dr Bismark Kuyon, a member of the IGNU and the former Speaker of the Interim National Assembly, was subsequently elected as Chairman of the Council of State. Shortly afterwards, however, Kuyon announced that the inauguration of the Council of State (originally scheduled to take place on 24 August) was to be postponed, pending the clear implementation of the process of disarmament. The NPFL criticized this decision, and accused Kuyon of violating the peace agreement, which required that the transitional institutions be installed within a period of 30 days. The resultant impasse continued for several months: Taylor refused to permit the disarmament of NPFL forces prior to the deployment of UN observers and the additional peace-keeping troops (although the NPFL, together with ULIMO, continued to demand the inauguration of the Council of State), while the IGNU insisted that the installation of the transitional authorities take place in conjunction with the disarmament process.

In September 1993 the IGNU expressed concern following an announcement by the new Nigerian administration that it was to withdraw its contingent from ECOMOG by the end of March 1994. Later in September a UN report concluded that AFL troops had perpetrated the massacre at Harbel (which had been widely attributed to the NPFL), and implied that ECOMOG had deliberately failed to identify those responsible. A number of AFL units were subsequently withdrawn to Monrovia and disarmed, while three members of the AFL were arrested for alleged participation in the massacre. (The IGNU disputed the results of the investigation.) In the same month the UN Security Council approved the establishment of a 300-member UN Observer Mission in Liberia (UNOMIL, see p. 50), which was to co-operate with ECOMOG and the OAU in overseeing the transitional process. In October the Transitional Legislative Assembly was established, in accordance with the peace agreement. Later in October it was announced that Tanzania, Uganda and Zimbabwe were to contribute troops to ECOMOG, in response to a request from the OAU. (Zimbabwe, however, failed to send a contingent, owing to financial difficulties.)

In October 1993 attempts to establish a council of ministers, as part of the proposed Liberian National Transitional Government (LNTG), were impeded by disagreements between the IGNU, the NPFL and ULIMO regarding the distribution of ministerial portfolios. Following a meeting in Cotonou in early November, however, the three factions agreed to the allocation of a number of portfolios. Later in November the NPFL accused the IGNU of further delaying the transitional process, after Sawyer dismissed Kuyon (who had reportedly dissociated himself from the IGNU's refusal to relinquish power prior to disarmament) and appointed Philip Banks, hitherto Minister of Justice, in his place. (Both the NPFL and ULIMO had previously replaced their representatives in the Council of State, apparently in an attempt to consolidate their political position.)

Meanwhile, it was feared that renewed hostilities in several areas of the country would jeopardize the peace accord. An armed faction known as the Liberia Peace Council (LPC), which reportedly comprised members of the Krahn ethnic group from Grand Gedeh County, joined by a number of disaffected AFL troops, emerged in September 1993, and subsequently entered into conflict with the NPFL in south-eastern Liberia. A large number of civilians fled to Buchanan from Rivercess and Grand Bassa Counties, in response to fighting in the region. The LPC claimed to be a non-partisan movement, established in response to what it claimed to be continued atrocities perpetrated by the NPFL. In December fighting between ULIMO and a newly-formed movement, the Lofa Defence Force (LDF), was also reported in Lofa County apparently in retaliation against alleged acts of violence committed by ULIMO forces in the region. The NPFL denied involvement with the LDF, which occupied territory previously controlled by ULIMO in north-western Liberia.

In December 1993 the additional contingents of ECOMOG troops began to arrive. In February 1994 further negotiations took place between the IGNU, the NPFL and ULIMO, with the aim of resolving outstanding differences regarding the implementation of the peace accord. At the end of February the Council of State elected David Kpomakpor, a representative of the IGNU, as its Chairman. In early March units belonging to UNOMIL and the new ECOMOG force were deployed, and the disarmament of all factions commenced. Following an ethnic dispute involving Kromah and the Chairman of ULIMO's military wing Maj.-Gen. Roosevelt Johnson (who had effectively replaced Seekie), however, some ULIMO troops refused to relinquish their armaments, on the grounds that they had received no instructions to do so. ECOMOG subsequently threatened to enforce the disarmament process if ULIMO continued to fail to co-operate with peace-keeping troops. On 7 March the Council of State was inaugurated; it was envisaged that the presidential and legislative elections (which were originally scheduled for February) would take place in September. However, the disarmament process was subsequently impeded by an increase in rebel activity: in addition to continuing hostilities involving the LDF and the LPC, more than 200 people were killed in clashes between members of the Krahn and Mandingo ethnic groups within ULIMO, particularly in the region of Tubmanburg (north of Monrovia, where the organization was officially located). The hostilities (which followed the dispute earlier that month between Kromah, a Mandingo, and Johnson, a Krahn) were prompted by resentment within the Krahn at the predominance of the Mandingo among ULIMO representatives in the transitional institutions. In early May, following continued fighting in western Liberia, the two factions agreed to a cease-fire, in response to the intervention by ECOMOG and UNOMIL (which, in April, had deployed troops in territory occupied by ULIMO); however, subsequent negotiations regarding the ethnic distribution of the posts allocated to ULIMO within the transitional institutions were unsuccessful, and it was reported that the cease-fire had not been implemented.

In April 1994 the mandate of UNOMIL to remain in Liberia (which was due to expire that month) was extended until October, pending the completion of the transitional process. Also in April the nomination of several cabinet ministers by the former IGNU, the NPFL and ULIMO was approved by the Transitional Legislative Assembly. The subsequent discovery that a letter (purportedly signed by President Nicéphore Soglo of Benin, who was then Chairman of the ECOWAS Conference of Heads of State and Government) upholding the allocation of the principal portfolios of justice and foreign affairs to members of the NPFL was a forgery prompted widespread speculation regarding the motivation of a number of elements involved in the peace process. Later in April, following continued controversy regarding the portfolios of justice and foreign affairs, Taylor declared that the NPFL would not participate in the LNTG unless all his ministerial nominees were accepted. In May a 19-member Cabinet was installed, comprising seven representatives of the NPFL (which held the disputed portfolios of justice and foreign affairs), seven of ULIMO and five of the former IGNU. Following a review of progress in the implementation of the peace settlement, the UN Security Council declared itself to be satisfied with the installation of the LNTG, but expressed concern at the persistent factional violence, which continued to impede the disarmament process.

In May 1994 the Nigerian Government threatened to commence the withdrawal of its troops from ECOMOG, following allegations by the NPFL of Nigerian support for the LPC. In June Tanzania indicated that it intended to withdraw its ECOMOG contingent from Liberia, owing to the failure of the UN to disburse funds that had been pledged to the Tanzanian Government. Later that month, following threats by the US Government to suspend assistance to Liberia, owing to the continued lack of progress in the implementation of the peace agreement, members of the Transitional Legislative Assembly met NPFL officials at Gbarnga to discuss the disarmament process. At the end of June some 50 people were killed in hostilities between the two ULIMO factions near the border with Sierra Leone; it was also reported that ECOMOG troops had clashed with Kromah's forces, after intervening to prevent a massacre of civilians. In early July Kromah's faction (henceforth referred to as ULIMO—K) initiated an offensive to recapture Tubmanburg, which was under the control of Roosevelt Johnson's forces (ULIMO—J). In mid-July the UN Security Council urged the LNTG to convene a meeting of the armed factions to discuss a programme for disarmament. Later that month the Minister of Labour in the LNTG, Tom Woewiyu (hitherto regarded as a close associate of Taylor), accused him of responsibility for atrocities perpetrated against civilians.

In early August 1994, following secret discussions, five of the factions involved in the civil conflict (the AFL, the LDF, the LPC, ULIMO—J and a section of the NPFL that was represented by Woewiyu) issued a joint statement undertaking to cease hostilities and to co-operate in the disarmament process; it was further agreed that the LPC and the LDF be allowed to join the LNTG. (However, Kromah and Taylor were not party to the accord, and further clashes between the LPC and the NPFL were subsequently reported in the region of Buchanan.) Shortly after the agreement was announced Taylor demanded that Woewiyu and two other members of the NPFL who supported him be removed from the Cabinet, on the grounds that they had refused to consult with the NPFL leadership on matters of state; Taylor further claimed that the three ministers were involved in the organization of attacks against NPFL positions by dissident members of the movement. Kpomakpor, however, refused to replace the ministers. At the end of August the NPFL announced that the movement's Chief of Staff had been killed, after staging an unsuccessful attempt to overthrow the NPFL leadership. Meanwhile, the President of Ghana, Jerry Rawlings (who had succeeded Soglo as the ECOWAS Chairman in early August), indicated that Ghanaian troops would be withdrawn from ECOMOG if the progress achieved in Liberia by the end of that year was judged to be insufficient.

In early September 1994 (when the original mandate of the LNTG was due to expire) a meeting, chaired by Rawlings, of the NPFL, the AFL and ULIMO—K took place in Akosombo, Ghana. On 12 September Taylor, Kromah and the Chief of Staff of the AFL, Lt-Gen. Hezekiah Bowen, signed a peace accord providing for the immediate cessation of hostilities and for the establishment later that month of a reconstituted Council of State, in which four of the members were to be nominated, respectively, by the three factions and a Liberian National Conference (LNC—comprising representatives of civilian organizations), while the fifth member was to be selected jointly by ULIMO (effectively ULIMO—K) and the NPFL from traditional chiefs; presidential and legislative elections were rescheduled for October 1995, and the new organs of government were to be installed in January 1996. However, the proposed installation of a principally military Council of State prompted widespread criticism, particularly from the LNC (which had been convened in Monrovia at the end of August). Meanwhile, following clashes in the Gbarnga region between dissident members of the NPFL and troops loyal to Taylor, the dissidents' Central Revolutionary Council (CRC) announced that Taylor had been deposed and replaced by Woewiyu, who indicated that he was not prepared to accept the Akosombo agreement. In mid-September disaffected members of the AFL, led by a former officer who had served in the Doe administration, Gen. Charles Julu, seized the presidential mansion, but were subsequently overpowered by ECOMOG forces. (Some 78 members of the AFL, including Julu, were later arrested, and a further 2,000 troops were disarmed by ECOMOG.) Later that month the NPFL dissidents (known as the NPFL—CRC), apparently in alliance with elements of the AFL, ULIMO, the LPC and the LDF, took control of Gbarnga; forces loyal to Taylor had retreated to the town of Palala, to the east of Gbarnga, while Taylor was said to have taken refuge in Côte d'Ivoire. (ULIMO, the LPC and the LDF subsequently accused the Ivorian Government of permitting NPFL forces to operate within its territory, after it was reported that Taylor had established a new base at Danané.) During September about 75,000 civilians fled to Côte d'Ivoire and Guinea, following the increase in factional hostilities.

In early October 1994 the Council of State removed Bowen from the post of AFL Chief of Staff, on the grounds that he had failed to respond effectively to the abortive coup attempt in September; Bowen, however, attributed his dismissal to his role as a signatory to the Akosombo agreement, which had been criticized by the LNTG, and refused to relinquish office. In the same month ECOMOG announced a reduction in its peace-keeping forces deployed in Liberia, citing a lack of financial resources, in conjunction with the failure of the international community to assist in the peace process; the UN Security Council extended the mandate of UNOMIL until January 1995, but also announced a reduction in personnel (which then numbered 368), in view of the lack of progress achieved. In early November 1994 Ghana reiterated its warning that it would withdraw from ECOMOG if the warring factions failed to reach a peace settlement, while the Nigerian Government withdrew military equipment from the peace-keeping force. Later that month a conference, attended by Bowen, Taylor, Woewiyu, the leader of the LPC, Dr George Boley, and the leader of the LDF, François Massaquoi, together with representatives of the LNC and the LNTG, was convened in the Ghanaian capital, Accra, to discuss preparations for the installation of a reconstituted Council of State, in accordance with the Akosombo agreement. However, a subsequent decision, endorsed by ECOWAS, that the AFL nominate a representative in conjunction with the 'Coalition Forces' (a loose alliance comprising the NPFL—CRC, the LPC, the LDF and elements of ULIMO—K) resulted in contention, with both Bowen and Boley claiming a seat in the proposed Council of State. Negotiations were adjourned at the end of November, after the participants failed to agree on the composition of the new transitional administration.

In early December 1994 the trial of Julu and 10 other members of the AFL, on charges of attempting to overthrow the LNTG, was adjourned for security reasons, following reports of armed attacks on ECOMOG positions. In the same month demonstrations were staged in Monrovia to protest at the failure to resolve the civil conflict by political means, after unidentified armed groups massacred some 48 civilians at Paynesville, on the outskirts of Monrovia. Meanwhile, it was reported that the NPFL had regained control of much of the territory, including Gbarnga, that the NPFL—CRC had captured in September. On 22 December, after the peace conference was reconvened in Accra, the participants reached agreement on a cease-fire, which was to enter into force later that month. The delegates also signed two accords that reaffirmed the terms of the Akosombo agreement, including provisions for the establishment of demilitarized zones throughout Liberia and for the installation of a reconstituted Council of State (which was to comprise a single representative of each of the NPFL, ULIMO, the AFL in conjunction with the Coalition Forces, and the LNC, with a fifth member elected jointly by the NPFL and ULIMO from traditional rulers); new institutions were to be installed on 1 January 1996, following multi-party elections, which were to take place by 14 November 1995. Later in December 1994 the UN Security Council extended the mandate of UNOMIL (now comprising 90 observers) until April 1995, while the Nigerian Government reduced its ECOMOG contingent to 6,000 (from about 10,000), in accordance with its stated aim gradually to withdraw from

Liberia. The cease-fire, which entered into force on 28 December, was widely observed, despite reports of skirmishes between supporters of ULIMO—J, the AFL and the NPFL around Monrovia.

In January 1995, following continuing disagreement between the AFL and the Coalition Forces regarding their joint representative in the Council of State, ECOWAS Heads of State submitted a proposal, which was accepted in principle by the armed factions, that the Council of State be expanded from five to six members (to include both Bowen and Woewiyu). However, subsequent negotiations were impeded by Taylor's persistent demands that he be granted the chairmanship of the Council of State, which was opposed by the other factional leaders. (A general perception that the Ghanaian mediators were prepared to comprise the principles of their mandate, in an effort to achieve a resolution, emerged following widespread allegations that they had urged Bowen to accept Taylor as Chairman.) In early February a compromise arrangement was negotiated, whereby Chief Tamba Taylor, the traditional ruler who had been nominated by ULIMO and the NPFL, would assume the office of Chairman, while Taylor and Kromah would become joint Vice-Chairmen; the three remaining seats in the Council of State were to be allocated to Bowen, Woewiyu and the representative of the LNC, Oscar Quiah. In the same month reports of renewed hostilities between the NPFL and the LPC in south-eastern Liberia prompted concern that any agreement reached by the armed factions would be undermined; ECOMOG also claimed that elements of the NPFL had infiltrated the outskirts of Monrovia in preparation for an attack on the capital. At the end of February Kpomakpor urged the factional leaders to establish a new transitional authority by 7 March (the first anniversary of the inauguration of the Council of State), and indicated that the LNC would otherwise reconvene to consider further proposals for the continuation of the peace process. Following the expiry of the stipulated date, however, the LNTG denied allegations that Kpomakpor intended to reconvene the LNC in order to obtain further executive powers. In early March the Tanzanian Government announced that its ECOMOG contingent (which numbered 800) was to be withdrawn from Liberia by the end of that month. However, Rawlings, who in that month met the US President, Bill Clinton, to request an intervention in the Liberian conflict, indicated that the Ghanaian contingent would remain in ECOMOG until peace was achieved. Later in March Kpomakpor and Chief Tamba Taylor met Ghanaian officials in Accra to discuss the continuing political impasse (which was apparently caused by Charles Taylor's reluctance to assume his seat in the new Council of State, in protest at Woewiyu's inclusion as a representative).

In April 1995 about 62 civilians were massacred by unidentified armed groups in the town of Yosi, near Buchanan, after hostilities between the NPFL and the LPC resumed in the region; renewed fighting in other parts of Liberia was also reported. Later that month a meeting between Taylor and an adviser to Rawlings took place in the Libyan capital, Tripoli, with mediation by the Libyan Head of State, Col Muammar Al-Qaddafi. At the end of April the withdrawal of the Tanzanian contingent of ECOMOG commenced. In May an ECOWAS summit meeting was convened in Abuja, Nigeria, to discuss the Liberian conflict; it was subsequently announced that the installation of the Council of State was to be postponed until the constituent factions demonstrated commitment to the observance of the cease-fire and to the disarmament process.

## Government

Under the Constitution of January 1986 (as amended in July 1988), legislative power is vested in the bicameral National Assembly, comprising the 26-member Senate and the 64-member House of Representatives. Executive power is vested in the President, who holds office for a six-year term (renewable more than once). The President, who appoints the Cabinet, is directly elected by universal adult suffrage, as are members of the Assembly. On 22 November 1990, following a period of civil conflict (see Recent History), an Interim President took office, and formed an Interim Government of National Unity (IGNU), which represented the principal political parties and the Liberian Council of Churches. Under the terms of the peace agreement that was signed in July 1993, the IGNU was replaced by an executive body known as the Council of State, and the Interim National Assembly by a Transitional Legislative Assembly, pending presidential and general elections. In September 1994, however, an agreement between the principal armed factions provided for the establishment of a reconstituted Council of State, and rescheduled the elections for October 1995. Under the terms of a further agreement between the factions, which was reached in December 1994, a new government was to be installed on 1 January 1996, following elections in November 1995. However, prolonged dissension between the factions regarding the composition of the proposed Council of State presented an impediment to the continuation of the peace process (see Recent History).

## Defence

In June 1994 the Armed Forces of Liberia (comprising troops of the late President Samuel Doe) were estimated to number 3,000–5,000, troops of the National Patriotic Front of Liberia 8,000–12,000, and those of the United Liberation Movement of Liberia for Democracy 5,000–6,000. In early 1995 troops of the ECOWAS Monitoring Group numbered 11,000; a 90-strong peace-keeping force, the UN Observer Mission in Liberia, was also present with a mandate to remain in the country until April of that year.

## Economic Affairs

In 1987, according to estimates by the World Bank, Liberia's gross national product (GNP), measured at average 1985–87 prices, was US $1,051m., equivalent to $450 per head. During 1980–87, it was estimated, GNP declined, in real terms, at an average annual rate of 2.1%, while real GNP per head declined by 5.2% per year. During 1985–93 the population increased by an annual average of 0.9%. During 1985–89, according to UN estimates, Liberia's gross domestic product (GDP) increased in real terms, by an annual average of 1.5%, compared with an average annual decline of 1.5% in 1980–85.

Agriculture (including forestry and fishing) contributed 36.7% of GDP in 1989. About 68.5% of the labour force were employed in the sector in 1993. The principal cash crops are rubber (which accounted for about 26% of export earnings in 1989), coffee and cocoa. The principal food crops are rice and cassava. However, yields of rice are relatively low, and some 70,000 metric tons of cereals were imported in 1990. Timber production is also important. Agricultural production, according to the FAO, increased by an annual average of 2.2% in 1980–89, but declined by 35.8% in 1990 and by 8.8% in 1991. Output increased by 5.5% in 1992, but fell by 11.0% in 1993.

Industry (including mining, manufacturing, construction and power) employed an estimated 9.4% of the labour force in 1980, and provided 22.3% of GDP in 1989. During 1985–89 industrial GDP increased by an annual average of 0.3%, compared with an average yearly decrease of 4.7% in 1980–85.

Mining employed 5.1% of the working population in 1980, and contributed 10.9% of GDP in 1989. The leading mineral export is iron ore (which accounted for 51% of export earnings in 1989), although production declined in the 1980s. Gold and diamonds are also mined, and Liberia possesses significant amounts of barytes and kyanite.

Manufacturing provided 7.3% of GDP in 1989, and employed about 1.2% of the working population in 1980. Measured by the value of output, the principal branches of manufacturing in 1984 were beverages (44.5% of the total), mineral products, chemicals and tobacco. Manufacturing GDP increased by an annual average of 3.2% in 1985–89, compared with an average increase of 0.2% per year in 1980–85.

Energy is derived principally from hydroelectric power. Imports of mineral fuels comprised an estimated 19.7% of the value of total imports in 1992.

Liberia's large open-registry ('flag of convenience') merchant shipping fleet has for many years been a significant source of foreign exchange: income from registration fees amounted to $17m. in 1988.

In 1987 Liberia recorded a visible trade surplus of US $63.2m., although there was a deficit of $117.6m. on the current account of the balance of payments. In 1992, according to World Bank estimates, a trade surplus of $152.2m. was recorded. In 1988 the principal source of imports (21.2%) was the USA; other major suppliers in that year were the Federal Republic of Germany, the Belgo-Luxembourg Economic Union (BLEU) and the Netherlands. The principal market for exports was the Federal Republic of Germany (which took 27.3% of the country's exports in that year); other significant purchasers were the USA, Italy, France and the BLEU. The principal exports in 1989 were iron ore, rubber, and logs. The principal imports in 1988 were machinery and transport equipment, mineral fuels, basic manufactures, and food and live animals.

In 1994 an estimated budgetary deficit of L$50m. was recorded. Liberia's external debt totalled US $1,926m. at the end of 1993, of which $1,070m. was long-term public debt. In 1987 the cost of servicing an external debt of $1,705m. was equivalent to 3.7% of the value of exports of goods and services. In 1980–89 the average annual rate of inflation was 4.6%. Consumer prices increased by an average of 8.1% in the first six months of 1990.

Liberia is a member of the Economic Community of West African States (ECOWAS, see p. 138) and the Mano River Union (see p. 239), both of which aim to promote closer economic co-operation in the region.

Liberia's economy is largely dependent on the export of primary products to industrial economies, and has been vulnerable to fluctuations in international commodity prices. The Government's failure to restrain budgetary expenditure and to pay its debts led, in 1986, to the suspension of assistance by the IMF and the World Bank. Civil conflict, which commenced at the end of 1989 (see Recent History), resulted in the suspension of much economic activity; the disruption of the agricultural sector has led to severe food shortages, necessitating substantial emergency assistance. Widespread looting of natural resources, particularly timber, by rebel factions was subsequently reported. Following the peace agreement that was signed in July 1993, hostilites were suspended in the greater part of the country; in view of the subsequent normalization of shipping activity, Liberia was expected to benefit from the resumption of exports of rubber and timber to increase foreign exchange revenue. However, continuing factional violence impeded reconstruction efforts, while additional large numbers of civilians fled to neighbouring countries or became internally displaced, necessitating an increase in emergency assistance. In August 1994 the Liberian National Transitional Government (LNTG) resumed dialogue with the IMF, after paying arrears of L$1m. to that organization. Following a visit by an IMF delegation at the end of that year, the LNTG announced that improvement of the fiscal situation was to be a priority; revenue was to be derived principally from taxes, particularly from funds generated by the merchant shipping register. It was feared, however, that insurance claims by foreign trading companies based in Monrovia would continue to deplete foreign exchange revenue.

## Social Welfare

Basic health services are limited, and there is no adequate state welfare system. In 1985 there were 227 physicians, 32 hospitals and 30 health centres. Of total budgetary expenditure by the central Government in 1988, L $14.5m. (5.1%) was for health, and a further L$2.9m. (1.0%) for social security and welfare. Medical care is provided free of charge to children who are less than two years of age. Since the outbreak of civil conflict in December 1989, health care has been administered by relief organizations.

## Education

Primary and secondary education are available free of charge, except for an annual registration fee, and the Government provides a 50% subsidy for university tuition. Education is officially compulsory for nine years, between seven and 16 years of age. Primary education begins at seven years of age and lasts for six years. Secondary education, beginning at 13 years of age, lasts for a further six years, divided into two cycles of three years each. In 1984 the total enrolment at primary schools was equivalent to only 40% of children in the relevant age-group (boys 51%; girls 28%), while the comparable ratio for secondary schools was 18%. The University in Monrovia had about 3,000 students in 1988. Other higher education institutes include the Cuttington University College (controlled by the Protestant Episcopal Church), a college of technology and a computer science institute. Expenditure on education by the central Government in 1988 was L$31.3m., representing 11.0% of total spending. UNESCO estimated that 60.5% of the adult population (males 50.2%; females 71.2%) remained illiterate in 1990.

## Public Holidays

**1995:** 1 January (New Year's Day), 11 February (Armed Forces Day), 12 March (Decoration Day), 15 March (J. J. Robert's Birthday), 11 April (Fast and Prayer Day), 12 April (National Redemption Day, Anniversary of the 1980 Coup), 14 April (Good Friday), 14 May (National Unification Day), 26 July (Independence Day), 24 August (Flag Day), 6 November (Thanksgiving Day), 12 November (National Memorial Day), 29 November (President Tubman's Birthday), 25 December (Christmas Day).

**1996:** 1 January (New Year's Day), 11 February (Armed Forces Day), 12 March (Decoration Day), 15 March (J. J. Robert's Birthday), 5 April (Good Friday), 11 April (Fast and Prayer Day), 12 April (National Redemption Day, Anniversary of the 1980 Coup), 14 May (National Unification Day), 26 July (Independence Day), 24 August (Flag Day), 6 November (Thanksgiving Day), 12 November (National Memorial Day), 29 November (President Tubman's Birthday), 25 December (Christmas Day).

## Weights and Measures

Imperial weights and measures, modified by US usage, are in force.

# Statistical Survey

Sources (unless otherwise stated): the former Ministry of Planning and Economic Affairs, POB 9016, Broad Street, Monrovia; tel. 222622.

## Area and Population

### AREA, POPULATION AND DENSITY

| | |
|---|---:|
| Area (sq km) | 97,754* |
| Population (census results) | |
| 1 February 1974 | |
|   Males | 759,109 |
|   Females | 744,259 |
|   Total | 1,503,368 |
| 1–14 February 1984 | 2,101,628 |
| Population (official estimates at mid-year) | |
| 1991 | 2,520,410 |
| 1992 | 2,580,236 |
| 1993 | 2,640,000 |
| Density (per sq km) at mid-1993 | 27.0 |

* 37,743 sq miles.

### ADMINISTRATIVE DIVISIONS (population at 1984 census)

| Counties: | | Nimba | 313,050 |
|---|---:|---|---:|
| Bomi | 66,420 | Rivercess | 37,849 |
| Bong | 255,813 | Sinoe | 64,147 |
| Grand Bassa | 159,648 | Territories: | |
| Grand Cape Mount | 79,322 | Gibi | 66,802 |
| Grand Gedeh | 102,810 | Kru Coast | 35,267 |
| Lofa | 247,641 | Marshall | 31,190 |
| Maryland | 85,267 | Sasstown | 11,524 |
| Montserrado | 544,878 | **Total** | 2,101,628 |

### PRINCIPAL TOWN

Monrovia (capital), population 421,058 at 1984 census.

LIBERIA

**BIRTHS AND DEATHS** (UN estimates, annual averages)

|  | 1975–80 | 1980–85 | 1985–90 |
|---|---|---|---|
| Birth rate (per 1,000) | 47.4 | 47.2 | 47.3 |
| Death rate (per 1,000) | 18.1 | 16.7 | 15.8 |

**Expectation of life** (UN estimates, years at birth, 1985–90): 53.0 (males 52.0; females 54.0).

Source: UN, *World Population Prospects: The 1992 Revision*.

**ECONOMICALLY ACTIVE POPULATION**

|  | 1978 | 1979 | 1980 |
|---|---|---|---|
| Agriculture, forestry, hunting and fishing | 355,467 | 366,834 | 392,926 |
| Mining | 25,374 | 26,184 | 28,047 |
| Manufacturing | 6,427 | 6,631 | 7,102 |
| Construction | 4,701 | 4,852 | 5,198 |
| Electricity, gas and water | 245 | 246 | 263 |
| Commerce | 18,668 | 19,266 | 20,636 |
| Transport and communications | 7,314 | 7,549 | 8,086 |
| Services | 49,567 | 51,154 | 54,783 |
| Others | 28,555 | 29,477 | 31,571 |
| **Total** | 496,318 | 512,193 | 548,615 |

**Mid-1993** (estimates in '000): Agriculture, etc. 702; Total 1,025 (Source: FAO, *Production Yearbook*).

## Agriculture

**PRINCIPAL CROPS** ('000 metric tons)

|  | 1991 | 1992 | 1993 |
|---|---|---|---|
| Rice (paddy)* | 109 | 102 | 71 |
| Sweet potatoes* | 18 | 18 | 18 |
| Cassava (Manioc)* | 300 | 300 | 310 |
| Yams* | 15 | 15 | 15 |
| Taro (Coco yam)* | 15 | 15 | 18 |
| Coconuts* | 7 | 7 | 7 |
| Palm kernels* | 7 | 7 | 7 |
| Vegetables and melons* | 71 | 71 | 71 |
| Sugar cane* | 225 | 225 | 234 |
| Oranges* | 7 | 7 | 7 |
| Pineapples* | 7 | 7 | 7 |
| Bananas* | 80 | 80 | 80 |
| Plantains* | 33 | 33 | 33 |
| Cocoa beans | 2 | 2 | 2 |
| Natural rubber (dry weight)† | 19† | 32† | 10* |

* FAO estimate(s).   † Unofficial figure.
Source: FAO, *Production Yearbook*.

**LIVESTOCK** (FAO estimates, '000 head, year ending September)

|  | 1991 | 1992 | 1993 |
|---|---|---|---|
| Cattle | 37 | 36 | 36 |
| Pigs | 120 | 120 | 120 |
| Sheep | 215 | 210 | 210 |
| Goats | 220 | 225 | 220 |

Poultry (FAO estimates, million): 4 in 1991; 4 in 1992; 4 in 1993.
Source: FAO, *Production Yearbook*.

**LIVESTOCK PRODUCTS** (FAO estimates, metric tons)

|  | 1991 | 1992 | 1993 |
|---|---|---|---|
| Pig meat | 4,000 | 4,000 | 4,000 |
| Poultry meat | 5,000 | 5,000 | 5,000 |
| Other meat | 8,000 | 8,000 | 8,000 |
| Cows' milk | 1,000 | 1,000 | 1,000 |
| Hen eggs | 3,840 | 3,600 | 3,600 |

Source; FAO, *Production Yearbook*.

## Forestry

**ROUNDWOOD REMOVALS** ('000 cubic metres, excluding bark)

|  | 1990* | 1991 | 1992 |
|---|---|---|---|
| Sawlogs, veneer logs and logs for sleepers | 1,008 | 593 | 890 |
| Other industrial wood* | 158 | 164 | 169 |
| Fuel wood* | 4,890 | 4,962 | 5,040 |
| **Total** | 6,056 | 5,719 | 6,099 |

* FAO estimates.
Source: FAO, *Yearbook of Forest Products*.

**SAWNWOOD PRODUCTION**
('000 cubic metres, including railway sleepers)

|  | 1985 | 1986 | 1987 |
|---|---|---|---|
| **Total** | 169 | 191 | 411 |

**1988–92**: Annual production as in 1987 (FAO estimates).
Source: FAO, *Yearbook of Forest Products*.

## Fishing

('000 metric tons, live weight)

|  | 1990 | 1991 | 1992 |
|---|---|---|---|
| Inland waters | 4.0 | 4.0 | 4.0 |
| Atlantic Ocean | 2.5 | 5.6 | 4.9 |
| **Total catch** | 6.5 | 9.6 | 8.9 |

Source: FAO, *Yearbook of Fishery Statistics*.

## Mining

|  | 1989 | 1990 | 1991 |
|---|---|---|---|
| Iron ore ('000 metric tons)* | 7,450 | 2,490 | n.a. |
| Industrial diamonds ('000 carats) | 93 | 60 | 60 |
| Gem diamonds ('000 carats)† | 62 | 40 | 40 |
| Gold (kilograms)* | 700 | 700 | 600 |

* Figures refer to the metal content of ores.
† Data from the US Bureau of Mines.
Source: UN, *Industrial Statistics Yearbook*.

## Industry

**SELECTED PRODUCTS**
('000 metric tons, unless otherwise indicated)

|  | 1988 | 1989 | 1990 |
|---|---|---|---|
| Palm oil* | 35 | 35 | 30 |
| Beer ('000 hectolitres) | 158 | n.a. | n.a. |
| Soft drinks ('000 hectolitres) | 171 | n.a. | n.a. |
| Cigarettes (million)† | 22 | 22 | 22 |
| Cement | 130 | 85‡ | 50 |
| Electric energy (million kWh) | 834 | 818 | 565 |

* FAO estimates.
† Data from the US Department of Agriculture.
‡ Provisional or estimated figure.
Source: mainly UN, *Industrial Statistics Yearbook*.
**1991**: Palm oil ('000 metric tons) 25 (unofficial figure); Cigarettes (million) 22; Electric energy (million kWh) 450.
**1992** ('000 metric tons): Palm oil 25 (unofficial figure).

# Finance

## CURRENCY AND EXCHANGE RATES

**Monetary Units**
100 cents = 1 Liberian dollar (L $).

**Sterling and Dollar Equivalents** (31 December 1994)
£1 sterling = L $1.5645;
US $1 = L $1.000;
L $100 = £63.92 = US $100.00.

**Exchange Rate**
Since 1940 the Liberian dollar has been officially at par with the US dollar.

## BUDGET (public sector accounts, L $ million, year ending 30 June)

| Revenue* | 1985/86 | 1986/87 | 1988† |
|---|---|---|---|
| Tax revenue | 172.7 | 172.4 | 203.8 |
| Taxes on income and profits | 71.7 | 61.5 | 72.1 |
| Taxes on property | 1.1 | 2.3 | 2.6 |
| Taxes on domestic transactions | 44.9 | 57.7 | 53.3 |
| Taxes on foreign trade | 51.6 | 48.6 | 73.6 |
| Other taxes | 3.4 | 2.3 | 2.2 |
| Other current revenue | 7.7 | 8.0 | 8.9 |
| Capital revenue | 0.3 | 0.2 | 0.1 |
| **Total** | **180.7** | **180.6** | **212.8** |

| Expenditure‡ | 1985/86 | 1986/87 | 1988† |
|---|---|---|---|
| General public services | 51.3 | 51.3 | 67.8 |
| Defence | 21.0 | 23.5 | 26.5 |
| Education | 38.8 | 42.8 | 31.3 |
| Health | 15.6 | 18.7 | 14.5 |
| Social security and welfare | 2.3 | 2.5 | 2.9 |
| Housing and community amenities | 2.7 | 2.6 | 2.1 |
| Recreational, cultural and religious affairs and services | 7.2 | 6.4 | 4.2 |
| Economic affairs and services | 94.4 | 72.8 | 79.8 |
| Fuel and energy | 7.3 | 4.5 | 17.4 |
| Agriculture, forestry, fishing and hunting | 21.0 | 23.6 | 14.1 |
| Mining, manufacturing and construction | 13.1 | 6.4 | 2.1 |
| Transport and communications | 19.8 | 18.2 | 15.0 |
| Other purposes | 40.6 | 42.9 | 54.3 |
| **Total** | **273.9** | **263.5** | **283.4** |
| Current§ | 205.3 | 226.1 | 244.7 |
| Capital | 68.6 | 37.4 | 38.7 |

* Excluding grants received from abroad (L $ million): 25.0 (current 17.0, capital 8.0) in 1985/86; 18.0 (current 12.2, capital 5.8) in 1986/87.
† Beginning in 1988, the fiscal year was changed to coincide with the calendar year.
‡ Excluding net lending (L $ million): 22.7 in 1985/86; 19.0 in 1986/87; 21.3 in 1988.
§ Including interest payments (L $ million): 40.6 in 1985/86; 42.9 in 1986/87; 41.2 in 1988.

Source: IMF, *Government Finance Statistics Yearbook*.

## INTERNATIONAL RESERVES (US $ million at 31 December)

| | 1991 | 1992 | 1993 |
|---|---|---|---|
| Reserve position in IMF | 0.04 | 0.04 | 0.04 |
| Foreign exchange | 1.27 | 0.94 | 2.33 |
| **Total** | **1.31** | **0.98** | **2.37** |

Source: IMF, *International Financial Statistics*.

## MONEY SUPPLY (L $ million at 31 December)

| | 1991 | 1992 | 1993 |
|---|---|---|---|
| Currency outside banks* | 189.28 | 154.94 | 274.11 |
| Demand deposits at commercial banks | 92.32 | 111.12 | 149.95 |

* Figures refer only to amounts of Liberian coin in circulation. US notes and coin also circulate, but the amount of these in private holdings is unknown. The amount of Liberian coin in circulation is small in comparison to US currency.

Source: IMF, *International Financial Statistics*.

## COST OF LIVING
(Consumer Price Index for Monrovia; base: 1980 = 100)

| | 1986 | 1987 | 1988 |
|---|---|---|---|
| Food | 107.8 | 108.0 | 128.8 |
| Fuel and light | 127.2 | 127.4 | 128.1 |
| Clothing | 124.9 | 144.8 | 157.5 |
| Rent | 103.8 | 104.1 | 105.1 |
| **All items** (incl. others) | 123.2 | 129.4 | 141.8 |

**1989:** Food 141.2 (average for January–October); All items 150.2.
**1990** (January–June): Food 160.7; All items 162.4.

Source: ILO, *Year Book of Labour Statistics*.

## NATIONAL ACCOUNTS (L $ million at current prices)
### Expenditure on the Gross Domestic Product

| | 1987 | 1988 | 1989 |
|---|---|---|---|
| Government final consumption expenditure | 143.9 | 136.3 | 141.6 |
| Private final consumption expenditure | 713.9 | 733.3 | 656.8 |
| Increase in stocks* | 7.0 | 3.5 | 4.0 |
| Gross fixed capital formation | 120.4 | 115.3 | 96.8 |
| Statistical discrepancy | 22.9 | 39.1 | 48.2 |
| **Total domestic expenditure** | **1,008.1** | **1,027.5** | **947.4** |
| Exports of goods and services | 438.2 | 452.3 | 521.4 |
| *Less* Imports of goods and services | 356.8 | 321.5 | 275.2 |
| **GDP in purchasers' values** | **1,089.5** | **1,158.3** | **1,193.6** |
| **GDP at constant 1981 prices** | **1,015.0** | **1,043.7** | **1,072.8** |

* Figures refer only to stocks of iron ore and rubber.

### Gross Domestic Product by Economic Activity

| | 1987 | 1988 | 1989 |
|---|---|---|---|
| Agriculture, hunting, forestry and fishing | 381.8 | 412.0 | 410.7 |
| Mining and quarrying | 105.0 | 115.0 | 122.3 |
| Manufacturing | 73.1 | 80.4 | 81.6 |
| Electricity, gas and water | 19.0 | 18.8 | 19.0 |
| Construction | 32.7 | 28.8 | 26.3 |
| Trade, restaurants and hotels | 60.1 | 64.2 | 63.3 |
| Transport, storage and communications | 75.3 | 79.1 | 79.1 |
| Finance, insurance, real estate and business services | 119.2 | 136.1 | 141.8 |
| Government services | 108.5 | 109.7 | 139.4 |
| Other community, social and personal services | 34.4 | 35.5 | 35.5 |
| **Sub-total** | **1,009.1** | **1,079.6** | **1,119.0** |
| *Less* Imputed bank service charge | 18.3 | 27.1 | 36.5 |
| **GDP at factor cost** | **990.8** | **1,052.5** | **1,082.5** |
| Indirect taxes, *less* subsidies | 99.0 | 105.8 | 111.3 |
| **GDP in purchasers' values** | **1,089.5** | **1,158.3** | **1,193.6** |

Source: UN, *National Accounts Statistics*.

LIBERIA

## BALANCE OF PAYMENTS (US $ million)

|  | 1985 | 1986 | 1987 |
|---|---|---|---|
| Merchandise exports f.o.b. | 430.4 | 407.9 | 374.9 |
| Merchandise imports f.o.b. | −263.8 | −258.8 | −311.7 |
| **Trade balance** | 166.6 | 149.1 | 63.2 |
| Exports of services | 34.6 | 56.9 | 52.5 |
| Imports of services | −80.2 | −80.5 | −74.2 |
| Other income received | 3.7 | 2.1 | 5.2 |
| Other income paid | −131.0 | −183.3 | −188.3 |
| Private unrequited transfers (net) | −28.0 | −25.4 | −21.4 |
| Official unrequited transfers (net) | 90.4 | 96.4 | 45.4 |
| **Current balance** | 56.1 | 15.3 | −117.6 |
| Direct investment (net) | −16.2 | −16.5 | 38.5 |
| Portfolio investment (net) | 4.4 | 5.6 | — |
| Other capital (net) | −139.0 | −191.6 | −223.8 |
| Net errors and omissions | −108.7 | −73.8 | 30.3 |
| **Overall balance** | −203.4 | −261.0 | −272.6 |

Source: IMF, *International Financial Statistics*.

# External Trade

## PRINCIPAL COMMODITIES (US $ million)

| Imports c.i.f. | 1986 | 1987 | 1988 |
|---|---|---|---|
| Food and live animals | 53.6 | 58.7 | 47.3 |
| Rice | 12.1 | 17.7 | 27.9 |
| Mineral fuels, lubricants, etc. | 52.9 | 69.8 | 55.3 |
| Refined petroleum products | 52.5 | 67.1 | n.a. |
| Motor spirit and other light fuels | 12.1 | 14.2 | n.a. |
| Chemicals and related products | 26.3 | 22.1 | 15.3 |
| Basic manufactures | 36.0 | 55.3 | 48.0 |
| Machinery and transport equipment | 59.1 | 73.5 | 82.3 |
| Miscellaneous manufactured articles | 18.1 | 14.2 | 15.4 |
| **Total** (incl. others) | 259.0 | 307.6 | 272.3 |

**1989** (US $ million): Total imports c.i.f. 323.0.

| Exports f.o.b. | 1986 | 1987 | 1988 |
|---|---|---|---|
| Coffee and substitutes | 16.3 | 9.0 | 5.6 |
| Cocoa | 9.0 | 5.9 | 6.3 |
| Natural rubber and gums | 70.9 | 89.4 | 110.2 |
| Wood in the rough or roughly squared | 33.1 | 35.5 | 32.0 |
| Iron ore and concentrates | 248.4 | 218.0 | 219.7 |
| Diamonds | 6.6 | 11.0 | 8.8 |
| **Total** (incl. others) | 408.4 | 382.2 | 396.3 |

Source: UN, *International Trade Statistics Yearbook*.

**1989** (L $ million): Total exports f.o.b. 461.16 (iron ore 235.05, rubber 119.93, logs 91.98). Source: National Bank of Liberia, *Quarterly Statistical Bulletin*.

## PRINCIPAL TRADING PARTNERS (US $ million)*

| Imports c.i.f. | 1986 | 1987 | 1988 |
|---|---|---|---|
| Belgium/Luxembourg | 8.5 | 11.2 | 15.0 |
| China, People's Republic | 7.1 | 14.7 | 4.8 |
| Denmark | 10.6 | 7.6 | 5.9 |
| France (incl. Monaco) | 6.5 | 6.4 | 4.7 |
| Germany, Federal Republic | 32.7 | 52.3 | 39.5 |
| Italy | 2.5 | 2.2 | 7.3 |
| Japan | 20.1 | 15.0 | 12.0 |
| Netherlands | 20.6 | 26.8 | 14.4 |
| Spain | 2.5 | 6.6 | 3.1 |
| Sweden | 2.4 | 0.6 | 4.6 |
| United Kingdom | 24.2 | 18.4 | 12.7 |
| USA | 42.5 | 58.0 | 57.7 |
| **Total** (incl. others) | 259.0 | 307.6 | 272.3 |

| Exports f.o.b. | 1986 | 1987 | 1988 |
|---|---|---|---|
| Belgium/Luxembourg | 29.2 | 23.2 | 28.2 |
| France (incl. Monaco) | 33.1 | 33.2 | 33.2 |
| Germany, Federal Republic | 114.5 | 109.2 | 108.1 |
| Italy | 70.3 | 63.4 | 63.2 |
| Japan | 4.9 | 1.0 | 4.8 |
| Netherlands | 14.4 | 11.5 | 10.5 |
| Spain | 16.4 | 17.8 | 13.4 |
| United Kingdom | 7.2 | 8.8 | 6.3 |
| USA | 93.2 | 73.9 | 74.6 |
| **Total** (incl. others) | 408.4 | 382.2 | 396.3 |

* Imports by country of origin; exports by country of last consignment.

Source: UN, *International Trade Statistics Yearbook*.

# Transport

## ROAD TRAFFIC (vehicles in use at 31 December)

|  | 1979 | 1986 | 1987 |
|---|---|---|---|
| Cars | 13,070 | 10,788 | 7,148 |
| Buses and coaches | 3,415 | 1,572 | 1,078 |
| Goods vehicles | 8,999 | 4,639 | 2,953 |
| **Total** | 25,484 | 16,999 | 11,179 |

Source: International Road Federation, *World Road Statistics*.

## SHIPPING

**Merchant Fleet** (at 30 June)

|  | 1991 | 1992 | 1993 |
|---|---|---|---|
| Number of vessels | 1,605 | 1,661 | 1,611 |
| Displacement ('000 gross registered tons) | 52,426.5 | 55,917.7 | 53,918.5 |

Source: Lloyd's Register of Shipping.

**International Sea-borne Freight Traffic** ('000 metric tons)

|  | 1988 | 1989 | 1990 |
|---|---|---|---|
| Goods loaded | 15,000 | 15,200 | 14,900 |
| Goods unloaded | 1,430 | 1,490 | 1,520 |

Source: UN, *Monthly Bulletin of Statistics*.

## CIVIL AVIATION (traffic on scheduled services)

|  | 1990 | 1991 | 1992 |
|---|---|---|---|
| Passengers carried ('000) | 32 | 32 | 32 |
| Passenger-km (million) | 7 | 7 | 7 |
| Total ton-km (million) | 1 | 1 | 1 |

Source: UN, *Statistical Yearbook*.

## Communications Media

|  | 1990 | 1991 | 1992 |
|---|---|---|---|
| Radio receivers ('000 in use) | 580 | 600 | 622 |
| Television receivers ('000 in use) | 47 | 49 | 51 |
| Telephones ('000 in use)* | 24 | 25 | n.a. |
| Daily newspapers (number) | 8 | n.a. | 8 |

* Estimates.

Sources: UNESCO, *Statistical Yearbook*; UN Economic Commission for Africa, *African Statistical Yearbook*.

## Education

|  | 1983 | 1984 | 1985 |
|---|---|---|---|
| Schools | 1,284 | 1,830 | 1,691 |
| Teachers | 7,202 | 9,817 | 9,856 |
| Students | 245,673 | 275,243 | 260,560 |

**1986:** Students 250,322.

Source: Ministry of Education, Monrovia.

# Directory

## The Constitution

The Constitution, promulgated on 6 January 1986 (and amended in July 1988), provides for the division of state authority into three independent branches: the executive, the legislature and the judiciary. Executive powers are vested in the President, who is Head of State, Head of Government and Commander-in-Chief of the Liberian armed forces, and who is elected by universal adult suffrage for a six-year term (renewable more than once). Legislative power is vested in the bicameral National Assembly, comprising the Senate and the House of Representatives. Members of both houses are directly elected by popular vote. The Constitution provides for a multi-party system of government, and incorporates powers to prevent the declaration of a one-party state, the dissolution of the legislature or the suspension of the judiciary. The Constitution may be amended by a two-thirds majority of both houses of the National Assembly.

An Interim President was inaugurated in November 1990, and an Interim Government of National Unity (IGNU) was appointed in Monrovia in January 1991. Under the terms of a peace agreement that was signed in July 1993, the IGNU was replaced by a Council of State, and the existing legislature by a Transitional Legislative Assembly, pending presidential and general elections (which were subsequently rescheduled for September 1994). In September 1994, however, an agreement between the principal warring factions provided for the establishment of a reconstituted Council of State, and rescheduled the elections for October 1995. Under the terms of a further agreement between the factions (concluded in December 1994), a new government was to be installed on 1 January 1996, following elections in November 1995.

## The Government

**LIBERIAN NATIONAL TRANSITIONAL GOVERNMENT**

### Council of State
(May 1995)

A transitional executive council, comprising representatives of the former Interim Government of National Unity (IGNU), the National Patriotic Forces of Liberia (NPFL) and the United Liberation Movement of Liberia for Democracy (ULIMO).

DAVID D. KPOMAKPOR (Chairman) (IGNU)
Gen. (retd) ISAAC MUSA (Vice-Chairman) (NPFL)
Dr EL-MOHAMED SHERIF (Vice-Chairman) (ULIMO)
PHILIP A. Z. BANKS (IGNU)
DEXTER TAHYOR (ULIMO)

### Cabinet
(May 1995)

An interim coalition of the IGNU, the NPFL and ULIMO.
**Minister of Foreign Affairs:** DOROTHY M. COOPER.
**Minister of Finance:** WILSON TARPEH (acting).
**Minister of Justice:** LAVELI SUPUWOOD.
**Minister of Defence:** Gen. SANDEE WARE.
**Minister of Posts and Telecommunications:** ROOSEVELT JAYJAY.
**Minister of Commerce and Industry:** LOSINEE F. KAMARA.
**Minister of Agriculture:** Dr ROLAND C. MASSAQUOI.
**Minister of Internal Affairs:** SAMUEL SAYE DOKIE.
**Minister of Health and Social Welfare:** Dr VAMBA KANNEH.
**Minister of Education:** Dr LEVI ZANGAI.
**Minister of Planning and Economic Affairs:** AMELIA WARD.
**Minister of Information, Culture and Tourism:** JOE W. MULBAH.
**Minister of Lands, Mines and Energy:** ZEHYEE KEKIE.
**Minister of Public Works:** Brig.-Gen. ACHEAPHON BESTMAN.
**Minister of Labour:** THOMAS J. WOEWEIYU.
**Minister of State for Presidential Affairs:** MANYU KAMARA.
**Minister of Youth and Sports:** COMMENY B. WESSEH.
**Minister of Rural Development:** SAMUEL BROWNELL.
**Minister of Transport:** SAM MAHN.
**Ministers without Portfolio:** MANYU KAMARA, ANSUMANA KROMAH.

### MINISTRIES

**Ministry of Agriculture:** Tubman Blvd, POB 9010, Monrovia.
**Ministry of Commerce and Industry:** Ashmun St, POB 9014, Monrovia.
**Ministry of Defence:** Benson St, POB 9007, Monrovia.
**Ministry of Education:** Broad St, POB 1545, Monrovia.
**Ministry of Finance:** Broad St, POB 9013, Monrovia.
**Ministry of Foreign Affairs:** Mamba Point, Monrovia.
**Ministry of Health and Social Welfare:** POB 9004, Sinkor, Monrovia.
**Ministry of Information, Culture and Tourism:** 110 United Nations Drive, POB 9021, Monrovia.
**Ministry of Internal Affairs:** cnr Warren and Benson Sts, POB 9008, Monrovia.
**Ministry of Justice:** Ashmun St, POB 9006, Monrovia.
**Ministry of Labour:** Mechlin St, POB 9040, Monrovia.
**Ministry of Lands, Mines and Energy:** Capitol Hill, POB 9024, Monrovia.
**Ministry of Planning and Economic Affairs:** Broad St, POB 9016, Monrovia.
**Ministry of Posts and Telecommunications:** Carey St, Monrovia.
**Ministry of Presidential Affairs:** Executive Mansion, Capitol Hill, Monrovia.
**Ministry of Public Affairs:** Lynch St, POB 9011, Monrovia.
**Ministry of Rural Development:** Monrovia.
**Ministry of Transport:** Monrovia.
**Ministry of Youth and Sports:** POB 9040, Sinkor, Monrovia.

## Legislature

### NATIONAL ASSEMBLY

The 1986 Constitution vests legislative authority in a bicameral National Assembly, comprising a Senate of 26 members and a House of Representatives of 64 members. Under the terms of the peace agreement that was signed in July 1993, the existing 28-member Interim National Assembly was replaced by a 35-member Transitional Legislative Assembly in October of that year (comprising representatives of the principal warring factions), pending legislative elections.

**Speaker of the Transitional Legislative Assembly:** MORRIS M. DUKULY.

LIBERIA
## Political Organizations

Under the terms of a peace agreement reached in December 1994, the following armed factions were to be represented in a new transitional authority:

**\*Liberia Peace Council (LPC):** f. 1993; predominantly Krahn support; has been engaged in conflict with NPFL forces in south-eastern Liberia; Chair. Dr GEORGE SIAGBE BOLEY; Sec.-Gen. OCTAVIUS WALKER.

**\*Lofa Defence Force (LDF):** f. 1993; has engaged in conflict with ULIMO forces in Lofa County; Leader FRANÇOIS MASSAQUOI.

**National Patriotic Front of Liberia (NPFL):** f. in Abidjan, Côte d'Ivoire; began mil. operations in Dec. 1989; based at Gbarnga, Bong County; Leader CHARLES GANKAY TAYLOR.

**\*Central Revolutionary Council (NPFL—CRC):** f. Sept. 1994 by dissident members of the NPFL; captured headquarters at Gbarnga and announced Taylor's deposition, but was reported to have lost territory to forces loyal to Taylor later that year; Leader TOM WOEWIYU.

**United Liberation Movement of Liberia for Democracy (ULIMO):** Tubmanburg; f. 1991 by supporters of the late Pres. Samuel Doe; split into two ethnic factions which have engaged in conflict: ULIMO—K (Mandingo, led by Alhaji G. V. KROMAH) and ULIMO—J (Krahn, led by Maj-Gen. ROOSEVELT JOHNSON).

\* The LPC, the LDF and the NPFL—CRC, together with elements of ULIMO—K, comprise a loose alliance, known as the Coalition Forces.

## Diplomatic Representation

Note: Following the advance of the NPFL on Monrovia in May 1990, all embassy staff were evacuated. Some embassies were subsequently reported to have reopened.

### EMBASSIES IN LIBERIA

**Algeria:** Capitol By-Pass, POB 2032, Monrovia; tel. 224311; telex 44475; Chargé d'affaires: MUHAMMAD AZZEDINE AZZOUZ.

**Cameroon:** 18th St and Payne Ave, Sinkor, POB 414, Monrovia; tel. 261374; telex 44240; Ambassador: VICTOR E. NDIBA.

**Côte d'Ivoire:** Tubman Blvd, Sinkor, POB 126, Monrovia; tel. 261123; telex 44273; Ambassador: CLÉMENT KAUL MELEDJE.

**Cuba:** 17 Kennedy Ave, Congotown, POB 3579, Monrovia; tel. 262600; Ambassador: M. GAUNEANO CARDOSO TOLEDO.

**Egypt:** POB 462, Monrovia; tel. 261953; telex 44308; Ambassador: MUHAMMAD SALEH EL-DIN EL-DAOUR.

**Germany:** Oldest Congotown, POB 34, Monrovia; tel. 261460; telex 44230; Ambassador: Dr JÜRGEN GEHL.

**Ghana:** cnr 11th St and Gardiner Ave, Sinkor, POB 471, Monrovia; tel. 261477; Ambassador: G. R. NIPAH.

**Guinea:** Tubman Blvd, Sinkor, POB 461, Monrovia; tel. 261182; Ambassador: (vacant).

**Holy See:** Apostolic Nunciature, Sinkor, POB 4211, Monrovia; tel. 262948; Apostolic Pro-Nuncio: Most Rev. LUIGI TRAVAGLINO, Titular Archbishop of Lettere (temporarily resident at 23 Jomo Keyatta Rd, POB 526, Freetown, Sierra Leone; tel. 242131; fax 240509).

**Israel:** Gardiner Ave, between 11th and 12th Sts, Sinkor, Monrovia; tel. 262861; telex 44415; Ambassador: MOSHE ITAN.

**Italy:** Mamba Point, POB 255, Monrovia; tel. 224580; telex 44438; Ambassador: Dr. ENRIC'ANGIOLO FERRONI-CARLI.

**Korea, Republic:** 10th St and Payne Ave, Sinkor, POB 2769, Monrovia; tel. 261532; telex 44241; Ambassador: KIM YONG-JIP.

**Lebanon:** 12th St, Monrovia; tel. 262537; telex 44208; Ambassador: MICHEL BITAR.

**Libya:** Monrovia.

**Morocco:** Tubman Blvd, Congotown, Monrovia; tel. 262767; telex 44540; Chargé d'affaires a.i.: Dr MOULAY ABBES AL-KADIRI.

**Nigeria:** Tubman Blvd, Sinkor, POB 366, Monrovia; tel. 261093; telex 44278; Ambassador: HENRY AJAKAIYE.

**Poland:** cnr 10th St and Gardiner Ave, Sinkor, POB 860, Monrovia; tel. 261113; Chargé d'affaires: ZBIGNIEW REJMAN.

**Romania:** 81 Sekou Touré Ave, Sinkor, POB 2598, Monrovia; tel. 261508; Chargé d'affaires: SILVESTRA ZUGRAV.

**Russia:** Payne Ave, Sinkor, POB 2010, Monrovia; tel. 261304; Ambassador: VASILI STEPANOVICH BEBKO.

**Senegal:** Monrovia, Ambassador MOCTAR TRAORÉ.

**Sierra Leone:** Tubman Blvd, POB 575, Monrovia; tel. 261301; Ambassador: DENNIS RANSFORD WOODE.

*Directory*

**Spain:** Capitol Hill, POB 275, Monrovia; tel. 221299; telex 44538; Ambassador: MANUEL DE LUNA.

**Sweden:** POB 335, Monrovia; tel. 261646; telex 44255; Chargé d'affaires: OVE SVENSSON.

**Switzerland:** Old Congo Rd, POB 283, Monrovia; tel. 261065; telex 44559; Chargé d'affaires: CHARLES HALLER.

**United Kingdom:** Mamba Point, POB 120, Monrovia; tel. 221491; telex 44287.

**USA:** 111 United Nations Drive, Mamba Point, POB 98, Monrovia; tel. 222994; Ambassador: WILLIAM H. TWADDELL.

**Zaire:** Spriggs Payne Airport, Sinkor, POB 1038, Monrovia; tel. 261326; Ambassador: MUABI M. S. KUMUANBA.

## Judicial System

In February 1982 the People's Supreme Tribunal (which had been established following the April 1980 coup) was renamed the People's Supreme Court, and its chairman and members became the Chief Justice and Associate Justices of the People's Supreme Court. The judicial system also comprised People's Circuit and Magistrate Courts. The five-member Supreme Court (composed of representatives of the interim Government and of the NPFL) was established in January 1992 to adjudicate in electoral disputes.

**Chief Justice of People's Supreme Court:** EMMANUEL GBALAZEH.

## Religion

Liberia is officially a Christian state, although complete religious freedom is guaranteed. Christianity and Islam are the two main religions. There are numerous religious sects, and many Liberians hold traditional beliefs.

### CHRISTIANITY

**Liberian Council of Churches:** 182 Tubman Blvd, POB 2191, Monrovia; tel. 262820; f. 1982; six full mems and two assoc. mems.; Pres. Bishop ARTHUR F. KULAH; Gen. Sec. IMOGENE M. COLLINS.

#### The Anglican Communion

Anglicans in Liberia are adherents of the Church of the Province of West Africa, incorporating the local Protestant Episcopal Church. Anglicanism was established in Liberia in 1836, and the diocese of Liberia was admitted into full membership of the Province in March 1982. In 1985 the Church had 125 congregations, 39 clergy, 26 schools and about 20,000 adherents in the country.

**Bishop of Liberia:** (vacant), POB 10-0277, Monrovia 10; tel. and fax 224760.

#### The Roman Catholic Church

Liberia comprises the archdiocese of Monrovia and the dioceses of Cape Palmas and Gbarnga. At 31 December 1992 there were an estimated 83,778 adherents in the country, equivalent to 2.9% of the total population. The Bishops participate in the Inter-territorial Catholic Bishops' Conference of the Gambia, Liberia and Sierra Leone (based in Freetown, Sierra Leone).

**Archbishop of Monrovia:** Most Rev. MICHAEL KPAKALA FRANCIS, Catholic Mission, POB 2078, Monrovia; tel. 221389; telex 44529; fax 221399.

#### Other Christian Churches

**Assemblies of God in Liberia:** POB 1297, Monrovia; f. 1908; 14,578 adherents, 287 churches; Gen. Supt JIMMIE K. DUGBE, Sr.

**Lutheran Church in Liberia:** POB 1046, Monrovia; 25,600 adherents; Pres. Bishop RONALD J. DIGGS.

**Providence Baptist Church:** cnr Broad and Center Sts, Monrovia; f. 1821; 2,500 adherents, 300 congregations, 6 ministers, 8 schools; Pastor Rev. A. MOMOLUE DIGGS; associated with:

**The Liberia Baptist Missionary and Educational Convention, Inc:** POB 390, Monrovia; tel. 222661; f. 1880; Pres. Rev. J. K. LEVEE MOULTON; Nat. Vice-Pres. Rev. J. GBANA HALL; Gen. Sec. CHARLES W. BLAKE.

**United Methodist Church in Liberia:** cnr 12th St and Tubman Blvd, POB 1010, 1000 Monrovia 10; tel. 223343; f. 1833; c. 70,000 adherents, 487 congregations, 450 ministers, 300 lay pastors, 38 schools; Resident Bishop Rev. ARTHUR F. KULAH; Sec. Rev. JULIUS SARWOLO NELSON.

Other active denominations include the National Baptist Mission, the Pentecostal Church, the Presbyterian Church in Liberia, the Prayer Band and the Church of the Lord Aladura.

# LIBERIA

## ISLAM

The total community numbers about 670,000.

**National Muslim Council of Liberia:** Monrovia; Leader Shaykh KAFUMBA KONNAH.

## The Press

### NEWSPAPERS

**Daily Observer:** 117 Broad St, Crown Hill, POB 1858, Monrovia; tel. 223545; f. 1981; independent; 5 a week; Editor-in-Chief STANTON B. PEABODY; circ. 30,000.

**Herald:** Monrovia; f. 1987; Catholic weekly; Editor RUFUS DARPOH.

**The Inquirer:** Monrovia; Man. Editor GABRIEL WILLIAMS.

**New Times:** Monrovia; Man. Editor RUFUS DARPOH; Editor JEFF MUTADA.

**Sunday Express:** Mamba Point, POB 3029, Monrovia; weekly; Editor JOHN F. SCOTLAND; circ. 5,000.

**Sunday People:** POB 3366, Monrovia; 2 a week; Editor D. G. PYNE-DRAPER.

### PERIODICALS

**Daily Listener:** POB 35, Monrovia; monthly; Man. CHARLES C. DENNIS; circ. 3,500.

**The Eye:** POB 4692, Monrovia; daily; Editor H. B. KINBAH.

**Journal of Commerce, Industry & Transportation:** POB 9041, Monrovia; tel. 222141; telex 44331.

**The Kpelle Messenger:** Kpelle Literacy Center, Lutheran Church, POB 1046, Monrovia; Kpelle-English monthly; Editor Rev. JOHN J. MANAWU.

**Liberian Star:** POB 691, Monrovia; f. 1954; monthly; Editor HENRY B. COLE; circ. 3,500.

**Palm:** Johnson and Carey Sts, POB 1110, Monrovia; 6 a year; Editor JAMES C. DENNIS.

**The People Magazine:** Bank of Liberia Bldg, Suite 214, Carey and Warren Sts, POB 3501, Monrovia; tel. 222743; f. 1985; monthly; Editor and Publr CHARLES A. SNETTER.

**Plain Talk:** POB 2108, Monrovia; daily; Editor-in-Chief N. MACAULAY PAYKUE.

**X-Ray Magazine:** c/o Liss Inc, POB 4196, Monrovia; tel. 221674; f. 1985; monthly; health; Man. Editor NMAH BROPLEH.

### PRESS ORGANIZATION

**Press Union of Liberia:** Monrovia; f. 1985; Pres. LAMINI A. WARITAY.

### NEWS AGENCIES

**Liberian News Agency (LINA):** POB 9021, Capitol Hill, Monrovia; tel. 222229; telex 44249; Dir-Gen. ERNEST KIAZOLY (acting).

#### Foreign Bureaux

**Agence France-Presse (AFP):** Monrovia; telex 44211; Rep. JAMES DORBOR.

**United Press International (UPI)** (USA): Monrovia; Correspondent T. K. SANNAH.

**Xinhua (New China) News Agency** (People's Republic of China): Adams St, Old Rd, Congotown, POB 3001, Monrovia; tel. 262821; telex 44547; Correspondent SUN BAOYU.

**Reuters** (UK) is also represented in Liberia.

## Publisher

### Government Publishing House

**Government Printer:** Government Printing Office, POB 9002, Monrovia; tel. 221029; telex 44224.

## Radio and Television

In 1992, according to UNESCO estimates, there were 622,000 radio receivers and 51,000 television receivers in use.

### RADIO

**ELBC—The Voice of Peace, Harmony and Reconciliation:** Liberian Broadcasting System, POB 594, Monrovia; tel. 224984; f. 1960; reorg. 1990, under the aegis of the interim Govt; broadcasts in English and Liberian vernaculars; Dir-Gen. WEADE KOBBAH WUREH; Asst Dir-Gen. (Radio) NOAH A. BORDOLO.

**LAMCO Broadcasting Station (ELNR):** LAMCO Information and Broadcasting Service, Nimba; Liberian news, music, cultural, political and educational programmes in English; carries national news and all nation-wide broadcasts from ELBC, and local news in English and African languages (Mano, Gio, Bassa, Vai, Lorma, Kru, Krahn, Grebo and Kpelle); also relays BBC World Service and African Service news programmes; Dir T. NELSON WILLIAMS.

**Liberia Rural Communications Network:** POB 10-02176, 1000 Monrovia 10; tel. 271368; f. 1981; govt-operated; rural development and entertainment programmes; operates three medium-wave stations and central administrative and programming unit; broadcasts in principal Liberian languages; Dir JEROME DAVIS.

**Radio ELWA:** POB 192, Monrovia; tel. 271669; f. 1954; operated by the Sudan Interior Mission; religious, cultural and educational broadcasts in English, French, Arabic and 42 west African vernaculars; Broadcasting Dir LEE J. SONIUS.

**Voice of America:** Monrovia; telex 44365; broadcasts in English, French, Swahili, Hausa and Portuguese.

### TELEVISION

**ELTV:** Liberian Broadcasting System, POB 594, Monrovia; tel. 224984; telex 44249; f. 1964; commercial station, partly govt-supported; broadcasts 5½ hours daily Mon.–Fri., 9½ hours daily Sat. and Sun.; Dir-Gen. WEADE KOBBAH WUREH.

## Finance

(cap. = capital; res = reserves; dep. = deposits; m. = million; br. = branch; amounts in Liberian dollars)

### BANKING

Most banking operations in Liberia were suspended in 1990, as a result of the disruption caused by the civil conflict, although several banks were subsequently reported to have reopened.

#### Central Bank

**National Bank of Liberia:** Broad St, POB 2048, Monrovia; tel. 222497; telex 44215; f. 1974; bank of issue; cap. and res 17.1m., dep. 70.7m. (1986); Gov. DAVID K. WINTER; Dep. Gov. LINDSAY M. HAINES.

#### Other Banks

**Agricultural and Co-operative Development Bank:** Carey and Warren Sts, POB 3585, Monrovia; tel. 224385; telex 44535; fax 221500; f. 1977; cap. 6.6m. (Dec. 1989), res. 6.7m., dep. 30.6m. (Dec. 1987); Chair. Dr NAH-DOE P. BROPLEM; Pres. and Gen. Man. JEROME M. HODGE; 6 brs.

**Citibank (Liberia):** Ashmun St, POB 280, Monrovia; tel. 224991; telex 44274; f. 1935; cap. 0.5m.; Gen. Man. THIERRY BUNGINER; 1 br.

**Eurobank Liberia Ltd:** Broad and Warren Sts, POB 2021, 1000 Monrovia; tel. 224873; telex 44455; fax 225921; Chair. GEORGES PHILIPPE; Pres. DONALD S. REYNOLDS; cap. 1m. (Dec. 1992).

**First Commercial and Investment Bank:** Cnr Ashmun and Mechlin Sts, POB 1442, Monrovia; tel. 222498; telex 44431; fax 222351; cap. 3.6m. (Dec. 1991); Chair. and Pres. EDWIN J. COOPER.

**International Trust Co of Liberia:** 80 Broad St, POB 292, Monrovia; tel. 221600; telex 44588; f. 1948; cap. 2m., dep. 30m. (Dec. 1989); Pres. DAVID CLARK; Gen. Man. RAYMOND M. ABOU SAMRA; 1 br.

**Liberia Finance and Trust Corporation:** Broad St, POB 3155, Monrovia; tel. 221020; telex 44386; cap. 790,487 (Dec. 1984); Chair. G. ALVIN JONES; Pres. C. T. O. KING, III.

**Liberian Bank for Development and Investment (LBDI):** Ashmun and Randall Sts, POB 0547, Monrovia; tel. 223998; telex 44345; fax 223044; f. 1961; cap. and res 1,832.1m., dep. 34.1m. (Dec. 1993); Chair. FRANCIS T. KARPEH; Pres. JAMES S. P. COOPER

**Liberian Trading and Development Bank Ltd (TRADEVCO):** 57 Ashmun St, POB 293, Monrovia; tel. 221800; telex 44270; fax 225035; f. 1955; wholly-owned subsidiary of Mediobanca SpA (Italy); cap. and res 3.2m., dep. 45.0m. (Dec. 1992). Chair. and Pres. GIORGIO PICOTTI.

**Meridien BIAO Bank Liberia Ltd:** Meridien House, Randall and Ashmun Sts, POB 0408, Monrovia; tel. 221500; telex 44565; fax 224087; cap. 7m. (Sept. 1993); Chair. J. C. KAPOTWE; Pres. RAHAMAT HOSEIN.

**National Housing and Savings Bank:** UN Drive, Waterside, POB 818, Monrovia; tel. 224985; telex 44337; fax 224498; f. 1972; priority financing for low-cost govt housing programmes; cap. 5.1m. (Dec. 1986); Pres. PATRICK D. KUTO-AKOI.

#### Banking Association

**Liberia Bankers' Association:** POB 292, Monrovia; an asscn of commercial and development banks; Pres. LEN MAESTRE.

## INSURANCE

**American International Underwriters, Inc:** Carter Bldg, 39 Broad St, POB 180, Monrovia; tel. 224921; telex 44389; general; Gen. Man. S. B. MENSAH.

**American Life Insurance Co:** Carter Bldg, 39 Broad St, POB 60, Monrovia; life and general; f. 1969; Vice-Pres. ALLEN BROWN.

**Insurance Co of Africa:** 80 Broad St, POB 292, Monrovia; f. 1969; life and general; Pres. GIZAW H. MARIAM.

**Lone Star Insurances Inc:** 51 Broad St, POB 1142, Monrovia; tel. 222257; telex 44394; non-life (property and casualty).

**Minet James Liberia Inc:** POB 541, Monrovia; Man. Dir EDWARD MILNE.

**National Insurance Corporation of Liberia (NICOL):** LBDI Bldg Complex, POB 1528, Sinkor, Monrovia; tel. 262429; telex 44228; f. 1984; state-owned; sole insurer for govt and parastatal bodies; also provides insurance for the Liberian-registered merchant shipping fleet; Man. Dir MIATTA EDITH SHERMAN.

**Royal Exchange Assurance:** Ashmun and Randall Sts, POB 666, Monrovia; all types of insurance; Man. RONALD WOODS.

**United Security Insurance Agencies Inc:** Randall St, POB 2071, Monrovia; telex 44568; personal (life, accident and medical); Dir EPHRAIM O. OKORO.

# Trade and Industry

## CHAMBER OF COMMERCE

**Liberia Chamber of Commerce:** POB 92, Monrovia; tel. 223738; telex 44211; f. 1951; Pres. DAVID A. B. JALLAH; Sec.-Gen. LUESETTE S. HOWELL.

## DEVELOPMENT ORGANIZATIONS

**Forestry Development Authority:** POB 3010, 1000 Monrovia; tel. 224940; responsible for forest management and conservation; Man. Dir BENSON S. GWYAN.

**Liberia Industrial Free Zone Authority:** Bushrod Island, POB 9047, Monrovia; f. 1975; 98 mems; Man. Dir GBAI M. GBALA.

**National Investment Commission (NIC):** Former Executive Mansion Bldg, POB 9043, Monrovia; tel. 225163; telex 44560; f. 1979; autonomous body negotiating investment incentives agreements on behalf of Govt; promotes agro-based and industrial development; Chair. G. E. SAIGBE BOLEY; Exec. Dir P. SEBASTIAN SMITH.

## MARKETING ORGANIZATION

**Liberian Produce Marketing Corporation:** POB 662, Monrovia; tel. 222447; telex 44590; f. 1961; govt-owned; exports Liberian produce, provides industrial facilities for processing of agricultural products and participates in agricultural development programmes; Man. Dir ALETHA JOHNSON-FRANCIS.

## EMPLOYERS' ASSOCIATION

**National Enterprises Corporation:** POB 518, Monrovia; tel. 261370; importer, wholesaler and distributor of foodstuffs, and wire and metal products for local industries; Pres. EMMANUEL SHAW, Sr.

## TRADE UNIONS

**Congress of Industrial Organizations:** 29 Ashmun St, POB 415, Monrovia; Pres. Gen. J. T. PRATT; Sec.-Gen. AMOS N. GRAY; 5 affiliated unions.

**Labor Congress of Liberia:** 71 Gurley St, Monrovia; Sec.-Gen. P. C. T. SONPON; 8 affiliated unions.

**Liberian Federation of Labor Unions:** J. B. McGill Labor Center, Gardnersville Freeway, POB 415, Monrovia; f. 1980 by merger; Sec.-Gen. AMOS GRAY; 10,000 mems (1983).

# Transport

## RAILWAYS

**Bong Mining Co Ltd:** POB 538, Monrovia; tel. 225222; telex 44269; fax 225770; operates 78 km of standard track, transporting iron ore concentrates and pellets from Bong mine to Monrovia; Gen. Man. H.-G. SCHNEIDER.

**Liberian Mining Co:** Monrovia; govt-owned; assumed control of LAMCO JV Operating Co in 1989; operates 267 track-km between Buchanan and the iron ore mine at Nimba; also operates a passenger railway between Buchanan and Yekepa.

**National Iron Ore Co Ltd:** POB 548, Monrovia; 145 km of track, Mano River to Monrovia, for transport of iron ore; Gen. Man. S. K. DATTA RAY.

## ROADS

In 1991 there were an estimated 6,095 km of classified roads, including 2,030 km of main roads and 1,540 km of secondary roads; about 2,400 km of the total network were paved. The main trunk road is the Monrovia–Sanniquellie motor road, extending north-east from the capital to the border with Guinea, near Ganta, and eastward through the hinterland to the border with Côte d'Ivoire. Trunk roads run through Tapita, in Nimba County, to Grand Gedeh County and from Monrovia to Buchanan. A bridge over the Mano river connects with the Sierra Leone road network, while a main road links Monrovia and Freetown (Sierra Leone). The principal roads in Liberia, which were closed throughout 1990 as a result of the armed conflict, were reported to have been reopened in early 1992.

## SHIPPING

In mid-1993 Liberia's open-registry fleet (1,611 vessels), the second largest in the world in terms of gross tonnage, had a total displacement of 53.9m. grt. In 1992 the resumption of armed conflict in Monrovia resulted in the suspension of most shipping activity. In mid-1993, however, the principal port of Buchanan was officially reopened to shipping.

**Liberia National Shipping Line (LNSL):** Monrovia; f. 1987; jt venture by the Liberian Govt and private German interests; routes to Europe, incl. the UK and Scandinavia.

**National Port Authority:** POB 1849, Monrovia; tel. 221454; telex 44275; f. 1967; administers Monrovia Free Port and the ports of Buchanan, Greenville and Harper; Man. L. A. KROMAH.

## CIVIL AVIATION

Liberia's principal airports are Roberts Field International Airport, at Harbel, 56 km east of Monrovia, and James Spriggs Payne Airport. There are more than 100 other airfields and airstrips. In 1992 the resumption of armed conflict in Monrovia resulted in the suspension of most air services.

**ADC Liberia Inc:** Monrovia; f. 1993; services to the United Kingdom, the USA and destinations in West Africa.

**Air Liberia:** POB 2076, Monrovia; telex 44298; f. 1974 by merger; state-owned; scheduled passenger and cargo services; Man. Dir JAMES K. KOFA.

# Tourism

**Bureau of Tourism:** Sinkor, Monrovia; Dir-Gen. JALLAH K. KAMARA.

# LIBYA

## Introductory Survey

**Location, Climate, Language, Religion, Flag, Capital**

The Great Socialist People's Libyan Arab Jamahiriya extends along the Mediterranean coast of North Africa. Its neighbours are Tunisia and Algeria to the west, Niger and Chad to the south, Egypt to the east, and Sudan to the south-east. The climate is very hot and dry. Most of the country is part of the Sahara, an arid desert, but the coastal regions are cooler. Average temperatures range from 13°C (55°F) to 38°C (100°F), but a maximum of 57.3°C (135°F) has been recorded in the interior. Arabic is the official language, but English and Italian are also used in trade. Almost all of the population are Sunni Muslims. The national flag (proportions 3 by 2) is plain green. The administrative capital was formerly Tripoli, but in September 1988 it was announced that most government departments were to be relocated, away from Tripoli.

**Recent History**

Formerly an Italian colony, Libya was occupied in 1942 by British and French troops. Cyrenaica and Tripolitania were subsequently governed by the United Kingdom, while Fezzan was administered by France. Following a UN resolution in 1949, the country became independent, as the United Kingdom of Libya, on 24 December 1951. Muhammad Idris as-Sanusi, Amir of Cyrenaica, became King Idris of Libya. The country enjoyed internal political stability and generally good relations with both the Arab world and the West.

The King was deposed in the bloodless revolution of September 1969. The perpetrators of the coup, a group of young nationalist army officers, established a Revolution Command Council (RCC), with Col Muammar al-Qaddafi as Chairman, and proclaimed the Libyan Arab Republic. In 1970, following agreements with the new regime, British and US military personnel were withdrawn from Libyan bases. In June 1971 the Arab Socialist Union (ASU) was established as the country's sole political party.

In April 1973 Col Qaddafi introduced a 'cultural revolution', involving the formation of 'people's committees' and an attempt to administer the country on an Islamic basis. Internal problems developed in 1975, with an attempted coup against Col Qaddafi. The General National Congress of the ASU held its first session in January 1976, and later became the General People's Congress (GPC), which first met in November 1976.

In March 1977 the GPC endorsed Qaddafi's plan to change the official name of the country to the Socialist People's Libyan Arab Jamahiriya. Power was vested in the people through People's Congresses and Popular Committees. The RCC disappeared, and the General Secretariat of the GPC (with Col Qaddafi as Secretary-General) was established. The GPC elected Col Qaddafi as Revolutionary Leader of the new state. The Council of Ministers was replaced by the General People's Committee, with 26 members, each a secretary of a department.

In March 1979 Qaddafi resigned from the post of Secretary-General of the General Secretariat of the GPC to devote more time to 'preserving the revolution'. The General Secretariat of the GPC was reorganized, while the membership of the General People's Committee was reduced to 21. The membership of the Committee was further reduced to 19 in March 1982, but increased to 20 in February 1984, when the post of Secretary for External Security was created, apparently to formalize Libya's activities in attempting to silence opponents of the Qaddafi regime at home and abroad. An office, attached to the Secretariat for Foreign Liaison, was also established in early 1984 to 'combat international terrorism'. These developments, combined with stern measures to curb the activity of dissidents, reflected Qaddafi's increasing sensitivity to the growth of opposition groups, principally the National Front for the Salvation of Libya (NFSL), which he accused foreign governments of fostering. In one of several such guerrilla operations during the first half of 1984, 15 NFSL commandos died in an attack on the Libyan leader's Tripoli residence.

At its annual meeting in February–March 1986, the GPC reduced the number of secretariats in the General People's Committee, apparently for greater administrative efficiency. The responsibilities of the defunct secretariats were, henceforth, to be handled by specially created national companies, such as already existed for the petroleum industry. In March 1987 the GPC elected the new General People's Committee, which retained only three Secretaries from the previous Committee.

In 1988, in an attempt to allay domestic dissatisfaction and international criticism, Col Qaddafi initiated a series of liberalizing economic and political reforms. In foreign policy he adopted a more pragmatic approach to his ambition of achieving union within the Maghreb (see below), and to his relations with other Arab and African countries. Within Libya he accused the Revolutionary Committees (young, pro-Qaddafi political activists) of murdering political opponents of his regime. In early March Qaddafi began to encourage the reopening of private businesses, in recognition of the inadequacy of state-sponsored supermarkets, and declared an amnesty for all prisoners, except those convicted of violent crimes or of conspiring with foreign powers. At the same time Libyan citizens were guaranteed freedom to travel abroad, and the powers of the Revolutionary Committees were curbed. Also in March the GPC created the People's Court and the People's Prosecution Bureau to replace the revolutionary courts. A new secretariat, for Jamahiri ('masses') Mobilization and Revolutionary Guidance, was established in May and in June the GPC approved a charter of human rights. In August Col Qaddafi announced that the army was to be replaced by a force of 'Jamahiri Guards', comprising conscripts and members of the existing army and police force, which would be supervised by 'people's defence committees'. In September it was decided to locate all except two of the secretariats of the GPC away from Tripoli, mostly in the town of Surt (Sirte), 400 km east of Tripoli. In January 1989 Col Qaddafi announced that all state institutions, including the state intelligence service and the official Libyan news agency, were to be abolished.

Despite the ongoing process of political and economic liberalization, evidence of popular discontent emerged in February 1989 in the form of anti-Government disturbances in Tripoli. While the principal focus of discontent was the management of the economy, Islamic fundamentalism was also reported to have played a part in the disturbances. Further clashes between Muslim fundamentalists and the security forces were reported in November 1989.

In October 1990 the GPC implemented the most extensive changes to the General People's Committee since March 1987. The number of secretariats was increased from 19 to 22, and a new Secretary-General, Abu Zayd Umar Durdah, and 11 new Secretaries were elected. The Secretariat for Jamahiri Mobilization and Revolutionary Guidance was abolished. At the same time, three of the five-member General Secretariat of the GPC were replaced, Abd ar-Raziq Sawsa becoming Secretary-General of the GPC in place of Dr Muftah al-Usta Omar.

In early October 1992 the GPC approved the reorganization of the secretariats within the General People's Committee, and in November new secretaries were appointed to the restructured Committee. The former Secretary for Economic Planning, Omar al-Muntasser, was named Secretary for Foreign Liaison and International Co-operation. Regarded as a moderate, al-Muntasser's appointment was viewed by some observers as a sign of Libya's willingness to resume dialogue with the West over the Lockerbie issue (see below).

Under Qaddafi, Libya assumed an active role in the Arab world. Various schemes for Arab unity led to the formation, in January 1972, of the Federation of Arab Republics, comprising Libya, Egypt and Syria. In 1972 Libya concluded an agreement with Egypt to merge the two countries in 1973. Neither union was effective, and proposals for union with Tunisia in 1974, with Syria in 1980 and with Chad in 1981 also proved abortive.

Relations with Egypt, already tense following the failure of the Libya-Egypt union, further deteriorated when President Sadat launched the October 1973 war against Israel without consulting Col Qaddafi. Relations with Egypt subsequently remained strained, with an outbreak of border fighting in July 1977. Libya objected very strongly to Sadat's peace initiative with Israel in November, and Tripoli was the venue for a summit of Arab 'rejectionist' states which immediately followed Sadat's visit to Jerusalem. Libya also strongly condemned the proposals for Middle East peace which were agreed by other Arab states in Fez, Morocco, in September 1982.

Libya has been accused of financing or directing subversive plots in a number of African countries, notably Chad (see chapter on Chad). In 1973 Libya occupied the 'Aozou strip' (a region of 114,000 sq km in the extreme north of Chad, reported to contain valuable reserves of minerals), to which it laid claim under the terms of an unratified treaty of 1935, whereby Italy and France altered their colonial frontiers. Colonel Qaddafi's intervention in the troubles in Chad temporarily secured the survival of President Goukouni Oueddei's Transitional Government of National Unity (GUNT) in N'Djamena during the fighting in late 1980. About 10,000 Libyan troops remained in Chad, however, and in October 1981 President Goukouni requested their removal. Libyan troops began withdrawing in November and were replaced by a peace-keeping force from the Organization of African Unity (OAU, see p. 200). In November 1982 the newly-installed President Hissène Habré of Chad, who had overthrown Goukouni, insisted that Libya was still interfering in Chad's internal affairs. In response to an appeal for assistance from President Habré, France deployed about 3,000 troops in Chad in August 1983. In September 1984, without consulting the Government of Chad, France and Libya concluded an agreement providing for the evacuation of both countries' forces, although Col Qaddafi subsequently acknowledged that some 3,000 Libyan troops remained in northern Chad.

In October 1986 Libya transferred its support from the rebels in Chad led by Goukouni to those belonging to another opposition faction. During the next year intense fighting took place for the control of north-western Chad. In August 1987 President Habré's forces advanced into the 'Aozou strip' and occupied the town of Aozou. Libya responded by bombing towns in northern Chad, and recaptured Aozou. In September Chadian forces destroyed an airbase 100 km inside Libya (claimed to be a base for Libyan raids on Chad). The French Government criticized the Chadian incursion into Libya, reiterating its opinion that the question of sovereignty over the Aozou strip should be determined by international arbitration. Later in September Chad and Libya agreed to observe a cease-fire proposed by the OAU. In October 1988 Libya and Chad restored diplomatic relations, although the question of sovereignty over the disputed region remained unresolved.

On 31 August 1989 the Libyan Secretary for Foreign Liaison and Chad's Minister of Foreign Affairs, meeting in the Algerian capital, signed an agreement concerning the 'Aozou strip'. The agreement, concluded with the help of Algerian mediation, envisaged that the parties would attempt to resolve their dispute through a political settlement within one year. If that failed, the issue was to be referred for arbitration by the International Court of Justice (ICJ). The 1989 agreement provided for the withdrawal of all forces from the disputed region, which was to be under the administration of a group of African observers, pending a settlement. All hostilities were to cease, and all prisoners being detained by both sides were to be released. In October Chad claimed that its forces had killed 600 members of the Libyan-backed Islamic Pan-African Legion near its border with Sudan. Libya denied Chadian claims that it was involved in the activities of the Legion, including border violations contrary to the peace accord signed in Algiers. In November a joint commission, composed of delegations from Chad and Libya, held its first meeting to consider the provisions of the Algiers agreement. In April 1990 the Chadian Government claimed to have intercepted and destroyed forces belonging to the Islamic Pan-African Legion within Chadian territory, and accused Libya of reinforcing its military presence in the 'Aozou strip' with Palestinian mercenaries. Libya again denied any involvement in the activities of the Legion. In September 1990 the territorial issue was submitted to the ICJ. Following the overthrow of President Habré in December 1990, there was speculation that Libya (which, it was widely alleged, had close links with the new administration) would acquire more influence in Chad and use the country as a base for the pursuit of its interests elsewhere in Africa. Shortly afterwards it was reported that some 2,000 Libyan prisoners of war had been repatriated. However, Col Qaddafi protested at the airlift from Chad (which was apparently overseen by the USA and France) of several hundred detainees, who had allegedly been trained by the USA to conduct military offensives against the Libyan leader, to Nigeria and Zaire. A two-day official visit to Libya by the new Chadian leader, Idriss Deby, in February 1991 consolidated relations between the two countries; however, neither party would abandon its claim to sovereignty over the 'Aozou strip', which remained under consideration by the ICJ until February 1994, when it rejected Libya's claim. Under UN supervision, all Libyan troops remaining in the 'Aozou strip' were withdrawn at the end of May. In early June Libya and Chad concluded a treaty of friendship, neighbourly terms and co-operation.

Libya's relations with the USA deteriorated in 1981. The Reagan administration had made plain that it objected to Libya's presence in Chad, and in August 1981 US fighter aircraft shot down two Libyan jets which had intercepted them over the Gulf of Surt (Sirte). In November the US oil company Exxon announced that it was closing down its Libyan operation (as, shortly afterwards, did Mobil), and in December President Reagan alleged that a Libyan 'hit-squad' had been sent to assassinate him. The discovery in February 1983 of an alleged Libyan coup plot against the Sudanese Government further soured relations. The United Kingdom severed diplomatic relations with Libya in April 1984, following a series of bomb attacks in the United Kingdom, believed to be aimed at Libyan dissidents.

In August 1984 Libya and Morocco unexpectedly signed a treaty of union in Oujda (Morocco). The proposed 'Arab-African Federation' of the two countries was approved by the GPC in Libya and by referendum in Morocco, but in August 1986 King Hassan of Morocco abrogated the treaty of union following violent criticism by Qaddafi of King Hassan's meeting in July with the Israeli Prime Minister. In December 1984 Libya and Malta signed a five-year treaty on security and military co-operation, requiring Libya to defend Malta if requested to do so by the Maltese Government. In June 1985 a ruling by the ICJ on a maritime boundary dispute between Libya and Malta, extended Libya's territorial waters 18 nautical miles (33 km) northwards towards Malta. The bilateral treaty was renewed for a further five years in February 1990, although military provisions (to which the USA had objected) were excluded.

Col Qaddafi visited Sudan in May 1985 to endorse the new regime of Lt-Gen. Abd ar-Rahman Swar ad-Dahab, who overthrew President Nimeri in a bloodless coup in April 1985. Qaddafi advised the rebels in southern Sudan (the Sudanese People's Liberation Army), whom he had supported against Nimeri, to disarm and to negotiate with the new Government. Diplomatic relations between Libya and Sudan were restored in the aftermath of the coup, and Libya agreed to assist Sudan in training its armed forces and to supply equipment. In March 1990 Libya and Sudan signed a pact of integration in order to facilitate a possible union of the two countries within four years. The union, however, did not materialize.

In July 1985 Col Qaddafi barred Egyptians from working in Libya, in retaliation for a similar measure preventing Libyans from working in Egypt. In August Tunisia expelled 283 Libyans (including 30 diplomats) for alleged spying. This followed a Libyan decision to expel Tunisian workers from Libya, officially as part of a campaign to achieve self-sufficiency in labour. About 30,000 Tunisians were actually deported between August and October. During 1985, it was estimated, Libya expelled or laid off more than 120,000 foreign workers, including workers from Mali, Mauritania, Niger and Syria. Tunisian imports were halted, and Libyan tourists were barred from visiting Tunisia, while Qaddafi urged the overthrow of the Government of President Bourguiba. In September Tunisia severed its diplomatic relations with Libya. In June Iraq had formally ended diplomatic links with Libya, after Qaddafi had signed a 'strategic alliance' agreement with Iran.

Details of a plan by the US Government's Central Intelligence Agency to undermine the Qaddafi regime in Libya were revealed in the US press in November 1985, and Libya's alleged involvement in international terrorism contributed to a serious worsening of relations between the two countries towards the end of 1985. Libya had already been accused by

Egypt of co-ordinating the hijack of an Egyptian airliner to Malta in November, as a result of which 61 people had died. In December the US Government accused Libya of harbouring and training Palestinian guerrillas, who were believed to be responsible for recent attacks on airports, and of being a centre for international terrorism. In January 1986 President Reagan ordered the severance of all economic and commercial relations with Libya, and froze Libyan assets in the USA.

A dispute over navigational rights led to a clash between US and Libyan armed forces in 1986. Since 1973 Libya had maintained that the entire Gulf of Surt (Sirte), and not merely the area within 12 nautical miles (22 km) of the Libyan coastline that was recognized under international law, constituted Libyan territorial waters. In December 1985 Col Qaddafi drew a notional 'line of death' across the Gulf, along latitude 32° 30′ N, which US and other foreign shipping were warned not to cross. At the end of January 1986 the US Navy deployed its Sixth Fleet off the Libyan coast, though it appears that at no time did any US vessel cross the 'line of death'. In March Libya fired missiles at US fighter aircraft flying over the Gulf of Surt (Sirte) and inside the 'line of death'. In two retaliatory attacks US fighters destroyed missile and radar facilities in the coastal town of Surt (Sirte), and four Libyan patrol boats in the Gulf. In April US military aircraft bombed military installations, airports, government buildings (including Qaddafi's own residential compound) and suspected terrorist training camps and communication centres in the Libyan cities of Tripoli and Benghazi. In justification of these attacks, the US Government claimed to have irrefutable proof of Libyan involvement in terrorist attacks and plots against US targets in Europe and the Middle East. A total of 101 people, including many civilians, were reported to have died in the raids.

In late 1988 tension between the USA and Libya increased after President Reagan stated that the US Government was considering military action against a factory at Rabta, outside Tripoli, where Libya was alleged by the USA to be preparing to produce chemical weapons. In January 1989 an encounter occurred over the Mediterranean between US and Libyan military aircraft, in which two Libyan fighter aircraft were shot down. In March 1990 both the USA and the Federal Republic of Germany claimed that Libya had commenced production of mustard gas at the factory at Rabta. When a fire broke out there during the same month, Libya accused these countries, together with Israel, of sabotage. All three countries denied any involvement. The Federal German Government stated that it would take measures, in accordance with international law, to halt the production of chemical weapons at Rabta, while the US Government refused to discount future military action against the factory. In June the US Government alleged that the plant at Rabta had not been destroyed by fire, as Libya had claimed, and voiced suspicions that a second such plant, for the production of chemical weapons, was under construction.

In June 1987 a Libyan proposal for a union of Libya and Algeria was submitted to President Chadli of Algeria, who, referring critically to Libya's intervention in Chad and to its policy towards Tunisia, suggested that a framework for a closer Algerian-Libyan relationship, short of actual union, was contained in the Maghreb Treaty of Fraternity and Co-operation of 1983, between Algeria, Mauritania and Tunisia. In October the Libyan and Algerian Governments agreed in principle on a treaty of political union. The accord was to be announced officially on 1 November, but, owing to political opposition in Algeria, the announcement was not made. Instead, the Algerian Government proposed that Libya should sign the Maghreb Treaty. This eventuality was made more likely by the re-establishment of diplomatic relations between Libya and Tunisia at the end of December. In February 1988 Col Qaddafi, President Chadli and President Ben Ali of Tunisia held discussions concerning a proposed regional political accord, following which the border between Libya and Tunisia was reopened.

In June 1988 the leaders of Algeria, Morocco, Tunisia, Libya, and Mauritania met in Algiers to discuss the prospects for a 'Maghreb without frontiers'. This meeting resulted in the creation of a Maghreb commission (to which each of the five countries contributed a delegation) to examine prospects for regional integration. At the end of June Libya and Algeria announced that they would each hold a referendum on a proposed union of the two countries. The union in question, however, envisaged a federation of the two states, within a 'Great Arab Maghreb', rather than the total merger for which Col Qaddafi had hoped. In August President Ben Ali of Tunisia visited Libya, where he and Col Qaddafi signed co-operation agreements and established a technical commission to examine means of accelerating co-operation, as a prelude to the creation of the 'Great Arab Maghreb'.

A summit meeting of North African Heads of State, held in Morocco in February 1989, concluded a treaty proclaiming the Union of the Arab Maghreb (UMA, see p. 241), comprising Algeria, Libya, Mauritania, Morocco and Tunisia. The treaty envisaged the establishment of a new body, the Council of Heads of State; regular meetings of ministers of foreign affairs; and the eventual free movement of goods, people, services and capital throughout the countries of the region. Between 1989 and 1992 the member states formulated 15 regional co-operation conventions. In February 1993, however, it was announced that, in view of the differing economic orientations of each signatory, no convention had actually been implemented, and the UMA's activities were to be 'frozen'. A meeting of UMA leaders was, however, convened in April 1994. In August Libya and Algeria signed an agreement to increase co-operation in security affairs.

In March 1987 Col Qaddafi was reconciled with Yasser Arafat's wing of the Palestine Liberation Organization (PLO), and sponsored efforts to reunify the divided Palestine liberation movement. It appeared that, after years of relative political isolation, Col Qaddafi found it expedient to realign Libyan policy with that of the majority of Arab states. After the beginning of the Palestinian uprising in the Israeli-occupied territories in December 1987, Col Qaddafi increased his efforts to reconcile the opposing factions within the PLO.

In September 1987 Libya re-established 'fraternal' links with Iraq, modifying its support for Iran in the Iran–Iraq War and urging the observance of a cease-fire (according to the terms of UN Security Council Resolution 598). Later in the same month Jordan restored its diplomatic relations with Libya. However, Libyan support for Iran had not completely ceased. Col Qaddafi refused to attend the extraordinary summit meeting of the League of Arab States (Arab League, see p. 182) which took place in Amman in November to discuss the Iran–Iraq War. His representative, Maj. Abd as-Salam Jalloud, quickly dissociated Libya from an apparently unanimously supported resolution, which censured Iran for its occupation of Arab (i.e. Iraqi) territory and for failing to accept UN cease-fire proposals. Libya also dissented from the League's decision to remove the prohibition on diplomatic relations between member states and Egypt.

Libya's relations with France improved in April 1990, after the release of three Europeans who had been held hostage in Lebanon. The French Government formally thanked the Libyan Government for its role in obtaining their release. In March France had returned to Libya three *Mirage* jet fighter aircraft which it had impounded in 1986, after their delivery to France for repairs. However, the French Government denied that the return of the aircraft had played any part in securing the release of the hostages. In September 1990, following an official investigation, France alleged that Col Qaddafi, together with President Assad of Syria and the leader of the Popular Front for the Liberation of Palestine—General Command (PFLP—GC), Ahmad Jibril, had been responsible for planning the bombing of a French passenger aircraft over Niger in September 1989.

Col Qaddafi attended the emergency Arab League summit meeting held in Cairo on 10 August 1990 to discuss Arab responses to the recent invasion of Kuwait by Iraq. Libya did not vote in favour of the proposal that individual member states should send troops to Saudi Arabia as part of an Arab deterrent force to support the USA in its attempt to forestall any military action against Saudi Arabia by Iraq. In early September Libyan aircraft were reported to be flying supplies of food to Iraq, in violation of the economic sanctions imposed on Iraq by the UN, and Libya announced that its ports were at Iraq's disposal for the purpose of importing food supplies. For the duration of the crisis in the region of the Persian (Arabian) Gulf, Libya both criticized Iraq's invasion of Kuwait and opposed the deployment (authorized by the UN) of a multinational force for the defence of Saudi Arabia and for the liberation of Kuwait.

Libya's relations with the USA and the United Kingdom deteriorated in November 1991, when the US and British Governments announced that they would seek to extradite two Libyan citizens who were alleged to have been responsible for an explosion which destroyed a Pan American World Airways passenger aircraft over Lockerbie, Scotland, in December 1988. The Libyan Government denied any involvement in the bombing, and recommended that the allegations be investigated by a neutral body, such as the ICJ. In January 1992 the UN Security Council adopted a resolution (No. 731) demanding Libya's compliance with requests for the extradition of its two nationals and its co-operation with a French inquiry into the 1989 aircraft bombing over Niger. Libya responded to the resolution by offering to try the two men accused of the Lockerbie bombing in Libya, a proposal which was rejected by the USA, the United Kingdom and France, which urged the UN to impose sanctions on Libya.

On 23 March 1992 Libya applied to the ICJ for an order confirming its right to refuse the extradition of the Lockerbie suspects by applying the terms of the 1971 Montreal Convention on airline terrorism. Judgment was not expected for another two years (the matter remained under consideration in early 1995), but the ICJ nevertheless ruled, on 14 April, that it had no power to prevent the UN from enacting sanctions against Libya.

An offer in late March 1992 by Col Qaddafi to place the two Lockerbie suspects under the jurisdiction of the Arab League was subsequently withdrawn. On 31 March the UN Security Council adopted a resolution (No. 748) imposing economic sanctions against Libya if the two accused Libyan nationals had not been extradited by 15 April 1992. In that event all international air links and arms trade with Libya were to be prohibited and its diplomatic representation reduced.

In Libya, in response to the decision of the UN Security Council, Col Qaddafi threatened to suspend petroleum supplies to, and withdraw all business from, those countries which complied with Resolution 748. On 2 April 1992 demonstrators besieged several Western embassies in Tripoli, and the Embassy of Venezuela (which had held the presidency of the UN Security Council when Resolution 748 was adopted) was ransacked and burnt. UN sanctions took effect on 15 April 1992. Prior to their imposition, Libya was reported to have been stockpiling food and medicines and to have transferred liquid capital from Europe to banking centres in the Persian (Arabian) Gulf region and the Far East.

In May 1992, at Col Qaddafi's instigation, 1,500 People's Congresses were convened in Libya and abroad, to enable ordinary citizens to decide the fate of the two Lockerbie suspects and their response to the UN sanctions. Arab diplomats and the more pragmatic associates of Qaddafi had begun to urge a compromise over the Lockerbie issue, fearing that the imposition of further UN sanctions, particularly an embargo on sales of petroleum, would be disastrous for Libya. In late June the GPC announced its decision to allow the two Lockerbie suspects to be tried abroad, provided that the proceedings were 'fair and just'. It suggested that such a trial might take place under the auspices of either the Arab League or the UN. In early August, at a meeting with Col Qaddafi, the UN Under-Secretary-General, Vladimir Petrovsky, warned that, if Libya continued to refuse to comply with Resolution 731, the UN might strengthen the sanctions already in force against it. On 12 August, however, the UN Security Council merely renewed the sanctions for a further 120 days.

In early Janary 1993 Libya closed all of its land borders for three days in protest at the UN's decision, taken in early December 1992, to renew the sanctions in force against Libya. In mid-February an article appeared in the US press that alleged that Libya was constructing an underground factory for the manufacture of chemical weapons at Tarhounah, west of Tripoli. In January Libya refused to sign a UN convention banning chemical weapons, on the grounds that not all Middle Eastern and North African states were party to the convention.

In August 1993 the USA, the United Kingdom and France announced that they would request the UN Security Council to strengthen the sanctions in force against Libya if, by 1 October, Libya had still not complied with UN Security Council Resolutions 731 and 748. The Libyan Government rejected this ultimatum, but stated its willingness to commence discussions with the USA, the United Kingdom and France on an appropriate venue for the trial of the two Lockerbie suspects. On 4 October the UN Secretary-General, Dr Boutros Boutros-Ghali, met the Libyan Secretary for Foreign Liaison and International Co-operation, Omar al-Muntasser, but failed to agree on a timetable for the surrender by the Libyan Government of the two Lockerbie suspects to either the USA or the United Kingdom. However, within the UN Security Council it proved impossible to obtain the essential co-operation of Russia in the imposition of stronger sanctions on Libya, and no further action was taken immediately.

It was reported in Western media in late October 1993 that a military *coup d'état* had been attempted against Col Qaddafi's regime by elements within the armed forces, amid general unrest. Elements loyal to Col Qaddafi were reported to have defeated the rebels, and Libya's Second-in-Command, Maj. Abd as-Salam Jalloud, was reported to have been placed under house arrest, together with many others. Qaddafi himself subsequently denied that a coup had been attempted.

On 11 November 1993 the UN Security Council adopted a resolution (No. 883) that provided for the strengthening of the economic sanctions in force against Libya in the event of the country's failure fully to comply with UN Security Council Resolutions 731 and 748 by 1 December. The sanctions, which were duly applied, included the closure of all Libyan Arab Airlines' offices abroad; a ban on the sale of equipment and services for the civil aviation sector; the sequestration of all Libyan financial resources overseas; a ban on the sale to Libya of specified items for use in the petroleum and gas industries; and a reduction in personnel levels at Libyan diplomatic missions abroad. In mid-December Pan American World Airways announced its intention to sue the State of Libya, Libyan Arab Airlines and the two Libyan citizens accused of the Lockerbie bombing for the destruction of its airliner and subsequent loss of business.

In January 1994 the Scottish lawyer representing the two Lockerbie suspects stated that they might be willing to stand trial in The Hague, the Netherlands. In late January the GPC convened in Surt (Sirte) and reorganized its General Secretariat and the General People's Committee. Col Qaddafi addressed the opening session of the GPC and referred to The Hague as an appropriate venue for the trial of the two Lockerbie suspects. In February, however, President Bill Clinton of the USA recommended that an embargo should be imposed on Libya's sales of petroleum (which accounted for some 98% of its export earnings and were unaffected by UN Security Council Resolution 883 of November 1993) if the country continued to defy the international community. In late February 1994 Libya indicated that it might withdraw from the Arab League, which it accused of having failed to defend Arab interests against those of the USA and Israel. At the beginning of May Col Qaddafi held talks with the Secretary-General of the Arab League, Dr Ahmad Esmat Abd al-Meguid, in Tripoli. The Arab League was reported now to favour a compromise solution to the Lockerbie affair.

On 12 June 1994 the Ministers of Foreign Affairs of the OAU member states adopted a resolution urging the UN Security Council to revoke the sanctions that it had imposed on Libya. The following day a member of the Palestinian Fatah Revolutionary Council, who was on trial in Lebanon, accused of the assassination of a Jordanian diplomat, claimed that the Council had been responsible for the explosion which destroyed the Pan American World Airways aircraft over Lockerbie in December 1988. At various times since February 1992 various parties had alleged that Iranian, Syrian and Palestinian agents—sometimes separately, sometimes in collaboration—had been responsible for the explosion. In December 1994 some members of the British Parliament viewed a documentary film that alleged Syrian, Iranian and Palestinian involvement in the attack, and that the US Central Intelligence Agency had known in advance that it would take place. In January 1995 British media published a US intelligence report, which had been compiled in March 1991, that again alleged that the attack had been carried out by Palestinian agents at the bidding of an Iranian former Minister of the Interior, in retaliation for the attack on the Iran Air Airbus A300B, mistakenly shot down by the *USS Vincennes* in July 1988. Nevertheless, both the US and the British authorities remained convinced that there was still sufficient evidence to continue to seek the extradition of the two Libyan suspects who had been formally indicted for the offence in the USA and Scotland.

In mid-February 1995 the Government announced that it would not assume the chairmanship of the UMA, as it was due to do later in the year, because other UMA member states were enforcing the sanctions which the UN had imposed on

# LIBYA

Libya. In late March the US Secretary of State announced that the USA would seek to persuade the UN Security Council to apply a ban on Libyan sales of petroleum before its forthcoming review of the sanctions already in force. At the end of the month, however, the Security Council did no more than renew the existing sanctions, prompting the USA to announce that it would impose more stringent unilateral sanctions on Libya. In April Libyan pilgrims were permitted by the UN to fly to Saudi Arabia for the annual *hajj*. Most of them were carried by Egypt Air airliners flying from Tripoli airport, but some were reported to have departed on Libyan Arab Airlines flights, in defiance of UN sanctions.

## Government

Power is vested in the people through People's Congresses, Popular Committees, Trade Unions, Vocational Syndicates, and the General People's Congress (GPC), with its General Secretariat. The Head of State is the Revolutionary Leader, elected by the GPC. Executive power is exercised by the General People's Committee, which comprises 17 Secretariats (the number having been raised from 14 in January 1994). The country is divided into three provinces, 10 governorates and 1,500 administrative communes.

## Defence

Libya's armed forces totalled 70,000 in June 1994. Military service is by selective conscription, lasting two years. The army, which numbers 40,000, is equipped with Soviet tanks, while the former USSR and France supplied jet fighters for the 22,000-strong air force. The navy numbers 8,000. Libya's defence budget in 1990 was an estimated LD421m.

## Economic Affairs

In 1989, according to estimates by the World Bank, Libya's gross national product (GNP), measured at average 1987–89 prices, was US $23,333m., equivalent to $5,310 per head. During 1980–89, it was estimated, GNP declined, in real terms, at an average annual rate of 5.4%, while GNP per head declined by 9.2% per year. During 1985–93 the population increased by an annual average of 3.6%. It was estimated that gross domestic product (GDP) declined, in real terms, by almost 4% annually in 1980–89. According to the UN Economic Commission for Africa, GDP rose by 6.9% in 1990. According to estimates by the British-based *Middle East Economic Digest*, Libya's GDP declined by 7%, to $28,000m., in 1993; and by a further 7%, to $26,000m., in 1994.

Agriculture (including forestry and fishing) contributed an estimated 7.2% of GDP in 1990. An estimated 12.9% of the labour force were employed in the sector in 1993. The principal subsistence crops are barley and wheat, but agriculture is based mainly on animal husbandry. The contribution of agricultural exports to total export earnings is negligible. During 1980–90 agricultural production increased by an annual average of 4%. In 1991 it rose by 9.4%, compared with the previous year, and in 1992 by 14.7%.

Industry (including mining, manufacturing, construction and power) employed an estimated 28.9% of the labour force in 1980. The sector provided an estimated 48% of GDP in 1990.

Mining contributed an estimated 25.7% of GDP in 1990. The sector employed only 2.6% of the working population in 1978. Crude petroleum is by far the most important mineral export. Libya also exports liquefied natural gas and has reserves of iron ore, potassium, magnesium, sulphur and gypsum.

Manufacturing provided an estimated 7.9% of GDP in 1990. The sector employed about 6.1% of the working population in 1978. The most important branches of manufacturing are petroleum refining, the processing of agricultural products and cement production.

Energy is derived principally from oil-fired power stations. Imports of mineral fuels and lubricants accounted for less than 1% of the value of total merchandise imports in 1991.

In 1990 Libya recorded a visible trade surplus of US $3,777m., and there was a surplus of $2,201m. on the current account of the balance of payments. In 1991 the principal sources of imports were Italy (21.5%), Germany (13.1%) and the United Kingdom (8.2%), while the principal markets for exports were Italy (41%), Germany (16.7%), France (7.7%) and Greece (5.2.%). Exports of crude petroleum accounted for about 94% of Libya's export earnings in 1991, while the principal imports were machinery and transport equipment, basic manufactures, miscellaneous manufactured articles, and food and live animals.

Projected budgetary expenditure for the year ending March 1993 amounted to LD2,823m., while revenue was projected at LD2,251m. The petroleum sector reportedly accounted for some 57% of total revenue. Libya's total external debt was US $2,100m. at the end of 1988. Consumer prices declined at an average rate of 2.7% per year during 1985–92. An estimated 2% of the labour force were unemployed in 1988.

Libya is a member of the Arab Monetary Fund (see p. 237), the Council of Arab Economic Unity (see p. 133), the Islamic Development Bank (see p. 180), the Organization of Arab Petroleum Exporting Countries (see p. 207), the Organization of the Petroleum Exporting Countries (see p. 210) and the Union of the Arab Maghreb (see p. 241).

Libya's fundamental economic difficulty is its dependence on exports of crude petroleum, and a UN embargo on Libyan sales of petroleum (see Recent History), if sustained for a long period of time, would be disastrous for the country's economy. Efforts to reduce the economy's dependence on exports of crude petroleum—through political and economic union with other North African states, and through the development of agriculture and the petroleum-refining sector—have yielded little success. Since the late 1980s the 'privatization' of public-sector activities has been officially encouraged, but there have been few signs of any substantial shift of emphasis in the economy. Foreign investment has been discouraged by Libya's political volatility, and the economic sanctions to which Libya has been subjected since April 1992 were reported—by Libyan officials—in November of that year to have already cost the economy some US $2,500m. New infrastructural and industrial projects have been suspended, petroleum revenues have been diverted to the purchase of supplies of food and medicine, in anticipation of harsher economic sanctions, and majority holdings in foreign companies have been reduced in order to prevent their sequestration.

## Social Welfare

The Government provides free health services, including two big hospitals in Benghazi and Tripoli. There is a scheme of pensions and national insurance. In 1985 there were an estimated 5,455 physicians, giving one of the best doctor-patient ratios of any country in Africa.

## Education

Education is compulsory for children between six and 15 years of age. Primary education begins at the age of six and lasts for nine years. Secondary education, from the age of 15, lasts for three years. Libya also has institutes for agricultural, technical and vocational training. In 1985 there were 4,164 primary schools, and in 1991 there were 99,623 teachers and 1,238,986 pupils. In 1991 215,508 pupils were receiving secondary education and the number of secondary school teachers was 18,501. Of the total number of pupils receiving secondary education in 1991, 138,860 were in general education, 39,491 in teacher training colleges and 37,157 were receiving vocational instruction. There are universities in Tripoli, Benghazi (two), Mersa Brega, Sebha and Ajdabia. Adult illiteracy among the Libyan population averaged 61% (males 38.7%; females 85.2%) in 1973. According to estimates by UNESCO, however, the rate of illiteracy among the whole adult population was 36.2% (males 24.6%; females 49.6%) in 1990.

## Public Holidays

**1995:** 3 March* (Id al-Fitr, end of Ramadan), 28 March (Evacuation Day), 10 May* (Id al-Adha, Feast of the Sacrifice), 31 May* (Islamic New Year), 9 June* (Ashoura), 11 June (Evacuation Day), 9 August* (Mouloud, Birth of Muhammad), 1 September (Revolution Day), 7 October (Evacuation Day), 20 December* (Leilat al-Meiraj, ascension of Muhammad).

**1996:** 21 February* (Id al-Fitr, end of Ramadan), 28 March (Evacuation Day), 29 April* (Id al-Adha, Feast of the Sacrifice), 19 May* (Islamic New Year), 28 May* (Ashoura), 11 June (Evacuation Day), 28 July* (Mouloud, Birth of Muhammad), 1 September (Revolution Day), 7 October (Evacuation Day), 8 December* (Leilat al-Meiraj, ascension of Muhammad).

* These holidays are dependent on the Islamic lunar calendar and may vary by one or two days from the dates given.
† This festival will occur twice (in the Islamic years A.H. 1414 and 1415) within the same Gregorian year.

## Weights and Measures

The metric system is in force.

LIBYA
*Statistical Survey*

# Statistical Survey

Source (unless otherwise stated): Census and Statistical Dept, Secretariat of Planning, 40 Sharia Damascus, 2nd Floor, Tripoli; tel. (21) 31731.

## Area and Population

### AREA, POPULATION AND DENSITY

| | |
|---|---:|
| Area (sq km) | 1,775,500* |
| Population (census results) | |
| 31 July 1973 | 2,249,237 |
| 31 July 1984† | |
| Males | 1,950,152 |
| Females | 1,687,336 |
| Total | 3,637,488 |
| Population (official estimates at mid-year)‡ | |
| 1992 | 4,509,000 |
| 1993 | 4,700,000 |
| Density (per sq km) at mid-1993 | 2.6 |

* 685,524 sq miles.
† Figures are provisional. The revised total is 3,642,576.
‡ Figures refer to the *de jure* population. At the 1984 census the *de jure* population was provisionally 3,237,160 (males 1,653,330; females 1,583,830).

### POPULATION BY BALADIYA (MUNICIPALITY)
(1984 census, provisional figures)

| | | | | |
|---|---:|---|---:|
| Tubruq (Tobruk) | 94,006 | Tarhuna | 84,640 |
| Darna | 105,031 | Tripoli | 990,697 |
| Jebel Akhdar | 120,662 | Al-Azizia | 85,068 |
| Al-Fatah | 102,763 | Az-Zawia (Azzawiya) | 220,075 |
| Benghazi | 485,386 | Nikat al-Khoms | 181,584 |
| Agedabia | 100,547 | Gharian | 117,073 |
| Sirte | 110,996 | Yefren | 73,420 |
| Sofuljeen | 45,195 | Ghadames | 52,247 |
| Al-Kufra | 25,139 | Sebha | 76,171 |
| Misurata | 178,29 | Ash-Shati | 46,749 |
| Zeleitin (Zliten) | 101,107 | Ubari | 48,701 |
| Al-Khoms | 149,642 | Murzuk | 42,294 |

### PRINCIPAL TOWNS (population at 1973 census)

| | | | | |
|---|---:|---|---:|
| Tripoli (capital) | 481,295 | Darna | 30,241 |
| Benghazi | 219,317 | Sebha | 28,714 |
| Misurata | 42,815 | Tubruq (Tobruk) | 28,061 |
| Az-Zawia (Azzawiya) | 39,382 | Al-Marj | 25,166 |
| Al-Beida | 31,796 | Zeleiten (Zliten) | 21,340 |
| Agedabia | 31,047 | | |

### BIRTHS, MARRIAGES AND DEATHS

| | Registered live births | | Registered marriages | | Registered deaths | |
|---|---:|---:|---:|---:|---:|---:|
| | Number | Rate (per 1,000) | Number | Rate (per 1,000) | Number | Rate (per 1,000) |
| 1986 | 160,750 | 46.0 | 17,252 | 4.9 | 24,460 | 7.0 |
| 1987 | 167,020 | 46.0 | 17,862 | 4.9 | 25,420 | 7.0 |
| 1988 | 173,530 | 46.0 | 16,989 | 4.5 | 26,410 | 7.0 |

**Expectation of life** (UN estimates, years at birth, 1985–90): 60.6 (males 59.1; females 62.5) (Source: UN, *World Population Prospects: The 1992 Revision*).

### EMPLOYMENT (official estimates, '000 persons)

| | 1976 | 1977 | 1978 |
|---|---:|---:|---:|
| Agriculture, forestry and fishing | 141.2 | 144.9 | 147.9 |
| Mining and quarrying | 18.5 | 19.2 | 20.4 |
| Manufacturing | 37.4 | 41.7 | 47.4 |
| Electricity, gas and water | 13.9 | 14.7 | 15.8 |
| Construction | 167.8 | 171.4 | 164.3 |
| Trade, restaurants and hotels | 52.0 | 52.3 | 47.5 |
| Transport, storage and communications | 57.9 | 63.1 | 67.5 |
| Financing, insurance, real estate and business services | 8.1 | 8.5 | 9.1 |
| Community, social and personal services | 175.8 | 185.9 | 191.2 |
| Activities not adequately defined | 60.1 | 63.3 | 62.1 |
| **Total** | **732.7** | **765.0** | **773.2** |

**Mid-1993** (estimates in '000): Agriculture, etc. 162; Total labour force 1,252 (Source: FAO, *Production Yearbook*).

## Agriculture

### PRINCIPAL CROPS (FAO estimates, '000 metric tons)

| | 1991 | 1992 | 1993 |
|---|---:|---:|---:|
| Barley | 145 | 150 | 150 |
| Wheat | 150 | 160 | 150 |
| Olives | 70 | 72 | 73 |
| Oranges | 95 | 98 | 100 |
| Tangerines, mandarins, clementines and satsumas | 4 | 4 | 4 |
| Lemons and limes | 4 | 4 | 4 |
| Almonds | 34.0 | 34.5 | 35.0 |
| Tomatoes | 170 | 175 | 175 |
| Dates | 75 | 76 | 77 |
| Potatoes | 138 | 152 | 155 |
| Grapes | 38 | 40 | 43 |

Source: FAO, *Production Yearbook*.

### LIVESTOCK (FAO estimates, '000 head, year ending September)

| | 1991 | 1992 | 1993 |
|---|---:|---:|---:|
| Cattle | 125 | 130 | 135 |
| Camels | 150 | 155 | 160 |
| Sheep | 5,500 | 5,600 | 5,650 |
| Goats | 1,200 | 1,250 | 1,260 |
| Poultry | 23,000 | 24,000 | 26,000 |

Source: FAO, *Production Yearbook*.

# LIBYA

**LIVESTOCK PRODUCTS** (FAO estimates, '000 metric tons)

|  | 1991 | 1992 | 1993 |
|---|---|---|---|
| Beef and veal | 25 | 20 | 22 |
| Mutton and lamb | 26 | 26 | 27 |
| Goat meat | 5 | 6 | 6 |
| Poultry meat | 68 | 70 | 72 |
| Cows' milk | 130 | 140 | 150 |
| Sheep's milk | 49 | 49 | 50 |
| Goats' milk | 21 | 21 | 22 |
| Hen eggs | 34.7 | 35.8 | 38.5 |
| Honey | 1.3 | 1.3 | 1.4 |
| Wool: |  |  |  |
|   greasy | 8.3 | 8.5 | 8.6 |
|   clean | 2.2 | 2.3 | 2.3 |
| Cattle and buffalo hides | 3.4 | 2.8 | 2.8 |
| Sheepskins | 6.0 | 6.1 | 6.3 |
| Goatskins | 0.9 | 1.0 | 1.0 |

Source: FAO, *Production Yearbook*.

## Forestry

**ROUNDWOOD REMOVALS**
(FAO estimates, '000 cubic metres, excl. bark)

|  | 1990 | 1991 | 1992 |
|---|---|---|---|
| Sawlogs, veneer logs and logs for sleepers* | 63 | 63 | 63 |
| Other industrial wood | 44 | 46 | 47 |
| Fuel wood* | 536 | 536 | 536 |
| **Total** | **643** | **645** | **646** |

* Assumed to be unchanged since 1978.

**Sawnwood production** (1978–92): 31,000 cubic metres per year (FAO estimates).

Source: FAO, *Yearbook of Forest Products*.

## Fishing

(FAO estimates, '000 metric tons, live weight)

|  | 1990 | 1991 | 1992 |
|---|---|---|---|
| Total catch | 8.7 | 8.0 | 8.4 |

Source: FAO, *Yearbook of Fishery Statistics*.

## Mining

|  | 1989 | 1990 | 1991 |
|---|---|---|---|
| Crude petroleum ('000 metric tons) | 54,320 | 67,162 | 71,815 |
| Natural gas ('000 terajoules) | 310 | 324 | 347 |

Source: UN, *Industrial Statistics Yearbook*.

**1992:** Crude petroleum 69.1 million metric tons (Source: UN, *Monthly Bulletin of Statistics*).

## Industry

**SELECTED PRODUCTS** ('000 metric tons, unless otherwise indicated)

|  | 1989 | 1990 | 1991 |
|---|---|---|---|
| Olive oil (crude)* | 10 | 10 | 10 |
| Cigarettes (million) | 3,500 | 3,500 | 3,500 |
| Jet fuels | 1,400 | 1,460 | 1,535 |
| Motor spirit (petrol) | 1,675 | 1,743 | 1,800 |
| Naphthas | 1,812 | 2,080 | 2,220 |
| Kerosene | 200 | 240 | 242 |
| Distillate fuel oils | 3,807 | 4,100 | 4,110 |
| Residual fuel oils | 4,581 | 4,800 | 4,810 |
| Liquefied petroleum gas: |  |  |  |
|   from natural gas plants | 248 | 260† | 300† |
|   from petroleum refineries† | 150 | 160 | 170 |
| Bitumen | 80 | 90 | 90 |
| Quicklime‡ | 263 | 263 | 263 |
| Cement‡ | 2,700 | 2,700 | 2,722 |
| Electric energy (million kWh) | 18,000 | 19,000 | 19,500 |

* FAO estimates.
† Provisional or estimated production.
‡ Estimates by the US Bureau of Mines.

Source: UN, *Industrial Statistics Yearbook*.

## Finance

**CURRENCY AND EXCHANGE RATES**

**Monetary Units**
1,000 dirhams = 1 Libyan dinar (LD).

**Sterling and Dollar Equivalents** (31 December 1994)
£1 sterling = 562.63 dirhams;
US $1 = 359.63 dirhams;
100 Libyan dinars = £177.74 = $278.07.

**Exchange Rate**
Between February 1973 and March 1986 the value of the Libyan dinar was fixed at US $3.37778 ($1 = 296.053 dirhams). In March 1986 the link with the US dollar was ended, and the currency was pegged to the IMF's special drawing right (SDR), initially at a rate of LD 1 = SDR 2.800. In May 1986 the rate was adjusted to LD 1 = SDR 2.60465 (SDR 1 = 383.929 dirhams). This remained in force until March 1992, when a new rate of LD 1 = SDR 2.52252 (SDR 1 = 396.429 dirhams) was introduced. Further devaluations were implemented in 1992, with the Libyan dinar set at SDR 2.46696 (SDR 1 = 405.357 dirhams) in July, and at SDR 2.41379 (SDR 1 = 414.286 dirhams) in August. The currency was devalued to SDR 2.2400 (SDR 1 = 446.429 dirhams) in August 1993. This valuation remained in effect until November 1994, when a new exchange rate of SDR 1 = 525 dirhams (LD 1 = SDR 1.90476) was introduced. For converting the value of external trade, the average exchange rate (US dollars per Libyan dinar) was: 3.5051 in 1988; 3.4229 in 1989; 3.7055 in 1990. In 1991 the conversion factor (dollars per dinar) for imports was 3.5587, while for exports it was 3.5551.

**CENTRAL BANK RESERVES** (US $ million at 31 December)

|  | 1990 | 1991 | 1992 |
|---|---|---|---|
| Gold | 152 | 152 | 152 |
| IMF special drawing rights | 409 | 461 | 383 |
| Reserve position in IMF | 346 | 348 | 439 |
| Foreign exchange* | 5,084 | 4,885 | 5,361 |
| **Total*** | **5,991** | **5,846** | **6,335** |

* Estimates.

**1993** (US $ million at 31 December): IMF special drawing rights 417; Reserve position in IMF 438.
**1994** (US $ million at 31 December): IMF special drawing rights 474; Reserve position in IMF 466.

Source: IMF, *International Financial Statistics*.

# LIBYA

*Statistical Survey*

## MONEY SUPPLY (LD million at 31 December)

|  | 1990 | 1991 | 1992 |
|---|---|---|---|
| Currency outside banks | 1,461.0 | 1,620.8 | 1,982.2 |
| Private sector deposits at Central Bank | 751.6 | 392.9 | 312.0 |
| Demand deposits at commercial banks | 2,239.6 | 2,279.1 | 2,693.0 |
| **Total money** | 4,452.2 | 4,292.8 | 4,987.2 |

Source: IMF, *International Financial Statistics*.

## COST OF LIVING
(Consumer Price Index, excluding rent, for Tripoli; base: 1979 = 100)

|  | 1982 | 1983 | 1984 |
|---|---|---|---|
| Food | 134.9 | 152.9 | 169.5 |
| Clothing | 141.1 | 150.6 | 169.4 |
| **All items** (incl. others) | 137.6 | 152.2 | 165.8 |

Source: International Labour Office, *Year Book of Labour Statistics*.

## NATIONAL ACCOUNTS (LD million at current prices)
### National Income and Product

|  | 1983 | 1984 | 1985 |
|---|---|---|---|
| Compensation of employees | 2,763.1 | 2,865.8 | 2,996.2 |
| Operating surplus | 5,282.7 | 4,357.8 | 4,572.4 |
| **Domestic factor incomes** | 8,045.8 | 7,223.6 | 7,568.6 |
| Consumption of fixed capital | 436.1 | 457.5 | 481.6 |
| **Gross domestic product (GDP) at factor cost** | 8,481.9 | 7,681.1 | 8,050.2 |
| Indirect taxes | 470.0 | 462.2 | 389.0 |
| *Less* Subsidies | 146.7 | 130.0 | 162.2 |
| **GDP in purchasers' values** | 8,805.2 | 8,013.3 | 8,277.0 |
| Factor income from abroad | 200.2 | 142.8 | 122.5 |
| *Less* Factor income paid abroad | 989.0 | 727.7 | 397.9 |
| **Gross national product** | 8,016.4 | 7,428.4 | 8,001.6 |
| *Less* Consumption of fixed capital | 436.1 | 457.5 | 481.6 |
| **National income in market prices** | 7,580.3 | 6,970.9 | 7,520.0 |
| Other current transfers from abroad | 8.6 | 2.3 | 2.6 |
| *Less* Other current transfers paid abroad | 25.2 | 27.9 | 16.0 |
| **National disposable income** | 7,563.7 | 6,945.3 | 7,506.6 |

Source: UN, *National Accounts Statistics*.

### Expenditure on the Gross Domestic Product
(estimates by the UN Economic Commission for Africa)

|  | 1985 | 1986 | 1987 |
|---|---|---|---|
| Government final consumption expenditure | 3,010 | 2,133 | 2,251 |
| Private final consumption expenditure | 3,433 | 2,523 | 2,669 |
| Increase in stocks | −41 | — | — |
| Gross fixed capital formation | 2,399 | 1,573 | 1,660 |
| **Total domestic expenditure** | 8,801 | 6,229 | 6,580 |
| Exports of goods and services | 2,865 | 2,275 | 2,401 |
| *Less* Imports of goods and services | 2,736 | 2,031 | 2,144 |
| **GDP in purchasers' values** | 8,930 | 6,473 | 6,837 |
| **GDP at constant 1980 prices** | 8,479 | 7,394 | 7,143 |

Source: UN Economic Commission for Africa, *African Statistical Yearbook*.

### Gross Domestic Product by Economic Activity

|  | 1988 | 1989 | 1990 |
|---|---|---|---|
| Agriculture, hunting, forestry and fishing | 367 | 396 | 643 |
| Mining and quarrying | 1,775 | 2,008 | 2,276 |
| Manufacturing | 488 | 561 | 702 |
| Electricity, gas and water | 139 | 153 | 200 |
| Construction | 893* | 920 | 1,083 |
| Wholesale and retail trade, restaurants and hotels | 440 | 491 | 752 |
| Transport, storage and communications | 391 | 440 | 578 |
| Finance, insurance, real estate and business services | 591 | 621 | 1,039 |
| Public administration and defence | 920* | 859 | 955 |
| Other services | 690* | 774 | 644 |
| **GDP at factor cost** | 6,694 | 7,224 | 8,872 |
| Indirect taxes, *less* subsidies | 364 | 392 | 480 |
| **GDP in purchasers' values** | 7,058 | 7,616 | 9,352 |

* Estimate.

Source: UN Economic Commission for Africa, *African Statistical Yearbook*

### BALANCE OF PAYMENTS (US $ million)

|  | 1988 | 1989 | 1990 |
|---|---|---|---|
| Merchandise exports f.o.b. | 5,653 | 7,274 | 11,352 |
| Merchandise imports f.o.b. | −5,762 | −6,509 | −7,575 |
| **Trade balance** | −109 | 765 | 3,777 |
| Exports of services | 128 | 117 | 117 |
| Imports of services | −1,637 | −1,481 | −1,385 |
| Other income received | 762 | 447 | 666 |
| Other income paid | −437 | −388 | −493 |
| Private unrequited transfers (net) | −497 | −472 | −446 |
| Official unrequited transfers (net) | −37 | −16 | −35 |
| **Current balance** | −1,826 | −1,026 | 2,201 |
| Direct investment (net) | 42 | 90 | 54 |
| Portfolio investment (net) | −222 | −52 | −115 |
| Other capital (net) | 343 | 1,150 | −945 |
| Net errors and omissions | 271 | 130 | −37 |
| **Overall balance** | −1,392 | 292 | 1,158 |

Source: IMF, *International Financial Statistics*.

## External Trade

### PRINCIPAL COMMODITIES (distribution by SITC, US $ '000)

| Imports c.i.f. | 1989 | 1990 | 1991 |
|---|---|---|---|
| Food and live animals | 911,593 | 1,155,174 | 1,123,869 |
| Beverages and tobacco | 18,439 | 7,797 | 24,445 |
| Crude materials (inedible) except fuels | 91,770 | 118,242 | 134,282 |
| Mineral fuels, lubricants, etc. | 16,651 | 16,049 | 20,641 |
| Animal and vegetable oils, fats and waxes | 89,797 | 106,554 | 172,132 |
| Chemicals and related products | 390,374 | 379,681 | 427,103 |
| Basic manufactures | 1,238,154 | 1,331,192 | 1,270,811 |
| Machinery and transport equipment | 1,715,808 | 1,936,551 | 1,898,485 |
| Miscellaneous manufactured articles | 547,878 | 527,953 | 518,147 |
| **Total** (incl. others) | 5,048,725 | 5,598,631 | 5,609,024 |

| Exports f.o.b. | 1989 | 1990 | 1991 |
|---|---|---|---|
| Mineral fuels, lubricants, etc. | 7,850,725 | 13,097,960 | 11,211,495 |
| Crude petroleum oils, etc. | 7,748,049 | 12,978,368 | 11,055,276 |
| Chemicals and related products | 387,985 | 524,710 | 393,892 |
| **Total** (incl. others) | 8,240,262 | 13,876,843 | 11,750,156 |

Source: UN, *International Trade Statistics Yearbook*.

**Total imports c.i.f.** (LD million, derived from IMF, *Direction of Trade Statistics*): 1,471.3 in 1992; 1,627.7 in 1993 (Source: IMF, *International Financial Statistics*).

# LIBYA

## PRINCIPAL TRADING PARTNERS (US $ '000)*

| Imports c.i.f. | 1989 | 1990 | 1991 |
|---|---|---|---|
| Austria | 96,626 | 108,452 | 162,490 |
| Belgium-Luxembourg | 136,839 | 156,065 | 115,694 |
| Brazil | 44,447 | 95,403 | 78,503 |
| Canada | 56,374 | 56,239 | 66,070 |
| China | 34,241 | 49,491 | 121,614 |
| France | 344,532 | 412,513 | 348,824 |
| Germany, Federal Republic | 745,055 | 819,436 | 733,878 |
| Greece | 53,285 | 81,209 | 68,219 |
| Ireland | 72,007 | 53,538 | 26,394 |
| Italy | 1,222,961 | 1,036,349 | 1,215,002 |
| Japan | 230,098 | 244,350 | 186,957 |
| Korea, Republic | 171,273 | 115,413 | 178,350 |
| Malta | 45,672 | 60,913 | 72,314 |
| Morocco | 83,115 | 120,941 | 200,005 |
| Netherlands | 167,215 | 313,237 | 216,756 |
| Poland | 68,772 | 36,913 | 21,107 |
| Spain | 62,047 | 53,751 | 50,194 |
| Sweden | 45,544 | 92,329 | 72,377 |
| Switzerland | 98,645 | 195,143 | 132,262 |
| Tunisia | 42,943 | 122,544 | 120,008 |
| Turkey | 243,053 | 290,231 | 356,227 |
| United Kingdom | 419,494 | 472,038 | 462,670 |
| USA | 76,932 | 69,962 | 72,910 |
| Yugoslavia | 74,163 | 74,724 | n.a. |
| **Total** (incl. others) | 5,048,725 | 5,598,631 | 5,609,024 |

| Exports f.o.b. | 1989 | 1990 | 1991 |
|---|---|---|---|
| Belgium-Luxembourg | 186,646 | 305,618 | 323,120 |
| Bulgaria | 176,252 | 242,489 | 88,450 |
| France | 805,193 | 1,187,634 | 906,845 |
| Germany, Federal Republic | 442,146 | 900,789 | 1,958,202 |
| Greece | 479,718 | 611,748 | 609,899 |
| Italy | 4,000,668 | 6,642,085 | 4,784,464 |
| Morocco | 8,431 | 115,392 | 128,320 |
| Netherlands | 454,529 | 387,915 | 203,939 |
| Portugal | 26,338 | 108,970 | 53,611 |
| Romania | 21,187 | 241,994 | 91,286 |
| Spain | 719,734 | 1,276,599 | 1,129,495 |
| Sudan | 68,143 | 150,732 | 160,317 |
| Switzerland | — | 4,453 | 225,336 |
| Tunisia | 13,367 | 72,138 | 100,708 |
| Turkey | 264,612 | 506,589 | 258,056 |
| USSR (former) | 129,808 | 203,502 | n.a. |
| United Kingdom | 157,142 | 247,657 | 151,845 |
| Yugoslavia | 149,750 | 369,874 | n.a. |
| **Total** (incl. others) | 8,240,262 | 13,876,843 | 11,750,156 |

* Imports by country of origin; exports by country of destination.
Source: UN, *International Trade Statistics Yearbook*.

## Transport

### ROAD TRAFFIC (motor vehicles in use)

|  | 1979 | 1980 | 1981 |
|---|---|---|---|
| Private cars | 308,746 | 415,531 | 473,383 |
| Taxis | 10,398 | 11,838 | 11,891 |
| Lorries | 167,748 | 208,464 | 271,815 |
| Buses | 2,835 | 2,658 | 3,990 |

### INTERNATIONAL SEA-BORNE SHIPPING
(freight traffic, estimates, '000 metric tons)

|  | 1989 | 1990 | 1991 |
|---|---|---|---|
| Goods loaded | 65,200 | 66,000 | 67,000 |
| Goods unloaded | 10,900 | 11,200 | 12,200 |

Source: UN Economic Commission for Africa, *African Statistical Yearbook*.

### CIVIL AVIATION (traffic on scheduled services)

|  | 1990 | 1991 | 1992 |
|---|---|---|---|
| Kilometres flown (million) | 19 | 19 | 11 |
| Passengers carried ('000) | 1,803 | 1,884 | 1,350 |
| Passenger-km (million) | 1,968 | 2,045 | 1,116 |
| Total ton-km (million) | 178 | 183 | 96 |

Source: UN, *Statistical Yearbook*.

## Communications Media

|  | 1990 | 1991 | 1992 |
|---|---|---|---|
| Radio receivers ('000 in use) | 1,020 | 1,060 | 1,100 |
| Television receivers ('000 in use) | 450 | 467 | 485 |
| Telephones ('000 in use)* | 84 | 85 | n.a. |
| Daily newspapers | 3 | n.a. | 4 |

Source: UNESCO, *Statistical Yearbook*.

* Source of these estimates: UN Economic Commission for Africa, *African Statistical Yearbook*.

## Education

|  | Teachers 1985 | Teachers 1991 | Pupils/Students 1985 | Pupils/Students 1991 |
|---|---|---|---|---|
| Pre-primary | 1,051 | n.a. | 15,028 | n.a. |
| Primary | 63,122 | 99,623 | 1,011,952 | 1,238,986 |
| Secondary: |  |  |  |  |
| General | 5,977 | 11,429 | 81,864 | 138,860 |
| Teacher training | 2,639 | 4,113 | 34,746 | 39,491 |
| Vocational | 2,149 | 2,959 | 26,503 | 37,157 |
| Universities, etc. | n.a. | n.a. | 30,000 | 72,899 |

Schools: Pre-primary 78 in 1985; Primary 4,164 in 1985.
Source: UNESCO, *Statistical Yearbook*.

# Directory

## The Constitution

The Libyan Arab People, meeting in the General People's Congress in Sebha from 2–28 March 1977, proclaimed its adherence to freedom and its readiness to defend it on its own land and anywhere else in the world. It also announced its adherence to socialism and its commitment to achieving total Arab Unity; its adherence to the moral human values, and confirmed the march of the revolution led by Col Muammar al-Qaddafi, the revolutionary leader, towards complete People's Authority.

The Libyan Arab People announced the following:

(i) The official name of Libya is henceforth The Socialist People's Libyan Arab Jamahiriya.

(ii) The Holy Koran is the social code in The Socialist People's Libyan Arab Jamahiriya.

(iii) The Direct People's Authority is the basis for the political order in The Socialist People's Libyan Arab Jamahiriya. The People shall practise its authority through People's Congresses, Popular Committees, Trade Unions, Vocational Syndicates, and The General People's Congress, in the presence of the law.

(iv) The defence of our homeland is the responsibility of every citizen. The whole people shall be trained militarily and armed by general military training, the preparation of which shall be specified by the law.

The General People's Congress in its extraordinary session held in Sebha issued four decrees:

The first decree announced the establishment of The People's Authority in compliance with the resolutions and recommendations of the People's Congresses and Trade Unions.

The second decree stipulated the choice of Col Muammar al-Qaddafi, the Revolutionary Leader, as Secretary-General of the General People's Congress.

The third decree stipulated the formation of the General Secretariat of the General People's Congress (see The Government, below).

The fourth decree stipulated the formation of the General People's Committee to carry out the tasks of the various former ministries (see The Government, below).

In 1986 it was announced that the country's official name was to be The Great Socialist People's Libyan Arab Jamahiriya.

## The Government

### HEAD OF STATE

**Revolutionary Leader:** Col MUAMMAR AL-QADDAFI (took office as Chairman of the Revolution Command Council 8 September 1969; he himself rejects this nomenclature and all other titles).

**Second-in-Command:** Maj. ABD AS-SALAM JALLOUD.

### GENERAL SECRETARIAT OF THE GENERAL PEOPLE'S CONGRESS

**Secretary-General:** ZENTANI MUHAMMAD ZENTANI.
**Assistant Secretary-General:** ABU ZAYD UMAR DURDAH.
**Secretary for Women's Affairs:** SALMA RASHID.
**Secretary for Affairs of the People's Congresses:** ALI MURSI ASH-SHAIRI.
**Secretary for Foreign Affairs:** SAAD MUJBIR.
**Secretary for Affairs of the People's Committees:** MAHMOUD AL-HITKI.
**Secretary for Affairs of the Trade Unions, Syndicates and Professional Associations:** ALI ASH-SHAMIKH.

### GENERAL PEOPLE'S COMMITTEE
(May 1995)

**Secretary-General of the General People's Committee:** ABD AL-MAJID AL-QAOUD.
**Secretary for Economic Planning and Finance:** MUHAMMAD BAIT AL-MAL.
**Secretary for Foreign Liaison and International Co-operation:** OMAR AL-MUNTASSER.
**Co-ordinators of the General Provisional Committee for Defence:** ABU BAKR JABER YUNES, MUSTAFA KHARRUBI, KHOUELDI HAMIDI.
**Secretary for Justice and Public Security:** MUHAMMAD AL-HIJAZI.
**Secretary for Energy:** ABDULLAH SALIM AL-BADRI.
**Secretary for the Economy and Trade:** AT-TAHER AL-JEHIMI.
**Secretary for Unity:** JOMAA AL-FEZZANI.
**Secretary for Industry:** FATHI BIN SHATWAN.
**Secretary for Education and Scientific Research:** MAATOUQ MUHAMMAD MAATOUQ.
**Secretary for Information and Culture:** AHMED IBRAHIM.
**Secretary for Marine Wealth:** MUFTAH MUHAMMAD KUAIBAH.
**Secretary for Agrarian Reform and Land Reclamation:** ISA ABD AL-KAFI AS-SID.
**Secretary for Transport and Communications:** AZZ AD-DIN AL-HINSHIRI.
**Secretary for Health and Social Security:** BAGHDADI ALI AL-MAHMOUDI.
**Secretary for Utilities and Housing:** MUBARAK ABDULLAH ASH-SHAMIKH.
**Secretary for the Great Man-made River:** JADALLAH AZIZ AT-TALHI.
**Secretary for the Supervision of Public Accounting and Control:** MAHMOUD BADI.

As part of a radical decentralization programme undertaken in September 1988, all General People's Committee secretariats (ministries), except those responsible for foreign liaison (foreign affairs) and information, were relocated away from Tripoli. According to diplomatic sources, the former Secretariat for Economy and Trade was moved to Benghazi; the Secretariat for Health to Kufra; and the remainder, excepting one, to Sirte, Col Qaddafi's birthplace. In early 1993 it was announced that the Secretariat for Foreign Liaison and International Co-operation was to be moved to Ras Lanouf.

## Legislature

### GENERAL PEOPLE'S CONGRESS

The Senate and House of Representatives were dissolved after the *coup d'état* of September 1969, and the provisional Constitution issued in December 1969 made no mention of elections or a return to parliamentary procedure. However, in January 1971 Col Qaddafi announced that a new legislature would be appointed, not elected; no date was mentioned. All political parties other than the Arab Socialist Union were banned. In November 1975 provision was made for the creation of the 1,112-member General National Congress of the Arab Socialist Union, which met officially in January 1976. This later became the General People's Congress (GPC), which met for the first time in November 1976 and in March 1977 began introducing the wide-ranging changes outlined in 'The Constitution' (above). The most recent Ordinary Session of the GPC took place in January 1994.

**Secretary-General:** ABD AR-RAZIQ SAWSA.

## Political Organizations

In June 1971 the Arab Socialist Union (ASU) was established as the country's sole authorized political party. The General National Congress of the ASU held its first session in January 1976 and later became the General People's Congress (see Legislature, above).

The following groups are in opposition to the Government:

**Libyan Baathist Party.**

**Libyan Democratic Movement:** f. 1977; external group.

**Libyan National Alliance:** f. 1980 in Cairo, Egypt; Leader: MANSOUR KIKHIA.

**National Front for the Salvation of Libya (NFSL):** f. 1981 in Khartoum, Sudan; aims to 'liberate Libya and save it from Qaddafi's rule', and to replace the existing regime by a democratically-elected government; Leader MUHAMMAD MEGARIEF.

## Diplomatic Representation

### EMBASSIES IN LIBYA

**Afghanistan:** POB 4245, Sharia Mozhar el-Aftes, Tripoli; tel. (21) 75192; Ambassador: (vacant).

**Algeria:** Sharia Kairauan 12, Tripoli; tel. (21) 40025; Ambassador: MOHAMMED SAIDI.
**Argentina:** POB 932, Sharia ibn Mufarrej al-Andaluz, Tripoli; tel. (21) 72160; telex 20190; Ambassador: ALFREDO CAMBACERES.
**Austria:** POB 3207, Sharia Khalid ibn al-Walid, Garden City, Tripoli; tel. (21) 43379; telex 20245; Ambassador: WILFRIED ALMOSLECHNER.
**Bangladesh:** POB 5086, Hadaba al-Khadra, Villa Omran al-Wershafani, Tripoli; tel. (21) 903807; telex 20970; Ambassador: M. AMINUL ISLAM.
**Belgium:** Tower 4, International Islamic Call Society Complex, Souk Ethulatnah, Tripoli; tel. (21) 37797; telex 20564; fax (21) 75618; Ambassador: L. DOYEN.
**Benin:** Tripoli; tel. (21) 72914; Ambassador: El-Hadj ALASSANE ABOUDOU.
**Brazil:** POB 2270, Sharia ben Ashur, Tripoli; tel. (21) 607970; telex 20082; Chargé d'affaires: REGIS NOVAES.
**Bulgaria:** POB 2945, Sharia Talha ben Abdullah 5-7, Tripoli; tel. (21) 4444260; Ambassador: KRASTIO ILOV.
**Burundi:** POB 2817, Sharia Ras Hassan, Tripoli; tel. (21) 608848; telex 20372; Ambassador: ZACHARIE BANYIYEZAKO.
**Chad:** POB 1078, Sharia Muhammad Mussadeq 25, Tripoli; tel. (21) 43955; Ambassador: IBRAHIM MAHAMAT TIDEI.
**China, People's Republic:** POB 5329, Gargaresh M 86, Tripoli; tel. (21) 830860; Ambassador: (vacant).
**Cuba:** POB 83738, Al-Andaluz District, Gargarech, Tripoli; tel. (21) 71346; telex 20513; Ambassador: RAÚL RODRÍGUEZ RÁMOS.
**Czech Republic:** POB 1097, Sharia Ahmad Lotfi Sayed, Ben Ashour Area, Tripoli; tel. (21) 603444; fax (21) 609608; Ambassador: ALEXANDR KARYCH.
**Egypt:** The Grand Hotel, Tripoli; tel. (21) 605500; telex 20780; fax (21) 45959; Ambassador: EL-SHAZLY.
**Ethiopia:** POB 12899, Sharia Jamahiriya, Tripoli; tel. (21) 608185; telex 20572; Ambassador: ABDULMENAN SHEKA.
**Finland:** POB 2508, Tripoli; tel. (21) 38057; Ambassador: ANTTI LASSILA.
**France:** POB 312, Sharia Saïd, Loutfi ben Achour, Tripoli; tel. (21) 607861; fax (21) 607864; Ambassador: JACQUES ROUQUETTE.
**Germany:** POB 302, Sharia Hassan al-Mashai, Tripoli; tel. (21) 30554; telex 20298; fax (21) 48968; Ambassador: CARL-DIETER HACH.
**Ghana:** POB 4169, Sharia as-Sway Khetumi, Tripoli; tel. (21) 44256; Ambassador: (vacant).
**Greece:** POB 5147, Sharia Jalal Bayar 18, Tripoli; tel. (21) 36978; telex 20409; fax (21) 41907; Ambassador: ELIAS DIMITRAKOPOULOS.
**Guinea:** POB 10657, Andalous, Tripoli; tel. (21) 72793; Ambassador: BAH KABA.
**Hungary:** POB 4010, Sharia Talha ben Abdullah, Tripoli; tel. (21) 605799; telex 20055; Ambassador: LÁSZLÓ FEHERVARI.
**India:** POB 3150, 16–18 Sharia Mahmud Shaltut, Tripoli; tel. (21) 4441835; telex 20115; fax (21) 3337560; Ambassador: SURENDRA KUMAR.
**Iran:** Sharia Gargaresh, Andalous, Tripoli; Ambassador: SEYYED MUHAMMAD QADEM KHUNSARI.
**Iraq:** Sharia ben Ashur, Tripoli.
**Italy:** POB 912, Sharia Uahran 1, Tripoli; tel. (21) 34131; telex 20602; Ambassador: GIORGIO REITANO; British interests section: POB 4206, Sharia Uahran, Tripoli; tel. (21) 31191; telex 20296; Consul: ALLEN BROWN.
**Japan:** Tower No. 4, That al-Imad Complex, Sharia Organization of African Unity, Tripoli; tel. (21) 607463; telex 20094; fax (21) 607462; Ambassador: AKIRA WATANABE.
**Korea, Democratic People's Republic:** Tripoli; Ambassador: O YONG RIN.
**Korea, Republic:** POB 4781/5160, Gargaresh 6 km, Travito Project, Tripoli; tel. (21) 833484; fax (21) 833503; Ambassador: PHILIPS CHOI.
**Kuwait:** POB 2225, Sharia Omar bin Yasser 8, Garden City, Tripoli; tel. (21) 40281; telex 20328; fax (21) 607053; Chargé d'affaires: ABD AL-AZIZ AL-DUAIJ.
**Lebanon:** POB 927, Sharia Omar bin Yasser Hadaek 20, Tripoli; tel. (21) 33733; telex 20609; Ambassador: MOUNIR KHOREISH.
**Malaysia:** POB 6309, Andalous, Tripoli; tel. (21) 833693; telex 20387; Chargé d'affaires a.i.: OTHMAN SAMIN.
**Mali:** Sharia Jaraba Saniet Zarrouk, Tripoli; tel. (21) 44924; Ambassador: EL BEKAYE SIDI MOCTAR KOUNTA.
**Malta:** POB 2534, Sharia Ubei ben Ka'ab, Tripoli; tel. (21) 3338081; telex 20273; fax (21) 4448401; Ambassador: GEORGE DOUBLESIN.

**Mauritania:** Sharia Eysa Wokwak, Tripoli; tel. (21) 43223; Ambassador: YAHIA MUHAMMAD EL-HADI.
**Morocco:** Sharia Bashir el-Ibrahim, Garden City, Tripoli; tel. (21) 34239; Chargé d'affaires: MEHDI MASDOUKI.
**Netherlands:** POB 3801, Sharia Jalal Bayar 20, Tripoli; tel. (21) 41549; telex 20279; fax 40386; Chargé d'affaires: B. F. TANGELDER.
**Nicaragua:** Beach Hotel, Andalous, Tripoli; tel. (21) 72641; Ambassador: GUILLERMO ESPINOSA.
**Niger:** POB 2251, Fachloun Area, Tripoli; tel. (21) 43104; Ambassador: KARIM ALIO.
**Nigeria:** POB 4417, Sharia Bashir el-Ibrahim, Tripoli; tel. (21) 43038; telex 20124; Ambassador: Prof. DANDATTI ABD AL-KADIR.
**Pakistan:** POB 2169, Sharia Abdul Karim al-Khattabi 16, Maidan Al-Qadasia, Tripoli; tel. (21) 40072; fax (21) 44698; Ambassador: KHAWAR RASHID PIRZADA.
**Philippines:** POB 12508, Sharia ed-Dul, Tripoli; tel. (21) 35607; telex 20304; Ambassador: ABDUL GHAFUUR MADKI ALONTO.
**Poland:** POB 519, Sharia ben Ashur 61, Tripoli; tel. (21) 607619; telex 20049; fax (21) 603641; Ambassador: STEFAN STANISZEWSKI.
**Qatar:** POB 3506, Sharia ben Ashur, Tripoli; tel. (21) 46660; Chargé d'affaires: HASAN AHMAD ABU HINDI.
**Romania:** POB 5085, Sharia Ahmad Lotfi Sayed, Tripoli; tel. (21) 45570; Ambassador: FLOREA RISTACHE.
**Russia:** POB 4792, Sharia Mustapha Kamel, Tripoli; tel. (21) 30545; telex 22029; Ambassador: VENYAMIN VIKTOROVICH POPOV.
**Rwanda:** POB 6677, Villa Ibrahim Musbah Missalati, Al-Andalous, Tripoli; tel. (21) 72864; telex 20236; fax (21) 70317; Chargé d'affaires: CHRISTOPHE HABIMANA.
**Saudi Arabia:** Sharia Kairauan 2, Tripoli; tel. (21) 30485; Chargé d'affaires: MUHAMMAD HASSAN BANDAH.
**Senegal:** Tripoli.
**Slovakia:** POB 2764, 1–3 Sharia Jallal Bayar, Tripoli; tel. (21) 3333312; fax (21) 3332568; Ambassador: (vacant).
**Spain:** POB 2302, Sharia el-Amir Abd al-Kader el-Jazairi 36, Tripoli; tel. (21) 36797; telex 20184; fax (21) 43743; Ambassador: PABLO BENAVIDES ORGAZ.
**Sudan:** Tripoli; Ambassador: ABD AL-MAJID BASHIR AL-AHMADI.
**Sweden:** POB 437, 5th Floor, Tower No. 5, That al-Imad, Tripoli; tel. (21) 47583; telex 20154; fax (21) 70357; Ambassador: NILS-ERIK SCHYBERG.
**Switzerland:** POB 439, Sharia ben Ashur, Tripoli; tel. (21) 607365; telex 20382; fax (21) 607487; Chargé d'affaires: JOSEF BUCHER.
**Syria:** POB 4219, Sharia Muhammad Rashid Reda 4, Tripoli (Relations Office); tel. 31783; Head: MUNIR BORKHAN.
**Togo:** POB 3420, Sharia Khaled ibn al-Walid, Tripoli; tel. (21) 4449565; telex 20373; fax (21) 3332423; Chargé d'affaires: OUYI KOFFI WOAKE.
**Tunisia:** POB 613, Sharia Bashir Ibrahimi, Tripoli; tel. (21) 31051; telex 20217; fax (21) 47600; High Representative: MANSOUR EZZEDDINE.
**Turkey:** POB 947, Sharia Jeraba, Tripoli; tel. (21) 3337717; telex 20031; fax (21) 3337686; Ambassador: ATEŞ BALKAN.
**Uganda:** POB 802015, Sharia ben Ashur, Tripoli; tel. (21) 604471; telex 20219; Chargé d'affaires a.i.: E. KWISENSHONI-MWEBIHIRE.
**United Kingdom:** (see Italy, above).
**Venezuela:** POB 2584, Sharia Abd ar-Rahman el-Kwakby, Tripoli; tel. (21) 36838; Ambassador: GONZALO SÁNCHEZ.
**Viet Nam:** POB 587, Sharia Talha ben Abdullah, Tripoli; tel. (21) 45753; Ambassador: DANG SAN.
**Yemen:** POB 4839, Sharia Ubei ben Ka'ab 36, Tripoli; tel. (21) 32323; Ambassador: ABD AL-WAHAB NASER JAHAF.
**Yugoslavia:** POB 1087, Sharia Turkia No. 14-16, Tripoli; tel. (21) 34114; Ambassador: DRAGO MIRŠIČ.
**Zaire:** POB 5066, Sharia Aziz al-Masri, Tripoli.

# Judicial System

The judicial system is composed, in order of seniority, of the Supreme Court, Courts of Appeal, and Courts of First Instance and Summary Courts.

All courts convene in open session, unless public morals or public order require a closed session; all judgments, however, are delivered in open session. Cases are heard in Arabic, with interpreters provided for aliens.

The courts apply the Libyan codes which include all the traditional branches of law, such as civil, commercial and penal codes, etc. Committees were formed in 1971 to examine Libyan law and ensure that it coincides with the rules of Islamic Shari'a. The proclamation of People's Authority in the Jamahiriya provides that the Holy Koran is the law of society.

### SUPREME COURT

The judgments of the Supreme Court are final. It is composed of the President and several Justices. Its judgments are issued by circuits of at least three Justices (the quorum is three). The Court hears appeals from the Courts of Appeal in civil, penal, administrative and civil status matters.

**President:** MUHAMMAD ALI AL-JADI.

### COURTS OF APPEAL

These courts settle appeals from Courts of First Instance; the quorum is three Justices. Each court of appeal has a court of assize.

### COURTS OF FIRST INSTANCE AND SUMMARY COURTS

These courts are first-stage courts in the Jamahiriya, and the cases heard in them are heard by one judge. Appeals against summary judgments are heard by the appellate court attached to the court of first instance, whose quorum is three judges.

### PEOPLE'S COURT

Established by order of the General People's Congress in March 1988.

**President:** Dr KHALIFAH SAID AL-QADHI.

### PEOPLE'S PROSECUTION BUREAU

Established by order of the General People's Congress in March 1988.

**President:** ABD AS-SALAM ALI AL-MIZIGHWI.

## Religion

### ISLAM

The vast majority of Libyan Arabs follow Sunni Muslim rites, although Col Qaddafi has rejected the Sunnah (i.e. the practice, course, way, manner or conduct of the Prophet Muhammad, as followed by Sunnis) as a basis for legislation.

**Chief Mufti of Libya:** Sheikh TAHER AHMAD AZ-ZAWI.

### CHRISTIANITY

#### The Roman Catholic Church

Libya comprises three Apostolic Vicariates and one Apostolic Prefecture. At 31 December 1993 there were an estimated 40,000 adherents in the country.

**Apostolic Vicariate of Benghazi:** POB 248, Benghazi; tel. (61) 96563; fax (61) 34696; Vicar Apostolic Mgr GIUSTINO GIULIO PASTORINO, Titular Bishop of Babra (absent).

**Apostolic Vicariate of Darna:** c/o POB 248, Benghazi; Vicar Apostolic (vacant).

**Apostolic Vicariate of Tripoli:** POB 365, Dahra, Tripoli; tel. (21) 31863; fax (21) 34696; Vicar Apostolic Mgr GIOVANNI INNOCENZO MARTINELLI, Titular Bishop of Tabuda; also Apostolic Administrator of Benghazi.

#### The Anglican Communion

Within the Episcopal Church in Jerusalem and the Middle East, Libya forms part of the diocese of Egypt (q.v.).

#### Other Christian Churches

The Coptic Orthodox Church is represented in Libya.

## The Press

Newspapers and periodicals are published either by the Jamahiriya News Agency (JANA), by government secretariats, by the Press Service or by trade unions.

### DAILIES

**Al-Fajr al-Jadid** (The New Dawn): POB 2303, Tripoli; tel. (21) 33056; f. 1969; since January 1978 published by JANA; circ. 40,000.

**Ash-Shams:** Tripoli.

### PERIODICALS

**Al-Amal** (Hope): Tripoli; weekly; social, for children; published by the Press Service.

**Ad-Daawa al-Islamia** (Islamic Call): POB 2682, Tanta St, Tripoli; tel. (21) 32055; telex 20480; fax (21) 38125; f. 1980; weekly (Wednesdays); Arabic, English, French; cultural; published by the World Islamic Call Society.

**Economic Bulletin:** POB 2303, Tripoli; monthly; published by JANA.

**Al-Jamahiriya:** POB 4814, Tripoli; tel. (21) 49294; f. 1980; weekly; Arabic; political; published by the revolutionary committees.

**Al-Jarida ar-Rasmiya** (The Official Newspaper): Tripoli; irregular; official state gazette.

**Libyan Arab Republic Gazette:** Tripoli; weekly; English; published by the Secretariat of Justice.

**Risalat al-Jihad** (Holy War Letter): POB 2682, Tripoli; tel. (21) 31021; telex 20407; f. 1983; monthly; Arabic, English, French; published by the World Islamic Call Society.

**Scientific Bulletin:** POB 2303, Tripoli; monthly; published by JANA.

**Ath-Thaqafa al-Arabiya** (Arab Culture): POB 4587, Tripoli; f. 1973; weekly; cultural; circ. 25,000.

**Al-Watan al-Arabi al-Kabir** (The Greater Arab Homeland): Tripoli; f. 1987.

**Az-Zahf al-Akhdar** (The Green Army): Tripoli; weekly; ideological journal of the revolutionary committees.

### NEWS AGENCIES

**Jamahiriya News Agency (JANA):** POB 2303, Sharia al-Fateh, Tripoli; tel. (21) 37106; telex 20841; branches and correspondents throughout Libya; main foreign bureaux: London, Paris, Rome, Beirut, Nairobi, Nouakchott and Kuwait; serves Libyan and foreign subscribers; Dir-Gen. IBRAHIM MUHAMMAD AL-BISHARI.

#### Foreign Bureaux

**Informatsionnoye Telegrafnoye Agentstvo Rossii—Telegrafnoye Agentstvo Suverennykh Stran (ITAR—TASS)** (Russia): Sharia Mustapha Kamel 10, Tripoli; Correspondent GEORG SHELENKOV.

ANSA (Italy) is also represented in Tripoli.

## Publishers

**Ad-Dar al-Arabia Lilkitab** (Maison Arabe du Livre): POB 3185, Tripoli; tel. (21) 47287; telex 20003; f. 1973 by Libya and Tunisia.

**Al-Fatah University, General Administration of Libraries, Printing and Publications:** POB 13543, Tripoli; tel. (21) 621988; telex 20629; f. 1955; academic books.

**General Co for Publishing, Advertising and Distribution:** POB 959, Souf al-Mahmudi, Tripoli; tel. (21) 45773; telex 20235; general, educational and academic books.

## Radio and Television

In 1992, according to UNESCO, there were an estimated 1,100,000 radio receivers and 485,000 television receivers in use.

**Great Socialist People's Libyan Arab Jamahiriya Broadcasting Corporation:** POB 3731, Tripoli; POB 119, el-Beida; tel. 32451; f. 1957 (TV 1968); broadcasts in Arabic and English from Tripoli and Benghazi; from September 1971 special daily broadcasts to Gaza and other Israeli-occupied territories were begun; External Service (Radio) and People's Revolution Broadcasting: POB 333, Tripoli; Dir-Gen. External Service ABDULLAH AL-MEGRI.

A national television service in Arabic was inaugurated in December 1968. Channels transmitting for limited hours in English, Italian and French have since been added.

## Finance

(cap. = capital; res = reserves; dep. = deposits;
LD = Libyan dinars; m. = million; brs = branches)

### BANKING

#### Central Bank

**Central Bank of Libya:** POB 1103, Sharia al-Malik Seoud, Tripoli; tel. (21) 33591; telex 20661; fax (21) 41488; f. 1955 as National Bank of Libya, name changed to Bank of Libya 1963, to Central Bank of Libya 1977; bank of issue and central bank carrying government accounts and operating exchange control; commercial operations transferred to National Commercial Bank 1970; cap.

LD100m., res LD131m., dep. LD2,193m., total assets LD4,648m. (June 1984); Governor Dr ABD AL-HAFIDH AL-ZILITNI.

### Other Banks

**Agricultural Bank:** POB 1100, 52 Sharia Omar Mukhtar, Tripoli; tel. (21) 38666; f. 1955; auth. cap. LD300m. (1981); Chair. AHMAD AL-AMIN AL-GADAMSI.

**Jamahiriya Bank:** POB 65155, Martyr St, Gharian; tel. (41) 31964; telex 20889; fax (41) 39402; f. 1969 as successor to Barclays Bank International in Libya; known as Masraf al-Jumhuriya until March 1977; wholly-owned subsidiary of the Central Bank; 42 brs throughout Libya; cap. LD25m., dep. LD946.8m., res LD22.1m., total assets LD1,446.6m. (Dec. 1987); Chair. MUSTAFA SALAH GEBRIL.

**Libyan Arab Foreign Bank:** POB 254, That al-Imad Administrative Complex, Tripoli; tel. (21) 41428; telex 20200; fax (21) 42970; f. 1972; offshore bank wholly owned by Central Bank of Libya; cap. and res LD240.1m., dep. LD890m., total assets LD1,398m. (Mar. 1993); Chair. and Gen. Man. REGED MISELLATI.

**National Commercial Bank SAL:** POB 4647, Shuhada Sq., Tripoli; tel. (21) 37191; telex 20169; f. 1970 to take over commercial banking division of Central Bank (then Bank of Libya) and brs of Aruba Bank and Istiklal Bank; 22 brs; cap. LD2.5m.; Chair. MUHAMMAD MUSTAFA GHADBAN.

**Sahara Bank:** POB 270, 10 Sharia 1 September, Tripoli; tel. (21) 32771; telex 20009; f. 1964 to take over br. of Banco di Sicilia; 20 brs; cap. LD525,000, res LD52.5m., dep. LD488.4m., total assets LD694m. (March 1988); Chair. and Gen. Man. OMAR ALI ASHABU.

**Savings and Real Estate Investment Bank:** POB 2297, Sharia Haite, Tripoli; tel. (21) 49306; telex 20309; f. 1975; 23 brs; cap. LD350m., dep. LD44m., res LD5m., total assets LD850m. (Dec. 1984); Chair. and Gen. Man. SAID LISHANI.

**Umma Bank SAL:** POB 685, 1 Giaddat Omar Mukhtar, Tripoli; tel. (21) 34031; telex 20256; fax (21) 32505; f. 1969 to take over brs of Banco di Roma; state-owned; 33 brs; cap. LD500,000, res LD96,712m., dep. LD556.2m. (Dec. 1982); Chair. and Gen. Man. SEDDIG OMAR EL-KABER.

**Wahda Bank:** POB 452, Fadiel Abu Omar Sq., El-Berkha, Benghazi; tel. (61) 24709; telex 40011; f. 1970 to take over Bank of North Africa, Commercial Bank, SAL, Nahda Arabia Bank, Société Africaine de Banque, Kafila al-Ahly Bank; state-owned; 49 brs; cap. LD36m., res LD77.1m., dep. LD935m., total assets LD1,463m. (March 1992); Chair. and Gen. Man. MUHAMMAD MUSTAFA GHADBAN.

### INSURANCE

**Libya Insurance Co:** POB 2438, Osama Bldg, Sharia 1 September, Tripoli; tel. (21) 44151; telex 20071; fax (21) 44178; POB 643, Benghazi; tel. (61) 99517; f. 1964 (merged with Al-Mukhtar Insurance Co in 1981); cap. LD30m.; all classes of insurance; Gen. Commr and Chair. K. M. SHERLALA.

## Petroleum

Until 1986 petroleum affairs in Libya were dealt with primarily by the Secretariat of the General People's Committee for Petroleum. This body was abolished in March 1986, and sole responsibility for the adminstration of the petroleum industry passed to the national companies which were already in existence. The Secretariat of the General People's Commitee for Petroleum was re-established in March 1989 and incorporated into the new Secretariat for the General People's Committee for Energy in October 1992. Since 1973 the Libyan Government has been entering into participation agreements with some of the foreign oil companies (concession holders), and nationalizing others. It has concluded 85%–15% production-sharing agreements with various oil companies.

### NATIONAL COMPANIES

**National Oil Corporation (NOC):** POB 2655, Tripoli; tel. (21) 46180; telex 61508; f. 1970 as successor to the Libyan General Petroleum Corporation, to undertake joint ventures with foreign companies; to build and operate refineries, storage tanks, petrochemical facilities, pipelines and tankers; to take part in arranging specifications for local and imported petroleum products; to participate in general planning of oil installations in Libya; to market crude oil and to establish and operate oil terminals; Chair. HAMOUDA AL-ASWAD.

**Agip (NAME) Ltd—Libyan Branch:** POB 346, Tripoli; tel. (21) 35135; telex 20282; fax (21) 35153; Sec. of People's Cttee A. M. CREUI.

**Arabian Gulf Oil Co:** POB 263, Benghazi; telex 40033; Sec. of People's Cttee H. A. LAYASS.

**Azzawiya Oil Refining Co:** affiliated with NOC, POB 6451, Tripoli (tel. 021 605389; telex 30423), and POB 15715, Azzawiya (tel. 023-20125); fax 605948; f. 1973; Gen. Commr HAMMOUDA M. AL-ASWAD.

**Brega Petroleum Marketing Co:** POB 402, Sharia Bashir es-Saidawi, Tripoli; tel. (21) 40830; telex 20090; f. 1971; Sec. of People's Cttee Dr DOKALI B. AL-MEGHARIEF.

**International Oil Investments Co:** Tripoli; f. 1988 with initial capital of $500m. to acquire 'downstream' facilities abroad; Chair. MUHAMMAD AL-JAWAD.

**National Drilling and Workover Co:** POB 1454, 208 Sharia Omar Mukhtar, Tripoli; tel. (21) 32411; telex 20332; f. 1986; Chair. IBRAHIM BAHI.

**Ras Lanouf Oil and Gas Processing Co:** Ras Lanouf, POB 2323, Tripoli; tel. (21) 607924; telex 50613; fax (21) 607924; f. 1978; Chair. MUHMUD ABDALLAH NAAS.

**Surt (Sirte) Oil Co:** POB 385, Tripoli; tel. (21) 602052; telex 30120; fax (21) 601487; f. 1955 as Esso Standard Libya, taken over by Surt Oil Co 1982; absorbed the National Petrochemicals Co in October 1990; exploration, production of crude oil, gas, and petrochemicals, liquefaction of natural gas.

**Umm al-Jawaby Petroleum Co:** POB 693, Tripoli; Chair. and Gen. Man. MUHAMMAD TENTTOUSH.

**Waha Oil Co:** POB 395, Tripoli; tel (21) 31116; telex 20158; fax (21) 37169; Sec. of People's Cttee ABDULLAH S. AL-BADRI.

**Zueitina Oil Co:** POB 2134, Tripoli; tel. (21) 3338011; telex 20130; fax (21) 3339109; Chair. of People's Cttee Dr N. A. ARIFI.

### FOREIGN COMPANIES

**Aquitaine Libya:** POB 282, Tripoli; tel. (21) 32411; telex 20148; Man. YVES PIROT.

**Wintershall-Libya:** POB 469 and 905, 9th Floor, Tower No. 4, That Al-Imad Complex, Tripoli; tel. (21) 4441494; telex 20103; fax (21) 4441493; Man. G. M. A. RENNER.

## Trade and Industry

There are state trade and industrial organizations responsible for the running of industries at all levels, which supervise production, distribution and sales. There are also central bodies responsible for the power generation industry, agriculture, land reclamation and transport.

### CHAMBERS OF COMMERCE

**Chamber of Commerce, Trade, Industry and Agriculture for the Eastern Province:** POB 208, Benghazi; tel. (61) 94526; telex 40077; f. 1953; Pres. Dr SADDEQ M. BUSNAINA; Gen. Man. YOUSUF AL-GIAMI; 5,400 mems.

**Tripoli Chamber of Commerce, Industry and Agriculture:** POB 2321, Sharia al-Fatah September, Tripoli; tel. (21) 33755; telex 20181; f. 1952; Pres. ABD AR-RAHMAN ABU SHOUASHI; Dir-Gen. MUHAMMAD SAAD KAYAT; 60,000 mems.

### DEVELOPMENT

**General National Organization for Industrialization:** POB 4388, Sharia San'a, Tripoli; tel. (21) 34995; telex 200990; f. 1970; a public organization responsible for the development of industry.

**Great Man-made River Authority (GMR):** Tripoli; supervises construction of pipeline carrying water to the Libyan coast from beneath the Sahara desert, to provide irrigation for agricultural projects; Sec.-Gen. MUHAMMAD AL-MANQOUSH.

**Kufra and Sarir Authority:** Council of Agricultural Development, Benghazi; f. 1972 to develop the Kufra Oasis and Sarir area in south-east Libya.

### TRADE UNIONS

**General Federation of Producers' Trade Unions:** POB 734, 2 Sharia Istanbul, Tripoli; tel. (21) 46011; telex 20229; f. 1952; affiliated to ICFTU; Sec.-Gen. BASHIR IHWIJ; 17 trade unions with 700,000 members.

**General Union for Oil and Petrochemicals:** Tripoli; Chair. MUHAMMAD MITHNANI.

**Pan-African Federation of Petroleum Energy and Allied Workers:** Tripoli; affiliated to the Organization of African Trade Union Unity.

## Transport

**Department of Road Transport and Railways:** POB 14527, Sharia az-Zawia, Secretariat of Communications and Transport

## LIBYA

Bldg, Tripoli; tel. (21) 609011-30; telex 20533; fax (21) 605605; Secretary for Public Works, Utilities, Transport and Communications MUBARAK ASH-SHAMIKH; Dir.-Gen. Projects and Research MUHAMMAD ABU ZIAN.

### RAILWAYS

There are, at present, no railways in Libya. An agreement was signed in 1983 with the People's Republic of China for the construction of a 170-km standard gauge line from Tripoli to Ras Jedir, on the Tunisian frontier. This was to be the first stage of a planned 364-km line along the coast from Ras Jedir to Tripoli and Misurata, and the first section in a proposed network totalling 3,000 km. Construction of a rapid transport system began in Tripoli in 1986. Owing to shortage of funds, neither of the above projects has been completed. In November 1990 Libya signed an agreement with Egypt to extend the Egyptian rail system westwards and link Benghazi to the Egyptian border. Work on the initial phase of the project—a rail link between As-Salum and Tubruq—commenced in October 1993.

### ROADS

The most important road is the 1,822-km national coast road from the Tunisian to the Egyptian border, passing through Tripoli and Benghazi. It has a second link between Barce and Lamluda, 141 km long. Another national road runs from a point on the coastal road 120 km south of Misurata through Sebha to Ghat near the Algerian border (total length 1,250 km). There is a branch 247 km long running from Vaddan to Surt (Sirte). A 690-km road, connecting Tripoli and Sebha, and another 626 km long, from Agedabia in the north to Kufra in the south-east, were opened in 1983. The Tripoli-to-Ghat section (941 km) of the third, 1,352-km long national road was opened in September 1984. There is a road crossing the desert from Sebha to the frontiers of Chad and Niger.

In addition to the national highways, the west of Libya has about 1,200 km of paved and macadamized roads and the east about 500 km. All the towns and villages of Libya, including the desert oases, are accessible by motor vehicle. In 1984 Libya had 25,675 km of paved roads.

### SHIPPING

The principal ports are Tripoli, Benghazi, Mersa Brega, Misurata and as-Sider. Zuetina, Ras Lanouf, Mersa Hariga, Mersa Brega and as-Sider are mainly oil ports. A 30-inch crude oil pipeline connects the Zelten oilfields with Mersa Brega. Another pipeline joins the Sarir oilfield with Mersa Hariga, the port of Tobruk, and a pipeline from the Sarir field to Zuetina was opened in 1968. A port is being developed at Darna. Libya also has the use of Tunisian port facilities at Sfax and Gabès, to alleviate congestion at Tripoli.

**General National Maritime Transport Company:** POB 80173, 2 Sharia Ahmad Sharif, Tripoli; tel. (21) 33155; telex 20208; f. 1970 to handle all projects dealing with maritime trade; in June 1994 Libya's merchant fleet consisted of 26 vessels (11 tankers, 1 chemical carrier and 14 general cargo and passenger vessels); Chair. SAID MILUD AL-AHRASH.

### CIVIL AVIATION

There are four civil airports: Tripoli International Airport, situated at Ben Gashir, 34 km (21 miles) from Tripoli; Benina Airport 19 km (12 miles) from Benghazi; Sebha Airport; Misurata Airport (domestic flights only). In the late 1980s there were plans for a new international airport to be built at Ras Lanouf and for airports at Brak and al-Waigh. Since April 1992 international civilian air links with Libya have been suspended, in accordance with UN Security Council Resolution 748 of 31 March 1992.

**Jamahiriya Libyan Arab Airlines:** POB 2555, Haiti St, Tripoli; tel. (21) 602083; telex 21093; f. 1989 by merger of Jamahiriya Air Transport (which in 1983 took over operations of United African Airlines) and Libyan Arab Airlines (f. 1964 as Kingdom of Libya Airlines and renamed 1969); passenger and cargo services from Tripoli, Benghazi and Sebha to destinations in Europe, North Africa and the Middle East; domestic services throughout Libya; Public relations Man. MUSTAFA A. BELKHIR.

## Tourism

The principal attractions for visitors to Libya are Tripoli, with its beaches and annual International Fair, the ancient Roman towns of Sabratha, Leptis Magna and Cyrene, and historic oases. Tourist arrivals totalled 120,000 in 1987.

**Department of Tourism and Fairs:** POB 891, Sharia Omar Mukhtar, Tripoli; tel. (21) 32255; telex 20179.

# LIECHTENSTEIN

## Introductory Survey

### Location, Climate, Language, Religion, Flag, Capital

The Principality of Liechtenstein is in central Europe. The country lies on the east bank of the Upper Rhine river, bordered by Switzerland to the west and south, and by Austria to the north and east. Liechtenstein has an Alpine climate, with mild winters. The official language is German, of which a dialect—Alemannish—is spoken. Almost all of the inhabitants profess Christianity, and about 81% are adherents of the Roman Catholic Church. The national flag (proportions five by three) consists of two equal horizontal stripes, of royal blue and red, with a golden princely crown, outlined in black, in the upper hoist. The capital is Vaduz.

### Recent History

Liechtenstein has been an independent state since 1719, except while under French domination in the early 19th century. In 1919 Switzerland assumed responsibility for Liechtenstein's diplomatic representation, replacing Austria. In 1920 a postal union with Switzerland was agreed, and in 1924 a treaty was concluded with Switzerland whereby Liechtenstein was incorporated in a joint customs union. Franz Josef II succeeded as ruling prince in 1938. In 1950 Liechtenstein became a party to the Statute of the International Court of Justice, and in 1978 it was admitted to the Council of Europe (see p. 134). Liechtenstein became a member of the UN in September 1990 (hitherto the country had been a member of some UN specialized agencies). In the following year Liechtenstein became a full member of the European Free Trade Association (EFTA, see p. 142).

After 42 years as the dominant party in government, the Fortschrittliche Bürgerpartei (FBP—Progressive Citizens' Party) was defeated by the Vaterländische Union (VU—Patriotic Union) at a general election to the Landtag (parliament) in February 1970, but it regained its majority four years later. At the election to the Landtag in February 1978 the VU, led by Hans Brunhart, won eight of the 15 seats, though with a minority of the votes cast, while the remaining seats were won by the FBP, led by Dr Walter Kieber, Head of Government since March 1974. After protracted negotiations Brunhart succeeded Kieber in April. The general election in February 1982 produced no change in the distribution of seats, although the VU did gain a majority of votes. Following a referendum in July 1984, women were granted the right to vote on a national basis. However, women were still not permitted to vote on communal affairs in three of Liechtenstein's 11 communes until April 1986, when they were finally accorded full voting rights. In December 1985 a proposal to add a new clause to the Constitution, on the principle of equality between men and women, was rejected by a large majority in a national referendum. In August 1984 Prince Franz Josef transferred executive power to his son, Prince Hans-Adam, although he remained titular Head of State. Following the death of Franz Josef in November 1989, Hans-Adam succeeded him as ruling Prince (Hans-Adam II).

The composition of the Landtag remained unchanged following a general election in February 1986, when women voted for the first time in a national poll. In January 1989 the Landtag was dissolved by Prince Hans-Adam, following a dispute between the VU and the FBP regarding the construction of a new museum to accommodate the royal art collection. At the subsequent general election, which took place in March, the number of seats in the Landtag was increased from 15 to 25; the VU retained its majority, securing 13 seats, while the FBP took the remaining 12 seats.

At the next general election, which took place in early February 1993, the VU lost its majority, taking only 11 of the Landtag's 25 seats. The FBP again returned 12 representatives, and two seats were won by an environmentalist party, the Freie Liste (FL—Free List). Lengthy negotiations resulted in the formation of a new FBP-led coalition with the VU, and Markus Büchel of the FBP became Head of Government. In September, however, following a unanimous vote in the Landtag expressing 'no confidence' in his leadership, Büchel was dismissed from his post, and Prince Hans-Adam dissolved parliament. At a further general election, which was held in late October, the VU regained its majority, winning 13 seats, while the FBP took 11 seats and the FL secured one. A VU-led coalition with the FBP was subsequently formed, with Mario Frick as Head of Government.

In October 1992 almost 2,000 people took part in a demonstration in Vaduz to protest against a threat by Prince Hans-Adam to dissolve the Landtag if deputies did not submit to his wish that a referendum to endorse Liechtenstein's entry to the nascent European Economic Area (EEA, see p. 142) take place in advance of a similar vote in Switzerland. The Prince believed that the outcome of the Swiss plebiscite might be prejudicial to that of the Liechtenstein vote, and that, in the event of voters' rejecting EEA membership at an early referendum, Liechtenstein might still be able to join other EFTA members in applying for admission to the European Community (EC—now European Union, see p. 143). A compromise was reached, whereby the referendum was scheduled to take place after the Swiss vote, while the Government agreed actively to promote a vote in favour of the EEA and to explore the possibility of applying to the EC should EEA membership be rejected. (The authorities subsequently decided that admission to the EU would not be beneficial to the Principality.) At the referendum, in mid-December, although Switzerland's voters had rejected accession to the EEA one week earlier, Liechtenstein's membership was approved by 55.8% of those who voted (about 87% of the Principality's electorate); consequently, a review of the two countries' joint customs union took place. In April 1995 a new national referendum was held, at which 55.9% of Liechtenstein's voters approved the revised customs arrangements. Liechtentstein thus joined the EEA at the beginning of May.

### Government

The Constitution of the hereditary Principality provides for a unicameral parliament (Landtag), composed of 25 members, elected, by universal adult suffrage, for four years (subject to dissolution), on the basis of proportional representation. A five-member government is elected by the Landtag, for its duration, and confirmed by the Sovereign.

### Defence

Although Liechtensteiners under the age of 60 years are liable to military service in an emergency, there has been no standing army since 1868 and there is only a small police force of 59 men and 19 auxiliaries.

### Economic Affairs

In terms of average gross national product (GNP), Liechtenstein is one of the richest nations in the world: GNP per head is comparable with that of Switzerland (which was US $36,410, at average 1991–93 prices, in 1993). In 1991 Liechtenstein's gross domestic product (GDP) per head, at current prices, was an estimated 89,474 Swiss francs.

Following the Second World War, the importance of agriculture declined in favour of industry. Within the agricultural sector the emphasis is on cattle-breeding, dairy-farming and arable farming. The principal crops are maize and potatoes. In 1993 1.7% of the working population were employed in agriculture.

In 1993 industrial activity, construction and commerce employed 48.1% of the working population. The metal, machinery and precision instruments industry is by far the most prominent sector. Other important areas are the chemical, furniture and ceramics industries.

In 1994 some 93% of energy requirements were imported from other countries.

In 1993 the services sector (excluding commerce) employed 50.2% of the working population. Within this sector, financial services are of great importance. Because of the stable political situation, the absolute bank secrecy and the low fiscal charges, many foreign corporations, holding companies and foundations (estimated to number about 70,000) have nominal offices in Liechtenstein. Such enterprises pay no tax on profit or income, contributing instead an annual levy on capital or net worth. These levies account for about 20% of the principality's yearly direct revenue. In 1980, however, Liechtenstein adopted legislation to increase controls on foreign firms, many of which were thereafter to be subject to audit and to be entered in the public register. The Principality has hitherto refused to permit the registration of foreign banks, in order not to overwhelm the small local population with further resident foreigners (see below). During the 1980s, in an attempt to promote the Bank in Liechtenstein AG internationally, the Prince of Liechtenstein Foundation (a coordinating financial organization which owns most of the bank's shares) began expanding its interests abroad by opening representative offices in other countries and by establishing a number of international ventures (mainly in the field of portfolio management and investment counselling). The building and hotel trades and other service industries are also highly developed.

With a very limited domestic market, Liechtenstein's industry is export-orientated. In 1993 total exports amounted to 2,417.1m. Swiss francs. Switzerland is the principal trading partner, receiving 13.8% of exports in 1993. In that year members of the EC and EFTA (including Switzerland) accounted for 41.6% and 20.0%, respectively, of total exports. Artificial teeth and other materials for dentistry are an important export, while the sale of postage stamps, mainly to tourists, provided about 4% of the national income in 1993.

The 1995 budget envisaged a surplus of 16.0m. Swiss francs. The average annual rate of inflation increased from 1.9% in 1988 to 5.9% in 1991, falling to 3.3% in 1993. Traditionally the unemployment rate has been negligible (in 1990 only 0.1% of the labour force were unemployed); by the end of 1993, however, the rate had risen to 1.4%. More than one-third of Liechtenstein's population are resident foreigners, many of whom provide the labour for industry, while about 6,500 workers cross the borders from Austria and Switzerland each day to work in Liechtenstein.

Liechtenstein has important economic links with neighbouring Switzerland. It is incorporated in a customs union with that country, and uses the Swiss franc as its currency. Liechtenstein became a member of EFTA in May 1991, and membership of the EEA was approved in a national referendum in December 1992. The Principality is also a member of the European Bank for Reconstruction and Development, inaugurated in April 1991 (see p. 140).

### Social Welfare
Accident insurance has been obligatory since 1910, and old-age and survivors' insurance since 1952. Family allowances were introduced in 1957, and unemployment benefits in 1970. Sickness insurance was made compulsory in 1910, and a pension fund was introduced in 1989.

### Education
Compulsory education begins at seven years of age. Basic instruction is given for five years at a primary school (Primarschule), after which a pupil may transfer to a lower secondary school (Oberschule) or secondary school (Realschule) for four years, or to the Liechtensteinisches Gymnasium (grammar school) for eight years. There is no university. Many Liechtensteiners continue their studies at universities in Austria, Germany or Switzerland. Liechtenstein has a further education college for the study of philosophy, a technical college (Fachhochschule), a music school and a school for mentally handicapped children.

### Public Holidays
**1995:** 1 January (New Year's Day), 6 January (Epiphany), 2 February (Candlemas), 19 March (St Joseph's Day), 14 April (Good Friday), 17 April (Easter Monday), 1 May (Labour Day), 25 May (Ascension), 5 June (Whit Monday), 15 June (Corpus Christi), 15 August (Assumption and National Holiday), 8 September (Nativity of the Virgin Mary), 1 November (All Saints' Day), 8 December (Immaculate Conception), 25 December (Christmas), 26 December (St Stephen's Day).

**1996:** 1 January (New Year's Day), 6 January (Epiphany), 2 February (Candlemas), 19 March (St Joseph's Day), 5 April (Good Friday), 8 April (Easter Monday), 1 May (Labour Day), 16 May (Ascension), 27 May (Whit Monday), 6 June (Corpus Christi), 15 August (Assumption and National Holiday), 8 September (Nativity of the Virgin Mary), 1 November (All Saints' Day), 8 December (Immaculate Conception), 25 December (Christmas), 26 December (St Stephen's Day).

### Weights and Measures
The metric system is in force.

# Statistical Survey

Source: Presse- und Informationsamt, Regierungsgebäude, 9490 Vaduz; tel. (75) 2366720; fax (75) 2366460.

### AREA AND POPULATION
**Area:** 160.0 sq km (61.8 sq miles).

**Population:** 29,868 (incl. 11,432 resident aliens) at census of December 1992; 30,310 (incl. 11,713 resident aliens) at December 1993.

**Density** (December 1993): 189 per sq km.

**Principal Towns** (population at December 1993): Vaduz (capital) 5,072; Schaan 5,129; Balzers 3,841; Triesen 3,776, Eschen 3,336; Mauren 2,938; Triesenberg 2,406.

**Births, Marriages and Deaths** (1993): Live births 415 (13.9 per 1,000); Marriages 445 (14.9 per 1,000); Deaths 178 (5.9 per 1,000).

**Employment** (1992): Agriculture and forestry 347; Industry, construction and commerce 9,982; Services 10,427; Total 20,756.

### AGRICULTURE, ETC.
**Principal Crops** (metric tons, 1987): Wheat 460; Oats 4; Barley 416; Silo-maize 27,880; Potatoes 1,040.

**Livestock** (1993): Cattle 5,675; Pigs 3,236; Horses 276; Sheep 2,641; Goats 181.

**Dairy Produce** (1993): Total production 12,494 metric tons.

**Forestry** (1993): Felling 14,759 cu m.

### FINANCE
**Currency and Exchange Rates:** Swiss currency: 100 Rappen (centimes) = 1 Franken (Swiss franc). *Sterling and Dollar Equivalents* (31 December 1994): £1 sterling = 2.047 Franken; US $1 = 1.309 Franken; 100 Franken = £48.84 = $76.41. For average exchange rate, see chapter on Switzerland.

**Budget** (estimates, '000 Swiss francs, 1995): Revenue 538,259; Expenditure 522,214.

### EXTERNAL TRADE
**Total Exports** (million Swiss francs, 1993): 2,417.1.

**Exports by Destination** (million Swiss francs, 1993): EFTA 484.6 (Switzerland 334.0); EC 1,004.4; Others 928.1; Total 2,417.1.

### TRANSPORT
**Road Traffic** (registered motor vehicles, December 1993): Passenger cars 17,767; Commercial vehicles 1,817; Motor cycles 2,573.

### TOURISM
**Foreign Tourist Arrivals** (1993, by country of origin): Austria 2,334; France 2,190; Germany 22,654; Italy 3,295; Netherlands 1,528; Switzerland 14,609; United Kingdom 1,557; USA 5,063; Others 11,750; Total 64,980.

### COMMUNICATIONS
**Media** (1993): Radio receivers 11,000; Television receivers 10,620; Telephones 18,916: Newspapers 3 (average circulation 10,470).

LIECHTENSTEIN

### EDUCATION
(1994/95)

**Kindergarten:** 52 schools; 57 teachers; 778 pupils.
**Primary:** 14 schools; 125 teachers; 1,914 pupils.
**Lower secondary:** 3 schools; 42 teachers; 458 pupils.
**Secondary:** 5 schools; 51 teachers; 796 pupils.
**Grammar:** 1 school; 35 teachers; 567 pupils.
**Music:** 1 school; 85 teachers; 2,200 pupils.

# Directory

## The Constitution

According to the Constitution of 5 October 1921, the monarchy is hereditary in the male line. The reigning Prince, who is constitutionally responsible for foreign affairs, exercises the legislative right jointly with the Landtag (parliament), with 25 members elected for four years (subject to dissolution) by general and secret ballot. Under the Constitution (as amended in 1969 and 1984), all citizens of over 20 years of age are eligible to vote. The voters participate directly in legislation by means of the initiative and the referendum.

In the case of adjournment or dissolution, the Landtag is replaced by a National Committee, consisting of the President of the Landtag and four deputies. The members of the Government are nominated by the Prince, on the proposition of the Landtag, for four years.

In accordance with a treaty concluded with Switzerland in 1924, Liechtenstein is incorporated in Swiss customs territory, and uses Swiss currency, customs and postal administration.

## The Government

### HEAD OF STATE

Prince HANS-ADAM II, Prince of Liechtenstein, Duke of Troppau, Count of Rietberg, succeeded 13 November 1989.

### GOVERNMENT
(May 1995)

A coalition of the Vaterländische Union (VU, Patriotic Union) and the Fortschrittliche Bürgerpartei (FBP, Progressive Citizens' Party).

**Head of Government:** Dr MARIO FRICK (VU).
**Deputy Head of Government:** THOMAS BÜCHEL (FBP).
**Government Councillors:** Dr ANDREA WILLI (VU), Dr MICHAEL RITTER (VU), Dr CORNELIA GASSNER (FBP).

### GOVERNMENT OFFICES

**Regierungsgebäude:** 9490 Vaduz; tel. (75) 2366111.

## Legislature

### LANDTAG

**President:** OTMAR HASLER (FBP).
**Vice-President:** PAUL KINDLE (VU).

**General Election, 24 October 1993**

| Party | Seats |
| --- | --- |
| VU (Patriotic Union) | 13 |
| FBP (Progressive Citizens' Party) | 11 |
| FL (Free List) | 1 |
| **Total** | **25** |

## Political Organizations

**Fortschrittliche Bürgerpartei (FBP)** (Progressive Citizens' Party): Feldkircherstr. 5, 9494 Schaan; tel. (75) 2333531; fax (75) 2322912; Chair. (vacant); Sec. HEIDI KINDLE.
**Freie Liste (FL)** (Free List): Postfach 177, 9494 Schaan; f. 1985; progressive ecological party.
**Vaterländische Union (VU)** (Patriotic Union): Fürst-Franz-Josef-Str. 13, 9490 Vaduz; tel. (75) 2361616; fax (75) 2361617; f. 1936 by merger of the People's Party (f. 1918) and the Heimatdienst movement; Chair. OSWALD KRANZ; Sec. MAGDA BATLINER.

## Diplomatic Representation

According to an arrangement concluded in 1919, Switzerland has agreed to represent Liechtenstein's interests in countries where it has diplomatic missions and where Liechtenstein is not represented in its own right. In so doing, Switzerland always acts only on the basis of mandates of a general or specific nature, which it may either refuse or accept, while Liechtenstein is free to enter into direct relations with foreign states or to establish its own additional missions. Liechtenstein has an embassy in Berne, a non-resident ambassador to Austria and a non-resident ambassador to the Holy See, as well as a permanent representative to the Council of Europe in Strasbourg and a permanent mission to the UN in New York. There are 37 consular representatives accredited to Liechtenstein.

## Judicial System

### CIVIL COURTS

**Landgericht** (County Court): 9490 Vaduz; tel. (75) 2366111; Court of First Instance; one presiding judge; Presiding Judge Dr FRANZ REDERER.
**Obergericht** (Superior Court): Court of Second Instance; bench of five judges; Presiding Judge Lic. Iur. MAX BIZOZZERO.
**Oberster Gerichtshof** (Supreme Court): Court of Third Instance; bench of five judges; Presiding Judge Dr KARL KOHLEGGER.

### CRIMINAL COURTS

**Landgericht** (Petty Sessions): for summary offences.
**Schöffengericht** (Court of Assizes): for minor misdemeanours; bench of three judges; Presiding Judge Dr BENEDIKT MARXER.
**Kriminalgericht** (Criminal Court): bench of five judges; Presiding Judge Dr FRANZ REDERER.
**Obergericht** (Superior Court): Court of Second Instance; bench of five judges; Presiding Judge Lic. Iur. MAX BIZOZZERO.
**Oberster Gerichtshof** (Supreme Court): Court of Third Instance: bench of five judges; Presiding Judge Dr KARL KOHLEGGER.

### ADMINISTRATIVE COURTS

**Verwaltungsbeschwerdeinstanz** (Administrative Court of Appeal): appeal against decrees and decisions of the Government may be made to this court; five members; Presiding Judge Dr HERBERT WILLE.
**State Court:** five members; exists for the protection of Public Law; Presiding Judge Lic. Iur. HARRY GSTÖHL.

## Religion

### CHRISTIANITY

About 81% of the inhabitants of Liechtenstein are Roman Catholics and belong to the Diocese of Chur, Switzerland. The few Protestants (7.3%) adhere to the parish of Vaduz.

**Diocese of Chur:** Bischöfliches Ordinariat, Hof 19, 7000 Chur, Switzerland; tel. (81) 222312; fax (81) 216140; Bishop: Rt Rev. WOLFGANG HAAS.

## The Press

**Liechtensteiner Vaterland:** Fürst-Franz-Josef-Str. 13, 9490 Vaduz; tel. (75) 2361616; telex 889442; fax (75) 2361617; f. 1913; daily (Monday to Saturday); organ of the VU; Editor GÜNTHER FRITZ; circ. 8,925.
**Liechtensteiner Volksblatt:** 9494 Schaan; tel. (75) 2324242; fax (75) 2322912; f. 1878; daily (Monday to Saturday); organ of the FBP; Editor GÜNTHER MEIER; circ. 8,600.

**Liechtensteiner Wochenzeitung:** 9494 Schaan; tel. (75) 2320885; fax (75) 2331340; f. 1993; weekly (Sunday); Dir INES WOHLWEND.

### PRESS AGENCY

**Presse- und Informationsamt** (Press and Information Office): Regierungsgebäude, 9490 Vaduz; tel. (75) 2366111; fax (75) 2366460; f. 1962; Dir ROLAND BÜCHEL.

## Publishers

**Buch und Verlagsdruckerei:** Im Städtle 32, 9490 Vaduz.

**Frank P. van Eck Publishers:** Haldenweg 8, 9495 Triesen; tel. and fax (75) 3922277; f. 1982; art, architecture, juvenile, golf; Man. Dir E. VAN ECK-SCHAEDLER.

**A. R. Gantner Verlag KG:** Beckagässle 4, Postfach 225, 9490 Vaduz; tel. (75) 2322735; telex 889373; fax (75) 2328554; botany; Dir BRUNI GANTNER.

**Verlag H.P. Gassner AG:** Austr. 7, Postfach 1222, 9490 Vaduz; tel. (75) 2327252; fax (75) 232720; f. 1979; Dir HANS PETER GASSNER.

**Liechtenstein-Verlag AG:** Schwefelstr. 33, Postfach 133, 9490 Vaduz; tel. (75) 2323925; telex 889326; fax (75) 2324340; f. 1947; belles-lettres and scientific books; agents for international literature; Man. ALBART SCHIKS.

**Litag Anstalt—Literarische, Medien und Künstler Agentur:** Beckagässle 4, Postfach 225, 9490 Vaduz; tel. (75) 2322735; telex 889373; fax (75) 2328554; f. 1956; Dir BRUNI GANTNER.

**Sändig Reprint Verlag Hans-Rainer Wohlwend:** Am Schrägen Weg 12, 9490 Vaduz; tel. and fax (75) 2323627; f. 1965; natural sciences, linguistics, freemasonry, fiction, folklore, music, history; Dir HANS-RAINER WOHLWEND.

**Topos Verlag AG:** Industriestr. 105, Postfach 551, 9491 Ruggell; tel. (75) 3734757; fax (75) 3736260; f. 1977; law, politics, literature, social science, periodicals; Dir GRAHAM A. P. SMITH.

## Finance

(cap. = capital; res = reserves; dep. = deposits; m. = millions; brs = branches; amounts in Swiss francs)

### BANKING

**Bank in Liechtenstein AG:** Herrengasse 12, Postfach 85, 9490 Vaduz; tel. (75) 2351122; telex 889222; fax (75) 2351522; f. 1920; cap. 291m., res 243m., dep. 6,490m. (Dec. 1993); Chair. FRITZ BÜHLER; CEO HEINZ NIPP.

**Centrum Bank AG:** Heiligkreuz 8, 9490 Vaduz; tel. (75) 2358585; fax 2358686.

**Liechtensteinische Landesbank** (State Bank): Städtle 44, Postfach 384, 9490 Vaduz; tel. (75) 2368811; fax (75) 2368822; f. 1861, present name since 1955; brs in Schaan, Triesenberg, Eschen and Balzers; cap. 190m., res 198.8m., dep. 5,862.6m. (Dec. 1993); Pres. ANDREAS VOGT; Gen. Man. KARLHEINZ HEEB.

**Neue Bank AG:** Kirchstr. 8, 9490 Vaduz; tel. (75) 2360808; fax (75) 2329260.

**Verwaltungs- und Privat-Bank AG** (Private Trust Bank Corporation): Im Zentrum, 9490 Vaduz; tel. (75) 2356655; fax (75) 2356500; f. 1956; cap. 90m., res 311.4m., dep. 3,700m. (Dec. 1993); Pres. Dr HEINZ BATLINER; Gen. Man. Dr ROLF KORMANN.

### STATE INSURANCE COMPANY

**Alters- und Hinterlassenen-Versicherung (AHV)** (Old Age and Survivors' Insurance): 9490 Vaduz; tel. (75) 2311252; fax (75) 2320406; Dir GERHARD BIEDERMANN.

## Trade and Industry

### CHAMBER OF COMMERCE

**Liechtensteinische Industrie-und Handelskammer** (Chamber of Industry and Commerce): Josef Rheinberger-Str. 11, Postfach 232, 9490 Vaduz; tel. (75) 2322744; fax (75) 2331503; aims to protect the industrial and commercial interests of Liechtenstein; Pres. Dipl. Ing. PETER FRICK; Dir WILLI FROMMELT.

### PRODUCERS' AND EMPLOYEES' ORGANIZATIONS

**Gewerbe- und Wirtschaftskammer für das Fürstentum Liechtenstein** (Trades Union): Zollstr. 23, 9494 Schaan; tel. (75) 2321864; fax (75) 2332304; f. 1936; aims to protect the interests of Liechtenstein artisans and tradespeople; Pres. GREGOR OTT; Sec. MANFRED BATLINER; 3,000 mems.

**Liechtensteiner Arbeitnehmer-Verband** (Employees' Association): 9490 Vaduz; tel. (75) 2324255; fax (75) 2329104; Pres. ALICE FEHR; Sec. ALBERT JEHLE.

**Vereinigung Bäuerlicher Organisationen** (Agricultural Union): Zollstr. 9, 9490 Vaduz; Pres. Dr ERNST WALCH; Sec. KLAUS BUCHEL.

## Transport

### RAILWAYS

There are 18.5 km of railway track in Liechtenstein. The Arlberg express (Paris to Vienna) passes through the Principality and a local line runs from Feldkirch in Austria to Buchs in Switzerland. The whole line is electrified and is administered by Austrian Federal Railways.

### ROADS

Modern roads connect the capital, Vaduz, with all the towns and villages in the Principality. The Rhine and Samina valleys are connected by a tunnel 740 m long. Public transport is provided by postal buses.

### INLAND WATERWAYS

A canal of 26 km, irrigating the Rhine valley, was opened in 1943.

## Tourism

Liechtenstein has an attractive Alpine setting in the Upper Rhine area. There is a celebrated postal museum, a National Museum and the Liechtenstein State Art Collection at Vaduz, as well as the Prince's castle. In 1993 Liechtenstein received 64,980 foreign visitors. There are about 50 hotels and inns, with a total of some 1,400 beds.

**Liechtenstein National Tourist Office:** Postfach 139, 9490 Vaduz; tel. (75) 3921111; fax (75) 3921618; Dir BERTHOLD KONRAD.

# LITHUANIA

## Introductory Survey

**Location, Climate, Language, Religion, Flag, Capital**

The Republic of Lithuania (formerly the Lithuanian Soviet Socialist Republic) is situated on the eastern coast of the Baltic Sea, in north-eastern Europe. It is bounded by Latvia to the north, by Belarus to the south-east, by Poland to the south-west and by the territory of the Russian Federation around Kaliningrad to the west. Lithuania's maritime position moderates an otherwise continental-type climate. Temperatures range from an average in January of −4.9°C (23.2°F) to a July mean of 17.0°C (62.6°F). The level of precipitation varies considerably from region to region. In the far west average annual rainfall is 700–850 mm, while in the central plain it is about 600 mm. The official state language is Lithuanian, a Baltic tongue which uses the Latin alphabet. The predominant religion is Christianity. Most ethnic Lithuanians are Roman Catholics by belief or tradition, but there are small communities of Lutherans and Calvinists, as well as a growing number of modern Protestant denominations. Adherents of Russian Orthodoxy are almost exclusively ethnic Slavs, while most Tatars have retained an adherence to Islam. The national flag (proportions 2 by 1) consists of three equal horizontal stripes of yellow, green and red. The capital is Vilnius.

**Recent History**

In 1569, to counter the threat from the Russian state of Muscovy, the Grand Duchy of Lithuania (established in the mid-13th century) united with Poland in the Union of Lublin, forming a Polish-Lithuanian Commonwealth. In 1795, at the third Partition of the Commonwealth, Lithuania was annexed by the Russian Empire. Uprisings against Russian rule were suppressed in 1830–31 and in 1863, and a policy of 'russification' was conducted, including the prohibition of publications in Lithuanian. Nevertheless, a strong nationalist movement evolved in the late 19th century.

In 1915, after the outbreak of the First World War, Lithuania was occupied by German troops. Despite the occupation, a 'Lithuanian Conference' was convened in September 1917. The Conference demanded the re-establishment of an independent Lithuanian state, and elected a 'Lithuanian Council', headed by Antanas Smetona; it proceeded to declare the independence of Lithuania on 16 February 1918. The new state survived both a Soviet attempt to create a Lithuanian-Belarusian (Byelorussian) Soviet republic and a Polish campaign aimed at reincorporating Lithuania within Poland. At the end of 1920 Poland annexed the region of Vilnius (Wilno), but was forced to recognize the rest of Lithuania as an independent state (with its temporary capital at Kaunas). Soviet Russia recognized Lithuanian independence in the Treaty of Moscow, signed on 12 July 1920.

Lithuania's first Constitution, which declared Lithuania a parliamentary democracy, was adopted on 1 August 1922. However, on 17 December 1926 Antanas Smetona seized power in a military *coup d'état* and established an authoritarian regime which lasted until 1940. Lithuania made important advances in the 1920s, introducing a comprehensive system of education and enjoying considerable success in agriculture, owing to the radical land reform of 1922.

According to the 'Secret Protocols' to the Treaty of Non-Aggression (the 'Molotov-Ribbentrop Pact') that was signed on 23 August 1939 by the USSR and Germany, Lithuania was to be part of the German sphere of influence. However, the Nazi-Soviet Treaty on Friendship and Existing Borders, which was agreed in September (following the outbreak of the Second World War), permitted the USSR to take control of Lithuania. On 10 October Lithuania was compelled to agree to the stationing of 20,000 Soviet troops on its territory. In return, the USSR granted the city of Vilnius (which had been seized by Soviet troops in September) to Lithuania. In June 1940 the USSR dispatched a further 100,000 troops to Lithuania and forced the Lithuanian Government to resign. A Soviet-approved 'People's Government' was formed. Elections to a 'People's Seim' (parliament), which only pro-Soviet candidates were permitted to contest, took place in July. The Seim proclaimed the Lithuanian Soviet Socialist Republic on 21 July. On 3 August Lithuania formally became a Union Republic of the USSR. The establishment of Soviet rule was followed by the arrest and imprisonment of many Lithuanian politicians and government officials.

Some 210,000 people, including 165,000 Jews, were killed during the Nazi occupation of Lithuania in 1941–44. The return of the Soviet Army, in 1944, was not welcomed by most Lithuanians, and anti-Soviet partisan warfare continued until 1952. After the defeat of Germany in 1945, traditional features of Soviet rule were swiftly introduced: Lithuanian agriculture was forcibly collectivized; rapid industrialization was implemented; some 150,000 people were deported; and leaders and members of the Catholic church were persecuted and imprisoned. Lithuanian political parties were disbanded, and exclusive political power became the preserve of the Lithuanian branch of the Communist Party of the Soviet Union (CPSU), the Communist Party of Lithuania (CPL). The CPL was led by Antanas Sniečkus (First Secretary 1940–74).

A significant dissident movement was established during the 1960s and 1970s. There were demonstrations in Kaunas in May 1972, in support of demands for religious and political freedom. With the introduction of the policy of *glasnost* (openness) by the Soviet leader, Mikhail Gorbachev, in the mid-1980s, a limited discussion of previously-censored aspects of Lithuanian history (notably the 'Molotov-Ribbentrop Pact') appeared in the press. Dissident groups sought to take advantage of a more tolerant attitude to political protests by staging a demonstration, in August 1987, which denounced the Pact. Although this demonstration was tolerated, security forces were used in February 1988 to prevent the public celebration of the 70th anniversary of Lithuanian independence. This, together with the dismay among the intelligentsia at the slow pace of reform in the republic, led to the establishment in June of the Lithuanian Movement for Reconstruction (Sąjūdis) by intellectuals. Throughout the remainder of 1988 Sąjūdis organized mass demonstrations to protest against environmental pollution, the suppression of national culture and 'russification', and, in August, to condemn the signing of the Molotov-Ribbentrop Pact. The movement appealed to the CPL to support a declaration of independence and recognition of Lithuanian as the state language. The latter demand was adopted by the Lithuanian Supreme Soviet (legislature) in November, together with restoration of traditional Lithuanian state symbols, but that body failed to declare the supremacy of Lithuania's laws over all-Union (USSR) legislation.

Despite these and other concessions made by the CPL to Lithuanian public opinion during 1988 (including the restoration of Independence Day as a public holiday and the return of church buildings to the Roman Catholic Church), Sąjūdis won the greatest number of seats at elections to the all-Union Congress of People's Deputies in March 1989. Of the 42 popularly-elected deputies, 36 were members of Sąjūdis. Thereafter, the CPL began to adopt a more radical position, in an attempt to retain some measure of popular support. On 18 May the CPL-dominated Supreme Soviet approved a declaration of Lithuanian sovereignty, which asserted the supremacy of Lithuania's laws over all-Union legislation. This was followed by increased public debate concerning the legitimacy of Soviet rule in Lithuania: a commission of the Lithuanian Supreme Soviet declared the establishment of Soviet power in 1940 to have been unconstitutional, and in August, on the 50th anniversary of the signing of the Pact with Nazi Germany, more than 1m. people participated in a 'human chain' extending from Tallinn in Estonia, through Latvia, to Vilnius.

Despite denunciations of Baltic nationalism by the all-Union authorities, the Lithuanian Supreme Soviet continued to adopt reformist legislation, including the establishment of freedom of religion and the legalization of a multi-party system. In December 1989 the CPL, despite an appeal from Gorbachev, declared itself an independent party, no longer subordinate to the CPSU. It also adopted a new programme that condemned communist policies of the past and declared support for multi-party democracy and independent statehood. Shortly afterwards a group of former CPL members who were opposed to independence formed a 'breakaway' movement, the Lithuanian Communist Party on the CPSU Platform (LCP). Meanwhile, Algirdas Brazauskas, First Secretary of the CPL since October 1988, was elected Chairman of the Presidium of the Lithuanian Supreme Soviet, defeating three other candidates, including Romualdas Ozolas, a leading member of Sąjūdis. None the less, Sąjūdis remained the dominant political force in the republic; its supporters won an overall majority in the elections to the Lithuanian Supreme Soviet in February and March 1990. This new pro-independence parliament elected Vytautas Landsbergis, the Chairman of Sąjūdis, to replace Brazauskas as its Chairman (*de facto* President of Lithuania), and on 11 March declared the restoration of Lithuanian independence. (Lithuania thus became the first of the Soviet republics to make such a declaration of independence.) The legislature (which was renamed the Supreme Council) also restored the pre-1940 name of the country (the Republic of Lithuania), and suspended the USSR Constitution on Lithuanian territory. On 17 March Kazimiera Prunskienė, a member of the CPL and hitherto a Deputy Chairman of the Council of Ministers, was appointed to be the first Prime Minister of the restored republic.

The Lithuanian declarations were condemned by a special session of the all-Union Congress of People's Deputies as 'unconstitutional', and Soviet forces occupied some CPL buildings in Vilnius and took control of newspaper-printing presses. In mid-April 1990 an economic embargo was imposed on Lithuania, whereby vital fuel supplies were suspended; it remained in force until late June, when Lithuania agreed to a six-month moratorium on the independence declaration, if formal negotiations began between the Soviet Government and Lithuania. Discussions began in August, but were soon ended by the Soviet Government.

In January 1991 Landsbergis announced that the suspension of the declaration of independence was ended, since substantive negotiations on Lithuania's status had not begun in the six-month period agreed. Tension increased in the republic when the Soviet Government, taking advantage of the crisis in the Persian (Arabian) Gulf region, dispatched to Vilnius troops of the Soviet Ministry of Internal Affairs (notably the special units, known as OMON), which occupied buildings that had previously belonged to the CPSU but had been nationalized by the Lithuanian Government. Meanwhile, there were policy differences within the Lithuanian leadership, and on 8 January Prunskienė and her Council of Ministers resigned after the Supreme Council refused to sanction proposed price increases. She was succeeded as Prime Minister by Gediminas Vagnorius, a member of the Supreme Council.

After more buildings were seized by OMON troops, Landsbergis mobilized popular support to help to defend the parliament building, which he believed to be under threat. On the night of 13–14 January 1991 Soviet troops seized the radio and television centre and the television tower. Thirteen civilians were killed in the attack, and some 500 were injured. The troops' actions were supported by a self-proclaimed National Salvation Committee, which demanded that it be granted full power to impose a state of emergency in the republic.

The military intervention in January 1991 strengthened popular support for independence. A referendum on Lithuanian independence took place in the republic on 9 February: 90.5% of the voters expressed support for the re-establishment of an independent Lithuania and for the withdrawal of the USSR army from the republic. In common with five other Soviet republics, Lithuania refused to conduct the all-Union referendum on the future of the USSR, which was held in the nine remaining republics in March. However, there was unofficial voting in predominantly Russian- and Polish-populated areas, with the overwhelming majority of people approving the preservation of the USSR.

In March 1991 Audrius Butkevičius, the Director-General of the Lithuanian Department of State Defence, was seized by OMON troops, and later in the month OMON troops opened fire on members of the nascent Lithuanian defence force, injuring several people. In May Landsbergis warned that Soviet troops might attempt further military intervention, following a series of attacks by OMON forces on Lithuania's newly-established customs posts on the border with Belarus. In July seven Lithuanian border guards died after being attacked by OMON troops.

In mid-August 1991 the seizure of power in Moscow by the State Committee for the State of Emergency (SCSE) prompted fears in Lithuania that there would be a renewed attempt to overthrow the Landsbergis administration and to reimpose Soviet rule. Soviet military vehicles entered Vilnius, but did not prevent the convening of an emergency session of the Supreme Council, which condemned the SCSE and issued a statement supporting Boris Yeltsin, President of the Russian Federation. There was sporadic violence in the republic when Soviet troops occupied broadcasting facilities and attacked customs posts. One member of the Lithuanian Department of State Defence was killed by Soviet forces.

As the Soviet coup collapsed, the Lithuanian Government ordered the withdrawal of Soviet forces from the republic and banned the LCP. (The CPL—now known as the Lithuanian Democratic Labour Party, LDLP—was not banned.) It also began to assume effective control of its borders, taking over customs posts at airports and on the Polish frontier. The collapse of the coup prompted the long-awaited recognition of Lithuanian independence by other states: by 30 August 1991 more than 40 states had announced the establishment or restoration of diplomatic ties with Lithuania. On 6 September the USSR State Council recognized the independence of Lithuania and the other Baltic republics (Estonia and Latvia), all three of which were admitted to the UN and the Conference on Security and Co-operation in Europe (subsequently renamed the OSCE, see p. 198) later in the month. Throughout the remainder of 1991 the Government continued to develop control over former Soviet institutions, and entered negotiations with Soviet and Russian representatives on matters related to the restoration of Lithuanian independence. Foremost among these was the issue of Soviet troops remaining in Lithuania (see below).

During the first half of 1992 there was an increasing polarity within the Supreme Council between deputies of the ruling Sąjūdis and mainly left-wing opposition parties, most prominently the LDLP, led by Brazauskas. The controversy largely centred on Landsbergis's attempts to institute a strong presidency, as well as what was perceived to be Vagnorius's increasingly authoritarian style of government and his mismanagement of the economy. At the same time there were accusations by some pro-Sąjūdis deputies that the LDLP was attempting to re-establish communist control. A crisis within the Council of Ministers emerged in April, when 10 of its members openly criticized Vagnorius's 'dictatorial' methods, which was followed by the resignation of two government ministers. In May a proposal to introduce an executive presidency was rejected in a referendum. In the same month Vagnorius tendered his resignation as Prime Minister; however, he remained in the post until July, when the legislature approved a motion expressing 'no confidence' in him. In that month the Seimas (as the Supreme Council had been renamed) appointed Aleksandras Abišala, a close associate of Landsbergis, to succeed Vagnorius. A new Council of Ministers was announced by Abišala shortly thereafter. Meanwhile, the growing division within the legislature had led to a boycott by pro-Sąjūdis deputies, rendering it frequently inquorate. In July, however, the Seimas approved a new electoral law, according to which Lithuania's first post-Soviet legislative elections, scheduled for October, would be held under a mixed system of majority voting and proportional representation.

Contrary to expectations, the LDLP emerged convincingly as the leading party in the elections to the Seimas (which took place, in two rounds, on 25 October and 15 November 1992), winning a total of 73 of the 141 seats. Sąjūdis, in alliance with the Citizens' Charter of Lithuania, secured only 30 seats. The defeat of Sąjūdis was attributed, in large part, to popular disenchantment with its management of economic reform and the deteriorating standard of living in the country. The Christian Democratic Party of Lithuania (CDPL), which was closely aligned with Sąjūdis, won 16 seats. Also on 25 October a new Constitution was overwhelmingly approved in a referendum. The new document resolved the controversy regarding presidential authority, stipulating that state powers were to be 'exercised by the Seimas, the President, the Government and the Judiciary', and was adopted by the Seimas on 6 November. Pending elections to the new post of President of the Republic (which were to be held by direct popular vote in early 1993),

Brazauskas was elected by the Seimas to be its Chairman, or acting Head of State.

Following the LDLP's electoral victory, Brazauskas stressed that the party's orientation was not (as some critics still claimed) 'neo-communist' but social democratic; he also advocated a broad coalition government 'of national consensus'. However, Sąjūdis refused to enter any such coalition, preferring to act in opposition. In December Brazauskas appointed Bronislovas Lubys (a Deputy Prime Minister in the outgoing administration) to the post of Prime Minister. A new coalition Council of Ministers was subsequently formed by Lubys; it retained six members of the previous Government, and included only three representatives of the LDLP.

The direct presidential election of 14 February 1993 was won by Brazauskas, with some 60% of the votes. His only rival was Stasys Lozoraitis, an *émigré* for more than 50 years and Lithuania's then ambassador to the USA (five other candidates, including Landsbergis, had withdrawn from the contest). Brazauskas subsequently announced his resignation from the LDLP. In March Adolfas Šleževičius, a former Deputy Minister of Agriculture, replaced Lubys as Prime Minister. In the following month Šleževičius was appointed Chairman of the LDLP. In May a new political organization, the Conservative Party of Lithuania (CP), was formed. It comprised mainly former members of Sąjūdis and was chaired by Landsbergis. Throughout the remainder of the year the CP established itself as the principal opposition party in the republic. In December Sąjūdis announced its transformation from a political organization into a 'public movement', a development which further reflected its diminishing influence in the political life of Lithuania.

During 1993 Lithuania experienced, in common with many other former Soviet republics, an alarming rise in organized crime (in particular, a proliferation of 'mafia' groups), which was attributed, in large part, to the country's general economic decline. Moreover, there were repeated allegations of high-level corruption, including within the Government. Such allegations, combined with reports of ideological divisions within the LDLP, suggested the growing instability of the Government, which was reflected in a number of ministerial resignations or dismissals during the course of the year. The right-wing opposition, led by the CP, consistently questioned the Government's competence and demanded the holding of legislative elections earlier than those scheduled for 1996.

Further resignations or dismissals of Government members continued throughout 1994, including a reshuffle of the Council of Ministers in June, in which three new ministries were created. In the same month the Government survived a vote of 'no confidence', which had been proposed by deputies of the Lithuanian Social Democratic Party in the Seimas. In early May the CP began to campaign for the halting of the country's already advanced privatization programme, claiming that members of the LDLP administration had illegally profited from the sale of state property. By late May more than 300,000 signatures (the requisite number) had been collected in favour of a referendum on the suspension of the privatization programme and the indexation of savings. The referendum was held in late August but was invalidated by an insufficient level of participation. In the following month Prime Minister Šleževičius began legal proceedings against Landsbergis, who had publicly accused the former of 'pursuing personal profit' in connection with the state privatization programme. Court hearings commenced in November, but were suspended in December. Increasing popular support for the CP was confirmed at local elections in March 1995, when the party won some 29% of the votes, while its close ally, the CDPL, received 17%. The LDLP gained only 20%.

Whereas Lithuania's Baltic neighbours, Estonia and Latvia, have large national minorities, ethnic Lithuanians constitute the overwhelming majority of the republic's population; in January 1992 ethnic Lithuanians represented some 80%, while the two largest minority groups, Russians and Poles, represented 9% and 7%, respectively, of the total population. As a result, the requirements for naturalization of non-ethnic Lithuanians have been less stringent than in the neighbouring Baltic republics, where national identity has been perceived as being under threat. Under Lithuania's new citizenship laws (adopted in late 1989), all residents, regardless of ethnic origin, were eligible to apply for naturalization; by early 1993 more than 90% of the country's non-ethnic-Lithuanian residents had been granted citizenship. Mainly because of its citizenship laws, Lithuania's relations with the Russian Federation have been less strained than those of its Baltic neighbours. During 1992 the Russian Government showed an increasing tendency to link the withdrawal of former Soviet troops from Estonia and Latvia with those countries' treatment of their Russian minorities. By contrast, real progress was achieved concerning the estimated 38,000 troops (now under Russian jurisdiction) remaining in Lithuania in early 1992. Negotiations for their withdrawal, which were held between the Lithuanian and Russian Governments during the first half of 1992, initially produced no tangible results, owing largely to Russia's claimed inability to accommodate all the returning troops. A referendum, held in Lithuania in June, overwhelmingly endorsed the immediate withdrawal of the troops. In September the Russian Government agreed to repatriate from Lithuania all the troops by the end of August 1993. There was considerable alarm in October 1992, when it was reported that the Russian President, Boris Yeltsin, had ordered the suspension of troop withdrawals from the Baltic republics, owing to the 'numerous violations of the rights of the Russian-speaking populations' there. However, the Russian Government subsequently appeared to have abandoned this position, and troop withdrawals were resumed.

In February 1993 it was reported that 14,000 former Soviet troops remained in Lithuania. The election in that month of Algirdas Brazauskas as President was expected to enhance future Russian-Lithuanian relations (his policies regarding the Russian Federation were widely believed to be more conciliatory than those of his predecessor). However, the troop withdrawals appeared jeopardized in mid-1993, owing to Lithuanian demands that the Russian Government pay compensation (of some US $166,000m.) for damages inflicted during the Soviet occupation. The Russian Federation declared its readiness to pay reparations only for damages caused after the dissolution of the USSR in December 1991. In mid-August 1993, moreover, the Russian Government suspended the withdrawal of the 2,500 troops remaining in Lithuania, also stating that it would use force if its servicemen were to suffer any harassment. The crisis was dispelled in late August, however, following intensive negotiations between Presidents Brazauskas and Yeltsin. The final troops left Lithuania, as scheduled, on 31 August, when full state sovereignty was perceived as having been restored. In November Lithuania and Russia signed several agreements, including an accord on 'most favoured nation' status in bilateral trade, and one on the transport via Lithuania of Russian military equipment and troops from the Russian exclave of Kaliningrad Oblast (region). However, there was disagreement between the two countries during 1994, following Lithuania's decision to introduce new regulations governing military transits across Lithuanian territory. In response, the Russian Government delayed the implementation of the trade agreement of November 1993. A compromise appeared to have been reached in January 1995, when the Lithuanian Government extended until 1 December the existing procedure for military transits, whereupon the Russian Government indicated that the agreement on bilateral trade would enter into force immediately. Meanwhile, in December 1994, it was announced that a draft treaty on the land border between Lithuania and Russia had been largely completed.

Lithuania's relations with neighbouring Poland have largely been concerned with the status of the Polish minority in Lithuania (and likewise with the ethnic Lithuanian population in Poland). Following the failed Soviet coup attempt of August 1991, leaders of councils in Polish-populated regions of Lithuania were dismissed, in response to their alleged support for the coup, and direct rule was introduced for six months (subsequently extended for a further six-month period). However, in January 1992 Lithuania and Poland signed a 'Declaration on Friendly Relations and Neighbourly Co-operation', which guaranteed the rights of the respective ethnic minorities and also recognized the existing border between the two countries. Negotiations were held during the following two years to formulate a proper treaty of friendship and co-operation. This was finally signed by the respective heads of state in April 1994. The Treaty, notably, did not include a condemnatory reference to Poland's occupation of Vilnius and the surrounding region in 1920-39 (a provision that had originally been demanded by Lithuania). The real improvement in relations between the two countries was confirmed by President Brazauskas's successful visit to Poland in February 1995.

# LITHUANIA

Lithuania has striven to maintain good relations with all the member states of the Commonwealth of Independent States (CIS, see p. 126), which succeeded the USSR upon its dissolution in December 1991. In 1992 and 1993 the majority of Lithuania's foreign trade was still conducted with member states of the CIS, although in 1994 trade with western countries exceeded that with the CIS for the first time. Among the former Soviet republics, Lithuania enjoys closest relations with its Baltic neighbours, Estonia and Latvia, with which it shares strong cultural and historical ties. Relations between the three states are co-ordinated through a consultative inter-parliamentary body, the Baltic Assembly, which was established in late 1991. Lithuania, Latvia and Estonia are also members of the Council of Baltic Sea States (see p. 238). In addition, Lithuania seeks to expand relations with the Scandinavian countries as well as with the member states of the Visegrad Group (the Czech Republic, Hungary, Poland and Slovakia), while pursuing a policy of close co-operation with, and eventual integration into, the political, economic and defence systems of western Europe.

## Government

Under the terms of the Constitution that was approved in a national referendum on 25 October 1992, supreme legislative authority resides with the Seimas (Parliament), which has 141 members, elected by universal adult suffrage for a four-year term. The President of the Republic (who is Head of State) is elected by direct popular vote for a period of five years (and a maximum of two consecutive terms). Executive power is vested in the Council of Ministers. This is headed by the Prime Minister, who is appointed by the President with the approval of the Seimas. For administrative purposes, Lithuania is divided into 10 districts (subdivided into 56 municipalities).

## Defence

Until independence Lithuania had no armed forces separate from those of the USSR. The Department of State Defence (established in April 1990) was reorganized as the Ministry of Defence in October 1991. In June 1994 Lithuania's armed forces totalled an estimated 8,900: army 4,300 (including conscripts), navy 350, air force 250, and a border guard of 4,000. Military service is compulsory and lasts for 12 months. Defence expenditure in 1994 was estimated to be equivalent to US $33m.

## Economic Affairs

In 1993, according to estimates by the World Bank, Lithuania's gross national product (GNP), measured at average 1991–93 prices, was US $4,891m., equivalent to $1,310 per head. During 1985–93, it was estimated, GNP per head declined, in real terms, at an average annual rate of 6.4%. Over the same period, the population increased by an annual average of 0.7%. Lithuania's gross domestic product (GDP) was estimated to have decreased, in real terms, by 13.4% in 1991, by 37.7% in 1992, and by 16.2% in 1993. However, a modest increase in overall GDP (of some 0.6%) was reported to have been achieved in 1994.

In 1992 agriculture (including forestry and fishing) contributed 24.0% of Lithuania's GDP and provided 19.0% of employment. The major agricultural sector is animal husbandry, which accounted for more than 50% of the value of total agricultural production in 1991. Principal crops are cereals, sugar beet, potatoes and vegetables. In 1991 legislation was adopted which permitted the restitution of land to its former owners. In that year the 'privatization' of state-owned farms and the reorganization of collective farms was initiated. By August 1993 some 80% of formerly state-owned agricultural assets had been transferred to private ownership. In 1993 agricultural production declined by an estimated 8%, compared with 1992.

Industry (including mining, manufacturing, construction and power) accounted for 33.9% of GDP, and provided 38.0% of employment, in 1992. The major industrial sectors are food-processing (31.5% of the total value of industrial output in 1991), light industry (21.3%) and machine-building and metal-working (18.3%). In 1993 mining provided only 0.2% of employment, while manufacturing provided 23.6%. In that year, however, industrial production was estimated to have declined by 47%, compared with 1992.

Lithuania is not richly endowed with mineral resources; however, there are small deposits of petroleum and natural gas, as well as reserves of peat and materials used in construction (limestone, gravel, clay and sand). Hence, Lithuania is highly dependent on imported raw materials and fuels (mostly petroleum, coal and natural gas), both for industry and for energy generation.

There is a nuclear power station at Ignalina. In 1993, according to preliminary estimates, nuclear power provided 86.9% of total electricity production, followed by thermal power (9.0%) and hydroelectric power (4.1%). Although a major importer of fuel products (which accounted for some 50% of the value of merchandise imports in 1993), Lithuania has substantial petroleum-refining and electricity-generating capacities, which enable it to export refined oil products and electricity. In 1991 Lithuania exported 44% of its gross electricity generation.

Services provided 42.7% of total employment, and 42.1% of GDP, in 1992. The GDP of the services sector declined, in real terms, by 17% in 1991.

In 1993 Lithuania recorded a visible trade deficit of US $267m., and there was a deficit of $84m. on the current account of the balance of payments. In the early 1990s the majority of Lithuania's trade was still conducted with republics of the former USSR, although trade with western countries increased steadily. In 1993 the Russian Federation was Lithuania's most important trading partner (accounting for 44% of its total trade turnover), followed by Ukraine and Germany. In 1993 the principal exports were energy products, light industrial and food products. The principal imports in that year were petroleum and natural gas products, machinery and metalworking products, chemicals and light industrial products.

In 1993 there was a budgetary surplus of 86.4m. litai. However, in the following year a budgetary deficit of 337.8m. litai was recorded. Lithuania's total external debt was US $291.2m. at the end of 1993, of which $163.5m. was long-term public debt. In 1992 the average annual rate of inflation was 1,020.8%; however, it declined to 410.2% in 1993 and to 45.1% in 1994. In March 1995 there were an estimated 107,000 people registered as unemployed (5.1% of the labour force).

In 1992 Lithuania became a member of the IMF and the World Bank. It also joined, as a 'Country of Operations', the European Bank for Reconstruction and Development (EBRD, see p. 140). An agreement on a free-trade area between Lithuania, Latvia and Estonia entered into force in April 1994. Lithuania became an associate member of the European Union in May 1995.

During the early 1990s the Government embarked upon a comprehensive programme of market-orientated reforms, including the transfer to private ownership of state-owned enterprises and the adoption of measures to encourage foreign investment. However, Lithuania's economic development was impeded by shortages of fuels and other essential commodities, arising from the disruption of trading relations with countries of the former USSR and the transition to payments in convertible currencies at world market prices. This resulted in a severe decline in industrial productivity and a consequent deterioration in living standards; in 1992 76% of families were officially reported to be living in poverty. Furthermore, the rate of inflation escalated dramatically during 1992, although, under the Government's stabilization programme, inflation was successfully curbed during 1993 and 1994, and the decline in real wages was also halted. An economic recovery appeared to have been achieved in 1994, when overall GDP increased by an estimated 0.6% (after four successive years of severe decline).

In May 1992 the Government initiated a programme of economic reform (in conjunction with, and supported by, the IMF), which envisaged greater stability of the national currency and economy, including a balanced budget, free market prices, banking reform and the 'privatization' of the state sector (by January 1995 78% of former state enterprises had been 'privatized'). In October 1992 the rouble was replaced by a provisional coupon currency, the talonas (which had been circulating in parallel with the rouble since May). A new national curency, the litas, was introduced in June 1993.

## Social Welfare

In pre-1940 Lithuania health care was provided by both state and private facilities. A comprehensive state-funded health system was introduced under Soviet rule. In October 1991, shortly after the re-establishment of Lithuanian independence, a National Health Concept was adopted, which strongly criticized the Soviet system and emphasized the need for far-reaching reforms. Although private practices had been legalized in 1990 and reforms in the health insurance system were subsequently implemented, by late 1993 the Lithuanian parliament had yet to adopt the necessary legislation to restructure the health care system. In 1993 there were 14,670 physicians and 39,896 paramedical personnel. In the following year there were 43,862 hospital beds, equivalent to 118 beds per 10,000 inhabitants. A national social insurance scheme covers all residents. The 1992 Constitution guarantees the right of citizens to old-age and disability pensions, as well as to social assistance in the event of unemployment, sickness, widowhood, etc. According to provisional official figures, 49.4% of budgetary spending (1,258m. litai) was to be allocated to the social and cultural spheres in 1994.

### Education

The reform of the Lithuanian educational system began to be planned in 1989, with major restructuring taking place after independence was restored in 1991. Under the terms of the 1992 Constitution, education, beginning at six years of age, is compulsory until the age of 16, and is available free of charge at all levels. There are three principal levels of education: general (from six or seven to 14 years of age), secondary general and secondary specialized (15–17) and higher. There are three types of general-education school: elementary, basic and secondary. In the 1993/94 academic year 510,500 students were enrolled in 2,317 general-education schools. In that year there were 15 institutions of higher education (including six universities), with a total enrolment of 53,000. In 1992 the total enrolment at general-education schools was equivalent to 83% of the population aged seven to 18 years. In 1991 the first seven private schools were opened (in 1994 there were 17). Lithuanian is the main language of instruction, although there are general-education schools in which the medium of instruction is Russian, Polish or Yiddish. There are also schools offering instruction in two or more languages. Expenditure on education by all levels of government in 1992 was 179m. litai (22.1% of total public spending). In 1989, according to census results, the average rate of adult illiteracy was only 1.6% (males 0.8%; females 2.2%).

### Public Holidays

**1995:** 1 January (New Year's Day), 16 February (Day of the Restoration of the Lithuanian State), 17 April (Easter Monday), 6 July (Anniversary of the Coronation of Grand Duke Mindaugas of Lithuania), 1 November (All Saints' Day), 25–26 December (Christmas).

**1996:** 1 January (New Year's Day), 16 February (Day of the Restoration of the Lithuanian State), 8 April (Easter Monday), 6 July (Anniversary of the Coronation of Grand Duke Mindaugas of Lithuania), 1 November (All Saints' Day), 25–26 December (Christmas).

### Weights and Measures

The metric system is in force.

# Statistical Survey

Source (unless otherwise indicated): Ministry of Culture, J. Basanavičiaus 5, Vilnius 2683; tel. (2) 619-486; fax (2) 623-120.

## Area and Population

### AREA, POPULATION AND DENSITY

| | |
|---|---|
| Area (sq km) | 65,300* |
| **Population (census results)†** | |
| 17 January 1979 | 3,391,490 |
| 12 January 1989 | |
|   Males | 1,738,953 |
|   Females | 1,935,849 |
|   Total | 3,674,802 |
| **Population (official estimates at 1 January)** | |
| 1993 | 3,751,400 |
| 1994 | 3,738,800 |
| 1995 | 3,717,000 |
| Density (per sq km) at 1 January 1995 | 56.9 |

\* 25,212 sq miles.

† Figures refer to the *de jure* population. The *de facto* total at the 1989 census was 3,689,779, comprising (in rounded figures) 1,747,200 males and 1,942,600 females.

### POPULATION BY NATIONALITY

(permanent inhabitants, official estimates at 1 January 1994)*

| | '000 | % |
|---|---|---|
| Lithuanian | 3,019.0 | 81.1 |
| Russian | 316.0 | 8.5 |
| Polish | 261.5 | 7.0 |
| Belarusian | 57.0 | 1.5 |
| Ukrainian | 38.5 | 1.0 |
| **Total** (incl. others) | 3,724.0 | 100.0 |

\* Figures are provisional. The revised total is 3,738,800.

### PRINCIPAL TOWNS (estimated population at 1 January 1994)

| | | | |
|---|---|---|---|
| Vilnius (capital) | 584,400 | Šiauliai | 146,600 |
| Kaunas | 423,900 | Panevėžys | 131,600 |
| Klaipėda | 204,600 | | |

### BIRTHS, MARRIAGES AND DEATHS

| | Registered live births | | Registered marriages | | Registered deaths | |
|---|---|---|---|---|---|---|
| | Number | Rate (per 1,000) | Number | Rate (per 1,000) | Number | Rate (per 1,000) |
| 1986 | 59,705 | 16.7 | n.a. | n.a. | 35,788 | 10.0 |
| 1987 | 59,360 | 16.4 | 35,122 | 9.7 | 36,917 | 10.2 |
| 1988 | 56,727 | 15.5 | 34,906 | 9.6 | 37,649 | 10.3 |
| 1989 | 55,782 | 15.1 | 34,630 | 9.4 | 38,150 | 10.3 |
| 1990 | 56,868 | 15.3 | 36,310 | 9.8 | 39,760 | 10.7 |
| 1991 | 56,219 | 15.0 | 34,241 | 9.2 | 41,013 | 11.0 |
| 1992 | 53,617 | 14.3 | 30,100 | 8.0 | 41,455 | 11.0 |
| 1993 | 46,727 | 12.5 | 23,709 | 6.3 | 46,107 | 12.3 |

**1994** (rates per 1,000): Births 12.0; Deaths 12.8.

**Expectation of life** (years at birth, 1993): 69.1 (males 63.3; females 75.0).

LITHUANIA

**EMPLOYMENT** (annual averages, '000 persons)

|  | 1990 | 1991 | 1992 |
|---|---|---|---|
| Agriculture, hunting, forestry and fishing | 350.2 | 337.5 | 353.1 |
| Mining and quarrying |  |  | 6.0 |
| Manufacturing | 555.1 | 566.9 | 498.9 |
| Electricity, gas and water |  |  | 30.5 |
| Construction | 209.0 | 182.7 | 169.4 |
| Trade, restaurants and hotels | 152.3 | 188.6 | 227.4 |
| Transport, storage and communications | 105.0 | 132.5 | 124.0 |
| Financing, insurance, real estate and business services | 12.0 | 10.7 | 33.2 |
| Community, social and personal services | 461.0 | 470.7 | 408.3 |
| Activities not adequately defined | 8.1 | 8.0 | 4.4 |
| **Total employed** | 1,852.7 | 1,897.6 | 1,855.2 |
| Males | 855.9 | 876.7 | 873.8 |
| Females | 996.8 | 1,020.9 | 981.4 |

**1989 census** (persons aged 15 years and over): Total labour force 1,901,232 (males 982,695; females 918,537).

Source: International Labour Office, *Year Book of Labour Statistics*.

# Agriculture

**PRINCIPAL CROPS** ('000 metric tons)

|  | 1991 | 1992 | 1993 |
|---|---|---|---|
| Wheat | 855 | 834 | 919* |
| Barley | 1,699 | 955 | 842* |
| Rye | 345 | 342 | 437* |
| Oats | 233 | 51 | 36* |
| Other cereals | 23 | 16 | 6 |
| Potatoes | 1,508 | 1,079 | 1,200† |
| Dry peas | 119 | 14 | 5† |
| Other pulses | 102 | 13 | 5† |
| Rapeseed | 13 | 8 | 8† |
| Cabbages | 145 | 112 | 130† |
| Cucumbers and gherkins | 34 | 10 | 10† |
| Onions (dry) | 22 | 13 | 13† |
| Carrots | 85 | 26 | 38† |
| Other vegetables | 180 | 100 | 89 |
| Sugar beets | 925 | 622 | 700† |
| Fruits and berries | 276 | 118* | 120 |
| Flax fibre and tow | 13.1 | 3.9 | 1.7 |

\* Unofficial figure.  † FAO estimate.

Source: mainly FAO, *Production Yearbook*.

**LIVESTOCK** ('000 head at 1 January)

|  | 1992 | 1993 | 1994 |
|---|---|---|---|
| Horses | 83 | 80 | 81.3 |
| Cattle | 2,197 | 1,701 | 1,384.3 |
| Pigs | 2,180 | 1,360 | 1,196.2 |
| Sheep | 58 | 52 | 45.0 |
| Goats | 6 | 9 | 10.4 |
| Poultry | 16,000* | 8,000 | 8,728.2 |

\* Unofficial figure.

Source: partly FAO, *Production Yearbook*.

**LIVESTOCK PRODUCTS**
('000 metric tons, unless otherwise indicated)

|  | 1991 | 1992 | 1993 |
|---|---|---|---|
| Beef and veal | 209 | 176 | 183* |
| Pig meat | 194 | 163 | 179* |
| Poultry meat | 44 | 37 | 40† |
| Cows' milk | 2,916 | 2,245 | 2,500* |
| Cheese | n.a. | 17.5 | 19.0† |
| Butter | 67.2 | 49.2 | 53.0* |
| Eggs | 69.2* | 53.2* | 55.0† |
| Honey | 2.7 | 3.0† | 3.0† |
| Wool (metric tons): |  |  |  |
| greasy | 128 | 120† | 125† |
| scoured | 77 | 72 | 75† |

\* Unofficial figure.  † FAO estimate.

Source: FAO, *Production Yearbook*.

# Forestry

**SAWNWOOD PRODUCTION** ('000 cubic metres)

|  | 1990 | 1991 | 1992 |
|---|---|---|---|
| **Total** (incl. railway sleepers) | 776 | 664 | 766 |

# Fishing

('000 metric tons, live weight)

|  | 1991 | 1992 |
|---|---|---|
| Common carp | 4.8 | 3.9 |
| Blue whiting | 6.4 | 13.8 |
| Silver hake | 11.7 | — |
| Atlantic redfishes | 3.4 | 10.5 |
| Needlefishes | — | 8.5 |
| Chilean jack mackerel | 109.3 | 7.8 |
| Other jack and horse mackerels | 75.7 | 45.5 |
| Atlantic herring | 6.6 | 5.8 |
| Round sardinella | 95.0 | 35.3 |
| European pilchard (sardine) | 47.6 | 6.8 |
| European anchovy | 10.3 | 0.0 |
| Largehead hairtail | 18.6 | 14.2 |
| Chub mackerel | 12.2 | 4.2 |
| **Total catch** (incl. others) | 475.0 | 192.5 |

Source: FAO, *Yearbook of Fishery Statistics*.
**1993:** Total catch 119,700 metric tons.

# Mining

('000 metric tons, unless otherwise indicated)

|  | 1989 | 1990 | 1991 |
|---|---|---|---|
| Dolomite ('000 cubic metres) | 1,390 | 1,200 | 990 |
| Peat | 1,745 | 763 | 650 |
| Limestone | 6,800 | 6,850 | 6,370 |
| Clay | 2,601 | 2,911 | 2,353 |
| Crude petroleum | n.a. | 11.7 | 33.0 |
| Sand |  |  |  |
| quartz | 120 | 110 | 110 |
| building | 5,020 | 3,591 | 3,280 |
| Gravel | 16,700 | 15,341 | 14,600 |

**1993:** Peat 144,000 metric tons; Quartz sand 86,000 cubic metres; Gravel 588,000 cubic metres.
**1994:** Peat 288,000 metric tons.

# LITHUANIA

## Industry

**SELECTED PRODUCTS**
('000 metric tons, unless otherwise indicated)

|  | 1992 | 1993 | 1994 |
|---|---|---|---|
| Refined sugar | 87.7 | 91.7 | 50.1 |
| Paper | 34.6 | 14.0 | 13.6 |
| Paperboard | 49.8 | 16.5 | 7.5 |
| Clay building bricks (million) | 1,049 | 425 | 343.6 |
| Television receivers ('000) | 444.8 | 423.1 | 177.4 |
| Domestic refrigerators ('000) | 137.4 | 276.3 | 265.7 |
| Electric energy (million kWh) | 18,707 | 14,138 | 9,961 |

## Finance

**CURRENCY AND EXCHANGE RATES**

**Monetary Units**
100 centas = 1 litas (plural: litai).

**Sterling and Dollar Equivalents** (31 December 1994)
£1 sterling = 6.26 litai;
US $1 = 4.00 litai;
100 litai = £15.98 = $25.00.

Note: In June 1993 Lithuania reintroduced its national currency, the litas, replacing a temporary coupon currency, the talonas, at a conversion rate of 1 litas = 100 talonai. The talonas had been introduced in May 1992, initially circulating alongside (and at par with) the Russian (formerly Soviet) rouble (for details of exchange rates for the rouble, see the chapter on Russia). From October 1992 the Russian rouble ceased to be legal tender in Lithuania. At 31 December 1992 the exchange rate was US $1 = 378.85 talonai. A rate of $1 = 4.00 litai was introduced on 1 April 1994.

**NATIONAL BUDGET** (million litai)*

| Revenue | 1991 | 1992 | 1993 |
|---|---|---|---|
| Taxation | 114.0 | 742.0 | 2,396.1 |
| Taxes on income and profits | 45.9 | 356.8 | 1,255.4 |
| Individual | 19.9 | 167.0 | 614.7 |
| Corporate | 26.0 | 189.8 | 640.7 |
| Taxes on goods and services | 57.8 | 359.9 | 981.1 |
| Excises | 49.8 | 111.1 | 212.3 |
| Value-added tax | 2.6 | 239.7 | 760.4 |
| Other current revenue | 8.5 | 33.1 | 337.1 |
| **Total** | 122.5 | 775.1 | 2,733.2 |

| Expenditure† | 1991 | 1992 | 1993 |
|---|---|---|---|
| General public services |  |  | 142.7 |
| Defence | 7.9 | 89.5 | 85.9 |
| Courts and police |  |  | 219.2 |
| Social welfare | 47.8 | 325.7 | 1,234.9 |
| Other purposes | 47.4 | 321.7 | 963.1 |
| **Total** | 103.1 | 736.9 | 2,645.8 |

**1994** (provisional, million litai): Revenue 2,393.6; Expenditure 2,527.3.

* Figures represent a consolidation of state and municipal budgets, excluding extrabudgetary accounts.

† Excluding lending minus repayments (million litai): 8.4 in 1991; –3.2 in 1992.

**Social Insurance Fund** (million litai): Revenue 38.3 in 1991, 261.0 in 1992, 774.2 in 1993; Expenditure 36.5 in 1991, 250.0 in 1992, 782 (provisional) in 1993.

**OFFICIAL RESERVES** (US $ million at 31 December)

|  | 1992 | 1993 |
|---|---|---|
| Gold* | 61.9 | 61.9 |
| Foreign exchange | 43.8 | 347.9 |
| **Total** | 105.7 | 409.8 |

* Valued at US $333 per troy ounce.

Sources: Bank of Lithuania and IMF.

**MONEY SUPPLY** (million litai at 31 December)

|  | 1991 | 1992 | 1993 |
|---|---|---|---|
| Currency outside banks | 73.8 | 183.9 | 792.2 |
| Demand deposits at banks | 128.0 | 452.8 | 982.7 |
| **Total money** | 201.8 | 636.7 | 1,774.9 |

**COST OF LIVING** (Consumer Price Index; base: 1992 = 100)

|  | 1993 |
|---|---|
| Food (excl. alcohol) | 531 |
| Alcoholic beverages | 334 |
| Non-food products | 504 |
| Services | 547 |
| **All items** | 510 |

**NATIONAL ACCOUNTS**

**Expenditure on the Gross Domestic Product**
(million litai at current prices)

|  | 1990 | 1991 | 1992 |
|---|---|---|---|
| Government final consumption expenditure | 25.2 | 64.2 | 426.6 |
| Private final consumption expenditure | 70.9 | 197.0 | 2,173.4 |
| Increase in stocks | 7.2 | 13.0 | 162.3 |
| Gross fixed capital formation | 37.1 | 71.8 | 429.8 |
| **Total domestic expenditure** | 140.3 | 346.0 | 3,192.1 |
| Net exports of goods and services | –11.4 | 35.9 | 76.5 |
| **GDP in purchasers' values** | 129.0 | 381.8 | 3,268.6 |

Source: IMF, *Lithuania, Economic Review*.
**1993**: GDP 8,350.7 million litai.

**Gross Domestic Product by Economic Activity**
(million roubles/talonai at current prices)

|  | 1989 | 1990 | 1991 |
|---|---|---|---|
| Agriculture | 3,339 | 3,558 | 8,100 |
| Forestry | 14 | 13 |  |
| Industry* | 4,225 | 4,228 | 18,199 |
| Construction | 1,277 | 1,356 | 1,861 |
| Transport and communications | 654 | 775 | 2,014 |
| Other material services | 957 | 1,074 | 3,634 |
| Non-material services | 1,791 | 1,893 | 5,296 |
| **Total** | 12,258 | 12,897 | 39,105 |

* Comprising manufacturing (except printing and publishing), mining and quarrying, electricity, gas, water, logging and fishing.

Source: World Bank, *Statistical Handbook: States of the Former USSR*.

**BALANCE OF PAYMENTS** (US $ million)

|  | 1991 | 1992 | 1993 |
|---|---|---|---|
| Merchandise exports f.o.b. | 6,783 | 1,145 | 1,877 |
| Merchandise imports f.o.b. | –4,937 | –1,084 | –2,144 |
| **Trade balance** | 1,846 | 61 | –267 |
| Services (net) | n.a. | –18 | 50 |
| Other income (net) | n.a. | 9 | 13 |
| Private unrequited transfers (net) | n.a. | 10 | 12 |
| Official unrequited transfers (net) | n.a. | 101 | 108 |
| **Current balance** | n.a. | 163 | –84 |
| Direct investment (net) | n.a. | 10 | 83 |
| Other capital (net) | n.a. | 84 | 122 |
| Net errors and omissions | n.a. | –132 | 35 |
| **Overall balance** | n.a. | 125 | 156 |

Source: IMF, mainly *Lithuania, Economic Review*.

LITHUANIA

## External Trade

**PRINCIPAL COMMODITIES** (million litai)*

| Imports | 1993 |
|---|---|
| Machinery and transport equipment | 499 |
| Mineral fuels and metals | 3,736 |
| Chemicals and fertilizers | 246 |
| Raw materials and intermediate products (non-food) | 264 |
| Raw materials for food and spices | 137 |
| Non-food consumer goods | 581 |
| **Total** (incl. others) | 5,609 |

| Exports | 1993 |
|---|---|
| Machinery and transport equipment | 564 |
| Mineral fuels and metals | 2,220 |
| Chemicals and fertilizers | 249 |
| Construction materials | 104 |
| Raw materials and intermediate products (non-food) | 258 |
| Food products | 620 |
| Non-food consumer goods | 896 |
| Material services | 395 |
| **Total** (incl. others) | 5,336 |

* Figures refer only to trade with the former USSR, western Europe and North America.

**PRINCIPAL TRADING PARTNERS** (million litai)

| Imports | 1993 |
|---|---|
| Belarus | 325.8 |
| Denmark | 239.3 |
| Estonia | 77.8 |
| Germany | 945.3 |
| Italy | 179.7 |
| Kazakhstan | 201.0 |
| Latvia | 143.4 |
| Netherlands | 223.9 |
| Poland | 214.5 |
| Russia | 5,256.5 |
| Ukraine | 609.3 |
| **Total** (incl. others) | 9,798.2 |

| Exports | 1993 |
|---|---|
| Belarus | 641.1 |
| Denmark | 130.4 |
| Estonia | 218.7 |
| Germany | 592.0 |
| Italy | 187.8 |
| Kazakhstan | 167.3 |
| Latvia | 635.7 |
| Netherlands | 243.7 |
| Poland | 608.0 |
| Russia | 2,884.7 |
| Ukraine | 977.5 |
| **Total** (incl. others) | 8,707.0 |

## Transport

**RAILWAYS** (traffic)

| | 1990 | 1991 | 1993* |
|---|---|---|---|
| Passenger journeys (million) | 32.6 | 24.2 | 25.1 |
| Passenger-km (million) | 3,640 | 3,225 | 2,700 |
| Freight transported (million metric tons) | 27.1 | 27.9 | 38.4 |
| Freight ton-km (million) | 19,258 | 17,748 | 11,030 |

* Figures for 1992 are not available.

**ROAD TRAFFIC** (public transport and freight)

| | 1993 |
|---|---|
| Passenger journeys (million) | 789.9 |
| Passenger-km (million) | 4,522 |
| Freight transported (million metric tons) | 170.2 |
| Freight ton-km (million) | 6,906 |

**ROAD TRAFFIC** (motor vehicles in use at 31 December)

| | 1991 | 1992 | 1993 |
|---|---|---|---|
| Passenger cars | 530,824 | 565,320 | 597,735 |
| Buses and coaches* | 4,886 | 4,735 | 4,390 |
| Lorries and vans | 84,341 | 87,321 | 89,530 |
| Motor cycles and mopeds | 196,075 | 192,148 | 180,452 |

* Public transport.

Source: International Road Federation, *World Road Statistics*.

**INLAND WATERWAYS**

| | 1993 | 1994 |
|---|---|---|
| Passenger journeys ('000) | 1,300 | 1,835.3 |
| Freight transported ('000 metric tons) | 700 | 655.5 |

**SHIPPING**

**Merchant Fleet** (vessels at 30 June)

| | 1992 |
|---|---|
| Displacement ('000 grt) | 668 |

Source: UN, *Statistical Yearbook*.

**Sea-borne Traffic**

| | 1993 |
|---|---|
| Passenger journeys ('000) | 15.9 |
| Passenger-km (million) | 8 |
| Freight transported (million metric tons) | 5.1 |
| Freight ton-km (million) | 15,821 |
| Goods loaded and unloaded ('000 metric tons) | 15,530 |

**CIVIL AVIATION** (traffic)

| | 1993 | 1994 |
|---|---|---|
| Passengers carried ('000) | 200 | 264.6 |
| Passenger-km (million) | 315 | 379.4 |
| Freight transported ('000 metric tons) | 2.8 | 4.4 |
| Freight ton-km ('000) | 200 | n.a. |

## Communications Media

|  | 1991 | 1992* | 1993 |
|---|---|---|---|
| Radio receivers ('000 in use) | 1,420* | 1,427 | 1,400 |
| Television receivers ('000 in use) | 1,400* | 1,410 | 1,770 |
| Telephones ('000 main lines in use) | 814 | n.a. | n.a. |
| Book production: titles† | 2,482 | 2,361 | 2,224 |
| Daily newspapers | 16 | 18 | 17 |
| Average circulation ('000) | n.a. | 836 | n.a. |
| Non-daily newspapers | n.a. | 395 | n.a. |
| Average circulation ('000) | n.a. | 2,851 | n.a. |
| Other periodicals | n.a. | 237 | 212 |
| Average circulation ('000) | n.a. | 2,602 | n.a. |

* Source: UNESCO, *Statistical Yearbook*.

## Education

(1993/94)

|  | Institutions | Students |
|---|---|---|
| General-education schools* | 2,317 | 510,500 |
| Secondary specialized institutions | 108 | 45,200 |
| College-type schools | 57 | 24,100 |
| Higher schools (incl. universities) | 15 | 53,000 |

* Including elementary (847), basic schools (576) and secondary schools (629).

Teachers (1992): Pre-primary schools 14,472; Primary and general secondary schools 47,504 (Source: UNESCO, *Statistical Yearbook*).

# Directory

## The Constitution

The Constitution was approved in a national referendum on 25 October 1992 and adopted by the Seimas on 6 November. The following is a summary of its main provisions:

### THE STATE

The Republic of Lithuania is an independent and democratic republic; its sovereignty is vested in the people, who exercise their supreme power either directly or through their democratically elected representatives. The powers of the State are exercised by the Seimas (Parliament), the President of the Republic, the Government and the Judiciary. The most significant issues concerning the State and the people are decided by referendum.

The territory of the republic is integral. Citizenship is acquired by birth or on other grounds determined by law. With certain exceptions established by law, no person may be a citizen of Lithuania and of another state at the same time. Lithuanian is the state languge.

### THE INDIVIDUAL AND THE STATE

The rights and freedoms of individuals are inviolable. Property is inviolable, and the rights of ownership are protected by law. Freedom of thought, conscience and religion are guaranteed. All persons are equal before the law. No one may be discriminated against on the basis of sex, race, nationality, language, origin, social status, religion or opinion. Citizens may choose their place of residence in Lithuania freely, and may leave the country at their own will. Citizens are guaranteed the right to form societies, political parties and associations. Citizens who belong to ethnic communities have the right to foster their language, culture and customs.

### SOCIETY AND THE STATE

The family is the basis of society and the State. Education is compulsory until the age of 16. Education at state and local government institutions is free of charge at all levels. State and local government establishments of education are secular, although, at the request of parents, they may offer classes in religious instruction. The State recognizes traditional Lithuanian and other churches and religious organizations, but there is no state religion. Censorship of mass media is prohibited. Ethnic communities may independently administer the affairs of their ethnic culture, education, organizations, etc. The State supports ethnic communities.

### NATIONAL ECONOMY AND LABOUR

Lithuania's economy is based on the right to private ownership and freedom of individual economic activity. Every person may freely choose an occupation, and has the right to adequate, safe and healthy working conditions, adequate compensation for work, and social security in the event of unemployment. Trade unions may be freely established and may function independently. Employees have the right to strike in order to protect their economic and social interests. The state guarantees the right of citizens to old-age and disability pensions, as well as to social assistance in the event of unemployment, sickness, widowhood, etc.

### THE SEIMAS

Legislative power rests with the Seimas. It comprises 141 members, elected for a four-year term on the basis of universal, equal and direct suffrage by secret ballot. Any citizen who has attained 25 years of age may be a candidate for the Seimas. Members of the Seimas may not be found criminally responsible, may not be arrested, and may not be subjected to any other restrictions of personal freedom, without the consent of the Seimas. The Seimas convenes for two regular four-months sessions every year.

The Seimas considers and enacts amendments to the Constitution; enacts laws; adopts resolutions for the organization of referendums; announces presidential elections; approves or rejects the candidature of the Prime Minister, as proposed by the President of the Republic; establishes or abolishes government ministries, upon the recommendation of the Government; supervises the activities of the Government, with the power to express a vote of 'no confidence' in the Prime Minister or individual ministers; appoints judges to the Constitutional Court and the Supreme Court; approves the state budget and supervises the implementation thereof; establishes state taxes and other obligatory payments; ratifies or denounces international treaties whereto the republic is a party, and considers other issues of foreign policy; establishes administrative divisions of the republic; issues acts of amnesty; imposes direct administration and martial law, declares states of emergency, announces mobilization, and adopts decisions to use the armed forces.

### THE PRESIDENT OF THE REPUBLIC

The President of the Republic is the Head of State. Any Lithuanian citizen by birth, who has lived in Lithuania for at least the three preceding years, who has reached 40 years of age and who is eligible for election to the Seimas, may be elected President of the Republic. The President is elected by the citizens of the republic, on the basis of universal, equal and direct suffrage by secret ballot, for a term of five years. No person may be elected to the office for more than two consecutive terms.

The President resolves basic issues of foreign policy and, in conjunction with the Government, implements foreign policy; signs international treaties and submits them to the Seimas for ratification; appoints or recalls, upon the recommendation of the Government, diplomatic representatives of Lithuania in foreign states and international organizations; appoints, upon the approval of the Seimas, the Prime Minister, and charges him/her with forming the Government, and approves its composition; removes, upon the approval of the Seimas, the Prime Minister from office; appoints or dismisses individual ministers, upon the recommendation of the Prime Minister; appoints or dismisses, upon the approval of the Seimas, the Commander-in-Chief of the armed forces and the head of the Security Service.

### THE GOVERNMENT

Executive power is held by the Government of the republic (Council of Ministers), which consists of the Prime Minister and other ministers. The Prime Minister is appointed and dismissed by the President of the Republic, with the approval of the Seimas. Ministers are appointed by the President, on the nomination of the Prime Minister.

# LITHUANIA

The Government administers the affairs of the country, protects the inviolability of the territory of Lithuania, and ensures state security and public order; implements laws and resolutions of the Seimas as well as presidential decrees; co-ordinates the activities of the ministries and other governmental institutions; prepares the draft state budget and submits it to the Seimas; executes the state budget and reports to the Seimas on its fulfilment; drafts legislative proposals and submits them to the Seimas for consideration; establishes and maintains diplomatic representation with foreign countries and international organizations.

### JUDICIAL SYSTEM

The judicial system is independent of the authority of the legislative and executive branches of government. It consists of a Constitutional Court, a Supreme Court, a Court of Appeal, and district and local courts (for details, see section on Judicial System below).

## The Government

### HEAD OF STATE

**President:** ALGIRDAS MYKOLAS BRAZAUSKAS (elected by direct popular vote 14 February 1993).

### COUNCIL OF MINISTERS
(May 1995)

**Prime Minister:** ADOLFAS ŠLEŽEVIČIUS.
**Minister of the Economy:** ALEKSANDRAS VASILIAUSKAS.
**Minister of Energy:** ARVYDAS KOSTAS LESCINSKAS.
**Minister of Finance:** REINOLDIJUS ŠARKINAS.
**Minister of Defence:** LINAS LINKEVIČIUS.
**Minister of Culture:** JUOZAS NEKROŠIUS.
**Minister of Forestry:** ALBERTAS VASILIAUSKAS.
**Minister of Industry and Trade:** KAZIMIERAS JUOZAS KLIMAŠAUSKAS.
**Minister of Communications and Information Technology:** GINTAUTAS ŽINTELIS.
**Minister of Social Welfare and Labour:** MINDAUGAS MIKAILA.
**Minister of Housing and Urban Development:** JULIUS LAICONAS.
**Minister of Justice:** JONAS PRAPIESTIS.
**Minister of Transport:** JONAS BIRŽIŠKIS.
**Minister of Health:** ANTANAS VINKUS.
**Minister of Foreign Affairs:** POVILAS GYLYS.
**Minister of the Interior:** ROMASIS VAITIEKŪNAS.
**Minister of Agriculture:** VYTAUTAS EINORIS.
**Minister of Education and Science:** VLADISLOVAS DOMARKAS.
**Minister of the Environment:** BRONIUS BRADAUSKAS.
**Minister of Government Reforms and Local Governments:** LAURYNAS MINDAUGAS STANKEVIČIUS.

### MINISTRIES

**Office of the President:** Gedimino pr. 53, Vilnius 2026; tel. (2) 612-811; fax (2) 226-210.
**Office of the Prime Minister:** Gedimino pr. 11, Vilnius 2039; tel. (2) 629-038; telex 261105; fax (2) 221-088.
**Ministry of Agriculture:** Gedimino pr. 19, Vilnius 2025; tel. (2) 625-654; telex 261181; fax (2) 224-440.
**Ministry of Communications and Information Technology:** Vilniaus 33, Vilnius 2008; tel. (2) 620-443; fax (2) 624-402.
**Ministry of Culture:** J. Basanavičiaus 5, Vilnius 2683; tel. (2) 619-486; fax (2) 623-120.
**Ministry of Defence:** Totorių 25/3, Vilnius 2001; tel. (2) 624-821; fax (2) 226-082.
**Ministry of the Economy:** Gedimino pr. 38/2, Vilnius 2600; tel. (2) 622-416; fax (2) 623-974.
**Ministry of Education and Science:** A. Volano 2/7, Vilnius 2691; tel. (2) 622-483; fax (2) 612-077.
**Ministry of Energy:** Vienuolio 8, Vilnius 2600; tel. (2) 615-140; fax (2) 626-845.
**Ministry of the Environment:** A. Juozapavičiaus 9, Vilnius 2600; tel. (2) 355-868; fax (2) 358-020.
**Ministry of Finance:** Šermukšnių 6, Vilnius 2696; tel. (2) 625-172; telex 261252; fax (2) 226-387.
**Ministry of Foreign Affairs:** J. Tumo-Vaižganto 2, Vilnius 2600; tel. (2) 618-537; telex 261144; fax (2) 620-752.
**Ministry of Forestry:** Gedimino pr. 56, Vilnius 2685; tel. (2) 626-864; fax (2) 622-178.
**Ministry of Government Reforms and Local Governments:** Gedimino pr. 11, Vilnius 2039; tel. (2) 628-518; fax (2) 226-935.
**Ministry of Health:** Gedimino pr. 27, Vilnius 2682; tel. (2) 621-625; fax (2) 224-601.
**Ministry of Housing and Urban Development:** A. Jakšto 4/9, Vilnius 2694; tel. (2) 610-558; fax (2) 220-847.
**Ministry of Industry and Trade:** J. Tumo-Vaižganto 8A/2, Vilnius 2739; tel. (2) 628-830; telex 261262; fax (2) 225-967.
**Ministry of the Interior:** Šventaragio 2, Vilnius 2600; tel. (2) 622-637; fax (2) 615-030.
**Ministry of Justice:** Gedimino pr. 30/1, Vilnius 2600; tel. (2) 624-670; fax (2) 625-940.
**Ministry of Social Welfare and Labour:** Vivulskio 11, Vilnius 2693; tel. (2) 651-236; telex 261152; fax (2) 224-601.
**Ministry of Transport:** Gedimino pr. 17, Vilnius 2679; tel. (2) 621-445; fax (2) 623-728.

## President and Legislature

### PRESIDENT

**Presidential Election, 14 February 1993**

| Candidates | Votes | % |
|---|---|---|
| ALGIRDAS MYKOLAS BRAZAUSKAS | 1,210,517 | 60.2 |
| STASYS LOZORAITIS | 767,345 | 38.1 |
| **Total\*** | 2,011,795 | 100.0 |

\* Including 33,933 spoilt voting papers (1.7% of the total).

### SEIMAS
(Parliament)

**Chairman:** ČESLOVAS JURŠENAS, Gedimino pr. 53, Vilnius 2026; tel. (2) 621-632; telex 261138; fax (2) 620-040.

**General Election, 25 October and 15 November 1992**

| Parties and Alliances | Seats |
|---|---|
| Lithuanian Democratic Labour Party | 73 |
| Sąjūdis/Citizens' Charter of Lithuania | 30 |
| Christian Democratic Party of Lithuania | 16 |
| Lithuanian Social Democratic Party | 8 |
| Polish Union | 4 |
| Others | 10 |
| **Total** | **141** |

## Political Organizations

**Christian Democratic Party of Lithuania:** Šv. Ignoto 14-6, Vilnius 2001; tel. (2) 227-327; f. 1905, re-est. 1989; Chair. POVILAS KATILIUS; 9,000 mems.

**Conservative Party of Lithuania:** Gedimino pr. 1-302, Vilnius 2001; tel. (2) 224-747; fax (2) 224-555; f. 1993 from elements of Sąjūdis; Chair. VYTAUTAS LANDSBERGIS; Chair. of Bd GEDIMINAS VAGNORIUS; 19,000 mems.

**Lithuanian Democratic Labour Party:** B. Radvilaitės 1, Vilnius 2600; tel. (2) 615-420; fax (2) 611-770; f. 1990, as a parliamentary social-democratic successor party to the Communist Party of Lithuania; Chair. ADOLFAS ŠLEŽEVIČIUS; 10,000 mems.

**Lithuanian Democratic Party:** A. Jakšto 9, Vilnius 2001; tel. (2) 626-033; fax (2) 469-671; f. 1902, re-est. 1989; Chair. SAULIUS PEČELIŪNAS; 2,200 mems.

**Lithuanian Farmers' Party:** Gedimino pr. 53, Vilnius 2026; tel. (2) 226-777; fax (2) 626-477; f. 1905 as Lithuanian Farmers' Union, re-est. 1990, renamed 1994; Chair. ALBINAS VAIŽMUŽIS; 1,000 mems.

**Lithuanian Green Party:** Pylimo 38-1, Vilnius 2024; tel. (2) 224-215; f. 1989; seeks a demilitarized, neutral and ecologically sound Lithuania; Chair. RIMANTAS ASTRAUSKAS; 450 mems.

**Lithuanian Independence Party:** Pylimo 38/1, Vilnius 2000; tel. (2) 614-721; f. 1990; Chair. VALENTINAS ŠAPALAS; 300 mems.

**Lithuanian Liberal Union:** B. Radvilaitės 1-210, Vilnius 2000; tel. (2) 612-635; f. 1990; Chair. GINUTIS VENCIUS; 700 mems.

**Lithuanian National Union:** Gedimino pr. 22, Vilnius 2600; tel. (2) 624-935; fax (2) 617-310; f. 1924, refounded 1989; Chair. RIMANTAS SMETONA; 2,000 mems.

**Lithuanian Poles' Electoral Action:** Didžioji 40, Vilnius 2024; tel. (2) 223-388; f. 1994; Chair. JAN SINKIEWICZ; 1,000 mems.

**Lithuanian Union of Political Prisoners and Deportees:** Laisvės al. 39, Kaunas 3000; tel. (7) 223-508; fax (7) 774-100; f. 1988, Pres. BALYS GAJAUSKAS; 85,000 mems.

# LITHUANIA

**Lithuanian Republican Party:** Pramonės pr. 3-62, Kaunas 3031; tel. (7) 752-214; active 1922-29; re-est. 1991; Chair. KAZIMIERAS PETRAITIS; 1,000 mems.

**Lithuanian Social Democratic Party:** J. Basanavičiaus 16/5, Vilnius 2009; tel. (2) 652-380; fax (2) 652-157; f. 1896, re-est. 1989; Chair. ALOYZAS SAKALAS; 600 mems.

## Diplomatic Representation

### EMBASSIES IN LITHUANIA

**Belarus:** P. Klimo 8, Vilnius 2009; tel. (2) 263-828; fax (2) 263-828; fax (2) 263-443; Ambassador: YAUGEN VAITOVICH.

**China, People's Republic:** Pergalės 15, Vilnius 4040; tel. (2) 651-197; Ambassador: WANG ZHADXIAN.

**Czech Republic:** A. Juozapavičiaus 11, Vilnius 2600; tel. (2) 351-631; fax (2) 354-843; Chargé d'affaires a.i.: JAROSLAVA JESLINKOVÁ.

**Denmark:** T. Kosciuškos 36, Vilnius 2600; tel. (2) 628-028; telex 612191; fax (2) 290-110; Ambassador: BIRGER DAN NIELSEN.

**Estonia:** Tilto 29, Vilnius 2001; tel. (2) 220-486; fax (2) 220-461; Ambassador: VALVI STRIKAITIENĖ.

**Finland:** Klaipėdos 6, Vilnius 2600; tel. (2) 221-621; fax (2) 222-441; Ambassador: TAISTO VEIKKO TOLVANEN.

**France:** Didžioji 1, Vilnius 2600; tel. (2) 222-979; fax (2) 223-530; Ambassador: PHILIPPE DE SUREMAIN.

**Germany:** Z. Sierakausko 24, Vilnius 2600; tel. (2) 650-272; Ambassador: REINHARDT KRAUS.

**Holy See:** T. Kosciuškos 28, Vilnius 2001; tel. (2) 223-696; fax (2) 224-228; Apostolic Nuncio: Most Rev. JUSTO MULLOR GARCÍA, Titular Archbishop of Bolsena.

**Italy:** Tauro 12, Vilnius 2600; tel. (2) 220-620; telex 261005; fax (2) 220-405; Ambassador: FRANCO TEMPESTA.

**Latvia:** M. K. Čurlionio 76, Vilnius 2600; tel. (2) 220-515; fax (2) 222-400; Ambassador: ALBERTS SARKANIS.

**Norway:** D. Poškos 59, Vilnius 2600; tel. (2) 754-202; telex 261096; fax (2) 754-149; Ambassador: PER GULLIK STAVNUM.

**Poland:** Aušros Vartų 7, Vilnius 2001; tel. (2) 224-444; fax (2) 223-454; Ambassador: JAN WIDACKI.

**Romania:** Turniškių 41, Vilnius 2016; tel. (2) 779-840; Chargé d'affaires a.i.: NICOLAE CRACIUN.

**Russia:** Latvių 53/54, Vilnius 2600; tel. (2) 351-763; fax (2) 353-877; Ambassador: NIKOLAY MIKHAILOVICH OBERTYSHEV.

**Sweden:** Jogailos 10, Vilnius 2000; tel. (2) 226-467; telex 261142; fax (2) 226-444; Ambassador: LARS MAGNUSSON.

**Turkey:** Didžioji 37, Vilnius 2001; tel. (2) 223-380; telex 261006; fax (2) 223-277; Ambassador: ERKAN GEZER.

**Ukraine:** Turniškių 22, Vilnius 2016; tel. (2) 763-626; Ambassador: ROSTISLAV BILODID.

**United Kingdom:** Antakalnio 2, Vilnius 2055; tel. (2) 222-070; fax (2) 357-579; Ambassador: THOMAS MACAN.

**USA:** Akmenų 6, Vilnius 2600; tel. (2) 223-031; fax (2) 222-779; Ambassador: JAMES W. SWIHART.

## Judicial System

The organs of justice are the Supreme Court, the Court of Appeal, district courts and local courts of administrative areas. The Seimas (legislature) appoints and dismisses from office the judges of the Supreme Court (including its Chairman) on the recommendation of the President of the Republic. Judges of the Court of Appeal are appointed by the President with the approval of the Seimas, while judges of district and local courts are appointed and dismissed by the President. All judges are appointed for a term of five years.

The Constitutional Court decides on the constitutionality of acts of the Seimas, as well as of the President and the Government. It consists of nine judges, who are appointed by the Seimas for a single term of nine years; one-third of the Court's members are replaced every three years.

The Office of the Prosecutor-General is an autonomous institution of the judiciary, comprising the Prosecutor-General and local prosecutors' offices which are subordinate to him. The Prosecutor-General and his deputies are appointed for terms of seven years by the Seimas on the recommendation of the President, while chief local prosecutors are appointed by the Prosecutor-General. The Office of the Prosecutor-General incorporates the Department for Crime Investigation. The State Arbitration decides cases of business litigation.

**Supreme Court:** Gynėjų 6, Vilnius 2725; tel. (2) 610-560; Chair. PRANAS KŪRIS.

**Office of the Prosecutor-General:** A. Smetonos 4, Vilnius 2709; tel. (2) 611-620; fax (2) 611-826; Prosecutor-General VLADAS NIKITINAS.

**Constitutional Court:** Gedimino pr. 36, Vilnius 2600; tel. (2) 226-398; fax (2) 227-975; Chair. JUOZAS ŽILYS.

**State Arbitration:** Gedimino pr. 39/1, Vilnius 2640; tel. (2) 622-843; Chief Arbitrator MARYTĖ MITKUVIENĖ.

## Religion

### CHRISTIANITY

#### The Roman Catholic Church

The Roman Catholic Church in Lithuania comprises two archdioceses and four dioceses. At 31 December 1993 there were an estimated 3,002,000 adherents in Lithuania. There are seminaries at Vilnius, Kaunas and Telšiai.

**Bishop's Conference** (Conferentia Episcopalis Lituaniae): Šventaragio 4, Vilnius 2001; tel. and fax (2) 225-455; Pres. Most Rev. AUDRYS JUOZAS BAČKIS, Archbishop of Vilnius.

**Archbishop of Kaunas:** Cardinal VINCENTAS SLADKEVIČIUS, M. Valančiaus 6, Kaunas 3000; tel. (7) 222-197; fax (7) 226-132.

**Archbishop of Vilnius:** Most Rev. AUDRYS JUOZAS BAČKIS, Šv. Mikalojaus 4, Vilnius 2001; tel. (2) 627-098; fax (2) 222-807.

#### Orthodox Churches

**Lithuanian Old Believers Pomor Church:** Naujininkų 24, Vilnius 2030; tel. (2) 695-271; 54 congregations; Chair. of Supreme Pomor Old Ritualists' Council VASILIJ VASILJEV.

**Vilnius and Lithuanian Eparchy of the Russian Orthodox Church:** Aušros Vartų 10, Vilnius 2001; tel. (2) 626-459; includes 43 congregations; Archbishop CHRIZOSTOM (Georgi Martishkin).

#### Protestant Churches

**Consistory of the Lithuanian Evangelical Lutheran Church:** Laisvės 68, Tauragė 5900; tel. (46) 52-345; Bishop JONAS KALVANAS.

**Evangelical Reformed Church in Lithuania:** POB 661, Vilnius 2049; tel. and fax (2) 450-656; Pres. of Collegium POVILAS A. JAŠINSKAS.

### ISLAM

**Lithuanian Muslims' Religious Community:** A. Vivulskio 3, Vilnius 2009; tel. (2) 655-120; Imam MIKAS CHALECKAS.

### JUDAISM

**Jewish Community:** Pylimo 4, Vilnius 2001; tel. (2) 613-003; fax (2) 227-915; f. 1992, to replace and expand the role of the Jewish Cultural Society; Chair. SIMONAS ALPERAVIČIUS; Chief Rabbi SAMUEL KAHN (Vilnius).

## The Press

In 1993 there were 393 newspapers published in Lithuania, including 333 published in Lithuanian, and 212 periodicals, including 191 in Lithuanian.

The publications listed below are in Lithuanian, except where otherwise indicated.

### PRINCIPAL NEWSPAPERS

**Diena** (Day): Laisvės pr. 60, Vilnius 2056; tel. (2) 429-933; fax (2) 421-790; f. 1994; 6 a week; independent; Editor-in-Chief RYTIS TARAILA; circ. 35,000.

**Ekho Litvy** (Echo of Lithuania): Laisvės pr. 60, Vilnius 2056; tel. (2) 428-463; fax (2) 428-636; f. 1940; 5 a week; in Russian; Editor VASILY YEMELYANOV; circ. 20,000.

**Kauno diena** (Kaunas Daily): Vytauto pr. 27, Kaunas 3687; tel. (7) 741-987; fax (7) 227-404; f. 1945; 6 a week; Editor-in-Chief TEKLĖ MAČIULIENĖ; circ. 72,000.

**Kurier Wileński** (Vilnius Express): Laisvės pr. 60, Vilnius 2056; tel. (2) 427-901; fax (2) 427-265; f. 1953; 5 a week; publ. by the Council of Ministers; in Polish; Editor ZBIGNIEW BALCEWICZ; circ. 10,000.

**Lietuvos aidas** (Echo of Lithuania): Maironio 1, Vilnius 2710; tel. (2) 615-208; fax (2) 224-876; f. 1917; re-est. 1990; 6 a week; Editor-in-Chief SAULIUS ŠALTENIS; circ. 36,000.

**Lietuvos rytas** (Lithuania's Morning): Gedimino pr. 12A, Vilnius 2001; tel. (2) 622-680; fax (2) 227-656; f. 1990; 6 a week in Lithuanian, with a weekly Russian edition; Editor GEDVYDAS VAINAUSKAS; circ. 100,000.

**Respublika** (Republic): A. Smetonos 2, Vilnius 2600; tel. (2) 223-112; fax (2) 223-538; f. 1989; 6 a week in Lithuanian, with 2

# LITHUANIA

*Directory*

Russian editions per week; Editor-in-Chief Vitas Tomkus; circ. 100,000.

**Vakarinės naujienos** (Evening News): Laisvės pr. 60, Vilnius 2056; tel. (2) 428-052; fax (2) 428-563; f. 1958; 6 a week; in Lithuanian and Russian; Editor Vytautas Žeimantas; circ. 50,000.

**Vakarų ekspresas** (Western Express): H. Manto 2, Klaipėda 5800; tel. and fax (61) 18-074; f. 1990; 6 a week; Editor-in-Chief Gintaras Tomkus; circ. 24,000.

## PRINCIPAL PERIODICALS

**Aitvaras** (Brownie): A. Smetonos 2, Vilnius 2600; tel. (2) 223-244; fax (2) 223-538; f. 1989; weekly; children's newspaper; Editor Jonas Kriščiūnas; circ. 8,000.

**Apžalga** (Review): Šv. Ignoto 14-6, Vilnius 2001; tel. (2) 611-151; fax (2) 610-503; f. 1990; weekly; publ. by Christian Democratic Party of Lithuania; Editor Audrone Škiudaitė; circ. 8,000.

**Caritas**: Vilniaus 29, Kaunas 3000; tel. (7) 209-683; fax (7) 205-549; f. 1989; monthly; Editor Vanda Ibianska; circ. 6,000.

**Dienovidis** (Midday): Pilies 23a, Vilnius 2001; tel. and fax (2) 223-101; f. 1990; weekly; Editor Aldona Žemaitytė; circ. 6,500.

**Genys** (Woodpecker): Bernardinų 8, Vilnius 2600; tel. (2) 616-334; fax (2) 227-656; f. 1940; monthly; illustrated; for 6–12-year-olds; Editor-in-Chief Vytautas Račickas; circ. 20,000.

**Gimtasis kraštas** (Native Land): Ž. Liauksmino 8/3, Vilnius 2600; tel. and fax (2) 628-171; f. 1967; weekly; independent; Editor-in-Chief Arvydas Praninskas; circ. 23,000.

**Hobby**: Rudens 33b, Vilnius 2600; tel. (2) 696-964; f. 1991; monthly; domestic animals; Editor-in-Chief Vytautas Klovas; circ. 10,000.

**Jaunimo gretos** (Ranks of Youth): Bernardinų 8, Vilnius 2600; tel. (2) 624-819; fax (2) 624-519; f. 1944; monthly; popular illustrated, youth issues; short stories and essays by beginners, translations; Editor-in-Chief Algis Petrulis; circ. 14,000.

**Kalba Vilnius** (Vilnius Calling): S. Konarskio 49, Vilnius 2674; tel. and fax (2) 661-022; f. 1956; weekly; Lithuanian TV and radio programmes; Editor Artūras Janušauskas; circ. 85,000.

**Katalikų pasaulis** (Catholic World): Pranciškonų 3/6, Vilnius 2001; tel. (2) 222-141; fax (2) 222-122; f. 1989; monthly; Editor-in-Chief Kastantas Lukėnas; circ. 13,000.

**Kinas** (Cinema): Bernardinų 8, Vilnius 2600; tel. (2) 613-039; f. 1972; monthly; Editor-in-Chief Linas Vildžiūnas; circ. 4,000.

**Kultūros barai** (Domains of Culture): Universiteto 6, Vilnius 2600; tel. (2) 616-696; fax (2) 610-538; f. 1965; monthly; Editor-in-Chief Bronys Savukynas; circ. 1,650.

**Lietuvos sportas** (Lithuanian Sports): Odminių 3, Vilnius 2600; tel. and fax (2) 616-757; f. 1922; re-est. 1992; 3 a week; Editor Bronius Čekanauskas; circ. 9,500.

**Lietuvos ūkis** (Lithuanian Economy): Algirdo 31, Vilnius 2600; tel. (2) 662-718; fax (2) 662-445; f. 1921; monthly; Editor-in-Chief Algirdas Jasionis; circ. 7,000.

**Literatūra ir menas** (Literature and Art): Universiteto 4, Vilnius 2600; tel. (2) 612-586; fax (2) 619-696; f. 1946; weekly; publ. by the Lithuanian Writers' Union; Editor-in-Chief Alvydas Šlepikas; circ. 3,300.

**Lithuania in the World**: T. Vrublevskio 6, Vilnius 2000; tel. and fax (2) 613-521; f. 1993; 6 a year; in English; Editor-in-Chief Stasys Kašauskas; circ. 20,000.

**Magazyn Wileński** (Vilnius Journal): Laisvės pr. 60, Vilnius 2019; tel. (2) 427-718; fax (2) 474-007; f. 1990; fortnightly; political, cultural; in Polish; Editor-in-Chief Michał Mackiewicz; circ. 5,000.

**Mokslas ir gyvenimas** (Science and Life): Antakalnio 36, Vilnius 2055; tel. (2) 741-572; f. 1957; monthly; popular science; Editor-in-Chief Juozas Baldauskas; circ. 10,000.

**Moksleivis** (Schoolmate): A. Jakšto 8/10, Vilnius 2600; tel. (2) 627-604; f. 1959; monthly; publ. by the Ministry of Education and Science; Editor-in-Chief Algimantas Zurba; circ. 7,000.

**Moteris** (Woman): Vykinto 7, Vilnius 2604; tel. and fax (2) 224-741; f. 1952; monthly; popular, for women; Editor-in-Chief Dalia Daugirdienė; circ. 75,000.

**Nemunas**: Gedimino 45, Kaunas 3000; tel. (7) 223-066; f. 1967; monthly; journal of the Lithuanian Writers' Union; Editor-in-Chief Algimantas Mikuta; circ. 3,000.

**Šluota** (Broom): Bernardinų 8/8, Vilnius 2722; tel. (2) 613-174; f. 1934; fortnightly; satirical; Editor-in-Chief Albertas Lukša; circ. 5,000.

**Švyturys** (Beacon): Maironio 1, Vilnius 2600; tel. (2) 627-488; f. 1949; monthly; politics, economics, history, culture, fiction; Editor-in-Chief Juozas Baušys; circ. 25,000.

**Tremtinys** (Deportee): Laisvės al. 39, Kaunas 3000; tel. (7) 223-508; fax (7) 774-100; f. 1988; fortnightly; publ. by the Lithuanian Union of Political Prisoners and Deportees; Editor-in-Chief Vanda Poderytė; circ. 8,000.

**Valstiečių laikraštis** (Farmer's Newspaper): Laisvės pr.60, Vilnius 2056; tel. (2) 429-942; fax (2) 421-281; f. 1940; 2 a week; Editor Jonas Švoba; circ. 100,000.

**Vasario 16** (16 February): A. Jakšto 9, Vilnius 2001; tel. (2) 626-033; fax (2) 469-671; f. 1988; fortnightly; journal of the Lithuanian Democratic Party; circ. 2,500.

### NEWS AGENCY

**ELTA** (Lithuanian Telegraph Agency): Gedimino pr. 21/2, Vilnius 2750; tel. (2) 613-667; telex 261296; fax (2) 619-507; f. 1920; Dir Algimantas Semaška.

## Publishers

**Alma littera**: Šermukšnių 3, Vilnius 2600; tel. and fax (2) 627-972; f. 1990; fiction, reference, dictionaries; Dir-Gen. Arvydas Andrijauskas.

**Baltos lankos** (White Sheets): Šv. Ignoto 14-5, Vilnius 2001; tel. (2) 616-174; fax (2) 223-222; f. 1992; literature, humanities, science, textbooks; Editor Saulius Žukas.

**Katalikų pasaulis** (Catholic World): Dominikonų 6, Vilnius 2001; tel. (2) 222-422; fax (2) 222-122; f. 1990; Dir Ričardas Černiauskas.

**Mintis** (Idea): Z. Sierakausko 15, Vilnius 2600; tel. (2) 632-943; fax (2) 637-426; f. 1949; philosophy, history, law, economics, tourist information; Dir Vytautas Visockas.

**Mokslo ir enciklopedijų leidykla** (Science and Encyclopedia Publishers): Žvaigždžių 23, Vilnius 2050; tel. (2) 458-525; fax (2) 458-537; f. 1992; science and reference books, dictionaries, encyclopedias, higher education textbooks, books for the general reader; Dir Zigmantas Pocius.

**Šviesa** (Light): Vytauto 25, Kaunas 3000; tel. (7) 741-634; fax (7) 741-632; f. 1945; textbooks and pedagogical literature; Dir Jonas Barcys.

**Vaga** (Furrow): Gedimino pr. 50, Vilnius 2600; tel. (2) 626-443; fax (2) 616-902; f. 1945; fiction, art; Dir Aleksandras Krasnovas.

**Vyturys** (Lark): Algirdo 31, Vilnius 2600; tel. (2) 660-665; fax (2) 263-449; f. 1985; fiction and non-fiction for children and youth; Dir Juozas Vaitkus.

### PUBLISHERS' ASSOCIATION

**Lithuanian Publishers' Association**: K. Sirvydo 6, Vilnius 2600; tel. (2) 628-945; fax (2) 619-696; f. 1989; Pres. Vincas Akelis.

## Radio and Television

In 1993 there were an estimated 1,400,000 radio receivers and 1,770,000 television receivers in use.

**Lithuanian Radio and Television**: S. Konarskio 49, Vilnius 2674; tel. (2) 263-383; telex 261151; fax (2) 263-282; f. 1940; govt-controlled; Dir-Gen. Juozas Neverauskas (acting).

**Lithuanian Radio**: f. 1926; broadcasts in Lithuanian, Russian, Polish, English, Yiddish, Belarusian and Ukrainian; Dir Virginijus Mičiulis.

**Lithuanian TV**: f. 1957; broadcasts in Lithuanian, Russian, Polish, Yiddish, Belarusian and Ukrainian; Dir Saulius Sondeckis.

## Finance

(cap. = capital; res = reserves; dep. = deposits; m. = million; brs = branches; amounts in litai, unless otherwise stated)

### BANKING

Before it regained independence, Lithuania was fully integrated into the economic and monetary systems of the USSR. In the early 1990s comprehensive reforms were made in Lithuania's banking system, beginning with the establishment of a central bank, the Bank of Lithuania. Apart from the Bank of Lithuania, in early 1995 the banking sector comprised the Agricultural Bank of Lithuania, the Lithuanian Savings Bank, the State Commercial Bank of Lithuania (in which 51% of the capital was state property), the Lithuanian Development Bank and 23 commercial banks.

### Central Bank

**Bank of Lithuania** (Lietuvos bankas): Gedimino pr. 6, Vilnius 2629; tel. (2) 224-008; telex 261090; fax (2) 221-501; f. 1922; re-est. 1990; central bank, responsible for bank supervision; cap. 5.0m., res 365.6m., dep. 362.7m. (Dec. 1993); Chair. of Bd Kazys Ratkevičius.

# LITHUANIA

## Commercial Banks

**Agricultural Bank of Lithuania:** Totorių 4, Vilnius 2600; tel. (2) 628-842; telex 261097; fax (2) 226-047; f. 1990; cap. 20m., dep. 497m.; Chair. of Bd VACLOVAS LITVINAS; 46 brs.

**Balticbank:** J. Basanavičiaus 26, Vilnius 2600; tel. (2) 623-151; telex 261163; fax (2) 623-583; f. 1991; cap. 13m., res 901,000, dep. 46m. (Dec. 1994); Chair. of Bd and Man. Dir GEDIMINAS RADZEVIČIUS.

**Bank of Commerce and Credit** (Komercijos ir kredito bankas): Savanorių 349, Kaunas 3042; tel. (7) 709-603; telex 269772; fax (7) 715-552; f. 1992; cap. 5.1m., res 1.2m., dep. 26.6m. (Dec. 1994); Pres. ARVYDAS KAZAKEVIČIUS.

**Bank Hermis:** Jogailos 9/1, Vilnius 2001; tel. (2) 224-757; telex 261210; fax (2) 224-477; f. 1991; cap. 72.4m., res 44.8m., dep. 972.0m. (Jan. 1993); Chair. NADIEŽDA NOVICKIENĖ; 3 brs.

**Bank of Vilnius** (Vilniaus bankas): Gedimino pr. 12, Vilnius 2600; tel. (2) 610-723; telex 261601; fax (2) 626-557; f. 1990; cap. 37.7m., dep. 256.7m. (Dec. 1994); Chair. JULIUS NIEDVARAS; 12 brs.

**Lithuanian Joint-Stock Innovation Bank** (Lietuvos akcinis inovacinis bankas): A. Jakšto 6, Vilnius 2600; tel. (2) 611-501; telex 261982; fax (2) 261-826; f. 1988; all general commercial banking services and investment banking; cap. 10.7m., res 6.1m., dep. 227.9m. (1994); Gen. Dir ARTŪRAS BALKEVIČIUS; 15 brs.

**Litimpex Bank:** Vilniaus 28, Vilnius 2600; tel. (2) 220-369; telex 261213; fax (2) 221-144; f. 1991; cap. 50m., res 18m., dep. 200m. (Dec. 1994); Chair. of Bd GINTAUTAS PREIDYS; 16 brs.

**State Commercial Bank of Lithuania:** J. Basanavičiaus 7, Vilnius 2631; tel. (2) 626-872; telex 261346; fax (2) 615-428; f. 1992; cap. US $5m., dep. US $589.7m. (1994); Chair. of Bd ALGIMANTAS BARUSEVIČIUS; 29 brs.

**Ūkio Bank:** J. Gruodžio 9, Kaunas 3000; tel. (7) 203-651; telex 269897; fax (7) 204-296; f. 1989; cap. 10.0m., res 4.6m., dep. 155.3m. (Dec. 1994); Chair. of Bd VALDIMARAS BŪTĖNAS; 14 brs.

## Development Bank

**Lithuanian Development Bank:** A. Stulginskio 4/7, Vilnius 2600; tel. (2) 617-031; fax (2) 225-259; f. 1994; Pres. JUOZAS ALIUKONIS.

## Savings Bank

**Lithuanian Savings Bank:** Savanorių pr.19, Vilnius 2015; tel. (2) 232-370; fax (2) 221-263; f. 1988; cap. 10m., dep. 188m. (1993); Chair. of Bd VYGINTAS BUBNYS; 53 brs.

## COMMODITY EXCHANGES

**National Commodity Exchange:** Savanorių pr. 124A, Vilnius 2600; tel. (2) 261-919; fax (2) 262-265; f. 1992; 18 mems; Pres. VYTAUTAS BAJORIŪNAS.

**Baltic Exchange:** Pylimo 2/6, Vilnius 2001; tel. (2) 619-981; fax (2) 620-726; f. 1991; 16 mems; Pres. VYTAUTAS SAKALAUSKAS.

## STOCK EXCHANGE

**National Stock Exchange:** Ukmergės 41, Vilnius 2600; tel. (2) 353-871; fax (2) 354-894; f. 1993; Dir-Gen. RIMANTAS BUSILA.

# Trade and Industry

## CHAMBERS OF COMMERCE

**Association of Lithuanian Chambers of Commerce and Industry:** V. Kudirkos 18, Vilnius 2600; tel. (2) 222-630; fax (2) 222-621; f. 1992; mem. of International Chamber of Commerce and of Asscn of European Chambers of Commerce and Industry; Pres. MINDAUGAS ČERNIAUSKAS.

**Kaunas Regional Chamber of Commerce and Industry:** J. Gruodžio 9, Kaunas 3000; tel. (7) 201-294; fax (7) 208-330; Pres. GINTARAS PETRIKAS.

**Klaipėda Regional Chamber of Commerce and Industry:** Danės 6, Klaipėda; tel (6) 253-811; fax (6) 250-984; Dir. VIKTORAS KROLIS.

**Marijampolė Regional Chamber of Commerce and Industry:** Kęstučio 9/20, Marijampolė; tel. (43) 55-568; fax (43) 51-893; Pres. VYGANDAS MATULIS.

**Panevėžys Regional Chamber of Commerce and Industry:** Respublikos 54, Panevėžys; tel. (54) 63-687; fax (54) 62-227; Pres. JUOZAS BEČELIS.

**Šiauliai Regional Chamber of Commerce and Industry:** Rūdės 17, Šiauliai 5400; tel. (1) 427-709; fax (1) 439-973; Pres. KASTYTIS VYŠNIAUSKAS.

**Vilnius Regional Chamber of Commerce and Industry:** Algirdo 31, Vilnius 2600; tel. (2) 661-550; fax (2) 661-542; f. 1991; 178 mems; Pres. ŠARŪNAS DAVAINIS.

## INDUSTRIAL ASSOCIATIONS

**Association of Lithuanian Businessmen:** A. Jakšto 9, Vilnius 2600; tel. (2) 614-963; fax (2) 628-702; f. 1989; Pres. JONAS VIESULAS.

**Lithuanian Manufacturers' Association:** Saltoniškių 19, Vilnius 2600; tel. (2) 751-278; fax (2) 353-320; f. 1989; Pres. BRONISLOVAS LUBYS.

## MAJOR STATE-OWNED INDUSTRIAL COMPANIES

**ACHEMA:** Taurosto 26, Jonava 5000; tel. (19) 56-624; telex 269845; fax (19) 56-911; f. 1965; produces chemical fertilizers; Pres. BRONISLOVAS LUBYS; 2,300 employees.

**Akmenės cementas:** Dalinkevičiaus 2, Naujoji Akmenė 5464; tel. (95) 58-323; telex 296419; fax (95) 52-198; f. 1952; produces cement, sorted limestone, etc.; Dir SIMONAS-VYTIS ANUŽIS; 1,670 employees.

**Alita:** Miškininkų 17, Alytus 4580; tel. (35) 52-337; telex 269841; fax (35) 54-467; produces wines, soft drinks, concentrated juices; Dir VYTAUTAS JUNEVIČIUS.

**Alytaus tekstile:** Pramonės 1, Alytus 4580; tel. (35) 57-357; fax (35) 35-566; f. 1965; cotton yarn and fabrics; Dir GINTAUTAS ANDRIUŠKEVIČIUS; 5,100 employees.

**Ekranas:** Elektronikos 1, Panevėžys 5319; tel. (54) 53-450; telex 287424; fax (54) 23-415; f. 1962; electronic components; Dir EIMUTIS ŽVYBAS; 5,700 employees.

**Kauno audiniai:** Griunvaldo 3/5, Kaunas 3697; tel. (7) 226-484; telex 269853; fax (7) 228-323; f. 1930; silk, fabrics; Dir ALGIMANTAS GUIGA.

**Kauno baldai:** Drobės 66, Kaunas 3002; tel. (7) 740-687; telex 269877; fax (7) 740-425; furniture products; Dir STEPONAS ARCIŠKEVIČIUS.

**Lelija:** Panerių, 43, Vilnius 2600; tel. (2) 630-761; telex 261225; fax (2) 661-577; f. 1947; garments; Dir-Gen. GENĖ ZAVECKIENE.

**NAFTA (Mažeikiai State Oil Refinery):** Juodeikiai District, Mažeikiai 5526; tel. (93) 70-639; telex 296416; fax (93) 92-525; f. 1980; petroleum derivatives, liquefied gas, sulphur; Dir-Gen. BRONISLOVAS VAINORAS.

**Neris:** Pramonės 97, Vilnius 2048; tel. (2) 674-848; telex 261256; fax (2) 671-815; f. 1958; repair and modernization of railway passenger carriages; Dir-Gen. RIMAS KELPŠA.

**Nuklonas:** Architektų 1, Šiauliai 5419; tel. (1) 452-235; telex 296426; fax (1) 450-280; f. 1968; electronic goods, incl. integrated circuits, household appliances; Dir VYTAUTAS SLANINA.

**Panevėžys Glass-Works:** Pramonės 10, Panevėžys 5319; tel. (54) 63-747; telex 287421; fax (54) 65-703; f. 1965; produces all kinds of glass; Dir ALFONSAS PABERALIS; 970 employees.

**Sirijus:** Artojų 7, Klaipėda 5799; tel. (6) 212-757; telex 278129; fax (6) 216-833; f. 1931; galvanic elements, batteries, wood-processing machine-tools; Dir-Gen. RIMVYDAS VAŠTAKAS.

**Snaigė:** Pramonės 6, Alytus 4580; tel. (35) 57-580; telex 269849; fax (35) 57-612; f. 1964; produces household refrigerators and thermo-insulation panels; Pres. ANTANAS ANDRIULIONIS; 2,900 employees.

**Vilniaus buitinė chemija:** Kirtimų 47, Vilnius 2028; tel. (2) 641-986; telex 261250; fax (2) 641-313; f. 1970; paints, solvents, glue, cosmetic products, insecticides; Dir-Gen. VYTAUTAS MILINAVIČIUS.

## TRADE UNIONS

**Community of Trade Unions:** V. Mykolaičio-Putino 5, Vilnius 2009; tel. (2) 635-460; fax (2) 615-246; f. 1990; 180,000 mems; Chair. GRAŽINA PALIOKIENĖ.

**Lithuanian Labour Federation:** Žirmūnų 48-25, Vilnius 2051; tel. (2) 737-944; f. 1919, re-est. 1991; 400 mems; Chair. LIONGINAS RADZEVIČIUS.

**Lithuanian Trade Unions Centre:** Basanavičiaus 29A, Vilnius 2600; tel. (2) 614-888; fax (2) 226-106; f. 1993; 14 affiliated unions with 258,000 mems; Chair. ALGIRDAS KVEDARAVIČIUS.

**Lithuanian Union of Free Trade Unions:** J. Jasinskio 9, Vilnius 2600; tel. (2) 610-921; fax (2) 619-078; f. 1992; 7 affiliated unions with 80,000 mems; Chair. ALGIRDAS SYSAS.

**Lithuanian Workers' Union:** V. Mykolaičio-Putino 5, Vilnius 2009; tel. (2) 621-743; fax (2) 615-253; f. 1989; 42 regional brs; 125,000 mems; Pres. ALDONA BALSIENĖ.

# Transport

## RAILWAYS

In 1994 there were 2,002 km of railway track in use in Lithuania, of which 122 km were electrified. Main lines link Vilnius with

# LITHUANIA

Rīga (Latvia), Minsk (Belarus) and Kaliningrad (Russian Federation), and Warsaw (Poland), via the Belarusian town of Grodno.

**Lithuanian Railways** (Lietuvos geležinkeliai): Mindaugo 12–14, Vilnius 2604; tel. (2) 660-041; fax (2) 618-323; f. 1991; Gen. Dir STASYS LABUTIS.

### ROADS

In 1994 the total length of the road network was 55,603 km, of which some 42,209 km were asphalted.

### SHIPPING

The main port is at Klaipėda. During the Soviet period the port was used as an important transit facility, with some 90% of its total traffic being transit trade to and from the republics of the USSR. This role diminished with the establishment of Lithuanian independence in 1991 and the disruption of traditional trading patterns following the dissolution of the USSR. The Lithuanian Shipping Company was formerly part of the Soviet merchant shipping system. In the early 1990s it was restructured as an independent enterprise, although it was adversely affected by declining trade and a largely obsolete fleet.

**Shipowning Company**

**Lithuanian Shipping Company:** J. Janonio 24, Klaipėda 5813; tel. (6) 219-824; telex 278111; fax (6) 218-069; f. 1969; transportation of cargo and passengers; Pres. ANTANAS ANILIONIS.

### CIVIL AVIATION

Lithuania has air links with Western European destinations and with cities in the former USSR. The state airline, Lietuvos avialinijos, is based at the international airport at Vilnius. A second airport, at Šiauliai, opened for international flights at the end of 1993.

**Lithuanian Airlines** (Lietuvos avialinijos): A. Gustaičio 4, Vilnius 2038; tel. (2) 630-116; telex 261165; fax (2) 266-828; f. 1991; Dir-Gen. STASYS DAILYDKA.

## Tourism

Tourist attractions in Lithuania include the historic cities of Vilnius, Kaunas, Kėdainiai, Trakai and Klaipėda, coastal resorts, such as Palanga and Kuršių Nerija, and picturesque countryside. There were some 300 private travel agencies in operation in 1994.

**State Touristic Service:** Gedimino pr. 30/1, Vilnius 2695; tel. (2) 226-706; fax (2) 226-819; Dir ANTANAS PETRAUSKAS.

# LUXEMBOURG

## Introductory Survey

### Location, Climate, Language, Religion, Flag, Capital

The Grand Duchy of Luxembourg is a land-locked country in western Europe. It is bordered by Belgium to the west and north, by France to the south, and by Germany to the east. The climate is temperate, with cool summers and mild winters. In Luxembourg-Ville the average temperature ranges from 1°C (33°F) in January to 18°C (64°F) in July. Letzeburgish, a German-Moselle-Frankish dialect, is the spoken language and became the official language in 1985. French is generally used for administrative purposes, while German is the principal written language of commerce and the press. Almost all of the inhabitants profess Christianity: about 94% are Roman Catholics and a small minority are Protestants. The national flag (proportions five by three) consists of three equal horizontal stripes, of red, white and blue. The capital is Luxembourg-Ville (Lützelburg).

### Recent History

As a founder member of the European Community (EC, known since November 1993 as the European Union—EU), of which Luxembourg-Ville is one of the main bases, Luxembourg has played a significant role in progress towards European integration since the Second World War. Luxembourg's commitment to such integration was exemplified by its status as one of the original signatories to the June 1990 Schengen Agreement (named after the town in Luxembourg where the accord was signed), which binds signatories to the abolition of internal border controls.

The Belgo-Luxembourg Economic Union (BLEU) has existed since 1921, except for the period from 1940 to 1944, when the Grand Duchy was subject to wartime occupation by Germany. In 1948 the Benelux Economic Union was inaugurated between Belgium, Luxembourg and the Netherlands, becoming effective in 1960, and establishing the three countries as a single customs area in 1970 (see p. 238).

In November 1964 Grand Duchess Charlotte abdicated, after a reign of 45 years, and was succeeded by her son, Prince Jean. The former Grand Duchess died in 1985.

Pierre Werner, leader of the Parti Chrétien Social (PCS), became Prime Minister in February 1959. After the fall of the Government in October 1968, Werner headed a coalition of the PCS and the Parti Démocratique ('Liberals') from January 1969 until May 1974. At a general election in May 1974 the PCS lost its political dominance for the first time since 1919, and in June a left-of-centre coalition between the Parti Ouvrier Socialiste Luxembourgeois (POSL) and the Parti Démocratique was formed under the premiership of Gaston Thorn, Minister for Foreign Affairs since 1969. At the next general election, in June 1979, the PCS increased its strength in the 59-member Chambre des Députés, from 18 to 24 seats. In July Pierre Werner again formed a coalition Government between his party and the Parti Démocratique, which held 15 seats.

A general election took place in June 1984, when the membership of the legislature was increased to 64. Once again, the PCS won the largest number of seats (25). However, the success of the POSL, which took 21 seats (compared with 14 in the previous legislature), was widely attributed to general dissatisfaction with an economic austerity programme which had been introduced during the early 1980s and with the rising level of unemployment. A centre-left coalition was formed in July between the PCS and the POSL, with Jacques Santer (hitherto Minister of Finance, Labour and Social Security) as Prime Minister, Pierre Werner having retired from politics. New elections to the Chambre des Députés (whose membership had been reduced to 60 in January 1989) took place in June 1989. The PCS, the POSL and the Parti Démocratique each lost three seats (returning, respectively, 22, 18 and 11 deputies). A new organization, the Comité d'Action 5/6 (which campaigned to secure improved pension rights for private-sector employees), enjoyed considerable success, obtaining four seats in the legislature. Two environmentalist groups, Déi Gréng Alternativ and Gréng Lëscht Ekologesch Initiativ, each acquired two seats. In the following month Santer was again sworn in as the head of a coalition Government, which comprised equal numbers of representatives from the PCS and the POSL. At the next general election, which took place (at the same time as elections to the European Parliament) on 12 June 1994, the PCS and the POSL each lost one representative in the Chambre de Députés, winning 21 and 17 seats respectively. The Party Démocratique secured 12 seats, Déi Gréng Alternativ and Gréng Lëscht Ekologesch Initiativ jointly secured five seats and the Comité d'Action pour la Démocratie et la Justice (formerly the Comité d'Action 5/6) also won five seats. The PSC-POSL coalition was immediately renewed, and Jacques Santer was reappointed Prime Minister.

In January 1995 Jacques Santer took office as President of the Commission of the European Union. He was succeeded as Prime Minister by Jean-Claude Juncker, hitherto Minister of the Budget, Minister of Finance and Minister of Labour. Soon afterwards a major reorganization of cabinet portfolios was undertaken.

Luxembourg's banking secrecy laws have for many years prompted international concern regarding the activities of banks and individual depositors benefiting from such legislation. In July 1989, in an attempt to prevent the 'laundering' of money gained from trafficking in illicit drugs, the Luxembourg Chambre des Députés adopted legislation requiring banks to identify the actual economic beneficiaries of accounts and holding companies. Attempts by the EC, in the early 1990s, to impose more uniform regulations on the conduct of financial services in its member countries, in conjunction with the world-wide liquidation, in July 1991, of the Bank of Credit and Commerce International (BCCI—for further details see the chapter on the United Arab Emirates), the holding company and a subsidiary of which were incorporated in Luxembourg, focused renewed attention on Luxembourg's regulatory procedures. Luxembourg was required to approve the compensation plan for the BCCI's creditors that had been formulated by the bank's liquidators and majority shareholders. Although this was granted, after some delay, by the Luxembourg District Court in October 1992, an appeal against the District Court's ruling (submitted on behalf of three prominent creditors, who objected to a clause in the plan which would require creditors to waive any further claims against the Abu Dhabi shareholders in respect of the BCCI collapse) was upheld in October 1993, considerably impeding the compensation process. In April 1993 legislation was introduced that permitted the confiscation of deposits in Luxembourg banks accruing from suspected illegal drugs-related activities.

In July 1992 the Chambre des Députés ratified, by an overwhelming majority, the Treaty on European Union, which had been approved by EC Heads of Government at Maastricht, the Netherlands, in December 1991 (see p. 149). Amendments to Luxembourg's Constitution would be necessitated by clauses in the treaty governing monetary union and foreigners' electoral rights.

### Government

Luxembourg is an hereditary and constitutional monarchy. Legislative power is exercised by the unicameral Chambre des Députés, with 60 members elected by universal adult suffrage for five years (subject to dissolution) on the basis of proportional representation. Some legislative functions are also entrusted to the advisory Conseil de l'Etat, with 21 members appointed for life by the Grand Duke, but decisions made by this body can be overruled by the legislature.

Executive power is vested in the Grand Duke, but is normally exercised by the Council of Ministers, led by the President of the Government (Prime Minister). The Grand Duke appoints ministers, but they are responsible to the legislature. Luxembourg is divided into 12 cantons.

### Defence

Luxembourg was a founder member of NATO in 1949. Compulsory military service was abolished in 1967, but Luxembourg maintains an army of volunteers, totalling 800, and a gendarmerie numbering 560 (June 1994). Defence expenditure in the budget for 1994 was about 3,700m. Luxembourg francs. In March 1987 the country became a signatory of the Benelux military convention, together with Belgium and the Netherlands. This aimed at the standardization of training methods and of military equipment in the three countries.

## Economic Affairs

In 1993, according to estimates by the World Bank, Luxembourg's gross national product (GNP), measured at average 1991-93 prices, was US $14,233m., equivalent to $35,850 per head. During 1985-93, it was estimated, GNP per head increased, in real terms, at an average annual rate of 2.7%. Over the same period the population increased by an annual average of 1.0%. Luxembourg's gross domestic product (GDP) increased, in real terms, by an annual average of 3.4% in 1980-90.

Agriculture (including forestry and fishing) contributed 2.2% of GDP in 1990. In 1993 about 3.0% of the working population were employed in the agricultural sector. The principal crops are cereals, potatoes and wine grapes. Livestock-rearing and dairy farming are also of some importance.

Industry (including mining, manufacturing, construction and power) provided 34.9% of GDP in 1990 and employed 29.4% of the working population in 1993. Manufacturing activities constitute the most important sector, contributing 25.9% of GDP in 1990. In 1993 17.2% of the working population were employed in extractive and manufacturing activities. Although the country's deposits of iron ore are no longer exploited, the iron and steel industry (which is dominated by a multinational corporation, Aciéries Réunies de Burbach-Esch-Dudelange SA—ARBED) remains one of the most important sectors of the Luxembourg economy, accounting for some 30% of all manufacturing output in 1990. Chemical, rubber and plastic products together provided a further 16% of the total. Other important branches of manufacturing are metal and machinery products, paper and printing and food products. During 1980-90 industrial GDP increased by an annual average of 3.0%, while manufacturing GDP increased by an average of 3.3% per year. In 1993 industrial production (excluding construction) declined by 3.3%.

A total of 1,378m. kWh of electrical energy was generated in 1990. Of the total, 820m. kWh (59.5%) were derived from hydroelectrical installations, and a further 559m. kWh from thermal power sources. Imports of petroleum products comprised 4.0% of the value of total imports in 1991.

Favourable laws governing banking secrecy and taxation have encouraged the development of Luxembourg as a major international financial centre. In 1990 the financial services sector (banking, finance and insurance) contributed 11.9% of GDP. At the end of 1993 there were 218 banks in Luxembourg, and 18,531 people were employed in banking activities in that year. At 1 January 1993 11,321 holding companies were registered in Luxembourg. Stock exchange activities (notably the 'Eurobond' market and investment portfolio management) are also prominent. Legislation adopted in 1984 has facilitated the establishment in Luxembourg, by major industrial companies, of 'captive' reinsurance companies. The data-processing and audio-visual industries have also become increasingly prominent. In 1992 overall profits in the banking sector increased by 18.5% (compared with an increase of 24.1% in 1991).

In 1993, according to provisional figures, Luxembourg recorded a visible trade deficit of 55,445m. Luxembourg francs; however, there was a surplus on the current account of the balance of payments of 61,600m. francs. Other members of the European Union (EU, see p. 143—formerly the European Community—EC) account for much of Luxembourg's foreign trade (supplying 86.9% of imports and purchasing 81.4% of exports, according to provisional figures for 1993). The most important trading partners in 1993 were Belgium (38.1% of imports; 15% of exports), Germany (28.5% of imports; 28.2% of exports) and France (11.0% of imports; 17.8% of exports). The principal exports in 1993 were base metals and manufactures, mechanical and electrical equipment, plastics, rubber and related products and textiles and clothing. The principal imports were machinery and electrical apparatus, transport equipment, base metals and manufactures and mineral products (including fuels).

In 1994 there was an overall budgetary deficit of 1,700m. Luxembourg francs. The annual rate of inflation averaged 3.3% in 1985-93; consumer prices increased by an annual average of 3.2% in 1992 and 3.6% in 1993, falling to 2.2% in 1994. About 2.4% of the labour force were unemployed in late 1994.

Luxembourg was a founder member of the EC and of the Benelux Economic Union (see p. 238). Luxembourg is also a member of the European Bank for Reconstruction and Development, inaugurated in 1991 (see p. 140).

The development of Luxembourg as an international financial centre during the 1970s coincided with a decline in the importance of the country's iron and steel sector, and has, in general, ensured sustained economic growth. Since the late 1980s Luxembourg has benefited from low levels of inflation and unemployment. ARBED (the country's largest single employer) suffered substantial losses in 1992 and 1993, owing to the adverse effects of the world-wide economic recession, including a downturn in international steel prices. However, the company returned to profitability in 1994. Luxembourg's annual visible trade deficit is offset by the contribution of the financial services sector to the overall current account surplus. Attempts by the EU to promote further economic integration among its member-countries, by abolishing restrictions on the movement of capital, could undermine Luxembourg's status as a centre for private and corporate investors, who have been attracted by the Grand Duchy's advantageous financial legislation. Prospects for continued growth are, therefore, largely dependent on the further diversification of Luxembourg's economy. The Government aims to profit from the exploitation of technological developments in the media and communications sectors.

## Social Welfare

Although virtually all types of employment are subject to compulsory social insurance, the Government does not itself operate the social services. They are administered by semi-public bodies, composed of government representatives and elected representatives of employers and employees. Social service benefits are also guaranteed to foreigners, in accordance with international conventions which have been agreed with individual countries. The comprehensive social insurance scheme covers accident insurance (compulsorily paid by all employers), health insurance (compulsory for employees and self-employed persons, but voluntary for others), invalidity and old-age pensions (contributions shared equally between employer and employee, the self-employed also making a compulsory contribution), family allowances and unemployment benefit, which amounts to 80% of gross earnings. At 31 December 1993 Luxembourg had 4,560 hospital beds, equivalent to 11.4 for every 1,000 inhabitants, and there were 848 physicians (2.1 per 1,000 inhabitants). Of total expenditure by the central Government in the general budget for 1991, 33,292.1m. Luxembourg francs (28.1%) was for social security, while 4,672.8m. francs (3.9%) was for public health.

## Education

Education in Luxembourg is compulsory from the age of six to 15 years. Primary education begins at six years of age and lasts for six years. German is the initial language of instruction at primary level. French is added to the programme in the second year, and replaces German as the language of instruction at secondary level.

At the age of 12, children can choose between secondary school (lycée) and technical education (enseignement secondaire technique). The first year of secondary school is a general orientation course on comprehensive lines, which is then followed by a choice between two sections: the Classical Section, with an emphasis on Latin, and the Modern Section, which stresses English and other modern languages. The completed secondary course lasts seven years, and leads to the Certificat de Fin d'Etudes Secondaires, which qualifies for university entrance. The technical education course, which leads to vocational and technical qualifications, is in three parts (each of three years): an orientation and observation course, an intermediate course and an upper course.

The Centre Universitaire was established in 1969, offering one-year courses in the humanities, sciences and law and economics, and also training courses for lawyers and teachers. It had more than 1,400 students in 1991/92. Many students also attend other European universities. Expenditure on education and scientific research by the central Government in the general budget for 1991 was 15,404.4m. Luxembourg francs (representing 13.0% of total spending).

LUXEMBOURG

## Public Holidays

**1995:** 1 January (New Year's Day), 17 April (Easter Monday), 1 May (Labour Day), 25 May (Ascension Day), 5 June (Whit Monday), 23 June (National Day), 15 August (Assumption), 1 November (All Saints' Day), 25 December (Christmas), 26 December (St Stephen's Day).

**1996:** 1 January (New Year's Day), 8 April (Easter Monday), 1 May (Labour Day), 16 May (Ascension Day), 27 May (Whit Monday), 23 June (National Day), 15 August (Asumption), 1 November (All Saint's Day), 25 December (Christmas), 26 December (St Stephen's Day).

## Weights and Measures

The metric system is in force.

# Statistical Survey

Source (unless otherwise stated): Service Central de la Statistique et des Etudes Economiques (STATEC), Ministère de l'Economie, 6 blvd Royal, BP 304, 2013 Luxembourg; tel. 478-1; telex 3464; fax 46-42-89.

## AREA AND POPULATION

**Area:** 2,586 sq km (999 sq miles).

**Population:** 384,634 (males 188,570; females 196,064) at census of 1 March 1991; 400,900 (males 196,904; females 203,996) at 1 January 1994 (official estimate).

**Density** (January 1994): 155.0 per sq km.

**Principal Municipalities** (population at 1 March 1991): Luxembourg-Ville (capital) 75,833; Esch-sur-Alzette 24,018; Differdange 15,740; Dudelange 14,677; Sanem 11,534.

**Births, Marriages and Deaths** (1993): Live births 5,353 (birth rate 13.4 per 1,000); Marriage rate 6.1 per 1,000; Deaths 3,915 (death rate 10.2 per 1,000).

**Immigration and Emigration** (1993): Arrivals 10,059; Departures 5,826.

**Employment** ('000 persons, incl. armed forces, 1992): Agriculture, hunting, forestry and fishing 6.0; Mining, quarrying and manufacturing 35.5; Electricity, gas and water 1.4; Construction 21.4; Trade, restaurants and hotels 40.7; Transport, storage and communications 13.3; Finance, insurance, real estate and business services 17.9; Other market services 35.9; Community, social and personal services 27.9; Total 200.4.

## AGRICULTURE, ETC.

**Principal Crops** (provisional figures, '000 metric tons, 1992): Wheat 39.5; Rye 2.1; Barley 65.0; Oats 17.2; Potatoes 19.2; Wine grapes 8.6.

**Livestock** (provisional figures, May 1993): Cattle 208,878; Horses 1,925; Pigs 71,800; Sheep 6,775; Poultry 63,444.

**Livestock Products** ('000 metric tons, 1991): Meat 25.3; Milk 262.3; Butter 3.6; Cheese 3.7.

**Forestry** ('000 cubic metres, 1991): Roundwood removals 598.9 (coniferous 203.8, broadleaved 395.1).

## INDUSTRY

**Selected Products** ('000 metric tons, 1993): Pig-iron 2,412; Crude steel 3,293.

## FINANCE

**Currency and Exchange Rates:** 100 centimes = 1 Luxembourg franc (Belgian currency is also legal tender). *Sterling and Dollar equivalents* (31 December 1994): £1 sterling = 49.80 francs; US $1 = 31.83 francs; 1,000 Luxembourg francs = £20.08 = $31.42. *Average Exchange Rate* (Luxembourg francs per US dollar): 32.150 in 1992; 34.597 in 1993; 33.456 in 1994. Note: The Luxembourg franc is at par with the Belgian franc.

**Budget** (million Luxembourg francs, 1991; general accounts): *Revenue:* Income tax 49,863.4; Other direct taxes 3,002.7; Turnover tax 17,687.9; Customs duties 11,930.8; Other indirect taxes 12,948.8; Other ordinary receipts 17,182.6; Other extraordinary receipts 156.3; Total 112,772.5. *Expenditure:* Administration, foreign affairs and co-operation 10,963.6; Defence 3,255.4; Public order and security 2,825.6; Education and scientific research 15,404.4; Social security 33,272.1; Public health 4,672.8; Housing, territorial planning and environment 6,256.7; Culture, leisure and religion 2,373.1; Power 126.0; Agriculture, hunting and fishing 4,293.3; General economic affairs, industry and commerce 4,519.1; Transport and communications 19,024.7; Public debt 1,827.3; Miscellaneous 9,599.8; Total 118,413.9. Source: Ministère des Finances. 1994 (million Luxembourg francs): Total revenue 133,200; Total expenditure 134,900.

**International Reserves** (US $ million at 31 December 1994): Gold 16.90; IMF special drawing rights 10.54, Reserve position in IMF 34.46; Foreign Exchange 30.73; Total 92.63. Source: IMF, *International Financial Statistics*.

**Cost of Living** (Consumer Price Index; averages for 1992; base: 1990 = 100): Food and drink 103.6, Housing 113.7, Household furniture and utensils 111.7, Clothing 111.0, Medical expenditure 113.5, Transport and communications 111.8, Leisure and education 106.1, Miscellaneous 114.1.

**National Accounts** (million Luxembourg francs at current prices): Gross domestic product (in purchasers' values) 377,458 in 1991; 406,300 in 1992; 432,578 in 1993.

**Balance of Payments** (estimates, '000 million Luxembourg francs, 1993): Merchandise exports f.o.b. 205.6; Merchandise imports f.o.b. 261.0; *Trade balance* −55.4; Exports of services 1,290.9; Imports of services 1,163.0; Unrequited transfers (net) −9.3; *Current balance* 61.6.

## EXTERNAL TRADE

**Principal Commodities** (provisional figures, million Luxembourg francs, 1993): *Imports:* Mineral products (incl. fuels) 32,067, Base metals and manufactures 35,267, Machinery and apparatus (incl. electrical) 42,179, Chemicals 21,411, Transport equipment 36,559, Total (incl. others) 261,033. *Exports:* Base metals and manufactures 69,607, Plastics, rubber and manufactures 27,159, Machinery and apparatus (incl. electrical) 33,331, Total (incl. others) 205,588.

**Principal Trading Partners** (provisional figures, million Luxembourg francs, 1993): *Imports:* Belgium 99,360; France 28,806; Germany 74,406; Netherlands 11,069; Total (incl. others) 261,033. *Exports:* Belgium 30,819; France 36,660; Germany 57,926; Italy 9,670; Netherlands 11,140; United Kingdom 13,368; USA 8,600; Total (incl. others) 205,588.

## TRANSPORT

**Railways** (traffic): Passenger-kilometres 282.4 million (estimate) in 1991; Freight ton-kilometres 647 million in 1993.

**Road Traffic** (motor vehicles in use at 1 January 1994): Private cars 217,754; Buses and coaches 850; Goods vehicles 14,641; Tractors 12,400; Total (incl. others) 263,333.

**Civil Aviation** (traffic on scheduled services, 1989): Passengers carried 296,000; Passenger-km 138 million. Source: UN, *Statistical Yearbook*.

## TOURISM

**Arrivals:** 538,471 in 1991; 508,870 in 1992; 525,707 in 1993 (figures refer to number of arrivals at hotels, etc.).

## COMMUNICATIONS MEDIA

**Telephones:** 214,821 in use (1993).

**Daily newspapers:** 5 (1994).

**Book production** (1992): 417* titles.

**Radio receivers:** 240,000 in use (1992)*.

**Television receivers:** 101,000 in use (1992)*.

* Source: UNESCO, *Statistical Yearbook*.

## EDUCATION

(1991/92)

**Nursery:** 467 teachers; 8,689 pupils.

**Primary:** 1,888 teachers; 26,197 pupils.

LUXEMBOURG

**Secondary:** 8,465 pupils.

**Middle, vocational and technical** (state sector only): 11,877 pupils.

**Higher Insitute of Technology:** 320 students.

**Teacher training:** 226 students.

**Other university-level:** 5,267 students (incl. 4,407 studying abroad).

# Directory

## The Constitution

The Constitution now in force dates back to 17 October 1868, but in 1919 a constituent assembly introduced into it some important changes, declaring that the sovereign power resided in the nation, that all secret treaties were denounced, and that deputies were to be elected, by 'scrutin de liste', and by proportional representation, on the basis of universal adult suffrage. Electors must be citizens of Luxembourg and must have attained 18 years of age. Candidates for election must have attained 21 years of age. The Grand Duke, who is Sovereign, chooses government ministers, may intervene in legislative questions, and has certain judicial powers. There is a single-chamber legislature, the Chambre des Députés, with 60 members elected for five years. There are four electoral districts, the North, the Centre, the South and East. By the law of 9 October 1956 the Constitution was further revised to the effect that: 'The exercise of prerogatives granted by the Constitution to the legislative, executive and judiciary powers, can, by treaty, be temporarily vested in institutions of international law.' In addition to the Council of Ministers, which consists of the President of the Government (Prime Minister) and at least three other ministers, The Conseil de l'Etat (which is the supreme administrative tribunal and which also fulfils certain legislative functions) comprises 21 members nominated by the Sovereign.

## The Government

### HEAD OF STATE

**Grand Duke:** HRH Jean Benoît Guillaume Marie Robert Louis Antoine Adolphe Marc d'Aviano (succeeded to the throne 12 November 1964).

### COUNCIL OF MINISTERS
(May 1995)

A coalition of the Parti Chrétien Social (C. Soc.) and the Parti Ouvrier Socialiste Luxembourgeois (Soc.).

**Prime Minister, Minister of State, Minister of the Treasury and Financial Affairs, Minister of State, Minister of Labour and Employment, Minister of Finance and the Treasury:** Jean-Claude Juncker (PCS).

**Deputy Prime Minister, Minister of Foreign Affairs, Foreign Trade and Co-operation:** Jacques Poos (POSL).

**Minister of Agriculture, Viticulture and Rural Development, Minister of Small Businesses, Minister of Housing, Minister of Tourism:** Fernand Boden (PCS).

**Minister of Justice, Minister of the Budget:** Marc Fischbach (PCS).

**Minister of the Family, Women's Affairs and the Disabled:** Josée Jacobs (PCS).

**Minister of National Education, Minister of Cultural and Religious Affairs:** Erna Hennicot-Schoepges (PCS).

**Minister of the Interior, Minister of the Civil Service:** Michel Wolter (PCS).

**Minister of the Economy and Trade, Minister of Public Works, Minister of Energy:** Robert Goebbels (POSL).

**Minister of the Environment and Minister of Health:** Johny Lahure (POSL).

**Minister of Territorial Administration, Minister of Defence and Minister of Youth and Sports:** Alex Bodry (POSL).

**Minister of Social Security, Minister of Transport, Minister of Post and Communications:** Mady Delvaux-Stehres (POSL).

### MINISTRIES

**Office of the Prime Minister and Ministry of State:** Hôtel de Bourgogne, 4 rue de la Congrégation, 2910 Luxembourg; tel. 478-1; telex 2790; fax 46-17-20.

**Ministry of Agriculture, Viticulture and Rural Development:** 1 rue de la Congrégation, 2913 Luxembourg; tel. 478-1; telex 2537; fax 46-40-27.

**Ministry of the Civil Service:** 12–14 ave Emile Reuter, 2420 Luxembourg; tel. 478-1; fax 478-31-22.

**Ministry of Post and Communications:** 18 montée de la Pétrusse, 2945 Luxembourg; tel. 478-1; telex 60482; fax 40-89-40.

**Ministry of Cultural and Religious Affairs:** 20 montée de la Pétrusse, 2912 Luxembourg; tel. 478-1; fax 40-24-27.

**Ministry of Defence:** Plateau du St Esprit, 2915 Luxembourg; tel. 478-1; telex 60751; fax 46-26-82.

**Ministry of the Economy and Trade:** 6 blvd Royal, 2914 Luxembourg; tel. 478-1; telex 3464; fax 46-04-48.

**Ministry of Energy:** 19–21 blvd Royal, 2449 Luxembourg; tel. 478-1.

**Ministry of the Environment:** 18 montée de la Pétrusse, 2918 Luxembourg; tel. 478-1; telex 2536; fax 40-04-10.

**Ministry of the Family, Women's Affairs and the Disabled:** 12–14 ave Emile Reuter, 2919 Luxembourg; tel. 478-1; fax 478-65-70.

**Ministry of Finance and the Treasury:** 3 rue de la Congrégation, 1352 Luxembourg; tel. 478-1; telex 2790; fax 47-52-41.

**Ministry of Foreign Affairs, Foreign Trade and Co-operation:** 5 rue Notre Dame, 2240 Luxembourg; tel. 478-1; telex 3405; fax 22-31-44.

**Ministry of Health:** 57 blvd de la Pétrusse, 2935 Luxembourg; tel. 478-1; telex 2546; fax 49-13-37.

**Ministry of the Interior:** 19 rue Beaumont, 2933 Luxembourg; tel. 478-1.

**Ministry of Justice:** 16 blvd Royal, 2934 Luxembourg; tel. 478-1; fax 22-76-61.

**Ministry of Labour and Employment:** 26 rue Zithe, 2939 Luxembourg; tel. 478-1; telex 2985; fax 478-63-25.

**Ministry of National Education:** 29 rue Aldringen, 2926 Luxembourg; tel. 478-5100; fax 47-85-11-0.

**Ministry of Physical Education, Sport and Youth:** 66 route de Trèves, BP 180, 2916 Luxembourg; tel. 478-1; fax 43-45-99.

**Ministry of Public Works:** 4 blvd F. D. Roosevelt, 2940 Luxembourg; tel. 478-1; fax 46-27-09.

**Ministry of Social Security:** 26 rue Zithe, 2936 Luxembourg; tel. 478-1; telex 2985; fax 478-63-28.

**Ministry of Territorial Administration:** 18 montée de la Petrusse, 2946 Luxembourg; tel. 478-1; fax 40-89-70.

**Ministry of Tourism:** 16 blvd Royal, 2937 Luxembourg; tel. 478-1; fax 47-40-11.

**Ministry of Transport:** 19–21 blvd Royal, 2938 Luxembourg; tel. 478-1; telex 1465; fax 46-43-15.

## Legislature

### CHAMBRE DES DÉPUTÉS
(Chamber of Deputies)

**President:** Jean Spautz (Parti Chrétien Social).

**General Election, 12 June 1994**

| Party | % of votes | Seats |
|---|---|---|
| Parti Chrétien Social | 31.41 | 21 |
| Parti Ouvrier Socialiste Luxembourgeois | 24.84 | 17 |
| Parti Démocratique | 18.85 | 12 |
| Déi Gréng Alternativ | } 10.94 { | 5 |
| Gréng Lëscht Ekologesch Initiativ | | |
| Comité d'Action pour la Démocratie et la Justice | } 13.96 { | 5 |
| Others | | |
| **Total** | 100.00 | 60 |

# LUXEMBOURG

## Political Organizations

**Comité d'Action pour la Démocratie et la Justice:** BP 365, 4004 Esch-sur-Alzette; tel. 46-37-42; fax 46-37-45; f. 1989, present name adopted 1994; campaigns to secure improved pension rights for private-sector employees.

**Déi Gréng Alternativ** (Green Alternative): BP 454, 2014 Luxembourg; tel. 46-37-40; fax 46-37-43; f. 1983; advocates 'grass-roots' democracy, environmental protection, social concern and increased aid to developing countries; Secs ABBES JACOBY, FELIX BRAZ.

**Gréng Lëscht Ekologesch Initiativ** (Green List Ecological Initiative): BP 1567, 1015 Luxembourg; tel. 22-77-67; fax 46-37-41; f. 1989; ecology party.

**Parti Chrétien Social (PCS)** (Christian Social Party): 4 rue de l'Eau, 1449 Luxembourg; tel. 22-57-31; fax 47-27-16; f. 1914; advocates political stability, sustained economic expansion, ecological and social progress; 9,500 mems; Pres. ERNA HENNICOT-SCHOEPGES; Sec.-Gen. CLAUDE WISELER.

**Parti Communiste Luxembourgeois** (Communist Party): 18 rue Christophe Plantin, 2339 Luxembourg; tel. 49-20-95; telex 2880; fax 49-37-47; f. 1921; pluralist and non-dogmatic Marxist party; advocates an independent economic policy, national sovereignty and eventual withdrawal from NATO; Pres. ALOYSE BISDORFF.

**Parti Démocratique Luxembourgeois** (Democratic Party): 46 Grand'rue, 1660 Luxembourg; tel. 22-10-21; telex 2978; fax 22-10-13; Liberal party; Leader LYDIE POLFER; Sec.-Gen. HENRI GRETHEN.

**Parti Ouvrier Socialiste Luxembourgeois (POSL)** (Socialist Workers' Party): 16 rue de Crécy, 1364 Luxembourg; tel. 45-59-91; fax 45-65-75; f. 1902; 6,000 mems; Pres. BEN FAYOT; Sec.-Gen. RAYMOND BECKER.

## Diplomatic Representation

### EMBASSIES IN LUXEMBOURG

**Austria:** 3 rue des Bains, 1212 Luxembourg; tel. 47-11-88; telex 2530; fax 46-39-74; Ambassador: JOHANN LEGTMANN.

**Belgium:** 4 rue des Girondins, 1626 Luxembourg; tel. 44-27-46; telex 2550; fax 45-42-82; Ambassador: PAUL DUQUE.

**China, People's Republic:** 2 rue Van Der Meulen, 2152 Luxembourg; tel. 43-69-91; fax 42-24-23; Ambassador SHI YANHUA.

**Denmark:** 4 bvld Royal, 2449 Luxembourg; tel. 22-21-22; telex 1705; fax 22-21-24; Ambassador: MICHAEL BENDIX.

**France:** 9 blvd Prince-Henri, 1724 Luxembourg, BP 359, 2013 Luxembourg; tel. 47-55-88; telex 2744; Ambassador: JACQUES LECLERC.

**Germany:** 20–22 ave Emile Reuter, 2420 Luxembourg; tel. 45-34-45-1; telex 3413; fax 45-56-04; Ambassador: ROLF-EBERHARD JUNG.

**Greece:** 117 val Ste Croix, 1371 Luxembourg; tel. 44-51-93; telex 2948; Ambassador: KONSTANTINOS IVRAKIS.

**Ireland:** 28 route d'Arlon, 1140 Luxembourg; tel. 45-06-10; fax 45-88-20; Ambassador: GERALDINE SKINNER.

**Italy:** 5 rue Marie-Adélaïde, 2128 Luxembourg; tel. 44-36-44; telex 2216; Ambassador: LEOPOLDO FORMICHELLA.

**Japan:** 17 rue Beaumont, 1219 Luxembourg; tel. 46-41-51; telex 1870; fax 46-41-76; Chargé d'affaires: JUNICHI NAKAMURA.

**Netherlands:** 5 rue C. M. Spoo, 2546 Luxembourg; tel. 22-75-70; telex 2204; fax 40-30-16; Ambassador: JOHAN G. W. FABER.

**Portugal:** 33 allée Scheffer, 2520 Luxembourg; tel. 47-39-55; telex 1782; Ambassador: MANUEL SYDER SANTIAGO.

**Russia:** Château de Beggen, 1719 Luxembourg; tel. 42-23-33; telex 60445; fax 42-23-34; Ambassador: ALEXEI GLOUKHOV.

**Spain:** 2–4 blvd E. Servais, 2535 Luxembourg; tel. 46-02-55; fax 47-48-50; Ambassador: ALONSO ALUDREZ DE TOLEDO.

**Switzerland:** 35 blvd Royal, BP 469, 2014 Luxembourg; tel. 22-74-74; fax 46-43-93; Ambassador: Dr FRANZ BIRRER.

**Turkey:** 20 rue Marie-Adélaïde, 2128 Luxembourg; tel. and fax 44-32-81; telex 2473; Ambassador: ERHAN TUNCEL.

**United Kingdom:** 14 blvd Roosevelt, 2450 Luxembourg; tel. 22-98-64; fax 22-98-67; Ambassador: JOHN NICHOLAS ELAM.

**USA:** 22 blvd E. Servais, 2535 Luxembourg; tel. 46-01-23; fax 46-14-01; Ambassador: CLAY CONSTANTINOU.

## Judicial System

The lowest courts in Luxembourg are those of the Justices of the Peace, of which there are three, at Luxembourg-Ville, Esch-sur-Alzette and Diekirch. These are competent to deal with civil, commercial and criminal cases of minor importance. Above these are the two District Courts, Luxembourg being divided into the judicial districts of Luxembourg and Diekirch. These are competent to deal with civil, commercial and criminal cases. The Superior Court of Justice includes both a court of appeal, hearing decisions made by District Courts, and the Cour de Cassation. As the judicial system of the Grand Duchy does not employ the jury system, a defendant is acquitted if a minority of the presiding judges find him or her guilty. The highest administrative court is the Comité du Contentieux du Conseil d'Etat. Special tribunals exist to adjudicate upon various matters of social administration such as social insurance. The department of the Procureur Général (Attorney-General) is responsible for the administration of the judiciary and the supervision of judicial police investigations.

Judges are appointed for life by the Grand Duke, and are not removable except by judicial sentence.

**Superior Court of Justice:** Pres. PAUL KAYSER.

**Attorney-General:** CAMILLE WAMPACH.

## Religion

### CHRISTIANITY

#### The Roman Catholic Church

For ecclesiastical purposes, Luxembourg comprises a single archdiocese, directly responsible to the Holy See. At 31 December 1993 there were, according to church data, an estimated 370,500 adherents in the country, representing about 94% of the total population.

**Archbishop of Luxembourg:** Most Rev. FERNAND FRANCK, Archevêché, 4 rue Génistre, BP 419, 2014 Luxembourg; tel. 46-20-23; fax 47-53-81.

#### The Anglican Communion

Within the Church of England, Luxembourg forms part of the diocese of Gibraltar in Europe.

**Chaplain:** Rev. C. G. POOLE, 11 rue Ernest Beres, 1232 Howald; tel. 48-53-97.

#### Protestant Church

**The Evangelical Church in the Grand Duchy of Luxembourg:** rue de la Congrégation, 1352 Luxembourg; tel. 22-96-70; fax 46-71-88; f. 1818 as Protestant Garnison Church, 1868 as community for the Grand Duchy; there are about 1,500 Evangelicals; Pres. Pasteur MICHEL FAULLIMMEL.

### JUDAISM

**Chief Rabbi:** JOSEPH SAYAGH, 15 blvd Grande-Duchesse Charlotte, 1331 Luxembourg; tel. 45-23-66; fax 25-04-30.

## The Press

### DAILIES

**Lëtzebuerger Journal:** 123 rue Adolphe Fischer, BP 2101, 1521 Luxembourg; tel. 49-30-33; fax 49-20-65; f. 1948; organ of the Democratic Party; Editor ROB ROEMEN; circ. 13,500 (1993).

**Luxemburger Wort/La Voix du Luxembourg:** 2 rue Christophe Plantin, 2988 Luxembourg; tel. 49-93-1; telex 3471; fax 49-10-78; f. 1848; German and French; Catholic; Christian Democrat; Publr PAUL ZIMMER; Chief Editor LÉON ZECHES; circ. 86,546 (1993).

**Le Républicain Lorrain:** 17B rue des Bains, 1212 Luxembourg; tel. 46-17-11; telex 1717; f. 1963; French; Publr/Editor V. DEMANGE (Metz, France); circ. 15,000 (1990).

**Tageblatt/Zeitung fir Letzebuerg:** 44 rue du Canal, 4050 Esch-sur-Alzette; tel. 54-71-31; fax 54-71-30; f. 1913; French and German; centre-left; Dir ALVIN SOLD; circ. 27,537 (1992).

**Zeitung vum Letzeburger Vollek:** 16 rue Christophe Plantin, BP 2106, 1021 Luxembourg; tel. 40-97-45; telex 2880; fax 49-69-20; f. 1946; organ of the Communist Party; Dir FRANÇOIS HOFFMANN; circ. 8,000 (1992).

### PERIODICALS

**AutoRevue:** BP 231, 2012 Luxembourg; tel. 22-99-3; f. 1948; monthly; illustrated; Publr PAUL NEYENS; circ. 12,000.

**Echo de l'Industrie:** 7 rue Alcide de Gasperi, BP 1304, 1013 Luxembourg; tel. 43-53-66; telex 60174; fax 43-23-28; f. 1920; monthly; industry, commerce; publ. by Fédération des Industriels Luxembourgeois; Dir LUCIEN JUNG; circ. 1,900.

**GréngeSpoun:** BP 684, 2016 Luxembourg; tel. 22-11-55; fax 22-11-53; f. 1988; weekly; social, ecological, environmental and general issues; Secs ROBERT GARCIA, RICHARD GRAF, RENÉE WAGENER; circ. 1,500.

**Handelsblad/Le Journal du Commerce:** 23 allée Scheffer, 2520 Luxembourg, BP 482, 2014 Luxembourg; tel. 47-31-25; fax 220059;

f. 1945; 6 a year; journal of the Confédération du Commerce Luxembourgeois; circ. 2,100.

**D'Handwierk:** BP 1604, 1016 Luxembourg; tel. 42-45-11-1; fax 42-45-25; monthly; organ of the Fédération des Artisans and the Chambre des Métiers; circ. 7,000.

**Horesca—Informations:** 9 rue des Trévires, BP 2524, 1025 Luxembourg; tel. 48-71-65; fax 48-71-56; monthly; hotel trade, tourism, gastronomy; Editor PHILIPPE ESCHENAUER; circ. 6,000.

**De Konsument:** 55 rue des Bruyères, 1274 Howald; tel. 49-60-22-1; telex 2966; fax 49-49-57; 18 a year; consumer affairs.

**De Letzeburger Bauer:** 16 blvd d'Avranches, 2980 Luxembourg; tel. 48-81-61; fax 40-03-75; weekly; journal of Luxembourg farming; circ. 7,500.

**D'Letzeburger Land:** 62 rue de Strasbourg, 2560 Luxembourg; tel. 48-57-57; fax 49-63-09; f. 1954; weekly; political, economic, cultural affairs; Man. Editors JEAN-MARIE MEYER, JEAN-PAUL HOFFMANN; circ. 6,500.

**Letzeburger Sonndesblad:** 2 rue Christophe Plantin, 2988 Luxembourg; weekly; Catholic; Dir Abbé ANDRÉ HEIDERSCHEID; circ. 8,000.

**Luxemburger Verbraucher-Zeitung:** 7 Grand'rue, Esch-sur-Alzette; 8 a year; consumer affairs.

**OGB-L Aktuell/Actualités:** 4002 Esch-sur-Alzette; tel. 54-05-45-1; telex 1368; fax 54-16-20; f. 1919; monthly; journal of the Confederation of Independent Trade Unions of Luxembourg; circ. 40,000.

**Revue/D'Letzebuerger Illustréiert:** BP 2755, 1027 Luxembourg; tel. 45-41-51; fax 45-88-74; f. 1945; weekly; illustrated; Man. Dir GUY LUDIG; Editor-in-Chief YOLANDE KIEFFER; circ. 28,000.

**Revue Technique Luxembourgeoise:** 4 blvd Grande-Duchesse Charlotte, Luxembourg; tel. 45-13-54; fax 45-09-32; f. 1908; quarterly; technology.

**Soziale Fortschrett (LCGB):** 11 rue du Commerce, BP 1208, Luxembourg; tel. 49-94-24-1; telex 2116; fax 49-94-24-49; f. 1921; fortnightly; journal of the Confederation of Christian Trade Unions of Luxembourg; Pres. MARCEL GLESENER; Gen. Sec. ROBERT WEBER; circ. 27,000.

**Tabou:** 131 rue des Muguets, 2167 Luxembourg; tel. and fax 438486; f. 1991; monthly; cultural affairs; circ. 50,000.

**Télécran:** 13 rue Bourbon, BP 1008, 1010 Luxembourg; tel. 49-94-50-1; fax 49-94-50-33; f. 1978; TV weekly; illustrated; Man. Editor CAREL SCHELTGEN; circ. 40,000.

**Transport:** 5 rue C. M. Spoo, 2546 Luxembourg; tel. 26-78-6; fortnightly; circ. 3,800.

### NEWS AGENCIES

Among the foreign bureaux in Luxembourg are:

**Agence Europe SA:** BP 428, 2014 Luxembourg; tel. 22-00-32; fax 46-22-77.

**Agence France-Presse (AFP):** 17B rue des Bains, 1212 Luxembourg; tel. 43-01-34-4; telex 2512; Correspondent CAMILLE MONTAIGU.

**Associated Press (AP)** (USA): Luxembourg-Eich; Correspondent JEAN-MARIE MEYER.

**Reuters Ltd:** 25C blvd Royal, 2449 Luxembourg; Bureau Chief CHRISTIAN SCHOCK.

**UPI** (USA) is also represented in Luxembourg.

### PRESS ASSOCIATION

**Association Luxembourgeoise des Editeurs de Journaux:** 2 rue Christophe Plantin, 2988 Luxembourg; tel. 49-93-1; telex 3471; fax 40-75-74; Pres. ALVIN SOLD; Sec. ANDRÉ HEIDERSCHEID.

## Publishers

**Joseph Beffort:** 18 rue de la Poste, BP 507, Luxembourg; tel. 22-66-19; f. 1869; scientific, economic reviews.

**Editions Emile Borschette:** 21 route de Larochette, 7640 Christnach; tel. 87-17-7; fax 87-95-99; f. 1987; belles-lettres, history, maps, law, languages, regional literature, theatre; CEO EMILE BORSCHETTE.

**Editpress Luxembourg:** 44 rue du Canal, BP 147, 4050 Esch-sur-Alzette; tel. 54-71-31; fax 54-71-30; Dir ALVIN SOLD.

**Imprimerie St-Paul SA:** 2 rue Christophe Plantin, 2988 Luxembourg; tel. 49-93-1; telex 3471; fax 40-75-74; f. 1887; general literature; Man. Dir PAUL ZIMMER.

**Edouard Kutter:** 17 rue des Bains, 1212 Luxembourg; tel. 23-57-1; fax 47-18-84; art, photography, facsimile editions on Luxembourg.

**Editions François Mersch:** BP 231, 2012 Luxembourg; tel. 22-99-3; history, photography.

**Editions Phi:** BP 66, 6400 Echternach; tel. 72-80-66; fax 72-83-25; f. 1980; fmrly Editions Francis van Maele; literature, art; Dir F. VAN MAELE.

**Editions-Reliures Schortgen:** 43 rue Marie Muller-Tesch, 4250 Esch-sur-Alzette; tel. 55-28-36; fax 57-20-12; art, history; Dir JEAN-PAUL SCHORTGEN.

### PUBLISHERS' ASSOCIATIONS

**Fédération Luxembourgeoise des Editeurs de Livres:** 23 allée Scheffer, 2520 Luxembourg; tel. 47-31-25; fax 220059; Pres. GASTON ZANGERLÉ.

**Fédération Luxembourgeoise des Travailleurs du Livre:** 26A rue de Pulvermühl, 2356 Luxembourg; tel. 42-24-18; fax 42-24-19; f. 1864; Pres. GUST STEFANETTI; Sec. CLAUDE BIEWESCH.

## Radio and Television

In 1992, according to UNESCO, there were an estimated 240,000 radio receivers and an estimated 101,000 television receivers in use. A medium-power television satellite, ASTRA 1A, to serve a pan-European audience, was launched on behalf of a privately-owned Luxembourg-based consortium, Société Européenne des Satellites (SES), in December 1988. A second spacecraft, ASTRA 1B, was sent into orbit in March 1991, and two further satellites (ASTRA 1C and ASTRA 1D) were launched on behalf of SES in May 1993 and November 1994 respectively.

**CLT Multi Media:** 45 blvd Pierre Frieden, 1543 Luxembourg; tel. 42-14-21; telex 3266; fax 42-142-27-60; f. 1931; fmrly Radio-Télé Luxembourg—Compagnie Luxembourgeoise de Télédiffusion; privately-owned; 13 radio stations (including services in Letzeburgish, French, German, English, Dutch and Italian) and nine television channels; also active in production, distribution, press and publishing; Pres. GASTON THORN.

**Société Européenne des Satellites (SES):** Château de Betzdorf, 6815 Betzdorf; tel. 71-0-72-51; telex 60625; fax 71-0-72-52-27; f. 1985; privately-owned; operates four satellites, broadcasting 64 channels: the ASTRA 1A television satellite (launched in December 1988), ASTRA 1B (March 1991), ASTRA 1C (May 1993), ASTRA 1D (November 1994); also operates 46 radio stations; Chair. PIERRE WERNER.

Radio frequencies were granted in July 1992 by the radio supervisory authority, the Commission Indépendante de la Radiodiffusion Luxembourgeoise, to the following operators:

**Alter Echos:** f. by environmentalist groups.

**Luxembourg Radio:** f. by Lëtzebuerger Journal, Tageblatt/Zeitung fir Letzebuerg, Revue/D'Letzebuerger Illustréiert and D'Letzeburger Land.

**Société Européenne de Communication Sociale:** f. by groups representing foreigners residing in Luxembourg.

**Société de Radio-diffusion Luxembourgeoise:** f. by Luxemburger Wort/La Voix du Luxembourg.

## Finance

(cap. = capital; res = reserves; dep. = deposits; m. = million; brs = branches; amounts in Luxembourg francs unless otherwise indicated).

**Institut Monétaire Luxembourgeois:** 63 ave de la Liberté, 2983 Luxembourg; tel. 40-29-29-203; telex 2766; fax 49-21-80; f. 1983 to represent Luxembourg in international monetary matters and to act as a banking supervisory authority; holds external assets and controls domestic loans; issues bank-notes and coins; responsible for the holding and management of official reserves; regulation of domestic credit; depositary institution for government funds; Dir-Gen. PIERRE JAANS; Dirs JEAN-NICOLAS SCHAUS, JEAN GUILL.

### BANKING

At the end of 1993 there were 221 banks in Luxembourg, most of which were subsidiaries or branches of foreign banks; a selection of the principal banks operating internationally is given below. The Banque Nationale de Belgique (see chapter on Belgium in Vol. I) acts as a central bank for Luxembourg.

#### Principal Banks

**Banco di Napoli International SA:** 10–12 ave Pasteur, 2310 Luxembourg, BP 1301, 1013 Luxembourg; tel. 47-59-59-1; telex 1533; fax 47-41-17; f. 1973; cap. ECU 144m., res ECU 10.5m., dep. ECU 3,874.3m., assets ECU 4,315.8m. (Dec. 1993); Chair. Prof. FERDINANDO VENTRIGLIA; Man. Dirs Prof. PIETRO GIOVANNINI, GIAN-PAOLO VIGLIAR.

**Banco di Roma International SA:** 26 blvd Royal, 2449 Luxembourg; tel. 47-08-51; telex 2436; fax 47-79-06-228; f. 1978; cap.

# LUXEMBOURG

and res 9,914.3m., dep. 133,146.1m., assets 146,179.1m. (Dec. 1991); Chair. Giuseppe Greco; Gen. Man. Antonio Ciocio.

**Banque et Caisse d'Epargne de l'Etat, Luxembourg:** 1 & 2 place de Metz, BP 2105, 2954 Luxembourg; tel. 40-15-1; telex 3417; fax 40-15-20-99; f. 1856 as Caisse de l'Epargne de l'Etat du Grand-Duché de Luxembourg—Banque de l'Etat, name changed 1989; govt-owned commercial, savings and state bank; cap. 7,000m., res 8,506m., dep. 620,888m. (Dec. 1993), assets 711,940m. (Dec. 1994); Chair. Victor Rod; CEO Raymond Kirsch.

**Banque Carnegie Luxembourg SA:** Centre Europe, 5 place de la Gare, 1616 Luxembourg, BP 1141, 1011 Luxembourg; tel. 40-40-301; telex 1558; fax 49-18-02; f. 1976 as PKbanken International (Luxembourg) SA, present name adopted 1993; wholly owned by Nordbanken (Sweden); cap. 350m., dep. 16,483m., assets 17,653m. (Dec. 1993); Chair. Lars Bertmar; Man. Dir Carl Uggla.

**Banque Colbert:** 1 rue Thomas Edison, 1445 Luxembourg, BP 736, 2017 Luxembourg; tel. 25-42-43; fax 25-42-57; f. 1983, present name adopted 1992; cap. 350m., res 6.2m., dep. 12,505.2m., assets 12,902.2m. (Dec. 1991); Chair. C. Franssens.

**Banque Continentale du Luxembourg SA:** 2 blvd Emmanuel Servais, 2535 Luxembourg; tel. 47-44-91; telex 2301; fax 47-76-88-529; f. 1967; cap. 1,785m., res 962m., dep. 82,789m., assets 87,878m. (Dec. 1993); Chair. Hubert de Saint-Amand; Gen. Man. Ullrich Günther Schubert.

**Banque Générale du Luxembourg SA:** 27 ave Monterey, 2951 Luxembourg; tel. 47-99-1; telex 3401; fax 47-99-25-79; f. 1919; cap. 3,500.1m., res 15,428.1m., dep. 681,267.5m., assets 742,429.3m. (Dec. 1993); Chair. Marcel Mart; 48 brs.

**Banque Internationale à Luxembourg SA:** 69 route d'Esch, 2953 Luxembourg; tel. 45-90-1; telex 3626; fax 45-90-20-10; f. 1856; bank of issue; cap. 4,098m., res 8,906m., dep. 756,434m., assets 819,642m. (Dec. 1994); Chair. Gaston Thorn; 47 brs.

**Banque Leu (Luxembourg) SA:** 16 rue Jean-Pierre Brasseur, BP 718, 2017 Luxembourg; tel. 45-32-22-1; telex 2492; fax 45-31-77; f. 1979; wholly owned by Leu Holding AG (Switzerland); cap. SFr 25m., res SFr 4.4m., dep. SFr 1,266.2m., assets SFr 1,432.2m. (Dec. 1993); Chair. Dr Werner Frey; Man. Dir Klaus Winkler.

**Banque de Luxembourg SA:** 14 blvd Royal, 2449 Luxembourg, BP 2221, 1022 Luxembourg; tel. 49-92-41; telex 2249; fax 49-51-85; f. 1936; cap. 3,000m., res 4,889m., dep. 220,244m., assets 233,899m. (Dec. 1993); Chair. Jean Weber; Vice-Chair. and Man. Dir Robert Reckinger; 4 brs.

**Banque Nationale de Paris (Luxembourg) SA:** 24 blvd Royal, BP 2463, 2952 Luxembourg; tel. 22-40-93; telex 60414; fax 22-64-80; f. 1921; cap. 1,020m., res 4,078.7m., dep. 158,107.5m., assets 174,322.9m. (Dec. 1992); Chair. Jacques-Henri Wahl; Man. Dir Thierry Dingreville.

**Banque Paribas Luxembourg:** 10A blvd Royal, 2093 Luxembourg; tel. 46-46-1; telex 2332; fax 46-46-41-41; f. 1964; cap. 2,250m., res 3,414m., dep. 200,082m., assets 225,514m. (Dec. 1993); Chair. Philippe Dulac; Man. Dir Claude Fauré.

**Berliner Bank International SA:** 60 Grand'rue, BP 71, 2010 Luxembourg; tel. 47-78-1; telex 1801; fax 47-78-26-9; f. 1977; cap. DM 50m., res DM 13m., dep. DM 2,374m., assets DM 2,485m. (Dec. 1993); Pres. Christoph Freiherr von Hammerstein-Loxten; Gen. Mans Konrad Reimann, Klaus A. Heiliger.

**BfG Bank Luxembourg SA:** 2 rue Jean Bertholet, 1233 Luxembourg, BP 1123, 1011 Luxembourg; tel. 45-22-55-1; telex 1415; fax 45-22-55-309; f. 1973; subsidiary of Bank für Gemeinwirtschaft AG, Frankfurt; cap. DM 160m., res DM 179m., dep. DM 5,990m., assets DM 7,402m. (Dec. 1993); Pres. Dr Paul Wieandt; Man. Dirs M. A. Lurz, Bernhard Müller, Reinhard Kornhaass.

**BHF-Bank International:** 283 route d'Arlon, BP 258, 2012 Luxembourg; tel. 45-76-76-1; telex 2661; fax 45-76-68; f. 1972; subsidiary of Berliner Handels- und Frankfurter Bank; cap. DM 50m., res DM 53m., dep. DM 4,389m., assets DM 4,711m. (Dec. 1993); Chair. Luis Graf von Zech; Man. Dirs Dr Hartmut Rothacker, Heinrich S. Wintzer.

**Christiania Bank Luxembourg SA:** 16 ave Pasteur, 2013 Luxembourg; tel. 47-44-70-1; telex 2843; fax 47-44-70-286; f. 1973; subsidiary of Christiana Bank og Kreditkasse (Norway); cap. 1,250m., res 2,523.8m., dep. 42,561.1m., assets 47,240m. (Dec. 1992); Chair. Jan Teksum; Man. Dir Hans J. Ødegaard.

**Citibank (Luxembourg) SA:** 49 blvd du Prince Henri, BP 1373, 1724 Luxembourg; tel. 47-79-57-1; telex 3798; fax 47-79-57-75; f. 1970; cap. 896m., res 916.4m., dep. 55,499.3m., assets 57,570m. (Dec. 1992); Man. Dirs Yves de Naurois, Paul Halloy.

**Commerzbank International SA:** 11 rue Notre Dame, 2240 Luxembourg, BP 303, 2013 Luxembourg; tel. 47-79-111; telex 1292; fax 47-79-11-270; f. 1969; cap. DM 225m., res DM 803m., dep. DM 19,017m., assets DM 21,317m. (Dec. 1993); Man. Dirs Wolfgang Möller, Klaus Tjaden.

**Crédit Suisse (Luxembourg) SA:** 56 Grand'rue, 1660 Luxembourg, BP 40, 2010 Luxembourg; tel. 46-00-11-1; telex 1356; fax 47-55-41; cap. 1,300m., res 6,575m., dep. 221,544m., assets 238,766m. (Dec. 1993); Pres. Dr Rudolf W. Hug; Man. Dir Rico Barandun.

**Den Danske Bank International SA:** 2 rue du Fossé, BP 173, 1536 Luxembourg; tel. 46-12-75; telex 1891; fax 47-30-78; f. 1976; in 1990 merged with Copenhagen HandelsBank International SA and Provinsbanken International (Luxembourg) SA; cap. 3,625m., res 2,762m., dep. 153,192m., assets 163,374m. (Dec. 1993); Man. Dir Henrik Hoffmann.

**Den norske Bank (Luxembourg) SA:** 6A route de Trèves, BP 297, 2012 Luxembourg; tel. 34-97-97-1; telex 1776; fax 34-97-97-700; f. 1974; cap. 1,200m., res 921.6m., dep. 27,030.9m., assets 39,674.3m. (Dec. 1993); Man. Dir Øivin Fjeldstad.

**Deutsche Bank Luxembourg SA:** 2 blvd Konrad Adenauer, 1115 Luxembourg, BP 586, 2015 Luxembourg; tel. 42-122-1; telex 60109; fax 42-122-449; cap. 8,600m., res 17,857m., dep. 677,855m., assets 733,254m. (Dec. 1993); Pres. Dr Ulrich Weiss; Man. Dir Dr Ekkehard Storck.

**Deutsche Girozentrale International SA:** 16 blvd Royal, 2449 Luxembourg, BP 19, 2010 Luxembourg; tel. 46-24-71-1; telex 2841; fax 46-24-77; f. 1971; cap. DM 50m., res DM 94m., dep. DM 8,009m., assets DM 8,409m. (Dec. 1993); Chair. Ernst-Otto Sandvoss; Man. Dir Bruno Stuckenbroeker.

**DG Bank Luxembourg SA:** 4 rue Thomas Edison, 1445 Luxembourg, BP 661, 2016 Luxembourg; tel. 44-90-31; telex 3747; fax 44-90-32-001; f. 1977; affiliate of DG Bank (Deutsche Genossenschaftsbank), Frankfurt; cap. DM 105m., res DM 641.4m., dep. DM 11,313.7m., assets DM 12,577m. (Dec. 1992); Chair. Dr Bernd Thiemann; Man. Dirs Detlef R. Baumert, Bernhard Singer.

**Dresdner Bank Luxembourg SA:** 26 rue du Marché-aux-Herbes, BP 355, 2097 Luxembourg; tel. 47-60-1; telex 2558; fax 47-60-33-1; f. 1967; fmrly Compagnie Luxembourgeoise de la Dresdner Bank AG; cap. DM 160m., res DM 646m., dep. DM 27,625m., assets DM 29,207m. (Dec. 1993); Chair. Jürgen Sarrazin; Man. Dirs Wolfgang A. Baertz, Walter H. Draisbach, F. Otto Wendt.

**East-West United Bank SA:** 10 blvd Joseph II, 1840 Luxembourg, BP 34, 2010 Luxembourg; tel. 45-30-61; telex 1373; fax 45-04-12; f. 1974; cap. 1,187m., res 443m., dep. 5,609m., assets 15,764m. (Dec. 1993); Chair. S. Rodionov.

**Fuji Bank (Luxembourg) SA:** 29 ave de la Porte-Neuve, 2227 Luxembourg; tel. 47-46-81; telex 3213; fax 47-46-88; f. 1980; cap. US $34.5m., res US $24.7m., dep. US $1,054.4m., assets US $1,136.5m. (Dec. 1992); Chair. Kusuo Shigyo; Man. Dir Shozaburo Shishido.

**Helaba Luxembourg Landesbank Hessen-Thüringen International SA:** 4 place de Paris, BP 1702, 1017 Luxembourg; tel. 49-94-01-1; telex 3295; fax 49-94-01-241; f. 1980; cap. DM 100m., res DM 35m., dep. DM 6,621m., assets DM 7,164m. (Dec. 1993); Dirs Rainer Kühn, Jürgen Völzer, Raymond Goebbels.

**Hypobank International SA:** 4 rue Alphonse Weicker, 2721 Luxembourg; tel. 4272-1; telex 2628; fax 4272-4500; f. 1972; subsidiary of Bayerische Hypotheken-und Wechsel-Bank AG, Munich; cap. DM 155m., res DM 267m., dep. DM 13,355m., assets DM 14,214m. (Dec. 1993); Chair. Dr Hans-Hubert Friedl; Man. Dirs Peter Binkowski, Klaus Fetzer.

**International Trade & Investment Bank SA:** Luxembourg; tel. 22-60-04; telex 1350; fax 46-28-29; f. 1973 as World Banking Corporation SA; cap. US $42.5m., res US $16.9m., dep. $113.6m., assets $173.0m. (Dec. 1991); Chair. Khalid S. bin Mahfooz; Man. Dir David Sharpin.

**Kansallis International Bank SA:** 1A rue Pierre d'Aspelt, BP 254, 2012 Luxembourg; tel. 252-020-1; telex 1819; fax 45-84-72; f. 1977; cap. 1,000m., res 313.9m., dep. 19,112.6m., assets 21,478.3m. (Dec. 1991); Chair. Jaakko Lassila; Man. Dir Gaudenz Prader.

**Kredietbank SA Luxembourgeoise:** 43 blvd Royal, 2955 Luxembourg; tel. 47-97-1; telex 3418; fax 47-26-67; f. 1949; cap. 6,361m., res 7,630m., dep. 494,819m., assets 541,654m. (Dec. 1993); Chair. Baron Luc Wauters; 5 brs.

**Lampebank International SA:** 2 rue de l'Eau, BP 164, 2011 Luxembourg; tel. 46-26-26-1; telex 3362; fax 22-01-34; f. 1979; cap. DM 25m., res DM 9.5m., dep. DM 965,914m., assets DM 1,012m. (Dec. 1993); Pres. Dr Helmut Nieland.

**Landesbank Rheinland-Pfalz International SA:** 6 rue de l'Ancien Athénée, 1144 Luxemland, BP 84, 2010 Luxembourg; tel. 47-59-21-1; telex 1835; fax 47-59-21-269; f. 1978; cap. DM 69m., res DM 54m., dep. DM 4,779m., assets DM 5,078m. (Dec. 1993); Chair. Hermann-Josef Bungarten; Man. Dirs Hans-Georg Stefan, Alain Baustert.

**Landesbank Schleswig-Holstein International SA:** 2 rue Jean Monnet, 2180 Luxembourg; tel. 42-41-411; telex 1806; fax 42-41-97; f. 1977; cap. DM 63.9m., res DM 45.1m., dep. DM 7,687.3m.,

# LUXEMBOURG

assets DM 8,119.7m. (Dec. 1993); Chair. WALTER SCHÄFER; Man. Dir Dr HANS-ALBRECHT SASSE.

**Norddeutsche Landesbank Luxembourg SA:** 26 route d'Arlon, BP 121, 1140 Luxembourg; tel. 45-22-11-1; telex 2485; fax 45-22-11-31-9; f. 1972; cap. DM 87.5m., res DM 151m., dep. DM 11,293m., assets DM 12,172m. (Dec. 1993); Man. Dir JOCHEN PETERMANN.

**Sanpaolo-Lariano Bank SA:** 12 ave de la Liberté, BP 2062, 1930 Luxembourg; tel. 40-37-60-1; telex 3168; fax 49-53-91; f. 1981; cap. ECU 35m., res ECU 2m., dep. ECU 1,529m., assets ECU 1,626m. (Dec. 1993); Chair. GIANNI ZANDANO; Gen. Man. STÉPHANE BOSI.

**Skandinaviska Enskilda Banken (Luxembourg) SA:** 31 rue Notre Dame, BP 621, 2016 Luxembourg; tel. 47-79-81-1; telex 1696; fax 47-31-37; f. 1977; cap. and res 1,961m., dep. 40,522m., assets 46,062m. (Dec. 1992); Pres. P. JEDEFORS; Man. Dir L. TÖRNQUIST.

**Société Européenne de Banque:** 19–21 blvd du Prince Henri, 1724 Luxembourg; tel. 46-14-11; telex 1274; fax 22-37-55; f. 1976; cap. 1,000m., res. 520m., dep. 73,464m., assets 77,651m. (Dec. 1993); Chair. CLAUDE DESCHENAUX; Man. Dir ARRIGO MANCINI.

**Svenska Handelsbanken SA:** 146 blvd de la Pétrusse, 2330 Luxembourg, BP 678, 2016 Luxembourg; tel. 49-98-11-1; telex 2405; fax 49-00-04; f. 1978; cap. 1,150m., res. 1,298.3m., dep. 38,594m., assets 42,074.3m. (Dec. 1993); Chair. MAGNUS UGGLA; Man. Dir FRANS HENRIK KOCKUM.

**Swiss Bank Corporation (Luxembourg) SA:** 26 route d'Arlon, BP 2, 2010 Luxembourg; tel. 45-20-301; telex 1481; fax 45-20-30-700; f. 1974; subsidiary of Swiss Bank Corpn.; cap. 2,800m., res 2,098m., dep. 121,439m., assets 134,536m. (Dec. 1993); Chair. JACQUES KAUFFMAN; Vice-Chair. ERNST BALSIGER.

**UBAE Arab German Bank SA:** Luxembourg; tel. 46-50-01-1; telex 2847; fax 47-48-88; f. 1973 as Union de Banques Arabes et Européennes; present name adopted 1979; cap. DM 50m., res DM 126.5m., dep. DM 434.9m., assets DM 641.4m. (Dec. 1991); Pres. ABDUL MAJEED SHOMAN; Man. Dir GÜNTER GROMMEK.

**Unibank SA:** 672 rue de Neudorf, BP 562, 2015 Luxembourg; tel. 43-88-71; telex 1590; fax 43-93-52; f. 1976 as Privatbanken International (Denmark) SA, Luxembourg; cap. 800m., res 2,155m., dep. 111,224m., assets 119,776m. (Dec. 1993); Chair. PETER SCHÜTZE; Man. Dir JHON MORTENSEN.

**Union Bank of Finland International SA:** 189 ave de la Faïencerie, 1511 Luxembourg, BP 569, 2015 Luxembourg; tel. 47-76-11-1; telex 1575; fax 47-76-11-25-1; f. 1976; cap. MCU 35m., res. MCU 15.4m., dep. MCU 260.9m., assets MCU 359m. (Dec. 1993); Chair. MIKAEL VON FRANCKELL; Man. Dir JAN-PETER REHN.

**Union Bank of Switzerland (Luxembourg) SA:** 36–38 Grand'rue BP 134, 2011 Luxembourg; tel. 45-12-11; telex 1280; fax 45-12-12-70-0; f. 1973; cap. SFr 150m., res SFr 628.7m., dep. SFr 16,283m., assets SFr 17,778.4m. (Dec. 1992); Chair. PIERRE DE WECK; Gen. Man. PETER FAES.

**Vereinsbank Internationale SA Luxembourg:** 38–40 ave Monterey, 2163 Luxembourg, BP 481, 2014 Luxembourg; tel. 45-10-11; telex 2654; fax 45-10-12-45; f. 1972 as Bayerische Vereinsbank International SA, name changed 1993; cap. DM 220m., res DM 397m., dep. DM 18,666m., assets DM 18,990m. (Dec. 1994); Pres. PETER REIMPELL; Man. Dirs ERNST-DIETER WIESNER, GUNNAR HOMANN, HOLGER MÖLLER.

**WestLB International SA:** 32–34 blvd Grande-Duchesse Charlotte, BP 420, 2014 Luxembourg; tel. 44-74-11; telex 2209; fax 44-741-210; f. 1972; subsid. of Westdeutsche Landesbank Girozentrale, Germany (75%), and Südwestdeutsche Landesbank Girozentrale, Germany (25%); cap. DM 126.5m., res DM 239.2m., dep. DM 18,456m., assets DM 19,800m. (Dec. 1993); Pres. HANS HENNING OFFEN; Gen. Man. FRANZ RUF.

**Westfalenbank International SA:** 31 blvd du Prince Henri, 2017 Luxembourg; tel. 47-59-01-1; telex 3358; fax 47-59-01-24; f. 1979; cap. DM 36m., res DM 16.1m., dep. DM 1,594.8m., assets DM 1,707.2m. (Dec. 1994); Pres. ROBERT K. GOGARTEN; Man. Dirs WALDEMAR E. GRAEWERT, PETER BINKOWSKI.

### Credit Institution

**Société Nationale de Crédit et d'Investissement (SNCI):** 7 rue du St-Esprit, BP 1207, 1012 Luxembourg; tel. 46-19-71-1; telex 60662; fax 46-19-79; f. 1978; cap. and res 7,319m., assets 25,280m. (1993); SNCI finances participations in certain cos, provides loans for investment and research and development projects, provides export credit; Pres. ROMAIN BAUSCH.

### Banking Association

**Association des Banques et Banquiers Luxembourg (ABBL):** 20 rue de la Poste, BP 13, 2010 Luxembourg; tel. 46-36-60-1; fax 46-09-21; f. 1939; Dir LUCIEN THIEL; Sec.-Gen. GEORGES GLESENER.

*Directory*

### STOCK EXCHANGE

**Société de la Bourse de Luxembourg SA:** 11 ave de la Porte-Neuve, BP 165, 2011 Luxembourg; tel. 47-79-36-1; telex 2559; fax 47-32-98; f. 1928; Pres. EDMOND ISRAEL; CEO MICHEL MAQUIL.

### INSURANCE

At 31 December 1992 there were 68 approved insurance companies, of which about one-half were Luxembourg companies; there were, in addition, 172 reinsurance companies. A selection of insurance companies is given below:

**Al Saudia Insurance and Reinsurance Co SA:** 11 blvd du Prince Henri, Luxembourg; f. 1977; Dir EDMOND RIES.

**Allianz Arab-German Insurance Co SA:** 13 blvd de la Foire, Luxembourg; f. 1979; Dir ARMAND HAAS.

**AXA Assurances Luxembourg:** 4–6 rue Adolphe, 1116 Luxembourg; tel. 44-24-24-1; telex 1779; fax 44-24-24-88; f. 1977; fmrly ASSURLUX (Assurances Réunies du Luxembourg); cap. 105m. (Dec. 1992); all branches and life; Chair. JEAN PRÜM.

**Le Foyer, Groupe d'Assurances:** 6 rue Albert Borschette, 2986 Luxembourg-Kirchberg; tel. 43-74-37; telex 2503; fax 42-22-23; f. 1922; all branches and life; Chair. MARC LAMBERT.

**La Luxembourgeoise SA d'Assurances:** 10 rue Aldringen, 1118 Luxembourg; tel. 47-61-1; telex 1450; fax 47-61-30-0; f. 1989; cap. 350m.; all branches of non-life; Chair. ROBERT HENTGEN; Dir GABRIEL DEIBENER.

**National Insurance Company SA:** 5 blvd de la Foire, Luxembourg; all branches; Gen. Man. RENÉ SCHMITTER.

**West of England Shipowners' Mutual Insurance Asscn (Luxembourg):** 33 blvd du Prince Henri, Luxembourg; tel. 47-00-67; telex 2702; f. 1970; marine mutual insurance; Gen. Man. P. A. ASPDEN.

# Trade and Industry

### CHAMBER OF COMMERCE

**Chambre de Commerce:** 7 rue Alcide de Gasperi, 2981 Luxembourg-Kirchberg; tel. 43-58-53; fax 43-83-26; Pres. JOSEPH KINSCH; Dir PAUL HIPPERT; 14,500 mems.

### INDUSTRIAL ASSOCIATIONS

**Centrale Paysanne Luxembourgeoise:** 16 blvd d'Avranches, 2980 Luxembourg; tel. 48-81-61-1; fax 40-03-75; f. 1945; Pres. CARLO RAUS; Sec. LUCIEN HALLER; groups all agricultural organizations.

**Confédération du Commerce Luxembourgeois:** 23 Centre Allée Scheffer, 2520 Luxembourg, BP 482, 2014 Luxembourg; tel. 47-31-25; fax 220059; f. 1909; Pres. NORBERT FRIOB; Sec.-Gen. THIERRY NOTHUM; 3,500 mems.

**Fédération des Artisans du Grand-Duché de Luxembourg:** BP 1604, 1016 Luxembourg; tel. 42-45-111; fax 42-45-25; f. 1905; Chair. LOUIS TOUSSAINT; Sec.-Gen. MARCEL SAUBER; 4,000 mems.

**Fédération des Industriels Luxembourgeois:** 7 rue Alcide de Gasperi, BP 1304, 1013 Luxembourg; tel. 43-53-66; telex 60174; fax 43-23-28; f. 1918; Pres. MARC ASSA; Adm. Dir LUCIEN JUNG; 350 mems.

**Groupement des Industries Sidérurgiques Luxembourgeoises** (Federation of Iron and Steel Industries in Luxembourg): BP 1704, 1017 Luxembourg; tel. 48-00-01; fax 48-35-32; f. 1927; Pres JOSEPH KINSCH (ARBED); Dir PIERRE SEIMETZ.

### TRADE UNIONS

**Confédération Générale du Travail du Luxembourg (CGT)** (Luxembourg General Confederation of Labour): 60 blvd J. F. Kennedy, BP 149, 4002 Esch-sur-Alzette; tel. 54-05-45; telex 1368; fax 54-16-20; f. 1927; Pres. JOHN CASTEGNARO; Sec.-Gen. JOSY KONZ; 48,000 mems (1994).

**Landsverband Luxemburger Eisenbahner, Transportarbeiter, Beamten und Angestellten** (National Union of Luxembourg Railway and Transport Workers and Employees): 63 rue de Bonnevoie, 1260 Luxembourg; tel. 48-70-44; fax 48-85-25; f. 1909; affiliated to CGT and International Transport Workers' Federation; Pres JOSY KONZ; Gen. Sec. RENÉ BLESER; 8,000 mems.

**Lëtzebuerger Chrëschtleche Gewerkschaftsbond (LCGB)** (Confederation of Christian Trade Unions): 11 rue du Commerce, BP 1208, 1012 Luxembourg; tel. 49-94-24-1; telex 2116; fax 49-94-24-49; f. 1921; affiliated to European Trade Union Confederation and World Confederation of Labour; Pres MARCEL GLESENER; Gen. Sec. ROBERT WEBER; 27,000 mems.

**Onofhaengege Gewerkschaftsbond-Letzeburg (OGB-L)** (Confederation of Independent Trade Unions): BP 149, 4002 Esch-sur-

## LUXEMBOURG

Alzette; tel. 54-05-45; telex 1368; fax 54-16-20; f. 1978; Pres. JOHN CASTEGNARO; 40,500 mems (1994).

## Transport

### RAILWAYS

At 31 December 1994 there were 275 km of electrified railway track.

**Société Nationale des Chemins de Fer Luxembourgeois:** 9 place de la Gare, BP 1803, 1018 Luxembourg; tel. 49-90-1; telex 2288; fax 49-90-44-70; Pres. Admin. Council JEANNOT SCHNEIDER; Dir-Gen. ROBERT MOLITOR.

### ROADS

At 31 December 1994 there were 5,134 km of roads, of which motorways comprised 121 km.

**Ministry of Public Works:** 4 blvd F. D. Roosevelt, 2940 Luxembourg; tel. 478-1; fax 46-27-09.

### INLAND WATERWAYS AND SHIPPING

The canalization of the Moselle river has given Rhine shipping direct access to Luxembourg. An 'offshore' shipping register was established in 1991.

### CIVIL AVIATION

There is an international airport near Luxembourg-Ville.

**Luxair** (Société Luxembourgeoise de Navigation Aérienne): Aéroport de Luxembourg, 2987 Luxembourg; tel. 48-98-1; telex 2372; fax 43-24-82; f. 1962; regular services to destinations in Europe and Africa; Dir and CEO ROGER SIETZEN.

**Cargolux Airlines International SA:** Aéroport de Luxembourg, 2990 Luxembourg; tel. 42-11-1; fax 43-54-46; f. 1970; regular all-freighter services between Europe, the Middle East, the Far East and the USA; world-wide charters; maintenance and sub-leasing services; Pres. ROGER SIETZEN.

## Tourism

Many tourist resorts have developed around the ruins of medieval castles such as Clerf, Esch/Sauer, Vianden and Wiltz. The Benedictine Abbey at Echternach is also much visited. There is a thermal centre at Mondorf-les-Bains, supplied by three mineralized springs. In addition, there are numerous footpaths and hiking trails. Luxembourg-Ville, with its many cultural events and historical monuments, is an important centre for congresses. In 1993 there were 525,707 tourist arrivals at hotels and similar establishments.

**Office National du Tourisme:** 77 rue d'Anvers, BP 1001, 1010 Luxembourg; tel. 40-08-08; fax 40-47-48; f. 1931; 170 mems; Chair. R. FRISCH; Dir ROBERT L. PHILIPPART.

# THE FORMER YUGOSLAV REPUBLIC OF MACEDONIA

## Introductory Survey

**Location, Climate, Language, Religion, Flag, Capital**

The former Yugoslav republic of Macedonia (FYRM) is situated in south-eastern Europe. The FYRM is a land-locked state and is bounded by Serbia to the north (the Serbian province of Kosovo to the north-west and Serbia proper to the north-east), Albania to the west, Greece to the south and Bulgaria to the east. The republic is predominantly mountainous with a continental climate, although the Vardar (Axiós) river valley, which bisects the country from north-west to south-east, across the centre of the republic and into Greece, has a mild Mediterranean climate with a mean summer-time temperature of 27°C (80°F). The official language of the republic, under the Constitution of November 1991, was originally stipulated as Macedonian (although this article was later removed—see Recent History). The Macedonian language is written in the Cyrillic script. Minority languages (notably Albanian) are used at local level. Most of the population is nominally Christian and of the Eastern Orthodox faith. The ethnic Macedonians (who accounted for 66.5% of the total population according to the 1994 census) are adherents of the Macedonian Orthodox Church, which is autocephalous or independent, but is not recognized by other Orthodox churches. Most of the ethnic Albanians (officially recorded as 22.9% of the population) are Muslims, although there are some Roman Catholic Albanians in Skopje and some Orthodox near Ohrid. Most of the remaining minority groups are also Muslims. The national flag (proportions 2 by 1) consists of a yellow disc (representing the sun), framed by eight long and eight short yellow rays, on a red field. The capital is Skopje.

**Recent History**

The ancient territory of Macedonia covered areas in northern Greece (Aegean Macedonia) and south-west Bulgaria (Pirin Macedonia), as well as the area comprising the present territory (Vardar Macedonia). Alexander III ('the Great'), who ruled the ancient kingdom of Macedonia, or Macedon, from 336 BC, consolidated Macedonian rule in Greece, and the campaign against the Persian Empire extended Macedonia's influence over Asia Minor, the Levant, Egypt, Mesopotamia, Persia and parts of India. The empire declined following the death of Alexander the Great in 323 BC, and Macedonia became a province of the Roman Empire in 148 BC. From the 12th century AD control of the area was contested between the Byzantine Empire, the Bulgarians and the Serbs, and the territory was under Ottoman rule from the 1370s until the 19th century. During the latter part of the 19th century the Greeks, Bulgarians and Serbs competed for influence in the territory, while a nationalist movement emerged, favouring a Southern Slav federation of Macedonians, Bulgarians and Serbs. After the First World War, during which Macedonia was occupied by the Bulgarians and the Central Powers, Vardar Macedonia, the area now known as the former Yugoslav republic of Macedonia (FYRM), became part of the new Kingdom of Serbs, Croats and Slovenes (formally named Yugoslavia in 1929). The territory was placed under the authority of the Serbian Church, and Serbian was made the official language, policies which helped to foster pro-Bulgarian sentiments. In the Second World War, however, the Bulgarian occupation of 1941–44 disillusioned many Yugoslav Macedonians. From 1943 Tito's Partisans (Josip Broz—alias Tito—was the General Secretary of the banned Communist Party of Yugoslavia) began to increase their support in the region, and after the war the new Federal People's Republic of Yugoslavia and its communist rulers resolved to include a Macedonian nation as a federal partner (having rejected the idea of a united Macedonia under Bulgaria). A distinct Macedonian identity was fostered (although largely to counter any residual pro-Bulgarian sentiment among the population), and a linguistic policy which encouraged the establishment of a Macedonian literary language distinct from Bulgarian and Serbian, together with the consolidation of a historical and cultural tradition, increased Macedonian self-awareness. In 1967 the Orthodox Church in Macedonia declared itself autocephalous, a move bitterly contested by the Serbian Orthodox Church, which refused to recognize it and succeeded in persuading the other Orthodox churches not to recognize it either. This Macedonian nationalism, surrounded by countries that denied its legitimacy, encouraged the republic's ambivalence towards the Yugoslav federation. Membership of Yugoslavia gave Macedonia a protected identity, but it feared resurgent Serbian nationalism in a federation without the balancing influence of Croatia and Slovenia.

The presence of a large ethnic Albanian minority (22.9% of the population, according to the 1994 census—although Albanian nationalist leaders in the FYRM claim that ethnic Albanians represent some 40% of the population) in western Macedonia added to Macedonian insecurities. The geographical and cultural proximity of neighbouring Kosovo (a province of Serbia with a majority ethnic Albanian population) and demands from the late 1960s for the creation of a Yugoslav Albanian republic alarmed the Macedonian authorities, who became particularly active against Albanian nationalism from 1981, mainly in the fields of education and language. There were also attempts to ban personal names of an 'Albanian-nationalist' nature and to discourage the high rate of births. In reaction to these measures, demonstrations were mounted in 1988 in which Albanian students played a prominent role. In the following year the ruling Communists responded by amending the republican Constitution, declaring Macedonia to be a 'nation-state' of the ethnic Macedonians and excluding mention of the 'Albanian and Turkish minorities'. Tension continued into the early 1990s, with the new Constitution of 1991 also refusing to specify the republic (with its new sovereign status) as a 'homeland' of the Albanians as well as the Macedonians, although it was enacted only by avoiding reference to official languages—a move designed to satisfy one of the requirements stipulated by the European Community (EC, known as the European Union, EU—see p. 143—from November 1993) for recognition of the new sovereign state. The main ethnic Albanian party in Macedonia, the Party for Democratic Prosperity (PDP), has repeatedly been accused of being an appendage of the Albanian nationalist movement in Kosovo, although the PDP has reiterated its commitment to the territorial integrity and sovereignty of the FYRM. In January 1992 an unofficial referendum (declared illegal by the Macedonian authorities) conducted among the ethnic Albanian population resulted in a 99.9% vote in favour of territorial and political autonomy for the Albanian population. In April of that year ethnic Albanians demonstrated in Skopje and north-western Macedonia, demanding the status of a constituent nation of Macedonia as a precondition for international recognition of Macedonia as an independent state.

In mid-1989 the Macedonian Communist regime conceded the introduction of a multi-party system in the Republic, and amended the Constitution accordingly. In February 1990 the Movement for All-Macedonian Action (MAMA) was founded by a group of intellectuals. It renounced any territorial claims, but discussed co-operation with the Macedonian-nationalist Ilinden movement in Bulgaria and held several large demonstrations to protest against the oppression of fellow nationals in Albania, Bulgaria and Greece. In June a more nationalist party, the Internal Macedonian Revolutionary Organization—Democratic Party for Macedonian National Unity (IMRO—DPMNU), was founded. There were delegates from the Macedonian diaspora at the founding congress, which elected Ljupčo Georgievski as leader. The congress declared the party's intention to seek the return of territories then within Serbia. The Communist authorities suspected elements of the

IMRO—DPMNU of favouring the Bulgarian cause and of fostering inter-ethnic tension with the Serbs. However, the republican Communist leader, Petar Gosev, President of what was now named the League of Communists of Macedonia—Party for Democratic Reform (LCM—PDR), also condemned the threat of Serbian nationalism, which made explicit claims later in the year when Serbia's main opposition leader, Vuk Drašković, revived the concept of 'South Serbia' and proposed a partition of Macedonia between a 'Greater Serbia' and Bulgaria.

In November and December 1990 the first multi-party elections to a new unicameral republican Sobranje (assembly) were held in Macedonia. The MAMA and the IMRO—DPMNU formed an electoral alliance, the Front for Macedonian National Unity, to counter the strong support for the ruling LCM—PDR. The first round of the elections was held on 11 November, and the nationalist Front alleged irregularities after it failed to win any seats. However, in subsequent rounds of voting (on 25 November and 9 December), the IMRO—DPMNU unexpectedly emerged as the single party with the most seats (a total of 37) in the 120-member Sobranje. The LCM—PDR won 31 seats and the two predominantly Albanian parties a total of 25. The republican branch of the federal Alliance of Reform Forces (ARF, subsequently the Liberal Party—LP) won 19 seats. These results were inconclusive, however, the uncertainty being amplified by a split in the IMRO—DPMNU, when Vladimir Golubovski challenged Georgievski for the leadership (none the less, the IMRO—DPMNU factions continued to vote as a single bloc in the Sobranje). A coalition administration for Macedonia was finally agreed in January 1991; Stojan Andov of the ARF was elected President of the republican Sobranje, Kiro Gligorov of the LCM—PDR was elected President of Macedonia, and Georgievski was elected Vice-President. Following some dispute over the allocation of portfolios, the three parties agreed to support a government largely consisting of members without political affiliation. In March the Sobranje approved a new Government, headed by an independent, Nikola Kljušev. This 'Government of Experts' committed itself to concentrating on the economic problems of Macedonia, which had been exacerbated by the Sobranje's inactivity in this area over the preceding months.

On 25 January 1991 the Sobranje unanimously adopted a motion declaring the republic a sovereign territory. In the months that followed the Macedonians were, none the less, active in attempts to mediate in the growing crisis in Yugoslavia. After the June declarations of Croatian and Slovenian 'dissociation' and the later escalation into civil war, Macedonia became wary of Serbian domination of the 'rump' federal institutions. It declared its neutrality and emphasized its sovereign status. On 8 September a referendum, boycotted by the Albanian population, overwhelmingly supported the sovereignty of Macedonia, which was again declared by the Sobranje. With war in the north of Yugoslavia, there was little federal reaction to this, and in October the evacuation of some 60% of the military bases in the republic was reported: the Macedonian authorities had received no official explanation, but it was believed that the forces were to be used in Croatia.

Georgievski resigned the vice-presidency in late October 1991, and the IMRO—DPMNU announced that it had joined the opposition. The party complained that, although it had the largest representation in the Assembly, it was being excluded from the decision-making process. However, the IMRO—DPMNU did participate in the passage of the new Constitution: its proposal for an introductory nationalist statement, which was strongly opposed by the predominantly Albanian parties, delayed the progress of the document. The Government favoured the exclusion of continual nationalist references, but did not support PDP demands to include educational and linguistic rights in the Constitution. The final version did not declare Macedonia to be the 'motherland' of the Macedonian people, but nor did it grant the Albanian language official equality with Macedonian. On 17 November the Constitution was endorsed by 96 of the 120 Assembly members: the majority of Albanian deputies and three IMRO—DPMNU deputies did not support its enactment.

Macedonian affairs were subsequently dominated by the question of international recognition. The republic, while no longer part of Yugoslavia, was unable to establish diplomatic and economic links, and was unable to take its place as an independent nation in the international community. The complete withdrawal of federal troops from Macedonia in March 1992, coupled with the adoption in April of a new Constitution in the Federal Republic of Yugoslavia (FRY), that referred only to Serbia and Montenegro, effectively signalled Yugoslav acceptance of Macedonian secession from the federation. In March Macedonia established diplomatic relations with Slovenia, and in April with Croatia.

Bulgaria recognized the state of Macedonia (although not the existence of a distinct Macedonian nationality or language) in January 1992, closely followed by Turkey, at the beginning of February, thus provoking huge demonstrations in Thessaloniki, the capital of the Greek region of Macedonia. The Greek Government insisted that 'Macedonia' was a purely geographical term (delineating an area that included a large part of northern Greece), and expressed fears that the adoption of such a name might foster a false claim to future territorial expansion. The Greek Government was instrumental in a decision, adopted by the EC in early 1992, that the republic should be awarded no formal recognition of independence by EC countries until stringent constitutional requirements had been fulfilled. In May, at a meeting in Lisbon, Portugal, EC ministers responsible for foreign affairs declared that the EC was 'willing to recognize Macedonia as a sovereign and independent state within its existing borders under a name that can be accepted by all concerned'. Gligorov described the declaration as 'injurious to the basic rights, feelings and dignity of a small and peaceful nation'. Negotiations in June, under the auspices of the EC, between the Macedonian Minister of Foreign Relations, Dr Denko Maleski, and the Greek Prime Minister, Konstantinos Mitsotakis, failed to resolve the problem, and Maleski resigned at the end of the month. Overwhelming parliamentary support, in July, for a motion expressing 'no confidence' in the Government was followed by mass demonstrations in Skopje to protest against the EC declaration and the Government's failure to gain international recognition for an independent Macedonia. The Government resigned in mid-July, and the IMRO—DPMNU, as the party with most seats in the Sobranje, was asked by President Gligorov to form a new coalition. It failed to do so, however, and eventually the Chairman of the Social Democratic Alliance of Macedonia (SDAM, as the LCM—PDR had now been renamed), Branko Crvenkovski, was installed as Prime Minister in early September at the head of a new coalition Government.

The republic formally commenced issuing passports and adopted a new flag in August 1992, a move which particularly aggravated the Greeks, who objected to the symbol of the 'Vergina Star' (which they regarded as a 2,300-year-old Greek symbol of Philip of Macedon and Alexander the Great) being used outside Greece. As a result of a blockade of petroleum deliveries imposed on Macedonia by Greece, fuel rationing was introduced in July, and by September stocks at the Skopje petroleum refinery were exhausted. In December Greece was criticized by the EC for withholding supplies of petroleum. In January 1993 the Danish Minister of Foreign Affairs, Uffe Ellemann-Jensen, in an address to the European Parliament, was severely critical of Greece's attempts to impede EC recognition of Macedonia. In the following month, reversing its previous position, Greece agreed to international arbitration over the issue of Macedonia's name, and pledged to honour any decision. A compromise was eventually reached when, on 8 April 1993, the republic was admitted to the UN under the temporary name of 'The Former Yugoslav Republic of Macedonia', pending settlement of the issue of a permanent name by international mediators. Shortly beforehand Italy had incurred Greek displeasure by unilaterally recognizing 'The Republic of Macedonia', apparently because of concern over the critical nature of the republic's economic problems. In mid-April the Macedonian Government survived a parliamentary vote of 'no confidence', proposed by the IMRO—DPMNU in protest at the Government's acceptance of the temporary name, which, they claimed, violated the Constitution, and at the economic crisis.

Despite the compromise decision on a temporary name, Greece continued to assert that the use of the 'Vergina Star' emblem and the name 'Macedonia' implied territorial claims on the northern Greek province of Macedonia, while the Macedonians denied any such intentions. A proposal, made in June 1993 by the joint UN-EC mediators on the former Yugoslavia, Cyrus Vance of the USA and Lord Owen of the United Kingdom, that 'Nova Macedonia' be adopted as a permanent name for the FYRM was rejected by the Greek Government, which reiterated its opposition to any name involving the term 'Macedonia'. In October the new Greek Prime Minister, Andreas Papandreou, announced that Greece was to withdraw from UN-sponsored negotiations with the FYRM on the issue of its name. In early January 1994 Greece requested that its EU partners exert their influence over the FYRM (other than Greece, all EU member states by now recognized the FYRM) to make concessions concerning its name, flag and Constitution, threatening to ban trade between itself and the FYRM if these three preconditions were not fulfilled. From mid-February (shortly after Russia and the USA had formally recognized the FYRM) Greece defied EU protests by blocking all shipments (excluding humanitarian aid and medical supplies) to the FYRM from the port of Thessaloniki, while road vehicles were also prevented from crossing the border into or from the FYRM; Greece subsequently closed its consulate in Skopje. Mediation efforts by the EU and the UN were unsuccessful, and in mid-April the European Commission, which contested that the Greek embargo was in violation of EU trade legislation, initiated legal proceedings against Greece at the Court of Justice of the European Communities. Further UN-sponsored negotiations failed to produce any significant concessions on the part of either the FYRM or Greece. In late June the European Court refused an attempt by the European Commission to secure an interim restraining order against the Greek blockade, pending a final ruling by the Court, which was not expected to be issued before the end of 1995. The Court began considering the case in early February 1995.

Relations between the Macedonian authorities and the ethnic Albanian minority deteriorated rapidly from late 1992. The Albanian Minister of Foreign Affairs made a formal protest to the FYRM Government after riots involving about 3,000 people in the Bit Pazar area of Skopje in November left four people dead (three ethnic Albanians and one Macedonian) and 23 injured. Further disturbances occurred in February 1993, when the construction of a refugee camp in Skopje led to four days of rioting by ethnic Macedonians, who feared the arrival of thousands of ethnic Albanian refugees from the Serbian province of Kosovo. The Government of Albania formally recognized the FYRM in April.

In November 1993 it was reported that several ethnic Albanians had been arrested in the western towns of Gostivar and Tetovo (both of which have predominantly Albanian populations) and in Skopje. The Government stated that the arrests had been made following the discovery of a plot to procure weapons and to form paramilitary groups (in collusion, it was implied, with Albania), with the eventual aim of establishing an Albanian republic in the west of the country. Among those implicated in the alleged conspiracy was a deputy government minister, Husein Haskaj. In late January 1994 Mithat Emini, the former General Secretary of the PDP, was arrested in connection with the plot. In late June Emini was sentenced to eight years' imprisonment, and Haskaj to six years in custody, after having been convicted of 'associating in order to engage in hostile activity'; eight others received custodial sentences of between five and eight years. (In mid-February 1995, following an appeal, all the sentences were reduced by two years.)

In mid-February 1994, after several months of disunity, the PDP split when a group of delegates withdrew from the party's congress. This group, led by Xheladin Murati (the Deputy President of the Sobranje) and styling itself the 'Party of Continuity', included the PDP's representatives in the Government and in parliament, and claimed to have retained the party's original programme. The other group, led by Arben Xhaferi, made more radical demands regarding the status of ethnic Albanians in the FYRM.

Groups representing ethnic Albanians protested that preparations for a national census, conducted in June–July 1994, were inadequate, and effectively prevented the full enumeration of the ethnic Albanian community. It was reported that many ethnic Albanians boycotted the census, despite appeals by their political leaders for full participation. Following the publication of the census results, ethnic Albanian groups continued to assert that their community was considerably larger than that officially indicated. The sentencing, in June, of Emini and his co-defendants prompted ethnic Albanian deputies to boycott the Sobranje in early July (although they resumed their seats to defeat a motion, proposed by the IMRO—DPMNU, expressing 'no confidence' in the Government). Murati resigned as leader of the 'moderate' PDP (and as a Deputy President of the Sobranje) in mid-July, reportedly in protest against the sentences; he was succeeded as party leader by Abdurahman Aliti.

Gligorov, representing the Alliance for Macedonia (an electoral coalition of the SDAM, the LP and the Socialist Party of Macedonia—SPM) was re-elected to the presidency on 16 October 1994, winning 78.37% of the valid votes cast; his only challenger was Ljubisa Georgievski of the IMRO—DPMNU. A first round of voting for a new Sobranje took place on the same day, at which the Alliance for Macedonia achieved considerable success. The IMRO—DPMNU, which failed to secure any seats at the first round, alleged widespread electoral fraud in both the presidential and parliamentary elections, and boycotted the second round of legislative voting, which took place on 30 October (a third round was necessary in 10 constituencies on 13 November, owing to irregularities in earlier rounds). The final results confirmed that the Alliance for Macedonia had won the majority of seats in the Sobranje (SDAM 58, LP 29, SPM eight). Aliti's PDP took 10 seats: the 'moderate' branch of the party had been legally recognized as the successor to the original PDP, and members of the 'radical' PDP had been obliged to stand as independent candidates (Xhaferi was among the independent candidates to be elected). In late November Gligorov asked Branko Crvenkovski to form a new government. The SDAM-led administration, which also included members of the LP, Aliti's PDP and the SPM, was approved by the Sobranje three weeks later.

The intention of the ethnic Albanian community to establish an Albanian-language university in Tetovo exacerbated ethnic tensions from late 1994. Ethnic Albanian groups claimed that the education system of the FYRM disadvantaged ethnic minorities; however, the Government asserted that to establish such an institution would be unconstitutional. In mid-December the authorities ordered the demolition of one of the buildings intended to house the university, stating that it had been constructed illegally, and a ban was imposed in Tetovo on all indoor meetings. The university was, none the less, formally established shortly afterwards. The opening of the academic year at the Tetovo university, in mid-February 1995, provoked considerable unrest. Police were reported to be disrupting classes, and an ethnic Albanian was killed in clashes between supporters of the university and security forces. Several people were arrested in connection with the violence, including the rector of the university, who was charged with incitement to resistance, and Nevzat Halili, a former PDP leader. Following negotiations between Aliti's PDP and the authorities, it was agreed that police reinforcements should be withdrawn from Tetovo, and later in the month it was reported that classes were to cease at the university (although all the ethnic Albanian parties reiterated their commitment to the establishment of an Albanian-language tertiary institution). However, some 2,000 students staged a demonstration in Skopje against the Tetovo university, and in late February it was reported that classes were taking place in private homes in the Tetovo region. In mid-March deputies of Xhaferi's PDP and the National Democratic Party withdrew from the Sobranje: among their demands for a return to its sessions were the introduction of Albanian as a working language of the parliament, together with concessions regarding the university in Tetovo. The rector of the Tetovo university was sentenced to two-and-a-half years' imprisonment in late April, but was provisionally released at the end of the following month.

Tensions involving other ethnic groups in the FYRM were also evident. In particular, the Democratic Alliance of Serbs in Macedonia claimed that the 1994 census discriminated against the ethnic Serb community (which constituted about 2% of the population, according to census results). In February 1995 ethnic Serb leaders indicated that the establishment of a Serbian university and assembly was under consideration.

In late 1992 the UN Security Council approved the deployment of members of the UN Protection Force (UNPROFOR, see p. 52 and Late Information) along the FYRM's border with the FRY and Albania, in an effort to protect the FYRM from any external threat to its security: accordingly, a 750-strong UNPROFOR contingent was deployed in the FYRM. In May 1993 Gligorov rejected a proposal made by his Serbian counterpart, Slobodan Milošević, for mutual recognition if the FYRM refused to accept proposed US forces on its territory. The deployment of US troops to reinforce the existing UNPROFOR

# THE FORMER YUGOSLAV REPUBLIC OF MACEDONIA

presence began in July. Under the reorganization of the UN force in March 1995, the operation in the FYRM was renamed the UN Preventive Deployment Force in the former Yugoslav republic of Macedonia (UNPREDEP).

Although agreement remained to be reached regarding a permanent name for the FYRM, by early 1995 the country had achieved wide international recognition and had established diplomatic relations with many countries. Following the imposition of the Greek embargo, from February 1994, Albania, Bulgaria, Italy and Turkey agreed to co-operate in providing trading routes for the FYRM. Relations with Bulgaria were, none the less, hindered by the question of the existence of a distinct Macedonian language, and the issue of the ethnic Albanian community in the FYRM was a frequent source of tension with Albania. While the FYRM formally supported the UN trade embargo on the FRY, there were frequent reports during the first half of 1993 that the FYRM was allowing trade to pass to or from Yugoslavia via its territory. The Gligorov administration claimed that the FYRM's economy had been severely damaged as a result of the blockade, and demanded that the country be compensated for losses suffered before sanctions against the FRY would be fully applied. There were subsequent indications that the FYRM was making greater efforts to prevent trade with the FRY, apparently linked to the republic's desire to achieve full international recognition. However, the FYRM responded to criticism during 1994 that violations of the blockade against the FRY had again increased by stating that the effects of the Greek sanctions against the FYRM necessitated some illegal transactions with the FRY.

## Government

According to the 1991 Constitution, legislative power is vested in the Sobranje (Assembly), with between 120 and 140 members, elected for a four-year term by universal adult suffrage. Executive power is held by the Ministers, including the Prime Minister, who is appointed by the President to head the Government. The Ministers are elected by the majority vote of all the deputies in the Sobranje.

## Defence

The army totalled 10,400 men in June 1994, with 8,000 conscripts, but possessed no heavy artillery. The air force numbered 50 men, yet, although the authorities planned to purchase helicopters, there were no aircraft. Conscription was introduced in April 1992, and military service lasts for nine months. There is a police force of 7,500 men, of which some 4,500 are armed. In June 1994 there were 938 UN peace-keeping troops in the FYRM.

## Economic Affairs

In 1993, according to World Bank estimates, the FYRM's gross national product (GNP), measured at average 1991–93 prices, was US $1,709m., equivalent to $780 per head. Between 1989 and 1993 the FYRM's gross domestic product (GDP) decreased by an estimated 40%. During 1991–94 the population declined by an annual average of 1.5%.

Agriculture, forestry and fishing engaged 8% of all employees in 1993. Agriculture contributed 13.0% of gross material product (GMP) in 1991, with dairy farming constituting the most important sector. The republic's principal agricultural exports are sugar beet, fruit, vegetables, cheese, lamb and tobacco. The wine industry is of considerable importance, and the FYRM is also a significant producer of rice and wheat.

Industry (comprising mining, manufacturing and utilities) represents the largest sector of the Macedonian economy, accounting for 40.4% of all employees in 1993 and contributing 42.1% of GDP in 1992. The construction sector contributed 6.6% of GDP in 1992. Mining engaged 2.4% of all employees in 1993. The only major mining activity is the production of coal, although there are also deposits of iron, zinc, chromium, manganese, lead and nickel. Manufacturing is dominated by metallurgy (which accounts for about 25% of total industrial output), chemicals and textile production. Footwear, food, beverages and tobacco are also important. About 35% of all employees were in manufacturing in 1993. Revenue from industrial production doubled between 1953 and 1988. However, the industrial sector was in decline prior to independence: in 1990 industrial output in the republic declined by 10.6%. Industrial activity has been further affected as a result of the international economic blockade of the Federal Republic of Yugoslavia (FRY) and by the disruption of petroleum sup-

plies from Greece. During 1993 industrial production fell by 11.9% (compared with the 1992 level), and in 1994 it declined by a further 10.5%, with the most severe decline being registered in the metallurgy and machine-building sectors. Industry continues to suffer in the FYRM, owing to supply problems caused by the Greek trade embargo.

The FYRM is able to produce 80% of its electricity requirements from its domestic coal and water resources. A pipeline to carry natural gas (from the territory of the former USSR) from the Bulgarian border is under construction.

In 1994 the FYRM recorded a trade deficit of US $374m. Before independence 50%–60% of the republic's trade was with the internal Yugoslav market (principally within Serbia). Trade with the FRY having formally ceased (in accordance with the international embargo on Serbia and Montenegro), the FYRM now conducts most of its trade with members of the European Union (principally Germany and Italy), and trading links have also been established with Slovenia, Russia, the USA, Bulgaria and Turkey.

In 1994 the Government aimed to restrict the general budget deficit to 6.6% of GMP, compared with 10.9% in 1993. The annual rate of inflation averaged 155% in 1981–91, rising to 1,511% in 1992. The average rise in consumer prices declined to 362% in 1993 and to about 120% in 1994. At the end of 1993 the FYRM's total external debt was estimated at US $866m., of which $528m. was long-term public debt. Some 32% of the labour force were unemployed in 1994.

The question of international recognition has impeded the FYRM's accession to regional and international organizations. The republic has, none the less, been admitted to the IMF and to other specialized agencies of the UN (see p. 58).

In mid-1994 FRY sources stated that the cost to the FYRM's economy of the international blockade of the FRY already amounted to some US $3,000m., with the loss of important trading markets undermining both the agricultural and industrial sectors. Economic activity has been further impeded by the Greek embargo, and the need to establish new trading routes has increased transport costs. Moreover, continuing uncertainty as to the FYRM's international status, together with an inadequate infrastructure, have tended to deter foreign investment. Political instability in neighbouring states has also prevented the redirection of trade. None the less, considerable success has been achieved in reducing the rate of inflation, notably since the introduction, in May 1993, of a national currency, the denar. Recent economic policy has emphasized rigid monetary policy and budgetary discipline, and the containment of the public-sector deficit through more efficient fiscal policies. A comprehensive rehabilitation programme is envisaged for the banking sector, to be implemented in co-operation with the World Bank. A major priority of the post-independence Government has been the development of the private sector as the main source of wealth and employment: more than 1,000 enterprises were scheduled for privatization by the end of the decade. However, it would appear that only by an easing of the regional situation will the FYRM's traditional trading routes and markets be restored, thereby alleviating the balance-of-payments deficit and enabling the FYRM to service its external debt, both of which remain major obstacles to sustained growth.

## Education

Elementary education is free and compulsory for all children between the ages of seven and 15. Various types of secondary education, beginning at 15 years of age and lasting for four years, are available to those who qualify. The Constitution guarantees nationals the right to elementary and secondary education in their mother tongue: there are Albanian-language schools, and a Serb-language school in Skopska Crna Gora. The University of Skopje, established in 1948, had some 24,000 students in the early 1990s. There is also a university in Bitola, established in 1979. An Albanian-language university was established in Tetovo by the ethnic Albanian minority in December 1994, but was declared illegal by the Government.

## Social Welfare

While Macedonia formed part of the former Yugoslav federation, the region benefited from the same welfare provisions as the rest of the country. There was an obligatory social insurance scheme for all persons in employment and their

## THE FORMER YUGOSLAV REPUBLIC OF MACEDONIA

families, which provided for health insurance, money payments and grants, in case of sickness, accident, disability and old age. All workers were entitled to annual leave, which varied between 18 and 36 days. In the 1980s the Yugoslav republics assumed increasing responsibility for social welfare, for which Macedonia, following its independence in 1991, assumed total responsibility. Thereafter, resources were more severely restricted. In 1993 there were an estimated 4,528 physicians, 52 hospitals and 10,834 hospital beds.

### Public Holidays

**1995:** 1–2 January (New Year), 1–2 May (Labour Day), 2 August, 11 October.
**1996:** 1–2 January (New Year), 1–2 May (Labour Day), 2 August, 11 October.

### Weights and Measures

The metric system is in force.

# Statistical Survey

Sources (unless otherwise indicated): Economic Chamber of Macedonia, 91000 Skopje, Dimitrie Čupovski 13, POB 324; tel. (91) 118088; telex 51438; fax (91) 116210; Statistical Office of Macedonia, 91000 Skopje, Dame Grueva 4, POB 506; tel. (91) 115022; fax (91) 111336; *Yugoslav Survey*, Belgrade, Moše Pijade 8/I, POB 677, Yugoslavia; tel. (11) 333610; fax (11) 332295.

## Area and Population

### AREA, POPULATION AND DENSITY

| | |
|---|---:|
| Area (sq km) | 25,713* |
| Population (census results) | |
| 31 March 1991 | 2,033,964 |
| 21 June–10 July 1994 | |
| Males | 976,051 |
| Females | 960,826 |
| Total | 1,936,877 |
| Density (per sq km) at June–July 1994 | 75.3 |

* 9,928 sq miles.

### PRINCIPAL ETHNIC GROUPS (census results)

| | 1991 | 1994 |
|---|---:|---:|
| Macedonian | 1,314,283 | 1,288,330 |
| Albanian | 427,313 | 442,914 |
| Turkish | 97,416 | 77,252 |
| Romany | 55,575 | 43,732 |
| Serbian | 44,159 | 39,260 |
| Muslim | 35,256 | n.a. |
| **Total** (incl. others) | 2,033,964 | 1,936,877 |

### PRINCIPAL TOWNS (population at 1994 census)

| | | | | |
|---|---:|---|---|---:|
| Skopje (capital) | 440,577 | | Kumanovo | 66,237 |
| Bitola | 75,386 | | Tetovo | 50,376 |
| Prilep | 67,371 | | | |

### BIRTHS, MARRIAGES AND DEATHS

**1990:** Registered live births 36,050 (birth rate 16.9 per 1,000); Registered deaths 14,926 (death rate 7.0 per 1,000).
**1992:** Registered live births 33,238; Registered marriages 15,354; Registered deaths 16,022.
**1993:** Registered live births 32,551 (provisional); Registered marriages 15,080; Registered deaths 15,591.

**Expectation of life**
(years at birth, 1990): Males 71; females 74.

### EMPLOYMENT
(ISIC Major Divisions, '000 employees, average of March and September)

| | 1991* | 1992 | 1993 |
|---|---:|---:|---:|
| Agriculture, hunting, forestry and fishing | 39 | 38 | 34 |
| Mining and quarrying | 9 | 10 | 10 |
| Manufacturing | 170 | 157 | 148 |
| Electricity, gas and water | 12 | 12 | 12 |
| Construction | 43 | 40 | 37 |
| Trade, restaurants and hotels | 58 | 55 | 49 |
| Transport, storage and communications | 24 | 22 | 21 |
| Financing, insurance, real estate and business services | 13 | 13 | 12 |
| Community, social and personal services | 87 | 85 | 85 |
| Activities not adequately defined | 13 | 14 | 13 |
| **Total** | 468 | 446 | 421 |
| Males | 294 | 278 | 263 |
| Females | 174 | 168 | 158 |

* Figures refer to state and co-operative sectors only.

Source: International Labour Office, *Year Book of Labour Statistics*.

## Agriculture

### PRINCIPAL CROPS ('000 metric tons)

| | 1991 | 1992 | 1993 |
|---|---:|---:|---:|
| Wheat | 341 | 300 | 240† |
| Rice (paddy) | 38 | 43 | 9 |
| Barley | 164 | 127 | 112† |
| Maize | 135 | 130 | 110† |
| Rye | 20 | 18 | 20* |
| Potatoes | 117 | 138 | 90* |
| Pulses | 25 | 34 | 26 |
| Sunflower seed | 37 | 38 | 18† |
| Cabbages | 62* | 56 | 45* |
| Tomatoes | 169 | 140 | 68* |
| Cucumbers and gherkins | 14† | 27 | 22* |
| Green peppers | 88* | 112 | 110* |
| Onions (dry) | 3 | 34 | 30* |
| Green beans | n.a. | 17 | 13* |
| Watermelons and melons | 105* | 119 | n.a. |
| Grapes | 264 | 265 | 205* |
| Apples | 48 | 88 | 40† |
| Pears | 15 | 17 | 16* |
| Plums | 24 | 28 | 16* |
| Other fruits and berries | 26 | 31 | 21 |
| Sugar beets | 82 | 61 | 43* |
| Tobacco (leaves) | 25 | 27 | 24† |

* FAO estimate.   † Unofficial figure.
Source: partly FAO, *Production Yearbook*.

**1994** ('000 metric tons): Wheat 336.1; Rice 8.7; Barley 149.4; Maize 133.2; Rye 15.5; Potatoes 131.4; Sunflower seed 17.9; Tomatoes 120.8; Green peppers 87.3; Grapes 205.5; Apples 70.1; Pears 11.6; Plums 25.2; Sugar beets 54.1; Tobacco 20.7.

**LIVESTOCK** ('000 head, year ending September)

|  | 1991 | 1992 | 1993 |
|---|---|---|---|
| Horses | 66 | 65 | 39* |
| Cattle | 287 | 285 | 285 |
| Pigs | 179 | 173 | 173 |
| Sheep | 2,297 | 2,251 | 2,351 |

* FAO estimate.

Source: FAO, *Production Yearbook*.

Poultry ('000 head): 4,297 in 1992; 4,393 in 1993.

**LIVESTOCK PRODUCTS** ('000 metric tons, unless otherwise indicated)

|  | 1991 | 1992 | 1993 |
|---|---|---|---|
| Beef and veal | 8 | 8 | 7* |
| Mutton and lamb | 13 | 12 | 11* |
| Pig meat | 15† | 10* | 12* |
| Poultry meat | 2 | 13* | 2* |
| Cows' milk | 123 | 117 | 100† |
| Sheep's milk | 62 | 58 | 52* |
| Cheese (metric tons) | 1,240 | 7,553 | 7,176* |
| Butter (metric tons) | 15 | 45* | 7,740* |
| Poultry eggs (metric tons)* | 27,700 | 25,900 | 18,600 |
| Honey (metric tons) | 1,719† | 1,608 | 870* |
| Wool: |  |  |  |
| greasy (metric tons) | 2,500 | 2,642 | 1,900* |
| clean (metric tons) | 1,484 | 1,321 | 1,140* |
| Cattle hides (metric tons)* | 1,800 | 1,134 | 954 |
| Sheepskins (metric tons)* | 1,264 | 1,200 | 1,100 |

* FAO estimate(s).   † Unofficial figure.

Source: FAO, *Production Yearbook*.

## Forestry

**SAWNWOOD PRODUCTION** ('000 cubic metres)

|  | 1992 |
|---|---|
| Coniferous (softwood) | 14.3 |
| Broadleaved (hardwood) | 48.2 |
| **Total** | 62.5 |

**1993** ('000 cubic metres): Timber harvested 1,107.

## Fishing

(FAO estimate, '000 metric tons, live weight)

|  | 1992 |
|---|---|
| **Total catch** (freshwater fishes) | 2.0 |

Source: FAO, *Yearbook of Fishery Statistics*.

## Mining

('000 metric tons)

|  | 1990 | 1991 | 1992 |
|---|---|---|---|
| Coal | 6,635 | 6,962 | 6,456 |

**1992** ('000 metric tons): Copper concentrates 39.1; Lead and zinc concentrates 93.9; Chromium concentrates 6.8.
**1994** ('000 metric tons): Copper concentrates 38.7; Lead and zinc concentrates 53.3; Chromium concentrates 4.2.

## Industry

**SELECTED PRODUCTS** ('000 metric tons, unless otherwise indicated)

|  | 1990 | 1991 | 1992 |
|---|---|---|---|
| Sugar | 14 | 9 | 9 |
| Wine ('000 hectolitres) | 690 | n.a. | 1,365 |
| Paper and paperboard | 43 | 35 | 29 |
| Cement | 639 | 606 | 516 |
| Crude steel | 504 | 221 | 171 |
| Aluminium (unwrought) | 6 | 8 | 6 |
| Motor coaches and buses (number)* | 9,501 | 12,091 | 10,100 |
| Lorries and vans (number) | 5,107 | 6,385 | 5,400 |
| Electric energy (million kWh) | 5,755 | 5,770 | 6,046 |

**1992** ('000 metric tons, unless otherwise indicated): Flour 158.4; Beer ('000 hectolitres) 860.8; Soft drinks ('000 hectolitres) 399.7; Cigarettes (million) 14,022; Wool yarn 7.5; Cotton yarn 9.1; Cotton fabrics ('000 sq metres) 29,009; Woollen fabrics ('000 sq metres) 10,059; Wood pulp 5.4; Sulphuric acid 95.1; Motor spirit (petrol) 104.5; Distillate fuel oils 173.7; Residual fuel oils 266.9; Building bricks (million) 346.9; Lead (unwrought) 24.6; Zinc (unwrought) 52.7; Refrigerators ('000) 147.4.
**1994** ('000 metric tons, unless otherwise indicated): Wine ('000 hectolitres) 811.3; Cigarettes (million) 13,600; Cotton yarn 7.6; Wood pulp 2.0; Sulphuric acid 72.1; Cement 486.5; Crude steel 2.5; Ferro-alloys 62.9; Aluminium (unwrought) 0.9; Electric energy (million kWh) 5,924.

* Vehicles assembled.

## Finance

**CURRENCY AND EXCHANGE RATES**

**Monetary Units**
100 deni = 1 new Macedonian denar.

**Sterling and Dollar Equivalents** (31 December 1994)
£1 sterling = 63.513 new denars;
US $1 = 40.596 new denars;
1,000 new denars = £15.745 = $24.633.

Note: The Macedonian denar was introduced in April 1992, replacing (initially at par) the Yugoslav dinar. In May 1993 a new Macedonian denar, equivalent to 100 of the former units, was established as the sole legal tender. Some of the figures in this survey are still in terms of Yugoslav dinars.

**COST OF LIVING** (Consumer price index; base: 1981=100)

|  | 1991 | 1992 | 1993 |
|---|---|---|---|
| Food | 1,079,200 | 18,270,400 | 81,449,400 |
| Fuel and light | 1,067,000 | 11,514,500 | 60,370,700 |
| Clothing | 1,116,500 | 22,832,500 | 96,147,600 |
| Rent* | 1,351,700 | 9,579,700 | 81,140,400 |
| **All items** (incl. others) | 1,166,200 | 18,790,300 | 86,811,000 |

* Including expenditure on the maintenance and repair of dwellings.

Source: International Labour Office, *Year Book of Labour Statistics*.

**NATIONAL ACCOUNTS** (million Yugoslav dinars* at current prices)

|  | 1989 | 1990 | 1991 |
|---|---|---|---|
| Gross material product | 12,623.9 | 55,070.6 | 113,646.7 |

* Figures are in terms of the new Yugoslav dinar, introduced on 1 January 1990 and equivalent to 10,000 former dinars.

**1992**: Gross material product US $1,678 million.

## External Trade

(US $million)

|  | 1993 | 1994 |
|---|---|---|
| Imports | 1,199 | 1,441.5 |
| Exports | 1,055 | 1,067.5 |

# THE FORMER YUGOSLAV REPUBLIC OF MACEDONIA

## Transport

**RAILWAYS** (traffic)

|  | 1991 |
|---|---|
| Passenger journeys ('000) | 3,122 |
| Freight carried ('000 metric tons) | 5,641 |
| Freight net ton-km (million) | 711.7 |

**1994:** Passenger journeys ('000): 1,230.

**ROAD TRAFFIC** (motor vehicles in use at 31 December)

|  | 1990 | 1991 | 1992 |
|---|---|---|---|
| Passenger cars | 230,774 | 249,654 | 279,861 |
| Buses and coaches | 2,320 | 2,576 | 2,828 |
| Lorries and vans | 18,300 | 19,757 | 22,746 |
| Road tractors | 7,811 | 6,869 | 8,898 |

Source: International Road Federation, *World Road Statistics*.

**CIVIL AVIATION** (traffic)

|  | 1991 |
|---|---|
| Aircraft movements | 8,283 |
| Passengers carried ('000) | 457.9 |
| Freight carried (metric tons) | 1,184 |

## Tourism

**FOREIGN TOURIST ARRIVALS** ('000)

|  | 1994 |
|---|---|
| Total | 623 |

## Communications Media

**Radio receivers** (1992): 369,000 in use.

**Television receivers** (1992): 338,000 in use.

**Telephones** (1990): 286,000 subscribers.

**Book production** (1990): 559 titles (incl. 67 pamphlets); 1,683,000 copies (incl. 146,000 pamphlets).

**Daily newspapers** (1990): 2 titles (combined average circulation estimated at 55,000 copies per issue).

**Non-daily newspapers** (estimate, 1991): 112 titles.

**Other periodicals** (estimates, 1991): 74 titles (combined average circulation 347,000 copies per issue).

Source: mainly UNESCO, *Statistical Yearbook*.

## Education

(1994/95)

|  | Institutions | Pupils |
|---|---|---|
| Pre-elementary | 486 | 36,895 |
| Elementary schools (general) | 1,050 | 258,955 |
| Secondary schools | 95 | 77,754 |
| Special schools (elementary) | 44 | 1,442 |
| Higher education | 2 | 27,340 |

**Teachers** (1992): Pre-primary 2,967; Primary 12,958; Secondary 4,345; Higher 2,273 (Source: UNESCO, *Statistical Yearbook*).

# Directory

## The Constitution

The Constitution of the former Yugoslav republic of Macedonia was promulgated on 17 November 1991. The following is a summary of the main provisions of the Constitution, which describes the country as the Republic of Macedonia:

### GENERAL PROVISIONS

The Republic of Macedonia is a sovereign, independent, democratic state, where sovereignty derives from democratically elected citizens, referendums and other forms of expression. The fundamental values defined by the Constitution are: basic human rights, free expression of nationality, the rule of law, a policy of pluralism and the free market, local self-government, entrepreneurship, social justice and solidarity, and respect for international law. State power is divided into legislative, executive and judicial power.

### BASIC RIGHTS

The following rights and freedoms are guaranteed and protected in the Republic: the right to life, the inviolability of each person's physical and moral integrity, the right to freedom of speech, public appearance, public information, belief, conscience and religion, and the freedom to organize and belong to a trade union or a political party. All forms of communication and personal data are secret, and the home is inviolable.

Military and semi-military associations, which do not belong to the Armed Forces of the Republic, are prohibited.

Any citizen who has reached the age of 18 years has the right to vote and to be elected to organs of government. The right to vote is equal, general and direct, and is realized in free elections by secret ballot. Citizens enjoy equal freedoms and rights without distinction as to sex, race, colour, national and social origin, political and religious conviction, material and social position.

### GOVERNMENT

**Legislature**

Legislative power resides with the Sobranje (assembly), which consists of between 120 and 140 deputies elected for four years. The Sobranje adopts and amends the Constitution, enacts laws and gives interpretations thereof, adopts the budget of the Republic, decides on war and peace, chooses the Government, elects judges and releases them from duty. The Sobranje may decide, by a majority vote, to call a referendum on issues within its competence. A decision is adopted at a referendum if the majority of voters taking part in the vote has voted in favour of it and if more than one-half of the electorate has participated in the vote. The Sobranje forms a Council for Inter-Nationality Relations, consisting of the President of the Republic and two representatives from each of the ethnic Macedonian, Albanian, Turkish and Roma communities and two representatives of other nationalities living in the state.

**President**

The President of the Republic represents the country and is responsible for ensuring respect for the Constitution and laws. He is commander of the Armed Forces and appoints the Prime Minister, appoints and recalls ambassadors, proposes members for the Judicial Council, appoints three members of the Security Council of the Republic (of which he is president) and proposes members for the Council of Inter-Nationality Relations.

# THE FORMER YUGOSLAV REPUBLIC OF MACEDONIA

## Ministers

Executive power in the Republic resides with the Prime Minister (Chairman of the Cabinet of Ministers) and Ministers, who cannot concurrently be deputies in the Sobranje. The Ministers are elected by the majority vote of all the deputies in the Sobranje. The Ministers implement laws and the state budget, and are responsible for foreign and diplomatic relations.

## Judiciary

Judicial power is vested in the courts, and is autonomous and independent. The Supreme Court is the highest court. The election and dismissal of judges is proposed by a Judicial Council. This body is composed of seven members, elected by the Sobranje from among the ranks of prominent lawyers.

## The Government

(May 1995)

**President of the Republic:** KIRO GLIGOROV (elected by the Sobranje 27 January 1991; elected by direct popular vote 16 October 1994).

### CABINET OF MINISTERS

A coalition of the Social Democratic Alliance of Macedonia (SDAM), the Party for Democratic Prosperity (PDP), the Liberal Party (LP), and the Socialist Party of Macedonia (SP).

**Chairman (Prime Minister):** BRANKO CRVENKOVSKI (SDAM).
**Minister of Foreign Affairs:** STEVO CRVENKOVSKI (LP).
**Minister of Internal Affairs:** Dr LJUBOMIR DANAILOV-FRČKOVSKI (Independent).
**Minister of Defence:** BLAGOJ HANDZISKI (SDAM).
**Minister of Justice:** Dr VLADO POPOVSKI (SDAM).
**Minister of Finance:** Dr JANE MILJOVSKI (SDAM).
**Minister of the Economy:** RISTO IVANOV (LP).
**Minister of Development:** BEKJIR ZUTA (PDP).
**Minister of Urbanization, Construction and Environment:** YORGO SHUNDOVSKI (SDAM).
**Minister of Transport and Communications:** DIMITAR BUZLEVSKI (SDAM).
**Minister of Agriculture, Forestry and Water Supply:** IVAN ANGELOV (LP).
**Minister of Labour and Social Policy:** ILIYAZ SABRIU (PDP).
**Minister of Education and Physical Culture:** EMILIA SIMOVSKA (SDAM)
**Minister of Science:** Dr SOFIA TODOROVA (SDAM).
**Minister of Culture:** ESTHREF ALIU (PDP)
**Minister of Health:** ILIYA FILIPCHE (SPM).
**Ministers without Portfolio:** Dr LJUBE TRPEVSKI (SP), GJUNER ISMAIL (SDAM), SASKO STEFKOV (LP), MUHAMED HALILI (PDP)

### MINISTRIES

**Office of the Prime Minister:** 91000 Skopje, Dame Gruev 6; tel. (91) 201211; fax (91) 211393.
**Ministry of Agriculture, Forestry and Water Supply:** 91000 Skopje, Leninova 2; tel. (91) 113045; fax (91) 211997.
**Ministry of Culture:** 91000 Skopje, Ilindenska bb; tel. (91) 220823; fax (91) 225810.
**Ministry of Defence:** 91000 Skopje, Orce Nikolov bb; tel. (91) 112872; fax (91) 221808.
**Ministry of Development:** 91000 Skopje, Bote Bocevski 9; tel. (91) 236318; fax (91) 223027.
**Ministry of the Economy:** 91000 Skopje, Bote Bocevski 9; tel. (91) 119628; fax (91) 111541.
**Ministry of Education and Physical Culture:** 91000 Skopje, Veljko Vlahovik bb; tel. (91) 236349; fax (91) 118414.
**Ministry of Finance:** 91000 Skopje, Dame Gruev 14; tel. (91) 232005; fax (91) 230466.
**Ministry of Foreign Affairs:** 91000 Skopje, Dame Gruev 4; tel. (91) 115832; fax (91) 115790.
**Ministry of Health:** 91000 Skopje, Vodnjanska bb; tel. (91) 231128; fax (91) 220163.
**Ministry of Information:** 91000 Skopje, 11 Oktomvri bb; tel. (91) 117703; fax (91) 114162.
**Ministry of Internal Affairs:** 91000 Skopje, Dimche Mirchev bb; tel. (91) 221972; fax (91) 116051.
**Ministry of Justice:** 91000 Skopje, Veljko Vlahovik 9; tel. (91) 117277; fax (91) 226975.
**Ministry of Labour and Social Policy:** 91000 Skopje, Dame Gruev 14; tel. (91) 238224; fax (91) 220408.
**Ministry of Science:** 91000 Skopje, Ilidenska bb; tel. (91) 238610; fax (91) 235573.
**Ministry of Transport and Communications:** 91000 Skopje.
**Ministry of Urbanization, Construction and Environment:** 91000 Skopje, Dame Gruev 14, tel. (91) 227204; fax (91) 117163.

## President and Legislature

### PRESIDENT

Election, 16 October 1994

| Candidate | Votes | % of votes |
|---|---|---|
| KIRO GLIGOROV (Alliance for Macedonia)* | 713,529 | 78.37 |
| LJUBISA GEORGIEVSKI (IMRO/DPMNU) | 196,936 | 21.63 |
| Total† | 910,465 | 100.00 |

* An electoral alliance of the Social Democratic Alliance of Macedonia, the Liberal Party and the Socialist Party of Macedonia.
† There were, in addition, 130,133 spoilt or invalid votes.

### SOBRANJE
(Assembly)

**President:** STOJAN ANDOV, 91000 Skopje, 11 Oktomvri bb; tel. (91) 227111.

**General Election, 16 and 30 October 1994***

| Party | Seats |
|---|---|
| Alliance for Macedonia: | |
|   Social Democratic Alliance of Macedonia | 58 |
|   Liberal Party | 29 |
|   Socialist Party of Macedonia | 8 |
| Party for Democratic Prosperity | 10 |
| National Democratic Party | 4 |
| Democratic Party of Macedonia | 1 |
| Social Democratic Party of Macedonia | 1 |
| Party for the Full Emancipation of Romanies in Macedonia | 1 |
| Democratic Party of Turks in Macedonia | } 1 |
| Party of Democratic Action—Islamic Way | |
| Independents | 7 |
| Total | 120 |

* A further round of voting took place in 10 electoral districts on 13 November 1994.

## Political Organizations

**Democratic Alliance of Serbs in Macedonia**/Demokratski Savez Srba u Makedoniji (DSSM): Skopje; f. 1994; Chair. BORIVOJE RISTIĆ.

**Democratic Party of Macedonia (DPM):** Skopje; Leader PETAR GOSEV.

**Democratic Party of Turks in Macedonia (DPTM):** Skopje; Leader ERDOGAN SARACH.

**Democratic Party of Yugoslavs of Macedonia (DPYM)**/Demokratska Partija Jugoslovena Makedonije (DPJM): Skopje; f. 1993; Chair. ZIVKO LEKOSKI; Gen. Sec. BOGDAN MICKOSKI.

**Internal Macedonian Revolutionary Organization—Democratic Party for Macedonian National Unity (IMRO—DPMNU)**/ Vnatresna Makedonska Revolucionerna Organizacija—Demokratska Partija za Makedonsko Nacionalno Edinstvo (VMRO—DPMNE): 91000 Skopje, Petar Drapshin br. 36; tel. (91) 211586; fax (91) 111441; nationalist; Pres. Prof. LJUPČO GEORGIEVSKI.

*****Liberal Party (LP):** Skopje, Ilinden bb; tel. (91) 213034; f. 1990 as republican br. of the all-Yugoslav Alliance of Reform Forces (ARF); Pres. STOJAN ANDOV.

**Macedonian Democratic Party:** Skopje; Leader TOMISLAV STOJANOVSKI.

**National Democratic Party**/Narodna Demokratska Partija (NDP): Tetovo, Gorna čaršija bb; tel. (94) 24604; f. 1990; predominantly ethnic Albanian and Muslim party; Gen.-Sec. ILJAZ HALILI.

**Party of Democratic Action—Islamic Way**/Stranka Demokratske Akcije—Islamski put: Skopje.

**Party for Democratic Prosperity (PDP)**/Partija za Demokratski Prosperitet: Tetovo, Dojce Stojcevski 14-a; tel. (94) 21380; f. 1990, split 1994; predominantly ethnic Albanian and Muslim party; Pres. ABDURAHMAN ALITI; Vice-Pres. DZEMAIL AJDARI, MUJDIM BAJRAMI.

**Party for the Full Emancipation of Romanies in Macedonia:** Skopje; Leader FAIK ABDIĆ.

**Party of Democratic Prosperity of Albanians in Macedonia:** Tetovo; f. 1994 by a split from the 'original' PDP; Chair. ARBEN XHAFERI.

*****Social Democratic Alliance of Macedonia (SDAM)**/Socijaldemokratski Sojuz na Makedonije (SDSM): 91000 Skopje, Bihačka 8; tel. (91) 231371; fax (91) 221071; f. 1943; name changed from League of Communists of Macedonia—Party of Democratic Reform in 1991; Leader BRANKO CRVENKOVSKI.

**Social Democratic Party of Macedonia:** Skopje; Leader ALEKSANDAR DONEV.

*****Socialist Party of Macedonia (SPM):** 91000 Skopje, Ilinden bb, POB 54; tel. (91) 228015; fax (91) 220025; f. 1990; left-wing.

* Denotes participants in the Alliance for Macedonia in the 1994 elections.

## Diplomatic Representation

**EMBASSIES IN THE FORMER YUGOSLAV REPUBLIC OF MACEDONIA**

**Albania:** 91000 Skopje, Tome Arsovski 29; tel. (91) 115878; fax (91) 226459.

**Bulgaria:** 91000 Skopje, Partizanski Odredi 17; tel. (91) 229444; fax (91) 233279; Ambassador: ANGEL SIMEONOV DIMITROV.

**France:** 91000 Skopje, Gradski zid, blok 5; tel. (91) 116734; fax (91) 118386.

**Germany:** 91000 Skopje, Veljko Vlahovic 26; tel. (91) 117799; fax (91) 117713.

**Italy:** 91000 Skopje, 8 Udarna brigada 22; tel. (91) 117686; fax (91) 117087.

**Romania:** 91000 Skopje, Londonska 11A; tel. (91) 315580; fax (91) 361130; Chargé d'affaires: NICOLAE MARES.

**Russia:** Skopje; Ambassador: YURY PETROVICH.

**Slovenia:** 91000 Skopje, Partizanski Odredi 3; tel. (91) 116213; fax (91) 118006; Chargé d'affaires: BORIS JELOVŠEK.

**Sweden:** 91000 Skopje, Orce Nikolov 119; tel. (91) 112065.

**Turkey:** 91000 Skopje, Slavej Planina bb; tel. (91) 113270; fax (91) 117024; Ambassador: SUHA NOYAN.

**United Kingdom:** 91000 Skopje, Veljko Vlahovic 26 (4th Floor); tel. (91) 116772; telex 51516; fax (91) 117005; Ambassador: TONY MILLSON.

## Judicial System

**Constitutional Court of the Republic of Macedonia:** 91000 Skopje, 12 Udarnas brig. bb; tel. (91) 233063; Pres. JORDAN ARSOV.

**Supreme Court:** 91000 Skopje, Borisa Kidriča bb; tel. (91) 234111; Pres. TIHOMIR VELKOVSKI.

**Office of the Public Prosecutor:** 91000 Skopje, Krste Misirkova bb; tel. (91) 229314; Public Prosecutor MARKO BUNDALEVSKI.

## Religion

Most ethnic Macedonians are adherents of the Eastern Orthodox Church, and since 1967 there has been an autocephalous Macedonian Orthodox Church. However, the Serbian Orthodox Church refuses to recognize it, and has persuaded the Ecumenical Patriarch and other Orthodox Churches not to do so either. There are some adherents of other Orthodox rites in the country. Those Macedonian (and Bulgarian) Slavs who converted to Islam during the Ottoman era are known as Pomaks and are included as an ethnic group of Muslims. The substantial Albanian population is mostly Muslim (mainly Sunni, but some adherents of a Dervish sect); there are a few Roman Catholic Christians and some Jews.

### CHRISTIANITY

**Macedonian Orthodox Church:** Skopje, POB 69; Metropolitan See of Ohrid revived in 1958; autocephaly declared 1967; 1m. mems; Head of Church and Archbishop of Ohrid and Macedonia: Metropolitan Archbishop MIHAIL RIĆ of Skopje.

#### The Roman Catholic Church

The diocese of Skopje-Prizren, suffragan to the archdiocese of Vrhbosna (Bosnia and Herzegovina), includes the FYRM and southern Yugoslavia (the Kosovo region of Serbia). At 31 December 1993 there were 64,000 adherents. Most adherents follow the Latin Rite, although there are a few adherents of the Byzantine Rite.

**Bishop of Skopje-Prizren:** Rt Rev. JOAKIM HERBUT, 91000 Skopje, Dimitrije Tucović 31; tel. and fax (91) 234123.

### ISLAM

**Islamic Community:** Skopje; formerly headquarters of the Skopje Region, one of the four administrative divisions of the Yugoslav Muslims.

## The Press

### PRINCIPAL NEWSPAPERS

**Birlik:** 91000 Skopje, Mito Hadživasilev bb; tel. (91) 116366; fax (91) 111146; f. 1944; Turkish-language newspaper; Editor-in-Chief DRITA KARAHASAN.

**Fljaka e Veljazerimit** (Torch of Brotherhood): 91000 Skopje, Mito Hadživasilev bb; tel. (91) 112095; fax (91) 224829; f. 1945, relaunched 1994; daily; Albanian-language newspaper; Editor-in-Chief ABDULJADI ZULFIĆARI; circ. 8,000.

**Nova Makedonija:** 91000 Skopje, Mito Hadživasilev bb; tel. (91) 113586; fax (91) 119416; f. 1944; daily; morning; in Macedonian; Dir PANDE KOLEMIŠEVSKI; Editor-in-Chief GEORGI AJANOVSKI; circ. 25,000.

**Puls:** 91000 Skopje, Mito Hadživasilev bb; tel. (91) 117479; f. 1991; Editor-in-Chief VASIL MISKOVSKI.

**Večer:** 91000 Skopje, Mito Hadživasilev bb; tel. (91) 111537; fax (91) 238329; f. 1963; daily; evening; in Macedonian; Editor-in-Chief STOJAN NASEV; circ. 29,200.

### PERIODICALS

**21:** 71000 Skopje, Ilinden bb; 2 a month; organ of the Social Democratic Union of Macedonia.

**Delo:** Skopje; f. 1993; weekly; nationalist.

**Puls:** Skopje; weekly; Editor-in-Chief SLOBOJAN PETROVIĆ.

**Republika:** Skopje; weekly.

**Trudbenik:** Skopje, Udarna brigada 12; weekly; organ of Macedonian Trade Unions; Editor SIMO IVANOVSKI.

### NEWS AGENCIES

**Makfaks:** Skopje.

## Publishers

**Detska radost/Nova Makedonija:** 91000 Skopje, Mito Hadživasilev Jasmin bb; tel. (91) 228757; fax (91) 225830; f. 1944; children's books; Dir PETAR BAKEVSKI.

**Kultura:** 91000 Skopje, Sv. Kliment Ohridski 68A; tel. (91) 111332; fax (91) 228608; f. 1945; history, philosophy, art, poetry, children's literature and fiction; in Macedonian; Dir DIMITAR BAŠEVSKI.

**Kulturen život:** 91000 Skopje, Ruzveltova 6; tel. (91) 239134; f. 1971; Editor LJUBICA ARSOVSKA.

**Makedonska kniga:** 91000 Skopje, 11 Oktomvri bb; tel. (91) 224055; telex 51637; fax (91) 236951; f. 1947; arts, non-fiction, novels, children's books; Dir SANDE STOJČEVSKI.

**Matica Makedonska:** 91000 Skopje, Gradski zid, blok 13; tel. and fax (91) 230358; f. 1991; Dir RADE SILJAN.

**Metaforum:** 91000 Skopje, Goce Delčev 6; tel. (91) 114890; fax (91) 115634; f. 1993; Dir RUŽICA BILKO.

**Misla:** 91000 Skopje, Partizanski odredi 1; tel. (91) 221844; fax (91) 118439; f. 1966; modern and classic Macedonian and translated literature; Dir VANČO SPASOVSKI.

**Naša kniga:** 91000 Skopje, Maksim Gorki 21, POB 132; tel. (91) 228066; fax (91) 116872; f. 1948; Dir STOJAN LEKOVSKI.

**Nova Makedonija:** 91000 Skopje, Mito Hadživasilev Jasmin bb; tel. (91) 116366; telex 51154; fax (91) 118238; newspapers, general publishing.

**Prosvetno delo:** 91000 Skopje, Dimitrie Čupovski 15; tel. (91) 117255; fax (91) 225434; f. 1945; works of domestic writers and textbooks in Macedonian for elementary, professional and high schools; fiction and scientific works; Dir Dr KRSTE ANGELOVSKI.

**Tabernakul:** 91000 Skopje, Kosturska niz 4–5; tel. and fax (91) 115329; f. 1989; Dir CVETAN VRADŽIVIRSKI.

## Radio and Television

At 31 December 1992 there were 369,000 radio receivers and 338,000 television receivers in use.

**Makedonska Radio-Televizija (MRT):** 91000 Skopje, Goce Delčev bb; tel. (91) 112200; telex 51157; fax (91) 111821; f. 1944 (radio), 1964 (TV); fmrly Radiotelevizija Skopje, name changed 1991; 3 radio and 3 TV programmes; broadcasts in Macedonian, Albanian and Turkish; Dir-Gen. MELPOMENI KORNETI; Dir of Radio GJORGI VAROSLIJA; Dir of TV SAŠO ORDANOSKI.

In the early 1990s there were 30 radio stations in the FYRM.

## Finance

The FYRM declared monetary independence in April 1992, introducing its own currency (in coupon form), the Macedonian denar (initially at par with the Yugoslav dinar; in May 1993 a new Macedonian denar, equivalent to 100 of the former units, was introduced).

(cap. = capital; res = reserves; dep. = deposits; m. = million; amounts in Macedonian denars; brs = branches)

### BANKS

#### National Bank

**Narodna Banka na Makedonija:** 91000 Skopje, Kompleks banki bb; tel. (91) 112177; telex 51415; fax (91) 111161; Gov. BORKO STANOEVSKI.

#### Selected Banks

**Komercijalna Banka a.d.—Skopje:** 91000 Skopje, Kej Dimitar Vlahov 4; tel. (91) 112077; telex 51162; fax (91) 111780; f. 1955; cap. 1,785m., res 653m., dep. 8,607m., total assets 16,819m. (Dec. 1994); Gen. Man. Dr ALEKSANDAR MANEVSKI.

**Stopanska Banka a.d.—Skopje:** 91000 Skopje, 11 Oktomvri 7; tel. (91) 115322; telex 51140; fax (91) 113263; f. 1944; cap. 3.6m., res 1.8m., dep. 54.6m. (Dec. 1993); Gen. Man. and Chief Exec. LJUBOMIR POPOVSKI; 24 brs.

## Trade and Industry

### CHAMBER OF COMMERCE

**Chamber of Economy of Macedonia:** 91000 Skopje, Dimitrie Čupovski 13; tel. (91) 233215; telex 51438; fax (91) 116210; f. 1962; Pres. DUŠAN PETRESKI.

## Transport

### RAILWAYS

In 1991 the rail network totalled 922 km, of which 231 km were electrified. Owing to the economic blockade against the Federal Republic of Yugoslavia, in force from September 1992, Macedonia suspended its freight railway traffic with the rest of Europe. In September 1993 it was announced by Germany that the Munich–Athens international train link via Skopje was to be suspended. This was Macedonia's last passenger railway link with central and western Europe. In February 1994 Albania, Bulgaria, Italy and Turkey agreed to co-operate to provide transport routes for the FYRM, including railway routes from Macedonia into Bulgaria and Albania.

**Macedonian Railways:** Skopje.

### ROADS

Macedonia's road network totalled 4,876 km in 1994. In February 1994 plans were announced for the construction of a 1,000-km highway between Istanbul (Turkey) and Durrës (Albania) via Skopje, which included the extension of the existing route into Bulgaria at a cost of US $5.5m.

**Makedonija Soobraćaj:** 91000 Skopje, Gradski zid blok 13; tel. (91) 118344; telex 51105; fax 233442; public road transport co.

### CIVIL AVIATION

Macedonia has two international airports, at Skopje and Ohrid.

**Palair Macedonian Airlines:** 91000 Skopje, Kuzman Jusifovski Pitu BB; tel. (91) 227877; telex 51364; fax (91) 222216; f. 1991; domestic services and flights to Germany, Slovenia, the CIS, the USA, Canada and Australia; Pres. BITOLJANA VANJA.

## Tourism

While part of the Yugoslav federation, tourism was a major source of foreign exchange in Macedonia. However, since independence in 1991, the tourist industry of the FYRM has declined, largely owing to the country's proximity to the conflict in other republics of the former Yugoslavia, its struggle to gain international recognition, the country's domestic instability and the intermittent sanctions imposed on the region by Greece. Nevertheless, the FYRM has a mountain climate, moderated by Mediterranean influences, and possesses some spectacular mountain scenery, suggesting considerable potential for the tourism industry should regional problems be eased. In 1994 623,000 tourists visited Macedonia.

# MADAGASCAR

## Introductory Survey

**Location, Climate, Language, Religion, Flag, Capital**

The Republic of Madagascar comprises the island of Madagascar, the fourth largest in the world, and several much smaller offshore islands, in the western Indian Ocean, about 500 km (300 miles) east of Mozambique, in southern Africa. The inland climate is temperate; temperatures in Antananarivo are generally between 8°C (48°F) and 27°C (81°F), with cooler, dryer weather between May and October. The coastal region is tropical with an average daily maximum temperature of 32°C (90°F). The rainy season extends from November to April in the highlands (average annual rainfall is 1,000 mm—1,500 mm) but is more prolonged on the coast, where average annual rainfall can reach 3,500 mm. The official languages are Malagasy and French. Hova and other dialects are also widely spoken. More than 50% of the population follow animist beliefs, while about 43% are Christians and the remainder are Muslims. The national flag (proportions 3 by 2) has a vertical white stripe (one-third of the length) at the hoist and two equal horizontal stripes, of red and green. The capital is Antananarivo (formerly Tananarive).

**Recent History**

A French possession since 1896, Madagascar became an autonomous state within the French Community in October 1958, as the Malagasy Republic. In May 1959 Philibert Tsiranana, leader of the Parti social démocrate (PSD), was elected President. The country achieved full independence on 26 June 1960. Prior to independence, France supported the PSD, which was identified with the majority coastal tribes (*côtiers*), as an alternative to the more nationalistic highland people, the Merina, the traditional ruling group in the island.

After 1967 the economy deteriorated, and there was growing opposition to the Government's alleged authoritarianism and subservience to French interests. In May 1972, following civil unrest, President Tsiranana transferred full powers to the Army Chief of Staff, Gen. Gabriel Ramanantsoa. In October 1973 pro-Government parties secured a decisive victory in legislative elections. A prolonged crisis, following an attempted military coup in December 1974, was resolved in early February 1975, when Ramanantsoa transferred power to Col Richard Ratsimandrava, hitherto Minister of the Interior. Shortly afterwards, however, Ratsimandrava was assassinated. On 12 February Brig.-Gen. Gilles Andriamahazo, who had been a member of the Ramanantsoa and Ratsimandrava Cabinets, assumed power and imposed martial law. All political parties were suspended.

In June 1975 Andriamahazo was succeeded as Head of State by Lt-Commdr Didier Ratsiraka, a *côtier* and a former Minister of Foreign Affairs, who became Chairman of the Supreme Revolutionary Council (SRC). In a referendum in December, more than 94% of voters approved a new Constitution, which provided for radical administrative and agrarian reforms, and the appointment of Ratsiraka as President of the Republic for a term of seven years. The country's name was changed to the Democratic Republic of Madagascar, and the 'Second Republic' was proclaimed. In January 1976 Col Joël Rakotomalala, a member of the SRC, was appointed Prime Minister, but the civilian element in the Cabinet was increased, and representatives of different regions and parties were included in the administration. In March the Avant-garde de la révolution malgache (AREMA—Antoky Ny Revolosiona Malagasy) was founded as the nucleus of the Front national pour la défense de la révolution socialiste malgache (FNDR), the only political organization permitted by the Constitution, and order was re-established. Following the death of Rakotomalala in July, Justin Rakotoniaina (hitherto the Minister of Education), was appointed Prime Minister in August.

At local government elections, which took place between March and June 1977, AREMA secured the majority of votes, resulting in division within the FNDR. The left-wing Mouvement national pour l'indépendance de Madagascar (Monima Ka Miviombio, known as Monima), led by Monja Jaona, withdrew from the FNDR, and was subsequently proscribed. At legislative elections in June, AREMA secured 112 of the 137 seats in the National People's Assembly. Rakotoniaina resigned in July, and was succeeded as Prime Minister by Lt-Col (later Col) Désiré Rakotoarijaona, a member of the SRC. A new Council of Ministers was formed in August, and the membership of the SRC was extended to include leaders of the former political parties, and more *côtiers*, in an effort to restore political equilibrium.

In October 1980 the arrest of Monja Jaona (who was accused of inciting resentment against the Government) prompted a number of demonstrations. Civil unrest, which was viewed, in part, as a response to increasing economic hardship in the country, continued in 1981, despite Monima's decision in March to rejoin the FNDR and Jaona's subsequent appointment to the SRC. In November 1982 Ratsiraka was re-elected to the presidency, receiving 80.17% of the votes cast. Jaona was removed from the SRC in December, following his appeal for a general strike in protest against the election results. At elections to the National People's Assembly, which took place in August 1983, AREMA secured 65% of the votes and won 117 of the 137 seats. Open dissatisfaction with the Government's policies continued, however, and in 1986–87 food shortages prompted widespread social unrest.

In 1987 opposition to President Ratsiraka increased within the FNDR. In April the Elan populaire pour l'unité nationale (Vonjy Iray Tsy Mivaky, known as Vonjy), one of the seven parties in the FNDR, announced that it would present a candidate for the presidential election, scheduled for November 1989. In August 1987 Jaona was selected as Monima's presidential candidate. In December 13 deputies from three constituent parties of the FNDR, Monima, Vonjy and the Mouvement pour le pouvoir prolétarien (Mpitolona ho amin'ny Fonjakan'ny Madinika—MFM), refused to approve the 1988/89 budget proposals. In February 1988 Rakotoarijaona resigned, owing to poor health, and was replaced as Prime Minister by Lt-Col Victor Ramahatra, formerly Minister of Public Works.

In December 1988 it was announced that legislative elections would take place in May of the following year. In January 1989 a constitutional amendment enabled Ratsiraka to bring forward the presidential election from November to March. In January the MFM, Vonjy and the Parti socialiste monima (Vondrona Sosialista Monima—VSM) announced the formation of an opposition alliance, the Alliance démocratique de Madagascar (ADM). In March Ratsiraka announced that press censorship was to be abolished.

In March 1989 Ratsiraka was re-elected to the presidency for a further seven-year term, with 62.7% of the total votes cast. He subsequently dismissed five members of the SRC who had opposed his re-election. In April riots occurred, following opposition allegations of electoral irregularities. However, a threat by the ADM to boycott the forthcoming legislative elections was averted when Ratsiraka agreed to allow representatives of opposition groups to observe polling procedures. At the elections, which duly took place in May, AREMA increased its majority in the National People's Assembly, winning 120 of the 137 seats (with 66.8% of the votes cast). The MFM, which obtained only seven seats, rejected the official results, alleging electoral misconduct. Vonjy secured four seats, the AKFM—Fanavaozana (a newly-formed group, comprising former members of the Parti du congrès de l'indépendance de Madagascar—AKFM), won three seats, the original AKFM two seats, and Monima only one seat. In July an abortive coup attempt was staged by a small group of armed men who temporarily took control of the national radio station and claimed that the Ratsiraka administration had been overthrown.

In August 1989 Ratsiraka assented to opposition demands for discussions about the future role and structure of the FNDR. In September AREMA secured the majority of votes in local government elections. In December, following discussions between the constituent parties of the FNDR, a constitutional amendment that abolished the requirement for political parties to be members of the FNDR (thus effectively dissolving the FNDR) was adopted by the National Assembly. (However, MFM deputies opposed the amendment, on the grounds that the principal tenets of the Constitution remained unchanged.)

In March 1990 the Government formally permitted the resumption of multi-party politics. Numerous organizations subsequently emerged, while other parties, which had hitherto operated within the FNDR, became official opposition movements. Several political associations which supported the Government joined AREMA to form a new coalition, the Mouvement militant pour le socialisme malagasy (MMSM). The principal opposition movements included the newly-formed Union nationale pour le développement et la démocratie (UNDD) and the MFM (now known as the Mouvement pour le progrès de Madagascar—Mpitolona ho amin'ny Fandrosoan'ny Madagasikara—MFM). Sixteen opposition factions, together with trade unions and other groups, established an informal alliance, the Comité des forces vives), which subsequently became known as Forces vives (FV—Hery Velona).

On 13 May 1990 a group of armed rebels seized the radio station at Antananarivo and announced that the Government had been overthrown. On the same day, however, government forces suppressed the revolt, during which about five people were reportedly killed. Eleven rebels, including two members of Vonjy, were subsequently arrested. In December several of those who had been accused of involvement in the attempted coup were acquitted, while others received short custodial sentences.

In November 1990 the National People's Assembly discussed a revision of the electoral code, which would permit all political organizations to participate in elections. In an attempt to restrict the number of opposition candidates, however, members of AREMA proposed an amendment stipulating that the printing of voting slips would be at each party's expense and that the cost would not be refunded unless the party obtained more than 10% of votes cast. In December the National People's Assembly approved legislation that provided for the abolition of press censorship, and permitted the establishment (in partnership with the Government) of private broadcasting stations. In February 1991 two close associates of President Ratsiraka resigned from the Council of Ministers.

At a meeting of the National People's Assembly in May 1991, the FV presented its proposals for constitutional reform. Beginning in mid-1991, the FV organized a series of national demonstrations, in support of its demands that the 1975 Constitution be abrogated and that a national conference be convened to draft a new document. Meanwhile, legislation that provided for extensive constitutional amendments was submitted to the National People's Assembly. However, opposition parties criticized the proposed amendments, on the grounds that the revised Constitution would retain references to socialism. In June 1991 opposition leaders applied to the Constitutional High Court to effect Ratsiraka's removal from office; Ratsiraka refused to resign, maintaining that he had been democratically elected. Later in that month the FV announced that it was to form a 'parallel' administration, which was to be known as the Provisional Government.

In July 1991 the FV organized a general strike, which, it threatened, would continue until the Government acceded to opposition demands for constitutional reform. Subsequent negotiations between the MMSM and the FV resulted in little progress, and proposals, submitted by a French intermediary, that Ratsiraka remain in office, with an opposition member as Prime Minister, were rejected by both parties. In response to Ratsiraka's continued refusal to resign, the FV threatened to suspend negotiations, and unilaterally appointed Jean Rakotoharison, a retired general, as President of the Provisional Government, and the leader of the UNDD, Albert Zafy, as its Prime Minister. However, Manandafy Rakotonirina, the leader of the MFM, rejected the formation of the Provisional Government, in favour of further negotiations, and announced the withdrawal of his party from the FV. Members of Zafy's Provisional Government subsequently occupied six official government ministries. Later in July, however, Ratsiraka ordered the detention of several members of the Provisional Government, including Zafy, and imposed a state of emergency in Antananarivo. (Although public meetings were prohibited under the state of emergency, demonstrations and rallies continued to take place.) The FV withdrew from negotiations with the MMSM, in protest against the arrests, while the Government of France appealed to Ratsiraka to release the opposition leaders. On 28 July, in response to increasing public pressure, Ratsiraka announced the dissolution of the Council of Ministers, and pledged to organize a constitutional referendum before the end of 1991. On the following day the members of the Provisional Government were released from custody, and Ratsiraka repealed legislation that authorized the detention of opponents of the Government. However, the FV deemed these concessions to be inadequate, and continued to demand Ratsiraka's resignation.

In early August 1991 Ratsiraka appointed Guy Razanamasy, the mayor of Antananarivo, as Prime Minister. In the same month a large number of demonstrators were killed when an anti-Government rally in the area of the presidential palace was violently suppressed by the presidential guard. Negotiations between the MMSM and the FV were again suspended, and the armed forces withdrew their support for Ratsiraka. Later that month Ratsiraka declared Madagascar to be a federation of six states, with himself as President, and claimed to command the support of five provinces, where AREMA continued to hold the majority of seats in regional councils. However, the FV disregarded the proclamation, and continued to demand that Ratsiraka relinquish the presidency. Razanamasy subsequently initiated discussions with the FV, in an attempt to resolve the conflict. It was reported that Ratsiraka had granted Razanamasy executive powers, which would enable him to implement democratic reforms. At the end of August Razanamasy announced the formation of a 24-member interim Government; however, the new administration, which did not include members of the FV or of the MFM, was condemned by opposition leaders.

In September 1991 Razanamasy announced that the salaries of striking civil servants would be suspended until work was resumed. In the same month negotiations between the Government and the opposition resulted in agreement on the proposed establishment of a public security committee, comprising representatives of the FV and the MMSM and church leaders, which would appoint a Prime Minister and supervise the organization of elections. However, opposition leaders objected to the suggested composition of the committee. Later in September the FV organized a one-day campaign of civil disobedience, which halted all economic activity in Antananarivo. In October several demonstrators were killed, following clashes between security forces and supporters of the opposition in the northern town of Antsiranana. Later that month civil servants returned to work; however, the FV announced that anti-Government demonstrations would continue.

On 31 October 1991 representatives of the Government, the FV, the MFM, church leaders and the armed forces signed an agreement providing for the suspension of the Constitution and the creation of a transitional Government, which was to remain in office for a maximum period of 18 months, pending the holding of presidential and legislative elections. Under the terms of the agreement, the SRC and the National People's Assembly were to be replaced by interim bodies, respectively the High State Authority for Transition to the Third Republic and the National Committee for Economic and Social Regeneration; however, other organs of the Second Republic, including the Constitutional High Court, were to be retained. On an interim basis, Ratsiraka was to remain as President of the Republic and Razanamasy as Prime Minister, while Zafy was designated President of the High State Authority, which was to comprise 18 representatives of the FV, seven of the MFM and six of the MMSM. Rakotonirina and Pastor Richard Andriamanjato, the leader of AKFM—Fanavaozana, were appointed as joint Presidents of the 131-member National Committee for Economic and Social Regeneration, which was to advise the Prime Minister on economic and social policy. The power to appoint or to dismiss ministers, hitherto vested in the President, was granted to Razanamasy. A new constitution, incorporating the reforms introduced under the agreement, was to be submitted to a national referendum by the end of 1991 (although the referendum was later postponed). Zafy subsequently rejected the agreement, on the grounds that it provided for Ratsiraka's retention of the nominal post of Commander-in-Chief of the Armed Forces. In mid-November Razanamasy announced the formation of a new, 25-member interim Government, which included three representatives of the MFM and one MMSM member. Francisque Ravony, one of the representatives of the MFM, was appointed to the newly-created post of Deputy Prime Minister. However, Zafy refused to participate in the new Government, and 10 portfolios that had been allocated to the FV remained vacant. Later in November, however, Zafy agreed to accept the presidency of the High State Authority for Transition to the Third Republic.

In December 1991 Razanamasy announced that the formation of the coalition Government had proved unsuccessful; shortly afterwards 11 ministers, including Ravony, resigned. Shortly afterwards Razanamasy appointed a 36-member Government of national consensus, in which 14 portfolios were allocated to the FV. Alfred Ramangasoavina, a member of the FV and a close associate of Zafy, was awarded the post of Second Deputy Prime Minister. In January 1992 Ratsiraka announced that all political factions (including all members of the FV) had now accepted the terms of the October 1991 agreement. The institutions which had been established by the accord were to prepare for the constitutional referendum, now scheduled for June 1992, and for local, presidential and legislative elections, which were to take place by the end of 1992.

In February 1992 a series of regional debates took place to compile a register of proposals for a new constitution, which was to be drafted by a National Forum. However, supporters of the MMSM disrupted debates in several towns. Also in February the High State Authority for Transition to the Third Republic announced the dissolution of the SRC and the National People's Assembly, in accordance with the October 1991 agreement. The High State Authority also indicated that a new body was to be created to supervise local elections, replacing the existing decentralized system of government, based on village assemblies (*fokontany*). However, the MMSM objected to this measure, and claimed that the High State Authority was not empowered to dissolve the local government structure. The Government subsequently announced that control of local government was to be transferred from elected councils to special delegations, and that security commissions were to be established to organize the *fokontany*. In March 1992 clashes were reported in Antsiranana between supporters of the FV and the MMSM, after the latter had attempted to prevent the assumption of power in the province by a special delegation. In the same month the Minister of the Economy resigned, reportedly as a result of pressure from the IMF and the World Bank.

At the National Forum, which was convened in late March 1992, the MMSM agreed to abandon its proposals for the creation of a federal republic, but continued to profess adherence to a decentralized system of government. The constituent commission of the National Forum also adopted provisions whereby the President of the Republic would not be permitted to receive foreign subsidies for, or to remain the leader of, a political party, and would be obliged to resign prior to a presidential election. Zafy subsequently demanded that Ratsiraka resign from the presidency, and stated that the proposed establishment of a federal system of government, which Ratsiraka supported, would allow the President to retain power. At the end of March, following a decision by the National Forum to include a provision in the draft Constitution that the President be restricted to two terms of office (thereby prohibiting Ratsiraka from contesting the presidential election), supporters of the MMSM staged an attack on the conference hall during a session of the Forum; several people, including a former government minister, were reported to have been killed in ensuing clashes with security forces.

In April 1992 the National Forum approved a draft Constitution and an electoral code, which were subsequently submitted for consideration by the Government. The proposed Constitution, of what was to be designated the Third Republic, envisaged a unitary state, and provided for a bicameral legislature, comprising a Senate and a National Assembly; two-thirds of the members of the Senate were to be selected by an electoral college for a term of four years, and the remaining third of the members were to be appointed by the President, while the National Assembly was to be elected by universal suffrage, under a system of proportional representation, for a four-year term of office. The authority of the constitutional President was subsequently reduced, and executive power was vested in the Prime Minister, who was to be appointed by the National Assembly. (The stipulation in the draft Constitution that the President be restricted to two terms of office had, however, been withdrawn.) Ratsiraka reiterated his intention to contest the presidential election, and demanded that a draft constitution providing for a federal system of government be submitted to the forthcoming referendum as an alternative to the Constitution that had been prepared by the National Forum. Continuing dissension within the Government regarding Ratsiraka's proposed exclusion from the presidential election and the extent of the constitutional President's authority subsequently delayed the publication of the draft Constitution, and resulted in the postponement of the referendum until August. (The presidential election was to take place two months after the publication of the official results of the referendum.)

In July 1992 a small group of armed men. who were believed to be members of an extremist faction of the FV, seized the radio station at Antananarivo, and announced that the Government had been overthrown. The coup attempt failed to attract popular support, however, and the rebels were subsequently arrested. In August supporters of a federal system of government took control of the airport and the radio and television stations at Antsiranana, and announced the establishment of a federal directorate in the town; similar incidents occurred at Toamasina, in the east, and Toliary, in the south-west of the country. On 19 August the new Constitution was approved by 72.2% of votes cast in the referendum; however, federalists forcibly prevented the electorate from voting in a number of regions, and it was reported that several people had been killed in clashes between supporters of the MMSM and members of the FV at Toamasina. Later that month the armed forces regained control of the towns that had been occupied by the federalists.

Following the publication of the official results of the referendum in September 1992, several prominent members of political organizations, including Zafy and Rakotonirina, announced that they were to contest the forthcoming presidential election. Division emerged within the FV, after a number of constituent parties in the alliance presented alternative candidates (notably Evariste Marson, the Minister of Finance and leader of the Rassemblement pour le socialisme et la démocratie) to Zafy, the officially elected candidate. Later in September the electoral code that had been drafted by the National Forum was submitted to a committee (comprising prominent government officials and church leaders), which proposed that the stipulation restricting the President to two terms of office be incorporated in the code. Shortly afterwards supporters of the MMSM unilaterally declared Antsiranana, Toliary, Toamasina and Fianarantsoa (in central Madagascar) to be federal states, and suspended infrastructural links between these provinces and Antananarivo. In early October federalists in Antsiranana, who were reportedly supported by members of the presidential guard, took hostage members of the FV, and seized control of the radio and television stations. However, a demonstration by federalists, who attempted to obstruct access to the airport at Antsiranana, was violently suppressed by security forces; eight people were reported to have been killed. Razanamasy subsequently declared the unilateral proclamation of independence of the four provinces to be illegal, but initiated negotiations with the federalists, in an effort to ensure that the forthcoming presidential election take place without disruption. Later that month further clashes took place in Toliary between supporters of the FV and federalists, led by Jaona, who had declared himself to be Governor of the province. At the end of October, however, the federalists agreed to participate in the presidential election, although the MMSM continued officially to reject the terms of the new Constitution.

In November 1992 10 of the 18 registered presidential candidates withdrew, apparently as a result of the substantial deposit stipulated in the newly ratified electoral code. In the presidential election, which took place on 25 November, Zafy secured 45.1% of votes cast, while Ratsiraka obtained 29.2% of the vote. Since an overall majority had not been achieved, a second round of voting was scheduled for January 1993, but was subsequently postponed until 10 February. Prior to the second round of the presidential election, the remaining six candidates withdrew in favour of Zafy, while an organization known as the Comité de soutien à la démocratie et au développement de Madagascar was established to co-ordinate his electoral campaign. On 10 February Zafy secured 66.74% of the votes cast in the second round of the presidential election. In early March, amid violent protests by federalists in Antsiranana and Toamasina, the Constitutional High Court officially declared that Zafy had been elected to the presidency. Shortly afterwards the Government announced that the legislative elections were to take place on 5 May. Several constituent parties of the FV that had not supported Zafy in the first round of the presidential election subsequently presented independent lists of candidates; the remaining parties in the alliance became known as the Cartel HVR (Hery Velona Rasalama—Forces vives Rasalama). At the end of March Zafy was inaugurated as President amid violent clashes between security forces and federalists in a number of towns in northern Madagascar. In April the Government postponed the legislative elections until June, to allow the authorities and the political parties further time for preparation, and announced that the number of seats in the National Assembly was to be reduced from 184 to 138. In accordance with the Constitution, Zafy resigned as President of the UNDD at a party congress in May, and Emmanuel Rakotovahiny, the Minister of State for Agriculture and Rural Development, was elected as his successor.

The legislative elections, which took place on 16 June 1993, were preceded by a period of increased violence: two people were killed and 40, including Jaona, were arrested, after security forces attacked federalists who had occupied the prefecture at Toliary; and an FV candidate was killed by unknown forces in Arivonimamo, to the south-west of the capital. At the elections to the National Assembly, which were contested by 121 political associations, the Cartel HVR secured 46 seats, while the MFM, led by Manandafy Rakotonirina, obtained 15 seats, and a newly-formed alliance of parties that supported Ratsiraka only 11 seats. Following the announcement of the official results, it appeared that the organizations that supported Zafy had won a majority of 75 of 134 seats in the National Assembly. (Results in four constituencies in northern Madagascar were declared invalid, as a result of alleged irregularities.) Prior to the first session of the National Assembly, however, intensive negotiations resulted in some realignment of party support for the various candidates who intended to contest the office of Prime Minister. In August Francisque Ravony, who had served as First Deputy Prime Minister in the transitional Government, was elected to the premiership (defeating 11 candidates, notably Rakotonirina and Roger Ralison, who was supported by the Cartel HVR. In the same month Andriamanjato was elected President of the National Assembly. Later in August a new Council of Ministers was formed. In October Ravony appointed a further three ministers to the Government.

In early 1994 reports emerged that Ravony no longer commanded a majority in the National Assembly, owing to the continual formation of new parliamentary alliances. In February Ravony announced that elections to establish new regional authorities (to be known as Collectivités Territoriales Décentralisées), which were originally scheduled for October 1993, had been postponed until July 1994. (In July, however, the elections were again postponed, owing to lack of agreement within the National Assembly, arising from the substantial cost involved, regarding proposals to decentralize local government.)

In April 1994 it was reported that the Malagasy authorities had demanded the expulsion of the French Ambassador in Antananarivo, alleging that he was involved in attempts to destabilize the Government. In June a programme of economic reforms, which had been drafted by the Government in agreement with the IMF and World Bank, was rejected by the National Assembly. (A number of deputies, who apparently included Andriamanjato, opposed the adoption of structural adjustment measures that had been imposed by the IMF and World Bank as a precondition to the approval of financial credit, in view of the increase in economic hardship that would ensue.) In July 31 deputies (including Razanamasy and Rakotonirina) belonging to a parliamentary coalition known as G6, proposed a motion of censure against Ravony's Government, which was, however, rejected by 94 of the 138 deputies. In August, following negotiations with a council that represented the constituent elements of the Cartel HVR, Ravony formed a new, 24-member Council of Ministers.

In October 1994 controversy over a local subsidiary enterprise, Flamco Madagascar, which had failed to reimburse funds advanced by the Government, prompted increased division between Ravony and Andriamanjato regarding the Government's economic policy; the Minister of Finance and the Budget, José Yvon Raserijaona, threatened to initiate legal proceedings against Flamco Madagascar's directors (who included two presidential counsellors and one of Andriamanjato's sons) on charges of misappropriating the funds, while Andriamanjato accused the Government of incompetence. Meanwhile, opposition leaders demanded the removal of Zafy, Ravony and Andriamanjato, amid general resentment towards the Government which had been precipitated by an increase in the rate of inflation resulting from the flotation of the Malagasy franc (see Economic Affairs). At a regional congress of AREMA, which took place at the end of October, Ratsiraka urged the resignation of Ravony and dissolution of the Government, and in early November the MFM and an opposition movement led by Razanamasy, known as Fihaonana, began a campaign in support of demands for the removal of the three government leaders. In the same month elements of the Cartel HVR that supported Andriamanjato demanded the dismissal of three government ministers, including Raserijaona, on the grounds of incompetence, subsequently joining the opposition in urging Ravony's resignation, after he failed to replace the three ministers concerned. In December, however, the budget for 1995, which incorporated austerity measures that had been imposed by the IMF and World Bank as a precondition to the continuation of negotiations, was approved by 68 of 90 votes cast in the National Assembly, despite opposition from the faction of the Cartel HVR that supported Andriamanjato.

In January 1995, following further demands from members of the Cartel HVR for Ravony's resignation, Andriamanjato claimed that opponents of the Government planned to stage a coup attempt. Later that month, in compliance with demands by the IMF and World Bank, Ravony dismissed the Governor of the Central Bank, Raoul Ravelomanana, who had approved the financial transaction with Flamco Madagascar, and, apparently as a concession to Andriamanjato, also removed Raserijaona from the post of Minister of Finance and the Budget, subsequently assuming the portfolio himself. The replacement of Ravelomanana fulfilled an important precondition for the resumption of financial credit from the IMF and World Bank; however, Zafy, who was apparently influenced by Andriamanjato, continued to insist that the Government was entitled to obtain financial assistance through transactions with private enterprises (despite a previous pledge to the Bretton Woods institutions by Ravony that such arrangements were to be suspended). Also in January international controversy emerged over a proposed mining project by a British company, Rio Tinto-Zinc, which was to take place in southern Madagascar; environmental organizations claimed that the enterprise would severely damage Madagascar's ecological balance. In March it was reported that members of the Cartel HVR had demonstrated in Madagascar in support of demands for Ravony's resignation. Later that month several members of a small opposition group were arrested, after announcing the establishment of a 'parallel government'.

Madagascar's foreign policy is officially non-aligned: while it formerly maintained close links with communist countries (particularly the People's Republic of China, the Democratic People's Republic of Korea and the former USSR), the Zafy Government has established relations with Israel, South Africa and the Republic of Korea. Relations with France have been affected by disputes over compensation for nationalized French assets and over the continuing French claim to the Iles Glorieuses, north of Madagascar, and three other islets in the Mozambique Channel. In 1980 the UN voted in favour of restoring all the disputed islets to Madagascar. In early 1986 the Government announced the extension of Madagascar's exclusive economic zone to include the Iles Glorieuses and the three islets. However, regular negotiations between Madagascar and France have taken place to settle the dispute, and France has continued to be Madagascar's principal trading partner and supplier of aid.

## Government

A new Constitution, which was endorsed by national referendum on 19 August 1992, provided for a unitary state, with a bicameral legislature, comprising a Senate and a 138-member National Assembly. Two-thirds of the members of the Senate are selected by an electoral college for a term of four years, and the remaining one-third of the members are appointed by the President, while the National Assembly is elected by universal suffrage, under a system of proportional representation, for a four-year term of office. The constitutional Head of State is the President, who is elected for a term of five years. Executive power is vested in the Prime Minister, who is elected by the National Assembly and appoints the Council of Ministers.

Local government has a four-tier structure, based on traditional village assemblies (*fokontany*). In early 1992 control of local government was transferred from elected councils to special delegations appointed by the central Government, pending elections to new regional authorities, to be known as Collectivités Territoriales Décentralisées (see Recent History).

### Defence

In June 1994 total armed forces numbered about 21,000 men: army 20,000, navy 500 and air force 500. There is a paramilitary gendarmerie of 7,500. The 1994 budget allocated an estimated 73,900m. francs MG to defence.

### Economic Affairs

In 1993, according to estimates by the World Bank, Madagascar's gross national product (GNP), measured at average 1991–93 prices, was US $3,039m., equivalent to about $240 per head. Between 1985 and 1993, it was estimated, GNP per head declined, in real terms, by an average of 1.7% per year, while the population increased by an annual average of 3.1%. Madagascar's gross domestic product (GDP) increased, in real terms, by an average of 1.1% per year in 1980–92, and by 1.9% in 1993.

In 1993 the agricultural sector (including forestry and fishing) accounted for 34% of GDP, and it employed an estimated 75.0% of the labour force. Rice, the staple food crop, is produced on some 50% of cultivated land. Since 1972, however, imports of rice have been necessary to supplement domestic production: some 103,000 metric tons of cereals were imported in 1989. The most important cash crop is vanilla (which accounted for 12.3% of total export revenue in 1993). Coffee, cloves, sugar, coconuts, tropical fruits, cotton and sisal are also cultivated. Cattle-farming is important. Sea fishing by coastal fishermen (particularly for crustaceans) is being expanded; vessels from EU countries fish for tuna and prawns in Madagascar's exclusive maritime zone, within 200 nautical miles (370 km) of the coast, in return for compensation. Agricultural GDP increased by an annual average of 2.4% in 1980–92, and by 3.3% in 1993.

Industry (including mining, manufacturing, construction and power) contributed 13.8% of Madagascar's GDP in 1993, and employed about 6% of the labour force in 1980. Industrial GDP increased by an annual average of 0.8% in 1980–92, and by 2.7% in 1993.

Madagascar has sizeable deposits of a wide range of minerals, principally chromite (chromium ore), which, with graphite and mica, is exported, together with small quantities of semi-precious stones. However, the mining sector provided only 0.3% of GDP in 1991. Plans were under way in the early 1990s to exploit deposits of bauxite and ilmenite (titanium ore) for export, and to attract foreign investment in coal-mining and the extraction of quartz. Offshore deposits of petroleum and natural gas were discovered in the late 1980s.

Manufacturing contributed 11.6% of GDP in 1991. The petroleum refinery at Toamasina, using imported petroleum, has contributed significantly to exports since 1967. Other important branches of manufacturing are textiles and clothing, food products, beverages and chemical products. Following the introduction of a new investment code in 1986, foreign private investors participated in the establishment of factories producing cement, textiles, fertilizers and pharmaceuticals.

Energy generation depends on imports of crude petroleum (which accounted for 12.0% of import costs in 1993) to fuel thermal installations, although hydroelectric resources have also been developed.

In 1992 Madagascar recorded a visible trade deficit of US $138m., and there was a deficit of $136m. on the current account of the balance of payments. The principal source of imports in 1993 was France (27.5%); other major suppliers were Japan, Germany and the USA. France was also the principal market for exports (accounting for 33.3% of exports in that year); other important purchasers were the USA, Germany and Japan. The principal exports in 1993 were coffee, shrimps and vanilla. The principal imports in that year included minerals (chiefly crude petroleum), chemicals, machinery and vehicles.

In 1991 there was a budgetary deficit of 272,400m. francs MG (equivalent to 5.5% of GDP). The estimated budgetary deficit for 1994 was equivalent to 6.8% of GDP. Madagascar's external debt totalled US $4,594m. at the end of 1993, of which $3,920m. was long-term public debt. In the same year the cost of debt-servicing was estimated to be equivalent to 14.3% of the value of exports of goods and services. The annual rate of inflation averaged 13.7% in 1985–93; in the year to September 1994, however, consumer prices increased by 32.1%.

Madagascar is a member of the Indian Ocean Commission (see p. 239), which promotes regional economic co-operation, and of the Preferential Trade Area for Eastern and Southern African States (PTA, see p. 240). In November 1993 Madagascar was among the PTA members to sign a treaty establishing a Common Market for Eastern and Southern Africa.

During the 1980s Madagascar's dominant agricultural sector was adversely affected by frequent cyclones and by fluctuations in the market prices of the country's principal exports, while industrial development was limited. Madagascar experienced severe balance-of-payments difficulties during the 1980s, and, under pressure from international aid donors, implemented economic reforms including measures to liberalize trade, adjustments of the exchange rate for the Malagasy franc, reductions in planned public spending and in price subsidies, and improvements in the management of public enterprises. In late 1993 the new Government initiated negotiations with financial institutions to obtain funding for a new economic reform programme. However, the IMF insisted that several economic reforms, which included the floating of the Malagasy franc, be implemented as a precondition to the disbursement of funding. In May 1994 the Government floated the Malagasy franc, precipitating substantial devaluation and a consequent increase in the rate of inflation. A 'framework agreement', signed by the Government and the Bretton Woods institutions in June, provided for the introduction of further reforms (including the removal of price controls and measures to reduce budgetary expenditure), prior to the adoption of a structural adjustment programme later that year. However, parliamentary opposition to the implementation of the economic austerity measures impeded subsequent progress (see Recent History). In October, in compliance with demands by the IMF and World Bank, the Prime Minister undertook to suspend arrangements with private enterprises whereby the Government obtained financial assistance independently from the Bretton Woods institutions, and the dismissal, in early 1995, of the Governor of the Central Bank fulfilled a further precondition to the resumption of credit from the World Bank and IMF. In February the Government accepted a number of economic reforms (similar to those agreed in June 1994), including the imposition of a new tax on petroleum products and restrictions on loans by the Central Bank to private enterprises; subject to the successful implementation of these measures, the IMF was to reschedule Madagascar's external debt arrears in mid-1995 and to resume financial disbursements later that year.

### Social Welfare

All medical services are free. The Government provides family allowances as well as benefits for industrial accidents and occupational diseases. A large proportion of welfare services is offered by Christian missions. In 1989 Madagascar had a total of 10,900 hospital beds. In the same year there were 1,416 physicians working in the country. Of total expenditure by the central Government in 1991, 48,700m. francs MG (6.0%) was allocated to health, and a further 10,900m. francs MG (1.4%) to social security and welfare.

### Education

Five years' education, to be undertaken usually between six and 13 years of age, is officially compulsory. Madagascar has both public and private schools, although legislation that was enacted in 1978 envisaged the progressive elimination of private education. Primary education generally begins at the age of six and lasts for five years. Secondary education, beginning at 11 years of age, lasts for a further seven years, comprising a first cycle of four years and a second of three years. In 1993 primary enrolment was equivalent to 79% of children in the relevant age-group (males 81%; females 77%), while the comparable ratio for secondary education was 15% (males 16%; females 15%). Enrolment in tertiary education in that year was equivalent to 3.9% of the relevant age-group (males 4.4%; females 3.4%). According to UNESCO estimates, 19.8% of the adult population (males 12.3%; females 27.1%) remained illiterate in 1990: one of the lowest rates of illiteracy in Africa. Expenditure on education by the central Govern-

## MADAGASCAR

ment was 127,500m. francs MG (15.8% of total expenditure) in 1991.

### Public Holidays

**1995:** 1 January (New Year), 29 March (Commemoration of 1947 Rebellion), 14 April (Good Friday), 17 April (Easter Monday), 1 May (Labour Day), 25 May (Ascension Day), 5 June (Whitsun), 26 June (Independence Day), 1 November (All Saints' Day), 25 December (Christmas), 30 December (Anniversary of the Democratic Republic of Madagascar).

**1996:** 1 January (New Year), 29 March (Commemoration of 1947 Rebellion), 5 April (Good Friday), 8 April (Easter Monday), 1 May (Labour Day), 16 May (Ascension Day), 27 May (Whitsun), 26 June (Independence Day), 1 November (All Saints' Day), 25 December (Christmas), 30 December (Anniversary of the Democratic Republic of Madagascar).

### Weights and Measures

The metric system is in force.

# Statistical Survey

Source (unless otherwise stated): Banque des Données de l'Etat, BP 485, Antananarivo; tel. 21613.

## Area and Population

**AREA, POPULATION AND DENSITY**

| | |
|---|---|
| Area (sq km) | 587,041* |
| Population (census results) | |
| 1974–75† | |
| Males | 3,805,288 |
| Females | 3,798,502 |
| Total | 7,603,790 |
| 1–19 August 1993 | 12,092,157 |
| Population (official estimates at mid-year) | |
| 1990 | 11,197,000 |
| 1991 | 11,493,000 |
| Density (per sq km) at August 1993 | 20.6 |

* 226,658 sq miles.
† The census took place in three stages: in provincial capitals on 1 December 1974; in Antananarivo and remaining urban areas on 17 February 1975; and in rural areas on 1 June 1975.

**PRINCIPAL ETHNIC GROUPS** (estimated population, 1974)

| | | | |
|---|---|---|---|
| Merina (Hova) | 1,993,000 | Sakalava | 470,156* |
| Betsimisaraka | 1,134,000 | Antandroy | 412,500 |
| Betsileo | 920,600 | Antaisaka | 406,468* |
| Tsimihety | 558,100 | | |

* 1972 figure.

**PRINCIPAL TOWNS** (population at 1975 census)

| | | | | |
|---|---|---|---|---|
| Antananarivo (capital) | 406,366 | Mahajanga (Majunga) | | 65,864 |
| Antsirabé | 78,941 | Toliary (Tuléar) | | 45,676 |
| Toamasina (Tamatave) | 77,395 | Antsiranana (Diégo-Suarez) | | 40,443 |
| Fianarantsoa | 68,054 | | | |

The population of Antananarivo was estimated to be 662,585 in 1985.

**BIRTHS AND DEATHS** (UN estimates, annual averages)

| | 1975–80 | 1980–85 | 1985–90 |
|---|---|---|---|
| Birth rate (per 1,000) | 45.7 | 45.9 | 45.8 |
| Death rate (per 1,000) | 16.7 | 15.4 | 14.0 |

**Expectation of life** (UN estimates, years at birth, 1985–90): 53.5 (males 52.0; females 55.0).

Source: UN, *World Population Prospects: The 1992 Revision.*

**ECONOMICALLY ACTIVE POPULATION**
(ILO estimates, '000 persons at mid-1980)

| | Males | Females | Total |
|---|---|---|---|
| Agriculture etc. | 1,731 | 1,583 | 3,314 |
| Industry | 216 | 28 | 244 |
| Services | 457 | 82 | 539 |
| **Total labour force** | 2,405 | 1,693 | 4,098 |

Source: ILO, *Economically Active Population Estimates and Projections, 1950–2025.*

**Mid-1985** (official estimates, '000 persons): Total labour force 3,929 (males 2,194; females 1,735) (Source: ILO, *Year Book of Labour Statistics*).

**Mid-1993** (estimates in '000): Agriculture, forestry and fishing 4,196; Total labour force 5,556 (Source: FAO, *Production Yearbook*).

## Agriculture

**PRINCIPAL CROPS** ('000 metric tons)

| | 1991 | 1992 | 1993 |
|---|---|---|---|
| Maize | 145 | 165 | 180 |
| Rice (paddy) | 2,342 | 2,450 | 2,550 |
| Sugar cane | 1,950 | 1,900 | 1,980 |
| Potatoes | 274 | 276 | 278 |
| Sweet potatoes* | 488 | 450 | 498 |
| Cassava (Manioc) | 2,307 | 2,320 | 2,350 |
| Taro (Coco yam)† | 115 | 120 | 125 |
| Dry beans† | 48 | 50 | 52 |
| Vegetables and melons† | 330 | 336 | 343 |
| Oranges† | 84 | 85 | 86 |
| Bananas† | 220 | 225 | 230 |
| Avocados† | 21 | 22 | 22 |
| Mangoes† | 205 | 200 | 205 |
| Pineapples† | 50 | 50 | 50 |
| Other fruits† | 213 | 217 | 220 |
| Groundnuts (in shell) | 29 | 34 | 32 |
| Cottonseed* | 16 | 17 | 16 |
| Cotton (lint)* | 10 | 10 | 10 |
| Coconuts† | 84 | 85 | 86 |
| Copra† | 10 | 10 | 10 |
| Coffee (green) | 85 | 87 | 88 |
| Cocoa beans | 4 | 4 | 4 |
| Tobacco (leaves)† | 4 | 4 | 4 |
| Sisal | 20 | 19 | 20 |

* Unofficial figures.   † FAO estimates.

Source: FAO, *Production Yearbook.*

# MADAGASCAR

**LIVESTOCK** ('000 head, year ending September)

|  | 1991* | 1992 | 1993† |
|---|---|---|---|
| Cattle | 10,265 | 10,276* | 10,280 |
| Pigs | 1,461 | 1,493* | 1,495 |
| Sheep | 721 | 730† | 735 |
| Goats | 1,229 | 1,250† | 1,270 |

* Unofficial figure(s).  † FAO estimate(s).

Chickens (FAO estimates, million): 20 in 1991; 21 in 1992; 22 in 1993.
Ducks (FAO estimates, million): 5 in 1991; 5 in 1992; 5 in 1993.
Turkeys (FAO estimates, million): 3 in 1991; 3 in 1992; 3 in 1993.

Source: FAO, *Production Yearbook*.

**LIVESTOCK PRODUCTS** (FAO estimates, '000 metric tons)

|  | 1991 | 1992 | 1993 |
|---|---|---|---|
| Cows' milk | 475 | 477 | 479 |
| Beef and veal | 143 | 143 | 143 |
| Pigs' meat | 47 | 48 | 48 |
| Poultry meat | 73 | 76 | 78 |
| Hen eggs | 15.9 | 16.7 | 17.4 |
| Honey | 3.8 | 3.8 | 3.8 |
| Cattle hides | 20.2 | 20.2 | 20.2 |

Source: FAO, *Production Yearbook*.

## Forestry

**ROUNDWOOD REMOVALS**
(FAO estimates, '000 cubic metres, excluding bark)

|  | 1990 | 1991 | 1992 |
|---|---|---|---|
| Sawlogs, veneer logs and logs for sleepers* | 468 | 468 | 468 |
| Other industrial wood* | 339 | 339 | 339 |
| Fuel wood | 7,293 | 7,537 | 7,790 |
| **Total** | 8,100 | 8,344 | 8,597 |

* Assumed to be unchanged since 1977.

Source: FAO, *Yearbook of Forest Products*.

**SAWNWOOD PRODUCTION**
('000 cubic metres, including railway sleepers)

|  | 1990 | 1991 | 1992 |
|---|---|---|---|
| **Total** | 234 | 233* | 233* |

* FAO estimate.

Source: FAO, *Yearbook of Forest Products*.

## Fishing

('000 metric tons, live weight)

|  | 1990 | 1991 | 1992 |
|---|---|---|---|
| Inland waters: |  |  |  |
| Freshwater fishes | 32.0 | 27.7 | 27.5 |
| Indian Ocean: |  |  |  |
| Marine fishes | 61.5 | 60.7 | 63.4 |
| Marine crabs | 1.2 | 1.0 | 0.8 |
| Tropical spiny lobsters | 0.3 | 0.4 | 0.5 |
| Shrimps and prawns | 9.2 | 10.2 | 13.5 |
| Molluscs | 0.2 | 0.5 | 0.5 |
| Other aquatic animals | 0.2 | 0.6 | 0.4 |
| **Total catch** | 104.6 | 101.2 | 106.6 |

Source: FAO, *Yearbook of Fishery Statistics*.

## Mining

(metric tons)

|  | 1988 | 1989 | 1990 |
|---|---|---|---|
| Graphite | 14,565 | 15,865 | 17,920 |
| Salt (unrefined) | 30,000* | 30,000 | 30,000 |
| Mica | 693 | 1,182 | 1,800 |
| Chromite† | 49,000 | 47,000 | 35,000 |

* Provisional figures.
† Figures refer to the chromium content of ores mined.

**1991**: Salt 30,000 metric tons.

Source: UN, *Industrial Statistics Yearbook*.

## Industry

**SELECTED PRODUCTS** (metric tons, unless otherwise indicated)

|  | 1989 | 1990 | 1991 |
|---|---|---|---|
| Raw sugar | 120,000 | 111,000 | 96,000 |
| Palm oil* | 3,800 | 3,800 | 3,800 |
| Beer (hectolitres) | 232,000 | 298,000 | n.a. |
| Cigarettes | 2,341 | 1,955 | n.a. |
| Woven cotton fabrics (million sq m) | 59.5 | 49.1 | n.a. |
| Cement | 24,000 | 20,000 | 23,000 |
| Liquefied petroleum gas | 1,000 | 1,000† | 1,000† |
| Motor spirit (petrol) | 29,000 | 25,000 | 35,000 |
| Kerosene | 19,000 | 20,000 | 21,000 |
| Distillate fuel oils | 46,000 | 43,000 | 45,000 |
| Residual fuel oils | 86,000 | 65,000 | 67,000 |
| Paints | 1,900 | 2,400 | n.a. |
| Soap | 14,500 | 14,900 | n.a. |
| Electric energy (for public use) (million kWh) | 447 | 450 | 452 |

* FAO estimates.  † Provisional figure.

Source: UN, *Industrial Statistics Yearbook*.

## Finance

**CURRENCY AND EXCHANGE RATES**

**Monetary Units**
100 centimes = 1 franc malgache (franc MG—Malagasy franc).

**Sterling and Dollar Equivalents** (30 November 1994)
£1 sterling = 5,901.1 francs MG;
US $1 = 3,770.2 francs MG;
10,000 francs MG = £1.695 = $2.652.

**Average Exchange Rate** (Malagasy francs per US $)
1991  1,835.4
1992  1,864.0
1993  1,913.8

# MADAGASCAR

## BUDGET ('000 million francs MG)

| Revenue* | 1989 | 1990 | 1991 |
|---|---|---|---|
| Taxation | 354.0 | 434.2 | 336.1 |
| Taxes on income, profits, etc. | 45.5 | 68.0 | 64.0 |
| General income tax | 16.2 | 22.5 | 21.6 |
| Corporate tax on profits | 25.1 | 37.2 | 35.2 |
| Domestic taxes on goods and services | 98.8 | 102.5 | 81.4 |
| Sales taxes | 44.0 | 47.5 | 28.4 |
| Excises | 35.3 | 34.0 | 20.8 |
| Profits on fiscal monopolies | 15.2 | 16.0 | 28.3 |
| Taxes on international trade and transactions | 201.7 | 254.6 | 186.0 |
| Import duties | 154.5 | 217.7 | 150.6 |
| Export duties | 47.2 | 36.9 | 35.4 |
| Other current revenue | 106.8 | 112.8 | 81.5 |
| Capital revenue | — | — | 11.6 |
| **Total** | 460.8 | 547.0 | 429.2 |

* Excluding grants received ('000 million francs MG): 55.8 in 1989; 66.8 in 1990; 38.2 in 1991.

| Expenditure | 1989 | 1990 | 1991 |
|---|---|---|---|
| General public services | 122.3 | 142.0 | 147.8 |
| Defence | 51.3 | 53.5 | 55.8 |
| Education | 92.5 | 110.6 | 127.5 |
| Health | 42.0 | 45.1 | 48.7 |
| Social security and welfare | 11.1 | 17.5 | 10.9 |
| Economic affairs and services | 338.1 | 295.4 | 265.8 |
| Agriculture, forestry, fishing and hunting | 135.8 | 122.6 | 95.7 |
| Mining, manufacturing and construction | 151.6 | 116.5 | 114.6 |
| Transportation and communication | 27.2 | 21.3 | 19.2 |
| Other purposes | 130.6 | 119.7 | 148.7 |
| **Sub-total** | 788.1 | 784.1 | 805.4 |
| Adjustment for expenditure financed by grants in kind | −108.2 | −135.4 | −65.6 |
| **Total** | 679.9 | 648.7 | 739.8 |
| Current | 399.8 | 418.8 | 480.0 |
| Capital | 280.1 | 229.9 | 259.8 |

Source: IMF, *Government Finance Statistics Yearbook*.

## INTERNATIONAL RESERVES (US $ million at 31 December)

| | 1989 | 1990 | 1991 |
|---|---|---|---|
| IMF special drawing rights | 0.1 | 0.2 | 0.1 |
| Foreign exchange | 245.2 | 91.9 | 88.8 |
| **Total** | 245.3 | 92.1 | 88.9 |

Source: IMF, *International Financial Statistics*.

## MONEY SUPPLY ('000 million francs MG at 31 December)

| | 1991 | 1992 | 1993 |
|---|---|---|---|
| Currency outside banks | 287.3 | 317.2 | 378.7 |
| Demand deposits at deposit money banks | 465.3 | 598.1 | 645.7 |
| **Total money** | 752.6 | 915.3 | 1,024.4 |

Source: IMF, *International Financial Statistics*.

## COST OF LIVING (Consumer Price Index for Madagascans in Antananarivo; base: 1980 = 100)

| | 1991 | 1992 | 1993 |
|---|---|---|---|
| Food | 523.2 | 610.2 | 660.9 |
| **All items*** | 511.0 | 631.1 | 694.3 |

* Excluding rent.

Source: ILO, *Year Book of Labour Statistics*.

## NATIONAL ACCOUNTS ('000 million francs MG at current prices)

### Expenditure on the Gross Domestic Product

| | 1991 | 1992 | 1993 |
|---|---|---|---|
| Government final consumption expenditure | 422.0 | 463.4 | 506.5 |
| Private final consumption expenditure | 4,529.1 | 4,973.0 | 5,801.9 |
| Increase in stocks / Gross fixed capital formation | 401.5 | 631.9 | 734.5 |
| **Total domestic expenditure** | 5,352.6 | 6,068.3 | 7,042.9 |
| Exports of goods and services | 846.4 | 929.9 | 987.9 |
| *Less* Imports of goods and services | 1,285.4 | 1,405.1 | 1,580.0 |
| **GDP in purchasers' values** | 4,913.6 | 5,593.1 | 6,450.9 |
| **GDP at constant 1990 prices** | 4,313.6 | 4,364.7 | 4,456.2 |

Source: IMF, *International Financial Statistics*.

### Gross Domestic Product by Economic Activity

| | 1989 | 1990 | 1991 |
|---|---|---|---|
| Agriculture, hunting, forestry and fishing | 1,181.7 | 1,334.3 | 1,488.4 |
| Mining and quarrying | 16.1 | 14.9 | 14.8 |
| Manufacturing | 471.6 | 492.6 | 530.6 |
| Electricity, gas and water | 42.7 | 78.7 | 87.0 |
| Construction | 48.7 | 61.7 | 52.6 |
| Trade, restaurants and hotels | 351.6 | 426.2 | 498.0 |
| Transport, storage and communications | 623.9 | 721.6 | 747.9 |
| Finance, insurance, real estate and business services | 58.7 | 64.6 | 70.0 |
| Public administration and defence | 190.9 | 240.7 | 284.4 |
| Other services | 658.7 | 756.9 | 791.9 |
| **GDP at factor cost** | 3,644.6 | 4,192.0 | 4,565.5 |
| Indirect taxes, *less* subsidies | 360.7 | 409.6 | 340.9 |
| **GDP in purchasers' values** | 4,005.3 | 4,601.6 | 4,906.4 |

Source: UN Economic Commission for Africa, *African Statistical Yearbook*.

## BALANCE OF PAYMENTS (US $ million)

| | 1990 | 1991 | 1992 |
|---|---|---|---|
| Merchandise exports f.o.b. | 319 | 338 | 328 |
| Merchandise imports f.o.b. | −566 | −440 | −466 |
| **Trade balance** | −248 | −102 | −138 |
| Exports of services | 194 | 147 | 172 |
| Imports of services | −274 | −239 | −266 |
| Other income received | 15 | 4 | 6 |
| Other income paid | −176 | −178 | −145 |
| Private unrequited transfers (net) | 49 | 52 | 88 |
| Official unrequited transfers (net) | 188 | 127 | 148 |
| **Current balance** | −251 | −188 | −136 |
| Direct investment (net) | 22 | 14 | 21 |
| Other capital (net) | −40 | −56 | −109 |
| Net errors and omissions | −9 | −4 | −52 |
| **Overall balance** | −278 | −235 | −276 |

Source: IMF, *International Financial Statistics*.

MADAGASCAR

# External Trade

**PRINCIPAL COMMODITIES**
(million francs MG, excluding gold and military goods)

| Imports | 1991 | 1992 | 1993 |
|---|---|---|---|
| Chemical products | 88,345.8 | 116,056.6 | 86,014.2 |
| Mineral products | 144,312.0 | 168,925.0 | 182,384.4 |
|   Crude petroleum | 91,076.9 | 95,880.9 | 105,389.8 |
| Textiles | 12,743.2 | 13,041.1 | 11,405.7 |
| Metal products | 53,232.1 | 59,571.3 | 60,204.1 |
| Machinery | 132,212.0 | 88,273.3 | 107,930.1 |
| Electrical equipment | 43,995.0 | 61,024.9 | 55,280.4 |
| Vehicles and parts | 98,527.0 | 81,502.0 | 103,984.5 |
| **Total** (incl. others) | 785,689.5 | 844,935.6 | 879,400.1 |

| Exports | 1991 | 1992 | 1993 |
|---|---|---|---|
| Coffee (green) | 51,902.0 | 58,844.1 | 76,888.2 |
| Vanilla | 84,887.0 | 95,540.7 | 59,323.5 |
| Sugar | 19,125.2 | 17,058.3 | 11,528.6 |
| Cloves and clove oil | 46,025.6 | 21,060.3 | 17,451.8 |
| Petroleum products | 20,551.5 | 17,412.9 | 16,291.7 |
| Shrimps | 74,772.5 | 70,581.0 | 76,410.3 |
| Lobsters | 6,901.9 | 5,941.1 | 4,431.0 |
| Cotton fabrics | 24,971.7 | 17,609.8 | 12,625.0 |
| Chromium | 17,288.1 | 14,373.7 | 14,791.8 |
| **Total** (incl. others) | 559,073.3 | 499,805.9 | 483,524.9 |

**PRINCIPAL TRADING PARTNERS** (million francs MG)

| Imports | 1991 | 1992 | 1993 |
|---|---|---|---|
| Belgium-Luxembourg | 17,390.5 | 14,946.6 | 18,147.5 |
| France | 246,479.2 | 256,193.2 | 241,994.0 |
| Germany | 65,947.0 | 51,253.1 | 60,562.9 |
| Italy | 25,367.0 | 24,839.4 | 19,724.8 |
| Japan | 51,722.3 | 49,352.7 | 78,474.4 |
| Netherlands | 14,528.8 | 18,539.9 | 10,153.4 |
| United Kingdom | 21,787.4 | 42,582.6 | 18,190.7 |
| USA | 53,689.0 | 49,683.2 | 55,929.0 |
| **Total** (incl. others) | 785,689.5 | 844,935.6 | 879,400.4 |

| Exports | 1991 | 1992 | 1993 |
|---|---|---|---|
| Belgium-Luxembourg | 5,483.2 | 16,469.3 | 16,210.0 |
| France | 143,531.9 | 133,064.2 | 161,400.4 |
| Germany | 55,810.3 | 49,592.8 | 60,721.5 |
| Italy | 15,788.9 | 15,647.3 | 16,538.9 |
| Japan | 47,526.9 | 42,974.0 | 31,918.3 |
| Netherlands | 16,365.1 | 10,890.4 | 9,102.4 |
| United Kingdom | 17,086.0 | 12,830.6 | 18,041.7 |
| USA | 78,009.9 | 77,617.0 | 32,444.3 |
| **Total** (incl. others) | 559,073.3 | 499,805.9 | 483,524.9 |

# Transport

**RAILWAYS** (traffic)

| | 1985 | 1986 | 1987 |
|---|---|---|---|
| Passengers carried ('000) | 2,564 | 3,161 | 2,974 |
| Passenger-km (millions) | 178 | 208 | 209 |
| Freight carried ('000 metric tons) | 808 | 735 | 693 |
| Ton-km (millions) | 208.5 | 188 | 174 |

Passenger-km (million): 242 in 1988; 204 in 1989; 198 in 1990. Ton-km (million): 174 in 1988; 207 in 1989; 209 in 1990 (Source: UN, *Statistical Yearbook*).

**ROAD TRAFFIC** (vehicles in use at 31 December)

| | 1990 | 1991 | 1992 |
|---|---|---|---|
| Cars | 41,900 | 44,272 | 47,711 |
| Buses and coaches | 2,700 | 2,980 | 3,145 |
| Goods vehicles | 7,900 } | 29,877 | 31,196 |
| Vans | 18,500 } | | |
| Tractors, trailers and semi-trailers | 290 | 342 | 380 |

Source: International Road Federation, *World Road Statistics*.

**INTERNATIONAL SEA-BORNE SHIPPING**
(freight traffic, '000 metric tons)

| | 1987 | 1988 | 1989 |
|---|---|---|---|
| Goods loaded: | | | |
|   Mahajanga | 17 | 18 | 29.4 |
|   Toamasina | 252 | 350 | 360.6 |
|   Other ports | 79 | 100 | 137.4 |
| **Total** | 348 | 468 | 527.4 |
| Goods unloaded: | | | |
|   Mahajanga | 37 | 32 | 30.8 |
|   Toamasina | 748 | 778 | 708.9 |
|   Other ports | 48 | 53 | 52.0 |
| **Total** | 833 | 863 | 791.7 |

**1990** ('000 metric tons): Goods loaded 540; Goods unloaded 984 (Source: UN, *Monthly Bulletin of Statistics*).

**CIVIL AVIATION** (traffic on scheduled services)

| | 1990 | 1991 | 1992 |
|---|---|---|---|
| Kilometres flown (million) | 6 | 6 | 6 |
| Passengers carried ('000) | 424 | 314 | 344 |
| Passenger-km (million) | 513 | 385 | 432 |
| Total ton-km (million) | 77 | 61 | 66 |

Source: UN, *Statistical Yearbook*.

# Tourism

| | 1990 | 1991 | 1992 |
|---|---|---|---|
| Tourist arrivals | 52,923 | 34,891 | 53,654 |
| Tourist receipts (US $ million) | 40 | 27 | 39 |

Source: UN, *Statistical Yearbook*.

MADAGASCAR

## Communications Media

|  | 1990 | 1991 | 1992 |
|---|---|---|---|
| Radio receivers ('000 in use) | 2,400 | 2,480 | 2,565 |
| Television receivers ('000 in use) | 240 | 248 | 260 |
| Telephones ('000 main lines in use) | 30 | 32* | n.a. |
| Book production†: |  |  |  |
| Titles | 154 | 46 | 85 |
| Copies ('000) | 541* | 111 | 402 |
| Daily newspapers: |  |  |  |
| Number | 5 | n.a. | 7 |
| Circulation ('000 copies) | 50 | n.a. | 48 |
| Non-daily newspapers: |  |  |  |
| Number | 27 | n.a. | 37 |
| Circulation | 105 | n.a. | 168 |

* Estimate.
† Including pamphlets (10 titles and 29,000 copies in 1991; 39 titles and 219,000 copies in 1992).

Sources: UNESCO, *Statistical Yearbook*; UN, *Statistical Yearbook*.

## Education

(1993, unless otherwise indicated)

|  | Insti-tutions | Teach-ers | Pupils Males | Pupils Females | Pupils Total |
|---|---|---|---|---|---|
| Primary | 13,508 | 38,743 | 763,905 | 726,412 | 1,490,317 |
| Secondary: |  |  |  |  |  |
| General | n.a. | 14,770 | 153,905 | 150,891 | 304,796 |
| Teacher training | n.a. | 15 | 34 | 56 | 90 |
| Vocational | n.a. | 1,091 | 5,348 | 2,705 | 8,053 |
| University level* | n.a. | 819 | 18,466 | 14,909 | 33,375 |

* 1992 figures.
Source: UNESCO, *Statistical Yearbook*.

# Directory

## The Constitution

The Constitution of the Republic of Madagascar, which was endorsed by national referendum on 19 August 1992, enshrines a unitary state, and provides for a bicameral legislature, comprising a Senate and a National Assembly. Two-thirds of the members of the Senate are selected by an electoral college for a term of four years, and the remaining one-third of the members are appointed by the President. The 138-member National Assembly is elected by universal adult suffrage, under a system of proportional representation, for a four-year term of office. The constitutional Head of State is the President, who is elected for a term of five years. If no candidate obtains an overall majority in the presidential election, a second round of voting is to take place a maximum of 30 days after the publication of the results of the first ballot. Executive power is vested in the Prime Minister, who is elected by the National Assembly, and appoints a Council of Ministers.

## The Government

### HEAD OF STATE

**President:** Prof. ALBERT ZAFY (took office 27 March 1993).

### COUNCIL OF MINISTERS
(May 1995)

**Prime Minister, and Minister of Finance and the Budget:** FRANCISQUE RAVONY.
**Minister of State for Agriculture and Rural Development:** EMMANUEL RAKOTOVAHINY.
**Minister of Foreign Affairs:** JACQUES SYLLA.
**Minister of Justice and Keeper of the Seals:** RABENIRAINY RAMANOELISON.
**Minister of the Interior and Decentralization:** CLÉMENT CHARLES SÉVÉRIN.
**Minister of Health:** DAMASY ANDRIAMBAO.
**Minister of the Civil Service, Labour and Social Legislation:** HENRI RAKOTOVOLOLONA.
**Minister of the Economy and Town Planning:** TOVONANAHARY RABETSITONTA.
**Minister of the Armed Forces:** Gen. CHARLES RABENJA.
**Minister of the National Police:** BERTHIN RAZAFINDRAZAKA.
**Minister of Transport and Meteorology:** DANIEL RAMAROMISA.
**Minister of Primary and Secondary Education:** FANONY FULGENCE.
**Minister of Public Works:** ROYAL RAOELFILS.
**Minister of Energy and Mining:** BETIANA BRUNO.
**Minister of Research and Development:** ROGER ANDRIANASOLO.
**Minister of Culture, Communications and Leisure Activities:** TSILAVINA RALAINDIMBY.
**Minister of Posts and Telecommunications:** NY HASINA ANDRIAMANJATO.
**Minister of Regional Planning:** HENRI RAKOTONIRAINY.
**Minister of Higher Education:** ADOLPHE RAKOTOMANGA.
**Minister of Industrial Promotion and Craftsmanship:** GÉDÉON RAJHONSON.
**Minister of Commerce and Supply:** JÉRÔME SAMBALIS.
**Minister of Tourism:** ALPHONSE RALISON.
**Minister of the Environment:** GEORGES ALDINE RABELAZA.
**Minister of Population, Youth and Sports:** THÉRÈSE RAVAO.

### MINISTRIES

**Office of the Prime Minister:** BP 248, Mahazoarivo, 101 Antananarivo; tel. (2) 25258; telex 22339; fax (2) 35258.
**Ministry of Agriculture and Rural Development:** BP 500, Anosy, 101 Antananarivo; tel. (2) 24710; telex 22508; fax (2) 26561.
**Ministry of the Armed Forces:** Ampahibe, Antananarivo; tel. (2) 22211.
**Ministry of the Civil Service, Labour and Social Legislation:** BP 270, 101 Antananarivo; tel. (2) 23581.
**Ministry of Commerce and Supply:** Ambohidahy, 101 Antananarivo; tel. (2) 27292; telex 22378; fax (2) 31280.
**Ministry of Culture, Communications and Leisure Activities:** BP 305, 101 Antananarivo; tel. (2) 27092; fax (2) 29448.
**Ministry of the Economy and Town Planning:** BP 674, Antananarivo 101; tel. (2) 20284.
**Ministry of Energy and Mining:** BP 527, Antananarivo; tel. (2) 25515; telex 22540.
**Ministry of the Environment:** Ampandrianomby, Antananarivo; tel. (2) 40908.
**Ministry of Foreign Affairs:** Anosy, 101 Antananarivo; tel. (2) 21198; telex 22236; fax (2) 34484.
**Ministry of Health:** Ambohidahy, 101 Antananarivo; tel. (2) 23697.
**Ministry of Higher Education:** BP 4163, Tsimbazana, 101 Antananarivo; tel. (2) 27185; fax (2) 23897.
**Ministry of Industrial Promotion and Craftsmanship:** BP 527, 101 Antananarivo; tel. (2) 25515; telex 22540.
**Ministry of the Interior and Decentralization:** Anosy, 101 Antananarivo; tel. (2) 23084.
**Ministry of Justice:** BP 231, Faravohitra, 101 Antananarivo; tel. (2) 24030.
**Ministry of National Police:** Anosy, 101 Antananarivo; tel. (2) 21029.
**Ministry of Population, Youth and Sports:** Ambohijatovo, 101 Antananarivo; tel. (2) 23075.
**Ministry of Posts and Telecommunications:** Antaninarenina, 101 Antananarivo; tel. (2) 26121; telex 22250.

MADAGASCAR

**Ministry of Primary and Secondary Education:** BP 267, Anosy, 101 Antananarivo; tel. (2) 21325.

**Ministry of Public Works:** Anosy, 101 Antananarivo; tel. (2) 24224; telex 22343.

**Ministry of Regional Planning:** BP 3378, Anosy, 101 Antananarivo; tel. (2) 35617.

**Ministry of Research and Development:** 27 rue Fernand Kasanga, BP 6224, Andoharano-Tsimbazaza, 101 Antananarivo; tel. (2) 33288; telex 22539; fax (2) 24075.

**Ministry of Tourism:** Tsimbazaza, BP 610, 101 Antananarivo; tel. (2) 26298; fax (2) 26710.

**Ministry of Transport and Meteorology:** Anosy, 101 Antananarivo; tel. (2) 24604; telex 22301; fax (2) 24001.

## President and Legislature

### PRESIDENT

**Presidential Election, First Ballot, 25 November 1992**

| Candidate | Votes | % |
| --- | --- | --- |
| Prof. ALBERT ZAFY (FV) | 1,846,842 | 45.16 |
| DIDIER RATSIRAKA (MMSM) | 1,195,026 | 29.22 |
| MANANDAFY RAKOTONIRINA (MFM) | 417,504 | 10.21 |
| EVARISTE MARSON (RPSD) | 188,235 | 4.60 |
| RUFFINE TSIRANANA (PSD) | 142,571 | 3.49 |
| JACQUES RABEMANANJARA (Independent) | 117,273 | 2.87 |
| RAZAFINDRAKOTO ANDRIAMANALINA (Independent) | 92,061 | 2.25 |
| TOVONANAHARY RABETSITONTA (Independent) | 89,715 | 2.19 |
| **Total** | **4,089,227** | **100.00** |

**Second Ballot, 10 February 1993**

| Candidate | Votes | % |
| --- | --- | --- |
| Prof. ALBERT ZAFY (FV) | 2,766,704 | 66.74 |
| DIDIER RATSIRAKA (MMSM) | 1,378,640 | 33.26 |
| **Total** | **4,145,344** | **100.00** |

### LEGISLATURE

The August 1992 Constitution provides for a bicameral legislature, comprising a Senate and a National Assembly.

#### National Assembly

**President:** Pastor RICHARD ANDRIAMANJATO.

**General Election, 16 June 1993**

| Party | Seats |
| --- | --- |
| Cartel HVR | 46 |
| MFM | 15 |
| Leader—Fanilo | 13 |
| FAMIMA | 11 |
| Fihaonana | 8 |
| RPSD | 8 |
| AKFM—Fanavaozana | 5 |
| UNDD—Cartel HVR | 5 |
| UNDD | 2 |
| CSDDM | 2 |
| Farimbona | 2 |
| Accord | 2 |
| Fivoarana | 2 |
| Teachers and Educators—Cartel HVR | 1 |
| GRAD—Iloafo | 1 |
| Vatomizana | 1 |
| Others | 14 |
| **Total** | **138** |

## Political Organizations

Legislation permitting the resumption of multi-party politics took effect in March 1990; more than 120 political associations subsequently emerged. The principal political organizations in 1995 were:

**AKFM—Fanavaozana:** Antananarivo; f. 1989 by a breakaway group from the former Parti du congrès de l'indépendance de Madagascar (AKFM); supports liberal policies; Leader Pastor RICHARD ANDRIAMANJATO.

**Cartel HVR (Hery Velona Rasalama—Forces vives Rasalama):** f. 1990 as Comité des forces vives; reconstituted in 1993, after a number of member parties broke away to contest elections; supported Prof. Albert Zafy in the presidential election; Pres. ALAIN RAMAROSON.

**Committee for the Support of Democracy and Development in Madagascar (CSDDM):** f. 1993; Leader FRANCISQUE RAVONY.

**Elan Populaire pour l'Unité Nationale (Vonjy Iray Tsy Mivaky—Vonjy):** 101 Antananarivo; f. 1973; centrist; Leader Dr JÉRÔME MAROJAMA RAZANABAHINY.

**FAMIMA:** f. 1993; supports fmr President Didier Ratsiraka.

**Fihaonana:** f. 1993; Leader GUY RAZANAMASY.

**Leader—Farito:** f. 1993; comprises 'non-politicians'; Leader HERIZO RAZAFIMAHALEO.

**Mouvement pour le progrès de Madagascar (Mpitolona ho amin'ny Fandrosoan'ny Madagasikara—MFM):** 101 Antananarivo; f. 1972 as Mouvement pour le pouvoir prolétarien (MFM), adopted present name in 1990; advocates liberal and market-orientated policies; Leader MANANDAFY RAKOTONIRINA; Sec.-Gen. GERMAIN RAKOTONIRAINY.

**Parti social démocrate (PSD):** Antananarivo; f. 1957, relaunched 1990; Sec.-Gen. RUFFINE TSIRANANA.

**Rassemblement pour le socialisme et la démocratie (RPSD):** breakaway faction from the PSD; Leader EVARISTE MARSON.

**Union nationale pour la démocratie et le développement (UNDD):** f. 1991 by Prof. ALBERT ZAFY; Leader EMMANUEL RAKOTOVAHINY.

Other parties represented in the legislature were Accord, Farimbona, Fivoarana, GRAD—Iloafa (Leader TOVONANAHARY RABETSITONJA), Teachers and Educators—Cartel HVR, and Vatomizana.

## Diplomatic Representation

### EMBASSIES IN MADAGASCAR

**China, People's Republic:** Ancien Hôtel Panorama, BP 1658, 101 Antananarivo; Ambassador: ZHAO BAOZHEN.

**Egypt:** 47 ave Lénine, BP 4082, Ankadifotsy, 101 Antananarivo; tel. (2) 25233; telex 22364; Ambassador: EL-GAMAL F. DAIEF.

**France:** 3 rue Jean Jaurès, BP 204, 101 Antananarivo; tel. (2) 23700; telex 22201; Ambassador: JEAN-DIDIER ROISIN.

**Germany:** 101 route circulaire, BP 516, Ambodirotra; tel. 23802; telex 22203; Ambassador: Dr HUBERT BEEMELMANS.

**Holy See:** Amboniloha Ivandry, BP 650, 101 Antananarivo; tel. (2) 42376; telex 22432; fax (2) 42384; Apostolic Pro-Nuncio: Most Rev. BLASCO FRANCISCO COLLAÇO, Titular Archbishop of Octava.

**India:** 4 làlana Emile Rajaonson, BP 1787, 101 Antananarivo; tel. (2) 23334; telex 22484; Ambassador: A. K. BASU.

**Indonesia:** 15 rue Radama I Tsaralalana, 101 Antananarivo; tel. (2) 24915; telex 22387; Chargé d'affaires a.i.: Dr SAMUSI.

**Iran:** route circulaire, Lot II L43 ter, 101 Antananarivo; tel. (2) 28639; telex 22510; fax (2) 22298; Chargé d'affaires a.i.: Dr MOSTAFA BOROUJERDI.

**Italy:** 22 rue Pasteur Rabary, BP 16, Ankadivato; tel. 21217; telex 22293; Ambassador: FRANCESCO SCIORTINO.

**Japan:** 8 rue du Dr Villette, BP 3863, Isoraka, 101 Antananarivo; tel. (2) 26102; telex 22308; fax (2) 21769; Ambassador: MASAHIKO IWASAKI.

**Korea, Democratic People's Republic:** Ambohibao; tel. 44442; telex 22494; Ambassador: KIM RYONG-YONG.

**Libya:** Lot IIB, 37A route Circulaire Ampandrana-Ouest, 101 Antananarivo; tel. (2) 21892; Secretary of People's Bureau: SALEM ALI SALEM DANNAH.

**Mauritius:** Antananarivo; Ambassador: (vacant).

**Russia:** Ampefiloha, Lot O, BP 4006; tel. 27070; Ambassador: YURI NIKOLAYEVICH MARZLIAKOV.

**South Africa:** Lot II J169, Ivandry, 101 Antananarivo; tel. (2) 42419; fax (2) 43504; Ambassador: ABRAHIM BRINK.

**Switzerland:** BP 118, 101 Antananarivo; tel. (2) 22846; telex 22300; fax (2) 28940; Chargé d'affaires: FRANCIS COUSIN.

**United Kingdom:** Immeuble 'Ny Havana', Cité de 67 Ha, BP 167, 101 Antananarivo; tel. (2) 27749; telex 22459; fax (2) 26690; Ambassador: PETER J. SMITH.

**USA:** 14–16 rue Rainitovo, Antsahavola, BP 620, 101 Antananarivo; tel. (2) 21257; telex 22202; fax (2) 34539; Ambassador: DENNIS BARRETT.

# Judicial System

### CONSTITUTIONAL HIGH COURT

**Haute Cour Constitutionnelle:** 101 Antananarivo; interprets the constitution and rules on constitutional issues; seven mems; Pres. NORBERT RATSIRAHONANA.

### SUPREME COURT

**Cour Suprême:** Palais de Justice, Anosy, 101 Antananarivo; Pres. ALICE RAJAONAH (interim); Attorney-General COLOMBE RAMANANTSOA (interim); Chamber Pres. YOLANDE RAMANGASOAVINA, FRANÇOIS RAMANANDRAIBE.

### COURT OF APPEAL

**Cour d'Appel:** Palais de Justice, Anosy, 101 Antananarivo; Pres. AIMÉE RAKOTONIRINA; Chamber Pres CHARLES RABETOKOTANY, PÉTRONILLE ANDRIAMIHAJA, BAKOLALAO RANAIVOHARIVONY, BERTHOLIER RAVELONTSALAMA, LUCIEN RABARIJHON, NELLY RAKOTOBE, ARLETTE RAMAROSON, CLÉMENTINE RAVANDISON, GISÈLE RABOTOVAO, JEAN-JACQUES RAJAONA.

### OTHER COURTS

**Tribunaux de Première Instance:** at Antananarivo, Toamasina, Antsiranana, Mahajanga, Fianarantsoa, Toliary, Antsirabé, Ambatondrazaka, Antalaha, Farafangana, Maintirano; for civil, commercial and social matters, and for registration.

**Cours Criminelles Ordinaires:** tries crimes of common law; attached to the Cour d'Appel in Antananarivo but may sit in any other large town. There are also 31 Cours Criminelles Spéciales dealing with cases concerning cattle.

**Tribunaux Spéciaux Economiques:** at Antananarivo, Toamasina, Mahajanga, Fianarantsoa, Antsiranana and Toliary; tries crimes specifically relating to economic matters.

**Tribunaux Criminels Spéciaux:** judges cases of looting and banditry; 31 courts.

# Religion

It is estimated that more than 50% of the population follow traditional animist beliefs, some 43% are Christians (about one-half of whom are Roman Catholics) and the remainder are Muslims.

### CHRISTIANITY

**Fiombonan'ny Fiangonana Kristiana eto Madagasikara (FFKM)/Conseil Chrétien des Eglises de Madagascar (Christian Council of Churches in Madagascar):** Vohipiraisama, Ambohijatovo-Atsimo, BP 798, 101 Antananarivo; tel. (2) 29052; f. 1980; four full mems and one assoc. mem.; Pres. Pastor EDMOND RAZAFIMEHELO; Gen. Sec. Rev. LALA ANDRIAMIHARISOA.

**Fiombonan'ny Fiangonana Protestanta eto Madagasikara (FFPM)/Fédération des Eglises Protestantes à Madagascar (Federation of the Protestant Churches in Madagascar):** VK 2 Vohipiraisana, Ambohijatovo-Atsimo, 101 Antananarivo; tel. (2) 20144; f. 1958; two mems; Pres. Rev. Dr PÉRI RASOLONDRAIMIBE; Gen. Sec. Rev. CHARLES RAKOTOSON.

#### The Anglican Communion

Anglicans are adherents of the Church of the Province of the Indian Ocean, comprising five dioceses (three in Madagascar, one in Mauritius and one in Seychelles). The Archbishop of the Province is the Bishop of Seychelles. The Church has about 160,000 adherents in Madagascar, where it embraces the Eklesia Episkopaly Malagasy (Malagasy Episcopal Church), founded in 1874.

**Bishop of Antananarivo:** Rt Rev. RÉMI JOSEPH RABENIRINA, Evêché Anglican, Ambohimanoro, 101 Antananarivo; tel. (2) 20827.

**Bishop of Antsiranana:** Rt Rev. KEITH BENZIES, Evêché Anglican, BP 278, Antsiranana; tel. (8) 22650.

**Bishop of Toamasina:** Rt Rev. DONALD SMITH, La Mission Anglicane, rue de la Fraternité, Toamasina; tel. (5) 32163.

#### The Roman Catholic Church

Madagascar comprises three archdioceses and 15 dioceses. At 31 December 1993 the number of adherents in the country represented about 21.4% of the total population.

**Bishops' Conference:** Conférence Episcopale de Madagascar, 102 bis ave Maréchal Joffre, Antanimena, BP 667, 101 Antananarivo; tel. (2) 20478; f. 1969; Pres. Rt Rev. JEAN-GUY RAKOTONDRAVAHATRA, Bishop of Ihosy.

**Archbishop of Antananarivo:** Cardinal ARMAND RAZAFINDRATANDRA, Archevêché, Andohalo, 101 Antananarivo; tel. (2) 20726.

**Archbishop of Antsiranana:** Most Rev. ALBERT JOSEPH TSIAHOANA, Archevêché, BP 415, 201 Antsiranana; tel. (8) 21605.

**Archbishop of Fianarantsoa:** Most Rev. PHILIBERT RANDRIAMBOLOLONA, Archevêché, place Mgr Givelet, BP 1440, 301 Fianarantsoa; tel. (7) 50672; fax (7) 24854.

#### Other Christian Churches

**Fiangonan' i Jesoa Kristy eto Madagasikara/Eglise de Jésus-Christ à Madagascar:** Lot 11 B18, Tohatohabato Ranavalona 1, Trano 'Ifanomezantsoa', BP 623, 101 Antananarivo; tel. (2) 26845; telex 22467; fax (2) 26372; f. 1968; Pres. Rev. EDMOND RAZAFIMAHEFA; Gen. Sec. Rev. LALA RASENDRAHASINA; 2m. mems.

**Fiangonana Loterana Malagasy** (Malagasy Lutheran Church): BP 1741, 101 Antananarivo; tel. (2) 22347; telex 22544; Pres. Rev. RANAIVOJAONA RAZAFIMANANTSOA; 600,000 mems.

# The Press

In December 1990 the National People's Assembly adopted legislation guaranteeing the freedom of the press and the right of newspapers to be established without prior authorization.

### PRINCIPAL DAILIES

**Bulletin de l'Agence Nationale d'Information 'Taratra' (ANTA):** 3 rue du R. P. Callet, Behoririka, BP 386, 101 Antananarivo; tel. (2) 21171; telex 22506; f. 1977; French; Man. Dir JEANNOT FENO.

**L'Express de Madagascar:** Antananarivo; f. 1995; French and Malagasy; Editor JEAN JACQUES RAMAMBRAZAFY.

**Imongo Vaovao:** 11K 4 bis Andravoahangy, BP 7014, 101 Antananarivo; tel. (2) 21053; f. 1955; Malagasy; Dir CLÉMENT RAMAMONJISOA; circ. 10,000.

**Madagascar Tribune:** Immeuble SME, rue Ravoninahitriniarivo, BP 659, Ankorondrano, 101 Antananarivo; tel. (2) 22635; telex 22340; fax (2) 22254; f. 1988; independent; French and Malagasy; Editor RAHAGA RAMAHOLIMIHASO; circ. 12,000.

**Maresaka:** 12 làlana Ratsimba John, Isotry, 101 Antananarivo; tel. (2) 23568; f. 1953; independent; Malagasy; Editor M. RALAIARIJAONA; circ. 5,000.

**Midi-Madagascar:** làlana Ravoninahitriniarivo, BP 1414, Ankorondrano, 101 Antananarivo; tel. (2) 30038; telex 22543; f. 1983; French; Dir JULIANA RAKOTOARIVELO; circ. 25,489.

### PRINCIPAL PERIODICALS

**Afaka:** BP 1475, 101 Antananarivo; Malagasy and French; Dir MAX RATSIMANDISA; circ. 5,000.

**Basy Vava:** Lot III E 96, Mahamasina Atsimo, 101 Antananarivo; tel. (2) 20448; f. 1959; Malagasy; Dir GABRIEL RAMANANJATO; circ. 3,000.

**Bulletin de la Société du Corps Médical Malgache:** Imprimerie Volamahitsy, 101 Antananarivo; Malagasy; monthly; Dir Dr RAKOTOMALALA.

**Dans les Media, Demain:** Immeuble Jeune Afrique, 58 rue Tsiombikibo, BP 1734, Ambatovinaky, 101 Antananarivo; tel. (2) 27788; telex 22225; fax (2) 30629; f. 1986; independent; weekly; Dir HONORÉ RAZAFINTSALAMA; circ. 2,500.

**Feon'ny Mpiasa:** Lot M8, Isotry, 101 Antananarivo; trade union affairs; Malagasy; monthly; Dir M. RAZAKANAIVO; circ. 2,000.

**Fiaraha-Miasa:** BP 1216, 101 Antananarivo; Malagasy; weekly; Dir SOLO NORBERT ANDRIAMORASATA; circ. 5,000.

**Gazetinao:** Lot IPA 37 ter, Anosimasina, 101 Antananarivo; tel. 33177; Malagasy; monthly; Dir ETIENNE M. RAKOTOMAHANINA; circ. 3,000.

**La Gazette d'Antsirabé:** Lot 12 C-190, Antsenakely, 110 Antsirabé; f. 1989; Dir VOLOLOHARIMANANA RAZAFIMANDIMBY; circ. 7,000.

**Gazety Medikaly:** Lot 12B, Ampahibe, 101 Antananarivo; tel. (2) 27898; f. 1965; medical; Dir PAUL RATSIMISETA; circ. 2,000.

**Isika Mianakavy:** Ambatomena, 301 Fianarantsoa; f. 1958; Roman Catholic; Malagasy; monthly; Dir J. RANAIVOMANANA; circ. 21,000.

**Journal Officiel de la République de Madagascar:** BP 248, 101 Antananarivo; tel. (2) 25258; f. 1883; official announcements; Malagasy and French; weekly; Dir SAMUEL RAMAROSON.

**Journal Scientifique de Madagascar:** Antananarivo; f. 1985; Dir Prof. MANAMBELONA; circ. 3,000.

**Jureco:** Immeuble SOMAGI, 120 rue Rainandriamampandry, 101 Antananarivo; tel. (2) 24145; fax (2) 20397; law and economics; monthly; Dir MBOARA ANDRIANARIMANANA.

**Lakroan'i Madagasikara:** Maison Jean XXIII, Mahamasina Sud, 101 Antananarivo; tel. (2) 21158; f. 1927; Roman Catholic; French and Malagasy; weekly; Dir LOUIS RASOLO; circ. 25,000.

**Mada-Économie:** 15 rue Ratsimilaho, BP 3464, 101 Antananarivo; tel. (2) 25634; f. 1977; reports events in south-east Africa; monthly; Editor RICHARD-CLAUDE RATOVONARIVO; circ. 5,000.

**Mpanolotsaina:** BP 623, 101 Antananarivo; tel. (2) 26845; religious, educational; Malagasy; quarterly; Dir PAUL SOLOHERY.

**Ny Mpamangy-FLM:** 9 rue Grandidier Isoraka, BP 538, Antsahamanitra, 101 Antananarivo; tel. (2) 32446; telex 22544; f. 1882; monthly; Dir Pastor MAMY ANDRIAMAHENINA; circ. 3,000.

**Ny Sakaizan'ny Tanora:** BP 538, Antsahaminitra, 101 Antananarivo; tel. (2) 32446; telex 22544; f. 1878; monthly; Editor-in-Chief DANIEL PROSPER ANDRIAMANJAKA; circ. 5,000.

**PME Madagascar:** rue Hugues Rabesahala, BP 953, Antsakaviro, 101 Antananarivo; tel. (2) 22536; telex 22261; fax (2) 34534; f. 1989; French; monthly; economic review; Dir ROMAIN ANDRIANARISOA; circ. 3,500.

**Recherche et Culture:** BP 907, 101 Antananarivo; tel. (2) 26600; f. 1985; publ. by French dept of the University of Antananarivo; 2 a year; Dir GINETTE RAMAROSON; circ. 1,000.

**Revue Ita:** BP 681, 101 Antananarivo; tel. (2) 30507; f. 1985; controlled by the Ministry of Population; quarterly; Dir FILS RAMALANJAONA; circ. 1,000.

**Revue de l'Océan Indien:** Communication et Médias Océan Indien, rue H. Rabesahala, BP 46, Antsakaviro, 101 Antananarivo; tel. (2) 22536; telex 22261; fax (2) 34534; f. 1980; quarterly; Man. Dir GEORGES RANAIVOSOA; Sec.-Gen. HERY M. A. RANAIVOSOA; circ. 5,000.

**Sahy:** Lot VD 42, Ambanidia, 101 Antananarivo; tel. (2) 22715; f. 1957; political; Malagasy; weekly; Editor ALINE RAKOTO; circ. 9,000.

**Sosialisma Mpiasa:** BP 1128, 101 Antananarivo; tel. (2) 21989; f. 1979; trade union affairs; Malagasy; monthly; Dir PAUL RABEMANANJARA; circ. 5,000.

**Valeurs—L'Hebdomadaire de Madagascar:** Antananarivo; f. 1995; weekly; Dir RIJA RASENDRATSIROFO.

**Vaovao:** BP 271, 101 Antananarivo; tel. (2) 21193; f. 1985; French and Malagasy; weekly; Dir MARC RAKOTONOELY; circ. 5,000.

### NEWS AGENCIES

**Agence Nationale d'Information 'Taratra' (ANTA):** 3 rue du R. P. Callet, Behoririka, BP 386, 101 Antananarivo; tel. (2) 21171; telex 22395; f 1977; Man. Dir JEANNOT FENO.

#### Foreign Bureaux

**Associated Press (AP)** (USA): BP 73, 101 Antananarivo; tel. (2) 40115; Correspondent CHRISTIAN CHADEFAUX.

**Korean Central News Agency (KCNA)** (Democratic People's Republic of Korea): BP 4276, 101 Antananarivo; tel. (2) 44795; Dir KIM YEUNG KYEUN.

**Xinhua (New China) News Agency** (People's Republic of China): BP 1656, 101 Antananarivo; tel. (2) 29927; telex 22360; Chief of Bureau WU HAIYUN.

Reuters (UK) is also represented in Madagascar.

## Publishers

**Editions Ambozontany:** BP 40, 301 Fianarantsoa; tel. (7) 50603; f. 1962; religious and school textbooks; Dir R. F. GIAMBRONE.

**Foibe Filankevitry Ny Mpampianatra (FOFIPA):** BP 202, 101 Antananarivo; tel. (2) 27500; f. 1971; school and educational texts; Dir Frère RAZAFINDRAKOTO.

**Madagascar Print and Press Co (MADPRINT):** rue Rabesahala, Antsakaviro, BP 953, 101 Antananarivo; tel. (2) 22536; telex 22226; fax (2) 34534; f. 1969; literary, technical and historical; Dir GEORGES RANAIVOSOA.

**Maison d'Edition Protestante Antso** (Librairie-Imprimerie): 19 rue Venance Manifatra, Imarivolanitra, BP 660, 101 Antananarivo; tel. (2) 20886; f. 1962; religious, school, social, political and general; Dir HANS ANDRIAMAMPIANINA.

**Imprimerie Nouvelle:** PK 2, Andranomahery, route de Majunga, 101 Antananarivo; tel. (2) 23330; Dir EUGÈNE RAHARIFIDY.

**Nouvelle Société de Presse et d'Edition (NSPE):** Immeuble Jeune Afrique, 58 rue Tsiombikibo, BP 1734, Ambatorinaky, 101 Antananarivo; tel. (2) 27788; telex 22225; fax (2) 30629.

**Office du Livre Malgache:** Lot 111 H29, Andrefan' Ambohijanahary, BP 617, 101 Antananarivo; tel. (2) 24449; f. 1970; children's and general; Sec.-Gen. JULIETTE RATSIMANDRAVA.

**Edisiona Salohy:** BP 7124, 101 Antananarivo; Dir JEAN RABENALISOA RAVALITERA.

**Société de Presse et d'Edition de Madagascar:** Antananarivo; non-fiction, reference, science, university textbooks; Man. Dir Mrs RAJAOFERA ANDRIAMBELO.

**Société Malgache d'Edition (SME):** BP 659, Ankorondrano, 101 Antananarivo; tel. (2) 22635; telex 22340; fax (2) 22254; f. 1943; general fiction; university and secondary textbooks; Man. Dir RAHAGA RAMAHOLIMIHASO.

**Société Nouvelle de l'Imprimerie Centrale (SNIC):** làlana Ravoninahitriniarivo, BP 1414, 101 Antananarivo; tel. (2) 21118; f. 1959; science, school textbooks; Man. Dir MARTHE ANDRIAMBELO.

**Imprimerie Takariva:** 4 rue Radley, BP 1029, Antanimena, 101 Antananarivo; tel. (2) 22128; f. 1933; fiction, languages, school textbooks; Man. Dir PAUL RAPATSALAHY.

**Trano Printy Fiangonana Loterana Malagasy (TPFLM):** BP 538, 9 ave Grandidier, Antsahamanitra, 101 Antananarivo; tel. (2) 23340; f. 1875; religious, educational and fiction; Man. ABEL ARNESA.

#### Government Publishing House

**Imprimerie Nationale:** BP 38, 101 Antananarivo; tel. (2) 23675; all official publs; Dir JEAN DENIS RANDRIANIRINA.

## Radio and Television

In December 1990 the state monopoly of broadcasting was abolished, and legislation authorizing the establishment of private radio and television stations 'in partnership with the Government or its agencies' was adopted; in early 1995 six independent radio stations were operating in Madagascar. According to UNESCO, there were an estimated 2,565,000 radio receivers and 260,000 television receivers in use in 1992.

### RADIO

**Radio Nationale Malagasy:** BP 442, 101 Antananarivo; tel. (2) 22066; state-controlled; broadcasts in French, Malagasy and English; Dir SIMON SEVA MBOINY.

**Le Messager Radio Evangélique:** BP 1374, 101 Antananarivo; tel. (2) 34495; broadcasts in French, English and Malagasy; Dir JOCELYN RANJARISON.

**Radio Antsiva:** Lot VA, 21 Ambohitantely, 101 Antananarivo; tel. (2) 34400; broadcasts in French, English and Malagasy; Dir SYLVAIN RAFIADANANTSOA.

**Radio Feon'ny Vahoaka (RFV):** 103 bldg Ramaroson, 8th Floor, 101 Antananarivo; tel. (2) 33820; broadcasts in French and Malagasy; Dir ALAIN RAMAROSON.

**Radio Korail:** Lot V III bis, Ankaditapaka Haute Ville; tel. 24494; broadcasts in French and Malagasy; Dir ALAIN RAJAONA.

**Radio Lazan'iarivo (RLI):** Lot V A49, Andafiavaratra, 101 Antananarivo; tel. (2) 29016; broadcasts in French, English and Malagasy; Dir IRÈNE RAVALISON.

**Radio Tsioka Vao (RTV):** Lot V T15/16, Ambohimitsimbona, Ankaditapaka; tel. 21749; broadcasts in French, English and Malagasy; Dir THOMAS BARNABE BETKOU DIEUDONNÉ.

### TELEVISION

**Télévision Nasionaly Malagasy:** BP 1202, 101 Antananarivo; tel. (2) 22381; telex 22506; f. 1931 as Radio-Télévision Malagasy; broadcasts in French and Malagasy; one transmitter; Dir-Gen. MAMY RAMIASINARIVO.

## Finance

(cap. = capital; res = reserves; dep. = deposits; m. = million; brs = branches; amounts in Malagasy francs)

All commercial banks and insurance companies were nationalized in 1975, but in 1988 a process of restructuring was begun, allowing private and foreign investment.

### BANKING
#### Central Bank

**Banque Centrale de la République Malgache:** ave de la Révolution Socialiste Malgache, BP 550, 101 Antananarivo; tel. (2) 21751; telex 22317; fax (2) 34532; f. 1973; bank of issue; cap. 1,000m.; Gov. GASTON RAVELOJAONA (acting).

#### Other Banks

**Bankin'ny Tantsaha Mpamokatra (BTM):** place de l'Indépendance, BP 183, 101 Antananarivo; tel. (2) 20251; telex 22208; fax (2) 33749; f. 1976 by merger; specializes in rural development; 90% state-owned; cap. 13,500m. (1992), dep. 193,485m. (1987); Man. BRUNO DISAINE; 75 brs.

**Banky Fampandrosoana ny Varotra (BFV):** 14 làlana Jeneraly Rabehevitra, BP 196, 101 Antananarivo; tel. (2) 20691; telex 22257; fax (2) 33645; 73.7% state-owned; f. 1977 by merger; cap.

# MADAGASCAR

11,500m. (1992), res 32,850.9m., dep. 246,257.1m. (1991); Chair. IGNACE RAMAROSON; Dir-Gen. JOSÉ YVON RASERIJAONA; 27 brs.

**Banque Malgache de l'Océan Indien (BMOI)** (Indian Ocean Malagasy Bank): place de l'Indépendance, BP 25, Antananarivo 101; tel. (2) 34609; telex 22381; fax (2) 34610; f. 1990; cap. 10,000m. (March 1993); Pres. GASTON RAMENASON; Dir-Gen. MICHEL LAFONT; 8 brs.

**BNI—Crédit Lyonnais Madagascar:** 74 rue du 26 Juin 1960, BP 174, 101 Antananarivo; tel. (2) 23951; telex 22205; fax (2) 33749; fmrly Bankin'ny Indostria; cap. 4,500m. (March 1993), dep. 239,811.5m. (1991); Pres. TANTELY ANDRIANARIVO; Dir-Gen. BERNARD FOURNIER; 27 brs.

**Union Commercial Bank (UCB):** 77 làlana Solombavambahoaka, BP 197, 101 Antananarivo; tel. (2) 27262; telex 22528; fax (2) 28740; f. 1992; cap. 1,500m. (March 1993); Pres. RAYMOND HEIN; Dir-Gen. JOCELYN THOMASSE.

## INSURANCE

**ARO (Assurances Réassurances Omnibranches):** Antsahavola, BP 42, 101 Antananarivo; tel. (2) 20154; telex 22265; fax (2) 34464; Pres. DÉSIRÉ RAJOBSON; Dir-Gen. HENRI RAJERISON.

**Assurance France-Madagascar:** 7 rue Rainitovo, BP 710, 101 Antananarivo; tel. (2) 23024; telex 22321; fax (2) 33673; f. 1951; Dir I. RATSIRA.

**Compagnie Malgache d'Assurances et de Réassurances:** Immeuble 'Ny Havana', Zone des 67 Ha, BP 3881, 101 Antananarivo; tel. (2) 26760; telex 22377; fax (2) 24303; f. 1968; cap. 13,482m. (1993); Pres. EVARISTE VAZAHA; Dir-Gen. JOCELYN RAKOTO-MAVO.

**Mutuelle d'Assurances Malagasy (MAMA):** 1F, 12 bis, rue Rainibetsimisaraka, Ambalavao-Isotry, BP 185, 101 Antananarivo; tel. (2) 22508; Pres. RAKOTOARIVONY ANDRIAMAROMANANA.

**Société Malgache d'Assurances, Faugère, Jutheau et Cie:** 13 rue Patrice Lumumba, BP 673, 101 Antananarivo; f. 1952; tel. (2) 23162; telex 22247; Dir ANDRIANJAKA RAVELONAHIANA.

# Trade and Industry

## CHAMBER OF COMMERCE

**Fédération des Chambres de Commerce, d'Industrie et d'Agriculture de Madagascar:** 20 rue Colbert, BP 166, 101 Antananarivo; tel. (2) 21567; 12 mem. chambers; Pres. HENRY RAZANATSHENEHO; Sec.-Gen. GEORGES RHEAL.

## TRADE ORGANIZATION

**Société d'Intérêt National des Produits Agricoles (SINPA):** BP 754, rue Fernand-Kasanga, Tsimbazaza, Antananarivo; tel. (2) 20558; telex 22309; fax (2) 20665; f. 1973; monopoly purchaser and distributor of agricultural produce; Chair. GUALBERT RAZANAJATOVO; Gen. Man. JEAN CLOVIS RALIJESY.

## DEVELOPMENT ORGANIZATIONS

**Office des mines nationales et des industries stratégiques (OMNIS):** 21 làlana Razanakombana, BP 1 bis, 101 Antananarivo; tel. (2) 24439; telex 22370; fax (2) 22985; f. 1976; fmrly Office militaire national pour les industries stratégiques; oversees the management of major industrial orgs and exploitation of mining resources; Dir-Gen. MAX DÉSIRÉ RAKOTO-ANDRIANTSILAVO.

**Société d'Etude et de Réalisation pour le Développement Industriel (SERDI):** 78 bis, ave Lénine Ankaditapaka, BP 3180, 101 Antananarivo; tel. (2) 21335; telex 22453; fax (2) 29669; f. 1966; Dir-Gen. DAVID RAFIDISON.

## PRINCIPAL EMPLOYERS' ORGANIZATIONS

**Groupement des Entreprises de Madagascar:** Kianja MDRM sy Tia Tanindrazana, BP 1338, 101 Antananarivo; f. 1973; 22 syndicates and 26 individual cos; Sec.-Gen. AUGUSTIN RAFIDISON.

**Syndicat des Exportateurs de Vanille de Madagascar:** Antalaha; 23 mems; Pres. M. BOURDILLON.

**Syndicat des Importateurs et Exportateurs de Madagascar:** 2 rue Georges Mandel, BP 188, 101 Antananarivo; Pres. M. FONTANA.

**Syndicat des Industries de Madagascar:** Kianja MDRM sy Tia Tanindrazana, BP 1695, 101 Antananarivo; tel. (2) 23608; f. 1958; Chair. CHARLES ANDRIANTSITOHAINA.

**Syndicat des Planteurs de Café:** 37 làlana Razafimahandry, BP 173, 101 Antananarivo.

**Syndicat Professionnel des Agents Généraux d'Assurances:** Antananarivo; f. 1949; Pres. SOLO RATSIMBAZAFY; Sec. IHANTA RANDRIAMANDRANTO.

## TRADE UNIONS

**Cartel National des Organisations Syndicales de Madagascar (CARNOSYAMA):** BP 1035, 101 Antananarivo.

**Confédération des Travailleurs Malgaches** (Fivomdronamben'ny Mpiasa Malagasy—FMM): 3 ave Lénine, Ambatomitsanga, 101 Antananarivo; tel. (2) 24565; f. 1957; Sec.-Gen. JEAN RASOLONDRAIBE; 30,000 mems.

**Fédération des Syndicats des Travailleurs de Madagascar** (Firaisan'ny Sendika eran'i Madagaskara—FISEMA): Lot III, rue Pasteur Isotry, 101 Antananarivo; f. 1956; Pres. DESIRÉ RALAMBOTAHINA; Sec.-Gen. M. RAZAKANAIVO; 8 affiliated unions; 60,000 mems.

**Fédération des Travailleurs Malagasy Révolutionnaires (FISEMARE):** Lot IV N 77, Ankadifots, BP 1128, Antananarivo-Befelatanana; tel. (2) 21989; f. 1985; Pres. PAUL RABEMANANJARA.

**Sendika Kristianina Malagasy—SEKRIMA** (Christian Confederation of Malagasy Trade Unions): Soarano, route de Mahajanga, BP 1035, 101 Antananarivo; tel. (2) 23174; f. 1937; Pres. MARIE RAKOTOANOSY; Gen. Sec. RAYMOND RAKOTOARISAONA; 158 affiliated unions; 40,000 mems.

**Sendika Revolisakionera Malagasy (SEREMA):** 101 Antananarivo.

**Union des Syndicats Autonomes de Madagascar (USAM):** Ampasadratsarahoby, Lot 11 H67, Faravohitra, BP 1038, 101 Antananarivo; Pres. NORBERT RAKOTOMANANA; Sec.-Gen. VICTOR RAHAGA; 46 affiliated unions; 30,000 mems.

# Transport

## RAILWAYS

In 1993 there were 1,095 km of railway, all 1-m gauge track. The northern system, which comprised 729 km of track, links Toamasina, on the east coast, with Antsirabé, in the interior, via Brikaville, Moramanga and Antananarivo, with a branch line from Moramanga to Vohidiala which divides to Lake Alaotra and Morarano to collect chromium ore. The southern system, which comprised 170 km of track, links Manakara, on the south-east coast, and Fianarantsoa.

**Réseau National des Chemins de Fer Malagasy:** 1 ave de l'Indépendance, BP 259, Soarano, 101 Antananarivo; tel. (2) 20521; telex 22233; fax (2) 22288; f. 1909; Dir-Gen. RANAIVOHARITAFIKA ANDRIANTSOAVINA.

## ROADS

In 1993 there were 34,739 km of classified roads, of which 8,528 km were main roads and 18,382 km were secondary roads; 5,350 km of the road network were paved. In 1987 there were 39,500 km of unclassified roads, used only in favourable weather.

## INLAND WATERWAYS

The Pangalanes Canal runs for 600 km near the east coast from Toamasina to Farafangana. In 1984 the Government initiated a development project which was to restore more than 200 km of the canal by 1988, at a cost of 18.5m. FMG. In early 1990 432 km of the canal between Toamasina and Mananjary were navigable.

## SHIPPING

There are 18 ports, the largest being at Toamasina, which handles about 70% of total traffic, and Mahajanga. In 1987 Madagascar received foreign loans totalling US $34.8m., including a credit of $16m. from the World Bank, to finance a project to rehabilitate 10 ports.

**Compagnie Générale Maritime (CGM):** BP 69, 501 Toamasina; tel. (5) 32312; telex 55612; f. 1976 by merger, Rep. J. P. BERGEROT.

**Compagnie Malgache de Navigation (CMN):** rue Toto Radona, BP 1621, 101 Antananarivo; tel. (2) 25516; telex 22263; f. 1960; coasters; 13,784 grt; transfer to private-sector ownership pending in 1994; Pres. Mme ELINAH BAKOLY RAJAONSON; Dir-Gen. ARISTIDE EMMANUEL.

**Navale et Commerciale Havraise Peninsulaire (NCHP):** rue Rabearivelo Antsahavola, BP 1021, 101 Antananarivo; tel. (2) 22502; telex 22273; Rep. JEAN PIERRE NOCKIN.

**Société Nationale Malgache des Transports Maritimes (SMTM):** 6 rue Indira Gandhi, BP 4077, 101 Antananarivo; tel. (2) 27342; telex 22277; fax (2) 33327; f. 1963; services to Europe; Chair. ALEXIS RAZAFINDRATSIRA; Dir-Gen. ANDRIONORO RAMANANTSOA.

**Solitany Malagasy (SOLIMA):** 2 ave Grandidier, BP 140, 101 Antananarivo; tel. (2) 20633; telex 22222; fax (2) 26693; f. 1976; transports and refines petroleum and its products; Chair. ALBERT ANDRIANTSOA RASOAMANAMA; Dir-Gen. CHRISTIAN LOUIS NTSAY.

## CIVIL AVIATION

The international airport is at Antananarivo, while the airports at Mahajanga, Toamasina and Nossi-Bé can also accommodate large jet aircraft. There are more than 200 airfields, of which 57 are open to public air traffic.

**Société Nationale Malgache des Transports Aériens (Air Madagascar):** 31 ave de l'Indépendance, BP 437, 101 Antananarivo; tel. (2) 22222; telex 22232; f. 1962; 89.58% state-owned; extensive internal routes connecting all the principal towns; external services to the Comoros, France, Mauritius and Réunion; Chair. EMMANUEL RAKOTOVAHINY; Dir-Gen. RANDRIAMASY ZACKY.

**Direction des Transports Aériens:** BP 921, Anosy, 101 Antananarivo; tel. (2) 24604; telex 22301; fax (2) 24001.

**Travaux Aériens de Madagascar:** BP 876; tel. 29691; fax 30540; Dir-Gen. SOLONAIVO RAKOTOMALALA.

# Tourism

Madagascar's attractions include unspoiled scenery and many unusual varieties of wildlife. In 1992 53,654 tourists visited Madagascar, and revenue from tourism was estimated at US $39m. In January 1989 a tourism investment programme was approved, in an effort to increase the number of visitors to 138,000 per year and to provide 5,000 extra hotel beds by 1995.

**Direction du Tourisme de Madagascar:** Ministry of Tourism, Tsimbazaza, BP 610, 101 Antananarivo; tel. (2) 26298; fax (2) 26710.

# MALAWI

## Introductory Survey

### Location, Climate, Language, Religion, Flag, Capital

The Republic of Malawi is a land-locked country in southern central Africa, with Zambia to the west, Mozambique to the south and east, and Tanzania to the north. Lake Malawi forms most of the eastern boundary. The climate is tropical, but much of the country is sufficiently high above sea-level to modify the heat. Temperatures range from 14°C (57°F) to 18°C (64°F) in mountain areas, but can reach 38°C (100°F) in low-lying regions. There is a rainy season between November and April. The official language is English, though Chichewa is being promoted as the basis for a 'Malawi Language'. Some 75% of the population profess Christianity, with 10% of inhabitants following traditional beliefs. A further 10% of Malawians, largely Asians, are Muslims, and there is also a Hindu minority. The national flag (proportions 3 by 2) has three equal horizontal stripes, of black, red and green, with a rising sun, in red, in the centre of the black stripe. The capital is Lilongwe.

### Recent History

Malawi was formerly the British protectorate of Nyasaland. In 1953 it was linked with two other British dependencies, Northern and Southern Rhodesia (now Zambia and Zimbabwe), to form the Federation of Rhodesia and Nyasaland. Elections in August 1961 gave the Malawi Congress Party (MCP), led by Dr Hastings Kamuzu Banda, a majority of seats in the Legislative Council. Dr Banda became Prime Minister in February 1963, and the Federation was dissolved in December. Nyasaland gained independence, as Malawi, on 6 July 1964. The country became a republic and a one-party state, with Banda as its first President, on 6 July 1966. In 1967 Malawi created a major controversy among African states by officially recognizing the Republic of South Africa. In 1971 Banda became Life President of Malawi and the first African head of state to visit South Africa. In 1976, however, Malawi recognized the communist-backed Government in Angola in preference to the South African-supported forces. Malawi later refused to recognize the 'independence' granted by South Africa to four of its African 'homelands'.

Until 1993 all Malawian citizens were obliged to be members of the MCP, and no political opposition was tolerated. In March 1979 Dr Banda openly admitted that a letter bomb that injured the exiled leader of the Socialist League of Malawi (LESOMA), Dr Attati Mpakati, had been sent on his instructions. In March 1983 Mpakati was assassinated in Zimbabwe, although the Malawi Government denied any responsibility for his death. In December 1981 Orton Chirwa and his wife, Vera, the leaders of the Malawi Freedom Movement (MAFREMO), were arrested. In May 1983 they were found guilty of treason and were sentenced to death, although Banda subsequently commuted the sentences to life imprisonment. (Orton Chirwa died in prison in October 1992, and Vera Chirwa was eventually released, 'on humanitarian grounds', in January 1993.)

Frequent reorganizations of the Cabinet effectively prevented the emergence of any political rival to Dr Banda. However, it was reported in 1983 that a conflict had developed between Dick Matenje, then Minister without Portfolio in the Cabinet and Secretary-General of the MCP, and John Tembo, then Governor of the Reserve Bank of Malawi, concerning the eventual succession to Banda. Matenje and three other senior politicians died in May; Malawian exiles claimed that the four men had been shot while attempting to flee the country, but the Government stated that they had died as the result of a road accident. (In January 1994 a former police officer claimed to have taken part in the shooting, under official orders, of the four; the Government, however, rejected calls for an official inquiry into the affair.) In spite of the political confusion arising from these deaths, elections to the National Assembly took place without incident in June 1983. As in 1978, only members of the MCP who had been approved by the President were allowed to contest the elections. Banda subsequently appointed several additional members to the National Assembly. In August 1984 Banda reorganized the MCP's Executive Committee; the important post of party Secretary-General was left unfilled, and remained vacant until the appointment of Gwanda Chakuamba in October 1993 (see below).

At elections to the National Assembly in May 1987 213 members of the MCP contested 69 of the 112 elective seats in the Assembly. Some 33 candidates were elected unopposed, and five elective seats were not filled. Banda subsequently nominated further members to the Assembly, bringing its total membership to 116 in 1989. In January 1992 Tembo (now widely perceived to be Banda's probable successor) was appointed Minister of State in the President's Office. At legislative elections in June 96 of the elective seats in the National Assembly (by then numbering 141) were contested by 630 members of the MCP, while 45 candidates were returned unopposed. Five seats remained vacant, following the disqualification of some candidates. An additional 10 members of the Assembly were nominated by Banda.

Political opposition to the Government by Malawi dissidents in exile continued throughout the 1980s and into the 1990s. In October 1989 10 people, including a senior official of MAFREMO and members of his family, were killed in a bomb attack in Lusaka, Zambia; the Malawi Government denied responsibility for the incident. In the following month the Government rejected allegations by the human rights group, Amnesty International, that several Malawian political detainees had been subjected to torture. In October 1990 another prominent international human rights organization accused the Malawi Government of using detention without trial, torture and assassination to suppress political opposition; it was also alleged that Malawi security forces had shot dead 20 anti-Government protesters in March of that year. In February 1991 a new opposition movement, the Malawi Socialist Labour Party, was formed by Malawians living in exile in Tanzania.

Opposition to the Government intensified during 1992: in March Malawi's Roman Catholic bishops published an open letter criticizing the Government's alleged abuses of human rights, and about 60 Malawian political exiles gathered in the Zambian capital to devise a strategy to precipitate political reforms. In early April Chakufwa Chihana, a prominent trade union leader who had demanded multi-party elections, was detained by the security forces. In May industrial unrest in the southern city of Blantyre escalated into violent anti-Government riots; these spread to the capital, Lilongwe, and reportedly resulted in 38 deaths. Later in the month Western donor nations suspended all but urgent humanitarian aid to Malawi, pending an improvement in the Government's human rights record. In July Chakufwa Chihana was charged with sedition, and in August the police detained 11 church leaders and prohibited a planned rally by pro-democracy supporters. In September opposition members formed the Alliance for Democracy (AFORD), a pressure group operating within Malawi under the chairmanship of Chihana, which aimed to campaign for democratic political reform. Another opposition grouping, the United Democratic Front (UDF), was formed in October. In that month Banda conceded that a referendum on the introduction of a multi-party system would take place; this was subsequently scheduled for June 1993. In November 1992, however, the Government banned AFORD. In the following month Chihana was found guilty of sedition and sentenced to two years' hard labour (reduced to nine months' in March 1993). In January 1993 more than 100,000 anti-Government demonstrators attended a rally in Blantyre. During that month LESOMA and another opposition party, the Malawi Democratic Union, merged to form the United Front for Multi-party Democracy. In March MAFREMO dissolved itself, and its membership joined AFORD.

The referendum on the introduction of a multi-party system was held, as scheduled, on 14 June 1993. Despite evidence of MCP attempts to disrupt the opposition's activities preceding the poll (which was monitored by UN observers), the opposition secured a decisive victory, with 63.2% of those who voted (some 63.5% of the electorate) supporting an end to single-party rule. Following the referendum, Banda rejected opposition demands for the immediate installation of an interim government of national unity. He agreed, however, to the establishment of a National Executive Council to oversee the transition to a democratic political system and the holding of free elections, and of a National Consultative Council to carry out the necessary amendments to the Constitution to provide for the introduction of a multi-party political system. Both were to be comprised of members of the Government and the opposition. Banda announced a general amnesty for thousands of political exiles, and stated that a general election would be held, on a multi-party basis, within a year. (Chihana had been released from prison a few days before the referendum, having served six months of his sentence.) In late June the Constitution was amended to allow the registration of political parties other than the MCP: by mid-August five organizations, including AFORD and the UDF, had been accorded official status. A UN-sponsored forum on the transition to democracy was held in Malawi in July; it was agreed that the UN would continue to play a supporting role in the country during the transitional period.

In September 1993 Banda carried out an extensive cabinet reshuffle, including the appointment of Hetherwick Ntaba as Minister of External Affairs, a post held by Banda himself since 1964. In early October 1994 Banda became seriously ill and underwent neurological surgery in South Africa. Having rejected opposition demands for the election of an interim neutral head of state, in mid-October the Office of the President announced the formation of a three-member Presidential Council, which was to assume executive power in Banda's absence. As required by the Constitution, the Council was chaired by the new Secretary-General of the MCP, Gwanda Chakuamba. (Chakuamba, a former government minister, had been sentenced to 22 years' imprisonment in 1981, after having been convicted of sedition; he was released in July 1993.) The two other members were also senior MCP officials, namely John Tembo and the Minister of Transport and Communications, Robson Chirwa. In early November the Presidential Council implemented a cabinet reshuffle, as a result of which Banda was without ministerial responsibilities for the first time since 1964. In mid-November the National Assembly passed the Constitutional Amendment Bill, which included the repeal of the institution of life presidency, the reduction of the qualifying age for a presidential candidate from 40 to 35 years, the repeal of the requirement that election candidates be members of the MCP, the repeal of the right of the President to nominate members of the legislature exclusively from the MCP, and the lowering of the minimum voting age from 21 to 18 years. The National Assembly also amended the Public Security Act, repealing all provisions relating to detention without trial.

Having made an unexpected and rapid recovery, Banda resumed full presidential powers on 7 December 1993 and the Presidential Council was dissolved. Shortly afterwards, in response to increasing pressure from the opposition, the Government amended the Constitution to provide for the appointment of an acting president in the event of the incumbent's being incapacitated. In February 1994 the MCP announced that Banda was to be the party's presidential candidate in the forthcoming general election, which was scheduled to take place on 17 May; Chakuamba was selected as the MCP's candidate for the vice-presidency. In the same month the National Assembly approved an increase in the number of elected legislative members in the approaching general election from 141 to 177.

Meanwhile, the MCP announced in September 1993 that the Malawi Young Pioneers (MYP), a widely-feared paramilitary section of the ruling party, were to be gradually disarmed. In early December, following the murder of three soldiers by MYP members, members of the regular army undertook a peremptory campaign to close MYP offices and camps. In the ensuing violence, which was believed to have been exacerbated by long-standing tensions between the army and the MYP, 32 people were reported to have been killed. Following his recovery from surgery, President Banda appointed a Minister of Defence (having hitherto held personal responsibility for defence) to oversee the MYP disarmament process and investigate army grievances. By early January 1994 it was reported that the disarmament of the MYP had been satisfactorily completed; it was also reported, however, that several thousand MYP members had crossed the border into Mozambique to take refuge in rebel bases. In late January 1994 the Governments of Malawi and Mozambique agreed to a programme for the repatriation of the MYP forces from Mozambican territory. In the following month the MYP was officially disbanded, although in May it was reported that at least 2,000 armed MYP members were in hiding in Mozambique.

On 16 May 1994 a provisional Constitution was adopted by the National Assembly. The new document included provisions for the appointment of a Constitutional Committee and of a human rights commission, and abolished the system of 'traditional' courts. Malawi's first multi-party parliamentary and presidential elections took place on 17 May. In the presidential election the Secretary-General of the UDF, (Elson) Bakili Muluzi (a former government minister and MCP Secretary-General), took 47.3% of the votes cast, defeating Banda (who won 33.6% of the votes), Chihana and Kampelo Kalua of the Malawi Democratic Party. Eight parties contested the legislative elections: of these, the UDF won 84 seats in the National Assembly, the MCP 55 and AFORD 36. (Voting was repeated in two constituencies where irregularities had been found, as a result of which the UDF and MCP each won a further seat.) The distribution of seats was strongly influenced by regional affiliations, with AFORD winning all of the Northern Region's seats, and the MCP and UDF particularly successful in the Central and Southern Regions, respectively. The Constitution was introduced for a one-year period on 18 May; it was to be subject to further review prior to official ratification one year later.

President Muluzi and his Vice-President, Justin Malewezi, were inaugurated on 21 May 1994. The principal aims of the new administration were defined as being to alleviate poverty and ensure food security, and to combat corruption and the mismanagement of resources. The closure was announced of three prisons where abuses of human rights were known to have taken place; an amnesty was announced for the country's remaining political prisoners, and all death sentences were commuted to terms of life imprisonment. The new Government, the composition of which was announced three days after the presidential investiture, was dominated by the UDF, but also included members of the Malawi National Democratic Party and the United Front for Multi-party Democracy. Attempts to recruit members of AFORD into a coalition administration failed, owing to disagreements regarding the allocation of senior portfolios, and in June AFORD and the MCP signed what was termed a memorandum of understanding whereby they would function as an opposition front. The Muluzi Government was thus deprived of a majority in the National Assembly, which was inaugurated at the end of June. In late August it was announced that Banda, while remaining honorary Life President of the MCP, was to retire from active involvement in politics. Chakuamba, as Vice-President of the Party, effectively became the leader of the MCP.

Government changes in late September 1994 included the appointment of Chihana to the post of Second Vice-President and Minister of Irrigation and Water Development; AFORD members were also allocated responsibility for agriculture, transport and research and the environment. None the less, the AFORD-MCP memorandum of understanding remained in force until January 1995, when AFORD, acknowledging that the new regime had made significant progress in the restoration of political stability and the establishment of democracy, announced an end to its co-operation with the MCP. The creation of the post of Second Vice-President necessitated a constitutional amendment, and provoked severe criticism from the MCP. Moreover, the National Constitutional Conference, which met in February to consider refinements to the document prior to its official promulgation, recommended that the post be abolished. In late March, however, the National Assembly (in the absence of MCP deputies, who boycotted the vote) approved the retention of the second vice-presidency; the Assembly also approved the establishment—although not before May 1999—of a second chamber of parliament, the Senate, as well as a constitutional clause requiring that senior state officials declare all personal assets within two months of assuming their post.

In June 1994 Muluzi announced the establishment of an independent commission of inquiry to investigate the deaths of Malenje and his associates in May 1983. In early January 1995, in accordance with the findings of the commission,

Banda was placed under house arrest; Tembo and two former police officers were arrested and detained, and the four were charged with murder and conspiracy to murder. A former inspector-general of the police, who was alleged, *inter alia*, to have destroyed evidence relating to the deaths, was charged later in the month. Cecilia Kadzamira, Tembo's niece and the former President's 'Official Hostess', was charged in early April with conspiracy to murder. The trial opened in late April, but was immediately adjourned, owing to Banda's failure to appear in court (his defence counsel asserted that he was too ill to stand trial), and to the non-adherence of the state prosecution to the requirement that they submit certain evidence to the defence. Banda failed to appear at a resumed hearing in early May.

Malawi, both economically and militarily, lies in the South African sphere of influence. Despite being the only African country to have maintained full diplomatic relations with South Africa during the apartheid era (a source of considerable tension with other countries of the region), Malawi joined the Southern African Development Co-ordination Conference (subsequently the Southern African Development Community, see p. 219), which for many years aimed to reduce the dependence of southern African countries on South Africa. Nevertheless, relations with Mozambique were frequently strained during the early and mid-1980s by the widely-held belief that the Banda regime was supporting the Resistência Nacional Moçambicana (Renamo—for further details, see the chapter on Mozambique). Following the death of President Machel of Mozambique in an aeroplane crash in South Africa in October 1986, the South African Government claimed that documents discovered in the crash wreckage revealed a plot by Mozambique and Zimbabwe to overthrow the Banda Government. Angry protests from Malawi to Mozambique and Zimbabwe were answered by denials of the accusations. In December, however, Malawi and Mozambique signed an agreement on defence and security matters, which was believed to include co-operation in eliminating Renamo operations. Malawian troops were subsequently stationed in Mozambique to protect the strategic railway line linking Malawi to the Mozambican port of Nacala. In July 1988, during an official visit to Malawi, President Chissano of Mozambique stated that he did not believe Malawi to be supporting Renamo and expressed gratitude for Malawi's military presence in his country. In December 1988 Malawi, Mozambique and the office of the UN High Commissioner for Refugees (UNHCR) signed an agreement to promote the voluntary repatriation of an estimated 650,000 Mozambican refugees, who had fled into Malawi during the previous two years and who were imposing a considerable burden on the country's resources. However, by mid-1992 the number of Mozambican refugees in Malawi had reportedly reached 1m. Under the provisions of the General Peace Agreement signed in Mozambique in October 1992, all Malawian troops were withdrawn from Mozambique by June 1993. It was reported by UNHCR that large numbers of Mozambican refugees had spontaneously left Malawi and returned to Mozambique throughout 1993 and in early 1994, although in mid-1994 it was estimated that some 600,000 Mozambican refugees remained in Malawi. The apparent continued presence in Mozambique of MYP units (many MYP members were said to have been harboured in Renamo bases) was a source of concern in the first months of the Muluzi administration. Chissano visited Malawi in March 1995, when the two countries agreed to review their joint defence and security co-operation accords to reflect current issues such as drugs-trafficking and arms-smuggling.

### Government
The Head of State is the President, who is elected by universal adult suffrage, in the context of a multi-party political system, for a term of five years. Executive power is vested in the President, and legislative power in the National Assembly, which has 177 elective seats. Members of the Assembly are elected for five years, by universal adult suffrage, in the context of a multi-party system. Cabinet Ministers are appointed by the President. The country is divided into three administrative regions (Northern, Central and Southern), subdivided into 24 districts.

### Defence
Malawi's defence forces numbered 10,400 men in June 1994, of which the army numbered 10,000, the air force 200 and the marines 200. All services form part of the army. There is also a paramilitary police force of 1,500. Government expenditure on defence in the financial year 1993/94 was an estimated K158m.

### Economic Affairs
In 1993, according to estimates by the World Bank, Malawi's gross national product (GNP), measured at average 1991–93 prices, was US $2,034m., equivalent to $220 per head. During 1985–93, it was estimated, GNP per head increased, in real terms, by an annual average of 0.4%. Over the same period the population increased by an annual average of 3.3%. Malawi's gross domestic product (GDP) increased, in real terms, by an annual average of 2.9% in 1980–92; real GDP increased by 10.8% in 1993, but declined by 12.3% in 1994.

Measured at constant 1978 prices, agriculture (including forestry and fishing) contributed 30.7% of GDP in 1994. An estimated 72.3% of the labour force were engaged in the sector in that year. The principal cash crops are tobacco (which accounted for 70.5% of domestic export earnings in 1994), tea and sugar cane. The principal food crops are cassava, maize, groundnuts and pulses. Severe drought conditions necessitated some 184,000 metric tons in food aid and the import of a further 270,000 tons of basic foods to be sold to stabilize prices and supplies in 1994/95. During 1980–92 agricultural GDP increased by an annual average of 1.4%; production increased by 31.4% in 1993 (following drought in 1992), but declined by 18.0% in 1994.

Industry (including manufacturing, construction and power) contributed 20.8% of GDP (at 1978 prices) in 1994, and engaged 4.7% of the employed labour force in 1987. During 1980–92 industrial GDP increased by an annual average of 3.5%.

Mining and quarrying engaged only 0.2% of the employed labour force in 1987. Limestone, coal and gemstones are mined, and there are plans to develop deposits of bauxite and graphite. There are also reserves of phosphates, uranium, glass sands, asbestos and vermiculite.

Manufacturing contributed 13.6% of GDP (at 1978 prices) in 1994, and engaged 2.9% of the employed labour force in 1987. The principal branches of manufacturing, measured by the value of output, in 1985 were food products (accounting for 34.9% of the total), chemical products (16.1%), textiles (11.0%) and beverages (9.9%). During 1980–92 manufacturing GDP increased by an annual average of 4.0%.

Production of electrical energy is by hydroelectric (principally) and thermal installations. Energy for domestic use is derived principally from fuel wood, although the Muluzi administration has announced that it intends to reduce dependence on this source. Imports of fuels comprised 15% of the value of total imports in 1992.

In 1994 Malawi recorded a visible trade surplus of US $304.1m., while there was a surplus of $164.2m. on the current account of the balance of payments. In 1990 the principal sources of imports were South Africa (30.7%) and the United Kingdom (22.9%); Japan and Germany were also notable suppliers. Germany was the principal market for exports (16.2%) in 1990; other important markets were the United Kingdom, Japan, the USA, South Africa and the Netherlands. Other members of the Preferential Trade Area for Eastern and Southern African States (PTA, see p. 240) supplied 7.8% of imports but took only 4.3% of exports in that year. The principal exports are tobacco, tea and sugar. The principal imports in 1990 were machinery and transport equipment, mineral fuels and miscellaneous manufactured articles.

In its programme for the financial year ending 31 March 1995 the Muluzi Government aimed to restrict the budgetary deficit (excluding grants and drought-related expenditure) to the equivalent of 6% of GDP. Malawi's external debt totalled US $1,821m. at the end of 1993, of which $1,724m. was long-term public debt. In that year the cost of debt-servicing was equivalent to 22.1% of exports of goods and services. The annual rate of inflation averaged 18.8% in 1985–93; consumer prices increased by an average of 22.8% in 1993, and by 34.6% in 1994. Some 1.3% of the labour force were unemployed in 1987.

Malawi is a member of the Southern African Development Community (see p. 219), of the International Tea Promotion Association (see p. 236) and of the International Tobacco Growers' Association (see p. 236). In November 1993 Malawi was among PTA members to sign a treaty establishing a Common Market for Eastern and Southern Africa (COMESA);

the first COMESA summit meeting took place in Malawi in December 1994.

Upon assuming office in May 1994, the Muluzi administration inherited an economy weakened not only by natural impediments to growth (including Malawi's land-locked position, the vulnerability of the dominant agricultural sector to drought, and a high rate of population growth), but also by what was perceived as mismanagement by the Banda regime. Agricultural diversification had failed to offset losses arising from the decline in the volume and value of tobacco exports, the manufacturing base remained narrow, and the civil service and parastatal sector were regarded as inefficient and, frequently, corrupt. The suspension of much foreign assistance in 1992–93 affected many sectors, and the easing of currency restrictions in February 1994 precipitated an effective devaluation of the kwacha, an accompanying increase in inflation and a serious depletion of official foreign-exchange reserves. The Muluzi Government was to continue policies of economic liberalization and diversification initiated under Banda in recent years, but pledged to combat corruption (many senior executives of parastatal organizations were removed from office) and inefficiency. A wide-ranging privatization programme was to include posts and telecommunications (responsibility for which was transferred to a commercially-operated statutory corporation in early 1995) and the ending of agricultural monopolies. With assistance from the IMF, it was aimed to achieve GDP growth of 4.5% by 1996/97, to limit inflation to about 5% by 1997, and to reduce the external current account deficit to 8.2% of GDP in 1997 (from about 13.7% in late 1994). Other multilateral and bilateral donors have responded favourably to the new regime, offering both financial and material assistance that will be essential to the success of its economic policies, and have praised Muluzi's undertaking to alleviate poverty and improve basic standards of health and education.

### Social Welfare

A social development agency, now part of the Ministry of Labour and Manpower Development, was formed in 1958. Its work includes care and protection of young people, the destitute and the physically handicapped. The agency also has responsibility for probation work, sport, community centres and women's clubs. Health services are provided by the central Government, as well as by local government, the Christian Health Authority of Malawi and other agencies. In 1993 Malawi had 52 hospitals, with 15,519 beds. There were, in addition, 270 health centres, 315 dispensaries, 91 maternity centres and 31 health posts. In 1984 there were 262 physicians and 1,286 nursing and midwifery personnel working in the country. The health sector was allocated 6% of recurrent government expenditure and 9% of development expenditure in the 1989/90 financial year.

### Education

Primary education, which is officially compulsory, begins at six years of age and lasts for eight years. Secondary education, which begins at 14 years of age, lasts for four years, comprising two cycles of two years. In 1990 primary school enrolment included 48% of children in the relevant age-group (males 50%, females 47%), but secondary enrolment included only 2% of children in the appropriate age-group. A programme to expand education at all levels has been undertaken; however, the introduction of free primary education in September 1994 was reported to have resulted in severe overcrowding in schools. The University of Malawi had 3,469 students in 1992/93. Some students attend institutions in the United Kingdom and the USA. Education was allocated 165m. kwacha (equivalent to 10.3% of total government expenditure) in 1990. In 1987, according to census results, the average rate of adult illiteracy was 51.5% (males 34.7%; females 66.5%).

### Public Holidays

**1995:** 1 January (New Year's Day), 3 March (Martyrs' Day), 14–17 April (Easter), 1 May (Labour Day), 6 July (Republic Day), 17 October (Mothers' Day), 21 December (National Tree Planting Day), 25–26 December (Christmas and Boxing Day).
**1996:** 1 January (New Year's Day), 3 March (Martyrs' Day), 5–8 April (Easter), 1 May (Labour Day), 6 July (Republic Day), 17 October (Mothers' Day), 21 December (National Tree Planting Day), 25–26 December (Christmas and Boxing Day).

### Weights and Measures

The metric system is in use.

# Statistical Survey

Sources (unless otherwise indicated): Ministry of Information and Tourism, POB 494, Blantyre; Reserve Bank of Malawi, POB 30063, Capital City, Lilongwe 3; tel. 780600; telex 44788; fax 782752.

## Area and Population

### AREA, POPULATION AND DENSITY

| | |
|---|---:|
| Area (sq km) | 118,484* |
| Population (census results) | |
| 20 September 1977 | 5,547,460 |
| 1–21 September 1987 | |
| Males | 3,867,136 |
| Females | 4,121,371 |
| Total | 7,988,507 |
| Population (official estimates at mid-year) | |
| 1992 | 9,344,600 |
| 1993 | 9,700,500 |
| 1994 | 10,032,600 |
| Density (per sq km) at mid-1994 | 84.7 |

* 45,747 sq miles. The area includes 24,208 sq km (9,347 sq miles) of inland water.

**Ethnic groups** (1977 census): Africans 5,532,298; Europeans 6,377; Asians 5,682; others 3,103.

### REGIONS (mid-1994)

| Region | Area (sq km)* | Estimated population | Density (per sq km) | Regional capital |
|---|---:|---:|---:|---|
| Southern | 31,753 | 4,980,500 | 156.9 | Blantyre |
| Central | 35,592 | 3,907,000 | 109.8 | Lilongwe |
| Northern | 26,931 | 1,145,100 | 42.5 | Mzuzu |
| **Total** | 94,276 | 10,032,600 | 106.4 | |

* Excluding inland waters, totalling 24,208 sq km.

### PRINCIPAL TOWNS (estimated population at mid-1994)

| | | | |
|---|---:|---|---:|
| Blantyre | 446,800* | Mzuzu | 62,700 |
| Lilongwe (capital) | 395,500 | Zomba | 62,700 |

* Including Limbe.

# MALAWI

*Statistical Survey*

**BIRTHS AND DEATHS** (UN estimates, annual averages)

|  | 1975–80 | 1980–85 | 1985–90 |
|---|---|---|---|
| Birth rate (per 1,000) | 57.2 | 56.6 | 55.6 |
| Death rate (per 1,000) | 24.0 | 22.3 | 21.4 |

**Expectation of life** (UN estimates, years at birth, 1985–90): 45.4 (males 44.6; females 46.2).

Source: UN, *World Population Prospects: The 1992 Revision.*

**ECONOMICALLY ACTIVE POPULATION***
(persons aged 10 to 64 years, 1987 census)

|  | Males | Females | Total |
|---|---|---|---|
| Agriculture, hunting, forestry and fishing | 1,293,606 | 1,674,327 | 2,967,933 |
| Mining and quarrying | 6,977 | 187 | 7,164 |
| Manufacturing | 79,293 | 18,483 | 97,776 |
| Electricity, gas and water | 8,306 | 527 | 8,833 |
| Construction | 45,006 | 1,869 | 46,875 |
| Trade, restaurants and hotels | 75,491 | 18,954 | 94,445 |
| Transport, storage and communications | 23,323 | 1,540 | 24,863 |
| Financing, insurance, real estate and business services | 4,418 | 1,172 | 5,590 |
| Community, social and personal services | 113,763 | 33,276 | 147,039 |
| Activities not adequately defined | 9,120 | 2,765 | 11,885 |
| **Total employed** | 1,659,303 | 1,753,100 | 3,412,403 |
| Unemployed | 36,549 | 8,801 | 45,350 |
| **Total labour force** | 1,695,852 | 1,761,901 | 3,457,753 |

* Excluding armed forces.

**Mid-1993** (estimates in '000): Agriculture, etc. 3,084; Total 4,267 (Source: FAO, *Production Yearbook*).

## Agriculture

**PRINCIPAL CROPS** ('000 metric tons)

|  | 1991 | 1992 | 1993 |
|---|---|---|---|
| Rice (paddy) | 63 | 50 | 65 |
| Maize | 1,589 | 612 | 2,034 |
| Sorghum | 19 | 4 | 22 |
| Potatoes† | 360 | 360 | 370 |
| Cassava (Manioc) | 168 | 129 | 216 |
| Dry beans† | 82 | 78 | 80 |
| Chick-peas† | 40 | 35 | 37 |
| Other pulses† | 231 | 223 | 227 |
| Groundnuts (in shell)* | 58 | 26 | 59 |
| Cottonseed* | 27 | 13 | 18 |
| Cotton (lint)* | 11 | 5 | 7 |
| Vegetables† | 255 | 237 | 251 |
| Bananas† | 90 | 85 | 90 |
| Plantains† | 190 | 185 | 195 |
| Other fruit† | 217 | 207 | 213 |
| Sugar cane† | 1,900 | 1,900 | 2,100 |
| Tea (made) | 41 | 28 | 40 |
| Tobacco (leaves) | 113 | 127 | 136* |

* Unofficial figure(s).   † FAO estimates.

Source: FAO, *Production Yearbook.*

**LIVESTOCK** ('000 head, year ending September)

|  | 1991* | 1992* | 1993† |
|---|---|---|---|
| Cattle | 899 | 967 | 970 |
| Pigs | 235 | 238 | 240 |
| Sheep | 186 | 195 | 195 |
| Goats | 846 | 887 | 888 |

* Unofficial figures.   † FAO estimates.

Poultry (FAO estimates, million, year ending September): 9 in 1991; 9 in 1992; 9 in 1993.

Source: FAO, *Production Yearbook.*

**LIVESTOCK PRODUCTS** (FAO estimates, '000 metric tons)

|  | 1991 | 1992 | 1993 |
|---|---|---|---|
| Beef and veal | 17 | 17 | 18 |
| Goat meat | 3 | 3 | 3 |
| Pig meat | 9 | 10 | 10 |
| Poultry meat | 9 | 9 | 9 |
| Cows' milk | 39 | 40 | 41 |
| Poultry eggs | 11.3 | 11.3 | 11.4 |

Source: FAO, *Production Yearbook.*

## Forestry

**ROUNDWOOD REMOVALS** ('000 cubic metres, excluding bark)

|  | 1990 | 1991* | 1992* |
|---|---|---|---|
| Sawlogs, veneer logs and logs for sleepers | 80 | 80 | 80 |
| Other industrial wood | 351 | 366 | 380 |
| Fuel wood | 8,554 | 8,912 | 9,246 |
| **Total** | 8,985 | 9,358 | 9,706 |

* FAO estimate(s).

Source: FAO, *Yearbook of Forest Products.*

**SAWNWOOD PRODUCTION**
(unofficial estimates, '000 cubic metres, incl. railway sleepers)

|  | 1989 | 1990 | 1991 |
|---|---|---|---|
| Coniferous (softwood) | 24 | 28 | 28 |
| Broadleaved (hardwood) | 15 | 15 | 15 |
| **Total** | 39 | 43 | 43 |

**1992:** Production as in 1991 (FAO estimates).

Source: FAO, *Yearbook of Forest Products.*

## Fishing

('000 metric tons, live weight)

|  | 1990 | 1991 | 1992* |
|---|---|---|---|
| Carps, barbels, etc. | 15.8 | 3.0 | 3.0 |
| Tilapias | 15.3 | 15.3 | 15.0 |
| Other freshwater fishes | 43.0 | 45.5 | 46.0 |
| **Total catch** | 74.1 | 63.7 | 64.0 |

* FAO estimates.

Source: FAO, *Yearbook of Fishery Statistics.*

## Mining

('000 metric tons, unless otherwise indicated)

|  | 1989 | 1990 | 1991 |
|---|---|---|---|
| Limestone | 125 | 143 | 184 |
| Coal | 37 | 41 | 52 |
| Lime | 3 | 4 | 5 |
| Quarry stone | 145 | 65 | 100 |
| Gemstones | 2 | 8 | 4 |

# MALAWI

## Industry

**SELECTED PRODUCTS** ('000 metric tons, unless otherwise indicated)

|  | 1989 | 1990 | 1991 |
|---|---|---|---|
| Raw sugar | 162 | 189 | 191 |
| Beer ('000 hectolitres) | 757 | 752 | 763 |
| Cigarettes (million) | 1,080* | 1,061 | 951 |
| Blankets ('000) | 836 | 988 | 1,126 |
| Cement | 79 | 101 | 112 |
| Electric energy (million kWh) | 586 | 718 | 750 |

* Data from the US Department of Agriculture.
Source: UN, *Industrial Statistics Yearbook*.

## Finance

**CURRENCY AND EXCHANGE RATES**

**Monetary Units**
100 tambala = 1 Malawi kwacha (K).

**Sterling and Dollar Equivalents** (31 December 1994)
£1 sterling = 23.847 kwacha;
US $1 = 15.299 kwacha;
1,000 Malawi kwacha = £41.93 = $65.37.

**Average Exchange Rate** (kwacha per US $)
1992  3.603
1993  4.403
1994  8.567

**RECURRENT BUDGET** (K million, year ending 31 March)

| Revenue | 1992/93 | 1993/94* | 1994/95† |
|---|---|---|---|
| Taxes on income and profits: | | | |
|   Companies | 222.6 | 250.1 | 327.2 |
|   Individuals | 226.9 | 262.3 | 344.3 |
| Taxes on goods and services: | | | |
|   Surtax | 372.3 | 468.5 | 734.8 |
|   Excise duties | 37.7 | 57.6 | 93.1 |
|   Licences | 11.7 | 12.3 | 18.4 |
| Import duties | 251.0 | 269.3 | 679.6 |
| Other tax revenue | 27.8 | 26.7 | 32.7 |
| **Total tax revenue** | 1,150.1 | 1,346.8 | 2,230.0 |
| Non-tax revenue | 240.0 | 309.2 | 485.4 |
| **Total** | 2,540.1 | 3,002.7 | 4,945.5 |

| Expenditure | 1992/93 | 1993/94* | 1994/95† |
|---|---|---|---|
| Wages and salaries | 415.6 | 533.7 | 838.6 |
| Goods and other services | 706.2 | 761.5 | 1,168.5 |
| Grants and subsidies to statutory bodies | 115.2 | 145.5 | 744.0 |
| Debt-servicing | 418.9 | 530.2 | 760.3 |
|   Interest payments | 254.1 | 272.9 | 581.2 |
|   Debt amortization | 164.8 | 257.4 | 179.1 |
| Other expenditure | 144.3 | 181.7 | 262.9 |
| **Total** (incl. extra-budgetary expenditure) | 1,800.2 | 2,152.7 | 3,774.4 |

* Provisional figures.  † Projected figures.

**DEVELOPMENT BUDGET** (K million, year ending 31 March)
**1992/93:** Total receipts 254.2; Total expenditure 467.7.
**1993/94** (provisional figures): Total receipts 424.1; Total expenditure 455.7.
**1994/95** (revised estimates): Total receipts 550.9; Total expenditure 958.9.

**INTERNATIONAL RESERVES** (US $ million at 31 December)

|  | 1992 | 1993 | 1994 |
|---|---|---|---|
| Gold | 0.54 | 0.54 | 0.55 |
| IMF special drawing rights | 0.08 | 0.23 | 6.20 |
| Reserve position in IMF | 3.05 | 3.05 | 3.25 |
| Foreign exchange | 36.82 | 53.59 | 33.35 |
| **Total** | 40.49 | 57.41 | 43.35 |

**MONEY SUPPLY** (K million at 31 December)

|  | 1992 | 1993 | 1994 |
|---|---|---|---|
| Currency outside banks | 289.79 | 414.21 | 624.74 |
| Official entities' deposits with monetary authorities | 22.01 | 45.58 | 14.54 |
| Demand deposits at commercial banks | 444.90 | 560.18 | 895.92 |
| **Total money** | 756.70 | 1,019.97 | 1,535.20 |

**COST OF LIVING** (National Consumer Price Index; base: 1990 = 100)

|  | 1992 | 1993 | 1994 |
|---|---|---|---|
| Food | 138.9 | 175.7 | 242.9 |
| Clothing | 114.4 | 126.2 | 149.3 |
| **All items** (incl. others) | 133.4 | 163.8 | 220.5 |

**NATIONAL ACCOUNTS**
**Expenditure on the Gross Domestic Product**
(K million in current prices)

|  | 1992 | 1993 | 1994 |
|---|---|---|---|
| Government final consumption expenditure | 1,240.9 | 1,529.0 | 2,565.3 |
| Private final consumption expenditure | 5,340.4 | 7,708.4 | 7,533.6 |
| Increase in stocks | 180.0 | 200.0 | 240.0 |
| Gross fixed capital formation | 1,077.0 | 890.0 | 1,243.0 |
| **Total domestic expenditure** | 7,838.3 | 10,327.4 | 11,581.9 |
| Exports of goods and services | 1,504.3 | 1,470.7 | 3,308.0 |
| *Less* Imports of goods and services | 2,648.8 | 2,855.9 | 3,912.0 |
| **GDP in purchasers' values** | 6,693.8 | 8,942.2 | 10,977.9 |

**Gross Domestic Product by Economic Activity**
(K million at constant 1978 prices)

|  | 1992 | 1993 | 1994 |
|---|---|---|---|
| Agriculture, forestry and fishing | 275.2 | 421.0 | 295.8 |
| Manufacturing | 141.6 | 126.8 | 130.8 |
| Electricity and water | 26.3 | 27.2 | 29.3 |
| Construction | 43.0 | 41.2 | 39.8 |
| Trade, restaurants and hotels | 129.5 | 118.4 | 112.6 |
| Transport and communications | 59.4 | 56.7 | 51.8 |
| Finance, insurance and business services | 71.4 | 67.3 | 62.3 |
| Ownership of dwellings | 44.4 | 44.9 | 45.9 |
| Private social services | 44.9 | 45.1 | 46.4 |
| Government services | 154.8 | 154.2 | 147.3 |
| **Sub-total** | 990.5 | 1,102.8 | 962.0 |
| *Less* Imputed bank service charges | 18.4 | 25.9 | 18.0 |
| **GDP at factor cost** | 972.1 | 1,076.9 | 944.0 |

MALAWI

## BALANCE OF PAYMENTS (US $ million)

|  | 1992 | 1993 | 1994 |
|---|---|---|---|
| Merchandise exports f.o.b. | 397.4 | 719.3 | 571.8 |
| Merchandise imports f.o.b. | -412.3 | -365.2 | -267.7 |
| **Trade balance** | -14.9 | 354.1 | 304.1 |
| Exports of services* | 26.5 | 19.0 | 18.3 |
| Imports of services* | -396.7 | -345.9 | -264.2 |
| Private unrequited transfers (net) | 13.7 | 29.8 | 18.5 |
| Official unrequited transfers (net) | 50.0 | 82.1 | 87.4 |
| **Current balance** | -321.4 | 139.1 | 164.2 |
| Long-term capital (net) | 89.2 | 197.4 | 42.3 |
| Short-term capital (net) | 0.3 | 0.0 | 0.0 |
| Net errors and omissions | -4.6 | 10.7 | -95.1 |
| **Overall balance** | -236.4 | 347.2 | 111.4 |

* Including other income.

# External Trade

## SELECTED COMMODITIES (K'000)

| Imports c.i.f. | 1988 | 1989 | 1990 |
|---|---|---|---|
| Piece goods | 21,064 | 29,864 | 31,811 |
| Other garments | 1,055 | 4,773 | 29,031 |
| Passenger cars and motorcycles | 13,226 | 31,600 | 67,534 |
| Commercial road vehicles | 47,886 | 69,098 | 78,175 |
| Medical and pharmaceutical goods | 24,967 | 28,247 | 35,212 |
| Petrol | 42,207 | 52,478 | 58,882 |
| Diesel fuel | 59,677 | 67,764 | 72,579 |
| **Total** (incl. others) | 1,080,151 | 1,398,803 | 1,584,218 |

**Total imports** (K million): 1,975.8 in 1991; 2,592.0 in 1992; 2,404.8 in 1993; 3,295.7 in 1994.

| Exports f.o.b. (excl. re-exports)* | 1992 | 1993 | 1994 |
|---|---|---|---|
| Tobacco | 1,029,820 | 938,010 | 2,184,380 |
| Tea | 106,730 | 156,690 | 231,700 |
| Sugar | 97,770 | 68,780 | 228,680 |
| **Total** (incl. others) | 1,391,230 | 1,356,350 | 3,098,460 |

* Total exports, including re-exports, were (K million): 1,431.6 in 1992; 1,396.6 in 1993; 3,167.4 in 1994.

## PRINCIPAL TRADING PARTNERS (K'000)

| Imports | 1988 | 1989 | 1990 |
|---|---|---|---|
| France | 30,187 | 17,035 | 45,502 |
| Germany, Federal Republic | 60,194 | 88,558 | 95,584 |
| Japan | 98,790 | 88,059 | 119,036 |
| Netherlands | 22,587 | 52,652 | 51,617 |
| South Africa | 337,765 | 514,373 | 486,222 |
| United Kingdom | 238,281 | 238,497 | 362,136 |
| USA | 55,069 | 47,801 | 33,808 |
| PTA* | 92,922 | 147,791 | 124,162 |
| **Total** (incl. others) | 1,080,151 | 1,398,803 | 1,584,218 |

| Exports (excl. re-exports) | 1988 | 1989 | 1990 |
|---|---|---|---|
| France | 26,028 | 26,857 | 37,178 |
| Germany, Federal Republic | 93,301 | 76,399 | 175,697 |
| Japan | 87,691 | 93,328 | 146,382 |
| Netherlands | 61,884 | 56,998 | 75,676 |
| South Africa | 88,710 | 70,679 | 77,733 |
| United Kingdom | 133,640 | 153,116 | 169,458 |
| USA | 83,611 | 93,265 | 129,523 |
| PTA* | 34,027 | 31,040 | 46,427 |
| **Total** (incl. others) | 742,031 | 730,169 | 1,083,861 |

* Preferential Trade Area for Eastern and Southern African States, which includes Malawi and 21 other countries.

# Transport

## RAILWAYS (traffic)

|  | 1991 | 1992 | 1993 |
|---|---|---|---|
| Passengers carried ('000) | 1,368 | 892 | 692 |
| Passenger-kilometres ('000) | 91,680 | 54,477 | 45,547 |
| Freight ('000 ton-km, net) | 59,569 | 68,186 | 42,264 |

Source: Malawi Railways, Limbe.

## ROAD TRAFFIC (motor vehicles in use at 31 December)

|  | 1990 | 1991 | 1992 |
|---|---|---|---|
| Cars | 11,266 | 11,548 | 13,898 |
| Goods vehicles | 9,807 | 10,052 | 12,113 |
| Tractors | 3,697 | 3,782 | 3,629 |
| Motor cycles | 3,536 | 3,624 | 3,580 |

Source: Road Traffic Commission, Blantyre.

## SHIPPING
### Inland waterways (lake transport)

|  | 1991 | 1992 | 1993 |
|---|---|---|---|
| Freight ('000 ton-km, net) | 6,818 | 5,933 | 3,682 |
| Passenger-kilometres ('000) | 18,606 | 20,379 | 10,332 |

Source: Malawi Railways, Limbe.

## CIVIL AVIATION (traffic)

|  | 1991 | 1992 | 1993 |
|---|---|---|---|
| Chileka Airport (Blantyre) |  |  |  |
| Passengers | 77,840 | 85,769 | 95,075 |
| Freight (metric tons) | 1,293 | 7,042 | 1,328 |
| Mail (metric tons) | 57 | 57 | 97 |
| Kamuzu International Airport (Lilongwe) |  |  |  |
| Passengers | 282,899 | 265,721 | 257,219 |
| Freight (metric tons) | 9,285 | 8,611 | 6,677 |
| Mail (metric tons) | 413 | 374 | 406 |

# Tourism

|  | 1989 | 1990 | 1991 |
|---|---|---|---|
| Number of departing visitors | 117,069 | 129,912 | 127,004 |
| Average expenditure per person (kwacha) | 299 | 331 | 387 |

MALAWI

## Communications Media

|  | 1990 | 1991 | 1992 |
|---|---|---|---|
| Radio receivers ('000 in use) | 2,080 | 2,200 | 2,285 |
| Telephones ('000 main lines in use) | 26 | 28 | n.a. |
| Daily newspapers: |  |  |  |
| Titles | 1 | n.a. | 1 |
| Average circulation ('000 copies) | 25 | n.a. | 25 |

Book production (1989): 141 titles (incl. 75 pamphlets).

Non-daily newspapers (1992): 4 titles (average circulation 133,000 copies).

Other periodicals (1986): 14 titles (average circulation 124,000 copies).

Sources: UNESCO, *Statistical Yearbook*; UN, *Statistical Yearbook*.

## Education

(Government, government-aided and unaided schools, 1989)

|  | Teachers | Pupils |
|---|---|---|
| Primary | 20,580 | 1,325,453 |
| Secondary (general) | 1,096 | 29,326 |
| Technical schools | 60 | 770 |
| Teacher training | 190 | 2,909 |
| University of Malawi | 235 | 2,685 |

**1990:** Primary schools 2,906; Primary pupils 1,400,682; Secondary (general) pupils 31,495; Technical school pupils 780.

Source: UNESCO, *Statistical Yearbook*.

# Directory

## The Constitution

A new Constitution, replacing the (amended) 1966 Constitution, was approved by the National Assembly on 16 May 1994, and took provisional effect for one year from 18 May. During this time the Constitution was to be subject to review, and the final document was promulgated on 18 May 1995.

### THE PRESIDENT

The President is both Head of State and Head of Government. The President is elected for five years, by universal adult suffrage, in the context of a multi-party political system. There are two Vice-Presidents.

### PARLIAMENT

Parliament comprises the President, the two Vice-Presidents and the National Assembly. The National Assembly has 177 elective seats, elections being by universal adult suffrage, in the context of a multi-party system. The Speaker is appointed from among the ordinary members of the Assembly. The parliamentary term is normally five years. The President has power to prorogue or dissolve Parliament.

### EXECUTIVE POWER

Executive power is exercised by the President.

## The Government

### HEAD OF STATE

**President:** (ELSON) BAKILI MULUZI (took office 21 May 1994).
**First Vice-President:** JUSTIN C. MALEWEZI.
**Second Vice-President:** CHAKUFWA TOM CHIHANA.

### CABINET
(May 1995)

A coalition of the United Democratic Front (UDF), the Alliance for Democracy (AFORD), the Malawi National Democratic Party (MNDP), and the United Front for Multi-party Democracy (UFMD).

**President and Head of Government:** BAKILI MULUZI (UDF).
**First Vice-President and Minister of Statutory Corporations:** JUSTIN MALEWEZI (UDF).
**Second Vice-President and Minister of Irrigation and Water Development:** CHAKUFWA CHIHANA (AFORD).
**Minister of Finance, Economic Planning and Development:** ALEKE BANDA (UDF).
**Minister of Commerce and Industry:** HARRY I. THOMSON (UDF).
**Minister of External Affairs:** EDWARD C. I. BWANALI (UDF).
**Minister of Information, Broadcasting, Posts and Telecommunications:** BROWN MPINGANJIRA (UDF).
**Minister of Justice and Constitutional Affairs:** PETER FACHI (UDF).
**Minister of Defence:** Dr CASSIM CHILUMPHA (UDF).
**Minister of Education, Science and Technology:** SAM MPASU (UDF).
**Minister of Home Affairs:** WENHAM NAKANGA (UDF).
**Minister of Transport and Civil Aviation:** Dr DENNIS NKHWAZI (AFORD).
**Minister of Agriculture and Livestock Development:** Dr MAPOPA CHIPETA (AFORD).
**Minister of Local Government and Rural Development:** JAMES L. MAKHUMULA (UDF).
**Minister of Works and Supplies:** PATRICK B. MBEWE (UDF).
**Minister of Women's and Children's Affairs, Community and Social Welfare:** EDDA E. CHITALO (UDF).
**Minister of Lands and Valuation:** Alhaji SHAIBU ITIMU (UDF).
**Minister of Energy and Mining:** ROLPH PATEL (UDF).
**Minister of Labour and Manpower Development:** ZILILO CHIBAMBO (UDF).
**Minister of Natural Resources:** Dr JOHN NKUMBA (UDF).
**Minister of Housing:** TIMOTHY MANGWAZU (MNDP).
**Minister of Wildlife and Tourism:** COLLINS CHIZUMIRA (UDF).
**Minister of Research and Environmental Affairs:** Dr MATEBO S. MZUNDA (AFORD).
**Minister of Relief and Rehabilitation Affairs:** GEORGE KANYANYA (UFMD).
**Minister of Physical Planning and Surveys:** Dr J. B. MPONDA MKANDAWIRE (AFORD).
**Minister of Youth, Sports and Culture:** A. CHILIVUMBO (AFORD).
**Minister of Health:** Dr GEORGE NTAFU (UDF).
**Attorney-General:** FRIDAY MAKUTA.

### MINISTRIES

**Office of the President:** Private Bag 301, Capital City, Lilongwe 3; telex 44389.
**Ministry of Agriculture and Livestock Development:** POB 30134, Capital City, Lilongwe 3; tel. 733300; telex 44648.
**Ministry of Commerce and Industry:** POB 30366, Capital City, Lilongwe 3; tel. 732711; telex 44873; fax 732551.
**Ministry for Education, Science and Technology:** Private Bag 328, Capital City, Lilongwe 3; tel. 733922; telex 44636; fax 782873.
**Ministry of Energy and Mining:** Private Bag 309, Capital City, Lilongwe 3.
**Ministry of External Affairs:** POB 30315, Capital City, Lilongwe 3; tel. 782211; telex 44113; fax 782434.
**Ministry of Finance, Economic Planning and Development:** POB 30049, Capital City, Lilongwe 3; tel. 7825333; telex 44407; fax 781679.
**Ministry of Forestry and Natural Resources:** Private Bag 350, Capital City, Lilongwe 3; telex 44465; fax 731452.
**Ministry of Health:** POB 30377, Capital City, Lilongwe 3; telex 44558.
**Ministry of Information and Tourism:** POB 494, Blantyre.

**Ministry of Justice and Constitutional Affairs:** Private Bag 333, Capital City, Lilongwe 3; tel. 731533; fax 731776.

**Ministry of Labour and Manpower Development:** Private Bag 344, Capital City, Lilongwe 3.

**Ministry of Local Government and Rural Development:** POB 30312, Capital City, Lilongwe 3.

**Ministry of Transport and Civil Aviation:** Private Bag 322, Capital City, Lilongwe 3; tel. 730122.

**Ministry of Women's and Children's Affairs, Community and Social Welfare:** Private Bag 330, Capital City, Lilongwe 3; tel. 732222; telex 44361.

**Ministry of Works and Supplies:** Private Bag 326, Capital City, Lilongwe 3; tel. 733188; telex 44285.

## President and Legislature

### PRESIDENT

**Presidential Election, 17 May 1994**

| Candidate | Votes | % of votes |
|---|---|---|
| BAKILI MULUZI (UDF) | 1,404,754 | 47.30 |
| Dr HASTINGS KAMUZU BANDA (MCP) | 996,363 | 33.55 |
| CHAKUFWA CHIHANA (AFORD) | 552,862 | 18.62 |
| KAMPELO KALUA (MDP) | 15,624 | 0.53 |
| **Total** | 2,969,603 | 100.00 |

### NATIONAL ASSEMBLY

**Speaker:** RODWELL T. C. MNYENYEMBE.

**General Election, 17 May 1994**

| Party | Seats |
|---|---|
| UDF | 84 |
| MCP | 55 |
| AFORD | 36 |
| **Total*** | 175 |

* Elections were repeated in two constituencies where irregularities had been found: as a result, the UDF and MCP each won an additional seat, bringing the total number of seats in the Assembly to 177.

## Political Organizations

The Malawi Congress Party was the sole party during 1966–93. In June 1993 the Constitution was amended to provide for the introduction of a multi-party political system. Eight political parties were authorized to participate in the multi-party elections of May 1994:

**Alliance for Democracy (AFORD):** Private Bag 28, Lilongwe; f. 1992 to secure democratic reforms; in March 1993 absorbed membership of fmr Malawi Freedom Movement; legalized mid-1993; Pres. CHAKUFWA CHIHANA.

**Congress for the Second Republic (CSR):** Leader KANYAMA CHIUME.

**Malawi Congress Party (MCP):** Private Bag 388, Lilongwe 3; tel. 730388; f. 1959; sole legal party 1966–93; Sec.-Gen. LOVEMORE MULO.

**Malawi Democratic Party (MDP):** Pres. KAMPELO KALUA.

**Malawi Democratic Union (MDU):** Sec.-Gen. M. DZIKOLIDO.

**Malawi National Democratic Party (MNDP):** Leader TIMOTHY MANGWAZU.

**United Democratic Front (UDF):** POB 3052, Limbe; f. 1992; leading party in May 1994 legislative elections; Pres. BAKILI MULUZI; Vice-Pres. ALEKE BANDA.

**United Front for Multi-party Democracy (UFMD):** f. 1992; Pres. EDMOND JIKA.

## Diplomatic Representation

### EMBASSIES AND HIGH COMMISSIONS IN MALAWI

**China (Taiwan):** Area 40, Plot No. 9, POB 30221, Capital City, Lilongwe 3; tel. 730611; telex 44317; Ambassador: ROBERT C. J. SHIH.

**Egypt:** POB 30451, Lilongwe 3; tel. 730300; telex 44538; Ambassador: F. M. Y. ELKHADI.

**France:** Area 40, Road No. 3, POB 30054, Lilongwe 3; tel. 783520; telex 44141; fax 780438; Ambassador: MICHEL AUCHÈRE.

**Germany:** POB 30046, Lilongwe 3; tel. 782555; telex 44124; fax 780250; Ambassador: ULRICH NITZSCHKE.

**Israel:** POB 30319, Lilongwe 3; tel. 782923; fax 780436; Ambassador: MOSHE ITAN.

**Korea, Republic:** POB 30583, Lilongwe 3; telex 44834; Ambassador: SON MYONG-SON.

**Mozambique:** POB 30579, Lilongwe 3; telex 44793; Ambassador: AMOS MAHANJANE.

**South Africa:** Mpico Bldg, City Centre, POB 30043, Lilongwe 3; tel. 783722; telex 44255; fax 782571; High Commissioner: LLEWELLYN CREWE-BROWN.

**United Kingdom:** POB 30042, Lilongwe 3; tel. 782400; telex 44727; fax 782657; High Commissioner: JOHN F. R. MARTIN.

**USA:** Area 40, Flat 18, POB 30016, Lilongwe 3; tel. 730166; telex 44627; Ambassador: MICHAEL T. F. PISTOR.

**Zambia:** POB 30138, Lilongwe 3; tel. 731911; telex 44181; High Commissioner: MITON CHIRU.

**Zimbabwe:** POB 30187, Lilongwe 3; tel. 733988; High Commissioner: Dr TENDAI MUTUNHU.

## Judicial System

The courts administering justice are the Supreme Court of Appeal, High Court and Magistrates' Courts.

The High Court, which has unlimited jurisdiction in civil and criminal matters, consists of the Chief Justice and five puisne judges. Traditional Courts were abolished under the 1994 Constitution. Appeals from the High Court are heard by the Supreme Court of Appeal in Blantyre.

**High Court of Malawi:** POB 30244, Chichiri, Blantyre 3; tel. 670255; Registrar D. F. MWAUNGULU.

**Chief Justice:** RICHARD A. BANDA.

**Puisne Judges:** H. M. MTEGHA, L. A. UNYOLO, M. P. MKANDAWIRE, D. G. TAMBALA, G. MUNLO.

## Religion

About 75% of the population profess Christianity. The Asian community includes Muslims and Hindus, and there is a small number of African Muslims. Traditional beliefs are followed by about 10% of the population.

### CHRISTIANITY

**Christian Council of Malawi:** POB 30068, Capital City, Lilongwe 3; tel. 730499; f. 1939; 13 mems and seven associates; Chair. Rev. Dr. S. D. CHIPHANGWI; Gen. Sec. Rev. M. M. MAPUTWA.

#### The Anglican Communion

The Church of the Province of Central Africa has about 80,000 adherents in its two dioceses in Malawi.

**Bishop of Lake Malawi:** Rt Rev. PETER NATHANIEL NYANJA, POB 30349, Capital City, Lilongwe 3; fax 731966.

**Bishop of Southern Malawi:** Rt Rev. NATHANIEL BENSON AIPA, PO Chilema, Zomba; fax 531243.

#### Protestant Churches

**The Baptist Convention in Malawi:** POB 51083, Limbe; tel. 643224; Chair. Rev. S. L. MALABWANYA; Gen. Sec. Rev. M. T. KACHASO GAMA.

**Church of Central Africa (Presbyterian):** comprises three synods in Malawi (Blantyre, Livingstonia and Nkhoma); Blantyre Synod: POB 413, Blantyre; tel. 636744; Gen. Sec. Rt Rev. Dr SILAS S. NCOZANA; 92,000 adherents in Malawi.

**Evangelical Fellowship of Malawi:** POB 2120, Blantyre; tel. 633543; Chair. K. M. LUWANI; Sec. W. C. MUSOPOLE.

**The Lutheran Church of Central Africa:** POB 748, Blantyre; tel. 630821; f. 1963; evangelical and medical work; Supt J. M. JANOSEK; 25,000 mems. in Malawi.

**Seventh-day Adventists:** POB 951, Blantyre; tel. 620264; telex 44216; Dir Mr MASOKA; Exec. Sec. Pastor D. W. KAPITAO.

The African Methodist Episcopal Church, the Churches of Christ, the Free Methodist Church, the Pentecostal Assemblies of God and the United Evangelical Church in Malawi are also active.

#### The Roman Catholic Church

Malawi comprises one archdiocese and six dioceses. At 31 December 1993 some 17% of the total population were adherents of the Roman Catholic Church.

**Episcopal Conference of Malawi:** Catholic Secretariat of Malawi, Chimutu Rd, POB 30384, Capital City, Lilongwe 3; tel. 782066; fax 782019; f. 1969; Pres. Most Rev. FELIX EUGENIO MKHORI, Bishop of Chikwawa.

**Archbishop of Blantyre:** Most Rev. JAMES CHIONA, Archbishop's House, POB 385, Blantyre; tel. 633905; fax 606107.

### BAHÁ'Í FAITH

**National Spiritual Assembly:** POB 5849, Limbe; tel. 640996; fax 640910; f. 1970; mems resident in nearly 1,500 localities.

## The Press

**ABA Today:** POB 5861, Limbe; f. 1982; monthly; publ. by African Businessmen's Association of Malawi.

**Boma Lathu:** POB 494, Blantyre; tel. 620266; f. 1973; monthly; Chichewa; publ. by the Ministry of Information and Tourism; circ. 80,000.

**Business and Development News:** POB 829, Blantyre; f. 1973; monthly.

**Chitukuko cha Amayi n'Malawi:** POB 494, Blantyre; tel. 620266; telex 44471; fax 620807; f. 1964; monthly; Chichewa (English—This is Malawi); circ. 12,000.

**The Daily Times:** Private Bag 39, Ginnery Corner, Blantyre; tel. 671566; telex 44112; fax 671114; f. 1895; Mon.–Fri.; English; Editor-in-Chief POULTON MTENJE; circ. 22,000.

**Financial Post:** Blantyre; f.1992; weekly; English; independent; Editor ALAUDIN OSMAN.

**The Independent:** Blantyre; f.1993; weekly; English; independent; Editor JANET KARIM.

**Kuunika:** PO Nkhoma, Lilongwe; f. 1909; monthly; Chichewa; Presbyterian; Editor Rev. M. C. NKHALAMBAYAUSI; circ. 6,000.

**Malawi Life:** Private Bag 39, Ginnery Corner, Blantyre; tel. 671566; f. 1991; monthly magazine; English.

**Malawi Government Gazette:** Government Printer, POB 37, Zomba; tel. 523155; f. 1894; weekly.

**Malawi News:** Private Bag 39, Ginnery Corner, Blantyre; tel. 671566; telex 44112; fax 671114; f. 1959; weekly; English, Chichewa; circ. 30,000.

**Moni:** POB 5592, Limbe; tel. 651139; telex 44814; f. 1964; monthly; Chichewa and English; circ. 40,000.

**Moyo:** POB 3, Blantyre; monthly; English; publ. by Ministry of Health.

**Nation:** Blantyre; f.1993; weekly; English; independent; Editor KEN LIPANGA.

**New Express:** Blantyre; f.1993; weekly; English; independent; Editors WILLIE ZINGANI, FELIX MPONDA.

**Odini:** POB 133, Lilongwe; tel. 721388; fax 721141; f. 1950; fortnightly; Chichewa and English; Roman Catholic; Dir S. P. KALILOMBE; circ. 12,000.

**OK Magazine:** POB 30125, Chichiri, Blantyre; f. 1974; monthly; English.

**This is Malawi:** POB 494, Blantyre; tel. 620266; telex 44471; fax 620807; f. 1964; monthly; English; also Chichewa edn: *Chitukuko cha Amayi n'Malawi* (see above); publ. by the Dept of Information; circ. 5,000.

### NEWS AGENCY

**Malawi News Agency (MANA):** Mzuza; tel. 636122; telex 44234; f. 1966.

## Publishers

**Christian Literature Association in Malawi:** POB 503, Blantyre; tel. 620839; f. 1968; general and religious books in Chichewa and English; Gen. Man. WILLIE ZINGANI.

**Likuni Press and Publishing House:** POB 133, Lilongwe; tel. 721388; fax 721141; f. 1949; publs in English and Chichewa; Gen. Man. (vacant).

**Popular Publications:** POB 5592, Limbe; tel. 651139; telex 44814; f. 1961; general and religious.

### Government Publishing House

**Government Printer:** POB 37, Zomba; tel. 523155.

## Radio and Television

There were an estimated 2,285,000 radio receivers in use (according to UNESCO) in 1992. In May 1994 the Government announced plans for the reintroduction of the Tumbuka language on national radio. In mid-1994 President Muluzi announced that a television service would be introduced in Malawi (television broadcasting had been banned under Dr Banda).

**Malawi Broadcasting Corporation:** POB 30133, Chichiri, Blantyre 3; tel. 671222; telex 44425; fax 671257; f. 1964; statutory body; semi-commercial, partly state-financed; domestic service in English, Chichewa and Chitumbuka; Gen. Man. HENRY R. CHIRWA; Head of Production THENNIS SINETA; Editor-in-Chief MOLLAND NKHATA.

## Finance

(cap. = capital; res = reserves; m. = million; dep. = deposits; brs = branches; amounts in kwacha)

### BANKING

#### Central Bank

**Reserve Bank of Malawi:** POB 30063, Capital City, Lilongwe 3; tel. 780600; telex 44788; fax 782752; f. 1965; bank of issue; cap. and res 88m., dep. 755m. (1991); Gov. FRANCIS PEREKAMOYO; Gen. Man. G. G. LENGU; br. in Blantyre.

#### Commercial Banks

**Commercial Bank of Malawi Ltd:** POB 1111, Blantyre; tel. 620144; telex 44340; fax 620360; f. 1970; cap. and res 100m., dep. 889m. (Dec. 1994); Chair. F. P. KALILOMBE; CEO DENNIS G. LAWRENCE; 13 brs; agencies throughout Malawi.

**National Bank of Malawi:** Victoria Ave, POB 945, Blantyre; tel. 620622; telex 44142; fax 620606; f. 1971; cap. and res 103.97m., dep. 932.33m. (Dec. 1993); Chair. C. W. FREYER; CEO E. G. BELL; 14 brs; agencies throughout Malawi.

#### Development Bank

**Investment and Development Bank of Malawi Ltd (INDEBANK):** Delamere House, Victoria Ave, POB 358, Blantyre; tel. 620055; telex 45201; fax 623353; f. 1972; cap. 17.4m. (Dec. 1992); provides loans to statutory corpns and to private enterprises in the agricultural, industrial, tourism, transport and commercial sectors, on a joint-financing basis; Gen. Man. C. L. MPHANDE.

#### Merchant Banks

**Leasing and Finance Co of Malawi Ltd:** Delamere House, 6th Floor, Victoria Ave, POB 1963, Blantyre; tel. 620233; telex 44179; fax 620275; f. 1986; cap. and res 14.7m. (1993); Gen. Man. M. J. TAYLOR.

**National Mercantile Credit Ltd:** Plantation House, POB 821, Blantyre; tel. 623670; fax 620549; f. 1958; cap. 4.2m. (Dec. 1993); Chair. E. G. BELL; Gen. Man. M. T. BAMFORD.

#### Savings Bank

**Post Office Savings Bank:** POB 521, Blantyre; tel. 620944; telex 44437.

### INSURANCE

**National Insurance Co Ltd:** NICO House, Private Bag 30421, Capital City, Lilongwe 3; tel. 783311; telex 44622; f. 1971; cap. and res 38.3m. (1994); offices at Blantyre, Lilongwe and Mzuzu, agencies country-wide; Gen. Man. F. L. MLUSU.

**Premier Life Office:** POB 393, Blantyre; tel. 620677; telex 44690.

## Trade and Industry

### CHAMBER OF COMMERCE

**Malawi Chamber of Commerce and Industry:** Chichiri Trade Fair Grounds, POB 258, Blantyre; tel. 671988; telex 43992; fax 671147; f. 1892; fmrly Associated Chambers of Commerce and Industry of Malawi; 400 mems; Chair. F. P. KALILOMBE.

### STATUTORY ORGANIZATIONS

**Agricultural Development and Marketing Corporation (ADMARC):** POB 5052, Limbe; tel. 640044; telex 44121; fax 640486; statutory trading org. that markets the agricultural crops produced by smallholder farmers; exporter of confectionery-grade groundnut kernels, maize, cassava and sunflower seed; primary marketing of tobacco, wheat and a wide variety of beans, peas and other seeds; co-operates with commercial cos in the cultivation and processing of agricultural produce; Gen. Man. E. B. KADZAKO.

**Malawi Posts and Telecommunications Corporation (MPTC):** Blantyre; f. 1995; frmly Department of Posts and Telecommunications.

MALAWI                                                                                                                                                                              *Directory*

### INDUSTRIAL AND COMMERCIAL ORGANIZATIONS

**Smallholder Coffee Authority:** POB 230, Mzuzu; tel. 332899; fax 332902; producers of arabica coffee.

**Smallholder Sugar Authority:** Blantyre; telex 44647.

**Smallholder Tea Authority:** POB 80, Thyolo.

**Tea Association of Malawi Ltd:** POB 930, Blantyre; tel. 671182; telex 44320; f. 1936; 20 mems.

**Tobacco Association of Malawi:** POB 31360, Lilongwe 3; tel. 783099; telex 44598; fax 783493; f. 1929; 25,000 mems; Chair. H. B. J. NTABA.

**Tobacco Exporters' Association of Malawi:** Private Bag 403, Kanengo, Lilongwe 4; tel. 765663; telex 44360; fax 765668; f. 1930; 9 mems; Exec. Sec. H. M. MBALE.

### DEVELOPMENT CORPORATIONS

**Malawi Development Corporation (MDC):** MDC House, Glyn Jones Rd, POB 566, Blantyre; tel. 620100; telex 44146; fax 620584; f. 1964; cap. 20m. kwacha (Dec. 1991); 100% state-owned; provides finance and management advice to commerce and industry; 15 subsidiary and assoc. cos; Chair. L. S. K. MSISKA; Gen. Man. P. D. PARTRIDGE.

**Malawi Export Promotion Council:** Delamere House, POB 1299, Blantyre; tel. 620499; telex 44589; fax 635429; f. 1974; Gen. Man. J. B. L. MALANGE.

**Malawi Investment Promotion Agency (MIPA):** Private Bag 302, Capital City, Lilongwe 3.

**Mining Investment and Development Corporation Ltd (MIDCOR):** POB 565, Lilongwe; f. 1985; state-owned; operates coal mines at Kaziwiziwi and Mchenga and explores for other mineral deposits; Gen. Man. STANLEY KALYATI.

**Small Enterprise Development Organization of Malawi (SEDOM):** POB 525, Blantyre; tel. 622555; telex 44666; fax 622781; f. 1982; tech. and management advice to indigenous small-scale businesses.

### EMPLOYERS' ASSOCIATIONS

**Employers' Consultative Association of Malawi (ECAM):** POB 2134, Blantyre; tel. 671337; f. 1963; 500 mems; Chair. D. KAMBAUWA; Exec. Dir T. CHIBWANA.

**Master Builders', Civil Engineering Contractors' and Allied Trades' Association:** POB 311, Blantyre; tel. 622966; f. 1955; 70 mems (1994); Chair. B. CLOW.

**Master Printers' Association of Malawi:** POB 2460, Blantyre; f. 1962; 21 mems; Chair. PAUL FREDERICK; Sec. W. E. THEU.

**Motor Traders' Association of Malawi:** POB 311, Blantyre; tel. 622966; fax 621215; f. 1954; 42 mems (1989); Chair. M. SCOTT.

### TRADE UNIONS

**Trades Union Congress of Malawi (TUCM):** POB 5094, Limbe; f. 1964; 6,500 mems; Chair. W. C. CHIMPHANGA; Gen. Sec. L. Y. MVULA; the following are among the principal affiliated unions:

**Building Construction, Civil Engineering and Allied Workers' Union:** POB 110, Limbe; tel. 650598; f. 1961; 6,000 mems; Chair. W. I. SOKO; Gen. Sec. G. SITIMA.

**Railway Workers' Union of Malawi:** POB 5393, Limbe; tel. 640844; f. 1954; 3,000 mems; Chair. W. C. CHIMPHANGA; Gen. Sec. F. L. MATTENJE.

Other unions affiliated to the TUCM are the Local Government Employees' Union, the Plantation and Agricultural Employees' Union, and the Transport and General Workers' Union.

### Unaffiliated Union

**Teachers' Association of Malawi:** Limbe; f. 1964; 3,000 mems.

## Transport

### RAILWAYS

Malawi Railways and the Central African Railway Co, its wholly-owned subsidiary, operate between Nsanje (near the southern border with Mozambique) and Mchinji (near the border with Zambia) via Blantyre, Salima and Lilongwe, and between Nkaya and Nayuci on the eastern border with Mozambique, covering a total of about 789 km. Malawi Railways and Mozambique State Railways provide the links from the Mozambique ports of Beira and Nacala to Malawi. These links, which traditionally form Malawi's principal trade routes, were effectively closed during 1983–85, owing to Mozambican insurgent activity. The rehabilitation of the rail link to Nacala was completed in October 1989. There is a rail/lake interchange station at Chipoka on Lake Malawi, from where Malawi Railways vessels operate services to other lake ports in Malawi. In March 1995 the International Development Association approved a credit of US$16.6m., in support of a project for the restructuring of the railway system which envisaged the eventual privatization of routes.

**Malawi Railways:** POB 5144, Limbe; tel. 640844; telex 44810; fax 640683; Chair. (vacant); Gen Man. F. W. MARKHAM.

### ROADS

The total length of roads in 1988 was 12,215 km, of which 2,662 km were bituminized. All main roads, and most secondary roads, are all-weather roads. Major routes link Lilongwe and Blantyre with Harare (Zimbabwe) Lusaka (Zambia) and Mbeya and Dar es Salaam (Tanzania). The 480-km highway along the western shore of Lake Malawi, linking the remote Northern Region with the Central and Southern Regions, is currently being upgraded. A project to create a new trade route, or 'Northern Corridor', through Tanzania involved road construction and improvements in Malawi, and was completed in 1992.

**Road Transport Operators' Association:** Makata Industrial Site, Manica Bldg, POB 30740, Chichiri, Blantyre 3; tel. 670422; telex 44275; fax 671423; f. 1956; 230 mems (1994); Chair. F. D. GHAMBI.

### CIVIL AVIATION

Kamuzu International Airport (at Lilongwe) was opened in 1982. There is another main airport, at Blantyre, which serves a number of regional airlines, and three domestic airports.

**Air Malawi Ltd:** Chibisa House, Glyn Jones Rd, POB 84, Blantyre; tel. 620177; telex 44245; fax 620042; f. 1967; domestic and scheduled regional services; charter flights are also operated; CEO Capt. LEWIS MBILIZI.

## Tourism

Fine scenery, beaches on Lake Malawi, big game and an excellent climate form the basis of the country's tourist potential. The number of departures by foreign visitors declined from 129,912 (including 105,366 visitors from other African countries) in 1990 to 127,004 in 1991.

**Department of Tourism:** POB 402, Blantyre; tel. 620300; telex 44645; fax 620947; f. 1969; responsible for Malawi tourist policy, administers govt rest-houses, sponsors training of hotel staff; publs tourist literature; Chief Tourism Officer M. M. MATOLA.

**Tourism Development and Investment Co (TDIC):** Blantyre; f. 1988 by Malawi Development Corpn to operate hotels and tours.

# MALAYSIA

## Introductory Survey

### Location, Climate, Language, Religion, Flag, Capital

The Federation of Malaysia, situated in South-East Asia, consists of 13 states. Eleven of these are in Peninsular Malaysia, in the southern part of the Kra peninsula (with Thailand to the north and the island of Singapore to the south), and two, Sabah and Sarawak, are on the north coast of the island of Borneo (Kalimantan), bordering Indonesia. Sarawak also borders Brunei, a coastal enclave in the north-east of the state. The climate is tropical, there is rain in all seasons and temperatures are generally between 22°C (72°F) and 33°C (92°F), with little variation throughout the year. The official language is Bahasa Malaysia, based on Malay, but English is also widely used. Chinese, Tamil and Iban are spoken by minorities. Islam is the established religion, practised by about 53% of the population (including virtually all Malays), while about 19%, including most of the Chinese community, follow Buddhism. The Indians are predominantly Hindus. There is a minority of Christians among all races, and traditional beliefs are practised, particularly in Sabah and Sarawak. Malaysia's national flag (proportions 2 by 1) has 14 horizontal stripes, alternating red and white, with a blue rectangular canton, containing a yellow crescent and a 14-pointed yellow star, in the upper hoist. The capital is Kuala Lumpur.

### Recent History

The 11 states of Malaya, under British protection, were united as the Malayan Union in April 1946 and became the Federation of Malaya in February 1948. An armed communist offensive began in 1948, and was not effectively suppressed until the mid-1950s. After 1960 the remainder of the banned Communist Party of Malaya (CPM) took refuge in southern Thailand. Meanwhile, Malaya was granted independence, within the Commonwealth, on 31 August 1957.

Malaysia was established on 16 September 1963, through the union of the independent Federation of Malaya (renamed the States of Malaya), the internally self-governing state of Singapore, and the former British colonies of Sarawak and Sabah (North Borneo). Singapore left the federation in August 1965, reducing the number of Malaysia's component states from 14 to 13. The States of Malaya were designated West Malaysia in 1966 and later styled Peninsular Malaysia.

In 1970 serious inter-communal rioting, engendered by Malay resentment of the Chinese community's economic dominance and of certain pro-Chinese electoral results, precipitated the resignation of Tunku Abdul Rahman, who had been Prime Minister of Malaya (and subsequently of Malaysia) since independence. The new Prime Minister, Tun Abdul Razak, widened the Government coalition, dominated by the United Malays National Organization (UMNO), to create a national front, Barisan Nasional (BN). The BN originally comprised 10 parties, absorbing most of the former opposition parties. In January 1976 the Prime Minister died and was succeeded by the Deputy Prime Minister, Dato' Hussein bin Onn.

Political stability was subsequently threatened by the resurgence of the communist guerrilla movement, which conducted a series of terrorist attacks in Peninsular Malaysia during 1976–78. However, CPM activity subsequently declined, owing to co-operation between Malaysia and Thailand in military operations along their common border. In 1987, in a Thai-sponsored amnesty, about 700 Malaysian communists surrendered to the Thai authorities. In December 1989, following a year of negotiations with the Thai Government, the remaining 1,188 rebels (including recruits from Thailand and Singapore) agreed to terminate all armed activities. The peace agreements, signed by the leader of the CPM and representatives of the Malaysian and Thai Governments, made provision for the resettlement of the insurgents in either Malaysia or Thailand and their eventual participation in legitimate political activity in Malaysia.

In October 1977 the expulsion of the Chief Minister of Kelantan from the dominant Parti Islam Sa-Malaysia (PAS—Pan-Malaysian Islamic Party) resulted in violent political disturbances in Kelantan and the declaration of a state of emergency by the federal Government. Direct rule was imposed in Kelantan, and the PAS was expelled from the BN coalition in December. In the federal and state elections of July 1978 Hussein consolidated the position of the BN, while the PAS, in opposition, suffered a serious reversal. In 1978, following the federal Government's rejection of proposals for a Chinese university, racial and religious tensions re-emerged.

In July 1981 Hussein was succeeded as Prime Minister by Dato' Seri Dr Mahathir Mohamad, Deputy Prime Minister since 1976. Mahathir called a general election in April 1982; the BN coalition won convincingly in all states and increased its overall strength in the House of Representatives.

At an election for the Sabah State Legislative Assembly in April 1985, a new political party, the Parti Bersatu Sabah (PBS—Sabah United Party) obtained more than one-half of the seats; Sabah thus became the only state that was not controlled by the BN. The legality of the new PBS Government was challenged by Muslim opponents, and in February 1986 the Chief Minister called a further election. In the May election the PBS won an increased majority of seats in the Assembly, and in June the BN agreed to admit the PBS into its ruling coalition, together with the United Sabah National Organization (USNO), which had been expelled in 1984.

In February 1986 Mahathir's leadership of the federal Government and of UMNO was challenged when Datuk Musa Hitam, the Deputy Prime Minister, resigned from the Government, owing to 'irreconcilable differences' with Mahathir. However, Musa retained his position as Deputy President of UMNO. During the following months Musa's supporters became increasingly critical of Mahathir, and divisions within the party widened. At an early general election in August, the BN coalition took 148 of the 177 seats in an enlarged House of Representatives: UMNO secured 83 seats, while the Malaysian Chinese Association (MCA) won 17. Of the opposition parties, the Democratic Action Party (DAP) won 24 seats, having gained support from ethnic Chinese voters who were disillusioned with the MCA. In state elections held simultaneously, the BN retained control of all the State Legislative Assemblies in Peninsular Malaysia. Several ministers who had supported Musa were subsequently demoted or removed from the Government.

In early 1987 there was a serious challenge for the presidency of UMNO from Tengku Razaleigh Hamzah, the Minister of Trade and Industry. At the UMNO General Assembly in April, none the less, Mahathir was elected UMNO President for the third time (and thus retained the position of Prime Minister at the head of the BN coalition), albeit with a greatly reduced majority. The General Assembly also narrowly elected Encik Abdul Ghafar Baba (who had replaced Musa as Deputy Prime Minister in February 1986) as UMNO Deputy President, a position that Musa had previously occupied. At the end of April 1987 Mahathir announced the resignation of Razaleigh and of Datuk Rais Yatim, the Minister of Foreign Affairs, from the Cabinet, and the dismissal of several other ministers who had supported Razaleigh.

Criticism of Mahathir's leadership persisted during 1987, both from within UMNO and from other political parties. At the same time, racial tensions intensified in various parts of the country over Chinese-language education, religion and other issues. Divisions within the ruling BN coalition Government in Sarawak resulted in the formation, in March, of a new political party, Persatuan Rakyat Malaysian Sarawak (PERMAS—Malaysian Sarawak Party), by disaffected members of the State Legislative Assembly. At an early election for the Sarawak Assembly in April, the BN was returned to power, although with a reduced majority.

In October–November 1987, allegedly to prevent violent racially-motivated riots between Chinese and Malays over politically sensitive issues, a total of 106 people were detained under the provisions of the Internal Security Act (ISA), which allows detention without trial on grounds of national security. Those detained included politicians from all parties (most notably the leader of the DAP, Lim Kit Siang), lawyers, journalists and leaders of pressure groups. Three newspapers were closed by the Government, and political rallies were prohibited. In November the Government introduced legislation to impose stringent penalties on editors and publishers disseminating what the Government regarded as 'false' news. Further new legislation, enacted in December, empowered the Minister of Information to monitor all radio and television broadcasts, and to revoke the licence of any private broadcasting company not conforming with 'Malaysian values'. By early 1989 all the detainees under the ISA had been released (although often under restrictive conditions) except Lim Kit Siang and his son, also a DAP member of parliament, who were not released until April.

In February 1988 the High Court gave a ruling on a suit filed in the previous June by dissatisfied members of UMNO, who claimed that, since some of the delegations taking part in the UMNO elections of April 1987 had not been legally registered, the elections should be declared null and void. The court ruled that, because of the irregularities, UMNO was an 'unlawful society' and that there had been 'no election at all'. Mahathir maintained that the ruling did not affect the legal status of the Government, and the Head of State, Tunku Mahmood Iskandar, expressed support for Mahathir. Later in February 1988 Mahathir announced that a 'New UMNO', UMNO Baru, had been formed and that members of the original party would have to re-register in order to join. In March it was announced that Razaleigh and his supporters were to be excluded from the new party. The assets of New UMNO (hereafter referred to as UMNO) were 'frozen' and placed under judicial control until the party's legal status had been resolved; they were finally returned in September 1994.

Also in March 1988 tension between the executive and the judiciary was intensified by Parliament's approval of constitutional amendments limiting the power of the judiciary to interpret laws. The Lord President of the Supreme Court, Tun Mohammed Salleh bin Abas, wrote to the Head of State to complain about government attempts to reduce the independence of the judiciary, and was subsequently dismissed from office. In June 1989 the Government further limited the powers of the judiciary when it introduced a security law, removing the right of persons being detained under provisions of the ISA to have recourse to the courts.

In late September 1988 Razaleigh and 12 others followed two earlier dissidents and left the BN coalition to join the opposition in the House of Representatives as independents. They were joined in early October by Musa. In December 1988 Musa and his supporters drafted a six-point resolution (the Johore Declaration), specifying the terms under which they would consent to join UMNO. These terms were accepted by UMNO in January 1989 but were binding only in the state of Johore. Following the defeat at a by-election in that month of an opposition representative by an MCA candidate with UMNO support, Musa announced his membership of UMNO, prompting a further eight dissident representatives in Johore to join the party.

In March 1989 Razaleigh's movement established an alliance with the fundamentalist PAS, which drew its support from conservative Muslims and which had been a member of the BN until its expulsion (arranged by Razaleigh) in 1977. In May 1989 Razaleigh's party registered as Semangat '46 (Spirit of 1946, a reference to the year of foundation of the original UMNO). The DAP, whose followers were largely urban Chinese, agreed to co-operate with Semangat '46 and the PAS, but refused to join a formal alliance, owing to their opposition to the PAS's proclaimed policy of forming an Islamic state in Malaysia. In June a former breakaway faction from the PAS, Barisan Jama'ah Islamiah Sa-Malaysia, left the BN coalition to join Semangat '46, the PAS and the Parti Hisbul Muslimin Malaysia in an opposition coalition, Angkatan Perpaduan Ummah (APU—Muslim Unity Movement). APU subsequently won a by-election by a small margin in Trengganu. In May and August, however, the BN won three by-elections. In December Mahathir held a cordial but unproductive meeting with Razaleigh, in an attempt to heal the rift in the ethnic Malay community.

In early October 1990 Mahathir announced that a general election would take place on 20–21 October. The opposition parties formed an informal electoral alliance, Gagasan Rakyat (People's Might). (Gagasan Rakyat was formally registered in April 1992, and Razaleigh was elected as Chairman in July.) Prior to the election the PBS withdrew from the BN and aligned itself with the opposition. Despite the defection of the PBS (which won the 14 seats that it contested), the BN controlled 127 of the 180 seats in the enlarged House of Representatives, thus retaining the two-thirds' majority necessary to amend the Constitution. The opposition's share of the seats increased from 37 to 53. However, Semangat '46 won only eight seats (compared with the 12 that it had held previously) of a total of 61 that it contested. Elections to 11 of the 13 State Legislative Assemblies (excluding Sabah and Sarawak) took place simultaneously. The BN obtained a majority of seats in every state except Kelantan, where APU won every seat in both the federal and state elections. Mahathir subsequently declared that it would be difficult for the federal Government to co-operate with the opposition state administrations in Sabah and Kelantan.

In November 1990, at a meeting of the UMNO General Assembly, Mahathir and Abdul Ghafar Baba were unanimously re-elected, respectively, as President and Deputy President of the party. Two incumbent Vice-Presidents of UMNO, Dato' Anwar Ibrahim, the Minister of Education, and Datuk Abdullah Ahmad Badawi, a former Minister of Defence (who had been dismissed in 1987 for supporting Razaleigh's leadership challenge), were re-elected; Datuk Seri Sanusi bin Junid, the Minister of Agriculture, was also elected a Vice-President. In February 1991 Mahathir announced cabinet changes, as a result of which Anwar, widely regarded as the probable future leader of UMNO, was appointed Minister of Finance and Abdullah, his long-standing rival, was named Minister of Foreign Affairs.

In January 1991 the Chief Minister of Sabah and President of the PBS, Datuk Seri Joseph Pairin Kitingan, was arrested and charged with corruption. (He was subsequently released on bail, and his trial opened in January 1992.) It was widely conjectured that his arrest and his press adviser's detention, under the ISA, were politically motivated. Following the defection of the PBS to the opposition in October 1990, Pairin Kitingan had been removed as chairman of two major federally-controlled state committees, and Sabah experienced delays in funding from the federal Government. Pairin Kitingan subsequently attended meetings with Mahathir, and in February 1991 the latter announced that the PBS state Government (which had secured 36 of 48 elective seats in the Sabah state election in July 1990) had proposed sharing power with USNO, which had won the remaining 12 elective seats. Later in February, at the annual General Assembly of USNO, the party's founder and President, Tun Mustapha Harun, announced that UMNO would henceforth be represented in Sabah; Mustapha subsequently resigned from USNO, and joined UMNO in Sabah. In May UMNO secured its first seat in Sabah, in a by-election necessitated by Mustapha's defection to UMNO. Shortly afterwards Jeffrey Kitingan (the brother of the Chief Minister) was detained under the ISA, accused of plotting Sabah's secession from Malaysia. In July two small ethnically-based parties in Sabah, the Kadazan-dominated Angkatan Keadilan Rakyat (AKAR—People's Justice Movement) and the predominantly Chinese Liberal Democratic Party, were permitted to join the BN to counter the influence of the PBS.

In elections to the enlarged Sarawak State Legislative Assembly on 27–28 September 1991, the BN coalition, calling itself the Barisan Tiga (Front of Three), secured 49 seats, while the opposition Parti Bansa Dayak Sarawak (PBDS—Sarawak Native People's Party), also a member of the BN at federal level, retained the remaining seven seats (compared with 15 in 1987). The decline in support for the PBDS allayed concern about the rise of Dayak nationalism, and effectively sanctioned the state Government's controversial logging and development policies (the PBDS had pledged to ban logging and to close plantations built on tribal land). In May 1992 the PBDS's application to join the BN at state level was formally rejected.

In December 1991 the High Court upheld a ruling by the Ministry of Home Affairs banning the public sale of party newspapers. As this principally affected the opposition journals, it was widely perceived to be a further government attempt to undermine the potential effectiveness of opposition parties.

In May 1992 Lim Kit Siang, was suspended from Parliament until the end of the year, after accusing the leader of the Malaysian Indian Congress (MIC—a member of the ruling BN coalition), Dato' Seri S. Samy Vellu, the Minister of Energy,

Telecommunications and Posts, of misappropriating 9m. Telekom Malaysia shares allocated by the Government to the Indian community. The charges against Samy Vellu were subsequently investigated by the Anti-Corruption Agency. In October, although the case had not been resolved, Samy Vellu was re-elected President of the MIC with a large majority. In August 1993 he was acquitted of all charges.

At the UMNO General Assembly in November 1991, Mahathir made reference to the nine hereditary rulers' supposed abuse of privilege for personal gain. In February 1992 a delegation of senior UMNO representatives (excluding Mahathir) presented the Sultans with a memorandum that alleged interference by the rulers in both political and commercial spheres. Such UMNO criticism of the Sultans was widely suspected to be due, in part, to the Sultan of Kelantan's open support for Razaleigh (a prince of Kelantan) in the 1990 general election. In July four of the nine Sultans approved a Proclamation of Constitutional Principles, drafted in consultation with UMNO, that established a code of conduct for the Sultans.

In November 1992 further controversy arose over the constitutional status of the Sultans when the Sultan of Johore assaulted a sports official. (In 1977, before he became Sultan, Mahmood Iskandar was convicted of 'culpable homicide' but was pardoned by his father the Sultan.) Mahathir, who in 1983 had successfully forced the Sultans to surrender their right to refuse assent to laws passed by Parliament, proposed to remove the rulers' immunity from prosecution, which was enshrined in the Constitution. In January 1993 Parliament approved constitutional amendments ending the Sultans' legal immunity, curtailing their power to pardon the offences of family members, and allowing parliamentary criticism of their misdeeds. Under the terms of the Constitution, however, the Sultans' privileges could not be restricted without the consent of the Conference of Rulers, comprising the nine Sultans. The Sultans, who were under intense pressure from the government-controlled media, indicated initially that they would approve the amendments, but, two hours before Parliament met, the rulers issued a statement rejecting the changes entirely. Mahathir responded by withdrawing from the Sultans various royal privileges (many of them financial), which, although customarily accorded, were not stipulated in the Constitution. In early February a constitutional crisis was averted when the Conference of Rulers agreed to the amendments with the inclusion of slight modifications. The amendments were thus finally adopted with royal consent in March.

In late February 1993 the Sultan of Kelantan belatedly opposed the accord reached between the Government and the Conference of Rulers. Mahathir responded in March by disputing the legitimacy of the Sultan's claim to the throne of Kelantan. A BN member of the House of Representatives subsequently named a brother of the Sultan, Tunku Ibrahim Petra, as the rightful claimant. In November the Kelantan State Legislative Assembly adopted the Islamic penal system, *hudud*. However, in order for Islamic law to take effect in Kelantan the federal Constitution would have to be amended by a two-thirds' majority of the House of Representatives.

At the UMNO Assembly, which took place in November 1992, Mahathir accused the PBS of conspiring to remove Sabah from the Federation of Malaysia. Shortly afterwards he suggested that the rights and privileges of Sabah, enshrined in the 1963 Twenty Points agreement (which delineated the terms of Sabah's membership of the Federation), should be reviewed. This was partly prompted by Sabah's recent decision to require Malaysians to produce passports to enter Sabah. Under the Twenty Points agreement, Sabah was given the right to choose its own official language and state religion and to control immigration. The federal Government continued to deny the opposition state Governments in both Sabah and Kelantan federal funds. It also announced a ban on the export of round logs from Sabah from 1 January 1993, thus depriving Sabah of nearly one-half of its budgeted income for 1993. The ban was, however, rescinded at federal level in May.

In April 1993 USNO, which had become increasingly marginalized within the BN coalition since the establishment of UMNO in Sabah, left the opposition in the Sabah State Legislative Assembly to form a coalition with the ruling PBS. Prior to the announcement, which was made by the new President of USNO, Tun Mustapha Amirkahar (the son of the former leader Tun Mustapha Harun), six of the 11 elected representatives of USNO joined UMNO. USNO's defection prompted the federal Government successfully to seek the party's deregistration in August, on the grounds that it had breached its own statutes. In the same month Tun Mustapha Harun was appointed to the federal post of Minister of Sabah Affairs.

In August 1993, despite earlier assertions that he would not challenge the incumbent Ghafar, Anwar announced his decision to contest the post of UMNO Deputy President in the party's divisional elections which Mahathir had postponed until November. The post was particularly significant as the Deputy President of UMNO was traditionally also accorded the position of Deputy Prime Minister and would be regarded as Dr Mahathir's probable successor. In October Mahathir was returned unopposed as President of UMNO and Ghafar submitted his resignation as Deputy Prime Minister, perhaps in protest against Mahathir's failure actively to support his candidacy for the deputy presidency of UMNO. By November Anwar, representing the *Malayu baru* (new Malays)—younger, urban, mainly professional Malays who had prospered as a result of economic expansion), had secured overwhelming support for his candidacy, prompting the more traditional Ghafar to withdraw from the contest (the latter also resigned from UMNO). Anwar was duly elected Deputy President of UMNO, and all three vice-presidential posts were won by his self-styled 'Vision Team', which comprised Tan Sri Haji Muhyiddin Yassim (the Menteri Besar of Johore), Datuk Seri Mohammed Najib bin Tun Abdul Razak (the Minister of Defence) and Tan Sri Dato' Mohammed Haji Mohammed Taib (the Menteri Besar of Selangor). Anwar was appointed Deputy Prime Minister in December.

In January 1994 Pairin Kitingan dissolved the Sabah State Legislative Assembly in preparation for elections, although the Assembly's mandate did not expire until 1995. Shortly afterwards Pairin Kitingan was convicted on charges of corruption by the High Court. He was, however, fined less than the minimum RM 2,000 that was required to disqualify him from office. Although Pairin Kitingan gained popular support owing to his perceived victimization concerning the corruption trial and to his resistance to federal encroachment on Sabahan authority, a faction emerged in the PBS that advocated more harmonious relations with the federal Government. In late January Datuk Yong Teck Lee, the Deputy President of the PBS and the Deputy Chief Minister of Sabah, resigned from the PBS and established the Sabah Progressive Party, which joined the BN in February to contest the Sabah state election. Former members of the deregistered USNO joined the PBS to contest the election, and the party also gained the support of Tun Mustapha Harun, who had resigned from his federal position of Minister of Sabah Affairs and as a member of UMNO in January (he died in January 1995). At the election, which took place on 18–19 February 1994, the PBS won a narrow majority, securing 25 of the 48 elective seats. Shortly before his inauguration as Chief Minister, however, Pairin Kitingan was informed that the state ruler, Tan Seri Mohamad Said Keruak, was too ill to carry out the ceremony. PBS leaders accused Said of allowing the BN time to persuade the PBS legislators to defect. Pairin Kitingan was finally sworn in as Chief Minister two days later. In March, however, several PBS members did defect to the opposition; among these was Jeffrey Kitingan, who announced the formation of a breakaway party, the Parti Demokratik Sabah Bersatu (PDSB—United Sabah Democratic Party). Jeffrey Kitingan had been released from detention under the ISA in December 1993, although he was initially confined to Seremban town in Negri Sembilan for two years. In January 1994, however, all restrictions on him had been revoked, encouraging suspicions of an agreement with the federal authorities. Pairin Kitingan tried to call new elections, but Said refused to sign the order of dissolution of the Assembly. On 17 March Pairin Kitingan resigned as Chief Minister, and on the following day Tan Sri Sakaran Dandai, a leader of the Sabah wing of UMNO, was sworn in at the head of a new administration. Jeffrey Kitingan's PDSB subsequently disintegrated, but he was elected Deputy President of AKAR.

On 4 February 1994 the Conference of Rulers designated the ruler (Yang di-Pertuan Besar) of Negri Sembilan, Tuanku Ja'afar ibni Al-Marhum Tuanku Abdul Rahman, as the new monarch (Yang di-Pertuan Agong). The Sultan of Selangor was elected as his deputy. The monarch assumed office on 26 April and was officially installed on 22 September.

In June 1994 the BN coalition agreed to admit two breakaway parties from the PBS, the Parti Demokratik Sabah (Sabah Democratic Party), led by Datuk Bernard Dompok, and the Parti Bersatu Rakyat Sabah (PBRS—United Sabah People's Party), led by Joseph Kurup, but refused to accept the application for membership of a third, Setia (Sabah People's United Democratic Party). In the same month it was announced that Dompok and Jeffrey Kitingan were to be appointed to the federal Government: in August Dompok became Minister in the Prime Minister's Department and Jeffrey Kitingan Deputy Minister for Housing and Local Government. Also in June Jeffrey Kitingan had been cleared of corruption in the High Court, following the unexplained withdrawal of several charges by the prosecution. In September five members of the PBRS, including the Deputy Chairman, left the BN to rejoin the PBS.

In late May 1994 the PBDS was readmitted to the ruling Barisan Tiga coalition in Sarawak. (The PBDS had been dismissed from the coalition prior to the state elections in 1987, although it had remained a member of the federal BN.)

In May 1994 the House of Representatives approved the 1994 Constitution (Amendment) Act, which further restricted the powers of the monarchy and provided for the restructuring of the judiciary. Hitherto the King had been competent to withhold his assent from legislation and return it, within 30 days, to Parliament for further consideration. The amendment required the King to give his assent to a bill within 30 days; if he failed to do so, the bill would, none the less, become law. The changes to the judiciary in the amendment included the creation of a Court of Appeal, the restyling of the Supreme Court as the Federal Court and of the Lord President as the Chief Justice. Provision for a mandatory code of ethics for judges, to be drawn up by the Government, caused some concern since, it was argued, the principle of the separation of the judiciary and the executive might thus be jeopardized.

From June 1994 the Government took action to suppress the activities of Al-Arqam, an Islamic sect which had been founded by Ashaari Muhammad in 1968. Al-Arqam was believed to have about 10,000 members in Malaysia, many of whom were public servants, and was alleged to control considerable assets. Although Al-Arqam had traditionally eschewed politics, the Government asserted that the group was a threat to national security and denounced its teachings as 'deviationist'; moreover, the Malaysian authorities accused it of training a military force in Thailand, although this was denied by both Al-Arqam and the Thai Government. In July UMNO threatened to expel party members who refused to leave Al-Arqam, and in early August the National Fatwa (Islamic Advisory) Council banned the sect on the grounds that its teachings contravened Islamic principles. Later in August the group was declared unlawful under the Societies Act 1956, and its 257 schools and 'Islamic villages' were closed. Large numbers of Al-Arqam members were arrested during August and September, and in early September Ashaari was deported from Thailand and detained on arrival in Malaysia under the ISA. Ashaari was released in October, whereupon he made a televised broadcast renouncing the teachings of Al-Arqam and appealing to his followers to adhere to correct Islamic principles; the movement was reported to have been disbanded in November.

During the second half of 1994 there was considerable controversy surrounding the Chief Minister of Malacca, Tan Sri Datuk Abdul Rahim bin Datuk Thamby Chik. In August Rahim (who was the leader of the powerful UMNO youth wing and a close associate of Anwar) was accused of having sexual relations with a minor, an offence constituting statutory rape. Rahim was also accused of having made large profits from dubious property deals, at a time of increasing concern about levels of corruption in public life (in June UMNO had held a special conference on the problem of corruption). In September he resigned as Chief Minister of Malacca, and was obliged to rescind his other party and administrative posts, pending investigations into his alleged misdeeds. Although the authorities decided in October that there was insufficient evidence to proceed with a prosecution against Rahim on the charge of statutory rape, in December he was charged on two counts of corruption (to which he pleaded not guilty). Also in December the official Anti-Corruption Agency began an investigation into share allocations made by the Minister of International Trade and Industry, Dato' Seri Paduka Rafidah Aziz, to her son-in-law: Rafidah, in her capacity as head of the state share allocation committee, had apparently awarded the shares under a scheme intended to increase the participation of native Malays in business. In retaliation for the allegations that she had broken conflict of interest rules, Rafidah read out a list in the House of Representatives of other prominent politicians (including Mahathir and Anwar) whose relatives were similarly said to have benefited from share issues; Rafidah contended, moreover, that the committee had been aware of the possible conflict of interest when the shares were allocated to her son-in-law.

In late December 1994 Sakaran retired as Chief Minister of Sabah and became state ruler. He was succeeded as Chief Minister by Tan Sri Datuk Mohamed Salleh Tun Said Keruak. In early 1995 the DAP withdrew from the Gagasan Rakyat, stating that it wished to prepare for the forthcoming general elections. It was, however, speculated in some quarters that the DAP's withdrawal from the opposition coalition was in reaction to the 'Islamicization' policies of the PAS, which is also a member. In March Ghafar rejoined UMNO.

Mahathir subsequently announced that general elections would take place on 24–25 April 1995. Administrative redivisions had entailed the creation of an additional 12 parliamentary and 43 state seats to be contested, and the borders of 100 constituencies had been altered to reflect demographic changes. Following an often acrimonious election campaign, in which opposition parties complained of biased coverage by the state-owned media and undemocratic practices by the Mahathir Government (including the manipulation of electoral boundaries to its own advantage), the BN won an overwhelming majority, taking 162 of the 192 seats in the House of Representatives (with approximately 64% of total votes cast). The DAP won only nine seats (compared with 20 in 1990); the PBS took eight of Sabah's federal seats (a loss of six), including those held by Jeffrey Kitingan and Dompok; the PAS won 7 seats (as in 1990) and Semangat '46 won 6 seats (a loss of two). The BN won 26 of Sarawak's 27 parliamentary seats. The BN also retained control of 10 of the 11 state assemblies for which voting took place, in most cases securing two-thirds' majorities. In Penang, notably, the DAP lost 13 of its 14 seats in the Penang state legislature, where it has been expecting to pose the greatest challenge to the BN. In Kelantan, which remained the only state under opposition control, a coalition of the PAS and Semangat '46 took 35 of the 43 state seats, although the BN none the less won the remaining seats in the state assembly (and had won two of the state's seats at the federal level). The overwhelming victory for the BN at both federal and state level (the largest since independence) was widely interpreted as a huge personal endorsement for Mahathir. A reorganization of the Cabinet followed.

In April 1992 Mahathir chaired a meeting on the environment held in Kuala Lumpur and attended by the developing countries. The meeting resulted in the adoption of the so-called Kuala Lumpur Declaration, which comprised demands for a halt to international environmental criticism of developing nations; an appeal to industrialized countries to adjust their own consumption and production patterns to avoid environmental pollution; and rejected the linking of development aid with improvements in human rights. Mahathir, as the effective international spokesperson for the developing countries, delivered this message at the UN Conference on Environment and Development in Rio de Janeiro, Brazil, in June of that year.

In January 1993 Gen. Fidel Ramos visited Malaysia, the first Philippine President to do so since 1968, owing to strained relations over the Philippines' claim to Sabah. Mahathir and Ramos agreed to establish a joint commission to address bilateral problems. In February 1994 Mahathir made the first official visit by a Malaysian head of government to the Philippines, and there was a marked increase in Malaysian investment in the Philippines during the mid-1990s. Relations with Indonesia also generally improved; during 1994 Indonesian and Malaysian officials attempted to resolve their conflicting claims to the sovereignty of two small islands off the coast of Borneo, Sipatan and Ligatan. In September a meeting ended without agreement as Malaysia advocated seeking binding arbitration by the international Court of Justice (ICJ), while Indonesia favoured a bilateral solution. Another territorial claim being pursued through negotiations was the dispute with Singapore over the island of Batu Puteh (Pedra Branca). In September 1994 the two countries agreed to refer the dispute to the ICJ, after they had failed to resolve the dispute through bilateral contacts.

# MALAYSIA

Mahathir's proposal to establish an East Asian Economic Caucus (EAEC), a trade group intended to exclude the USA, met with considerable resistance from the US Government (which continued to promote the US-dominated Asia-Pacific Economic Co-operation Forum—APEC, see p. 237) and Australia. In July 1993 the Association of South East Asian Nations (ASEAN, p. 109), of which Malaysia is a member, agreed, despite the continuing reluctance of Japan to participate, that the EAEC should operate as an East Asian interest group within APEC. On an official visit to Malaysia in November 1994 the Chinese President, Jiang Zemin, expressed support for the EAEC.

In November 1993 Malaysia suspended normal relations with Australia, following an incident in which the Australian Prime Minister, Paul Keating, referred to Mahathir as a 'recalcitrant' for not attending the APEC informal summit in the USA in that month. Mahathir's absence was thought to be due to earlier US attacks on the EAEC. Following a letter from Keating expressing regret, normal relations with Australia were resumed. Relations with the USA were strengthened following a visit by Mahathir to Washington, DC, in May 1994, during which he met the US President, Bill Clinton. Mahathir subsequently attended the APEC summit meeting held in Indonesia in November, and, despite having reservations about some aspects of the agreement to increase trade liberalization and investment between member states, offered to host the 1998 summit in Malaysia.

In February 1994 the Malaysian Government announced its decision not to award new government contracts to British firms, in protest at allegations in the British media that certain Malaysian politicians, including Mahathir, were corrupt. The British press reports followed revelations in the United Kingdom that British development aid of £234m. for the allegedly uneconomical Pergau dam project in Kelantan had been used as a means of securing a defence contract from Malaysia worth £1,300m. The ban on British firms was ended in September 1994.

## Government

Malaysia is a federation of 13 states. The capital, Kuala Lumpur, is a separate Federal Territory, as is the island of Labuan. The Head of State, or Supreme Head of Malaysia, is a monarch, elected for a five-year term (with a Deputy Head of State) by and from the hereditary rulers of nine of the states. The monarch acts on the advice of Parliament and the Cabinet. Parliament consists of the Dewan Negara (Senate) and the Dewan Rakyat (House of Representatives). The Senate has 70 members, including 40 appointed by the Head of State and 30 elected members, 26 chosen by State Legislative Assemblies (two from each) and four from the two Federal Territories. The House of Representatives consists of 192 members, elected for five years by universal adult suffrage: 144 from Peninsular Malaysia, 27 from Sarawak, 20 from Sabah and one from Labuan. The Head of State appoints the Prime Minister and, on the latter's recommendation, other ministers. The Cabinet is responsible to Parliament. The country is divided into 130 administrative districts, and the Federal Territories of Kuala Lumpur and Labuan.

## Defence

In June 1994 the active armed forces totalled 114,500 men: army 90,000, navy 12,000 and air force 12,500. Military service is voluntary. There was also a reserve force of 58,300 (army 55,000, navy 2,700, air force 600). Paramilitary forces in 1994 included a Police Field Force of 18,000 men and a People's Volunteer Corps with about 168,000 members. Federal budget estimates for 1994 allocated RM5,367m. to defence (about 11.8% of total government expenditure).

## Economic Affairs

In 1993, according to estimates by the World Bank, Malaysia's gross national product (GNP), measured at average 1991–93 prices, was US $60,061m., equivalent to US $3,160 per head. During 1985–93, it was estimated, GNP per head increased, in real terms, at an average annual rate of 5.7%. Over the same period the population increased by an annual average of 2.4%. Malaysia's gross domestic product (GDP) increased, in real terms, by an annual average of 5.9% in 1980–92; GDP increased by an estimated 8.5% in 1993, and by 8.7% in 1994.

Measured at constant 1978 prices, agriculture (including forestry and fishing) contributed an estimated 14.6% of GDP in 1994, and engaged an estimated 21.4% of the employed labour force in 1993. The principal subsistence crop is rice, although in 1991 national production satisfied only about 60% of domestic requirements. Malaysia is the world's leading producer of palm oil, exports of which contributed 4.8% of the value of total merchandise exports in 1993. It was also formerly the world's leading producer of natural rubber, but by 1992 both Thailand and Indonesia had surpassed Malaysian production levels; in 1994 rubber accounted for less than 2% of total exports. Other important cash crops include cocoa, pepper, coconuts, tea and pineapples. Sawlogs remained an important source of foreign exchange following the introduction of limited conservation measures in the mid-1980s. In 1993, however, exports of sawlogs declined by more than 50%, in volume terms, owing to the Government's policy of sustainable management and to the restrictions on exports of logs imposed in January of that year (there was, none the less, a marked increase in both the volume and value of exports of sawn timber in 1993). During 1980–92 agricultural GDP increased by an annual average of 3.6%; agricultural GDP increased by 3.9% in 1993.

Industry (including mining, manufacturing, construction and power) contributed an estimated 44.2% of GDP (at 1978 prices) in 1994, and—excluding utilities—engaged about 31.9% of the employed labour force in 1993. During 1980–92 industrial GDP increased by an annual average of 8.0%.

Mining contributed an estimated 7.3% of GDP in 1994, although it engaged only an estimated 0.5% of the employed labour force in 1993. In 1993 estimated proven gas reserves stood at 2,170,000m. cu m, and petroleum reserves at 4,300m. barrels. Exports of mineral fuels and lubricants provided 10.3% of total export earnings in 1994. Malaysia is one of the world's leading producers of tin, although in 1993 sales of this commodity accounted for only 0.4% of total export revenue. Bauxite, copper and iron are also mined. The GDP of the mining sector declined by 1.3% in 1993, compared with an increase of 1.7% in 1992.

Manufacturing (the largest export sector) contributed an estimated 30.7% of GDP (at 1978 prices) in 1994, and engaged 24.0% of the employed labour force in 1993. The most important branches, measured by gross value of output, are electrical and electronic appliances (particularly radio and television receivers), food products, rubber products, industrial chemicals, wood products, petroleum-refining and motor vehicles. During 1980–92 manufacturing GDP increased by an annual average of 10.0%; manufacturing GDP increased by 12.8% in 1993.

Energy is derived principally from Malaysia's own reserves of petroleum. The country's dependence on petroleum as its principal source of commercial energy declined from 71% in 1985 to 38% in 1993. The share contributed by natural gas increased from 19% to 33% over the same period. In 1993 hydropower and coal accounted for 15% and 14%, respectively, of the country's generating capacity. In 1995 construction was expected to begin on a 2,400-MW hydroelectric dam at Bakun in Sarawak; completion of the project was anticipated by 2001. Imports of mineral fuels comprised 3.6% of the value of merchandise imports in 1993.

Tourism makes a significant contribution to the economy. In 1994 about 7.2m. tourists visited Malaysia, contributing about US $3,600m. in foreign exchange receipts (compared with $1,700m. in 1993). In 1994 the financial sector contributed 10.7% of GDP (at 1978 prices). The Kuala Lumpur Stock Exchange was capitalized at RM 619,637m. in 1994 (compared with $156,100m. in 1993); the number of listed companies rose from 307 in 1989 to 413 in 1993.

In 1993 Malaysia recorded a visible trade surplus of US $3,183m., and there was a deficit of $2,466m. on the current account of the balance of payments; in 1994 there was a deficit of RM 11,600m. on the current account. In 1993 the principal source of imports (27.4%) was Japan; other major suppliers were the USA, Singapore and Taiwan. The principal market for exports (21.7%) was Singapore; other significant purchasers were the USA, Japan and the United Kingdom. The principal imports in 1993 were machinery and transport equipment, basic manufactures, chemicals and miscellaneous manufactured articles. The principal exports were machinery and transport equipment, miscellaneous manufactured articles, mineral fuels and related products, other inedible crude materials and basic manufactures.

For 1994 there was a projected federal budgetary deficit of RM 298m. In 1993 Malaysia's external debt totalled

US $23,335m., of which $13,863m. was long-term public debt The cost of servicing debt in that year was equivalent to 7.9% of the value of exports of goods and services. The annual rate of inflation averaged 2.7% in 1985–93; in 1994 it averaged 3.7%. An estimated 3.6% of the labour force were unemployed in 1993; in 1994 unemployment was 2.9%, according to official estimates.

Malaysia is a member of the Asian Development Bank (see p. 107), the Association of South East Asian Nations (ASEAN—see p. 109), the Colombo Plan (see p. 238) and Asia-Pacific Economic Co-operation (APEC—see p. 237), all of which aim to accelerate economic progress in the region. In January 1992 the member-states of ASEAN agreed to establish a free trade zone, the ASEAN Free Trade Area, within 15 years from January 1993. In the early 1990s Malaysia was attempting to establish a new regional body, the 'East Asian Economic Caucus', which would complement ASEAN and widen the area of economic co-operation to include Japan and the People's Republic of China.

In June 1991 the successor to Malaysia's 20-year New Economic Policy (NEP), the New Development Policy (NDP), was inaugurated. The emphasis on 'racial' economic restructuring in the NEP shifted towards economic growth and the eradication of poverty under the NDP. During the 1990s the economy continued to expand rapidly under the policies introduced in the 1980s: the liberalization of foreign investment legislation; tax reforms; a reduction in trade tariffs; and the privatization of state enterprises (by April 1994 a total of 107 enterprises had been privatized). Inflationary pressures in the early 1990s had been effectively relieved by high interest rates and the imposition of some credit controls, although there were concerns that long-term growth might be jeopardized by a decline in foreign investment (owing to increased competition for funds from neighbouring China and Viet Nam), infrastructural constraints and a shortage of skilled labour—issues which the Mahathir Government was seeking to address in the mid-1990s. At the end of 1994 Malaysia continued to experience strong growth, together with low rates of inflation and of employment. Increasingly export-orientated, the Malaysian economy has, none the less, witnessed a sustained reduction in the trade surplus in recent years, while concern regarding inflationary pressures concomitant with high levels of growth has increased. The 1995–2000 Malaysia economic plan, to be detailed in late 1995, was expected to address these issues and to emphasize the introduction of more technology-intensive industries, with the aim of alleviating some of the demand for labour and of improving the country's technological capacity.

### Social Welfare

Social welfare is the responsibility of the Ministry of Health and the Ministry of National Unity and Community Development. Employers and employees contribute to the Employees' Provident Fund for retirement benefits. The independent Social Welfare Lotteries Board contributes large sums to welfare schemes. Government-sponsored social work among aged and disabled people is supported by many voluntary societies. In 1992 there were an estimated 107 government hospitals (72 in Peninsular Malaysia, 16 in Sabah and 19 in Sarawak), served by 7,719 physicians. In 1987 there were 152 private hospitals and nursing homes, with a total of 4,215 beds. Federal budget estimates for 1994 allocated RM 2.418m. to health and RM 2,355m. to social security (constituting 5.3% and 5.2%, respectively, of total planned current expenditure by the Federal Government).

### Education

Under the Malaysian education system, free schooling is provided at government-assisted schools for children between the ages of six and 18 years. There are also private schools, which receive no government financial aid. Education is compulsory for nine years between the ages of six and 14 years. Bahasa Malaysia is the main medium of instruction, while English is taught as a second language; Chinese and Tamil are used for instruction only in primary institutions. Primary education begins at six years of age and lasts for six years. In 1992 the number of pupils attending primary schools was equivalent to 93% of children in the relevant age-group (males 93%; females 94%). Secondary education, beginning at the age of 12, lasts for seven years, comprising a first cycle of three years and a second of four. Pupils may attend vocational and technical secondary schools instead of the final four years of academic education. In 1992 the total enrolment at secondary schools was equivalent to 60% of the school-age population (males 58%; females 62%). In 1994 Malaysia had eight universities; in 1992 there was an estimated total of 66,460 students at seven universities. In August 1994 the construction was announced of a ninth university outside Kota Kinabalu in Sabah. In October the Government introduced a bill that would allow foreign universities to establish branch campuses in Malaysia. From the end of that year the Government permitted the use of English as a medium of instruction in science and engineering subjects at the tertiary level.

Federal budget estimates for 1994 allocated RM 9,550m. to education (21.0% of total projected expenditure). In 1980 the average rate of adult illiteracy was 30.4% but in 1990, according to UNESCO estimates, the rate had declined to 21.6% (males 13.5%; females 29.6%).

### Public Holidays

Each state has its own public holidays, and the following federal holidays are also observed:

**1995:** 31 January–1 February* (Chinese New Year), 3 March† (Hari Raya Puasa, end of Ramadan), 1 May (Labour Day), 10 May† (Hari Raya Haji, Feast of the Sacrifice), 13 May (Vesak Day), 3 June (Official Birthday of HM the Yang di-Pertuan Agong), 9 August† (Mouloud, Prophet Muhammad's Birthday), 31 August (National Day), 23 October (Deepavali)‡, 25 December (Christmas Day).

**1996:** 19–20 February* (Chinese New Year), 21–22 February† (Hari Raya Puasa, end of Ramadan), 29 April (Vesak Day), 1 May (Labour Day), 21 May† (Hari Raya Haji, Feast of the Sacrifice), 3 June (Official Birthday of HM the Yang di-Pertuan Agong), 28 July† (Mouloud, Prophet Muhammad's Birthday), 31 August (National Day), November (Deepavali)‡, 25 December (Christmas Day).

* The first two days of the first moon of the lunar calendar.
† These holidays are dependent on the Islamic lunar calendar and may vary by one or two days from the dates given.
‡ Except Sabah and Sarawak.

### Weights and Measures

The metric system is in force. There is also a local system of weights and measures:

1 cupak = 1 quart (1.1365 litres)
1 gantang = 1 gallon (4.5461 litres)
1 tahil = 1+ ounces (37.8 grams)
16 tahils = 1 kati = 1+ lb (604.8 grams)
100 katis = 1 picul = 133+ lb (60.48 kg)
40 piculs = 1 koyan = 5,333+ lb (2,419.2 kg)

# Statistical Survey

Sources (unless otherwise stated): Department of Statistics, Wisma Statistik, Jalan Cenderasari, 50514 Kuala Lumpur, tel. (3) 2944264; fax (3) 2931132; Departments of Statistics, Kuching and Kota Kinabalu.

Note: Unless otherwise indicated, statistics refer to all states of Malaysia.

## Area and Population

### AREA, POPULATION AND DENSITY

| | |
|---|---:|
| Area (sq km) | |
| Peninsular Malaysia | 131,598 |
| Sabah (incl. Labuan) | 73,711 |
| Sarawak | 124,449 |
| Total | 329,758* |
| Population (census results)† | |
| 10 June 1980 | 13,435,588 |
| 14 August 1991 | |
| Males | 8,861,124 |
| Females | 8,705,858 |
| Total | 17,566,982 |
| Population (official estimates at mid-year) | |
| 1992 | 18,606,300 |
| 1993 | 19,046,900 |
| Density (per sq km) at mid-1993 | 57.8 |

* 127,320 sq miles.
† The figures have not been adjusted for underenumeration. The revised total for 1980 is 13,745,241, of which: Peninsular Malaysia 11,426,613; Sabah 1,011,046; Sarawak 1,307,582.

### PRINCIPAL ETHNIC GROUPS*
(estimates, '000 persons at 30 June 1991)

| | Peninsular Malaysia | Sabah | Sarawak |
|---|---:|---:|---:|
| Malays and other indigenous groups | 8,744.9 | 1,322.9 | 1,215.8 |
| Chinese | 4,640.3 | | |
| Indians | 1,462.3 | 206.5 | 493.0 |
| Others | 95.3 | | |
| **Total** | 14,942.7 | 1,529.4 | 1,708.8 |

* Not revised to take account of the results of the August 1991 census.

### STATES (at census of August 1991)

| | Area (sq km) | Population |
|---|---:|---:|
| Johor (Johore) | 18,986 | 2,074,297 |
| Kedah | 9,426 | 1,304,800 |
| Kelantan | 14,943 | 1,181,680 |
| Melaka (Malacca) | 1,650 | 504,502 |
| Negeri Sembilan (Negri Sembilan) | 6,643 | 691,150 |
| Pahang | 35,965 | 1,036,724 |
| Perak | 21,005 | 1,880,016 |
| Perlis | 795 | 184,070 |
| Pulau Pinang (Penang) | 1,031 | 1,065,075 |
| Sabah | 73,620 | 1,736,902 |
| Sarawak | 124,449 | 1,648,217 |
| Selangor | 7,956 | 2,289,236 |
| Terengganu (Trengganu) | 12,955 | 770,931 |
| Federal Territory of Kuala Lumpur | 243 | 1,145,075 |
| Federal Territory of Labuan | 91 | 54,307 |
| **Total** | 329,758 | 17,566,982 |

### PRINCIPAL TOWNS
(population, excluding underenumeration, at 1991 census)

| | | | | |
|---|---:|---|---:|
| Kuala Lumpur (capital) | 1,145,075 | Kota Baharu (Kota Bahru) | 219,713 |
| Ipoh | 382,633 | Georgetown | 219,376 |
| Johor Baharu (Johore Bahru) | 328,646 | Kota Kinabalu | 208,484 |
| Melaka (Malacca) | 295,999 | Kuantan | 198,356 |
| Petaling Jaya | 254,849 | Taiping | 183,165 |
| Tawai | 244,765 | Seremban | 182,584 |
| Kelang (Klang) | 243,698 | Kuching | 147,729 |
| Kuala Terengganu (Kuala Trengganu) | 228,659 | Sibu | 126,384 |
| Sandakan | 223,432 | Alor Setar | 125,026 |
| | | Seloyang Baru | 124,606 |
| | | Shah Alam | 101,733 |

### BIRTHS AND DEATHS*

| | Registered live births | | Registered deaths | |
|---|---:|---:|---:|---:|
| | Number | Rate (per 1,000) | Number | Rate (per 1,000) |
| 1989 | 472,989 | 27.3 | 81,521 | 4.7 |
| 1990 | 505,039 | 28.4 | 83,644 | 4.7 |
| 1991 | 507,889 | 27.8 | 83,851 | 4.6 |
| 1992† | 516,800 | 27.8 | 85,800 | 4.6 |
| 1993† | 544,700 | 28.6 | 85,700 | 4.5 |

* Registration is reported to be complete for Peninsular Malaysia, but is incomplete for Sabah and Sarawak.
† Figures are provisional.

**Expectation of life** (years at birth, Peninsular Malaysia only, 1992, provisional): Males 69.0; Females 73.7.

### ECONOMICALLY ACTIVE POPULATION
(labour force surveys, ISIC Major Divisions, '000 persons)

| | 1991 | 1992 | 1993* |
|---|---:|---:|---:|
| Agriculture, forestry and fishing | 1,680 | 1,630 | 1,580 |
| Mining and quarrying | 36 | 36 | 35 |
| Manufacturing | 1,500 | 1,640 | 1,766 |
| Construction | 465 | 507 | 550 |
| Transport, storage and communications | 314 | 326 | 342 |
| Finance, insurance, real estate and business services | 279 | 300 | 315 |
| Government services | 854 | 858 | 862 |
| Other services† | 1,798 | 1,851 | 1,920 |
| **Total employed** | 6,926 | 7,148 | 7,371 |
| Unemployed | 315 | 293 | 275 |
| **Total labour force** | 7,241 | 7,441 | 7,646 |

* Estimates.
† Including employment in electricity, gas and water and trade, hotels and restaurants.

Source: Economic Planning Unit.

MALAYSIA

## Agriculture

**PRINCIPAL CROPS** ('000 metric tons)

|  | 1991 | 1992 | 1993 |
|---|---|---|---|
| Rice (paddy) | 2,141 | 2,070 | 2,100* |
| Maize* | 35 | 36 | 37 |
| Sweet potatoes† | 42 | 44 | 48 |
| Cassava (Manioc) | 420† | 430† | 435 |
| Other roots and tubers† | 50 | 50 | 50 |
| Groundnuts (in shell)† | 5 | 5 | 4 |
| Coconuts* | 984 | 1,084 | 1,030 |
| Copra† | 73 | 80 | 76 |
| Palm kernels | 1,786 | 1,874 | 2,266 |
| Vegetables and melons† | 351 | 366 | 383 |
| Pineapples† | 32 | 33 | 34 |
| Bananas | 509† | 510† | 520 |
| Other fruit (excl. melons)† | 579 | 586 | 630 |
| Sugar cane† | 1,024 | 1,125 | 1,137 |
| Coffee (green) | 8† | 8† | 9 |
| Cocoa beans | 230 | 220* | 226 |
| Tea (made)† | 5† | 3 | 4† |
| Tobacco (leaves) | 11 | 12 | 10† |
| Natural rubber | 1,256 | 1,218 | 1,210* |

* Unofficial figure(s).   † FAO estimate(s).

Source: FAO, *Production Yearbook*.

Pepper ('000 metric tons): 20 in 1988; 25 in 1989.

**LIVESTOCK** ('000 head, year ending September)

|  | 1991 | 1992* | 1993 |
|---|---|---|---|
| Cattle | 701 | 718 | 735 |
| Buffaloes | 202 | 194 | 186 |
| Goats | 346 | 349 | 352 |
| Sheep | 247 | 276 | 308 |
| Pigs | 2,708 | 2,843 | 2,983 |

* FAO estimates.

Chickens (FAO estimates, million): 74 in 1991; 84 in 1992; 95 in 1993.

Source: FAO, *Production Yearbook*.

**LIVESTOCK PRODUCTS** ('000 metric tons)

|  | 1991 | 1992 | 1993 |
|---|---|---|---|
| Beef and veal* | 13 | 13 | 14 |
| Buffalo meat* | 5 | 4 | 4 |
| Pig meat* | 225 | 222 | 219 |
| Poultry meat | 473 | 539* | 606* |
| Cow's milk | 31 | 32 | 33 |
| Hen eggs | 319.8 | 336.0* | 350.0* |
| Cattle and buffalo hides* | 2.7 | 2.7 | 2.8 |

* FAO estimate(s).   † Unofficial figure.

Source: FAO, *Production Yearbook*.

## Forestry

**ROUNDWOOD REMOVALS** ('000 cubic metres, excl. bark)

|  | 1990 | 1991 | 1992 |
|---|---|---|---|
| Sawlogs, veneer logs and logs for sleepers | 39,666 | 39,871 | 43,511 |
| Pulpwood* | 613 | 613 | 613 |
| Other industrial wood* | 692 | 709 | 727 |
| Fuel wood* | 8,719 | 8,938 | 9,157 |
| Total | 46,690 | 50,131 | 54,008 |

* FAO estimates (figures for pulpwood are assumed to be unchanged since 1978).

Source: FAO, *Yearbook of Forest Products*.

**SAWNWOOD PRODUCTION**
('000 cubic metres, incl. railway sleepers)

|  | 1990 | 1991 | 1992 |
|---|---|---|---|
| Coniferous (softwood)* | 69 | 69 | 69 |
| Broadleaved (hardwood)† | 8,780 | 8,924 | 9,300 |
| Total | 8,849 | 8,993 | 9,369 |

* FAO estimates.   † Unofficial figures.

Source: FAO, *Yearbook of Forest Products*.

## Fishing

(FAO estimates, '000 metric tons, live weight)

|  | 1990 | 1991 | 1992 |
|---|---|---|---|
| Inland waters | 14.6 | 14.5 | 16.0 |
| Pacific Ocean | 589.4 | 605.5 | 624.0 |
| Total | 604.0 | 620.0 | 640.0 |

Source: FAO, *Yearbook of Fishery Statistics*.

## Mining

**PRODUCTION** (metric tons, unless otherwise indicated)

|  | 1990 | 1991* | 1992* |
|---|---|---|---|
| Tin-in-concentrates | 28,468 | 20,710 | 14,339 |
| Copper concentrates† | 101,931 | 98,347 | 111,593 |
| Bauxite | 398,180 | 376,418 | 330,593 |
| Iron ore† | 344,186 | 375,869 | 314,819 |
| Kaolin | 152,972 | 186,699 | 244,623 |
| Gold (kg) | 1,586 | 1,615 | 2,215 |
| Silver (kg) | 12,451 | 13,440 | 16,325 |
| Barytes | 48,291 | 16,600 | 10,525 |
| Crude petroleum ('000 metric tons) | 29,556 | 30,765 | 31,292 |
| Natural gas (million cu ft)‡ | 502,538 | 574,235 | 642,241 |
| Ilmenite† | 530,237 | 336,347 | 337,744 |
| Zirconium† | 4,279 | 5,579 | 2,608 |

* Provisional.

† Figures refer to the gross weight of ores and concentrates. The metal content (in '000 metric tons) was: Copper 24.3 in 1990, 25.6 in 1991 (Source: Metallgesellschaft AG, Germany); Iron 192 in 1990, 215 in 1991 (Source: UN, *Industrial Statistics Yearbook*).

‡ Includes quantity reinjected, flared and lost.

**1993:** Crude petroleum 32,210,000 metric tons (Sabah and Sarawak only) (Source: UN, *Monthly Bulletin of Statistics*).

## Industry

**SELECTED PRODUCTS** (Peninsular Malaysia)
(metric tons, unless otherwise indicated)

|  | 1990 | 1991 | 1992 |
|---|---|---|---|
| Rubber: |  |  |  |
|   Processed latex | 255,947 | 285,921 | 263,892 |
|   Rubber compound | 19,437 | 19,232 | 16,995 |
|   Inner tubes ('000) | 12,224 | 13,918 | 12,775 |
|   Rubber sheeting | 7,042 | 7,072 | 6,994 |
|   Pneumatic tyres ('000) | 6,764 | 7,970 | 8,540 |
|   Rubber bands | 3,785 | 3,665 | 3,567 |
|   Rubber gloves ('000 pairs) | 1,793,741 | 2,398,738 | 3,473,004 |
| Cement ('000 metric tons) | 5,881 | 7,451 | 8,366 |
| Cigarettes | 17,331 | 17,498 | 16,574 |
| Tin metal—primary* | 49,002 | 42,718 | 45,598 |
| Palm oil—crude ('000 metric tons)† | 6,094.6‡ | 6,141 | 6,373 |
| Semiconductors (million) | 2,565 | 2,689 | 3,121 |

* Source: *International Tin Statistics*.

† Production in all Malaysia.

‡ Estimate.

MALAYSIA

# Finance

## CURRENCY AND EXCHANGE RATES

**Monetary Units**
100 sen = 1 ringgit Malaysia (RM—also formerly Malaysian dollar).

**Sterling and US Dollar Equivalents** (31 December 1994)
£1 sterling = RM 3.9950;
US $1 = RM 2.5535;
RM 100 = £25.03 = US $39.16.

**Average Exchange Rate** (RM per US $)
1992  2.5474
1993  2.5741
1994  2.6243

## FEDERAL BUDGET (RM million)

| Revenue | 1992 | 1993 | 1994* |
|---|---|---|---|
| Tax revenue | 30,181 | 33,235 | 37,186 |
| Direct taxes | 14,386 | 15,661 | 18,391 |
| Companies | 10,941 | 11,410 | 13,214 |
| Individuals | 3,441 | 4,248 | 5,172 |
| Indirect taxes | 15,795 | 17,574 | 18,795 |
| Goods and services | 8,410 | 9,986 | 10,436 |
| Sales tax | 3,082 | 3,468 | 3,668 |
| Excises | 5,328 | 5,798 | 6,768 |
| International trade | 6,073 | 6,030 | 6,482 |
| Import duties | 4,384 | 4,566 | 5,036 |
| Export duties | 1,689 | 1,464 | 1,446 |
| Other current revenue | 8,934 | 8,761 | 7,941 |
| Property income | 7,816 | 7,205 | 6,523 |
| Capital revenue | 57 | 37 | 29 |
| **Total** | **39,172** | **42,033** | **45,156** |

| Expenditure | 1992 | 1993 | 1994* |
|---|---|---|---|
| General services | 25,978 | 27,127 | 29,149 |
| General administration | 3,886 | 4,147 | 4,017 |
| Internal security | 2,469 | 2,437 | 2,261 |
| Defence | 4,500 | 4,951 | 5,367 |
| Education | 8,059 | 8,538 | 9,550 |
| Health | 2,414 | 2,407 | 2,418 |
| Social security | 2,183 | 2,320 | 2,355 |
| Economic services | 8,002 | 7,776 | 9,848 |
| Agriculture, forestry and rural development | 2,389 | 2,442 | 2,675 |
| Transport and communication | 3,517 | 3,464 | 4,409 |
| Other purposes | 6,791 | 6,868 | 6,457 |
| **Total** | **40,508†** | **41,714†** | **45,454** |

* Budget estimates.
† Including adjustment for accounts payable (RM million): −262 in 1992; −57 in 1993.

Source: IMF, *Malaysia—Recent Economic Developments* (1994).

## PUBLIC DEVELOPMENT EXPENDITURE (RM million)

| | 1992* | 1993† | 1994‡ |
|---|---|---|---|
| Security | 2,173 | 2,240 | 2,567 |
| Defence | 1,629 | 1,672 | 2,211 |
| Social Services | 2,653 | 2,398 | 3,206 |
| Education | 1,205 | 1,196 | 1,587 |
| Health | 602 | 490 | 342 |
| Housing | 94 | 163 | 504 |
| Economic Services | 4,504 | 4,873 | 7,049 |
| Agriculture and rural development | 1,098 | 1,102 | 1,528 |
| Public utilities | 834 | 617 | 940 |
| Commerce and industry | 648 | 728 | 1,106 |
| Transport | 1,896 | 2,390 | 3,425 |
| General administration | 358 | 410 | 528 |
| **Total** | **9,688** | **9,921** | **13,350** |

* Estimated actual.   † Estimates.   ‡ Budget allocation.

## INTERNATIONAL RESERVES (US $ million at 31 December)

| | 1991 | 1992 | 1993 |
|---|---|---|---|
| Gold* | 118 | 115 | 115 |
| IMF special drawing rights | 207 | 113 | 121 |
| Reserve position in IMF | 257 | 330 | 315 |
| Foreign exchange | 10,421 | 16,784 | 26,814 |
| **Total** | **11,004** | **17,343** | **27,364** |

* Valued at 35 SDRs per troy ounce.
Source: IMF, *International Financial Statistics*.

## MONEY SUPPLY (RM million at 31 December)

| | 1991 | 1992 | 1993 |
|---|---|---|---|
| Currency outside banks | 12,070 | 12,124 | 13,506 |
| Demand deposits at commercial banks | 15,758 | 18,931 | 29,128 |
| **Total money** (incl. others) | **27,928** | **35,544** | **48,077** |

Source: IMF, *International Financial Statistics*.

## COST OF LIVING
(Peninsular Malaysia, Consumer Price Index; base: 1990 = 100)

| | 1991 | 1992 | 1993 |
|---|---|---|---|
| Food | 104.8 | 111.7 | 114.2 |
| Beverages and tobacco | 107.8 | 117.1 | 134.4 |
| Clothing and footwear | 106.2 | 109.4 | 109.9 |
| Gross rent, fuel and power | 103.0 | 106.8 | 110.5 |
| **All items** (incl. others) | **104.4** | **109.3** | **113.2** |

**1994:** All items 117.4 (Source: IMF, *International Financial Statistics*).

## NATIONAL ACCOUNTS (RM million)
**Expenditure on the Gross Domestic Product** (in current prices)

| | 1991 | 1992 | 1993* |
|---|---|---|---|
| Government final consumption expenditure | 18,391 | 19,304 | 20,864 |
| Private final consumption expenditure | 70,929 | 76,046 | 84,850 |
| Increase in stocks | 1,698 | −813 | 1,574 |
| Gross fixed capital formation | 46,181 | 50,697 | 57,007 |
| **Total domestic expenditure** | **137,199** | **145,234** | **164,295** |
| Exports of goods and services | 105,468 | 115,231 | 132,545 |
| *Less* Imports of goods and services | 113,108 | 112,681 | 130,967 |
| **GDP in purchasers' values** | **129,559** | **147,784** | **165,873** |
| Net factor income from abroad | −6,011 | −7,517 | −8,113 |
| **GNP in purchasers' values** | **123,548** | **140,267** | **157,760** |

* Estimates.

**Gross Domestic Product by Economic Activity**
(at constant 1978 prices)

| | 1992 | 1993 | 1994* |
|---|---|---|---|
| Agriculture, livestock, forestry and fishing | 15,432 | 16,040 | 16,337 |
| Mining and quarrying | 8,088 | 7,971 | 8,142 |
| Manufacturing | 26,859 | 30,361 | 34,293 |
| Construction | 3,615 | 4,032 | 4,514 |
| Electricity, gas and water | 1,931 | 2,182 | 2,467 |
| Transport, storage and communications | 6,579 | 7,171 | 7,820 |
| Wholesale and retail trade, hotels and restaurants | 11,165 | 12,304 | 13,551 |
| Finance, insurance, real estate and business services | 9,607 | 10,764 | 11,898 |
| Government services | 9,466 | 9,943 | 10,395 |
| Other services | 1,977 | 2,124 | 2,274 |
| **Sub-total** | **94,719** | **102,892** | **111,691** |
| Import duties | 3,728 | 4,105 | 4,474 |
| *Less* Imputed bank service charges | 5,376 | 6,045 | 6,783 |
| **GDP in purchasers' values** | **983,071** | **100,950** | **109,381** |

* Provisional.

## MALAYSIA

### BALANCE OF PAYMENTS (US $ million)

| | 1991 | 1992 | 1993 |
|---|---|---|---|
| Merchandise exports f.o.b. | 33,534 | 39,613 | 45,984 |
| Merchandise imports f.o.b. | -33,007 | -36,238 | -42,801 |
| **Trade balance** | 527 | 3,375 | 3,183 |
| Exports of services | 4,553 | 5,437 | 5,607 |
| Imports of services | -6,878 | -7,637 | -8,208 |
| Other income received | 1,425 | 1,605 | 1,987 |
| Other income paid | -3,898 | -4,748 | -5,194 |
| Private unrequited transfers (net) | 29 | 65 | 84 |
| Government unrequited transfers (net) | 8 | 67 | 75 |
| **Current balance** | -4,234 | -1,836 | -2,466 |
| Direct capital investment (net) | 3,998 | 5,183 | 5,206 |
| Portfolio investment | 170 | -1,108 | -984 |
| Other capital (net) | 1,454 | 4,708 | 6,785 |
| Net errors and omissions | -151 | -292 | 2,802 |
| **Overall balance** | 1,238 | 6,655 | 11,343 |

Source: IMF, *International Financial Statistics*.

## External Trade

### PRINCIPAL COMMODITIES (RM million)

| Imports | 1991 | 1992 | 1993 |
|---|---|---|---|
| Food and live animals | 5,139 | 5,470 | 5,816 |
| Beverages and tobacco | 424 | 399 | 390 |
| Crude materials, inedible, excluding fuels | 2,810 | 2,630 | 3,261 |
| Mineral fuels, lubricants and related materials | 4,253 | 4,243 | 4,243 |
| Animal and vegetable oils and fats | 395 | 331 | 404 |
| Chemicals | 7,663 | 8,163 | 8,941 |
| Basic manufactures | 15,924 | 16,270 | 17,726 |
| Machinery and transport equipment | 54,165 | 55,711 | 65,323 |
| Miscellaneous manufactured articles | 5,650 | 5,869 | 6,526 |
| Other commodities and transactions | 4,409 | 2,354 | 4,793 |
| **Total** | 100,831 | 101,440 | 117,423 |

| Exports | 1991 | 1992 | 1993 |
|---|---|---|---|
| Food and live animals | 3,652 | 3,762 | 3,963 |
| Beverages and tobacco | 169 | 192 | 185 |
| Crude materials, inedible, excluding fuels | 11,140 | 11,081 | 10,987 |
| Mineral fuels, lubricants and related materials | 14,659 | 13,418 | 12,484 |
| Crude petroleum | 10,184 | 9,147 | n.a. |
| Animal and vegetable oils and fats | 6,227 | 6,875 | 7,240 |
| Chemicals | 1,667 | 2,123 | 2,651 |
| Basic manufactures | 7,360 | 8,831 | 11,610 |
| Machinery and transport equipment | 38,866 | 45,411 | 58,751 |
| Miscellaneous manufactured articles | 10,320 | 11,505 | 12,532 |
| Other commodities and transactions | 439 | 460 | 811 |
| **Total** | 94,497 | 103,657 | 121,214 |

### PRINCIPAL TRADING PARTNERS (RM million)

| Imports | 1991 | 1992 | 1993 |
|---|---|---|---|
| Australia | 3,233 | 2,699 | 3,325 |
| China, People's Republic | 2,213 | 2,482 | 2,818 |
| France | 1,384 | 1,322 | 1,674 |
| Germany | 4,397 | 4,271 | 4,483 |
| Hong Kong | 2,061 | 2,302 | 2,369 |
| Indonesia | 1,390 | 1,621 | 1,846 |
| Italy | 1,223 | 1,338 | 1,507 |
| Japan | 26,289 | 26,366 | 32,230 |
| Korea, Republic | 2,743 | 3,103 | 3,576 |
| Singapore | 15,714 | 15,970 | 17,886 |
| Sweden | 1,162 | 663 | 757 |
| Switzerland | 1,314 | 1,446 | 1,487 |
| Taiwan | 5,506 | 5,760 | 6,293 |
| Thailand | 2,452 | 2,516 | 2,916 |
| United Kingdom | 4,669 | 3,466 | 3,667 |
| USA | 15,458 | 16,024 | 19,854 |
| **Total** (incl. others) | 100,831 | 101,440 | 117,423 |

| Exports | 1991 | 1992 | 1993 |
|---|---|---|---|
| Australia | 1,614 | 1,732 | 1,617 |
| Belgium | 1,047 | 1,218 | 1,450 |
| Canada | 736 | 895 | 1,172 |
| China, People's Republic | 1,761 | 1,961 | 3,094 |
| France | 1,309 | 1,438 | 1,713 |
| Germany* | 3,421 | 4,156 | 4,431 |
| Hong Kong | 3,172 | 3,925 | 4,994 |
| Indonesia | 1,386 | 1,289 | 1,398 |
| Japan | 14,840 | 13,921 | 15,729 |
| Korea, Republic | 4,168 | 3,549 | 4,115 |
| Netherlands | 2,280 | 2,524 | 2,949 |
| Philippines | 908 | 1,215 | 1,235 |
| Singapore* | 22,030 | 23,860 | 26,307 |
| Taiwan | 2,566 | 3,229 | 3,888 |
| Thailand | 3,013 | 3,785 | 4,359 |
| United Kingdom | 4,139 | 4,176 | 5,102 |
| USA | 15,984 | 19,279 | 24,631 |
| **Total** (incl. others) | 94,497 | 103,657 | 121,214 |

* Including re-exports.

## Transport

### RAILWAYS (traffic)
**Peninsular Malaysia**

| | 1990 | 1991 | 1992 |
|---|---|---|---|
| Freight ('000 metric tons) | 4,649 | 4,360 | 3,314 |
| Passenger journeys ('000) | 8,476 | 8,527 | 7,456 |

**Sabah**

| | 1990 | 1991 | 1992 |
|---|---|---|---|
| Freight ('000 metric tons) | 19 | 17 | 17 |
| Passenger journeys ('000) | 457 | 503 | 440 |

### ROAD TRAFFIC (registered vehicles in use)

| | 1989 | 1990 | 1991 |
|---|---|---|---|
| Private motor cycles | 2,848,717 | 3,035,930 | 3,257,542 |
| Private motor cars | 1,658,567 | 1,811,141 | 1,986,751 |
| Buses | 24,828 | 26,803 | 28,661 |
| Lorries and vans | 349,737 | 380,330 | 418,142 |
| Taxis | 30,803 | 34,477 | 28,091 |
| Others | 159,134 | 174,048 | 188,508 |

**31 December 1992:** Motor cycles 3,473,643; Passenger motor cars 2,147,974; Buses and coaches 30,013; Lorries and vans 442,401
(Source: IRF, *World Road Statistics*).

## MALAYSIA

### SHIPPING

**Merchant Fleet** (at 30 June)

|  | 1990 | 1991 | 1992 |
|---|---|---|---|
| Number of vessels | 498 | 508 | 552 |
| Displacement (grt) | 1,717,479 | 1,755,279 | 2,015,562 |

Source: Lloyd's Register of Shipping.

**Foreign Trade (Peninsular Malaysia)**
(vessels over 75 net registered tons)

|  | 1988 | 1989 | 1990 |
|---|---|---|---|
| Entered: |  |  |  |
| No. of vessels | 7,248 | 8,120 | 9,620 |
| '000 net registered tons | 47,909 | 51,540 | 57,050 |
| Cleared: |  |  |  |
| No. of vessels | 7,201 | 8,048 | 9,497 |
| '000 net registered tons | 47,943 | 51,244 | 55,973 |

**Sabah** (1988, '000 nrt): Tonnage entered 16,237; tonnage cleared 16,237.
**Sarawak** (1988, '000 nrt): Tonnage entered 16,870; tonnage cleared 17,478.

Source: Marine Department.

**Coastal Trade (Peninsular Malaysia)**
(vessels over 75 net registered tons)

|  | 1988 | 1989 | 1990 |
|---|---|---|---|
| Entered: |  |  |  |
| No. of vessels | 9,583 | 10,583 | 10,874 |
| Net registered tons | 7,654,681 | 8,162,154 | 8,917,369 |
| Cleared: |  |  |  |
| No. of vessels | 9,531 | 10,537 | 10,828 |
| Net registered tons | 7,624,028 | 8,177,818 | 9,087,016 |

### CIVIL AVIATION (traffic)

|  | 1988 | 1989 | 1990 |
|---|---|---|---|
| Passengers: |  |  |  |
| Embarked | 6,068,756 | 7,119,333 | 8,717,899 |
| Disembarked | 6,072,950 | 6,987,821 | 8,605,474 |
| Cargo (metric tons): |  |  |  |
| Landed | 81,016 | 90,643 | 113,266 |
| Dispatched | 86,507 | 98,708 | 128,324 |

## Tourism

|  | 1989 | 1990 | 1991 |
|---|---|---|---|
| Tourist arrivals ('000) | 4,846 | 7,446 | 5,847 |
| Total receipts from tourism (US $ million) | 1,038 | 1,667 | 1,530 |

**1993:** Tourist arrivals ('000) 6,450; Total receipts from tourism (US $ million) 1,700.
**1994:** Tourist arrivals ('000) 7,200; Total receipts from tourism (US $ million) 3,600.

Source: UN, *Statistical Yearbook for Asia and the Pacific*.

## Communications Media

|  | 1990 | 1991 | 1992 |
|---|---|---|---|
| Radio receivers ('000 in use) | 7,680 | 7,880 | 8,080 |
| Television receivers ('000 in use) | 2,640 | 2,724 | 2,820 |
| Telephones ('000 main lines in use)* | 1,586 | 1,817 | n.a. |
| Book production†: |  |  |  |
| Titles | 4,578 | 3,748 | n.a. |
| Copies ('000) | 23,233 | 13,620 | n.a. |
| Daily Newspapers: |  |  |  |
| Titles | 45 | n.a. | 39 |
| Average circulation ('000 copies) | 2,500‡ | n.a. | 2,200‡ |

**Non-daily newspapers** (1988, estimate): 19 (circulation 4,500,00 copies).
**Other periodicals** 1,631 (circulation 1,689,000 copies).

\* Telekom Malaysia only.
† Including pamphlets (208 titles and 1,707,000 copies in 1990; 66 titles and 171,000 copies in 1991).
‡ Estimate.

Sources: UNESCO, *Statistical Yearbook*; UN, *Statistical Yearbook*.

## Education

(Government-assisted schools, 1990)

|  | Establishments | Teachers | Students |
|---|---|---|---|
| Total primary | 6,828 | 120,025 | 2,447,206 |
| Total secondary | 1,342 | 73,395 | 1,374,564 |
| of which: |  |  |  |
| Academic secondary | 1,261 | 69,493 | 1,335,377 |
| Vocational secondary | 57 | 2,570 | 24,845 |
| Technical secondary | 9 | 392 | 5,846 |
| MARA junior science colleges | 15 | 940 | 8,496 |
| Institutes of Higher Education: |  |  |  |
| Teacher-training colleges | 28 | 2,183 | 23,006 |
| Universities | 7 | 5,250 | 55,248 |
| Polytechnics and colleges | 9 | 2,670 | 39,013 |
| Total higher | 44 | 10,103 | 117,267 |

Note: In Sabah, in 1990, there were 962 primary establishments (with 236,619 students), 126 secondary establishments (including 7 vocational schools) and four teacher-training colleges.

In Sarawak, in 1990, there were 1,266 primary establishments (with 223,348 students), 128 secondary establishments (including 5 vocational schools) and three teacher-training colleges.

In 1989 there were 447 private secondary schools, with a total of 115,903 students.

Source: Ministry of Education.

Pre-primary (1992): 6,352 schools; 11,341 teachers; 383,715 pupils (males 195,499; females 188,216).
Primary (1992): 6,946 schools; 130,482 teachers; 2,652,397 pupils (males 1,390,631; females 1,261,766).
General secondary (1992): 81,250 teachers; 1,536,080 pupils (males 750,758; females 785,322).
Vocational (1992): 3,494 teachers; 30,710 pupils (males 21,780; females 8,924).

Source: UNESCO, *Statistical Yearbook*.

# Directory

## The Constitution

The Constitution of the Federation of Malaya became effective at independence on 31 August 1957. As subsequently amended, it is now the Constitution of Malaysia. The main provisions are summarized below.

### SUPREME HEAD OF STATE

The Yang di-Pertuan Agong (King or Supreme Sovereign) is the Supreme Head of Malaysia.

Every act of government is derived from his authority, although he acts on the advice of Parliament and the Cabinet. The appointment of a Prime Minister lies within his discretion, and he has the right to refuse to dissolve Parliament even against the advice of the Prime Minister. He appoints the Judges of the Federal Court and the High Courts on the advice of the Prime Minister. He is the Supreme Commander of the Armed Forces. The Yang di-Pertuan Agong is elected by the Conference of Rulers, and to qualify for election he must be one of the nine hereditary Rulers. He holds office for five years or until his earlier resignation or death. Election is by secret ballot on each Ruler in turn, starting with the Ruler next in precedence after the late or former Yang di-Pertuan Agong. The first Ruler to obtain not fewer than five votes is declared elected. The Deputy Supreme Head of State (the Timbalan Yang di-Pertuan Agong) is elected by a similar process. On election the Yang di-Pertuan Agong relinquishes, for his tenure of office, all his functions as Ruler of his own state and may appoint a Regent. The Timbalan Yang di-Pertuan Agong exercises no powers in the ordinary course, but is immediately available to fill the post of Yang di-Pertuan Agong and carry out his functions in the latter's absence or disability. In the event of the Yang di-Pertuan Agong's death or resignation he takes over the exercise of sovereignty until the Conference of Rulers has elected a successor.

### CONFERENCE OF RULERS

The Conference of Rulers consists of the Rulers and the heads of the other states. Its prime duty is the election by the Rulers only of the Yang di-Pertuan Agong and his deputy. The Conference must be consulted in the appointment of judges, the Auditor-General, the Election Commission and the Services Commissions. It must also be consulted and concur in the alteration of state boundaries, the extension to the federation as a whole, of Islamic religious acts and observances, and in any bill to amend the Constitution. Consultation is mandatory in matters affecting public policy or the special position of the Malays and natives of Sabah and Sarawak. The Conference also considers matters affecting the rights, prerogatives and privileges of the Rulers themselves.

### FEDERAL PARLIAMENT

Parliament has two Houses—the Dewan Negara (Senate) and the Dewan Rakyat (House of Representatives). The Senate has a membership of 70, comprising 30 elected and 40 appointed members. Each state legislature, acting as an electoral college, elects two Senators; these may be members of the State Legislative Assembly or otherwise. The remaining four Senators represent the two Federal Territories, Kuala Lumpur and the island of Labuan. The Yang di-Pertuan Agong appoints the other 40 members of the Senate. Members of the Senate must be at least 30 years old. The Senate elects its President and Deputy President from among its members. It may initiate legislation, but all proposed legislation for the granting of funds must be introduced in the first instance in the House of Representatives. All legislative measures require approval by both Houses of Parliament before being presented to the Yang di-Pertuan Agong for the Royal Assent in order to become law. A bill originating in the Senate cannot receive Royal Assent until it has been approved by the House of Representatives, but the Senate has delaying powers only over a bill originating from and approved by the House of Representatives. Senators serve for a period of three years, but the Senate is not subject to dissolution. Parliament can, by statute, increase the number of Senators elected from each state to three. The House of Representatives consists of 180 elected members (see Amendments). Of these, 132 are from Peninsular Malaysia (including seven from Kuala Lumpur), 27 from Sarawak and 21 from Sabah (including one from Labuan). Members are returned from single-member constituencies on the basis of universal adult franchise. The life of the House of Representatives is limited to five years, after which time a fresh general election must be held.

The Yang di-Pertuan Agong may dissolve Parliament before then if the Prime Minister so advises.

### THE CABINET

To advise him in the exercise of his functions, the Yang di-Pertuan Agong appoints the Cabinet, consisting of the Prime Minister and an unspecified number of Ministers (who must all be Members of Parliament). The Prime Minister must be a citizen born in Malaysia and a member of the House of Representatives who, in the opinion of the Yang di-Pertuan Agong, commands the confidence of that House. Ministers are appointed on the advice of the Prime Minister. A number of Deputy Ministers (who are not members of the Cabinet) are also appointed from among Members of Parliament. The Cabinet meets regularly under the chairmanship of the Prime Minister to formulate policy.

### PUBLIC SERVICES

The Public Services, civilian and military, are non-political and owe their loyalty not to the party in power but to the Yang di-Pertuan Agong and the Rulers. They serve whichever government may be in power, irrespective of the latter's political affiliation. To ensure the impartiality of the service, and its protection from political interference, the Constitution provides for a number of Services Commissions to select and appoint officers, to place them on the pensionable establishment, to determine promotion, and to maintain discipline.

### THE STATES

The heads of nine of the 13 states are hereditary Rulers. The Ruler of Perlis has the title of Raja, and the Ruler of Negri Sembilan that of Yang di-Pertuan Besar. The rest of the Rulers are Sultans. The heads of the States of Malacca, Penang, Sabah and Sarawak are each designated Yang di-Pertua Negeri and do not participate in the election of the Yang di-Pertuan Agong. Each of the 13 states has its own written Constitution, and a single Legislative Assembly. Every state legislature has powers to legislate on matters not reserved for the Federal Parliament. Each State Legislative Assembly has the right to order its own procedure, and the members enjoy parliamentary privilege. All members of the Legislative Assemblies are directly elected from single-member constituencies. The head of the state acts on the advice of the State Government. This advice is tendered by the State Executive Council or Cabinet in precisely the same manner in which the Federal Cabinet tenders advice to the Yang di-Pertuan Agong.

The legislative authority of the state is vested in the head of the state in the State Legislative Assembly. The executive authority of the state is vested in the head of the state, but executive functions may be conferred on other persons by law. Every state has its own Executive Council or Cabinet to advise the head of the state, headed by its Chief Minister (in Malacca, Penang, Sabah and Sarawak) or Menteri Besar (in other states), and collectively responsible to the state legislature. Each state in Peninsular Malaysia is divided into administrative districts, each with its District Officer. Sabah is divided into four residencies: West Coast, Interior, Sandakan and Tawau with headquarters at Kota Kinabalu, Keningua, Sandakan and Tawau respectively. Sarawak is divided into five Divisions, each in charge of a Resident—the First Division, with headquarters at Kuching; the Second Division, with headquarters at Simanggang; the Third Division, with headquarters at Sibu; the Fourth Division, with headquarters at Miri; the Fifth Division, with headquarters at Limbang.

### AMENDMENTS

From 1 February 1974, the city of Kuala Lumpur, formerly the seat of the Federal Government and capital of Selangor State, is designated the Federal Territory of Kuala Lumpur. It is administered directly by the Federal Government and returns five members to the House of Representatives.

In April 1981 the legislature approved an amendment empowering the Yang di-Pertuan Agong to declare a state of emergency on the grounds of imminent danger of a breakdown in law and order or a threat to national security.

In August 1983 the legislature approved an amendment empowering the Prime Minister, instead of the Yang di-Pertuan Agong, to declare a state of emergency.

The island of Labuan, formerly part of Sabah State, was designated a Federal Territory as from 16 April 1984.

The legislature approved an amendment increasing the number of parliamentary constituencies in Sarawak from 24 to 27. The amendment took effect at the general election of 20–21 October

# MALAYSIA

1990. The total number of seats in the House of Representatives, which had increased to 177 following an amendment in August 1983, was thus expanded to 180.

In March 1988 the legislature approved two amendments relating to the judiciary (see Judicial System).

In October 1992 the legislature adopted an amendment increasing the number of parliamentary constituencies from 180 to 192. The Kuala Lumpur Federal Territory and Selangor each gained three seats, Johore two, and Perlis, Kedah, Kelantan and Pahang one. The amendment was to take effect at the next general election.

In March 1993 an amendment was approved which removed the immunity from prosecution of the hereditary Rulers.

In May 1994 the House of Representatives approved an amendment which ended the right of the Yang di-Pertuan Agong to delay legislation by withholding his assent from legislation and returning it to Parliament for further consideration. Under the amendment, the Yang di-Pertuan Agong was obliged to give his assent to a bill within 30 days; if he failed to do so, the bill would, none the less, become law. An amendment was simultaneously approved restructuring the judiciary and introducing a mandatory code of ethics for judges, to be drawn up by the Government.

## The Government

### SUPREME HEAD OF STATE
(HM the Yang di-Pertuan Agong)

HM Tuanku JA'AFAR IBNI AL-MARHUM Tuanku ABDUL RAHMAN (Yang di-Pertuan Besar of Negri Sembilan) (took office 26 April 1994).

### Deputy Supreme Head of State
(Timbalan Yang di-Pertuan Agong)

HRH Sultan SALAHUDDIN ABDUL AZIZ SHAH Al-Haj IBNI AL-MARHUM Sultan HISAMUDDIN ALAM SHAH Al-Haj (Sultan of Selangor).

### THE CABINET
(May 1995)

**Prime Minister and Minister of Home Affairs:** Dato' Seri Dr MAHATHIR MOHAMAD.
**Deputy Prime Minister and Minister of Finance:** Dato' Seri ANWAR IBRAHIM.
**Minister of Housing and Local Government:** Dr TING CHEW PEH.
**Minister of Foreign Affairs:** Datuk ABDULLAH BIN Haji AHMAD BADAWI.
**Minister of International Trade and Industry:** Dato' Seri Paduka RAFIDAH AZIZ.
**Minister of Domestic Trade and Consumer Affairs:** Dato' Haji ABU HASSAN BIN Haji OMAR.
**Minister of Defence:** Datuk SYED HAMID ALBAR.
**Minister of Transport:** Datuk Seri Dr LING LIONG SIK.
**Minister of National Unity and Community Development:** Datin Paduka ZALEHA ISMAIL.
**Minister of Primary Industries:** Dato' Seri Dr LIM KENG YAIK.
**Minister of Energy, Telecommunications and Posts:** Dato' LEO MOGGIE ANAK IROK.
**Minister of Works:** Dato' Seri S. SAMY VELLU.
**Minister of Public Enterprises:** Datuk Dr MOHAMAD YUSOF MOHAMAD NOR.
**Minister of Youth and Sports:** Tan Sri MUHYIDDIN YASSIN.
**Minister of Education:** Datuk Seri NAJIB Tun RAZAK.
**Minister of Information:** Dato' MOHAMAD BIN RAHMAT.
**Minister of Human Resources:** Datuk LIM AH LEK.
**Minister of Land and Co-operative Development:** OSU BIN Haji SUKAM.
**Minister of Culture, Arts and Tourism:** Dato' SABBARUDDIN CHIK.
**Minister of Science, Technology and the Environment:** LAW HIENG DING.
**Minister of Health:** CHUA JUI MENG.
**Minister of Agriculture:** Datuk Amar Dr SULAIMAN DAUD.
**Minister of Rural Development:** Dato' Haji ANNUAR BIN MUSA.
**Minister of Entrepreneur Development:** Datuk MUSTAPA MOHAMED.
**Ministers in the Prime Minister's Department:** Datuk ABANG ABU BAKAR BIN Datu BANDAR ABANG Haji MUSTAPHA, Dr ABDUL HAMID OTHMAN, Datuk CHON KAH KIAT.
**Minister of Justice and Minister in the Prime Minister's Department:** SYED HAMID SYED JAAFAR ALBAR.

## MINISTRIES

**Prime Minister's Department** (Jabatan Perdana Menteri): Jalan Dato' Onn, 50502 Kuala Lumpur; tel. (3) 2321957; telex 33099; fax (3) 2329227.

**Ministry of Agriculture** (Kementerian Pertanian): Wisma Tani, Jalan Sultan Salahuddin, 50624 Kuala Lumpur; tel. (3) 2982011; telex 33045; fax (3) 2913758.

**Ministry of Culture, Arts and Tourism** (Kementerian Kebudayaan, Kesenian dan Pelancongan): Menara Dato' Onn, 34th–36th Floor, POB 5–7, Putra World Trade Centre, 50694 Kuala Lumpur; tel. (3) 2937111; telex 28222; fax (3) 2910951.

**Ministry of Defence** (Kementerian Pertahanan): Jalan Padang Tembak, 50634 Kuala Lumpur; tel. (3) 2921333; telex 30289; fax (3) 2980484.

**Ministry of Domestic Trade and Consumer Affairs** (Kementerian Perdagangan Dalam Negeri dan Hal Ehival Pengguna): Block 10, Kompleks Pejabat Kerajaan, Jalan Duta, 50622 Kuala Lumpur; tel. (3) 2546022; telex 30634; fax (3) 2550827.

**Ministry of Education** (Kementerian Pendidikan): Block J, Pusat Bandar Damansara, 50604 Kuala Lumpur; tel. (3) 2556900; fax (3) 2554994.

**Ministry of Energy, Telecommunications and Posts** (Kementerian Tenaga, Telekom dan Pos): Wisma Damansara, Ground Floor, Jalan Semantan, 50668 Kuala Lumpur; tel. (3) 2546677; telex 30777; fax (3) 2557901.

**Ministry of Finance** (Kementerian Kewangan): Block 9, Kompleks Pejabat Kerajaan, Jalan Duta, 50592 Kuala Lumpur; tel. (3) 2546066; telex 30242; fax (3) 2556264.

**Ministry of Foreign Affairs** (Kementerian Luar Negeri): Wisma Putra, Jalan Wisma Putra, 50602 Kuala Lumpur; tel. (3) 2488088; telex 30310; fax (3) 2424551.

**Ministry of Health** (Kementerian Kesihatan): Jalan Cenderasari, 50590 Kuala Lumpur; tel. (3) 2985077; telex 28102; fax (3) 2911436.

**Ministry of Home Affairs** (Kementerian Dalam Negeri): Jalan Dato' Onn, 50546 Kuala Lumpur; tel. (3) 2309344; fax (3) 2301051.

**Ministry of Housing and Local Government** (Kementerian Perumahan dan Kerajaan Tempatan): Blok K, Pusat Bandar Damansara, 50782 Kuala Lumpur; tel. (3) 2547033; fax (3) 2547380.

**Ministry of Human Resources** (Kementerian Sumber Manusia): Block B, Utara, Pusat Bandar Damansara, Jalan Damanlela, Bukit Damansara, 50530 Kuala Lumpur; tel. (3) 2557200; fax (3) 2554700.

**Ministry of Information** (Kementerian Penerangan): Angkasapuri, Bukit Putra, 50610 Kuala Lumpur; tel. (3) 2825333; telex 31383; fax (3) 2821255.

**Ministry of International Trade and Industry** (Kementerian Perdagangan Antarabangsa dan Industri): Block 10, Kompleks Pejabat Kerajaan, Jalan Duta, 50622 Kuala Lumpur; tel. (3) 2540033; telex 28017; fax (3) 2550827.

**Ministry of Justice** (Kementerian Undang-undang): Bangunan Kuwasa, 21st–22nd Floors, Jalan Raja Laut, 50506 Kuala Lumpur; tel. (3) 2935733; telex 33548.

**Ministry of Land and Co-operative Development** (Kementerian Tanah dan Pembangunan Koperasi): Wisma Keramat, 13th Floor, Jalan Gurney, 50574 Kuala Lumpur; tel. (3) 2921566; fax (3) 2918641.

**Ministry of National Unity and Community Development** (Kementerian Kebajikan Masyarakat): Wisma Shen, 6th–16th Floors, Jalan Masjid India, 50562 Kuala Lumpur; tel. (3) 2925011.

**Ministry of Primary Industries** (Kementerian Perusahaan Utama): Menara Daya Bumi, 6th–8th Floors, Jalan Sultan Hishamuddin, 50654 Kuala Lumpur; tel. (3) 2747511; telex 30808; fax (3) 2745014.

**Ministry of Public Enterprises** (Kementerian Perusahaan Awam): Wisma PKNS, 3rd Floor, Jalan Raja Laut, 50652 Kuala Lumpur; tel. (3) 2985022; telex 33069; fax (3) 2917623.

**Ministry of Rural Development** (Kementerian Pembangunan Luar Bandar): Kompleks Kewangan, 5th Floor, Jalan Raja Laut, 50606 Kuala Lumpur; tel. (3) 2910255; fax (3) 2611339.

**Ministry of Science, Technology and the Environment** (Kementerian Sains, Teknologi dan Alam Sekitar): Wisma Sime Darby, 14th Floor, Jalan Raja Laut, 50662 Kuala Lumpur; tel. (3) 2938955; telex 28154; fax (3) 2936006.

**Ministry of Transport** (Kementerian Pengangkutan): Wisma Perdana, 5th–7th Floors, 50616 Kuala Lumpur; tel. (3) 2548122; telex 30999; fax (3) 2557041.

**Ministry of Works** (Kementerian Kerja Raya): Jalan Sultan Salahuddin, 50580 Kuala Lumpur; tel. (3) 2919011; telex 30415; fax (3) 2921202.

MALAYSIA

**Ministry of Youth and Sports** (Kementerian Belia dan Sukan): Block K, Pusat Bandar Damansara, 7th Floor, 50570 Kuala Lumpur; tel. (3) 2552255; fax (3) 2556506.

## Legislature

### PARLIAMENT

#### Dewan Negara
(Senate)

The Senate has 70 members, of whom 30 are elected. Each State Legislative Assembly and Federal Territory elects two members. The Supreme Head of State appoints the remaining 40 members.

**Speaker:** Tan Sri BENEDICT STEPHENS.

#### Dewan Rakyat
(House of Representatives)

The House of Representatives has a total of 180 members; 132 from Peninsular Malaysia (including seven from Kuala Lumpur), 27 from Sarawak and 21 from Sabah (including one from the island of Labuan).

In October 1992 the legislature approved an amendment to the Constitution, which was to take effect at the next general election, increasing the number of parliamentary constituencies from 180 to 192.

**Speaker:** Tan Sri MUHAMMAD ZAHIR ISMAIL.
**Deputy Speaker:** ONG TEE KEAT.

**General Election, 24–25 April 1995**

| Party | Seats |
|---|---|
| Barisan Nasional (National Front) | 162 |
|    United Malays National Organization | 88 |
|    Malaysian Chinese Association | 30 |
|    Sarawak National Front parties | 26 |
|    Malaysian Indian Congress | 7 |
|    Gerakan Rakyat Malaysia | 7 |
|    Sabah National Front parties | 4 |
| Democratic Action Party | 9 |
| Parti Bersatu Sabah | 8 |
| Parti Islam Sa-Malaysia | 7 |
| Semangat '46 | 6 |
| **Total** | **192** |

## The States

### JOHORE
(Capital: Johore Bahru)

**Sultan:** HRH Tunku MAHMOOD ISKANDAR IBNI AL-MARHUM Sultan ISMAIL.
**Menteri Besar:** Haji ABDUL GHANI OTHMAN.
**State Legislative Assembly:** 40 seats: Barisan Nasional 40; elected April 1995.

### KEDAH
(Capital: Alor Star)

**Sultan:** HRH Tunku Haji ABDUL HALIM MU'ADZAM SHAH IBNI AL-MARHUM Sultan BADLISHAH.
**Menteri Besar:** Tan Sri Datuk Paduka Haji OSMAN AROFF.
**State Legislative Assembly:** 36 seats: Barisan Nasional 34; Parti Islam Sa-Malaysia 2; elected April 1995.

### KELANTAN
(Capital: Kota Bahru)

**Sultan:** HRH Tuanku ISMAIL PETRA IBNI AL-MARHUM Sultan YAHAYA PETRA.
**Menteri Besar:** Datuk Haji NIK ABDUL AZIZ NIK MAT.
**State Legislative Assembly:** 43 seats: Parti Islam Sa-Malaysia 24; Semangat '46 11; Barisan Nasional 8; elected April 1995.

### MALACCA
(Capital: Malacca)

**Yang di-Pertua Negeri:** HE Tan Sri Datuk Sri UTAMA SYED AHMAD Al-Haj BIN SYED MAHMUD SHAHABUDIN.
**Chief Minister:** Datuk MOHD ZIN ABDUL GHANI.
**State Legislative Assembly:** 25 seats: Barisan Nasional 22; Democratic Action Party 3; elected April 1995.

### NEGRI SEMBILAN
(Capital: Seremban)

**Regent:** Tunku Laksamana Tunku NAQUIYUDDIN IBNI Tuanku JA'AFAR.
**Menteri Besar:** Tan Sri Datuk MOHAMMED ISA BIN Datuk Haji ABDUL SAMAD.
**State Legislative Assembly:** 32 seats: Barisan Nasional 30; Democratic Action Party 2; elected April 1995.

### PAHANG
(Capital: Kuantan)

**Sultan:** HRH Haji AHMAD SHAH AL-MUSTA'IN BILLAH IBNI AL-MARHUM Sultan ABU BAKAR RI'AYATUDDIN AL-MU'ADZAM SHAH.
**Menteri Besar:** Tan Sri MOHD KHALIL YAACOB.
**State Legislative Assembly:** 38 seats: Barisan Nasional 37; Democratic Action Party 1; elected April 1995.

### PENANG
(Capital: George Town)

**Yang di-Pertua Negeri:** HE Tun Haji HAMDAN SHEIKH TAHIR.
**Chief Minister:** Dr KOH TSU KOON.
**State Legislative Assembly:** 33 seats: Barisan Nasional 32; Democratic Action Party 1; elected April 1995.

### PERAK
(Capital: Ipoh)

**Sultan:** HRH Sultan AZLAN SHAH.
**Menteri Besar:** Tan Sri Datuk Seri RAMLI NGAH BIN TALIB.
**State Legislative Assembly:** 52 seats: Barisan Nasional 51; Democratic Action Party 1; elected April 1995.

### PERLIS
(Capital: Kangar)

**Raja:** HRH Tuanku SYED PUTRA IBNI AL-MARHUM SYED HASSAN JAMALULLAIL.
**Chief Minister:** Encik SAHIDAN KASSIM.
**State Legislative Assembly:** 15 seats: all held by the Barisan Nasional; elected April 1995.

### SABAH
(Capital: Kota Kinabalu)

**Yang di-Pertua Negeri:** HE Tan Sri SAKARAN DANDAI.
**Chief Minister:** Tan Sri Datuk MOHAMED SALLEH Tun SAID KERUAK.
**State Legislative Assembly:** 54 seats: Parti Bersatu Sabah 25; Barisan Nasional 23; Nominated 6; elected February 1994. (On 18 March, owing to a series of defections from the Parti Bersatu Sabah, the Barisan Nasional formed a new administration.)

### SARAWAK
(Capital: Kuching)

**Yang di-Pertua Negeri:** HE Datuk Patinggi Haji AHMAD ZAIDI ADRUCE BIN MUHAMMED NOOR.
**Chief Minister:** Tan Sri Datuk Patinggi Amar Haji ABDUL TAIB MAHMUD.
**State Legislative Assembly:** 56 seats: all held by the Barisan Nasional; elected September 1991.

### SELANGOR
(Capital: Shah Alam)

**Sultan:** HRH Sultan SALAHUDDIN ABDUL AZIZ SHAH Al-Haj IBNI AL-MARHUM Sultan HISAMUDDIN ALAM SHAH Al-Haj.
**Menteri Besar:** Tan Sri Dato' MOHAMMED Haji MOHAMMED TAIB.
**State Legislative Assembly:** 48 seats: Barisan Nasional 45; Democratic Action Party 3; elected April 1995.

### TRENGGANU
(Capital: Kuala Trengganu)

**Sultan:** HRH MAHMUD AL-MUKTAFI BILLAH SHAH IBNI AL-MARHUM Tuanku Sultan ISMAIL NASIRUDDIN SHAH.
**Menteri Besar:** Tan Sri Datuk Amar Seri Di Raja Haji WAN MOKHTAR BIN AHMAD.
**State Legislative Assembly:** 32 seats: Barisan Nasional 25; Parti Islam Sa-Malaysia 7; elected April 1995.

MALAYSIA

## Political Organizations

**Angkatan Perpaduan Ummah (APU)** (Muslim Unity Movement): f. 1989; an opposition coalition of four parties:

**Barisan Jama'ah Islamiah Sa-Malaysia (Berjasa)** (Front Malaysian Islamic Council—FMIC): Kelantan; f. 1977; pro-Islamic; 50,000 mems; Pres. Dato' Haji WAN HASHIM BIN Haji WAN ACHMED; Sec.-Gen. MAHMUD ZUHDI BIN Haji ABDUL MAJID.

* **Parti Hisbul Muslimin Malaysia (Hamim)** (Islamic Front of Malaysia): Kota Bahru, Kelantan; f. 1983 as an alternative party to PAS; Pres. Datuk ASRI MUDA.

**Parti Islam Sa-Malaysia (PAS)** (Pan-Malaysian Islamic Party): Markaz Tarbiyyah PAS Pusat, Lorong Haji Hassan, off Jalan Batu Geliga, Kuala Lumpur; tel. (3) 6895612; f. 1951; seeks to establish an Islamic state; 300,000 mems; Pres. FADZIL NOR; Sec.-Gen. HALIM ARSHAT.

* **Semangat '46** (Spirit of 1946): f. 1989; 'breakaway' group from UMNO after its deregistration in 1988; Pres. Tunku RAZALEIGH HAMZAH.

**Barisan Nasional (BN)** (National Front): Pejabat Timbalan Perdana Menteri, Jabatan Perdanan Menteri, Jalan Dato' Onn, 50502 Kuala Lumpur; tel. (3) 984895; f. 1973; the governing multiracial coalition of 14 parties; Sec.-Gen. Dato' MOHAMED RAHMAT. Comprises:

**Angkatan Keadilan Rakyat (AKAR)** (People's Justice Movement): Paramount Industrial Centre, Lot 3, Ground Floor, Kolombong Rd, 88100 Kota Kinabalu, Sabah; tel. (88) 428779; Dusun-based breakaway faction of the PBS; Leaders Dato' MARK KODING, KALAKAU UNTOL, PENDIKAR AMIN Haji MULIA.

**Gerakan Rakyat Malaysia (GERAKAN)** (Malaysian People's Movement): 10–12, Jalan 1/77B, off Changkat Thambi Dollah, 55100 Kuala Lumpur; tel. (3) 2417855; fax (3) 2485648; f. 1968; 140,000 mems; Pres. Dato' Seri Dr LIM KENG YAIK; Sec.-Gen. Tan Sri Dato' CHAN CHOONG TAK.

**Liberal Democratic Party:** Sabah; Chinese-dominated.

**Malaysian Chinese Association (MCA):** Wisma MCA, 8th Floor, 163 Jalan Ampang, POB 10626, 50720 Kuala Lumpur; tel. (3) 2618044; telex 33278; fax (3) 2619772; f. 1949; c. 500,000 mems; Pres. Datuk Seri Dr LING LIONG SIK.

**Malaysian Indian Congress (MIC):** Menara Manickavasagam, 6th Floor, 1 Jalan Rahmat, 50350 Kuala Lumpur; tel. (3) 4424377; f. 1946; 401,000 mems (1992); Pres. Dato' Seri S. SAMY VELLU; Sec.-Gen. Dato' G. VADIVELOO.

**Parti Bansa Dayak Sarawak (PBDS)** (Sarawak Native People's Party): Kuching, Sarawak; f. 1983 by fmr mems of Sarawak National Party; Pres. Dato' LEO MOGGIE ANAK IROK; Vice-Pres. Datuk DANIEL TAJEM.

**Parti Bersatu Rakyat Sabah (PBRS)** (United Sabah People's Party): Kota Kinabalu, Sabah; f. 1994; breakaway faction of PBS; mostly Christian Kadazans; Leader Datuk JOSEPH KURUP.

**Parti Demokratik Sabah (PDS)** (Sabah Democratic Party): Kota Kinabalu, Sabah; f. 1994; breakaway faction of PBS; mostly Christian Kadazans; Leader Datuk BERNARD DOMPOK.

**Parti Pesaka Bumiputera Bersatu (PBB)** (United Bumiputra Party): Jalan Satok/Kulas, 93400 Kuching, Sarawak; f. 1983; Pres. Tan Sri Datuk Patinggi Amar Haji ABDUL TAIB MAHMUD; Dep. Pres. Datuk ALFRED JABU AK NUMPANG.

**People's Progressive Party of Malaysia (PPP):** 43 Jalan Station, 1st Floor, 3000 Ipoh, Perak; tel. (5) 518837; f. 1955; Pres. MAK HON KAM.

**Sabah Progressive Party (SAPP):** Kota Kinabalu, Sabah; f. 1994; breakaway faction of PBS; Chinese-dominated; Pres. Datuk YONG TECK LEE.

**Sarawak National Action Party (SNAP):** 304–305 Mei Jun Bldg, Rubber Rd, POB 2960, 93758 Kuching, Sarawak; tel. (82) 254244; f. 1961; Pres. Datuk Amar JAMES WONG KIM MIN; Sec.-Gen. Encik PETER GANI AK KIAI.

**Sarawak United People's Party (SUPP):** 7 Central Rd West, POB 454, 93710 Kuching, Sarawak; tel. (82) 246999; fax (82) 256510; f. 1959; Pres. Tan Sri Datuk Amar Dr WONG SOON KAI; Sec.-Gen. Datuk Dr GEORGE CHAN HONG NAM.

**United Malays National Organization** (Pertubuhan Kebangsaan Melayu Bersatu)—**UMNO Baru** (New UMNO): Menara Dato' Onn, 38th Floor, Jalan Tun Dr Ismail, 50480 Kuala Lumpur; fax (3) 4420273; f. 1988 to replace the original UMNO (f. 1946) which had been declared an illegal organization, owing to the participation of unregistered branches in party elections in April 1987; Supreme Council of 42 mems; 1.7m. mems; Pres. Dato' Seri Dr MAHATHIR MOHAMAD; Dep. Pres. Dato' Seri ANWAR IBRAHIM; Sec.-Gen. Dato' MOHAMED RAHMAT.

**Angkatan Democratic Liberal Sabah (Adil):** Sabah; intended primarily to attract Malay Muslims.

**Angkatan Keadilan Insan Malaysia (AKIM)** (Malaysian Justice Movement): f.1995; formed by former members of PAS and Semangat '46; Pres. CHE GU MUSA SALIH.

**Bersatu Rakyat Jelata Sabah (BERJAYA)** (Sabah People's Union): Natikar Bldg, 1st Floor, POB 2130, Kota Kinabalu, Sabah; f. 1975; 400,000 mems; Pres. Haji MOHAMMED NOOR MANSOOR.

* **Democratic Action Party (DAP):** 24 Rd 20/9, Petaling Jaya, Selangor; tel. (3) 7578022; fax (3) 7575718; f. 1966; main opposition party; advocates multiracial society based on democratic socialism; 12,000 mems; Chair. Dr CHEN MAN HIN; Sec.-Gen. LIM KIT SIANG.

**Democratic Malaysia Indian Party (DMIP):** f. 1985; Leader V. GOVINDARAJ.

* **Indian Progressive Front (IPF):** Kuala Lumpur.

* **Kongres Indian Muslim Malaysia (KIMMA):** Kuala Lumpur; tel. (3) 2324759; f. 1977; aims to unite Malaysian Indian Muslims politically; 25,000 mems; Pres. AHAMED ELIAS; Sec.-Gen. MOHAMMED ALI BIN Haji NAINA MOHAMMED.

* **Malaysian Solidarity Party:** Kuala Lumpur.

**Parti Bersatu Sabah (PBS)** (Sabah United Party): Kota Kinabalu, Sabah; f. 1985; mostly Christian Kadazans; Pres. Datuk Seri JOSEPH PAIRIN KITINGAN.

**Parti Ikatan Masyarakat Islam** (Islamic Alliance Party): Trengganu.

**Parti Kadazan Asli Sabah (PKAS):** Sabah; f. 1985.

**Parti Keadilan Masyarakat (PEKEMAS)** (Social Justice Party): Kuala Lumpur; f. 1971 by fmr mems of GERAKAN; Chair. SHAHARYDDIN DAHALAN.

**Parti Kongres Sarawak (PKS):** Sarawak; f. 1985.

**Parti Nasionalis Malaysia (NasMa):** f. 1985; multiracial; Leader ZAINAB YANG.

**Parti Rakyat Jati Sarawak (PAJAR)** (Sarawak Native People's Party): 22A Bampeylde Rd, 93200 Kuching, Sarawak; f. 1978; Leader ALI KAWI.

**Parti Rakyat Sabah** (Sabah People's Party): Kota Kinabalu, Sabah; f. 1989; Leader Datuk JAMES ONGKILI.

* **Parti Rakyat Malaysia (PRM):** Kuala Lumpur; f. 1955; named Parti Sosialis Rakyat Malaya from 1970–90; Pres. SYED HUSIN ALI.

**Persatuan Rakyat Malaysian Sarawak (PERMAS)** (Malaysian Sarawak Party): Kuching, Sarawak; f. March 1987 by fmr mems of PBB; Leader Haji BUJANG ULIS.

**Pertubuhan Bumiputera Bersatu Sarawak (PBBS)** (United Sarawak National Association): Kuala Lumpur; f. 1986; Chair. Haji WAN HABIB SYED MAHMUD.

**Pertubuhan Rakyat Sabah Bersatu** (United Sabah People's Organization—USPO): Tingkat 3, 9 Jalan Bendahara, Berjaya, Kampong Ayer, POB 993, Kota Kinabalu, Sabah.

**Sabah Chinese Party (PCS):** Kota Kinabalu, Sabah; f. 1986; Pres. Encik FRANCIS LEONG.

**Sabah Chinese Consolidated Party (SCCP):** POB 704, Kota Kinabalu, Sabah; f. 1964; 14,000 mems; Pres. JOHNNY SOON; Sec.-Gen. CHAN TET ON.

**Sarawak People's Organization (SAPO):** Miri, Sarawak; mainly Chinese support; Sec.-Gen. RAYMOND SEZTU.

**Setia** (Sabah People's United Democratic Party): Sabah; f. 1994.

**United Malaysian Indian Party:** aims to promote unity and economic and social advancement of the Indian community; Sec. KUMAR MANOHARAN.

* Member of the **Gagasan Rakyat** (People's Might), an opposition coalition comprising six parties; Chair. Tunku RAZALEIGH HAMZAH.

## Diplomatic Representation

### EMBASSIES AND HIGH COMMISSIONS IN MALAYSIA

**Argentina:** 3 Jalan Semantan 2, Damansara Heights, POB 11200, 50738 Kuala Lumpur; tel. (3) 2550176; telex 31854; fax (3) 2552706; Ambassador: Dr EDUARDO ALBERTO SADOUS.

**Australia:** 6 Jalan Yap Kwan Seng, 50450 Kuala Lumpur; tel. (3) 2423122; telex 30260; fax (3) 2415773; High Commissioner: JOHN DAUTH.

**Austria:** MUI Plaza Bldg, 7th Floor, Jalan P. Ramlee, POB 10154, 50704 Kuala Lumpur; tel. (3) 2484277; telex 31263; fax (3) 2489813; Ambassador: Dr UDO EHRLICH-ADAM.

**Bangladesh:** 204–1 Jalan Ampang, 50450 Kuala Lumpur; tel. (3) 2423271; telex 31593; High Commissioner: FAROOQ SOBHAN.

**Belgium:** 12 Lorong Yap Kwan Seng, 50450 Kuala Lumpur; POB 10558, 50718 Kuala Lumpur; tel. (3) 2625733; telex 30044; fax (3) 2625922; Ambassador: ERIC DUCHÊNE.

## MALAYSIA

**Bolivia:** 12 Lorong Yap Kwan Seng, Kuala Lumpur; tel. (3) 2425146; Chargé d'affaires: Dr Francisco Blacutt.

**Brazil:** 22 Pesiaran Damansara Endah, Damansara Heights, 50490 Kuala Lumpur; tel. (3) 2548607; telex 31574; fax (3) 2555086; Ambassador: Sergio Damasceno Vieira.

**Brunei:** Wisma Sin Heap Lee, 8th Floor, Jalan Tun Razak, 50400 Kuala Lumpur; tel. (3) 2612800; fax (3) 2612898; High Commissioner: Pengiran Haji Vaya bin Pengiran Haji Rajid.

**Canada:** Plaza MBf, 7th Floor, Jalan Ampang, POB 10990, 50732 Kuala Lumpur; tel. (3) 261-2000; telex 30269; fax (3) 2613428; High Commissioner: John P. Bell.

**China, People's Republic:** 229 Jalan Ampang, 50450 Kuala Lumpur; tel. (3) 2428495; Ambassador: Qian Jinchang.

**Czech Republic:** 32 Jalan Mesra, off Jalan Ampang, 55000 Kuala Lumpur; tel. (3) 2427185; telex 30669; fax (3) 2412727; Chargé d'affaires: Jaromir Deyl.

**Denmark:** Wisma Angkasa Raya, 22nd Floor, 123 Jalan Ampang, POB 10908, 50728 Kuala Lumpur; tel. (3) 2416088; telex 30427; fax (3) 2423732; Ambassador: Henning Kristiansen.

**Egypt:** 28 Lingkungan U Thant, POB 12004, 55000 Kuala Lumpur; tel. (3) 4568184; telex 31196; fax (3) 4573515; Ambassador: Ahmed Nazmi Moustafa.

**Finland:** Plaza MBf, 15th Floor, Jalan Ampang, POB 10909, 50728 Kuala Lumpur; tel. (3) 261-1088; telex 31535; fax (3) 2615354; Ambassador: Ilkka Vilho Ruso.

**France:** 192 Jalan Ampang, 50450 Kuala Lumpur; tel. (3) 2484122; telex 30436; Ambassador: Thierry Reynard.

**Germany:** 3 Jalan U Thant, POB 10023, 50700 Kuala Lumpur; tel. (3) 2429666; telex 30380; fax (3) 2413943; Ambassador: Wilfried Vogeler.

**India:** Wisma Selangor Dredging, 20th Floor, West Block, 142c, Jalan Ampang, 50450 Kuala Lumpur; tel. (3) 261700; telex 30317; fax (3) 2617301; High Commissioner: Rajendra Singh Rathore.

**Indonesia:** 233 Jalan Tun Razak, POB 10889, 50400 Kuala Lumpur; tel. (3) 9842011; telex 30258; fax (3) 9847908; Ambassador: Sudarmadi.

**Iran:** 1 Lorong U Thant Satu, 55000 Kuala Lumpur; tel. (3) 4514824; telex 02117; Ambassador: Mohammed-Reza Morshedzadeh.

**Iraq:** 2 Jalan Langgak Golf, off Jalan Tun Razak, POB 12022, 55000 Kuala Lumpur; tel. (3) 2480555; telex 30328; fax (3) 2414331; Ambassador: Hisham Tabaqchali.

**Italy:** 99 Jalan U Thant, 55000 Kuala Lumpur; tel. (3) 4565122; telex 30797; fax (3) 4573199; Ambassador: Luca Daniele Biolato.

**Japan:** 11 Pesiaran Stonor, off Jalan Tun Razak, 50450 Kuala Lumpur; tel. (3) 2427044; telex 30385; fax (3) 2426570; Ambassador: Fukuda Hiroshi.

**Kazakhstan:** Kuala Lumpur; Chargé d'affaires: Murat Munataev.

**Korea, Democratic People's Republic:** 203 Jalan Ampang, Kuala Lumpur; tel. (3) 2420650; telex 30995; Ambassador: Kim Jin Ok.

**Korea, Republic:** Wisma MCA, 22nd Floor, 163 Jalan Ampang, 50450 Kuala Lumpur; tel. (3) 2621385; fax (3) 2623108; Ambassador: Chung Kyung Yil.

**Libya:** 6 Jalan Madge, Kuala Lumpur; tel. (3) 2432112; Secretary: Ali Suleiman Alaujali.

**Myanmar:** 7 Jalan U Thant, 55000 Kuala Lumpur; tel. (3) 2423863; Ambassador: U Ko.

**Netherlands:** 4 Jalan Mesra, POB 10543, 50716 Kuala Lumpur; tel. (3) 2485151; telex 30330; fax (3) 2411959; Ambassador: G. Th. E. R. Arnold.

**New Zealand:** Menara IMC, 21st Floor, 8 Jalan Sultan Ismail, POB 12003, 50764 Kuala Lumpur; tel. (3) 2382533; fax (3) 2380387; High Commissioner: Timothy J. Hannah.

**Nigeria:** 14 Jalan U Thant, off Jalan Tun Razak, 55000 Kuala Lumpur; tel. (3) 2484526; High Commissioner: Alhaji Abdulrahman Gara.

**Pakistan:** 132 Jalan Ampang, 50450 Kuala Lumpur; tel. (3) 2418877; telex 33289; fax (3) 2415958; High Commissioner: K. A. Aziz Khan.

**Philippines:** 1 Changkat Kia Peng, 50450 Kuala Lumpur; tel. (3) 2484233; fax (3) 2483576; Ambassador: Alberto Encomienda.

**Poland:** 495, Bt 4½, Jalan Ampang, 68000 Ampang; tel. (3) 4576733; telex 33291; fax (3) 4570123; Chargé d'affaires: Tomasz Kozlowski.

**Romania:** 114 Jalan Damai, off Jalan Ampang, 55000 Kuala Lumpur; tel. (3) 2423172; telex 30362; fax (3) 2448713; Ambassador: Eugen Popa.

**Russia:** 263 Jalan Ampang, 50450 Kuala Lumpur; tel. (3) 4560009; telex 26073; fax (3) 4576091; Ambassador: Vitaliy Vorobyev.

**Saudi Arabia:** 11 Jalan Ampang, 55000 Kuala Lumpur; tel. (3) 4579433; telex 30795; Ambassador: Sheikh Muhammad al-Hamad al-Shubaili.

**Singapore:** 209 Jalan Tun Razak, 50400 Kuala Lumpur; tel. (3) 2616277; telex 30320; High Commissioner: Low Choon Ming.

**South Africa:** c/o Kuala Lumpur Hilton Hotel, Lower Lobby, Jalan Sultan Ismail, POB 10577, Kuala Lumpur 50718; tel. (3) 2455841; Chargé d'affaires: Henry Raubenheimer.

**Sri Lanka:** 2A Jalan Ampang Hilir, 55000 Kuala Lumpur; tel. (3) 4510000; telex 31534; fax (3) 4513850; High Commissioner: C. Raajadurai.

**Sweden:** Wisma Angkasa Raya, 6th Floor, Jalan Ampang, POB 10239, 50708 Kuala Lumpur; tel. (3) 2485433; telex 30315; fax (3) 2486325; Ambassador: Percy Westerlund.

**Switzerland:** POB 12008, 50764 Kuala Lumpur; tel. (3) 2480622; telex 31155; fax (3) 2480935; Ambassador: Henri Cuennet.

**Thailand:** 206 Jalan Ampang, Kuala Lumpur; tel. (3) 2488222; telex 31566; Ambassador: Dr Chawan Chawanid.

**Turkey:** 118 Jalan U Thant, 55000 Kuala Lumpur; tel. (3) 4572225; telex 31245; Ambassador: Yalcin Tug.

**United Kingdom:** 185 Jalan Ampang, 50450 Kuala Lumpur; tel. (3) 2482122; fax (3) 2480880; High Commissioner: David J. Moss.

**USA:** 376 Jalan Tun Razak, POB 10035, 50700 Kuala Lumpur; tel. (3) 2489011; telex 32956; fax (3) 2435207; Ambassador: Paul M. Cleveland.

**Viet Nam:** 4 Pesiaran Stonor, 50450 Kuala Lumpur; tel. (3) 2484036; Ambassador: Ngo Tat To.

**Zimbabwe:** 85 Jalan Ampang, Hilir, 55000 Kuala Lumpur; tel. (3) 4516779; fax (3) 4517252; Ambassador: D. C. Chigiga.

# Judicial System

The two High Courts, one in Peninsular Malaysia and the other in Sabah and Sarawak, have original, appellate and revisional jurisdiction as the federal law provides. Above these two High Courts is the Federal Court (formerly the Supreme Court) which has, to the exclusion of any other court, jurisdiction in any dispute between states or between the Federation and any state; and has special jurisdiction as to the interpretation of the Constitution. In 1994 a 10-member Court of Appeal was created under a constitutional amendment, replacing the right of appeal to the Privy Council in the United Kingdom; which was ended in 1985. There is also a right of appeal from the High Courts to the Federal Court. The High Courts each consist of the Chief Judge (formerly Chief Justice) and a number of Judges. The Federal Court consists of the Chief Justice (formerly the Lord President) together with the two Chief Judges of the High Courts and seven Federal Court Judges. The Chief Justice and Judges of the Federal Court, and the Chief Judges and Judges of the High Courts, are appointed by the Yang di-Pertuan Agong on the advice of the Prime Minister, after consulting the Conference of Rulers.

The Sessions Courts, which are situated in the principal urban and rural centres, are presided over by a Sessions Judge, who is a member of the Federation Legal and Judicial Service and is a qualified barrister or a Bachelor of Law from any of the recognized universities. Their criminal jurisdiction covers the less serious indictable offences, excluding those that carry the death penalty. Civil cases are heard without a jury. Civil jurisdiction of a Sessions Judge's Court is up to RM 100,000. The Sessions Judges are appointed by the Yang di-Pertuan Agong.

The Magistrates' Courts are also found in the main urban and rural centres and have both civil and criminal jurisdiction, although of a more restricted nature than that of the Sessions Courts. The Magistrates consist of officers from the Federation Legal and Judicial Service. They are appointed by the heads of the states in which they officiate on the recommendation of the Chief Judge.

In March 1988 the Government obtained parliamentary approval for two constitutional amendments: allowing the State to choose which judges should consider a certain case; and forbidding judges and magistrates from interpreting the law, but restricting them to apportioning guilt and applying precise penalties, as determined by the legislature. The Supreme Court (now the Federal Court) was not mentioned in the amendments, and is assumed to be exempt from their provisions.

**Federal Court of Malaysia:** Bangunan Sultan Abdul Samad, Jalan Raja, 50506 Kuala Lumpur; tel. (3) 2939011; telex 33548; fax (3) 2932582.

**Chief Justice of the Federal Court:** Tun Abdul Hamid Omar.

**Chief Judge of the High Court in Peninsular Malaysia:** Tan Sri Mohd Eusoff Chin.

**Chief Judge of the High Court in Sabah and Sarawak:** Tan Sri Datuk Mohd Jemuri Serjan.

**Attorney-General:** Datuk Mohtar Abdullah.

MALAYSIA

## Religion

Islam is the established religion but freedom of religious practice is guaranteed. Almost all ethnic Malays are Muslims, representing 53% of the total population in 1985. In Peninsular Malaysia 19% followed Buddhism (19% in Sarawak and 8% in Sabah), 7% were Christians (29% in Sarawak and 24% in Sabah), and Chinese faiths, including Confucianism and Daoism, were followed by 11.6%. Sikhs and other religions accounted for 0.5%, while 2%, mostly in Sabah and Sarawak, were animists.

**Malaysian Consultative Council of Buddhism, Christianity, Hinduism and Sikhism:** a non-Muslim group.

### ISLAM

**President of the Majlis Islam:** Datuk Haji MOHD FAUZI BIN Haji ABDUL HAMID, Kuching, Sarawak.

### CHRISTIANITY

**Majlis Gereja-Gereja Malaysia** (Council of Churches of Malaysia): 26 Jalan University, 46200 Petaling Jaya, Selangor; tel. (3) 7567092; fax (3) 7560353; f. 1947; 17 mem. churches; 7 associate mems; Pres. Dr DENIS C. DUTTON; Hon. Gen. Sec. VARGHESE GEORGE.

#### The Anglican Communion

Malaysia comprises three Anglican dioceses, all subordinate to the Archbishop of Canterbury, the Primate of All England.

**Bishop of Kuching:** Rt Rev. Datuk JOHN LEONG CHEE YUN, Bishop's House, POB 347, 93704 Kuching, Sarawak; tel. (82) 240187; fax (82) 426488; has jurisdiction over Sarawak, Brunei and part of Indonesian Kalimantan (Borneo).

**Bishop of Sabah:** Rt Rev. YONG PING CHUNG, Bishop's House, Jalan Tangki, POB 10811, 88809 Kota Kinabalu, Sabah; fax (88) 245942.

**Bishop of West Malaysia:** (vacant) Bishop's House, 14 Pesiaran Stonor, 50450 Kuala Lumpur; tel. (3) 2427303; fax (3) 2416460.

#### The Baptist Church

**Malaysia Baptist Convention:** 2 Jalan 2/38, 46000 Petaling Jaya, Selangor; tel. (3) 7923564; fax (3) 7933603; Chair. LEOW KAM FATT.

#### The Methodist Church

**Methodist Church in Malaysia:** 23 Jalan Mayang, 50450 Kuala Lumpur; tel. (3) 2622444; fax (3) 2611388; 100,000 mems; Bishop Dr DENIS C. DUTTON.

#### The Presbyterian Church

**Presbyterian Church in Malaysia:** Joyful Grace Church, Jalan Alsagoff, 82000 Pontian, Johore; tel. (7) 711390; fax (7) 324384; Pastor TITUS KIM KAH TECK.

#### The Roman Catholic Church

Malaysia comprises two archdioceses and six dioceses, with an estimated 592,251 adherents at the end of December 1993, approximately 3.1% of the population.

**Catholic Bishops' Conference of Malaysia, Singapore and Brunei:** 2 km Jalan Subang, Batu Tiga, 40000 Shah Alam, Selangor; tel. and fax (3) 5596803; Pres. Most Rev. PETER CHUNG HOAN TING, Archbishop of Kuching.

**Archbishop of Kuala Lumpur:** Most Rev. ANTHONY SOTER FERNANDEZ, Archbishop's House, 528 Jalan Bukit Nanas, 50250 Kuala Lumpur; tel. (3) 2388828; fax (3) 2012815.

**Archbishop of Kuching:** Most Rev. PETER CHUNG HOAN TING, Archbishop's Office, 118 Jalan Tun Abang Haji Openg, POB 940, 93781 Kuching, Sarawak; tel. (82) 242634; fax (82) 425724.

### BAHÁ'Í FAITH

**Spiritual Assembly of the Bahá'ís of Malaysia:** 4 Lorong Titiwangsa 5, off Jalan Pahang, 53200 Kuala Lumpur; tel. (3) 4235183; fax (3) 4226277; mems resident in 2,057 localities.

## The Press

### PENINSULAR MALAYSIA

#### DAILIES

##### English Language

**Business Times:** 31 Jalan Riong, 59100 Kuala Lumpur; tel. (3) 2822628; telex 30259; fax (3) 2825424; f. 1976; morning; Editor HARDEV KAUR; circ. 13,000.

*Directory*

**Malay Mail:** 31 Jalan Riong, 59100 Kuala Lumpur; tel. (3) 2745444; fax (3) 2749434; f. 1896; afternoon; Editor K. C. BOEY; circ. 70,000.

**New Straits Times:** 31 Jalan Riong, 59100 Kuala Lumpur; tel. (3) 2823322; fax (3) 2821434; f. 1945; morning; Editor A. KADIR JASIN; circ. 167,868.

**The Star:** 13 Jalan 13/6, 46200 Petaling Jaya, POB 12474, Selangor; tel. (3) 7578811; telex 37373; fax (3) 7554039; f. 1971; morning; Editor-in-Chief V. K. CHIN; circ. 161,459.

**The Sun:** Kuala Lumpur; f. 1993; Editor-in-Chief PHILEMON SOON; Editor CHEAM TOON LEE.

##### Chinese Language

**Chung Kuo Pao** (China Press): 40 Jalan Lima, off Jalan Chan Sow Lin, 55200 Kuala Lumpur; tel. (3) 2218855; fax (3) 2212810; f. 1946; Editor WONG AH LEK; Gen. Man. CHIEW POH GUAN; circ. 110,000.

**Kwong Wah Yit Poh:** 19 Presgrave St, 10300 Penang; tel. (4) 612312; fax (4) 628540; f. 1910; morning; Chief Editor SZE TOH TGAM; circ. 39,000 (weekdays), 47,000 (Sunday).

**Nanyang Siang Pau (Malaysia):** 80 Jalan Riong, 59100 Kuala Lumpur; tel. (3) 2745133; telex 30338; fax (3) 2748991; f. 1923; morning; Editor-in-Chief TEO BAK KIM; circ. 145,000 (Mon.–Sat.), 165,000 (Sunday).

**Shin Min Daily News:** 31 Jalan Riong, Bangsar, 59100 Kuala Lumpur; tel. (3) 2826363; fax (3) 2821812; f. 1966; morning; Editor-in-Chief CHENG SONG HUAT; circ. 82,000.

**Sin Chew Jit Poh (Malaysia):** 19 Jalan Semangat, POB 367, Jalan Sultan, Petaling Jaya, Selangor; tel. (3) 7582888; telex 37697; fax (3) 7570527; f. 1929; morning; Chief Editor LIEW CHEN CHUAN; circ. 210,000 (daily), 230,000 (Sunday).

##### Malay Language

**Berita Harian:** 31 Jalan Riong, 59100 Kuala Lumpur; tel. (3) 2745444; fax (3) 2749434; f. 1957; morning; Editor Encik AHMAD NAZRI ABDULLAH; circ. 250,000.

**Mingguan Perdana:** Kuala Lumpur; tel. (3) 619133; Group Chief Editor KHALID JAFRI.

**Utusan Malaysia:** 46M Jalan Lima, off Jalan Chan Sow Lin, POB 671, Kuala Lumpur; tel. (3) 2787055; fax (3) 2227876; f. 1965; morning; Editor-in-Chief ZAINUDIN MAIDIN; circ. 240,000.

##### Tamil Language

**Tamil Nesan:** 37 Jalan Ampang, POB 299, Kuala Lumpur 01-17; tel. (3) 284439; f. 1924; morning; Editor V. VIVEKANANTHAN; circ. 30,000 (daily), 60,000 (Sunday).

**Tamil Osai:** 19 Jalan Murai Dua, Batu Kompleks, Jalan Ipoh, Kuala Lumpur; tel. (3) 671644; circ. 21,000 (daily), 40,000 (Sunday).

**Tamil Thinamani:** 9 Jalan Murai Dua, Batu Kompleks, Jalan Ipoh, Kuala Lumpur; tel. (3) 66719; Editor S. NACHIAPPAN; circ. 18,000 (daily), 39,000 (Sunday).

#### SUNDAY PAPERS

##### English Language

**New Sunday Times:** 31 Jalan Riong, 59100 Kuala Lumpur; tel. (3) 2823322; fax (3) 2821434; f. 1845; morning; Editor Encik A. KADIR JASIN; circ. 225,000.

**Sunday Mail:** 31 Jalan Riong, 59100 Kuala Lumpur; tel. (3) 2822829; telex 30259; fax (3) 2821434; f. 1896; morning; Editor JOACHIM S. P. NG; circ. 99,000.

**Sunday Star:** 13 Jalan 13/6, 46200 Petaling Jaya, POB 12474, Selangor; tel. (3) 7578811; telex 37373; fax (3) 7554039; f. 1971; Editor-in-Chief V. K. CHIN; Editor MICHAEL AERIA; circ. 182,000.

##### Chinese Language

**Shin Min Sunday:** 31 Jalan Riong, 59100 Kuala Lumpur; tel. (3) 2826363; fax (3) 2821812; morning; Editor-in-Chief CHENG SONG HUAT; circ. 90,000.

##### Malay Language

**Berita Minggu:** 31 Jalan Riong, 59100 Kuala Lumpur; tel. (3) 2745444; fax (3) 2749434; f. 1957; morning; Editor Encik AHMAD NAZRI ABDULLAH; circ. 360,000.

**Mingguan Malaysia:** 46M Jalan Lima, off Jalan Chan Sow Lin, POB 671, Kuala Lumpur; tel. (3) 2787055; fax (3) 2227876; f. 1964; Editor-in-Chief ZAINUDIN MAIDIN; circ. 403,000.

**Utusan Zaman:** 46M Jalan Lima, off Jalan Chan Sow Lin, POB 671, Kuala Lumpur; tel. (3) 2787055; fax (3) 2227876; f. 1939; Editor MUSTAFA FADULA SUHAIMI; circ. 57,000.

#### PERIODICALS

##### English Language

**Aliran Monthly:** Penang; monthly; social and political; Editor P. RAMAKRISHNAN.

# MALAYSIA

**Her World:** Berita Publishing Sdn Bhd, 22 Jalan Liku, 59100 Kuala Lumpur; tel. (3) 2824322; telex 30259; fax (3) 2821605; monthly; Editor ALICE CHEE LAN NEO; circ. 35,000.

**Malaysia Warta Kerajaan Seri Paduka Baginda** (HM Government Gazette): Government Printing Dept, Jalan Chan Sow Lin, 50554 Kuala Lumpur; fortnightly.

**Malaysian Agricultural Journal:** Ministry of Agriculture, Publications Unit, Wisma Tani, Jalan Sultan Salahuddin, 50624 Kuala Lumpur; tel. (3) 2982011; telex 33045; fax (3) 2913758; f. 1901; 2 a year.

**Malaysian Digest:** c/o Ministry of Foreign Affairs, Jalan Wisma Putra, 50602 Kuala Lumpur; tel. (3) 2488088; monthly.

**Malaysian Forester:** Faculty of Forestry, Universiti Pertanian Malaysia, 43400 Serdang, Selangor; tel. (3) 9486101; telex 37454; f. 1931; quarterly; Editors NIK MUHAMAD MAJID, YUSUF HADI, ONG MENG SENG.

**The Planter:** Wisma ISP, 29–33 Jalan U Thant, POB 10262, 50708 Kuala Lumpur; tel. (3) 2425561; fax (3) 2426898; f. 1919; publ. by Inc Soc. of Planters; monthly; Editor W. T. PERERA; circ. 3,700.

### Chinese Language

**Mister Weekly:** 80M Jalan SS21/39, Damansara Utama, 47400 Petaling Jaya, Selangor; tel. (3) 7190355; telex 37122; fax (3) 7172163; f. 1976; weekly; Editor WONG AH TAI; circ. 60,000.

**New Life Post:** 80M Jalan SS21/39, Damansara Utama, 47400 Petaling Jaya, Selangor; tel. (3) 7190355; fax (3) 7172163; f. 1972; bi-weekly; Editor LOW BENG CHEE; circ. 140,000.

**New Tide Magazine:** 2 Jalan 19/1, Petaling Jaya, Selangor; f. 1974; every 3 weeks; Editor CHEONG SAW LAN; circ. 53,000.

### Malay Language

**Dewan Masyarakat:** Dewan Bahasa dan Pustaka, POB 10803, 50926 Kuala Lumpur; tel. (3) 2481011; telex 32683; f. 1963; monthly; current affairs; Editor NIK ZAINAL ABIDIN HASSAN; circ. 65,000.

**Dewan Pelajar:** Dewan Bahasa dan Pustaka, Jalan Wisma Putra, POB 10803, 50926 Kuala Lumpur; tel. (3) 2481011; fax (3) 2484208; f. 1967; monthly; children's; Editor ZALEHA HASHIM; circ. 148,000.

**Jelita:** Berita Publishing Sdn, 22 Jalan Liku, 59100 Kuala Lumpur; tel. (3) 2824322; fax (3) 2740605; monthly; fashion and beauty magazine; Editor ROHANI PA' WAN CHIK; circ. 80,000.

**Mastika:** 46M Jalan Lima, off Jalan Chan Sow Lin, Kuala Lumpur; tel. (3) 487055; monthly; Malayan illustrated magazine; Editor AZIZAH ALI; circ. 40,000.

**Pengasoh:** Majlis Ugama Islam, Kota Bahru, Kelantan; f. 1918; monthly; Editor YUSOFF ZAKY YACOB; circ. 15,000.

**Utusan Filem dan Feshen:** 46M Jalan Lima, off Jalan Chan Sow Lin, Kuala Lumpur; tel. (3) 487055; fortnightly; cinema; Editor MUSTAFA BIN ABDUL RAHIM; circ. 35,000.

**Utusan Radio dan TV:** 46M Jalan Lima, off Jalan Chan Sow Lin, Kuala Lumpur; tel. (3) 2787055; fax (3) 2227876; fortnightly; Editor NORSHAH TAMBY; circ. 89,000.

**Wanita:** 46M Jalan Lima, off Jalan Chan Sow Lin, Kuala Lumpur; tel. (3) 2787055; fax (3) 2227876; weekly; women; Editor NIK RAHIMAH HASSAN; circ. 107,000.

**Watan:** Kumpulan Akhbar Watan (KJ) Sdn Bhd, 50–52 Lorong Rahim Kajai 14, Taman Tun Dr Ismail, 60000 Kuala Lumpur; f. 1977; every three weeks; Malay and English; Editor Encik HISHAMUDDIN HAJI YAACUB; circ. 80,000.

### Punjabi Language

**Navjiwan Punjabi News:** 52 Jalan 8/18, Jalan Toman, Petaling Jaya, 46050 Selangor; tel. (3) 7565725; f. 1950; weekly; Assoc. Editor TARA SINGH; circ. 9,000.

## SABAH

### DAILIES

**Api Siang Pau** (Kota Kinabalu Commercial Press): 24 Lorong Dewan, POB 170, Kota Kinabalu; f. 1954; morning; Chinese; Editor Datuk LO KWOCK CHUEN; circ. 3,000.

**Daily Express:** News House, 16 Jalan Pasar Baru, POB 10139, 88801 Kota Kinabalu; tel. (88) 56422; telex 81134; fax (88) 238420; f. 1963; morning; English, Bahasa Malaysia and Kadazan; Editor-in-Chief EDDY AUN KHENG LOK; circ. 30,000.

**Hwa Chiaw Jit Pao** (Overseas Chinese Daily News): News House, 16 Jalan Pasar Baru, POB 10139, 88801 Kota Kinabalu; tel. (88) 52216; telex 81134; f. 1936; morning; Chinese; Editor HII YUK SENG; circ. 28,000.

**Merdeka Daily News:** POB 332, 90007 Sandakan; tel. (89) 214517; fax (89) 275537; f. 1968; morning; Chinese; Editor-in-Chief KWAN KUH HANG; circ. 19,000.

**Sabah Times:** 76 Jalan Gaya, POB 10525, 88805 Kota Kinabalu; tel. (88) 249111; fax (88) 249222; English, Malay and Kadazan; Editor-in-Chief LEE WENG CHUNG; circ. 30,000.

**Syarikat Sabah Times:** POB 10525, 88805 Kota Kinabalu; tel. (88) 52217; telex 80230; f. 1952; English, Malay and Kadazan; circ. 25,000.

**Tawau Jih Pao:** POB 464, 1072 Jalan Kuhara, Tawau; tel. (89) 72576; Chinese; Editor-in-Chief STEPHEN LAI KIM YEAN.

## SARAWAK

### DAILIES

**Berita Petang Sarawak:** 13 Jalan Gedung, 93450 Kuching; POB 1315, 93726 Kuching; tel. (82) 480771; fax (82) 489006; f. 1972; evening; Chinese; Chief Editor HWANG YU CHAI; circ. 12,000.

**Borneo Post:** 11 Island Rd, 1st Floor, POB 20, 96000 Sibu; tel. (84) 332055; telex 72070; fax (84) 310702; morning; English; Man. Dir LAU HUI SIANG; Editor NGUOI HOW YIEN; circ. 21,037.

**Chinese Daily News:** Jalan Nipah, POB 138, Kuching; tel. (82) 52036; fax (82) 420358; f. 1945; Chinese; Editor T. T. CHOW; circ. 8,000.

**International Times:** International Weekly, Lot 7778, Jalan Tun Abdul Razak, POB 1158, 93724 Kuching; tel. (82) 487778; fax (82) 480996; f. 1968; morning; Chinese; Editor LEE FOOK ONN; circ. 25,000.

**Malaysia Daily News:** 7 Island Rd, POB 237, 96009 Sibu; tel. (84) 324373; tel. (84) 326790; f. 1968; morning; Chinese; Editor WONG SENG KWONG; circ. 27,000.

**Miri Daily News:** Lot 88, Piasau Industrial Estate, POB 377, 98007 Miri; tel. (85) 652777; fax (85) 655655; f. 1957; morning; Chinese; Editor KU KIANG FAH; Man. HWANG JUN HIEN; circ. 17,000.

**The People's Mirror Sdn Bhd:** Lot 316–318, Tabuan Laru Commercial Centre, 93350 Kuching; tel. (82) 360030; fax (82) 363278; English; Editor-in-Chief B. R. ADAI; circ. 14,000.

**Sarawak Tribune and Sunday Tribune:** Jalan Nipah, Padungan, POB 138, 93700 Kuching; tel. (82) 424411; telex 70213; fax (82) 428330; f. 1945; English; Editor FRANCIS SIAH; circ. 22,000.

**See Hua Daily News:** 40 Jalan Tuanku Osman, POB 20, 96007 Sibu; tel. (84) 332055; telex 72070; fax (84) 321255; f. 1952; morning; Chinese; Man. Editor LAU HUI SIONG; circ. 60,000.

### PERIODICALS

**Pedoman Rakyat:** Malaysian Information Services, Mosque Rd, 93612, Kuching; tel. (82) 240141; f. 1956; monthly; Malay; Editor Haji MOHD RAKAWI BIN Tan Sr IKHWAN; circ. 30,000.

**Pembrita:** Malaysian Information Services, Mosque Rd, 93612 Kuching; tel. (82) 247231; f. 1950; monthly; Iban; Editor ALBAN JAWA; circ. 20,000.

**Sarawak Gazette:** Sarawak Museum, Jalan Tun Abang Haji Openg, 93566 Kuching; tel. (82) 244232; fax (82) 246680; f. 1870; quarterly; English; Chief Editor Datuk Haji TAHA ARIFFIN; circ. 1,000.

**Utusan Sarawak:** Abell Rd, POB 138, 93700 Kuching; tel. (82) 424411; fax (82) 420358; f. 1949; Malay; Editor Haji ABDUL AZIZ Haji MALIM; circ. 3,000.

### NEWS AGENCIES

**Bernama** (Malaysian National News Agency): Wisma Bernama, 28 Jalan 1/65A, off Jalan Tun Razak, POB 10024, 50700 Kuala Lumpur; tel. (3) 2939933; telex 30461; fax (3) 2981102; f. 1967; general and foreign news, economic features and photo services, public relations wire, screen information and data services, stock market on-line equities service, real-time commodity and monetary information services; daily output in Malay and English; in June 1990 Bernama was given the exclusive right to receive and distribute news in Malaysia; the process of incorporating Bernama as a company under government control was initiated in mid-1994 and was due for completion in 1996; Gen. Man. MOHAMED RAUS BORHAN; Editor-in-Chief ABDUL RAHMAN BIN Haji SULAIMAN.

### Foreign Bureaux

**Agence France-Presse (AFP):** 26 Hotel Equatorial, 1st Floor, Jalan Treacher, 2610520 Kuala Lumpur; tel. (3) 2691906; fax (3) 2615606; Correspondent MERVIN NAMBIAR.

**Associated Press (AP)** (USA): Wisma Bernama, 28 Rd 1/65A, off Jalan Tun Razak, POB 12219, Kuala Lumpur; tel. (3) 2926155; Correspondent HARI SUBRAMANIAM.

MALAYSIA — Directory

**Inter Press Service (IPS)** (Italy): 32 Jalan Mudah Barat, Taman Midah, 56000 Kuala Lumpur; tel. (3) 9716830; telex 31030; fax (3) 2612872; Correspondent (vacant).

**Press Trust of India:** 114 Jalan Limau Manis, Bangsar Park, Kuala Lumpur; tel. (3) 940673; Correspondent T. V. VENKITACHALAM.

**Thai News Agency:** 124F Burmah Rd, Penang; also Kuala Lumpur; Rep. SOOK BURANAKUL.

**United Press International (UPI)** (USA): Room 1, Ground Floor, Wisma Bernama Jalan 1/65A, 50400 Kuala Lumpur; tel. (3) 2933393; fax (3) 2913876; Rep. MARY LEIGH.

Reuters (UK) and Xinhua (People's Republic of China) are also represented in Malaysia.

### PRESS ASSOCIATION

**Persatuan Penerbit-Penerbit Akhbar Malaysia** (Malaysian Newspaper Publishers' Asscn): 75B Jalan SS21/1A, Damansara Utama, 47400 Petaling Jaya, Selangor Darul Ehsan; tel. (3) 7198195; fax (3) 7197394; Chair. ISMAIL HUSIN (1994/95).

## Publishers

### KUALA LUMPUR

**Anthonian Publishing Sdn Bhd:** 235 Jalan Brickfields, 2nd Floor, 50470 Kuala Lumpur; tel. (3) 2747166; telex 30463; f. 1949; textbooks, children's, reference, languages, fiction; Man. Dir CHEE MIN.

**Berita Publishing Sdn Bhd:** 22 Jalan Liku, Bangsar, 59100 Kuala Lumpur; tel. (3) 2824322; fax (3) 2821605; educational, professional, religious; Gen. Man. ABDUL MANAF SAAD.

**Dewan Bahasa dan Pustaka** (National Language and Literature Agency): POB 10803, 50926 Kuala Lumpur; tel. (3) 2481011; fax (3) 2442081; f. 1956; textbooks, general and children's, Malay language and literature, foreign translations; Dir-Gen. Haji SHAARI ABDULLAH (acting).

**Geetha Sdn Bhd:** 13A Jalan Kovil Hilir, Sentul, 51100 Kuala Lumpur; tel. (3) 4417073; Tamil; history, education, reference and textbooks; Man. Dir P. V. SETHU.

**Golden Books Centre Sdn Bhd:** 14 Lorong Bunus Enam, 1st Floor, off Jalan Masjid India, 50100 Kuala Lumpur; tel. (3) 2939862; fax (3) 2928035; f. 1981; legal and professional, children's books, fiction, biographies, dictionaries; Man. Dir Dr SYED IBRAHIM.

**Jabatan Penerbitan Universiti Malaya** (University of Malaya Press): University of Malaya, Lembah Pantai, 59100 Kuala Lumpur; tel. (3) 7574361; telex 39845; fax (3) 7574473; f. 1954; general fiction, literature, economics, history, medicine, politics, general and social science; Head of Dept Dr M. SIDIN AHMAD ISHAK.

**Malaya Press Sdn Bhd:** 22–24 Jalan Bukit Bintang, 55100 Kuala Lumpur; tel. (3) 2425764; f. 1958; magazines, children's, guidebooks, textbooks; Man. Dir LAI WING CHUN.

**Marican Sdn Bhd:** Kuala Lumpur; tel. (3) 2740146; telex 31697; politics, anthropology, sociology, labour, religion, history, guidebooks, dictionaries; Gen. Man. Dr Y. MANSOOR MARICAN.

**Pustaka Antara:** 399A Jalan Tuanku Abdul Rahman, 50100 Kuala Lumpur; tel. (3) 2980044; fax (3) 2917997; textbooks, children's, languages, fiction; Man. Dir Datuk ABDUL AZIZ BIN AHMAD; Gen. Man. FADZILLAH ABDUL AZIZ.

**Teks Publishing Sdn Bhd:** Kuala Lumpur; tel. (3) 7186619; school textbooks, children's, languages, fiction, general; Man. Dir TAN HAI.

**Utusan Publications and Distributors Sdn Bhd:** 46M Jalan Lima, off Jalan Chan Sow Lin, 55200 Kuala Lumpur; tel. (3) 2413945; telex 30489; school textbooks, children's, languages, fiction, general; Man. Dir Encik MAZLAN NORDIN; Man. Encik SHAMUGHIL BIN ISMAIL.

### JOHORE

**Pelangi Educational Enterprise:** 28A Jalan Abiad, Taman Tebrau Jaya, Johore Bahru, Johore; tel. (7) 323060; school textbooks, children's, languages; Mans LAI CHIN HENG, SAM CHIN YAN.

**Penerbitan Pelangi Sdn Bhd:** 64966 Jalan Pingai, Taman Pelgani, 80400 Johore Bahru; tel. (7) 3316288; fax (7) 3329201; guidebooks and reference; Man. Dir SAMUEL SUM KOWN CHEEK.

**Textbooks Malaysia Sdn Bhd:** 39 Jalan Buloh Kasap, POB 30, 85007 Segamat, Johore; tel. and fax (7) 9311181; school textbooks, children's fiction, guidebooks and reference; Man. Dir FREDDIE KHOO.

### NEGRI SEMBILAN

**Bharathi Press:** 23–24 Jalan Dato' Sheikh Ahmad, POB 74, 70700 Seremban, Negri Sembilan; tel. (6) 722911; f. 1939; Partners M. R. N. MUTHURENGAM, M. SUBRAMANIA BHARATHI.

**Minerva Publications:** 96 Jalan Dato, Bandar Tunggal, 70000 Seremban, Negri Sembilan; tel. and fax (6) 734439; f. 1964; English; Man. Dir TAJUDDIN MUHAMMED.

### PENANG

**Sino-Malay Publishing Co Ltd:** 141 Lebuh Carnarvon, 10100 Pulau Pinang; tel. (4) 22534.

**Syarikat United Book Sdn Bhd:** 187–189 Lebuh Carnarvon, 10100 Pulau Pinang; tel. (4) 61635; telex 40119; fax (4) 615063; textbooks, children's, reference, fiction, guidebooks; Man. Dir CHEW SING GUAN.

### SELANGOR

**Academia Publications:** 10 Jalan 217, Petaling Jaya, Selangor; tel. (3) 572455; textbooks; Man. CHONG THIM SIN.

**Eastview Productions Sdn Bhd:** 11 Lorong 51A/227C, 46100 Petaling Jaya, Selangor; tel. (3) 7556639; fax (3) 7550731; f. 1980; school textbooks, children's, fiction, reference, general; Man. Dir K. L. SEOW; Asst Gen. Man. T. F. PHANG.

**Federal Publications Sdn Bhd:** Lot 46, Subang Hi Tech Industrial Park, Batu Tiga, 40000 Shah Alam, Selangor; tel. (3) 7351511; fax (3) 7364620; educational, trade directories, children's magazines, guidebooks, general; Gen. Man. STEPHEN K. S. LIM.

**FEP International Sdn Bhd:** 2 Jalan SS 4D/14, POB 1091, 47301 Petaling Jaya, Selangor; tel. (3) 7036150; fax (3) 7036989; f. 1969; children's, languages, fiction, dictionaries, textbooks and reference; Man. Dir LIM MOK-HAI.

**Kompas Publishing Sdn Bhd:** 3A Jalan SS14/1, Subang Jaya, 47500 Petaling Jaya, Selangor; tel. (3) 7338892; fax (3) 7338895; Man. Dir KHOO HOCK SEE.

**Longman Malaysia Sdn Bhd:** 3 Jalan Kilang A, off Jalan Penchala, 46050 Petaling Jaya, Selangor; tel. (3) 7920466; telex 37600; fax (3) 7918005; fiction, textbooks, children's, reference, general, educational materials; Dir WONG WEE WOON.

**Macmillan Publishers (M) Sdn Bhd:** 126B, Jalan SS 24/2, Taman Megah, 47301 Petaling Jaya, Selangor; tel. (3) 7751220; fax (3) 7771971; Sales Man. LIM KUAN SENG.

**Oxford University Press:** Selangor; tel. (3) 7551744; telex 37283; fax (3) 7568119; f. 1957; academic and general; Man. NOOR AZLINA YUNUS.

**Penerbit Fajar Bakti Sdn Bhd:** 3 Jalan 13/3, Jalan Semangat, POB 1050, 46860 Petaling Jaya, Selangor; tel. (3) 7563415; fax (3) 7552190; school, college and university textbooks, children's, fiction, general; Man. Dir M. SOCKALINGAM.

**Pustaka Delta Pelajaran Sdn Bhd:** Wisma Delta, Lot 18 Jalan 51A/223, 46100 Petaling Jaya, Selangor; tel. (3) 7570000; telex 20382; fax (3) 7576688; Man. Dir LIM KIM WAH.

**Times Editions Pte Ltd:** 1st Floor, Bangunan Times Publishing, Lot 46, Subang Hi-Tech Industrial Park, Batu Tiga, 40000 Shah Alam, Selangor; tel. (3) 7363517; fax (3) 7364620; a subsidiary of Times Publishing Group; children's, languages, fiction, biography, cooking, general; Commissioning Editor CHRISTINE CHONG.

**Times Educational Sdn Bhd:** 22 Jalan 19/3, 46300 Petaling Jaya, Selangor; tel. (3) 7571766; fax (3) 7573607; textbooks, general and reference; Man. FOONG CHUI LIN.

### GOVERNMENT PUBLISHING HOUSE

**Percetakan Nasional Malaysia Bhd (Malaysia National Printing Ltd):** Jalan Chan Sow Lin, 50554 Kuala Lumpur; tel. (3) 2212022; fax (3) 2220690; fmrly the National Printing Department, incorporated as a company under govt control in January 1993.

### PUBLISHERS' ASSOCIATION

**Malaysian Book Publishers' Association:** 10 Jalan 217, 46050 Petaling Jaya, Selangor; tel. (3) 7914108; fax (3) 7910416; f. 1968; Pres. Encik HASROM BIN HARON; 105 mems.

## Radio and Television

In 1992, according to UNESCO, there were about 8,080,000 radio receivers and an estimated 2,820,000 television receivers in use.

Under the Broadcasting Act (approved in December 1987), the Minister of Information is empowered to control and monitor all radio and television broadcasting, and to revoke the licence of any private company violating the Act by broadcasting material 'conflicting with Malaysian values'.

**Radio Television Malaysia (RTM):** Dept of Broadcasting, Angkasapuri, Bukit Putra, 50614 Kuala Lumpur; tel. (3) 2825333; telex 30283 (radio), 31383 (television); fax (3) 2824735; f. 1946 (television introduced 1963); supervises radio and television broad-

MALAYSIA

casting; Dir-Gen. Jaafar Kamin; Dep. Dir-Gen. Tamimuddin Abdul Karim.

**Radio Television Malaysia (Sabah):** Jalan Tuaran, 88614 Kota Kinabalu; tel. (88) 213444; telex 80061; fax (88) 223493; f. 1955 (television introduced 1971); a dept of RTM; broadcasts programmes over two networks for 280 hours a week in Malay, English, Chinese (two dialects), Kadazan, Murut, Dusun and Bajau; Dir of Broadcasting Haji Mohd Mokhtar bin Abdul Kadir.

**Radio Television Malaysia (Sarawak):** Broadcasting House, Jalan Satok, 93614 Kuching; tel. (82) 248422; telex 70084; f. 1954; a dept of RTM; broadcasts 483 hours per week in Malay, English, Chinese, Iban, Bidayuh, Melanau, Kayan, Kenyah, Bisayah and Murut; Dir of Broadcasting Encik Amran Abdul Hamid.

### RADIO

**Radio Malaysia:** Radio Television Malaysia, POB 11272, 50740 Kuala Lumpur; tel. (3) 2823991; fax (3) 2825859; f. 1946; domestic service; operates six networks; broadcasts in Bahasa Malaysia, English, Chinese (Mandarin and other dialects), Tamil and Aborigine (Temiar and Semai dialects); Dir of Radio Madzhi Johari.

  **Suara Islam** (Voice of Islam): Islamic Affairs Division, Prime Minister's Department, Jalan Dato' Onn, 50502, Kuala Lumpur; tel. (3) 2321957; telex 33099; fax (3) 2388374; Asia-Pacific region; broadcasts in Bahasa Malaysia on Islam.

  **Suara Malaysia** (Voice of Malaysia): Radio Television Malaysia, POB 11272, 50740 Kuala Lumpur; tel. (3) 2824976; telex 30283; fax (3) 2825859; f. 1963; overseas service in Arabic, Burmese, English, Bahasa Indonesia, Chinese (Mandarin), Bahasa Malaysia, Tagalog and Thai; Controller of Overseas Service Yong Rafidah Yaacob.

**Rediffusion (Malaya) Sdn Bhd:** Rediffusion House, 17 Jalan Pahang, POB 570, 53000 Kuala Lumpur; tel. (3) 4424544; telex 30080; fax (3) 4424614; f. 1949; two programmes; 41,901 subscribers in Kuala Lumpur; 10,856 subscribers in Penang; 6,146 subscribers in Province Wellesley; 20,253 subscribers in Ipoh; Gen. Man. James Chiam Shuh Min.

**Time Highway Radio:** Kuala Lumpur; f. 1994; serves Kuala Lumpur region; broadcasts in English; Chief Exec. Hisham Rahman.

### TELEVISION

**Television Malaysia:** Radio Television Malaysia, Angkasapuri, Kuala Lumpur 22-10; tel. (3) 2745333; telex 31383; fax (3) 2304735; f. 1963; operates two national networks; Controller of Programmes Ismail Mohamed Jah.

**TV 3 (Sistem Televisyen Malaysia Bhd):** Bangunan KUB, 7th–9th Floors, No. 1 Lorong Kapar, off Jalan Syed Putra, 58000 Kuala Lumpur; tel. (3) 2743111; telex 33014; fax (3) 2748896; f. 1983; Malaysia's first private television network, began broadcasting in 1984; Chair. Dato' M. Noor Azam; Chief Operating Officer Shamsul Khalid Ismail.

In June 1993 the Government selected four local companies to form a consortium to operate a second commercial station, TV4. Malaysia's first satellite, Measat 1, was scheduled to be launched in September 1995.

## Finance

(cap. = capital; auth. = authorized; res = reserves; dep. = deposits; m. = million; brs = branches; amounts in ringgit Malaysia)

### BANKING

At 31 December 1990 there were 23 domestic commercial banks, 12 merchant banks, 16 foreign banks and 44 local finance companies operating in Malaysia.

#### Central Bank

**Bank Negara Malaysia:** Jalan Dato' Onn, POB 10922, 50480 Kuala Lumpur; tel. (3) 2988044; telex 30201; fax (3) 2912990; f. 1959; bank of issue; cap. 100m., dep. 40,612.7m. (Dec. 1992); Gov.Tan Sri Dato' Jaffar bin Hussein; Dep. Gov. Tan Sri Dato' Dr Lin See Yan; 11 brs.

#### Commercial Banks
Peninsular Malaysia

**Ban Hin Lee Bank Bhd:** 43 Lebuh Pantai, 10300 Penang; POB 232, 10720 Penang; tel. (4) 2623434; telex 40087; fax (4) 2623601; f. 1935; cap. 112m., dep. 2,600m. (Dec. 1994); Chair. and Chief Exec. Dato' Goh Eng Toon; 35 brs.

**Bank Bumiputra Malaysia Bhd:** Menara Bumiputra, Jalan Melaka, 50100 Kuala Lumpur; POB 10407, 50913 Kuala Lumpur; tel. (3) 2988011; telex 30445; fax (3) 2987264; f. 1965; state-owned; cap. 1,150m., dep. 20,754m. (March 1993); Chair. Tan Sri Datuk Abdul Khalid Sahan; Exec. Dir. Abdul Aziz Othman; 168 brs.

**Bank Buruh (Malaysia) Bhd:** Bangunan Kuwasa, 24th Floor, 5 Jalan Raja Laut, 50350 Kuala Lumpur; tel. (3) 2934566; telex 31269; fax (3) 2936308; f. 1975; cap. 49.1m., dep. 925.2m. (June 1992); Chair. Tan Sri Datuk Haji Rozhan bin Haji Kuntom; Exec. Dir Tan Sri Dato' R. V. Navaratnam; 4 brs.

**Bank of Commerce (M) Bhd:** 6 Jalan Tun Perak, POB 10753, 50724 Kuala Lumpur; tel. (3) 2931722; telex 30454; fax (3) 2912030; f. 1991, following merger of the United Asian Bank and Bank of Commerce; cap. 356.3m., dep. 9,041.2m. (Dec. 1993); Chair. Tan Sri Radin Soenarno Al-Haj; Pres. Mohamed Nor bin Mohamed Yusof; 41 brs.

**Bank Pembangunan Malaysia Bhd:** Menara Bank Pembangunan, POB 12352, Jalan Sultan Ismail, 50774 Kuala Lumpur; tel. (3) 2913399; telex 30058; fax (3) 2928520; f. 1973; cap. 105.5m., dep. 476.2m. (Dec. 1993); Chair. Tan Sri Dato' Dr Haji A. Hamid Haji A. Rahman; Man Dir. and CEO Nik Ibrahim bin Nik Abdullah; 13 brs.

**Development and Commercial Bank Bhd:** Wisma On-Tai, 18th Floor, 161B, Jalan Ampang, 50450 Kuala Lumpur; POB 10145, 50907 Kuala Lumpur; tel. (3) 2617177; telex 31032; fax (3) 2619541; f. 1965; cap. 386.4m., dep. 9,527.9m. (Dec. 1993); Chair. Tan Sri Geh Ik Cheong; CEO Tuan Haji Ismail bin Zakaria; 52 brs.

**EON Bank Bhd:** Wisma Cyclecarri, 11th Floor, 288 Jalan Raja Laut, 50350, Kuala Lumpur; POB 12996, 50796 Kuala Lumpur; tel. (3) 2941188; telex 36835; fax (3) 2985163; f. 1963; fmrly Kong Ming Bank Bhd; cap. 100m., dep. 664.0m. (Dec. 1993); Chair. Rin Kei Mei; Dir and CEO Kok Nam Soon; 19 brs.

**Kwong Yik Bank Bhd:** 75 Jalan Tun H. S. Lee, 50000 Kuala Lumpur; tel. (3) 2325633; fax (3) 2387227; f. 1913; cap. 250.0m., dep. 3,574.7m. (June 1993); Chair. Dato' Mohamed Basir bin Ahmad; Exec. Dir Dato' Mohamed Yusof Haji Nassir; 53 brs.

**Malayan Banking Bhd:** 100 Jalan Tun Perak, 50050 Kuala Lumpur; tel. (3) 2347783; telex 30438; fax (3) 2322504; f. 1960; cap. 758.3m., dep. 35,693.0m. (June 1993); Chair. Tan Sri Hashim bin Aman; Man. Dir Ahmad Mohd Don; 253 brs.

**Malaysian French Bank Bhd:** MFB Bldg, 11A Jalan Raja Chulan, POB 10069, 50704 Kuala Lumpur; tel. (3) 2301322; telex 30251; fax (3) 2300193; f. 1982; cap. 55m., dep. 1,452.8m. (Dec. 1990); Chair. Hooi Kam Sooi; CEO Lee Chen Chong; 17 brs.

**MUI Bank Bhd:** MUI Plaza, 21st Floor, Jalan P. Ramlee, 50250 Kuala Lumpur; tel. (3) 2411533; telex 32590; fax (3) 2416306; f. 1905; fmrly Malayan United Bank Bhd; cap. 120m., dep. 2,271m. (Dec. 1992); Chair. Tunku Osman Ahmad; Man. Dir Nik Hashim bin Nik Yusoff; 36 brs.

**Oriental Bank Bhd:** Menara Promet, 14th Floor, Jalan Sultan Ismail, 50250 Kuala Lumpur; tel. (3) 2437088; telex 30778; fax (3) 2420744; f. 1936; cap. 135.4m., dep. 2,520.9m. (March 1993); Chair. Tan Sri Dato' Jaffar bin Abdul; CEO Dato' Ramli bin Ahmad; 18 brs.

**The Pacific Bank Bhd:** Wisma Genting, 2nd Floor, Jalan Sultan Ismail, POB 10930, 50730 Kuala Lumpur; tel. (3) 2614822; telex 21153; fax (3) 2618253; f. 1963; cap. 101m., dep. 2,458m.(Dec. 1993); Chair. Tan Sri Dato' Dr Lin See Yan; Gen. Man. Lai Wan; 38 brs.

**Perwira Affin Bank Bhd:** Wisma SPK, 3rd Floor, Jalan Sultan Ismail, POB 10459, 50915 Kuala Lumpur; tel. (3) 2410000; telex 30448; fax (3) 2428197; f. 1975; fmrly Perwira Habib Bank Malaysia Bhd; cap. 50.2m., dep. 4,537.0m. (Dec. 1993); Chair. Gen. Tan Sri Dato' Zain Hashim; Exec. Dir Wan Salleh Mohammad; 48 brs.

**Public Bank Bhd:** Bangunan Public Bank, 6 Jalan Sultan Sulaiman, 50000 Kuala Lumpur; tel. (3) 2733333; telex 30780; fax (3) 2742179; f. 1965; cap. 565m., dep. 13,634m. (Dec. 1993); Chair. Tan Sri Dato' Thong Yaw Hong; Pres. Tan Sri Dato' Teh Hong Piow; 138 brs.

**Southern Bank Bhd:** Wisma Genting, 28 Jalan Sultan Ismail, 50250 Kuala Lumpur; POB 12281, 50772 Kuala Lumpur; tel. (3) 2637000; telex 31023; fax (3) 2484314; f. 1963; cap. 116.9m., dep. 2,523.6m. (Dec. 1992); Chair. Tan Sri Osman S. Cassim; CEO Dato' Tan Teong Hean; 51 brs.

**United Malayan Banking Corpn Bhd:** Bangunan UMBC, Jalan Sultan Sulaiman, POB 12006, 50935 Kuala Lumpur; tel. (3) 2309866; telex 30484; fax (3) 2322627; f. 1959; cap. 583.5m., dep. 12,412.4m. (Jan. 1993); Chair. Datuk Mohd Noor bin Yusof; CEO Azimuddin bin Abd Ghani; 82 brs.

Sabah

**Hock Hua Bank (Sabah) Bhd:** Hock Hua Bldg, 5th Floor, 22 Jalan Pantai, 88000 Kota Kinabalu; tel. (88) 218922; telex 80684; f. 1961; subsidiary of Hock Hua Bank Bhd (Sarawak); cap. 121m., dep. 2,126m. (Dec. 1993); Chair. Tan Sri Datuk Amar Ling Beng Siew; CEO Ting Sik Kang; 27 brs.

# MALAYSIA

*Directory*

**Sabah Bank Bhd:** Wisma Tun Fuad Stephens, 8th–11th Floor, Jalan Tuaran, Karamunsing, 88100 Kota Kinabalu; tel. (88) 218911; telex 80294; fax (88) 231184; f. 1979; cap. 178.5m., dep. 877.5m. (Dec. 1993); Exec. Chair. Datuk Nicholas Fung; 17 brs.

### Sarawak

**Bank Utama (Malaysia) Bhd:** 18B Jalan Haji Taha, 937400 Kuching; tel. (82) 419294; telex 70101; fax (82) 424954; f. 1976; cap. 99m., dep. 1,587.7m. (Dec. 1992); Chair. Datuk Effendi Norwawi; Senior Vice-Pres. Joseph Ling Kuok Hua; 14 brs.

**Hock Hua Bank Bhd:** 3 Central Rd, 96000 Sibu; tel. (84) 335677; telex 72042; fax (84) 337888; f. 1951; cap. 121m., dep. 2,417.2m. (Dec. 1993); Chair. Tan Sri Datuk Amar Ling Beng Siew; Exec. Dir Ting Sik Kang; 27 brs.

**Wah Tat Bank Bhd:** 15 Bank Rd, POB 87, 96007 Sibu; tel. (84) 336733; telex 72024; fax (84) 332803; f. 1929; cap. 13m., dep. 311.5m. (Dec. 1993); Chair. Dr Chew Peng Hong; Man. Dir Chew Peng Cheng; 12 brs.

### Merchant Banks

**Amanah Merchant Bank Bhd:** Bangunan Kompleks Kewangan, 19th Floor, 82 Jalan Raja Chulan, 50200 Kuala Lumpur; tel. (3) 2610155; telex 30602; fax (3) 2615770; f. 1974; cap. 19m., dep. 452m. (Dec. 1992); Chair. Dato' Abdul Khalid bin Ibrahim; CEO Osman Mohammed Isa.

**Arab-Malaysian Merchant Bank Bhd:** Bangunan Arab-Malaysian, 22nd Floor, 55 Jalan Raja Chulan, 50200 Kuala Lumpur; tel. (3) 2382633; telex 31167; fax (3) 2382842; cap. 192.5m., dep. 3,723m. (March 1993); Chair. Tan Sri Dato' Azman Hashim; Man. Dir Dato' Malek Merican.

**Aseambankers Malaysia Bhd:** Menara Maybank, 33rd Floor, 100 Jalan Tun Perak, 50050 Kuala Lumpur; tel. (3) 2384211; telex 20227; fax (3) 2384194; f. 1973; cap. 23.4m., dep. 480.5m. (Dec. 1990); Man. Dir Izham Mahmud; Gen. Man. Puan Ishah Ismail.

**Asian International Merchant Bankers Bhd:** UMBC Annexe, 10th Floor, Jalan Sultan Sulaiman, 50000 Kuala Lumpur; tel. (3) 2012022; telex 30205; fax (3) 2740304; cap. 15m., dep. 669.3m. (Jan. 1994); Chair. Dato' Mohamed Noor bin Yusof; Senior Vice-Pres. Tee Keng Joo.

**Bumiputra Merchant Bankers Bhd:** Menara Aetna-Universal, 15th Floor, 84 Jalan Raja Chulan, POB 10890, 50928 Kuala Lumpur; tel. (3) 2615266; telex 30282; fax (3) 2615051; f. 1972; a subsidiary of Bank Bumiputra Malaysia Bhd; cap. 98,133m., dep. 954m. (March 1993); Chair. Tan Sri Datuk Dr Abdul Khalid Sahan; Exec. Dir Yap Chee Keong.

**Commerce International Merchant Bankers Bhd:** Pernas International, 20th Floor, Jalan Sultan Ismail, 50250 Kuala Lumpur; tel. (3) 2613411; telex 30903; dep. 411.2m. (Dec. 1992); CEO Robert Cheim Dau Meng.

**DCB Sakura Merchant Bankers Bhd:** Menara TR, 22nd Floor, 161B Jalan Ampang, 50450 Kuala Lumpur; tel. (3) 2612444; fax (3) 2619241; f. 1974; cap. 60m., dep. 1,673m. (Dec. 1994); Chair. Tan Sri Geh Ik Cheong; Man. Dir Heah Sieu Lay.

**Malaysian International Merchant Bankers Bhd:** Bangunan MIDF, 4th Floor, 195A Jalan Tun Razak, 50400 Kuala Lumpur; tel. (3) 2611200; telex 30299; fax (3) 2635022; f. 1970; cap. 25m., dep. 712m. (March 1993); Chair. Tan Sri Dato' Seri Zain Azraai bin Zainal Abidin; Exec. Dir and CEO Lai Yang Shu-Yin.

**Perdana Merchant Bankers Bhd:** Wisma Genting, 11th Floor, Jalan Sultan Ismail, 50250 Kuala Lumpur; tel. (3) 2324188; fax (3) 2322964; cap. 20m., dep. 500.2m. (Sept. 1993); Exec. Vice-Pres. and CEO Ong Meng Teck.

**Permata Merchant Bank Bhd:** Menara Boustead, 27th Floor, 69 Jalan Raja Chulan, POB 11424, 50744 Kuala Lumpur; tel. (3) 2438700; telex 30294; fax (3) 2438701; cap. 12.5m., dep. 335.7m. (Dec. 1988); Chair. Tengku Tan Sri Dato' Ngah Mohamed; Chief Exec. Datuk Abdul Samad bin Yahaya.

**Rakyat First Merchant Bankers Bhd:** Bangunan Angkasa Raya, 5th Floor, Jalan Ampang, 50450 Kuala Lumpur; tel. (3) 2487011; telex 30658; fax (3) 2410123; f. 1974; cap. 15m., dep. 161m. (Dec. 1988); Chair. Encik Anuar Jaafar; Chief Gen. Man. Bjorn C. W. Jonker.

**Utama Wardley Bhd:** Plaza See Hoy Chan, 17th Floor, Jalan Raja Chulan, 50200 Kuala Lumpur; POB 12406, 50776 Kuala Lumpur; tel. (3) 2388644; telex 32250; fax (3) 2304372; f. 1975; cap. 33m., dep. 539m. (Dec. 1993); Chair. Datuk Effendi Norwawi; Gen. Man. Lau Kim Wing.

### Co-operative Bank

**Bank Kerjasama Rakyat Malaysia Bhd:** Bangunan Bank Rakyat, Jalan Tangsi, Petí Surat 11024, 50732 Kuala Lumpur; tel. (3) 2985011; telex 30667; f. 1954; 29,002 mems, of which 868 were rural co-operatives (1983); Chair. Sha'aya Basheer; Man. Dir Anuar Jaafar; 23 brs.

### Development Banks

**Bank Industri Malaysia Bhd** (Industrial Development Bank of Malaysia): Bangunan Bank Industri, 14th–18th Floors, Jalan Sultan Ismail, 50250 Kuala Lumpur; tel. (3) 2929088; telex 31546; fax (3) 2985701; POB 10788, 50724, Kuala Lumpur; f. 1979; govt-owned; finances long-term, high-technology projects, shipping and shipyards, engineering (metal-based, electrical and electronic) and export credit industries; cap. 120.4m., dep. 52.6m. (Dec. 1993); Chair. Tan Sri Dato' Wira Abdul Rahman Arshad; Gen. Man. Encik Abdul Rahman Mohamed Noor.

**Development Bank of Malaysia:** Bangunan MOCCIS, 17 Jalan Melaka, 50100 Kuala Lumpur; tel. (3) 2320633; telex 30058.

**Sabah Development Bank Bhd:** SDB Tower, Wisma Tun Fuad Stephens, Kilometre 2.4, Jalan Tuaran, Karamunsing, 88300, Kota Kinabalu, Sabah; tel. (88) 232177; telex 80214; fax (88) 222852; f. 1977; wholly owned by state Govt of Sabah; cap. 200m., dep. 505.2m. (Dec. 1993); Chair. Datuk Haji Hassan Ibrahim; Man. Dir and CEO Jimmy Duis.

### Islamic Bank

**Bank Islam Malaysia Bhd:** Menara Tun Razak, 9th and 20th Floors, Jalan Raja Laut 50350, Kuala Lumpur; POB 11080, 50734 Kuala Lumpur; tel. (3) 2935566; telex 31783; fax (3) 2922153; f. 1983; 16% govt-owned; cap. 133.4m., dep. 1,612.2m. (June 1993); Chair. Raja Tan Sri Dato' Shamsuddin bin Abdel Kadir; Man. Dir Ahmad Tajudin Abdul Rahman; 32 brs.

### Foreign Banks

Foreign banks with branches in Malaysia were given until October 1994 to incorporate their operations locally under the provisions of the Banking and Financial Institutions Act 1989.

**Algemene Bank Nederland NV** (Netherlands): Wisma Sachdev 16–2, Jalan Raja Laut, POB 10094, 50704 Kuala Lumpur; tel. (3) 2416800; telex 30372; fax (3) 2417087; f. 1888; dep. 282m. (1990); Man. R. G. Nieuwenhuijs; 2 brs.

**Bangkok Bank Ltd** (Thailand): 105 Jalan Tun H. S. Lee, 50000 Kuala Lumpur; tel. (3) 2324555; telex 30359; fax (3) 2388569; f. 1958; dep. 280.2m. (1991); CEO Wong Chee Leong; 1 br.

**Bank of America Malaysia Bhd:** Wisma Goldhill, Jalan Raja Chulan, 50730 Kuala Lumpur; tel. (3) 2021133; telex 30253; fax (3) 2019087; f. 1959; dep. 150m. (1993); Vice-Pres. and Man. Dir Frederick Chino.

**Bank of Tokyo Ltd** (Japan): 1 Leboh Ampang, POB 10955, 50931 Kuala Lumpur; tel. (3) 2326436; telex 30616; f. 1959; dep. 260.2m. (1988); Gen. Man. Hajime Shinohara; 1 br.

**Chase Manhattan Bank, NA** (USA): Pernas International, Jalan Sultan Ismail, 50250 Kuala Lumpur; tel. (3) 2610011; telex 30224; fax (3) 2615505; f. 1964; dep. 577m. (Dec. 1990); Gen. Man. and Vice-Pres. Edward T. Nocco; 1 br.

**Chung Khiaw Bank Malaysia Bhd:** Chung Khiaw Bank Bldg, Jalan Raja Laut, POB 12405, 50944 Kuala Lumpur; tel. (3) 2924511; telex 30350; fax (3) 2989546; f. 1947; dep. 1,548m. (Dec. 1990); CEO Yoong Yan Pin; 16 brs.

**Citibank NA** (USA): 28 Medan Pasar, POB 10112, 50904 Kuala Lumpur; tel. (3) 2325334; telex 31165; fax (3) 2328763; f. 1959; dep. 795m. (1983); Vice-Pres. N. N. Hariharan; 3 brs.

**Deutsche Bank Aktiengesellschaft** (Germany): Apera-ULG Centre, 84 Jalan Raja Chulan, 50200 Kuala Lumpur; tel. (3) 2610799; telex 20367; fax (3) 2610828; f. 1972; dep. 116.6m. (Dec. 1988); Man. Heinz Poehlsen; 1 br.

**Hongkong Bank Malaysia Bhd** (Hong Kong): 2 Leboh Ampang, POB 10244, 50912 Kuala Lumpur; tel. (3) 2300744; telex 30381; f. 1860; CEO (Malaysia) Richard Orgill; 36 brs.

**OCBC Bank Malaysia:** Wisma Lee Rubber, Jalan Melaka, POB 10197, 50911 Kuala Lumpur; tel. (3) 2920344; telex 30358; fax (3) 2926518; f. 1932; cap. 559.4m., dep. 2,211.5m. (Dec. 1988); Exec. Vice-Pres. Fong Weng Phak; 25 brs.

**Overseas Union Bank Ltd** (Singapore): OUB Bldg, Leboh Pasar Besar, 50050 Kuala Lumpur; tel. (3) 2328642; telex 30356; fax (3) 2307540; f. 1959; dep. 597m. (Dec. 1985); Vice-Pres. and Man. Chan Gong Ping; 12 brs.

**Standard Chartered Bank** (United Kingdom): 2 Jalan Ampang, POB 11001, 50732 Kuala Lumpur; tel. (3) 2326555; telex 30266; fax (3) 2383295; f. 1875; dep. 4,645m. (Dec. 1991); Chief Exec. A. G. Rogers; 36 brs.

**United Overseas Bank (Malaysia) Bhd:** Chung Khiaw Bank Bldg, Jalan Raja Laut, POB 11212, 50738 Kuala Lumpur; tel. (3) 2927722; telex 31877; fax (3) 2981228; f. 1920; dep. 971m. (Dec. 1990); Dir and CEO Tan Siak Tee; 9 brs.

### Bankers' Associations

**Association of Banks in Malaysia:** UBN Tower, 17th Floor, 10 Jalan P. Ramlee, 50250 Kuala Lumpur; tel. (3) 2388041; telex

# MALAYSIA

20235; fax (3) 2388004; Chair. Tuan Haji ISMAIL BIN ZAKARIA; Exec. Dir WONG SUAN LYE.

**Institute of Bankers:** The Amoda, 5th Floor, 22 Jalan Imbi, 55100 Kuala Lumpur; tel. (3) 2426722; fax (3) 2420615; Chair. Tan Sri Dato' JAFFAR HUSSEIN.

## STOCK EXCHANGES

**Kuala Lumpur Commodity Exchange:** Citypoint, Dayabumi Complex, 4th Floor, Jalan Sultan Hishamuddin, POB 11260, 50740 Kuala Lumpur; tel. (3) 2936822; telex 31472; fax (3) 2742215; f. 1980; trades in palm oil, palm kernel oil, two grades of rubber futures, tin futures and cocoa futures; CEO Dato' SYED ABDUL JABBAR SHAHABUDIN.

**Kuala Lumpur Stock Exchange (KLSE):** Exchange Sq., 4th Floor, off Jalan Semantan, Damansara Heights, 50490 Kuala Lumpur; tel. (3) 2546433; telex 30241; fax (3) 2557463; f. 1973; in 1994 KLSE authorized the ownership of up to 49% of Malaysian stockbroking companies by foreign interests; 147 mems; Exec. Chair. Encik NIK MOHAMED DIN BIN Datuk NIK YUSOFF; Gen. Man. Encik MOHAMED SALLEH BIN ABDUL MAJID.

**Securities Commission (SC):** Kuala Lumpur; f. 1993; Exec. Chair. Datuk Dr MUNIR MAJID.

## INSURANCE

From 1988 onwards, all insurance companies were placed under the authority of the Central Bank, Bank Negara Malaysia. In 1991 there were 58 insurance companies operating in Malaysia.

### Principal Insurance Companies

**Amanah South British Insurance Sdn Bhd:** Jalan Sultan Ismail, 50250 Kuala Lumpur; tel. (3) 488277; Gen. Man. G. J. DOBSON.

**Asia Insurance Co Ltd:** Bangunan Asia Insurance, 2 Jalan Raja Chulan, 50200 Kuala Lumpur; tel. (3) 2302511; telex 32935; f. 1923; general.

**British American Life & General Insurance Bhd:** Bangunan British American, 6th Floor, Jalan Semantan, Damansara Heights, 50490 Kuala Lumpur; tel. (3) 2548055; telex 30337.

**Capital Insurance Bhd:** 38 Jalan Ampang, POB 12338, 50774 Kuala Lumpur; tel. (3) 2308033; telex 31360.

**D. & C. Insurance Sdn Bhd:** RHBI, 4th Floor, 424 Jalan Tun Razak, 50400 Kuala Lumpur; tel. (3) 9812731; fax (3) 9812729; fmrly NEM Insurance (Malaysia) Sdn Bhd; Gen. Man. K. W. HOO.

**Hong Leong Assurance Sdn Bhd:** Wisma Hla, 18th Floor, Jalan Raja Chulan, 50200 Kuala Lumpur; tel. (3) 2414022; telex 31205; fax (3) 2421267.

**Jerneh Insurance Corpn Sdn Bhd:** Wisma Jerneh, 12th Floor, 38 Jalan Sultan Ismail, POB 12420, 50788 Kuala Lumpur; tel. (3) 2427066; telex 32190; f. 1970; general; Gen. Man. KUOK KHOON PING.

**Kompas Insurans Bhd:** See Hoy Chan Plaza, 16th Floor, Jalan Raja Chulan, 50200 Kuala Lumpur; tel. (3) 2300399; telex 31448; fax (3) 2306016.

**Malaysia National Insurance Sdn Bhd:** 19th–25th Floors, Menara PNB, 201A Jalan Tun Razak, 50400 Kuala Lumpur; tel. (3) 2617311; telex 30624; fax (3) 2618010; f. 1970; life and general; Exec. Chair. ANNUAR SENAWI.

**Malaysian Co-operative Insurance Society Ltd:** Wisma MCIS, Jalan Barat, 46200 Petaling Jaya, Selangor; tel. (3) 7552577; telex 37493; fax (3) 7575964; f. 1954; CEO AHMAD SUBRI ABDULLAH; Gen. Man. L. MEYYAPPAN.

**MBA Life Assurance Sdn Bhd:** Wisma MBA, Ground Floor, 33 Jalan Gereja, 50100 Kuala Lumpur, POB 10939, 50730 Kuala Lumpur; tel. (3) 2300421; telex 30888; fax (3) 2380260.

**MBf Insurans Sdn Bhd:** Plaza MBf, 5th Floor, Jalan Ampang, POB 10345, 50710 Kuala Lumpur.

**Overseas Assurance Corpn Ltd:** OCBC Bldg, 1st Floor, 2 Jalan Hang Kasturi, 50050 Kuala Lumpur; tel. (3) 2388000; telex 32910; fax (3) 2387642; Dep. Gen. Man. G. K. TAN.

**Progressive Insurance Sdn Bhd:** Nagaria Complex, 9th–10th Floors, 12 Jalan Imbi, POB 10028, 50700 Kuala Lumpur; tel. (3) 2410044; telex 31396; fax (3) 2418257.

**Sime East West Insurance Bhd:** Wisma Sime Darby, 15th Floor, Jalan Raja Laut, 50350 Kuala Lumpur; tel. (3) 2937888; telex 33528; fax (3) 2914672; Gen. Man. HOW LIAN KOO.

**South-East Asia Insurance Bhd:** Bangunan Yayasan Selangor, 9th Floor, Jalan Bukit Bintang, 55100 Kuala Lumpur; tel. (3) 2428111; telex 30066; fax (3) 2429820.

**Straits and Island General Insurance Sdn Bhd:** Wisma Equity, 4th Floor, Jalan Ampang, Kuala Lumpur; tel. (3) 2489033; fax (3) 2486429; Gen. Man. SONG YAM LIM.

**Trust International Insurance (M) Sdn Bhd:** Menara Kewangan, 21st Floor, Jalan Sultan Ismail, 50250 Kuala Lumpur; tel. (3) 2304055; telex 33652; CEO A. SUBRI ABDULLAH.

**UMBC Insurans Sdn Bhd:** Bangunan UMBC, 16th Floor, Jalan Sultan Sulaiman, 50000 Kuala Lumpur; tel. (3) 2328733; telex 30666; fax (3) 2322181; f. 1961; CEO ABDULLAH ABDUL SAMAD.

**United Continental Insurance Sdn Bhd:** MUI Plaza, 4th Floor, Jalan Parry, Kuala Lumpur 04-01; tel. (3) 433611; telex 30459; Chair. Tan Sri Haji MUHAMMAD NOAH BIN OMAR.

**United Oriental Assurance Sdn Bhd:** 36 Wisma UOA, 36 Jalan Ampang, 50450 Kuala Lumpur; tel. (3) 202844; telex 31354; fax (3) 2324150.

**Zürich Insurance (Malaysia) Sdn Bhd:** Wisma Selangor Dredging, 4th Floor, East Block, 142B Jalan Ampang, 50450 Kuala Lumpur; tel. (3) 2617031; fax (3) 2617014; Man. Dir. JUERG RUECKMAR.

# Trade and Industry

## PENINSULAR MALAYSIA

### CHAMBERS OF COMMERCE

**Associated Chinese Chambers of Commerce and Industry of Malaysia:** Office Tower, Plaza Berjaya (Kompleks Nagaria), 8th Floor, 12 Jalan Imbi, 55100 Kuala Lumpur; tel. (3) 2452503; fax (3) 2452562; Pres. Tan Sri Datuk AMAR WEE BOON PING; Exec. Sec. ONG KIM SENG.

**Malay Chamber of Commerce and Industry of Malaysia:** Kuala Lumpur; tel. (3) 433090; Chair. Dr NAWAWI BIN MAT AWIN; Exec. Dir ZULKIPLI Haji ABDUL GHANI.

**Malaysian Associated Indian Chambers of Commerce and Industry:** 116 Jalan Tuanku Abdul Rahman, 50100 Kuala Lumpur; tel. (3) 2924817; fax (3) 2911670; f. 1950; Pres. Dato' V. K. K. TEAGARAJAN; Hon. Sec. LACHMAN NARAINDAS; 8 brs

**Malaysian International Chamber of Commerce and Industry (MICCI)** (Dewan Perniagaan dan Perindustrian Antarabangsa Malaysia): Wisma Damansara, 10th Floor, Jalan Semantan, POB 12921, 50792 Kuala Lumpur; tel. (3) 2542677; fax (3) 2554946; f. 1837; brs in Penang, Perak, Johore and Sabah; 890 corporate mems; Pres. LIM SAY CHONG; Exec. Dir P. J. L. JENKINS.

**National Chamber of Commerce and Industry of Malaysia:** 37 Jalan Kia Peng, 50450 Kuala Lumpur; tel. (3) 2419600; telex 33642; fax (3) 2413775; f. 1962; Pres. Tan Sri WAN AZMI WAN HAMZAH; Sec.-Gen. Dato' MOHD RAMLI KUSHAIRI.

### INVESTMENT ORGANIZATION

**Khazanah Nasional:** Kuala Lumpur; f. 1994; state-controlled investment co; assumed responsibility for certain assets formerly under control of the Minister of Finance Inc.; holds 40% of Telekom Malaysia Bhd, 40% of Tenaga Nasional Bhd, 38.6% of HICOM Bhd and 17.8% of PROTON; Chair. Datuk Seri Dr MAHATHIR MOHAMAD.

### PRINCIPAL DEVELOPMENT ORGANIZATIONS AND PUBLIC CORPORATIONS

**Federal Agricultural Marketing Authority (FAMA):** Bangunan KUWASA, 5th–8th Floors, Jalan Raja Laut, 50350 Kuala Lumpur; tel. (3) 2932622; telex 31669; fax (3) 2910494; f. 1965 to supervise, co-ordinate and improve existing markets and methods of marketing agricultural produce and to seek and promote new markets and outlets for agricultural produce; Chair. Encik SHAHIDAN KASSIM; Dir-Gen. Dr ABDUL AZIZ MOHAMED YAACOB.

**Federal Land Development Authority (FELDA):** Jalan Maktab, 54000 Kuala Lumpur; tel. (3) 2935066; telex 32159; fax (3) 2920087; f. 1956; govt statutory body formed to develop land into agricultural smallholdings to eradicate rural poverty; 893,150 ha of land developed (1994); involved in rubber, oil palm and sugarcane cultivation; Chair. RAJA Tan Sri MUHAMMAD ALIAS; Dir-Gen. MOHAMED FADZIL YUNUS.

**Fisheries Development Authority (Malaysia) (MAJUIKAN):** Bangunan PKNS, 7th Floor, Jalan Raja Laut, 50350 Kuala Lumpur; tel. (3) 2924044; telex 31560; Chair. Datuk ARSHAD BIN AYUB.

**Gas Malaysia:** Kuala Lumpur; Chair. IBRAHIM ZAINUDDIN.

**Heavy Industries Corporation of Malaysia (HICOM) Bhd:** Kuala Lumpur; heavy industries group; Chair. Tan Sri JAMIL MOHD JAN.

**Kumpulan FIMA Bhd** (Food Industries of Malaysia): Kompleks FIMA, International Airport, Subang, Selangor; tel. (3) 7462199; telex 37933; f. 1972; fmrly govt corpn, transferred to private sector in 1991; promotes food and related industry through investment on its own or by co-ventures with local or foreign entrepreneurs; oil palm, cocoa and fruit plantation developments; manufacturing and packaging, trading, supermarkets and restaurants; Man. Dir Dato' MOHD NOOR BIN ISMAIL; 1,189 employees.

**Majlis Amanah Rakyat (MARA)** (Trust Council for the People): MEDAN MARA Bldg, 13th Floor, Jalan Raja Laut, 50609 Kuala

# MALAYSIA

Lumpur; tel. (3) 2915111; telex 30316; fax (3) 2913620; f. 1966 to promote, stimulate, facilitate and undertake economic and social development; to participate in industrial and commercial undertakings and jt ventures; Chair. Tan Sri NAZRI AZIZ.

**Malaysia Export Credit Insurance Bhd:** Bangunan Bank Industri, 13th Floor, Jalan Sultan Ismail, POB 11048, 50734 Kuala Lumpur; tel. (3) 2910677; telex 31190; fax (3) 2910353; f. 1977; jt govt and private sector venture to provide insurance for exporters of locally manufactured products; cap. RM150m., sales RM1.5m.; Gen. Man. ABDUL RAHMAN MOHAMED NOOR; 55 employees.

**Malaysia External Trade Development Corp. (Matrade):** Kuala Lumpur; f. 1993; national exports promotion agency.

**Malaysian Industrial Development Authority (MIDA):** Wisma Damansara, ground, 3rd–6th, 9th and 11th Floors, Jalan Semantan, POB 10618, 50720 Kuala Lumpur; tel. (3) 2553633; telex 30752; fax (3) 2557970; f. 1967; Chair. Tan Sri Dato' ZAINAL ABIDIN BIN SULONG; Dir-Gen. ZAINUN AISHAH AHMAD.

**Malaysian Industrial Development Finance Bhd:** 195A Jalan Tun Razak, POB 12110, 50939 Kuala Lumpur; tel. (3) 2610066; fax (3) 2615973; f. 1960 by the Govt, banks, insurance cos; industrial financing, advisory services, project development, merchant and commercial banking services; Chair. Tan Sri Dato' Seri ZAIN AZRAAI BIN ZAINAL ABIDIN; Gen. Man. Encik DARWIS BIN MOHD DAEK.

**Malaysian Timber Industry Board** (Lembaga Perindustrian Kayu Malaysia): Kuala Lumpur; tel. 2486233; telex 30993; fax (3) 2418416; f. 1968; to promote and regulate the export of timber and timber products from Peninsular Malaysia; Chair. Tan Sri Dato' WONG KUM CHOON; Dir-Gen. Dato' BAHARUDDIN BIN Haji GHAZALI.

**Muda Agricultural Development Authority (MADA):** MADA HQ, Ampang Jajar, 05990 Alor Setar, Kedah; tel. (4) 728255; fax (4) 712667; Chair. Tan Sri Dato' Seri Haji OSMAN BIN Haji AROFF.

**National Land Finance Co-operative Society Ltd:** Bangunan UMBC, 20th Floor, 2 Jalan Sulaiman, POB 12133, 50768 Kuala Lumpur; tel. (3) 2307044; f. 1960 to raise funds from rubber industry workers and others to purchase rubber estates; 65,000 mems; owns rubber, tea, oil palm, cocoa and coconut plantations (15,168 ha); cap. p.u. RM35m.; Chief Exec. K. R. SOMASUNDRAM.

**Palm Oil Registration and Licensing Authority (PORLA):** Block A, 5th–7th Floors, Damansara Town Centre, Damansara Heights, POB 12184, 50770 Kuala Lumpur; tel. (3) 2547122; telex 30087; f. 1977 to regulate and promote all aspects of the palm oil industry; Dir-Gen. RAHIM ZAIN.

**Perbadanan Nasional Bhd (PERNAS):** Kuala Lumpur; tel. (3) 2935177; telex 30399; f. 1969; govt-sponsored; promotes trade, banking, property and plantation development, construction, mineral exploration, steel manufacturing, inland container transportation, mining, insurance, industrial development, engineering services, telecommunication equipment, hotels and shipping; cap. p.u. RM 116.25m.; 10 wholly-owned subsidiaries, over 60 jointly-owned subsidiaries and 18 assoc. cos; Chair. Tunku Dato' SHAHRIMAN BIN Tunku SULAIMAN; Man. Dir Dato' A. RAHMAN BIN HAMIDON.

**Perodua:** Kuala Lumpur; joint Government and foreign-owned (Daihatsu) car manufacturer; Chair. Raja Tun MOHAR Raja BADIOZAMAN.

**Perusahaan Otomobil Nasional (PROTON):** Kawasan Perindustrian HICOM, Batu Tiga, 40000 Shah Alam, Selangor Darul Ehsan; fax (3) 2305195; f. 1983; national car co; partially transferred to the private sector in 1992; cap. 500m., sales 2,287m. (1993); Chair. Tan Sri Dato' JAMIL BIN MOHAMED JAN; Man. Dir Datuk MOHAMED NADZMI SALLEH.

**Perwaja Steel Sdn Bhd:** Ubn Tower, 13th Floor, 10 Jalan P. Ramlee, 50250 Kuala Lumpur; national steel project; Man. Dir Tan Sri ERIC CHIA.

**Petroleum Nasional Bhd (PETRONAS):** Menara Dayabumi, Kompleks Dayabumi, Jalan Sultan Hishamuddin, POB 12444, 50778 Kuala Lumpur; tel. (3) 2743833; telex 31123; f. 1974; national oil co engaged in exploration, production, refining and marketing; Chair. Tan Sri Datuk AZIZAN ZAINUL ABIDIN; Pres. and CEO Dato' MOHAMED HASSAN MARICAN; 13,000 employees.

**Rubber Industry Smallholders Development Authority (RISDA):** 4½ miles, Jalan Ampang, 50450 Kuala Lumpur; tel. (3) 4564022; telex 30369; Dir-Gen. Encik MOHD ZAIN BIN Haji YAHYA.

**Telekom Malaysia Bhd:** Ibupejabat Telekom Malaysia, Jalan Pantai Baharu, 59200 Kuala Lumpur; fax (3) 2418463; provision of telecommunications and related services; partially privatized in 1990; cap. 1,986m., sales 3,931m. (1993); Chair. Tan Sri Dato' Dr MOHAMED RASHDAN BIN Haji BABA.

**Tenaga Nasional Bhd:** 129 Jalan Bangsar, 59200 Kuala Lumpur; fax (3) 2418463; generation, transmission, distribution and sales of electricity; partially transferred to the private sector in 1992; cap. 3,002m., sales 5,030m. (1993). Chair. Tan Sri Dato' Haji Dr ANI BIN AROPE.

## INDUSTRIAL AND TRADE ASSOCIATIONS

**Federation of Malaysian Manufacturers:** Wisma Sime Darby, 17th Floor, Jalan Raja Laut, POB 12194, 50770 Kuala Lumpur; tel. (3) 2931244; telex 32437; fax (3) 2935105; f. 1968; 1,677 mems (March 1995); Pres. Dato' MOHAMED SOPIEE bin Sheikh IBRAHIM; CEO Tan KEOK YIN.

**Federation of Rubber Trade Associations of Malaysia:** 138 Jalan Bandar, 50000 Kuala Lumpur; tel. (3) 2384006.

**Malaysian Chamber of Mines:** West Block, 8th Floor, Wisma Selangor Dredging, 142c Jalan Ampang, POB 12560, 50782 Kuala Lumpur; tel. (3) 2616171; fax (3) 2616179; f. 1914; Chair. Tuan Haji ABDUL SUKOR BIN SHAHAR; Sec. MUHAMAD NOR MUHAMAD; 161 mems.

**Malaysian Employers' Federation:** Exchange Sq., 11th Floor, off Jalan Semantan, 50490 Kuala Lumpur; tel. (3) 2549422; telex 31862; fax (3) 2550830; f. 1959; Pres. Dato' Dr MOKHZANI BIN ABDUL RAHIM; private-sector org. incorporating eight employer organizations and 2,435 individual enterprises, including:

**Association of Insurance Employers:** POB 10395, 50712 Kuala Lumpur; tel. (3) 2302422; telex 33204; fax (3) 2303261; fmrly States of Malaysia Insurance Asscn; 32 mems; Pres. NG KIM HOONG.

**Commercial Employers' Association of Peninsular Malaysia:** Kuala Lumpur; 12 mems; Pres. Tuan Haji ABDUL AZIZ MOHAMAD.

**Johore Plantation Employers' Asscn.**

**Malayan Agricultural Producers' Association:** Kuala Lumpur; tel. (3) 4573988; fax (3) 4573113; f. 1980; 480 mem. estates and 131 factories; Pres. Tan Sri Dato' Haji Dr ANI BIN AROPE; Dir S. J. CHELLIAH.

**Malayan Commercial Banks' Association:** POB 12001, 50764 Kuala Lumpur; tel. 2328002.

**Malayan Mining Employers' Association:** West Block, 8th Floor, Wisma Selangor Dredging, Jalan Ampang, POB 12560, 50782 Kuala Lumpur; tel. (3) 2616171; fax (3) 2616179; Pres. SUKOR BIN SHAHAR; Sec. KAM CHENG ENG.

**Pan Malayan Road Transport Operators Association.**

**Malaysian Iron & Steel Industry Federation:** Wisma MCIS, 6th Floor, Secondary Tower Block, Jalan Barat, 46200 Petaling Jaya, Selangor; tel. (3) 7586031; fax (3) 7586016; Chair. Dato' SOONG SIEW HOONG; 75 mems.

**Malaysian Oil Palm Growers' Council:** Wisma Getah Asli I, 3rd Floor, North Wing, 148 Jalan Ampang, POB 10747, 50724 Kuala Lumpur; tel. (3) 2615088; telex 31356; fax (3) 2612504; f. 1953.

**The Malaysian Pineapple Industry Board:** Wisma SBBU, 2nd Floor, Jalan Padi Mahsuri 12, Bandar Baru UDA, 81200 Johore Bahru; tel. (7) 2361211; fax (7) 2365694; Dir Gen. Tuan Haji ISMAIL BIN ABD JAMAL.

**The Malaysian Rubber Products Manufacturers' Association:** 1 Jalan USJ 11/1J, Subang Jaya, 47620 Petaling Jaya, Selangor; tel. (3) 7316150; fax (3) 7316152; f. 1952; Pres. Tan Sri Datuk ARSHAD AYUB; 140 mems.

**Malaysian Rubber Research and Development Board:** Bangunan Getah Asli (Menara), 16th–19th Floors, 148 Jalan Ampang, POB 10508, 50716 Kuala Lumpur; tel. (3) 2614422; fax (3) 2613139; f. 1958; plans and determines policies and programmes of natural rubber research, technical development and promotion work nationally and worldwide; co-ordinates all research activities; Chair. and Controller of Rubber Research Tan Sri Dato' Dr OTHMAN YEOP ABDULLAH.

**Malaysian Textile Manufacturers' Association:** Wisma Selangor Dredging, 9th Floor, West Block, 142C Jalan Ampang, 50450 Kuala Lumpur; tel. (3) 2621587; fax (3) 2625148; Pres. Datuk Haji ALI BIN ESA; Exec. Dir M. B. CHOY; 290 mems.

**National Tobacco Board:** POB 198, 15720 Kota Bahru, Kelantan; tel. (9) 7652933; fax (9) 7655640.

**Northern Malaya Rubber Millers and Packers Association:** 22 Pitt St, 3rd Floor, Suites 301–303, 10200 Penang; tel. (4) 620037; f. 1919; 153 mems; Pres. HWANG SING LUE; Hon. Sec. LEE SENG KEOK; Hon. Treas. NG KWENG HAI.

**Palm Oil Refiners Association of Malaysia (PORAM):** 50200 Kuala Lumpur; tel. (3) 2488893; telex 31483; f. 1975 to promote the palm oil refining industry; Chair. Datuk ROBERT W. K. CHAN; 27 mems.

**Rubber Trade Association of Malacca:** 128A Wolferston Rd, Malacca.

**Rubber Trade Association of Perak:** 1–3 Jalan Chua Cheng Bok, Ipoh; tel. (5) 549212.

**Rubber Trade Association of Selangor and Pahang:** 138 Jalan Bandar, 50000 Kuala Lumpur; tel. (3) 2384006.

**Timber Trade Federation of Malaysia:** 2 Lorong Haji Taib Satu, POB 11099, Kuala Lumpur 02-07.

**Tin Industry Research and Development Board:** West Block, 8th Floor, Wisma Selangor Dredging, Jalan Ampang, POB 12560, 50782

# MALAYSIA

Kuala Lumpur; tel. (3) 2616171; fax (3) 2616179; Chair. SUKOR BIN SHAHAR; Sec. MUHAMAD NOR MUHAMAD.

## TRADE UNIONS

In 1988 there were 414 trades unions, 47% of which were from the private sector. About 10.3% of the Malaysian work-force of 5.9m. belonged to unions. In 1989 15 unions, including several affiliated to the Malaysian Trades Union Congress, formed the Malaysian Labour Organization. The organization was granted official registration in 1990.

**Congress of Unions of Employees in the Public Administrative and Civil Services (CUEPACS):** a nat. fed. with 53 affiliates, representing 115,000 govt workers (1985).

**Malaysian Labour Organization (MLO):** f. 1989 by 15 unions; 100,000 mems; Gen. Sec. K. SANMUGAM.

**Malaysian Trades Union Congress:** MTUC Bldg, 4th Floor, 19 Jalan Barat, POB 38, 46700 Petaling Jaya, Selangor; tel. (3) 7560224; fax (3) 7562773; f. 1949; 180 affiliated unions, about 500,000 mems; Pres. ZAINAL RAMPAK (arrested Oct. 1994); Sec.-Gen. G. RAJASEKARAN.

Principal affiliated unions:

**All Malayan Estate Staff Union:** POB 12, University Garden, 46700 Petaling Jaya; tel. 7741554; 2,654 mems.; Pres. R. KRISHNAN; Gen. Sec. S. THAMOTHARAN.

**Amalgamated Union of Employees in Government Clerical and Allied Services:** 32A Jalan Gajah, off Jalan Yew, Pudu, 55100 Kuala Lumpur; tel. (3) 9859613; fax (3) 9838632; 6,703 mems; Pres. IBRAHIM BIN ABDUL WAHAB; Gen. Sec. MOHAMED IBRAHIM BIN ABDUL WAHAB.

**Chemical Workers Union:** Petaling Jaya, Selangor; 1,886 mems; Pres. RUSIAN HITAM; Gen. Sec. JOHN MATHEWS.

**Electricity Industry Workers' Union:** 55-2 Jalan SS 15/8A, Subang Jaya, 47500 Petaling Jaya, Selangor; tel. (3) 7335243; 8,775 mems; Pres. ABDUL MANAB; Gen. Sec. P. ARUNASALAM.

**Harbour Workers Union, Port Kelang:** 106 Persiaran Raja Muda Musa, Port Kelang; 2,426 mems; Pres. MOHAMED SHARIFF BIN YAMIN; Gen. Sec. MOHAMED HAYAT BIN AWANG.

**Kesatuan Pekerja Tenaga Nasional Bhd:** 30 Jalan Liku Bangsar, POB 10400, 59100 Kuala Lumpur; tel. (3) 2745657; 10,456 mems; Pres. MOHAMED ABU BAKAR; Gen. Sec. IDRIS BIN ISMAIL.

**Kesatuan Pekerja-Pekerja FELDA:** 2 Jalan Maktab Enam, Melelui Jalan Perumahaan, Gurney, Kuala Lumpur; tel. (3) 2929972; 6,131 mems; Pres. INDERA PUTERA; Gen. Sec. MAULOT BIN MANAS.

**Kesatuan Pekerja-Pekerja Perusahaan Membuat Tekstil dan Pakaian Pulau Pinang dan Seberang Prai:** 23 Lorong Talang Satu, Prai Gardens, 13600 Prai; tel. 301397; 3,900 mems; Pres. ABDUL RAZAK HAMID; Gen. Sec. KENNETH STEPHEN PERKINS.

**Metal Industry Employees' Union:** Metalworkers' House, 5 Lorong Utara Kecil, 46200 Petaling Jaya, Selangor; tel. (3) 7567214; fax (3) 7550854; 11,625 mems; Pres. KAMARUSZAMAN BIN MANSOR; Gen. Sec. JACOB ENGKATESU.

**National Union of Commercial Workers:** Bangunan NUCW, 98A–D Jalan Masjid India, 50100 Kuala Lumpur; POB 12059, 50780 Kuala Lumpur; tel. (3) 2927385; fax (3) 2925930; f. 1959; 11,937 mems; Pres. Tuan Haji ABDUL AZIZ BIN ISMAIL; Gen. Sec. S. RAJENDRA PARSHAD.

**National Union of Plantation Workers in Malaysia:** 2 Jalan Templer, POB 73, 46700 Petaling Jaya, Selangor; tel. 7927622; telex 37566; fax (3) 7915321; f. 1954; 81,991 mems; Pres. YUSOF MAMAT; Gen. Sec. (vacant).

**National Union of PWD Employees:** 32B Jalan Gajah, off Jalan Yew, 55100 Kuala Lumpur; tel. (3) 9850149; 5,869 mems; Pres. KULOP IBRAHIM; Gen. Sec. S. SANTHANASAMY.

**National Union of Telecoms Employees:** Wisma NUTE, 17A Jalan Bangsar, 59200 Kuala Lumpur; tel. (3) 2821599; fax (3) 2821015; 17,155 mems; Pres. MOHAMED SHAFIE B.P. MAMMAL; Gen. Sec. MOHD JAFAR BIN ABDUL MAJID.

**Railwaymen's Union of Malaya:** Bangunan Tong Nam, 1st Floor, Jalan Tun Sambathan (Travers), 50470 Kuala Lumpur; tel. (3) 2741107; fax (3) 2731805; 5,500 mems; Pres. ABDUL GAFFOR BIN IBRAHIM; Gen. Sec. S. VEERASINGAM.

**Rubber Research Institute Staff Union:** POB 10150, 50908 Kuala Lumpur; tel. (3) 4565102; 1,509 mems; Pres. MURALEE NAIR; Gen. Sec. A. J. PATRICK.

**Technical Services Union—Tenaga Nasional Berhad:** Bangunan Keselamatan, POB 11003, Bangsar, Kuala Lumpur; tel. 2823581; 3,690 mems; Pres. RAMLY YATIM; Gen. Sec. CLIFFORD SEN.

**Timber Employees Union :** 10 Jalan AU 5C/14, Ampang, Ulu Kelang, Selangor; 7,174 mems; Pres. ABDULLAH METON; Gen. Sec. MINHAT SULAIMAN.

**Transport Workers' Union:** 21 Jalan Barat, Petaling Jaya, 46200 Selangor; tel. (3) 7566567; 10,447 mems; Pres. ZAINAL RAMPAK; Gen. Sec. Dr V. DAVID.

### Independent Federations and Unions

**Federation of Unions in the Textile, Garment and Leather Industry:** c/o Selangor Textile and Garment Manufacturing Employees Union, 9D Jalan Travers, 50470 Kuala Lumpur; tel. (3) 2742578; f. 1989; four affiliates; Pres. ABDUL RAHIM BIN MUSIRAN; Gen. Sec. MOHAMED ZIN BIN ABDUL KADIR.

**Kongres Kesatuan Guru-Guru Dalam Perkhidmatan Pelajaran** (Congress of Unions of Employees in the Teaching Services): Wisma Amar, Jalan Abdullah, Muar, Johor; seven affiliates; Pres. RAMLI BIN MOHD JOHAN; Sec.-Gen. KASSIM BIN Haji HARON.

**Malaysian Medical Assistants Association:** Kuala Lumpur; tel. (3) 981044; 10 affiliates; Pres. MOHAMED ESA HITAM.

**Malaysian Technical Services Union:** 3A Jalan Menteri, off Jalan Cochrane, 55100 Kuala Lumpur; tel. (3) 9851778; fax (3) 9811875; 7,233 mems; Pres. MOHAMED YUSOF Haji HARMAIN SHAH; Gen. Sec. SAMUEL DEVADASAN.

**National Union of Bank Employees:** Bangunan NUBE, Rooms 501 and 502, 114 Jalan Tuanku Abdul Rahman, POB 12488, 50780 Kuala Lumpur; tel. (3) 2988592; fax (3) 2910050; 27,000 mems; Gen. Sec. K. SANMUGAM.

**National Union of Journalists:** 30B Jalan Padang Belia, 50470 Kuala Lumpur; tel. (3) 2742867; fax (3) 2744776; f. 1962; 1,700 mems; Gen. Sec. ONN EE SENG.

**National Union of Newspaper Workers:** 11B Jalan 20/14, Paramount Garden, 46300 Petaling Jaya, Selangor; tel. (3) 7768118; fax (3) 7751490; 4,000 mems; Pres. ZULKIFLEE MOHD SAID; Gen. Sec. SUPPIAH VELLAISAMY.

**Non-Metallic Mineral Products Manufacturing Employees' Union:** 99A Jalan SS 14/1, Subang Jaya, 47500 Petaling Jaya, Selangor; tel. (3) 7339006; 6,716 mems; Sec. ABDULLAH BIN ABU BAKAR.

## CO-OPERATIVES

In 1982 there was a total of 2,326 registered co-operatives involved in housing, agriculture and industry in Malaysia, with 1.86m. mems.

## SABAH

### CHAMBERS OF COMMERCE

**Sabah Chamber of Commerce and Industry:** Jalan Tiga, Sandakan; tel. (89) 2141; Pres. T. H. WONG.

### TRADE UNIONS AND ASSOCIATIONS

**Chinese School Teachers' Association:** POB 10, Tenom; f. 1956; 74 mems; Sec. VUN CHAU CHOI.

**Sabah Banking Employees Union:** POB 503, Sandakan; 729 mems; Gen. Sec. LEE CHI HONG.

**Sabah Civil Service Union:** Kota Kinabalu; f. 1952; 1,356 mems; Pres. J. K. K. VOON; Sec. STEPHEN WONG.

**Sabah Commercial Employees' Union:** Sinsuran Shopping Complex, Lot 3, Blok N, 2nd Floor, POB 10357, 88803 Kota Kinabalu; tel. (88) 225971; f. 1957; 1,030 mems; Gen. Sec. KING BEE SIEW.

**Sabah Medical Services Union:** POB 11257, 88720 Kota Kinabalu; tel. (88) 204109; 1,030 mems; Pres. VISVALINGAM SUPPIAH; Gen. Sec. DENNIS LIM.

**Sabah Petroleum Industry Workers' Union:** POB 1087, Kota Kinabalu; 168 mems; Gen. Sec. THIEN FOOK SHIN.

**Sabah Teachers' Union:** POB 10912, 88810 Kota Kinabalu; tel. (88) 420034; fax (88) 431633; f. 1962; 1,079 mems; Pres. JOHN NG AH KIAN; Sec.-Gen. PATRICK Y. C. CHOK.

## SARAWAK

### CHAMBERS OF COMMERCE

**The Associated Chinese Chamber of Commerce:** 24 Jalan Green Hill, 1st Floor, Kuching; tel. (82) 428815; fax (82) 429950; f. 1965; Pres. WEE BOON PING; Sec. Gen. SIM TECK KUI.

**South Indian Chamber of Commerce of Sarawak:** 37C India St, Kuching; f. 1952; Pres. ABDUL MAJEED; Vice-Pres. SYED AHMAD.

**Sarawak Chamber of Commerce and Industry (SCCI):** POB 64, 93700 Kuching; tel. (82) 237148; fax (82) 237186; f. 1950; Chair. Datuk Haji MOHAMED AMIN BIN Haji SATEM; Dep. Chair. Encik MOHAMED SHOOKRY GANI.

### DEVELOPMENT ORGANIZATIONS

**Borneo Development Corpn Sdn Bhd:** Head Office: Electra House, Top Floor, Power St, POB 342, 93704 Kuching, Sarawak; tel. (82)

244241; telex 70188; fax (82) 428786; Sabah Office: Penthouse, 12th Floor, Wisma Merdeka, Jalan Tun Razak, POB 10721, 88807 Kota Kinabalu; tel. (88) 238816; telex 81145; fax (88) 230450; f. 1958; shareholders: State Govts of Sarawak and Sabah; cap. p.u. RM 30m. (1991); CEO and Gen. Man. SALLEH Haji SULAIMAN; Sec. KUSHAIRI Haji ZAIDEL.

**Malaysian Pepper Marketing Board:** Tanah Putih, POB 1653, 93916 Kuching; tel. (82) 331811; telex 70987; fax (82) 336877; f. 1972; responsible for the statutory grading of all Sarawak pepper for export, licensing of pepper dealers and exporters and the development and promotion of pepper grading, storage and processing facilities; Gen. Man. ADNANDAN BIN ABDULLAH.

**Sarawak Economic Development Corpn:** Menara SEDC, 6th–11th Floors, Sarawak Plaza, Jalan Tunku Abdul Rahman, POB 400, 93902 Kuching; tel. (82) 416777; telex 70063; fax (82) 424330; f. 1972; statutory org. responsible for commercial and industrial development in Sarawak either solely or jtly with foreign and local entrepreneurs; responsible for the development of tourism infrastructure; Chair. Datuk Effendi NORWAWI.

### TRADE UNIONS

**Sarawak Bank Employees Union:** POB 1343, 98008 Miri; tel. (85) 31236; fax (85) 418111; 1,430 mems; Gen. Sec. DOMINIC CH'NG YUNG TED.

**Sarawak Commercial Employees Union:** POB 807, Kuching; 1,636 mems; Gen. Sec. SONG SWEE LIAP.

**Sarawak Teachers' Union:** 139A Jalan Rock, 1st Floor, 93200 Kuching; tel. (82) 245727; fax (82) 245757; f. 1965; 6,500 mems; Pres. WILLIAM GHANI BINA; Sec.-Gen. THOMAS HUO KOK SEN.

## Transport

### RAILWAYS

#### Peninsular Malaysia

The state-owned Malayan Railway had a total length of 1,672 km in Peninsular Malaysia in 1992. The main railway line follows the west coast and extends 782 km from Singapore, south of Peninsular Malaysia, to Butterworth (opposite Penang Island) in the north. From Bukit Mertajam, close to Butterworth, the Kedah line runs north to the Thai border at Padang Besar where connection is made with the State Railway of Thailand. The East Coast Line, 526 km long, runs from Gemas to Tumpat (in Kelantan). A 21-km branch line from Pasir Mas (27 km south of Tumpat) connects with the State Railway of Thailand at the border station of Sungei Golok. Branch lines serve railway-operated ports at Port Dickson and Telok Anson as well as Port Klang and Jurong (Singapore).

The construction of a privately-owned light-rail network in Kuala Lumpur was scheduled for completion by 1996. The project is the first phase of a planned transit system of upgraded light-rail and railbus services encircling Kuala Lumpur, which has been postponed since the mid-1980s.

Under the Sixth Malaysia Plan (1991–95), RM 1,370m. was allocated to improving the railway system.

**Keretapi Tanah Melayu (KTM)** (Malayan Railways): Jalan Sultan Hishamuddin, 50621 Kuala Lumpur; tel. (3) 2749422; telex 32925; fax (3) 2749424; f. 1885; incorporated as a co under govt control in Aug. 1992; Man. Dir ABDUL RAHIM OSMAN.

#### Sabah

**Sabah State Railway:** 88999 Kota Kinabalu; tel. (88) 254611; fax (88) 236395; 134 track-km of 1-m gauge (1995); goods and passenger services from Tanjong Aru to Tenom, serving part of the west coast and the interior; diesel trains are used; Gen. Man. Datuk Haji H. A. MAJIN.

### ROADS

#### Peninsular Malaysia

Peninsular Malaysia's road system is extensive, in contrast to those of Sabah and Sarawak. In 1992 the road network in Malaysia totalled at least 92,545 km, of which 574 km was motorway, 13,983 km highways and 42,988 km secondary roads; 75% of the network was paved. A main trunk road runs from the Thai border in the north to Singapore in the south. Construction of a second Malaysia–Singapore bridge was scheduled for completion in 1995. Work was completed in 1992 on a 928-km inter-urban toll expressway, including the 13.5-km Penang bridge, linking Penang Island and Peninsular Malaysia (opened in 1985), and forming the last link of the east–west highway. The 848-km North–South Highway, a toll road extending from the Thai border in the north to the causeway to Singapore in the south, was opened in September 1994. In 1991 construction began on a second east–west highway which was expected to cost RM 270m.

Under the Sixth Malaysia Plan (1991–95), RM 7,600m. was allocated to the expansion and upgrading of the road system.

#### Sabah

**Jabatan Kerja Raya** (Public Works Department): 88582 Kota Kinabalu, Sabah; tel. (88) 244333; telex 80339; fax (88) 237234; maintains a network totalling 9,782 km, of which 1,066 km were trunk roads in 1993; the total included 2,544 km of sealed roads; Dir Ir. HIEW THIEN CHOI.

#### Sarawak

**Jabatan Kerja Raya** (Public Works Department): Bangunan Wisma Saberkas, Jalan Tun Abang Haji Openg, 93582 Kuching; tel. (82) 244041; telex 70112; fax (82) 429679; total length of roads (Dec. 1991) 3,997 km, including 1,486 km of trunk roads, 1,430 km of feeder/development roads, 888 km of rural and 193 km of other roads; Dir Dato' MICHAEL PARKER; Dep. Dir KHO KWANG HUI.

### SHIPPING

The ports in Malaysia are classified as federal ports, under the jurisdiction of the Federal Ministry of Transport, or state ports, responsible to the state ministries of Sabah and Sarawak.

At 30 June 1992 the Malaysian merchant fleet totalled 552 vessels, with a combined displacement of 2.0m. grt.

#### Peninsular Malaysia

The federal ports in Peninsular Malaysia are Klang (the principal port), Penang, Johore, Kuantan and Bintulu. In the early 1990s the port authorities were in the process of being transferred to the private sector. The Government had earlier approved a plan to build a RM 500m. port next to Klang Port by 1995. A project to expand the capacity of Johore Port was scheduled for completion by 1995.

**Johore Port Authority:** POB 66, 81707 Pasir Gudang, Johore; tel. (7) 517721; telex 60192; fax (7) 517684; f. 1973; Gen. Man. DAMON NORI MASO'OD.

**Johore Port Sdn Bhd:** POB 151, Pasir Gudang, 81707 Johore; tel. (7) 2525888; telex 60192; fax (7) 510291; Man. Dir Dato' Haji YAHYA BIN Haji ABDUL GHANI.

**Klang Port Authority:** POB 202, Jalan Pelabuhan, 42005 Port Klang, Selangor; tel. (3) 3688211; telex 39524; fax (3) 3670211; f. 1963; Gen. Man. M. RAJASINGAM.

**Kuantan Port Authority:** Tanjung Gelang, POB 161, 25720 Kuantan, Pahang; tel. (9) 433201; telex 50234; fax (9) 433866; f. 1974; Gen. Man. Dato' TIK MUSTAFFA.

**Penang Port Commission:** 3A-6 Bangunan Sri Weld, Pangkalan Weld, 10300 Pulau Pinang; tel. (4) 6579636; fax (4) 626211; f. 1956; Chair. Dato' ZAINOL ABIDIN BIN Dato' Haji SALLEH; Gen. Man. AZMI BIN OSMAN.

#### Sabah

The chief ports are Kota Kinabalu, Sandakan, Tawau, Lahad Datu, Kudat, Semporna and Kunak and are administered by the Sabah Ports Authority. Many international shipping lines serve Sabah. Local services are operated by smaller vessels. The Sapangar Bay oil terminal, 25 km from Kota Kinabalu wharf, can accommodate oil tankers of up to 30,000 dwt.

**Sabah Ports Authority:** Bangunan Ibu Pejabat LPS, Jalan Tun Fuad, Tanjung Lipat, 88617 Kota Kinabalu, Sabah; tel. (88) 56155; telex 80074; fax (88) 223036.

#### Sarawak

There are four port authorities in Sarawak: Kuching, Rajang, Miri and Bintulu. Kuching, Rajang and Miri are independent statutory institutions, while Bintulu is a federal port. Kuching port serves the southern region of Sarawak, Rajang port the central region, and Miri port the northern region.

**Kuching Port Authority:** Jalan Pelabuhan, Pending, POB 530, 93710 Kuching, Sarawak; tel. (82) 482144; telex 70420; fax (82) 481696; f. 1961.

**Rajang Port Authority:** 96000 Sibu, Sarawak; tel. (84) 319009; telex 72121; fax (84) 318754; f. 1970; Gen. Man. Tuan Haji MOHIDIN Haji SEMAN.

#### Principal Shipping Companies

**Achipelego Shipping (Sarawak) Sdn Bhd:** Lot 267/270, Jalan Chan Chin Ann, POB 2998, 93758 Kuching; tel. (82) 412581; telex 70294; fax (82) 416249; Gen. Man. MICHAEL M. AMAN.

**Haj Shipping Sdn Bhd:** 33 Jalan Cunggah, 42000 Kuala Lumpur; tel. (3) 380966; telex 39646; Chair. H. BIN ABDUL JAMIL; Gen. Man. T. J. TOONG.

**Malaysia Shipping Corpn Sdn Bhd:** Office Tower, Plaza Berjaya (Kompleks Nagaria), Suite 14C, 14th Floor, 12 Jalan Imbi, 55100 Kuala Lumpur; tel. (3) 2418788; telex 21249; fax (3) 2429214.

**Malaysian International Shipping Corpn Bhd** (National Shipping Line of Malaysia): Wisma MISC, 2nd Floor, 2 Jalan Conlay, POB 10371, 50712 Kuala Lumpur; tel. (3) 2428088; telex 30325; fax (3) 2486602; f. 1968; regular sailings between the Far East, South-East Asia, Australia and Japan and Europe; also operates chartering, tanker and agency services; substantial shareholder, Kumpulan Wang Amanah Pencen; Man. Dir ARIFFIN ALIAS.

**Perbadanan Nasional Shipping Line Bhd (PNSL):** Annexe Block, 3rd Floor, Menara Tun Razak, Jalan Raja Laut, POB 10457, 50714 Kuala Lumpur; tel. (3) 2932211; telex 31670; fax (3) 2932423; f. 1982; specializes in bulk cargoes; Exec. Dep. Chair. Dato' SULAIMAN ABDULLAH.

**Perkapalan Shamelin Jaya Sdn Bhd:** Bangunan Mayban Trust, Penthouse Suite, Penang St, 10200 Penang; tel. (4) 612400; telex 40321; fax (4) 623122; Man. Dir MOHD NOOR MD KAMALUDIN.

**Syarikat Perkapalan Kris Sdn Bhd** (The Kris Shipping Co Ltd): Block A, 309-609 Glomac Business Centre, 10 Jalan SS6/1, POB 8428 Kelana Jaya, 46789 Petaling Jaya, Selangor; tel. (3) 7046477; telex 30635; fax (3) 7048007; domestic services; Gen. Man. ROHANY TALIB; Dep. Gen. Man. THO TEIT CHANG.

**Trans-Asia Shipping Corpn Sdn Bhd:** Yee Song Bldg, 11th Floor, 15 Jalan Raja Chulan, Kuala Lumpur; tel. (3) 209177; telex 30655.

### CIVIL AVIATION

Malaysia's major international airport, Subang, is situated in Kuala Lumpur, and there are regional airports at Kota Kinabalu, Penang, Johore Bahru, Kuching and Pulau Langkawi. In addition, there are airports catering for domestic services at Alor Star, Ipoh, Kota Bahru, Kuala Trengganu, Kuantan and Malacca in Peninsular Malaysia, Sibu, Bintulu and Miri in Sarawak and Sandakan, Tawau, Lahad Datu and Labuan in Sabah. There are also numerous smaller airstrips. In September 1988 India's International Airport Authority won a contract to build a new airport in Sibu, Sarawak. A new international airport in Sepang, Selangor (70 km south of Kuala Lumpur), the Kuala Lumpur International Airport, was scheduled to begin operations in 1998.

**Department of Civil Aviation:** (Jabatan Penerbangan Awam Malaysia): Wisma DCA, Bangunan Yen San, Lot 13A, Jalan 225, 46100 Petaling Jaya, Selangor; tel. (3) 7576666; telex 20394; fax (3) 7571144; Dir. Gen. (vacant).

**Air Asia Sdn Bhd:** Kuala Lumpur; f. 1994; a second national airline, with a licence to operate domestic and regional flights; 85%-owned by HICOM.

**Malaysia Airlines:** 33F Bangunan MAS, Jalan Sultan Ismail, 50250 Kuala Lumpur; tel. (3) 2610555; telex 37614; fax (3) 2613472; f. 1971 as the Malaysian successor to the Malaysia Singapore Airlines (MSA); known as Malaysian Airline System (MAS) until Oct. 1987; services to 36 domestic points and to 52 international destinations; Chair. Datuk TAJUDIN RAMLI; Man. Dir WAN MALEK IBRAHIM.

**Pelangi Air:** Apprentice Training Bldg, 2nd Floor, MAS Complex B, Subang International Airport, 47200 Subang, Selangor; tel. (3) 2624446; fax (3) 2624515; f. 1988; regional carrier.

## Tourism

Malaysia has a rapidly-growing tourist industry and the cultures of the many ethnic groups in the country provide a particular attraction. In 1990, designated 'Visit Malaysia Year', 7.5m. tourists visited Malaysia (of whom some 7.1m. visited Peninsular Malaysia), contributing US $1,657m. in receipts of foreign exchange. The year 1994 was also designated 'Visit Malaysia Year', owing to the success of the previous campaign: some 7.2m. tourists visited, and tourist receipts totalled $3,600m.

**Tourist Development Corpn of Malaysia:** Menara Dato' Onn, 24th–27th Floors, Putra World Trade Centre, Jalan Tun Ismail, 50480 Kuala Lumpur; tel. (3) 2935188; telex 30093; fax (3) 2935884; f. 1972 to co-ordinate and promote activities relating to tourism; information centres in London, Frankfurt, Paris, Los Angeles, San Francisco, Sydney, Perth, Tokyo, Hong Kong, Bangkok, Singapore, Taipei and Vancouver; Chair. Raja Tan Sri MOHAR BIN Raja BADIOZAMAN; Dep. Chair. and Dir-Gen. Encik BADRI BIN MASRI.

**Sabah Tourist Association:** POB 946, Kota Kinabalu; tel. (88) 211484; f. 1962; 55 mems; parastatal promotional org.; Chair. ALBERT TEO; Exec. Sec. AGNES HO.

**Sarawak Tourist Association:** Sarawak Tourist Information Centre, Main Bazaar, 93000 Kuching; POB 887, 93718 Kuching; tel. (82) 240620; fax (82) 427151; f. 1964; Chair. PHILIP YONG KHI LIANG; Hon. Sec. S. C. CHAN.

# MALDIVES

## Introductory Survey

### Location, Climate, Language, Religion, Flag, Capital

The Republic of Maldives is in southern Asia. The country, lying about 675 km (420 miles) south-west of Sri Lanka, consists of 1,190 small coral islands (of which 198 are inhabited), grouped in 26 natural atolls (but divided, for administrative purposes, into 19 atolls), in the Indian Ocean. The climate is hot and humid. The average annual temperature is 27°C (80°F), with little daily or seasonal variation, while annual rainfall is generally between 2,540 mm and 3,800 mm (100 ins to 150 ins). The national language is Dhivehi (Maldivian), which is related to Sinhala. Islam is the state religion, and most Maldivians are Sunni Muslims. The national flag (proportions 3 by 2) is red, with a green rectangle, containing a white crescent, in the centre. The capital is Malé.

### Recent History

Maldives, called the Maldive Islands until April 1969, formerly had an elected Sultan as head of state. The islands were placed under British protection, with internal self-government, in 1887. They became a republic in January 1953 but the sultanate was restored in February 1954. Maldives became fully independent, outside the Commonwealth, on 26 July 1965. Following a referendum, the country became a republic again in November 1968, with Amir Ibrahim Nasir, Prime Minister since 1957, as President.

In 1956 the Maldivian and British Governments agreed to the establishment of a Royal Air Force staging post on Gan, an island in the southernmost atoll, Addu. In 1975 the British Government's decision to close the base and to evacuate British forces created a large commercial and military vacuum. In October 1977 President Nasir rejected an offer of an annual payment of US $1m. from the USSR to lease the former base on Gan, announcing that he would not lease the island for military purposes, nor lease it to a superpower. In 1981 the President announced plans to establish an industrial zone on Gan. By 1990 there were two factories (producing ready-made garments) operating on Gan. The airport on Gan, which links the capital, Malé, with the south, is now fully operational and is due to become an international airport in the near future.

A new Constitution, promulgated in 1968, vested considerable powers in the President, including the right to appoint and dismiss the Prime Minister and the Cabinet.

In March 1975, following rumours of a coup conspiracy, President Nasir dismissed the Prime Minister, Ahmed Zaki, and the premiership was abolished. Unexpectedly, President Nasir announced that he would not seek re-election at the end of his second term in 1978. To succeed him, the legislature chose Maumoon Abdul Gayoom, Minister of Transport under Nasir, who was approved by referendum in July 1978 and took office in November. President Gayoom announced that his main priority would be the development of the poor rural regions, while in foreign affairs the existing policy of non-alignment would continue.

Ex-President Nasir left the country after his resignation, but the authorities subsequently sought his return to Maldives, where he was required to answer charges of misappropriating government funds. In 1980 President Gayoom confirmed an attempted coup against the Government and implicated Nasir in the alleged plot. Nasir was to stand trial, in his absence, on these and other charges. In April 1981 Ahmed Naseem, former Deputy Fisheries Minister and brother-in-law of Nasir, was sentenced to life imprisonment for plotting to overthrow President Gayoom. Nasir himself denied any involvement in the coup, and attempts to extradite him from Singapore were unsuccessful. (In July 1990, however, President Gayoom officially pardoned Nasir *in absentia*, in recognition of the role that he had played in winning national independence.) In 1983 another unsuccessful plot against President Gayoom was reported. In September he was re-elected as President, for a further five years, by a national referendum (with 95.6% of the popular vote). In September 1988 Gayoom was again re-elected unopposed, for a third five-year term, obtaining a record 96.4% of the popular vote.

A third, and more serious, attempt to depose President Gayoom took place in November 1988, when a sea-borne mercenary force, which was composed of around 80 alleged Sri Lankan Tamil separatists (led by a disaffected Maldivian businessman, Abdullah Luthufi), landed in Malé and endeavoured to seize control of important government installations. At the request of President Gayoom, however, the Indian Government dispatched an emergency contingent of 1,600 troops, which rapidly and successfully suppressed the attempted coup. Nineteen people were reported to have been killed in the fighting. In September 1989 the President commuted to life imprisonment the death sentences imposed on 12 Sri Lankans and four Maldivians, who took part in the aborted coup. The Indian Government withdrew its remaining 160 troops from Maldives in early November.

In November 1989 Maldives hosted an international conference, with delegates from other small islands, to discuss the threat posed to low-lying island countries by the predicted rise in sea-level caused by heating of the earth's atmosphere as a result of pollution (the 'greenhouse effect'). In June 1990 an Environmental Research Unit, which was to operate under the Ministry of Planning and the Environment (now the Ministry of Planning, Human Resources and Environment), was established in Maldives.

In February 1990, despite alleged opposition from powerful members of the privileged élite, President Gayoom announced that, as part of proposals for a broad new policy of liberalization and democratic reform, he was planning to introduce legislation, in the near future, enabling him to distribute powers, currently enjoyed by the President alone, amongst other official bodies. A further sign of growing democratization in Maldives was the holding of discussions by the President's Consultative Council, in early 1990, concerning freedom of speech (particularly in the local press). In April, however, it became apparent that some Maldivians opposed political change, when three pro-reform members of the Majlis received anonymous death threats. A few months later, following the emergence of several politically outspoken magazines, including *Sangu* (The Conchshell), there was an abrupt reversal of the Government's policy regarding the liberalization of the press. All publications not sanctioned by the Government were banned, and a number of leading writers and publishers were arrested.

As part of a major cabinet reshuffle in late May 1990, President Gayoom dismissed the Minister of State for Defence and National Security, Ilyas Ibrahim (who also held the Trade and Industries portfolio and headed the State Trading Corporation), from his post, following the latter's abrupt and unannounced departure from the country. The Government later disclosed that Ibrahim (Gayoom's brother-in-law) was to have appeared before a presidential special commission investigating alleged embezzlement and misappropriation of government funds. On his return to Maldives in August, Ibrahim was placed under house arrest. In March 1991, however, the special commission concluded that there was no evidence of involvement, either direct or indirect, by Ibrahim in the alleged financial misdeeds; in the same month the President appointed Ilyas Ibrahim as Minister of Atolls Administration. In April the President established an anti-corruption board, which was to investigate allegations of corruption, bribery, fraud, misappropriation of government funds and property, and misuse of government office.

In early August 1993, a few weeks before the Majlis vote on the presidential candidate, Gayoom was informed that Ilyas Ibrahim, whose position as Minister of Atolls Administration had afforded him the opportunity to build a political base outside Malé (where he already enjoyed considerable popularity), was seeking the presidency and attempting to influence members of the Majlis (the Majlis chooses by secret ballot a single candidate, who is presented to the country in a referendum). In the Majlis vote, held in late August, the incumbent President, who had previously been unanimously nominated for the presidency by the legislature, obtained 28 votes, against 18 for his brother-in-law. For his allegedly unconstitutional behaviour, however, Ibrahim was charged with attempting to 'influence the members of the Majlis' and he promptly left the country. Ibrahim was subsequently tried *in absentia* and sentenced to 15 years' imprisonment. In addition, his brother, Abbas Ibrahim, was removed from his post as Minister of Fisheries and Agriculture.

In October 1993 Gayoom was re-elected as President, for a further five years, by a national referendum in which he obtained 92.8% of the popular vote. Following his re-election, the President carried out an extensive cabinet reshuffle and a far-reaching reorganization of government bodies, including the establishment of two new ministries (that of Youth, Women's Affairs and Sports and that of Information and Culture), in order to increase efficiency and further democratic reform. In his inaugural address to the Majlis, Gayoom pledged to introduce constitutional reform to enable more than one candidate to contest the presidency (by direct vote of the people).

In November 1994, at an official ceremony marking Republic Day, President Gayoom outlined various measures intended to strengthen the political system and to further democratization. These included the granting of greater autonomy and responsibilities to members of the Cabinet, the introduction of regulations governing the conduct of civil servants (in order to increase their accountability), the introduction of democratic elections to island development committees and atoll committees, and the establishment of a Law Commission to carry out reforms to the judicial system.

Maldives is a founder member of the South Asian Association for Regional Co-operation (SAARC, see p. 241), which was formally constituted in December 1985, and became a full member of the Commonwealth in June 1985. In February 1995 Maldives had diplomatic relations with 118 countries. Maldives' international standing was enhanced in November 1990, when it successfully hosted the fifth SAARC summit meeting, which was held in Malé.

## Government

Legislative power is held by the unicameral Citizens' Council (Majlis), with 48 members, including 40 elected for five years by universal adult suffrage (two by the National Capital Island and two from each of the 19 atolls) and eight appointed by the President. Executive power is vested in the President, elected by popular vote (on nomination by the Majlis) for five years. He governs with the assistance of an appointed Cabinet, responsible to the Majlis. The country has 20 administrative districts: the capital is under direct central administration while the 19 atolls are each under an atoll chief (verin) who is appointed by the President, under the general guidance of the Minister of Atolls Administration. There are no political parties.

## Economic Affairs

In 1993, according to estimates by the World Bank, Maldives' gross national product (GNP), measured at average 1991–93 prices, was US $194m., equivalent to $820 per head. During 1985–92, it was estimated, GNP per head increased, in real terms, at an average annual rate of 8.5%. During 1985–93 the population increased by an annual average of 3.3%. According to official estimates, Maldives' gross domestic product (GDP) increased, in real terms, by an annual average of 10.3% in 1985–91, by 6.3% in 1992, by 6.2% in 1993 and by 6.6% in 1994.

Agriculture (including fishing) contributed 23.7% of GDP in 1991 (15.1% was provided by fishing). About 25% of the total working population were employed in the sector (more than 20% in fishing) in 1990. In 1992 fishing was Maldives' second largest source of foreign exchange, after tourism. Dried and frozen skipjack tuna accounted for about 49% of total export earnings in 1986. The value of canned tuna exports in 1992 totalled about US $16m. Small quantities of various fruits, vegetables and cereals are produced, but virtually all of the principal staple foods have to be imported. The dominant agricultural activity (not including fishing) in Maldives is coconut production. Agricultural GDP (not including fishing) increased by 6.2% in 1991, compared with the previous year. The GDP of the fisheries sector grew by 15% in 1994, compared with 1993.

Industry (including mining, manufacturing, power and construction) employed about 22% of the working population in 1990 and provided 16.8% of GDP in 1992.

Mining and quarrying contributed 1.8% of GDP in 1992, and employed 0.9% of the working population in 1990. In February 1989 the Government and a Netherlands company signed a contract permitting exploration for petroleum in Maldives. However, by late 1991, despite the drilling of an offshore test well earlier that year, no reserves of petroleum or natural gas had been discovered in Maldivian waters.

The manufacturing and power sectors together employed 15.9% of the working population in 1990, but provided only 6.0% of GDP in 1992. There are only a small number of 'modern' manufacturing enterprises in Maldives, including fish-canning, garment-making and soft-drink bottling. Although cottage industries (such as the weaving of coir yarn and boat-building) employ nearly one-quarter of the total labour force, there is little scope for expansion, owing to the limited size of the domestic market. Because of its lack of manufacturing industries, Maldives has to import most essential consumer and capital goods. In the late 1980s and early 1990s traditional handicrafts, such as lacquer work and shell craft, revived as a result of the tourist market.

Energy is derived principally from petroleum, imports of which comprised 14.6% of the cost of imports in 1991. Owing to a surge in commercial activities and a significant increase in construction projects in Malé, demand for electricity in the capital grew rapidly in the late 1980s and early 1990s. Accordingly, plans were formulated in late 1991 to augment the generating capacity of the power station in Malé and to improve the distribution network.

Following the decline of the shipping industry in the 1980s, tourism gained in importance as an economic sector, and by 1989 it had overtaken the fishing industry as Maldives' largest source of foreign exchange. In 1992 revenue from tourism totalled about 198.2m. rufiyaa, and tourist arrivals reached 235,852 (compared with only 29,325 in 1978). In 1992 the tourism sector provided 17.7% of GDP. The total number of tourist arrivals rose to 278,000 in 1994.

In 1993 Maldives recorded a visible trade deficit of US $139.3m., and there was a deficit of $47.6m. on the current account of the balance of payments. Major trading partners with Maldives are the United Kingdom, the USA, Sri Lanka and Singapore. The principal exports in 1992 were marine products (tuna being the largest export commodity) and clothing. The principal imports were manufactured goods, petroleum products and food items. In that year the cost of imports exceeded total GDP.

In early 1995 the 1994 budgetary deficit was estimated at about 127m. rufiyaa. Foreign grant aid in 1994 was projected to total an estimated 207m. rufiyaa. In 1991 Japan was Maldives' largest aid donor. Maldives' total external debt was US $114.6m. at the end of 1993, of which $111.6m. was long-term public debt. In that year the cost of debt-servicing was equivalent to 3.8% of revenue from exports of goods and services. During 1990–91 the average annual rate of inflation was 14.7%, rising to 17.2% in 1992. In 1993 the rate of inflation increased to 20% as a result of higher money supply growth, depreciation of the exchange rate and rises in certain administered prices and in the procurement price of fish. Around 1.6% of the labour force were unemployed in early 1985.

Maldives is a member of the Asian Development Bank (see p. 107), the Colombo Plan (see p. 238), and the South Asian Association for Regional Co-operation (SAARC, see p. 241).

One result of the rapid growth and increasing importance of the tourism sector in Maldives in the 1980s and the early 1990s was the Government's efforts to improve the infrastructure (including development of communication systems, sanitation and water supply). By 1993 postal services were available to all the inhabited islands, telephone facilities were provided in the major islands of seven of the southern atolls and three of the northern atolls and facsimile services were available to some islands. The numerous development projects undertaken during the 1980s and early 1990s resulted in a shortage of labour, which was partly alleviated by employing workers from abroad and by the establishment of vocational training courses. In late 1994 more than 17,000 expatriate workers were employed in Maldives. In the first half of the 1990s the trade deficit increased annually as fish exports declined and imports grew. The decrease in fish exports reflected the slump in global demand, more intense competition from foreign producers and falling prices in the principal European markets. At the same time, imports were boosted by import liberalization measures and by expansionary monetary

## Social Welfare

The country's main hospital, the 200-bed Indira Gandhi Memorial Hospital in Malé, which was built with Indian aid, was opened in 1994. There are also four regional hospitals—one in the north and three in the south—with a combined total of 61 beds, and 21 primary health care centres. A Family Planning Centre was opened in Malé in 1994. In 1992 30 duty physicians and 17 medical specialists were working in the Central Hospital in Malé (which was closed following the inauguration of the Indira Gandhi Memorial Hospital in late 1994). In 1992 there were 2.3 community health workers per 10,000 inhabitants in Maldives. The Institute for Health Sciences was inaugurated in late 1992. Of total projected expenditure by the central Government in 1995, 216m. rufiyaa (11.5%) was allocated to the health and welfare sector.

## Education

Education is not compulsory. There are three types of formal education: traditional Koranic schools (Makthab), Dhivehi-language primary schools (Madhrasa) and English-language primary and secondary schools. Schools of the third category are the only ones equipped to teach a standard curriculum. In 1984 a national curriculum was introduced in all schools. Primary education begins at six years of age and lasts for five years. Secondary education, beginning at the age of 11, lasts for up to seven years, comprising a first cycle of five years and a second of two years. In 1983 it was estimated that only about 65% of the school-age population attended school. School enrolment grew by 9.5%, however, between 1984 and 1986. At the end of 1992 there were 57 government schools (with a total of 32,475 pupils), and at the end of 1989 there were 211 community and private schools (with 36,504 pupils). The construction of the first secondary school outside Malé was completed, on Hithadoo Island in Addu Atoll, in 1992. There is a full-time vocational training centre, a teacher-training institute, an institute of hotel and catering services (opened in 1987), a Centre for Management and Administration, a Science Education Centre, and an Islamic education centre. Construction work on the Maldives Institute of Technical Education, which, when completed, was expected to alleviate the problem of the lack of local skilled labour, was begun in mid-1993. In 1980, when the rate of adult literacy stood at 63%, a Basic Education Programme was launched, and an estimated 11,000 adults attended classes during 1983. In 1991 the Government estimated that the islands' rate of adult literacy was 98.2%, the highest literacy rate in South Asia. In January 1989 the Government established a National Council on Education to oversee the development of education in Maldives. Projected budgetary expenditure on education by the central Government in 1995 was 257m. rufiyaa, representing 13.7% of total spending.

## Public Holidays

**1995:** 7 January (National Day), 3 March* (Id al-Fitr, end of Ramadan), 10 May* (Id al-Adha, feast of the Sacrifice), 31 May* (Islamic New Year), 26 July (Independence Day), 9 August* (Birth of the Prophet Muhammad), 3 November (Victory Day), 11 November (Republic Day), 2 December (Martyrs' Day), 10 December (Fishermens' Day).

**1996:** 7 January (National Day), 21 February* (Id al-Fitr, end of Ramadan), 29 April* (Id al-Adha, feast of the Sacrifice), 19 May* (Islamic New Year), 26 July (Independence Day), 28 July* (Birth of the Prophet Muhammad), 3 November (Victory Day), 11 November (Republic Day), 2 December (Martyrs' Day), 10 December (Fishermens' Day).

* These holidays are dependent on the Islamic lunar calendar and may vary by one or two days from the dates given.

# Statistical Survey

Source (unless otherwise stated): Ministry of Information and Culture, Huravee Bldg, Ameer Ahmed Magu, Malé 20–05; tel. 323836; telex 66085; fax 326211.

## AREA AND POPULATION

**Area:** 298 sq km (115 sq miles).

**Population:** 181,453 (males 94,060, females 87,393) at census of 25–28 March 1985; 213,215 (males 109,336, females 103,879) at census of 2–8 March 1990; 231,000 (official estimate) at mid-1992; 238,363 (official estimate) at mid-1993.

**Density** (mid-1993): 799.9 per sq km.

**Principal Town:** Malé (capital), population 60,105 (at 31 December 1992).

**Births and Deaths** (1992): Registered live births 8,139 (birth rate 35.3 per 1,000), Registered deaths 1,330 (death rate 5.8 per 1,000). Source: UN, *Population and Vital Statistics Report*.

**Expectation of Life** (years at birth, 1991): Males 66.18; females 65.20. Source: UN, *Demographic Yearbook*.

**Economically Active Population** (persons aged 14 years and over, census of March 1990): Agriculture, hunting, forestry and fishing 14,117; Mining and quarrying 496; Manufacturing 8,441; Electricity, gas and water 445; Construction 3,151; Trade, restaurants and hotels 8,884; Transport, storage and communications 5,321; Financing, insurance, real estate and business services 1,058; Community, social and personal services 11,848; Activities not adequately defined 2,188; Total employed 55,949 (males 44,858; females 11,091); Unemployed persons previously employed 486 (males 340; females 146); Total labour force 56,435. Figures exclude members of the armed forces and persons seeking work for the first time. Source: ILO, *Year Book of Labour Statistics*.

## AGRICULTURE, ETC.

**Principal Crops** (metric tons, 1992): Coconuts (number of nuts) 13,442,737, Finger millet 5.7, Maize 1.6, Cassava 31.6, Sweet potatoes 13.8, Taro (Colocasia) 141.7, Alocasia 522.3, Onions 0.1, Chillies 40.3, Sorghum 2.0.

**Sea Fishing** ('000 metric tons, 1992): Skipjack tuna (Oceanic skipjack) 58.6, Yellowfin tuna 8.7, Other tuna-related species 6.2, Other marine fishes 8.6, Total catch 82.0. *Total Catch* (metric tons): 90,000 in 1993; 104,000 in 1994. Source: Ministry of Fisheries and Agriculture.

## INDUSTRY

**Selected Products** ('000 metric tons, unless otherwise indicated, 1991): Frozen fish 10.1; Salted, dried or smoked fish 6.8; Canned fish 7.2; Electric energy 28 million kWh. Source: UN, *Industrial Statistics Yearbook*. **1992** ('000 metric tons): Frozen fish 5.5; Salted, dried or smoked fish 5.4; Canned fish 7.4; Fish meal 5.5.

## FINANCE

**Currency and Exchange Rates:** 100 laari (larees) = 1 rufiyaa (Maldivian rupee). *Sterling and Dollar Equivalents* (31 December 1994): £1 sterling = 18.41 rufiyaa; US $1 = 11.77 rufiyaa; 1,000 rufiyaa = £54.31 = $84.96. *Average Exchange Rate* (rufiyaa per $): 10.569 in 1992; 10.957 in 1993; 11.586 in 1994.

**Budget** (million rufiyaa): *1994* (estimates): Revenue: Taxation 505, Non-tax revenue 330 (Revenue from resort leases 124, Entrepreneurial income 85), Loan assistance for development projects 382, Grant aid 136, Food and financial aid 20; Total 1,373. Expenditure: Social development 428 (Education 241, Health and welfare 130), Economic development 472.2 (Fisheries 340, Tourism 19.5), Loan repayments 155; Total (incl. others) 1,570.2 (Recurrent 794, Capital 776.2). *1995* (estimates): Revenue: Taxation 613 (Import duties 375, Tourism taxes 178), Non-tax revenue 442 (Revenue from resort leases 135, Entrepreneurial income 123), Loans from abroad 542, Grant aid 207; Total 1,804. Expenditure: Social development 559 (Education 257, Health and welfare 216), Economic development 633 (Fisheries 220); Total (incl. others) 1,881 (Recurrent 855, Capital 1,026).

**International Reserves** (US $ million at 31 December 1993): Gold 0.04; IMF special drawing rights 0.03; Reserve position in IMF 1.21; Foreign exchange 24.92; Total 26.20. (US $ million at 31

## MALDIVES

December 1994): IMF special drawing rights 0.05; Reserve position in IMF 1.28; Foreign exchange 29.89. Source: IMF, *International Financial Statistics*.

**Money Supply** (million rufiyaa at 31 December 1993): Currency outside banks 330.38; Demand deposits at commercial banks 281.13; Total money (incl. others) 694.54. Source: IMF, *International Financial Statistics*.

**Gross Domestic Product by Economic Activity** (US $ million at constant 1985 prices, 1992): Fishing 21.4; Coral and sand mining 2.9; Manufacturing (incl. electricity) 9.4; Construction 14.3; Distribution 28.6; Tourism 27.9; Transport 10.1; Real estate 6.6; Government administration 14.1; Services 9.5; Other 13.1; *Total* 157.9.

**Balance of Payments** (US $ million, 1993): Merchandise exports f.o.b. 38.5; Merchandise imports f.o.b. −177.8; *Trade balance* −139.3; Exports of services 178.2; Imports of services −55.8; Other income received 3.0; Other income paid −22.0; Private unrequited transfers (net) −20.0; Official unrequited transfers (net) 8.3; *Current balance* −47.6; Direct investment (net) 6.9; Other capital (net) 18.0; Net errors and omissions 22.6; *Overall balance* −0.1. Source: IMF, *International Financial Statistics*.

### EXTERNAL TRADE

**Total Trade** (US $ million): *Imports c.i.f.:* 161.2 in 1991; 189.3 in 1992; 185.1 in 1993. *Exports f.o.b.:* 53.7 in 1991; 40.0 in 1992; 34.6 in 1993. Source: IMF, *International Financial Statistics*.

**Principal Commodities** (million rufiyaa, 1992): *Imports:* Consumer goods 997.5; Petroleum products 242.1; Intermediate and capital goods 761.8. *Exports:* Frozen skipjack tuna 35.9; Apparel and clothing accessories 84.1; Canned tuna 161.6; Dried skipjack tuna 73.1; Dried sharkfins 11.1; Fish meal 10.6; Salted and dried fish 26.9.

**Principal Trading Partners** (million rufiyaa, 1991): *Exports:* United Kingdom 135.3; USA 125.6; Sri Lanka 104.0; Thailand 59.4; Germany 35.7; Singapore 27.9; Japan 21.3; Netherlands 11.4; Hong Kong 10.0. *Imports:* India 127.9; Sri Lanka 126.1; Singapore 94.3; United Kingdom 95.3; Japan 66.9; Thailand 46.5; Hong Kong 36.6; United Arab Emirates 32.8; Germany 28.8.

### TRANSPORT

**Road Traffic** (1992): Passenger cars 725, Bicycles 38,252, Taxis 985, Motorcycles 4,126, Lorries, trucks and tractors 455, Vans and buses 110, Jeeps 267, Hand carts 284.

**Merchant Shipping Fleet** (displacement, '000 gross registered tons at 30 June): 78 in 1990; 42 in 1991; 52 in 1992. Source: UN, *Statistical Yearbook*.

**International Shipping** (freight traffic, '000 metric tons, 1990): Goods loaded 27; Goods unloaded 78. Source: UN, *Monthly Bulletin of Statistics*.

**Civil Aviation** (traffic on scheduled services, 1990): Passengers carried 9,000; Passenger-km (million) 3. Source: UN, *Statistical Yearbook*.

### TOURISM

**Foreign Visitors by Country of Origin** (1992): Australia 2,884, Austria 8,328, France 14,018, Germany 52,141, India 7,805, Italy 49,149, Japan 18,379, Sri Lanka 13,695, Switzerland 11,309, United Kingdom 15,500; Total (incl. others) 235,852.

**Tourist Arrivals:** 241,000 in 1993; 278,000 in 1994.

**Tourist Receipts** (million rufiyaa): 141 in 1990; 157 in 1991; 198.2 in 1992.

**Tourist Resorts:** (1994): 73.

**Hotel Beds** (1994): 9,500.

### COMMUNICATIONS MEDIA

At the end of March 1992 there were 27,848 radio receivers and 6,591 television receivers in use.

**Telephones** ('000 main lines in use): 5 (estimate) in 1989; 6 in 1990; 8 in 1991. Source: UN, *Statistical Yearbook*.

### EDUCATION

**Primary** (1986): 243 schools, 41,812 pupils, 1,138 teachers.
**Secondary** (1986): 9 schools, 3,581 pupils, 291 teachers.
**Vocational** (1986): 11 schools, 544 pupils, 54 teachers.
**Total Number of Teachers** (1989): 1,833 (1,412 local; 421 from overseas).
**Total Number of Pupils** (1992): 73,642 (32,475 in state schools; 41,167 in private schools).

# Directory

## The Constitution

Following a referendum in March 1968, the Maldive Islands (renamed Maldives in April 1969) became a republic on 11 November 1968. The main provisions of the 1968 Constitution are:

The President is Head of State and is vested with full executive powers.

Every five years the Majlis, or Citizens' Council, elects by secret ballot a single candidate to be the President, who is presented to the country at a referendum. If the candidate does not secure a minimum 51% endorsement of the national vote at the referendum, the Majlis is required to present another candidate.

The President appoints a Cabinet.

The members of the Cabinet are individually responsible to the Majlis.

The Majlis has 48 members, including 40 elected for five years by universal adult suffrage (two by the National Capital Island and two from each of the 19 atolls) and eight appointed by the President. The Majlis is empowered to enact laws within the framework of the Constitution and to sanction the annual national budget.

The powers of the President, the Cabinet and the legislature are laid down in the Constitution.

Within the provisions of Islam, freedom of 'life movement', speech and development are guaranteed as basic rights of the people.

## The Government

**President and Head of State:** MAUMOON ABDUL GAYOOM (took office 11 November 1978; re-elected 30 September 1983, 23 September 1988 and 1 October 1993).

### THE CABINET
(May 1995)

**President, Minister of Defence and National Security, and of Finance and Treasury:** MAUMOON ABDUL GAYOOM.
**Minister of Fisheries and Agriculture:** HASSAN SAABIR.
**Minister of Foreign Affairs:** FATHULLA JAMEEL.
**Minister of Education:** Dr MOHAMED LATHEEF.
**Minister of Trade and Industries:** ABDULLA YAAMEEN.
**Minister of Health and Welfare:** AHMED ABDULLA.
**Minister of Justice and Islamic Affairs:** MOHAMED RASHEED IBRAHIM.
**Minister of Tourism:** IBRAHIM HUSSAIN ZAKI.
**Minister of Transport and Communications:** AHMED ZAHIR.
**Minister of Planning, Human Resources and Environment:** ISMAIL SHAFEEU.
**Minister of Home Affairs:** ABDULLA JAMEEL.
**Minister of Construction and Public Works:** UMAR ZAHIR.
**Minister of Atolls Administration:** ABDUL RASHEED HUSSAIN.
**Minister of Youth, Women's Affairs and Sports:** RASHIDA YOOSUF.
**Minister of Information and Culture:** IBRAHIM MANIK.
**Minister at the President's Office:** MOHAMED ZAHIR HUSSAIN.
**Minister of State for Presidential Affairs:** MOHAMED HUSSAIN.
**Attorney-General:** Dr MOHAMED MUNAWWAR.

There were, in addition, two Ministers of State and two Ministers of State without Independent Charge.

In July 1985 a Consultative Council, comprising 15 members, was appointed by the President to advise him on a wide variety of issues. In early 1990 the membership of the Council was increased to 55 (Chair. MOOSA FATHY; Vice-Chair. Sheikh MOHAMED RASHEED IBRAHIM).

# MALDIVES

## MINISTRIES

**The President's Office:** Boduthakurufaanu Magu, Malé 20-05; tel. 323701; telex 66013; fax 325500.

**The Attorney-General's Office:** Huravee Bldg, Malé 20-05; tel. 323809; fax 314109.

**Ministry of Atolls Administration:** Faashana Bldg, Boduthakurufaanu Magu (North), Malé 20-05; tel. 322825; fax 327750.

**Ministry of Construction and Public Works:** Izzuddeen Magu, Malé 20-01; tel. 323234; telex 77071; fax 326637.

**Ministry of Defence and National Security:** Bandeyrige, Ameer Ahmed Magu, Malé 20-05; tel. 322601; telex 66056; fax 313281.

**Ministry of Education:** Ghaazee Bldg, Ameer Ahmed Magu, Malé 20-02; tel. 323262; telex 66032; fax 321201.

**Ministry of Finance and Treasury:** Ghaazee Bldg, 2nd Floor, Ameer Ahmed Magu, Malé 20-05; tel. 325908; telex 66032; fax 324432.

**Ministry of Fisheries and Agriculture:** Ghaazee Bldg, Ameer Ahmed Magu, Malé 20-05; tel. 322625; telex 77033; fax 326558.

**Ministry of Foreign Affairs:** Boduthakurufaanu Magu, Malé 20-05; tel. 323400; telex 66008; fax 323841.

**Ministry of Health and Welfare:** Ghaazee Bldg, Ameer Ahmed Magu, Malé 20-05; tel. 323138; telex 66181; fax 328889.

**Ministry of Home Affairs:** Huravee Bldg, Ameer Ahmed Magu, Malé 20-05; tel. 323820; telex 77039; fax 324739.

**Ministry of Information and Culture:** Buruzu Magu, Malé 20-04; tel. 323836; telex 66085; fax 326211.

**Ministry of Justice and Islamic Affairs:** Justice Bldg, Orchid Magu, Malé 20-05; tel. 322303; fax 324103.

**Ministry of Planning, Human Resources and Environment:** Ghaazee Bldg, Ameer Ahmed Magu, Malé 20-05; tel. 322919; telex 66110; fax 327351.

**Ministry of Tourism:** Boduthakurufaanu Magu, Malé 20–05; tel. 323224; telex 66019; fax 322512.

**Ministry of Trade and Industries:** Ghaazee Bldg, Ameer Ahmed Magu, Malé 20-05; tel. 323668; telex 77076; fax 323756.

**Ministry of Transport and Communications:** Huravee Bldg, Ameer Ahmed Magu, Henveyru, Malé 20-05; tel. 323991; telex 77066; fax 323994.

**Ministry of Youth, Women's Affairs and Sports:** Umar Shopping Arcade, Chaandhanee Magu, Malé 20-02; tel. 325527; fax 316237.

## Legislature

### MAJLIS

The Majlis (Citizens' Council) comprises 48 members, of whom eight are appointed by the President, two elected by the people of Malé and two elected from each of the 19 atolls.

**Speaker:** ABDULLA HAMEED.
**Deputy Speaker:** AHMED ZAHIR.

### CITIZENS' SPECIAL MAJLIS

This is a special council with power to legislate in matters concerning the Constitution, financial activities and the protection of citizens' rights. It also considers any law changing the administrative structure or related to the leasing of land to foreigners. It comprises all the members of the Majlis, the Cabinet, 40 elected members (two from each atoll, two from Malé) and eight nominated by the President.

**Chairman:** ABDULLA HAMEED.

## Political Organizations

There are no political parties in Maldives.

## Diplomatic Representation

### HIGH COMMISSIONS IN MALDIVES

**India:** Maafannuaage, Malé; tel. 323015; telex 66044; fax 324778; High Commissioner: Dr HAR SWARUP SINGH.

**Pakistan:** 2 Moonimaage, Galolhu, POB 2006, Malé; tel. 322024; telex 66087; fax 321832; High Commissioner: AMANULLAH GICHKEE.

**Sri Lanka:** Sakeena Manzil, Medhuziyaaraiyh Magu, Malé 20-05; tel. 322845; telex 66061; fax 321652; High Commissioner: C. S. POOLOKASINGHAM.

## Judicial System

The administration of justice is undertaken in accordance with Islamic (Shari'a) law, through a body appointed by the President. In 1980 the Maldives High Court was established. There are four courts in Malé, and 200 Island Courts, one in every inhabited island. All courts, with the exception of the High Court, are under the control of the Ministry of Justice and Islamic Affairs.

### HIGH COURT

**Chief Justice:** MOOSA FATHY.
**Judges:** IBRAHIM NASEER, AHMED HAMEED FAHMY, YOOSUF MOOSA.

In February 1995 the President established a five-member Advisory Council on Judicial Affairs. The Council was to function under the President's Office and was to study and offer counsel to the President on appeals made to the President by either the appellant or the respondent in cases adjudicated by the High Court. The Council was also to offer such counsel as and when requested by the President on other judicial matters.

### ADVISORY COUNCIL ON JUDICIAL AFFAIRS

**Members:** MOOSA FATHY, ABDULLA HAMEED, Dr MOHAMED MUNAWWAR, Prof. MOHAMED RASHEED IBRAHIM, AL-SHEIKH HASSAN YOOSUF.

## Religion

Islam is the state religion, and the Maldivians are Sunni Muslims. In mid-1991 there were 724 mosques and 266 women's mosques throughout the country.

## The Press

In December 1993 the Government established a National Press Council to review, monitor and further develop journalism in Maldives.

**Aafathis:** Silver Star 4, Handhuvaree Higun, Malé; tel. 328730; fax 328906; daily; Dhivehi and English; Editor ABDUL SATTAR; circ. 300.

**Cricket Scene:** Machchangolhi Kibigasdhoshuge; f. 1987; 2 a year; publ. by the Maldives Cricket Foundation; Editor President MAUMOON ABDUL GAYOOM.

**Dheenuge Magu** (The Path of Religion): The President's Office, Boduthakurufaanu Magu, Malé 20-05; tel. 323701; telex 66013; fax 325500; f. 1986; weekly; Dhivehi; religious; publ. by the President's Office; Editor MAUMOON ABDUL GAYOOM; Dep. Editor MOHAMED RASHEED IBRAHIM; circ. 7,000.

**Faiythoora:** National Council for Linguistic and Historical Research, Soasun Magu, Malé 20-05; tel. 323066; f. 1979; monthly magazine; Dhivehi; Maldivian history, culture and language; Editor UZ. ABDULLA HAMEED; circ. 800.

**Furadhaana:** Ministry of Information and Culture, Buruzu Magu, Malé 20-04; tel. 321749; telex 66085; fax 326211; f. 1990; fortnightly; Dhivehi; Editor IBRAHIM MANIK; circ. 1,000.

**Haveeru:** G. Olympus (North Side), POB 20103, Malé 20-04; tel. 323685; fax 323103; f. 1979; daily; Dhivehi and English; Chair. MOHAMED ZAHIR HUSSAIN; Editor ALI RAFEEQ; circ. 4,500.

**Jamaathuge Khabaru** (Community News): Non-Formal Education Centre, Salahudeen Bldg, Malé 20-04; tel. 328772; fax 322231; monthly; Dhivehi; Editor AHMED ZAHIR; circ. 1,500.

**Maldives News Bulletin:** Maldives News Bureau, Buruzu Magu, Malé 20-04; tel. 323836; telex 66085; fax 326211; weekly; English; Editor ALI SHAREEF; circ. 300.

**Our Environment:** Forum of Writers on the Environment, c/o Ministry of Planning, Human Resources and Environment, Ghaazee Bldg, Ameer Ahmed Magu, Malé 20-05; tel. 324861; telex 66110; fax 327351; f. 1990; monthly; Dhivehi; Editor FAROUQ AHMED.

**Rasain:** Ministry of Fisheries and Agriculture, Ghaazee Bldg, Ameer Ahmed Magu, Malé 20-05; tel. 322625; telex 77033; fax 326558; f. 1980; annual; fisheries development.

### NEWS AGENCIES

**Haveeru News Service (HNS):** Husnuheena Magu, POB 20103, Malé 20-04; tel. 323685; fax 323103; f. 1979; Chair. MOHAMED ZAHIR HUSSAIN.

**Hiyama News Agency:** H. Navaagan, Malé 20-05; tel. 322588.

**Maldives News Bureau (MNB):** Ministry of Information and Culture, Buruzu Magu, Malé 20-04; tel. 323836; telex 66085; fax 326211.

## PUBLISHERS

**Corona Press:** Faamudheyri Magu, Malé; tel. 314741.

**Cyprea Print:** Raiydhebai Magu, Malé 20-03; tel. 328381; telex 66026; fax 328380; f. 1984; Man. Dir ABDULLA SAEED.

**Haveeru Printers and Publishers:** POB 20103, Malé; tel. 323685; fax 323103.

**Novelty Printers and Publishers:** Malé 20-01; tel. 322490; telex 66045; fax 327039; general and reference books; Sr Exec. ALI HUSSAIN.

**Ummeedhee Press:** M. Vani, Fareedhee Magu, Malé 20-01; tel. 326412; f. 1986; printing and publishing; Principal Officers ABDUL SHAKOOR ALI, ALI MOHAMED.

## Radio and Television

At the end of March 1992 there were 27,848 radio receivers and 6,591 television receivers in use.

**Voice of Maldives (VOM)** (Dhivehi Raajjeyge Adu): Moonlight Higun, Malé 20-06; tel. 325577; telex 66085; fax 328357; radio broadcasting began in 1962; home service in Dhivehi and English; broadcasts for an average of 16 hrs daily; Dir-Gen. BADRUL NASEER.

**Television Maldives:** Buruzu Magu, Malé 20-04; tel. 323106; telex 66085; television broadcasting began in 1978; broadcasts for an average of 6–7 hrs daily; covers a 40-km radius around Malé; Dir-Gen. HUSSAIN MOHAMED.

## Finance

(cap. = capital; brs = branches; amounts in rufiyaa)

### CENTRAL BANK

**Maldives Monetary Authority (MMA):** Umar Shopping Arcade, 1st & 3rd Floor, Chandhanee Magu, Maafannu, Malé 20-02; tel. 323783; telex 66144; fax 323862; f. 1981; bank of issue; supervises and regulates commercial bank and foreign exchange dealings and advises the Govt on banking and monetary matters; Gov. President MAUMOON ABDUL GAYOOM; Vice-Gov. ARIF HILMY; Gen. Man. KHADHEEJA HASSAN.

### COMMERCIAL BANK

**Bank of Maldives Ltd (BML):** 11 Boduthakurufaanu Magu, Malé 20-05; tel. 314876; telex 77030; fax 328233; f. 1982; 75% state-owned, 25% publicly-owned; cap. 20.4m. (1994); Chair. ABDULLA HAMEED; Gen. Man. and Chief Exec. B. RATHUNAMA; 10 brs.

### FOREIGN BANKS

**Bank of Ceylon** (Sri Lanka): 2 Orchid Magu, Malé; tel. 323045; telex 66080; fax 320575; Sr Exec. ARTHUR PERERA; 2 brs.

**Habib Bank Ltd** (Pakistan): Ground Floor, Ship Plaza, 1/6 Orchid Magu, Malé; tel. 322051; telex 66016; fax 326791; Vice-Pres. and Chief Man. AHEED BAKHSH QUADRI.

**State Bank of India:** Boduthakurufaanu Magu, Malé; tel. 323054; telex 66015; fax 323053; CEO J. PRASAD.

### INSURANCE

**Allied Insurance Co of the Maldives (Pte) Ltd:** 04–06 STO Trade Centre, Orchid Magu, Malé; tel. 324612; telex 77063; fax 325035; f. 1985; all classes of non-life insurance; operated by State Trading Organisation (see below); Chief Exec. MOHAMED MANIKU; Dir of Admin. IBRAHIM ATHIF SHAKOOR.

## Trade and Industry

**Maldives Traders' Association (MTA):** 4th Floor, Metropolis Bldg, Ibrahim Hassan Didi Magu, Malé 20-02; tel. 326634; fax 321889; f. 1979; Pres. GASIM IBRAHIM.

**Sri Lankan Trade Centre:** Malé; f. 1993 to encourage and facilitate trade and investment between Sri Lanka and Maldives.

### CHAMBERS OF COMMERCE AND INDUSTRIES

**Maldives National Chambers of Commerce and Industries:** Malé; f. 1994.

### GOVERNMENT ORGANIZATIONS

**Maldives Industrial Fisheries Co Ltd (MIFCO):** STO Trade Centre, Malé 20-02; telex 77014; fax 323955; f. 1993 to replace the Fisheries Projects Implementation Department (f. 1984); 80% owned by Govt, 20% owned by STO; under administration of Ministry of Fisheries and Agriculture; commercial enterprise engaged in fish purchasing, processing, canning and export; operates Felivaru Tuna Processing Plant; Chair. and Man. Dir IBRAHIM SHAKEEB; Dep. Dirs ADNAN ALI, HASSAN HALEEM.

**Felivaru Tuna Processing Plant:** Felivaru, Lhaviyani Atoll; tel. 230376; fax 230375; capacity to produce 50 metric tons of canned fish per day; Man. ABDUL FATHTHAH.

**State Trading Organisation (STO):** STO Bldg, 7 Haveeree Higun, Malé 20-02; tel. 323279; telex 66006; fax 325218; f. 1964 as Athirimaafannuge Trading Account, renamed as above in 1976; state-owned commercial organization; under administration of independent Board of Directors; imports and distributes staple foods, fuels, pharmaceuticals and general consumer items; handles the majority of the country's trading imports in addition to acting as purchaser for govt requirements; undertakes long-term development projects; Man. Dir MOHAMED MANIKU.

## Transport

**Maldives Transport and Contracting Co Ltd (MTCC):** MTCC Bldg, 3rd Floor, Boduthakurufaanu Magu, POB 2063, Malé 20-02; tel. 324135; telex 77038; fax 323221; f. 1981; 60% state-owned, 40% publicly owned; marine transport, civil and technical contracting, harbour development, shipping agents for general cargo, passenger liners and oil tankers; Man. Dir BANDHU IBRAHIM SALEEM; Dirs ADAM SALEEM, MOHAMED SHIHAB.

### SHIPPING

Vessels operate from Maldives to Sri Lanka and Singapore at frequent intervals, also calling at points in India, Pakistan, Myanmar (formerly Burma), Malaysia, Bangladesh, Thailand, Indonesia and the Middle East. In 1988 the ocean-going fleet of Maldives had a total displacement of 104,000 gross tons. Smaller vessels provide services between the islands on an irregular basis. Malé is the only port handling international traffic. In September 1986 a new commercial harbour was opened in Malé. In July 1991 the First Malé Port Development Project was inaugurated, with the aim of improving and increasing the capacity and efficiency of Malé Port. The second phase of the US $13.5m. project was completed in late 1992. The Second Malé Port Development Project, which was to be partly financed by a loan from the ADB and which involved the construction of an alongside berth and the provision of complementary port facilities, was inaugurated in late 1993 and was expected to be completed in 1996. It was estimated that the project would cost a total of US $10.4m.

**Maldives Ports Authority:** Commercial Harbour, Malé 20-02; tel. 327228; telex 66109; fax 325293; f. 1986; under administration of Ministry of Transport and Communications; Man. Dir ALI ABDULLAH.

**Huvadhoo Shipping (Pvt) Ltd:** Oceanic Store No. 3, Malé; tel. 322083; telex 66089; Man. Dir MOHAMED SALEEM.

**Island Enterprises (Pvt) Ltd:** 24 Boduthakurufaanu Magu, Malé; tel. 322747; telex 66042; fleet of two vessels (capacity 22,003 dwt); Sr Exec. MAIZAN UMAR MANIK.

**Madihaa Co (Pvt) Ltd:** 1/40 Shaheed Ali Higun, Malé; tel. 327812; fax 322251; Man. Dir MOOSA AHMED.

**Maldives National Ship Management Ltd:** MSL Bldg, Orchid Magu, Malé 20-02; tel. 322021; telex 66001; fax 324323; f. 1965 as Maldives Shipping Ltd; 100% state-owned; fleet of eight general cargo vessels and two container vessels; br. in Bombay; Dir (vacant); Man. MOHAMED MOOSA MANIK.

**Matrana Enterprises (Pvt) Ltd:** 97 Majeedhee Magu, Malé; tel. 321733; fax 322832; Sr Exec. MOHAMED ABDULLA.

**Mega-Speed Liners:** Malé; f. 1994; operates high-speed passenger service between Malé and the southern atolls.

**Villa Shipping and Trading:** Villa Bldg, Malé; tel. 321326; fax 325177.

### CIVIL AVIATION

The existing airport on Hululé Island near Malé, which was first opened in 1966, was expanded and improved to international standard with financial assistance from Kuwait, Abu Dhabi, Saudi Arabia and OPEC and, as Malé International Airport, was officially opened in November 1981. Charter flights from Europe subsequently began. In addition, there are four domestic airports covering different regions of the country: one on Gan Island, Addu Atoll, another on Kadhdhoo Island, Hadhdhummathi Atoll (opened in December 1986), another on Hanimaadhoo Island, South Thiladhummathi Atoll (opened in October 1990), and another on

Kaadedhdhoo Island, South Huvadhu Atoll (opened in December 1993). The airport on Gan Island was expected to be capable of servicing international flights in the near future. Construction of a fifth domestic airport, in Raa Atoll Dhuvaafaru, was scheduled to begin in 1994. In early 1995 there were 10 helipads being used in Maldives.

**Air Maldives Ltd:** Faashana Bldg, Boduthakurufaanu Magu, Malé; tel. 322436; telex 77058; fax 325066; f. 1974; 51% govt-owned, 49% owned by Malaysian Helicopter Services; under administration of Ministry of Transport and Communications; domestic flights; international flights to Sri Lanka, India and Malaysia; ground handling agent for 18 international airlines; passenger-handling services; general sales agent for all scheduled carriers operating to Maldives; organizes tours, hotel-booking, etc.; Chair. and Man. Dir ANBAREE ABDUL SATTAR; Dep. Man. Dir IBRAHIM ZUHAIR.

**Hummingbird Helicopters (Maldives) Pvt Ltd:** MHA Bldg, 4th Floor, 1 Orchid Magu, POB 6, Malé; tel. 325708; telex 66185; fax 323161; f. 1989; operates 5 helicopters; Man. Dir C. H. CHAMBERS; Dir (Commercial and Operations) HEINZ FROEHLICH.

**Seagull Airways (Pvt) Ltd:** 02-00, MTCC Bldg, Boduthakurufaanu Magu, Malé 20-02; tel. 315234; fax 315123; f. 1993; operates four helicopters (with capacity of 20 passengers each).

## Tourism

The tourist industry brings considerable foreign exchange to Maldives, and receipts from tourism amounted to 198.2m. rufiyaa in 1992. The islands' attractions include white sandy beaches and multi-coloured coral formations. By 1994 there were 73 island resorts and there was a total of 9,500 beds. The annual total of foreign visitors increased from only 29,325 in 1978 to 278,000 in 1994.

**Maldives Association of Tourism Industry (MATI):** H. Deems Villa, Meheli Goalhi, POB 23, Malé; tel. 326640; fax 326641; f. 1984; promotes and develops tourism; Chair. MOHAMED UMAR MANIK; Sec.-Gen. AHMED MUJUTHABA.

**Tourist Information Unit:** Malé International Airport, Hululé Island; tel. 325511 (Ext. 648).

# MALI

## Introductory Survey

### Location, Climate, Language, Religion, Flag, Capital

The Republic of Mali is a land-locked country in West Africa, with Algeria to the north, Mauritania and Senegal to the west, Guinea and Côte d'Ivoire to the south, and Burkina Faso and Niger to the east. The climate is hot throughout the country. The northern region of Mali is part of the Sahara, an arid desert. It is wetter in the south, where the rainy season is from June to October. Temperatures in Bamako are generally between 16°C (61°F) and 39°C (103°F). The official language is French but a number of other languages, including Bambara, Fulfulde, Sonrai, Tamashek, Soninke and Dogon, are widely spoken. About 80% of the population are Muslims and an estimated 18% follow traditional animist beliefs; about 1.2% are Christians. The national flag (proportions 3 by 2) has three equal vertical stripes, of green, gold and red. The capital is Bamako.

### Recent History

Mali was formerly French Sudan (Soudan), a part of French West Africa. In April 1959 it merged with Senegal to form the Federation of Mali, which became independent on 20 June 1960. Senegal seceded two months later, and the remnant of the Federation was proclaimed the Republic of Mali on 22 September 1960. Its first President was Modibo Keita, the leader of the Union soudanaise party, who pursued authoritarian socialist policies and severed Mali's links with the French political and financial bloc. Mali withdrew from the Franc Zone (see p. 168) in 1962, and developed close economic links with the USSR and the other communist states. Rapid inflation and the increasing incidence of smuggling caused Mali to return to the Franc Zone in 1968; however, the country did not become fully reintegrated into the Zone's monetary union until 1984.

The elected Assemblée nationale was dissolved in January 1968. Following a series of purges of Union soudanaise and public officials, Keita was overthrown in November of that year by a group of junior army officers, who assumed power as the Comité militaire pour la libération nationale (CMLN). The Constitution was abrogated, and all political activity was banned. Lt (later Gen.) Moussa Traoré became Head of State and President of the CMLN, while Capt. Yoro Diakité became President of the Government (Prime Minister). The Government gave assurances that a return to civilian rule would be permitted when Mali's severe economic problems (largely arising from the drought in the Sahel region) had been overcome and when new political institutions had been created. In September 1969 Traoré assumed the presidency of the Government, demoting Diakité to a lesser ministerial post.

In April 1974 the CMLN published a proposed new Constitution, providing for the establishment of a one-party state, with the military regime remaining in power for a transitional period of five years. The document was approved by a referendum in June. Proposals for the formation of a new ruling party, the Union démocratique du peuple malien (UDPM), were announced in September 1976. The proposals encountered persistent opposition from politicians who had been active before the 1968 coup, and from those (particularly students) who advocated the establishment of a multi-party democracy. Hostile anti-Government demonstrations followed Keita's death in custody in 1977, and there was also reported to be resistance to civilian rule from within the army. The influence of civilians in Traoré's administration was increased following the arrest, in February 1978, of the four members of the CMLN who were most closely associated with the repressive machinery of military rule. Together with 32 senior members of the police and armed forces, they were accused of undermining state security, of embezzlement and of corruption. Two of the former officials were sentenced to death in September (one sentence was later revised to 10 years' hard labour); 25 other defendants received custodial sentences.

The UDPM was officially constituted in March 1979, and presidential and legislative elections took place in June. President Traoré, the sole candidate in the former, was elected for a five-year term, reportedly receiving more than 99% of the votes cast; the single list of UDPM candidates for the 82-member Assemblée nationale was similarly elected for a four-year term.

In January 1980, following student protests concerning examinations and grants, the Government dissolved the students' union because it refused to affiliate to the UDPM. Hundreds of students were detained, and in March the death in custody of the student union leader resulted in further disruption. In December 1980 a plot to overthrow the Government was discovered, and several junior police officers were arrested. Three people were later condemned to death for their part in the conspiracy.

A constitutional amendment, adopted in September 1981, increased the presidential term of office to six years and reduced that of the legislature to three years. Elections to the Assemblée nationale were held in June 1982 and June 1985, with UDPM candidates being elected unopposed on both occasions. In June 1985 Gen. Traoré was re-elected to the presidency, reportedly obtaining 99.94% of the votes cast. In June 1986 Traoré relinquished the defence portfolio to a close associate, Gen. Sékou Ly, and appointed Dr Mamadou Dembélé (hitherto Minister of Public Health and Social Affairs) to the recreated office of Prime Minister.

A long-standing territorial dispute between Mali and Burkina Faso, concerning the 'Agacher strip' (an area extending for 160 km along their common border and believed to contain valuable deposits of minerals), escalated into armed conflict in December 1985: fighting lasted for six days, and resulted in some 50 deaths. The International Court of Justice (ICJ), to which the issue had been referred in 1983, urged both countries to withdraw their troops from the disputed zone, and in January 1986, following regional mediation, troops were withdrawn from the Agacher area. The two states resumed full diplomatic relations in June, and accepted as binding the ICJ's final ruling on the dispute in December, whereby they were each awarded sovereignty over one-half of the territory.

The office of Prime Minister was again abolished in June 1988; Dembélé returned to his former position within the Council of Ministers (he was dismissed from the Government one year later), and Traoré resumed responsibility for defence, transferring Ly to the Ministry of National Education. At legislative elections later in June 1988, provision was made for as many as three candidates, nominated by UDPM regional party offices, to contest each seat. It was reported that the UDPM candidates were endorsed by 98.56% of those who voted, although only about one-half of the incumbent deputies were returned to the Assemblée nationale. In September Traoré announced the closure of the Taoudenni prison, in northern Mali, and reduced the sentences of (or released) its 78 detainees. Among the persons to be released were several of those who had been implicated in the 1978 coup attempt.

In March 1990 Traoré initiated a nation-wide series of conferences to consider the exercise of democracy within and by the UDPM. Although the role of the ruling party was generally upheld outside the capital, many speakers at the Bamako conference disclosed support for multi-party politics. In response, Traoré stated that diverse political opinions must be expressed within the framework of the UDPM. Mali's first cohesive opposition movements began to emerge later in the year. The most influential were the Comité national d'initiative démocratique (CNID, which included many lawyers) and the Alliance pour la démocratie au Mali (ADEMA, a group that in August had published an open letter demanding that a national conference be convened to draft a new constitution and to determine a programme for a transition to a multi-party system). ADEMA and the CNID organized mass pro-democracy demonstrations in December, and in January 1991 the UDPM-affiliated trade union federation, the Union nationale des travailleurs du Mali, which also made clear its support for a transition to multi-party politics, co-ordinated a 48-hour general strike as part of a campaign for significant increases in levels of pay. The industrial action coincided with a reorganization of the Council of Ministers, in which Traoré assigned the defence portfolio to Brig.-Gen. Mamadou Coulibaly and transferred Ly to the Ministry of the Interior and Basic Development.

One of Ly's first actions in his new post was to issue warnings to the CNID and ADEMA, as well as to a recently-formed unofficial students' organization, the Association des élèves et étudiants du Mali (AEEM), that their political activities must cease. Rallies were organized in protest against the restrictions, and unrest intensified following the arrest of the leader of the AEEM, Oumar Mariko. Students, school pupils and lawyers led violent anti-Government demonstrations in Bamako: according to official reports, two demonstrators were killed, and 35 injured, when security forces intervened to suppress the protests. Educational establishments throughout the country were closed by the authorities, in response to violence in other regions, and the Government deployed armoured vehicles in the capital. Some 250 demonstrators were reported to have been arrested at the time of the disturbances, although officials stated that Mariko had been released from custody before the outbreak of violence. Further arrests were made in late January 1991: by the end of the month 32 protesters remained in detention. The Government ordered the resumption of classes in mid-February.

Violent pro-democracy demonstrations, on 22–24 March 1991, were harshly repressed by the security forces: official figures later revealed that 106 people were killed, and 708 injured, at this time. Traoré promised political reforms, but refused to accede to demands for his resignation, and on 26 March it was announced that Traoré had been arrested. A military Conseil national de réconciliation (CNR), led by Lt-Col (later Brig.-Gen.) Amadou Toumani Touré (the commander of the army's parachute regiment), assumed power, and the Constitution, the Government, the legislature and the UDPM were dissolved. On 31 March, following negotiations between the CNR and representatives of those organizations that had opposed Traoré, a 25-member Comité de transition pour le salut du peuple (CTSP) was established, chaired by Touré, to oversee the transition to democracy: a national conference would be convened to determine the country's political evolution, and it was envisaged that the armed forces would withdraw from political life on 20 January 1992 (the date of the annual 'Armed Forces Day' national holiday), relinquishing power to newly-elected organs of State. In early April Soumana Sacko, who had briefly been Minister of Finance and Trade in 1987, was appointed Prime Minister. Sacko, a UN development official who had been working in the Central African Republic, returned to Mali, whereupon he nominated a civilian-dominated Council of Ministers.

The CTSP, while affirming its commitment to the economic adjustment efforts that had been adopted in the latter years of the Traoré administration, undertook the reform of Malian political life, seeking to remove from positions of influence officials who were believed to have been associated with corruption under the previous regime. Among those who were arrested in subsequent months were Mamadou Coulibaly and Ousmane Coulibaly (the Chief of Staff of the Army, who was detained in connection with the brutality of the security forces in repressing the unrest that had preceded Traoré's downfall), while some close associates of the former President who had initially been appointed to the CTSP were later dismissed. In June 1991 it was announced that Traoré and other members of his regime would be tried in connection with the repression of the unrest in March, as well as illegal self-enrichment. (The new administration pledged to recover Traoré's personal fortune, rumoured to total some US $2,000m., which was said to have been deposited in overseas bank accounts.) In July it was announced that a coup attempt, led by Maj. Lamine Diabira (the Minister of Territorial Administration in the new Government), had been foiled; Diabira and his associates were arrested, and the Council of Ministers and the CTSP were reorganized. Military personnel and civil servants were promised immediate salary increases, and an amnesty was proclaimed for most political prisoners who had been detained under the previous regime.

Provision was made for the registration of political parties, and by the time of the National Conference, which was convened in late July 1991, some 36 organizations had been accorded official status. The CNID was registered as the Congrès national d'initiative démocratique, and ADEMA adopted the additional title of Parti africain pour la solidarité et la justice (while generally retaining its original acronym). Pre-independence parties, banned for many years, re-emerged, most notably the Union soudanaise, now known formally as the Union soudanaise—Rassemblement démocratique africain (US—RDA, in recognition of the party's original links with the Ivorian-dominated regional RDA).

The National Conference, which took place in Bamako on 29 July–12 August 1991, was attended by some 1,800 delegates, who duly adopted a draft Constitution for what was to be designated the Third Republic of Mali, together with an electoral code and a charter governing the activities of political parties. The draft made provision for the separation of the powers of the executive, legislative and judicial organs of state, with the President (in whom executive power would be vested) and legislature each being elected for five years, by universal suffrage, in the context of a multi-party political system. A timetable for the transition to democratic rule was subsequently announced: a constitutional referendum was to take place on 1 December, to be followed (if adopted) by municipal, legislative and presidential elections before 20 January 1992. In late August 1991 seven government ministers and about one-half of the members of the CTSP were replaced, following allegations that many had been implicated in the security forces' repressive actions earlier in the year. A further, minor reorganization of the Council of Ministers followed in December.

In November 1991 it was announced that the period of transition to democratic rule was to be extended until 26 March 1992. The delay was attributed principally to the CTSP's desire first to conclude an agreement with Tuareg rebels in the north of the country (see below); however, it was also admitted that the foreign assistance that had hitherto been granted was insufficient to finance the electoral processes. The constitutional referendum thus took place on 12 January 1992: the draft document was endorsed by 99.76% of those who voted (only about 43% of the registered electorate). Municipal elections proceeded one week later, at which 23 of the 48 authorized parties presented candidates. ADEMA enjoyed the greatest success, winning 214 of the total of 751 municipal seats; the US—RDA secured 130 seats, and the CNID 96. Less than 35% of the electorate were reported to have participated. Five of the 21 parties registered to contest the legislative elections (the first round of which was scheduled for 26 January) threatened to boycott the poll, alleging irregularities in the conduct of the municipal voting, and the Government subsequently announced that the elections would be postponed for four weeks. At the elections to the Assemblée nationale, on 23 February and 8 March, the level of participation by voters was again low (little more than 20%). Many parties alleged malpractice by ADEMA, which won 76 of the 129 seats; the CNID took nine seats, and the US–RDA eight.

The date for the transition to civilian rule was again postponed, and nine candidates eventually contested the first round of the presidential election on 12 April 1992. Although the ADEMA leader, Alpha Oumar Konaré, won the largest share of the votes cast (44.95%), he failed to secure an overall majority. A second round of voting, contested by Konaré and his nearest rival, Tiéoulé Mamadou Konaté (of the US—RDA), thus followed two weeks later, at which Konaré secured 69.01% of the votes, and was duly elected President. Overall, only about one-fifth of the electorate were reported to have voted.

Immediately upon his inauguration as President of the Third Republic, on 8 June 1992, Konaré appointed Younoussi Touré (hitherto the national director of the Banque centrale des états de l'Afrique de l'ouest) as Prime Minister. Touré's first Council of Ministers, the composition of which was announced shortly afterwards, was dominated by members of ADEMA, although the national education and the justice and human rights portfolios were allocated, respectively, to representatives of the US—RDA and of the Parti pour la démocratie et le progrès (PDP).

The trial of Moussa Traoré and his associates began, after considerable delay, in November 1992. In February 1993 Traoré, Ly, Mamadou Coulibaly and Ousmane Coulibaly were sentenced to death, after having been convicted by Bamako's Criminal Court of 'premeditated murder, battery and voluntary manslaughter' at the time of the March 1991 unrest; 28 others, who had been accused of complicity in the repression, were acquitted. Appeal proceedings were immediately initiated against all four sentences, but the death sentences were upheld by the Supreme Court in May 1993. (None the less, it was expected that Konaré would commute them to terms of life imprisonment—until this time, it was believed that no death sentence had been implemented since 1980.) Charges remained against Traoré, his wife and several others, in connection with the 'economic crimes' of the former regime. In June 1993 it was reported that the authorities had denied legal status to a revived UDPM.

Widespread dissatisfaction at the consequences of economic austerity (as agreements with international creditors necessitated severe restrictions on public expenditure) were reflected in the education sector in the first part of 1993. In March students and school pupils attacked public buildings and vehicles in Bamako, and security forces intervened when protesters besieged the offices of the state radio service. In early April at least one person was killed in clashes with the security forces, who had again intervened when students set fire to public buildings, including the seat of the legislature, the official residence of the Minister of State for National Education and the headquarters of ADEMA. Younoussi Touré resigned shortly afterwards; he was replaced as Prime Minister by Abdoulaye Sekou Sow, the Minister of State for Defence in the outgoing administration, who, while not a member of any political party, was reported to be sympathetic to Konaré's policies. Sow implemented an extensive reorganization of the Government: his administration remained dominated by ADEMA, but also included representatives of other parties (among them the CNID, which was allocated three ministries, including the justice portfolio).

During the latter part of 1993 there was evidence of discontent among the parties participating in government. Members of ADEMA, the CNID and the US—RDA expressed dissatisfaction at their exclusion from the decision-making process, which was, they alleged, excessively controlled by Konaré and the Council of Ministers. Moreover, there was concern that members of the Traoré regime still held positions of influence, and parties outside the government coalition protested that the trials for 'economic crimes' of the former President and his associates had not yet begun. A reorganization and 'streamlining' of the Government, in November, included the appointment of new ministers responsible for finance (a major programme of economic austerity measures, announced in September, had been the subject of considerable political controversy, and had failed to prevent the suspension of assistance by the IMF and the World Bank) and foreign affairs. ADEMA remained the most prominent party in the Council of Ministers: among other represented parties were the CNID, the PDP and the Rassemblement pour la démocratie et le progrès (RDP). The USA—RDA, while initially a participant in the new Government, withdrew from the coalition shortly afterwards. In December it was revealed that a coup atttempt, orchestrated by Oumar Diallo (Traoré's former aide-de-camp, who had been detained since July, accused of the misappropriation of state funds), had been thwarted. The Government confirmed that five junior armed forces officers had been arrested for their part in the plot, which had aimed to assassinate Konaré, Sow and the President of the Assemblée nationale.

Following the devaluation, in January 1994, of the CFA franc, the Government announced plans to offset the immediate adverse effects of the measure. In early February differences between Sow and ministers belonging to ADEMA's radical wing, regarding the conduct of economic policy, prompted the Prime Minister to resign. He was replaced by Ibrahim Boubacar Keita, since November 1993 the Minister of Foreign Affairs, Malians Abroad and African Integration, who was said to be a member of ADEMA's radical tendency. Konaré and Keita initially intended that the composition of the Council of Ministers should remain largely unchanged; however, the CNID and the RDP withdrew from the coalition, protesting that they had not been consulted about the recent changes. A new Government, again dominated by ADEMA, was appointed; the PDP subsequently withdrew, although its representative in the Council of Ministers resigned from the party, in order that he might retain his portfolio.

Sow's resignation coincided with renewed unrest in the education sector. Protests against the effects of the currency devaluation and to demand compensatory grant increases culminated in mid-February 1994 in violent demonstrations in Bamako, as a result of which many arrests were made. Educational establishments were closed, and an independent radio station was ordered by the authorities to cease transmissions. The arrest, in early March, of the leader of the AEEM, Yehia Oud Zarawana, prompted further disturbances, during which public buildings were attacked. A day of 'inaction', organized by opposition groups in late March, in an attempt to secure the reopening of secondary and tertiary establishments (the resumption of classes at primary schools had been announced shortly beforehand) and the release of Zarawana and about 30 other students, was deemed by the authorities to have been poorly observed, although the opposition claimed that many economic activities in the capital had been disrupted. An attack, the same day, on the residence of the French Consul-General in Bamako (attributed by some sources to a self-styled 'armed resistance group', which had recently distributed tracts threatening attacks on Western interests in Mali) was followed in early May by an assault by about 100 students and school pupils on the Bamako offices of the official French development agency. In mid-July the Government permitted the release on bail of Zarawana and his co-defendants, shortly after they had begun a hunger strike in an attempt to secure their unconditional release.

The salaries of state employees were increased by 10% with effect from April 1994, and by a further 5% six months later. However, dissatisfaction at the consequences of economic austerity was evident in the armed forces, and junior army officers staged a brief strike in early August, demanding the 'necessary means' to fulfil their duties. In mid-November cadets who had been dismissed from the gendarmerie, following a strike prompted by the delayed payment of arrears, seized weapons and erected barricades in Bamako: one person was killed, and about 300 cadets were arrested, following army intervention to suppress the protest.

Persistent rumours of divisions within ADEMA were apparently confirmed in late September 1994, when the election of Keita to the party presidency precipitated the resignation of prominent figures, including the outgoing Vice-President, Mamadou Lamine Traoré, and Secretary-General, Mouhamedou Dicko, from the governing party. Former members of ADEMA formed a new organization, the Mouvement pour l'indépendance, la renaissance et l'intégration africaines, in December. Despite predictions that the split would necessitate wide-ranging government changes, the membership of the Council of Ministers was largely unaltered by a reorganization of portfolios in late October. Boubacar Sadassi, who was appointed Minister of the Armed Forces and Veterans in the reshuffle, was killed in a motor accident in mid-February 1995; he was replaced in the Government by Mamadou Ba. In November, the editor of an independent newspaper was arrested and charged with defamation and the propagation of false information, following the publication of an article alleging that Konaré, deeming the country to be ungovernable, wished to resign; legal proceedings were, however, withdrawn in early January 1995. Also in January a further attempt to secure legal status for the UDPM was rejected by the Supreme Court. None the less, the Mouvement patriotique pour le renouveau, established by several of those who had sought to revive the UDPM, was granted official status later in the month.

Ethnic unrest emerged in north-eastern Mali in mid-1990, as large numbers of light-skinnned Tuareg nomads, who had migrated to Algeria and Libya at times of drought, began to return to West Africa (see also the Recent History of Niger). A Tuareg attack in June on the sub-prefecture of Menaka (in north-eastern Mali, near the border with Niger), as a result of which 14 deaths were reported, prompted the authorities to impose a state of emergency in the Gao and Tombouctou regions, and the armed forces began a repressive campaign against the nomads. The Traoré Government's assertions that the perpetrators of the rebellion had received ideological and military training in Libya, and were attempting to establish an independent Tuareg state in north-eastern Mali, were strenuously denied by both the Government of Libya and Tuareg leaders. Rebel forces staged a further offensive near Bouressa in September, as a result of which 200 members of the Malian armed forces were said to have been killed. In the same month the Heads of State of Algeria, Libya, Mali and Niger, meeting in Algeria, agreed, in principle, measures governing border controls and facilitating the return of refugees to their region of origin. Also in September it was announced that a new administrative district was to be established in the Kidal area of north-eastern Mali, in an attempt to promote economic development in that region. In January 1991 representatives of the Traoré Government met delegates from two Tuareg groups, the Mouvement populaire de l'Azaouad (MPA) and the Front islamique-arabe de l'Azaouad (FIAA), at Tamanrasset, Algeria: a peace accord was signed, providing for an immediate cease-fire and for the eventual granting of a status of 'internal autonomy' for the Adrar region of northern Mali. The state of emergency was revoked, and in March 24 Tuaregs who had been captured during clashes with the Malian armed forces in 1990 were released from custody.

Following the overthrow of the Traoré regime, the Touré administration affirmed its commitment to the Tamanrasset accord, and Tuareg groups were represented in the CTSP. However, unrest continued in the north. At the time of the National Conference it was reported that at least 150 members of the armed forces had been killed since the outbreak of the rebellion; meanwhile, thousands of Tuaregs, Moors and Bella (the descendants of the Tuaregs' black slaves, some of whom remained with the nomads) had fled to Algeria, Mauritania and Burkina Faso, in order to escape the armed forces' punitive actions. In August 1991 the Malian transitional leadership proposed a dialogue with the rebels, inviting Tuareg leaders to attend a conference in Tombouctou in November. Although the MPA agreed to send delegates, the FIAA rejected Tombouctou as a venue for the conference, and attacks and skirmishes continued throughout the second half of the year. (The conference was later postponed.) Meanwhile, the MPA lost the support of more militant members, who formed the Front populaire de libération de l'Azaouad (FPLA), which claimed responsibility for several attacks in northern Mali.

In December 1991 a preparatory conference in Mopti (in anticipation of negotiations that were to take place in Algeria) was attended by representatives of the Malian Government and of four Tuareg groups, the MPA, the FIAA, the FPLA and the Armée révolutionnaire de l'Azaouad (ARLA). With Algerian mediation, the delegates agreed in principle to a peace settlement that envisaged an end to hostilities, the establishment of a commission of inquiry to examine the acts of violence perpetrated and losses suffered in areas affected by the conflict, and a reciprocal exchange of prisoners. The negotiations continued in the Algerian capital in January 1992, when the Malian authorities and the MPA, the FIAA and the ARLA (now negotiating together as the Mouvements et fronts unifiés de l'Azaouad—MFUA) formally agreed to implement the Mopti accord; the FPLA was not reported to have attended the talks. A truce entered into force in February, and the commission of inquiry was inaugurated in Gao shortly afterwards. Further talks in Algiers culminated, in March, in the drafting of a 'National Pact', which was signed by the Malian authorities and the MFUA on 11 April. Meanwhile, an exchange of prisoners was undertaken, and measures to facilitate the repatriation of refugees were initiated. In addition to the provisions of the Mopti accord, the National Pact envisaged special administrative structures for the northern regions, the eventual incorporation of Tuareg fighters into the national army, the demilitarization of the north (and the establishment of joint government-Tuareg patrols to enforce security in the area) and the reinforcement of efforts to integrate Tuaregs into the national political and economic fields.

Sporadic attacks, particularly against members of the northern majority Songhai group, continued. None the less, provisions of the National Pact were implemented in the second half of 1992 and the early part of 1993. Joint patrols were established, and in November 1992 President Konaré visited the north to inaugurate the new administrative structures. In February 1993 the Malian Government and the MFUA signed an accord facilitating the integration of an initial 600 Tuaregs into the national army. However, the refusal of the FPLA (whose leadership was based in Burkina) to participate in the application of the National Pact undermined the peace process until May 1993, when the dissident movement's secretary-general, Rhissa Ag Sidi Mohamed, expressed satisfaction at the success of early efforts to repatriate refugees. He and his supporters subsequently returned to Mali, apparently willing to observe the provisions of the Pact.

The Algerian Government continued to play an active role in the application of the Pact, and in February 1993 an agreement was signed regarding the repatriation of Malian refugees from southern Algeria. Konaré and senior members of his administration also entered into negotiations with the Burkinabè and Mauritanian authorities, with a view to facilitating the return of refugees from those countries. In May the office of the UN High Commissioner for Refugees (UNHCR) announced that it was to oversee a two-year voluntary repatriation programme, whereby it was envisaged that 12,000 refugees would be resettled in Mali before the end of 1993. During the second half of the year, however, Tuareg leaders expressed concern that difficulties in repatriating refugees and in the implementation of other provisions of the National Pact were the cause of occasional attacks in the north. The assassination (allegedly by members of the ARLA) in the Kidal region, in February 1994, of Col Bilal Saloum (the military leader of the MPA, regarded as a principal architect of the peace process, who had joined the Malian army in accordance with the Pact), and hostilities in subsequent weeks involving the MPA and the ARLA, indicated a deterioration in the situation in the north, although the MPA and the ARLA signed a peace agreement in April. A meeting in Tamanrasset, in mid-April, between representatives of the Malian Government and the MFUA (with Algerian mediation), intended to assess progress in the implementation of the National Pact, was complicated by new demands, made by the MFUA, regarding the full integration of Tuaregs into Mali's civilian and military structures—which was, the Malian authorities maintained, governed by the constraints of the austerity programme. In mid-May, none the less, agreement was reached in Algiers regarding the integration of 1,500 former rebels into the regular army and of a further 4,860 Tuaregs into civilian sectors; the MFUA undertook to dismantle its military bases in the north, while the Government reaffirmed its commitment to the pursuit of development projects in northern areas.

The success of the Algiers agreement was, however, undermined by an intensification of clashes and acts of banditry in the north, as a result of which several hundred people, including many civilians, were reported to have been killed in the first half of 1994. Tensions, periodically escalating into violence, were reported between the so-called integrated Tuareg fighters and regular members of the Malian armed forces, while the emergence of a Songhai-dominated black resistance movement, the Mouvement patriotique malien Ghanda Koy ('Masters of the Land'), further threatened the restoration of calm. Malian trade union leaders, moreover, expressed their opposition to the recruitment of Tuaregs into the civil service at a time of economic austerity. Violence continued, despite the stated commitment of the Malian Government and the MFUA to the National Pact, with the adherence of the FIAA increasingly being called into question after the death of one of its leaders, in early June, as a result of a clash with members of the armed forces. In the same month the Assemblée nationale adopted a resolution demanding that the MFUA exert its authority over the rebel movement, and urging the Government to bring an end to the insecurity in the north. Meeting in Tamanrasset, in late June, the Malian authorities and the MFUA agreed on the need for the reinforcement (initiated in previous weeks) of the army presence in areas affected by the violence, and established modalities for the more effective integration of Tuareg fighters. None the less, there was considerable concern regarding the future of the National Pact following a serious escalation of violence in July. At the end of that month security forces acted to disperse an unauthorized anti-Tuareg demonstration in Bamako (there were similar protests in Gao, Kayes and Mopti at this time), and in early August there was a grenade attack on the home of a prominent Tuareg official in the capital.

In late August 1994, at a meeting in Bamako to discuss the Tuareg issue (attended by the ministers responsible for foreign affairs of Mali, Algeria, Burkina, Libya, Mauritania and Niger), an agreement was reached by Mali, Algeria, UNHCR and the International Fund for Agricultural Development regarding the voluntary repatriation from Algeria of Malian refugees. The accord, whereby the Malian authorities undertook to protect the fundamental rights and dignity of the Tuaregs, and which guaranteed international protection for Tuareg refugees, was welcomed by MFUA leaders who were meeting in Tamanrasset at the same time. At the Tuaregs' meeting, the MFUA pledged the reconciliation of the Tuareg movements and reiterated its commitment to the National Pact; however, the talks were not attended by representatives of the 'dissident' Tuaregs, and unrest continued. In September the human rights organization, Amnesty International, published a report expressing concern at the deaths of increasing numbers of civilians as a result of the conflict, and denouncing a cycle of violence whereby attacks by armed Tuareg and Moorish groups were followed by retaliatory attacks, identified as summary executions, by the Malian armed forces on light-skinned civilians. Hostilities intensified, and in late October, following an attack (for which the FIAA claimed responsibility) on Gao and retaliatory action by the army, as a result of which, according to official figures, 66 people were killed, both the Government and the MFUA appealed for an end to the violence.

Following the appointment of a new Minister of the Armed Forces and Veterans, shortly after the Gao attack, the authorities were widely regarded as having adopted a less conciliatory approach towards the Tuareg rebels, and in subsequent weeks the army claimed to have captured several rebel bases. The FIAA appeared increasingly marginalized in the peace process: although the group stated, in late November 1994, that it had agreed to an Algerian request to observe a two-week truce, the Algerian-based FIAA leader, Zahabi Ould Sidi Mohamed (held by Keita to be personally responsible for endangering the National Pact) protested that the Algerian authorities were co-operating with Mali in preventing him from travelling to Belgium to attend a debate—organized in mid-December by the Development and Co-operation Committee of the European Parliament—on the Tuareg issue. (The session was attended by representatives of the MFUA and by a Malian parliamentary delegation).

In mid-January 1995 representatives of the FPLA and Ghanda Koy, meeting in Bourem, issued a joint statement appealing for an end to hostilities in the north, and for the implementation of the National Pact. Shortly afterwards Zahabi Ould Sidi Mohamed asserted that the FIAA, again observing a truce, was willing to co-operate with the Government and with other Tuareg groups in the restoration of peace, and stated that he was willing, if necessary, to withdraw from the political process in the interests of promoting stability. At the end of the month representatives of Ghanda Koy, the FPLA and local communities held talks in Gao.

The presence in neighbouring countries of large numbers of refugees from the conflict in northern Mali, and the attendant issue of border security, dominated Mali's regional relations during the first years of the Konaré administration. Estimates of the total number of Malian refugees varied, but in late 1994 there were reported to be as many as 45,000 in Algeria, some 50,000 in Burkina, and up to 118,000 in Mauritania. Some 10,000 Tuaregs were also, according to some reports, members of the Libyan armed forces. Prior to the agreement signed with Algeria in August, repatriation accords had been reached with Mauritania in April of that year, and with Burkina in July.

## Government

The Constitution of the Third Republic, which was approved in a national referendum on 12 January 1992, provides for the separation of the powers of the executive, legislative and judicial organs of state. Executive power is vested in the President of the Republic, who is elected for five years by universal suffrage. The President appoints a Prime Minister, who, in turn, appoints a Council of Ministers. Legislative power is vested in the unicameral, 129-member Assemblée nationale, elected for five years by universal suffrage (13 deputies are elected to represent Malians resident abroad). Elections take place in the context of a multi-party political system.

Mali has eight administrative regions, and a district government in Bamako. The Constitution makes provision for the establishment of a High Council of Local Communities.

## Defence

In June 1994 the Malian army numbered about 7,350 men: land army 6,900, naval force about 50 (with three patrol boats on the River Niger), air force 400. A further 7,800 men were members of paramilitary forces. In addition, 20 Russian military advisers were in Mali in mid-1994. Military service is by selective conscription and lasts for two years. The estimated defence budget for 1994 was 18,600m. francs CFA.

## Economic Affairs

In 1993, according to estimates by the World Bank, Mali's gross national product (GNP), measured at average 1991–93 prices, was US $2,744m., equivalent to $300 per head. During 1985–93, it was estimated, GNP per head declined, in real terms, at an average annual rate of 4.3%. Over the same period the population increased by an annual average of 2.8%. Mali's gross domestic product (GDP) increased, in real terms, by an annual average of 2.9% in 1980–92; GDP declined by 0.8% in 1993, but increased by an estimated 2.4% in 1994.

Agriculture (including forestry and fishing) contributed about 42.4% of GDP in 1993. Some 79.2% of the labour force were employed in the sector in that year. The principal cash crops are cotton (exports of ginned cotton accounted for 57.0% of the value of merchandise exports in 1990) and groundnuts; exports of vegetables and mangoes are also of some significance. The principal subsistence crops are millet, sorghum, fonio, rice and maize. A high rate of population growth necessitates cereal imports (estimated at 90,000 metric tons in 1992/93) in most years. Although severely affected by drought in the early 1980s, by the end of the decade the livestock-rearing and fishing sectors had recovered sufficiently to make an important contribution to the domestic food supply and to export revenue, accounting for about one-fifth of GDP in the early 1990s. Agricultural GDP increased by an annual average of 5.5% in 1985–93, compared with an average annual decline of 5.3% in 1980–85.

Industry (including mining, manufacturing, construction and power) contributed an estimated 11.0% of GDP in 1993. Only about 2% of the labour force were employed in industrial activities in 1980. Industrial GDP increased by an annual average of 0.9% in 1985–93, compared with an average increase of 10.9% per year in 1980–85.

Mining contributed only 1.6% of GDP in 1990. However, the importance of the sector was expected to increase with the successful exploitation (from the latter part of the 1980s) of the country's gold reserves: exports of gold contributed an estimated 17.5% of the value of total exports in 1992. Salt, marble and phosphate rock are also mined. The eventual exploitation of deposits of iron ore, diamonds and uranium is envisaged, and reserves of several other minerals, including petroleum, bauxite, manganese, zinc, copper and lithium, have also been detected.

The manufacturing sector, which (together with mining) contributed an estimated 8.9% of GDP in 1993, is based on the processing of agricultural products (principally cotton, sugar and rice). Brewing and tobacco industries are represented, and the production of construction materials is also notable. Manufacturing GDP increased by an annual average of 9.4% in 1980–85, but the rate of growth slowed to 1.1% per year in 1985–90.

Of total electric energy generated in 1990, about two-thirds was derived from hydroelectric installations. Imports of fuels comprised some 30% of the value of merchandise imports in 1992.

In 1993 Mali recorded a visible trade deficit of US $119.9m., while there was a deficit of $102.6m. on the current account of the balance of payments. In 1990 the principal source of imports (22.7%) was France; other major suppliers in that year were Côte d'Ivoire, Senegal and the Federal Republic of Germany. The principal market for exports in 1990 was Côte d'Ivoire (49.0%); other significant purchasers were France, Senegal and Switzerland. The principal exports in 1990 were ginned cotton, live animals and miscellaneous manufactured articles. The principal imports were machinery and transport equipment, food products, petroleum products, other raw materials, chemicals and miscellaneous manufactured articles.

In 1993 Mali recorded a budgetary deficit (excluding grants) equivalent to 9.6% of GDP. Mali's total external debt was US $2,650m. at the end of 1993, of which $2,506m. was long-term public debt. In that year the cost of debt-servicing was equivalent to 6.1% of the value of exports of goods and services. Consumer prices declined by an annual average of 0.9% in 1988–93; prices declined by an average of 0.6% in 1993, and it was aimed to restrict inflation to about 35% in 1994.

Mali is a member of numerous international and regional organizations, including the Economic Community of West African States (ECOWAS, see p. 138), the West African organs of the Franc Zone (see p. 168), the African Groundnut Council (see p. 234), the Liptako–Gourma Integrated Development Authority (see p. 239), the Niger Basin Authority (see p. 240) and the Organisation pour la mise en valeur du fleuve Sénégal (OMVS, see p. 240).

Economic adjustment efforts implemented (with support from multilateral and bilateral creditors) in the later years of the Traoré regime ensured real GDP growth and low rates of inflation. However, severe structural weaknesses, exacerbated by many years of systematic corruption, undermined economic viability. Although the Konaré administration undertook to consolidate policies of economic liberalization initiated under Traoré, the Government's failure in 1992–93 to reconcile creditors' requirements with domestic demands provoked social tensions and undermined relations with the IMF and the World Bank. A return to GDP growth in 1994 was largely attributed to the positive effects of the devaluation, in January of that year, of the CFA franc (with the enhanced competitiveness of cotton, in particular, generating improved export revenue). With assistance from the IMF, it is aimed to achieve real GDP growth averaging 4.9% annually in 1995–97, and to restore the rate of inflation and the budgetary and external current-account deficits to pre-devaluation levels during this period. The pursuit of economic diversification, accelerated privatization and the restructuring of enterprises remaining under state control are to be accompanied by greater investment in social projects, and the Government has expressed particular optimism regarding prospects for the further development, with foreign investors, of gold mining. However, Mali's narrow export base and high dependence on imports continue to check growth, as do the substantial foreign and domestic debts. Moreover, the need for increased expenditure on the military that has arisen from the conflict in the north, together with the costs accompanying efforts more effectively to integrate Tuareg communities (and eventually to accommodate repatriated refugees) will represent a considerable burden on domestic finances in the mid-1990s.

### Social Welfare

In 1977 Mali had 192 hospital establishments, with a total of 3,512 beds. In 1983 there were 339 physicians and 3,662 nursing personnel working in the country. A minimum wage is in force. Budget estimates for 1990 allocated 9,154m. francs CFA to health services (3.5% of consolidated budget expenditure).

### Education

Education is provided free of charge and is officially compulsory between seven and 16 years of age. Primary education usually begins at the age of seven and lasts for a minimum of six years and a maximum of eight years. Secondary education, from 13 years of age, lasts for a further six years, comprising two cycles of three years each. The rate of school enrolment in Mali is among the lowest in the world, and in 1991 enrolment at primary schools included only 19% of children in the relevant age-group (males 23%; females 14%). Secondary enrolment in that year was equivalent to only 7% of children in that age-group (males 10%; females 5%). Although some higher education facilities are available in Mali, many students receive higher education abroad, mainly in France and Senegal. In 1988, according to official estimates, adult illiteracy averaged 81.2% (males 73.6%; females 88.6%). Budget estimates for 1990 allocated 17,201m. francs CFA to the education sector (6.6% of consolidated budget expenditure).

### Public Holidays

**1995:** 1 January (New Year's Day), 20 January (Armed Forces Day), 3 March* (Korité, end of Ramadan), 17 April (Easter Monday), 1 May (Labour Day), 10 May* (Tabaski, Feast of the Sacrifice), 25 May (Africa Day, anniversary of the OAU's foundation), 9 August* (Mouloud, Birth of the Prophet), 8 September* (Baptism of the Prophet), 22 September (Independence Day), 19 November (Anniversary of the 1968 *coup d'état*), 25 December (Christmas).
**1996:** 1 January (New Year's Day), 20 January (Armed Forces Day), 21 February* (Korité, end of Ramadan), 8 April (Easter Monday), 29 April* (Tabaski, Feast of the Sacrifice), 1 May (Labour Day), 25 May (Africa Day, anniversary of the OAU's foundation), 28 July* (Mouloud, Birth of the Prophet), 27 August* (Baptism of the Prophet), 22 September (Independence Day), 19 November (Anniversary of the 1968 *coup d'état*), 25 December (Christmas).

* These holidays are determined by the Islamic lunar calendar and may vary by one or two days from the dates given.

### Weights and Measures

The metric system is in force.

# Statistical Survey

Source (unless otherwise stated): Direction de la Statistique et de l'Informatique, Ministère des Finances et du Commerce, BP 234, Koulouba, Bamako; tel. 22-56-87; telex 2559; fax 22-88-53.

## Area and Population

### AREA, POPULATION AND DENSITY

| | |
|---|---|
| Area (sq km) | 1,240,192* |
| Population (census results) | |
| 16 December 1976 | 6,394,918 |
| 1–30 April 1987 | |
| Males | 3,760,711 |
| Females | 3,935,637 |
| Total | 7,696,348 |
| Population (official estimates at mid-year) | |
| 1989 | 7,960,000 |
| 1990 | 8,156,000 |
| Density (per sq km) at mid-1990 | 6.6 |

*478,841 sq miles.

### PRINCIPAL ETHNIC GROUPS (estimates, 1963)

| | | | | |
|---|---|---|---|---|
| Bambara | 1,000,000 | Malinke | | 200,000 |
| Fulani | 450,000 | Tuareg | | 240,000 |
| Marka | 280,000 | Sénoufo | | 375,000 |
| Songhai | 230,000 | Dogon | | 130,000 |

### ADMINISTRATIVE DIVISIONS
(estimated population at 1987 census)

District
Bamako . . . 646,163

Regions*
| | | | |
|---|---|---|---|
| Ségou | 1,328,250 | Kayes | 1,058,575 |
| Sikasso | 1,308,828 | Tombouctou | 453,032 |
| Mopti | 1,261,383 | Gao | 383,734 |
| Koulikoro | 1,180,260 | | |

* A new region, Kidal, was formally established on 15 May 1991.

### PRINCIPAL TOWNS
(population at 1976 census)

| | | | |
|---|---|---|---|
| Bamako (capital) | 404,000 | Sikasso | 47,000 |
| Ségou | 65,000 | Kayes | 45,000 |
| Mopti | 54,000 | | |

(population at 1987 census)
Bamako . . . 658,275

# MALI

*Statistical Survey*

**BIRTHS AND DEATHS** (UN estimates, annual averages)

|  | 1975–80 | 1980–85 | 1985–90 |
|---|---|---|---|
| Birth rate (per 1,000) | 50.7 | 50.8 | 51.0 |
| Death rate (per 1,000) | 24.1 | 22.3 | 20.7 |

**Expectation of life** (UN estimates, years at birth, 1985–90): 44.0 (males 42.4; females 45.6).

Source: UN, *World Population Prospects: The 1992 Revision*.

**ECONOMICALLY ACTIVE POPULATION**
(ILO estimates, '000 persons at mid-1980)

|  | Males | Females | Total |
|---|---|---|---|
| Agriculture, etc. | 1,649 | 314 | 1,963 |
| Industry | 32 | 14 | 46 |
| Services | 214 | 72 | 287 |
| **Total labour force** | 1,896 | 400 | 2,296 |

Source: ILO, *Economically Active Population Estimates and Projections, 1950–2025*.

**Mid-1993** (estimates in '000): Agriculture, etc. 2,524; Total 3,187 (Source: FAO, *Production Yearbook*).

## Agriculture

**PRINCIPAL CROPS** ('000 metric tons)

|  | 1991 | 1992 | 1993 |
|---|---|---|---|
| Millet, sorghum and fonio | 1,660 | 1,184 | 1,385 |
| Rice (paddy) | 454 | 410 | 388 |
| Maize | 257 | 193 | 275 |
| Other cereals | 44 | 32 | 26 |
| Sugar cane* | 309 | 305 | 311 |
| Sweet potatoes† | 55 | 55 | 55 |
| Cassava (Manioc)† | 73 | 73 | 73 |
| Other roots and tubers† | 17 | 17 | 17 |
| Vegetables† | 257 | 262 | 267 |
| Fruit† | 15 | 16 | 16 |
| Pulses† | 61 | 62 | 64 |
| Groundnuts (in shell) | 151 | 112 | 135† |
| Cottonseed† | 157 | 180 | 178 |
| Cotton (lint) | 115 | 135† | 135* |

* Unofficial figure(s).  † FAO estimate(s).

Source: FAO, *Production Yearbook*.

**LIVESTOCK** ('000 head, year ending September)

|  | 1991 | 1992 | 1993 |
|---|---|---|---|
| Cattle | 5,198 | 5,373 | 5,554 |
| Sheep | 6,359 | 6,658 | 6,971 |
| Goats | 6,359 | 6,658 | 6,971 |
| Pigs | 67 | 75 | 84 |
| Horses | 83 | 85 | 87* |
| Asses | 590 | 600 | 610* |
| Camels | 246 | 250 | 250* |

Poultry (million): 22 in 1991; 22 in 1992; 22* in 1993.

* FAO estimate.

Source: FAO, *Production Yearbook*.

**LIVESTOCK PRODUCTS** (FAO estimates, '000 metric tons)

|  | 1991 | 1992 | 1993 |
|---|---|---|---|
| Cows' milk | 127 | 132 | 136 |
| Sheep's milk | 73 | 77 | 80 |
| Goats' milk | 147 | 154 | 161 |
| Beef and veal | 74 | 78 | 81 |
| Mutton and lamb | 22 | 23 | 24 |
| Goat meat | 24 | 25 | 27 |
| Poultry meat | 24 | 24 | 24 |
| Poultry eggs | 11.9 | 11.9 | 11.9 |
| Cattle hides | 11.4 | 12.0 | 12.4 |
| Sheepskins | 5.1 | 5.2 | 5.5 |
| Goatskins | 3.5 | 3.6 | 3.8 |

Source: FAO, *Production Yearbook*.

## Forestry

**ROUNDWOOD REMOVALS**
(FAO estimates, '000 cubic metres, excluding bark)

|  | 1990 | 1991 | 1992 |
|---|---|---|---|
| Sawlogs, veneer logs and logs for sleepers* | 13 | 13 | 13 |
| Other industrial wood | 344 | 355 | 367 |
| Fuel wood | 5,232 | 5,399 | 5,573 |
| **Total** | 5,589 | 5,767 | 5,953 |

* Estimated to be unchaged since 1988.

Source: FAO, *Yearbook of Forest Products*.

## Fishing

('000 metric tons, live weight)

|  | 1990 | 1991 | 1992 |
|---|---|---|---|
| **Total catch** (freshwater fishes) | 70.5 | 68.8 | 68.5 |

* FAO estimate.

Source: FAO, *Yearbook of Fishery Statistics*.

## Mining

|  | 1990 | 1991 | 1992 |
|---|---|---|---|
| Gold (kilograms)* | 2,355 | 2,597 | 3,467 |
| Salt ('000 metric tons)† | 5 | 5 | n.a. |

* Source: Secrétariat du Comité Monétaire de la Zone Franc, *Rapport 1992*.
† Data from the US Bureau of Mines in UN, *Industrial Statistics Yearbook*.

## Industry

**SELECTED PRODUCTS** ('000 metric tons, unless otherwise indicated)

|  | 1989 | 1990 | 1991 |
|---|---|---|---|
| Salted, dried or smoked fish* | 3.4 | 3.5 | n.a. |
| Raw sugar* | 22 | 24 | 27 |
| Cement† | 20 | 20 | 22 |
| Electric energy (million kWh) | 246 | 273 | 276 |

* Data from the FAO.  † Data from the US Bureau of Mines.

Source: UN, *Industrial Statistics Yearbook*.

MALI

# Finance

## CURRENCY AND EXCHANGE RATES

**Monetary Units**
100 centimes = 1 franc de la Communauté financière africaine (CFA).

**French Franc, Sterling and Dollar Equivalents** (31 December 1994)
1 French franc = 100 francs CFA;
£1 sterling = 834.94 francs CFA;
US $1 = 533.68 francs CFA;
1,000 francs CFA = £1.198 = $1.874.

**Average Exchange Rate** (francs CFA per US $)
1992   264.69
1993   283.16
1994   555.20

Note: An exchange rate of 1 French franc = 50 francs CFA, established in 1948, remained in force until January 1994, when the CFA franc was devalued by 50%, with the exchange rate adjusted to 1 French franc = 100 francs CFA.

## BUDGET ESTIMATES ('000 million francs CFA)

| Revenue | 1992 | 1993 | 1994 |
|---|---|---|---|
| Current revenue | 139.1 | 121.6 | 142.8 |
| Tax receipts | 112.2 | 113.1 | 131.7 |
| Other current revenue | 26.9 | 8.6 | 11.1 |
| Capital receipts | 0.7 | 1.0 | — |
| External grants, aid and subsidies | 36.7 | 35.8 | 70.4 |
| Borrowing | 38.3 | 29.9 | 78.1 |
| **Total** | 214.8 | 188.3 | 291.3 |

| Expenditure | 1992 | 1993 | 1994 |
|---|---|---|---|
| Administrative expenditure | 100.8 | 97.7 | 130.7 |
| Investment expenditure | 102.0 | 73.7 | 159.6 |
| Debt-servicing | 19.7 | 21.0 | 71.4 |
| **Total** | 222.5 | 192.4 | 361.7 |

Source: Banque centrale des états de l'Afrique de l'ouest.

**1995** (Budget estimates, '000 million francs CFA): Revenue 297.8; Expenditure 354.0.

## INTERNATIONAL RESERVES (US $ million at 31 December)

|  | 1991 | 1992 | 1993 |
|---|---|---|---|
| Gold* | 6.7 | 6.5 | 7.0 |
| IMF special drawing rights | 0.4 | 0.1 | 0.1 |
| Reserve position in IMF | 12.4 | 11.9 | 12.0 |
| Foreign exchange | 306.5 | 295.9 | 320.3 |
| **Total** | 326.0 | 314.4 | 339.4 |

* Valued at market-related prices.

Source: IMF, *International Financial Statistics*.

## MONEY SUPPLY ('000 million francs CFA at 31 December)

|  | 1991 | 1992 | 1993 |
|---|---|---|---|
| Currency outside banks | 59.97 | 60.84 | 65.07 |
| Demand deposits | 47.40 | 47.36 | 52.72 |
| **Total money** | 107.37 | 108.20 | 117.79 |

Source: IMF, *International Financial Statistics*.

## COST OF LIVING
(National Consumer Price Index; base: 1988 = 100)

|  | 1991 | 1992 | 1993 |
|---|---|---|---|
| Food | 101.8 | 92.0 | 91.4 |
| **All items** (incl. others) | 101.9 | 95.9 | 95.3 |

Source: ILO, *Year Book of Labour Statistics*.

## NATIONAL ACCOUNTS
('000 million francs CFA at current prices)

### Expenditure on the Gross Domestic Product

|  | 1989* | 1990 | 1991* |
|---|---|---|---|
| Government final consumption expenditure | 98.5 | 96.4 | 118.3 |
| Private final consumption expenditure | 499.6 | 562.0 | 591.2 |
| Increase in stocks | 15.4 | 13.3 | −14.5 |
| Gross fixed capital formation | 122.0 | 123.3 | 122.9 |
| **Total domestic expenditure** | 735.5 | 795.0 | 817.9 |
| Exports of goods and services | 106.6 | 114.8 | 120.0 |
| *Less* Imports of goods and services | 207.4 | 225.6 | 225.6 |
| **GDP in purchasers' values** | 634.7 | 684.2 | 712.3 |

* Provisional.

Source: Banque centrale des états de l'Afrique de l'ouest.

### Gross Domestic Product by Economic Activity

|  | 1989* | 1990 | 1991* |
|---|---|---|---|
| Agriculture, hunting, forestry and fishing | 275.9 | 305.4 | 322.2 |
| Manufacturing and mining | 53.3 | 57.4 | 58.8 |
| Water and electricity | 7.8 | 8.6 | 9.5 |
| Construction and public works | 28.4 | 27.9 | 27.9 |
| Transport and telecommunications | 31.2 | 32.7 | 35.9 |
| Trade | 99.2 | 113.2 | 108.7 |
| Other services | 43.0 | 45.6 | 45.6 |
| Public administration | 65.9 | 60.4 | 70.6 |
| **Sub-total** | 604.7 | 651.2 | 679.2 |
| Import duties | 34.8 | 37.9 | 38.1 |
| *Less* Imputed bank service charge | 4.8 | 4.9 | 5.0 |
| **Total** | 634.7 | 684.2 | 712.3 |

* Provisional.

Source: Banque centrale des états de l'Afrique de l'ouest.

## BALANCE OF PAYMENTS (US $ million)

|  | 1991 | 1992 | 1993 |
|---|---|---|---|
| Merchandise exports f.o.b. | 354.5 | 339.3 | 343.6 |
| Merchandise imports f.o.b. | −447.1 | −484.0 | −463.5 |
| **Trade balance** | −92.7 | −144.7 | −119.9 |
| Exports of services | 85.4 | 74.4 | 78.4 |
| Imports of services | −378.4 | −406.5 | −394.5 |
| Other income received | 20.9 | 24.6 | 24.4 |
| Other income paid | −59.2 | −54.8 | −47.0 |
| Private unrequited transfers (net) | 70.0 | 88.0 | 84.8 |
| Official unrequited transfers (net) | 312.9 | 312.8 | 271.2 |
| **Current balance** | −41.1 | −106.2 | −102.6 |
| Direct investment (net) | 3.5 | −7.6 | — |
| Other capital (net) | 49.3 | 10.6 | −5.7 |
| Net errors and omissions | 29.0 | −22.7 | 22.7 |
| **Overall balance** | 40.7 | −125.8 | −85.5 |

Source: IMF, *International Financial Statistics*.

MALI

## External Trade

**PRINCIPAL COMMODITIES** (million francs CFA)

| Imports c.i.f. | 1988 | 1989 | 1990 |
|---|---|---|---|
| **Food and live animals** | 33,673 | 18,585 | 34,368 |
| Food products of animal origin | 6,895 | 3,426 | 7,225 |
| Dairy products | 6,558 | 2,957 | 6,817 |
| Food products of plant origin | 7,682 | 4,786 | 10,725 |
| Cereals | 3,958 | 2,420 | 6,463 |
| Processed foodstuffs | 19,096 | 10,373 | 16,418 |
| Sugar and confectionery | 10,518 | 5,577 | 9,641 |
| **Beverages and tobacco** | 3,183 | 5,301 | 5,880 |
| **Energy products** | 11,688 | 19,419 | 31,920 |
| Petroleum products | 10,926 | 19,199 | 31,827 |
| **Other raw materials (inedible)** | 21,653 | 13,776 | 23,587 |
| **Machinery and transport equipment** | 32,670 | 21,781 | 35,953 |
| Non-electrical machinery | 15,867 | 10,361 | 15,467 |
| Electrical machinery | 6,319 | 4,091 | 8,764 |
| Transport equipment | 10,484 | 7,329 | 11,722 |
| **Other industrial products** | 44,866 | 27,122 | 29,815 |
| Chemical products | 16,628 | 14,181 | 18,174 |
| Miscellaneous manufactured articles | 28,238 | 12,941 | 11,641 |
| Cotton yarn and fabrics | 2,211 | 890 | 2,826 |
| **Total** (incl. others) | 150,230 | 108,468 | 164,020 |

| Exports f.o.b. | 1988 | 1989 | 1990 |
|---|---|---|---|
| **Food and live animals** | 7,864 | 27,496 | 28,792 |
| Food products of animal origin | 5,356 | 26,918 | 27,653 |
| Live animals | 5,031 | 26,785 | 27,455 |
| Food products of plant origin | 1,799 | 481 | 886 |
| **Raw materials (inedible)** | 40,675 | 47,350 | 59,028 |
| Cotton (ginned) | 37,844 | 44,309 | 55,684 |
| **Oils and fats** | 4,621 | 20 | 1,104 |
| **Other industrial products** | 10,543 | 3,862 | 7,815 |
| Miscellaneous manufactured articles | 10,542 | 3,862 | 7,805 |
| **Total** (incl. others) | 63,888 | 78,777 | 97,683 |

Source: Banque centrale des états de l'Afrique de l'ouest.

**Gold** (exports f.o.b., '000 million francs CFA): 11.9 in 1990; 14.0 in 1991; 15.2 (provisional) in 1992 (Source: Secrétariat du Comité Monétaire de la Zone Franc, *Rapport 1992*).

**PRINCIPAL TRADING PARTNERS** (million francs CFA)

| Imports | 1988 | 1989 | 1990 |
|---|---|---|---|
| Austria | 2,098 | 112 | 263 |
| Belgium-Luxembourg | 7,997 | 4,513 | 7,771 |
| Canada | 95 | 1,952 | 2,328 |
| China, People's Republic | 3,927 | 2,057 | 5,366 |
| Côte d'Ivoire | 12,467 | 21,793 | 29,720 |
| France | 44,725 | 26,599 | 37,163 |
| Germany, Fed. Republic | 10,504 | 7,394 | 9,128 |
| Hong Kong | 2,223 | 460 | 2,118 |
| Italy | 8,795 | 3,014 | 5,257 |
| Japan | 3,677 | 3,337 | 7,016 |
| Netherlands | 9,552 | 5,384 | 6,183 |
| Nigeria | 2,663 | 3,310 | 3,416 |
| Poland | 1,744 | 51 | 250 |
| Senegal | 7,379 | 7,611 | 15,275 |
| Spain | 6,502 | 2,636 | 4,482 |
| Switzerland | 2,317 | 1,173 | 1,491 |
| Thailand | 870 | 747 | 1,273 |
| USSR | 1,764 | 996 | 1,457 |
| United Kingdom | 2,821 | 3,713 | 4,721 |
| USA | 3,432 | 4,104 | 7,886 |
| **Total** (incl. others) | 150,230 | 108,468 | 164,019 |

| Exports | 1988 | 1989 | 1990 |
|---|---|---|---|
| Belgium-Luxembourg | 5,960 | 892 | 463 |
| Canada | 2,364 | 2,414 | — |
| China, People's Republic | 4,959 | 5,803 | 396 |
| Côte d'Ivoire | 4,824 | 21,831 | 47,855 |
| France | 5,740 | 3,871 | 23,981 |
| Germany, Fed. Republic | 3,469 | 3,416 | 9 |
| Ireland | 2,622 | 2,234 | — |
| Italy | 1,027 | 948 | 72 |
| Japan | 843 | 851 | — |
| Morocco | 2,083 | 1,789 | — |
| Netherlands | 1,334 | 615 | 126 |
| Portugal | 3,254 | 2,671 | — |
| Senegal | 1,577 | 7,914 | 16,991 |
| Spain | 1,140 | 1,625 | 33 |
| Switzerland | 8,627 | 3,612 | 6,678 |
| Thailand | 1,134 | 1,835 | — |
| Tunisia | 743 | 1,302 | — |
| United Kingdom | 1,563 | 1,546 | 114 |
| **Total** (incl. others) | 63,888 | 78,777 | 97,683 |

Source: Banque centrale des états de l'Afrique de l'ouest.

## Transport

**RAILWAYS** (traffic)

| | 1986 | 1987 | 1988 |
|---|---|---|---|
| Passenger-km (million) | 176.9 | 772.8 | 731.9 |
| Freight ton-km (million) | 225.1 | 429.3 | 432.2 |

**1993:** Passenger-km (million) 845.9; Freight ton-km (million) 460.9.
Source: Banque centrale des états de l'Afrique de l'ouest.

**ROAD TRAFFIC** (estimates, '000 motor vehicles in use)

| | 1989 | 1990 | 1991 |
|---|---|---|---|
| Passenger cars | 22 | 23 | 24 |
| Commercial vehicles | 13 | 13 | 14 |

Source: UN Economic Commission for Africa, *African Statistical Yearbook*.

**CIVIL AVIATION** (traffic handled at Bamako Airport)

| | 1990 | 1991 | 1992 |
|---|---|---|---|
| Passengers (number)* | 278,573 | 253,012 | 230,971 |
| Freight (metric tons) | 8,290 | 7,894 | 4,909 |
| Mail (metric tons) | 76 | 80 | 74 |

* Includes passengers in transit.

Source: Banque centrale des états de l'Afrique de l'ouest.

## Communications Media

| | 1990 | 1991 | 1992 |
|---|---|---|---|
| Radio receivers ('000 in use) | 400 | 415 | 430 |
| Television receivers ('000 in use) | 10 | 11 | 11 |
| Telephones ('000 in use)* | 17 | 18 | n.a. |
| Daily newspapers | | | |
| Number | 2 | n.a. | 2 |
| Average circulation ('000 copies)* | 10 | n.a. | 41 |

* Estimate(s).

**Book production** (textbooks, government publications and university theses, including pamphlets): 160 titles (92,000 copies) in 1984.

Sources: UNESCO, *Statistical Yearbook*; UN Economic Commission for Africa, *African Statistical Yearbook*.

MALI

## Tourism

|  | 1988 | 1989 | 1990 |
|---|---|---|---|
| Tourist arrivals ('000) . . . | 36 | 32 | 44 |
| Tourist receipts (US $ million) | 38 | 28 | 32 |

Source: UN, *Statistical Yearbook*.

## Education

(1991, unless otherwise indicated)

|  | Institu- tions | Teach- ers | Students Males | Students Females | Students Total |
|---|---|---|---|---|---|
| Primary. . . . | 1,514 | 7,963 | 236,004 | 139,127 | 375,131 |
| Secondary |  |  |  |  |  |
| General . . . | n.a. | 4,854 | 52,473 | 26,447 | 78,920 |
| Teacher training* | n.a. | 182 | 721 | 173 | 894 |
| Vocational . | n.a. | 762* | 5,798 | 2,917 | 8,715 |
| University level* | n.a. | 701 | 5,798 | 905 | 6,703 |

* 1990 figure(s).
Source: UNESCO, *Statistical Yearbook*.

**1993:** Teacher training: Institutions 3; Teachers 73; Students 439 (males 368; females 73) (Source: Ministère de l'Education Nationale, Bamako).

# Directory

## The Constitution

Following the overthrow of President Moussa Traoré in March 1991, the Constitution of June 1979 was suspended. A new Constitution was approved in a national referendum on 12 January 1992:

The Constitution of the Third Republic of Mali upholds the principles of national sovereignty and the rule of law in a secular, multi-party state. The document provides for the separation of the powers of the executive, legislative and judicial organs of state.

Executive power is vested in the President of the Republic, who is elected for five years by universal adult suffrage. The President appoints the Prime Minister, who, in turn, appoints other members of the Council of Ministers.

Legislative authority is exercised by the unicameral Assemblée nationale, which is elected for five years by universal adult suffrage. Of the chamber's 129 deputies, 13 are elected to represent the interests of Malians resident abroad.

The Constitution guarantees the independence of the judiciary. Final jurisdiction in constitutional matters is vested in a Constitutional Court.

The rights, freedoms and obligations of Malian citizens are enshrined in the Constitution. Freedom of the press and of association are guaranteed.

## The Government

### HEAD OF STATE

**President:** ALPHA OUMAR KONARÉ (took office 8 June 1992).

### COUNCIL OF MINISTERS
(May 1995)

**Prime Minister:** IBRAHIM BOUBACAR KEITA.

**Minister of State for Foreign Affairs, Malians Abroad and African Integration:** DJONKOUMA TRAORÉ.

**Minister of Public Works and Transport:** MOHAMED AG ERLAF.

**Minister of Health, Solidarity and the Elderly:** Maj. MODIBO SIDIBÉ.

**Minister of Industry, Handicrafts and Tourism:** FATOU HAIDARA.

**Minister of Youth and Sports:** BOUBACAR KARAMOKO COULIBALY.

**Minister of the Armed Forces and Veterans:** MAMADOU BA.

**Minister of Secondary and Higher Education and Scientific Research:** MOUSTAPHA DICKO.

**Minister of Territorial Administration and Security:** Lt-Col SADA SAMAKÉ.

**Minister of Justice and Keeper of the Seals:** CHEIKNA DETTEBA KAMISSOKO.

**Minister of Culture and Communications, Spokesperson for the Government:** BAKARY KONIMBA TRAORÉ.

**Minister of Finance and Trade:** SOUMEYLA CISSÉ.

**Minister of Basic Education:** ADAMA SAMASSEKOU.

**Minister of Urban Development and Housing:** SY KADIATOU SOW.

**Minister of Mines, Energy and Water Resources:** CHEIKNA SEYDOU TIDIANI DIAWARA.

**Minister of Employment, the Civil Service and Labour:** BOUBACAR GAOUSSOU DIARRA.

**Minister of Rural Development and the Environment:** MODIBO TRAORÉ.

### MINISTRIES

**Office of the President:** BP 1463, Bamako; tel. 22-24-61; telex 2521.

**Office of the Prime Minister:** BP 97, Bamako.

**Ministry of the Armed Forces and Veterans:** BP 215, Bamako; tel. 22-26-17.

**Ministry of Culture and Communications:** Bamako.

**Ministry of Employment, the Civil Service and Labour:** BP 80, Bamako; tel. 22-59-51.

**Ministry of Finance and Trade:** BP 234, Koulouba, Bamako; tel. 22-56-87; telex 2559; fax 22-88-53.

**Ministry of Foreign Affairs, Malians Abroad and African Integration:** Koulouba, Bamako; tel. 22-54-89; telex 2560.

**Ministry of Health, Solidarity and the Elderly:** Koulouba, Bamako; tel. 22-53-01.

**Ministry of Industry, Handicrafts and Tourism:** BP 1759, Bamako; tel. 22-80-58; fax 23-02-61.

**Ministry of Justice:** BP 97, Bamako; tel. 22-24-36.

**Ministry of Mines, Energy and Water Resources:** BP 238, Bamako; tel. 22-35-47.

**Ministry of National Education:** BP 71, Bamako; tel. 22-24-50.

**Ministry of Public Works and Transport:** c/o World Bank Resident Mission, BP 1864, Bamako; tel. 22-66-82.

**Ministry of Rural Development and the Environment:** BP 1676, Bamako; tel. 22-60-24.

**Ministry of Territorial Administration and Security:** BP 78, Bamako; tel. 22-39-37.

**Ministry of Urban Development and Housing:** Bamako.

**Ministry of Youth and Sports:** Bamako.

MALI

## President and Legislature

### PRESIDENT

**Presidential Election, First Ballot, 12 April 1992**

| Candidate | % of votes |
| --- | --- |
| Alpha Oumar Konaré | 44.95 |
| Tiéoulé Mamadou Konaté | 14.51 |
| Mountaga Tall | 11.41 |
| Alamy Sylla | 9.44 |
| Baba Akhib Haidarra | 7.37 |
| Idrissa Traoré | 4.10 |
| Amadou Ali Niagandou | 4.01 |
| Mamadou (Maribato) Diaby | 2.16 |
| Bamba Moussa Diallo | 2.04 |
| Total | 100.00 |

**Second Ballot, 26 April 1992**

| Candidate | % of votes |
| --- | --- |
| Alpha Oumar Konaré | 69.01 |
| Tiéoulé Mamadou Konaté | 30.99 |
| Total | 100.00 |

### ASSEMBLÉE NATIONALE

**President:** Aly Nouhoun Diallo.

**General Election, 23 February and 8 March 1992**

| Party | Seats |
| --- | --- |
| ADEMA | 76 |
| CNID | 9 |
| US—RDA | 8 |
| PMD | 6 |
| RDP | 4 |
| UDD | 4 |
| UFDP | 3 |
| RDT | 3 |
| PDP | 2 |
| UMDD | 1 |
| Total | 116* |

* An additional 13 deputies were to be elected to represent the interests of Malians resident abroad.

## Advisory Councils

**Conseil Economique et Social:** Bamako; f. 1987.
**Cour Constitutionnelle:** Bamako; f. 1994.

## Political Organizations

Following the dissolution in March 1991 of the Union démocratique du peuple malien (UDPM), which had been the sole legal party since 1979 provision was made for the registration of an unlimited number of political parties. At the 1992 municipal and legislative elections some 48 organizations had been officially registered. The following parties were among the most prominent in these elections:

**Alliance pour la démocratie au Mali—Parti africain pour la solidarité et la justice (ADEMA):** BP 1791, Bamako; tel. 22-03-68; f. 1990 as Alliance pour la démocratie au Mali; Chair. Ibrahim Boubacar Keita.

**Congrès national d'initiative démocratique (CNID):** Bamako; f. 1990 as Comité national d'initiative démocratique; Chair. Me Mountaga Tall; Sec.-Gen. Amida Diabaté.

**Parti pour la démocratie et le progrès (PDP):** BP 1823, Bamako; tel. and fax 22-64-52; f. 1991; Leader: Me Idrissa Traoré.

**Parti malien pour le développement (PMD):** Bamako.

**Rassemblement pour la démocratie et le progrès (RDP):** BP 2110, Bamako; tel. 22-30-92; fax 22-67-95; f. 1990; Leader Almamy Sylla.

**Rassemblement pour la démocratie et le travail (RDT):** Bamako.

**Union pour la démocratie et le développement (UDD):** Bamako; f. 1991 by fmr supporters of ex-President Traoré; Leader Moussa Balla Coulibaly.

**Union des forces démocratiques pour le progrès (UFDP):** f. 1991; Sec.-Gen. Me Demba Diallo.

**Union malienne pour la démocratie et le développement (UMDD):** Bamako.

**Union soudanaise—Rassemblement démocratique africain (US—RDA):** Bamako; sole legal party 1960–68; revived 1991; Sec.-Gen. Mamadou Bechir Gologo.

Disaffected members of ADEMA formed the **Mouvement pour l'indépendance, la renaissance et l'intégration africaines (MIRIA)** in December 1994. The **Mouvement patriotique pour le renouveau (MPR)**, established by former members of the UDPM, was legalized in January 1995. A split was reported in the CNID in March 1995.

## Diplomatic Representation

### EMBASSIES IN MALI

**Algeria:** route de Daoudabougou; tel. 22-51-76; telex 2414; fax 22-93-74; Ambassador: Ahmed Ferhat Zerhouni.

**Burkina Faso:** BP 9022, Bamako; Ambassador: Hamadou Kone.

**Canada:** route de Koulikoro, BP 198, Bamako; telex 2530; Chargé d'affaires a.i.: Guy Gagnon.

**China, People's Republic:** BP 112, Bamako; telex 2455; Ambassador: Wu Donghe.

**Egypt:** BP 44, Badalabougou; tel. 22-35-03; fax 22-08-91; Ambassador: Abdelsalam Yehia el-Tawil.

**France:** square Patrice Lumumba, BP 17, Bamako; tel. 22-29-51; telex 2569; fax 22-03-29; Ambassador: Gabriel Regnault de Bellescize.

**Germany:** Badalabougou-Est, Lotissement A6, BP 100, Bamako; tel. 22-32-99; telex 2529; fax 22-96-50; Ambassador: Harro Adt.

**Guinea:** BP 118, Bamako; tel. 22-29-75; telex 2576; Ambassador: Mamadou Mass Diallo.

**Iran:** quartier de l'Hippodrome, BP 2136, Bamako; Ambassador: Mojtaba Shafii.

**Iraq:** BP 2512, Bamako-Badalabougou; tel. 22-38-06; telex 2416; Chargé d'affaires a.i.: Jassim N. Msawil.

**Korea, Democratic People's Republic:** BP 765, Sogoniko, Bamako; Ambassador: Kim Gi Han.

**Libya:** quartier de l'Hippodrome, Bamako; telex 2420; Ambassador: Farage Inaya.

**Malaysia:** Badalabougou-Ouest, BP 98, Bamako; tel. 22-27-83; telex 2423; fax 22-32-32; Ambassador: Choo Siew-Kioh.

**Mauritania:** BP 135, Bamako; telex 2415; Ambassador: Bilal Ould Werzeg.

**Morocco:** BP 2013, Bamako; tel. 22-21-23; telex 22430; fax 22-77-87; Ambassador: Larbi Roudiés.

**Nigeria:** BP 57, Badalabougou; tel. 22-57-71; Chargé d'affaires: M. O. Kuforiji.

**Russia:** BP 300, Bamako; Ambassador: Pavel Petrovski.

**Saudi Arabia:** BP 81, Badalabougou; telex 2408; Chargé d'affaires Muhammad Rajamiri.

**Senegal:** ave Kassé Keïta, BP 42, Bamako; tel. 22-82-74; fax 23-17-80; Ambassador: Mamadou Laity Ndiaye.

**USA:** angle rue Rochester NY et rue Mohamed V, BP 34, Bamako; tel. 22-54-70; telex 2248; fax 22-37-12; Ambassador: William H. Damerion, III.

## Judicial System

The 1992 Constitution guarantees the independence of the judiciary.

**Supreme Court:** BP 7, Bamako; tel. 22-24-06; f. 1969; 25 mems; judicial section comprises two civil chambers, one commercial chamber, one social chamber and one criminal chamber; in addition, there are administrative and financial regulatory sections; Pres. Louis Bastide; Sec.-Gen. Henriette Bounsly.

**Court of Appeal:** Bamako.

**President of the Bar:** Me Magatté Sèye.

There are two Tribunaux de première instance (Magistrates' Courts) and also courts for labour disputes.

## Religion

It is estimated that about 80% of the population are Muslims, while 18% follow traditional animist beliefs and 1.2% are Christians.

## ISLAM

**Chief Mosque:** Bagadadji, place de la République, Bamako.

## CHRISTIANITY

### The Roman Catholic Church

Mali comprises one archdiocese and five dioceses. At 31 December 1992 there were an estimated 98,334 adherents in the country (1.1% of the total population).

**Bishops' Conference:** Conférence Episcopale du Mali, BP 298, Bamako; tel. 22-67-84; fax 22-67-00; f. 1973; Pres. Rt Rev. JEAN-MARIE CISSÉ, Bishop of Sikasso.

**Archbishop of Bamako:** Most Rev. LUC AUGUSTE SANGARÉ, Archevêché, BP 298, Bamako; tel. 22-54-99; fax 22-52-14.

### Other Christian Churches

There are numerous Protestant mission centres, mainly administered by US societies, with a total personnel of about 370.

# The Press

Restrictions on press freedom were formally ended under a new statute which entered force during December 1992 and January 1993.

### DAILY NEWSPAPER

**L'Essor—La Voix du Peuple:** BP 141, Bamako; tel. 22-47-97; f. 1949; pro-Government newspaper; Editor SOULEYMANE DRABO; circ. 3,500.

### PERIODICALS

There were some 60 periodicals in late 1993.

**L'Afro-Arabe Revue:** rue Mohamed V, BP 2044, Bamako; quarterly; Editor MOHAMED BEN BABA AHMED; circ. 1,000.

**L'Aurore:** BP 2043, Bamako; f. 1990; fortnightly; independent; Editor CHOUAHIBOU TRAORÉ.

**Barakela:** Bamako; monthly; publ. by the Union nationale des travailleurs du Mali.

**Citoyen:** Bamako; f. 1992; fortnightly; independent.

**Concorde:** BP 2043, Bamako; weekly; French and Arabic; Editor AL-MAMOUN KEITA; circ. 500.

**Danbe:** Bamako; f. 1990; organ of the CNID.

**Les Echos:** BP 2043, Bamako; f. 1989; fortnightly; publ. by Jamana cultural co-operative; circ. 25,000.

**Jamana—Revue Culturelle Malienne:** BP 2043, Bamako; f. 1983; quarterly; organ of Jamana cultural co-operative (f. by ALPHA OUMAR KONARÉ).

**Kabaaru:** Mopti; monthly; Fulbé language; rural interest; Editor BADAMA DOUCOURÉ; circ. 5,000.

**Kibaru:** BP 1463, Bamako; monthly; Bambara and three other languages; rural interest; Editor AMADOU GAGNY KANTÉ; circ. 5,000.

**Journal Officiel de la République du Mali:** BP 1463, Bamako; official announcements.

**Mali Muso** (Women of Mali): Bamako; quarterly; publ. by the Union des femmes du Mali; circ. 5,000.

**Podium:** BP 141, Bamako; weekly; culture and sports.

**Nouvel Horizon:** BP 942, Bamako; weekly; independent; Editor SEMBI TOURÉ.

**Le Républicain:** BP 1484, Bamako; f. 1992; weekly; independent; Publr TIÉBILÉ DRAME.

**La Roue:** Quinzambougou, BP 2043, Bamako; pre-independence journal, revived 1990; independent.

**Sunjata:** BP 141, Bamako; monthly; social, economic and political affairs; Editor SOUMEYLOU MAÏGA; circ. 3,000.

**Yiriwa:** BP 2043, Bamako; f. 1990; independent.

### NEWS AGENCIES

**Agence Malienne de Presse et Publicité (AMAPP):** BP 116, Bamako; tel. 22-26-47; telex 2421; f. 1977; Dir GAOUSSOU DRABO.

### Foreign Bureaux

**Agence France-Presse (AFP):** BP 778, Bamako; telex 2480; Correspondent CHOUAÏBOU BONKANE.

**Rossiyskoye Informatsionnoye Agentstvo—Novosti (RIA—Novosti)** (Russia): BP 193, Bamako; tel. 22-45-25; telex 2528; Correspondent BORIS TARASOV.

**Xinhua (New China) News Agency** (People's Republic of China): c/o Ambassade de la République Populaire de Chine, BP 112, Bamako; telex 2455; Correspondent NI MANHE.

IPS (Italy) and Reuters (UK) are also represented in Mali.

# Publisher

**EDIM SA:** ave Kassé Keïta, BP 21, Bamako; tel. 22-40-41; f. 1972 as Editions Imprimeries du Mali, reorg. 1987; general fiction and non-fiction, textbooks; Chair. and Man. Dir IBRAHIMA BERTHE.

# Radio and Television

In 1992, according to UNESCO, there were an estimated 430,000 radio receivers and 11,000 television receivers in use. Legislation authorizing the establishment of private radio and television stations was promulgated in early 1992. Radio France International and the Gabonese-based Africa No. 1 began FM broadcasts in Mali in March 1993.

**Office de Radiodiffusion-Télévision Malienne (ORTM):** BP 171, Bamako; tel. 22-24-74; f. 1957; state-owned; radio programmes in French, English, Bambara, Peulh, Sarakolé, Tamachek, Sonrai, Moorish, Wolof; about 37 hours weekly of television broadcasts; Man. Dir ABDOULAYE SIDIBE; Dir of Television CHEICK HAMALLA TOURÉ.

**Chaîne 2:** Bamako; f. 1993; radio broadcasts to Bamako.

**Fréquence 3:** Bamako; f. 1992; commercial radio station.

**Radio-Bamakan:** Bamako; f. 1991; pro-ADEMA.

**Radio Kayira:** Bamako; f. 1992; pro-CNID.

**Radio Kledu:** Bamako; f. 1992; commercial; Prop. MAMADOU COULIBALY.

**Radio Liberté:** Nouveau Marché de Médine, BP 5015, Bamako; tel. 22-05-81; f. 1991; commercial station broadcasting 14 hours daily.

**Radio Tabalé:** BP 697, Bamako; tel. and fax 22-78-70; f. 1991; independent public service station broadcasting 57 hours weekly; Dir TIÉMOKO KONÉ.

# Finance

(cap. = capital; res = reserves; m. = million; brs = branches; amounts in francs CFA)

### BANKING

#### Central Bank

**Banque Centrale des Etats de l'Afrique de l'Ouest (BCEAO):** BP 206, Bamako; tel. 22-37-56; telex 2574; fax 22-47-86; headquarters in Dakar, Senegal; bank of issue and central bank for the seven states of Union économique et monétaire ouest-africaine (UEMOA), comprising Benin, Burkina Faso, Côte d'Ivoire, Mali, Niger, Senegal and Togo; cap. and res 530,827m. (Sept. 1993); Gov. CHARLES KONAN BANNY; Dir in Mali MANDÉ SIDIBÉ; br. at Mopti.

#### Commercial Banks

**Bank of Africa-Mali (BOA):** ave Kassé Keïta, BP 2249, Bamako; tel. 22-46-72; telex 2581; fax 22-46-53; f. 1982; 73% owned by private Malian interests; cap. 1,400m. (Sept. 1993); Chair. BOUREIMA SYLLA; Man. Dir XAVIER ALIBERT; 4 brs.

**Banque Commerciale du Sahel (BCS):** ave Kassé Keïta, BP 2372, Bamako; tel. 22-55-20; telex 2580; fax 22-55-43; f. 1982; fmrly Banque Arabe Libyo-Malienne pour le Commerce Extérieur et le Développement; 76.9% owned by Libyan Arab Foreign Bank, 22.6% state-owned; cap. 1,100m. (Sept. 1993); Chair. SEDDIK EL HAJJAJI; Man. Dir MOHAMED OMAR JABALLAH.

**Banque Malienne de Crédit et de Dépôts SA (BMCD):** ave du Fleuve, BP 45, Bamako; tel. 22-53-36; telex 2572; fax 22-79-50; f. 1961; 50.02% state-owned, 49.98% owned by Crédit Lyonnais (France); cap. 1,000m. (Sept. 1992); Chair. and Man. Dir AMIDOU OUMAR SY.

**Banque Meridien BIAO Mali SA:** Immeuble de Bolibana, blvd de l'Indépendance, BP 15, Bamako; tel. 22-50–66; telex 2501; fax 22-45-66; f. 1981; 51% owned by Meridien BIAO SA (Luxembourg), 49% by private Malian interests; cap. 3,403m. (Sept. 1993); Man. Dir ASSAMA SY; 4 brs.

**Financial Bank Mali:** ave Kassé Keïta, BP 1813, Bamako; tel. 22-72-00; telex 2713; fax 22-51-15; f. 1990; 100% Swiss-owned; Chair. and Man. Dir CHARLES BAYSSET.

#### Development Banks

**Banque de Développement du Mali SA (BDM):** ave du Fleuve, BP 94, Bamako; tel. 22-20-50; telex 2522; fax 22-50-85; f. 1968;

# MALI

*Directory*

23% owned by private Malian interests, 20% state-owned, 20% owned by BCEAO, 20% by Banque ouest-africaine de développement; cap. 3,000m. (Sept. 1992); Chair. Minister of Finance and Trade; Man. Dir Mohamed Slaoui; 11 brs.

**Banque Nationale de Développement Agricole (BNDA):** Immeuble Caisse Autonome d'Amortissement, quartier du Fleuve, BP 2424, Bamako; tel. 22-64-64; telex 2638; fax 22-29-61; f. 1981; 39.5% state-owned; cap. 3,772m. (March 1993); Chair. Minister of Finance and Trade; Man. Dir Bakary Traoré; 2 brs.

### Financial Institution

**Caisse Autonome d'Amortissement du Mali:** Immeuble Caisse Autonome d'Amortissement, Quartier du Fleuve, BP 1617, Bamako; telex 2676; management of state funds; Dir Minister of Finance and Trade.

### INSURANCE

**Caisse Nationale d'Assurance et de Réassurance (CNAR):** Immeuble CNAR, square Patrice Lumumba, BP 568, Bamako; tel. 22-64-54; telex 2549; fax 22-23-29; state-owned; cap. 50m.; Man. Dir Founeke Keita; 10 brs.

**La Soutra:** BP 52, Bamako; telex 2469; fax 22-55-23; f. 1979; cap. 150m.; Chair. Amadou Niono.

## Trade and Industry

### DEVELOPMENT ORGANIZATIONS

**Caisse Française de Développement (CFD):** BP 32, Bamako; tel. 22-28-42; telex 2502; fmrly Caisse Centrale de Coopération Economique, name changed 1992; Dir Robert Chahinian.

**Compagnie Malienne pour le Développement des Textiles (CMDT):** BP 487, Bamako; tel. 22-24-62; telex 2554; fax 22-81-41; f. 1975; cap. 1,000m. francs CFA; 60% state-owned, 40% owned by Cie Française pour le Développement des Fibres Textiles; restructuring in progress in 1994; cotton cultivation, ginning and marketing; Chair. and Man. Dir Drissa Keita.

**Mission Française de Coopération et d'Action Culturelle:** BP 84, Bamako; tel. 22-64-29; telex 2653; fax 22-83-39; administers bilateral aid from France; Dir Jean Monlaü.

**Office de Développement Intégré du Mali-Ouest (ODIMO):** square Patrice Lumumba, BP 72, Bamako; tel. 22-57-59; fmrly office de Développement Intégré des Productions Arachidières et Céréalières; development of diversified forms of agricultural production; Man. Dir Zana Sanogo.

**Office du Niger:** BP 106, Ségou; tel. 32-00-93; fax 32-01-43; f. 1932; taken over from the French authorities in 1958; restructuring in progress in 1993–94; cap. 7,139m. francs CFA; the original project involved a major dam, 72 km above Ségou, directing water into irrigation networks covering 1m. ha on the left bank of the Niger; since 1960 the irrigated area has been extended to only 53,300 ha, but a rehabilitation scheme, announced in 1986, was to upgrade the existing networks and increase the total cultivable area; the scheme is being executed with assistance from several international donor organizations; the Office du Niger also operates four rice-processing plants; Pres. and Man. Dir Fernand Traoré.

**Office des Produits Agricoles du Mali (OPAM):** BP 132, Bamako; tel. 22-37-55; telex 2509; fax 22-04-06; f. 1965; cap. 5,800m. francs CFA; state-owned; manages National (Cereals) Security Stock, administers food aid, responsible for sales of cereals and distribution to deficit areas; Man. Dir Abdoulaye Koita.

**Société Nationale de Recherches et d'Exploitation des Ressources Minières du Mali (SONAREM):** BP 2, Kati; tel. 27-20-42; state-owned; Man. Dir Makan Kayentao.

### CHAMBER OF COMMERCE

**Chambre de Commerce et d'Industrie du Mali:** place de la Liberté, BP 46, Bamako; tel. 22-50-36; telex 2435; fax 22-21-20; f. 1906; Pres. Drahamane Hamidou Touré; Sec.-Gen. Daba Traoré.

### EMPLOYERS' ASSOCIATIONS

**Association Malienne des Exportateurs de Légumes (AMELEF):** BP 1996, Bamako; f. 1984; Pres. Badara Faganda Traoré; Sec.-Gen. Birama Traoré.

**Association Malienne des Exportateurs de Ressources Animales (AMERA):** Centre Malien de Commerce Extérieur, BP 1996, Bamako; tel. 22-56-83; f. 1985; Pres. Ambarké Yermangore; Admin. Sec. Ali Hacko.

### TRADE UNION FEDERATION

**Union nationale des travailleurs du Mali (UNTM):** Bourse du Travail, blvd de l'Indépendance, BP 169, Bamako; tel. 22-20-31; f. 1963; Sec.-Gen. Issé Doucouré; mems in 12 affiliated national industrial-sector unions.

## Transport

### RAILWAYS

Mali's only railway runs from Koulikoro, via Bamako, to the Senegal border (642 track-km). The line continues to Dakar, a total distance of 1,286 km. Some 500,000 tons of freight were handled on the Malian railway in 1990. Plans exist for the construction of a new rail line linking Bamako with Kouroussa and Kankan, in Guinea.

**Régie du Chemin de Fer du Mali (RCFM):** rue Baba Diarra, BP 260, Bamako; tel. 22-29-68; telex 2586; fax 22-83-88; f. 1960; Pres. Diakaridia Sidibé; Man. Dir Mme Cisse Oumou.

### ROADS

The Malian road network in the early 1990s totalled some 18,000 km, of which about 6,000 km were all-weather roads and some 2,000 km were tarred. A bituminized road between Bamako and Abidjan (Côte d'Ivoire) provides Mali's main economic link to the coast.

**Compagnie Malienne de Transports Routiers (CMTR):** BP 208, Bamako; tel. 22-33-64; telex 2539; f. 1970; state-owned; Man. Dir Mamadou Touré.

### INLAND WATERWAYS

The River Niger is navigable in parts of its course through Mali (1,693 km) during the rainy season from July to late December. The River Senegal was, until the early 1990s, navigable from Kayes to Saint-Louis (Senegal) only between August and November, but its navigability was expected to improve following the inauguration, in October 1992, of the Manantali dam, and the completion of works to deepen the river-bed.

**Compagnie Malienne de Navigation (CMN):** BP 10, Koulikoro; tel. 26-20-94; telex 3002; f. 1968; state-owned; river transport and shipbuilding; Pres. and Man. Dir Lassiné Mariko (Koné).

**Société Navale Malienne (SONAM):** Bamako; f. 1981; transferred to private ownership in 1986; Chair. Alioune Keïta.

### CIVIL AVIATION

The principal airport is at Bamako-Senou. The other major airports are at Bourem, Gao, Goundam, Kayes, Kita, Mopti, Nioro, Ségou, Tessalit and Tombouctou. There are about 40 small airfields.

**Air Afrique:** BP 2651, Bamako; tel. 22-76-86; fax 22-61-36; see under Côte d'Ivoire; Dir in Mali B. Djibo.

**Mali Tombouctou Air Service (MALITAS):** Bamako; f. 1988 to succeed Air Mali; 20% state-owned, 80% owned by private Malian interests; domestic services; Chair. Amadou Ousmane Simaga.

**Société des Transports Aériens (STA):** BP 1809, Bamako; f. 1984; privately-owned; local services; Man. Dir Melhem Elie Sabbague.

## Tourism

Some 44,000 tourists visited Mali in 1990; receipts from tourism in that year totalled US $32m. Mali's cultural heritage is promoted as a tourist attraction, although unrest in the north after 1990 adversely affected the sector.

**Société Malienne d'Exploitation des Ressources Touristiques (SMERT):** place de la République, BP 222, Bamako; tel. 22-59-42; telex 2433; f. 1975; 25% state-owned; Man. Dir Hamady Sow.

# MALTA

## Introductory Survey

**Location, Climate, Language, Religion, Flag, Capital**

The Republic of Malta is in southern Europe. The country comprises an archipelago (the largest and only inhabited islands being Malta, Gozo and Comino) in the central Mediterranean Sea. The main island, Malta, lies 93 km (58 miles) south of the Italian island of Sicily and 290 km (180 miles) north of the Libyan coast, with Tunisia to the west. The climate is warm, with average temperatures of 22.6°C (72.7°F) in summer and 13.7°C (56.6°F) in winter. Average annual rainfall is 559 mm (22 in). Maltese and English are the official languages, though Italian is widely spoken. About 91% of the inhabitants are Christians belonging to the Roman Catholic Church. The national flag (proportions 3 by 2) consists of two equal vertical stripes, white in the hoist and red in the fly, with a representation of the George Cross, edged with red, in the upper hoist. The capital is Valletta, on the island of Malta.

**Recent History**

Malta became a Crown Colony of the United Kingdom in 1814. Constitutions that gave the islands limited self-government, but which reserved defence, foreign affairs and other matters to the representative of the British Government, were in force in 1921–36, 1947–59 and 1962–64. In the intervening periods the representative of the British Government exercised executive authority. During the Second World War Malta suffered severe aerial bombardment and was awarded the George Cross in 1942 by King George VI.

Dom Mintoff, leader of the Malta Labour Party (MLP) since 1949, became Prime Minister in 1955. At a referendum, held in February 1956, 75% of those voting supported integration with the United Kingdom, as favoured by the MLP. The conservative Nationalist Party (Partit Nazzjonalista—PN), led by Dr Giorgio Borg Olivier, boycotted the referendum. Mintoff resigned in 1958, after rejecting British proposals. As a result of the subsequent disturbances, a state of emergency was declared, and the Constitution suspended.

By 1961 both major parties advocated Malta's independence. The PN, which had the support of the Roman Catholic Church, won legislative elections in February 1962; Borg Olivier became Prime Minister, and negotiations concerning independence began. Malta became an independent sovereign state, within the Commonwealth, on 21 September 1964. At the same time defence and financial aid agreements, effective over a 10-year period, were reached with the United Kingdom.

In June 1971 an MLP Government, led by Dom Mintoff, took office. Pursuing a policy of non-alignment, the Government concluded agreements for cultural, economic and commercial co-operation with Italy, Libya, Tunisia, the USSR, several East European countries, the USA, the People's Republic of China and others, and received technical assistance, notably from Libya. On taking office, the MLP Government abrogated the 1964 Mutual Defence and Assistance Agreement between Malta and the United Kingdom. This agreement was eventually replaced in 1972 by a new seven-year agreement, under which Malta was to receive substantially increased rental payments for the use of military facilities by the United Kingdom and other NATO countries. British troops were finally withdrawn in March 1979.

Malta became a republic on 13 December 1974. Sir Anthony Mamo, hitherto the Governor-General, became President and Head of State. At a general election in September 1976 the MLP was returned to power with a narrow legislative majority. In December 1976 Mamo was succeeded as President by Dr Anton Buttigieg, a former Minister of Justice. In February 1982 he, in turn, was replaced as Head of State by Agatha Barbara, previously Minister of Labour.

Measures introduced in 1977 to regulate industry, and proposals adopted in January 1978 by Malta's largest trade union and the MLP for close co-operation, were criticized by the PN and by the other unions. Legislation enacted in 1981, restricting the power of the law courts to challenge government action, further increased tension between the two parties.

The MLP was again returned to power in the December 1981 elections, with a majority of three seats in the House of Representatives, although it obtained only 49.1% of the votes. The PN, which had obtained 50.9% of the votes, contested the result, refused to take its seats as the opposition party, and organized a campaign of civil disobedience. Complaints about the pro-Government bias of the broadcasting services led to a boycott of advertising by supporters of the PN during 1982 and 1983. In August 1982 the House of Representatives approved legislation forbidding any citizen to broadcast to Malta from abroad, and a further measure in January 1983 banned contacts between foreign diplomats on the island and the opposition—a law that was withdrawn a month later, after it had been rejected as illegal by the diplomatic community. In February 1984 Dr Carmelo Mifsud Bonnici, the leader-designate of the MLP, threatened to cancel future elections if there was evidence of 'foreign interference' on behalf of Maltese political parties.

In March 1983 the Nationalists resumed their seats in the House, ending a 15-month boycott, but immediately withdrew, protesting against a government resolution to loosen ties with the European Community (EC, known as the European Union, EU—see p. 143—from November 1993). Following intervention by President Barbara, Mintoff promised constitutional amendments and weekly consultations with the opposition; however, these collapsed in June, when the Government blamed the PN for the bombing of government offices. Relations between the two major parties worsened in November, when a government-authorized raid on the PN headquarters was alleged to have discovered a cache of arms and ammunition.

In June 1983 the House of Representatives approved controversial legislation, designed to expropriate some 75% of church property in order to finance the provision of universal free education and the abolition of fee-paying church schools. Opponents of the measure denounced it as both unconstitutional and a violation of religious liberty, and in September 1984 the courts declared the legislation to be null and void. In April 1984 the House approved legislation forbidding any school to accept fees (including voluntary gifts and donations). The Roman Catholic Archbishop of Malta refused to accept government conditions, and closed all church schools in the autumn term, in response to outbreaks of violence and growing tensions; a strike by state school teachers in October and November further polarized opinion, but an agreement was reached in November, allowing the schools to re-open.

At the end of December 1984 Mintoff announced his retirement, and was replaced by Mifsud Bonnici as Prime Minister. In April 1985 the Maltese Government, the Archbishop and a Vatican representative signed an agreement providing for the introduction of free education in church secondary schools, over a three-year period, while guaranteeing the autonomy of church schools. In July 1986 the Government and the Vatican signed a temporary agreement whereby the Government would pay one-half of the cost of operating the church schools in the school years 1985/86 and 1986/87. In July 1988 the enactment of legislation that introduced new procedures for licensing church schools led to a dispute in which the Roman Catholic Church claimed that the State should reduce its supervisory powers over church education.

In February 1987 the House of Representatives was dissolved, and in the same month Agatha Barbara relinquished the presidency, at the end of her five-year term of office. Paul Xuereb, the former Speaker of the House of Representatives, was appointed as acting President. At a general election, in May, the PN obtained 50.9% of the votes but won only 31 of the 65 seats in the House of Representatives, while the MLP, with 48.9% of the votes, won the remaining 34 seats. However, in accordance with a constitutional amendment that had been adopted in January (see Government, below), the PN was allocated four additional seats, giving it a majority of one in the legislature, thus ending the MLP's 16-year period of rule.

The leader of the PN, Dr Edward Fenech-Adami, became Prime Minister.

In April 1989 Dr Vincent Tabone, hitherto the Minister of Foreign Affairs, took office as President. At a general election to the House of Representatives in February 1992 the PN was returned to power with an increased majority over the MLP of three seats. This result was widely viewed as confirmation of public support for the PN's pro-EC policies. In April 1994 Tabone was succeeded as President by Dr Ugo Mifsud Bonnici, hitherto Minister of Education and Human Resources.

Malta has maintained a policy of non-alignment in its international relations, and has negotiated economic co-operation agreements with many countries. In 1980 Italy agreed to guarantee Malta's neutrality and to provide financial and technical aid over five years. Another agreement guaranteeing Malta's neutrality was concluded with the USSR in 1981. In 1984 the Governments of Malta and Libya signed a five-year treaty of co-operation, which included an undertaking by Libya to provide military training. The treaty signified a return to the previously close relations between the two countries, which had deteriorated in 1980, owing to a dispute over a maritime boundary (finally resolved by the International Court of Justice in 1985). Malta has an association agreement with the EU (see p. 163), originally signed in 1970 and periodically renewed. In 1985–86 the Mifsud Bonnici Government renegotiated the agreements with Italy and with the EC, which had been allowed to lapse by Mintoff. On becoming Prime Minister in May 1987, Fenech-Adami declared that the Government, while retaining Malta's non-aligned status and its links with Libya, would seek closer relations with the USA and other Western countries, and would apply for full membership of the EC (see below).

In June 1988 four British Navy warships visited Malta. A strike was organized by the General Workers' Union, and meetings were held throughout the island by the MLP in protest against the visit, as the ships were believed to be carrying nuclear weapons, and thereby compromised Malta's non-aligned status.

Links between Malta and Libya were strengthened when a radio station, 'Voice of the Mediterranean', was established in Malta in September 1988. The station was to be administered jointly by the Governments of the two countries. In the same month it was announced that visa requirements between Malta and Libya were to be abolished. In February 1990 the two countries' bilateral co-operation treaty was renewed until 1995, albeit without the military component (which had impeded good relations with the USA).

A formal application for full membership of the EC (with which Malta conducts almost three-quarters of its trade) was submitted by the Maltese Government in July 1990. In June 1993 the EC Commission recommended that, subject to the Government of Malta's satisfying EC requirements for regulatory reforms in financial services, competition and consumer protection, favourable consideration should be given to the future accession of Malta to the EU. These recommendations were endorsed in October by the EC General Affairs Council. In June 1994 the Council affirmed that the next phase of enlargement, following the (then) expected accession to the EU in January 1995 of Austria, Finland, Norway and Sweden, would involve Malta and Cyprus.

In April 1995 the House of Representatives approved a government proposal that Malta participate in the NATO 'partnership for peace' programme (see p. 192).

### Government

Under the 1974 Constitution, legislative power is held by the unicameral House of Representatives, whose 65 members are elected by universal adult suffrage for five years (subject to dissolution) on the basis of proportional representation. A constitutional amendment was adopted in January 1987 to ensure that a party which received more than 50% of the total votes cast in a general election would obtain a majority of seats in the legislature. The President is the constitutional Head of State, elected for a five-year term by the House, and executive power is exercised by the Cabinet. The President appoints the Prime Minister and, on the latter's recommendation, other Ministers. The Cabinet is responsible to the House.

### Defence

In June 1994 the armed forces of Malta consisted of a regular army of 1,850. Military service is voluntary. The defence budget for 1995 was estimated to be LM10.9m. Military assistance and training is provided by Italy, Germany, the United Kingdom and the USA.

### Economic Affairs

In 1992, according to estimates by the World Bank, Malta's gross national product (GNP), measured at average 1990–92 prices, was US $2,606m.; GNP per head in 1991 was $7,300. During 1985–92, it was estimated, GNP per head increased, in real terms, at an average annual rate of 5.4%. During 1985–93 the population increased by an annual average of 0.7%. Malta's gross domestic product (GDP) increased, in real terms, at an average annual rate of 4.1% in 1980–92 and by 4.5% in 1993. GDP, at current prices, was estimated at $2,455m. in 1993.

Agriculture (including hunting, forestry and fishing) contributed 3.0% of GDP in 1993. Some 2.3% of the working population were employed in the sector at November 1994. The principal export crop is potatoes. Tomatoes and other vegetables, cereals (principally wheat and barley) and fruit are also cultivated. Livestock and livestock products are also important, and efforts are being made to develop the fishing industry. Exports of food and live animals accounted for 2.1% of total exports in 1993. Agricultural production increased at an average rate of 1.4% per year in 1980–92 and by 5.8% in 1993.

Industry (including mining, manufacturing, construction and power) accounted for 33.9% of total employment in December 1991 and provided 34.6% of GDP in 1993. Industrial production increased by an average of 5.6% per year in 1980–89.

Mining and quarrying, together with construction, contributed 3.1% of GDP in 1993, and employed 3.9% of the working population at November 1994. The mining sector alone accounted for only 0.5% of total employment in December 1991. The sector's output expanded at an average annual rate of 6.1% in 1980–89. The principal activities are stone and sand quarrying. There are reserves of petroleum in Maltese offshore waters, and petroleum and gas exploration is currently under way.

Manufacturing contributed 24.0% of GDP in 1993. Some 27.5% of the working population were employed in the manufacturing sector at December 1991. Based on the gross value of output, the principal branches of manufacturing in 1991 were transport equipment and machinery, food and beverages, and textiles, footwear and clothing. Manufacturing production increased by 5.6% per year, on average, in 1980–89.

Energy is derived principally from imports of crude petroleum (the majority of which is purchased, at preferential rates, from Libya) and coal. Imports of mineral fuels comprised 4.7% of the value of total imports in 1993.

Tourism is a major source of foreign exchange earnings; in 1993 revenue from the sector accounted for 25.8% of the total value of exports of goods and services. In that year some 6.5% of the working population were directly employed in the tourism industry. In 1994 an estimated 1,175,000 tourists visited Malta, while revenue from tourism reached LM250m. In 1992 the United Kingdom accounted for 52.4% of tourist arrivals.

In 1993 Malta recorded a visible trade deficit of US $602.2m., and there was a deficit of $67.5m. on the current account of the balance of payments. More than 70% of Malta's trade is with the countries of the European Union (EU, see p. 143). In 1993 the principal source of imports (27.2%) was Italy; other major suppliers were Germany, the United Kingdom, the USA and France. Italy was also the principal market for exports (taking 32.2% of the total); other significant purchasers were Germany, the United Kingdom, the USA, Libya and the Netherlands. The principal exports in 1993 were machinery and transport equipment, manufactured articles (including clothing), and basic manufactures. The principal imports were machinery and transport equipment, basic manufactures (including textile yarn and fabrics), and food and live animals.

In 1993 Malta recorded a budgetary deficit of US $80.9m. (equivalent to 3.4% of GDP in that year). Malta's external debt totalled $746.1m. at the end of 1993, of which $127.9m. was long-term public debt. In 1992, when the total debt was $603.3m., the cost of debt-servicing was equivalent to 1.9% of the value of exports of goods and services. The annual rate of inflation averaged 2.7% in 1985–93; consumer prices increased by an annual average of 4.1% in 1994. In November 1994 4.0% of the labour force were unemployed.

Malta has an association agreement with the European Community (EC, now European Union—EU), originally signed in 1970, allowing favourable trading conditions for Malta, together with economic assistance from the Community (see p. 163). In July 1990 the Government formally applied for full Maltese membership of the EC, and in June 1993 the European Commission confirmed Malta's eligibility for eventual accession to the EU. In March 1995 the Commission gave its endorsement to measures being undertaken by the Maltese Government to align its economy more closely with the EU. Negotiations on the terms of Malta's entry to the EU were expected to begin in 1997.

After the closure, in 1979, of the British military base and naval docks, on which Malta's economy had been largely dependent, the Maltese Government pursued a successful policy of restructuring and diversification. The domestic market is limited, owing to the small population. There are few natural resources, and almost all raw materials have to be imported. Malta's development has therefore been based on the promotion of manufacturing for export and on tourism. A series of measures, implemented by the Government from 1987 onwards, reduced the role of the State in the economy and encouraged private enterprise. Legislation that was enacted in 1988 resulted in the expansion of foreign investment in manufacturing industry (particularly in non-traditional fields, such as electronics, information technology and pharmaceuticals). Other important developments have included the establishment of a major 'offshore' business centre, the opening of Malta's first stock exchange and the construction of a free port. In November 1992 the Maltese lira was devalued by 10%, in an attempt by the Government to minimize the adverse effects of world-wide recession on Malta's developing economy through retaining the islands' attractions as a base for foreign investment and as a popular tourist destination and through preserving the competitiveness of its exports. In 1994 the Government adopted extensive legislation that provided for Malta's further development as an international financial centre.

## Social Welfare

A comprehensive scheme of social insurance and other benefits is in operation. Non-contributory social welfare programmes include social work with families, care and protection of children, vocational and social rehabilitation centres and services for disabled persons. In 1994 Malta had five government hospitals, with a total of 2,126 beds, and there were 910 physicians working in the country. Of total recurrent budgetary expenditure projected for 1995, about LM 40.8m. (9.1%) was allocated to health services (including care of the elderly), and a further LM 125.7m. (28.1%) to social security.

## Education

Education is compulsory between the ages of five and 16 years, and is available free of charge in government schools and institutions, from kindergarten to university. Primary education begins at five years of age. Secondary education begins at the age of 11, and lasts for up to seven years, comprising a first cycle of five years and a second of two years. The first cycle is generally based on courses leading to examinations at the Ordinary Level of the British General Certificate of Education (GCE) or equivalent. However, after the second year, students may opt for craft courses of three or four years' duration in trade schools. Higher Secondary education provides two courses leading to the Advanced Level of the GCE. In 1992/93 there were also 67 private primary and secondary schools, administered by the Roman Catholic Church. Under an agreement between the Government and the Roman Catholic Church (signed in 1985), free education for pupils in church secondary schools was introduced in stages between 1985 and 1988. In 1990 enrolment at primary schools included 99% of children in the relevant age-group (boys 100%; girls 96%), while secondary enrolment included 80% of the appropriate age-group (boys 81%; girls 80%). Higher education is available at the University of Malta, which comprises 10 faculties. There are also a number of technical institutes, specialist schools and an extended skill-training scheme for trade-school leavers. About 5,000 full-time students were enrolled in tertiary institutions for the 1993/94 academic year. The Government also provides adult education courses. The 1994 budget proposals allocated LM37.2m. to education (representing 9.6% of total recurrent expenditure for that year). In 1986 the average rate of adult illiteracy was 12.1%.

## Public Holidays

**1995:** 1 January (New Year's Day), 10 February (St Paul's Shipwreck), 19 March (St Joseph), 31 March (Freedom Day), 14 April (Good Friday), 1 May (St Joseph the Worker and May Day), 7 June (Memorial of 1919 riot), 29 June (St Peter and St Paul), 15 August (Assumption), 8 September (Our Lady of Victories), 21 September (Independence Day), 8 December (Immaculate Conception), 13 December (Republic Day), 25 December (Christmas Day).

**1996:** 1 January (New Year's Day), 10 February (St Paul's Shipwreck), 19 March (St Joseph), 31 March (Freedom Day), 5 April (Good Friday), 1 May (St Joseph the Worker and May Day), 7 June (Memorial of 1919 riot), 29 June (St Peter and St Paul), 15 August (Assumption), 8 September (Our Lady of Victories), 21 September (Independence Day), 8 December (Immaculate Conception), 13 December (Republic Day), 25 December (Christmas Day).

## Weights and Measures

The metric system is in force.

# Statistical Survey

Source (unless otherwise stated): Central Office of Statistics, Auberge d'Italie, Merchants St, Valletta; tel. 224597; fax 248483.

### AREA, POPULATION AND DENSITY

**Area:** 316 sq km (122 sq miles).

**Population:** 345,418 (males 169,832, females 175,586) at census of 16 November 1985 (figures refer to *de jure* population); 369,135 (males 182,653, females 186,482) at 31 December 1994 (official estimate, excluding non-Maltese).

**Density:** 1,168 per sq km (Maltese population only) at 31 December 1994.

**Principal Towns** (estimated population at 31 March 1994): Birkirkara 21,551; Qormi 17,928; Mosta 15,887; Sliema 13,823; Zabbar 13,772; Valletta (capital) 7,953.

**Births and Deaths** (1994): Live births 4,784 (birth rate 13.0 per 1,000); Deaths 2,666 (death rate 7.2 per 1,000).

**Expectation of Life** (years at birth, 1993): Males 74.7; Females 78.6.

**Economically Active Population** (official estimates, '000 persons, 30 November 1994): Agriculture and fishing 3.1; Quarrying, construction and oil drilling 5.2; Manufacturing 29.5; Wholesale and retail trade 14.3; Finance, insurance and real estate 1.5; Transport, storage and communications 5.8; Hotels and catering establishments 9.0; Other personal services 10.0; Public sector (incl. armed forces) 51.1; Others 4.4; Total employed 134.0; Unemployed 5.6; Total labour force 139.6 (males 102.9, females 36.7).

### AGRICULTURE, ETC

**Principal Crops** (FAO estimates, '000 metric tons, 1993): Wheat 5; Barley 4; Potatoes 24; Tomatoes 20; Other vegetables and melons 33; Fruit (excl. melons) 12. Source: FAO, *Production Yearbook*.

**Livestock** (FAO estimates, '000 head, year ending September 1993): Cattle 24; Pigs 109; Goats 5; Sheep 6; Poultry 1,000. Source: FAO, *Production Yearbook*.

# MALTA

**Livestock Products** (FAO estimates, '000 metric tons, 1993): Beef 2; Pig meat 9; Poultry meat 4; Cows' milk 24; Goats' milk 2; Poultry eggs 6.8. Source: FAO, *Production Yearbook*.

**Fishing** (metric tons, live weight): Total catch 708 in 1991; 540 in 1992; 683 in 1993.

## INDUSTRY

**Production** (gross output, LM '000, 1991): Stone quarrying and sand pits 4,305; Food and beverages 87,039; Tobacco products 17,197; Textiles, footwear and clothing 79,710; Wood and cork products and furniture 17,010; Printing, publishing and allied trades 29,664; Rubber, chemicals, and non-metallic products 55,770; Metals 22,843; Transport equipment and machinery 238,843; Construction 47,013; Miscellaneous industries 36,622; Total 636,016.

## FINANCE

**Currency and Exchange rates:** 1,000 mils = 100 cents = 1 Maltese lira (LM; plural: liri). *Sterling and Dollar Equivalents* (31 December 1994): £1 sterling = 575.3 mils; US $1 = 368.1 mils; LM100 = £173.81 = $271.66. *Average Exchange Rate* (US $ per Maltese lira): 3.1459 in 1992; 2.6171 in 1993; 2.6486 in 1994.

**Budget** (estimates, LM million, 1994): *Revenue:* Income tax 91.9; Customs and excise 82.7; Social security 103.9; Grants and loans 52.5; Total (incl. others) 479.4. *Expenditure:* Recurrent expenditure 385.9 (of which Social security 117.4; Health, incl. care of the elderly 43.5; Education 37.2; Defence 10.3); Public debt servicing 21.4; Capital expenditure 114.7; Total 522.0.

**International Reserves** (US $ million at 31 December 1994): Gold 40.0; IMF special drawing rights 52.0; Reserve position in IMF 37.1; Foreign exchange 1,760.5; Total 1,889.6. Source: IMF, *International Financial Statistics*.

**Money Supply** (LM million at 31 December 1994): Currency outside banks 365.9; Demand deposits at commercial banks 72.4; Total money (incl. others) 463.5. Source: IMF, *International Financial Statistics*.

**Cost of Living** (Retail Price Index; base: 1991 = 100): *1994:* Food 109.2; Fuel and light 100.3; Clothing 110.2; Rent (incl. expenditure on maintenance and repairs of dwelling and water) 104.1; All items (incl. others) 110.2.

**Gross Domestic Product** (LM million at current market prices): 806.9 in 1991; 874.8 in 1992; 938.2 in 1993.

**Gross Domestic Product by Economic Activity** (LM '000, 1993): Agriculture, hunting, forestry and fishing 25,277; Mining and quarrying (incl. construction) 25,446; Manufacturing 199,978; Government enterprises 62,555; Wholesale and retail trade 114,692; Transport, storage and communications 59,428; Finance, insurance, real estate and business services 125,604; Community, social and personal services 84,233; Government and other services 135,048; Sub-total 832,261; Indirect taxes, *less* subsidies 105,937; Total 938,198.

**Balance of Payments** (US $ million): *1992:* Merchandise exports f.o.b. 1,557.1; Merchandise imports f.o.b. −2,104.0; *Trade Balance* −546.8; Exports of services 936.3; Imports of services −604.2; Other income received 271.2; Other income paid −119.8; Private unrequited transfers (net) 9.4; Official unrequited transfers (net) 84.3; *Current Balance* −30.4; Direct investment (net) 39.5; Portfolio investment (net) 209.5; Other capital (net) 247.1; Net errors and omissions −62.8; *Overall balance* 44.8. *1993:* Merchandise exports f.o.b. 1,351.1; Merchandise imports f.o.b. −1,953.2m. *Trade Balance* −602.2; Exports of services 946.7; Imports of services −618.1; Other income received 244.8; Other income paid −99.7; Private unrequited transfers (net) 7.3; Official unrequited transfers (net) 53.6; *Current Balance* −67.5. Source: IMF, *International Financial Statistics*.

## EXTERNAL TRADE

**Principal Commodities** (LM '000, 1993): *Imports c.i.f.:* Food and live animals 70,509; Beverages and tobacco 8,772; Crude materials (inedible) except fuels 13,935; Mineral fuels, lubricants, etc. 38,973 (Petroleum products and gas 35,706); Chemicals 56,393; Basic manufactures 130,374 (Textile yarn, fabrics, etc. 41,917); Machinery and transport equipment 416,097; Miscellaneous manufactured articles 86,819; Total (incl. others) 830,920. *Exports f.o.b.:* Food and live animals 10,868; Beverages and tobacco 4,865; Mineral fuels, lubricants, etc. 11,461; Basic manufactures 34,808; Machinery and transport equipment 296,154; Miscellaneous manufactured articles 142,426 (Clothing 58,106); Total (incl. others) 518,325.

**Principal Trading Partners** (LM '000, 1993): *Imports:* France 69,765, Germany 118,711, Italy 225,929, United Kingdom 111,396, USA 72,765; Total (incl. others) 830,920. *Exports:* Germany 81,010, Italy 167,139, Libya 25,137, Netherlands 12,976, United Kingdom 41,827, USA 38,896; Total (incl. others) 518,325. Figures for exports to individual countries exclude stores and bunkers for ships and aircraft.

## TRANSPORT

**Road Traffic** (motor vehicles in use, 1992): Private cars 120,320, Commercial vehicles 27,978, Motorcycles 6,636; Public service vehicles 5,212; Total 160,146.

**Shipping:** *Merchant fleet* (1994): Vessels 1,086; Displacement (million grt) 15.5. *International freight traffic* (metric tons, 1994): Goods loaded 309,124; Goods unloaded 1,780,629.

**Civil Aviation** (traffic on scheduled services, 1991): Civil aircraft movements 21,410; Passengers carried 2,174,125 (1993); Freight 8,875 metric tons; Mail 685 tons.

## TOURISM

**Tourist Arrivals:** 1,002,381 in 1992; 1,063,069 in 1993; 1,175,000 in 1994.

## COMMUNICATIONS MEDIA

*__Radio Receivers__ (1992): 189,000 in use.

*__Television Receivers__ (1992): 267,000 in use.

**Telephones** (December 1991): 191,876 in use.

*__Book Production__ (1992): 395 titles (incl. 112 pamphlets).

*__Daily newspapers__ (1992): 3 titles (combined average circulation 54,000 copies per issue).

*__Non-daily newspapers__ (1992): 8 titles.

*__Other periodicals__ (1992): 359 titles.

*Source: UNESCO, *Statistical Yearbook*.

## EDUCATION

**Pre-primary** (1990): 58 schools; 688 teachers; 11,313 students.

**Primary** (1990): 115 schools; 1,780 teachers; 36,899 students.

**Secondary** (1990): *General:* 43 schools; 1,978 teachers; 25,891 students; *Vocational:* 33 schools; 710 teachers; 6,653 students.

**University** (1990): 128 lecturers; 2,525 students.

# Directory

## The Constitution

On 13 December 1974 the Independence Constitution of 1964 was substantially amended to bring into effect a Republican Constitution, under the terms of which Malta became a democratic republic within the Commonwealth, founded on work and on respect for the fundamental rights and freedoms of the individual. The new Constitution provided for the creation of the office of President of Malta to replace that of Governor-General.

The religion of the Maltese people is recognized to be the Roman Catholic Apostolic Religion, and the Church Authorities have the constitutional right and duty to teach according to its principles. The religious teaching of the Roman Catholic Church is provided in all State schools as part of compulsory education.

The Constitution provides that the national language and the language of the Courts is Maltese but that both Maltese and English are official languages.

An independent Public Services Commission, consisting of three to five members, is appointed by the President, on the advice of the Prime Minister, to make recommendations to the Prime Minister concerning appointments to public office and the dismissal and disciplinary control of persons holding public office.

The Constitution also provides for an Employment Commission, consisting of a chairman and four other members, the function of which is to ensure that, in respect of employment, no distinction, exclusion or preference that is not justifiable is made or given in favour of or against any person by reason of his or her political opinion.

The Judicature is independent.

Radio and television broadcasting is controlled by an independent authority.

### DECLARATION OF PRINCIPLES

The Constitution upholds the right to work and to reasonable hours of work, the safeguarding of rights of women workers, the encouragement of private economic enterprise, the encouragement of co-operatives, the provision of free and compulsory primary education, and the provision of social assistance and insurance.

### FUNDAMENTAL RIGHTS AND FREEDOMS OF THE INDIVIDUAL

The Constitution provides for the protection of the right to life, freedom from arbitrary arrest or detention, protection of freedom of conscience, protection from discrimination on the grounds of race, etc.

### THE PRESIDENT

Under the Constitution, the office of President becomes vacant after five years from the date of appointment made by resolution of the House of Representatives. The President appoints the Prime Minister, choosing the member of the House of Representatives who is judged to be ablest to command the confidence of a majority of the members. On the advice of the Prime Minister, the President appoints the other ministers, the Chief Justice, the Judges and the Attorney-General.

### THE CABINET

The Cabinet consists of the Prime Minister and such number of other ministers as recommended by the Prime Minister.

### PARLIAMENT

The House of Representatives consists of such number of members, being an odd number and divisible by the number of divisions, as Parliament by law determines from time to time. In future the electoral divisions are not to be fewer than nine and not more than 15, as Parliament may from time to time determine. The normal life of the House of Representatives is five years, after which a general election is held. Election is by universal adult suffrage on the basis of proportional representation. The age of majority is 18 years. Under a constitutional amendment adopted in January 1987, it was ensured that a party receiving more than 50% of the total votes cast in a general election would obtain a majority of seats in the House of Representatives, by the allocation (if necessary) of extra seats to that party.

### NEUTRALITY AND NON-ALIGNMENT

In January 1987 a constitutional amendment was adopted, aiming to entrench in the Constitution Malta's status of neutrality and adherence to a policy of non-alignment, and stipulating that no foreign military base will be permitted on Maltese territory.

## The Government

### HEAD OF STATE

**President:** Dr UGO MIFSUD BONNICI (took office 4 April 1994).

### THE CABINET
(May 1995)

**Prime Minister:** Dr EDWARD FENECH-ADAMI.

**Deputy Prime Minister and Minister of Foreign Affairs:** Prof. GUIDO DE MARCO.

**Minister of Education and Human Resources:** MICHAEL FALZON.

**Minister for Home Affairs and Social Development:** Dr LOUIS GALEA.

**Minister for Economic Services:** Dr GEORGE BONELLO DU PUIS.

**Minister for the Environment:** Dr FRANCIS ZAMMIT DIMECH.

**Minister for Gozo:** ANTON TABONE.

**Minister of Finance:** JOHN DALLI.

**Minister for Social Security:** Dr GEORGE HYZLER.

**Minister of Justice:** Dr JOSEPH FENECH.

**Minister for Transport, Communications and Technology:** Dr MICHAEL FRENDO.

**Minister for Youth and the Arts:** Dr MICHAEL REFALO.

**Minister for Food, Agriculture and Fisheries:** CENSU GALEA.

### PARLIAMENTARY SECRETARIES (ATTACHED TO MINISTRIES)

**Ministry of Education and Human Resources:** Dr JOSEPH CASSAR.

**Ministry for Home Affairs and Social Development:** Prof. JOHN RIZZO NAUDI, Dr ANTOINE MIFSUD BONNICI.

**Ministry for Economic Services:** Dr JOSEPH PSAILA SAVONA.

**Ministry for the Environment:** NINU ZAMMIT, Dr STANLEY ZAMMIT.

**Ministry of Finance:** Prof. JOSEF BONNICI.

### MINISTRIES

**Office of the President:** The Palace, Valletta CMR 02; tel. 221221; telex 1471; fax 241241.

**Office of the Prime Minister:** Auberge de Castille (Kastilja), Valletta CMR 02; tel. 242560; telex 1531; fax 243303.

**Office of the Deputy Prime Minister and of the Minister of Foreign Affairs:** Palazzo Parisio, Merchants St, Valletta CMR 02; tel. 242191; telex 1497; fax 237822.

**Ministry for Economic Services:** Auberge d'Aragon, Valletta CMR 02; tel. 245391; fax 241494.

**Ministry of Education and Human Resources:** Floriana CMR 02; tel. 231385; fax 221634.

**Ministry for the Environment:** Floriana CMR 02; tel. 222378; fax 231293.

**Ministry of Finance:** Maison Demandols, South St, Valletta CMR 02; tel. 232646; telex 1512; fax 224667.

**Ministry for Food, Agriculture and Fisheries:** Barriera Wharf, Valletta CMR 02; tel. 225236; telex 1790; fax 231294.

**Ministry for Gozo:** St Francis Sq., Victoria, Gozo; tel. 561482; telex 1715; fax 561755.

**Ministry for Home Affairs and Social Development:** Casa Leoni, St Venera CMR 02; tel. 485100; fax 443595.

**Ministry of Justice:** House of Four Winds, Valletta CMR 02; tel. 242960; telex 1397; fax 243024.

**Ministry for Social Security:** Palazzo Ferreria, Republic St, Valletta CMR 02; tel. 243166; telex 1893; fax 243017.

**Ministry for Transport, Communications and Technology:** Lascaris, Valletta CMR 02; tel. 243880; telex 1108; fax 243758.

**Ministry for Youth and the Arts:** Floriana CMR 02; tel. 244041; fax 243025.

## Legislature

### HOUSE OF REPRESENTATIVES

**Speaker:** Dr LAWRENCE GONZI.

**General Election, 22 February 1992**

| Party | Votes | % | Seats |
|---|---|---|---|
| Nationalist Party | 127,932 | 51.77 | 34 |
| Malta Labour Party | 114,911 | 46.50 | 31 |
| Alternattiva Demokratika | 4,186 | 1.69 | — |
| Independent | 110 | 0.04 | — |
| Total | 247,139 | 100.00 | 65 |

## Political Organizations

**Alternattiva Demokratika:** 12 Antonio Agius St, Floriana VLT 14; tel. 240334; fax 224745; f. 1989; emphasizes environmental and human rights issues; Chair. Dr WENZU MINTOFF; Co-ordinator SAVIOUR BALZAN.

**Communist Party:** 14/8 Vincenti Bldgs, Strait St, Valletta VLT 08; tel. 232311; f. 1969; Marxist-Leninist; advocates dismantling of military bases in the Mediterranean region; Pres. CHARLES ZAMMIT; Gen. Sec. ANTHONY VASSALLO.

**Malta Democratic Party** (Partit Demokratiku Malti—PDM): 3 Spencer Bldg, Preca St, POB 27, Blata I-Bajda; tel. 220339; fax 240679; f. 1985; advocates decentralized government and a plural society; Pres. MICHAEL VELLA; Gen. Sec. LINO BRIGUGLIO.

**Malta Labour Party (MLP)** (Partit tal-Haddiema): March 31st St, Senglea CSP 06; tel. 690129; fax 690145; f. 1921; democratic socialist; mem. of Socialist International; Leader Dr ALFRED SANT; Pres. Dr MARIO VELLA; Gen. Sec. JIMMY MAGRO; 39,000 mems.

**Nationalist Party** (Partit Nazzjonalista—PN): Dar Centrali PN, Pietà; tel. 243641; telex 1941; fax 242886; f. 1880; Christian democratic; advocates full membership of the EU; mem. of European Union of Christian Democratic Parties; Leader Dr EDWARD FENECH-ADAMI; Gen. Sec. Dr AUSTIN GATT; 31,000 mems.

## Diplomatic Representation

### EMBASSIES AND HIGH COMMISSIONS IN MALTA

**Australia:** Ta'Xbiex Terrace, Ta'Xbiex MSD 11; tel. 338201; fax 344059; High Commissioner: CHRISTOPHER FREEMAN.

**China, People's Republic:** Karmnu Court, Lapsi St, St Julian's; tel. 334695; telex 1385; fax 344730; Ambassador: YIN YUFU.

**Egypt:** Villa Mon Rêve, 11 Sir Temi Zammit St, Ta'Xbiex MSD 11; tel. 333259; telex 1300; fax 319230; Ambassador: MAHER EL KASHEF.

**France:** Villa Seminia, 12 Sir Temi Zammit St, Ta'Xbiex; tel. 331107; telex 1381; fax 334640; Ambassador: PATRICK AMIOT.

**Germany:** 'Il-Piazzetta', Entrance B, 1st Floor, Tower Rd, Sliema; tel. 336531; telex 1224; fax 333976; Ambassador: Dr MARTIN FLORIN.

**Holy See:** Villa Cor Jesu, Pitkali Rd, Attard BZN 04 (Apostolic Nunciature); tel. 414732; fax 484120; Apostolic Nuncio: (vacant).

**India:** Regional Rd, St Julian's SGN 02; tel. 344302; telex 1618; fax 344259; High Commissioner: PRAVEEN L. GOYAL.

**Italy:** 5 Vilhena St, Floriana; tel. 233157; telex 1388; fax 235339; Ambassador: Dr MARCO COLOMBO.

**Libya:** Dar il-Jamahariya, Notabile Rd, Balzan; tel. 486347; telex 1258; fax 483939; Ambassador: Dr HEND ABU-BAKER SIALA.

**Russia:** Ariel House, Anthony Schembri St, Kappara, San Gwann; tel. 371905; telex 1545; fax 372131; Ambassador: YEVGENY N. MIKHAILOV.

**Spain:** 145/10 Tower Rd, Sliema; tel. 314164; telex 1686; fax 333732; Ambassador: JOSÉ MANUEL CERVERA DE GONGORA.

**Tunisia:** Dar Carthage, Qormi Rd, Attard BZN 02; tel. 435175; telex 1835; fax 435102; Ambassador: FAROUK LADJIMI.

**United Kingdom:** 7 St Anne St, Floriana VLT 15; tel. 233134; fax 242001; High Commissioner: GRAHAM ARCHER.

**USA:** Development House, 3rd Floor, St Anne St, Floriana; tel. 235960; fax 243229; Ambassador: JOSEPH R. PAOLINO, Jr.

## Judicial System

The legal system consists of enactments of the Parliament of Malta, and those of the British Parliament not repealed or replaced by enactments of the Maltese legislature. Maltese Civil Law derives largely from Roman Law, while British Law has had great influence on public law.

The Courts are: Constitutional Court, Court of Appeal, Civil Court, Commercial Court, Court of Magistrates, Court of Criminal Appeal, Criminal Court and Juvenile Court.

**Chief Justice, President of the Court of Appeal and the Constitutional Court:** Prof. GIUSEPPE MIFSUD BONNICI.

**Judges:** CARMEL A. AGIUS, JOSEPH D. CAMILLERI, JOSEPH A. FILLETTI, VICTOR CARUANA COLOMBO, ALBERT MANCHE, FRANCO DEPASQUALE, ANTON DEPASQUALE, JOSEPH SAID PULLICINO, FRANK G. CAMILLERI, ALBERTO J. MAGRI, NOEL ARRIGO.

**Attorney-General:** ANTHONY BORG BARTHET.

## Religion

### CHRISTIANITY

#### The Roman Catholic Church

Malta comprises one archdiocese and one diocese. At 31 December 1993 there were an estimated 350,800 adherents in the country, representing about 93.3% of the total population.

**Bishops' Conference:** Conferenza Episcopale Maltese, Archbishop's Curia, POB 29, Valletta CMR 01; tel. 605350; fax 622971; f. 1971; Pres. Most Rev. JOSEPH MERCIECA, Archbishop of Malta.

**Archbishop of Malta:** Most Rev. JOSEPH MERCIECA, Archbishop's Curia, POB 29, Valletta CMR 01; tel. 245350; fax 242173.

**Bishop of Gozo:** Rt Rev. NIKOL JOSEPH CAUCHI, Chancery Office, Republic St, Victoria VCT 103, Gozo; tel. 556661; fax 551278.

#### The Anglican Communion

Malta forms part of the diocese of Gibraltar in Europe.

**Church of England:** Pro-Cathedral of St Paul, Independence Sq., Valletta VLT 12; tel. 225714; Bishop of Gibraltar in Europe Rt Rev. JOHN HIND (resident in England); Chancellor of the Pro-Cathedral Rev. Canon PHILIP COUSINS.

## The Press

### DAILIES

**In-Nazzjon:** Independence Print, Herbert Ganado St, POB 37, Peità HMR 06; tel. 243641; telex 1941; fax 242886; f. 1970; Maltese; Editor JOE ZAHRA; circ. 20,000.

**L-Orizzont:** Union Press, Workers' Memorial Bldg, South St, Valletta VLT 11; tel. 244451; telex 1307; fax 238484; f. 1962; Maltese; Editor FRANS GHIRXI; circ. 25,000.

**The Times:** Allied Newspapers Ltd, Strickland House, 341 St Paul St, POB 328, Valletta VLT 07; tel. 241464; telex 1341; fax 247901; f. 1935; English; Editor VICTOR AQUILINA; circ. 23,000.

### WEEKLIES

**The Financial and Business Post:** 92 Swieqi Rd, Apartment 4, Swieqi STJ 02; tel. 338774; fax 338276; f. 1994; English; Editor JOHN SHEPHERD.

**Gwida:** Mercury Publicity Services, POB 83, Valletta CMR 01; tel. and fax 220932; Maltese and English; radio, television and entertainment guide; Editor JOE CALLEJA; circ. 12,000.

**Il-Gens:** Media Centre, National Rd, Blata L-Bajda HMR 02; tel. 246677; fax 234057; f. 1988; Maltese; Editor CARMEL ATTARD; circ. 13,000.

**Il-Mument:** Independence Print, Herbert Ganado St, POB 37, Pietà HMR 06; tel. 243641; telex 1941; fax 242886; f. 1972; Maltese; Editor VICTOR CAMILLERI; circ. 25,000.

**It-Tórca** (The Torch): Union Press, Workers' Memorial Bldg, South St, Valletta VLT 11; tel. 244451; telex 1307; fax 238484; f. 1944; Maltese; Editor LOUIS CAUCHI; circ. 30,000.

**Lehen Is-Sewwa:** Catholic Institute, Floriana VLT 16; tel. 225847; f. 1928; Roman Catholic; Editor PAUL SALIBA; circ. 10,000.

**Kull Hadd:** Marsa Press, Industrial Estate, Marsa HMR 15; tel. 235313; fax 240717; f. 1993; Maltese; Editor EVARIST BARTOLO.

**The Malta Business Weekly:** Airways House, 6th Floor, High St, Sliema SLM 15; tel. 345888; fax 346062; f. 1994; English; Editor JEFFREY BEZZINA.

**The Malta Independent:** Airways House, 6th Floor, High St, Sliema SLM 15; tel. 345888; fax 346062; f. 1992; English; Editor RAYMOND BUGEJA.

**The Sunday Times:** Allied Newspapers Ltd, Strickland House, 341 St Paul St, POB 328, Valletta VLT 07; tel. 241464; telex 1341; fax 240806; f. 1922; English; Editor LAURENCE GRECH; circ. 30,000.

MALTA

## SELECTED PERIODICALS

**Alternattiva:** 12 Antonio Agius St, Floriana; tel. 240334; fax 224745; f. 1989; fortnightly; Maltese; organ of Alternattiva Demokratika; Editor STEPHEN CACHIA.

**Base:** Foundation for Human Resources Development, 76 Old Theatre St, Valletta; tel. 245779; fax 245778; quarterly; Editor HILARY CARUANA.

**Commercial Courier:** Malta Chamber of Commerce, Exchange Bldgs, Republic St, Valletta VLT 05; tel. 247233; fax 245223; monthly; Editor STEFANO MALLIA; circ. 1,500.

**The Employer:** Malta Employers' Association, 35/1 South St, Valletta VLT 11; tel. 222992; fax 230227; Editor ALFRED J. BELLIZZI.

**Industry Today:** Development House, St Anne St, Floriana VLT 01; tel. 234428; fax 240702; quarterly; journal of the Malta Fed. of Industry; Editor EDWIN CALLEJA; circ. 1,000.

**Kultura:** J. P. Publications, POB 9, Old Bakery St, Valletta; tel. 344794; fax 344797; Editor-in-Chief TONY MALLIA; circ. 12,000.

**Malta Economic Indicators:** Central Office of Statistics, Auberge d'Italie, Merchants St, Valletta; tel. 224597; fax 248483; and the Economic Planning Division, Ministry of Finance; monthly.

**Malta Economic Update:** J.P. Publications, POB 9, Old Bakery St, Valletta; tel. 344794; fax 344797; monthly; English; Editor-in-Chief TONY MALLIA; circ. 16,000.

**Malta Government Gazette:** Department of Information, 3 Castille Place, Valletta CMR 02; tel. 225231; telex 1448; fax 237170; f. 1813; 2 a week; Maltese and English; circ. 3,000.

**Malta This Month:** Advantage Advertising Ltd, Regency House, Republic St, Valletta; tel. 249924; fax 249927; monthly; publication of Air Malta; Editor PETER DARMANIN.

**Pajjizna:** Department of Information, 3 Castille Place, Valletta CMR 02; tel. 224901; telex 1448; fax 237170; f. 1988; every two months; Maltese; circ. 20,000.

**The Retailer:** Association of General Retailers and Traders, Exchange Bldgs, Republic St, Valletta VLT 05; tel. 230459; fax 246925; monthly; Editor VINCENT FARRUGIA.

**The Teacher:** Teachers' Institute, 213 Republic St, Valletta; tel. 222663; every 2 months; journal of the Malta Union of Teachers; Editor JOHN JONES.

## NEWS AGENCIES

**Agence France-Presse (AFP):** 370 Zabbar Rd, Fgura PLA 16; tel. 801491; Correspondent MARIA INGUANEZ.

**Agenzia Nazionale Stampa Associata (ANSA)** (Italy) and **Deutsche Presse-Agentur (dpa)** (Germany): c/o The Sunday Times, Strickland House, Allied Newspapers Ltd, 341 St Paul St, POB 328, Valletta VLT 07; tel. 241464; telex 1341; fax 240806; Correspondent LAURENCE GRECH.

**Associated Press (AP)** (USA): 'Carmen', Valletta Rd, Paola PLA 02; tel. 821868; fax 247901; Correspondent VICTOR AQUILINA; and 'Thyme', Geronimo Abos St, Lija BZN 11; tel. 241464; Correspondent CHRISTOPHER SCICLUNA.

**Deutsche Presse-Agentur (dpa):** see Agenzia Nazionale Stampa Associata.

**Jamahiriya News Agency (JANA)** (Libya): Dar il-Jamaharija, Balzan; tel. 486347; Correspondent MOHAMED ABDALLA EMSEEK.

**Reuters** (United Kingdom): Sylvia House, Laurent Ropa St, Birkirkara BKR 02; tel. 442281; Correspondent JOSEPH P. SCICLUNA.

**United Press International (UPI):** 'Carmen', Valletta Rd, Paola PLA 02; tel. 821868; fax 247901; Correspondent VICTOR AQUILINA.

## Publishers

**A.C. Aquilina and Co Ltd:** c/o Guga Bookshops, 'Gug', Tria It-Jiben, St Andrews STS 64; tel. 233774; fax 235072; general; Dir RITA PORTELLI.

**Progress Press Co. Ltd:** Strickland House, 341 St Paul St, POB 328, Valletta VLT 07; tel. 241464; telex 1341; fax 237150; f. 1957; educational and text books, fiction, guidebooks; Chair. RONALD AGIUS; Man. Dir WILFRID B. ASCIAK.

**Publishers' Enterprises Group (PEG) Ltd:** PEG Bldg, UB7, San Gwann Industrial Estate, San Gwann; tel. 448359; fax 488908; f. 1983; educational, children's, cookery, technical, tourism, leisure; Man. Editor EMANUEL DEBATTISTA.

**University of Malta Press:** The University, Msida; tel. 336451; telex 407; fax 336450; f. 1953; Maltese folklore, history, law, bibliography and language.

**A. Vassallo and Sons Ltd:** Main Gate St, POB 6, Victoria, Gozo; tel. 556609; school text books, maps, guides.

*Directory*

## Radio and Television

In 1992, according to UNESCO estimates, there were 189,000 radio receivers and 267,000 television receivers in use. In December 1994 there were an estimated 147,200 licensed colour television receivers. All broadcasting services are subject to the provisions of the Constitution and the Broadcasting Ordinance and are under the overall supervision of the Broadcasting Authority. In early 1995 there were 12 radio stations, two television stations and a cable television service.

**Malta Broadcasting Authority:** National Rd, Blata I-Bajda; tel. 247908; telex 1100; fax 240855; f. 1961; statutory body responsible for the supervision and regulation of sound and television broadcasting; Chair. Dr JOSEPH PIROTTA; CEO ANTOINE J. ELLUL.

### RADIO AND TELEVISION COMPANIES

**Bay Radio:** St George's Bay, St Julians STJ 02; tel. 373813; telex 920; fax 376113; Station Man. CLEM DALTON.

**Island Sound Radio:** 46 Robert Samut Sq., Floriana VLT 14; tel. 249141; fax 243770; Head of News DON DURBRIDGE.

**Live FM Radio:** 70 Capuchins St, Floriana; tel. 249151; fax 250369; Head of News JOE GRIMA.

**Melita Cable TV Ltd:** 'Highrise', Imradd St, Ta'Xbiex MSD 12; tel. 345470; fax 345435; CEO MICHAEL J. ANZIANO.

**Public Broadcasting Services Ltd:** POB 82, G'Mangia, Valletta CMR 01; tel. 225051; fax 244601; f. 1991; govt-owned; operates national radio and television services: Radio Malta (broadcasts on one MW and one VHF frequency with combined programme output of 34 hours daily); and Television Malta (transmits scheduled programmes for 68 hours per week, with a further 28 hours of satellite re-transmissions); Chair. Dr PHILIP FARRUGIA RANDON; Man. Dir ROLAND FLAMINI; Head of Programmes (Radio Malta) JOHN INGWANEZ.

**Radio 101:** St Andrew St, San Gwann SGN 05; tel. 345101; fax 345008; Head of News JOHN ZAMMIT.

**Radio Calypso:** 12 Fortunato Mizzi St, Victoria VCT 111, Gozo; tel. 563000; fax 563565; News Editor SIMON LUMSDEN.

**Radju MAS:** 15 Old Mint St, Valletta VLT 12; tel. 237755; fax 247246.

**Rainbow Productions Ltd:** A28B Industrial Estate, Marsa HMR 15; tel. 244903; fax 248249; operates radio and television services; Head of News (Super ITV) ETIENNE ST JOHN; Head of Programmes (Radio Super 1) Rev. DAVID AZZOPARDI.

**RTK:** Media Centre, National Rd, Blata I-Bajda HMR 02; tel. 243783; fax 234057; Head of News CARMEL ATTARD.

**Smash Radio:** Smash Communications, Thistle Lane, Paola PLA 19; tel. 697829; fax 697830; f. 1992; Man. JESMOND SALIBA.

**University Radio:** Old Humanities Bldg, University of Malta, Tal-Qroqq MSD 06; tel. 333313; fax 314485.

**Voice of the Mediterranean (VOM):** POB 143, Valetta; tel. 248080; fax 241501; f. 1988; jtly owned by Maltese and Libyan Govts; broadcasts programmes in English and Arabic for six hours daily on one MW and two short-wave frequencies; transmits to more than 55 countries; Man. Dir Dr RICHARD VELLA LAURENTI.

## Finance

(cap. = capital; res = reserves; dep. = deposits; m. = million; br. = branch; amounts in Maltese liri)

### BANKING
#### Central Bank

**Central Bank of Malta:** Castille Place, Valletta CMR 01; tel. 247480; telex 1262; fax 243051; f. 1968; bank of issue; cap. and res 41m., dep. 233.7m. (Dec. 1994); Gov. FRANCIS J. VASSALLO.

#### Commercial Banks

**APS Bank Ltd:** 24 St Anne St, Floriana; tel. 226644; telex 1426; fax 226202; f. 1910; cap. and res 3m., dep. 31.6m. (Dec. 1994); Chair. ALFRED P. FARRUGIA; Gen. Mans EDWIN GRUPETTA, EDWARD CACHIA.

**Bank of Valletta Ltd:** 58 Zachary St, Valletta VLT 04; tel. 243261; telex 1235; fax 230894; f. 1974; cap. and res 39.8m., dep. 522.5m. (Sept. 1994); Chair. Dr JOHN C. GRECH; Gen. Man. (Operations) FRANK XERRI DE CARO; 50 brs in Malta and Gozo.

**Lombard Bank (Malta) Ltd:** Lombard House, 67 Republic St, POB 584, Valletta CMR 01; tel. 248411; telex 1379; fax 246600; f. 1969; cap. and res 3m., dep. 30.2m. (Sept. 1994); Chair. ALFRED MALLIA; Gen. Man. (Operations) F. BONELLO; 5 brs.

**Mid-Med Bank Ltd:** 233 Republic St, POB 428, Valletta VLT 05; tel. 245281; telex 1370; fax 485857; f. 1975; cap. and res 43.5m.,

# MALTA

dep. 681.8m. (Sept. 1994); Chair. Norman P. Mifsud; Gen. Mans John Melillo, Joseph C. Caruana; 50 brs and agencies.

### Other Financial Institutions

**First International Merchant Bank (Malta) Ltd:** Plaza Commercial Centre, 7th Floor, Bisazza St, Sliema SLM 15; tel. 322100; fax 322122; f. 1994; Gen. Man. J. Fletcher.

**Investment Finance Bank Ltd:** 168 Strait St, Valletta VLT 08; tel. 232017; telex 1744; fax 242014; f. 1976; subsidiary of Mid-Med Bank Ltd; cap. and res 6.3m. (Sept. 1993); medium- and long-term finance for business enterprises; Chair. Norman P. Mifsud; Gen. Man. Alfred Sladden.

**Izola Bank:** 53 St Dominic St, Valletta VLT 06; tel. 241258; fax 241250; Gen. Man. Peter Muscat.

**Lohombus Bank:** Spencer Gardens, Blata l-Bajda HMR 12; tel. 226055; fax 242669; cap. and res 7m. (Sept. 1994); Chair. Joseph Sammut; Gen. Man. J. M. Formosa.

**Valletta Investment Bank Ltd:** 144 St Christopher St, Valletta VLT 03; tel. 235241; fax 234419; f. 1990; cap. and res 5m. (Sept. 1994); Chair. John Grech; Gen. Man. A. Bencini.

### 'Offshore' Banks

**Bank of Valletta International:** 86 South St, Valletta VLT 11; tel. 244970; fax 222132; f. 1992; Chair. Dr John C. Grech.

**First Austrian Bank:** 136 Christopher St, Valletta; tel. 230624; fax 243219; f. 1993; Chair. Dr Patrick Galea.

**Mid-Med Bank (Overseas) Ltd:** 15 Republic St, Valletta VLT 04; tel. 249801; fax 249805; f. 1992; Chair. Norman P. Mifsud.

### STOCK EXCHANGE

**Maltese Stock Exchange:** Pope Pius V St, Valletta; tel. 244051; fax 244071; f. 1992; Chair. Frederick Mifsud Bonnici.

### INSURANCE

**Mediterranean Insurance Brokers Ltd:** Mediterranean Bldg, Abate Rigord St, Ta'Xbiex MSD 12; tel. 340530; telex 1528; fax 341597; f. 1976; CEO L. Ciantar.

**Middle Sea Insurance Co Ltd:** Middle Sea House, POB 337, Floriana VLT 16; tel. 246262; telex 1862; fax 248195; f. 1981; Man. Dir Mario C. Grech.

Numerous foreign insurance companies, principally British, Canadian and Italian, are represented in Malta by local agents.

## Trade and Industry

### DEVELOPMENT ORGANIZATIONS

**Malta Development Corporation (MDC):** Notabile Rd, Mrietiel, POB 571, Valletta CMR 01; tel. 448944; fax 448966; f. 1967; administers govt programme of investment incentives; liaises between industry and the Govt and assists foreign cos; Chair. Prof. J. V. Bannister.

**Malta Financial Services Centre:** Attard; tel. 441155; fax 441188; promotes and supervises Malta's 'offshore' financial and trading centre; Chair. Dr Mario Felice; CEO Dr Andre Camilleri.

**Malta Investment Management Co Ltd (MIMCOL):** Trade Centre, Industrial Estate, San Gwann SGN 09; tel. 497970; fax 499568; f. 1988 by the Govt to manage its investments in domestic commercial enterprises; Chair. Anthony S. Diacono.

### INDUSTRIAL AND COMMERCIAL ORGANIZATIONS

**Department of Industry:** Kukkanja St, St Venera CMR 02; tel. 446250; fax 446257; f. 1964; monitors the performance of established private industries; aids development of local, especially small-scale, industry; ensures high quality of manufactured goods, both imported and locally-made; assists in marketing and monitors latest achievements in international technology; also encourages and promotes Maltese handicrafts, and operates two crafts villages and two craft centres; Dir Mario Farrugia.

**Department of Trade:** Lascaris, Valletta CMR 02; tel. 231365; fax 246800; f. 1955; functions include import, export, trading licensing, consumer protection, price enforcement, foreign trade relations and the registration of partnerships, trade marks, patents and designs; Dir Lawrence C. Coppini.

**Malta Chamber of Commerce:** Exchange Bldgs, Republic St, Valletta VLT 05; tel. 247233; fax 245223; f. 1848; Pres. Francis T. Gera; 1,100 mems.

**Malta Export Trade Corporation Ltd (METCO):** Trade Centre, Industrial Estate, San Gwann SGN 09; POB 8, San Gwann SGN 01; tel. 446186; telex 1966; fax 496687; Chair. John L. Bonello; Man. Dir Alexander Agius Cesareo.

**Malta Federation of Industry:** Development House, St Anne St, Floriana VLT 01; tel. 234428; fax 240702; f. 1946; national organization for industry; 360 corporate mems; Pres. Franco Masini; Sec.-Gen. Edwin Calleja.

**Malta Freeport Corporation:** Freeport Centre, Kalafrana BBG 05; tel. 650200; fax 684814; f. 1988; container distribution centre; also operates oil products terminal and general warehousing facilities; Chair. Marin Hili.

### MAJOR STATE-OWNED ENTERPRISES

**Enemalta Corpn:** Central Administration Bldg, Church Wharf, POB 6, Hamrun HMR 01; tel. 223601; fax 243055; f. 1977; state energy corpn; purchases and distributes petroleum products and steam coal for electricity generation; transmits and distributes electricity, petroleum products and gas; Chair. J. Ellul Vincenti.

**Malta Drydocks:** The Docks, POB 581, Valletta; tel. 822451; fax 824027; f. 1959; ship repairing and shipbuilding; heavy industrial engineering; operates seven dry docks and nine deepwater berths; Chair. Sammy Meilaq.

> **Manoel Island Yacht Yard:** Manoel Island GZR 03; tel. 334453; telex 1310; fax 343900; yacht and small craft repairs; boat park; Man. Victor Seguna.

**Malta Shipbuilding Co Ltd:** Marsa Shipyard, Marsa, POB 5, Valletta CMR 01; tel. 826251; fax 240930; f. 1976; shipbuilding facilities, structural steel fabrication and other projects in offshore petroleum industry; 61% owned by Maltese Govt; Chair. Albert Mizzi; CEO Carm L. Farrugia.

**Telemalta Corporation:** Spencer Hill, Marsa; tel. 247770; telex 1357; fax 240761; f. 1975 by the Govt to operate all telecommunications services; Chair. Dr Richard Galea Debono; Gen. Man. Anthony De Bono.

### EMPLOYERS' ASSOCIATION

**Malta Employers' Association:** 35/1 South St, Valletta VLT 11; tel. 222992; fax 230227; f. 1965; Pres. John E. Sullivan; Sec.-Gen. A. J. Bellizzi.

### TRADE UNIONS

In June 1994 there were 32 trade unions (with a membership of 76,734).

**Confederation of Malta Trade Unions (CMTU):** 13 South St, POB 467, Valletta CMR 01; tel. 237313; telex 1593; fax 250146; f. 1958; affiliated to the World Confed. of Labour, to the Commonwealth Trade Union Council and to the European Trade Union Confed.; Pres. Salvinu Spiteri; Gen. Sec. Charles V. Naudi; 31,000 mems.

The principal affiliated unions include:

> **Association of General Retailers & Traders Union (GRTU):** Exchange Bldgs, Republic St, Valletta VLT 05; tel. 230459; fax 246925; f. 1948; Pres. Carlo Cini; Dir-Gen. Dr Vincent Farrugia; 7,032 mems.
>
> **Malta Union of Teachers:** Teachers' Institute, 213 Republic St, Valletta; tel. 222663; fax 244074; f. 1919; Pres. A. Buhagiar; Gen. Sec. J. P. Degiovani; 4,040 mems.
>
> **Union Haddiema Maghqudin (UHM):** 'Dar Reggie Miller', St Thomas St, Floriana VLT 15; tel. 220847; fax 246091; f. 1966; Pres. S. Spiteri; Sec.-Gen. M. Agius; 23,261 mems.

**The General Workers' Union (GWU):** Workers' Memorial Bldg, South St, Valletta; tel. 241996; telex 1307; fax 242975; f. 1946; affiliated to ICFTU; Pres. L. Lautier; Gen. Sec. Angelo Fenech; 43,750 mems.

## Transport

### RAILWAYS

There are no railways in Malta.

### ROADS

In 1993 there were 1,582 km of roads, including 1,410 km of main roads. About 93% of roads are paved. Bus services run to all parts of the main island and to most parts of Gozo. Capital expenditure on roads was LM5.8m. in 1993.

**Roads Department:** Cannon Rd, St Venera HMR 07; tel. 484634; fax 243753.

**Public Transport Authority:** B'Kara Rd, Msida MSD 13; tel. 486927; fax 483443; supervisory body; Chair. Michael Seychell.

### SHIPPING

In 1990 a total of 2,921 ships, with a registered displacement of 13,140,007 gross tons, entered Maltese ports. In the late 1980s

# MALTA

Malta opened its national shipping register to ships of all countries, in an attempt to generate revenue. In 1994 Malta's merchant fleet was the 10th largest in the world in terms of gross tonnage, comprising 1,086 vessels, with a total displacement of 15.5m. gross registered tons. The island's dry dock facilities are an important source of revenue.

**Malta Maritime Authority:** Maritime House, Lascaris Wharf, Valletta VLT 01; tel. 250360; fax 250365; supervises the administration and operation of ports and yachting centres, and of vessel registrations under the Maltese flag; Chair. JOSEPH GRIOLI.

**Blanchi & Co Ltd:** Palazzo Marina, 143 St Christopher St, Valletta VLT 02; tel. 232241; telex 1257; fax 232991; Man. Dir R. BIANCHI.

**Cassar & Cooper Ltd:** Valletta Bldgs, 54 South St, Valletta; tel. 238372; telex 1270; fax 237864; Dir MICHAEL COOPER.

**Medserv Ltd:** Manoel Island, Gzira GZA 03; tel. 336408; telex 1485; fax 339511; Chair. F. H. SAID.

**Mifsud Brothers (Shipping and Travel) Ltd:** 66 South St, POB 294, Valletta; tel. 232157; telex 1230; fax 221331; agents for Lloyd Triestino, Sloman Neptune, Bremen, Cunard Line, Southampton and Iraqi Line, Basra.

**O. F. Gollcher & Sons Ltd:** 19 Zachary St, POB 268, Valletta VLT 10; tel. 231851; telex 1227; fax 234195; Dir MARK GOLLCHER.

**Ripard, Larvan & Ripard Ltd:** 156 Ta'Xbiex Seafront, Gzira GZR 03; tel. 331563; fax 343419; Man. Dir CHRISTIAN RIPARD.

**Sea Malta Co Ltd:** Sea Malta Bldg, Flagstone Wharf, Marsa HMR 12; tel. 232230; telex 1210; fax 225776; f. 1973; national shipping line; operates services to and from the United Kingdom and Northern Europe; also roll-on/roll-off services between Malta, southern Italy, Sicily, Marseille and Libya; agency services, ship management, freight forwarding, ship-broking, bunkering, warehouse and passenger services; Chair. J. A. SCICLUNA; Man. Dir G. XERRI; Sec. J. T. APPS.

**S. Mifsud & Sons Ltd (SMS):** 131 East St, Valletta VLT 06; tel. 233127; telex 1277; fax 234180; car-ferry services three times weekly between Malta and Reggio di Calabria via Syracuse and Catania; weekly between Malta and Naples via Syracuse, Catania and Reggio di Calabria; also agents for Tirrenia Lines of Naples; Dir ADRIAN S. MIFSUD.

**Sullivan Shipping Agencies Ltd:** Exchange Bldgs, Republic St, Valletta VLT 05; tel. 245127; telex 1301; fax 233417; Man. Dir ERNEST SULLIVAN.

**Thos C. Smith:** 12 St Christopher St, Valletta VLT 06; tel. 245071; telex 1272; fax 220078; Man. Dir JOE GERADA.

**Virtu Steamship Co Ltd:** POB 315, Valletta; 'Virtu', 3 Princess Elizabeth Terrace, Ta'Xbiex MSD 11; tel. 316766; telex 1214; fax 314533; f. 1945; ship-owners; ship agents; shipbrokers; Malta-Sicily express passenger ferry service; travel agents; Man. Dir F. A. PORTELLI.

## CIVIL AVIATION

Malta International Airport, which is situated at Luqa (8 km from Valletta), has a capacity of 5m. passengers per year. In 1993 a total of 2,174,125 passengers passed through the airport.

**Air Malta Co Ltd:** Luqa LQA 05; tel. 824330; telex 1389; fax 673241; f. 1973; national airline with a 96.4% state shareholding; scheduled passenger and cargo services to mainland Europe, the United Kingdom, Scandinavia, Sicily, North Africa and the Middle East; charter services to the United Kingdom and mainland Europe; Chair. and CEO JOSEPH N. TABONE.

# Tourism

Malta has climatic, scenic and historical attractions, including fine beaches. Tourism is a major sector of Malta's economy, generating foreign exchange earnings of LM250m. in 1994, when there were 1,175,000 visitors.

**National Tourism Organisation—Malta (NTOM):** 280 Republic St, Valletta CMR 02; tel. 224444; fax 220401; publs tourist information brochures and hotel lists; Chair. Dr JOSEPH GALEA DEBONO.

# THE MARSHALL ISLANDS

## Introductory Survey

**Location, Climate, Language, Religion, Flag, Capital**

The Republic of the Marshall Islands consists of two groups of islands, the Ratak and Ralik chains, comprising 31 atolls and covering about 180 sq km (70 sq miles) of land. The territory lies within the area of the Pacific Ocean known as Micronesia (which includes Kiribati, Tuvalu and other territories). The islands lie about 3,200 km (2,000 miles) south-west of Hawaii and about 2,100 km (1,300 miles) south-east of Guam. Rainfall decreases from south to north, with January, February and March being the driest months, although seasonal variations in rainfall and temperature are generally small. The native population comprises various ethno-linguistic groups, but English is widely understood. The principal religion is Christianity, much of the population being Roman Catholic. The national flag (proportions 190 by 100) is dark blue, with a representation of a white star (with 20 short and four long rays) in the upper hoist; superimposed across the field are two progressively-wider stripes (orange above white), running from near the lower hoist corner to near the upper fly corner. The capital is the Dalap-Uliga-Darrit Municipality, on Majuro atoll.

**Recent History**

The first European contact with the Marshall and Caroline Islands was by Spanish expeditions in the 16th century, including those led by the Portuguese navigator Fernão de Magalhães (Ferdinand Magellan) and the Spaniard Miguel de Saavedra. Spanish influence in the islands was eroded towards the end of the 19th century. German trading companies were active in the Marshall Islands from the 1850s onwards. Spanish sovereignty over the Marshall Islands was recognized in 1886 by the Papal Bull of Pope Leo XIII, which also gave Germany trading rights there. In 1899 Germany bought from Spain the Caroline Islands and the Northern Mariana Islands (except Guam, which had been ceded to the USA after the Spanish–American War of 1898). In 1914, at the beginning of the First World War, Japan occupied the islands, receiving a mandate for its administration from the League of Nations in 1920. After the capture of the islands by US military forces in 1944 and 1945, most of the Japanese settlers were repatriated, and in 1947 the United Nations established the Trust Territory of the Pacific Islands (comprising the Caroline Islands, the Marshall Islands and the Northern Mariana Islands), to allow the USA to administer the region. The territory was governed by the US Navy from 1947 until 1951, when control passed to a civil administration—although the Northern Mariana Islands remained under military control until 1962.

From 1965 onwards there were increasing demands for local autonomy. In that year the Congress of Micronesia was formed, and in 1967 a commission was established to examine the future political status of the islands. In 1970 it declared Micronesians' rights to sovereignty over their own lands, of self-determination, to their own constitution and to revoke any form of free association with the USA. In May 1977, after eight years of negotiations, President Jimmy Carter announced that his administration intended to adopt measures to terminate the trusteeship agreement by 1981.

On 9 January 1978 the Marianas District achieved separate status as the Commonwealth of the Northern Mariana Islands (q.v.), but remained legally a part of the Trusteeship until 1986. The Marshall Islands District drafted its own Constitution, which came into effect on 1 May 1979, and the four districts of Yap, Truk (now Chuuk), Ponape (now Pohnpei) and Kosrae ratified a new Constitution, to become the Federated States of Micronesia (q.v.), on 10 May 1979. In the Palau District a referendum in July 1979 approved a proposed local constitution, which came into effect on 1 January 1981, when the district became the Republic of Palau (q.v.).

The USA signed the Compact of Free Association with the Republic of Palau in August 1982, and with the Marshall Islands and the Federated States of Micronesia in October. The trusteeship of the islands was due to end after the principle and terms of the Compacts had been approved by the respective peoples and legislatures of the new countries, by the US Congress and by the UN Security Council. Under the Compacts, the four countries (including the Northern Mariana Islands) would be independent of each other and would manage their internal and foreign affairs separately, while the USA would be responsible for defence and security. The Compacts with the Federated States of Micronesia and the Marshall Islands were approved in plebiscites in June and September 1983 respectively. The Congress of the Federated States of Micronesia ratified the country's decision in September. Under the Compact with the Marshall Islands, the USA was to retain its military bases in the Marshall Islands for at least 15 years and, over the same period, was to provide annual aid of US $30m.

On 21 October 1986 the Compact between the Marshall Islands and the USA came into effect, following its approval by the islands' Government. In November President Ronald Reagan issued a proclamation that formally ended US administration of Micronesia. The first President of the Republic of the Marshall Islands was Amata Kabua, who was re-elected for further four-year terms of office in 1984, 1988 and in January 1992, following the success of his supporters at the legislative elections of November 1991. In December 1990 the UN Security Council finally voted formally to ratify the termination of the trusteeship agreement; the Marshall Islands became a member of the UN in September 1991.

The Marshall Islands' atolls of Bikini and Eniwetak were used by the US Government for experiments with nuclear weapons, Bikini in 1946–58 and Eniwetak in 1948–58. The native inhabitants of Eniwetak were evacuated before tests began, and were allowed to return to the atoll in 1980, after much of the contaminated area had supposedly been rendered safe. The inhabitants of Bikini atoll campaigned for similar treatment, and in 1985 the US administration agreed to decontaminate Bikini atoll over a period of between 10 and 15 years. Under the terms of the Compact, the US administration consented to establish a US $150m. trust fund to settle claims against the USA resulting from the testing of nuclear devices in the Marshall Islands during the 1940s and 1950s. In 1989 the US Supreme Court ruled that the Compact of 1983 and subsequent US legislation in 1986 prevented the islanders from suing the USA for any additional compensation, but in January 1990 a panel of judges approved further compensation for the islanders. By mid-1993 $112m. had been paid to the victims of the nuclear testing out of interest from the trust fund. In 1992 more than 400 Marshall Islanders received the first nuclear test compensation for personal injury, from a fund of $45m., to be paid over 15 years.

Another atoll in the Marshall Islands, Kwajalein, has been used since 1947 as a target for the testing of missiles fired from California, USA. Under the terms of the Compact, the US Government is committed to providing an estimated US $170m. in rent, over a period of 30 years, for land used as the site of a missile-tracking station, and a further $80m. for development projects. The inhabitants of Kwajalein atoll were concentrated on the small island of Ebeye, adjacent to the US base on Kwajalein Island, before a new programme of weapons-testing began in 1961. Consequent overcrowding led to numerous social problems on Ebeye, including (according to a government report) an increase in crime, suicide and the rate of deaths from malnutrition in children between 1983 and 1989. In 1985 the entire population of Rongelap atoll (which had been engulfed in nuclear fall-out from the tests at Bikini in 1954) was forced to resettle on Mejato atoll, after surveys suggested that levels of radiation there remained dangerous. Similar tests, carried out by US scientists in 1992, revealed that Bikini atoll also remained contaminated. In January 1994 several senior members of the Marshall Islands' legislature, the Nitijela, demanded that the US Government release detailed information on the effects of its nuclear testing programme in the islands. The Minister of Foreign Affairs, Tom Kijiner, claimed that the fact that information relating to the tests had remained 'classified' had resulted in the payment of inadequate compensation to the islanders. In July documentation was released by the US Department of Energy, giving conclusive evidence that Marshall Islanders had been deliberately exposed to high levels of radiation in order that its effects on their health could be studied by US medical researchers. A report by Japanese scientists published in early 1995 indicated that some 40% of the former inhabitants of Rongelap atoll were suffering from cancer.

In February 1989 it was announced that Marshall Islands' passports were to be offered for sale at a price of US $250,000 (reduced to $100,000 in September of that year), in an attempt to stimulate Asian investment. In March 1993 an Australian national was convicted on 15 forgery charges, in connection with the offer of Marshall Islands passports to Taiwanese nationals.

In December 1993 the Government announced that it was considering plans to reduce the number of employees in the 3,000-strong public-service sector by up to 25%. Further reforms of the sector were announced in 1994.

The Marshall Islands has established diplomatic relations with numerous countries world-wide, and maintains an embassy in Washington, DC (USA), Suva (Fiji), Tokyo (Japan) and Beijing (People's Republic of China). The Marshall Islands Government has made clear its belief that its links with Australia (with which diplomatic relations were established in 1987) would be greatly enhanced by an Australian embassy on its territory (currently served by an ambassador based in the Federated States of Micronesia).

A UN report, in 1989, on the 'greenhouse effect' (heating of the earth's atmosphere) predicted a possible resultant rise in sea-level of some 3.7 m by 2030, which would completely submerge the Marshall Islands. In May 1993 the Australian Government commissioned the construction of a station for the monitoring of sea-level and climate change, to be based on Majuro. However, policies of the Marshall Islands Government have, at times, caused regional concerns regarding pollution. A series of proposed projects in the early 1990s (involving, for example, the use of imported domestic waste as landfill and the burning of disused car tyres to generate energy) promoted concern among environmentalists. Most controversial, however, was the announcement, in May 1994, that a feasibility study was to be conducted into the establishment of large-scale facilities for the storage of nuclear waste on one or more of the country's contaminated islands. US government criticism of the plans was strongly denounced by the Marshall Islands authorities, who claimed that the project constituted the only opportunity for the country to generate sufficient income for the rehabilitation of contaminated islands and the provision of treatment for illnesses caused by the US nuclear-test programme. In late 1994 a US company offered the Marshall Islands Government US $160m. over five years for the right to develop an undergound nuclear storage site.

In June 1990, during a visit to Washington, DC, President Kabua emphasized the Marshall Islands' opposition to proposals before the US Congress that involved the inclusion of Wake Island, or Enenkio atoll, in the Territory of Guam. Kabua claimed the atoll for the Marshall Islands, stating that Enenkio was a traditional site for Marshallese chiefly rituals. The claim was repeated in July 1993, when the Marshall Islands' Government requested that its fishing vessels be allowed access to Enenkio's waters, and again in late 1994, following an announcement by the US Air Force that it was to cease its military operations on the atoll. Another territorial dispute, involving the chiefly rights to a group of islands including Kwajalein atoll, was resolved with the signing of an agreement in October of that year. The dispute between two branches of the Kabua family originated at the beginning of the 20th century, when two brothers both claimed rightful inheritance of the title Iroijlaplap (paramount chief).

### Government

The Constitution of the Republic of the Marshall Islands, which became effective on 1 May 1979, provides for a parliamentary form of government, with legislative authority vested in the 33-member Nitijela. The Nitijela (members of which are elected, by popular vote, for a four-year term) elects the President of the Marshall Islands (also a four-year mandate) from among its own members. Under the terms of the Compact of Free Association (which was signed by the Governments of the Marshall Islands and the USA on 25 June 1983, and which was effectively ratified by the US Congress on 14 January 1986) the Republic of the Marshall Islands is a sovereign, self-governing state.

Local governmental units are the municipalities and villages. Elected Magistrates and Councils govern the municipalities. Village government is largely traditional.

### Defence

The defence of the Marshall Islands is the responsibility of the USA, which maintains a military presence on Kwajalein atoll.

### Economic Affairs

During 1985–93, according to estimates by the World Bank, the population of the Marshall Islands increased by an annual average of 3.9%. Agriculture is mainly on a subsistence level, the principal crops being coconuts, cassava and sweet potatoes. In 1993 some 12,000 metric tons of copra were produced; coconut products provided some 49% of exports in 1991, and earned US $1.4m. in foreign exchange. A commercial tuna-fishing industry is being developed. In April 1992 the Guam Fishing Co signed an agreement with the USA for the construction of a tuna-canning factory on Majuro, which was expected to create some 900 jobs. A further agreement, with the People's Republic of China, signed in mid-1993, envisaged a major expansion of the islands' fishing industry, with the provision of up to 100 long-line vessels (the country's existing fleet comprised 13 vessels). The cultivation of seaweed was developed extensively in 1992, and in 1994 a project to cultivate blacklip pearl oysters was undertaken with US funding. There are few mineral resources, although high-grade phosphate deposits exist on Ailinglaplap atoll.

In March 1989 legislation was proposed to increase personal and business income taxes on a sliding scale. The legislation also included tax concessions to encourage foreign investment, and the international shipping registry experienced considerable expansion following the political troubles in Panama in 1989. An 'offshore' banking system also operates. The construction of a floating dry-dock on Majuro in early 1995 was expected to encourage expansion in the domestic shipping industry.

In 1991 the Marshall Islands recorded a trade deficit of US $53.6m. The major exports in that year were coconut oil and trochus. The principal imports included basic manufactures (which accounted for 29.0% of total expenditure on merchandise imports), food and live animals (24.3%), machinery and transport equipment (16.3%), mineral fuels, etc. (11.1%) and beverages and tobacco (9.9%).

Budgetary estimates for 1992 envisaged a recurrent deficit of US $27.5m. Financial assistance from the USA, in accordance with the terms stipulated in the Compact of Free Association, contributes a large part of the islands' revenue. In 1990 this source of aid accounted for two-thirds of the $69m. revenue. However, in 1991 expenditure was limited by a decrease of some 15% in funding from the agreement with the USA. Aid is also provided by Taiwan, Japan and Australia.

The Marshall Islands is a member of the South Pacific Commission (see p. 215), the South Pacific Forum (p. 217), the South Pacific Regional Trade and Economic Co-operation Agreement (SPARTECA—see p. 218) and the Asian Development Bank (ADB—see p. 107).

In June 1992 the Marshall Islands Government approved a five-year development plan, which aimed at increasing activity in the fishing and tourist industries, as well as creating employment and developing the outer islands. (However, economic development was severely hampered by typhoon damage (Typhoons Axel and Gay) and drought during 1992.) The Government's proposals for retrenchment in the public-service sector, announced in 1993–94, have notably been welcomed by the ADB. Apparently attracted by the prospect of unrestricted access to the US market, the People's Republic of China announced plans for major investment in the islands in mid-1993: proposed projects included the intensive development of the fishing industry and the establishment of an industrial park. The announcement, in late 1994, that operations at the Kwajalein missiles-testing base were to be severely curtailed, owing to reductions in the US defence budget, caused considerable concern in the Marshall Islands. (Activities at the base have hitherto contributed an estimated US $25m. annually to the islands' economy and provided employment for some 1,500 islanders.) Further dissatisfaction was expressed in late 1994 and early 1995 surrounding allegations that the US Government had not fulfilled many of its financial obligations to the Marshall Islands as defined under the Compact of Free

# THE MARSHALL ISLANDS

Association. The Kabua Government hoped, however, to obtain a degree of financial security if its project to construct a storage facility for nuclear waste were realized (see Recent History).

### Social Welfare

In 1987 there were 19 physicians and 88 nurses working in the Marshall Islands. According to a UNICEF report of May 1991, two-thirds of Marshallese children were malnourished, and by March 1992 3% were suffering from vitamin A deficiency (1% is considered an epidemic). The islands high rate of population growth (see Economic Affairs) is also a source of social problems. In late 1994 a loan of US $5.7m. was received from the Asian Development Bank to improve health services.

### Education

Education is compulsory between the ages of six and 14. In 1987 a total of 9,692 children attended the 90 primary schools of the Marshall Islands, while 1,743 pupils were enrolled at eight secondary schools. The College of the Marshall Islands (which became independent from the College of Micronesia in 1993) is based on Majuro. In early 1995 the islands received a grant of US $6m. from Japan to fund projects to improve secondary education, as well as a loan of US $2m from the People's Republic of China to finance the construction of a new secondary school on Majuro. Government expenditure on education in 1995 was estimated at US $12.3m., equivalent to 14.7% of total budgetary spending.

### Weights and Measures

With certain exceptions, the imperial system is in force. One US cwt equals 100 lb; one long ton equals 2,240 lb; one short ton equals 2,000 lb. A policy of gradual voluntary conversion to the metric system is being undertaken.

# Statistical Survey

## AREA AND POPULATION

**Area:** 180 sq km (70 sq miles) (land only); two island groups, the Ratak and Ralik Chains.

**Population:** 43,380 at census of 13 November 1988; 52,000 (official estimate) at mid-1993.

**Density** (mid-1993): 289 per sq km.

**Births and Deaths** (1989): Live births 1,429 (birth rate 32.2 per 1,000); Deaths 151 (death rate 3.4 per 1,000).

**Expectation of Life** (estimates, years at birth, 1991): 66.1 (males 64.1; females 68.0). Source: UN, *Statistical Yearbook for Asia and the Pacific*.

## AGRICULTURE, ETC.

**Principal Crops*** (FAO estimates, '000 metric tons, 1993): Coconuts 140; Copra 18; Cassava 12; Sweet potatoes 3; Vegetables and melons 3; Bananas 2; Other fruit 1. Source: FAO, *Production Yearbook*.

**Livestock*** (FAO estimates, '000 head, year ending September 1993): Pigs 32; Cattle 14; Goats 4. Source: FAO, *Production Yearbook*.

**Livestock Products*** (FAO estimates, metric tons, 1993): Pigmeat 1,000; Hen eggs 170; Cattle and buffalo hides 45. Source: FAO, *Production Yearbook*.

* Includes the Federated States of Micronesia and Palau.

**Fishing** (metric tons, live weight): Total catch 200 (FAO estimate) in 1990; 200 in 1991; 204 in 1992. Source: FAO, *Yearbook of Fishery Statistics*.

## FINANCE

(including the Federated States of Micronesia and Palau, unless otherwise indicated)

**Currency and Exchange Rates:** United States currency is used: 100 cents = 1 United States dollar (US $). *Sterling Equivalents* (31 December 1994): £1 sterling = US $1.5645; US $100 = £63.92.

**Budget** (1982, US $'000): *Revenue:* Reimbursements and other operating income 26,523; Grant from US Congress 98,614; Total funds available 125,137. *Expenditure:* Resources and development 7,891; General administration 9,048; Construction 8,544; Health 13,809; Education 28,296; Public Works 23,932; Other 27,349; Total 118,869. **1990** (estimates, US $ million): *Expenditure:* Health, education and social services 3.9; Recurrent expenditure 42.1; Development 9.1; Debt repayments 13.9; Total (incl. others) 69.4. **1992*** (estimates, US $ million): *Revenue:* Recurrent 20.1 (Tax 14.1). *Expenditure:* Recurrent 47.6; Capital 5.8.

* Figures relate exclusively to the Marshall Islands.

## EXTERNAL TRADE

**Principal Commodities:** (US $'000, 1991): *Imports:* Food and live animals 13,717; Beverages and tobacco 5,575; Crude materials, inedible, except fuels 3,677; Mineral fuels, lubricants and related materials 6,288; Animal and vegetable oils and fats 109; Chemicals 1,508; Basic manufactures 16,395; Machinery and transport equipment 9,172; Total 56,441. *Exports:* Coconut oil 1,396; Copra 18; Handicrafts 4; Trochus 176; Total (incl. others) 2,890.

Source: UN, *Statistical Yearbook for Asia and the Pacific*.

## TRANSPORT

**Road Traffic*** (vehicles in use, 1977): Trucks 273; Pickups 2,038; Sedans 4,002; Jeeps 335; Motor cycles, etc. 468; Other motor vehicles 107.

**Merchant Shipping Fleet** (at 30 June 1993): Vessels 57; Displacement ('000 gross registered tons) 2,198.0. Source: Lloyd's Register of Shipping.

**International Shipping*** (estimated freight traffic, '000 metric tons, 1990): Goods loaded 29; Goods unloaded 123. Source: UN, *Monthly Bulletin of Statistics*.

* Includes the Northern Mariana Islands, the Federated States of Micronesia and Palau.

**Civil Aviation** (1990): Passengers carried 66,000; Passenger-km 52 million. Freight ton-km 3,000. Source: UN, *Statistical Yearbook*.

## EDUCATION

**Primary** (1987): 90 schools; 444 teachers; 9,962 pupils.
**Secondary** (1987): 8 schools; 1,743 pupils.
Source: UN, *Statistical Yearbook for Asia and the Pacific*.

# Directory

## The Constitution

On 1 May 1979 the locally-drafted Constitution of the Republic of the Marshall Islands became effective. The Constitution provides for a parliamentary form of government, with legislative authority vested in the 33-member Nitijela. Members of the Nitijela are elected by a popular vote, from 25 districts, for a four-year term. There is an advisory council of 12 high chiefs, or Iroij. The Nitijela elects the President of the Marshall Islands (who also has a four-year mandate) from among its own members. The President then selects members of the Cabinet from among the members of the Nitijela. On 25 June 1983 the final draft of the Compact of Free Association was signed by the Governments of the Marshall Islands and the USA and the Compact was effectively ratified by the US Congress on 14 January 1986. By the terms of the Compact, free association recognizes the Republic of the Marshall Islands as an internally sovereign, self-governing state, whose policy concerning foreign affairs must be consistent with guidelines laid down in the Compact. Full responsibility for defence lies with the USA, which undertakes to provide regular economic assistance. The economic and defence provisions of the Compact are renewable after 15 years, but the status of free association continues indefinitely.

## The Government

### HEAD OF STATE

**President:** AMATA KABUA (took office 1980; re-elected 1984, 1988 and 1992).

### THE CABINET
(May 1995)

**Minister of Education:** EVELYN KONOU.
**Minister of Finance:** RUBEN ZACKHRAS.
**Minister of Foreign Affairs:** PHILLIP MULLER.
**Minister of Health and Environment:** TOM KIJINER.
**Minister of Internal Affairs:** BRENSON WASE.
**Minister of Justice:** LUCKNER ABNER.
**Minister of Public Works:** HIROSHI YAMAMURA.
**Minister of Resources and Development:** LOMES MCKAY.
**Minister of Social Services:** CHRISTOPHER LOEAK.
**Minister of Transportation and Communications:** KUNIO LEMARI.
**Attorney-General:** BOYD SPREHN.
**Auditor-General:** BRIAN RIORADAN.

### GOVERNMENT OFFICES

All ministries are based on Majuro. Work on a new Capitol building began in 1990.

**Office of the President:** Govt of the Republic of the Marshall Islands, POB 2, Majuro, MH 96960; tel. (625) 3445; fax (625) 4020.

## Legislature

### THE NITIJELA

The Nitijela consists of 33 elected members, known as Senators. The most recent elections were held in November 1991. The Nitijela is advised by the House of Iroij, comprised of 12 traditional leaders.

**Speaker:** Senator KESSAI NOTE.

## Political Organization

**Ralik Ratak Democratic Party:** f. 1991; opposes President Kabua; Founder TONY DEBRUM.

## Diplomatic Representation

### EMBASSIES IN THE MARSHALL ISLANDS

**China, People's Republic:** Majuro, MH 96960; Ambassador: ZHOU JINMING.
**Japan:** Majuro, MH 96960; Ambassador: TAKAKAZU KURIYAMA.
**USA:** POB 680, Majuro, MH 96960; tel. (625) 4011; fax (625) 4012; Ambassador: DAVID C. FIELDS.

## Judicial System

The judicial system consists of the Supreme Court and the High Court, which preside over District and Community Courts, and the Traditional Rights Court.

**Supreme Court of the Republic of the Marshall Islands:** Majuro, MH 96960; tel. (625) 3201; fax (625) 3323; Chief Justice CLINTON R. ASHFORD.
**High Court of the Republic of the Marshall Islands:** Majuro, MH 96960; tel. (625) 3201; Chief Justice NEIL RUTLEDGE.
**Traditional Rights Court of the Marshall Islands:** Majuro, MH 96960; customary law only; Chief Judge (vacant).

## Religion

The population is predominantly Christian, mainly Roman Catholic. The Assembly of God, Jehovah's Witnesses, Seventh-day Adventists, the Church of Jesus Christ of Latter-day Saints (Mormons), the United Church of Christ, Baptists and the Bahá'í Faith are also represented.

### CHRISTIANITY

#### The Roman Catholic Church

The Apostolic Prefecture of the Marshall Islands included 4,000 adherents at 31 December 1993.

**Prefect Apostolic of the Marshall Islands:** Rev. Fr JAMES C. GOULD, POB 8, Majuro, MH 96960; tel. (625) 3307; fax (625) 5520.

#### Protestant Churches

The Marshall Islands come under the auspices of the United Church Board for World Ministries (475 Riverside Drive, New York, NY 10115, USA); Sec. for Latin America, Caribbean and Oceania Dr PATRICIA RUMER.

### BAHÁ'Í FAITH

**National Spiritual Assembly:** POB 1017, Majuro, MH 96960; mems resident in 48 localities.

## The Press

**Kwajalein Hourglass:** POB 23, Kwajalein, MH 96555; tel. (238) 7994; f. 1954; 2 a week; Editor PAT CATALOO; circ. 2,000.
**Marshall Islands Gazette:** Office of the Chief Secretary, Marshall Islands Government, Majuro, MH 96960; tel. (625) 3143; f. 1982; Editor GIFF JOHNSON.
**Marshall Islands Journal:** POB 14, Majuro, MH 96960; tel. (625) 3143; fax (625) 3136; f. 1970; weekly; Editor JOE MURPHY; circ. 3,700.

## Radio

**Radio Marshalls V7AB:** POB 3250, Majuro, MH 96960; tel. (625) 3411; fax (625) 3412; govt-owned; commercial; programmes in English and Marshallese; Station Man. PETER BOONE.
**Marshall Broadcasting Co:** POB 19, Majuro, MH 96960; tel. (625) 3383; privately-owned.

The US Dept of Defense operates a radio station (24 hours a day) and a television station for the military base on Kwajalein atoll.

## Finance

(cap. = capital; res = reserves; dep. = deposits; amounts in US dollars)

### BANKING

**Bank of Guam** (USA): POB C, Majuro, MH 96960; Man. JOE C. AYUYU; brs in Ebeye, Kwajalein and Majuro.
**Bank of Hawaii** (USA): Majuro, MH 96960.
**Bank of the Marshall Islands:** POB J, Majuro, MH 96960; tel. (625) 3662; telex 0938; fax (625) 3661; f. 1982; 40% govt-owned; dep. 5.4m., total assets 7.1m. (Dec. 1992); Chair. GRANT LABAUN; Man. PATRICK CHEN.
**Marshall Islands Development Bank:** Majuro, MH 96960.

# Trade and Industry

## CHAMBER OF COMMERCE

**Majuro Chamber of Commerce:** Majuro, MH 96960; Pres. JERRY KRAMER.

## DEVELOPMENT ORGANIZATIONS AND STATE AUTHORITIES

**Marshall Islands Environmental Protection Agency:** Majuro, MH 96960; Dir JIBA KABUA.

**Marshall Islands Development Authority:** Majuro, MH 96960; Gen. Man. JUSTIN DEBRUM.

**Marshall Islands Marine Resources Authority:** Majuro, MH 96960; Dir DANNY WASE.

**Kwajalein Atoll Development Authority (KADA):** POB 5159, Ebeye Island, Kwajalein, MH 96970; Dir JEBAN RIKLON.

**Tobolar Copra Processing Authority:** POB G, Majuro, MH 96960; tel. (625) 3494; fax (625) 7206.

## CO-OPERATIVES

These include the Ebeye Co-op, Farmers' Market Co-operative, Kwajalein Employees' Credit Union, Marshall Is Credit Union, Marshall Is Fishermen's Co-operative, Marshall Is Handicraft Co-operative.

# Transport

## ROADS

Macadam and concrete roads are found in the more important islands. Other islands have stone and coral-surfaced roads and tracks.

## SHIPPING

Most shipping is government-organized. However, Nauru Pacific Line operates a regular container service from Melbourne (Australia) to Majuro and other services from San Francisco (USA) and Honolulu (Hawaii) to Majuro. Other commercial carriers include Pacific Micronesian Lines, Philippine Micronesia and Orient Navigation (PM & O), Tiger Line, Nippon Yusen Kaisha, and Matson Line. In 1989 the Republic of the Marshall Islands became a shareholder in the regional shipping company, Pacific Forum Line (see under South Pacific Forum Secretariat), which operates a service between Fiji and Australia, via the Marshall Islands. In August 1993 a Swedish company announced that it was to operate a monthly cargo service between Australia and the USA, via the Marshall Islands.

The Marshall Islands operates an 'offshore' shipping register. At 30 June 1993 the merchant fleet comprised 57 vessels, with a combined displacement of 2.2m. grt.

**Vessel Registry:**

**Marshall Islands Maritime and Corporate Administrators Inc:** c/o International Registries Inc, Reston International Center, 11800 Sunrise Valley Drive, 6th Floor, Reston, VA 22091, USA; tel. (703) 620-4880; fax (703) 476-8522; Senior Deputy Commissioner: GUY E. C. MAITLAND; Local Office: **The Trust Company of the Marshall Islands Inc:** POB 1405, Majuro, MH 96960; tel. (625) 3018; fax (625) 3017; Deputy Registrar of Corporations: EDWARD BARON BIGLER.

## CIVIL AVIATION

**Air Marshall Islands (AMI):** POB 1319, Majuro, MH 96960; tel. (625) 3731; fax (625) 3730; f. 1980; internal services for the Marshall Islands and international flights to Honolulu (USA), Nadi (Fiji), Tarawa (Kiribati) and Funafuti (Tuvalu); also charter, air ambulance and maritime surveillance operations; Chair. President of the Marshall Islands; Man. Dir and CEO STEPHEN FULK.

# Tourism

Tourism is hindered by a lack of transport facilities. There were an estimated 7,000 visitors in 1990, of whom some 900 were tourists.

**Tourist Authority:** POB 1727, Majuro, MH 96960; tel. (625) 3206; fax (625) 3218; Tourism Officer WALLACE PETER.

# MAURITANIA

## Introductory Survey

### Location, Climate, Language, Religion, Flag, Capital

The Islamic Republic of Mauritania lies in north-west Africa, with the Atlantic Ocean to the west, Algeria and the disputed territory of Western Sahara (occupied by Morocco) to the north, Mali to the east and south, and Senegal to the south. The climate is hot and dry, particularly in the north, which is mainly desert. Average annual rainfall in the early 1990s was reported to be only 100 mm (3.9 ins). The 1991 Constitution designates Arabic (which is spoken by the Moorish majority) as the official language, and Arabic, Poular, Wolof and Solinke as the national languages. The black population in the south is mainly French-speaking, and French is widely used in commercial and business circles. Islam is the state religion, and the inhabitants are almost all Muslims. The national flag (proportions 3 by 2) comprises a green field, bearing, on the vertical median, a yellow five-pointed star between the upward-pointing horns of a yellow crescent moon. The capital is Nouakchott, although Nouadhibou is the main centre for economic activity.

### Recent History

Mauritania, formerly part of French West Africa, achieved full independence on 28 November 1960 (having become a self-governing member of the French Community two years earlier). Moktar Ould Daddah, leader of the Parti du regroupement mauritanien (PRM) and Prime Minister since June 1959, became Head of State at independence, and was elected President in August 1961. After independence all parties merged with the PRM to form the Parti du peuple mauritanien (PPM), with Ould Daddah as Secretary-General, and Mauritania became a one-party state in 1964. The country moved away from the French sphere of influence and towards closer relations with Arab nations.

Under a tripartite agreement of November 1975, Spain ceded Spanish (now Western) Sahara to Mauritania and Morocco, to be apportioned between them. The agreement took effect in February 1976, when Mauritania occupied the southern portion of the territory (which it named Tiris el Gharbia). Guerrilla fighting ensued, with Moroccan and Mauritanian troops in action against the forces of the Frente Popular para la Liberación de Sakiet el Hamra y Río de Oro (the Polisario Front), a national liberation movement advocating independence for Western Sahara. Attacks within Mauritania by Polisario forces, particularly on the railway line that is essential for the transport of iron ore from Zouérate (in the west of the interior) to the coast, were highly damaging to the economy. Diplomatic links with Algeria, which was supporting Polisario bases within its borders, were severed in March 1976. At the same time relations with Morocco, which had been poor until that country renounced territorial claims that included Mauritania, improved, and in June 1977 a joint defence pact was formed.

By 1977 Mauritania was spending two-thirds of its budget on defending territory that promised no economic benefits. The disruption of iron-ore exports, combined with the effects of drought, had brought the country almost to bankruptcy. In July 1978 Ould Daddah was deposed in a bloodless coup, led by the armed forces Chief of Staff, Lt-Col (later Col) Moustapha Ould Mohamed Salek, who took power as Chairman of what was named the Military Committee for National Recovery (CMRN). The Constitution was suspended, and the Government, National Assembly and PPM were dissolved: a 'constitutional charter' vested executive authority in the Chairman of the CMRN. Polisario immediately declared a cease-fire with Mauritania, but the continuing presence of several thousand Moroccan troops in Mauritania impeded progress towards a full settlement. The deadlock led to internal political instability, and in April 1979 the CMRN was replaced by the Military Committee for National Salvation (CMSN). Salek continued to head the CMSN, but relinquished the post of Prime Minister to another member of his administration, Lt-Col Ahmed Ould Bouceif. The CMSN adopted a new charter, assuming legislative power for itself and separating the roles of Head of State and Head of Government. Bouceif was killed in an air crash in May, and the CMSN appointed Lt-Col Mohamed Khouna Ould Haidalla, the Minister of Defence since April, in his place. Salek resigned in June, and was replaced as titular Head of State by Lt-Col Mohamed Mahmoud Ould Ahmed Louly, hitherto Minister of Public Services. In July Polisario announced a resumption of hostilities against Mauritania. Later that month the Organization of African Unity (OAU, see p. 200) recommended that a referendum be held to determine the future of the disputed region. These events provided the impetus for Mauritania's final withdrawal from the war: Haidalla renounced Mauritania's territorial claims in Western Sahara, and a peace treaty was signed with Polisario in August. Morocco announced its annexation of the territory (in addition to the northern part of Western Sahara, which it already held). At the same time diplomatic relations between Mauritania and Algeria were re-established.

Haidalla consolidated his position in January 1980, when he succeeded Louly as Head of State, while retaining the post of Prime Minister; he retained the posts of Prime Minister and Minister of Defence until December, when Sid Ahmed Ould Bneijara was appointed Prime Minister in a largely civilian Council of Ministers. A draft Constitution, envisaging a multiparty system, was prepared, with a view to approval in a national referendum. However, an attempted coup in March 1981 prompted Haidalla to end civilian participation in the Government. The defence portfolio was assumed in April by the new Prime Minister, Lt-Col (later Col) Maawiya Ould Sid'Ahmed Taya (a prominent member of the CMSN, and the Chief of Staff of the Army since April 1980), and the draft Constitution was abandoned. Another coup plot was discovered in February 1982, resulting in the arrest and subsequent imprisonment of its leaders, ex-President Salek and former Prime Minister Bneijara.

In March 1984 widespread student unrest was denounced by the Government as a Libyan-backed 'destabilization plot'. All student union activities were suspended, and there were many arrests. Haidalla once again assumed the positions of Prime Minister and Minister of Defence, reassigning Col Taya to his former position as army Chief of Staff. On 12 December, while Haidalla was attending a Franco-African 'summit' meeting in Burundi, Taya assumed the presidency in a bloodless coup. A new Government was formed, in which Taya, the President of the Council of Ministers, also took the defence portfolio. An amnesty was proclaimed for all political prisoners and exiles, including Ould Daddah (then in exile in Tunisia), Salek and Bneijara. Haidalla was detained upon his return to Mauritania.

Diplomatic relations with Morocco were severed in 1981, with Mauritania accusing its neighbour of involvement in the attempted coup in March, and Morocco claiming in October that the Polisario Front was launching attacks on Moroccan territory from bases in Mauritania. Both countries denied the accusations. In 1983 Mauritania sought to improve relations between the Maghreb countries (Algeria, Morocco, Mauritania, Tunisia and Libya) and was a signatory of the Maghreb Fraternity and Co-operation Treaty, drawn up by Algeria and Tunisia. However, relations with Morocco deteriorated again when, in February 1984, Mauritania announced its recognition of the Sahrawi Arab Democratic Republic, the Western Saharan state that had been proclaimed by Polisario in 1976. Taya restored diplomatic relations with Morocco in April 1985.

Although the Taya administration instituted important economic and (to a lesser extent) political changes, an escalation of ethnic tensions presented a major threat to domestic harmony. The publication, in April 1986, of a document entitled the 'Oppressed Black African Manifesto' resulted in the arrest, in September, of about 40 prominent black dissidents. The subsequent conviction of 20 of those detained, on charges of 'undermining national unity', led to civil disturbances (including arson attacks in the capital, Nouakchott, and in the northern port city of Nouadhibou), and to increased activity by organizations opposed to what they claimed to be the oppression of black Mauritanians by the light-skinned Moorish community. In October 1987 51 members of the black Toucouleur ethnic group were arrested, following the discovery of a coup plot. Following a trial (held in camera) in December, three black armed forces officers were sentenced to death and executed, and 41 prison sentences were imposed. Allegations that some detainees had been tortured were subsequently made by a Senegalese-based opposition movement, the Forces de libération africaine de Mauritanie (FLAM—a group which conducted a sporadic campaign of attacks on official targets during the late 1980s and early 1990s). In January 1988 it was reported that more than 500 black NCOs had been expelled from the army, gendarmerie and national guard, as a result of disturbances following the executions. Reports in mid-1988 stated that some 600 people, including members of the armed forces, had been arrested, as part of a short-lived purge of light-skinned supporters of the pro-Iraqi Baathist movement (which had hitherto been influential in Mauritanian public life and was also known to be sympathetic to Moroccan interests). In September 13 opponents of the Taya Government, all of whom were alleged to have links with that movement, were given prison sentences of between two and five years, after having been convicted of undermining the internal and external security of the state, and of recruiting military personnel on behalf of an unnamed country. In December Haidalla and five of his associates were released from detention. In December 1989 it was announced that the sentences of all those who had been convicted of undermining the internal or external security of the state, or of participating in illegal organizations, were to be reduced by one year.

The persistence of ethnic divisions within Mauritania was exemplified by the conduct of the country's three-year border dispute with Senegal. The deaths, in April 1989, of two Senegalese farmers, following a disagreement with Mauritanian livestock-breeders regarding grazing rights in the border-region between the two countries, provoked a crisis that reflected long-standing mutual ethnic and economic rivalries. Mauritanian nationals resident in Senegal were attacked, and their businesses looted (the retail trade in Senegal had hitherto been dominated by some 300,000 mainly light-skinned Mauritanian expatriates). Senegalese nationals in Mauritania (an estimated 30,000, many of whom were employed in the manufacturing sector), together with black Mauritanians, suffered similar aggression. Estimates of the number of casualties and deaths varied, but it was believed that by early May several hundred people, mostly Senegalese, had been killed. Operations to repatriate nationals of both countries were conducted, with international assistance. It was believed that the Mauritanian authorities had taken advantage of the crisis to expel members of its black indigenous population to Senegal, and the human rights organization, Amnesty International, expressed concern that violations of black Mauritanians' rights were taking place. In addition, many black Mauritanians fled, or were expelled, to Mali.

Mediation attempts were initiated shortly after the conflict erupted, notably by the OAU, but, although both parties expressed their commitment to the principle of a negotiated settlement, Senegal's insistence on the inviolability of the border, defined at the time of French colonial rule, and Mauritania's demand that its nationals who had lost property in Senegal be compensated by the Diouf Government remained the major impediments to a solution. The two countries suspended diplomatic relations in August. Further outbreaks of violence occurred in late 1989, when black Mauritanians sheltering in Senegal crossed into their former homeland to recover their property. The Taya Government accused the Senegalese armed forces of collaborating in these incursions. In early 1990 attempts at mediation by representatives of the OAU were thwarted by military skirmishes in the border region, as a result of which several deaths were reported.

Hopes of a *rapprochement* were undermined in late 1990, when the Mauritanian authorities accused the Government of Senegal of complicity in an alleged attempt to overthrow the Taya Government. In December several sources, including Amnesty International, drew attention to the arrests of large numbers of black Mauritanians. Government officials confirmed that many arrests (of military personnel and civilians) had been made, in connection with a foiled coup plot, but refuted suggestions that detainees had been tortured. The Senegalese Government denied any involvement in the alleged plot, and relations between the two countries subsequently deteriorated. In January and February 1991 incidents were reported in which Mauritanian naval vessels had opened fire on Senegalese fishing boats, apparently in Senegal's territorial waters; in March several deaths were reported to have resulted from a military engagement, on Senegalese territory, between the two countries' armed forces, following an incursion by Senegalese troops into Mauritania.

In March 1991 60 of those who had been detained following the alleged discovery of the 1990 coup plot were released. Further clemency measures were announced shortly thereafter, as a result of which all those who had been convicted of undermining state security were officially said to have been released from custody. Although the Taya Government claimed that almost all the country's political prisoners had thus been freed, other sources asserted that several hundred of those who had been arrested in late 1990 remained, uncharged, in detention. Moreover, Amnesty International cited reports that some 200 recent detainees had been tortured and summarily executed.

In April 1991 President Taya announced that a new constitution, which would allow for the installation of a multi-party political system, would be drafted and, upon completion, be submitted for approval in a national referendum. This unexpected announcement coincided with an upsurge of overt political opposition. In May and June women who were demanding to know the fate of relatives who had 'disappeared' following the alleged disclosure of the 1990 plot staged a demonstration in Nouakchott, and in June 1991 the arrest of demonstrators who were protesting against increases in the price of bread provoked rioting in Nouadhibou. Tracts and open letters circulated, condemning the Taya Government and demanding that a national conference be convened to consider the country's political evolution.

The draft Constitution was submitted to a national referendum on 12 July 1991. Official reports stated that 97.9% of those who voted (85.3% of the registered electorate) approved the new document, which accorded extensive powers to the President of the Republic. However, opposition groups contested this result, stating that electoral participation had been as low as 8% of registered voters. It was envisaged that, pending the installation of the organs of state provided for in the new document (see Government, below), the CMSN, under Taya's leadership, would remain in power on an interim basis. Under the Constitution, Arabic was designated as the sole official language. Shortly after the adoption of the Constitution legislation to permit the registration of political parties was promulgated: among the first organizations to be accorded official status was the Democratic and Social Republican Party (DSRP), which was closely linked with Taya and was strongly criticized by opposition movements for its privileged access to the state apparatus.

Amnesty measures were announced in late July 1991 for all those (including exiles) who had been accused or convicted of undermining state security. In mid-August, none the less, a further women's demonstration was violently dispersed by the security forces. Later in the same month Amnesty International published a list of 339 detainees who were reported to have died in detention since late 1990, alleging that most deaths had been as a result of torture.

The presidential election, which took place on 17 January 1992, was contested by four candidates, including Taya, Ahmed Ould Daddah (the half-brother of Mauritania's first President) and Salek (who had deposed President Ould Daddah in 1978). Taya was elected President by 62.7% of those who voted (the rate of participation was 51.7% of the registered electorate); his nearest rival was Ahmed Ould Daddah, who was supported by 32.8% of voters. The defeated candidates alleged electoral fraud, and appealed unsuccessfully to the Supreme Court to declare the election invalid. (Independent observers, while admitting that some 'administrative' errors had undoubtedly occurred, would not condemn the poll as fraudulent.) Unrest in the aftermath of the election resulted in at least two deaths and about 160 arrests.

By the time of the legislative elections, which took place on 6 and 13 March 1992, six opposition parties had withdrawn their candidates, in protest against electoral procedures which, they claimed, were unduly favourable to the DSRP. Taya's party thus took 67 of the 79 seats in the National Assembly, and all but two of the remaining seats were won by independent candidates. The rate of participation by voters was reported to have been low. All ethnic groups were said by the authorities to be represented in the legislature. Other than the DSRP, only one (unsuccessful) party presented candidates at elections to the Senate, which took place on 3 and 10 April. The new, 56-member upper house (which was elected by municipal leaders) thus included 36 DSRP members; 17 independent candidates were elected, the remaining seats being reserved for representatives of Mauritanians resident abroad.

Taya was inaugurated as President of the Republic on 18 April 1992. He immediately named a civilian Prime Minister, Sidi Mohamed Ould Boubacar (the Minister of Finance since October 1990). Included in the new Government were three black ministers and one opposition representative, and only one member of the military. There were further government changes in January, June and November 1993, and in May 1994.

The devaluation of the national currency, the ouguiya, in October 1992 (as part of a major programme of economic adjustment—see Economic Affairs) precipitated violent protests in Nouakchott, as traders immediately imposed sharp increases in the prices of basic household commodities. Security forces intervened to restore order, and a night-time curfew was enforced in the Nouakchott region for a period of two weeks. The Government gave assurances that measures would be taken to offset the adverse social consequences of the currency's depreciation, and, to this end, compensatory salary increases were introduced in all sectors in January 1993. None the less, opposition groups continued to denounce the extent and effects of the devaluation.

In May 1993 the National Assembly approved legislation pardoning all those (specifically including members of the army and security forces) who had been convicted of offences perpetrated in connection with 'armed operations and acts of violence and terrorism' during the three years preceding Taya's inauguration as elected President. Security forces subsequently intervened to disperse a demonstration in Nouakchott that had been organized by opponents of the measure, which, they claimed, exonerated members of the armed forces for crimes committed during a period of severe repression of the black community.

Influence over local government, following Mauritania's first multi-party municipal elections (which took place in January and February 1994), was won overwhelmingly by the DSRP, which took control of 172 of the country's 208 administrative districts. Opposition groups, including Ahmed Ould Daddah's Union of Democratic Forces—New Era (UDF—NE, which took control of 17 districts, the remainder being won by independent candidates), protested that the elections had been conducted fraudulently, and had been unduly favourable to the DSRP.

Shortly before the first round of municipal voting the President of the unauthorized Mauritanian Human Rights Association (MHRA), Cheikh Sadibou Camara (who was also a member of a prominent opposition party, the Union for Democracy and Progress—UDP), was arrested and detained for several days, reportedly on charges of incitement to agitation. Camara was believed to have reported to a visiting delegation of international human rights organizations that children of Harratin (black Moors, who had formerly been slaves) had been abducted and sold into slavery: Mauritanian law regards any reference to a return to slavery as injurious to national unity. Overseas human rights monitors, who appealed for Camara's release, protested that the Government's assertion that he belonged to an unrecognized organization was invalid, since the MHRA had on several occasions applied for legal status, which had been withheld despite the fact that the right of free association is enshrined in the Constitution. Earlier in January 1994 Mauritania's first independent trade union confederation had been legalized, after a protracted dispute between its leaders and the Government. In June the authorities suspended publication of an independent journal, Le Calame, for a period of one month, apparently due to the inclusion of a report by the International Federation of Human Rights that was severely critical of the Government; similarly, publication of another journal, Eveil-Hebdo, was temporarily suspended by the Government in the following month. In September seven independent journals suspended publication, in protest at what they claimed were increased censorship measures. In February 1995 an international conference on the press, which was to have been held in Nouakchott, was prohibited by the Government.

Beginning in the final months of 1993 there was increasing evidence of the Government's desire to counter activities by fundamentalist Islamic organizations. During September 1994 more than 90 alleged members of illicit fundamentalist organizations were arrested: among those detained were a former government minister, 10 religious leaders and several foreign nationals. In the following month an amnesty was granted to the detainees after several of their number had made broadcast 'confessions' regarding their membership of extremist groups. Among those who confessed to belonging to an Islamic Movement in Mauritania (Hasim) were prominent members of the UDF—NE, whose leadership had condemned, and questioned the justification for, the arrests. The Taya Government, which accused foreign Islamic groups of promoting extremism in Mauritania, subsequently prohibited the delivery of political speeches in places of worship and outlawed certain Islamic organizations. In February 1995 Mauritania, Morocco, Tunisia, Egypt and Israel participated in discussions with NATO regarding the future co-ordination of efforts to counter the rise of Islamic fundamentalism and weapons proliferation in the Middle East and North Africa.

The Taya administration encountered growing domestic tension in early 1995. An increase of some 25% in the price of bread in January (following the imposition of value-added tax of 5% on food products and of 14% on industrial supplies) led to riots in Nouakchott in the second half of the month. Several prominent opposition figures, including Ahmed Ould Daddah and the UDP leader, Hamdi Ould Mouknass, were arrested and placed under house arrest, accused of organizing the disturbances; a night-time curfew was imposed in the capital, and public gatherings were temporarily banned. The curfew was revoked at the end of January, and the opposition leaders were released in early February. In that month the Government (which asserted that, since the new taxes had replaced other levies, prices should not have been significantly affected) adopted measures aimed at controlling the prices of essential consumer goods.

Government changes in late February 1995 included the appointment of new Ministers of Finance and of Defence. In March the Movement of Independent Democrats, which until 1994 had been a member of the UDF—NE, announced that it was to join the DSRP, claiming that the alliance would afford it greater influence in government and enable it to monitor respect for human rights.

Renewed diplomatic activity in the second half of 1991 and the early months of 1992 finally culminated in the resumption, in late April 1992, of diplomatic relations with Senegal. The process of reopening the border began in May. However, many of the issues that had hitherto impeded the normalization of relations (including the demarcation of the border and the problem of refugees) remained unresolved. Moreover, Mauritanian refugees in Senegal insisted that, as long as their national identity (*Mauritanité*) and land and property rights were not recognized by the Taya Government, they would not return to Mauritania. Tensions were reported in September 1993, after the Mauritanian authorities announced that Senegalese nationals would henceforth be required to fulfil certain criteria, including currency-exchange requirements, before being allowed to remain in (or to enter) Mauritania. Although concern was expressed that such conditions might be used to prevent black Mauritanians who had fled to Senegal in 1989 from returning to Mauritania, in late 1994 the Governments of Mauritania and Senegal agreed new measures to facilitate the free movement of goods and people between the two countries, and in early 1995 it was reported that diplomatic initiatives with a view to the repatriation of some 70,000 black Mauritanians from Senegal were in progress.

Relations with Mali were also dominated at this time by the issue of refugees, which was the subject of senior-level negotiations between the two countries in 1992–94. The problem of Mauritanian refugees in Mali (numbering about 15,000 in early 1995) was compounded by the presence in Mauritania of light-skinned Malian Tuaregs and Moors, as well as Bella (the descendants of the Tuaregs' black slaves, some of whom remained with the Tuaregs). In April 1994 an agreement was signed by Mauritania, Mali and representatives of the UN High Commissioner for Refugees regarding the voluntary repatriation of Malian refugees from Mauritania. Later in the month the Governments of Mauritania, Mali and Senegal agreed to strengthen military co-operation in order to improve joint border security. In July, however, Mauritania dispatched military reinforcements to the border with Mali, in an attempt to prevent a fresh influx of refugees following an escalation of unrest in the north of that country. None the less, by December it was reported that there were as many as 118,000 Malian refugees in Mauritania. In January 1995 the Governments of Mauritania, Mali and Senegal issued a communiqué in which they pledged to co-operate in resolving joint border issues and in combating extremism, arms-smuggling and drugs-trafficking.

In February 1989 Mauritania was a founder member, with Algeria, Libya, Morocco and Tunisia, of the Union of the Arab Maghreb (UMA, see p. 241). The member states subsequently formulated 15 regional co-operation conventions. In February 1993, however, it was announced that, given the differing economic orientations of each signatory, no convention had actually been implemented, and the UMA's activities were to be 'frozen'. Meetings of UMA leaders were, none the less, convened in 1994–95.

Mauritania's relations with France improved significantly in the early 1990s, following the introduction of multi-party institutions. Taya made an official visit to France in December 1993, during which he held discussions, described as 'fruitful' with President Mitterrand and the Prime Minister, Edouard Balladur. The Mauritanian authorities expressed the hope that bilateral co-operation would be improved as a result of such contacts. Conversely, in mid-1993 the USA suspended Mauritania's benefits under its generalized system of preferences—a programme whereby developing nations enjoy privileged access to US markets—on account of the Taya administration's poor record on workers' rights.

## Government

The Constitution that was approved in a national referendum on 12 July 1991 vests executive power in the President of the Republic (who is elected by universal adult suffrage for a period of six years). The bicameral legislature comprises a 79-member National Assembly (elected by universal suffrage for five years) and a 56-member Senate (elected by municipal leaders with a six-year mandate—part of its membership being elected every two years). All elections are conducted in the context of a multi-party political system. The President of the Republic is empowered to appoint a Prime Minister, who is designated Head of Government.

For the purpose of local administration, Mauritania is divided into 13 provinces, comprising a total of 208 districts.

## Defence

In June 1994 the total armed forces were estimated to number 15,650 men: army 15,000, navy about 500, air force 150. Full-time membership of paramilitary forces totalled about 5,000. Military service is by authorized conscription, and lasts for two years. Defence expenditure was estimated at 4,500m. UM in 1994.

## Economic Affairs

In 1993, according to estimates by the World Bank, Mauritania's gross national product (GNP), measured at average 1991–93 prices, was US $1,087m., equivalent to $510 per head. During 1985–93, it was estimated, GNP per head declined, in real terms, at an average annual rate of 0.1%. Over the same period the population increased by an annual average of 2.7%. Mauritania's gross domestic product (GDP) increased, in real terms, by an annual average of 1.9% in 1980–92. The IMF estimated GDP growth of 4.9% in 1993, and projected growth of 4.2% in 1994.

Agriculture (including forestry and fishing) contributed 27% of GDP in 1993. About 63.1% of the labour force were employed in the agricultural sector in that year. Owing to the unsuitability of much of the land for crop cultivation, output of staple foods (millet, sorghum, rice and pulses) is insufficient for the country's needs: a cereals deficit of 210,000 metric tons was forecast in the 1992/93 agricultural season. Livestock-rearing is the principal occupation of the rural population. Fishing, which in 1990 provided 46% of export earnings, supplies 5%–10% of annual GDP and up to 25% of budgetary revenue, and also makes a significant contribution to domestic food requirements. During 1980–92 agricultural GDP increased by an annual average of 1.5%.

Industry (including mining, manufacturing, construction and power) provided 27% of GDP in 1992. An estimated 8.9% of the labour force were employed in the industrial sector in 1980. During 1980–92 industrial GDP increased by an annual average of 3.9%.

Mining contributed 11.7% of GDP in 1991. The principal activity in this sector is the extraction of iron ore, exports of which contributed 41.4% of total export earnings in 1989. Gypsum and gold are also mined, and there are plans to revive the exploitation of copper reserves. Other exploitable mineral resources include phosphates, sulphur and peat. Prospecting for offshore reserves of petroleum began in 1989. The GDP of the mining sector declined by an annual average of 3.4% in 1982–91.

The manufacturing sector contributed 11% of GDP in 1992. Fish-processing (which contributes as much as 4% of annual GDP) is the most important activity. The processing of minerals (including imported petroleum) is also of some significance. Manufacturing GDP increased by an annual average of 6.2% in 1982–91.

Mauritania is expected eventually to utilize electricity generated at hydroelectric installations that have been constructed on the Senegal river, thus reducing the country's dependence on power generated at thermal stations. Imports of fuels comprised 6% of the value of merchandise imports in 1992.

In 1992 Mauritania recorded a visible trade deficit of US $54.5m. (the first deficit since 1984), and there was a deficit of $117.2m. on the current account of the balance of payments. The principal sources of imports are France (which supplied 25.8% of the total in 1991) and Spain. Important markets for exports include Japan and countries of the European Union (see p. 143). The principal exports are fish and fish products and iron ore. The principal imports are foodstuffs, machinery and transport equipment and building materials.

In its economic programme for 1994 the Taya administration aimed to reduce the overall deficit on consolidated government operations to 2.4% of GDP (compared with 11.0% in 1993). Mauritania's total external debt was US $2,203m. at the end of 1993, of which $1,960m. was long-term public debt. In that year the cost of debt-servicing was equivalent to 27.3% of the value of exports of goods and services. The annual rate of inflation averaged 7.6% in 1985–93; consumer prices increased by an average of 9.3% in 1993.

Mauritania is a member of the Economic Community of West African States (ECOWAS, see p. 138), of the Islamic Development Bank (see p. 180), of the Organisation pour la mise en valeur du fleuve Sénégal (OMVS, see p. 240) and of the Union of the Arab Maghreb (UMA, see p. 241).

Favourable results of the economic adjustment efforts undertaken by the Taya regime in the second half of the 1980s were subsequently undermined, principally by a decline in productivity in the agricultural and iron sectors, by the border dispute with Senegal, and by the withdrawal of funding by several important Islamic donor nations, in response to Mauritania's support for Iraq during the 1990–91 crisis in the region of the Persian (Arabian) Gulf. Moreover, a lack of diversification has led to an over-dependence on the iron and fishing sectors (the latter having itself suffered from under-investment and insufficient monitoring of stocks). A new programme of economic reform was undertaken in late 1992 (formulated in consultation with, and with funding from, the IMF and the World Bank), resulting in the restoration of real GDP growth in 1992–94. A devaluation (by 28%) of the ouguiya in October 1992, as part of the programme, was intended to improve Mauritania's international competitiveness, and the rate of inflation was stabilized in 1993. In its (IMF-supported) programme for 1995–97, the Government was to continue to implement policies of economic liberalization, including the restructuring of the banking sector and the civil service, a revision of the tax system, and the improved management of fish resources. The overall budget deficit was to be eliminated by 1996, by means of tight controls on expenditure, combined with increased revenue generated by measures including the accelerated privatization of state-owned enterprises. Important debt-relief concessions were granted by official creditors in 1993 and 1994, in recognition of the Government's adjustment efforts hitherto. None the less, Mauritania remains heavily dependent on external borrowing, and its vulnerability to drought and the high rate of population growth will continue to make demands on public finances during the 1990s.

# MAURITANIA

## Social Welfare
The National Social Insurance Fund administers family allowances, industrial accident benefits, insurance against occupational diseases, and old-age benefits. In 1987 Mauritania had 14 hospitals, and there were 197 physicians. There were 142 health centres in 1985, with a total of 1,325 beds. It was envisaged that investment in the health sector would amount to 1,042m. UM in 1993.

## Education
Formal education is not compulsory in Mauritania. Primary education begins at six years of age and lasts for six years. In 1992 total enrolment at primary schools was equivalent to only 62% of children in the relevant age-group (70% of boys; 55% of girls). It is aimed to increase primary enrolment to 90% of all children by 2000. Secondary education begins at 12 years of age and lasts for six years, comprising two cycles of three years each. The total enrolment at secondary schools in 1992 was equivalent to only 15% of children in the appropriate age-group (20% of boys; 10% of girls). At the time of the 1988 census adult illiteracy averaged 64.9% (males 53.9%; females 75.4%). A plan to make Arabic the compulsory first language in all schools (which had been postponed in 1979, following protests from the French-speaking south) was reintroduced in April 1988. In 1991/92 a total of 5,850 students were enrolled at Mauritania's four higher education institutions (including the University of Nouakchott, opened in 1983). Expenditure on education in 1988 was 3,188m. UM (22% of current expenditure in that year). Some 1,050m. UM was to be invested in education in 1993.

## Public Holidays
**1995:** 1 January (New Year's Day), 3 March* (Korité—Id al-Fitr, end of Ramadan), 1 May (Labour Day), 10 May* (Tabaski—Id al-Adha, Feast of the Sacrifice), 25 May (African Liberation Day, anniversary of the OAU's foundation), 31 May* (Islamic New Year), 9 August* (Mouloud, Birth of Muhammad), 28 November (National Day), 20 December* (Leilat al-Meiraj, Ascension of Muhammad).

**1996:** 1 January (New Year's Day), 21 February* (Korité—Id al-Fitr, end of Ramadan), 29 April* (Tabaski—Id al-Adha, Feast of the Sacrifice), 1 May (Labour Day), 19 May* (Islamic New Year), 25 May (African Liberation Day, anniversary of the OAU's foundation), 28 July* (Mouloud, Birth of Muhammad), 28 November (National Day), 8 December* (Leilat al-Meiraj, Ascension of Muhammad).

* These holidays are determined by the Islamic lunar calendar and may vary by one or two days from the dates given.

## Weights and Measures
The metric system is in force.

# Statistical Survey

Figures exclude Mauritania's section of Western Sahara, annexed in 1976 and relinquished in 1979.
Source (unless otherwise stated): Office National de la Statistique, BP 240, Nouakchott; tel. 514-77.

## Area and Population

### AREA, POPULATION AND DENSITY

| | |
|---|---|
| Area (sq km) | 1,030,700* |
| Population (census results)† | |
| 1 January 1977 | 1,338,830 |
| 5–20 April 1988 | |
| Males | 923,175 |
| Females | 941,061 |
| Total | 1,864,236 |
| Population (official estimates at mid-year) | |
| 1989 | 1,919,858 |
| 1991‡ | 2,036,000 |
| Density (per sq km) at mid-1991 | 2.0 |

* 397,950 sq miles.
† Figures include estimates for Mauritania's nomad population (444,020 in 1977; 224,095 in 1988).
‡ No estimate is available for mid-1990.

### REGIONS

| Region | Chief town | Area ('000 sq km) | Population (1977 census, '000) |
|---|---|---|---|
| Hodh el Charqui | Néma | 183 | 157 |
| Hodh el Gharbi | Aïoun el Atrous | 53 | 124 |
| Assaba | Kiffa | 37 | 129 |
| Gorgol | Kaédi | 14 | 149 |
| Brakna | Aleg | 33 | 151 |
| Trarza | Rosso | 68 | 216 |
| Adrar | Atar | 215 | 55 |
| Dakhlet-Nouadhibou | Nouadhibou | 22 | 23 |
| Tagant | Tidjikja | 95 | 75 |
| Guidimaka | Sélibaby | 10 | 83 |
| Tiris Zemmour | F'Derik | 253 | 23 |
| Inchiri | Akjoujt | 47 | 18 |
| Nouakchott | Nouakchott | 1 | 135 |
| **Total** | | **1,030** | **1,338** |

**PRINCIPAL TOWNS** (population at census of January 1977)

| | | | | |
|---|---|---|---|---|
| Nouakchott (capital) | 134,986* | Zouérate | | 17,947 |
| Nouadhibou | | Atar | | 16,394 |
| (Port-Etienne) | 22,365 | Rosso | | 15,888 |
| Kaédi | 20,356 | | | |

* Estimated at 350,000 in 1984.

**BIRTHS AND DEATHS** (UN estimates, annual averages)

| | 1975–80 | 1980–85 | 1985–90 |
|---|---|---|---|
| Birth rate (per 1,000) | 46.7 | 46.5 | 46.2 |
| Death rate (per 1,000) | 22.1 | 20.5 | 19.0 |

**Expectation of life** (UN estimates, years at birth, 1985–90): 46.0 (males 44.4; females 47.6).

Source: UN, *World Population Prospects: The 1992 Revision*.

**ECONOMICALLY ACTIVE POPULATION**
(ILO estimates, '000 persons at mid-1980)

| | Males | Females | Total |
|---|---|---|---|
| Agriculture, etc. | 268 | 90 | 358 |
| Industry | 43 | 3 | 46 |
| Services | 101 | 11 | 112 |
| **Total** | **413** | **103** | **516** |

Source: ILO, *Economically Active Population Estimates and Projections, 1950–2025*.

**Mid-1993** (estimates in '000): Agriculture, etc. 445; Total 705 (Source: FAO, *Production Yearbook*).

# MAURITANIA

## Agriculture

**PRINCIPAL CROPS** ('000 metric tons)

|  | 1991 | 1992 | 1993 |
|---|---|---|---|
| Millet and sorghum | 60 | 53* | 118 |
| Rice (paddy) | 42 | 51† | 40† |
| Maize | 2 | 2* | 5 |
| Potatoes† | 1 | 1 | n.a. |
| Sweet potatoes† | 3 | 2 | 2 |
| Yams† | 3 | 3 | 2 |
| Pulses | 28 | 21† | 15† |
| Dates† | 14 | 12 | 10 |
| Watermelons | 7 | 7† | 5† |
| Groundnuts (in shell)† | 2 | 2 | 2 |

* Unofficial figure.   † FAO estimate(s).

Source: FAO, *Production Yearbook*.

**LIVESTOCK** ('000 head, year ending September)

|  | 1991 | 1992* | 1993* |
|---|---|---|---|
| Cattle | 1,400 | 1,000 | 1,000 |
| Goats* | 3,500 | 3,200 | 3,100 |
| Sheep* | 5,300 | 5,000 | 4,800 |
| Asses* | 153 | 154 | 155 |
| Horses* | 18 | 18 | 18 |
| Camels | 990 | 900 | 950 |

Poultry (million)*: 4 in 1991; 4 in 1992; 4 in 1993.

* FAO estimates.

Source: FAO, *Production Yearbook*.

**LIVESTOCK PRODUCTS**
(FAO estimates unless otherwise indicated, '000 metric tons)

|  | 1991 | 1992 | 1993 |
|---|---|---|---|
| Beef and veal | 20* | 20 | 20 |
| Mutton and lamb | 13 | 12 | 12 |
| Goat meat | 8 | 8 | 8 |
| Poultry meat | 4 | 4 | 4 |
| Other meat | 21 | 22 | 23 |
| Cows' milk | 98 | 96 | 87 |
| Sheep's milk | 70 | 70 | 61 |
| Goats' milk | 81 | 80 | 76 |
| Poultry eggs | 4.4 | 4.3 | 4.4 |
| Cattle hides | 2.5 | 1.8 | 1.8 |
| Sheepskins | 1.8 | 1.6 | 1.6 |
| Goatskins | 1.0 | 0.9 | 0.9 |

* Unofficial figure.

Source: FAO, *Production Yearbook*.

## Forestry

**ROUNDWOOD REMOVALS**
(FAO estimates, '000 cubic metres, excluding bark)

|  | 1990 | 1991 | 1992 |
|---|---|---|---|
| Sawlogs, veneer logs and logs for sleepers* | 1 | 1 | 1 |
| Other industrial wood† | 4 | 4 | 4 |
| Fuel wood | 7 | 8 | 8 |
| **Total** | 12 | 13 | 13 |

* Assumed by the FAO to be unchanged since 1977.
† Assumed by the FAO to be unchanged since 1987.

Source: FAO, *Yearbook of Forest Products*.

## Fishing

(FAO estimates, '000 metric tons, live weight)

|  | 1990 | 1991 | 1992 |
|---|---|---|---|
| Freshwater fishes | 6.0 | 6.0 | 6.0 |
| Flatfishes | 2.0 | 2.0 | 1.9 |
| Groupers and seabasses | 6.6 | 6.5 | 6.2 |
| Meagre | 5.5 | 5.5 | 5.2 |
| Porgies, seabreams, etc. | 6.5 | 6.4 | 6.2 |
| Sardinellas | 2.8 | 2.7 | 2.6 |
| Other marine fishes (incl. unspecified) | 21.7 | 21.4 | 20.5 |
| **Total fish** | 51.1 | 50.5 | 48.5 |
| Marine crustaceans | 0.3 | 0.3 | 0.3 |
| Cuttlefishes and bobtail squids | 3.1 | 4.0 | 3.8 |
| Octopuses | 21.9 | 28.3 | 27.1 |
| Other cephalopods | 4.3 | 5.5 | 5.3 |
| **Total catch** | 80.5 | 88.7 | 85.0 |

Source: FAO, *Yearbook of Fishery Statistics*.

## Mining

('000 metric tons)

|  | 1989 | 1990 | 1991 |
|---|---|---|---|
| Iron ore: gross weight* | 11,300 | 11,600 | 10,300 |
| metal content† | 7,874 | 7,250 | n.a. |
| Gypsum (crude)† | 6 | 8 | 3 |

* Estimates.
† Data from the US Bureau of Mines.

Sources: UN, *Monthly Bulletin of Statistics* and *Industrial Statistics Yearbook*.

## Industry

**SELECTED PRODUCTS** ('000 metric tons, unless otherwise indicated)

|  | 1988 | 1989 | 1990 |
|---|---|---|---|
| Frozen and chilled fish* | 33.7 | 34.0 | 34.0 |
| Salted, dried and smoked fish* | 0.7 | 0.8 | 1.2 |
| Fish oils | 2 | 2 | 3 |
| Electric energy (million kWh) | 121 | 129 | 140 |

* Data from the FAO.

**1991:** Electric energy (million kWh) 143.

Sources: UN, *Industrial Statistics Yearbook*; UN Economic Commission for Africa, *African Statistical Yearbook*.

## Finance

**CURRENCY AND EXCHANGE RATES**

**Monetary Units**
  5 khoums = 1 ouguiya (UM).

**Sterling and Dollar Equivalents** (31 December 1994)
  £1 sterling = 200.83 ouguiyas;
  US $1 = 128.37 ouguiyas;
  1,000 ouguiyas = £4.979 = $7.790.

**Average Exchange Rate** (ouguiyas per US $)
  1992  87.027
  1993  120.806
  1994  123.575

# MAURITANIA

## BUDGET* (million ouguiyas)

| Revenue | 1978 | 1979 |
|---|---|---|
| Tax revenue | 3,875 | 4,937 |
| Taxes on income and profits | 1,049 | 1,551 |
| Social security contributions | 385 | 426 |
| Taxes on goods and services | 850 | 1,177 |
| Turnover taxes | 590 | 740 |
| Excises | 204 | 188 |
| Taxes on services | 35 | 213 |
| Import duties | 1,461 | 1,678 |
| Other current revenue | 1,810 | 768 |
| Property income | 141 | 176 |
| Fines and forfeits | 788 | 282 |
| Capital revenue | 862 | 679 |
| Sales of fishing rights | 816 | 662 |
| Other items (net)† | −118 | 97 |
| Grants from abroad | 3,341 | 3,182 |
| **Total** | **9,770** | **9,663** |

| Expenditure | 1978 | 1979 |
|---|---|---|
| General public services | 2,405 | 2,490 |
| Defence | 3,541 | 3,238 |
| Education | 1,036 | 1,147 |
| Health | 318 | 310 |
| Social security and welfare | 379 | 423 |
| Other community and social services | 153 | 172 |
| Economic services | 1,125 | 1,485 |
| Agriculture, forestry and fishing | 631 | 781 |
| Roads | 132 | 261 |
| Other transport | 263 | 281 |
| Other purposes | 728 | 627 |
| **Sub-total** | **9,685** | **9,892** |
| *Less:* Contributions to social security | −69 | −78 |
| Other items (net)† | −545 | 1,199 |
| Lending (minus repayments) | 1,570 | 114 |
| **Total** | **10,641** | **11,127** |

* Figures refer to the consolidated accounts of the general budget, the National Social Security Fund, the Mauritanian Red Crescent and the Ecole Nationale d'Administration.

† Including adjustment of accounts to a cash basis.

**1983** (general budget only, million ouguiyas): Revenue 8,963 (excluding grants 161); Expenditure 10,109 (excluding net lending 233).

Source: IMF, *Government Finance Statistics Yearbook*.

**1984** (estimates, million ouguiyas): Revenue 11,056; Expenditure 13,741.
**1986**‡ (revised estimates, million ouguiyas): Revenue 14,655; Expenditure 19,742 (recurrent 12,949; debt-servicing 4,516).
**1987** (estimates, million ouguiyas): Budget balanced at 19,842.
**1988** (estimates, million ouguiyas): Budget balanced at 20,504.
**1989** (estimates, million ouguiyas): Budget balanced at 22,000.
**1990** (estimates, million ouguiyas): Budget balanced at 22,119.
**1991** (estimates, million ouguiyas): Budget balanced at 23,200.
**1992** (estimates, million ouguiyas): Budget balanced at 24,723.
**1993** (estimates, million ouguiyas): Budget balanced at 32,200.
**1994** (estimates, million ouguiyas): Budget balanced at 38,169 (investment expenditure 19,781).

‡ Figures for 1985 are not available.

## INTERNATIONAL RESERVES (US $ million at 31 December)

| | 1991 | 1992 | 1993 |
|---|---|---|---|
| Gold* | 4.2 | 3.8 | 4.5 |
| IMF special drawing rights | 0.1 | 0.1 | 0.1 |
| Foreign exchange | 67.5 | 61.1 | 44.4 |
| **Total** | **71.8** | **65.0** | **49.1** |

* Valued at market-related prices.

Source: IMF, *International Financial Statistics*.

## MONEY SUPPLY (million ouguiyas at 31 December)

| | 1991 | 1992 | 1993 |
|---|---|---|---|
| Currency outside banks | 7,335 | 7,898 | 9,097 |
| Demand deposits at deposit money banks | 11,646 | 11,986 | 11,508 |
| **Total money** (incl. others) | **19,376** | **20,202** | **20,938** |

Source: IMF, *International Financial Statistics*.

## COST OF LIVING (Consumer Price Index for Mauritanian households in Nouakchott; base: 1990 = 100)

| | 1991 | 1992 | 1993 |
|---|---|---|---|
| **All items** | 105.6 | 116.3 | 127.2 |

Source: IMF, *International Financial Statistics*.

## NATIONAL ACCOUNTS
(million ouguiyas in current prices)

### Expenditure on the Gross Domestic Product

| | 1989 | 1990 | 1991 |
|---|---|---|---|
| Government final consumption expenditure | 15,000 | 16,748 | 17,619 |
| Private final consumption expenditure | 54,580 | 60,582 | 65,065 |
| Increase in stocks | 200 | 228 | 222 |
| Gross fixed capital formation | 14,670 | 16,363 | 17,091 |
| **Total domestic expenditure** | **84,450** | **93,921** | **99,997** |
| Exports of goods and services | 46,350 | 51,404 | 56,647 |
| *Less* Imports of goods and services | 48,300 | 53,625 | 59,194 |
| **GDP in purchasers' values** | **82,500** | **91,700** | **97,450** |
| **GDP at constant 1980 prices** | **38,609** | **40,154** | **41,681** |

### Gross Domestic Product by Economic Activity

| | 1989 | 1990 | 1991 |
|---|---|---|---|
| Agriculture, hunting, forestry and fishing | 19,500 | 21,100 | 23,421 |
| Mining and quarrying | 6,290 | 8,590 | 9,234 |
| Manufacturing | 3,600 | 4,700 | 5,264 |
| Electricity, gas and water | 650 | 720 | 809 |
| Construction | 3,770 | 4,020 | 4,193 |
| Trade, restaurants and hotels | 8,670 | 9,670 | 10,608 |
| Transport, storage and communications | 6,800 | 7,400 | 8,140 |
| Finance, insurance, real estate and business services | 3,480 | 4,080 | 4,525 |
| Government services | 8,620 | 9,520 | 10,129 |
| Other services | 2,070 | 2,260 | 2,446 |
| **GDP at factor cost** | **63,450** | **72,060** | **78,770** |
| Indirect taxes, *less* subsidies | 19,050 | 19,640 | 18,680 |
| **GDP in purchasers' values** | **82,500** | **91,700** | **97,450** |

Source: UN Economic Commission for Africa, *African Statistical Yearbook*.

MAURITANIA

**BALANCE OF PAYMENTS** (US $ million)

|  | 1990 | 1991 | 1992 |
|---|---|---|---|
| Merchandise exports f.o.b. | 443.9 | 435.8 | 406.8 |
| Merchandise imports f.o.b. | −382.9 | −399.1 | −461.3 |
| **Trade balance** | 61.0 | 36.7 | −54.5 |
| Exports of services | 26.8 | 31.2 | 20.2 |
| Imports of services | −136.8 | −151.0 | −179.1 |
| Other income received | 3.8 | 2.0 | 1.1 |
| Other income paid | −50.2 | −34.9 | −29.9 |
| Private unrequited transfers (net) | −15.6 | −17.2 | 24.5 |
| Official unrequited transfers (net) | 101.5 | 103.3 | 100.6 |
| **Current balance** | −9.6 | −29.9 | −117.2 |
| Direct investment (net) | 6.7 | 2.3 | 5.0 |
| Other capital (net) | −7.2 | 24.4 | 70.4 |
| Net errors and omissions | −62.3 | 19.5 | 58.8 |
| **Overall balance** | −72.5 | 16.3 | 17.0 |

Source: IMF, *International Financial Statistics*.

# External Trade

**PRINCIPAL COMMODITIES** (million ouguiyas)

| Imports c.i.f. | 1978 | 1979 | 1980 |
|---|---|---|---|
| Consumer goods | 3,999.4 | 5,438.4 | 6,111.0 |
| Tea, sugar and rice | 1,530.8 | 1,604.6 | 2,275.0 |
| Other foodstuffs | 1,196.9 | 2,308.8 | 2,132.0 |
| Other consumer goods | 1,271.7 | 1,524.6 | 1,704.0 |
| Transport equipment | 657.8 | 795.6 | 1,332.6 |
| Vehicles | 351.8 | 268.6 | 569.4 |
| Spare parts and tyres | 306.0 | 527.0 | 704.7 |
| Investment goods | 1,023.9 | 1,475.7 | 2,320.4 |
| Building materials | 609.8 | 670.7 | 778.9 |
| Capital goods | 414.1 | 805.0 | 1,541.5 |
| Fuels | 606.1 | 2,053.8 | 1,557.0 |
| Others | 2,077.6 | 2,456.5 | 1,797.0 |
| **Total** | 8,364.8 | 12,219.6 | 13,118.9 |

**Total imports** (million ouguiyas): 12,793 (Petroleum 1,773) in 1981; 14,213 (Petroleum 3,334) in 1982; 12,411 (Petroleum 2,278) in 1983; 13,201 (Petroleum 3,161) in 1984; 17,806 (Petroleum 2,487) in 1985; 16,429 (Petroleum 3,439) in 1986; 17,392 (Petroleum 2,639) in 1987; 18,029 (Petroleum 2,074) in 1988; 18,462 (Petroleum 2,630) in 1989.
**1990** (imports, million ouguiyas): Petroleum 4,493.
Source (for 1981–90): IMF, *International Financial Statistics*.
**Total imports** (million ouguiyas): 18,412 in 1991.

| Exports f.o.b. | 1987 | 1988 | 1989 |
|---|---|---|---|
| Iron ore | 9,815 | 10,599 | 15,035 |
| Fish and fish products | 20,088 | 16,056 | 21,297 |
| **Total** (incl. others) | 31,608 | 26,655 | 36,332 |

**1990** (exports, million ouguiyas): Iron ore 11,355; Fish and fish products 26,373.
Source: IMF, *International Financial Statistics*.
**1991** (total exports, million ouguiyas): 18,231.

**PRINCIPAL TRADING PARTNERS** (US $'000)

| Imports c.i.f. | 1982 | 1983 | 1984 |
|---|---|---|---|
| France | 45,632 | 52,929 | 39,435 |
| Senegal | 21,082 | 20,201 | 18,570 |
| Spain | 25,792 | 22,850 | 31,694 |
| Other Europe | 40,338 | 33,837 | 38,304 |
| Others | 140,177 | 96,687 | 85,368 |
| **Total** | 273,021 | 226,504 | 213,371 |

| Exports f.o.b. | 1982 | 1983 | 1984 |
|---|---|---|---|
| France | 41,751 | 29,205 | 35,221 |
| Japan | 14,846 | 34,859 | 37,239 |
| Senegal | 2,055 | 1,153 | 540 |
| Spain | 25,333 | 35,031 | 29,613 |
| Others | 149,283 | 204,453 | 189,712 |
| **Total** | 233,268 | 304,701 | 297,325 |

Source: UN, *International Trade Statistics Yearbook*.

# Transport

**RAILWAYS**

**1984:** Passengers carried 19,353; Passenger-km 7m.; Freight carried 9.1m. metric tons; Freight ton-km 6,142m.

**Freight ton-km** (million): 6,365 in 1985; 6,411 in 1986; 6,473 in 1987; 6,535 in 1988; 6,610 in 1989; 6,690 in 1990; 6,720 in 1991 (figures for 1988–91 are estimates) (Source: UN Economic Commission for Africa, *African Statistical Yearbook*).

**ROAD TRAFFIC** (estimates, '000 motor vehicles in use)

|  | 1989 | 1990 | 1991 |
|---|---|---|---|
| Passenger cars | 13 | 13 | 14 |
| Commercial vehicles | 6 | 6 | 7 |

Source: UN Economic Commission for Africa, *African Statistical Yearbook*.

**INTERNATIONAL SEA-BORNE SHIPPING**
(estimated freight traffic, '000 metric tons)

|  | 1988 | 1989 | 1990 |
|---|---|---|---|
| Goods loaded | 8,960 | 9,010 | 10,037 |
| Goods unloaded | 610 | 616 | 674 |

Source: UN, *Monthly Bulletin of Statistics*.

**CIVIL AVIATION** (traffic on scheduled services)*

|  | 1990 | 1991 | 1992 |
|---|---|---|---|
| Kilometres flown (million) | 4 | 3 | 3 |
| Passengers carried ('000) | 223 | 213 | 213 |
| Passenger-km (million) | 307 | 282 | 275 |
| Total ton-km (million) | 46 | 43 | 41 |

* Including an apportionment of the traffic of Air Afrique.
Source: UN, *Statistical Yearbook*.

# Tourism

**Tourist Arrivals** (estimates, '000): 12 in 1984; 13 in 1985; 13 in 1986.
**Receipts from Tourism** (US $ million): 7 in 1984; 5 in 1985; 8 in 1986; 14 in 1987; 14 in 1988; 15 in 1989; 14 in 1990; 13 in 1991 (figures for 1989–91 are estimates).
Source: UN Economic Commission for Africa, *African Statistical Yearbook*.

## Communications Media

|  | 1990 | 1991 | 1992 |
|---|---|---|---|
| Radio receivers ('000 in use) | 291 | 300 | 309 |
| Television receivers ('000 in use) | 47 | 49 | 50 |
| Telephones ('000 in use)* | 16 | 17 | n.a. |
| Daily newspapers |  |  |  |
| Number | 1 | n.a. | 1 |
| Average circulation ('000 copies) | 1* | n.a. | 1* |

* Estimate(s).

Sources: UNESCO, *Statistical Yearbook*; UN Economic Commission for Africa, *African Statistical Yearbook*.

## Education

(1992/93, unless otherwise indicated)

|  | Institutions | Teachers | Students Males | Students Females | Students Total |
|---|---|---|---|---|---|
| Pre-primary | 36 | 108 | n.a. | n.a. | 800 |
| Primary | 1,451 | 4,276 | 121,981 | 97,277 | 219,258 |
| Secondary |  |  |  |  |  |
| General | n.a. | 2,071 | 27,162 | 13,909 | 41,071 |
| Teacher training | 2* | 49 | 560 | 231 | 791 |
| Vocational | 3* | 116 | 978 | 194 | 1,172 |
| University level* | 4 | 250 | 4,791 | 789 | 5,580 |
| Other higher* |  |  | 192 | 78 | 270 |

* 1991/92 figure(s).

Source: Mainly UNESCO, *Statistical Yearbook*.

# Directory

While no longer an official language under the terms of the 1991 Constitution (see below), French is still widely used in Mauritania, especially in the commercial sector. Many organizations are therefore listed under their French names, by which they are generally known.

## The Constitution

The Constitution of the Arab and African Islamic Republic of Mauritania was approved in a national referendum on 12 July 1991.

The Constitution provides for the establishment of a multi-party political system. The President of the Republic is elected, by universal adult suffrage (the minimum age for voters being 18 years), for a period of six years: no limitations regarding the renewal of the presidential mandate are stipulated. Legislative power is vested in a National Assembly (elected by universal suffrage for a period of five years) and in a Senate (elected by municipal leaders with a six-year mandate—part of its membership being elected every two years). The President of the Republic is empowered to appoint a head of government. Provision is also made for the establishment of a Constitutional Council and a Supreme Islamic Council (both of which were inaugurated in 1992), as well as an Economic and Social Council.

The Constitution states that the official language is Arabic, and that the national languages are Arabic, Poular, Wolof and Solinke.

## The Government

### HEAD OF STATE

**President:** Col MAAWIYA OULD SID'AHMED TAYA (took office 12 December 1984; elected President 17 January 1992).

### COUNCIL OF MINISTERS
(May 1995)

**Prime Minister:** SIDI MOHAMED OULD BOUBACAR.
**Minister of State Control:** ETHMANE SID'AHMED YESSA.
**Minister of Foreign Affairs and Co-operation:** MOHAMED SALEM OULD LEKHEL.
**Minister of Defence:** ABDALLAHI OULD ABDI.
**Minister of Justice:** ADAMA SAMBA SOW.
**Minister of the Interior, Posts and Telecommunications:** MOHAMED LEMINE SALEM OULD DAH.
**Minister of Finance:** SIDI MOHAMED OULD BIYA.
**Minister of Fisheries and Marine Economy:** CHEIKH AFIA OULD MOHAMED KHOUNA.
**Minister of Planning and Employment:** MOHAMED LEMINE CH'BIH OULD CHEIKA MALAININE.
**Minister of Trade, Handicrafts and Tourism:** DIAGANA MOUSSA.
**Minister of Industry and Mines:** N'GUE DAH LEMINE.
**Minister of Equipment and Transport:** SOW MOHAMED DEYNA.
**Minister of National Education:** Dr LOULID OUEIDAD.
**Minister of the Civil Service, Labour, Youth and Sports:** SIDI MOHAMED OULD MOHAMED FALL.
**Minister of Water and Energy:** MOHAMED LEMINE OULD AHMED.
**Minister of Rural Development and the Environment:** SGHAIER OULD MBAREK.
**Minister of Health and Social Affairs:** MOHAMED OULD LAMAR.
**Minister of Culture and Islamic Orientation:** LIMAM OULD TAGADDI.
**Minister of Information:** AHMED OULD KHALIFAH OULD JIDDOU.
**Minister of Women's Affairs:** MARIAM BINT AHMED AICHE.
**Minister in charge of Relations with Parliament:** RACHID OULD SALEH.
**Minister, Secretary-General of the Presidency:** Col AHMED OULD MINNH.
**Secretary of State for Literacy and Basic Education and for the Union of the Arab Maghreb Affairs:** CHEIKH OULD ALI.
**Secretary of State, in charge of Civil Status:** KHATTAR OULD CHEIKH AHMED.

### MINISTRIES

**Office of the President:** Présidence de la République, BP 184, Nouakchott; tel. 523-17; telex 580.
**Ministry of the Civil Service, Labour, Youth and Sports:** Nouakchott.
**Ministry of Culture and Islamic Orientation:** BP 223, Nouakchott; tel. 511-30; telex 585.
**Ministry of Defence:** BP 184, Nouakchott; tel. 520-20; telex 566.
**Ministry of Finance:** BP 181, Nouakchott; tel. 520-20; telex 572.
**Ministry of Equipment and Transport:** BP 237, Nouakchott; telex 585.
**Ministry of Fisheries and Marine Economy:** BP 137, Nouakchott; tel. 524-76; telex 595; fax 531-46.
**Ministry of Foreign Affairs and Co-operation:** BP 230, Nouakchott; tel. 520-20; telex 585.
**Ministry of Health and Social Affairs:** BP 177, Nouakchott; tel. 518-58.
**Ministry of Industry and Mines:** BP 183, Nouakchott; tel. 513-18.
**Ministry of Information:** BP 223, Nouakchott.
**Ministry of the Interior, Posts and Telecommunications:** Nouakchott; tel. 529-34; telex 844.
**Ministry of Justice:** BP 350, Nouakchott; tel. 510-83.
**Ministry of National Education:** BP 387, Nouakchott; tel. 518-98.
**Ministry of Planning and Employment:** Nouakchott.
**Ministry of Rural Development and the Environment:** BP 366, Nouakchott; tel. 520-20 (ext. 386).
**Ministry of State Control:** Nouakchott.
**Ministry of Trade, Handicrafts and Tourism:** Nouakchott.
**Ministry of Water and Energy:** Nouakchott.

# MAURITANIA

**Office of the Secretary-General of the Government:** BP 184, Nouakchott.

## President and Legislature

### PRESIDENT

**Election, 17 January 1992**

|  | Votes | % of total |
|---|---:|---:|
| Maawiya Ould Sid'Ahmed Taya | 345,583 | 62.65 |
| Ahmed Ould Daddah | 180,658 | 32.75 |
| Moustapha Ould Mohamed Salek | 15,735 | 2.85 |
| Mohamed Mahmoud Ould Mah | 7,506 | 1.36 |
| Total* | 551,575 | 100.00 |

* Included in the total number of valid votes are 2,093 'neutral votes'.

### SENATE

**President:** Dieng Boubou Farba.

Elections to the 56-member Senate took place on 3 and 10 April 1992. It was reported that 36 candidates of the Democratic and Social Republican Party (DSRP) were elected; 17 seats were won by independent candidates, and a further three senators were to represent the interests of Mauritanians resident abroad. Part of the Senate is subject to re-election every two years: accordingly, elections for 17 senators took place on 15 and 22 April 1994, while elections for the three representatives of Mauritanians abroad were conducted by the Senate on 14 May. The DSRP retained its majority in the upper house following the elections.

### NATIONAL ASSEMBLY

**President:** Commdt (retd) Cheikh Sid'Ahmed Ould Baba.

**General Election, 6 and 13 March 1992**

|  | Seats |
|---|---:|
| Democratic and Social Republican Party | 67 |
| Mauritanian Party for Renewal | 1 |
| Rally for Democracy and National Unity | 1 |
| Independent | 10 |
| Total | 79 |

## Advisory Councils

**Constitutional Council:** f. 1992; includes six mems, three nominated by the Head of State and three designated by the Presidents of the Senate and National Assembly; Pres. Didi Ould Bounaama; Sec.-Gen. Mohamed Ould Mrehib.

**Supreme Islamic Council** (al-Majlis al-Islamiya al-A'la'): f. 1992.

The 1991 Constitution also provides for the establishment of an Economic and Social Council.

## Political Organizations

Following the adoption of the July 1991 Constitution, legislation to permit the authorization of political parties was promulgated. By early 1995 at least 18 parties had been accorded official status. Among these were:

**Democratic Centre Party (DCP):** Leader Moulaye Mohamed.

**Democratic and Social Republican Party (DSRP):** f. 1991; absorbed Movement of Independent Democrats in 1995; party of President Taya; Leader Cheikh Sid'Ahmed Ould Baba.

**El Hor:** split from UDF—NE in 1994; Leader Messaoud Ould Boulkheir.

**Mauritanian Party for Renewal (MPR):** f. 1991; Leader Moulaye el Hassan Ould Jeyid.

**People's Progressive Party (PPP):** f. 1991; Leader Taleb Ould Jiddou.

**Rally for Democracy and National Unity (RDNU):** f. 1991; Chair. Ahmed Ould Sidi Baba.

**Socialist and Democratic People's Union (SDPU):** f. 1991; Leader Mohamed Mahmoud Ould Mah.

**Union for Democracy and Progress (UDP):** f. 1993; Pres. Hamdi Ould Mouknass; Sec.-Gen. Ahmed Ould Menaya.

**Union of Democratic Forces—New Era (UDF—NE):** f. 1991 as Union of Democratic Forces, renamed 1992, restructured (following splits) 1994; Sec.-Gen. Ahmed Ould Daddah.

Unauthorized but influential is the Islamic **Ummah Party** (the Constitution prohibits the authorization of religious political organizations), founded in 1991 and led by Imam Sidi Yahya. The clandestine anti-Government **Forces de libération africaine de Mauritanie (FLAM)**, formed in 1983 to represent black Africans in Mauritania, remained active in 1993, while a further outlawed group, the **Rassemblement pour la renaissance des nègres-africains de la Mauritanie**, has conducted a sporadic campaign of violence against the Government and its supporters.

## Diplomatic Representation

### EMBASSIES IN MAURITANIA

**Algeria:** Nouakchott; telex 871; Ambassador: Abdelkrim ben Hocine.

**China, People's Republic:** BP 196, Nouakchott; Ambassador: Zhane Junqi.

**Egypt:** BP 176, Nouakchott; telex 520; Ambassador: (vacant).

**France:** BP 231, rue Ahmed Ould M'Hamed, Nouakchott; tel. 517-40; telex 582; Ambassador: Michel Raimbaud.

**Gabon:** BP 38, Nouakchott; tel. 529-19; telex 593; Ambassador: Jacques Bonaventure Essonghe.

**Germany:** BP 372, Nouakchott; tel. 510-32; telex 5555; fax 517-22; Ambassador: Dr Johannes E. Westerhoff.

**Korea, Republic:** BP 324, Nouakchott; tel. 537-86; fax 544-43; Chargé d'affaires a.i.: Won Chol-Kim.

**Libya:** Nouakchott; telex 534; Ambassador: Nasser Abass Othmane.

**Morocco:** BP 621, Nouakchott; tel. 514-11; telex 550; Ambassador: Abderrahmane el Kouhen.

**Nigeria:** BP 367, Nouakchott; telex 869; Ambassador: Abubacar Mahamed.

**Russia:** BP 251, Nouakchott; tel. 519-73; Ambassador: Vladimir S. Shishov.

**Saudi Arabia:** Nouakchott; telex 813; Ambassador: Mohamed Al Fadh el Issa.

**Senegal:** BP 611, Nouakchott; Ambassador: Doudou Diop.

**Spain:** BP 232, Nouakchott; tel. 520-80; telex 5563; fax 540-88; Ambassador: Juan María López-Aguilar.

**Tunisia:** BP 681, Nouakchott; tel. 528-71; telex 857; Ambassador: Mohamed H'Sairi.

**USA:** BP 222, Nouakchott; tel. 526-60; telex 558; fax 525-89; Ambassador: Gordon S. Brown.

**Zaire:** BP 487, Nouakchott; tel. 528-36; telex 812; Ambassador: Kyalwe Mihambo.

## Judicial System

The Code of Law was promulgated in 1961 and subsequently modified to integrate modern law with Islamic institutions and practices. The main courts comprise a magistrate's court with six regional sections, 42 departmental civil courts and labour courts.

Shari'a (Islamic) law was introduced in February 1980. A special Islamic court was established in March of that year, presided over by a magistrate of Islamic law, assisted by two counsellors and two *ulemas* (Muslim jurists and interpreters of the Koran).

**Supreme Court:** Palais de Justice, Nouakchott; tel. 521-20; f. 1961; intended to ensure the independence of the judiciary; the court is competent in juridical, administrative and electoral matters; Pres. Ahmedou Ould Abdelkader.

## Religion

### ISLAM

Islam is the official religion, and the population are almost entirely Muslims of the Malekite rite. The major religious groups are the Tijaniya and the Qadiriya. Chinguetti, in the district of Adrar, is the seventh Holy Place in Islam.

### CHRISTIANITY

#### Roman Catholic Church

Mauritania comprises the single diocese of Nouakchott, directly responsible to the Holy See. The Bishop participates in the Bishops' Conference of Senegal, Mauritania, Cape Verde and Guinea-Bissau, based in Dakar, Senegal. At 31 December 1992 there were an estimated 4,500 adherents, mainly non-nationals, in the country.

MAURITANIA

**Bishop of Nouakchott:** Mgr ROBERT DE CHEVIGNY, Evêché, BP 5377, Nouakchott; tel. 515-15; fax 537-51.

## The Press

**Bulletin de la Chambre de Commerce:** BP 215, Nouakchott; tel. 522-14; telex 581.

**Ach-Chaab:** BP 371, Nouakchott; tel. 535-23; telex 583; daily; French and Arabic; publ. by Agence Mauritanienne de l'Information; Dir-Gen. HADEMINE OULD SADY.

**Al-Bayane:** Nouakchott; f. 1991; independent; Arabic and French; Dir YAHYA OULD BECHIR.

**Le Calame:** Nouakchott; weekly; French and Arabic; independent.

**Eveil-Hebdo:** BP 587, Nouakchott; weekly; independent.

**Journal Officiel:** Ministry of Justice, BP 350, Nouakchott; fortnightly.

**Mauritanie Demain:** Nouakchott; monthly; independent; Editor MUBARAK OULD BEIROUK.

**Le Peuple:** BP 371, Nouakchott; 6 a year; French and Arabic.

### NEWS AGENCIES

**Agence Mauritanienne de l'Information (AMI):** BP 371, Nouakchott; tel. 529-70; telex 525; fmrly Agence Mauritanienne de Presse, name changed 1990; state-controlled; Dir RACHID OULD SALEH.

#### Foreign Bureau

**Xinhua (New China) News Agency** (People's Republic of China): Nouakchott; telex 541; Correspondent WANG TIANRUI.

Agence France-Presse and Reuters (UK) are also represented in Mauritania.

## Publishers

**Imprimerie Commerciale et Administrative de Mauritanie:** BP 164, Nouakchott; textbooks, educational.

**Société Mauritanienne de Presse et d'Impression (SMPI):** BP 371, Nouakchott; tel. 527-19; telex 877; f. 1978; state-owned; Pres. MOHAMED OULD BOUBACAR; Man. Dir MOUSSA OULD EBNOU.

**Société Nationale d'Impression:** BP 618, Nouakchott; govt publishing house; Pres. MOUSTAPHA SALECK OULD AHMED BRIHIM.

**Société Nouvelle d'Impression et de Presse Professionnelles:** Nouakchott.

## Radio and Television

In 1992, according to estimates by UNESCO, there were 309,000 radio receivers and 50,000 television receivers in use.

**Office de Radiodiffusion et Télévision de Mauritanie (ORTM):** BP 200, Nouakchott; tel. 521-64; telex 515; f. 1958; state-owned; five transmitters; radio broadcasts in Arabic, French, Sarakolé, Toucouleur and Wolof; Dir SIDI OULD CHEIKH.

## Finance

(cap. = capital; res = reserves; dep. = deposits; m. = million; br. = branch; amounts in UM)

### BANKING

#### Central Bank

**Banque Centrale de Mauritanie (BCM):** ave de l'Indépendance, BP 623, Nouakchott; tel. 522-06; telex 532; fax 527-59; f. 1973; bank of issue; cap. 200m.; Gov. MOUHAMEDOU OULD MICHEL; 4 brs.

#### Commercial Banks

**Banque al-Baraka Mauritanienne Islamique (BAMIS):** ave du Roi Fayçal, BP 650, Nouakchott; tel. 514-24; telex 535; fax 516-21; f. 1985; 84% owned by al-Baraka Group (Saudi Arabia); cap. 3,000m. (1994); Chair. Dr HASSAN ABDALLAH KAMEL; Man. Dir MOHAMED LEMINE JEILANI.

**Banque Mauritanienne pour le Commerce International (BMCI):** Immeuble BMCI, ave Gamal-Abdel-Nasser, BP 622, Nouakchott; tel. 524-69; telex 5543; fax 520-45; f. 1974; privately-owned; cap. 1,000m., res 2,284m., dep. 12,080m. (Dec. 1993); Chair. and Man. Dir SIDI MOHAMED ABASS; brs at Nouadhibou, Nema and Aioun.

**Banque Nationale de Mauritanie (BNM):** ave Gamal-Abdel-Nasser, BP 614, Nouakchott; tel. 526-02; telex 567; fax 533-95; f. 1988 by merger; privately-owned; cap. 500m., res 109m., dep. 9,061m. (Dec. 1992); Man. Dir MOHAMED O. A. O. NOUEIGUED.

**Chinguitty Bank:** ave Gamal-Abdel-Nasser, BP 626, Nouakchott; tel. 521-42; telex 5562; fax 533-82; f. 1972 as Banque Arabe Libyenne-Mauritanienne pour le Commerce Extérieur et le Développement, name changed 1993; 50% state-owned, 50% owned by Libyan Arab Foreign Bank; cap. 1,500m. (Dec. 1993); Chair. HASSEN OULD SALEH; Man. Dir OMAR MOHAMED SEGHAYER; br. at Nouadhibou.

### INSURANCE

**Société Mauritanienne d'Assurances et de Réassurances (SMAR):** 12 ave Gamal-Abdel-Nasser, BP 163, Nouakchott; tel. 526-50; telex 527; fax 518-18; f. 1974; 51% govt-owned, 49% owned by BCM; cap. 1,000m.; Chair. MAOULOUD OULD SIDI ABDALLA; Man. Dir ANNE AMADOU BABALY.

In late 1992 the Government approved proposals to end SMAR's insurance monopoly.

## Trade and Industry

### CHAMBER OF COMMERCE

**Chambre de Commerce, d'Agriculture, d'Elevage, d'Industrie et des Mines de Mauritanie:** BP 215, Nouakchott; tel. 522-14; telex 581; f. 1954; Chair. KANE YAYA.

### DEVELOPMENT ORGANIZATIONS

**Caisse Française de Développement (CFD):** quartier des Ambassades, BP 211, Nouakchott; fmrly Caisse Centrale de Coopération Economique, name changed 1992; tel. 523-09; telex 516; Dir M. CATTIN.

**Mission Française de Coopération:** BP 203, Nouakchott; tel. 521-21; telex 582; administers bilateral aid; Dir JEAN HABERT.

**Office Mauritanien des Céréales (OMC):** BP 368, Nouakchott; tel. 528-30; telex 513; f. 1975; state-owned; Pres. WALY N'DAO; Dir MOHAMED BOCOUM.

**Société Arabe Mauritano-Libyenne de Développement Agricole (SAMALIDA):** BP 658, Nouakchott; tel. 537-15; f. 1980; cap. 350m. UM; 51% state-owned, 49% owned by Govt of Libya; Dir-Gen. O. TURKI.

**Société Nationale de Développement Rural (SONADER):** BP 321, Nouakchott; tel. 521-61; telex 807; Dir-Gen. MOHAMED OULD BABETTA.

### TRADE ORGANIZATIONS

**Bureau d'Achats pour la République Islamique de Mauritanie (BARIM):** ave du Président J. F. Kennedy, BP 272, Nouakchott; tel. 510-57; telex 810; f. 1969; cap. 6m. UM; importer and exporter; Dir-Gen. D. DIABIRA.

**Société Mauritanienne de Commercialisation du Poisson (SMCP):** BP 259, Nouadhibou; tel. 452-81; telex 420; f. 1984; cap. 500m. UM; state-owned; partial transfer to private ownership pending in 1994; until 1992 monopoly exporter of demersal fish and crustaceans; Pres. MOHAMED SALEM OULD LEKHAL; Dir-Gen. MOHAMED OULD MOCTAR.

**Société Mauritanienne de Commercialisation des Produits Pétroliers (SMCPP):** BP 679, Nouakchott; tel. 526-61; telex 849; f. 1980; cap. 120m. UM; state-owned; partial transfer to private ownership pending in 1994; import and distribution of petroleum products; Dir-Gen. ABDALLAHI OULD MOUHAMADEN.

**Société Nationale d'Importation et d'Exportation (SONIMEX):** BP 290, Nouakchott; tel. 514-72; telex 561; f. 1966; cap. 914m. UM; 74% state-owned; import of foodstuffs and textiles, distribution of essential consumer goods, export of gum-arabic; Pres. MOHAMED KHATTRY OULD SEGANE; Dir-Gen. MOUSSA FALL.

### EMPLOYERS' ORGANIZATIONS

**Confédération Générale des Employeurs de Mauritanie (CGEM):** BP 383, Nouakchott; telex 859; f. 1974; professional assen for all employers active in Mauritania; Sec.-Gen. MOHAMED ALI OULD SIDI MOHAMED.

**Union Nationale des Industries et Entreprises de Mauritanie (UNIEMA):** BP 215, Nouakchott.

### TRADE UNIONS

**Confédération Générale des Travailleurs de Mauritanie:** Nouakchott; f. 1992, officially recognized as Mauritania's first independent trade union confederation January 1994.

**Union des Travailleurs de Mauritanie (UTM):** Bourse du Travail, BP 630, Nouakchott; f. 1961; Sec.-Gen. MOHAMED BRAHIM (acting); 45,000 mems.

MAURITANIA

## Transport

### RAILWAYS

A 670-km railway connects the iron-ore deposits at Zouérate with Nouadhibou; a 40-km extension services the reserves at El Rhein, and a 30-km extension those at M'Haoudat. Motive power is diesel-electric. The Société Nationale Industrielle et Minière—Société d'Economie Mixte (SNIM—SEM) operates one of the longest (2.4 km) and heaviest (22,000 metric tons) trains in the world.

**SNIM—Direction du Chemin de Fer et du Port:** BP 42, Nouadhibou; tel. 451-74; telex 426; fax 453-96; f. 1963, present ownership (SNIM—SEM) since 1974; Gen. Man. MOHAMED SALECK OULD HEYINE; Dir KHALIA OULD BEYAH.

### ROADS

In 1986 there were about 7,500 km of roads and tracks, of which main roads comprised some 2,700 km, and 22.5% of the road network (about 1,686 km) was tarred. The 1,100-km TransMauritania highway, completed in 1985, links Nouakchott with Néma in the east of the country. Plans exist for the construction of a 7,400-km highway, linking Nouakchott with the Libyan port of Tubruq (Tobruk).

**Société des Transports Publics de Nouakchott:** BP 342, Nouakchott; tel. 529-53; f. 1975; Pres. CHEIKH MALAININE ROBERT; Dir-Gen. MAMADOU SOULEYMANE KANE.

### INLAND WATERWAYS

The River Senegal is navigable in the wet season by small coastal vessels as far as Kayes (Mali) and by river vessels as far as Kaédi; in the dry season as far as Rosso and Boghé, respectively. The major river ports are at Rosso, Kaédi and Gouraye.

### SHIPPING

The principal port is at Point-Central, 10 km south of Nouadhibou. Operational since 1963, it is almost wholly occupied with mineral exports. There is a commercial and fishing port at Nouadhibou, which handled 393,716 metric tons in 1983. The deep-water Port de l'Amitié at Nouakchott, built and maintained with assistance from the People's Republic of China, was inaugurated in 1986. The port, which has a total capacity of 1m. tons annually, handled 636,842 tons in 1991 (compared with 479,791 tons in 1990); the number of ships using the port in 1991 was 281 (compared with 244 in 1990).

**Port de l'Amitié de Nouakchott:** BP 267, Nouakchott; tel. 514-53; telex 538; f. 1986; deep-water port; Dir-Gen. KONÉ OULD MAHMOUD.

**Port Autonome de Nouadhibou:** BP 236, Nouadhibou; tel. 451-34; telex 441; f. 1973; state-owned; Pres. HABIB ELY; Dir-Gen. AMAR OULD H'MOÏDHA.

#### Shipping Companies

**Compagnie Mauritanienne de Navigation Maritime (COMAUNAM):** 119 ave Gamal-Abdel-Nasser, BP 799, Nouakchott; tel. 536-34; telex 5862; fax 525-04; f. 1973; 51% state-owned, 49% owned by Govt of Algeria; nat. shipping co; forwarding agent, stevedoring; Chair. MOHAND TIGHILT; Dir-Gen. KAMIL ABDELKADER.

**Société d'Acconage et de Manutention en Mauritanie (SAMMA):** BP 258, Nouadhibou; tel. 452-63; telex 433; f. 1960; freight and handling, shipping agent, forwarding agent, stevedoring; Chair. MOHAMED OULD ZEÏDANE; Man. Dir MOHAMED MAHMOUD OULD MATY.

**Société Générale de Consignation et d'Entreprises Maritimes (SOGECO):** BP 351, Nouakchott; tel. 522-02; telex 5502; fax 539-03; f. 1973; Chair. and Man. Dir ISMAIL OULD ABEIDNA.

### CIVIL AVIATION

There are international airports at Nouakchott and Nouadhibou, an airport at Néma, and 23 smaller airstrips. Facilities at Nouakchott were expanded considerably in the late 1980s and early 1990s.

**Air Afrique:** BP 51, Nouakchott; tel. 525-45; fax 549-44; see under Côte d'Ivoire.

**Société d'Economie Mixte Air Mauritanie:** BP 41, Nouakchott; tel. 521-46; telex 573; fax 538-15; f. 1974; 60% state-owned, 20% owned by Air Afrique; domestic and regional passenger and cargo services; Dir-Gen. SIDI OULD ZEIN.

## Tourism

Mauritania's principal tourist attractions are its historical sites, several of which have been listed by UNESCO under its World Heritage Programme, and its game reserves and national parks. Some 13,000 tourists visited Mauritania in 1986. Receipts from tourism in 1991 totalled an estimated US $13m.

**Direction du Tourisme:** BP 246, Nouakchott; tel. 535-72; f. 1988; Dir KANE ISMAILA.

**Société Mauritanienne de Tourisme et d'Hôtellerie (SMTH):** BP 552, Nouakchott; tel. 533-51; f. 1969; 50% owned by Air Afrique; promotes tourism, manages hotels and organizes tours; Man. Dir OULD CHEIKH ABDALLAHI.

# MAURITIUS

## Introductory Survey

### Location, Climate, Language, Religion, Flag, Capital

The Republic of Mauritius lies in the Indian Ocean. The principal island, from which the country takes its name, lies about 800 km (500 miles) east of Madagascar. The other main islands are Rodrigues, the Agalega Islands and the Cargados Carajos Shoals (St Brandon Islands). The climate is sub-tropical and generally humid. The average annual temperature is 23°C (73°F) at sea-level, falling to 19°C (66°F) at an altitude of 600m (about 2,000 ft). Average annual rainfall varies from 890 mm (35 ins) at sea-level to 5,080 mm (200 ins) on the highest parts. Tropical cyclones, which may be severe, occur between September and May. Most of the islands' inhabitants are of Indian descent. On the island of Mauritius the most widely spoken languages in 1983 were Creole (29.1%), Hindi (21.6%) and Bhojpuri (18.8%). Almost all of the population of Rodrigues speak Creole. English is the country's official language, and Creole (derived from French) the lingua franca. In 1972 the principal religious groups on the island of Mauritius were Hindus (51.0%), Christians (31.3%) and Muslims (16.6%). Almost all of Rodrigues' inhabitants profess Christianity. The national flag (proportions 3 by 2) has four equal horizontal stripes, of red, blue, yellow and green. The capital is Port Louis.

### Recent History

The islands of Mauritius and Rodrigues, formerly French possessions, were captured by British forces in 1810. France formally ceded the islands to the United Kingdom in 1814. Subsequent settlers came mainly from East Africa and India, and the European population remained largely French-speaking.

A ministerial form of government was introduced in 1957. The first elections under universal adult suffrage, held in 1959, were won by the Mauritius Labour Party (MLP), whose leader, Dr (later Sir) Seewoosagur Ramgoolam, became Chief Minister in 1961 and Premier in 1964. In November 1965 the United Kingdom transferred the Chagos Archipelago (including the atoll of Diego Garcia), a Mauritian dependency about 2,000 km (1,250 miles) north-east of the main island, to the newly-created British Indian Ocean Territory (q.v.). Mauritius' subsequent campaign for the return of the islands was intensified, following the development of Diego Garcia as a major US military base in 1980. Mauritius also claims sovereignty of the French-held island of Tromelin, about 550 km (340 miles) to the north-west.

An electoral alliance led by Ramgoolam secured a legislative majority at elections held in August 1967, and a new Constitution, providing for self-government, was introduced. Mauritius became independent, within the Commonwealth, on 12 March 1968, with Ramgoolam as Prime Minister.

During the 1970s political opposition to Ramgoolam's coalition governments emerged, following the establishment of a left-wing organization, the Mouvement Militant Mauricien (MMM), led by Paul Bérenger. In response to a prolonged general strike in 1971, a state of emergency was declared, and legislative elections, scheduled for 1972, were postponed. The coalition of the MLP and the Parti Mauricien Social-Démocrate (PMSD) was dissolved in December 1973, following disagreement over foreign policy and increases in taxation; the MLP continued in office in coalition with the Comité d'Action Musulman (CAM). At the delayed general election, which took place in December 1976, the MMM became the largest single party in the Legislative Assembly, but Ramgoolam formed a new coalition Government incorporating the Independence Party (an electoral alliance of the MLP and the CAM) and the PMSD. However, industrial unrest and growing unemployment led to widespread disenchantment with the Government. At a general election in June 1982 the MMM, in alliance with the Parti Socialiste Mauricien (PSM), won all 60 contested seats on the main island. Aneerood (later Sir Aneerood) Jugnauth became Prime Minister, and Paul Bérenger Minister of Finance.

The MMM/PSM coalition collapsed in March 1983, when 12 ministers, including Bérenger, resigned, following differences concerning economic policy and the status of Creole (which Bérenger's supporters sought to make the national language). Jugnauth appointed a new Government, and he and his supporters were subsequently excluded from MMM meetings. At the end of March Bérenger was officially designated leader of the opposition. In April Jugnauth formed a new political party, the Mouvement Socialiste Militant, and in May the PSM was dissolved and incorporated into the new party, which was renamed the Mouvement Socialiste Mauricien (MSM). The new Government was unable to command a majority in the legislature, which was dissolved in June. A general election took place in August, at which an electoral alliance of the MSM, the MLP and the PMSD (led by Sir Gaëtan Duval, until March the leader of the parliamentary opposition), won 41 of the 62 elective seats in the Assembly. The MMM took only 19 seats, and the Organisation du Peuple Rodriguais (OPR) the remaining two seats. Bérenger was defeated in his home constituency, but was awarded a seat in the Assembly under the 'additional' members' allocation system (see Government). Following the election, Jugnauth (who remained Prime Minister) formed a new Council of Ministers, in which Duval became Deputy Prime Minister. Relations between the MLP and the MSM subsequently deteriorated, and in February 1984 Jugnauth dismissed Sir Satcam Boolell (who had become leader of the MLP, following Ramgoolam's appointment as Governor-General of Mauritius in December 1983) from the Government. In response, the MLP officially withdrew from the ruling coalition; however, 11 MLP deputies continued to support the Government, forming a faction within the party, the Rassemblement des Travaillistes Mauriciens (RTM).

In December 1985 four members of the Legislative Assembly were arrested in the Netherlands, accused of involvement in the smuggling of illegal drugs. Four ministers resigned after Jugnauth failed publicly to name other deputies who were believed to be implicated in the affair. An extensive reshuffle of the Council of Ministers followed in January 1986. In the same month Sir Veerasamy Ringadoo, a member of the MSM and former Minister of Finance, succeeded Ramgoolam (who had died in December 1985) as Governor-General.

In response to a temporary parliamentary boycott by the MMM and increasing criticism from within the MSM, Jugnauth established a commission of inquiry in mid-1986 to investigate the alleged involvement of members of the Government in drugs-trafficking. In July three ministers resigned, citing lack of confidence in Jugnauth's leadership of the country and of the MSM. The Government retaliated by expelling 11 MSM dissidents from the party. In August there was a further reshuffle of the Council of Ministers, in which Boolell rejoined the Government as a Deputy Prime Minister, with responsibility for foreign affairs (the MLP was thus reintegrated with the government coalition).

In November 1986 three members of the Legislative Assembly, all of whom supported the government alliance, resigned their posts, after having been implicated by the commission of inquiry into the drugs scandal. The ruling coalition's strength in the legislature was thus reduced to 30 seats. In January 1987 Jugnauth announced that a general election would take place within the year, rather than in 1988 (as scheduled). In March 1987 the commission of inquiry named six further coalition deputies who had been directly involved in drugs-trafficking. The Government subsequently refused to accept the parliamentary support of the six. In the same month new allegations implicated Duval in the affair. Duval's subsequent offer of resignation was rejected by Jugnauth, who declared his complete confidence in the Deputy Prime Minister.

Jugnauth dissolved the legislature in July 1987, and a general election followed on 30 August. The MSM again formed an electoral alliance with the PMSD and the MLP, the three parties having won 39 of the 62 elective seats (although they received only 49.8% of the total votes). The MMM, which campaigned as an opposition 'union' with two small parties (the Mouvement des Travaillistes Démocrates and the Front des Travailleurs Socialistes), won 21 seats, with 48.1% of the votes, while the OPR took the two remaining seats. Of the eight 'additional' seats, five were allocated to the MSM/PMSD/MLP alliance and three to the MMM. Bérenger failed to secure a seat, and his functions as President of the MMM and leader of the opposition in the Legislative Assembly were assumed by Dr Paramhansa Nababsing (while Bérenger himself took Nababsing's former post of MMM Secretary-General). A new Council of Ministers took office in September, and the Government subsequently announced plans to make Mauritius a republic within the Commonwealth.

In July 1988 Harish Boodhoo, the leader of the PSM until its dissolution in 1983, announced the revival of that party, which left the MSM. In the following month, after a disagreement over employment policies, the coalition was weakened by the withdrawal of support by the PMSD, whose leader, Duval, left the Government. Two attempts on Jugnauth's life (in November 1988 and March 1989) were ascribed by the Prime Minister to criminals involved in drugs-trafficking. In June 1989 the government coalition gained a seat in the Legislative Assembly as a result of a by-election. In the same month Duval was arrested (and subsequently released) for alleged involvement in a political assassination in 1971.

In July 1990 the MSM and the MMM agreed to form an alliance to contest the next general election, and to promote constitutional measures that would allow Mauritius to become a republic, while remaining within the Commonwealth. It was proposed that Bérenger would assume the presidency of the proposed republic (replacing the British monarch, Queen Elizabeth II, as Head of State), while Jugnauth would retain the position of Prime Minister. However, the draft amendments, which were presented to the Legislative Assembly in mid-August, were opposed by members of the MLP, who formed an alliance with the PMSD. Following his failure to secure the requisite majority support, Jugnauth subsequently dismissed Boolell from the Government, together with two MSM ministers who had refused to support the proposals. A further three ministers belonging to the MLP resigned, leaving only one MLP member in the Government. Boolell subsequently relinquished the leadership of the MLP to Dr Navin Ramgoolam (the son of Sir Seewoosagur). In September Jugnauth announced the formation of a new coalition Government, in which the six vacant ministerial portfolios were allocated to members of the MMM. Nababsing was appointed a Deputy Prime Minister in the new administration. In late November, despite strong objections by the MLP, the Legislative Assembly adopted a constitutional amendment that would facilitate the dismissal of its Speaker. (The incumbent Speaker, Chattradhari Daby, had expressed opposition to the MSM/MMM-sponsored proposals for a republican constitution.)

Jugnauth dissolved the Legislative Assembly in August 1991. At the subsequent general election, which took place on 15 September, an alliance of the MSM, the MMM and the Mouvement des Travaillistes Démocrates (MTD), won 57 of the 62 directly elected seats, while the MLP/PMSD alliance obtained three seats. The two remaining seats were secured by the OPR. Four 'additional' seats were subsequently allocated to members of the MLP/PMSD alliance. However, the seven opposition members, including Duval and Dr Ramgoolam, alleged electoral malpractice, and refused to attend the inaugural session of the Legislative Assembly. In late September Jugnauth formed a new 24-member Government, to which nine representatives of the MMM (including Bérenger, who became Minister of External Affairs) and one representative of the MTD were appointed. Shortly afterwards Duval resigned from the Legislative Assembly. Municipal elections in the following month were boycotted by the MLP/PMSD alliance; accordingly, the MSM/MMM/MTD alliance secured 125 of the 126 contested seats.

In October 1991 Jugnauth announced that, subject to the adoption by the legislature of constitutional amendments, Mauritius would become a republic within the Commonwealth on 12 March 1992. A majority of three-quarters of the members of the Legislative Assembly would be required to approve the amendments. In the event, the constitutional changes were approved by the 59 MSM, MMM, MTD and OPR deputies on 10 December 1991. (The seven members of the MLP/PMSD alliance refused to vote, protesting that the amendments provided for an increase in executive power, to the detriment of the legislature.) Under the terms of the revised Constitution, the Governor-General, Sir Veerasamy Ringadoo (nominated by Jugnauth), was to assume the presidency on an interim basis, pending the election of a president and vice-president, for a five-year term, by a simple majority of the Legislative Assembly, which was to be renamed the National Assembly. (The MLP/PMSD alliance criticized the provisions for the selection of the Head of State, and demanded that the President be elected by universal suffrage.) Executive power was to be vested in the Prime Minister, who would be appointed by the President, and would be the member of the National Assembly best able to command a majority in the legislature. (The terms of the MSM's alliance with the MMM effectively confirmed Jugnauth in the office of premier.) The Constitution also reaffirmed Mauritius' claim of sovereignty over the Chagos Archipelago and the island of Tromelin (see above). On 12 March 1992 Ringadoo took office as interim President. In the same month the Government announced that Cassam Uteem, the Minister of Industry and Industrial Technology and a member of the MMM, was, subject to legislative approval, to assume the presidency after a period of three months.

In April 1992 opposition deputies in the National Assembly demanded that Jugnauth resign, following controversy over the depiction of his wife, Sarojni Jugnauth, on a new issue of bank note. It was reported that subsequent widespread criticism of Jugnauth had adversely affected the MSM/MMM alliance. In June Ringadoo resigned as President, officially on grounds of ill health, and the National Assembly duly elected Uteem to the presidency; Sir Rabindrah Ghurburrun, a member of the MMM, was nominated as Vice-President.

In the second half of 1992 disputes between the Government and members of the opposition continued. In November Jugnauth allegedly issued threats against Boodhoo at a meeting of the MSM, in response to plans for a demonstration by the PSM, which was to take place near Jugnauth's residence. Boodhoo formally protested to the security forces, and members of the PSM, supported by the MLP, subsequently demanded that Jugnauth be arrested.

In October 1992 Dr Ramgoolam announced that he was to return to the United Kingdom to complete legal studies (although he was to retain the leadership of the MLP), despite a constitutional stipulation that the mandate of a parliamentary deputy who failed to attend sessions of the National Assembly for a period of more than three months would be suspended. Plans by Ramgoolam to return to Mauritius to attend subsequent parliamentary meetings were thwarted by Jugnauth, who, in December, unexpectedly curtailed a session of the National Assembly, and, in January 1993, convened a further session without prior notice (contrary to usual practice). Legal proceedings, initiated by the MSM, to exclude Dr Ramgoolam from the National Assembly were subsequently disallowed by the Supreme Court.

The government coalition came under increasing pressure during 1993, amid intensifying disputes between the MSM and the MMM. In August, following an unexpected success by the PMSD in municipal by-elections in a constituency that traditionally supported the MMM, a meeting between Bérenger and Dr Ramgoolam prompted speculation that an MMM/MLP alliance was contemplated. Shortly afterwards Jugnauth dismissed Bérenger from the Council of Ministers, on the grounds that he had repeatedly criticized government policy.

The removal of Bérenger precipitated a serious crisis within the MMM, whose political bureau decided that the other nine members of the party who held ministerial portfolios should remain in the coalition Government. Led by the Deputy Prime Minister, Paramhansa Nababsing, and the Minister of Industry and Industrial Technology, Jean-Claude de l'Estrac, supporters of the pro-coalition faction announced in October 1993 that Bérenger had been suspended as Secretary-General of the MMM. Bérenger and his supporters responded by expelling 11 MMM officials from the party, and seeking a legal ban on Nababsing and de l'Estrac from using the party name. The split in the MMM led in November to a government reshuffle, in which the remaining two MMM ministers supporting Bérenger were replaced by members of the party's pro-coalition faction.

In April 1994 the MLP and the MMM announced that they had agreed terms for an alliance to contest the next general elections. Under its provisions, Ramgoolam was to be Prime Minister and Bérenger the Deputy Prime Minister, with Cabinet portfolios allocated on the basis of 12 ministries to the MLP and nine to the MMM. In the same month, three MPs from the MSM, who had been close associates of a former Minister of Agriculture who had been dismissed two months earlier, withdrew their support from the Government.

Nababsing and the dissident faction of the MMM, having lost Bérenger's legal challenge for the use of the party name, formed a new party, the Renouveau Militant Mauricien (RMM), which formally commenced political activity in June 1994. In the same month, Jugnauth declared that the Government, which retained a cohesive parliamentary majority, would remain in office to the conclusion of its mandate in September 1996. In August 1994 a number of Cabinet posts were reallocated.

In November 1994, during the course of a parliamentary debate on electoral issues, Bérenger and de l'Estrac accepted a mutual challenge to resign their seats in the National Assembly and to contest by-elections. In the following month the MSM indicated that it would not oppose RMM candidates in the two polls. In January 1995, however, Jugnauth unsuccessfully sought to undermine the MLP/MMM alliance by offering electoral support to the MLP. The by-elections, held in February, were both won by MLP/MMM candidates, and Bérenger was returned to the National Assembly. Following these results, Jugnauth opened political negotiations with the PMSD, whose leader, Luc Xavier Duval (the son of Sir Gaëtan Duval), agreed to enter the coalition as Minister of Industry and Industrial Technology and Minister of Tourism. The cabinet post of Attorney-General and Minister of Justice, previously held by Jugnauth, was also allocated to the PMSD, and Sir Gaëtan Duval accepted an appointment as an economic adviser to the Prime Minister.

### Government

Constitutional amendments, which were approved by the Legislative Assembly (henceforth known as the National Assembly) in December 1991 and came into effect on 12 March 1992, provided for the establishment of a republic. The constitutional Head of State is the President of the Republic, who is elected by a simple majority of the National Assembly for a five-year term of office. Legislative power is vested in the unicameral National Assembly, which comprises the Speaker, 62 members elected by universal adult suffrage for a term of five years, up to eight 'additional' members (unsuccessful candidates who receive the largest number of votes at a legislative election, to whom seats are allocated by the Electoral Supervisory Commission to ensure a balance in representation of the different ethnic groups), and the Attorney-General (if not an elected member). Executive power is vested in the Prime Minister, who is appointed by the President and is the member of the National Assembly best able to command a majority in the Assembly. The President appoints other ministers, on the recommendation of the Prime Minister.

### Defence

The country has no standing defence forces, although there is a special 1,300-strong police mobile unit to ensure internal security. Government expenditure on defence in the financial year 1992/93 totalled Rs 180.1m.

### Economic Affairs

In 1993, according to estimates by the World Bank, Mauritius' gross national product (GNP), measured at average 1991–93 prices, was US $3,309m., equivalent to $2,980 per head. During 1985–93, it was estimated, GNP per head increased, in real terms, by 5.8% per year. Over the same period the population increased by an annual average of 1.1%. Mauritius' gross domestic product (GDP) increased, in real terms, by an annual average of 6.2% in 1980–92 and by 5.0% in 1993.

Agriculture (including hunting, forestry and fishing) contributed an estimated 10.0% of GDP, and engaged 14.8% of the employed labour force, in 1993. The principal cash crops are sugar cane (raw sugar and molasses accounted for 25.5% of total export earnings in 1993), tea and tobacco. Food crops include potatoes and maize. Poultry farming is also important. During 1980–92 agricultural GDP increased by an annual average of 2.1% in real terms.

Industry (including mining, manufacturing, construction and power) contributed an estimated 32.6% of GDP in 1993, and engaged 36.9% of the employed labour force in that year. During 1980–92 industrial GDP increased, in real terms, by an annual average of 9.2%. Mining is negligible, accounting for less than 1% of employment and GDP.

Manufacturing contributed an estimated 22.3% of GDP, and engaged 29.0% of the employed labour force, in 1993. The principal branches of manufacturing, based on the value of output, in 1990 were wearing apparel (accounting for 38.0% of the total) and food products (30.6%). Clothing (excluding footwear) provided 51.2% of total export earnings in 1992. The Export Processing Zone (EPZ) processes imported raw materials to produce goods for the export market: the principal EPZ products are textiles and clothing, while other important products include electrical components and diamonds. Manufacturing in the EPZ provided 14.4% of GDP in 1988. The non-EPZ sector, excluding sugar-milling, contributed 7.8% of GDP, and its output grew by 6%, in 1988. During 1980–92 manufacturing GDP increased by an annual average of 10.1%.

Electric energy is derived principally from hydroelectric and thermal (oil-fired) power stations; bagasse (a by-product of sugar cane) is also used as fuel for generating electricity: in 1992 a programme was initiated to enable Mauritius eventually to derive 15% of its energy requirements from bagasse. Imports of petroleum products comprised about 5.8% of the value of merchandise imports in 1993.

The services sector contributed an estimated 57.4% of GDP in 1993, and engaged 47.7% of the employed labour force. Tourism is the third most important source of revenue, after agriculture and manufacturing. In 1993 the number of tourists increased to 375,000 from 335,400 in 1992, when receipts from tourism totalled Rs 4,400m. An 'offshore' banking sector and a stock exchange were inaugurated in 1989. The GDP of the services sector increased by an annual average of 5.6% in 1980–92.

In 1993 Mauritius recorded a visible trade deficit of US $254.2m., and there was a deficit of $92.0m. on the current account of the balance of payments. In 1993 the principal source of imports (13.5%) was South Africa; other major suppliers were France, the United Kingdom and Japan. The principal market for exports (taking 32.4% of exports in that year) was the United Kingdom; other significant purchasers were France and the USA. The principal domestic exports in 1993 were clothing and raw sugar. The principal imports in that year were textile yarn and fabrics, petroleum products, industrial machinery and motor vehicles.

In the financial year ending 30 June 1993 there was an estimated budgetary surplus of Rs 24.7m. Mauritius' external debt totalled US $999m. at the end of 1993, of which $717m. was long-term public debt. In that year the cost of debt-servicing was equivalent to 6.0% of the value of exports of goods and services. The annual rate of inflation averaged 9.3% in 1981–92. The average rise in consumer prices was 4.6% in 1992, but increased to 10.6% in 1993, as a consequence of the removal of government subsidies on flour and rice imports. The inflation rate declined to 7.4% in 1994. It was estimated that only 2% of the labour force were unemployed in 1991.

Mauritius is a member of the Indian Ocean Commission (IOC, see p. 239), which aims to promote regional economic co-operation.

Mauritius' economy was traditionally dependent on sugar production, and economic growth was therefore vulnerable to adverse climatic conditions and changes in international prices for sugar. However, since the 1980s the Government has pursued a successful policy of diversification, encouraging labour-intensive manufacturing (particularly of clothing) for export, and extensive reforms have been implemented with IMF support. As a result, a high rate of economic growth was achieved, but by the early 1990s this had led to an increase in the rate of inflation, shortages of labour, and industrial pollution. Port Louis has been established as a free port. In April 1993 the Government initiated a three-year economic development plan, with the objective of achieving further diversification and modernization of the economy. The plan included measures that were designed to promote foreign investment, to increase export revenue and to reduce the rate of inflation. In 1986 controls on the movement of foreign exchange were relaxed, as part of a strategy to establish Mauritius as an international financial centre, with the ancillary aim of attracting capital from Hong Kong, after that territory's return to Chinese sovereignty in 1997.

### Social Welfare

The social infrastructure includes a well-developed public health service, with (in 1993) 14 hospitals, 29 health centres, 126 primary care units, 10 maternal and child health centres, 142 vaccination centres and 33 government dental clinics. In

MAURITIUS

*Introductory Survey, Statistical Survey*

the private sector there were nine clinics providing in-patient and out-patient care. In 1993 there were 1,100 physicians, 130 dentists, and 2,732 nurses and midwives working in Mauritius. Health services are provided free of charge by the Government and are accessible to all the population. Relief is payable to unemployed heads of families under the Unemployment Hardship Relief Scheme. The Social Aid Scheme provides means-tested benefit and a monthly allowance for families with three children under 15 years of age. A national pension scheme was introduced in 1978. Of total expenditure by the central Government (excluding transfers to local government) in the financial year 1992/93, Rs 1,145.8m. (9.8%) was for health, and a further Rs 1,966.2m. (16.8%) for social security and welfare.

### Education

Educational standards are relatively high, and in 1990, according to census results, the average rate of adult illiteracy was only 20.1% (males 14.8%; females 25.3%), although education is not compulsory. Primary education begins at five years of age and lasts for six years. Secondary education, beginning at the age of 11, lasts for up to seven years, comprising a first cycle of three years and a second of four years. Primary and secondary education are available free of charge. In 1991 an estimated 89% of children in the relevant age-group (males 87%; females 90%) were attending primary school. In the same year the number of children attending secondary schools was equivalent to 54% of the appropriate age-group (males 52%; females 56%). Control of the large private sector in secondary education was indirectly assumed by the Government in 1977. The University of Mauritius, founded in 1965, had 2,161 students in 1993/94; in addition many students receive further education abroad. Of total expenditure by the central Government (excluding transfers to local government) in 1992/93, Rs 1,810.3m. (15.5%) was for education.

### Public Holidays

**1995:** 1–2 January (New Year), 31 January (Chinese Spring Festival), 3 March* (Id al-Fitr, end of Ramadan), 12 March (National Day), 14 April (Good Friday), 1 May (Labour Day), 1 November (All Saints' Day), 25 December (Christmas Day) (also the Hindu festivals of Thaipoosam Cavadee, Maha Shivaratree, Ougadi, Ganesh Chaturti and Divali).

**1996:** 1–2 January (New Year), 19 February (Chinese Spring Festival), 21 Feb.* (Id al-Fitr, end of Ramadan), 12 March (National Day), 5 April (Good Friday), 1 May (Labour Day), 1 November (All Saints' Day), 25 December (Christmas Day) (also the Hindu festivals of Thaipoosam Cavadee, Maha Shivaratree, Ougadi, Ganesh Chaturti and Divali).

* This holiday is dependent on the Islamic lunar calendar and may vary by one or two days from the dates given.

### Weights and Measures

The metric system is in standard use.

# Statistical Survey

Source (unless otherwise stated): Central Statistical Office, Toorawa Centre, cnr Sir Seewoosagur Ramgoolam and J. Mosque Sts, Port Louis; tel. 2122316.

## Area and Population

### AREA, POPULATION AND DENSITY

| | |
|---|---|
| Area (sq km) | 2,040* |
| Population (census results) | |
| 2 July 1983† | |
|   Males | 499,360 |
|   Females | 502,818 |
|   Total | 1,002,178 |
| 1 July 1990‡ | 1,058,942 |
| Population (official estimates at mid-year)§ | |
| 1991 | 1,070,128 |
| 1992 | 1,084,000 |
| 1993 | 1,098,000 |
| Density (per sq km) at mid-1993§ | 557.6 |

* 788 sq miles.
† Including an adjustment of 1,746 for underenumeration.
‡ Including an adjustment of 2,115 for underenumeration on the island of Mauritius (enumerated total 1,022,456, comprising 510,676 males and 511,780 females). The population of the island of Rodrigues was 34,204 (males 17,084; females 17,120).
§ Islands of Mauritius and Rodrigues only (area 1,969 sq km, population 1,058,775 at 1990 census).

### ISLANDS

| | | Population | |
|---|---|---|---|
| | Area (sq km) | 2 July 1983 Census* | 1 July 1990 Census† |
| Mauritius | 1,865 | 968,609‡ | 1,024,571‡ |
| Rodrigues | 104 | 33,082 | 34,204 |
| Other islands | 71 | 487 | 167 |

* Figures relate to the *de facto* population.
† Figures relate to the *de jure* population.
‡ Including adjustment for underenumeration.

### ETHNIC GROUPS

Island of Mauritius, mid-1982: 664,480 Indo-Mauritians (507,985 Hindus, 156,495 Muslims), 264,537 general population (incl. Creole and Franco-Mauritian communities), 20,669 Chinese.

### LANGUAGE GROUPS (census of 1 July 1990)*

| | |
|---|---|
| Arabic | 1,686 |
| Bhojpuri | 343,832 |
| Chinese | 17,652 |
| Creole | 379,288 |
| English | 888 |
| French | 22,367 |
| Hindi | 38,181 |
| Marathi | 17,732 |
| Tamil | 47,953 |
| Telegu | 21,033 |
| Urdu | 45,311 |
| Other languages | 120,737 |
| **Total** | **1,056,660** |

* Figures refer to the usual languages spoken by the population on the islands of Mauritius and Rodrigues only. The data exclude an adjustment for underenumeration. The adjusted total was 1,058,775.

### PRINCIPAL TOWNS (estimated population at mid-1993)

| | | | |
|---|---|---|---|
| Port Louis (capital) | 143,509 | Curepipe | 75,483 |
| Beau Bassin/Rose Hill | 95,140 | Quatre Bornes | 72,402 |
| Vacoas-Phoenix | 93,288 | | |

# MAURITIUS

## BIRTHS, MARRIAGES AND DEATHS*

|  | Registered live births | | Registered marriages | | Registered deaths | |
|---|---|---|---|---|---|---|
|  | Number | Rate (per 1,000) | Number | Rate (per 1,000) | Number | Rate (per 1,000) |
| 1990 | 22,369 | 21.1 | 11,425 | 10.8 | 7,031 | 6.6 |
| 1991 | 22,197 | 20.7 | 11,295 | 10.6 | 7,027 | 6.6 |
| 1992 | 22,902 | 21.1 | 11,408 | 10.5 | 7,023 | 6.5 |
| 1993 | 22,329 | 20.3 | 11,579 | 10.5 | 7,433 | 6.8 |

* Figures refer to the islands of Mauritius and Rodrigues only. The data are tabulated by year of registration, rather than by year of occurrence.

## EMPLOYMENT (persons aged 12 years and over)

|  | 1991 | 1992 | 1993 |
|---|---|---|---|
| Agriculture, hunting, forestry and fishing | 72,000 | 71,500 | 71,000 |
| Mining and quarrying | 1,000 | 1,200 | 1,200 |
| Manufacturing | 139,400 | 141,300 | 139,100 |
| Electricity, gas and water | 3,400 | 3,400 | 3,500 |
| Construction | 30,700 | 31,700 | 32,900 |
| Trade, restaurants and hotels | 56,900 | 61,300 | 66,800 |
| Transport, storage and communications | 31,000 | 33,500 | 34,700 |
| Financing, insurance, real estate and business services | 12,100 | 12,900 | 14,100 |
| Community, social and personal services | 105,200 | 107,800 | 113,200 |
| Activities not adequately defined | 4,400 | 3,600 | 3,000 |
| **Total employed** | **456,100** | **468,200** | **479,500** |
| Males | 303,400 | 310,100 | 314,500 |
| Females | 152,700 | 158,100 | 165,000 |

# Agriculture

## PRINCIPAL CROPS ('000 metric tons)

|  | 1991 | 1992 | 1993* |
|---|---|---|---|
| Maize | 2 | 2 | 2 |
| Potatoes | 16 | 19 | 20 |
| Coconuts | 2 | 2 | 2 |
| Tomatoes | 9 | 10 | 11 |
| Sugar cane | 6,430 | 5,650 | 6,300 |
| Bananas | 6 | 9 | 9 |
| Tobacco (leaves) | 1 | 1 | 1 |
| Groundnuts (in shell) | 1 | 1 | 1 |

* FAO estimates.

Source: FAO, *Production Yearbook*.

Tea (made) ('000 metric tons): 5.9 in 1991; 5.8 in 1992; 5.9 in 1993 (Source: International Tea Committee).

## LIVESTOCK ('000 head, year ending September)

|  | 1991 | 1992 | 1993* |
|---|---|---|---|
| Cattle | 34* | 33 | 34 |
| Pigs | 14 | 14 | 14 |
| Sheep | 6 | 7 | 7 |
| Goats* | 96 | 95 | 95 |

* FAO estimate(s).

Source: FAO, *Production Yearbook*.

## LIVESTOCK PRODUCTS ('000 metric tons)

|  | 1991 | 1992 | 1993* |
|---|---|---|---|
| Meat | 15 | 14 | 14 |
| Cows' milk* | 25 | 25 | 25 |
| Hen eggs* | 4.2 | 4.3 | 44 |

* FAO estimates.

Source: FAO, *Production Yearbook*.

# Forestry

## ROUNDWOOD REMOVALS ('000 cubic metres, excluding bark)

|  | 1990 | 1991 | 1992 |
|---|---|---|---|
| Sawlogs, veneer logs and logs for sleepers | 6 | 9 | 7 |
| Other industrial wood | 5 | 5 | 3 |
| Fuel wood | 16 | 3 | 2 |
| **Total** | **27** | **17** | **12** |

Source: FAO, *Yearbook of Forest Products*.

## SAWNWOOD PRODUCTION ('000 cubic metres)

|  | 1990 | 1991 | 1992 |
|---|---|---|---|
| **Total** | 4 | 5 | 4 |

Source: FAO, *Yearbook of Forest Products*.

# Fishing

('000 metric tons, live weight)

|  | 1990 | 1991 | 1992 |
|---|---|---|---|
| Emperors (Scavengers) | 3.7 | 4.0 | 5.3 |
| Skipjack tuna | 4.1 | 6.5 | 6.0 |
| Yellowfin tuna | 1.4 | 2.7 | 2.2 |
| Other fishes (incl. unspecified) | 5.1 | 5.2 | 5.2 |
| Crustaceans and molluscs | 0.4 | 0.4 | 0.5 |
| **Total catch** | **14.7** | **18.9** | **19.2** |

Source: FAO, *Yearbook of Fishery Statistics*.

# Industry

## SELECTED PRODUCTS (metric tons, unless otherwise indicated)

|  | 1990 | 1991 | 1992 |
|---|---|---|---|
| Raw sugar | 624,302 | 611,340 | 643,168 |
| Molasses | 168,023 | 174,933 | 173,000 |
| Manufactured tea | 5,751 | 5,918 | 5,828 |
| Beer and stout (hectolitres) | 281,243 | 291,453 | 295,100 |
| Electric energy (million kWh) | 667 | 737 | n.a. |

**Rum** (hectolitres): 53,000 in 1987; 59,000 in 1988; 64,000 in 1989 (Source: UN, *Industrial Statistics Yearbook*).

**Ethyl alcohol** (hectolitres): 22,292 in 1987; 29,000 in 1988; 26,000 in 1989 (Source: mainly UN, *Industrial Statistics Yearbook*).

# MAURITIUS

## Finance

**CURRENCY AND EXCHANGE RATES**

**Monetary Units**
100 cents = 1 Mauritian rupee.

**Sterling and Dollar Equivalents** (31 December 1994)
£1 sterling = 27.95 rupees;
US $1 = 17.86 rupees;
1,000 Mauritian rupees = £35.78 = $55.98.

**Average Exchange Rate** (Mauritian rupees per US $)
1992   15.563
1993   17.648
1994   17.960

**BUDGET** (million rupees, year ending 30 June)*

| Revenue† | 1990/91 | 1991/92 | 1992/93 |
|---|---|---|---|
| Taxation | 9,516.7 | 9,957.1 | 11,013.8 |
| Taxes on income, profits and capital gains | 1,387.1 | 1,565.4 | 1,464.7 |
| Individual taxes | 544.1 | 552.2 | 696.8 |
| Corporate taxes | 843.0 | 1,013.2 | 767.9 |
| Social security contributions | 419.1 | 574.3 | 690.5 |
| Taxes on property | 609.8 | 568.7 | 716.1 |
| Taxes on financial and capital transactions | 599.3 | 559.1 | 704.8 |
| Domestic taxes on goods and services | 2,297.9 | 2,585.3 | 2,939.8 |
| General sales, turnover or value-added taxes | 846.0 | 951.2 | 1,044.5 |
| Excises | 831.3 | 886.2 | 1,075.6 |
| Alcoholic beverages | 492.6 | 536.7 | 620.0 |
| Taxes on specific services | 471.5 | 576.6 | 573.7 |
| Taxes on international trade and transactions | 4,719.2 | 4,587.6 | 5,119.1 |
| Import duties | 4,247.9 | 4,159.5 | 4,685.2 |
| Customs duties | 2,789.4 | 2,708.6 | 3,222.4 |
| Other import charges | 1,458.5 | 1,450.9 | 1,462.8 |
| Export duties | 427.6 | 416.3 | 433.8 |
| Other current revenue | 598.2 | 1,420.9 | 1,366.4 |
| Entrepreneurial and property income | 248.1 | 991.4 | 957.2 |
| From non-financial public enterprises and public financial institutions | 213.1 | 934.8 | 896.3 |
| Administrative fees and charges, non-industrial and incidental sales | 260.1 | 314.8 | 306.4 |
| **Total** | 10,114.9 | 11,378.0 | 12,363.2 |

| Expenditure‡ | 1990/91 | 1991/92 | 1992/93 |
|---|---|---|---|
| General public services | 1,042.8 | 1,226.1 | 1,240.3 |
| Defence | 153.0 | 175.6 | 180.1 |
| Public order and safety | 901.9 | 882.9 | 1,093.8 |
| Education | 1,444.0 | 1,684.0 | 1,810.3 |
| Health | 870.6 | 930.9 | 1,145.8 |
| Social security and welfare | 1,458.4 | 1,764.7 | 1,966.2 |
| Housing and community amenities | 328.3 | 500.4 | 738.7 |
| Recreational, cultural and religious affairs and services | 164.5 | 340.3 | 234.4 |
| Economic affairs and services | 1,489.5 | 1,880.8 | 1,886.1 |
| Agriculture, forestry, fishing and hunting | 623.9 | 683.0 | 715.2 |
| Mining, manufacturing and construction | 35.3 | 40.5 | 67.1 |
| Transport and communication | 433.1 | 689.4 | 665.2 |
| Other purposes | 2,090.5 | 2,131.9 | 1,846.1 |
| Public debt interest | 1,564.0 | 1,469.8 | 1,182.3 |
| Transfers to local government | 353.6 | 409.6 | 437.5 |
| Development works | 100.2 | 114.0 | 106.5 |
| **Total** | 9,943.5 | 11,517.6 | 12,141.8 |
| Current | 8,218.2 | 9,246.4 | 9,779.5 |
| Capital | 1,725.3 | 2,271.2 | 2,362.3 |

* Figures represent a consolidation of the General Budget, the National Pensions Fund and the operations of 13 extrabudgetary units of the central Government. The accounts of local government councils are excluded.
† Excluding grants received from abroad (million rupees): 25.2 in 1991/92; 78.0 in 1992/93.
‡ Excluding net lending (million rupees): 244.0 in 1991/92; 274.7 in 1992/93.

**INTERNATIONAL RESERVES** (US $ million at 31 December)

|  | 1992 | 1993 | 1994 |
|---|---|---|---|
| Gold* | 4.2 | 3.9 | 4.0 |
| IMF special drawing rights | 24.3 | 28.9 | 31.2 |
| Reserve position in IMF | 8.6 | 10.1 | 10.7 |
| Foreign exchange | 787.3 | 718.1 | 705.7 |
| **Total** | 824.3 | 760.9 | 751.6 |

* Valued at market-related prices.
Source: IMF, *International Financial Statistics*.

**MONEY SUPPLY** (million rupees at 31 December)

|  | 1991 | 1992 | 1993 |
|---|---|---|---|
| Currency outside banks | 3,407.5 | 3,820.1 | 4,230.9 |
| Demand deposits at deposit money banks | 3,262.8 | 3,383.4 | 3,188.3 |
| **Total money** (incl. others) | 6,676.5 | 7,209.2 | 7,423.2 |

Source: IMF, *International Financial Statistics*.

**COST OF LIVING** (Consumer Price Index, average of monthly figures. Base: June 1992 = 100)

|  | 1991* | 1992 | 1993 |
|---|---|---|---|
| Food | 149.2 | 102.4 | 116.5 |
| Fuel and light | 118.3 | 103.2 | 107.4 |
| Rent | 126.4 | 102.9 | 106.4 |
| **All items** (incl. others) | 149.5 | 103.5 | 114.4 |

* Base: 1987 = 100.

# MAURITIUS

*Statistical Survey*

## NATIONAL ACCOUNTS (million rupees in current prices)
### Components of the Gross National Product

|  | 1991 | 1992 | 1993* |
|---|---|---|---|
| Compensation of employees | 17,228 | 19,455 | 22,800 |
| Operating surplus } | 18,720 | 20,960 | 23,550 |
| Consumption of fixed capital } |  |  |  |
| **Gross domestic product (GDP) at factor cost** | 35,948 | 40,415 | 46,350 |
| Indirect taxes | 7,221 | 7.765 | 8,630 |
| *Less* Subsidies | 403 | 465 | 330 |
| **GDP in purchasers' values** | 42,766 | 47,715 | 54,650 |
| Factor income received from abroad | 1,292 } | 180 | 50 |
| *Less* Factor income paid abroad | 1,203 } |  |  |
| **Gross national product (GNP) at market prices** | 42,855 | 47,895 | 54,700 |

### Expenditure on the Gross Domestic Product

|  | 1991 | 1992 | 1993* |
|---|---|---|---|
| Government final consumption expenditure | 5,005 | 5,560 | 6,600 |
| Private final consumption expenditure | 27,500 | 30,156 | 34,400 |
| Increase in stocks | −453 | 140 | 310 |
| Gross fixed capital formation | 12,385 | 13,630 | 15,600 |
| **Total domestic expenditure** | 44,437 | 49,486 | 56,910 |
| Exports of goods and services | 27,861 | 29,902 | 33,350 |
| *Less* Imports of goods and services | 29,532 | 31,673 | 35,610 |
| **GDP in purchasers' values** | 42,766 | 47,715 | 54,650 |
| **GDP at constant 1987 prices** | 29,367 | 31,164 | 32,721 |

### Gross Domestic Product by Economic Activity (at factor cost)

|  | 1991 | 1992 | 1993* |
|---|---|---|---|
| Agriculture, forestry, hunting and fishing | 4,093 | 4,495 | 4,625 |
| Mining and quarrying | 45 | 55 | 70 |
| Manufacturing | 8,274 | 9,200 | 10,315 |
| Electricity, gas and water | 775 | 975 | 1,240 |
| Construction | 2,590 | 3,005 | 3,500 |
| Trade, restaurants and hotels | 6,100 | 6,900 | 8,150 |
| Transport, storage and communications | 4,200 | 4,810 | 5,550 |
| Financing, insurance, real estate and business services | 4,354 | 4,825 | 5,500 |
| Government services | 3,640 | 3,985 | 4,825 |
| Other services | 1,877 | 2,165 | 2,575 |
| **Total** | 35,948 | 40,415 | 46,350 |

* Figures are provisional.

## BALANCE OF PAYMENTS (US $ million)

|  | 1991 | 1992 | 1993 |
|---|---|---|---|
| Merchandise exports f.o.b. | 1,215.1 | 1,302.6 | 1,304.4 |
| Merchandise imports f.o.b. | −1,419.1 | −1,473.4 | −1,558.6 |
| **Trade balance** | −204.0 | −170.9 | −254.2 |
| Exports of services | 566.6 | 609.6 | 609.9 |
| Imports of services | −467.9 | −543.3 | −547.4 |
| Other income received | 82.5 | 91.0 | 70.0 |
| Other income paid | −76.9 | −80.1 | −66.4 |
| Private unrequited transfers (net) | 79.5 | 86.6 | 91.7 |
| Official unrequited transfers (net) | 1.9 | 5.4 | 4.4 |
| **Current balance** | −18.2 | −1.5 | −92.0 |
| Direct investment (net) | 8.1 | −28.6 | −25.5 |
| Portfolio investment (net) | −0.4 | — | −2.2 |
| Other capital (net) | 34.2 | 13.8 | 39.9 |
| Net errors and omissions | 167.2 | 59.7 | 86.8 |
| **Overall balance** | 190.8 | 43.3 | 7.0 |

Source: IMF, *International Financial Statistics*.

# External Trade

## PRINCIPAL COMMODITIES (million rupees)

| Imports c.i.f.* | 1991 | 1992 | 1993 |
|---|---|---|---|
| Dairy products | 547 | 598 | 667 |
| Rice | 314 | 277 | 464 |
| Petroleum products | 1,783 | 1,766 | 1,771 |
| Textile yarn and thread | 1,717 | 1,825 | 2,256 |
| Textile fabrics | 2,910 | 3,174 | 4,300 |
| Cement | 523 | 554 | 630 |
| Iron and steel goods | 700 | 689 | 777 |
| Power-generating machinery | 843 | 531 | 179 |
| Machinery for particular industries | 1,149 | 977 | 1,601 |
| General industrial machinery | 739 | 793 | 918 |
| Road motor vehicles | 1,188 | 1,310 | 1,396 |
| **Total** (incl. others) | 24,383 | 25,313 | 30,342 |

| Exports f.o.b.† | 1991 | 1992 | 1993 |
|---|---|---|---|
| Sugar, raw | 5,298 | 5,668 | 5,770 |
| Molasses | 96 | 91 | 93 |
| Tea | 83 | 95 | 113 |
| **Total** (incl. others) | 5,948 | 6,432 | 6,622 |

* Figures are provisional.
† Figures refer to domestic exports, excluding exports (mainly clothing) from the Export Processing Zone (EPZ), totalling (in million rupees): 12,136 in 1991; 13,081 in 1992; 15,821 in 1993.

## PRINCIPAL TRADING PARTNERS (million rupees)

| Imports c.i.f.* | 1991 | 1992 | 1993 |
|---|---|---|---|
| Australia | 795 | 804 | 897 |
| Bahrain | 628 | 240 | 13 |
| Belgium | 306 | 362 | 747 |
| China, People's Repub. | 949 | 844 | 1,276 |
| France | 3,283 | 3,372 | 3,831 |
| Germany | 1,358 | 1,249 | 1,457 |
| Hong Kong | 1,068 | 1,082 | 1,393 |
| India | 1,115 | 1,323 | 1,773 |
| Indonesia | 144 | 227 | 403 |
| Italy | 781 | 744 | 1,026 |
| Japan | 1,770 | 2,176 | 1,792 |
| Korea, Repub. | 277 | 367 | 447 |
| Malaysia | 539 | 664 | 835 |
| New Zealand | 337 | 337 | 361 |
| Pakistan | 309 | 305 | 462 |
| Singapore | 730 | 808 | 894 |
| South Africa | 2,870 | 3,272 | 4,112 |
| Switzerland | 349 | 433 | 556 |
| Taiwan | 1,104 | 948 | 1,262 |
| United Kingdom | 1,677 | 1,834 | 2,143 |
| USA | 530 | 553 | 707 |
| **Total** (incl. others) | 24,363 | 25,313 | 30,542 |

| Exports f.o.b.* | 1991 | 1992 | 1993 |
|---|---|---|---|
| Belgium | 328 | 357 | 496 |
| France | 3,727 | 4,207 | 4,709 |
| Germany | 2,055 | 1,778 | 1,633 |
| Italy | 918 | 937 | 917 |
| Netherlands | 368 | 368 | 480 |
| Réunion | 364 | 453 | 483 |
| United Kingdom | 6,750 | 6,992 | 7,440 |
| USA | 2,209 | 2,500 | 4,117 |
| **Total** (incl. others) | 18,700 | 20,072 | 22,992 |

* Figures are provisional.

MAURITIUS

*Statistical Survey*

## Transport

**ROAD TRAFFIC**

|  | 1991 | 1992 | 1993 |
|---|---|---|---|
| Private vehicles: |  |  |  |
|   Cars | 30,882 | 32,751 | 34,449 |
|   Motorcycles and mopeds | 68,090 | 77,227 | 85,540 |
| Commercial vehicles: |  |  |  |
|   Buses | 2,021 | 2,097 | 2,217 |
|   Taxis | 3,965 | 4,014 | 4,050 |
|   Goods vehicles | 27,425 | 30,952 | 33,829 |
| Government vehicles | 3,912 | 4,136 | 4,378 |

Source: Ministry of Works, Port Louis.

**SHIPPING**

**Merchant Fleet** (vessels registered at 30 June)

|  | 1990 | 1991 | 1992 |
|---|---|---|---|
| Displacement ('000 grt) | 99 | 82 | 122 |

Source: UN, *Statistical Yearbook*.

**Sea-borne Freight Traffic** ('000 metric tons)

|  | 1991 | 1992 | 1993 |
|---|---|---|---|
| Goods unloaded | 2,024 | 2,232 | 2,375 |
| Goods loaded | 851 | 956 | 830 |

Source: Ministry of Works, Port Louis.

**CIVIL AVIATION** (traffic)

|  | 1991 | 1992 | 1993 |
|---|---|---|---|
| Aircraft landings | 5,265 | 5,322 | 5,577 |
| Passenger arrivals | 426,680 | 475,920 | 526,000* |
| Freight unloaded (metric tons) | 11,198 | 11,200 | 11,066 |
| Freight loaded (metric tons) | 18,191 | 15,704 | 14,674 |

* Provisional.

Source: Ministry of Works, Port Louis.

## Tourism

**FOREIGN TOURIST ARRIVALS**

| Country of Residence | 1991 | 1992 | 1993* |
|---|---|---|---|
| France | 58,370 | 74,300 | 86,300 |
| Germany | 24,140 | 29,800 | 40,600 |
| Italy | 13,290 | 14,990 | 15,000 |
| Madagascar | 6,010 | 7,260 | 7,600 |
| Réunion | 77,890 | 81,260 | 89,000 |
| South Africa | 43,020 | 39,790 | 42,000 |
| Switzerland | 8,930 | 10,150 | 11,000 |
| United Kingdom | 20,660 | 24,510 | 29,100 |
| **Total** (incl. others) | 300,670 | 335,400 | 375,000 |

* Provisional.

## Communications Media

|  | 1990 | 1991 | 1992 |
|---|---|---|---|
| Radio receivers ('000 in use) | 385 | 390 | 395 |
| Television receivers ('000 in use) | 233 | 236 | 239 |
| Book production*: |  |  |  |
|   Titles | 75 | 56 | 80 |
|   Copies ('000) | 216 | 157 | 99 |
| Daily newspapers: |  |  |  |
|   Number | 7 | n.a. | 6 |
|   Average circulation ('000 copies) | 80 | n.a. | 80 |
| Non-daily newspapers: |  |  |  |
|   Number | 24 | n.a. | 25 |
|   Average circulation ('000 copies) | 75 | n.a. | n.a. |
| Other periodicals: |  |  |  |
|   Number | 48 | n.a. | 62 |

* Including pamphlets (22 titles and 109,000 copies 1990; 20 titles and 92,000 copies in 1991; 24 titles and 14,000 copies in 1992).

Source: UNESCO, *Statistical Yearbook*.

**Telephones** ('000 main lines in use): 53 in 1989; 60 in 1990; 65 (estimate) in 1991 (Source: UN *Statistical Yearbook*).

## Education

(1993)

|  | Institutions | Students |
|---|---|---|
| Primary | 281 | 125,543 |
| Secondary | 123 | 87,661 |
| University | 1 | 2,161 |
| Institute of Education | 1 | 2,645 |
| Lycée Polytechnique | 1 | 395 |

Teachers (1991): Primary 6,369; General Secondary 3,949 (Source: UNESCO, *Statistical Yearbook*).

# Directory

## The Constitution

The Mauritius Independence Order, which established a self-governing state, came into force on 12 March 1968, and was subsequently amended. Constitutional amendments providing for the adoption of republican status were approved by the Legislative Assembly (henceforth known as the National Assembly) on 10 December 1991, and came into effect on 12 March 1992. The main provisions of the revised Constitution are listed below:

### HEAD OF STATE

The Head of State is the President of the Republic, who is elected by a simple majority of the National Assembly for a five-year term of office. The President appoints the Prime Minister (in whom executive power is vested) and, on the latter's recommendation, other ministers.

### COUNCIL OF MINISTERS

The Council of Ministers, which is headed by the Prime Minister, is appointed by the President and is responsible to the National Assembly.

### THE NATIONAL ASSEMBLY

The National Assembly, which has a term of five years, comprises the Speaker, 62 members elected by universal adult suffrage, a maximum of eight additional members and the Attorney-General (if not an elected member). The island of Mauritius is divided into 20 three-member constituencies for legislative elections. Rodrigues returns two members to the National Assembly, one of whom is designated Minister for Rodrigues. The official language of the National Assembly is English, but any member may address the Speaker in French.

## The Government

### HEAD OF STATE

**President:** CASSAM UTEEM (took office 30 June 1992).
**Vice-President:** Sir RABINDRAH GHURBURRUN.

### COUNCIL OF MINISTERS
(May 1995)

A coalition of the Mouvement Socialiste Mauricien (MSM), the Renouveau Militant Mauricien (RMM), the Parti Mauricien Social-Démocrate (PMSD) and the Mouvement des Travaillistes Démocrates (MTD). The Organisation du Peuple Rodriguais (OPR) is also represented.

**Prime Minister, Minister of Defence and Internal Security, and Reform Institutions and the Outer Islands:** Sir ANEROOD JUGNAUTH (MSM).
**Deputy Prime Minister and Minister of Economic Planning and Development, Minister of Information and of Internal and External Communications:** Dr PARAMHANSA NABABSING (RMM).
**Minister of Health:** JEAN RÉGIS FINETTE (MSM).
**Minister of Trade and Shipping:** DWARKANATH GUNGAH (MSM).
**Minister of Women's Rights, Child Development and Family Welfare:** Mrs SHEILABHAI BAPPOO (MSM).
**Minister of External Affairs:** RAMDATHSING JADDOO (MSM).
**Minister of Arts, Culture and Youth Development:** MOOKHESSWUR CHOONEE (MSM).
**Minister for Rodrigues:** LOUIS SERGE CLAIR (OPR).
**Minister of Housing, Lands and Town and Country Planning:** LOUIS AMÉDÉE DARGA (RMM).
**Minister of Agriculture and Natural Resources:** KEERTEE COOMAR RUHEE (RMM).
**Minister of Local Government:** PREMDUT KOONJOO (RMM).
**Minister of Labour and Industrial Relations:** KARL AUGUSTE OFFMANN (MSM).
**Minister of Sports and Leisure:** MICHAEL GLOVER (MSM).
**Minister of Co-operatives and Handicraft:** JAGDISHWAR GOBURDHUN (MSM).
**Minister of Works:** ANIL KUMAR BACHOO (MTD).
**Minister of Manpower Resources and Vocational and Technical Training:** NOEL AH-QWET LEE CHEONG LEM (RMM).
**Minister of the Environment and Quality of Life:** BASHIR AHMUD KHODABUX (RMM).
**Minister of Social Security and National Solidarity:** DHARMANAND GOOPT FOKEER (RMM).
**Minister of Education and Science:** ARMOOGUM PARSURAMEN (MSM).
**Minister of Civil Service Affairs and Employment:** ASHOK KUMAR JUGNAUTH (MSM).
**Minister of Finance:** RAMAKRISHNA SITHANEN (MSM).
**Minister of Energy, Water Resources and Postal Services, and of Scientific Research and Technology:** Dr AHMUD SWALAY KASENALLY (RMM).
**Minister of Industry and Industrial Technology, and of Tourism:** LUC XAVIER DUVAL (PMSD).
**Minister of Fisheries and Marine Resources:** MATHIEU ANGE LACLÉ (RMM).
**Attorney-General and Minister of Justice:** Sir MAURICE RAULT (PMSD).

### MINISTRIES

**Prime Minister's Office:** Government Centre, Port Louis; tel. 2011001; telex 4249; fax 2088619.
**Ministry of Agriculture and Natural Resources:** NPF Bldg, 9th Floor, Port Louis; tel. 2127946; fax 2124427.
**Ministry of Arts, Culture, Leisure and Reform Institutions:** Government Centre, Port Louis; tel. 2012032.
**Ministry of Civil Service Affairs and Employment:** Government Centre, Port Louis; tel. 2011035; fax 2129528.
**Ministry of Co-operatives and Handicraft:** Life Insurance Corpn of India Bldg, 3rd Floor, John Kennedy St, Port Louis; tel. 2084812; fax 2089265.
**Ministry of Economic Planning and Development:** Emmanuel Anquetil Bldg, Sir Seewoosagur Ramgoolam St, Port Louis; tel. 2011576; fax 2124124.
**Ministry of Education and Science:** Sun Trust Bldg, Edith Cavell St, Port Louis; tel. 2128411; fax 2123783.
**Ministry of Energy, Water Resources and Postal Services:** Government Centre, Port Louis; tel. 2011087; fax 2086497.
**Ministry of the Environment and Quality of Life:** Barracks St, Port Louis; tel. 2128332; fax 2129407.
**Ministry of External Affairs:** Government Centre, Port Louis; tel. 2011416; fax 2088087.
**Ministry of Finance:** Government Centre, Port Louis; tel. 2011145; fax 2088622.
**Ministry of Fisheries and Marine Resources:** Port Louis.
**Ministry of Health:** Emmanuel Anquetil Bldg, Sir Seewoosagur Ramgoolam St, Port Louis; tel. 2011910; fax 2080376.
**Ministry of Housing, Lands and Town and Country Planning:** Moorgate House, Port Louis; tel. 2126022; fax 2127482.
**Ministry of Industry and Industrial Technology:** Government Centre, Port Louis; tel. 2011221; fax 2128201.
**Ministry of Information:** Government Centre, Port Louis; tel. 2011278; fax 2088243.
**Ministry of Internal and External Communications:** Emmanuel Anquetil Bldg, 10th Floor, Sir Seewoosagur Ramgoolam St, Port Louis; tel. 2011089; fax 2121673.
**Ministry of Justice:** Jules Koenig St, Port Louis; tel. 2085321.
**Ministry of Labour and Industrial Relations:** Ming Court, cnr Eugène Laurent and GMD Atchia Sts, Port Louis; tel. 2123049; fax 2123070.
**Ministry of Local Government:** Government Centre, Port Louis; tel. 2011215.
**Ministry of Manpower Resources and Vocational and Technical Training:** Jade House, Remy Ollier St, Port Louis; tel. 2421462.
**Ministry for Rodrigues:** Fon Sing Bldg, Edith Cavell St, Port Louis; tel. 2088472; fax 2126329.
**Ministry of Social Security and National Solidarity:** cnr Maillard and Jules Koenig Sts, Port Louis; tel. 2123006.
**Ministry of Tourism:** Emmanuel Anquetil Bldg, Sir Seewoosagur Ramgoolam St, Port Louis; tel. 2012286; fax 2086776.
**Ministry of Trade and Shipping:** Government Centre, Port Louis; tel. 2011067; fax 2126368.

# MAURITIUS

**Ministry of Women's Rights, Child Development and Family Welfare:** Rainbow House, cnr Edith Cavell and Brown Sequard Sts, Port Louis; tel. 2082061; fax 2088250.

**Ministry of Works:** Treasury Bldg, Port Louis; tel. 2080281; fax 2128373.

**Ministry of Youth and Sports:** Emmanuel Anquetil Bldg, Sir Seewoosagur Ramgoolam St, Port Louis; tel. 2011242; fax 2126506.

## Legislature

### NATIONAL ASSEMBLY*

**Speaker:** ISWARDEO SEETARAM.

**General Election, 15 September 1991**

| Party | Seats† |
| --- | --- |
| Mouvement Socialiste Mauricien | 29 |
| Mouvement Militant Mauricien‡ | 26 |
| Mauritius Labour Party | } 3 |
| Parti Mauricien Social-Démocrate | |
| Mouvement des Travaillistes Démocrates | 2 |
| Organisation du Peuple Rodriguais | 2 |

\* The legislature was elected as the Legislative Assembly. It was renamed the National Assembly in accordance with the constitutional amendments that took effect in March 1992.

† Four additional members (unsuccessful candidates who attracted the largest number of votes) were appointed from the MLP/PMSD alliance.

‡ Split in Oct. 1993. The faction supporting the coalition Government was reconstituted in June 1994 as the Renouveau Militant Mauricien.

## Political Organizations

**Comité d'Action Musulman (CAM):** POB 882, Port Louis; f. 1958; Indo-Mauritian Muslim support; Pres. YOUSSUF MOHAMMED.

**Mauritius Labour Party (MLP):** 7 Guy Rozemont Sq., Port Louis; tel. 2126691; f. 1936; Leader Dr NAVIN RAMGOOLAM; Sec.-Gen. JOSEPH TSANG MAN KIN.

**Mouvement des Démocrates Libéraux (MDL):** f. 1994 by VISHNU LUTCHMEENARAIDOO; seeks to replace the MLP in an electoral alliance with the PMSD to contest parl. elections in 1996.

**Mouvement des Travaillistes Démocrates (MTD):** Port Louis; Leader ANIL KUMAR BACHOO.

**Mouvement Militant Mauricien (MMM):** Port Louis; f. 1969; Socialist; Leader PAUL BÉRENGER.

**Mouvement Socialiste Mauricien (MSM):** Port Louis; f. 1983 by breakaway group from MMM; dominant party in subsequent coalition govts; Leader Sir ANEROOD JUGNAUTH; Sec.-Gen. V. SAJADAH.

**Organisation du Peuple Rodriguais (OPR):** Port Mathurin, Rodrigues; represents the interests of Rodrigues; Leader LOUIS SERGE CLAIR.

**Parti Mauricien Social-Démocrate (PMSD):** POB 599, Port Louis; Pres. ALAN DRIVER; Leader LUC XAVIER DUVAL.

**Parti Socialiste Mauricien (PSM):** Port Louis; breakaway faction from the Mauritius Labour Party; joined the MSM in 1983; reconstituted as a separate party in 1988; Leader HARISH BOODHOO.

**Renouveau Militant Mauricien (RMM):** Port Louis; f. 1994 by breakaway faction of Mouvement Militant Mauricien; Chair. DHARMANAND FOKEER; Leader Dr PARAMHANSA (PREM) NABABSING; Gen. Sec. J. BOULLÉ.

**Union Démocratique Mauricienne (UDM):** 10 Barracks St, Port Louis; tel. 2124945; advocates proportional representation; affiliated to International Christian Democrats; Leader GUY OLLIVRY; Sec.-Gen. ELWYN CHUTEL.

Minor left-wing parties include the **Front des Travailleurs Socialistes** and **Lalit**, a Marxist-Leninist party.

## Diplomatic Representation

### EMBASSIES AND HIGH COMMISSIONS IN MAURITIUS

**Australia:** Port Louis; tel. 2081700; telex 4414; fax 2088878; High Commissioner: MARY L. MCCARTER.

**China, People's Republic:** Royal Rd, Belle Rose, Quatre Bornes, Port Louis; tel. 4549111; Ambassador: YANG YIHUAI.

**Egypt:** King George V Ave, Floreal, Port Louis; tel. 6965012; telex 4332; Ambassador: H. ELBITAR.

**France:** St George's St, Port Louis; tel. 2083755; telex 4233; fax 2088145; Ambassador: JOËL DE ZORZI.

**India:** Life Insurance Corporation of India Bldg, President John F. Kennedy St, Port Louis; tel. 2083775; telex 4523; fax 2086859; High Commissioner: SHYAM SARAN.

**Madagascar:** Queen Mary Ave, Floreal, Port Louis; tel. 6865015; Ambassador: C. ZENY.

**Pakistan:** Anglo-Mauritius House, Intendance St, Port Louis; tel. 2126547; telex 4609; fax 2126548; High Commissioner: NASEER MIAN.

**Russia:** Queen Mary Ave, Floreal, POB 509, Port Louis; tel. 6961545; telex 4826; Ambassador: N. KALAEVICH ASSATOUR AGARON.

**South Africa:** Port Louis; High Commissioner: JOHN SUNDE.

**United Kingdom:** POB 1063, Port Louis; tel. 2111361; telex 4861; fax 2111369; High Commissioner: JOHN C. HARRISON.

**USA:** Rogers House, President John F. Kennedy St, Port Louis; tel. 2082347; fax 2089534; Ambassador: LESLIE M. ALEXANDER.

## Judicial System

The laws of Mauritius are derived both from the old French Codes, suitably amended, and from English Law. The Judicial Department consists of the Supreme Court, presided over by the Chief Justice and eight other Judges who are also Judges of the Court of Criminal Appeal and the Court of Civil Appeal, the Intermediate Court, the Industrial Court and 10 District Courts. There is a right of appeal in certain cases to the Judicial Committee of the Privy Council in the United Kingdom.

**Chief Justice:** RAJSOOMER LALLAH.

**Senior Puisne Judge:** J. FORGET.

**Puisne Judges:** A. G. PILLAY, V. BOOLELL, Y. K. J. YEUNG SIK YUEN, K. P. MATADEEN, Mrs R. N. NARAYEN, E. BALANCY, P. LAM SHANG LEEN.

## Religion

At the 1972 census, Hindus comprised 51.0% of the population on the island of Mauritius, with Christians accounting for 31.3%, Muslims 16.6% and Buddhists 0.6%.

### CHRISTIANITY

#### The Anglican Communion

Anglicans in Mauritius are within the Church of the Province of the Indian Ocean, comprising five dioceses (three in Madagascar, one in Mauritius and one in Seychelles). The Archbishop of the Province is the Bishop of Seychelles. In 1983 the Church had 5,438 members in Mauritius.

**Bishop of Mauritius:** Rt Rev. REX DONAT, Bishop's House, Phoenix; tel. 6865158.

#### Presbyterian Church of Mauritius

**Minister:** Pasteur ANDRÉ DE RÉLAND, 11 Poudrière St, Port Louis; tel. 2082386; f. 1814.

#### The Roman Catholic Church

Mauritius comprises a single diocese, directly responsible to the Holy See. At 31 December 1993 there were an estimated 287,853 adherents in the country, representing about 26% of the total population.

**Bishop of Port Louis:** Rt Rev. MAURICE PIAT, Evêché, 13 Mgr Gonin St, Port Louis; tel. 2083068; fax 2086607.

### BAHÁ'Í FAITH

**National Spiritual Assembly:** POB 538, Port Louis; tel. 2122179; mems resident in 190 localities.

### ISLAM

**Mauritius Islamic Mission:** Noor-e-Islam Mosque, Port Louis; Imam S. M. BEEHARRY.

## The Press

### DAILIES

**China Times:** 24 Emmanuel Anquetil St, POB 325, Port Louis; tel. 2403067; f. 1953; Chinese; Editor-in-Chief LONG SIONG AH KENG; circ. 3,000.

**Chinese Daily News:** 32 Rémy Ollier St, POB 316, Port Louis; tel. 2400472; f. 1932; Chinese; Editor-in-Chief WONG YUEN MOY; circ. 5,000.

# MAURITIUS

**L'Express:** 3 Brown Sequard St, POB 247, Port Louis; tel. 2124365; telex 4384; fax 2088174; f. 1963; English and French; Editor-in-Chief PATRICK MICHEL; circ. 30,000.

**Le Mauricien:** 8 St George St, POB 7, Port Louis; tel. 2083251; fax 2087059; f. 1908; English and French; Editor-in-Chief GAËTAN SENEQUE (acting); circ. 30,000.

**Le Socialiste:** Manilall Bldg, 3rd Floor, Brabant St, Port Louis; tel. 2088003; English and French; Editor-in-Chief Dr MONAF KHEDARUN; circ. 6,000.

**The Sun:** 31 Edith Cavell St, Port Louis; tel. 2124820; fax 2089517; English and French; Editor-in-Chief SUBASH GOBIN; circ. 22,000.

### WEEKLIES AND FORTNIGHTLIES

**5-Plus Magazine:** Résidence des Palmiers, 198 Royal Rd, Beau Bassin; tel. 4543353; fax 4543420; f. 1988; English and French; Editor-in-Chief PIERRE BENOÎT; circ. 10,000.

**5-Plus Dimanche:** Résidence des Palmiers, 198 Royal Rd, Beau Bassin; tel. 4543353; fax 4543420; f. 1994; English and French; Editor-in-Chief FINLAY SALESSE; circ. 30,000.

**Business Magazine:** TN Tower, 1st Floor, 13 St George St, Port Louis; tel. 2111925; fax 2111926; f. 1993; English and French; Editor-in-Chief LYNDSAY RIVIÈRE; circ. 6,000.

**Le Croissant:** cnr Velore and Noor Essan Mosque Sts, Port Louis; tel. 2407105; English and French; Editor-in-Chief B. A. OOZEER.

**Le Dimanche:** 5 Jemmapes St, Port Louis; tel. 2121177; f. 1961; English and French; Editor RAYMOND RICHARD NAUVEL; circ. 25,000.

**Impact News:** 6 Grandcourt, Port Louis; tel. 2408567; English and French; Editor-in-Chief CADER SAIB.

**Lalit de Klas:** 153B Royal Rd, G.R.N.W., Port Louis; tel. 2082132; English, French and Creole; Editor ASHOK SUBRON.

**Le Lotus:** 73 Prince of Wales St, Rose Hill; tel. 2084068; English and French; Editor-in-Chief MOGANADEN PILLAY.

**Le Mag:** Industrial Zone, Tombeay Bay; tel. 2471005; fax 2471061; f. 1993; English and French; Editor-in-Chief ALAN GORDON-GENTIL; circ. 8,000.

**Mauritius Times:** 23 Bourbon St, POB 202, Port Louis; tel. 2121313; telex 4409; fax 4643445; f. 1954; English and French; Editor-in-Chief BICKRAMSINGH RAMLALLAH; circ. 15,000.

**Le Message de L'Ahmadiyyat:** POB 6, Rose Hill; English and French; Editor-in-Chief M. A. ZAFRULLAH.

**Le Militant Magazine:** 7 Lord Kitchener St, Port Louis; tel. 2126050; fax 2082291; f. 1989; English and French; Editor-in-Chief MITRADEV PEERTHUM; circ. 2,000.

**Mirror:** 39 Emmanuel Anqueitil St, Port Louis; tel. 2403298; Chinese; Editor-in-Chief NG KEE SIONG; circ. 4,000.

**Le Nouveau Défi:** 43 Lord Kitchener St, Port Louis; tel. 2110843; Editor-in-Chief YVON BRÛLECOEUR.

**Le Nouveau Militant:** 21 Poudrière St, Port Louis; tel. 2126553; fax 2082291; f. 1979; publ. by the Mouvement Militant Mauricien; English and French; Editor-in-Chief J. RAUMIAH.

**Le Rodriguais:** Saint Gabriel, Rodrigues; tel. 8311613; fax 8311484; f. 1989; Creole, English and French; Editor JACQUES EDOUARD; circ. 2,000.

**Star:** 14 Orléans St, Port Louis; tel. 2122736; English and French; Editor-in-Chief Dr HASSAM RUHOMALLY.

**Sunday:** 31 Edith Cavell St, Port Louis; tel. 2089516; fax 2087059; f. 1966; English and French; Editor-in-Chief SUBASH GOBIN.

**Le Trident:** 6 Industrial Zone, Coromandel; tel. and fax 2334430; English and French; Editor-in-Chief P. C. DEWOCHAND.

**La Vie Catholique:** 28 Nicolay Rd, Port Louis; tel. and fax 2420975; f. 1930; English and French; Editor-in-Chief MONIQUE DINAN; circ. 15,000.

**Vision:** Rm 402, 3rd Floor, Chancery House, Lislet Geoffroy St, Port Louis; tel. 2113337; fax 2113339; f. 1994; English and French; Editor-in-Chief SHAFICK OSMAN; circ. 6,000.

**Week-End:** 8 St George St, Port Louis; tel. 2083252; fax 2087059; f. 1966; French and English; Editor-in-Chief GÉRARD CATEAU; circ. 35,000.

**Week-End Scope:** 8 St George St, Port Louis; tel. 2083251; fax 2087059; English and French; Editor-in-Chief AHMAD SALARBUX.

**Weekly:** Lake Thoune Min Bldg, 8 Corderie St, Port Louis; tel. 2127034; English and French; Editor-in-Chief TEKLALL GUNESH.

### OTHER SELECTED PERIODICALS

**Adaava:** 29 Paul and Virginie St, Port Louis; tel. 2421621; English and French; editor-in-Chief ADAM MAHMADE ALLY.

**CCI-INFO:** 3 Royal St, Port Louis; tel. 2083301; telex 4277; fax 2080076; English and French; f. 1995; publication of the Mauritius Chamber of Commerce and Industry.

**Ciné Star Magazine:** 64 Sir Seewoosagur Ramgoolam St, Port Louis; tel. 2401447; English and French; Editor-in-Chief RAOUF SOOBRATTY.

**Education News:** Edith Cavell St, Port Louis; tel. 2121303; English and French; monthly; Editor-in-Chief GIAN AUBEELUCK.

**Le Message:** c/o Ahmadiyya Muslim Asscn, Dar es Salaam, POB 6, Rose Hill; tel. 4641747; fax 4542223; French; monthly; Editor ZAFRULLAH DOMUN.

**La Nouvelle Mauricienne:** 43 Lord Kitchener St, Port Louis; tel. 2110843; English and French; Editor-in-Chief YVON BRÛLECOEUR.

**Perspectives:** 13 Jemmapes St, Port Louis; tel. 2081754; English and French; monthly; Editor T. TSANG KWAI KEW.

**Le Progrès Islamique:** 51 Solferino St, Rose Hill; f. 1948; English and French; monthly; Editor N. SOOKIA.

**PROSI:** Plantation House, Port Louis; tel. 2123302; telex 4214; fax 2128710; f. 1969; sugar industry journal; monthly; circ. 2,750.

**La Voix d'Islam:** Parisot Rd, Mesnil, Phoenix; f. 1951; English and French; monthly.

## Publishers

**Best Graphics Ltd:** Le Mauricien Bldg, 2nd Floor, 8 St George St, Port Louis; tel. 2086183; fax 2126143; English and French; Gen. Man. CLIFFORD LILYMAN.

**Bukié Banané:** 5 Edwin Ythier St, Rose Hill; tel. 4542327; f. 1979; Creole literature, poetry and drama; Man. Dir DEV VIRAHSAWMY.

**Business Publications Ltd:** TN Tower, 1st Floor, St George St, Port Louis; tel. 2111925; fax 2111926; f. 1993; English and French; Dir LYNDSAY RIVIÈRE.

**Editions du Dattier:** 6 Bois Chéri Rd, Moka; tel. and fax 4330875; English and French; Man. Dir VÉRONIQUE LAGESSE.

**Editions Nassau:** Barclay St, Rose Hill; f. 1970; general fiction and paperbacks; Gen. Man. E. H. DENNEMONT.

**Editions de l'Océan Indien Ltée:** Stanley, Rose Hill; tel. 4643959; telex 4739; fax 4643445; f. 1977; textbooks, literature; English and French; Chair. S. BISSOONDOYAL.

**Editions Le Printemps:** 4 Club Rd, Vacoas; tel. 6961017; fax 6867302; Man. Dir ISLAM SULLIVAN.

**Précigraph Ltd:** St Vincent de Paul Ave, Les Pailles; tel. 2085049; fax 2085050; English and French; Man. Dir FRANCE DE LABAUVE D'ARIFAT.

## Radio and Television

In 1992, according to UNESCO estimates, there were 395,000 radio receivers and 239,000 television receivers in use. In 1993 159,712 licensed television receivers were in use.

**Mauritius Broadcasting Corporation:** Broadcasting House, Louis Pasteur St, Forest Side; tel. 6755001; telex 4230; fax 6767332; f. 1964; independent corpn operating the national radio and television services; Dir-Gen. BIJAY COOMAR MADHOU.

## Finance

(cap. = capital; p.u. = paid up; res = reserves; m. = million; dep. = deposits; br. = branch; amounts in Mauritian rupees)

### BANKING

#### Central Bank

**Bank of Mauritius:** Sir William Newton St, POB 29, Port Louis; tel. 2084164; telex 4253; fax 2089204; f. 1967; bank of issue; cap. and res 33m., dep. 5,109.1m. (June 1993); Gov. Sir INDURDUTH RAMPHUL; Man. Dir RANAPARTAB TACOURI.

#### Commercial Banks

**Bank of Baroda:** Sir William Newton St, POB 553, Port Louis; tel. 2081504; telex 4237; fax 2083892; Vice-Pres. B. L. NAIK.

**Banque Nationale de Paris Intercontinentale:** 1 Sir William Newton St, POB 494, Port Louis; tel. 2084147; telex 4231; fax 2088143; Pres. MICHEL PÉBEREAU; Man. Dir YANN OZANNE.

**Barclays Bank PLC, Mauritius:** Sir William Newton St, POB 284, Port Louis; tel. 2121816; telex 4347; fax 2082720; Gen. Man. PATRICK H. NOBLE; 21 brs.

**Delphis Bank Ltd:** 16 Sir William Newton St, POB 485, Port Louis; tel. 2085061; telex 4294; fax 2085388; Man. Dir VIJAY KUMAR RAMPHUL.

## MAURITIUS

**Habib Bank Ltd:** 26 Sir William Newton St, POB 505, Port Louis; tel. 2080848; telex 4226; fax 2123829; Sr Vice-Pres. MOHAMMAD PARVEZ.

**Hongkong and Shanghai Banking Corporation Ltd:** Place d'Armes, POB 50, Port Louis; tel. 2081801; telex 4235; fax 2085187; Man. RICHARD INGILS.

**Indian Ocean International Bank Ltd:** 34 Sir William Newton St, POB 863, Port Louis; tel. 2080121; telex 4390; fax 2080127; f. 1978; cap. and res 59.9m., dep. 803.4m. (June 1993); Chair. and Man. Dir SAM CUNDEN; Gen. Man. H. BHASKAR KEDLAYA.

**Mauritius Commercial Bank Ltd:** 9–15 Sir William Newton St, POB 52, Port Louis; tel. 2082801; telex 4218; fax 2087054; f. 1838; cap. 582.6m., dep. 27,211.7m. (June 1994); Pres. ADOLPHE VALLET; Gen. Man. YVAN LAGESSE; 41 brs.

**MCC Ltd:** 3 Dumas St, POB 572, Port Louis; tel. 2081059; telex 4248; fax 2087698; f. 1948; cap. p.u. 26.8m. (Feb. 1990), dep. 605.3m. (1989); assumed control of Mauritius Co-operative Central Bank Ltd in 1992; Deputy Mans P. AUCKLE, A. GUJADHUR.

**South East Asian Bank Ltd:** 26 Bourbon St, POB 13, Port Louis; tel. 2088826; telex 5328; fax 2088825; f. 1989; cap. and res 76.2m., dep. 289.5m. (Dec. 1992); Chair. Dr ABDUL KHALID BIN SAHAN; Gen. Man. RAMLI AWANGAM.

**State Bank of Mauritius Ltd:** Chancery House, 4th Floor, Lislet Geoffroy St, POB 152, Port Louis; tel. 2088903; telex 4910; fax 2088209; f. 1973; cap. and res 1,309.7m., dep. 10,416.3m. (June 1993); Chair. D. D. MANRAJ; Man. Dir THUKIVAKAM MUNI KRISHNA REDDY; 46 brs.

**Union International Bank Ltd:** 22 Sir William Newton St, POB 1076, Port Louis; tel. 2088080; telex 4894; fax 2088085; f. 1987; cap. and res 36.6m., dep. 547.6m. (Dec. 1993); Chair. VIVEK CHADHA; Man. Dir and CEO KAUP PRAKASH CHANDRA HEGDE.

### Development Bank

**Development Bank of Mauritius Ltd:** La Chaussée St, POB 157, Port Louis; tel. 2080241; telex 4248; fax 2088498; f. 1964; cap. and res 738m., dep. 579.2m. (June 1993); 65% govt-owned; Chair. Sir B. GHURBURRUN; Exec. Dir RADHA LUXMUN PRABHU.

### 'Offshore' Banks

'Offshore' banking operations commenced in 1989.

**Banque Internationale des Mascareignes:** Moorgate House, 4th Floor, Sir William Newton St, POB 489, Port Louis; tel. 2124978; telex 4701; fax. 2124983; f. 1991; cap. p.u. 6m. (1993); joint venture between Crédit Lyonnais de France and Mauritius Commercial Bank Ltd; Chair. A. WOLKENSTEIN; Gen. Man. FRÉDÉRIC DUNTZE.

**Banque Privée Edmond de Rothschild (Océan Indien) Ltée:** Chancery House, 3rd Floor, Lislet Geoffroy St, Port Louis; tel. 2122784; telex 4547; fax 2084561; Man. Dir ADRIEN WEHRLI.

**State Bank International Ltd:** SICOM Bldg, 10th Floor, Sir Célicourt Antelme St, Port Louis; tel. 2122054; fax 2122050; joint venture between the State Bank of Mauritius and the State Bank of India; Man. Dir M. MADHUKAR.

Bank of Baroda, Banque Nationale de Paris Intercontinentale, Barclays Bank PLC and Hong Kong and Shanghai Banking Corporation also operate 'offshore' banking units.

### STOCK EXCHANGE

**Stock Exchange Commission:** SICOM Bldg, Sir Célicourt Antelme St, Port Louis; tel. 2088735; telex 5291; fax 2088676; f. 1993; Chair. DHIREN DABEE (acting); CEO Ms SHARDA DINDOYAL.

**Stock Exchange of Mauritius:** Cascades Bldg, 6th Floor, Edith Cavell St, Port Louis; tel. 2129541; fax 2088409; f. 1989; Chair. BRUNO HARDY; Man. DARMANAND VIRAHSAWMY.

### INSURANCE

**Albatross Insurance Co Ltd:** 22 St George St, POB 116, Port Louis; tel. 2122874; telex 4299; fax 2084800; f. 1975; Chair. DEREK TAYLOR; Man. Dir JEAN DE LA HOGUE.

**Anglo-Mauritius Assurance Society Ltd:** Swan Group Centre, 12 Intendance St, Port Louis; tel. 2112312; fax 2088956; inc. 1951; Chair. J. M. ANTOINE HAREL; Gen. Man. JEAN DE FONDAUMIÈRE.

**British American Insurance Co (Mauritius) Ltd:** BAI Bldg, 25 Pope Hennessy St, POB 331, Port Louis; tel. 2083637; fax 2083713; Chair. DAWOOD RAWAT; Man. Dir ALAIN C. Y. CHEONG.

**Indian Ocean General Assurance Ltd:** cnr Rémy Ollier and Corderie Sts, Port Louis; tel. 2124125; fax 2125850; f. 1970; Chair. SAM CUNDEN; Man. Dir Mrs D. A. CUNDEN.

**Island Insurance Co Ltd:** 27 St Louis St, Port Louis; tel. 2124860; fax 2088762; Chair. CARRIM A. CURRIMJEE; Man. OLIVIER LAGESSE.

**Jubilee Insurance Co Ltd:** 9 Corderie St, Port Louis; tel. 2123113; fax 2407643; Man. Dir HAMID PATEL.

**Lamco International Insurance Ltd:** 12 Barracks St, Port Louis; tel. 2120233; fax 2080630; f. 1978; Chair. S. M. LATIFF; Gen. Man. A. S. KARKHANIS.

**Life Insurance Corporation of India:** LIC Centre, President John Kennedy St, Port Louis; tel. 2125316; telex 4726; fax 2086392; Chief Man. Mr ATIMBAH.

**Mauritian Eagle Insurance Co Ltd:** 10 Dr Ferrière St, POB 854, Port Louis; tel. 2124877; telex 4867; fax 2088608; f. 1973; Chair. CHRISTIAN DALAIS; Exec. Dir GUY LEROUX.

**Mauritius Union Assurance Co Ltd:** 4 Léoville l'Homme St, POB 233, Port Louis; tel. 2084185; telex 4310; fax 2122962; f. 1948; Chair. Sir MAURICE LATOUR-ADRIEN; Man. Dir GERVAIS SALAÜN.

**The New India Assurance Co Ltd:** Bank of Baroda Bldg, 3rd Floor, 32 Sir William Newton St, POB 398, Port Louis; tel. 2081442; telex 4834; fax 2082160; Man. Dir S. A. KUMAR.

**La Prudence Mauricienne Assurances Ltée:** Fon Sing Bldg, 1st Floor, Edith Cavell St, POB 882, Port Louis; tel. 2088935; fax 2088936; Chair. ROBERT DE FROBERVILLE; Man. Dir FELIX MAUREL.

**Rainbow Insurance Co Ltd:** 23 Edith Cavell St, POB 389, Port Louis; tel. 2125767; telex 4356; fax 2088750; f. 1976; Chair. B. GOKULSING; Gen. Man. LATIF KUMAR RAMBURN.

**Seagull Insurance Ltd:** Blendax House, 3rd Floor, Dumas St, Port Louis; tel. 2120867; telex 4593; fax 2082417; Chair. Y. V. LAI FAT FUR; Man. Dir O. GUNGABISSOON.

**SICOM Ltd:** SICOM Bldg, Sir Célicourt Antelme St, Port Louis; tel. 2085406; telex 4396; fax 2087662; f. 1975; Chair. R. JUGURNAUTH; Man. Dir JACQUES BLACKBURN.

**Stella Insurance Co Ltd:** 17 Sir Seewoosagur Ramgoolam St, POB 852, Port Louis; tel. 2086051; telex 4719; fax 2081639; f. 1977; Chair. and Man. Dir R. KRESHAN JHOBOO.

**Sun Insurance Co Ltd:** 2 St George St, Port Louis; tel. 2122522; telex 4452; fax 2082052; f. 1981; Chair. Sir KAILASH RAMDANEE; Man. Dir Lady (URSULA) RAMDANEE.

**Swan Insurance Co Ltd:** Swan Group Centre, 10 Intendance St, POB 364, Port Louis; tel. 2112001; telex 4393; fax 2086898; incorp. 1955; Chair. J. M. ANTOINE HAREL; Gen. Man. GILLES DE SORNAY.

**L. and H. Vigier de Latour Ltd:** Les Jamalacs Bldg, Old Council St, Port Louis; tel. 2122034; telex 4386; fax 2126056; Chair. and Man. Dir L. J. D. HENRI VIGIER DE LATOUR.

## Trade and Industry

### CHAMBER OF COMMERCE

**Mauritius Chamber of Commerce and Industry:** 3 Royal St, Port Louis; tel. 2083301; telex 4277; fax 2080076; f. 1850; 380 mems; Pres. MARDAY VENKATASAMY; Sec.-Gen. JEAN-CLAUDE MONTOCCHIO.

### TRADING ORGANIZATIONS

**Chinese Chamber of Commerce:** 35 Dr Joseph Rivière St, Port Louis; tel. 2080946; fax 2421193; Pres. JEAN KOK SHUN.

**Indian Traders' Association:** POB 231, Port Louis; tel. 2403509.

**Mauritius Chamber of Merchants:** Louis Pasteur St, Port Louis; tel. 2121477; telex 4619; fax 2087088; Pres. AHMED ABDULLA AHMED.

**State Trading Corpn:** Fon Sing Bldg, Edith Cavell St, Port Louis; tel. 2085440; telex 4537; fax 2088359; f. 1982 to manage import and distribution of rice, wheat, flour, petroleum products and cement; cap. Rs 10m.; 99% state-owned; Pres. (vacant); Gen. Man. BEEJAYE GOORAH.

### DEVELOPMENT ORGANIZATIONS

**Mauritius Export Development and Investment Authority (MEDIA):** BAI Bldg, 2nd Floor, 25 Pope Hennessy St, POB 1184, Port Louis; tel. 2087750; telex 4597; fax 2085965; f. 1985 to promote exports of goods and services and to encourage export-orientated investment; Chair. FAKHRU CURRIMJEE; CEO CHAND BHADAIN.

**Mauritius Freeport Authority:** Deramann Tower, 3rd Floor, 30 Sir William Newton St, Port Louis; tel. 2129627; fax 2129626; f. 1990 to promote freeport activities; Chair. Prof. EDOUARD LIM FAT; Dir-Gen. GÉRARD SANSPEUR.

# MAURITIUS

**Mauritius Offshore Business Activities Authority:** Deramann Tower, 1st Floor, 30 Sir William Newton St, Port Louis; tel. 2110143; fax 2129459; manages and promotes 'offshore' commercial activities; Pres. Ramakrishna Sithanen; Dir Iqbal Rajahballee.

**State Investment Corporation Ltd (SIC):** Fon Sing Bldg, 2nd Floor, 12 Edith Cavell St, Port Louis; tel. 2122978; telex 4635; fax 2088948; provides support for new investment and transfer of technology, in agriculture, industry and tourism; Chair. Dev Manraj; Man. Dir Mardaymootoo Naker.

## EMPLOYERS' ASSOCIATION

**Mauritius Employers' Federation:** Cerné House, Chaussée St, Port Louis; tel. 2121599; fax 2126725; f. 1962; Pres. Paul R. de Chasteigner du Mée; Dir Dr Azad Jeetun.

## TRADE UNIONS

### Federations

**Federation of Civil Service Unions (FCSU):** 33 Corderie St, Port Louis; tel. 2426621; f. 1975; 52 affiliated unions with 16,500 mems (1992); Pres. D. Bhuruth; Gen.-Sec. R. Sungkur.

**General Workers' Federation:** 19b Poudrière St, Port Louis; tel. 2123338; Pres. Beedianand Jhurry; Sec.-Gen. Farook Auchoybur.

**Mauritius Federation of Trade Unions:** Etienne Pellereau St, Port Louis; tel 2401486; f. 1958; four affiliated unions; Pres. Farook Hossenbux; Sec.-Gen. R. Mareemootoo.

**Mauritius Labour Congress:** 8 Louis Victor de la Faye St, Port Louis; tel. 2124343; telex 4611; fax 2088945; f. 1963; 55 affiliated unions with 70,000 mems (1992); Pres. R. Allgoo; Gen. Sec. K. Hurrynag.

### Principal Unions

**Government Servants' Association:** 107a Royal Rd, Beau Bassin; tel. 4644242; f. 1945; 14,000 mems (1984); Pres. A. H. Malleck-Amode; Sec.-Gen. S. P. Torul.

**Government Teachers' Union:** 3 Mgr Gonin St, POB 1111, Port Louis; tel. 2080047; f. 1945; 4,625 mems (1992); Pres. Jugdish Lollbeeharry; Sec. Shivcoomar Baichoo.

**Nursing Association:** Royal Rd, Beau Bassin; tel. 4645850; f. 1955; 2,040 mems (1980); Pres. Cassam Kureeman; Sec.-Gen. Francis Supparayen.

**Organization of Artisans' Unity:** 42 Sir William Newton St, Port Louis; tel. 2124557; f. 1973; 2,874 mems (1994); Pres. Auguste Follet; Sec. Roy Ramchurn.

**Plantation Workers' Union:** 8 Louis Victor de la Faye St, Port Louis; tel. 2121735; f. 1955; 13,726 mems (1990); Pres. C. Bhagirutty; Sec. N. L. Roy.

**Port Louis Harbour and Docks Workers' Union:** 19b Poudrière St, Port Louis; tel. 2082276; 2,198 mems (1980); Pres. M. Veerabadren; Sec.-Gen. Gerard Bertrand.

**Sugar Industry Staff Employees' Association:** 1 Rémy Ollier St, Port Louis; tel. 2121947; f. 1947; 1,472 mems (1987); Chair. R. de Chasteauneuf; Sec.-Gen. Jean Maclou.

**Textile, Clothes and Other Manufactures Workers' Union:** Thomy d'Arifat St, Curepipe; tel. 6765280; Pres. Padmatee Teeluck; Sec.-Gen. Désiré Guildaree.

**Union of Bus Industry Workers:** 19b Poudrière St, Port Louis; tel. 2123338; 1,783 mems (1980); Pres. Babooa; Sec.-Gen. F. Auchoybur.

**Union of Employees of the Ministry of Agriculture and other Ministries:** Royal Rd, Curepipe; tel. 6861847; f. 1989; 2,131 mems (1988); Sec. P. Jagarnath.

**Union of Labourers of the Sugar and Tea Industry:** Royal Rd, Curepipe; f. 1969; 2,150 mems (1980); Sec. P. Ramchurn.

**Union of Municipality Workers:** 23 Brabant St, Port Louis; 1,991 mems (1980); Sec. M. V. Ramsamy.

**Union of Workers of the Development Works Corporation:** 23 Brabant St, Port Louis; 2,651 mems; Sec. E. Varden.

## CO-OPERATIVE SOCIETIES

**Mauritius Co-operative Agricultural Federation Ltd:** Co-operation House, 3 Dumas St, Port Louis; tel. 2121360; f. 1950; supplies agricultural materials; promotes the interests of 209 mem. socs; Chair. R. Seeruttun; Sec. R. Hemoo.

**Mauritius Co-operative Union Ltd:** Co-operation House, 3 Dumas St, Port Louis; tel. 2122922; telex 4348; f. 1952; educational and promotional activities; 303 mem. socs (1983); Pres. Toovan Ramphul; Sec.-Gen. Dharamjeet Bucktower.

# Transport

### RAILWAYS

There are no railways in Mauritius.

### ROADS

In 1991 there were 1,831 km of classified roads, of which 886 km were main roads, and 577 km were secondary roads. About 93% of the road network is paved. The construction of an urban highway, linking the motorways approaching Port Louis, and the extension of one of the motorways to Plaisance airport were completed in 1988. Of total projected expenditure by the Government in 1990/91, Rs 190m. was allocated to the rehabilitation of roads.

### SHIPPING

Mauritius is served by numerous foreign shipping lines. In 1990 Port Louis was established as a free port to expedite the development of Mauritius as an entrepôt centre. In 1995 the World Bank approved a loan of US $20m. for a programme to develop the port.

**Mauritius Marine Authority:** Port Administration Bldg, POB 379, Mer Rouge, Port Louis; tel. 2400415; telex 4238; fax 2400856; f. 1976; port and maritime authority; Chair. H. Ramnarain; Dir-Gen. J. H. Nagdan.

**Islands Services Ltd:** Rogers House, 5 President John Kennedy St, POB 60, Port Louis; tel. 2086801; telex 4312; fax 2085045; services to Indian Ocean islands; Chair. Sir René Maingard; Exec. Dir Capt. René Sanson.

**Mauritius Shipping Corporation Ltd:** Nova Bldg, 1 Military Rd, Port Lous; tel. 2425255; telex 4874; fax 2425245; Pres. Hervé Duval; Dir Suren Ramphul.

**Société Mauricienne de Navigation Ltée:** 1 rue de la Reine, POB 53, Port Louis; tel. 2083241; telex 4213; fax 2088931; Dir Yves Bellepeau.

### CIVIL AVIATION

Sir Seewoosagur Ramgoolam international airport is at Plaisance, 4 km from Mahébourg; work on upgrading the airport started in 1984 and was completed in 1987. A further expansion programme, which was projected to cost more than US $30m., was initiated in 1993, when the airport handled 1.06m. passengers. Plans were announced in early 1995 for the construction of additional runway and air traffic control facilities, at an estimated cost of Rs 800m.; the programme was due to commence later that year.

**Air Mauritius:** Air Mauritius Centre, 2 President John Kennedy St, POB 441, Port Louis; tel. 2087700; telex 4415; fax 2088331; f. 1967; 51% state-owned; services to destinations in Europe, Asia, Australia and Africa; Chair. and Man. Dir Sir Harry Tirvengadum.

# Tourism

Tourists are attracted to Mauritius by its scenery and beaches, the pleasant climate and the blend of cultures. Accommodation capacity totalled 11,200 beds in 1994. The number of visitors increased from 139,670 in 1984 to 400,526 in 1994, when receipts totalled an estimated Rs 6,052m. In 1994 the greatest numbers of visitors were from France (26%), Réunion (19%) and South Africa (9.9).

**Mauritius Government Tourist Office:** Emmanuel Anquetil Bldg, Sir Seewoosagur Ramgoolam St, Port Louis; tel. 2011703; telex 4249; fax 2125142; Gen. Man. Cyril Vadamootoo.

# MEXICO

## Introductory Survey

### Location, Climate, Language, Religion, Flag, Capital

The United Mexican States is, by far, the largest country in Central America. It is bordered to the north by the USA, and to the south by Guatemala and Belize. The Gulf of Mexico and the Caribbean Sea lie to the east, and the Pacific Ocean and Gulf of California to the west. The climate varies with altitude. The tropical southern region and the coastal lowlands are hot and wet, with an average annual temperature of 18°C (64°F), while the highlands of the central plateau are temperate. Much of the north and west is arid desert. In Mexico City, which lies at about 2,250 m (nearly 7,400 ft) above sea-level, temperatures are generally between 5°C (42°F) and 25°C (78°F). The country's highest recorded temperature is 58°C (136°F). The principal language is Spanish, spoken by more than 90% of the population in 1990, while about 8% speak indigenous languages, of which náhuatl is the most widely spoken. Almost all of Mexico's inhabitants profess Christianity, and about 90% are adherents of the Roman Catholic Church. The national flag (proportions 7 by 4) has three equal vertical stripes from hoist to fly, of green, white and red, with the state emblem (a brown eagle, holding a snake in its beak, on a green cactus, with a wreath of oak and laurel beneath) in the centre of the white stripe. The capital is Mexico City.

### Recent History

Conquered by Hernán Cortés in the 16th century, Mexico was ruled by Spain until the wars of independence of 1810–21. After the war of 1846, Mexico ceded about one-half of its territory to the USA. Attempts at political and social reform by the anti-clerical Benito Juárez led to civil war in 1857–60, and the repudiation of Mexico's external debts by Juárez in 1860 led to war with Britain, the USA and France. The Austrian Archduke Maximilian, whom France tried to install as Emperor of Mexico, was executed, on the orders of Juárez, in 1867. Order was restored during the dictatorship of Porfirio Díaz, which lasted from 1876 until the Revolution of 1910. The Constitution of 1917 embodied the aims of the Revolution by revising land ownership, by drafting a labour code and by curtailing the power of the Roman Catholic Church.

Since 1929 the country has been dominated by the Partido Revolucionario Institucional (PRI) in an effective one-party system, while maintaining a democratic form of election. However, allegations of widespread electoral malpractice have persistently undermined PRI victories. The President from 1934 until 1940, Lázaro Cárdenas, accelerated the land reform which had been initiated under the 1917 Constitution, and nationalized the petroleum sector. He was succeeded by Gen. Manuel Avila Camacho, who embarked on a programme of industrialization. Avila's successor, President Miguel Alemán Valdés (1946–52), concentrated on expanding educational services. President Adolfo Ruiz Cortines held office from 1952 to 1958, and President Adolfo López Mateos from 1958 to 1964, when Gustavo Díaz Ordaz was elected President. Luis Echeverría Alvarez won the presidential election of 1970 and pledged to extend the benefits of Mexico's prosperity to all sectors of the population.

In the July 1976 elections, the PRI candidate, José López Portillo, was elected President with almost 95% of the votes cast. In 1977 President López Portillo initiated reforms to improve minority party representation in the legislature and to increase democratic participation. The Government's mismanagement of the economy, combined with the President's reluctance to make testing political decisions, brought the country to the verge of bankruptcy in 1982. The high level of political participation in the presidential election of July 1982 was without precedent, with left-wing groups taking part for the first time. Elections to the Cámara Federal de Diputados (Federal Chamber of Deputies), conducted concurrently, were also open but, as three-quarters of the seats in the Cámara were contested under the single-member constituency system, the PRI achieved another overwhelming victory. On taking office in December, the new President, Miguel de la Madrid Hurtado embarked on a programme of major economic reform and actively sought to reduce institutionalized corruption in public services. The Government's economic programme gave precedence to the repayment of Mexico's debts, a policy which imposed severe financial constraints upon the middle and lower classes and which led to growing disaffection among traditional PRI supporters, including the influential trade union, the Confederación de Trabajadores de México (CTM). Opposition to the Government was demonstrated by the important gains which were made by the Partido Acción Nacional (PAN) at municipal elections in the state capitals of Durango and Chihuahua during July 1983. The PRI's effective response ensured success at the remaining elections, but provoked opposition allegations of widespread electoral fraud. Contrary to expectations, at gubernatorial and congressional elections conducted in July 1985, the PRI secured all seven state governorships and won 288 of the 300 directly elective seats in the Cámara. The PAN's objections to the results were dismissed by the Federal Electoral Commission, but violent clashes between protesting PAN supporters and the police continued in northern Mexico for several weeks.

The formation of a major left-wing alliance, the Partido Mexicano Socialista—PMS (comprising six parties), in 1987 and, in particular, the emergence of a dissident faction, the Corriente Democrática (CD), within the PRI in 1986 were disturbing political developments for the ruling party. In October 1987 it was disclosed that Carlos Salinas de Gortari, the Secretary of Planning and Financial Budget and one of the principal architects of the Government's economic policy, had been selected as the PRI's presidential candidate for the election, scheduled for July 1988. In early 1988 the CD and four other left-wing parties (including the PMS coalition) formed an electoral alliance, the Frente Democrático Nacional (FDN), headed by CD leader Cuauhtémoc Cárdenas Solórzano. The legitimacy of the PRI victory at the presidential and congressional elections, conducted on 6 July, was fiercely challenged by the opposition groups, following a delay in the publication of any official results, reports of electoral fraud at more than 7,000 polling stations and the failure of the Federal Electoral Commission to release details of results from almost 50% of polling stations. Moreover, Cuauhtémoc Cárdenas claimed victory on behalf of the broad-left coalition; for the first time ever, the opposition secured seats in the Senado (Senate), while the PRI suffered clear defeats in the Distrito Federal and at least three other states.

In August the new Congreso de la Unión (Congress) was installed and immediately assumed the function of an electoral college, in order to investigate the claims of both sides. In September, the allocation of 200 seats in the Cámara by proportional representation afforded the PRI a congressional majority and effective control of the electoral college. Opposition members withdrew from the Cámara in protest at the PRI's obstruction of the investigation, enabling the ruling party to ratify Salinas as the new President with 50.7% of the votes cast. Cárdenas was credited with 31.1% of the votes. The results, although widely regarded as having been manipulated by the PRI, nevertheless revealed a considerable erosion in support for the party, particularly among the traditional bastions of the trade unions, peasant groups and bureaucracy.

President Salinas took office on 1 December 1988, declaring that among his administration's priorities would be the renegotiation of the foreign debt, a new initiative to combat poverty and a campaign to eradicate fraud and corruption. During 1989, despite the Government's active reinforcement of its commitment to the elimination of corruption (particularly in the industrial and business sectors and in trade unions), the implication of police and security forces in a succession of abuses of human rights threatened to undermine the success of this initiative. In February 1990 an official Mexican research institute published a report which concluded that the majority of Mexico's violent crimes involved current or former members of the police force, and that violations of human rights and arbitrary detention, particularly in order to extract a confession, were widespread.

Negotiations to reduce Mexico's vast foreign debt were given priority by the new Government in 1989. Agreements on rescheduling were reached with the 'Paris Club' of creditor governments in May, and with some 450 commercial banks in February 1990. Success for the Government in financial negotiations with banks, international organizations and foreign governments was largely dependent upon its ability to provide evidence of a stable and developing domestic economy. In January 1989 a Pact for Economic Stability and Growth (PECE) was implemented, with the agreement of employers' organizations and trade unions (replacing an earlier agreement, concluded in December 1987): it aimed to control inflation and restrict public expenditure, and was subsequently extended, in November 1991 and October 1993 (until the end of 1994). In May 1989 Salinas announced a National Development Plan which identified political and economic objectives for 1989–94 as the defence of Mexican interests and sovereignty, the strengthening of democratic life, the recovery of economic growth and price stability, and improvement in the standard of living.

In 1989 trade union disputes and demands for pay increases led to strikes by teachers, bus-drivers, steel-workers and motor-industry workers. A further cause of labour unrest was the extensive divestment programme, initiated by the Government in 1989. Although certain companies were reserved for state and national investment only, incentives to foreign investment were provided by a liberalization of laws previously protecting certain sectors, including the petroleum, pharmaceuticals and computer industries.

In May 1989, following the dissolution of the FDN earlier in the year, supporters of the CD, together with the PMS, formed a new party, the Partido de la Revolución Democrática (PRD), under the leadership of Cuauhtémoc Cárdenas. Throughout 1989 political opposition to the PRI was strengthened by success in gubernatorial and municipal elections, and by further accusations that electoral fraud had been committed by the PRI. In October 1989 proposed constitutional amendments, drafted in order to facilitate the future adoption of the PRI's Federal Electoral Code (COPIFE), were finally adopted with the unexpected support of the PAN. A 'governability clause' whereby an absolute majority of seats in the Cámara would be awarded to the leading party, should it receive at least 35% of the votes at a general election, was critized by the PRD for leading to 'over-representation'.

Throughout 1990 the PRI recorded impressive victories in state and local elections in the state of México, and in municipal elections in the states of Coahuila, Hidalgo and Yucatán. The PRD denounced all election results as grossly misrepresentative and alleged that electoral malpractices, particularly the deliberate duplication of names on electoral registers, remained widespread. In July the new Federal Electoral Code was approved by the Cámara with support from all represented parties, with the exception of the PRD. The new legislation contained provisions for the compilation of a new national electoral roll, the issue of more detailed identification cards for voters, the modification of the Federal Electoral Institute (IFE), and the creation of a new 21-member Federal Electoral Tribunal (TFE). Although the PRI insisted that the overall emphasis of the reform was to allow greater public access to the electoral process at every level, the PRD was highly critical of many of the provisions of the new law, including alleged procedural obstacles to the formation of political alliances, and the power given to the President to appoint both the head of the IFE (the Secretary of the Interior) and to nominate six 'independent' lawyers to its executive.

At the 14th National Assembly of the PRI, convened in September 1990, the party suffered a serious reversal following the emergence of significant internal differences. Expectations of widespread party reform and democratization (in an attempt to foster a more politically legitimate image, both domestically and internationally) were largely frustrated by PRI traditionalists, and reforms to existing party statutes were almost exclusively confined to matters of procedure and internal structure.

In June 1990, in response to continuing allegations of federal police complicity in abuses of human rights, President Salinas announced the creation of the National Commission for Human Rights (CNDH). Opposition groups and private human rights organizations, however, were critical of the Government's stipulation that the Commission should be excluded from addressing cases relating to political campaigns or electoral processes. In October the Government announced proposals for legislation transferring responsibility for the interrogation of suspected criminals from the federal judicial police to the public magistrate's office. The proposed legislation also sought to undermine the validity of confession alone (often allegedly extracted under torture) as sufficient grounds for conviction.

In 1991 the PRI continued to secure disputed electoral success. The party won controversial victories in mayoral and legislative elections in the state of Morelos in March, and in gubernatorial and congressional elections in Nuevo León in July. The PRI achieved considerable success at mid-term congressional elections conducted in August, receiving 61.5% of the votes cast and thereby winning 290 of the 300 directly-elective seats in the Cámara (plus 30 of the 200 seats awarded by proportional representation) and 31 of the 32 contested seats in the Senado. The return to the level of support that the PRI had enjoyed prior to the 1988 elections was largely attributed to the success of the Government's programme of economic reform. The election results were less encouraging for the opposition (although the PAN secured 10 directly-elective seats in the Cámara and its first seat in the Senado) and were particularly disappointing for the PRD, which failed to secure a directly-elective seat in either congressional house. Initial results from gubernatorial elections in six states, conducted simultaneously with the congressional ballot, indicated a similar level of support for the PRI, which claimed victory in all six states. Although opposition allegations of electoral malpractice had become inevitable, President Salinas was anxious to avoid attracting international attention to the failings of the electoral system and was reported to have intervened personally in the vociferously disputed gubernatorial contests in the states of Guanajuato and San Luis Potosí, where newly-elected PRI governors were eventually replaced with interim governors, pending fresh elections. (In January 1992 a dispute prompted by the success of the PRI at elections in the state of Tabasco, conducted in November 1991, was similarly resolved.)

In early November 1991, bolstered by a significant increase in popular and congressional support, President Salinas announced ambitious proposals for constitutional reform with regard to agriculture, education and religion. Concern was expressed by PRI traditionalists that the agricultural reform programme (which envisaged the liberalization and development of the sector through the abolition of the land-distribution programme, established by the 1917 Constitution, and by the effective 'privatization' of the inefficient *ejido* system of rural worker tenants, who would be allowed the opportunity to buy and sell their plots, and to enter into joint ventures with private investors) and the proposals for the devolution of federal responsibility for education, to state and municipal bodies, might jeopardize the PRI's broad base of support from the rural community and from the 1.2m.-strong teachers' union. Legislation to enact the agrarian reform was submitted to Congress later in the month and the amendments were formally adopted in March 1992. Reform proposals to grant legal recognition to the Roman Catholic Church received congressional approval in December 1991, and constitutional restrictions on the Church were ended by a new law, promulgated by the President in January 1992. A National Agreement for the Modernization of Basic Education, encompassing the future implementation of the Government's education reform proposals, was agreed between the Federal Government, state governments and the national teachers' union in May 1992.

In early January 1992 President Salinas effected a minor re-organization of the Cabinet, with the appointment of a new Secretary of Public Education, and the amalgamation of the budget and finance secretariats, in order to facilitate more continuity in economic policy.

During 1992, elections for governors, legislative bodies and local mayors in 14 states produced few unexpected results, with PRI candidates enjoying success in almost all contests (with the notable exception of a gubernatorial victory for the PAN in the state of Chihuahua in July). Opposition groups, most notably the PRD, continued to level accusations of procedural malpractice against the PRI. In early October, following repeated denunciation of the legitimacy of his election in July, the newly-elected Governor of the state of Michoacán was forced temporarily to resign in favour of a less controversial PRI official. Tensions arising from the disputed outcome of municipal elections, conducted in the states of Michoacán and Oaxaca in December 1992, erupted into violence in January in 1993 when angry PRD supporters clashed with security forces while attempting to occupy municipal buildings.

In May 1992 an interim governor for the state of Jalisco was elected by the state legislature, following the resignation of Guillermo Cosio Vidaurri, who had provoked public outrage by attempting to exonerate state and local officials indentified (together with local employees of the state petroleum company, PEMEX), by the Attorney-General, as being responsible (through negligence) for a series of explosions which had devastated the state capital, Guadalajara, in April, resulting in the deaths of more than 200 inhabitants.

Several cabinet changes, implemented by President Salinas in January and March 1993, were widely interpreted as an attempt to consolidate the Government's position in preparation for the selection of the PRI candidate for the presidential election, scheduled for August 1994. PRI victories at gubernatorial and legislative elections to several states, during 1993, were inevitably denounced by the opposition as having been fraudulently won. In July, in an attempt to curtail persistent domestic and international criticism of the country's inefficient electoral system, President Salinas presented an electoral reform proposal, which received draft approval from the Congreso in August, and was finalized in mid-September. Among the provisions of the proposal were guarantees of greater access to the media for all parties, of restrictions on party funding, and of improved impartiality of supervision. Other measures sought to increase the representation of minority parties in the Senado, and to end over-representation of larger parties in the Cámara. The 'governability clause' introduced in 1989 was to be removed. While the reforms were welcomed by most opposition groups, many PRI members expressed concern that the party's position would be dangerously compromised by the proposals, which were considered to have been assembled without due consultation within the party. Further divisions within the PRI were anticipated in late November, following the selection of Luis Donaldo Colosio, the Secretary of Social Development, as the party's candidate for the August 1994 presidential elections. The Mayor of Mexico City, Víctor Manuel Camacho Solís, who had been widely expected to secure the candidacy, immediately resigned his post (seemingly in frustration at having been overlooked) but subsequently accepted the foreign affairs portfolio in a reorganized Cabinet. Additional reforms to the electoral system, which claimed to end PRI domination and effective control of the IFE, received congressional approval in March 1994, but failed to appease PRD leaders, who had demanded that the incumbent head of the IFE, the Secretary of the Interior, should be replaced by an impartial president elected by the IFE's newly-created six-member commission.

On 1 January 1994 armed Indian groups numbering 1,000-3,000 took control of four municipalities of the southern state of Chiapas. The rebels issued the Declaration of the Lacandona Jungle, identifying themselves as the previously unknown Ejército Zapatista de Liberación Nacional—EZLN (after Emiliano Zapata, who championed the land rights of Mexican peasants during the 1910-17 Revolution), and detailed a series of demands for economic and social change in the region, culminating in a declaration of war against the Government and a statement of intent to depose the 'dictator', President Salinas. A charismatic rebel spokesman indentified as 'Sub-comandante Marcos', stated that the insurgency had been deliberately timed to coincide with the implementation of the North American Free Trade Agreement (NAFTA—see below), which the rebels considered to be the latest in a series of segregative government intitiatives, adopted at the expense of indigenous groups. During the first day of the uprising the insurgents killed several police officials and abducted some prominent local figures, including a former Chiapas state governor. However, the armed forces were slow to respond, engaging the rebels in battle for the first time on 3 January in the town of Ocosingo. A subsequent military campaign of heavy and seemingly inaccurate bombardment of guerrilla positions in the surrounding mountains did much to enhance the popularity of the guerrilla cause, and was abandoned on 10 January, when the Government announced a unilateral cease-fire and an amnesty (effective from 22 January) for those EZLN members prepared to surrender arms. A cabinet reshuffle effected on the same day facilitated the appointment of Manuel Camacho Solís, a politician popular with centre-left elements of the PRI, as head of a peace and reconciliation commission in Chiapas. Camacho immediately enlisted the help of Samuel Ruiz, Bishop of San Cristóbal de las Casas, one of Chiapas' largest towns, in an attempt to foster a peaceful dialogue with the EZLN, although sporadic fighting continued throughout January. Negotiations between Camacho and the rebels began on 22 February, with the mediation of Ruiz, and were concluded on 2 March with the publication of a document detailing 34 demands of the EZLN, and the Government's response to them. A preliminary accord was subsequently reached following the Government's loose acceptance of many of the rebels' stipulations, including an acceleration of the Solidarity anti-poverty programme in the region (see section on Social Welfare), the incorporation of traditional Indian structures of justice and political organization, and a commitment from the Government to investigate the impact of NAFTA and recent land reform legislation on Indian communities. Official figures suggested that 100-150 guerrillas, soldiers and civilians had been killed during the conflict, while estimates by the Roman Catholic Church indicated that there had been as many as 400 casualties.

While Camacho's swift negotiation of a somewhat tenuous agreement with the EZLN went some way to limit the damage inflicted on the Government by the Chiapas insurrection, the PRI was plunged into further political chaos by the assassination, on 23 March 1994, of its presidential candidate, Luis Donaldo Colosio, at a campaign rally in the north-western border town of Tijuana. Mario Aburto Martínez, a suspect arrested at the scene of the murder, was later identified as the apparently motiveless assassin. However, speculation that Colosio had been the victim of a conspiracy within the PRI establishment increased following the arrest, in connection with the incident, of a number of party members associated with police and intelligence agencies. The delicate task of selecting Colosio's successor as presidential candidate was complicated by a constitutional stipulation that candidates should not have held public office during the six-month period prior to the election, thereby eliminating the possible candidature of many of the PRI's most experienced politicians. In late March the PRI named Ernesto Zedillo Ponce de León, a former cabinet minister who had most recently been acting as Colosio's campaign manager, as the party's new presidential candidate.

At presidential elections conducted on 21 August 1994 Zedillo was elected President with 48.8% of the votes, ahead of the PAN candidate, Diego Fernández de Cevallos, with 25.9%, and the PRD candidate, Cuauhtémoc Cárdenas, who received 16.6% of the votes cast. The PRI also achieved considerable success at congressional elections conducted concurrently, securing all of the directly-elective seats in the Senado and all but 23 of the directly-elective seats in the Cámara. Governorship of the state of Chiapas, also contested on the 21 August, was also won by the PRI candidate. Although Zedillo was considered to have conducted an unremarkable electoral campaign (during which he had promised to suspend the privilege of the *dedazo*—the presidential right to nominate PRI officials, and to increase the rate of economic growth to twice that of population growth by the end of 1995) and was the first PRI presidential candidate to receive less than 50% of the votes, his margin of victory was greater than had been predicted, and support for the PRI in the congressional poll had also exceeded expectations. Despite the participation of some 70,000 impartial monitors and the attendance, at the invitation of President Salinas, of a UN advisory technical team, numerous incidents of electoral malpractice were again reported. However, opposition protests against the level of procedural irregularities were more muted than in previous contests.

At his formal inauguration on 1 December 1994 Zedillo identified the immediate aims of his administration as the promotion of the independence of the judiciary, the separation of party political activity from the functions of federal government and the further reform of the electoral system. Public confidence in the impartiality and ability of the judiciary had been seriously undermined by the inconsistency and confusion surrounding recent investigations into the deaths of Colosio and José Francisco Ruiz Massieu (see below). Zedillo's appointment of a senior member of the PAN to the post of Attorney-General, in a new Cabinet announced at the end of November, together with the announcement, on 5 December, of more detailed plans for judicial reform (including proposals to prevent politicians from securing judicial office), sought to restore the prestige of the judiciary. The remainder of the Cabinet was composed of PRI members and one independent. In late December a sudden financial crisis (see below) prompted the replacement of the Secretary of Finance and Public Credit, and in late January a number of government portfolios were redistributed after the dismissal of the Secretary of Public Education, Fausto Alzati, following the disclosure that he had lied about his professional qualifications. Renewed allegations of widespread corruption in public office and the deterioration of the state of the economy contributed to a dramatic defeat for the PRI in gubernatorial elections to the state of Jalisco, conducted in February 1995, where the PAN candidate was elected.

The report of a special investigation into Colosio's murder, conducted by Miguel Montes García, was published in July 1994, and concluded that Mario Aburto Martínez had acted alone in the assassination, reversing the findings of a preliminary investigation which had suggested the existence of a number of conspirators. The report provoked widespread public incredulity, and President Salinas immediately commissioned a further independent investigation to be conducted by a newly-appointed special prosecutor. Speculation that Colosio had been the first victim of a politically-motivated campaign of violence, conducted by a cabal of reactionary PRI veterans in order to check the advance of the party's reformist wing, was intensified following the murder, in September, of the PRI Secretary-General, José Francisco Ruiz Massieu, although responsibility for Ruiz Massieu's death was initially attributed to the powerful Golfo drugs cartel (allegedly based on the north-eastern state of Tamaulipas, and responsible for the bulk of cross-border trafficking of cocaine to the USA). At the end of October Aburto Martínez was sentenced to 42 years imprisonment for Colosio's murder. By February 1995, however, a report issued by the Attorney-General, Fernando Antonio Lozano García, was highly critical of all previous investigations into the incident, concluding that the assassination had involved at least two gunmen. Meanwhile, in November 1994 Ruiz Massieu's brother, Mario, resigned his post as Deputy Attorney-General, claiming that senior PRI officials, including the party President and the Secretary-General, had impeded his investigation into his brother's death, in an attempt to protect the identities of those responsible for the assassination. In late February 1995 Raúl Salinas de Gortari, brother of former President Salinas, was arrested on charges of complicity in Ruiz Massieu's murder, and in April Fernando Rodríguez González (a former employee at the Cámara Federal de Diputados, who was charged with hiring the assassins) implicated several new conspirators, including five state Governors.

In early March 1995, following the arrest of his brother, former President Salinas began a solitary public campaign to discredit the new administration and to defend himself from accusations of responsibility for the country's economic crisis (see below) and from allegations that he had obstructed attempts to bring to justice those responsible for Colosio's death. Salinas' efforts culminated in a highly-publicized but brief hunger strike which prompted the Attorney-General to issue a statement confirming that there was no evidence that Salinas had impeded the Colosio murder inquiry. Some days later, allegedly at the suggestion of Zedillo, Salinas left the country, accompanied by his family.

Meanwhile, in June 1994 the EZLN announced that, following lengthy consultation, the Government's peace proposal had been rejected by an overwhelming majority of the movement's supporters. However, a similar majority had rejected the resumption of hostilities with the security forces, and had endorsed the extension of the cease-fire, pending renewed bilateral discussions. In response President Zedillo was critical of the work of the peace and reconciliation commission, prompting the resignation of Camacho Solís, who was replaced with Jorge Madrazo Cuéllar, the head of the national human rights commission. A national democratic convention, convened by the EZLN in August, and attended by some 5,000 representatives of popular organizations throughout the country, resolved to seek a peaceful transition to democracy, to oppose the PRI at the forthcoming elections and to organize a campaign of civil disobediance in the event of a fraudulently-won contest. By October tensions in Chiapas had increased (partly as a result of a conflict of interests between evangelical Christian Indian groups and Indian traditionalists) and the EZLN announced its withdrawal from increasingly entrenched negotiations with the Government, citing an increase in the military presence in the area and the controversial victory of the PRI candidate, Eduardo Robledo Rincón, in gubernatorial elections to the state, as reasons for the escalation in civil unrest. Violent confrontations between left- and right-wing groups, peasants and landowners and EZLN supporters and security forces increased in the weeks preceeding Robledo Rincón's inauguration. A second national democratic convention, organized in November, endorsed a campaign of civil disorder to disrupt the Governor's inauguration, but voted to resume negotiations with the Government. Fears that the Government might again seek a military solution to the crisis were aroused in December following the installation, by opposition groups, of a parallel state administration for Chiapas, on 8 December. Such concerns were initially dispelled by both sides' adoption of a more conciliatory approach to negotiations during December and January 1995 and by the EZLN's support for a Government initiative to establish a national mediation commission. However, in early February President Zedillo announced the resumption of a Government military offensive against EZLN positions in Chiapas, following the discovery of a number of illegal arsenals in Mexico City and Veracruz, which Zedillo claimed had been amassed by the EZLN (with deliberate disrespect for the cease-fire agreement) in preparation for a nationwide offensive. Zedillo also issued warrants for the arrest of several EZLN leaders including Subcomandante Marcos, who was identified as Rafael Sebastián Guillén Vicente. Some days later, however, the Government appeared to adjust this uncompromising stance, and further confrontational military operations in the region were suspended on the same day that Robledo Rincón's decision to take a temporary leave of absence from the post of Governor of Chiapas was announced. The warrants for the arrest of EZLN leaders were subsequently suspended, and in March the Law for Dialogue, Conciliation and Honourable Peace in Chiapas was enacted by the Government, with the support of all major political parties. Support for the Law, which seeks to facilitate future negotiations and to establish commissions to instigate and monitor the peace process, was welcomed by EZLN spokesmen, who, in turn, conveyed their willingness to renew a dialogue with the authorities. Formal discussions between the two sides began in San Andrés Larraínzar on 22 April but were promptly adjourned until mid-May, following the failure of both sides to agree on an emergency programme to defuse regional tension.

The new Zedilo administration encountered immediate economic difficulties, largely inherited from the previous administration's failure to address effectively the long-term problems of a burgeoning current account deficit. Although in September 1994 the Salinas administration had announced the successful conclusion of the Pact for Welfare, Stability and Growth (PABEC-largely based on the old PECE) with the trade unions and the business community, which envisaged inflation and economic growth of 4% for 1995, by mid-December the value of the peso was declining so rapidly that the new administration was forced to undertake a series of dramatic economic adjustments (including an unsuccessful attempt to re-establish financial stability through a 15% devaluation of the currency which resulted in the resignation of Zedillo's first Secretary of Finance and Public Credit, Jaime Serra Puche). A number of emergency economic austerity programmes, announced in quick succession, failed to halt a spectacular loss in the value of the peso against the US dollar, and confidence in the financial markets was only restored by US President Bill Clinton's announcement, at the end of January 1995, that a credit facility of almost US $51,000m. would be extended to the Mexican Government by the US Government's foreign exchange fund, the IMF, the Bank for International Settlements (BIS) and a number of other organizations. A new economic austerity plan, announced in March, provided for a 10% reduction in public expenditure and an increase, from 10% to 15%, in the rate of value-added tax, effective from 1 April. Revised economic forecasts for the year envisaged a 2% contraction of the economy, a rate of inflation of 42% and the loss of some 500,000 jobs in the six month period to September 1995.

Mexico's foreign policy has been determined largely by relations with the USA. The rapid expansion of petroleum production, from the mid-1970s onwards, gave Mexico a new independence. In its relations with Central American countries, Mexico favoured the left-wing regimes in Cuba and

Nicaragua during the 1980s. In 1982 the US Government rejected López Portillo's peace plan, which offered Mexican mediation between the USA, Cuba and Nicaragua. As a member of the Contadora group (with Colombia, Panama and Venezuela), Mexico advocated a negotiated settlement to the conflicts in Central America, and urged the withdrawal of all foreign advisers in the region.

In February 1985 relations between Mexico and the USA deteriorated, following the murder of an agent of the US Drug Enforcement Administration (DEA) by Mexican drugs-traffickers. The situation was exacerbated in April 1990 when a Mexican physician, Humberto Alvarez Machaín, was abducted, in Mexico, by agents employed by the DEA, and transported to the USA where he was arrested on charges relating to the murder. The Mexican authorities considered this action to be in violation of the existing US-Mexican extradition treaty, and refused to recognize the legality of the trial, despite a ruling by the US Supreme Court, in June 1992, that such action could be legally justified. In December, however, the situation was largely defused when the case was dismissed, owing to lack of evidence, and Dr Alvarez was allowed to return to Mexico. Meanwhile, throughout the late 1980s relations between Mexico and the USA remained tense, largely because of disagreement over the problem of illegal immigration from Mexico into the USA and Mexico's failure to take effective action against the illegal drugs trade.

In November 1990 President Salinas confirmed Mexico's commitment to proceed with proposals made by President Bush of the USA for the development of a free trade agreement between the two countries and the creation of a free trade area by 1993 (possibly embracing Canada at a later date). Negotiations with US and Canadian representatives continued during 1992, and in August a draft of the North American Free Trade Agreement (NAFTA) was produced, and was formally approved by all three countries in December 1992. Implementation of the Agreement, however, remained dependent upon its ratification by the three national legislatures. In August 1993 hopes for the prompt implementation of the Agreement were encouraged by the successful conclusion of negotiations between the three signatory nations on the outstanding issues of labour and environmental protection. A final obstacle was overcome in November 1993 when the final draft was ratified by the US House of Representatives (and subsequently by the Mexican Senado and the US Senate), and the Agreement duly took effect from the 1 January 1994. Among the provisions of the Agreement are the gradual reduction of tariffs on 50% of products over a period of 10–15 years (some 57% of tariffs on agricultural trade between the US and Mexico was removed immediately), and the establishment, by Mexico and the USA, of a North American Development Bank (Nadbank) charged with the funding of initiatives for the rehabilitation of the two countries' common border.

President Salinas attempted to improve official relations with the Roman Catholic Church by inviting members of the Catholic hierarchy to his inauguration in 1988. In February 1990 Salinas appointed a personal envoy to the Vatican. Following the promulgation, in January 1992, of constitutional amendments whereby institutionalized restrictions on the Catholic Church were formally ended, full diplomatic relations with the Vatican were restored in September 1992.

In January 1991 a preliminary free trade agreement was signed with Honduras, Guatemala, El Salvador, Nicaragua and Costa Rica, in order to facilitate the negotiation of bilateral agreements between Mexico and each of the five countries, leading to free trade in an increasing range of products over a six-year period.

During the early 1990s Mexico negotiated agreements for greater economic co-operation and increased bilateral trade with Colombia and Venezuela (as the Group of Three), with Chile, Costa Rica and with the European Union.

### Government

Mexico is a federal republic comprising 31 states and a Distrito Federal—Federal District (around the capital). Under the 1917 Constitution, legislative power is vested in the bicameral Congreso de la Unión, elected by universal adult suffrage. The Senado has 128 members (four from each state and the Distrito Federal), serving a six-year term. The Cámara Federal de Diputados, directly elected for three years, has 500 seats, of which 300 are filled from single-member constituencies. The remaining 200 seats, allocated so as to achieve proportional representation, are filled from parties' lists of candidates.

Executive power is held by the President, directly elected for six years at the same time as the Senado. He governs with the assistance of an appointed Cabinet. Each state has its own constitution and is administered by a Governor (elected for six years) and an elected chamber of deputies.

### Defence

Military service, on a part-time basis (four hours per week), is compulsory for conscripts selected by lottery, for one year. In June 1994 the active armed forces totalled 175,000: 130,000 in the army, 37,000 in the navy (including naval air force and marines) and 8,000 in the air force. There is a rural defence militia numbering 14,000. Defence expenditure for 1994 was budgeted at 4,900m. new pesos.

### Economic Affairs

In 1993, according to estimates by the World Bank, Mexico's gross national product (GNP), measured at average 1991–93 prices, was US $324,951m., equivalent to $3,750 per head. During 1985–93, it was estimated, GNP per head increased, in real terms, at an average annual rate of 0.9%. Over the same period, the population increased by an annual average of 1.8%. Mexico's gross domestic product (GDP) increased, in real terms, by an annual average of 1.9% in 1980–92.

Agriculture (including forestry and fishing) contributed an estimated 6.8% of GDP in 1992. About 28.1% of the employed labour force were engaged in the sector in 1993. The staple food crops are maize, wheat, sorghum, barley, rice, beans and potatoes. The principal cash crops are coffee (which accounted for an estimated 1.1% of total export earnings in 1992), cotton, sugar cane, fruit and vegetables (particularly tomatoes). Livestock-raising and fisheries are also important. During 1980–92 agricultural GDP increased by an annual average of 0.6%.

Industry (including mining, manufacturing, construction and power) engaged 27.8% of the employed labour force in 1990, and provided 28.9% of GDP in 1992. During 1980–92 industrial GDP increased by an annual average of 1.6%.

Mining contributed an estimated 2.1% of GDP in 1992, and 1.1% of the employed labour force were engaged in the sector in 1990. Mexico has large reserves of petroleum (which accounted for an estimated 27.3% of total export earnings in 1992) and natural gas. Zinc, salt, silver, copper, celestite and fluorite are also major mineral exports. Mercury, bismuth, antimony, cadmium, manganese, and phosphates are also mined, and there are significant reserves of uranium. A four-year plan to develop the mining sector through privatization and reclassification was initiated by the Government in 1990.

Manufacturing provided an estimated 20.7% of GDP in 1992, and an estimated 19.2% of the employed labour force were engaged in the sector in 1990. In 1991 the most important branches of manufacturing (based on value of output) were motor vehicles, food products, iron and steel, chemicals, beverages and electrical machinery. Petroleum refineries also contribute significantly to the sector. Mexico's more than 2,000 *maquiladora* export plants, where intermediate materials produced on US territory are processed or assembled on the Mexican side of the border, provide an estimated half a million jobs and make an increasingly significant contribution to the sector (more than 50% of total manufacturing revenues for 1993).

Energy is derived principally from mineral fuels and lubricants and hydroelectric power. In 1992, of total output of electricity by state-operated power installations, 78.6% was generated by thermoelectric power plants; (including 6.8% by coal-powered plants, 4.8% by gas thermal power plants and 3.2% by the country's nuclear electric power plant–which became operational in 1989); and 21.4% by hydro-electric plants.

Tourism is one of Mexico's principal sources of foreign exchange. In 1992 there were an estimated 6.4m. visitors to Mexico (mostly from the USA and Canada), providing revenue of US $3,868m. In 1991 receipts from tourism represented an estimated 3% of GDP.

In 1993 Mexico recorded a visible trade deficit of US $18,891m. (excluding transactions proceeding from the *maquiladora* sector) and there was a deficit of $23,390m. on the current account of the balance of payments. In 1992 the principal source of imports (62.9%) was the USA, which was also the principal market for exports (68.7%). Other major trading partners are Japan, Spain, France, Germany, Brazil and Canada. The principal exports in 1992 were crude petroleum, engines and spare parts for road vehicles, passenger cars, electrical goods and fresh or simply preserved vegetables. The principal imports were motor vehicle chassis, industrial machinery and equipment, iron and steel, telecommunications apparatus, organic chemicals, cereals and cereal preparations, and petroleum and petroleum products.

Preliminary budget figures for 1990 indicated a surplus of 5,104,000m. pesos. Mexico's external debt totalled US $118,028m. at the end of 1993, of which US $74,450m. was long-term public debt. In that year the cost of debt-servicing was equivalent to 32.7% of the value of exports of goods and services. The average annual rate of inflation was 47.1% in 1985–93, and stood at 9.8% in 1993. Some 2.7% of the total labour force were officially recorded as unemployed at the 1990 census.

Mexico is a member of the Inter-American Development Bank (see p. 170), and of the Latin American Integration Association (see p. 181). Mexico was admitted to the Asia Pacific Economic Co-operation group–APEC (see p.106) in 1993, and joined the Organisation of Economic Co-operation and Development—OECD (see p. 194) in 1994. Mexico is also a signatory nation to the North American Free Trade Agreement–NAFTA (see p.190).

Since the mid-1970s, the expansion of Mexico's petroleum industry has provided the main stimulus to the country's economic development, but the fall in world petroleum prices in the mid-1980s stifled economic activity, resulting in a decline in real per capita income of almost 50%. Agriculture has remained, for the most part, at subsistence level. Growth in the sector was hampered by the inefficient *ejido* land-holding system (dating from the 1917 Constitution) which concerned around 30,000 farm communities and some 103m. ha of land in 1991, and was finally abolished in 1992. An agricultural development plan, Procampo, announced in October 1993, aims to reactivate the sector through a programme of modernization and subsidies. During the 1980s industrial development was impeded by the flight of capital, the depreciation of the peso and a shortage of foreign exchange, and Mexico's vast foreign debt proved a serious obstacle to economic stability, despite successive rescheduling agreements. An ambitious debt-reduction programme, proposed by the US Government and supported by the World Bank and the IMF, was finalized in 1990 and was expected to allow the economy to expand. Mexico's eligibility for debt relief was enhanced by the Government's economic measures, which from 1987 (supported by pacts with trade unions and employers: see Recent History) aimed to encourage exports by a steady devaluation of the peso, and to limit inflation by restricting increases in prices and wages. By mid-1992 Mexico's domestic and foreign debt represented 38% of GDP, compared with more than 70% in 1988. The Salinas administration undertook tax reforms, removed many restrictions on foreign investment, and continued the extensive privatization programme begun by the previous administration. Import permits were replaced with competitive tariffs to encourage foreign participation, while the divestment programme reduced the state sector from 1,155 concerns, in 1982, to less than 300 in 1992. According to official estimates, economic growth for 1994 was 3.5%. Initial predictions of economic growth and inflation of 4% for 1995 were revised significantly following the dramatic loss in the value of the peso against the US dollar in late 1994 and early 1995 (see Recent History).

## Social Welfare

Social welfare is administered by the Mexican Social Security Institute (IMSS) and financed by contributions from employers, employees and the Government. An estimated 11,316,000 individuals were directly insured by the IMSS in 1991. In the same year, the Institute of Social Security and Services for State Employees (ISSSTE), provided cover for around 8,509,000 public-sector workers. There is no unemployment benefit. In 1991 there were 59,913 beds, 81,593 physicians and 122,623 nursing personnel distributed among 12,682 medical units within the national health system. Of total expenditure by the central Government in 1990, an estimated 2,279,000m. old pesos (1.9%) was for health services, and a further 14,776,000m. old pesos (12.3%) for social security and welfare. In December 1988 President Salinas announced the implementation of a new initiative to attempt to combat widespread poverty. The Programa Nacional de Solidaridad—Pronasol (National Solidarity Programme) was to provide funds for agricultural inputs, education, drinking-water, electricity, food distribution and basic infrastructure throughout Mexico. In November 1994 Salinas claimed that the six-year programme had cost US $16,000m. (20% of which had been spent in the most impoverished states of Chiapas, Oaxaca and Guerrero) and had provided 19,230 villages with electricity for the first time. Three hundred and fifty-five hospitals, 4,373 medical centres and 1,241 clinics had been built or refurbished under the scheme, while 81,350 schools had been constructed and a further 120,000 had been rehabilitated.

## Education

Education in state schools is provided free of charge and is officially compulsory. It covers six years of primary education, beginning at six years of age. Secondary education, which is not compulsory, begins at the age of 12 and lasts for up to six years. In 1992 the total enrolment at primary and secondary schools was equivalent to 85% of the school-age population. In 1992 an estimated 100% of children in the relevant age-group were enrolled in primary education, while the total enrolment at secondary schools was equivalent to 56% of students in the relevant age-group. Much is being carried out in the field of adult education, and the average rate of adult illiteracy declined from 34.6% in 1960 to 17% (males 13.8%; females 20.1%) in 1980. According to UNESCO estimates, the rate of adult illiteracy in 1990 was 12.4% (males 9.6%; females 15.0%). In 1993/94 there were some 13,000 institutes of higher education. There were 82 universities in 1985. Initiatives for education, implemented as part of the National Solidarity programme (see above), have included the construction of more than 37,000 new educational facilities in 1989–91, and a scholarship scheme to encourage continued school attendance by indigenous and rural children. The National Agreement for the Modernization of Basic Education, agreed between the Federal Government, state governments and the national teachers' union in May 1992, envisaged the future devolution of federal responsibility for education, to state and municipal bodies. Of total expenditure by the central Government in 1990, an estimated 16,527,000m. old pesos (13.7%) was for education.

## Public Holidays

**1995:** 1 January (New Year's Day), 5 February (Constitution Day), 21 March (Birthday of Benito Juárez), 14–17 April (Easter), 1 May (Labour Day), 5 May (Anniversary of the Battle of Puebla)*, 16 September (Independence Day), 12 October (Discovery of America), 1 November (All Saints' Day)*, 2 November (All Souls' Day)*, 20 November (Anniversary of the Revolution), 12 December (Day of Our Lady of Guadalupe)*, 25 December (Christmas).

**1996:** 1 January (New Year's Day), 5 February (Constitution Day), 21 March (Birthday of Benito Juárez), 5–8 April (Easter), 1 May (Labour Day), 5 May (Anniversary of the Battle of Puebla)*, 16 September (Independence Day), 12 October (Discovery of America), 1 November (All Saints' Day)*, 2 November (All Souls' Day)*, 20 November (Anniversary of the Revolution), 12 December (Day of Our Lady of Guadalupe)*, 25 December (Christmas).

* Widely-celebrated unofficial holidays.

## Weights and Measures

The metric system is in force.

# Statistical Survey

Sources (unless otherwise stated): Dirección General de Estadística, Instituto Nacional de Estadística, Geografía e Informática (INEGI), Edif. Sede, Avda Prolongación Héroe de Nacozari 2301 Sur, 20290 Aguascalientes, Ags.; Banco de México, Avda 5 de Mayo 2, Apdo 98 bis, 06059 México, DF; tel. (5) 709-0044; telex 1772669; Banco Nacional de Comercio Exterior, Camino a Santa Teresa 1679, Col. Jardines del Pedregal, 01900 México, DF; tel. (5) 568-2122; telex 176-0243.

## Area and Population

### AREA, POPULATION AND DENSITY

| | |
|---|---:|
| **Area (sq km)** | |
| Land | 1,908,691 |
| Inland water | 49,510 |
| Total | 1,958,201* |
| **Population (census results)†** | |
| 4 June 1980 | 66,846,833 |
| 12–16 March 1990 | |
| Males | 39,893,969 |
| Females | 41,355,676 |
| Total | 81,249,645 |
| **Population (official estimate at mid-year)** | |
| 1993 | 87,341,000 |
| Density (per sq km) at mid-1993 | 44.6 |

* 756,066 sq miles.
† Excluding adjustment for underenumeration, estimated to have been approximately 2,700,000 in 1980.

### ADMINISTRATIVE DIVISIONS (at census of March 1990)

| States | Area (sq km) | Estimated Population | Density (per sq km) | Capital |
|---|---:|---:|---:|---|
| Aguascalientes (Ags) | 5,471 | 719,659 | 131.54 | Aguascalientes |
| Baja California Norte (BCN) | 69,921 | 1,660,855 | 23.75 | Mexicali |
| Baja California Sur (BCS) | 73,475 | 317,764 | 4.32 | La Paz |
| Campeche (Camp.) | 50,812 | 535,185 | 10.53 | Campeche |
| Chiapas (Chis) | 74,211 | 3,210,496 | 43.26 | Tuxtla Gutiérrez |
| Chihuahua (Chih.) | 244,938 | 2,441,873 | 9.97 | Chihuahua |
| Coahuila (Coah.) | 149,982 | 1,972,340 | 13.15 | Saltillo |
| Colima (Col.) | 5,191 | 428,510 | 82.55 | Colima |
| Distrito Federal (DF) | 1,479 | 8,235,744 | 5,568.45 | Mexico City |
| Durango (Dgo) | 123,181 | 1,349,378 | 10.95 | Victoria de Durango |
| Guanajuato (Gto) | 30,491 | 3,982,593 | 130.62 | Guanajuato |
| Guerrero (Gro) | 64,281 | 2,620,637 | 40.77 | Chilpancingo de los Bravos |
| Hidalgo (Hgo) | 20,813 | 1,888,366 | 90.73 | Pachuca de Soto |
| Jalisco (Jal.) | 80,836 | 5,302,689 | 65.60 | Guadalajara |
| México (Méx.) | 21,355 | 9,815,795 | 459.65 | Toluca de Lerdo |
| Michoacán (Mich.) | 59,928 | 3,548,199 | 59.21 | Morelia |
| Morelos (Mor.) | 4,950 | 1,195,059 | 241.43 | Cuernavaca |
| Nayarit (Nay.) | 26,979 | 824,643 | 30.57 | Tepic |
| Nuevo León (NL) | 64,924 | 3,098,736 | 47.73 | Monterrey |
| Oaxaca (Oax.) | 93,952 | 3,019,560 | 32.14 | Oaxaca de Juárez |
| Puebla (Pue.) | 33,902 | 4,126,101 | 121.71 | Heróica Puebla de Zaragoza |
| Querétaro (Qro) | 11,449 | 1,051,235 | 91.82 | Querétaro |
| Quintana Roo (Q.Roo) | 50,212 | 493,277 | 9.82 | Ciudad Chetumal |
| San Luis Potosí (SLP) | 63,068 | 2,003,187 | 31.76 | San Luis Potosí |
| Sinaloa (Sin.) | 58,328 | 2,204,054 | 37.79 | Culiacán Rosales |
| Sonora (Son.) | 182,052 | 1,823,606 | 10.02 | Hermosillo |
| Tabasco (Tab.) | 25,267 | 1,501,744 | 59.43 | Villahermosa |
| Tamaulipas (Tamps) | 79,384 | 2,249,581 | 28.34 | Ciudad Victoria |
| Tlaxcala (Tlax.) | 4,016 | 761,277 | 189.56 | Tlaxcala de Xicohténcatl |
| Veracruz (Ver.) | 71,699 | 6,228,239 | 86.87 | Jalapa Enríquez |
| Yucatán (Yuc.) | 38,402 | 1,362.940 | 35.49 | Mérida |
| Zacatecas (Zac.) | 73,252 | 1,276,323 | 17.42 | Zacatecas |
| **Total** | 1,958,201 | 81,249,645 | 41.49 | — |

### PRINCIPAL TOWNS (population at census of March 1990)*

| | |
|---|---:|
| Ciudad de México (Mexico City—capital) | 8,236,960 |
| Guadalajara | 1,628,617 |
| Nezahualcóyotl | 1,259,543 |
| Monterrey | 1,064,197 |
| Heróica Puebla de Zaragoza (Puebla) | 1,054,921 |
| León | 872,453 |
| Ciudad Juárez | 797,679 |
| Tijuana | 742,686 |
| Mexicali | 602,390 |
| Culiacán Rosales (Culiacán) | 602,114 |
| Acapulco de Juárez (Acapulco) | 592,187 |
| Mérida | 557,340 |
| Chihuahua | 530,487 |
| San Luis Potosí | 525,819 |
| Aguascalientes | 506,384 |
| Morelia | 489,756 |
| Toluca de Lerdo (Toluca) | 487,630 |
| Torreón | 459,809 |
| Querétaro | 454,049 |
| Hermosillo | 449,472 |
| Saltillo | 440,845 |
| Victoria de Durango (Durango) | 414,015 |
| Villahermosa | 390,161 |
| Irapuato | 362,471 |
| Veracruz Llave (Veracruz) | 327,522 |
| Celaya | 315,577 |
| Atizapán de Zarogoza | 315,413 |
| Mazatlán | 314,249 |
| Ciudad Obregón | 311,078 |
| Los Mochis | 305,507 |
| Matamoros | 303,392 |
| Tuxtla Gutiérrez | 295,615 |
| Jalapa Enríquez (Jalapa) | 288,331 |
| Reynosa | 281,392 |
| Cuernavaca | 281,752 |
| Tampico | 271,636 |
| Ensenada | 260,905 |
| Guasave | 257,821 |

* Preliminary results.

### BIRTHS, MARRIAGES AND DEATHS*

| | Registered live births | Rate (per 1,000) | Registered marriages | Rate (per 1,000) | Registered deaths | Rate (per 1,000) |
|---|---:|---:|---:|---:|---:|---:|
| | Number | | Number | | Number | |
| 1986 | 2,579,301 | 32.4 | 579,887 | 7.3 | 400,079 | 5.0 |
| 1987 | 2,794,390 | 34.4 | 617,248 | 7.6 | 406,913 | 5.0 |
| 1988 | 2,622,031 | 31.7 | 630,106 | 7.6 | 412,987 | 5.0 |
| 1989 | 2,620,262 | 31.0 | 632,020 | 7.5 | 423,304 | 5.0 |
| 1990 | 2,735,312 | 31.7 | 642,201 | 7.5 | 422,803 | 4.9 |
| 1991 | 2,756,447 | 31.4 | 652,172 | 7.4 | 411,131 | 4.7 |
| 1992 | 2,797,397 | 31.2 | 667,598 | 7.5 | 409,814 | 4.6 |
| 1993 | 2,765,580 | 30.3 | 679,911 | 7.5 | 413,756 | 4.5 |

* Data are tabulated by year of registration rather than by year of occurrence. However, birth registration is incomplete. According to UN estimates, the average annual rates in 1985–90 were: births 30.0 per 1,000; deaths 5.9 per 1,000.

**Expectation of life** (UN estimates, years at birth, 1985–90): 68.8 (males 65.7; females 72.1) (Source: UN, *World Population Prospects, 1992 Revision*).

# MEXICO

*Statistical Survey*

## ECONOMICALLY ACTIVE POPULATION
(persons aged 12 years and over, 1990 census)

|  | Males | Females | Total |
|---|---|---|---|
| Agriculture, hunting, forestry and fishing | 5,110,964 | 189,150 | 5,300,114 |
| Mining and quarrying | 232,972 | 27,543 | 260,515 |
| Manufacturing | 3,436,220 | 1,057,059 | 4,493,279 |
| Electricity, gas and water | 135,518 | 18,951 | 154,469 |
| Construction | 1,551,059 | 43,902 | 1,594,961 |
| Trade, restaurants and hotels | 2,558,832 | 1,316,268 | 3,875,100 |
| Transport, storage and communications | 948,994 | 96,398 | 1,045,392 |
| Financing, insurance, real estate and business services | 516,918 | 275,014 | 791,932 |
| Community, social and personal services | 2,891,575 | 2,192,204 | 5,083,779 |
| Activities not adequately defined | 499,090 | 304,782 | 803,872 |
| **Total employed** | 17,882,142 | 5,521,271 | 23,403,413 |
| Unemployed | 536,553 | 123,317 | 659,870 |
| **Total labour force** | 18,418,695 | 5,644,588 | 24,063,283 |

**1993** (sample survey, April–June, persons aged 12 years and over): Total employed 32,832,680; Unemployed 819,132; Total labour force 33,651,812.

Source: ILO, *Year Book of Labour Statistics*.

## Agriculture

### PRINCIPAL CROPS ('000 metric tons)

|  | 1991 | 1992 | 1993 |
|---|---|---|---|
| Wheat | 4,061 | 3,626 | 3,622* |
| Rice (paddy) | 347 | 361 | 325* |
| Barley | 580 | 536 | 551* |
| Maize | 14,253 | 17,003 | 18,600* |
| Oats | 121 | 100* | 120† |
| Sorghum | 4,250 | 5,345 | 2,602* |
| Potatoes | 1,211 | 1,230† | 1,210† |
| Sweet potatoes | 35 | 35† | 35† |
| Other roots and tubers† | 75 | 77† | 78† |
| Dry beans | 1,379 | 804 | 700* |
| Dry broad beans | 26 | 26† | 26† |
| Chick-peas | 195 | 195† | 196† |
| Soybeans | 725 | 594 | 520* |
| Groundnuts (in shell) | 115 | 110* | 120† |
| Sesame seed | 37 | 24 | 50* |
| Safflower seed | 88 | 82* | 120† |
| Cottonseed | 307 | 52 | 40* |
| Cotton (lint) | 202 | 33* | 23* |
| Coconuts† | 1,005 | 1,122 | 990 |
| Copra | 175 | 200 | 173 |
| Sugar cane | 38,387 | 39,955 | 41,652 |
| Tomatoes | 2,122 | 1,413 | 1,780* |
| Green chillies | 761 | 760 | 760† |
| Green beans† | 45 | 46 | 46 |
| Green peas† | 40 | 40† | 40† |
| Watermelons | 393 | 393† | 394† |
| Melons | 645 | 646† | 647† |
| Grapes | 530 | 520† | 525† |
| Apples | 527 | 598* | 580* |
| Pears | 44 | 30* | 32* |
| Peaches and nectarines | 132 | 155* | 150† |
| Plums | 58 | 59† | 59† |
| Oranges | 2,369 | 2,541 | 2,530* |
| Lemons and limes | 717 | 777 | 700† |
| Grapefruit | 98 | 118* | 120† |
| Avocados | 780 | 725 | 786† |
| Mangoes | 1,118 | 1,120† | 1,130† |
| Pineapples | 299 | 299† | 300† |
| Bananas | 1,889 | 2,095 | 1,650† |
| Strawberries | 88.2 | 75.7 | 67.0† |
| Coffee (green) | 334 | 360 | 184* |
| Cocoa beans | 44 | 44 | 43* |
| Tobacco (leaves) | 29 | 30* | 30* |

* Unofficial figure.  † FAO estimate(s).

Source: FAO, *Production Yearbook*.

### LIVESTOCK ('000 head, year ending September)

|  | 1991 | 1992 | 1993 |
|---|---|---|---|
| Cattle | 31,460 | 30,157* | 30,649* |
| Pigs | 15,786 | 16,502 | 16,832 |
| Sheep | 5,000† | 5,300* | 5,876 |
| Goats | 10,532 | 11,008 | 11,066† |
| Horses† | 6,175 | 6,180 | 6,185 |
| Mules† | 3,190 | 3,200 | 3,210 |
| Asses† | 3,188 | 3,189 | 3,190 |

Chickens (million): 248 in 1991; 282* in 1992; 285† in 1993.
Ducks (million)†: 7 in 1991; 7 in 1992; 8 in 1993.
Turkeys (million): 6 in 1991; 6† in 1992; 6† in 1993.

* Unofficial figure.  † FAO estimate(s).

Source: FAO, *Production Yearbook*.

### LIVESTOCK PRODUCTS ('000 metric tons)

|  | 1991 | 1992 | 1993 |
|---|---|---|---|
| Beef and veal | 1,189 | 1,247 | 1,300* |
| Mutton and lamb | 26 | 28 | 32* |
| Goat meat* | 31 | 31 | 32 |
| Pig meat | 812 | 820 | 830 |
| Horse meat† | 74 | 76 | 78 |
| Poultry meat | 897 | 936 | 923 |
| Cows' milk | 6,925 | 7,204 | 7,450* |
| Goats' milk | 131 | 148 | 136† |
| Butter* | 31.0 | 28.0 | 28.0 |
| Cheese† | 114.5 | 117.5 | 116.4 |
| Evaporated and condensed milk† | 164.4 | 166.3 | 166.3 |
| Hen eggs | 1,141.4 | 1,160.6 | 1,190.0 |
| Cattle hides* | 155.0 | 160.0 | 161.0 |
| Honey | 69.5 | 63.9 | 55.0* |

* Unofficial figure(s).  † FAO estimate(s).

Source: FAO, *Production Yearbook*.

## Forestry

### ROUNDWOOD REMOVALS
('000 cubic metres, excluding bark)

|  | 1990 | 1991 | 1992 |
|---|---|---|---|
| Sawlogs, veneer logs and logs for sleepers | 5,793 | 5,390 | 5,477 |
| Pulpwood* | 1,954 | 1,954 | 1,954 |
| Other industrial wood* | 139 | 98 | 85 |
| Fuel wood* | 14,805 | 15,127 | 15,450 |
| **Total** | 22,691 | 22,569 | 22,966 |

* FAO estimate(s).

Source: FAO, *Yearbook of Forest Products*.

### SAWNWOOD PRODUCTION
('000 cubic metres, incl. railway sleepers)

|  | 1990 | 1991† | 1992* |
|---|---|---|---|
| Coniferous (softwood) | 2,028* | 2,345 | 2,345 |
| Broadleaved (hardwood) | 339† | 351 | 351 |
| **Total** | 2,366 | 2,696 | 2,696 |

* FAO estimate(s).  † Unofficial figure(s).

Source: FAO, *Yearbook of Forest Products*.

MEXICO

## Fishing

('000 metric tons, live weight)

|  | 1990 | 1991 | 1992 |
|---|---|---|---|
| Cichlids | 83.8 | 75.2 | 77.0 |
| Other freshwater fishes | 105.4 | 92.2 | 88.1 |
| California pilchard (sardine) | 398.7 | 467.4 | 251.5 |
| Californian anchoveta | 0.6 | 12.1 | 3.4 |
| Yellowfin tuna | 117.7 | 116.4 | 122.2 |
| Marine shrimps and prawns | 62.3 | 70.6 | 66.2 |
| American cupped oyster | 47.7 | 34.6 | 29.2 |
| **Total catch** (incl. others)* | 1,400.9 | 1,453.3 | 1,247.6 |

* Including unspecified marine fishes ('000 metric tons): 286.4 in 1990; 312.1 in 1991; 347.7 in 1992.

Source: FAO, *Yearbook of Fishery Statistics*.

## Mining*

(metric tons, unless otherwise indicated)

|  | 1991 | 1992 | 1993 |
|---|---|---|---|
| Antimony | 2,752 | 1,064 | 1,494 |
| Arsenic | 4,922 | 4,293 | 4,447 |
| Barytes | 191,962 | 443,782 | 123,158 |
| Bismuth | 651 | 807 | 911 |
| Cadmium | 1,253 | 1,323 | 1,436 |
| Coal | 4,790,185 | 5,059,947 | 5,483,536 |
| Coke | 2,153,117 | 2,033,003 | 1,929,728 |
| Copper | 267,039 | 277,129 | 301,097 |
| Crude petroleum ('000 cu m)† | 137,562 | 138,191 | n.a. |
| Dolomite | 435,214 | 466,490 | 459,938 |
| Feldspar | 138,732 | 159,718 | 122,752 |
| Fluorite | 324,320 | 286,640 | 282,228 |
| Gas (million cu m)† | 37,556 | 37,141 | 36,703 |
| Gold (kg) | 8,858 | 10,857 | 11,413 |
| Graphite | 30,165 | 31,470 | 40,353 |
| Gypsum | 2,318,165 | 2,960,126 | 2,837,185 |
| Iron | 6,390,436 | 6,544,956 | 6,755,104 |
| Lead | 158,831 | 173,014 | 179,675 |
| Manganese | 79,206 | 137,146 | 122,166 |
| Molybdenum | 2,597 | 2,347 | 2,577 |
| Phosphate rock | 416,426 | 338,744 | 228,306 |
| Silver | 2,207 | 2,325 | 2,368 |
| Sulphur | 1,791,841 | 1,484,497 | 905,713 |
| Tungsten | 194 | 162 | 0 |
| Zinc | 301,685 | 340,681 | 334,232 |

* Figures for metallic minerals refer to the metal content of ores.
† Preliminary figures.

## Industry

**SELECTED PRODUCTS**
('000 metric tons, unless otherwise indicated)

|  | 1990 | 1991 | 1992* |
|---|---|---|---|
| Wheat flour | 2,510 | 2,488 | 2,477 |
| Corn flour | 932 | 914 | 960 |
| Sugar | 3,174 | 3,661 | 3,291 |
| Beer ('000 hectolitres) | 38,734 | 41,092 | 40,162 |
| Cigarettes (million cartons) | 2,769 | 2,734 | 2,799 |
| Lubricating oils | 199 | 217 | 211 |
| Sulphuric acid | 440 | 338 | 167 |
| Tyres ('000 units) | 13,628 | 14,547 | 16,168 |
| Cement | 24,289 | 24,785 | 26,033 |
| Gas stoves—household ('000 units) | 370 | 458 | 490 |
| Refrigerators—household ('000 units) | 302 | 396 | 429 |
| Washing machines—household ('000 units) | 558 | 611 | 642 |
| Television receivers ('000 units) | 633 | 490 | 435 |
| Cotton yarn | 12.2 | 10.2 | 8.0 |
| Electric energy (million kWh) | 122,749 | 126,958 | 131,501 |

* Provisional.

## Finance

**CURRENCY AND EXCHANGE RATES**

**Monetary Units**
100 centavos = 1 Mexican nuevo peso.

**Sterling and US Dollar Equivalents** (31 December 1994)
£1 sterling = 8.331 nuevos pesos;
US $1 = 5.325 nuevos pesos;
100 Mexican nuevos pesos = £12.003 = $18.779.

**Average Exchange Rate** (nuevos pesos per US $)
1992   3.0949
1993   3.1156
1994   3.3751

Note: Figures are given in terms of the nuevo (new) peso, introduced on 1 January 1993 and equivalent to 1,000 former pesos.

**BUDGET** ('000 million old pesos)*

| Revenue | 1988 | 1989 | 1990† |
|---|---|---|---|
| Taxation‡ | 56,859 | 77,493 | 88,965 |
| Taxes on income, profits and capital gains | 20,103 | 27,285 | 35,181 |
| Social security contributions | 7,731 | 10,628 | 13,086 |
| Taxes on payroll and work force | 499 | 605 | 718 |
| Value-added tax | 13,574 | 17,482 | 19,882 |
| Excises | 10,254 | 11,879 | 8,610 |
| Sales of gasoline | 6,812 | 7,954 | 4,320 |
| Taxes on specific services | 831 | 1,279 | 1,410 |
| Motor vehicle taxes | 346 | 444 | 493 |
| Taxes on hydrocarbons | 13,338 | 17,915 | 23,587 |
| Import duties | 2,194 | 4,654 | 4,302 |
| Other current revenue | 10,606 | 15,344 | 7,392 |
| Property income | 5,271 | 5,993 | 5,504 |
| Fines and forfeits | 747 | 1,238 | 1,128 |
| Capital revenue | 11 | 4 | 50 |
| **Total revenue** | 67,476 | 92,841 | 96,407 |

# MEXICO

## Statistical Survey

| Expenditure§ | 1988 | 1989 | 1990† |
|---|---|---|---|
| General public services | 1,802 | 2,673 | 3,423 |
| Defence | 2,077 | 2,642 | 2,815 |
| Public order and safety | 395 | 524 | 556 |
| Education | 9,716 | 13,972 | 16,527 |
| Health | 1,435 | 1,810 | 2,279 |
| Social security and welfare | 8,188 | 11,183 | 14,776 |
| Housing and community amenities | 549 | 891 | 722 |
| Recreational, cultural and religious affairs and services | 353 | 36 | 346 |
| Economic affairs and services | 10,908 | 17,024 | 15,930 |
| Fuel and energy | 1,371 | 1,996 | 2,178 |
| Agriculture, forestry and fishing | 2,222 | 3,445 | 3,451 |
| Mining, manufacturing and construction | 2,409 | 2,749 | 2,047 |
| Roads | 831 | 944 | 1,105 |
| Other transport and communications | 1,585 | 1,795 | 1,247 |
| Other purposes | 72,349 | 68,609 | 63,026 |
| Interest on public debt | 63,256 | 62,602 | 52,715 |
| **Sub-total** | 107,772 | 119,364 | 120,400 |
| Contributions to social security | −446 | −680 | −948 |
| Adjustment to cash basis | −53 | −65 | −200 |
| **Total expenditure** | 107,273 | 118,619 | 119,252 |
| Current | 97,031 | 103,795 | 102,384 |
| Capital | 10,242 | 14,824 | 16,868 |

\* Figures refer to the consolidated accounts of the central Government, including government agencies and the national social security system. The budgets of state and local governments are excluded.
† Preliminary figures.
‡ After deducting payments in certificates ('000 million old pesos): 53 in 1988; 65 in 1989; 200 in 1990; taxes collected for states ('000 million old pesos): 12,063 in 1988; 14,553 in 1989; 18,200 in 1990; and tax refunds ('000 million old pesos): 204 in 1988; 477 in 1989.
§ Excluding net lending ('000 million old pesos): 546 in 1988; 716 in 1989; −27,949 in 1990.
Source: IMF, *Government Finance Statistics Yearbook*.

### INTERNATIONAL RESERVES (US $ million at 31 December)*

| | 1992 | 1993 | 1994 |
|---|---|---|---|
| IMF special drawing rights | 548 | 223 | 177 |
| Foreign exchange | 18,394 | 24,886 | 6.101 |
| **Total** | 18,942 | 25,109 | 6,278 |

\* Excluding gold reserves ($357 million at 30 September 1989).
Source: IMF, *International Financial Statistics*.

### MONEY SUPPLY ('000 million old pesos at 31 December)

| | 1991 | 1992 | 1993 |
|---|---|---|---|
| Currency outside banks | 32,513 | 38,116 | 43,351 |
| Demand deposits at deposit money banks | 72,772 | 82,604 | 98,308 |
| **Total money** (incl. others) | 106,227 | 122,220 | 143,485 |

Source: IMF, *International Financial Statistics*.

### COST OF LIVING (Consumer Price Index; base: 1978 = 100)

| | 1991 | 1992 | 1993 |
|---|---|---|---|
| Food, beverages and tobacco | 24,945.7 | 27,747.4 | 29,574.1 |
| Clothing, footwear and accessories | 25,859.6 | 28,748.3 | 31,294.6 |
| Housing | 25,776.9 | 30,388.3 | 33,830.8 |
| Furniture and domestic appliances | 22,887.8 | 25,265.0 | 27,199.0 |
| Health and personal care | 28,883.1 | 33,772.1 | 37,965.8 |
| Transport | 29,508.8 | 37,010.4 | 40,638.7 |
| Education and recreation | 30,551.7 | 37,172.4 | 44,487.1 |
| Other services | 45,598.5 | 52,024.2 | 57,894.9 |
| **All items** | 27,576.3 | 31,852.8 | 34,959.0 |

## NATIONAL ACCOUNTS
(million new pesos at current prices)

### National Income and Product

| | 1990 | 1991 | 1992 |
|---|---|---|---|
| Compensation of employees | 171,415.5 | 222,959.7 | 278,553.6 |
| Operating surplus | 382,538.0 | 473,394.5 | 539,514.6 |
| **Domestic factor incomes** | 553,953.5 | 696,354.2 | 818,068.2 |
| Consumption of fixed capital | 66,238.8 | 82,702.8 | 98,237.1 |
| **Gross domestic product at factor cost** | 620,192.3 | 779,057.0 | 916,305.3 |
| Indirect taxes | 74,873.4 | 93,851.5 | 111,889.5 |
| *Less* Subsidies | 8,660.0 | 7,742.8 | 9,038.9 |
| **GDP in purchasers' values** | 686,405.7 | 865,165.7 | 1,019,155.9 |

### Expenditure on the Gross Domestic Product

| | 1990 | 1991 | 1992 |
|---|---|---|---|
| Government final consumption expenditure | 57,798.5 | 77,971.4 | 102,750.7 |
| Private final consumption expenditure | 486,354.4 | 621,208.4 | 736,137.1 |
| Increase in stocks | 22,544.2 | 25,327.1 | 25,253.7 |
| Gross fixed capital formation | 127,727.6 | 168,486.5 | 211,933.5 |
| **Total domestic expenditure** | 694,424.7 | 892,993.4 | 1,076,075.0 |
| Exports of goods and services | 108,299.0 | 119,535.2 | 128,052.6 |
| *Less* Imports of goods and services | 116,317.9 | 147,362.8 | 184,971.7 |
| **GDP in purchasers' values** | 686,405.7 | 865,165.7 | 1,019,155.9 |

### Gross Domestic Product by Economic Activity

| | 1990 | 1991 | 1992 |
|---|---|---|---|
| Agriculture, forestry and fishing | 54,810.9 | 66,682.3 | 71,139.6 |
| Mining and quarrying | 17,695.7 | 18,120.4 | 21,423.7 |
| Manufacturing | 156,179.7 | 192,526.5 | 215,711.0 |
| Electricity, gas and water | 9,479.6 | 13,068.0 | 15,721.1 |
| Construction | 27,230.0 | 36,216.7 | 48,490.7 |
| Trade, restaurants and hotels | 178,782.9 | 214,150.3 | 244,150.0 |
| Transport, storage and communications | 56,505.4 | 76,544.8 | 95,104.9 |
| Finance, insurance, real estate and business services | 80,973.1 | 108,409.5 | 136,127.0 |
| Community, social and personal services | 112,300.7 | 150,462.2 | 194,879.8 |
| **Sub-total** | 693,957.6 | 876,180.8 | 1,042,747.8 |
| *Less* Imputed bank service charges | 7,551.9 | 11,015.1 | 23,591.8 |
| **Total** | 686,405.7 | 865,165.7 | 1,019,155.9 |

### BALANCE OF PAYMENTS (US $ million)

| | 1991 | 1992 | 1993 |
|---|---|---|---|
| Merchandise exports f.o.b. | 26,855 | 27,516 | 30,033 |
| Merchandise imports f.o.b. | −38,184 | −48,193 | −48,924 |
| **Trade balance** | −11,329 | −20,677 | −18,891 |
| Exports of services | 12,841 | 13,933 | 14,766 |
| Imports of services | −10,540 | −11,487 | −11,030 |
| Other income received | 3,601 | 2,874 | 2,703 |
| Other income paid | −12,207 | −12,470 | −13,625 |
| Private unrequited transfers (net) | 2,633 | 2,908 | 2,591 |
| Official unrequited transfers (net) | 105 | 113 | 96 |
| **Current balance** | −14,896 | −24,806 | −23,390 |
| Direct investment (net) | 4,742 | 4,393 | 4,901 |
| Portfolio investment (net) | 12,138 | 19,175 | 27,867 |
| Other capital (net) | 8,241 | 3,438 | −709 |
| Net errors and omissions | −2,252 | −455 | 1,437 |
| **Overall balance** | 7,973 | 1,745 | 7,232 |

Source: IMF, *International Financial Statistics*.

MEXICO

# External Trade

Note: Data exclude imports into free zones and exports from bonded factories, mostly to the USA.

**PRINCIPAL COMMODITIES**
(distribution by SITC, US $ million)

| Imports f.o.b. | 1990 | 1991 | 1992 |
|---|---|---|---|
| **Food and live animals** | 3,504.0 | 3,041.1 | 4,096.2 |
| Cereals and cereal preparations | 944.2 | 757.8 | 1,239.7 |
| **Crude materials (inedible) except fuels** | 1,898.1 | 2,109.8 | 2,431.1 |
| **Mineral fuels, lubricants, etc.** | 1,133.5 | 1,402.2 | 1,674.5 |
| Petroleum and petroleum products | 898.9 | 1,158.1 | 1,210.4 |
| **Chemicals and related products** | 2,967.4 | 3,739.2 | 4,397.2 |
| Organic chemicals | 1,063.4 | 1,347.0 | 1,461.0 |
| Plastic materials, etc. | 684.4 | 860.5 | 906.9 |
| **Basic manufactures** | 3,901.8 | 5,455.7 | 6,654.7 |
| Iron and steel | 1,117.0 | 1,607.7 | 1,791.0 |
| Manufacturers of metals, n.e.s. | 746.8 | 1,074.7 | 1,287.3 |
| **Machinery and transport equipment** | 13,052.2 | 18,134.0 | 23,012.2 |
| Power-generating machinery and equipment | 574.2 | 798.5 | 1,097.9 |
| Machinery specialized for particular industries | 1,862.1 | 2,069.1 | 2,627.2 |
| General industrial machinery and equipment | 1,911.9 | 2,464.8 | 3,257.1 |
| Non-electric parts and accessories | 659.1 | 833.2 | 1,018.0 |
| Office machines and automatic data-processing equipment | 1,120.0 | 1,455.0 | 1,759.3 |
| Telecommunications and sound recording and reproducing apparatus and equipment | 1,383.0 | 1,779.4 | 2,085.1 |
| Other electrical machinery, apparatus, etc. | 1,558.3 | 2,056.2 | 2,578.4 |
| Road vehicles | 3,592.7 | 6,351.2 | 7,938.0 |
| Motor vehicle parts and accessories | 3,029.5 | 5,726.6 | 6,846.4 |
| Motor vehicle chassis | 2,620.9 | 5,213.5 | 6,171.1 |
| **Miscellaneous manufactured articles** | 2,597.7 | 3,574.0 | 4,870.1 |
| Professional, scientific and controlling instruments and apparatus | 535.9 | 799.5 | 1,045.34 |
| **Total** (incl. others) | 29,559.5 | 38,073.3 | 47,877.9 |

| Exports f.o.b. | 1990 | 1991 | 1992 |
|---|---|---|---|
| **Food and live animals** | 2,710.6 | 2,967.4 | 2,681.8 |
| Fruit and vegetables | 1,463.9 | 1,532.3 | 1,488.1 |
| Fresh or simply preserved vegetables | 1,009.7 | 893.7 | 905.6 |
| **Crude materials (inedible) except fuels** | 1,096.8 | 1,102.6 | 1,052.3 |
| **Mineral fuels, lubricants, etc.** | 9,868.9 | 8,091.4 | 8,114.3 |
| Petroleum and petroleum products | 9,545.5 | 7,822.4 | 7,932.3 |
| Crude petroleum | 8,918.7 | 7,388.9 | 7,416.0 |
| **Chemicals and related products** | 1,763.3 | 1,995.5 | 2,079.3 |
| Organic chemicals | 574.2 | 734.3 | 732.6 |
| **Basic manufactures** | 2,997.2 | 3,003.1 | 3,104.6 |
| Iron and steel | 756.6 | 749.2 | 687.7 |
| Non-ferrous metals | 844.0 | 688.9 | 714.5 |
| **Machinery and transport equipment** | 6,602.2 | 8,312.7 | 8,603.9 |
| Power-generating machinery | 1,510.9 | 1,545.1 | 1,576.5 |
| Internal combustion piston engines | 1,394.4 | 1,353.4 | 1,378.9 |
| Office machines and automatic data-processing equipment | 560.4 | 745.8 | 757.9 |
| Electrical machinery, apparatus, etc. | 614.5 | 737.7 | 991.0 |
| Road vehicles | 3,086.2 | 4,463.9 | 4,442.1 |
| Passenger motor vehicles, except buses | 2,614.1 | 3,784.4 | 3,293.3 |
| **Miscellaneous manufactured articles** | 894.3 | 1,074.0 | 1,152.0 |
| **Total** (incl. others) | 26,344.7 | 26,956.7 | 27,207.1 |

Source: UN, *International Trade Statistics Yearbook*.

**PRINCIPAL TRADING PARTNERS** (US $ million)

| Imports f.o.b. | 1990 | 1991 | 1992 |
|---|---|---|---|
| Brazil | 357.8 | 753.2 | 1,109.1 |
| Canada | 390.7 | 780.4 | 1,044.0 |
| China, People's Rep. | 218.4 | 428.5 | 541.8 |
| France | 716.3 | 979.8 | 1,304.0 |
| Germany | 1,645.6 | 2,328.0 | 2,476.6 |
| Italy | 446.9 | 621.2 | 983.3 |
| Japan | 1,283.1 | 2,061.5 | 3,040.0 |
| Korea, Democratic People's Republic | 25.8 | 350.0 | 608.7 |
| Spain | 503.8 | 572.3 | 873.9 |
| Switzerland-Liechtenstein | 406.5 | 376.5 | 472.0 |
| United Kingdom | 590.3 | 495.9 | 616.7 |
| USA | 19,845.6 | 24,651.7 | 30,128.8 |
| **Total** (incl. others) | 29,556.8 | 38,072.4 | 47,876.9 |

| Exports f.o.b. | 1990 | 1991 | 1992 |
|---|---|---|---|
| Belgium-Luxembourg | 209.7 | 301.8 | 275.6 |
| Brazil | 165.3 | 184.0 | 427.3 |
| Canada | 219.9 | 561.2 | 785.0 |
| France | 546.3 | 606.0 | 546.8 |
| Germany | 321.2 | 557.4 | 482.0 |
| Japan | 1,442.3 | 1,229.8 | 883.6 |
| Spain | 1,439.8 | 1,184.0 | 1,216.5 |
| United Kingdom | 182.3 | 223.9 | 245.6 |
| USA | 18,491.3 | 18,728.7 | 18,656.7 |
| **Total** (incl. others) | 26,247.4 | 26,939.2 | 27,165.6 |

Source: UN, *International Trade Statistics Yearbook*.

## Transport

**RAILWAYS** ('000)

|  | 1991 | 1992* | 1993 |
|---|---|---|---|
| Passengers carried | 14,901 | 14,740 | 10,878 |
| Passenger-kilometres | 4,686,017 | 4,793,936 | 3,793,936 |
| Freight ton-kilometres | 32,944,487 | 34,216,146 | 35,671,951 |

* Preliminary figures.

**ROAD TRAFFIC** (motor vehicles in use at 31 December)

|  | 1991 | 1992 | 1993* |
|---|---|---|---|
| Cars | 7,219,887 | 7,749,641 | 8,014,143 |
| Buses | 98,109 | 95,350 | 96,552 |
| Lorries | 3,306,375 | 3,505,733 | 3,661,482 |
| Motor cycles | 262,355 | 275,394 | 283,653 |

* Provisional figures.

**SHIPPING**

**Merchant Fleet** (at 30 June)

|  | 1990 | 1991 | 1992 |
|---|---|---|---|
| Number of vessels | 640 | 649 | 635 |
| Displacement ('000 grt) | 1,320 | 1,196 | 1,110 |

Source: Lloyd's Register of Shipping.

**Sea-Borne Shipping**
(domestic and international freight traffic, '000 metric tons)

|  | 1991 | 1992 | 1993* |
|---|---|---|---|
| Goods loaded | 128,011 | 130,172 | 129,091 |
| Goods unloaded | 52,540 | 53,702 | 53,121 |

* Provisional figures.

**CIVIL AVIATION** (traffic on scheduled services)

|  | 1991 | 1992 | 1993 |
|---|---|---|---|
| Kilometres flown (million) | 242 | 292 | 325 |
| Passengers carried ('000) | 16,987 | 19,513 | 20,022 |
| Passenger-km (million) | 20,226 | 22,138 | 23,721 |
| Total ton-km (million)* | 1,709 | 1,726 | n.a. |

* Source: UN, *Statistical Yearbook*.

## Tourism

|  | 1990 | 1991 | 1992† |
|---|---|---|---|
| Tourists ('000) | 6,392.7 | 6,371.7 | 6,352.3 |
| Total expenditure (US $ million) | 3,400.9 | 3,783.7 | 3,867.8 |

* Figures exclude excursionists and cruise-ship passengers.

Source: Secretaría de Turismo.

## Communications Media

|  | 1990 | 1991 | 1992 |
|---|---|---|---|
| Radio receivers ('000 in use) | 21,500 | 22,000 | 22,500 |
| Television receivers ('000 in use) | 12,350 | 12,750 | 13,100 |
| Telephones ('000 in use)* | 10,350 | 11,113 | 11,891 |
| Book production: titles | 2,608† | n.a. | n.a. |
| Daily newspapers | 285 | n.a. | 292 |

* Source: INEGI.
† Including pamphlets: 21.

Source: mainly UNESCO, *Statistical Yearbook*.

## Education

(estimates, 1993/94)

|  | Institutions | Students* | Teachers |
|---|---|---|---|
| Nursery | 52,325 | 2,901.5 | 116,039 |
| Primary | 85,503 | 14,468.7 | 488,139 |
| Secondary | 20,550 | 4,311.8 | 243,877 |
| Higher | 13,000 | 3,961.0 | 324,148 |

* Figures are in thousands.

Source: Secretaría de Educación Pública.

# Directory

## The Constitution

The present Mexican Constitution was proclaimed on 5 February 1917, at the end of the revolution, which began in 1910, against the regime of Porfirio Díaz. Its provisions regarding religion, education and the ownership and exploitation of mineral wealth reflect the long revolutionary struggle against the concentration of power in the hands of the Roman Catholic Church and the large landowners, and the struggle which culminated, in the 1930s, in the expropriation of the properties of the foreign petroleum companies. It has been amended from time to time.

### GOVERNMENT

**The President and Congress.**
The President of the Republic, in agreement with the Cabinet and with the approval of the Congreso de la Unión (Congress) or of the Permanent Committee when the Congreso is not in session, may suspend constitutional guarantees in case of foreign invasion, serious disturbance, or any other emergency endangering the people.

The exercise of supreme executive authority is vested in the President, who is elected for six years and enters office on 1 December of the year of election. The presidential powers include the right to appoint and remove members of the Cabinet, the Attorney-General and the Governor of the Distrito Federal (Federal District); to appoint, with the approval of the Senado (Senate), diplomatic officials, the higher officers of the army, and ministers of the supreme and higher courts of justice. The President is also empowered to dispose of the armed forces for the internal and external security of the federation.

The Congreso is composed of the Cámara Federal de Diputados (Federal Chamber of Deputies) elected every three years, and the Senado whose members hold office for six years. There is one deputy for every 250,000 people and for every fraction of over 125,000 people. The Senado is composed of two members for each state and two for the Distrito Federal. Regular sessions of the Congreso begin on 1 September and may not continue beyond 31 December of the same year. Extraordinary sessions may be convened by the Permanent Committee.

The powers of the Congreso include the right to: pass laws and regulations; impose taxes; specify the criteria on which the Executive may negotiate loans; declare war; raise, maintain and regulate the organization of the armed forces; establish and maintain schools of various types throughout the country; approve or reject the budget; sanction appointments submitted by the President of the Supreme Court and magistrates of the superior court of the Distrito Federal; approve or reject treaties and conventions made with foreign powers; and ratify diplomatic appointments.

The Permanent Committee, consisting of 29 members of the Congreso (15 of whom are deputies and 14 senators), officiates when the Congreso is in recess, and is responsible for the convening of extraordinary sessions of the Congreso.

### The States

Governors are elected by popular vote in a general election every six years. The local legislature is formed by deputies, who are changed every three years. The judicature is specially appointed under the Constitution by the competent authority (it is never subject to the popular vote).

Each state is a separate unit, with the right to levy taxes and to legislate in certain matters. The states are not allowed to levy inter-state customs duties.

### The Federal District

The Distrito Federal consists of Mexico City and several neighbouring small towns and villages. The Governor is appointed by the President.

## EDUCATION

According to the Constitution, the provision of educational facilities is the joint responsibility of the federation, the states and the municipalities. Education shall be democratic, and shall be directed to developing all the faculties of the individual students, while imbuing them with love of their country and a consciousness of international solidarity and justice. Religious bodies may not provide education, except training for the priesthood. Private educational institutions must conform to the requirements of the Constitution with regard to the nature of the teaching given. The education provided by the states shall be free of charge.

## RELIGION

Religious bodies of whatever denomination shall not have the capacity to possess or administer real estate or capital invested therein. Churches are the property of the nation; the headquarters of bishops, seminaries, convents and other property used for the propagation of a religious creed shall pass into the hands of the state, to be dedicated to the public service of the federation or of the respective state. Institutions of charity, provided they are not connected with a religious body, may hold real property. The establishment of monastic orders is prohibited. Ministers of religion must be Mexican; they may not criticize the fundamental laws of the country in a public or private meeting; they may not vote or form associations for political purposes. Political meetings may not be held in places of worship.

A reform proposal, whereby constitutional restrictions on the Catholic Church were formally ended, received congressional approval in December 1991 and was promulgated as law in January 1992.

## LAND AND MINERAL OWNERSHIP

Article 27 of the Constitution vests direct ownership of minerals and other products of the subsoil, including petroleum and water, in the nation, and reserves to the Federal Government alone the right to grant concessions in accordance with the laws to individuals and companies, on the condition that they establish regular work for the exploitation of the materials. At the same time, the right to acquire ownership of lands and waters belonging to the nation, or concessions for their exploitation, is limited to Mexican individuals and companies, although the State may concede similar rights to foreigners who agree not to invoke the protection of their governments to enforce such rights. No alien may acquire direct ownership over lands and waters within an area 100 kilometres wide along the frontiers or 50 kilometres along the coast.

The same article declares null all alienations of lands, waters and forests belonging to towns or communities made by political chiefs or other local authorities in violation of the provisions of the law of 25 June 1856,* and all concessions or sales of communally-held lands, waters and forests made by the federal authorities after 1 December 1876. The population settlements which lack *ejidos* (state-owned smallholdings), or cannot obtain restitution of lands previously held, shall be granted lands in proportion to the needs of the population. The area of land granted to the individual may not be less than 10 hectares of irrigated or watered land, or the equivalent in other kinds of land.

The owners affected by decisions to divide and redistribute land (with the exception of the owners of farming or cattle-rearing properties) shall not have any right of redress, nor may they invoke the right of amparo† in protection of their interests. They may, however, apply to the Government for indemnification. Small properties, the areas of which are defined in the Constitution, will not be subject to expropriation. The Constitution leaves to the Congreso the duty of determining the maximum size of rural properties.

In March 1992 an agrarian reform amendment, whereby the programme of land-distribution established by the 1917 Constitution was abolished and the terms of the *ejido* system of tenant farmers were relaxed, was formally adopted.

Monopolies and measures to restrict competition in industry, commerce or public services are prohibited.

A section of the Constitution deals with work and social security.

On 30 December 1977 a Federal Law on Political Organizations and Electoral Procedure was promulgated. It includes the following provisions:

Legislative power is vested in the Congreso de la Unión which comprises the Cámara Federal de Diputados and the Senado. The Cámara shall comprise 300 deputies elected by majority vote within single-member electoral districts and up to 100 deputies (increased to 200 for the legislative elections of July 1988) elected by a system of proportional representation from regional lists within multi-member constituencies. The Senado comprises two members for each state and two for the Distrito Federal, elected by majority vote.

Executive power is exercised by the President of the Republic of the United Mexican States, elected by majority vote.

Ordinary elections will be held every three years for the federal deputies and every six years for the senators and the President of the Republic on the first Sunday of July of the year in question. When a vacancy occurs among members of the Congreso elected by majority vote, the house in question shall call extraordinary elections, and when a vacancy occurs among members of the Cámara elected by proportional representation it shall be filled by the candidate of the same party who received the next highest number of votes at the last ordinary election.

Voting is the right and duty of every citizen, male or female, over the age of 18 years.

A political party shall be registered if it has at least 3,000 members in each one of at least half the states in Mexico or at least 300 members in each one of at least half of the single-member constituencies. In either case the total number of members must be no less than 65,000. A party can also obtain conditional registration if it has been active for at least four years. Registration is confirmed if the party obtains at least 1.5% of the popular vote. All political parties shall have free access to the media.

In September 1993 an amendment to the Law on Electoral Procedure provided for the expansion of the Senado to 128 seats, representing four members for each state and the Distrito Federal, three to be elected by majority vote and one by proportional representation.

\* The Lerdo Law against ecclesiastical privilege, which became the basis of the Liberal Constitution of 1857.

† The Constitution provides for the procedure known as juicio de amparo, a wider form of habeas corpus, which the individual may invoke in protection of his constitutional rights.

# The Government

## HEAD OF STATE

**President:** Ernesto Zedillo Ponce de León (took office 1 December 1994).

## THE CABINET
(May 1995)

**Secretary of the Interior:** Esteban Moctezuma Barragán.
**Secretary of Foreign Affairs:** José Angel Treviño.
**Secretary of National Defence:** Gen. Enrique Cervantes Aguirre.
**Secretary of the Navy:** Adm. José Ramón Lorenzo Franco.
**Secretary of Finance and Public Credit:** Guillermo Ortiz Martínez.
**Secretary of Energy:** Ignacio Pichardo Pagaza.
**Secretary of Trade and Industrial Promotion:** Herminio Blanco.
**Secretary of Agriculture and Water Resources:** Francisco Labastida Ochoa.
**Secretary of Transport and Communications:** Carlos Ruiz Sacristán.

MEXICO

**Secretary of Social Development:** CARLOS ROJAS GUTIÉRREZ.
**Secretary of the Environment, Natural Resources and Fisheries:** JULIA CARABIAS LILLO.
**Secretary of Public Education:** MIGUEL LIMÓN ROJAS.
**Secretary of Health:** JUAN RAMÓN DE LA FUENTE.
**Secretary of Labour and Social Welfare:** SANTIAGO OÑATE LABORDE.
**Comptroller-General:** NORMA SAMANIEGO.
**Secretary of Agrarian Reform:** ARTURO WARMAN GRYJ.
**Secretary of Tourism:** SILVIA HERNÁNDEZ.
**Governor of Federal District:** MANUEL AGUILERA GÓMEZ.
**Attorney-General:** FERNANDO ANTONIO LOZANO GARCÍA.

### SECRETARIATS OF STATE

**Office of the President:** Los Pinos, Puerta 1, Col. San Miguel Chapultepec, 11850 México, DF; tel. (5) 515-3717; telex 1760010; fax (5) 510-8713.
**Secretariat of State for Agrarian Reform:** Torre B, 15°, Calzada de la Viga 1174, Col. Apatlaco, 09430 México, DF; tel. (5) 650-5001; telex 1772505; fax (5) 650-6100.
**Secretariat of State for Agriculture and Water Resources:** Insurgentes Sur 476, 13°, Col. Roma Sur, 06760 México, DF; tel. (5) 584-0010; telex 1775890; fax (5) 584-1887.
**Secretariat of State for Energy:** Insurgentes Sur 552, 3°, Col. Roma Sur, 06769 México, DF; tel. (5) 584-4304; telex 1775690; fax (5) 574-3396.
**Secretariat of State for the Environment, Natural Resources and Fisheries:** Avda Alvaro Obregón 269, 6°, Col. Roma Sur, 06700 México, DF; tel. (5) 208-1291; telex 1777483; fax (5) 208-1834.
**Secretariat of State for Finance and Public Credit:** Palacio Nacional, Patio Central, 3°, 06066 México, DF; tel. (5) 518-2711; telex 1776397; fax (5) 510-3796.
**Secretariat of State for Foreign Affairs:** Avda Ricardo Flores Magón 1, 19°, Col. Guerrero, 06995 México, DF; tel. (5) 782-3660; telex 1763478; fax (5) 782-3511.
**Secretariat of State for Health:** Lieja 7, 1° Col. Juárez, 06600 México, DF; tel. (5) 553-7670; telex 1773429; fax (5) 286-5497.
**Secretariat of State for the Interior:** Bucareli 99, 1°, Col. Juárez, 06069 México, DF; tel. (5) 566-0245; telex 1774375; fax (5) 546-8120.
**Secretariat of State for Labour and Social Welfare:** Edif. A, 4°, Periférico Sur 4271, Col. Fuentes del Pedregal, 14140 México, DF; tel. (5) 645-3969.
**Secretariat of State for National Defence:** Blvd Manuel, Avila Camacho y Avda Industria Militar, Col. Lomas de Sotelo, 11640 México, DF; tel. (5) 395-6766; telex 1776312; fax (5) 557-1370.
**Secretariat of State for the Navy:** Eje 2 Oriente, Tramo H, Escuela Naval Militar 861, Col. Los Cipreses, 04830 México, DF; tel. (5) 684-4188; telex 1773646; fax (5) 679-6411.
**Secretariat of State for Public Education:** República de Argentina y González Obregón 28, 2°, Puerta 3010 y 3011, Col. Centro, 06029 México, DF; tel. (5) 328-1000.
**Secretariat of State for Social Development:** Edif. 'B', planta alta, Avda Constituyentes 947, Col. Belém de las Flores, 01110 México, DF; tel. (5) 271-8765; telex 1771198; fax (5) 271-8217.
**Secretariat of State for Tourism:** Presidente Masarik 172, 8°, Col. Polanco, 11587 México, DF; tel. (5) 250-8604; telex 1777566; fax (5) 254-0014.
**Secretariat of State for Trade and Industrial Promotion:** Alfonso Reyes 30, 10°, Col. Condesa, 06170 México, DF; tel. (5) 286-1757; telex 1775718; fax (5) 286-1543.
**Secretariat of State for Transport and Communications:** Avda Universidad y Xola, Cuerpo C, 1°, Col. Narvarte, 03028 México, DF; tel. (5) 538-5148; fax (5) 519-9748.
**Office of the Comptroller-General:** Insurgentes Sur 1735, 10°, Col. Guadalupe Insurgentes, 01028 México DF; tel. (5) 682-4580; telex 1764014; fax (5) 524-8306.
**Department of the Federal District:** Plaza de la Constitución 1, 1°, Centro, 06068 México, DF; tel. (5) 510-0349; fax (5) 518-2998.
**Office of the Attorney-General:** Reforma Norte y Violeta, 2°, Col. Guerrero, 06300 México, DF; tel. (5) 526-7025; telex 1772701; fax (5) 526-7992.

## State Governors

**Federal District:** MANUEL AGUILERA GÓMEZ.
**Aguascalientes:** Ing. OTTO GRANADOS ROLDÁN.
**Baja California Norte:** Lic. ERNESTO RUFFO APPEL.
**Baja California Sur:** Lic. GUILLERMO MERCADO ROMERO.
**Campeche:** Ing. JORGE SALOMÓN AZAR GARCÍA.
**Chiapas:** JULIO CÉSAR RUIZ FERRO.
**Chihuahua:** Lic. FRANCISCO BARRIO TERRAZAS.
**Coahuila:** ROGELIO MONTEMAYOR SEGUY.
**Colima:** Lic. CARLOS DE LA MADRID VIRGEN.
**Durango:** Lic. MAXIMILIANO SILLERIO ESPARZA.
**Guanajuato:** VICENTE FOX QUESADA.
**Guerrero:** Lic. RUBÉN FIGUEROA ALCOCER.
**Hidalgo:** Lic. JESÚS MURILLO KARAM.
**Jalisco:** ALBERTO CÁRDENAS.
**México:** EMILIO CHAYFFET CHEMOR.
**Michoacán:** Lic. AUSENCIO CHÁVEZ HERNÁNDEZ (a.i.).
**Morelos:** JORGE CARRILLO OLEA.
**Nayarit:** RIGOBERTO OCHOA ZARAGOZA.
**Nuevo León:** Lic. SÓCRATES RIZZO GARCÍA.
**Oaxaca:** Lic. DIODORO CARRASCO ALTAMIRANO.
**Puebla:** Lic. MANUEL BARTLETT DÍAZ.
**Querétaro:** Lic. ENRIQUE BURGOS GARCÍA.
**Quintana Roo:** MARIO ERNESTO VILLANUEVA MADRID.
**San Luis Potosí:** Lic. HORACIO SÁNCHEZ UNZUETA.
**Sinaloa:** Lic. RENATO VEGA ALVARADO.
**Sonora:** Lic. MANLIO FABIO BELTRONES RIVERA.
**Tabasco:** Lic. ROBERTO MADRAZO PINTADO.
**Tamaulipas:** Ing. MANUEL CAVAZOS LERMA.
**Tlaxcala:** Lic. JOSÉ ANTONIO ALVAREZ LIMA.
**Veracruz:** Lic. PATRICIO CHIRINOS CALERO.
**Yucatán:** VÍCTOR CERVERA PACHECO.
**Zacatecas:** Lic. ARTURO ROMO GUTIÉRREZ.

## President and Legislature

### PRESIDENT

**Election, 21 August 1994**

| Candidate | Number of votes | Percentage of votes |
|---|---|---|
| ERNESTO ZEDILLO PONCE DE LEÓN (PRI) | 17,336,325 | 48.77 |
| DIEGO FERNÁNDEZ DE CEVALLOS (PAN) | 9,222,899 | 25.94 |
| CUAUHTÉMOC CÁRDENAS SOLÓRZANO (PRD) | 5,901,557 | 16.60 |
| CECILIA DE SOTO (PT) | 975,356 | 2.74 |
| Others | 2,114,146 | 5.95 |
| **Total** | **35,550,283** | **100.00** |

### CONGRESO DE LA UNIÓN

#### Senado
(Senate)

**President of the Senate:** EMILIO M. GONZÁLEZ.

**Elections, 21 August 1994**

In August 1994 the Partido Revolucionario Institucional (PRI) won 64 seats in the 128-seat Senate, which, in addition to its 31 sitting members, gave it a total of 95 seats. The Partido Acción Nacional (PAN) did not gain any seats by direct election, but won 24 seats through proportional representation. This gave the PAN a total of 25 seats, including one existing senator. The Partido de la Revolución Democrática (PRD) (successor to the FDN) gained eight seats through proportional representation.

#### Cámara Federal de Diputados
(Federal Chamber of Deputies)

**President of the Federal Chamber of Deputies:** GUILLERMO JIMÉNEZ MORALES.

**Elections, 21 August 1994**

| Party | Directly-elected seats | Proportionally-elected seats | Total seats |
|---|---|---|---|
| Partido Revolucionario Institucional (PRI) | 277 | 23 | 300 |
| Partido Acción Nacional (PAN) | 18 | 101 | 119 |
| Partido de la Revolución Democrática (PRD) | 5 | 64 | 69 |
| Partido del Trabajo (PT) | — | 12 | 12 |
| **Total** | **300** | **200** | **500** |

MEXICO                                                                                                    *Directory*

## Political Organizations

To retain legal political registration, parties must secure at least 1.5% of total votes at two consecutive federal elections. Several of the parties listed below are no longer officially registered but continue to be politically active.

**Partido Revolucionario Institucional (PRI):** Insurgentes Norte 61, 06350 México, DF; telex 1776561; f. 1929 as the Partido Nacional Revolucionario, but is regarded as the natural successor to the victorious parties of the revolutionary period; broadly based and centre government party; Pres. María de los Angeles Moreno; Sec.-Gen. Pedro Joaquín Coldwell; dissident factions within the PRI include:

**Corriente Crítica (CC):** Leader (vacant).

**Movimiento por el Cambio Democrático (MCD):** Leader Julio Hernández López.

**Acción Comunitaria (Acomac):** México, DF; registered as a political party in 1978.

**Movimiento al Socialismo (MAS):** México, DF; left-wing; Leader Adolfo Gilly.

**Partido Acción Nacional (PAN):** Angel Urraza 812, Col. del Valle, 03100 México, DF; tel. (5) 559-0802; telex 1764164; fax (5) 559-0975; f. 1939; democratic party; 130,000 mems; Pres. Carlos Castillo Peraza; Gen. Sec. Felipe Calderón Hinojosa.

**Partido Auténtico de la Revolución Mexicana (PARM):** México, DF; f. 1954 to sustain the ideology of the Mexican Political Constitution of 1917; 191,500 mems; Pres. Jesús Guzmán Rubio; Sec.-Gen. Carlos Cantú Rosas.

**Partido Demócrata Mexicano (PDM):** Edisón 89, Col. Revolución o Tabacalera, 06030 México, DF; tel. (5) 592-5688; fax (5) 535-0031; f. 1975; Christian Democrat party; 450,000 mems; Pres. Marcelo Gaxiola Félix.

**Partido del Foro Democrático:** México, DF; f. 1993 by dissident PAN members; Christian Democrat party; Chair. Pablo Emilio Madero.

**Partido del Frente Cardenista de Reconstrucción Nacional (PFCRN):** Avda México 199, Col. Hipódromo Condesa, 06170 México, DF; f. 1972; Marxist-Leninist; fmrly Partido Socialista de los Trabajadores; 132,000 mems; Pres. Rafael Aguilar Talamantes; Sec.-Gen. Graco Ramírez Abreu.

**Partido Popular Socialista (PPS):** Avda Alvaro Obregón 185, Col. Roma, 06977 México, DF; tel. (5) 533-0816; f. 1948; left-wing party; Sec.-Gen. Jorge Cruickshank García.

**Partido de la Revolución Democrática (PRD):** México, DF; f. 1989 by the Corriente Democrática (CD) and elements of the Partido Mexicano Socialista (PMS); centre-left; Chair. Porfirio Muñoz Ledo.

**Partido Revolucionario Socialista (PRS):** México, DF; officially registered as a party in 1985; left-wing.

**Partido Revolucionario de los Trabajadores (PRT):** México, DF; Trotskyist; Co-ordinator Pedro Peñaloza.

**Partido del Trabajo (PT):** México, DF; f. 1991; labour party; Leader Cecilia de Soto.

**Partido Verde Ecologista Mexicano (PVEM):** México, DF; f. 1990; ecologist party.

**Unificación y Progreso (UPAC):** México, DF; officially registered as a political party in 1978; liberal.

The 1988 presidential and congressional elections were contested by the **Frente Democrático Nacional (FDN)**, an electoral alliance formed, in 1988, by the Corriente Democrática—CD (f. 1986 by Porfirio Muñoz Ledo and Cuauhtémoc Cárdenas Solórzano as a dissident faction of the PRI), the MAS, PARM, PMS and PPS.

The following party is not legally recognized:

**Partido Social Demócrata (PSD):** México, DF; lost its registration after the 1982 elections; Leader Manuel Moreno Sánchez.

The following illegal organizations are active:

**Ejército de los Pobres:** left-wing guerrilla group; military wing of the Partido de los Pobres; Leader Felipe Martínez Soriano.

**Frente Democrático Oriental de México Emiliano Zapata (FDOMEZ):** peasant organization.

**Los Tecos:** based at the University of Guadalajara; extreme right-wing terrorist group.

**Partido Revolucionario Obrerista y Clandestino de Unión Popular (PROCUP):** peasant organization.

## Diplomatic Representation

### EMBASSIES IN MEXICO

**Albania:** Solón 337, Col. Los Morales, 11510 México, DF; tel. (5) 540-0461; telex 1771391; Ambassador: Gëzim Arapi.

**Algeria:** Sierra Madre 540, Col. Lomas de Chapultepec, 11000 México, DF; tel. (5) 540-7577; telex 1774310; fax (5) 540-7579; Chargé d'affaires: Ahmed Saadi.

**Argentina:** Avila Camacho 1, 7°, Col. Lomas de Chapultepec, 11000 México, DF; tel. (5) 540-4867; telex 1774214; Ambassador: Facundo Roberto Suárez.

**Australia:** Jaime Balmes 11, Plaza Polanco, Torre B, 10°, Col. Los Morales, 11510 México, DF; tel. (5) 395-9988; telex 1773920; fax (5) 395-7153; Ambassador: Keith Baker.

**Austria:** Campos Elíseos 305, Col. Polanco, 11560 México, DF; tel. (5) 280-6919; telex 1774448; fax (5) 280-2227; Ambassador: Klas Daublebsky.

**Belgium:** Musset 41, Col. Polanco, 11550 México, DF; tel. (5) 280-0758; telex 1771030; fax (5) 280-0208; Ambassador: Willy Verriest.

**Belize:** México, DF; Ambassador: Atlay Morales.

**Bolivia:** Campos Elíseos 169, 3°, Col. Polanco, 11560 México, DF; tel. (5) 254-1998; Chargé d'affaires a.i.: Raúl Alfonso García.

**Brazil:** Lope de Armendariz 130, Col. Lomas Virreyes, 11000 México, DF; tel. (5) 202-7500; telex 1771334; fax (5) 520-4929; Ambassador: Luis Felipe de Seixas Corrêa.

**Canada:** Schiller 529, Col. Polanco, 11560 México, DF; tel. (5) 724-7900; telex 1771191; fax (5) 724-7980; Ambassador: David J. S. Winfield.

**Chile:** México, DF; Ambassador: Carlos Portales Cifuentes.

**China, People's Republic:** Avda Río Magdalena 172, Col. Tizapán, 01090 México, DF; tel. (5) 548-0898; telex 1773907; Ambassador: Huang Shikang.

**Colombia:** Génova 2-105, Col. Juárez, 06600 México, DF; tel. (5) 528-9290; telex 1772951; Ambassador: Ing. Ignacio Umaña de Brigard.

**Costa Rica:** Sierra Gorda 89, Col. Lomas Barrilaco, 11010, México, DF; tel. (5) 520-1718; telex 1763134; Ambassador: Ángel Edmundo Solano Calderón.

**Côte d'Ivoire:** Tennyson 67, Col. Polanco, 11550 México, DF; tel. (5) 254-4398; telex 1763115; Ambassador: Ahoussi Julian Kacou.

**Cuba:** Presidente Mazaryk 554, Col. Polanco, 11560 México, DF; tel. (5) 280-8039; telex 1774472; fax (5) 280-0839; Ambassador: Abelardo Curbelo Padrón.

**Cyprus:** Sierra Paracaima 1305, Col. Lomas de Chapultepec, 11000 México, DF; tel. (5) 596-0960; fax (5) 251-1623; Ambassador: Stavros Orphanou.

**Czech Republic:** Cuvier 22, esq. Kepler, Col. Anzures, 11590 México, DF; tel. (5) 531-1837; telex 1773092.

**Denmark:** Tres Picos 43, Apdo 105-105, Col. Polanco, 11560 México, DF; tel. (5) 255-3405; telex 1773049; fax (5) 545-5797; Ambassador: Martin Kofod.

**Dominican Republic:** Avda Insurgentes Sur 216–301, Col. Roma Sur, 06170 México, DF; tel. (5) 533-0215; Ambassador: Alfonso Canto Dinzey.

**Ecuador:** Tennyson 217, Col. Polanco, 11550 México, DF; tel. (5) 545-7041; Chargé d'affaires: Gustavo Bucheli Garcés.

**Egypt:** Alejandro Dumas 131, Col. Polanco, 11560 México, DF; tel. (5) 531-9028; telex 1775660; Ambassador: Aziz Seif el Nasr.

**El Salvador:** Aristóteles 153, Col. Polanco, 11550 México, DF; tel. (5) 250-1391; telex 1777399; Ambassador: Sigfrido Antonio Muñez Cruz.

**Ethiopia:** Miguel de Cervantes de Saavedra 465-602, Col. Irrigación, 11500 México, DF; tel. (5) 557-2238; telex 1771825; Chargé d'affaires: Fesesha Masresha.

**Finland:** Monte Pelvoux 111, 4°, Col. Lomas de Chapultepec, Del. Miguel Hidalgo, 11000 México, DF; tel. (5) 540-6036; telex 1771187; fax (5) 540-0114; Ambassador: Kimmo Pulkkinen.

**France:** Havre 15, Col. Juárez, 06600 México, DF; tel. (5) 533-1360; telex 1771302; fax (5) 514-7311; Ambassador: Paul Dijoud.

**Germany:** Lord Byron 737, Col. Polanco Chapultepec, Apdo 107-92, 11560 México, DF; tel. (5) 545-6655; telex 1773089; fax (5) 255-3180; Ambassador: (vacant).

**Greece:** Paseo de las Palmas 2060, Col. Lomas Reforma, 11020 México, DF; tel. (5) 596-6333; telex 1777319; Ambassador: Constantinos Vassis.

**Guatemala:** Esplanada 1025, Col. Lomas de Chapultepec, 11000 México, DF; tel. (5) 520-2794; Ambassador: Julio César Méndez Montenegro.

**Haiti:** Taine 229, 4°, Col. Chapultepec Morales, 11570 México, DF; tel. (5) 250-7913; Ambassador: Antoine Bernard.

**Holy See:** Calle Juan Pablo II 118, Col. Guadalupe Inn., Deleg. Alvaro Obregón, 01020 México, DF; tel. (5) 663-3999; fax (5)

# MEXICO

663-5308; Apostolic Nuncio: Most Rev. GIROLAMO PRIGIONE, Titular Archbishop of Lauriacum.

**Honduras:** Paseo Las Palmas 765–202, Col. Lomas de Chapultepec, 11000 México, DF; tel. (5) 658-4855; telex 1762222; Ambassador: ROBERTO SUAZO TOMÉ.

**Hungary:** Paseo de las Palmas 2005, Col. Lomas Reforma, 11020 México, DF; tel. (5) 596-0523; telex 1774503; Ambassador: ANTAL SOLYOM.

**India:** Musset 325, Col. Polanco, 11550 México, DF; tel. (5) 531-1050; telex 1775864; fax (5) 254-2349; Ambassador: ALAN NAZARETH.

**Indonesia:** Julio Verne 27, Col. Polanco, 11560 México, DF; tel. (5) 540-4167; telex 1772712; Ambassador: SUMADI.

**Iran:** Paseo de la Reforma 2350, Col. Lomas Altas, 11950 México, DF; tel. (5) 596-5399; telex 1774205; Ambassador: Dr ALIREZA DEIHIM.

**Iraq:** Paseo de la Reforma 1875, Col. Lomas, 11020 México, DF; tel. (5) 596-0254; telex 1777680; Ambassador: ABDUL KARIM MOHAMED NAJIM AL-TAI.

**Israel:** Sierra Madre 215, Del. Miguel Hidalgo, 11000 México, DF; tel. (5) 540-6340; telex 1773094; fax (5) 282-4825; Ambassador: DAVID TOURGEMAN.

**Italy:** Paseo de las Palmas 1994, Col. Lomas de Chapultepec, 11020 México, DF; tel. (5) 596-3655; telex 1772717; Ambassador: SERGIO CATTANI.

**Jamaica:** Monte Líbano 885, Lomas de Chapultepec, 11000 México, DF; tel. (5) 520-1421; telex 1771338; fax (5) 520-4704; Ambassador: THOMAS ALVIN STIMPSON.

**Japan:** Paseo de la Reforma 395, Col. Cuauhtémoc, Apdo 5-101, 06500 México, DF; tel. (5) 211-0028; telex 1772420; fax (5) 207-7743; Ambassador: TSUNEO TANAKA.

**Korea, Democratic People's Republic:** México, DF; Ambassador: KIM CHAN SIK.

**Korea, Republic:** Lope de Almendariz 110, Col. Lomas Virreyes, 11000 México, DF; tel. (5) 596-7131; telex 1773102; Ambassador: KOO CHOONG-WHEY.

**Lebanon:** Julio Verne 8, Col. Polanco, 11560 México, DF; tel. (5) 540-3295; telex 1763169; Ambassador: AMINE EL-KHAZEN.

**Netherlands:** Montes Urales Sur 635, 2°, Col. Lomas de Chapultepec, 11000 México, DF; tel. (5) 540-7788; telex 1774366; fax (5) 202-6148; Ambassador: ADRIËN F. TIELEMAN.

**New Zealand:** Homero 229, 8°, Col. Chapultepec Morales, 11570 México, DF; tel. (5) 250-5999; telex 1763154; fax (5) 255-4142; Ambassador: BRUCE W. MIDDLETON.

**Nicaragua:** Ahumada Villagrán 36, Col. Lomas de Chapultepec, 11000 México, DF; tel. (5) 540-5625; telex 1772381; Ambassador: Dr EDMUNDO JARQUÍN CALDERÓN.

**Norway:** Avda Virreyes 1460, Col. Lomas de Chapultepec, 11000 México, DF; tel. (5) 540-3486; telex 1772996; Ambassador: ROLF BERG.

**Pakistan:** Hegel 512, Col. Chapultepec Morales, 11570 México, DF; tel. (5) 203-3636; telex 1763355; fax (5) 203-9907; Ambassador: MANSOOR ALAM.

**Panama:** Campos Elíseos 111, Col. Bosque de Chapultepec, 11580 México, DF; tel. (5) 250-4045; Ambassador: EZEQUIEL RODRIGUES.

**Paraguay:** Avda Taine 713, Col. Bosque de Chapultepec, 11580 México, DF; tel. (5) 545-8155; Ambassador: RAÚL ARMIN GÓMEZ NÚÑEZ.

**Peru:** Paseo de las Palmas 2030, Col. Lomas Reforma, 11020 México, DF; tel. (5) 596-0521; telex 1773087; Ambassador: Dr JUAN DE LA PIEDRA VILLALONGA.

**Philippines:** Calderón de la Barca 240, Col. Reforma-Polanco, Del. Miguel Hidalgo, 11550 México, DF; tel. (5) 254-8055; telex 1772058; fax (5) 545-8631; Ambassador: SAMUEL T. RAMEL.

**Poland:** Cracovia 40, Col. San Ángel, 01000 México, DF; tel. (5) 550-4700; telex 1773090; Ambassador: IRENA GABOR-JATCZAK.

**Portugal:** Alejandro Dumas 311, Col. Polanco, 11550 México, DF; tel. (5) 545-6213; telex 1772533; fax (5) 203-0790; Ambassador: ANTONIO CABRITA MATIAS.

**Romania:** Sofocles 311, Col. Los Morales, 11510 México, DF; tel. (5) 52-0984; telex 1775868; Ambassador: CONSTANTIN BABALAU.

**Russia:** José Vasconcelos 204, Col. Hipódromo Condesa, 06140 México, DF; tel. (5) 273-1305; telex 1777570; fax (5) 273-1545; Ambassador: YEVGUENI A. AMBARTSUMOV.

**Saudi Arabia:** Reforma 607, Col. Lomas de Chapultepec, 11000 México, DF; tel. (5) 540-0240; telex 1775714; Chargé d'Affaires: ALTAYEB T. ALHAZZAZI.

**Slovakia:** Julio Verne 35, Col. Polanco, 11481 México, DF; tel. (5) 280-6451; fax (5) 280-6669; Ambassador (vacant).

**Spain:** Parque Vía Reforma 2105, Col. Lomas de Chapultepec, 11000 México, DF; tel. 596-2652; telex 1776295; fax (5) 596-0646; Ambassador: ALBERTO AZA.

**Suriname:** Calle Cicerón 609, Col. Los Morales, 11510 México, DF; tel. (5) 540-4371; telex 1763120; Ambassador: HARVEY NAARENDORP.

**Sweden:** Edif. Plaza Comermex, 6°, Blvd Manuel Avila Camacho 1, 11000 México, DF; tel. (5) 540-6393; telex 1771115; Ambassador: BO HENRIKSON.

**Switzerland:** Hamburgo 66, 4°, Col. Juárez, Apdo 1027, 06600 México, DF; tel. (5) 533-0735; telex 1774396; fax (5) 514-7083; Ambassador: PAUL A. RAMSEYER.

**Thailand:** Sierra Vertientes 1030, Col. Lomas de Chapultepec, 11000 México, DF; tel. (5) 596-1290; telex 1772910; fax (5) 596-8236; Ambassador: SIRAJAYA BUDDHI-BAEDYA.

**Turkey:** Paseo de las Palmas 1525, Col. Lomas de Chapultepec, 11000 México, DF; tel. (5) 520-2344; telex 1774495; fax (5) 540-3185; Ambassador: NURVER NUREŞ.

**United Kingdom:** Lerma 71, Col. Cuauhtémoc, Apdo 96 bis, 06500 México, DF; tel. (5) 207-2089; fax (5) 207-7672; Ambassador: ADRIAN J. BEAMISH.

**USA:** Paseo de la Reforma 305, Col. Cuauhtémoc, 06500 México, DF; tel. (5) 211-0042; telex 1773091; fax (5) 208-4178; Ambassador: JAMES R. JONES.

**Uruguay:** Hegel 149, 1°, Col. Chapultepec Morales, 11570 México, DF; tel. (5) 531-0880; telex 1771396; fax (5) 531-4029; Ambassador: JUAN PEDRO AMESTOY.

**Venezuela:** Edif. Simón Bolivar, Londres 167, Col. Juárez, 06600 México, DF; tel. (5) 525-0364; telex 1775813; Ambassador: GUIDO GROOSCORS.

**Viet Nam:** Sierra Ventana 255, Col. Lomas de Chapultepec, 11000 México, DF; tel. (5) 540-1612; telex 1771079; Chargé d'affaires: HOANG HIEP.

**Yugoslavia:** Montañas Rocallosas Ote 515, Col. Lomas de Chapultepec, 11000 México, DF; tel. (5) 259-1332; telex 1771331; fax (5) 520-9927; Ambassador: IGNAC GOLOB.

## Judicial System

The principle of the separation of the judiciary from the legislative and executive powers is embodied in the 1917 Constitution. The judicial system is divided into two areas: the federal, dealing with federal law, and the state, dealing only with state law within each state.

The federal judicial system has both ordinary and constitutional jurisdiction and judicial power is exercised by the Supreme Court of Justice, Circuit Courts (Tribunales de Circuito) and District Courts (Juzgados de Distrito). The Supreme Court comprises 21 numerary ministers and five supernumeraries and may meet in joint session or in its separate chambers: Penal Affairs, Administrative Affairs, Civil Affairs and Labour Affairs.

The Circuit Courts may be collegiate, when dealing with the derecho de amparo (protection of constitutional rights of an individual), or unitary, when dealing with appeal cases. The Collegiate Circuit Courts comprise three magistrates and there are 23 circuits with residence in the cities of México, Toluca, Guadalajara, Monterrey, Hermosillo, Puebla, Veracruz, Torreón, San Luis Potosí, Villahermosa, Morelia, Mazatlán, Oaxaca, Mérida, Mexicali, Guanajuato, Chihuahua, Cuernavaca, Ciudad Victoria, Tuxtla Gutiérrez, Chilpancingo, Querétaro and Zacatecas. The Unitary Circuit Courts comprise one magistrate and there are 23 circuits with residence in the same cities as given above.

There are 158 District Courts.

### SUPREME COURT

Pino Suárez 2, Centro, Deleg. Cuauhtémoc, 06065 México, DF; tel. (5) 522-1500; fax (5) 522-0152.

**President:** Lic. ULISES SCHMILL ORDÓÑEZ.

#### First Chamber—Penal Affairs
**President:** IGNACIO M. CAL Y MAYOR GUTIÉRREZ. Four other judges.

#### Second Chamber—Administrative Affairs
**President:** NOÉ CASTAÑÓN LEÓN. Four other judges.

#### Third Chamber—Civil Affairs
**President:** JOSÉ TRINIDAD LANZ CÁRDENAS. Four other judges.

#### Fourth Chamber—Labour Affairs
**President:** CARLOS GARCÍA VÁZQUEZ. Four other judges.

#### Auxiliary Chamber
**President:** GUILLERMO GUZMÁN OROZCO. Four other judges.

# Religion

## CHRISTIANITY

### The Roman Catholic Church

The prevailing religion is Roman Catholicism, but the Church, disestablished in 1857, was for many years, under the Constitution of 1917, subject to state control. A constitutional amendment, promulgated in January 1992, officially removed all restrictions on the Church. For ecclesiastical purposes, Mexico comprises 14 archdioceses, 58 dioceses and seven territorial prelatures. An estimated 90% of the population are adherents.

**Bishops' Conference:** Conferencia del Episcopado Mexicano (CEM), Prolongación Río Acatlán, Lago de Guadalupe, 54760 Cuautitlán Izcalli, México, DF; tel. (5) 877-2663; fax (5) 877-2603; f. 1979; Pres. Sergio Obeso Rivera, Archbishop of Jalapa.

**Archbishop of Acapulco:** Rafael Bello Ruiz, Arzobispado, Quebrada 16, Apdo 201, 39300 Acapulco, Gro; tel. (748) 20763.

**Archbishop of Antequera/Oaxaca:** Hector González Martínez, Independencia 700, Apdo 31, 68000 Oaxaca, Oax.; tel. (951) 64401; fax (951) 62493.

**Archbishop of Chihuahua:** José Fernández Arteaga, Arzobispado, Avda Cuauhtémoc 1828, Apdo 7, 31000 Chihuahua, Chih.; tel. (14) 10-3202; fax (14) 10-5621.

**Archbishop of Durango:** José Trinidad Medel Pérez, Arzobispado, 20 de Noviembre 306 Pte, Apdo 116, 34000 Durango, Dgo; tel. (181) 14242; fax (181) 28881.

**Archbishop of Guadalajara:** Cardinal Juan Sandoval Iñíguez, Arzobispado, Liceo 17, Apdo 1-331, 44100 Guadalajara, Jal.; tel. (3) 614-5504; fax (3) 658-2300.

**Archbishop of Hermosillo/Sonora:** Carlos Quintero Arce, Arzobispado, Dr Paliza 81, Apdo 1, 83260 Hermosillo, Son.; tel. (621) 32138; fax (621) 31327.

**Archbishop of Jalapa:** Sergio Obeso Rivera, Arzobispado, Avda Manuel Avila Camacho 73, Apdo 359, 91000 Jalapa, Ver.; tel. (281) 75578.

**Archbishop of Mexico City:** (vacant), Curia del Arzobispado de México, Durango 90, planta baja, 7°, Col. Roma, Apdo 24433, 06700 México, DF; tel. (5) 208-3200; fax (5) 208-5350.

**Archbishop of Monterrey:** Cardinal Adolfo Antonio Suárez Rivera, Zuazua 1100 con Ocampo, Apdo 7, 64000 Monterrey, NL; tel. (8) 345-2466; telex 383392; fax (8) 345-3557.

**Archbishop of Morelia:** Alberto Suárez Inda, Arzobispado, Apdo 17, 58000 Morelia, Mich.; tel. (451) 20523; fax (451) 23744.

**Archbishop of Puebla de los Angeles:** Rosendo Huesca Pacheco, Avda 2 Sur 305, Apdo 235, 72000 Puebla, Pue.; tel. (22) 32-4591; fax (22) 46-2277.

**Archbishop of San Luis Potosí:** Arturo A. Szymanski Ramírez, Arzobispado, Calle Francisco Madero 300, Apdo 1, 78000 San Luis Potosí, SLP; tel. (481) 24555; fax (481) 27979.

**Archbishop of Tlalnepantla:** Manuel Pérez-Gil González, Arzobispado, Avda Juárez 42, Apdo 268, 54000 Tlalnepantla, Méx.; tel. (5) 565-5944; fax (5) 565-2751.

**Archbishop of Yucatán:** Emilio C. Berlie Belaunzarán, Arzobispado, Calle 58 501, 97000 Mérida, Yuc.; tel. (99) 28-5720; fax (99) 23-7983.

### The Anglican Communion

Mexico is divided into five dioceses, which form the Province of the Anglican Church in Mexico, established in 1995.

**Bishop of Cuernavaca:** José Guadalupe Saucedo, Apdo 192, Admon. 4, 62431 Cuernavaca, Mor.; tel. (73) 15-2870.

**Bishop of Mexico City:** Sergio Carranza Gómez, Avda San Jerónimo 117, Col. San Angel, 01000 México, DF; tel. (5) 616-2205.

**Bishop of Northern Mexico:** Germán Martínez Márquez, Simón Bolívar 2005 Nte, Col. Mitras Centro, 64460 Monterrey, NL; tel. (83) 48-7362.

**Bishop of South-Eastern Mexico:** Claro Huerta Ramas, Avda Las Américas 73, Col. Aguacatl, 91130 Jalapa, Ver.; tel. (281) 44387.

**Bishop of Western Mexico:** Samuel Espinoza Venegas, Apdo 2-1220, 44280 Guadalajara, Jal.; tel. (3) 615-5070.

### Other Protestant Churches

**Federación Evangélica de México:** Motolinia 8, Of. 107, Del. Cuauhtémoc, 1830, 06002, México, DF; tel. (5) 585-0594; f. 1926; Pres. Prof. Moises Méndez; Exec. Sec. Rev. Israel Ortiz Murrieta.

**Iglesia Evangélica Luterana de México:** Mina Pte 5808, Nuevo Larado, Tamps; Pres. Encarnación Estrada; 3,000 mems.

**Iglesia Metodista de México:** Central Area: Miravalle 209, Col. Portales, 03570 México, DF; tel. (5) 539-3674; fax (5) 672-4278; f. 1930; 55,000 mems; 370 congregations; Bishop: Ulises Hernández Bautista.; Northern Area: Fray Bartolomé de Olmedo 149, Quintas del Márquez, 76050 Querétaro, Qro; tel. (42) 13-3089; Bishop: Raúl Ruiz Avila; South-eastern Area: Poniente 311, 4°, 72000 Puebla, Pue.; tel. (22) 42-1895; Bishop: Fidel Ramírez Sánchez; Central Area: Avda Morelos 524 Pte, Torreón, Coah.: tel. (17) 12-3471; fax (17) 16-2697; Bishop Baltasar González Carrillo; North-eastern Area: Cuernavaca 116, Col. San Benito, 83190 Hermosillo, Son.; tel. (62) 14-2780; Bishop: Daniel de la Cruz Areyzaga; Eastern Area: Galeana 430 Norte, 64000 Monterrey, NL; tel. (8) 342-5376; fax (8) 344-0055; Bishop Ricardo Esparza Zuno.

**National Baptist Convention of Mexico:** Vizcaínas Ote No 16, Altos, 06080 Mexico, DF; tel. (5) 518-2691; f. 1903; Pres. Jorge Munguía Martínez.

## BAHÁ'Í FAITH

**National Spiritual Assembly of the Bahá'ís of Mexico:** Emerson 421, Col. Chapultepec Morales, Del. Miguel Hidalgo, 11570 México, DF; tel. (5) 545-2155; fax (5) 255-5972; mems resident in 1,000 localities.

# The Press

## DAILY NEWSPAPERS

### México, DF

**La Afición:** Ignacio Mariscal 23, Apdo 64 bis, 06030 México, DF; tel. (5) 546-4780; f. 1930; sport, entertainment, news; Pres. Juan Ealy Ortiz; Gen. Man. Jesús Christian Ramírez R.; circ. 98,500.

**Cuestión:** Laguna de Mayrán 410, Col. Anáhuac, 11320 México, DF; tel. (5) 250-4055; f. 1980; midday; Dir-Gen. Lic. Alberto González Parra; Gen. Man. Carlos Martínez González; circ. 60,000.

**El Día:** Avda Insurgentes Norte 1210, Col. Capukiklan, 07370 México, DF; tel. (5) 546-0456; telex 1771029; fax (5) 537-6629; f. 1962; morning; Editor José de Villa; circ. 75,000.

**Diario de México:** Chimalpopoca 38, Col. Obrera, 06800 México, DF; tel. (5) 578-8437; fax (5) 578-7650; f. 1948; morning; Dir-Gen. Federico Bracamontes Gálvez; Gen. Man. Benigno Vázquez Olazo; circ. 63,000.

**Esto:** Guillermo Prieto 9, 1°, 06470 México, DF; tel. (5) 535-2722; telex 1772615; fax (5) 535-5560; f. 1941; morning; Pres. Lic. Mario Vázquez Raña; Man. Arnulfo García Ramírez; circ. 400,200, Mondays 450,000.

**Excélsior:** Reforma 18, Apdo 120 bis, 06600 México, DF; tel. (5) 535-6552; f. 1917; morning; independent; Dir Regino Díaz Redondo; Gen. Man. Juventuno Olivera López; circ. 200,000.

**El Financiero:** Lago Bolsena 176, Col. Anáhuac entre Lago Peipus y Lago Onega, 11320 México, DF; tel. (5) 254-6299; fax (5) 255-1881; f. 1981; financial; Dir Lic. Rogelio Cárdenas; circ. 135,000.

**El Heraldo de México:** Dr Carmona y Valle 150, Col. Doctores, 06720 México, DF; tel. (5) 578-3632; telex 1771219; f. 1965; morning; Dir-Gen. Gabriel Alarcón; Gen. Man. Gabriel Alarcón, Jr; circ. 209,600.

**El Nacional:** Ignacio Mariscal 25, 3°, Col. Tabacalera, Apdo 446, 06030 México, DF; tel. (5) 535-3074; telex 1777551; fax (5) 705-5615; f. 1929; morning; Dir José Carreño Carlón; Gen. Man. Luis Lara Rubio; circ. 120,000.

**Novedades:** Balderas 87, esq. Morelas, 06040 México, DF; tel. (5) 510-9707; telex 1773031; fax (5) 521-4505; f. 1936; morning; independent; Pres. and Editor-in-Chief Rómulo O'Farrill, Jr; Vice-Pres. Lic. Miguel Alemán Velasco; circ. 210,000, Sundays 220,000, Mondays 240,000.

**Ovaciones:** Lago Zirahuén 279, 20°, Col. Anáhuac, 11320 México, DF; tel. (5) 399-8211; f. 1947; morning and evening editions; Pres. Lic. Fernando González Parra; Gen. Man. Alberto González Parra; circ. 205,000; evening circ. 220,000.

**La Prensa:** Basilio Badillo 40, 06030 México, DF; tel. (5) 512-0799; telex 1774253; f. 1928; morning; Pres. and Dir-Gen. Mario Santaella de la Cajiga; circ. 300,000.

**El Sol de México:** Guillermo Prieto 7, 20°, Col. San Rafael, 06470 México, DF; tel. (5) 566-1511; f. 1965; morning and midday; Pres. and Dir-Gen. Lic. Mario Vázquez Raña; Dir Pilar Ferreira García; circ. 110,000.

**El Universal:** Iturbide 7 y Bucareli 8, Apdo 909, 06040 México, DF; tel. (5) 709-1313; f. 1916; morning; independent; centre-left; Pres. and Dir-Gen. Juan Francisco Ealy Ortiz; circ. 121,968, Sundays 119,837.

**Uno Más Uno:** Retorno de Correggio 12, 03720 México 19, DF; tel. (5) 563-9911; f. 1977; morning; left-wing; Dir Luis Gutiérrez Rodríguez; Gen. Man. Lic. Carlos Vázquez García; circ. 90,000.

## PROVINCIAL DAILY NEWSPAPERS
(circ. over 50,000)

### Baja California Norte, BCN

**ABC—Tijuana:** Agua Caliente 2700, Col. Cacho, 22150 Tijuana, BCN; tel. (66) 84-0971; telex 566532; f. 1977; morning; Dir-Gen. Rogelio Lozoya Godoy; circ. 50,000.

**El Mexicano:** Carretera al Aeropuerto s/n, Fracc. Alamar, Apdo 2333, Tijuana, BCN; tel. (66) 26-1602; fax (66) 26-1612; f. 1959; morning; Dir and Gen. Man. Eligio Valencia Roque; circ. 75,000.

**El Sol de Tijuana:** Rufino Tamayo 4, Zona Río, 22320 Tijuana, BCN; tel. (66) 34-2193; f. 1989; morning; Dir Lic. Rubén Téllez Fuentes; circ. 50,000.

**La Voz de la Frontera:** Avda Francisco I. Madero 1545, Col. Nueva, Apdo 946, 21100 Mexicali, BCN; tel. (65) 53-4545; telex 569708; fax (65) 53-6912; f. 1964; morning; independent; Pres. and Dir-Gen. Mario Vázquez Raña; Gen. Man. Lic. Mario Valdés Hernández; circ. 65,000.

### Chihuahua, Chih.

**El Heraldo de Chihuahua:** Avda Universidad 2507, Apdo 1515, 31240 Chihuahua, Chih.; tel. (14) 13-1086; telex 349836; f. 1927; morning; Dir. Alejandro Irigoyen Páez; circ. 52,000.

**El Tiempo:** Avda 16 de Septiembre 337, 4, Ciudad Juárez, Chih.; tel. (16) 14-8560; morning; Pres. and Dir-Gen. José Luis Boone Menchaca; circ. 50,000.

### Guanajuato, Gto

**Contacto de Léon:** Blvd Cerrito de Jerez 103, esq. Blvd A. López Mateos Ote, Apdo 1005, 37000 León, Gto; tel. (471) 62757; telex 120686; fax (471) 69600; f. 1983; evening; Dir-Gen. Lic. Juan Ignacio Morales Castañeda; circ. 50,000.

**El Heraldo de León:** Hermanos Aldama 222, Apdo 299, 37530 León, Gto; tel. (471) 33528; fax (471) 35411; f. 1957; morning; Dir.-Gen. Mauricio Bercún Melnic; circ. 67,000.

### Jalisco, Jal.

**El Diario de Guadalajara:** Calle 14 2550, Zona Industrial, 44940, Guadalajara, Jal.; tel. (3) 612-0043; telex 774579; fax (3) 612-0818; f. 1969; morning; Pres. and Dir-Gen. Luis A. González Becerra; circ. 78,000.

**El Informador:** Independencia 300, Apdo 3 bis, 44100 Guadalajara, Jal.; tel. (3) 614-6340; telex 682764; fax (3) 614-4653; f. 1917; morning; Editor Jorge Alvarez del Castillo; circ. 60,000.

**El Occidental:** Calzada Independencia Sur 324, Apdo 1-699, 44100 Guadalajara, Jal.; tel. (3) 613-0690; telex 681799; fax (3) 613-6796; f. 1942; morning; Dir Lic. Ricardo del Valle del Peral; circ. 85,000.

### México, Méx.

**ABC:** Avda Hidalgo Ote 1339, Centro Comercial, 50000 Toluca, Méx.; tel. (721) 79880; fax (721) 79646; f. 1984; morning; Pres. and Editor Miled Libien Kaui; circ. 65,000.

**Diario de Toluca:** Allende Sur 205, 50000 Toluca, Méx.; tel. (721) 42403; fax (721) 41523; f. 1980; morning; Editor Anuar Maccise Uribe; circ. 65,000.

**El Heraldo de Toluca:** Salvador Díaz Mirón 700, Col. Sánchez Colín, 50150 Toluca, Méx.; tel. (721) 73453; fax (721) 22535; f. 1955; morning; Editor Alberto Baraza Sánchez A.; circ. 72,000.

**El Mañana:** Avda Hidalgo Ote 1339, Toluca, Méx.; tel. (721) 79880; f. 1986; morning; Dir Guillermo Padilla Cruz; circ. 65,000.

**El Mundo:** Allende Sur 205, Toluca, Méx.; tel. (721) 42403; fax (721) 41523; f. 1986; evening; Dir-Gen. Jorge Ortiz Arrieta; circ. 50,000.

**Rumbo:** Paseo Tollocan, Carretera México-Toluca km 57.5, 50000 Toluca, Méx.; tel. (721) 61444; f. 1968; morning; Editor Lic. Esteban Rivera Rivera; circ. 65,000.

### Michoacán, Mich.

**La Voz de Michoacán:** Blvd del Periodismo 1270, Col. Arriaga Rivera, Apdo 121, 58190 Morelia, Mich.; tel. (43) 16-0730; telex 69823; fax (43) 16-1151; f. 1948; morning; Dir-Gen. Miguel Medina Robles; circ. 50,000.

### Morelos, Mor.

**El Diario de Morelos:** Morelos Sur 817, Col. Las Palmas, 62000 Cuernavaca, Mor.; tel. (73) 14-2660; fax (73) 14-1253; morning; circ. 50,000.

### Nayarit, Nay.

**El Meridiano de Nayarit:** E. Zapata 73 Pte, Apdo 65, 63000 Tepic, Nay.; tel. (321) 20145; telex 61135; fax (321) 29418; f. 1942; morning; Dir Dr David Alfaro; circ. 50,000.

**El Observador:** Allende 110 Ote, Despachos 203-204, 63000 Tepic, Nay.; tel. (321) 24309; fax (321) 24309; morning; Pres. and Dir-Gen. Lic. Luis A. González Becerra; circ. 55,000.

### Nuevo León, NL

**ABC:** Platón Sánchez Sur 411, 64000 Monterrey, NL; tel. (8) 344-4480; telex 382056; fax (8) 344-5990; f. 1985; morning; Pres. and Dir-Gen. Gonzalo Estrada Cruz; circ. 75,000, Sundays 80,000.

**El Diario de Monterrey:** Eugenio Garza Sada 2245, Col. Roma Sur, Apdo 3128, 647000 Monterrey, NL; tel. (8) 359-2525; telex 382605; f. 1974; morning; Dir-Gen. Lic. Jorge Villegas; circ. 75,000.

**El Norte:** Washington Ote 629, Apdo 186, 64000 Monterrey, NL; tel. (8) 345-5100; telex 382642; fax (8) 345-0264; f. 1938; morning; Man. Dir Alejandro Junco de la Vega; circ. 125,000, Sundays 165,000.

**El Porvenir:** Galeana Sur 344, Apdo 218, 64000 Monterrey, NL; tel. (8) 345-4080; telex 382739; fax (8) 345-7795; f. 1919; morning; Dir-Gen. Lic. Jesús Cantú Escalante; circ. 75,000.

**El Sol:** Washington Ote 629, Apdo 186, 64000 Monterrey, NL; tel. (8) 345-3388; telex 382642; fax (8) 345-0264; f. 1922; evening (except Sundays); Man. Dir Alejandro Junco de la Vega; circ. 80,000.

### Oaxaca, Oax.

**El Imparcial:** Armenta y López 312, Apdo 322, 68000 Oaxaca, Oax.; tel. (951) 62812; telex 18821; fax (951) 60050; f. 1951; morning; Dir-Gen. Lic. Benjamín Fernández Pichardo; circ. 55,000.

### Puebla, Pue.

**El Sol de Puebla:** Avda 3 Ote 201, Apdo 190, 72000 Puebla, Pue.; tel. (22) 42-4560; telex 178242; fax (22) 42-0370; f. 1944; morning; Man. Rodolfo Sierra Sánchez; circ. 67,000.

### San Luis Potosí, SLP

**El Heraldo:** Villerías 305, 78000 San Luis Potosí, SLP; tel. (481) 23312; telex 13694; fax (481) 22081; f. 1954; morning; Dir-Gen. Alejandro Villasana Mena; circ. 60,620.

**Momento:** Zenón Fernández y Leandro Valle, Col. Jardines del Estadio, 78280 San Luis Potosí, SLP; tel. (481) 44444; telex 13865; fax (481) 12-2020; f. 1975; morning; Dir-Gen. Ramón Pedroza Langarica; circ. 63,000, Sundays 68,000.

**Pulso:** Galeana 485, 78000 San Luis Potosí, SLP; tel. (481) 27575; telex 13667; fax (481) 23525; morning; Dir-Gen. Miguel Valladares García; circ. 60,000.

**El Sol de San Luis:** Avda Universidad 565, Apdo 342, 78000 San Luis Potosí, SLP; tel. (481) 24412; fax (481) 21368; f. 1952; morning; Dir José Angel Martínez Limón; Man. Francisco López Espinosa; circ. 60,000.

### Sinaloa, Sin.

**El Debate de Culiacán:** Colón y Rivapalacio, 80000 Culiacán, Sin.; tel. (671) 53911; telex 665727; fax (671) 57131; f. 1972; morning; Dir Rosario I. Oropeza; circ. 50,000.

**El Debate de Los Mochis:** Obregón 8 y Degollado Pte, 81200 Los Mochis, Sin.; tel. (681) 29894; telex 53233; fax (681) 57454; f. 1941; morning; Dir-Gen. José Isabel Ramos Santos; circ. 50,000.

**Noreste Culiacán:** Angel Flores 282 Ote, 80000 Culiacán, Sin.; tel. (671) 32100; fax (671) 28006; f. 1973; morning; Pres. and Dir-Gen. Lic. Silvino Silva Lozano; circ. 50,000.

### Sonora, Son.

**El Imparcial:** Mina y Sufragio Efectivo 71, Apdo 66, 83000 Hermosillo, Son.; tel. (621) 74700; telex 58850; fax (621) 74483; f. 1937; morning; Pres. and Editor José Alberto Healy N.; circ. 68,000, Sundays 72,000.

### Tamaulipas, Tamps

**El Bravo:** Morelos y Primera 129, Apdo 483, 87300 Matamoros, Tamps; tel. (891) 60100; telex 35848; fax (891) 62007; f. 1951; morning; Dir Isauro Rodríguez Garza; circ. 60,000.

**El Diario de Nuevo Laredo:** González 2409, Apdo 101, 88000 Nuevo Laredo, Tamps; tel. (871) 28444; telex 36627; fax (871) 28221; f. 1948; morning; Editor Ruperto Villarreal Montemayor; circ. 68,130, Sundays 73,495.

**Expressión:** Calle 3a y Novedades 1, Col. Periodistas, 87300 Matamoros, Tamps; tel. (891) 25248; morning; circ. 50,000.

**El Mañana de Reynosa:** Prof. Lauro Aguirre con Matías Canales, Apdo 14, 88620 Ciudad Reynosa, Tamps; tel. (892) 36363; telex 35762; fax (892) 30198; f. 1949; morning; Dir-Gen. Heriberto Deandar Martínez; circ. 65,000.

**El Mundo:** Ejército Nacional 201, Col. Guadalupe, 89120 Tampico, Tamps; tel. (12) 34570; f. 1918; Dir-Gen. Antonio Manzur Marón; circ. 75,000.

# MEXICO

**La Opinión de Matamoros:** Blvd Lauro Villar 200, Apdo 486, 87400 Matamoros, Tamps; tel. (891) 37757; fax (891) 22132; f. 1971; Dir-Gen. JUAN B. GARCÍA GÓMEZ; circ. 68,000.

**Prensa de Reynosa:** Matamoros y González Ortega, 88500 Reynosa, Tamps; tel. (892) 23515; telex 35722; f. 1963; morning; Dir-Gen. FÉLIX GARZA ELIZONDO; circ. 60,000.

**El Sol de Tampico:** Altamira 311 Pte, Apdo 434, 89000 Tampico, Tamps; tel. (12) 12-1718; telex 14848; fax (12) 12-6986; f. 1950; morning; Dir-Gen. Lic. RUBÉN DÍAZ DE LA GARZA; circ. 77,000.

### Veracruz, Ver.

**Diario del Istmo:** Avda Hidalgo 1115, 96400 Coatzacoalcos, Ver.; tel. (921) 48800; telex 78891; fax (921) 83514; f. 1979; morning; Dir-Gen. Lic. JOSÉ PABLO ROBLES MARTÍNEZ; circ. 63,200.

### Yucatán, Yuc.

**Diario de Yucatán:** Calle 60, No 521, Apdo 64, 97000 Mérida, Yuc.; tel. (99) 23-8444; telex 75889; fax (99) 28-2850; f. 1925; morning; Dir-Gen. CARLOS R. MENÉNDEZ NAVARRETE; circ. 60,181, Sundays 66,427.

**Novedades de Yucatán:** Calle 62, No 514A, 97000 Mérida Yuc.; tel. (99) 23-9933; telex 753722; fax (99) 24-9629; f. 1964; morning; Pres. RÓMULO O'FARRILL, Jr; Gen. Man. GERARDO GARCÍA GAMBOA; circ. 50,000.

**¡Por Esto!:** Calle 60 624-2, 97000 Mérida, Yuc.; f. 1991; morning; circ. 80,000.

### SELECTED WEEKLY NEWSPAPERS

**Bolsa de Trabajo:** San Francisco 657, 9A, Col. del Valle, 03100 México, DF; tel. (5) 536-8387; f. 1988; employment; Pres. and Dir-Gen. MÓNICA ELÍAS CALLES; circ. 30,000.

**Segundamano:** Loma del Parque 24, Lomas de Vista Hermosa, 05100 México, DF; tel. (5) 514-9343; f. 1986; Dir-Gen. LUIS MAGAÑA M.; circ. 70,000.

### PERIODICALS
(general interest, circ. over 65,000)

**Automundo Deportivo:** Morelos 16, 4°, 06040 México, DF; tel. (5) 521-1255; fax (5) 521-7798; f. 1970; monthly; sport; Dir JESÚS GONZÁLEZ DÍAZ; circ. 100,000.

**Barbie:** Insurgentes Sur 605-906, Col. Nápoles, 03810 México, DF; tel. (5) 536-6654; telex 1764640; fax (5) 523-1042; monthly; girls' magazine; Dir Lic. LILIANA MORENO G.; circ. 92,371.

**Cancionero del Fénix:** Lago Trasimeno 36c, Col. Anáhuac, 11320 México, DF; tel. (5) 399-9862; f. 1986; monthly; entertainment; Dir Lic. GABRIEL CANTÓN ELÍAS CALLES; circ. 100,000.

**Capricho:** Morelos 16, planta baja, 06040 México, DF; tel. (5) 510-9151; telex 1773031; weekly; Pres. RÓMULO O'FARRILL, Jr; Gen. Man. SAMUEL PODOLSKY RAPOPORT; circ. 320,000.

**Conozca:** Lucio Blanco 435, Azcapotzalco, 02400 México, DF; tel. (5) 352-6444; telex 1771598; fax (5) 561-9176; f. 1991; monthly; Dir-Gen. SERGIO GARCÉS SOLÍS DE OVANDO; circ. 70,000.

**Contenido:** Darwin 101, Col. Anzures, 11590 México, DF; tel. (5) 531-3162; fax (5) 531-3164; f. 1963; monthly; popular appeal; Dir ARMANDO AYALA A.; circ. 135,763.

**Cosmopolitan (México):** Lucio Blanco 435, Azcapotzalco, 02400 México, DF; tel. (5) 352-6444; fax (5) 561-9176; f. 1973; monthly; women's magazine; Dir SARA MARÍA CASTANY; circ. 150,000.

**Estrellas:** Torcuato Tasso 231, Col. Polanco, 11560 México, DF; tel. (5) 250-2222; telex 1763081; fax (5) 250-3535; f. 1986; fortnightly; show business; Pres. LUIS CARLOS MENDIOLA; circ. 200,000.

**Fama:** Avda Eugenio Garza Sada Sur 2245, Col. Roma, Apdo 3128, 64700 Monterrey, NL; tel. (8) 359-2525; fortnightly; show business; Pres. JESÚS D. GONZÁLEZ; Editorial Dir RAMIRO GARZA; circ. 250,000.

**La Familia Cristiana:** Apdo 69-766, Coyoacán, 04460 México, DF; tel. (5) 549-1454; fax (5) 670-9392; f. 1952; monthly; Dir GREGORIO EMMANUEL HIDALGO; circ. 75,000.

**Impacto:** Avda Ceylán 517, Col. Industrial Vallejo, Apdo 2986, 02300 México, DF; tel. (5) 587-3855; telex 1762055; fax (5) 567-7781; f. 1949; weekly; politics; Dir CARLOS MONCADA OCHOA; circ. 115,000.

**Kena:** Avda Insurgentes Sur 605-906, Col. Nápoles, 03810 México, DF; tel. (5) 536-6654; telex 1764640; fax (5) 682-3037; f. 1977; fortnightly; women's interest; Dir LILIANA MORENO; circ. 98,038.

**Mecánica Popular:** Lucio Blanco 435, Azcapotzalco, 02400 México, DF; tel. (5) 352-6444; telex 1771598; fax (5) 561-9176; f. 1947; monthly; crafts and home improvements; Dir SANTIAGO J. VILLAZÓN; circ. 101,000.

**Medix:** Lucio Blanco 435, Azcapotzalco, 02400 México, DF; tel. (5) 352-0771; telex 1771598; fax (5) 561-9176; f. 1989; monthly; health; Dir-Gen. JAVIER ORTIZ CAMORLINGA; circ. 87,000.

**Muy Interesante:** Lucio Blanco 435, Azcapotzalco, 02400 México, DF; tel. (5) 352-6444; telex 1771598; fax (5) 561-9176; f. 1984; monthly; scientific development; Dir GUSTAVO GONZÁLEZ LEWIS; circ. 192,126.

**La Pequeña Diana:** Cereales 189, Col. Granjas Esmeralda, 09810 México, DF; tel. (5) 581-0660; fax (5) 670-6734; f. 1984; monthly; crafts; Dir-Gen. ARTHUR W. HONEGGER W.; circ. 30,000.

**Rutas de Pasión:** Morelos 16, 4°, 06040 México, DF; tel. (5) 521-4690; fax (5) 521-7798; f. 1965; weekly; Pres. RÓMULO O'FARRILL, Jr; Gen. Man. DEA MARÍA REVILLA; circ. 115,000.

**Selecciones del Reader's Digest:** Avda Lomas de Sotelo 1102, Col. Lomas Hermosa, Apdo 552, Naucalpan, 11200 México, DF; tel. (5) 358-9155; telex 1774213; fax (5) 395-3835; f. 1940; monthly; Dir JOSÉ ANGEL MENÉNDEZ; circ. 700,000.

**Shape:** Mier y Pesado 126, Col. del Valle, 03100 México, DF; tel. (5) 687-4699; fax (5) 523-7045; monthly; health and fitness; Editor DIANA DE RAMERY; circ. 75,000.

**¡Siempre!:** Vallarta 20, Apdo 4-033, 06470 México, DF; tel. (5) 566-9355; fax (5) 546-5130; f. 1953; weekly; left of centre; Dir Lic. BEATRÍZ PAGÉS LLERGO; circ. 100,000.

**Teenager International:** Mier y Pesado 126, Col. del Valle, 03100 México, DF; tel. (5) 687-4699; fax (5) 523-7045; quarterly; young people's interests; Editor MARÍA LUISA GALVÁN DE SAYROLS; circ. 100,000.

**Tele-Guía:** Lucio Blanco 435, Azcapotzalco, 02400 México, DF; tel. (5) 352-6444; telex 1771598; fax (5) 561-9176; f. 1952; weekly; television guide; Pres. GUSTAVO GONZÁLEZ LEWIS; Dir RAFAEL MARTÍNEZ; circ. 750,000.

**Tiempo Libre:** Holbein 75 bis, Col. Nochebuena Mixcoac, 03720 México, DF; tel. (5) 611-3874; fax (5) 611-2884; f. 1980; weekly; entertainment guide; Dir-Gen. ANGELES AGUILAR ZINSER; circ. 90,000.

**Tú:** Lucio Blanco 435, Azcapotzalco, 02400 México, DF; tel. (5) 352-6444; telex 1771598; fax (5) 561-9176; f. 1980; monthly; Pres. GUSTAVO GONZÁLEZ LEWIS; circ. 150,000.

**TV y Novelas:** Lucio Blanco 435, Azcapotzalco, 02400 México, DF; tel. (5) 352-6444; telex 1771598; fax (5) 561-9176; f. 1979; fortnightly; television guide and short stories; Pres. GUSTAVO GONZÁLEZ LEWIS; circ. 900,000.

**Ultima Moda:** Balderas 87, 2°, 06040 México, DF; tel. (5) 518-5481; f. 1966; fortnightly; fashion; Pres. RÓMULO O'FARRILL, Jr; Gen. Man. Lic. SAMUEL PODOLSKY RAPOPORT; circ. 230,000.

**Vanidades:** Lucio Blanco 435, Azcapotzalco, 02400 México, DF; tel. (5) 352-3266; telex 1771598; fax (5) 561-9176; f. 1961; fortnightly; women's magazine; Dir SARA BARCELÓ DE CASTANY; circ. 180,000.

### SPECIALIST PERIODICALS
(circ. over 30,000)

**Auto-industria:** Querétaro 229-402, Col. Roma, 06700 México, DF; tel. (5) 264-2848; fax (5) 584-4821; f. 1971; monthly; motoring; Dir-Gen. ALFREDO VILLAGRÁN ARÉVALO; circ. 30,386.

**Boletín Industrial:** Goldsmith 37-403, Col. Polanco, 11550 México, DF; tel. (5) 280-6463; fax (5) 280-3194; f. 1983; monthly; Dir-Gen. HUMBERTO VALADÉS DÍAZ; circ. 36,000.

**El Campo:** Mar Negro 147, Col. Tacuba, 11410 México, DF; tel. (5) 527-4554; monthly; farming; circ. 35,000.

**Ciencia y Desarrollo:** Edif. del S.N.I., Avda San Fernando 1, Col. Niño Jesús, Del. Tlalpan, 14080 México, DF; tel. (5) 655-1221; fax (5) 626-0370; f. 1975; every 2 months; scientific; Dir ALFREDO GÓMEZ RODRÍGUEZ; circ. 8,000.

**Comercio:** Río Tíber 87, 06500 México, DF; tel. (5) 514-0873; fax (5) 514-1008; f. 1960; monthly; business review; Dir RAÚL HORTA; circ. 40,000.

**Gaceta Médica de México:** Academia Nacional de Medicina, Unidad de Congresos del Centro Médico Nacional Siglo XXI, Bloque B, Avda Cuauhtémoc 330, Col. Doctores, 06725 México, DF; tel. (5) 578-2044; fax (5) 578-4271; f. 1864; every 2 months; medicine; Editor Dr HÉCTOR PÉREZ-RINCÓN; circ. 40,000.

**Hércules Moderno:** Avda Rodolfo Gaona, Edif. 82-B-203, Lomas de Sotelo, 11200 México, DF; tel. (5) 557-0792; fax (5) 395-6564; f. 1980; fortnightly; physical exercise; Dir VÍCTOR ARZATE; circ. 45,000.

**Información Científica y Tecnológica (ICyT):** Edif. CONACYT, Circuito Cultural Universitario, Ciudad Universitaria, 04515 México, DF; tel. (5) 655-6366; telex 1774521; f. 1979; monthly; organ of the Consejo Nacional de Ciencia y Tecnología; Dir-Gen. Dr MANUEL ORTEGA O.; circ. 30,000.

**Intercambio Internacional:** Nicolás 1154, Col. San Juan, México, DF; weekly; commerce; circ. 50,000.

**Negobancos (Negocios y Bancos):** Bolívar 8-601, Apdo 1907, 06000 México, DF; tel. (5) 510-1884; fax (5) 512-9411; f. 1951;

# MEXICO

fortnightly; business, economics; Dir ALFREDO FARRUGIA REED; circ. 35,000.

**Noticiario Industrial:** Goldsmith 38-302, Col. Polanco, 11560 México, DF; tel. (5) 259-1448; telex 1763259; fax (5) 540-0673; f. 1988; monthly; Dir NEAL W. BAKER; circ. 34,144.

**Opinión Agropecuaria:** Edif. Sallquer, Avda Alvaro Obregon 12, México, DF; weekly; circ. 60,000.

**Visión:** Arquímedes 199, 6° y 7°, Col. Polanco, 11570 México, DF; tel. (5) 203-6091; telex 1763168; offices in Santa Fe de Bogotá, Buenos Aires and Santiago de Chile; f. 1950; fortnightly; politics and economics; Gen. Man. ROBERTO BELLO; circ. 42,810.

## ASSOCIATIONS

**Asociación de Diarios Independientes:** Nueva York 228, Col. Nápoles, 03810 México, DF; tel. (5) 687-1200; Pres. MAURICIO BERCÚN.

**Asociación Nacional de Periodistas A.C.:** Luis G. Obregón 17, Desp. 209, Centro, 06020 México, DF; tel. (5) 702-1546.

**Federación Latinoamericana de Periodistas (FELAP):** Nuevo Leon 144, 1°, Col. Condesa, 06170 México, DF; tel. (5) 286-6055; fax (5) 286-6085.

## NEWS AGENCIES

**Agencia Mexicana de Información (AMI):** Avda Cuauhtémoc 16, Col. Doctores, 06720 México, DF; tel. (5) 761-9933; telex 75646; Gen.-Man. EVA VÁZQUEZ LÓPEZ.

**Noti-Acción:** Blvd de los Virreyes 1030, Lomas de Chapultepec, 11000 México, DF; tel. (5) 520-0951; Gen. Co-ordinator RUTH J. BARRIENTOS GARZÓN.

**Notimex, SA de CV:** Morena 110, 3°, Col. del Valle, 03100 México, DF; tel. (5) 687-0500; telex 1771162; fax (5) 687-4324; f. 1968; services to press, radio and TV in Mexico and throughout the world; Dir-Gen. RUBÉN ALVAREZ MENDIOLA.

### Foreign Bureaux

**Agence France-Presse (AFP):** Torre Latinoamericana, 28°, Lázaro Cárdenas y Madero, Apdo M10330, 06007 México, DF; tel. (5) 518-5494; telex 1773095; Bureau Chief FRANÇOIS CAMPREDON.

**Agenzia Nazionale Stampa Associata (ANSA)** (Italy): Avda Cuauhtémoc 16, 3°, Of. 304-305, Col. Doctores, 06720 México, DF; tel. (5) 761-2223; telex 1773497; fax (5) 761-2326; Bureau Chief GIULIO GELIBTER.

**Associated Press (AP)** (USA): Edif. Bank of America, 8°, Of. 902-804, Paseo de la Reforma 116, Apdo 1181, México, DF; tel. (5) 566-3488; telex 1771064; Bureau Chief ELOY O. AGUILAR.

**Deutsche Presse-Agentur (dpa)** (Germany): Avda Cuauhtémoc 16, Col. Doctores, 06720 México, DF; tel. (5) 578-4829; fax (5) 761-0762; Bureau Chief THOMAS VON MONILLARD.

**EFE** (Spain): Lafayette 69, Col. Anzures, 11590 México, DF; tel. (5) 545-8256; telex 1760002; Bureau Chief FRANCISCO OSABA ARRANZ.

**Informatsionnoye Telegrafnoye Agentstvo Rossii—Telegrafnoye Agentsvo Suverennykh Stran (ITAR—TASS)** (Russia): Avda Amsterdam 218, Dpto 103, México 11, DF; Correspondent IGOR GOLUBEV.

**Inter Press Service (IPS)** (Italy): Avda Cuauhtémoc 16-403, Col. Doctores, Del. Cuauhtémoc, 06720 México, DF; tel. (5) 578-0417; telex 61219; fax (5) 578-0099; Chief Correspondent JOSÉ L. ALCAZAR DE LA RIVA.

**Jiji Tsushin-Sha** (Japan): Savilla 9, 2°, Col. Juárez, Del. Cuauhtémoc, 06600 México, DF; tel. (5) 528-9651; telex 1761267; fax (5) 511-0062; Bureau Chief FUJIO IKEDA.

**Kyodo Tsushin** (Japan): Jardín 13, Col. Tlacopac, 01040 México, DF; tel. (5) 548-3295; telex 1763380; Correspondent SEIICHI TODA.

**Prensa Latina** (Cuba): Edif. B, Dpto 504, Avda Insurgentes Centro 125, Col. San Rafael, Del. Cuauhtémoc, 06470 México, DF; tel. (5) 546-6015; telex 1773979; fax (5) 592-0570; Chief Correspondent Lic. MIGUEL LOZANO ALEMÁN.

**Reuters Ltd** (UK): Monte Pelvoux 110, 3rd Floor, Lomas de Chapultepec, 11000 México, DF; Bureau Chief MICHAEL MAZZOLA.

**United Press International (UPI)** (USA): Avda Cuauhtémoc 16, Col. Dóctores, Del. Cuauhtémoc, 06700 México, DF; tel. (5) 761-5365; telex 1773957; Bureau Chief EDWIN VIDAL.

**Xinhua (New China) News Agency** (People's Republic of China): Francisco I, Madero 17, Col. Tlacopac, 01040 México, DF; tel. (5) 550-9860; telex 1773096; Correspondents SHEN JIASONG, XUE HONG.

### ASSOCIATION

**Asociación de Corresponsales Extranjeros en México (ACEM):** Avda Cuauhtémoc 16, 1°, Col. Doctores, Del. Cuauhtémoc, 06720 México, DF; tel. (5) 588-3241; telex 1772383; fax (5) 588-6382.

## Publishers

### México, DF

**Addison-Wesley Iberoamericana, SA de CV:** Blvd de las Cataratas 3, 2°, Col. Jardines del Pedregal, 01900 México, DF; tel. (5) 568-3618; telex 1771410; fax (5) 660-4930; f. 1986; educational textbooks; Pres. JUAN JOSÉ FERNÁNDEZ GAOS.

**M. Aguilar Editor, SA:** Avda Universidad 767, 03100 México, DF; tel. (5) 688-8966; telex 1771582; fax (5) 604-2304; f. 1965; general literature; Man. Dir ANTONIO RUANO FERNÁNDEZ.

**Arbol Editorial, SA de CV:** Avda Cuauhtémoc 1430, Col. Sta Cruz Atoyac, 03310 México, DF; tel. (5) 688-4828; fax (5) 605-7600; f. 1979; health, philosophy, theatre; Man. Dir GERARDO GALLY.

**Editorial Avante, SA:** Luis González Obregón 9-altos, Apdo 45-796, México, DF; tel. (5) 521-7563; fax (5) 521-5245; f. 1950; educational, drama, linguistics; Man. Dir MARIO HINOJOSA SAENZ.

**Editorial Azteca, SA:** Calle de la Luna 225–227, México 3, DF; tel. (5) 526-1157; f. 1956; religion, literature and technical; Man. Dir ALFONSO ALEMÓN JALOMO.

**Librería y Ediciones Botas, SA:** Justo Sierra 52, Apdo 941, 06020 México, DF; tel. (5) 702-4083; fax (5) 702-5403; f. 1910; history, law, philosophy, literature, fine arts, science, language, economics, medicine; Dir ERNESTO BOTAS H.

**Cía Editorial Continental, SA de CV (CECSA):** Renacimiento 180, Col. San Juan Tlihuaca, 02400 México, DF; tel. (5) 561-8399; telex 1760261; fax (5) 561-5477; f. 1954; science, technology, general textbooks; Gen. Man. C.P. VICTÓRICO ALBORES S.

**Ediciones de Cultura Popular, SA:** Odontología 76, Copilco Universidad, México 20, DF; f. 1969; history, politics, social sciences; Man. Dir URIEL JARQUÍN GALVEZ.

**Ediciones CUPSA:** Centro de Comunicación Cultural CUPSA, Apdo 97 bis, 06000 México, DF; tel. (5) 546-2100; f. 1958; Biblical studies, theology, church history, devotional materials, hymnbooks; Dir ELISA TOSTADO.

**Editorial Diana, SA de CV:** Roberto Gayol 1219, Col. del Valle, Apdo 44986, 03100 México, DF; tel. (5) 575-0711; fax (5) 575-3211; f. 1946; general trade and technical books; Exec. Pres. JOSÉ LUIS RAMÍREZ C.

**Ediciones Era, SA:** Calle del Trabajo 31, Col. La Fama, Tlalpan, 14269 México, DF; tel. (5) 528-1221; fax (5) 606-2904; f. 1960; general and social science, art and literature; Gen. Man. NIEVES ESPRESATE XIRAU.

**Editorial Everest Mexicana, SA:** Avda Río Tuxpan 23, México 13, DF; tel. (5) 686-1431; f. 1980; general textbooks; Gen. Man. JUAN JESÚS OVEJERO SANZ.

**Espasa Calpe Mexicana, SA:** Pitágoras 1139, Col. del Valle, 03100 México, DF; tel. (5) 575-5022; f. 1948; literature, music, economics, philosophy, encyclopaedia; Man. FRANCISCO CRUZ RUBIO.

**Fernández Editores, SA de CV:** Eje 1 Pte México-Coyoacán 321, Col. Xoco, 03330 México, DF; tel. (5) 605-6557; telex 1773630; fax (5) 688-9173; f. 1943; children's literature, text-books, education, educational toys, didactic material; Man. Dir LUIS GERARDO FERNÁNDEZ PÉREZ.

**Editorial Fondo de Cultura Económica, SA de CV:** Avda Universidad 975, Del. Benito Juárez, 03100 México, DF; tel. (5) 524-1820; telex 1775866; fax (5) 534-4319; f. 1934; economics, history, philosophy, science, politics, psychology, sociology, literature; Dir Lic. MIGUEL DE LA MADRID.

**Editorial Grijalbo, SA de CV:** Calzada San Bartolo-Naucalpan 282, Col. Argentina, Apdo 17-568, 11230 México, DF; tel. (5) 358-4355; telex 1771415; f. 1954; general fiction, history, sciences, philosophy, children's books; Man. Dir ROGELIO CARVAJAL DÁVILA.

**Nueva Editorial Interamericana, SA de CV:** Cedro 512, Apdo 26370, 06450 México, DF; tel. (5) 541-3155; telex 1771196; f. 1944; sciences and technology; Gen. Man. JOSÉ LUIS ROSAS RIVERO.

**Editorial Joaquín Mortiz, SA de CV:** Insurgentes sur 1162, 3°, Col. Del Valle, 03100 México, DF; tel. (5) 575-8585; telex 1764458; fax (5) 575-8980; f. 1962; general literature; Man. Dir JORGE LÓPEZ ALBA.

**Editorial Jus, SA de CV:** Plaza de Abasolo 14, Col. Guerrero, 06300 México, DF; tel. (5) 526-0616; fax (5) 529-1444; f. 1938; history of Mexico, law, philosophy, economy, religion; Man. TOMÁS G. REYNOSO.

**Ediciones Larousse, SA de CV:** Marsella 53 esq. Nápoles, Col. Juárez, 06600 México, DF; tel. (5) 208–2005; telex 1771746; fax (5) 208-6255; f. 1965; Man. Dir DOMINIQUE BERTÍN.

**Editora Latino Americana, SA:** Guatemala 10-220, México 1, DF; popular literature; Dir JORGE H. YÉPEZ.

**Editorial Limusa, SA:** Balderas 95, 1°, Col. Centro, 06040 México, DF; tel. (5) 542-4500; telex 1762410; fax (5) 512-2903; f. 1962; science, general, textbooks; Man. Dir CARLOS NORIEGA ARIAS.

# MEXICO

**Editorial Nuestro Tiempo, SA:** Avda Universidad 771, Desp. 103-104, Col. del Valle, 03100 México, DF; tel. (5) 688-8768; fax (5) 688-6868; f. 1966; social sciences; Man. Dir ESPERANZA NACIF BARQUET.

**Editorial Oasis, SA:** Avda Oaxaca 28, B°, 06700 México, DF; tel. (5) 528-8293; f. 1954; literature, pedagogy, poetry; Man. MARÍA TERESA ESTRADA DE FERNÁNDEZ DEL BUSTO.

**Editorial Orión:** Sierra Mojada 325, 11000 México, DF; tel. (5) 520-0224; f. 1942; archaeology, philosophy, psychology, literature, fiction; Man. Dir Sra SILVA HERNÁNDEZ VIUDA DE CÁRDENAS.

**Editorial Patria, SA de CV:** Renacimiento 180, Col. San Juan Tlihuaca, Azcapotzalco, 02400 México, DF; tel. (5) 561-9299; telex 1764172; fax (5) 561-3218; f. 1933; sociology, general literature, children's books; Man. Dir MA ISABEL LASA DE LA MORA.

**Editorial Porrúa Hnos, SA:** Argentina 15, 5°, México 1, DF; tel. 522-4866; f. 1944; general literature; Man. Dir J. A. PÉREZ PORRÚA.

**Editorial Posada, SA de CV:** La Otra Banda 74, Col. Tizapan San Angel, 01090 México, DF; tel. (5) 548-2109; f. 1968; general; Dir-Gen. GUILLERMO MENDIZÁBAL LIZALDE.

**Editorial Quetzacoatl, SA:** Medicina 37, Local 1 y 2, México 20, DF; tel. (5) 548-6180; Man. Dir ALBERTO RODRÍGUEZ VALDÉS.

**Harmex, SA de CV:** Lucio Blanco 435, Azcapotzalco, 02400 México, DF; tel. (5) 352-6538; fax (5) 352-8218; romantic fiction; Pres. GUSTAVO GONZÁLEZ LEWIS.

**Medios Publicitarios Mexicanos, SA de CV:** Avda México 99-103, Col. Hip. Condesa, 06170 México, DF; tel. (5) 574-2858; fax (5) 574-2668; f. 1958; advertising media rates and data; Man. FERNANDO VILLAMIL AVILA.

**Reverté Ediciones, SA de CV:** Río Pánuco 141-A, 06500 México, DF; tel. (5) 533-5658; fax (5) 514-6799; f. 1955; science, technical; Man. Dir JAVIER REVERTÉ MASCÓ.

**Salvat Mexicana de Ediciones, SA de CV:** Pres. Masaryk 101, 5°, 11570 México, DF; tel. (5) 250-6041; telex 1763096; fax (5) 250-6861; medicine, encyclopaedic works; Dir GUILLERMO HERNÁNDEZ PÉREZ.

**Siglo XXI Editores, SA de CV:** Avda Cerro del Agua 248, Col. Romero de Terreros, Del. Coyoacán, 04310 México, DF; tel. (5) 658-7999; fax (5) 658-7599; f. 1966; art, economics, education, history, social sciences, literature, philology and linguistics, philosophy and political science; Dir-Gen. Lic. JAIME LABASTIDA OCHOA; Gen. Man. Ing. GUADALUPE ORTIZ ELGUEA.

**Editorial Trillas, SA:** Avda Río Churubusco 385 Pte, Col. Xoco, Apdo 10534, 03330 México, DF; tel. (5) 688-4233; telex 1762109; f. 1954; science, technical, textbooks, children's books; Man. Dir FRANCISCO TRILLAS MERCADER.

**Universidad Nacional Autónoma de México:** Dirección General de Fomento Editorial, Avda del Iman 5, Ciudad Universitaria, 04510 México, DF; tel. (5) 550-7473; fax (5) 550-7428; f. 1935; publications in all fields; Dir-Gen. ARTURO VELÁZQUEZ JIMÉNEZ.

### ASSOCIATIONS

**Cámara Nacional de la Industria Editorial Mexicana:** Holanda 13, Col. San Diego Churubusco, 04120 México, DF; tel. (5) 688-2011; fax (5) 604-3147; f. 1964; Pres. JULIO SANZ CRESPO; Gen. Man. FEDERICO KRAFFT VERA.

**Instituto Mexicano del Libro, AC:** México, DF; tel. (5) 535-2061; Pres. KLAUS THIELE; Sec.-Gen. ISABEL RUIZ GONZÁLEZ.

**Organización Editorial Mexicana, SA:** Guillermo Prieto 7, 06470 México, DF; tel. (5) 566-1511; telex 1772657; fax (5) 566-0694.

**Prensa Nacional Asociada, SA (PRENASA):** Avda Insurgentes Centro 114-411, 06030 México, DF; tel. (5) 546-7389.

## Radio and Television

In 1992 there were an estimated 22,500,000 radio receivers and 13,100,000 television receivers in use.

### REGULATORY BODIES

**Cámara Nacional de la Industria de Radio y Televisión (CIRT):** Avda Horacio 1013, Col. Polanco, 11550 México, DF; tel. (5) 726-9909; fax (5) 545-6767; f. 1942; Pres. JAVIER PÉREZ DE ANDA; Gen. Man. CÉSAR HERNÁNDEZ ESPEJO.

**Dirección General de Radio, Televisión y Cine (RTC):** Atletas 2, Col. Country Club, Del. Coyoacán, 04220 México, DF; tel. (5) 544-3768; telex 1760298; Dir-Gen. Lic. MANUEL VILLA AGUILERA.

**Dirección General de Telecomunicaciones:** Lázaro Cárdenas 567, 11°, Ala Norte, Narvarte, 03020 México, DF; tel. (5) 519-9161; Dir-Gen. Ing. ENRIQUE LUENGAS H.

**Dirección de Normas de Radiodifusión:** Eugenia 197, 1°, Col. Vértiz Narvarte, 03020 México, DF; tel. (5) 590-4372; licence issuing authority; Dir Dr ALFONSO AMILPAS.

### RADIO

In 1993 there were 1,040 commercial radio stations in Mexico. Among the most important commercial networks are:

**ARTSA:** Avda de Los Virreyes 1030, Col. Lomas de Chapultepec, 11000 México, DF; tel. (5) 202-3344; telex 1772779; fax (5) 202-6940; Dir-Gen. Lic. GUSTAVO ECHEVARRÍA ARCE.

**Cadena Crystal Cima, SA de CV:** Montecito 59, Col. Nápoles, 03810 México, DF; tel. (5) 682-4370; Dir-Gen. Lic. FRANCISCO J. SÁNCHEZ CAMPUZANO.

**Corporación Mexicana de Radiodifusion:** Callo Tetitla 23, esq. Calle Coapa, Col. Toriello Guerra, 14050 México, DF; tel. (5) 666-4422; fax (5) 207-6503; Pres. and Dir-Gen. ENRIQUE BERNAL SERVÍN.

**Firme, SA:** Gauss 10, Col. Nueva Anzures, 11590 México, DF; tel. (5) 250-7788; fax (5) 531-9880; Dir-Gen. LUIS IGNACIO SANTIBÁÑEZ.

**Frecuencia Modulada Mexicana, SA de CV, Grupo Stereorey y FM Globo:** Mariano Escobedo 532, Col. Anzures, 11590 México, DF; tel. (5) 203-4520; telex 1762128; fax (5) 203-4574; Pres. JOAQUÍN VARGAS G.; Dir-Gen. JOSÉ VARGAS S.

**Grupo Acir, SA:** Monte Pirineos 770, Col. Lomas de Chapultepec, 11000 México, DF; tel. (5) 540-4291; telex 1773947; fax (5) 540-4106; f. 1965; comprises 140 stations; Pres. FRANCISCO IBARRA LÓPEZ.

**Instituto Mexicano de la Radio (IMER):** Mayorazgo 83, Col. Yoco, 03330 México, DF; tel. (5) 604-7741; Dir-Gen. ALEJANDRO MONTAÑO MARTÍNEZ.

**Núcleo Radio Mil:** Insurgentes Sur 1870, 01030 México, DF; tel. (5) 662-6060; telex 1775751; f. 1960; comprises seven radio stations in Mexico City and three provincial radio stations; Pres. and Dir-Gen. Lic. E. GUILLERMO SALAS PEYRÓ.

**Organización Impulsora de Radio, SA de CV:** Avda Nuevo León 16, 2°, Col. Hipódromo Condesa, Del. Cuauhtémoc, 06170 México, DF; tel. (5) 286-5844; telex 1761008; fax (5) 207-5778; f. 1965; comprises 81 radio stations; Pres. ADRIÁN AGUIRRE GÓMEZ; Dir-Gen. ROBERTO PLIEGO GONZÁLEZ.

**Organización Radio Centro:** Artículo 123, N° 90 Centro, 06050 México, DF; tel. (5) 709-2220; fax (5) 512-8588; nine stations in Mexico City; Pres. MARÍA ESTHER GÓMEZ DE AGUIRRE.

**Organización Radiofónica de México, SA:** Tuxpan 39, 8°, Col. Roma Sur, 06760 México, DF; tel. (5) 264-2025; fax (5) 264-5720; Pres. JAIME FERNÁNDEZ ARMENDÁRIZ.

**Radio Cadena Nacional, SA (RCN):** Avda Coyoacán 1899, Col. Acacias, 03240 México, DF; tel. (5) 534-2300; fax (5) 524-2753; f. 1948; Pres. RAFAEL NAVARRO ARRONTE; Dir-Gen. Lic. SERGIO FAJARDO ORTIZ.

**Radio Comerciales, SA de CV:** Avda México y López Mateos, 44680 Guadalajara, Jal.; tel. (3) 615-0852; fax (3) 630-3487; 7 major commercial stations.

**Radio Educación:** Angel Urraza 622, Col. del Valle, 03100 México, DF; tel. (5) 559-6169; fax (5) 575-6566; f. 1924; Gen. Dir LUIS ERNESTO PI OROZCO.

**Radio Fórmula, SA:** Privada de Horacio 10, Col. Polanco, 11560 México, DF; tel. (5) 282-1016; Dir Lic. ROGERIO AZCARRAGA.

**Radiodifusoras Asociadas, SA de CV (RASA):** Durango 341, 1° y 2°, Col. Roma, 06700 México, DF; tel. (5) 286-1222; telex 1760219; fax (5) 286-2774; f. 1956; Pres. JOSÉ LARIS ITURBIDE; Dir-Gen. JOSÉ LARIS RODRÍGUEZ.

**Radiodifusores Asociados de Innovación y Organización, SA:** Emerson 412, Chapultepec Morales, 11560 México, DF; tel. (5) 203-5577; telex 1773797; fax (5) 254-2302; Dir-Gen. Lic. CARLOS QUIÑONES ARMENDÁRIZ.

**Radiorama, SA:** Reforma 51, 11°, 06030 México, DF; tel. (5) 566-0471; telex 1761072; Dir JOSÉ LUIS C. RESÉNDIZ.

**Representaciones Comerciales Integrales:** Avda Chapultepec 431, Col. Juárez, 06600 México, DF; tel. (5) 533-6185; Dir-Gen. ALFONSO PALMA V.

**Sistema Radio Juventud:** Pablo Casals 567, Prados Providencia, 44670 Guadalajara, Jal.; tel. (3) 641-6677; fax (3) 641-3413; f. 1975; network of several stations including Estereo Soul 89.9 FM; Dirs ALBERTO LEAL A., J. JESÚS OROZCO G., GABRIEL ARREGUI V.

**Sistema Radiofónico Nacional, SA:** Baja California 163, Of. 602, 06760 México, DF; tel. (5) 574-0298; f. 1971; represents commercial radio networks; Dir-Gen. RENÉ C. DE LA ROSA.

**Sociedad Mexicana de Radio, SA de CV (SOMER):** Gutenberg 89, Col. Anzures, 11590 México, DF; tel. (5) 255-5297; fax (5) 545-0310; Dir-Gen. EDILBERTO HUESCA PERROTIN.

### TELEVISION

In 1992 there were 752 television stations, including 115 cable television stations.

MEXICO — Directory

Among the most important are:

**Asesoramiento y Servicios Técnicos Industriales, SA (ASTISA):** Niños Héroes 15, México 7, DF; tel. (5) 585-3333; telex 1773994; commercial; Dir ROBERTO CHÁVEZ TINAJERO.

**MVS (Multivisión):** Blvd Puerto Aéreo 486, Col. Moctezuma, 15500 México, DF; tel. (5) 571-2835; subscriber-funded.

**Tele Cadena Mexicana, SA:** Avda Chapultepec 18, 06724 México, DF; tel. (5) 535-1679; commercial, comprises about 80 stations; Dir Lic. JORGE ARMANDO PIÑA MEDINA.

**Televisa, SA:** Edif. Televicentro, Avda Chapultepec 28, Col. Doctores, 06724 México, DF; tel. (5) 709-3333; telex 1773154; fax (5) 709-2136; f. 1973; commercial; began broadcasts to Europe via satellite in Dec. 1988 through its subsidiary, Galavisión; 406 affiliated stations; Exec. Pres. EMILIO AZCÁRRAGA MILMO; Chair. RÓMULO O'FARRILL, Jr.

**Televisión Azteca, SA de CV:** Avda Periférico Sur 4121, Col. Fuentes del Pedregal, 14141 México, DF; tel. (5) 420-1313; f. 1993 to assume responsibility for former state-owned channels 7 and 13; Pres. RICARDO B. SALINAS.

**Televisión de la República Mexicana:** Mina 24, Col. Guerrero, México, DF; tel. (5) 528-6321; cultural; Dir EDUARDO LIZALDE.

**XEIPN-TV:** Instituto Politécnico Nacional, Carpio 476, Col. Casco de Santo Tomás, México 17, DF; tel. (5) 396-8177; telex 1777554; Dir-Gen. Lic. ALEJANDRA LAJOUR.

As a member of the Intelsat international consortium, Mexico has received communications via satellite since the 1960s. The launch of the Morelos I and Morelos II satellites, in 1985, provided Mexico with its own satellite communications system. The Morelos satellites were superseded by a new satellite network, Solidaridad, which was inaugurated in early 1994.

# Finance

(cap. = capital; dep. = deposits; m. = million; res = reserves; amounts in old pesos unless otherwise stated)

### BANKING

The Mexican banking system is comprised of the Banco de México (the central bank of issue), multiple or commercial banking institutions and development banking institutions. Banking activity, regulated by the Federal Government, seeks to encourage saving in all sectors and regions, to channel resources, where appropriate, to a broad-based system of institutionalized credit, resulting in the decentralization of the system and of the economy in general.

Commercial banking institutions are constituted as *Sociedades Anónimas*, with wholly private social capital. Development banking institutions exist as *Sociedades Nacionales de Crédito*, participation in their capital is exclusive to the Federal Government, notwithstanding the possibility of accepting limited amounts of private capital.

The financial authorities of the Federal Government are empowered to approve the establishment of representative offices and branches of foreign financial institutions in Mexico, providing that the active and passive operations of such entities are conducted exclusively with foreign residents. The successful implementation of NAFTA is expected to facilitate the full participation of financial entities from the USA, Canada and Mexico in the banking systems of each of the signatory nations.

All private banks were nationalized in September 1982. By July 1992, however, the banking system had been completely returned to the private sector, with total revenue from the sale of 18 banks amounting to US $12,900m.

Total bank deposits, as at June 1994, were estimated at 625,000m. new pesos.

In October 1994 the Government approved the application for operating licences within Mexico of 18 foreign banks.

### Supervisory Authority

**Comisión Nacional Bancaria** (National Banking Commission): Insurgentes Sur 1971, Torre Norte, 10°, México, DF; tel. (5) 724-6961; fax (5) 724-6963; f. 1924; government commission controlling all credit institutions in Mexico; 6 mems; Pres. GUILLERMO PRIETO FORTÚN.

### Central Bank

**Banco de México (BANXICO):** Avda 5 de Mayo 2, Apdo 98 bis, 06059 México, DF; tel. (5) 237-2000; telex 1773050; fax (5) 237-2370; f. 1925; currency issuing authority; became autonomous on 1 April 1994; broad powers to regulate monetary policy in all areas except for the exchange rate, which remains the responsibility of the Finance and Public Credit Secretariat; res US $7,854m. (March 1995); Gov. MIGUEL MANCERA AGUAYO; 9 brs.

### Commercial Banks

**Banca Confía, SA:** Paseo de la Reforma 450, Col. Juárez, 06600 México, DF; tel. (5) 207-0197; telex 1776494; fax (5) 525-7370; f. 1977, fmrly Banco de Industria y Comercio; transferred to private ownership in August 1991; cap. 337,000m., res 224,000m., dep. 5,467,000m. (Dec. 1992); Dir-Gen. Ing. JORGE LANKENAU ROCHA; 137 brs.

**Banca Cremi, SA:** Paseo de la Reforma 93, 15°, Col. Tabacalora, 06030 México, DF; tel. (5) 227-7000; telex 1771213; fax (5) 535-4778; f. 1978; multiple bank merged with Fomento y Promoción in 1985; transferred to private ownership in June 1991; operations assumed by federal regulators in Sept. 1994, pending investigation; cap. 463,000m., res 144,000m., dep. 9,030,000m. (Dec. 1992); Dir-Gen. Lic. ANTONIO MIJARES RICCI; 114 brs.

**Banca Promex, SA:** Avda La Paz 875, 44100 Guadalajara, Jal.; tel. (3) 679-5000; telex 17681847; fax (3) 613-1188; f. 1940; multiple bank; cap. 250,000m., res. 237,000m., dep. 2,519,000m. (Dec. 1992); CEO EDUARDO A. CARRILLO; 153 brs.

**Banca Serfín, SA:** 16 de Septiembre 38, 06000 México, DF; tel. (5) 709-7644; telex 1771130; fax (5) 512-1173; f. 1864; merged with Banco Continental Ganadero in 1985; transferred to private ownership in January 1992; cap. 59.5m. new pesos, res 3,076.1m. new pesos, dep. 61,063.9m. new pesos (Dec. 1993); CEO Lic. ABELARDO MORALES PURÓN; 650 brs.

**Banco del Atlántico, SA:** Avda Hidalgo 128, Coyoacán, 04030 México, DF; tel. (5) 626-1778; telex 1772456; fax (5) 544-5096; f. 1952; merged with Banco Monterrey in 1985; cap. 839,000m., res 26,000m., dep. 7,285,000m. (Dec. 1992); Dir-Gen. Lic. FERNANDO RAMOS GONZÁLEZ DE CASTILLA; 207 brs.

**Banco BCH, SA:** Paseo de la Reforma 364, 2°, Col. Juárez, 06694 México, DF; tel. (5) 533-0434; telex 1776230; fax (5) 533-4701; f. 1941; merged with Banco Sofimex in 1985; transferred to private ownership in 1991; cap. 605,000m., res 419,000m., dep. 6,685m. (Dec. 1992); Chair. FRANCISCO SUÁREZ DÁVILA; 130 brs.

**Banco del Centro, SA (Bancen):** Venustiano Carranza 235, 78000 San Luis Potosí, SLP; tel. (481) 21316; telex 1772476; fax (481) 43094; f. 1935; merged with Banca de Provincias in 1985; cap. 150m. new pesos, res 314m. new pesos, dep. 4,971m. new pesos (Dec. 1993); Dir-Gen. HUGO VILLA MANSO; 130 brs.

**Banco de Crédito y Servicio, SA (Bancreser):** Paseo de la Reforma 116, 18°, Col. Juárez, 06600 México, DF; tel. (5) 546-3459; telex 1774564; fax (5) 592-3582; f. 1976; transferred to private ownership in 1991; cap. 229,000m., res 300,000m., dep. 4,619,000m. (Dec. 1992); Dir-Gen. RUBÉN ACOSTA CARRASCO; 74 brs.

**Banco Internacional, SA:** Paseo de la Reforma 156, 3°, Col. Juárez, 06600 México, DF; tel. (5) 721-2222; telex 1776341; fax (5) 721-2193; f. 1976; cap. 976,000m., res 432,000m., dep. 12,981,000m. (Dec. 1992); Dir-Gen. Lic. ANTONIO DEL VALLE RUIZ; 326 brs.

**Banco Mercantil del Norte, SA:** Zaragoza Sur 920, 64000 Monterrey, NL; tel. (8) 319-5200; telex 383382; fax (8) 319-5221; f. 1899; merged with Banco Regional del Norte in 1985; cap. 283.0m. new pesos, res 761.6m. new pesos, dep. 10,740.8m. new pesos (Dec. 1993); Dir-Gen. ROBERTO GONZÁLEZ BARRERA; 141 brs.

**Banco Mexicano, Somex, SNC:** Paseo de la Reforma 211, 17°, México, DF; tel. (5) 591-1611; telex 1772789; fax (5) 566-8493; f. 1981 (from merger of Banco Somex and Banco Mexicano); multiple bank; cap. 639,000m., res 758,000m., dep. 10,989m. (Dec. 1992); Pres. JULIO RODOLFO MOCTEZUMA CID; 329 brs.

**Banco Nacional de México, SA (Banamex):** Avda Isabel la Católica 44, 1°, 06089 México, DF; tel. (5) 225-4623; telex 1772611; fax (5) 225-4810; f. 1884; transferred to private ownership in August 1991; cap. 5,298,000m., res 2,037,000m., dep. 73,063,000m. (Dec. 1992); Dir-Gen. ALFREDO HARP HELÚ; 630 brs.

**Banco Obrero, SA:** Viena 4, 5°, Col. Juárez, 06600 México, DF; tel. (5) 627-0785; telex 1777450; fax (5) 705-6217; f. 1977; cap. 125,000m., res 6,000m., dep. 2,181,000m. (Dec. 1992); Dir-Gen. (vacant); 24 brs.

**Banco de Oriente, SA (Banorie):** Avda 2 Oriente 10, Apdo 30, 72000 Puebla, Pue.; tel. (22) 46-2801; telex 178209; fax (22) 42-0401; f. 1944; transferred to private ownership in 1991; cap. 49.9m. new pesos, res 119.9m. new pesos, dep. 2,266.5m. new pesos (Sept. 1993); Chair. RICARDO MARGAÍN BERLANGA; 48 brs.

**Banco Unión:** México, DF; operations assumed by federal regulators in Sept. 1994 pending investigation.

**Bancomer, SA:** Centro Bancomer, Avda Universidad 1200, Apdo 9 bis, 03339 México, DF; tel. (5) 534-0034; telex 1775781; fax (5) 621-3230; f. 1864; multiple bank; transferred to private ownership in October 1991; cap. 1,000m. new pesos, res 6,107.6m. new pesos, dep. 83,699.8m. new pesos (Dec. 1993); Dir-Gen. Ing. RICARDO GUAJARDO TOUCHÉ; 900 brs.

**Banoro (Banco del Noroeste) SA:** Obregón y Angel Flores, Culiacán, Sin.; tel. (671) 34062; telex 665882; fax (671) 53871; f. 1939;

cap. 383,000m., res 57,000m., dep. 3,422,000m. (Dec. 1992); Gen. Man. Francisco Gurria Lacroix; 97 brs.

**Banpaís, SA:** Avda Morelos 110 Pte, Monterrey, NL; tel. (83) 43-8730; telex 0382844; fax (83) 43-3461; f. 1892 as Banco de Nuevo León, present name 1978; merged with Banco Latino in 1985; transferred to private ownership in June 1991; cap. 636,000m., res 28,000m., dep. 8,390,000m. (Dec. 1992); Chair. Carlos Sales Gutiérrez; 118 brs.

**Mercantil Probursa, SA:** Montes Urales 620, 3°, Lomas de Chapultepec, México, DF; tel. (5) 325-8001; telex 1775837; fax (5) 325-8054; f. 1977 as Multibanco Mercantil de México, merged with Bancam in 1985; transferred to private ownership in June 1991; adopted current name in 1993; cap. 430,000m., res 167,000m., dep. 7,677,000m. (Dec. 1992); Dir-Gen. Lic. José Madariaga Lomelin; 110 brs.

**Multibanco Comermex, SA:** Plaza Comermex, Blvd Miguel Avila Camacho 1, Col. Chapultepec Polanco, Mexico 10, DF; tel. (5) 229-2929; telex 1775837; fax (5) 229-2695; f. 1977; cap. 82.5m. new pesos, res 1,113.0m. new pesos, dep. 35,712.4m. new pesos (Dec. 1993); Dir-Gen. José Luis Espinosa; 333 brs.

### Development Banks

**Banco Nacional de Comercio Exterior, SNC (BANCOMEXT):** Avda Camino Santa Teresa 1679, Col. Jardines del Pedregal, Del. Alvaro Obregón, 01900 México, DF; tel. (5) 327-6000; telex 1764393; fax (5) 327-6206; f. 1937; cap. 2,532,871m., res 858,934m., dep. 35m. (Sept. 1992); Gen. Dir José Angel Gurrí; 3 brs.

**Banco Nacional de Crédito Rural, SNC (BANRURAL):** Agrarismo 227, Col. Escandón, 11800 México, DF; tel. (5) 273-1945; telex 1772904; fax (5) 271-5519; f. 1975; provides financing for agriculture and normal banking services; cap. 1,791,569m., res −155,439m., dep. 623,402m. (Sep. 1992); Dir-Gen. Ing. Jaime de la Mora Gómez; 187 brs.

**Banco Nacional del Ejército, Fuerza Aérea y Armada, SNC (BANJERCITO):** Avda Industria Militar 1055, 2°, Lomas de Sotelo, 11200 México, DF; tel. (5) 557-8661; telex 1763307; fax (5) 557-6249; f. 1947; cap. 11,035m., res 1,780.7m., dep. 139,184.5m. (Sept. 1990); Dir-Gen. José Luis Coronel Guzmán; 17 brs.

**Banco Nacional de Obras y Servicios Públicos, SNC (BANOBRAS):** Tecoyotitla 100, 4°, Col. Flórida, Apdo 7133, 06900 México, DF; tel. (5) 583-1449; telex 1772619; fax (5) 723-6248; f. 1933; cap. 858,371m., res 1,730,298m., dep. 1,132,681m. (Sept. 1992); Chair. Jesús Silva Herzog Flores.

**Banco del Pequeño Comercio, SNC (BANPECO):** Paseo de la Reforma 262, México, DF; tel. (5) 533-6095; telex 1760119; fax (5) 512-2771; f. 1943; cap. 24,036m., res 2,632m., dep. 575,432m. (Sept. 1990); Dir-Gen. Roberto Diéguez Armas; 108 brs.

**Financiera Nacional Azucarera, SNC (FINA, SNC):** Insurgentes Sur 716, Col. del Valle, Apdo 10764, 03100 México, DF; tel. (5) 682-8846; fax (5) 543-5490; f. 1953; cap. 159,662m., res 52,724m., dep. 2,252,660m. (Sept. 1992); Dir-Gen. Lic. Andrés Gilberto Treviño Moreno.

**Nacional Financiera, SNC (NAFIN):** Insurgentes Sur 1971, Torre Sur, 10°, Col. Guadalupe Inn, 01020 México, DF; tel. (5) 548-3306; telex 1772659; fax (5) 664-0742; f. 1934; government industrial development bank; provides loans, guarantees and investments; contracts and handles development loans from abroad; cap. 483,974m., res 2,212,322m., dep. 2,386,479m. (Sept. 1990); Dir-Gen. Lic. Oscar Espinoza Villarreal; 50 brs; administers:

**Fondo de Equipamiento Industrial (FONEI):** México, DF; tel. (5) 559-8702; f. 1971 to finance industrial investment projects; Dir Lic. Jesús Villaseñor G.

**Fondo de Garantía y Fomento a la Industria Mediana y Pequeña (FOGAIN):** Insurgentes Sur 1480, 4°, Col. Insurgentes Mixcoac, México, DF; tel. (5) 535-1974; telex 1773363; f. 1953 to supply credit to and encourage the development of small-and medium-sized industries; Dir Lic. Héctor Arangua Morales.

**Fondo Nacional de Fomento Industrial (FOMIN):** Paseo de la Reforma 295, 9°, Col. Cuauhtémoc, 06500 México, DF; tel. (5) 514-2430; f. 1972 to promote industrial improvement and initiative with venture capital; Dir Lic. Ronaldo Poucel van der Mersch.

### Foreign Bank

**Citibank NA** (USA): Paseo de la Reforma 390, 18°, 06030 México, DF; tel. (5) 211-3030; telex 1772769; fax (5) 208-0250; cap. 102,000m., res 6,000m., dep. 1,005,000m. (Dec. 1992); Dir-Gen. Gabriel Jaramillo; 6 brs.

## BANKERS' ASSOCIATION

**Asociación Mexicana de Bancos:** Torre Latinoamericana, 9°, Madero y Lázaro Cárdenas, Apdo 89 bis, 06007 México, DF; tel. (5) 521-4080; telex 1774510; fax (5) 521-5229; f. 1928; Pres. Ing. Ricardo Guajardo Touché; Dir-Gen. Rafael Olivera Escalona; 52 mems.

## STOCK EXCHANGE

**Comisión Nacional de Valores** (National Securities Commission): Barranca del Muerto 275, Col. San José Insurgentes, 03900 México, DF; tel. (5) 651-0129; f. 1946; a federal commission to regulate the stock exchange system; Pres. Lic. Patricio Ayala; Vice-Pres. Guillermo Núñez Herrera.

In 1976 the three stock exchanges of Mexico City, Guadalajara and Monterrey were amalgamated into a single organization:

**Bolsa Mexicana de Valores, SA de CV:** Paseo de la Reforma 255, Col. Cuauhtémoc, 06500 México, DF; tel. (5) 726-6600; telex 1762233; fax (5) 591-0642; f. 1894; Pres. Lic. Manuel Robleda Gonzales de Castilla; Dir-Gen. Lic. Guillermo Núñez Herrera.

## INSURANCE
### México, DF

**Aseguradora Banpaís, SA:** Insurgentes Sur 1443, 7°, México 19, DF; f. 1958; Pres. Lic. Adrián Sada González; Dir-Gen. Rodrigo M. Sada Gómez.

**Aseguradora Cuauhtémoc, SA:** Blvd Manuel Avila Camacho 164, 11570 México, DF; tel. (5) 250-9800; telex 1773917; fax (5) 540-3204; f. 1944; general; Exec. Pres. Juan B. Riveroll; Dir-Gen. Javier Compeán Amezcua.

**Aseguradora Hidalgo, SA:** Avda Presidente Masarik 111, Col. Polanco, Del. Miguel Hidalgo, 11570 México, DF; f. 1931; life; Dir-Gen. Lic. José Gómez Gordoa; Dep. Dir-Gen. Lic. Sergio Morales Bustos.

**Aseguradora Mexicana (Asemex):** México, DF; general, except life; transferred to private ownership in 1990.

**La Continental Seguros, SA:** Avda Francisco I Madero, 1, 10°, 06007 México, DF; tel. (5) 518-1670; telex 1771210; fax (5) 510-3259; f. 1936; general; Pres. Ing. Teodoro Amerlinck y Zirión; Vice-Pres. Ing. Rodrigo Amerlinck y Assereto.

**La Nacional, Cía de Seguros, SA:** Dom. Miguel Angel de Quevedo 915, 04339 México, DF; telex 1760006; f. 1901; life, etc.; Pres. Clemente Cabello; Chair. Lic. Alberto Bailleres.

**Pan American de México, Cía de Seguros, SA:** México, DF; f. 1940; Pres. Lic. Jess N. Dalton; Dir-Gen. Gilberto Escobeda Paz.

**Previsión Obrera, Sociedad Mutualista de Seguros sobre la Vida:** Ricardo Flores Magón 206, México, DF; f. 1934; life; Man. Antonio Castellanos Tovar.

**Seguros América Banamex, SA:** Avda Revolución 1508, Col. Guadalupe Inn, 01020 México, DF; f. 1933; Pres. Agustín F. Legorreta; Dir-Gen. Juan Orozco Gómez Portugal.

**Seguros Atlántida Multiba, SA:** Independencia 37, 2°, Apdo 152, 06050 México, DF; tel. (5) 510-8810; telex 1771125; fax (5) 512-4091; f. 1941; general, except life; Pres. Boris Sigal Boulayevsky; Dir-Gen. Alfonso de Orduña y Pérez.

**Seguros Azteca, SA:** Insurgentes 102, México 6, DF; f. 1933; general including life; Pres. Juan Campo Rodríguez.

**Seguros Cigna, SA:** Arquimedes 199, 10°, Col. Polanco, 11560 México, DF; f. 1944; Pres. Eduardo Carrillo; Dir-Gen. Luis E. Maurette.

**Seguros La Comercial, SA:** Insurgentes Sur 3900, Del. Tlalpan, 14000 México, DF; f. 1936; life, etc.; Pres. Eloy S. Vallina; Dir-Gen. Héctor González Valenzuela.

**Seguros Constitución, SA:** Avda Revolución 2042, Col. La Otra Banda, 01090 México, DF; tel. (5) 550-7910; telex 1764504; f. 1937; life, accident; Pres. Isidoro Rodríguez Ruiz; Dir-Gen. Alfonso de Orduña y Pérez.

**Seguros el Fénix, SA:** México, DF; f. 1937; Pres. Victoriano Olazábal E.; Dir-Gen. Jaime Matute Labrador.

**Seguros Internacional, SA:** Abraham González 67, México, DF; f. 1945; general; Pres. Lic. Gustavo Romero Kolbeck.

**Seguros de México, SA:** Insurgentes Sur 3496, Col. Peña Pobre, 14060 México, DF; tel. (5) 679-3855; telex 1771936; f. 1957; life, etc.; Dir-Gen. Lic. Antonio Mijares Ricci.

**Seguros Protección Mutua, SA:** Constituyentes 357, 11830 México DF; tel. (5) 277-7100; telex 1761933; f. 1933; general; Dir-Gen. Gustavo González Nogués.

**Seguros La Provincial, SA:** Miguel Ángel de Quevedo 915, 04339 México, DF; telex 1760006; f. 1936; general; Pres. Clemente Cabello; Chair. Alberto Bailleres.

**Seguros La República, SA:** Paseo de la Reforma 383, México, DF; f. 1966; general; 43% owned by Commercial Union (UK); Pres. Luciano Arechederra Quintana; Gen. Man. Juan Antonio de Arrieta Mendizábal.

MEXICO                                                                                                              *Directory*

**Seguros Tepeyac, SA:** Humboldt 56, Col. Centro, 06040 México, DF; tel. (5) 521-8684; telex 1771289; fax (5) 510-1347; f. 1944; general; Dir-Gen. José Luis Llamosas Portilla.

### Guadalajara, Jal.
**Nueva Galicia, Compañía de Seguros Generales, SA:** Guadalajara, Jal.; f. 1946; fire; Pres. Salvador Veytia y Veytia.

**Seguros La Comercial, SA, División Centro:** Avda Lerdo de Tejada 2007, 3°, Guadalajara, Jal.; tel. (36) 16-4460; telex 0682856; f. 1940; fire; Pres. Eloy S. Vallina; Dir-Gen. Héctor González Valenzuela.

### Monterrey, NL
**Seguros Monterrey Aetna, SA:** Avda Diagonal Sta Engracia 221 Oriente, Col. Lomas de San Francisco, 64710 Monterrey, NL; tel. (8) 319-1111; fax (8) 363-0428; f. 1940; casualty, life, etc.; Dir-Gen. Federico Reyes Garcia.

**Seguros La Comercial del Norte, SA:** Zaragoza Sur 1000, 1°, Condominio 'Acero Monterrey', Apdo 944, Monterrey, NL; f. 1939; general; Pres. Manuel L. Barragán; Dir-Gen. Salim Farah Sessin.

**Seguros Monterrey del Círculo Mercantil, SA, Sociedad General de Seguros:** Padre Mier Pte 276, Monterrey, NL; f. 1941; life; Gen. Man. Carmen G. Masso de Navarro.

### Insurance Association
**Asociación Mexicana de Instituciones de Seguros, AC:** Ejército Nacional 904, 6°, México, DF; f. 1946; all insurance companies operating in Mexico are members; Pres. Kurt Vogt Sartorius.

## Trade and Industry

### CHAMBERS OF COMMERCE

**Confederación de Cámaras Nacionales de Comercio, Servicios y Turismo—CONCANACO** (Confederation of National Chambers of Commerce): Balderas 144, 3°, Col. Centro, 06079 México, DF; tel. (5) 709-1559; telex 1777318; fax (5) 709-1152; f. 1917; Pres. Ing. Hugo Villalobos González; Dir-Gen. Lic. José de Jesús Castellanos López; comprises 283 regional Chambers.

**Cámara Nacional de Comercio de la Ciudad de México (CANACO)** (National Chamber of Commerce of Mexico City): Paseo de la Reforma 42, 3°, Col. Centro, Apdo 32005, 06048 México, DF; tel. (5) 592-2677; telex 1777262; fax (5) 592-2279; f. 1874; 50,000 mems; Pres. Vicente Mayo García; Dir-Gen. Ing. Marcos Pérez Arenas.

**Cámara Nacional de la Industria y de la Transformación (CANACINTRA):** Calle Vallarta 21, 3°, México, DF; tel. (5) 566-9333; represents majority of smaller manufacturing businesses; Pres. Víctor Manuel Terrones López.

Chambers of Commerce exist in the chief town of each State as well as in the larger centres of commercial activity.

### CHAMBERS OF INDUSTRY

The 64 Industrial Chambers and 32 Associations, many of which are located in the Federal District, are representative of the major industries of the country.

#### Central Confederation
**Confederación de Cámaras Industriales de los Estados Unidos Mexicanos—CONCAMIN** (Confed. of Industrial Chambers): Manuel María Contreras 133, 8°, Col. Cuauhtémoc, 06500 México, DF; tel. (5) 566-7822; fax (5) 535-6871; f. 1918; represents and promotes the activities of the entire industrial sector; Pres. Fernando Cortina Legarreta; Dir-Gen. Lic. Alvaro Torre Prieto.

### DEVELOPMENT ORGANIZATIONS AND STATE AUTHORITIES

**Asociación Nacional de Importadores y Exportadores de la República Mexicana (ANIERM)** (National Association of Importers and Exporters): Monterrey 130, Col. Roma-Cuauhtémoc, 06700 México, DF; tel. (5) 564-8618; telex 1772443; fax (5) 584-5317; f. 1944; Pres. Rodrigo Guerra B.; Vice-Pres. Lic. Humberto Simoneen Ardila.

**Azúcar, SA de CV:** Insurgentes Sur 1079, Col. Nochebuena, 03910 México, DF; tel. (5) 563-7100; telex 1772554; f. 1983 to develop the sugar industry; Dir Ing. Eduardo A. MacGregor Beltrán.

**Comisión Coordinadora de la Industria Siderúrgica:** México, DF; f. 1972; co-ordinating commission for the development of the iron and steel industries; Dir-Gen. Lic. Alfredo Ade Tomasini.

**Comisión Federal de Electricidad (CFE):** Río Ródano 14, 7°, Col. Cuauhtémoc, 06568 México, DF; tel. (5) 533-2033; telex 171031; fax (5) 553-6490; Dir-Gen. Ing. Guillermo Guerrero Villalobos.

**Comisión de Fomento Minero:** Puente de Tecamachalco 26, Lomas de Chapultepec, 11000 México, DF; tel. (5) 540-2906; telex 1771382; f. 1934; to promote the development of the mining sector; Dir Lic. Luis de Pablo Serna.

**Comisión Nacional del Cacao (Conadeca):** Calle Tlaxcala 208, Col. Hipódromo, 06100 México, DF; tel. (5) 286-9495; telex 1771397; f. 1973 to promote the cultivation, industrialization and the marketing of cocoa; Dir-Gen. Lic. Julio Derbez del Pino.

**Comisión Nacional de Energía:** Francisco Márquez 160, Col. Condesa, México, DF; f. 1973; commission to control energy policy and planning; Chair. Fernando Hiriart Valderrama.

**Comisión Nacional de Fruticultura (Conafrut):** Allende 8 Sur, 76007 Querétaro, Qro; tel. (463) 570-2499; telex 1776351; f. 1961 to develop the production, industrialization and marketing of fruits; Dir Lic. Francisco Merino Rábago.

**Comisión Nacional de Inversiones Extranjeras:** Blvd Avila Camacho1, 11°, 11000 México, DF; tel. (5) 540-1426; telex 1763158; fax (5) 286-1551; f. 1973; commission to co-ordinate foreign investment; Exec. Sec. Dr Carlos Camacho Gaos.

**Comisión Nacional de Seguridad Nuclear y Salvaguardias (CNSNS):** Dr Barragán 779 México, DF; tel. (5) 590-1481; telex 1764413; fax (5) 590-6103; f. 1979 to establish standards for the development of the nuclear industry and guarantee its safety; Dir-Gen. Ing. Miguel Medina Vaillard.

**Comisión Nacional de las Zonas Aridas:** México, DF; tel. (5) 525-9360; f. 1970; commission to co-ordinate the development and use of arid areas; Dir Ing. José Ignacio Navarro González.

**Comisión Petroquímica Mexicana:** México, DF; to promote the development of the petrochemical industry; Tech. Sec. Ing. Juan Antonio Bargés Mestres.

**Compañía Nacional de Subsistencias Populares (CONASUPO):** Avda Insurgentes Sur 489, 4°, Col. Hipódromo Condesa, 06100 México, DF; tel. (5) 272-0472; fax (5) 272-0607; f. 1965 to protect the income of small farmers, improve the marketing of basic farm commodities and supervise the operation of rural co-operative stores; cap. 3,700m.; Dir Lic. Javier Bonilla García.

**Consejo Empresarial Mexicano para Asuntos Internacionales (CEMAI):** Homero 517, 7°, Col. Polanco, 11570 Mexico, DF; tel. (5) 531-7636; fax (5) 531-1590.

**Consejo Nacional de Comercio Exterior (CONACEX):** Tlaxcala 177-803, Col. Cuauhtémoc, 06100 México, DF; tel. (5) 286-8744; fax (5) 211-8465; promotes national exports.

**Consejo Nacional de Comercio Exterior del Noreste, AC (CONACEX NORESTE):** Edif. de las Instituciones, 7°, Ocampo 250 Pte, Apdo 2067, Monterrey, NL; tel. (8) 342-2143; telex 383050; fax (8) 342-8207; f. 1962; to promote national exports; Pres. Ing. José R. Treviño Salinas; Dir-Gen. Guillermo Díaz de la Garza.

**Consejo Nacional de Recursos Minerales:** Avda Niños Héroes 139, 06720 México, DF; tel. (5) 568-6112; f. 1957; government agency for the development of mineral resources; Dir Ing. Fernando Castillo Nieto.

**Dirección General de Política e Inversiones Industriales:** Insurgentes Sur 546, México, DF; government body established to direct industrial policy; took over the functions of the Comisión Coordinadora para el Desarrollo de la Industria de Maquinaria y Equipo, Comisión Nacional Coordinadora para el Desarrollo Industrial; Dir-Gen. Lic. Vladimiro Brailovsky F.

**Instituto del Fondo Nacional de la Vivienda para los Trabajadores (INFONAVIT):** Barranca del Muerto 280, 4°, Col. Guadalupe Inn., Del. Alvaro Obregón, 01029 México, DF; tel. (5) 660-2423; f. 1972 to finance the construction of low-cost housing for the working classes; Dir José Juan de Olloqui y Labastida.

**Instituto Mexicano del Café (Inmecafé):** Carretera Jalapa-Veracruz Km 4, Campo Experimental Garnica, Jalapa, Ver.; Lago Merú 32, Col. Granada, México, DF; tel. (5) 250-5543; telex 15536; f. 1958; sponsors cultivation to increase domestic and foreign sales of coffee; Dir-Gen. Jesús Salazar Toledano.

**Instituto Mexicano del Petróleo (IMP):** Avda Eje Central Lázaro Cárdenas 152, Apdo 14-805, 07730 México, DF; tel. (5) 567-6600; telex 1773116; fax (5) 567-6047; f. 1965 to foster development of the petroleum, chemical and petrochemical industries; Dir Víctor Manuel Alcerreca (acting).

**Instituto Nacional de Investigaciones Forestales y Agropecuarios—INIFAP** (National Forestry and Agricultural Research Institute): Apdo 6-882, 06600 México, DF; tel. (5) 687-7451; f. 1985; conducts research into plant genetics, management of species and conservation; operates under auspices of the Secretariat of State for Agriculture and Water Resources; Exec. Dir Dr Manuel R. Villa Issa.

**Instituto Nacional de Investigaciones Nucleares (ININ):** Sierra Mojada 447, 2°, Col. Lomas de Barrilaco, Sección Vertientes, 11010 México, DF; tel. (5) 521-9402; telex 1773824; fax (5) 521-3798; f.

1979 to plan research and development of nuclear science and technology, as well as the peaceful uses of nuclear energy, for the social, scientific and technological development of the country; administers the Secondary Standard Dosimetry Laboratory, the Centro de Información y Documentación Nuclear (CIDN), which serves Mexico's entire scientific community; the 1 MW research reactor which came into operation, in 1967, supplies part of Mexico's requirements for radioactive isotopes; also operates a 12 MeV Tandem Van de Graaf. Mexico's first nuclear reactor, at Laguna Verde (generating capacity 654 MW) became operational in 1989 and is administered by the Comisión Federal de Electricidad (CFE); a second 654 MW reactor is being commissioned; Dir-Gen. Dr JULIÁN SÁNCHEZ GUTIÉRREZ.

**Instituto Nacional de Pesca** (National Fishery Institute): Alvaro Obregón 269, 10°, Col. Roma, 06709 México, DF; tel. (5) 211-0063; f. 1962; Dir ALICIA BARCENA IBARRA.

**Laboratorios Nacionales de Fomento Industrial:** Avda Industria Militar 261, Col. Lomas de Tecamachalco, Naucalpan de Juárez, 53390 México, DF; tel. (5) 589-0199; telex 1771996; fax (5) 589-7162; f. 1948; conducts scientific research for industrial development; Dir Dr MANUEL RUIZ DE CHÁVEZ.

**Petróleos Mexicanos—PEMEX:** Avda Marina Nacional 329, 44°, Col. Anáhuac, 11300 México, DF; tel. (5) 254-2249; telex 1774286; fax (5) 531-0616; f. 1938; government agency for the exploitation of Mexico's petroleum resources (see also under Shipping); Dir-Gen. ADRIÁN LAJOUS; 190,157 employees.

**Tabacos Mexicanos, SA de CV (TABAMEX):** Avda Ejército Nacional 862, Col. Chapultapec de los Morales, Del. Miguel Hidalgo, 11510 México, DF; tel. (5) 395-5477; telex 1773904; fax (5) 395-6836; f. 1972 to foster the cultivation, industrialization and marketing of tobacco; Dir-Gen. GUSTAVO CARVAJAL MORENO.

**Uranio Mexicano (URAMEX):** Insurgentes Sur 1079, 3°, México, DF; tel. (5) 563-7100; telex 349702 (Chihuahua); supervises the use of uranium; Dir-Gen. ALBERTO ESCOGET ARTIGAS.

### GOVERNMENT ADVISORY BODIES

**Comisión Nacional de Precios:** Avda Juárez 101, 17°, México 1, DF; tel. (5) 510-0436; f. 1977; national prices commission; Dir-Gen. JESÚS SÁNCHEZ JIMÉNEZ.

**Comisión Nacional de Salarios Mínimos:** Avda Cuauhtémoc 14, Col. Doctores, 06720 México 7, DF; tel. (5) 578-9021; fax (5) 578-5775; f. 1962 in accordance with Section VI of Article 123 of the Constitution; national commission on minimum salaries; Pres. Lic. BASILIO GONZÁLEZ-NUÑEZ; Tech. Dir ALIDA BERNAL COSIO.

**Instituto Nacional del Consumidor:** Insurgentes Sur 1228, 10°, Col. del Valle Tlacoquemecatl, 03210 México, DF; tel. (5) 559-2478; fax (5) 559-0123; f. 1976; national institute for consumer protection; Dir-Gen. MARGARITA ORTEGA VILLA.

**Procuraduría Federal del Consumidor:** Dr Carmona y Valle 11, Col. Doctores, 06720 México, DF; tel. (5) 761-3021; f. 1975; consumer protection; Dir IGNACIO PICHARDO PAGAZA.

### DEVELOPMENT FUNDS

The following funds were established under the auspices of the Banco de México:

**Fideicomiso Instituído en Relación con la Agricultura (FIRA):** México, DF; tel. (5) 550-7011; Dir Ing. ANTONIO BACA DÍAZ; a group of funds to aid agricultural financing, comprising:

**Fondo de Garantía y Fomento para la Agricultura, Ganadería y Avicultura (FOGAGA):** f. 1954.

**Fondo Especial para Financiamientos Agropecuarios (FEFA):** f. 1965.

**Fondo Especial de Asistencia Técnica y Garantía para Créditos Agropecuarios (FEGA):** f. 1972.

**Fondo Nacional de Fomento al Turismo (FONATUR):** (see under Tourism).

**Fondo de Operación y Financiamiento Bancario a la Vivienda:** Ejército Nacional 180, 7°, 8° y 11°, Col. Anzures, 11590 México, DF; tel. (5) 255-4199; fax (5) 203-7304; f. 1963 to promote the construction of low-cost housing through savings and credit schemes; Dir-Gen. Lic. MANUEL ZEPEDA PAYERAS.

### EMPLOYERS' ORGANIZATIONS

**Confederación Patronal de la República Mexicana (COPARMEX)** (Employers' Federation): Insurgentes Sur 950, 2°, Col. del Valle, 03100 México, DF; tel. (5) 687-6493; telex 7401667; f. 1929; national syndicate of free affiliated businesspeople organized to promote economic development; Pres. Ing. JORGE OCEJO MORENO; Sec. and Dir-Gen. Lic. GUSTAVO J. SERRANO; 34,000 mems.

**Consejo Coordinador Empresarial (CCE):** Paseo de la Reforma 255, Floor 11, Col. Cuauhtémoc, 06500 México, DF; tel. (5) 592-3910; fax (5) 592-3857; f. 1974; co-ordinating body of private sector; Pres. LUIS GERMÁN CÁRCOBA; Dir FRANCISCO CALDERÓN.

**Consejo Mexicano de Hombres de Negocios (CMHN):** México, DF; represents leading businesspeople; affiliated to CCE.

### TRADE UNIONS

**Congreso del Trabajo—CT:** Ricardo Flores Magón 44, Col. Guerrero, México 13, DF; tel. (5) 597-8088; f. 1966; part of PRI (government party); trade union congress which is made up of trade union federations, confederations, etc.; supervised establishment of welfare organization FONACOT; Pres. JORGE SÁNCHEZ GARCÍA; Chair. FIDEL VELÁZQUEZ.

**Confederación Regional Obrera Mexicana—CROM** (Regional Confederation of Mexican Workers): República de Cuba 60, México, DF; f. 1918; Sec.-Gen. IGNACIO CUAUHTÉMOC PALETA; 120,000 mems, 900 affiliated syndicates.

**Confederación Revolucionaria de Obreros y Campesinos—CROC** (Revolutionary Confederation of Workers and Farmers): Hamburgo 250, Col. Juárez, 06600 México, DF; f. 1952; Pres. and Sec.-Gen. JOSÉ DE JESÚS PÉREZ; 120,000 mems in 22 state federations and 8 national unions.

**Confederación Revolucionaria de Trabajadores—CRT** (Revolutionary Confederation of Workers): Dr Jiménez 218, Col. Doctores, México, DF; f. 1954; Sec.-Gen. MARIO SUÁREZ GARCÍA; 10,000 mems; 10 federations and 192 syndicates.

**Confederación de Trabajadores de México—CTM** (Confederation of Mexican Workers): Vallarta 8, México, DF; f. 1936; admitted to ICFTU; Sec.-Gen. FIDEL VELÁZQUEZ; 5.5m. mems.

**Federación Obrera de Organizaciones Femeniles—FOOF** (Workers' Federation of Women's Organizations): Vallarta 8, México, DF; f. 1950; a women workers' union within CTM; Sec.-Gen. HILDA ANDERSON NEVÁREZ; 400,000 mems.

**Federación Nacional de Sindicatos Independientes** (National Federation of Independent Trade Unions): Isaac Garza 311, Oriente, Monterrey, NL; f. 1936; Sec.-Gen. ISAAC TREVIÑO FRÍAS; 1,760,000 mems; 960 unions.

**Federación de Sindicatos de Trabajadores al Servicio del Estado—FSTSE** (Federation of Unions of Government Workers): Maestro Antonio Caso 35, México 4, DF; f. 1938; Sec.-Gen. Dr HUGO DOMENZAÍN GUZMÁN; 800,000 mems; 91 unions.

**Frente Unida Sindical por la Defensa de los Trabajadores y la Constitución** (United Union Front in Defence of the Workers and the Constitution): f. 1990; established by more than 120 trade organizations to support the implementation of workers' constitutional rights.

**Unión General de Obreros y Campesinos de México—UGOCM** (General Union of Workers and Farmers of Mexico): José María Marroquí 8, 2°, 06050 México, DF; tel. (5) 518-3015; f. 1949; admitted to WFTU/CSTAL; Sec.-Gen. JUAN RODRÍGUEZ GONZÁLEZ; 7,500 mems, over 2,500 syndicates.

A number of major unions are non-affiliated; they include:

**Frente Auténtico de los Trabajadores (FAT).**

**Pacto de Unidad Sindical Solidaridad (PAUSS):** comprises 10 independent trade unions.

**Sindicato Industrial de Trabajadores Mineros, Metalúrgicos y Similares de la República Mexicana** (Industrial Union of Mine, Metallurgical and Related Workers of the Republic of Mexico): La Barranca s/n, 51030 México, DF; tel. (5) 565-5596; f. 1933; Sec.-Gen. NAPOLEON GÓMEZ SADA; 86,000 mems.

**Sindicato Nacional de Trabajadores de la Educación (SNTE):** Venezuela 44 Centro, México, DF; tel. (5) 702-0005; fax (5) 702-6303; teachers' union; Leader ELBA ESTHER GORDILLO MORALES; 1.2m. mems.

**Coordinadora Nacional de Trabajadores de la Educación (CNTE):** dissident faction; Leader TEODORO PALOMINO.

**Sindicato Revolucionario de Trabajadores Petroleros de la República Mexicana (SRTPRM)** (Union of Petroleum Workers of the Republic of Mexico): close links with PEMEX; Sec.-Gen. SEBASTIÁN GUZMÁN CABRERA; 110,000 mems; includes:

**Movimiento Nacional Petrolero:** reformist faction; Leader HEBRAÍCAZ VÁSQUEZ.

**Sindicato de Trabajadores Ferrocarrileros de la República Mexicana** (Union of Railroad Workers of the Republic of Mexico): Calzada Ricardo Flores Magón 206, Col. Guerrero, México 3, DF; tel. (5) 597-1011; f. 1933; Sec.-Gen. JORGE PERALTA VARGAS; 100,000 mems.

**Sindicato Unico de Trabajadores Electricistas de la República Mexicana** (Sole Union of Electricity Workers of the Republic of Mexico): México, DF; Sec.-Gen. LEONARDO RODRÍGUEZ ALCAINE.

**Sindicato Unico de Trabajadores de la Industria Nuclear (SUTIN):** Leader ANTONIO PONCE.

# MEXICO

**Unión Obrera Independiente (UOI):** non-aligned.

The major agricultural unions are:

**Central Campesina Independiente:** Dr E. González Martínez 101, México, DF; Leader Senator ALFONSO GARZÓN SANTIBÁÑEZ.

**Confederación Nacional de Campesinos—CNC:** Mariano Azuela 121, México, DF; Leader Prof. HÉCTOR HUGO OLIVARES VENTURA.

**Confederación Nacional Ganadera:** Calzada Mariano Escobedo 714, México 5, DF; Pres. M. V. Z. ARCADIO LEÓN ESTRADA; 300,000 mems.

**Consejo Agrarista Mexicano:** México, DF; Sec.-Gen. HUMBERTO SERRANO.

**Unión Nacional de Trabajadores Agriculturas (UNTA).**

# Transport

Road transport accounts for about 98% of all public passenger traffic and for about 80% of freight traffic (approximately 12.3m. passengers and 35,001m. ton-kilometres of freight in 1993). Mexico's terrain is difficult for overland travel. As a result, there has been an expansion of air transport and there were 83 international and national airports, plus 2,418 landing fields and feeder airports, in 1992. International flights are provided by a large number of national and foreign airlines. In 1990 Mexico's Airports and Auxiliary Services agency (ASA) announced that, as part of a long-term policy of decentralization, landing rights for wide-bodied civil airliners could be transferred from the capital's Benito Juárez airport to a vastly expanded facility at Toluca, some 65 km from the capital, by 1991. Mexico has 140 seaports, 29 river docks and a further 29 lake shelters. More than 85% of Mexico's foreign trade is conducted through maritime transport. Between 1984 and 1988 the Government developed the main industrial ports of Tampico, Coatzacoalcos, Lázaro Cárdenas, Altamira, Laguna de Ostión and Salina Cruz in an attempt to redirect growth and to facilitate exports. The port at Dos Bocas, on the Gulf of Mexico, is intended to be the largest in Latin America when it is opened. A 300-km railway link across the isthmus of Tehuantepec connects the Caribbean port of Coatzacoalcos with the Pacific port of Salina Cruz.

In 1992, as part of an ambitious divestment programme, the Government announced that concessions would be offered for sale to the private sector, in 1993, to operate nine ports and 61 of the country's airports. ASA was to be absorbed by the finance secretariat in early 1993 while the national ports authority was to be disbanded, responsibility for each port being transferred to Administraciones Portuarias Integrales (APIs).

**Secretaría de Transportes y Comunicaciones:** Avda Universidad y Xola, Cuerpo C, 1°, Col. Narvarte, 03028 México, DF; tel. (5) 538-5148; fax (5) 519-9748.

**Aeropuertos y Servicios Auxiliares (ASA):** Dir LUIS MARTÍNEZ VILLICANA.

**Caminos y Puentes Federales de Ingresos (CPFI):** Dir GUSTAVO PETRICIOLI.

## STATE RAILWAYS

In 1993 there were 26,445 km of main line track. In the same year the railway system carried 50.8m. metric tons of freight and an estimated 10.9m. passengers.

**Ferrocarriles Nacionales de México** (National Railways of Mexico): Centro Administrativo, Avda Jesús García Corona 140, 13°, Ala 'A', Col. Buenavista, 06358 México, DF; tel. (5) 547-9060; telex 1773999; fax (5) 177-3111; f. 1873; government-owned since 1937; in 1977 merged with Ferrocarril del Pacífico, Ferrocarril Chihuahua al Pacífico and Ferrocarril Sonora–Baja California; operates in five regions: north-east (4,189 km), north-west (4,573 km), centre (3,676 km), Pacific (3,839 km) and south-west (3,629 km); system extends from the US border at Mexicali (Calexico), Nogales (Nogales), Ciudad Juárez (El Paso), Piedras Negras (Eagle Pass), Nuevo Laredo (Laredo), and Matamoros (Brownsville) to Guatemalan frontier; investment budget of US $300m. for 1991; Gen. Dir LUIS DE PABLOS.

**Sistema de Transporte Colectivo:** Delicias 67, 06070 México, DF; tel. (5) 709-1133; telex 1774267; fax (5) 512-3601; f. 1967; the first stage of a combined underground and surface railway system in Mexico City was opened in 1969; ten lines, covering 158 km, were operating, in 1994, and five new lines, bringing the total distance to 315 km, are to be completed by the year 2010; the system is wholly state-owned and the fares are partially subsidized; Gen. Man. Lic. ALFONSO CASO AGUILAR.

## ROADS

In 1993 there were 245,433 km of roads, of which some 36% were paved, including 4,286 km of motorways and 45,727 km of highways. The construction of some 4,000 km of new four-lane toll highways, through the granting of government concessions to the private sector, was undertaken during 1989–93.

Long-distance buses form one of the principal methods of transport in Mexico, and there are some 600 lines operating services throughout the country.

**Dirección General de Autotransporte Federal:** Calzada de las Bombas 411, 11°, Col. San Bartolo Coapa, 04800 México, DF; tel. (5) 684-0757; co-ordinates long distance bus services.

## SHIPPING

In 1992 Mexico's merchant fleet numbered 635 vessels, with a total displacement of 1,109,683m. grt. The Government operates the facilities of seaports. In early 1988 the Government announced a US $92.5m. project to rehabilitate the ports of Guaymas, Tampico-Altamira, Manzanillo and Veracruz. New ports were planned for the early 1990s at Progreso, on the Gulf of Mexico, and at Pichilingue and Topolobampo on the Pacific coast.

**Comisión Nacional Coordinadora de Puertos:** Edif. Zona Franca, Antiguo Puerto Libre, Coatzacoalcos, Ver.; tel. (921) 25077; telex 78842; f. 1970; government agency to co-ordinate all maritime port operations; Supt C. MORALES.

**Port of Acapulco:** Puertos Mexicanos, Malecón Fiscal s/n, Acapulco, Gro.; tel. (748) 22067; telex 16925; fax (748) 31648; Harbour Master Capt. RENÉ F. NOVALES BETANZOS.

**Port of Coatzacoalcos:** Edif. Zona Franca, Antiguo Puerto Libra, Coatzacoalcos, Ver.; tel. (921) 25077; telex 78842; Harbour Master Capt. FLORENCIO GUTIÉRREZ.

**Port of Manzanillo:** Superintendencia de Operación Portuaria, Edif. Federal, Avda Tte Azueta s/n, Apdo 126, Manzanillo, Col.; tel. (333) 23470; telex 62513; Port Supt FERNANDO CASTILLO MENÉNDEZ.

**Port of Tampico:** Puertos Mexicanos, Recinto Portuario, 1°, Del. Tampico-Altamira, 89000 Tampico, Tamps; tel. (12) 12-5430; telex 14887; fax (12) 12-5744; Harbour Master Capt. ARISTIDES PALMA P.

**Administración Portuaria Integral de Veracruz, SA de CV:** Marina Mercante 210, 7°, 91700 Veracruz, Ver.; tel. (29) 32-1319; fax (29) 32-3040; privatized in 1993; Gen.-Man. ANGEL GONZÁLEZ RUL.

**Petróleos Mexicanos—PEMEX:** Edif. 1917, 2°, Avda Marina Nacional 329, Col. Huasteca, Miguel Hidalgo, México 17, DF; tel. (5) 531-6053; telex 1773986; Dir-Gen. J. R. MOCTEZUMA.

**Transportación Marítima Mexicana, SA:** Avda de la Cúspide 4755, Col. Parques del Pedregal, Del. Tlalpan, 14010 México, DF; tel. (5) 652-4111; telex 1771383; fax (5) 665-3566; f. 1955; cargo services to Europe, the Mediterranean, Scandinavia, the USA, South and Central America, the Caribbean and the Far East; Pres. MANUEL MONROY; Man. Dir ALEJANDRO ROJAS.

## CIVIL AVIATION

**Aero California:** Hidalgo 316, Apdo 555, La Paz, Baja California Sur, BCS; tel. (682) 22109; telex 53993; f. 1960; regional carrier with scheduled passenger and cargo services to most major Mexican cities.

**Aero Cozumel:** Aeropuerto Internacional, Apdo 322, Cozumel, Q. Roo; tel. (987) 23456; fax (987) 20877; charter airline; subsidiary of Mexicana; Dir JAMIE VALENZUELA TAMARIZ.

**Aerocaribe:** Avda Tulum y Uxmal 29, Locales 13 y 14, Cancún 77500, Q. Roo; tel. (99) 46-1307; fax (99) 46-1330; f. 1975; operates a network of domestic passenger flights from Cancún and Merida; subsidiary of Mexicana; Dir-Gen. JAIME VALENZUELA TAMARIZ.

**Aerocancún:** Edif. Oasis 29, Avda Kukulcan esq Cenzontle, Zona Hotelera, 77500 Cancún, Q. Roo; tel. (988) 32474; fax (988) 32558; charter services to the USA, South America, the Caribbean and Europe; Dir-Gen. JAVIER MARANON.

**Aeromar, Transportes Aeromar:** Aeropuerto Internacional, Zona E, Hangar 7, 15620 México, DF; tel. (5) 627-0205; fax (5) 758-1303; f. 1987; scheduled domestic passenger and cargo services; Pres. JUAN I. STETA.

**Aerovías de México (Aeromexico):** Paseo de la Reforma 445, 12°, Col. Juarez, 06500 México, DF; tel. (5) 327-4000; telex 1772765; fax (5) 511-5359; f. 1934 as Aeronaves de México, nationalized 1959; fmrly Aeroméxico until 1988, when, following bankruptcy, the Government sold a 75% stake to private investors and a 25% stake to the Asociación Sindical de Pilotos de México; services between most principal cities of Mexico and the USA, Canada, Colombia, Panama, Venezuela, France and Spain; Pres. ERNESTO MARTENS REBOLLEDO; Dir-Gen. ALFONSO PASQUEL.

**Mexicana (Compañía Mexicana de Aviación, SA de CV):** Xola 535, 30°, Col. del Valle, Apdo 12813, 03100 México, DF; tel. (5) 227-0260; telex 1771247; fax (5) 687-8786; f. 1921; operated as private company, until July 1982, when the Government took a

58% stake; in 1989 it was returned to private ownership; in February 1993 Aerovías de México took a majority share (55%) in the company; international services between Mexico City and the USA, Central America and Caribbean; domestic services; Chair. (vacant).

## Tourism

Tourism remains one of Mexico's principal sources of foreign exchange. Mexico received an estimated 6,352,300 visitors in 1992, and receipts from tourists, in that year, were estimated at US $3,867.8m. More than 90% of visitors come from the USA and Canada. The country is famous for volcanoes, coastal scenery and the great Sierra Nevada (Sierra Madre) mountain range. The relics of the Mayan and Aztec civilizations and of Spanish Colonial Mexico are of historic and artistic interest. Zihuatanejo, on the Pacific coast, and Cancún, on the Caribbean, were developed as tourist resorts by the Government. In 1992 there were 344,000 hotel rooms in Mexico. The government tourism agency, FONATUR, encourages the renovation and expansion of old hotels and provides attractive incentives for the industry. FONATUR is also the main developer of major resorts in Mexico.

**Secretaría de Turismo** (Secretariat of State for Tourism): Avda Presidente Masarik 172, 8°, 11587 México, DF; tel. (5) 250-8228; telex 1777566; fax (5) 250-4406; Dir-Gen. SILVIA HERNÁNDEZ.

**Fondo Nacional de Fomento al Turismo (FONATUR):** Insurgentes Sur 800, 17°, Col. Del Valle, 03100 México, DF; tel. (5) 687-2697; telex 1777636; f. 1956 to finance and promote the development of tourism; Dir-Gen. Dr KEMIL A. RIZK.

# THE FEDERATED STATES OF MICRONESIA

## Introductory Survey

**Location, Climate, Language, Religion, Flag, Capital**

The Federated States of Micronesia forms (with Palau, q.v.) the archipelago of the Caroline Islands, about 800 km east of the Philippines. The Federated States of Micronesia includes (from west to east) the states of Yap, Chuuk (formerly Truk), Pohnpei (formerly Ponape) and Kosrae. The islands are subject to heavy rainfall, although precipitation decreases from east to west. January, February and March are the driest months, although seasonal variations in rainfall and temperature are generally small. Average annual temperature is 27°C (81°F). The native population consists of various ethno-linguistic groups, but English is widely understood. The principal religion is Christianity, much of the population being Roman Catholic. The national flag (proportions 19 by 10) consists of four five-pointed white stars, arranged as a circle, situated centrally on a light blue field. The capital is Kolonia, on Pohnpei.

**Recent History**

The Federated States of Micronesia was formerly part of the US-administered Trust Territory of the Pacific Islands (for history up to 1965, see chapter on the Marshall Islands).

From 1965 there were increasing demands for local autonomy within the Trust Territory of the Pacific Islands. In that year the Congress of Micronesia was formed, and in 1967 a commission to examine the future political status of the islands was established. In 1970 it declared Micronesians' rights to sovereignty over their own lands, to self-determination, to devise their own constitution and to revoke any form of free association with the USA. In May 1977, after eight years of negotiations, US President Carter announced that his administration intended to adopt measures to terminate the trusteeship agreement by 1981. Until 1979 the four districts of Yap, Truk (Chuuk since 1990), Ponape (Pohnpei since 1984) and Kosrae were governed by a local administrator, appointed by the President of the USA. However, on 10 May 1979 the four districts ratified a new Constitution to become the Federated States of Micronesia. The Constitution was promulgated in 1980.

The USA signed the Compact of Free Association with the Republic of Palau in August 1982, and with the Marshall Islands and the Federated States of Micronesia in October. Under the Compacts, the four countries (including the Northern Mariana Islands) became independent of each other and took charge of both their internal and foreign affairs separately, while the USA remained responsible for defence and security. The Compact was approved by plebiscite in the Federated States of Micronesia in June 1983, and was ratified by the islands' Congress in September.

In May 1986 the UN Trusteeship Council endorsed the US Government's request for the termination of the existing trusteeship agreement with the islands. US administration of the Federated States of Micronesia was formally ended in November of that year. The UN Security Council ratified the termination of the trusteeship agreement in December 1990. Ponape was renamed Pohnpei in November 1984, when its Constitution came into effect. Truk was renamed Chuuk in January 1990, when its new Constitution was proposed (being later adopted).

At an election to the federal Congress in March 1991, the incumbent President (since 1987), John Haglelgam, failed to secure re-election as Senator-at-Large for Yap, and was therefore prevented from contesting the presidency for a second term. In May 1991 the Congress elected Bailey Olter, a former Vice-President, to the presidency. At congressional elections in March 1995 Olter was re-elected to the Pohnpei Senator-at-Large seat. Presidential elections were due to take place in May. A proposed constitutional amendment, which sought to extend the Senator's term in office from two to four years, was expected to be defeated in early 1995.

The Federated States of Micronesia was admitted to the UN in September 1991, and became a member of the International Monetary Fund in June 1993.

**Government**

On 10 May 1979 the locally-drafted Constitution of the Federated States of Micronesia, incorporating the four states of Kosrae, Yap, Ponape (later Pohnpei) and Truk (later Chuuk), became effective. The federal legislature, the Congress, comprises 14 members (Senators). The four states each elect one 'Senator-at-Large', for a four-year term. The remaining 10 Senators are elected for two-year terms: their seats are distributed in proportion to the population of each state. Each of the four states also has its own Constitution, Governor and legislature. The federal President and Vice-President are elected by the Congress from among the four Senators-at-Large; the offices rotate among the four states. (By-elections are then held for the seats to which the President and Vice-President had been elected.) In November 1986 the Compact of Free Association was signed by the Governments of the Federated States of Micronesia and the USA. By the terms of the Compact, the Federated States of Micronesia is a sovereign, self-governing state.

Local government units are the municipalities and villages. Elected Magistrates and Councils govern the municipalities. Village government is largely traditional.

**Defence**

The USA is responsible for the defence of the Federated States of Micronesia.

**Economic Affairs**

In 1990, according to Asian Development Bank (ADB) estimates, gross domestic product (GDP) in the Federated States of Micronesia amounted to some US $160m. In 1988 gross national product (GNP) per head was reported to be $1,500. Farming and fishing are mainly on a subsistence level, although their importance is diminishing, and the principal agricultural crops are coconuts, cassava and sweet potatoes. White peppercorns are produced on Pohnpei. The sector accounted for 40% of exports in 1988, and was to be developed further in 1991 with a grant from the ADB. In 1993 the Federated States of Micronesia received $17.6m. in fees from foreign fisheries licensing agreements, mainly with Japan (compared with $10.3m. in 1989). In 1991 more than 400 vessels were licensed to fish in the islands' waters, and in that year a tuna-processing plant was established on Kosrae. A loan of some $6.5m. and a grant of $0.5m., received from the ADB in late 1993, were to be used in projects aimed at ensuring the efficient management and conservation of the islands' marine resources. However, a report published in early 1995 expressed concern at the significant decline in the total catch since 1991.

The tourist industry is of some significance, with 20,475 tourists visiting the islands in 1990. It was hoped that improved communications, which included the construction of two new airfields on Onoun and Ta Islands (in the state of Chuuk) in 1991, would further stimulate tourism, hitherto hindered by the territory's remote situation.

In the late 1970s a capital improvement programme was initiated by the US Government to build major infrastructures in each of the four districts. These included the construction of an airport and harbour on Kosrae, for which the US Government provided US $21m. The US Government pledged to contribute a further $1,000m. in aid to the territory before the year 2000 (although the islands announced their intention to reduce dependence on US aid, over the same period, from 90%

# THE FEDERATED STATES OF MICRONESIA

*Introductory Survey, Statistical Survey*

of the total budget to between 70% and 80%). Funding for the project was completed in 1985. Grants from external sources amounted to $130m. in 1990, and total budgetary expenditure in that year was estimated to be $128m. In 1988 the rate of unemployment was reported to be 80%.

The Federated States of Micronesia is a member of the South Pacific Commission (see p. 215), the South Pacific Forum (see p. 217) and the South Pacific Regional Trade and Economic Co-operation Agreement (SPARTECA—see p. 218).

In November 1990 the islands were severely affected by Typhoon Owen, which left 4,500 people homeless and destroyed an estimated 90% of subsistence crops. A state of emergency was declared in April 1992, as the islands experienced severe drought. An extremely high rate of population growth (which averaged 2.4% per year in 1985–93 and more than 3% in the early 1990s) has exacerbated certain economic problems, but is, however, partially offset by an annual emigration rate of more than 2%. In mid-1994 the ADB recommended a programme of major structural adjustment of the economy, in preparation for the cessation of US assistance under the Compact of Free Association at the beginning of the 21st century. A trade and investment mission to Australia, conducted by business and government representatives in late 1994, resulted in several proposed projects for the islands, involving tourism, sand and aggregate mining, citrus processing and small-scale farming.

## Social Welfare

In 1989 there were a total of four hospitals, with 319 beds, in the Federated States of Micronesia. In that year 32 physicians and 291 nurses were working in the islands. According to a report by the World Health Organization in early 1995, a high proportion of the population suffers from cardio-vascular diseases, diabetes, obesity and other conditions attributable to social and dietary problems, particularly an increase in the consumption of imported foods.

## Education

Primary education, which begins at six years of age and lasts for eight years, is compulsory. Secondary education, beginning at 14 years of age, comprises two cycles, each of two years. The Micronesia Maritime and Fisheries Academy, which was opened in Yap in 1990, provides education and training in fisheries technology at secondary and tertiary levels.

## Public Holidays

**1995:** 1 January (New Year's Day), 10 May (Constitution Day), 24 October (United Nations Day), 3 November (Independence Day), 25 December (Christmas Day).

**1996:** 1 January (New Year's Day), 10 May (Constitution Day), 24 October (United Nations Day), 3 November (Independence Day), 25 December (Christmas Day).

## Weights and Measures

With certain exceptions, the imperial system is in force. One US cwt equals 100 lb; one long ton equals 2,240 lb; one short ton equals 2,000 lb. A policy of gradual voluntary conversion to the metric system is being undertaken.

# Statistical Survey

Note: Further statistics relating to the Federated States of Micronesia are to be found in the chapter on the Marshall Islands.

## AREA AND POPULATION

**Area:** 700 sq km (270.3 sq miles): Chuuk (294 islands) 127 sq km; Kosrae (5 islands) 110 sq km; Pohnpei (163 islands) 344 sq km; Yap (145 islands) 119 sq km.

**Population:** 100,520 at census of 1991; 105,000 (official estimate) at mid-1993. *By State (1991):* Chuuk 48,853; Kosrae 7,435; Pohnpei 33,346; Yap 10,886.

**Density** (1993): 150.0 per sq km. *By State* (1991, per sq km): Chuuk 384.7; Kosrae 67.6; Pohnpei 96.9; Yap 91.5.

**Births and Deaths** (1992): Birth rate 36.7 per 1,000; Death rate 7.8 per 1,000. Source: UN, *Statistical Yearbook for Asia and the Pacific.*

**Expectation of Life** (World Bank estimate, years at birth, 1992): 71.

## AGRICULTURE, ETC.

**Fishing** (metric tons, live weight): Total catch 2,140 (FAO estimate) in 1990; 1,411 in 1991; 1,505 (FAO estimate) in 1992. Source: FAO, *Yearbook of Fishery Statistics.*

## FINANCE

**Currency and Exchange Rates:** United States currency is used: 100 cents = 1 United States dollar (US $). *Sterling Equivalents* (31 December 1994): £1 sterling = US $1.5645; US $100 = £63.92.

**Budget** (1990, US $ million): Recurrent Revenue 43.49; Recurrent Expenditure 101.48; Capital Expenditure 26.30. Source: UN, *Statistical Yearbook for Asia and the Pacific.*

## EXTERNAL TRADE

**1991:** *Imports* US $88.63m. *Exports* $11.63m. (including copra, coconut oil, fish, pepper and handicrafts).

Source: UN, *Statistical Yearbook for Asia and the Pacific.*

## TOURISM

**Tourist Arrivals:** 20,475 in 1990.

## COMMUNICATIONS MEDIA

**Telephones** ('000 main lines in use, 1991): 3*.

**Radio Receivers** (1988): 17,500 in use.

**Television Receivers** (1988): 1,125 in use.

* Source: UN, *Statistical Yearbook.*

## EDUCATION

**Primary** (1987): 177 schools; 1,051 teachers (1984); 25,139 pupils.

**Secondary** (1987): 17 schools; 314 teachers (1984); 5,385 pupils.

**Tertiary** (1986): 861 students.

Source: UN, *Statistical Yearbook for Asia and the Pacific.*

# Directory

## The Constitution

On 10 May 1979 the locally-drafted Constitution of the Federated States of Micronesia, incorporating the four states of Kosrae, Yap, Ponape (formally renamed Pohnpei in November 1984) and Truk (renamed Chuuk in January 1990), became effective. Each of the four states has its own Constitution, elected legislature and Governor. The Constitution guarantees fundamental human rights and establishes a separation of the judicial, executive and legislative powers. The federal legislature, the Congress of the Federated States of Micronesia, is a unicameral parliament with 14 members, popularly elected. The executive consists of the President, elected by the Congress, and a Cabinet. The Constitution provides for a review of the governmental and federal system every 10 years.

In November 1986 the Compact of Free Association was signed by the Governments of the Federated States of Micronesia and the USA. By the terms of the Compact, the Federated States of Micronesia is an internally sovereign, self-governing state, whose policy concerning foreign affairs must be consistent with guidelines laid down in the Compact. Full responsibility for defence lies with the USA, which also undertakes to provide regular economic assistance. The security arrangements may be terminated only by mutual agreement. The economic and defence provisions of the Compact are renewable after 15 years, but the status of free association continues indefinitely.

## The Government

### HEAD OF STATE

**President:** BAILEY OLTER (took office 21 May 1991).
**Vice-President:** JACOB NENA.

#### THE CABINET
(May 1995)

**Secretary of the Department of External Affairs:** RESIO MOSES.
**Secretary of the Department of Resources and Development:** ASTERIO TAKESY.
**Secretary of the Department of Finance:** ALOYSIUS TUUTH.
**Secretary of the Department of Social Services:** Dr ELIUEL PRETRICK.
**Attorney-General:** BILL MANN.

#### GOVERNMENT OFFICES

**Department of Finance:** POB PS-158, Palikir, Pohnpei, Eastern Caroline Islands, FM 96941; tel. 320-2640; fax 320-2380.
**National Government of the Federated States of Micronesia:** POB PS-53, Palikir, Pohnpei, Eastern Caroline Islands, FM 96941; tel. 320-2649; telex 729-6807; fax 320-2785.
**Public Information Office:** POB PS-34, Palikir, Pohnpei, Eastern Caroline Islands, FM 96941.

## Legislature

### CONGRESS OF THE FEDERATED STATES OF MICRONESIA

The Congress comprises 14 members (Senators), of whom four are elected for a four-year term and 10 for a two-year term.
**Speaker:** JACK FRITZ.

#### STATE LEGISLATURES

**Chuuk State Legislature:** Wenn, Chuuk Lagoon, Chuuk, Eastern Caroline Islands, FM 96942; Senate of 10 mems and House of Representatives of 28 mems elected for four years; Gov. SASAO GOULAND.
**Kosrae State Legislature:** POB 187, Tofol, Kosrae, Eastern Caroline Islands, FM 96944; tel. 370-3019; fax 370-2177; unicameral body of 14 mems serving for four years.
**Pohnpei State Legislature:** Kolonia, Pohnpei, Eastern Caroline Islands, FM 96941; 27 representatives elected for four years (terms staggered); Gov. RESIO MOSES.
**Yap State Legislature:** Colonia, Yap, Western Caroline Islands, FM 96943; 10 mems, six elected from the Yap Islands proper and four elected from the Outer Islands of Ulithi and Woleai, for a four-year term; Gov. PETRUS TUN.

## Diplomatic Representation

### EMBASSIES IN MICRONESIA

**Australia:** POB S, Kolonia, Pohnpei, Eastern Caroline Islands, FM 96941; tel. 320-5448; fax 320-5449; Ambassador: PETER STANFORD.
**China, People's Republic:** Kolonia, Pohnpei, Eastern Caroline Islands, FM 96941; Ambassador: CHEN YONGCHENG.
**USA:** POB 1286, Kolonia, Pohnpei, Eastern Caroline Islands, FM 96941; tel. 320-2187; fax 320-2186; Ambassador: MARCH FONG EU.

## Judicial System

**Supreme Court of the Federated States of Micronesia:** POB P5-J, Kolonia, Pohnpei, Eastern Caroline Islands, FM 96941; tel. 320-2357; fax 320-2756; Chief Justice EDWARD C. KING.

State Courts and Appellate Courts have been established in Yap, Chuuk, Kosrae and Pohnpei.

## Religion

The population is predominantly Christian, mainly Roman Catholic. The Assembly of God, Jehovah's Witnesses, Seventh-day Adventists, the Church of Jesus Christ of Latter-day Saints (Mormons), the United Church of Christ, Baptists and the Bahá'í Faith are also represented.

### CHRISTIANITY

#### The Roman Catholic Church

The Federated States of Micronesia forms a part of the diocese of the Caroline Islands, suffragan to the archdiocese of Agaña (Guam). The Bishop participates in the Catholic Bishops' Conference of the Pacific, based in Fiji. At 31 December 1993 there were 73,041 adherents in the diocese.

**Bishop of the Caroline Islands:** Most Rev. MARTIN JOSEPH NEYLON, Bishop's House, POB 250, Weno, Chuuk, Eastern Caroline Islands, FM 96942; tel. 330-2313; fax 330-4394.

#### Other Churches

**United Church of Christ in Pohnpei:** Kolonia, Pohnpei, Eastern Caroline Islands, FM 96941.
**Liebenzell Mission:** Rev. ERNST SENG, POB 9, Chuuk, Eastern Caroline Islands, FM 96942.

## The Press

**Chuuk News Chronicle:** POB 244, Wenn, Chuuk, Eastern Caroline Islands, FM 96942; f. 1983; Editor MARCIANA AKASY.
**FSM—Job Training Partnership Act News:** Pohnpei, Eastern Caroline Islands, FM 96941; f. 1994; monthly; US-funded.
**Micronesia Focus:** Pohnpei, Eastern Caroline Islands, FM 96941; Editor KETSON JOHNSON.
**The National Union:** FSM Information, POB 490, Kolonia, Pohnpei, Eastern Caroline Islands, FM 96941; tel. 320-2548; telex 6807; f. 1980; 2 a month; Public Information Officer KETSON JOHNSON; circ. 5,000.

## Radio and Television

There were an estimated 17,500 radio receivers and 1,125 television receivers in use in 1988.

### RADIO

**Federated States of Micronesia Public Information Office:** POB 34, Palikir, Pohnpei, Eastern Caroline Islands, FM 96941; tel. 320-2548; telex 6807; fax 320-2785; govt-operated; four regional stations, each broadcasting 18 hours daily; Information Officer TERRY M. GAMABRUW; Liaison Officer ESIKIEL A. LIPPWE.

**Station V6AJ:** POB 147, Lelu, Kosrae, Eastern Caroline Islands, FM 96944; tel. 370-3040; telex 6874; programmes in English and Kosraean; Man. McDonald Ittu.

**Station WSZA:** POB 117, Colonia, Yap, Western Caroline Islands, FM 96943; tel. 350-2174; fax 350-4113; programmes in English, Yapese, Ulithian and Satawalese; Man. Peter Garamfel.

**Station WSZC:** Wenn, Chuuk, Eastern Caroline Islands, FM 96942; programmes in Chuukese and English; Man. P. J. Maipi.

**Station WSZD:** POB 1086, Kolonia, Pohnpei, Eastern Caroline Islands, FM 96941; programmes in English and Ponapean; Man. Dusty Frederick.

### TELEVISION

**Island Cable TV—Pohnpei:** POB 1628, Pohnpei, Eastern Caroline Islands, FM 96941; tel. 320-2641; fax 320-2670; f. 1991; Pres. Bernard Helgenberger; Gen. Man. Poya Shakibaee.

**TV Station Chuuk—TTKK:** Wenn, Chuuk, Eastern Caroline Islands, FM 96942; commercial.

**TV Station Pohnpei—KPON:** Central Micronesia Communications, POB 460, Kolonia, Pohnpei, Eastern Caroline Islands, FM 96941; f. 1977; commercial; Pres. Bernard Helgenberger; Tech. Dir David Cliffe.

**TV Station Yap—WAAB:** Colonia, Yap, Western Caroline Islands, FM 96943; tel. 350-2160; fax 350-4113; govt-owned; Man. Lou Defngin.

## Finance

### BANKING

#### Commercial Banks

**Bank of the Federated States of Micronesia:** Pohnpei, Eastern Caroline Islands, FM 96941.

**Bank of Guam** (USA): 367, Kolonia, Pohnpei, Eastern Caroline Islands, FM 96941; tel. 320-2446; fax 320-2562; Man. Vida B. Moors; brs in Chuuk, Majuro, Ebeye and Kwajalein.

**Bank of Hawaii** (USA): POB 280, Kolonia, Pohnpei, Eastern Caroline Islands FM 96941; tel. 320-543; Man. Christina Michelsen. POB 309, Yap, Western Caroline Islands FM 96943; tel. 350-2129; telex 6853; Man. Al Azuma.

#### Development Bank

**Federated States of Micronesia Development Bank:** POB M, Kolonia, Pohnpei, Eastern Caroline Islands, FM 96941; tel. 320-2480; fax 320-2482; f. 1979; Pres. Manny Mori; 4 brs.

Banking services for the rest of the territory are available in Guam, Hawaii and on the US mainland.

## Trade and Industry

### DEVELOPMENT AUTHORITY

**Economic Development Authority:** Kolonia, Pohnpei, Eastern Caroline Islands, FM 96941; Chair. President of the Federated States of Micronesia.

### GOVERNMENT CORPORATION

**FSM National Fisheries Corpn:** Kolonia, Pohnpei, Eastern Caroline Islands, FM 96941; f. 1984; in 1990 it set up, with the Economic Devt Authority and an Australian co, the Caroline Fishing Co (three vessels); exists to promote fisheries development; Pres. Peter Sitan; Chair. Reed Nena.

### CO-OPERATIVES

**Chuuk:** Chuuk Co-operative, Faichuk Cacao and Copra Co-operative Asscn, Pis Fishermen's Co-operative, Fefan Women's Co-operative.

**Pohnpei:** Pohnpei Federation of Co-operative Asscns (POB 100, Pohnpei, Eastern Caroline Islands, FM 96941), Pohnpei Handicraft Co-operative, Pohnpei Fishermen's Co-operative, Uh Soumwet Co-operative Asscn, Kolonia Consumers' and Producers' Co-operative Asscn, Kitti Minimum Co-operative Asscn, Kapingamarangi Copra Producers' Asscn, Metalanim Copra Co-operative Asscn, PICS Co-operative Asscn, Mokil Island Co-operative Asscn, Ngatik Island Co-operative Asscn, Nukuoro Island Co-operative Asscn, Kosrae Island Co-operative Asscn, Pingelap Consumers' Co-operative Asscn.

**Yap:** Yap Co-operative Asscn, POB 159, Colonia, Yap, Western Caroline Islands, FM 96943; tel. 350-2209; fax 350-4114; f. 1952; Pres. James Gilmar; Gen. Man. Tony Ganngiyan; 1,200 mems.

## Transport

### ROADS

Macadam and concrete roads are found in the more important islands. Other islands have stone and coral-surfaced roads and tracks.

### SHIPPING

**Micronesian Maritime Authority:** Chair. Jesse Raglmar-Subolmar; Vice-Chair. Gerson Jackson; Exec. Dir Bernard Thoulag.

Most shipping in the territory is government-organized. However, Nauru Pacific Line operates a regular container service from Melbourne (Australia) to Chuuk, Pohnpei, Kosrae and other services from San Francisco (USA) and Honolulu (Hawaii) to Pohnpei and Chuuk. The Kyowa Line operates a monthly service from Hong Kong, Taiwan, the Republic of Korea and Japan to Chuuk and Pohnpei. The Micronesia Transport Line operates a service from Sydney (Australia) to Yap, Chuuk and Pohnpei.

### CIVIL AVIATION

The Federated States of Micronesia is served by Air Micronesia, Air Nauru and Continental Airlines (USA). Pacific Missionary Aviation, based in Pohnpei and Yap, provides domestic air services. There are international airports on Pohnpei, Chuuk, Yap and Kosrae, and airstrips in the outer islands of Onoun and Ta in Chuuk.

## Tourism

The tourist industry is a significant source of revenue, although it has been hampered by the lack of infrastructure. Visitor attractions include excellent conditions for scuba-diving (notably in Chuuk Lagoon), Second World War battle sites and relics (many underwater) and the ancient ruined city of Nan Madol on Pohnpei. In 1990 tourist arrivals numbered 20,475; in that year there was a total of 362 hotel rooms.

# MOLDOVA

## Introductory Survey

**Location, Climate, Language, Religion, Flag, Capital**

The Republic of Moldova (formerly the Moldovan Soviet Socialist Republic) is a small land-locked country situated in south-eastern Europe. It includes only a small proportion of the historical territories of Moldova (or Moldavia, in its Russian form), most of which are in Romania, while others (southern Bessarabia and northern Bucovina) are in Ukraine. The republic is bounded to the north, east and south by Ukraine. To the west it borders Romania. The climate is very favourable for agriculture, with long, warm summers and relatively mild winters. Average temperatures in Chişinău (Kishinev) range from 21°C (70°F) in July to −4°C (24°F) in January. The Constitution of July 1994 describes the official language as 'Moldovan' (although this is widely considered to be identical to Romanian). Most of the inhabitants of Moldova profess Christianity, the largest denomination being the Eastern Orthodox Church. The Gagauz, despite their Turkish origins, are also adherents of Orthodox Christianity. The Russian Orthodox Church (Moscow Patriarchy) has jurisdiction in Moldova, but there are Romanian and Turkish liturgies. The national flag (proportions 2 by 1) consists of three equal vertical stripes, of light blue, yellow and red; the yellow stripe has at its centre the arms of Moldova (a shield bearing a stylized bull's head in yellow, set between an eight-pointed yellow star, a five-petalled yellow flower, and a yellow crescent, the shield being set on the breast of an eagle, in gold and red, which holds a green olive branch in its dexter talons, a yellow sceptre in its sinister talons, and a yellow cross in its beak). The capital is Chişinău (Kishinev).

**Recent History**

The area of the present-day Republic of Moldova corresponds to only part of the medieval principality of Moldova (also known as Moldavia), which emerged as an important regional power in the 15th century. In the following century, however, the principality came under Ottoman domination. Following a period of conflict between the Ottoman and Russian Empires in the late 18th century, Moldova was divided into two parts under the Treaty of Bucharest of 1812: the eastern territory of Bessarabia, situated between the Prut and Dnestr rivers (and which roughly corresponds to modern Moldova), was ceded to Russia, while the Ottomans retained control of western Moldova. A Romanian nationalist movement evolved in western Moldova and the neighbouring region of Wallachia during the 19th century, culminating in the proclamation of a sovereign Romanian state in 1877, independent of the Ottoman Empire. In 1881 Romania became a kingdom. In June 1918, after the collapse of the Russian Empire, Bessarabia was proclaimed an independent republic, although in November it voted to become part of Romania. The union of Bessarabia with Romania was recognized in the Treaty of Paris (1920). However, the USSR (established in December 1922) refused to recognize Romania's claims to the territory, and, in October 1924, formed a Moldovan Autonomous Soviet Socialist Republic (ASSR) on the eastern side of the Dnestr, in the Ukrainian Soviet Socialist Republic (SSR). In June 1940 Romania was forced to cede Bessarabia and northern Bucovina to the USSR, the annexation having been agreed with Germany in the Treaty of Non-Aggression (the 'Molotov-Ribbentrop Pact') of August 1939. Northern Bucovina, southern Bessarabia and the Kotovsk-Balta region of the Moldovan ASSR were incorporated into the Ukrainian SSR. The remaining parts of the Moldovan ASSR and of Bessarabia were merged to form the Moldovan SSR, which formally joined the USSR on 2 August 1940. Political power in the republic became the preserve of the Communist Party of Moldova (CPM), itself a subsidiary of the Communist Party of the Soviet Union (CPSU).

Between July 1941 and August 1944 the Moldovan SSR was reunited with Romania. However, the Soviet Army reannexed the region in 1944, and the Moldovan SSR was re-established. Soviet policy in Moldova concentrated on isolating the region from its historical links with Romania: cross-border traffic virtually ceased; the Cyrillic script was imposed on the Romanian language (which was referred to as 'Moldovan'); and Russian and Ukrainian immigration was encouraged. In the 1950s thousands of ethnic Romanians were deported to Central Asia. Moldova remained among the more conservative republics of the USSR. Two future Soviet leaders, Leonid Brezhnev and Konstantin Chernenko, held prominent positions in the CPM during their early years of CPSU service: Brezhnev as First Secretary (leader) of the CPM in 1950–52, and Chernenko as head of the party's propaganda department in 1948–56.

The policy of *glasnost* (openness), introduced by the Soviet leader, Mikhail Gorbachev, in 1986, allowed the expression of opposition to the process of 'russification'. In May 1987 the CPM issued a decree increasing provision for the teaching of Romanian in schools, but this did little to satisfy public opinion. In 1988 there were demands for an immediate halt to immigration, for the restoration of the Latin alphabet and for Romanian to be declared the official language of the republic.

In May 1989 a number of independent cultural and political groups, which had emerged in 1988–89 but were denied legal status by the authorities, allied to form the Popular Front of Moldova (PFM). In June some 70,000 people attended a protest demonstration, organized by the PFM, on the anniversary of the Soviet annexation of Bessarabia in 1940. This was followed, in August 1989, by large demonstrations in the capital, Chişinău (Kishinev), in support of proposals by the Moldovan Supreme Soviet (legislature) to make Romanian the official language of the republic. Following protests by non-ethnic-Romanians and a strike, on 29 August, by ethnic Russians and Ukrainians, the proposals were amended. On 1 September a law was enacted which provided for Russian to be retained as a language of inter-ethnic communication, but the official language was to be Romanian and the Latin script reintroduced.

Disturbances during the Revolution Day celebrations in Chişinău, on 7 November 1989, and rioting three days later, led to the dismissal of the First Secretary of the CPM, Semion Grossu. He was replaced by Petru Lucinschi, a young ethnic Romanian considered to be more supportive of Gorbachev's reforms.

The increasing influence of the Romanian-speaking population was strongly opposed by other inhabitants of the republic (who, at the 1989 census, comprised some 35% of the total population). In the areas east of the Dnestr, where Russians and Ukrainians predominated, the local authorities refused to implement the language law. Opposition to growing Moldovan nationalism was led by the Yedinstvo (Unity) Movement, a group dominated by leading CPM members, and the United Work Collectives, an organization based among the working-class Slavs of the towns east of the Dnestr. These two organizations acted in close co-operation, and had strong links with Gagauz Halky (Gagauz People), the most prominent of the political groups representing the 150,000-strong Gagauz minority (a Turkic people). On 28 January 1990 a referendum took place in the eastern town of Tiraspol, in which the predominantly Russian-speaking population voted overwhelmingly to seek greater autonomy for the region beyond the Dnestr (Transdnestria).

None of the independent political groups was officially allowed to support candidates in the elections to the Moldovan Supreme Soviet, which took place on 25 February 1990, but individual candidates made clear where their sympathies lay. About 80% of the 380 deputies elected were members of the CPM, but many were also sympathetic to the aims of the PFM. Approximately 40% of the new deputies were supported by the PFM, and a further 30% were estimated to be broadly in favour of its main aims. The remaining 30% were mostly representatives of the non-ethnic-Romanian population. When the new Supreme Soviet convened in April, Mircea Snegur, a CPM member supported by the PFM, was elected Chairman of the Supreme Soviet. (In September he was elected to the newly-instituted post of President of the Republic, and the

Chairman of the Supreme Soviet became solely a parliamentary speaker.) Another of the nationalists' proposals, the adoption of the blue, yellow and red tricolour of Romania as the republic's official flag (although with a Moldovan coat of arms to distinguish it from that of the Romanian state), was also approved.

On 24 May 1990 the Government of Petr Paskar resigned after losing a vote of 'no confidence'. A leading reformist economist, Mircea Druc, was appointed Chairman of a Council of Ministers, which was dominated by radical reformers. The new Government implemented far-reaching changes to political life in Moldova. The CPM's constitutional right to power was revoked, and interference by any political party in the management of state institutions, the media and law-enforcement agencies was forbidden. Printing presses, newspapers and radio stations belonging to the CPM were transferred to state control. On 23 June the Supreme Soviet adopted a declaration of sovereignty asserting the supremacy of Moldova's Constitution and laws throughout the republic, which was to be known only as the Soviet Socialist Republic of Moldova (as opposed to the russified 'Moldavia'). The Supreme Soviet also declared the 1940 annexation of Bessarabia to have been illegal, and on the following day thousands of Moldovans and Romanians assembled at the border for a ceremony to commemorate the 50th anniversary of the annexation.

The actions of the increasingly radical Romanian majority in the legislature provoked further anxiety among the country's ethnic minorities during 1990. In August the Gagauz proclaimed a separate 'Gagauz SSR' in the southern region around Comrat. In the following month east-bank Slavs proclaimed their secession from Moldova and the establishment of the 'Transdnestrian SSR', comprising Moldovan territory east of the Dnestr, with its self-styled capital at Tiraspol. Both declarations were immediately annulled by the Moldovan Supreme Soviet. On 25 October, none the less, the Gagauz held elections to a Gagauz Supreme Soviet. Moldovan nationalists sought to thwart this by sending some 50,000 armed volunteers to the area. Violence was prevented only by the dispatch of Soviet troops to the region. The elections proceeded, and on 31 October the new Gagauz Supreme Soviet convened in Comrat. Stepan Topal was elected its President. Further inter-ethnic violence occurred east of the Dnestr in November, when elections were announced to a Transdnestrian Supreme Soviet. Four people were killed, and at least 16 injured, when Moldovan police attempted to regain control of the east-bank town of Dubăsari (Dubossary), where the local authorities had announced a state of emergency. Negotiations in Moscow, between the Moldovan Government, the east-bank Slavs and the Gagauz, failed to resolve the crisis, but the elections proceeded without further violence.

The Moldovan leadership refused to attend further tripartite talks, proposed in December 1990. Instead, on 16 December an estimated 800,000 people, attending a 'Grand National Assembly', voted by acclamation to reject any new union treaty (which was being negotiated by other Soviet republics). Furthermore, on 19 February 1991 the Moldovan Supreme Soviet resolved not to conduct the all-Union referendum on the future of the USSR, which was scheduled for 17 March, and to endorse proposals for a confederation of states without central control as the preferred replacement for the USSR. Despite the official boycott, some 650,000 people, mostly Russians, Ukrainians and Gagauz, participated in the referendum: they voted almost unanimously for the preservation of the USSR.

Despite opposition by the republic's ethnic minorities, the ethnic-Romanian-dominated Government and legislature continued the process of *de facto* secession from the USSR. All-Union enterprises were placed under republican jurisdiction, a Moldovan state bank was established (independent of the USSR Gosbank), the CPM was prohibited from activities in state and government organs, and conscription to the USSR armed forces was not implemented.

In May 1991 the words 'Soviet Socialist' were removed from the republic's name, and the Supreme Soviet was renamed the Moldovan Parliament. In the same month, following a vote of 'no confidence' by the legislature, Mircea Druc was removed from the post of Prime Minister; he was succeeded by Valeriu Muravschi, hitherto Deputy Prime Minister.

Following the seizure of power in Moscow by the State Committee for the State of Emergency, on 19 August 1991, the commanders of the USSR's South-Western Military District attempted to impose a state of emergency in Moldova. Their demands were rejected by the republican leadership, which immediately announced its support for the Russian President, Boris Yeltsin, in his opposition to the coup, and demanded the reinstatement of Gorbachev as President of the USSR. On 27 August, after the coup had collapsed, the Moldovan Parliament and a 'Grand National Assembly' proclaimed Moldova's independence from the USSR. The independence proclamation committed Moldova to adhere to international agreements on human rights, declared the exclusive validity of Moldovan legislation in the republic, and demanded the withdrawal of Soviet troops from Moldovan territory. The CPM was banned.

The declaration of independence was followed by practical measures to implement Moldovan secession from the USSR. The Moldovan Government asserted its jurisdiction over the border with Romania, including all customs installations. Customs posts were also introduced on the border with Ukraine. In September 1991 President Snegur ordered the creation of national armed forces, and took control of the republican KGB (state security service), transforming it into a Ministry of National Security. In the same month the Government announced that it would no longer participate in any all-Union structures or in negotiations for a new political union. However, in November the leadership did sign a treaty to establish an economic community. When in December the Commonwealth of Independent States (CIS, see p. 126) was proposed as a replacement for the USSR, Moldova expressed a willingness to participate, on condition that such an organization did not impinge on Moldovan independence. Support for independence was further demonstrated when elections were held to the republican presidency on 8 December. Mircea Snegur was the only candidate, and received 98.2% of the votes cast. On 21 December Moldova was among the 11 signatories to the Alma-Ata Declaration (see p. 127). The Declaration was to be ratified by a new Moldovan Parliament, following its election. The establishment of the CIS led to wider international recognition of Moldova's independence, which had been somewhat delayed by concern regarding inter-ethnic tension within the republic. By August 1992 some 110 states had accorded recognition to Moldova; of these, 60 had established diplomatic relations with the republic. In early 1992 Moldova joined both the UN and the Conference on Security and Co-operation in Europe (later renamed the OSCE, see p. 198).

Moldovan affairs during the first half of 1992 were dominated by the armed conflict in Transdnestria (see below), and by the question of possible unification with Romania. This position was strongly advocated by the ruling PFM (which, in February, was re-formed as the Christian Democratic Popular Front—CDPF). Moreover, a National Council for Reintegration had been established in December 1991, comprising legislators from both Moldova and Romania who were committed to the idea of a unified Romanian state. However, in Moldova itself popular support for unification remained insubstantial, with most citizens considering themselves Moldovan rather than Romanian. In June 1992 the CDPF-dominated Government announced its resignation (with the exception of four ministers). This development was attributed largely to popular opposition to the Government's pro-unification policies as well as to its failure to fulfil its promised economic and other reforms. The severe decline in the standard of living and the Government's inability to curb the increase in corruption and lawlessness also contributed to the fall of the CDPF administration.

Andrei Sangheli, a Deputy Prime Minister and the Minister of Agriculture and the Food Industry in the outgoing Government, was appointed Prime Minister. A new Government 'of national accord' was formed in late July–early August 1992. It was led by the Agrarian Democratic Party (ADP), which largely comprised members of the former communist leadership, in particular collective farm managers. Several government portfolios, which had been reserved for representatives from Transdnestria and Gagauzia, were in fact not accepted by the separatists. The CDPF became the leading party in opposition. The ADP declared its commitment to consolidating Moldovan statehood, rejecting any future union with Romania in favour of a closer alignment with Russia and the member states of the CIS. The ADP's anti-unification policies were strongly supported by President Snegur, who, in January 1993, proposed that the issue be resolved in a referendum, confident that it would be rejected. Contrary to expectations, Snegur's proposal was defeated by Parliament (by a margin of only one vote). The ensuing political crisis led to the resignations of both supporters and opponents of union with Romania, including the pro-unification Chairman of Parliament, Alexandru Moşanu. Moşanu was replaced in February by Petru Lucinschi, the former leader of the CPM.

Following the fall of the CDPF Government in mid-1992 and the subsequent resignation of many CDPF deputies from Parliament, the ADP was able to make substantial progress with the drafting of the new Moldovan Constitution during 1993. By the end of that year the draft was nearing completion, although it could only be ratified by the new Parliament that was due to be elected in early 1994. The draft Constitution provided, inter alia, for a reduced, 104-member legislature. In October 1993 Parliament recessed, having adopted a new electoral law. Sangheli and eight members of the Government were 'temporarily suspended' by Snegur in January 1994, in anticipation of the election of the new Parliament.

The first multi-party elections in Moldova's history were held on 27 February 1994, with the participation of more than 73% of the electorate. On the eve of the election, the authorities in Gagauzia rescinded their decision to boycott the poll, and the turn-out in the region was reported to be high. In the Transdnestr region the local leadership did not permit polling stations to open; however, residents were not prevented from voting on the left bank of the Dnestr. Thirteen parties and blocs contested the election, the result of which demonstrated widespread popular support for parties advocating continued Moldovan independence. The ADP emerged with the largest share of the votes (43.2%); as a result, it gained an overall majority in the Parliament (56 of the 104 seats). The successor party of the CPM, the Socialist Party (SP), in alliance with the Slav-based Yedinstvo (Unity) Movement, won 28 seats. Two pro-unification groups shared the remaining 20 seats: the Peasants' Party of Moldova/Congress of Intelligentsia alliance (11) and the CDPF alliance (nine). Apart from minor irregularities, the election was declared 'democratic and well-organized' by approximately 150 international observers.

The overwhelming lack of support for the pro-unification parties was confirmed in a national referendum on Moldova's statehood, held on 6 March 1994. Of the 75% of the electorate which participated, more than 95% were in favour of continued independence.

In late March 1994 Andrei Sangheli was re-elected Prime Minister, while Petru Lucinschi was re-elected Chairman of Parliament. A new, smaller Council of Ministers, comprising solely members of the ADP, was appointed in early April. The new Government pledged to strengthen ties with the CIS, in an attempt to prevent further economic decline. In late March the Ministry of Justice refused registration to the CPM, despite the fact that in September 1993 Parliament had voted to relegalize the party. However, in early May 1994 the party was finally permitted to register, as the Moldovan Party of Communists (MPC).

The new Constitution was adopted by Parliament in late July 1994 (it entered into force in late August). It described Moldova as a 'presidential parliamentary republic . . . based on the rule of law . . ., in which human rights are of supreme value'. As well as establishing the country's 'permanent neutrality', the Constitution also provided for a 'special legal status' for Transdnestria and Gagauzia within Moldova (the exact terms of which were to be determined at a later date). The official state language was described as 'Moldovan' (rather than Romanian), although the two languages were acknowledged to be identical. This prompted criticism by the CDPF and other pro-unification groups. In March–April 1995 thousands of students participated in a series of daily rallies in Chişinău, at which their principal demand was that Romanian be redesignated the official state language. In response, President Snegur decreed a six-month moratorium on the language issue, during which time a special committee would examine the matter. Parliament was to determine the official name of the language subsequently.

At local elections, held in April 1995, the ADP retained its leading position in most districts (in total, winning control of some 62% of the republic's municipalities). In Gagauzia, however, the MCP and the SP won the largest representation. The elections were boycotted in Transdnestria.

Following the proclamation of Transdnestria's secession in September 1990, relations between the region and the central Government in Chişinău remained tense. Armed conflict broke out in December 1991, as the leadership of the self-proclaimed republic, opposed to the PFM-led Government's objective of reunification with Romania, launched a campaign to gain control of the Transdnestr region (with the ultimate aim of unity with the Russian Federation). More than six months of military conflict ensued, as Moldovan government troops were dispatched to combat the local Slav militia. The Moldovan Government claimed that the east-bank forces were actively supported by the Russian Government, while the Moldovans were, in turn, accused of receiving military and other assistance from Romania. The situation was complicated by the presence (and alleged involvement in support of the east-bank Slavs) of the former Soviet 14th Army, which was still stationed in the region and jurisdiction over which had been transferred to the Russian Federation. Peace negotiations were held at regular intervals, with the participation of Moldova, Russia, Ukraine and Romania; however, none of the agreed cease-fires was observed. By June 1992 some 700 people were believed to have been killed in the conflict, with a further estimated 50,000 people forced to take refuge in neighbouring Ukraine. On 21 July, however, a peace agreement was finally negotiated by Presidents Snegur and Yeltsin, whereby Transdnestria was accorded 'special status' within Moldova (the terms of which were to be formulated later). The region was also given the right to determine its future in the event of Moldova's reintegration into Romania. Later in July Russian, Moldovan and Dnestrian peace-keeping troops were deployed in the region to monitor the cease-fire. However, Moldova's relations with the Russian Federation remained strained during the remainder of 1992, and no agreement was reached regarding the eventual withdrawal of the 14th Army.

During the period of the Transdnestrian conflict, the situation in Gagauzia remained peaceful. However, during 1993 the two separatist regions continued to demand full statehood, although they both subsequently came to accept the principle of sovereignty within a loose confederation with Moldova. The authorities in both regions also appeared intent on preserving the political and administrative structures of the Soviet period. By late 1993 neither republic had been recognized by any foreign state. In January 1994 the Moldovan Government accepted proposals by the CSCE for greater autonomy, including economic independence, for Transdnestria, within a Moldovan confederation. The Transdnestrian leadership expressed its approval of the proposals, and the result of the Moldovan parliamentary election of the following month (which eliminated the possibility of Moldova's future unification with Romania) further enhanced the prospects for peace in the region. In late April President Snegur and the Transdnestrian leader, Igor Smirnov, pledged their commitment to holding negotiations for a peaceful resolution of the conflict, based on the CSCE recommendations.

Prospects for a peaceful settlement of the conflicts in Transdnestria and Gagauzia appeared even closer following the adoption in July 1994 of the new Moldovan Constitution, which provided for a 'special legal status' for both regions. Negotiations duly commenced on the details of Transdnestria's and Gagauzia's future status within Moldova. Agreement was quickly reached between the Government and the Gagauz authorities, and in December the Moldovan Parliament adopted legislation on the 'special status of Gagauz-Eri' (or Gagauzia). The regions of southern Moldova populated by the Gagauz were to enjoy broad self-administrative powers, and Gagauz was to be one of three official languages (with Moldovan and Russian). Legislative power was to be vested in a regional assembly, while a directly-elected 'bashkan' was to hold a quasi-presidential position. The law on the status of Gagauz-Eri entered into force in February 1995, and in the following month a referendum was held in the region to determine which settlements would form part of Gagauz-Eri. Elections to the 35-seat regional assembly ('halk toplusu') took place in late May–early June. Elections, held simultaneously, to the post of bashkan were won by Gheorghe Tabunshchik, the First Secretary of the Comrat branch of the MPC. Under the new Constitution, Tabunshchik, as Gagauz leader, became a member of the Council of Ministers.

Negotiations on defining the 'special status' of Transdnestria were less successful. Progress was hampered, in particular, by disagreement over the future of the 15,000-strong 14th Army. The Transdnestrian leadership demanded the continued presence of the Army in the region as a guarantor of security. In October 1994, however, following two years of negotiations, the Moldovan and Russian Governments reached an agreement, under which Russia pledged to withdraw the 14th Army within a period of three years. The agreement was subsequently criticized by the Army's commander, Gen. Aleksandr Lebed, who warned that the withdrawal might be followed by renewed hostilities, as no political settlement of the conflict had been reached. A referendum was held in Transdnestria in late March, in which some 91% of participants voted against the agreed withdrawal of the 14th Army. Local elections, held simultaneously, confirmed the supremacy of the socialist Union of Patriotic Forces, which had led the self-proclaimed republic during the preceding four years. The elections and the referendum were both declared illegal by President Snegur. In late May Gen. Lebed tendered his resignation, and his successor, Maj.-Gen. Valery Yevnevich, was announced in the following month. In late June the withdrawal of weapons and ammunition of the 14th Army was reportedly begun.

Owing to the changing domestic situation, Moldova's membership of the CIS was equivocal from its signature of the Alma-Ata Declaration in December 1991 until early 1994. The republic did not become a party to the treaty on collective security (the Tashkent Agreement of May 1992), and in January 1993 Moldova was one of three CIS member states that did not sign a charter on closer political and economic integration. In August of that year the Moldovan Parliament failed by four votes to ratify the Alma-Ata Declaration, thus technically removing Moldova from the CIS. This development was largely due to the influence of deputies favouring unification with Romania. However, it was increasingly recognized that Moldova's economic survival depended on the CIS, and at a summit meeting of the Commonwealth held in Moscow in September, President Snegur signed a treaty to join the new CIS economic union. Following Moldova's parliamentary election of February 1994 and the referendum in March which strongly endorsed continued independence, Parliament reversed its earlier decision, and in late April it finally ratified membership of the CIS by 76 votes to 18. However, the legislature indicated that Moldova would participate neither in CIS military structures nor in monetary union.

### Government
Under the Constitution of 1994, supreme legislative power is held by the unicameral 104-member Moldovan Parliament, which is directly elected every four years. The directly-elected President is Head of State and holds executive power in conjunction with the Council of Ministers, led by the Prime Minister. For administrative purposes, Moldova is divided into 40 districts and four cities. The Constitution provided for broad self-administrative powers for the formerly separatist regions of Transdnestria and Gagauzia (see Recent History).

### Defence
Following independence from the USSR (declared in August 1991), the Moldovan Government initiated the creation of national armed forces. By June 1994 these were estimated to number 11,100: army 9,800 and air force 1,300. There are paramilitary forces (of an estimated 3,400), attached to the Ministry of the Interior. Military service is compulsory and lasts for up to 18 months. In mid-1995 the former Soviet 14th Army was still stationed (under Russian jurisdiction) in the separatist Transdnestr region of Moldova; under an agreement concluded by the Moldovan and Russian Governments in late 1994, the 14th Army was to have been withdrawn from Transdnestr within three years. In early 1994 Moldova joined NATO's 'partnership for peace' programme (see p. 192). In 1994 budgetary spending on defence was an estimated US $51m.

### Economic Affairs
In 1993, according to estimates by the World Bank, Moldova's gross national product (GNP), measured at average 1991–93 prices, was US $5,160m., equivalent to $1,180 per head. During 1985–93, it was estimated, GNP per head declined, in real terms, by an average annual rate of 5.4%. During the same period the population increased by an annual average of 0.5%. In 1991 Moldova's net material product (NMP) declined, in real terms, by 18.0%, compared with 1990. In 1992 NMP decreased further, by 28.8%, although in 1993 a less severe decline (of an estimated 3.9%) was registered. In 1994 NMP was reported to have declined by 31.0%.

As a result of its extremely fertile land and temperate climate, Moldova's economy is dominated by agriculture and related industries. Some 85% of the country's terrain is cultivated. In 1993, according to preliminary data, agriculture (including forestry) contributed about 42% of NMP; in the previous year the sector provided 40% of employment. Principal crops include wine grapes and other fruit, tobacco, vegetables and grain. In 1992 fruits, vegetables and tobacco accounted for 39% of total agricultural output. The wine industry has traditionally occupied a central role in the economy; although it was seriously disrupted by the Soviet Government's anti-alcohol campaign of the mid-1980s (with some vineyards being uprooted and replaced by other crops), the industry has since been revived. The principal animal products are milk, pork and beef. The private ownership of land was legalized in 1991. In the same year agricultural NMP fell by 28.0%, compared with 1990. It declined by a further 56.9% in 1992; however, in 1993 agricultural NMP increased by an estimated 5.8%. This positive trend was reversed in 1994, when a decline of 26.0% was recorded.

In 1993, according to preliminary figures, industry (including mining, manufacturing, construction and power) contributed 49% of NMP; in the previous year industry provided 26% of employment. The sector is dominated by food-processing, wine and tobacco production, light industry, machine-building and metalworking. In 1993 food-processing accounted for 36.7% of the value of total industrial output (excluding the Transdnestr region), followed by machinery and metalworking (22.7%) and light industry (21.4%). In 1992 industrial output declined by 29.5%, compared with the previous year; however, in 1993, it was estimated to have increased by 3.9%. A decline of 34.0% was registered in 1994.

Moldova has extremely limited mineral resources, and there is no domestic production of fuel or non-ferrous metals. Deposits of petroleum and natural gas were discovered in southern Moldova in the early 1990s, but have not as yet been exploited.

The manufacturing sector contributed 19% of employment in 1992. In 1991 the principal branches, measured by gross value of output, were food-processsing (46.3%), metal products and machinery (15.9%), textiles (11.9%), garments (6.7%) and leather products and footwear (4.2%).

Firewood and a small hydroelectric power station on the River Dnestr provide the only sources of domestic energy (satisfying only 1.4% of domestic consumption in 1992). Consequently the country relies heavily on imported fuels and raw materials (principally from the Russian Federation and Ukraine), both for energy generation and for industry. The value of energy imports in 1990 was equivalent to about 5% of gross domestic product (GDP); this share had increased to some 24% by 1993. Natural gas accounts for about 40% of all fuel consumption. In 1992 98.2% of Moldova's domestic electricity generation came from thermal power stations, while the remaining 1.8% was derived from the country's hydroelectric station. Moldova re-exports some of the electricity that it generates.

In 1993 Moldova recorded a visible trade deficit of an estimated US $162m., while there was a deficit of $177m. on the current account of the balance of payments. In the early 1990s republics of the (former) USSR remained Moldova's principal trading partners, although trade with western countries increased steadily. In 1994 the Russian Federation continued to be the leading trading partner (accounting for 46.1% of Moldova's total trade turnover), followed in importance by Ukraine (16.4%), Romania (11.0%), Germany (4.1%) and Belarus (3.6%). In 1991 food and agricultural products accounted for 46% of the value of total exports, followed by light industrial products (22%) and machinery and metalworking products (19%). Moldova's principal imports reflect the requirements of its agro-industrial complex: in 1991 light industrial products accounted for 26% of the value of all imports, while energy products and machinery and metalworking products accounted for 16% and 15%, respectively.

In 1993, according to preliminary data, the state budget (excluding the Transdnestr region) showed a deficit of 189m. Moldovan lei. Moldova's external debt totalled US $289.0m. at the end of 1993, of which $201.6m. was long-term public debt. In that year the cost of debt-servicing was equivalent to 0.4% of the value of exports of goods and services. Consumer prices increased by an annual average of 1,804% in 1993, and by 487% in 1994. In the year to December 1994 the rate of inflation was 104.7%. In December 1992 some 80,000 people were registered as unemployed; however, the level of 'hidden unemployment' was reported to be considerably higher.

Moldova became a member of the IMF and the World Bank in 1992. It also joined the European Bank for Reconstruction and Development (EBRD, see p. 140). It subsequently joined the International Development Association (see p. 74).

In common with other former Soviet republics following independence, Moldova's planned transition to a market economic system has been hampered by numerous factors, most prominently the serious disruptions in inter-republican trade. As a consequence, there have been severe shortfalls in deliveries of the fuels and raw materials on which Moldova's economy depends, and production in all sectors (in particular the crucial agricultural sector) has declined drastically. Another factor that adversely affected economic performance was the armed conflict in the Transdnestr region (the main industrial centre) in the first half of 1992 and the region's subsequent attempts to secede from Moldova (see Recent History), compounded by a devastating drought in that year. In order to counteract the negative effects of remaining in the rouble area (such as a rapidly increasing annual rate of inflation), Moldova introduced its own national currency (the Moldovan leu) in November 1993, replacing the temporary coupon currency (the Moldovan rouble) that had been in operation since mid-1992.

In May 1994 the IMF reported that the first stage of Moldova's economic reform programme (devised in consultation with the IMF) had achieved considerable success: the leu had remained stable over a period of several months, while inflation had been dramatically curbed in early 1994. After two years of considerable decline, agricultural and industrial growth was recorded in 1993. However, production in both sectors decreased severely again in 1994, largely as a result of a number of natural disasters that affected Moldova during the year. In early 1995 it was reported that some 32% of the population were living below the poverty line.

### Social Welfare

The social security and health systems provide a comprehensive service, which is fully funded by the State. Social security provides allowances for families, especially those with low incomes, pensioners and invalids. Pensions and invalid allowances are funded by the extrabudgetary Social Security Fund, established in 1991, which collects taxes from enterprises, organizations and institutions to fund the social security system. The Social Security Fund includes the following funds: the Special Pension and Allowances Fund, from which pensions and allowances for pensioners and large families are paid; the Special Insurance Fund, which provides allowances for temporary incapacity for work, pregnancy and maternity leave, allowances for childbirth, funeral allowances, etc.; and the Special Employment Fund, which provides unemployment payments. In early 1995 746,700 people were in receipt of pensions; in the previous year expenditure on pensions totalled 354.9m. lei.

In January 1992 the National Social Assistance Fund was established (as well as local extrabudgetary funds) to provide financial aid to the most vulnerable groups of the population. In 1994 a total of 7.1m. lei was provided as financial assistance for such groups, including invalids, pensioners, large families, one-parent families and the disabled.

In 1994 there were 122.2 hospital beds per 10,000 inhabitants. In the following year the state budget allocated 315m. lei to health care (some 15% of total budgetary expenditure).

### Education

Until the late 1980s the system of education was an integral part of the Soviet system, with most education in the Russian language. In 1990 and 1991 there were extensive changes to the education system, with Romanian literature and history added to the curriculum. In the period 1980–88 the proportion of pupils in general day-schools taught in Russian increased from 36.9% to 40.9%, although this trend was reversed in the early 1990s, with many Russian-language schools being closed. In 1989, according to census results, the rate of adult illiteracy in Moldova was 3.6% (males 1.4%; females 5.6%). In 1993, according to preliminary figures, the state budget allocated 127m. lei (or 23.4% of total budgetary spending) to education.

### Public Holidays

**1995:** 1 January (New Year's Day), 7–8 January (Christmas), 8 March (International Women's Day), 21 April (Good Friday), 24 April (Easter Monday), 9 May (Victory and Commemoration Day), 27 August (Independence Day), 31 August ('Limbă Noastră', National Language Day).

**1996:** 1 January (New Year's Day), 7–8 January (Christmas), 8 March (International Women's Day), 12 April (Good Friday), 15 April (Easter Monday), 9 May (Victory and Commemoration Day), 27 August (Independence Day), 31 August ('Limbă Noastră', National Language Day).

### Weights and Measures

The metric system is in force.

# Statistical Survey

Principal sources (unless otherwise indicated): IMF, *Moldova, Economic Review* and *International Financial Statistics: Supplement on Countries of the Former Soviet Union*; World Bank, *Statistical Handbook: States of the Former USSR*.

## Area and Population

### AREA, POPULATION AND DENSITY

| | |
|---|---:|
| Area (sq km) | 33,700* |
| Population (census results)† | |
|   17 January 1979 | 3,949,756 |
|   12 January 1989 | |
|     Males | 2,063,192 |
|     Females | 2,272,168 |
|     Total | 4,335,360 |
| Population (official estimates at mid-year) | |
|   1991 | 4,363,000 |
|   1992 | 4,348,000 |
|   1993 | 4,356,000 |
| Density (per sq km) at mid-1993 | 129.3 |

* 13,010 sq miles.

† Figures refer to the *de jure* population. The *de facto* total at the 1989 census was 4,337,592.

### PRINCIPAL ETHNIC GROUPS (permanent inhabitants, 1989 census)

| | Number ('000) | % |
|---|---:|---:|
| Moldovan | 2,795 | 64.5 |
| Ukrainian | 600 | 13.8 |
| Russian | 562 | 13.0 |
| Gagauzi | 153 | 3.5 |
| Bulgarian | 88 | 2.0 |
| Jewish | 66 | 1.5 |
| Other | 71 | 1.6 |
| **Total** | **4,335** | **100.0** |

### PRINCIPAL TOWNS (estimated population at 1 July 1992)

| | | | |
|---|---:|---|---:|
| Chișinău (Kishinev) (capital) | 667,100 | Bălți (Beltsy) | 159,000 |
| Tiraspol | 186,200 | Bender (Benderi) | 132,700 |

Source: UN, *Demographic Yearbook*.

# MOLDOVA

## BIRTHS, MARRIAGES AND DEATHS

|  | Registered live births | | Registered marriages | | Registered deaths | |
|---|---|---|---|---|---|---|
|  | Number | Rate (per 1,000) | Number | Rate (per 1,000) | Number | Rate (per 1,000) |
| 1987 | 91,762 | 21.4 | 39,084 | 9.1 | 40,185 | 9.4 |
| 1988 | 88,568 | 20.5 | 39,745 | 9.2 | 40,912 | 9.5 |
| 1989 | 82,221 | 18.9 | 39,928 | 9.2 | 40,113 | 9.2 |

**1992** (provisional): Live births 70,102 (birth rate 16.1 per 1,000); Marriages 39,340 (marriage rate 9.0 per 1,000); Deaths 44,637 (death rate 10.2 per 1,000).

Source: UN, *Demographic Yearbook*.

**Expectation of life** (years at birth, 1989): 69.0 (males 65.5; females 72.3) (Source: Goskomstat USSR).

## EMPLOYMENT (annual averages, '000 persons)

|  | 1990 | 1991 | 1992 |
|---|---|---|---|
| Agriculture, hunting, forestry and fishing | 700 | 865 | 820 |
| Manufacturing | 443 | 363 | 394 |
| Electricity, gas and water | 13 | 13 | 14 |
| Construction | 144 | 121 | 120 |
| Trade, restaurants and hotels | 138 | 111 | 111 |
| Transport, storage and communications | 111 | 105 | 102 |
| Financing, insurance, real estate and business services | 9 | 10 | 9 |
| Community, social and personal services | 444 | 422 | 422 |
| Activities not adequately defined | 69 | 60 | 58 |
| **Total employed** | **2,071** | **2,070** | **2,050** |

**1989 census** (persons aged 15 years and over): Total labour force 2,117,592 (males 1,084,504; females 1,033,088).

Source: ILO, *Year Book of Labour Statistics*.

# Agriculture

## PRINCIPAL CROPS ('000 metric tons)

|  | 1991 | 1992 | 1993 |
|---|---|---|---|
| Wheat | 1,056 | 926 | 1,394 |
| Barley | 427 | 405 | 481 |
| Maize | 1,501 | 634 | 1,360 |
| Potatoes | 291 | 311 | 300* |
| Peas (dry) | n.a. | 104 | 90† |
| Soybeans (Soya beans) | 33 | 8 | 30† |
| Sunflower seed | 169 | 197 | 216* |
| Cabbages | n.a. | 300* | 300* |
| Tomatoes | n.a. | 164* | 180* |
| Cucumbers and gherkins | n.a. | 100* | 122* |
| Onions (dry) | n.a. | 65* | 65* |
| Carrots | n.a. | 50* | 38* |
| Watermelons† | 454 | 650 | 550 |
| Grapes | 774 | 824 | 730† |
| Sugar beets | 2,262 | 1,973 | 1,900* |
| Apples | n.a. | 337* | 390† |
| Pears | n.a. | 25* | 25† |
| Peaches and nectarines | n.a. | 37* | 86† |
| Plums | n.a. | 61* | 62† |
| Tobacco (leaves) | 69 | 42 | 60† |

* Unofficial figure.

† FAO estimate(s). Figures for watermelons include melons, pumpkins and squash.

Sources: FAO, *Production Yearbook*; World Bank, *Statistical Handbook: States of the Former USSR*.

## LIVESTOCK ('000 head at 1 January)

|  | 1991 | 1992 | 1993 |
|---|---|---|---|
| Horses | 47 | 49 | 51 |
| Cattle | 1,061 | 1,000 | 970 |
| Pigs | 1,850 | 1,753 | 1,487 |
| Sheep | 1,245 | 1,239 | 1,294 |
| Goats | 37 | 40 | 63 |
| Poultry | 24,814 | 23,614 | 22,000* |

* FAO estimate.

## LIVESTOCK PRODUCTS ('000 metric tons)

|  | 1991 | 1992 | 1993 |
|---|---|---|---|
| Beef and veal | 96 | 75 | 67* |
| Pig meat | 145 | 114 | 95† |
| Poultry meat | 56 | 39 | 35† |
| Cows' milk | 1,292 | 1,128 | 1,000† |
| Butter | 21.8 | 19.0 | 18.0* |
| Cheese | 10.0 | 4.6 | 6.0† |
| Poultry eggs | 72.4 | 44.8* | 45.0† |
| Wool: |  |  |  |
| greasy | 2.9 | 2.6 | 3.0† |
| scoured | 1.8 | 1.5 | 1.8† |

* Unofficial figure.   † FAO estimate.

Sources: mainly FAO, *Production Yearbook*, and World Bank, *Statistical Handbook: States of the Former USSR*.

# Fishing

('000 metric tons, live weight)

|  | 1991 | 1992* |
|---|---|---|
| Silver carp | 2.5 | 2.4 |
| Hoven's carp | 2.6 | 2.5 |
| Other fishes | 0.1 | 0.1 |
| **Total catch** | **5.2** | **5.0** |

* FAO estimates.

Source: FAO, *Yearbook of Fishery Statistics*.

# Industry

## SELECTED PRODUCTS ('000 metric tons, unless otherwise indicated)

|  | 1991 | 1992 | 1993* |
|---|---|---|---|
| Vegetable oil | 117.9 | 57.9 | 53.9 |
| Flour | 576.7 | 500.4 | 357.4 |
| Raw sugar | 236.9 | 208.1 | 195.0 |
| Wine from grapes (million litres) | 143.4 | 141.1 | 92.9 |
| Mineral water (million litres) | 32.8 | 13.7 | 8.0 |
| Soft drinks (million litres) | 86.4 | 29.0 | 15.2 |
| Cigarettes (million) | 9,200 | 8,600 | 8,800 |
| Cloth (million sq m) | 228.1 | 183.0 | 31.0 |
| Knitted articles (million) | 52.3 | 35.3 | 18.5 |
| Carpets (million sq m) | 4.2 | 2.8 | 2.6 |
| Footwear (million pairs) | 20.8 | 14.5 | 11.9 |
| Refrigerators and freezers ('000) | 117.7 | 54.8 | 57.6 |
| Washing machines ('000) | 194.0 | 102.0 | 122.7 |
| Television receivers ('000) | 172.5 | 176.1 | 166.7 |
| Tractors ('000) | 6.6 | 5.4 | 4.2 |
| Electric energy (million kWh) | 13,100 | 11,200 | n.a. |

* Excluding the Transdnestr region.

# MOLDOVA

# Finance

## CURRENCY AND EXCHANGE RATES

**Monetary Units**
 100 bani (singular: ban) = 1 Moldovan leu (plural: lei).

**Sterling and Dollar Equivalents** (31 December 1994)
 £1 sterling = 6.680 lei;
 US $1 = 4.270 lei;
 100 Moldovan lei = £14.97 = $23.42.

Note: The Moldovan leu was introduced (except in the Transdnestr region) on 29 November 1993, replacing the Moldovan rouble at a rate of 1 leu = 1,000 roubles. The Moldovan rouble had been introduced in June 1992, as a temporaray coupon currency, and was initially at par with the Russian (formerly Soviet) rouble. Based on the official rate of exchange, the average value of the Soviet currency (roubles per US dollar) was: 0.6274 in 1989; 0.5856 in 1990; 0.5819 in 1991. However, a multiple exchange rate system was in operation, with separate non-commercial and tourist rates. A commercial exchange rate was introduced on 1 November 1990, replacing the official rate for most transactions. The commercial rate (roubles per US dollar) was: 1.692 at 31 December 1990; 1.671 at 31 December 1991. Between November 1989 and April 1991 the tourist exchange rate valued the rouble at one-tenth of the official rate. In April 1991 this rate, renamed the 'special rate', was set at $1 = 27.6 roubles. It was subsequently adjusted. Following the dissolution of the USSR in December 1991, Russia and several other former Soviet republics retained the rouble as their monetary unit. The average interbank market rate in 1992 was $1 = 222.1 Russian roubles. In July 1993 all pre-1993 Russian roubles were withdrawn from circulation in Moldova (except in the Transdnestr region), and from August a distinction was introduced between Moldovan roubles and the currencies of other countries in the rouble area. Some of the figures in this Survey are still expressed in terms of roubles.

## STATE BUDGET (million lei)*

| Revenue | 1992 | 1993† |
|---|---|---|
| Direct taxes | 14 | 132 |
| Taxes on profits | 10 | 97 |
| Taxes on personal incomes | 4 | 35 |
| Domestic taxes on goods and services | 24 | 158 |
| Value-added tax | 14 | 95 |
| Excises | 10 | 63 |
| Taxes on international trade | 1 | 19 |
| Land tax | — | 14 |
| Other taxes | — | 3 |
| Other revenues | 4 | 38 |
| Road fees | — | 10 |
| **Total** | 43 | 364 |

| Expenditure‡ | 1992 | 1993† |
|---|---|---|
| Current expenditure | 48 | 484 |
| National economy | 3 | 27 |
| Education | 14 | 127 |
| Health care | 7 | 80 |
| Food subsidies | 8 | 50 |
| Other subsidies | 3 | 13 |
| Cash compensation | — | 18 |
| Law and defence | 5 | 58 |
| Interest payments | 1 | 23 |
| Capital expenditure | 7 | 59 |
| **Total** | 55 | 543 |

* Figures refer to a consolidation of the operations of central (republican) and local governments, excluding the accounts of social security schemes and other extrabudgetary funds. Data exclude the Transdnestr region.
† Preliminary.
‡ Excluding net lending (million lei): 39 in 1992; 10 in 1993

## INTERNATIONAL RESERVES (US $ million at 31 December)

| | 1992 | 1993 | 1994 |
|---|---|---|---|
| IMF special drawing rights | — | 34.41 | 21.34 |
| Reserve position in IMF | 0.01 | 0.01 | 0.01 |
| Foreign exchange | 2.44 | 41.92 | 174.09 |
| **Total** (excl. gold) | 2.45 | 76.34 | 195.44 |

Source: IMF, *International Financial Statistics*.

## MONEY SUPPLY (million roubles at 31 December)

| | 1991 | 1992 |
|---|---|---|
| Currency outside banks | 1,827 | 9,444 |
| Demand deposits at banks | 7,260 | 51,808 |

**1993** (million lei at 31 December): Currency outside banks 119.4.

## COST OF LIVING (Consumer Price Index; base: 1991 = 100)

| | 1992 | 1993 |
|---|---|---|
| Food | 1,188.4 | 20,382 |
| Clothing | 951.9 | n.a. |
| **All items** (incl. others) | 1,208.7 | 23,014 |

**1994:** All items 135,087.

Sources: ILO, *Year Book of Labour Statistics*; UN, *Monthly Bulletin of Statistics*.

## NATIONAL ACCOUNTS ('000 lei at current prices)

**Net Material Product by Use**

| | 1990 | 1991 | 1992 |
|---|---|---|---|
| Personal consumption | 6,907 | 13,862 | 77,124 |
| Material consumption in the units of the non-material sphere serving individuals | 680 | 1,108 | 10,845 |
| **Consumption of the population** | 7,587 | 14,970 | 87,969 |
| Material consumption in the units of the non-material sphere serving the community as a whole | 190 | 170 | 2,233 |
| Net fixed capital formation | 1,065 | 1,280 | 11,195 |
| Increase in material circulating assets and in stocks | 824 | 3,662 | 115,651 |
| Losses | 141 | 226 | 1,289 |
| Net exports of goods and material services / Net errors and omissions | −364 | −1,555 | −51,448 |
| **Total** | 9,443 | 18,753 | 166,889 |

**Net Material Product by Economic Activity**

| | 1991 | 1992 | 1993* |
|---|---|---|---|
| Agriculture | 7,822 | 72,351 | 680,681 |
| Forestry | 13 | 143 | 1,538 |
| Industry† | 7,048 | 55,289 | 676,871 |
| Construction | 1,296 | 14,868 | 123,389 |
| Transport and communications | 711 | 7,981 | 15,252 |
| Trade and catering | 1,757 | 15,700 | 126,892 |
| Other activities of the material sphere | 106 | 557 | 5,553 |
| **Total** | 18,753 | 166,889 | 1,630,176 |

* Preliminary figures.
† Comprising manufacturing (except printing and publishing), mining and quarrying, electricity, gas, water, logging and fishing.

## BALANCE OF PAYMENTS (US $ million)

| | 1991 | 1992 | 1993* |
|---|---|---|---|
| Merchandise exports f.o.b. | 4,646 | 868 | 449 |
| Merchandise imports f.o.b. | −4,643 | −905 | −611 |
| **Trade balance** | 3 | −37 | −162 |
| Services and other income (net) | — | −2 | −36 |
| Unrequited transfers (net) | — | — | 22 |
| **Current balance** | 3 | −39 | −177 |
| Long-term capital (net) | 25 | 34 | 83 |
| Other capital (net) | — | — | 53 |
| Net errors and omissions | 167 | −9 | 29 |
| **Overall balance** | 196 | −14 | −12 |

* Estimates.

Sources: IMF and World Bank.

# MOLDOVA

## External Trade

**TRADE WITH THE FORMER USSR**
**PRINCIPAL COMMODITIES** (million roubles)

| Imports | 1989 | 1990 | 1991 |
|---|---|---|---|
| Industrial products | 4,883.2 | 4,618.9 | 7,063 |
| Petroleum and gas | 519.6 | 424.6 | 1,218 |
| Coal | 128.6 | 119.1 | 146 |
| Iron and steel | 310.8 | 285.8 | 263 |
| Non-ferrous metallurgy | 154.7 | 150.4 | 264 |
| Chemical and petroleum products | 588.9 | 581.3 | 1,069 |
| Machine-building and metalworking | 1,610.4 | 1,504.4 | 1,134 |
| Wood and paper products | 223.6 | 205.0 | 351 |
| Construction materials | 119.2 | 117.3 | 116 |
| Light industry | 704.3 | 769.0 | 1,768 |
| Food and beverages | 364.6 | 256.6 | 492 |
| Agricultural products (unprocessed) | 90.3 | 149.6 | 166 |
| Other commodities | 218.0 | 223.1 | 8 |
| **Total** | **5,191.5** | **4,991.6** | **7,237** |

| Exports | 1989 | 1990 | 1991 |
|---|---|---|---|
| Industrial products | 4,822.7 | 5,388.3 | 6,980 |
| Chemical and petroleum products | 195.5 | 206.2 | 181 |
| Machine-building and metalworking | 983.1 | 978.0 | 1,532 |
| Wood and paper products | 109.3 | 80.8 | 135 |
| Light industry | 1,148.7 | 1,165.5 | 1,659 |
| Food and beverages | 2,101.5 | 2,621.1 | 2,790 |
| Agricultural products (unprocessed) | 319.4 | 426.5 | 805 |
| **Total** (incl. others) | **5,186.4** | **5,853.3** | **7,809** |

**PRINCIPAL TRADING PARTNERS** (million roubles)

| | 1991 Imports | 1991 Exports | 1992 Imports | 1992 Exports |
|---|---|---|---|---|
| Azerbaijan | 81.7 | 106.2 | 1,124.8 | 1,259.5 |
| Belarus | 598.2 | 508.7 | 9,506.8 | 2,776.0 |
| Georgia | 122.6 | 60.9 | 367.9 | 291.4 |
| Kazakhstan | 260.6 | 180.2 | 760.8 | 1,232.3 |
| Kyrgyzstan | 39.6 | 55.8 | 255.0 | 350.9 |
| Latvia | 100.5 | 150.1 | 382.0 | 578.3 |
| Lithuania | 160.5 | 170.1 | 869.0 | 761.6 |
| Russia | 3,269.8 | 4,724.7 | 42,787.4 | 25,015.7 |
| Turkmenistan | 50.1 | 36.5 | 1,725.6 | 1,696.4 |
| Ukraine | 1,863.0 | 1,418.8 | 14,331.2 | 12,466.3 |
| Uzbekistan | 258.9 | 166.4 | 1,522.3 | 958.3 |
| **Total** (incl. others) | **7,237.3** | **7,809.0** | **73,929.7** | **47,841.7** |

**TRADE WITH OTHER COUNTRIES**
**PRINCIPAL COMMODITIES** (million roubles)

| Imports | 1989 | 1990 | 1991 |
|---|---|---|---|
| Industrial products | 1,292.6 | 1,347.6 | 812 |
| Chemical and petroleum products | 122.3 | 150.1 | 92 |
| Machine-building and metalworking | 250.6 | 356.7 | 160 |
| Wood and paper products | 37.9 | 19.1 | 25 |
| Construction materials | 31.5 | 26.3 | 8 |
| Light industry | 570.1 | 538.4 | 429 |
| Food and beverages | 239.4 | 204.5 | 89 |
| Agricultural products (unprocessed) | 126.3 | 121.2 | 389 |
| **Total** (incl. others) | **1,420.0** | **1,469.8** | **1,207** |

| Exports | 1989 | 1990 | 1991 |
|---|---|---|---|
| Industrial products | 266.8 | 300.4 | 313 |
| Electric power | 87.9 | 58.8 | 36 |
| Iron and steel | 7.2 | 10.9 | n.a. |
| Chemical and petroleum products | 2.1 | 4.2 | 7 |
| Machine-building and metalworking | 50.3 | 67.1 | 21 |
| Light industry | 34.0 | 41.8 | 99 |
| Food and beverages | 81.2 | 111.7 | 134 |
| Agricultural products (unprocessed) | 2.6 | 22.6 | 16 |
| **Total** (incl. others) | **270.0** | **323.4** | **332** |

**PRINCIPAL TRADING PARTNERS**

| | 1991 (million roubles) Imports | Exports | 1992 (US $ million) Imports | Exports |
|---|---|---|---|---|
| Austria | 78.6 | 49.5 | 3.4 | 0.4 |
| Bulgaria | 48.1 | 37.3 | 19.3 | 13.0 |
| Canada | 53.5 | 8.1 | 0.2 | 2.2 |
| Czechoslovakia | 52.6 | 9.5 | 1.3 | 0.6 |
| France | 53.5 | 6.4 | 1.7 | 0.5 |
| Germany | 64.6 | 58.3 | 18.7 | 8.3 |
| Hungary | 14.4 | 18.3 | 1.4 | 2.8 |
| Italy | 19.4 | 11.2 | 6.3 | 1.6 |
| Japan | 27.9 | 10.0 | 0.3 | 0.1 |
| Poland | 22.8 | 8.7 | 3.9 | 2.7 |
| Romania | 261.8 | 55.3 | 62.5 | 102.3 |
| United Kingdom | 6.8 | 14.0 | 0.7 | 0.3 |
| USA | 239.0 | 4.7 | 36.5 | — |
| **Total** (incl. others) | **1,206.5** | **331.8** | **170.3** | **156.5** |

## Transport

**RAILWAYS** (traffic)

| | 1989 | 1990 | 1991 |
|---|---|---|---|
| Passenger-km (million) | 1,514 | 1,464 | 1,280 |
| Freight net ton-km (million) | 15,632 | 15,007 | 11,883 |

Source: UN, *Statistical Yearbook*.

**ROAD TRAFFIC** (motor vehicles registered at 31 December)

| | 1990 | 1991 | 1992 |
|---|---|---|---|
| Passenger cars | 209,013 | 218,059 | 221,883 |
| Goods vehicles | 11,060 | 10,528 | 9,297 |
| Buses and coaches | 11,308 | 11,226 | 11,112 |
| Motor cycles and scooters | 196,354 | 198,809 | n.a. |

Source: International Road Federation, *World Road Statistics*.

MOLDOVA

## Communications Media

|  | 1989 | 1990 | 1991 |
|---|---|---|---|
| Telephones ('000 main lines in use) | 430* | 460* | 495 |

* Estimate.

Source: UN, *Statistical Yearbook*.

**1992:** Book production: 802 titles (363,000 copies); Daily newspapers 5 (combined estimated circulation 205,000); Non-daily newspapers 212 (combined estimated circulation 1,269,000); Other periodicals 68 (combined circulation 351,000) (Source: UNESCO, *Statistical Yearbook*).

## Education

(1991)

|  | Institutions | Teachers | Students |
|---|---|---|---|
| Primary | 1,595 | 16,853 | 306,933 |
| General secondary | n.a. | 32,254* | 407,596 |
| Vocational | n.a. | n.a. | 38,253 |
| Higher | 9† | n.a. | 54,700‡ |

* Estimate.   † 1987/88.   ‡ 1990.

Source: mainly UNESCO, *Statistical Yearbook*.

# Directory

## The Constitution

A new Constitution was adopted by the Moldovan Parliament on 28 July 1994; it entered into force on 27 August. The Constitution describes Moldova as a 'presidential parliamentary republic', which is a 'sovereign, independent and indivisible state, based on the rule of law', in which 'human rights and freedoms are of supreme value'. The official state language is Moldovan (which is acknowledged to be identical to Romanian). Supreme legislative power resides with the unicameral 104-member Moldovan Parliament, which is directly elected for a four-year term. The President of the Republic (also directly elected for four years) is Head of State and holds executive power in conjunction with the Council of Ministers, headed by the Prime Minister. The provisions of the Constitution are protected by a Constitutional Court.

The Constitution granted the hitherto separatist regions of Transdnestria and Gagauzia 'special legal status' (see Recent History).

## The Government

### HEAD OF STATE

**President:** MIRCEA SNEGUR (directly elected 8 December 1991).

### COUNCIL OF MINISTERS
(June 1995)

**Prime Minister:** ANDREI SANGHELI.
**Deputy Prime Ministers:** VALENTIN CUNEV, ION GUȚU, VALERIU BULGARI, GRIGORE OJOG.
**Minister of State:** GHEORGHE GUSAC.
**Minister of the Economy:** VALERIU BOBUȚAC.
**Minister of Finance:** VALERIU CHIȚAN.
**Minister of Privatization and Administration of State Property:** CESLAV CIOBANU.
**Minister of Industry:** GRIGORE TRIBOI.
**Minister of Agriculture and Food:** VITALIE GORINCIOI.
**Minister of Communications and Informatics:** ION CASIAN.
**Minister of Labour and Social Security:** DUMITRU NEDELCU.
**Minister of Health:** TIMOFEI MOȘNEAGA.
**Minister of Education:** PETRU GAUGAȘ.
**Minister of Culture:** MIHAI CIBOTARU.
**Minister of Justice:** VASILE STURZA.
**Minister of Defence:** PAVEL CREANGĂ.
**Minister of the Interior:** CONSTANTIN ANTOCI.
**Minister of National Security:** VASILE CALMOI.
**Minister of Foreign Affairs:** MIHAI POPOV.
**Minister of Transport:** VASILE IOVV.
**Minister of Public Works:** MIHAI SEVEROVAN.
**Minister of Relations with Parliament:** VICTOR PUȘCAȘ.
**Bashkan (Leader) of Gagauzia:** GHEORGHE TABUNSHCHIK.

### CHAIRMEN OF STATE DEPARTMENTS

**Chairman of the State Department for Customs:** GHEORGHE HIOARĂ.

**Chairman of the State Department for Energy and Energy Resources:** VALERIU ICONNICOV.
**Chairman of the State Department for Environmental Protection:** ION DEDIU.
**Chairman of the State Department for the Gas Industry:** BORIS CARANDIUC.
**Chairman of the State Department for Privatization:** VISARION CEȘUEV.
**Chairman of the State Department for Publishing:** AUREL SCOBIOALĂ.
**Chairman of the State Department for Technology:** DUMITRU CIMPOIEȘ.

### MINISTRIES

**Ministry of Agriculture and Food:** Chișinău, Ștefan cel Mare; tel. (2) 23-35-36.
**Ministry of Communications and Informatics:** 277012 Chișinău, Ștefan cel Mare 134; tel. (2) 22-10-01; telex 163227; fax (2) 24-15-53.
**Ministry of Culture:** 277033 Chișinău, Piața Marii Adunări Naționale 1; tel. (2) 23-39-56; telex 136137; fax (2) 23-23-88.
**Ministry of Defence:** 277048 Chișinău, str. Hîncești 84; tel. (2) 23-26-31; fax (2) 23-45-35.
**Ministry of the Economy:** 277033 Chișinău, Piața Marii Adunări Naționale 1; tel. (2) 23-31-35; fax (2) 23-40-64.
**Ministry of Education:** 277033 Chișinău, Piața Marii Adunări Naționale 1; tel. (2) 23-35-15; fax (2) 23-34-74.
**Ministry of Finance:** 277033 Chișinău, Cosmonauților 7; tel. (2) 23-35-75.
**Ministry of Foreign Affairs:** 277033 Chișinău, Piața Marii Adunări Naționale 1; tel. (2) 23-39-40; telex 163130; fax (2) 23-23-02.
**Ministry of Health:** Chișinău, str. Hîncești 1; tel. (2) 72-10-10.
**Ministry of Industry:** 277001 Chișinău, Ștefan cel Mare 69; tel. (2) 23-35-56; telex 163177; fax (2) 22-24-73.
**Ministry of the Interior:** Chișinău, Ștefan cel Mare 67; tel. (2) 23-35-69.
**Ministry of Justice:** 277012 Chișinău, str. 23 August 82; tel. (2) 23-33-15; fax (2) 23-47-97.
**Ministry of Labour and Social Security:** 277009 Chișinău, str. Hîncești 1; tel. (2) 72-99-86; fax (2) 72-30-00.
**Ministry of National Security:** Chișinău, Ștefan cel Mare 166; tel. (2) 23-93-09.
**Ministry of Privatization and Administration of State Property:** Chișinău.
**Ministry of Public Works:** 277028 Chișinău, str. Gh. Tudor 3; tel. (2) 25-91-11; telex 163133; fax (2) 25-94-99.
**Ministry of Relations with Parliament:** Chișinău.
**Ministry of Transport:** 277004 Chișinău, Bucuriey 12A; tel. (2) 62-05-70; fax (2) 62-48-75.

### State Departments

**State Department for Customs:** Chișinău.
**State Department for Energy and Energy Resources:** 277012 Chișinău, M. Eminescu 50; tel. (2) 22-40-30; fax (2) 22-22-64.

MOLDOVA                                                                                                                                              *Directory*

**State Department for Environmental Protection:** 277001 Chişinău, Ştefan cel Mare 73; tel. (2) 22-61-61; fax (2) 23-38-06.

**State Department for the Gas Industry:** Chişinău, str. Albisoara 38; tel. (2) 24-05-29.

**State Department for Privatization:** Chişinău.

**State Department for Publishing:** 277004 Chişinău, Ştefan cel Mare 180; tel. (2) 24-65-25; fax (2) 24-64-12.

**State Department for Technology:** Chişinău.

## Legislature

### MOLDOVAN PARLIAMENT

**Chairman:** PETRU LUCINSCHI.

**Deputy Chairmen:** DUMITRU MOTPAN, NICOLAE ANDRONIC.

**General Election, 27 February 1994**

| Parties and alliances | % of votes | Seats |
| --- | --- | --- |
| Agrarian Democratic Party | 43.2 | 56 |
| Socialist Party/Yedinstvo (Unity) Movement | 22.0 | 28 |
| Peasants' Party of Moldova/Congress of Intelligentsia | 9.2 | 11 |
| Christian Democratic Popular Front alliance | 7.5 | 9 |
| Other parties* | 18.1 | — |
| **Total** | **100.0** | **104** |

* Including the Social Democratic Party of Moldova, the Democratic Labour Party of Moldova and the Reform Party.

## Political Organizations

**Agrarian Democratic Party (ADP):** Chişinău; f. by moderates from both the Popular Front of Moldova and the Communist Party of Moldova; supports Moldovan independence, CIS membership and economic and agricultural reform; Leader PETRU LUCINSCHI; Chair. DUMITRU MOTPAN.

**Christian Democratic Popular Front (CDPF):** 277014 Chişinău, str. Nicolae Iorga 5; tel. (2) 22-50-64; fax (2) 23-44-80; f. 1989 as the Popular Front of Moldova, renamed 1992; advocates Moldova's reintegration into Romania; Chair. IURIE ROSCA.

**Congress of Intelligentsia:** Chişinău; f. 1993 by former Popular Front of Moldova members; favours union with Romania.

**Democratic Labour Party of Moldova:** Chişinău; f. 1993; Pres. ALEXANDRU ARSENI.

**Liberal Democracy Party:** Chişinău; Co-Chair. NICOLAE CHIRTOACA.

**Moldovan Party of Communists:** Chişinău; fmrly the Communist Party of Moldova (banned Aug. 1991); revived as above 1994; First Sec. VLADIMIR VORONIN.

**Peasants' Party of Moldova:** Chişinău; nationalist, moderate party.

**Reform Party:** Chişinău; f. 1993; centre-right party which seeks to represent middle-class interests; Leader ANATOL SALARU; Chair. ŞTEFAN GORDA.

**Social Democratic Party of Moldova:** Chişinău; f. 1990; centrist party advocating full Moldovan independence and rejecting any forms of extremism or violence; Chair. ANATOL TARANU.

**Socialist Party:** Chişinău; successor to the former Communist Party of Moldova; favours socialist economic and social policies, defends the rights of Russian and other minorities and advocates CIS membership; Leader VALERIU SENIC.

**Yedinstvo (Unity) Movement:** 277009 Chişinău, str. Hînceşti 35; tel. (2) 23-79-52; f. 1989; represents interests of ethnic minorities in Moldova; Chair. PETR SHORNIKOV.

Parties and organizations in Transdnestria include: the Union of Patriotic Forces (Tiraspol; radical socialist; Leader VASILY YAKOVLEV); the United Council of Workers' Collectives (Tiraspol; radical); 'For Accord and Stability' (Tiraspol; moderate); and 'Position' (Tiraspol; moderate; Leader SVETLANA MIGULEA).

Parties and organizations in Gagauzia include: the Vatan (Motherland) Party (Comrat; Leader ANDREI CHESHMEJI) and Gagauz Halky (Gagauz People) (Comrat).

## Diplomatic Representation

### EMBASSIES IN MOLDOVA

**Bulgaria:** Chişinău, str. 31 August 135, Hotel Dacia; tel. (2) 23-79-83; fax (2) 23-24-01; Ambassador: BRONIMIR RADEV.

**China, People's Republic:** Chişinău, str. Cireşilor 66; tel. (2) 73-36-04; fax (2) 73-35-67; Ambassador: DENG CHAOCONG.

**Germany:** 277012 Chişinău, str. Maria Ciubotaru 37, Hotel Seabeco, Suite 622; tel. (2) 23-28-72; fax (2) 23-46-80; Chargé d'affaires a.i.: JOHANNES GIFFELS.

**Hungary:** Chişinău, Ştefan cel Mare 131; tel. (2) 22-83-53; fax (2) 22-83-94; Ambassador: JÓZSEF NAGY.

**Poland:** Chişinău, str. 31 August 135, Hotel Dacia; tel. and fax (2) 23-34-38; Ambassador: VIKTOR ROSS.

**Romania:** Chişinău, str. Bucureşti 66/1; tel. (2) 23-34-69; fax (2) 23-75-83; Ambassador: MARIAN ENACHE.

**Russia:** Chişinău, str. Mateevici 78; tel. (2) 22-85-73; fax (2) 23-26-00; Ambassador: ALEKSANDR PAPKIN.

**Turkey:** Chişinău, str. Mateevici 67; tel. (2) 24-52-92; fax (2) 22-55-28; Ambassador: TANIN SARP TEVFIC.

**Ukraine:** 277012 Chişinău, str. 31 August 127; tel. (2) 23-79-19; fax (2) 23-79-22; Chargé d'affaires a.i.: EUGEN LEVITSKY.

**USA:** Chişinău, str. Mateevici 103; tel. (2) 23-37-72; fax (2) 23-24-94; Ambassador: MARY C. PENDLETON.

## Judicial System

**Chairman of the Supreme Court:** VICTOR PUŞCAŞ.

**Chairman of the Constitutional Court:** PAVEL BARBALAT.

**Procurator-General:** DUMITRU POSTOVAN.

## Religion

The majority of the inhabitants of Moldova profess Christianity, the largest denomination being the Eastern Orthodox Church. The Gagauz, although of Turkic descent, are also adherents of Orthodox Christianity.

### Roman Catholic Church

The diocese of Tiraspol was founded in 1848, but has been inoperative for many years. In 1993 there were an estimated 15,000 Catholics in Moldova.

**Apostolic Administrator of Moldova:** Mgr ANTON COŞA, 277012 Chişinău, str. Mitropolit Dosoftei 85; tel. (2) 22-85-84.

### Russian Orthodox Church

In December 1992 the Patriarch of Moscow and All Russia issued a decree altering the status of the Eparchy of Chişinău and Moldova to that of a Metropolitan See. The Government accepted this decree, thus tacitly rejecting the claims of the Metropolitan of Bessarabia.

**Archbishop of Chişinău and Moldova:** VLADIMIR.

## The Press

In 1989 there were 200 officially-registered newspapers published in Moldova (including 85 published in Romanian), and 65 periodicals (including 30 in Romanian). In 1990 the number of Romanian-language newspapers and periodicals increased, and most publications began using the Latin script.

The publications listed below are in Romanian, except where otherwise indicated.

### PRINCIPAL NEWSPAPERS

**Curierul de Seară** (Evening Herald): Chişinău.

**Dnestrovskaya Pravda** (Dnestr Truth): Tiraspol; Russian.

**Glasul Naţiunii** (Voice of the Nation): Chişinău; weekly.

**Kishinyovskiye Novosti** (Chişinău News): Chişinău; Russian.

**Moldova Suverană** (Sovereign Moldova): 277012 Chişinău, str. Puşkin 22; tel. (2) 23-35-38; fax (2) 23-31-10; f. 1924; 4 a week; organ of the Govt of Moldova; Editor ANDREI HROPOTINSCHI; circ. 100,000.

**Nezavisimaya Moldova** (Independent Moldova): 277612 Chişinău, str. Puşkin 22; tel. (2) 23-36-05; fax (2) 23-36-08; f. 1925; 5 a week; independent; Russian; Editor BORIS MARIAN; circ. 60,692.

**Ţara** (Homeland): Chişinău; organ of the Christian Democratic Popular Front; circ. 8,000.

**Tinerimya Moldovei/Molodezh Moldovy** (Youth of Moldova): Chişinău; f. 1928; 3 a week; editions in Romanian (circ. 12,212) and Russian (circ. 4,274); Editor V. BOTNARU.

**Trudovoy Tiraspol** (Working Tiraspol): Tiraspol, str. 25 October 101; tel. (33) 3-04-12; f. 1989; main newspaper of the east-bank Slavs; Russian; Editor DIMA KONDRATOVICH; circ. 7,500.

# MOLDOVA

*Directory*

**Viaţă Satului** (Life of the Village): 277612 Chişinău, str. Puşkin 22, Casa presei, et. 4; tel. (2) 23-03-68; f. 1945; 3 a week; govt publ.; Editor V. S. Spiney; circ. 50,000.

### PRINCIPAL PERIODICALS

**Basarabia** (Bessarabia): Chişinău; f. 1931; fmrly *Nistru*; monthly; journal of the Union of Writers of Moldova; fiction; Editor-in-Chief D. Matkovsky; circ. 4,500.

**Chipăruş** (Peppercorn): 277612 Chişinău, str. Puşkin 22; tel. (2) 23-38-16; f. 1958; fortnightly; satirical; Editor-in-Chief Ion Vikol; circ. 6,000.

**Femeia Moldovei** (Moldovan Woman): 233470 Chişinău, str. 28 June 45; tel. (2) 23-31-64; f. 1951; monthly; popular, for women; circ. 25,468.

**Lanterna Magică** (Magic Lantern): Chişinău, str. Bucureşti 39; tel. (2) 26-51-77; telex 163137; fax (2) 23-23-88; f. 1990; publ. by the Ministry of Culture; 6 a year; art, culture; circ. 2,500.

**Literatură şi Artă:** 277009 Chişinău, str. Sfatul Ţării; tel. (2) 24-92-96; f. 1954; weekly; organ of the Union of Writers of Moldova; literary; Editor Nicolae Dabija; circ. 100,000.

**Moldova:** Chişinău; f. 1966; monthly; illustrated popular and fiction; circ. 4,855.

**Noi** (Us): Chişinău; tel. (2) 23-31-10; f. 1930; fmrly *Scînteia Leninista*; monthly; fiction; for 10–15-year-olds; Man. Valeriu Volontir; circ. 8,900.

**Sud-Est** (South East): Chişinău, str. Maria Ciubotaru 16; tel. (2) 23-26-05; fax (2) 23-22-42; f. 1990; publ. by the Ministry of Culture; quarterly; art, culture; Editor-in-Chief Valentina Taslauana; circ. 5,000.

### NEWS AGENCY

**Moldovan Information Agency—Bassapres:** 277012 Chişinău, str. Hînceşti 72; tel. (2) 22-84-41; fax (2) 22-13-96.

**State Information Agency—Moldpres:** 277012 Chişinău, str. Puşkin 22; tel. (2) 23-34-28; telex 163140; fax (2) 23-43-71; f. 1990 as Moldovapres, reorganized 1994.

## Publishers

In 1989 there were 1,479 titles (books and pamphlets) published in Moldova (21.3m. copies), of which 522 titles were in Romanian (9.5m. copies).

**Editura Enciclopedică:** 277612 Chişinău, Ştefan cel Mare 180; tel. (2) 24-68-92; Editor-in-Chief Ion Grosu.

**Humanitas:** Chişinău, Ştefan cel Mare; political and fiction; Romanian, Russian, Ukrainian, Gagauz and Bulgarian; Dir N. N. Mumzhi.

**Hyperion:** 277004 Chişinău, Ştefan cel Mare; tel. (2) 24-64-14; f. 1977; fiction, non-fiction, poetry, art books; Romanian, Russian, English, French, Spanish, Gagauz and Bulgarian; Dir Valeriu Matei.

**Lumina** (Light): Chişinău, Ştefan cel Mare 180; tel. (2) 24-63-95; f. 1966; educational textbooks; Man. Vladimir I. Kistruga; Editor-in-Chief Chiril T. Vakulovsky.

**Ştiinţa:** Chişinău, str. Academic 3; tel. (2) 73-96-16; f. 1959; scientific literature; Romanian and Russian; Dir G. N. Prini.

**Universitas:** 277009 Chişinău, str. Mateevici 60; tel. (2) 24-00-41; fax 24-06-55; Editor-in-Chief Iurie Kolesnik.

### GOVERNMENT AGENCY

**State Department for Publishing:** 277004 Chişinău, Ştefan cel Mare 180; tel. (2) 24-65-25; fax (2) 24-64-12; Chair. Aurel Scobioală.

## Radio and Television

**State Radio and Television Company of Moldova** (Compania de Stat Teleradio-Moldova): 277028 Chişinău, str. Mioriţa 1; tel. (2) 72-10-77; telex 163210; fax (2) 72-33-52; f. 1994; Pres. Adrian Usatîi.

**Radio Chişinău:** 277028 Chişinău, str. Mioriţa 1; tel. (2) 72-10-77; f. 1930; broadcasts in Romanian, Russian, Ukrainian, Gagauz and Yiddish; Dir-Gen. Alexandru Dorogan.

**Chişinău Television:** 277028 Chişinău, str. Hînceşti 64; tel. (2) 73-94-70; f. 1958; Dir-Gen. Dumitru Ţurcanu.

## Finance

(cap. = capital; res = reserves; dep. = deposits; m. = million; brs = branches; amounts in Moldovan lei, unless otherwise stated)

### BANKING

Restructuring of Moldova's banking system was begun in 1991 with the establishment of a central bank, the National Bank of Moldova (NBM), which was formerly a branch of the USSR Gosbank (state bank). The NBM is independent of the Government (but subordinate to Parliament) and has the power to regulate monetary policy and the financial system. In 1993, apart from the NBM, the banking system comprised the Savings Bank of Moldova (with a total of 4.5m. accounts) and 17 other commercial banks.

### Central Bank

**National Bank of Moldova:** 277006 Chişinău, Renasterii 7; tel. (2) 22-16-79; telex 163213; fax (2) 22-95-91; f. 1991; res 1.7m., dep. 725.6m. (Jan. 1994); Dir Leonid Talmaci.

### Commercial Banks

**Banca socială:** 277006 Chişinău, str. Banulescu Bodony 61; tel. (2) 22-86-02; telex 163265; fax (2) 22-31-32; f. 1991; joint-stock commercial bank; cap. 3.4m., dep. 1.5m. (1993); Pres. Vladimir Suetnov; First Vice-Pres. Aglaya Krivchanskaya; 13 brs.

**Bancosind:** 277036 Chişinău, str. Puşkin 26; tel. (2) 22-36-31; fax (2) 22-55-86; trade-union bank; Chair. Boris Cojuhari.

**Commercial Besarabiabank:** 277006 Chişinău, str. Puşkin 42; tel. (2) 24-07-57; fax (2) 24-47-54; Chair. Gheorghe Andries.

**Intreprinzbank:** 277036 Chişinău, str. Sfatul Ţării 16; tel. (2) 47-11-89; fax (2) 22-51-70; Chair. Pavel Vizer.

**Moldmebelbank:** 277001 Chişinău, str. Tighina 65; tel. (2) 22-89-50; telex 163169; fax (2) 22-50-11; Chair. Nicolai Dorin.

**Moldindconbanc SA:** 277006 Chişinău, Renasterii 7; tel. (2) 22-55-21; telex 163228; fax (2) 22-93-82; f. 1991; joint-stock commercial bank; cap. 5.5m. (March 1995); Chair. Anatol I. Ţurcanu; 24 brs.

**Moldova-Agroindbanc SA:** 277006 Chişinău, Renasterii 7; tel. (2) 22-83-17; telex 163263; fax (2) 23-27-06; f. 1991; joint-stock commercial bank; cap. 2,725m. roubles, dep. 1,030m. roubles (Aug. 1993); Chair. Grigore Furtună; 43 brs.

**Promstroibank:** 129700 Ribniţa, Promislennii 2; tel. (55) 5-00-39; fax (55) 3-23-95; Chair. Nina Iusupova.

**Victoriabank:** 277004 Chişinău, str. 31 August 141; tel. (2) 23-30-65; telex 163188; fax (2) 23-39-33; Chair. Victor Ţurcanu; 3 brs.

### Savings Bank

**Savings Bank of Moldova** (Banca de economii a Moldovei): 277006 Chişinău, Cosmonauţilor 9; tel. (2) 22-52-27; fax (2) 24-47-31; f. 1992; cap 5.4m., res 1.2m., dep. 64.2m. (March 1995); Chair. Constantin Bulgac; 46 brs.

### Foreign Bank

**Finist Bank** (Russia): 278000 Tiraspol, str. K. Liebknecht; tel. (33) 3-64-75.

## Trade and Industry

### CHAMBER OF COMMERCE

**Chamber of Commerce and Industry of the Republic of Moldova:** 277012 Chişinău, M. Eminescu 28; tel. (2) 22-15-52; telex 163118; fax (2) 23-38-10; f. 1969; Chair. Vasily D. Gandrabura.

### FOREIGN TRADE ORGANIZATIONS

**Moldimpex:** 277018 Chişinău, Botanicheskaya 15; tel. (2) 55-70-36; Gen. Dir V. D. Volodin.

### CONSUMER ORGANIZATION

**Union of Consumers' Societies of Moldova:** 277001 Chişinău, Ştefan cel Mare 67; tel. (2) 23-35-95; telex 163155; fax (2) 26-24-84; f. 1925; Chair. Pavel G. Dubalar.

### TRADE UNIONS

**Federation of Independent Trade Unions of Moldova:** Chişinău, str. 31 August 129; tel. (2) 23-74-92; fax (2) 23-76-98; f. 1990; Pres. Ion Godonoga.

## Transport

### RAILWAYS

**Moldovan Railways:** 277012 Chişinău, str. Vlaicu Pîrcălab 48; tel. (2) 23-25-83; fax (2) 22-13-80; f. 1992 following the dissolution of the former Soviet Railways (SZD) organization; total network 1,300 km; Pres. G. Mikenberg.

### ROADS

At the end of 1992 Moldova's total network of roads (including urban roads) was 14,508 km, of which some 12,330 km were hard-surfaced. The total network included 5,006 km of highways or main roads and 5,604 km of secondary or regional roads. In that

# MOLDOVA

year there was a total of 242,292 passenger cars, buses and goods vehicles in use.

### INLAND WATERWAYS

In 1994 the total length of navigable waterways in Moldova was 424 km. The main river ports are at Bender (Benderi), Ribniţa and Ungeni.

### SHIPPING

**Joint-Stock Shipping Co Neptun:** 277012 Chişinău, str. Hînceşti 119; tel. and fax (2) 22-69-54; Gen. Dir Victor Andruşca.

### CIVIL AVIATION

**Department of Civil Aviation:** 277026 Chişinău Airport; tel. (2) 52-60-82; fax (2) 52-49-25; Dir Pavel Leşan.

**Air Moldova:** 277026 Chişinău Airport; tel. (2) 52-60-82; telex 163169; fax (2) 52-49-25; scheduled and charter passenger and cargo flights to destinations in Europe and the CIS; Dir-Gen. Pavel Leşan.

**Moldavian Airlines:** 277026 Chişinău Airport; f. 1994; scheduled and charter passenger and cargo flights to destinations in the CIS.

## Tourism

**Moldova-Tur:** 277058 Chişinău, Ştefan cel Mare 4; tel. (2) 26-66-79; telex 162112; fax (2) 26-25-86; f. 1990; Dir-Gen. Nicolae Chernomaz.

# MONACO

## Introductory Survey

### Location, Climate, Language, Religion, Flag

The Principality of Monaco lies in western Europe. The country is a small enclave in south-eastern France, about 15 km east of Nice. It has a coastline on the Mediterranean Sea but is otherwise surrounded by French territory. The climate is Mediterranean, with warm summers and very mild winters. The official language is French, but Monégasque (a mixture of the French Provençal and Italian Ligurian dialects), Italian and English are also spoken. Most of the population profess Christianity, with more than 90% belonging to the Roman Catholic Church. The national flag (proportions officially 5 by 4) has two equal horizontal stripes, of red and white. The state flag (proportions 5 by 4) displays the princely arms of Monaco (a white shield, held by two monks and superimposed on a pavilion of ermine) on a white background.

### History

The Principality of Monaco is an hereditary monarchy, which has been ruled by the Grimaldi dynasty since 1297. It was abolished during the French Revolution but re-established in 1814. In 1861 Monaco became an independent state under the protection of France. The Constitution, which was promulgated in January 1911, vested legislative power jointly in the Prince and an 18-member Conseil National, selected for a term of five years by a panel comprising nine delegates of the municipality and 21 members elected by universal suffrage. Agreements in 1918 and 1919 between France and Monaco provided for Monaco's incorporation into France should the reigning prince die without leaving a male heir. Prince Louis II, the ruler of Monaco since 1922, died in May 1949, and was succeeded by his grandson, Prince Rainier III. A new Constitution, introduced in December 1962, abolished the formerly-held principle of the divine right of the ruler, and stipulated that the Conseil National be elected by universal adult suffrage.

At legislative elections in 1963 a grouping of candidates who supported Prince Rainier, known as the Union Nationale et Démocratique (UND), won 17 of the 18 seats on the Conseil National, while an opposition grouping, the Mouvement d'Union Démocratique (MUD), secured the remaining seat. At elections in 1968 the UND obtained all 18 seats; in 1973, however, the MUD and another opposition grouping, Action Monégasque, won a seat each (but both later became inactive). At subsequent elections, which took place in 1978, 1983 and 1988, the UND secured all 18 seats on the Conseil National. At elections in January 1993, however, two lists of candidates, known as the Liste Campora and the Liste Médecin, secured 15 and two seats respectively, while an independent candidate won the remaining seat.

In October 1994 an agreement between the French and Monégasque authorities, providing for the official exchange of financial information that would assist in the detection of criminal activities, was designed to reduce the illegal transfer of funds to banks in Monaco. In December of that year the Minister of State was replaced. In early 1995 rumours emerged that Prince Rainier (who had undergone surgery in late 1994) intended to abdicate in favour of his son, Prince Albert.

Monaco participates in the work of a number of international organizations, and in May 1993 was admitted to membership of the UN.

### Government

Legislative power is vested jointly in the Prince, an hereditary ruler, and the 18-member Conseil National, which is elected by universal adult suffrage, under a system of proportional representation, for a term of five years. The electorate comprises only Monégasque citizens aged 21 years or over. Executive power is exercised, under the authority of the Prince, by the four-member Council of Government, headed by the Minister of State (a French civil servant selected by the Prince from a list of three candidates presented by the French Government). The Prince represents the Principality in its relations with foreign powers, and signs and ratifies treaties.

### Economic Affairs

There are no available data for gross national product (GNP) or gross domestic product (GDP) in Monaco separate from the figures for France. Monaco has the highest population density of all the independent states in the world.

There is no agricultural land in Monaco. In 1990 a Belgian enterprise established an offshore fish farm for sea bass and sea bream; production was projected to reach 1,000 tons in 1993.

Industry accounted for 27% of economic activity in 1990, and employed 25% of the labour force in 1986. Industry is mainly light in Monaco. The principal sectors, measured by gross value of output, are chemicals and pharmaceuticals, plastics, micro-electronics and electrical goods, paper and card manufacture, and clothing and textiles.

Service industries represent the most significant sector of the economy in Monaco. Banking and finance accounted for more than 38% of the services sector and employed 5.7% of the labour force in 1988. At mid-1994 the total value of deposits in Monaco's private banking sector was estimated at 80,000m. French francs. Real estate accounted for 26% of the sector in 1991.

Tourism is also an important source of income, providing an estimated 25% of total government revenue in 1991. In 1993 208,206 tourists (excluding excursionists) visited Monaco, representing a decline of 15%, compared with 1992. Including excursionists, some 4m. people visited the Principality in 1992, and in that year revenue from tourism totalled US $1,300m. The greatest number of visitors in 1993 were from Italy (33%) and France (17%). In 1994 the conference industry accounted for about one-third of Monaco's foreign visitors.

Monaco's external trade is included in the figures for France. Revenue is derived principally from real estate, light and medium industry, indirect taxation and tourism.

In 1993 there was a budgetary deficit of 29.7m. francs: expenditure amounted to 3,327.9m. francs. In 1987 value-added tax contributed 55% to total government revenue. At the end of March 1994 about 700 people were unemployed in the Principality.

Monaco is largely dependent on imports from France, owing to its lack of natural resources. There is a severe labour shortage in the Principality, and the economy is reliant on migrant workers (many of whom are from France and Italy). Following the establishment of a casino in the 1860s, tourism became the dominant sector in the economy. In the 1980s, however, the sectors of industry and real estate expanded, after a series of land reclamation projects increased Monaco's area by 20%. In addition, a number of foreign companies and banks are registered in Monaco in order to take advantage of the low rates of taxation on company profits. Since the removal of French restrictions on foreign exchange in 1987 Monaco's banking industry (which includes an offshore banking sector) has expanded. In the early 1990s, however, the tourism and property-development sectors contracted (despite the comparative overall stability of the economy); the Government continued its policy of promoting economic diversification, with the implementation of a programme of public works, which was designed to encourage the establishment of small industrial enterprises. In 1994 several land reclamation projects were under way, while the construction of a new conference and cultural centre, scheduled for completion in 1998, was expected to result in the further expansion of Monaco's business conference industry.

### Public Holidays

**1995:** 1 January (New Year's Day), 27 January (Feast of St Dévote, Patron Saint of the Principality), 17 April (Easter Monday), 1 May (Fête du Travail), 25 May (Ascension Day), 5 June (Whit Monday), 15 August (Assumption), 1 November (All Saints' Day), 19 November (National Day/Fête du Prince), 8 December (Immaculate Conception), 25–26 December (Christmas).

**1996:** 1 January (New Year's Day), 27 January (Feast of St Dévote, Patron Saint of the Principality), 8 April (Easter Monday), 1 May (Fête du Travail), 16 May (Ascension Day), 27 May (Whit Monday), 15 August (Assumption), 1 November (All Saints' Day), 19 November (National Day/Fête du Prince), 8 December (Immaculate Conception), 25–26 December (Christmas).

**Weights and Measures**
The metric system is in force.

# Statistical Survey

Source: Centre de Presse de la Principauté de Monaco; tel. 93-30-42-27; fax 93-15-01-54.

### AREA AND POPULATION
**Area:** 1.95 sq km.
**Population:** 27,063 (males 12,598; females 14,465) at census of 4 March 1982; 29,876 at census of July 1990.
**Density** (1990): 15,321 per sq km.
**Births, Marriages and Deaths** (1990): Live births 717; Marriages 187; Deaths 536.

### FINANCE
**Currency and Exchange Rates:** French currency: 100 centimes = 1 franc. *Sterling and Dollar Equivalents* (31 December 1994): £1 sterling = 8.349 francs; US $1 = 5.337 francs; 1,000 French francs = £119.77 = $187.38. *Average Exchange Rate* (French francs per US dollar): 5.294 in 1992; 5.663 in 1993; 5.552 in 1994.
*Note:* Some Monégasque currency, at par with the French, also circulates.
**Budget** (million francs, 1993): Revenue 3,298.2; Expenditure 3,327.9.

### EXTERNAL TRADE
Monaco's imports and exports are included in the figures for France.

### TRANSPORT
**Road Traffic** (vehicles in use at 31 December 1988): Cars 16,851; Buses and coaches 62; Goods vehicles 614; Vans 2,995; Total 20,482. Source: International Road Federation, *World Road Statistics*.

### TOURISM
**Visitor Arrivals** (1993): 208,206 (excluding excursionists).

### COMMUNICATIONS MEDIA
**Radio Receivers** (1992): 30,000 in use.
**Television Receivers** (1992): 22,000 in use.
Source: UNESCO, *Statistical Yearbook*.
**Telephones** (1991, estimate) 26,000 main lines in use. Source: UN, *Statistical Yearbook*.

### EDUCATION
(1991)
**Primary:** 7 schools; 60 teachers; 1,761 pupils (males 892; females 869).
**General Secondary:** 181 teachers; 2,383 pupils (males 1,163; females 1,220).
**Vocational:** 145 teachers (1990); 475 pupils (males 304; females 171).
Source: UNESCO, *Statistical Yearbook*.

# Directory

## The Constitution

The Constitution of 17 December 1962 vests legislative power jointly in the Prince and the 18-member Conseil National, which is elected by universal adult suffrage, under a system of proportional representation, for a term of five years. Executive power is exercised, under the authority of the Prince, by the four-member Council of Government, headed by the Minister of State. The Constitution maintains the traditional hereditary monarchy, although the principle of the divine right of the ruler is renounced. The right of association, trade union freedom and the right to strike are guaranteed. The Supreme Tribunal safeguards fundamental liberties. Any future constitutional amendments are to be submitted for approval by the Conseil National.

## The Government

### HEAD OF STATE
HSH Prince RAINIER III (succeeded 9 May 1949).

### MINISTERS
(May 1995)
**Chief of the Cabinet:** DENIS RAVERA.
**Minister of State:** PAUL DIJOUD.

### Government Councillors
**Interior:** JEAN ARIBAUD.
**Finance and Economic Affairs:** ETIENNE FRANZI.
**Public Works and Social Affairs:** JOSÉ BADIA.

### MINISTRIES
The address for all Ministries is: BP 522, MC 98015; tel. 93-15-80-00; telex 469942; fax 93-15-82-17.

## Legislature

### CONSEIL NATIONAL
The Conseil National has 18 members. At the most recent elections, which took place on 24 January and 31 January 1993, the **Liste Campora** secured 15 seats, the **Liste Médecin** two seats, and an independent candidate the remaining seat.
**President:** JEAN-LOUIS CAMPORA.
**Vice-President:** JEAN-JOSEPH PASTOR.

## Political Organizations

There are no political parties as such in Monaco; however, candidates are generally grouped into lists to contest elections to the Conseil National. Between 1963 and 1992 the Conseil National was dominated by representatives of the **Union Nationale et Démocratique** (National and Democratic Union). At the 1993 elections, however, the two main groupings were the **Liste Campora**, led by JEAN-LOUIS CAMPORA, and the **Liste Médecin**, led by JEAN-LOUIS MÉDECIN.

## Diplomatic Representation

There are no embassies in Monaco, but diplomatic relations are maintained at consular level with 48 countries.

MONACO
*Directory*

## Judicial System

The organization of the legal system is similar to that of France. There is one Justice of the Peace, a Tribunal de Première Instance (Court of First Instance), a Cour d'Appel (Court of Appeal), a Cour de Révision (High Court of Appeal), a Tribunal Criminel (Crown Court) and finally the Tribunal Suprême (Supreme Tribunal), which deals with infringements of the rights and liberties provided by the Constitution, and also with legal actions aiming at the annulment of administrative decisions for abusive exercise of power.

**Palais de Justice:** rue Col Bellando de Castro, BP 513, MC 98025 Monaco Cedex; tel. 93-15-80-00; fax 93-50-05-68.
**Director of Judicial Services:** NOËL MUSEUX.
**President of the Supreme Tribunal:** RENÉ-JEAN DUPUY.
**President of the High Court of Appeal:** JEAN BEL.
**President of the Court of Appeal:** HENRI CHARLIAC.
**President of the Court of First Instance:** JEAN-FRANÇOIS LANDWERLIN.

## Religion

### CHRISTIANITY

#### The Roman Catholic Church

Monaco comprises a single archdiocese, directly responsible to the Holy See. At 31 December 1993 there were an estimated 27,000 adherents in the country, representing more than 90% of the total population.

**Archbishop of Monaco:** Most Rev. JOSEPH-MARIE SARDOU, Archevêché, 1 rue de l'Abbaye, BP 517, MC 98015; tel. 93-30-88-10; fax 92-16-73-88.

#### The Anglican Communion

Within the Church of England, Monaco forms part of the diocese of Gibraltar in Europe.
**Chaplain:** Rev. BARRY W. THOMAS, St Paul's Church House, ave de Grande Bretagne, MC 98000; tel. 93-30-71-06.

There are also a Protestant church and a synagogue in the Principality.

## The Press

**Gazette Monaco—Côte d'Azur:** 25 blvd Albert 1er, MC 98000; tel. 93-25-20-36; fax 93-25-14-64; f. 1976; monthly; regional information; Dir-Gen. JEAN CLAUDE MARSAN; Chief Editor NOËLLE BINE-MULLER; circ. 10,000.
**Journal de Monaco:** BP 522, MC 98015; tel. 92-16-60-30; fax 93-30-36-49; f. 1858; edited at the Ministry of State; official weekly; contains texts of laws and decrees; Man. Editor RAINIER IMPERTI.
**Monaco Actualité:** 2 rue du Gabia, MC 98000; tel. 92-05-75-36; fax 92-05-75-34; Dir-Gen. MAURICE RICCOBONO; circ. 15,000.
**Monte Carlo Méditerranée:** 9 ave des Castelans, MC 98000 Monaco; tel. 92-05-67-67; fax 92-05-37-01; Dir-Gen. GÉRARD COMMAN; Chief Editor CAROLE CHABRIER.

French newspapers are widely read and a special Monaco edition of *Nice Matin* is published in Nice, France.

### NEWS AGENCY

**Agence France-Presse (AFP):** 2 blvd des Moulins, MC 98000; tel. 93-30-36-49; telex 469760; fax 93-50-92-80; Rep. GEORGES BERTELOTTI.

## Publishers

**Avenir Publications:** 25 blvd d'Italie, MC 98005; tel. 93-05-53-63; telex 489994; fax 93-25-87-99; scientific and technical.
**EDIPROM:** 9 ave des Castelans, MC 98000; tel. 92-05-67-67; fax 92-05-37-01; advertising material, official publications; Pres. GÉRARD COMMAN.
**Editions Latino-Americaines SAM:** 1 rue Bel Respiro, MC 98000; tel. 93-50-56-52; medical; Pres. MICHÈLE GHIENA; Dir PAUL DUCARTERON.
**Editions de l'Oiseau-Lyre SAM:** 20 rue des Remparts, MC 98015 Monaco Cedex; tel. 93-30-09-44; fax 93-30-19-15; f. 1932; music publishers; Dir MARGARITA M. HANSON.
**Editions de Radio Monte Carlo SAM:** 16 blvd Princesse Charlotte, MC 98080; tel. 93-50-52-52; general; Dir ROBERT PINTO.
**Editions Regain S.N.C. Boy et Cie:** 10 blvd d'Italie, MC 98000; tel. 93-50-62-04; f. 1946; fiction, essays, autobiography, travel, religion philosophy, poetry; Dir-Gen. M.-G. BOY.
**Editions du Rocher:** 28 rue Comte Félix Gastaldi, MC 98000; tel. 93-30-33-41; fax 93-50-73-71; scientific, medical, detective and general; Dir JEAN PAUL BERTRAND.
**Les Editions André Sauret SAM:** 8 quai Antoine 1er, BP 48, MC 98000; tel. 93-50-68-84; art, fiction; Dir RAYMOND LEVY.
**Société Mediterranéenne d'Edition SAM:** 1 ave Henri Dunant, Palais de la Scala, MC 98000; tel. 93-50-85-33; history; Dir ANTOINE PEYRAT.

## Radio and Television

In 1992 there were an estimated 30,000 radio receivers and 22,000 television receivers in use.

### RADIO

**Radio Monte Carlo SAM (RMC):** 16 blvd Princesse Charlotte, BP 128, MC 98080; tel. 93-15-16-17; telex 469926; fax 93-15-16-60; the official programme of RMC is broadcast in French on 1,400 metres (218 kHz); programmes in French and Italian are broadcast on 205 metres (1,467 kHz); foreign programmes are broadcast in 12 languages on 205 metres (1,467 kHz) and on short-wave frequencies; programmes on RMC may be backed by commercials or by sponsors; 83% owned by the French Government; Pres. CÉSAR C. SOLAMITO; Dir-Gen. JEAN-NOËL TASSEZ.
**Société Monégasque d'Exploitation et d'Études de Radiodiffusion (SOMERA):** 16 blvd Princesse Charlotte, MC 98000; tel. 93-15-16-17; telex 469926; fax 93-15-16-60; subsidiary of RMC; in French and Arabic; Pres. CÉSAR C. SOLAMITO; Dir-Gen. JACQUES TAQUET.
**Trans World Radio SC:** POB 349, MC 98007; tel. 92-16-56-00; fax 92-16-56-01; f. 1955; broadcasts evangelical programmes in 29 languages; Pres. THOMAS J. LOWELL; Station Man. RICHARD OLSON.

### TELEVISION

**Globo Monte-Carlo:** 19 ave des Castelans, MC 98000; tel. 92-05-74-56; telex 479606; fax 92-05-24-37; programmes in Italian; Pres. ALEXANDRA ZINGALÈS.
**Société Spéciale d'Entreprises Télé Monte-Carlo:** 16 blvd Princesse Charlotte, BP 279, MC 98090 Monaco Cedex; tel. 93-15-14-15; telex 469823; fax 93-50-66-97; f. 1954; Pres. JEAN PASTORELLI.

## Finance

(cap. = capital, res = reserves, dep. = deposits, brs = branches, m. = million, amounts in French francs)

### BANKS

In 1994 a total of 39 banks, including major French, Italian, US and British banks, were represented in the Principality.

**ABC Banque Internationale de Monaco:** place du Casino, BP 147, MC 98003; tel. 93-50-06-08; telex 469163; fax 93-25-61-37; f. 1980; 49% owned by Arab Banking Corporation, Bahrain, 32% by Arab Banking Corporation-International Holding B.V., Netherlands, 19% by Arab Banking Corporation-Daus and Co., GmbH, Frankfurt; cap. 75m., res 19.5m., dep. 1,333.6 (Dec. 1992); Pres. HATEM ABU SAID; Gen. Man. PAUL GOUSLISTY.
**Banque Centrale Monégasque de Crédit:** 4 blvd du Jardin Exotique, BP 227, MC 98004; tel. 92-16-52-00; telex 469623; fax 93-30-91-93; f. 1969; cap. 25m., res. 31m., dep. 352.2m. (Dec. 1992); Pres. JEAN DEFLASSIEUX; Dir-Gen. MARC LANZERINI.
**Banque Sudameris:** 2 blvd des Moulins, MC 98000; tel. 92-16-51-00; telex 489480; fax 92-16-51-13; Man. ALBERTO CORDERO DI MONTEZEMOLO.
**Barclays Bank SA:** 31 ave de la Costa, MC 98000; tel. 93-15-35-35; telex 469951; fax 93-25-15-68; 3 brs.
**Caixabank Monaco:** 9 blvd d'Italie, MC 98000; tel. 93-15-23-23; telex 469802; fax 93-15-23-30; f. 1953; cap. 120m., res. 7.1m., dep. 1,748.7m. (Dec. 1993); Chair. JUAN JOSÉ TORIBIO; Gen. Man. JUAN BOVEDA.
**Compagnie Financière Edmond de Rothschild Banque:** 2 ave de Monte-Carlo, MC 98000; tel. 93-25-09-09; telex 479501; fax 93-25-75-57.
**Compagnie Monégasque de Banque SAM:** 23 ave de la Costa, BP 167, MC 98003; tel. 93-15-77-77; telex 479269; fax 93-25-08-69; f. 1976; cap. p.u. 560m., res 105.8m., dep. 9,359.3m. (Dec. 1994); Chair. ENRICO BRAGGIOTTI; Man. Dir FRANCESCO MORABITO.
**Crédit de Monaco pour le Commerce:** 1 square Théodore Gastaud, MC 98000; tel. 93-50-10-50; telex 469520; fax 93-30-41-37;

f. 1980; cap. 25m., res 22.1m., dep. 579.7m. (1988); Dir Jean-Véran Souffron.

**Crédit Foncier de Monaco SAM:** 11 blvd Albert 1er, MC 98000; tel. 93-15-45-00; telex 469738; fax 93-15-46-00; f. 1922; subsidiary of Banque Indosuez; cap. 135m., res 113.5m., dep. 11,768.4m. (Dec. 1992); Chair. Michel de Robillard; Gen. Man. Yves Max; 6 brs.

**Société de Banque Suisse (Monaco):** 2 ave de Grande Bretagne, BP 189, MC 98007; tel. 93-15-58-15; telex 469955; fax 93-15-58-00; f. 1956; cap. 60m., res 27.0m., dep. 5,581.5m. (Dec. 1992); Chair. Pierre Louis Bosshart; Man. Dir Alain Roux.

**Société de Banques et d'Investissements SAM:** 26 blvd d'Italie, MC 98000; tel. 93-15-74-74; telex 479464; fax 90-50-15-37; f. 1956; deposit bank; cap. 70m., res 2.9m., dep. 1,197m. (1992); Chair. and Man. Dir François Charron.

### INSURANCE COMPANIES

**Gramaglia AGF:** 9 ave Princesse Alice, BP 153, MC 98003; tel. 93-50-55-16; telex 479406; fax 93-50-35-81; Dir Antoine Gramaglia.

**Monaco Insurance Services:** 3 ave Saint-Charles, BP 113, MC 98008; tel. 93-25-38-58; fax 93-25-74-37; Dir Pierre Aoun.

**Mourenon et Giannotti:** 22 blvd Princesse Charlotte, MC 98000; tel. 93-25-04-05; fax 93-50-55-39; Dirs Jean-Philippe Mourenon, José Giannotti.

**J.P. Sassi-Drouot Assurances:** 28 blvd Princesse Charlotte, MC 98000; tel. 93-30-45-88; Dir Jean-Pierre Sassi.

**Silvain Assurances:** 33 blvd Princesse Charlotte, BP 267, MC 98005; tel. 93-25-54-45; telex 489485; fax 93-50-39-05; Dir Philippe Silvain.

**Société Française de Recours Cie d'Assurances:** 28 blvd Princesse Charlotte, MC 98000; tel. 93-50-52-63; telex 469748; fax 93-50-54-49; Dir Floriano Conte.

## Trade and Industry

### EMPLOYERS' ASSOCIATION

**Fédération Patronale Monégasque (FPM)** (Employers' Federation of Monaco): Immeuble 'Le Coronado', 20 ave de Fontvieille, MC 98000; tel. 92-05-38-92; fax 92-05-20-04; f. 1944; Pres. Victor Pastor; 19 member unions, with 1,000 individual mems.

### TRADE UNION

**Union des Syndicats de Monaco (USM)** (Union of Monaco Trade Unions): 18 rue de la Turbie; tel. 93-30-19-30; f. 1944; Pres. Charles Soccal; Sec.-Gen. Angèle Braquetti; 35 member unions with 5,000 individual mems.

### OTHER ORGANIZATIONS

**Conseil Economique:** 8 rue Louis Notari, Monte-Carlo; tel. 93-30-20-82; consultative organization in six sections dealing with all aspects of Monaco's economy; comprises 30 members who represent, in equal proportions, employers, workers and the Government; named by the Head of State every three years from all nationalities; President must be Monégasque national; Pres. René Clerissi; Vice-Pres Charles Manni, André Morra.

**Jeune Chambre Economique de Monaco:** POB 13, MC 98001; tel. 92-05-54-00; telex 469870; fax 92-05-31-29; f. 1963; 90 mems; Pres. Claus Thonbo.

## Transport

### RAILWAYS

There is 1.7 km of railway track in Monaco running from France to Monte-Carlo. It is operated by the French state railway, the Société Nationale des Chemins de fer Français (see chapter on France). In 1994 the construction of an underground railway station was envisaged under the Government's continuing policy of land reclamation.

### ROADS

In 1988 there were 50 km of major roads in the Principality.

### SHIPPING

Monaco has an estimated docking capacity of 100 cruise ships. In 1993 a programme to expand the Principality's main harbour, Port Hercule, at a projected cost of US $254m., was initiated.

### CIVIL AVIATION

There is a helicopter shuttle service between the international airport at Nice, France, and Monaco's heliport at Fontvieille.

**Heli-Air Monaco SAM:** Héliport de Monaco, MC 98000; tel. 92-05-00-50; telex 479343; fax 92-05-76-17; Pres. Jacques Crovetto.

## Tourism

Tourists are attracted to Monaco by the Mediterranean climate, dramatic scenery and numerous entertainment facilities, including a casino. In 1993 208,206 tourists (excluding excursionists) visited Monaco. In 1992, when (including excursionists) an estimated 4m. people visited the Principality, revenue from tourism totalled US $1,300m. In that year there were 18 hotels in the Principality.

**Académie Internationale du Tourisme:** Monte-Carlo; tel. 93-30-97-68; f. 1951 under the patronage of Prince Rainier III; promotes the development of tourism; Pres. Mario Grego; Treas. Louis Nagel; 108 mems.

**Direction du Tourisme et des Congrès:** 2A blvd des Moulins, MC 98030; tel. 92-16-61-16; telex 469760; fax 92-16-60-00; there are also international conference centres in Monte-Carlo at: Centre de Congrès Auditorium de Monte-Carlo, blvd Louis II and at Centre de Rencontres Internationales, ave d'Ostende; Dir Régine May.

**Société des Bains de Mer (SBM):** place du Casino, BP 139, MC 98007; tel. 92-16-20-00; telex 469925; fax 92-16-38-60; f. 1863; corporation in which the Government holds a 69% interest; controls the entertainment facilities of Monaco, including the casino and numerous hotels, clubs, restaurants and sporting facilities; Chair. Raoul Biancheri.

# MONGOLIA

## Introductory Survey

### Location, Climate, Language, Religion, Flag, Capital

Mongolia is a land-locked country in central Asia, with the Russian Federation to the north and the People's Republic of China to the south, east and west. The climate is dry, with generally mild summers but very cold winters. Temperatures in Ulan Bator are usually between −32°C (−26°F) and 22°C (71°F). The principal language is Khalkha Mongolian. Kazakh is spoken in the province of Bayan-ölgiy. There is no state religion, but Buddhist Lamaism is being encouraged once again. The national flag (proportions 2 by 1) has three equal vertical stripes, of red, blue and red, with the 'soyombo' symbol (a combination of abstract devices) in gold on the red stripe at the hoist. The capital is Ulan Bator (Ulaanbaatar).

### Recent History

The country was formerly the Manchu province of Outer Mongolia. In 1911, following the republican revolution in China, Mongolian princes declared the province's independence. With backing from Tsarist Russia, Outer Mongolia gained autonomy, as a feudal Buddhist monarchy, but Russia accepted Chinese suzerainty over the province in 1915. Following the Russian revolution of 1917, China began to re-establish control in Mongolia in 1919. In 1920 Mongol nationalists appealed to the new Soviet regime for help, and in March 1921 they met in the USSR to found the Mongolian People's Party, called the Mongolian People's Revolutionary Party (MPRP) since 1924, and established a Provisional People's Government. After nationalist forces, with Soviet help, drove the anti-Bolshevik forces of Baron von Ungern-Sternberg from the Mongolian capital, independence was proclaimed on 11 July 1921. The USSR recognized the People's Government in November of that year. In November 1924, after the death of Bogd Haan (King) Javdzandamba Hutagt VIII, the Mongolian People's Republic (MPR) was proclaimed.

Soviet troops left in 1925, but the MPR became increasingly dependent on the USSR's support. The Government conducted campaigns to collectivize the economy and to destroy the power of the nobility and Buddhist priests. In 1932 an armed uprising was suppressed with Soviet help. Following a purge of the MPRP and army leadership in 1936–39, power was concentrated in the hands of Marshal Horloogiyn Choybalsan as Prime Minister and MPRP leader. The dictatorship of Choybalsan closely followed the pattern of Stalin's regime in the USSR, and its thousands of victims included eminent politicians, military officers, religious leaders and intellectuals. In 1939 a Japanese invasion from Manchuria was repelled by Soviet and Mongolian forces at Halhyn Gol (Nomonhan). The resultant truce lasted until war was declared on Japan in August 1945, four days before the Japanese surrender, and northern China was invaded. In a plebiscite in October 1945, it was reported that 100% of the votes were cast in favour of independence, and this was recognized by China in January 1946.

Choybalsan died in January 1952 and was succeeded as Prime Minister by Yumjaagiyn Tsedenbal, who had been the Party's First Secretary (leader) since 1940. Dashiyn Damba became First Secretary of the MPRP in April 1954. During the 1950s Mongolia was recognized only by other communist countries. Tsedenbal replaced Damba as First Secretary of the MPRP in November 1958, and a new constitution was adopted in July 1960. Mongolia became a member of the UN in October 1961 and was subsequently accorded diplomatic recognition by the United Kingdom and other western European and developing countries. By January 1987, when Mongolia was finally granted diplomatic recognition by the USA, it had diplomatic relations with more than 100 states.

For many years, Mongolia depended on economic, military and political support from the USSR, and the Mongolian leadership loyally endorsed Soviet policies. Mongolia became a member of the Soviet-dominated Council for Mutual Economic Assistance (CMEA) in 1962. Relations with the People's Republic of China were good until the onset of the Sino–Soviet dispute in the 1960s, when Mongolia renewed accusations of China's intention to annex Mongolia. In the early 1970s Mongolia accused the Chinese leadership of ill-treating the Mongol population of Chinese Inner Mongolia, and also protested on several occasions at cross-border incursions by Chinese troops. In 1983 it was reported that 2,000 ethnic Chinese immigrants had been expelled from Mongolia, and there were signs that the Mongolian Government wished to eject almost the entire resident Chinese community (estimated at 7,000), despite protests from Beijing. In 1986, however, Sino-Mongolian relations improved significantly, when the Chinese Vice-Minister of Foreign Affairs visited Ulan Bator, and the two countries signed agreements on consular relations and trade. In June 1987 a delegation from the Chinese National People's Congress (NPC), led by Peng Chong (a Vice-Chairman of the NPC Standing Committee), visited Ulan Bator, and in the same month a treaty concerning the resolution of border disputes was initialled by representatives of the two governments. In January 1987 the Soviet Government announced that, between April and June, it was to withdraw about one-fifth of its military forces from Mongolia, in a move acknowledged by the Mongolian Government as an 'act of goodwill' towards stability in the region. The process continued during the late 1980s, and by late September 1992 all former Soviet troops and military equipment had been withdrawn from Mongolia.

Jamsrangiyn Sambuu, Head of State since July 1954, died in May 1972. He was replaced in June 1974 by Tsedenbal, who remained as First Secretary of the MPRP (restyled General Secretary in 1981) but relinquished the post of Chairman of the Council of Ministers to Jambyn Batmönh. In August 1984 Tsedenbal was removed from the Party leadership and state presidency, apparently owing to ill health, and Batmönh replaced him as General Secretary of the MPRP. In December Batmönh also became Head of State, while Dumaagiyn Sodnom, hitherto a Deputy Chairman of the Council of Ministers and the Chairman of the State Planning Commission, was appointed Chairman of the Council of Ministers. At elections for the 11th People's Great Hural (legislature), held in June 1986, there was an official turn-out of 99.99% for the unopposed election of the 370 deputies.

In late 1986 government ministries dealing with agriculture, water supply and construction were reorganized, and in late 1987–early 1988 more extensive restructuring took place, with the aim of improving the efficiency and productivity of the country's economy. However, by late 1988 the MPRP Political Bureau was obliged to admit that economic renewal was not succeeding because of the need for social reforms. Batmönh advocated greater openness and offered the prospect of multi-candidate elections. He criticized Tsedenbal for the country's 'stagnation', also stating that the former leader had belittled collective leadership.

Between December 1989 and March 1990 there was a great upsurge in public political activity, as several newly-formed opposition movements and parties organized a series of peaceful demonstrations in Ulan Bator, demanding political and economic reforms. The most prominent of the new opposition groups was the Mongolian Democratic Union (MDU), which was founded in December 1989 and accorded official recognition by the Government in January 1990. In that month dialogue was initiated between MPRP officials and representatives of the MDU, including its chief co-ordinator, Sanjaasürengiyn Dzorig (a lecturer at the Mongolian State University).

The emergence of further opposition groups, together with escalating public demonstrations (involving as many as 20,000 people), led to a crisis of confidence within the MPRP. At a party plenum, held in mid-March 1990, Batmönh announced the resignation of the entire Political Bureau as well as of the Secretariat of the Central Committee. Gombojavyn Ochirbat, a former head of the Ideological Department of the Central Committee and a former Chairman of the Central Council of Mongolian Trade Unions, was elected the new General Secretary of the party, replacing Batmönh. A new five-member Political Bureau was formed. The plenum voted to expel the former MPRP General Secretary, Yumjaagiyn Tsedenbal, from the party and to rehabilitate several prominent victims of Tsedenbal's purges of the 1960s.

At a session of the People's Great Hural, which was held shortly after the MPRP plenum, Punsalmaagiyn Ochirbat, hitherto the Minister of Foreign Economic Relations and Supply, was elected to the post of Chairman of the Presidium (Head of State), replacing Batmönh, and other senior positions in the Presidium were reorganized. Dumaagiyn Sodnom was dismissed from his post as Chairman of the Council of Ministers and was replaced by Sharavyn Gungaadorj, a Deputy Chairman and Minister of Agriculture and the Food Industry. The Hural also adopted amendments to the Constitution, including the removal of references to the MPRP as the 'guiding force' in Mongolian society, and approved a new electoral law. It was decided that the next elections to the Hural would be held in mid-1990, and not in 1991 as originally planned. Meanwhile, all limits on personal livestock holdings were removed, and new regulations were introduced to encourage foreign investment in Mongolia. However, in late March 1990 an estimated 13,000 people, dissatisfied with the results of the Hural's session, demonstrated in Ulan Bator, demanding the dissolution of the Hural. Opposition leaders declared that the changes which the legislature had introduced were not far-reaching enough, and demanded the introduction of a multi-party electoral law, allowing opposition parties to present candidates for election to the legislature.

In April 1990 the MPRP held an extraordinary congress, at which more than three-quarters of the membership of the Central Committee was renewed. General Secretary Gombojavyn Ochirbat was elected to the restyled post of Chairman of the party. The Political Bureau was renamed the Presidium, and a new four-member Secretariat of the Central Committee was appointed.

In May 1990 the People's Great Hural adopted a law on political parties, which legalized the new 'informal' parties through official registration, and also adopted further amendments to the Constitution, introducing a presidential system with a standing legislature called the State Little Hural, elected by proportional representation of parties.

At the July 1990 general election and consequent re-elections, 430 deputies were elected to serve a five-year term: 357 from the MPRP (in some instances unopposed), 16 from the Mongolian Democratic Party (MDP, the political wing of the MDU), nine from the Mongolian Revolutionary Youth League, six from the Mongolian National Progress Party (MNPP), four from the Mongolian Social-Democratic Party (MSDP), and 39 without party affiliation. Under constitutional amendments adopted in May 1990, the People's Great Hural was required to convene at least four times in the five years of its term.

In September 1990 the People's Great Hural elected Punsalmaagiyn Ochirbat to be the country's first President, with a five-year term of office; his previous post of Chairman of the Presidium lapsed. Jambyn Gombojav was elected Chairman (speaker) of the Great Hural, with four Vice-Chairmen from various parties. Radnaasümbereliyn Gonchigdorj of the MSDP was subsequently elected Chairman of the State Little Hural, *ex officio* becoming Vice-President of Mongolia. Dashiyn Byambasüren was appointed Prime Minister (equivalent to the former post of Chairman of the Council of Ministers) and began consultations on the formation of a multi-party government. The newly restyled Cabinet was elected by the State Little Hural in September and October. Under the amended Constitution, the President, Vice-President and Ministers were not permitted to remain concurrently deputies of the People's Great Hural; therefore, re-elections of deputies to the People's Great Hural were held in mid-November.

The 20th Congress of the MPRP, which was held in February 1991, elected a new 99-member Central Committee, which, in turn, appointed a new Presidium. The Central Committee also elected a new Chairman, Büdragchaagiyn Dash-Yondon, the Chairman of the Ulan Bator City Party Committee, who had become a Presidium member in November 1990.

A new Constitution was adopted by an almost unanimous vote of the Great Hural in January 1992, and entered into force in the following month. It provided for a unicameral Mongolian Great Hural, comprising 76 members, to replace the People's Great Hural following legislative elections, to be held in June. (The State Little Hural was to be abolished following the elections.) The country's official name was changed from the Mongolian People's Republic to Mongolia, and the communist gold star was removed from the national flag.

The 21st Congress of the MPRP, held in February 1992, elected 147 members to the Central Committee. The post of MPRP Secretary was abolished, and the three incumbent Secretaries were appointed Vice-Chairmen. Dash-Yondon was re-elected party Chairman.

At the elections to the Mongolian Great Hural in June 1992, a total of 293 candidates stood in 26 constituencies, comprising the 18 *aymag* (provinces), the towns of Darhan and Erdenet, and Ulan Bator City (six). The constituencies had two, three or four seats, according to the size of the local electorate. The MPRP presented 82 candidates, compared with 51 put forward by an alliance of the MDP, the MNPP and the United Party (UP), and 30 by the MSDP; six other parties and another alliance also took part, although with fewer candidates.

A total of 1,037,392 voters (95.6% of the electorate) participated in the elections, although 62,738 ballots were declared invalid. Candidates were elected by a simple majority, provided that they obtained the support of at least 50% of the electorate in their constituency. The MPRP candidates received altogether 1,719,887 votes (some 57%), while the candidates of the other parties (excluding independents) achieved a combined total of 1,205,350 votes (40%), of which the MDP-MNPP-UP alliance won 521,883 votes and the MSDP 304,548. The outcome of the election was disproportionate, however, with the MPRP taking 70 seats (71, if a pro-MPRP independent is included). The remaining seats went to the MDP (two, including an independent), the MSDP, MNPP and UP (one each).

The first session of the Mongolian Great Hural opened in July 1992 with the election of officers, the nomination of Puntsagiyn Jasray, a prominent economist, to the post of Prime Minister, and the approval of his Cabinet. Natsagiyn Bagabandi, a Vice-Chairman of the MPRP Central Committee, was elected Chairman of the Great Hural. Jambyn Gombojav (Chairman of the People's Great Hural from late 1990 to late 1991) was elected Vice-Chairman of the new Hural. Meanwhile, a National Security Council was established, with the country's President as its Chairman, and the Prime Minister and Chairman of the Great Hural as its members.

In October 1992 the MDP, MNPP, UP and the Mongolian Renewal Party amalgamated to form the Mongolian National Democratic Party (MNDP), with a General Council headed by the MNPP leader, Davaadorjiyn Ganbold, and including Sanjaasürengiyn Dzorig and other prominent opposition politicians. In the same month the MPRP Central Committee was renamed the MPRP Little Hural, and its membership was increased to 169 (and subsequently to 198). The Presidium was replaced by a nine-member Party Leadership Council, headed by Büdragchaagiyn Dash-Yondon as its General Secretary.

In December 1992 the former Prime Minister, Dashiyn Byambasüren, resigned from the Great Hural and the MPRP to establish the non-political Mongolian Development Society, which was joined by several former ministers and current members of the Great Hural. In early 1993 the MDU, New Progressive Union, Mongolian Youth Union and Mongolian Students' Union allied to form the Coalition of Four Unions. Headed by a youth leader, Sangajavyn Bayartsogt, the Coalition began to pressurize the Government for the acceleration of reform and the improvement of living conditions. In early March 1993 several thousand supporters of opposition parties staged a protest demonstration in Ulan Bator, demanding that the MPRP Government resign over its failure to improve the economic situation. The demonstration commemorated the third anniversary of the protest actions that brought about the collapse of old-style communist rule in Mongolia.

The Great Hural adopted a Presidential Election Law in March 1993, and direct elections to the presidency were called for 6 June; the three parliamentary parties (the MPRP, MNDP and MSDP) were obliged to nominate their candidates by mid-April. In the event, Lodongiyn Tüdev, a member of the Party Leadership Council and Editor-in-Chief of the MPRP organ, *Ünen*, was chosen as the MPRP's candidate, while President Ochirbat was nominated by a coalition of the MNDP and the MSDP. The result of the election was a convincing popular victory for Ochirbat: he received 57.8% of the votes cast, compared with 38.7% for Tüdev.

# MONGOLIA

A new political party, the United Heritage Party (UHP), was formed in December 1993 by the amalgamation of the United Herdsmen's and Farmers' Party, the United Private Owners' Party, the Capitalist Party and the Independence Party. The UHP, not represented in the Great Hural, claimed to have a membership of 20,000. In mid-1994 another new political formation emerged, the Mongolian Democratic Renewal Party, with the former Prime Minister, Dashiyn Byambasüren, as its Chairman.

In early 1994 the MPRP's political credibility was undermined by allegations of corruption directed against the party leadership both in government and in the legislature. The allegations, which were originally made by a Mongolian counter-intelligence officer, were pursued by the opposition parties, although no specific charges emerged. The Prime Minister, Puntsagiyn Jasray, denied the allegations and rejected demands for the Government's resignation. Opposition deputies boycotted sessions of the Great Hural. A number of anti-Government demonstrations were staged by the Mongolian Democratic Association, and a hunger strike began in Ulan Bator's main square. These actions came to an end only in late April, when the Great Hural agreed to draft legislation to prevent corruption among government officials and to free the media from government control. (Under the Law on the Government of May 1993, Mongolian radio and television had been transformed into a government organization.)

In mid-1994 the Great Hural approved the formation of three new provinces, named Darhan-Uul, Orhon and Gov'-Sümber, around the towns of Darhan and Erdenet and the former Soviet Army base of Choyr, respectively.

In July 1994 the Great Hural adopted a resolution postponing until 2001 implementation of the 1990 decision to reintroduce (in 1994) the classical Mongolian language and script for official publications. The resolution, which confirmed the continued use of the Cyrillic (Russian) script, was vetoed by President Ochirbat, but the Hural rejected his veto. There was, in any case, too little public and material support for such a change.

During an official visit to the Russian Federation in January 1993, President Ochirbat and the Russian President, Boris Yeltsin, issued a joint statement expressing regret at the execution and imprisonment of Mongolian citizens in the USSR during the Stalinist purges. Details were released about the fate of 32 prominent Mongolian officials, including a former Prime Minister, Butachiyn Genden, who was executed in 1937. Ochirbat and Yeltsin also signed a new 20-year Mongolian-Russian Treaty of Friendship and Co-operation to replace the defunct Mongolian-Soviet treaty of 1986. A similar treaty had been signed in November 1992, during the official visit to Mongolia by Leonid Kravchuk, the President of Ukraine.

Relations between Mongolia and China deteriorated somewhat during 1993, following the publication in China of a book entitled *The Secret of Mongolia's Independence*, which was condemned by the Mongolian Government as an attempt to assert Chinese territorial claims on Mongolia, despite Chinese denials that the book represented official policy. Nevertheless, relations had improved by April 1994, when a new Treaty of Friendship and Co-operation was concluded during a visit to Ulan Bator by the Chinese Premier, Li Peng. An agreement on cultural, economic and technical co-operation was also signed.

Two important documents outlining Mongolian foreign policy objectives were published in July 1994. Advocating 'political realism', *The Mongolian National Security Concept* gave top priority to maintaining a 'balanced relationship' with Russia and China, while 'strengthening trust and developing all-round good-neighbourly relations and mutually beneficial co-operation with both'. *The Mongolian Foreign Policy Concept* also described as the 'foremost objective' of the country's foreign policy the pursuit of 'friendly relations with Russia and China, and without favouring one or the other to develop co-operation with them in complete equality'. Traditional features and specific aspects of economic co-operation were to be safeguarded. Other priorities listed were: friendly relations with the USA, Japan, Germany and other highly developed nations of West and East; consolidation of political and economic integration in the Asian region; co-operation with the UN and its various bodies; and friendly relations with the newly independent states of eastern Europe and the CIS, as well as with developing countries.

### Government

Supreme legislative power is vested in the 76-member Mongolian Great Hural (Assembly), elected by universal adult suffrage for four years. The Great Hural recognizes the President on his election and appoints the Prime Minister and members of the Cabinet, which is the highest executive body. The President is Head of State and Commander-in-Chief of the Armed Forces. The President is directly elected for a term of four years.

Since May 1994 Mongolia has been divided into 21 provinces (*aymag*) and one municipality (Ulan Bator), with appointed governors and elected local assemblies.

### Defence

In June 1994 Mongolia's defence forces numbered 21,250, comprising an army of 20,000 (of whom 12,000 were thought to be conscripts) and 1,250 air force personnel. There was a paramilitary force of about 10,000, in addition to internal security troops and frontier guards. Military service is for 12 months (for males aged 18–28 years). Weapons, ammunition and vehicles were traditionally supplied by the USSR. The withdrawal of all former Soviet troops and military equipment had been completed by late September 1992. Defence expenditure for 1995 was projected at 9,050.8m. tögrög, about 9.4% of total budgetary expenditure.

### Economic Affairs

In 1991, according to official sources, gross national product (GNP) per head was US $112. During 1985–93 the population increased by an annual average of 2.8%. During 1980–87 Mongolia's net material product (NMP) increased, in real terms, at an average rate of 6.0% per year. In 1988 real NMP grew by 4.3%, compared with 1987. In 1992 NMP declined by 16.0%, compared with 1991.

At mid-1993 about 28% of the labour force were employed in agriculture (including forestry), which contributed 18.8% of NMP in 1987. Animal herding is the main economic activity and is practised throughout the country. In 1994 there were 26.8m. sheep, goats, horses, cattle and camels. By mid-1993 some 80% of all livestock was privately owned. State farms, of which there were 52 in 1988, practise agriculture on a large scale. The principal crops are cereals (330,700 metric tons in 1994), potatoes and vegetables. Agricultural production increased at an average rate of 1.5% per year in 1980–90, but declined by 6.3% in 1991 and by 11.9% in 1992.

Industrial activity (including construction) provided 40.4% of NMP in 1987 and employed about 21% of the labour force at mid-1980. Industrial production (excluding gas and construction) increased at an average annual rate of 7.2% over the period 1980–89, but decreased by about 2% in 1990 and by 15% in 1991. Reflecting the country's general economic decline, gross industrial production fell by 14.8% in 1992, compared with the previous year.

The most important minerals are coal, copper, fluorspar, tungsten, tin, gold and lead. The copper-molybdenum works at Erdenet provided almost 50% of the value of Mongolia's exports in 1993. The discovery of further reserves of petroleum at Tsagaan Els, East Gobi province, in late 1994, raised hopes that Mongolia's own resources might in future meet part of the demand for petroleum products (although a domestic refinery would be needed).

Measured by the value of output, textiles, leather products (including footwear), wood products (including furniture) and foodstuffs form the major branches of manufacturing.

Energy is derived principally from thermal power stations, fuelled by coal. Most provincial centres have thermal power stations or diesel generators, while smaller rural centres generally rely on small diesel generators. In more isolated areas wood, roots, bushes and dried animal dung are used for domestic fuel. The Ulan Bator No. 4 power station, the largest in the country, went into operation in 1985. Its capacity of 380 MW doubled Mongolia's generating capacity.

In 1992, according to provisional figures, Mongolia recorded a visible trade deficit of US $44.2m., while there was a deficit of $31.3m. on the current account of the balance of payments. In the same year about 74% of Mongolia's foreign trade was conducted with other former socialist countries. In 1994 the principal source of imports (59%) was the Russian Federation, followed in importance by the People's Republic of China (10%) and Japan (6%). The Russian Federation was also the principal market for exports (28%), followed by China (19%)

and Japan and Kazakhstan (both about 13%). The principal imports in 1993 were industrial goods (75.4%) and consumer goods (24.6%). Fuel and petroleum accounted for 32.6% of industrial imports. The principal exports in 1989 were fuels, minerals and metals (42.8%), raw materials (including foodstuffs, 35.7%) and industrial consumer goods (17.5%).

The 1995 budget envisaged a deficit of 12,903.4m. tögrög. Mongolia's total external debt was US $391.2m. at the end of 1993, of which $344.4m. was long-term public debt. In that year the cost of debt-servicing was equivalent to 4.4% of the value of exports of goods and services. However, this sum excluded the 9,700m. roubles claimed by Russia for aid granted during the Soviet period. In 1994, according to IMF estimates, the annual rate of inflation averaged 66%. In January 1995 some 74,900 people were unemployed.

Mongolia was a member of the Council for Mutual Economic Assistance (CMEA) until that body's dissolution in mid-1991. In 1989 Mongolia joined the Group of 77 (an organization of developing countries, founded under the auspices of UNCTAD, to promote economic co-operation). In February 1991 Mongolia became a member of the Asian Development Bank (see p. 107) as well as of the IMF and World Bank. In 1994 the European Union (EU) announced the inclusion of Mongolia in TACIS, the EU's programme of technical assistance to the Commonwealth of Independent States.

Mongolia's regular pattern of Five-Year Plans and CMEA-orientated trade was disrupted in 1990–91 by the collapse of command economies in the USSR and eastern European countries, by the transition to payments in convertible currencies and by the first steps towards 'privatization' and a market economy in Mongolia itself. There ensued a rapid decline in Mongolia's foreign trade, which, with traditional (formerly socialist) partners, was largely reduced, by the shortage of convertible currencies, to barter transactions. Industrial production declined sharply, as a result of widespread fuel shortages and problems of distribution. The rationing of basic foodstuffs was introduced for the urban population. However, during 1993 Mongolia stabilized the economy, liberalizing prices while reducing inflation, also cutting current expenditure and implementing a new exchange rate mechanism. The first signs of economic growth emerged in 1994. The World Bank welcomed these developments, although it estimated that Mongolia would still need aid worth US $150m.–$200m. per year for the foreseeable future. Among the Government's immediate priorities are to minimize the social impact of the transition to a market economy, to reduce the government sector in agriculture and to improve the environment.

**Social Welfare**

In 1990 there were 26,427 hospital beds and 6,180 physicians, with ratios of 126 hospital beds and 29.5 physicians per 10,000 of the population. By 1992 the ratio of physicians had fallen to 26 per 10,000 inhabitants, and that of trained medical personnel from 88 (in 1990) to 76 per 10,000. The infant mortality rate in 1992 was 60 per 1,000 live births. Projected expenditure on health by central and local budgets in 1995 was 13,500m. tögrög (14.0% of total budgetary spending). In the previous year 10,945m. tögrög (13.9% of expenditure) was allocated to pensions and support for low-income households.

With monthly incomes averaging 12,100 tögrög for an urban family and 11,000 tögrög for a rural family at the end of 1993, the subsistence minimum was estimated at 3,200 and 2,900 tögrög (1,580 and 1,040 tögrög per head) respectively. On this basis, 137,300 families (587,300 people) were classified as 'poor', 32,245 families (137,400 people) as 'very poor', and more than 100,000 people were below the subsistence level.

**Education**

Ten-year general education is compulsory, beginning at six years of age. Pupils may attend vocational-technical schools from the age of 16 to 18 years. In 1994/95 enrolment in general schools was 381,204. There are nine universities, 18 special secondary schools and 32 vocational-technical schools, with a total enrolment of 34,045 in 1994/95. Many Mongolian students continue their academic careers at universities and technical schools in Russia and Germany. Projected expenditure on education by central and local budgets in 1995 was 22,300m. tögrög (23.1% of total budgetary spending).

**Public Holidays**

**1995:** 1 January (New Year), 1–2 February (Tsagaan Sar, lunar new year), 11–13 July (National Days).

**1996:** 1 January (New Year), 19–21 February (Tsagaan Sar, lunar new year), 11–13 July (National Days).

**Weights and Measures**

The metric system is in force.

MONGOLIA

# Statistical Survey

Revised by Alan J. K. Sanders.

Note: As a result of the reform of the Central Statistical Directorate and the publication of a new Law on Statistics in early 1994, the methods of collecting and reporting socio-economic statistics were changed. The Directorate was, for the first time, commissioned to collect data on the operation of private industrial, agricultural and transport enterprises, as well as state and co-operative ones. No annual statistical report for 1993 was published.

## Area and Population

### AREA, POPULATION AND DENSITY

| | |
|---|---|
| Area (sq km) | 1,565,000* |
| Population (census results) | |
| 5 January 1979 | 1,594,800 |
| 5 January 1989 | |
| Males | 1,020,300 |
| Females | 1,023,100 |
| Total | 2,043,400 |
| Population (official estimates at 1 January) | |
| 1993 | 2,200,000 |
| 1994 | 2,250,000 |
| 1995 | 2,288,000 |
| Density (per sq km) at 1 January 1995 | 1.5 |

* 604,250 sq miles.

### ADMINISTRATIVE DIVISIONS (end of 1990)

| Province (Aymag)* | Area ('000 sq km) | Population ('000) | Provincial Centre |
|---|---|---|---|
| Arhangay | 55 | 89.2 | Tsetserleg |
| Bayanhongor | 116 | 78.7 | Bayanhongor |
| Bayan-ölgiy | 46 | 99.3 | Ölgiy |
| Bulgan | 49 | 56.7 | Bulgan |
| Dornod (Eastern) | 123.5 | 82.6 | Choybalsan |
| Dornogov' (East Gobi) | 111 | 58.6 | Saynshand |
| Dundgov' (Central Gobi) | 78 | 51.9 | Mandalgov' |
| Dzavhan | 82 | 93.6 | Uliastay |
| Gov'-altay | 142 | 65.1 | Altay |
| Hentiy | 82 | 76.7 | Öndörhaan |
| Hovd | 76 | 81.1 | Hovd |
| Hövsgöl | 101 | 106.9 | Mörön |
| Ömnögov' (South Gobi) | 165 | 43.5 | Dalandzadgad |
| Övörhangay | 63 | 100.4 | Arvayheer |
| Selenge | 42.8 | 92.0 | Sühbaatar |
| Sühbaatar | 82 | 53.5 | Baruun urt |
| Töv | 78.2 | 108.0† | Dzuun mod |
| Uvs | 69 | 91.8 | Ulaangom |

* Three new provinces were created in May 1994: Darhan-Uul, Orhon and Gov'-Sümber. The respective provincial centres were Darhan, Erdenet and Choyr, previously towns under state jurisdiction.
† 1993.

### ETHNIC GROUPS (1989 census)

| | Number | % |
|---|---|---|
| Halh (Khalkha) | 1,610,200 | 78.8 |
| Kazakh (Hasag) | 120,500 | 5.9 |
| Dörvöd (Durbet) | 55,200 | 2.7 |
| Bayad (Bayat) | 38,800 | 1.9 |
| Buryat (Buriat) | 34,700 | 1.7 |
| Dariganga | 28,600 | 1.4 |
| Dzahchin (Zakhchin) | 22,500 | 1.1 |
| Urianhay | 20,400 | 1.0 |
| Darhad | 14,300 | 0.7 |
| Torguud (Torgut) | 10,200 | 0.5 |
| Ööld (Eleuth) | 8,100 | 0.4 |
| Hoton | 4,000 | 0.2 |
| Myangad (Mingat) | 4,000 | 0.2 |
| Barga | 2,000 | 0.1 |
| Others | 69,900 | 3.4 |
| **Total** | **2,043,400** | **100.0** |

### PRINCIPAL TOWNS (population, 1994)

| | | | |
|---|---|---|---|
| Ulan Bator | 680,000 | Erdenet | 63,000 |
| Darhan | 85,800 | Choybalsan | 46,000 |

### BIRTHS, MARRIAGES AND DEATHS

Birth rate (per 1,000): 35.5 in 1989, 35.3 in 1990, 24.0 in 1994; marriage rate (per 1,000): 7.5 in 1989; death rate (per 1,000): 8.2 in 1989, 8.5 in 1990, 8.5 in 1994.

### EXPECTATION OF LIFE

62.5 years at birth (1994).

### ECONOMICALLY ACTIVE POPULATION

(ILO estimates, '000 persons at mid-1980)

| | Males | Females | Total |
|---|---|---|---|
| Agriculture, etc. | 181 | 126 | 308 |
| Industry | 89 | 74 | 162 |
| Services | 152 | 151 | 303 |
| **Total labour force** | **421** | **351** | **772** |

Source: ILO, *Economically Active Population Estimates and Projections, 1950–2025.*
**Mid-1993** (estimates in '000): Agriculture, etc. 310; Total 1,115 (Source: FAO, *Production Yearbook*).

### EMPLOYMENT (state and co-operative sector)

| | 1988 | 1989 | 1990 |
|---|---|---|---|
| Industry | 116,500 | 119,700 | 123,400 |
| Construction | 38,600 | 41,700 | 44,600 |
| Agriculture | 183,100 | 185,900 | 189,400 |
| Transport | 47,400 | 53,900 | 48,000 |
| Trade and supply | 46,800 | 47,500 | 49,200 |
| Services | 24,400 | 26,400 | 28,900 |
| Science | 11,200 | 14,100 | 14,100 |
| Education and arts | 70,100 | 74,500 | 75,500 |
| Health, social services and tourism | 42,800 | 44,700 | 46,700 |
| Administration | 12,700 | 12,300 | 10,900 |
| Other | 17,700 | 12,400 | 18,000 |
| **Total employed** | **611,300** | **633,100** | **648,700** |

**Unemployed:** 54,000 in January 1993; 72,300 in March 1994; 74,900 in January 1995.

## Agriculture

### PRINCIPAL CROPS (metric tons)

| | 1992 | 1993 | 1994 |
|---|---|---|---|
| Cereals* | 493,900 | 479,500 | 330,700 |
| Potatoes | 78,500 | 60,100 | 54,000 |
| Other vegetables | 16,400 | 22,700 | 22,800 |
| Fodder and silage | 171,900 | n.a. | n.a. |
| Hay | 668,500 | n.a. | 672,200 |

* Mostly wheat, but also small quantities of barley and oats.

# MONGOLIA

## LIVESTOCK

|  | 1992 | 1993 | 1994 |
|---|---|---|---|
| Sheep | 14,634,700 | 13,779,193 | 13,779,400 |
| Goats | 5,598,100 | 6,107,041 | 7,239,100 |
| Horses | 2,197,800 | 2,190,325 | 2,408,400 |
| Cattle | 2,814,000 | 2,730,456 | 3,003,700 |
| Camels | 414,900 | 367,673 | 366,100 |
| **Total** | 25,659,500 | 25,174,688 | 26,796,700 |

**1995:** Pigs 28,000; Poultry 180,000.

Livestock raised from birth totalled 8.7m. in 1992; 7.6m. in 1993; and 8.5m. in 1994.

## AGRICULTURAL PROCUREMENTS ('000 metric tons, unless otherwise indicated)

|  | 1990 | 1991 | 1992 |
|---|---|---|---|
| Livestock and meat (live weight)* | 176.3 | 173.8 | 102.5 |
| Butter | 4.4 | 2.8 | 1.3 |
| Milk (million litres) | 48.1 | 38.3 | 25.0 |
| Pig meat | 5.1 | 4.9 | 0.8 |
| Eggs (million) | 34.8 | 24.2 | 16.8 |
| Wool (all sorts) | 26.8 | 25.0 | 17.6 |
| Large hides ('000)† | 474.4 | 452.5 | 387.8 |
| Small hides ('000)‡ | 3,885.6 | 3,754.9 | 3,147.1 |
| Grain | 399.6 | 327.7 | 256.5 |
| Potatoes | 72.6 | 56.9 | 35.3 |
| Green vegetables | 29.7 | 16.5 | 7.3 |

* Mainly cattle, sheep and goats.
† Cattle and horse.
‡ Sheep and goat.

**1993** ('000 metric tons, unless otherwise indicated): Pig meat 0.7; Eggs (million) 10.0.

**1994** ('000 metric tons, unless otherwise indicated): Pig meat 0.6; Eggs (million) 3.6; Grain 191.1; Potatoes 11.1; Green vegetables 8.3.

## PROCUREMENT OF WOOL, HIDES AND SKINS

|  | 1988 | 1989 | 1990 |
|---|---|---|---|
| Sheep's wool (metric tons) | 18,700 | 19,500 | 20,000 |
| Camels' wool (metric tons) | 2,800 | 2,600 | 2,300 |
| Goats' wool (metric tons) | 800 | 800 | 800 |
| Goats' hair (metric tons) | 1,300 | 1,300 | 1,400 |
| Cattle hides (units) | 502,400 | 472,000 | 462,100 |
| Horse hides (units) | 137,300 | 120,200 | 115,100 |
| Camel skins (units) | 32,500 | 33,400 | 26,500 |
| Sheep skins (units) | 4,098,800 | 4,237,600 | 3,869,500 |
| Goat skins (units) | 1,100,900 | 1,069,700 | 1,228,400 |
| Marmot pelts (units) | 1,108,800 | 925,900 | 846,200 |
| Squirrel skins (units) | 17,700 | 10,700 | 8,000 |
| Wolf skins (units) | 4,000 | 4,500 | 3,700 |

# Forestry

## ROUNDWOOD REMOVALS
('000 cubic metres, excluding bark)

|  | 1990* | 1991 | 1992 |
|---|---|---|---|
| Industrial wood | 1,040 | 720 | 610 |
| Fuel wood | 1,350 | 1,350* | 1,350* |
| **Total** | 2,390 | 2,070 | 1,960 |

* FAO estimate(s).

Source: FAO, *Yearbook of Forest Products*.

**Sawnwood Production** ('000 cubic metres, including boxboards): 124.0 in 1992; 84.5 in 1993; 50.3 in 1994.

# Fishing
(metric tons, live weight)

|  | 1991 | 1992 | 1993 |
|---|---|---|---|
| **Total catch** (freshwater fishes) | 100.1 | 19.7 | 16.6 |

# Mining
(metric tons, unless otherwise indicated)

|  | 1992 | 1993 | 1994 |
|---|---|---|---|
| Hard coal and lignite | 6,247,300 | 5,608,500 | 5,012,400 |
| Fluorspar | 622,000 | 536,800 | 383,200 |
| Copper concentrate | 300,200 | 334,300 | 343,300 |
| Molybdenum concentrate | 3,500 | 4,367 | 4,396 |
| Gold (kilograms) | 800 | 1,117 | 1,975 |

# Industry

## SELECTED PRODUCTS

|  | 1992 | 1993 | 1994 |
|---|---|---|---|
| Electricity (million kWh) | 2,357.8 | 2,131.7 | 2,122.7 |
| Railway sleepers ('000 cu metres) | 8.1 | 11.3 | 11.0 |
| Plywood (cu metres) | 1,054.5 | 221.0 | n.a. |
| Chipboard (cu metres) | 880.2 | 140.2 | n.a. |
| Matches (million boxes) | 17.6 | 22.3 | 17.1 |
| Cement ('000 metric tons) | 132.5 | 82.3 | 85.8 |
| Lime ('000 metric tons) | 67.8 | 51.2 | 66.4 |
| Ferroconcrete ('000 cu metres) | 42.0 | 17.1 | 16.0 |
| Bricks (million) | 39.1 | 23.7 | 27.3 |
| Breeze-blocks (million) | 14.9 | 9.7 | 6.3 |
| Woollen cloth ('000 metres) | 705.8 | 289.9 | 76.7 |
| Carpets ('000 sq metres) | 1,037.0 | 1,000.1 | 681.5 |
| Knitwear ('000 garments) | 1,411.7 | 990.7 | 515.7 |
| Cashmere (metric tons) | 97.6 | 121.5 | 232.1 |
| Camelhair blankets ('000) | 90.6 | 48.7 | 24.1 |
| Washed wool (metric tons) | 7,057.3 | 3,466.4 | 2,062.5 |
| Felt ('000 metres) | 494.8 | 241.4 | 107.7 |
| Felt footwear ('000 pairs) | 409.1 | 252.1 | 90.1 |
| Leather footwear ('000 pairs) | 2,244.7 | 1,030.8 | 604.6 |
| Leather coats and jackets ('000) | 181.2 | 169.5 | 70.3 |
| Mongolian *deel* ('000) | 44.3 | 8.4 | 13.8 |
| Two-piece suits ('000) | 11.8 | 2.7 | 2.5 |
| Sheepskin coats ('000) | 99.4 | 86.6 | 57.1 |
| Raw hides ('000 sq metres) | 439.9 | 99.4 | n.a. |
| Lambskin ('000 sq metres) | 994.9 | 287.2 | 316.4 |
| Kid leather ('000 sq metres) | 494.5 | 64.4 | 115.0 |
| Chinaware ('000 pieces) | 3,337.2 | 1,789.2 | 1,582.4 |
| Flour ('000 metric tons) | 181.9 | 138.8 | 124.3 |
| Canned meat (metric tons) | 568.9 | 358.3 | 243.1 |
| Preserved vegetables (metric tons) | 270.0 | 110.2 | 115.5 |
| Bread (metric tons) | 60,860.2 | 46,007.3 | 33,908.8 |
| Molasses (metric tons) | 1,243.1 | 398.7 | 711.1 |
| Confectionery (metric tons) | 10,720.2 | 6,172.9 | 6,149.3 |
| Pasta (metric tons) | 3,304.6 | 1,540.0 | 1,319.3 |
| Vodka ('000 litres) | 6,686.6 | 5,250.8 | 3,626.0 |
| Beer ('000 litres) | 3,042.8 | 2,287.2 | 821.5 |
| Soft drinks ('000 litres) | 9,666.1 | 6,697.1 | 5,768.0 |
| Household soap (metric tons) | 373.5 | 179.5 | 473.4 |
| Toilet soap (metric tons) | 393.8 | 171.3 | 93.4 |
| Candles ('000) | 5,237.2 | 6,428.1 | 3,100.0 |

MONGOLIA
*Statistical Survey*

## Finance

### CURRENCY AND EXCHANGE RATES

**Monetary Units**
100 möngö = 1 tögrög (tughrik).

**Sterling and Dollar Equivalents** (31 December 1994)
£1 sterling = 647.8 tögrög;
US $1 = 414.1 tögrög;
1,000 tögrög = £1.544 = $2.415.

**Average Exchange Rate** (tögrög per US $)
1994 412.72.

### BUDGET (forecasts, million tögrög)

| Revenue* | 1994† | 1995‡ |
|---|---:|---:|
| Taxation | 42,347.6 | 67,082.2 |
| Income tax | 15,281.5 | 18,904.2 |
| Tax on foreign activities | 12,540.3 | — |
| Customs duty | — | 7,799.7 |
| Sales tax | 11,151.5 | 10,459.5 |
| Special taxes | 3,151.8 | 7,656.1 |
| Other taxes | 222.5 | n.a. |
| Non-tax revenue | 8,761.5 | 13,723.5 |
| Sales of shares | 3,431.2 | 3,539.0 |
| Road fund | 3,866.3 | 4,094.6 |
| Other non-tax revenue | 1,463.9 | n.a. |
| Capital revenue (privatization) | 115.8 | 2,800.0 |
| Pensions | 2,577.0 | — |
| Health insurance | 2,131.9 | — |
| **Total** | **55,933.8** | **83,605.7** |

* Excluding receipts of foreign aid (million tögrög): 7,371 in 1994; 6,020 in 1995.
† As published, but, according to the budget speech by the Minister of Finance, business tax was to be 15,300m., customs duty 10,100m. and sales tax 7,900m.
‡ Figures are based on a revised classification. Total revenue includes (million tögrög): Social security 17,735.6; Revenue from budgeted organizations 2,564.5.

| Expenditure | 1994 | 1995* |
|---|---:|---:|
| Wages (state enterprises) | 5,158.9 | 10,228.6 |
| Capital investment | 6,000.0 | 7,350.0 |
| Construction projects | 2,195.9 | n.a. |
| Defence | 7,214.1 | 9,050.8 |
| General social services | 2,262.3 | 3,979.0 |
| Presidency | 60.5 | 62.4 |
| Mongolian Great Hural | 105.3 | 237.3 |
| Constitutional Court | 4.5 | 9.7 |
| Law courts | 238.6 | 456.7 |
| Procuracy | 176.8 | 232.3 |
| State security | 390.8 | 515.8 |
| Special purpose fund | 15,981.8 | — |
| Pensions | 10,384.6 | — |
| Support for low incomes | 560.0 | — |
| Health insurance | 2,891.1 | — |
| State training | 2,146.1 | — |
| Pensions and insurance | — | 6,000.0 |
| Local budgets | 10,865.3 | 13,481.1 |
| Other purposes† | | |
| Education | 15,300.0 | 22,300.0 |
| Health | 10,200.0 | 13,500.0 |
| Culture and arts | 1,200.0 | — |
| Science | 912.0 | 1,200.0 |
| Radio and television | 1,700.0 | — |
| Environment | 900.0 | — |
| Administration | 6,460.0 | n.a. |
| Police and prisons | 4,200.0 | n.a. |
| Culture, sports and media | — | 4,100.0 |
| **Total** | **78,468.1** | **96,509.1** |

* Figures are based on a revised classification.
† Expenditure shared between central and local budgets.

### NATIONAL ACCOUNTS
(million tögrög at current prices)

| | 1988 | 1989 | 1990 |
|---|---:|---:|---:|
| Net material product | 7,899.6 | 8,646.0 | 8,327.5 |

Source: UN, *National Accounts Statistics*.

### BALANCE OF PAYMENTS (US $ million)

| | 1990 | 1991 | 1992* |
|---|---:|---:|---:|
| Merchandise exports f.o.b. | 444.8 | 346.5 | 355.8 |
| Merchandise imports f.o.b. | -1,023.6 | -501.2 | -400.0 |
| **Trade balance** | **-578.8** | **-154.7** | **-44.2** |
| Exports of services | 48.0 | 23.6 | 35.0 |
| Imports of services | -77.0 | -26.9 | -33.4 |
| Other income received | 5.1 | 2.9 | 0.2 |
| Other income paid | -48.7 | -5.4 | -27.2 |
| Private unrequited transfers (net) | 0.0 | 0.0 | -2.9 |
| Official unrequited transfers (net) | 7.4 | 43.6 | 41.2 |
| **Current balance** | **-644.0** | **-116.9** | **-31.3** |
| Direct investment (net) | 0.0 | 0.0 | 2.0 |
| Other long-term capital (net) | 516.7 | 130.3 | 86.3 |
| Short-term capital (net) | 74.0 | -105.6 | -69.6 |
| Net errors and omissions | | | |
| **Overall balance** | **-53.3** | **-92.2** | **-12.6** |

* Figures are provisional.
Source: World Bank, *World Tables*.

## External Trade

### SELECTED COMMODITIES

| Imports | 1991 | 1992 | 1993 |
|---|---:|---:|---:|
| Industrial technical goods (US $ million) | 283.7 | 349.1 | 272.6 |
| Fuel and petroleum (US $ million) | 130.1 | 88.3 | 87.0 |
| Consumer goods (US $ million) | 77.2 | 69.2 | 88.9 |
| Sugar ('000 metric tons) | 32.0 | 17.6 | 19.4 |
| Butter ('000 metric tons) | 1.7 | 1.6 | 7.0 |
| Flour ('000 metric tons) | 39.0 | 20.3 | 84.7 |
| Rice ('000 metric tons) | 14.7 | 4.6 | 30.2 |
| Cotton cloth ('000 metres) | 1,408.0 | 10,127.7 | 6,384.7 |
| Silk ('000 metres) | 667.5 | 444.7 | 1,078.8 |
| Footwear ('000 pairs) | 193.9 | 212.5 | 209.8 |
| Tarpaulin ('000 metres) | 80.0 | 738.7 | 1,624.0 |
| Batteries (US $ '000) | 223.1 | 2,348.5 | 841.8 |
| Tobacco (metric tons) | 486.6 | 722.2 | 235.1 |
| Matches (million boxes) | n.a. | 37.7 | 8.4 |
| Sewing machines (units) | 2,000 | 335 | 7,448 |
| Refrigerators (units) | 6,700 | 19 | 1,391 |
| Vacuum cleaners (units) | 4,000 | 29 | 1,674 |
| Television receivers (units) | n.a. | 6,250 | 7,991 |
| Motorcycles (units) | 1,050 | 775 | 2,533 |
| Household soap (metric tons) | 58.4 | 4,078.3 | 2,288.2 |
| Fresh fruit (metric tons) | 3,070.0 | 529.2 | 812.6 |
| Candles (US $ '000) | 164.3 | 706.2 | 91.2 |

## MONGOLIA

| Exports | 1992 | 1993 | 1994 |
|---|---|---|---|
| Copper concentrate ('000 metric tons) | 346.0 | 394.5 | 406.9 |
| Molybdenum concentrate (metric tons) | 2,975.1 | 2,908.7 | 5,200.0 |
| Fluorspar concentrate ('000 metric tons) | 97.2 | 77.2 | 88.0 |
| Sawn timber ('000 metric tons) | 87.6 | 78.2 | 47.0 |
| Washed wool (metric tons) | 7,320.6 | 2,638.2 | 752.1 |
| Woollen yarn (metric tons) | 108.4 | 94.5 | n.a. |
| Camel wool (metric tons) | 1,735.1 | 3,063.4 | 2,504.5 |
| Camel wool goods ('000 articles) | 44.9 | 12.2 | n.a. |
| Processed cashmere (metric tons) | n.a. | 1,450.7 | 1,323.5 |
| Cashmere tops and goods (metric tons) | n.a. | 65.0 | 252.0 |
| Leather jackets ('000 articles) | 108.6 | 68.0 | n.a. |
| Sheepskin coats ('000 articles) | 38.7 | 12.3 | n.a. |
| Carpets ('000 sq metres) | 405.7 | 481.1 | 68.6 |
| Guts ('000 bunches) | 3,523.8 | 1,361.8 | 914.0 |
| Horse hides ('000) | 13.5 | 153.5 | 39.1 |
| Cow hides ('000) | 68.9 | 465.7 | 313.0 |
| Sheep skins ('000) | 1,633.6 | 4,151.2 | 1,992.9 |
| Goat skins ('000) | 265.0 | 681.9 | 494.7 |
| Horn, antler (metric tons) | 347.3 | 272.7 | n.a. |
| Waste bone (metric tons) | 3,233.0 | 1,630.6 | 4,929.8 |
| Scrap iron ('000 metric tons) | 32.1 | 39.3 | 22.7 |
| Non-ferrous scrap (metric tons) | 4,408.0 | 3,284.1 | 505.9 |

**PRINCIPAL TRADING PARTNERS** (US $ '000)

| Imports | 1994 |
|---|---|
| Belgium | 888.1 |
| China, People's Republic | 21,379.2 |
| Czech Republic | 2,804.2 |
| Germany | 8,802.7 |
| Hong Kong | 9,608.7 |
| Italy | 246.4 |
| Japan | 13,702.4 |
| Kazakhstan | 147.2 |
| Korea, Republic | 9,430.1 |
| Netherlands | 126.6 |
| Russia | 128,306.8 |
| Switzerland | 3,347.7 |
| United Kingdom | 1,081.8 |
| USA | 8,216.4 |
| **Total** (incl. others) | 218,662.1 |

| Exports | 1994 |
|---|---|
| Belgium | 1,615.8 |
| China, People's Republic | 62,811.6 |
| Czech Republic | 515.5 |
| Germany | 2,027.2 |
| Hong Kong | 2,280.9 |
| Italy | 8,716.4 |
| Japan | 42,344.9 |
| Kazakhstan | 40,729.0 |
| Korea, Republic | 19,131.5 |
| Netherlands | 3,036.2 |
| Russia | 89,869.8 |
| Switzerland | 20,692.5 |
| United Kingdom | 4,690.6 |
| USA | 11,938.0 |
| **Total** (incl. others) | 324,294.5 |

## Transport

**FREIGHT TRAFFIC** (million metric ton-km)

| | 1991 | 1992 | 1993 |
|---|---|---|---|
| Rail | 2,957.9 | 2,756.4 | 2,531.0 |
| Road | 1,271.0 | 559.1 | 268.4 |
| Air | 3.8 | 5.4 | 5.8 |
| **Total** | 4,232.7 | 3,320.9 | 2,805.2 |

**Total freight carried:** 15,200,000 tons in 1992; 11,400,000 tons in 1993; 9,900,000 in 1994.

**PASSENGER TRAFFIC** (million passenger/km)

| | 1991 | 1992 | 1993 |
|---|---|---|---|
| Rail | 598.0 | 629.5 | 582.5 |
| Road | 913.4 | 963.0 | 700.5 |
| Air | 408.1 | 364.0 | 289.6 |
| **Total** | 1,919.5 | 1,956.5 | 1,572.7 |

**Total passengers carried:** 252,000,000 in 1992; 192,000,000 in 1993; 146,900,000 in 1994.

## Communications Media

| | 1988 | 1989 | 1990 |
|---|---|---|---|
| Telephones ('000 in use) | 58.3 | 62.6 | 66.4 |
| Radio receivers ('000 in use) | 226.2 | 222.5 | 205.6 |
| Television receivers ('000 in use) | 122.8 | 132.9 | 137.4 |

**Book production** (1990): 717 titles; 6,397,000 copies. Figures include pamphlets (524 titles).

**Telephones** ('000 in use): 104.5 in 1994.

## Education

(1994/95)

| | Institutions | Teachers | Students |
|---|---|---|---|
| General schools | 659 | 19,097 | 381,204 |
| Vocational-technical | 32 | 1,800* | 7,555 |
| Special secondary | 18 | 1,300* | 12,690 |
| Higher | 9 | 1,465* | 13,800 |

* 1990/91.

# Directory

## The Constitution

The Constitution was adopted on 13 January 1992 and came into force on 12 February of that year. It proclaims Mongolia (*Mongol Uls*), with its capital at Ulan Bator (Ulaanbaatar), to be an independent sovereign republic which ensures for its people democracy, justice, freedom, equality and national unity. It recognizes all forms of ownership of property, including land, and affirms that a 'multi-structured economy' will take account of 'universal trends of world economic development and national conditions'.

The 'citizen's right to life' is qualified by the death penalty for serious crimes, and the law provides for the imposition of forced labour. Freedom of residence and travel within the country and abroad may be limited for security reasons. The citizens' duties are to respect the Constitution and the rights and interests of others, pay taxes, and serve in the armed forces, as well as the 'sacred duty' to work, safeguard one's health, bring up one's children and protect the environment.

Supreme legislative power is vested in the Mongolian Great Hural (Assembly), a single chamber with 76 members elected by universal adult suffrage for a four-year term, with a Chairman and Vice-Chairman elected from amongst the members. The Great Hural recognizes the President on his election and appoints the Prime Minister and members of the Cabinet. A presidential veto of a decision of the Great Hural can be overruled by a two-thirds majority of the Hural. Sessions are held once every six months for at least 65 working days; decisions are taken by a simple majority.

The President is Head of State and Commander-in-Chief of the Armed Forces. He must be an indigenous citizen at least 45 years old who has resided continuously in Mongolia for the five years before election. Presidential candidates are nominated by parties with seats in the Great Hural; the winning candidate in general presidential elections is President for a four-year term.

The Cabinet is the highest executive body and drafts economic, social and financial policy, takes environmental protection measures, strengthens defence and security, protects human rights and implements foreign policy for a four-year term.

The Supreme Court, headed by the Chief Justice, is the highest judicial organ. Judicial independence is protected by the General Council of Courts. The Procurator General, nominated by the President, serves a six-year term.

Local administration in the 21 *aymag* (provinces) and Ulan Bator is effected on the basis of 'self-government and central guidance', comprising local hurals of representatives elected by citizens and governors (*dzasag darga*), nominated by the Prime Minister to serve four-year terms.

The Constitutional Court, which guarantees 'strict observance' of the Constitution, consists of nine members nominated for a six-year term, three each by the Great Hural, the President and the Supreme Court.

## The Government

### PRESIDENCY

**President and Commander-in-Chief of the Armed Forces:** PUNSALMAAGIYN OCHIRBAT (elected Chairman of the Presidium of the People's Great Hural 21 March 1990; elected President of Mongolia 3 September 1990; re-elected President of Mongolia by direct vote 6 June 1993).
**Presidential Chancellor:** MENDSAYHANY ENHSAYHAN.
**Director of the Presidential Information Service:** CHUNTYN CHULUUNBAATAR.

### NATIONAL SECURITY COUNCIL

The President heads the National Security Council; the Prime Minister and the Chairman of the Mongolian Great Hural are its members (the Secretary is the President's national security adviser).
**Chairman:** PUNSALMAAGIYN OCHIRBAT.
**Members:** PUNTSAGIYN JASRAY, NATSAGIYN BAGABANDI.
**Secretary:** JARGALSAYHANY ENHSAYHAN.

### CABINET
(June 1995)

**Prime Minister:** PUNTSAGIYN JASRAY.
**Deputy Prime Minister:** LHAMSÜRENGIYN ENEBISH.
**Deputy Prime Minister:** CHOYJILSÜRENGIYN PÜREVDORJ.
**Minister of Culture:** NAMBARYN ENHBAYAR.
**Minister of Defence:** Lt-Gen. SHAGALYN JADAMBAA.
**Minister of Demography and Labour:** ERDENIYN GOMBOJAV.
**Minister of the Environment:** DZAMBYN BATJARGAL.
**Minister of Finance:** ERDENIYN BYAMBAJAV.
**Minister of Food and Agriculture:** TSEVEENJAVYN ÖÖLD.
**Minister of Foreign Relations:** TSERENPILIYN GOMBOSÜREN.
**Minister of Power, Geology and Mining:** BYAMBYN JIGJID.
**Minister of Health:** PAGVAJAVYN NYAMDAVAA.
**Minister of Law:** NAMSRAYJAVYN LUVSANJAV.
**Minister of Infrastructure Development:** RADZDAKIYN SANDALHAN.
**Minister of Science and Education:** SANJBEGDZIYN TÖMÖR-OCHIR.
**Minister of Trade and Industry:** TSEVEGMIDIYN TSOGT.
**Head of Administration:** SAMDANGIYN BANDZRAGCH.

### GOVERNMENT DEPARTMENTS
(June 1995)

#### Basic Structure Directorates

**Chairman of the National Development Board:** CHÜLTEMIYN ULAAN.
**Head of the Central Intelligence Directorate:** Lt-Col DALHJAVYN SANDAG.
**Head of the Chief Directorate of Police:** Maj.-Gen. BAASTYN PÜREV.
**Head of the Radio and Television Affairs Directorate:** BYAMBAJAVYN ÖVGÖNHÜÜ.
**Head of the Statistics Directorate:** BADAMTSEDENGIYN TSEND-AYUUSH.
**Head of the Montsame News Agency:** CHULUUNBATYN ERDENE.

#### Infrastructure Directorates

**Head of the Chief Directorate of Customs:** BADRAHYN SHARAVSAMBUU.
**Head of the Chief Directorate of Taxation:** LHANAASÜRENGIYN PÜREVDORJ.
**Head of the Border Troops Directorate:** Maj.-Gen. P. SÜNDEV.
**Head of the Civil Defence Directorate*:** Maj.-Gen. GOMBOSÜRENGIYN DAMDINSÜREN.
* Directly subordinate to the Prime Minister.

### MINISTRIES AND GOVERNMENT DEPARTMENTS

All Ministries and Government Departments are in Ulan Bator.
**Ministry of Foreign Relations:** Ulan Bator; tel. 321870; telex 245.
**Ministry of Trade and Industry:** Ulan Bator 11; tel. 323454; telex 221; fax 326325.

## President and Legislature

### PRESIDENT

**Election, 6 June 1993**

| Candidate | Votes | % |
|---|---|---|
| PUNSALMAAGIYN OCHIRBAT (MNDP/MSDP) | 592,622 | 57.8 |
| LODONGIYN TÜDEV (MPRP) | 396,870 | 38.7 |

### MONGOLIAN GREAT HURAL

Under the fourth Constitution, which came into force in February 1992, the single-chamber Mongolian Great Hural is the state's supreme legislative body. Its Chairman may act as President of Mongolia when the President is indisposed. At the June 1992 general election 76 members from 26 constituencies were elected to serve a four-year term: 70 from the Mongolian People's Revolutionary Party (MPRP), one independent (pro-MPRP), one from the Mongolian Democratic Party (MDP), one independent (pro-MDP), and one each from the Mongolian National Progress Party (MNPP), the Mongolian Social-Democratic Party and the United Party (UP). (In late 1992 the MDP, MNPP and UP merged with the Mongolian Renewal Party to form the Mongolian National Democratic Party.) The Great Hural must meet for at least 65 working days in every six months. There are six Standing Committees.
**Chairman:** NATSAGIYN BAGABANDI.

MONGOLIA

Vice-Chairman: JAMBYN GOMBOJAV.
General Secretary: NAMSRAYN RINCHINDORJ.

## Political Organizations

**Mongolian People's Revolutionary Party (MPRP):** Baga Toyruu 37/1, Ulan Bator 11; tel. 323245; fax 320368; f. 1921; 81,400 mems (March 1995).

### Little Hural

At the 21st congress of the MPRP, in February 1992, 147 members were elected to the Central Committee. In October 1992 the Central Committee was renamed the Little Hural and its membership was increased to 169 (and subsequently to 198). The Presidium was renamed the Party Leadership Council.

### Party Leadership Council

**General Secretary:** BÜDRAGCHAAGIYN DASH-YONDON.
**Secretaries:** BALDANGIYN ENHMANDAH, DAMDINGIYN DEMBEREL.
**Members:**
NADMIDIYN BAYARTSAYHAN
JANLAVYN BYAMBAJAV
SANDUYJAVYN DASHDAVAA
LHAMSÜRENGIYN ENEBISH
ERDENIYN GOMBOJAV
GÜNTEVIYN ÖLDZIY
TSERENHÜÜGIYN SHARAVDORJ
LODONGIYN TÜDEV

#### OTHER PARTIES

**Believers' Democratic Party:** Ulan Bator; f. 1990 (registered in 1991); Buddhist; 2,000 mems (May 1991); Leader TS. BAYARSÜREN.
**Mongolian Democratic Renewal Party:** Ulan Bator; f. 1994; Chair. DASHIYN BYAMBASÜREN.
**Mongolian Greens Party:** CPOB 1089, Ulan Bator; tel. 323871; telex 79236; f. 1990; political wing of the Alliance of Greens; 3,500 mems (1993); Chair. L. NYAM.
**Mongolian National Democratic Party (MNDP):** Chingisiyn örgön chölöö 1, Ulan Bator; tel. 324221; fax 325170; f. 1992, following a merger of the Mongolian Democratic Party, the Mongolian National Progress Party, the Mongolian Renewal Party and the United Party; 40,000 mems (Nov. 1993); Pres. DAVAADORJIYN GANBOLD.
**Mongolian People's Party:** Ulan Bator; f. 1991; its establishment forestalled plans by MPRP to revert to its original name, MPP; Chair. Lama D. BAASAN.
**Mongolian Social-Democratic Party (MSDP):** POB 578, Ulan Bator 11; tel. 329469; f. 1990; political wing of the Democratic Socialist Movement; consultative mem. of the Socialist International; 20,000 mems (Feb. 1993); Chair. RADNAASÜMBERELIYN GONCHIGDORJ.
**United Heritage Party:** Ulan Bator; f. 1993 as an amalgamation of the United Private Owners' Party, United Herdsmen's and Farmers' Party, Capitalist Party and Independence Party; 20,000 mems (Jan. 1994); Chair. BAASANJAVYN JAMTS.

## Diplomatic Representation

### EMBASSIES IN MONGOLIA

**Bulgaria:** POB 702, Ulan Bator; tel. 321119; telex 220; Ambassador: (vacant).
**China, People's Republic:** Ulan Bator; tel. 322778; Ambassador: PEI JIAYI.
**Cuba:** Ulan Bator; tel. 327008; telex 228; Ambassador: ESTEBAN LOBAINA ROMERO.
**Germany:** POB 708, Ulan Bator; tel. 323325; telex 79242; fax 323905; Ambassador: Dr CORNEL METTERNICH.
**Hungary:** Enh Tayvny Gudamj 1, Ulan Bator; tel. 323973; telex 79322; fax 311793; Ambassador: MIKLÓS JACZKOVITS.
**India:** POB 691, Ulan Bator; tel. 358122; telex 79325; fax 358171; Ambassador: KUSHOK BAKULA.
**Japan:** Zaluuchuudyn Gudamj 12, Ulan Bator 13; tel. 324408; telex 79229; fax 323745; Ambassador: YOSHIHIRO HASUMI.
**Korea, Democratic People's Republic:** Ulan Bator; Ambassador: CHONG CHUNG HO.
**Korea, Republic:** Ulan Bator; Ambassador: KIM CHONG-SUNG.
**Poland:** Zaluuchuudyn Örgön Chölöö 10, Ulan Bator 13 (PO Box 706); tel. 323365; Ambassador: STANISŁAW GODZIŃSKI.
**Romania:** Ulan Bator; telex 252; Ambassador: (vacant).
**Russia:** Ulan Bator; Ambassador: SERGEI RAZOV.
**United Kingdom:** Enh Tayvny Gudamj 30 (PO Box 703), Ulan Bator 13; tel. 358133; telex 79261; fax 358036; Ambassador: IAN SLOANE.
**USA:** Ulan Bator; tel. 329639; telex 79253; fax 320776; Ambassador: DONALD C. JOHNSON.
**Viet Nam:** Ulan Bator; telex 249; Ambassador: VU VAN VACH.
**Yugoslavia:** Ulan Bator; telex 259; Ambassador: (vacant).

## Judicial System

Under the fourth Constitution, judicial independence is protected by the General Council of Courts, consisting of the Chief Justice (Chairman of the Supreme Court), the Chairman of the Constitutional Court, Procurator General, Minister of Law and others. The Council nominates the members of the Supreme Court for approval by the Great Hural. The Chief Justice is chosen from among the members of the Supreme Court and approved by the President for a six-year term. Civil, criminal and administrative cases are handled by Ulan Bator City court, the 18 *aymag* (provincial) courts, *sum* (rural district) and urban district courts, while the system of special courts (military, railway, etc.) is still in place. The Procurator General and his deputies, who play an investigatory role, are nominated by the President and approved by the Great Hural for six-year terms. The Constitutional Court safeguards the constitutional legality of legislation. It consists of nine members, three nominated each by the President, Great Hural and Supreme Court, and elects a Chairman from among its number.

**Chief Justice:** DASHDORJIYN DEMBERELTSEREN.
**Procurator General:** NANDZADYN GANBAYAR.
**Chairman of Constitutional Court:** GALDANGIYN SOVD.

## Religion

The 1992 Constitution maintains the separation of Church and State but forbids any discrimination, declaring that 'the State shall respect religion and religion shall honour the State'. During the early years of communist rule Mongolia's traditional Mahayana Buddhism was virtually destroyed, then exploited as a 'show-piece' for visiting dignitaries (although the Dalai Lama himself was not permitted to visit Mongolia until the early 1980s). The national Buddhist centre is Gandantegchinlen Hiyd (monastery) in Ulan Bator, with about 100 lamas and a seminary; it is the headquarters of the Asian Buddhist Conference for Peace. In the early 1990s some 2,000 lamas established small communities at the sites of 120 former monasteries, temples and religious schools, some of which were being restored. These included two other important monasteries, Erdene Dzuu and Amarbayasgalant. The Kazakhs of western Mongolia are nominally Sunni Muslims, but their mosques, also destroyed in the 1930s or closed subsequently, are only now being rebuilt or reopened. Traces of shamanism from the pre-Buddhist period still survive. In recent years there has been a new upsurge in Christian missionary activity in Mongolia. However, the Law on State-Church Relations (of November 1993) sought to make Buddhism the predominant religion and restricted the dissemination of beliefs other than Buddhism, Islam and shamanism. The law was challenged by human rights campaigners and Mongolian Christians as unconstitutional.

### BUDDHISM

**Hamba Lama:** Ulan Bator 38; tel. 60354; Head of the Gandantegchinlen Monastery, Centre of Mongolian Buddhists: DEMBERELIYN CHOYJAMTS.
**Union of Mongolian Believers:** Pres. S. BAYANTSAGAAN.

### CHRISTIANITY
#### Roman Catholic Church

**Catholic Mission:** POB 694, Ulan Bator; Superior Rev. WENS PADILLA.

#### Protestant Churches

**Association of Mongolian Protestants:** f. 1990; Pastor M. BOLDBAATAR.

### ISLAM

**Muslim Society:** f. 1990; Chair. of Central Council Haji HADIRYN SAYRAAN.

## The Press

### PRINCIPAL NATIONAL NEWSPAPERS

**Ardchilal** (Democracy): Democratic Association, Erhüügiyn 5, Sühbaatar Düüreg, Ulan Bator; tel. 56193; 3 a month; Editor S. AMARSANAA.

# MONGOLIA

**Ardyn Erh** (People's Power): Dzasgiyn Gadzryn Ordon, Ulan Bator 12; tel. and fax 329281; f. 1924, restored 1990; publ. by Mongolian Great Hural and Cabinet; 312 a year; Editor-in-Chief Ts. Baldorj; circ. 77,500.

**Bagsh** (Teacher): Ulan Bator; f. 1989; publ. by Ministry of Science and Education; 36 a year; subscription circ. 17,636.

**Chölööt Inder** (Free Tribune): CPO Box 855, Ulan Bator 210646; tel. 324936; telex 79258; f. 1991; publ. by United Asscn of Free Trade Unions; 36 a year; Editor R. Battömör; circ. 10,000.

**Dzohist Ayalgüü** (Harmony): CPO Box 310, Ulan Bator; tel. 328497; f. 1990; publ. by National Association of Free Writers and Translators; 24 a year; Editor J. Saruulbuyan.

**Erh Chölöö** (Freedom): MÜAN-yn töv bayr, Chingisiyn örgön chölöö, Ulan Bator; tel. 310717; fax 325170; f. 1992; organ of the Mongolian National Democratic Party; 36 a year; Editor Sh. Altangerel; circ. 2,000.

**Hödölmör** (Labour): Sühbaataryn Talbay 3, Ulan Bator 210664; tel. 323026; f. 1928; publ. by Confederation of Mongolian Trade Unions; 80 a year; Editor-in-Chief N. Myagmar; subscription circ. 64,920.

**Il Tovchoo** (Openness): Ulan Bator; tel. 321653; f. 1990; publ. by Montsame news agency; current affairs; 36 a year; Editor G. Akim; circ. 15,000.

**Mongol Horshoo** (Mongolian Co-operative): Huv'sgalchdyn Örgön Chölöö 24, Ulan Bator 11; tel. 320567; f. 1990; publ. by Association of Production and Services Co-operatives and Horshooimpeks; 24 a year; Editor Ch. Alagsay; circ. 15,000.

**Mongolyn Dzaluuchuud** (Mongolian Youth): Baga Toyruu 10, MZH ordon 207, Ulan Bator 210611; tel. 321921; f. 1924; publ. by Revolutionary Youth League; 36 a year; Editor N. Lutbayar; subscription circ. 76,278.

**Mongolyn Hödöö** (Mongolian Countryside): Ulan Bator; tel. 55577; f. 1961; publ. by Association of Herdsmen, Association of Cropgrowers and National Association of Agricultural Co-operative Members; 36 a year; Editor-in-Chief Ts. Mönhbaatar; subscription circ. 21,523.

**Mongolyn Sport** (Mongolian Sport): Baga Toyrog 55, Ulan Bator 11; tel. 324052; publ. by National Olympic Committee; 56 a year; Editor S. Tüvdenyam; subscription circ. 27,359.

**Niysleliyn Sonin Bichig** (Capital's Newspaper): Ulan Bator; f. 1954; fmrly *Ulaanbaataryn Medee*; publ. by Ulan Bator City People's Revolutionary Party Cttee; weekly; Editor L. Chuluunbat; subscription circ. 39,650.

**Tonshuul** (Woodpecker): Huv'sgalchdyn Örgön Chölöö 24, Ulan Bator; tel. 322385; f. 1935; publ. by Union of Writers; satirical; 16 a year; Responsible Editor J. Baramsay; subscription circ. 54,192.

**Tusgaar Togtnol** (Independence): Ulan Bator; f. 1930; fmrly *Ulaan Od*; publ. by Ministry of Defence; 36 a year; Editor-in-Chief A. Bayarmagnay; subscription circ. 24,659.

**Ulaanbaatar** (Ulan Bator): Baga Toyrog, Ulan Bator 11; tel. 322215; f. 1990; publ. by Ulan Bator City Executive Administration; 248 a year; Responsible Editor Ü. Hürelbaatar; subscription circ. 31,000.

**Utga Dzohiol** (Literature): Union of Writers, Sühbaataryn Gudamj 11, Ulan Bator 46; tel. 321863; f. 1955; 24 a year; Editor-in-Chief Ts. Enhbat; circ. 3,000.

**Üg** (The Word): CPO Box 578, Ulan Bator; tel. 321204; f. 1990; publ. by Mongolian Social-Democratic Party; 24 a year; Editor S. Idshinnorov; subscription circ. 30,331.

**Ünen** (Truth): Huv'sgalchdyn Örgön Chölöö 24, Ulan Bator 11; tel. 323223; f. 1920; publ. by the MPRP; 96 a year; Editor-in-Chief Lodongiyn Tüdev; circ. 150,000.

## PRINCIPAL PERIODICALS

**Birjiyn Medee** (Stockmarket News): Ulan Bator; f. 1991; weekly.

**Bodlyn Solbitsol** (Cross Opinions): Ulan Bator; f. 1991; publ. by *Ünen*; 24 a year.

**Bodrol Byasalgal** (Interpretation and Contemplation): Ulan Bator; theoretical and political magazine; publ. by MPRP; 4 a year; Editor G. Törtogtoh; circ. 15,000.

**Bolovsrol** (Education): Ulan Bator; publ. by Ministry of Science and Education; 8 a year.

**Dorno-Örnö** (East-West): POB 48/17, Ulan Bator; fax 322613; f. 1978; publ. by Institute of Oriental and International Studies of Acad. of Sciences; scientific and socio-political journal; history, culture, foreign relations; articles in Mongolian, with summaries in English; two a year; Editor-in-Chief Dr Ts. Batbayar.

**Dzah Dzeel** (Market): Ulan Bator; f. 1990; publ. by Ministry of Trade and Industry; weekly.

**Dzar Bichig** (Publicity Herald): Ulan Bator; f. 1991; free journal publ. by National Information Centre containing theatre, cinema and television programmes and advertisements; 104 a year.

*Directory*

**Dzar Medee** (Business Times): POB 584, Ulan Bator 210646; tel. 322073; f. 1991; advertising paper publ. by Günnü Inc., National Information Centre; Editors V. Baatarchuluun, D. Ganbaatar.

**Dzasgiyn Gadzryn Medee** (Government News): Ulan Bator; f. 1991; presidential and government decrees and resolutions; 3 a week; Editor-in-Chief H. Tsevlee.

**Erüül Mend** (Health): Ulan Bator; publ. by Ministry of Health; quarterly; Editor-in-Chief Sh. Jigjidsüren.

**Gal** (Fire): CPO Box 527, Ulan Bator 210611; f. 1991; non-political cultural journal publ. by the Mongolian Cultural Foundation; Editor-in-Chief Y. Baatar.

**Goo Maral** (Beautiful Doe): POB 1058/46, Ulan Bator; tel. 328060; fax 327723; f. 1925; publ. by Federation of Women; quarterly; Editor-in-Chief J. Erdenechimeg; circ. 4,000.

**Haluun Hönjil** (Warm Blanket): POB 44/587, Ulan Bator; tel. 325115; 'erotic' fortnightly; Owners S. Bayarmönh, L. Zorigt.

**Höh Ineed** (Ironic Laugh): PO 46, Box 971, Ulan Bator; tel. 321425; f. 1990; satirical independent; monthly; Editor J. Chimedtseren.

**Huul' Dzüyn Medeelel** (Legal Information): Ministry of Law, Ulan Bator; f. 1990; monthly.

**Huul' Yos** (Legality): Ulan Bator; publ. by Procurator's Office, Supreme Court and Ministry of Law; quarterly; Editor B. Hatanbaatar.

**Hün Boloh Bagaasaa** (Growing Up): Ulan Bator; publ. by Ministry of Science and Education; 24 a year; Editor N. Tsevgee; circ. 23,400.

**Hüniy Erh** (Human Rights): POB 107, Ulan Bator 24; tel. 324573; f. 1991; publ. by Voluntary Committee for Defence of Human Rights and Mongolian Section of Amnesty International; quarterly.

**Itgel + T** (Hope Plus Technology): Room 221, 2nd floor, Design Institute, Barilgachdyn Talbay, Ulan Bator; f. 1991; publ. by Association of Private Manufacturers; monthly.

**Malchin** (Herdsman): Ulan Bator; quarterly.

**Mongol Roman** (Mongolian Novel): Union of Writers, Sühbaataryn Gudamj 11, Ulan Bator 46; tel. 321863; f. 1989; 2 a year; Editor-in-Chief Ts. Enhbat; circ. 2,000.

**Mongoljin Goo** (Mongolian Beauty): POB 1058/46, Ulan Bator; tel. 328060; fax 327723; f. 1990; 36 a year; supplement of *Goo Maral*; Editor J. Erdenechimeg; circ. 3,000.

**Mongol Times**: D. Natsagdorjiyn Gudamj, Ulan Bator; tel. 310665; monthly; Editor Ch. Kulanda.

**Mongolyn Anagaah Uhaan** (Mongolian Medicine): Ulan Bator; publ. by Ministry of Health and Scientific Society of Physicians; quarterly; Editor Sh. Jigjidsüren.

**Mongolyn Hödöö Aj Ahuy** (Mongolian Agriculture): Ulan Bator; tel. 55577; publ. by Ministry of Food and Agriculture and Union of Agricultural Production Associations; quarterly; Editor-in-Chief Ts. Mönhbaatar.

**Setgüülch** (Journalist): Ulan Bator; tel. 325388; f. 1982; publ. by Union of Journalists; journalism, politics, literature, art, economy; quarterly; Editor T. Baasansüren; circ. 4,000.

**Shinjleh Uhaany Akademiyn Medee** (Academy of Sciences News): Sühbaataryn Talbay 3, Ulan Bator; telex 305; f. 1961; publ. by Academy of Sciences; quarterly; Editor S. Norovsambuu.

**Töriyn Medeelel** (State Information): Government House, Ulan Bator 12; tel. 324460; f. 1990; presidential and governmental decrees, state laws, parliamentary news; 10 a year; circ. 10,000.

**Tsog** (Spark): Union of Writers, Sühbaataryn Gudamj 11, Ulan Bator 46; tel. 321863; f. 1944; 2 a year; Editor-in-Chief Ts. Enhbat; circ. 2,000.

## FOREIGN LANGUAGE PUBLICATIONS

**Evt Shaadzgay** (Friendly Magpies): POB 971, Ulan Bator 46; f. 1991; for students of English; with parallel texts in English and Mongolian; monthly; Editor B. Pürevdorj.

**Foreign Trade of Mongolia:** Chamber of Commerce and Industry, Sambuugiyn Gudamj 11, Ulan Bator 38; telex 79336; fax 324620; 2 a year; in English.

**The Mongolian Independent:** Ulan Bator; f. 1993; fortnightly; in English; Editor-in-Chief Ch. Buyannemeh.

**The Mongol Messenger:** Montsame News Agency, POB 1514, Ulan Bator; tel. 325512; telex 230; fax 327857; f. 1991; weekly newspaper in English; Editor-in-Chief Chanravyn Bürenbayar; circ. 1,200.

**Novosti Mongolii** (News from Mongolia): POB 1514, Ulan Bator; tel. 310157; fax 327857; f. 1942; fortnightly; in Russian; Editor-in-Chief Ch. Tümendelger.

## NEWS AGENCIES

**Montsame (Mongol Tsahilgaan Medeeniy Agentlag)** (Mongolian News Agency): Jigjidjavyn Gudamj 1, Ulan Bator 13; tel. 320077;

telex 230; fax 327857; f. 1957; govt-controlled; Dir-Gen. Chuluun-batyn Erdene.

### Foreign Bureaux

**Informatsionnoye Telegrafnoye Agentstvo Rossii—Telegrafnoe Agentstvo Suverennykh Stran (ITAR—TASS)** (Russia): October 4, Rm 323, Ulan Bator; telex 242; Bureau Chief V. B. Ionov; Correspondent Dugar Sanzhiyev.

**Rossiyskoye Informatsionnoye Agentstvo—Novosti (RIA—Novosti)** (Russia): POB 686, Ulan Bator; tel. 327384; telex 240; Bureau Chief V. Oganov.

**Xinhua (New China) News Agency** (People's Republic of China): Ulan Bator; tel. 322718; Correspondents Wang Yimin, Chang Wanlong, Lu Guodong.

## Publishers

### Government Publishing House

**Sühbaatar Publishing House:** Ulan Bator; produces 70% of Mongolia's printed matter, including 12 central newspapers, 32 magazines and, in 1988, 6,699 books and brochures (7.8m. copies; 8.4m. copies in 1989).

There are also publishing houses in each province, and other publishing houses in Ulan Bator. Newspaper publishing fell from 134.1m. copies in 1990 to 20.5m. copies in 1993. Book printing likewise declined, from 96.3m. printer's sheets (each of 16 pages) in 1990 to 19.2m. in 1993.

## Radio and Television

In 1990 there were 205,600 radio receivers and 137,400 television receivers in use, as well as 443,200 wired radio outlets in urban areas. A 1,900-km radio relay line from Ulan Bator to Altay and Ölgiy also provides direct-dialling telephone links as well as television services for western Mongolia. New radio relay lines have been built from Ulan Bator to Choybalsan and from Ulan Bator to Sühbaatar and Saynshand. Most of the population is in the zone of television reception, following the inauguration of relays via Asiasat.

**Head of Mongolian Government Radio and Television Affairs Directorate:** Byambajavyn Övgönhüü.

### RADIO

**Mongolradio:** Huv'sgalyn Dzam 3, Ulan Bator 11; tel. 321624; f. 1934; under govt control; programmes in Mongolian (two), Russian, Chinese, English, Japanese and Kazakh; Dir Urtnasangiyn Sarantuyaa.

### TELEVISION

**Mongoltelevidz:** Huv'sgalyn Dzam 3, Ulan Bator 11; f. 1967; under govt control; morning and evening transmissions, five days per week, of locally-originated material relayed by land-line and Asiasat; programmes received from the former USSR via the Molniya satellite and the Orbita ground station in Ulan Bator and via the Ekran satellite system in several hundred other population centres; US programmes also relayed for 2–3 hours daily; Kazakh television received in Bayan-ölgiy; Dir Shirbadzaryn Altansüh.

**Medeelel, Ariljaany Chölöö Suvag** (Free Channel of Information and Exchange): Ulan Bator; f. 1992; home and foreign news, press comments, interviews, entertainment and advertising on radio and television; Dirs D. Altangerel, D. Garam-Ochir.

## Finance

(cap. = capital; m. = million; amounts in tögrög)

### BANKING

#### Central Bank

**Mongolbank:** Hudaldaany Gudamj 6, Ulan Bator; tel. 322173; telex 79333; fax 311471; f. 1924 as the State Bank of the Mongolian People's Republic; Pres. Demchigjavyn Molomjamts.

#### Other Banks

**Ardyn Bank** (People's Bank): Mongolbank Building, Ulan Bator; tel. 327467; f. 1991; cap. 15,100m.; Dir-Gen. A. Tserendorj; 14 brs.

**Avtodzam Bank** (Motor Roads Bank): Bridge-Building Office, Ulan Bator; tel. 381744; f. 1990; cap. 95m.; Dir-Gen. Ts. Sangidorj.

**Bayan Bogd Bank:** Ulan Bator; Owner D. Adyaa.

**Ediyn Tenger Bank:** Ulan Bator; Dir-Gen. V. Baatar.

**Hödöö Aj Ahuyn Bank** (Agricultural Bank): Agricultural Co-operatives Association Building, Ulan Bator 240149; telex 79384; fax 358670; f. 1991; cap. 5,300m.; Dir-Gen. Ch. Chuluunbaatar; 342 brs.

**Höröngö Oruulalt Tehnologiyn Shinechleltiyn Bank** (Bank for Capital Investment and Technological Innovation): Hudaldaany Gudamj, Ulan Bator 11; tel. 381125; telex 79245; fax 381115; f. 1990; cap. 1,300m.; Dir N. Chuluunbaatar; 31 brs.

**Hudaldaa Högjliyn Bank** (Trade and Development Bank): Hudaldaany Gudamj 6, Ulan Bator; tel. 326729; telex 79334; fax 325449; f. 1991; carries out Mongolbank's foreign operations; Dir-Gen. E. Sandagdorj.

**Mongol Biznes Bank** (Mongolian Business Bank): Ulan Bator; Dir-Gen. A. Davaanyam.

**Mongol Daatgal Bank** (Mongolian Insurance Bank): Sühbaataryn Talbay 20A, Ulan Bator 11; tel. 310827; telex 79366; fax 323614; f. 1990; cap. 1,121m.; Dir-Gen. Sh. Goohüü; 22 brs.

**Mongol Horshoo Bank** (Mongolian Co-operative Bank): Karl Marksyn Gudamj 4, Ulan Bator 48; tel. 325239; telex 79221; f. 1990; cap. 95.8m.; Chair. of Board Mijdiyn Terbish; 5 brs.

**Mongol Shuudan Bank** (Mongolian Post Bank): Ulan Bator; Dir-Gen. D. Bayar.

**Töv Adzi Bank** (Central Asia Bank): Ulan Bator; tel. 311645; f. 1992; Dir-Gen. D. Süh-Erdene.

**Tülsh-Erchim Bank** (Fuel and Power Bank): Ulan Bator; f. 1992; Dir M. Myagmarsüren.

**Ulaanbaatar Bank** (Ulan Bator Bank): Ulan Bator; Dir-Gen. A. Myagmar.

**Üyldveriyn Huv' Niylüülsen Bank** (Industrial Shares Bank): Ulan Bator 120646; tel. 310833; f. 1990; cap. 418m.; Dir-Gen. Gendendorjiyn Yansanjav.

### STOCK EXCHANGE

**Stock Exchange:** Sühbaataryn Talbay 14, Ulan Bator; tel. 310501; telex 246; fax 325170; f. 1991; Dir N. Dzoljargal.

### INSURANCE

**Agricultural Insurance Co:** Nayramdal District, Ulan Bator; tel. 54026; f. 1992; insurance of farm stock, equipment and buildings.

**Mongol Daatgal** (National Insurance and Reinsurance Co): Ih Toyruu 11, Ulan Bator; tel. 313025; telex 79367; fax 310347; f. 1934; national insurance and reinsurance enterprise; Pres. Ts. Tsend.

## Trade and Industry

**International Trade and Co-operation Department:** Ministry of Trade and Industry, Ulan Bator 11; tel. 323028; Gen. Dir P. Narangua.

**Market Research Institute:** Ministry of Trade and Industry, Ulan Bator 11; tel. 327472; telex 221; fax 326325; market information collection, analysis and dissemination, consultancy, business opportunity development, organization of international conferences, publication of lists of Mongolian foreign trade bodies; trade library; Dir Sambuugiyn Demberel.

### CO-OPERATIVES

**Association of Consumer Co-operatives:** Ulan Bator; Chair. of Central Council P. Erdenehuyag.

**Association of Production and Services Co-operatives:** Ulan Bator; tel. 77293; Pres. of Supreme Council Dandzangiyn Radnaaragchaa.

### PRIVATE ASSOCIATIONS

**Association of Individual Herdsmen:** Ulan Bator; f. 1991; Chair. Ts. Ganhuyag.

**Association of Owners of Private Enterprises:** Ulan Bator; f. 1992; Pres. T. Nyamdorj.

**Association of Owners of Private Industry:** Ulan Bator; f. 1990 with 39 mems; Pres. Luvsanbaldangiyn Nyamsambuu.

### FOREIGN TRADE

Mongolia has trading relations with over 30 countries.

**Mongolian Chamber of Commerce and Industry:** Sambuugiyn Gudamj 11, Ulan Bator 38; tel. 324620; telex 79336; f. 1960; responsible for establishing economic and trading relations, contacts between trade and industrial organizations, both at home and abroad, and for generating foreign trade; organizes commodity inspection, press information and international exhbns and fairs at

# MONGOLIA

home and abroad; registration of trademarks and patents; Chair. DAMDINDORJIYN HURTS.

### Import and Export Firms and Corporations

**Agrotekhimpeks:** Ulan Bator 32; tel. 50543; imports agricultural machinery and implements, seed, fertilizer, veterinary medicines and irrigation equipment.

**Ar'simpeks:** Ulan Bator 52; tel. 343007; telex 301; fax 343008; exports hides and skins, fur and leather goods; imports machinery, chemicals and accessories for leather, fur and shoe industries; Pres. A. TSERENBALJID.

**Avtoneftimport:** Tolgoyt, Ulan Bator; tel. 32643; imports motor vehicles, aircraft and railway rolling stock, spare parts, petroleum and petroleum products and tyres.

**Barter and Border:** Huv'sgalchdyn Örgön Chölöö, Ulan Bator 11; tel. 324848; barter and border trade operations.

**Bolovsrol:** POB 982, Ulan Bator 46; tel. 320674; telex 236; educational and medical services; produces industrial goods; Dir-Gen. S. BYAMBADORJ.

**Horshooimpeks:** Negdsen Ündesniy Gudamj 11, Ulan Bator; tel. 320116; telex 79221; fax 325717; commercial firm of Association of Production and Services Co-operatives; exports raw materials and manufactures produced by co-operatives; imports industrial machinery, consumer goods and goods for duty-free shops in Mongolia; Gen. Dir S. PÜREVDORJ.

**Horshoololimpeks:** Tolgoyt 37, Ulan Bator (PO Box 262); tel. 332926; fax 331128; f. 1964; exports sub-standard skins, hides, wool and furs, handicrafts, and finished products; imports equipment and materials for housing and for clothing and leather goods; Dir L. ÖLDZIYBUYAN.

**Kompleksimport:** Ulan Bator; tel. 32169; imports sets of equipment and turnkey projects; training of Mongolians abroad.

**Materialimpeks:** Teeverchdiyn Gudamj, Ulan Bator 35; tel. 369176; telex 79310; fax 369172; exports cement, lime, mineral pigments, sawn timber, ceramic tiles, window and door fittings; imports cement, glass, roofing material, dyes, sanitary ware, metals and metalware; Gen. Man. MOGOLDOYN NYAMJAV.

**Monel:** Science and Culture Building, 8th floor, Sühbaataryn Talbay, Ulan Bator 11; tel. 327546; telex 79311; electronics corporation, manufacturer and trader; exports and imports electronic equipment.

**Monenzym:** Research and Production Association of Enzymology and Microbiology, Tolgoyt 25, Ulan Bator; tel. 32431; telex 307; research, testing and production of enzymes and microbiological products.

**Mongol An Corporation:** Ulan Bator 38; tel. 360237; telex 79230; fax 360067; exports hunting products; imports hunting equipment and technology; organizes hunting and trekking tours; Dir-Gen. U. BUYANDELGER.

**Mongoleksport Co Ltd:** Ministry of Trade and Industry Bldg, Erh Chölööniy Talbay, Ulan Bator 11; tel. 323035; telex 79244; fax 329234; exports wool, hair, cashmere, casings, mining products, antler, skins and hides.

**Mongolimpeks:** Huv'sgalchdyn Örgön Chölöö, Ulan Bator 11; tel. 326081; telex 221; exports cashmere, camels' wool, hair, fur, casings, powdered blood and horn, antler, wheat gluten, alcoholic drinks, cashmere and camels' wool knitwear, blankets, copper concentrate, souvenirs, stamps and coins; imports light and mining industry machinery, scientific instruments, chemicals, pharmaceuticals and consumer goods.

**Mongol Gadzryn Tos:** Üyldverchniy Gudamj, Ulan Bator 37; tel. 61584; telex 79235; petroleum company engaged in petroleum exploration and development in Mongolia; Dir D. SENGEE.

**Mongol Mark:** POB 13/794, Ulan Bator; tel. 360509; fax 314124; exports and imports postage stamps, postcards and envelopes.

**Monos:** Ulan Bator 461370; tel. 64057; science and production firm; exports food protein and peptones; imports industrial goods and products.

**Noosimpeks:** Ulan Bator 52; tel. 342611; telex 302; fax 343057; exports scoured sheep's wool, yarn, carpets, fabrics, blankets, mohair and felt boots; imports machinery and chemicals for wool industry.

**Nüürs:** Ulan Bator 46; tel. 327428; telex 323; firm of the Ministry of Power; exports and imports in coal-mining field.

**Packaging:** Tolgoyt, Ulan Bator; tel. 31053; telex 221; company of the Ministry of Trade and Industry; exports raw materials of agricultural origin, sawn timber, consumer goods, unused spare parts and equipment and non-ferrous scrap; imports machinery and materials for packaging industry and consumer goods.

**Raznoimpeks:** Ulan Bator; tel. 329670; telex 317; exports canned meat, powdered bone, alcoholic drinks, macaroni and confectionery; imports cotton and woollen fabrics, silk, knitwear, shoes, fresh and canned fruit, vegetables, tea, milk powder, acids, paints, safety equipment, protective clothing, printing and packaging paper.

**Servisimpeks:** Chamber of Commerce and Industry, Sambuugiyn Gudamj, Ulan Bator 11; tel. 324620; telex 79336; printing and advertising services, international fairs, barter trade, economic co-operation and information.

**Tehnikimport:** Ulan Bator; tel. 32336; telex 314; imports machinery, instruments and spare parts for light, food, wood, building, power and mining industries, road-building and communications.

**Tuushin Co Ltd:** Ulan Bator 210628; tel. 325510; telex 231; fax 322800; foreign trade transport firm; transport and forwarding policy and services, warehousing, customs agent.

### TRADE UNIONS

**Confederation of Mongolian Trade Unions:** Sühbaataryn Talbay 3, Ulan Bator 11; tel. 327253; fax 322128; brs throughout the country; Chair. GORCHINSÜRENGIYN ADYAA; International Relations Adviser TS. NATSAGDORJ; 450,000 mems (1994).

**'Höh Mongol' (Blue Mongolia) Free Trade Unions:** Ulan Bator; f. 1991 by Mongolian Democratic Union; Leader SH. TÖMÖRBAATAR.

**United Association of Free Trade Unions:** f. 1990; Co-ordinator V. SANDAGDORJ.

# Transport

## RAILWAYS

In 1993 the Mongolian Railway had a total route length of 1,807 km (track length of 2,325 km). In 1990 it carried 2.6m. passengers and 14.5m. tons of freight (about 70% of total freight traffic). However, traffic by rail later declined, owing to fuel shortages; in 1991 rail freight carriage was 10.3m. tons, falling to 8.6m. tons in 1992.

**Ulan Bator Railway:** POB 376, Ulan Bator; Dir RADNAABADZARYN RASH.

External Lines: from the Russian frontier at Naushki/Sühbaatar (connecting with the Trans-Siberian Railway) to Ulan Bator and on to the Chinese frontier at Dzamyn-üüd/Erhlien, connecting with Beijing (total length 1,110 km).

Branches: from Darhan to Sharyn Gol coalfield (length 63 km); branch from Salhit near Darhan, westwards to Erdenet (Erdenetiyn-ovoo open-cast copper mine) in Bulgan Province (length 164 km); from Bagahangay to Baga nuur coal-mine, southeast of Ulan Bator (96 km); from Har-ayrag to Bor-öndör fluorspar mines (60 km); from Saynshand to Dzüünbayan oilfield (63 km).

Planned branches (1988): Erdenet to Mörön (length 400 km) and Tavan-tolgoy to Ayrag (length 400 km).

**Eastern Railway:** Choybalsan; from the Russian frontier at Borzya/Ereentsav to Choybalsan (length 238 km); Chingis Dalan to Marday uranium mine, near Dashbalbar (110 km).

## ROADS

Main roads link Ulan Bator with the Chinese frontier at Dzamyn üüd/Erhlien and with the Russian frontier at Altanbulag/Kyakhta. A road from Chita in Russia crosses the frontier in the east at Mangut/Onon (Öldziy) and branches for Choybalsan and Öndörhaan. In the west and north-west, roads from Biysk and Irkutsk in Russia go to Tsagaannuur, Bayan-ölgiy Aymag, and Hanh, on Lake Hövsgöl, respectively. The total length of these roads was 3,949.5 km in 1988. In the early 1990s the length of asphalted roads approached 1,200 km, almost entirely in towns. The first section of a hard-surfaced road between Ulan Bator and Bayanhongor was completed in 1975. The road from Darhan to Erdenet was also to be surfaced. Mongolia divides its road system into state-grade and country-grade roads. State-grade roads run from Ulan Bator to provincial centres and from provincial centres to the border. There are 11,200 km of state-grade roads, of which 10% are hard-surfaced and a further 13% gravel-surfaced. Country-grade roads (also 13% gravel-surfaced) account for the remaining 38,000 km, but they are mostly rough cross-country tracks.

According to a vehicle census reported in December 1994, Mongolia had 54,053 motor vehicles, including 25,378 goods vehicles, 2,736 tankers, 2,776 specialized vehicles (such as ambulances and fire engines), 2,500 buses and trolleybuses and 20,663 cars. Of these vehicles, 20,246 were privately-owned, including 12,670 cars.

There are bus services in Ulan Bator and other large towns, and road haulage services throughout the country on the basis of motor transport depots, mostly situated in provincial centres. However, in 1991 and 1992 services were truncated, owing to fuel shortages.

## MONGOLIA

### INLAND WATERWAYS

Water transport plies Lake Hövsgöl and the River Selenge (397 km navigable) in the northern part of the country. Tugs and barges on Lake Hövsgöl transport goods brought in by road to Hanh from Russia to Hatgal on the southern shore.

### CIVIL AVIATION

**Mongolian Civil Air Transport (MIAT):** Ulan Bator; tel. 72240; f. 1956; internal services to most provincial centres and some district centres; services to destinations in Russia, Kazakhstan and China; total route length: 42,900 km; Dir of Civil Aviation LHAGVASÜREN-GIYN LHAGVAA.

## Tourism

A foreign tourist service bureau was established in 1954, but tourism is not very developed. There are three hotels for foreign tourists in Ulan Bator, with a total of 900 beds, and the outlying tourist centres (Terelj, South Gobi, Öndör-Dov and Hujirt) have basic facilities. The country's main attractions are its scenery, wildlife and historical relics. In 1994 Mongolia received 7,000 tourists.

**Mongolian Foreign Tourism Co ('Juulchin'):** Chingis Haany Örgön Chölöö, Ulan Bator 210543; tel. 328428; telex 79318; fax 320246; f. 1954; Dir-Gen. BEGDZSÜRENGIYN DELGERSÜREN.

There are also several co-operative travel bureaux, including 'Bayalag', 'Jangar' and 'Bumba'.

# MOROCCO

## Introductory Survey

**Location, Climate, Language, Religion, Flag, Capital**

The Kingdom of Morocco is situated in the extreme north-west of Africa. It has a long coastline on the shores of the Atlantic Ocean and, east of the Strait of Gibraltar, on the Mediterranean Sea, facing southern Spain. Morocco's eastern frontier is with Algeria, while to the south lies the disputed territory of Western Sahara (under Moroccan occupation), which has a lengthy Atlantic coastline and borders Mauritania to the east and south. Morocco's climate is semi-tropical. It is warm and sunny on the coast, while the plains of the interior are intensely hot in summer. Average temperatures are 27°C (81°F) in summer and 7°C (45°F) in winter for Rabat, and 38°C (101°F) and 4°C (40°F) respectively for Marrakesh. The rainy season in the north is from November to April. The official language is Arabic, but a large minority speak Berber. Spanish is widely spoken in the northern regions, and French in the rest of Morocco. The established religion is Islam, and most of the country's inhabitants are Muslims. There are Christian and Jewish minorities. The national flag (proportions 3 by 2) is red, with a green pentagram (intersecting lines in the form of a five-pointed star), known as 'Solomon's Seal', in the centre. The capital is Rabat.

**Recent History**

In 1912, under the terms of the Treaty of Fez, most of Morocco became a French protectorate, while a smaller Spanish protectorate was instituted in the north and far south of the country. Spain also retained control of Spanish Sahara (now Western Sahara), and Tangier became an international zone in 1923. A nationalist movement developed in Morocco during the 1930s and 1940s, led by the Istiqlal (Independence) grouping, and on 2 March 1956 the French protectorate achieved independence as the Sultanate of Morocco. The first Head of State of independent Morocco was Sultan Mohammad V, who had reigned since 1927 (although he had been temporarily removed from office by the French authorities between 1953 and 1955). The northern zone of the Spanish protectorate joined the new state in April 1956, and Tangier's international status was abolished in October of that year. The southern zone of the Spanish protectorate was ceded to Morocco in 1958, but no agreement was reached on the Spanish enclaves of Ceuta and Melilla, in the north, the Ifni region in the south, or the Spanish Saharan territories to the south of Morocco, which all remained under Spanish control. The Sultan was restyled King of Morocco in August 1957, and became Prime Minister in May 1960. He died in February 1961, and was succeeded by his son, Moulay Hassan, who took the title of Hassan II.

For the first 13 years of his reign King Hassan's position was unstable. Successive constitutions attempted to balance royal power with demands for greater political freedom. In May 1963 elections to Morocco's first House of Representatives took place, and six months later the King relinquished the post of Prime Minister. In June 1965, however, increasing political fragmentation, compounded by popular dissatisfaction with prevailing social conditions, prompted Hassan to declare a 'state of exception', and to resume full legislative and executive powers. Although he again relinquished the premiership in June 1967, the emergency provisions remained in force until July 1970, when a new Constitution was approved. In August a general election resulted in a pro-Government majority in the new Chamber of Representatives.

In July 1971 an attempted *coup d'état* was quickly suppressed by forces loyal to the King. Among those arrested in the aftermath of the failed coup were numerous members of the left-wing Union Nationale des Forces Populaires (UNFP), five of whom were sentenced to death in September. In August 1972 air force personnel attempted to shoot down an aircraft in which King Hassan was travelling. Among those implicated in the plot was Gen. Muhammad Oufkir, the Minister of National Defence and head of the armed forces, who committed suicide soon afterwards.

Although a revised Constitution (which provided for a new unicameral legislature) had been approved in March 1972 by popular referendum, a general election did not take place until June 1977, ending 12 years of direct rule. Two-thirds of the deputies in the Chamber of Representatives were directly elected, and the remainder were elected by local government councils, professional associations and labour organizations. Supporters of King Hassan's policies won a majority of seats in the new legislature, and a Government of national unity was formed, which included several opposition leaders from Istiqlal and the Mouvement Populaire (MP), in addition to the pro-monarchist independents.

Substantial increases in the price of staple foods precipitated strikes and rioting in June 1981, and several trade union and opposition leaders were detained for their alleged involvement in the disturbances. Further opposition was aroused in October, when it was announced that the term of office of the Chamber of Representatives was to be extended from four to six years. In protest, all 14 deputies belonging to the Union Socialiste des Forces Populaires (USFP—formed as a result of a split in the UNFP) withdrew from the Chamber. Elections to the legislature were further postponed in November 1983, owing to the Western Saharan dispute (see below). Meanwhile, an interim Government of national unity was appointed, headed by Mohamed Karim Lamrani (Prime Minister in 1971–72), who was chosen for his lack of party affiliation. The new Government included members of the six main political parties: Istiqlal, the MP, the Parti Nationale Démocrate (PND), the Rassemblement National des Indépendants (RNI), the Union Constitutionelle (UC) and the USFP.

In January 1984 there was serious rioting in several northern towns, prompted by imminent increases in food prices and rumours of planned increases in education fees. According to unofficial sources, some 110 people were killed after troops opened fire on demonstrators. The rioting subsided when King Hassan cancelled the price increases. Legislative elections (postponed from the previous year) took place in September and October. Despite significant gains by the USFP, which won 36 seats, the Chamber of Representatives was again dominated by the centre-right parties, which together controlled 206 of the 306 seats. A new Cabinet, appointed in April 1985, included members of the MP, the PND, the RNI and the UC. Lamrani, who remained as Prime Minister, announced a programme of reforms in industry, the civil service and the health and education systems. Lamrani resigned in September 1986, owing to ill health, and was replaced by Az ad-Dine Laraki (hitherto Deputy Prime Minister and Minister of National Education).

During the second half of the 1980s the Government dealt severely with organizations that, it believed, were a threat to internal stability. During 1985 and 1986 members of Islamic fundamentalist and radical left-wing groups were imprisoned. In late 1986 and 1987, however, King Hassan granted a series of amnesties for both political and non-political detainees. In 1988 a newly-formed human rights group, the Organisation Marocaine des Droits de l'Homme (OMDH), was initially banned, but in December it succeeded in holding its inaugural assembly, having received official authorization. In 1989 more than 1,000 prisoners were released by royal pardon. In January 1990 the Government ordered the dissolution of an illegal Islamic fundamentalist movement, Al Adl-wa-'l Ihsan (Justice and Charity), whose leader, Abd es-Salam Yassine, was placed under house arrest in December 1989. In February 1990 the human rights organization, Amnesty International, appealed to King Hassan to end the alleged violations of the human rights of detainees. In November human rights groups demanded a public inquiry into reports that hundreds of suspected opponents of the Government had 'disappeared' in the past 15 years.

In December 1990 unrest erupted in several cities during a 24-hour general strike, which had been organized to demand wage rises commensurate with rapidly rising prices. In Fez at least 20 people were reported to have been killed, and demonstrations in other cities degenerated into violence. Security forces were deployed in Fez and Rabat to restore order, and an estimated 1,500 demonstrators were arrested (more than 100 of whom subsequently received prison sentences). It was widely accepted that growing frustration at the country's socio-economic problems, notably the lack of job opportunities for the young and the unequal distribution of wealth, had precipitated the riots. In January 1991, following negotiations with leading trade unions, the Government announced that minimum wages in most sectors were to increase by 15%. However, those trade unions that had organized the December general strike condemned the increase as insufficient.

In late 1991 clashes were reported on several university campuses between Islamic fundamentalist and left-wing, secular students. Several Algerian fundamentalists were reported to have been among those arrested in connection with the death of a left-wing student, who had been abducted, with two others, from the university at Oujda. The proscribed Al Adl wa-'l Ihsan movement was also alleged to have been involved in the disturbances.

In October 1991 Mahjoubi Aherdane, the founder of the MP, established a new political organization, the Mouvement National Populaire. In the following month Istiqlal and the USFP announced that they would form a united front to campaign for a programme of democratic reforms, including the separation and redefinition of the powers of the executive and legislative branches of government, and a more independent judiciary. They also advocated the establishment of a neutral authority to oversee the next general election (which had been postponed since 1990, pending a settlement of the Western Sahara dispute).

The release of political detainees continued during the second half of 1991, indicating the Moroccan Government's desire to improve its international reputation regarding human rights. In September Abraham Serfaty, a prominent left-wing dissident detained since 1974, was released and deported to France. In November 26 former military personnel who had been detained at the Tazmamart military prison for more than 18 years (for their alleged involvement in the coup attempts in 1971 and 1972) were released. In December three French nationals were released from Tazmamart, where they had been held, apparently without trial, since 1975. Furthermore, in January 1992 three associates of Serfaty were released from detention, while the sentences of 260 other offenders were annulled or reduced. In April, however, Noubir Amaoui—the Secretary-General of the pro-USFP trade union, the Confédération Démocratique du Travail (CDT), and a senior member of the USFP—was sentenced to two years' imprisonment, following his conviction on charges of making 'insulting and defamatory' remarks about the Moroccan Government during an interview with a leading Spanish newspaper. Several Moroccan newspapers were proscribed in the aftermath of the conviction.

In March 1992 King Hassan announced that the Constitution was to be revised, with the principal aim of redefining the competences of, and relationship between, the executive and legislative organs of state. Upon completion, the amended document would be submitted for approval in a national referendum, and would be followed by national legislative elections. In June legislation providing for a minimum voting age of 20 years and equal funding and access to the media for all parties was adopted by pro-Government deputies in the Chamber; opposition deputies boycotted the vote, in support of their demands to lower the minimum voting age to 18 years. Later that month, in order to forestall an opposition boycott of the elections, an electoral commission was created, comprising delegates from all the political parties represented in the Chamber of Representatives. Also in June five opposition parties, Istiqlal, the USFP, the Parti du Progrès et du Socialisme (PPS), the Organisation de l'Action Démocratique et Populaire (OADP) and the UNFP, united to form the Bloc Démocratique to present a unified position on common demands.

In July 1992 King Hassan indicated that legislative elections would take place in November, and that voting would be extended to include Western Sahara, irrespective of the UN's progress in organizing a referendum on the territory's status (see below). He also denied the existence of any political prisoners (although this claim was refuted by human rights organizations). In August the King dissolved the Government, and nominated Lamrani as Prime Minister in an interim, politically independent Government, the principal task of which would be to oversee the forthcoming elections. Ministers with formal party political affiliations were removed from the Cabinet.

The revised Constitution was overwhelmingly approved in a national referendum on 4 September 1992: according to official figures, 99.96% of those who voted (97.29% of the electorate) endorsed the new document. Approval for the Constitution was reported to be unanimous in major cities and in three of the four provinces of Western Sahara. Opposition groups, who had advocated a boycott of the referendum, denounced the official results. Under the terms of the new Constitution, the King would retain strong executive powers, including the right to appoint the Prime Minister, although the nomination of government members would henceforth be the prerogative of the Prime Minister. The Government would be required to reflect the composition of the Chamber of Representatives, and was obliged to submit its legislative programme for the Chamber's approval; new legislation would automatically be promulgated one month after having been endorsed by parliament, regardless of whether royal assent had yet been received. Provision was also made for the establishment of a Constitutional Council and of an Economic and Social Council, and guarantees of human rights were enshrined in the Constitution.

Elections took place in some 1,540 communes on 16 October 1992. The greatest success was enjoyed by the RNI, which, with 18.1% of the votes cast, won 21.7% of the total of 22,282 seats. The UC received 13.4% of the votes, while nominally independent, but largely pro-Government, candidates, took 13.8% of the votes. Although the USFP and Istiqlal were widely supported in urban areas, the two parties together won only 20.6% of the total votes cast (securing 19.4% of the available seats). Berber candidates, including representatives of the MP, together took about 22% of the overall votes, and were particularly successful in the Rif and Moyen and Haut Atlas regions. The main opposition parties denounced what they claimed to be widespread instances of bribery and electoral malpractice.

In November 1992 security forces dispersed trade union activists who had gathered outside the prison at Salé to demand the release of Noubir Amaoui; an appeal against his sentence was rejected in January 1993. (He was finally released following a government amnesty in July.) In late 1992 a leading member of the Association Marocaine des Droits de l'Homme (AMDH), Ahmed Belaichi, was sentenced to three years' imprisonment for making derogatory remarks about the armed forces. In February 1993 the AMDH alleged that some 750 political prisoners were being detained in Morocco.

In November 1992 it was announced that elections to the new Chamber of Representatives would take place in April 1993. In February, however, the USFP, Istiqlal, the PPS and the OADP withdrew from the electoral commission, in protest against the terms of the electoral code. In March the Government announced that the legislative elections would be postponed until June, in order that opposition grievances might be addressed. The decision was welcomed by the opposition parties, and in May the Bloc Démocratique rejoined the electoral commission. Moreover, the USFP and Istiqlal agreed to present a joint list of candidates at the forthcoming elections.

The legislative elections, which took place on 25 June 1993, were widely accepted, even by opposition parties, as the most equitable since independence. Of the 222 directly elective seats in the enlarged Chamber of Representatives, the USFP won 48 and Istiqlal 43. (The combined total of seats of the Bloc Démocratique was 99.) The MP won 33 seats, the RNI 28, and the UC 27. The indirect election, by an electoral college, of the remaining 111 members of the Chamber of Representatives took place on 17 September, and was less favourable to the Bloc Démocratique, which won only 21 seats. Of the combined total of 333 seats in the Chamber of Representatives, the USFP controlled 56, the UC 54, Istiqlal 52, the MP 51, and the RNI 41. The USFP and Istiqlal protested against irregularities in the procedure of the electoral college voting, and demanded the annulment of the indirect election results. At the end of September Abd ar-Rahman al-Yousifi resigned as First Secretary of the USFP, purportedly in protest at the conduct of the electoral college. At the beginning of October the USFP and Istiqlal, as the main components of the Bloc Démocratique, rejected an offer from the King to participate in a coalition government with the loyalist, centre-right parties that, grouped in the Entente Nationale, controlled the largest number of seats in the Chamber of Representatives: their refusal was due to the King's insistence that the post of Prime Minister and responsibility for foreign affairs, justice and the interior should not be conferred upon opposition groups, on the grounds that they lacked experience of government. In mid-November the King reappointed Lamrani as Prime Minister. The new Government (which included a Minister Delegate to the Prime Minister, in charge of Human Rights) was composed of technocrats and independents, and did not include any representatives of the parties that had contested the legislative elections. By-elections took place in 14 constituencies in late April 1994 (all except one of them occasioned by a decision of the Constitutional Council to annul the results of the legislative elections, owing to electoral irregularities).

In December 1993 the Conseil Consultatif des Droits de l'Homme, established by the King in April 1990, substantiated allegations by human rights organizations of the 'disappearance' and detention of political activists, while denying the existence of secret detention centres. In February 1994 security forces intervened following violent clashes between radical Islamic and left-wing students at the University of Fez; 26 students were later imprisoned for their part in the disturbances. In the same month the Government banned a proposed general strike, organized by the CDT to protest against low wages and the general decline of living standards. All the main trade unions and most of the opposition parties united in condemning the prohibition order. Subsequently 11 CDT activists were detained and charged with incitement. In late May 1994 the King replaced Lamrani as Prime Minister with Abd al-Latif Filali, hitherto the Minister of State for Foreign Affairs and Co-operation. Although Filali held consultations with the political groupings represented in parliament, the composition of the new Government, formed in early June, in which Filali retained the foreign affairs and co-operation portfolio, was unchanged. However, the Minister of Finance, Mohamed Segou, was dismissed in mid-July. The PPS was renamed the Parti du Renouveau et du Progrès in mid-June.

In early July 1994 King Hassan appealed to all political parties to participate in a government of national unity. A royal amnesty, later in the month, for 424 prisoners (most of whom had been detained on political grounds) was broadly welcomed by opposition and human rights groups: among those released were Morocco's longest serving political prisoner and about 100 members of Al Adlwa-'l Ihsan. In mid-October, moreover, King Hassan announced his intention to select a Prime Minister from the ranks of the opposition. By early 1995, however, negotiations on the formation of a coalition government had failed, apparently owing to the Bloc Démocratique's refusal to join an administration in which Driss Basri (a long-serving government minister and close associate of the King) remained as Minister of the Interior and Information, and in late January King Hassan instructed Filali to form a new cabinet. In late February the King approved Filali's new Government, composed of technocrats and members of the centre-right Entente Nationale (nine from the UC, eight from the MP, and three from the PND). The portfolios of the interior and of information were, notably, separated: Driss Basri remained as Minister of the Interior, while Driss Alaoui M'Daghri, regarded as a 'liberal' technocrat, took responsibility for the newly-named Ministry of Communications. The selection of an uncompromising member of the UC, Mohamed Ziane, as Minister Delegate to the Prime Minister, in charge of Human Rights, was criticized by the OMDH, which accused the Government of insincerity with regard to its expressed commitment to respect for human rights.

In the early 1970s (following the cession of the Spanish enclave of Ifni to Morocco in 1969) political opinion in Morocco was united in opposing the continued occupation by Spain of areas considered to be historically parts of Moroccan territory: namely Spanish Sahara and Spanish North Africa (q.v.), which consisted of a number of small enclaves on Morocco's Mediterranean coast. A campaign to annex Spanish Sahara, initiated in July 1974, received active support from all Moroccan political parties. In October 1975 Hassan ordered a 'green march' by more than 300,000 unarmed Moroccans to occupy the territory. The marchers were stopped by the Spanish authorities when they had barely crossed the border, but on 14 November Spain agreed to cede the territory to Morocco and Mauritania, to be apportioned equally between them. Spain formally relinquished sovereignty of Spanish Sahara on 28 February 1976. Moroccan troops moved into the territory to confront a guerrilla uprising, led by the Frente Popular Para la Liberación de Sakiet el Hamra y Río de Oro (the Polisario Front), a national liberation movement, supported by Algeria and (later) Libya, that aimed to achieve an independent Western Saharan state. On 27 February the Polisario Front declared the 'Sahrawi Arab Democratic Republic' (SADR), and shortly afterwards established a Government-in-exile in Algeria. In protest, Morocco severed diplomatic relations with Algeria.

Guerrilla warfare in Western Sahara continued from 1976 onwards. Moroccan troops (some 30,000 were deployed in the region by June 1977) inflicted heavy casualties, and ensured the security of the few major towns, but they could not prevent constant infiltration, harassment and sabotage by Polisario forces. Moreover, Polisario had considerable success against Mauritanian troops, and in August 1979 Mauritania renounced its claim to Saharan territory and signed a peace treaty with the Polisario Front. Morocco immmediately asserted its claim to the whole of the Western Sahara and annexed the region.

In July 1980 the SADR applied to join the Organization of African Unity (OAU, see p. 200) as a sovereign state. Although 26 of the 50 member states recognized the Polisario Front as the rightful government of Western Sahara, Morocco insisted that a two-thirds majority was needed to confer membership. An OAU proposal for a cease-fire and a referendum on the territory failed to gain Moroccan support, and in 1981 heavy fighting resumed in the region. In early 1982 the OAU announced that the SADR had been accepted as the organization's 51st member. However, when 18 member states threatened to leave the OAU in protest, a compromise was reached whereby the SADR, while remaining a member, agreed not to attend meetings of the organization. Nevertheless, in November 1984 the SADR delegation attended an OAU summit meeting, with little opposition from other states; Morocco resigned from the OAU in protest, thus becoming the first state to leave the organization. Meanwhile, fighting continued in Western Sahara, and the Polisario Front claimed to have killed 5,673 Moroccan soliders between 1982 and 1985. However, decisive victories proved impossible, owing to Morocco's defensive strategy of building a 2,500-km wall of sand, equipped with electronic detectors, to surround Western Sahara.

In October 1985 Morocco announced a unilateral cease-fire in Western Sahara, and invited the UN to supervise a referendum there in the following January. The Polisario Front continued to insist that direct negotiations with Morocco were necessary before a referendum could be held, but the Moroccan Government still refused to attend such talks with Polisario. A series of 'proximity' (indirect) talks between the two sides, arranged by the UN and the OAU in 1986 and 1987, failed to achieve a solution, and in January 1988 Polisario forces renewed their offensive on Moroccan positions in Western Sahara. In August, however, it was announced that the Polisario Front and Morocco had provisionally accepted a peace plan, proposed by the UN Secretary-General. The plan envisaged the conclusion of a formal cease-fire, to be followed by a referendum on self-determination in Western Sahara. Among the conditions stipulated for the holding of the referendum were a reduction in Moroccan military forces in Western Sahara and the withdrawal of Polisario forces to their bases. A list of eligible voters was to be based on the Spanish census of 1974. In September 1988 implementation of the peace process was impeded by a renewed Polisario offensive. Muhammad Abd al-Aziz, President of the SADR, reiterated that the peace plan was accepted in principle only, and that direct negotiations with Morocco were still necessary.

In January 1989 a meeting finally took place, in Marrakesh, between King Hassan and officials of the Polisario Front and the SADR, the first direct contact for 13 years. The meeting was reported to have been limited to exchanges of goodwill, but it was followed, in February, by the announcement of a unilateral cease-fire by the Polisario Front. However, a further meeting, scheduled for February, was postponed by King Hassan, and in September Hassan rejected the possibility of official negotiations with the SADR. Later in the month the Polisario Front renewed its military attacks on Moroccan positions. In early March 1990 the Polisario Front announced that it would suspend military operations until the end of the month, to facilitate visits to the area by a special representative of the UN and the UN Secretary-General, Javier Pérez de

Cuéllar. Both the Moroccan Government and Polisario expressed the hope that the referendum could take place within six months, but remained divided over the extent of the franchise, the maintenance of security during the voting process, and the question of which Moroccan forces would withdraw. In April 1991 the UN established a special peace-keeping force, the UN Mission for the Referendum in Western Sahara (MINURSO, see p. 49), which was to implement the 1988 plan for a referendum on self-determination.

In June 1991 the Polisario Front agreed to the enforcement of a formal cease-fire, with effect from 6 September, from which date the 2,000-strong MINURSO delegation would undertake its duties in the region. In August, however, the peace process was undermined by renewed fighting in Western Sahara. Nevertheless, the cease-fire came into effect as scheduled, and the MINURSO deployment began.

In late September 1991 reports suggested that some 30,000 people had entered Western Sahara from Morocco, prompting claims that the Moroccan authorities were attempting to alter the region's demography in advance of the referendum. There were also reports that more than 170,000 Sahrawis who had fled the region since 1976 were being repatriated, in order that they might participate in the referendum. Meanwhile, it was becoming evident that difficulties were being encountered in the deployment of MINURSO personnel in the region: by early November only 200 had been deployed in Western Sahara, while Morocco had not withdrawn any forces from the region (under the terms of the cease-fire agreement, Morocco was to have withdrawn one-half of its 130,000 troops from Western Sahara by mid-September). The peace process was further discredited when, in November, it was revealed that the UN might agree to modify the list of those eligible to vote in the referendum to include as many as 40,000 people who were not registered under the 1974 census. The UN's role as a mediator was further damaged by the resignation, in mid-December, of Johannes Manz, the UN's special envoy appointed to oversee MINURSO, who claimed that the timetable for the referendum and the funding allocated to the peace process were inadequate. Further doubts as to the impartiality of the UN arose when Pérez de Cuéllar recommended to the UN Security Council that the franchise be widened in Western Sahara, apparently to the advantage of Morocco. His proposals were rejected by the Security Council, and it became evident that the referendum would have to be postponed.

In early 1992 it was alleged that Morocco had repeatedly violated the September 1991 cease-fire agreement: of 77 violations recorded by the UN, all but two were attributed to Moroccan forces. Claims also persisted that Morocco was hindering the work of MINURSO. In March a Pakistani diplomatist, Lt-Gen. (retd.) Sahabzada Yaqub Khan, was appointed to succeed Johannes Manz as the UN's special envoy to Western Sahara. In May Dr Boutros Boutros-Ghali (the UN Secretary-General since January) announced that Morocco and Polisario representatives were to begin indirect talks under his auspices. In the same month, however, Morocco appeared to prejudge the result of the proposed referendum by including the population of Western Sahara in the voting lists for its own regional and local elections (see above). In June further UN-sponsored indirect talks took place in Geneva, Switzerland.

At the end of June 1992 the SADR Government, which by this time was recognized by 75 countries, appealed to the international community and the UN to condemn alleged Moroccan violations of the cease-fire and to exert pressure for the implementation of the UN peace plan. In August, however, Ibrahim Hakim, of late the SADR ambassador to Algeria and a former Sahrawi minister of foreign affairs, defected to Morocco, claiming that Algeria was no longer committed to the establishment of an independent state in Western Sahara; Hakim was subsequently appointed as the King's itinerant ambassador.

UN-sponsored negotiations in New York, USA, in September 1992 again failed to formulate acceptable criteria for the drafting of lists of persons eligible to vote in an eventual referendum. The peace process was further frustrated by Polisario reports of major disturbances in the disputed region. Polisario alleged that, in late September, Moroccan security forces had killed 15 people and made hundreds of arrests in Assa, in southern Morocco; moreover, it was claimed that security forces had used violence to disperse demonstrators in the Western Saharan capital, el-Aaiún, and in Samara (which, Polisario asserted, was under a state of siege). The Moroccan authorities denied all allegations of repression. Polisario made renewed threats to resume its armed struggle, and protested at continuing violations by Morocco of the cease-fire terms. Further talks in Geneva, which were to have begun in November, failed when no agreement could be reached regarding the composition of the delegations.

In February 1993 Amnesty International denounced what it alleged to be violations of human rights by both the Moroccan authorities and the Polisario Front. In early March the UN Security Council approved a new timetable for a resolution to the dispute, whereby the referendum would take place by the end of 1993. In July the first direct negotiations took place between the Moroccan Government and the Polisario Front, although little progress was achieved. In September, in a reorganization of the SADR Government, Bouchraya Hammoudi Bayoune replaced Mahfoud Ali Beïba as Prime Minister. Discussions that had been scheduled to be held in the USA in October were postponed, following Polisario's refusal to participate in the talks, owing to the Moroccan Government's inclusion of former Polisario members in its delegation. In September it was reported that only 360 of the proposed 2,000 UN military personnel were in place in Western Sahara. In mid-March 1994 Boutros-Ghali submitted a report to the Security Council that detailed three possible procedures for overcoming the impasse on the Western Saharan issue: the continuation of negotiations until the end of June, in an attempt to secure the agreement of both Morocco and the Polisario Front on an electoral list; the organization of a referendum in December 1994, irrespective of Polisario reservations; and the effective withdrawal of the UN from the peace process. In late March the Security Council agreed to a continuation of negotiations for a further three months, and undertook to review the future of MINURSO if a referendum were not organized before the end of the year.

In late April 1994 the Polisario Front accepted the UN programme for the registration of voters. However, the work of a UN voter identification commission, which had been due to commence in June, was delayed, owing to the Moroccan Government's objection to the inclusion of OAU observers (whose impartiality it doubted) in the process. The registration of the electorate finally began in late August, for a referendum scheduled to take place in February 1995. In early November 1994, however, Boutros-Ghali reported to the Security Council that the registration of voters was proceeding only slowly (owing, the Polisario Front alleged, to dilatory tactics on the part of the Moroccan Government). In January 1995 the Security Council voted to extend the mandate of MINURSO until the end of May. In March 1995 Muhammad Abd al-Aziz appealed to the European Parliament to exert pressure on the UN to accelerate the identification process, since, Polisario believed, it could take several years to complete if it continued at its present pace. At the end of the month Boutros-Ghali announced that the referendum, then scheduled to take place in October, would not now take place until January 1996 at the earliest.

Relations with other North African states improved significantly in the late 1980s. In May 1988 Algeria and Morocco agreed to re-establish diplomatic relations. (Diplomatic relations with Mauritania had been suspended in 1981 and resumed in April 1985.) In February 1989 North African heads of state, meeting in Marrakesh, signed a treaty establishing the Union of the Arab Maghreb (UMA, see p. 241). The new body, which included Morocco, Algeria, Libya, Mauritania and Tunisia, aimed to promote trade by allowing the free movement of goods, services and workers. During 1990 bilateral agreements on economic co-operation were concluded by Morocco with Algeria and Libya, and there were further discussions within the UMA on the formation of a North African free trade area. However, there were political disagreements over Algeria's continued support for the Polisario Front, and over Morocco's condemnation of Iraq, following the Iraqi invasion of Kuwait in August 1990. Relations between Morocco and Algeria improved in early 1992, following the nomination of Muhammad Boudiaf as Chairman of Algeria's High Council of State, and remained apparently cordial despite the assassination of Boudiaf in June. However, relations with Algeria deteriorated in August 1994, following the murder, apparently by Islamic fundamentalists, of two Spanish tourists in Marrakesh, which the Moroccan authorities attributed in part to Algerian nationals. The imposition by Morocco of entry restrictions on Algerian citizens prompted the Algerian Government to introduce reciprocal visa restrictions and announce the temporary closure of its border with Morocco. Tensions eased slightly in September, when Algeria announced the appointment of a new Ambassador to Morocco, and in October the Moroccan Minister of Energy and Mines attended ceremonies in Algeria to mark the commencement of work on a Maghreb–Europe gas pipeline. In late January 1995 three people, including one Algerian, were sentenced to death for their part in acts of terrorism including the August 1994 murders; three other defendants were sentenced to life imprisonment.

In February 1993 Filali, then Minister of State for Foreign Affairs and Co-operation, announced that, at a recent meeting of the foreign ministers of the five UMA countries, it had been decided that there should be a 'pause' in the development of a closer union; it was noted that, of the 15 conventions signed since the inauguration of the UMA, none had as yet been fully applied. However, meetings of the organization took place in 1994–95. In late October and early November 1994 King Hassan hosted the first Middle East and North African Economic Summit, held in Casablanca. Matters under discussion included methods of financing a new regional bank for the Middle East.

Following the invasion of Kuwait by Iraq, in August 1990, the Moroccan Government condemned the action and announced that it would provide troops to defend Saudi Arabia against any possible further aggression. By December some 1,500 Moroccan troops were stationed in Saudi Arabia as part of the multinational alliance that was authorized by the UN to enforce the withdrawal of Iraq from Kuwait. However, in late January 1991, in response to pro-Iraqi demonstrations in Morocco, the Government gave implicit support to a one-day general strike, organized by the principal Moroccan trade unions to express solidarity with the Iraqi people. In early February 1991 an estimated 300,000 people demonstrated in Rabat, where they denounced the war against Iraq and demanded the withdrawal of the Moroccan contingent from the multinational force. The Government, however, dismissed criticism of its military policy in the region of the Persian (Arabian) Gulf, and stressed that its troops were in the region to defend Saudi Arabia and not to force Iraq to withdraw from Kuwait. In September 1993 the Israeli Prime Minister visited Rabat, an indication of improved relations between Morocco and Israel, and of the role played by King Hassan in the Middle East peace process. In September 1994 Morocco became only the second Arab country (after Egypt) to establish direct links with Israel, when Morocco and Israel agreed to open liaison offices, respectively, in Tel Aviv and Rabat. The Israeli Minister of Foreign Affairs, Shimon Peres, inaugurated the liaison office in Morocco in November, and in March 1995 Morocco became the third Arab country to establish a diplomatic presence in Israel when it opened its liaison office in Tel Aviv.

Morocco has generally maintained close relations with France. The release from detention of Abraham Serfaty and of three French nationals during the second half of 1991 (see above) received wide publicity in France. However, the French Government expressed considerable concern following the imposition of death sentences on three defendants in January 1995 (see above), all of whom had been resident in France prior to their arrest. As the development of a Maghreb union slowed, Morocco attempted to improve relations with the European Community (EC, now European Union—EU—see p. 143), which was critical of Morocco's human rights record. In March 1993, however, the EC announced that negotiations on a form of partnership, which would include permanent political dialogue, economic co-operation, financial aid and progressive moves towards the establishment of a free trade zone, would start within a year. Disputes concerning fishing rights in Moroccan waters undermined relations with the EU in late 1994 and early 1995. In March 1995 negotiations commenced (apparently with little success) between Morocco and the EU for the renewal of fishing licences. A joint agricultural accord had been concluded in January.

In March 1994 it was reported that the Spanish legislature was considering the conferment of autonomous status, similar to that enjoyed by Spain's mainland regions, on the Spanish enclaves of Ceuta and Melilla. In February 1995, following the final approval by the Spanish parliament of the statutes of autonomy for the two enclaves, the Moroccan Government intensified its diplomatic campaign to obtain sovereignty over the territories.

### Government

The 1992 Constitution provides for a modified constitutional monarchy, with an hereditary King as Head of State. Legislative power is vested in the unicameral Chamber of Representatives, whose 333 members are elected for six years. Of the total membership, 222 are directly elected, on the basis of universal adult suffrage, while the remainder are chosen by an electoral college composed of local councillors and representatives of professional bodies. Executive power is vested in the King, who appoints (and may dismiss) the Prime Minister, who, in turn, appoints other members of the Cabinet. The King may also dissolve the Chamber.

### Defence

In June 1994 Morocco's armed forces numbered 195,500, consisting of an army of 175,000, a navy of 7,000 and an air force of 13,500. In addition, there is a paramilitary 'gendarmerie royale' of 12,000, and a paramilitary 'force auxiliaire' of 30,000 men (including a mobile intervention corps of 5,000). There is obligatory military service of 18 months. Under the 1995 budget, government expenditure on defence was projected at 10,100m. dirhams (9.2% of total expenditure).

### Economic Affairs

In 1993, according to estimates by the World Bank, Morocco's gross national product (GNP), measured at average 1991–93 prices, was US $27,645m., equivalent to $1,030 per head. During 1985–93, it was estimated, GNP per head increased, in real terms, by 0.9% per year. Over the same period the population increased by an annual average of 2.4%. Morocco's gross domestic product (GDP) increased, in real terms, by an annual average of 4.0% in 1980–92. Real GDP declined by an estimated 4.1% in 1992, and increased by only about 0.2% in 1993, largely owing to the effects of drought; however an increase of some 11% was forecast for 1994.

Agriculture (including forestry and fishing) contributed 15.0% of GDP in 1993. In the same year an estimated 34.0% of the labour force were employed in the sector. The principal crops are cereals (mainly wheat and barley), sugar beet, citrus fruit, tomatoes and potatoes. The effects of drought on domestic production necessitated the import of 2.7m. tons of cereals in 1993. Almost all of the country's meat requirements are produced domestically. The sale of licences to foreign fishing fleets is an important source of revenue. In 1993 seafoods and seafood products accounted for 14.6% of total exports, while citrus fruits accounted for 4.2% of all exports. During 1980–92 agricultural GDP increased by an annual average of 5.3%. Food production increased by an average of 8.5% per year in 1985–91; output declined by 25.0% in 1992, and showed little improvement in 1993, but increased by 37.9% in 1994.

Industry (including mining, manufacturing, construction and power) employed 24.2% of the labour force in 1982, and provided 33.9% of GDP in 1993. During 1980–92 industrial GDP increased by an annual average of 3.0%.

Mining and quarrying contributed 2.2% of GDP in 1993, and employed 1.1% of the labour force in 1982. The major mineral exports are phosphate rock and phosphoric acid, which together earned some 16.5% of export revenues in 1993. Morocco is the world's largest exporter of phosphate rock. Crude petroleum is produced in small quantities, and gas is also extracted. Coal, iron ore, barytes, lead, copper, zinc and manganese are mined. Deposits of nickel, cobalt and bauxite have been discovered.

Manufacturing employed 15.5% of the labour force in 1982 and contributed 23.7% of GDP in 1993. The most important branches, measured by gross value of output, are phosphate products (chiefly fertilizers), petroleum-refining, food-processing and textiles. During 1980–92 manufacturing GDP increased by an annual average of 4.2%.

Electric energy is derived principally from thermal power stations using imported petroleum and gas (85% in 1989) and hydroelectricity (15%). Coal-fired power stations were being developed in the late 1980s and early 1990s, while plans exist for the development of nuclear power. Imports of fuel products comprised 14.4% of the value of total merchandise imports in 1993.

The services sector contributed 51.1% of GDP in 1993. The tourist industry is generally a major source of revenue, although it was adversely affected by the 1990–91 crisis in the region of the Persian (Arabian) Gulf. In 1992 tourist receipts were reported to have increased by 40%, and there were an estimated 3,252,062 visitors in that year. In 1993 migrant workers' remittances, another important source of income, totalled about US $2,200m.

In 1993 Morocco recorded a visible trade deficit of US $2,380m., and there was a deficit of $525m. on the current account of the balance of payments. In 1993 the principal source of imports (23.0%) was France; other major suppliers in that year were Spain and the USA. France was also the principal market for exports (33.2%) in 1993; Spain was also an important purchaser of Moroccan exports. The principal exports in 1993 were phosphates and phosphoric acid, seafoods and seafood products, clothing, fertilizers and hosiery. The principal imports in that year were crude petroleum, wheat and chemicals.

The 1992 budget deficit was equivalent to 1.7% of GDP. The 1995 budget envisaged a deficit of 3,600m. dirhams, compared with a deficit of some 5,200m. in 1994. Morocco's total external debt in 1993 was US $21,430m., of which $20,310m. was long-term public debt. The cost of servicing debt in that year was equivalent to 30.7% of exports of goods and services. The annual rate of inflation averaged 5.3% in 1985–93. The rate was 5.2% in 1993 and 5.1% in 1994. An estimated 16% of the urban labour force were unemployed in 1994.

Morocco is a member of the African Development Bank (see p. 102), the Islamic Development Bank (see p. 180) and of the Arab Fund for Economic and Social Development (see p. 237). It is a founder member of the Union of the Arab Maghreb (see p. 241).

Factors impeding Morocco's economic performance include high rates of population growth and of unemployment, a cumbersome public sector, the vulnerability of agricultural production to drought and over-reliance on exports of phosphates. Economic reforms (undertaken since 1980 under the auspices of the IMF), including the reduction of taxes, tariffs and subsidies and the introduction of a more efficient tax system, have resulted in the reduction of the budget deficit, of the rate of inflation and of the external current account deficit. Efforts to stimulate foreign investment have had considerable success, and in 1992 the value of such investments exceeded the current account deficit for the first time. A major privatization programme produced receipts of an estimated 6,000m. dirhams in 1993–94 from the sale of 30 state enterprises, and was to be pursued beyond the end of 1995 (the original deadline for the sale of more than 100 enterprises), with further state interests being included in the programme. The sale of such concerns as the Société Nationale d'Investissements and the Banque Marocaine du Commerce Extérieur has increased the international status of the flourishing Casablanca stock exchange, and the establishment of a foreign exchange market, planned for the mid-1990s, was expected to entail the full convertibility of the dirham. Future development depends on the expansion of export activity, the further diversification of sources of foreign investment and the development of higher value-added manufacturing industries. Moreover, the external debt remains substantial, despite a series of rescheduling agreements with both official and commercial creditors, and the cost of debt-servicing continues to represent a considerable burden on public finances.

### Social Welfare

All employees are required to contribute to a Social Welfare Fund, which operates a system of benefits in the event of illness, occupational accidents and old age. In 1978 Morocco had 161 hospitals, and in 1984 there were 25,807 hospital beds, and 3,882 physicians working in the country. In 1987 there were 4,908 physicians employed in Morocco. Under the 1981–85 development programme 12 hospitals and 238 clinics were constructed. Of total expenditure by the central Government in 1987, 1,342m. dirhams (3.0%) was for health, and 3,061m. dirhams (6.9%) for social security and welfare. A priority of the 1993 budget was to increase expenditure on social sectors by an average of 12%.

### Education

Morocco has state-controlled primary, secondary and technical schools, and there are also private schools. Education is compulsory for six years, to be undertaken between the ages of seven and 16 years. Primary education begins at seven years of age and lasts for six years. Secondary education, beginning at the age of 13, lasts for up to six years (comprising two cycles of three years). Primary enrolment in 1992 included 59% of children in the relevant age-group (69% of boys; 50% of girls), while secondary enrolment included 29% of the relevant age-group (boys 33%; girls 24%). In 1988 the secondary school graduation examination, the *baccalauréat*, was replaced by a system of continuous assessment. There were 11 universities, with a total of 230,000 students in 1992/93, as well as several other institutions for higher education. An English-language university, funded by Saudi Arabia, was inaugurated at Ifrane in January 1995. In 1990, according to UNESCO estimates, adult illiteracy averaged 50.5% (males 38.7%, females 62.0%). Under the 1995 budget, expenditure on education by the central Government was projected at 14,700m. dirhams (13.4% of total spending).

### Public Holidays

**1995:** 1 January (New Year), 1 February* (Beginning of Ramadan), 3 March (Festival of the Throne, anniversary of King Hassan's accession), 3 March* (Eid el Seghir—Id al-Fitr, end of Ramadan), 1 May (Labour Day), 10 May* (Eid el Kebir—Id al-Adha, Feast of the Sacrifice), 31 May* (Islamic New Year), 9 June* (Ashoura), 9 August* (Mouloud, Birth of the Prophet), 14 August (Oued ed-Dahab Day, anniversary of 1979 annexation), 6 November (Anniversary of the Green March), 18 November (Independence Day).

**1996:** 1 January (New Year), 22 January* (Beginning of Ramadan), 21 February* (Eid el Seghir—Id al-Fitr, end of Ramadan), 3 March (Festival of the Throne, anniversary of King Hassan's accession), 29 April* (Eid el Kebir—Id al-Adha, Feast of the Sacrifice), 1 May (Labour Day), 19 May* (Islamic New Year), 28 May* (Ashoura), 28 July* (Mouloud, Birth of the Prophet), 14 August (Oued ed-Dahab Day, anniversary of 1979 annexation), 6 November (Anniversary of the Green March), 18 November (Independence Day).

* These holidays are dependent on the Islamic lunar calendar and may vary by one or two days from the dates given.

### Weights and Measures

The metric system is in force.

# Statistical Survey

Source (unless otherwise stated): Direction de la Statistique, Ministère du Plan, BP 178, Rabat; tel. 73606; telex 32714.

Note: Unless otherwise indicated, the data exclude Western (formerly Spanish) Sahara, a disputed territory under Moroccan occupation.

## Area and Population

### AREA, POPULATION AND DENSITY

| | |
|---|---:|
| Area (sq km) | 710,850* |
| Population (census results) | |
| 20 July 1971 | 15,321,210 |
| 3 September 1982† | |
| Males | 10,205,859 |
| Females | 10,182,358 |
| Total | 20,388,217 |
| Population (official estimates at mid-year)† | |
| 1992 | 25,547,000 |
| 1993 | 26,069,000 |
| Density (per sq km) at mid-1993 | 36.7 |

* 274,461 sq miles. This area includes the disputed territory of Western Sahara, which covers 252,120 sq km (97,344 sq miles).

† Including Western Sahara, with a population of 163,868 (provisional) at the 1982 census.

### PROVINCES AND PREFECTURES
(estimated population at mid-1993)

| | Area (sq km) | Population ('000)* | Density (per sq km) |
|---|---:|---:|---:|
| Agadir | 5,910 | 831 | 140.6 |
| al-Hocima | 3,550 | 377 | 106.2 |
| Azizal | 10,050 | 421 | 41.9 |
| Beni Mellal | 7,075 | 966 | 136.5 |
| Ben Slimane | 2,760 | 206 | 74.6 |
| Boujdour† | 100,120 | 10 | 0.1 |
| Boulemane | 14,395 | 158 | 11.0 |
| Chaouen | 4,350 | 369 | 84.8 |
| el-Aaiún† | 39,360 | 144 | 3.7 |
| el-Jadida | 6,000 | 944 | 157.3 |
| el-Kellaa Srarhna | 10,070 | 694 | 68.9 |
| er-Rachidia | 59,585 | 511 | 8.6 |
| es-Saouira | 6,335 | 431 | 68.0 |
| es-Smara† | 61,760 | 26 | 0.4 |
| Fès | 5,400 | 1,051 | 194.6 |
| Figuig | 55,990 | 108 | 1.9 |
| Guelmim | 28,750 | 171 | 5.9 |
| Ifrane | 3,310 | 118 | 35.6 |
| Kénitra | 4,745 | 940 | 198.1 |
| Khemisset | 8,305 | 480 | 57.8 |
| Khenifra | 12,320 | 450 | 36.5 |
| Khouribga | 4,250 | 558 | 131.3 |
| Marrakech | 14,755 | 1,549 | 105.0 |
| Meknès | 3,995 | 765 | 191.5 |
| Nador | 6,130 | 817 | 133.3 |
| Ouarzazate | 41,550 | 661 | 15.9 |
| Oued ed-Dahab† | 50,880 | 28 | 0.6 |
| Oujda | 20,700 | 992 | 47.9 |
| Safi | 7,285 | 862 | 118.3 |
| Settat | 9,750 | 799 | 81.9 |
| Sidi Kacem | 4,060 | 610 | 150.2 |
| Tanger | 1,195 | 579 | 484.5 |
| Tan-Tan | 17,295 | 56 | 3.2 |
| Taounate | 5,585 | 609 | 109.0 |
| Taroudant | 16,460 | 668 | 40.6 |
| Tata | 25,925 | 107 | 4.1 |
| Taza | 15,020 | 724 | 48.2 |
| Tétouan-Larache | 6,025 | 878 | 145.7 |
| Tiznit | 6,960 | 387 | 55.6 |

| — continued | Area (sq km) | Population ('000)* | Density (per sq km) |
|---|---:|---:|---:|
| Casablanca } Aïn Chok-Hay Hassani } Aïn Sebaa-H' Mohammadi } Ben M'sick-S. Othmane } Mohammadia-Znata | 1,615 | 3,406 | 2,109.0 |
| Rabat-Salé } Skwrate-Temara | 1,275 | 1,608 | 1,261.2 |
| **Total** | 710,850 | 26,069 | 36.7 |

* Figures are provisional.

† The provinces of Boujdour, el-Aaiún, es-Smara and Oued ed-Dahab form the disputed territory of Western Sahara.

**PRINCIPAL TOWNS** (estimated population at mid-1993)

| | | | |
|---|---:|---|---:|
| Casablanca | 3,163,000 | Meknès | 505,000 |
| Rabat (capital)* | 1,397,000 | Beni-Mellal | 474,000 |
| Fès (Fez) | 753,000 | Agadir | 459,000 |
| Marrakech (Marrakesh) | 688,000 | Kénitra | 457,000 |
| | | Tanger (Tangier) | 428,000 |
| Oujda | 676,000 | Safi | 412,000 |
| Tétouan | 508,000 | Khouribga | 354,000 |

* Including Salé.

**BIRTHS AND DEATHS** (UN estimates, annual averages)

| | 1975–80 | 1980–85 | 1985–90 |
|---|---:|---:|---:|
| Birth rate (per 1,000) | 39.4 | 37.3 | 35.6 |
| Death rate (per 1,000) | 13.0 | 11.4 | 9.8 |

**Expectation of life** (UN estimates, years at birth, 1985–90): 60.7 (males 59.1; females 62.5).

Source: UN, *World Population Prospects: The 1992 Revision*.

**ECONOMICALLY ACTIVE POPULATION** (1982 census)*

| | Males | Females | Total |
|---|---:|---:|---:|
| Agriculture, hunting, forestry and fishing | 1,989,203 | 362,426 | 2,351,629 |
| Mining and quarrying | 61,110 | 2,250 | 63,360 |
| Manufacturing | 593,738 | 336,877 | 930,615 |
| Electricity, gas and water | 21,165 | 1,300 | 22,465 |
| Construction | 434,093 | 3,371 | 437,464 |
| Trade, restaurants and hotels | 474,392 | 23,738 | 498,130 |
| Transport, storage and communications | 136,853 | 4,128 | 140,981 |
| Financing, insurance, real estate and business services } Community, social and personal services | 725,938 | 280,974 | 1,006,912 |
| Activities not adequately defined | 381,488 | 166,216 | 547,704 |
| **Total** | 4,817,980 | 1,181,280 | 5,999,260 |

* Figures are based on a 5% sample tabulation of census returns. The data relate to employed persons aged 7 years and over and unemployed persons (excluding those seeking work for the first time) aged 15 years and over.

**Mid-1993** (estimates in '000): Agriculture, etc. 2,868; Total 8,441 (Source: FAO, *Production Yearbook*).

MOROCCO

*Statistical Survey*

## Agriculture

**PRINCIPAL CROPS** ('000 metric tons)

|  | 1991 | 1992 | 1993 |
|---|---|---|---|
| Wheat | 4,939 | 1,562 | 1,573 |
| Rice (paddy) | 25 | 22 | 54 |
| Barley | 3,253 | 1,081 | 1,027 |
| Maize | 335 | 216 | 202 |
| Oats | 76 | 29 | 32 |
| Sorghum | 15 | 18 | 21 |
| Other cereals | 25 | 24 | 21 |
| Potatoes | 1,074 | 918 | 869 |
| Sweet potatoes | 20 | 12 | 15* |
| Dry broad beans | 204 | 68 | 160 |
| Dry peas | 68 | 10 | 49 |
| Chick-peas | 67 | 26 | 22 |
| Lentils | 51 | 19 | 8 |
| Other pulses | 67 | 40 | 38 |
| Soybeans (Soya beans) | 20 | 4 | 4* |
| Groundnuts (in shell) | 20 | 35 | 34 |
| Sunflower seed | 87 | 146 | 200† |
| Cottonseed | 14 | 6 | n.a. |
| Olives† | 390 | 500 | 550 |
| Artichokes | 24 | 24 | 24 |
| Tomatoes | 803 | 894 | 917 |
| Cauliflowers | 51 | 21 | 11 |
| Pumpkins, squash and gourds | 113 | 120 | 100* |
| Cucumbers and gherkins | 30 | 16 | 19 |
| Aubergines (Eggplants) | 32 | 29 | 28 |
| Green peppers | 76 | 97 | 86 |
| Onions (dry) | 413 | 351 | 324 |
| Green beans | 23 | 25 | 25 |
| Green peas | 47 | 24 | 36 |
| Carrots | 187 | 161 | 172 |
| Other vegetables | 565 | 440 | 480 |
| Watermelons | 369 | 238 | 248 |
| Melons | 326 | 313 | 230* |
| Grapes | 259 | 294 | 230 |
| Dates | 107 | 82 | 111 |
| Sugar cane | 1,028 | 994 | 946 |
| Sugar beets | 3,036 | 2,754 | 3,162 |
| Apples | 249 | 278 | 320 |
| Pears | 31 | 30 | 50 |
| Peaches and nectarines | 25 | 33 | 34 |
| Plums | 41 | 45 | 42 |
| Oranges | 1,097 | 784 | 860* |
| Tangerines, mandarins, clementines and satsumas | 311 | 273 | 300 |
| Lemons and limes | 20 | 15 | 16* |
| Apricots | 92 | 66 | 120 |
| Bananas | 62 | 74 | 93 |
| Other fruits and berries | 153 | 151 | 153 |
| Almonds | 70 | 55 | 55 |
| Tobacco (leaves) | 7† | 7* | 7* |
| Cotton (lint)† | 7 | 3 | n.a. |

* FAO estimate.   † Unofficial figure(s).
Source: FAO, *Production Yearbook*.

**LIVESTOCK** ('000 head, year ending September)

|  | 1991 | 1992 | 1993 |
|---|---|---|---|
| Cattle | 3,183 | 3,269 | 2,924 |
| Sheep | 13,308 | 17,201 | 16,302 |
| Goats | 4,561 | 5,340 | 4,773 |
| Camels | 33 | 36 | 36 |
| Horses | 188 | 186 | 180 |
| Mules | 528 | 536 | 547 |
| Asses | 896 | 940 | 946 |

**Poultry** (FAO estimates, million): 72 in 1991; 76 in 1992; 78 in 1993.
Source: FAO, *Production Yearbook*.

**LIVESTOCK PRODUCTS** ('000 metric tons)

|  | 1991 | 1992 | 1993 |
|---|---|---|---|
| Beef and veal | 165 | 160 | 154 |
| Mutton and lamb | 90 | 90 | 66 |
| Goat meat | 14* | 17* | 20 |
| Poultry meat | 143 | 152 | 155 |
| Other meat | 35 | 35 | 37 |
| Cows' milk | 962 | 920* | 814 |
| Sheep's milk* | 27 | 28 | 27 |
| Goats' milk* | 35 | 36 | 37 |
| Butter* | 15.2 | 14.6 | 13.1 |
| Cheese* | 7.3 | 7.4 | 7.2 |
| Poultry eggs* | 171.6 | 182.4 | 187.2 |
| Honey* | 2.6 | 2.8 | 3.4 |
| Wool (greasy) | 35.0† | 36.0* | 35.0 |
| Wool (clean) | 16.8† | 17.3* | 16.8* |
| Cattle hides (fresh)* | 18.2 | 27.0 | 22.6 |
| Sheepskins (fresh)* | 10.6 | 12.0 | 10.2 |
| Goatskins (fresh)* | 2.2 | 2.6 | 2.8 |

* FAO estimate(s).   † Unofficial figure.
Source: FAO, *Production Yearbook*.

## Forestry

**ROUNDWOOD REMOVALS** ('000 cubic metres, excluding bark)

|  | 1990 | 1991 | 1992 |
|---|---|---|---|
| Sawlogs, veneer logs and logs for sleepers | 149 | 225 | 156 |
| Pulpwood | 158 | 597 | 472 |
| Other industrial wood* | 288 | 295 | 302 |
| Fuel wood* | 1,382 | 1,405 | 1,426 |
| **Total** | 1,977 | 2,522 | 2,356 |

* FAO estimates.
Source: FAO, *Yearbook of Forest Products*.

**SAWNWOOD PRODUCTION**
('000 cubic metres, including railway sleepers)

|  | 1987* | 1988 | 1989 |
|---|---|---|---|
| Coniferous (soft wood)* | 40 | 26 | 43 |
| Broadleaved (hard wood) | 40 | 27 | 40 |
| **Total** | 80 | 53 | 83 |

* FAO estimates.
**1990–92:** Annual production as in 1989 (FAO estimates).
Source: FAO, *Yearbook of Forest Products*.

## Fishing

('000 metric tons, live weight)

|  | 1990 | 1991 | 1992 |
|---|---|---|---|
| Jack and horse mackerels | 17.4 | 14.7 | 21.6 |
| European pilchard (sardine) | 345.9 | 370.6 | 322.2 |
| European anchovy | 10.5 | 19.6 | 17.1 |
| Chub mackerel | 27.7 | 11.2 | 15.9 |
| Other fishes (incl. unspecified) | 83.7 | 77.9 | 82.6 |
| **Total fish** | 485.3 | 494.1 | 459.5 |
| Crustaceans | 5.4 | 6.1 | 5.9 |
| Cuttlefishes and bobtail squids | 13.8 | 17.2 | 9.0 |
| Octopuses | 52.3 | 65.1 | 60.4 |
| Other molluscs | 8.6 | 10.6 | 13.3 |
| **Total catch** | 565.5 | 593.1 | 548.1 |
| Inland waters | 1.4 | 1.4 | 2.0 |
| Atlantic Ocean | 530.7 | 562.2 | 509.2 |
| Mediterranean Sea | 33.4 | 29.5 | 36.9 |

Source: FAO, *Yearbook of Fishery Statistics*.

MOROCCO
*Statistical Survey*

## Mining

('000 metric tons)

|  | 1991 | 1992 | 1993 |
|---|---|---|---|
| Hard coal | 550.8 | 575.8 | 603.8 |
| Crude petroleum | 11.8 | 10.8 | 10.2 |
| Iron ore* | 98.7 | 84.7 | 66.3 |
| Copper concentrates* | 39.0 | 34.3 | 35.7 |
| Lead concentrates* | 103.4 | 105.0 | 111.9 |
| Manganese ore* | 59.3 | 49.1 | 42.6 |
| Zinc concentrates* | 51.5 | 42.4 | 125.7 |
| Phosphate rock | 17,900 | 19,145 | 18,305 |
| Fluorspar (acid grade) | 74.6 | 85.5 | 70.0 |
| Barytes | 434.7 | 401.6 | 349.6 |
| Salt (unrefined) | 143.9 | 164.5 | 147.0 |
| Clay | 37.6 | 38.1 | 8.7 |

\* Figures refer to the gross weight of ores and concentrates. The estimated metal content (in '000 metric tons) was: Iron 58 in 1991; Copper 10.9 in 1991, 9.6 in 1992, 11.5 in 1993; Lead 70.6 in 1991, 72.4 in 1992, 77.2 in 1993; Manganese 30.4 in 1991; Zinc 26.8 in 1991 (Source: UN, *Industrial Statistics Yearbook* and *Monthly Bulletin of Statistics*).

## Industry

**SELECTED PRODUCTS***
('000 metric tons, unless otherwise indicated)

|  | 1991 | 1992 | 1993 |
|---|---|---|---|
| Cement | 5,777 | 6,223 | n.a. |
| Electric energy (million kWh) | 9,205 | 9,720 | 9,895 |
| Passenger motor cars ('000)† | 23 | 17 | n.a. |
| Phosphate fertilizers‡ | 1,180 | 1,070 | 997 |
| Carpets and rugs ('000 sq m) | 1,156 | 879 | 900 |
| Wine ('000 hl) | 390 | 430 | 330 |
| Olive oil (crude) | 55 | 38 | 40 |
| Motor spirit—petrol | 352 | 403 | 397 |
| Naphthas | 465 | 542 | 301 |
| Kerosene | 47 | 45 | 43 |
| Distillate fuel oils | 1,797 | 2,080 | 1,919 |
| Residual fuel oils | 2,027 | 2,143 | 2,459 |
| Jet fuel | 183 | 206 | 223 |
| Petroleum bitumen—asphalt | 114 | 116 | 101 |
| Liquefied petroleum gas | 225 | 233 | 247 |

\* Major industrial establishments only.
† Assembly only.
‡ Estimated production in terms of phosphoric acid (Source: FAO, *Quarterly Bulletin of Statistics*).

## Finance

**CURRENCY AND EXCHANGE RATES**
**Monetary Units**
100 centimes (santimat) = 1 Moroccan dirham.

**Sterling and Dollar Equivalents** (31 December 1994)
£1 sterling = 14.02 dirhams;
US $1 = 8.96 dirhams;
1,000 Moroccan dirhams = £71.34 = $111.61.

**Average Exchange Rate** (dirhams per US $)
1992   8.538
1993   9.299
1994   9.203

**BUDGET** (estimates, million dirhams)

| Revenue | 1991 | 1992 | 1993 |
|---|---|---|---|
| Direct taxes | 13,505 | 16,694 | 15,342 |
| Customs duties | 12,908 | 14,470 | 14,743 |
| Indirect taxes | 17,328 | 19,336 | 20,359 |
| Registration fees and stamp duties | 2,591 | 2,650 | 2,567 |
| Government property | 118 | 152 | 117 |
| State monopolies | 2,668 | 2,811 | 2,980 |
| Income carried in from adjusted expenditure | 114 | 81 | 361 |
| Gross borrowings | 5,331 | 14,394 | 14,858 |
| Nominal receipts | 7 | 3 | 2 |
| **Total** (incl. others) | 57,562 | 73,465 | 75,919 |

| Expenditure | 1990 | 1991 | 1992 |
|---|---|---|---|
| Current expenditure |  |  |  |
| Administration | 278 | 291 | 318 |
| Personnel | 21,873 | 22,754 | 25,430 |
| Material and supplies | 5,868 | 6,667 | 7,500 |
| Common expenses | 2,078 | 2,412 | 2,959 |
| Debt-servicing | 22,433 | 24,604 | 22,437 |
| Contingencies | 250 | 996 | 1,081 |
| **Sub-total** | 52,780 | 57,724 | 59,725 |
| Capital expenditure | 12,675 | 12,900 | 13,592 |
| **Total** | 65,455 | 70,624 | 73,317 |

Source: Banque Al-Maghrib.

**1993** (estimate, million dirhams): Expenditure 80,000.

**INTERNATIONAL RESERVES** (US $ million at 31 December)

|  | 1992 | 1993 | 1994 |
|---|---|---|---|
| Gold* | 14 | 202 | n.a. |
| IMF special drawing rights | 77 | 34 | 26 |
| Reserve position in IMF | 42 | 42 | 44 |
| Foreign exchange | 3,465 | 3,579 | 4,281 |
| **Total** | 3,598 | 3,857 | n.a. |

\* National valuation of gold reserves (704,000 troy ounces in each year).
Source: IMF, *International Financial Statistics*.

**MONEY SUPPLY** (million dirhams at 31 December)

|  | 1991 | 1992 | 1993 |
|---|---|---|---|
| Currency outside banks | 34,269 | 35,745 | 37,202 |
| Private sector deposits at Bank of Morocco | 1,184 | 1,140 | 1,692 |
| Demand deposits at deposit money banks | 61,757 | 66,636 | 70,033 |
| Checking deposits at post office | 1,777 | 1,520 | 1,625 |
| Private sector checking deposits at treasury | 4,693 | 5,041 | 6,020 |
| **Total money** | 103,680 | 110,082 | 116,572 |

**COST OF LIVING** (Consumer Price Index; base: 1980 = 100)

|  | 1990 | 1991 | 1992 |
|---|---|---|---|
| Food | 200.3 | 217.3 | 228.0 |
| Clothing | 176.9 | 189.5 | 198.6 |
| **All items** (incl. others) | 201.3 | 217.7 | 228.5 |

**1993** (base: 1989 = 100): Food 133.2; Fuel and light 120.8; Clothing 128.2; Rent 123.2; All items (incl. others) 128.5.

Source: ILO, *Year Book of Labour Statistics*.

# MOROCCO

*Statistical Survey*

## NATIONAL ACCOUNTS

**Gross Domestic Product by Economic Activity**
(million dirhams at current prices)

|  | 1991 | 1992 | 1993* |
|---|---:|---:|---:|
| Agriculture, hunting, forestry and fishing | 48,010.1 | 36,031.3 | 35,418.8 |
| Mining and quarrying | 5,640.1 | 5,430.5 | 5,269.3 |
| Manufacturing | 50,438.7 | 54,253.9 | 56,060.5 |
| Electricity and water | 6,487.6 | 6,863.9 | 7,172.8 |
| Construction | 12,060.1 | 12,040.1 | 11,640.6 |
| Trade, restaurants and hotels | 30,623.6 | 32,427.9 | 33,559.5 |
| Transport, storage and communications | 14,065.9 | 15,191.1 | 16,621.7 |
| Finance, insurance, real estate and business services | 9,313.5 | 10,590.2 | 11,113.8 |
| Government services | 29,258.0 | 30,979.0 | 32,507.0 |
| Other community, social and personal services | 23,122.1 | 25,201.4 | 26,900.4 |
| **Sub-total** | 229,019.7 | 229,009.3 | 236,264.4 |
| Import duties | 22,031.0 | 23,156.0 | 22,932.0 |
| *Less* Imputed bank service charge | 9,644.1 | 10,941.7 | 11,513.9 |
| **GDP in purchasers' values** | 241,406.6 | 241,223.6 | 247,682.5 |

* Figures are provisional.

## BALANCE OF PAYMENTS (US $ million)

|  | 1991 | 1992 | 1993 |
|---|---:|---:|---:|
| Merchandise exports f.o.b. | 4,277 | 3,956 | 3,682 |
| Merchandise imports f.o.b. | −6,253 | −6,692 | −6,062 |
| **Trade balance** | −1,976 | −2,736 | −2,380 |
| Exports of services | 1,771 | 2,349 | 2,379 |
| Imports of services | −1,313 | −1,457 | −1,536 |
| Other income received | 203 | 293 | 229 |
| Other income paid | −1,375 | −1,416 | −1,509 |
| Private unrequited transfers (net) | 2,013 | 2,179 | 2,138 |
| Official unrequited transfers (net) | 280 | 360 | 154 |
| **Current balance** | −396 | −427 | −525 |
| Direct investment (net) | 320 | 424 | 493 |
| Other capital (net) | 1,155 | 947 | 473 |
| Net errors and omissions | 88 | 2 | −372 |
| **Overall balance** | 1,167 | 946 | 70 |

Source: IMF, *International Financial Statistics*.

# External Trade

## PRINCIPAL COMMODITIES (million dirhams)

| Imports c.i.f. | 1991 | 1992 | 1993 |
|---|---:|---:|---:|
| Crude petroleum | 6,580 | 8,007 | 6,693 |
| Chemical products | 2,529 | 2,393 | 2,718 |
| Boilers | 49 | 622 | 2,436 |
| Industrial vehicles | 1,220 | 1,311 | 922 |
| Wood | 1,343 | 1,666 | 1,400 |
| Wheat | 1,314 | 2,736 | 3,267 |
| Sulphur | 2,191 | 1,829 | 1,071 |
| Fabrics | 1,615 | 1,396 | 1,327 |
| Synthetic plastics | 1,433 | 1,459 | 1,484 |
| **Total** (incl. others) | 59,730 | 62,805 | 61,908 |

| Exports f.o.b. | 1991 | 1992 | 1993 |
|---|---:|---:|---:|
| Phosphates | 3,016 | 2,621 | 2,416 |
| Phosphoric acid | 3,716 | 3,425 | 3,256 |
| Fertilizers | 3,316 | 2,446 | 2,895 |
| Clothing | 4,187 | 4,137 | 4,012 |
| Crustaceans and molluscs | 2,729 | 2,501 | 2,924 |
| Citrus fruits | 1,819 | 1,461 | 1,443 |
| Hosiery | 2,165 | 2,406 | 2,732 |
| Canned fish | 1,347 | 1,360 | 1,354 |
| Fresh fish | 1,205 | 871 | 738 |
| **Total** (incl. others) | 37,283 | 33,959 | 34,366 |

Source: Office des Changes, Rabat.

## PRINCIPAL TRADING PARTNERS (million dirhams)*

| Imports c.i.f. | 1991 | 1992 | 1993 |
|---|---:|---:|---:|
| Algeria | 480 | 779 | 1,003 |
| Belgium-Luxembourg | 1,721 | 1,703 | 1,434 |
| Brazil | 1,408 | 1,300 | 1,335 |
| Canada | 1,966 | 1,339 | 953 |
| China, People's Republic | 1,238 | 1,246 | 1,169 |
| France | 14,449 | 14,948 | 14,210 |
| Germany | 3,529 | 3,727 | 3,674 |
| Iran | 214 | 1,468 | 1,551 |
| Italy | 4,153 | 3,902 | 3,886 |
| Japan | 1,282 | 1,317 | 1,060 |
| Kuwait | — | 306 | 747 |
| Libya† | 1,215 | 870 | n.a. |
| Netherlands | 1,576 | 1,530 | 1,353 |
| Poland | 749 | 718 | 642 |
| Saudi Arabia | 2,927 | 3,459 | 3,474 |
| Spain | 4,940 | 5,361 | 6,500 |
| Sweden | 1,202 | 1,135 | 1,108 |
| Switzerland | 845 | 878 | 697 |
| Turkey† | 322 | 741 | n.a. |
| USSR (former) | 1,276 | 876‡ | n.a. |
| United Arab Emirates | 2,270 | 2,218 | 1,031 |
| United Kingdom | 2,065 | 1,720 | 1,684 |
| USA | 3,485 | 3,714 | 6,250 |
| **Total** (incl. others) | 59,720 | 62,805 | 61,908 |

| Exports f.o.b. | 1991 | 1992 | 1993 |
|---|---:|---:|---:|
| Algeria | 640 | 612 | 723 |
| Belgium-Luxembourg | 1,273 | 1,176 | 1,026 |
| France | 11,855 | 11,130 | 11,414 |
| Germany | 1,819 | 1,605 | 1,519 |
| India | 2,609 | 2,024 | 1,336 |
| Iran | 251 | 217 | 502 |
| Italy | 2,309 | 1,894 | 1,797 |
| Japan | 1,949 | 1,678 | 2,021 |
| Liberia | 1 | 1 | 389 |
| Libya | 1,710 | 1,120 | 1,273 |
| Mexico | 226 | 264 | 363 |
| Netherlands | 922 | 1,062 | 898 |
| Saudi Arabia | 994 | 558 | 449 |
| Spain | 3,283 | 3,066 | 3,037 |
| Tunisia | 543 | 423 | 365 |
| Turkey | 533 | 255 | 385 |
| United Kingdom | 1,022 | 1,137 | 1,244 |
| USA | 937 | 1,272 | 1,171 |
| **Total** (incl. others) | 37,283 | 33,959 | 34,366 |

* Imports by country of production; exports by country of last consignment.
† Source: UN, *International Trade Statistics Yearbook*.
‡ Imports from Russia only.

MOROCCO

## Transport

**RAILWAYS** (traffic)*

|  | 1991 | 1992 | 1993 |
|---|---|---|---|
| Passenger-km (million) | 2,345 | 2,233 | 1,904 |
| Freight ton-km (million) | 4,523 | 5,001 | 4,415 |

* Figures refer to principal railways only.

**ROAD TRAFFIC** (motor vehicles in use at 31 December)

|  | 1991 | 1992 | 1993 |
|---|---|---|---|
| Passenger cars | 707,148 | 778,880 | 849,344 |
| Buses and coaches | 11,292 | 11,660 | 11,967 |
| Goods vehicles | 223,726 | 232,699 | 239,975 |
| Motorcycles and scooters | 19,487 | 19,592 | 19,689 |

**SHIPPING**

Merchant Fleet Displacement (vessels registered at 30 June, '000 grt)

|  | 1990 | 1991 | 1992 |
|---|---|---|---|
| Total | 488 | 483 | 479 |

Source: UN, *Statistical Yearbook*.

International Sea-borne Freight Traffic ('000 metric tons)

|  | 1988 | 1989 | 1990 |
|---|---|---|---|
| Goods loaded | 23,900 | 21,450 | 20,257 |
| Goods unloaded | 11,850 | 12,209 | 12,454 |

Source: UN, *Monthly Bulletin of Statistics*.

**CIVIL AVIATION** (traffic on scheduled services)

|  | 1990 | 1991 | 1992 |
|---|---|---|---|
| Kilometres flown (million) | 30 | 27 | 42 |
| Passengers carried ('000) | 1,580 | 1,430 | 2,169 |
| Passenger-km (million) | 2,889 | 2,533 | 4,297 |
| Total ton-km (million) | 255 | 257 | 399 |

Source: UN, *Statistical Yearbook*.

## Tourism

**FOREIGN TOURIST ARRIVALS**

| Country of Origin | 1990 | 1991 | 1992 |
|---|---|---|---|
| Algeria | 1,452,645 | 2,048,616 | 1,659,634 |
| France | 451,817 | 290,630 | 428,983 |
| Germany | 161,186 | 108,462 | 184,645 |
| Italy | 80,372 | 67,505 | 113,348 |
| Spain | 210,802 | 193,207 | 276,988 |
| United Kingdom | 89,467 | 58,473 | 95,267 |
| USA | 83,816 | 48,034 | 89,536 |
| **Total** (incl. others) | 2,978,366 | 3,190,384 | 3,252,062 |

Source: Direction Générale de la Sûreté Nationale.

## Communications Media

|  | 1990 | 1991 | 1992 |
|---|---|---|---|
| Radio receivers ('000 in use) | 5,250 | 5,385 | 5,527 |
| Television receivers ('000 in use) | 1,850 | 1,900 | 1,950 |
| Telephones ('000 main lines in use) | 402 | 497 | n.a. |
| Daily newspapers | 13 | n.a. | 14 |

Sources: UNESCO, *Statistical Yearbook*; UN, *Statistical Yearbook*.

## Education

(1994/95, unless otherwise indicated)

|  | Institutions | Teachers | Males | Females | Total |
|---|---|---|---|---|---|
| Pre-primary | 32,021 | 36,553 | 555,392 | 241,277 | 796,669 |
| Primary | 4,740 | 102,163 | 1,698,398 | 1,197,339 | 2,895,737 |
| Secondary |  |  |  |  |  |
| General* | 1,172 | 73,726 | 725,858 | 521,750 | 1,247,608 |
| Vocational† | 55 | 2,951 | 10,466 | 7,119 | 17,585 |
| University level‡ | 50 | 6,877 | 140,453 | 89,559 | 230,012 |

* State schools only.
† Data exclude professional schools.
‡ 1992/93 figures.

Source: Ministère de l'Education Nationale, Rabat.

# Directory

## The Constitution

The following is a summary of the main provisions of the Constitution, as approved in a national referendum on 4 September 1992.

### PREAMBLE

The Kingdom of Morocco, a sovereign Islamic State, shall be a part of the Great Maghreb. As an African State, one of its aims shall be the realization of African unity. It will adhere to the principles, rights and obligations of those international organizations of which it is a member and will work for the preservation of peace and security in the world.

### GENERAL PRINCIPLES

Morocco shall be a constitutional, democratic and social monarchy. Sovereignty shall pertain to the nation and be exercised directly by means of the referendum and indirectly by the constitutional institutions. All Moroccans shall be equal before the law, and all adults shall enjoy equal political rights including the franchise. Freedoms of movement, opinion and speech and the right of assembly shall be guaranteed. Islam shall be the state religion. All Moroccans shall have equal rights in seeking education and employment. The right to strike, and to private property, shall be guaranteed. All Moroccans shall contribute to the defence of the Kingdom and to public costs. Neither the state, system of monarchy nor the prescriptions related to the religion of Islam may be subject to a constitutional revision. There shall be no one-party system.

### THE MONARCHY

The Crown of Morocco and its attendant constitutional rights shall be hereditary in the line of HM King Hassan II, and shall be transmitted to the oldest son, unless during his lifetime the King has appointed as his successor another of his sons. The King is the symbol of unity, guarantees the continuity of the state, and safeguards respect for Islam and the Constitution. The King shall have the power to appoint and dismiss the Prime Minister and other Cabinet Ministers (who are nominated by the Prime Minister), and shall preside over the Cabinet. He shall promulgate legislation that has been approved by the Chamber of Representatives within a 30-day period, and have the power to dissolve the Chamber; and is empowered to initiate revisions to the Constitution. The Sovereign is the Commander-in-Chief of the Armed Forces; makes appointments to civil and military posts; appoints Ambassadors; signs and ratifies treaties; presides over the Supreme Council of the Magistracy, the Supreme Council of Education and the Supreme Council for National Reconstruction; and exercises the right of pardon. In cases of threat to the national territory or to the action of constitutional institutions, the King, having consulted the President of the Chamber of Representatives and the Chairman of the Constitutional Council, and after addressing the nation, shall have the right to declare a State of Emergency by royal decree. The State of Emergency shall not entail the dissolution of the Chamber of Representatives and shall be terminated by the same procedure followed in its proclamation.

### LEGISLATURE

This shall consist of a single assembly, the Chamber of Representatives, whose members are to be elected for a six-year term. Two-thirds of the members shall be elected by direct universal suffrage, and one-third by an electoral college composed of councillors in local government and employers' and employees' representatives. The Chamber shall adopt legislation, which may be initiated by its members or by the Prime Minister; authorize any declaration of war; initiate a revision of the Constitution; and approve any extension beyond 30 days of a state of emergency. The Chamber of Representatives shall hold its meetings during two sessions each year, which shall commence on the second Friday in April and the second Friday in October.

### GOVERNMENT

The Government, composed of the Prime Minister and his Ministers, shall be responsible to the King and the Chamber of Representatives and shall ensure the execution of laws. The Prime Minister shall be empowered to initiate legislation and to exercise statutory powers except where these are reserved to the King. He shall present to the Chamber the Government's intended programme and shall be responsible for co-ordinating ministerial work.

### RELATIONS BETWEEN THE AUTHORITIES

The King may request a second reading, by the Chamber of Representatives, of any draft bill or proposed law. In addition he may submit proposed legislation to a referendum by decree; and dissolve the Chamber if a proposal that has been rejected by it is approved by referendum. He may also dissolve the Chamber by decree after consulting the Chairman of the Constitutional Council, and addressing the nation, but the succeeding Chamber may not be dissolved within a year of its election. The Chamber of Representatives may force the collective resignation of the Government either by refusing a vote of confidence or by adopting a censure motion.

### THE CONSTITUTIONAL COUNCIL

A Constitutional Council shall be established, consisting of a Chairman, four members appointed by the King for a period of six years, and four members appointed by the President of the Chamber of Representatives for the same period. Half of each category of the Council shall be renewed every three years. The Council shall be empowered to judge the validity of legislative elections and referendums, as well as that of organic laws and the Rules of Procedure of the Chamber of Representatives, submitted to it.

### THE ECONOMIC AND SOCIAL COUNCIL

An Economic and Social Council shall be established to give its opinion on all matters of an economic or social nature. Its constitution, organization, prerogatives and rules of procedure shall be determined by an organic law.

### JUDICIARY

The Judiciary shall be independent. Judges shall be appointed on the recommendation of the Supreme Council of the Judiciary presided over by the King.

# The Government

### HEAD OF STATE

HM King HASSAN II (acceded 3 March 1961).

### CABINET
(June 1995)

UC—Union Constitutionnelle; MP—Mouvement Populaire; PND—Parti Nationale Démocrate.

Prime Minister and Minister of Foreign Affairs and Co-operation: ABD AL-LATIF FILALI.
Minister of State: MOULAY AHMAD ALAOUI.
Minister of State for the Interior: DRISS BASRI.
Minister of Justice: ABDERRAHMANE AMALOU (UC).
Minister of Public Health: AHMED ALAMI (PND).
Minister of Finance and Foreign Investments: MOHAMED KABBAJ (UC).
Minister of National Education: RACHID BEN MOKHTAR.
Minister of Agriculture and Agricultural Investments: HASSAN ABOU AYOUB (MP).
Minister of Ocean Fisheries and the Merchant Navy: MUSTAPHA SAHEL.
Minister of Public Works: ABD AL-AZIZ MEZZIANE BELFKIH.
Minister of Communications and Spokesman of the Government: DRISS ALAOUI M'DAGHRI.
Minister of Trade, Industry and Handicrafts: DRISS JETTOU.
Minister of Religious Endowments (Awqaf) and Islamic Affairs: ABD AL-KAEBIR ALAOUI M'DAGHRI.
Minister of Energy and Mines: ABD AL-LATIF GUERRAOUI.
Minister of Privatization: ABDERRAHMANE SAAIDI.
Minister of Cultural Affairs: ABD AL-AZMANI (UC).
Secretary-General of the Government: ABDESSADEK RABI.
Minister of Transport: SAID AMESKANE (MP).
Minister of Posts and Telecommunications: HAMZA KETTANI (UC).
Minister of Youth and Sports: AHMED MEZZIANE (MP).
Minister of Employment and Social Affairs: AMINE DAMNATI (MP).
Minister of Housing: SAID FASSI.
Minister of Tourism: MOHAMED ALAOUI MOHAMADI (UC).
Minister of the Environment: NOUREDDINE BENOMAR ALAMI (UC).
Minister of Vocational Training: ABDESSALEM BAROUAL (MP).
Minister of Higher Education, Professional Training and Scientific Research: DRISS KHALIL.
Minister Foreign Trade: MOHAMED ALAMI (MP).
Minister Delegate to the Prime Minister: ABDERRAHMANE SBAI.
Minister Delegate to the Prime Minister, in charge of Relations with the Chamber of Representatives: ABDESSALAM BARAKA (UC).
Minister Delegate to the Prime Minister, in charge of Administrative Affairs: MESSAOUD MANSOURI (MP).
Minister Delegate to the Prime Minister, in charge of Promoting the Economy: MOHAMED HAMMA (MP).
Minister Delegate to the Prime Minister, in charge of Human Rights: MOHAMED ZIANE (UC).
Minister Delegate to the Prime Minister, in charge of Population: LAMINE BENOMAR (PND).
Secretary of State for Foreign Affairs and Co-operation: TAIEB EL-FASSI FIHRI.
Deputy Secretary of State to the Minister of Foreign Affairs, in charge of the Affairs of the Moroccan Community Abroad: LAHSENE GABON (PND).
Deputy Secretary of State to the Minister of Foreign Affairs, in charge of Relations with the Arab Maghreb Union: ABD AL-AZIZ MSIOUI (UC).

### MINISTRIES

**Ministry of Agriculture and Agricultural Investments:** Cité Ministérielle, Rabat; tel. (7) 290808; fax 290800.

**Ministry of Cultural Affairs:** rue Gandhi, Rabat; tel. (7) 66054.

**Ministry of Employment and Social Affairs:** Quartier Administratif, Rabat; tel. (7) 60521; telex 31057.

**Ministry of Energy and Mines:** ave Maa al-Ainane, Rabat; tel. (7) 77924; telex 32761.

**Ministry of Finance:** ave Muhammad V, Quartier Administratif, Rabat; tel. (7) 62171; telex 31820.

**Ministry of Foreign Affairs and Co-operation:** ave Franklin Roosevelt, Rabat; tel. (7) 62841; telex 31007.

**Ministry of Housing:** Quartier Administratif, Rabat; tel. (7) 60263; telex 32744.

**Ministry of the Interior:** place de la Poste Centrale, Rabat; tel. (7) 66016; telex 31015.

**Ministry of Justice:** 485 blvd Muhammad V, Rabat; tel. (7) 60041; telex 31888.

**Ministry of National Education:** place de la Victoire, Rabat; tel. (7) 771822; telex 36016.

# MOROCCO

**Ministry of Ocean Fisheries and the Merchant Navy:** 63 blvd Moulay Youssef, Rabat; tel. (7) 63366; telex 32679.

**Ministry of Posts and Telecommunications:** ave Moulay Hassan, Rabat; tel. (7) 702091; telex 36043; fax (7) 705641.

**Ministry of Privatization:** 47 ave Ibn Sina, BP 6552, Agdal, Rabat; tel. (7) 672017; fax (7) 673299.

**Ministry of Public Health:** 335 ave Muhammad V, Rabat; tel. (7) 61121; telex 31642.

**Ministry of Religious Endowments (Awqaf) and Islamic Affairs:** Enceinte du Palais Royal, Rabat; tel. (7) 62703; telex 31771.

**Ministry of Tourism:** Rabat.

**Ministry of Trade, Industry and Handicrafts:** Quartier Administratif, Rabat; tel. (7) 61701; telex 36641.

**Ministry of Transport:** rue Maa al-Ainane, Casier Officiel, Rabat-Chellah; tel. (7) 73486; telex 31626.

**Ministry of Vocational Training:** Quartier Administratif, Rabat; tel. (7) 65473; telex 31613.

**Ministry of Youth and Sports:** 485 blvd Muhammad V, Rabat; tel. (7) 60041; telex 32652.

## Legislature

### MAJLIS AN-NUWAB
(Chamber of Representatives)

**President:** AHMAD OSMAN.

**1993 Elections**
(direct voting on 25 June; electoral college voting took place on 17 September).

| | Seats by Direct Election | Seats by Indirect Election | Total Seats |
|---|---|---|---|
| Union Socialiste des Forces Populaires | 48 | 8 | 56 |
| Union Constitutionnelle | 27 | 27 | 54 |
| Istiqlal | 43 | 9 | 52 |
| Mouvement Populaire | 33 | 18 | 51 |
| Rassemblement National des Indépendants | 28 | 13 | 41 |
| Mouvement National Populaire | 14 | 11 | 25 |
| Parti National Démocrate | 14 | 10 | 24 |
| Parti du Progrès et du Socialisme* | 6 | 4 | 10 |
| Parti Démocratique pour l'Indépendance | 3 | 6 | 9 |
| Union Marocaine du Travail† | — | 3 | 3 |
| Organisation de l'Action Démocratique et Populaire | 2 | — | 2 |
| Parti de l'Action | 2 | — | 2 |
| Independents | 2 | 2 | 4 |
| **Total** | **222** | **111** | **333** |

* Name changed to Parti du Renouveau et du Progrès in 1994.
† A trade union federation.

Note: By-elections were necessitated in 13 constituencies where the election result had been invalidated by the Constitutional Council.

## Political Organizations

**Bloc Démocratique (Koutla Dimocratya):** f. 1992; opposition alliance comprising the USFP, Istiqlal, the OADP, the PRP and the UNFP; supported by trade unions and other groupings.

**Entente Nationale (Wifaq):** loyalist, centre-right coalition comprising the UC, the MP, the RNI, the MNP and the PND.

**Istiqlal:** 4 charia Ibnou Toumert, Rabat; tel. (7) 730951; fax (7) 725354; f. 1944; aims to raise living standards and to confer equal rights on all; stresses the Moroccan claim to Western Sahara; Sec.-Gen. M'HAMED BOUCETTA.

**Mouvement National Populaire (MNP):** f. 1991; Leader MAHJOUBI AHERDANE.

**Mouvement Populaire (MP):** 12 rue Marinin Hassan, Rabat; tel. (7) 730808; fax (7) 200165; f. 1959; conservative; Sec. Gen. MUHAMMAD LAENSER.

**Mouvement Populaire Constitutionnel et Démocratique (MPCD):** 352 blvd Muhammad V, Rabat; tel. (7) 702347; f. 1967; breakaway party from Mouvement Populaire; Leader Dr ABD AL-KARIM KHATIB.

**Organisation de l'Action Démocratique et Populaire (OADP):** 29 blvd Lalla Yakout, BP 15797, Casablanca; tel. (2) 278442; f. 1983; Sec.-Gen. MUHAMMAD BEN SAÏD.

**Parti de l'Action:** 113 ave Allal ben Abdallah, Rabat; tel. (7) 24973; f. 1974; advocates democracy and progress; Sec.-Gen. ABDALLAH SENHAJI.

**Parti de l'Avant-garde Démocratique Socialiste (PADS):** an offshoot of the USFP; legalized in April 1992.

**Parti du Centre Social:** Centre socialist party.

**Parti Démocratique pour l'Indépendance:** Casablanca; tel. (2) 223359; f. 1946; Leader THAMI EL-OUAZZANI.

**Parti Libéral Progressiste (PLP):** Casablanca; f. 1974; advocates individual freedom and free enterprise; Leader AKHMOUCH AHMAD OULHAJ.

**Parti National Démocrate (PND):** 18 rue de Tunis, Rabat; tel. (7) 30754; f. 1981 from split within RNI; working within the framework of the constitutional monarchy, aims to support the democratic process, defend Morocco's territorial integrity and reduce social and economic disparities; Leader ARSALANE EL-JADIDI.

**Parti National pour l'Unité et la Solidarité:** Casablanca; tel. (2) 370501; f. 1982; Sec.-Gen. MUHAMMAD ASMAR.

**Parti du Renouveau et du Progrès (PRP):** 32 rue Lédru Rollin, BP 13152, Casablanca; tel. (2) 222238; f. 1974; successor to the Parti Communiste Marocain (banned in 1952), and the Parti de la Libération et du Socialisme (banned in 1969); name changed from Parti du Progrès et du Socialisme in 1994; left-wing; advocates nationalization and democracy; 35,000 mems; Sec.-Gen. ALI YATA.

**Rassemblement National des Indépendants (RNI):** rue Erfour, Rabat; tel. (7) 65418; f. 1978 from the pro-government independents' group that formed the majority in the Chamber of Representatives; Leader MOULAY AHMAD ALAOUI.

**Union Constitutionnelle (UC):** 4 ave Bin El Ouidane, Rabat; tel. (7) 76935; telex 24645; f. 1983; 25-member Political Bureau; Leader MAATI BOUABID.

**Union Nationale des Forces Populaires (UNFP):** 28–30 rue Magellan, BP 747, Casablanca 01; tel. (2) 302023; fax (2) 319301; f. 1959 by MEHDI BEN BARKA from a group within Istiqlal; left-wing; in 1972 a split occurred between the Casablanca and Rabat sections of the party; Leader MOULAY ABDALLAH IBRAHIM.

**Union Socialiste des Forces Populaires (USFP):** 17 rue Oued Souss, Agdal, Rabat; tel. (7) 73905; telex 31966; f. 1959 as UNFP, became USFP in 1974; left-wing progressive party, has consistently boycotted elections; 100,000 mems; First Sec. FATHALLAH OULAALOU.

The following group is active in the disputed territory of Western Sahara:

**Frente Popular para la Liberación de Saguia el Hamra y Rio de Oro (Frente Polisario)** (Polisario Front): BP 10, El-Mouradia, Algiers; f. 1973 to gain independence for Western Sahara, first from Spain and then from Morocco and Mauritania; signed peace treaty with Mauritanian Government in 1979; supported by the Algerian Government; in February 1976 proclaimed the Sahrawi Arab Democratic Republic (SADR), since recognized by 30 member-states of the OAU (to which it was admitted in February 1982 as the 51st member) and by more than 70 countries worldwide; its main organs are a seven-member executive committee, a 27-member Political Bureau and a 45-member Sahrawi National Council; Sec.-Gen. of the Polisario Front and Pres. of the SADR MUHAMMAD ABD AL-AZIZ; Prime Minister of the SADR BOUCHRAYA HAMMOUDI BAYOUNE.

## Diplomatic Representation

### EMBASSIES IN MOROCCO

**Algeria:** 46 blvd Tariq Ibn Ziad, Rabat; tel. (7) 65092; Ambassador: BELAID MOHAMED LAKHDAR.

**Argentina:** 12 rue Mekki Bitaouri Souissi, Rabat; tel. (7) 55120; telex 31017; Ambassador: MARCELO DELPECHE.

**Austria:** 2 Zankat Tiddas, BP 135, Rabat; tel. (7) 764003; telex 31623; fax (7) 765425; Ambassador: TASSILO F. OGRINZ.

**Belgium:** 6 ave de Marrakech, BP 163, Rabat; tel. (7) 64746; telex 31087; Ambassador: ANDRÉ FONTAINE.

**Brazil:** 1 charia Marrakech, Rabat; tel. (7) 765522; telex 31628; fax (7) 766705; Ambassador: ANTÔNIO S. CANTUARIA GUIMARÃES.

**Bulgaria:** 4 ave de Meknès, Rabat; tel. (7) 764082; telex 31761; fax (7) 763201; Ambassador: KOSSIO PROYKOV KITIPOV.

# MOROCCO

**Cameroon:** 20 rue du Rif, Souissi, Rabat; Ambassador: Mahamat Paba Sale.
**Canada:** 13 bis rue Jaafar as-Sadik, BP 709, Agdal, Rabat; tel. (7) 772880; telex 31964; fax (7) 772887; Ambassador: Robert Kenneth Higham.
**Central African Republic:** Villa 42, ave Pasteur, Agdal, Rabat; tel. (7) 70203; telex 31920; Ambassador: Jules Koualeyaboro.
**China, People's Republic:** 16 charia al-Fahs, Rabat; tel. (7) 54056; telex 31023; Ambassador: An Guozheng.
**Côte d'Ivoire:** 21 Zankat Tiddas, BP 192, Rabat; tel. (7) 63151; telex 31070; Ambassador: Amadou Thiam.
**Czech Republic:** Zankat Ait Melloul, BP 410, Souissi, Rabat; tel. (7) 55421; telex 32941; fax (7) 55420; Ambassador: Vladimir Sattran.
**Denmark:** 4 rue de Khémisset, BP 203, Rabat; tel. (7) 767986; telex 31077; fax (7) 769709; Ambassador: Peter Branner.
**Egypt:** 31 Zankat Al Jazair, Rabat; tel. (7) 31833; Ambassador: Muhammad Beshr.
**Equatorial Guinea:** 30 ave des Nations Unies, BP 723, Agdal, Rabat; tel. (7) 74205; telex 31796; Ambassador: Resurrección Bita.
**Finland:** 18 rue de Khémisset, Rabat; tel. (7) 62352; Ambassador: Heikki Kalha.
**France:** 3 rue Sahnoun, Rabat; tel. (7) 777822; telex 31013; fax (7) 777752; Ambassador: Henri de Coignac.
**Gabon:** ave des Zaërs, Km 3.5, Rabat; tel. (7) 51968; telex 31999; Ambassador: Claude Roger Owansango.
**Germany:** 7 Zankat Madnine, BP 235, Rabat; tel. (7) 709662; telex 36026; fax (7) 706851; Ambassador: Dr Herwig Bartels.
**Greece:** 23 rue d'Oujda, Rabat; tel. (7) 23839; telex 31953; Ambassador: Dimitri Skouroliakos.
**Guinea:** 15 rue Hamzah, Rabat; tel. (7) 674148; telex 31796; fax (7) 672513; Ambassador: El-Haj Guirane Nidiaye.
**Holy See:** rue Béni M'tir, BP 1303, Souissi, Rabat (Apostolic Nunciature); tel. (7) 772277; fax (7) 756213; Apostolic Nuncio: Most Rev. Domenico de Luca, Titular Archbishop of Teglata in Numidia.
**Hungary:** BP 5026, Souissi II, Rabat; tel. (7) 750757; telex 32718; fax (7) 775423; Ambassador: Béla Bényei.
**Indonesia:** 63 rue Béni Boufrah, Rabat; tel. (7) 57860; telex 32783; fax (7) 57859; Ambassador: Tawfiq Rachman Soedarbo.
**Iran:** route de Zair, Kacem, Souissi, Rabat; tel. (7) 52167; fax (7) 50353; Ambassador: Ja'far Shamsian.
**Iraq:** 39 rue Béni Iznassen, Souissi, Rabat; tel. (7) 54466; telex 31663; Ambassador: Fadhil al-Shahir.
**Italy:** 2 Zankat Idriss el-Azhar, BP 111, Rabat; tel. (7) 766597; telex 32731; fax (7) 766882; Ambassador: Emilio De Stefanis.
**Japan:** 70 ave des Nations Unies, Agdal, Rabat; tel. (7) 674163; telex 31901; fax 672274; Ambassador: Kyoichi Omura.
**Jordan:** Villa al-Wafae, Lot 5, Souissi II, Rabat; tel. (7) 59270; telex 31085; fax (7) 58722; Ambassador: Hussein Hammami.
**Korea, Republic:** 41 ave Bani Iznassen, Souissi, Rabat; tel. (7) 751767; telex 31698; fax (7) 750189; Ambassador: Kim Dong-Ho.
**Kuwait:** Rm 413, charia Iman Malik, Rabat; tel. (7) 56423; telex 31955; Ambassador: Abd al-Muhsin Salem al-Haroun.
**Lebanon:** 19 ave de Fès, Rabat; tel. (7) 60728; telex 31060; Ambassador: Sami Omar Kronfol.
**Libya:** 1 rue Chouaïb Doukkali, BP 225, Rabat; tel. (7) 68828; telex 31957; Chargé d'affaires a.i.: Muhammad Zwai.
**Mauritania:** 9 rue Taza, Souissi, Rabat; Ambassador: Sidna Ould Cheikh Taleb Bouya.
**Mexico:** 10 ave de Marrakech, Rabat; tel. (7) 767956; telex 36248; fax (7) 758583; Ambassador: Salvador Campos Icardo.
**Netherlands:** 40 rue de Tunis, BP 329, Rabat; tel. (7) 733512; telex 31962; fax (7) 733333; Ambassador: Jonkheer D. M. Schorer.
**Nigeria:** 70 ave Omar ibn al-Khattab, BP 347, Agdal, Rabat; tel. (7) 671857; telex 31976; fax (7) 672739; Ambassador: Y. Usman.
**Oman:** 21 rue Hamza, Agdal, Rabat; tel. (7) 71064; telex 31747; Ambassador: Muhammad bin Salim al-Shanfari.
**Pakistan:** 2 blvd Soomat Hassan, Rabat; tel. (7) 31791; telex 31918; Ambassador: Muhammad Safdar.
**Peru:** 16 rue d'Ifrane, Rabat; tel. (7) 723236; telex 32659; fax (7) 702803; Chargé d'affaires: Enrique Zañartu.
**Poland:** 23 Zankat Oqbah, Agdal, BP 425, Rabat; tel. (7) 771791; telex 31003; fax (7) 775320; Ambassador: Piotr Szymanowski.
**Portugal:** 5 rue Thami Lamdouar, Souissi, Rabat; tel. (7) 56446; telex 31711; Ambassador: Jorge Ritto.
**Qatar:** 4 charia Tarik ibn Ziad, BP 1220, Rabat; tel. (7) 65681; telex 31624; Ambassador: Ali Ahmed as-Sulaiti.
**Romania:** 10 rue d'Ouezzane, Rabat; tel. (7) 27899; Ambassador: Dr Emilian Manciur.
**Russia:** Km 4, route des Zaërs, Rabat; tel. (7) 53581; telex 31602; Ambassador: Yuri M. Rybakov.
**Saudi Arabia:** 43 place de l'Unité Africaine, Rabat; tel. (7) 30171; telex 32875; Ambassador: Ali Majed Kabbani.
**Senegal:** 17 rue Cadi ben Hamadi Senhaji, Souissi, Rabat; tel. (7) 54148; telex 31048; Ambassador: Gen. Coumba Diouf Niang.
**Spain:** 3 Zankat Madnine, Rabat; tel. (7) 68638; telex 31073; Ambassador: Joaquín Ortega Salinas.
**Sudan:** 5 ave Ghomara, Souissi, Rabat; tel. (7) 52863; Ambassador: Abdalla Maghoub.
**Sweden:** 159 ave John Kennedy, BP 428, Rabat; tel. (7) 759303; telex 36541; fax (7) 758048; Ambassador: Mathias Mossberg.
**Switzerland:** Sq de Berkane, BP 169, Rabat; tel. (7) 66974; telex 31996; fax (7) 05749; Ambassador: Gérard Franel.
**Tunisia:** 6 ave de Fès, Rabat; tel. (7) 30636; telex 31009; Ambassador: Abderrazak Kefi.
**Turkey:** 7 ave de Fès, Rabat; tel. (7) 762605; telex 36164; fax (7) 704980; Ambassador: Onder Ozar.
**United Arab Emirates:** 11 ave des Alaouines, Rabat; tel. (7) 30975; telex 31697; Ambassador: Issaa Hamad Bushahab.
**United Kingdom:** 17 blvd de la Tour Hassan, BP 45, Rabat; tel. (7) 720905; telex 31022; fax (7) 704531; Ambassador: Sir Allan Ramsay.
**USA:** 2 charia Marrakech, Rabat; tel. (7) 762265; telex 31005; fax (7) 765661; Ambassador: Marc Charles Ginsberg.
**Yemen:** 11 rue Abou-Hanifa, Agdal, Rabat; tel. (7) 74363; telex 32855; Ambassador: (vacant).
**Yugoslavia:** 23 ave Bni Znassen, Souissi, BP 5014, Rabat; tel. (7) 52201; telex 31760; Ambassador: Dimitrije Babić.
**Zaire:** 34 ave de la Victoire, BP 537, Rabat-Chellah; tel. (7) 734862; telex 31954; Ambassador: Tomona Bate Tangale.

## Judicial System

The **Supreme Court** (al-Majlis al-Aala) is responsible for the interpretation of the law and regulates the jurisprudence of the courts and tribunals of the Kingdom. The Supreme Court sits at Rabat and is divided into six Chambers.
**First President:** Muhammad Mikou.
**Attorney-General:** Ahmad Zeghari.

The 15 **Courts of Appeal** hear appeals from lower courts and also comprise a criminal division.

The **Courts of First Instance** pass judgment on offences punishable by up to five years' imprisonment. These courts also pass judgment, without possibility of appeal, in personal, civil and commercial cases involving up to 3,000 dirhams.

The **Regional Tribunals** pass judgment in the first and last resort in cases of personal property of 1,000 dirhams. The Regional Tribunals also pass judgment, subject to appeal before the Court of Appeal, in cases of minor offences in penal matters, punishable by a fine of 10 to 800 dirhams.

**Labour Tribunals** settle, by means of conciliation, disputes arising from rental contracts or services between employers and employees engaged in private industry. There are 14 labour tribunals in the Kingdom.

The **High Court of Justice**, comprising members elected from the Chamber of Representatives and a president appointed by royal decree, considers crimes and felonies allegedly committed by government members in the exercise of their functions.

## Religion

### ISLAM

About 99% of Moroccans are Muslims (of whom about 90% are of the Sunni sect), and Islam is the state religion.

### CHRISTIANITY

There are about 69,000 Christians, mostly Roman Catholics.

#### The Roman Catholic Church

Morocco (excluding the disputed territory of Western Sahara) comprises two archdioceses, directly responsible to the Holy See. At 31 December 1993 there were an estimated 24,747 adherents in the country, representing 0.1% of the population. The Moroccan archbishops participate in the Conférence Episcopale Régionale du Nord de l'Afrique (f. 1985), based in Algiers (Algeria).

MOROCCO

**Archbishop of Rabat:** Most Rev. HUBERT MICHON, Archevêché, 1 rue Henri Dunant, BP 258, Rabat; tel. (7) 709239; fax (7) 706282.
**Archbishop of Tangier:** Most Rev. JOSÉ ANTONIO PETEIRO FREIRE, Archevêché, 55 rue Sidi Bouabid, BP 2116, Tangier; tel. (9) 932762; fax (9) 949117.

Western Sahara comprises a single Apostolic Prefecture, with an estimated 160 Catholics (1993).

**Prefect Apostolic of Western Sahara:** Fr ACACIO VALBUENA, Misión Católica, BP 31, el-Aaiún; tel. 893270.

### The Anglican Communion

Within the Church of England, Morocco forms part of the diocese of Gibraltar in Europe. There are Anglican churches in Casablanca and Tangier.

### Protestant Church

**Evangelical Church:** 33 rue d'Azilal, Casablanca 20000; tel. (2) 302151; f. 1920; established in 9 towns; Pres. Pastor ETIENNE QUINCHE; 1,000 mems.

### JUDAISM

There is a Jewish community of 6,000–7,000.

**Grand Rabbi of Casablanca:** CHALOM MESSAS, President of the Rabbinical Court of Casablanca, Palais de Justice, place des Nations Unies.

## The Press

### DAILIES

#### Casablanca

**Al-Bayane** (The Manifesto): 62 blvd de la Gironde, BP 13152, Casablanca; tel. (2) 307666; Arabic and French; organ of the Parti du Progrès et du Socialisme; Dir ALI YATA; circ. 5,000.

**Al-Ittihad al-Ichtiraki** (Socialist Unity): 33 rue Emir Abdelkader, Casablanca 05; tel. (2) 241538; telex 24961; Arabic; organ of the Union Socialiste des Forces Populaires; Dir ABDALLAH BOUHLAL.

**Maroc Soir:** 34 rue Muhammad Smiha, Casablanca; tel. (2) 268860; telex 23845; fax (2) 262969; f. 1971; French; Dir DRISSI EL-ALAMI; circ. 50,000.

**Le Matin du Sahara et du Maghreb:** 88 blvd Muhammad V, Casablanca; tel. (2) 268860; telex 23845; fax (2) 262969; f. 1971; French; Dir ABD AL-HAFID ROUISSI; circ. 100,000.

**Rissalat al-Oumma** (The Message of the Nation): 158 ave des Forces Armées Royales, Casablanca; tel. (2) 310427; Arabic; weekly edition in French; organ of the Union Constitutionnelle; Dir MUHAMMAD ALAOUI MUHAMMADI.

#### Rabat

**Al-Alam** (The Flag): 11 ave Allal ben Abdallah, BP 141, Rabat; tel. (7) 32419; fax (7) 733896; f. 1946; organ of the Istiqlal party; Arabic; literary supplement on Fridays; weekly edition on Mondays; monthly edition on foreign policy; Dir ABD AL-KRIM GHALLAB; circ. 100,000.

**Al-Anba'a** (Information): 21 rue Patrice Lumumba, Rabat; tel. (7) 24644; f. 1970; Arabic; publ. by Ministry of Information; Dir AHMAD AL-YAAKOUBI; circ. 15,000.

**Al-Maghrib:** 6 rue Laos, Rabat; tel. (7) 22708; telex 31916; fax (7) 22765; f. 1977; French; organ of the Rassemblement National des Indépendants; Dir MUSTAPHA IZNASNI; circ. 15,000.

**Al-Mithaq al-Watani** (The National Charter): 6 rue Laos, Rabat; tel. (7) 22708; telex 31916; fax (7) 22765; f. 1977; Arabic; organ of the Rassemblement National des Indépendants; Dir MUSTAPHA IZNASNI; circ. 15,000.

**An-Nidal Ad-Dimokrati** (The Democratic Struggle): 18 rue Tunis, Rabat; tel. (7) 30754; Arabic; organ of the Parti National Démocrate; Dir MUHAMMAD ARSALANE AL-JADIDI.

**L'Opinion:** 11 ave Allal ben Abdallah, Rabat; tel. (7) 27812; fax (7) 32182; f. 1965; French; organ of the Istiqlal party; Dir MUHAMMAD IDRISSI KAÏTOUNI; circ. 60,000.

### SELECTED PERIODICALS

#### Casablanca

**Bulletin Mensuel de la Chambre de Commerce et d'Industrie de la Wilaya du Grand Casablanca:** 98 blvd Muhammad V, BP 423, Casablanca; tel. (2) 264327; telex 24630; monthly; French; Pres. LAHCEN EL-WAFI.

**Cedies Informations:** 23 blvd Muhammad Abdouh, Casablanca; tel. (2) 252696; telex 23835; fax (2) 253839; weekly; French; Admin. A. OUALI.

**Construire:** 25 rue d'Azilal, Immeuble Ortiba, Casablanca; tel. (2) 305721; fax (2) 317577; f. 1940; weekly; French; Dir TALAL BOUCHAIB.

**Les Echos Africains:** Immeuble SONIR, angle blvd Smiha, rue d'Anjou, BP 13140, Casablanca; tel. (2) 307271; telex 27905; f. 1972; monthly; French; news, economics; Dir MUHAMMAD CHOUFFANI EL-FASSI; Editor Mme SOODIA FARIDI; circ. 5,000.

**FLASH-économie:** 28 ave des Forces Armées Royales, Casablanca; tel. (2) 203031; weekly; French; Dir KHODIJA IDRISSI.

**Al-Ittihad al-Watani Lilkouate ach-Chaabia** (National Union of Popular Forces): 28-30 rue Magellan, Casablanca 01; tel. (2) 302023; fax (2) 319301; weekly; Arabic; organ of the Union Nationale des Forces Populaires; Dir MOULAY ABDALLAH IBRAHIM.

**Lamalif:** 6 bis rue Defly Dieude, Casablanca; tel. (2) 220032; f. 1966; monthly; French; economic, social and cultural magazine; Dir MUHAMMAD LOGHLAM.

**Maroc Fruits:** 22 rue Al-Messaoudi, Casablanca 02; tel. (2) 363946; fax (2) 364041; f. 1958; fortnightly; Arabic, French; organ of the Association des Producteurs d'Agrumes du Maroc; Dir NEJJAI AHMED MANSOUR; circ. 6,000.

**Maroc Soir:** 88 blvd Muhammad V, Casablanca; tel. (2) 301271; telex 23845; fax (2) 317535; f. 1971; French; Dir ABD AL-HAFID ROUISSI.

**Matin Hebdo:** 34 rue Muhammad Smiha, Casablanca; tel. (2) 301271; telex 27794; weekly; French; Dir AHMAD AL-ALAMI.

**Matin Magazine:** 88 blvd Muhammad V, Casablanca; tel. (2) 268860; telex 23845; fax (2) 262969; f. 1971; weekly; French; Dir ABD AL-HAFID ROUISSI.

**An-Nidal** (The Struggle): 10 rue Cols Bleus, Sidi Bousmara, Médina Kédima, Casablanca; f. 1973; weekly; Dir IBRAHIMI AHMAD.

**Al-Ousbouaa al-Maghribia:** 158 ave des Forces Armées Royales, Casablanca; f. 1984; organ of the Union Constitutionnelle; Dir A. MUHAMMADI.

**Panorama Interview:** 17 rue Lapebie, Casablanca; tel. (2) 277396; monthly; French; Dir BOUJEMAÀ AMARA.

**La Quinzaine du Maroc:** 53 rue Dumont d'Urville, Casablanca; tel. (2) 302482; fax (2) 440426; monthly; English/French; Dir HUBERT MAURO.

**Revue Douanes Marocaines:** 69 rue Muhammad Smiha, Casablanca; tel. (2) 301613; f. 1959; monthly; French; general economic review; Dir MUHAMMAD KABOUS.

**Revue Marocaine de Droit:** 24 rue Nolly, Casablanca; tel. (2) 273673; telex 22644; quarterly; French and Arabic; Dirs J. P. RAZON, A. KETTANI.

**La Vie Economique:** 5 blvd ben Yacine, Casablanca; tel. (2) 443868; telex 28045; fax (2) 304542; f. 1921; weekly; French; Pres. and Dir JEAN LOUIS SERVAN-SCHREIBER.

**La Vie Industrielle et Agricole:** 142 blvd Muhammad V, Casablanca; tel. (2) 274407; 2 a month; French; Dir AHMAD ZAGHARI.

**La Vie Touristique Africaine:** 142 blvd Muhammad V, Casablanca; tel. (2) 274407; telex 21721; fortnightly; French; tourist information; Dir AHMAD ZAGHARI.

#### Rabat

**Al-Aklam** (The Pens): BP 2229, Rabat; monthly; Arabic; Dir ABD AR-RAHMAN BEN AMAR.

**Anoual:** 5 bis ave Hassan II, BP 1385, Rabat; tel. (7) 26733; fax (7) 738259; f. 1979; weekly; Arabic; organ of the Organisation de l'Action Démocratique et Populaire; Dir ABD AL-LATIF AOUAD.

**Ach-Chorta** (The Police): BP 437, Rabat; tel. (7) 23194; monthly; Arabic; Dir MUHAMMAD AD-DRIF.

**Da'ouat Al-Haqq** (Call of the Truth): al-Michwar as-Said, Rabat; publ. by Ministry of Religious Endowments (Awqaf) and Islamic Affairs; tel. (7) 60810; f. 1957; monthly; Arabic.

**Al-Haraka:** 8 Sahat al-Alaouiyine, Rabat; tel. (7) 64493; weekly; Arabic; organ of the Mouvement Populaire; Dir ALI ALAOUI.

**Al-Imane:** rue Akenssous, BP 356, Rabat; f. 1963; monthly; Arabic; Dir ABOU BAKER AL-KADIRI.

**Al-Irchad** (Spiritual Guidance): al-Michwar as-Said, Rabat; publ. by Ministry of Religious Endowments (Awqaf) and Islamic Affairs; tel. (7) 60810; f. 1967; monthly; Arabic.

**Al-Khansa:** 154 ave Souss Mohamedia, Rabat; monthly; Arabic; Dir ABOUZAL AICHA.

**Al-Maghribi:** 113 ave Allal ben Abdallah, Rabat; tel. (7) 68139; weekly; Arabic; organ of the Parti de l'Action; Dir ABDALLAH AL-HANANI.

**At-Tadamoun:** 23 ave Allal ben Abdallah, Rabat; monthly; Arabic; Dir ABD AL-MAJID SEMLALI EL-HASANI.

#### Tangier

**Actualités Touristiques:** 80 rue de la Liberté, Tangier; monthly; French; Dir TAYEB ALAMI.

# MOROCCO

**Le Journal de Tanger:** 11 ave Moulay Abd al-Aziz, BP 420, Tangier; tel. (9) 46051; fax (9) 45709; f. 1904; weekly; French, English, Spanish and Arabic; Dir BAKHAT ABD AL-HAQ; circ. 10,000.

### NEWS AGENCIES

**Wikalat al-Maghreb al-Arabi (WMA):** 122 ave Allal ben Abdallah, BP 1049, Rabat 10000; tel. (7) 764083; telex 36044; fax (7) 765005; f. 1959 as Maghreb Arabe Presse; Arabic, French, English and Spanish; government-owned; Man. Dir ABD AL-JALIL FENJIRO.

### Foreign Bureaux

**Agence France-Presse (AFP):** 2 bis rue du Caire, BP 118, Rabat; tel. (7) 768943; telex 31903; fax (7) 700357; f. 1920; Dir IGNACE DALLE.

**Agencia EFE** (Spain): 14 ave du Kairouane, Rabat; tel. (7) 23218; telex 32806; fax (7) 32195; Bureau Chief ALBERTO MASEGOSA.

**Agenzia Nazionale Stampa Associata (ANSA)** (Italy): 10 rue el Yamana, Rabat; tel. (7) 311083; telex 31044; Dir RAFFA HOUCINE.

**Austria Presse-Agentur (APA):** 28 ave des Forces Armées Royales, BP 13906, Casablanca; tel. (2) 275762; telex 23959; Dir MUKAROVSKY GEZA.

**Informatsionnoye Telegrafnoye Agentstvo Rossii—Telegrafnoye Agentstvo Suverennykh Stran (ITAR—TASS)** (Russia): 30 charia Muhammed Mazha, 32 rue de la Somme, Rabat; tel. (7) 750315; telex 31018; Dir OLEG CHIROKOV.

**Inter Press Service (IPS)** (Italy): 46 rue Abou Derr, Rabat; tel. (7) 756869; fax (7) 727183; Dir BOULOUIZ BOUCHRA.

**Reuters** (United Kingdom): 509 Immeuble es-Saada, ave Hassan II, Rabat; tel. (7) 726518; fax (7) 722499; Correspondent KATE DOURIAN.

**Rossiyskoye Informatsionnoye Agentstvo—Novosti (RIA—Novosti)** (Russia): BP 281, Rabat; tel. (7) 69784; telex 31069; Dir BORIS BOUKAREV.

**Xinhua (New China) News Agency** (People's Republic of China): 4 rue Kadi Mekki el-Bitaouri, Rabat; tel. (7) 55320; telex 31674; Dir LIU ZUOWEN.

## Publishers

**Dar el-Kitab:** place de la Mosquée, quartier des Habous, BP 4018, Casablanca; tel. (2) 246326; telex 26630; fax (2) 244484; f. 1948; philosophy, history, Africana, general and social science; Arabic and French; Dir BOUTALEB ABDOU ABD AL-HAY; Gen. Man. SOAD KADIRI.

**Editions La Porte:** 281 ave Muhammad V, Rabat; tel. (7) 709958; fax (7) 706478; law, guides, economics, educational books; Man. Dir MUHAMMAD RAFII DOUKKALI.

**Editions Maghrébines:** 5–13 rue Soldat Roch, Casablanca; tel. (2) 245148; telex 22994; f. 1962; general non-fiction.

### Government Publishing House

**Imprimerie Officielle:** ave Jean Mermoz, Rabat-Chellah; tel. (7) 65024.

## Radio and Television

In 1992, according to UNESCO estimates, there were 5.5m. radio receivers and 2.0m. television receivers in use. Morocco can receive broadcasts from Spanish radio stations, and the main Spanish television channels can also be received in northern Morocco.

**Radiodiffusion Télévision Marocaine:** 1 Zenkat el-Brihi, BP 1042, Rabat; tel. (7) 64951; telex 31010; government station; *Radio:* Network A in Arabic, Network B in French, Network C in Berber, Spanish and English; Foreign Service in Arabic, French and English; *Television:* began 1962; 45 hours weekly; French and Arabic; carries commercial advertising; Dir-Gen. MUHAMMAD TRICHA; Dir Television MUHAMMAD LISSARI; Dir Radio ABD AR-RAHMAN ACHOUR; Dir Foreign Service AHMAD RAYANE.

**2M International:** Société d'études et de réalisations audiovisuelles, km 7, 3 route de Rabat, Ain-Sebaa, Casablanca; tel. (2) 354444; fax (2) 354071; f. 1988, transmission commenced 1989; private television channel, jointly owned by Moroccan interests (85%) and by foreign concerns; broadcasting in French and Arabic; Dir-Gen. TAWFIK BENNANI-SMIRES.

**Radio Méditerranée Internationale:** 3 et 5 rue Emsallah, BP 2055, Tangier; tel. (9) 936363; telex 33711; fax (9) 936363; Arabic and French; Man. Dir PIERRE CASALTA.

**Voice of America Radio Station in Tangier:** c/o US Consulate General, Chemin des Amoureux, Tangier.

## Finance

(cap. = capital; res = reserves; dep. = deposits; m. = million; brs = branches; amounts in dirhams unless otherwise indicated)

### BANKING

#### Central Bank

**Bank Al-Maghrib:** 277 ave Muhammad V, BP 445, Rabat; tel. (7) 702626; telex 31006; fax (7) 706677; f. 1959 as Banque du Maroc; bank of issue; cap. 500m., res. 3,857m., dep. 10,172.9m., total assets 59,426m. (Dec. 1993); Gov. MUHAMMAD SEQAT.

#### Other Banks

**ABM Bank SA:** Immeuble des Habous, place du 16 Novembre, BP 13478, Casablanca 21000; tel. (2) 221275; telex 21709; fax (2) 204124; f. 1948 as Algemene Bank Marokko; 50% owned by ABN AMRO Bank NV (Netherlands), 50% owned by Moroccan interests; cap. 155,000, res 197.5m., dep. 1,496.5m., total assets 2,109.8m. (Dec. 1991); Pres. Hadj ABDERRAHMANE BOUFTAS; Gen. Man. AZZEDDINE MAÂCH; 17 brs.

**Arab Bank Maroc:** 174 blvd Muhammad V, BP 13810, Casablanca; tel. (2) 223152; telex 22942; fax (2) 200233; f. 1975; 50% owned by Arab Bank PLC, 50% by Banque Centrale Populaire; total assets 1,240m. (Dec. 1993); Pres. ABD AL-LATIF LARAKI; Gen. Man. SALAH HAROUN; 3 brs.

**Banque Commerciale du Maroc SA:** 2 blvd Moulay Youssef, BP 20000, Casablanca; tel. (2) 224169; telex 22863; fax (2) 268829; f. 1911; 20.3% owned by Banco Credito Hispano; cap. 1,067.1m., res 1,223.1m., dep. 17,156m., total assets 23,555m. (Dec. 1993); Chair. and CEO ABD AL-AZIZ ALAMI; Dir and Gen. Man. ALI IBN MANSOUR; 112 brs.

**Banque Marocaine du Commerce Extérieur SA:** 140 ave Hassan II, BP 13425, Casablanca 01; tel. (2) 200456; telex 21635; fax (2) 200490; f. 1959; transferred to majority private ownership in 1995; cap. 1,000m., res 1,276.8m., dep. 25,673m., total assets 28,150.6m. (Dec. 1993); Chair. and Chief Exec. ABD AL-LATIF JOUAHRI; Gen. Dir MOHAMED JOUAHRI; 170 brs.

**Banque Marocaine pour l'Afrique et l'Orient:** 1 place Bandoeng, Casablanca; tel. (2) 307070; telex 26720; fax (2) 301673; f. 1975 to take over British Bank of the Middle East (Morocco); cap. 200m., res 1.4m., dep. 1,589.0m. (Dec. 1993); Chair. FARID DELLERO; Gen. Man. ABD AL-HAMID BENANI DAKHAMA; 32 brs.

**Banque Marocaine pour le Commerce et l'Industrie SA:** 26 place des Nations Unies, BP 13573, Casablanca; tel. (2) 224101; telex 21967; fax (2) 208978; f. 1964; transfer to private ownership pending in 1995; cap. 515m., res 470m., dep. 7,325m. (Dec. 1994); Chair. MUSTAPHA FARIS; Gen. Man. JEAN-CLAUDE TREMOSA; 80 brs.

**Banque Nationale pour le Développement Economique:** 12 place des Alaouites, BP 407, Rabat; tel. (7) 706040; telex 31942; fax (7) 703706; f. 1959; cap. 336m., res 495m., dep. 7,611.5m., total assets 8,493.2m. (1992); Gen. Man. FARID DELLERO; 2 brs.

**Crédit Immobilier et Hôtelier:** 187 ave Hassan II, Casablanca; tel. (2) 202480; telex 22839; fax (2) 266303; f. 1920; transfer to private ownership pending in 1995; cap. 785m., res 1,051.2m., dep. 15,997.2m., total assets 17,961.9m. (Dec. 1992); Pres. MOULAY ZAHIDI; Gen. Man. ABD AL-HAK BEN KIRANE; 72 brs.

**Crédit du Maroc SA:** 48–58 blvd Muhammad V, BP 13579, Casablanca; tel. (2) 224142; telex 21054; fax (2) 277127; f. 1963; cap. 833.8m., dep. 8,813m., total assets 10,271m. (Dec. 1993); Chair. JAWAD BEN BRAHIM; Gen. Man. MUHAMMAD TAZI MEZALEK; 105 brs.

**Crédit Populaire du Maroc:** 101 blvd Muhammad Zerktouni, BP 10622, Casablanca 02; tel. (2) 202533; telex 21723; fax (2) 267889; 51% state-owned, 49% privately-owned; cap. 286m., res 2,174.4m., dep. 32,515.2m., total assets 35,135.8m. (Dec. 1990); Chair. ABD AL-LATIF LARAKI; Gen. Man. ABD AL-HAK AL-ABDI.

**Société Générale Marocaine de Banques SA:** 55 blvd Abd al-Moumen, Casablanca; tel. (2) 200972; telex 24076; fax (2) 200961; f. 1962; cap. 520m., dep. 7,341m. (Dec. 1993); Pres. MUHAMMAD BARGACH; Gen. Man. ABD AL-AZIZ TAZI; 94 brs.

**Société Marocaine de Dépôt et Crédit:** 79 ave Hassan II, BP 296, Casablanca; tel. (2) 224114; telex 21013; fax (2) 271590; f. 1974; cap. 101.25m., res 64.6m., dep. 1,958.7m. (Dec. 1989); Pres. ABD AL-KADER BEN SALAH; Gen. Man. MOHAMED TAZI; 21 brs.

**Unión Bancaria Hispano Marroquí (UNIBAN):** 69 rue du Prince Moulay Abdellah, Casablanca; tel. (2) 220230; telex 24997; fax (2) 207584; f. 1958; 50% participation of Banco Bilbao Vizcaya, Spain; cap. 246.4m., res 129.9m., dep. 2,435m., total assets 3,176.1m. (Dec. 1994); Chair. ENRIQUE MAS; Gen. Man. PEDRO GILA; 30 brs.

**Wafabank:** 163 ave Hassan II, Casablanca 01; tel. (2) 224105; telex 21051; fax (2) 266202; f. 1964 as Compagnie Marocaine de Crédit et de Banque; cap. 553.2m., res 1,045.1m., dep. 13,386.9m., total assets 15,162.0m. (Dec. 1993); Pres. ABD AL-HAK BENNANI; 89 brs.

### Bank Organizations

**Association Professionnelle des Intermédiaires de Bourse du Maroc:** 71 ave des l'Armées Royales, Casablanca; tel. (2) 314824; telex 22821; fax (2) 314903; f. 1967; groups all banks and brokers in the stock exchange of Casablanca, for studies, inquiries of general interest and contacts with official authorities; 11 mems; Pres. ABD AL-LATIF JOUAHRI.

**Groupement Professionnel des Banques du Maroc:** 71 ave des Forces Armées Royales, Casablanca; tel. (2) 314824; telex 22821; fax (2) 314903; f. 1967; groups all commercial banks for studies, inquiries of general interest, and contacts with official authorities; 18 mems; Pres. ABD AL-LATIF JOUAHRI.

### STOCK EXCHANGE

**Bourse des Valeurs de Casablanca:** 98 blvd Muhammad V, Casablanca; tel. (2) 279354; telex 23698; fax (2) 200365; f. 1929; Pres. (vacant); Dir ABD AR-RAZAQ LARAKI.

### INSURANCE

**Al-Amane:** 298 blvd Muhammad V, Casablanca; tel. (2) 304571; telex 27726; f. 1975; cap. 30m.; Vice Pres. and Dir-Gen. M. BOUGHALEB.

**Al-Wataniya:** 83 ave de l'Armée Royale, Casablanca; tel. (2) 314850; telex 21877; fax (2) 313043; Dir-Gen. M. ABD AL-JALIL CHRAIBI.

**Alliance Africaine:** 63 blvd Moulay Youssef, Casablanca; tel. (2) 200694; telex 45737; fax (2) 200694; f. 1975; cap. 8m.; Pres. ABD AR-RAHIM CHERKAOUI; Dir-Gen. KHALID CHEDDADI.

**Atlanta:** 49 angle rues Lafuente et Longwy, Casablanca; tel. (2) 260289; telex 21644; fax (2) 203011; f. 1947; cap. 12m.; Dir MOHAMED REYAD; Dir-Gen. OMAR BENNANI.

**Cie Africaine d'Assurances:** 120 ave Hassan II, Casablanca; tel. (2) 224185; telex 21661; fax (2) 260150; f. 1950; Pres. FOUAD FILALI; Dir-Gen. HAFID EL-ALAMY.

**Cie Arabia:** 123 rue Rahal El Meskini, Casablanca; tel. (2) 200766; Dir M. ABD AL-JALIL CHRAIBI.

**Cie Atlantique d'Assurances (CADA):** 3 rue des Hirondelles, Rond Point Racine, Casablanca; tel. (2) 390033; telex 22042; fax (2) 223664; f. 1931; cap. 2.8m.; Dir-Gen. AMAL KANOUNI.

**Cie d'Assurances SANAD:** 3 blvd Muhammad V, BP 13438, Casablanca; tel. (2) 260591; telex 21927; fax (2) 293813; f. 1975; Chair. MUHAMMAD AOUAD; Dir-Gen. ABDELTIF TAHIRI.

**Cie Nordafricaine et Intercontinentale d'Assurances (CNIA):** 157 ave Hassan II, Casablanca; tel. (2) 224118; telex 21096; fax (2) 267866; cap. 30m.; Dir-Gen. AHMED ZINOUN; Man. Dir SAAD KANOUNI.

**L'Entente:** 122 ave Hassan II, Casablanca; tel. (2) 267272; telex 46480; fax (2) 267023; f. 1950; cap. 60m.; Pres. Dir-Gen. MUHAMMAD EL-MEHDI BOUGHALEB.

**Garantie Générale Marocaine:** 106 rue Abd ar-Rahman Sahraoui, Casablanca; tel. (2) 279015; telex 24885; Dir-Gen. HABIB BELRHITI.

**La Marocaine Vie:** 37 blvd Moulay Youssef, Casablanca; tel. (2) 206320; telex 46462; fax (2) 261971; f. 1978; cap. 12m.; Pres. and Dir-Gen. H. KETTANI.

**Mutuelle Centrale Marocaine d'Assurances:** 16 rue Abou Inane, BP 27, Rabat; tel. (7) 766960; telex 31739; Pres. ABD AS-SALAM CHERIF D'OUEZZANE; Dir-Gen. YACOUBI SOUSSANE.

**Mutuelle d'Assurances des Transporteurs Unis (MATU):** 215 blvd Zerktouni, Casablanca; tel. (2) 367097; Dir-Gen. M. BENYAMNA MOHAMED.

**Remar:** angle blvd Muhammad V, Casablanca; tel. (2) 305166; telex 45887; fax (2) 305305; f. 1970; cap. 6m.; Dir-Gen. MUHAMMAD CHERKAOUI.

**La Renaissance:** Siège Social, 197 ave Hassan II, Casablanca; tel. (2) 221613; telex 21680; fax (2) 276563; f. 1980; cap. 3m.; Dir-Gen. SELLAM SEKKAT.

**La Royale Marocaine d'Assurances (RMA):** 67–69 ave de l'Armée Royale, Casablanca; tel. (2) 312163; telex 21818; fax (2) 313884; f. 1949; cap. 30m.; Chair. OTHMAN BEN JELLOUN; Dir SÉBASTIEN CASTRO.

**Es-Saada, Cie d'Assurances et de Réassurances:** 123 ave Hassan II, BP 13860, Casablanca; tel. (2) 222525; telex 21791; fax (2) 262655; f. 1961; cap. 50m.; Pres. MEHDI OUAZZANI; Man. Dir SAÏD OUAZZANI.

**Société Centrale de Réassurance:** Tour Atlas, place Zallaqa, BP 13183, Casablanca; tel. (7) 308585; telex 28084; fax (2) 308672; f. 1960; cap. 30m.; Chair. FAROUK BENNIS; CEO YAHIA FILALI.

**Société Marocaine d'Assurances à l'Exportation:** 24 rue Ali Bnou, Abderrazak, BP 15953, Casablanca; tel. (2) 294811; telex 45951; fax (2) 294816; f. 1988; insurance for exporters in the public and private sectors; assistance for export promotion; Pres., Dir-Gen. ABD AL-HAMID JOUAHRI; Asst. Dir-Gen. ABD EL-KADER DRIOUACHE.

**Victoire:** 50 ave Mers-Sultan, Casablanca; tel. (2) 297808; telex 23993; fax (2) 203076; f. 1982; Chair. ABAHMAOUI MUHAMMAD.

**WAFA Assurance:** 1–3 blvd Abd al-Moumen, Casablanca; tel. (2) 224575; telex 21867; fax (2) 209103; Dir-Gen. JAOUAD KETTANI.

### INSURANCE ASSOCIATION

**Fédération Marocaine des Sociétés d'Assurances et de Réassurances:** 154 blvd d'Anfa, Casablanca; tel. (2) 391850; telex 45524; fax (2) 391854; f. 1958; 22 mem. companies; Pres. ABD AL-JALIL CHRAIBI; Dir ABD AL-FETTAH ALAMI.

## Trade and Industry

### CHAMBERS OF COMMERCE

**La Fédération des Chambres de Commerce et d'Industrie du Maroc:** 6 rue d'Erfoud, Rabat-Agdal; tel. (7) 767078; telex 36662; fax (7) 767076; f. 1962; groups the 25 Chambers of Commerce and Industry; Pres. MOULAY LAHCEN EL-IDRISSI; Dir-Gen. KAMAL BOUHAMDI.

**Chambre de Commerce et d'Industrie de Rabat-Salé et de Skhirat-Temara:** 1 rue Gandhi, BP 131, Rabat; tel. (7) 706444; telex 36898; fax (7) 706768; Pres. MOULAY LAHCEN EL-IDRISSI; Dir MUHAMMAD NAJIB AFFANE.

**Chambre de Commerce et d'Industrie de la Wilaya du Grand Casablanca:** 98 blvd Muhammad V, BP 423, Casablanca; tel. (2) 264327; telex 24630; Pres. LAHCEN EL-WAFI.

### DEVELOPMENT ORGANIZATIONS

**Bureau de Recherches et de Participations Minières (BRPM):** 5 charia Moulay Hassan, BP 99, Rabat; tel. (7) 05005; telex 31066; fax (7) 09411; f. 1928; a state agency conducting exploration, valorization and exploitation of mineral resources; Gen. Man. ASSOU LHATOUTE; Sec.-Gen. ALI BENNANI.

**Caisse de Dépôt et de Gestion:** Sahat Moulay El-Hassan, BP 408, Rabat; tel. (7) 765520; telex 31072; fax (7) 763849; f. 1959; finances small-scale projects; Gen. Man. MUHAMMAD FADEL LAHLOU.

**Caisse Marocaine des Marchés** (Marketing Fund): Résidence El Manar, blvd Abd al-Moumen, Casablanca; tel. (2) 259118; telex 24740; fax (2) 259120; f. 1950; cap. 10m. dirhams; Man. HASSAN KISSI.

**Caisse Nationale de Crédit Agricole** (Agricultural Credit Fund): 2 ave d'Alger, BP 49, Rabat; tel. (7) 725920; telex 31657; fax (7) 732580; f. 1961; cap. 1,575m. dirhams, dep. 2,710m. dirhams; Man. Dir MOULAY RACHID HADDAOUI.

**Centre Marocain de Promotion des Exportations (CMPE):** 23 blvd Bnou Majid el-Bahar, BP 10937, Casablanca; tel. (2) 302210; telex 27847; fax (2) 301793; f. 1980; state organization for promotion of exports; Dir-Gen. MOUNIR M. BENSAID.

**Office National Interprofessionnel des Céréales et des Légumineuses:** 25 ave Hassan I, BP 154, Rabat; tel. (7) 61735; telex 31930; f. 1937; Dir-Gen. MUHAMMAD GUERRAOUI.

**Office pour le Développement Industriel (ODI):** 10 rue Gandhi, BP 211, Rabat; tel. (7) 708460; telex 31053; fax (7) 67695; f. 1973; a state agency to develop industry; Man. Dir ABD AL-HAMID BELAHSEN.

**Société de Développement Agricole (SODEA):** ave Hadj Ahmed Cherkaoui, BP 6280, Rabat; tel. (7) 70813; telex 31675; fax (7) 74798; f. 1972; state agricultural development organization; Man. Dir M. SABBARI HASSANI LARBI.

**Société de Gestion des Terres Agricoles (SOGETA):** 35 rue Daïet-Erroumi, BP 731, Agdal, Rabat; tel. (7) 72834; telex 31704; f. 1973; oversees use of agricultural land; Man. Dir OMAR AL-HEBIL.

**Société Nationale d'Investissement (SNI):** 43 rue Aspirant Lafuenté, BP 38, Casablanca; tel. (2) 223081; telex 22736; f. 1966; cap. 150m. dirhams; Pres. MUHAMMAD BARGACH; Dir-Gen. ABDALLAH BELKZIZ.

### PRINCIPAL STATE ENTERPRISES

**Office Chérifien des Phosphates (OCP):** blvd de la Grande Ceinture, route d'el Jadida, Casablanca; tel. (2) 360025; telex 21630; f. 1921; a state company to produce and market rock phosphates and derivatives; Dir-Gen. MUHAMMAD FETTAH.

**Office National de l'Eau Potable (ONEP):** 6 bis rue Patrice Lumumba, Rabat; tel. (7) 734004; telex 31982; fax (7) 731355; responsible for drinking-water supply; Dir HOUCINE TIJANI.

**Office National de l'Electricité (ONE):** 65 rue Othman Ben Affan, BP 13498, Casablanca 20100; tel. (2) 224165; telex 22780; fax (2) 220038; f. 1963; state electricity authority; Dir-Gen. ABERRAHMANE NAJI.

# MOROCCO

**Office National des Pêches:** 13/15 rue Chevalier Bayard, BP 21, Casablanca; tel. (2) 240551; telex 25708; f. 1969; state fishing organization; Man. Dir ABD AL-AZIZ EL-BELGHETI.

**Société d'Exploitation des Mines du Rif (SEFERIF):** 30 Abou-Faris el-Marini, BP 436, Rabat; tel. (7) 66350; telex 31708; nationalized 1967; open and underground mines produce iron ore for export and for the projected Nador iron and steel complex; Man. Dir MUHAMMAD HARRAK.

**Société Nationale de Sidérurgie (SONASID):** Route RP 18, Mont Arouit, BP 151, Nador; tel. (6) 609441; telex 65787; fax (6) 609442; f. 1974; iron and steel projects; cap. 390m. dirhams; transfer to private ownership pending in 1995; Dir-Gen. ABDALLAH SOUIBRI.

### EMPLOYERS' ORGANIZATIONS

**Association Marocaine des Industries Textiles et de l'Habillement (AMITH):** 58 rue Lughérini, Casablanca; tel. (2) 300393; telex 45502; fax (2) 300442; f. 1958; mems 700 textile, knitwear and ready-made garment factories; Pres. LAHLOU MUHAMMAD; Sec.-Gen. ALI BERRADA.

**Association des Producteurs d'Agrumes du Maroc (ASPAM):** 22 rue al-Messaoudi, Casablanca; tel. (2) 363946; fax (2) 364041; f. 1958; links Moroccan citrus and vegetable growers; has its own processing plants; Chair. AHMED MANSOUR NEJJAI.

**Association Professionnelle des Cimentiers:** 239 blvd Moulay Ismail, BP 3096, Casablanca; cement manufacturers.

**Confédération Générale Economique Marocaine (CGEM):** 23 blvd Muhammad Abdou, Casablanca 20100; tel. (2) 252696; telex 23835; fax (2) 253839; Pres. ABD AR-RAHIM LAHJOUJI; Sec.-Gen. ABD AR-RAHMAN OUALI.

**Union Marocaine de l'Agriculture (UMA):** 12 place des Alaouites, Rabat; Pres. M. NEJJAI.

### TRADE UNIONS

**Confédération Démocratique du Travail (CDT):** 51 rue Abdallah Medyouni, BP 13576, Casablanca; tel. (2) 313432; telex 22662; fax (2) 310307; f. 1978; associated with USFP; 300,000 mems; Sec.-Gen. NOUBIR AMAOUI.

**Union Générale des Travailleurs Marocains (UGTM):** 9 rue du Rif, angle Route de Médiouna, Casablanca; tel. (2) 282144; f. 1960; associated with Istiqlal; supported by unions not affiliated to UMT; 673,000 mems; Sec.-Gen. ABD AR-RAZZAQ AFILAL.

**Union Marocaine du Travail (UMT):** Bourse du Travail, 232 ave des Forces Armées Royales, Casablanca; tel. 302292; telex 27825; left-wing and associated with the UNFP; most unions are affiliated; 700,000 mems; Sec. MAHJOUB BEN SEDDIQ.

**Union Syndicale Agricole (USA):** agricultural section of UMT.

**Union Marocaine du Travail Autonome:** Rabat; breakaway union from UMT.

### TRADE FAIRS

**Office National des Foires et des Expositions de Casablanca (OFEC):** Casablanca.

**Salon International du Matériel pour l'Industrie du Textile et du Cuir:** 11 rue Boukraa, Casablanca; tel. (2) 222871; telex 22093; fax (2) 264949; f. 1991; textiles and leather; annually for three days in March.

## Transport

**Office National des Transports (ONT):** rue al-Fadila, Quartier-Industriel, BP 596, Rabat-Chellah; tel. (7) 797842; telex 36090; fax (7) 797850; f. 1958; Man. Dir MOHAMED EL YOUSFI AHMED.

### RAILWAYS

In 1992 there were 1,907 km of railways, of which 271 km were double track; 988 km of lines were electrified and diesel locomotives were used on the rest. The network carried some 9.5m. passengers and 25.5m. metric tons of freight in 1993 (compared with more than 11m. passengers and 28m. tons of freight in 1992). All services are nationalized.

**Office National des Chemins de Fer du Maroc (ONCFM):** rue Abderrahmane El Ghafiki, Rabat-Agdal; tel. (7) 774747; telex 31907; fax (7) 774480; f. 1963; administers all Morocco's railways; Pres. Minister of Transport; Dir-Gen. MOHAMED LAÂLEJ.

### ROADS

In 1991 there were 59,474 km of classified roads, of which 49.5% were paved. There were 73 km of motorway, 10,906 km of main roads and 9,391 km of regional roads.

**Compagnie de Transports au Maroc 'Lignes Nationales' (CTM—LN):** 23 rue Léon l'Africain, Casablanca; tel. (2) 312061; telex 28962; agencies in Tangier, Rabat, Meknès, Oujda, Marrakesh, Agadir, el-Jadida, Safi, Casablanca, es-Saouira, Ksar es-Souk, Fez and Ouarzazate; privatized in mid-1993 with 40% of shares reserved for Moroccan citizens; Man. Dir MUHAMMAD AL-ALJ.

### SHIPPING

Morocco's 21 ports handled 40.5m. tons of goods in 1993, an increase of 4.8% compared with the previous year's total. The most important ports, in terms of the volume of goods handled, are Casablanca, Muhammadia, Jorf Lasfar and Safi. Tangier is the principal port for passenger services. In 1992 ODEP announced a five-year investment programme (1993–97), costing a projected 1,595m. dirhams, that included plans for a container terminal at Casablanca (scheduled to be operational by the end of 1994).

**Office d'Exploitation des Ports (ODEP):** 175–177 blvd Zerktouni, Casablanca; tel. (2) 232324; telex 46790; fax (2) 232335; f. 1985; Man. Dir MUHAMMAD HALAB.

#### Principal Shipping Companies

**Agence Gibmar SA:** 3 rue Henri Regnault, Tangier; tel. (9) 35875; telex 33091; fax (9) 33239; also at Casablanca; regular services from Tangier to Gibraltar; Chair. DRISS TAZI; Gen. Man. YOUSSEF BENYAHIA.

**Compagnie Chérifienne d'Armement:** 5 blvd Abdallah ben Yacine, Casablanca 21700; tel. (2) 309455; telex 27030; fax (2) 301186; f. 1929; regular services to Europe; Chair. ABD AL-WAHAB LARAKI; Dir ABD AL-AZIZ MANTRACH.

**Compagnie Marocaine d'Agences Maritimes (COMARINE):** 45 ave des Forces Armées Royales, 21000, Casablanca; tel. (2) 311941; telex 21851; fax (2) 312570; f. 1969; Pres. AHMAD EL-OUALI EL-ALAMI; Dir-Gen. THIERRY LABAUE.

**Compagnie Marocaine de Navigation (COMANAV):** 7 blvd de la Résistance, BP 628, Casablanca; tel. (2) 303012; telex 26093; fax (2) 308455; f. 1946; regular services to Mediterranean, Northwest European, Middle Eastern and West African ports; tramping; Pres. A. ALAOUI KACIMI; Dir-Gen. YAHIA SAOUDI.

**Générale Maritime SA:** 12 rue Foucauld, BP 746, Casablanca; tel. (2) 279590; telex 23802; f. 1974; chemicals; Dir-Gen. ABD AL-WAHAB BEN KIRANE.

**Intercona SA (Transmediterránea and Isleña de Navegación):** 31 ave de la Résistance, Tangier; tel. (9) 41101; telex 33005; fax (9) 43863; f. 1943; daily services from Algeciras (Spain) to Tangier and Ceuta (Spanish North Africa); Dir-Gen. ANTONIO FERRE CASALS.

**Limadet-ferry:** 3 rue Ibn Rochd, Tangier; tel. (9) 33639; telex 33013; fax (9) 37173; f. 1966; operates between Algeciras (Spain) and Tangier, six daily; Dir-Gen. RACHID BEN MANSOUR.

**Messageries Marocaines:** 65 ave des Forces Armées Royales, BP 69, Casablanca; telex 23762; Dir-Gen. MUHAMMAD EL-OUALI EL-ALAMI.

**Société Marocaine de Navigation Atlas:** 81 ave Houmane el-Fatouaki, Casablanca 21000; tel. (2) 224190; telex 23067; fax (2) 274401; f. 1976; Chair. HASSAN CHAMI; Man. Dir M. SLAOUI.

**Société Marocaine de Navigation Fruitière (SOFRUMA):** 18 rue Colbert, Casablanca; tel. (2) 310003; telex 23097; fax (2) 310031; f. 1962; Dir-Gen. KHAMMAL ABD EL-HAMID.

**Voyages Paquet:** 65 ave des Forces Armées Royales, Casablanca; tel. (2) 311065; telex 24649; fax (2) 442108; f. 1970; Pres. MUHAMMAD EL-OUALI EL-ALAMI; Man. Dir BAKALI EL-OUALI EL-ALAMI.

### CIVIL AVIATION

The main international airports are at Casablanca (King Muhammad V), Rabat, Tangier, Marrakesh, Agadir, Oujda, Al-Hocima and Fez.

**Royal Air Maroc:** Aéroport de Casablanca-Anfa; tel. (2) 912000; telex 21880; fax (2) 912397; f. 1953; 94% state-owned; domestic flights and services to 35 countries in Western Europe, Scandinavia, the Americas, North and West Africa, the Canary Islands and the Middle East; Chair. MUHAMMAD MEKOUAR; Man. Dir MOHAMED HASSAN.

## Tourism

Tourism is Morocco's second main source of convertible currency. The country's attractions for tourists include its sunny climate, ancient sites (notably the cities of Fez, Marrakesh, Meknès and Rabat) and spectacular scenery. There are popular holiday resorts on the Atlantic and Mediterranean coasts. In 1992 tourist arrivals increased by 1.9%, compared with the previous year, to 3,252,062.

**Office National Marocain du Tourisme:** 31 angle ave al-Abtal and rue Oved Fas, Agdal, Rabat; tel. (7) 775171; telex 31933; fax (7) 777437; f. 1918; Dir ABDERRAOUF LAHRESH.

# MOZAMBIQUE
## Introductory Survey

**Location, Climate, Language, Religion, Flag, Capital**

The Republic of Mozambique lies on the east coast of Africa, bordered to the north by Tanzania, to the west by Malawi, Zambia and Zimbabwe, and to the south by South Africa and Swaziland. The country has a coastline of about 2,470 km (1,535 miles) on the shores of the Indian Ocean, and is separated from Madagascar, to the east, by the Mozambique Channel. Except in a few upland areas, the climate varies from tropical to sub-tropical. Rainfall is irregular, but the rainy season is usually from November to March, when average temperatures in Maputo are between 26°C (79°F) and 30°C (86°F). In the cooler dry season the average temperatures are 18°C (64°F) to 20°C (68°F) in June and July. Portuguese is the official language, while numerous African languages, including Ronga, Shangaan and Muchope, are widely spoken. Many of the inhabitants follow traditional beliefs. There are about 5m. Christians, the majority of whom are Roman Catholics, and 4m. Muslims. The national flag (proportions 3 by 2) has three equal horizontal stripes, of green, black and yellow, separated by narrow white stripes. At the hoist is a red triangle containing a five-pointed yellow star, on which are superimposed an open book, a hoe and a rifle. The capital is Maputo (formerly Lourenço Marques).

**Recent History**

Mozambique became a Portuguese colony in the 19th century and an overseas province in 1951. Nationalist groups began to form in the 1960s. The Frente de Libertação de Moçambique (Frelimo—Mozambique Liberation Front) was formed in 1962 and launched a military campaign in 1964. After the coup in Portugal in April 1974 (see chapter on Portugal), negotiations between Frelimo and the new Portuguese Government resulted in a period of rule in Mozambique by a transitional Government, followed by full independence on 25 June 1975. Samora Machel, leader of Frelimo since the murder of its founding leader, Eduardo Mondlane, in 1969, became the first President of Mozambique. At its third Congress, in February 1977, Frelimo was reconstituted as the Frelimo Party, a 'Marxist-Leninist vanguard party', with restricted membership. Between September and December elections took place to local, district and provincial assemblies and, finally, at national level, to the Assembléia Popular (People's Assembly).

In March 1976 Mozambique closed its border with Rhodesia (now Zimbabwe) and applied economic sanctions against that country. Mozambique was the principal base for Rhodesian nationalist guerrillas, and consequently suffered considerable devastation as a result of offensives launched by Rhodesian government forces against guerrilla camps. The border was reopened in January 1980.

After Zimbabwean independence in April 1980, South Africa adopted Rhodesia's role as supporter of the Mozambican opposition guerrilla group, Resistência Nacional Moçambicana (Renamo), also known as the Movimento Nacional da Resistência de Moçambique. The activities of Renamo subsequently increased, causing persistent disruption to road, rail and oil pipeline links from Mozambican ports, which were vital to the economic independence of southern African nations from South Africa. In 1982 Zimbabwean troops were deployed along the oil pipeline that runs from Mutare, in Zimbabwe, to Beira, Mozambique, to prevent sabotage attempts by Renamo.

In 1983 South African forces launched two separate attacks against targets in Maputo that were allegedly occupied by the then banned African National Congress of South Africa (ANC). In March 1984, however, Mozambique and South Africa signed a formal joint non-aggression pact, known as the Nkomati accord, whereby each Government undertook to prevent opposition forces on its territory from launching attacks against the other, and a Joint Security Commission was established. The accord effectively implied that South Africa would withdraw its covert support for Renamo in return for a guarantee by Mozambique that it would prevent any further use of its territory by the ANC.

During 1984 the Frelimo Government effectively reduced ANC activity in Mozambique. Renamo activity, however, intensified, although the South African Government denied that it had continued to support the rebels. The gravity of the security situation led the Frelimo Government to appeal to foreign powers for increased military assistance in 1985, and in June it was agreed that Zimbabwe would augment its military presence in Mozambique. A major military offensive against Renamo in July resulted in the capture, in August, of the rebels' national operational command centre, 'Casa Banana' in Sofala province, and of other major rebel bases in the area. In September Mozambique alleged that documents, discovered at one of the captured Renamo bases, revealed that South Africa had repeatedly violated the Nkomati accord by providing material support for the rebels, and that a South African government representative had held several meetings with Renamo officials. South Africa eventually confirmed the allegations, but claimed that the continued contacts with Renamo were designed to promote peace talks between the guerrillas and the Frelimo Government. The Joint Security Commission ceased to meet in 1985. In October 1986 the South African Government announced its decision to ban recruitment of migrant Mozambican mineworkers, in retaliation for an alleged increase in activity by ANC guerrillas in the Mozambique border region.

In February 1986 Renamo recaptured 'Casa Banana' but it was regained by Zimbabwean troops in April. In October Renamo declared war on Zimbabwe, in response to a statement by Robert Mugabe, the Zimbabwean Prime Minister (later President), that his Government would strengthen its support for the Frelimo forces. Renamo rebels consolidated their position during 1986, although the Frelimo forces, with increased reinforcements from Tanzania and Zimbabwe, captured several rebel bases in December.

General elections were scheduled to take place in 1982, but were postponed several times because of the security situation. In March 1986, in an attempt to strengthen Frelimo's control of the country, the Council of Ministers was divided into three sections, each supervised by a senior Frelimo official. The post of Prime Minister, which was allocated to Mário Machungo (previously the Minister of Planning), was created in July. Legislative elections were eventually begun in August 1986, but were subject to delays, owing to the intensity of the internal conflict.

On 19 October 1986 President Machel died in an aviation accident in South Africa. The causes of the incident were unclear, and the Mozambican Ministry of Information declared that it did not exclude the possibility that South Africa had been responsible for the crash. In November the South African Government claimed that documents discovered in the crash wreckage revealed a plot by Mozambique and Zimbabwe to overthrow the Government of Malawi. These accusations were denied by both Mozambique and Zimbabwe.

In November 1986 the Central Committee of Frelimo appointed Joaquim Alberto Chissano, hitherto Minister for Foreign Affairs, as President. The elections were then resumed. In contrast to the 1977 elections, the voters were given a choice of candidates, with 299 Frelimo nominees for the 250 seats in the Assembléia Popular; nevertheless, all government and party leaders had been re-elected when the poll was completed in December 1986.

In July 1987, following the massacre, allegedly by Renamo rebels, of 424 people in the southern Mozambican town of Homoine, Mozambique accused South Africa of continuing to support Renamo. South Africa strongly denied any involvement in the massacre, however, and the two countries agreed to conduct a joint investigation into the incident. Further talks were held in September in an attempt to revive the Nkomati accord, and in November Mozambique, South Africa and Portugal signed an agreement to restore the Cahora Bassa hydro-electric plant in Mozambique (potentially one of the greatest sources of electricity in southern Africa). In May 1988 Mozambican and South African officials agreed to reactivate the

Nkomati accord and to re-establish the Joint Security Commission, and in September Chissano met the South African President, P. W. Botha, in Mozambique. As a result of this meeting, Mozambique and South Africa established a joint commission for co-operation and development, and South Africa agreed to provide 'non-lethal' military aid for the protection of electricity transmission lines running between Cahora Bassa and South Africa. In addition, South Africa agreed to give assistance for improvements to Maputo harbour and to the road and rail links between Mozambique and South Africa, and in November restrictions on the recruitment of Mozambican mineworkers in South Africa were withdrawn.

Renamo announced a unilateral cease-fire in April 1989, in order to allow aid to reach people affected by famine, but this was reportedly not observed. In June the Frelimo Government publicized proposals for a negotiated resolution of the conflict; these offered 'dialogue' to all 'individuals' who chose to renounce violence and to respect the Constitution. (The Government emphasized that amendments to the Constitution were being considered at that time.) At Frelimo's fifth Congress, held in July, the party's exclusively Marxist-Leninist orientation was renounced; more pragmatic policies were approved, and party membership was opened to Mozambicans from all sectors of society, including business executives and religious leaders. In January 1990 President Chissano announced the drafting of a new constitution, to be presented to the Assembléia Popular for approval later in the year.

It was announced in mid-1989 that President Daniel arap Moi of Kenya and President Mugabe of Zimbabwe had agreed to mediate between the Mozambique Government and Renamo. In August Renamo rejected the Government's peace proposals, and demanded recognition as a political entity, the introduction of multi-party elections and the withdrawal of Zimbabwean troops from Mozambique as preconditions for peace. Nevertheless, there was indirect contact between the Government and Renamo during the second half of 1989, and in December Presidents Moi and Mugabe invited both parties to hold direct negotiations. The Government agreed to this offer in principle, but it continued to deny official recognition to Renamo. The role of Mugabe and Moi as mediators came to an end after Renamo refused to attend a meeting between the protagonists that had been arranged to take place in Malawi in June 1990. However, direct talks were held in July in Rome, Italy, between delegations from the Mozambican Government, led by the Minister of Transport and Communications, Lt-Gen. Armando Emílio Guebuza, and Renamo, headed by Raul Domingos. In August the Frelimo Central Committee voted unanimously in favour of introducing a multi-party system, with a view to elections, planned for 1991, thus removing a major obstacle to progress in the negotiations with Renamo. Further talks between the Government and the rebels took place in August and November 1990, the latter session resulting in an agreement at the beginning of December, for a partial cease-fire. Under the terms of the agreement, all Zimbabwean troops present in Mozambique were required to retire to the Beira and Limpopo transport 'corridors' which link Zimbabwe to the Mozambican ports of Beira and Maputo, on the Indian Ocean. The cease-fire was confined to these areas.

The agreement in Rome followed the introduction, on 30 November 1990, of a new Mozambican Constitution, formally ending Frelimo's single-party rule and committing the State to political pluralism and a free-market economy, and including private property rights and guarantees of press freedom. The official name of the country was changed from the People's Republic of Mozambique to the Republic of Mozambique. Renamo refused to recognize the new Constitution, declaring that it had been drafted without democratic consultation. Presidential and legislative elections, to take place under the terms of the new Constitution, were scheduled for mid-1991. The President was henceforth to be elected by direct universal suffrage, and the legislature was renamed the Assembléia da República (Assembly of the Republic). A new law concerning the formation, structure and function of political parties came into effect in February. In accordance with Article 30 of the Constitution, Renamo would not be recognized as a legitimate political party until it had renounced violence completely.

In late December 1990 negotiations between the Government and Renamo were resumed in Rome, and a Joint Verification Commission, comprising independent representatives from 10 nations, in addition to those of the Government and Renamo, was established to monitor the partial cease-fire. In the areas not covered by the cease-fire Renamo offensives escalated as rebels attempted to take control of positions previously held by the Zimbabwean armed forces. A fifth round of talks took place in Rome in January 1991, but collapsed following the presentation of a report by the Joint Verification Commission containing accusations that Renamo had violated the cease-fire agreement. Renamo questioned the impartiality of the Commission and, in turn, accused Zimbabwean troops of contravening the accord by operating outside of the designated areas. In February Renamo announced that it would resume guerrilla activities within the areas covered by the cease-fire accord. Further talks were scheduled to take place in April but were repeatedly postponed by Renamo, which proposed the introduction of new subjects of discussion to a previously agreed agenda. Renamo also increased the intensity of its military offensives to coincide with the talks (which finally took place in May) in an attempt to strengthen its negotiating position.

In June 1991 the Government announced that it had uncovered a plot, involving several members of the armed forces, to overthrow Chissano. Among those detained were former Chief-of-Staff of the Armed Forces, Col-Gen. Sebastião Mabote, and three brothers of the late President Michel. The leaders of the coup were believed to be opposed to the introduction of a multi-party system and to negotiations with Renamo. In August the Minister of the Interior, Col Manuel José António Mucananda, was detained in connection with the attempted coup. He was, however, exonerated in February 1992, on the grounds that he had been instrumental in bringing the coup attempt to the attention of the authorities. (He resumed his ministerial duties as Minister of the Interior in April.)

In August 1991 a Frelimo party congress undertook further structural changes. The Political Bureau was restyled the Political Commission; Chissano was re-elected as President of the party, while Feliciano Salomão Gundana, Minister of the Presidency, was appointed to the newly-created position of Secretary-General. As part of the democratization of the party, members of the Central Committee were for the first time elected by secret ballot.

In October 1991, in an eighth round of talks (following the suspension of discussions in August), Renamo and the Government signed a protocol agreeing fundamental principles and containing a set of mutual guarantees as a basis for a peace accord. It was suspected that Renamo's compliance was prompted by its failure to seize the military initiative following the withdrawal of the Zimbabwean troops to the transport 'corridors'. Throughout the discussions Renamo continued guerrilla attacks, many of which were launched from South Africa despite the Nkomati accord. Under the terms of the protocol, Renamo effectively recognized the legitimacy of the Government, and agreed to enter the multi-party political framework. In addition, it abandoned previous demands for UN representatives to take governmental control in the period between the signing of a cease-fire accord and the holding of elections. In return, the Government pledged not to legislate on any of the points under negotiation in Rome (including electoral provisions and the future integration of rebels into the armed forces) until a general peace accord had been signed. In early November discussions were interrupted, following the presentation by Renamo of a document casting doubt on its recognition of the Government's legitimacy. Later in the month, however, a second protocol, concerning party law, was signed by both parties, enabling Renamo to begin functioning as a political party immediately after the signing of a general peace accord. Further talks, held in December, led to an agreement that a general election should take place one year after the signing of such an accord, but failed to reach agreement on a permanent truce.

Despite an attempt by President Mugabe and President Hastings Banda of Malawi to accelerate the progress of the peace talks by holding direct discussions with Renamo leader, Afonso Macacho Marceta Dhlakama, in Malawi in early January 1992, talks, which began in Rome later that month, proved inconclusive. However, a third protocol, establishing the principles for the country's future electoral system, was signed in mid-March 1992. Under the terms of the protocol, the elections, to be held (one year after the signing of the general peace accord) under a system of proportional representation, were to be supervised by international observers. An electoral commission was to be established, with one-third of its members to be appointed by Renamo. Following a series of delays, talks were resumed in Rome in June. The discussions were intended to address issues concerning security and the military. However, the insistence of Renamo representatives on introducing constitutional issues to the agreed agenda resulted in an impasse. In July, following meetings with President Mugabe and President F. W. de Klerk of South Africa, Chissano announced that he was prepared to meet Dhlakama for direct talks. On 7 August, following three days of discussions in Rome (in the presence of President Mugabe, representatives of the Italian Government and of the Roman Catholic Church), Chissano and Dhlakama signed a joint declaration committing the two sides to a total cease-fire by 1 October, as part of a General Peace Agreement which would provide for presidential and legislative elections within one year. Dhlakama rejected Chissano's offer of an immediate armistice, on the grounds that the mechanisms necessary to guarantee such a truce had first to be implemented.

In September 1992 Chissano and Dhlakama met in Gaborone, Botswana, to attempt to resolve the deadlocked military and security issues. Chissano offered to establish an independent commission to monitor and guarantee the impartiality of the Serviço de Informação e Segurança do Estado (SISE—State Information and Security Service), a body which Renamo claimed to be merely a continuation of the disbanded political police, the Serviço Nacional de Segurança Popular (National Service of People's Security). In addition, the figure of 30,000 was agreed upon as the number of troops to comprise the joint national defence force.

Following a slight delay (during which Dhlakama raised further questions regarding the commission to monitor the SISE and the administration of Renamo-occupied territory pending elections), the General Peace Agreement was finally signed on 4 October 1992. Under the terms of the agreement, a general cease-fire was to come into force immediately after ratification of the treaty by the Assembléia da República. Both the Renamo troops and the government forces were to withdraw to assembly points within seven days of ratification. The new 30,000-strong national defence force, the Forças Armadas de Defesa de Moçambique (FADM), would then be created, drawing on equal numbers from each side, with the remaining troops surrendering their weapons to a UN peace-keeping force within six months. A Cease-Fire Commission, incorporating representatives from the Government, Renamo and the UN, was to be established to assume responsibility for supervising the implementation of the truce regulations. In overall political control of the peace process would be the Comissão de Supervisão e Controle (CSC—Supervision and Control Commission), comprising representatives of the Government, Renamo and the UN, with responsibilities including the supervision of the Cease-Fire Commission and other commissions charged with establishing the joint armed forces, reintegrating demobilized soldiers into society, and verifying the withdrawal of foreign troops from Mozambique. In addition, Chissano was to appoint a National Information Commission (COMINFO) with responsibilities including the supervision of the SISE. Presidential and legislative elections were to take place, under UN supervision, one year after the signing of the General Peace Agreement, provided that it had been fully implemented and the demobilization process completed.

The General Peace Agreement was duly ratified by the Assembléia da República, and came into force on 15 October 1992. On that day some 20 UN observers arrived in Maputo to supervise the first phase of the cease-fire. However, the mutual recriminations that were to characterize the period leading up to the elections began in the following week, when the Government accused Renamo of systematically violating the accord: the rebels had reportedly occupied four strategically-positioned towns in central and northern Mozambique. Dhlakama subsequently claimed that Renamo's actions had been defensive manoeuvres, and, in turn, accused government forces of violating the accord by advancing into Renamo territory.

In November 1992, owing to considerable delays in the formation of the various peace commissions that were envisaged in the General Peace Agreement, the timetable for the cease-fire operations was redrafted. In December the UN Security Council finally approved a plan for the establishment of the UN Operation in Mozambique (ONUMOZ, see p. 51), providing for the deployment of some 7,500 troops, police and civilian observers to oversee the process of demobilization and formation of the FADM, and to supervise the forthcoming elections. A meeting of international aid donors, held in Rome, agreed to commit some US $400m. towards the cost of the operation. However, there were continued delays in the deployment of the peace-keeping force, since the UN was experiencing difficulty in persuading its member nations to commit troops. Renamo, for its part, refused to begin confining its forces to assembly points until 65% of the UN force was in place. The location of the 49 assembly points was not agreed until February 1993. In March the peace process was effectively halted when Renamo withdrew from the CSC and the Cease-Fire Commission, protesting that proper provisions had not been made to accommodate its officials. In early April Dhlakama announced that his forces would begin to report to assembly points only when Renamo received US $15m. to finance its transition into a political party. The first UN troops (an Italian battalion) became operational in the Beira 'corridor' on 1 April, and in mid-April the Zimbabwean troops guarding the Beira and Limpopo 'corridors' finally withdrew, six months behind schedule, following their replacement by UN forces. On 14 April the UN Security Council unanimously adopted a resolution expressing serious concern at the delays in the peace process, and calling for the timetable for implementation of the General Peace Agreement to be finalized and for both sides to guarantee freedom of movement for ONUMOZ. In late April the Special Representative of the UN Secretary-General to Mozambique, Aldo Ajello, confirmed that, owing to the delays, the elections were unlikely to be held before mid-1994.

By early May 1993 the ONUMOZ force was approaching full strength, with units contributed by 19 countries totalling 4,721 armed and 150 unarmed personnel. Renamo, meanwhile, continued to use its demands for finance to delay the demobilization process, claiming that it needed US $100m. from the international community. In June, however, Renamo returned to the CSC. At a subsequent meeting of the commission in Maputo, agreement was reached on a formal postponement of the election date to October 1994. A revised timetable for the peace process, published by ONUMOZ, envisaged the opening of assembly points in July and August 1993, with demobilization beginning in September. Training of the FADM would take place between September 1993 and February 1994. Electoral registers would be prepared in April–June 1994, the election campaign would be conducted between 1 September and 14 October, to be followed by the elections in mid-October. A meeting in Maputo of international aid donors, also in June 1993, revealed growing impatience among the international community with the repeated delays in the peace process and with Renamo's escalating demands for logistical and financial support. The meeting produced promises of additional support for the peace process, bringing the total pledged by donors to US $520m., including support for the repatriation of 1.5m. refugees from neighbouring countries, the resettlement of 4m.–5m. displaced people and the reintegration of some 80,000 former combatants into civilian life. The UN also agreed to establish a trust fund of $10m. to finance Renamo's transformation into a political party, with the disbursement of funds dependent on UN approval. A second trust fund, accessible to all political parties other than Frelimo and Renamo, was to be established after the National Electoral Commission had been formed, following the eventual approval of a new electoral law.

In July 1993 Renamo announced new preconditions to the advancement of the peace process, initially insisting on the recognition of its own administration, to operate parallel to that of the Government. This demand was later revised, with Renamo asking for its members to be appointed to five of the country's 11 provincial governorships. In September, however, following direct talks between Chissano and Dhlakama, an agreement was signed resolving the question of the control of provincial administrations. Under the terms of the agreement, Renamo was to appoint three advisers to each of the incumbent provincial governors to make recommendations relating to the reintegration of areas under Renamo control into a single state administration. It was also agreed that a request be made to the UN to send a police corps to supervise the activities of the national police and ensure neutrality in areas under Renamo control. (However, Dhlakama was later reported to have said that he would await evidence that the measures were effective before beginning the demobilization of his troops.)

In October 1993 the CSC approved a new timetable covering all aspects of the peace process, including the elections in October 1994. The timetable stipulated the approval of the new electoral law by the end of November 1993. Troops were to be confined to assembly points between November and December, with demobilization to take place in January–May 1994. Training of the FADM was to begin in January and it was to be fully operational by September. However, at the time of announcement of the new timetable only 36 of the 49 designated assembly points had been approved, and only 23 were ready to begin accommodating troops.

In November 1993 the UN Security Council adopted a resolution renewing the mandate of ONUMOZ for a further six months. In addition, it responded to the joint request by the Government and Renamo for a UN police corps by authorizing the deployment of 128 police observers. In the same month consensus was finally reached on the text of the electoral law, and this was promulgated at the end of December.

At a meeting of the CSC in mid-November 1993 an agreement was signed providing for the confinement of troops to begin on 30 November. The process was to have been concluded by the end of the year. However, less than 15% of the total number of troops for confinement entered assembly points, and in January 1994 the UN expressed concern at the slow pace at which government troops were assembling. Also in January 540 military instructors (comprising government and Renamo troops who had been trained by British instructors in Zimbabwe) arrived in Mozambique to begin training the FADM. However, owing to logistical problems, the formal date for the initial cycle of training to begin was repeatedly postponed: the definitive date was finally set for 21 March, some two months later than envisaged in the revised timetable for the peace process agreed in October 1993.

The National Electoral Commission was inaugurated in early February 1994. The composition of the commission, which had finally been agreed (after protracted dispute) in October 1993, included 10 members from the Government, seven from Renamo, three from the other opposition parties and an independent chairman. Later in February 1994 the UN Security Council announced that, in response to demands made by Dhlakama for a reinforcement of the UN police corps monitoring the confinement areas, it would be increasing its membership from 128 to 1,144 (with simultaneous reductions in the number of UN military personnel, to avoid extrabudgetary expenditure). In addition, the Security Council urged the Government and Renamo to set a specific date for the October general election and appealed for an early start to voter registration, as well as a rapid conclusion to the demobilization process. By the end of February only 50% of troops had entered assembly points and none had officially been demobilized. In early March, in an effort to expedite the confinement process (which, to an extent, had been hampered by the inadequate capacity of assembly points), the Government announced its decision to begin the unilateral demobilization of its troops. Renamo responded by beginning the demobilization of its troops in mid-March. In early April Lt-Gen. Lagos Lidimo, the nominee of the Government, and former Renamo guerrilla commander Lt-Gen. Mateus Ngonhamo were inaugurated as the high command of the FADM.

In mid-April 1994 Chissano issued a decree establishing the date of the presidential and legislative elections as 27–28 October. In early May the UN Security Council adopted a resolution renewing the mandate of ONUMOZ for the final period, ending on 15 November, subject to review in July and September. Voter registration for the elections began on 1 June and was due to continue until 15 August, with an additional period of five days for special cases, such as returning refugees and demobilized soldiers (however, voter registration was later reopened between 24 August and 2 September). In late July the National Electoral Commission announced that, as a consensus could not be reached on the issue of the enfranchisement of Mozambicans living abroad, emigrants would not be granted the right to vote in the forthcoming elections. Also in July, despite international pressure, Chissano publicly dismissed the possibility of a pre-election agreement providing for a government of national unity involving representatives of Renamo and other opposition parties.

The confinement and demobilization processes continued to make slow progress, and the deadline for the completion of confinement was consequently extended, beyond the beginning of the electoral process, to 8 July 1994, with demobilization to be completed by 15 August. On that date, according to figures issued by ONUMOZ, a total of 64,277 government troops had registered at confinement points, of which 48,237 had been demobilized. The total number of Renamo troops registered was 22,790, of which 14,925 had been demobilized, thus making it impossible for Renamo to supply its quota of 15,000 troops to the FADM. At that point only 7,375 troops from both sides had enlisted in the FADM (4,134 government troops; 3,241 Renamo troops). The deadline for registration at confinement points was subsequently extended to 31 August, after which date it was to continue at three centres in the north, centre and south of the country. On 16 August, in accordance with the provisions of the General Peace Agreement, the government Forças Armadas de Moçambique were formally dissolved and their assets transferred to the FADM, which was duly inaugurated as the country's official armed forces on the same day. During July and August a series of mutinies and demonstrations occurred involving troops from both sides stationed in confinement areas. The soldiers were protesting at poor conditions and the slow pace of demobilization. In August Renamo formally registered as a political party. In the same month the Partido Liberal e Democrático de Moçambique, the Partido Nacional Democrático and the Partido Nacional de Moçambique formed an electoral coalition, the União Democrático (UD).

Election campaigning began in September 1994. However, in that month Renamo issued a statement demanding further funding—it had already exhausted the US $11.6m. made available by the UN trust fund established to transform Renamo into a political party—and threatened to withdraw from the electoral process should finance not be forthcoming. Subsequently the USA pledged $1m. towards Renamo's election campaign.

Presidential and legislative elections were held on 27–29 October 1994. The extension of the voting to a third day had become necessary following the withdrawal of Renamo from the elections only hours before the beginning of the poll, claiming that conditions were not in place to ensure free and fair elections. However, following concerted international pressure, Renamo abandoned its boycott in the early hours of 28 October.

The official election results were issued by the National Electoral Commission on 19 November 1994. In the presidential election Chissano secured an outright majority (53.30%) of the votes, thus avoiding the need for a second round of voting. His closest rival was Dhlakama, who received 33.73% of the votes. In the legislative election Frelimo also secured an overall majority, winning 129 of the 250 seats, while Renamo obtained 112 and the UD the remaining nine seats. Renamo received considerable support in central and northern Mozambique, and won a majority of the votes in five of the country's 11 provinces (including the most economically important in the country). The level of participation by the electorate was considerable, with some 80% of the total 6.1m. registered voters exercising their right to vote. Dhlakama subsequently accepted the results of the elections, although he maintained that there had been irregularities. The UN recognized the occurrence of irregularities, but asserted that these were insufficient to have affected the overall credibility of the poll, which it declared to have been free and fair. (This view was endorsed by international observers at the elections, who numbered some 2,300.) According to the UN Development Programme the total cost of Mozambique's first multi-party elections was US $63.53m., of which the vast majority (some $59m.) was funded by international donors. In mid-November the UN Security Council adopted a resolution extending the mandate of ONUMOZ until the inauguration of the new Government: the withdrawal of ONUMOZ troops and police was to be completed by 31 January 1995. In December 1994 the Cease-Fire Commission issued its final report, according to which ONUMOZ had registered a combined total of 91,691 government and Renamo troops during the confinement process, of whom 11,579 had enlisted in the FADM (compared with the 30,000 envisaged in the General Peace Accord). In practice, demobilization had continued until 15 September, with special cases still being processed the day before the elections.

Chissano was inaugurated as President on 9 December 1994, and the new Government was sworn in on 23 December. All the portfolios were assigned to members of Frelimo. Demands by Renamo that it be awarded governorships in the five provinces where it won a majority of the votes in the legislative elections were rejected by Chissano—three new provincial Governors appointed in January 1995 were all members of Frelimo. At the first session of the new Assembléia da República, which began on 8 December 1994, a dispute concerning the voting procedure employed to elect the new Chairman of the legislature resulted in the withdrawal of the Renamo and UD deputies, who had unsuccessfully demanded a secret ballot; both parties had abandoned the legislative boycott by the end of December, although not before the conclusion of the first session. In that month seven small opposition parties without representation in the legislature announced the formation of an alliance, the Frente Unida de Salvação, which aimed to influence the legislature on social, political and economic issues.

In March 1995 the Minister of National Defence announced that, once legislation had been enacted allowing for the reintroduction of compulsory military service, a further 4,500 troops would be drafted into the FADM in that year. The total strength of the FADM would be defined by government policy, and the figure of 30,000 envisaged in the General Peace Accord would not necessarily be observed. During that month there were several incidents of insurrection involving members of the FADM who were demanding salary increases. By the end of March all ONUMOZ troops and police had withdrawn from Mozambique, two months later than originally envisaged, and only a small unit of ONUMOZ officials remained in the country.

As a result of the civil war, it was estimated that some 4.3m. Mozambicans were threatened by starvation in early 1990. Increased Renamo activity during 1991 and early 1992 exacerbated both the famine and refugee problems. In July 1992 the Government and Renamo signed a joint declaration allowing unrestricted passage in Renamo territory for relief workers providing aid and assistance to the millions threatened by starvation. However, according to reports in September, Renamo had failed to guarantee safe passage to the aid workers, thus obstructing a major relief programme. In January 1993 the office of the United Nations High Commissioner for Refugees (UNHCR) estimated that there were 1.7m. Mozambican refugees in neighbouring countries. As a consequence of the signing of the General Peace Agreement in October 1992, an estimated 800,000 refugees were expected to return to the country in 1993. In June 1993 UNHCR began its official voluntary repatriation programme with the return of a small group from an estimated total of 140,000 refugees in Zimbabwe. In August Mozambique, UNHCR and Swaziland signed a tripartite agreement providing for the return of 24,000 refugees from Swaziland, and in October the first contingent arrived in Mozambique. The first group from an estimated 25,000 refugees in Zambia also returned in October. In the same month a tripartite agreement was signed with South Africa, providing for the voluntary repatriation of some 350,000 Mozambican refugees. However, in January 1994 it was reported that South Africa had expressed its intention to begin expelling refugees from April. In February UNHCR reported that some 600,000 refugees had returned from neighbouring countries in 1993, although the majority had done so spontaneously—with the largest number of voluntary returnees coming from Malawi. (By January 1994 only 20,167 refugees were reported to have returned through UNHCR repatriation schemes.) In 1994 a further 600,000–700,000 refugees were expected to return. The complete repatriation programme was expected to last a total of three years and to cost US $203m. In March 1995 UNHCR reportedly announced that it would cease repatriating Mozambican refugees from South Africa at the end of that month because the process had become too expensive. According to a report by the International Organization for Migration, issued in November 1994, there were still 684,000 'internally displaced' people in Mozambique at that time. However, an estimated 3m. had been successfully resettled since the signing of the General Peace Agreement.

Relations between Mozambique and Malawi deteriorated in 1986. In September Machel threatened to close the border between the two countries if Malawi's alleged assistance to the Renamo rebels continued. However, despite the revelation of the alleged plot by Mozambique and Zimbabwe against the Government of Malawi in November, a joint co-operation agreement between Mozambique and Malawi was signed in December. In April 1987 it was confirmed that some 300 Malawian troops were in Mozambique, guarding the railway line linking Malawi to the Mozambican port of Nacala; the number of Malawian troops in Mozambique was subsequently increased to 600. In July 1988, during a state visit to Malawi, Chissano praised the country for its support of his Government. In December 1988 Mozambique, Malawi, and UNHCR signed an agreement to promote the voluntary repatriation of Mozambican refugees in Malawi. In accordance with the provisions of the General Peace Agreement, which required all Malawian troops to be withdrawn from the country prior to the holding of elections, Malawi withdrew its troops in June 1993.

Most of the 250,000 Portuguese who had remained in Mozambique after independence had left by June 1977. In 1985 Portugal agreed to adopt measures to curb the activities of Renamo in Lisbon. After independence, Mozambique developed strong international links with the USSR and other countries of the communist bloc, and with neighbouring African states: it is a member of the Southern African Development Community (SADC, see p. 219), which was founded in 1979, as the Southern African Development Co-ordination Conference, to reduce the region's economic dependence on South Africa, principally by developing alternative trade routes through Mozambique. During the 1980s Mozambique developed stronger links with Western countries, particularly the USA, the United Kingdom and other members of the EC (now the European Union), and in October 1987 it was granted observer status at a meeting of Commonwealth Heads of Government. In 1993 full diplomatic relations were established with South Africa and the Republic of Korea. In July 1994 Mozambique and South Africa established a new Joint Defence and Security Commission, replacing the Joint Security Commission originally established in 1984. In January 1995 a Joint Mozambique-Swaziland Security Subcommission met for discussions following violations of Mozambique's border by the Swaziland armed forces.

### Government

On 30 November 1990 a new Constitution was introduced, providing for multi-party democracy. Under the Constitution, legislative power is vested in the Assembly of the Republic, with 250 members, who are elected for a five-year term. Members are elected by universal, direct adult suffrage in a secret ballot, according to a system of proportional representation. The President of the Republic, who is Head of State, is directly elected for a five-year term; the President holds executive power and governs with the assistance of an appointed Council of Ministers. Provincial Governors, appointed by the President, have overall responsibility for the functions of government within each of the 11 Provinces. Directly-elected local assemblies choose delegates to district assemblies, which, in turn, elect delegates to provincial assemblies. Multi-party municipal elections were due to be held no later than October 1996.

### Defence

In June 1990 the National Defence Force (Forças Armadas de Moçambique—FAM) totalled an estimated 72,000, with 60,000 in the army, 1,000 in the navy and 6,000 in the air force, and a paramilitary force of 5,000; there were also provincial and people's militias in villages. In December 1991 the Government announced plans to reduce the FAM by 45,000, in anticipation of the signing of a cease-fire agreement, whereupon, it was proposed, a single body of armed forces, incorporating Renamo guerrillas, would be created. Under the provisions of the General Peace Agreement of October 1992, the joint armed forces (Forças Armadas de Defesa de Moçambique—FADM), were to number 30,000, comprising equal numbers of government and Renamo troops. All troops from both sides were to register at assembly points throughout the country; those not enlisting in the FADM were to be demobilized. In accordance with the provisions of the General Peace Agreement, all Zimbabwean and Malawian troops stationed in Mozambique to guard the 'transport corridors' linking the land-locked southern African states with the Indian Ocean were withdrawn—in April 1993 and July 1993, respectively—prior to the holding of presidential and legislative elections in October 1994. On 16 August the FAM were formally dissolved and the FADM inaugurated as the country's official armed forces. According to the final report, issued in December 1994, of the Cease-Fire Commission (established under the General Peace Agreement to supervise the implementation of truce regulations), a combined total of only 11,579 government and Renamo troops (from a total of 91,691 troops registered at assembly points) had enlisted in the FADM. In 1995 the Government was seeking to introduce legislation providing for the reintroduction of compulsory military service, which had been suspended under the General Peace Accord, in order to increase the strength of the FADM. In March the Minister of National Defence announced that, once enabling legislation had been introduced, a further 4,500 troops would be drafted into the FADM in 1995. The total strength of the FADM was to be defined by government policy, and the figure of 30,000 envisaged in the General Peace Accord would not necessarily be observed. By the end of March all troops and police belonging to the UN Operation in Mozambique (ONUMOZ), stationed in the country to facilitate the pacification and electoral processes, had withdrawn. After that date only a small unit of ONUMOZ officials remained in the country. Expenditure on defence and security, including the demobilization process and the formation of the FADM, totalled US $84.3m. in 1994, and was to be reduced considerably in 1995.

## Economic Affairs

In 1993, according to estimates by the World Bank, Mozambique's gross national product (GNP), measured at average 1991–93 prices, was US $1,375m., equivalent to only about $80 per head. During 1985–93, it was estimated, GNP per head increased, in real terms, by an average of 1.9% per year. Over the same period the population increased by an annual average of 2.6%. Mozambique's gross domestic product (GDP) increased, in real terms, by 0.4% per year in 1980–92, by an estimated 19.1% in 1993 and an estimated 4.3% in 1994.

Agriculture (including forestry and fishing) contributed an estimated 39.1% of GDP in 1991. At mid-1993 an estimated 80.7% of the working population were employed in the sector. Fishing is the principal export activity: shrimps, prawns and lobsters accounted for 54.6% of total export earnings in 1993. The principal cash crops are cashew nuts (accounting for 6.2% of export earnings in 1993), cotton (8.4%) and sugar cane. The main subsistence crop is cassava. During 1980–92 agricultural GDP increased by an estimated annual average of 1.3%.

Industry (including mining, manufacturing, construction and power) employed an estimated 9.1% of the working population and provided an estimated 42.4% of GDP in 1991. During 1980–92 industrial GDP declined by an estimated annual average of 0.4%.

Mining and quarrying contributed an estimated 0.2% of GDP in 1991. Only coal and salt are exploited in significant quantities, although bauxite is also mined and the exploitation of commercially viable levels of graphite was expected to begin in the mid-1990s. There are also reserves of high-grade iron ore, tantalite, fluorspar, zirconium, asbestos, uranium, copper, nickel, ilmenite, rutile, moazite, gold, platinum, diamonds, emeralds, bismuth, mica, semi-precious stones and natural gas. Plans began in 1994 to develop a natural gas field at Pande, in the province of Inhambane, where reserves were estimated at 55m. cu m. Sales of the gas to South Africa, which was expected to be the principal consumer, were due to begin in 1998, following the construction of a 600-km pipeline.

Manufacturing contributed an estimated 24.6% of GDP in 1991. Manufacturing and mining engaged 6.2% of the working population in 1980. Based on the value of output, the most important branches of manufacturing in 1992 were food products (accounting for 30.2% of the total), textiles and clothing (15.8%), beverages and tobacco (11.6%) and chemical products (9.2%).

Electrical energy is derived principally from hydroelectric power. In 1988 about one-third of the electricity supply was imported from South Africa. In 1987 Mozambique, Portugal and South Africa signed an agreement to rehabilitate Mozambique's important Cahora Bassa hydroelectric plant on the Zambezi River and to repair transmission lines linking the plant to the South African electricity grid. Upon completion of the project, Mozambique was to export hydroelectric power to South Africa. However, work was continually delayed as a result of the security situation. Following the signing of the General Peace Agreement in October 1992, funding was sought to resume work on the project. Rehabilitation of the plant and transmission lines was expected to resume in March 1995 and to be completed in 1997. Plans to construct transmission lines for the export of electricity to Zimbabwe were under way in 1995, and plans for the construction of further lines to supply Malawi and Swaziland were being pursued following the signing of agreements between Mozambique and those countries in 1994. Mozambique imports all of its petroleum requirements.

In 1992 Mozambique recorded a trade deficit of US $659m., and there was a deficit of $381m. on the current account of the balance of payments. In 1989 the principal source of imports (23.2%) was South Africa; other major suppliers were the USSR, the USA and Portugal. In 1992 the principal market for exports was Spain (29.5%); other significant purchasers were South Africa, the USA and Portugal. The principal exports are crustaceans (principally shrimps and prawns), cashew nuts, raw cotton, sugar and copra. The principal imports in 1990 were foodstuffs, capital goods, crude petroleum and petroleum products and machinery and spare parts.

In 1993 there was a budgetary deficit of 1,215,200m. meticais. Mozambique's total external debt was estimated at US $5,263m. at the end of 1993, of which $4,650m. was long-term public debt. In that year the cost of debt-servicing was equivalent to 20.6% of the total value of exports of goods and services. The average annual rate of inflation was 53.5% in 1985–93; consumer prices increased by an average of 42.2% in 1993 and by 77.8% in the year to August 1994.

Mozambique is a member of the Southern African Development Community (SADC, see p. 219) and of the Preferential Trade Area for Eastern and Southern African States (PTA, see p. 240). In November 1993 Mozambique was among PTA members to sign a treaty establishing a Common Market for Eastern and Southern Africa.

In terms of average income, Mozambique is one of the poorest countries in the world. During the 1980s economic development was severely frustrated by the effects of the civil war (in particular the disruption of agriculture and the sabotage of transport routes and power lines). A shortage of skilled labour and the pursuit of rigid centrally-planned economic policies were also deemed to have contributed to sharply declining production, increasing foreign debt and widespread poverty. In 1987 the Government adopted an Economic and Social Rehabilitation Programme, comprising measures aimed at stabilization and structural adjustment, supported by the IMF and the World Bank. Since 1990 there has been considerable progress in liberalizing the economy, including the introduction of legislation facilitating investment, the reform of the financial sector, the restructuring and privatization of state enterprises and the removal of most price controls. Such measures have served to curb inflation and reduce the fiscal deficit. With the signing of the General Peace Agreement in 1992, production in rural areas, particularly small-scale farming began to increase. This, in addition to continued structural reform and the partial restoration of the infrastructure, contributed to significant GDP growth in 1993. Foreign assistance continues to play a fundamental role in the Mozambican economy (56% of total projected expenditure in the 1994 budget was to be funded by donations and credits from the international community). In early 1995 donor nations pledged US $783.5m. in grants and loans for investment, balance-of-payments support and food aid, and an additional $326m. in debt relief. A significant and sustained increase in export growth is necessary in order to reduce Mozambique's dependency on foreign assistance. In a five-year plan submitted to the legislature in early 1995, the Government identified rural development as its main priority, with the aim of both creating employment and boosting production for export. Other important areas for export development are the services sector (in particular the ports, roads and railways that service neighbouring countries) and the energy sector.

## Social Welfare

Most of the European medical personnel left the country at independence. In 1991 there were 39 hospitals, with a total of 7,564 beds, and 932 health posts and centres, with a total of 5,003 beds. In the same year there were only 435 physicians (one per 37,141 inhabitants) working in Mozambique. Health care was allocated 2.8% of total planned expenditure in the 1990 budget.

## MOZAMBIQUE

### Education

At independence, between 85% and 95% of the adult population were illiterate. In the early 1980s there was a major emphasis on campaigns for adult literacy and other adult education. By 1990, according to estimates by UNESCO, 67.1% of the adult population were illiterate (males 54.9%; females 78.7%). Education is officially compulsory for seven years from the age of seven. Primary schooling begins at six years of age and lasts for five years. Secondary schooling, which begins at 12 years of age, lasts for seven years and comprises a first cycle of two years and a further cycle of five years. The number of children receiving primary education increased from 634,000 in 1973 to 1,495,000 in 1979, but declined to 1,199,476 in 1992, owing to the security situation. As a proportion of the school-age population, the total enrolment at primary and secondary schools increased from 30% in 1972 to 52% in 1979, but declined to the equivalent of 32% in 1992 (males 37%; females 27%). There were 3,482 students at the university in 1992. Expenditure on education by all levels of government in 1990, including foreign aid received for the purpose, was 72,264m. meticais (12.0% of total government expenditure). In early 1991 the Government introduced a programme to improve primary education and strengthen the overall management of the education sector, at a cost of US $67.9m. (to be provided mostly by the World Bank).

### Public Holidays

**1995:** 1 January (New Year's Day), 3 February (Heroes' Day, anniversary of the assassination of Eduardo Mondlane), 7 April (Day of the Mozambican Woman), 1 May (Workers' Day), 25 June (Independence Day), 7 September (Victory Day—anniversary of the end of the Armed Struggle), 25 September (Anniversary of the launching of the Armed Struggle for National Liberation, and Day of the Armed Forces of Mozambique), 25 December (National Family Day).

**1996:** 1 January (New Year's Day), 3 February (Heroes' Day, anniversary of the assassination of Eduardo Mondlane), 7 April (Day of the Mozambican Woman), 1 May (Workers' Day), 25 June (Independence Day), 7 September (Victory Day—anniversary of the end of the Armed Struggle), 25 September (Anniversary of the launching of the Armed Struggle for National Liberation, and Day of the Armed Forces of Mozambique), 25 December (National Family Day).

### Weights and Measures

The metric system is in force.

# Statistical Survey

Source (unless otherwise stated): Direcção Nacional de Estatística, Commissão Nacional do Plano, Avda Ahmed Sekou Touré 21, CP 493, Maputo; tel. 743117.

## Area and Population

### AREA, POPULATION AND DENSITY

| | |
|---|---:|
| Area (sq km) | 799,380* |
| Population (census results) | |
| 15 December 1970 | 8,168,933† |
| 1 August 1980‡ | |
| Males | 5,670,484 |
| Females | 6,003,241 |
| Total | 11,673,725 |
| Population (official estimates at mid-year) | |
| 1991 | 14,420,000 |
| 1992 | 14,790,000 |
| 1993 | 15,583,000 |
| Density (per sq km) at mid-1993 | 19.5 |

* 308,641 sq miles. The area includes 13,000 sq km (5,019 sq miles) of inland water.
† Covering only those areas under Portuguese control.
‡ Excluding an adjustment for underenumeration, estimated at 3.8%. The adjusted total is 12,130,000 (males 5,908,500; females 6,221,500).

### PROVINCES (at 1 January 1987)

| Province | Area (sq km) | Population (provisional) | Density (per sq km) |
|---|---:|---:|---:|
| Cabo Delgado | 82,625 | 1,109,921 | 13.4 |
| Gaza | 75,709 | 1,138,724 | 15.0 |
| Inhambane | 68,615 | 1,167,022 | 17.0 |
| Manica | 61,661 | 756,886 | 12.3 |
| City of Maputo | 602 | 1,006,765 | 1,672.4 |
| Maputo province | 25,756 | 544,692 | 21.1 |
| Nampula | 81,606 | 2,837,856 | 34.8 |
| Niassa | 129,056 | 607,670 | 4.7 |
| Sofala | 68,018 | 1,257,710 | 18.5 |
| Tete | 100,724 | 981,319 | 9.7 |
| Zambézia | 105,008 | 2,952,251 | 28.1 |
| **Total** | 799,380 | 14,360,816 | 18.0 |

### PRINCIPAL TOWN

Maputo (capital), population 755,300 (including adjustment) at census of 1 August 1980; estimated population 1,006,765 at 1 January 1987.

### BIRTHS AND DEATHS (UN estimates, annual averages)

| | 1975–80 | 1980–85 | 1985–90 |
|---|---:|---:|---:|
| Birth rate (per 1,000) | 45.4 | 45.7 | 45.0 |
| Death rate (per 1,000) | 20.8 | 20.0 | 18.8 |

**Expectation of life** (UN estimates, years at birth, 1985–90): 46.1 (males 44.5; females 47.8).

Source: UN, *World Population Prospects: The 1992 Revision*.

### ECONOMICALLY ACTIVE POPULATION
(persons aged 12 years and over, 1980 census)

| | Males | Females | Total |
|---|---:|---:|---:|
| Agriculture, forestry, hunting and fishing | 1,887,779 | 2,867,052 | 4,754,831 |
| Mining and quarrying | } 323,730 | 23,064 | 346,794 |
| Manufacturing | | | |
| Construction | 41,611 | 510 | 42,121 |
| Commerce | 90,654 | 21,590 | 112,244 |
| Transport, storage and communications | 74,817 | 2,208 | 77,025 |
| Other services* | 203,629 | 39,820 | 243,449 |
| **Total employed** | 2,622,220 | 2,954,244 | 5,576,464 |
| Unemployed | 75,505 | 19,321 | 94,826 |
| **Total labour force** | 2,697,725 | 2,973,565 | 5,671,290 |

* Including electricity, gas and water.

Source: ILO, *Year Book of Labour Statistics*.

**1991** (estimates, '000 persons): Agriculture 6,870; Industry 766; Services 798; Total labour force 8,434 (Source: UN Economic Commission for Africa, *African Statistical Yearbook*).

MOZAMBIQUE

## Agriculture

**PRINCIPAL CROPS** ('000 metric tons)

|  | 1991 | 1992 | 1993 |
|---|---|---|---|
| Rice (paddy) | 56 | 33† | 66† |
| Maize | 327 | 133† | 533† |
| Sorghum | 155 | 66 | 143 |
| Potatoes* | 71 | 72 | 72 |
| Sweet potatoes* | 55 | 55 | 55 |
| Cassava (Manioc) | 3,690 | 3,239† | 3,511† |
| Pulses | 78 | 56† | 79† |
| Groundnuts (in shell) | 115* | 87† | 84† |
| Sunflower seed | 10 | 10 | 10* |
| Cottonseed† | 24 | 26 | 26 |
| Cotton (lint)† | 12 | 13† | 13 |
| Coconuts* | 425 | 425 | 425 |
| Copra | 72† | 72† | 72* |
| Vegetables and melons* | 165 | 112 | 114 |
| Sugar cane* | 280 | 330 | 330 |
| Oranges | 20 | 12 | 12* |
| Mangoes* | 32 | 25 | 30 |
| Bananas* | 80 | 70 | 80 |
| Papayas* | 44 | 35 | 40 |
| Other fruits* | 172 | 118 | 130 |
| Cashew nuts | 31 | 54 | 54* |
| Tea (made) | 5 | 1 | 1* |
| Tobacco (leaves) | 3† | 3* | 3* |
| Jute and jute-like fibres* | 4 | 4 | 4 |
| Sisal* | 1 | 1 | 1 |

\* FAO estimate(s).   † Unofficial estimate(s).

Source: FAO, *Production Yearbook*.

**LIVESTOCK** (FAO estimates, '000 head, year ending September)

|  | 1991 | 1992 | 1993 |
|---|---|---|---|
| Asses | 20 | 20 | 20 |
| Cattle | 1,370 | 1,250 | 1,250 |
| Pigs | 165 | 170 | 170 |
| Sheep | 118 | 118 | 118 |
| Goats | 380 | 385 | 385 |

Chickens (FAO estimates, million): 22 in 1991; 22 in 1992; 22 in 1993.

Source: FAO, *Production Yearbook*.

**LIVESTOCK PRODUCTS** (FAO estimates, '000 metric tons)

|  | 1991 | 1992 | 1993 |
|---|---|---|---|
| Beef and veal | 47 | 36 | 36 |
| Goat meat | 2 | 2 | 2 |
| Pig meat | 12 | 12 | 12 |
| Poultry meat | 28 | 28 | 28 |
| Cows' milk | 63 | 57 | 57 |
| Goats' milk | 10 | 10 | 10 |
| Hen eggs | 11.4 | 11.4 | 11.4 |
| Cattle hides | 6.3 | 4.8 | 4.8 |

Source: FAO, *Production Yearbook*.

## Forestry

**ROUNDWOOD REMOVALS** ('000 cubic metres)

|  | 1990 | 1991 | 1992 |
|---|---|---|---|
| Sawlogs, veneer logs and logs for sleepers | 47 | 46 | 52 |
| Other industrial wood* | 877 | 895 | 919 |
| Fuel wood* | 15,022 | 15,022 | 15,022 |
| **Total** | 15,946 | 15,963 | 15,993 |

\* FAO estimates (the annual figure for fuel wood is assumed to be unchanged since 1987).

Source: FAO, *Yearbook of Forest Products*.

**SAWNWOOD PRODUCTION** ('000 cubic metres, incl. railway sleepers)

|  | 1990 | 1991 | 1992 |
|---|---|---|---|
| Coniferous (softwood) | 8 | 7 | 6* |
| Broadleaved (hardwood) | 18 | 10 | 11 |
| **Total** | 26 | 17 | 17 |

\* FAO estimate.

Source: FAO, *Yearbook of Forest Products*.

## Fishing

('000 metric tons, live weight)

|  | 1990 | 1991 | 1992 |
|---|---|---|---|
| Inland waters: |  |  |  |
| Freshwater fishes* | 4.0 | 3.5 | 4.0 |
| Indian Ocean: |  |  |  |
| Marine fishes* | 28.3 | 27.3 | 26.8 |
| Shrimps and prawns | 6.8 | 7.7 | 6.3 |
| Other crustaceans* | 0.2 | 0.2 | 0.2 |
| Molluscs* | 0.2 | 0.2 | 0.2 |
| **Total catch*** | 39.5 | 38.9 | 37.5 |

\* FAO estimates.

Source: FAO, *Yearbook of Fishery Statistics*.

## Mining

('000 metric tons)

|  | 1990 | 1991 | 1992 |
|---|---|---|---|
| Coal | 122.2 | 112.0 | 27.0 |
| Bauxite | 6.6 | 7.9 | 9.3 |
| Salt (unrefined) | 46.9 | 45.3 | 22.8 |

Source: Ministry of Mineral Resources.

## Industry

**SELECTED PRODUCTS** ('000 metric tons, unless otherwise indicated)

|  | 1988 | 1989 | 1990 |
|---|---|---|---|
| Margarine | 6 | 6 | 6 |
| Wheat flour | 61 | 56 | 50 |
| Raw sugar | 19 | 24 | 33 |
| Beer ('000 hl) | 297 | 158 | 117 |
| Cigarettes (million) | 670 | 3,500 | 1,864 |
| Footwear (thousand pairs) | 477 | 347 | 217 |
| Sulphuric acid | 13 | 13 | 13 |
| Cement | 64 | 80 | 100 |
| Radio receivers ('000) | 91 | 103 | 103 |
| Electric energy (million kWh) | 475 | 485 | 485 |

Source: UN Economic Commission for Africa, *African Statistical Yearbook*.

**1991** ('000 metric tons, unless otherwise indicated): Raw sugar 33 (FAO figure); Cigarettes (million) 1,060; Cement 80 (estimate); Electric energy (million kWh) 490 (Source: UN, *Industrial Statistics Yearbook*).

# MOZAMBIQUE

## Finance

### CURRENCY AND EXCHANGE RATES

**Monetary Units**
100 centavos = 1 metical (plural: meticais).

**Sterling and Dollar Equivalents** (31 December 1994)
£1 sterling = 10,405.5 meticais;
US $1 = 6,651.0 meticais;
100,000 meticais = £9.610 = $15.035.

**Average Exchange Rate** (meticais per US $)
1992  2,550.4
1993  3,874.2
1994  6,038.6

### BUDGET ('000 million meticais)

| Revenue | 1991 | 1992 | 1993 |
|---|---|---|---|
| Taxation | 379.9 | 574.1 | 995.0 |
| On income | 79.0 | 102.9 | 156.6 |
| On goods and services | 177.3 | 281.5 | 534.6 |
| Customs duties | 108.9 | 168.8 | 278.7 |
| Import duties | 68.0 | 112.3 | 172.9 |
| Other taxes | 14.6 | 20.8 | 25.2 |
| Non-tax revenue | 67.3 | 86.9 | 97.6 |
| **Total** | 447.1 | 661.0 | 1,092.6 |

| Expenditure | 1991 | 1992 | 1993 |
|---|---|---|---|
| Current expenditure* | 457.4 | 764.7 | 1,170.8 |
| Defence and security | 178.0 | 259.3 | 416.8 |
| Civil service salaries | 101.0 | 142.5 | 238.8 |
| Goods and services | 89.6 | 172.4 | 230.0 |
| Interest on public debt | 46.2 | 120.1 | 198.0 |
| Others | 50.4 | 69.3 | 89.5 |
| Investment expenditure† | 464.9 | 694.0 | 1,097.0 |
| Liquidation of debt of enterprises | 36.0 | 37.4 | 40.0 |
| **Total** | 958.3 | 1,496.1 | 2,307.8 |

* Including adjustments relating to preceding or following periods ('000 million meticais): −7.8 in 1991; 1.1 in 1992; −2.3 in 1993.
† Including adjustments relating to preceding or following periods ('000 million meticais): −26.0 in 1991; −60.0 in 1992; −42.0 in 1993.

Source: the former Ministry of Finance, Maputo.

### CENTRAL BANK RESERVES (US $ million at 31 December)

|  | 1989 | 1990 | 1991 |
|---|---|---|---|
| IMF special drawing rights | 0.03 | 0.03 | 0.04 |
| Reserve position in IMF | 0.01 | 0.01 | 0.01 |
| Foreign exchange | 162.34 | 207.43 | 217.53 |
| **Total** | 162.38 | 207.48 | 217.58 |

Source: IMF, *International Financial Statistics*.

### MONEY SUPPLY ('000 million meticais at 31 December)

|  | 1989 | 1990 | 1991 |
|---|---|---|---|
| Currency outside banks | 94.1 | 147.1 | 189.6 |
| Demand deposits at commercial banks | 129.3 | 178.2 | 224.1 |

Source: IMF, *International Financial Statistics*.

### COST OF LIVING
(Consumer Price Index for Maputo; base: 1990=100)

|  | 1991 | 1992 | 1993 |
|---|---|---|---|
| All items | 132.9 | 193.4 | 275.0 |

Source: IMF, *International Financial Statistics*.

## NATIONAL ACCOUNTS

**National Income and Product** ('000 million meticais at current prices)

|  | 1984 | 1985 | 1986 |
|---|---|---|---|
| Domestic factor incomes* | 95.7 | 137.2 | 146.3 |
| Consumption of fixed capital | 4.0 | 4.0 | 4.0 |
| **Gross domestic product (GDP) at factor cost** | 99.7 | 141.2 | 150.3 |
| Indirect taxes | 9.8 | 6.9 | 8.7 |
| *Less* Subsidies | 0.4 | 0.5 | 0.5 |
| **GDP in purchasers' values** | 109.1 | 147.6 | 158.4 |
| Net factor income from abroad | 0.3 | 0.2 | 0.6 |
| **Gross national product** | 109.4 | 147.8 | 159.0 |
| *Less* Consumption of fixed capital | 4.0 | 4.0 | 4.0 |
| **National income in market prices** | 105.4 | 143.8 | 155.0 |

* Compensation of employees and the operating surplus of enterprises.

Source: UN, *National Accounts Statistics*.

**Expenditure on the Gross Domestic Product**
('000 million meticais at current prices)

|  | 1991 | 1992 | 1993 |
|---|---|---|---|
| Government final consumption expenditure | 378 | 598 | 919 |
| Private final consumption expenditure | 1,420 | 2,131 | 3,834 |
| Gross capital formation | 1,250 | 2,016 | 3,759 |
| **Total domestic expenditure** | 3,048 | 4,745 | 8,512 |
| Exports of goods and services | 444 | 739 | 1,162 |
| *Less* Imports of goods and services | 1,436 | 2,359 | 4,031 |
| **GDP in purchasers' values** | 2,056 | 3,126 | 5,643 |

Source: IMF, *International Financial Statistics*.

**Gross Domestic Product by Economic Activity**
(estimates, million meticais at current prices)

|  | 1989 | 1990 | 1991 |
|---|---|---|---|
| Agriculture, hunting, forestry and fishing | 555,480 | 668,150 | 801,780 |
| Mining and quarrying | 2,610 | 3,600 | 4,320 |
| Manufacturing | 305,240 | 420,700 | 504,840 |
| Electricity, gas and water | 54,360 | 74,920 | 89,910 |
| Construction | 86,030 | 225,000 | 270,000 |
| Trade, restaurants and hotels | 60,920 | 83,970 | 100,760 |
| Transport and communications | 124,350 | 162,400 | 194,880 |
| Finance, insurance, real estate, etc. | 4,460 | 6,140 | 7,370 |
| Public administration and defence | 37,730 | 52,000 | 62,410 |
| Other services | 7,120 | 9,810 | 11,770 |
| **GDP at factor cost** | 1,238,300 | 1,706,700 | 2,048,040 |
| Indirect taxes, *less* subsidies | 106,570 | 146,540 | 175,840 |
| **GDP in purchasers' values** | 1,344,870 | 1,853,240 | 2,223,880 |

Source: UN Economic Commission for Africa, *African Statistical Yearbook*.

MOZAMBIQUE

## BALANCE OF PAYMENTS (US $ million)

|  | 1990 | 1991 | 1992 |
|---|---|---|---|
| Merchandise exports f.o.b. | 126 | 162 | 139 |
| Merchandise imports f.o.b. | −790 | −809 | −799 |
| **Trade balance** | **−663** | **−647** | **−659** |
| Exports of services | 103 | 147 | 165 |
| Imports of services | −206 | −237 | −246 |
| Other income received | 70 | 56 | 58 |
| Other income paid | −168 | −166 | −198 |
| Official unrequited transfers (net) | 448 | 502 | 499 |
| **Current balance** | **−415** | **−344** | **−381** |
| Direct investment (net) | 9 | 23 | 25 |
| Other capital (net) | −93 | −210 | −148 |
| Net errors and omissions | 66 | −4 | 32 |
| **Overall balance** | **−433** | **−536** | **−472** |

Source: IMF, *International Financial Statistics*.

# External Trade

## PRINCIPAL COMMODITIES (US $'000)

| Imports c.i.f. | 1988 | 1989 | 1990 |
|---|---|---|---|
| Consumer goods: | | | |
| Foodstuffs | 176,298 | 173,629 | 253,924 |
| Other | 104,597 | 155,927 | 83,888 |
| Primary materials: | | | |
| Chemicals | 48,547 | 52,185 | 31,953 |
| Metals | 35,465 | 42,472 | 29,808 |
| Crude petroleum and petroleum products | 61,104 | 71,523 | 95,860 |
| Other | 70,893 | 81,693 | 97,723 |
| Machinery and spare parts | 101,183 | 87,509 | 83,628 |
| Capital goods | 137,513 | 142,736 | 200,736 |
| **Total** | **735,600** | **807,674** | **877,520** |

**Total imports** (US $ million): 899 in 1991; 855 in 1992; 955 in 1993 (Source: UN, *Monthly Bulletin of Statistics*).

| Exports f.o.b. | 1991 | 1992 | 1993 |
|---|---|---|---|
| Cashew nuts | 16,033 | 17,592 | 8,151 |
| Shrimps, prawns, etc. | 60,779 | 64,550 | 68,793 |
| Raw cotton | 8,777 | 10,805 | 11,055 |
| Sugar | 9,765 | 6,655 | — |
| Copra | 4,657 | 4,188 | 2,500 |
| Lobsters | 2,814 | 4,885 | 3,188 |
| **Total** (incl. others) | **162,350** | **139,304** | **131,899** |

## PRINCIPAL TRADING PARTNERS (US $'000)

| Imports c.i.f. | 1987 | 1988 | 1989 |
|---|---|---|---|
| Belgium-Luxembourg | 4,824 | 9,668 | 8,148 |
| Canada | 4,917 | 24,027 | 11,504 |
| France | 35,558 | 29,200 | 32,789 |
| German Democratic Republic | 8,677 | 17,093 | 29,140 |
| Germany, Federal Republic | 31,547 | 31,831 | 30,594 |
| Italy | 85,023 | 68,092 | 48,355 |
| Japan | 34,581 | 24,011 | 45,309 |
| Portugal | 31,049 | 42,627 | 55,130 |
| Netherlands | 27,398 | 29,313 | 16,475 |
| South Africa | 85,809 | 110,179 | 187,652 |
| Sweden | 27,653 | 28,875 | 24,406 |
| Switzerland | 9,685 | 5,024 | 4,590 |
| USSR | 54,896 | 73,228 | 78,842 |
| United Kingdom | 29,228 | 39,750 | 38,533 |
| USA | 62,888 | 56,222 | 57,279 |
| Zimbabwe | 15,366 | 31,337 | 22,858 |
| **Total** (incl. others) | **642,000** | **735,600** | **807,676** |

| Exports f.o.b. | 1990 | 1991 | 1992 |
|---|---|---|---|
| German Democratic Republic | 1,229 | 1,732 | 949 |
| Germany, Federal Republic | 1,407* | | |
| Japan | 13,092 | 19,635 | 13,163 |
| Portugal | 7,061 | 9,745 | 18,221 |
| South Africa | 8,868 | 14,148 | 23,033 |
| Spain | 22,634 | 31,238 | 41,028 |
| USSR (former) | 2,635 | 4,580 | 296† |
| United Kingdom | 5,067 | 743 | 681 |
| USA | 14,553 | 21,409 | 18,610 |
| Zimbabwe | 273 | 5,283 | 8,270 |
| **Total** (incl. others) | **126,427** | **162,350** | **139,305** |

* Figure includes trade with the former German Democratic Republic from October 1990.
† Exports to Russia only.

# Transport

## RAILWAYS (traffic)

|  | 1984 | 1985 | 1986 |
|---|---|---|---|
| Freight carried ('000 metric tons) | 3,698.6 | 2,899.5 | 2,949.3 |
| Freight ton-km (million) | 536.3 | 289.6 | 303.3 |
| Passengers carried ('000) | 5,296.0 | 6,723.0 | 6,619.0 |
| Passenger-km (million) | 284.1 | 225.4 | 263.6 |

**1987:** Passenger-km 105m.; Freight ton-km 353m.
**1988:** Passenger-km 75m.; Freight ton-km 306m.
Source: UN, *Statistical Yearbook*.
**1989:** Passenger-km 73.5m.; Freight ton-km 402.2m.
**1990:** Passenger-km 78.9m.; Freight ton-km 421.4m.
**1991:** Passenger-km 79.0m.; Freight ton-km 306.7m.
**1992:** Passenger-km 26.0m.; Freight ton-km 616.0m.

## ROAD TRAFFIC (motor vehicles in use at 31 December)

|  | 1987 | 1988 |
|---|---|---|
| Passenger cars | 23,810 | 24,700 |
| Buses and coaches | 1,641 | 1,380 |
| Goods vehicles | 10,250 | 11,300 |
| Vans | 28,370 | 29,500 |

Source: International Road Federation, *World Road Statistics*.

## SHIPPING

**Merchant Fleet** ('000 gross registered tons at 30 June)

|  | 1990 | 1991 | 1992 |
|---|---|---|---|
| Total displacement | 40 | 37 | 39 |

Source: UN, *Statistical Yearbook*.

**International Sea-borne Shipping** (freight traffic, '000 metric tons)

|  | 1989 | 1990 | 1991* |
|---|---|---|---|
| Goods loaded | 2,430 | 2,578 | 2,800 |
| Goods unloaded | 3,254 | 3,379 | 3,400 |

* Estimates.
Sources: UN, *Monthly Bulletin of Statistics*; UN Economic Commission for Africa, *African Statistical Yearbook*.

## CIVIL AVIATION (traffic on scheduled services)

|  | 1990 | 1991 | 1992 |
|---|---|---|---|
| Kilometres flown (million) | 5 | 5 | 5 |
| Passengers carried ('000) | 280 | 283 | 225 |
| Passenger-km (million) | 502 | 465 | 387 |
| Total ton-km (million) | 56 | 52 | 44 |

Source: UN, *Statistical Yearbook*.

MOZAMBIQUE
Statistical Survey, Directory

## Communications Media

|  | 1990 | 1991 | 1992 |
|---|---|---|---|
| Radio receivers ('000 in use) | 650 | 680 | 700 |
| Television receivers ('000 in use) | 40 | 42 | 44 |
| Telephones ('000 main lines in use) | 47 | 53 | n.a. |
| Daily newspapers: |  |  |  |
| Number | 2 | n.a. | 2 |
| Average circulation ('000) | 81 | n.a. | 81 |

**Non-daily newspapers** (1988): 2 (estimated average circulation 85,000).
**Periodicals** (1988): 3 (average circulation 1,828,000).
**Book Production** (1984): 66 titles (including 37 pamphlets); 3,490,000 copies (including 360,000 pamphlets).
Source: mainly UNESCO, *Statistical Yearbook*.

## Education

(1992, unless otherwise indicated)

|  | Institutions | Teachers | Males | Females | Total |
|---|---|---|---|---|---|
| Pre-primary* | n.a. | n.a. | 24,278 | 20,822 | 45,100 |
| Primary | 3,384 | 22,474 | 685,314 | 514,162 | 1,199,476 |
| Secondary: |  |  |  |  |  |
| General | n.a. | 3,614 | 88,120 | 57,278 | 145,398 |
| Vocational | n.a. | 846† | 7,299 | 2,485 | 9,784 |
| Teacher training | n.a. | 280 | 2,589 | 1,431 | 4,020 |
| Higher | 2 | 577 | 2,584 | 898 | 3,482 |

* 1986 figures; data refer to initiation classes.
† 1991 figure.
Source: mainly UNESCO, *Statistical Yearbook*.

# Directory

## The Constitution

The Constitution came into force on 30 November 1990, replacing the previous version, introduced at independence on 25 June 1975 and revised in 1978. It is summarized below.

### GENERAL PRINCIPLES

The Republic of Mozambique is an independent, sovereign, unitary and democratic state of social justice. Sovereignty resides in the people, who exercise it according to the forms laid down in the Constitution. The fundamental objectives of the Republic include:

The defence of independence and sovereignty;

the defence and promotion of human rights and of the equality of citizens before the law; and

the strengthening of democracy, of freedom and of social and individual stability.

### POLITICAL PARTICIPATION

The people exercise power through universal, direct, equal, secret, personal and periodic suffrage to elect their representatives, by referenda and through permanent democratic participation. Political parties are prohibited from advocating or resorting to violence.

### FUNDAMENTAL RIGHTS AND DUTIES OF CITIZENS

All citizens enjoy the same rights and are subject to the same duties, irrespective of colour, race, sex, ethnic origin, place of birth, religion, level of education, social position or occupation. In realizing the objectives of the Constitution, all citizens enjoy freedom of opinion, assembly and association. All citizens over 18 years of age are entitled to vote and be elected. Active participation in the defence of the country is the duty of every citizen. Individual freedoms are guaranteed by the State, including freedom of expression, of the press, of assembly, of association and of religion. The State guarantees accused persons the right to a legal defence. No Court or Tribunal has the power to impose a sentence of death upon any person.

### STATE ORGANS

Public elective officers are chosen by elections through universal, direct, secret, personal and periodic vote. Legally-recognized political parties may participate in elections.

### THE PRESIDENT

The President is the Head of State and of the Government, and Commander-in-Chief of the armed forces. The President is elected by direct, equal, secret and personal universal suffrage on a majority vote, and must be proposed by at least 10,000 voters, of whom at least 200 must reside in each province. The term of office is five years. A candidate may be re-elected on only two consecutive occasions, or again after an interval of five years between terms.

### THE ASSEMBLY OF THE REPUBLIC

Legislative power is vested in the Assembly of the Republic. The Assembly is elected by universal direct adult suffrage on a secret ballot, and is composed of 250 Deputies. The Assembly is elected for a maximum term of five years, but may be dissolved by the President before the expiry of its term. The Assembly holds two ordinary sessions each year.

### THE COUNCIL OF MINISTERS

The Council of Ministers is the Government of the Republic. The Prime Minister assists and advises the President in the leadership of the Government and presents the Government's programme, budget and policies to the Assembly, assisted by other ministers.

### LOCAL STATE ORGANS

The Republic is administered in provinces, districts, cities and localities. The highest state organ in a province is the provincial government, presided over by a governor, who is answerable to the central Government. There shall be assemblies at each administrative level.

### THE JUDICIARY

Judicial functions shall be exercised through the Supreme Court and other courts provided for in the law on the judiciary, which also subordinates them to the Assembly of the Republic. Courts must safeguard the principles of the Constitution and defend the rights and legitimate interests of citizens. Judges are independent, subject only to the law.

## The Government

### HEAD OF STATE

**President of the Republic and Commander-in-Chief of the Armed Forces:** JOAQUIM ALBERTO CHISSANO (took office 6 November 1986; elected President 27–29 October 1994).

### COUNCIL OF MINISTERS
(June 1995)

**Prime Minister:** Dr PASCOAL MANUEL MOCUMBI.
**Minister for Foreign Affairs and Co-operation:** Dr LEONARD SANTOS SIMÃO.
**Minister of National Defence:** AGUIAR JONASSANE REGINALDO REAL MAZULA.
**Minister of the Interior:** Col MANUEL JOSÉ ANTÓNIO MUCANANDA.
**Minister of State Administration:** ALFREDO GAMITO.
**Minister of Economic and Social Affairs:** Dr ENEAS DA CONCEIÇÃO COMICHE.
**Minister of Justice:** JOSÉ IBRAIMO ABUDO.
**Minister of Planning and Finance:** TOMÁS AUGUSTO SALOMÃO.
**Minister of Education:** ARNALDO VALENTE NHAVOTO.
**Minister of Parliamentary Affairs:** FRANCISCO CAETANO J. MADEIRA.

# MOZAMBIQUE

**Minister of Health:** AURELIO ARMANDO ZILHÃO.
**Minister of Mineral Resources and Energy:** JOHN WILLIAM KACHAMILA.
**Minister of Public Works and Housing:** ROBERTO COSTLEY WHITE.
**Minister of Environmental Co-ordination:** BERNARDO PEDRO FERRAZ.
**Minister of Culture, Youth and Sports:** JOSÉ MATEUS MUARIA KATUPHA.
**Minister of Labour:** GUILHERME LUIS MAVILA.
**Minister of Agriculture and Fisheries:** CARLOS AGOSTINHO DO ROSÁRIO.
**Minister of Industry, Commerce and Tourism:** OLDEMIRO J. BALOI.
**Minister of Transport and Communications:** PAULO MUXANGA.
**Minister of Social Action Co-ordination:** ALCINDA A. DE ABREU.
**Minister in the President's Office, with responsibility for Defence and Security Affairs:** ARMIRINHO DA CRUZ MARCOS MANHAZE.

## MINISTRIES

**Office of the President:** Avda Julius Nyerere, Maputo; tel. 491121; telex 6243.
**Ministry of Agriculture and Fisheries:** Praça dos Heróis Moçambicanos, CP 1406, Maputo; tel. 460010; telex 6195; fax 460145.
**Ministry of Culture, Youth and Sports:** Avda Patrice Lumumba 1217, CP 1742, Maputo; tel. 420068; telex 6621.
**Ministry of Economic and Social Affairs:** Maputo.
**Ministry of Education:** Avda 24 de Julho 167, Maputo; tel. 492006; telex 6148; fax 492196.
**Ministry of Environmental Co-ordination:** Maputo.
**Ministry of Foreign Affairs and Co-operation:** Avda Julius Nyerere 4, Maputo; tel. 490218; telex 6418.
**Ministry of Health:** Avdas Eduardo Mondlane e Salvador Allende, CP 264, Maputo; tel. 430814; telex 6239.
**Ministry of Industry, Commerce and Tourism:** Avda 25 de Setembro 1218, Maputo; tel. 431029; telex 6235.
**Ministry of Information:** Avda Francisco Orlando Magumbwe 780, Maputo; tel. 491087; telex 6487.
**Ministry of the Interior:** Avda Olof Palme 46/48, Maputo; tel. 420130; telex 6487.
**Ministry of Justice:** Avda Julius Nyerere 33, Maputo; tel. 490940; telex 6594; fax 492106.
**Ministry of Labour:** Avda 24 de Julho 2351-2365, CP 281, Maputo; tel. 427051; telex 6392.
**Ministry of Mineral Resources and Energy:** Avda Fernão de Magalhães 34, Maputo; tel. 429615.
**Ministry of National Defence:** Avda Mártires de Mueda, Maputo; tel. 492081; telex 6331.
**Ministry of Parliamentary Affairs:** Maputo.
**Ministry of Planning and Finance:** Praça da Marinha Popular, CP 272, Maputo; tel. 425071; telex 6569.
**Ministry of Public Works and Housing:** Maputo.
**Ministry of Social Action Co-ordination:** Maputo.
**Ministry of State Administration:** Maputo.
**Ministry of Transport and Communications:** Avda Mártires de Inhaminga 306, Maputo; tel. 430151; telex 6466.

### PROVINCIAL GOVERNORS

**Cabo Delgado Province:** JORGE MUANAHUMO.
**Gaza Province:** EUGÉNIO NUMAIO.
**Inhambane Province:** FRANCISCO JOÃO PATEGUANA.
**Manica Province:** ARTUR USSENE CANANA.
**Maputo Province:** RAIMUNDO MANUEL BILA.
**Nampula Province:** ROSÁRIO MUALEIA.
**Niassa Province:** AIRES BONIFACIO.
**Sofala Province:** ORLANDO CANDUA.
**Tete Province:** VIRGILIO FERRÃO.
**Zambézia Province:** FELISBERTO PAULINO TOMÁS.
**City of Maputo:** JOÃO BAPTISTA COSMÉ.

# President and Legislature

## PRESIDENT

Presidential Election, 27–29 October 1994

|  | Votes | % of votes |
|---|---|---|
| JOAQUIM ALBERTO CHISSANO (Frelimo) | 2,633,740 | 53.30 |
| AFONSO MACHACO MARCETA DHLAKAMA (Renamo) | 1,666,965 | 33.73 |
| WEHIA MONAKACHO RIPUA (Pademo) | 141,905 | 2.87 |
| CARLOS ALEXANDRE DOS REIS (Unamo) | 120,708 | 2.44 |
| Dr MÁXIMO DIOGO JOSÉ DIAS (Monamo—PMSD) | 115,442 | 2.34 |
| VASCO CAMPIRA MAMBOYA ALFAZEMA (Pacode) | 58,848 | 1.19 |
| YAQUB NEVES SALOMÃO SIBINDY (Pimo) | 51,070 | 1.03 |
| Dr DOMINGOS ANTÓNIO MASCARENHAS AROUCA (Fumo—PCD) | 37,767 | 0.76 |
| CARLOS JOSÉ MARIA JEQUE (Independent) | 34,588 | 0.70 |
| CASIMIRO MIGUEL NHAMITHAMBO (Sol) | 32,036 | 0.65 |
| MARIO CARLOS MACHEL (Independent) | 24,238 | 0.49 |
| Dr PADIMBE MAHOSE KAMATI ANDREA (PPPM) | 24,208 | 0.49 |
| Total* | 4,941,515 | 100.00 |

* Excluding 312,143 blank votes and 147,282 spoilt votes.

## ASSEMBLÉIA DA REPÚBLICA

**Chairman:** EDUARDO MULEMBUE.

General Election, 27–29 October 1994

|  | Votes | % of votes | Seats |
|---|---|---|---|
| Frente de Libertação de Moçambique (Frelimo) | 2,115,793 | 44.33 | 129 |
| Resistência Nacional Moçambicana (Renamo) | 1,803,506 | 37.78 | 112 |
| União Democrática (UD) | 245,793 | 5.15 | 9 |
| Aliança Patriótica (AP) | 93,051 | 1.95 | — |
| Partido Social, Liberal e Democrático (Sol) | 79,622 | 1.67 | — |
| Frente Unida de Moçambique—Partido de Convergência Democrática (Fumo—PCD) | 66,527 | 1.39 | — |
| Partido de Convenção Nacional (PCN) | 60,635 | 1.27 | — |
| Partido Independente de Moçambique (Pimo) | 58,590 | 1.23 | — |
| Partido de Congresso Democrático (Pacode) | 52,446 | 1.10 | — |
| Partido de Progresso Popular de Moçambique (PPPM) | 50,793 | 1.06 | — |
| Partido de Renovação Democrático (PRD) | 48,030 | 1.01 | — |
| Partido Democrático de Moçambique (Pademo) | 36,689 | 0.77 | — |
| União Nacional Moçambicana (Unamo) | 34,809 | 0.73 | — |
| Partido do Trabalho (PT) | 26,961 | 0.56 | — |
| Total* | 4,773,245 | 100.00 | 250 |

* Excluding 457,382 blank votes and 173,592 spoilt votes.

# Political Organizations

**Aliança Democrática de Moçambique (ADM):** f. 1994; Co-ordinator JOSÉ PEREIRA BRANQUINHO.

**Aliança Patriótica (AP):** f. 1994; electoral alliance comprising:
  **Movimento Nacionalista Moçambicana—Partido Moçambicano da Social Democracia (Monamo—PMSD):** Sec.-Gen. Dr MÁXIMO DIOGO JOSÉ DIAS.
  **Frente de Ação Patriótica (FAP):** f. 1991; Pres. JOSÉ CARLOS PALAÇO; Sec.-Gen. RAUL DA CONCEIÇÃO.

**Confederação Democrática de Moçambique (Codemo):** f. 1991; Leader DOMINGOS CARDOSO.

**Congresso Independente de Moçambique (Coinmo):** Pres. VÍTOR MARCOS SAENE; Sec.-Gen. HILDA RABECA TSININE.

**Frente de Libertação de Moçambique (Frelimo):** Rua Pereiro do Lago, Maputo; f. 1962 by the merger of three nationalist parties: the União Democrática Nacional de Moçambique, the União Nacionalista Africana de Moçambique and the União Africana de Moçambique Independente; reorg. 1977 as a 'Marxist-Leninist vanguard party'; in July 1989 abandoned its exclusive Marxist-

Leninist orientation; Chair. JOAQUIM ALBERTO CHISSANO; Sec.-Gen. FELICIANO SALOMÃO GUNDANA.

**Frente Unida de Moçambique—Partido de Convergência Democrática (Fumo—PCD):** Pres. Dr DOMINGOS ANTÓNIO MASCARENHAS AROUCA.

**Frente Unida de Salvação (FUS):** f. 1994; alliance comprising:

**Partido do Congresso Democrático (Pacode):** Leader VASCO CAMPIRA MAMBOYA ALFAZEMA.

**Partido Independente de Moçambique (Pimo):** f. 1993; Pres. YAQUB NEVES SALOMÃO SIBINDY.

**Partido de Progresso do Povo Moçambicano (PPPM):** f. 1991; obtained legal status 1992; Pres. Dr PADIMBE MAHOSE KAMATI ANDREA; Sec.-Gen. CHE ABDALA.

**Partido Renovador Democrático (PRD):** obtained legal status 1994; Pres. MANECA DANIEL.

**Partido do Trabalho (PT):** f. 1993; breakaway faction of PPPM; Pres. MIGUEL MABOTE.

**Partido Social, Liberal e Democrático (Sol):** breakaway faction of Palmo; Leader CASIMIRO MIGUEL NHAMITHAMBO.

**União Nacional Moçambicana (Unamo):** f. 1987; breakaway faction of Renamo; social democratic; obtained legal status 1992; Pres. CARLOS ALEXANDRE DOS REIS; Sec.-Gen. FLORENCIA JOÃO DA SILVA.

**Partido Agrário de Moçambique (PAM):** f. 1991.

**Partido Comunista de Moçambique (Pacomo):** f. 1995.

**Partido de Convenção Nacional (PCN):** obtained legal status Dec. 1992; Chair. LUTERO CHIMBIRIMBIRI SIMANGO; Sec.-Gen. Dr GABRIEL MABUNDA.

**Partido Democrático de Libertação de Moçambique (Padelimo):** based in Kenya; Pres. JOAQUIM JOSÉ NIOTA.

**Partido Democrático de Moçambique (Pademo):** f. 1991; obtained legal status 1993; Co-ordinator WEHIA MONAKACHO RIPUA.

**Partido Internacionalista Democrático de Moçambique (Pidemo):** f. 1993; Leader JOÃO KAMACHO.

**Partido Patriótico Independente de Moçambique:** f. 1995; breakaway faction of Pimo; Leader MUSSAGY ABDUL MUSSAGY.

**Partido Progressivo e Liberal Federalista das Comunidades Religiosas de Moçambique (PPLFCRM):** f. 1992; Pres. NEVES SERRANO.

**Partido Revolucionário do Povo Socialista Unido de Moçambique (Prepsumo):** f. 1992.

**Partido Social Democrático (PSD):** Leader CARLOS MACHEL.

**Regedores e Camponeses de Moçambique (Recamo):** f. by ARONE SIJAMO.

**Resistência Nacional Moçambicana (Renamo):** also known as Movimento Nacional da Resistência de Moçambique (MNR); f. 1976; former guerrilla group, in conflict with the Government between 1976 and the signing of the General Peace Agreement in October 1992; registered as a political party August 1994; operates 'Voz da Renamo' radio station; Pres. and C-in-C AFONSO MACACHO MARCETA DHLAKAMA; Sec.-Gen. FRANCISCO XAVIER MARCELINO.

**União Democrática (UD):** f. 1994; Gen. Sec. ANTÓNIO PALANGE; coalition comprising:

**Partido Liberal e Democrático de Moçambique (Palmo):** obtained legal status 1993; Chair. MARTINS BILAL; Pres. ANTÓNIO PALANGE.

**Partido Nacional Democrático (Panade):** obtained legal status 1993; Leader JOSÉ CHICUARRA MASSINGA.

**Partido Nacional de Moçambique (Panamo):** Pres. MARCOS JUMA.

**União Democrática de Moçambique (Udemo):** f. 1987 as the mil. wing of Unamo, from which it broke away in 1991; adopted present name in April 1992; Leader GIMO PHIRI.

In 1994 the government confirmed reports that the following armed separatist group was operating in Zambézia province.

**Rombézia:** aims to establish separate state in northern Mozambique between Rovuma and Zambezi rivers; reported to receive support from Malawi-based Portuguese; Leader MANUEL ROCHA.

## Diplomatic Representation

### EMBASSIES IN MOZAMBIQUE

**Algeria:** CP 1709, Maputo; tel. 492070; telex 6554; fax 490582; Ambassador: BRAHIM TAÏBI.

**Angola:** Maputo; Ambassador: PAULO CONDENÇA DE CARVALHO.

**Belgium:** CP 1500, Maputo; tel. 490077; telex 6511; Ambassador: MICHEL VANTROYEN.

**Brazil:** Avda Kenneth Kaunda 296, CP 1167, Maputo; tel. 492388; fax 490986; Ambassador: LUCIANO OZORIO ROSA.

**Bulgaria:** CP 4689, Maputo; tel. 491471; telex 6324; Ambassador: IVAN MARINOV SOKOLARSKI.

**China, People's Republic:** CP 4668, Maputo; tel. 491560; Ambassador: MI SHIHENG.

**Congo:** Avda Kenneth Kaunda 783, CP 4743, Maputo; tel. 490142; telex 6207; Ambassador: EMILIENNE BOTOKA.

**Cuba:** CP 387, Maputo; tel. 491905; telex 6359; Ambassador: JOSÉ ESPINOSA.

**Czech Republic:** CP 1463, Maputo; tel. 491484; telex 6216.

**Denmark:** Avda 24 de Julho 1500, CP 4588, Maputo; tel. 420172; telex 6164; fax 420557; Chargé d'affaires: STIG BARLYNG.

**Egypt:** CP 4662, Maputo; tel. 491118; telex 6417; Ambassador: MOHAMED HINDAM.

**France:** Avda Julius Nyerere 2361, CP 4781, Maputo; tel. 490444; telex 6307; Ambassador: ROBERT PUISSANT.

**Germany:** Rua de Mapulangwene 506, CP 1595; Maputo; tel. 492714; telex 6489; fax 494888; Ambassador: HELMUT RAU.

**Greece:** CP 714, Maputo; tel. 490481; telex 6299; fax 491397; Ambassador: ALEXANDROS SANDIS.

**Guinea:** CP 1125, Maputo; tel. 491478; telex 6527; Ambassador: (vacant).

**Holy See:** Avda Julius Nyerere 882, CP 2738, Maputo; tel. 491144; fax 492217; Apostolic Delegate: Most Rev. PETER STEPHAN ZURBRIGGEN, Titular Archbishop of Glastonia (Glastonbury).

**Hungary:** Avda Kenneth Kaunda 714, CP 1245, Maputo; tel. 492953; telex 6431; fax 490880; Ambassador: MIHÁLY TERJÉK.

**India:** Avda Kenneth Kaunda 167, Maputo; tel. 490584; telex 6452; fax 492364; Ambassador: P. S. RANDHAWA.

**Iran:** Avda Mártires da Machava 1630, Maputo; tel. 490700; telex 6159; fax 492005; Chargé d'affaires: MOHAMMAD ALI SADEGHI.

**Italy:** Avda Kenneth Kaunda 387, CP 976, Maputo; tel. 491605; telex 6442; Ambassador: MANFREDO INCISCA DI CAMERANA.

**Korea, Democratic People's Republic:** CP 4694, Maputo; tel. 491482; Ambassador: RYANG KI RAK.

**Lesotho:** CP 1477, Maputo; tel. 492473; telex 6439; Ambassador: B. NTS'OHI.

**Libya:** CP 4434, Maputo; tel. 490662; telex 6475; Ambassador: MUHAMMAD AHMAD AL-AMARY.

**Malawi:** CP 4148, Maputo; tel. 491468; telex 6300; Ambassador: Rev. E. CHINKWITA-PHIRI.

**Netherlands:** CP 1163, Maputo; tel. 490031; telex 6178; fax 490429; Ambassador: R. A. VORNIS.

**Nicaragua:** Maputo; tel. 490810; telex 6245; Ambassador: CARLOS JOSÉ GARCÍA CASTILLO.

**Nigeria:** CP 4693, Maputo; tel. 490105; telex 6414; Ambassador: S. O. OGUNDELE.

**Pakistan:** CP 4745, Maputo; tel. 491265; Ambassador: MOHAMMAD NASSER KHAN.

**Poland:** Rua D. João IV 22, Maputo; tel. 490284; Ambassador: MIROSŁAW DACKIEWICZ.

**Portugal:** Avda Julius Nyerere 730, CP 4696, Maputo; tel. 490431; telex 1172; fax 491127; Ambassador: RUI GONÇALO CHAVES DE BRITO E CUNHA.

**Romania:** CP 4648, Maputo; tel. 492999; telex 6397; Chargé d'affaires a.i.: TOMAS BALASOIU.

**Russia:** Avda Agostinho Neto 1103, CP 4666, Maputo; tel. 420091; telex 6635; Ambassador: VLADIMIR KORNEYEV.

**Somalia:** CP 4715, Maputo; telex 6354; Ambassador: YUSUF HASSAN IBRAHIM.

**South Africa:** Avda Julius Nyerere 745, CP 1120, Maputo; tel. 493030; telex 6376; fax 493029; Ambassador: M. ZITHA.

**Spain:** Rua Damião de Gois 347, CP 1331, Maputo; tel. 492025; telex 6579; fax 492055; Ambassador: FRANCISCO J. VIQUEIRA.

**Swaziland:** CP 4711, Maputo; tel. 492117; telex 6353; Ambassador: ALPHABET NKAMBULE.

**Sweden:** CP 338, Maputo; tel. 490091; telex 6272; fax 490056; Ambassador: LARS-OLOF EDSTRÖM.

**Switzerland:** CP 135, Maputo; tel. 492432; telex 6233; Chargé d'affaires: JEAN PIERRE BALLAMAR.

**United Kingdom:** Avda Vladimir I. Lénine 310, CP 55, Maputo; tel. 420111; telex 6265; fax 421666; Ambassador: RICHARD EDIS.

**USA:** CP 783, Maputo; tel. 492797; Ambassador: DENNIS C. JETT.

**Zaire:** CP 2407, Maputo; tel. 492354; telex 6316; Ambassador: W'EBER M.-B. ANGELO.

# MOZAMBIQUE

**Zambia:** CP 4655, Maputo; tel. 492452; telex 6415; fax 491893; Ambassador: Maj.-Gen. B. CHISUTA.

**Zimbabwe:** CP 743, Maputo; tel. 490404; telex 6542; Ambassador: JOHN MAYOWE.

## Judicial System

The Constitution of November 1990 provides for a Supreme Court and other judicial courts, an Administrative Court, courts-martial, customs courts, maritime courts and labour courts. The Supreme Court consists of professional judges, appointed by the President of the Republic, and judges elected by the Assembly of the Republic. It acts in sections, as a trial court of primary and appellate jurisdiction, and in plenary session, as a court of final appeal. The Administrative Court controls the legality of administrative acts and supervises public expenditure.

**President of the Supreme Court:** MARIO MANGAZE.

## Religion

Many inhabitants follow traditional beliefs, but there are an estimated 5m. Christians and 4m. Muslims. There is a small Hindu community.

### CHRISTIANITY

In 1975 educational and medical facilities that had hitherto been administered by churches were acquired by the State. In June 1988 the Government announced that these facilities were to be returned.

**Conselho Cristão de Moçambique** (Christian Council of Mozambique): Avda Ahmed Sekou Touré 1822, Maputo; tel. 422836; telex 6119; f. 1948; 18 mems; Pres. Rev. LUÍS WANELA; Gen. Sec. Rev. FILIPE SIQUE MBANZE.

#### The Roman Catholic Church

Mozambique comprises three archdioceses and nine dioceses. At 31 December 1993 adherents represented some 14.4% of the total population.

**Bishops' Conference:** Conferência Episcopal de Moçambique, Secretariado Geral, CP 286, Maputo; tel. 490766; telex 6101; f. 1982; Pres. Rt Rev. FRANCISCO JOÃO SILOTA, Bishop of Chimoio.

**Archbishop of Beira:** Most Rev. JAIME PEDRO GONÇALVES, Cúria Arquiepiscopal, CP 544, Beira; tel. 322313; fax 327639.

**Archbishop of Maputo:** Cardinal ALEXANDRE JOSÉ MARIA DOS SANTOS, Paço Arquiepiscopal, Avda Eduardo Mondlane 1448, CP 258, Maputo; tel. 426240; fax 421873.

**Archbishop of Nampula:** Most Rev. MANUEL VIEIRA PINTO, Paço Arquiepiscopal, CP 84, Nampula; tel. 213025; fax 214194.

#### The Anglican Communion

Anglicans in Mozambique are adherents of the Church of the Province of Southern Africa. There are two dioceses in Mozambique. The Metropolitan of the Province is the Archbishop of Cape Town, South Africa.

**Bishop of Lebombo:** Rt Rev. DINIS SALOMÃO SENGULANE, CP 120, Maputo; tel. 734364; telex 6119; fax 401093.

**Bishop of Niassa:** Rt Rev. PAULINO TOMÁS MANHIQUE, Missão Anglicana de Messumba, Metangula, CP 264, Lichinga, Niassa.

#### Other Churches

**Baptist Convention of Mozambique:** Avda Maguiguane 386, CP 852, Maputo; tel. 26852; Pres. Rev. BENTO BARTOLOMEU MATUSSE.

**Free Methodist Church:** Pres. Rev. LUÍS WANELA.

**Presbyterian Church of Mozambique:** Avda Ahmed Sekou Touré 1822, CP 21, Maputo; tel. 423139; telex 6119; fax 430332; 60,000 adherents; Pres. of Synodal Council Rev. AMOSSE BALTAZAR ZITA.

Other denominations active in Mozambique include the Church of Christ, the Church of the Nazarene, the Reformed Church in Mozambique, the United Congregational Church of Mozambique, the United Methodist Church of Mozambique, and the Wesleyan Methodist Church.

### ISLAM

**Islamic Congress of Mozambique:** represents Sunni Muslims; Chair. HASSANE MAKDÁ.

**Islamic Council of Mozambique:** Leader Sheikh ABOOBACAR ISMAEL MANGIRÁ.

## The Press

### DAILIES

**Diário de Moçambique:** Rua D. João de Mascarenhas, CP 81, Beira; tel. 322501; telex 7347; f. 1981; under state management since Sept. 1991; Dir EZEQUIEL AMBROSIO; Editor FARUCO SADIQUE; circ. 16,000.

**Imparcial:** news-sheet; sympathetic to Renamo.

**Mediafax:** Avda Mártires da Machava 1002, Maputo; tel. 490906; telex 6233; fax 490063; f. by co-operative of independent journalists Mediacoop; news-sheet by subscription only, distribution by fax; Editor CARLOS CARDOSO.

**Notícias:** Rua Joaquim Lapa, CP 327, Maputo; tel. 420119; telex 6453; f. 1926; morning; under state management since Sept. 1991; Dir-Gen. and Editor ALBINO MAGAIA; circ. 33,000.

### WEEKLIES

**Boletim da República:** Avda Vladimir Lénine, CP 275, Maputo; govt and official notices; publ. by Imprensa Nacional da Moçambique.

**Domingo:** Rua Joaquim Lapa, CP 327, Maputo; tel. 431026; telex 6453; f. 1981; Sun.; Dir BENJAMIN FADUCO; Editor JORGE MATINE; circ. 40,000.

**Savana:** c/o Mediacoop, Avda Amílcar Cabral 1049, CP 73, Maputo; tel. 430106; fax 430721; f. 1994; Dir KOK NAM; Editor SALOMÃO MOYOANA.

**Tempo:** Avda Ahmed Sekou Touré 1078, CP 2917, Maputo; tel. 26191; telex 6486; f. 1970; magazine; under state management since Sept. 1991; Dir SIMEÃO CACHAMBA; circ. 40,000.

### PERIODICALS

**Agricultura:** Instituto Nacional de Investigação Agronómica, CP 3658, Maputo; tel. 30091; f. 1982; quarterly; publ. by Centro de Documentação de Agricultura, Silvicultura, Pecuária e Pescas.

**Moçambique—Informação Estatística:** Comissão Nacional do Plano, CP 2051, Maputo; f. 1982; publ. by Centro de Documentação Económica.

**Novos Tempos:** monthly; Renamo-owned.

**Portos e Caminhos de Ferro:** CP 276, Maputo; English and Portuguese; ports and railways; quarterly.

**Revista Médica de Moçambique:** Instituto Nacional de Saúde, Ministério da Saúde e Faculdade de Medicina, Universidade Eduardo Mondlane, CP 264, Maputo; tel. 420368; telex 6239; fax 423726; f. 1982; 4 a year; medical journal; Editor RUI GAMA VAZ.

### NEWS AGENCIES

**Agência de Informação de Moçambique (AIM):** Rua da Radio Moçambique, CP 896, Maputo; tel. 430795; telex 6430; fax 421906; f. 1975; daily reports in Portuguese and English; monthly bulletin in English; Dir RICARDO MALATE.

#### Foreign Bureaux

**Agence France-Press (AFP):** c/o AIM, Rua da Radio Moçambique, CP 896, Maputo; tel. 430723; telex 6430; fax 421906; Correspondent PAUL FAUVET.

**Agência Lusa de Informação** (Portugal): Avda Ho Chi Min 111, Maputo; tel. 427591; fax 421690; Bureau Chief CARLOS LOBATO.

**Agenzia Nazionale Stampa Associata (ANSA)** (Italy): c/o AIM, Rua da Radio Moçambique, CP 896, Maputo; tel. 430723; telex 6252; fax 421906; Correspondent PAUL FAUVET.

**Allgemeiner Deutscher Nachrichtendienst (ADN)** (Germany): Rua Damião de Gois 177, CP 1144, Maputo; telex 6416; Correspondent MATTHIAS KUNERT.

**Inter Press Service (IPS) Italy:** c/o AIM, Rua da Radio Moçambique, CP 896, Maputo; tel. 430795; telex 6430; fax 429253; Correspondent GIL LAURENCIANO.

**Rossiyskoye Informatsionnoye Agentstvo—Novosti (RIA—Novosti)** (Russia): CP 4692, Maputo; tel. 491034; telex 6285; Correspondent YURI BOGOMOLOV.

**Xinhua (New China) News Agency** (People's Republic of China): Avda Mártires da Machava 1309, CP 4675, Maputo; tel. 741560; telex 6449; Correspondent YANG ZHIGANG.

**Reuters (UK)** is also represented in Mozambique.

## Publishers

**Editora Minerva Central:** Rua Consiglieri Pedroso 84, CP 212, Maputo; telex 6561; f. 1908; stationers and printers, educational, technical and medical textbooks; Man. Dir J. F. CARVALHO.

MOZAMBIQUE                                                                                                                                          *Directory*

**Empresa Moderna Lda:** Avda 25 de Setembro, CP 473, Maputo; tel. 424594; f. 1937; fiction, history, textbooks; Gen. Dir Fernando Henrique dos Santos António.

**Instituto Nacional do Livro e do Disco:** Avda 24 de Julho 1921, CP 4030, Maputo; tel. 34870; telex 6288; govt publishing and purchasing agency; Dir Arménio Correia.

### Government Publishing House
**Imprensa Nacional de Moçambique:** CP 275, Maputo.

## Radio and Television

According to UNESCO, there were an estimated 700,000 radio receivers and 44,000 television receivers in use in 1992.

### RADIO

**Rádio Moçambique:** CP 2000, Maputo; tel. 421814; telex 6712; fax 421816; f. 1975; programmes in Portuguese, English and vernacular languages; Chair. Manuel Fernando Veterano.

By January 1995 the Government had issued licences to 13 private radio stations. Of those, only three were broadcasting at that time.

**Voz da Renamo:** owned by former rebel movement Renamo; transmitters in Maputo and Gorongosa, Sofala province.

**Radio Miramar:** owned by Brazilian religious sect, the Universal Church of the Kingdom of God.

**Radio RTK:** owner Carlos Klint.

### TELEVISION

**Televisão Experimental (TVE):** Avda Julius Nyerere 930, CP 2675, Maputo; tel. 744788; telex 6346; f. 1981; transmissions on Wed., Thurs., Sat. and Sun. only; Dir António Júlio Botelho Moniz.

## Finance

(cap. = capital; res = reserves; dep. = deposits; m. = million; brs = branches; amounts in meticais)

### BANKING
#### Central Bank

**Banco de Moçambique:** Avda 25 de Setembro 1695, CP 423, Maputo; tel. 428151; telex 6251; fax 421233; f. 1975; bank of issue; cap. 50,000m. (1994); Gov. Adriano Afonso Maleiane.

#### Commercial Banks

**Banco Comercial de Moçambique:** Avda 25 de Setembro 1695, CP 865, Maputo; tel. 421711; telex 6358; fax 433247; f. 1992 to take over commercial banking activities of Central Bank; cap. 30,000m., dep. 1,054,445m. (1993); Pres. Augusto Joaquim Cândida; Exec. Dir and Gen. Man. Alberto da Costa Calú; 47 brs and agencies.

**Banco Popular de Desenvolvimento:** Avda 25 de Setembro 1184, CP 757, Maputo; tel. 428125; telex 6250; fax 423470; f. 1977; state-owned; cap. 16,000m., res 2,765m., dep. 441,203m. (1993); Chair. Hermenegildo Maria Cepêda Gamito; 193 brs and agencies.

**Banco Standard Totta de Moçambique, SARL:** Praça 25 de Junho 45, CP 2086, Maputo; tel. 423041; telex 6223; fax 421933; f. 1966; 20% Mozambican owned; cap. 9,375m., res 2,014,528m., dep. 199,502m. (1993); Man. Dir Dr António José Martins Galamba; 13 brs and agencies.

The relaxation of the banking laws in the early 1990s facilitated the establishment in Mozambique of branches of foreign banks including Banco de Fomento e Exterior SA and Banco Português do Atlântico. In 1994 the Government authorized a joint venture between Banco de Moçambique and the Portuguese Banco Comercial Português SA to create the Banco Internacional de Moçambique (BIM). The new bank was expected to concentrate on the management of foreign currency remittances from Mozambicans working in South Africa.

### DEVELOPMENT FUND

**Fundo de Desenvolvimento Agrícola e Rural:** CP 1406, Maputo; tel. 460349; fax 460157; f. 1987 to provide credit for small farmers and rural co-operatives; promotes agricultural and rural development; Sec. Eduardo Oliveira.

### INSURANCE

In December 1991 the Assembléia da República approved legislation terminating the state monopoly of insurance and reinsurance activities.

**Empresa Moçambicana de Seguros, EE (EMOSE):** Avda 25 de Setembro 1383, CP 1165, Maputo; tel. 422095; telex 6280; f. 1977 as state insurance monopoly; took over business of 24 fmr cos; cap. 150m.; Gen. Dir Venancio Mondlane.

## Trade and Industry

### CHAMBER OF COMMERCE

**Câmara de Comércio de Moçambique:** Rua Mateus Sansão Mutemba 452, CP 1836, Maputo; tel. 491970; telex 6498; Pres. Américo Magaia; Sec.-Gen. João Albasini.

### INVESTMENT ORGANIZATION

**Centro de Promoção de Investimentos (CPI):** POB 4635, Maputo; tel. 422456; telex 6876; fax 422459; encourages foreign investment and jt ventures with foreign firms; evaluates and negotiates investment proposals; Dir Augusto Sumburane.

### STATE FOREIGN-TRADING ENTERPRISES

**Citrinos de Manica, EE:** Avda 25 de Setembro, Chimoio, CP 15, Manica; tel. 42316; exports citrus and tropical fruit; Dir Osias M. Manjate.

**Citrinos de Maputo, EE:** Avda 25 de Setembro 1509, 6° Andar, CP 1659, Maputo; tel. 421857; telex 6538; exports citrus fruits; Dir Gen. Maurício Moty Carimo.

**Companhia de Desenvolvimento Mineiro (CDM):** Avda 24 de Julho 1895, 1°—2° Andares, CP 1152, Maputo; tel. 429170; telex 6413; fax 428921; exports marble, tantalite, asbestos anthophylite, beryl, bentonite, agates, precious and semi-precious stones; Dir Luís Jossene.

**Companhia Industrial de Cordoarias de Moçambique (CICOMO), SARL:** Avda Zedequias Manganhela 520, 4° Andar, CP 4113, Maputo; tel. 427272; telex 6347; sisal; Dir Carlos Cordeiro.

**Distribuidora de Materiais de Construção (DIMAC):** Avda Zedequias Manganhela 520, 11° Andar, CP 222, Maputo; tel. 423308; telex 6343; fax 422805; f. 1979; building materials; transfer to private ownership pending; Dir Rui Fernandes.

**Empresa de Comércio Externo de Equipamentos Industriais (INTERMÁQUINA):** Rua Consiglieri Pedroso 165, CP 808, Maputo; tel. 424056; telex 6543; industrial equipment and accessories; Dir Kong Lam.

**Empresa Distribuidora de Equipamento Eléctrico e Electrónico e Componentes (INTERELECTRA):** Avda Samora Machel 162, CP 1159, Maputo; tel. 427091; telex 6203; fax 420723; electrical equipment and components; Dir Francisco Paulo Cuche.

**Empresa Distribuidora e Importadora de Metais (INTERMETAL):** Rua Com. Baeta Neves 53, CP 1162, Maputo; tel. 422770; telex 6372; metals and metal products; Man. Dir Jorge Silvestre Luís Guinda.

**Empresa Estatal de Hidráulica (HIDROMOC):** Avda do Trabalho 1501, CP 193, Maputo; tel. 400181; telex 6234; fax 400043; irrigation equipment and chemicals for water treatment; transfer to private ownership pending; Dir Eduardo J. Nhacule.

**Empresa Estatal de Importação e Exportação de Medicamentos (MEDIMOC):** Avda Julius Nyerere 500, 1° Andar, CP 600, Maputo; tel. 491211; telex 6260; fax 490168; pharmaceuticals, medical equipment and supplies; Gen. Dir Renato Ronda.

**Empresa Moçambicana de Apetrechamento da Indústria Pesqueira (EQUIPESCA):** Avda Zedequias Manganhela 520, CP 2342, Maputo; tel. 27630; telex 6284; fishing equipment; Dir Joaquim Martins da Cruz.

**Empresa Moçambicana de Importação e Exportação de Produtos Pesqueiros (PESCOM Internacional):** Rua Consiglieri Pedroso 343, 4° Andar, CP 1570, Maputo; tel. 421734; telex 6409; fax 24961; f. 1978; imports and exports fish products; Dir Felisberto Manuel.

**Empresa Moçambicana de Importação e Exportação de Produtos Químicos e Plásticos (INTERQUIMICA):** Rua de Bagamoyo 333, CP 2268, Maputo; tel. 423168; telex 6274; fax 21229; chemicals, fertilizers, pesticides, plastics, paper; Dir Aurélio Ricardo Chiziane.

**Empresa Nacional de Carvão de Moçambique (CARBOMOC):** Rua Joaquim Lapa 108, CP 1773, Maputo; tel. 427625; telex 6413; fax 424714; f. 1948; mineral extraction and export; Dir Jaime Ribeiro.

**Empresa Nacional de Importação e Exportação de Veículos Motorizadas (INTERMECANO):** Rua Consiglieri Pedroso 165, CP 1280, Maputo; tel. 430221; telex 6505; motor cycles, cars, trucks, buses, construction plant, agricultural machinery, spare parts; Dir Rodrigo de Oliveira.

# MOZAMBIQUE

**Empresa Nacional Petróleos de Moçambique (PETROMOC):** Praça dos Trabalhadores 9, CP 417, Maputo; tel. 427191; telex 6382; fax 430181; f. 1977 to take over the Sonarep oil refinery and its associated distribution co; state directorate for liquid fuels within Mozambique, including petroleum products passing through Mozambique to inland countries; Dir MANUEL PATRÍCIO DA CRUZ VIOLA.

**ENACOMO, SARL (Empresa Nacional de Comércio):** Avda Samora Machel 285, 1° Andar, CP 698, Maputo; tel. 430172; telex 6387; fax 427754; f. 1976; imports, exports, procurement, investment; Man. Dir CARLOS PACHECO FARIA.

**Importadora de Bens de Consumo (IMBEC):** Rua da Mesquita 33, CP 4229, Maputo; tel. 421455; telex 6350; fax 423650; f. 1982; import of consumer goods; Man. Dir CARLOS COSSA.

**Lojas Francas de Moçambique (INTERFRANCA):** Rua Timor Leste 106, CP 1206, Maputo; tel. 425199; telex 6403; fax 431044; music equipment, motor cars, handicrafts, furniture; Gen. Dir CARLOS E. N. RIBEIRO.

**Riopele Têxteis de Moçambique, SARL:** Rua Joaquim Lapa 21, CP 1658, Maputo; tel. 31331; telex 6371; fax 422902; textiles; Dir CARLOS RIBEIRO.

## OTHER MAJOR STATE ENTERPRISES

**Comércio Grossista de Produtos Alimentares (COGROPA):** Avda 25 de Setembro 874–896, CP 308, Maputo; tel. 428655; telex 6370; food supplies; transfer to private ownership pending; Dir ANTÓNIO BAPTISTA DO AMARAL.

**Companhia da Zambézia, SARL:** Avda Samora Machel 245, 4° Andar, CP 617, Maputo; tel. 420639; telex 6380; fax 421507; f. 1892; agriculture; Dirs JOSÉ BENTO VEDOR, JOÃO FORTE, CARLOS DE MATOS.

**Companhia do Cajú do Monapo, SARL:** Avda do Trabalho 2106, CP 1248, Maputo; tel. 400290; telex 6249; fax 401164; cashew nuts; CEO Dr LACERDA FERREIRA.

**Companhia Siderurgica de Moçambique (CSM), SARL:** Avda Nuno Alvares 566, CP 441, Maputo; tel. 401281; telex 6262; fax 400400; steel; Technical Man. HERLANDER PEDROSO.

**Companhia Industrial do Monapo, SARL:** Avda do Trabalho 2106, CP 1248, Maputo; tel. 400290; telex 6249; fax 401164; animal and vegetable oils and soap; CEO CARMEN RAMOS.

**Electricidade de Moçambique:** Avda Agostinho Neto 70, CP 2447, Maputo; tel. 492011; telex 6407; production and distribution of electric energy; Dir FERNANDO RAMOS JULIÃO.

**Empresa de Construções Metálicas (ECOME):** Avda das Industrias-Machava, CP 1358, Maputo; tel. 752282; agricultural equipment; Dir JUSTINO LUCAS.

**Empresa Estatal de Maquinaria Agrícola (AGRO-ALFA):** Avda 24 de Julho 2755, CP 1318, Maputo; tel. 422928; telex 6405; fax 30889; f. 1978; agricultural equipment; Dir ALFREDO MACAMO.

**Empresa de Gestão e Assistência Técnica ao Equipamento Agrícola (MECANAGRO):** Avda das FPLM 184, CP 2727, Maputo; tel. 460016; telex 6344; agricultural machinery; Dir RAGENDRA DE SOUSA.

**Empresa Metalúrgica de Moçambique, SARL:** Avda de Moçambique 1500, CP 1316, Maputo; tel. 475189; telex 6499; fax 475149; f. 1951; metallurgical products; Dir JOÃO GARROCHINHO.

**Empresa Moçambicana de Malhas (EMMA), SARL:** Avda Zedequias Manganhela 488, CP 2603, Maputo; tel. 423112; telex 6813; textiles; Admin. AMADE OSSUMANE.

**Empresa Moçambicana de Chá (EMOCHÁ):** Avda Zedequias Manganhela 250, Maputo; tel. 424779; telex 6519; tea production; Dir MARCOS BASTOS.

**Empresa Nacional de Cajú (CAJÚ):** Avda das Industrias, CP 124, Maputo; tel. 753009; telex 6326; cashew nuts; Dir JÚLIO CUAMBA.

**Empresa Nacional de Calçado e Têxteis (ENCATEX):** Avda 24 de Julho 2969, CP 67, Maputo; tel. 731258; telex 6421; footwear and textiles; Dir SOVERANO BELCHIOR.

**Empresa Nacional de Hidrocarbonetos de Moçambique (ENHM):** Avda Fernão de Magalhães 34, CP 2904, Maputo; tel. 460083; telex 6478; controls concessions for petroleum exploration and production; Dir MÁRIO MARQUES.

**Empresa Provincial (AVICOLA) EE:** Avda 25 de Setembro 1676, CP 4202, Maputo; tel. 34738; Dir MÁRIO BERNARDO.

**Fábricas Associadas de Óleos (FASOL), SARL:** Avda de Namaacha, CP 1128, Maputo; tel. 723186; telex 6070; oils; transfer to private ownership pending; Dir CARLOS COSTA.

**Forjadora, SARL—Fábrica Moçambicana de Equipamentos Industriais:** Avda de Angola 2850, CP 3078, Maputo; tel. 465537; telex 6107; fax 465211; metal structures; Man. Dir. JORGE MORGADO.

**Indústria Moçambicana de Aço (IMA), SARL:** Avda 24 de Julho 2373, 12° Andar, CP 2566, Maputo; tel. 421141; telex 6323; fax 423446; steel; Dir MANUEL JOSÉ SEREJO.

**Moçambique-Industrial, SARL:** Rua Aruangua 39, 1° Andar, CP 432, Beira; tel. 322123; telex 7352; fax 325347; oils; Dir JORGE SOEIRO.

**Química-Geral, SARL:** Língamo-Matola, CP 15, Maputo; tel. 424713; telex 6448; fertilizers; Dir ALFREDO BADURU.

**Sena Sugar Estate Lda:** Avda 25 de Setembro 2801, CP 361, Maputo; tel. 427610; telex 6422; fax 426753; fmrly British-owned; govt-administered since 1978; plantations and mills in Sofala and Zambézia provinces; Dir HERMINIO MACHADO.

**Texlom, SARL:** Avda Filipe Samuel Magaia 514, CP 194, Maputo; telex 6289; textiles; Dir JOSÉ AUGUSTO TOMO PSICO.

## TRADE UNIONS

Freedom to form trade unions, and the right to strike, are guaranteed under the 1990 Constitution.

**Organização Nacional dos Jornalistas (OJN):** Avda 24 de Julho, 231, Maputo; tel. 492031; f. 1978; Sec.-Gen. HILÁRIO M. E. MATUSSE.

**Organização dos Trabalhadores de Moçambique—Central Sindical (OTM—CS)** (Mozambique Workers' Organization—Trade Union Headquarters): Rua Manuel António de Sousa 36, Maputo; tel. 426477; telex 6116; fax 421671; f. 1983 as trade union fed. to replace fmr production councils; officially recognized in 1990; 200,000 mems (1993); Pres. JOAQUIM FANHEIRO; Secs-Gen. AUGUSTO MACAMO, SOARES BUNHAZA NHACA.

**Sindicato Nacional dos Trabalhadores Agro-Pecuários e Florestais (SINTAF):** Avda 25 de Setembro 1676, 1°, Maputo; tel. 431182; Sec.-Gen. EUSÉBIO LUÍS CHIVULELE.

**Sindicato Nacional dos Trabalhadores da Aviação Civil, Correios e Comunicações (SINTAC):** Avda 25 de Setembro 1509, 2° andar, No 5, Maputo; tel. 30996; Sec.-Gen. MANUEL SANTOS DOS REIS.

**Sindicato Nacional dos Trabalhadores do Comércio, Banca e Seguros (SINTCOBASE):** Avda Ho Chi Min 365, 1° andar, CP 2142, Maputo; tel. 426271; Sec.-Gen. AMÓS JÚNIOR MATSINHE.

**Sindicato Nacional dos Trabalhadores da Indústria do Açúcar (SINTIA):** Avda das FPLM 1912, Maputo; tel. 460108; f. 1989; Sec.-Gen. ALEXANDRE CÂNDIDO MUNGUAMBE.

**Sindicato Nacional dos Trabalhadores da Indústria Alimentar e Bebidas (SINTIAB):** Avda Eduardo Mondlane 1267, CP 394, Maputo; tel. 424709; Sec.-Gen. SAMUEL FENIAS MATSINHE.

**Sindicato Nacional dos Trabalhadores da Indústria de Cajú (SINTIC):** Rua do Jardim 574, 1° andar, Maputo; tel. 475300; Sec.-Gen. BOAVENTURA MONDLANE.

**Sindicato Nacional dos Trabalhadores da Indústria de Construção Civil, Madeira e Minas (SINTICIM):** Avda 24 de Julho 2341, 5° andar dt°, Maputo; tel. 421159; Sec.-Gen. JOSÉ ALBINO.

**Sindicato Nacional dos Trabalhadores da Indústria Hoteleira, Turismo e Similares (SINTHOTS):** Avda Eduardo Mondlane 1267, CP 394, Maputo; tel. 420409; Sec.-Gen. ALBERTO MANUEL NHAPOSSE.

**Sindicato Nacional dos Trabalhadores da Indústria Metalúrgica, Metalomecânica e Energia (SINTIME):** Avda Samora Machel 30, 6° andar, No 6, CP 1868, Maputo; tel. 428588; fax 421671; Sec.-Gen. RUI BENJAMIM COSTA.

**Sindicato Nacional dos Trabalhadores da Indústria Química, Borracha, Papel e Gráfica (SINTIQUIGRA):** Avda Karl Marx 414, 1° andar, CP 4433, Maputo; tel. 421553; Sec.-Gen. JOAQUIM M. FANHEIRO.

**Sindicato Nacional dos Trabalhadores da Indústria Têxtil Vestuário, Couro e Calçado (SINTEVEC):** Avda Maria José de Albuquerque 70, 11° andar, CP 2613, Maputo; tel. 415623; Sec.-Gen. PEDRO JOAQUIM MANDLAZE.

**Sindicato Nacional dos Trabalhadores da Marinha Mercante e Pesca (SINTMAP):** Rua Joaquim Lapa 4° 22-5° andar, No 6, Maputo; tel. 421148; Sec.-Gen. DANIEL MANUEL NGOQUE.

**Sindicato Nacional dos Trabalhadores dos Portos e Caminhos de Ferro (SINPOCAF):** Avda Guerra Popular, CP 2158, Maputo; tel. 420531; Sec.-Gen. DINIS EFRAIME FRANCISCO NHANGUMBE.

**Sindicato Nacional dos Trabalhadores dos Transportes Rodoviários e Assistência Técnica (SINTRAT):** Avda Paulo Samuel Kankhomba 1568, 1° andar, 14, Maputo; tel. 402390; Sec.-Gen. ALCANO HORÁCIO MULA.

**Sindicatos Livres e Independentes de Moçambique (SLIM):** Sec.-Gen. JEREMIAS TIMANE.

# Transport

The 'Beira Corridor', where rail and road links and a petroleum pipeline run from Manica, on the Zimbabwean border, to the Mozambican port of Beira, forms a vital outlet for the landlocked southern African countries, particularly Zimbabwe. The

# MOZAMBIQUE

development of this route is a major priority of the Southern African Development Community (SADC). Following the General Peace Agreement in 1992, rehabilitation of the transport network, which had been continually disrupted by guerrilla attacks and sabotage, began, funded principally by the SADC. By 1994 the 'Beira Corridor' was fully operational.

### RAILWAYS

In 1987 the total length of track was 3,131 km, excluding the Sena Sugar Estates Railway (90 km), which serves only the company's properties. The railways are all state-owned. There are both internal routes and rail links between Mozambican ports and South Africa, Zimbabwe and Malawi. During the hostilities many lines and services were disrupted by Renamo guerrilla operations. Improvement work on most of the principal railway lines began in the early 1980s. The rehabilitation of the 534-km Limpopo railway, linking Chicualacuala, at the Zimbabwe border, with the port of Maputo, was completed in March 1993. In September 1993 it was announced that the implementation of plans, initiated in 1990 but later disrupted, to rehabilitate the railway linking the port of Beira with the coal-mining centre of Moatize had resumed. In November 1993, following the rehabilitation of some 538 km of the 610-km railway linking the port of Nacala with Blantyre, in Malawi, the completed section, which runs from Nacala to Entre Lagos on the Malawi border, was reopened. In early 1995 rehabilitation of the Machava–Goba section of the railway linking Mozambique and Swaziland, which began in 1993, was nearing completion.

**Direcção Nacional dos Portos e Caminhos de Ferro de Moçambique (CFM):** Avda Mártires de Inhaminga 336, CP 276, Maputo; tel. 430151; telex 6438; f. 1929; 3,131 km open; there are five separate systems linking Mozambican ports with the country's hinterland, and with other southern African countries, including Malawi, Zimbabwe and South Africa. These systems are administered from Nampula, Beira, Maputo, Inhambane and Quelimane respectively; Dir MÁRIO ANTÓNIO DIMANDE.

**Empresa Nacional dos Portos e Caminhos de Ferro de Moçambique (CFM), SARL:** Praça dos Trabalhadores, CP 2158, Maputo; tel. 427173; telex 6208; Dir-Gen. MÁRIO ANTÓNIO DIMANDE.

### ROADS

In 1991 there were 27,287 km of roads in Mozambique, of which 4,693 km were paved. In that year a major programme, supervised by the SADCC (now SADC), was in progress to improve the road links between Mozambique and neighbouring countries. In early 1994 the Government announced a five-year road rehabilitation programme to reopen 11,000 km of roads closed during the hostilities, and to upgrade 3,000 km of paved roads and 13,000 km of secondary and tertiary roads. The programme, which was to cost an estimated US $24,000m., was to be financed mainly by international donors and the World Bank.

### SHIPPING

The main ports are Maputo, Beira, Nacala and Quelimane. Some 6.2m. tons of cargo were handled in 1991. The modernization and expansion of the port of Beira, which began in 1991, was completed in 1994. The construction of a new petroleum terminal doubled the port's capacity, thus facilitating the transportation of petroleum products along the 'Beira Corridor' to Zimbabwe. Rehabilitation of the port of Maputo was completed in 1989, as part of the SADCC (now SADC) transport programme. Repairs to the port of Nacala, damaged by a cyclone in early 1994, were to cost an estimated $14m. In late 1994 the port was reported to be operating at only 25%–30% of its capacity. Foreign assistance was being sought to finance the repairs.

**Agência Nacional de Frete e Navegação (ANFRENA):** Rua Consiglieri Pedroso 396, CP 492, Maputo; tel. 428111; telex 6258; fax 427822; Dir FERDINAND WILSON.

**Companhia Nacional de Navegação:** CP 2064, Maputo; telex 6237.

**Companhia Portuguesa de Transportes Marítimos:** Avda Samora Machel 239, CP 2, Maputo; tel. 426912.

**Empresa Moçambicana de Cargas (MOCARGO):** Rua Consiglieri Pedroso 430, 1°–4° Andar, CP 888, Maputo; tel. 431022; telex 6581; fax 421438; f. 1984; shipping, chartering and road transport; Man. Dir MANUEL DE SOUSA AMARAL.

**Manica Freight Services, SARL:** Praça dos Trabalhadores 51, CP 557, Maputo; tel. 425048; telex 6221; fax 431084; international shipping agents; Dir W. A. VERPLOEGH.

**Navique EE (Empresa Moçambicana de Navegação):** Rua de Bagamoyo 366, CP 145, Maputo; tel. 425316; telex 6424; fax 426310; Chair. DANIEL C. LAMPIAO; Man. Dir JORGE DE SOUSA COELHO.

### CIVIL AVIATION

There are 16 airports, of which three are international airports.

**Aerocondor Moçambique:** Beira.

**Empresa Nacional de Transporte e Trabalho Aéreo, EE (TTA):** Aeroporto Internacional de Maputo, CP 2054, Maputo; tel. 465292; telex 6539; fax 465484; scheduled services to 35 domestic points; also operates air taxi services, agricultural and special aviation services; Dir ESTEVÃO ALBERTO JUNIOR.

**Linhas Aéreas de Moçambique (LAM):** Aeroporto Internacional de Maputo, CP 2060, Maputo; tel. 465137; telex 6386; fax 735601; f. 1980; operates domestic services and international services within Africa and to Europe; Chair. and Dir-Gen. JOSÉ RICARDO ZUZARTE VIEGAS.

## Tourism

Tourism, formerly a significant source of foreign exchange, ceased completely following independence, and was resumed on a limited scale in 1980. There were 1,000 visitors in 1981 (compared with 292,000 in 1972 and 69,000 in 1974). In 1984 a joint-venture company was established with South Africa in order to develop tourism on Inhaca island. With the successful conduct of multi-party elections in 1994 and the prospect of continued peace, tourism became once again a potentially viable sector of the Mozambican economy.

**Empresa Nacional de Turismo (ENT):** Avda 25 de Setembro 1203, CP 2446, Maputo; tel. 421794; telex 6303; fax 421795; f. 1985; hotels and tourism; Gen. Dir GILDO NEVES.

# MYANMAR

## Introductory Survey

**Location, Climate, Language, Religion, Flag, Capital**

The Union of Myanmar (Myanma Naing-ngan—formerly Burma) lies in the north-west region of South-East Asia, between the Tibetan plateau and the Malay peninsula. The country is bordered by Bangladesh and India to the north-west, by the People's Republic of China and Laos to the north-east and by Thailand to the south-east. The climate is tropical, with an average temperature of 27°C (80°F) and monsoon rains from May to October. Average annual rainfall is between 2,500mm and 5,000mm in the coastal and mountainous regions of the north and east, but reaches a maximum of only 1,000mm in the lowlands of the interior. Temperatures in Yangon (Rangoon) are generally between 18°C (65°F) and 36°C (97°F). The official language is Myanmar (Burmese), and there are also a number of tribal languages. About 87% of the population are Buddhists. There are animist, Muslim, Hindu and Christian minorities, and there is a Chinese community of some 350,000. The national flag is red, with a blue canton, in the upper hoist, bearing two ears of rice within a cogwheel and a ring of 14 five-pointed stars (one for each state), all in white. The capital is Yangon.

**Recent History**

Burma (now Myanmar) was annexed to British India during the 19th century, and became a separate British dependency, with a limited measure of self-government, in 1937. Japanese forces invaded and occupied the country in February 1942, and Japan granted nominal independence under a government of anti-British nationalists. The Burmese nationalists later turned against Japan and aided Allied forces to reoccupy the country in May 1945. They formed a resistance movement, the Anti-Fascist People's Freedom League (AFPFL), led by Gen. Aung San, which became the main political force after the defeat of Japan. Aung San was assassinated in July 1947 and was succeeded by U Nu. On 4 January 1948 the Union of Burma became independent, outside the Commonwealth, with U Nu as the first Prime Minister.

During the first decade of independence Burma was a parliamentary democracy, and the Government successfully resisted revolts by communists and other insurgent groups. In 1958 the ruling AFPFL split into two wings, the 'Clean' AFPFL and the 'Stable' AFPFL, and U Nu invited the Army Chief of Staff, Gen. Ne Win, to head a caretaker Government. Elections to the Chamber of Deputies in February 1960 gave an overwhelming majority to U Nu, leading the 'Clean' AFPFL (which was renamed the Union Party in March), and he resumed office in April. Despite its popularity, however, the U Nu administration proved ineffective, and in March 1962 Gen. Ne Win intervened again, staging a coup to depose U Nu (who was subsequently detained until 1966). The new Revolutionary Council suspended the Constitution and instituted authoritarian control through the government-sponsored Burma Socialist Programme Party (BSPP). All other political parties were outlawed in March 1964.

The next decade saw the creation of a more centralized system of government, attempting to win popular support and nationalizing important sectors of the economy. A new Constitution, aiming to transform Burma into a democratic socialist state, was approved in a national referendum in December 1973. The Constitution of the renamed Socialist Republic of the Union of Burma, which came into force in January 1974, confirmed the BSPP as the sole authorized political party, and provided for the establishment of new organs of state. Elections to a new legislative body, the People's Assembly, took place in January 1974, and in March the Revolutionary Council was dissolved. U Ne Win (who, together with other senior army officers, had become a civilian in 1972) was elected President by the newly-created State Council. Burma's economic problems increased, however, and in 1974 there were riots over food shortages and social injustices. Student demonstrations took place in 1976, as social problems increased. Following an attempted coup by members of the armed forces in July, the BSPP reviewed its economic policies, and in 1977 a new economic programme was adopted in an attempt to quell unrest.

An election in January 1978 gave U Ne Win a mandate to rule for a further four years, and in March he was re-elected Chairman of the State Council. In May 1980 a general amnesty was declared for political dissidents, including exiles (as a result of which U Nu, who had been living abroad since 1969, returned to Burma in July). Gen. San Yu, formerly the Army Chief of Staff, was elected Chairman of the State Council in November 1981; U Ne Win, however, remained Chairman of the BSPP. The Citizenship Law of 1982 provided for three categories of citizen, and precluded members of non-indigenous races from holding important positions. At the fifth Congress of the BSPP, in August 1985, U Ne Win was re-elected for a further four-year term as Chairman. Elections for a new People's Assembly were held in November.

In August 1987, owing to the country's increasing economic problems, an unprecedented extraordinary meeting, comprising the BSPP Central Committee, the organs of the State Council and other state organs, was convened. U Ne Win proposed a review of the policies of the past 25 years, and acknowledged the need to correct any shortcomings. In September the announcement of the withdrawal from circulation of high-denomination banknotes, coupled with rice shortages following a poor harvest, provoked student riots, the first public display of civil unrest since 1976. Owing to continued economic deprivation, further student unrest in Rangoon (now Yangon) in March 1988 culminated in serious riots which were violently suppressed by the *lon htein* (riot police), under the direct command of U Sein Lwin, the BSPP Joint General Secretary. Further demonstrations, to demand the release of persons who had been detained in March, started in June. The Government's response was again extremely brutal, and many demonstrators were killed. In July vain attempts were made to counter the growing unpopularity of the Government, including the removal from office of Maj.-Gen. Min Gaung, the Minister of Home and Religious Affairs, and U Thien Aung, the head of the People's Police Force in Rangoon, for their alleged responsibility for events during March and June. (The Prime Minister, also, was subsequently dismissed.) Finally, at an extraordinary meeting of the BSPP Congress in July, U Ne Win resigned as party Chairman and asked the Congress to approve the holding of a national referendum on the issue of a multi-party system. The Congress rejected the referendum proposal and the resignation of four other senior members of the BSPP, including that of U Sein Lwin, but accepted the resignation of U San Yu, the BSPP Vice-Chairman.

The subsequent election of U Sein Lwin to the chairmanship of the BSPP by the party's Central Executive Committee, and his appointment as Chairman of the State Council and as state President, increased popular discontent and provoked further student-led riots. Martial law was imposed on Rangoon, and thousands of unarmed demonstrators were reportedly massacred by the armed forces throughout the country. In August 1988 students appealed for a general strike, and U Sein Lwin was forced to resign after only 17 days in office. He was replaced by the more moderate Dr Maung Maung, hitherto the Attorney-General, whose response to the continued rioting was conciliatory. Martial law was revoked; Brig.-Gen. Aung Gyi (a former close colleague of U Ne Win but subsequently an outspoken critic of the regime), who had been detained under U Sein Lwin, was released; and permission was given for the formation of the All Burma Students' Union. Demonstrations continued, however, and by September students and Buddhist monks had assumed control of the municipal government of many towns. In early September U Nu, the former Prime Minister, requested foreign support for his formation of an 'alternative government'. The emerging opposition leaders, Aung Gyi, Aung San Suu Kyi (daughter of Gen. Aung San) and Gen. (retd) Tin U (a former Chief of Staff and Minister of Defence), then formed the National United Front for Democracy, which was subsequently renamed the League for Democracy and later the National League for Democracy (NLD).

At an emergency meeting of the BSPP Congress in September 1988, it was decided that free elections would be held within three months and that members of the armed forces, police and civil service could no longer be affiliated to a political party. Now distanced from the BSPP, the armed forces, led by Gen. (later Senior Gen.) Saw Maung, seized power on 18 September, ostensibly to maintain order until multi-party elections could be arranged. The State Law and Order Restoration Council (SLORC) was formed, all state organs (including the People's Assembly, the State Council and the Council of Ministers) were abolished, demonstrations were banned and a nationwide dusk-to-dawn curfew was imposed. Despite these measures, opposition movements demonstrated in favour of an interim civilian government, and it was estimated that more than 1,000 demonstrators were killed in the first few days following the coup. The SLORC announced the formation of a nine-member government, with Saw Maung as Minister of Defence and of Foreign Affairs and subsequently also Prime Minister. It was widely believed, however, that U Ne Win, although ostensibly in retirement, retained a controlling influence over the new leaders, all of whom, including Saw Maung, were known to be his supporters. The new Government changed the official name of the country to the Union of Burma (as it had been before 1973). The law maintaining the BSPP as the sole party was abrogated, and new parties were encouraged to register for the forthcoming elections. The BSPP registered under a new name, the National Unity Party (NUP), with U Tha Kyaw, the former Minister of Transport, as Chairman. In December, owing to disagreements with Aung San Suu Kyi, Aung Gyi was expelled from the NLD, after he had founded the Union National Democracy Party. Tin U was elected as the new NLD Chairman. The former Prime Minister, U Nu, returned to prominence as the leader of a new party, the League for Democracy and Peace (LDP), and also commanded the support of the newly-formed Democracy Party.

From October 1988 to January 1989 Aung San Suu Kyi campaigned in townships and rural areas across the nation, and elicited much popular support, despite the martial law regulations which remained in force, banning public gatherings of five or more people. In March 1989 anti-Government demonstrations took place in many cities, in protest at the increasing harassment of Aung San Suu Kyi and the arrest of many NLD supporters and activists. In July Aung San Suu Kyi cancelled a rally to commemorate the anniversary of the assassination (in 1947) of her father, Aung San, owing to the threat of government violence; two days later, both she and Tin U were placed under house arrest, accused of 'endangering the State' by their activities.

In May 1989 electoral legislation, which had been promulgated in March, was ratified. It provided for the holding of multi-party elections on 27 May 1990, and permitted campaigning only in the three months prior to the election date. In June 1989 the SLORC changed the official name of the country to the Union of Myanmar (Myanma Naing-ngan), on the grounds that the previous title conveyed the impression that the population consisted solely of ethnic Burmans. The transliteration to the Roman alphabet of many other place-names was changed, to correspond more closely with pronunciation.

In December 1989 Tin U was sentenced by a military tribunal to three years' imprisonment, with hard labour, for taking part in the anti-Government uprising in 1988. Later in the same month, U Nu was disqualified from contesting the forthcoming general election, owing to his refusal to announce the dissolution of the 'alternative government' whose formation he had proclaimed in September 1988. In January 1990 U Nu and 13 members of the 'alternative government' were placed under house arrest. Five members subsequently resigned and were released. Later in January, Aung San Suu Kyi was barred from contesting the election, owing to her 'entitlement to the privileges of a foreigner' (a reference to her marriage to a British citizen) and her alleged involvement with insurgents.

In February 1990 martial law was revoked in 10 townships, following the repeal of similar restrictions in eight townships in November 1989. It was reported that during 1989 tens of thousands of Myanma citizens had been forcibly evicted from densely-populated areas in major cities, where anti-Government demonstrations had received much support, and resettled in rural areas. In January and April 1989 the human rights organization, Amnesty International, published information regarding violations of human rights in Myanmar, including the torture and summary execution of dissident students. This was followed by criticism from the UN later in the year.

In May 1990 93 parties presented a total of 2,296 candidates to contest 492 seats at the general election for the new assembly. There were also 87 independent candidates. Despite previous efforts to weaken the influence of known leaders and to eliminate dissidents, the voting was reported to be free and orderly. The NLD received 59.9% of the total votes and won 396 of the 485 seats that were, in the event, contested, while the NUP obtained 21.2% of the votes but won only 10 seats. The NLD demanded the immediate opening of negotiations with the SLORC, and progress towards popular rule. However, the SLORC announced that the election had been intended to provide not a legislature but a constituent assembly, which was to draft a constitution establishing a 'strong government', and was to be under the direction of a national convention to be established by the SLORC. The resulting draft constitution would have to be endorsed by referendum, and subsequently approved by the SLORC, before a transfer of power could take place. In July the SLORC announced Order 1/90, which stated that the SLORC would continue as the *de facto* Government until a new constitution was drafted. Elected members of the NLD responded (independently of their leadership) with the 'Gandhi Hall Declaration', which appealed for the convening of an assembly of all elected representatives by September.

In early August 1990, at an anti-Government protest held in Mandalay to commemorate the killing of thousands of demonstrators in 1988, troops killed four protesters, including two Buddhist monks. In early September the SLORC arrested six members of the NLD, including the acting Chairman, Kyi Maung, and the acting Secretary-General, Chit Hlaing, on charges of passing state secrets to unauthorized persons. Kyi Maung was replaced as acting NLD Chairman by U Aung Shwe, a former ambassador to Australia and an original member of the NLD Central Executive Committee. Also in September, NLD representatives discussed plans to declare a provisional government in Mandalay, without the support of the party's Central Executive Committee. Influential monks agreed to support the declaration, which was to take place in October. However, the plan was abandoned after government troops surrounded monasteries. The SLORC subsequently ordered the dissolution of all Buddhist organizations involved in anti-Government activities (all except nine sects) and empowered military commanders to impose death sentences on rebellious monks. More than 50 senior members of the NLD were arrested, and in late October and early November members of all political parties were required to endorse Order 1/90. In acquiescing, the NLD effectively nullified its demand for an immediate transfer of power.

In mid-December 1990 a group of candidates who had been elected to the constituent assembly fled to Manerplaw, on the Thai border, and announced a 'parallel government', the National Coalition Government of the Union of Burma (NCGUB), with the support of the Democratic Alliance of Burma (DAB), a 21-member organization uniting ethnic rebel forces with student dissidents and monks. The self-styled Prime Minister of the eight-member NCGUB was Sein Win, the leader of the Party for National Democracy (PND) and a cousin of Aung San Suu Kyi. The NLD leadership expelled members who had taken part in the formation of the 'parallel government', despite broad support for the move in the NLD. The SLORC annulled the PND's registration as a political party and, subsequently, the elected status of the eight members of the NCGUB.

In February 1991 the SLORC annulled the registration of the LDP. Two other political parties were also banned in early 1991. In April Gen. (later Senior Gen.) Than Shwe, the Vice-Chairman of the SLORC and the Deputy Chief of Staff of the armed forces, officially announced that the SLORC would not transfer power to the Assembly elected in May 1990, as the political parties involved were 'subversive' and 'unfit to rule'. On the following day, in response to continued pressure from the SLORC, the NLD effected a complete reshuffle of the party's Central Executive Committee, replacing Suu Kyi as General Secretary by the previously unknown U Lwin, and Tin U by the former acting Chairman, U Aung Shwe.

In July 1991 the SLORC retroactively amended electoral legislation adopted in May 1989 extending the grounds on which representatives of the Assembly could be disqualified or disbarred from contesting future elections to include convictions for breaches of law and order. Under measures implemented by the SLORC more than 80 elected representatives had already died, been imprisoned or been forced into exile since the election in May 1990. In early September the SLORC declared its intention to remain in charge of state administration for a further five or 10 years. In mid-September U Ohn Gyaw, the Vice-Minister for Foreign Affairs, was appointed Minister for Foreign Affairs in place of Saw Maung, becoming the first civilian in the Cabinet.

In October 1991 Aung San Suu Kyi was awarded the Nobel Peace Prize. The leader of the NCGUB, Sein Win, attended the presentation of the award to Suu Kyi's family in Oslo, Norway, in December and gained the Norwegian Government's *de facto* recognition of the NCGUB. In Myanmar students staged the first demonstrations since 1989 to coincide with the ceremony, protesting against Suu Kyi's continued detention and demanding progress towards democracy. The students were dispersed by the security forces. Universities and colleges, which had reopened in May 1991, were closed, and thousands of teaching staff were dismissed or sent on re-education courses. The day after the demonstrations it was announced that Suu Kyi had been expelled from the NLD. Also in December Amnesty International issued a report detailing the arrests of 200 political prisoners in the first seven months of 1991, bringing the total detained since 1988 to 1,500. In January 1992 Tin U's expulsion from the NLD was broadcast.

At the end of January 1992 three additional members were appointed to the SLORC and the Cabinet was expanded to include seven new ministers, four of whom were civilians. The changes, together with a reorganization of senior ministers which took place in February, were widely perceived to benefit the 'hardline' Chief of Military Intelligence, Maj.-Gen. (later Lt-Gen.) Khin Nyunt (First Secretary of the SLORC). Khin Nyunt was widely regarded as the most powerful member of the SLORC, owing to U Ne Win's continued patronage. Divisions within the ruling junta between the younger Khin Nyunt and the more senior officers were becoming increasingly evident. The ministerial reorganization took place amid unconfirmed reports of a deterioration in Saw Maung's health, following rumours of a nervous collapse in December 1991. In March 1992 Than Shwe replaced Saw Maung as Minister of Defence. In late April the increasingly erratic Saw Maung retired as Chairman of the SLORC and Prime Minister for reasons of ill health. Than Shwe was subsequently appointed to both these posts. The SLORC promptly ordered the release of several political prisoners, including U Nu, and announced that Suu Kyi could receive a visit from her family. Than Shwe indicated that he was prepared to meet Suu Kyi personally to discuss her future. In June the first meeting took place between members of the SLORC and opposition representatives from the remaining 10 legal parties, in preparation for the holding of a national convention, which was to draft a new constitution. Public discontent concerning the SLORC's domination of the constitutional negotiations increased, and the NLD delegation to the co-ordinating committee was urged to demand the release of Suu Kyi and her participation in discussions.

In mid-August 1992 universities and colleges were reopened, and in early September the night curfew, imposed four years previously, was repealed. In the same month a reorganization of the Cabinet included the appointment of two Deputy Prime Ministers and the promotion to ministerial posts of four northern commanders of the armed forces who were known to oppose Khin Nyunt. These appointments, which ended the first overt power struggle under the SLORC, strengthened Khin Nyunt's position by effectively depriving the commanders of power. Following the government reshuffle, the SLORC revoked two martial law decrees, which had been in force for three years, although a ban on gatherings of more than five people remained in place. In late September further political prisoners were granted an amnesty, bringing the total released to 534. It was estimated, however, that a further 1,600 prisoners remained in detention.

In January 1993 the National Convention finally assembled, but was swiftly adjourned, owing to the objections of the opposition members to the SLORC's demand that the armed forces be allocated a leading role in government under a new constitution. When the National Convention reconvened at the beginning of February, the NLD issued a statement opposing military dominance and proposing a national referendum on whether it should be incorporated in a new constitution. The National Convention was again adjourned. The SLORC reacted to opposition intransigence by suspending its conciliatory gestures; many arrests were reported during January and February. (In April Aung Gyi was sentenced to six months' imprisonment.) At the end of February discussions on a draft constitution were resumed. The National Convention was adjourned, however, in early April, following the unexpected submission of a proposal by Yo E La of the Lahu National Development Party. Yo E La advocated the readoption of the basic principles of the federal and democratic Constitution that was in effect prior to 1962. The Lahus also proposed the introduction of extensive provisions for local autonomy for all national minorities.

When the National Convention reconvened in June 1993, Maj.-Gen. (subsequently Lt-Gen.) Myo Nyunt, a member of the SLORC, offended many ethnic minorities by suggesting that the names of Myanmar's states, which reflected the ethnic composition of the regions, be changed. Owing to continuing intransigence on the part of opposition groupings, the National Convention was adjourned in August, reconvened in September and adjourned once more later that month. U Aung Shwe, the Chairman of the NLD, and U Khun Tun Oo, the leader of the Shan Nationalities League for Democracy, were both severely reprimanded by the SLORC for their refusal to co-operate. The Chairman of the National Convention's Convening Committee, U Aung Toe (the Chief Justice), subsequently announced (seemingly without grounds) that a consensus existed in favour of the SLORC's demands, which comprised: the inclusion, in both the lower and upper chambers of a proposed parliament, of military personnel (to be appointed by the Commander-in-Chief of the Armed Forces); the election of the President by an electoral college; the independent self-administration of the armed forces; and the right of the Commander-in-Chief to exercise state power in an emergency (effectively granting legitimate status to a future coup).

In September 1993 an alternative mass movement to the NUP (which had lost credibility through its election defeat) was formed to establish a civilian front through which the armed forces could exercise control. The Union Solidarity and Development Association (USDA), whose aims were indistinguishable from those of the SLORC, was not officially registered as a political party, thus enabling civil servants to join the organization, with the incentive of considerable privileges. In January 1994 large numbers of people were coerced into joining USDA rallies to demonstrate support for the constitutional proposals presented by the SLORC. In that month the National Convention reconvened for discussions on the draft Constitution. In February a delegation led by a member of the US Congress was granted permission to visit Aung San Suu Kyi. Suu Kyi sent an encouraging message to the democracy movement and appealed for a meeting with the SLORC, expressing her willingness to negotiate on all issues except her exile. On the following day the SLORC announced that Suu Kyi would be detained until at least 1995 (despite the legal maximum of five years under house arrest, whereby Suu Kyi would be released in July 1994), since her first year in detention had only been an 'arrest period'.

In April 1994 the National Convention was adjourned, having adopted guidelines for three significant chapters of the future Constitution. According to these guidelines, Myanmar was to be renamed the Republic of the Union of Myanmar, comprising seven states (associated with some of the country's minority ethnic groups) and seven regions (largely representing the majority Bamar-populated areas). The Republic would be headed by an executive president, elected for five years; proposals for the disqualification of any candidate with a foreign spouse or children were clearly designed to prevent Suu Kyi from entering any future presidential election.

Reconvening in early September 1994, the Convention again stressed that the central role of the military (as 'permanent representatives of the people') be enshrined in the new Constitution. Proposals by six ethnic minority groups for the establishment of their own self-administered 'national zones' were considered favourably, although comparable demands by several other minority groups were rejected. In his report to the National Convention, U Aung Toe submitted proposals for key chapters of the Constitution, covering the legislature, judiciary and Government, at Union, state and regional level.

It was proposed that legislative power be shared between a bicameral Pyidaungsu Hluttaw (Union Parliament) and regional and state assemblies, all of which were to include representatives of the military. The Pyidaungsu Hluttaw was to comprise the Pyithu Hluttaw and the Amyotha Hluttaw (House of Nationalities): the former would comprise 330 elected deputies and 110 members of the 'Tatmadaw' (Defence Services) and would be elected for five years. The latter would be constituted with equal numbers of representatives from the proposed seven regions and seven states of the Republic, as well as members of the 'Tatmadaw', and was to comprise a maximum of 224 deputies. A provisional date for the next general election was sheduled for 2 September 1997. Meetings of the National Convention continued in early 1995, by which time a set of basic principles had been announced, on the basis of which areas were to be designated for self-administration. In early April the Convention was adjourned until October.

Meanwhile, in July 1994, Khin Nyunt announced what appeared to be a major change of policy: that the SLORC was prepared to hold talks with Aung San Suu Kyi. In the same month the Minister for Foreign Affairs, U Ohn Gyaw, attending the ASEAN meeting in Bangkok (see below), stated that his Government would accept the invitation of the UN Secretary-General, Dr Boutros Boutros-Ghali, to discuss issues of democratization, national reconciliation and human rights in Myanmar. In August a second US Congressman led a delegation to Yangon, meeting with Khin Nyunt. Following mediation by a senior Buddhist monk between Suu Kyi and leading members of the SLORC, in mid-September Suu Kyi was permitted to leave her house for the first time to meet Than Shwe and Khin Nyunt. Parts of the meeting were broadcast on state television, although no specific details of the talks were reported. In late October Suu Kyi held a second meeting with senior members of the SLORC. It was widely believed that the meetings represented an acknowledgement by the SLORC of Suu Kyi's position as the leading opposition figure. In early November, however, a delegation led by the US Deputy Assistant Secretary of State for East Asian and Pacific Affairs was not permitted to visit Suu Kyi. In the same month it was reported that Suu Kyi had met other detained members of the NLD, including its former Chairman Tin U. In January 1995 the SLORC announced that Suu Kyi would be freed only when the new Constitution had been completed; Suu Kyi simultaneously rejected suggestions that she might reach a compromise with the SLORC on terms for her release. None the less, in late March a senior SLORC official suggested that Suu Kyi could be released in July, when her legal detention had expired. In mid-March the Government released 31 political prisoners, including Tin U and Kyi Maung. In the previous month leading members of the SLORC had held talks in Yangon with an envoy of the UN Secretary-General on the range of issues agreed in mid-1994. In early July 1995 it was reported that Suu Kyi had been released from house arrest.

After Burma gained independence in 1948, various groups conducted armed insurgency campaigns against government forces. The most effective of the ethnic-based insurgency groups was the Karen National Union (KNU), founded in 1948, which led a protracted campaign for the establishment of an independent state for the Karen ethnic group, partly through the activities of its military wing, the Karen National Liberation Army (KNLA). The KNU was a member of the National Democratic Front (NDF), an organization which at one time comprised 11 ethnic minority groups (including Kachin, Karenni, Mon, Shan, Pa-O, Palaung, Wa, Arakanese and Lahu parties), formed in 1975 (by five groups, originally) with the aim of making Burma a federal union and opposing both the Government and, initially, the Communist Party of Burma (CPB). The CPB was one of the most well-organized insurgent movements, in military terms, and gained control of significant areas in northern Burma. By May 1986 the various minority groups in the NDF had agreed to relinquish their individual demands for autonomy, in favour of a unified demand for a federal system of government. At the same time, the CPB withdrew its demand for a 'one-party' government and entered into an alliance with the NDF. At the second NDF Congress in June 1987, Maj.-Gen. Bo Mya, the President of the KNU and Chief of Staff of the KNLA, was replaced as NDF President by Saw Maw Reh, a former Chairman of the Karenni National Progressive Party, and further leadership changes removed all KNU representatives from senior NDF positions. The new NDF leaders advocated the establishment, mainly through political means, of autonomous, ethnic-based states within a Burmese union.

The insurgent groups were sympathetic to the anti-Government movements in the major cities. Continued attacks throughout 1988 engaged the government forces in the border areas, leaving fewer of them to impose order in the towns. In late September the Karens announced plans to co-operate with protesting students and Buddhist monks to work towards the achievement of democracy. After the armed forces seized power, insurgents intensified operations, aided by at least 3,000 students whom the Karen rebels agreed to train and arm. In November 22 anti-Government groups, led by members of the NDF, formed the Democratic Alliance of Burma (DAB). The KNU leader, Maj.-Gen. Bo Mya, was elected President, while Brang Seng (Chairman of the Kachin Independence Organization) and Nai Shwe Kyin (a Mon) were elected Vice-Presidents.

In April 1989 dissatisfaction with the leadership of the CPB led to a mutiny by Wa tribesmen, who constituted an estimated 80%–90% of the CPB's membership. Rebellious Wa soldiers captured the CPB headquarters, and the party's leaders were forced into exile in the People's Republic of China. The leaders of the mutiny subsequently accepted SLORC proposals for the former forces of the CPB army to become government-controlled militia forces in exchange for supplies of rice, financial support and development aid. The former CPB troops agreed to use their main forces against the 25,000-strong rebel separatist Mong Tai (Shan State) Army (formerly the Shan United Army), whose leader, Khun Sa, controlled much of the drug trade in the 'Golden Triangle', the world's major opium-producing area, where the borders of Myanmar, Laos and Thailand meet. The SLORC also approached members of the NDF, and was successful in securing agreements with the Shan State Progressive Party in September 1989, the Pa-O National Organization in March 1991 and the Palaung State Liberation Organization in May 1991. In July 1991, at the third NDF Congress, these three movements were expelled, reducing the NDF's membership to eight organizations, and Nai Shwe Kyin was elected as the NDF's new President.

In December 1988, following a visit by the Prime Minister of Thailand, the SLORC granted licences to Thai business interests to exploit raw materials in Burma, in return for much-needed foreign exchange. Although there was no announcement of any official Thai-Burmese agreement, subsequent offensives by government forces against rebel groups achieved unprecedented success, with troops frequently entering Thai territory and attacking insurgent bases from the rear. By December 1989 six KNU bases along the Thai border had been captured, and in January 1990 two more camps, sheltering a large number of student dissidents, were seized. In January 1990 the armed forces launched an offensive against Mon separatists. In February they succeeded in capturing Three Pagodas Pass, a principal 'black market' trade route between Thailand and Myanmar, and the headquarters of the New Mon State Party.

In 1991 intense fighting between government and rebel forces continued as the KNLA advanced into the lower central Irrawaddy (Ayeyarwady) Delta in October and November. This potentially diversionary tactic failed to prevent a concerted attempt by government troops to seize control of the KNU and DAB headquarters, which was also the seat of the NCGUB. The SLORC aimed to capture Manerplaw before Armed Forces Day, at the end of March 1992. However, despite sophisticated weaponry purchased from the People's Republic of China for an estimated US $1,200m., government troops failed to seize control of the camp. This was partly due to a belated Thai reaction to the threat of Thai sovereignty posed by the incursion of Myanma soldiers into Thailand. Following repeated border violations the Thai Government fulfilled prior threats of strong retaliation and in mid-March forced hundreds of Myanma troops out of entrenched positions in Thailand, which they had taken up in order to attack the KNU headquarters from the rear. In April the SLORC, having failed in its objective, officially suspended its offensive against the KNU, 'in the interests of national unity'. In October, however, government troops resumed hostilities and made several incursions into Thai territory. In December the Thai and Myanma Governments reached agreement to 'relocate' the Myanma armed forces, and in February 1993 they resolved to demarcate their common border.

In February and March 1993 the Kachin Independence Organization (KIO) attended peace talks with the Government in the Kachin state capital of Myitkyina. The discussions were the result of pressure exerted by the People's Republic of China and Thailand, which wished to facilitate the exploitation of the area's extensive timber and jade resources. The Kachins were in a vulnerable position, since they were no longer able to obtain arms from the practically defunct CPB or through Thailand (as the Mong Tai Army controlled the territory between Kachin encampments and the Thai boder). The SLORC was anxious to reach an accommodation with the Kachins, as the NCGUB would be severely weakened by the loss of their support (although a *de facto* national cease-fire had been in effect since October 1992). The KIO appeared to have signed a peace agreement in April but, owing to attempts by the Kachins to persuade other members of the DAB to enter discussions with the SLORC, the cease-fire agreement was not announced until October. The agreement was ratified in Yangon in February 1994. The KIO were suspended from the DAB in October 1993 for negotiating separately with the SLORC, and the DAB reiterated its conditions for discussions with the SLORC in a series of open letters. The DAB stipulations included the recognition of the DAB as a single negotiating body (the SLORC insisted on meeting each ethnic group separately); the location of the negotiating process in a neutral country; an immediate end to the forcible mass relocation of villagers; a new body to draft a constitution; and the release of all political detainees, beginning with Suu Kyi. Under Thai pressure, however, the DAB policy of negotiating as a front was unofficially abandoned. The Mons began talks with the SLORC in December, and the Karennis were engaged in discussions with the junta in early 1994. The KNU was also involved in negotiations with the SLORC in early 1994, but insisted that it was representing the DAB.

The process of reconciliation continued with the 'return to the legal fold' in May 1994 of the Karenni National People's Liberation Front, reportedly the 11th insurgent group to conclude a cease-fire agreement with the SLORC. This was followed, in October, by the declaration of a cease-fire by the Shan State Nationalities Liberation Organization. In late December government forces launched a new offensive against the KNU, recapturing its headquarters at Manerplaw in January 1995, forcing many hundreds of Karen fighters across the border into Thailand. The virtual defeat of the Karen forces was attributed to their reportedly severe lack of ammunition and funds and also to the defection from the KNU in December 1994 of a mainly Buddhist faction, which established itself as the Democratic Karen Buddhist Organization (DKBO). The DKBO, which had comprised an estimated 10% of the strength of the KNLA, allegedly supported the government forces in their offensive. In February 1995 the Myanma army captured the KNU's last stronghold, and in the following month Bo Mya resigned as the commander-in-chief of the KNLA (although he remained the leader of the KNU). In late March the KNU declared a unilateral cease-fire with the aim of initiating negotiations with the SLORC. Earlier in the month a second Karenni organization, the Karenni National Progressive Party, reportedly became the 14th ethnic insurgent group to abandon its armed struggle against the SLORC.

Following the effective defeat of the KNU, Khun Sa's Mong Tai Army remained the only ethnic force still representing a military threat to the SLORC. Khun Sa's position had been strengthened by greater control of the 'Golden Triangle', where opium cultivation had expanded considerably. In December 1993, in order to improve its international reputation, the SLORC initiated a major offensive against Mong Tai Army encampments on the Thai border. During that month Khun Sa convened a Shan 'parliament' in his base of Homong, which was attended by hundreds of delegates. This was followed, in May 1994, by Khun Sa's declaration of an independent Shan State, of which he declared himself 'president'. In the same month fighting intensified between Government forces and the Mong Tai Army near the Thai border, with heavy losses reported on both sides. However, Khun Sa claimed that his army retained control of two-thirds of the Shan State. It was reported that Khun Sa had been successful in persuading some insurgent groups still forming part of the NDF to co-operate with the Mong Tai Army in a loose alliance against the SLORC. In July Khun Sa was reported to have offered to end opium cultivation and to surrender to the government forces in exchange for their withdrawal from the Shan State and a guarantee of Shan independence. In early 1995, following its successful offensive against the Karens, the Myanma army renewed attacks against the Mong Tai Army: fighting was still continuing in May.

In late 1989 the SLORC began resettling Burman Buddhists in the predominantly Muslim areas of Arakan (renamed Rakhine), displacing the local Rohingya Muslims. In April 1991 Rohingya refugees were forced over the border into Bangladesh, as a result of the brutal operations of the Myanma armed forces, including the destruction of villages, widespread killings and pillaging. The Rohingyas had been similarly persecuted in 1976–78, when more than 200,000 of them had sought refuge in Bangladesh. The Rohingyas had finally been repatriated, only to lose their citizenship following the introduction of new nationality legislation in 1982. In late November 1991 the SLORC pledged to repatriate genuine Myanma citizens but claimed that many of the refugees were illegal Bengali immigrants. In December tension was heightened by an attack by Myanma troops on a Bangladeshi border post, in which one Bangladeshi guard was killed. Myanmar had begun to amass troops on the border, accusing the Government of Bangladesh of providing sanctuary for the Muslim guerrillas campaigning for autonomy in Arakan. In late April 1992 the Myanma and Bangladeshi Governments signed an agreement providing for the repatriation of those Rohingya refugees who possessed official documentation to begin in May. The repatriation programme was delayed, however, owing to the continuing flow of refugees to Bangladesh. The first group of Rohingya refugees were returned to Myanmar in late September, without the supervision of the Office of the UN High Commissioner for Refugees. Despite demonstrations by Rohingyas in Bangladesh against forced repatriation, refugees continued to be returned to Myanmar. In November 1993 the SLORC agreed to give the UN access to repatriated Rohingya refugees, which was expected to accelerate the programme. By the end of 1994 approximately 60,000 Rohingya refugees (of a total of about 265,000) had been repatriated. In late April 1994 guerrillas of the Rohingya Solidarity Organization carried out attacks in the Maungdaw area of Arakan State. In October, none the less, a Government representative stated that all of the refugees would be repatriated by the end of 1995.

The People's Republic of China restored diplomatic relations with Burma in 1978. From 1988, as Burma's international isolation intensified, China assumed an increasingly important role. It became Myanmar's principal aid donor, arms supplier and source of consumer goods, and delayed the passage of UN resolutions that were strongly critical of the SLORC's violations of human rights. In an attempt to counter China's increasing influence in Myanmar, in late 1992 India, which had initially been strongly critical of the SLORC, began to improve relations with Myanmar. This trend was also evident in the country's relations with other Asian neighbours, which wished to expand economic links with Myanmar. Trade between Myanmar and the Association of South East Asian Nations (ASEAN, see p. 109) expanded in the early 1990s, and in July 1994 the Myanma Minister for Foreign Affairs attended the annual meeting of ASEAN foreign ministers (the first time that Myanmar had been invited to attend). Myanmar's relations with Thailand had been strained during the 1980s, owing to incursions into Thai territory by Myanma government forces seeking to suppress Myanma insurgent groups, and to the many thousands of Myanma citizens who had taken refuge in Thailand. However, in 1993 it was agreed to delineate the Thai-Myanma border, and in the following year construction began of a 'friendship bridge' across the border.

**Government**

Following the military coup of September 1988, all state organs, including the People's Assembly, the State Council and the Council of Ministers, were abolished by the State Law and Order Restoration Council (SLORC), and the country was placed under martial law. A constituent assembly was elected in May 1990, but this body was accorded no legislative power. In September 1991 the SLORC announced that it would remain the governing authority for a further period of between five and 10 years. During September 1992 a night curfew, imposed in 1988, and two martial law decrees, in force for three years, were revoked. A ban remained, however, on gatherings of more than five people. In early 1993 a national convention, comprising members of the SLORC and representatives of the oppposition parties, met to draft a new constitution; discussions continued during 1994 and in early 1995. Legislative elections were provisionally scheduled for September 1997.

### Defence

Myanmar maintains a policy of neutrality and has no external defence treaties. The armed forces are largely engaged in internal security duties. In June 1994 the armed services totalled about 286,000 men, of whom 265,000 were in the army, 12,000–15,000 in the navy and 9,000 in the air force. Paramilitary forces comprised the People's Police Force of 50,000 men and the People's Militia of 35,000 men. Government expenditure on defence in 1991/92 was 6,086m. kyats (22.0% of total expenditure by the central Government).

### Economic Affairs

In 1986, according to estimates by the World Bank, Myanmar's gross national product (GNP), measured at average 1984–86 prices, was US $7,450m., equivalent to $200 per head. During 1973–86, it was estimated, GNP increased, in real terms, at an annual average of 5.7%, while real GNP per head rose by 3.6% per year. In 1985–93 the population increased by an annual average of 2.2%. Myanmar's gross domestic product (GDP), measured in constant prices, increased by an annual average of 5.0% in 1980–85, but declined by an annual average of 3.2% in 1985–89. GDP was officially estimated to have increased by 1.3% in 1991/92, by 10.9% in 1992/93 and by 5.6% in 1993/94.

Agriculture (including forestry and fishing) contributed 58.9% of GDP in 1992/93, according to provisional estimates. In 1992 the sector engaged an estimated 69.2% of the employed labour force. Rice is the staple crop, and in most years it is the second largest export commodity. Other crops include sugar cane, maize, groundnuts, pulses, rubber and tobacco. There was speculation that the Government was involved in the export of opium in 1989–94. The fishing sector is also important. In 1991 49.3% of Myanmar was under forest cover. In 1992/93 forest products, including logs, sawn timber and processed goods, accounted for 32% of total export earnings. (Teak is frequently felled illegally and smuggled across the border into Thailand.) The output of the agricultural sector expanded by 15.2% in 1992/93.

Industry (including mining, manufacturing, construction and power) provided 9.8% of GDP in 1992/93. In 1992 the sector engaged an estimated 9.4% of the employed labour force.

Mining and quarrying contributed an estimated 0.7% of GDP in 1992/93 and engaged about 0.5% of the employed labour force in 1992. Production of crude petroleum decreased steadily from 1980, and in 1988 Myanmar was obliged to import petroleum. In 1989 Myanmar concluded its first petroleum exploration and production-sharing agreements with foreign companies. (By the end of 1992 16 such agreements had been signed.) Crude petroleum production rose from 5.3m. barrels in 1990/91 to 7.3m. barrels in 1993/94. In 1991 proven onshore reserves of natural gas totalled about 250,000m. cu m. Other important minerals that are commercially exploited include tin, zinc, copper, tungsten, coal, lead, gems and silver. The output of the mining sector reportedly increased by 5.6% in 1993/94.

Manufacturing contributed an estimated 7.4% of GDP in 1992/93 and engaged about 7.0% of the employed labour force in 1992. The most important branches are food and beverage processing (which accounted for 77% of gross manufacturing output in 1988/90), the production of industrial raw materials (cement, plywood and fertilizers), petroleum refining and textiles. The sector is adversely affected by shortages of electricity and the high price of machinery and spare parts. In 1992/93, however, the output of the manufacturing sector expanded by 13.7%.

Energy is derived principally from natural gas, which accounted for 43% of electricity production in 1992/93. Hydroelectric power contributed 34%, diesel generators 12% and thermal energy the remaining 11%. In 1990 energy imports were equivalent to 3% of merchandise exports.

In 1990 Myanmar recorded a visible trade deficit of US $301.7m., and there was a deficit of $431.3m. on the current account of the balance of payments. In 1991 the principal individual source of imports (about 29.3%) was the People's Republic of China; other major suppliers were Singapore, Western Europe and Japan. China was also the principal market for exports (16.3%); other significant purchasers were Singapore, India, Thailand and Japan. Illegal trade is widespread, and was estimated to be equivalent to 50% of official trade in 1985. The principal imports include machinery and transport equipment, chemicals and consumer goods. The principal exports include teak, rice, base metals, gems and cement.

In the financial year ending 31 March 1992 there was a budgetary deficit of 9,582m. kyats. Myanmar's external debt totalled US $5,478m. at the end of 1993, of which $5,135m. was long-term public debt. In 1991 the cost of servicing the total debt (which was $4,853m.) was equivalent to 11.3% of exports of goods and services. The annual rate of inflation averaged 22.4% in 1985–93; the rate averaged 21.9% in 1992, but increased to 29.6% in 1993. In 1990, according to official estimates, 3.5% of the labour force were unemployed.

Myanmar is a member of the Asian Development Bank (see p. 107) and the Colombo Plan (see p. 238), both of which provide assistance for economic development in the region.

Economic progress in Myanmar is impeded by numerous problems: substantial debt arrears, which have been exacerbated by the appreciation of the Japanese yen in which much of the debt is denominated; a shortage of foreign exchange; a lack of foreign aid, owing to international criticism of continued violations of human rights; an artificially high official exchange rate (and, consequently, a high level of transactions at a 'black-market' rate); inadequate infrastructure; and widespread corruption. In the late 1980s a limited liberalization of the economy took place, including the abolition of restraints on internal and external trade in 1988 (although the Government retained a monopoly on exports of teak, gems, pearls, natural gas and petroleum). In the same year a liberal law regulating foreign investment was promulgated and, in order to procure foreign exchange, licences were sold, mostly to Thailand, for extensive exploitation of the country's resources. Foreign investment was almost exclusively in projects to exploit timber or to extract petroleum and other minerals. Despite the considerable impediments, these measures stimulated an expansion of the economy in the early 1990s, as neighbouring Asian countries, particularly the People's Republic of China, competed for access to Myanmar's markets. In late 1994 the Government announced that state-owned enterprises would gradually be privatized, and in March 1995 it proclaimed its commitment to an 'open-door' liberalized economic system.

### Social Welfare

Myanmar has fairly well-developed health facilities but they are not comprehensive. In 1986/87 the country had 10,579 physicians and 7,895 nurses. There were 636 hospitals, with a total of 25,839 beds. Health treatment is available free of charge. Of total expenditure by the central Government in the financial year 1991/92, 1,886m. kyats (6.8%) was for health, and a further 1,319m. kyats (4.8%) for social security and welfare. Certain workers are covered by social security insurance, and all workers are entitled to state pensions.

### Education

Education is provided free of charge, where available, and is compulsory at primary level. In 1990, according to UNESCO estimates, adult illiteracy averaged 19.4% (males 10.9%, females 27.7%), a relatively small proportion for a low-income country. Primary education begins at five years of age and lasts for five years. Secondary education, beginning at 10 years of age, lasts for a further six years, comprising a first cycle of four years and a second of two years. In 1990 the total enrolment at primary and secondary schools was equivalent to 62% of the school-age population (male 63%; females 61%). In that year enrolment at secondary schools was equivalent to 23% of children in the relevant age-group (males 23%; females 23%). Emphasis is placed on vocational and technical training. Expenditure on education by the central Government in 1991/92 was 4,810m. kyats, representing 17.4% of total expenditure.

### Public Holidays

**1995:** 4 January (Independence Day), 12 February (Union Day), 2 March (Peasants' Day, anniversary of the 1962 coup), March* (Full Moon of Tabaung), 27 March (Armed Forces Day), April* (Maha Thingyan—Water Festival), 17 April (New Year), 1 May (Workers' Day), 10 May† (Id al-Adha—Feast of the Sacrifice), May* (Full Moon of Kason), 19 July (Martyrs' Day), July/August* (Full Moon of Waso), October* (Full Moon of Thadingyut), October* (Devali), November* (Tazaungdaing

## MYANMAR

Festival), November/December* (National Day), 25 December (Christmas Day).

**1996:** 4 January (Independence Day), 12 February (Union Day), 2 March (Peasants' Day, anniversary of the 1962 coup), March* (Full Moon of Tabaung), 27 March (Armed Forces Day), April* (Maha Thingyan—Water Festival), 17 April (New Year), 29 April† (Id al-Adha—Feast of the Sacrifice), 1 May (Workers' Day), May* (Full Moon of Kason), 19 July (Martyrs' Day), July/August* (Full Moon of Waso), October* (Full Moon of Thadingyut), October* (Devali), November* (Tazaungdaing Festival), November/December* (National Day), 25 December (Christmas Day).

* A number of holidays depend on lunar sightings.
† This holiday is regulated by the Islamic calendar and may vary by one or two days from the dates given.

**Weights and Measures**

The imperial system is in force.

# Statistical Survey

Source (unless otherwise stated): Ministry of National Planning and Economic Development, Merchant St, Yangon; tel. (1) 72159; fax (1) 82101.

## Area and Population

**AREA, POPULATION AND DENSITY**

| | |
|---|---:|
| Area (sq km) | 676,552* |
| Population (census results) | |
| 31 March 1973 | 28,885,867 |
| 31 March 1983† | |
| Males | 17,507,837 |
| Females | 17,798,352 |
| Total | 35,306,189 |
| Population (official estimates at 1 October) | |
| 1989 | 40,030,000 |
| 1990 | 40,790,000 |
| 1991 | 41,550,000 |
| Density (per sq km) at 1 October 1991 | 61.4 |

* 261,218 sq miles.
† Figures exclude adjustment for underenumeration. Also excluded are 7,716 Myanma citizens (5,704 males; 2,012 females) abroad.

**PRINCIPAL TOWNS** (census of 31 March 1983)

| | | | |
|---|---:|---|---:|
| Yangon (Rangoon) | 2,513,023 | Pathein (Bassein) | 144,096 |
| Mandalay | 532,949 | Taunggyi | 108,231 |
| Mawlamyine (Moulmein) | 219,961 | Sittwe (Akyab) | 107,621 |
| Bago (Pegu) | 150,528 | Manywa | 106,843 |

Source: UN, *Demographic Yearbook*.

**BIRTHS AND DEATHS** (UN estimates, annual averages)

| | 1975–80 | 1980–85 | 1985–90 |
|---|---:|---:|---:|
| Birth rate (per 1,000) | 37.5 | 35.5 | 34.1 |
| Death rate (per 1,000) | 14.9 | 14.1 | 12.5 |

Source: UN, *World Population Prospects: The 1992 Revision*.

**Expectation of life** (years at birth, 1991): Males 60.0; Females 63.5 (Source: UN, *Statistical Yearbook for Asia and the Pacific*).

**EMPLOYMENT** *
('000 persons)

| | 1990 | 1991 | 1992 |
|---|---:|---:|---:|
| Agriculture, hunting, forestry and fishing | 10,614 | 10,867 | 11,076 |
| Mining and quarrying | 78 | 79 | 79 |
| Manufacturing | 1,137 | 1,132 | 1,124 |
| Electricity, gas and water | 17 | 17 | 17 |
| Construction | 174 | 188 | 283 |
| Trade, restaurants and hotels | 1,409 | 1,396 | 1,355 |
| Transport, storage and communications | 385 | 388 | 394 |
| Financing, insurance, real estate and business services | 956 | 1,205 | 1,205 |
| Community, social and personal services† | 455 | 465 | 474 |
| **Total employed** | 15,221 | 15,737 | 16,007 |

* Excluding armed forces.
† Including activities not adequately defined.

Source: UN, *Statistical Yearbook for Asia and the Pacific*.

## Agriculture

**PRINCIPAL CROPS** ('000 metric tons)

| | 1991 | 1992 | 1993 |
|---|---:|---:|---:|
| Wheat | 123 | 143 | 139 |
| Rice (paddy) | 13,199 | 14,835 | 17,434 |
| Maize | 216 | 212 | 220* |
| Millet | 119 | 137 | 140* |
| Potatoes | 136 | 156 | 143 |
| Sugar cane | 2,105 | 2,431 | 3,410 |
| Pulses | 526 | 677 | 842 |
| Groundnuts (in shell) | 472 | 378 | 433 |
| Cottonseed | 42 | 42 | 45 |
| Cotton (lint) | 21 | 21 | 23 |
| Sesame seed | 216 | 170 | 237 |
| Tobacco (leaves) | 43 | 53 | 50 |
| Jute and substitutes | 26 | 27 | 48 |
| Natural rubber | 15 | 15 | 16 |
| Vegetables (incl. melons) | 2,181 | 2,202 | 2,225 |
| Fruit (excl. melons) | 976 | 964 | 1,013 |

* FAO estimate.

Source: FAO, *Production Yearbook*.

# MYANMAR

## LIVESTOCK ('000 head, year ending September)

|  | 1991 | 1992 | 1993 |
|---|---|---|---|
| Horses | 118 | 116 | 120 |
| Cattle | 9,382 | 9,470 | 9,584 |
| Buffaloes | 2,100 | 2,099 | 2,110 |
| Pigs | 2,372 | 2,514 | 2,529 |
| Sheep | 279 | 284 | 305 |
| Goats | 1,011 | 1,076 | 1,092 |

Chickens (million): 25 in 1991; 25 in 1992; 25 in 1993.
Ducks (million): 4 in 1991; 4 in 1992; 4 in 1993.
Source: FAO, *Production Yearbook*.

## LIVESTOCK PRODUCTS ('000 metric tons)

|  | 1991 | 1992 | 1993 |
|---|---|---|---|
| Beef and veal* | 86 | 88 | 89 |
| Buffalo meat* | 22 | 22 | 22 |
| Mutton and lamb | 1 | 1 | 2 |
| Goats' meat | 5 | 5 | 6 |
| Pig meat* | 82 | 88 | 91 |
| Poultry meat | 84 | 89 | 90 |
| Cows' milk | 427 | 431 | 435 |
| Buffaloes' milk | 94 | 95 | 97 |
| Goats' milk* | 5 | 5 | 5 |
| Butter and ghee* | 9.4 | 9.5 | 9.6 |
| Cheese* | 26.8 | 27.0 | 27.3 |
| Hen eggs | 35.9 | 36.6 | 37.3 |
| Other poultry eggs | 6.2 | 7.3 | 6.9 |
| Cattle and buffalo hides* | 23.1 | 23.2 | 23.3 |

* FAO estimates.

Source: FAO, *Production Yearbook*.

## Forestry

### ROUNDWOOD REMOVALS ('000 cu m, excl. bark)

|  | 1990 | 1991 | 1992 |
|---|---|---|---|
| Sawlogs, veneer logs and logs for sleepers | 2,413 | 2,783 | 2,791 |
| Other industrial wood* | 1,254 | 1,282 | 1,310 |
| Fuel wood* | 17,846 | 18,236 | 18,632 |
| **Total** | 21,513 | 22,301 | 22,733 |

* FAO estimates.
Source: FAO, *Yearbook of Forest Products*.

### SAWNWOOD PRODUCTION ('000 cu m, incl. railway sleepers)

|  | 1990 | 1991 | 1992 |
|---|---|---|---|
| **Total** | 296 | 239 | 282 |

Source: FAO, *Yearbook of Forest Products*.

## Fishing

(metric tons)

|  | 1990 | 1991 | 1992* |
|---|---|---|---|
| Inland waters | 144,586 | 175,149 | 182,400 |
| Indian Ocean | 599,232 | 594,087 | 617,600 |
| **Total catch** | 743,818 | 769,236 | 800,000 |

* FAO estimates.
Source: FAO, *Yearbook of Fishery Statistics*.

## Mining

(metric tons, unless otherwise indicated)

|  | 1989 | 1990 | 1991 |
|---|---|---|---|
| Coal | 39,000 | 42,000 | 44,000* |
| Crude petroleum | 889,000 | 875,000 | 920,000* |
| Natural gas (petajoules) | 42 | 42 | 39 |
| Lead† | 5,200 | 2,300 | 2,700 |
| Tin†‡ | 276 | 292 | 179 |
| Tungsten | 300* | 311 | 300* |
| Zinc†‡ | 2,200 | 2,200 | 1,500 |
| Silver‡ | 6 | 7 | 5 |

* Provisional.
† Figures refer to the metal content of ores and concentrates.
‡ Government production only.
Source: mainly UN, *Industrial Statistics Yearbook*.

## Industry

### SELECTED PRODUCTS
('000 metric tons, unless otherwise indicated)

|  | 1989 | 1990 | 1991 |
|---|---|---|---|
| Raw sugar | 31 | 36 | 21 |
| Refined sugar* | 32 | 29 | 36 |
| Beer ('000 hectolitres)* | 21 | 24 | 30 |
| Cigarettes (million)* | 505 | 979 | 682 |
| Cotton yarn* | 6.9 | 9.3 | 5.4 |
| Woven cotton fabrics (million sq m)† | 21 | n.a. | n.a. |
| Plywood ('000 cu m) | 15 | 15 | 15 |
| Printing and writing paper | 7 | 5 | 5 |
| Nitrogenous fertilizers‡ | 112 | 88 | n.a. |
| Jet fuels | 22 | 22 | 20 |
| Motor spirit (petrol) | 126 | 124 | 122 |
| Kerosene | 13 | 12 | 11 |
| Distillate fuel oils | 289 | 285 | 275 |
| Residual fuel oils | 120 | 118 | 115 |
| Lubricating oils | 16 | 15 | 14 |
| Clay building bricks (million)* | 61 | 61 | 61 |
| Cement* | 441 | 420 | 443 |
| Tin-unwrought (metric tons)§ | 500‖ | 500‖ | 309 |
| Bicycles ('000)* | 8 | 5 | 6 |
| Electric energy (million kWh) | 2,472 | 2,601 | 2,400 |

* Government production only.
† Production by government-owned enterprises only.
‡ Twelve months ending 30 June of year stated.
§ Primary metal production (Source: *International Tin Statistics*, Geneva, Switzerland).
‖ Estimate.
Source: UN, *Industrial Statistics Yearbook*.

## Finance

**CURRENCY AND EXCHANGE RATES**

**Monetary Units**
100 pyas = 1 kyat.

**Sterling and Dollar Equivalents** (31 December 1994)
£1 sterling = 9.235 kyats;
US $1 = 5.903 kyats;
1,000 kyats = £108.28 = $169.41.

**Average Exchange Rate** (kyats per US $)
1992   6.1045
1993   6.1570
1994   5.9749

Note: Since January 1975 the value of the kyat has been linked to the IMF's special drawing right (SDR). Since May 1977 the exchange rate has been fixed at a mid-point of SDR 1 = 8.5085 kyats.

# MYANMAR

*Statistical Survey*

### CENTRAL GOVERNMENT BUDGET
(million kyats, year ending 31 March)

| Revenue* | 1989/90 | 1990/91 | 1991/92 |
|---|---|---|---|
| Taxes on income and profits | 877 | 2,806 | 1,970 |
| Domestic taxes on goods and services | 2,989 | 4,418 | 5,646 |
| Import duties | 1,447 | 2,193 | 2,864 |
| Property income | 2,142 | 3,434 | 3,342 |
| Fees, charges and sales | 2,289 | 3,047 | 3,521 |
| Sale of fixed assets | 2,098 | 150 | 696 |
| **Total** | 11,842 | 16,048 | 18,039 |

* Excluding grants received from abroad (million kyats): 152 in 1989/90; 140 in 1990/91; 300 in 1991/92.

| Expenditure* | 1989/90 | 1990/91 | 1991/92 |
|---|---|---|---|
| General public services | 2,775 | 5,035 | 4,717 |
| Defence | 4,331 | 5,436 | 6,086 |
| Education | 2,947 | 3,875 | 4,810 |
| Health | 816 | 1,588 | 1,886 |
| Social security and welfare | 1,226 | 1,075 | 1,319 |
| Housing and community amenities | 1,477 | 2,031 | 2,020 |
| Recreational, cultural and religious affairs and services | 265 | 378 | 782 |
| Economic affairs and services | 3,593 | 4,772 | 5,390 |
| Agriculture, forestry and fishing | 1,971 | 2,271 | 2,028 |
| Road transport | 1,051 | 1,769 | 2,621 |
| **Total** (incl. others) | 17,566 | 24,349 | 27,621 |
| Current | 13,927 | 17,323 | 18,361 |
| Capital | 3,639 | 7,026 | 9,260 |

* Excluding net lending (million kyats): −383 in 1989/90; −372 in 1990/91; −289 in 1991/92.

Source: IMF, *Government Finance Statistics Yearbook*.

### INTERNATIONAL RESERVES (US $ million at 31 December)

|  | 1992 | 1993 | 1994 |
|---|---|---|---|
| Gold* | 12.1 | 12.1 | 12.8 |
| IMF special drawing rights | — | 0.3 | 0.1 |
| Foreign exchange | 280.1 | 302.6 | 421.9 |
| **Total** | 292.2 | 315.0 | 434.8 |

* Valued at SDR 35 per troy ounce.

Source: IMF, *International Financial Statistics*.

### MONEY SUPPLY (million kyats at 31 December)

|  | 1988 | 1989 | 1990 |
|---|---|---|---|
| Currency outside banks | 14,659 | 19,926 | 29,211 |
| Demand deposits at banks | 1,009 | 1,391 | 1,376 |
| **Total money** | 15,668 | 21,317 | 30,587 |

Source: IMF, *International Financial Statistics*.

### COST OF LIVING
(Consumer Price Index for Yangon; base: 1980 = 100)

|  | 1991 | 1992 | 1993 |
|---|---|---|---|
| Food | 412.5 | 505.2 | 701.6 |
| Fuel and light | 483.1 | 607.4 | 685.8 |
| Clothing | 327.8 | 433.8 | 518.3 |
| Rent* | 245.7 | 284.2 | 322.9 |
| **All items** (incl. others) | 386.8 | 471.6 | 611.4 |

* Including expenditure on maintenance and repairs of dwellings.

Source: ILO, *Year Book of Labour Statistics*.

### NATIONAL ACCOUNTS
(million kyats at current prices, year ending 31 March)

**National Income and Product**

|  | 1989/90 | 1990/91 | 1991/92 |
|---|---|---|---|
| Compensation of employees | 52,535 | 64,414 | 76,526 |
| Operating surplus | 60,177 | 70,641 | 84,333 |
| **Domestic factor incomes** | 112,712 | 135,055 | 160,859 |
| Consumption of fixed capital | 7,519 | 8,309 | 9,251 |
| **Gross domestic product (GDP) at factor cost** | 120,231 | 143,364 | 170,110 |
| Indirect taxes, *less* subsidies | 4,435 | 6,610 | 6,461 |
| **GDP in purchasers' values** | 124,666 | 149,974 | 176,571 |
| Net factor income from abroad | −304 | 47 | −269 |
| **Gross national product** | 124,362 | 150,021 | 176,302 |
| *Less* Consumption of fixed capital | 7,519 | 8,309 | 9,251 |
| **National income in market prices** | 116,843 | 141,712 | 167,051 |

Source: UN, *National Accounts Statistics*.

**Expenditure on the Gross Domestic Product**

|  | 1991/92 | 1992/93 | 1993/94 |
|---|---|---|---|
| Final consumption expenditure | 160,610 | 216,062 | 301,335 |
| Increase in stocks | 1,032 | 2,601 | 5,226 |
| Gross fixed capital formation | 27,571 | 31,028 | 35,670 |
| **Total domestic expenditure** | 189,213 | 249,691 | 342,231 |
| Exports of goods and services | 2,926 | 3,590 | 4,071 |
| *Less* Imports of goods and services | 5,337 | 5,365 | 7,218 |
| **GDP in purchasers' values** | 186,802 | 247,917 | 339,084 |
| **GDP at constant 1990/91 prices** | 148,232 | 164,977 | 174,811 |

Source: IMF, *International Financial Statistics*.

**Gross Domestic Product by Economic Activity***

|  | 1990/91 | 1991/92 | 1992/93 |
|---|---|---|---|
| Agriculture, hunting, forestry and fishing | 86,800 | 103,598 | 110,859 |
| Mining and quarrying | 1,040 | 1,076 | 1,264 |
| Manufacturing | 11,115 | 12,206 | 13,928 |
| Electricity, gas and water | 402 | 372 | 392 |
| Construction | 2,478 | 3,073 | 2,887 |
| Wholesale and retail trade | 33,731 | 40,096 | 42,355 |
| Transport, storage and communications | 4,053 | 4,316 | 4,642 |
| Finance | 276 | 295 | 326 |
| Government services | 6,095 | 6,477 | 11,693 |
| Other services | 3,984 | 5,062 | |
| **GDP in purchasers' values** | 149,974 | 176,571 | 188,346 |

* Provisional.

Sources: UN, *National Accounts Statistics* and *Statistical Yearbook for Asia and the Pacific*.

# MYANMAR

## BALANCE OF PAYMENTS (US $ million)

|  | 1988 | 1989 | 1990 |
|---|---|---|---|
| Merchandise exports f.o.b. | 165.7 | 222.8 | 222.6 |
| Merchandise imports f.o.b. | −370.2 | −304.3 | −524.3 |
| **Trade balance** | **−204.5** | **−81.5** | **−301.7** |
| Exports of services | 46.5 | 56.4 | 93.3 |
| Imports of services | −34.2 | −44.3 | −72.2 |
| Other income received | 3.2 | 2.9 | 2.6 |
| Other income paid | −79.4 | −57.1 | −192.3 |
| Private unrequited transfers (net) | 8.6 | 14.3 | 10.2 |
| Government unrequited transfers (net) | 83.9 | 41.4 | 28.8 |
| **Current balance** | **−175.9** | **−68.0** | **−431.3** |
| Direct investment (net) | — | 7.8 | 161.1 |
| Portfolio investment (net) | — | 84.0 | 232.9 |
| Other capital (net) | 139.7 | 74.2 | 24.6 |
| Net errors and omissions | 116.7 | 52.7 | 21.3 |
| **Overall balance** | **80.5** | **150.6** | **8.7** |

Source: IMF, *International Financial Statistics*.

# External Trade

## PRINCIPAL COMMODITIES*
(distribution by SITC, million kyats, year ending 31 March)

| Imports c.i.f. | 1989/90 | 1990/91 | 1991/92 |
|---|---|---|---|
| **Food and live animals** | 27.5 | 104.8 | 192.3 |
| Milk, condensed or evaporated, incl. milk cream | 10.5 | 46.5 | 17.6 |
| **Beverages and tobacco** | 2.2 | 10.3 | 12.2 |
| **Crude materials (inedible) except fuels** | 17.9 | 29.4 | 10.6 |
| **Mineral fuels, lubricants, etc** | 113.7 | 239.4 | 185.4 |
| Refined mineral oil | 66.7 | 201.3 | 77.5 |
| **Animal and vegetable oils, fats and waxes** | 73.3 | 433.7 | 384.5 |
| Edible vegetable oil and hydrogenated oils | 65.0 | 406.1 | 350.1 |
| **Chemicals and related products** | 373.7 | 311.8 | 384.3 |
| Pharmaceutical products | 75.4 | 94.2 | 121.0 |
| Fertilizers, manufactured | 87.1 | 27.1 | 64.5 |
| **Basic manufactures** | 370.9 | 673.8 | 620.7 |
| Paper, paper board and manufactures | 31.5 | 77.0 | 110.9 |
| Base metals and manufactures | 230.1 | 463.3 | 363.4 |
| Cotton yarn | 10.2 | 12.9 | 9.2 |
| Cotton fabrics | 1.4 | 3.0 | 23.6 |
| **Machinery and transport equipment** | 1,207.6 | 2,045.5 | 1,721.0 |
| **Miscellaneous manufactured articles** | 138.4 | 205.6 | 162.3 |

| Exports f.o.b. | 1989/90 | 1990/91 | 1991/92 |
|---|---|---|---|
| **Food and live animals** | 571.4 | 866.6 | 906.3 |
| Fish and fish products | 131.8 | 150.2 | 145.0 |
| Rice and rice products | 266.3 | 172.1 | 251.0 |
| Matpe | 57.0 | 147.4 | 185.7 |
| Oilcakes | 14.8 | 12.1 | 13.7 |
| **Beverages and tobacco** | — | 11.0 | 2.4 |
| **Crude materials (inedible) except fuels** | 968.1 | 1,270.6 | 1,246.5 |
| Raw rubber | 8.4 | 3.3 | 34.1 |
| Teak and other hardwood | 890.7 | 999.0 | 749.0 |
| Base metals and ores | 67.5 | 71.6 | 48.4 |
| **Mineral fuels, lubricants, etc.** | 46.7 | 8.3 | 7.0 |
| **Chemicals and related products** | 32.8 | 9.0 | 0.5 |
| **Basic manufactures** | 117.0 | 205.5 | 61.4 |
| **Machinery and transport equipment** | 1.2 | — | — |
| **Miscellaneous manufactured articles** | 23.7 | 16.6 | 69.3 |

* Figures exclude border trade.

Source: UN, *Statistical Yearbook for Asia and the Pacific*.

## PRINCIPAL TRADING PARTNERS
(US $ million)

| Imports | 1989* | 1990* | 1991 |
|---|---|---|---|
| Australia | 3.1 | 24.2 | 3.4 |
| China, People's Republic | 6.1 | 137.7 | 314.4 |
| Eastern Europe and Former USSR | 17.4 | 30.8 | 60.8 |
| Hong Kong | 1.2 | 8.6 | 14.7 |
| Japan | 75.8 | 110.8 | 90.8 |
| Korea, Republic | 0.4 | 19.1 | 33.1 |
| Malaysia | 5.1 | 31.6 | 73.7 |
| Singapore | 11.3 | 119.2 | 295.8 |
| Thailand | 1.1 | 19.8 | 20.2 |
| USA | 11.7 | 19.3 | 26.2 |
| Western Europe | 51.4 | 125.2 | 114.7 |
| **Total** (incl. others) | **194.3** | **663.4** | **1,073.1** |

| Exports | 1989* | 1990* | 1991 |
|---|---|---|---|
| China, People's Republic | 2.6 | 33.3 | 96.1 |
| Eastern Europe and Former USSR | 10.8 | 11.7 | 10.6 |
| Hong Kong | 19.6 | 22.9 | 33.7 |
| India | 4.9 | 44.2 | 53.6 |
| Indonesia | 15.0 | 10.1 | 2.6 |
| Japan | 18.0 | 28.3 | 44.9 |
| Korea, Republic | 11.4 | 8.9 | 4.3 |
| Malaysia | 4.7 | 8.6 | 15.6 |
| Singapore | 20.9 | 46.2 | 81.0 |
| Sri Lanka | 12.6 | 12.5 | 13.8 |
| Thailand | 1.7 | 48.9 | 52.5 |
| USA | 1.6 | 9.4 | 26.6 |
| Western Europe | 22.3 | 31.1 | 37.9 |
| **Total** (incl. others) | **214.5** | **402.1** | **588.1** |

* Provisional.

Source: UN, *Statistical Yearbook for Asia and the Pacific*.

# Transport

## RAILWAYS (traffic, year ending 31 March)

|  | 1988/89 | 1989/90 | 1990/91* |
|---|---|---|---|
| Passengers carried ('000) | 36,680 | 48,486 | 54,573 |
| Passenger-miles (million) | 1,870 | 2,295 | 2,685 |
| Freight carried ('000 tons) | 1,270 | 1,731 | 1,930 |
| Freight ton-miles (million) | 197 | 265 | 307 |

* Provisional.

MYANMAR

## ROAD TRAFFIC*
('000 motor vehicles in use)

|  | 1989 | 1990 | 1991 |
|---|---|---|---|
| Passenger cars | 71.3 | 78.1 | 88.6 |
| Commercial vehicles | 53.7 | 54.9 | 56.6 |

* Including vehicles operated by police or other governmental security organizations.

Source: UN, *Statistical Yearbook*.

## INLAND WATERWAYS (traffic by state-owned vessels)

|  | 1988/89 | 1989/90 | 1990/91* |
|---|---|---|---|
| Passengers carried ('000) | 14,552 | 20,566 | 27,481 |
| Passenger-miles (million) | 345 | 423 | 482 |
| Freight carried ('000 tons) | 1,839 | 2,512 | 2,491 |
| Freight ton-miles (million) | 267 | 325 | 326 |

* Provisional.

## SHIPPING

**Merchant Fleet**
('000 gross registered tons at 30 June)

|  | 1990 | 1991 | 1992 |
|---|---|---|---|
| Total | 827 | 1,046 | 947 |

Source: UN, *Statistical Yearbook*.

**International Sea-Borne Freight Traffic**
('000 metric tons)

|  | 1988 | 1989 | 1990 |
|---|---|---|---|
| Goods loaded | 1,198 | 800 | 765 |
| Goods unloaded | 676 | 350 | 645 |

Source: UN, *Monthly Bulletin of Statistics*.

## CIVIL AVIATION (internal and external flights)

|  | 1988/89 | 1989/90 | 1990/91* |
|---|---|---|---|
| Passengers carried ('000) | 308 | 361 | 466 |
| Passenger-miles (million) | 84 | 103 | 128 |
| Freight carried ('000 tons) | 2.4 | 3.1 | 4.4 |
| Freight ton-miles ('000) | 708 | 806 | 1,373 |

* Provisional.

# Tourism

**FOREIGN TOURIST ARRIVALS**

|  | 1989 | 1990 | 1991* |
|---|---|---|---|
| Number of visitors | 5,044 | 8,968 | 8,061 |
| Tourist revenue (million kyats) | 29.9 | 56.6 | 81.6 |

* Provisional.

# Communications Media

|  | 1990 | 1991 | 1992 |
|---|---|---|---|
| Radio receivers ('000 in use) | 3,425 | 3,500 | 3,580 |
| Television receivers ('000 in use) | 80 | 80 | 88 |
| Telephones ('000 main lines in use) | 71 | 76 | n.a. |
| Daily newspapers |  |  |  |
| Number | 2 | n.a. | 2 |
| Average circulation ('000 copies) | 200* | n.a. | 324 |

* Estimate.

Sources: UNESCO, *Statistical Yearbook*; UN, *Statistical Yearbook*.

# Education

(provisional, 1992/93)

|  | Institutions | Teachers | Students |
|---|---|---|---|
| Primary schools | 36,499 | 198,909 | 6,518,800 |
| Secondary schools | 3,032 | 69,697 | 1,661,900 |
| General | 2,920 | 67,503 | 1,633,700 |
| Vocational | 94 | 1,738 | 24,100 |
| Teacher training | 18 | 456 | 4,100 |
| Higher education | 40 | 6,696 | 260,300 |

Source: UN, *Statistical Yearbook for Asia and the Pacific*.

# Directory

## The Constitution

On 18 September 1988 a military junta, the State Law and Order Restoration Council (SLORC), assumed power and abolished all state organs created under the Constitution of 3 January 1974. The country was placed under martial law. The state organs were superseded by the SLORC at all levels with the Division, Township and Village State Law and Order Restoration Councils. The SLORC announced that a new constitution was to be drafted by the 485-member Constituent Assembly that was elected in May 1990. In early 1993 a national convention, comprising members of the SLORC and representatives of opposition parties, met to draft a new constitution. Negotiations were still in progress in early 1995.

## The Government

### HEAD OF STATE

**Chairman of the State Law and Order Restoration Council:** Senior Gen. THAN SHWE (took office 23 April 1992).

### STATE LAW AND ORDER RESTORATION COUNCIL
(June 1995)

Senior Gen. THAN SHWE (Chairman)
Lt-Gen. MAUNG AYE (Vice-Chairman)
Lt-Gen. KHIN NYUNT (First Secretary)
Lt-Gen. TIN U (Second Secretary)
Vice-Adm. MAUNG MAUNG KHIN
Lt-Gen. TIN TUN
Lt-Gen. AUNG YE KYAW
Lt-Gen. PHONE MYINT
Lt-Gen. SEIN AUNG
Lt-Gen. CHIT SWE
Lt-Gen. KYAW BA
Lt-Gen. MAUNG THINT
Maj.-Gen. NYAN LIN
Lt-Gen. MYINT AUNG
Lt-Gen. MYA THINN
Lt-Gen. TUN KYI
Lt-Gen. AYE THAUNG
Lt-Gen. MYO NYUNT
Lt-Gen. MAUNG HLA
Lt-Gen. KYAW MIN
Maj.-Gen. SOE MYINT

### CABINET
(June 1995)

**Prime Minister and Minister for Defence:** Senior Gen. THAN SHWE.
**Deputy Prime Ministers:** Vice-Adm. MAUNG MAUNG KHIN, Lt-Gen. TIN TUN.

# MYANMAR

Minister for Mines: Lt-Gen. KYAW MIN.
Minister for Transport: Lt-Gen. THEIN WIN.
Minister for Home Affairs: Lt-Gen. MYA THINN.
Minister for Co-operatives: U THAN AUNG.
Minister for Industry (No. I): Lt-Gen. SEIN AUNG.
Minister for Forestry: Lt-Gen. CHIT SWE.
Minister for Agriculture: Lt-Gen. MYINT AUNG.
Minister for National Planning and Economic Development: Brig.-Gen. DAVID ABEL.
Minister of Finance and Revenue: Brig.-Gen. WIN TIN.
Minister for Health: Vice-Adm. THAN NYUNT.
Minister for Education: U PAN AUNG.
Minister for Foreign Affairs: U OHN GYAW.
Minister for Culture: Lt-Gen. AUNG YE KYAW.
Minister for Information: Brig.-Gen. MYO THANT.
Minister for Livestock Breeding and Fisheries: Brig.-Gen. MAUNG MAUNG.
Minister for Energy: U KHIN MAUNG THEIN.
Minister for Rail Transportation: U WIN SEIN.
Minister for Industry (No. II): U THAN SHWE.
Minister for Construction: U KHIN MAUNG YIN.
Minister for Communications, Posts and Telegraphs: U SOE THA.
Minister for Social Welfare, Relief and Resettlement: Brig.-Gen. THAUNG MYINT.
Minister for Religious Affairs: Lt-Gen. MYO NYUNT.
Minister for Labour: Lt-Gen. AYE THAUNG.
Minister for Hotels and Tourism: Lt-Gen. KYAW BA.
Minister for Trade: Lt-Gen. TUN KYI.
Minister for the Development of Border Areas and National Races: Lt-Gen. MAUNG THINT.
Ministers at the Prime Minister's Office: Brig.-Gen. LUN MAUNG, Col PE THEIN.

## MINISTRIES

**Prime Minister's Office:** Ministers' Office, Yangon; tel. (1) 83742.
**Ministry of Agriculture and Forestry:** Thiri Mingala Lane, Kaba Aye Pagoda Rd, Yangon; tel. (1) 65587; fax (1) 53984.
**Ministry of Communications, Posts and Telegraphs:** Corner of Merchant and Theinbyu Sts, Yangon; tel. (1) 92019; fax (1) 92977.
**Ministry of Construction:** Ministers' Office, Yangon; tel. (1) 85899; fax (1) 89531.
**Ministry of Co-operatives:** 259–263 Bogyoke Aung San St, Yangon; tel. (1) 77096; fax (1) 83063.
**Ministry of Culture:** 26–42 Pansodan St, Yangon; tel. (1) 75175.
**Ministry of Defence:** Signal Pagoda Rd, Yangon; tel. (1) 81611; telex 21316.
**Ministry of the Development of Border Areas and National Races:** Ministers' Office, Yangon.
**Ministry of Education:** Ministers' Office, Yangon; tel. (1) 86726.
**Ministry of Energy:** 74–80 Minye Kyawswa Rd, Yangon; tel. (1) 21060; telex 21307; fax (1) 22964.
**Ministry of Finance and Revenue:** Ministers' Office, Yangon; tel. (1) 84763; fax (1) 80688.
**Ministry of Foreign Affairs:** Prome Court, Prome Rd, Yangon; tel. (1) 22844; telex 21313; fax (1) 22950.
**Ministry of Health:** Ministers' Office, Yangon; tel. (1) 82834; fax (1) 90581.
**Ministry of Home Affairs:** New Saya Sari Rd, Yangon; tel. (1) 71952.
**Ministry of Hotels and Tourism:** 77–91 Sule Pagoda Rd, Yangon; tel. (1) 78228; telex 21330; fax (1) 89604.
**Ministry of Industry (No. I):** 192 Kaba Aye Pagoda Rd, Yangon; tel. (1) 56064; telex 21513.
**Ministry of Industry (No. II):** Ministers' Office, Yangon; tel. (1) 82826; telex 21503.
**Ministry of Information:** Bo Sung Kyaw St, Yangon; tel. (1) 94827; fax (1) 89274.
**Ministry of Labour:** Ministers' Office, Yangon; tel. (1) 78320.
**Ministry of Livestock Breeding and Fisheries:** Ministers' Office, Yangon; tel. (1) 80398; fax (1) 89711.
**Ministry of Mines:** 90 Kanbe Rd, Yankin, Yangon; tel. (1) 57316; fax (1) 57455.
**Ministry of National Planning and Economic Development:** Merchant St, Yangon; tel. (1) 72159; fax (1) 82101.
**Ministry of Rail Transportation:** Corner of Merchant and Theinbyu Sts, Yangon; tel. (1) 92775.
**Ministry of Religious Affairs:** Yangon.
**Ministry of Social Welfare, Relief and Resettlement:** Ministers' Office; tel. (1) 78299.
**Ministry of Trade:** 228–240 Strand Rd, Yangon; tel. (1) 84299; telex 21338; fax (1) 89578.
**Ministry of Transport:** Ministers' Office, Yangon; tel. (1) 96811; fax (1) 96824.

# Legislature

## CONSTITUENT ASSEMBLY

Following the military coup of 18 September 1988, the 489-member Pyithu Hluttaw (People's Assembly), together with all other state organs, was abolished. A general election was held on 27 May 1990. It was subsequently announced, however, that the new body was to serve as a constituent assembly, responsible for the drafting of a new constitution, and that it was to have no legislative power. The next legislative election was provisionally scheduled for September 1997.

**General Election, 27 May 1990**

| Party | % of Votes | Seats |
|---|---|---|
| National League for Democracy | 59.9 | 392 |
| Shan Nationalities League for Democracy | 1.7 | 23 |
| Arakan League for Democracy | 1.2 | 11 |
| National Unity Party | 21.2 | 10 |
| Mon National Democratic Front | 1.0 | 5 |
| National Democratic Party for Human Rights | 0.9 | 4 |
| Chin National League for Democracy | 0.4 | 3 |
| Kachin State National Congress for Democracy | 0.1 | 3 |
| Party for National Democracy | 0.5 | 3 |
| Union Pa-O National Organization | 0.3 | 3 |
| Zomi National Congress | | 2 |
| National Hill Regional Progressive Party | | 2 |
| Kayah State Nationalities League for Democracy | | 2 |
| Ta-ang (Palaung) National League for Democracy | | 2 |
| Democratic Organization for Kayan National Unity | | 2 |
| Democracy Party | | 1 |
| Graduates' and Old Students' Democratic Association | | 1 |
| Patriotic Old Comrades' League | 12.8 | 1 |
| Shan State Kokang Democratic Party | | 1 |
| Union Danu League for Democracy Party | | 1 |
| Kamans National League for Democracy | | 1 |
| Mara People's Party | | 1 |
| Union Nationals Democracy Party | | 1 |
| Mro (or) Khami National Solidarity Organization | | 1 |
| Lisu National Solidarity Party | | 1 |
| United Nationalities League for Democracy | | 1 |
| Karen State National Organization | | 1 |
| Independents | | 6 |
| **Total** | **100.0** | **485** |

# Political Organizations

A total of 93 parties contested the general election of May 1990. By September 1993 the SLORC had deregistered all except 10 political parties:

**Kokang Democracy and Unity Party:** Yangon.
**Lahu National Development Party:** f. 1988; Leader U DANIEL AUNG.
**Mro (or) Khami National Solidarity Organization:** f. 1988; Leader U SAN THA AUNG.
**National League for Democracy (NLD):** 97B West Shwegondine Rd, Bahan Township, Yangon; f. 1988; initially known as the National United Front for Democracy, and subsequently as the League for Democracy; present name adopted in Sept. 1988; exec. cttee of 16 mems; Chair. U AUNG SHWE; Gen. Sec. U LWIN.
**National Unity Party (NUP):** 93C Windermere Rd, Kamayut, Yangon; tel. 78180; f. 1962 as the Burma Socialist Programme Party; sole legal political party until Sept. 1988, when present

name was adopted; 15-mem. Cen. Exec. Cttee and 280-mem. Cen. Cttee; Chair. U THA KYAW; Jt Gen. Secs U TUN YI, U THAN TIN.

**Shan Nationalities League for Democracy:** f. 1988; Leader U KHUN TUN OO.

**Shan State Kokang Democratic Party:** f. 1988; Leader U YAN-KYIN MAW.

**Union Kayin League:** Yangon.

**Union Pa-O National Organization:** f. 1988; Leader U SAN HLA.

**Wa National Development Party:** Yangon.

The following parties contested the general election of March 1990 but subsequently had their legal status annulled:

**Anti-Fascist People's Freedom League:** 95A Shwegondine Rd, Bahan Township, Yangon; f. 1988; assumed name of wartime resistance movement which became Myanmar's major political force after independence; formed by those who separated from U NU in 1958; Chair. BO KYAW NYUNT; Gen. Sec. CHO CHO KYAW NYEIN.

**Democracy Party:** f. 1988; comprises supporters of fmr Prime Minister U NU; Chair. U THU WAI; Vice-Chair. U KHUN YE NAUNG.

**Democratic Front for National Reconstruction:** Yangon; f. 1988; left-wing; Leader Thakin CHIT MAUNG.

**League for Democracy and Peace (LDP):** 10 Wingaba Rd, Bahan Township, Yangon; f. 1988; Gen. Sec. U THEIN SEIN.

**Party for National Democracy:** Yangon; f. 1988; Chair. SEIN WIN.

**People's Democratic Party:** 150 Lewis St, Kyauktada Township, Yangon; f. 1988; initially known as the National Democratic Party; Chair. Thakin LWIN; Gen. Sec. U TIN SHWE.

**Union National Democracy Party (UNDP):** 2–4 Shin Saw Pu Rd, Sanchaung Township, Yangon; f. 1988 by Brig.-Gen. AUNG GYI (fmr Chair. of the National League for Democracy); Chair. U KYAW MYINT LAY.

**United League of Democratic Parties:** 875 Compound 21, Ledauntkan St, Sa-Hsa Ward, Thingangyun Township, Yangon; f. 1989.

**United Nationalities League for Democracy:** Yangon; an alliance of 21 parties.

Other deregistered parties included the Arakan League for Democracy, the Mon National Democratic Front, the National Democratic Party for Human Rights, the Chin National League for Democracy, the Kachin State National Congress for Democracy, the Zomi National Congress, the Naga Hill Regional Progressive Party, the Kayah State Nationalities League for Democracy, the Ta-ang (Palaung) National League for Democracy, the Democratic Organization for Kayan National Unity, the Graduates' and Old Students' Democratic Association, the Patriotic Old Comrades' League, the Union Danu League for Democracy, the Kamans National League for Democracy, the Mara People's Party, the Lisu National Solidarity Party and the Karen State National Organization.

The following groups are in armed conflict with the Government:

**Arakan Rohingya Islamic Front:** seeks self-determination for Arakan; Leader NURUL ISLAM.

**Communist Party of Burma (CPB):** f. 1939, reorg. 1946; has operated clandestinely since 1948; has participated since 1986 in jt military operations with sections of the NDF; in 1989 internal dissent resulted in the rebellion of about 80% of CPB members, mostly Wa hill tribesmen and Kokang Chinese; the CPB's military efficacy was thus almost destroyed; Chair. of Cen. Cttee Thakin BA THEIN TIN (exiled).

**Democratic Alliance of Burma (DAB):** Manerplaw; f. 1988; formed by members of the NDF to incorporate dissident students, monks and expatriates; Pres. Maj.-Gen. BO MYA; Gen. Sec. U TIN MAUNG WIN. Remaining organizations include:

**All-Burma Student Democratic Front:** Dagwin; f. 1988; split into two factions, the Moe Thi Zun faction and the Naing Aung faction, in 1990.

**Karen National Union (KNU):** f. 1948; Pres. Maj.-Gen. BO MYA; Sec.-Gen. BA THIN/**Karen National Liberation Army (KNLA):** c. 6,000 troops.

**New Mon State Party (NMSP):** Chair. NAI SHWE KYIN/**Mon National Liberation Army (MNLA):** c. 300 troops; Chief of Staff NAI NOL LAR.

**Mong Tai Army:** Homong, Shan State; fmrly the Shan United Army; comprises 25,000 men to protect and control the trade in illicit drugs; controlled by KHUN SA; Leader Maj.-Gen. DE WIN.

**National Democratic Front (NDF):** f. 1975; aims to establish a federal union based on national self-determination; Pres. NAI SHWE KYIN (NMSP); Vice-Pres. NOR MONG ONN (SSPP).

By mid-1995 the following groups had signed cease-fire agreements, or had reached other means of accommodation with the SLORC:

**Arakan Liberation Party (ALP)/Arakan Liberation Army (ALA):** f. 1974; Chair. and Chief of Staff Maj. KHAING YE KHAING.

**Chin National Front (CNF)/Chin National Army (CNA):** Chin State; 3,000 troops; Leader JOHN KAW KIM THANG.

**Democratic Karen Buddhist Organization (DKBO):** Manerplaw; f. 1994; splinter group of the KNU; Chair. U THA HTOO KYAW/**Democratic Karen Buddhist Army (DKBA):** f. 1994; c. 600 troops; Chief of Staff Maj.-Gen. YWAR HAY.

**Kachin Independence Organization (KIO):** Myitkyina; Chair. Maj.-Gen. ZAU MAI (acting)/**Kachin Independence Army (KIA):** f. 1961; c. 8,000 troops; Chief of Staff Maj.-Gen. ZAU MAI.

**Karenni National People's Liberation Front (KNPLF):** Leader U TUN KYAW.

**Karenni National Progressive Party (KNPP):** Chair. BYA REH/**Karenni Revolutionary Army (KRA):** c. 400 troops; Chief of Staff Brig.-Gen. BEE HTOO.

**Kayan New Land Party:** Leader U THAN SOE NAING.

**Lahu National Army (LNA).**

**Palaung State Liberation Organization (PSLO):** Vice-Chair. KHRUS SANGAI (acting)/**Palaung State Liberation Army (PSLA):** c. 500 troops; Chief of Staff Maj. AI MONG.

**Pa-O National Organization (PNO):** Chair. AUNG KHAM HTI/**Pa-O National Army (PNA):** c. 300–400 troops; Chief of Staff Col HTOON YI.

**Rohingya Solidarity Organization:** 5,000 mems; Pres. MOHAMMAD YUNUS.

**Shan State Nationalities Liberation Organization (SSNLO):** Chair. U THA KALEI.

**Shan State Progressive Party (SSPP):** f. 1971; Gen. Sec. Col SAI LAK/**Shan State Army (SSA):** c. 2,500 troops; Chief of Staff Lt-Col GAW LIN DA.

**Wa National Organization (WNO)/Wa National Army (WNA):** c. 600–700 troops; Chair. and Chief of Staff AI CHAU HSEU.

## Diplomatic Representation
### EMBASSIES IN MYANMAR

**Australia:** 88 Strand Rd, Yangon; tel. (1) 80711; telex 21301; fax (1) 71434; Ambassador: STUART HUME.

**Bangladesh:** 56 Kaba Aye Pagoda Rd, Yangon; tel. (1) 39556; telex 21320; Ambassador: Brig. (retd) CHOWDHURY KHALEQUZZAMAN.

**China, People's Republic:** 1 Pyidaungsu Yeiktha Rd, Yangon; tel. (1) 21280; telex 21346; Ambassador: CHEN BAOLIU.

**Egypt:** 81 Pyidaungsu Yeiktha Rd, Yangon; tel. (1) 22886; telex 21315; fax (1) 22865; Ambassador: MOHAMAD HASSAN GHANEM.

**France:** 102 Pyidaungsu Yeiktha Rd, POB 858, Yangon; tel. (1) 82122; telex 21314; fax (1) 87759; Ambassador: BERNARD POTTIER.

**Germany:** 32 Natmauk Rd, POB 12, Yangon; tel. (1) 38951; telex 21401; fax (1) 38899; Ambassador: Dr Baron WALTHER VON MARSCHALL.

**India:** 545–547 Merchant St, Yangon; tel. (1) 82933; telex 21201; fax (1) 89562; Ambassador: GOPALASWAMI PARTHASARATHY.

**Indonesia:** 100 Pyidaungsu Yeiktha Rd, Yangon; tel. (1) 81714; Ambassador: MOCHAMAD SANOESI.

**Iran:** Yangon; Ambassador: GHOLAMREZA YUSOFI.

**Israel:** 49 Pyay Rd, Yangon; tel. (1) 22290; fax (1) 22463; Ambassador: MORDECHAY KARNI.

**Italy:** 3 Inya Myaing Rd, Golden Valley, Yangon; tel. (1) 30966; telex 21317; fax (1) 33670; Ambassador: Dr GIORGIO BOSCO.

**Japan:** 100 Natmauk Rd, Yangon; tel. (1) 39644; telex 21400; fax (1) 39643; Ambassador: TAKASHI TAJIMA.

**Korea, Republic:** 97 University Ave, Yangon; tel. (1) 30655; telex 21324; Ambassador: JUNG HWAN KIM.

**Laos:** POB 1550; A1 Diplomatic Quarters, Taw Win Rd, Yangon; tel. (1) 22482; telex 21519; Ambassador: LY BOLINKHAM.

**Malaysia:** 82 Pyidaungsu Yeiktha Rd, Yangon; tel. (1) 20249; telex 21321; fax (1) 21840; Ambassador: Datuk JOHN TENEWI NUEK.

**Nepal:** 16 Natmauk Yeiktha Rd, Yangon; tel. (1) 50633; telex 21402; Chargé d'affaires: BASANTA BIDARI.

**Pakistan:** A4 Diplomatic Quarters, Pyi Rd, Yangon; tel. (1) 22881; Ambassador: Air Vice-Marshal (retd) ABBAS MIRZA.

**Philippines:** 50 Pyi Rd, 6½ Mile, Yangon; tel. (1) 64010; Chargé d'affaires: VIRGILIO REYES, Jr.

**Russia:** 38 Sagawa Rd, Yangon; tel. (1) 89730; telex 21367; fax (1) 73891; Ambassador: VALERY V. NAZAROV.

**Singapore:** 287 Pyi Rd, Yangon; tel. (1) 35688; telex 21356; fax (1) 33129; Ambassador: CALVIN EIJ MUN HOO.

# MYANMAR

**Sri Lanka:** 34 Taw Win Rd, POB 1150, Yangon; tel. (1) 22812; telex 21352; fax (1) 21509; Ambassador: K. B. FERNANDO.
**Thailand:** 45 Pyi Rd, Yangon; tel. (1) 21713; telex 21341; Ambassador: POKSAK NIN-UBON.
**United Kingdom:** 80 Strand Rd, POB 638, Yangon; tel. (1) 95300; fax (1) 89566; Ambassador: JULIAN HARTLAND-SWANN.
**USA:** 581 Merchant St, POB 521, Yangon; tel. (1) 82055; telex 21230; fax (1) 80409; Chargé d'affaires: MARILYN A. MEYERS.
**Viet Nam:** 36 Wingaba Rd, Yangon; tel. (1) 38905; Ambassador: TRAN VIET TAN.
**Yugoslavia:** 114A Inya Rd, POB 943, Yangon; tel. (1) 32655; fax (1) 32831; Chargé d'affaires a.i.: MILOS BELJIĆ.

## Judicial System

A new judicial structure was established in March 1974. Its highest organ, composed of members of the People's Assembly, was the Council of People's Justices, which functioned as the central Court of Justice. Below this Council were the state, divisional, township, ward and village tract courts formed with members of local People's Councils. These arrangements ceased to operate following the imposition of military rule in September 1988, when a Supreme Court with five members was appointed. A chief justice, an attorney-general and a deputy attorney-general were also appointed.

**Chief Justice:** U AUNG TOE.
**Attorney-General:** U THA DUN.

## Religion

Freedom of religious belief and practice is guaranteed. In 1992 an estimated 87.2% of the population were Buddhists, 5.6% Christians, 3.6% Muslims, 1.0% Hindus and 2.6% animists or adherents of other religions.

### CHRISTIANITY

**Myanmar Naing-ngan Khrityan Athin-daw-mya Kaung-si** (Myanmar Council of Churches): Central YMCA Bldg, 263 Maha Bandoola St, POB 1400, Yangon; tel. (1) 96219; fax (1) 96848; f. 1974 to succeed the Burma Christian Council; 12 mem. churches; Pres. Rev. M. ZAU YAW; Gen. Sec. Rt Rev. MAHN SAN SI HTAY.

#### The Roman Catholic Church

Myanmar comprises two archdioceses and 10 dioceses. At 31 December 1993 an estimated 1.2% of the total population were adherents.

**Catholic Bishops' Conference of Myanmar:** 292 Pyi Rd, Sanchaung PO, Yangon 11111; tel. (1) 30268; f. 1988; Pres. Most Rev. ALPHONSE U THAN AUNG, Archbishop of Mandalay.

**Archbishop of Mandalay:** Most Rev. ALPHONSE U THAN AUNG, Archbishop's House, 82nd and 25th St, Mandalay 05071; tel. (2) 21997.

**Archbishop of Yangon:** Most Rev. GABRIEL THOHEY MAHN GABY, Archbishop's House, 289 Theinbyu St, Botataung, Yangon; tel. (1) 94899.

#### The Anglican Communion

Anglicans are adherents of the Church of the Province of Myanmar, comprising five dioceses. The Province was formed in February 1970, and contained an estimated 45,000 adherents in 1985.

**Archbishop of Myanmar and Bishop of Yangon:** Most Rev. ANDREW MYA HAN, Bishopscourt, 140 Pyidaungsu Yeiktha Rd, Dagon PO, Yangon; tel. (1) 85379; postal address: c/o Rev Monty Morris, 11 Convent Rd, Bangkok, Thailand.

#### Protestant Churches

**Lutheran Bethlehem Church:** 181–183 Theinbyu St, Kandawgalay PO 11221, POB 773, Yangon; tel. (1) 78148; Pres. Rev. JOSEPH JOHN ANDREWS.

**Myanmar Baptist Convention:** 143 Minye Kyawswa Rd, POB 506, Yangon; tel. (1) 21465; f. 1865 as Burma Baptist Missionary Convention; present name adopted 1954; 522,215 mems (1993); Pres. Rev. DANIEL HTOO; Gen. Sec. Rev. SAW MAR GAY GYI.

**Myanmar Methodist Church:** Methodist Headquarters, 22 Signal Pagoda Rd, Yangon; Bishop C. F. CHU.

**Presbyterian Church of Myanmar:** Synod Office, Falam, Chin State; 22,000 mems; Rev. SUN KANGLO.

Other denominations active in Myanmar include the **Lisu Christian Church** and the **Salvation Army**.

## The Press

### DAILIES

**Myanma Alin** (New Light of Myanmar): 212 Theinbyu Rd, Botahtaung PO, POB 40, Yangon; tel. (1) 73182; f. 1963; fmrly Loktha Pyithu Nezin (Working People's Daily); organ of the SLORC; morning; Myanmar; Chief Editor U SOE MYINT; circ. 400,000.

**New Light of Myanmar:** 22–30 Strand Rd, Yangon; tel. (1) 89190; f. 1963; fmrly Working People's Daily; organ of the SLORC; morning; English; Chief Editor U KYAW MIN; circ. 14,000.

### PERIODICALS

**Do Kyaung Tha:** Myawaddy Press, 181-3 Sule Pagoda Rd, Yangon; f. 1965; monthly; Myanmar and English; circ. 17,000.

**Gita Padetha:** Yangon; journal of Myanma Music Council; circ. 10,000.

**Guardian Magazine:** 392/396 Merchant St, Botahtaung PO, POB 1522, Yangon; tel. (1) 70150; f. 1953; nationalized 1964; monthly; English; literary; circ. 11,600.

**Moethaukpan** (Aurora): Myawaddy Press, 181-3 Sule Pagoda Rd, Yangon; f. 1980; monthly; Myanmar and English; circ. 27,500.

**Myawaddy Journal:** Myawaddy Press, 181-3 Sule Pagoda Rd, Yangon; f. 1989; fortnightly; news; circ. 8,700.

**Myawaddy Magazine:** Myawaddy Press, 181-3 Sule Pagoda Rd, Yangon; tel. (1) 82669; f. 1952; monthly; literary magazine; circ. 4,200.

**Ngwetaryi Magazine:** Myawaddy Press, 181-3 Sule Pagoda Rd, Yangon; tel. (1) 82669; f. 1961; monthly; cultural; circ. 3,400.

**Pyinnya Lawka Journal:** 529 Merchant St, Yangon; publ. by Sarpay Beikman Management Board; quarterly; circ. 18,000.

**Shwe Thwe:** 529 Merchant St, Yangon; weekly; bilingual children's journal; publ. by Sarpay Beikman Management Board; circ. 100,000.

**Teza:** Myawaddy Press, 181-3 Sule Pagoda Rd, Yangon; f. 1965; monthly; English and Myanmar; pictorial publication for children; circ. 29,500.

**Thwe/Thauk Magazine:** 185 48th St, Yangon; f. 1946; monthly; literary.

### NEWS AGENCIES

**Myanmar News Agency (MNA):** 212 Theinbyu Rd, Yangon; tel. (1) 70893; f. 1963; govt-controlled; Chief Editors U ZAW MIN THEIN (domestic section), U KYAW MIN (external section).

#### Foreign Bureaux

**Agence France-Presse (AFP)** (France): 12L Pyithu Lane, 7th Mile, Yangon; tel. (1) 61069; telex 21314; Correspondent U KHIN MAUNG THWIN.

**Agenzia Nazionale Stampa Associata (ANSA)** (Italy): POB 270, Yangon; tel. (1) 90039; telex 21201; fax (1) 90804; Rep. (vacant).

**Associated Press (AP)** (USA): 283 U Wisara Rd, Sanchaung PO 11111, Yangon; tel. (1) 30176; telex 21327; Rep. Daw AYE AYE WIN.

**Xinhua (New China) News Agency** (People's Republic of China): 105 Leeds Rd, Yangon; tel. (1) 21400; telex 21351; Correspondent ZHANG YUHFEI.

**Reuters** (UK) and UPI (USA) are also represented in Myanmar.

## Publishers

**Hanthawaddy Press:** 157 Bo Aung Gyaw St, Yangon; f. 1889; textbooks, multilingual dictionaries; Man. Editor U ZAW WIN.

**Knowledge Publishing House:** 130 Bo Gyoke Aung San St, Yegyaw, Yangon; travel, fiction, religion, politics and directories.

**Kyipwaye Press:** 84th St, Letsaigan, Mandalay; arts, travel, religion, fiction and children's.

**Myawaddy Press:** 181–183 Sule Pagoda Rd, Yangon; tel. (1) 78510; journals and magazines; CEO U THEIN SEIN.

**Sarpay Beikman Management Board:** 529 Merchant St, Yangon; tel. (1) 83611; f. 1947; encyclopaedias, literature, fine arts and general; also magazines and translations; Chair. U TAIK SOE; Vice-Chair. U MAUNG MAUNG KHIN.

**Shumawa Press:** 146 West Wing, Bogyoke Market, Yangon; non-fiction.

**Shwepyidan:** 12A Haiaban, Yegwaw Quarter, Yangon; politics, religion, law.

**Smart and Mookerdum:** 221 Sule Pagoda Rd, Yangon; arts, cookery, popular science.

**Thu Dhama Wadi Press:** 55–56 Maung Khine St, POB 419, Yangon; f. 1903; religious; Propr U TIN HTOO; Man. U PAN MAUNG.

### Government Publishing House

**Printing and Publishing Enterprise:** 228 Theinbyu St, Yangon; tel. (1) 81527; Man. Dir U AUNG NAING.

### PUBLISHERS' ASSOCIATION

**Myanma Publishers' Union:** 146 Bogyoke Market, Yangon.

## Radio and Television

In 1992, according to UNESCO estimates, there were 3,580,000 radio receivers and 88,000 television receivers in use.

**Myanma TV and Radio Department (MTRD):** GPOB 1432, Yangon Taing, Yangon; tel. (1) 31355; telex 21360; fax (1) 30211; f. 1946; fmrly Burma (later Myanma) Broadcasting Service; broadcasts in Myanmar, Arakanese (Rakhine), Shan, Karen (Kayin), Chin, Kachin, Kayah, Mon and English; colour television transmissions began in 1980; Dir-Gen. U KYI LWIN; Dir of Radio Broadcasting U KO KO HTWE; Dir of Television Broadcasting U PHONE MYINT.

**TV Myawaddy:** Yangon; f. 1995; military broadcasting station transmitting programmes via satellite.

In 1992 the National Coalition Government of the Union of Burma began broadcasting to Myanmar from Norway under the name **Democratic Voice of Burma**.

## Finance

(cap. = capital; res = reserves; dep. = deposits; m. = million; brs = branches; amounts in kyats)

### BANKING

In July 1990 new banking legislation was promulgated, reorganizing the operations of the Central Bank, establishing a state-owned development institution, the Myanma Agricultural and Rural Development Bank, and providing for the formation of private-sector banks and the opening of branches of foreign banks.

#### Central Bank

**Central Bank of Myanmar:** 24–26 Sule Pagoda Rd, POB 184, Yangon; tel. (1) 85300; telex 21213; f. 1968; bank of issue; cap. 200m.; dep. 13,955m.; Gov. U MAUNG MAUNG HAN; 37 brs.

#### State Banks

**Myanma Economic Bank (MEB):** 1–19 Sule Pagoda Rd, Yangon; tel. (1) 81819; telex 21214; provides domestic banking network throughout the country; Man. Dir U KYAW KYAW.

**Myanma Foreign Trade Bank:** 80–86 Maha Bandoola Garden St, POB 203, Yangon; tel. (1) 83129; telex 21300; fax (1) 89585; f. 1976; cap. and res 86.5m., dep. 10,791m. (March 1989); handles all foreign exchange and international banking transactions; Man. Dir U HLA THEIN; Sec. U TIN MAUNG AYE.

#### Development Banks

**Myanma Agricultural and Rural Development Bank (MARDB):** 1-7 Latha St, Yangon; tel. (1) 26905; f. 1953 as State Agricultural Bank, reconstituted as above 1990; state-owned; cap. 60.0m., dep. 615.6m. (Sept. 1993); Man. Dir U CHIT SWE.

**Myanma Investment and Commercial Bank (MICB):** 526/532 Merchant St, Yangon; tel. (1) 87156; state-owned; Man Dir U KHIN MAUNG.

#### Private Banks

**Asian Yangon International Bank Ltd:** 319–328 Maha Bandoola St, Yangon.

**Co-operative Bank Ltd:** 334–336 Strand Rd, Yangon; tel. (1) 72641; Gen. Man. U NYUNT HLAING.

**First Private Bank Ltd (FPB):** Theingyizay (C) Bldg, 3rd Floor, Yangon; tel. (1) 89929; telex 21201; fax (1) 89960; f. 1992 as the first publicly-subscribed bank; fmrly the Commercial and Development Bank Ltd; provides loans to private business and small-scale industrial sectors; cap. 156.1m. (Feb. 1995); Chair. Dr SEIN MAUNG; 1 br.

**Kanbawza Bank Ltd:** Taunggyi.

**Myanma Citizens Bank(MCB):** 383 Maha Bandoola St, Yangon; tel. (1) 73512; f. 1991; Chair. U HLA TIN.

**Myanma National Bank Ltd:** Yangon; f. 1992.

**Myanma Oriental Bank Ltd:** 809 Corner of Maha Bandoola St and 11th St, Yangon; tel. (1) 24408; Chair. U BA SEIN.

**Myanma Universal Bank:** 81 Theinbyu Rd, Yangon; f. 1995.

**Myanmar May Flower Bank Ltd:** 159/161 Myanma Gonyi Rd, Yangon; tel. (1) 86948; Chair. U KYAW WIN.

**Myawaddy Bank:** 189 Sule Pagoda Rd, Yangon; tel. (1) 87900.

**Prime Commercial Bank Ltd:** 437 Pyay Rd, Kamayut Township, Yangon; tel. (1) 35990.

**Tun Foundation Bank Ltd:** 165–167 Bo Aung Gyaw St, Yangon; tel. (1) 92020; Chair. U THEIN TUN.

**Yadanabon Bank Ltd:** 58A Bayintnaung St, between 84-85 St, Mandalay.

**Yangon City Bank Ltd:** 12–18 Sepin St, Kyauktada Township, Yangon; tel. (1) 89231; f. 1993; auth. cap. 500m.; 100% owned by the Yangon City Development Committee; Chair. U. KYAW WIN.

**Yoma Bank Ltd:** 1 Kwunchan St, Mingalataungnyunt Township, Yangon; tel. (1) 77460; Chair. U AUNG KHIN.

#### Foreign Banks

By May 1995 a total of 11 foreign banks had opened representative offices in Yangon and a further 13 banks were preparing to open offices.

### INSURANCE

**Myanma Insurance:** 163–167 Pansodan St, Yangon; tel. (1) 83656; telex 21203; fax (1) 89596; f. 1975; govt-controlled; Man. Dir U BA TUN.

## Trade and Industry

### CHAMBER OF COMMERCE

**Chamber of Commerce and Industry:** Yangon.

### STATE ECONOMIC ENTERPRISES

**Inspection and Agency Service:** 383 Maha Bandoola St, Yangon; tel. (1) 76048; telex 21215; fax (1) 84823; works on behalf of state-owned enterprises to promote business with foreign companies; Man. Dir U OHN KHIN.

**Livestock Feedstuff and Milk Products Enterprise:** 10th Mile, Pyay Rd, Yangon; tel. (1) 65178; telex 21310; Man. Dir U KHIN MYINT.

**Myanma Agricultural Produce Trading:** 70 Pansodan St, Yangon; tel. (1) 82891; telex 21227; fax (1) 89578; Man. Dir U THEIN MYINT.

**Myanma Agricultural Service:** 72–74 Shwedagon Pagoda Rd, Yangon; tel. (1) 86034; telex 21311; fax (1) 83651; Man. Dir Dr MYA MAUNG.

**Myanma Ceramic Industries:** 196 Kaba Aye Pagoda Rd, Yangon; tel. (1) 56077; telex 21500; fax (1) 56063; produces cement, glass, pottery, marble, asbestos sheets and refactory bricks; Man. Dir Dr MYA MAUNG.

**Myanma Electric Power Enterprise:** 197–199 Lower Kyimyindine Rd, Yangon; tel. (1) 22866; telex 21306; Man. Dir U THAUNG SEIN.

**Myanma Export-Import Services:** 622–624 Merchant St, Yangon; tel. (1) 80266; telex 21305; fax (1) 89587; Man. Dir U THAUNG SEIN.

**Myanma Farms Enterprise:** Pyi Rd, 9th Mile, Yangon; tel. (1) 63044; telex 21217; Man. Dir Col KHIN MAUNG AYE.

**Myanma Foodstuff Industries:** 192 Kaba Aye Pagoda Rd, Yangon; tel. (1) 56533; telex 21513; fax (1) 56053; Man. Dir U THAN SHWE.

**Myanma Gems Enterprise:** 66 Kaba Aye Pagoda Rd, POB 1397, Yangon; tel. (1) 60363; telex 21506; fax (1) 65092; Man. Dir U KHIN OO.

**Myanma General Industries:** 192 Kaba Aye Pagoda Rd, Yangon; telex 21500; fax (1) 56053; Man. Dir U TUN ZAW.

**Myanma Heavy Industries:** 56 Kaba Aye Pagoda Rd, POB 370, Yangon; tel. (1) 62880; telex 21503; fax (1) 60465; f. 1960; mfr of vehicles, electrical appliances, electronic goods and agricultural machinery; Man. Dir U MYINT THEIN LWIN.

**Myanma Jute Industries:** 275 Yangon-Insein Rd, Yangon; tel. (1) 61794; telex 21513; Man. Dir Lt-Col MYINT MAUNG.

**Myanma Metal Industries:** 192 Kaba Aye Pagoda Rd, Yangon; tel. (1) 56841; telex 21500; Man. Dir U KYAW MYINT.

**Myanma Oil and Gas Enterprise:** 74–80 Minye Kyawswa Rd, Yangon; tel. (1) 22874; telex 21307; fax (1) 22964; fmrly Myanma Oil Corpn (previously Burma Oil Co); nationalized 1963; Man. Dir U PE KYI.

**Myanma Paper and Chemical Industries:** 192 Kaba Aye Pagoda Rd, Yangon; tel. (1) 55776; telex 21500; fax (1) 57744; Man. Dir U TIN AUNG.

# MYANMAR

**Myanma Petrochemical Enterprise:** 23 Minye Kyawswa Rd, Yangon; tel. (1) 22822; telex 21329; fax (1) 22960; f. 1975; govt-controlled; Man. Dir U HLAING MYINT SAN.

**Myanma Petroleum Products Enterprise:** 7A Thanlyetsun Rd, Yangon; tel. (1) 21097; telex 21329; Man. Dir U AUNG HLAING.

**Myanma Pharmaceutical Industries:** 192 Kaba Aye Pagoda Rd, Yangon; tel. (1) 56742; telex 21500; fax (1) 56053; Man. Dir U TIN HLAING.

**Myanma Posts and Telecommunications:** 43 Bo Aung Gyaw St, Yangon; tel. (1) 87991; telex 21222; fax (1) 89911; Man. Dir U HTAY AUNG.

**Myanma Textile Industries:** 192 Kaba Aye Pagoda Rd, Yangon; tel. (1) 56333; telex 21500; fax (1) 56053; Man. Dir U WIN ZAW NYUNT.

**Myanma Timber Enterprise:** POB 206, Ahlone, Yangon; tel. (1) 20650; telex 21312; fax (1) 21816; f. 1948; extraction, processing, and main exporter of teak and other timber, veneers, plywood and other forest products; Man. Dir U MYAT WIN.

**No. 1 Mining Enterprise:** Kanbe Rd, Yankin, Yangon; tel. (1) 57457; telex 21511; fax (1) 52615; fmrly Myanma Bawdwin Corpn; govt-controlled; development and mining of non-ferrous metals; Man. Dir Col TIN WIN.

**No. 2 Mining Enterprise:** Kanbe Rd, Yankin, Yangon; tel. (1) 51421; telex 21511; fax (1) 52615; fmrly Myanma Tin Tungsten Development Corpn; govt-controlled; development and mining of tin, tungsten and antimony; Man. Dir Col TIN WIN.

**No. 3 Mining Enterprise:** 90 Kanbe Rd, Yankin, Yangon; tel. (1) 57444; telex 21511; fax (1) 56224; govt-controlled; production of pig iron, carbon steel, steel grinding balls, coal, barytes, gypsum, limestone, chromite, antimony, various clays and granite, etc.; Man. Dir U MYA SOE.

## HOLDING COMPANY

**Union of Myanmar Economic Holdings:** Yangon; f. 1990; public holding company; auth. cap. 10,000m. kyats; 40% of the share capital was to be subscribed by the Ministry of Defence and 60% by members of the armed forces.

## CO-OPERATIVES

There were 20,594 co-operative societies in 1988/89.

**Central Co-operative Society (CCS) Council:** 334/336 Strand Rd, Yangon; tel. (1) 74550; Chair. U THAN HLANG; Sec. U TIN LATT.

**Co-operative Department:** 259–263 Bogyoke Aung San Rd, Yangon; tel. (1) 71024; telex 21201; Dir-Gen. U MAUNG HTI.

## WORKERS' AND PEASANTS' COUNCILS

Conditions of work are stipulated in the Workers' Rights and Responsibilities Law, enacted in 1964. Regional workers' councils ensure that government directives are complied with, and that targets are met on a regional basis. In January 1985 there were 293 workers' councils in towns, with more than 1.8m. members. They are co-ordinated by a central workers' organization in Yangon, formed in 1968 to replace trades union organizations which had been abolished in 1964.

**Peasants' Asiayone (Organization):** Yangon; tel. (1) 82819; f. 1977; peasants' representative org.; Chair. Brig.-Gen. U THAN NYUNT; Sec. U SAN TUN.

**Workers' Unity Organization:** Central Organizing Committee, 61 Thein Byu St, Yangon; tel. (1) 84043; f. 1968; workers' representative org.; Chair. U OHN KYAW; Sec. U NYUNT THEIN.

# Transport

All railways, domestic air services, passenger and freight road transport services and inland water facilities are owned and operated by state-controlled enterprises.

## RAILWAYS

The railway network comprised 4,740 km of track in 1992/93.

**Myanma Railways:** Bogyoke Aung San St, POB 118, Yangon; tel. (1) 84455; telex 21361; f. 1877; govt-operated; Man. Dir U AUNG THEIN; Gen. Man. U THAUNG LWIN.

## ROADS

In 1988 the total length of roads in Myanmar was 23,463 km, of which 8,927 km were bituminized and 2,643 km were metalled roads.

**Road Transportation Department:** 375 Bogyoke Aung San St, Yangon; tel. (1) 82252; telex 21201; f. 1963 to implement phased nationalization of passenger and freight road transport; in 1989/90 operated 2,233 haulage trucks and 1,258 passenger buses; Man. Dir U OHN MYINT.

## INLAND WATERWAYS

The principal artery of traffic is the River Ayeyarwady (Irrawaddy), which is navigable as far as Bhamo, about 1,450 km inland, while parts of the Thanlwin and Chindwinn rivers are also navigable.

**Inland Water Transport:** 50 Pansodan St, Yangon; tel. (1) 82614; telex 21331; fax (1) 86500; govt-owned; operates cargo and passenger services throughout Myanmar; 36m. passengers and 3.1m. tons of freight were carried in 1993/94; Man. Dir U HLA MIN.

## SHIPPING

Yangon is the chief port. Vessels with a displacement of up to 15,000 tons can be accommodated. Plans were being considered for the development, in the late 1990s, of a new international port at Thilawa, 13 km from Yangon.

In 1991 the Myanma merchant fleet totalled 154 vessels, with a combined displacement of 1,046,029 grt.

**Myanma Port Authority:** 10 Pansodan St, POB 1, Yangon; tel. (1) 83122; telex 21208; fax (1) 95134; f. 1880; general port and harbour duties; Man. Dir U TIN OO; Gen. Man. U HLAING SOON.

**Myanma Five Star Line:** 132–136 Theinbyu Rd, POB 1221, Yangon; tel. (1) 95279; telex 21210; fax (1) 89567; f. 1959; cargo services to the Far East, South-East Asia and Europe; Man. Dir U KHIN MAUNG HTOO; Gen. Man. U KYAW ZAW; fleet of 22 coastal and ocean-going vessels.

## CIVIL AVIATION

Mingaladon Airport, near Yangon, is equipped to international standards. In December 1993 Kyauktheingan in Bago (Pegu) was selected as the location of the proposed Hanthawaddy international airport.

**Department of Civil Aviation:** Mingaladon Airport, Yangon; telex 21228; Dir-Gen. U TIN AYE.

**Myanma Airways (MA):** 104 Strand Rd, Yangon; tel. (1) 82678; telex 21204; fax (1) 89583; f. 1948; govt-controlled; internal network operates services to 25 airports; Man. Dir Lt-Col THURA WIN MYINT; Gen. Man. U ZAW WIN.

**Myanma Airways International (MAI):** Yangon; tel. (1) 89772; f. 1993; transferred to the private sector in September 1993; 70% owned by a private consortium, 30% by the SLORC; operates services to Bangkok, Dhaka, Hong Kong, Jakarta, Kuala Lumpur and Singapore.

# Tourism

Tourism is relatively undeveloped. Yangon, Mandalay, Taunggyi and Pagan possess outstanding palaces, Buddhist temples and shrines. In 1992 Myanmar received an estimated 11,430 foreign visitors, an increase of 41.8% compared with 1991 but still considerably less than the total of 41,904 visitors in 1987. In 1994, however, 67,000 tourist arrivals were recorded, reflecting the Government's recent promotion of the industry (with 1995 designated 'Visit Myanmar Year'). In June 1990 the Myanmar Tourism Law was enacted, delineating the basic principles to be followed in the tourism industry and providing for foreign companies to obtain licences to establish any enterprise connected with tourism.

**Myanmar Hotels and Tourism Services:** 77–91 Sule Pagoda Rd, POB 1398, Yangon 11141; tel. (1) 83363; telex 21330; fax (1) 89588; govt-controlled; manages all hotels, tourist offices, tourist department stores and duty-free shops; Man. Dir Lt-Col SOE THEIN.

**Myanmar Travels and Tours:** 77–91 Sule Pagoda Rd, POB 559, Yangon 11141; tel. (1) 75828; telex 21330; fax (1) 89588; sole tour operator and travel agent; handles all travel arrangements for groups and individuals; Man. U MYO LWIN.

# NAMIBIA

## Introductory Survey

### Location, Climate, Language, Religion, Flag, Capital

The Republic of Namibia (formerly known as South West Africa) lies in south-western Africa, with South Africa to the south and south-east, Botswana to the east and Angola to the north. The country has a long coastline on the Atlantic Ocean. The narrow Caprivi Strip, between Angola and Botswana in the north-east, extends Namibia to the Zambezi river, giving it a border with Zambia. The climate is generally hot, although coastal areas have relatively mild temperatures. Most of the country is subject to droughts and unreliable rainfall. The average annual rainfall varies from about 50 mm on the coast to 550 mm in the north. The arid Namib Desert stretches along the west coast, while the easternmost area is part of the Kalahari Desert. The official language is English; however, most of the African ethnic groups have their own languages, and Afrikaans and German are widely used. About 90% of the population are Christians. The national flag (proportions 3 by 2) comprises a blue triangle in the upper hoist corner, bearing a yellow sun (a blue-bordered disc, surrounded by 12 triangular rays), separated from a green triangle in the lower fly corner by a white-bordered, broad red stripe. The capital is Windhoek.

### Recent History

South West Africa became a German possession in 1884. The territory excluded the port of Walvis Bay and 12 small offshore islands, previously annexed by the United Kingdom and subsequently incorporated in South Africa. In 1914, when the First World War broke out, South African forces occupied South West Africa, and in 1915 Germany surrendered the territory. In 1920 the League of Nations entrusted South Africa with a mandate to administer South West Africa. In 1925 South Africa granted a Constitution giving limited self-government to European inhabitants only. No trusteeship agreement was concluded with the UN after the Second World War, and in 1946 the UN refused South Africa's request for permission to annex South West Africa. In 1949 the territory's European (white) voters were granted representation in the South African Parliament. In 1950 the International Court of Justice (ICJ) issued a ruling that the area should remain under international mandate and that South Africa should submit it to the control of the UN. South Africa refused to comply with this judgment. In October 1966 South Africa's security and apartheid laws were extended to South West Africa, retrospective to 1950.

Opposition within South West Africa to South African rule led to the establishment (in 1957 and 1959 respectively) of two African nationalist organizations, the South West Africa People's Organisation (SWAPO) and the South West African National Union (SWANU). During 1966 SWAPO's military arm, the People's Liberation Army of Namibia (PLAN), launched an armed struggle for the liberation of the territory. PLAN operated from bases in Angola and Zambia, and was controlled by the external wing of SWAPO (led by Sam Nujoma—the President of SWAPO from 1959). SWAPO also had a legal wing, which was tolerated in South West Africa.

South Africa was consistently criticized at the UN over its extension of apartheid to the territory. The UN General Assembly voted to terminate South Africa's mandate in October 1966, established a UN Council for South West Africa in May 1967, and changed the name of the territory to Namibia in June 1968. In 1971 the ICJ ruled that South Africa's presence was illegal. In 1973 the UN General Assembly recognized SWAPO as 'the authentic representative of the Namibian people' and appointed the first UN Commissioner for Namibia to undertake 'executive and administrative tasks'.

In 1973 South Africa established a short-lived multiracial Advisory Council for the territory, but this was boycotted by SWAPO and most influential Africans. In November 1974 the all-white South West Africa Legislative Assembly organized a multiracial constitutional conference on the territory's future, which began in Windhoek in September 1975, attended by representatives of the territory's 11 main ethnic groups. However, neither the UN nor the Organization of African Unity (OAU, see p. 200) recognized the so-called Turnhalle Conference, owing to its ethnic and non-democratic basis, and the legal wing of SWAPO refused to attend. In 1976 and 1977 proposals for procedures whereby Namibia was to achieve independence and formulate a constitution were made by the Turnhalle Conference, but rejected by SWAPO, the UN and the OAU. In September 1977 South Africa appointed an Administrator-General to govern the territory. In November the Turnhalle Conference was dissolved; during that month the Democratic Turnhalle Alliance (DTA), a coalition of conservative political groups representing the ethnic groups involved in the Turnhalle Conference, was formed.

In early 1978 talks were held between South Africa, SWAPO and a 'contact group' comprising Canada, France, the Federal Republic of Germany, the United Kingdom and the USA (at the time the five Western members of the UN Security Council). In March the Western powers presented proposals for a Namibian settlement, including the holding of UN-supervised elections, a reduction in the numbers of South African troops in Namibia and the release of political prisoners. The proposals, conditionally accepted by both South Africa and SWAPO, were incorporated in the UN Security Council's Resolution 435 in September. However, South Africa continued to implement its own internal solution for Namibia by holding an election for a Constituent Assembly in December. The election was contested by five parties, but boycotted by SWAPO, the SWAPO-Democrats (comprising activists who opposed Nujoma's leadership of the main organization) and the Namibian National Front. Of the 50 seats in the Assembly, 41 were won by the DTA. In May 1979 South Africa unilaterally established a legislative National Assembly, without executive powers, from the existing Constituent Assembly. In June, following the detention of about 40 of its prominent members, the legal wing of SWAPO closed its offices in Windhoek and dissolved its executive council.

The UN brought all parties to a conference at Geneva in January 1981, but negotiations to reach a cease-fire and to proceed to UN-supervised elections failed. Later in 1981 the Western powers attempted to secure support for a three-phase independence plan. However, South Africa's insistence (supported by the US Government) that any withdrawal of South African forces must be linked to the withdrawal of Cuban troops from Angola was unacceptable at that time to both Angola and the UN.

Meanwhile, the Pretoria Government proceeded with attempts to consolidate the interim administration in Namibia, in pursuit of an internal settlement. The Ministerial Council, formed in July 1980 and chaired by Dirk Mudge (also Chairman of the DTA), assumed much of the Administrator-General's executive power in September 1981. However, the DTA was seriously weakened in February 1982 by the resignation of its President, Peter Kalangula, the leader of the only significant movement supported by the Ovambo (the largest ethnic group in Namibia) other than SWAPO. Mudge, after several months of disagreement with the South African Government over the future role of the DTA in the territory, resigned the chairmanship of the Ministerial Council in January 1983, causing the dissolution of the Council. South Africa, through the Administrator-General, disbanded the National Assembly and resumed direct rule of Namibia. In February Dr Willem van Niekerk took office as Administrator-General.

In November 1983 the Multi-Party Conference (MPC), a grouping initially comprising seven internal political parties (but boycotted by SWAPO), was established. The MPC appeared to be promoted by South Africa as a means of reaching a settlement on the independence issue outside the framework of Resolution 435, and of reducing SWAPO's dominance in any future post-independence government for Namibia.

South Africa continued, however, to negotiate on the independence issue with SWAPO and Angola. In February 1984 South Africa and Angola agreed to a cease-fire on the

Angola–Namibia border, and set up a joint commission to monitor the withdrawal of all South African troops from Angola. Under the agreement, Angola undertook to ensure that neither Cuban nor SWAPO forces would move into the areas vacated by the South African troops. Nujoma pledged support for the agreement, but stated that SWAPO would not abandon the armed conflict until there was a cease-fire in Namibia itself and until South Africa had agreed to UN-supervised elections. Discussions on the independence issue in mid-1984, involving van Niekerk, SWAPO representatives and members of the MPC, ended inconclusively. Negotiations in 1984–86 between the South African Government and the US Assistant Secretary of State for African Affairs proved equally unproductive.

In April 1985 the South African Government accepted a proposal by the MPC for a 'Transitional Government of National Unity' (TGNU) in Namibia, which was formally established in Windhoek in June, although the arrangement was condemned in advance by the Western 'contact group' and was declared 'null and void' by the UN Secretary-General. The TGNU consisted of an executive Cabinet, drawn from a National Assembly of 62 members who were appointed from among the parties constituting the MPC. The establishment of the TGNU was accompanied by the proclamation of a 'bill of rights', drawn up by the MPC, which prohibited racial discrimination. A Constitutional Council was also established, to prepare a constitution for an independent Namibia. The South African Government retained responsibility for foreign affairs, defence and internal security, and all legislation was to be subject to approval by the Administrator-General. Louis Pienaar replaced van Niekerk in this post in July.

In March 1986 the South African Government announced a deadline of 1 August 1986 for implementation of UN Security Council Resolution 435, on condition that the Cuban troops be withdrawn from Angola; in June it abandoned this deadline, on the grounds that no discernible preparation to withdraw the troops had been made. In January 1987 SWAPO guerrillas resumed operations in white-owned farming areas for the first time since 1983. During 1987, following the liberalization of labour laws and the legalization of trade unions for African workers in 1986, the trade union movement became increasingly active. In mid-1987 the Constitutional Council published a draft Constitution; however, the South African Government indicated that it could not accept the lack of a guarantee of minority rights in the proposal, thus preventing its adoption. In March 1988 the Namibian Supreme Court declared the 'AG8' law of 1980 (which provided for the election of 'second-tier' legislative assemblies and for the administration of education and health facilities on an ethnic, rather than a geographical, basis) to be in conflict with the 1985 'bill of rights'. In April 1988, however, President P. W. Botha of South Africa expressed impatience at the slow progress that was being made towards establishing a permanent constitution, and announced that he was granting the Administrator-General powers to restrict newspapers that were deemed to promote 'subversion and terrorism', and to organize ethnically-based local elections.

In January 1988, following negotiations between representatives of the US, Angolan and Cuban Governments, both Angola and Cuba were reported to have accepted, in principle, the US demand for a complete withdrawal of Cuban troops from Angola, but they reiterated that this would be conditional on the cessation of South African support for the União Nacional para a Independência Total de Angola (UNITA), which was in conflict with the Angolan Government. In March proposals for the withdrawal of all Cuban troops, presented by Angola and Cuba, were rejected by the South African Government as being insufficiently detailed. In May negotiations between Angola, Cuba and South Africa recommenced, with the USA acting as mediator. By mid-July a document containing 14 'essential principles' for a peaceful settlement had been accepted by the participants, and in early August it was agreed that the implementation of Resolution 435 would begin on 1 November 1988. In the same month the Governments of South Africa, Cuba and Angola announced a cease-fire, to which SWAPO agreed, and South Africa undertook to withdraw all its forces from Angola. However, the November deadline was not fulfilled, owing to failure to agree on an exact schedule for the evacuation of Cuban troops from Angola. In mid-November the terms of the Cuban troop withdrawal were agreed in principle, although official ratification of the agreement did not take place until mid-December.

On 22 December 1988 Angola, Cuba and South Africa signed a formal treaty designating 1 April 1989 as the implementation date for Resolution 435 and establishing a joint commission to monitor the treaty's implementation; another agreement was signed by Angola and Cuba, requiring the evacuation of all Cuban troops from Angola by July 1991. A Constituent Assembly was to be elected in Namibia on 1 November 1989. South African forces in Namibia were to be confined to their bases, and their numbers reduced to 1,500 by 1 July 1989; all South African troops were to have been withdrawn from Namibia one week after the November election. The SWAPO forces were to be confined to bases in Angola in April, before being disarmed and repatriated. A multinational military observer force, the UN Transition Assistance Group (UNTAG), was to monitor the South African withdrawal, and civilian administrators and an international police force were to supervise the election. The UNTAG forces began to arrive in February. At the end of that month the TGNU was formally disbanded, and on 1 March the National Assembly voted to dissolve itself: from then until independence the territory was governed by the Administrator-General (Pienaar), in consultation, from 1 April, with the Special Representative of the UN Secretary-General, Martti Ahtisaari. Pienaar and Ahtisaari were jointly responsible for arranging the November election.

The scheduled implementation of Resolution 435 was disrupted by large-scale movements, beginning on 1 April 1989, of SWAPO guerrillas into Namibia from Angola, as a result of which the South African security forces, with the consent of the UN, suspended the cease-fire. About 280 SWAPO troops were reported to have been killed in the subsequent conflict. Following negotiations by the joint monitoring commission, conditions were arranged for an evacuation of the SWAPO forces to Angola. At a meeting of the joint commission in May, the cease-fire was certified to be once more in force. In June most racially discriminatory legislation was repealed, and an amnesty was granted to Namibian refugees and exiles: by late September nearly 42,000 people, including Nujoma, had returned to Namibia. Meanwhile, South Africa completed its troop reduction ahead of schedule.

The election was conducted peacefully on 7–11 November 1989; more than 95% of the electorate voted. The 72 seats in the Constituent Assembly were contested by candidates from 10 political parties and alliances, and representatives of seven parties and fronts were elected. SWAPO received 57.3% of all votes cast and won 41 seats, thus obtaining a majority of the seats in the Assembly but failing to achieve the two-thirds' majority that would have enabled the party to impose its own draft constitution on the emergent nation. The DTA, with 28.6% of the votes, secured 21 seats.

Following the election, South Africa's remaining troops were evacuated from Namibia, while SWAPO's bases in Angola were disbanded. SWAPO's popularity appeared to have been adversely affected by allegations that the organization had imprisoned and tortured some of its opponents: these allegations were consolidated by a ruling of the Supreme Court, in September 1989, that SWAPO was illegally detaining Namibian citizens abroad.

In February 1990 the Constituent Assembly adopted a draft Constitution, providing for a multi-party democracy, based on universal adult suffrage (see Government, below). Later in the month the Constituent Assembly elected Nujoma to be Namibia's first President. On 21 March Namibia became independent: the Constituent Assembly was redesignated the National Assembly, and Nujoma assumed executive power. A Cabinet, headed by Hage Geingob, was also sworn in. In April British military advisers arrived in Namibia to assist in training the Namibian Defence Force (NDF), comprising former members of the demobilized PLAN and the disbanded South West Africa Territory Force.

In July 1990 it was announced that a plot to overthrow the Government had been discovered, reportedly involving former members of the national police force and of the disbanded counter-insurgency unit, Koevoet; in July 1991 three people who had been arrested in connection with the plot were convicted of high treason, with two of them receiving terms of imprisonment. In October 1990 the appointment as Commander of the Army of a former SWAPO Head of Security, who, it was alleged, had been responsible for atrocities committed during the struggle for independence, caused much protest among opposition groups. During that month the human rights organization, Amnesty International, recommended that the Namibian Government conduct an inquiry into alleged violations of human rights by SWAPO prior to the country's independence; at least 350 people who had been imprisoned by SWAPO at that time were reportedly unaccounted for in late 1990.

In July 1991 the South African Government admitted that it had provided some R100m. in funding for the DTA and several other political parties opposed to SWAPO prior to the election of November 1989. In November 1991 the DTA, formerly a coalition of ethnically-based political groupings, voted to reconstitute itself as a single party, known as the DTA of Namibia (retaining Dirk Mudge as its Chairman). In the following month, at SWAPO's first Congress, Nujoma was re-elected as the party's President.

In late November and early December 1992 SWAPO won an overwhelming majority of the votes at elections to the country's 13 Regional Councils, taking control of nine councils. An advisory National Council, comprising two members from each of the Regional Councils, was inaugurated as the second chamber of parliament in early 1993, and its first session began in May of that year.

Namibia's first post-independence presidential and legislative elections took place on 7–8 December 1994, and resulted in overwhelming victories for Nujoma and SWAPO. Nujoma was elected for a second term as President, securing 76.3% of the votes cast; his only challenger was the President of the DTA, Mishake Muyongo (Mudge having retired from active politics). SWAPO secured 53 of the elective seats in the National Assembly, winning 73.9% of the valid votes cast. The DTA retained 15 seats (with 20.8% of the votes), and the United Democratic Front two. The remaining two seats were won by the Democratic Coalition of Namibia (DCN—an alliance of the National Patriotic Front and the German Union) and the Monitor Action Group. SWANU, which had been a founder member of the DCN in August, but subsequently withdrew to contest the elections in its own right, failed to secure representation in the legislature. Although SWAPO thus had a two-thirds' majority in the National Assembly, Nujoma gave assurances that no amendments would be made to the Constitution without prior approval by national referendum. The election results were released despite evidence of irregularities in four constituencies (three results were the subject of High Court adjudication in early 1995), and the DTA led opposition claims of 'gross irregularities' in electoral procedures—international observers had, however, expressed satisfaction with the conduct of voting. The success of Nujoma and SWAPO was, in part, attributed to the popularity of land reform legislation recently approved by the National Assembly.

Nujoma was sworn in for his second presidential term on 21 March 1995. The previous day, as part of a major reorganization of Cabinet portfolios, he had assumed personal responsibility for home affairs and the police, in what was interpreted as an attempt to curb an increase in crime and in discontent within the police force. Geingob remained as Prime Minister, with Hendrik Witbooi, previously Minister of Labour, Public Services and Manpower Development, as his deputy. Helmut Angula (hitherto Minister of Fisheries and Marine Resources) became Minister of Finance.

Following Namibia's independence, the port of Walvis Bay, its surrounding territory of 1,124 sq km and the 12 offshore Penguin Islands remained under South African jurisdiction. In March 1991 the Namibian and South African Governments held unproductive talks on Namibia's claim to the territories. In September, however, the two Governments agreed to administer the disputed territories jointly, pending a final settlement on sovereignty. In August 1992 Namibia and South Africa announced the forthcoming establishment of the Walvis Bay Joint Administration Authority, comprising an equal number of representatives from both countries. In August 1993, however, the South African multi-party constitutional negotiating committee instructed the de Klerk Government to prepare legislation for the transfer of sovereignty over Walvis Bay to Namibia. Accordingly, negotiations between Namibia and South Africa began in the following month, and bilateral agreements were subsequently formulated regarding the future of South African interests in the Walvis Bay area. Namibia formally took control of Walvis Bay and its islands with effect from 1 March 1994. In August SWAPO won eight seats, and the DTA two seats, in Walvis Bay's first non-racial local elections.

In March 1993 UNITA alleged that members of the NDF had crossed the border into southern Angola to assist Angolan government forces in offensives against UNITA. Later in the month UNITA claimed that some 2,000 Cuban troops had landed at Namibia's southern port of Lüderitz, from where they had been transferred to Angola to assist the government forces. The Namibian authorities denied any involvement in the Angolan civil conflict. In the following month it was disclosed that, following a series of border incursions and the reported intimidation of Namibian citizens, NDF troops had been dispatched to the border region to protect two hospitals that were said to be under threat of attack by UNITA. That organization continued to allege Namibian support for the Angolan government forces, and, although the Nujoma Government continued to deny involvement in Angola, it was reported in July that members of Namibia's parliamentary opposition had accused the NDF of collaborating with Angola in the abduction of Namibians from the border region into Angola to join the Angolan government forces: in response, the Namibian Government stated that all those transported to Angola from Namibia were, in fact, illegal immigrants. A 550-km stretch of the border was closed from September 1994, following an attack, attributed by the Namibian authorities to UNITA, as a result of which three Namibian nationals were killed.

Following independence, Namibia became a member of the UN, the Commonwealth and the OAU. In June 1993 Nujoma travelled to the USA, where he was the first black African Head of State to be received by President Bill Clinton. In 1994 SWAPO contributed funds for the electoral campaigns of the African National Congress of South Africa and the Pan-Africanist Congress. President Nelson Mandela visited Namibia in August of that year, and in December South Africa announced the cancellation of Namibia's pre-independence bilateral debt, estimated at some R800m; South African property in Namibia was also transferred to the Namibian authorities.

In February 1995 it was reported that, following the failure of a mediation attempt by President Robert Mugabe of Zimbabwe, Namibia and Botswana were to refer a dispute regarding the demarcation of their joint border on the Chobe river (specifically, the issue of the sovereignty of the uninhabited island of Kasikili-Sududu) for adjudication by the ICJ.

### Government

On 21 March 1990 Namibia became independent, and the Constitution took effect. Executive authority is held by the President, who is the Head of State. According to the Constitution, the President shall be directly elected by universal adult suffrage for a term of five years, and permitted to hold office for a maximum of two terms. Legislative power is vested in the National Assembly, comprising 72 members directly elected by universal adult suffrage and as many as six non-voting members nominated by the President. Elections to the National Assembly are to be held at least every five years. An advisory National Council, comprising two representatives from each of the country's 13 Regional Councils, elected for a six-year period, operates as the second chamber of parliament.

### Defence

In June 1994 the armed forces numbered 8,100 men (army 8,000; marines 100). A coast guard is currently being formed. Budget estimates for 1993/94 allocated R180m. to the Ministry of Defence (representing 5.4% of total projected budgetary expenditure for that year).

### Economic Affairs

In 1993, according to estimates by the World Bank, Namibia's gross national product (GNP), measured at average 1991–93 prices, was US $2,594m., equivalent to $1,660 per head. During 1985–93, it was estimated, GNP per head increased, in real terms, at an average annual rate of 2.3%. Over the same period the population increased by an annual average of 3.0%. Namibia's gross domestic product (GDP) increased, in real terms, by an average of 3.0% in 1986–93.

Agriculture (including fishing) contributed 9.8% of GDP in 1993, and employed an estimated 32.7% of the labour force (many of whom were engaged in subsistence farming) in that year. Namibia has potentially one of the richest fisheries in the world, although concerns were revived in the mid-1990s regarding overfishing in Namibia's coastal waters. Government revenue from sales of fishing concessions was projected at R91m. in 1993, while exports of fish and fish products in that year provided 22.5% of total export earnings. The principal agricultural activity is beef production, which contributes approximately 87% of Namibia's gross non-fishing agricultural income. The production of pelts from karakul sheep is also important. The fastest growing sector in Namibian agriculture is currently ostrich farming. The main crops cultivated in Namibia are maize, millet and root crops. Drought conditions in 1992 led to shortages, and a cereals deficit of 98,200 metric tons was forecast for 1993/94. Agricultural GDP increased by an annual average of 5.2% in 1986–93.

Industry (including mining, manufacturing, construction and power) contributed 31.2% of GDP in 1993, and engaged 15.0% of the employed labour force in 1991. During 1986–93 industrial GDP decreased, in real terms, by an annual average of 1.3%.

Mining contributed 17.6% of GDP in 1993; the sector engaged 3.7% of the employed labour force in 1991. Namibia has rich deposits of many minerals, producing, most notably, some 30% of total world output of gem diamonds (more than 90% of diamonds mined in Namibia are of gem quality). Diamonds contribute some 60% of Namibia's mining GDP, and are the prinicipal mineral export, accounting for an estimated 35.6% of export earnings in 1993. The mining of diamond deposits off shore is of increasing importance. In late 1994 the dominant mining concern in Namibia, CDM (Pty) Ltd, hitherto a wholly-owned subsidiary of the De Beers group, was restructured as Namdeb Diamond Corporation, and one-half of its interests transferred to the Namibian State. Uranium is also an important mineral export. In addition, copper, lead, zinc, silver, tin, gold, salt and semi-precious stones are mined, and Namibia has considerable deposits of hydrocarbons, lithium, manganese, tungsten, cadmium and vanadium. The country is also believed to have significant reserves of coal, iron ore and platinum, while there is considerable potential for the development of limestone and marble resources. The GDP of the mining sector declined by an average of 3.2% per year in 1986–93, although that of diamond mining increased by 1.9%.

Manufacturing contributed 9.3% of GDP in 1993, and engaged 5.8% of the employed labour force in 1991. The sector has remained underdeveloped, largely owing to Namibia's economic dependence on South Africa. The principal manufacturing activities are the processing of fish (which contributed 45.9% of manufacturing GDP in 1993) and minerals for export; brewing, meat-processing and the production of chemicals are also significant. During 1986–93 manufacturing GDP increased, in real terms, by an annual average of 6.6%.

Energy is currently derived principally from imported coal and petroleum products. However, Namibia has considerable potential to produce hydroelectric power. There is a hydroelectric station at Ruacana, on the Cunene river at the border with Angola, and construction of a second hydroelectric station at Epupa is planned. Offshore deposits of natural gas have yet to be exploited on a commercial basis. Imports of mineral fuels accounted for 7.5% of the value of total merchandise imports in 1993.

The services sector contributed 59.0% of GDP in 1993. Tourism is expanding rapidly, and was to be the focus of a major privatization initiative in the mid-1990s. The acquisition of Walvis Bay in March 1994, and subsequent establishment there of a free-trade zone, was expected to enhance Namibia's status as an entrepôt for regional trade.

In 1992 Namibia recorded a visible trade surplus of US $110m., while there was a surplus of US $142m. on the current account of the balance of payments. South Africa is the dominant source of imports, providing 86.9% of the total in 1993. The principal exports in 1993 were minerals (chiefly diamonds), fish and fish products, live animals and meat. The principal import groups in that year included machinery and transport equipment; food, live animals, beverages and tobacco; chemical products; mineral fuels; textiles, clothing and footwear.

Budget estimates for the financial year ending 31 March 1996 envisaged an overall deficit of some N$511 (equivalent to 3.5% of GDP, compared with 4.2% in 1994/95). At independence in 1990 Namibia inherited a total external public debt of R826.6m., which was to be repaid in 17 annual instalments from April 1995; in December 1994, however, South Africa agreed to cancel the debt. The annual rate of inflation averaged 13.0% in 1985–93; consumer prices increased by an average of 10.8% in 1993. Some 38% of the labour force were unemployed in early 1995.

Namibia is a full member of the Southern African Development Community (see p. 219) and of the Southern African Customs Union (with Botswana, Lesotho, South Africa and Swaziland). In November 1993 Namibia was among members of the Preferential Trade Area for Eastern and Southern African States (see p. 240) to sign a treaty providing for the establishment of a Common Market for Eastern and Southern Africa (COMESA), although in October 1994 Namibia announced its withdrawal from COMESA.

Despite the country's vulnerability to drought, Namibia's potential for economic prosperity is high, given its abundant mineral reserves and rich fisheries, as well as a well-developed infrastructure inherited at independence, all of which will have been enhanced by the acquisition, in 1994, of sovereignty over Walvis Bay (and some R84m. in related assets) and of important diamond-mining rights. In an attempt to prevent potential over-dependence on the mining and fishing sectors, the Nujoma administration has identified the need to diversify agriculture and manufacturing, emphasizing the promotion of import-substitution and export-orientated activities, and to exploit the potential of sectors such as tourism. The Government reported growth in all sectors during 1994; the country benefited from the cancellation of debt by South Africa, and the rate of inflation was regarded as manageable. However, despite the introduction (at par with the South African rand) of a new national currency, the Nambian dollar, in September 1993, Namibia's economic progress will continue to be largely influenced by its dependence on South Africa. The success of attempts to attract much-needed foreign investment has been limited by perceptions of corruption in public life, while expenditure on the civil service (the size of which had doubled since independence) is regarded as a considerable drain on public funds. There remain, moreover, wide disparities in the distribution of wealth, although the approval of land-reform legislation in late 1994 signified the initiation of attempts to address this problem; other social impediments to growth that must be overcome include the high rate of unemployment, as well as poor levels of education and health care.

## Social Welfare

In 1988 there were 61 hospitals and 156 clinics, with 250 general medical practitioners and specialist physicians. The ratio of hospital beds to population was 6 per 1,000. In the budget proposals for 1993/94 R440m. (13.1% of total projected expenditure) was allocated to the Ministry of Health and Social Services. The 1995/96 budget allocated some 17% of total expenditure (approximately N$738m.) to health.

## Education

Under the Constitution, education is compulsory between the ages of six and 16 years, or until primary education has been completed (whichever is the sooner). Primary education consists of seven grades, and secondary education of five. In 1992 enrolment at primary schools included 83.0% of children in the relevant age-group (males 81.0%; females 85.1%). Enrolment at secondary schools in the same year was equivalent to 42.8% of the secondary school-age population (males 38.6%; females 47.0%). Higher education is provided by the University of Namibia, the Technicon of Namibia, a vocational college and four teacher-training colleges. In 1993 8,652 students were enrolled at these institutions. Various schemes for informal adult education are also in operation in an effort to combat illiteracy; since 1992 some 42,000 Namibians have followed such programmes. An estimated 62% of the adult population was literate in the mid-1990s. In 1993/94 N$913m. (some 24% of total government expenditure) was allocated to the Ministry of Education and Culture; the 1995/96 budget allocated some 28% of total expenditure (approximately N$1,215m.) to education.

## Public Holidays

**1995:** 1 January (New Year's Day), 21 March (Independence Day), 14–17 April (Easter), 1 May (Workers' Day), 4 May (Casinga Day), 25 May (Ascension Day and Africa Day, anniversary of the OAU's foundation), 26 August (Heroes' Day), 7 October (Day of Goodwill), 10 December (Human Rights Day), 25–26 December (Christmas).

**1996:** 1 January (New Year's Day), 21 March (Independence Day), 5–8 April (Easter), 1 May (Workers' Day), 4 May (Cas-

# NAMIBIA

inga Day), 16 May (Ascension Day), 25 May (Africa Day, anniversary of the OAU's foundation), 26 August (Heroes' Day), 7 October (Day of Goodwill), 10 December (Human Rights Day), 25–26 December (Christmas).

## Weights and Measures

The metric system is in use.

# Statistical Survey

Source (unless otherwise stated): Strategy Network International Ltd, The Namibia Office, Clutha House, 10 Storey's Gate, London, SW1P 3AY, England (no longer in operation).

## Area and Population

### AREA, POPULATION AND DENSITY*

| | |
|---|---:|
| Area (sq km) | 824,292† |
| Population (census results) | |
| May 1981 | 1,033,196 |
| 21 October 1991‡ | |
| Males | 680,927 |
| Females | 720,784 |
| Total | 1,401,711 |
| Population (official estimates at mid-year) | |
| 1992 | 1,445,000 |
| 1993 | 1,490,000 |
| Density (per sq km) at mid-1993 | 1.8 |

* Including data for Walvis Bay, sovereignty over which was transferred from South Africa to Namibia with effect from March 1994. Walvis Bay has an area of 1,124 sq km (434 sq miles) and had a population of 20,800 in 1981.

† 318,261 sq miles.

‡ Figures are provisional. The revised total is 1,409,920.

### ETHNIC GROUPS (population, 1988 estimate)

| | | | | |
|---|---:|---|---|---:|
| Ovambo | 623,000 | | Caprivian | 47,000 |
| Kavango | 117,000 | | Bushmen | 36,000 |
| Damara | 94,000 | | Baster | 31,000 |
| Herero | 94,000 | | Tswana | 7,000 |
| White | 80,000 | | Others | 12,000 |
| Nama | 60,000 | | **Total** | 1,252,000 |
| Coloured | 51,000 | | | |

### PRINCIPAL TOWN

Windhoek (capital), estimated population 114,500 in December 1988.

### BIRTHS AND DEATHS (UN estimates, annual averages)

| | 1975–80 | 1980–85 | 1985–90 |
|---|---:|---:|---:|
| Birth rate (per 1,000) | 43.9 | 43.0 | 42.7 |
| Death rate (per 1,000) | 15.2 | 13.6 | 12.1 |

**Expectation of life** (UN estimates, years at birth, 1985–90): 56.2 (males 55.0; females 57.5).

Source: UN, *World Population Prospects: The 1992 Revision*.

### ECONOMICALLY ACTIVE POPULATION
(persons aged 10 years and over, 1991 census)

| | Males | Females | Total |
|---|---:|---:|---:|
| Agriculture, hunting, forestry and fishing | 99,987 | 89,942 | 189,929 |
| Mining and quarrying | 13,837 | 849 | 14,686 |
| Manufacturing | 10,773 | 12,111 | 22,884 |
| Electricity, gas and water | 2,826 | 148 | 2,974 |
| Construction | 18,137 | 501 | 18,638 |
| Trade, restaurants and hotels | 19,678 | 18,142 | 37,820 |
| Transport, storage and communications | 8,003 | 1,319 | 9,322 |
| Financing, insurance, real estate and business services | 5,180 | 3,367 | 8,547 |
| Community, social and personal services | 3,664 | 2,163 | 5,827 |
| Activities not adequately defined | 39,224 | 44,490 | 83,714 |
| **Total employed** | 221,309 | 173,032 | 394,341 |
| Unemployed | 57,263 | 41,976 | 99,239 |
| **Total labour force** | 278,572 | 215,008 | 493,580 |

Source: ILO, *Year Book of Labour Statistics*.

## Agriculture

### PRINCIPAL CROPS ('000 metric tons)

| | 1991 | 1992 | 1993 |
|---|---:|---:|---:|
| Maize | 50 | 13 | 32 |
| Millet | 50 | 12 | 36† |
| Roots and tubers* | 275 | 220 | 250 |
| Vegetables* | 8 | 8 | 8 |
| Fruit* | 10 | 10 | 10 |

* FAO estimates.   † Unofficial figure.

Source: FAO, *Production Yearbook*.

### LIVESTOCK ('000 head, year ending September)

| | 1991 | 1992 | 1993* |
|---|---:|---:|---:|
| Horses | 53* | 55 | 55 |
| Mules | 6* | 7† | 7 |
| Asses | 68* | 70† | 71 |
| Cattle | 2,212 | 2,206 | 2,300 |
| Pigs | 17 | 15 | 15 |
| Sheep | 3,295 | 2,863 | 2,900 |
| Goats | 1,886 | 1,750 | 1,800 |

* FAO estimate(s).   † Unofficial figure.

Source: FAO, *Production Yearbook*.

# NAMIBIA

**LIVESTOCK PRODUCTS** ('000 metric tons)

|  | 1991 | 1992 | 1993 |
|---|---|---|---|
| Beef and veal* | 45 | 46 | 48 |
| Mutton and lamb* | 14 | 15 | 15 |
| Goat meat* | 5 | 4 | 4 |
| Pig meat* | 2 | 2 | 2 |
| Other meat* | 4 | 5 | 5 |
| Cows' milk* | 71 | 70 | 71 |
| Wool: | | | |
| greasy | 1.2 | 1.0* | 1.0* |
| scoured* | 0.8 | 0.6 | 0.6 |

* FAO estimate(s).

Source: FAO, *Production Yearbook*.

## Forestry

Separate figures are not yet available. Data for Namibia are included in those for South Africa.

## Fishing*

('000 metric tons, live weight)

|  | 1990 | 1991 | 1992 |
|---|---|---|---|
| Cape hakes | 28.0 | 29.5 | 49.1 |
| Cape monk | 1.5 | 4.1 | 6.1 |
| Cape horse mackerel | 85.1 | 83.2 | 116.3 |
| Southern African pilchard | 89.4 | 68.9 | 80.8 |
| Southern African anchovy | 50.5 | 17.1 | 38.8 |
| Other fishes (incl. unspecified) | 2.1 | 1.6 | 1.9 |
| **Total fish** | 256.6 | 204.2 | 292.9 |
| Crustaceans and molluscs | 0.5 | 0.4 | 0.2 |
| **Total catch** | 257.1 | 204.7 | 293.1 |

* Figures include quantities caught by licensed foreign vessels in Namibian waters and processed in Lüderitz and Walvis Bay.

Source: FAO, *Yearbook of Fishery Statistics*.

## Mining

('000 metric tons, unless otherwise indicated)

|  | 1991 | 1992 | 1993 |
|---|---|---|---|
| Copper concentrates* | 35.1 | 35.6 | 32.9 |
| Lead concentrates* | 15.2 | 14.9 | 10.9 |
| Zinc concentrates* | 35.4 | 35.7 | 18.0 |
| Silver ore (metric tons)* | 91 | 89 | 72 |
| Uranium ore (metric tons)* | n.a. | 2,148 | 1,961 |
| Gold ore (kilograms)* | 1,850 | 2,025 | 1,953 |
| Marble | 10.0 | — | 18.4 |
| Fluorspar† | 27.8 | 37.7 | 43.5 |
| Arsenic trioxide (metric tons)‡ | 1,804 | 2,300 | 2,290 |
| Salt (unrefined): | | | |
| Sea salt | 132.7 | 113.6 | 126.5 |
| Rock salt | 6.4 | 5.4 | 4.1 |
| Diamonds ('000 carats) | 1,186.9 | 1,549.3 | 1,141.1 |
| Amethyst (metric tons) | 110 | 8,575 | 180 |

**1994** (provisional, '000 metric tons, unless otherwise indicated): Silver ore (metric tons)* 64; Gold ore (kilograms)* 2,445; Fluorspar† 52.7; Sea salt 351.8; Rock salt 4.6; Amethyst (metric tons) 50.

* Figures refer to the metal content of ores and concentrates.
† 98% calcium fluoride.
‡ 75% arsenic.

Sources: Ministry of Mines and Energy; Ministry of Trade and Industry.

## Industry

**SELECTED PRODUCTS** (metric tons)

|  | 1991 | 1992 | 1993 |
|---|---|---|---|
| Unrefined copper (unwrought) | 31,923 | 37,531 | 34,788 |
| Refined lead (unwrought)* | 33,367 | 31,655 | 31,236 |
| Refined cadmium (unwrought) | 67 | 29 | 13 |

**1994** (provisional, metric tons): Refined cadmium 19.

Sources: Ministry of Mines and Energy; Ministry of Trade and Industry.

## Finance

**CURRENCY AND EXCHANGE RATES**

**Monetary Units**
100 cents = 1 Namibian dollar (N $).

**Sterling and US Dollar Equivalents** (31 December 1994)
£1 sterling = N $5.545;
US $1 = N $3.544;
N $100 = £18.03 = US $28.21.

**Average Exchange Rate** (N $ per US $)
1992  2.8520
1993  3.2677
1994  3.5508

Note: The Namibian dollar was introduced in September 1993, replacing (at par) the South African rand. The rand remained legal tender in Namibia. Some of the figures in this Survey are still in terms of rand.

**CENTRAL GOVERNMENT BUDGET**
(million rand, year ending 31 March)

| Revenue* | 1989/90 | 1990/91† | 1991/92‡ |
|---|---|---|---|
| Taxation | 1,768.7 | 1,538.0 | 1,985.1 |
| Taxes on income, profits and capital gains | 796.4 | 740.7 | 536.4 |
| Individual taxes | 336.8 | 408.5 | 335.0 |
| Corporate taxes | 459.6 | 332.2 | 201.4 |
| Diamond-mining | 131.6 | 62.3 | — |
| Other mining | 157.3 | 100.8 | 51.0 |
| Non-mining companies | 170.4 | 167.6 | 150.0 |
| Domestic taxes on goods and services | 454.7 | 494.7 | 576.3 |
| General sales tax | 310.4 | 359.3 | 390.0 |
| Excises | 127.8 | 120.0 | 140.0 |
| Taxes on international trade and transactions | 498.2 | 283.8 | 860.4 |
| Import duties | 447.8 | 223.5 | 810.0 |
| Export duties | 50.4 | 60.3 | 50.4 |
| Other current revenue | 239.7 | 196.8 | 310.1 |
| Entrepreneurial and property income | 117.3 | 89.9 | 186.0 |
| Administrative fees and charges, non-industrial and incidental sales | 83.3 | 100.4 | 118.5 |
| Capital revenue | 3.4 | 0.1 | 3.7 |
| **Total** | 2,011.8 | 1,734.9 | 2,298.9 |

# NAMIBIA

*Statistical Survey*

| Expenditure§ | 1990/91† | 1991/92‡ |
|---|---|---|
| General public services | 323.3 | 460.0 |
| Defence | 113.0 | 184.0 |
| Public order and safety | 159.1 | 210.9 |
| Education | 423.5 | 628.2 |
| Health | 225.9 | 275.2 |
| Social security and welfare | 131.5 | 192.9 |
| Housing and community amenities | 175.3 | 225.4 |
| Recreational, cultural and religious affairs and services | 68.5 | 83.5 |
| Economic affairs and services | 294.1 | 491.0 |
|   Agriculture, forestry, fishing and hunting | 95.1 | 189.5 |
|   Transport and communications | 154.6 | 232.4 |
| Other purposes | 126.5 | 79.2 |
| **Total** | **2,040.8** | **2,830.3** |
| Current | 1,784.5 | 2,327.4 |
| Capital | 256.3 | 502.9 |

\* Excluding grants received (million rand): 280.9 in 1989/90; 100.0 in 1990/91; 105.0 in 1991/92.
† Provisional figures.
‡ Estimates.
§ Excluding lending minus repayments (million rand): 3.2 in 1990/91; 17.7 in 1991/92.

Source: IMF, *Government Finance Statistics Yearbook*.

**INTERNATIONAL RESERVES** (US $ million at 31 December)*

| | 1992 | 1993 | 1994 |
|---|---|---|---|
| IMF special drawing rights | 0.01 | 0.02 | 0.02 |
| Reserve position in IMF | 0.01 | 0.01 | 0.01 |
| Foreign exchange | 49.69 | 133.67 | 202.59 |
| **Total** | **49.72** | **133.70** | **202.62** |

\* Excluding gold, of which there were no official reserves in 1992–94.

Source: IMF, *International Financial Statistics*.

**MONEY SUPPLY** (N $ million at 31 December)

| | 1992 | 1993 | 1994 |
|---|---|---|---|
| Demand deposits at commercial banks | 1,002.4 | 1,333.1 | 1,465.3 |
| Total money | 1,002.4 | 1,466.8 | 1,682.8 |

Source: IMF, *International Financial Statistics*.

**COST OF LIVING**
(Consumer Price Index for Windhoek; base: 1990 = 100)

| | 1992 | 1993 | 1994 |
|---|---|---|---|
| **All items** | 131.7 | 143.0 | 158.4 |

Source: IMF, *International Financial Statistics*.

**NATIONAL ACCOUNTS** (N $ million at current prices)
**National Income and Product**

| | 1991 | 1992 | 1993 |
|---|---|---|---|
| Compensation of employees | 3,217.8 | 3,714.7 | 4,093.6 |
| Operating surplus | 1,852.3 | 2,149.2 | 2,457.6 |
| **Domestic factor incomes** | **5,070.1** | **5,863.9** | **6,551.2** |
| Consumption of fixed capital | 288.7 | 318.1 | 341.4 |
| **Gross domestic product (GDP) at factor cost** | **5,358.8** | **6,182.0** | **6,892.6** |
| Indirect taxes | 961.8 | 1,209.2 | 1,403.1 |
| *Less* Subsidies | 68.4 | 122.7 | 101.3 |
| **GDP in purchasers' values** | **6,252.2** | **7,268.5** | **8,194.4** |
| Net factor income from abroad | 278.0 | 120.0 | 178.0 |
| **Gross national product** | **6,530.2** | **7,388.5** | **8,372.4** |
| *Less* Consumption of fixed capital | 288.7 | 318.1 | 341.4 |
| **National income in market prices** | **6,241.5** | **7,070.4** | **8,031.0** |

**Expenditure on the Gross Domestic Product**

| | 1991 | 1992 | 1993 |
|---|---|---|---|
| Government final consumption expenditure | 2,148.5 | 2,617.7 | 2,708.4 |
| Private final consumption expenditure | 4,073.8 | 4,588.8 | 5,181.5 |
| Increase in stocks | −3.5 | −73.0 | −80.4 |
| Gross fixed capital formation | 653.1 | 907.4 | 868.2 |
| **Total domestic expenditure** | **6,871.9** | **8,040.9** | **8,677.7** |
| Exports of goods and services | 3,766.6 | 4,223.0 | 4,803.0 |
| *Less* Imports of goods and services | 4,386.3 | 4,995.4 | 5,286.3 |
| **GDP in purchasers' values** | **6,252.2** | **7,268.5** | **8,194.4** |
| **GDP at constant 1985 prices** | **3,541.1** | **3,766.6** | **3,684.8** |

**Gross Domestic Product by Economic Activity** (at factor cost)

| | 1991 | 1992 | 1993 |
|---|---|---|---|
| Agriculture, hunting, forestry and fishing | 546.6 | 558.6 | 678.1 |
| Mining and quarrying | 1,098.9 | 1,200.3 | 1,216.3 |
| Manufacturing | 400.4 | 492.1 | 637.9 |
| Electricity, gas and water | 114.2 | 126.6 | 134.7 |
| Construction | 111.0 | 143.5 | 161.0 |
| Trade, restaurants and hotels | 673.3 | 731.5 | 816.7 |
| Transport, storage and communications | 363.7 | 419.5 | 475.4 |
| Finance, insurance, real estate and business services | 422.1 | 492.7 | 552.7 |
| Government services | 1,343.6 | 1,691.6 | 1,857.1 |
| Other community, social and personal services | 112.5 | 128.4 | 142.2 |
| Other services | 172.5 | 197.2 | 220.5 |
| **Total** | **5,358.8** | **6,182.0** | **6,892.6** |

Source: Ministry of Finance.

**BALANCE OF PAYMENTS** (US $ million)

| | 1990 | 1991 | 1992 |
|---|---|---|---|
| Merchandise exports f.o.b. | 1,101 | 1,252 | 1,288 |
| Merchandise imports f.o.b. | −1,117 | −1,108 | −1,177 |
| **Trade balance** | **−16** | **144** | **110** |
| Exports of services | 107 | 117 | 131 |
| Imports of services | −385 | −457 | −468 |
| Other income received | 201 | 261 | 215 |
| Other income paid | −162 | −148 | −150 |
| Private unrequited transfers (net) | 25 | 24 | 24 |
| Official unrequited transfers (net) | 192 | 311 | 280 |
| **Current balance** | **−38** | **251** | **142** |
| Direct investment (net) | 36 | 100 | 53 |
| Portfolio investment (net) | 11 | −26 | 4 |
| Other capital (net) | −244 | −285 | −173 |
| Net errors and omissions | 275 | −54 | −33 |
| **Overall balance** | **39** | **−14** | **−7** |

Source: IMF, *International Financial Statistics*.

# External Trade

**PRINCIPAL COMMODITIES** (N $ million)

| Imports c.i.f. | 1991 | 1992 | 1993* |
|---|---|---|---|
| Food and live animals } Beverages and tobacco } | 768 | 959 | 1,065 |
| Mineral fuels and lubricants | 302 | 280 | 285 |
| Chemicals and related products | 246 | 286 | 304 |
| Wood, paper and paper products (incl. furniture) | 183 | 200 | 209 |
| Textiles, clothing and footwear | 217 | 211 | 228 |
| Machinery (incl. electrical) | 434 | 471 | 514 |
| Transport equipment | 482 | 605 | 666 |
| **Total** (incl. others) | **3,173** | **3,553** | **3,804** |

# NAMIBIA

| Exports f.o.b. | 1991 | 1992 | 1993* |
|---|---|---|---|
| Food and live animals | 966 | 1,131 | 1,146 |
| Live animals chiefly for food | 211 | 259 | 258 |
| Cattle | 106 | 107 | 135 |
| Sheep and goats | 100 | 136 | 112 |
| Meat and meat preparations | 277 | 308 | 309 |
| Beef and veal | 239 | 256 | 238 |
| Fish, crustaceans and molluscs | 450 | 534 | 549 |
| Mineral products | 2,030 | 2,097 | 2,342 |
| Diamonds | 1,222 | 1,334 | 1,504 |
| Copper | 192 | 222 | 188 |
| Zinc | 82 | 60 | 40 |
| Manufactured products | 357 | 556 | 683 |
| Canned fish, fish meal and fish oil | 220 | 311 | 403 |
| **Total** (incl. others) | 3,401 | 3,826 | 4,224 |

* Figures are provisional.

**PRINCIPAL TRADING PARTNERS**

The principal source of imports is South Africa (N $ million): 2,852 in 1991; 3,133 in 1992; 3,304 (provisional) in 1993.

Source: Bank of Namibia.

## Transport

**RAILWAYS**

|  | 1993 |
|---|---|
| Freight (million net ton-km) | 1,097.3 |
| Passengers carried ('000) | 88.8 |

Source: Bank of Namibia.

**ROAD TRAFFIC**

**1993:** Registered vehicles 138,005.

Source: Ministry of Works, Transport and Communications, Windhoek.

**CIVIL AVIATION** (traffic on scheduled services)

|  | 1991 | 1992 |
|---|---|---|
| Kilometres flown (million) | 4 | 6 |
| Passengers carried ('000) | 149 | 163 |
| Passenger-km (million) | 464 | 535 |
| Total ton-km (million) | 55 | 59 |

Source: UN, *Statistical Yearbook*.

**SHIPPING**
(sea-borne freight traffic at Walvis Bay, '000 metric tons)

|  | 1994 |
|---|---|
| Goods loaded | 623 |
| Goods unloaded | 477 |

Source: Ministry of Works, Transport and Communications, Windhoek.

## Communications Media

|  | 1990 | 1991 | 1992 |
|---|---|---|---|
| Radio receivers ('000 in use) | n.a. | 188 | 195 |
| Television receivers ('000 in use) | 30 | 31 | 32 |
| Daily newspapers |  |  |  |
| Number | 6 | n.a. | 4 |
| Average circulation ('000 copies) | 220 | n.a. | 209 |
| Non-daily newspapers |  |  |  |
| Number | 18 | n.a. | n.a. |
| Average circulation ('000 copies) | 71 | n.a. | n.a. |
| Book production (titles published) | 106 | 193 | n.a. |

Source: UNESCO, *Statistical Yearbook*.

Telephones ('000 main lines in use, year ending 31 March): 53 in 1990/91; 57 in 1991/92 (Source: UN, *Statistical Yearbook*).

## Education

(1993)

|  | Institutions | Males | Females | Total |
|---|---|---|---|---|
| Pre-primary | 12 | 2,424 | 2,476 | 4,900 |
| Primary | 933 | 175,312 | 176,788 | 352,100 |
| Secondary: |  |  |  |  |
| General | 97 | 41,418 | 50,718 | 92,136 |
| Other* | 17 | 1,023 | 480 | 1,503 |
| Tertiary | 7 | 2,737 | 3,786 | 6,523 |

* Including technical, vocational, agricultural and special schools.

# Directory

## The Constitution

The Constitution of the Republic of Namibia took effect at independence on 21 March 1990. Its principal provisions are summarized below:

### THE REPUBLIC

The Republic of Namibia is a sovereign, secular, democratic and unitary State and the Constitution is the supreme law.

### FUNDAMENTAL HUMAN RIGHTS AND FREEDOMS

The fundamental rights and freedoms of the individual are guaranteed regardless of sex, race, colour, ethnic origin, religion, creed or social or economic status. All citizens shall have the right to form and join political parties. The practice of racial discrimination shall be prohibited.

### THE PRESIDENT

Executive power shall be vested in the President and the Cabinet. The President shall be the Head of State and of the Government and the Commander-in-Chief of the Defence Force. The President shall be directly elected by universal and equal adult suffrage, and must receive more than 50% of the votes cast. The term of office shall be five years; one person may not hold the office of President for more than two terms.

### THE CABINET

The Cabinet shall consist of the President, the Prime Minister and such other ministers as the President may appoint from members of the National Assembly. The President may also appoint a Deputy Prime Minister. The functions of the members of the Cabinet shall include directing the activities of ministries and government departments, initiating bills for submission to the National Assembly, formulating, explaining and assessing for the National Assembly the budget of the State and its economic development plans, formulating, explaining and analysing for the National Assembly Namibia's foreign policy and foreign trade policy and advising the President on the state of national defence.

### THE NATIONAL ASSEMBLY

Legislative power shall be vested in the National Assembly, which shall be composed of 72 members elected by general, direct and secret ballots and not more than six non-voting members appointed by the President by virtue of their special expertise, status, skill or experience. Every National Assembly shall continue for a maximum period of five years, but it may be dissolved by the President before the expiry of its term.

### THE NATIONAL COUNCIL

The National Council shall consist of two members from each region (elected by Regional Councils from among their members) and shall have a life of six years. The functions of the National Council shall include considering all bills passed by the National Assembly, investigating any subordinate legislation referred to it by the National Assembly for advice, and recommending legislation to the National Assembly on matters of regional concern.

### OTHER PROVISIONS

Other provisions relate to the administration of justice (see under Judicial System), regional and local government, the public service commission, the security commission, the police, defence forces and prison service, finance, and the central bank and national planning commission. The repeal of, or amendments to, the Constitution require the approval of two-thirds of the members of the National Assembly and two-thirds of the members of the National Council; if the proposed repeal or amendment secures a majority of two-thirds of the members of the National Assembly, but not a majority of two-thirds of the members of the National Council, the President may make the proposals the subject of a national referendum, in which a two-thirds majority is needed for approval of the legislation.

## The Government

### HEAD OF STATE

**President and Commander-in-Chief of the Defence Force:** SAMUEL (SAM) DANIEL NUJOMA (took office 21 March 1990; elected by direct suffrage 7–8 December 1994).

### CABINET
(June 1995)

**President and Minister of Home Affairs:** SAMUEL (SAM) DANIEL NUJOMA.
**Prime Minister:** HAGE GEINGOB.
**Deputy Prime Minister:** V. HENDRIK WITBOOI.
**Minister of Foreign Affairs:** THEO-BEN GURIRAB.
**Minister of Basic Education and Culture:** JOHN MUTORWA.
**Minister of Tertiary Education and Vocational Training:** NAHAS ANGULA.
**Minister of Information and Broadcasting:** BEN AMADHILA.
**Minister of Mines and Energy:** ANDIMBA TOIVO JA TOIVO.
**Minister of Justice:** Dr NGARIKUTUKE TJIRIANGE.
**Minister of Trade and Industry:** HIDIPO HAMUTENYA.
**Minister of Agriculture, Water and Rural Development:** NANGOLO MBUMBA.
**Minister of Defence:** PHILLEMON MALIMA.
**Minister of Finance:** HELMUT ANGULA.
**Minister of Health and Social Services:** NICKY IYAMBO.
**Minister of Labour, Public Services and Manpower Development:** MOSES GAROEB.
**Minister of Regional and Local Government and Housing:** Dr LIBERTINE AMATHILA.
**Minister of Environment and Tourism:** GERT HANEKOM.
**Minister of Works, Transport and Communications:** HAMPIE PLICHTA.
**Minister of Lands, Resettlement and Rehabilitation:** RICHARD KAPELWA KABAJANI.
**Minister of Fisheries and Marine Resources:** HIFIKEPUNYE POHAMBA.
**Minister of Youth and Sports:** PENDUKENI ITHANA.
**Minister of Prisons and Correctional Services:** MARCO HAUSIKO.

### MINISTRIES

**Office of the President:** State House, Private Bag 13339, Windhoek; tel. (61) 220010; telex 3222; fax (61) 221780.
**Office of the Prime Minister:** Private Bag 13338, Windhoek; tel. (61) 2879111; fax (61) 226189.
**Ministry of Agriculture, Water and Rural Development:** Private Bag 13184, Windhoek; tel. (61) 396911; telex 3109; fax (61) 229861.
**Ministry of Defence:** Private Bag 13307, Windhoek; tel. (61) 221920; fax (61) 224277.
**Ministry of Education and Culture:** Private Bag 13186, Windhoek; tel. (61) 221327; fax (61) 36236.
**Ministry of Environment and Tourism:** Govt Bldgs, 5th Floor, Private Bag 13346, Windhoek; tel. (61) 2849111; fax (61) 229936.
**Ministry of Finance:** Fiscus Bldg, John Meinert St, Private Bag 13295, Windhoek; tel. (61) 3099111; telex 3369; fax (61) 36454.
**Ministry of Fisheries and Marine Resources:** Private Bag 13355, Windhoek; tel. (61) 3969111; fax (61) 224566.
**Ministry of Foreign Affairs:** Govt Bldgs, East Wing, 4th Floor, Private Bag 13347, Windhoek; tel. (61) 2829111; telex 655; fax (61) 223937.
**Ministry of Health and Social Services:** Old State Hospital, Nightingale St, Private Bag 13198, Windhoek; tel. (61) 32170; telex 3366; fax (61) 33419.
**Ministry of Home Affairs:** Cohen Bldg, Kasino St, Windhoek; tel. (61) 221361; telex 403; fax (61) 223817.
**Ministry of Information and Broadcasting:** Govt Bldgs, 2nd Floor, Private Bag 13344, Windhoek; tel. (61) 222302; telex 2123; fax (61) 222343.
**Ministry of Justice:** Justitia Bldg, Independence Ave, Private Bag 13302, Windhoek; tel. (61) 239280; telex 635; fax (61) 221233.
**Ministry of Labour, Public Services and Manpower Development:** Mercedes St, POB 23115, Windhoek; tel. (61) 212956; telex 496; fax (61) 212323.
**Ministry of Lands, Resettlement and Rehabilitation:** Private Bag 13343, Windhoek; tel. (61) 220241; telex 826; fax (61) 228240.
**Ministry of Mines and Energy:** Trust Centre Bldg, Independence Ave, Windhoek; tel. (61) 226571; telex 487; fax (61) 38643.

NAMIBIA

**Ministry of Regional and Local Government and Housing:** Private Bag 13289, Windhoek; tel. (61) 225898; telex 603; fax (61) 226049.

**Ministry of Trade and Industry:** Govt Bldgs, Private Bag 13340, Windhoek; tel. (61) 2849111; telex 808; fax (61) 220227.

**Ministry of Works, Transport and Communications:** Private Bag 13341, Windhoek; tel. (61) 2089111; telex 709; fax (61) 228560.

**Ministry of Youth and Sports:** Edcom Bldg, 6th Floor, Private Bag 13359, Windhoek; tel. (61) 220066; fax (61) 221304.

## President and Legislature

### PRESIDENT
Presidential Election, 7–8 December 1994.

| Candidate | Votes | % of Votes |
|---|---|---|
| Samuel Nujoma (SWAPO) | 370,452 | 76.34 |
| Mishake Muyongo (DTA) | 114,843 | 23.66 |
| Total | 485,295 | 100.00 |

### NATIONAL ASSEMBLY
**Speaker:** Dr Moses Tjitendero.

**General Election, 7–8 December 1994**

| Party | Votes | % | Seats* |
|---|---|---|---|
| South West Africa People's Organisation of Namibia | 361,800 | 73.89 | 53 |
| Democratic Turnhalle Alliance of Namibia | 101,748 | 20.78 | 15 |
| United Democratic Front | 13,309 | 2.72 | 2 |
| Democratic Coalition of Namibia | 4,058 | 0.83 | 1 |
| Monitor Action Group | 4,005 | 0.82 | 1 |
| South West African National Union | 2,598 | 0.53 | — |
| Federal Convention of Namibia | 1,166 | 0.24 | — |
| Workers' Revolutionary Party | 952 | 0.19 | — |
| Total | 489,636 | 100.00 | 72 |

* In addition to the 72 directly-elected members, six non-voting members were nominated by the President.

## Political Organizations

**Action Christian National:** POB 294, Windhoek; tel. (61) 226159; white support; Leader Kosie Pretorius.

**Christian Democratic Action for Social Justice (CDA):** Ondwangwa; telex 3143; f. 1982; supported by Ovambos and fmr supporters of National Democratic Party; Leader Rev. Peter Kalangula.

**Democratic Coalition of Namibia (DCN):** Windhoek; f. 1994 as coalition of the National Patriotic Front, the South West African National Union (withdrew from coalition in Nov. 1994) and the German Union; Leader Moses Katjiuongua.

**Democratic Turnhalle Alliance of Namibia (DTA):** POB 173, Windhoek; telex 3217; f. 1977 as a coalition of ethnically-based political groupings; reorg. as a single party Nov. 1991; Pres. Mishake Muyongo; Chair. Piet Junius.

**Federal Convention of Namibia (FCN):** Windhoek; f. 1988; Leader Johannes Diergaardt; federalist, opposing unitary form of govt for Namibia; an alliance of ethnically-based parties, including:

**NUDO—Progressive Party Jo'Horongo:** f. 1987; Pres. Mburumba Kerina.

**Rehoboth Bevryde Demokratiese Party (Rehoboth Free Democratic Party** or **Liberation Front) (RBDP):** Leader Johannes Diergaardt; coalition of the **Rehoboth Bevrydingsparty** (Leader Johannes Diergaardt) and the **Rehoboth Democratic Party** (Leader K. G. Freigang).

**Monitor Action Group (MAG):** Windhoek; f. 1991 (formerly National Party of South West Africa; Leader Kosie Pretorius.

**Namibia National Democratic Party:** Windhoek; Leader Paul Helmuth.

**Namibia National Front:** Windhoek; Leader Vekuii Rukoro.

**South West Africa People's Organisation of Namibia (SWAPO):** Windhoek; f. 1957 as the Ovamboland People's Congress; renamed South West Africa People's Organisation in 1960; adopted present name in 1968; recognized by the UN, from Dec. 1973 until April 1989, as the 'sole and authentic representative of the Namibian people'; obtained majority of seats at Nov. 1989 election for the Constituent Assembly, and formed a Govt following independence in March 1990; Pres. Samuel (Sam) Daniel Nujoma; Sec.-Gen. Moses Garoeb.

**South West African National Union (SWANU):** Windhoek; f. 1959; Leader Hitjevi Veii.

**United Democratic Front (UDF):** Windhoek; f. 1989 as a centrist coalition of eight parties; Nat. Chair. Reggie Diergaardt; Leader Justus Garoeb.

**Workers' Revolutionary Party:** Windhoek; f. 1989; Trotskyist; Leaders Werner Mamugwe, Hewat Beukes.

## Diplomatic Representation

### EMBASSIES AND HIGH COMMISSIONS IN NAMIBIA

**Algeria:** 95 John Meinert St, Windhoek; tel. (61) 229896; Chargé d'affaires a.i.: A. I. Bengueuedda.

**Angola:** Angola House, 3 Ausspann St, Private Bag 12020, Windhoek; tel. (61) 227535; telex 897; fax (61) 221498; Ambassador: Dr Alberto D. C. B. Ribeiro.

**Bangladesh:** Windhoek; tel. (61) 32301; telex 650; High Commissioner: A. Y. B. I. Siddiqi (acting).

**Botswana:** 101 Klein Windhoek Rd, POB 20359, Windhoek; tel. (61) 221942; telex 894; fax (61) 36034; High Commissioner: Tuelenyana Rosemary Ditlhabi-Oliphant.

**Brazil:** 52 Bismarck St, POB 24166, Windhoek; tel. (61) 37368; telex 498; fax (61) 33389; Chargé d'affaires a.i.: José Augusto Lindgren Alves.

**Canada:** POB 2147, Windhoek; tel. (61) 222941; telex 402; fax (61) 224204; High Commissioner: Wayne Hammond.

**China, People's Republic:** 39 Beethoven St, POB 22777, Windhoek; tel. (61) 222089; telex 675; fax (61) 225544; Ambassador: Ji Peiding.

**Congo:** 9 Corner St, POB 22970, Windhoek; tel. (61) 226958; telex 405; fax (61) 228642; Ambassador: A. Kondho.

**Cuba:** 31 Omuramba Rd, Eros, POB 23866, Windhoek; tel. (61) 227153; telex 406; fax (61) 31584; Ambassador: Angel Dalmau Fernández.

**Denmark:** Sanlam Centre, 154 Independence Ave, POB 20126, Windhoek; tel. (61) 224923; telex 461; fax (61) 35807; Chargé d'affaires a.i.: Sven Bille Bjerregaard.

**Egypt:** 10 Berg St, POB 11853, Windhoek; tel. (61) 221501; telex 421; fax (61) 228856; Ambassador: Mohammed Hussein Elsadr.

**Finland:** POB 3649, Windhoek; tel. (61) 221355; telex 671; fax (61) 221349; Ambassador: Kirsti Lintonen.

**France:** 1 Goethe St, POB 20484, Windhoek; tel. (61) 229021; telex 715; fax (61) 31436; Ambassador: Alain Dementhon.

**Germany:** POB 231, Windhoek; tel. (61) 229217; telex 482; fax (61) 222981; Ambassador: Dr Hanns Schumacher.

**Ghana:** 5 Klein Windhoek Rd, POB 24165, Windhoek; tel. (61) 221341; fax (61) 221343; High Commissioner: Dr Keli Nordor.

**India:** 97 Klein Windhoek Rd, POB 1209, Windhoek; tel. (61) 228433; telex 832; fax (61) 37320; High Commissioner: Kanwar Singh Jasrotia.

**Iran:** 81 Klein Windhoek Rd, Windhoek; tel. (61) 229974; telex 637; fax (61) 220016; Chargé d'affaires a.i.: Ahmad Amoozadeh.

**Italy:** POB 24065, Windhoek; tel. (61) 228602; telex 620; fax (61) 229860; Ambassador: Piero De Masi.

**Japan:** Windhoek; tel. (61) 727500; fax (61) 727769; Chargé d'affaires a.i.: Yukio Rokujo.

**Kenya:** Kenya House, 134 Robert Mugabe St, POB 2889, Windhoek; tel. (61) 226836; telex 823; fax (61) 221409; High Commissioner: Joseph Sefu.

**Korea, Democratic People's Republic:** 2 Jenner St, POB 22927, Windhoek; tel. (61) 41967; telex 631; Chargé d'affaires a.i.: Kim Pyong Gi.

**Korea, Republic:** Sanlam Centre, 154 Independence Ave, 10th Floor, POB 3788, Windhoek; tel. (61) 229286; telex 801; fax (61) 229847; Ambassador: Soong Chull-Chin.

**Libya:** 69 Burg St, Luxury Hill, POB 124, Windhoek; tel. (61) 221139; telex 868; fax (61) 34471; Chargé d'affaires a.i.: H. O. Alshaoshi.

# NAMIBIA

**Malawi:** 56 Bismarck St, POB 23384, Windhoek; tel. (61) 221291; telex 469; fax (61) 221392; High Commissioner: JAMES KALILANGWE (acting).
**Nigeria:** 4 Omuramba Rd, POB 23547, Windhoek; tel. (61) 32103; fax (61) 221639; High Commissioner: EDWARD AINA.
**Norway:** POB 9936, Windhoek; tel. (61) 227812; telex 432; fax (61) 222226; Ambassador: ARILD OYEN.
**Portugal:** 28 Garten St, POB 443, Windhoek; tel. (61) 228736; telex 409; Chargé d'affaires a.i.: JOÃO JOSÉ GOMES.
**Romania:** 1 Kestrell St, Hochland Park, POB 6827, Windhoek; tel. (61) 224630; telex 435; fax (61) 221564; Ambassador: P. VLASCEANU.
**Russia:** 4 Christian St, POB 3826, Windhoek; tel. (61) 228671; telex 865; fax (61) 229061; Ambassador: BAKHTIER M. KHAKIMOV.
**Spain:** 58 Bismarck St, POB 21811, Windhoek; tel. (61) 223066; fax (61) 223046; Ambassador: CARLOS SÁNCHEZ DE BOADO.
**Sudan:** POB 3708, Windhoek; tel. (61) 228544; Ambassador: ABD ELMONIEM MUSTAFA ELAMIN.
**Sweden:** POB 23087, Windhoek; tel. (61) 222905; telex 463; fax (61) 222774; Ambassador: STEN RYLANDER.
**United Kingdom:** 116 Robert Mugabe Ave, POB 22202, Windhoek; tel. (61) 223022; telex 2343; fax (61) 228895; High Commissioner: HENRY HOGGER.
**USA:** 14 Lossen St, Private Bag 12029, Windhoek; tel. (61) 221601; fax (61) 229792; Ambassador: MARSHALL MCCALLIE.
**Venezuela:** Southern Life Tower, 3rd Floor, Post Street Mall, Private Bag 13353, Windhoek; tel. (61) 227905; telex 862; fax (61) 227804; Chargé d'affaires a.i.: ALBERTO VALERO.
**Yugoslavia:** 10 Chateau St, POB 3705, Windhoek; tel. (61) 36900; telex 3174; fax (61) 222260; Chargé d'affaires: PETKO DELIĆ.
**Zambia:** 22 Sam Nujoma Dr., POB 22882, Windhoek; tel. (61) 37610; telex 485; fax (61) 228162; High Commissioner: (vacant).
**Zimbabwe:** cnr Independence Ave and Grimm St, POB 23056, Windhoek; tel. (61) 228134; telex 866; fax (61) 228659; High Commissioner: ALBAN TAKA KANENGONI DETE.

# Judicial System

Judicial power is exercised by the Supreme Court, the High Court and a number of Magistrate and Lower Courts. The Constitution provides for the appointment of an Ombudsman.

**Chief Justice:** ISMAIL MAHOMED.
**Attorney-General:** REINHARD RUKORO.

# Religion

It is estimated that about 90% of the population are Christians. The principal denominations in 1981 were the Lutheran (528,323 adherents), Roman Catholic (195,000), Dutch Reformed (63,322), Anglican (57,560) and Methodist (10,558).

## CHRISTIANITY

**Council of Churches in Namibia:** 8 Mont Blanc St, POB 41, Windhoek; tel. (61) 217621; telex 834; fax (61) 62786; f. 1978; eight mem. churches; Pres. Bishop HENDRIK FREDERIK; Gen. Sec. Dr ABISAI SHEJAVALI.

### The Anglican Communion

Namibia comprises a single diocese in the Church of the Province of Southern Africa. The Metropolitan of the Province is the Archbishop of Cape Town, South Africa.

**Bishop of Namibia:** Rt Rev. JAMES HAMUPANDA KAULUMA, POB 57, Windhoek; tel. (61) 38920; fax (61) 225903.

### Dutch Reformed Church

**Dutch Reformed Church of South West Africa/Namibia:** POB 389, Windhoek; tel. (61) 41144; Moderator Rev. A. J. DE KLERK.

### Evangelical Lutheran

**Evangelical Lutheran Church in Namibia:** Bishop Dr KLEOPAS DUMENI, Private Bag 2018, Ondangwa; tel. (6756) 40241; telex 3257; fax (6756) 272.
**Evangelical Lutheran Church (Rhenish Mission Church):** POB 5069, Windhoek; tel. (61) 224531; telex 3107; f. 1967; Pres. Bishop HENDRIK FREDERIK.
**German Evangelical-Lutheran Church in Namibia:** POB 233, Windhoek; tel. (61) 224294; fax (61) 221470; mems 8,200; Pres. Rev. Landespropst REINHARD KEDING.

### Methodist

**African Methodist Episcopal Church:** Rev. B. G. KARUAERA, Windhoek; tel. (61) 62757.
**Methodist Church of Southern Africa:** POB 143, Windhoek; tel. (61) 228921.

### The Roman Catholic Church

Namibia comprises one archdiocese, one diocese and one apostolic vicariate. At 31 December 1993 there were an estimated 251,885 adherents in Namibia, representing about 15.1% of the total population.

**Archbishop of Windhoek:** Most Rev. BONIFATIUS HAUSHIKU, POB 272, Windhoek; tel. (61) 227595; fax (61) 229836.

### Other Christian Churches

Among other denominations active in Namibia are the Evangelical Reformed Church in Africa, the Presbyterian Church of Southern Africa and the United Congregational Church of Southern Africa.

## BAHÁ'Í FAITH

**National Spiritual Assembly:** POB 20372, Windhoek; tel. (61) 227961; mems resident in 208 localities.

# The Press

**Abacus:** POB 22791, Windhoek; tel. (61) 35596; fax (61) 36497; weekly; English; educational; Editor HEIDI VON EGIDY; circ. 45,000.
**Acoda Info:** POB 20549, Windhoek; tel. (61) 37623; fax (61) 31583; monthly; English, French.
**Action:** POB 20500, Windhoek; tel. (61) 62957; fax (61) 216375; 2 a month; Afrikaans, English; religious; Editor FRANS VAN DER MERWE; circ. 12,000.
**AgriForum:** 114 Robert Mugabe St, Private Bag 13255, Windhoek; tel. (61) 37838; fax (61) 220193; monthly; Afrikaans, English; Editor PEDRO STEENKAMP; circ. 5,000.
**Allgemeine Zeitung:** 49 Stuebel St, POB 56, Windhoek; tel. (61) 225411; fax (61) 224843; f. 1915; daily; German; Editor-in-Chief HANS FEDDERSEN; circ. 5,000.
**Aloe:** POB 59, Windhoek; tel. (61) 3912353; fax (61) 3912091; monthly; English; Edited by the Windhoek Municipality; circ. 35,000.
**Bargain Post:** POB 23000, Windhoek; tel. (61) 227182; fax (61) 220226; 2 a month; English; business and advertisments; Editor JOHAN ENGELBRECHT; circ. 15,000.
**Bricks Community Newspaper:** POB 20642, Windhoek; tel. (61) 62726; fax (61) 63510; bi-monthly; English; Editor ANDRÉ STRAUSS; circ. 2,000.
**Monitor:** POB 2196, Windhoek; tel. (61) 34141; fax (61) 32802; monthly; Afrikaans, English; Editor EWERT BENADE; circ. 4,100.
**Namib Times:** 7th St., POB 706, Walvis Bay; tel. (642) 5854; telex 844; fax (642) 4813; 2 a week; Afrikaans, English, German and Portuguese; Editor PAUL VINCENT; circ. 4,500.
**Namibia Brief:** POB 2123, Windhoek; tel. (61) 37250; fax (61) 37251; quarterly; English; Editor CATHY BLATT; circ. 10,000.
**Namibia Business Update:** POB 11602, Windhoek; tel. (61) 38898; fax (61) 220104; monthly; English; Editor MOLLY CURRY; circ. 1,500.
**Namibia Development Briefing:** POB 20642, Windhoek; tel. (61) 62726; fax (61) 63510; bi-monthly; English; circ. 1,000.
**Namibia Economist:** POB 49, Windhoek; tel. (61) 221925; fax (61) 220615; monthly; Afrikaans, English; Editor DANIEL STEINMANN; circ. 7,000.
**Namibia Focus:** POB 23000, Windhoek; tel. (61) 227182; fax (61) 220226; monthly; English; business; Editor JOHAN ENGELBRECHT; circ. 30,000.
**Namibia Today:** POB 24669, Windhoek; tel. (61) 229150; fax (61) 229150; 2 a week; Afrikaans, English, Oshiherero, Oshiwambo; publ. by SWAPO; Editor KAOMO-VIJINDA TJOMBE; circ. 5,000.
**The Namibian:** John Mernest St., POB 20783, Windhoek; tel. (61) 36970; telex 3032; fax (61) 33980; daily; Afrikaans, English, Oshiwambo; left-wing; Editor GWEN LISTER; circ. 9,500.
**The Namibian Worker:** POB 61208, Windhoek; tel. (61) 216186; fax (61) 216186; Afrikaans, English, Owambo; publ. by National Union of Namibian Workers; Editor CHRIS NDIVANGA; circ. 4,000.
**New Era:** Private Bag 13344, Windhoek; tel. (61) 3082180; fax (61) 224937; weekly; English; Editor RAJAH MUNAMAVA; circ. 25,000.
**Otjikoto Journal:** POB 40, Tsumeb; tel. (671) 21115; fax (671) 21710; monthly; English; Editor JIM KASTELIC; circ. 3,600.
**Rössing News:** Private Bag 5005, Swakopmund; tel. (641) 592382; fax (641) 592301; weekly; English; Editor MAGGI BARNARD; circ. 2,400.

# NAMIBIA

**Die Republikein** (The Republican): POB 3436, Windhoek; tel. (61) 230331; telex 3201; fax (61) 35674; f. 1977; daily; Afrikaans, English and German; organ of DTA of Namibia; Editor CHRIS JACOBIE; circ. 12,000.

**Sperrgebiet Gazette:** POB 35, Oranjemund; tel. (6332) 2470; weekly; English, Oshiwambo; Editor CHARLOTTE BEWS.

**Die Suidwester:** POB 2196, Windhoek; tel. and fax (61) 34141; telex 600; f. 1944; weekly; Afrikaans.

**Tempo:** POB 1794, Windhoek; tel. (61) 230331; fax (61) 22110; f. 1992; weekly; Afrikaans, English and German; Editor GERRIT LLOETE; circ. 11,500.

**Visitor:** POB 23000, Windhoek; tel. (61) 227182; fax (61) 220226; monthly; English; tourist information; Editor JOHAN ENGELBRECHT; circ. 10,000.

**Welcome:** POB 11854, Windhoek; tel. (61) 227001; fax (61) 224317; 2 a month; English; tourist information; Editors JENS SCHNEIDER, MARITA POTGIETER; circ. 5,000.

**The Windhoek Advertiser:** 49 Stuebel St, POB 2255, Windhoek; tel. (61) 225464; fax (61) 221737; f. 1919; daily; English; Editor HANNES SMITH; circ. 1,800 (Mon.–Thur.), 10,000 (Sat.).

**Windhoek Observer:** POB 2384, Windhoek; tel. (61) 224511; fax (61) 229839; f. 1978; weekly; English; Editor TED MCGILL; circ. 9,600.

### NEWS AGENCIES

**Namibian Press Agency (Nampa):** POB 613541, Windhoek; tel. (61) 221711; fax (61) 221713; Editor-in-Chief MOCKS SHIVUTE.

#### Foreign Bureaux

**Associated Press (AP)** (USA): POB 22791, Windhoek; tel. (61) 225715; fax (61) 36467; Correspondent HEIDI VON EGIDY.

**Informatsionnoye Telegrafnoye Agentstvo Rossii—Telegrafnoye Agentstvo Suverennykh Stran (ITAR—TASS)** (Russia): POB 24821, Windhoek; tel. (61) 32909; telex 713; fax (61) 32909; Correspondent ALEKSANDR P. PROSVETOV.

**Inter Press Service (IPS)** (Italy): POB 20783, Windhoek; tel. (61) 226645; telex 3032; Correspondent MARK VERBAAN.

**South African Press Association (SAPA):** POB 2032, Windhoek; tel. (61) 226339; Bureau Chief JOHANN VAN HEERDEN.

**Xinhua (New China) News Agency** (People's Republic of China): POB 22130, Windhoek; tel. (61) 226484; fax (61) 226484; Bureau Chief TENG WENVI.

Reuters (UK) is also represented in Namibia.

## Publishers

**Deutscher Verlag (Pty) Ltd:** POB 56, Windhoek; fax (61) 224843; f. 1939; newspaper publr.

**Gamsberg Publishers:** POB 22830, Windhoek; tel. (61) 28714; telex 3108; f. 1977; textbooks, fiction and non-fiction; Man. Dir Dr HANS VILJOEN.

**Interface (Pty) Ltd:** Windhoek; tel. (61) 228652; fax (61) 224402; f. 1987; Man. Dir MARÉ MOUTON.

**John Meinert (Pty) Ltd:** POB 56, Windhoek; f. 1924; newspapers.

**Namibia Scientific Society:** POB 67, Windhoek; tel. (61) 225372; f. 1925; Man. Dir A. HENRICHSEN.

## Radio and Television

In 1992, according to UNESCO, there were an estimated 195,000 radio receivers and 32,000 television receivers in use.

**Namibian Broadcasting Corporation (NBC):** POB 321, Windhoek; tel. (61) 215811; telex 622; fax (61) 217760; f. 1990; broadcasts on eight radio channels in 11 languages; television programmes are broadcast in English; Dir-Gen. NAHUM J. GORELICK. Namibia's first commercial radio station began broadcasts in April 1994.

## Finance

(cap. = capital; res = reserves; dep. = deposits; m. = million; brs = branches; amounts in rand)

### BANKING
#### Central Bank

**Bank of Namibia:** 10 Göring St, POB 2882, Windhoek; tel. (61) 226401; telex 710; fax (61) 229874; f. 1990; Gov. Dr JAAFAR AHMAD; Deputy Gov. TOM K. ALWEENDO.

#### Commercial Banks

**Bank Windhoek Ltd:** 262 Independence Ave, POB 15, Windhoek; tel. (61) 31850; telex 908660; fax (61) 225813; f. 1982; cap. and res 23.4m., dep. 629.0m. (March 1994); Chair. J. C. BRANDT; Man. Dir D. P. DE LANGE; 15 brs.

**Commercial Bank of Namibia Ltd:** 12–20 Bülow St, POB 1, Windhoek; tel. (61) 2959111; telex 898; fax (61) 224417; f. 1973 as Bank of Namibia, name changed in 1990; 92.7%-owned by Namibian Banking Corporation Ltd; cap. and res 26.5m., dep. 482.9m. (June 1993); Chair. V. BURGHAGEN; Man. Dir HANS-JÜRGEN STEUBER.

**First National Bank of Namibia Ltd:** 207 Independence Ave, POB 195, Windhoek; tel. (61) 229610; telex 479; fax (61) 225604; f. 1986; cap. and res 103.7m., dep. 1,093.9m. (Sept. 1993); Chair. H. D. VOIGTS; Man. Dir G. S. VAN STADEN; 28 brs and 11 agencies.

**Namibian Banking Corporation:** Carl List Haus, Independence Ave, POB 370, Windhoek; tel. (61) 225946; telex 629; fax (61) 223741; Chair. J. C. WESTRAAT; Man. Dir P. P. NIEHAUS; 3 brs.

**Standard Bank Namibia Ltd:** Mutual Platz, POB 3327, Windhoek; tel. (61) 2949111; telex 3079; fax (61) 224481; f. 1915 as Standard Bank SWA, name changed in 1990; controlled by the Standard Bank of South Africa; cap. and res 43.7m., dep. 1,074.2m. (Dec. 1993); Chair. C. J. F. BRAND; Man. Dir V. B. MOLL; 33 brs.

### STOCK EXCHANGE

**Namibia Stock Exchange:** Nimrod Bldg, Kasino St, POB 2401, Windhoek; tel. (61) 227647; fax (61) 32513; f. 1992; Chair. Exec. Cttee HANS-JÜRGEN STEUBER.

### INSURANCE

**W. Biederlack & Co:** Independence Ave, POB 365, Windhoek; tel. (61) 33177; fax (61) 34874; f. 1990.

**Commercial Union Insurance Ltd:** Bülow St, POB 1599, Windhoek; tel. (61) 37137; telex 3096.

**Incorporated General Insurance Ltd:** 10 Bülow St, POB 2516, Windhoek; tel. (61) 37453; telex 415; fax (61) 35647.

**Lifegro Assurance Ltd:** Independence Ave, POB 23055, Windhoek; tel. (61) 33068.

**Metropolitan Life Ltd:** Goethe St, POB 3785, Windhoek; tel. (61) 37840.

**Mutual and Federal Insurance Co Ltd:** Mutual Bldg, Independence Ave, POB 151, Windhoek; tel. (61) 37730; telex 3084; Man. H. K. BORCHARDT.

**Namibia National Insurance Co Ltd:** Bülow St, POB 23053, Windhoek; tel. (61) 224539; fax (61) 38737; fmrly Federated Insurance Co Ltd.

**Protea Assurance Co Ltd:** Windhoek; tel. (61) 225891; telex 414.

**Prudential Assurance Co of South Africa:** Independence Ave, POB 365, Windhoek; tel. (61) 33176; telex 481.

**SA Mutual Life Assurance Soc.:** Independence Ave, POB 165, Windhoek; tel. (61) 36620; fax (61) 34874.

**Sanlam Life Assurance Ltd:** Bülow St, POB 317, Windhoek; tel. (61) 36680.

**Santam Insurance Ltd:** Independence Ave, POB 204, Windhoek; tel. (61) 38214.

**Southern Life Assurance Ltd:** Southern Tower, Post Street Mall, POB 637, Windhoek; tel. (61) 34056; fax (61) 31574.

## Trade and Industry

### STATE HOLDING

**Namdeb Diamond Corporation:** Windhoek; f. 1994, following reorganization of CDM (Pty) Ltd; 50% state-owned, 50% owned by De Beers Centenary AG; diamond mining.

### CHAMBERS OF COMMERCE

**Namibia National Chamber of Commerce and Industry:** POB 9355, Windhoek; tel. (61) 228809; fax (61) 228009.

**Windhoek Chamber of Commerce and Industries:** SWA Building Society Bldg, 3rd Floor, POB 191, Windhoek; tel. (61) 222000; fax (61) 33690; f. 1920; Pres. D. DE LANGE; Gen. Man. H. H. SCHMIDT; 230 mems.

### CHAMBER OF MINES

**Chamber of Mines of Namibia:** POB 2895, Windhoek; tel. (61) 37925; fax (61) 222638; f. 1979; Pres. TONY DE BEER.

### DEVELOPMENT ORGANIZATIONS

**Investment Centre:** Ministry of Trade and Industry, Govt Bldgs, Private Bag 13340, Windhoek; tel. (61) 2892431; telex 870; fax (61) 220227.

**Namibia Development Corporation:** Private Bag 13252, Windhoek; tel. (61) 306911; telex 870; fax (61) 33943; f. 1993 to replace First National Development Corpn; promotes foreign investment and provides concessional loans and equity to new enterprises; manages agricultural projects; Chair. H.-G. STIER; Man. Dir A. J. BOTES.

**Namibian International Business Development Organization (NIBDO):** POB 82, Windhoek; tel. (61) 37970; fax (61) 33690; Pres. DES MATHEWS.

**National Building and Investment Corporation:** POB 20192, Windhoek; tel. (61) 37224; fax (61) 222301.

**National Housing Enterprise:** POB 20192, Windhoek; tel. (61) 225518; fax (61) 222301; Chair. N. SCHOOMBE; CEO A. M. TSOWASELO.

### PUBLIC BOARDS AND CORPORATIONS

**Meat Board of Namibia:** POB 38, Windhoek; tel. (61) 33180; telex 679; fax (61) 228310; f. 1935; Gen. Man. H. W. KREFT.

**Meat Corporation of Namibia (MEATCO NAMIBIA):** POB 3881, Windhoek; tel. (61) 216810; fax (61) 217045.

**Namibian Agronomic Board:** POB 5096, Windhoek; tel. (61) 224741; fax (61) 225371; Gen. Man. Dr KOBUS KOTZE.

**Namibian Karakul Board:** Private Bag 13300, Windhoek; tel. (61) 37750; fax (61) 36122.

**National Petroleum Corporation of Namibia (NAMCOR):** Windhoek; Chair. SKERF POTTAS.

**South West Africa Water and Electricity Corporation (SWAWEK):** Swawek Centre, 147 Robert Mugabe St, POB 2864, Windhoek; tel. (61) 31830; fax (61) 32805; Chair. and Man. Dir J. P. BRAND.

### EMPLOYERS' ORGANIZATIONS

**Construction Industries Federation of Namibia:** POB 1479, Windhoek; tel. (61) 230028; fax (61) 224534; Pres. NEIL THOMPSON.

**Electrical Contractors' Association:** POB 3163, Windhoek; tel. (61) 37920; Pres. F. PFAFFENTHALER.

**Motor Industries Federation of Namibia:** POB 1503, Windhoek; tel. (61) 37970; fax (61) 33690.

**Namibia Agricultural Union (NAU):** Private Bag 13255, Windhoek; tel. (61) 37838; fax (61) 220193; Pres. PAUL SMIT.

**Namibia Chamber of Printing:** POB 363, Windhoek; tel. (61) 37905; fax (61) 222927; Sec. S. G. TIMM.

### LABOUR ORGANIZATIONS

There are several union federations, and a number of independent unions.

#### Trade Union Federations

**Confederation of Labour:** POB 22060, Windhoek.

**National Allied Unions (NANAU):** Windhoek; f. 1987; an alliance of trade unions, representing c. 7,600 mems, incl. Namibia Wholesale and Retail Workers' Union (f. 1986; Gen. Sec. T. NGAUJAKE; 6,000 mems), and Namibia Women Support Cttee; Pres. HENOCH HANDURA.

**Namibia Trade Union (NTU):** Windhoek; f. 1985; represents 6,700 domestic, farm and metal workers; Pres. ALPHA KANGUEEHI; Sec.-Gen. BEAU TJISESETA.

**Namibia Trade Union Council (NTUC):** Windhoek; f. 1981; affiliates include Northern Builders' Asscn.

**National Union of Namibian Workers (NUNW):** POB 50034, Windhoek; tel. (61) 215037; fax (61) 215589; f. 1971; Sec.-Gen. BERNHARDT ESAU; 87,600 mems; affiliates include:

**Mineworkers' Union of Namibia (MUN):** f. 1986; Chair. ASSER KAPERE; Pres. JOHN SHAETON HODI; Gen. Sec. PETER NAHOLO (acting); 12,500 mems.

**Namibia Food and Allied Workers' Union:** f. 1986; Chair. MATHEUS LIBEREKI; Chair. ELIFAS NANGOLO; Gen. Sec. MAGDALENA IPINGE (acting); 12,000 mems.

**Namibia Metal and Allied Workers' Union:** f. 1987; Chair. ANDRIES TEMBA; Gen. Sec. MOSES SHIKWA (acting); 5,500 mems.

**Namibia Public Workers' Union:** f. 1987; Chair. STEVEN IMMANUEL; Gen. Sec. PETER ILONGA; 11,000 mems.

**Namibia Transport and Allied Workers' Union:** f. 1988; Gen. Sec. IMMANUEL KAVAA; Chair. TYLVES GIDEON; 7,500 mems.

#### Other Unions

**Association for Government Service Officials:** Windhoek; f. 1981; Chair. ALLAN HATTLE; 9,000 mems.

**Namibia Building Workers' Association:** Windhoek; Sec. H. BOCK.

**Public Service Union of Namibia:** POB 21662, Windhoek; tel. (61) 213083; fax (61) 213047; f. 1981; Sec.-Gen. S. LAWRENCE.

**Society for Officials of Financial Unions:** Windhoek; Sec. Mrs A. CARMEN; 1,050 mems.

**South West Africa Municipal Association:** Windhoek; f. 1968; Gen. Sec. HANS SCHOEMAN; 3,000 mems.

## Transport

### RAILWAYS

The main line runs from Nakop, at the border with South Africa, via Keetmanshoop to Windhoek, Kranzberg, Grootfontein, Tsumeb, Swakopmund and Walvis Bay, while there are three branch lines, from Windhoek to Gobabis, Otjiwarongo to Outjo and Keetmanshoop to Lüderitz. Total rail tracks in Namibia are 2,382 route-km.

**TransNamib Ltd:** TransNamib Bldg, cnr Independence Ave and Bahnhof St, Private Bag 13204, Windhoek; tel. (61) 2982109; telex 465; fax (61) 2982386; state-owned; Chair. J. A. BRÜCKNER; Man. Dir FRANÇOIS UYS.

### ROADS

In 1994 the road network comprised 42,594 km of roads, including 5,010 km of tarred roads, 26,646 km of gravel roads, 235 km of salt/gypsum roads and 10,682 km of natural roads. Road maintenance and construction was allocated N$194m. in the 1994/95 budget. A major road link with central Botswana, the Trans-Kalahari Highway, was scheduled for completion by 1995, and construction of the Trans-Caprivi highway linking Namibia with Northern Botswana, Zambia and Zimbabwe, is scheduled for completion by 1996. The Government is also engaged in upgrading and expanding the road network in northern Namibia.

### SHIPPING

Walvis Bay and Lüderitz are the only ports, although the development of other harbours is planned. Walvis Bay harbour, the region's only deep-water port, is linked to the main overseas shipping routes and handles almost one-half of Namibia's external trade. The port is under the jurisdiction of the Namibian Ports Authority (NAMPORT).

### CIVIL AVIATION

The international airport, which is 47 km from Windhoek, registered 308,690 passenger arrivals and departures in 1993. There are a number of other airports dispersed throughout Namibia, as well as numerous landing strips.

**Air Namibia:** TransNamib Bldg, cnr Independence ave and Bahnhof St, POB 731, Windhoek; tel. and fax (61) 221910; telex 657; f. 1959 as Namib Air; state-owned; domestic flights and services to Southern Africa and Western Europe; Chair. J. A. BRÜCKNER; Gen. Man. KEITH PETCH.

## Tourism

In the mid-1990s tourism was reported to be the fastest growing sector of the Namibian economy. Nambia's principal tourist attractions are its game parks and nature reserves (at independence in 1990 the protection of wildlife and the sustainable utilization of the environment were enshrined in the Namibian Constitution). A total of 288,000 tourist arrivals was recorded in Namibia in 1993, including 38,000 excursionists; the majority (more than 60%) originated from South Africa. In 1992 receipts from tourism totalled R394m. Under a five-year programme for the expansion and privatization of the tourist industry, announced in mid-1993, the Government aimed to invest some R547m. in the sector, and projected that foreign tourist arrivals would reach 396,000 per year by 1997.

**Namibia Tourism:** Private Bag 13346, Windhoek; tel. (61) 2849111; fax (61) 221930.

# NAURU

## Introductory Survey

**Location, Climate, Language, Religion, Flag, Capital**

The Republic of Nauru is a small island in the central Pacific Ocean, lying about 40 km (25 miles) south of the Equator and about 4,000 km (2,500 miles) north-east of Sydney, Australia. Its nearest neighbour is Banaba (Ocean Island), in Kiribati, about 300 km (186 miles) to the east. The climate is tropical, with a westerly monsoon season from November to February. The average annual rainfall is about 1,500 mm (59 ins), but actual rainfall is extremely variable. Of the total population in 1983, 61.7% were Nauruans. Their language is Nauruan, but English is also widely understood. The majority of Nauruans are Christians, mostly adherents of the Nauruan Protestant Church. The national flag (proportions 2 by 1) is royal blue, divided by a narrow horizontal yellow stripe, with a 12-pointed white star at the lower hoist. The island state has no official capital.

**Recent History**

Nauru, inhabited by a predominantly Polynesian people, organized in 12 clans, was annexed by Germany in 1888. In 1914, shortly after the outbreak of the First World War, the island was captured by Australian forces. It continued to be administered by Australia under a League of Nations mandate (granted in 1920) which also named the United Kingdom and New Zealand as co-trustees. Between 1942 and 1945 Nauru was occupied by the Japanese, who deported 1,200 islanders to Truk (now Chuuk), Micronesia, where many died in bombing raids or from starvation. In 1947 the island was placed under United Nations Trusteeship, with Australia as the administering power on behalf of the Governments of Australia, New Zealand and the United Kingdom. The UN Trusteeship Council proposed in 1964 that the indigenous people of Nauru be resettled on Curtis Island, off the Queensland coast. This offer was made in anticipation of the progressive exhaustion of the island's phosphate deposits, and because of the environmental devastation resulting from the mining operations. However, the Nauruans elected to remain on the island. Between 1906 and 1968 41m. metric tons of phosphate were mined. Nauru was accorded a considerable measure of self-government in January 1966, with the establishment of Legislative and Executive Councils, and proceeded to independence on 31 January 1968 (exactly 22 years after the surviving Nauruans returned to the island from exile in Micronesia). Under an agreement announced in November 1968, Nauru became a 'special member' of the Commonwealth, not represented at meetings of Heads of Government. Nauru is not a member of the UN.

The Head Chief of Nauru, Hammer DeRoburt, was elected President in May 1968 and re-elected in 1971 and 1973. Dissatisfaction with his increasingly personal rule led to the election, by Parliament, to the presidency of Bernard Dowiyogo (leader of the recently-established, informal Nauru Party) in December 1976, and the formation of a new Cabinet. Dowiyogo was re-elected President after a general election in November 1977. However, DeRoburt's supporters adopted tactics of obstruction in Parliament, and in December 1977 Dowiyogo resigned, in response to Parliament's refusal to approve budgetary legislation; he was re-elected shortly afterwards, but was again forced to resign in April, following the defeat of a legislative proposal concerning phosphate royalties. Lagumot Harris, another member of the Nauru Party, succeeded him, but resigned three weeks later, when Parliament rejected a finance measure, and DeRoburt was again elected President. He was re-elected in December 1978, in December 1980 and in May and December 1983.

In September 1986 DeRoburt resigned, following the defeat of a government proposal for an amendment to the annual budget legislation; he was replaced as President by Kennan Adeang, who was elected in Parliament by nine votes to DeRoburt's eight. However, after holding office for only 14 days, Adeang was defeated by a parliamentary vote expressing 'no confidence', following an unsuccessful attempt by his Government to enact new budget proposals, and DeRoburt subsequently resumed the presidency.

At parliamentary elections in December 1986 supporters of DeRoburt secured eight seats, as did those of Adeang, while independent candidates (including the country's first woman member) secured the remaining two. Adeang was elected President, once more gaining a majority of one vote in Parliament, but was subsequently ousted by another vote expressing 'no confidence', and DeRoburt was again reinstated as President. The atmosphere of political uncertainty, generated by the absence of a clear majority in Parliament, led DeRoburt to dissolve Parliament in preparation for another general election in January 1987, at which DeRoburt was re-elected to the presidency, by 11 votes to six. In February Adeang announced the establishment of the Democratic Party of Nauru, which was in essence a revival of the Nauru Party. Eight members of Parliament subsequently joined the new party, which declared that its aim was to curtail the extension of presidential powers and to promote democracy.

In August 1989, expressing dissatisfaction with the budget and fears over prospects for the rehabilitation of the island (see below), Adeang proposed a parliamentary motion of 'no confidence' in DeRoburt. The motion was approved by 10 votes to five, and Kenas Aroi, a former Minister for Finance, was subsequently elected President. In December Aroi resigned, owing to ill health, and after a general election, held in the same month, Bernard Dowiyogo was re-elected President, defeating DeRoburt by 10 votes to six. The next presidential election, held shortly after a general election in November 1992, was contested largely on the issue of financial management. Initially, support for Dowiyogo and his challenger, Buraro Detudamo, was divided equally; however, a final vote resulted in victory for Dowiyogo by 10 votes to seven.

In February 1987 representatives of the British, Australian and New Zealand Governments signed documents effecting the official demise of the British Phosphate Commissioners, who from 1919 until 1970 had overseen the mining of Nauru's phosphate deposits. President DeRoburt subsequently expressed concern about the distribution of the Commissioners' accumulated assets, which were estimated to be worth $A55m. His proposal that part of this sum be spent on the rehabilitation of areas of the island that had been mined before independence was rejected by the three Governments involved. In August 1987 DeRoburt established a commission of inquiry to investigate proposals for rehabilitation. The commission, which completed its investigation in December 1988, proposed that the three Governments provide one-third ($A72m.) of the estimated rehabilitation costs. In May 1989 Australia's refusal to contribute to the rehabilitation of former phosphate mining areas prompted Nauru to institute proceedings, claiming compensation from Australia for damage to its environment, at the International Court of Justice. However, in August 1993, following negotiations between President Dowiyogo and the Australian Prime Minister, Paul Keating, a Compact of Settlement was signed, under which the Australian Government was to pay a total of $A107m. to Nauru. New Zealand and the United Kingdom subsequently agreed to contribute $A12m. each towards the settlement.

As a result of a strike by pilots of Air Nauru, begun in May 1988, the Governments of Australia and New Zealand withdrew certification of the airline, concerned that it was not complying with safety standards. The Australian High Commissioner was subsequently declared *persona non grata* in Nauru for communicating confidential information about Air Nauru to the Australian Government. In November 1989 Air Nauru resumed operations, and in December normal diplomatic relations with Australia were restored. In early 1994 the Supreme Court of Victoria, Australia, which in 1992 had agreed to hear a case brought against the Nauruan Government by former pilots of Air Nauru who had been dismissed following the industrial action of 1988–89, awarded damages to all except one of the pilots for wrongful dismissal and loss of salary. The Government announced its intention to appeal against the judgment.

Allegations, made in 1989 by a Western Samoan government minister, that the Nauru Government had secretly contributed to the campaign funds of the opposition in Western Samoa before a general election there in 1988 led to a deterioration in relations between the two countries. In January 1990 the Nauru Government recalled its consul from Western Samoa, halted work on an important hotel project in Apia and sold all its assets there.

In late 1992 the eight island nations that were parties to the Nauru Agreement (a sub-group of the South Pacific Forum Fisheries Agency—see p. 218) signed a fisheries management treaty. The action, which aimed to reduce excessive exploitation of tuna stocks by restricting the number of fishing licences granted to foreign fleets, was prompted by an increase in the incidence of vessels operating illegally in the islands' waters. In late 1994 the signatories endorsed a reduction of 10% in the number of licences issued to foreign vessels, and reiterated their intention to promote more locally-based fishing activity.

In 1989 a UN report on the 'greenhouse effect' (the heating of the earth's atmosphere and a resultant rise in sea-level) listed Nauru as one of the countries that might disappear beneath the sea in the 21st century, unless drastic action were taken. Another issue provoking concern for the environment was raised in late 1992, when it was announced that a vessel carrying plutonium would pass close to Nauru *en route* to Japan from France. Dowiyogo travelled to Japan to protest at the proposal and to urge other Pacific island nations to refuse the vessel entry into their Exclusive Economic Zones.

## Government

Legislative power is vested in the unicameral Parliament, with 18 members elected by universal adult suffrage for up to three years. Executive authority is vested in a Cabinet, which consists of the President of the Republic, elected by the Parliament, and ministers appointed by him. The Cabinet is collectively responsible to Parliament. Responsibilities for administration are divided between the Nauru Local Government Council and the Government. The Council, an elected body of nine members from the country's 14 districts, elects one of its members to be Head Chief.

## Defence

Nauru has no defence forces: under an informal arrangement, Australia is responsible for the country's defence.

## Economic Affairs

In 1985, according to estimates by the OECD, Nauru's gross national product (GNP), measured at current prices, was US $80.7m., equivalent to US $8,070 per head. During 1975–85, it was estimated, GNP increased, in real terms, at an average annual rate of 6.4%, while real GNP per head rose by 4.9% per year. The population increased by an annual average of 1.8% between 1982 and 1992.

Agricultural activity is limited to the small-scale production of tropical fruit, vegetables and livestock. Coconuts are the principal crop. Bananas, pineapples and the screw-pine (*Pandanus*) are also cultivated as food crops, while the islanders keep pigs and chickens. However, almost all Nauru's requirements (including most of its drinking water) are imported.

Until the early 1990s Nauru's economy was based on the extraction of phosphate rock, which constituted four-fifths of the island's surface area. In 1983 the phosphate industry employed around 1,400 people, of whom only 295 were Nauruans. Phosphate mining is a major source of government revenue and almost the only source of export earnings. Of total exports to Australia and New Zealand in the financial year 1987/88, phosphates were valued at $A92.7m. (99.0%). However, the Government's phosphate royalties for the financial year 1990/91 declined sharply from the previous year's figure of $A35m. to an estimated $A25m., owing to a decline in demand: exports to Australia, Nauru's principal customer, were reduced by some 50%, to an estimated 500,000 metric tons, in that year. Revenue from phosphate sales has been invested in a long-term trust fund (the Nauru Phosphate Royalties Trust, whose assets totalled about US $900m. in 1992), in the development of shipping and aviation services, and in property purchases in Australia and elsewhere. However, not all investments have been successful, and some Pacific hotel ventures, as well as the staging of a lavish musical production in the United Kingdom, have been described as disastrous. Criticism regarding the inefficient management of Nauru's funds intensified following the conviction, in October 1994, of an accountant employed by the Nauru Phosphate Royalties Trust for the theft of $A1.2m. from the Trust. New construction projects in Hawaii and Fiji were announced in early 1995.

The principal markets for phosphates (the only export) are Australia, New Zealand and Japan. Energy is derived principally from imported petroleum.

For the financial year ending 30 June 1991 there was an estimated budgetary deficit of $A5.6m.; expenditure was estimated at $A71.2m. The economy is reliant on imported labour, notably from Kiribati and Tuvalu.

Nauru is a member of the South Pacific Commission (see p. 215), of the South Pacific Forum (see p. 217) and of the UN Economic and Social Commission for Asia and the Pacific (see p. 27), all of which aim to promote regional development. In addition, Nauru became a member of the Asian Development Bank (ADB—see p. 107) in September 1991.

After gaining independence, Nauru benefited from sole control of phosphate earnings and, as a result, its income per head has been among the highest in the world. This, however, had serious repercussions for the country, which became excessively dependent on imported labour, imports of consumer goods and convenience foods, precipitating severe social problems. Another effect of phosphate mining was to render 80% of the island uninhabitable and impossible to cultivate, leading to chronic overcrowding. Deposits of phosphates are expected to be exhausted by the late 1990s, by which time it is hoped that Nauru will be able to derive economic security from its shipping and aviation services, its role as a 'tax haven' for international business, and the revenue accruing from its foreign investments. Methods for the rehabilitation of the damaged areas of the island were being investigated, following the achievement of a $A107m. compensation settlement from the Australian Government in August 1993. Plans to use landfill envisaged the restoration of vegetation to the mined areas, and the re-establishment of many of the species of flora and fauna, previously abundant on the island.

## Social Welfare

The Government maintains a comprehensive social welfare system which provides housing and free medical treatment (abroad if necessary) for all citizens. In 1980 there was one hospital bed for every 34 citizens, and, in 1989, one physician for every 700. According to a report on mortality, published in 1989, one-third of the adult Nauruan population suffer from diabetes (the worst incidence of the disease anywhere in the world), while obesity, heart disease, alcoholism and other illnesses attributable to social and dietary problems are also prevalent.

## Education

Education is free and compulsory for Nauruan children between six and 16 years of age. Primary education begins at the age of six and lasts for six years. Secondary education, beginning at 12 years of age, lasts for up to five years. In 1985 there were four infant schools, seven primary schools, two secondary schools and four vocational schools; the total number of teachers was 131. In 1984 Nauruans studying overseas at secondary and tertiary levels numbered 88. There is a university extension centre, linked with the University of the South Pacific in Suva, Fiji.

## Public Holidays

**1995:** 1 January (New Year's Day), 31 January (Independence Day), 14–17 April (Easter), 26 October (Angam Day), 25–26 December (Christmas).

**1996:** 1 January (New Year's Day), 31 January (Independence Day), 5–8 April (Easter), 26 October (Angam Day), 25–26 December (Christmas).

# Statistical Survey

Source (unless otherwise stated): General Statistician, Nauru Government Offices, Yaren.

### AREA AND POPULATION

**Area:** 21.3 sq km (8.2 sq miles).

**Population:** 8,042 (Nauruan 4,964; Other Pacific Islanders 2,134; Asians 682; Caucasians—mainly Australians and New Zealanders—262) at census of 13 May 1983; 9,919 at census of 1992.

**Density:** 465.7 per sq km (1992 census).

**Births and Deaths** (1983): Live births 251 (birth rate 31.2 per 1,000); Deaths 47 (death rate 5.8 per 1,000).

**Economically Active Population** (census of 30 June 1966): 2,473 (Administration 845, Phosphate mining 1,408, Other activities 220).

### AGRICULTURE, ETC.

**Principal Crop and Livestock** (1993): Coconuts 2,000 metric tons; Pigs 3,000 head (FAO estimates). Source: FAO, *Production Yearbook*.

**Fishing** (metric tons, live weight): Total catch 180 (FAO estimate) in 1990; 190 in 1991; 377 in 1992. Source: FAO, *Yearbook of Fishery Statistics*.

### MINING

**Phosphate Rock** ('000 metric tons): 1,181 in 1989; 926 in 1990; 530 in 1991. The phosphoric acid content is estimated at 38.3%. Source: UN, *Industrial Statistics Yearbook*.

### INDUSTRY

**Electric energy** (million kWh): 29 per year in 1986–91. Source: UN, *Industrial Statistics Yearbook*.

### FINANCE

**Currency and Exchange Rates:** Australian currency: 100 cents = 1 Australian dollar ($A). *Sterling and US Dollar Equivalents* (31 December 1994): £1 sterling = $A2.017; US $1 = $A1.289; $A100 = £49.58 = US $77.57. *Average Exchange Rate* (US $ per Australian dollar): 0.7353 in 1992; 0.6801 in 1993; 0.7317 in 1994.

**Budget** (estimates, $A '000, year ending 30 June 1991): *Revenue:* Nauru Phosphate Corporation 25,000; Air Nauru 34,400; Total (incl. others) 65,600. *Expenditure:* 71,200.

### EXTERNAL TRADE

**1988/89** ($A '000, year ending 30 June): *Imports:* 17,564. *Exports:* 101,292. Source: UN, *Statistical Yearbook for Asia and the Pacific*.

Note: Figures refer to trade with Australia and New Zealand only.

### TRANSPORT

**Road Traffic** (1989): 1,448 registered motor vehicles.

**Shipping:** *Merchant Fleet* (displacement, '000 grt at 30 June): 32 in 1990; 15 in 1991; 5 in 1992. Source: UN, *Statistical Yearbook*. *International Freight Traffic* (estimates, '000 metric tons, 1990): Goods loaded 1,650; Goods unloaded 59. Source: UN, *Monthly Bulletin of Statistics*.

**Civil Aviation** (traffic on scheduled services, 1990): Kilometres flown (million) 2; Passengers carried ('000) 55; Passenger-km (million) 103; Total ton-km (million) 11. Source: UN, *Statistical Yearbook*.

### COMMUNICATIONS MEDIA

**Radio Receivers** (1992): 6,000 in use. Source: UNESCO, *Statistical Yearbook*.

**Telephones** (1988): 2,000 in use. Source: UN, *Statistical Yearbook*.

### EDUCATION

**Pre-primary** (1985): 4 schools; 20 teachers; 383 pupils.

**Primary** (1985): 7 schools; 71 teachers; 1,451 pupils.

**General Secondary** (1985): 2 schools; 36 teachers; 465 pupils.

**Vocational** (1985): 4 teachers; 17 students.

Source: UNESCO, *Statistical Yearbook*.

Nauruans studying at secondary and tertiary levels overseas in 1984 numbered 88.

# Directory

## The Constitution

The Constitution of the Republic of Nauru came into force at independence on 31 January 1968, having been adopted two days previously. It protects fundamental rights and freedoms, and vests executive authority in the Cabinet, which is responsible to a popularly elected parliament. The President of the Republic is elected by Parliament from among its members. The Cabinet is composed of five or six members, including the President, who presides. There are 18 members of Parliament, including the Cabinet. Voting is compulsory for all Nauruans who are more than 20 years of age, except in certain specified instances.

The highest judicial organ is the Supreme Court and there is provision for the creation of subordinate courts with designated jurisdiction.

There is a Treasury Fund from which monies may be taken by Appropriation Acts.

A Public Service is provided for, with the person designated as the Chief Secretary being the Commissioner of the Public Service.

Special mention is given to the allocation of profits and royalties from the sale of phosphates.

## The Government

### HEAD OF STATE

**President:** BERNARD DOWIYOGO (elected 12 December 1989; re-elected 18 November 1992).

### CABINET
(June 1995)

**President, Minister for Island Development and Industry, External Affairs, Public Service and Civil Aviation:** BERNARD DOWIYOGO.

**Minister for Finance, Internal Affairs and Minister Assisting the President:** VINSON DETENAMO.

**Minister for Public Works and Community Services:** VINCI CLODUMAR.

**Minister for Education:** PRES NIMES EKWONA.

**Minister for Justice:** DEROG GIOURA.

**Minister for Health:** LUDWIG SCOTTY.

### MINISTRIES

**Office of the President:** Yaren, Nauru; telex 33100.

**Ministry of Education:** Yaren, Nauru; tel. 3130; fax 3718.

**Ministry of Health:** Yaren, Nauru; tel. 4095; telex 33081; fax 4170.

**Ministry of Finance:** Aiwo, Nauru; tel. 3140; telex 33081; fax 4477.

**Ministry of Justice:** Yaren, Nauru; tel. 3747; telex 33081; fax 3108.

**Ministry of Public Works and Community Services:** Yaren, Nauru; telex 33081.

## Legislature

### PARLIAMENT

Parliament comprises 18 members. The most recent general election took place on 14 November 1992. All members were elected as independents.

**Speaker:** PAUL JEREAMIA.

## Political Organization

**Democratic Party of Nauru:** c/o Parliament House, Yaren, Nauru; f. 1987; revival of Nauru Party (f. 1975); Leader KENNAN RANIBOK ADEANG.

## Diplomatic Representation

### HIGH COMMISSION AND EMBASSY IN NAURU

**Australia:** Civic Centre, POB 6, Aiwo, Nauru; tel. 3232; fax 3227; High Commissioner: TOM SINKOVITS.

**China (Taiwan):** POB 294, Nauru; Chargé d'affaires: HSIUNG KIEN.

## Judicial System

The Chief Justice presides over the Supreme Court, which exercises both original and appellate jurisdiction. The Resident Magistrate presides over the District Court, and he also acts as Coroner under the Inquests Act 1977. The Supreme Court and the District Court are courts of record. The Family Court consists of three members, one being the Resident Magistrate as Chairman, and two other members drawn from a panel of Nauruans. The Chief Justice is Chairman of the Public Services Appeals Board and of the Police Appeals Board.

### SUPREME COURT
tel. 3163; fax 3104.

**Chief Justice:** Sir GAVEN JOHN DONNE (non-resident).

### DISTRICT COURT

**Resident Magistrate:** G. N. SAKSENA.

### FAMILY COURT

**Chairman:** G. N. SAKSENA.

## Religion

Nauruans are predominantly Christians, adhering either to the Nauruan Protestant Church or to the Roman Catholic Church.

**Nauruan Protestant Church:** Head Office, Nauru; Moderator (vacant).

**Roman Catholic Church:** Nauru; tel. 4486; fax 6229; Nauru forms part of the diocese of Tarawa and Nauru, comprising Kiribati and Nauru. The Bishop resides on Tarawa Atoll, Kiribati.

## The Press

**Bulletin:** Nauru; tel. 3090; weekly; Nauruan and English; local and overseas news; Editor J. E. HEINE; circ. 750.

**Central Star News:** Nauru; f. 1991; fortnightly.

**The Nauru Chronicle:** Nauru; Editor RUBY DEDIYA.

## Radio and Television

According to UNESCO, there were an estimated 6,000 radio receivers in use in 1992.

**Nauru Broadcasting Service:** Nauru; tel. 3109; fax 3195; f. 1968; state-owned and non-commercial; broadcasts in the mornings in English and Nauruan; Station Man. RIN TSITSI; Technical Dirs NATHAN DEDIYA, NOEL KAMTAURA.

In May 1991 a television service began operating on the island. Television New Zealand Ltd supplies most of the programmes via satellite or on video-tape.

## Finance

(cap. = capital; res = reserves; dep. = deposits; m. = million; amounts in Australian dollars unless otherwise stated.)

### BANKING

#### State Bank

**Bank of Nauru:** Civic Centre, POB 289, Nauru; tel. 3238; fax 3203; f. 1976; state-owned; cap. 12.0m., res 123.0m., dep. 115.0m. (Dec. 1993); Chair. L. SCOTTY; Gen. Man. N. GOSWAMI; 2 brs.

#### Commercial Banks

**Allied Bank Corporation:** POB 300, Aiwo, Nauru; tel. 3347; telex 33090; fax 3347; f. 1990; cap. US $3.0m., res US $46.4m., dep. US $5,926.2m. (Dec. 1993); Gen. Man. S. A. PICCI; Dir J. C. MAHER.

**Hampshire Bank and Trust Inc:** POB 300, Aiwo, Nauru; tel. 3349; fax 3347; f. 1986; cap. 32.3m., res 54.6m., dep. 540.4m. (Dec. 1994); Gen. Man. R. VAN ZANTEN.

### INSURANCE

**Nauru Insurance Corporation:** POB 82, Nauru; tel. 3346; telex 33088; fax 3731; f. 1974; sole licensed insurer and reinsurer in Nauru.

## Trade and Industry

**Nauru Agency Corporation:** POB 300, Aiwo, Nauru; tel. 3348; telex 33090; fax 3730; functions as a merchant bank to assist entrepreneurs in the registration of holding and trading corporations and the procurement of banking, trust and insurance licences; Vice-Chair. KELLY D. EMIU; Gen. Man. K. DEENABANDHU.

**Nauru Corporation:** Civic Centre, Yaren, Nauru; f. 1925; operated by the Nauru Council; the major retailer in Nauru; Chair. BERNARD DOWIYOGO; Gen. Man. A. EPHRAIM.

**Nauru Fishing Corporation:** Aiwo, Nauru; tel. 5291; telex 33091; fax 3261; f. 1979; owned by Nauru Local Government Council; one 600-ton purse-seine vessel.

**Nauru Phosphate Corporation:** Aiwo, Nauru; tel. 4170; telex 33082; fax 3787; f. 1970; operates the phosphate industry and several public services of the Republic of Nauru (including provision of electricity and fresh water) on behalf of the Nauruan people; responsible for the mining and marketing of phosphate; Chair. RENE HARRIS; Gen. Man. B. L. BLUNDELL.

**Nauru Phosphate Royalties Trust:** Nauru; statutory corpn; invests phosphate royalties to achieve govt revenue; extensive international interests, esp. hotels and real estate; Sec. MALCOLM REID.

## Transport

### RAILWAYS

There are 5.2 km of 0.9-m gauge railway serving the phosphate workings.

### ROADS

A sealed road, 16 km long, circles the island, and another serves Buada District. There were 1,448 registered vehicles in 1989.

### SHIPPING

As Nauru has no wharves, passenger and cargo handling are operated by barge.

**Nauru Pacific:** Civic Centre, Yaren, Nauru; tel. 4581; telex 33083; f. 1969; operates cargo charter services to ports in Australia, New Zealand, Asia, the Pacific and the west coast of the USA; Man. Dir (vacant).

### CIVIL AVIATION

**Air Nauru:** Directorate of Civil Aviation, Government of Nauru Offices, Yaren, Nauru; tel. 3141; telex 33081; fax 3170; f. 1970; operates services to Kiribati, Fiji, New Caledonia, Solomon Islands, Guam, the Philippines, Micronesia, Hawaii (USA), Australia and New Zealand; Chair. BERNARD DOWIYOGO; CEO FELIX KUN; Dir of Civil Aviation Capt. BARRY CRANSTON.

# NEPAL

## Introductory Survey

**Location, Climate, Language, Religion, Flag, Capital**

The Kingdom of Nepal is a land-locked Asian country in the Himalaya mountain range, with India to the east, south and west, and Tibet (the Xizang Autonomous Region), in the People's Republic of China, to the north. The climate varies sharply with altitude, from arctic on the higher peaks of the Himalaya mountains (where the air temperature is permanently below freezing point) to humid sub-tropical in the central valley of Kathmandu, which is warm and sunny in summer. Temperatures in Kathmandu, which is 1,337 m (4,386 ft) above sea-level, are generally between 2°C (35°F) and 30°C (86°F), with an annual average of 11°C (52°F). The rainy season is between June and October. Average annual rainfall varies from about 1,000 mm (40 ins) in western Nepal to about 2,500 mm (100 ins) in the east. The official language is Nepali, which was spoken by 58.4% of the population in 1981. Other languages include Maithir (11.1% in 1981) and Bhojpuri (7.6%). Nearly 90% of the population were Hindus in 1981, with 5.3% Buddhists and 2.7% Muslims. The national flag (proportions 3 by 4) is composed of two crimson pennants, each with a blue border. The upper section contains a white crescent moon (horns upwards and surmounted by a disc with eight rays) and the lower section a white sun in splendour. The capital is Kathmandu.

**Recent History**

Nepal is an hereditary monarchy, but for more than 100 years, until 1951, effective power was held by the Rana family, who created the post of hereditary Prime Minister. A popular revolution, led by the Nepali Congress Party (NCP), toppled the Ranas and restored King Tribhuvan to power. A limited constitutional monarchy was established in 1951. During most of the 1950s government was controlled by the monarchy, first under Tribhuvan and then, after his death in 1955, under his son, Mahendra. In February 1959 King Mahendra promulgated Nepal's first Constitution, providing for a bicameral parliament, including a popularly-elected lower house. Elections, held later that month, resulted in victory for the NCP, led by B. P. Koirala, who became Prime Minister.

However, the King retained a certain degree of power, and persistent differences between the King and the Prime Minister led to a royal coup in December 1960: Nepal's first brief period of democracy was thus brought to an abrupt end. The King dismissed the Cabinet and dissolved Parliament. A royal decree of January 1961 banned political parties. King Mahendra accused the Koirala administration of corruption, and in December 1962 he introduced a new Constitution, reasserting absolute royal power and providing for a 'partyless' system of government, based on the Panchayat (village council), with a Prime Minister appointed by the King. This office was filled successively by Dr Tulsi Giri (1962–65), Surya Bahadur Thapa (1965–69) and Kirti Nidhi Bista (1969–70, 1971–73). King Mahendra himself was Prime Minister from April 1970 to April 1971. In January 1972 King Mahendra died and was succeeded by his son, Birendra. Nagendra Prasad Rijal became Prime Minister in July 1973, and held office until December 1975, when Dr Giri was reappointed. The new Government made major changes to the Constitution which allowed for a widening of the franchise and more frequent elections to the Rashtriya Panchayat (National Assembly), but in no way were the King's powers eroded. In September 1977 Dr Giri resigned and was succeeded by Bista.

B. P. Koirala, the former Prime Minister and an advocate of parliamentary democracy, was acquitted of treason in February 1978. Returning from abroad a year later, he was placed under house arrest in April 1979, but then released, partly to appease students who had been demonstrating for reforms. National unrest grew and, after King Birendra announced in May that there would be a national referendum on whether to restore multi-party democracy, Bista resigned and was succeeded as Prime Minister by Thapa. In the referendum, held in May 1980, 54.8% of the voters supported the Panchayat system with reforms. As a result, the King formed a Constitutional Reforms Commission, and in December 1980 he issued a decree under which amendments to the Constitution were made, including the proviso that the appointment of the Prime Minister by the King would henceforth be on the recommendation of the Rashtriya Panchayat. In accordance with the new provisions, direct legislative elections were held in May 1981, the first of their kind since 1959, although still on a non-party basis. Thapa was re-elected by the Rashtriya Panchayat as Prime Minister in June, and the King installed a new Council of Ministers. An extensive ministerial reshuffle took place in October 1982, but this failed to stem increasing official corruption and economic mismanagement. A new Press Act, approved in November, increased censorship. The lateness of the monsoon led to droughts and severe food shortages, and the economic situation worsened. In July 1983, for the first time in the 23-year history of the Panchayat system, the incumbent Prime Minister, Surya Bahadur Thapa, was ousted, and a new Council of Ministers was formed by a former Chairman of the Rashtriya Panchayat, Lokendra Bahadur Chand, who had successfully introduced a motion expressing 'no confidence' in Thapa.

In September 1984 a motion expressing 'no confidence' in Chand was proposed in the Rashtriya Panchayat by Thapa, the former Prime Minister, in protest against increasing corruption in the Government. The motion failed, however, to reach a vote because of the intervention of a group of 'neutralist' members who feared that repeated votes on motions of 'no confidence' would undermine the Panchayat system. A government reshuffle ensued, and several allegedly corrupt ministers were removed, while all factions in the Panchayat were accommodated. Disappointment with the reshuffle led to the emergence of a new anti-Chand group from within the 'neutralists', led by Badra Sharma, a former Secretary-General of the NCP. In March 1985 the NCP held a convention in Kathmandu, and in May it embarked upon a campaign of civil disobedience, aimed at restoring a multi-party political system and parliamentary rule under a constitutional monarchy. In June there was a series of bomb explosions, resulting in loss of life. The explosions were apparently co-ordinated by two newly-formed anti-monarchist and anti-Government groups, the Janawadi Morcha (Democratic Front), led by the exiled Ram Raja Prasad Singh, and the Samyukta Mukti Bahini (United Liberation Torch-bearers). These bombings united an otherwise seriously divided legislature against the terrorists, and forced the predominantly moderate opposition to abandon the campaign of civil disobedience and to disclaim any responsibility for the explosions. In August the Rashtriya Panchayat approved a stringent anti-terrorist law, and more than 1,000 people were arrested in connection with the unrest. In January 1986 the Government announced that a general election would be held in May.

In March 1986 the King accepted the resignation of the Prime Minister and the Council of Ministers, and appointed an interim Government for the pre-election period, led by a former Prime Minister, Nagendra Prasad Rijal. About 64% of the electorate voted in the election, in spite of appeals by the NCP and the pro-Beijing faction of the Communist Party of Nepal (CPN) (neither of which presented candidates) for a boycott of the polls. All the candidates in the election were nominally independents, but it was reported that among the 72 new entrants to the Rashtriya Panchayat (40 members retained their seats) were at least 16 members of the Marxist-Leninist faction of the CPN. In June the King nominated 25 additional members of the new Rashtriya Panchayat, and Marich Man Singh Shrestha (previously Chairman of the Rashtriya Panchayat) was elected unopposed by the Assembly as the new Prime Minister. A few days later, on the recommendation of the Prime Minister, the King appointed a new 17-member Council of Ministers. In late 1986, to counter the growing influence of the communist faction in the Rashtriya Panchayat, several senior figures (including Jog Meher Shrestha, a former government minister, and Lokendra

Bahadur Chand) established a 'Democratic Panchayat Forum' which expressed full support for the non-party system.

Members of the NCP and the Marxist-Leninist faction of the CPN participated (as independents) in local elections in March–April 1987. The opposition achieved only limited success, with the NCP candidates winning 15% of the local seats and the communist candidates 20%, while pro-Government candidates won 65% of the seats. The NCP subsequently claimed that there had been extensive electoral fraud and intimidation of voters by supporters of the Panchayat system. NCP candidates, however, were elected to the important posts of mayor and deputy mayor in Kathmandu, and the party won three further mayorships and eight deputy mayorships.

In 1986–87 the Nepalese Government continued its policy of press censorship, in an effort to curb anti-Government criticism. In June 1987, in an apparent attempt to improve the image of the Panchayat system, the Government initiated an anti-corruption campaign, during the course of which several senior officials were arrested for drug-smuggling and other offences. In December the Government announced plans to reorganize government ministries and departments, in an effort to make them more efficient. As part of this reorganization, more than 160 officials were dismissed from their posts. In early 1988 the Government continued its policy of suppressing opposition. In January the President of the NCP was arrested, and in February more than 100 people, who were planning to demonstrate in support of the NCP mayor of Kathmandu (who had been suspended from office for his anti-Panchayat stance), were also detained. In March an extensive government reshuffle included the establishment of a new Ministry of Housing and Physical Planning. In June a motion expressing 'no confidence' in Shrestha's Government was presented by 53 members of the Rashtriya Panchayat, including two former Prime Ministers, Surya Bahadur Thapa and Lokendra Bahadur Chand. They accused the Government of failing to curb corruption and of pursuing a misguided economic policy. The Chairman of the Rashtriya Panchayat rejected the motion, however, on 'technical grounds' in the name of Panchayat unity. In October there was another major reshuffle of the Council of Ministers, which included the dismissal of 11 ministers.

In early September 1989 the Government arrested more than 900 supporters of the NCP, in an apparent attempt to prevent them from celebrating the anniversary of the birth of Nepal's first elected Prime Minister, B. P. Koirala. During these celebrations the NCP demonstrated in protest against the failings of the country's non-party political system. In early November the leaders of the NCP held a meeting in Kathmandu with members of several other left-wing and communist political groups, to discuss the proposed formation of a country-wide peaceful 'movement for the restoration of democracy'. At the meeting they stated that the aims of the movement would be the alleviation of Nepal's severe economic problems (including the trade dispute with India, see below), the restoration of full democracy, the transfer from absolute to constitutional monarchy, the immediate replacement of the Panchayat Government by an interim national government, the removal of the ban on political activities, and the introduction of a multi-party system. At the end of January 1990 a co-ordination committee to conduct the *Jana Andolan* (People's Movement) was formed by the NCP and the newly-formed United Left Front (ULF, led by Sahana Pradhan, comprising six factions of the CPN and a labour group), despite the Government's efforts to pre-empt its inauguration by arresting hundreds of activists (including many students) and by banning, or heavily censoring, more newspapers. During the consequent violent confrontations between protesters and police that took place in the later half of February, it was officially estimated that 12 people were killed and hundreds more were arrested. Violent demonstrations, strikes and mass arrests continued throughout March. At the end of the month the Minister of Foreign Affairs, Shailendra Kumar Upadhayaya, resigned from his post, following differences with the Prime Minister regarding the Government's management of the crisis. A few days later, there was an extensive government reshuffle, including the dismissal of nine ministers, who allegedly opposed the Government's acts of repression against the pro-democracy movement. In an effort to end the political unrest, the King dismissed Marich Man Singh Shrestha's Government on 6 April and nominated a restricted four-member Council of Ministers, under the leadership of the more moderate Lokendra Bahadur Chand. He also offered to establish a committee to study the possibility of altering the Constitution and to hold discussions with the opposition, and he promised to initiate an official enquiry into the 20 deaths that had occurred during demonstrations since February. Despite these concessions, the situation worsened later the same day, when troops opened fire on a crowd of 100,000–200,000 demonstrators who were marching towards the royal palace in Kathmandu, killing at least 50 people. A temporary curfew was imposed on the capital, and many political agitators were arrested. The Government immediately initiated talks with the opposition, and on 8 April the King announced that the 30-year ban on political parties was to be ended, thus enabling the future holding of multi-party elections, and that a commission to study constitutional reform was to be established. At the same time, the *Jana Andolan* suspended its campaign of demonstrations. Many political activists continued to agitate, however, in demand of the removal of the formal structure of the Panchayat system. A week later, the King accepted the resignation of Lokendra Bahadur Chand from his post as Prime Minister, dismissed the Council of Ministers and announced the dissolution of the Rashtriya Panchayat. King Birendra then invited the opposition alliance of the NCP and the ULF to form an interim government. On 19 April a new 11-member coalition Council of Ministers (including two ministers nominated by the King and two independents), under the premiership of the President of the NCP, Krishna Prasad Bhattarai, was sworn in.

The new Prime Minister announced that a general election would be held, on a multi-party basis, within a year. The principal task of the interim Government was to prepare a new constitution in accordance with the spirit of multi-party democracy and constitutional monarchy. King Birendra stated that he was committed to transforming his role into that of a constitutional monarch, and following further violent clashes in Kathmandu between anti-royalists and police, he ordered the army and the police to comply with the orders of the interim Government in order to facilitate a smooth transition to democracy.

In mid-May 1990 King Birendra announced a general amnesty for all religious and political prisoners. On 21 May he delegated the legislative powers of the dissolved Rashtriya Panchayat to the new Council of Ministers, so that the Council was empowered to enact, amend and repeal legislation in order to bring about the introduction of a multi-party democracy. At the end of the month the King formed a nine-member Constitutional Recommendation Commission, based on the suggestions of the Prime Minister, which, after consulting the various parties, was to prepare a draft constitution and present it to the King within three months. At the end of July the death sentence was abolished in Nepal, and the laws restricting freedom of the press and freedom of association were repealed. The King suspended almost one-half of the articles in the Constitution to enable the interim Government to function smoothly. The draft of the new Constitution, which was published at the end of August, recommended the introduction of a constitutional monarchy; a democratic multi-party system and a bicameral legislature composed of a 205-member House of Representatives (Pratinidhi Sabha) and a 60-member National Council (Rashtriya Sabha); the official guarantee of fundamental rights (including freedom of expression); an independent judiciary; and the placing of the army under the control of a three-member National Defence Council, headed by the Prime Minister. The draft Constitution recognized Hinduism as the country's dominant religion. It also, however, guaranteed freedom for religious minorities to practise their beliefs (although restrictions on proselytizing were to remain in force). Under the draft Constitution, the King would be allowed to declare a state of emergency on the advice of the Council of Ministers, but such declarations would have to be approved by the House of Representatives within three months. A crucial clause in the new Constitution required the King 'to obey and protect' the Constitution: under the old regime, the King was considered to be above the Constitution. The draft Constitution was approved by the Council of Ministers on 15 October and sent to the King for his endorsement. King Birendra, however, amended the draft in a final effort to retain sovereign authority and full emergency powers. This attempt provoked violent protests. The Council of Ministers rejected most of the proposed amendments in the royal counter-draft, but agreed to the King's proposal to establish a council of state (Raj Parishad), with a standing committee headed by a royal appointee. The 15-member committee was to be composed of eight royal appointees and seven other members, including the Prime Minister, the Ministers of Defence and Foreign Affairs, the Chief Justice of the Supreme Court and the Chief of Army Staff. Bhattarai stressed, however, that the formation of this committee would not alter the democratic nature of the new Constitution, since it would not function as a parallel body to the Council of Ministers. He also emphasized that the King would only be permitted to act on judicial, executive and legislative matters on the advice of the Council of Ministers. The new Constitution was officially promulgated by the King on 9 November.

The communist movement in Nepal suffered a set-back in December 1990, when four of the seven constituents of the ULF broke away from the front. Sahana Pradhan stated, however, that the three remaining factions would continue to operate as the ULF. The main reason given for the split was that the four breakaway groups were not represented in the interim coalition Council of Ministers. In early January 1991 two major factions of the CPN (the Marxist and Marxist-Leninist factions) merged to form the CPN (Unified Marxist-Leninist—UML).

The process for the holding of a successful general election began with the registration of political parties and the delimitation of 205 constituencies. Of the 44 political parties registered by the election commission, however, only 20 actually participated in the general election, which was held on 12 May 1991. The NCP decided to contest the election alone and not on the basis of an electoral alignment with any of its former *Jana Andolan* partners. The communists interpreted the NCP's move as the result of an increased understanding between the palace and the NCP on the basis that both wanted to forestall the rise of communism in the country. Consequently, relations between the NCP and the CPN (UML) became strained and competitive. The general election was not only peaceful, but was also characterized by a good turn-out (65.2% of the electorate). The NCP won a comfortable majority (110 seats), but it was soundly defeated by the CPN (UML) in the eastern hill districts and in some parts of the Terai. In Kathmandu, supposedly an NCP stronghold, the party lost all of the seats but one. By winning 69 seats, the CPN (UML) established itself as the second largest party in the House of Representatives, followed by the United People's Front (UPF), an amalgam of radical, Maoist groups, with nine seats. Two other communist organizations—the Nepal Workers' and Peasants' Party and a faction of the CPN—received two seats each, thus making a total communist tally in the House of Representatives of 82 seats. The Nepali Sadbhavana Party, which, despite the constitutional prohibition against regional-based parties, was a plains- or Terai-based party, obtained six seats, all of which were in the Terai. The National Democratic Party (Chand) and the National Democratic Party (Thapa), led by the former Prime Ministers, fared badly in the election, winning only four seats—the latter one and the former three. All of the three independent candidates who won seats subsequently joined the NCP. The acting Prime Minister, K. P. Bhattarai, lost his seat in the capital, and was replaced in the premiership by Girija Prasad Koirala, the General Secretary of the NCP.

By the end of 1991 unity within the ruling NCP was threatened by growing internal dissent amongst its leadership, particularly between the senior leader, Ganesh Man Singh, and G. P. Koirala. In late December the Prime Minister carried out a reshuffle of the Council of Ministers introducing more of his own supporters as new ministers in an apparent attempt to strengthen his hold on power. The Government suffered a further set-back in early April 1992 when a *bandh* (general strike), organized by the communist and other opposition parties in Kathmandu in protest against price rises, water shortages and alleged government corruption, resulted in the deaths of at least seven anti-Government demonstrators (according to government sources) following violent clashes with the police. Despite the consequent imposition of curfews in the capital and in the neighbouring town of Lalitpur, the opposition staged a number of anti-Government protest marches and demonstrations during the following week. The success of a second general strike, which was held in early May, demonstrated the continuing strength of the radical left. It brought Kathmandu to a standstill and, unlike the earlier general strike, passed off without violent incidents. Despite the strikes and the rising cost of living, the NCP performed well in the local elections held throughout the country in May and June; of especial note was the party's strong showing in the Kathmandu valley where it had performed so badly in the 1991 general election. There were, however, widespread reports of ballot-rigging and vote-purchasing, features that had apparently been absent from the 1991 general election.

Under the leadership of G. P. Koirala, the centrist NCP Government shifted to the right. The public image of the monarchy and leading members of the former Panchayat regime were rehabilitated with government support. No charges were brought against senior officials of the former administration for corruption or human rights violations. Replicating the patronage system of the Panchayat regime, the NCP rapidly began to dominate the public administration structure. The ruling party's persistent failure to democratize its internal bodies and the absence of open election to posts in the party leadership met with criticism both within and without the NCP.

In addition to opposition from the leadership of his own party, Koirala was faced with increasing criticism from the opposition parties themselves, which focused on an agreement drawn up by the Prime Minister in December 1991 granting India access to water from the Tanakpur barrage in the Terai, the terms of which were only subsequently revealed to the Nepalese House of Representatives. Alleging that the agreement constituted a treaty affecting national sovereignty, and therefore requiring a two-thirds' majority in the House of Representatives, the opposition launched a campaign calling for the resignation of Koirala on the grounds of unconstitutional behaviour.

In January–February 1993 the national UML congress jettisoned much of the party's Marxist dogma and tacitly acknowledged the party's commitment to working within a democratic multi-party system. However, the untimely deaths of the party's General Secretary, Madan Bhandari, and Politburo member Jiv Raj Ashrit, following a mysterious road accident in mid-May, threw the UML into disarray, leading to fears of an open split. The rejection by the UML of the findings of a government inquiry, which concluded that the deaths had been accidental, provoked nation-wide protests in support of demands for an independent inquiry into the so-called 'Dhasdunga Incident'. In late May Madhav Kumar Nepal was appointed as the new General Secretary of the UML.

In the mean time, the rehabilitation of officials of the former Panchayat regime continued. In January 1993 the King appointed senior figures of the old administration, including former Prime Ministers, Lokendra Bahadur Chand and Marich Man Singh Shrestha, to the 121-member Council of State (Raj Parishad), in a move designed both to rehabilitate former Panchayat officials and to reassert his leadership role over them. In June the right-wing National Democratic Party (NDP, formed in February 1992, following a merger of the Chand and Thapa factions) held its first national conference in Kathmandu, an event that would have been inconceivable three years previously, when its leaders were forced into hiding by the democracy movement. A resurgence in the popularity of the monarchy contributed to this process.

In July 1993 heavy monsoon rains caused extensive flash floods, the worst for 40 years, affecting 21 of the country's 75 districts. Tens of thousands were left homeless and about 2,000 people were killed.

In mid-August 1993 the UML signed an agreement with the NCP, providing for the permanent withdrawal of the UML from anti-Government agitation in return for the ruling party's pledge to establish an independent commission to investigate the 'Dhasdunga Incident'. The UPF and other left-wing groups, however, continued their campaign of nation-wide general strikes and demonstrations demanding, amongst other things, the Prime Minister's resignation over the Tanakpur controversy and a curb on the NCP's increasing hold on power over public life. The Government was also criticized for its apparent inability to resolve the deteriorating economic situation, for its perceived subservience to India, and for its alleged involvement in corruption. To compound its growing number of problems, further serious rifts became apparent within the ruling NCP when the party's President, Krishna Prasad Bhattarai, lost a legislative by-election to the UML candidate in Kathmandu in February 1994; his defeat was widely attributed to Koirala's public opposition to his candidature. At the end of the month the Prime Minister rejected demands for his resignation made by supporters of Bhattarai in the NCP's Central Executive Committee. In early March, however, the Government survived a vote of no confidence (by 113 votes to 81) presented to the House of Representatives by the UML. The opposition itself suffered from internal dissension in mid-1994 when both the UPF and the CPN (Unity Centre) split into competing factions, while the UML continued to be divided between radical and conservative camps. The crisis within the NCP came to a head on 10 July when followers of Ganesh Man Singh withdrew their support for Koirala, who thereby lost his parliamentary majority. Consequently the defeated Prime Minister offered his resignation and on the following day the King dissolved the House of Representatives. Koirala was appointed as interim Prime Minister pending the holding of a general election, which was brought forward from mid-1996 to 13 November 1994 (later postponed until 15 November). At the general election, which attracted a relatively low turn-out of 58%, the UML unexpectedly emerged as the single largest party, winning 88 seats, while the NCP came a close second, with 85 seats. At the end of the month, following two weeks of political deadlock, the UML formed a minority Government under the premiership of its moderate Chairman, Man Mohan Adhikari. In late December the communist Government won a vote of confidence in the House of Representatives.

On 11 June 1995 the NCP registered a parliamentary motion of no confidence against the communist Government and, in conjunction with the NDP and the Nepali Sadbhavana Party, submitted a memorandum to King Birendra, staking their claim to form an alternative government. On the recommendation of the Prime Minister, the King dissolved the legislature on 13 June and announced that fresh elections were to be held on 23 November. Man Mohan Adhikari and his Council of Ministers were to function as a caretaker Government, pending the general election.

In 1978 the old Trade and Transit Treaty between Nepal and India was replaced by two treaties (renewed in the mid-1980s), the one concerning bilateral trade between the two countries, the other allowing Nepal to develop trade with other countries via India. Relations with India deteriorated considerably in March 1989, however, when India decided not to renew the treaties, insisting that a common treaty covering both issues be negotiated. Nepal refused, however, stressing the importance of keeping the treaties separate, on the grounds that trade issues are negotiable, whereas the right of transit is a recognized basic right of land-locked countries. In response, India closed 13 of the 15 transit points through which most of Nepal's trade is conducted. Severe shortages of food and fuel ensued, and the prices of basic products increased significantly. It was widely believed that a major issue aggravating the dispute was Nepal's purchase of weapons (including anti-aircraft guns) from the People's Republic of China in 1988, which, according to India, violated the Treaty of Peace and Friendship concluded by India and Nepal in 1950. Diplomatic relations between Nepal and India remained strained throughout 1989, with trade at a virtual standstill. Following several rounds of senior-level talks, a joint communiqué was signed by the two countries during a visit by Prime Minister Bhattarai to India in June 1990, restoring trade relations and reopening the transit points, and assuring mutual consultations on matters of security. A few days earlier, as an apparent gesture of goodwill to India, the Nepalese Government had told the Chinese Government to defer indefinitely the delivery of the final consignment of arms destined for Nepal. Bhattarai's visit to India received enthusiastic support from the Nepalese people, although a small left-wing minority accused the Government of conceding too much to India. It was generally agreed that the visit to Kathmandu by the Indian Prime Minister, Chandra Shekhar, in February 1991 (the first official visit to Nepal by an Indian Premier since 1977), shortly after it was announced that the first free elections there were to be held in May, helped to reaffirm the traditionally amicable ties between the two countries. Separate trade and transit treaties (valid for five and seven years respectively) were signed during a visit by Prime Minister Koirala to India in December 1991. In April 1995 the new communist Prime Minister, Man Mohan Adhikari, during his first official visit to India, insisted that, despite earlier indications to the contrary, his Government did not wish to abrogate the 1950 Treaty of Peace and Friendship, but would, rather, seek to modify it and introduce new clauses regarding security and migration.

The People's Republic of China has contributed a considerable amount to the Nepalese economy, and the first meeting of a joint committee on economic co-operation took place in December 1984. This committee met for a second time (and thenceforth annually) in Kathmandu in March 1986, when China agreed to increase its imports from Nepal in order to minimize trade imbalances. Relations between Nepal and China improved further in November 1989, when the Chinese Premier, Li Peng, paid an official three-day visit to Kathmandu. This visit was viewed with some misgiving by India as emphasizing Nepal's increasingly friendly relations with China. In March 1992 the Nepalese Prime Minister, G. P. Koirala, paid a week-long official goodwill visit to Beijing.

In 1985 it was agreed that Nepal's border with Tibet (the Xizang Autonomous Region) should be opened. Following the outbreak of ethnic violence in Tibet in March 1989, however, the border between Nepal and Tibet was closed temporarily. In February 1991 the interim Government of Nepal cancelled a visit by the Dalai Lama, the Tibetan leader in exile, on 'technical grounds'. The cancellation followed Chinese protests made to the Nepalese Government against the proposed visit. The Nepalese authorities have been consistent in their efforts to repatriate refugees fleeing from Tibet. In October 1993 G. P. Koirala paid an informal visit to Tibet—the first visit to the region by a Nepalese premier since the 1950s.

Ties with Bangladesh are also significant, particularly regarding the utilization of joint water resources. In December 1982 Pakistan and Nepal strengthened their trade links by renewing a 1962 agreement, and in 1983 they established a joint economic commission and a regular air link.

In late 1991 and throughout 1992 thousands of Bhutanese of Nepalese origin arrived at refugee camps in eastern Nepal, following the outbreak of political and ethnic unrest in Bhutan. By the end of July 1994 more than 85,000 refugees were living in seven camps in the districts of Jhapa and Morang. In the first half of 1993 talks were held between Bhutanese and Nepalese government officials regarding proposals to resolve the issues at stake. The Nepalese Government steadfastly refused to consider any solution that did not include the resettlement in Bhutan of all ethnic Nepalese refugees living in the camps. This proposal was rejected by the Bhutan Government, which claimed that the majority of the camp population were not actually Bhutanese. The apparent deadlock was broken, however, when a joint statement was signed by the Ministers of Home Affairs of Bhutan and Nepal in mid-July 1993, which committed each side to establishing a 'high-level joint committee' to work towards a settlement. By April 1995 the committee had held numerous meetings but had made no substantial progress as regards the refugee problem.

Nepal pursues a non-aligned foreign policy, and had diplomatic relations with 108 countries in early 1995. Nepal (with six other countries) is a founder member of the South Asian Association for Regional Co-operation (SAARC, see p. 241), formally established in 1985; the Association's permanent secretariat was established in Kathmandu in 1987.

## Government

Under the provisions of the Constitution promulgated in November 1990, Nepal is a constitutional monarchy. The Constitution provides for a bicameral Parliament, comprising a 205-member House of Representatives (Pratinidhi Sabha) and a 60-member National Council (Rashtriya Sabha), as the supreme legislative body. The House of Representatives is elected for a five-year term, and members of the National Council hold office for a six-year term. Executive power is vested in the King and the Council of Ministers, which is answerable to the House of Representatives. The King appoints the leader of the party that commands a majority in the House of Representatives as Prime Minister, while other ministers are appointed, from among the members of Parliament, on the recommendation of the Prime Minister.

For the purposes of local administration, Nepal is divided into 14 zones.

## Defence

In June 1994 Nepal's total armed forces numbered 35,000 men (to be increased to 40,000 in the near future)—army 34,800, air force 200. Military service is voluntary. The defence budget for 1994 was an estimated 2,100m. rupees.

## Economic Affairs

In 1993, according to estimates by the World Bank, Nepal's gross national product (GNP), measured at average 1991–93 prices, was US $3,174m., equivalent to $160 per head. During 1985–93, it was estimated, GNP per head increased, in real terms, at an average annual rate of 1.8%. Over the same period, the population increased by an annual average of 2.6%. Nepal's gross domestic product (GDP) increased, in real terms, by an annual average of 5.0% in 1980–92, by 2.9% in the year ending 15 July 1993 and, despite the disastrous 1993 monsoon, by an estimated 6.9% in 1993/94.

Agriculture (including hunting, forestry and fishing) contributed an estimated 50.1% of GDP in 1992/93. About 81% of the labour force were employed in the sector, according to the 1991 census. The principal crops are rice, maize, barley, millet, wheat, sugar cane, tobacco, potatoes, cardamom, fruits and oilseeds. During 1980–92 agricultural GDP increased by an annual average of 4.8%, but in 1992/93 it fell by 1.2%, as a result of a severe drought in mid-1992. Partly as a result of the heavy rains in 1993, the agricultural sector expanded in 1993/94 after two years of contraction, and food production increased by 20%.

Industry (comprising mining, manufacturing, construction and utilities) employed only 0.6% of the labour force in 1981, but provided an estimated 19.8% of GDP in 1992/93. About 60% of Nepal's industrial output comes from traditional cottage industries, and the remainder from modern industries. The official index of industrial production declined by 0.4% during 1992/93, compared with a 4.8% increase during the previous year, reflecting power shortages caused by load-shedding.

Mining employed only 0.01% of the labour force in 1981, and contributed an estimated 0.1% of GDP in 1992/93. Mica is mined east of Kathmandu, and there are also small deposits of lignite, copper, cobalt and iron ore. In 1986 Nepal signed an agreement allowing two foreign companies to explore for petroleum in the extreme south-east of the country.

Manufacturing contributed an estimated 9.1% of GDP in 1992/93, and employed about 0.5% of the labour force in 1981. The most important modern branches of manufacturing are the production of bricks and tiles, carpets and ready-made garments (accounting for 55% and 23%, respectively, of the value of Nepal's exports in 1992/93) and paper. Traditional cottage industries include basket-making and the production of cotton fabrics and edible oils.

Energy is derived principally from traditional sources (particularly fuelwood). Imports of mineral fuel and lubricants (mainly for the transport sector), however, comprised an estimated 10.9% of the cost of total imports in 1992/93. In addition, Nepal's rivers are exploited for hydroelectric power production, but in 1994 it was estimated that only about 0.3% of the country's huge potential generating capacity (i.e. only about 241,000 kW of a potential 83m. kW) was being utilized.

Tourism is an important source of foreign exchange. In 1992 the number of foreign visitors reached 334,353, and receipts from tourism amounted to US $61.1m.

In 1993 Nepal recorded a visible trade deficit of US $461.6m., and there was a deficit of $222.5m. on the current account of the balance of payments. In 1990/91 the principal source of imports (an estimated 32.1%) was India, while Germany was the principal market for exports (35.9%). Other major trading partners were Japan, Singapore and the USA. The principal exports in 1992/93 were manufactured goods and articles and food and live animals. The principal imports were basic manufactures, machinery and transport equipment, and chemicals and pharmaceuticals.

Budget proposals for the financial year ending 15 July 1995 envisaged total expenditure (regular and development) of NRs 39,914m. Total recurrent revenue was expected to reach NRs 22,385m, while foreign loans and grants were projected to total NRs 15,628m. Nepal's total external debt was US $2,009m. at the end of 1993, of which $1,938m. was long-term public debt. In 1992 the cost of debt-servicing was equivalent to 11.7% of receipts from exports of goods and services. The annual rate of inflation averaged 10.4% in 1985–93. The national consumer price index rose by 8.1% in 1993/94, compared with 9.6% in the previous year.

Nepal is a member of the Asian Development Bank (see p. 107) and the Colombo Plan (see p. 238), both of which seek to encourage regional economic development.

With an inhospitable terrain, comprising isolated valleys and very high mountains, Nepal is among the least developed countries in the world. In 1985 the Government initiated a 15-year Basic Needs Programme, one of the aims of which was to double agricultural production by the end of the century (particularly by means of greater utilization of fertilizers). In the late 1980s an increase in industrial production was helped by the introduction of more liberal import policies, by an increase in foreign (particularly Indian) investment, by the Government's encouragement of new industries using domestic and imported raw materials and machinery, and by the promotion of import-substitution industries such as textiles and paper. In 1987, in a further attempt to improve domestic production, the Government abolished export duty and income tax on revenue from exports. Nepal's Eighth Five-Year Plan (1992–97) was announced in December 1991 with planned expenditure of NRs 190,000m.—64% of the revenue was to be provided by the private sector and the remainder by the public sector (including foreign loans and grants). The Plan aimed to achieve annual GDP growth of 5.1%, create 1.4m. new jobs and address the serious problem of rural poverty. In March 1992 the Government announced that the Nepalese rupee was to be made partially convertible (in foreign exchange transactions), as part of a series of economic reforms introduced in an attempt to develop industry further and to increase exports to countries other than India. A five-day 'Investment Forum' was held in Kathmandu in late 1992 in an attempt to attract further foreign investment (on more liberal terms) in Nepal. The Forum, which was sponsored by the UN, placed particular emphasis on agro-based, hotel and mining industries. During the five days local and foreign businessmen pledged to undertake 119 industrial projects worth a total of $900m. In February 1993 the Nepalese rupee was made fully convertible for current account transactions, with the currency's value pegged at the rate of 1.60 per Indian rupee. The communist Government, which came to power in November 1994, stated that it intended to continue the process of economic liberalization (with only minor adjustments) and to adhere to free-market policies. One of the Government's main priorities was land reform; a land commission was established in January 1995 to investigate tenancy rights and ceilings on land holdings. Among the Government's other aims was the transfer to private ownership of 80 state-owned companies.

## Social Welfare

In 1986 there were about 600 physicians working in Nepal. In 1982 there were 73 hospitals, with a total of 2,586 beds: one for every 5,483 of the population. Of total projected expenditure by the central Government in the financial year 1990/91, NRs 884.7m. (4.7%) was for health. A 300-bed teaching hospital for 500 students, built with Japanese government assistance, was opened in 1984. In 1985 the Government instigated an ambitious Basic Needs Programme, which aimed to eradicate rural poverty by the year 2000. In 1994 India signed a NRs 800m. agreement to establish an Institute of Health Sciences at Dharan in eastern Nepal; the Institute is to have a 350-bed hospital and a 30-seat medical college.

## Education

Primary education, beginning at six years of age and lasting for five years, is officially compulsory and is provided free of charge in government schools. Secondary education, beginning at the age of 11, lasts for a further five years, comprising a first cycle of two years and a second of three years. In 1992 the total enrolment at primary and secondary schools was equivalent to 72% of the school-age population (boys 88%; girls 55%). Primary enrolment in that year was equivalent to 102% of children in the relevant age-group (boys 121%; girls 81%), while the comparable ratio for secondary enrolment was 36% (boys 47%; girls 24%). There are two state universities, the Tribhuvan University in Kathmandu and the Mahendra Sanskrit Viswavidyalaya in Beljhundi, Dang (founded in 1986), and one private university in Banepa, which, together, had a total of 110,239 students in 1992. Proposed development expenditure on education by the central Government in the 1992/93 budget was NRs 3,550m. (10.6% of total spending). The Eighth Five-Year Plan (1992–97) included proposals to introduce free compulsory secondary education in phases over the next 10 years. According to the 1991 census, the average rate of adult illiteracy was 60% (males 45%; females 75%).

## NEPAL

### Public Holidays

**1995:** 11 January (National Unity Day), 30 January (Martyrs' Day), 19 February (Rashtriya Prajatantra Divas—National Democracy Day), 27 February (Shivaratri—in honour of Lord Shiva), 5 March (Holi Festival), 8 March (Nepalese Women's Day), 9 April (Birthday of Lord Ram), 14 April (Navabarsha—New Year's Day), 14 May (Baishakh Purnima—Birthday of Lord Buddha), 8 September (Indra Jatra—Festival of Rain God), 25 September–7 October (Dasain—Durga Puja Festival), 21–25 October (Deepawali—Festival of Lights), 8 November (Queen Aishworya's Birthday), 9 November (Constitution Day), 29 December (King Birendra's Birthday).

**1996:** 11 January (National Unity Day), 30 January (Martyrs' Day), 17 February (Shivaratri—in honour of Lord Shiva), 19 February (Rashtriya Prajatantra Divas—National Democracy Day), 5 March (Holi Festival), 8 March (Nepalese Women's Day), 28 March (Birthday of Lord Ram), 14 April (Navabarsha—New Year's Day), April/May (Baishakh Purnima—Birthday of Lord Buddha), September (Indra Jatra—Festival of Rain God), September/October, over a week (Dasain—Durga Puja Festival), October/November, three days (Deepawali—Festival of Lights), 8 November (Queen Aishworya's Birthday), 9 November (Constitution Day), 29 December (King Birendra's Birthday).

### Weights and Measures

The metric system has been officially adopted but traditional local and Indian systems of weights and measures are widely used.

# Statistical Survey

Source (unless otherwise stated): National Planning Commission Secretariat, Singha Durbar, POB 1284, Kathmandu; tel. 215000.

## Area and Population

### AREA, POPULATION AND DENSITY

| | |
|---|---:|
| Area (sq km) | 147,181* |
| Population (census results) | |
| 22 June 1981 | 15,022,839 |
| 22 June 1991† | |
| Males | 9,220,914 |
| Females | 9,241,167 |
| Total | 18,462,081 |
| Population (official estimates at mid-year)‡ | |
| 1988 | 17,994,000 |
| 1989 | 18,442,000 |
| 1990 | 18,916,000 |
| Density (per sq km) at 22 June 1991 | 125.4 |

* 56,827 sq miles.
† Figures are provisional.
‡ Not revised to take account of the results of the 1991 census.

**Capital:** Kathmandu, population 235,160 at 1981 census.

### BIRTHS AND DEATHS (UN estimates, annual averages)

| | 1975–80 | 1980–85 | 1985–90 |
|---|---:|---:|---:|
| Birth rate (per 1,000) | 44.6 | 42.9 | 39.6 |
| Death rate (per 1,000) | 19.0 | 17.0 | 14.8 |

**Expectation of life** (UN estimates, years at birth, 1985–90): 50.9 (males 51.5; females 50.3).

Source: UN, *World Population Prospects: The 1992 Revision*.

### ECONOMICALLY ACTIVE POPULATION (1981 census)

| | Males | Females | Total |
|---|---:|---:|---:|
| Agriculture, hunting, forestry and fishing | 3,974,119 | 2,270,170 | 6,244,289 |
| Mining and quarrying | 712 | 259 | 971 |
| Manufacturing | 28,115 | 4,914 | 33,029 |
| Electricity, gas and water | 2,867 | 146 | 3,013 |
| Construction | 1,903 | 119 | 2,022 |
| Trade, restaurants and hotels | 93,020 | 16,426 | 109,446 |
| Transport, storage and communications | 7,080 | 344 | 7,424 |
| Financing, insurance, real estate and business service | 8,846 | 1,004 | 9,850 |
| Community, social and personal services | 268,062 | 45,508 | 313,570 |
| Activities not adequately defined | 95,220 | 32,052 | 127,272 |
| **Total** | **4,479,944** | **2,370,942** | **6,850,886** |

Source: ILO, *Year Book of Labour Statistics*.

## Agriculture

### PRINCIPAL CROPS ('000 metric tons)

| | 1991 | 1992 | 1993 |
|---|---:|---:|---:|
| Wheat | 836 | 779 | 765 |
| Rice (paddy) | 3,223 | 2,585 | 3,100* |
| Barley | 28 | 28 | 28 |
| Maize | 1,205 | 1,291 | 1,200* |
| Millet | 229 | 237 | 232† |
| Potatoes | 738 | 733 | 733 |
| Other roots and tubers | 141 | 141 | 142 |
| Lentils | 73 | 73 | 105 |
| Other pulses | 91 | 84 | 101 |
| Linseed† | 31 | 31 | 31 |
| Vegetables | 1,075 | 1,128 | 1,179 |
| Fruit | 504 | 516 | 542 |
| Sugar cane | 1,106 | 1,291 | 1,366 |
| Tobacco (leaves) | 7 | 6 | 6 |
| Jute and jute-like fibres | 19 | 10 | 12† |

* Unofficial figure.   † FAO estimate(s).

### LIVESTOCK ('000 head, year ending September)

| | 1991 | 1992 | 1993 |
|---|---:|---:|---:|
| Cattle | 6,255 | 6,246 | 6,237 |
| Buffaloes | 3,044 | 3,058 | 3,073 |
| Pigs | 592 | 599 | 630 |
| Sheep | 906 | 912 | 911 |
| Goats | 5,367 | 5,406 | 5,452 |

Poultry (FAO estimates, million): 7 in 1991; 7 in 1992; 7 in 1993.

Source: FAO, *Production Yearbook*.

### LIVESTOCK PRODUCTS ('000 metric tons)

| | 1991 | 1992 | 1993 |
|---|---:|---:|---:|
| Beef and veal* | 4 | 4 | 4 |
| Buffalo meat | 95 | 96 | 97 |
| Mutton and lamb | 3 | 3 | 3 |
| Goat meat | 30 | 30 | 30 |
| Pig meat | 10 | 10 | 10 |
| Poultry meat | 9 | 9 | 9 |
| Cows' milk | 256 | 259 | 261 |
| Buffaloes' milk | 608 | 612 | 616 |
| Goats' milk* | 51 | 52 | 52 |
| Butter and ghee* | 16.1 | 16.4 | 17.1 |
| Poultry eggs | 18.8† | 18.8† | 19.1* |
| Wool: | | | |
| greasy | 0.8 | 0.6 | 0.6 |
| clean* | 0.4 | 0.3 | 0.3 |

* FAO estimate(s).   † Unofficial figure.

Source: FAO, *Production Yearbook*.

# Forestry

**ROUNDWOOD REMOVALS** ('000 cu m, excluding bark)

|  | 1990 | 1991 | 1992* |
|---|---|---|---|
| Industrial wood | 570 | 620 | 620 |
| Fuel wood | 18,052* | 18,513* | 18,971 |
| **Total** | 18,622 | 19,133 | 19,591 |

* FAO estimate(s).
Source: FAO, *Yearbook of Forest Products*.

**SAWNWOOD PRODUCTION** ('000 cu m, including railway sleepers)

|  | 1990 | 1991 | 1992* |
|---|---|---|---|
| Coniferous (softwood) | 20 | 20 | 20 |
| Broadleaved (hardwood) | 550 | 600 | 600 |
| **Total** | 570 | 620 | 620 |

* FAO estimates.
Source: FAO, *Yearbook of Forest Products*.

# Fishing

('000 metric tons, live weight)

|  | 1990 | 1991 | 1992 |
|---|---|---|---|
| Total catch | 14.5 | 15.6 | 16.5 |

Source: FAO, *Yearbook of Fishery Statistics*.

# Industry

**SELECTED PRODUCTS** (metric tons, unless otherwise indicated)

|  | 1991 | 1992 | 1993 |
|---|---|---|---|
| Vegetable ghee | n.a. | 12,242 | 10,424 |
| Raw sugar | 41,399 | 55,365 | 48,621 |
| Beer and liquor (hectolitres) | 13,300 | 15,300 | 17,080 |
| Cigarettes (million) | 8,780 | 7,000 | 7,700 |
| Jute goods | 20,064 | 17,639 | 17,172 |
| Cotton textiles (million sq metres) | 6.4 | 7.2 | 7.1 |
| Synthetic textiles (million sq metres) | 21.3 | 11.4 | 12.2 |
| Cement | 184,000 | 237,327 | 273,532 |
| Steel rods | 56,704 | 59,661 | 60,683 |
| Tea | 1,930 | 1,476 | 1,621 |
| Soap | 28,553 | 20,903 | 27,215 |

# Finance

**CURRENCY AND EXCHANGE RATES**

**Monetary Units**
100 paisa (pice) = 1 Nepalese rupee (NR).

**Sterling and Dollar Equivalents** (31 December 1994)
£1 sterling = NRs 78.04;
US $1 = NRs 49.88;
1,000 Nepalese rupees = £12.81 = $20.05.

**Average Exchange Rate** (rupees per US $)
1992  42.718
1993  48.607
1994  49.398

**BUDGET** (NRs million, year ending 15 July)*

| Revenue† | 1988/89 | 1989/90‡ | 1990/91‡ |
|---|---|---|---|
| Taxation | 6,301.1 | 7,235.6 | 8,130.0 |
| Taxes on income, profits and capital gains | 879.7 | 942.9 | 975.0 |
| Individual | 641.2 | 712.0 | 714.5 |
| Corporate | 220.0 | 218.0 | 224.5 |
| Taxes on property | 420.0 | 461.1 | 533.0 |
| Taxes on financial and capital transactions | 320.6 | 368.3 | 435.0 |
| Domestic taxes on goods and services | 2,710.8 | 3,118.9 | 3,598.5 |
| General sales, turnover or value-added taxes | 1,379.7 | 1,608.9 | 1,800.5 |
| Excises | 877.6 | 1,045.2 | 1,235.0 |
| Taxes on specific services | 215.3 | 249.6 | 315.0 |
| Taxes on the use of goods or on permission to use goods or to perform activities | 238.2 | 215.2 | 248.0 |
| Taxes on international trade and transactions | 2,289.9 | 2,707.0 | 3,017.0 |
| Import duties | 2,227.2 | 2,674.8 | 2,952.0 |
| Export duties | 62.7 | 32.2 | 65.0 |
| Other current revenue | 1,214.0 | 1,498.2 | 1,672.2 |
| Entrepreneurial and property income | 376.0 | 459.3 | 497.5 |
| Dividends and interest | 362.7 | 447.3 | 483.5 |
| Administrative fees and charges, non-industrial and incidental sales | 795.2 | 992.8 | 1,129.3 |
| Civil administration | 500.7 | 659.7 | 650.0 |
| Capital revenue | 25.3 | 33.6 | 45.0 |
| **Total** | 7,540.4 | 8,767.4 | 9,847.2 |

| Expenditure § | 1988/89 | 1989/90‡ | 1990/91‡ |
|---|---|---|---|
| General public services | 1,333.6 | 1,487.2 | 1,524.6 |
| Defence | 898.7 | 1,076.9 | 1,113.9 |
| Education | 1,741.7 | 1,950.1 | 2,078.7 |
| Health | 867.2 | 855.4 | 884.7 |
| Housing and community amenities | 877.5 | 1,488.5 | 1,283.6 |
| Economic affairs and services | 8,535.3 | 7,340.9 | 8,161.3 |
| Agriculture, forestry, fishing and hunting | 1,618.3 | 1,509.4 | 1,832.2 |
| Mining and mineral resources, manufacturing and construction | 570.0 | 796.5 | 844.9 |
| Transport and communications | 2,421.9 | 2,300.9 | 2,397.1 |
| Road transport | 1,482.4 | 1,210.8 | 1,621.8 |
| Communications | 448.8 | 226.3 | 143.2 |
| Other purposes | 3,150.4 | 3,611.7 | 3,942.2 |
| Interest payments | 1,186.6 | 1,517.2 | 1,581.4 |
| General transfers to panchayats | 488.6 | 477.4 | 375.7 |
| Contingency and miscellaneous | 1,475.2 | 1,617.1 | 1,985.1 |
| **Total** | 17,404.5 | 17,810.7 | 18,989.0 |
| Current | 5,075.7 | 5,914.2 | 6,662.2 |
| Capital | 12,328.8 | 11,896.5 | 12,326.8 |

* The data represent a consolidation of the regular and development budgets of the central Government.
† Excluding grants (all capital) received from abroad (NRs million): 1,680.6 in 1988/89; 1,828.6 in 1989/90; 2,509.4 in 1990/91.
‡ Figures are provisional or projected.
§ Excluding lending minus repayments (NRs million): −170.0 in 1988/89; −201.5 in 1989/90; −205.0 in 1990/91.

Source: IMF, *Government Finance Statistics Yearbook*.

**1991/92** (provisional, NRs million, year ending 15 July): Recurrent revenue 12,557.1, Foreign loans 8,317.1, Foreign grants 3,511.4; *Total revenue* 24,385.6; Regular expenditure 9,745.9, Development expenditure 16,895.0; *Total expenditure* 26,640.9.
**1992/93** (provisional, NRs million, year ending 15 July): Recurrent revenue 17,001, Foreign loans 10,353, Foreign grants 4,621; *Total revenue* 31,975; Regular expenditure 12,000, Development expenditure 21,595; *Total expenditure* 33,595.
**1993/94** (provisional, NRs million, year ending 15 July): Recurrent revenue 18,084, Foreign loans 11,281, Foreign grants 4,328; *Total revenue* 33,693; Regular expenditure 12,888, Development expenditure 22,626; *Total expenditure* 35,514.
**1994/95** (provisional, NRs million, year ending 15 July): Recurrent revenue 22,385, Foreign loans and grants 15,628; *Total revenue* 38,013; Regular expenditure 18,767, Development expenditure 21,147; *Total expenditure* 39,914.

# NEPAL

*Statistical Survey*

**OFFICIAL RESERVES** (US $ million at mid-December)

|  | 1992 | 1993 | 1994 |
|---|---|---|---|
| Gold* | 6.5 | 6.5 | 6.5 |
| IMF special drawing rights | 0.2 | — | 0.1 |
| Reserve position in IMF | 7.9 | 7.9 | 8.4 |
| Foreign exchange | 459.4 | 632.3 | 685.1 |
| **Total** | 474.0 | 646.7 | 700.1 |

* Valued at $42.22 per troy ounce.

Source: IMF, *International Financial Statistics*.

**MONEY SUPPLY** (NRs million at mid-December)*

|  | 1991 | 1992 | 1993 |
|---|---|---|---|
| Currency outside banks | 12,465 | 14,201 | 17,390 |
| Private sector deposits with monetary authorities | 864 | 897 | 1,307 |
| Demand deposits at commercial banks | 4,286 | 5,331 | 6,622 |
| **Total money** | 17,614 | 20,428 | 25,320 |

* Excluding Indian currency in circulation.

Source: IMF, *International Financial Statistics*.

**COST OF LIVING**
(National Consumer Price Index; base: 1980 = 100)

|  | 1985 | 1986 | 1987 |
|---|---|---|---|
| Food | 152.4 | 186.9 | 210.0 |
| Fuel and light | 195.8 | 207.7 | 214.2 |
| Clothing | 142.5 | 161.4 | 172.4 |
| Rent | 186.7 | 214.4 | 244.0 |
| **All items** (incl. others) | 155.0 | 184.5 | 204.3 |

**1988:** All items 222.7.
**1989:** Food 249.8; All items 241.8.
**1990:** Food 267.9; All items 264.4.
**1991:** Food 316.7; All items 305.5.
**1992:** Food 373.6; All items 357.9.

Source: ILO, *Year Book of Labour Statistics*.

**1993:** All items 384.7 (Source: UN, *Monthly Bulletin of Statistics*).

**NATIONAL ACCOUNTS**
(NRs million at current prices, year ending 15 July)
**Composition of the Gross National Product** (provisional)

|  | 1987/88 | 1988/89 | 1989/90 |
|---|---|---|---|
| **Gross domestic product (GDP) at factor cost** | 63,600 | 72,822 | 82,466 |
| Indirect taxes, *less* subsidies | 5,258 | 5,437 | 6,245 |
| **GDP in purchasers' values** | 68,858 | 78,259 | 88,711 |
| Factor income from abroad | 1,804 | 2,111 | 2,435 |
| *Less* Factor income paid abroad | 229 | 397 | 501 |
| **Gross national product (GNP)** | 70,433 | 79,973 | 90,645 |

Source: UN, *National Accounts Statistics*.

**Expenditure on the Gross Domestic Product**

|  | 1990/91 | 1991/92 | 1992/93 |
|---|---|---|---|
| Government final consumption expenditure | 11,085 | 11,908 | 14,900 |
| Private final consumption expenditure | 97,901 | 121,370 | 135,279 |
| Increase in stocks | 2,294 | 2,342 | 2,375 |
| Gross fixed capital formation | 22,780 | 29,277 | 33,928 |
| Statistical discrepancy | −4,373 | −4,554 | −5,367 |
| **Total domestic expenditure** | 129,687 | 160,343 | 181,115 |
| Exports of goods and services | 14,226 | 23,909 | 30,948 |
| *Less* Imports of goods and services | 27,785 | 39,321 | 47,429 |
| **GDP in purchasers' values** | 116,128 | 144,931 | 164,634 |
| **GDP at constant 1989/90 prices** | 106,124 | 111,030 | 114,303 |

Source: IMF, *International Financial Statistics*.

**Gross Domestic Product by Economic Activity**

|  | 1990/91 | 1991/92 | 1992/93* |
|---|---|---|---|
| Agriculture, hunting, forestry and fishing | 52,047 | 61,486 | 66,155 |
| Mining and quarrying | 131 | 162 | 178 |
| Manufacturing | 6,333 | 9,330 | 11,990 |
| Electricity, gas and water | 652 | 994 | 1,137 |
| Construction | 8,155 | 10,193 | 12,765 |
| Trade, restaurants and hotels | 5,901 | 7,536 | 7,164 |
| Transport, storage and communications | 5,894 | 7,652 | 8,916 |
| Finance, insurance, real estate and business services | 9,517 | 11,372 | 13,573 |
| Community, social and personal services | 8,314 | 9,196 | 10,115 |
| **GDP at factor cost** | 96,944 | 117,921 | 131,993 |
| Indirect taxes, *less* subsidies | 7,004 | 8,265 | 9,549 |
| **GDP in purchasers' values** | 103,948 | 126,186 | 141,542 |

* Estimates.

Source: IMF, *Nepal, Economic Review*.

**BALANCE OF PAYMENTS** (US $ million)

|  | 1991 | 1992 | 1993 |
|---|---|---|---|
| Merchandise exports f.o.b. | 274.5 | 376.3 | 397.0 |
| Merchandise imports f.o.b. | −756.9 | −752.1 | −858.6 |
| **Trade balance** | −482.4 | −375.8 | −461.6 |
| Exports of services | 239.8 | 273.8 | 333.2 |
| Imports of services | −183.9 | −225.0 | −251.8 |
| Other income received | 27.0 | 33.5 | 28.9 |
| Other income paid | −16.2 | −16.8 | −23.7 |
| Private unrequited transfers (net) | 53.7 | 45.7 | 74.3 |
| Official unrequited transfers (net) | 57.5 | 83.2 | 78.2 |
| **Current balance** | −304.4 | −181.3 | −222.5 |
| Capital (net) | 457.1 | 335.9 | 283.5 |
| Net errors and omissions | 10.7 | 0.8 | 4.6 |
| **Overall balance** | 163.4 | 155.4 | 65.6 |

Source: IMF, *International Financial Statistics*.

**FOREIGN AID RECEIVED** (NRs million, year ending 15 July)

|  | Grants 1989/90 | Grants 1990/91 | Grants 1991/92 | Loans 1989/90 | Loans 1990/91 | Loans 1991/92 | Total 1989/90 | Total 1990/91 | Total 1991/92 |
|---|---|---|---|---|---|---|---|---|---|
| Bilateral | 1,553.3 | 1,337.1 | 1,207.5 | 1,000.6 | 1,602.8 | 2,389.8 | 2,553.9 | 2,939.9 | 3,597.3 |
| Multilateral | 254.5 | 292.8 | 323.5 | 3,637.7 | 4,653.9 | 3,879.6 | 3,892.2 | 4,946.7 | 4,203.1 |
| **Total** | 1,807.8 | 1,629.9 | 1,531.0 | 4,638.3 | 6,256.7 | 6,269.4 | 6,446.1 | 7,886.6 | 7,800.4 |

Source: IMF, *Nepal, Economic Review*.

# NEPAL

## External Trade

**PRINCIPAL COMMODITIES** (NRs million, year ending 15 July)

| Imports c.i.f. | 1990/91 | 1991/92 | 1992/93* |
|---|---|---|---|
| Food and live animals | 1,821 | 3,670 | 3,559 |
| Beverages and tobacco | 257 | 152 | 276 |
| Crude materials (inedible) except fuels | 2,013 | 3,751 | 4,289 |
| Mineral fuels and lubricants | 2,278 | 3,673 | 4,135 |
| Animal and vegetable oils and fats | 742 | 814 | 882 |
| Chemicals and drugs | 3,051 | 4,437 | 4,979 |
| Basic manufactures | 5,951 | 8,751 | 10,147 |
| Machinery and transport equipment | 5,990 | 5,873 | 6,444 |
| Miscellaneous manufactured articles | 1,121 | 1,657 | 1,955 |
| Other commodities and transactions | 32 | 221 | 1,221 |
| **Total** | **23,256** | **32,998** | **37,888** |

| Exports f.o.b. | 1990/91 | 1991/92 | 1992/93* |
|---|---|---|---|
| Food and live animals | 986 | 2,096 | 2,343 |
| Beverages and tobacco | 12 | 4 | 7 |
| Crude materials (inedible) except fuels | 312 | 478 | 431 |
| Animal and vegetable oils and fats | 202 | 120 | 157 |
| Chemicals and drugs | 18 | 31 | 31 |
| Basic manufactures | 4,312 | 7,628 | 10,116 |
| Machinery and transport equipment | — | — | 3 |
| Miscellaneous manufactured articles | 1,546 | 3,582 | 3,959 |
| Other commodities and transactions | 15 | 19 | 676 |
| **Total** | **7,403** | **13,959** | **17,722** |

* Estimates.

Source: IMF, *Nepal, Economic Review*.

**PRINCIPAL TRADING PARTNERS** (NRs million, year ending 15 July)

| Imports | 1988/89 | 1989/90 | 1990/91 |
|---|---|---|---|
| Bangladesh | n.a. | 415.4 | n.a. |
| China, People's Republic | 439.1 | 891.6 | 1,102.4 |
| France | 286.1 | 595.9 | 725.6 |
| Germany, Federal Republic | 900.3 | 516.2 | 495.7 |
| Hong Kong | n.a. | 343.4 | n.a. |
| India | 4,238.7 | 4,674.5 | 7,772.4* |
| Japan | 1,740.3 | 1,628.8 | 3,128.5 |
| Korea, Republic | 606.5 | 787.4 | 518.1 |
| Kuwait | 557.6 | n.a. | n.a. |
| New Zealand | 341.3 | 830.4 | 1,215.3 |
| Poland | n.a. | n.a. | 363.8 |
| Singapore | 1,470.5 | 2,944.2 | 3,377.1 |
| Taiwan | n.a. | n.a. | 389.3 |
| United Kingdom | 365.2 | n.a. | n.a. |

| Exports | 1988/89 | 1989/90 | 1990/91 |
|---|---|---|---|
| Bangladesh | n.a. | 71.3 | n.a. |
| Belgium | 93.6 | 152.9 | 174.5 |
| Czechoslovakia | 26.9 | n.a. | n.a. |
| France | n.a. | n.a. | 59.1 |
| Germany, Federal Republic | 871.7 | 1,368.0 | 2,728.8 |
| India | 1,034.9 | 602.5 | 1,701.2* |
| Iraq | 49.2 | 122.4 | n.a. |
| Italy | 69.0 | 108.7 | 146.2 |
| Netherlands | 29.9 | n.a. | 75.4 |
| Sri Lanka | n.a. | n.a. | 101.4 |
| Switzerland | 315.2 | 422.5 | 497.1 |
| USSR | n.a. | 88.6 | n.a. |
| United Kingdom | 240.2 | 254.2 | 169.0 |
| USA | 1,171.7 | 1,442.2 | 1,400.5 |

* Provisional figure.

Source: Nepal Rastra Bank, Trade Promotion Centre.

## Transport

**ROAD TRAFFIC** (vehicles in use at 31 December)

| | 1976 | 1977 | 1978 |
|---|---|---|---|
| Private cars | 11,526 | 12,679 | 14,201 |
| Buses and coaches | 1,484 | 1,662 | 2,001 |
| Goods vehicles | 5,848 | 6,608 | 7,987 |
| Motorcycles and scooters | 6,485 | 7,523 | 9,521 |

Source: International Road Federation, *World Road Statistics*.

**CIVIL AVIATION**
**Royal Nepal Airlines Corporation** (year ending 15 July)

| | 1989/90 | 1990/91 | 1991/92 |
|---|---|---|---|
| Passengers | 607,640 | 633,925 | 654,076 |
| Freight (metric tons)* | 7,156 | 4,855 | 4,900 |

* Including excess baggage and mail.

Source: Royal Nepal Airlines Corporation.

## Tourism

| | 1990 | 1991 | 1992 |
|---|---|---|---|
| Tourist arrivals | 254,885 | 292,995 | 334,353 |
| Tourist receipts (US $ million) | 63.7 | 58.6 | 61.1 |
| Number of hotel beds* | 10,244 | 11,384 | 11,772 |

* Recognized by Department of Tourism.

Source: Department of Tourism.

**1993:** Tourist arrivals 280,000.

**Hotel beds:** 12,547 in 1993; 13,322 in 1994.

## Communications Media

| | 1990 | 1991 | 1992 |
|---|---|---|---|
| Radio receivers ('000 in use) | 650 | 670 | 690 |
| Television receivers ('000 in use) | 35 | 40 | 45 |
| Daily newspapers | 28 | n.a. | 25 |
| Average circulation ('000 copies) | 150* | n.a. | 140* |

* Estimate.

Source: UNESCO, *Statistical Yearbook*.

**Telephones** ('000 main lines in use): 45 in 1989; 57 in 1990; 65 in 1991 (Source: UN, *Statistical Yearbook*).

## Education

(1992)

| | Institutions | Teachers | Students |
|---|---|---|---|
| Primary | 19,498 | 77,948 | 3,034,710 |
| Secondary | 5,917* | 25,357 | 855,137 |
| University | 3 | 4,925 | 110,239 |

* 1990 figure.

Pre-primary (1984): 176 schools, 733 teachers, 16,864 students.

Source: UNESCO, *Statistical Yearbook*.

# Directory

## The Constitution

Following the political unrest in early 1990 and the consequent dissolution of the Panchayat system in April–May 1990, political parties were legalized. At the end of May the King formed a nine-member Constitutional Recommendation Commission, which presented the draft of a new constitution at the end of August. The new Constitution, limiting the King's powers and guaranteeing fundamental rights, was promulgated by the King on 9 November.

The main provisions of the Constitution are summarized below:

The preamble to the Constitution envisages the guarantee of the fundamental rights of every citizen and the protection of his liberty, the consolidation of parliamentary government, the constitutional monarchy and the multi-party system, and the provision of an independent judicial system. Sovereignty resides in the Nepalese people. The Constitution is the fundamental law of the land.

Nepal is a multi-ethnic, multi-lingual, democratic, independent, indivisible, sovereign, Hindu and constitutional monarchical kingdom. Nepali is recognized as the national and official language.

### FUNDAMENTAL RIGHTS

Part Three of the Constitution provides for the fundamental rights of the citizen: all citizens are equal before the law; no discrimination is to be practised on the basis of religion, race, sex, caste, tribe or ideology; no person can be deprived of his liberty except in accordance with the law; capital punishment remains abolished; freedom of expression, freedom to assemble peaceably and without arms, freedom to form trade unions and associations, and freedom of movement are also guaranteed. Similarly, pre-censorship of publications is prohibited and, thus, the right to press and publications is ensured. In the sphere of criminal justice, the following rights are specified in the Constitution: no person is to be punished unless made punishable by law; no person may be tried more than once for the same offence; no one is compelled to testify against himself; no one is to be given punishment greater than that which the law at the time of the offence has prescribed; cruelty to detainees is prohibited; no person is to be detained without having first been informed about the grounds for such an action; and the detainee must appear before the judicial authorities within 24 hours of his arrest. In addition, provision has also been made to compensate any person who is wrongfully detained. A person's right to property is ensured, and the right to protect and promote one's own language, script and culture, as well as the right to education up to primary level in the child's mother tongue, have been safeguarded. Similarly, the right to practise religion and to manage and protect religious places and trusts has been granted to the country's various religious groups. The right to secrecy and inviolability of the person, residence, property, documents, letters and other information is also guaranteed.

### GOVERNMENT AND LEGISLATURE

His Majesty the King is the symbol of Nepalese nationality and of the unity of the people of Nepal. The expenditures and the privileges relating to His Majesty and the royal family are determined by law. His Majesty's income and property are exempt from tax.

The executive powers of the country are vested in His Majesty and the Council of Ministers. The direction, supervision and conduct of the general administration of the Kingdom of Nepal are the responsibility of the Council of Ministers. All official duties undertaken by His Majesty, except those which are within his exclusive domain or which are performed on the recommendation of some other institutions or officials, are discharged only on the advice of, and with the consent of, the Council of Ministers. His Majesty appoints the leader of the party that commands a majority in the House of Representatives as Prime Minister, while other Ministers are appointed, from among the members of Parliament, on the recommendation of the Prime Minister. The Council of Ministers is answerable to the House of Representatives. In the event that no single party holds an outright majority in the House, the member who commands a working majority on the basis of the support of two or more parties shall be asked to form the Government. Should this also not be the case, His Majesty may ask a member of the party with the largest number of deputies to form the Government. In the event of these exceptional circumstances, the leader forming the Government must obtain a vote of confidence in the House within 30 days. If such confidence is lacking, His Majesty is to dissolve the House and to order a fresh election to be held within six months. The Parliament is bicameral, comprising the House of Representatives and the National Council. His Majesty, the House of Representatives and the National Council together form the Parliament of the country. The House of Representatives has 205 members, and all persons who have attained the age of 18 years are eligible to vote for candidates, on the basis of adult franchise. The National Council has 60 members, consisting of 10 nominees of His Majesty, 35 members, including three female members, elected by the House of Representatives, and 15 members elected by the electoral college, which includes the heads of the local committees of various development regions. The tenure of office of the members of the House of Representatives is five years, and that of the members of the National Council six years.

### THE JUDICIARY

The judicial system has three tiers: the Supreme Court, the Appellate Courts and the District Courts. The Supreme Court is the principal Court and is also a Court of Record. The Supreme Court consists of a Chief Justice and 14 other Judges. The appointment of the Chief Justice is made on the recommendation of the Constitutional Council, while other Judges of the Supreme Court, the Appellate Courts and the District Courts are nominated on the recommendation of the Judicial Council. All Judges are appointed by His Majesty on such recommendations.

### OTHER INSTITUTIONS

The Constitution also makes provisions for the establishment of a Council of State (Raj Parishad) and its standing committee, a Public Service Commission, Auditor General, Election Commission, Attorney-General, Abuse of Authority Investigation Commission, etc.

### POLITICAL PARTIES

Political parties are required to register with the Election Commission, and, to be officially recognized, at least 5% of the candidates presented by a party must be female and the party should obtain at least 3% of the total votes cast at the election to the House of Representatives. It has been specifically provided that no law that bans, or imposes restrictions on, political parties may be enacted.

### EMERGENCY PROVISIONS

If and when there is a grave emergency in the country, caused by threat to the sovereignty, indivisibility or security of the country (owing to war, foreign aggression, armed revolt or extreme economic depression), His Majesty may declare a state of emergency in the country. Such a declaration must obtain the approval of the House of Representatives within three months. During the period of emergency, fundamental rights, with the exception of the right of recourse to *habeas corpus*, may be suspended.

### AMENDMENTS

The Constitution may be amended by a two-thirds majority in each House of Parliament. No changes, however, would be allowed to alter the spirit of the preamble.

### DEFENCE

His Majesty is the Supreme Commander-in-Chief of the Royal Nepal Army. The Royal Nepal Army is administered and deployed by His Majesty on the recommendation of the National Defence Council. The Commander-in-Chief is appointed on the recommendation of the Prime Minister. The National Defence Council consists of the Prime Minister, as Chairman, the Defence Minister and the Commander-in-Chief.

Official matters that involve, *inter alia*, the subjects of defence and strategic alliance, the boundaries of the Kingdom of Nepal, agreements on peace and friendship, and treaties concerning the utilization and distribution of natural resources, have to be approved by a two-thirds majority of the members of both Houses in a joint session of Parliament.

## The Government

### HEAD OF STATE

HM King BIRENDRA BIR BIKRAM SHAH DEV (succeeded to the throne 31 January 1972; crowned 24 February 1975).

## INTERIM COUNCIL OF MINISTERS
(June 1995)

**Prime Minister and Minister of Royal Palace Affairs:** MAN MOHAN ADHIKARI.
**Deputy Prime Minister and Minister of Defence and of Foreign Affairs:** MADHAV KUMAR NEPAL.
**Minister of Finance:** BHARAT MOHAN ADHIKARI.
**Minister of Home Affairs:** KHADGA PRASAD OLI.
**Minister of Local Development and Supplies:** CHANDRA PRAKASH MAINALI.
**Minister of Agriculture, Land Reform and Management:** RADHA KRISHNA MAINALI.
**Minister of Education, Culture and Social Welfare:** MODNATH PRASHRIT.
**Minister of Communications:** PRADIP NEPAL.
**Minister of Labour and Health:** PADMA RATNA TULADHAR.
**Minister of State for Works and Transport:** ASHOK KUMAR RAI.
**Minister of State for Forests and the Environment:** SALIM MIYA ANSARI.
**Minister of State for Housing and Physical Planning:** PREM SINGH DHAMI.
**Minister of State for Law, Justice, Parliamentary Affairs and General Administration:** SUBASH CHANDRA NEMBANG.
**Minister of State for Commerce, Tourism and Civil Aviation:** BHIM BAHADUR RAWAL.
**Minister of State for Industry and Water Resources:** HARI PRASAD PANDEY.

## MINISTRIES

All Ministries are in Kathmandu.
**Office of the Prime Minister:** Central Secretariat, Singha Durbar, Kathmandu; tel. 228555; fax 228286.
**Ministry of Communications:** Singha Durbar, Kathmandu.
**Ministry of Education, Culture and Social Welfare:** Keshar Mahal, Kanti Path, Kathmandu; tel. 411599; fax 412460.
**Ministry of Finance:** Bagdurbar, Kathmandu; tel. 215099; telex 2249.
**Ministry of Foreign Affairs:** Shital Niwas, Maharajganj, Kathmandu; tel. 416011; telex 2224; fax 416016.
**Ministry of Water Resources:** Kathmandu; telex 2312.
**Ministry of Works and Transport:** Babar Mahal, Kathmandu; tel. 226537.

# Legislature*

### NATIONAL COUNCIL

The National Council (Rashtriya Sabha) has 60 members, consisting of 10 nominees of the King, 35 members (including three women) elected by the House of Representatives, and 15 members elected by the electoral college, which includes the heads of the local committees of various development regions. The tenure of office of the members of the National Council is six years.
**Chairman:** BENI BAHADUR KARKI.

### HOUSE OF REPRESENTATIVES

The 205-member House of Representatives (Pratinidhi Sabha) is elected, on the basis of adult franchise, for five years.
**Speaker:** RAM CHANDRA PAUDYEL.

**General Election, 15 November 1994**

| Party | Seats |
|---|---|
| Communist Party of Nepal (Unified Marxist-Leninist—UML) | 88 |
| Nepali Congress Party (NCP) | 83 |
| National Democratic Party (NDP) | 20 |
| Nepal Workers' and Peasants' Party | 4 |
| Nepali Sadbhavana Party | 3 |
| Independents | 7 |
| **Total** | **205** |

* Following the dissolution of the legislature on 13 June 1995, it was announced that a fresh general election was to be held on 23 November.

# Political Organizations

After the political upheaval in early 1990, the establishment and operation of political parties, which had been prohibited under the Panchayat system, were legalized. According to the 1990 Constitution, political parties are required to register with the Election Commission, and, in order to be officially recognized, 5% of the candidates presented by a party must be female and the party should obtain at least 3% of the total votes cast in the election to the House of Representatives. The Constitution also specifies that no law may be adopted that bans, or imposes restrictions on, political parties.

**Communist Party of Nepal (Unified Marxist-Leninist—UML):** Bag Bazar, POB 5471, Kathmandu; tel. 223639; fax 221411; f. 1991, when two major factions of the Communist Party of Nepal (CPN; f. 1949; banned 1960; legalized 1990)—the Marxist and Marxist-Leninist factions—merged; Chair. MAN MOHAN ADHIKARI; Gen. Sec. MADHAV KUMAR NEPAL.

**Communist Party of Nepal (Unity Centre):** Kathmandu; f. 1990; members include the Maoist United People's Front (UPF); Chair. TULSI LAL AMATYA.

**National Democratic Party (NDP)** (Rashtriya Prajatantra Party): Kathmandu; f. 1992 following merger of National Democratic Party (Chand) and National Democratic Party (Thapa); centre-right; Leader LOKENDRA BAHADUR CHAND; Pres. SURYA BAHADUR THAPA.

**National People's Council** (Rashtriya Janata Parishad): Kathmandu; f. 1992; royalist; aims to defend democracy, nationalism and sovereignty; Pres. MAITRIKA PRASAD KOIRALA; Vice-Pres. KIRTI NIDHI BISTA.

**National People's Liberation Forum:** Kathmandu; left-wing; rejects 1990 Constitution as reactionary; Chair. M. S. THAPA.

**Nepal Praja Parishad:** Battisputali, Kathmandu; tel. 471616; f. 1936; banned 1961; legalized 1990; Pres. RAM HARI SHARMA.

**Nepal Workers' and Peasants' Party:** Kathmandu; communist; Chair. NARAYAN MAN BIJUKCHE.

**Nepali Congress Party (NCP):** Kathmandu; tel. 227748; fax 227747; f. 1947; banned 1960; legalized 1990; Pres. KRISHNA PRASAD BHATTARAI; Supreme Leader GANESH MAN SINGH; Gen. Sec. MAHENDRA NARAYAN NIDHI; 50,000 active members, 500,000 ordinary members.

**Nepali Janata Dal:** Kathmandu; f. 1990; advocates the consolidation of the multi-party democratic system and supports the campaign against corruption; Leader HARI PRASAD POKHAREL.

**Nepali National Congress:** Kathmandu; Pres. DILLI RAMAN REGMI.

**Nepali Sadbhavana Party:** f. 1990; promotes the rights of the Madhesiya community, who are of Indian origin and reside in the Terai; demands that the Government recognize Hindi as an official language, that constituencies in the Terai be allocated on the basis of population, and that the Government grant citizenship to those who settled in Nepal before April 1990; Pres. GAJENDRA NARAYAN SINGH; Gen. Sec. HRIDAYESH TRIPATHI.

**United Left Front (ULF):** Kathmandu; f. 1990 by six factions of the CPN and a labour group, which then, in alliance with the NCP, initiated a campaign known as the Movement for the Restoration of Democracy; four of the seven constituents of the ULF left the front in Dec. 1990; Leader SAHANA PRADHAN.

Anti-Government terrorist campaigns were launched within Nepal in 1985 by two insurgent groups, the Samyukta Mukti Bahini (United Liberation Torch-bearers) and the Janawadi Morcha (Democratic Front; Pres. RAM RAJA PRASAD SINGH), both of which have been banned.

# Diplomatic Representation

### EMBASSIES IN NEPAL

**Australia:** Bansbari, Kathmandu; tel. 411578; telex 2395; fax 417533; Ambassador: LES DOUGLAS.

**Bangladesh:** Naxal, Bhagawati Bahal, POB 789, Kathmandu; tel. 414943; telex 2420; fax 414265; Ambassador: SYED MUHAMMAD HUSSAIN.

**China, People's Republic:** Baluwatar, Kathmandu; tel. 211289; Ambassador: SHAO JIONGCHU.

**Denmark:** Baluwatar, Lalita Niwas Rd, POB 6332, Kathmandu; tel. 413010; telex 2771; fax 411409; Chargé d'affaires a.i.: K. V. JOHANSEN.

**Egypt:** Pulchowk, Patan, POB 792, Kathmandu; tel. 524844; telex 2225; fax 522975; Ambassador: ABD EL-HAMID MOHAMED TABAK.

**France:** Lazimpat, POB 452, Kathmandu; tel. 412332; telex 2209; fax 419968; Ambassador: DANIEL DUPONT.

**Germany:** Gyaneshwar, POB 226, Kathmandu; tel. 416832; telex 2213; fax 416899; Ambassador: Dr KARL-HEINZ SCHOLTYSSEK.

**India:** Lainchaur, Kathmandu; tel. 211300; telex 2449; Ambassador: K. V. RAJAN.

# NEPAL

**Israel:** Lazimpat, POB 371, Kathmandu; tel. 411811; fax 413920; Ambassador: Esther Efrat-Smilg.
**Italy:** Baluwatar, POB 1097, Kathmandu; tel. 412743; telex 2311; fax 413879; Ambassador: Sergio Grimaldi.
**Japan:** Panipokhari, POB 264, Kathmandu; tel. 414083; telex 2208; fax 419238; Ambassador: Arichi Kazuaki.
**Korea, Democratic People's Republic:** Lalitpur, Kathmandu; tel. 521084; telex 2330; Ambassador: Rim Hoe Song.
**Korea, Republic:** Himshah, Red Cross Marg, Tahachal, Kathmandu; tel. 270172; telex 2222; Ambassador: Lee Joung-Binn.
**Myanmar:** Chakupat, Patan Gate, Lalipur, Kathmandu; tel. 521788; telex 2396; fax 523402; Ambassador: U Khin Maung Ohn.
**Pakistan:** Panipokhari, POB 202, Kathmandu; tel. 410565; Ambassador: Muhammad Nasser Mian.
**Russia:** Baluwatar, Kathmandu; tel. 211255; Ambassador: (vacant).
**Thailand:** Jyoti Kendra, Thapathali, Kathmandu; tel. 213910; telex 2373; Ambassador: Sirajaya Buddhi-Baedya.
**United Kingdom:** Lainchaur, POB 106, Kathmandu; tel. 410583; telex 2343; fax 411789; Ambassador: Timothy J. B. George.
**USA:** Panipokhari, Kathmandu; tel. 411179; telex 2381; fax 419963; Ambassador: Sandy Vogelgesang.

## Judicial System

According to the Constitution promulgated in November 1990, the judicial system is composed of three tiers: the Supreme Court (which is also a Court of Record), the Appellate Courts and the District Courts. The Supreme Court consists of a Chief Justice and 14 other judges. The Chief Justice is appointed by the King on the recommendation of the Constitutional Council, while all other judges are appointed on the recommendation of the Judicial Council.

**Chief Justice:** Biswonath Upadhaya.
**Attorney-General:** Moti Kazi Sthapit.

## Religion

At the 1981 census, 89.5% of the population professed Hinduism (the religion of the Royal Family), while 5.3% were Buddhists and 2.7% Muslims. In 1990 there were an estimated 50,000 Christians in Nepal.

Under the Constitution promulgated in November 1990, the right to practise religion and to manage and protect religious places and trusts was granted to Nepal's various religious groups.

### BUDDHISM

**All Nepal Bhikkhu Council:** Anandakuti Vihar, Swayambhu, POB 3007, Kathmandu; tel. 271420; fax 227058.
**Nepal Buddhist Association:** Kathmandu; tel. 5214420; Sec. Rev. Bhikkhu Amritananda, Ananda Kuti, Kathmandu.

### CHRISTIANITY
#### The Roman Catholic Church

The Church is represented in Nepal by a single mission. At 31 December 1993 there were an estimated 4,443 adherents in the country.

**Catholic Mission:** c/o St Francis Xavier's School, Jawlakhel, POB 50, Kathmandu; tel. 521710; fax 525620; f. 1983; Ecclesiastical Superior Fr Anthony Francis Sharma.

## The Press

Under provisions incorporated in the 1990 Constitution, press freedom is ensured in Nepal.

### PRINCIPAL DAILIES

**The Commoner:** Naradevi, POB 203, Kathmandu; tel. 228236; f. 1956; English; Publr and Chief Editor Gopal Dass Shrestha; circ. 7,000.
**Daily News:** 7/358 Kohity Bahal, POB 171, Kathmandu; tel. 223131; telex 2634; fax 225544; f. 1983; Nepali; Chief Editor Manju Ratna Sakya; Publr Subha Luxmi Sakya; circ. 13,500.
**Dainik Nirnaya:** Bhairawa; tel. 20117; Nepali; Editor P. K. Bhattachan.
**Gorkhapatra:** Dharma Path, POB 23, Kathmandu; tel. 221478; fax 222921; f. 1901; Nepali; Editor-in-Chief Krishna Bhakta Shrestha; circ. 75,000.
**Janadoot:** Ga-2, 549, Kamal Pokhari (In front of the Police Station), Kathmandu; tel. 412501; Nepali; Editor Govinda Biyogi; circ. 6,500.
**The Motherland:** POB 1184, Kathmandu; English; Editor Manindra Raj Shrestha; circ. 5,000.
**Nepal Times:** Maruhiti; f. 1955; Nepali; Publr and Editor Chandra Lal Jha; circ. 3,000.
**Nepali Hindi Daily:** Maitidevi, POB 49, Kathmandu; tel. 411374; fax 414324; f. 1958; evening; Hindi; Chief Editor Uma Kant Das; Dep. Editor V. K. Das; circ. 43,000.
**Rising Nepal:** Dharma Path, Kathmandu; tel. 222252; telex 2294; f. 1965; English; Editor-in-Chief Shyam Bahadur; circ. 20,000.
**Samaj:** National Printing Press, Dilli Bazar, Kathmandu; f. 1954; Nepali; Editor Mani Raj Upadhyaya; circ. 5,000.
**Samaya:** Kamal Press, Ramshah Path, Kathmandu; Nepali; Editor Manik Lal Shrestha; circ. 18,000.

### SELECTED PERIODICALS

**Agricultural Credit:** Agricultural Credit Training Institute, Agricultural Development Bank, Ramshah Path, Panchayat Plaza, Kathmandu; tel. 216075; telex 2267; quarterly; publ. by the Agricultural Development Bank; Chair. Pravu Prasad Parajuli; Editor Prem Nath Ojha.
**Arpan:** Kohity Bahal, POB 285, Kathmandu; tel. 220531; telex 2634; fax 225544; f. 1964; weekly; Nepali; Publr and Chief Editor Manju Ratna Sakya; Editor Mewa Kazi Kansakar; circ. 16,000.
**Commerce:** 7/358 Kohity Bahal, POB 171, Kathmandu; tel. 216636; telex 2634; fax 225544; f. 1971; monthly; English; Publr and Chief Editor Manju Ratna Sakya; Editor Subha Luxmi Sakya; circ. 10,000.
**Current:** Kamalpokhari, POB 191, Kathmandu; tel. 413554; f. 1982; weekly; Nepali; Publr and Editor Devendra Gautam; Foreign Editor Upendra Gautam; circ. 7,000.
**Deshanter:** Kathmandu; weekly; Editor Shiva Adhikari.
**Foreign Affairs Journal:** 5/287 Lagon, Kathmandu; f. 1976; 3 a year; articles on Nepalese foreign relations and diary of main news events; Publr and Editor Bhola Bikrum Rana; circ. 5,000.
**Himal:** POB 42, Lalitpur; tel. 523845; fax 521013; f. 1988; bimonthly; development and environment issues throughout the Himalaya; Editor Kanak Mani Dixit.
**Independent:** Ramkuti-4, Kamaladi, POB 3543, Kathmandu; tel. 223836; fax 226293; f. 1990; weekly; English; Editor Ram Pradhan.
**Janmabhumi:** Janmabhumi Press, Tahachal, Kathmandu; weekly; Nepali; Publr and Editor Ganesh Ballav Pradhan.
**Madhuparka:** Dharma Path, POB 23, Kathmandu; tel. 222278; telex 2294; f. 1986; monthly; Nepali; literary; Editor-in-Chief Krishna Bhakta Shrestha; circ. 20,000.
**Matribhoomi** (Nepali Weekly): GA 2-549, Kamal Pokhai (in front of the Police Station), Kathmandu; tel. 412501; weekly; Nepali; Editor Govinda Biyogi.
**Nepal Chronicle:** Maruhiti; weekly; English; Publr and Editor Chandra Lal Jha.
**Nepal Trade Bulletin:** Trade Promotion Centre, Kopundol, Lalitpur, POB 825, Kathmandu; tel. 524771; telex 2302; fax 521637; 3 a year; English; Editors Bijaya Vaidya, Sushila Shakya.
**Spotlight:** POB 7256, Kathmandu; tel. 410772; f. 1991; weekly; English; Editor Madhav Kumar Rimal.
**Vashudha:** Makhan, Kathmandu; monthly; English; social, political and economic affairs; Publr and Editor T. L. Shrestha.
**Yugantar:** Kathmandu; weekly.

### NEWS AGENCIES

**Nepal Sangbad Samiti Co Pvt Ltd:** Kathmandu; f. 1992.
**Rastriya Samachar Samiti (RSS):** Prithivi Path, POB 220, Kathmandu; tel. 227912; telex 2234; fax 227698; f. 1962; state-operated; Gen. Man. Mukunda Parajuli.

#### Foreign Bureaux

**Agence France-Presse (AFP):** Bhote Bahal South, Hansa Marg, POB 402, Kathmandu; tel. 221541; telex 2226; fax 222998; Correspondent Kedar Man Singh.
**Associated Press (AP)** (USA): Thapathli Panchayan, POB 513, Kathmandu; tel. 212767; telex 2252; Correspondent Binaya Guracharya.
**Deutsche Presse-Agentur (dpa)** (Germany): KH 1-27 Tebahal Tole, POB 680, Kathmandu 44601; tel. 224557; telex 2240; Correspondent K. C. Shyam Bahadur.

NEPAL
Directory

**Inter Press Service (IPS)** (Italy): c/o Nepal Press Institute, POB 4128, Kathmandu; tel. and fax 228943; Correspondent Dhruba Adhikary.

**Kyodo News Service** (Japan): GA 2-502, Battisputali, POB 3772, Kathmandu; tel. 470106; telex 2646; Correspondent Madhav Acharya.

**Reuters** (UK): Dilli Bazar, POB 224, Kathmandu; tel. 412436; telex 2284.

**United Press International (UPI)** (USA): POB 802, Kathmandu; tel. 215684; telex 2424; Correspondent Bhola Bikram Rana.

### PRESS ASSOCIATIONS

**Nepal Journalists Association (NJA):** Maitighar, POB 285, Kathmandu; tel. 225226; telex 2634; fax 225544; 3,430 mems; Pres. Manju Ratna Sakya; Gen. Sec. Madan Sharma.

**Press Council:** RSS Bldg, Prithvi Path, POB 3077, Kathmandu; tel. 215521; fax 227698; f. 1969; Pres. Justice B. P. Singh; Sec. S. R. Sharma.

## Publishers

**Educational Enterprise:** Mahankalsthan, Kathmandu; tel. 223749; educational and technical.

**International Standards Books and Periodicals (Pvt) Ltd:** POB 3000, Kathmandu 3-30; tel. 224005; telex 3000; fax 229071; f. 1991; Sr Man. Dir Suindra Lall Chhipa; Chief Exec. Man. Dir Ganesh Lall Singh Chhipa.

**Lakoul Press:** Palpa-Tansen, Kathmandu; educational and physical sciences.

**Mahabir Singh Chiniya Main:** Makhan Tola, Kathmandu.

**Ratna Pustak Bhandar:** Bhotahity Tole, POB 98, Kathmandu; tel. 223026; f. 1945; textbooks, general, non-fiction and fiction; Propr Ratna Prasad Shrestha.

**Royal Nepal Academy:** Kamaladi, Kathmandu; tel. 221241; f. 1957; languages, literature, social sciences, art and philosophy.

**Sajha Prakashan:** Pulchowk, Kathmandu; tel. 521023; f. 1964; educational, literary and general; Chair. Tej Bahadur Panta; Gen. Man. Dr Tulsi Prasad Bhattarai.

### Government Publishing House

**Department of Information:** Ministry of Communications, Singh Durbar, Kathmandu.

## Radio and Television

In March 1986 Nepal's first television station began broadcasting within the Kathmandu valley. In 1992, according to UNESCO, there were an estimated 690,000 radio receivers, and 45,000 television receivers in use. In that year radio broadcasts reached about 90% of Nepal's population. In October 1994 a television satellite transmission service, Space Time Network, was established in Kathmandu.

**Radio Nepal:** Radio Broadcasting Service, HM Government of Nepal, Singha Durbar, POB 634, Kathmandu; tel. 223910; telex 2590; fax 221952; f. 1951; broadcasts on short and medium wave in Nepali and English; short-wave station at Khumaltar and medium-wave stations at Bhaisepati, Pokhara, Surkhet, Dipayal, Bardibas and Dharan; Exec. Dir S. R. Sharma.

**Nepalese Television Corporation:** Singha Durbar, POB 3826, Kathmandu; tel. 228447; telex 2548; fax 228312; broadcasts 32 hours a week; Gen. Man. Tapa Nath Shukla; Dep. Gen. Man. (Technical) Ravindra S. Rana.

## Finance

(auth. = authorized; cap. = capital; p.u. = paid up; m. = million; dep. = deposits; res = reserves; brs = branches; amounts in Nepalese rupees)

### BANKING

#### Central Bank

**Nepal Rastra Bank:** Lalita Niwas, Baluwatar, Kathmandu; tel. 419084; telex 2207; fax 417553; f. 1956; bank of issue; cap. 10m., res 10,562.4m., dep. 6,611.7m. (Jan. 1994); Gov. and Chair. Harishankher Tripathi; 9 brs.

#### Commercial Banks

**Everest Bank Ltd:** Kathmandu; f. 1994.

**Himalayan Bank Ltd:** Tridevi Marg, Kathmandu; tel. 227019; telex 2789; fax 222800.

**Nepal Bank Ltd:** Dharma Path, Juddha Rd, POB 36, Kathmandu; tel. 221185; telex 2220; fax 222383; f. 1937; 51% state-owned; cap. 680.5m., res 217.0m., dep. 12,880.2m. (April 1992); Chair. Durga Prakash Pandey; Gen. Man. Bishwambhar Man Singh Pradhan; 226 brs and sub-brs.

**Rastriya Banijya Bank** (National Commercial Bank): Tangal Bhatbhateni Rd, Kathmandu; tel. 411164; telex 2247; f. 1966; 100% state-owned; cap. 20m., res 95.1m., dep. 6,426.2m. (July 1989); Chair. Damodar Prasad Gautam; Gen. Man. Prithivi Bahadur Pande; 193 brs, 4 regional offices.

#### Foreign Banks

The following foreign banks have opened branches in Nepal, in partnership with local business interests, as part of a gradual deregulation of Nepal's financial institutions and industry, in order to encourage foreign investment.

**Nepal Arab Bank Ltd (Nabil):** Jyoti Bhavan, Kanti Path, POB 3729, Kathmandu; tel. 227181; telex 2385; fax 226905; f. 1984; 50% owned by Emirates Bank International Ltd (Dubai, United Arab Emirates), 30% by the Nepalese public and 20% by Nepalese financial institutions; cap. 65m., res 126m., dep. 3,347m. (July 1993); Chair. B. R. S. Malla; Exec. Dir S. C. Kabadkar; 8 brs.

**Nepal Bangladesh Bank:** Kathmandu; f. 1994.

**Nepal Grindlays Bank Ltd:** Naya Baneshwar, POB 3990, Kathmandu; tel. 212683; telex 2531; fax 226762; f. 1986; 50% owned by ANZ Grindlays Bank PLC (United Kingdom), 35% by Nepal Bank Ltd and 15% by the Nepalese public; cap. 50.0m., res 138.8m., dep. 4,407.9m. (July 1993); Chair. Dr B. N. Chalise; Gen. Man. J. F. Murray; 7 brs.

**Nepal Indosuez Bank Ltd:** Durbar Marg, POB 3412, Kathmandu; tel. 228229; telex 2435; fax 226349; f. 1986; 50% owned by Banque Indosuez (France), 50% by Nepal Rastra Bank; cap. 60.0m., res 78.0m., dep. 1,442.8m. (July 1993); Chair. Dipendra Purush Dhakal; Man. André Monclar.

**Nepal SBI Bank Ltd:** 26 Durbar Marg, POB 6049, Kathmandu; tel: 225326; telex 2796; fax 221268; f. 1993; 50% owned by State Bank of India, 30% by Nepalese public, 15% by Employees' Provident Fund (Nepal) and 5% by Agricultural Development Bank (Nepal); Chair. Narayan Raj Tiwari; Man. Dir A. B. Chakravarty.

#### Development Finance Organizations

**Agricultural Development Bank:** Ramshah Path, Kathmandu; tel. 211744; telex 2267; fax 225329; f. 1968; 74% state-owned, 21% owned by the Nepal Rastra Bank, and 5% by co-operatives and private individuals; specialized agricultural credit institution providing credit for agricultural development to co-operatives, individuals and asscns; receives deposits from individuals, co-operatives and other asscns to generate savings in the agricultural sector; acts as Government's implementing agency for small farmers' group development project, assisted by the Asian Development Bank and financed by the UN Development Programme; operational networks include 14 zonal offices, 37 brs, 92 sub-brs, 52 depots and 160 small farmers' development projects, 3 Zonal Training Centres, 2 Appropriate Technology Units; total assets 2,171m., cap. p.u. 249m., dep. 199m. (July 1986); Chair. and Gen. Man. S. Krishna Upadhyaya.

**National Finance Co Ltd:** Basantapur, POB 6942, Kathmandu; tel. 215769; telex 2241; fax 222920; f. 1992; financial and merchant banking; auth. cap. 60m., res 1.2m., dep. 211m. (1995); Chair. H. B. Malla; Man. Dir B. L. Shrestha; 1 rep. office.

**Nepal Industrial Development Corporation (NIDC):** NIDC Bldg, Durbar Marga, POB 10, Kathmandu; tel. 228322; telex 2369; f. 1959; state-owned; holds investments of 110.9m. in 36 industrial enterprises; offers financial and technical assistance to private sector industries; in 1987/88 approved a total of 126.5m. in loans, working capital and share investment, and disbursed 150.3m.; cap. p.u. 218.4m. (July 1987); Gen. Man. Ajit Narayan Singh Thapa.

### STOCK EXCHANGE

**Nepal Stock Exchange Ltd:** Dillibazar, POB 1550, Kathmandu; tel. 415210; f. 1976, reorg. 1984; converted in June 1993 from Securities Exchange Centre to Nepal Stock Exchange; 66 listed cos; Gen. Man. Madan Raj Joshi; Chief Officer (Admin. and Market Operations) M. P. Sharma; Chief Officer (Information, Planning and Development) M. P. Dhungel.

### INSURANCE

**Rastriya Beema Sansthan** (National Insurance Corpn): RBS Bldg, Ramshah Path, POB 527, Kathmandu; telex 2219; fax 227110; f. 1967; Gen. Man. Indra Prasad Karmacharya.

## Trade and Industry

**National Planning Commission (NPC):** Singh Durbar, POB 1284, Kathmandu; tel. 226879; fax 226500; Chair. the Prime Minister;

Vice-Chair. Dr Ram Sharan Mahat; Member Sec. Dr Rabindra Kumar Shakya.

## CHAMBERS OF COMMERCE

**Federation of Nepalese Chambers of Commerce and Industry (FNCCI):** TNT Bldg, Teenkune, Koteswor, POB 269, Kathmandu; tel. 475032; telex 2786; fax 474051; f. 1965; comprises 62 District Chambers of Commerce and Industries, 36 Commodity Associations, 250 leading industrial and commercial undertakings in both the public and private sector, and three Bi-National Chambers; Pres. Binod K. Chaudhary; Sec.-Gen. Badri Prasad Ojha.

**Nepal Chamber of Commerce:** Chamber Bhavan, Kanti Path, POB 198, Kathmandu; tel. 222890; telex 2349; fax 229998; f. 1952; non-profit organization promoting industrial and commercial development; 1,500 regd mems and 4,500 enrolled mems; Pres. I. L. Shrestha; Sec.-Gen. R. K. Shrestha.

## DEVELOPMENT ORGANIZATIONS

**Agriculture Inputs Corporation:** Teku, Kuleswor, POB 195, Kathmandu; f. 1972; govt-owned; sole supplier of inputs for agricultural development (procuring and distribution of chemical fertilizers, improved seeds, agricultural tools and plant protection material) at national level; operates seeds multiplication programme (paddy, wheat, maize and vegetable); seed processing plants at Hetauda, Itahari, Janakpur, Nepalgunj and Sidharthanagar; Chair. Prithu Narshing Rana; Gen. Man. Narayan Bahadur Shrestha; Planning Chief Amrit Man Tamrakar.

**National Trading Ltd:** Teku, POB 128, Kathmandu; tel. 227924; telex 2211; fax 225151; f. 1962; govt-owned; imports and distributes construction materials and raw materials for industry; also machinery, vehicles and consumer goods; operates bonded warehouse, duty-free shop and related activities; brs in all major towns; Chair. Shambhu Sharan Prasad; Gen. Man. Pramod Kumar Upadhyaya.

**Nepal Foreign Trade Association:** Kathmandu; Pres. Gajananda Agrawal.

**Nepal Resettlement Co:** Kathmandu; f. 1963; govt-owned; engaged in resettling people from the densely-populated hill country to the western Terai plain.

**Salt Trading Corporation Ltd:** Kalimati, POB 483, Kathmandu; tel. 271208; telex 2241; fax 271704; f. 1963 as a joint venture of the public and private sectors (30% and 70% respectively) to manage the import and distribution of salt; also deals in sugar, edible oils, cereals, pulses and spices; deals in the export of tyres, inner tubes and spinning yarn; Chair. A. M. Sherchan; Chief Exec. H. B. Malla.

**Trade Promotion Centre (TPC):** Kopundol, Lalitpur, POB 825, Kathmandu; tel. 524771; telex 2302; fax 521637; f. 1971 to encourage exports; govt-owned; Gen. Man. Hari Prasad Sharma (acting).

## TRADE ASSOCIATIONS

**Nepal Carpet Industries Association:** Kathmandu; Pres. Kamal Singh Karki.

**Readymade Garment Association of Nepal:** Kopundol, Lalitpur, Kathmandu; tel. 523372; telex 2478; Pres. Kedar Amatya.

## TRADE UNIONS

Trade unions were banned in Nepal in 1961, but were legalized again in early 1990, following the success of the pro-democracy movement and the collapse of the Panchayat system.

**Nepal Trade Union Centre:** Tinkune Koteshower, POB 9667, Kathmandu; tel. 477105; fax 419148; f. 1986; Pres. Mohan Lal Acharya; Sec.-Gen. Laxman Prasad Pandey.

# Transport

**Ministry of Works and Transport:** Babar Mahal, Kathmandu; tel. 226537; Sec. Mukti Prasad Kafle.

**Nepal Yatayat Sansthan** (Nepal Transport Corpn): Teku, POB 309, Kathmandu; tel. 222547; f. 1966; controls the operation of road transport facilities, railways, ropeway, trucks, trolley buses and container services; Gen. Man. A. B. Shrestha.

## RAILWAYS

**Janakpur Railway:** Khajuri; tel. 2082; HQ Jayanagar, India; f. 1937; 53 km open, linking Jayanagar with Janakpur and Bijalpura; narrow gauge; 11 steam engines, 25 coaches and vans, and 20 wagons; Man. J. B. Thapa.

**Nepal Government Railway:** Birganj; f. 1927; 48 km linking Raxaul in India to Amlekhganj, of which the 6 km between Raxaul and Birganj are used for goods traffic; 7 steam engines, 12 coaches and 82 wagons; Man. D. Singh (acting).

## ROADS

In April 1994 there were 9,608 km of roads, of which 3,436 km were black-topped. Around Kathmandu there are short sections of roads suitable for motor vehicles, and there is a 28-km ring road round the valley. A 190-km mountain road, Tribhuwana Rajpath, links the capital with the Indian railhead at Raxaul. The Siddhartha Highway, constructed with Indian assistance, connects the Pokhara valley, in mid-west Nepal, with Sonauli, on the Indian border in Uttar Pradesh. The 114-km Arniko Highway, constructed with Chinese help, connects Kathmandu with Kodari, on the Chinese border. In the early 1990s the final section of the 1,030-km East–West Highway was under construction. A number of north–south roads were also being constructed to connect the district headquarters with the East–West Highway. In March 1994 the International Development Association approved credit of US$ 50.5m., which was to help finance Nepal's $81.1m. road maintenance and rehabilitation programme.

A fleet of container trucks operates between Calcutta and Raxaul and other points in Nepal for transporting exports to, and imports from, third countries. Trolley buses provide a passenger service over the 13 km between Kathmandu and Bhaktapur.

## ROPEWAY

A 42-km ropeway links Hetauda and Kathmandu and can carry 22 tons of freight per hour throughout the year. Food grains, construction goods and heavy goods on this route are transported by this ropeway.

## CIVIL AVIATION

Tribhuvan international airport is situated about 6 km from Kathmandu.

**Royal Nepal Airlines Corporation (RNAC):** RNAC Bldg, Kanti Path, POB 401, Kathmandu 711000; tel. 220757; telex 2212; fax 225348; f. 1958; 100% state-owned; scheduled services to 37 domestic airfields and international scheduled flights to Europe, the Middle East and the Far East; Chair. Bala Ram Singh Malla; Man. Dir Kalyan Dev Bhattarai.

The monopoly of the RNAC in domestic air services came to an end in mid-1992, when three private companies, **Everest Air, Nepal Airways** and **Nicon Air,** commenced serving internal routes. By early 1995 there were six private airline companies operating in Nepal.

# Tourism

Tourism is being developed through the construction of new tourist centres in the Kathmandu valley, Pokhara valley and Chitwan. Regular air services link Kathmandu with Pokhara and Chitwan. Major tourist attractions include Lumbini, the birthplace of Buddha, the lake city of Pokhara, and the Himalaya mountain range, including Mt Everest, the world's highest peak. In May 1989, in an effort to increase tourism, the Government abolished travel restrictions in 18 areas of north-western Nepal which had previously been inaccessible to foreigners. As expected, following the restoration of parliamentary democracy in 1990, tourist arrivals in Nepal rose considerably. Further travel restrictions in the remote areas of the kingdom were abolished in 1991, and efforts have been made to attract foreign investment in the Nepalese tourism industry. In March 1992 the Asian Development Bank approved a loan of US $10.4m. for Nepal for a tourism infrastructure development project. Nepal received 334,353 tourists in 1992, compared with 292,995 in 1991. In 1993, however, tourist arrivals declined to 280,000. Tourist receipts rose from US $58.6m. in 1991 to US $61.1m. in 1992. The number of hotel beds increased from 11,384 in 1991 to 11,772 (the majority of which were in Kathmandu) in 1992 and to 12,547 in 1993.

**Department of Tourism:** HM Government of Nepal, Patan Dhoka, Lalitpur, Kathmandu; tel. 523692; telex 2693; fax 527852; Dir-Gen. Sushil Kant Jha.

# THE NETHERLANDS

## Introductory Survey

**Location, Climate, Language, Religion, Flag, Capital**

The Kingdom of the Netherlands is situated in western Europe. The country is bordered to the east by Germany and to the south by Belgium. Its northern and western shores face the North Sea. The climate is temperate: the average temperature in January is 0°C (32°F), and the summer average is 21°C (70°F). The national language is Dutch. Nearly two-thirds of the inhabitants are adherents of Christian churches (36% are Roman Catholics and 26% Protestants), while most of the remainder do not profess any religion. The national flag (proportions three by two) has three equal horizontal stripes, of red, white and blue. The capital is Amsterdam, but the seat of government is The Hague ('s-Gravenhage).

**Recent History**

The Netherlands was occupied by Germany during the Second World War. Following its liberation in 1945, the country chose to abandon its traditional policy of neutrality, subsequently becoming a member of Western European Union (see p. 221) and NATO (see p. 191). The Treaty establishing the Benelux Economic Union between the Netherlands, Belgium and Luxembourg was signed in 1958 and came into force in 1960 (see p. 238). The Netherlands was a founder member of the European Community (EC—known as the European Union, see p. 143, since November 1993). Indonesia, formerly the Netherlands East Indies, was granted independence in 1949, except for West New Guinea, which was transferred in 1963. In 1975 Suriname became independent, leaving the Netherlands Antilles as the only remaining Dutch dependency. Aruba, formerly part of the Netherlands Antilles, was granted separate status within the Kingdom of the Netherlands in January 1986.

Queen Juliana, who had reigned since 1948, abdicated in favour of her eldest daughter, Beatrix, in April 1980, following the adoption in February of a constitutional amendment which allowed for the accession of the reigning monarch's eldest child, regardless of sex.

All post-war governments have been formed by various coalitions between the several Catholic and Protestant ('confessional') and 'progressive' Socialist and Liberal parties. At a general election held in April 1971 the left made substantial gains. In July 1972 the Government was forced to resign after losing its working majority in the Second Chamber of the States-General (see Government, below). Another general election took place in November 1972, at which the 'confessional' parties suffered a major setback, and in May 1973 a new Government was formed by a left-of-centre coalition of three 'progressive' parties (the Labour Party—PvdA, the Political Party of Radical Democrats, and Democraten '66) and two 'confessional' parties (the Catholic People's Party and the Anti-Revolutionary Party), under the leadership of Dr Johannes (Joop) den Uyl of the PvdA. This administration made progress towards its principal aim of redistribution of wealth, by modifying the fiscal structure and by guaranteeing minimum wage levels for all adult workers.

The coalition collapsed in March 1977, following disagreement over land-reform legislation; a general election followed in May. Attempts to form a left-of-centre coalition between the PvdA, the Christian Democratic Appeal (CDA)—an alliance of 'confessional' parties which united in 1980 to form a single party—and Democraten '66 were unsuccessful, and in December 1977 Andries van Agt (CDA) formed a centre-right coalition Government between the CDA and the right-wing People's Party for Freedom and Democracy (VVD). The new coalition was supported by only 77 of the 150 members of the Second Chamber and was weakened by, among other factors, Cabinet disagreements on NATO policy and the extent of spending cuts. Nevertheless, the Government survived its full term of office. A general election was held in May 1981: after some delay, caused by disagreements regarding economic policy and the proposed siting of NATO 'cruise' missiles in the Netherlands, a centre-left coalition was formed in September, led by van Agt and comprising the CDA (which had become the largest party in the Second Chamber), the PvdA and Democraten '66. The Council of Ministers resigned after only five weeks of office, owing to its failure to agree on economic strategy. In November the three-party coalition accepted a compromise economic programme, but deep divisions within the Government continued to delay effective action on economic problems. The coalition collapsed again in May 1982: all six PvdA ministers resigned when their ambitious job-creation plan was cut, after which van Agt led a minority interim Government of the CDA and Democraten '66.

A general election, held in September 1982, did not immediately resolve the political stalemate. Although the PvdA secured the greatest number of seats in the Second Chamber (47), the election produced a swing to the right, potentially giving the combined CDA and VVD a workable majority. An attempt to form a centre-left administration failed, on account of the PvdA's rejection of the proposed deployment of 'cruise' missiles, and the long-standing hostility between the leaders of the CDA and the PvdA. Talks on the formation of a new administration continued until November, when a centre-right CDA-VVD coalition was established under the leadership of Rudolphus (Ruud) Lubbers, a former Minister for Economic Affairs, who had recently succeeded van Agt as Chairman of the CDA. During 1983 the implementation of a programme of economic austerity measures precipitated severely disruptive strikes in the public sector. Meanwhile, the Government also encountered much public criticism over the issue of siting 'cruise' missiles in the Netherlands. A decision on deployment of the missiles was repeatedly deferred until, in February 1986, the Second Chamber approved the deployment of 48 missiles by the end of 1988; this decision was, however, superseded by the conclusion, in December 1987, of a treaty on intermediate-range nuclear forces, whereby the USA and the USSR agreed to eliminate weapons of this category based in Europe.

The ruling CDA-VVD coalition was returned to power at a general election in May 1986, with (as in 1982) the two parties winning 81 of the 150 seats in the Second Chamber. A loss of nine seats by the VVD was offset by a corresponding gain by the CDA, which, with 54 seats, became the largest party in the Second Chamber. The election did, none the less, produce a shift towards the centrist parties, with the PvdA and Democraten 66 (D66—whose name was thus amended during 1986) both gaining seats at the expense of smaller radical groups. Following the election, Joop den Uyl was replaced as parliamentary leader of the PvdA by Wim Kok, a former trade union leader. The CDA-VVD coalition, formed in July, included nine Ministers from the previous administration; its programme provided for further reductions in public expenditure.

The unity of the CDA-VVD coalition was challenged during 1988, when Lubbers' proposals for extensive reforms of the tax system were approved by coalition members only after the Prime Minister had conceded to demands from within his own party that any reductions in levels of taxation would not be to the detriment of the welfare system. In May 1989 the VVD caused the collapse of the Government by refusing to support Lubbers' proposals for the financing of a 20-year environmental protection programme, the National Environment Policy (NEP), which would involve a reduction in government spending in other sectors (such as defence and housing), an increase in taxes on motor fuels, and the abolition of tax concessions for commuters using private transport. The VVD proposed a motion of 'no confidence' in the Government, and Lubbers tendered the resignation of the Council of Ministers before a vote was taken in the Second Chamber. Lubbers remained in office as leader of an interim Government, pending a general election which took place in September. At the election the CDA again secured 54 seats in the Second Chamber, while the PvdA took 49 seats (three fewer than in 1986). The VVD suffered considerable losses, ceding five seats to rival parties. An alliance of left-wing organizations, Groen Links, won six seats.

In October 1989 negotiations between the CDA and the PvdA culminated in the formation of a centre-left coalition. (Earlier discussions involving the CDA, the VVD and D66, with a view to forming a new centre-right administration, had ended in failure, and D66 had also withdrawn from negotiations with the CDA and the PvdA.) The coalition accord envisaged increases in welfare provisions, to be funded by reductions in defence expenditure (see below). A job-creation programme was announced, while reductions in certain categories of taxation were planned. The new administration also affirmed its commitment to the NEP. In November Lubbers was sworn in as Prime Minister in charge of his third administration: the new Government was composed of equal numbers of representatives of the CDA and the PvdA. Wim Kok was appointed Deputy Prime Minister and Minister of Finance; his party also secured the defence portfolio.

In August 1990 the Government introduced an enhanced version of the NEP, which was designated the National Environment Policy Plus (NEPP). The NEPP was to represent an accelerated implementation of the previous plan, so that the long-term objectives might be achieved earlier. The new plan emphasized energy conservation and improvements in waste disposal and recycling. Instead of abolishing the system of tax deductions for car commuters (an unpopular proposal under the NEP), the NEPP advocated limiting the standard tax allowance for motorists and increasing excise duties on fuel. The plan would be financed by both the Government and the industrial sector.

The stability of the governing coalition was threatened in mid-1991, following proposals by the CDA to limit government expenditure by reforming the controversial extensive disability benefit programme of the national welfare system. Despite its initial rejection of the proposals, the PvdA eventually agreed to a compromise whereby the number of years of entitlement to full disability payments was to be limited. The Government's decision led to protest actions, including strikes, in many parts of the country in September of that year.

In November 1992 the Second Chamber ratified the Treaty on European Union, which had been signed by EC Heads of Government at Maastricht in December 1991 (see p. 149); the Treaty was similarly approved by the First Chamber in December 1992. Social legislation, approved by the Second Chamber in the same year and by the First Chamber in 1993, codified a procedure for the practice of euthanasia, in circumstances where it was repeatedly requested by an incurably ill patient.

At the beginning of 1994 legislation restricting the grounds on which foreigners would be awarded refugee status in the Netherlands came into force; during 1993 nearly 35,500 requests for political asylum had been received.

At a general election to the Second Chamber, held in May 1994, the CDA lost its leading position in the Government, winning only 34 seats, while conceding 20 seats to rival parties. The PvdA, which had focused its election manifesto on unemployment and reductions in social welfare, won 37 seats, representing a loss of 15 seats. Both the VVD and D66 improved upon their performances at the previous general election, securing 31 and 24 seats respectively. The remaining 24 seats were distributed among eight smaller parties and special issue groups, including two organizations representing the interests of the elderly population. The results of the election represented a decisive rejection of the political *status quo* that had prevailed since 1982. As the combined seats of the CDA and PvdA amounted to less than an absolute majority, negotiations on a three-party coalition agreement commenced in mid-May between the PvdA (now the largest party in the Second Chamber), the VVD and D66. Progress was initially retarded by deeply-entrenched disagreement between the VVD and PvdA over the latter party's reluctance to sanction severe cuts in social welfare spending, as part of a necessary overall reduction in public expenditure. Eventually, in mid-August, following several concessions by the PvdA (including the proposed privatization of some social benefits), a PvdA-VVD-D66 coalition was agreed. Wim Kok was appointed Prime Minister, in charge of a Cabinet comprising five representatives of the PvdA, five of the VVD and four D66 members. The CDA (now led by Enneüs Heerma, Ruud Lubbers having retired from domestic politics following the May election) was excluded from the Cabinet for the first time since 1917. The party did, however, win 10 of the country's 31 seats at elections to the European Parliament in June 1994; the PvdA won eight, and the VVD six.

In late January and early February 1995 the Netherlands suffered severe storms, resulting in heavy flooding along the Rivers Waal, Meuse and Rhine, which required the temporary evacuation from their homes of some 250,000 people. After the floods had subsided, the Prime Minister announced the inauguration of a top-priority five-year programme to improve and strengthen the nation's river dikes defence system.

During the crisis in the Persian (Arabian) Gulf region, which followed the invasion and annexation of Kuwait by Iraq in August 1990, the Lubbers Government firmly supported military action by a multinational force opposing Iraq and sent warships to the region, as well as defensive missiles to Turkey. In April 1995 Turkey recalled its ambassador to the Netherlands, in protest at the establishment by separatist Turkish Kurds of a parliament-in-exile in the Netherlands.

### Government

The Netherlands is a constitutional and hereditary monarchy. Legislative power is held by the bicameral States-General. The First Chamber has 75 members and is indirectly elected for four years by members of the 12 Provincial Councils. The Second Chamber comprises 150 members and is directly elected by universal adult suffrage for four years (subject to dissolution), on the basis of proportional representation. The Head of State has mainly formal prerogatives, and executive power is exercised by the Council of Ministers, led by the Prime Minister, which is responsible to the States-General. The monarch appoints the Prime Minister and, on the latter's recommendation, other ministers. Each of the 12 provinces is administered by a directly-elected Provincial Council, a Provincial Executive and a Sovereign Commissioner, who is appointed by Royal Decree.

### Defence

The Netherlands is a member of NATO. The duration of military service (which is compulsory between the ages of 20 and 35 years) is nine months. The Government plans to abolish conscription by 1998 and to reduce substantially the number of military personnel and the level of defence expenditure by 2000. Total strength of the armed forces in June 1994 was 70,900 (2,600 women; 29,500 conscripts), including army 43,200, navy 14,300, air force 9,000, Royal Military Constabulary 3,600, Inter-Service Organization 800. Defence budget estimates for 1995 totalled 13,600m. guilders.

### Economic Affairs

In 1993, according to estimates by the World Bank, the Netherlands' gross national product (GNP), measured at average 1991–93 prices, was US $316,404m., equivalent to $20,710 per head. During 1985–93, it was estimated, GNP per head increased, in real terms, at an average annual rate of 1.3%. Over the same period the population increased by an annual average of 0.7%. The Netherlands' gross domestic product (GDP) increased, in real terms, by an annual average of 2.3% in 1980–92, by just 0.4% in 1993, and by 2.2% in 1994.

Agriculture (including forestry and fishing) contributed 3.8% of GDP in 1992. Although only 3.9% of the working population were employed in the sector in 1993, the Netherlands is a net exporter of agricultural products: in 1992 exports of food and live animals provided 18.0% of total export earnings. The principal crops are sugar beet, potatoes, cereals, vegetables and fruit. Dairy farming is of particular importance. The horticulture industry is highly developed (plants and cut flowers provided 3.1% of export earnings in 1991). During 1985–92 agricultural production increased by an annual average of 1.6%.

Industry (including mining, manufacturing, construction and power) contributed 29.7% of GDP in 1992. About 25.4% of the working population were employed in the sector in 1993. Industrial output declined by 1.5% in 1993; however, the sector reportedly expanded in 1994.

Extractive activities provided 3.1% of GDP in 1992. In 1993 about 0.2% of the working population were employed in mining and quarrying. The principal mineral resource is natural gas (of which the Netherlands was the world's fifth largest producer in 1990). Reserves of petroleum are also exploited.

Manufacturing contributed 19.3% of GDP in 1992. The sector employed 18.0% of the working population in 1993. Measured by the value of output, the principal branches of manufacturing in 1992 were metal products (accounting for 34.5% of the total), food products (17.5%) and chemical, rubber and plastic products (15.9%). Several multinational companies are domiciled in the Netherlands. During 1980–90 manufacturing output increased by an annual average of 2.6%.

The Netherlands' reserves of natural gas provided about one-half of the country's energy requirements in the early 1990s. Imports of mineral fuels comprised 8.6% of the value of total imports in 1992. During the 1980s and early 1990s successive governments sought to promote the utilization of 'renewable' energy resources.

In 1993 the Netherlands recorded a visible trade surplus of US $12,908m., while there was a surplus of $9,775m. on the current account of the balance of payments. In 1992 the principal source of imports (25.2%) was Germany, which was also the principal market for exports (28.8%). Other major trading partners are the Belgo-Luxembourg Economic Union, the United Kingdom, France, the USA and Italy. The principal exports in 1992 were machinery and transport equipment, food and live animals, chemicals and basic manufactures. The principal imports in that year were machinery and transport equipment, basic manufactures, miscellaneous manufactured articles, food and live animals, chemicals and mineral fuels.

In 1995 there was a projected budgetary deficit of 18,600m. guilders; the actual budgetary deficit for 1994 was equivalent to 2.2% of GDP. In 1985–93 the annual rate of inflation averaged 1.6%. The average annual rate of inflation was 3.2% in 1992, declining to 2.6% in 1993; in 1994 the rate was 2.8%. Some 7.6% of the labour force were unemployed in early 1995.

The Netherlands is a founder member of the European Union (see p. 143), of the Benelux Economic Union (see p. 238), and of the European Bank for Reconstruction and Development (see p. 140).

By the late 1980s the Netherlands' economy was characterized by buoyant, export-led growth, a persistent balance-of-payments surplus, a negligible rate of inflation, strong business investment and a high level of public expenditure. It was planned to enhance the status of the country as a centre for both international trade and financial activity during the next decade. However, growth in the early 1990s was undermined by a series of budget deficits and a high level of unemployment. Moreover, the contribution to government revenue of sales of natural gas has been subject to fluctuations in international prices for petroleum (to which the price of this resource is indexed). A rise in European interest rates, following German unification, and a slight slowing of the Dutch economy's rate of growth prompted the Lubbers administration, in February 1991, to introduce measures aimed at reducing the budgetary deficit (with appreciable results). Budget proposals for 1995 included several measures that aimed to stimulate job creation over a period of four years. The programme of the coalition Government that was inaugurated in mid-1994 envisaged a substantial reduction in public expenditure.

### Social Welfare

The Netherlands allots an unusually high proportion of its national income to social security and public health. There are five general National Insurance acts covering old-age pensions, widows' and orphans' pensions, children's allowances, disablement pensions and exceptional medical expenses. A further four acts, applicable specifically to workers, cover sickness benefits, health insurance, working incapacity insurance and unemployment benefits. The General Disablement Act of 1967 covers incapacity to work for up to one year, regardless of cause. After this time, compensation is paid (up to 80% of the previous income). In 1991 the Government announced that the disablement benefit scheme was to be reformed, in an attempt to reduce the country's annual budget deficit. Further planned reforms to the benefits system were announced in 1994. Health insurance is compulsory for wage earners with an income below an annually fixed level, and for elderly persons who were insured prior to retirement. Contributions are paid jointly by employer and employee, while retired persons pay a percentage of their pensions. In 1987 there were 32,193 physicians in the Netherlands, and in 1986 the country had 729 hospital establishments. In 1994 the number of hospital beds was equivalent to one for every 244 inhabitants. Provisional budget figures for 1993 allocated 51,689m. guilders to social security and health (24.1% of total expenditure by the central Government).

### Education

There are two types of school in the Netherlands: (1) public schools, which are maintained by municipalities, and attended by about 30% of all school children; (2) private schools, which are, for the most part, denominational and are attended by almost 70% of the school-going population; both types are fully subsidized by the state. Schools are administered by school boards, responsible to the local authorities or to the private organizations that operate them, thus providing teachers with considerable freedom. The Minister of Education and Science, advised by an education council, is responsible for educational legislation and its enforcement.

Full-time education is compulsory in the Netherlands from five to 16 years of age, and part-time education is compulsory for a further two years. Some 98% of four-year-old children also attend primary schools. Primary education lasts for eight years and is followed by various types of secondary education. Pre-university schools provide various six-year courses that prepare pupils for university education. General secondary education comprises senior and junior secondary schools, providing five- and four-year courses that prepare pupils for higher vocational institutes and senior secondary vocational education respectively. In all types there is latitude in the choice of subjects taken. In 1992/93 about 162,000 students were enrolled at the Netherlands' 13 universities. In addition, the Open University had some 36,000 students. Some 210,000 full-time students were enrolled at the 83 institutes of higher vocational education. Education and culture were provisionally allocated 15% of total expenditure by the central Government in the 1993 budget.

### Public Holidays

**1995:** 1 January (New Year's Day), 14 April (Good Friday), 17 April (Easter Monday), 30 April (Queen's Day), 5 May (National Liberation Day), 25 May (Ascension Day), 5 June (Whit Monday), 25–26 December (Christmas).

**1996:** 1 January (New Year's Day), 5 April (Good Friday), 8 April (Easter Monday), 30 April (Queen's Day), 5 May (National Liberation Day), 16 May (Ascension Day), 27 May (Whit Monday), 25–26 December (Christmas).

### Weights and Measures

The metric system is in force.

# Statistical Survey

Source: Netherlands Central Bureau of Statistics, Prinses Beatrixlaan 428, POB 959, 2270 AZ Voorburg; tel. (70) 3373800; telex 32692; fax (70) 3877429.

## Area and Population

### AREA, POPULATION AND DENSITY

| | |
|---|---:|
| Area (sq km, land only) | 33,939* |
| Population (census results)† | |
| 31 May 1960 | 11,461,964 |
| 28 February 1971 | 13,060,115 |
| Population (official estimates at mid-year)† | |
| 1992 | 15,183,700 |
| 1993 | 15,297,670 |
| 1994 | 15,385,000 |
| Density (per sq km) at mid-1994 | 453 |

* 13,104 sq miles.   † Population is *de jure*.

### PRINCIPAL TOWNS (population of municipalities at 1 January 1993)

| | |
|---|---:|
| Amsterdam (capital)* | 719,856 |
| Rotterdam | 596,023 |
| 's-Gravenhage (The Hague)* | 444,661 |
| Utrecht | 234,170 |
| Eindhoven | 195,267 |
| Groningen | 170,038 |
| Tilburg | 162,398 |
| Apeldoorn | 149,504 |
| Haarlem | 149,315 |
| Enschede | 147,349 |
| Nijmegen | 146,993 |
| Arnhem | 133,272 |
| Zaanstad | 131,785 |
| Breda | 128,185 |
| Maastricht | 118,285 |
| Leiden | 113,838 |
| Dordrecht | 112,687 |
| Amersfoort | 106,923 |
| Zoetermeer | 102,937 |
| Haarlemmermeer | 102,781 |

* Amsterdam is the capital, while The Hague is the seat of government.

### BIRTHS, MARRIAGES AND DEATHS

| | Live births* Number | Rate (per 1,000) | Marriages Number | Rate (per 1,000) | Deaths* Number | Rate (per 1,000) |
|---|---:|---:|---:|---:|---:|---:|
| 1985 | 178,136 | 12.3 | 82,747 | 5.7 | 122,704 | 8.5 |
| 1986 | 184,513 | 12.7 | 87,337 | 6.0 | 125,307 | 8.6 |
| 1987 | 186,667 | 12.7 | 87,400 | 6.0 | 122,199 | 8.3 |
| 1988 | 186,647 | 12.6 | 87,843 | 6.0 | 124,163 | 8.4 |
| 1989 | 188,979 | 12.7 | 90,248 | 6.1 | 128,905 | 8.7 |
| 1990 | 197,965 | 13.2 | 95,649 | 6.4 | 128,824 | 8.6 |
| 1991 | 198,655 | 13.2 | 94,932 | 6.3 | 129,958 | 8.6 |
| 1992 | 196,734 | 13.0 | 93,638 | 6.2 | 129,887 | 8.6 |

* Including residents outside the country if listed in a Netherlands population register.

### IMMIGRATION AND EMIGRATION

| Immigrants from | 1990 | 1991 | 1992 |
|---|---:|---:|---:|
| EC countries | 31,864 | 33,892 | 35,332 |
| Europe (unspecified) | 20,298 | 21,684 | 21,337 |
| Canada | 1,220 | 1,330 | 1,240 |
| Netherlands Antilles | 7,058 | 6,694 | 4,679 |
| Suriname | 8,416 | 8,288 | 8,328 |
| USA | 4,997 | 5,349 | 5,698 |
| America (unspecified) | 5,104 | 5,042 | 4,676 |
| Indonesia | 1,768 | 1,809 | 1,927 |
| Asia (unspecified) | 12,715 | 13,550 | 13,384 |
| Africa | 21,717 | 20,288 | 17,964 |
| Australia | 1,402 | 1,492 | 1,454 |
| Oceania (unspecified) | 791 | 831 | 907 |
| **Total** | 117,350 | 120,249 | 116,926 |

| Emigrants to | 1990 | 1991 | 1992 |
|---|---:|---:|---:|
| EC countries | 26,151 | 26,250 | 26,820 |
| Europe (unspecified) | 6,159 | 5,907 | 6,188 |
| Canada | 1,256 | 1,120 | 1,117 |
| Netherlands Antilles | 3,310 | 3,460 | 3,917 |
| Suriname | 1,604 | 1,853 | 1,696 |
| USA | 4,804 | 4,619 | 4,679 |
| America (unspecified) | 2,807 | 2,799 | 2,818 |
| Indonesia | 899 | 972 | 869 |
| Asia (unspecified) | 4,339 | 4,586 | 4,966 |
| Africa | 4,102 | 4,076 | 4,058 |
| Australia | 1,104 | 1,013 | 1,034 |
| Oceania (unspecified) | 809 | 673 | 672 |
| **Total** | 57,344 | 57,328 | 58,834 |

### EMPLOYMENT ('000 persons aged 15 to 64 years)

| | 1991 | 1992 | 1993* |
|---|---:|---:|---:|
| Agriculture, hunting, forestry and fishing | 293 | 261 | 232 |
| Mining and quarrying | 14 | 9 | 12 |
| Manufacturing | 1,169 | 1,171 | 1,064 |
| Electricity, gas and water | 44 | 45 | 41 |
| Construction | 418 | 392 | 389 |
| Trade, restaurants and hotels | 1,138 | 1,139 | 958 |
| Transport, storage and communications | 403 | 416 | 379 |
| Financing, insurance, real estate and business services | 682 | 710 | 669 |
| Community, social and personal services | 2,313 | 2,281 | 2,097 |
| Activities not adequately defined | 47 | 152 | 85 |
| **Total** | 6,521 | 6,576 | 5,925 |
| Males | 4,004 | 3,979 | 3,771 |
| Females | 2,517 | 2,598 | 2,154 |

* Data exclude persons working for less than 12 hours per week. Source for 1993 figures: ILO, *Year Book of Labour Statistics*.

# THE NETHERLANDS

## Agriculture

**PRINCIPAL CROPS** ('000 metric tons)

|  | 1991 | 1992 | 1993 |
|---|---|---|---|
| Wheat | 944 | 1,017 | 1,035 |
| Rye | 34 | 34 | 41 |
| Barley | 238 | 204 | 252 |
| Oats | 18 | 19 | 30 |
| Potatoes (a) | 4,843 | 5,261 | 5,063 |
| Potatoes (b) | 2,106 | 2,380 | 2,637 |
| Sugar beet | 7,189 | 8,251 | 7,478 |
| Linseed | } 35 | 25 | 27 |
| Flax (unrippled) | | | |
| Vegetables and fruit | 4,027 | 4,405 | n.a. |

(a) Consumption—includes early potatoes.  (b) For factories.

**LIVESTOCK** ('000 head)

|  | 1991 | 1992 | 1993 |
|---|---|---|---|
| Horses and ponies* | 77 | 86 | 92 |
| Cattle | 5,062 | 4,920 | 4,797 |
| Sheep | 1,882 | 1,954 | 1,916 |
| Pigs | 13,217 | 14,161 | 14,964 |
| Chickens | 93,596 | 99,372 | 95,919 |

* Aged three years and over.

**LIVESTOCK PRODUCTS** ('000 metric tons)

|  | 1991 | 1992 | 1993* |
|---|---|---|---|
| Beef and veal | 567 | 569 | 604† |
| Mutton and lamb | 31 | 28 | 18† |
| Pig meat | 1,806 | 1,864 | 1,749† |
| Poultry meat | 547 | 575 | 509 |
| Cows' milk | 11,085 | 10,974 | 11,010† |
| Butter | 163 | 149 | 148† |
| Cheese | 634 | 662 | 632 |
| Hen eggs | 661 | 639 | 600† |

* Source: FAO, *Production Yearbook*.   † Estimate.

## Fishing

('000 metric tons, live weight)

|  | 1990 | 1991 | 1992 |
|---|---|---|---|
| European plaice | 78.2 | 67.9 | 51.1 |
| Atlantic horse mackerel | 98.4 | 123.7 | 122.6 |
| Atlantic herring | 82.8 | 85.4 | 85.8 |
| Atlantic mackerel | 31.9 | 39.7 | 38.9 |
| Blue mussel | 98.8 | 49.3 | 51.0 |
| **Total catch** (incl. others) | 459.0 | 443.1 | 438.0 |
| Inland waters | 3.1 | 4.1 | 2.8 |
| Atlantic Ocean | 455.9 | 439.0 | 435.2 |

Source: FAO, *Yearbook of Fishery Statistics*.

## Mining

|  | 1990 | 1991 | 1992 |
|---|---|---|---|
| Crude petroleum ('000 metric tons) | 3,533 | 3,258 | 2,845 |
| Natural gas (million cu m) | 72,238 | 81,666 | 82,020 |

## Industry

**SELECTED PRODUCTS** ('000 metric tons, unless otherwise indicated)

|  | 1990 | 1991 | 1992 |
|---|---|---|---|
| Sugar | 1,231 | 1,047 | 1,149 |
| Margarine | 208 | 211 | 209 |
| Coke | 2,736 | 2,933 | 2,918 |
| Electricity (million kWh) | 71,852 | 74,553 | 77,196 |
| Gas—manufactured ('000 terajoules) | 325 | 303 | 340 |
| Pig-iron | 4,960 | 4,697 | 4,849 |
| Ingot steel | 5,412 | 5,171 | 5,439 |
| Rolled steel products | 3,608 | 3,652 | 3,720 |
| Tinplate | 528 | 549 | 550 |
| Cotton yarn (metric tons) | 5,000 | 3,800 | 3,400 |
| Wool yarn—hand-knitted (metric tons) | 2,600 | 2,600 | 1,800 |
| Woven cotton fabrics (metric tons) | 10,525 | 10,200 | 8,800 |
| Footwear ('000 pairs)* | 5,438 | 5,250 | 4,400 |
| Building bricks (million) | 1,630 | 1,556 | 1,489 |
| Cement | 3,729 | 3,546 | 3,301 |
| Dwelling units—completed (number) | 97,384 | 82,888 | 86,164 |
| Phosphate fertilizers (a)† | 378 | 365 | 345 |
| Nitrogen fertilizers (b)† | 1,848 | 1,875 | 1,840 |
| Merchant ships launched ('000 gross registered tons) | 163 | 173 | 163 |
| Paper and paperboard | 2,732 | 2,754 | 2,811 |

* Excluding indoor footwear.
† Production during 12 months ending 30 June of the year stated. Figures are in terms of (a) phosphoric acid or (b) nitrogen (Source: FAO, *Quarterly Bulletin of Statistics*).

## Finance

**CURRENCY AND EXCHANGE RATES**

**Monetary Units:**
100 cents = 1 Netherlands gulden (guilder) or florin.

**Sterling and Dollar Equivalents** (31 December 1994)
£1 sterling = 2.715 guilders;
US $1 = 1.735 guilders;
100 Netherlands guilders = £36.83 = $57.63.

**Average Exchange Rate** (guilders per US $)
1992  1.7585
1993  1.8573
1994  1.8200

**BUDGET** (million guilders)

| Revenue | 1991* | 1992* | 1993† |
|---|---|---|---|
| Income tax | 66,843 | 65,644 | 69,530 |
| Corporation tax | 18,566 | 17,373 | 17,100 |
| Import duties | 3,345 | 3,304 | 3,275 |
| Excise duties | 10,349 | 11,638 | 12,125 |
| Turnover tax | 39,930 | 40,637 | 39,150 |
| Motor vehicle tax | 3,733 | 3,982 | 4,870 |
| Tax on legal transactions | 3,135 | 3,375 | 3,325 |
| Other taxes | 7,195 | 7,695 | 8,360 |
| Shares in profits from Netherlands Bank | 2,410 | 1,893 | 1,825 |
| Interest from loans (Housing Act dwellings) | 3,716 | 3,734 | 3,667 |
| Capital transfers, Postal and Telecomm. Service | 1,046 | 1,466 | 1,459 |
| Natural gas revenues | 7,264 | 7,488 | 6,418 |
| Others | 19,970 | 20,526 | 30,771 |
| **Total** | 187,502 | 188,755 | 201,875 |

# THE NETHERLANDS

## Statistical Survey

| Expenditure | 1991* | 1992* | 1993† |
|---|---|---|---|
| Social security and public health | 51,948 | 50,416 | 51,689 |
| Education and culture | 34,870 | 36,976 | 36,217 |
| Defence | 14,144 | 14,456 | 13,697 |
| Transport and public works | 12,066 | 12,504 | 12,079 |
| Housing, town and country planning | 12,298 | 12,613 | 11,516 |
| Interest on public debt | 24,975 | 26,656 | 28,238 |
| Agriculture and fishery‡ | 8,513 | 8,523 | 8,530 |
| Local authorities' shares in taxes | 15,520 | 16,473 | 17,854 |
| European Communities' shares in taxes | 7,304 | 7,199 | 7,716 |
| Public order and security | 6,395 | 6,911 | 7,257 |
| Foreign relations | 1,222 | 1,365 | 1,580 |
| Foreign aid | 5,623 | 5,950 | 5,945 |
| Trade and handicraft | 5,098 | 3,887 | 4,723 |
| Others | 6,865 | 7,410 | 7,435 |
| **Total** | 206,841 | 211,339 | 214,476 |

* Account figures.   † Provisional figures.
‡ The Netherlands' share of the levies of the EC's Agriculture Equalization Fund is included in the expenditure on agriculture and excluded from the European Communities' shares in taxes.

### INTERNATIONAL RESERVES (US $ million at 31 December)*

|  | 1992 | 1993 | 1994 |
|---|---|---|---|
| Gold† | 13,712 | 7,639 | 8,477 |
| IMF special drawing rights | 554 | 583 | 645 |
| Reserve position in IMF | 1,147 | 1,092 | 1,171 |
| Foreign exchange | 20,237 | 29,669 | 32,787 |
| **Total** | 35,649 | 38,983 | 43,080 |

* Excluding deposits made with the European Monetary Co-operation Fund.
† Gold reserves were valued at 18,200 guilders per kg in 1992 and at 13,600 guilders per kg in 1993 and 1994.

Source: IMF, *International Financial Statistics*.

### MONEY SUPPLY (million guilders at 31 December)*

|  | 1992 | 1993 | 1994 |
|---|---|---|---|
| Currency outside banks | 36,990 | 37,590 | 38,110 |
| Demand deposits at deposit money banks | 98,000 | 111,920 | 114,040 |
| **Total money** (incl. others) | 135,070 | 149,640 | 152,240 |

* Figures are rounded to the nearest 10 million guilders.

Source: IMF, *International Financial Statistics*.

### COST OF LIVING (Consumer Price Index. Base: 1985 = 100)

|  | 1991 | 1992 | 1993 |
|---|---|---|---|
| Food, beverages and tobacco | 104.4 | 107.5 | 108.3 |
| Clothing and footwear | 92.8 | 93.4 | 94.7 |
| Rent and other housing cost, heating and lighting | 108.9 | 113.0 | 116.6 |
| Furniture, domestic appliances, tools and maintenance | 109.0 | 111.8 | 113.2 |
| Medical care | 119.3 | 127.3 | 129.8 |
| Transport and communications | 110.8 | 114.9 | 117.6 |
| Education and leisure | 104.4 | 106.7 | 109.2 |
| Other goods and services | 110.8 | 115.3 | 118.5 |
| **All items** | 108.5 | 112.5 | 114.9 |

### NATIONAL ACCOUNTS (million guilders at current prices)
#### National Income and Product

|  | 1990 | 1991* | 1992* |
|---|---|---|---|
| Compensation of employees | 267,740 | 283,940 | 299,620 |
| Operating surplus | 142,310 | 146,520 | 142,270 |
| **Domestic factor incomes** | 410,050 | 430,460 | 441,890 |
| Consumption of fixed capital | 58,230 | 61,600 | 65,320 |
| **Gross domestic product (GDP) at factor cost** | 468,280 | 492,060 | 507,210 |
| Indirect taxes | 63,720 | 67,750 | 73,540 |
| Less Subsidies | 15,730 | 17,930 | 17,530 |
| **GDP in purchasers' values** | 516,270 | 541,880 | 563,220 |
| Net factor income from abroad | −910 | −1,170 | −1,370 |
| **Gross national product** | 515,360 | 540,710 | 561,850 |
| Less Consumption of fixed capital | 58,230 | 61,600 | 65,320 |
| **National income in market prices** | 457,130 | 479,110 | 496,530 |
| Other current transfers from abroad (net) | −3,250 | −6,120 | −5,490 |
| **National disposable income** | 453,880 | 472,990 | 491,040 |

* Figures are provisional.

#### Expenditure on the Gross Domestic Product

|  | 1990 | 1991* | 1992* |
|---|---|---|---|
| Government final consumption expenditure | 74,800 | 77,940 | 81,500 |
| Private final consumption expenditure | 303,100 | 323,000 | 339,520 |
| Increase in stocks | 6,520 | 3,480 | 2,060 |
| Gross fixed capital formation | 107,940 | 110,830 | 114,980 |
| **Total domestic expenditure** | 492,360 | 515,250 | 538,060 |
| Exports of goods and services | 279,740 | 294,420 | 294,430 |
| Less Imports of goods and services | 255,830 | 267,790 | 269,270 |
| **GDP in purchasers' values** | 516,270 | 541,880 | 563,220 |

* Figures are provisional.

#### Gross Domestic Product by Economic Activity (provisional)

|  | 1990 | 1991* | 1992* |
|---|---|---|---|
| Agriculture, hunting, forestry and fishing | 20,841 | 21,168 | 20,466 |
| Mining and quarrying | 15,421 | 18,264 | 16,523 |
| Manufacturing | 97,971 | 99,581 | 102,853 |
| Electricity, gas and water | 8,597 | 8,994 | 8,961 |
| Construction | 27,056 | 27,871 | 30,126 |
| Trade, restaurants and hotels (excl. repair services) | 76,635 | 80,346 | 83,093 |
| Transport, storage and communications | 32,203 | 34,921 | 36,013 |
| Finance, insurance, real estate and business services | 110,716 | 118,668 | 126,431 |
| Government services | 51,593 | 53,258 | 55,760 |
| Other services | 46,548 | 49,851 | 52,490 |
| **Sub-total** | 487,581 | 512,922 | 532,716 |
| Statistical discrepancy | — | −13 | 8 |
| Import duties, value-added tax and selective investment levy | 46,750 | 48,740 | 50,990 |
| Less Imputed bank service charge | 18,061 | 19,769 | 20,494 |
| **GDP in purchasers' values** | 516,270 | 541,880 | 563,220 |

* Figures are provisional.

THE NETHERLANDS

*Statistical Survey*

## BALANCE OF PAYMENTS (US $ million)

|  | 1991 | 1992 | 1993 |
|---|---|---|---|
| Merchandise exports f.o.b. | 122,625 | 129,195 | 120,295 |
| Merchandise imports f.o.b. | −111,885 | −117,855 | −107,387 |
| **Trade balance** | 10,740 | 11,340 | 12,908 |
| Exports of services | 31,818 | 35,593 | 35,552 |
| Imports of services | −30,482 | −34,395 | −33,591 |
| Other income received | 29,326 | 29,408 | 29,347 |
| Other income paid | −29,463 | −30,561 | −29,323 |
| Private unrequited transfers (net) | −1,222 | −1,619 | −1,650 |
| Official unrequited transfers (net) | −3,189 | −3,261 | −3,468 |
| **Current balance** | 7,529 | 6,504 | 9,775 |
| Direct investment (net) | −7,262 | −6,789 | −4,561 |
| Portfolio investment (net) | −859 | −9,213 | 1,670 |
| Other capital (net) | 1,789 | 8,606 | −9,237 |
| Net errors and omissions | −1,121 | 7,318 | 8,896 |
| **Overall balance** | 77 | 6,427 | 6,542 |

Source: IMF, *International Financial Statistics*.

## FOREIGN AID (million guilders)

|  | 1990 | 1991 | 1992 |
|---|---|---|---|
| **Total** | 5,265 | 5,623 | 5,950 |

# External Trade

## PRINCIPAL COMMODITIES (distribution by SITC, million guilders)

| Imports c.i.f. | 1990 | 1991 | 1992 |
|---|---|---|---|
| **Food and live animals** | 22,198 | 24,264 | 25,522 |
| Fruit and vegetables | 5,963 | 6,803 | 6,794 |
| **Crude materials (inedible) except fuels** | 12,225 | 11,118 | 11,193 |
| **Mineral fuels, lubricants, etc.** | 23,972 | 22,487 | 20,303 |
| Petroleum and petroleum products | 20,482 | 18,987 | 17,294 |
| Crude petroleum | 14,738 | 14,043 | 13,500 |
| **Chemicals and related products** | 24,077 | 24,904 | 25,378 |
| Organic chemicals | 6,523 | 6,625 | 6,458 |
| **Basic manufactures** | 39,421 | 39,064 | 38,135 |
| Paper, paperboard and manufactures | 6,822 | 7,127 | 7,006 |
| Textile yarn, fabrics, etc. | 6,581 | 6,603 | 6,386 |
| Iron and steel | 7,388 | 6,861 | 6,135 |
| **Machinery and transport equipment** | 71,107 | 75,665 | 74,559 |
| Non-electric machinery | 34,437 | 35,913 | 35,515 |
| Electrical machinery, apparatus, etc. | 16,641 | 17,647 | 17,383 |
| Telecommunications equipment | 6,224 | 6,555 | 6,163 |
| Transport equipment | 20,031 | 22,105 | 21,661 |
| Road motor vehicles and parts (excl. tyres, engines and electrical parts) | 16,265 | 17,949 | 17,198 |
| Passenger cars (excl. buses) | 8,126 | 9,461 | 8,812 |
| **Miscellaneous manufactured articles** | 32,018 | 34,651 | 33,648 |
| Clothing (excl. footwear) | 8,684 | 9,830 | 10,125 |
| **Total** (incl. others)* | 229,707 | 237,117 | 236,159 |

* Including victuals and stores of foreign origin supplied to Netherlands ships and aircraft.

| Exports f.o.b. | 1990 | 1991 | 1992 |
|---|---|---|---|
| **Food and live animals** | 41,089 | 43,013 | 44,195 |
| Meat and meat preparations | 9,289 | 9,593 | 10,086 |
| Fresh, chilled or frozen meat and edible offals | n.a. | 7,988 | 8,487 |
| Dairy products and eggs | 7,975 | 8,138 | 8,417 |
| Fruit and vegetables | 9,530 | 10,721 | 10,127 |
| Fresh or simply preserved vegetables | 5,202 | 5,920 | 5,442 |
| **Beverages and tobacco** | 5,335 | 5,921 | 6,272 |
| **Crude materials (inedible) except fuels** | 13,561 | 14,241 | 14,164 |
| Live plants (incl. bulbs), cut flowers, etc. | 6,982 | 7,643 | n.a. |
| **Mineral fuels, lubricants, etc.** | 23,157 | 24,610 | 21,149 |
| Petroleum and petroleum products | 16,526 | 16,306 | 13,694 |
| Petroleum products | 16,157 | 15,218 | 12,799 |
| Natural gas | 5,798 | 7,761 | 6,909 |
| **Chemicals and related products** | 40,596 | 40,163 | 39,021 |
| Organic chemicals | 11,425 | 10,823 | 9,927 |
| Plastics in primary forms | n.a. | 10,317 | 9,647 |
| **Basic manufactures** | 33,954 | 35,087 | 33,671 |
| Paper, paperboard and manufactures | 5,694 | 5,763 | 5,621 |
| Textile, yarn, fabrics, etc. | 7,028 | 7,108 | 6,961 |
| Iron and steel | 5,980 | 6,040 | 5,565 |
| **Machinery and transport equipment** | 56,437 | 58,841 | 58,603 |
| Non-electric machinery | 28,695 | 30,089 | 30,114 |
| Electrical machinery, apparatus, etc. | 13,671 | 14,480 | 14,212 |
| Transport equipment | 14,069 | 14,273 | 14,278 |
| Road motor vehicles and parts (excl. tyres, engines and electrical parts) | n.a. | 9,616 | 9,008 |
| **Miscellaneous manufactured articles** | 22,830 | 24,880 | 26,398 |
| **Total** (incl. others)* | 239,181 | 249,051 | 245,861 |

* Includes victuals and stores supplied to foreign ships and aircraft.

## PRINCIPAL TRADING PARTNERS (million guilders)*

| Imports c.i.f. | 1990 | 1991 | 1992 |
|---|---|---|---|
| Belgium-Luxembourg | 32,105 | 33,504 | 33,581 |
| Denmark | 2,763 | 2,867 | 3,115 |
| France | 17,708 | 17,882 | 18,658 |
| Germany, Federal Republic† | 58,876 | 60,475 | 59,586 |
| Iran | 1,859 | 2,180 | 2,466 |
| Ireland | n.a. | n.a. | 2,540 |
| Italy | 8,594 | 8,770 | 8,542 |
| Japan | 7,314 | 8,596 | 8,575 |
| Saudi Arabia | 2,546 | 4,962 | 3,972 |
| Spain | 3,344 | 3,422 | 3,674 |
| Sweden | 4,963 | 4,842 | 4,936 |
| Switzerland | 3,203 | 3,194 | 3,333 |
| Taiwan | n.a. | n.a. | 2,450 |
| United Kingdom | 18,782 | 20,513 | 20,420 |
| USA | 18,058 | 19,154 | 18,322 |
| **Total** (incl. others) | 229,707 | 236,565 | 236,159 |

## THE NETHERLANDS

| Exports f.o.b.‡ | 1990 | 1991 | 1992 |
|---|---|---|---|
| Austria | 2,823 | 2,796 | 2,923 |
| Belgium-Luxembourg | 34,939 | 35,658 | 35,123 |
| Denmark | 3,964 | 4,013 | 3,704 |
| France | 26,739 | 26,533 | 25,953 |
| Germany, Federal Republic† | 66,031 | 73,197 | 70,809 |
| Greece | n.a. | n.a. | 2,623 |
| Italy | 15,893 | 15,939 | 15,743 |
| Spain | 5,917 | 6,173 | 6,381 |
| Sweden | 4,298 | 4,234 | 3,943 |
| Switzerland | 4,361 | 4,409 | 4,565 |
| United Kingdom | 24,357 | 23,260 | 22,615 |
| USA | 9,630 | 9,716 | 9,983 |
| **Total** (incl. others) | 239,181 | 249,051 | 245,861 |

\* Imports by country of consignment; exports by country of destination.
† Including the former German Democratic Republic from 1991.
‡ Figures for individual countries exclude stores and bunkers for foreign ships and aircraft (1,643 million guilders in 1992).

## Transport

**RAILWAYS** (traffic)

| | 1990 | 1991 | 1992 |
|---|---|---|---|
| Passenger-km (million) | 11,060 | 15,195 | 15,350 |
| Freight ton-km (million) | 3,070 | 3,038 | 2,764 |

**ROAD TRAFFIC** ('000 motor vehicles in use at 1 August)

| | 1991 | 1992 | 1993 |
|---|---|---|---|
| Passenger cars | 5,569 | 5,658 | 5,755 |
| Lorries or trucks | 565 | 606 | 641 |
| Motor buses | 12 | 12 | 12 |
| Special vehicles | 27 | 26 | 26 |
| Motor cycles | 191 | 232 | 275 |
| Cycles with auxiliary motor | 458 | 770 | n.a. |

**SHIPPING**
**Inland Waterways** (transport fleet at 1 January)

| | 1991 | 1992 | 1993 |
|---|---|---|---|
| Number of vessels | 6,011 | 5,681 | 5,524 |
| Carrying capacity ('000 metric tons) | 5,994 | 5,840 | 5,842 |

**Inland Waterways** (freight traffic, '000 metric tons)

| | 1990 | 1991 | 1992 |
|---|---|---|---|
| Internal transport | 84,032 | 74,734 | 66,392 |
| International transport | 202,115 | 199,075 | 194,705 |
| of which: | | | |
| Rhine traffic | 129,677 | 125,187 | 121,407 |

**Merchant Fleet** (at 30 June)

| | 1991 | 1992 | 1993 |
|---|---|---|---|
| Number of vessels | 1,249 | 1,027 | 1,006 |
| Displacement ('000 gross registered tons) | 3,872 | 3,346 | 3,086 |

Source: Lloyd's Register of Shipping.

**Sea-borne Freight Traffic** ('000 metric tons)

| | 1990 | 1991 | 1992 |
|---|---|---|---|
| Goods loaded | 91,839 | 90,505 | 89,013 |
| Goods unloaded | 281,251 | 286,713 | 289,177 |

**CIVIL AVIATION**\* (Netherlands scheduled air services—million)

| | 1990/91 | 1991/92 | 1992/93 |
|---|---|---|---|
| Kilometres flown | 163 | 188 | 220 |
| Passenger-kilometres | 26,504 | 28,736 | 33,064 |
| Cargo ton-kilometres | } 2,250 | 2,354 | 2,562 |
| Mail ton-kilometres | | | |

\* Figures refer to KLM operations only. Years from 1 April to 31 March.

## Tourism

**FOREIGN TOURIST ARRIVALS** ('000)\*

| Country of Origin | 1990 | 1991 | 1992 |
|---|---|---|---|
| Belgium | 160.4 | 159.8 | 170.0 |
| Denmark | 69.6 | 60.8 | 63.1 |
| Finland | 35.8 | 31.8 | 26.9 |
| France | 304.3 | 259.8 | 287.8 |
| Germany, Federal Republic | 731.6 | 798.6 | 813.9 |
| Ireland | 24.9 | 27.2 | 25.9 |
| Italy | 299.2 | 276.8 | 244.2 |
| Japan | 95.8 | 87.3 | 111.7 |
| Luxembourg | 13.3 | 13.1 | 14.6 |
| Norway | 46.0 | 46.0 | 49.8 |
| Spain and Portugal | 151.9 | 154.2 | 146.8 |
| Sweden | 114.7 | 113.1 | 118.8 |
| Switzerland | 100.3 | 95.0 | 92.5 |
| United Kingdom | 716.3 | 703.4 | 745.5 |
| USA | 455.6 | 366.2 | 408.8 |
| **Total** (incl. others) | 3,902.7 | 3,686.6 | 3,931.7 |

\* Arrivals at hotels and boarding houses with more than 20 beds.

## Communications Media

| | 1990 | 1991 | 1992 |
|---|---|---|---|
| Telephones in use ('000)\* | 6,940 | 7,175 | n.a. |
| Radio receivers ('000) | 13,550 | 13,650 | 13,755 |
| Television receivers ('000) | n.a. | n.a. | 7,400 |
| Book production: titles† | 13,691 | 11,613 | 11,844 |

\* Number of connections irrespective of number of instruments.
† Excluding pamphlets.
Sources: mainly UNESCO, *Statistical Yearbook*; UN, *Statistical Yearbook*.

## Education

(1992/93—Full-time)

| | Institutions | Students ('000) |
|---|---|---|
| Primary education | 8,331 | 1,415 |
| Special education | 1,002 | 111 |
| General secondary | 1,134 | 667 |
| Vocational | 527 | 498 |
| Junior | 394 | 215 |
| Senior | 133 | 283 |
| Higher vocational | 83 | 210 |
| University status | 13 | 162 |

\* Excluding agricultural institutions.

# Directory

## The Constitution

The Netherlands' first Constitution was adopted in 1814–15. The present Constitution, the first since 1848, came into force on 17 February 1983. Its main provisions are summarized below:

### THE KINGDOM OF THE NETHERLANDS

The Kingdom of the Netherlands consists of territories in Europe (the Netherlands) and in the Caribbean (the Netherlands Antilles and Aruba). Suriname, formerly an overseas territory of the Netherlands, gained independence in 1975. Under the Charter for the Kingdom of the Netherlands, signed by Queen Juliana in 1954, the Netherlands and the Netherlands Antilles constitute a single realm, ruled by the House of Orange-Nassau. In January 1986 Aruba, formerly part of the Netherlands Antilles, was granted separate status within the Kingdom of the Netherlands.

### THE MONARCHY

The Netherlands is a constitutional monarchy with a parliamentary system of government. The Constitution regulates the royal succession and the regency in great detail. A successor to the Throne may be appointed by Act of Parliament if it appears that there will otherwise be no successor. The Bill for this purpose shall be discussed and decided upon in a joint session of the two Chambers of the States-General. The Sovereign is succeeded by his or her eldest child. The age of majority of the Sovereign is 18 years. Until the Sovereign has attained that age, the royal prerogative shall be exercised by a Regent.

### ELECTORAL SYSTEM

The Parliament of the Netherlands is called the States-General and is composed of two Chambers, a First and a Second Chamber. The Second Chamber, which is the more important politically, consists of 150 members, and is directly elected for four years on the basis of proportional representation. The First Chamber comprises 75 members and is elected by the (directly-elected) members of the provincial councils.

Nearly all Dutch nationals who have attained the age of 18 years are entitled to take part in the election for the Second Chamber. Those not entitled to vote are certain groups of non-resident nationals, mentally-disordered and legally incompetent persons.

To be eligible for membership of the States-General, a person must be a Dutch national, must have attained the age of 18 years and must not have been disqualified from voting.

### MINISTERIAL RESPONSIBILITY

The Ministers, led by the Prime Minister, are responsible to the States-General for all acts of government. This means, for example, that the power of the Government (Sovereign and Ministers) to dissolve one or both Chambers of the States-General is ultimately subject to the judgment of the States-General. The right to declare war and conclude treaties can, in principle, only be exercised subject to prior parliamentary approval. The Constitution contains provisions concerning the transferral of legislative, executive and judicial power to international institutions and on the legal supremacy of self-executing provisions of treaties.

The Prime Minister and the other Ministers are appointed and dismissed by Royal Decree. Ministries are established by Royal Decree.

A Cabinet is formed by a so-called 'formateur' (usually the future Prime Minister), who will have been assured of the support of a majority in the Second Chamber of the States-General.

A Minister may not be a member of the States-General. However, Ministers have the right to attend sittings of the Chambers and may take part in the deliberations. They must supply the Chambers, either orally or in writing, with any information requested, provided that this cannot be deemed to conflict with the interests of the State.

A statement of the policy which is to be pursued by the Government is given by the Sovereign every year on the third Tuesday in September before a joint session of the two Chambers of the States-General.

Acts of Parliament are passed jointly by the Government and the States-General. Bills, including the draft budget, must be introduced into the Second Chamber. The Second Chamber has the right to amend bills; the First Chamber can only accept or reject a bill. Revision of the Constitution requires two parliamentary readings of the bills that contain the proposed changes. In between the two readings, the States-General must be dissolved and elections held.

### THE COUNCIL OF STATE

The Council of State is the Government's oldest and most important advisory body. It must be consulted on all bills and draft general administrative orders. The Council is also an important court for administrative disputes.

The Sovereign is President of the Council of State, but the day-to-day running of the Council is the responsibility of its Vice-President. Its other members—usually former politicians, scholars, judges and business executives—are appointed for life.

### LOCAL GOVERNMENT

The Netherlands is divided into 12 provinces. Provinces may be dissolved and established by Act of Parliament. The provincial administrative organs are the Provincial Council, the Provincial Executive and the Sovereign's Commissioner. The Provincial Council—directly elected, as is the Second Chamber, on the basis of proportional representation—forms the provincial equivalent of the Parliament. Each Provincial Council elects, from among its members, a Provincial Executive.

The Sovereign's Commissioner is appointed and dismissed by Royal Decree. Each Commissioner presides over both the Provincial Council and the Provincial Executive. The provincial administrative organs have the constitutionally guaranteed power to regulate and administer their own internal affairs. They may also be required by, or pursuant to, Act of Parliament to provide regulation and administration. At present there are 636 municipalities in the Netherlands. The municipal administrative organs are the Municipal Council (directly elected by the local inhabitants), the Municipal Executive (chosen by the Council from among its members) and the Burgomaster (appointed and dismissed by Royal Decree). The Burgomaster (Mayor) presides over both the Municipal Council and the Municipal Executive. The Municipal Council has the power to make local regulations.

## The Government

### HEAD OF STATE

**Queen of the Netherlands:** HM Queen BEATRIX WILHELMINA ARMGARD (succeeded to the throne 30 April 1980).

### COUNCIL OF MINISTERS
(June 1995)

A coalition of the Labour Party (PvdA), the People's Party for Freedom and Democracy (VVD) and the Democraten 66 (D66).

**Prime Minister:** WIM KOK (PvdA).

**First Deputy Prime Minister and Minister for Home Affairs:** HANS DIJKSTAL (VVD).

**Second Deputy Prime Minister and Minister of Foreign Affairs:** HANS VAN MIERLO (D66).

**Minister for Development Co-operation:** JAN P. PRONK (PvdA).

**Minister of Finance:** GERRIT ZALM (VVD).

**Minister of Defence:** JORIS VOORHOEVE (VVD).

**Minister of Economic Affairs:** G. J. WIJERS (D66).

**Minister for Justice:** WINNIE SORGDRAGER (D66).

**Minister of Agriculture, Nature Management and Fisheries:** J. VAN AARTSEN (VVD).

**Minister of Education, Culture and Science:** JO RITZEN (PvdA).

**Minister for Social Affairs and Employment:** AD MELKERT (PvdA).

**Minister of Transport, Public Works and Water Management:** ANNEMARIE JORRITSMA-LEBBINK (VVD).

**Minister of Welfare, Public Health and Sport:** E. BORST-EILERS (D66).

**Minister of Housing, Spatial Planning and Environment:** M. DE BOER (PvdA).

### MINISTRIES

**Office of the Prime Minister:** Binnenhof 20, POB 20001, 2500 EA The Hague; tel. (70) 3614031; telex 32473.

**Ministry of Agriculture, Nature Management and Fisheries:** POB 20401, 2500 EK The Hague; tel. (70) 3793911; telex 32040.

# THE NETHERLANDS

**Ministry of Defence:** Plein 4, POB 20701, 2500 ES The Hague; tel. (70) 3188188; telex 31337.

**Ministry of Development Co-operation:** operates under Ministry of Foreign Affairs (see below).

**Ministry of Economic Affairs:** Bezuidenhoutseweg 67, POB 20101, 2500 EC The Hague; tel. (70) 3796110; fax (70) 3797001.

**Ministry of Education, Culture and Science:** Europaweg 4, POB 25000, 2700 LZ Zoetermeer; tel. (79) 531911; telex 32636; fax (79) 531953.

**Ministry of Finance:** POB 20201, 2500 EE The Hague; tel. (70) 3427540; fax (70) 3427900.

**Ministry of Foreign Affairs:** Bezuidenhoutseweg 67, POB 20061, 2500 EB The Hague; tel. (70) 3486486; telex 31326.

**Ministry of Home Affairs:** Schedeldoekshaven 200, POB 20011, 2500 EA The Hague; tel. (70) 3026302; telex 32109; fax (70) 3639153.

**Ministry of Housing, Spatial Planning and the Environment:** Rijnstraat 8, POB 20951, 2500 EZ, The Hague; tel. (70) 3393939.

**Ministry of Justice:** Schedeldoekshaven 100, POB 20301, 2500 EH The Hague; tel. (70) 3707911; telex 34554.

**Ministry of Social Affairs and Employment:** Anna van Hannoverstraat 4, POB 90801, 2509 LV The Hague; tel. (70) 3334444; telex 331250; fax (70) 3334023.

**Ministry of Transport, Public Works and Water Management:** Plesmanweg 1, POB 20901, 2500 EX The Hague; tel. (70) 3516171; telex 32562; fax (70) 3517895.

**Ministry of Welfare, Public Health and Sport:** Sir Winston Churchilllaan 370, POB 5406, 2280 HK Rijswijk; tel. (70) 3407911; telex 31680; fax (70) 3407340.

## Legislature

### STATEN GENERAAL
(States-General)

**President of the First Chamber:** H. D. TJEENK WILLINK.
**President of the Second Chamber:** W. J. DEETMAN.

#### First Chamber
Election, 29 May 1995

| | Seats |
|---|---|
| Volkspartij voor Vrijheid en Democratie | 23 |
| Partij van de Arbeid | 14 |
| Christen-Democratisch Appel | 19 |
| Democraten 66 | 7 |
| Groen Links | 4 |
| Staatkundig Gereformeerde Partij | 2 |
| Algemeen Ouderen Verbond | 2 |
| Gereformeerd Politiek Verbond | 1 |
| Reformatorische Politieke Federatie | 1 |
| Socialistische Partij | 1 |
| De Groenen | 1 |
| **Total** | **75** |

#### Second Chamber
General Election, 3 May 1994

| | Seats |
|---|---|
| Partij van de Arbeid | 37 |
| Christen-Democratisch Appel | 34 |
| Volkspartij voor Vrijheid en Democratie | 31 |
| Democraten 66 | 24 |
| Algemeen Ouderen Verbond | 6 |
| Groen Links | 5 |
| Centrumdemocraten | 3 |
| Reformatorische Politieke Federatie | 3 |
| Staatkundig Gereformeerde Partij | 2 |
| Gereformeerd Politiek Verbond | 2 |
| Socialistische Partij | 2 |
| Union 55+ | 1 |
| **Total** | **150** |

## Political Organizations

**Algemeen Ouderen Verbond (AOV)** (General Union of the Elderly): Eindhoven; tel. (40) 433961; Leader JET NIJPELS.

**Centrumdemocraten (CD)** (Centre Democrats): POB 84, 2501 CB The Hague; tel. (70) 3469264; right-wing nationalist party; Chair. and Parliamentary Leader JOHANNES JANMAAT; Sec. W. B. SCHUURMAN; 1,500 mems.

**Centrumpartij 86 (CP86)** (Centre Party 86): right-wing nationalist party.

**Christen-Democratisch Appel (CDA)** (Christian Democratic Appeal): Dr Kuyperstraat 5, 2514 BA The Hague; tel. (70) 3924461; telex 31050; fax (70) 3643417; f. 1980 by merger of three 'confessional' parties; Chair. (vacant); Parliamentary Leader ENNEÜS HEERMA; Gen. Sec. C. BREMMER; c. 120,000 mems.

**Democraten 66 (D66):** Noordwal 10, 2513 EA The Hague; tel. (70) 3621515; fax (70) 3641917; f. 1966 as Democraten '66, name amended 1986; Chair. HANS VAN MIERLO; Parliamentary Leader GERRIT-JAN WOLFENSPERGER; 13,500 mems.

**Gereformeerd Politiek Verbond (GPV)** (Reformed Political Asscn): POB 439, 3800 AK Amersfoort; tel. (33) 613546; fax (33) 610132; f. 1948; Chair. J. BLOKLAND; Parliamentary Leader GERT J. SCHUTTE; Sec. S. J. C. CNOSSEN; 13,000 mems.

**Groen Links** (The Green Left): POB 700, 1000 AS Amsterdam; tel. (20) 6202212; fax (20) 6251849; f. 1991 by merger of the Communistische Partij van Nederland, Evangelische Volkspartij, Pacifistisch Socialistische Partij and Politieke Partij Radikalen; Chair. A. HARREWIJN; Parliamentary Leader PAUL ROSENMULLER.

**De Groenen** (Green Party): POB 540, 3500 AM Utrecht; tel. (30) 304248; fax (30) 302380; f. 1983; Chair. KIRSTEN KUIPERS.

**Partij van de Arbeid (PvdA)** (Labour Party): Nicolaas Witsenkade 30, 1017 ZT Amsterdam; tel. (20) 5512155; fax (20) 5512330; f. 1946 by merger of progressive and liberal organizations; democratic socialist; Chair. FELIX ROTTENBERG; Party Leader WIM KOK; Parliamentary Leader JACQUES WALLAGE; c. 60,000 mems.

**Reformatorische Politieke Federatie (RPF)** (Evangelical Political Federation): POB 302, 8070 AH Nunspeet; tel. (3412) 56744; f. 1975; interdenominational, based on biblical precepts; Chair. A. VAN DEN BERG; Parliamentary Leader LEEN C. VAN DIJKE; Sec. W. VAN GROOTHEEST; 11,000 mems.

**Socialistiese Arbeiderspartij (SAP)** (Socialist Workers' Party): Sint Jacobstraat 10–20, 1012 NC Amsterdam; tel. (20) 6259272; fax (20) 6203774; f. 1974; Trotskyist.

**Socialistische Partij** (Socialist Party): Rotterdam; tel. (10) 4673222; Leader JAN MARIJNISSEN.

**Staatkundig Gereformeerde Partij (SGP)** (Political Reformed Party): Laan van Meerdervoort 165, 2517 AZ The Hague; tel. (70) 3456226; fax (70) 3655959; f. 1918; Calvinist, female membership banned in 1993; Chair. Rev. D. J. BUDDING; Parliamentary Leader BAS J. VAN DER VLIES; Sec. A. DE BOER; 24,000 mems.

**Union 55+:** POB 111, 72450 EC Holten; tel. (5483) 62422; party representing the elderly; Leader BERT LEERKES.

**Volkspartij voor Vrijheid en Democratie (VVD)** (People's Party for Freedom and Democracy—Netherlands Liberal Party): POB 30836, 2500 GV The Hague; tel. (70) 3613061; fax (70) 3608276; f. 1948; advocates free enterprise, individual freedom and responsibility, but its programme also supports social security and recommends the participation of workers in profits and management; Chair. WILLEM HOEKZEMA; Parliamentary Leader FRITS BOLKESTEIN; Sec. (vacant); 68,000 mems.

## Diplomatic Representation

### EMBASSIES IN THE NETHERLANDS

**Algeria:** Van Stolklaan 1–3, 2585 JS The Hague; tel. (70) 3522954; telex 30991; fax (70) 3540222; Ambassador: MOSTEFA BOUAKAZ.

**Argentina:** Javastraat 20, 2585 AN The Hague; tel. (70) 3654836; fax (70) 3924900; Ambassador: GUSTAVO E. FIGUEROA.

**Australia:** Carnegielaan 12, 2517 KH The Hague; tel. (70) 3108200; fax (70) 3107863; Ambassador: MICHAEL TATE.

**Austria:** van Alkemadelaan 342, 2597 AS The Hague; tel. (70) 3245470; telex 32236; Ambassador: Dr HEINRICH PFUSTERSCHMID-HARDTENSTEIN.

**Belgium:** Lange Vijverberg 12, 2513 AC The Hague; tel. (70) 3644910; telex 31035; fax (70) 3645579; Ambassador: JAN F. WILLEMS.

**Brazil:** Mauritskade 19, 2514 HD The Hague; tel. (70) 3469229; telex 32444; fax (70) 3561273; Ambassador: ALFONSO ARINOS DE MELLO-FRANCO.

**Bulgaria:** Duinrooseweg 9, 2597 KJ The Hague; tel. (70) 3503051; Ambassador: LJUBEN GOTSEV.

**Canada:** Sophialaan 7, 2514 JP The Hague; tel. (70) 3614111; telex 31270; fax (70) 3561111; Ambassador: MICHAEL R. BELL.

**Cape Verde:** Koninginnegracht 44, 2514 AD The Hague; tel. (70) 3469623; telex 34321; fax (70) 3467702; Ambassador: TERÊNCIO G. ALVES.

**Chile:** Mauritskade 51, 2514 HG The Hague; tel. (70) 3642748; telex 34199; fax (70) 3616227; Ambassador: JORGE ANTONIO TAPIA VALDÉS.
**China, People's Republic:** Adriaan Goekooplaan 7, 2517 JX The Hague; tel. (70) 3551515; telex 32018; fax (70) 3551651; Ambassador: WU JIANMIN.
**Colombia:** Groot Hertoginnelaan 14, 2517 EG The Hague; tel. (70) 3614545; telex 31357; fax (70) 3614636; Ambassador: FRANCISCO POSADA DE LA PEÑA.
**Costa Rica:** Statenlaan 28, 2582 GM The Hague; tel. (70) 3540780; fax (70) 3584754; Ambassador: J. FRANCISCO OREAMUNO.
**Cuba:** Prins Mauritslaan 6, 2582 LR The Hague; tel. (70) 3541417; telex 31318; fax (70) 3520159; Ambassador: MARTA GUZMÁN PASCUAL.
**Czech Republic:** Paleisstraat 4, 2514 JA The Hague; tel. (70) 3469712; fax (70) 3563349; Chargé d'affaires: JOZEF BRAUN.
**Denmark:** Koninginnegracht 30, 2514 AB The Hague; tel. (70) 3655830; telex 32075; fax (70) 3602150; Ambassador: TORBEN FROST.
**Egypt:** Borweg 1, 2597 LR The Hague; tel. (70) 3542000; telex 32529; fax (70) 3543304; Ambassador: MOHAMED ABD-EL-AZIZ SHARARA.
**El Salvador:** Catsheuvel 117, 2517 KA The Hague; tel. (70) 3520712; fax (70) 3584141; Ambassador: ROBERTO ARTURO CASTRILLO HIDALGO.
**Finland:** Groot Hertoginnelaan 16, 2517 EG The Hague; tel. (70) 3469754; fax (70) 3107174; Ambassador: ERKKI MÄENTAKANEN.
**France:** Smidsplein 1, 2514 BT The Hague; tel. (70) 3560606; telex 31465; Ambassador: JEAN-RENÉ BERNARD.
**Germany:** Groot Hertoginnelaan 18–20, 2517 EG The Hague; tel. (70) 3420600; telex 31012; fax (70) 3651957; Ambassador: Dr KLAUS JÜRGEN CITRON.
**Greece:** Koninginnegracht 37, 2514 AD The Hague; tel. (70) 3638700; telex 34112; fax (70) 3563040; Ambassador: PETROS D. ANGHELAKIS.
**Holy See:** Carnegielaan 5 (Apostolic Nunciature), 2517 KH The Hague; tel. (70) 3503363; fax (70) 3521461; Apostolic Nuncio: Most Rev. HENRI LEMAÎTRE, Titular Archbishop of Tongeren (Tongres).
**Honduras:** J. van Oldenbarneveltlaan 85, 2582 NK The Hague; tel. (70) 3523728; fax (70) 3504183; Chargé d'affaires a.i.: A. DE SAAVEDRA Y MUGUELAR.
**Hungary:** Hogeweg 14, 2585 JD The Hague; tel. (70) 3500404; telex 32147; fax (70) 3521749; Ambassador: Dr ISTVÁN CSEJTEI.
**India:** Buitenrustweg 2, 2517 KD The Hague; tel. (70) 3469771; telex 33543; fax (70) 3617072; Ambassador: I. P. KHOSLA.
**Indonesia:** Tobias Asserlaan 8, 2517 KC The Hague; tel. (70) 3108100; telex 32356; fax (70) 3643331; Ambassador: BINTORO TJOKROAMIDJOJO.
**Iran:** Duinweg 24, 2587 AD The Hague; tel. (70) 3548483; telex 33016; fax (70) 3503224; Ambassador: BEHZAD MAZAHERI.
**Iraq:** Johan de Wittlaan 16, 2517 JR The Hague; tel. (70) 3469683; telex 34353; Ambassador: (vacant).
**Ireland:** Dr Kuyperstraat 9, 2514 BA The Hague; tel. (70) 3630993; telex 31352; fax (70) 3617604; Ambassador: DENIS O'LEARY.
**Israel:** Buitenhof 47, 2513 AH The Hague; tel. (70) 3760500; fax (70) 3760555; Ambassador: M. N. BAVLY.
**Italy:** Alexanderstraat 12, 2514 JL The Hague; tel. (70) 3469249; telex 31530; fax (70) 3614932; Ambassador: RANIERI TALLARIGO.
**Japan:** Tobias Asserlaan 2, 2517 KC The Hague; tel. (70) 3469544; telex 32105; fax (70) 3106341; Ambassador: TATSUO ARIMA.
**Kenya:** Nieuwe Parklaan 21, 2597 LA The Hague; tel. (70) 3504215; telex 33354; fax (70) 3553594; Ambassador: S. O. MAGETO.
**Korea, Republic:** The Hague; tel. (70) 3520621; telex 33291; fax (70) 3523426; Ambassador: IN JO-LIM.
**Kuwait:** Carnegielaan 9, 2517 KH The Hague; tel. (70) 3603813; fax (70) 3924588; Ambassador: ALI H. AL-SAMMAK.
**Lebanon:** Frederikstraat 2, 2514 LK The Hague; tel. (70) 3658906; telex 32462; fax (70) 3620779; Chargé d'affaires: GHARAMY AYOUB.
**Luxembourg:** Nassaulaan 8, 2514 JS The Hague; tel. (70) 3647589; telex 33174; fax (70) 3563303; Ambassador: HUBERT WURTH.
**Malaysia:** Rustenburgweg 2, 2517 KE The Hague; tel. (70) 3506506; telex 33024; fax (70) 3506536; Ambassador: SALLEHUDDIN ABDULLAH.
**Mexico:** Nassauplein 17, 2585 EB The Hague; tel. (70) 3602900; telex 33235; fax (70) 3560543; Ambassador: EZEQUIEL PADILLA.
**Morocco:** Oranjestraat 9, 2514 JB The Hague; tel. (70) 3469617; telex 34163; fax (70) 3614503; Ambassador: MEHDI ALAOUI.
**New Zealand:** Carnegielaan 10, 2517 KH The Hague; tel. (70) 3469324; telex 31557; fax (70) 3632983; Ambassador: GRAEME AMMUNDSEN.
**Nicaragua:** Zoutmannstraat 53E, 2518 GM The Hague; tel. (70) 3630967; fax (70) 3479049; Ambassador: CARLOS J. ARGÜELLO.
**Nigeria:** Wagenaarweg 5, 2597 LL The Hague; tel. (70) 3501703; telex 31785; Ambassador: IBRAHIM M. BINDAWA.
**Norway:** Prinsessegracht 6A, 2514 AN The Hague; tel. (70) 3451900; telex 32265; fax (70) 3659630; Ambassador: ARNE LANGELAND.
**Oman:** Koninginnegracht 27, 2514 AB The Hague; tel. (70) 3615800; telex 30965; fax (70) 3605364; Ambassador: ABDULAZIZ BIN ABDULLAH BIN ZAHOR AL-HINAI.
**Pakistan:** Amaliastraat 8, 2514 JC The Hague; tel. (70) 3648948; telex 33696; fax (70) 3106047; Ambassador: JAVID HUSAIN.
**Peru:** van Alkemadelaan 189, 2597 AE The Hague; tel. (70) 3280506; telex 33568; fax (70) 3282091; Ambassador: JORGE COLUNGE VILLACORTA.
**Philippines:** Laan Copes van Cattenburch 125, 2585 EZ The Hague; tel. (70) 3604820; telex 33103; Ambassador: EDILBERTO CANOS DE JESUS.
**Poland:** Alexanderstraat 25, 2514 JM The Hague; tel. (70) 3602806; telex 31286; fax (70) 3602810; Ambassador: Dr FRANCISZEK MORAWSKI.
**Portugal:** Bazarstraat 21, 2518 AG The Hague; tel. (70) 3630217; telex 33204; fax (70) 3615589; Ambassador: ANTÓNIO CASCAIS.
**Romania:** Catsheuvel 55, 2517 KA The Hague; tel. (70) 3543796; telex 32189; fax (70) 3541587; Ambassador: MARIN BUHOARA.
**Russia:** Andries Bickerweg 2, 2517 JP The Hague; tel. (70) 3451300; telex 34585; fax (70) 3617960; Ambassador: ALEKSANDR DAVIDOVICH CHIKVAIDZE.
**Saudi Arabia:** Alexanderstraat 19, 2514 JM The Hague; tel. (70) 3614391; Ambassador: ABDELMOHSEN MOHAMMED AL-SUDEARI.
**Slovakia:** Parkweg 1, 2585 JG The Hague; tel. (70) 3557566; fax (70) 3514769; Ambassador: Dr STEFAN PAULÍNY.
**South Africa:** Wassenaarseweg 40, 2596 CJ The Hague; tel. (70) 3924501; telex 33610; fax (70) 3460669; Ambassador: Dr ZACHARIAS JOHANNES DE BEER.
**Spain:** Lange Voorhout 50, 2514 EG The Hague; tel. (70) 3643814; telex 32373; fax (70) 3617959; Ambassador: ANTONIO JOSÉ FOURNIER.
**Sudan:** Laan Copes van Cattenburch 81, 2585 EW The Hague; tel. (70) 3605300; telex 32213; fax (70) 3617975; Ambassador: NURI K. SIDDIG.
**Suriname:** Alexander Gogelweg 2, 2517 JH The Hague; tel. (70) 3650844; telex 32220; fax (70) 3617445; Ambassador: EVERT AZIMULLAH.
**Sweden:** Neuhuyskade 40, POB 90648, 2509 LP The Hague; tel. (70) 3245424; telex 31291; fax (70) 3247911; Ambassador: JAN AF SILLÉN.
**Switzerland:** Lange Voorhout 42, 2514 EE The Hague; tel. (70) 3642831; telex 32705; fax (70) 3561238; Ambassador: ALFRED RÜEGG.
**Tanzania:** Prinsessegracht 32, 2514 AP The Hague; tel. (70) 3653800; telex 32065; fax (70) 3106686; Ambassador: ASTERIUS MAGNUS IDDI.
**Thailand:** Buitenrustweg 1, 2517 KD The Hague; tel. (70) 3459703; telex 34207; Ambassador: ABINANT NA RANONG.
**Tunisia:** Gentsestraat 98, 2587 HX The Hague; tel. (70) 3512251; telex 31271; fax (70) 3514323; Ambassador: ANOUAR BERRAÏES.
**Turkey:** Jan Evertstraat 15, 2514 BS The Hague; tel. (70) 3604912; telex 32623; fax (70) 3617969; Ambassador: (vacant).
**United Kingdom:** Lange Voorhout 10, 2514 ED The Hague; tel. (70) 4270427; fax (70) 4270345; Ambassador: Sir DAVID MIERS.
**USA:** Lange Voorhout 102, 2514 EJ The Hague; tel. (70) 3624911; fax (70) 3614688; Ambassador: K. TERRY DORNBUSH, Jr.
**Uruguay:** Nassaulaan 1, 2514 JS The Hague; tel. (70) 3609815; telex 32139; fax (70) 3562826; Ambassador: JUAN ANDRÉS PACHECO.
**Venezuela:** Nassaulaan 2, 2514 JS The Hague; tel. (70) 3523851; telex 34058; fax (70) 3656954; Ambassador: FRANCISCO PAPARONI.
**Yemen:** Surinamestraat 9, 2585 GG The Hague; tel. (70) 3653936; telex 33290; fax (70) 3563312; Ambassador: (vacant).
**Yugoslavia:** Groot Hertoginnelaan 30, 2517 EG The Hague; tel. (70) 3632397; telex 33199; fax (70) 3602421; Ambassador: Prof. Dr BORUT BOHTE.
**Zaire:** Violenweg 2, 2597 KL The Hague; tel. (70) 3547904; telex 32246; fax (70) 3541373; Ambassador: KIMBULU MOYANSO WA LOKWA.

# Judicial System

Justices and judges must have graduated in law at a Dutch university, and are nominated for life by the Crown. The justices of the

# THE NETHERLANDS

Supreme Court are nominated from a list of three compiled by the Second Chamber of the States-General.

### SUPREME COURT

**De Hoge Raad der Nederlanden:** POB 20303, 2500 EH The Hague; tel. (70) 3611311; fax (70) 3617484; f. 1838. For appeals in cassation against decisions of courts of lower jurisdiction. As a court of first instance, the Supreme Court tries offences committed in their official capacity by members of the States-General and Ministers. Dealing with appeals in cassation a court is composed of three or five justices (Raadsheren).

**President of the Supreme Court:** S. ROYER.
**Procurator-General:** TH. B. TEN KATE.
**Secretary of the Court:** W. J. C. M. VAN NISPEN TOT SEVENAER.

### COURTS OF APPEAL

**Gerechtshoven:** Five courts: Amsterdam, Arnhem, 's-Hertogenbosch, Leeuwarden, The Hague. A court is composed of three judges (Raadsheren); appeal is from decisions of the District Courts of Justice. Fiscal Divisions (Belastingkamers) of the Courts of Appeal deal with appeals against decisions relating to the enforcement of the fiscal laws (administrative jurisdiction). The court of Arnhem has a Tenancy Division (Pachtkamer) composed of three judges and two assessors (a tenant and a landlord) and a Penitentiary Division (Penitentiaire Kamer) composed of three judges and two experts. The Tenancy Division hears appeals from decisions of all Canton Tenancy Divisions. The Penitentiary Division hears appeals against refusals of release on license, which is usually granted after two-thirds of a prison sentence longer than one year, unless there are special objections from the Minister of Justice. A Companies Division (Ondernemingskamer) is attached to the court at Amsterdam, consisting of three judges and two experts as assessors.

### DISTRICT COURTS OF JUSTICE

**Arrondissementsrechtbanken:** There are 19 courts for important civil and penal cases and for appeals from decisions of the Canton Judges. A court is composed of three judges (Rechter); no jury; summary jurisdiction in civil cases by the President of the Court; simple penal cases, including economic offences, generally by a single judge (Politierechter). Offences committed by juveniles are (with certain exceptions) tried by a specialized judge (Kinderrechter), who is also competent to take certain legal steps when the upbringing of a juvenile is endangered.

### CANTON COURTS

**Kantongerechten:** There are 62 courts for civil and penal cases of minor importance. A court consists of a single judge, the Canton Judge (Kantonrechter). Each Canton Court has a Tenancy Division (Pachtkamer), presided over by the Canton Judge who is assisted by two assessors (a landlord and a tenant).

### ADMINISTRATIVE JURISDICTION

**Ambtenarengerechten** (Civil Service Courts): 10 courts for civil service arbitration. The Civil Service Court at The Hague also acts as Military Service Court for military service arbitration, and hears appeals against decisions on pensions for ex-civil and military servants.

**Raden van Beroep** (Appeal Councils): 10 courts to hear appeals against decisions enforcing social insurance legislation.

**Centrale Raad van Beroep** (Central Appeal Council): Utrecht; tries in supreme instance appeals against decisions of the Appeal Councils and the Civil Service Courts.

**College van Beroep voor het Bedrijfsleven** (Board of Appeal for Trade Industry): Hears in first and last instances appeals against decisions enforcing social-economic legislation.

**Afdeling Rechtspraak van de Raad van State** (Judicial Section of the Council of State): Hears appeals from private persons against administrative decisions.

# Religion

### CHRISTIANITY

About 36% of the population are Roman Catholics and about 26% are Protestants.

**Raad van Kerken in Nederland** (Council of Churches in the Netherlands): Kon. Wilhelminalaan 5, 3818 Amersfoort; tel. (33) 633844; f. 1968; 10 mem. churches; Pres. Prof. Dr R. G. W. HUYSMANS; Gen. Sec. Rev. E. VAN STRATEN.

### The Roman Catholic Church

The Netherlands comprises one archdiocese and six dioceses. At 31 December 1993 there were an estimated 5,512,195 adherents in the country.

**Bishops' Conference:** Nederlandse Bisschoppenconferentie, Biltstraat 121, POB 13049, 3507 LA Utrecht; tel. (30) 334244; fax (30) 332103; f. 1980; Pres. Cardinal Dr ADRIANUS J. SIMONIS, Archbishop of Utrecht.

**Archbishop of Utrecht:** Cardinal Dr ADRIANUS J. SIMONIS, Aartsbisdom, Maliebaan 40, POB 14019, 3508 SB Utrecht; tel. (30) 316956; fax (30) 311962.

### Protestant Churches

**Christelijke Gereformeerde Kerken in Nederland** (Christian Reformed Churches in the Netherlands): Vijftien Morgen 31, POB 334, 3900 AH Veenendaal; tel. (8385) 29176; f. 1834; Sec. of Foreign Relations Cttee Rev. P. DEN BUTTER; about 75,000 mems; 180 churches.

**Churches of Christ, Scientist:** c/o MARIUS W. VERHULST, De Bogerd 3, 4132 GJ Vianen ZH, tel. (3473) 71836; fax (3473) 74735; churches at Amsterdam, Haarlem and The Hague.

**Deutsche Evangelische Gemeinde** (German Evangelical Church): Bleijenburg 3B, 2511 VC, The Hague; tel. (70) 3465727; Pastor D. OSTHUS.

**Doopsgezinde Broederschap (Gemeenten)** (Mennonite Brotherhood): Algemene Doopsgezinde Sociëteit, Singel 454, 1017 AN Amsterdam; tel. (20) 6230914; fax (20) 6278919; f. 1811; Pres. P. A. BEUN; Sec.-Gen. B. STENVERS-DE BOER; 16,500 mems; 136 parishes.

**Evangelische Broedergemeente (Hernhutters):** Rotterdam; tel. (10) 4219188; f. 1746; Pastor J. W. TL. RAPPARLIÉ; 3,000 mems in Holland; six parishes.

**Evangelisch-Lutherse Kerk** (Evangelical Lutheran Church): Jan de Bakkerstraat 13/15, 3441 ED Woerden; tel. (3480) 12183; fax (3480) 12183; Pres. Rev. K. VAN DER HORST; Sec. Rev. R. E. VAN DEN BERG; 28,600 mems; 61 parishes.

**De Gereformeerde Kerken in Nederland** (The Reformed Churches in the Netherlands): Burg de Beaufortweg 18, POB 202, 3830 AE Leusden; tel. (33) 960360; fax (33) 948707; f. 1892; vigorously Calvinistic; has a General Synod which is elected every two years by the 13 Particular (district) Synods; Sec. for Foreign Affairs Dr L. J. KOFFEMAN; 852 churches, 1,260 officiating ministers, 763,000 mems.

**Hersteld Apostolische Zendingkerk** (Restored Apostolic Missionary Church): Hogerbeetstraat 32, 2242 TR Wassenaar; tel. (1751) 13995; f. 1863; Apostle for the Netherlands H. F. RIJNDERS; Sec. J. L. M. STRAETEMANS; 500 mems; 10 parishes.

**Nederlandse Hervormde Kerk** (Netherlands Reformed Church): Overgoo 11, POB 405, 2260 AK Leidschendam; tel. (70) 3131131; fax (70) 3131202; was from 16th to 18th century the State Church. Its 9 church provinces are subdivided into 74 districts, 144 fraternals and 1,400 parishes, under the jurisdiction of the General Synod; Sec.-Gen. Rev. Dr K. BLEI; 2.5m. mems.

**Remonstrantse Broederschap** (Remonstrant Brotherhood): Nieuwe Gracht 27, 3512 LC Utrecht; tel. (30) 316970; fax (30) 311055; f. 1619; Pres. W. E. R. VAN HERWIJNA; Gen. Sec. M. A. BOSMAN-HUIZINGA; 10,000 mems; 46 parishes.

**Unie van Baptistengemeenten in Nederland** (Union of Baptist Churches in The Netherlands): Biltseweg 10, 3735 MC Bosch en Duin; tel. (30) 284457; fax (30) 251798; f. 1881; Pres. C. EIJER; Treasurer A. VAN DEN HOEF; 12,300 mems.

### Other Christian Churches

**Anglikaans Kerkgenootschap** (Anglican Church): Riouwstraat 2, 2585 HA The Hague; tel. (70) 3555359; f. 1698; British Chaplain Rev. JOHN WALLIS.

**Katholiek Apostolische Gemeenten** (Catholic Apostolic Church): 1 De Riemerstraat 3, 2513 CT The Hague; tel. (70) 3555018; f. 1867; seven parishes in the Netherlands and three in Belgium.

**Oud-katholieke Kerk van Nederland** (Old Catholic Church): Kon. Wilhelminalaan 3, 3818 HN Amersfoort; tel. (33) 630442; fax (33) 619348; f. 1723 in the Netherlands with Jansenist influence; a group of Catholics who refuse to accept papal infallibility and other new dogmas of the Roman Catholic Church, and have therefore set up a separate ecclesiastical organization based upon the Episcopal model; full communion with the Anglican Churches since 1931; Archbishop of Utrecht Mgr A. J. GLAZEMAKER (18 parishes); Bishop of Haarlem Mgr Dr J. L. WIRIX-SPEETJENS (12 parishes); Bishop of Deventer (vacant); 10,000 mems; also churches in Europe and USA.

**Vrij-Katholieke Kerk** (Liberal Catholic Church): Centraal Bureau, Apollolaan 456, 2324 CG Leiden; tel. (71) 763048; f. 1916; Bishop Rt Rev. J. PH. DRAAISMA, Goudvinklaan 92, 3722 VE Bilthoven; 12 congregations; 40 priests; 1,400 mems.

THE NETHERLANDS                                                                                                                                          *Directory*

### JUDAISM

**Portugees-Israëlietisch Kerkgenootschap** (Portuguese-Israelite Federation): mr Visserplein 3, 1011 RD Amsterdam; tel. (20) 6245351; fax (20) 6254680; Pres. Dr J. Z. BARUCH; Hon. Sec. D. L. RODRIGUES-LOPES.

### BAHÁ'Í FAITH

**National Spiritual Assembly:** Riouwstraat 27, 2585 GR The Hague; tel. (70) 3554017; fax (70) 3506161; mems resident in 174 locations.

## The Press

Newspapers first appeared in Amsterdam in the early seventeenth century and were soon established in other cities. The Constitution guarantees the freedom of the press.

There are eight dailies which circulate throughout the country and about 50 provincial newspapers. Some papers appear in several different regional versions. A distinguishing feature of the Dutch press is that it is aimed at the family and most of the papers are read in the home. Nearly all of the total circulation is sold by subscription. There is practically no 'sensationalist' press.

### PRINCIPAL DAILIES

#### Alkmaar
**Noordhollands Dagblad:** POB 2, 1800 AA Alkmaar; tel. (72) 196196; fax (72) 126183; f. 1799; morning; Editor D. P. J. VAN REEUWYK; circ. 154,300.

#### Alphen aan den Rijn
**Rijn en Gouwe:** POB 1, 2400 AA Alphen a/d Rijn; tel. (1720) 87444; fax (1720) 87408; f. 1876; morning; Editor L. M. HESKES; circ. 36,900.

#### Amersfoort
**Amersfoortse Courant:** POB 43, 3800 AA Amersfoort; tel. (33) 647911; fax (33) 647334; f. 1887; evening; Editor H. GOESSENS; circ. 42,000.

#### Amsterdam
**De Courant Nieuws van de Dag** (The Courier Daily News): POB 376, 1000 EB Amsterdam; tel. (20) 5859111; fax (20) 5854130; f. 1923; evening; Editor P. H. H. WYNANS; circ. 51,100.
**Het Financieele Dagblad** (Financial Daily): POB 216, 1000 AE Amsterdam; tel. (20) 5574511; telex 18326; fax (20) 5574400; f. 1796; morning; Editor CHRISTIAAN BERENDSEN; circ. 41,000.
**Het Parool:** POB 433, 1000 AK Amsterdam; tel. (20) 5629333; fax (20) 6681608; f. 1940; evening; Editor S. VAN DER ZEE; circ. 102,500.
**De Telegraaf:** POB 376, 1000 EB Amsterdam; tel. (20) 5859111; telex 14436; fax (20) 5852113; f. 1893; morning; Editors E. BOS, J. OLDE KALTER; circ. 775,000.
**Trouw:** POB 859, 1000 AW Amsterdam; tel. (20) 5629444; telex 13006; fax (20) 6681608; f. 1943; morning; Editor J. GREVEN; circ. 121,000.
**De Volkskrant** (The People's Journal): POB 1002, 1000 BA Amsterdam; tel. (20) 5629222; fax (20) 6681608; f. 1919; morning; Editor P. I. BROERTJES; circ. 358,200.

#### Apeldoorn
**Apeldoornse Courant:** POB 99, 7300 AB Apeldoorn; tel. (55) 388388; fax (55) 388333; f. 1903; evening; Chief Editor D. W. H. VAN DER MOER; circ. 40,300.
**Arnhemse Courant:** POB 99, 7300 AB Apeldoorn; tel. (55) 388388; fax (55) 388333; f. 1814; evening; Editor G. DIELESSEN; circ. 31,400.
**Deventer Dagblad:** POB 99, 7300 AB Apeldoorn; tel. (55) 388388; fax (55) 388333; f. 1869; Editor L. ENTHOVEN; circ. 52,400.
**Reformatorisch Dagblad:** POB 613, 7300 AR Apeldoorn; tel. (55) 495222; telex 36445; fax (55) 417450; f. 1971; evening; Editor C. S. L. JANSE; circ. 56,000.

#### Assen
**Drentse Courant:** POB 36, 9400 AA Assen; tel. (5920) 29500; f. 1823; morning; Editor G. VOGELAAR.

#### Barneveld
**Barneveldse Krant:** POB 67, 3770 AB Barneveld; tel. (3420) 94911; fax (3420) 13141; f. 1871; evening; Editor J. VAN GINKEL; circ. 10,800.
**Nederlands Dagblad/Gereformeerd Gezinsblad:** POB 111, 3770 AC Barneveld; tel. (3420) 10720; fax (3420) 92619; f. 1944; morning; Editors J. P. DE VRIES, P. A. BERGWERFF; circ. 28,500.

#### Breda
**De Stem** (The Voice): POB 3229, 4800 MB Breda; tel. (76) 236911; fax (76) 236200; f. 1860; morning; Dir Editor H. COUMANS; circ. 110,100.

#### Dordrecht
**De Dordtenaar:** POB 54, 3300 AB Dordrecht; tel. (78) 324711; fax (78) 324709; f. 1946; morning; Editor H. KERSTIENS; circ. 38,700.

#### Enschede
**Dagblad Tubantia:** POB 28, 7500 AA Enschede; tel. (53) 842842; fax (53) 842230; f. 1872; evening; Editor W. P. TIMMERS; circ. 152,600 (incl. *Twentsche Courant* below).
**Twentsche Courant:** POB 28, 7500 AA Enschede; tel. (53) 842842; fax (53) 842230; f. 1844; circ. see *Dagblad Tubantia* above.

#### Groningen
**Nieuwsblad van het Noorden:** POB 60, 9700 MC Groningen; tel. (50) 844844; fax (50) 844109; f. 1888; evening; Editor A. A. M. SCHUURMANS.

#### Haarlem
**Haarlems Dagblad:** POB 507, 2003 PA Haarlem; tel. (23) 150150; fax (23) 310296; f. 1656; evening; Editor F. NYPELS; circ. 61,300.
**Leidsch Dagblad:** POB 507, 2003 PA Haarlem; tel. (23) 150150; fax (23) 310296; f. 1860; evening; Editor J. G. C. MAJOOR; circ. 47,000.

#### The Hague
**Haagsche Courant:** POB 16050, 2500 AA The Hague; tel. (70) 3190911; fax (70) 3906447; f. 1883; evening; Editor J. SCHINKELSHOEK; circ. 148,000.
**Nederlandse Staatscourant:** POB 20014, 2500 EA The Hague; tel. (70) 3789911; fax (70) 3475575; f. 1813; morning; Editor A. M. DEN HAAN; circ. 14,600.

#### Heerlen
**Limburgs Dagblad:** POB 3100, 6401 DP Heerlen; tel. (45) 739911; fax (45) 710698; f. 1918; morning; Editor R. A. M. BROWN; circ. 79,800.

#### 's-Hertogenbosch
**Eindhovens Dagblad:** POB 235, 5201 HB 's-Hertogenbosch; tel. (73) 157157; fax (73) 132229; circ. see *Brabants Dagblad* below.
**Brabants Dagblad:** POB 235, 5201 HB 's-Hertogenbosch; tel. (73) 157157; fax (73) 132229; f. 1771; morning; Editor T. VAN DER MEULEN; circ. 296,600 (incl. *Eindhovens Dagblad* above).

#### Hilversum
**De Gooi- en Eemlander:** POB 15, 1200 AA Hilversum; tel. (35) 257911; fax (35) 257201; f. 1871; evening; Editor H. VAN ZENDEREN; circ. 52,600.

#### Houten
**Utrechts Nieuwsblad:** POB 500, 3990 DM Houten; tel. (3403) 99911; fax (3403) 99226; f. 1893; evening; Chief Editor Drs G. SELLES; circ. 148,000.

#### Leeuwarden
**Friesch Dagblad:** POB 412, 8901 BE Leeuwarden; tel. (58) 987654; fax (58) 987540; f. 1903; evening; Editor K. JANSMA; circ. 22,200.
**Leeuwarder Courant:** POB 394, 8901 BD Leeuwarden; tel. (58) 845845; fax (58) 845209; f. 1752; evening; Editors R. MULDER, H. SPEERSTRA; circ. 111,400.

#### Maastricht
**De Limburger:** POB 1056, 6201 MK Maastricht; tel. (43) 821234; fax (43) 670320; f. 1845; morning; Editor G. KESSELS; circ. 144,800.

#### Nijmegen
**De Gelderlander:** POB 36, 6500 DA Nijmegen; tel. (80) 650611; fax (80) 650209; f. 1848; morning; Editor H. J. KUYT; circ. 175,000.

#### Roosendaal
**Brabants Nieuwsblad:** POB 1052, 4700 BB Roosendaal; tel. (1650) 35970; fax (1650) 58905; f. 1863; morning; Editor G. BIELDERMAN; circ. 54,100.

#### Rotterdam
**Algemeen Dagblad:** POB 8983, 3009 TC Rotterdam; tel. (10) 4066677; fax (10) 4066969; f. 1946; morning; Editor P. R. VAN DIJK; circ. 413,900.
**NRC Handelsblad:** POB 8987, 3009 TH Rotterdam; tel. (10) 4066111; fax (10) 4066967; f. 1970; evening; Editor B. KNAPEN; circ. 268,300.

# THE NETHERLANDS

**Rotterdams Dagblad:** POB 1162, 3000 BD Rotterdam; tel. (10) 4004320; fax (10) 4004323; f. 1991; evening; Editors J. Prins, L. P. Pronk; circ. 118,300.

### Venlo

**Dagblad voor Noord-Limburg:** POB 65, 5900 AB Venlo; tel. (77) 551234; fax (77) 517916; f. 1863; morning; Editor A. Brattinga; circ. 53,900.

### Vlissingen

**Provinciale Zeeuwse Courant:** POB 18, 4380 AA Vlissingen; tel. (1184) 84000; fax (1184) 70102; f. 1758; morning; Editors C. van der Maas, A. Oosthoek; circ. 62,400.

### Zwolle

**Zwolse Courant:** POB 67, 8000 AB Zwolle; tel. (38) 275275; fax (38) 213648; f. 1790; evening; Editor J. Bartelds; circ. 70,400.

## SELECTED WEEKLIES

**Adformatie;** POB 75462, 1070 AL Amsterdam; tel. (20) 5733644; fax (20) 6793581; advertising, marketing; circ. 44,210.

**Aktueel:** POB 94210, 1090 GE Amsterdam; tel. (20) 5979600; fax (20) 5979682.

**AVRO bode:** POB 5000, 1200 EW Hilversum; tel. (35) 717911; telex 43012; fax (35) 717443; publ. by Algemene Omroepvereniging; radio and TV guide; circ. 920,710.

**De Boerderij:** POB 4, 7000 BA Doetinchem; tel. (8340) 49911; telex 45481; fax (8340) 43839; f. 1915; farming; Dir G. Noorman; circ. 89,050.

**Donald Duck:** Haarlem-Schalkwijk; tel. (23) 304304; telex 41371; fax (23) 352554; children's interest; Dir J. P. Sträter; circ. 342,240.

**Elsevier:** POB 152, 1000 AD Amsterdam; tel. (20) 5674911; telex 15301; fax (20) 5674398; f. 1945; current affairs; Chief Editor Drs A. S. Spoor; circ. 113,520.

**HP/De Tijd** (The Times): POB 348, 1000 AH Amsterdam; tel. (20) 5734811; telex 16597; fax (20) 5734406; f. 1845 as daily; changed to weekly in 1974; Christian progressive; current affairs; Dir A. Visser; circ. 37,580.

**Libelle:** POB 1, 2000 MA Haarlem-Schalkwijk; tel. (23) 304304; telex 41371; fax (23) 350911; f. 1934; women's interest; Editor-in-Chief Els Loesberg; circ. 757,900.

**Margriet:** POB 497, 1000 AL Amsterdam; tel. (20) 4306300; fax (20) 4300666; f. 1939; women's interest; Dir A. Visser; circ. 587,390.

**Mikro-Gids:** POB 10050, 1201 DB Hilversum; tel. (35) 713911; fax (35) 219058; publ. by Katholieke Radio Omroep; radio and TV guide; Dir Dr C. Zwaan; circ. 460,000.

**NCRV-Gids:** POB 121, 1200 JE Hilversum; tel. (35) 719911; telex 43249; fax (35) 719661; f. 1924; publ. by Nederlandse Christelijke Radio Vereniging; radio and TV guide; Dir J. Wytema; circ. 473,730.

**Nederlands Tijdschrift voor Geneeskunde** (Dutch Medical Journal): POB 75971, 1070 AZ Amsterdam; tel. (20) 6620150; fax (20) 6735481; f. 1856; Pres. Prof. Dr A. J. Dunning; Vice-Pres. Prof. Dr H. G. M. Rooijmans; Secs Dr A. J. P. M. Overbeke, Dr J. H. M. Lockefeer; circ. 32,000.

**Nieuwe Revu:** POB 497, 1000 AL Amsterdam; tel. (20) 5734509; telex 16597; fax (20) 5734534; f. 1968; general interest; Editors-in-Chief J. Mentens, H. Verstraaten; circ. 164,170.

**Panorama:** POB 1, 2000 MA Haarlem-Schalkwijk; tel. (23) 304304; telex 41371; fax (23) 350382; f. 1913; general interest; Dir R. van Vuure; circ. 198,000.

**Popfoto:** Ceylonpoort 5-25, 2037 AA Haarlem-Schalkwijk; tel. (23) 304304; fax (23) 304704; teenage interest; circ. 120,000.

**Privé:** POB 127, 1000 AC Amsterdam; tel. (20) 5853340; telex 10449; fax (20) 5854111; f. 1977; women's interest; Editors W. P. J. Smitt, H. van der Meyden; circ. 472,030.

**Story:** POB 1, 2000 MA Haarlem-Schalkwijk; tel. (23) 304304; telex 41371; fax (23) 367904; f. 1974; general interest; circ. 419,130.

**Studio:** POB 10050, 1201 DB Hilversum; tel. (35) 714911; fax (35) 714655; publ. by Katholieke Radio Omroep; radio and TV guide; Dir C. Zwaan; circ. 280,000.

**TeleVizier:** POB 5000, 1200 EW Hilversum; tel. (35) 717911; telex 43012; fax (35) 717443; publ. by Algemene Omroepvereniging; radio and TV guide; circ. 308,170.

**Tina:** Ceylonpoort 5-25, 2037 AA Haarlem-Schalkwijk; tel. (23) 304304; telex 41371; fax (23) 304704; teenage interest; circ. 117,840.

**TrosKompas:** Radarweg 50, 1042 AP Amsterdam; tel. (20) 5853238; telex 10449; fax (20) 5854111; publ. by Televisie Radio Omroep Stichting; radio and TV guide; Editor Wim Koesen; circ. 717,690.

**Vara TV Magazine:** POB 175, 1200 AD Hilversum; tel. (35) 711911; fax (35) 711429; radio and TV guide; Editor Hans Wilbrink; circ. 545,000.

**Veronica:** POB 22418, 1202 CJ Hilversum; tel. (35) 723723; telex 73012; fax (35) 214495; f. 1971; radio and TV guide; Editor R. Briel; circ. 1,250,000.

**Viva:** POB 497, 1000 AL Amsterdam; tel. (20) 5734811; telex 16597; fax (20) 5734406; women's interest; Dir A. Visser; circ. 124,300.

**Voetbal International:** POB 1050, 1000 BB Amsterdam; tel. (20) 5518711; telex 16307; fax (20) 6229141; football; Gen. Man. T. G. G. Bouwman; circ. 199,190.

**VPRO-Gids:** POB 11, 1200 JC Hilversum; tel. (35) 712911; fax (35) 712285; radio and TV guide; circ. 220,000.

**Vrij Nederland:** POB 1254, 1000 BG Amsterdam; tel. (20) 5518711; telex 16307; fax (20) 6229141; f. 1940; current affairs; Editors R. Ferdinandusse, J. van Tijn; circ. 128,820.

**Yes:** Ceylonpoort 5-25, 2037 AA Haarlem, POB 1, 2000 MA Haarlem; tel. (23) 304304; fax (23) 350382; circ. 174,250.

## SELECTED PERIODICALS
### Art, History and Literature

**Antiek:** POB 274, 7240 AG Lochem; tel. (5730) 52276; fax (5730) 54906; f. 1965; 10 a year; arts and antiques; Dir J. Bottema.

**De Architect:** POB 34, 2501 AG The Hague; tel. (70) 3569100; fax (70) 3614264; Dir A. H. Th. Muller; circ. 6,580.

**Kunstbeeld:** POB 246, 3990 GA Houten; tel. (3403) 95711; telex 39682; fax (3403) 50903; monthly; Dir H. J. Demoet; circ. 12,500.

**Spiegel Historiael:** Linnaeusparkweg 156, 1098 EM Amsterdam; tel. (20) 6652759; fax (20) 6657831; f. 1966; monthly; history and archaeology; circ. 9,500.

**Tableau Fine Arts Magazine:** Oranje Nassaulaan 17, 1075 AH Amsterdam; tel. (20) 6648681; fax (20) 6641872; every 2 months; Gen. Editor Bob van den Burg; circ. 20,000.

**Tijdschrift voor Geschiedenis** (Historical Review): POB 716, 9700 AS Groningen; f. 1886; quarterly; Editor Prof. K. van Berkel.

### Economic and Business

**Bedrijfsdocumentaire:** Hettenheuvelweg 41–43, POB 1198, 1000 BD Amsterdam; tel. (20) 916666; fax (20) 960396; 10 a year; management; publ. by Koggeschip Vakbladen BV; circ. 110,000.

**Computable:** POB 9194, 1006 CC Amsterdam; tel. (20) 5102911; telex 14407; fax (20) 6175137; Dir W. de Wit; circ. 82,580.

**Elektronica/Databus:** POB 23, 7400 GA Deventer; tel. (5700) 48699; fax (5700) 10918; f. 1953; 21 a year; computing and electronics; Editor Th. van Gelder; circ. 12,000.

**Export Channel (Import/Export):** Stolbergstraat 14, 2012 EP Haarlem; tel. (23) 319022; fax (23) 317974; f. 1945; monthly; 2 editions; export promotion of consumer and industrial goods; circ. 50,000 (consumer edition), 70,000 (technical edition).

**Informatie Management:** POB 34, 2501 AG The Hague; tel. (70) 3045700; fax (70) 3045800; monthly; computing, data-processing, management; circ. 5,000.

**Intermediair:** POB 9194, 1006 CC Amsterdam; tel. (20) 5102911; telex 14407; fax (20) 6175137; monthly; management; Dir G. J. Laurman; circ. 213,990.

**Management Team:** POB 397, 3900 AJ Veenendaal; tel. (8385) 21422; telex 30485; fax (8385) 23136; f. 1980; monthly; management; Editor T. Lucas; circ. 138,110.

**Ondernemersvisie:** POB 4, 2400 MA Alphen a/d Rijn; tel. (1720) 66633; telex 39682; fax (1720) 75933; f. 1979; 16 a year; commerce; Editor Joster Horst; circ. 80,000.

**PC Magazine:** POB 9194, 1006 CC Amsterdam; tel. (20) 5102911; telex 14407; fax (20) 175137; monthly; computing; circ. 91,500.

### Home, Fashion and General

**Ariadne:** POB 2252, 3500 HD Utrecht; tel. (30) 822511; fax (30) 898388; f. 1946; monthly; home decoration, fashion, beauty, crafts; Editor Rozemarijn de Witte; circ. 150,020.

**Het Beste uit Reader's Digest:** POB 13600, 1100 KA Amsterdam; tel. (20) 5678911; telex 13295; fax (20) 6976422; f. 1957; monthly; general interest; Gen. Man. Drs C. R. Rog; circ. 394,000.

**Cosmopolitan:** POB 497, 1000 AL Amsterdam; tel. (20) 65734811; telex 16597; fax (20) 65734406; f. 1982; monthly; women's interest; Dir P. Middeldorp; circ. 135,200.

**Kijk:** Haaksbergweg 75, 1101 BR Amsterdam; tel. (20) 4300455; fax (20) 4300450; popular science and history; circ. 115,000.

**Knip:** POB 2252, 3500 HD Utrecht; tel. (30) 822511; fax (30) 898388; monthly; fashion and needlework; Publisher J. Martens; circ. 153,610.

THE NETHERLANDS                                                                                                              *Directory*

**Nouveau:** Ceylonpoort 5-25, 2037 AA Haarlem; tel. (23) 304304; fax (23) 350621; women's interest; Dir K. P. M. VAN DE PAS; circ. 155,590.

**Opzij:** POB 1311, 1000 BH Amsterdam; tel. (20) 5518525; fax (20) 6251288; circ. 70,000.

**Ouders van Nu:** POB 1918, 2003 BA Haarlem; tel. (23) 304304; telex 40349; fax (23) 339248; f. 1967; monthly; childcare; Editor M. DE GROOT; circ. 156,720.

**Playboy:** POB 1, 2000 MA Haarlem-Schalkwijk; tel. (23) 304304; fax 350621; f. 1903; monthly; Dir K. P. M. VAN DE PAS; circ. 129,460.

**TIP Culinair:** POB 1, 2000 MA Haarlem-Schalkwijk; tel. (23) 304304; fax (23) 350621; f. 1977; monthly; home interest, cookery; Dir K. P. M. VAN DE PAS; circ. 100,000.

**VT-Wonen:** Europalaan 93, 3526 KP Utrecht; tel. (30) 822511; fax (30) 898388; circ. 163,410.

### Leisure Interests and Sport

**Autokampioen:** POB 93200, 2509 BA The Hague; tel. (70) 3146688; telex 32032; fax (70) 3146279; f. 1908; publ. by Royal Dutch Touring Club (ANWB); motoring; fortnightly; Editor J. VROOMANS; circ. 85,000.

**DoehetZelf-Woonideeën:** POB 1, 2000 MA Haarlem; tel. (23) 304272; fax (23) 400414; f. 1957; monthly; DIY; Editor J. HOFFMANS; circ. 153,400.

**Golfjournal:** POB 9943, 1006 AP Amsterdam; tel. (20) 5182773; fax (20) 5182707; f. 1937; 10 a year; Dir JAN KEES VAN DER VELDEN; circ. 55,000.

**Kampeer & Caravan Kampioen:** POB 93200, 2509 BA The Hague; tel. (70) 3146691; fax (70) 3242509; f. 1941; monthly; camping and caravanning; publ. by Royal Dutch Touring Club (ANWB); Dir F. VOORBERGEN; circ. 140,000.

**Kampioen:** POB 93200, 2509 BA The Hague; tel. (70) 3146676; telex 34590; fax (70) 3242509; f. 1885; monthly; recreation and tourism; publ. by Royal Dutch Touring Club (ANWB); Editor J. KARSEMEIJER; circ. 3,000,000.

**Reizen:** POB 93200, 2509 BA The Hague; tel. (70) 3146670; fax (70) 3147610; monthly; tourism, travel; publ. by Royal Dutch Touring Club (ANWB); Editor-in-Chief MIKE BISSCHOPS; circ. 50,000.

**Sport International:** POB 817, 2900 AV Capelle-IJssel; tel. (10) 4421600; fax (10) 4422250; f. 1981; monthly; Editor-in-Chief JOHN LINSE; circ. 47,350.

**Waterkampioen:** POB 93200, 2509 BA The Hague; tel. (70) 3147247; fax (70) 3242509; f. 1927; fortnightly; water sports and yachting; publ. by Royal Dutch Touring Club (ANWB); Editor ROB OLIEROOCK; circ. 60,000.

### Scientific and Medical

**Grasduinen:** Ceylonpoort 5-25, 2037 AA Haarlem-Schalkwijk; tel. (23) 304205; telex 41371; fax (23) 352554; monthly; natural history; circ. 60,000.

**Huisarts en Wetenschap:** POB 3176, 3502 GD Utrecht; tel. (30) 2881700; fax (30) 2870668; monthly; medical; Editor FRANS J. MEIJMAN; circ. 8,500.

**Natuur en Techniek:** Centrale Uitg. en Adviesbureau, POB 415, 6200 AK Maastricht; tel. (43) 254044; telex 56642; fax (43) 216124; f. 1932; monthly; Dir JOHAN H. BOERMANN; circ. 47,360.

**Technische Revue:** POB 4, 7000 BA Doetinchem; tel. (8340) 49911; telex 45481; fortnightly; review of new products; Dir D. J. HAANK; circ. 14,500.

### Statistics

**Statistisch Jaarboek van het Centraal Bureau voor de Statistiek** (Statistical Year Book of the Netherlands Central Bureau of Statistics): Prinses Beatrixlaan 428, POB 4000, 2270 JM Voorburg; tel. (70) 3373800; fax (70) 3877429; f. 1899; also *Netherlands Official Statistics* (quarterly) and 300 other publs; Dir-Gen. Prof. Dr A. P. J. ABRAHAMSE.

### NEWS AGENCY

**Algemeen Nederlands Persbureau (ANP)** (Netherlands News Agency): Eisenhowerlaan 128, 2517 KM The Hague; tel. (70) 3520520; telex 30206; fax (70) 3512900; f. 1934; Photo Dept (ANP-FOTO): Wibautstraat 129, 1091 GL Amsterdam; tel. (20) 5685685; telex 12747; official agency of the Netherlands Daily Press Asscn; Man. Dir C. N. F. VAN DITSHUIZEN; Editor-in-Chief R. H. G. MEIJER.

### Foreign Bureaux

**Agence France-Presse (AFP):** Eisenhowerlaan 128, 2517 KM The Hague, POB 1, 2501 AA The Hague; tel. (70) 3500978; telex 33538; Bureau Man. ODILE MEUVRET.

**Agenzia Nazionale Stampa Associata (ANSA)** (Italy): Tulpentuin 62, 2272 Voorburg; tel. (70) 873761; Correspondent BRUNO RIGUTTO.

**Associated Press (AP)** (USA): Keizersgracht 205, POB 1016, 1000 BA Amsterdam; tel. (20) 235057; telex 12218; Bureau Chief ABNER KATZMAN.

**Deutsche Presse-Agentur (dpa)** (Germany): Eisenhowerlaan 128, 2517 KM The Hague; tel. (70) 3551468; fax (70) 3521637; Correspondent MICHAEL SEGBERS.

**Informatsionnoye Telegrafnoye Agentstvo Rossii—Telegrafnoye Agentstvo Suverennykh Stran (ITAR—TASS)** (Russia): J. van Oldenbarneveltlaan 96, 2582 NZ The Hague; tel. and fax (70) 3553876; f. 1945; Correspondent VALENTIN VOLKOV.

**Inter Press Service (IPS)** (Italy): van Eeghenstraat 77, 1071 EX Amsterdam; tel. (20) 6640817; telex 18377; fax (20) 6719701; Dir BOUDEWIJN J. M. POELMANN.

**Reuters** (UK): Hobbemastraat 20, 1071 ZC Amsterdam, POB 74733, 1070 BS Amsterdam; tel. (20) 5708500; fax (20) 6645133; Chief Correspondent I. GEOGHEGAN.

**Rossiyskoe Informatsionnoye Agentstvo—Novosti (RIA—Novosti)** (Russia): Nieuwe Parklaan 15, 2597 LA, The Hague; tel. (70) 3523360; fax (70) 3512108; Dir A. POSKAKUKHIN.

UPI (USA) is also represented in the Netherlands.

### PRESS ORGANIZATIONS

**Buitenlandse Persvereniging in Nederland** (Foreign Press Asscn in the Netherlands): POB 61072, 2506 AB The Hague; tel. (70) 3460055; fax (70) 3456039; f. 1925; Pres. HELMUT HETZEL; Sec. FRISO ENDT; 100 mems.

**Centraal Bureau voor Courantenpubliciteit van de Ned. Dagbladpers (CEBUCO)** (Central Advertising Bureau of the Netherlands Daily Press): POB 20112, 1000 HC Amsterdam; tel. (20) 6242316; fax (20) 6278775; f. 1935; Dir Dr M. J. KUIP.

**De Nederlandse Nieuwsbladpers (NNP)** (Netherlands Newspaper Press): Van Blankenburgstraat 74, 2517 XT The Hague; tel. (70) 3459530; fax (70) 3655052; f. 1945; org. of publrs of non-daily newspapers; Pres. C. R. REBEL; 57 mems.

**Nederlandse Organisatie van Tijdschrift-Uitgevers** (Netherlands Asscn of Periodical Publrs): POB 100, 1243 ZJ s'Graveland; tel. (35) 6559100; fax (35) 6563254; f. 1945; Chair. R. F. J. H. VAN ROOIJ; 100 mems.

**Nederlandse Vereniging van Journalisten** (Netherlands Union of Journalists): Joh. Vermeerstraat 22, POB 75997, 1070 AZ Amsterdam; tel. (20) 6766771; fax (20) 6624901; f. 1884; 6,700 mems.

**Vereniging De Nederlandse Dagbladpers (NDP)** (Dutch Asscn of Daily Newspaper Publrs): Joh. Vermeerstraat 14, 1071 DR Amsterdam, POB 75111, 1070 AC Amsterdam; tel. (20) 6763366; fax (20) 6766777; f. 1908; Chair. W. F. DE PAGTER; Gen. Sec. J. W. D. GAST; 34 mems.

# Publishers

**Uitgeverij Ankh-Hermes BV:** Smyrnastraat 5, POB 125, 7400 AC Deventer; tel. (5700) 33355; fax (5700) 24632; health, herbs, eastern wisdom, astrology, acupuncture, alternative medicine, philosophy, psychotherapy, parapsychology; Dir N. H. DE HAAS.

**Anthos:** Parkstraat 7, POB 1, 3740 AA Baarn; tel. (2154) 18441; fax (2154) 15433; social issues, politics, biographies, literature, feminism; Dir. R. AMMERLAAN.

**APA (Academic Publishers Associated):** POB 122, 3600 AC Maarssen; tel. (30) 436166; f. 1966; subsidiaries: Holland University Press, Fontes Pers, Oriental Press, Philo Press, van Heusden, Hissink; new and reprint editions in the arts, humanities and science; Dir G. VAN HEUSDEN.

**BV Uitgeverij De Arbeiderspers:** Singel 262, POB 3879, 1001 AR Amsterdam; tel (020) 5511262; telex 11556; fax (20) 6224937; participant in Singel 262 holdings group; general, fiction and non-fiction; Dir R. J. W. DIETZ.

**A. Asher & Co BV:** Keizersgracht 489–491I, 1017 DM Amsterdam; tel. (20) 6222255; fax (20) 6382666; f. 1830; natural history; Dir N. ISRAEL.

**Bert Bakker BV:** Herengracht 406, 1017 BX Amsterdam; tel. (20) 6241934; fax (20) 6225461; f. 1893; Dutch and international literature, sociology, history, politics, science; Dir MAI SPIJKERS.

**John Benjamins BV:** Amsteldijk 44, POB 75577, 1070 AN Amsterdam; tel. (20) 6738156; telex 15798; fax (20) 6739773; f. 1964; linguistics, philology; antiquarian scholarly periodicals; Man. Dirs J. L. BENJAMINS, Mrs C. L. BENJAMINS-SCHALEKAMP.

**C.V. De Bezige Bij u.a.:** Van Miereveldstraat 1–3, POB 75184, 1070 AD Amsterdam; tel. (20) 6735731; fax (20) 6761948; f. 1945; Publr ALBERT VOSTER.

**Erven J. Bijleveld:** Janskerkhof 7, 3512 BK Utrecht; tel. (30) 317008; fax (30) 368675; f. 1865; psychology, sociology, philosophy, religion and history; Man. J. B. BOMMELJÉ.

# THE NETHERLANDS

**Boekencentrum BV:** Goudstraat 50, POB 29, 2700 AA Zoetermeer; tel. (79) 615481; fax (79) 615489; bibles, theology; Dir N. A. DE WAAL.

**Bohn Stafleu Van Hoghum BV:** De Molen 77, POB 246, 3990 GA Houten; tel. (3403) 95711; fax (3403) 50903; mem. of Wolters Kluwer NV holdings group; social sciences, humanities, medical, dental and nursing; Dir H. J. DEMOET; Man. H. R. SCHLICK.

**Boom Pers Boeken en Tijdschriftenuitgeverij BV:** Amsterdam (fmrly Boom-Pers BV, Meppel); tel. (20) 6226107; fax (20) 6253327; f. 1842; philosophy, educational and social sciences, environment, history; Man. Dir K. VAN DER SCHEER.

**Uitgeverij Bosch & Keuning:** Parkstraat 7, POB 1, 3740 AA Baarn; tel. (2154) 18441; fax (2154) 15433; f. 1925; mem. of Combo holdings group; general fiction and non-fiction, literature, reference; *Sesam* series; Dir R. AMMERLAAN.

**E. J. Brill NV:** Plantijnstraat 2, POB 9000, 2300 PA Leiden; tel. (71) 312624; fax (71) 317532; f. 1683; academic books and periodicals (mainly in English); classics, medieval, renaissance and oriental studies, comparative religion, biology; Pres. R. J. KASTELEYN; Dir M. G. E. VENEKAMP.

**Uitgeverij De Brink/Uitgeverij Ploegsma BV:** Keizersgracht 616, POB 19857, 1000 GW Amsterdam; tel. (20) 6262907; fax (20) 6242994; Dir H. BRINKMAN-HEIKENS.

**A. W. Bruna Uitgevers BV:** Kobaltweg 23-25, POB 8411, 3503 RK Utrecht; tel. (30) 470411; telex 70245; fax (30) 410018; f. 1868; general literature; Dir M. J. J. VAN DER BEEK.

**Uitgeverij J. H. de Bussy BV:** POB 162, 1000 AD Amsterdam; tel. (20) 6606464; fax (20) 6952076; finance; Man. A. DEKKER.

**Uitgeverij G. F. Callenbach BV:** Ambachtsstraat 13A, POB 1086, 3860 BB Nijkerk; tel. (3494) 51241; fax (3494) 59727; mem. of Combo holdings group; f. 1854; Publr J. P. A. WISSINK.

**Uitgeverij Cantecleer BV:** Dorpsstraat 74, POB 24, 3730 AA De Bilt; tel. (30) 204014; fax (30) 210106; mem. of Combo holdings group; f. 1949; Man. Dir J. A. J. JUNGERHANS.

**Combo Uitgeversgroep:** Parkstraat 7, POB 1, 3740 AA Baarn; tel. (2154) 18441; fax (2154) 15433; f. 1925; holdings group, Dir W. VAN DE WILLIGE.

**Uitgeverij Dekker & Van de Vegt:** Industrieweg 38, POB 574, 9400 AN Assen; tel. (5920) 40995; fax (5920) 72064; f. 1856; mem. of Van Gorcum holdings group; social sciences, psychology, medicine; Man. R. M. MEIJERING.

**Elsevier NV:** Van de Sande Bakhuyzenstraat 4, 1061 AG Amsterdam, POB 470, 1000 AL Amsterdam; tel. (20) 5159111; telex 16479; fax (20) 6832617; f. 1979 by merger; Pres. Prof. PIERRE J. VINKEN; Vice-Pres. L. VAN VOLLENHOVENN; subholdings include some 60 subsidiaries in the Netherlands and abroad specializing in: reference works, handbooks, weekly magazines, newspapers, trade and technical pubs, (postgraduate) scientific books and journals, audiovisual materials, further education study courses, databases; also includes:

   **Excerpta Medica Medical Communications:** Van de Sande Bakhuyzenstraat 4, 1061 AG Amsterdam; tel. (20) 5159222; fax (20) 6854171.

   **Elsevier Science BV (Academic Publishing Division):** Sara Burgerhartstraat 25, 1055 KV Amsterdam, POB 2400, 1000 CK Amsterdam; tel. (20) 4853911; fax (20) 4852457; incorporates the following divisions: life sciences, geology, economics, physics, chemistry, computer science, engineering and technology.

**Uitgeverij De Prom BV:** Pr. Marielaan 8, POB 1, 3740 AA Baarn; tel. (2154) 22141; fax (2154) 23855; f. 1981; mem. of Combo holdings group; literature and art books; Dir W. HAZEU.

**Van Gennep BV:** Spuistraat 283, 1012 VR Amsterdam; tel. (20) 6247033; fax (20) 6247035; history, social theory, political science, biographies, literature; Man. Dirs ROB VAN GENNEP, JAAP JANSEN.

**Uitgeverij J. H. Gottmer/H. J. W. Becht BV:** Prof. van Vlotenweg 1A, POB 160, 2060 AD Bloemendaal; tel. (23) 257150; fax (23) 274404; f. 1937; fiction, non-fiction, children's books, religion, travel guides; Dirs Mrs H. V. M. W. GOTTMER, C. G. A. VAN WIJK.

**Gouda Quint BV:** Willemsplein 2, POB 1148, 6801 MK Arnhem; tel. (85) 454762; fax (85) 514509; f. 1735; mem. of Wolters Kluwer NV holdings group; law and taxation; Dir K. H. MULDER.

**Ten Have BV:** Pr. Marielaan 8, POB 1, 3740 AA Baarn; tel. (2154) 22144; fax (2154) 23855; f. 1831; mem. of Combo holdings group; religious; Dir A. VAN DER WORP.

**Uitgeversmaatschappij Holland BV:** Spaarne 110, 2011 CM Haarlem; tel. (23) 323061; fax (23) 342908; f. 1922; literature, reference, science, children's books; Dir R. VAN ULZEN.

**Uitgeverij Hollandia BV:** Beukenlaan 20, POB 70, 3740 AB Baarn; tel. (2154) 18941; fax (2154) 21917; f. 1899; travel, yachting and nautical books; Dir TONNIS MUNTINGA.

**Kluwer Academic Publishers BV:** Spuiboulevard 50, POB 17, 3300 AA Dordrecht; tel. (78) 334911; telex 29245; fax (78) 334254; f. 1988; mem. of Wolters Kluwer NV holdings group; publrs of books and journals on, *inter alia*, philosophy, logic, mathematics, linguistics, Soviet philosophy, sinology and oriental studies, social history, economics, econometrics, geophysics, space research, astronomy, chemistry, physics, energy, life and environmental sciences; Dirs F. W. B. VAN HUMALDA VAN EYSINGA, A. VISSER, J. F. HATTINK.

**Uitgeversmaatschappij J. H. Kok BV:** Gildestraat 5, POB 130, 8260 AC Kampen; tel. (5202) 92555; fax (5202) 27331; f. 1894; holdings group; theology, belles-lettres, education, science, periodicals; 15 subsidiaries; Dirs B. A. ENDEDIJK, A. C. VAN DAM.

**Lemniscaat BV:** Vijverlaan 48, POB 4066, 3006 AB Rotterdam; tel. (10) 4141744; fax (10) 4141560; f. 1963; psychology, care of the disabled and retarded, books for juveniles and young adults, picture books; Dir J. C. BOELE VAN HENSBROEK.

**Uitgeverij Leopold BV:** Singel 262, POB 3879, 1001 AR Amsterdam; tel. (20) 5511262; telex 11556; fax (20) 6203509; f. 1923; participant in Singel 262 holdings group; children's books; Dir Mrs E. W. M. TEN HOUTEN.

**Uitgeverij Luitingh Sijthoff BV:** Vinkenburgstraat 2A, POB 14095, 3508 SC Utrecht; tel. (30) 349211; telex 70684; fax (30) 349208; f. 1946; mem. of Wolters Kluwer NV holdings group; fiction and popular non-fiction; Man. Dir A. DE GROOT.

**Malmberg BV:** Leeghwaterlaan 16, POB 233, 5201 AE Den Bosch; tel. (73) 288811; fax (73) 210512; f. 1885; mem. of VNU group; educational; Dir J. A. M. VAN VELTHOVEN.

**J.M. Meulenhoff BV:** Herengracht 507, POB 100, 1000 AC Amsterdam; tel. (20) 6267555; telex 16234; fax (20) 6205516; f. 1895; literature, historical, political, social/cultural, art, paperbacks and pocket books; Dir M. W. B. ASSCHER.

**Nienhuis Montessori International BV:** Industriepark 14, POB 16, 7020 AA Zelhem; tel. (8342) 1841; telex 45925; fax (8342) 3909; f. 1800; holdings group; publrs and printers specializing in scientific books and periodicals; Dir A. J. NIENHUIS.

**Nijgh & van Ditmar Educatief:** Patrijsweg 32, POB 3075, 2280 GB Rijswijk; tel. (70) 3952324; fax (70) 3191284; f. 1837; textbooks, technical books; Dir W. J. OERLEMANS.

**Em. Querido's Uitgeverij BV:** Singel 262, POB 3879, 1001 AR Amsterdam; tel. (20) 5511262; fax (20) 6203509; f. 1915; participant in 'Singel 262' holdings group; general fiction, history, children's books, translations from Latin and Greek texts; Dir ARY T. LANGBROEK.

**Uitgeversmij. La Rivière & Voorhoeve Kampen:** Gildestraat 5, POB 130, 8260 AC Kampen; tel. (5202) 92555; fax (5020) 27331; f. 1876; mem. of Kok holdings group; general non-fiction, children's books; Dirs B. A. ENDEDIJK, A. C. VAN DAM; Man. Editors J. WEGGEMANS, J. VAN BEUSEKOM.

**Editions Rodopi BV:** Keizersgracht 302-304, 1016 EX Amsterdam; tel. (20) 6227507; fax (20) 6380948; f. 1966; Dir F. A. VAN DER ZEE.

**Samsom/H. D. Tjeenk Willink BV:** Prinses Margrietlaan 3, POB 316, 2400 AH Alphen a/d Rijn; tel. (1720) 66633; fax (1720) 93270; f. 1874; mem. of Wolters Kluwer NV holdings group; books and periodicals on law, education, environment; Man. N. W. J. VAN DER KLEY.

**Samsom Bedrijfs Informatie BV:** Prinses Margrietlaan 3, POB 4, 2400 MA Alphen a/d Rijn; tel. (1720) 66321; telex 39682; fax (1720) 75933; f. 1882; mem. of Wolters Kluwer NV holdings group; periodicals and books on business, social and marketing management, financial management and administration; Dir C. J. STEUR.

**SDU:** Christoffel Plantijnstraat 2, POB 20014, 2500 JV The Hague; tel. (70) 3789911; fax (70) 3475778; fmrly Staatsdrukkerij-en Uitgeverijbedrijf; Dir R. E. MULDER.

**BV Uitgeverijen 'Singel 262':** Singel 262, POB 3879, 1001 AR Amsterdam; tel. (20) 5511262; telex 11556; fax (20) 6203509; holding group; Man. Dir P. F. M. DE JONG.

**A.J.G. Strengholt Boeken, Anno 1928 BV:** Hofstede Oud-Bussem, Flevolaan 41, POB 338, 1400 AH Bussum; tel (02159) 58411; fax (2159) 46173; f. 1928; health, biography, music, current affairs; Dir C. I. C. BAKKER.

**Swets & Zeitlinger, BV:** Heereweg 347B, POB 825, 2160 SZ Lisse; tel. (2521) 35111; telex 41325; fax (2521) 15888; f. 1901; subscription agent for periodicals worldwide; publr of books and journals; Dirs A. SWETS, C. SCHUURMAN.

**Theatrum Orbis Terrarum BV:** Keizersgracht 489-491I, 1017 DM Amsterdam; tel. (20) 6222255; fax (20) 6382666; f. 1963; biography, history, religion, science, the arts; Dir N. ISRAËL.

**BV W. J. Thieme & Cie:** Industrieweg 85, POB 7, 7200 AA Zutphen; tel. (5750) 94911; fax (5750) 19970; f. 1863; educational and general books; Dirs K. SCHILLEMANS, M. E. A. BEX-DERKS.

THE NETHERLANDS

**Uitgeverij De Tijdstroom BV:** Postbus 19135, 3501 DC Utrecht; tel. (30) 586900; fax (30) 586950; f. 1921; schoolbooks, medical, periodicals in these fields; Dir C. H. J. STAVENUITER.

**Tijl Data BV:** POB 9943, 1006 AP Amsterdam; tel. (20) 5182888; fax (20) 6155646; f. 1777; financial database publishing; Man. Dir N. M. J. HAASNOOT.

**Unieboek BV:** Gebouw Spoorgaard, Onderdoor 7, POB 97, 3990 DB Houten; tel. (3403) 77660; fax (3403) 77600; f. 1890; holdings group incorporating 10 publishing houses; general and juvenile literature, fiction, popular science, history, art, social, economics, religion, textbooks, etc.; Dir Y. R. C. VAN OORT.

**Uitgeverij L. J. Veen BV:** Herengracht 481, 1017 BT Amsterdam; tel. (20) 5249800; fax (20) 6276851; f. 1887; literature, fiction, non-fiction; Man. Dir A. DE GROOT.

**VNU Business Publications BV:** Rijnsburgstraat 11, POB 9194, 1006 CC Amsterdam; tel. (20) 5102911; telex 14407; fax (20) 6175137; technical, computer management, textiles, careers; Dir J. BEUVERY.

**Wereldvenster, Het:** Gebouw Spoorgaard, Onderdoor 7, POB 97, 3990 DB Houten; tel. (3403) 77660; fax (3403) 77600; f. 1947; mem. of Unieboek BV holdings group; 'Third World' literature, politics, cinematography, Black American literature; Dir A. C. AKVELD.

**West Friesland BV:** Zuiddijk 2A, POB 23, 5700 AA Helmond; tel. (4920) 45268; fax (4920) 28635; f. 1944; novels, biographies, children's books, paperbacks, young adults; Man. Dir M. H. J. HENDRIKS; Editor-in-Chief F. H. JONKERS.

**Wolters Kluwer NV:** Stadhouderskade 1, POB 818, 1000 AV Amsterdam; tel. (20) 6070400; fax (20) 6070490; international publishing group; Chair. Dr C. J. BRAKEL; Dirs Dr R. PIETERSE, C. H. VAN KEMPEL, P. W. VAN WEL.

**Wolters-Noordhoff BV:** Damsport 157, POB 58, 9700 MB Groningen; tel. (50) 226888; fax (50) 264866; f. 1836; educational books, dictionaries, geographical and historical atlases and maps; Dir Prof. Dr B. P. F. AL.

**Zomer & Keuning Boeken BV:** Kernhemseweg 7, POB 235, 6710 BE Ede; tel. (8380) 57676; telex 37095; fax (8380) 50114; f. 1919; mem. of Wolters Kluwer NV holdings group; nature, gardening, cookery, juvenile, history, archaeology, health, handicrafts, reference books, religion, international co-productions, book club; Dir P. I. A. P. M. ZWAGA.

### PUBLISHERS' ASSOCIATIONS

**Koninklijke Nederlandse Uitgeversbond** (Royal Dutch Publrs' Asscn): Keizersgracht 391, 1016 EJ Amsterdam; tel. (20) 6267736; fax (20) 6203859; f. 1880; Chair. K. J. LEEFLANG; Sec. R. M. VRIJ; 196 mems.

**Koninklijke Vereeniging ter bevordering van de belangen des Boekhandels** (Royal Netherlands Book Trade Society): Frederiksplein 1, POB 15007, 1001 MA Amsterdam; tel. (20) 6240212; fax (20) 6208871; f. 1815; Chair. D. W. VAN KREVELEN; Sec.-Gen. M. VAN VOLLENHOVEN-NAGEL; 956 mems.

## Radio and Television

According to UNESCO estimates, there were 13.8m. radio receivers and 7.4m. television receivers in use in 1992.

Radio and television programmes in the Netherlands are broadcast by about 30 organizations, with the majority of services being provided by the eight broadcasting associations listed below. These are independent bodies, each with a particular political, social or religious character: they are allocated transmission time by the Commissariaat van de Media (National Media Board) in accordance with the size of their respective memberships.

There are five privately-owned national radio stations that are operated on a public service basis, as well as 13 regional stations and about 330 local stations. Five national commercial radio stations were due to start broadcasting in 1994. Television programmes are transmitted on three public channels, each of which is allocated to a different combination of broadcasting associations and other organizations, and on the commercially-funded channels RTL4 and RTL5. By 1987 more than 76% of Dutch households were able to receive cable television, and some 60% were also able to receive at least one satellite station.

Until the end of 1987 radio and television broadcasting was co-ordinated by the state-owned Nederlandse Omroep Stichting (NOS—Netherlands Broadcasting Corporation), which also provided technical facilities, archives and other services to broadcasting organizations as well as transmitting programmes in its own right. Following the entry into force of a new Media Act on 1 January 1988, the NOS was divided into two separate organizations with differing functions, as follows:

*Directory*

**Nederlandse Omroepprogramma Stichting (NOS):** POB 26444, 1202 JJ Hilversum; tel. (35) 779222; telex 43312; transmission of programmes of general interest and promotion of Dutch broadcasting interests; Management Board comprises one mem. from each of the eight broadcasting asscns, four mems appointed by the Minister of Education, Culture and Science, and a Chair. appointed by the Crown; Chair. Dr M. DE JONG; Vice-Chair. A. H. VAN DEN HEUVEL.

**Nederlandse Omroepproduktie Bedrijf (NOB):** POB 10, 1200 JB Hilversum; tel. (35) 779111; independent co providing production facilities to broadcasters; Pres. P. PORSIUS; Vice-Pres. A. N. T. TEKSTRA.

### Broadcasting Associations

**Algemene Omroepvereniging AVRO:** POB 2, 1200 JA Hilversum; tel. (35) 717911; telex 43012; fax (35) 717461; f. 1923; independent; 800,000 mems; Pres. G. C. WALLIS DE VRIES; Dirs B. K. KLAP (Radio and TV), F. MARÉCHAL (Finance).

**Evangelische Omroep (EO):** Oude Amersfoortseweg 79A, POB 21000, 1202 BB Hilversum; tel. (35) 882411; telex 43325; fax (35) 882685; f. 1967; Chair. A. VAN DER VEER; Man. Dir J. DE KOSTER.

**Katholieke Radio Omroep (KRO):** Emmastraat 52, POB 23000, 1202 EA Hilversum; tel. (35) 713911; fax (35) 217158; f. 1925; Catholic; 620,000 mems; Pres G. J. M. BRAKS, G. J. HULSHOF, L. J. M. TER STEEG.

**Nederlandse Christelijke Radio Vereniging (NCRV):** Bergweg 30, POB 25000, 1202 HB Hilversum; tel. (35) 719911; telex 43249; f. 1924; Protestant; over 530,000 mems; Pres. A. HERSTEL; Dir A. DUIJSER.

**Omroepvereniging VARA:** Heuvellaan 33, POB 175, 1200 AD Hilversum; telex 43105; f. 1925; socialist and progressive; 515,000 mems; Pres. M. P. H. VAN DAM; Radio and TV Sec. H. VAN WIJK.

**Omroepvereniging VPRO:** 's-Gravelandseweg 63-73, POB 11, 1200 JC Hilversum; telex 43014; fax (35) 712500; f. 1926; 602,353 mems; Pres. A. J. HEERMA VAN VOSS; Dir H. VAN BEERS.

**Televisie Radio Omroep Stichting (TROS):** POB 28450 Hilversum; tel. (35) 715715; fax (35) 715775; f. 1964; independent; 713,025 mems; Chair. C. WOLZAK.

**Veronica Omroep Organisatie (VOO):** Laapersveld 75, 1213 VB Hilversum; tel. (35) 716716; telex 43027; fax (35) 249771; f. 1976; 1,031,000 mems; Chair. Dr J. P. VAN DER REIJDEN; Man. Dir R. S. OUT.

### OVERSEAS BROADCASTING

**Radio Nederland Wereldomroep** (Radio Netherlands International): Witte Kruislaan 55, POB 222, 1200 JG Hilversum; f. 1947; tel. (35) 724211; telex 43336; fax (35) 724352; daily transmissions in Dutch, English, Spanish, Indonesian, Sranan Tongo and Papiamento; transcription service for foreign radio and TV stations; Radio Nederland Training Centre (for students from developing countries); Pres. LODEWIJK BOUWENS.

## Finance

(cap. = capital; res = reserves; dep. = deposits; m. = million; brs = branches; all values are given in guilders unless otherwise stated)

### BANKING

#### Central Bank

**De Nederlandsche Bank NV:** Westeinde 1, POB 98, 1000 AB Amsterdam; tel. (20) 5249111; f. 1814; nationalized 1948; cap. 20m., res 2,468.9m., notes in circ. 38,300m. (Dec. 1994); Pres. Dr WIM F. DUISENBERG; Dir J. KONING; 12 brs.

#### Principal Commercial Banks

**ABN AMRO Bank NV:** POB 600, 1000 AP Amsterdam; tel. (20) 6289898; fax (20) 6287740; f. 1990 by merger of Algemene Bank Nederland NV and Amsterdam-Rotterdam Bank NV; cap. 3,380m., res 15,760m., dep. 461,561m. (Dec. 1993); Chair. P. J. KALFF; 1,450 brs.

**The Bank of Tokyo (Holland) NV:** POB 792, 1000 AT Amsterdam; tel. (20) 5737737; telex 14497; fax (20) 6791016; f. 1972; cap. 93.6m., res 86.3m., dep. 3,968m. (Dec. 1993); Chair. T. KURACHI; Gen. Man. H. SAITO.

**Banque Paribas Nederland NV:** Herengracht 539-543, POB 274, 1000 AG Amsterdam; tel. (20) 5204911; telex 11488; fax (20) 6247502; f. 1872 in Netherlands; fmrly Banque de Paris et des Pays-Bas; cap. 163.9m., res 58.4m., dep. 6,862m. (Dec. 1993); Chair. D. SCHNEITER; 9 brs.

**Coöperatieve Centrale Raiffeisen-Boerenleenbank BA (Rabobank Nederland):** Croeselaan 18, POB 17100, 3500 HG Utrecht; tel. (30) 909111; telex 40200; fax (30) 901973; f. 1898; res

# THE NETHERLANDS

15,232m., dep. 238,000m. (Dec. 1993); Chair. H. H. F. WIJFFELS; 2,090 brs.

**Crédit Lyonnais Bank Nederland NV:** 63 Coolsingel, POB 1045, Rotterdam; tel. (10) 4695911; telex 21366; fax (10) 4148391; f. 1925 as Slavenburg's Bank, assumed present name 1983; cap. 800m., res 166m., dep. 30,544m. (Dec. 1993); Chair. W. VAN DRIEL; 80 brs.

**Dai-Ichi Kangyo Bank Nederland NV:** Apollolaan 171, 1077 AS Amsterdam; tel. (20) 5740200; telex 15717; fax (20) 6760301; f. 1974; cap. 198m., res 31.3m., dep. 9,760m. (Dec. 1993); Gen. Man. K. TAKAGI.

**Deutsche Bank de Bary & Co NV:** Herengracht 448–460, 1017 CA Amsterdam, POB 268, 1000 AG Amsterdam; tel. (20) 5554911; telex 12029; fax (20) 5554428; f. 1919; fmrly H. Albert de Bary & Co; cap. 44.3m., res 144m., dep. 6,061m. (Dec. 1993); Man. Dirs H. FONTEIN, Baron A. F. VAN LIJNDEN, L. N. DEGLE; 2 brs.

**Friesland Bank:** Zuiderstraat 1, Leeuwarden; tel. (58) 994499; telex 46120; fax (58) 994591; f. 1913 as Coöperatieve Zuivel-Bank; cap. 3.5m., res 280m., dep. 5,577m. (Dec. 1993); Chair. H. J. BIERMA; 61 brs.

**Indonesische Overzeese Bank NV:** Stadhouderskade 84, 1073 AT Amsterdam; tel. (20) 5700700; telex 11327; fax (20) 6626119; f. 1965; cap. 104m., res 134m., dep. 3,518m. (March 1994); Chair. Dr J. SOEDRADJAD DJIWANDONO; Man. Dirs SIDHARTA S. P. SOERJADI, H. J. BUSS, A. DARSANA.

**ING Bank Internationale Nederlanden Bank NV:** POB 810, 1000 AV Amsterdam; tel. (20) 5415411; fax (20) 5415444; f. 1991; cap. 1,058m., res 6,856m., dep. 193,536m. (Dec. 1993); Chair. G. J. A. VAN DER LUGT.

**F. van Lanschot Bankiers NV:** POB 1021, 5200 HC 's-Hertogenbosch; tel. (73) 153911; telex 50641; fax (73) 153066; f. 1737; cap. 85m., res 257m., dep. 6,276m. (Dec. 1993); Chair. H. HEEMSKERK; Deputy Chair. C. L. M. DE QUAY; 23 brs.

**Mees Pierson NV:** POB 243, 1000 AE Amsterdam; tel. (20) 5279111; telex 11424; fax (20) 5274592; f. 1993 by merger of Bank Mees & Hope NV and Pierson, Heldring & Pierson NV; cap. 434m., res 1,510m., dep. 33,998m. (Dec. 1993).

**Nomura Bank Nederland NV:** De Boelelaan 7, 1083 HJ Amsterdam; tel. (20) 5496969; telex 16406; fax (20) 6461642; f. 1972 as Nomura Europe NV; cap. 120m., res 146m., dep. 3,540m. (March 1994); Pres. and Man. Dir N. ANDO.

**Yamaichi Bank Nederland NV:** World Trade Center, Strawinskylaan 1057, 1077 XX Amsterdam; tel. (20) 6649966; telex 15772; fax (20) 6628415; f. 1973; cap. 70m., res 117m., dep. 1,772m. (March 1994); Pres. T. NISHIMURA; Man. Dir K. L. KREFFER.

### Bankers' Associations

**Amsterdamse Bankiersvereniging** (Asscn of Amsterdam Bankers): POB 19870, 1000 GW Amsterdam; tel. (20) 5502821; fax (20) 6239748; Pres. Dr TH. A. J. MEYS; Sec. A. VAN HELLENBERG HUBAR.

**Nederlandse Bankiersvereniging** (Netherlands Bankers' Asscn): POB 19870, 1000 GW Amsterdam; tel. (20) 5502888; telex 16785; fax (20) 6239748; f. 1989; Pres. H. H. F. WIJFFELS; Gen. Man. L. M. OVERMARS.

### STOCK EXCHANGES

A supervisory authority, the Netherlands Securities Board, commenced activities in 1989.

**European Options Exchange:** POB 19164, 1000 GD Amsterdam; tel. (20) 5504550; fax (20) 6230012; f. 1978; operates as an exchange for stock, index, bond, currency and precious metals options and futures under supervision of the Netherlands Securities Board; Pres. JOOST KUIPER.

**Rotterdam Energy Futures Exchange (ROEFEX):** Rotterdam; f. 1989; Pres. TJERK E. WESTERTERP.

**Vereniging voor de Effectenhandel** (Amsterdam Stock Exchange): Beursplein 5, 1012 JW Amsterdam; tel. (20) 5234567; telex 12302; fax (20) 6248062; f. 1876; Chair. Baron BOUDEWIJN F. VAN ITTERSUM; Sec.-Gen. P. ARLMAN.

There are also financial futures, grain, citrus fruits and insurance bourses in the Netherlands; the 'spot' market for petroleum operates from Rotterdam.

### INSURANCE COMPANIES

**AEGON Insurance Group:** Mariahoeveplein 50, POB 202, 2501 CE The Hague; tel. (70) 3443210; telex 31657; fax (70) 3475238; f. 1983 by merger; life, accident, health, general and linked activities; gross premium income 12,351m. (1993); Chair. K. J. STORM.

**AMEV Levensverzekering NV:** Archimedeslaan 10, 3584 BA Utrecht; tel. (30) 579111; fax (30) 578300; f. 1883; Man. Dirs L. J. BEUGELSDIJK (Chair.), J. A. DE JONGH, H. J. RUTTEN; Sec. E. J. C. M. MULDERS.

*Directory*

**Delta Lloyd Verzekeringsgroep NV:** Spaklerweg 4, POB 1000, 1000 BA Amsterdam; tel. (20) 5949111; telex 18678; fax (20) 937968; f. 1807; subsidiary of Commercial Union PLC (UK); Dirs A. A. ANBEEK VAN DER MEIJDEN, G. W. Baron VAN DER FELTZ, J. E. JANSEN.

**Internationale-Nederlanden Verzekeringen NV:** Strawinskylaan 2631, 1077 ZZ Amsterdam; tel. (70) 5415411; fax (70) 5415423; f. 1963; Chair. of Exec. Board A. G. JACOBS.

**Nationale-Nederlanden Levensverzekering Maatschappij NV** (Life Assurance): Weena 505, 3013 AL Rotterdam; tel. (10) 4449111; fax (10) 4449222; f. 1863; Chairs A. W. SLOOTWEG, G. M. A. M. VAN STAVEREN.

**Nationale-Nederlanden Schadeverzekering Maatschappij NV** (General Insurance): POB 90504, 2509 LM The Hague; tel. (70) 3418080; telex 31585; fax (70) 3416551; f. 1970; Chair. R. C. J. RICHAERS.

**RVS Levensverzekering, NV:** Weena 505, 3013 AL Rotterdam; tel. (10) 4012922; telex 23372; fax (10) 4011880; f. 1838; mem. of Internationale-Nederlanden group; life; Chair. D. J. M. BLOK.

**RVS Schadeverzekering NV** (Fire and Casualty Insurance): Lange Voorhout 3, 2514 EA The Hague; tel. (70) 3750750; telex 31034; mem. of Internationale-Nederlanden group; Man. Dirs D. J. M. BLOK, Drs J. J. VAN DAM, W. VAN ES, M. A. HUENDER, H. W. SMID, H. C. VAN SCHIE, P. VERHAAGEN.

**Stad Rotterdam:** Weena 70, 3012 CM Rotterdam; tel. (10) 4017200; telex 23266; fax (10) 4125490; f. 1720; Chair. C. J. DE SWART.

### Insurance Associations

**Verbond van Verzekeraars, Sector Levensverzekering** (Asscn of Insurers, Life Insurance Section): Groothertoginnelaan 8, POB 990, 2501 CZ The Hague; tel. (70) 3614731; telex 34053; fax (70) 3623607; f. 1923; Chair. R. VAN DER SMEEDE; Gen. Man. W. A. MOOIJ.

**Verzekeringskamer** (Chamber of Insurance): POB 929, 7301 BD Apeldoorn; tel. (55) 3550000; fax (55) 3557240; f. 1923; Pres. Dr A. J. VERMAAT.

## Trade and Industry

### CHAMBERS OF COMMERCE

There are numerous Chambers of Commerce and Industry in the Netherlands. The most important are:

**Kamer van Koophandel en Fabrieken voor Amsterdam** (Amsterdam Chamber of Commerce and Industry): De Ruyterkade 5, 1013 AA Amsterdam, POB 2852, 1000 CW Amsterdam; tel. (20) 5236600; fax (20) 5236677; f. 1811; Dep. Sec.-Gen. J. BEVAART.

**Kamer van Koophandel en Fabrieken voor Rotterdam en de Beneden-Maas** (Rotterdam and Lower Maas Chamber of Commerce and Industry): Beursgebouw World Trade Center, Beursplein 37, 3011 AA Rotterdam, POB 30025, 3001 DA Rotterdam; tel. (10) 4057777; fax (10) 4145754; f. 1803; Pres. R. P. M. DE BOK; Sec.-Gen. A. P. A. J. BORG.

**Kamer van Koophandel en Fabrieken voor 's-Gravenhage** (The Hague Chamber of Commerce and Industry): Koningskade 30, 2596 AA The Hague, POB 29718, 2502 LS The Hague; tel. (70) 3287100; fax (70) 3240684; Pres. J. P. VAN IERSEL; Sec.-Gen. Drs CHR. W. L. DE BOUTER.

### TRADE ORGANIZATION

**Nederlands Centrum voor Handelsbevordering** (Netherlands Council for Trade Promotion): Bezuidenhoutseweg 181, POB 10, 2501 CA The Hague; tel. (70) 3441544; telex 32306; fax (70) 3853531; Man. Dir A. F. M. VAN DORP.

### EMPLOYERS' ORGANIZATIONS

**Koninklijke Nederlandse Landbouw Comité** (Royal Netherlands Agricultural Board): Rooseveldplantsoen 4, 2515 KR The Hague; tel. (70) 3382700; fax (70) 3520121; f. 1884; Chair. M. J. VAREKAMP; 45,000 mems.

**Koninklijke Nederlandse Zuivelbond FNZ** (Royal Netherlands Dairy Federation): Volmerlaan 7, POB 5831, 2280 HV Rijswijk; tel. (70) 3953100; fax (70) 3903897; f. 1900; fed. of 23 co-operative dairies with 92 plants; Chair. Dr M. L. DE HEER; Sec. Dr E. E. BOLHUIS.

**Nederlands Christelijk Werkgeversverbond (NCW)** (Netherlands Christian Federation of Employers): Johan de Wittlaan 15, POB 84100, 2508 AC The Hague; tel. (70) 3519519; fax (70) 3522059; f. 1970; Chair. Dr J. C. BLANKERT; Dir Prof. Drs J. WEITENBERG; 11,000 mems.

**Nederlands Elektronica-en Radiogenootschap:** POB 39, 2260 AK Leidschendam; tel. (70) 3325112; fax (70) 3326477; f. 1921; Pres. Prof. J. H. GEELS; Sec. G. DE GROOT; 700 mems.

## THE NETHERLANDS

**Nederlandsche Maatschappij voor Nijverheid en Handel** (Netherlands Society for Industry and Trade): Spaarne 17, POB 205, 2000 AE Haarlem; tel. (23) 360624; fax (23) 360122; f. 1777; Chair. Prof. Dr H. H. van den Kroonenberg; Sec.-Gen. R. C. Kolff; more than 9,500 mems.

**Nederlandse Tuinbouwraad** (Netherlands Horticultural Council): Schiefbaanstraat 29, 2596 RC The Hague; tel. (70) 3450600; telex 32185; fax (70) 3453902; f. 1908; Chair. J. J. J. Langeslag; Sec. Ir J. M. Gerritsen.

**Verbond van Nederlandse Ondernemingen VNO** (Federation of Netherlands Industry): Prinses Beatrixlaan 5, POB 93093, 2509 AB The Hague; tel. (70) 3497373; fax (70) 3819508; f. 1968; covers industry, transport, finance, trade and fisheries; Pres. Dr A. H. G. Rinnooy Kan; Dir-Gen. J. J. H. Jacobs; mems: 100 asscns representing more than 25,000 enterprises.

### TRADE UNIONS

Central Federations and affiliated unions are mainly organized on a religious, political or economic basis. The most important unions are those of the transport, metal, building and textile industries, the civil service and agriculture.

#### Central Federations

**Christelijk Nationaal Vakverbond in Nederland (CNV)** (Christian National Federation of Trade Unions): Ravellaan 1, 3533 JE Utrecht; tel. (30) 913911; fax (30) 946544; f. 1909; Pres. A. A. Westerlaken; Gen. Sec. J. Brüning; 342,000 mems.

Seventeen affiliated unions, of which the principal are:

**CFO-CNV-bond voor Overheid, Zorgsector en Verzelfstandigde Overheidsinstellingen (CFO)** (Civil Servants): Zeekant 35, 2586 AA The Hague; tel. (70) 3582582; fax (70) 3547163; Pres. L. G. L. M. Poell; Sec. K. Kruithof; 89,000 mems.

**Dienstenbond CNV** (Service Industries, Media and Printing): Polarisave 175, 2132 JJ Hoofddorp; tel. (2503) 51052; fax (2503) 50150; f. 1894; Pres. D. Swagerman; Sec. R. J. Rotshuizen; 30,000 mems.

**Hout-en Bouwbond CNV** (Wood and Building): Oude Haven 1, 3984 KT Odijk; tel. (3405) 97711; fax (3405) 71101; Pres. F. van der Meulen; Sec. D. van de Kamp; 45,000 mems.

**Industrie- en Voedingsbond CNV:** Rietgors 1, POB 2080, Nieuwegein; tel. (3402) 44124; fax (3402) 42774; Pres. D. Terpstra; Sec. A. Bruggeman; 61,000 mems.

**Vervoersbond CNV** (Transport): Stationsweg 5, 3445 AA Woerden; tel. (3480) 20014; fax (3480) 23488; f. 1903; Pres. E. Jongsma; Sec. J. van der Kamp; 19,000 mems.

**Federatie Nederlandse Vakbeweging (FNV)** (Netherlands Trade Union Confederation): POB 8456, 1005 AL Amsterdam; tel. (20) 5816300; telex 16660; fax (20) 6844541; f. 1975 as confederation of the Netherlands Federation of Trade Unions (f. 1906) and the Netherlands Catholic Trade Union Federation (f. 1909); Pres. J. Stekelenburg; Vice-Pres. C. P. Vogelaar; Gen. Sec. A. J. A. Groen; 1,092,780 mems.

Nineteen affiliated unions, of which the principal are:

**Algemene Bond van Onderwijzend Personeel** (Teachers): Herengracht 54, 1015 BN Amsterdam; tel. (20) 5206799; fax (20) 6274205; f. 1966; Pres. J. Tichelaar; Sec. H. Verheggen; 50,300 mems.

**Bouw-en Houtbond FNV** (Building): Houttuinlaan 3, POB 520, 3447 AM Woerden; tel. (3480) 75911; fax (3480) 23610; f. 1917; Pres. R. de Vries; Sec.-Gen. A. L. M. Kamp; 163,100 mems.

**Druk en Papier FNV** (Printing and Allied Trades): J. Tooropstraat, 1062 BK Amsterdam; tel. (20) 6143105; fax (20) 6151091; Pres. R. von Tilburg; Vice-Pres. P. de Lange; Gen. Sec. J. Aalder.

**FNV Dienstenbond** (Retail, Banking, Insurance and Trade): Houttuinlaan 6, POB 550, 3440 AN Woerden; tel. (3480) 87788; fax (3480) 31498; f. 1882; Pres. M. P. F. Spanjers; Gen. Sec. W. Drijver; 90,000 mems.

**AbvaKabo** (Government Personnel, Civil Servants, Private Health Workers, Social Workers, Post and Telecom Workers, Public Utility Workers): Bredewater 16, POB 3010, 2700 KT Zoetermeer; tel. (79) 536161; fax (79) 521226; f. 1982; Pres. C. Vrins; Gen. Sec. A. J. M. van Huygevoort; 296,290 mems.

**Industriebond FNV** (Metal, Electrical and Electronic Workers, General Factory Workers, Textile and Clothing Workers, Chemical Workers, etc.): Slotermeerlaan 80, POB 8107, 1005 AC Amsterdam; tel. (20) 5061234; fax (20) 5061115; Pres. B. van der Weg; Gen. Sec. D. Nas; 230,000 mems.

**Nederlandse Politiebond** (Police): Naritaweg 12, 1043 BZ Amsterdam; tel. (20) 6820301; fax (20) 6868146; f. 1946; Pres. J. F. W. van Duijn; Gen. Sec. A. Lok; 18,900 mems.

**Vervoersbond FNV** (Railway, Tram, Inland Waterways, Civil Aviation, Dock and Transport Workers): Goeman Borgesiuslaan 77, POB 9208, 3506 GE Utrecht; tel. (30) 738222; telex 40693; fax (30) 738225; Pres. W. Waleson; Gen. Sec. J. Smeets; 63,900 mems.

**Voedingsbond FNV** (Agricultural and Food Workers): Goeman Borgesiuslaan 77, POB 9750, 3515 ET Utrecht; tel. (30) 738333; telex 40693; fax (30) 738313; Pres. P. A. Andela; Sec. A. Kruis; 64,800 mems.

**VHP—Vakorganisatie voor Middelbaar en Hoger Personeel** (Netherlands Federation of Managerial Personnel): Randhoeve 223, POB 300, 3990 DH Houten; tel. (3403) 94811; fax (3403) 79825; fmrly NCHP; Vice-Pres. J. H. Hensen; 30,000 mems in 150 affiliated organizations.

### CONSULTATIVE ORGANIZATIONS

**Stichting van de Arbeid** (Labour Foundation): Bezuidenhoutseweg 60, 2594 AW The Hague; tel. (70) 3499577; fax (70) 3832535; f. 1945; central organ of co-operation and consultation between employers and employees; 20 board mems; Joint Pres Dr A. H. G. Rinnooy Kan, J. Stekelenburg; Sec. Drs E. H. Broekema.

**Sociaal-Economische Raad** (Socio-Economic Council): Bezuidenhoutseweg 60, 2594 AW The Hague; POB 90405, 2509 LK The Hague; tel. (70) 3499499; telex 32377; fax (70) 3832535; tripartite advisory body; f. 1950 to advise the Govt on social and economic problems; 45 mems, of which 15 belong to the Netherlands trade union federations, 15 belong to the employers' organizations, and 15 are independent experts in social and economic affairs appointed by the Crown; Pres. Th. Quené; Sec.-Gen. R. Gerritse.

## Land Reclamation and Development

Without intensive land-protection schemes, nearly the whole of the north and west of the Netherlands (about half of the total area of the country) would be inundated by sea-water twice a day. A large part of the country (including part of the former Zuiderzee, now the IJsselmeer) has already been drained.

The Delta Plan, which was adopted in 1958 and provided for the construction of eight dams, a major canal, several locks and a system of dikes, aimed to shorten the southern coastline by 700 km and to protect the estuaries of Zeeland and Southern Holland. The final cost of the delta works project, which had originally been projected at 2,500m. guilders, totalled around 14,000m. guilders, as the result of a complex adaptation to ensure the preservation of the delta's ecological balance.

The Ministry of Transport, Public Works and Water Management is responsible for land reclamation and waterways.

## Transport

### RAILWAYS

Most of the Dutch railway network is electrified; the remaining track carries diesel electric and diesel stock. There were 2,798 km of state-operated railways in 1991, providing mainly passenger services.

**NV Nederlandse Spoorwegen:** Moreelsepark 1, POB 2025, 3500 HA Utrecht; tel. (30) 359111; telex 47257; fax (30) 332458; f. 1937; limited liability co of which the State is the sole shareholder; operates all railway lines in the Netherlands; Pres. and Chief Exec. L. F. Ploeger.

### ROADS

In 1992 there were about 2,118 km of motorway and some 104,590 km of roads in the Netherlands. It was announced in 1988 that five tunnels were to be constructed in the 'western corridor' of the Netherlands (at a projected cost of 3,500m. guilders, to be provided by private investors), in an attempt to alleviate severe traffic congestion in that region. The construction of the first tunnel, under the river De Noord, was under way in the early 1990s.

### INLAND WATERWAYS

An extensive network of rivers and canals navigable for ships of 50 tons and over, totalling 4,832 km, has led to the outstanding development of Dutch inland shipping. About one-third of goods transported inside the Netherlands are carried on the canals and waterways. Dutch inland shipping has access to Germany and France along the Rhine and its branch rivers, and to France and Belgium along the Meuse and Scheldt (including the Rhine-Scheldt link). Ocean traffic reaches Rotterdam via the New Waterway, and Amsterdam is connected to the North Sea by the

# THE NETHERLANDS

21-km long North Sea Canal. Following severe river flooding in early 1995, the Government announced the inauguration of an urgent five-year programme to improve and strengthen the Netherlands' river dikes defence system.

## SHIPPING

The Netherlands is one of the world's leading shipping countries. At mid-1993 the merchant fleet comprised 1,006 vessels, with a combined displacement of 3,085,644 gross registered tons. The Rotterdam complex, incorporating the Europoort for large oil tankers and bulk carriers, is the main EU port and the busiest port in the world, handling some 293.2m. metric tons of traffic in 1992.

### Principal Companies

**Hudig & Veder's Stoomvaart Maatschappij BV:** Willemskade 23, 3016 DM Rotterdam; tel. (10) 4143322; telex 22115; fax (10) 4333618; f. 1882; liner service to Ireland; Man. Dir J. G. A. FONTEIN.

**KNSM-Kroonburgh BV:** Coolsingel 139, POB 958, 3000 AZ Rotterdam; tel. (10) 4117532; telex 23045; fax (10) 4149400; liner services from Antwerp to the Baltic ports, the Channel Islands, southern Iberia and North Africa and from the Hamburg/Antwerp range to the Mediterranean and Levant ports; Man. Dir H. DEKKER.

**Koninklijke Nedlloyd Groep NV** (Royal Nedlloyd Group): POB 487, 3000 AL Rotterdam; tel. (10) 4007111; telex 27087; divisions: Nedlloyd Lines, Neddrill, Logistics Services, Mammoet Transport, Van Gend & Loos, Nedlloyd Road Cargo; controls more than 100 subsidiaries in ocean shipping, non-shipping transport, energy sector, etc.; Chair. LEO J. M. BERNDSEN; Dirs H. J. HELB, H. H. MEIJER.

**Nederlandsche Stoomvaart Maatschappij 'Oceaan' BV:** Scheepmakershaven 25, POB 776, 3000 AT Rotterdam; tel. (10) 4117580; fax (10) 4117629; associated with Ocean Transport and Trading PLC (UK); Man. Dir J. W. DIETRICH.

**Shell Tankers BV:** Folkert Elsingastraat 34, 3067 NW Rotterdam; tel. (10) 4071899; telex 36529; fax (10) 4564889; Man. Dir J. A. M. ELIAS.

**Stena Line:** Stationsweg 10, POB 2, 3150 AA Hoek van Holland; tel. (1747) 89333; telex 31272; fax (1747) 87047; took over activities of Crown Line 1989; operates daily (day and night) ferry services for accompanied private cars, commercial freight vehicles and trailers between Hoek van Holland and Harwich (UK); Man. Dir JAN HEPPENER (acting).

**Van Ommeren Ceteco NV:** Westerlaan 10, 3016 CK Rotterdam; tel. (10) 4649111; telex 21435; f. 1839; transport, storage and trading; Chair. C. J. VAN DEN DRIEST.

**Van Uden Maritime BV:** Veerhaven 14, 3016 CJ Rotterdam; tel. (10) 2416161; telex 24095; fax (10) 4367950; agencies in Rotterdam, Antwerp, Amsterdam; liner operators; international chartering; Man. T. O. M. VAN T'HOFF.

**Vinke and Co:** Rotterdam; tel. (10) 4365500; fax (10) 4129859; f. 1860; shipowners, shipbrokers, forwarding and passenger agents; Dir B. K. BROUWERENS.

### Shipping Association

**Koninklijke Nederlandse Redersvereniging** (Royal Netherlands Shipowners' Asscn): Rotterdam; Van Vollenhovenstraat 3, 3016 BE Rotterdam; tel. (10) 4360400; fax (10) 4360376; f. 1905; Chair. M. A. BUSKER; Man. Dir C. B. H. STAL; 33 mems.

## CIVIL AVIATION

The main Dutch airport is at Schiphol, near Amsterdam. There are also international airports at Zestienhoven for Rotterdam, Beek for Maastricht and at Eelde for Groningen. During the mid-1990s a long-term programme was under way to expand the capacity of Schiphol Airport; it was hoped that the airport would handle 40m. passengers annually by 2015 (compared with 21.3m. passengers in 1993).

In 1992 the Netherlands signed an 'open skies' agreement with the USA, providing Dutch carriers with unrestricted access to the US aviation market.

**Air Holland Charter BV:** POB 75116, 1117 ZR Schiphol; tel. (20) 6584444; telex 11808; fax (20) 6598176; f. 1985; passenger charter flights; Pres. P. P. F. LANGENDIJK.

**KLM (Koninklijke Luchtvaart Maatschappij NV)** (Royal Dutch Airlines): Schiphol Airport, POB 7700, 1117 ZL Schiphol; head office: Amsterdamseweg 55, 1182 GP Amstelveen; tel. (20) 6499123; telex 11252; fax (20) 6412872; f. 1919; world's oldest commercial airline; regular air services throughout Europe; inter-Continental services between Europe, Near, Middle and Far East, Australia, North, Central and South America, Africa; 38.2% state-owned; subsidiary: KLM Cityhopper, f. 1991; Pres. P. BOUW; Deputy Pres. C. DEN HARTOG.

**Martinair Holland NV:** POB 7507, 1118 ZG Schiphol Airport; tel. (20) 6011222; telex 11678; fax (20) 6011303; f. 1958; worldwide passenger and cargo charter services; 49.2% owned by Koninklijke Nedlloyd Groep NV, 33.8% by KLM; Pres. J. MARTIN SCHRÖDER; Exec. Vice-Pres. F. C. PEDERSEN.

**Transavia Airlines:** POB 7777, 1118 ZM Schiphol Airport; tel. (20) 6046518; telex 18138; fax (20) 6015093; f. 1966; charter services; world-wide wet and dry leases; scheduled services; 80% owned by KLM; Pres. P. J. LEGRO.

# Tourism

The principal tourist attractions in the Netherlands are the outlying islands, the old towns, the canals, the cultivated fields of spring flowers, the art galleries and modern architecture. The city of Amsterdam receives nearly one-half of all tourist visits. In 1989 about 6% of the working population were employed in tourism. Some 3,931,700 foreign tourists stayed in hotels and boarding houses in the Netherlands in 1992.

**Nederlands Bureau voor Toerisme** (Netherlands Board of Tourism): POB 458, 2260 MG Leidschendam; tel. (70) 3705705; fax (70) 3201654; f. 1968; Man. Dir. J. A. T. CORNELISSEN.

**Royal Dutch Touring Club ANWB:** Wassenaarseweg 220, 2509 BA The Hague; tel. (70) 3147147; telex 32032; fax (70) 3146969; f. 1883; Dir-Gen. P. A. NOUWEN; 50 brs in Europe; 3m. mems.

# NETHERLANDS DEPENDENCIES

## ARUBA

### Introductory Survey

**Location, Climate, Language, Religion, Flag, Capital**

Aruba is one of the group of Benedenwindse Eilands or 'Leeward Islands', which it forms with part of the Netherlands Antilles (q.v.), and lies in the southern Caribbean Sea, 25 km north of Venezuela and 68 km west of the island of Curaçao (Netherlands Antilles). The climate is tropical, with an average annual temperature of 27°C (81°F), but is tempered by north-easterly winds. Rainfall is very low, averaging only about 510 mm annually. The official language is Dutch, but the dominant language is Papiamento (a mixture of Dutch, Spanish, English, Arawak Indian and several West African dialects). Spanish and English are also spoken. Most of the inhabitants profess Christianity and belong to the Roman Catholic Church, although a wide variety of other denominations are represented. The national flag (proportions 3 by 2) is blue, with two narrow yellow horizontal stripes in the lower section and a white-bordered four-pointed red star in the upper hoist. The capital is Oranjestad.

**Recent History**

The island is one of the few in the Caribbean where the original Indian (Arawak) population was not entirely exterminated following its discovery by Europeans. Aruba was claimed for Spain in 1499, but was first colonized by the Dutch in 1636 and formed part of the Dutch possessions in the West Indies. Administered from Curaçao after 1845, in 1954 Aruba became a member of the autonomous federation of the Netherlands Antilles (see p. 2230). The establishment of a large petroleum refinery on the island, at San Nicolaas, in 1929 led to the rapid expansion of the economy and a high standard of living for the islanders. However, many Arubans resented the administrative dominance of Curaçao, and what they regarded as the excessive demands made upon Aruban wealth and resources by the other five islands within the Netherlands Antilles. The island's principal political party, the Movimentu Electoral di Pueblo (MEP), campaigned, from its foundation in 1971 onwards, for Aruban independence and separation from the other islands. In a referendum held in Aruba in March 1977 82% of voters supported independence and withdrawal from the Antillean federation. The MEP used its position in the coalition Government of the Netherlands Antilles, formed in 1979, to press for concessions from the other islands towards early independence for Aruba. In 1981 (after the MEP had withdrawn from the Government of the Netherlands Antilles) a provisional agreement was reached between the Dutch and Antillean Governments on Aruba's future. Following the report of a commission, and tripartite discussions between the two Governments and representatives of the Staten (parliament) of Aruba, it was agreed in March 1983 that Aruba should receive separate status (*status aparte*), within the Kingdom of the Netherlands, from 1 January 1986, achieving full independence in 1996. The Dutch Government would remain responsible for defence and external relations until independence, while Aruba was to form a co-operative union with the Netherlands Antilles (the Antilles of the Five) in economic and monetary affairs.

At local elections in April 1983 the MEP increased its representation to 13 of the 21 seats in the Staten, and the leader of the MEP, Gilberto F. (Betico) Croes, remained as leader of the island Government. The austerity measures that the MEP administration introduced in an attempt to alleviate the adverse effects of the closure of the San Nicolaas petroleum refinery, which had been announced in October 1984, provoked a series of strikes and demonstrations by civil servants in protest at wage reductions and price rises. The MEP suffered a consequent loss of popularity. As a result of elections to the Staten in November 1985, the MEP was succeeded in government by a coalition of four opposition parties led by the Arubaanse Volkspartij (AVP). Aruba achieved separate status, as planned, on 1 January 1986, and Jan Hendrik A. (Henny) Eman, leader of the AVP, became the island's first Prime Minister. Croes, who was seriously injured in a car accident only hours before Aruba's transition to separate status, died in November 1986: he was succeeded as leader of the MEP by Nelson O. Oduber.

From 1988 Aruba began to enjoy an economic recovery, based on tourism. However, the opposition MEP claimed that the benefits to the whole community were limited, and also criticized Eman's stated reservations about independence in 1996 and his refusal to negotiate with the Netherlands about transitional arrangements.

At a general election in January 1989 the MEP came within 28 votes of securing an absolute majority in the Staten. The number of seats held by the MEP increased from eight to 10, and in February Oduber formed a Government in coalition with the Partido Patriótico Arubano (PPA) and the Accion Democratico Nacional (ADN). (Both these parties had been in the previous Government, and retained one seat each at the election.) The AVP itself, however, increased the number of its seats from seven to eight, but its other coalition partners lost their representation. The remaining seat was won by the Partido Patriótico Nobo, which gained a place in the Staten for the first time.

The MEP and the AVP each secured nine seats in the Staten at the January 1993 general election, while the three remaining seats were won by the ADN, the PPA and the Organisacion Liberal Arubano (OLA). Despite gaining fewer votes than the AVP, the MEP administration remained in office, renewing the coalition with the ADN and the PPA. In April 1994, however, Oduber announced his Government's resignation, following the withdrawal of the ADN and the PPA from the coalition. In early May, following lengthy inter-party negotiations, it was agreed that a fresh general election would be held by August. Government functions were to be undertaken in the interim by the MEP. The general election was held on 29 July and resulted in the AVP's securing 10 seats, while the MEP won nine seats and the OLA obtained the remaining two seats. On 30 August the leader of the AVP, Jan Hendrik A. (Henny) Eman, formed a Government in coalition with the OLA.

Aruba's relations with the Antilles of the Five improved after 1986. In 1987 Aruba agreed to undertake economic co-operation, and in 1988 the three Dutch 'Leeward Islands' initiated a joint project for the development of tourism. Aruba's relations with the 'metropolitan' Netherlands were dominated at this time by the latter's pressure for more control to be exercised over the large amount of aid that it gave to Aruba, and by the issue of independence, in particular the future arrangements for the island's security: Aruba's strategic position, close to the South American mainland, and the possibility of its being used as a base for drugs-trafficking, were matters of particular concern. The Oduber Government which took office in February 1989 requested a full defence commitment from the Netherlands, and favoured a continued association with the Netherlands in a Dutch 'commonwealth'. In mid-1990 the Dutch Government made proposals for a commonwealth structure that would ensure autonomy for Aruba while retaining the territory as a part of the Kingdom of the Netherlands. In September 1990 the Aruban Minister of Justice announced that Aruba was to adopt the 1988 UN Convention on measures to combat trade in illegal drugs; a joint Dutch and Aruban team was formed to conduct investigations.

In March 1994, at a meeting in The Hague, the Netherlands, of the Governments of Aruba, the Netherlands and the Netherlands Antilles, it was decided to cancel plans for Aruba's transition to full independence, due to take place in 1996. While the possibility of a transition to full independence at a later date was not excluded, this was not considered a priority, and would, moreover, require the approval of the Aruban people, by referendum, as well as the support of a two-thirds' majority in the Staten.

After acquiring separate status, Aruba fostered relations with some of its Caribbean neighbours and with countries in

Latin America. This included the development of ties with Venezuela, despite popular suspicion of Venezuela, which had traditionally laid claim to the Dutch 'Leeward Islands', including Aruba.

### Government

Aruba has separate status within the Kingdom of the Netherlands. Legislative power is held by the unicameral Staten (parliament) of 21 members, elected by universal adult suffrage for four years (subject to dissolution). Executive power in all domestic affairs is vested in the Council of Ministers (led by the Prime Minister), responsible to the Staten. The Governor, appointed by the Dutch Crown for a term of six years, represents the monarch of the Netherlands on Aruba and holds responsibility for external affairs and defence. The Governor is assisted by an advisory council.

### Defence

The Netherlands is responsible for Aruba's defence. Military service is compulsory. The Governor is Commander-in-Chief of the armed forces on the island. A Dutch naval contingent is stationed in Aruba.

### Economic Affairs

In 1993, according to the World Bank, Aruba's gross national product (GNP) per head (measured at average 1991–93 prices) was estimated to be in the upper-middle-income group (US $2,786–$8,625). Gross domestic product (GDP), in current prices, was A Fl. 2,002m., or A Fl. 25,700 per head, in 1993. In that year GDP increased by 9.0%, compared with the year before. In 1985–93 the population increased by an annual average of 0.4%.

Agriculture (including forestry and fishing) contributed 15% of GDP in 1970. The only significant agricultural activity is the cultivation of aloes (used in the manufacture of cosmetics and pharmaceuticals); aloe-based products are exported. Some livestock is raised and there is a small fishing industry.

The industrial sector, and the island's economy, was formerly based on the refining and transhipment of imported petroleum and petroleum products. In the early 1980s this sector accounted for one-quarter of GDP, and in 1984 it provided 98.9% of Aruba's exports. The San Nicolaas petroleum refinery ceased operations in 1985; in 1989 an agreement was signed with a US company for the partial rehabilitation of the plant, which reopened in October 1990. Production was an estimated 140,000 barrels per day in 1993, and plans were under discussion in 1994 for a phased expansion, over a period of three years, aimed at doubling the output of the refinery. There is a large petroleum transhipment terminal on Aruba, and a small petrochemicals industry. There are believed to be exploitable reserves of hydrocarbons within Aruban territory, and Aruba also has reserves of salt.

Light industry is limited to the production of tobacco, beverages and some consumer goods. There is a 'free zone', and the ports of Oranjestad and Barcadera provide bunkering and repair facilities for ships. In the 1980s an extensive programme of hotel-building maintained an active construction sector.

Since the mid-1980s service industries have become Aruba's principal economic activity. Financial services are well established in Aruba, and in the late 1980s facilities were improved to encourage the growth of a data-processing industry, an important service to US companies in particular. Aruba's principal source of income is tourism. In 1994 the number of stop-over visitors increased by 3.6%, to 582,136, while cruise-ship tourists increased by 2.4%, to 257,138. In that year tourist spending totalled US $466.7m.

In 1994 Aruba recorded a visible trade deficit of A Fl. 555.9m., while in that year there was a surplus on the current account of the balance of payments of A Fl. 119.3m. Aruba is obliged to import most of its requirements, particularly machinery and transport equipment, basic manufactures and foodstuffs. The USA, the Netherlands, the United Kingdom and Venezuela are important trading partners.

In 1988 it was estimated that the budget deficit would be A Fl. 18m., taking into account budgetary assistance from the Netherlands (this ceased during 1988). The level of Dutch aid in general was reduced from almost A Fl. 70m. in 1986 to about A Fl. 55m. in 1989. In 1993 the total public external debt had reached US $180.4m. The average annual rate of inflation was 4.0% in 1985–93. The rate averaged 5.3% in 1993. Only 0.5% of the labour force were unemployed in 1993.

As part of the Kingdom of the Netherlands, Aruba is classed as an Overseas Territory in association with the European Union (see p. 143). It forms a co-operative union with the Antilles of the Five in monetary and economic affairs. Aruba also has observer status with the Caribbean Community and Common Market (CARICOM, see p. 114).

The development of agriculture on Aruba is prevented by the poor quality of the soil and the prohibitive cost of using desalinated water. The island suffered from some disinvestment following its separation from the rest of the Netherlands Antilles in 1986. Changes in US taxation regulations and the abrogation of taxation treaties by the USA and the United Kingdom imperilled the financial services industry, but in 1988 the Aruban Government introduced new measures to strengthen the 'offshore' financial sector. Following the unexpected closure of the San Nicolaas petroleum refinery in 1985, the Aruban administration instituted a policy of retrenchment and austerity, except for investment in tourism development (relying particularly on its share of Antillean assets, of which it had received 30%, and on Dutch assistance). By the end of the 1980s the economy was performing strongly, although there was some dissatisfaction that the benefits were not shared by enough of the population, and the reopening of the refinery in 1990 offered further potential for growth. Since 1985 successive Governments have favoured continued stringency in public finance, and investment in diversification, concentrating on services and light industry, and aiming to reduce dependence on tourism, particularly from the USA. In 1992, following six consecutive years of growth, during which period there was a threefold increase in hotel capacity, a moratorium was imposed on construction in the tourism industry, partly in recognition of the environmental impact on the island and also to allow for the necessary infrastructural development to support the sector.

### Social Welfare

Medical care is provided, free of charge, by the Government. There is a modern hospital on the island, constructed, with financial aid from the Netherlands, in 1976.

### Education

Education is not compulsory. The education system is similar to that of the Netherlands. Primary education begins at six years of age and lasts for six years. Secondary education, beginning at the age of 12, lasts for up to five years. The main language of instruction is Dutch, but Papiamento is being introduced (using a different spelling system from that of the Antilles of the Five). The University of Aruba had 137 enrolled students in 1994. The Government allocated 16.8% of budget expenditure to education in 1992. The estimated rate of adult literacy is 97.5%.

### Public Holidays

**1995:** 1 January (New Year's Day), 27 February (Lenten Carnival), 18 March (Aruba Flag Day), 14–17 April (Easter), 30 April (Queen's Day), 1 May (Labour Day), 25 May (Ascension Day), 5 June (Whit Monday), 25–26 December (Christmas).

**1996:** 1 January (New Year's Day), 19 February (Lenten Carnival), 18 March (Aruba Flag Day), 5–8 April (Easter), 30 April (Queen's Day), 1 May (Labour Day), 16 May (Ascension Day), 27 May (Whit Monday), 25–26 December (Christmas).

### Weights and Measures

The metric system is in force.

## Statistical Survey

Sources (unless otherwise stated): Department of Economic Affairs, Commerce and Industry (Direktie Economische Zaken, Handel en Industrie), Sun Plaza Bldg, L.G. Smith Blvd 160, Oranjestad; tel. (8) 21181; fax (8) 34494; Centrale Bank van Aruba, Havenstraat 2, Oranjestad; tel. (8) 22509; telex 5045; fax (8) 32251.

### AREA, POPULATION AND DENSITY

**Area:** 193 sq km (74.5 sq miles).

**Population:** 66,687 (males 32,821, females 33,866) at census of 6 October 1991; 77,898 (males 38,702, females 39,196) at mid-1993 (official estimate).

**Density** (mid-1993): 403.6 per sq km.
**Births and Deaths** (1993): Registered live births 1,337 (birth rate 17.2 per 1,000); Registered deaths 406 (death rate 5.2 per 1,000).

### FISHING

**Total catch** (metric tons, live weight): 420 in 1990 (FAO estimate); 350 in 1991 (FAO estimate); 300 in 1992. Source: FAO, *Yearbook of Fishery Statistics*.

### INDUSTRY

**Electric Energy** (million kWh, 1991): 340. Source: UN, *Industrial Statistics Yearbook*.

### FINANCE

**Currency and Exchange Rates:** 100 cents = 1 Aruban gulden (guilder) or florin (A Fl.). *Sterling and Dollar Equivalents* (31 December 1994): £1 sterling = A Fl. 2.800; US $1 = A Fl. 1.790; A Fl. 100 = £35.71 = $55.87. Note: The Aruban florin was introduced in January 1986, replacing (at par) the Netherlands Antilles guilder or florin (NA Fl.). Since its introduction, the currency has had a fixed exchange rate of US $1 = A Fl. 1.79.
**International Reserves** (US $ million at 31 December 1994): Gold 25.63; Foreign exchange 177.59; Total 203.22. Source: IMF, *International Financial Statistics*.
**Money Supply** (A Fl. million at 31 December 1994): Currency outside banks 87.57; Demand deposits at commercial banks 345.87; Total money (incl. others) 437.24. Source: IMF, *International Financial Statistics*.
**Cost of Living** (Consumer Price Index, excl. compulsory social security; base: 1990 = 100): 105.6 in 1991; 109.6 in 1992; 115.4 in 1993. Source: IMF, *International Financial Statistics*.
**Gross Domestic Product** (A Fl. million at current prices): 1,703 in 1991; 1,837 in 1992; 2,002 1993.
**Balance of Payments** (A Fl. million, 1994): Merchandise exports c.i.f. 2,321.2; Merchandise imports c.i.f. −2,877.1; *Trade Balance* −555.9; Exports of services 1,116.6; Imports of services −408.3; Other income received 17.1; Other income paid −38.4; Unrequited transfers −11.8; *Current Balance* 119.3; Direct investment (net) −138.9; Portfolio investment (net) −16.7; Other capital (net) 60.1; Net errors and omissions 3.7; *Overall Balance* 27.5.

### EXTERNAL TRADE

**Principal Commodities** (US $ million, 1990): *Imports c.i.f.*: Food and live animals 78.9; Beverages and tobacco 18.2; Mineral fuels, lubricants, etc. 15.7; Chemicals 45.9; Basic manufactures 116.5; Machinery and transport equipment 159.0; Total (incl. others) 550.4. *Exports f.o.b.*: Food and live animals 3.5; Beverages and tobacco 8.5; Chemicals 1.3; Basic manufactures 1.7; Machinery and transport equipment 4.0; Total (incl. others) 28.3.

### TRANSPORT

**Road Traffic** (motor vehicles in use, December 1994): Passenger cars 31,817; Lorries 718; Buses 217; Taxis 351; Other cars 3,511; Motor cycles 599; Total 37,213.
**Shipping** (1993): *Arrivals:* Oil tankers 591; Cruise ships 352.
**Civil Aviation:** *Aircraft movements:* 34,751 in 1991; 33,457 in 1992; 32,850 in 1993.

### TOURISM

**Tourist Arrivals:** 758,301 (541,714 stop-over visitors, 216,587 cruise-ship passengers) in 1992; 813,138 (562,034 stop-over visitors, 251,104 cruise-ship passengers) in 1993; 839,274 (582,136 stop-over visitors, 257,138 cruise-ship passengers) in 1994.

### COMMUNICATIONS MEDIA

**Radio Receivers** (1988): 40,000 in use.
**Television Receivers** (1988): 20,000 in use.
**Telephones** (1993): 22,922 in use.

### EDUCATION

**Pre-primary** (1993/4): 23 schools; 2,242 pupils; 85 teachers.
**Primary** (1993/4): 32 schools; 7,433 pupils; 349 teachers.
**Junior High** (1993/4): 9 schools; 2,006 pupils; 114 teachers.
**Senior High** (1993/4): 1 school; 1,211 pupils; 69 teachers.
**Technical and Vocational** (1993/4): 15 institutions; 2,793 pupils; 229 teachers.
**Teacher Training** (1993/4): 1 institution; 71 students; 22 teachers.
**Special Education** (1993/4): 3 schools; 241 pupils; 36 teachers.

# Directory

## The Constitution

On 1 January 1986 Aruba acquired separate status (*status aparte*) within the Kingdom of the Netherlands. The form of government is similar to that for the Netherlands Antilles, which is embodied in the Charter of the Kingdom of the Netherlands (operational from 20 December 1954). The Netherlands, the Netherlands Antilles (Antilles of the Five) and Aruba each enjoy full autonomy in domestic and internal affairs and are united on a basis of equality for the protection of their common interests and the granting of mutual assistance. In economic and monetary affairs there is a co-operative union between Aruba and the Antilles of the Five, known as the 'Union of the Netherlands Antilles and Aruba'.

The monarch of the Netherlands is represented in Aruba by the Governor, who is appointed by the Dutch Crown for a term of six years. The Government of Aruba appoints a minister plenipotentiary to represent it in the Government of the Kingdom. Whenever the Netherlands Council of Ministers is dealing with matters coming under the heading of joint affairs of the realm (in practice mainly foreign affairs and defence), the Council assumes the status of Council of Ministers of the Kingdom. In that event, Aruba's Minister Plenipotentiary takes part, with full voting powers, in the deliberations.

A legislative proposal regarding affairs of the realm and applying to Aruba as well as to the 'metropolitan' Netherlands is sent, simultaneously with its submission, to the Staten Generaal (the Netherlands parliament) and to the Staten (parliament) of Aruba. The latter body can report in writing to the Staten Generaal on the draft Kingdom Statute and designate one or more special delegates to attend the debates and furnish information in the meetings of the Chambers of the Staten Generaal. Before the final vote on a draft the Minister Plenipotentiary has the right to express an opinion on it. If he disapproves of the draft, and if in the Second Chamber a three-fifths' majority of the votes cast is not obtained, the discussions on the draft are suspended and further deliberations take place in the Council of Ministers of the Kingdom. When special delegates attend the meetings of the Chambers this right devolves upon the delegates of the parliamentary body designated for this purpose.

The Governor has executive power in external affairs, which he exercises in co-operation with the Council of Ministers. He is assisted by an advisory council which consists of at least five members appointed by him.

Executive power in internal affairs is vested in a nominated Council of Ministers, responsible to the Staten. The Aruban Staten consists of 21 members, who are elected by universal adult suffrage for four years (subject to dissolution), on the basis of proportional representation. Inhabitants have the right to vote if they have Dutch nationality and have reached 18 years of age. Voting is not compulsory.

## The Government

### HEAD OF STATE

HM Queen BEATRIX of the Netherlands.
**Governor:** OLINDO KOOLMAN (took office in 1992).

### COUNCIL OF MINISTERS

A coalition of the Arubaanse Volkspartij (AVP) and the Organisacion Liberal Arubano (OLA).

(June 1995)

**Prime Minister and Minister of General Affairs:** JAN HENDRIK A. (HENNY) EMAN (AVP).
**Deputy Prime Minister and Minister of Transport, Communications and Utilities:** GLENBERT F. CROES (OLA).
**Minister of Finance:** ARMAND W. ENGELBRECHT (AVP).
**Minister of Justice and Public Works:** EDGAR J. VOS (AVP).
**Minister of Education and Labour:** PEDRO E. CROES (AVP).
**Minister of Economic Affairs and Tourism:** ROBERTICO R. CROES (AVP).
**Minister of Public Health and Social Affairs:** LILIA G. BEKE-MARTÍNEZ (OLA).
**Minister Plenipotentiary and Member of the Council of Ministers of the Realm for Aruba in the Netherlands:** ANTONIO G. CROES (AVP).
**Minister Plenipotentiary of the Realm for Aruba in Washington, DC (USA):** T. MONZON.

## MINISTRIES

**Office of the Governor:** Plaza Henny Eman 3, Oranjestad.
**Office of the Prime Minister:** Government Offices, L. G. Smith Blvd 76, Oranjestad; tel. (8) 39022; telex 5191; fax (8) 38958.
**Ministry of Economic Affairs and Tourism:** L. G. Smith Blvd 76, Oranjestad; tel. (8) 39017; telex 5191; fax (8) 35985.
**Ministry of Education and Labour:** L. G. Smith Blvd 76, Oranjestad; tel. (8) 30937; fax (8) 28328.
**Ministry of Finance:** L. G. Smith Blvd 76, Oranjestad; tel. (8) 39148; fax (8) 39147.
**Ministry of General Affairs:** L. G. Smith Blvd 76, Oranjestad; tel. (8) 24900; fax (8) 38958.
**Ministry of Public Health and Social Affairs:** L. G. Smith Blvd 76, Oranjestad; tel. (8) 39079; telex 5060; fax (8) 39693.
**Ministry of Justice and Public Works:** L. G. Smith Blvd 76, Oranjestad; tel. (8) 39131; fax (8) 25388.
**Ministry of Transport, Communications and Utilities:** L. G. Smith Blvd 76, Oranjestad; tel. (8) 39002; fax (8) 35985.

**Office of the Minister Plenipotentiary for Aruba:** Schimmelpennicklaan 1, 2517 JN The Hague, the Netherlands; tel. (70) 365-9824; fax (70) 345-1446.

## Legislature

### STATEN

**Speaker:** M. V. CHRISTIAANS (AVP), Staten, L. G. Smith Blvd, Oranjestad.
**Clerk:** R. P. SOMMER.

**General Election, 29 July 1994**

| Party | Seats |
| --- | --- |
| Arubaanse Volkspartij | 10 |
| Movimentu Electoral di Pueblo | 9 |
| Organisacion Liberal Arubano | 2 |
| Partido Patriótico Arubano | — |
| Accion Democratico Nacional | — |
| **Total** | **21** |

## Political Organizations

**Accion Democratico Nacional (ADN)** (National Democratic Action): Oranjestad; f. 1985; Leader PEDRO P. KELLY.
**Arubaanse Volkspartij (AVP)** (Aruba People's Party): Oranjestad; tel. (8) 33500; fax (8) 37870; f. 1942; advocates Aruba's separate status; Leader JAN HENDRIK A. (HENNY) EMAN.
**Movimentu Electoral di Pueblo (MEP)** (People's Electoral Movement): Cumana 84, Oranjestad; f. 1971; socialist; 1,200 mems; Pres. and Leader NELSON O. ODUBER.
**Organisacion Liberal Arubano (OLA)** (Aruban Liberal Organization): Oranjestad.
**Partido Democratico Arubano (PDA)** (Democratic Party of Aruba): Oranjestad; f. 1983; Leader LÉONARD BERLINSKI.
**Partido Patriótico Arubano (PPA)** (Patriotic Party of Aruba): Oranjestad; f. 1949; opposed to complete independence for Aruba; Leader BENNY NISBETT.
**Partido Patriótico Nobo (PPN)** (New Patriotic Party): Oranjestad; split from PPA in 1987; Leader EDDY WERLEMAN.

## Religion

Roman Catholics form the largest religious community, numbering more than 80% of the population. The Anglicans and the Methodist, Dutch Protestant and other Protestant churches have a total membership of about 6,500. There are approximately 130 Jews.

### CHRISTIANITY

#### The Roman Catholic Church

Aruba forms part of the diocese of Willemstad, comprising the Netherlands Antilles and Aruba. The Bishop resides in Willemstad (Curaçao, Netherlands Antilles).
**Roman Catholic Church:** J. Yrausquin Plein 3, POB 702, Oranjestad; tel. (8) 21434; fax (8) 21409.

#### The Anglican Communion

Within the Church in the Province of the West Indies, Aruba forms part of the diocese of the North Eastern Caribbean and Aruba. The Bishop, who is also Archbishop of the Province, is resident in St John's, Antigua.
**Anglican Church:** Weg Seroe Pretoe 31, San Nicolaas; tel. (8) 45142.

#### Protestant Churches

**Dutch Protestant Church:** Wilhelminaplein, Oranjestad; tel. (8) 21435.
**Evangelical Church:** C. Huygenstraat 17, Oranjestad; tel. (8) 22058.
**Jehovah's Witnesses:** Guyabastraat 3, Oranjestad; tel. (8) 21615.
**Methodist Church:** Longfellowstraat, Oranjestad; tel. (8) 25243.
**Seventh-day Adventist:** Weststraat, Oranjestad; tel. (8) 27295.

### JUDAISM

**Beth Israel Synagogue:** A. Lacle Blvd, Oranjestad; tel. (8) 23272; fax (8) 23534.

## Judicial System

(see Netherlands Antilles, p. 2235)

**Attorney-General of Aruba:** Dr FLORENCIO WERNET.
**Courts of Justice:** Hendrikstraat, Oranjestad.

## The Press

### DAILIES

**Amigoe di Aruba:** Caya G. F. (Betico) Croes 110, POB 323, Oranjestad; tel. (8) 24333; fax (8) 22368; f. 1884; Dutch; Gen. Man. and Editor-in-Chief MICHAEL O. WILLEMSE; circ. 12,000 (in Aruba and Netherlands Antilles).
**Beurs-en Nieuwsberichten:** Bachstraat 6, Oranjestad; tel. (8) 21465; f. 1935; Dutch.
**Corant:** Newtonstraat 14, Oranjestad; tel. (8) 28628; fax (8) 34834; f.1986; Papiamento; Dir STANLEY ARENDS.
**Diario:** Wilhelminastraat 81, Oranjestad; tel. (8) 22207; f. 1980; Papiamento; morning; Editor/Man. JOSSY MANSUR.
**Extra:** Margrietstraat 3, Oranjestad; tel. (8) 28820; fax (8) 27800; Papiamento; Editor/Dir VICTOR (TOKO) WINKLAAR.
**Meridiano:** Wilhelminastraat 81, Oranjestad; tel. (8) 22207; f. 1980; Papiamento; midday; Editor/Man. JOSSY MANSUR.
**The News:** Italiestraat 5, Oranjestad; tel. (8) 24725; telex 5171; fax (8) 26125; f. 1951; English; Publr GERARDUS J. SCHOUTEN; Man. Editor W. BEN BENNETT; circ. 8,228.
**La Prensa:** Bachstraat 6, POB 566 Oranjestad; tel. (8) 21199; fax (8) 28634; f. 1929; Papiamento; Editor THOMAS C. PIETERSZ.

### NEWS AGENCIES

**Algemeen Nederlands Persbureau (ANP)** (The Netherlands): Caya G. F. (Betico) Croes 110, POB 323, Oranjestad; tel. (8) 24333; fax (8) 22368.
**Aruba News Agencies:** Bachstraat 6, Oranjestad; tel. (8) 21243.

### Foreign Bureau

**United Press International (UPI)** (USA): Italiestraat 5, Oranjestad; tel. (8) 24725.

## Publishers

**De Wit Stores NV:** L. G. Smith Blvd 110, POB 386, Oranjestad; tel. (8) 23500; fax (8) 21575; f. 1948; Man. Dirs M. PONSON, F. OLMTAK.
**Oranjestad Printing NV:** Italiestraat 5, POB 300, Oranjestad; Man. Dir GERARDUS J. SCHOUTEN.
**Publicidad Aruba NV:** Wilhelminastraat 101, Oranjestad; tel. (8) 25132.
**Publicidad Exito Aruba SA:** Domenicanessenstraat 17, POB 142, Oranjestad; tel. (8) 22020; fax (8) 24242; f. 1958.
**Rozenstand Publishing Co:** Cuquisastraat 1, Oranjestad; tel. (8) 24482.
**VAD Printers Inc.:** L. G. Smith Blvd 110, POB 201, Oranjestad; tel. (8) 24550; fax (8) 33072; fmrly Verenigde Antilliaanse Drukkerijen NV.

NETHERLANDS DEPENDENCIES                                                                                                                      *Aruba*

## Radio and Television

In 1988 there were an estimated 40,000 radio receivers and 20,000 television receivers in use on the island.

### RADIO

**Radio 1270:** Bernardstraat 138, POB 28, St Nicolaas; tel. (8) 45602; fax (8) 27753; commercial station; programmes in Dutch, English, Spanish and Papiamento; Dir F. A. LEAVER; Station Man. J. A. C. ALDERS.

**Radio Carina FM:** J. G. Emanstraat 49, Oranjestad; tel. (8) 26433; commercial station; programmes in Dutch, English, Spanish and Papiamento; Dir-Gen. ALBERT DIEVENTHALER.

**Radio Caruso Booi FM:** G. M. De Bruynewijk 49, Savaneta; tel. (8) 47752; fax (8) 43351; commercial station; broadcasts for 24 hrs a day; programmes in Dutch, English, Spanish and Papiamento; Pres. HUBERT E. A. BOOI; Gen. Man. SIRA BOOI.

**Radio Kelkboom:** Bloemond 14, POB 146, Oranjestad; tel. (8) 21899; fax (8) 34825; f. 1954; commercial radio station; programmes in Dutch, English, Spanish and Papiamento; Owner and Dir CARLOS A. KELKBOOM; Station Man. EMILE A. M. KELKBOOM.

**Radio Victoria:** Pos Chiquito, POB 410, Oranjestad; tel. (8) 57090; fax (8) 59052; f. 1958; religious and cultural station owned by the Evangelical Alliance Mission; AM and FM service; programmes in Dutch, English, Spanish and Papiamento; Man. Dir EFRAIM R. ANGELA.

**Voz di Aruba** (Voice of Aruba): Van Leeuwenhoekstraat 26, POB 219, Oranjestad; tel. (8) 24134; commercial radio station; programmes in Dutch, English, Spanish and Papiamento; also operates Canal 90 on FM; Dir A. M. ARENDS, Jr.

### TELEVISION

**Tele-Aruba NV:** POB 392, Oranjestad; tel. (8) 57302; fax (8) 51683; f. 1963; formerly operated by Netherlands Antilles Television Co; commercial; govt-owned; Gen. Man. JANE LAMPKIN.

## Finance

(cap. = capital; res = reserves; dep. = deposits; m. = million; brs = branches; amounts in Aruban guilders).

### BANKING

#### Central Bank

**Centrale Bank van Aruba:** Havenstraat 2, Oranjestad; tel. (8) 22509; telex 5045; fax (8) 32251; f. 1986; cap. 10.0m., res 14.9m., dep. 218.1m. (Dec. 1994); Pres. J. H. DU MARCHIE SARVAAS; Dir K. A. H. POLVLIET.

#### Commercial Banks

**ABN AMRO Bank NV:** Caya G. F. (Betico) Croes 89, Oranjestad; tel. (8) 21515; telex 5032; fax (8) 21856; Man. A. R. HARMSEN; 3 brs.

**Aruba Bank NV:** Caya G. F. (Betico) Croes 41, POB 192, Oranjestad; tel. (8) 21550; telex 5103; fax (8) 29152; f. 1936; cap. and res 10m., dep. 158m. (1986); Man. Dir I. A. DURAND; 8 brs.

**Banco di Caribe NV:** Caya G. F. (Betico) Croes 90, Oranjestad; tel. (8) 32168; telex 5157; fax (8) 32422; f. 1987; Man. Dir N. R. ARENDSZ; 1 br.

**Caribbean Mercantile Bank NV:** Caya G. F. (Betico) Croes 53, POB 28, Oranjestad; tel. (8) 23118; telex 5041; fax (8) 24373; f. 1963; cap. and res 10.5m., dep. 89.7m. (Dec. 1984); Man. Dir D. A. MACVICAR; 6 brs.

**First National Bank of Aruba NV:** Caya G. F. (Betico) Croes 67, Oranjestad; tel. (8) 33221; telex 5034; fax (8) 21756; f. 1987; Man. Dir. E. TROMP; Gen. Man. CHARLES RUND; 3 brs.

**Interbank Aruba NV:** Caya G. F. (Betico) Croes 38, Oranjestad; tel. (8) 31080; telex 5224; fax (8) 24058; f. 1987; Man. Dir CARLO R. MANSUR; 3 brs.

#### Investment Bank

**Aruban Investment Bank NV:** Middenweg 20, POB 1011, Oranjestad; tel. (8) 27327; fax (8) 27461; f. 1987; Pres. JOS J. SCHOOLMEESTERS.

### INSURANCE

A number of foreign companies have offices in Oranjestad, mainly British, Dutch and US firms.

## Trade and Industry

### CHAMBER OF COMMERCE AND INDUSTRY

**Aruba Chamber of Commerce and Industry:** Zoutmanstraat 21, POB 140, Oranjestad; tel. (8) 21566; telex 5174; fax (8) 33962; f. 1930; Pres. R. F. CROES; Exec. Dir L. C. DE SOUZA.

### TRADE ASSOCIATION

**Aruba Trade and Industry Association:** ATIA Bldg, Pedro Gallegostraat 6, POB 562, Oranjestad; tel. (8) 27593; fax (8) 33068; f. 1945; Pres. ROBERT W. CROES.

### DEVELOPMENT ORGANIZATION

**Department of Economic Affairs, Commerce and Industry** (Direktie Economische Zaken, Handel en Industrie): Sun Plaza Bldg, L. G. Smith Blvd 160, Oranjestad; tel. (8) 21181; fax 34494; Dir HUMPHREY VAN TRIKT.

### TRADE UNIONS

**Federashon di Trahadonan Arubano—FTA** (Aruban Workers' Federation): Bernardstraat 23, San Nicolaas; tel. (8) 45448; fax (8) 45504; f. 1964; independent; affiliated to World Confederation of Labour; Sec.-Gen. ANSELMO PONTILIUS.

There are also several unions for government and semi-government workers and employees.

## Transport

There are no railways, but Aruba has a network of all-weather roads.

**Arubus NV:** Sabana Blanco 67, Oranjestad; tel. (8) 27089; fax (8) 28633; state-owned company providing public transport services.

### SHIPPING

The island's principal seaport is Oranjestad, whose harbour can accommodate ocean-going vessels. There are also ports at Barcadera and San Nicolaas.

**Aruba Ports Authority NV:** L. G. Smith Blvd 23, Oranjestad; tel. (8) 26633; fax (8) 32896; f. 1981; Dir M. H. HENRÍQUEZ.

**Officina Maritima de Aruba:** Plaza Shopping Centre, L. G. Smith Blvd 94, Oranjestad; tel. (8) 21622; telex 5022.

#### Principal Shipping Companies

**Magna Shipping Co:** Koningstraat 52, Oranjestad; tel. (8) 24349.

**Rodoca Shipping and Trading SA:** Franklinstraat 2, Oranjestad; tel. (8) 23016; telex 2076; fax (8) 27041; formerly Aruba Shipping and Chartering Co NV.

### CIVIL AVIATION

The Queen Beatrix International Airport, about 2.5 km from Oranjestad, is served by numerous airlines, linking the island with destinations in the Caribbean, Europe, the USA and Central and South America. A project to upgrade the airport was due to be completed in 1995

**Air Aruba:** Wayaka 31-A, POB 1017, Oranjestad; tel. (8) 30005; telex 5189; fax (8) 25867; f. 1986, began flying operations 1988; fmrly state-owned; services to destinations in North and South America, Europe and within the Caribbean; Chair. A. R. ARENDS; Pres. PETER LOOK-HONG.

## Tourism

Aruba's white sandy beaches, particularly along the southern coast, are an attraction for foreign visitors. Tourism is a major industry. The number of hotel rooms increased from 2,385 in January 1986 to 6,313 by the end of 1994. In 1994 there were 582,136 stop-over visitors. In that year most stop-over visitors came from the USA (55.7%), Venezuela (12.9%), the Netherlands (5.5%), Brazil (5.1%) and Canada (4.1%). In the same year 257,138 cruise-ship passengers visited Aruba. Tourism receipts totalled US $466.7m in 1993.

**Aruba Tourism Authority:** L. G. Smith Blvd 172, Oranjestad; tel. (8) 21019; fax (8) 34702; offices in North America, Latin America and Europe; Man. Dir R. WEVER.

**Aruba Hotel and Tourism Association:** POB 542, Oranjestad; tel. (8) 22607; fax (8) 24202; Chief Exec. Officer RORY ARENDS.

# THE NETHERLANDS ANTILLES

## Introductory Survey

**Location, Climate, Language, Religion, Flag, Capital**

The Netherlands Antilles (Antilles of the Five) consists of two groups of islands in the Caribbean Sea, about 800 km (500 miles) apart. The main group, lying off the coast of Venezuela, consists of Bonaire and Curaçao which (together with Aruba, 68 km to the east of Curaçao) are known as the Benedenwindse Eilands or 'Leeward Islands'; to the north-east lie the small volcanic islands of St (Sint) Eustatius (also known as Statia), Saba and St (Sint) Maarten (the northern half of the last island being a dependency of the French overseas department of Guadeloupe), known as the Bovenwindse Eilands or 'Windward Islands' (although actually in the Leeward group of the Lesser Antilles). The climate is tropical, moderated by the sea, with an average annual temperature of 27.5°C (81°F) and little rainfall. The official languages are Dutch and Papiamento (a mixture of Dutch, Spanish, Portuguese, English, Arawak Indian and several West African dialects), which is the dominant language of the 'Leeward Islands'. English is the official and principal language of the 'Windward Islands'. Spanish is also widely spoken. Almost all of the inhabitants profess Christianity: the people of the 'Leeward Islands' and Saba are predominantly Roman Catholics, while those of St Eustatius and St Maarten are predominantly Protestants. The state flag (proportions 3 by 2) is white, with a red vertical stripe in the centre, crossed by a horizontal blue stripe on which there are five white five-pointed stars (one for each of the main islands) arranged in an oval. The capital is Willemstad, on the island of Curaçao.

**Recent History**

The 'Leeward Islands', already settled by communities of Arawak Indians, were discovered by the Spanish in 1499 and were seized by the Dutch in the 1630s. Curaçao became prosperous in the late 17th and 18th centuries as an entrepôt for trade in the Caribbean. The 'Windward Islands', once settled by Carib Indians and believed to have been sighted by Columbus in 1493, were settled by the Dutch in the mid-17th century. After frequent changes in possession, the islands (including Aruba) were finally confirmed as Dutch territory in 1816. The two groups were administered as Curaçao and Dependencies between 1845 and 1948. Slavery was abolished in 1863, and the islands suffered from an economic decline until the establishment of petroleum refineries on Curaçao and Aruba, in 1918 and 1929 respectively. During the Second World War Queen Wilhelmina of the Netherlands promised independence, and in 1954 a Charter gave the federation of six islands full autonomy in domestic affairs, and declared it to be an integral part of the Kingdom of the Netherlands.

Divisions of political allegiance within the territory have been along island, rather than policy, lines, and a series of coalition governments has frequently paralysed decision-making. In 1969 serious rioting and looting broke out in Willemstad after a demonstration by workers in the petroleum industry. Troops had to be sent from the Netherlands to quell the disturbances and to restore order. In February 1970 the socialist Government of Ciro Kroon resigned over the nomination of a new Governor, and in 1971 the Government of E. Petronia resigned over the rejection by the Staten (parliament) of new financial measures.

Following elections to the Staten in June 1977, a coalition government, excluding the Movimentu Electoral di Pueblo (MEP) of Aruba, was formed, with the leader of the Democratische Partij (DP), Silvio Rozendal, as Prime Minister. After a boycott of the session by the MEP and the Frente Obrero i Liberashon 30 di mei (FOL), the Staten was eventually convened by a Governor's decree in October. Rozendal resigned in April 1979, and elections were held in July. A coalition administration was formed by the Movimentu Antiyas Nobo (MAN), the MEP and the Unión Patriótico Bonairiano (UPB), with Dominico (Don) Martina, the leader of the MAN, as Prime Minister. The DP joined the coalition Government in December 1980.

In Aruba resentment of the administrative dominance of Curaçao had led in 1971 to the formation of the MEP, to seek indepenence for the island. In 1981 a series of talks began with the Netherlands Government over Aruba's future. However, in September the MEP representatives in the Staten withdrew their support for the Government over Aruba's rights to possible discoveries of petroleum off its coast. The Government's majority was restored by the inclusion of the DP—St Maarten (DP—StM) member for the 'Windward Islands' in the coalition, but a DP resignation in January 1982 precipitated a further crisis. A general election in June failed to resolve the situation, and it was not until October that agreement was reached on the formation of a new coalition, which excluded the MEP. Martina remained as Prime Minister.

In March 1983 agreement was finally reached whereby Aruba would be given separate status (*status aparte*) within the Kingdom of the Netherlands from January 1986, with the prospect of achieving full independence in 1996 (for further details, see the chapter on Aruba, p. 2225). Arguments continued over the division of the Antilles' financial reserves, and over rights to explore for petroleum and other minerals. In June 1984 Martina's coalition Government resigned, precipitating a three-month political crisis. In September a five-party coalition was formed, with Maria Liberia-Peters of the conservative Partido Nashonal di Pueblo (PNP) as Prime Minister. The new Government, anticipating the curtailment of its mandate (by the planned withdrawal of the Aruban MEP members in January 1986), concentrated on measures designed to counter the worsening economic situation on the islands.

At a general election held in November 1985 the PNP gained the largest number of seats in the Staten for the Antilles of the Five (six out of 22), but was unable to secure enough support from other parties to form a government. Martina once again became Prime Minister and formed a coalition Government. During 1986 and 1987 the Government was forced to introduce a series of economic austerity measures, following Aruba's separation from the Netherlands Antilles and the decline of both the petroleum-refining industry and 'offshore' financial services. The Martina coalition resigned in March 1988, after losing the support of the DP—StM and the FOL. In May Liberia-Peters formed a new coalition with all the parties represented in the Staten except for the MAN and the DP—Curaçao (DP—C). The new Government controlled 13 of the 22 seats but depended on the support of the DP—StM and the FOL, which had caused the defeat of the Martina administration. In 1988 the Netherlands exerted pressure for more control to be exercised over the large amount of aid that it provided for the Netherlands Antilles. In January 1989 Martina revealed that successive Curaçao administrations had been diverting some revenues from the 'offshore' financial sector into a fund that had not been declared to The Hague during negotiations for budget support. This caused some anger in the Netherlands, as well as domestic tension in the Staten.

From 1986 Claude Wathey, leader of the DP—StM, became the principal advocate of independence or separate status for St Maarten. He also favoured the formation of a Dutch 'commonwealth'. The 'metropolitan' Netherlands, however, which had initially been reluctant to permit separate status for Aruba, was anxious to prevent any further fragmentation of the Antillean federation. Such a development would delay settlement of a timetable for eventual independence. The PNP, which sought to reduce Curaçao's financial obligations within the federation, supported a less centralized system of government. The four smaller islands are all net recipients of funds from the central treasury, and the volatility of island politics does not encourage financial caution. In 1988 Bonaire was without an administration for six weeks before a coalition was formed in December, under the threat of intervention by The Hague.

Agreement on a looser structure of federation appeared more probable from January 1989, when Martina expressed support for it in principle. In early 1990 the Dutch Government indicated that it would not insist upon progress towards independence if the population did not support it. Furthermore, while the 'metropolitan' Government was unwilling to allow the complete disintegration of the federation, it was prepared to consider a less centralized system or the creation of two federations in the separate island groups. At a general election in March 1990 the PNP increased the number of its seats (all on Curaçao) to seven, again making it the largest single party in the Staten, and, after some weeks of negotiations, Maria Liberia-Peters assumed the leadership of a broad-based coalition Government.

Proposals made by the 'metropolitan' Government in mid-1990 for constitutional reform envisaged a commonwealth structure that would replace the two-tier system of federal and island governments currently in operation in the Antilles. The proposals included the division of the Antilles of the Five into two parts, one comprising Curaçao and Bonaire, the other the islands of St Maarten, Saba and St Eustatius. Although the majority of the inhabitants of both Curaçao and St Maarten were understood to favour independence, the commonwealth structure would have the advantage of including guarantees concerning defence, representation overseas, financial assistance and nationality. It would also ensure associate membership of the European Community (known as the European Union—see p. 143—from November 1993).

In late March 1992 the FOL and its partner at the 1990 election, the Social Independiente, withdrew from the Government. In the following month Liberia-Peters formed a new coalition with the DP—StM, the UPB and the DP—C. In September 1993 the DP—StM withdrew from the coalition, although the Government maintained its majority in the Staten with the support of an independent deputy. In November the Windward Islands People's Movement (WIPM) also lent its support to the Government in the Staten, although it did not join the coalition.

On 19 November 1993 a referendum was conducted on Curaçao on that island's constitutional status, with the result that 73.6% of the electorate voted for a continuance of the island's status as a member of the Antillean federation. The option favoured by the Government, that of separate status, received only 17.9% of the votes cast. As a result of this defeat, the WIPM and the UPB withdrew their support from the Government, thereby reducing its seats in the Staten from 13 to nine and leaving it without a majority. In the following week Liberia-Peters resigned, and the Minister of Justice, Susanne F. C. Römer, assumed the position of acting Prime Minister. At the request of Liberia-Peters, Alejandro Felippe Paula, a professor at the University of the Netherlands Antilles, subsequently agreed to be nominated to head an interim Government, pending a general election in February 1994, on condition that he receive the support of all the parties of the previous coalition. Paula's nomination gained the support of 16 members of the Staten, and on 28 December 1993 he was inaugurated as interim Prime Minister.

At the general election in February 1994 a new party based in Curaçao, the Partido Antía Restrukturá, led by Miguel A. Pourier, secured eight seats—making it the largest single party in the Staten. Following negotiations, Pourier assumed the leadership of a broadly-based coalition Government, which was inaugurated in late March.

On 14 October 1994 referendums were conducted on St Maarten, St Eustatius and Saba concerning the islands' constitutional status. A referendum on the same issue was conducted on Bonaire on 21 October. In each case the electorate voted to continue as members of the Antillean federation. On Bonaire 88% of the electorate voted for this option, while the equivalent vote on St Eustatius was 86.3% and on Saba was 90.6%. On St Maarten 59.8% of the electorate voted to remain within the Antillean federation, while the option of autonomy within the Kingdom of the Netherlands received 32% of the vote.

In July 1992, following an inquiry into the administration of St Maarten, the 'metropolitan' Government placed the island under 'higher supervision', limiting the island Government's power to make decisions on expenditure. In addition to having incurred a budget deficit of some US $100m., the island's administration was also alleged to be guilty of corruption. In February 1993, as a result of continuing pressure from the USA to act on reports of drugs-trafficking and organized crime on the island, the 'metropolitan' Government announced that it would be intensifying its supervision of the administration of St Maarten and that all major government decisions would require the approval of the Lieutenant-Governor of the island. In mid-1993 several prominent politicians and businessmen, including Claude Wathey and a former Lieutenant-Governor of St Maarten, Ralph Richardson, were placed under judicial investigation in connection with alleged corrupt practices on the island. In early November, following the arrest (in the previous month) of Wathey and Richardson and their subsequent transfer to Curaçao—a one-day protest strike was organized on St Maarten and a petition was raised, appealing for the detainees to be returned to the island. In December the period of 'higher supervision' of St Maarten by the 'metropolitan' Government was extended to 1 June 1994. However, following its election in February 1994, the Pourier administration expressed its intention to demand the withdrawal of the 'metropolitan' Government's measures and to implement even more stringent policies of its own. In mid-1994 Wathey was sentenced to 18 months' imprisonment for corrupt practices in relation to expansion projects at Princess Juliana airport and St Maarten's Great Bay harbour. Richardson was also imprisoned on similar charges. The Government was to establish a fiscal corruption unit to combat financial crime.

Venezuela, the Antilles' closest neighbour in the south, has territorial claims to the 'Leeward Islands', but since 1983 has endeavoured to maintain political and social stability on the islands by continuing to support Curaçao's petroleum-refining industry (see below). The 'metropolitan' Government usually delegates negotiations about regional issues to the Antillean and Aruban governments. Relations with Aruba improved after it had gained separate status. Aruba agreed to economic co-operation in 1987 and, in 1988, to a joint tourism development project.

### Government

The Governor of the Netherlands Antilles, appointed by the Dutch Crown for a term of six years, represents the monarch of the Netherlands in the territory, and has executive power over external affairs. The Governor is assisted by an advisory council. Executive power in internal affairs is vested in the Council of Ministers. The Council is responsible to the Staten (parliament), which has 22 members elected by universal adult suffrage for four years (subject to dissolution). The administration of each island is conducted by its own Island Council, Executive Council and Lieutenant-Governor.

### Defence

Although defence is the responsibility of the Netherlands, compulsory military service is laid down in an Antilles Ordinance. The Governor is the Commander-in-Chief of the armed forces in the islands, and a Dutch naval contingent is stationed in the Netherlands Antilles.

### Economic Affairs

In 1988, according to official sources, the gross national product (GNP) of the Antilles of the Five, measured at current prices, was US $1,407m., equivalent to $7,395 per head. GNP per head increased at an average rate of 0.3% per year, in real terms, between 1985 and 1988. In 1985–93 the population increased by an annual average of 0.9%. Gross domestic product (GDP) increased, in real terms, at an average annual rate of 3.6% in the period 1985–88, and stood at NA Fl. 3,395.7m. in 1991. However, GDP declined by 1.8% in 1993, following six years of growth. The relative isolation of the individual islands has led to the development of semi-independent economies, and economic conditions vary greatly between them.

Agriculture, together with forestry, fishing and mining, contributed only 0.7% of GDP in 1991. Agriculture, forestry and fishing employed 1.1% of the working population in 1992. Less than 5% of the total land area is cultivated. The chief products are aloes (Bonaire is a major exporter), sorghum, divi-divi, groundnuts, beans, fresh vegetables and tropical fruit. A bitter variety of orange is grown, for use in the production of Curaçao liqueur. There is also some fishing.

Industry (including manufacturing, construction, power and water, but excluding the petroleum-refining industry) contributed 17.8% of GDP in 1991. Industry employed 19.8% of the working population in 1992.

The mining and quarrying sector employed less than 1.0% of the working population in 1988, mainly on Bonaire, producing salt. Apart from some phosphates on Curaçao (exploited until the mid-1980s), the islands have no other significant mineral reserves.

Manufacturing contributed 7.6% of GDP in 1991, and employed 9.3% of the working population in 1992; activities include food-processing, production of Curaçao liqueur, and the manufacture of paint, paper, soap and cigarettes. Bonaire has a textile factory, and there is a 'free zone' on Curaçao, but the 'Windward Islands' have very few manufacturing activities. Petroleum-refining (using petroleum imported from Venezuela) is the islands' principal industrial activity. After the closure of the Aruban refinery (see section on Aruba), the loss-making Curaçao refinery was leased to the Venezuelan state petroleum company until 1994; the lease was subsequently renewed for a period of 20 years. Production at the refinery increased from 173m. barrels in 1986 to 220m. barrels in 1991, before declining to 196m. barrels in 1992. In 1986 mineral fuels accounted for some 65% of imports and for some 95% of exports (Curaçao and Bonaire only). Petroleum transhipment is also important, and ship repairs at the Curaçao dry dock make a significant contribution to the economy.

The Netherlands Antilles is a major 'offshore' financial centre. The financial and business services sector contributed 20.1% of GDP in 1991, and employed 11.0% of the working population in 1992. There are over 30,000 companies registered in the Netherlands Antilles; official revenues from this sector declined, however, from NA Fl. 465.3m. in 1986 to NA Fl. 185m. in 1992. Most financial services are based in Curaçao, but St Maarten is also important. A major industry for all the islands (particularly St Maarten) is tourism, which is the largest employer (28.1% in 1992) after the public sector. Government services (excluding social services, etc.) contributed 15.0% of GDP in 1992 and, during the early 1980s, were the largest employer in the islands.

In 1993 the Antilles of the Five recorded a visible trade deficit of US $904.0m., much of which was offset by revenue from services: there was a deficit of $15.9m. on the current account of the balance of payments. The petroleum industry dominates the trade figures of the Netherlands Antilles, particularly of the 'Leeward Islands'. In 1990 the principal source of imports was Venezuela (which provides crude petroleum), and the principal market for exports was the USA. The USA is an important trading partner for all the islands of the Netherlands Antilles, as are the Netherlands and other Caribbean countries. Petroleum is the principal commodity for both import and export, but the Netherlands Antilles also imports manufactured goods, machinery and transport equipment, and food and live animals, while it exports aloes, Curaçao liqueur and some light manufactures.

In 1993 there was a surplus of NA Fl. 14.5m. on the central Government's budget. In 1992 there was an estimated deficit of NA Fl. 128.2m. on the budget of the island Government of Curaçao. The administrations of the small islands tend to operate with deficits. In 1992 the total public domestic debts of the central Government and the island Government of Curaçao were NA Fl. 442.5m. and NA Fl. 524.9m., respectively. Total foreign debt was NA Fl. 626.3m., owed chiefly to the Netherlands. The average annual rates of inflation in Curaçao and Bonaire were 2.0% and 2.1%, respectively, in 1993. In the same year the average annual rate of inflation in St Maarten was 0.8%. The rate of unemployment in the labour force was 15.3% for the Netherlands Antilles as a whole in 1992, and 13.4% for Curaçao in 1993.

The Netherlands Antilles, as part of the Kingdom of the Netherlands, has the status of an Overseas Territory in association with the European Union (see p. 143). In 1988 the Netherlands Antilles was accorded observer status by the Caribbean Community and Common Market (CARICOM, see p. 114).

The relative economic diversity of Curaçao and Bonaire contrasts with the other islands' dependence on tourism and on public-sector employment. The economic fragmentation of the islands contributes to strains on the federation of the Netherlands Antilles. From 1986 St Maarten and Curaçao appeared increasingly unwilling to subsidize the smaller islands. Bonaire, Saba and St Eustatius are net recipients of funds from the central treasury. The three islands incur large budget deficits each year, despite grants from the federal Government. The economy of the Netherlands Antilles was adversely affected during the 1980s by a reduction in income from petroleum-refining (as the result of a decline in international prices, restrictions imposed by the Organization of the Petroleum Exporting Countries on production by Venezuela—the chief source of crude petroleum for the Netherlands Antilles—and a reduction in demand by the USA). Changes in legislation in the USA and the United Kingdom during the decade reduced the attraction of the islands as a 'tax haven', and affected income from 'offshore' financial activities. Economic assistance from the Netherlands was reduced during the late 1980s, and the Antillean Government was forced to introduce austerity measures and to increase its efforts to diversify the economy.

### Social Welfare

The Government provides free medical care and supplementary food supplies for poor persons. There are seven hospitals on Curaçao and one on each of the other islands, with a total of 1,436 beds. There were some 273 physicians in the Antilles of the Five in 1992. Of total expenditure by the central Government in 1991, NA Fl. 38.8m. (7.1%) was for health, and a further NA Fl. 199.3m. (36.4%) for social security and welfare.

### Education

Education was made compulsory in 1992. The Government allocates about one-third of budget expenditure to education, and the islands' educational facilities are generally of a high standard. The education system is the same as that of the Netherlands. Dutch is used as the principal language of instruction in schools on the 'Leeward Islands', while English is used in schools on the 'Windward Islands'. Instruction in Papiamento (using a different spelling system from that adopted by Aruba) has been introduced in primary schools. Primary education begins at six years of age and lasts for six years. Secondary education lasts for a further five years. The University of the Netherlands Antilles, sited on Curaçao, had 620 students in 1991. The estimated rate of adult literacy is 95%. In 1991 public expenditure on education in the Antilles of the Five included NA Fl. 30.7m. by the central Government and NA Fl. 148.8m. by local governments.

### Public Holidays

**1995:** 1 January (New Year's Day), 27 February (Curaçao and Bonaire only: Lenten Carnival), 14–17 April (Easter), 30 April (Queen's Day), 1 May (Labour Day), 25 May (Ascension Day), 5 June (St Maarten, Saba and St Eustatius only: Whit Monday), 2 July (Curaçao Day), 6 September (Bonaire Day), 11 November (St Maarten Day), 16 November (St Eustatius Day), 6 December (Saba Day), 25–26 December (Christmas).

**1996:** 1 January (New Year's Day), 19 February (Curaçao and Bonaire only: Lenten Carnival), 5–8 April (Easter), 30 April (Queen's Day), 1 May (Labour Day), 16 May (Ascension Day), 27 May (St Maarten, Saba and St Eustatius only: Whit Monday), 2 July (Curaçao Day), 6 September (Bonaire Day), 11 November (St Maarten Day), 16 November (St Eustatius Day), 6 December (Saba Day), 25–26 December (Christmas).

### Weights and Measures

The metric system is in force.

## Statistical Survey

Sources (unless otherwise stated): Centraal Bureau voor de Statistiek, Fort Amsterdam, Willemstad, Curaçao; tel. (9) 61-1329; Bank van de Nederlandse Antillen, Breedestraat 1, Willemstad, Curaçao; tel. (9) 61-3600; telex 1155; fax (9) 61-5004.

### AREA, POPULATION AND DENSITY

**Area** (sq km): Curaçao 444; Bonaire 288; St Maarten (Dutch sector) 34; St Eustatius 21; Saba 13; Total 800 (309 sq miles).

**Population:** 171,620 (males 82,808, females 88,812) at census of 1 February 1981 (excluding adjustment for underenumeration); 189,474 (males 90,707; females 98,767) at census of 27 January 1992 (excluding adjustment for underenumeration); 197,069 at mid-1993 (official estimate). *By island* (at census of 1992): Curaçao 144,097; Bonaire 10,187; St Maarten (Dutch sector) 32,221; St Eustatius 1,839; Saba 1,130.

**Density** (per sq km, 1992): Curaçao 324.5; Bonaire 35.4; St Maarten (Dutch sector) 947.7; St Eustatius 87.6; Saba 86.9; Total 236.8.

**Births, Marriages and Deaths** (1993): Registered live births 3,854; Registered marriages 1,223; Registered deaths 1,379.

**Expectation of Life** (years at birth, 1981): males 71.13; females 75.75. Source: UN, *Demographic Yearbook*.

**Economically Active Population** (1992 census): Agriculture, fishing and mining 798; Manufacturing 6,949; Electricity, gas and water 1,243; Construction 6,497; Trade, restaurants and hotels 20,879; Transport, storage and communications 4,991; Financing, insurance, real estate and business services 8,204; Other services 24,761. Total employed 74,322; Unemployed 13,434; Total labour force 87,756.

## AGRICULTURE, ETC.

**Livestock** (FAO estimates, '000 head, year ending September 1993, incl. Aruba): Asses 3; Cattle 1; Pigs 3; Goats 13; Sheep 7. Source: FAO, *Production Yearbook*.

**Livestock Products** (FAO estimates, '000 metric tons, 1993, incl. Aruba): Meat 1; Hen eggs 0.5. Source: FAO, *Production Yearbook*.

**Fishing** (FAO estimates, metric tons, live weight): Total catch 1,200 in 1990; 1,100 in 1991; 1,150 in 1992. Source: FAO, *Yearbook of Fishery Statistics*.

## MINING

**Production** (estimate, incl. Aruba, '000 metric tons, 1990): Salt (unrefined) 354. Source: US Bureau of Mines.

## INDUSTRY

**Production** (estimates, excl. Aruba, '000 metric tons, unless otherwise indicated, 1991): Kerosene 25; Jet fuel 750; Residual fuel oils 4,675; Lubricating oils 300; Petroleum bitumen (asphalt) 455; Liquefied petroleum gas 40; Motor spirit (petrol) 1,300; Aviation gasoline 10; Distillate fuel oils (gas oil) 2,000; Sulphur (recovered) 60; Electric energy (million kWh) 800. Source: UN, *Industrial Statistics Yearbook*.

## FINANCE

**Currency and Exchange Rates:** 100 cents = 1 Netherlands Antilles gulden (guilder) or florin (NA Fl.). *Sterling and Dollar Equivalents* (31 December 1994): £1 sterling = NA Fl. 2.800; US $1 = NA Fl. 1.790; NA Fl. 100 = £35.71 = $55.87. *Exchange Rate:* In December 1971 the central bank's mid-point rate was fixed at US $1 = NA Fl. 1.80. In 1989 this was adjusted to $1 = NA Fl. 1.79.

**Central Government Budget** (NA Fl. million, 1993): Revenue 571.6 (Current 446.2, Capital 125.4), excl. grants received (94.8); Expenditure 614.7 (Current 453.3, Capital 161.4), excl. net lending (37.2).

**International Reserves** (US $ million at 31 December 1994): Gold (national valuation) 38, Foreign exchange 179; Total 217. Source: IMF, *International Financial Statistics*.

**Money Supply** (NA Fl. million at 31 December 1993): Currency outside banks 183.4; Demand deposits at commercial banks 501.9; Private sector deposits at Girosystem Curaçao 60.1; Total (incl. others) 785.0. Source: IMF, *International Financial Statistics*.

**Cost of Living** (Consumer Price Index, year ending 31 December, excl. compulsory social security; base: Oct. 1990 = 100): *Bonaire:* 103.8 in 1992; 106.0 in 1993. *Curaçao:* 103.1 in 1992; 105.2 in 1993. *St Maarten:* 103.2 in 1992; 104.0 in 1993.

**Gross Domestic Product** (excl. Aruba, million NA Fl. at current prices, 1991): Agriculture, fishing, mining, etc. 25.0; Manufacturing 273.4; Electricity, gas and water 132.6; Construction 234.6; Trade, restaurants and hotels 933.2; Transport, storage and communications 391.2; Finance, insurance, real estate and business services 722.5; Community, social and personal services 340.0; Government services 537.8; *Sub-total* 3,590.3; *Less* Imputed bank service charge 194.6; *Gross domestic product* 3,395.7.

**Balance of Payments** (US $ million, 1993): Merchandise exports f.o.b. 226.3; Merchandise imports f.o.b. −1,130.3; *Trade Balance* −904.0; Exports of services 1,284.6; Imports of services −615.3; Other income received 356.4; Other income paid −132.1; Private unrequited transfers (net) −61.6; Official unrequited transfers (net) 56.0; *Current Balance* −15.9; Direct investment (net) 13.2; Portfolio investment (net) −12.5; Other capital (net) 21.5; Net errors and omissions 37.8; *Overall balance* 44.0. Source: IMF, *International Financial Statistics*.

## EXTERNAL TRADE

**Principal Commodities** (Curaçao and Bonaire, NA Fl. million, 1992): *Imports c.i.f.:* Food and live animals 260; Beverages and tobacco 29; Mineral fuels, lubricants, etc. and crude materials 1,965; Chemicals 123; Basic manufactures 221; Machinery and transport equipment 457; Miscellaneous manufactured articles 271; Total (incl. others) 3,344. *Exports f.o.b.:* Food, beverages and tobacco 84; Crude materials (inedible) except fuels 19; Mineral fuels, lubricants, etc. 2,545; Chemical products 25; Manufactured goods 16; Machinery and transport equipment 89; Others 13; Total 2,790.

**Principal Trading Partners** (Curaçao and Bonaire, excl. petroleum and petroleum products, NA Fl. million, 1990): *Imports:* North America 445 (USA 414); EC 316 (Netherlands 218); South America 89; Japan 83; Caribbean 43; Total (incl. others) 1,138. *Exports:* EC 40.6 (Netherlands 28.3, United Kingdom 3.5); Caribbean 35.0; North America 20.6 (USA 20.4); Total (incl. others) 117.3.

## TRANSPORT

**Road Traffic** (motor vehicles registered, 1993): Passenger cars 61,952, Lorries 13,416, Buses 641, Taxis 413, Other cars 3,962, Motor cycles (excl. Saba) 832, Total 81,216.

**International Shipping** (estimated freight traffic, '000 metric tons, 1990, incl. Aruba): Goods loaded 13,905; Goods unloaded 10,462. Source: UN, *Monthly Bulletin of Statistics*.

## TOURISM

**Tourists** (1994): *Stop-over Tourists* (in hotels): Bonaire 60,700; Curaçao 238,310; St Maarten 565,386; St Eustatius (provisional, 1993) 15,500; Saba (provisional, 1993) 27,000. *Cruise Tourists:* Bonaire 10,182; Curaçao 157,230; St Maarten 659,943; St Eustatius (1988) 3,351; Saba (1989) 14,354.

## COMMUNICATIONS MEDIA

**Radio Receivers** (1992): 205,000 in use.
**Television Receivers** (1992): 64,000 in use.
**Telephones** (1993): 67,984 subscriber lines.
**Daily Newspapers** (1992): 6 titles (estimated circulation 53,000 copies per issue).
Source: mainly UNESCO, *Statistical Yearbook*.

## EDUCATION

**Pre-primary** (1991): 74 schools; 7,462 pupils; 314 teachers.
**Primary** (1991): 86 schools; 22,410 pupils; 1,077 teachers.
**Junior High** (1991): 17 schools; 4,941 pupils; 348 teachers.
**Senior High** (1991): 6 schools; 3,134 pupils; 298 teachers.
**Technical and Vocational** (1991): 37 institutions; 6,247 pupils; 431 teachers.
**Teacher Training** (1991): 1 institution; 107 students; 28 teachers (1983).
**University of the Netherlands Antilles** (1991): 620 students; 53 teachers (1983).
**Special Education** (1991): 19 schools; 1,538 pupils; 182 teachers.

# Directory

## The Constitution

The form of government for the Netherlands Antilles is embodied in the Charter of the Kingdom of the Netherlands, which came into force on 20 December 1954. The Netherlands, the Netherlands Antilles and, since 1986, Aruba each enjoy full autonomy in domestic and internal affairs and are united on a basis of equality for the protection of their common interests and the granting of mutual assistance.

The monarch of the Netherlands is represented in the Netherlands Antilles by the Governor, who is appointed by the Dutch Crown for a term of six years. The central Government of the Netherlands Antilles appoints a Minister Plenipotentiary to represent the Antilles in the Government of the Kingdom. Whenever the Netherlands Council of Ministers is dealing with matters coming under the heading of joint affairs of the realm (in practice mainly foreign affairs and defence), the Council assumes the status of Council of Ministers of the Kingdom. In that event, the Minister Plenipotentiary appointed by the Government of the Netherlands Antilles takes part, with full voting powers, in the deliberations.

A legislative proposal regarding affairs of the realm and applying to the Netherlands Antilles as well as to the 'metropolitan' Netherlands is sent, simultaneously with its submission, to the Staten Generaal (the Netherlands parliament) and to the Staten (parliament) of the Netherlands Antilles. The latter body can report in writing to the Staten Generaal on the draft Kingdom Statute and designate one or more special delegates to attend the debates and furnish information in the meetings of the Chambers of the Staten Generaal. Before the final vote on a draft the Minister Plenipotentiary has the right to express an opinion on it. If he disapproves of the draft, and if in the Second Chamber a three-fifths' majority of the votes cast is not obtained, the discussions on the draft are suspended and further deliberations take place in the Council of Ministers of the Kingdom. When special delegates attend the meetings of the Chambers this right devolves upon the delegates of the parliamentary body designated for this purpose.

The Governor has executive power in external affairs, which he exercises in co-operation with the Council of Ministers. He is assisted by an advisory council which consists of at least five members appointed by him.

Executive power in internal affairs is vested in the nominated Council of Ministers, responsible to the Staten. The Netherlands Antilles Staten consists of 22 members, who are elected by universal adult suffrage for four years (subject to dissolution). Each island forms an electoral district. Curaçao elects 14 members, Bonaire three members, St Maarten three members and Saba and St Eustatius one member each. In the islands where more than one member is elected, the election is by proportional representation. Inhabitants have the right to vote if they have Dutch nationality and have reached 18 years of age. Voting is not compulsory. Each island territory also elects its Island Council (Curaçao 21 members, Bonaire 9, St Maarten 7, St Eustatius and Saba 5), and its internal affairs are managed by an executive council, consisting of the Gezaghebber (Lieutenant-Governor), and a number of commissioners. The central Government of the Netherlands Antilles has the right to annul any local island decision which is in conflict with the public interest or the Constitution. Control of the police, communications, monetary affairs, health and education remain under the jurisdiction of the central Government.

On 1 January 1986 Aruba acquired separate status (*status aparte*) within the Kingdom of the Netherlands. However, in economic and monetary affairs there is a co-operative union between Aruba and the Antilles of the Five, known as the 'Union of the Netherlands Antilles and Aruba'.

## The Government

### HEAD OF STATE

HM Queen BEATRIX of the Netherlands.
**Governor:** JAIME M. SALEH.

### COUNCIL OF MINISTERS

A coalition of the Partido Antía Restrukturá (PAR), the Movimentu Antiyas Nobo (MAN), the Democratische Partij—Bonaire (DP—B), the St Maarten Patriotic Alliance (SPA), the Windward Islands People's Movement (WIPM), the Democratic Party—Statia (DP—Ste) and an independent member.

(June 1995)

**Prime Minister and Minister of General Affairs:** MIGUEL A. POURIER (PAR).
**Deputy Prime Minister and Minister of Economic Affairs and of Transport and Communications:** LEO A. I. CHANCE (SPA).
**Minister of Development, Co-operation, Women's Affairs and Humanitarian Affairs:** SIMONA EDITH STRAUSS-MARCERA (DP—B).
**Minister of Finance:** ETIENNE N. YS (PAR).
**Minister of Public Health and Environmental Affairs:** STANLEY H. INDERSON (MAN).
**Minister of Justice:** PEDRO J. ATACHO (PAR).
**Minister of Education, Sport, Culture and Youth Affairs:** MARTA B. VAN DEN KROEF-DIJKHOFF (PAR).
**Minister of Labour and Social Affairs:** JEFFREY A. CORION (independent).

There are three Secretaries of State.

**Minister Plenipotentiary and Member of the Council of Ministers of the Realm for the Netherlands Antilles:** Dr CAREL PIETER DE HASETH (PAR).

### GEZAGHEBBERS
(Lieutenant-Governors)

**Bonaire:** Dr FRITZ GOEDGEDRAG, Kralendijk, Bonaire; tel. (7) 5330.
**Curaçao:** STANLEY BETRIAN, Centraal Bestuurskantoor, Concordiastraat 24, Willemstad, Curaçao; tel. (9) 61-2900.
**Saba:** SYDNEY A. E. SORTON, The Bottom, Saba; tel. (4) 3311.
**St Eustatius:** IRWIN E. TEMMER, Oranjestad, St Eustatius; tel. (3) 2213.
**St Maarten:** DENNIS RICHARDSON, Central Administration, Secretariat, Philipsburg, St Maarten; tel. (5) 22233.

### MINISTRIES

**Office of the Governor:** Fort Amsterdam 2, Willemstad, Curaçao; tel. (9) 61-2000; telex 1119; fax (9) 61-1412.

**Ministry of Development, Co-operation, Women's Affairs and Humanitarian Affairs:** Fort Amsterdam 17, Willemstad, Curaçao; tel. (9) 61-1866; fax (9) 61-1268.
**Ministry of Economic Affairs:** De Rouvilleweg 7, Willemstad, Curaçao; tel. (9) 62-6400; telex 1233.
**Ministry of Education, Sport, Culture and Youth Affairs:** Fort Amsterdam 17, Willemstad, Curaçao; tel. (9) 61-6033; fax (9) 61-8941.
**Ministry of Finance:** Pietermaai 4–4A, Willemstad, Curaçao; tel. (9) 61-2052.
**Ministry of Public Health and Environmental Affairs:** Heelsumstraat, Willemstad, Curaçao; tel. (9) 61-4555; fax (9) 61-2388.
**Ministry of Justice:** Fort Amsterdam 17, Willemstad, Curaçao; tel. (9) 61-2494; telex 1079.
**Ministry of Labour and Social Affairs:** Fort Amsterdam 17, Willemstad, Curaçao; tel. (9) 61-3988.
**Ministry of Transport and Communications:** Fort Amsterdam 17, Willemstad, Curaçao; tel. (9) 61-3988; telex 1079.

**Office of the Minister Plenipotentiary for the Netherlands Antilles:** Antillenhuis, Badhuisweg 173–175, 2597 JP The Hague, the Netherlands; tel. (70) 351-2811; fax (70) 351-2722.

## Legislature

### STATEN

**Speaker:** LUCILLE A. GEORGE-WOUT.

**General Election, 25 February 1994**

| Party | Votes | Seats |
|---|---|---|
| Partido Antía Restrukturá | 33,996 | 8 |
| Partido Nashonal di Pueblo | 16,049 | 3 |
| Movimentu Antiyas Nobo | 10,949 | 2 |
| St Maarten Patriotic Alliance | 3,369 | 2 |
| Democratische Partij—Bonaire | 2,590 | 2 |
| Democratische Partij—Curaçao | 5,856 | 1 |
| Democratic Party—St Maarten | 2,964 | 1 |
| Unión Patriótico Bonairiano | 2,110 | 1 |
| Windward Islands People's Movement | 453 | 1 |
| Democratic Party—Statia | 438 | 1 |
| Others | 8,537 | — |
| **Total** | **87,311** | **22** |

## Political Organizations

**Democratische Partij—Bonaire (DP—B)** (Democratic Party—Bonaire): Kaya America 13A, POB 294, Kralendijk, Bonaire; tel. (7) 5923; fax (7) 7341; f. 1954; also known as Partido Democratico Boneriano; Leader JOPIE ABRAHAM.

**Democratische Partij—Curaçao (DP—C)** (Democratic Party—Curaçao): Neptunusweg 28, Willemstad, Curaçao; tel. (9) 75432; telex 1171; f. 1944; Leader RAYMOND BENTOERA.

**Democratic Party—St Maarten (DP—StM):** Philipsburg, POB 414, St Maarten; tel. (5) 30050; fax (5) 22455; Leader CLAUDE WATHEY.

**Democratic Party—Statia (DP—StE):** Oranjestad, St Eustatius; Leader KENNETH VAN PUTTEN.

**Frente Obrero i Liberashon 30 di mei (FOL)** (Workers' Liberation Front of 30 May): Fensohnstr. 14, Willemstad, Curaçao; tel. (9) 61-8105; f. 1969; formed alliance with SI for 1990 election; Leaders WILSON GODETT, STANLEY INDERSEN, TOLINCHI PIETERSZ.

**Movimentu Antiyas Nobo (MAN)** (Movement for a New Antilles): Landhuis Morgenster, Willemstad, Curaçao; tel. (9) 68-4781; f. 1971; socialist; Leader DOMINICO (DON) F. MARTINA.

**Nos Patria:** Willemstad, Curaçao; Leader CHIN BEHILIA.

**People's Democratic Party (PDP):** Philipsburg, St Maarten; tel. (5) 22696; Leader MILLICENT DE WEEVER.

**Partido Antía Restrukturá (PAR)** (Restructured Antilles Party): Fokkerweg 26, Unit 3, Curaçao; tel. (9) 65-2566; fax (9) 65-2622; f. 1993; social-Christian ideology; Pres. MIGUEL A. POURIER; Sec. PEDRO J. ATACHO.

**Partido Nashonal di Pueblo (PNP)** (National People's Party): Willemstad, Curaçao; f. 1948; also known as Nationale Volkspartij; Social Christian Party; Leader MARIA PH. LIBERIA-PETERS.

**Partido Obrero di Bonaire** (Bonaire Workers' Party): Kralendijk, Bonaire.

**St Maarten Patriotic Alliance (SPA):** Frontstraat 69, Philipsburg, St Maarten; tel. (5) 31064; fax (5) 31065; Leader VANCE JAMES, Jr.

**Social Independiente (SI):** Willemstad, Curaçao, f. 1986 by fmr PNP mems in Curaçao; formed electoral alliance with FOL for 1990 election; Leader GEORGE HUECK.

**Unión Patriótico Bonairiano (UPB)** (Patriotic Union of Bonaire): POB 55, Kralendijk, Bonaire; 2,134 mems; Leader CH. L. R. (RUDI) ELLIS; Sec.-Gen. C. V. WINKLAAR.

**Windward Islands People's Movement (WIPM):** Windwardside, POB 525, Saba; tel. (4) 2244; Chair. and Leader WILL JOHNSTON; Sec.-Gen. DAVE LEVENSTONE.

## Religion

### CHRISTIANITY

Most of the population were Christian, the predominant denomination being Roman Catholicism. According to the 1992 census, Roman Catholics formed the largest single group on four of the five islands: 82% of the population of Bonaire, 81% on Curaçao, 65% on Saba and 41% on St Maarten. On St Eustatius the Methodists formed the largest single denomination (31%). Of the other denominations, the main ones were the Anglicans and the Dutch Reformed Church. There were also small communities of Jews, Muslims and Bahá'ís.

**Curaçaose Raad van Kerken** (Curaçao Council of Churches): Ronde Klipweg 11, Willemstad, Curaçao; tel. (9) 37-9672; fax (9) 362183; f. 1958; six member churches; Chair. ANNA T. KELIE; Exec. Sec. PAUL VAN DER WAAL.

#### The Roman Catholic Church

The Netherlands Antilles and Aruba together form the diocese of Willemstad, suffragan to the archdiocese of Port of Spain (Trinidad and Tobago). At 31 December 1993 the diocese numbered an estimated 197,481 adherents. Some 80% of the population of the Antilles of the Five were Roman Catholics in 1993. The Bishop participates in the Antilles Episcopal Conference, currently based in Port of Spain, Trinidad and Tobago.

**Bishop of Willemstad:** Rt Rev. WILLEM MICHEL ELLIS, Breedestraat 31, Otrobanda, Willemstad, Curaçao; tel. (9) 62-5876; fax (9) 62-7437.

#### The Anglican Communion

Saba, St Eustatius and St Maarten form part of the diocese of the North Eastern Caribbean and Aruba, within the Church in the Province of the West Indies. The Bishop, who is also Archbishop of the Province, is resident in St John's, Antigua.

#### Other Churches

**Iglesia Protestant Uni** (United Protestant Church): Fortkerk, Fort Amsterdam, Willemstad, Curaçao; f. 1825 by union of Dutch Reformed and Evangelical Lutheran Churches; Pres. Rev. G. J. SCHÜSSLER; 8 congregations; 11,280 adherents.

**Methodist Church:** Oranjestad, St Eustatius.

Other denominations active in the islands include the Moravian, Apostolic Faith, Wesleyan Holiness and Norwegian Seamen's Churches, the Baptists, Calvinists, Jehovah's Witnesses, Evangelists, Seventh-day Adventists, the Church of Christ and the New Testament Church of God.

### JUDAISM

**The Jewish Community:** Congregation Mikvé Israel-Emanuel, Hanchi di Snoa 29, POB 322, Willemstad, Curaçao; tel. (9) 61-1067; fax (9) 61-1214; f. 1732 on present site; about 350 mems.

## Judicial System

Legal authority is exercised by the Court of First Instance (which sits in all the islands) and in appeal by the Joint High Court of Justice of the Netherlands Antilles and Aruba. The members of the Joint High Court of Justice sit singly as judges in the Courts of First Instance. The Chief Justice of the Joint High Court of Justice, its members (a maximum of 30) and the Attorneys-General of the Netherlands Antilles and of Aruba are appointed for life by the Dutch monarch, after consultation with the Governments of the Netherlands Antilles and Aruba.

**Joint High Court of Justice:** Wilhelminaplein 4, Willemstad, Curaçao; tel. (9) 63-4111.

**Chief Justice of the Joint High Court:** Dr L. A. J. DE LANNOY.

**Attorney-General of the Netherlands Antilles:** Dr R. F. PIETERSZ.

## The Press

**Amigoe:** Scherpenheuvel z/n, POB 577, Willemstad, Curaçao; tel. (9) 67-2000; fax (9) 67-4524; f. 1884; Christian; daily; evening; Dutch; Dir INGRID DE MAAYER-HOLLANDER; Chief Editor NORBERT HENDRIKSE; circ. 10,000.

**Bala:** Noord Zapateer nst 13, Willemstad, Curaçao; tel. (9) 67-1646; fax (9) 67-1041; daily; Papiamento.

**Beurs-en Nieuwsberichten:** W. I. Compagniestraat 41, POB 215, Willemstad, Curaçao; tel. (9) 62-4680; fax (9) 62-8411; f. 1935; daily; evening; Dutch; Editor H. O. VAN DELDEN; circ. 8,000.

**The Business Journal:** Indjuweg 30A, Willemstad, Curaçao; tel. (9) 61-1367; fax (9) 61-1955; monthly; English.

**The Chronicle:** Pointe Blanche, Philipsburg, St Maarten; tel. (5) 25462; daily; English.

**De Curaçaosche Courant:** Frederikstraat 123, POB 15, Willemstad, Curaçao; tel. (9) 61-2766; fax (9) 62-6535; f. 1812; weekly; Dutch; Editor J. KORIDON.

**Extra:** W. I. Compagniestraat 41, Willemstad, Curaçao; tel. (9) 62-4595; fax (9) 62-7575; daily; morning; Papiamento; Man. R. YRAUSQUIN; Editor MIKE OEHLERS; circ. 20,000.

**Know-How:** Schottegatweg Oost 56, POB 473, Willemstad, Curaçao; tel. (9) 36-7079; fax (9) 36-7080; monthly; English.

**Newsletter of Curaçao Trade and Industry Association:** Kaya Junior Salas 1, POB 49, Willemstad, Curaçao; tel. (9) 61-1210; telex 1055; fax (9) 61-5422; f. 1972; monthly; English and Dutch; economic and industrial paper.

**Nobo:** Scherpenheuvel w/n, POB 323, Willemstad, Curaçao; tel. (9) 67-3500; fax (9) 67-2783; daily; evening; Papiamento; Editor CARLOS DAANTJE; circ. 15,000.

**Nos Isla:** Refineria Isla (Curazao) SA, Emmastad, Curaçao; 2 a month; Papiamento; circ. 2,000.

**Noticiero:** Mamayaweg 4, Willemstad, Curaçao; tel. (9) 61-7744; fax (9) 61-7811; daily; Papiamento; Editor RIGOBERTO GALAN MELENDREZ.

**La Prensa:** W. I. Compagniestraat 41, Willemstad, Curaçao; tel. (9) 62-4086; fax (9) 62-5983; f. 1929; daily; evening; Papiamento; Man. R. YRAUSQUIN; Editor SIGFRIED RIGAUD; circ. 10,750.

**Saba Herald:** The Level, Saba; tel. (4) 2244; f. 1968; monthly; news, local history; Editor WILL JOHNSON; circ. 500.

**St Maarten Guardian:** Vlaun Bldg, Pondfill, POB 1046, Philipsburg, St Maarten; tel. (5) 26022; fax (5) 26043; f. 1989; daily; English; Man. Dir RICHARD F. GIBSON; Man. Editor JOSEPH DOMINIQUE; circ. 4,000.

**Ultimo Noticia:** Frederikstraat 123, Willemstad, Curaçao; tel. (9) 62-3444; fax (9) 62-6535; daily; morning; Papiamento; Editor A. A. JONCKHEER.

**La Unión:** Rotaprint NV, Willemstad, Curaçao; weekly; Papiamento.

### NEWS AGENCIES

**Algemeen Nederlands Persbureau (ANP)** (The Netherlands): Panoramaweg 5, POB 439, Willemstad, Curaçao; tel. (9) 61-2233; telex 1100; fax (9) 61-7431; Representative RONNIE RENS.

**Associated Press (AP)** (USA): Roodeweg 64, Willemstad, Curaçao; tel. (9) 62-6586; Representative ORLANDO CUALES.

## Publishers

**Curaçao Drukkerij en Uitgevers Maatschappij:** Pietermaaiweg, Willemstad, Curaçao.

**Ediciones Populares:** W. I. Compagniestraat 41, Willemstad, Curaçao; f. 1929; Dir RONALD YRAUSQUIN.

**Drukkerij Scherpenheuvel, NV:** Scherpenheuvel, POB 60, Willemstad, Curaçao; tel. (9) 67-1134.

**Drukkerij de Stad NV:** W. I. Compagniestraat 41, Willemstad, Curaçao; tel. (9) 62-3878; fax (9) 62-5983; f. 1929; Dir RONALD YRAUSQUIN.

**Offsetdrukkerij Intergrafia, NV:** Essoweg 54, Willemstad, Curaçao; tel. (9) 64-3180.

## Radio and Television

In 1992, according to UNESCO, there were an estimated 205,000 radio receivers and 64,000 television receivers in use in the Antilles of the Five.

**Landsradio—Telecommunications Administration:** Schouburgweg 22, POB 103, Willemstad, Curaçao; tel. (9) 63-1111; telex 1075.

NETHERLANDS DEPENDENCIES                                                    *The Netherlands Antilles*

## RADIO

**Radio Caribe:** Ledaweg 35, Brievengat, Willemstad, Curaçao; tel. (9) 36-9564; fax (9) 36-9569; f. 1955; commercial station; programmes in Dutch, English, Spanish and Papiamento; Dir-Gen. C. R. HEILLEGGER.

**Radio Curom Z 86** (Curaçaose Radio-Omroep Vereniging): Roodeweg 64, POB 2169, Willemstad, Curaçao; tel. (9) 62-6586; fax (9) 62-5796; f. 1933; broadcasts in Papiamento; also operates **Radio Curom Z FM**; Pres. C. G. GROOTENS; Dir ORLANDO CUALES.

**Radio Exito:** Wolkstraat 15, Willemstad, Curaçao; tel. (9) 65-8884; fax (9) 65-8886.

**Radio Hoyer:** Plasa Horacio Hoyer 21, Willemstad, Curaçao; tel. (9) 61-1678; fax (9) 61-6528; commercial; two stations: Radio Hoyer I (mainly Papiamento, also Spanish) and II (mainly Dutch, also English) in Curaçao; Dir HELEN HOYER.

**Radio Korsou FM:** Bataljonweg 7, POB 3250, Willemstad, Curaçao; tel. (9) 37-3012; fax (9) 37-2888; 24 hrs a day; programmes in Papiamento and Dutch; Owner J. P. C. OOSTERHOF.

    **Laser 101 (101.1 FM):** tel. (9) 37-7139; fax (9) 37-5215; 24 hours a day; music; English and Papiamento; Gen. Man. ALAN H. EVERTSZ.

**Radio Paradise:** ITC Building, Piscadera Bay, POB 6103, Curaçao; tel. (9) 63-6107; fax (9) 63-6404; Man. Dir J. A. VISSER.

**Radio Statia—PJE3:** St Eustatius Broadcasting NV, Korthalweg, St Eustatius; tel. (3) 82262; 12½ hrs daily.

**Semiya Broadcasting:** Klipstraat 2, Willemstad, Curaçao; tel. (9) 62-8287; fax (9) 62-8390.

**Trans World Radio (TWR):** Kaya Gouverneur N. Debrotweg 64, Kralendijk, Bonaire; tel. (7) 8800; telex 446421; fax (7) 8808; religious, educational and cultural station; programmes to South, Central and North America, Caribbean in four languages; Pres. THOMAS J. LOWELL, II; Station Dir THOMAS F. CORCORAN.

**The Voice of St Maarten—PJD2 Radio:** Plaza 21, Backstreet, POB 366, Philipsburg, St Maarten; tel. (5) 22580; fax (5) 24905; also operates **PJD3** on FM (24 hrs); commercial; programmes in English; Gen. Man. DON R. HUGHES.

**Voice of Saba—PJF1:** The Bottom, POB 1, Saba; studio in St Maarten; tel. (5) 63213; also operates The Voice of Saba FM; Man. MAX W. NICHOLSON.

**Voz di Bonaire—PJB2** (Voice of Bonaire): Kaya Gobernador Debrot 2, Kralendijk, Bonaire; tel. (7) 5971; fax (7) 5000; owned by Radiodifucion Boneriano; programmes in Papiamento, Spanish and Dutch; Owner F. DA SILVA PILOTO.

There is a relay station for Radio Nederland on Bonaire.

## TELEVISION

**Leeward Broadcasting Corporation—Television:** POB 375, Philipsburg, St Maarten; tel. (5) 23491; transmissions for 10½ hours daily.

**Antilliaanse Televisie Mij NV** (Antilles Television Co): Berg Arraret, POB 415, Willemstad, Curaçao; tel. (9) 61-1288; telex 3332; fax (9) 61-4138; f. 1960; operates Tele-Curaçao (formerly operated Tele-Aruba); commercial; govt-owned; also operates cable service, offering programmes from US satellite television and two Venezuelan channels; Dir JOSÉ M. CIJNTJE.

Five television channels can be received on Curaçao, in total. Relay stations provide Bonaire with programmes from Curaçao, St Maarten with programmes from Puerto Rico, and Saba and St Eustatius with programmes from St Maarten and neighbouring islands. Curaçao has a publicly-owned cable television service, TDS.

# Finance

(cap. = capital; res = reserves; dep. = deposits; m. = million; brs = branches; amounts in Netherlands Antilles guilders unless otherwise stated)

## BANKING
### Central Bank

**Bank van de Nederlandse Antillen** (Bank of the Netherlands Antilles): Breedestraat 1, Willemstad, Curaçao; tel. (9) 61-3600; telex 1155; fax (9) 61-5004; f. 1828 as Curaçaosche Bank; name changed as above 1962; cap. and res 66m. (Dec. 1991); Chair. M. NICOLINA; Pres. EMSLEY TROMP; Dirs R. REYNAERT, W. BENARD; 1 br in Philipsburg (St Maarten).

### Commercial Banks

**ABN AMRO Bank NV:** Kaya Flamboyan 1, POB 3144, Willemstad, Curaçao; tel. (9) 63-8000; telex 1121; fax (9) 37-0620; f. 1964; Gen. Man H. V. IGNACIO; 6 brs.

**Banco di Caribe NV:** Schottegatweg Oost 205, POB 3785, Willemstad, Curaçao; tel. (9) 61-6588; telex 1266; fax (9) 61-5220; f. 1973; cap. 2.0m., res 11.9m., dep. 315.1m. (Dec. 1992); Man. Dirs E. DE KORT, R. HENRÍQUEZ; 3 brs.

**Banco Industrial de Venezuela:** Handelskade 12, Willemstad, Curaçao; tel. (9) 61-1612; telex 1103; fax (9) 61-6534; f. 1973; Gen. Man. CRISTÓBAL ORLANDO PACHECO MERCHÁN.

**Banco Mercantil CA, SACA (Curaçao):** Abraham de Veerstraat 1, POB 565, Willemstad, Curaçao; tel. (9) 61-1706; telex 1252; fax (9) 61-1828; f. 1988; Gen. Man. FULVIO FERRARO.

**Banco de Venezuela NV:** Hanchi di Snoa 16, POB 131, Curaçao; tel. (9) 61-1777; telex 3041; fax (9) 61-2053; f. 1993; Man. Dirs H. P. F. VON AESCH, R. YANES V., E. BORBERG.

**Bank of Nova Scotia NV** (Canada): Backstreet 62, POB 303, Philipsburg, St Maarten; tel. (5) 22262; telex 8036; fax (5) 22435; f. 1969; Man. ROBERT G. JUDD.

**Barclays Bank plc** (UK): 29 Front St, POB 141, Philipsburg, St Maarten; tel. (5) 23511; telex 8022; fax (5) 24531; f. 1959; Man. EDWARD ARMOGAN; offices in Saba and St Eustatius.

**Chase Manhattan Bank NA** (USA): Chase Financial Center, Soualiga Building, Cannegieter Road (Pondfill) and Mullet Bay Hotel, POB 921, Philipsburg, St Maarten; tel. (5) 53801; telex 8003; fax (5) 53692; f. 1971; Gen. Man. K. BUTLER.

**CITCO Bank Antilles NV:** Schottegatweg Oost 44, POB 707, Willemstad, Curaçao; tel. (9) 37-0388; telex 3394; fax (9) 37-7902; f. 1980 as Curaçao Banking Corporation NV; name changed as above 1985; Man. Dirs R. CAPWELL, L. C. LUCKMAN, Jr; 2 brs.

**Girodienst (Curaçao):** Scharlooweg 35, Curaçao; tel. (9) 61-4999; Gen. Man. H. J. SILVANO.

**Interbank Antilles NV:** Caya Grandi 49, Kralendijk, Bonaire; tel. (7) 5997; fax (7) 7665; f. 1991 as Interbank Bonaire NV, name changed as above 1994; Man. Dirs H. L. MARCHANT, C. R. MANSUR.

**ING Bank NV (Internationale Nederlanden Bank NV):** Kaya W. F. G. (Jombi) Mensing 14, POB 3895, Willemstad, Curaçao; tel. (9) 32-7000; telex 1047; fax (9) 32-7580; f. 1989 as Nederlandse Middenstandsbank NV: name changed as above 1992; Gen. Man. B. KLEIN.

**Maduro & Curiel's Bank NV:** Plaza Jojo Correa 2–4, POB 305, Willemstad, Curaçao; tel. (9) 66-1100; telex 1127; fax (9) 66-1122; f. 1916 as NV Maduro's Bank, 1931 merged with Curiel's Bank; affiliated with Bank of Nova Scotia NV, Toronto; cap. 20.0m., res 92.5m., dep. 1,596.4m. (Dec. 1993); Man. Dir L. K. LYNCH; Chair. and Gen. Man. LIONEL CAPRILES; 12 brs.

**McLaughlin Bank NV:** Wilhelminaplein 14–16, POB 763, Willemstad, Curaçao; tel. (9) 61-2822; telex 3302; fax (9) 61-2820; f. 1989; Man. Dir EDGARD V. LOTMAN; 2 brs.

**MeesPierson (Nederlandse Antillen) NV:** Berg Arrarat 1, POB 3889, Willemstad, Curaçao; tel. (9) 63-9300; telex 3303; fax (9) 61-3943; f. 1952 as Pierson, Heldring and Pierson (Curação) NV; name changed as above 1993; international banking/trust company; Man. Dir J. C. A. BIJLOOS.

**Orco Bank NV:** Dr Henry Fergusonweg 10, POB 4928, Willemstad, Curaçao; tel. (9) 37-2000; telex 3374; fax (9) 37-6741; f. 1986; cap. 52.2m., res 442.0m., dep. 619.8m. (Dec. 1993); Chair. W. GUIS; Pres. C. BROERE.

**St Maarten Commercial Bank NV:** Cannegieterstreet, POB 465, Philipsburg, St Maarten; tel. (5) 25908; telex 8181; fax (5) 25964; f. 1988; Gen. Man. B. CLARKE.

**The Windward Islands Bank Ltd:** Clem Labega Square 7, POB 220, Philipsburg, St Maarten; affiliated to Maduro and Curiel's Bank NV; tel. (5) 22335; telex 8016; fax (5) 24761; f. 1960; cap. and res 3.6m., dep. 53.6m. (Dec. 1984); Man. Dirs V. P. HENRÍQUEZ, W. G. H. STRIJBOSCH.

### 'Offshore' Banks
(without permission to operate locally)

**ABN AMRO Bank Asset Management (Curaçao) NV:** Schottegatweg Zuid Blok E, POB 469, Willemstad, Curaçao; tel. (9) 65-8555; fax (9) 65-6097; f. 1976; Man. B. RENNER.

**Abu Dhabi International Bank NV:** Schottegatweg Oost 130, POB 3141, Willemstad, Curaçao; tel. (9) 61-1299; fax (9) 61-5392; f. 1979; cap. US $20.0m., res $5.0m., dep. $261.7m. (Dec. 1993); Man. Dir JAMES P. STEELE III.

**Banco Caracas NV:** Kaya W.F.G. (Jombi) Mensing 36, POB 3141, Willemstad, Curaçao; tel. (9) 61-1299; fax (9) 61-5392; f. 1984; Pres. GEORGE L. REEVES.

**Banco Consolidado NV:** Handelskrade 12, POB 3141, Willemstad, Curaçao; tel. (9) 61-3423; f. 1978.

**Banco Continental Overseas NV:** Kaya Urdal 3, POB 508, Willemstad, Curaçao; tel. (9) 36-7299; telex 1206; fax (9) 37-8146; f. 1981; Man. Dir HENDRIK SCHUTTE.

**Banco Latino NV:** De Ruyterkade 61, POB 785, Willemstad, Curaçao; tel. (9) 61-2987; telex 3031; fax (9) 61-6163; f. 1978; cap. US $25.0m., res $12.3m., dep. $450.8m. (Nov. 1992); Chair. Dr Gustavo Gómez López; Pres. Folco Falchi.

**Banco Provincial Overseas NV:** Santa Rosaweg 53/55, POB 5312, Willemstad, Curaçao; tel. (9) 37-6011; telex 1425; fax (9) 37-6346; Man. E. Suares.

**Banco Real SA:** Kaya W.F.G. (Jombi) Mensing 36, POB 3141, Willemstad, Curaçao; tel. (9) 61-1299; (9) fax (9) 61-5392; f. 1974.

**Banque Paribas Curaçao NV:** Polarisweg 35, POB 767, Willemstad, Curaçao; tel. (9) 61-8061; fax (9) 61-5151; f. 1976.

**Caribbean American Bank NV:** Kaya Flamboyan 7, Rooi Catootje, POB 2096, Willemstad, Curaçao; tel. (9) 32-5200; telex 3272; fax (9) 32-5325; Man. Dir Dr Marco Tulio Henríquez.

**Crédit Lyonnais Bank Nederland NV:** Office Park Zeelandia, Kaya W.F.G. (Jombi) Mensing 18, POB 599, Willemstad, Curaçao; tel. (9) 61-1122; telex 1170; fax (9) 65-6265; Gen. Man. J. A. Brouwer.

**FGH Finance NV:** ITC Building, Piscadera Bay, POB 6100, Curaçao; tel. (9) 63-6300; telex 1479; fax (9) 63-6430; Man. Dir J. D. Overberg.

**F. Van Lanschot Bankiers (Curaçao) NV:** Schottegatweg Oost 32, POB 4799, Willemstad, Curaçao; tel. (9) 37-1011; telex 3255; fax (9) 37-1086; f. 1962; Man. A. van Geest.

**First Curaçao International Bank NV:** Office Park Zeelandia, Kaya W.F.G. (Jombi) Mensing 18, POB 299, Willemstad, Curaçao; tel. (9) 37-2100; telex 1058; fax (9) 37-2018; f. 1973; cap. and res US $55m., dep. $244m. (1988); Pres. and CEO J. Ch. Deuss; Man. M. Neuman-Rouira.

**Rabobank Curaçao NV:** Scharloweg 55, POB 3876, Willemstad, Curaçao; tel. (9) 65-2011; telex 3422; fax (9) 65-2066; f. 1978; cap. 100.0m., res 83.7m., dep. 1,352.3m. (Dec. 1993); Chair. H. W. E. Riedlin; Gen. Man. Donald F. Heukels.

**Toronto Dominion (Curaçao) NV:** c/o SCRIBA NV, Polarisweg 31–33, POB 703, Willemstad, Curaçao; tel. (9) 61-3199; fax (9) 61-1099; f. 1981; Man. E. L. Goulding.

**Union Bancaire Privée—CBI-TDB:** John B. Gorsiraweg 6, POB 3889, Willemstad, Curaçao; tel. (9) 63-9300; fax (9) 61-4129; fmrly Compagnie de Banque et d'Investissements.

Other 'offshore' banks in the Netherlands Antilles include American Express Overseas Credit Corporation NV, Banco Aliado NV, Banco del Orinoco (Bonaire) NV, Banco Mercantil Venezolano NV, Banco Principal NV, Banco Provincial International NV, Banco Tequendama (Curaçao) NV, Banque de Suez Nederland International NV, Banrey Banking and Trust Company NV, Banunion NV, Citco Banking Corporation NV, Compagnie Bancaire des Antilles NV, Deutche Bank Finance NV, De Nationale Investeringsbank NA, NV, Exprinter International Bank NV, Ebna Bank NV, FGH Bank (Antilles) NV, Granite Structure Bank NV, Integra Bank (Overseas) NV, Lavoro Bank Overseas NV, Lombard-Atlantic Bank NV, Middenbank (Curaçao) NV, Netherlands Caribbean Bank NV, Noro Bank NV, Premier Bank International NV, Safra Bank NV, The Caribbean American Bank NV.

### Other Banks

**Ontwikkelingsbank van de Nederlandse Antillen:** Salinja 206, Willemstad, Curaçao; tel. (9) 61-5551; f. 1981; provides long-term credit for export-oriented development projects.

**Postspaarbank:** Waaigatplein 1, Willemstad, Curaçao; tel. (9) 61-1126; fax (9) 61-7851; f. 1905; post office savings' bank; Chair. H. J. J. Victoria; cap. 21m.; 20 brs.

There are also several mortgage banks.

### Banking Associations

**Association of Offshore Bankers of the Netherlands Antilles:** c/o CITCO Bank Antilles NV, Schottegatweg Oost 44, POB 707, Willemstad, Curaçao; tel. (9) 32-2322; fax (9) 37-7902; Pres. L. C.Luckmann.

**Curaçao Bankers' Association (CBA):** Plaza Jojo Correa 2–4, Willemstad, Curaçao; tel. (9) 66-1100; fax (9) 66-1122; Pres. L. Capriles.

### INSURANCE

A number of foreign companies have offices in Curaçao, mainly British, Canadian, Dutch and US firms.

**Netherlands Antilles Insurers Union (NAVV):** c/o ING-Fatum, Cas Coraweg 2, Willemstad, Curaçao; tel. (9) 33-3333; fax (9) 37-0176; Pres. S. C. Bakmeijer.

## Trade and Industry

### CHAMBERS OF COMMERCE AND INDUSTRY

**Bonaire Chamber of Commerce and Industry:** Princess Mariestraat, POB 52, Kralendijk, Bonaire; tel. (7) 5595; fax (7) 8995.

**Curaçao Chamber of Commerce and Industry:** Kaya Junior Salas 1, POB 10, Willemstad, Curaçao; tel. (9) 61-1455; fax (9) 61-5652; Pres. Richard N. Hart; Exec. Dir Michael Hellburg.

**St Maarten Chamber of Commerce and Industry:** W. J. A. Nisbeth Rd, POB 454, Philipsburg, St Maarten; tel. (5) 23590; telex 8063; fax (5) 23512; f. 1979; Exec. Dir Oswald Francis.

### MARKETING ASSOCIATION

**Curaçao Inc.:** ITC Bldg, Piscadera Bay, POB 6112, Curaçao; tel. (9) 63-6250; fax (9) 63-6485; f. 1988; 10 mems, including Antillean Airlines, Curaçao Chamber of Commerce, Curaçao Bankers Association, and tourism and trade asscns; Man. Dir Richard López-Ramírez.

### DEVELOPMENT ORGANIZATIONS

**Curaçao Industrial and International Trade Development Company—CURINDE:** Emancipatie Blvd 7, Willemstad, Curaçao; tel. (9) 37-6000; telex 1459; fax (9) 37-1336; f. 1980; manages the 68-acre Free Zone and the Brievengat Industrial Park; Man. Dir E. R. Smeulders.

**Foreign Investment Agency Curaçao—FIAC:** Scharlooweg 174, Curaçao; tel. (9) 65-7044; telex 1456; fax (9) 61-5788.

**International Trade Center Curaçao:** ITC Bldg, POB 6005, Piscadera Bay, Curaçao; tel. (9) 63-6100; fax (9) 62-4408.

### COMMERCIAL AND INDUSTRIAL ASSOCIATIONS

**Association of Industrialists of the Netherlands Antilles (ASINA):** Kaya Junior Salas 1, Willemstad, Curaçao; tel. (9) 61-2353; fax (9) 65-8040; Pres. R. M. Lucia.

**Bonaire Trade and Industry Asscn** (Vereniging Bedrijfsleven Bonaire): POB 371, Kralendijk, Bonaire.

**Curaçao Exporters' Association:** Distribution Centre, ITC Bldg, Piscadera Bay, Willemstad, Curaçao; tel. (9) 62-8666; fax (9) 62-8681; Pres. O. Ergun.

**Curaçao Trade and Industry Asscn** (Vereniging Bedrijfsleven Curaçao—VBC): Kaya Junior Salas 1, POB 49, Willemstad, Curaçao; tel. (9) 61-1210; telex 1055; fax (9) 61-5652; Pres. Deanna Chemaly; Exec. Dir R. P. J. Lieuw.

**Offshore Association of the Netherlands Antilles (VOB):** c/o Holland Intertrust (Antilles) NV, De Ruyterkade 58A, Willemstad, Curaçao; tel. (9) 61-3277; fax (9) 61-1061; Pres. G. E. Elias.

### TRADE UNIONS

**Algemene Bond van Overheidspersoneel—ABVO** (General Union of Civil Servants): POB 3604, Willemstad, Curaçao; tel. (9) 76097; f. 1936; Pres. F. S. Britto; Sec. S. J. Heerenveen; 5,000 mems.

**Algemene Federatie van Bonaireaanse Werknemers (AFBW):** Kralendijk, Bonaire.

**Central General di Trahado di Corsow—CGTC** (General Headquarters for Workers of Curaçao): POB 2078, Willemstad, Curaçao; tel. (9) 62-3995; fax (9) 62-7700; f. 1949; Sec.-Gen. Oscar I. Semerel.

**Curaçaosche Federatie van Werknemers** (Curaçao Federation of Workers): Schouwburgweg 44, Willemstad, Curaçao; tel. (9) 76300; f. 1964; Pres. Wilfred Spencer; Sec.-Gen. Ronchi Isenia; 204 affiliated unions; about 2,000 mems.

**Federashon Bonaireana di Trabou (FEDEBON):** Kaya Krabè 6, Nikiboko, POB 324, Bonaire; tel. and fax (7) 8845; Pres. Gerold Bernabela.

**Petroleum Workers' Federation of Curaçao:** Willemstad, Curaçao; affiliated to Int. Petroleum and Chemical Workers' Fed.; tel. (9) 37-0255; fax (9) 37-5250; f. 1955; Pres. R. G. Gijsbertha; about 1,500 mems.

**Sentral di Sindikatonan di Korsou—SSK** (Confederation of Curaçao Trade Unions): Schouwburgweg 44, POB 3036, Willemstad; tel. (9) 76300; 6,000 mems.

**Sindikato di Trahado den Edukashon na Korsou—SITEK** (Curaçao Schoolteachers' Trade Union): Landhuis Stenen Koraal, Willemstad, Curaçao; tel. (9) 682902; fax (9) 690552; 1,234 mems.

**Windward Islands' Federation of Labour (WIFOL):** Convention Centre, Pond Fill, Long Wall Rd, Prince Bernard Bridge, POB 1097, St Maarten; Pres. Theophilus Thompson.

## Transport

### RAILWAYS

There are no railways.

# NETHERLANDS DEPENDENCIES — The Netherlands Antilles

## ROADS

All the islands have a good system of all-weather roads. There were 590 km of roads in 1992, of which 300 km were paved.

## SHIPPING

Curaçao is an important centre for the refining and transhipment of Venezuelan and Middle Eastern petroleum. Willemstad is served by the Schottegat harbour, set in a wide bay with a long channel and deep water. Facilities for handling containerized traffic at Willemstad were inaugurated in 1984. Curaçao is also served by ports at Bullen Bay and Caracas Bay. St Maarten is one of the Caribbean's leading ports for visits by cruise ships. Each of the other islands has a good harbour, except for Saba which has one inlet, equipped with a large pier. Many foreign shipping lines call at ports in the Netherlands Antilles.

**Curaçao Ports Authority:** Werf de Wilde, POB 689, Willemstad, Curaçao; tel. (9) 61-4422; telex 3339; fax (9) 61-3907; Man. Dir E. Voges.

**Harbour Corporation of St Maarten:** Emmaplein, Philipsburg, St Maarten; tel. (5) 22472; port authority.

**Curaçao Shippers' Association:** Kaya Flamboyan 11, Willemstad, Curaçao; tel. (9) 37-0600; fax (9) 37-3875; Pres. A. Beaujon.

### Principal Shipping Companies

**Caribbean Cargo Services NV:** Jan Thiel w/n, POB 442, Willemstad, Curaçao; tel. (9) 67-2588; telex 3438.

**Curaçao Ports Services Inc. NV—CPS.** Curaçao Container Terminal, POB 170, Curaçao; tel. (9) 61-5177; fax (9) 61-3732; Man. Dir Karel Jan. O. Aster.

**Dammers & van der Heide, Shipping and Trading (Antilles) Inc.:** Kaya Flamboyan 11, POB 3018, Willemstad, Curaçao; tel. (9) 37-0600; telex 3306; fax (9) 37-3875; Man. Dir J. J. Ponsen.

**Gomez Transport NV:** Schottegatweg Oost 128, Willemstad, Curaçao; tel. (9) 61-5882; telex 3002; Man. Fernando da Costa Gomez.

**Hal Antillen NV:** De Ruyterkade 63, POB 812, Curaçao.

**Intermodal Container Services NV:** Fokkerweg 30, Willemstad, POB 3747, Curaçao; tel. (9) 61-3330; telex 3038; Mans A. R. Beaujon, N. N. Harms.

**S. E. L. Maduro & Sons (Curaçao) Inc:** Maduro Plaza, Dokweg 19, Willemstad, POB 3304, Curaçao; tel. (9) 37-6564; telex 1092; fax (9) 37-1266; Pres. H. A. van der Kwast; Vice-Pres. E. E. Stassart.

**Anthony Veder & Co NV:** Zeelandia, POB 3677, Curaçao; tel. (9) 61-4700; telex 3338; fax (9) 61-2576; Man. Dir Joop van Vliet.

## CIVIL AVIATION

There are international airports at Curaçao (Dr A. Plesman, or Hato, 12 km (7.5 miles) from Willemstad), Bonaire (Flamingo Field) and St Maarten (Princess Juliana, 16 km (10 miles) from Philipsburg); and airfields for inter-island flights at St Eustatius and Saba.

**ALM—Antilliaanse Luchtvaart Maatschappij** (Antillean Airlines): Hato International Airport, Curaçao; tel. (9) 33-8888; telex 1114; fax (9) 33-8300; f. 1964 to assume responsibilities of the Caribbean division of KLM (The Netherlands); majority govt-owned since 1969; internal services between Bonaire, Curaçao and St Maarten; external services to destinations in North and South America and within the Caribbean; Pres. K. J. Chong.

**Windward Islands Airways International (WIA—Winair) NV:** Princess Juliana Airport, POB 2088, Philipsburg, St Maarten; tel. (5) 52568; fax (5) 44229; f. 1961; govt-owned since 1974; scheduled flights to Lesser Antilles and charter flights throughout Eastern Caribbean; Chair. G. Damoen; Man. Dir H. M. Smith.

# Tourism

Tourism is a major industry on all the islands. The principal attractions for tourists are the white, sandy beaches, marine wildlife and diving facilities. There are marine parks in the waters around Curaçao, Bonaire and Saba. The numerous historic sites are of interest to visitors. The largest number of tourists visit St Maarten, Curaçao and Bonaire. In 1994 these three islands received 864,396 stop-over visitors (of whom 65.4% were on St Maarten) and 827,355 cruise-ship passengers (of whom 79.8% were on St Maarten). Saba had an estimated 27,000 stop-over visitors in 1993 and 14,354 cruise-ship passengers in 1989; St Eustatius received an estimated 15,500 stop-over visitors in 1993 and 3,351 cruise-ship passengers in 1988. Receipts from tourism totalled some NA Fl. 1,000m. in 1993.

**Bonaire Government Tourist Board:** Kaya Simon Bolivar 12, Kralendijk, Bonaire; tel. (7) 8322; fax (7) 8408; Dir Ronnie Pieters.

**Curaçao Tourism Development Foundation (Tourism Development Bureau):** Pietermaai 19, POB 3266, Willemstad, Curaçao; tel. (9) 61-6000; fax (9) 61-2305; Dir Pieter Sampson.

**Saba Tourist Office:** Windwardside, POB 527, Saba; tel. (4) 62231; telex 8006; fax (4) 62350; Dir Glenn C. Holm.

**St Eustatius Tourism Development Foundation:** Fort Oranje Straat z/n, Oranjestad, St Eustatius; tel. (3) 82433; fax (3) 82433; Dir Alida Francis.

**St Maarten Tourist Board:** Walter Nisbeth Rd 23, Philipsburg, St Maarten; tel. (5) 22337; fax (5) 22734; Dir Cornelius de Weever.

### HOTEL ASSOCIATIONS

**Bonaire Hotel and Tourism Association:** Kralendijk, Bonaire; Man. Dir Hugo Gerharts.

**Curaçao Hotel and Tourism Association (CHATA):** ITC Building, Piscadera Bay, POB 6115, Curaçao; tel. (9) 63-6260; fax (9) 63-6445; Pres. F. N. Moller.

**St Maarten Hotel Association:** Promenade 14, POB 486, Philipsburg, St Maarten; tel. (5) 23133; telex 8014.

# NEW ZEALAND

## Introductory Survey

### Location, Climate, Language, Religion, Flag, Capital

The Dominion of New Zealand lies in the South Pacific Ocean, about 1,750 km (1,100 miles) south-east of Australia. It consists of North Island and South Island, separated by the narrow Cook Strait, and several smaller islands, including Stewart Island in the south. The climate is temperate and moist, with an average temperature of 12°C (52°F), except in the far north, where higher temperatures are reached. The official language is English, but the indigenous Maori inhabitants (an estimated 9.6% of the total population in 1991) also use their own language. At the 1991 census, 62.1% of the inhabitants professed Christianity: 22.1% were Anglicans, 16.3% Presbyterians and 15.0% Roman Catholics. The national flag (proportions 2 by 1) is dark blue, with a representation of the United Kingdom flag as a canton in the upper hoist. In the fly are four five-pointed red stars, edged in white, in the form of the Southern Cross constellation. The capital is Wellington, on North Island.

### Recent History

New Zealand is a former British colony. It became a dominion, under the British Crown, in 1907 and achieved full independence by the Statute of Westminster, adopted by the British Parliament in 1931 and accepted by New Zealand in 1947.

In 1962 Western Samoa (q.v.), formerly administered by New Zealand, achieved independence, and in 1965 the Cook Islands attained full internal self-government, but retained many links, including common citizenship, with New Zealand. In October 1974 Niue, one of New Zealand's island territories, obtained similar status 'in free association with New Zealand'. New Zealand retains two Dependent Territories, Ross Dependency and Tokelau (for details of New Zealand's Dependent and Associated Territories, see p. 2257).

In December 1972 the first Labour Government for more than 12 years came to power, under the leadership of Norman Kirk, after a succession of New Zealand National Party administrations. The Labour Party took office at a time when the economy was thriving, mainly as a result of a sharp increase in international prices for agricultural commodities. However, this prosperity was accompanied by inflation, and soaring domestic demand and the international energy crisis of 1973–74 led to a rapid rise in imports, a reduction in exchange reserves and a severe balance-of-payments problem.

The Labour Government's foreign policy was more independent than that of its predecessors. It phased out New Zealand's military commitments under the South-East Asia Treaty Organization and established diplomatic relations with the People's Republic of China.

Norman Kirk died in August 1974, and Wallace Rowling, hitherto Minister of Finance, became Prime Minister in September. The economic recession worsened, and in November 1975 a general election resulted in victory for the National Party, which won 55 of the 87 seats in the House of Representatives, while the Labour Party took the remaining 32 seats. The new Government, under Robert (from January 1984, Sir Robert) Muldoon, who had led the National Party since July 1974, introduced austere economic policies, including a 'freeze' on wages, and in 1976 reduced the annual intake of migrants from 30,000 to 5,000, while conducting a campaign against illegal immigrants.

New Zealand continued to suffer a very low rate of economic growth and increasing unemployment. Popular dissatisfaction with Muldoon's sometimes controversial leadership was reflected at the general election in November 1978. The National Party retained power, with 50 of the 92 seats in the enlarged House of Representatives, but its share of the total vote fell from 47.2% in 1975 to 39.8%. Labour won more votes (40.4% of the total) but fewer seats (41). The Social Credit Party received 17.1% of the total votes, compared with only 7.4% in 1975, but obtained only one seat. In the November 1981 election Muldoon's majority was further reduced. The National Party won 47 of the 92 seats in the House, while Labour, which again received more votes, won 43 seats and Social Credit (despite obtaining 20.6% of votes cast) only two.

In February 1984 Muldoon's Government antagonized New Zealand's trade unions by effecting legislation to ban 'closed shop' agreements with employers, thus giving employees the right to choose whether or not to join a trade union. Further legislation was used in June to compel striking construction workers to return to work. In the same month, faced with dissent within his own party (which threatened its working majority in the House of Representatives), Muldoon called an early general election for July. The Labour Party obtained 43% of the total votes and secured 56 of the 95 seats in an enlarged House of Representatives, while the National Party, with 36% of the votes, took 37 seats: it was thought that the National Party had lost considerable support to the newly-formed New Zealand Party, a right-wing party which won 12.3% of the votes (but no seats) after campaigning for a minimum of government intervention in the economy. David Lange (the leader of the Labour Party since February 1983) became Prime Minister. James McLay, who had been deputy leader of the National Party since March 1984, defeated Muldoon in an election for the leadership of the party in November 1984 (but he was replaced as party leader by his deputy, James Bolger, in March 1986).

The Labour Government introduced controversial deregulatory measures to improve the country's economic situation. The initial success of these measures, together with widespread popular support for the Government's anti-nuclear policy (see below), contributed to a second victory for the Labour Party in a general election in August 1987. Of the 97 seats in the enlarged House of Representatives, the Labour Party secured 58, and the National Party 39. (The Democratic Party lost both the seats that its predecessor, the Social Credit Party, had won at the 1984 election.) Of the votes cast, the Labour Party received 47.4%, and the National Party 42.8%.

In 1987 Lange's Government initiated a policy of 'privatization' of state-owned enterprises. The policy proved to be an immediate source of controversy within the Labour Party. In November 1988 policy disagreements prompted Lange to dismiss the Minister responsible for the privatization programme, Richard Prebble. Lange was accused by Cabinet colleagues of acting without consultation, and in December Roger (later Sir Roger) Douglas, the Minister of Finance, declared that he would not serve another term under Lange. Douglas was promptly dismissed from office, and later that month unsuccessfully challenged Lange for the leadership of the Labour Party. In May 1989 the formation of the NewLabour Party (led by a former president of the Labour Party, Jim Anderton) was announced: the party aimed to appeal to Labour supporters who had become disillusioned with the Government's advocacy of privatization. In early August Douglas was elected by Labour MPs to a vacant Cabinet post, thus prompting Lange to resign. Shortly afterwards, Geoffrey Palmer, hitherto the deputy leader of the Labour Party, was elected the Labour Party's parliamentary leader and Prime Minister.

In January 1990 Palmer undertook a wide-ranging government reshuffle. The return of Richard Prebble to the Cabinet, in his former post as Minister for State-Owned Enterprises, provoked considerable anger within the Labour Party. The Government also aroused hostility by its introduction of a substantial fee for tertiary-level students, together with a proposal to end the autonomy of the universities. The continued sale of state assets, especially that of the telecommunications company, Telecom, was also unpopular (although a portion of the proceeds from the Telecom sales was to be invested in education and health).

On 4 September 1990, less than eight weeks before the next general election, Palmer resigned as Prime Minister. Public opinion polls had indicated that Labour, under his leadership, had lost support to the National Party, and members of the Cabinet had consequently urged him to resign. Michael Moore, the Minister of External Relations and Trade (who had also contested the August 1989 leadership election), replaced Palmer as Prime Minister and Labour Party leader. Moore promised to act promptly to avert the enormous budget deficit forecast for 1991/92, and, two weeks later, he secured an agreement with the country's trade union leaders regarding restricted pay settlements. In October 1990, none the less, the National Party won 47.8% of the votes at the general election, taking 67 of the 97 seats in the House of Representatives. The Labour Party, with 35.1% of the votes, won 29 seats, while the NewLabour Party retained its sole seat, obtaining 5.2% of the votes. James Bolger, as leader of the National Party, thus became Prime Minister at the head of a government that promised to continue Labour's strict budgetary and monetary controls, and to undertake further deregulation, notably of the labour market, while pledging selective assistance for industry. The sale of state assets would also continue.

In November 1990 the new Government's first economic proposals were outlined. They included the repeal of legislation on equal pay for women, and envisaged reductions in public spending, particularly in the field of social welfare. In December the Government announced measures that entailed proposed reductions in unemployment benefit, family benefits, and in medical and sickness payments, and prepared for the introduction of a system whereby users of medical and educational services (hitherto provided free of charge) would be required to pay, according to a means test. These measures were received with anger by social and church groups. Protest marches took place in April 1991, and plans for a 'freeze' in the levels of old-age pensions prompted groups representing the elderly unsuccessfully to petition the British Monarch (through the Governor-General) to dismiss the Bolger Government.

Two National Party members of the House of Representatives resigned from the party in August 1991, in protest against the proposals, and the Minister of Maori Affairs, Winston Peters (who had openly criticized the Government's economic strategy), was dismissed in early October. In November Sir Robert Muldoon announced that he would resign from the legislature in early 1992, in protest against the Government's economic policies and failure to honour pre-election promises, particularly its pledge not to lower the real value of pensions. Earlier in the month protests and criticism had prompted the Government to withdraw its stringent means-testing measures for the allocation of state pensions, but the overall level of payments remained lower than previously.

In December 1992 a coalition was formed by minor parties as a challenge to the two main parties. The grouping, known as the Alliance, consisted of the NewLabour Party, the New Zealand Democratic Party, the Green Party of Aotearoa—New Zealand and Mana Motuhake. In its first electoral test (the by-election in February 1992 that had been precipitated by Muldoon's resignation) the Alliance campaigned for the provision of education and health care free of charge and the return to the public sector of 'privatized' state assets. The National Party retained the seat in the by-election, but with a greatly reduced majority. The Alliance secured 38% of the votes, only 5% less than the share received by the National Party.

In September 1992 a preliminary referendum on proposed electoral reform was held. The electorate voted overwhelmingly in favour of the abolition of the 'first-past-the-post' system and for its replacement by a form of proportional representation; of the four alternatives offered, the mixed member proportional system (similar to that used in Germany) received the greatest support. A second, binding referendum was to be arranged to coincide with the next general election, scheduled for late 1993. The new rules were to be implemented at the 1996 election.

In March 1993, in an attempt to improve the National Party's chances of re-election, a minor reorganization of the Government was carried out. Changes included the replacement of Simon Upton, Minister of Health responsible for the implementation of unpopular hospital reforms, by Bill Birch, a close associate of Bolger. The highly controversial charges for hospital beds were abolished by the new Minister. In the same month the outspoken Winston Peters, who had continued to embarrass the Government, resigned from his parliamentary seat in order to stand for re-election as an independent candidate. The by-election in April resulted in an overwhelming victory for Peters, the major political parties having declined to present candidates. In July Peters established New Zealand First, and announced that the party would contest all 99 seats at the forthcoming general election.

At the election, held on 6 November 1993, the National Party, which had campaigned mainly on the Government's record of economic recovery, was narrowly returned to office, receiving 35.2% of the total votes cast and securing 50 seats in the House of Representatives. The Labour Party, with 34.7% of the votes, won 45 seats, the Alliance two and New Zealand First two. At the concurrent, second referendum on electoral reform, 54% of voters favoured the adoption of the mixed member system of proportional representation. A new Government was appointed in late November. Changes included the replacement of Ruth Richardson as Minister of Finance by Bill Birch, the latter being succeeded as Minister of Health by Jenny Shipley. Michael Moore, the parliamentary leader of the Labour Party, was replaced by Helen Clark, the former Deputy Prime Minister and Minister of Health.

In August 1994 the Government narrowly retained its majority at a by-election brought about by the unexpected resignation of Ruth Richardson from the House of Representatives. In the following month Ross Meurant, a junior minister, announced his decision to leave the National Party and to found the Right of Centre (ROC). The Prime Minister, therefore, was effectively obliged to form a coalition Government. In October a former Cabinet minister, Peter Dunne, resigned from the Labour Party, following differences over the party's policy on taxation, and declared his intention to remain in the House of Representatives as an independent member. He subsequently established a new party, Future New Zealand. The traditional two-party system was further challenged in early 1995, when support for ACT New Zealand, co-founded by Sir Roger Douglas (reformist Minister of Finance in 1984–88) who had recently announced his return to politics, began to increase rapidly.

During 1987 there were protests by the Maoris (the aboriginal inhabitants of New Zealand) concerning their cultural and economic rights and, in particular, their claims to land in accordance with the Treaty of Waitangi, concluded in 1840 by the British Government and Maori leaders, whereby sovereignty had been ceded to the United Kingdom in return for the Maoris' retention of their hunting and fishing grounds. In November 1987 a ruling by the Waitangi Tribunal, reconvened in 1975 to consider retrospectively the claims of Maori land rights activists, recommended the restoration of an Auckland harbour headland to the Maori people. By 1994 about 75% of the country was subject to land claims by Maori groups. In December of that year the Government offered the sum of $NZ1,000m., payable over a 10-year period from September 1992, in full and final settlement of outstanding claims for compensation.The condition that all future land claims be renounced, however, was rejected by most Maori groups. In the same month a historic agreement between the Government and the Tainui people of Waikato provided for the return of 14,164 ha of land, confiscated in 1863 and now valued at $NZ100m., and also for the deposit over a period of five years of $NZ65m. in a land acquisition trust. In February 1995 the Waitangi Day celebrations were disrupted by Maori protesters, as a result of which the annual ceremony to commemorate the signing of the 1840 Treaty, attended by the Prime Minister and the Governor-General, had to be abandoned.

In response to Maori grievances over fishing rights, the Government introduced, in 1988, a Maori Fisheries Bill, under the provisions of which 2.5% of current fishing quotas were to be restored to the Maori people annually for the following 19 years. However, Maori activists alleged that the proposed legislation was racially discriminatory, since it stipulated that no other Maori fishing claim would be considered by the Waitangi Tribunal until the 19 years had elapsed. The bill was also condemned by some white New Zealanders, as, if implemented as proposed, it would guarantee the Maori people about 50% of the country's entire fishing rights by the year 2008. In August 1992, finding that the Government had failed to honour its obligations under the Treaty of 1840, the Waitangi Tribunal recommended that ownership of most of the fisheries of South Island be transferred to the Ngai Tahu, one of New Zealand's smallest Maori tribes. In November 1992, in the hope of reaching a permanent settlement, the Government advanced the sum of $NZ150m. to a Maori consortium to enable the latter's purchase of a 50% stake in the country's biggest inshore fishing company. In early 1995 the Treaty of

Waitangi Fisheries Commission, established to resolve the issue of the allocation among Maoris of resources valued at $NZ200m., had yet to deliver its recommendations.

From 1984 the Lange Government's pledge to ban from New Zealand's ports all vessels believed to be carrying nuclear weapons or powered by nuclear energy caused considerable strain in the country's relations with Australia and the USA, its partners in the ANZUS military pact (see p. 247). In July 1986 the US Government announced its intention to devise new, bilateral defence arrangements with Australia, and in August the USA's military obligations to New Zealand under the ANZUS Treaty were formally suspended, pending 'adequate corrective measures'. In February 1987 the US Government announced its decision not to renew a 1982 memorandum of understanding (due to be renegotiated in June of that year), whereby New Zealand was able to purchase military equipment from the USA at favourable prices. The Lange Government subsequently defined a new defence strategy, based on increased self-reliance for the country's military forces, in conjunction with continuing co-operation with Australia and greater involvement in the affairs of the South Pacific region. In June 1987 legislation banning nuclear-armed ships was formally enacted by the House of Representatives, despite strong opposition from the National Party. In September 1989 New Zealand agreed the terms for a joint venture with Australia to build as many as 12 naval frigates to patrol the South Pacific. The decision proved to be highly contentious within New Zealand, both because of the high costs that would be incurred at a time of economic austerity, and because of allegations that the Government was succumbing to political pressure from Australia to return to the ANZUS alliance and abandon its independent anti-nuclear stance. In March 1990 the opposition National Party announced its support for the anti-nuclear policy, a position that it retained after its election to government office in October of the same year. Following the US Government's decision, in September 1991, to remove nuclear weapons from surface naval vessels, Bolger announced that his administration would reconsider the law banning visits from nuclear-armed and nuclear-propelled warships. The review would focus on the nuclear propulsion ban, which was seen as the obstacle to a renegotiated alliance with Australia and the USA. In July 1992 the USA announced that its warships no longer carried tactical nuclear weapons. In December the report commissioned by the Prime Minister was released. The committee of scientists concluded that the dangers of permitting nuclear-powered vessels to enter New Zealand waters were minimal. Despite these findings, no immediate change to the anti-nuclear legislation was envisaged. In February 1994 the New Zealand Prime Minister welcomed the US decision to resume senior-level contacts with Wellington, suspended since 1985. As relations continued to improve, in December 1994 the USA announced that nuclear-armed warships would not be dispatched to New Zealand, thus acknowledging the latter's ban. In early 1995 the Prime Minister was warmly received in Washington by President Clinton.

In July 1985 the trawler *Rainbow Warrior*, the flagship of the anti-nuclear environmentalist group Greenpeace (which was to have led a flotilla to Mururoa Atoll, in French Polynesia, to protest against French testing of nuclear weapons in the Pacific), was blown up and sunk in Auckland Harbour. One member of the crew was killed as a result of the explosion. Two agents of the French secret service were tried for manslaughter in November and sentenced to 10 years' imprisonment, initially in Auckland. The French Government made repeated requests for the release or repatriation of the agents, and in July 1986 the two Governments eventually reached an agreement, whereby the agents were to be transferred to detention on Hao Atoll, in French Polynesia, for three years. The French Government made a formal apology for its part in the sabotage operation, and paid the New Zealand Government $NZ7m. in compensation. By May 1988, however, both the agents had been taken back to France, ostensibly for medical reasons. When neither agent was returned to the atoll, Lange referred the matter to the UN for arbitration in October: in May 1990 an arbitration panel ruled that France's repatriation of the agents constituted a substantial violation of the 1986 agreement, but it announced that the agents would not be required to return to Hao Atoll. In accordance with a recommendation by the panel, France agreed to pay an initial US $2m. into a joint fund intended to foster close and friendly relations between the two countries. In April 1991 the French Prime Minister, Michel Rocard, visited New Zealand and again apologized for the sinking of the *Rainbow Warrior*, while reiterating that French testing of nuclear weapons in the Pacific was to continue. However, relations between the two countries deteriorated in July, following the French Government's announcement that it had conferred an honour for distinguished service on one of the two agents responsible for the sabotage of the *Rainbow Warrior*. The issue re-emerged in November, when a third French agent, also suspected of involvement in the 1985 incident, was arrested, at New Zealand's instigation, in Switzerland. In December 1991, however, the New Zealand Government decided against seeking the man's extradition, on the grounds that the case was now considered to be closed. France announced the suspension of its nuclear testing in the South Pacific in April 1992. In May 1993 the first French warship to visit New Zealand since 1985 entered Auckland.

### Government

Executive power is vested in the British monarch, as Head of State, and is exercisable by an appointed representative, the Governor-General, who must be guided by the advice of the Executive Council (Cabinet), led by the Prime Minister. In March 1994 the Prime Minister indicated that New Zealand might become a republic by the year 2000. Legislative power is vested in the unicameral House of Representatives, with 99 members (including four Maoris) elected for three years by universal adult suffrage from single-member constituencies. A system of mixed member proportional representation was to be introduced in 1996, when the legislature was to be expanded to 120 seats (65 electorate members, including five seats reserved for Maoris, the remaining 55 being chosen from party lists). The Governor-General appoints the Prime Minister and, on the latter's recommendation, other Ministers. The Cabinet is responsible to the House.

### Defence

The ANZUS Security Treaty was signed by New Zealand in 1951 (see p. 247). The total strength of active forces in June 1994 was 10,000: army 4,500, navy 2,200, air force 3,300. Reserves totalled 7,850. The defence budget for 1994 was $NZ1,300m.

### Economic Affairs

In 1993, according to estimates by the World Bank, New Zealand's gross national product (GNP), measured at average 1991–93 prices, was US $44,674m., equivalent to US $12,900 per head. During 1985–93, it was estimated, GNP per head increased, in real terms, at an average annual rate of 0.2%. Over the same period, the population increased by 0.8% annually. New Zealand's gross domestic product (GDP) increased, in real terms, by an annual average of 1.4% in 1980–92.

Agriculture (including forestry, hunting and fishing) contributed 5.2% of GDP in the year ending March 1994. About 10.4% of the working population were employed in the sector in 1994. The principal crops are barley, wheat and maize. Fruit (particularly kiwifruit, apples and pears) and vegetables are also cultivated. New Zealand is a major producer of wool. Meat and dairy products are important, contributing 14.6% and 14.4% of export earnings, respectively, in the year ending June 1994. The forestry industry continued to show strong expansion in 1993/94, when exports of cork and wood reached $NZ1,355.1m. The fisheries sector is of increasing significance, exports in 1993/94 being worth an estimated $NZ1,206.6m. During 1980–88 agricultural production increased by an annual average of 1.1%; however, output declined by 3.7% in 1989 and by 3.4% in 1990. Production was affected by drought in late 1992. In the 12 months to September 1993 the agricultural sector contracted by 0.4%, compared with the corresponding period of 1991/92.

Industry (including mining, manufacturing, construction and power) employed 25.0% of the working population in 1994, and provided 22.9% of GDP in the year ending March 1991. During 1980–89 industrial GDP increased by an annual average of 1.8%. After declining by 5.0% in 1991, industrial production rose by 1.3% in 1992.

Mining contributed only 1.4% of GDP in the year ending March 1991, and employed less than 0.3% of the working population in 1994. New Zealand has substantial coal reserves; petroleum, natural gas, iron, gold and silica are also exploited.

A considerable amount of natural gas is used to produce synthetic petrol.

Manufacturing contributed 17.5% of GDP in the year ending March 1991. The sector employed 18.1% of the working population in 1994. Measured by the value of output, the principal branches of manufacturing in the year ending March 1990 were food products (22.8% of the total), printing and publishing, wood and paper products, chemicals, metals and metal products, machinery and transport equipment. During 1980–89 manufacturing GDP increased by an annual average of 1.6%. Manufacturing output rose by 6.7% in the year to September 1993, compared with the corresponding 12 months of 1991/92.

Energy is derived from domestic supplies of natural gas, petroleum and coal. Hydroelectric power supplied about 75% of the electricity output in the early 1990s. Imports of mineral fuels comprised 5.7% of the total value of merchandise imports in 1993/94.

In the year ending March 1988 tourism became the single largest source of foreign exchange. Receipts totalled $NZ3,560m. in 1993/94, when visitor arrivals exceeded 1.2m.

In 1993 New Zealand recorded a visible trade surplus of US $1,714m., but there was a deficit of US $932m. on the current account of the balance of payments. The trade surplus decreased in 1994. In the year ending June 1994 the principal sources of imports were Australia (21.5%), the USA (18.1%) and Japan (15.8%), which were also the principal markets for exports in that year (Australia 21.0%, Japan 14.6% and the USA 11.2%). The United Kingdom, other members of the European Union and Asian countries are also important trading partners. The principal exports in 1993/94 were meat, dairy products, fruit and vegetables, fish, cork and wood and machinery. The principal imports were machinery and transport equipment, minerals, chemicals and plastic materials.

Budget estimates for the year ending June 1995 envisaged a surplus of $NZ2,300m. (equivalent to 2.6% of GDP). In mid-1994 New Zealand's external debt stood at $NZ65,800m. The average rate of unemployment declined from 9.6% of the labour force in 1993 to 8.1% in 1994. The average annual rate of inflation was 5.9% in 1985–93. Consumer prices increased by an annual average of 1.8% in 1994, compared with 1.3% in 1993.

New Zealand is a member of the OECD (see p. 194), APEC (p. 106), the South Pacific Commission (p. 215) and the South Pacific Forum (p. 217). In 1982 New Zealand signed an agreement for a 'closer economic relationship' (CER) with Australia, aiming to eliminate trade barriers between the two countries by 1995. These were, in fact, eliminated in July 1990.

The Bolger Government, elected in October 1990 and re-elected in November 1993, aimed to reduce the budgetary deficit and the rates of inflation and unemployment. However, popular dissatisfaction with some of the more stringent adjustment measures obliged the Government to abandon elements of its programme (see Recent History). Nevertheless, the first budget surplus since 1978 was achieved in mid-1994. Assisted by higher tax revenues, this surplus was expected to increase and to enable the Government to repay most of its external debt by 1998. The annual rate of inflation had been substantially reduced by 1992, rising slightly in 1993 and again in 1994, but unemployment, although declining, remained at a relatively high level. The economy began to emerge from recession in 1992, when, following four years of contraction, GDP grew by 3.1%. In 1993 the growth rate rose to 4.6%, with a rate of almost 7.0% estimated for 1994. This strong expansion was expected to continue in 1995.

### Social Welfare

New Zealand has a targeted system of social welfare, administered by the Department of Social Welfare. The system, which is financed from general taxation, provides superannuation for senior citizens and income-tested benefits for eligible people who are unemployed, sick, single parents or invalids. Certain supplementary services are provided. The Department also incorporates the NZ Children and Young Persons Service (social work with children and families) and the NZ Community Funding Agency (which administers government funding to approved organizations and community groups). In 1992 there were 18,823 public and 7,149 private hospital beds in New Zealand, and 7,170 practising physicians. Of total net budgetary expenditure by the central Government in the financial year ending 30 June 1993, $NZ3,898m. (13.1%) was for health and $NZ10,747m. (36.2%) was for social services.

### Education

State education is free and, for children between six and 16 years of age, compulsory. Primary education lasts from five to 11 years of age, after which children transfer to secondary schools until a maximum age of 18. Primary enrolment and secondary enrolment up to the age of 15 years in 1994 was 100% of children in the relevant age-group, while the comparable ratio for secondary enrolment of those aged 16 was about 94%. In July 1994 a total of 408,544 students were enrolled in primary schools and 228,445 in secondary schools. In addition, 33,512 pupils attended composite schools, providing both primary and secondary education. There are seven universities, as well as 25 polytechnics, offering education at the post-secondary level. Changes introduced in 1991 obliged most students to pay part of their fees: parental income is tested to determine the level of allowances. Budgetary expenditure on education by the central Government in the financial year ending 30 June 1994 was $NZ4,763m., representing 15.8% of total net spending.

### Public Holidays

**1995:** 1-2 January (New Year), 6 February (Waitangi Day, anniversary of 1840 treaty), 14–17 April (Easter), 25 April (ANZAC Day, anniversary of 1915 landing at Gallipoli), 5 June (Queen's Official Birthday), 23 October (Labour Day), 25 December (Christmas Day), 26 December (Boxing Day).

**1996:** 1-2 January (New Year), 6 February (Waitangi Day, anniversary of 1840 treaty), 5–8 April (Easter), 25 April (ANZAC Day, anniversary of 1915 landing at Gallipoli), 3 June (Queen's Official Birthday), 28 October (Labour Day), 25 December (Christmas Day), 26 December (Boxing Day).

### Weights and Measures

The metric system is in force.

# Statistical Survey

Source (unless otherwise stated): Statistics New Zealand, Aorangi House, 85 Molesworth St, POB 2922, Wellington 1; tel. (4) 495-4600; telex 31313; fax (4) 472-9135.

## Area and Population

**AREA, POPULATION AND DENSITY**

| | |
|---|---:|
| Area (sq km) | 270,534* |
| Population (census results) | |
| 4 March 1986 | 3,307,084 |
| 5 March 1991 | |
| Males | 1,693,200 |
| Females | 1,741,750 |
| Total | 3,434,950 |
| Population (official estimates at 31 March) | |
| 1992 | 3,454,900 |
| 1993 | 3,494,300 |
| 1994 | 3,541,700 |
| Density (per sq km) at 31 March 1994 | 13.1 |

* 104,454 sq miles.

**Population** (official estimate at 31 December 1994): 3,577,300.

**PRINCIPAL CENTRES OF POPULATION**
(estimates, 31 March 1993)

| | | | |
|---|---:|---|---:|
| Auckland | 910,200 | Napier-Hastings | 111,200 |
| Wellington (capital) | 326,900 | Dunedin | 110,800 |
| Christchurch | 312,600 | Palmerston North | 74,100 |
| Hamilton | 151,800 | Tauranga | 73,800 |

**BIRTHS, MARRIAGES AND DEATHS**

| | Live births* | | Marriages | | Deaths* | |
|---|---:|---:|---:|---:|---:|---:|
| | Number | Rate (per '000) | Number | Rate (per '000) | Number | Rate (per '000) |
| 1986 | 52,824 | 16.1 | 24,037 | 7.3 | 27,045 | 8.3 |
| 1987 | 55,254 | 16.7 | 24,443 | 7.4 | 27,419 | 8.3 |
| 1988 | 57,546 | 17.3 | 23,485 | 7.1 | 27,408 | 8.3 |
| 1989 | 58,091 | 17.4 | 22,733 | 6.8 | 27,042 | 8.1 |
| 1990 | 60,153 | 17.9 | 23,341 | 6.9 | 26,531 | 7.9 |
| 1991 | 60,001 | 17.6 | 23,065 | 6.8 | 26,501 | 7.8 |
| 1992 | 59,266 | 17.2 | 22,018 | 6.4 | 27,249 | 7.9 |
| 1993† | 58,868 | 16.9 | 22,056 | 6.3 | 27,240 | 7.8 |

* Data for births and deaths are tabulated by year of registration rather than by year of occurrence.
† Provisional.

**1994:** Live births: 57,439; Marriages 21,858.

**Expectation of life** (years at birth, 1992–94): males 73.4; females 79.1.

**IMMIGRATION AND EMIGRATION** (year ending 31 March)*

| | 1990/91 | 1991/92 | 1992/93 |
|---|---:|---:|---:|
| Long-term immigrants | 57,088 | 49,010 | 49,562 |
| Long-term emigrants | 45,472 | 44,723 | 42,714 |

* Figures refer to persons intending to remain in New Zealand, or New Zealand residents intending to remain abroad, for 12 months or more.

**EMPLOYMENT**
('000 persons aged 15 years and over, excl. armed forces)

| | 1992 | 1993 | 1994 |
|---|---:|---:|---:|
| Agriculture, hunting, forestry and fishing | 159.1 | 157.7 | 161.7 |
| Mining and quarrying | 3.5 | 4.0 | 4.5 |
| Manufacturing | 240.2 | 255.0 | 282.9 |
| Electricity, gas and water | 11.1 | 10.9 | 10.3 |
| Construction | 79.6 | 80.9 | 92.4 |
| Trade, restaurants and hotels | 308.3 | 316.1 | 327.3 |
| Transport, storage and communications | 89.0 | 90.6 | 91.7 |
| Finance, insurance, real estate and business services | 157.7 | 149.0 | 159.0 |
| Community, social and personal services | 416.0 | 429.3 | 427.8 |
| Activities not adequately defined | 2.1 | 2.5 | 1.9 |
| **Total** | **1,466.6** | **1,495.8** | **1,559.5** |
| Males | 820.8 | 838.5 | 870.6 |
| Females | 645.8 | 657.4 | 688.9 |

**1994** (persons aged 15 years and over): Total labour force 1,697,900 (males 951,400; females 746,500), including 138,400 unemployed (males 80,900; females 57,500).

Source: *Household Labour Force Survey*.

## Agriculture

**PRINCIPAL CROPS** ('000 metric tons, year ending 30 June)

| | 1990/91 | 1991/92 | 1992/93 |
|---|---:|---:|---:|
| Wheat | 181 | 191 | 181 |
| Oats | 57 | 58 | 73 |
| Barley | 382 | 319 | 347 |
| Maize | 183 | 164 | 171 |
| Field peas | 65 | 78 | 80* |

* FAO estimate.
Source: FAO, *Production Yearbook*.

**LIVESTOCK** ('000 head at 30 June)

| | 1991 | 1992 | 1993 |
|---|---:|---:|---:|
| Cattle | 8,100 | 8,145 | 8,675 |
| Sheep | 55,162 | 52,571 | 51,000 |
| Goats | 793 | 533 | 470 |
| Pigs | 407 | 411 | 430 |
| Horses | 91 | 88 | 80 |
| Deer | 1,130 | 1,135 | n.a. |
| Poultry (million)* | 10 | 10 | 10 |

* FAO estimates.
Source: mainly FAO, *Production Yearbook*.

NEW ZEALAND

**LIVESTOCK PRODUCTS** ('000 metric tons)

|  | 1990/91 | 1991/92 | 1992/93 |
|---|---|---|---|
| Beef* | 523.9 | 522.5 | 558.1 |
| Veal* | 13.0 | 14.0 | 14.1 |
| Mutton* | 145.4 | 157.8 | 134.5 |
| Lamb* | 383.2 | 400.0 | 351.8 |
| Pig meat* | 43.1 | 47.2 | 48.6 |
| Liquid milk (million litres)† | 7,077.0 | 7,455.0 | 7,629.0 |
| Butter (creamery)† | 215.7 | 213.6 | 206.6 |
| Cheese† | 127.0 | 142.3 | 144.5 |
| Preserved milk†‡ | 421.0 | 431.4 | 458.0 |
| Casein† | 65.7 | 73.3 | 74.2 |
| Wool (greasy)§ | 305.3 | 255.5 | 255.5 |

\* Year ended 30 September. Figures are for meat from slaughter at meat export works and abattoirs for the local market.
† Year ended 31 May.
‡ Skim-milk, butter-milk, whole-milk powder and infant milk food.
§ Year ended 30 June. The estimated ratio of clean to greasy wool was 75% in each year.

## Forestry

**ROUNDWOOD REMOVALS**
('000 cu m, excluding bark, year ending 31 March)

|  | 1990/91 | 1991/92 | 1992/93 |
|---|---|---|---|
| Sawlogs | 5,004 | 4,995 | 5,722 |
| Pulp logs | 4,194 | 4,176 | 3,943 |
| Export logs and chips | 3,645 | 4,407 | 5,138 |
| Other | 651 | 653 | 757 |
| **Total** | 13,494 | 14,231 | 15,560 |

Source: Ministry of Forestry.

**SAWNWOOD PRODUCTION** ('000 cu m, year ending 31 March)

| Species | 1990/91 | 1991/92 | 1992/93 |
|---|---|---|---|
| Rimu and miro | 69 | 51 | 55 |
| Tawa | 5 | 4 | 2 |
| Douglas fir | 224 | 221 | 160 |
| Kahikatea | 2 | 2 | 3 |
| Exotic pines | 1,946 | 1,996 | 2,379 |
| Beech | 7 | 4 | 4 |
| Kauri | 1 | — | 2 |
| Eucalyptus | 1 | 1 | 2 |
| **Total** (incl. others) | 2,283 | 2,301 | 2,634 |

Source: Ministry of Forestry.

## Fishing*

(landings, '000 metric tons)

|  | 1991 | 1992 | 1993 |
|---|---|---|---|
| Snoek (Barracouta) | 25.2 | 20.1 | 31.0 |
| Blue grenadier (Hoki) | 226.0 | 212.2 | 177.3 |
| Ruff (Kahawai) | 5.0 | 4.8 | 6.6 |
| Orange roughy | 32.6 | 36.3 | 34.6 |
| Oreo dories | 17.1 | 19.8 | 20.8 |
| Jack mackerels | 31.3 | 38.1 | 49.4 |
| Tunas | 11.2 | 6.4 | 5.4 |
| Southern blue whiting | 34.2 | 76.2 | 27.1 |
| **Total fish** (incl. others) | 499.7 | 539.1 | 493.1 |
| Squids | 40.7 | 59.7 | 37.0 |
| Other shellfish† | 8.7 | 9.9 | 9.8 |
| **Total** | 549.1 | 608.8 | 539.8 |

\* Includes catches made by vessels chartered by NZ companies.
† No farmed mussels or oysters are included.
Source: Ministry of Agriculture and Fisheries.

## Mining

('000 metric tons, unless otherwise indicated)

|  | 1991 | 1992 | 1993 |
|---|---|---|---|
| Coal (incl. lignite) | 2,684.1 | 2,948.6 | 3,101.1 |
| Gold (kg) | 6,758.3 | 10,531.2 | 11,161.4 |
| Crude petroleum and condensate ('000 cu m) | 2,185.3 | 2,056.7 | 2,170.4 |
| Gross natural gas (terajoules) | 227,470 | 242,540 | 236,410 |
| Liquid petroleum gas ('000 cu m)* | 273.0 | 317.9 | 351.6 |
| Iron sands | 2,264.8 | 2,934.1 | 2,388.8 |
| Silica sand | 99.1 | 71.9 | 48.6 |
| Limestone | 3,107.7 | 3,692.0 | 4,242.3 |

**1994:** Crude petroleum and condensate ('000 cu m) 2,093.3; Natural gas (terajoules) 227,140; Liquid petroleum gas ('000 cu m)* 343.9.
\* Including natural gas liquid.
Source: Ministry of Commerce.

## Industry

**SELECTED PRODUCTS**
(metric tons, unless otherwise indicated)

|  | 1990 | 1991 | 1992 |
|---|---|---|---|
| Chicken (fresh and frozen)* | 56,261 | 58,287 | 60,944 |
| Beer ('000 litres) | 388,969 | 362,656 | 363,705 |
| Soft drinks ('000 litres) | 167,106 | 173,940 | 180,861 |
| Wool yarn (pure and mixed) | 18,282 | n.a. | 18,564 |
| Knitted fabrics | 6,180 | 6,820 | 6,700 |
| Footwear ('000 pairs)† | 4,977 | 4,022 | 3,308 |
| Wood pulp ('000 metric tons)‡ | 1,348.7 | 1,343.3 | 1,280.6§ |
| Paper and paperboard ('000 metric tons)‡ | 822.4 | 779.9 | 746.7§ |
| Fibre board ('000 metric tons)‡ | 326.1 | 361.5 | 375.1§ |
| Particle board ('000 cu m)‡ | 159.9 | 155.4 | 164.9§ |
| Plywood (cu m)‡ | 60,726 | 57,864 | 86,426§ |
| Jet fuels ('000 metric tons) | 786 | 716 | n.a. |
| Motor spirit—petrol ('000 metric tons) | 1,733 | 1,565 | 1,472 |
| Distillate fuel oils ('000 metric tons) | 1,351 | 1,432 | 1,405 |
| Residual fuel oils ('000 metric tons) | 390 | 381 | 415 |
| Cement ('000 metric tons)[1] | 681 | 581 | 599 |
| Ready-mixed concrete ('000 cu m) | 1,545 | 1,355 | 1,383 |
| Chemical fertilizers ('000 metric tons)[2] | 1,246 | 994 | 1,178 |
| Wine ('000 hectolitres)[3] | 379 | 424 | 455 |

\* Twelve months ending September of year stated.
† From September 1990 the survey was limited to the 50 largest manufacturers, which, at the June 1990 quarter, represented 93% of total production.
‡ Twelve months beginning 1 April of year stated.
§ Provisional.
[1] Excluding exported cement.
[2] Figures relate only to the operations of super-phosphate manufacturing works.
[3] Domestic sales of grape wine.

Aluminium ('000 metric tons, primary metal): 259.7 in 1990; 258.5 in 1991; 242.4 in 1992; 296.1 in 1993. Source: *World Metal Statistics* (London).

**1993:** Chicken (fresh and frozen, metric tons) 68,214; Motor spirit ('000 metric tons) 1,433; Distillate fuel oils ('000 metric tons) 1,278; Residual fuel oils ('000 metric tons) 359; Cement ('000 metric tons) 688; Ready-mixed concrete ('000 cu m) 1,631; Chemical fertilizers ('000 metric tons) 1,450.

NEW ZEALAND

# Finance

## CURRENCY AND EXCHANGE RATES

**Monetary Units**
100 cents = 1 New Zealand dollar ($NZ).

**Sterling and US Dollar Equivalents** (31 December 1994)
£1 sterling = $NZ2.444;
US $1 = $NZ1.562;
$NZ100 = £40.92 = US $64.02.

**Exchange Rate** (US $ per New Zealand dollar)
1992   0.5381
1993   0.5407
1994   0.5937

### BUDGET ($NZ million, year ending 30 June)

| Revenue | 1990/91 | 1991/92 | 1992/93 |
|---|---|---|---|
| Income tax (incl. corporate) | 16,370 | 15,421 | 15,913 |
| Other direct taxation | 252 | 87 | 89 |
| Excise duty | 1,821 | 1,811 | 1,857 |
| Goods and services tax | 6,163 | 6,268 | 6,545 |
| Other indirect taxation | 1,191 | 1,256 | 1,353 |
| Interest, profit and miscellaneous receipts | 3,213 | 2,792 | 1,585 |
| **Total net receipts** | 29,010 | 27,635 | 27,342 |

| Expenditure | 1990/91 | 1991/92 | 1992/93 |
|---|---|---|---|
| Administration | 3,090.0 | 2,732 | 3,177 |
| Foreign relations | 1,640.8 | 1,627 | 1,547 |
| Development of industry | 1,373.7 | 910 | 1,127 |
| Education | 4,401.1 | 4,467 | 4,548 |
| Social services | 11,005.0 | 10,620 | 10,747 |
| Health | 3,986.0 | 3,855 | 3,898 |
| Transport | 826.4 | 816 | 725 |
| Debt services | 4,624.2 | 4,147 | 3,913 |
| Other expenditure | −3,694.8 | −390 | — |
| **Total net expenditure** | 27,252.4 | 28,784 | 29,682 |

### OVERSEAS RESERVES ($NZ million at 31 March)

| | 1991 | 1992 | 1993 |
|---|---|---|---|
| Reserve Bank overseas reserves | 4,055.7 | 4,426.0 | 4,526.6 |
| Treasury overseas reserves | 2,447.6 | 1,213.5 | 1,364.5 |
| Reserve position in the IMF | 104.1 | 147.5 | 279.3 |
| IMF special drawing rights | 0.6 | 2.2 | 0.4 |
| **Total official reserves** | 6,608.0 | 5,789.2 | 6,170.8 |

### MONEY SUPPLY ($NZ million at 31 December)

| | 1991 | 1992 | 1993 |
|---|---|---|---|
| Currency outside banks | 1,118 | 1,173 | 1,199 |

Source: IMF, *International Financial Statistics*.

### COST OF LIVING
(Annual averages; Consumers' Price Index; base: Oct.–Dec. 1988 = 100)

| | 1991 | 1992 | 1993 |
|---|---|---|---|
| Food | 115.0 | 115.2 | 116.4 |
| Housing | 112.0 | 107.7 | 109.4 |
| Household operation | 108.6 | 109.8 | 111.3 |
| Apparel | 109.0 | 110.3 | 111.4 |
| Transportation | 107.0 | 109.2 | 110.9 |
| Miscellaneous | 122.5 | 130.9 | 131.8 |
| **All items** | 113.4 | 114.5 | 116.0 |

## NATIONAL ACCOUNTS
($NZ million at current prices, year ending 31 March)

**National Income and Product**

| | 1990/91 | 1991/92 | 1992/93 |
|---|---|---|---|
| Compensation of employees | 33,202 | 32,697 | 33,426 |
| Operating surplus | 23,168 | 23,360 | 25,744 |
| **Domestic factor incomes** | 56,370 | 56,057 | 59,170 |
| Consumption of fixed capital | 6,444 | 6,774 | 7,191 |
| **Gross domestic product (GDP) at factor cost** | 62,814 | 62,831 | 66,361 |
| Indirect taxes | 10,982 | 10,720 | 10,923 |
| Less Subsidies | 194 | 172 | 218 |
| **GDP in purchasers' values** | 73,602 | 73,379 | 77,066 |
| Net factor income from abroad | −3,957 | −3,538 | −2,785 |
| **Gross national product** | 69,645 | 69,841 | 74,281 |
| Less Consumption of fixed capital | 6,444 | 6,774 | 7,191 |
| **National income in market prices** | 63,201 | 63,067 | 67,090 |

**Expenditure on the Gross Domestic Product**

| | 1990/91 | 1991/92 | 1992/93 |
|---|---|---|---|
| Government final consumption expenditure | 12,529 | 12,417 | 12,445 |
| Private final consumption expenditure | 45,456 | 45,886 | 47,282 |
| Increase in stocks | 1,013 | 548 | 1,650 |
| Gross fixed capital formation | 14,570 | 12,222 | 13,350 |
| Statistical discrepancy | −88 | 191 | 625 |
| **Total domestic expenditure** | 73,480 | 71,264 | 75,352 |
| Exports of goods and services | 19,949 | 21,485 | 23,753 |
| Less Imports of goods and services | 19,827 | 19,370 | 22,038 |
| **GDP in purchasers' values** | 73,602 | 73,379 | 77,067 |
| **GDP at constant 1982/83 prices** | 35,465 | 35,119 | 36,052 |

**Gross Domestic Product by Economic Activity\***

| | 1988/89 | 1989/90 | 1990/91 |
|---|---|---|---|
| Agriculture | 3,832 | 4,247 | 3,535 |
| Hunting and fishing | 240 | 213 | 210 |
| Forestry and logging | 645 | 727 | 1,013 |
| Mining and quarrying | 696 | 835 | 1,006 |
| Manufacturing | 11,208 | 12,145 | 12,485 |
| Electricity, gas and water | 145 | 148 | 144 |
| Construction | 2,830 | 2,878 | 2,748 |
| Trade, restaurants and hotels | 10,639 | 11,395 | 12,393 |
| Transport, storage and communications | 2,205 | 2,862 | 3,902 |
| Finance, insurance, real estate and business services | 8,341 | 9,405 | 9,569 |
| Government industries and services | 17,001 | 16,778 | 15,731 |
| Other community, social and personal services | 1,955 | 1,974 | 2,149 |
| Other services | 5,482 | 5,900 | 6,595 |
| **Sub-total** | 65,219 | 69,507 | 71,480 |
| Goods and services tax on production | 3,454 | 4,411 | 4,705 |
| Import duties | 507 | 629 | 556 |
| Other indirect taxes | 89 | 82 | 69 |
| Less Imputed bank service charge | 2,866 | 3,194 | 3,208 |
| **Total** | 66,403 | 71,435 | 73,602 |

\* Apart from government industries and services, the contributions to GDP from the different kinds of economic activity refer only to the private sector.

# NEW ZEALAND

## BALANCE OF PAYMENTS (US $ million)

|  | 1991 | 1992 | 1993 |
|---|---|---|---|
| Merchandise exports f.o.b. | 9,555 | 9,781 | 10,463 |
| Merchandise imports f.o.b. | −7,483 | −8,108 | −8,749 |
| **Trade balance** | 2,072 | 1,674 | 1,714 |
| Exports of services | 2,532 | 2,557 | 2,749 |
| Imports of services | −3,413 | −3,568 | −3,474 |
| Other income received | 32 | −95 | 143 |
| Other income paid | −2,566 | −2,121 | −2,592 |
| Private unrequited transfers (net) | 728 | 740 | 575 |
| Official unrequited transfers (net) | −43 | −56 | −46 |
| **Current balance** | −658 | −869 | −932 |
| Capital (net) | −1,239 | −2,352 | −2,774 |
| Net errors and omissions | 386 | 1,743 | 1,933 |
| **Overall balance** | −1,511 | −1,477 | −1,773 |

Source: IMF, *International Financial Statistics*.

# External Trade

**PRINCIPAL COMMODITIES** ($NZ million, year ending 30 June)

| Imports (value for duty) | 1991/92 | 1992/93 | 1993/94 |
|---|---|---|---|
| **Food and live animals** | 767.7 | 872.7 | 968.2 |
| Fruit and vegetables | 194.3 | 211.9 | 223.1 |
| **Beverages and tobacco** | 153.5 | 167.3 | 179.2 |
| **Crude materials (inedible) except fuels** | 528.6 | 509.2 | 556.9 |
| Metalliferous ores and metal scrap | 250.5 | 188.5 | 215.6 |
| **Mineral fuels, lubricants, etc.** | 995.0 | 1,081.9 | 968.2 |
| Petroleum and petroleum products | 992.4 | 1,079.5 | 965.4 |
| **Animal and vegetable oils, fats and waxes** | 58.8 | 68.4 | 72.4 |
| **Chemicals and related products** | 1,867.7 | 2,126.4 | 2,315.8 |
| Medicinal and pharmaceutical products | 465.0 | 527.1 | 549.1 |
| Plastics in primary forms | 281.5 | 340.5 | 350.1 |
| Plastics in non-primary forms | 179.6 | 211.3 | 233.1 |
| **Basic manufactures** | 2,390.3 | 2,656.3 | 2,662.0 |
| Paper, paperboard and its articles | 383.5 | 474.1 | 419.6 |
| Textile yarn, fabrics and made-up articles | 646.5 | 703.2 | 693.6 |
| Iron and steel | 323.5 | 339.9 | 372.1 |
| Non-ferrous metals | 214.5 | 281.1 | 276.0 |
| Other metal manufactures | 414.8 | 392.9 | 402.1 |
| **Machinery and transport equipment** | 5,481.6 | 6,265.3 | 6,943.4 |
| Machinery | 3,437.2 | 4,012.9 | 4,572.7 |
| Transport equipment | 2,044.4 | 2,252.5 | 2,370.7 |
| **Miscellaneous manufactured articles** | 1,962.7 | 2,221.2 | 2,342.0 |
| Clothing, apparel and footwear | 388.7 | 474.7 | 488.8 |
| Scientific instruments and apparatus | 297.3 | 329.2 | 345.0 |
| Other manufactured articles | 951.9 | 1,047.4 | 1,087.2 |
| **Other commodities and transactions** | 9.0 | 10.7 | 11.1 |
| **Total** | 14,215.0 | 15,979.4 | 17,019.3 |

* Provisional.

**Total imports c.i.f.** ($NZ million): 15,483.4 in 1991/92; 17,332.8 in 1992/93; 18,468.9 in 1993/94.

| Exports f.o.b | 1991/92 | 1992/93 | 1993/94 |
|---|---|---|---|
| **Food and live animals** | 8,225.4 | 8,493.0 | 8,634.2 |
| Meat and meat preparations | 3,013.6 | 3,078.0 | 2,902.3 |
| Dairy products and birds' eggs | 2,386.9 | 2,679.7 | 2,849.0 |
| Fish, crustaceans and molluscs | 1,140.2 | 1,157.6 | 1,206.6 |
| Fruit and vegetables | 1,224.7 | 1,095.0 | 1,181.3 |
| **Beverages and tobacco** | 75.8 | 93.3 | 90.0 |
| **Crude materials (inedible) except fuels** | 3,058.4 | 3,332.7 | 3,657.8 |
| Raw hides, skins and furskins | 355.2 | 378.1 | 421.0 |
| Cork and wood | 738.0 | 1,192.5 | 1,355.1 |
| Paper, pulp and waste | 385.9 | 361.1 | 335.5 |
| Textile fibres | 1,103.3 | 918.7 | 1,071.9 |
| **Mineral fuels, lubricants, etc.** | 500.6 | 485.4 | 455.0 |
| Petroleum and petroleum products | 422.1 | 400.9 | 362.0 |
| **Animal and vegetable oils, fats and waxes** | 118.9 | 120.9 | 122.3 |
| **Chemicals and related products** | 1,003.6 | 1,110.5 | 1,293.7 |
| **Basic manufactures** | 2,504.3 | 2,598.1 | 2,678.8 |
| Paper, paperboard and its articles | 418.0 | 424.1 | 407.9 |
| Iron and steel | 322.1 | 312.8 | 311.0 |
| Non-ferrous metals | 719.6 | 695.0 | 706.5 |
| **Machinery and transport equipment** | 1,257.5 | 1,423.4 | 1,535.4 |
| Machinery | 868.9 | 1,048.9 | 1,231.8 |
| Transport equipment | 388.5 | 374.5 | 303.7 |
| **Miscellaneous manufactured articles** | 658.4 | 833.1 | 857.5 |
| **Other commodities and transactions** | 437.3 | 480.9 | 502.3 |
| **Total*** | 17,840.3 | 18,971.2 | 19,827.1 |

* Including re-exports ($NZ million): 684.7 in 1991/92; 730.3 in 1992/93; 660.7 in 1993/94.

**PRINCIPAL TRADING PARTNERS**
($NZ million, year ending 30 June)

| Imports (value for duty)* | 1991/92 | 1992/93 | 1993/94 |
|---|---|---|---|
| Australia | 3,162.6 | 3,466.5 | 3,656.9 |
| Canada | 229.9 | 230.4 | 263.1 |
| China, People's Republic | 319.8 | 458.6 | 516.6 |
| France | 251.5 | 284.4 | 295.1 |
| Germany, Federal Republic | 592.3 | 680.3 | 754.2 |
| Hong Kong | 195.0 | 217.9 | 207.0 |
| Italy | 328.8 | 361.6 | 448.4 |
| Japan | 2,159.8 | 2,442.4 | 2,693.9 |
| Korea, Republic | 224.8 | 258.3 | 272.6 |
| Malaysia | 135.1 | 218.0 | 202.7 |
| Netherlands | 153.5 | 180.4 | 195.3 |
| Saudi Arabia | 458.7 | 362.9 | 339.0 |
| Singapore | 340.1 | 224.9 | 279.6 |
| Sweden | 177.2 | 219.8 | 301.3 |
| Switzerland | 155.6 | 184.4 | 200.7 |
| Taiwan | 399.9 | 453.0 | 487.1 |
| Thailand | 105.7 | 123.5 | 134.4 |
| United Arab Emirates | 166.9 | 233.0 | 184.0 |
| United Kingdom | 874.4 | 995.7 | 1,036.5 |
| USA | 2,597.4 | 2,966.1 | 3,072.5 |
| **Total** (incl. others) | 14,215.0 | 15,979.4 | 17,019.3 |

* Excluding specie and gold.

# NEW ZEALAND

| Exports* | 1991/92 | 1992/93 | 1993/94 |
|---|---|---|---|
| Australia | 3,387.8 | 3,785.6 | 4,162.3 |
| Belgium | 237.7 | 224.8 | 239.1 |
| Canada | 268.1 | 311.9 | 361.9 |
| China, People's Republic | 361.5 | 368.1 | 528.6 |
| Fiji | 178.5 | 220.8 | 215.7 |
| France | 217.3 | 221.6 | 211.6 |
| Germany, Federal Republic | 415.4 | 488.8 | 490.8 |
| Hong Kong | 363.2 | 412.7 | 481.9 |
| Indonesia | 232.8 | 246.5 | 210.1 |
| Iran | 183.8 | 131.6 | 72.8 |
| Italy | 213.7 | 200.3 | 265.3 |
| Japan | 2,738.6 | 2,759.1 | 2,886.8 |
| Korea, Republic | 767.5 | 857.1 | 928.6 |
| Malaysia | 470.5 | 382.6 | 392.8 |
| Mexico | 188.0 | 246.8 | 279.6 |
| Saudi Arabia | 205.7 | 227.7 | 215.9 |
| Singapore | 286.7 | 289.7 | 269.6 |
| Taiwan | 431.5 | 486.7 | 507.3 |
| Thailand | 177.0 | 208.5 | 192.2 |
| USSR | 99.5 | 107.6† | 134.4† |
| United Kingdom | 1,165.1 | 1,216.8 | 1,182.3 |
| USA | 2,295.2 | 2,256.6 | 2,228.7 |
| **Total** (incl. others) | 17,926.5 | 18,971.2 | 19,827.1 |

\* Including re-exports. Excluding specie and gold.
† Exports to Russia.

# Transport

**RAILWAYS** (traffic, year ending 30 June)

| | 1990/91 | 1991/92 | 1992/93 |
|---|---|---|---|
| Freight ('000 metric tons) | 8,127 | 8,777 | 8,500 |
| Freight metric ton-km (million) | 2,408 | 2,475 | 2,500 |

**1993/94:** Freight ('000 metric tons): 9,444.
Source: New Zealand Rail.

**ROAD TRAFFIC** (vehicles licensed at 31 March)

| | 1992 | 1993 | 1994 |
|---|---|---|---|
| Passenger cars | 1,542,912 | 1,562,134 | 1,600,499 |
| Goods service vehicles | 309,290 | 322,400 | 340,261 |
| Taxis | 3,572 | 3,803 | 4,079 |
| Buses and service coaches | 7,328 | 8,227 | 8,657 |
| Trailers and caravans | 369,048 | 368,846 | 374,110 |
| Motor cycles and mopeds | 66,676 | 61,245 | 59,061 |
| Other vehicles | 53,042 | 52,762 | 50,848 |
| **Total** | 2,351,868 | 2,379,417 | 2,437,515 |

\* Including contract vehicles.

## SHIPPING

**Merchant Fleet** (at 30 June)

| | 1990 | 1991 | 1992 |
|---|---|---|---|
| Displacement ('000 grt) | 260 | 275 | 242 |

Source: UN, *Statistical Yearbook*.

**Vessels Entered and Cleared** (year ending 30 June)

| | Overseas Number | Overseas Displacement ('000 gross tons) | Coastwise Number | Coastwise Displacement ('000 gross tons) |
|---|---|---|---|---|
| Entered | | | | |
| 1990/91 | 4,365 | 38,069 | 7,844 | 59,946 |
| 1991/92 | 3,282 | 27,983 | 6,319 | 47,301 |
| 1992/93 | 4,012 | 35,138 | 9,447 | 68,624 |
| Cleared | | | | |
| 1990/91 | 4,166 | 36,158 | 7,950 | 62,483 |
| 1991/92 | 3,298 | 27,508 | 6,265 | 47,105 |
| 1992/93 | 4,226 | 37,593 | 9,338 | 66,911 |

**International Sea-borne Freight Traffic**
('000 metric tons, year ending 30 June)

| | 1991/92 | 1992/93 | 1993/94 |
|---|---|---|---|
| Goods loaded | 15,778 | 16,233 | 16,500 |
| Goods unloaded | 8,291 | 8,935 | 9,000 |

**CIVIL AVIATION** (domestic and international traffic on scheduled services)

| | 1990 | 1991 | 1992 |
|---|---|---|---|
| Kilometres flown (million) | 95 | 107 | 110 |
| Passengers carried ('000) | 5,866 | 5,371 | 5,328 |
| Passenger-km (million) | 11,279 | 11,299 | 12,551 |
| Total metric ton-km (million) | 1,404 | 1,454 | 1,606 |

Source: UN, *Statistical Yearbook*.

# Tourism

('000 visitors, year ending 31 March)

| From | 1991/92 | 1992/93 | 1993/94 |
|---|---|---|---|
| Australia | 341 | 362 | 369 |
| Canada | 30 | 26 | 28 |
| Germany | 38 | 51 | 59 |
| Japan | 125 | 131 | 140 |
| Korea, Republic | 9 | 16 | 38 |
| Taiwan | 19 | 32 | 48 |
| United Kingdom | 93 | 97 | 111 |
| USA | 135 | 134 | 151 |
| **Total** (incl. others) | 1,000 | 1,087 | 1,213 |

Source: New Zealand Tourism Board.

## Communications Media

|  | 1990 | 1991 | 1992 |
|---|---|---|---|
| Radio receivers ('000 in use) | 3,150 | 3,180 | 3,215 |
| Television receivers ('000 in use) | 1,500 | 1,515 | 1,530 |
| Telephones ('000 in use)*† | 1,444 | 1,469 | 1,493 |
| Daily newspapers: |  |  |  |
| Number | 35 | n.a. | 31 |
| Circulation ('000 copies) | 1,100‡ | n.a. | 1,050‡ |

\* At 31 March.   † Main lines.   ‡ Provisional.

Non-daily newspapers (number, 1988): 139.

Book production (1984): 3,452 titles (books 1,601; pamphlets 1,851).

Sources: UNESCO, *Statistical Yearbook;* UN, *Statistical Yearbook*.

## Education
(July 1994)

|  | Institutions | Teachers (full-time equivalent) | Students |
|---|---|---|---|
| Early childhood services | 3,751 | 10,930 | 153,634* |
| Primary | 2,326 | 19,864 | 408,544 |
| Composite schools† | 91 | 1,584 | 33,512 |
| Secondary‡ | 335 | 14,774 | 228,445 |
| Special schools | 56 | 562 | 2,070 |
| Polytechnic | 25 | 4,801 | 86,128 |
| Colleges of education | 5 | 571 | 12,474 |
| University | 7 | 4,411 | 103,087 |
| Private training establishments receiving government grants | 40 | n.a. | 2,100 |

\* Includes children on the regular roll of the Correspondence School, kindergartens, playcentres, Te Kohanga Reo, Early Childhood Development Unit funded playgroups, Early Childhood Development Units, Pacific Island Early Childhood Centres and childcare centres.

† Composite schools provide both primary and secondary education (includes area schools and the Correspondence School).

‡ Secondary includes schools covering forms 3 to 7, forms 1 to 7, forms 3 to 7 with attached intermediates.

Source: Ministry of Education, Wellington.

# Directory

## The Constitution

New Zealand has no written constitution. The political system is closely modelled on that of the United Kingdom. As in the latter country, constitutional practice is an accumulation of convention, precedent and tradition. A brief description of New Zealand's principal organs of government is given below:

### HEAD OF STATE

Executive power is vested in the monarch and is exercisable in New Zealand by the monarch's personal representative, the Governor-General.

In the execution of the powers and authorities vested in him, the Governor-General must be guided by the advice of the Executive Council.

### EXECUTIVE COUNCIL

The Executive Council consists of the Governor-General and all the Ministers. Two members, exclusive of the Governor-General or the presiding member, constitute a quorum. The Governor-General appoints the Prime Minister and, on the latter's recommendation, the other Ministers.

### HOUSE OF REPRESENTATIVES

Parliament comprises the Crown and the House of Representatives.

The number of members constituting the House of Representatives is 99, each representing a single constituency. Of the total members, 95 are drawn from general seats and four from Maori seats.* They are designated 'Members of Parliament' and are elected for three years, subject to the dissolution of the House before the completion of their term.

Everyone over the age of 18 years may vote in the election of members for the House of Representatives. Since August 1975 any person, regardless of nationality, ordinarily resident in New Zealand for 12 months or more and resident in an electoral district for at least one month is qualified to be registered as a voter. Compulsory registration of all electors except Maoris was introduced at the end of 1924; it was introduced for Maoris in 1956.

There are 95 general electoral districts and four Maori electoral districts. As from August 1975, any person of the Maori race, which includes any descendant of such a person, may enrol on the Maori roll for that particular Maori electoral district in which that person resides.

By the Electoral Amendment Act, 1937, which made provision for a secret ballot in Maori elections, Maori electors were granted the same privileges, in the exercise of their vote, as general electors.

In local government the electoral franchise is the same.

Note: A system of mixed member proportional representation was to be introduced at the 1996 general election. The House of Representatives was to be expanded to 120 members: 65 electorate members (five seats being reserved for Maoris) and 55 members chosen from party lists.

## The Government

**Head of State:** HM Queen ELIZABETH II (acceded to the throne 6 February 1952).

**Governor-General and Commander-in-Chief:** Dame CATHERINE TIZARD (took office 20 November 1990).

### CABINET
(June 1995)

**Prime Minister and Minister in charge of the NZ Security Intelligence Service:** JAMES B. BOLGER.

**Deputy Prime Minister, Leader of the House, Minister of Foreign Affairs and Trade and of Pacific Island Affairs:** DON MCKINNON.

**Minister of Finance and Minister responsible for Government Superannuation Fund Department:** BILL BIRCH.

**Attorney-General, Minister of State Services, for Crown Health Enterprises, Minister in charge of the Audit Department and Minister responsible for Serious Fraud Office:** PAUL EAST.

**Minister of Health and of Women's Affairs:** JENNY SHIPLEY.

**Minister of Labour, of Fisheries and Energy:** DOUG KIDD.

**Minister of Commerce, for Industry, for Trade Negotiations, Associate Minister of Foreign Affairs and Trade, Minister for State Owned Enterprises, of Railways and Minister in charge of the Public Trust Office:** PHILIP BURDON.

**Minister for the Environment, of Research, Science and Technology and for Crown Research Institutes:** SIMON UPTON.

# NEW ZEALAND

**Minister of Education and Minister responsible for Education Review Office and National Library:** Dr LOCKWOOD SMITH.
**Minister of Agriculture, for Forestry and for Racing:** JOHN FALLOON.
**Minister of Employment, of Revenue and Deputy Minister of Finance:** WYATT CREECH.
**Minister of Justice, Minister in charge of Treaty of Waitangi Negotiations, Minister for Disarmament and Arms Control and of Cultural Affairs:** DOUGLAS GRAHAM.
**Minister of Tourism, for Sport, Fitness and Leisure and of Local Government:** JOHN BANKS.
**Minister of Conservation, of Lands, of Survey and Land Information, Minister in charge of the Valuation Department, Associate Minister of Employment and of Agriculture:** DENIS MARSHALL.
**Minister of Maori Development, of Police and Associate Minister of Education:** JOHN LUXTON.
**Minister of Defence, Minister in charge of War Pensions, Minister of Internal Affairs and Civil Defence:** WARREN COOPER.
**Minister of Transport, of Statistics, of Communications, for Information Technology, of Broadcasting and Associate Minister of Health:** MAURICE WILLIAMSON.
**Minister of Housing, of Customs and Associate Minister of Tourism:** MURRAY MCCULLY.
**Minister of Social Welfare and for Senior Citizens:** P. J. GRESHAM.
**Minister for Accident Rehabilitation and Compensation Insurance, Associate Minister of Finance and Minister responsible for Radio New Zealand Ltd and Television New Zealand Ltd:** B. W. CLIFFE.
**Minister of State and Associate Minister of Foreign Affairs and Trade:** ROBIN GRAY.
**Minister of Immigration, of Business Development and Associate Minister of Employment:** ROGER MAXWELL.
**Minister of Youth Affairs, Associate Minister of Education, of Social Welfare and of Pacific Island Affairs:** ROGER MCCLAY.
**Minister of Consumer Affairs, Associate Minister of Health, of Social Welfare and of Women's Affairs:** KATHERINE O'REGAN.

## MINISTRIES AND GOVERNMENT DEPARTMENTS

**Department of the Prime Minister and Cabinet:** Executive Wing, Parliament House, Wellington; tel. (4) 471-9700; fax (4) 473-2508.
**Ministry of Agriculture:** POB 2526, Wellington; tel. (4) 472-0367; telex 31532; fax (4) 472-9071.
**Ministry of Civil Defence:** POB 5010, Wellington; tel. (4) 473-7363; fax (4) 473-7369.
**Ministry of Commerce:** POB 1473, Wellington; tel. (4) 472-0030; fax (4) 473-4638.
**Department of Conservation:** POB 10-420, Wellington; tel. (4) 471-0726; fax (4) 471-1082.
**Ministry of Consumer Affairs:** POB 1473, Wellington; tel. (4) 474-2750; fax (4) 473-9400.
**Ministry of Cultural Affairs:** POB 5364, Wellington; tel. (4) 499-4229; fax (4) 499-4490.
**Customs Department:** POB 2218, Wellington; tel. (4) 473-6099; fax (4) 473-7370.
**Ministry of Defence:** POB 5347, Wellington; tel. (4) 496-0999; fax (4) 496-0859.
**Ministry of Education:** Private Box 1666, Wellington; tel. (4) 473-5544; fax (4) 499-1327.
**Ministry for the Environment:** POB 10-362, Wellington; tel. (4) 473-4090; fax (4) 471-0195.
**Ministry of Fisheries:** Wellington; to be established on 1 July 1995.
**Ministry of Foreign Affairs and Trade:** Private Bag 18901, Wellington; tel. (4) 472-8877; fax (4) 472-9596.
**Ministry of Forestry:** POB 1610, Wellington; tel. (4) 472-1569; fax (4) 472-2314.
**Ministry of Health:** POB 5013, Wellington; tel. (4) 496-2000; fax (4) 496-2340.
**Department of Internal Affairs:** POB 805, Wellington; tel. (4) 495-7200; fax (4) 495-7222.
**Department of Justice:** POB 180, Wellington; tel. (4) 472-5980; fax (4) 499-2295. (To become Ministry of Justice on 1 October 1995.)
**Department of Labour:** POB 3705, Wellington; tel. (4) 473-7800; fax (4) 471-1906.

**Ministry of Maori Development:** POB 3943, Wellington; tel. (4) 494-7000; fax (4) 494-7010.
**Ministry of Pacific Island Affairs:** POB 833, Wellington; tel. (4) 473-4493; fax (4) 473-4301.
**Ministry of Research, Science and Technology:** POB 5336, Wellington; tel. (4) 472-6400; fax (4) 471-1284.
**Department of Social Welfare:** Private Bag 21, Wellington 1; tel. (4) 472-7666; fax (4) 472-6873.
**State Services Commission:** POB 329, Wellington; tel. (4) 472-5639; fax (4) 472-5979.
**Statistics New Zealand:** POB 2922, Wellington; tel. (4) 495-4600; fax (4) 472-9135.
**Department of Survey and Land Information:** Private Box 170, Wellington; tel. (4) 473-5022; fax (4) 472-2244.
**Ministry of Transport:** POB 3175, Wellington; tel. (4) 472-1253; fax (4) 473-3697.
**Treasury:** POB 3724, Wellington; tel. (4) 472-2733; telex 31198; fax (4) 473-0982.
**Ministry of Women's Affairs:** PO 10-049, Wellington; tel. (4) 473-4112; fax (4) 472-0961.
**Ministry of Youth Affairs:** POB 10-300, Wellington; tel. (4) 471-2158; fax (4) 471-2233.

# Legislature

## HOUSE OF REPRESENTATIVES

**Speaker:** PETER TAPSELL.
**Leader of the House:** DON MCKINNON.

**General Election, 6 November 1993**

| Party | Number of votes | % of votes | Seats |
|---|---|---|---|
| National Party | 673,892 | 35.05 | 50* |
| Labour Party | 666,800 | 34.68 | 45† |
| The Alliance | 350,063 | 18.21 | 2 |
| New Zealand First | 161,481 | 8.40 | 2 |
| Others | 70,560 | 3.67 | – |
| Total | 1,922,796 | 100.00 | 99 |

* In September 1994 a National Party member departed to found a new party, Right of Centre, but continued to support the Government.

† In October 1994 a Labour Party member resigned, declaring his intention to remain in the House as an independent member. He subsequently established Future New Zealand

# Political Organizations

**ACT New Zealand:** f. 1994 as Association of Consumers and Taxpayers; aims to end hospital waiting-lists, establish flexible education system and implement tax reforms; Co-founder Sir ROGER DOUGLAS; Pres. RODNEY HIDE; Chair. DEREK QUIGLEY.

**Future New Zealand:** c/o House of Representatives, Wellington; f. 1994 by fmr Labour Party mem.; Leader PETER DUNNE.

**Green Party of Aotearoa—New Zealand:** POB 11-652, Wellington; tel. (9) 520-5656; fax (9) 520-5649; f. 1990 (fmrly Values Party, f. 1972); ecologist socialist party; Gen. Sec. VIVIENNE STEPHENS.

**Labour Party:** 160–162 Willis St, Wellington; tel. (4) 384-7649; fax (4) 384-8060; f. 1916; advocates an organized economy guaranteeing an adequate standard of living to every person able and willing to work; Pres. MARYANN STREET; Parl. Leader HELEN CLARK; Gen. Sec. ANTHONY TIMMS.

**Liberal Party:** c/o House of Representatives, Wellington; f. 1991 by dissident National Party mems; Pres. MALCOLM WRIGHT; Leader GILBERT MYLES.

**Mana Motuhake o Aotearoa** (New Zealand Self-Government Party): f. 1980; pro-Maori; promotes bicultural policies; Pres. PETER MOEAHU; Leader SANDRA LEE.

**NewLabour Party:** Private Bag 5, Newton, Auckland; tel. (9) 360-1918; fax (9) 360-0744; f. 1989; Leader JIM ANDERTON.

**New Zealand Democratic Party:** 2 Gillies Ave, POB 9967, Auckland 2; tel. (9) 523-1888; fax (9) 524-0798; f. 1953 as Social Credit Political League; adopted present name 1985; liberal; Pres. MARGARET COOK; Leader JOHN WRIGHT.

**New Zealand First:** c/o House of Representatives, Wellington; f. 1993 by fmr National Party mems; Leader WINSTON PETERS.

# NEW ZEALAND

**New Zealand National Party:** 14th Floor, Willbank House, 57 Willis St, POB 1155, Wellington 1; tel. (4) 472-5211; fax (4) 478-1622; f. 1936; centrist; supports private enterprise and competitive business, together with maximum personal freedom; Pres. GEOFF THOMPSON; Parl. Leader JAMES B. BOLGER.

**Right of Centre (ROC):** c/o House of Representatives, Wellington; f. 1994 by fmr National Party mem.; Leader ROSS MEURANT; Chair. CLIFF HEATH.

**Socialist Unity Party:** POB 11-478, Wellington; tel. (4) 382-9074; fax (4) 236-8857; f. 1966; Marxist; Pres. GEORGE E. JACKSON; Gen. Sec. MARILYN TUCKER.

**Socialist Workers Organisation:** POB 8851, Auckland; tel. and fax (9) 634-3984; f. 1995 by merger of Communist Party of New Zealand (f. 1921) and International Socialist Organisation; Nat. Organizer BARRY LEE.

In December 1991 a new centrist coalition of parties was established: the **Alliance** (Leader JIM ANDERTON) comprises the New Zealand Democratic Party, the NewLabour Party, the Green Party of Aotearoa, Mana Motuhake o Aotearoa and also the Liberal Party. By late 1993 the grouping had 18,000 members.

## Diplomatic Representation

### EMBASSIES AND HIGH COMMISSIONS IN NEW ZEALAND

**Australia:** 72–78 Hobson St, Thorndon, POB 4036, Wellington; tel. (4) 473-6411; telex 3375; fax (4) 473-6420; High Commissioner: R. J. GREET.

**Belgium:** 12th Floor, Willis Corroon House, 1–3 Willeston St, Wellington; tel. (4) 472-9558; telex 31452; fax (4) 471-2764; Ambassador: JAN HELLEMANS.

**Canada:** 61 Molesworth St, POB 12049, Wellington 1; tel. (4) 473-9577; fax (4) 471-2082; High Commissioner: ROBERT WRIGHT.

**Chile:** Willis Corroon House, 7th Floor, 1–3 Willeston St, POB 3861, Wellington; tel. (4) 472-5180; telex 31034; fax (4) 472-5324; Ambassador: DEMETRIO INFANTE.

**China, People's Republic:** 2–6 Glenmore St, Wellington; tel. (4) 472-1382; telex 3843; fax (4) 499-0419; Ambassador: HUANG GUI-FANG (designate).

**Colombia:** Level 11, Wool House, 10 Brandon St, POB 798, Wellington; tel. (4) 472-1080; fax (4) 472-1087; Ambassador: LUIS CARLOS LONDOÑO IRAGORRI.

**Fiji:** 31 Pipitea St, Thorndon, POB 3940, Wellington; tel. (4) 473-5401; fax (4) 499-1011; Ambassador: JIOJI N. GUIVALU.

**France:** Willis Corroon House, 13th Floor, 1–3 Willeston St, POB 1695, Wellington; tel. (4) 472-0200; telex 3580; fax (4) 472-5887; Ambassador: JACQUES LE BLANC.

**Germany:** 90–92 Hobson St, POB 1687, Wellington; tel. (4) 473-6063; telex 30131; fax (4) 473-6069; Ambassador: Dr GERHARD WEBER.

**Holy See:** Apostolic Nunciature, 112 Queen's Drive, Lyall Bay, Wellington 3, POB 14-044; tel. (4) 387-3470; fax (4) 387-8170; Apostolic Nuncio: Most Rev. THOMAS A. WHITE, Titular Archbishop of Sabiona.

**India:** FAI House, 10th Floor, 180 Molesworth St, POB 4045, Wellington 1; tel. (4) 473-6390; telex 31676; fax (4) 499-0665; High Commissioner: K. M. MEENA.

**Indonesia:** 70 Glen Road, Kelburn, POB 3543, Wellington; tel. (4) 475-8699; telex 3892; fax (4) 475-9374; Ambassador: Tengku DAHLIA SOEMOLANG.

**Iran:** POB 10-249, The Terrace, Wellington; tel. (4) 386-2983; telex 31226; fax (4) 386-3065; Ambassador: ABOLFAZL KHAZAEE TORSHIZI.

**Israel:** DB Towers, 111 The Terrace, POB 2171, Wellington; tel. (4) 472-2362; fax (4) 499-0632; Ambassador: NISSAN KOREN KRUPSKY.

**Italy:** 34–38 Grant Rd, Thorndon, POB 463, Wellington 1; tel. (4) 473-5339; telex 31571; fax (4) 472-7255; Ambassador: Dr OTTONE MATTEI.

**Japan:** Norwich Insurance House, 7th–8th Floors, 3–11 Hunter St, POB 6340, Wellington 1; tel. (4) 473-1540; telex 3544; fax (4) 471-2951; Ambassador: SADAKAZU TANIGUCHI.

**Korea, Republic:** Level 11, ASB Bank Tower, 2 Hunter St, POB 11-143, Wellington; tel. (4) 473-9073; telex 3352; fax (4) 472-3865; Ambassador: DONG IK LEE.

**Malaysia:** 10 Washington Ave, Brooklyn, POB 9422, Wellington; tel. (4) 385-2019; fax (4) 385-6973; High Commissioner: MAHALIL Hj. BAHARAM (acting).

**Mexico:** Level 8, GRE House, 111–115 Customhouse Quay, POB 11-510, Manners St, Wellington; tel. (4) 472-5555; fax (4) 472-5800; Ambassador: JOSÉ CABALLERO-BAZÁN.

**Netherlands:** Investment Centre, 10th Floor, Cnr Featherston and Ballance Sts, POB 840, Wellington; tel. (4) 473-8652; telex 3987; fax (4) 471-2923; Ambassador: G. J. DU MARCHIE SARVAAS.

**Papua New Guinea:** 279 Willis St, POB 197, Wellington; tel. (4) 385-2474; fax (4) 385-2477; High Commissioner: DAMIEN GAMIANDU.

**Peru:** Level 8, Cigna House, 40 Mercer St, POB 2566, Wellington; tel. (4) 499-8087; fax (4) 499-8057; Chargé d'affaires: JAVIER CUADROS.

**Philippines:** 50 Hobson St, Thorndon, POB 12042, Wellington; tel. (4) 472-9921; fax (4) 472-5170; Ambassador: VESTA I. CUYUGAN.

**Poland:** 17 Upland Rd, Kelburn, Wellington; tel. (4) 471-2456; fax (4) 471-2455; Chargé d'affaires: STANISŁAW AMANOWICZ.

**Russia:** 57 Messines Rd, Karori, Wellington; tel. (4) 476-6113; telex 36727; fax (4) 476-3843; Ambassador: (vacant).

**Singapore:** 17 Kabul St, Khandallah, POB 13140, Wellington; tel. (4) 479-2076; fax (4) 479-2315; High Commissioner: Brig.-Gen. MICHAEL ENG CHENG TEO.

**Switzerland:** Panama House, 22 Panama St, Wellington; tel. (4) 472-1593; telex 31539; fax (4) 499-6302; Ambassador: ERNST THURNHEER.

**Thailand:** 2 Cook St, Karori, POB 17-226, Wellington; tel. (4) 476-8618; telex 30162; fax (4) 476-3677; Ambassador: NIKHOM TANTEMSAPYA.

**Turkey:** 15–17 Murphy St, POB 12-248, Wellington; tel. (4) 472-1292; telex 30050; fax (4) 472-1277; Ambassador: TEOMAN SÜRENKÖK.

**United Kingdom:** 44 Hill St, POB 1812, Wellington; tel. (4) 472-6049; fax (4) 471-1974; High Commissioner: ROBERT ALSTON.

**USA:** 29 Fitzherbert Terrace, POB 1190, Wellington; tel. (4) 472-2068; fax (4) 471-2380; Ambassador: JOSIAH BEEMAN.

**Western Samoa:** 1A Wesley Rd, Kelburn, POB 1430, Wellington; tel. (4) 472-0953; fax (4) 471-2479; High Commissioner: LA'ULU FETAUIMALEMAU MATA'AFA.

## Judicial System

The Judicial System of New Zealand comprises a Court of Appeal, a High Court and District Courts, all of which have civil and criminal jurisdiction, and the specialist courts, the Employment Court, the Family Court, the Youth Court and the Maori Land Court. Final appeal (which was under review in 1995) is to the Judicial Committee of the Privy Council in the United Kingdom. In civil cases parties have an appeal to the Privy Council from the Court of Appeal as a matter of right if the case involves $NZ5,000 or more; leave to appeal is not automatically granted for criminal cases.

The Court of Appeal hears appeals from the High Court, although it does have some original jurisdiction. Its decisions are final, except in cases that may be appealed to the Privy Council. Appeals regarding convictions and sentences handed down by the High Court or District Trial Courts are by leave only.

The High Court has jurisdiction to hear cases involving major crimes, admiralty law and civil matters of more than $NZ200,000 (more than $NZ62,500 per year for rent and more than $NZ500,000 for real estate). It hears appeals from lower courts and tribunals, and reviews administrative actions.

District Courts have an extensive criminal and civil law jurisdiction. They hear civil cases up to $NZ200,000, unless the parties agree to litigate a larger sum (up to $NZ62,500 per year for rent and up to $NZ500,000 for real estate). Justices of the Peace can hear minor criminal and traffic matters if less than $NZ5,000. The Family Court, which is a division of the District Courts, has the jurisdiction to deal with dissolution of marriages, adoption, guardianship applications, domestic actions, matrimonial property, child support, care and protection applications regarding children and young persons, and similar matters.

The tribunals are as follows: the Employment Tribunal, Disputes Tribunal, Equal Opportunities Tribunal, Residential Tenancies Tribunal, Waitangi Tribunal and Planning Tribunal. The Disputes Tribunal has the jurisdiction to hear civil matters involving sums up to $NZ3,000. If the parties agree, it can hear cases involving sums up to $NZ5,000.

In criminal cases involving indictable offences (major crimes), the defendant has the right to a jury. In criminal cases involving summary offences (minor crimes), the defendant may elect to have a jury if the sentence corresponding to the charge is three months or greater.

**Attorney-General:** PAUL EAST.

**Chief Justice:** Sir THOMAS EICHELBAUM.

NEW ZEALAND

### THE COURT OF APPEAL
**President:** Sir ROBIN BRUNSKILL COOKE.

**Judges:** Sir THOMAS EICHELBAUM (ex officio), Sir IVOR LLOYD MORGAN RICHARDSON, Sir MAURICE EUGENE CASEY, MICHAEL HARDIE BOYS, THOMAS MUNRO GAULT, IAN LLOYD MCKAY.

### THE HIGH COURT
**Judges:** Sir RICHARD IAN BARKER, THOMAS MURRAY THORP, LAURENCE MURRAY GREIG, JOHN HAMILTON WALLACE, DAVID LANCE TOMPKINS, RODNEY GERALD GALLEN, JOHN STEELE HENRY, RICHARD ALEXANDER HERON, ANTHONY ARTHUR TRAVERS ELLIS, NEIL WILLIAM WILLIAMSON, ROBERT PHILIP SMELLIE, ROBERT ANDREW MCGECHAN, JOHN ANTHONY DOOGUE, ANDREW PATRICK CHARLES TIPPING, NOEL CROSSLEY ANDERSON, JAMES BRUCE ROBERTSON, ROBERT LLOYD FISHER, COLIN CAMPBELL FRASER, DANIEL PAUL NEAZOR, EDMUND WALTER THOMAS, PETER GEORGE SPENSER PENLINGTON, PAUL BASIL TEMM, PETER BLANCHARD, ROBERT GRANT HAMMOND, Dame SILVIA ROSE CARTWRIGHT, DAVID STEWART MORRIS, JOHN DAVID RABONE.

## Religion
### CHRISTIANITY
**Conference of Churches in Aotearoa New Zealand:** POB 9573, Newmarket, Auckland; tel. (9) 525-4179; fax (9) 525-4346; f. 1987 to replace the National Council of Churches in New Zealand (f. 1941); 11 mem. churches, 1 assoc. mem.; Pres JOHN FITZMAURICE, GLADYS MEAD, NIK CREE; Administrator JUDITH CRIMMINS.

**Te Runanga Whakawhanaunga i Nga Hahi o Aotearoa** (Maori Council of Churches in New Zealand): POB 9573, Newmarket, Auckland; tel. (9) 525-4179; fax (9) 525-4346; f. 1982; four mem. churches; Administrator TE RUA GRETHA.

#### The Anglican Communion
The Anglican Church in Aotearoa, New Zealand and Polynesia comprises Te Pihopatanga o Aotearoa and eight dioceses (one of which is Polynesia). In 1991 the Church had an estimated 732,048 members (22.1% of the total population) in New Zealand.

**Primate of the Anglican Church in Aotearoa, New Zealand and Polynesia, and Bishop of Wellington:** Most Rev. BRIAN NEWTON DAVIS, POB 12-046, Wellington; tel. (4) 472-1057; fax (4) 499-1360.

**General Secretary and Treasurer:** ROBIN NAIRN, POB 885, Hastings; tel. (6) 878-7902; fax (6) 878-7905.

#### The Roman Catholic Church
For ecclesiastical purposes, New Zealand comprises one archdiocese and five dioceses. At 31 December 1993 there were an estimated 488,842 adherents.

**Bishops' Conference:** New Zealand Catholic Bishops' Conference, POB 1937, Wellington; tel. (4) 496-1795; fax (4) 499-2519; f. 1974; Pres. Rt Rev. LEONARD A. BOYLE, Bishop of Dunedin; Sec. Cardinal THOMAS STAFFORD WILLIAMS, Archbishop of Wellington.

**Archbishop of Wellington:** HE Cardinal THOMAS STAFFORD WILLIAMS, POB 1937, Wellington 1; tel. (4) 496-1795; fax (4) 499-2519.

#### Other Christian Churches
**Baptist Churches of New Zealand:** 90 Russell Rd, Manurewa, POB 97-543, South Auckland; tel. (9) 266-1101; fax (9) 266-1095; f. 1882; 23,557 mems; Pres. Rev. TOM FREW; Exec. Sec. Rev. IAN BROWN.

**Congregational Union of New Zealand:** Gen. Sec.: Rev. ALESANA MCCARTHY, 14 St Catherine Cres., West Harbour, Auckland; f. 1884; 352 mems, 12 churches.

**Methodist Church of New Zealand:** Connexional Office, POB 931, Christchurch; tel. (3) 366-6049; fax (3) 366-6009; 13,056 mems; Gen. Sec. Rev. S. J. WEST.

**Presbyterian Church of Aotearoa New Zealand:** 100 Tory St, POB 9049, Wellington; tel. (4) 801-6000; fax (4) 801-6001; 550,000 mems; Moderator Rt Rev. MARGARET E. SCHRADER; Assembly Exec. Sec. Rev. MICHAEL D. THAWLEY.

There are several Maori Churches in New Zealand, with a total membership of over 30,000. These include the Ratana Church of New Zealand, Ringatu Church, Church of Te Kooti Rikirangi, Absolute Maori Established Church and United Maori Mission. The Antiochian Orthodox Church, the Assemblies of God, the Greek Orthodox Church of New Zealand, the Liberal Catholic Church, and the Society of Friends (Quakers) are also active.

### BAHÁ'Í FAITH
**National Spiritual Assembly of the Bahá'ís of New Zealand:** POB 21-551, Henderson, Auckland 8; tel. (9) 837-4866; fax (9) 837-4898.

## The Press
### NEWSPAPERS AND PERIODICALS
#### Principal Dailies
**Bay of Plenty Times:** 108 Durham St, Private Bag TG12002, Tauranga; tel. (7) 578-3059; fax (7) 578-0047; f. 1872; evening; Gen. Man. WI POMANA; Editor J. G. PETTIT; circ. 20,336.

**The Daily News:** POB 444, New Plymouth; tel. (6) 758-0559; fax (6) 758-6849; morning; Gen. Man. KEVIN NIELSON; Editor MURRAY GOSTON; circ. 29,114.

**The Daily Post:** 61 Hinemoa St, POB 1442, Rotorua; tel. (7) 348 6199; fax (7) 346 0153; f. 1885; evening; Gen. Man. G. CAULFIELD; Editor R. G. MAYSTON; circ. 12,884.

**Daily Telegraph:** 27 Tennyson St, POB 343, Napier; tel. (6) 835-4488; fax (6) 835-6786; f. 1871; evening; Gen. Man. J. A. SILVESTER; Editor K. R. HAWKER; circ. 16,834.

**The Dominion:** 40 Boulcott St, POB 1297, Wellington; tel. (4) 474-0000; fax (4) 474-0350; f. 1907; morning; Gen. Man. I. D. WELLS; Editor RICHARD LONG; circ. 64,296.

**Evening Post:** Press House, 40 Boulcott St, POB 3740, Wellington; tel. (4) 474-0444; fax (4) 474-0237; f. 1865; Gen. Man. I. D. WELLS; Editor P. R. CAVANAGH; circ. 72,000.

**Evening Standard:** POB 3, Palmerston North; tel. (6) 356-9009; fax (6) 350-9836; f. 1880; evening; Gen. Man. A. P. BROAD; Editor J. R. HARVEY; circ. 24,437.

**Gisborne Herald:** 64 Gladstone Rd, POB 1143, Gisborne; tel. (6) 867-2099; fax (6) 867-8048; f. 1874; evening; Man. Dir M. C. MUIR; Editor IAIN GILLIES; circ. 9,587.

**The Hawke's Bay Herald Tribune:** 113 Karamu Rd, POB 180, Hastings; tel. (6) 878-5155; fax (6) 876-4000; f. 1857; evening; conservative; Gen. Man. R. D. HALL; Editor J. E. MORGAN; circ. 19,828.

**Marlborough Express:** 62 Arthur St, POB 242, Blenheim; tel. (3) 578-6059; fax (3) 578-0497; f. 1866; Man. Dir ROGER G. ROSE; Editor BRENDON BURNS; circ. 10,719.

**The National Business Review:** Level 26, United Bank Tower, 125 Queen St, POB 145, Auckland; tel. (9) 307-1629; fax (9) 307-9060; f. 1987; Editor FRANCES O'SULLIVAN; circ. 19,600.

**Nelson Evening Mail:** 15 Bridge St, POB 244, Nelson; tel. (3) 548-7079; fax (3) 546-2802; f. 1866; evening; Gen. Man. NIGEL WATT; Editor DAVID J. MITCHELL; circ. 19,069.

**New Zealand Herald:** 46 Albert St, POB 32, Auckland; tel. (9) 379-5050; fax (9) 366-0146; f. 1863; morning; Man. Dir H. M. HORTON; Editor P. J. SCHERER; circ. 250,000.

**Northern Advocate:** Water St, POB 210, Whangarei; tel. (9) 438-2399; fax (9) 430-5669; f. 1875; evening; Man. Dir W. K. CRAWFORD; Editor G. A. BARROW; circ. 15,772.

**Otago Daily Times:** Lower Stuart St, POB 517, Dunedin; tel. (3) 477-4760; telex 5692; fax (3) 477-1313; f. 1861; morning; Man. Dir JULIAN C. S. SMITH; Editor GEOFF ADAMS; circ. 51,113.

**The Press:** Cathedral Sq., Private Bag 4722, Christchurch; tel. (3) 379-0940; fax (3) 364-8492; f. 1861; morning; Gen. Man. R. A. BARKER; Editor D. W. C. WILSON; circ. 102,066.

**Southland Times:** 67 Esk St, POB 805, Invercargill; tel. (3) 218-1909; fax (3) 214-9905; f. 1862; morning; Gen. Man. ROBIN D. WATSON; Editor CLIVE A. LIND; circ. 33,300.

**Taranaki Daily News:** Currie St, POB 444, New Plymouth; tel. (6) 758-0559; fax (6) 758-6849; f. 1857; Editor MURRAY GOSTON; circ. 29,432.

**Timaru Herald:** 52 Bank St, POB 46, Timaru; tel. (3) 684-4129; fax (3) 688-1042; f. 1864; morning; Gen. Man. CHRIS JAGUSCH; Editor B. R. APPLEBY; circ. 15,287.

**Waikato Times:** Private Bag 3086, Hamilton; tel. (7) 849-6180; fax (7) 849-9603; f. 1872; evening; independent; Gen. Man. P. G. HENSON; Editor SUZANNE CARTY; circ. 40,923.

**Wanganui Chronicle:** 59 Taupo Quay, POB 433, Wanganui; tel. (6) 345-3919; fax (6) 345-3232; f. 1856; morning; Gen. Man. R. A. JARDEN; Editor J. McLEES; circ. 15,265.

#### Weeklies and Other Newspapers
**Best Bets:** POB 1327, Auckland; telex 2574; horse-racing and trotting; Editor BOB LOVETT; circ. 45,000.

**Christchurch Star:** 293 Tuam St, POB 1467, Christchurch; tel. (3) 379-7100; fax (3) 366-0180; f. 1868; 2 a week; independent; Man. Editor M. A. FLETCHER; circ. 120,232.

**Mercantile Gazette:** 8 Sheffield Crescent, Christchurch 8005; tel. (3) 358-3219; fax (3) 358-4490; f. 1876; fortnightly; Mon.; economics, finance, management, stock market, politics; Editor BILL HORSLEY; circ. 16,300.

NEW ZEALAND
*Directory*

**New Truth:** News Media (Auckland) Ltd, Glenside Crescent, POB 1327, Auckland; tel. (9) 379-7626; fax (9) 309-2279; f. 1905; Friday; local news and features; TV and entertainment; sports; Editor Hedley Mortlock; circ. 112,000.

**New Zealand Gazette:** Dept of Internal Affairs, POB 805, Wellington; tel. (4) 495-7200; fax (4) 495-7289; f. 1840; weekly; circ. 1,000.

**New Zealand Tablet:** 39 Crawford St, POB 1285, Dunedin; tel. (3) 477-8010; fax (3) 477-8245; f. 1873; Sun.; Roman Catholic; Editor Fr J. M. Hill; circ. 4,500.

**North Shore Times Advertiser:** POB 33-235, Takapuna, Auckland 9; tel. (9) 489-4189; fax (9) 486-1950; 3 a week; Editor I. Dunn; circ. 56,368.

**Paeroa Gazette:** Belmont Rd, POB 130, Paeroa; tel. (7) 862-8662; fax (7) 862-8661; Wed.; Editor Peter Shand; circ. 2,800.

**Sunday Star-Times:** POB 1409, Auckland; tel. (9) 379-7626; fax (9) 309-0258; f. 1994 by merger; Gen. Man. Alan Hitchens; circ. 101,369.

**Taieri Herald:** POB 105, Mosgiel; tel. (3) 489-7123; fax (3) 489-7668; f. 1962; weekly; Man. Editor Steve McAlister; circ. 9,962.

**Waihi Gazette:** Seddon St, Waihi; tel. (7) 863-8674; fax (7) 863-8103; weekly; Editor Peter Shand; circ. 7,116.

**Wairarapa News:** POB 18, Carterton; tel. (6) 379-8039; fax (6) 379-6481; f. 1869; Editor Eric Turner; circ. 16,000.

### Other Periodicals

**AA Directions:** AA Centre, 342 Lambton Quay, POB 1, Wellington; tel. (4) 473-8738; fax (4) 471-2080; every two months, excl. Jan./Feb.; official magazine of the New Zealand Automobile Association; Editor R. J. Smithies; circ. 533,341.

**Architecture/New Zealand:** AGM Publishing Ltd, Private Bag 99-915, Newmarket, Auckland; tel. (9) 379-5393; fax (9) 308-9523; f. 1987; every 2 months; Editor Steve Bohling; circ. 9,000.

**Australian Women's Weekly** (NZ edition): Private Bag 92512, Wellesley St, Auckland; tel. (9) 373-5408; fax (9) 308-9498; monthly; circ. 120,795.

**Landfall:** University of Otago Press, POB 56, Dunedin; tel. (3) 479-8807; fax (3) 479-8385; 2 a year; literary; Editor Chris Price.

**Management:** POB 5544, Wellesley St, Auckland; tel. (9) 358-5455; fax (9) 358-5462; f. 1954; monthly; business; Editor Carroll du Chateau; circ. 11,000.

**More Magazine:** Private Bag, Wellesley St, Auckland; tel. (9) 373-5408; fax (9) 309-8718; monthly; Editor Shelley Clement; circ. 50,000.

**New Truth and TV Extra:** 155 New North Rd, Auckland 1; tel. (9) 302-1300; fax (9) 309-2279; weekly; Editor Hedley Mortlock; circ. 41,000.

**New Zealand Dairy Exporter:** POB 299, Wellington; tel. (4) 499-0300; fax (4) 499-0330; f. 1925; monthly; Man. Editor L. McEldowney; circ. 22,800.

**The New Zealand Farmer:** Great South Rd, POB 4233, Auckland; tel. (9) 520-9451; fax (9) 520-9459; f. 1882; weekly; Editor Tony Leggett; circ. 18,000.

**New Zealand Forest Industries:** POB 5544, Auckland; tel. (9) 358-5455; fax (9) 358-5462; f. 1960; monthly; forestry; Editor Vicki Jayne; circ. 2,500.

**New Zealand Gardener:** POB 6341, Wellesley St, Auckland; tel. (4) 293-4495; f. 1944; monthly; Editor J. Matthews; circ. 65,000.

**New Zealand Horse & Pony:** POB 1327, Auckland; tel. (9) 379-7626; fax (9) 309-2279; f. 1959; monthly; Editor Joan E. Gilchrist; circ. 7,000.

**New Zealand Medical Journal:** University of Otago Medical School, POB 913, Dunedin; tel. (3) 474-1060; fax (3) 479-0401; f. 1887; 2 a month; Editor Prof. R. G. Robinson; circ. 5,000.

**New Zealand Official Yearbook:** Statistics New Zealand, POB 2922, Wellington; tel. (4) 495-4600; fax (4) 472-9135; f. 1893; Editor Jane Evans; circ. 4,900.

**New Zealand Science Review:** POB 1874, Wellington; fax (63) 505-623; f. 1942; 4 a year; reviews, policy and philosophy of science; Editor F. B. Shorland.

**New Zealand Wings:** POB 120, Otaki; tel. (6) 364-6423; fax (6) 364-7797; f. 1932; monthly; Editor Ross Macpherson; circ. 20,000.

**New Zealand Woman's Day:** Private Bag 92512, Wellesley St, Auckland; tel. (9) 373-5408; fax (9) 357-0978; weekly; Editor Louise Wright; circ. 220,363.

**New Zealand Woman's Weekly:** 360 Dominion Rd, Private Bag, Auckland 3; tel. (9) 638-8105; fax (9) 630-9128; f. 1932; Mon.; women's issues and general interest; Editor Sarah-Kate Lynch; circ. 145,309.

**New Zealandia:** POB 845, Auckland; tel. (9) 378-4380; fax (9) 360-3065; f. 1934; monthly; Roman Catholic; Editor Paul Freedman; circ. 12,500.

**NZ Business:** 22 Heather St, Private Bag 93218, Parnell, Auckland; tel. (9) 379-4233; fax (9) 309-3575; f. 1938; monthly; Editor Ena Hutchinson; circ. 8,871.

**NZ Listener:** 360 Dominion Rd, Mount Eden, POB 7, Auckland; tel. (9) 623-1002; fax (9) 623-1011; f. 1939; weekly; general features, politics, arts, TV, radio; Editor Jenny Wheeler; circ. 116,000.

**NZ Turf Digest:** News Media (Auckland) Ltd, Glenside Crescent, POB 1327, Auckland; tel. (9) 379-4207; fax (9) 366-4565; Sun./Thur.; Editor Bob Lovett; circ. 22,000.

**NZRSA Review:** 181 Willis St, POB 27248, Wellington; tel. (4) 384-7994; fax (4) 385-3325; every 2 months; magazine of the NZ Returned Services' Asscn; circ. 86,005.

**Otago Southland Farmer:** POB 45, Balclutha; tel. (3) 418-1115; fax (3) 418-1173; fortnightly; Editor T. Carson; circ. 17,000.

**Pacific Way Magazine:** Private Bag, Wellesley St, Auckland; tel. (9) 373-5408; fax (9) 309-8718; monthly; circ. 80,000.

**PSA Journal:** c/o NZPSA, Private Bag, Wellington; tel. (4) 494-2000; fax (4) 494-2010; f. 1913; 10 a year; journal of the NZ Public Service Asscn; Editor Pat Martin; circ. 63,500.

**Reader's Digest:** POB 3372, Auckland 1015; tel. (9) 360-0434; fax (9) 360-0584; monthly; Editor Bruce Heilbuth; circ. 151,626.

**Straight Furrow:** POB 715, Wellington; tel. (4) 473-7269; fax (4) 473-1081; f. 1933; fortnightly; Editor Susan Grant; circ. 86,000.

**Time New Zealand:** Tandem House, 18 St Martins Lane, POB 198, Auckland; telex 21429; fax (9) 366-4706; weekly; circ. 42,765.

**World Affairs:** UN Asscn of NZ, POB 11-750, Wellington; tel. (4) 382-8783; f. 1945; 3 a year; Editor David Zwartz.

### NEWS AGENCIES

**New Zealand Press Association:** Newspaper House, 93 Boulcott St, POB 1599, Wellington; tel. (4) 472-7910; telex 3515; fax (4) 478-1625; f. 1879; non-political; Chair. M. Robson; Man. Editor P. O'Hara.

**South Pacific News Service Ltd (Sopacnews):** POB 5026, Lambton Quay, Wellington; tel. (4) 472-4451; fax (4) 499-0405; f. 1948; Man. Editor Neale McMillan.

### Foreign Bureaux

**Agence France-Presse (AFP):** Newspaper House, 1st Floor, 93 Boulcott St, POB 11-420, Wellington; tel. (4) 473-3666; fax (4) 471-0185; Correspondent Michael Field.

**Reuters (UK):** POB 11-744, Wellington; tel. (4) 473-4746; telex 30330; fax (4) 473-6212; Correspondent Mark Trevelyan.

**United Press International (UPI)** (USA): Press Gallery, Parliament Bldgs, Wellington; tel. (4) 471-9552; fax (4) 472-7604; Correspondent Brendon Burns.

**Xinhua (New China) News Agency** (People's Republic of China): 136 Northland Rd, Northland, Wellington; tel. (4) 475-7607; telex 30043; fax (4) 475-7607; Correspondent Yang Guojun.

### PRESS COUNCIL

**New Zealand Press Council:** POB 1066, Wellington; tel. (4) 473-5220; fax (4) 471-0987; f. 1972; Chair. Sir Joseph Ongley; Sec. G. W. Jenkins.

### PRESS ASSOCIATIONS

**Commonwealth Press Union (New Zealand Section):** POB 1066, Wellington; tel. (4) 472-6223; fax (4) 471-0987; Chair. G. T. Adams; Sec. P. O'Reilly.

**New Zealand Community Newspapers Association (Inc):** POB 1066, Wellington; tel. (4) 499-2153; fax (4) 499-1075; Exec. Dir Keith Berry.

**Newspaper Publishers' Association of New Zealand (Inc):** Newspaper House, POB 1066, 93 Boulcott St, Wellington 1; tel. (4) 472-6223; fax (4) 471-0987; f. 1898; 34 mems; Pres. J. M. Robson; Exec. Dir P. O'Reilly; Exec. Officer A. Shepherd.

# Publishers

**Auckland University Press:** Private Bag 92019, University of Auckland, Auckland; tel. (9) 373-7528; fax (9) 373-7465; f. 1966; scholarly; Man. Editor Elizabeth P. Caffin.

**Butterworths of New Zealand Ltd:** 203–207 Victoria St, POB 472, Wellington; tel. (4) 385-1479; fax (4) 385-1598; taxation, legal; Man. Dir P. G. Kirk.

# NEW ZEALAND

**Christchurch Caxton Press Ltd:** 113 Victoria St, Christchurch 1; tel. (3) 366-8516; fax (3) 365-7840; f. 1935; history, prose, gardening, human interest, tourist pictorial; Man. Dir BRUCE BASCAND.

**Dunmore Press Ltd:** POB 5115, Palmerston North; tel. (6) 358-7169; fax (6) 357-9242; f. 1975; history, general, academic; Chair. VALERIE GATENBY; Editor MURRAY R. GATENBY.

**G.P. Publications Ltd:** Archives House, 10 Mulgrave St, POB 12-052, Wellington; tel. (4) 473-7211; fax (4) 496-5698; general publishers and leading distributor of government publs; fmrly Govt Printing Office; Gen. Man. (vacant)

**HarperCollins Publishers (New Zealand) Ltd:** 31 View Rd, Glenfield, Auckland; tel. (9) 443-9400; fax (9) 443-9403; f. 1888; general and educational; Man. Dir BARRIE HITCHON.

**Hodder Moa Beckett Publishers:** POB 3858, Auckland 1; tel. (9) 444-3640; fax (9) 444-3646; f. 1971; Man. Dir NEIL ASTON.

**Longman Paul Ltd:** Private Bag 102908, North Shore Mail Centre, Glenfield, Auckland 10; tel. (9) 444-4968; fax (9) 444-4957; f. 1968; educational; Dirs ROSEMARY STAGG, ELIZABETH NELSON, R. W. FISHER, B. V. ASHCROFT-HAWLEY.

**McGraw-Hill Publishing Co, New Zealand Ltd:** 5 Joval Pl., Manukau City, POB 97082, Wiri; tel. (9) 262-2537; fax (9) 262-2540; f. 1974; educational; Man. JANET POWELL.

**New Zealand Council for Educational Research:** POB 3237, Wellington; tel. (4) 384-7939; fax (4) 384-7933; f. 1934; scholarly, research monographs, educational, academic, periodicals; Chair. Dr COLIN KNIGHT; Dir Dr ANNE MEADE.

**Oxford University Press:** 540 Great South Rd, Greenlane, POB 11-149, Ellerslie, Auckland 5; tel. (9) 525-8020; fax (9) 525-1072; f. 1948; literature, history, law, Maori and Pacific, social science, reference, agriculture, business, etc.; Publr LINDA CASSELLS.

**Penguin Books (NZ) Ltd:** 182–190 Wairau Rd, Auckland 10; tel. (9) 444-4965; fax (9) 444-1470; f. 1973; Dir GEOFF WALKER.

**Wendy Pye Ltd:** Private Bag 17-905, Greenlane, Auckland; tel. (9) 525-3575; fax (9) 525-4205; children's fiction and educational; Man. Dir WENDY PYE.

**Random House New Zealand Ltd:** Private Bag 102950, North Shore Mail Centre, Glenfield, Auckland; tel. (9) 444-7197; fax (9) 444-7524; f. 1977; general; Man. Dir JULIET ROGERS.

**Reed Publishing (NZ) Ltd:** Private Bag 34901, Birkenhead, Auckland 10; tel. (9) 480-4950; fax (9) 480-4999; fiction and general non-fiction; Man. Dir ALAN L. SMITH.

**University of Otago Press:** POB 56, Dunedin; tel. (3) 479-8807; fax (3) 479-8385; f. 1958; academic, trade publs.; Man. Editor WENDY HARREX.

**Whitcoulls Ltd:** 3rd Floor, 186 Queen St, Private Bag 92098, Auckland 1; tel. (9) 309-2233; fax (9) 302-2608; NZ, general and educational; Gen. Man. D. K. WORLEY.

### PUBLISHERS' ASSOCIATION

**Book Publishers' Association of New Zealand Inc.:** Norwich Bldg, 8th Floor, cnr Queen and Durham Sts, Auckland 1; tel. (9) 309-2561; fax (9) 309-7798; f. 1977; Pres. TONY HARKINS; Dir DEAN REYNOLDS.

## Radio and Television

In 1988 two state-owned enterprises, Radio New Zealand Ltd and Television New Zealand Ltd, were formed to replace the Broadcasting Corporation of New Zealand, a public corporation. Revenue for non-commercial television production and public broadcasting is derived from the public broadcasting fee, payable by owners of all operating television receivers. Commercial radio has been operating in New Zealand since 1936.

In 1992 there were an estimated 3.2m. radio receivers and 1.5m. television receivers in use.

### RADIO

**Radio New Zealand Ltd:** Gleneagles Bldg, The Terrace, POB 2092, Wellington; tel. (4) 474-1555; telex 31031; fax (4) 474-1340; f. 1936; operates 40 commercial/community stations in New Zealand, a commercial linking network and one part-commercial network; provides consultancy and engineering services within New Zealand and overseas; CEO NIGEL MILAN.

**New Zealand Public Radio Ltd:** wholly-owned subsidiary of Radio New Zealand Ltd; operates two non-commercial networks, a 24-hour news and current affairs service, and Radio New Zealand Archives; directs short-wave service to the South Pacific.

### TELEVISION

**Television New Zealand Ltd:** Television Centre, Cnr Hobson and Victoria Sts, POB 3819, Auckland; tel. (9) 377-0630; fax (9) 375-0979; f. 1960; the television service is responsible for the production of programmes for the two TV networks, Television One and Channel 2, and for the sale of all local productions; networks are commercial all week and transmit in colour; Television One covers the whole population, while Channel 2 has 99% coverage; both networks transmit morning, afternoon and evening, seven days a week, and about 28% of programme content is locally produced; CEO BRENT HARMAN.

#### Private Television

A national private television service, TV3, was inaugurated in November 1989. Four more companies were awarded television broadcasting licences in February 1990, including Sky Network Television Ltd, which commenced operation of three 'pay channels' transmitting news, films and sports programmes in May 1990. Canterbury Television, the country's first 'free-to-air' regional operator, began transmission to the Canterbury region in June 1991.

**Canterbury Television:** POB 3741, Christchurch; tel. (3) 365-5505; fax (3) 365-5773; wholly owned by Fogarty McMenamin Trust.

**TV3 Network Holdings Ltd:** Private Bag 92624, Auckland; tel. (9) 377-9730; fax (9) 302-2321; f. 1989; 40% owned by Westpac Banking Corpn, 40% by TV3 Network Ltd and 20% by CanWest.

**Sky Network Television Limited:** POB 9059, Newmarket, Auckland; tel. (9) 579-9999; fax (9) 579-0910; f. 1990; 51% owned by Bell Atlantic Ameritech, TCI, and Time Warner, 9% Todd Group, 16% Craig Heatley and Terry Jarvis, 16% Television New Zealand Limited, 9% Alan Gibbs and Trevor Farmer, 0.4% ESPN.

## Finance

(cap. = capital; res = reserves; dep. = deposits; m. = million; amounts in New Zealand dollars)

### BANKING

#### Central Bank

**Reserve Bank of New Zealand:** 2 The Terrace, POB 2498, Wellington; tel. (4) 472-2029; telex 3368; fax (4) 473-8554; f. 1934; bank of issue; cap. and res 363.8m., serviced liabilities 6,580.6m. (June 1994); Gov. Dr DONALD BRASH; Dep. Govs P. W. E. NICHOLL, R. J. LANG.

#### Registered Banks

As a result of legislation which took effect in April 1987, several foreign banks were incorporated into the domestic banking system.

**ANZ Banking Group (New Zealand) Ltd:** 215–229 Lambton Quay, POB 1492, Wellington; tel. (4) 496-7000; telex 3385; fax (4) 473-6919; f. 1979; subsidiary of Australia and New Zealand Banking Group Ltd of Melbourne, Australia; cap. and res 977m., dep. 11,869m. (Sept. 1994); Chair. D. P. MERCER; Man. Dir W. S. STEVENS; 131 brs and sub-brs.

**ASB Bank Ltd:** ASB Bank Centre, Cnr Wellesley and Albert Sts, POB 35, Auckland 1; tel. (9) 377-8930; telex 60881; fax (9) 3078010; f. 1847 as Auckland Savings Bank, name changed 1988; res 276m., dep. 4,841m. (Dec. 1993); Chair. G. J. JUDD; Man. Dir R. J. NORRIS; 130 brs.

**Bank of New Zealand (BNZ):** BNZ Centre, 1 Willis St, POB 2392, Wellington; tel. (4) 474-6999; telex 3344; fax (4) 474-6563; f. 1861; owned by National Australia Bank; cap. 913.5m., res −279.9m., dep. 15,715.2m. (Sept. 1993); Chair. R. W. STANNARD; Man. Dir R. M. C. PROWSE; 309 brs and sub-brs.

**Bankers Trust New Zealand Ltd:** POB 6900, Wellesley St, Auckland; tel. (9) 309-3226; telex 63612; fax (9) 303-1851; f. 1986; cap. and res 139.1m. (Dec. 1994); Chair. R. FERGUSON; CEO G. R. WALKER.

**Banque Indosuez** (France): Level 14, ASB Tower, 2 Hunter St, POB 10-112, Wellington; tel. (4) 495-3555; telex 31143; fax (4) 495-3535; f. 1981; CEO for NZ DUNCAN WYLIE.

**BNZ Finance Ltd:** Norwich Insurance House, 100 Willis St, POB 401, Wellington; tel. (4) 472-4306; fax (4) 472-8970; subsidiary of Bank of New Zealand; cap. and res 175m., dep. 621m. (Sept. 1993); Man. Dir R. A. BONIFANT.

**Citibank NA** (USA): POB 3429, Auckland; tel. (9) 302-3128; fax (9) 308-9928; CEO R. A. WILKS; 2 brs.

**Countrywide Banking Corpn Ltd:** POB 5445, Auckland; tel. (9) 309-8900; fax (9) 377-9550; f. 1897; cap. 385m., dep. 4,776m. (Feb. 1995); Chair. P. F. CLAPSHAW; Man. Dir D. J. WOLFENDEN; 75 brs.

# NEW ZEALAND

**Hongkong and Shanghai Banking Corporation Ltd** (Hong Kong): POB 5947, 4/F Hongkong Bank House, 290 Queen St, Auckland; tel. (9) 309-3800; telex 63427; fax (9) 309-6681; Man. S. WALLIS; 3 brs.

**National Australia Bank (NZ) Ltd:** 160 Grafton Rd, Private Bag 92107, Auckland; tel. (9) 309-2300; telex 60726; fax (9) 391-477; f. 1987; cap. and res 157m., dep. 1,562m. (Sept. 1992); Chair. P. A. JEFFERIES; Exec. Dir R. P. MCCRACKEN; 37 brs.

**National Bank of New Zealand Ltd:** 170–186 Featherston St, POB 1791, Wellington 1; tel. (4) 494-4000; telex 31388; fax (4) 494-4010; f. 1873; cap. and res 800m., dep. 13,414m. (Dec. 1994); Chair. P. M. MCCAW; Dir and CEO Sir JOHN ANDERSON; 190 brs.

**Post Office Bank Ltd:** 215–229 Lambton Quay, POB 1492, Wellington; tel. (4) 496-7000; fax (4) 473-6919; f. 1987; subsidiary of Australia and New Zealand Banking Group Ltd of Melbourne, Australia; cap. and res 346m., dep. 3,050m. (Sept. 1992); Chair. P. J. O. HAWKINS; CEO C. J. CAMM; 180 brs and sub-brs.

**Primary Industry Bank of Australia Ltd:** POB 1069 Auckland; tel. (9) 302-1728; fax (9) 303-1420; Man. R. B. LANDER.

**Trust Bank Central Ltd:** cnr Heretaunga St and Railway Rd, POB 348, Hastings; tel. (6) 878-2094; fax (6) 878-3392; f. 1972; cap. and res 20m., dep. 880m. (July 1993); Pres. M. A. SEWELL.

**TSB Bank Ltd:** POB 240, New Plymouth; tel. (6) 759-9280; fax (6) 759-9280; f. 1850; fmrly Taranaki Savings Bank Ltd; dep. 456m. (March 1994); Man. Dir K. W. RIMMINGTON; 15 brs.

**Westland Bank Ltd:** 99 Revell St, POB 103, Hokitika; tel. (3) 755-8680; fax (3) 755-8277; full subsidiary of ASB Bank Ltd; cap. and res 6,176m., dep. 108m. (June 1992); Man. Dir K. J. BEAMS; 9 brs.

**Westpac Banking Corporation** (Australia): 318–324 Lambton Quay, Wellington; tel. (4) 498-1000; telex 3365; fax (4) 473-7115; cap. and res 412m., dep. 6,184m. (Sept. 1992); Gen. Man. H. M. PRICE; 167 brs.

### Other Banks

**Maori Development Corpn:** MDC House, 142 Broadway, POB 9845, Newmarket, Auckland; tel. (9) 520-6282; fax (9) 520-6804; f. 1987 to provide financial and advisory services to Maori-owned enterprises; cap. p.u. 26m.; Chair. R. H. MAHUTA; CEO W. G. WARD-HOLMES.

**Postbank:** 58–66 Willis St, Wellington 1; tel. (4) 729-809; f. 1987; owned by Australia and New Zealand Banking Corpn; total assets 3,720m. (Sept. 1988); 550 brs.

### Association

**New Zealand Bankers' Association:** POB 3043, Wellington; tel. (4) 472-8838; fax (4) 473-1698; Exec. Dir S. S. CARLAW.

## STOCK EXCHANGES

**Dunedin Stock Exchange:** POB 298, Dunedin; tel. (3) 477-5900; Chair. E. S. EDGAR; Sec. R. P. LEWIS.

**New Zealand Stock Exchange:** Caltex Tower, 286–292 Lambton Quay, POB 2959, Wellington 1; tel. (4) 472-7599; fax (4) 473-1470; Man. Dir W. P. FOSTER.

### Supervisory Body

**New Zealand Securities Commission:** POB 1179, Wellington; tel. (4) 472-9830; fax (4) 472-8076; f. 1979; Chair. EUAN ABERNETHY.

## INSURANCE

**AA-GIO Insurance Ltd:** POB 992, Auckland; tel. (9) 357-9999; fax (9) 358-4044; Chief Exec. PETER ROSE.

**Allied Mutual Insurance (AMI) Ltd:** 29–35 Latimer Sq., POB 2116, Christchurch; tel. (3) 371-9000; fax (3) 371-8314; f. 1926; Chair. K. G. L. NOLAN; CEO E. B. MCKESSAR.

**AMP Fire and General Insurance Co (NZ) Ltd:** 86/90 Customhouse Quay, POB 1093, Wellington; tel. (4) 498-8000; fax (4) 471-2312; f. 1958; fire, accident, marine, general; Chair. GRAEME W. VALENTINE; Man. K. SHAW.

**ANZ Life Assurance Co Ltd:** POB 1492, Wellington; tel. and fax (4) 496-7666; Man. R. A. DEAN.

**BNZ Life Insurance Ltd:** POB 11-544, Wellington; tel. (4) 382-2577; fax (4) 474-6883; Man. N. K. FAIRLESS.

**Cigna Insurance NZ Ltd:** POB 734, Auckland; tel. (9) 377-1459; fax (9) 303-1909; Gen. Man. ALEX ROBERTSON.

**Colonial Mutual Life Assurance Society Ltd:** 117 Customhouse Quay, POB 191, Wellington 6000; tel. (4) 471-4000; fax (4) 471-1079; life, accident, investment, sickness and disability, staff superannuation; Gen. Man. D. J. MAY.

**Commercial Union General Insurance Co Ltd:** 142 Featherston St, POB 2797, Wellington; tel. (4) 473-9177; fax (4) 473-7424; fire, accident, travel, engineering; Gen. Man. T. WAKEFIELD.

**EXGO:** POB 5037, Wellington 1; tel. (4) 496-9600; fax (4) 496-9670; f. 1964; credit insurance unit of State Insurance Ltd (see below); Man. Dir D. J. PRITCHARD; Man. A. J. H. REDWOOD.

**FAI Metropolitan Life Assurance Co of New Zealand Ltd:** FAI House, 46 Parnell Rd, Parnell, Private Bag, Auckland 1; tel. (9) 308-9900; fax (9) 307-0911; f. 1962; life; Man. Dir PETER W. FITZSIMMONS.

**Farmers' Mutual Group:** 68 The Square, POB 1943, Palmerston North 5301; fax (6) 356-4603; comprises Farmers' Mutual Insurance Asscn and Farmers' Mutual Insurance Ltd; fire, accident, motor vehicle, marine, life; Gen. Man. M. MILLAR.

**The National Insurance Co of New Zealand, Ltd:** 67–73 Hurstmere Rd, POB 33-144, Takapuna; tel. (9) 486-9340; fax (9) 486-9368; f. 1873; Chair. Sir C. J. MAIDEN; Man. Dir P. R. HUNT.

**National Mutual Group:** National Mutual Centre, 80 The Terrace, POB 1692, Wellington; tel. (4) 474-4500; telex 3597; fax (4) 473-0716; life, disability, superannuation and business insurance and investments, statutory trustee services; Gen. Man. W. A. RACTLIFFE.

**The New Zealand Local Government Insurance Corporation Ltd:** Local Government Bldg, 114–118 Lambton Quay, POB 1214, Wellington; tel. (4) 472-6437; f. 1960; fire, motor, all risks, accident; Chair. I. W. LAWRENCE; Gen. Man. R. D. MEAD.

**Norwich Union Life Insurance (NZ) Ltd:** cnr Hunter and Victoria Sts, Wellington 1; tel. (4) 472-0488; fax (4) 471-6970; life and superannuation; Man. Dir V. E. ARKINSTALL.

**NZI Insurance New Zealand Ltd:** NZI House, 3–13 Shortland St, Private Bag 92130, Auckland 1; tel. (9) 309-7000; telex 2928; fax (9) 309-7097; Gen. Man. H. D. SMITH.

**The Prudential Assurance Co New Zealand Ltd:** 332–340 Lambton Quay, POB 291, Wellington; tel. (4) 473-9209; fax (4) 478-1788; Gen. Man. A. J. MOLLOY.

**QBE Insurance (International) Ltd:** POB 44, Auckland; tel. (9) 303-2699; fax (9) 303-3070; Man. GRAEME EVANS.

**State Insurance Ltd:** Hunter St, Wellington 1; tel. (4) 496-9600; fax (4) 472-5824; f. 1905; mem. Norwich Union Insurance Group; Man. Dir D. J. PRITCHARD.

**Sun Alliance Life Ltd:** 139 The Terrace, POB 894, Wellington; tel. (4) 495-8700; fax (4) 495-8850; f. 1889; Man. Dir. T. C. SOLE.

**Tower Corporation:** Level 5, 50–64 Customhouse Quay, POB 352, Wellington; tel. (4) 472-6059; fax (4) 498-7903; f. 1869; Group Man. Dir JAMES BOONZAIER.

### Associations

**Insurance Council of New Zealand:** POB 474, Wellington; tel. (4) 472-5230; fax (4) 473-3011; CEO DAVID SARGEANT.

**Life Office Association of New Zealand Inc:** POB 1514, Wellington; Chief Exec. ARTHUR C. DAVIS; Exec. Officer DEBORAH KEATING.

# Trade and Industry

## CHAMBERS OF COMMERCE

**Auckland Regional Chamber of Commerce and Industry:** POB 47, Auckland; tel. (9) 309-6100; fax (9) 309-0081; CEO MICHAEL BARNETT; Pres. NORMAN JOHNSTON.

**Chamber of Commerce and International Trade (Canterbury):** Christchurch; tel. (3) 664-992; fax (3) 798-658; CEO PHIL FALLOON; Pres. JOHN FRANCIS.

**New Zealand Chambers of Commerce and Industry:** POB 11-043, Wellington; tel. (4) 472-3376; fax (4) 472-3375; Exec. Dir ELIZABETH GRIFFIN; Pres. DON BREADEN.

**Otago Chamber of Commerce and Industry Inc:** 2 Stafford St, POB 5713, Dunedin; tel. (3) 479-0181; fax (3) 477-0341; CEO J. S. THORN; Pres. JULIAN SMITH.

**Wellington Chamber of Commerce:** 9th Floor, 109 Featherston St, POB 1590, Wellington; tel. (4) 472-2725; fax (4) 471-1767; f. 1856; Chief Exec. R. R. HARDING; 1,050 mems.

## ENTERPRISE AND DEVELOPMENT BOARDS

**New Zealand Enterprise Board Ltd:** POB 11-480, Wellington; tel. (4) 499-0100; fax (4) 499-0101; Chair. DONALD SIMCOCK; Exec. Dir TONY HASSED.

**New Zealand Trade Development Board (TRADENZ):** POB 10-341, Wellington; tel. (4) 499-2244; fax (4) 473-3193; CEO RICK CHRISTIE; Chair. GAVIN CORMACK.

## MANUFACTURERS' ORGANIZATIONS

**The Auckland Manufacturers' Association:** 247 Remuera Rd, POB 28-245, Remuera, Auckland 5; tel. (9) 520-2044; fax (9) 523-3613; f. 1886; Pres. M. A. RAE; CEO B. GOLDSWORTHY; 1,150 mems.

NEW ZEALAND                                                                                                                                       *Directory*

**Canterbury Manufacturers' Association:** POB 13-152, Armagh, Christchurch; tel. (3) 366-5993; fax (3) 366-6815; f. 1879; CEO MICHAEL HANNAH; 550 mems.

**New Zealand Manufacturers' Federation (Inc):** Enterprise House, 3–9 Church St, Wellington, POB 11-543, Wellington; tel. (4) 473-3000; fax (4) 473-3004; f. 1926; Chief Exec. SIMON ARNOLD.

**Wellington Manufacturers' Association:** Enterprise House, 3–9 Church St, POB 11-748, Wellington; tel. (4) 473-3092; fax (4) 473-3004; f. 1895; Pres. D. KELLY; 350 mems.

### PRODUCERS' AND EXPORTERS' ORGANIZATIONS

**Federated Farmers of New Zealand (Inc):** 6th Floor, Agriculture House, 12 Johnston St, Wellington 1; POB 715, Wellington; tel. (4) 473-7269; fax (4) 473-1081; f. 1946; Pres. GRAHAM B. ROBERTSON; CEO THEO SIMEONIDIS; 21,500 mems.

**National Beekeepers' Association of New Zealand (Inc):** Farming House, 211–213 Market St, POB 307, Hastings; tel. (6) 878-5385; fax (6) 878-6007; f. 1913; 1,400 mems; Pres. NICK WALLINGFORD; Sec. HARRY BROWN.

**New Zealand Animal By-Products Exporters' Association:** POB 2804, 11 Longhurst Terrace, Christchurch; tel. (3) 332-2895; fax (3) 337-2571; 25 mems; Sec. J. L. NAYSMITH.

**New Zealand Apple and Pear Marketing Board:** POB 3328, Wellington; tel. (4) 473-1420; fax (4) 472-2980; CEO JOE POPE; Chair. JOHN MCCLISKIE.

**New Zealand Berryfruit Growers' Federation (Inc):** Agriculture House, 12 Johnston St, POB 10-050, Wellington; tel. (4) 473-5387; fax (4) 471-2861; 530 mems; Pres. BOB TEAL; Exec. Officer VAL FOLEY.

**New Zealand Council of Wool Exporters Inc:** POB 536, Christchurch; tel. (3) 379-7484; fax (3) 366-6061; Exec. Man. R. H. F. NICHOLSON; Pres. D. E. QUESTED.

**New Zealand Dairy Board:** Pastoral House, Lambton Quay, POB 417, Wellington 1; tel. (4) 471-8300; telex 3348; fax (4) 471-8600; f. 1961; Chair. Sir DRYDEN SPRING; Sec. J. MURRAY.

**New Zealand Fishing Industry Board:** Private Bag 24-901, Wellington; tel. (4) 385-4005; fax (4) 384-2727; CEO RAY DOBSON; Chair. C. T. HORTON.

**New Zealand Fruit Wine Makers:** Agriculture House, POB 10050, Wellington; tel. (4) 473-5387; fax (4) 471-2861; 37 mems; Chair. BRIAN SHANKS; Exec. Officer VAL FOLEY.

**New Zealand Kiwifruit Marketing Board:** POB 9906, Auckland 1; tel. (9) 366-1200; fax (9) 366-1206; Chair. JOHN L. PALMER; Exec. Dir ERIC V. HENRY.

**New Zealand Meat Marketing Corpn Ltd:** POB 9440, Wellington; tel. (4) 385-2368; fax (4) 385-2387; Gen. Man. WAYNE GEARY; Chair. BRUCE BISHOP.

**New Zealand Meat Producers' Board:** Seabridge House, 110 Featherston St, POB 121, Wellington; tel. (4) 473-9150; fax (4) 472-3172; f. 1922; Chair. DAVID FRITH; Sec. C. L. CRAIG; 11 mems.

**New Zealand Pork Industry Board:** POB 4048, Wellington; tel. (4) 385-4229; fax (4) 385-8522; f. 1937; Chair. R. E. JEFFREY; Gen. Man. B. J. MILNE.

**New Zealand Vegetable and Potato Growers' Federation (Inc):** Agriculture House, Johnston St, POB 10232, Wellington 1; tel. (4) 472-3795; fax (4) 471-2861; 5,000 mems; Pres. M. LILLEY; Exec. Officer P. R. SILCOCK.

**New Zealand Wool Board/Wools of New Zealand:** 10 Brandon St, Box 3225, Wellington; tel. (4) 472-6888; telex 3472; fax (4) 473-7872; assists research, development, production and marketing of NZ wool; Chair. P. G. MORRISON; CEO Dr J. G. SINCLAIR.

### PRINCIPAL EMPLOYERS' ASSOCIATIONS

**New Zealand Employers' Federation (Inc):** 15–17 Murphy St, POB 1786, Wellington; tel. (4) 499-4111; fax (4) 499-4112; f. 1902; links dist. employers' asscns and other nat. industrial orgs; Pres. RICHARD G. TWEEDIE; CEO S. MARSHALL.

**New Zealand Master Builders' Federation (Inc):** 80–82 Kent Terrace, POB 1796, Wellington; tel. (4) 385-8999; fax (4) 385-8995; Chief Exec. T. R. ALLSEBROOK.

**New Zealand Timber Industry Federation:** 219 Thorndon Quay, POB 308, Wellington; tel. (4) 473-5200; fax (4) 473-6536; 350 mems; Exec. Dir W. S. COFFEY.

**NZ Fruitgrowers' Federation:** Huddart Parker Bldg, POB 2175, Wellington, 6015; tel. (4) 472-6559; fax (4) 472-6409; f. 1916; 5,500 mems; Exec. Dir M. T. GAFFANEY.

**Retail and Wholesale Merchants' Association of New Zealand (Inc):** 101–103 Molesworth St, POB 12-086, Wellington 6000; tel. (4) 472-3733; fax (4) 472-1071; f. 1920 as the NZ Retailers' Fed. (Inc); present name adopted in 1987, following merger with the NZ Wholesale Hardware Fed.; direct membership 2,200 stores, 1,500 affiliated mems; Pres. CHRIS JAMES; CEO DOUG MCLAREN.

### TRADE UNIONS

In 1993 a total of 67 unions were in operation, comprising 409,112 members.

**The New Zealand Council of Trade Unions:** POB 6645, Union House, 169 Willis St, Wellington 1; tel. (4) 385-1334; fax (4) 385-6051; f. 1937, present name since 1987; affiliated to ICFTU; 357,000 mems; Pres. KEN G. DOUGLAS; Sec. ANGELA FOULKES.

#### Principal Affiliated Unions

**Communication and Energy Workers' Union:** POB 6254, Wellington; tel. (4) 384-4099; fax (4) 385-4355; Pres. J. CROWLEY; CEO D. A. UDY.

**FinSec Finance Sector Union:** POB 27-355, Wellington; tel. (4) 385-7723; fax (4) 385-2214; Pres. DAVE PEARCE; Sec. PAUL GOULTER.

**National Distribution Union:** Private Bag 68-902, Grey Lynn, Auckland; tel. (9) 378-0220; fax (9) 376-6238; Pres. BILL ANDERSEN; Sec. MIKE JACKSON.

**New Zealand Dairy Workers Union, Inc:** POB 9046, Hamilton; tel. (7) 839-0239; fax (7) 838-0398; f. 1992; 5,300 mems; Sec. RAY POTROZ; Pres. G. CAMPBELL.

**New Zealand Educational Institute/Te Riu Roa:** POB 466, Wellington; tel. (4) 384-9689; fax (4) 385-1772; f. 1883; Pres. HELEN DUNCAN; Sec. ROSSLYN NOONAN.

**New Zealand Engineering Union Inc:** 37–39 Marjoribanks St, Wellington; tel. (4) 384-8195; fax (4) 384-9110; 35,000 mems; Pres. KENNY BARCLAY; Sec. REX JONES.

**New Zealand Harbour Workers' Union:** POB 1103, Wellington; tel. (4) 499-2066; fax (4) 471-0896; Pres. J. R. MURFITT; Sec. J. R. WILSON.

**New Zealand Meat Workers and Related Trades Union:** POB 13-048, Armagh, Christchurch; tel. (3) 366-5105; fax (3) 379-7763; 12,500 mems; Pres. D. WILSON; Gen. Sec. R. G. KIRK.

**New Zealand Nurses' Organization:** POB 2128, Wellington; tel. (4) 385-0847; fax (4) 382-9993; Nat. Dir BRENDA WILSON.

**New Zealand Post Primary Teachers' Association:** POB 2119, Wellington; tel. (4) 384-9964; fax (4) 382-8763; Pres. ROGER TOBIN; Sec. KEVIN BUNKER.

**New Zealand Public Service Association:** PSA House, 11 Aurora Terrace, POB 3817, Wellington 1; tel. (4) 494-2000; fax (4) 494-2019; 68,000 mems; Pres. TONY SIMPSON; Gen. Sec. DAVID THORP.

**Service Workers' Union of Aotearoa:** POB 6649, Te Aro, Wellington; tel. (4) 385-0992; fax (4) 384-8631; 72,000 mems; Pres. WINNIE WATENE; Sec. MARK GOSCHE.

**The Wood Industries Union of Aotearoa:** POB 93, Rotorua; tel. (7) 348-9176; fax (7) 348-7901; 4,000 mems; Pres. PHIL WHITE; Sec. JIM JONES.

#### Other Unions

**New Zealand Amalgamated Workers' Union:** Central Chambers, 3 Eva St, POB 11-761, Wellington; tel. (4) 385-0525; fax (4) 384-7537; 12,500 mems in shearing and agriculture, forestry and highway and power construction; Pres. E. ANSLOW; Sec. C. CLAYTON.

**New Zealand Building Trades Union:** Manners St, POB 11-356, Wellington; tel. (4) 385-1178; fax (4) 385-1177; 6,000 mems; Pres. P. REIDY; Sec. A. RUSS.

**New Zealand Police Association:** POB 12-344, Wellington; tel. (4) 472-0198; fax (4) 471-1309; f. 1936; Pres. STEVE HINDS; Sec. GRAHAM HARDING.

**New Zealand Printing, Packaging and Media Union:** 3 Eva St, Wellington 1; tel. (4) 384-9498; fax (4) 382-8577; f. 1995; Pres. TREVOR ATKINSON; Sec. PAUL TOLICH.

**New Zealand Seafarers' Union:** POB 1103, Te Aro, Wellington; tel. (4) 499-3560; fax (4) 471-0896; f. 1993; Pres. (vacant); Sec. M. H. WILLIAMS.

**United Food, Beverage and General Workers' Union:** POB 27361, Wellington; tel. (4) 385-6439; fax (4) 385-8982; Nat. Sec. TERRY O'SHEA.

# Transport

## RAILWAYS

There were 3,973 km of railways in New Zealand in 1993.

**New Zealand Rail Ltd:** Private Bag, Bunny St, Wellington 1; tel. (4) 498-2000; fax (4) 498-3259; f. 1990; transferred to private ownership in 1993; rail and ferry services; Man. Dir Dr FRANCIS SMALL.

## ROADS

In 1993 there were 92,700 km of roads in New Zealand, including both state highways and local roads. Responsibility for road management, road safety, construction and maintenance and passenger transport on a national basis belongs to Transit New Zealand, a Crown-owned entity established in 1989 to replace the former National Roads Board and Urban Transport Council, with the overall aim of promoting policies and allocating resources to achieve a safe and efficient land transport system, maximizing national economic and social benefits.

**Transit New Zealand:** POB 5084, 20–26 Ballance St, Wellington; tel. (4) 499-6600; fax (4) 496-6666; Crown agency responsible for road management, safety and passenger transport; Chair. IAN MCCUTCHEON; Gen. Man. Dr ROBERT DUNLOP.

## SHIPPING

There are about 13 main seaports, of which the most important are Auckland, Tauranga, Wellington, Lyttleton (the port of Christchurch) and Port Chalmers (Dunedin).

### Principal Companies

**Nedlloyd New Zealand Ltd:** Investment House, Cnr Featherston and Ballance Sts, Box 890, Wellington; tel. (4) 474-7800; fax (4) 474-7829; worldwide services; Man. Dir PETER DEKKER.

**P & O Containers New Zealand Ltd:** 2–10 Customhouse Quay, POB 1699, Wellington; tel. (4) 473-6477; fax (4) 472-1906; worldwide shipping services; Man. Dir P. A. WINDFIELD.

**Union Shipping New Zealand Ltd:** Union House, 36 Quay St, Private Bag 92097, Auckland; tel. (9) 377-4730; telex 2534; fax (9) 309-1504; f. 1875, present name since 1988; roll on/roll off and containerized cargo services between NZ and Australia; CEO JAMES BRYANT; Gen. Man. IAN NEWMAN.

Other major shipping companies operating services to New Zealand include Blue Star Line (NZ) Ltd, Columbus Line and Sofrana-Unilines, which link New Zealand with Australia, the Pacific Islands, South-East Asia and the USA.

## CIVIL AVIATION

There are international airports at Auckland, Christchurch and Wellington.

**Air Nelson:** Private Bag 32, Nelson; tel. (3) 546-7484; fax (3) 546-6272; f. 1979, changed to present name 1986; operates services throughout New Zealand; Man. Dir ROBERT INGLIS.

**Air New Zealand:** Quay Tower, 29 Customs St West, Private Bag, Auckland 1; tel. (9) 366-2400; telex 2541; fax (9) 366-2759; f. 1978 by merger; privatized in 1989; 35.2% owned by Brierley Investments Ltd, 20% by Qantas, 5% by Japan Air Lines; services to Australia, the Pacific Islands, Asia, Europe and North America, as well as regular daily services to 25 cities and towns in New Zealand; Chair. BOB MATTHEW; Man. Dir JIM MCCREA.

**Ansett New Zealand:** 50 Grafton Rd, POB 4168, Auckland; tel. (9) 309-6235; fax (9) 309-6434; f. 1987; operates services between Auckland, Christchurch, Wellington, Dunedin, Queenstown, Invercargill, Nelson, Palmerston North and Rotorua; commuter services to Whangarei, Whakatane, Blenheim and Nelson; CEO CRAIG WALLACE.

**Mount Cook Airline:** 47 Riccarton Rd, POB 4644, Christchurch; tel. (3) 348-2099; telex 4297; fax (3) 343-8159; f. 1921; domestic services throughout NZ; Gen. Man. P. J. CLARK.

# Tourism

New Zealand's principal tourist attractions are its high mountains, lakes, forests, hot springs and beaches, and it is particularly well-known for its trout and deep-sea fishing. In the 12 months to March 1994 New Zealand received 1,213,318 visitors. Receipts from tourism totalled $NZ3,560m. in 1993/94.

**New Zealand Tourism Board:** Fletcher Challenge House, 89 The Terrace, Wellington; tel. (4) 472-8860; fax (4) 478-1736; f. 1901; responsible for development and marketing of New Zealand as a tourism destination; Chair. NORMAN GEARY; Chief Exec. IAN KEAN; offices in Auckland, Wellington, Christchurch, Rotorua and Queenstown; 15 offices overseas.

# NEW ZEALAND'S DEPENDENT AND ASSOCIATED TERRITORIES

New Zealand's Associated Territories are the Dependent Territories
of Tokelau and the Ross Dependency and the self-governing Cook Islands and Niue.

## ROSS DEPENDENCY

The Ross Dependency comprises the sector of Antarctica between 160°E and 150°W (moving eastward) and the islands lying between those degrees of longitude and south of latitude 60°S. It has been administered by New Zealand since 1923 and has a total area of 750,310 sq km (289,700 sq miles), comprising a land area of 413,540 sq km and an ice shelf of 336,770 sq km.

Scott Base was established in 1957 on Ross Island and in the following year the Ross Dependency Research Committee was formed to supervise New Zealand activity on the Territory. In 1968 a new scientific station was set up at Lake Vanda, about 130 km (80 miles) west of Scott Base. In 1986 traces of petroleum were discovered in the Territory, more than 600m. below the sea-bed.

**Ross Dependency Research Committee:** c/o Ministry of Research, Science and Technology, POB 5336, Wellington, New Zealand; tel. (4) 472-6400; fax (4) 471-1284; f. 1958; responsible to the Minister of Research, Science and Technology for co-ordinating all New Zealand activity in the Dependency; Chair. R. G. NORMAN; Exec. Officer K. E. CARPINTER.

## TOKELAU

### Introductory Survey

**Location, Climate, Language, Religion, Flag, Capital**

Tokelau consists of three atolls (Atafu, Nukunonu and Fakaofo) which lie about 480 km (300 miles) north of Western Samoa, in the Pacific Ocean. The average annual temperature is 28°C (82°F), July being the coolest month and May the warmest; rainfall is heavy but inconsistent. The principal language is Tokelauan (a Polynesian language), although English is also widely spoken. The population is almost entirely Christian, with 67.2% adhering to the Congregational Christian Church of Samoa (a Protestant denomination) and 30% to the Roman Catholic Church. The New Zealand flag is used in the Territory (see p. 2239). Tokelau has no capital, each atoll having its own administrative centre.

**Recent History**

The Tokelau (formerly Union) Islands became a British protectorate in 1877. At the request of the inhabitants, the United Kingdom annexed the islands in 1916 and included them within the Gilbert and Ellice Islands Colony (now Kiribati and Tuvalu). The British Government transferred administrative control of the islands to New Zealand by legislation enacted in 1925, effective from February 1926. The group was officially designated the Tokelau Islands in 1946, and sovereignty was transferred to New Zealand by legislation of 1948, effective from January 1949. From 1962 until the end of 1971 the High Commissioner for New Zealand in Western Samoa was also the Administrator of the Tokelau Islands. In November 1974 the administration of the Tokelau Islands was transferred to the Ministry of Foreign Affairs in New Zealand. In 1976 the Tokelau Islands were officially redesignated Tokelau.

New Zealand has undertaken to assist Tokelau towards increased self-government and economic self-sufficiency. The Territory was visited by the United Nations Special Committee on Decolonization in 1976 and 1981, but on both occasions the missions reported that the people of Tokelau did not wish to change the nature of the existing relationship between Tokelau and New Zealand. In June 1987, however, in a statement to the UN Special Committee, Tokelau expressed a desire to achieve greater political autonomy, while maintaining its relationship with New Zealand.

In December 1980 New Zealand and the USA signed a treaty whereby a US claim to Tokelau, dating from 1856, was relinquished. At the same time New Zealand relinquished a claim, on behalf of Tokelau, to Swain's Island, administered by the USA since 1925 as part of American Samoa. The treaty was ratified in August 1983.

In 1989 Tokelau supported efforts by the South Pacific Forum to impose a regional ban on drift-net fishing (which was believed to have resulted in a serious depletion in tuna stocks). In November New Zealand prohibited drift-net fishing within Tokelau's exclusive economic zone, extending to 200 nautical miles (370 km) from the islands' coastline.

In 1989 a UN report on the 'greenhouse effect' (the heating of the earth's atmosphere as a result of pollution) listed Tokelau as one of the island groups that would completely disappear beneath the sea in the 21st century, unless drastic action were taken.

Cyclone damage in February 1990 destroyed all banana trees and 80% of coconut and breadfruit trees, and wrecked two hospitals, schools, housing and bridges.

In late 1991 Tokelau obtained a catamaran, which provided the first passenger service linking the three atolls for 40 years. In February 1993 it was announced that the Office for Tokelau Affairs (hitherto based in Apia, Western Samoa) was to be relocated to the Territory; however, this was not thought likely to imply any change in Tokelau's dependent status, the popularity of which was reiterated by the Official Secretary in late 1992.

**Government**

The administration of Tokelau is the responsibility of the Minister of Foreign Affairs of New Zealand, who is empowered to appoint an administrator to the Territory. In practice, most of the Administrator's powers are delegated to the Official Secretary, who heads the Tokelau Apia Liaison Office. Each atoll has its own Council of Elders, or Taupulega, which comprises the heads of family groups together with two elected members, the Faipule and the Pulenuku. The Faipule represents the atoll in its dealings with the administering power and the public service, and presides over the Council and the court. The Pulenuku is responsible for the administration of village affairs. The Faipule and the Pulenuku are democratically elected by universal adult suffrage every three years. Twice a year the representatives of all three Councils of Elders meet at the General Fono, which is attended by 15 delegates from each atoll and chaired by the three Faipules.

**Economic Affairs**

Agriculture (including fishing) is, excluding copra production, of a basic subsistence nature. Coconuts (the source of copra) are the only cash crop. Pulaka, breadfruit, papayas, the screw-pine (*Pandanus*) and bananas are cultivated as food crops. Livestock comprises pigs, poultry and goats. Ocean and lagoon fish and shellfish are staple constituents of the islanders' diet. The sale of fishing licences for Tokelau's exclusive economic zone to foreign fleets provides an important source of income, as do fees from shipping and customs duties.

Manufacturing chiefly comprises the production of copra and handicrafts. However, the opening, in late 1990, of a factory processing highly-priced yellowfin tuna seemed likely to provide another important source of income. The principal markets for the product are New Zealand and Japan. The sale of postage stamps and souvenir coins (which are legal tender, although New Zealand currency is in general use) also makes a significant contribution to the Territory's income, as does revenue provided by remittances from Tokelauans working abroad, mainly in New Zealand.

The public service, which is the principal employer, engaged 195 people at the end of June 1991.

In 1983/84 the principal source of imports was Western Samoa, which was also the sole importer of Tokelauan goods. In that year copra and handicrafts were the only exports. The principal imports are generally foodstuffs, building materials and fuel.

In the financial year ending 31 March 1991 New Zealand budgetary assistance amounted to $NZ4.3m. (of a total of $NZ4.6m. in subsidies) and there was a total budgetary deficit of $NZ0.8m. Total revenue amounted to $NZ5.3m. in 1992/93, of which $NZ4.3m. was in the form of subsidies from New Zealand.

Tokelau is a member of the South Pacific Commission (see p. 215), and, as a Dependent Territory of New Zealand, is represented by that country in the South Pacific Forum and other international organizations.

During the 1980s and early 1990s Tokelau's agricultural development was adversely affected by inclement weather. The Territory's small size, remote situation, lack of land-based resources and the population's continuing migration to New Zealand severely hinder economic development. The New Zealand budget for 1989 allowed the payment of 50% of retirement income for people residing abroad, in an attempt to persuade Tokelauans to return to the islands and to contribute to the Territory's economic development. The improvement of shipping links in the late 1980s and early 1990s, although of general economic benefit, resulted in an increase in imported foods, which, according to a report published in 1992, has contributed to serious social and dietary problems in the islands.

### Social Welfare

In 1986 Tokelau had three government hospitals, with a total of 39 beds, and there were four government physicians working in the Territory.

### Education

Education is provided free of charge, and is compulsory between the ages of five and 16 years: nine years of primary education are followed by two years at secondary level. There are three schools, one on each atoll. Government expenditure on education in 1989/90 was equivalent to 14% of total budgetary expenditure. The New Zealand Department of Education provides advisory services and some educational equipment. Scholarships are awarded for secondary and tertiary education and vocational training in Western Samoa, Fiji, Niue, Tonga and New Zealand. There was a total of 97 Tokelauan students at overseas institutions in 1990.

### Public Holidays

**1995:** 1 January (New Year's Day), 6 February (Waitangi Day, anniversary of 1840 treaty), 14–17 April (Easter), 25 April (ANZAC Day, anniversary of 1915 landing at Gallipoli), 17 June (Queen's Official Birthday), 16 October (Labour Day), 25 December (Christmas Day), 26 December (Boxing Day).

**1996:** 1 January (New Year's Day), 6 February (Waitangi Day, anniversary of 1840 treaty), 5–8 April (Easter), 25 April (ANZAC Day, anniversary of 1915 landing at Gallipoli), 15 June (Queen's Official Birthday), 14 October (Labour Day), 25 December (Christmas Day), 26 December (Boxing Day).

### Weights and Measures

The metric system is in force.

## Statistical Survey

### AREA AND POPULATION

**Area:** Atafu 2.03 sq km; Nukunonu 5.46 sq km; Fakaofo 2.63 sq km; Total 10.12 sq km (3.9 sq miles).
**Population** (census of March 1991): Atafu 543; Nukunonu 437; Fakaofo 597; Total 1,577. *Tokelauans resident in New Zealand* 2,802.
**Density** (1991): 155.8 per sq km.
**Births and Deaths** (1983): Live births 36 (birth rate 22 per 1,000); Deaths 11 (death rate 7 per 1,000).

### AGRICULTURE, ETC.

**Crop Production** (FAO estimates, metric tons): Coconuts 3,000 (1993); Copra 1,000 (1980). Source: FAO, *Production Yearbook*.
**Livestock** (1993): Pigs 1,000 (FAO estimate). Source: FAO, *Production Yearbook*.
**Fishing** (metric tons, live weight): 200 (FAO estimate) in 1990; 231 in 1991; 191 in 1992. Source: FAO, *Yearbook of Fishery Statistics*.

### FINANCE

**Currency and Exchange Rates:** New Zealand currency is legal tender. Tokelau souvenir coins have also been issued. New Zealand currency: 100 cents = 1 New Zealand dollar ($NZ); *Sterling and US Dollar Equivalents* (31 December 1994): £1 sterling = $NZ2.444; US $1 = $NZ1.562; $NZ100 = £40.92 = US $64.02. *Average Exchange Rate* (US $ per $NZ): 0.5381 in 1992; 0.5407 in 1993; 0.5937 in 1994.

**Budget** ($NZ, year ending 30 June 1991): *Revenue:* Local 1,158,471; New Zealand subsidy 4,564,429 (Budgetary assistance 4,338,000); Total 5,772,900. *Expenditure:* Total 6,512,247. *1992/93* ($NZ): *Revenue:* Local 1,032,880; New Zealand subsidy 4,300,000; Total 5,332,880.

### EXTERNAL TRADE

**Principal Commodities:** *Imports:* Foodstuffs; Building materials WS $104,953 (1983/84), Fuel. *Exports:* Copra $NZ43,542 (1982/83); Handicrafts WS $10,348 (1983/84); there were no other exports.

### COMMUNICATIONS

**Radio Receivers** (estimate, 1992): 1,000 in use.
**Non-daily Newspapers** (estimates, 1988): 1, circulation 2,000.
Source: UNESCO, *Statistical Yearbook*.

### EDUCATION

**Schools** (1990): 3 (one school for all levels on each atoll).
**Teachers** (1990): Qualified 43; Aides 8; Adult Learning Centre Co-ordinators 3.
**Pupils** (1991): Pre-primary 133; Primary 361; Secondary 221 (1987).
**Students Overseas** (1990): Secondary 42; Technical and vocational 36; Teacher training 3; University 16.

## Directory
### The Constitution

Tokelau is administered under the authority of the Tokelau Islands Act 1948 and subsequent amendments and regulations. The Act declared Tokelau (then known as the Tokelau Islands) to be within the territorial boundaries of New Zealand. All executive and administrative functions are vested in the Administrator, the representative of the Crown, who is responsible to the Minister of Foreign Affairs and Trade in the New Zealand Government. The office of Administrator is normally held conjointly with that of New Zealand's Secretary of Foreign Affairs and Trade, but provision is made for the offices to be held separately. Most of the powers of the Administrator are delegated to the Official Secretary, who heads the Tokelau Apia Liaison Office. The Official Secretary is also the head and co-ordinator of the Tokelau Public Service, and so exercises authority delegated from the State Services Commission. The chief representative of the Administrator (and the Crown) on each atoll is the highest elected official, the Faipule, who exercises executive, political and judicial powers. The three Faipules act as the representatives of the Territory in dealings with the administration and at international meetings, and choose one of their number to hold the title Ulu-O-Tokelau (Head of Tokelau) for a term of one year. The Ulu-O-Tokelau chairs sessions of the territorial assembly, the General Fono. The General Fono is a meeting of delegates, 15 from each atoll (including the Faipule and the Pulenuku—Village Mayor), to represent the entire Territory. There are two or three meetings each year, which may take place on any of the atolls. The General Fono is the highest advisory body and the administration must consult it about all policy affecting the Territory. The assembly has limited legislative functions and has responsibility for the territorial budget. There are a number of specialist committees, such as the Budget Committee and the Law Committee.

Tokelau is an association of three autonomous atoll communities. Local government consists of the Faipule, the Pulenuku and the Taupulega (Island Council or Council of Elders). The Faipule and the Pulenuku are elected every three years on the basis of universal adult suffrage (the age of majority being 21). The Faipule represents the atoll community, liaises with the administration and the officers of the Tokelau Public Service, acts as a judicial commissioner and presides over meetings of the Taupulega. The Pulenuku is responsible for the administration of village affairs, including the maintenance of water supplies and the inspection of plantations, and, in some instances, the resolution of land disputes (practically all land is held by customary title, by the head of a family group, and may not be alienated to non-Tokelauans). The Taupulega is the principal organ of local government. The Taupulega also appoints the Failautuhi (Island Clerk), to record its meetings and transactions, and chooses its atoll's delegates to the General Fono. The Taupulega council in Atafu consists of the Faipule, the Pulenuku and the head of every family group; in Nukunonu it consists of the Faipule, the Pulenuku, the elders of the community and the nominated heads of extended families; in Fakaofo it consists of the Faipule, the Pulenuku and the elders (meetings of all the heads of family groups take place only infrequently).

## The Government

(June 1995)

**Administrator:** LINDSAY WATT (took office March 1993).
**Official Secretary, Office for Tokelau Affairs:** CASIMILO J. PEREZ.

### FAIPULES

At elections in January 1993, the Faipule of Nukunonu was re-elected for his second term and the two others were elected for a first term.

**Faipule of Fakaofo:** KELI NEEMIA.
**Faipule of Nukunonu:** SALESIO LUI.
**Faipule of Atafu:** LEPAIO SIMI.

### GOVERNMENT OFFICES

**Tokelau Apia Liaison Office/Ofiha o na Matakupu Tokelau:** POB 865, Apia, Western Samoa; tel. 20822; fax 21761.

Each atoll has an office of the Tokelau Public Service, with a supervising administrative official, located in its village.

## Judicial System

Tokelau's legislative and judicial systems are based on the Tokelau Islands Act 1948 and subsequent amendments and regulations. The Act provided for a variety of British regulations to continue in force and, where no other legislation applies, the law of England and Wales in 1840 (the year in which British sovereignty over New Zealand was established) was to be applicable. New Zealand statute law applies in Tokelau only if specifically extended there. In 1986 legislation formalized the transfer of High Court civil and criminal jurisdiction from Niue to New Zealand. Most cases are judged by the Tokelau Commissioner (currently the Faipule) established on each atoll.

## Religion

On Atafu almost all inhabitants are members of the Congregational Christian Church in Samoa (the General Secretary is based in Apia, Western Samoa); on Nukunonu all are Roman Catholic, while both denominations are represented on Fakaofo. In 1986 some 67% of the total population adhered to the Congregational Christian Church, and 30% to the Roman Catholic Church.

### CHRISTIANITY
#### Roman Catholic Church

The Church is represented in Tokelau by a Mission, established in June 1992. There were an estimated 530 adherents at 31 December 1992.
**Superior:** Fr PATRICK EDWARD O'CONNOR, Catholic Mission, Nukunonu.

## Radio

Each atoll has a radio station to broadcast shipping and weather reports. Radio-telephone provides the main communications link with other areas. Telecommunication services were upgraded in 1993.

## Finance

In 1977 a savings bank was established on each island; commercial and other banking facilities are available in Apia, Western Samoa.

## Trade and Industry

A village co-operative store was established on each island in 1977. Local industries include copra production, woodwork and plaited craft goods, and the processing of tuna.

## Transport

There are no roads or motor vehicles. Unscheduled inter-atoll voyages, by sea, are forbidden because the risk of missing landfall is too great. Passengers and cargo are transported by vessels which anchor off shore, as there are no harbour facilities. Most links are with Western Samoa, but a monthly service from Fiji was introduced in 1986. Plans to construct an airstrip on each atoll have been postponed in favour of the development of shipping links. A New Zealand-funded inter-atoll vessel commenced service in November 1991, providing the first regular link between the atolls for 40 years.

# COOK ISLANDS

## Introductory Survey

### Location, Climate, Language, Religion, Flag, Capital

The 13 inhabited and two uninhabited islands of the Cook Islands are located in the southern Pacific Ocean. The Territory lies between American Samoa, to the west, and French Polynesia, to the east. The islands extend over about 2m. sq km (more than 750,000 sq miles) of ocean, and form two groups: the Northern Cooks, which are all atolls and include Pukapuka, Rakahanga and Manihiki, and the Southern Cooks, including Aitutaki, Mangaia and Rarotonga, which are all volcanic islands. From December to March the climate is warm and humid, with the possibility of severe storms; from April to November the climate is mild and equable. The average annual rainfall on Rarotonga is 2,012 mm (79 ins). The official languages are English and Cook Islands Maori. The principal religion is Christianity, with about 70% of the population adhering to the Cook Islands Congregational Christian Church. The islands' flag (proportions 2 by 1) displays 15 five-pointed white stars (representing the islands of the group) on a royal blue field, with the United Kingdom's Union Flag as a canton in the upper hoist. The capital is Avarua, on Rarotonga.

### Recent History

The first Europeans to visit the islands were members of a British expedition, led by Capt. James Cook (after whom the islands are named), in 1773. The Cook Islands were proclaimed a British protectorate in 1888, and a part of New Zealand in 1901.

On 5 August 1965 the Cook Islands became a self-governing Territory in free association with New Zealand. The people are New Zealand citizens. Sir Albert Henry, leader of the Cook Islands Party (CIP), was elected Premier in 1965 and re-elected in 1971, 1974 and March 1978. However, in July 1978, following an inquiry into alleged electoral malpractice, the Chief Justice disallowed votes cast in the elections to the Legislative Assembly (later renamed Parliament) by Cook Islands expatriates who had been flown from New Zealand, with their fares paid from public funds. The amended ballot gave a majority to the Democratic Party (DP), and its leader, Dr (later Sir) Thomas Davis, was sworn in as Premier by the Chief Justice. In August 1979 Sir Albert Henry was convicted of conspiracy to defraud, and was formally stripped of his knighthood.

In May 1981 the Cook Islands' Constitution was amended to increase the membership of Parliament from 22 to 24, and to extend the parliamentary term from four to five years.

In March 1983 Sir Thomas Davis lost power to the CIP, under Geoffrey Henry, cousin of the former Premier. However, with one seat already subject to re-election, Henry's majority of three was reduced by the death of one CIP member of Parliament and the transfer of allegiance to the DP by another. Geoffrey Henry resigned in August, but continued with an interim administration until a general election in November returned the DP to power under Davis. In August 1984 Davis announced important government changes, with three of the seven posts going to members of the CIP, to form a coalition Government, with Geoffrey Henry as Deputy Prime Minister.

In mid-1985 Davis dismissed Henry, who had endorsed an unsuccessful motion expressing 'no confidence' in the Government, and Henry's supporters withdrew from the coalition. Henry's successor as Deputy Prime Minister was Dr Terepai Maoate, one of four CIP members who continued to support the Davis Government, in defiance of the CIP central committee.

In August 1985 eight members of the South Pacific Forum (see p. 217), including the Cook Islands, signed a treaty on Rarotonga, designating a 'nuclear-free' zone in the South Pacific. The treaty imposed a ban on the manufacture, testing, storage and use of nuclear weapons, and the dumping of nuclear waste, in the region.

In January 1986, following the rift between New Zealand and the USA in respect of the ANZUS security arrangements (see p. 247), Davis declared the Cook Islands a neutral country, because he considered that New Zealand (which has control over the islands' defence and foreign policy) was no longer in a position to defend the Territory. The proclamation of neutrality meant that the Cook Islands would not enter into a military relationship with any foreign power, and, in particular, would prohibit visits by US warships.

In July 1987 Davis was forced to resign from the post of Prime Minister when a parliamentary motion expressing 'no confidence' in his administration was approved, following protracted controversy over his unsuccessful attempts to gain approval in the legislature for contentious budget proposals. He was succeeded by Dr Pupuke Robati, a member of the Cabinet and a leading figure in the DP.

At a general election, held in January 1989, the CIP secured 13 of the 24 seats in Parliament, the DP won eight seats, the Democratic Tumu Party (DTP), which had been formed in 1985 as a result of a split in the DP, two seats, and an independent candidate one seat. Geoffrey Henry again became Prime Minister and formed a new Cabinet, on the basis of a political alliance with the DTP. (The independent member joined the CIP in August, thereby increasing the number of seats held by the party to 14.)

In mid-1990 the defection of a member of Parliament, Ben Toma, from the DP to the CIP prompted the DP to challenge his eligibility for Parliament, following which the Cook Islands High Court ruled that, since he was normally resident in Australia, Toma was ineligible to represent Cook Islanders in the legislature. Toma appealed unsuccessfully against the decision, but, after returning to live in the Cook Islands, he was re-elected at a by-election in January 1991. This provided the CIP with 15 seats in Parliament and thus the minimum two-thirds majority support necessary to amend the Constitution, should it so wish. In August 1991 a constitutional amendment was passed, which increased the number of members of Parliament to 25, and at an election to the newly-created seat a CIP candidate was successful. The amendment also provided for an increase in the number of cabinet members from seven to nine (including the Prime Minister).

In May 1992 a fire destroyed most of the government administration centre in Rarotonga. Two men were convicted of arson in the following month, one of whom admitted to hoping to avoid being charged in connection with an incident of petty larceny by burning down the Department of Justice. The damage caused was estimated at $NZ10m. The Asian Development Bank provided a loan of US $500,000 for the emergency restoration of telecommunication services, and in May 1993 agreed to lend the Government a further US $5m. for the reconstruction of the administrative centre.

In mid-1992 Norman George (parliamentary whip of the DP) was dismissed from the party, following a dispute over government spending, and in October he formed the Alliance Party.

At a general election on 24 March 1994 the CIP increased its majority, winning 20 seats in Parliament, while the DP secured three and the Alliance Party two. Davis, who failed to win a seat, subsequently resigned as leader of the DP. A referendum, held simultaneously, revealed that a majority of the electorate favoured retaining the current name (69.8% of voters), national anthem (80.2%) and flag (48.5%) of the Cook Islands.

A financial scandal was narrowly averted following reports that during 1994 the Government had issued loan guarantees for foreign companies worth more than $NZ1,200m. (the island's total revenue for 1994/95 was estimated to total $NZ50m.). An investigation into the affair by the New Zealand Reserve Bank in early 1995 found that the Government had not been guilty of fraud, but rather had been coerced into the activity by unscrupulous foreign business interests.

Visits by US naval vessels were allowed to resume by Henry's Government. In 1989, as a result of the serious depletion of tuna stocks in its waters, the Government agreed to participate in Australia's regional fisheries programme, and received a patrol boat from Australia to monitor the Cook Islands' exclusive economic zone (EEZ), within 200 nautical miles (370 km) of the islands' coastline. In November a regional convention banning drift-net fishing in the South Pacific was adopted by members of the South Pacific Forum, including the Cook Islands. In October 1991 the Cook Islands signed a treaty of friendship and co-operation with France, covering economic development, trade and surveillance of the islands' EEZ. The establishment of closer relations with France was widely regarded as an expression of the Cook Islands' Government's dissatisfaction with existing arrangements with New Zealand.

### Government

The Cook Islands is an internally self-governing state in free association with New Zealand, which is responsible for the Cook Islands' external affairs and defence (although the Territory has progressively assumed control over much of its foreign policy). Executive authority is vested in the British monarch, who is Head of State, and is exercised through her official representative; a representative of the New Zealand Government (redesignated High Commissioner in 1994) resides on Rarotonga. Executive government is carried out by the Cabinet, consisting of the Prime Minister and eight other ministers. The Cabinet is collectively responsible to the Parliament, which is formed of 25 members who are elected by universal adult suffrage every five years (including one member elected by non-resident voters). The House of Ariki, which comprises up to 15 members who are hereditary chiefs, can advise the Government, but has no legislative powers. Each of the main islands, except Rarotonga, has an elected island council, and a government representative who is appointed by the Prime Minister.

### Economic Affairs

In 1983–93, according to estimates by the Asian Development Bank, gross domestic product (GDP) increased, in real terms, by an annual average of 6.3%, and rose by some 11% in 1992 alone. GDP, at current prices, was estimated at $NZ110.2m. in 1990/91, while GDP per head stood at some $NZ5,938 in that year. In 1993 GDP per head was estimated at $NZ6,329.

Agriculture (including hunting, forestry and fishing) contributed 17.1% of GDP in 1990/91, and engaged 12.5% of the employed labour force in 1991. In that year the sector provided 16.8% of export earnings, with exports of papayas alone accounting for 12.5% of the total. Other important cash crops are coconuts and tropical and citrus fruits. Cassava, sweet potatoes and vegetables are cultivated as food crops. Pigs and poultry are kept. The sale of fishing licences to foreign fleets provides an important source of income, and totalled $NZ0.7m. in 1990/91 (an increase of almost 70% compared with the previous year). Aquaculture, in the form of giant clam farming and pearl oyster farming, was developed during the 1980s. In 1991 exports of pearl shells earned $NZ0.2m., while exports of trochus shells earned $NZ0.3m. In the same year sales of black pearls from Manihiki atoll earned some $NZ3.2m. Pearl oyster farms in the lagoons of Manihiki and Penrhyn atolls were expected to contribute significantly to production levels in the industry, revenue from which was projected to total some $NZ40m. by the late 1990s. The Government has also announced plans to develop cattle-ranching, ostrich farming and the cultivation of vanilla, taro, coffee and arrowroot on Atiu, Mangaia and Mauke.

Industry (including mining and quarrying, manufacturing, construction and power) provided 6.4% of GDP in 1990/91, and engaged 14.0% of employees in 1991. Manufacturing contributed 2.8% of GDP in 1990/91, and engaged 4.2% of employees in 1991. The most important industrial activities are fruit-processing and handicrafts. Mineral fuels accounted for 11.8% of total imports in 1991. In mid-1993 the Japanese Government expressed interest in extracting valuable minerals, including cobalt and manganese, from deep-sea nodules found in the islands' EEZ.

Tourism expanded considerably in the late 1980s and early 1990s, and earned some $NZ40m. in 1992. The sector engages an estimated 30% of the employed labour force. 'Offshore' banking, introduced to the islands in 1982, expanded rapidly, with more than 2,000 international companies registered in 1987. In 1992 the islands were established as an alternative domicile for companies listed on the Hong Kong Stock Exchange. A significant proportion of the islands' revenue is provided by remittances from migrants (who outnumber the residents of the islands).

In 1991 the Cook Islands recorded a trade deficit of $NZ85.1m. The principal source of imports in 1990 was New Zealand (42% of the total), while Hong Kong was the principal market for exports (33%). Other major trading partners are Japan, Italy and Australia. The principal exports in 1991 were papayas, pearl shells and black pearls. The principal imports in that year were foodstuffs, manufactures, machinery and transport equipment and mineral fuels.

In the financial year ending 31 March 1991 there was an estimated budgetary deficit of $NZ10.8m. Budgetary aid from New Zealand, however, (which represented some 14% of total revenue) transformed the deficit into a surplus of $NZ0.2m. There was a projected budgetary deficit of $NZ5.9m. for the 1992/93 financial year. Development assistance from New Zealand totalled $NZ14.0m. in 1992/93. It was estimated that the islands' external debt, which amounted to 22% of GDP in 1990, increased to the equivalent of total GDP in 1993. The annual rate of inflation averaged 12.2% in 1980–87, but decreased to some 6% in 1990 and 1991.

The Cook Islands is a member of the South Pacific Commission (see p. 215) and the South Pacific Forum (see p. 217).

Development plans in the 1980s aimed to stimulate the economy through the private sector, by offering incentives for investors and by developing the infrastructure. In the early 1990s the Government encouraged closer trade links with other territories of the region, particularly French Polynesia. The Cook Islands' aspirations for economic development were seriously undermined in 1992, when the administrative centre in Rarotonga was destroyed by fire. A reconstruction programme was initiated in mid-1993 with a loan from the Asian Development Bank. Following its re-election in March 1994, the Government announced plans for several projects aimed at further promoting economic growth. These included the construction of at least two new tourist resorts in the outer islands, the rehabilitation of the coconut industry, the initiation of a deep-sea mining programme and the expansion of the black pearl industry.

### Social Welfare

In 1991 the Cook Islands had 13 government hospitals, with a total of 154 beds, in that year there were 20 physicians and 88 nurses working in the islands. All medical treatment is available free of charge for Cook Islanders.

### Education

Free secular education is compulsory for a period of ten years between five and 15 years of age. Primary education, from the age of five, lasts for six years. Secondary education, beginning at 11 years of age, comprises two cycles, each of three years. In 1994 there were 20 primary schools, eight high schools (which provide education leading to the Cook Islands School Certificate) and seven secondary schools (which teach up to New Zealand School Certificate level). In that year 4,707 pupils were enrolled in primary and secondary schools and there was a total of 355 teachers (including pre-primary school teachers). Tertiary education is provided at a teacher-training college, a nursing school and through an apprenticeship scheme. Under the New Zealand Training Scheme, the New Zealand Government offers overseas scholarships in New Zealand, Fiji, Papua New Guinea, Australia and Western Samoa for secondary and tertiary education, career-training and short-term in-service training. There is an extension centre of the University of the South Pacific (based in Fiji) in the Cook Islands. According to UNESCO, budgetary expenditure on education in 1991 was $NZ8,236,000 (12.4% of total expenditure in that year).

### Public Holidays

**1995:** 1 January (New Year's Day), 14–17 April (Easter), 25 April (ANZAC Day, anniversary of 1915 landing at Gallipoli), 17 June (Queen's Official Birthday), 25 December (Christmas Day), 26 December (Boxing Day).

**1996:** 1 January (New Year's Day), 5–8 April (Easter), 25 April (ANZAC Day, anniversary of 1915 landing at Gallipoli), 15 June (Queen's Official Birthday), 25 December (Christmas Day), 26 December (Boxing Day).

### Weights and Measures

The metric system is in force.

## Statistical Survey

Sources (unless otherwise stated): Statistics Office, POB 125, Rarotonga; tel. 29390; Prime Minister's Department, Government of the Cook Islands, Avarua, Rarotonga; tel. 29300; fax 22856.

### AREA AND POPULATION

**Area:** 237 sq km (91.5 sq miles).

**Population:** 17,610 (males 9,185; females 8,425) at census of 1 December 1986; 18,552 (males 9,666; females 8,886) at census of 1 December 1991. *By island* (provisional, 1991 census): Rarotonga (including the capital, Avarua) 10,918; Aitutaki 2,366; Atiu 1,003; Mangaia 1,105; Manihiki 666; Mauke 639; Mitiaro 249; Nassau 103; Palmerston (Avarua) 49; Penrhyn (Tongareva) 503; Pukapuka 670; Rakahanga 262; Suwarrow 10; At sea 9. *Cook Island Maoris Resident in New Zealand* (1992): 31,092.

**Density** (1991): 78 per sq km.

**Births, Marriages and Deaths** (registrations, 1992): Births 510 (birth rate 28.3 per 1,000); (1990) Marriages 129 (marriage rate 14.5 per 1,000); Deaths 104 (death rate 5.8 per 1,000).

**Employment** (September 1991): Agriculture, hunting, forestry and fishing 823; Mining and quarrying 28; Manufacturing 280; Electricity, gas and water 226; Construction 394; Trade, restaurants and hotels 1,289; Transport, storage and communications 527; Financing, insurance, real estate and business services 268; Community, social and personal services 2,772; Total 6,607. Source: UN, *Statistical Yearbook for Asia and the Pacific*.

### AGRICULTURE, ETC.

**Principal Crops** (mainly FAO estimates, metric tons, 1993): Cassava 4,000; Sweet potatoes 2,000; Coconuts 5,000; Copra 1,000 (1991); Vegetables and melons 2,000; Citrus fruits 4,000; Mangoes 2,000; Papayas 1,000; Pineapples 1,000 (1990); Bananas 1,000 (1990); Avocados 1,000 (1991). Source: FAO, *Production Yearbook*.

**Livestock** ('000 head, year ending September 1993): Pigs 25; Goats 7; Poultry 44,687 (1988); Horses 9 (1990). Source: mainly FAO, *Production Yearbook*.

**Fishing** (metric tons, live weight): Total catch 1,200 (FAO estimate) in 1990; 1,100 in 1991; 982 in 1992. Source: FAO, *Yearbook of Fishery Statistics*.

### FINANCE

**Currency and Exchange Rates:** New Zealand and Cook Islands currencies, which are at par with each other, are both legal tender. New Zealand currency: 100 cents = 1 New Zealand dollar ($NZ); for details of exchange rates, see Tokelau, p. 2258. Cook Islands currency: 100 cents = 1 Cook Islands dollar ($CI).

**Budget** ($NZ million, year ending 31 March 1991): *Revenue:* Total (recurrent) revenue 79.7 (Taxes 40.0, New Zealand budgetary aid 11.0, Other non-tax revenue 28.7). *Expenditure:* Current expenditure 76.9 (principal items are education, public health and public works); Capital expenditure 2.6; Total 79.5. *1992/93* (estimates, $NZ million): Revenue 74.6; Expenditure 80.5. *1993/94* (estimates, $NZ million): Recurrent Revenue 71.0; Recurrent Expenditure 80.2.

**Cost of Living** (Consumer Price Index for Rarotonga; base: 1989 = 100): 106.1 in 1990; 112.3 in 1991.

**Gross Domestic Product by Economic Activity** (estimates, $NZ '000 in current prices, 1990/91): Agriculture and fishing 18,891; Mining and quarrying 404; Manufacturing 3,046; Electricity, gas and water 1,086; Construction 2,485; Trade, restaurants and hotels 23,409; Transport and communications 12,652; Financial and business services 12,679; Community, social and personal services 1,893; Public administration 28,242; Ownership of dwellings 5,404; Sub-total 110,191; *Less* Imputed bank service charge 3,302; GDP at factor cost 106,889.

### EXTERNAL TRADE

**Principal Commodities** (distribution by SITC, $NZ '000, 1991): *Imports c.i.f.:* Food and live animals 19,525; Beverages and tobacco 5,614; Mineral fuels, etc. 11,189; Chemicals 6,691; Basic manufactures 18,731; Machinery and transport equipment 17,011; Miscellaneous manufactured articles 12,975; Total (incl. others) 94,505. *Exports f.o.b.:* Food and live animals 1,588 (Papaya 1,175); Crude materials, excl. fuels 416; Basic manufactures 6,635; Machinery and transport equipment 56; Miscellaneous manufactured articles 714; Total (incl. others) 9,428.

**Principal Trading Partners** ($NZ '000): *Imports* (1990): New Zealand 36,295; Italy 27,626; Australia 4,316; Total (incl. others) 86,330. *Exports*: Hong Kong 2,683; New Zealand 2,531; Japan 1,998; Total (incl. others) 8,173.

### TRANSPORT

**Road Traffic** (registered vehicles, April 1983): 6,555.

**International Shipping** (estimated freight traffic, '000 metric tons, 1990): Goods loaded 9; Goods unloaded 32. Source: UN, *Monthly Bulletin of Statistics*.

**Civil Aviation** (1992): *Aircraft Movements:* 546. *Freight Traffic* (metric tons): Goods loaded 977.3; Good unloaded 1,007.8.

### TOURISM

**Foreign Visitor Arrivals:** 39,984 in 1991; 50,009 in 1992; 52,868 in 1993.

### COMMUNICATIONS MEDIA

**Radio Receivers** (1992): 13,000.
**Television Receivers** (1992): 3,000.
**Telephones** (1994): 4,180.
**Daily Newspaper** (1990): 1, circ. (estimate) 2,000.
Source: UNESCO, *Statistical Yearbook*.

### EDUCATION

**Pre-primary** (1994): 27 schools; 23 teachers (1988); 529 pupils.
**Primary** (1994): 20 schools; 141 teachers (1989); 2,537 pupils.
**Secondary*** (1994): 15 schools; 159 teachers (1989); 2,170 pupils.
**Higher** (1980): 41 teachers; 360 pupils†.
* Includes high school education.
† Source: UNESCO, *Statistical Yearbook*.

# Directory

## The Constitution

On 5 August 1965 a new Constitution was proclaimed, whereby the people of the Cook Islands have complete control over their own affairs in free association with New Zealand, but they can at any time move into full independence by a unilateral act if they so wish.

Executive authority is vested in the British monarch, who is Head of State, and exercised through an official representative. The New Zealand Government also appoints a representative (from 1994 redesignated High Commissioner), resident on Rarotonga.

Executive powers are exercised by a Cabinet consisting of the Prime Minister and eight ministers including a Deputy Prime Minister. The Cabinet is collectively responsible to Parliament.

Parliament consists of 25 members who are elected by universal suffrage every five years (including one member elected by voters living overseas), and is presided over by the Speaker. The House of Ariki comprises up to 15 members who are hereditary chiefs; it can advise the Government, particularly on matters relating to land and indigenous people but has no legislative powers.

Each of the main islands, except Rarotonga (which is divided into three tribal districts or *vaka*), has an elected mayor and a government representative who is appointed by the Prime Minister.

## The Government

**Queen's Representative:** APENERA SHORT.
**New Zealand High Commissioner:** DARRYL DUNN (took office in 1994).

### THE CABINET
(June 1995)

**Prime Minister and Minister of Finance and the Police:** Sir GEOFFREY A. HENRY.
**Deputy Prime Minister and Minister of Foreign Affairs, Immigration and Energy:** INATIO AKARURU.
**Minister of Agriculture, Conservation, Post and Telecommunications, Customs, Inland Revenue and the Public Service Commission:** VAINE TAIREA.
**Minister of Education, Cultural Development and Legislative Services:** NGERETEINA PUNA.
**Minister of Home Affairs, Trade, Labour, Transport and Shipping, Outer Islands' Development and Corrective Services:** PAPAMAMA POKINO.
**Minister of Health, Economic Development and Planning, Tourism, Civil Aviation and State-owned Enterprises:** Dr JOSEPH WILLIAMS.
**Minister of Information Services, Marine Resources and the General Licensing Authority:** TEPURE TAPAITAU.
**Minister of Justice, Lands and Survey, Youth and Sports, with responsibility for Electoral Office, Religious Advisory Council and the Aronga Mana:** TEKAOTIKI MATOPO.
**Minister of Public Works, Housing, Water Supply and Te Apanga Uira:** TIHINA TOM MARSTERS.

### GOVERNMENT OFFICES

All ministries are in Avarua, Rarotonga.
**Office of the Queen's Representative:** POB 134, Titikaveka, Rarotonga; tel. 29311.
**Office of the New Zealand High Commissioner:** Philatelic Bureau Bldg, Takuvaine Rd, POB 21, Avarua, Rarotonga; tel. 22201; fax 21241.
**Prime Minister's Department:** Government of the Cook Islands, Avarua, Rarotonga; tel. 29304; fax 22856.

### HOUSE OF ARIKI

**House of Ariki and Koutu Nui:** POB 59, Rarotonga; tel. 29317; fax 29318.
**President:** PA TEPAERU UPOKOTINI MARIE ARIKI.
**Vice-President:** TINOMANA TUORO RUTA ARIKI.

## Legislature

### PARLIAMENT

**Legislative Service:** POB 13, Rarotonga; tel. 26500; fax 21260.
**Speaker:** RAUTUTI TARINGA.

**General Election, 24 March 1994**

| Party | Seats |
|---|---|
| Cook Islands Party (CIP) | 20 |
| Democratic Party (Coalition) | 3 |
| Alliance Party | 2 |
| **Total** | **25** |

NEW ZEALAND'S DEPENDENT AND ASSOCIATED TERRITORIES *Cook Islands*

## Political Organizations

**Alliance Party:** Rarotonga; f. 1992 from split with Democratic Party (Coalition); Leader NORMAN GEORGE.

**Cook Islands Labour Party:** Rarotonga; f. 1988; anti-nuclear; Leader RENA ARIKI JONASSEN.

**Cook Islands Party (CIP):** Rarotonga; f. 1965; Leader Sir GEOFFREY A. HENRY.

**Democratic Party:** POB 492, Rarotonga; tel. 21224; f. 1971; Leader Dr TEREPAI MAOATE.

**Democratic Tumu Party:** POB 492, Rarotonga; tel. 21224; telex 00682; fax 22520; split from Democratic Party in 1985; Leader VINCENT A. K. T. INGRAM.

## Judicial System

**Department of Justice:** POB 111, Avarua, Rarotonga; tel. 29410; fax 29610.

The judiciary comprises the Privy Council, the Court of Appeal and the High Court.

The High Court exercises jurisdiction in respect of civil, criminal and land titles cases on all the islands, except for Mangaia, Pukapuka and Mitiaro, where disputes over land titles are settled locally. The Court of Appeal hears appeals against decisions of the High Court. The Privy Council, sitting in the United Kingdom, is the final appellate tribunal for the country.

**Attorney-General:** Sir GEOFFREY A. HENRY.
**Solicitor-General:** JOHN MCFADZIEN.
**Chief Justice of the High Court:** Sir CLINTON MARCUS ROPER.
**Judges of the High Court:** JOHN DOUGLAS DILLON, Sir PETER J. QUILLIAM, Sir GRAHAM DAVIES SPEIGHT, RICHARD IAN BARKER, PETER GORDON HILLYER, JOHN STEELE HENRY, RONALD GILBERT.

## Religion

### CHRISTIANITY

The principal denomination is the Cook Islands (Congregational) Christian Church, to which about 70% of the territory's population belong.

**Religious Advisory Council of the Cook Islands:** POB 31, Rarotonga; tel. 22851; fax 22852; f. 1968; four mem. churches; Pres. KEVIN GEELAN; Gen. Sec. TUNGANE POKURA.

#### The Roman Catholic Church

The Cook Islands and Niue form the diocese of Rarotonga, suffragan to the archdiocese of Suva (Fiji). At 31 December 1994 the diocese contained an estimated 3,086 adherents. The Bishop participates in the Catholic Bishops' Conference of the Pacific, based in Suva.

**Bishop of Rarotonga:** Rt Rev. ROBIN WALSH LEAMY, Catholic Mission, POB 147, Rarotonga; tel. 20817; fax 26174.

#### The Anglican Communion

The Cook Islands are within the diocese of Polynesia, part of the Church of the Province of New Zealand. The Bishop of Polynesia is resident in Fiji.

#### Protestant Churches

**Cook Islands Christian Church:** Takamoa, POB 93, Rarotonga; tel. 26452; 11,193 mems (1986); Pres. Rev. TEKERE PEREITI; Gen. Sec. TERE MATAIO.

**Seventh-day Adventists:** POB 31, Rarotonga; tel. 22851; fax 22852; 1,267 mems (1986); Pres. KEVIN GEELAN.

Other churches active in the territory include the Assembly of God, the Church of Latter-day Saints (Mormons), the Apostolic Church, the Bahá'í faith, the Jehovah's Witnesses and the Baptist Church.

### BAHÁ'Í FAITH

**National Spiritual Assembly:** POB 1, Rarotonga; tel. 20658; mems resident in eight localities.

## The Press

**Beach News:** POB 692, Rarotonga; tel. 23490; fax 23490; monthly; Editor COLIN HALL.

**Cook Islands News:** POB 15, Avarua, Rarotonga; tel. 22999; fax 25303; f. 1954 by Govt, transferred to private ownership 1989; daily; mainly English; Man. Dir PHIL EVANS; Editor ALEX SWORD; circ. 2,000.

**Cook Islands Sun:** POB 753, Snowbird Laundry, Arorangi, Rarotonga; f. 1988; tourist newspaper; twice a year; Editor WARREN ATKINSON.

## Radio and Television

In 1992, according to UNESCO, there were an estimated 13,000 radio receivers and 3,000 television receivers in use.

**Cook Islands Broadcasting Corpn (CIBC):** POB 126, Avarua, Rarotonga; tel. 29460; fax 21907; f. 1989 to operate new television service, and radio service of former Broadcasting and Newspaper Corpn; state-owned; Gen. Man. EMILE KAIRUA.

**Radio Cook Islands:** tel. 20100; broadcasts in English and Maori 18 hours daily.

**Cook Islands TV:** tel. 29460; f. 1989; broadcasts nightly, in English and Maori, from 5 p.m. to 10.15 p.m.; 10 hours of local programmes per week; remainder provided by Television New Zealand.

**KC Radio:** POB 521, Avarua, Rarotonga; tel. 23203; f. 1979 as Radio Ikurangi; commercial; operates station ZK1ZD; broadcasts 18 hours daily on FM; Man. Dir and Gen. Man. DAVID SCHMIDT.

## Finance

**Cook Islands Monetary Board:** POB 594, Rarotonga; tel. 21074; fax 21798; f. 1981; exercises control of currency; controlling body for trade and industry as well as finance; registers companies, financial institutions, etc.; Sec. M. BROWN.

### BANKING

#### Development Bank

**Cook Islands Development Bank:** POB 113, Avarua, Rarotonga; tel. 29341; fax 29343; f. 1978 to replace Nat. Devt Corpn and Housing Corpn; finances development projects in all areas of the economy and helps islanders establish small businesses and industries by providing loans and management advisory assistance; cap. p.u. $NZ4.5m.; total assets $NZ9,139,437 (Mar. 1991); Gen. Man. UNAKEA KAUVAI; brs on Rarotonga and Aitutaki.

#### Commercial Banks

**Cook Islands Savings Bank:** Private Bag, Rarotonga; tel. 29471; fax 28471.

**Australia and New Zealand (ANZ) Banking Corpn:** POB 21750, Rarotonga; tel. 21750; fax 21760.

**Westpac Banking Corpn (Australia):** Main Rd, Avarua, POB 42, Rarotonga; tel 22014; fax 20802; Man. D. MCKENZIE.

Legislation was adopted in 1981 to facilitate the establishment of 'offshore' banking operations.

## Trade and Industry

**Chamber of Commerce:** POB 242, Rarotonga; tel. 20295; fax 20969; f. 1956.

**Cook Islands Trading Corporation:** Avarua, Rarotonga; telex 62013; fax 20857.

### TRADE UNIONS

**Airport Workers Union:** Rarotonga Int. Airport, POB 90, Rarotonga; tel. 25890; fax 21890; f. 1985; Pres. NGA JESSIE; Gen. Sec. SIONA PAKU.

**Cook Islands Industrial Union of Waterside Workers:** Avarua, Rarotonga.

**Public Service Association:** POB 403, Avarua, Rarotonga; tel. 24422; fax 24423; largest union in the Cook Islands.

## Transport

### ROADS

On Rarotonga a 33-km sealed road encircles the island's coastline. A partly-sealed inland road, known as the Ara Metua, is suitable for vehicles. Roads on the other islands are mainly unsealed.

### SHIPPING

The main ports are on Rarotonga (Avatiu), Mangaia and Aitutaki. The Rarotonga Line (part of the Sofara Group) operates regular cargo services between the Cook Islands, Niue, and Auckland, New Zealand.

**Apex Maritime:** POB 378, Rarotonga; tel. 27651; fax 21138.

**Cook Islands National Line:** POB 264, Rarotonga; tel. 20374; fax 20855; operates three fleet cargo services between the Cook

Islands, Niue, Western Samoa, Norfolk Island, Tonga and New Zealand; Dirs Chris Vaile, George Ellis.

**Cook Islands Shipping Ltd:** POB 2001, Arorangi, Rarotonga; tel. 24905; fax 24906.

**Cook Islands Waterfront Commission:** Rarotonga; tel. 21921; operates internal services on behalf of the Government.

**Mainline Brown:** POB 139, Rarotonga; tel. 22305; operates internal services.

**Pelorus Maritime Ltd:** POB 128, Rarotonga; tel. 22369; fax 22369.

### CIVIL AVIATION

An international airport was opened on Rarotonga in 1974. Polynesian Airlines and Air New Zealand operate services linking Rarotonga with other airports in the region. Survey work on the possible construction of a new international airport on Aitutaki started in April 1990.

**Air Rarotonga:** POB 79, Panama, Rarotonga; tel. 22888; fax 20979; f. 1978; privately owned; operates internal passenger and cargo services and charter services to Niue and French Polynesia; Man. Dir Ewan F. Smith.

**Cook Airlines:** Rarotonga; f. 1991 as Aviaki Air; Chair. Norman George.

## Tourism

Tourism is the most important industry in the Cook Islands, and there were 52,868 arrivals of foreign visitors in 1993, compared with 25,615 in 1984. Of total visitors in 1993, 33.2% came from Europe, 27.0% from New Zealand, 14.7% from the USA, 11.0% from Australia and 7.6% from Canada; 7.4% were Cook Islanders residing overseas. There were a total of 1,505 hotel beds in the islands in 1991. Most of the tourist facilities are to be found on Rarotonga and Aitutaki, but the outer islands also offer attractive scenery. Revenue from tourism on Rarotonga was estimated at some $NZ40m. in 1993.

**Cook Islands Tourist Authority:** POB 14, Rarotonga; tel. 29435; fax 21435; Dir Chris Wong.

# NIUE

## Introductory Survey

### Location, Climate, Language, Religion, Flag, Capital

Niue is a coral island, located in the Pacific Ocean, about 480 km (300 miles) east of Tonga and 930 km (580 miles) west of the southern Cook Islands. Rainfall occurs predominantly during the hottest months, from December to March, when the average temperature is 27°C (81°F). Average annual rainfall is 7,715mm (298 ins). Niuean, a Polynesian language, and English are spoken. The population is predominantly Christian, with 66% belonging to the Ekalesia Niue, a Protestant church, in 1991. Niue's flag (proportions 2 by 1) is yellow, bearing, in the upper hoist corner, the United Kingdom's Union Flag with a yellow five-pointed star on each arm of the cross of St George and a slightly larger yellow five-pointed star on a blue disc in the centre of the cross. Some 30% of the population resides in Alofi, which is the capital and administrative centre of Niue.

### Recent History

The first Europeans to discover Niue were members of a British expedition, led by Capt. James Cook, in 1774. Missionaries visited the island throughout the 19th century, and in 1900 Niue was declared a British protectorate. In 1901 Niue was formally annexed to New Zealand as part of the Cook Islands, but in 1904 it was granted a separate administration.

In October 1974 Niue attained 'self-government in free association with New Zealand'. Niueans retain New Zealand citizenship, and a sizeable resident Niuean community exists in New Zealand. The 1991 population census revealed an 11.5% decrease since 1986, and many more Niueans live in New Zealand than on Niue. Robert (from 1982, Sir Robert) Rex, who had been the island's political leader since the early 1950s, was Niue's Premier when it became self-governing, and retained the post at three-yearly general elections in 1975–90.

The migration of Niueans to New Zealand has been a cause of concern, and in October 1985 the Government of New Zealand announced its intention to review New Zealand's constitutional relationship with Niue, with the express aim of preventing further depopulation of the island. In 1987 a six-member committee, comprising four New Zealanders and two Niueans, was formed to examine Niue's economic and social conditions, and to consider the possibility of the island's reverting to the status of a New Zealand-administered territory.

At a general election in March 1987 all except three of the 20 members of the Niue Assembly were re-elected. The Niue People's Action Party (NPAP), founded in 1987, secured one seat. The NPAP, Niue's only political party, criticized the Government's economic policy, and in particular its apparent inability to account for a substantial amount of the budgetary aid received from New Zealand. A declared aim of the party was to persuade Niueans residing in New Zealand to invest in projects on Niue.

In April 1989 the New Zealand Auditor-General issued a report which was highly critical of the Niuean Government's use of aid money from New Zealand, in particular Rex's preferential treatment of public servants in the allocation of grants. In June Young Vivian, leader of the unofficial NPAP opposition in the Niue Assembly, proposed a motion expressing 'no confidence' in the Government, which was defeated by 13 votes to seven. In November proposed legislation which included the replacement of New Zealand's Governor-General by a Niuean citizen was rejected by the Niue Assembly, owing to the implications for relations with New Zealand.

At a general election held in April 1990 candidates of the NPAP and its sympathizers won 12 of the 20 seats. Earlier disagreements in the NPAP leadership, however, allowed Rex to secure the support of four members previously opposed to his Government. Rex therefore remained Premier. In September there was disagreement within the Cabinet about reconstruction policy (following Cyclone Ofa, which had struck the island in February), and two ministers supported a proposal for a change of Premier. Rex dismissed the two, appointing Young Vivian and another member of the unofficial opposition to their posts.

The announcement in mid-1991 by the New Zealand Government that it was to reduce its aid payments to Niue by about $NZ1m. (a decrease of some 10% on the average annual allocation) caused considerable concern on the island. More than a quarter of the paid labour force on Niue were employed by the Niue Government, and, following the reduction in aid in July 1991, about 150 (some 25%) lost their jobs. Members of the Government subsequently travelled to New Zealand to appeal against the decision and to request the provision of redundancy payments for the dismissed employees. Their attempts failed, however, with the New Zealand Government reiterating its claim that aid had been inefficiently used in the past. By 1993 aid provided by New Zealand was some 30% lower than in 1990.

In December 1992 Sir Robert Rex died, and Young Vivian (who had been serving as acting Premier at the time of Rex's death) was unanimously elected Premier by the Government. A reallocation of cabinet portfolios was announced shortly after the election. Legislative elections took place on 27 February 1993, and on 9 March the Niue Assembly elected Frank Lui, a former cabinet minister, as Premier. Lui, who defeated Young Vivian by 11 votes to nine, announced a new Cabinet following the election; among the new Premier's stated objectives were the development of tourism and plans to encourage Niueans resident in New Zealand to return to the island.

In March 1994 Vivian proposed a motion of 'no confidence' in the Government, alleging that too few cabinet meetings had been convened. The motion, however, was defeated. A further attempt by the opposition to propose a 'no-confidence' motion in the Government was invalidated in the High Court in October on a procedural matter. However, during the ensuing debate, the Minister for National Planning and Economic Development, Sani Lakatani, resigned in order to join the opposition as its deputy leader, thus leaving the Government with only 10 official supporters in the Assembly. Subsequent opposition demands for the intervention of the Governor-General of New Zealand in dissolving the legislature, in preparation for a general election, were rejected. However, in March 1995, Lui announced that an early election would take place, in order to end the atmosphere of increasing political uncertainty in the island.

### Government

Niue enjoys self-government in free association with New Zealand. The New Zealand Government, however, remains responsible for the island's defence and external affairs. Executive government is carried out by the Premier and three other ministers. Legislation is the responsibility of the Niue Assembly, which has 20 members (14 village representatives and six elected on a common roll), but New Zealand, if called upon to do so by the Assembly, will also legislate for the island. There is a New Zealand representative in Niue, whose status was upgraded to that of High Commissioner in August 1993.

### Economic Affairs

Agriculture (including fishing) employs only a small minority of the labour force as a full-time occupation, although a majority of households practise subsistence gardening. The principal crops are coconuts and root crops. Honey is also produced for export. Coconut cream was the island's major export until the closure of the coconut cream processing factory in 1989. The main subsistence crops are taro, yams, cassava and sweet potatoes. A taro export scheme was successfully introduced in the early 1990s, and production of the crop increased by more than 500% in 1993. Pigs, poultry, goats and beef cattle are raised, mainly for local consumption. A small forestry project has been undertaken.

Tourism was severely affected in 1989 by the suspension of air transport, while cyclone damage (which destroyed the island's only hotel) prevented a recovery in 1990. However, a proposed increase in the frequency of flights between Niue and Auckland from April 1992 was expected to enhance prospects for tourism, as was a project to construct 60 hotel rooms by the mid-1990s. A total of 1,668 tourists (mainly from New Zealand) visited Niue in 1992.

Niue records an annual trade deficit, with imports in 1993 exceeding exports by around 1,300%. In 1985 the principal source of imports (59.5%) was New Zealand, which was also the principal market for exports (88.4%). In 1993 New Zealand provided 86.1% of imports. The principal exports in 1993 were root crops, coconuts, honey and handicrafts. The principal imports were foodstuffs, manufactured goods, machinery, equipment, fuels and chemicals.

For the financial year ending 30 June 1990 there was a projected budgetary deficit of $NZ8.06m. Aid from New Zealand, however, reduced the deficit to $NZ434,600. In 1991/92 the budgetary deficit was estimated to exceed US $1.5m. Development assistance from New Zealand totalled $NZ7.51m. in 1992/93. The annual rate of inflation averaged 11.0% in 1980–87; consumer prices increased by an average of 5.1% in 1991, and by 4.9% in 1992.

Niue is a member of the South Pacific Commission (see p. 215) and the South Pacific Forum (see p. 217).

During the 1980s and early 1990s Niue's economic development was adversely affected by inclement weather, inadequate transport services and the annual migration of about 10% of the population to New Zealand. Two-thirds of the land surface is uncultivable, and marine resources are variable. The 1991/92 budget envisaged the development of tourism, and also included incentives to prevent school-leavers from migrating to New Zealand to seek employment. However, further development of potentially successful sectors of the economy was threatened by the reduction in budgetary aid from New Zealand in 1991 (see Recent History). In an attempt to diversify Niue's aid sources, efforts were made to improve relations with Australia in 1992, and in mid-1993 Papua New Guinea responded to requests for assistance by providing the island with some $A0.2m. Premier Frank Lui announced further measures in 1993 (including the establishment of the Population Development Committee), aimed at encouraging the return to the island of Niueans resident in New Zealand. It was hoped that, by increasing the resident population, Niue's economy could be stimulated and its chances for self-sufficiency improved. The policy appeared to be succeeding according to the provisional results of a census, carried out in October 1994, which recorded the first population increase in 20 years. In early 1994 the Niue Assembly approved legislation allowing the island to become an 'offshore' financial centre. The Government predicted that Niue could earn up to $NZ11m. annually in fees from its financial services.

### Social Welfare

In 1992 the Niue Government maintained one hospital with 24 beds and one dental clinic, and in 1980 there were two government physicians and 23 nurses working on the island.

### Education

Education is provided free of charge, and is compulsory for 10 years between five and 14 years of age. Primary education, from the age of five, lasts for eight years, and is followed by four years of secondary education. A total of 641 pupils were enrolled in primary and secondary education in 1991. A number of school-leavers take up tertiary education, mainly in the Pacific region and, to a lesser extent, in New Zealand. There is an extension centre of the University of the South Pacific in Niue. An estimated 50 students were engaged in tertiary education in 1991. The budget for 1991 allocated $NZ1,454,000 to education (10.2% of total expenditure).

### Public Holidays

**1995:** 1 January (New Year's Day), 6 February (Waitangi Day, anniversary of 1840 treaty), 14–17 April (Easter), 25 April (ANZAC Day, anniversary of 1915 landing at Gallipoli), 17 June (Queen's Official Birthday), 9–10 October (Constitution Day celebrations), 16 October (Peniamina's Day), 25 December (Christmas Day), 26 December (Boxing Day).

**1996:** 1 January (New Year's Day), 6 February (Waitangi Day, anniversary of 1840 treaty), 5–8 April (Easter), 25 April (ANZAC Day, anniversary of 1915 landing at Gallipoli), 15 June (Queen's Official Birthday), 7–8 October (Constitution Day celebrations), 14 October (Peniamina's Day), 25 December (Christmas Day), 26 December (Boxing Day).

### Weights and Measures

The metric system is in force.

# Statistical Survey

Source (unless otherwise stated): Statistics/Immigration Unit, Administrative Department, POB 67, Alofi; tel. 4018; telex 67014; fax 4010.

### AREA AND POPULATION

**Area:** 262.7 sq km (101.4 sq miles).
**Population:** 2,531 (males 1,271; females 1,260) at census of 29 September 1986; 2,239 (males 1,134; females 1,105) at census of 3 November 1991; 2,321 (provisional) at census of October 1994. A total of 14,556 Niueans lived in New Zealand in 1991.
**Density** (1994): 8.8 per sq km.
**Ethnic Groups** (1986): Niueans 2,219; Tongans (Polynesians) 102; Europeans (mainly New Zealanders) 98; Others (esp. Samoans and Asians) 112; Total 2,531 (only 242 were not New Zealand citizens). 1991: Niueans 1,962; Non-Niueans 277.
**Births, Marriages and Deaths** (1992): Births 43 (birth rate 16.6 per 1,000); Marriages 13; Deaths 13 (death rate 5.0 per 1,000).
**Expectation of Life** (official estimates, years at birth, 1991): 62.5 (males 60.0; females 65.0).

**Employment** (1991): Agriculture, forestry and fishing 45; Manufacturing 27; Construction 36; Trade 58; Restaurants and hotels 19; Transport 40; Finance 27; Real estate, etc. 43; Public administration 242; Education 66; Health, etc. 61; Total (incl. others) 701.

### AGRICULTURE, ETC.

**Principal Crops** (FAO estimates, '000 metric tons, 1993): Taro 3; Coconuts 2; Bananas 1 (1989). Source: FAO, *Production Yearbook*.
**Livestock** (1987, unless otherwise indicated): Cattle 450; Pigs 2,000 (1993); Chickens 9,716 (1989); Ducks 50; Goats 47.
**Forestry** (cu m, 1985): Roundwood removals 613; Sawnwood 201.
**Fishing** (metric tons): Total catch 115 in 1990; 120 in 1991; 115 in 1992. Source: FAO, *Yearbook of Fishery Statistics*.

### INDUSTRY

**Production** (1992): Electrical energy 2.7 million kWh.

### FINANCE

**Currency and Exchange Rates:** 100 cents = 1 New Zealand dollar ($NZ). For details, see Tokelau, p. 2258.
**Budget** ($NZ '000, year ending 30 June 1990; Revenue 11,296 (New Zealand budgetary support 7,625, Niue Govt Revenue 3,671); Expenditure 11,730.6; (year ending 30 June 1993): Revenue 14,927 (New Zealand budgetary support 7,509, Niue Govt Revenue 7,418).
**Overseas Aid** ($NZ, 1989/90): New Zealand budgetary support 7,625,000; Total 8,375,438.
**Cost of Living** (Consumer Price Index in March; base: 1990 = 100): 105.1 in 1991; 110.3 in 1992.
**Gross Domestic Product** ($NZ '000 in current prices): 11,751 in 1991.

### EXTERNAL TRADE

**Principal Commodities** ($NZ '000, 1993): *Imports c.i.f.:* Food and live animals 1,949.7; Beverages, spirits and vinegar 334.0; Mineral fuels 228.5; Wood and cork products 345.3; Iron and steel and articles thereof 278.3; Machinery and parts 374.6; Electrical goods 819.1; Motor vehicles 739.0; Total (incl. others) 6,962.1. *Exports f.o.b.:* Taro 450.5; Yams 22.6; Coconuts 10.2; Others (incl. honey and handicrafts) 50.0; Re-exports 10.0; Total 543.2.
**Principal Trading Partners** ($NZ '000, 1993): *Imports c.i.f.:* Australia 101.7; Fiji 140.9; Japan 358.3; New Zealand 5,993.8; USA 197.2; Western Samoa 47.2; Total (incl. others) 6,962.1. *Exports f.o.b.:* Total 543.2.

### TRANSPORT

**Road Traffic** (registrations, 1992): Passenger cars 130; Motorcycles 301; Vans, etc. 177; Heavy lorries 36; Buses 11; Total motor vehicles 655.
**International Shipping:** *Ship Arrivals* (1989): Yachts 20; Merchant vessels 22; Total 42. *Freight Traffic* (official estimates, metric tons, 1989): Unloaded 3,410; Loaded 10.
**Civil Aviation:** *Passengers* (1992): Arrivals 3,500; Departures 3,345; Transit n.a. *Freight Traffic* (metric tons, 1992): Unloaded 41.6; Loaded 15.7.

### TOURISM

**Visitor Arrivals** (1992): Pacific islands 286; Australia 81; New Zealand 1,163; USA 70; Europe 42; Canada 11; Total (incl. others) 1,668.

### COMMUNICATIONS MEDIA

**Telephones** (1991): 376 in use.
**Radio Receivers** (1991): 414 in use.
**Television Receivers** (1991): 312 in use.
**Newspaper** (1991): 1 weekly, circulation (estimate) 400.

### EDUCATION

**Primary** (March 1991): 1 school; 22 teachers; 337 pupils.
**Secondary** (March 1991): 1 school; 27 teachers; 304 pupils.
**Post-secondary** (March 1991): 50 students (estimate).

# Directory
## The Constitution

In October 1974 Niue gained self-government in free association with New Zealand. The latter, however, remains responsible for

NEW ZEALAND'S DEPENDENT AND ASSOCIATED TERRITORIES

Niue's defence and external affairs and will continue economic and administrative assistance. Executive authority in Niue is vested in the British monarch as sovereign of New Zealand but exercised through the government of the Premier, assisted by three ministers. Legislative power is vested in the Niue Assembly or Fono Ekepule, which comprises 20 members (14 village representatives and six elected on a common roll), but New Zealand, if requested to do so by the Assembly, will also legislate for the island. There is a New Zealand representative in Niue, the High Commissioner, who is charged with liaising between the Governments of Niue and New Zealand.

## The Government

**New Zealand High Commissioner:** WARREN SEARELL.
**Secretary to Government:** BRADLEY PUNU.

### THE CABINET
(June 1995)

**Premier and Minister for External Relations, Finance, Trade, Justice and Lands, Police and Immigration, Transport, Civil Aviation and Shipping, Public Service Commission and Administrative Services:** FRANK FAKAOTIMANAVA LUI.
**Minister for National Planning and Economic Development, Inland Revenue, Customs, Business Relations and Private Sector Development:** AUKUSO PAVIHI.
**Minister for Education, Health, Community, Youth and Sport, Tourism, Art and Culture, Religious Affairs, Women's Affairs and the Environment:** O'LOVE TAUVEVE JACOBSEN.
**Minister for Agriculture, Forestry and Fisheries, Public Works, Posts and Telecommunications and Broadcasting:** TERRY DONALD COE.

### GOVERNMENT OFFICES

All ministries are in Alofi.
**Office of the New Zealand High Commissioner:** POB 78, Tapeu, Alofi; tel. 4022; fax 4173.
**Office of the Secretary to Government:** POB 42, Alofi; tel. 4224; telex 67014; fax 4232.

## Legislature

### ASSEMBLY

The Niue Assembly or Fono Ekepule has 20 members (14 village representatives and six members elected on a common roll). The most recent general election was held on 27 February 1993.
**Speaker:** SAM P. E. TAGELAGI.

## Political Organization

**Niue People's Action Party (NPAP):** Alofi; f. 1987 in opposition to Govt of Sir Robert Rex; Leader YOUNG VIVIAN.

## Judicial System

The Chief Justice of the High Court and the Land Court Judge visit Niue quarterly. In addition, lay justices are locally appointed and exercise limited criminal and civil jurisdiction. Appeals against High Court judgments are heard in the Court of Appeal of Niue (created in 1992).
**The High Court:** exercises civil and criminal jurisdiction.
**The Land Court:** is concerned with litigation over land and titles.
**Land Appellate Court:** hears appeals over decisions of the Land Court.
**Chief Justice:** JOHN DILLON.

## Religion

About 66% of the population belong to the Ekalesia Niue, a Protestant organization, which had 1,487 adherents at the time of the 1991 census. Within the Roman Catholic Church, Niue forms part of the diocese of Rarotonga (see the Cook Islands). The Church of Jesus Christ of Latter-day Saints (Mormon), the Seventh-day Adventists, the Jehovah's Witnesses and the Church of God of Jerusalem are also represented.
**Ekalesia Niue:** Head Office, POB 25, Alofi; tel. 4012; fax 4196; f. 1846 by London Missionary Society, became Ekalesia Niue in 1966; Pres. Rev. PAHETOGIA FAITALA; Gen. Sec. Rev. LIVA TUKUTAMA.

## The Press

**Niue Star:** Alofi; weekly; publ. by Jackson's Photography and Video; circ. 400.

## Radio and Television

There were an estimated 414 radio receivers and 312 television receivers in use in 1991. Construction of a new television and radio station for the Niue Broadcasting Corporation began in 1992, with Australian aid.
**Niue Broadcasting Corporation:** POB 23, Alofi; tel. 4026; telex 67013; fax 4217; operates television service and radio service; govt-owned; CEO TREVOR TIAKIA; Gen. Man. HIMA DOUGLAS.
  **Radio Sunshine:** broadcasts in English and Niuean; Gen. Man. HIMA DOUGLAS.
  **Television Niue:** broadcasts in English and Niuean, six days a week from 5 p.m. to 11 p.m.

## Finance

### DEVELOPMENT BANK

**Fale Tupe Atihake Ha Niue** (Development Bank of Niue): POB 34, Alofi; tel. 4335; fax 4010; f. 1993 began operations July 1994; Gen. Man. DAVID C. COTTINGHAM.

### COMMERCIAL BANK

**Westpac Banking Corpn:** Main St, Alofi; tel. 4221; fax 4043; Man. P. A. DICK.

## Transport

### ROADS

There are 123 km of all-weather roads and 106 km of access and plantation roads. A total of 655 motor vehicles were registered in 1992.

### SHIPPING

The best anchorage is an open roadstead at Alofi, the largest of Niue's 14 villages. Under a three-year agreement with the Niue Government, signed in August 1989, the Cook Islands National Line began to operate a monthly cargo shipping service between New Zealand, the Cook Islands and Niue. Since the same year Niue has received a service from Kingurra Nominees (a Warner Trust co) every six weeks. Fuel supplies are delivered by a tanker (the *Pacific Explorer*) from Fiji.

### CIVIL AVIATION

Hanan International Airport has a total sealed runway of 1,650 m. Air links were seriously affected by the cessation of the Air Nauru service in 1989. In mid-1992 the Government suspended the licence of Niue Airways, and flights between Niue, the Cook Islands, Western Samoa and New Zealand were operated by Polynesian Airlines (under charter to the Niue Government). In early 1993 Air Nauru began operating a weekly service between Niue and Auckland, New Zealand. Work to extend the runway by 700 m was to commence in late 1994 with New Zealand assistance.
**Niue Airways Ltd (NAL):** Hanan International Airport; f. 1990; registered in New Zealand; Dir RAY YOUNG.

## Tourism

Niue has a small but significant tourist industry, which was enhanced by an increase in the frequency of flights between the island and New Zealand in the early 1990s. A total of 1,668 people visited the island in 1992, of whom some 40% were tourists. In that year 70% of visitors came from New Zealand.

# NICARAGUA

## Introductory Survey

### Location, Climate, Language, Religion, Flag, Capital

The Republic of Nicaragua lies in the Central American isthmus, bounded by the Pacific Ocean to the west and by the Caribbean Sea to the east. Its neighbours are Honduras, to the north, and Costa Rica, to the south. The climate is tropical, with an average annual temperature of 25.5°C (78°F). The rainy season extends from May to October. The national language is Spanish, although English is spoken by some indigenous Indians along the Caribbean coast. Almost all of the inhabitants profess Christianity, and the great majority are Roman Catholics. The national flag (proportions 5 by 3) has three equal horizontal stripes, of blue, white and blue, with the state emblem (a triangle enclosing a dark blue sea from which rise five volcanoes, in green, surmounted by a Phrygian cap from which extend white rays and, at the top, a rainbow, all encircled by the words, in gold capitals, 'República de Nicaragua' and 'América Central') in the centre of the white stripe; the same flag without the state emblem is an alternative version of the civil flag. The capital is Managua.

### Recent History

Nicaragua was under Spanish rule from the 16th century until 1821. It then became part of the Central American Federation until 1838. From 1927 US troops were based in Nicaragua at the request of the Government, which was opposed by a guerrilla group, led by Augusto César Sandino. In 1933, following the establishment of the National Guard (commanded by Gen. Anastasio Somoza García), the US troops left Nicaragua. Sandino was assassinated in 1934, but some of his followers ('Sandinistas') continued to oppose actively the new regime. Somoza seized power in a coup in 1935 and took office as President in 1936. Apart from a brief interlude in the late 1940s, Somoza remained as President until September 1956, when he was assassinated. However, the Somoza family continued to dominate Nicaraguan politics until 1979.

In 1962 the left-wing Frente Sandinista de Liberación Nacional (FSLN, the Sandinista National Liberation Front) was formed with the object of overthrowing the Somozas by revolution. General Anastasio Somoza Debayle, son of the former dictator, became President in May 1967, holding office until April 1972. He retained his command of the National Guard. The Congreso Nacional (National Congress) was dissolved, and a triumvirate ruled until Gen. Somoza was re-elected President in September 1974. In January 1978 the murder of Pedro Joaquín Chamorro Cardenal, the leader of the opposition coalition and the editor of *La Prensa* (the country's only independent newspaper), provoked violent demonstrations against the Government and demands for President Somoza's resignation.

In June 1979 the FSLN announced the formation of a provisional Junta of National Reconstruction, with five members. With the FSLN in command of many towns and preparing for the final onslaught on Managua, President Somoza resigned and left the country on 17 July 1979. (He was assassinated in Paraguay in September 1980.) After the Sandinistas had gained control of the capital, the Junta and its Provisional Governing Council took power on 20 July as the Government of National Reconstruction. The 1974 Constitution was abrogated, and the bicameral Congreso Nacional dissolved. The National Guard was disbanded and replaced by the Ejército Popular Sandinista (EPS—Sandinista People's Army), officially established in August. Between 40,000 and 50,000 people were estimated to have died during the revolution. In August the Junta issued a 'Statute on Rights and Guarantees for the Citizens of Nicaragua', providing for basic personal freedoms and restoring freedom of the press and broadcasting. Civil rights were restored in January 1980.

On taking office, the Junta had issued a Basic Statute, providing for the creation of an appointed Council of State to act as an interim legislature. In March 1981 the Junta was reduced from five to three members. At the same time, Commdr Daniel Ortega Saavedra was appointed Co-ordinator of the Junta and of its new consultative body, the Council of Government.

By 1981 discontent at the postponement of elections and the increasing hegemony of the Sandinistas had led to the creation of counter-revolutionary forces ('Contras'), who were mostly members of the former National Guard and operated from camps in Honduras. Faced with the prospect of forced resettlement, some 120,000 English-speaking Miskito Indians, who were hoping to establish the province of Zelaya as an independent territory, allied themselves with the Contras. At the same time, relations between the US and Nicaraguan Governments had seriously deteriorated, culminating in the suspension of US economic aid in April 1981. In the same year the US Government donated US $10m. in support of the Contras, while covert operations by the US Central Intelligence Agency (CIA) attempted to destabilize the Sandinista regime.

In March 1982 the Sandinista Government responded to the growing attacks by declaring a state of emergency. However, the intensity of attacks on economic targets, border towns and the Nicaraguan army by the Fuerzas Democráticas Nicaragüenses (FDN), anti-Sandinista guerrillas based in Honduras, increased. A Contra group, the Alianza Revolucionaria Democrática (ARDE), was also established in Costa Rica, led by Edén Pastora Gómez, a prominent figure in the revolution who had become disillusioned with the Sandinistas. In December the Sandinistas reaffirmed their support for the initiatives of the 'Contadora group' (Colombia, Mexico, Panama and Venezuela), which was attempting to find peaceful solutions to the disputes involving Central America, and adopted a more conciliatory approach towards the opposition.

In January 1984 the Government announced that a presidential election and elections to a constituent assembly would be held on 4 November 1984. The elections would be free and open, and voting would be based on a system of proportional representation. The constituent assembly was to draw up a constitution within two years of taking office. In August the Government restored the majority of the civil rights that had been suspended in September 1982, in order to permit parties to campaign without restrictions.

At the elections in November 1984 the FSLN candidate, Daniel Ortega Saavedra, received 67% of the votes cast in the presidential election, and the party won 61 of the 96 seats in the National Constituent Assembly, which replaced the Council of State. The new Government took office in January 1985, under President Ortega (hitherto Co-ordinator of the Junta, which ceased to exist).

Meanwhile, in June 1984 talks had commenced between the Nicaraguan and US Governments in order to foster the peace negotiations proposed by the Contadora group. However, although the Sandinistas agreed in September to sign a peace agreement, the US Government rejected the agreement on the grounds that the forthcoming Nicaraguan elections would not be fairly conducted. In February 1985 President Ortega launched an independent peace initiative, announcing the expulsion of 100 Cuban military advisers from Nicaragua and imposing an indefinite moratorium on the acquisition of armaments. Ortega's reforms were rejected by the US President, Ronald Reagan, who reaffirmed his Government's commitment to removing the Sandinistas from power in Nicaragua.

In June 1985 leaders of the FDN and of more moderate opposition groups announced the formation of the Unión Nicaragüense Opositora, a co-ordinating opposition movement, which also included Miskito Indian opponents of the Government. In the same month the US Congress voted to allocate US $27m. in non-military aid to the Contras. In spite of this set-back, the Nicaraguan Government reaffirmed its desire to resume negotiations with the USA. Concurrently, however, the Government revoked its moratorium on purchases of armaments and declared a state of alert. The fighting escalated, and clashes along Nicaragua's borders with Costa Rica and Honduras became increasingly frequent. In July thousands of Miskito Indians began to return to their ancestral homelands in northern Nicaragua, following talks between the

Government and the leading Indian organizations concerning autonomy for the region. Agreement was also reached between the Sandinistas and several Miskito military commanders on a cease-fire. Draft legislation on autonomy for the communities of the Caribbean coast was presented to the Asamblea Nacional (National Assembly) in 1987.

In August 1986 the US Congress approved assistance for the Contras worth US $100m. (although this had twice been rejected by the House of Representatives earlier in the year). In November the US Government disclosed that funds accruing from its clandestine sales of military equipment to Iran had been used to support the Contras. In May 1987 the Unión Nicaragüense Opositora and a rival Contra faction, the Bloque Opositor del Sur (BOS), based in Costa Rica, agreed to form a new coalition grouping, to be known as the Resistencia Nicaragüense. The agreement also included the integration of the resistance forces into a single unit, the Ejército de la Resistencia Nicaragüense (Nicaraguan Resistance Army).

In November 1986 the legislature adopted a new Constitution, which was promulgated in January 1987; on the same day, however, civil liberties, guaranteed in the Constitution, were again suspended by the renewal of the five-year-old state of emergency.

In April 1986 the Governments of Costa Rica, El Salvador, Guatemala and Honduras agreed to sign a peace settlement which had been proposed by the Contadora group in September 1984. This accord agreed on limiting the acquisition of weapons, the withdrawal of all external and irregular forces and the holding of democratic elections. Nicaragua did not endorse the agreement. In February 1987 the same four Governments approved a new peace plan, submitted by the President of Costa Rica and largely based on the Contadora proposals, but placing greater emphasis on democratization within Nicaragua, including the lifting of the state of emergency. The proposal subsequently underwent some modification, and in August the peace plan was signed by the Presidents of Costa Rica, El Salvador, Guatemala, Honduras and Nicaragua, at a summit meeting in Guatemala. In accordance with the plan's requirements, a four-member National Commission for Reconciliation was created in Nicaragua in August: it was chaired by Cardinal Miguel Obando y Bravo, the Archbishop of Managua, a leading critic of the Government. However, President Ortega declared repeatedly that the state of emergency would not be revoked until US aggression against the people of Nicaragua ceased, and he refused to negotiate directly with the Contras. In September President Reagan pledged that he would continue to campaign to secure US $270m. in aid for the Contras in 1987/88.

In January 1988, following a summit meeting of the five Central American Presidents, the Nicaraguan Government ended the state of emergency, and consented to participate directly in negotiations with the Contras. The first direct discussions between the Contras and the Sandinistas took place in San José, Costa Rica, in January, but ended without agreement on the Contras' demand for a programme of broad democratic reform. In February the US House of Representatives rejected President Reagan's request for US $36.2m. in aid to the Contras (including $3.6m. in military aid), and in March a further proposal for humanitarian aid worth $30.8m. was also rejected. In March, however, a further round of negotiations was held in Nicaragua itself, between representatives of the Government and of the Contras. A 60-day cease-fire was agreed (with effect from 1 April), as a prelude to detailed peace negotiations (and was later unilaterally extended by the Government, until November 1989). The Government agreed to release political prisoners (in stages) and to permit the participation of the Contras in domestic political dialogue and (eventually) in elections. In April the US Congress agreed to provide $48m. in non-military aid for the Contras.

In May 1988 the Nicaraguan Government signed an agreement on a permanent cease-fire with the Yatama group of Miskito Indian rebels. In August the US Senate approved the provision of US $27m. in humanitarian aid for the Contras. As the hope of further military aid diminished, the Contra fighters retreated into Honduras.

In February 1989 the five Central American Presidents met in El Salvador to discuss the reactivation of the regional peace plan. At the meeting it was agreed that, in return for the dismantling of Contra bases in Honduras, there would be moves towards greater democracy in Nicaragua. These included pledges to hold a general election, open to opposition parties, by February 1990; the abolition of constraints on the press; and unrestricted access for all political parties to the media. In March 1989 1,894 former members of Somoza's National Guard were released from prison in accordance with the agreement reached at the February meeting. In the same month the US Government agreed to supply the Contras with US $4.5m. of humanitarian aid per month until February 1990. In April 1989 the Government announced that a general election would be held on 25 February 1990. A number of electoral reforms were introduced: Contra rebels were permitted to return to vote, on condition that they relinquished their armed struggle under a proposed demobilization plan.

In June 1989 the Unión Nacional Opositora (UNO) was formed by 14 opposition parties of varying political views: they decided to present a joint presidential candidate and a single programme in the forthcoming elections. Discussions, held in August, between the opposition parties and the Government led to an agreement on electoral procedures and guarantees.

In August 1989 the five Central American Presidents met in Tela, Honduras, where they signed the Tela agreement. This provided for the voluntary demobilization, repatriation or relocation of the Contra forces within a 90-day period. To facilitate this process, an International Commission of Support and Verification (CIAV) was established by the UN and the Organization of American States. Following mediation (conducted by the former US President, Jimmy Carter), the Government concluded an agreement with the leaders of the Miskito Indians of the Caribbean coast. The rebels agreed to renounce their armed struggle and to join the political process, and decided to support the presidential candidate of the Partido Social Cristiano Nicaragüense (PSCN), Erick Ramírez, in the February elections. Meanwhile, the UNO designated Violeta Barrios de Chamorro (the owner and director of the opposition daily newspaper, *La Prensa*, since the assassination of her husband, Pedro Chamorro, in 1978), to be its presidential candidate. Daniel Ortega was nominated as the presidential candidate for the FSLN.

In November 1989 President Ortega declared the ending of the cease-fire with the Contra rebels, on the grounds that not enough was being done to implement the Tela agreement and disband Contra forces stationed in Honduras. In response to these events, the UN Security Council established the UN Observer Group in Central America (ONUCA) to monitor compliance with the Tela agreement, to prevent cross-border incursions by rebel groups and to assist in supervising the forthcoming Nicaraguan elections.

In February 1990 some 2,500 foreign observers monitored the elections, which were agreed to be 'free and fair' and resulted in an unexpected victory for Violeta Chamorro, the UNO candidate, who obtained some 55% of votes in the presidential election, while Ortega received 41%. After the elections, the Sandinista Government decreed an immediate cease-fire. The president-elect pledged to 'depoliticize' the military and security forces, and urged the Contra rebels to disband and return to civilian life.

By March 1990 it had become clear that the UNO had not secured a sufficient majority of seats in the Asamblea Nacional to make amendments to the Constitution. Consequently, the new Government would be prevented from radically reforming the armed forces, which, under the Constitution, bore the name Ejército Popular Sandinista (EPS—Sandinista People's Army) and were mandated to protect the Sandinista revolution.

During the interim period before the transfer of power, which was to take place on 25 April 1990, President Ortega introduced a number of reforms. A General Amnesty and National Reconciliation Law was adopted: it was designed to pre-empt retaliatory measures against outgoing officials and to quash legal proceedings against those who had committed politically-motivated crimes against the State since 1979. In addition, a civil service law was introduced to protect the rights of public-sector employees.

In March 1990 the US President, George Bush, announced his intention to abolish the USA's five-year trade embargo on Nicaragua, and requested congressional approval for US $500m. in aid to Nicaragua over the next two years. On 19 April a cease-fire was agreed by the Contras and the Sandinista armed forces. The Contras agreed to surrender their weapons by 10 June, and to assemble in 'security zones' supervised by UN troops. A transitional agreement between the outgoing

Sandinista Government and the newly-elected UNO coalition provided for a reduction in the strength of the security forces and their subordination to civilian authority. Upon taking office on 25 April, President Chamorro assumed the post of Minister of National Defence, but allowed the previous minister, Gen. Humberto Ortega Saavedra, temporarily to retain the post of Chief of the EPS: this provoked considerable controversy within the UNO and the Contra leadership. However, in return for a commitment from the Contras to sign the demobilization accords, the Government agreed to the establishment of a special police force, composed of former Contra rebels, in order to guarantee security within the demobilization zones. On 27 June the demobilization of the Contra rebels was officially concluded, signifying the end of 11 years of civil war in Nicaragua.

On assuming office, the UNO Government immediately attempted to reverse much Sandinista policy. The suspension of the civil service law in May 1990 provoked a public-sector strike, which brought the country to a standstill. President Chamorro was forced to concede wage increases of 100% and the establishment of a joint trade union and government commission to revise the civil service law. In July another general strike, involving 100,000 workers, was held in support of demands for wage increases and also in protest at the implementation of legislation allowing the restoration to private ownership of land that had been nationalized and redistributed under the Sandinista Government. Once again the Government granted concessions, including a 43% wage increase, the promise of a further rise in August, and the suspension of the programme to privatize land. The agreement was condemned by the Vice-President, Virgilio Godoy Reyes, who accused President Chamorro of capitulating too readily to the demands of the FSLN.

During 1990 there were numerous violent incidents arising from conflicts over the ownership of land. In mid-October the Government announced the formation of a National Agrarian Commission to study the problems of land distribution and illegal land seizures. The commission was to include members of the trade unions and former Contras.

In June 1991 the emergence of groups of re-armed Contra rebels (known as Re-contras) became apparent with the reported occupation of several cities in the northern province of Jinotega. The Re-contras' stated aim was to publicize the grievances of thousands of demobilized Contras in the north of the country who had not received land and aid promised them under the terms of the resettlement plan introduced by the Government following demobilization. Many demobilized Contras considered the presence of a predominantly Sandinista police force a threat to their security.

In late August 1991 a supervisory body, the National Security Commission, including a 150-strong Brigada Especial de Desarme (BED—special disarmament brigade), was established to disarm civilians. In the same month Radio Sandino acknowledged the existence of groups of re-armed Sandinistas (Re-compas) which, it claimed, had been formed to counter the military operations of the Re-contras. In spite of the efforts of the National Security Commission, reports of hostilities between Re-contras and Re-compas continued. The phased disarmament of the Re-contras and the Re-compas began in late January 1992. However, in mid-April groups of the former combatants began to join forces, forming the 'Revueltos', to demand land and credit promised to them prior to demobilization. The groups, acting predominantly in the north of the country, blockaded roads and occupied public and private property. In mid-May the Government attempted to placate the Revueltos, allocating them 800 plots of land outside the capital as a gesture of its intent to address seriously the groups' grievances. Rebel activity continued, however, throughout 1992, prompting the Government to issue an ultimatum to the rebels, requiring them to retire to designated areas for disarmament by the end of January 1993 or be subjected to a concerted military onslaught. However, this deadline passed without military intervention. In May 1993, following renewed attacks by rearmed rebel groups, the Government implemented a partial suspension of constitutional gaurantees in five northern departments and issued a further ultimatum to the rebels to disarm and accept an amnesty within 30 days.

In late July 1993 the Government deployed more than 2,000 troops to quell an uprising by a group of Re-compas, the Frente Revolucionario de Obreros y Campesinos, in the northern town of Estelí. The rebels had seized the town to support their demands that the Government honour its commitment to provide land and credit to demobilized soldiers. The ensuing hostilities resulted in the deaths of some 45 people, including several civilians, and the Government was subsequently accused of using undue force. Later that month the Government issued a further ultimatum to all remaining rearmed rebels in the country (estimated to number as many as 2,500) to enter designated security areas by 31 July and disarm by the end of August. On 17 August the legislature approved an amnesty, covering all political crimes committed before 15 August. On 19 August a group of some 150 Re-contras, the Frente Norte 3-80 (FN 3-80), seized 38 hostages in the village of El Zúngano in the municipality of Quilalí, some 300 km north of the capital. The hostages, who included three members of the legislature, were members of the BED who had been sent to discuss the Government's amnesty proposals with the rebels. The FN 3-80's demands included the dismissal of the Minister of the Presidency, Antonio Lacayo Oyanguren, and Humberto Ortega. In response, on 20 August, a group of Re-compas, the Comando 40 por la Dignidad de la Soberanía, seized the offices of the Alianza Política Opositora (APO—formerly the UNO, see below) in the capital and took 33 hostages, including the political council of the APO. Two commissions were immediately established by the Government to negotiate a settlement, and by 26 August all the hostages had been released. In return, both rebel groups were offered an amnesty. The FN 3-80 received assurances that the Government would review its grievances, and a temporary truce was declared, pending the group's disarmament, which was to be completed by 12 October. However, the FN 3-80 failed to comply with the deadline, and in mid-October more than 2,500 government troops were deployed against them. In early February 1994 a cease-fire was agreed, and on 24 February, following the mediation of Cardinal Miguel Obando y Bravo and the Organization of American States, a peace agreement was signed, providing for the demobilization of the FN 3-80 by mid-April. In return, the rebels were granted an amnesty and the right to be incorporated into the national police force. Demobilization was completed on 15 April. However, violent incidents involving further groups of armed rebels, identified as Re-contras, continued in northern and central Nicaragua. In response the Government deployed the security forces to combat the rebels' activities, which, it asserted, were criminal and not related to legitimate demands for land. In June 1994, in separate incidents, groups of Re-compas and Re-contras staged occupations in Managua. In early June a group of Re-compas occupied the Venezuelan embassy and Managua cathedral; later that month Re-contras occupied the Colombian embassy and the headquarters of the International Commission of Support and Verification of the OAS. Both groups were acting in support of demands that the Government honour its commitment to provide land and credit to demobilized soldiers.

In mid-June 1991 the FSLN withdrew indefinitely its 39 deputies from the Asamblea Nacional, in protest against the introduction by conservative deputies of a draft bill revoking two laws concerning redistribution of property. The laws (commonly known as the *piñata* laws) had been introduced by the FSLN in March 1990, immediately prior to the transfer of power to the newly-elected Government of Violeta Chamorro. They guaranteed the property rights of the thousands of people who had benefited from the land expropriation that had been conducted by the Sandinistas. Supporters of the FSLN reacted violently to the situation, occupying several radio stations and government office buildings in Managua and elsewhere in the country and perpetrating bomb attacks against the homes and offices of several politicians who were alleged to support the draft bill. In August 1991 the legislature approved the abrogation of the *piñata* laws, but in the following month President Chamorro vetoed parts of the bill that she deemed to be unconstitutional. In response, right-wing supporters of Godoy accused Chamorro of yielding to pressure exerted by the Sandinistas. By this stage, disagreement over the property issue had led to the alienation by Chamorro of the majority of UNO deputies, and the legislature only narrowly failed to overturn the veto in December.

In July 1991 the FSLN convened its first-ever congress. In what was described as a move to safeguard party unity, the leadership secured its re-election to the National Directorate *en bloc*, with Daniel Ortega appointed to the newly-created post of General Secretary.

In early January 1992 President Chamorro reorganized the Cabinet, with the aim of promoting social peace and economic growth. Members of the UNO coalition were replaced by new ministers, who were described as 'pragmatic technocrats', in an attempt to reinforce Chamorro's policy of national reconciliation. However, in April Lacayo (son-in-law of Violeta Chamorro and widely considered to be the principal architect of government policy) announced that the Government was seeking 'fundamental agreements' with the FSLN. This announcement served to fuel the anger of right-wing and liberal members of the UNO coalition who, led by Godoy and the President of the Asamblea Nacional, Alfredo César Aguirre, accused both Lacayo and Chamorro of being in league with the Sandinistas. In May Gen. Ortega was summoned to appear before the Asamblea Nacional to answer charges that he was maintaining a second, clandestine and pro-Sandinista army in the country. A possible vote of censure against Ortega was avoided when the Government secured a court injunction in early June.

In late May 1992, at the instigation of Republican US Senator Jesse Helms (a fervent anti-Sandinista), the US Congress suspended the release of US $116m. in aid to Nicaragua, on the grounds that the Nicaraguan Government had failed to compensate US citizens for land expropriated under the Sandinista regime. In addition, objections were raised concerning the influence enjoyed by the Sandinistas over the Government, and the alleged channelling of US funds to Sandinista organizations.

In July 1992, in a further attempt by right-wing members of the UNO to discredit the Government, the ComptrollerGeneral, Guillermo Potoy, released a document implicating Lacayo in the alleged illegal diversion of more than US $1m. of public funds, of which $400,000 had reportedly been used to bribe UNO deputies to support the Government on crucial issues, including the *piñata* laws.

In late August 1992 the imminent release of the suspended US aid was again postponed, following the publication of a report by the US Senate's Foreign Relations Committee which claimed that the *de facto* rulers of Nicaragua were the Sandinistas, who, it maintained, controlled the army, police and judiciary as well as much of the public administrative system. As a result of the suspension of US aid, the Government was forced to implement a series of compensatory austerity measures. In early September, in response to US and UNO criticism on the issue of the return of property expropriated under the Sandinista Government, Chamorro signed decrees establishing a property ombudsman's office and other provisions to expedite the processing of property claims. In addition, the President signed an agreement specifying that all unjustly confiscated property would be returned (or the rightful owners compensated).

A serious legislative crisis began in early September 1992, when César convened the legislature and—in the absence of the deputies of the FSLN and the Grupo de Centro (GC), a group of eight dissident UNO deputies who had maintained their allegiance to the Government, thus depriving the UNO of its parliamentary majority—irregularly recruited substitute deputies in order to elect new legislative authorities. Chamorro subsequently announced that no laws approved by the legislature would be promulgated until it recognized a Supreme Court decision ruling César's actions to be unconstitutional and declaring all subsequent rulings by the legislature null and void. On 29 December Chamorro ordered the army to occupy the assembly building and appointed a provisional administration to manage assembly affairs, pending the election of new legislative authorities. On 9 January 1993 the legislature, which was quorate despite a boycott by the UNO deputies, elected Gustavo Tablada Zelaya of the GC, who was Secretary-General of the Partido Socialista Nicaragüense (PSN), to be the new President of the Asamblea Nacional, replacing César. The six remaining legislative posts were shared equally by the GC and the FSLN. On the same day, Chamorro announced a cabinet reshuffle in which two new ministries, of Tourism and of Social Action, were created. The new appointments included a Sandinista, Fernando Guzmán Cuadra, as Minister of Tourism. The UNO responded to its exclusion from the new Cabinet by declaring itself in open opposition to the Government and announcing its formation as an opposition party, expelling four member parties (including the PSN) for their involvement with the GC and changing its title to the Alianza Política Opositora (APO). The APO continued to boycott the Asamblea Nacional and in February threatened a nationwide campaign of civil disobedience if Chamorro should fail to heed its demands for the expulsion of Sandinistas from the Government.

In early May 1993, in an attempt to resolve the legislative dispute and address the country's social and economic problems, the Government held separate talks with the APO, the FSLN and representatives of the trade unions and the private sector, with a view to establishing an agenda for multilateral discussions. However, the APO insisted that it would not participate in a national dialogue until its parliamentary majority had been restored and Lacayo and Humberto Ortega had been dismissed, and in late May it abandoned the talks. Bilateral discussions between the APO and the Government resumed in early September, following the announcement by Chamorro that Gen. Humberto Ortega would be replaced as Chief of the EPS in 1994. However, the APO continued to demand the dismissal of Lacayo and of the deputies of the GC, whose allegiance to the Government, they alleged, had been obtained by bribery. Talks were suspended in late September.

In early October 1993 unprecedented discussions between the APO and the FSLN resulted in a joint demand for a complete restructuring of the Government's economic policy. In addition, it was agreed that Humberto Ortega should resign as soon as a new law regulating the armed forces was enacted. Constitutional issues were also discussed, with the APO proposing the election of a constituent assembly, while the FSLN favoured the implementation of partial constitutional reform by the incumbent legislature. Talks were suspended in mid-October, when the FSLN and the GC signed an agreement endorsing the latter's position in the legislature. The APO subsequently resumed discussions with the Government. However, following further talks between the APO and the FLSN, an agreement was signed in late October, providing for the implementation of partial constitutional reforms on condition that a consensus was reached on the substance of the reforms by 30 November. This concession by the APO followed a serious internal dispute in which three parties, the Unión Demócrata Cristiana (UDC), the Movimiento Democrático Nicaragüense (MDN) and the Alianza Popular Conservadora (APC), emerged in favour of partial constitutional reform, in apparent opposition to the majority of the parties of the APO, which continued to demand the election of a constituent assembly. With regard to the agreement with the FSLN, the political council of the APO stipulated that it would support the reforms (which required endorsement by 60% of deputies to be enacted) only on condition that its parliamentary majority be restored (through the dismissal of the GC deputies and their replacement by APO members) and that it gain control of the legislative authorities.

In late November 1993 talks between the APO and the FSLN on the draft constitutional reform bill resulted in the signing of an initial agreement covering a series of issues, including provisions for the creation of a council of ministers to review budget expenditure and advise on policy matters, and a planning and economic council to operate with the participation of representatives of the private sector and labour organizations. In early December the APO extended the deadline for a consensus on the reforms to 15 December, the end of the current legislative session, but reiterated its demands for the dismissal of the deputies of the GC. That month the divisions within the APO resulted in the UDC, the MDN and the APC breaking away from the alliance. On 20 December the UDC formally allied itself to the FSLN and the GC, and on 4 January 1994 the APO formally expelled the UDC, the MDN and the APC. On 10 January the Asamblea Nacional reconvened, and a new working alliance (with more than the 60% majority necessary to approve constitutional reform), including the FSLN, the GC, the UDC, the MDN and the APC, elected new legislative authorities. In addition, it was announced that a political council would be established to expedite the enactment of new legislation. By mid-January the political council of the APO had abandoned its boycott of the legislature, and its remaining deputies returned.

In early January 1994 Chamorro conducted a minor reorganization of the Cabinet, upgrading the environment and natural resources institute to the status of ministry. In early February evidence of a widening division within the FSLN became apparent when Daniel Ortega founded the Izquierda Democrática Sandinista, an internal faction of the FSLN comprising 'orthodox revolutionaries' and intended to maintain the party's role as a revolutionary force, openly supporting 'all forms of struggle', aims not shared by the party's 'renewalist' faction, led by Sergio Ramírez Mercado. In the same month the Partido Social Demócrata left the APO. Following the departure of the Partido Liberal Constitucionalista from the alliance in April, the APO was reduced to just four parties.

In early 1994 a conflict emerged between the legislature and the presidency concerning legislative jurisdiction in matters of fiscal policy following the approval by the Asamblea Nacional of legislation repealing a tax that had been imposed by executive decree. An attempt by Chamorro to veto the legislation prompted the legislature to publish it in La Gaceta, Diario Oficial, thereby enacting it. These events followed a similar confrontation concerning the authority to grant fishing licences, and signalled growing tension between the presidency and the legislature in advance of the debate on constitutional reform.

In April 1994 Gen. Humberto Ortega officially announced his retirement as Chief of the EPS. The date of his retirement was to be specified in new legislation on the reorganization of the armed forces, on which consensus had been reached between the Government and the military command in mid-April, and which remained to be approved by the legislature.

In May 1994, in the light of increasing party disunity, the FSLN held an extraordinary congress to conduct internal elections and establish the party's political direction. The result was a victory for the orthodox faction of the party, which secured control of the party's national directorate— expanded from nine to 15 members—winning eight seats, while the renewalist faction obtained four seats and the remaining three seats were gained by centrist candidates. The orthodox faction also gained dominance in elections to the party assembly, the Asamblea Sandinista, which subsequently voted in favour of a policy of opposition to the Government. Daniel Ortega was re-elected as Secretary-General of the FSLN, while Ramírez was excluded from the party's national directorate, although he retained his position as leader of the FSLN bloc of deputies in the legislature.

In August 1994 the Asamblea Nacional approved the new legislation regulating the armed forces. The legislation, which was intended to depoliticize the armed forces and make them fully accountable to the civilian authorities, included stipulations for the replacement of Gen. Humberto Ortega as Chief of the EPS, who was to retire on 21 February 1995. His successor would be nominated by a military council and approved by the President. The position would in future carry a limited term of office of five years.

In September 1994 there was further evidence of division within the FSLN when the Asamblea Sandinista dismissed Ramírez as leader of the FSLN bloc of deputies in the legislature. This was prompted by the decision of the FSLN deputies, the majority of whom belonged to the renewalist faction of the party, to present a package of constitutional reform proposals to the legislature, without consulting the party proper. The Asamblea Sandinista ordered the withdrawal of the proposals and, when the deputies refused to do so, announced that Daniel Ortega was to assume his seat in the legislature, replacing Ramírez who, since 1990, had occupied the seat as Ortega's reserve. The FSLN deputies subsequently elected Dora María Téllez to head the bloc, despite a party directive to elect Daniel Ortega to the position.

On 24 November 1994, despite opposition from Chamorro, who questioned the legitimacy of such an extensive reform of the Constitution by the legislature and demanded the establishment of a constitutional assembly to conduct the reforms, the Asamblea Nacional approved amendments to some 67 of the Constitution's 202 articles. The emphasis of the reforms was to adjust the balance of authority in favour of the legislature, and to the disadvantage of the Government. In particular, the Government would be required to seek legislative approval for external loans, debt negotiations and international trade agreements; the legislature would also have greater powers in the allocation of the budget. A further amendment, prohibiting close relatives of a serving president from contesting the presidential election, was widely considered to be intended specifically to prevent Chamorro's son-in-law and Minister of the Presidency, Antonio Lacayo Oyanguren, from securing presidential office in the next election, due in 1996. Other reforms included a reduction in the presidential and legislative terms, from six to five years, and the withdrawal of the absolute ban on presidential re-election, although consecutive terms remained prohibited. The reform package was described as illegal by the FSLN leadership but gained the support of 32 of the 39 deputies in the FSLN bloc, reflecting the irreconcilable division within the party. Of particular concern to the FSLN leadership was the introduction of a second round of presidential elections should a single candidate fail to secure the necessary 45% of the votes to win outright in the initial round. It maintained that this was intended to allow right-wing parties to ally in order to prevent an FSLN victory. In the light of the recent legislation regulating the armed forces, amendments were also introduced enshrining civilian authority over the depoliticized security forces. The armed forces, which under the Constitution had previously been entitled the Ejército Popular Sandinista, were thenceforth referred to as the Ejército de Nicaragua (Nicaraguan Army). In that month the Minister of Environment and Natural Resources, Jaime Incer Barquero, was dismissed following allegations of corruption. He was replaced the following month by Milton Caldera Cardenal. In December 1994 Chamorro announced the appointment of Maj.-Gen. Joaquín Cuadra Lacayo as the new Commander-in-Chief of the armed forces, with effect from 21 February 1995.

In January 1995 the disunity within the FSLN finally resulted in members of the renewalist faction, led by Sergio Ramírez Mercado, breaking away to form a separate political party, the Movimiento de Renovación Sandinista (MRS). The rupture followed the resignation of the moderate Dora María Téllez as leader of the FSLN bloc in the legislature. Téllez had complained that the FSLN-controlled press had been conducting a defamatory campaign against her. On the following day Ramírez resigned from the FSLN to begin the process of transforming the renewalist faction into a political party. In February Téllez was one of three members of the 15-member FSLN national directorate who left the party to join the MRS; the other members were Luis Carrión and Mirna Cunningham. In early January the Minister of Government, Alfredo Mendieta Artola, resigned, prompting a reorganization of the cabinet.

On 7 February 1995 the constitutional amendments, which had been ratified by the legislature at the beginning of the month, were signed and submitted to Chamorro for approval within 15 days. However, following Chamorro's refusal to promulgate the reforms, on 24 February the Asamblea Nacional released the amendments for publication, thereby enacting them. Chamorro condemned the decision as unconstitutional and contested the legitimacy of the amendments. In the meantime an application made by Antonio Lacayo to the Court of Appeal, contesting the constitutional amendment preventing him from entering the next presidential election, was rejected. On 21 February Gen. Humberto Ortega was officially succeeded as Commander-in-Chief of the armed forces by Joaquín Cuadra Lacayo, who was promoted to the rank of General. In mid-June a resolution to the dispute concerning the constitutional amendments was achieved by the signing of a political accord between the Government and the legislature. Under the terms of the agreement, many of the amendments intended to reduce presidential authority were to be moderated. Legislation defining the interpretation and implementation of the amendments was approved by the Asamblea Nacional in early July, thus enabling the promulgation, by Chamorro, of the amendments, which was expected to occur later that month.

In September 1993 a nationwide strike was called by transport unions, in protest at the introduction of a new vehicle tax and petroleum price increases. Following four days of hostilities, during which demonstrations escalated into a general protest against prevailing economic and social conditions, an agreement was signed with transport co-operatives providing for the abolition of the new tax and a freeze on petroleum prices until the end of 1993. In January 1994 renewed demands for a reduction in petroleum prices were supported by another nationwide transport strike. The protest was resolved in early February following further concessions by the Government. In August, following the introduction of increased petroleum prices, a further strike lasting eight days and affecting some 90% of the country's transport system, was conducted in support of demands for the suspension of the petroleum price increases and for a review of transport fares. The dispute, which was estimated to have cost $20m. in lost production, was resolved when the Government agreed to a reduction in petroleum prices and the introduction of a subsidy on bus fares.

In 1994 delays in the resolution of claims by US citizens for compensation for, or the restitution of, property expropriated under the Sandinista Government, threatened to undermine relations with, and jeopardize inflows of aid from, the USA. In April the US Congress approved the Helms-González Amendment providing for the suspension of bilateral aid to countries where the property of US citizens had been confiscated. The amendment also obliged the US Government to veto applications by those countries to international lending agencies. However, Nicaraguan efforts to resolve US property claims prior to the July deadline stipulated in the amendment proved sufficient to avoid the suspension of aid.

### Government

Executive power is vested in the President, who is elected by popular vote for a six-year term. The President is assisted by a Vice-President and an appointed Cabinet. Legislative power is held by the Asamblea Nacional (National Assembly), elected by universal adult suffrage, under a system of proportional representation. Following the elections of February 1990, the National Assembly was reduced from 96 to 92 members, as, apart from the FSLN and UNO, only two parties obtained sufficient votes in the presidential election to be entitled to an extra seat in the Assembly.

Note: Constitutional reforms, due to be enacted in July 1995, provided for a reduction in the presidential and legislative terms, to five years.

### Defence

In June 1990 the professional armed forces numbered 63,500, of whom 57,000 were in the army, 3,500 in the navy and 3,000 in the air force. Following the electoral defeat of the FSLN in February 1990 and the signing of a cease-fire agreement with the Contra rebels in April the new Government introduced a policy of 'professionalization and institutionalization' of the Sandinista-dominated armed forces. In June 1994 the armed forces were estimated to total 15,200 (army 13,500, navy 500, air-force 1,200). Compulsory military service was abolished in April 1990. The defence budget for 1994 totalled US $72.9m., compared with $1,890m. in 1987.

### Economic Affairs

In 1993, according to estimates by the World Bank, Nicaragua's gross national product (GNP), measured at average 1991–93 prices, was US $1,421m., equivalent to $360 per head. During 1985–93, it was estimated, GNP per head declined, in real terms, by 6.2% per year. Over the same period, the population increased by an annual average of 2.6%. Nicaragua's gross domestic product (GDP) decreased, in real terms, by an annual average of 1.7% in 1980–92, and was estimated to have declined by 0.7% in 1993 before increasing by 3.2% in 1994.

Agriculture (including forestry and fishing) contributed about 30% of GDP in 1993, and employed an estimated 34.6% of the economically active population in 1993. The principal cash crops are coffee (which accounted for an estimated 20.8% of export earnings in 1992), cotton, sugar cane and bananas. Maize, beans and rice are the principal food crops. Livestock products accounted for an estimated 18.8% of export earnings in 1992. Production of timber and shellfish is also important. During 1980–92 agricultural GDP decreased by an annual average of 2.0%.

Industry (including mining, manufacturing, construction and power) employed about 16% of the labour force in 1980 and provided about 20% of GDP in 1993. During 1980–92 industrial GDP decreased by an annual average of 3.0%.

Mining contributed 0.8% of GDP in 1990, and employed 0.8% of the labour force in 1980. Nicaragua has workable deposits of gold, silver, lead and zinc.

Manufacturing contributed about 17% of GDP in 1993, and employed about 11% of the labour force in 1980. Measured by the value of output, the principal branches of manufacturing in 1985 were food products (about 34% of the total), beverages, petroleum-refining and chemicals. During 1980–92 manufacturing GDP declined by an annual average of 3.2%.

Energy is derived principally from imported petroleum, although two hydroelectric plants in the department of Jinotega account for one-third of the electrical energy generated in the country. Imports of mineral fuels comprised an estimated 13.7% of the total value of imports in 1992.

In 1993 Nicaragua recorded a visible trade deficit of US $392.4m., and there was a deficit of $644.3m. on the current account of the balance of payments. Nicaragua has established important trading links with European countries, and formerly maintained close trading relations with the USSR. (A trade embargo was imposed by the USA, formerly an important trading partner, betweeen 1985 and 1990.) The principal exports in 1992 were coffee, meat, cotton, sugar, seafood and bananas. The principal imports were non-durable consumer goods, primary materials for industry, capital goods for industry and petroleum products.

In 1992 Nicaragua recorded an estimated budgetary deficit of 179.9m. gold córdobas. At the end of 1993 Nicaragua's total external debt was US $10,445m., of which $8,773m. was long-term public debt. The cost of servicing external debt in that year was equivalent to 29.2% of the total value of exports of goods and services. The annual rate of inflation averaged 2,533.8% in 1985–92, and stood at about 35,000% in 1988; the official figure for 1989 was 1,689%, and the official estimate for 1990 was 12,000%. However, the annual rate of inflation declined in 1991 to 674%, and declined further in 1992 to 9.9% before increasing to an estimated 25.9% in 1993 and then declining to an estimated 13.0% in 1994. According to official figures, some 66% of the labour force were unemployed in 1994.

Nicaragua is a member of the Central American Common Market (see p. 117), which aims eventually to liberalize intra-regional trade, and of the Inter-American Development Bank (see p. 170).

On assuming power in 1990, the Chamorro administration inherited an economy devastated by the effects of a prolonged civil war and characterized by extremely low output, hyperinflation and a large foreign debt burden. With the implementation of a comprehensive economic reform programme, supported by the IMF, inflation was brought under control, levels of foreign reserves were greatly improved, and the fiscal deficit significantly reduced. In 1994 the Government secured a three-year Enhanced Structural Adjustment Facility with the IMF, providing US $173m. in loans to support its economic programme. The agreement was also expected to facilitate the disbursement of at least a further $600m. in donations and loans from international donors and lending agencies. Among the measures envisaged in the agreement were improved taxation and customs administration, increased public-sector tariffs, further reductions in public-sector employment levels, the rationalization of government entities, continued privatization of state enterprises and reduced public spending. Despite curbs on expenditure, there was to be increased social provision, in particular in health and education, and in the alleviation of poverty, which was estimated to affect as many as 70% of the population, although these measures were to be largely dependent on foreign financing. Disputes concerning the ownership of property that had been expropriated under the Sandinista Government continued to represent a significant obstacle to both private investment and agricultural-sector growth, and a swift resolution of the issue was identified as a major priority by the Government. Efforts were also being made to secure reductions of up to 75% of the country's external debt; in 1994 both Germany and Russia agreed to cancel significant amounts of Nicaraguan debt. Positive GDP growth in 1994 reflected a strong export performance, led by the agricultural sector. Continued improvements in export levels and increasing inflows of foreign aid were expected to contribute to further expansion in 1995.

### Social Welfare

The standard of health care improved substantially under the Sandinista Government. In 1980 Nicaragua had 50 hospitals, with a total of 4,573 beds, and there were 1,562 physicians working in the country. By 1984 the number of physicians had increased to 2,110. Of total expenditure by the central Government in 1980, 923m. córdobas (14.6%) was for health, and a further 281m. córdobas (4.4%) for social security and welfare.

### Education

Primary and secondary education have been provided free of charge since 1979. Primary education, which is officially

# NICARAGUA

compulsory, begins at seven years of age and lasts for six years. Secondary education, beginning at the age of 13, lasts for up to five years, comprising a first cycle of three years and a second of two years. In 1992 the total enrolment at primary and secondary schools was equivalent to 78% of the school-age population (boys 76%; girls 80%). Of children in the relevant age-group, primary enrolment in 1992 was 80% (boys 79%; girls 82%), while secondary enrolment in that year was equivalent to 42% (boys 40%; girls 45%). There are many commercial schools and four universities. In 1991 a total of 31,499 students attended universities and other higher education institutes. Expenditure by the Ministry of Education was 140.2m. new córdobas (13.1% of total government spending) in 1987, and 393,109m. new córdobas in 1989. Government expenditure on primary and secondary education was 275m. gold córdobas (10.6% of total expenditure) in 1992.

## Public Holidays

**1995:** 1 January (New Year's Day), 13 April (Maundy Thursday), 14 April (Good Friday), 1 May (Labour Day), 19 July (Liberation Day), 10 August (Managua local holiday), 14 September (Battle of San Jacinto), 15 September (Independence Day), 2 November (All Souls' Day), 25 December (Christmas).

**1996:** 1 January (New Year's Day), 4 April (Maundy Thursday), 5 April (Good Friday), 1 May (Labour Day), 19 July (Liberation Day), 10 August (Managua local holiday), 14 September (Battle of San Jacinto), 15 September (Independence Day), 2 November (All Souls' Day), 25 December (Christmas).

A considerable number of local holidays are also observed.

## Weights and Measures

The metric system is officially used, although some Spanish and local units are also in general use.

# Statistical Survey

Source (unless otherwise stated): Instituto Nacional de Estadísticas y Censos (INEC), Las Brisas, Frente Hospital Fonseca, Managua; tel. (2) 66-2031.

## Area and Population

### AREA, POPULATION AND DENSITY

| | |
|---|---:|
| Area (sq km) | |
| Land | 109,004 |
| Inland water | 11,250 |
| Total | 120,254* |
| Population (census of 20 April 1971) | |
| Males | 921,543 |
| Females | 956,409 |
| Total | 1,877,952 |
| Population (official estimates at mid-year)† | |
| 1992 | 4,130,000 |
| 1993 | 4,265,000 |
| 1994 | 4,401,000 |
| Density (per sq km) at mid-1994 | 36.6 |

* 46,430 sq miles. † Figures are provisional.

### DEPARTMENTS (estimated population at mid-1981)

| | | | |
|---|---:|---|---:|
| Boaco | 88,662 | Managua | 819,679 |
| Carazo | 109,450 | Masaya | 149,015 |
| Chinandega | 228,573 | Matagalpa | 220,548 |
| Chontales | 98,462 | Nueva Segovia | 97,765 |
| Estelí | 110,076 | Río San Juan | 29,001 |
| Granada | 113,102 | Rivas | 108,913 |
| Jinotega | 127,159 | Zelaya | 202,462 |
| León | 248,704 | **Total** | **2,823,979** |
| Madríz | 72,408 | | |

### PRINCIPAL TOWN

Managua (capital), estimated population 608,020 at mid-1979.

### BIRTHS, MARRIAGES AND DEATHS

| | Births | Marriages | Deaths |
|---|---:|---:|---:|
| 1979 | 114,069 | 10,373 | 32,206 |
| 1980 | 120,560 | 17,174 | 28,599 |
| 1981* | 104,113 | 16,237 | 10,133 |

* Registration was incomplete.

**1983** (provisional): Births 135,132 (birth rate 44.2 per 1,000); Deaths 29,045 (death rate 9.7 per 1,000).

**1986** (registrations): Births 141,039 (birth rate 41.7 per 1,000); Marriages 11,919 (marriage rate 3.5 per 1,000); Deaths 27,008 (death rate 8.0 per 1,000).

**1990** (provisional): Births 93,093 (birth rate 24.0 per 1,000); Deaths 14,264 (death rate 3.7 per 1,000).

**Expectation of life** (years at birth, 1990–95): males 64.80; females 67.71 (Source: UN, *Demographic Yearbook*).

### ECONOMICALLY ACTIVE POPULATION

| | 1978 | 1979 | 1980* |
|---|---:|---:|---:|
| Agriculture, hunting and fishing | 325,001 | 353,663 | 391,963 |
| Mining and quarrying | 4,990 | 5,914 | 6,566 |
| Manufacturing | 115,090 | 82,529 | 91,403 |
| Construction | 28,200 | 33,715 | 6,652 |
| Electricity, gas and water | 4,815 | 6,043 | 37,322 |
| Commerce | 103,940 | 94,822 | 105,053 |
| Transport, storage and communications | 21,500 | 27,069 | 30,064 |
| Other services | 152,465 | 158,466 | 175,550 |
| Unspecified activities | 4,370 | 17,470 | 19,352 |
| **Total** | **760,371** | **779,691** | **863,925** |

* Official estimate.

**1991** (estimates, persons aged 10 years and over): Total labour force 1,386,300 (males 925,604; females 460,696).
Source: ILO, *Year Book of Labour Statistics*.

**Mid-1992** (estimates, '000 persons): Agriculture, etc 406; Total 1,147.

**Mid-1993** (estimates, '000 persons): Agriculture, etc 418; Total 1,206 (source: FAO, *Production Yearbook*).

# Agriculture

**PRINCIPAL CROPS** ('000 metric tons)

|  | 1991 | 1992 | 1993 |
|---|---|---|---|
| Rice (paddy)† | 119 | 154 | 178 |
| Maize | 199 | 252 | 283 |
| Sorghum | 71 | 92 | 105 |
| Cassava (Manioc)* | 52 | 51 | 52 |
| Dry beans | 72 | 64 | 73 |
| Seed cotton | 81 | 67 | 4* |
| Cottonseed | 40 | 36 | 2* |
| Cotton (lint) | 30 | 26 | 1† |
| Tomatoes* | 31 | 31 | 33 |
| Oranges* | 68 | 68 | 70 |
| Pineapples* | 43 | 43 | 45 |
| Bananas | 133 | 135 | 136* |
| Plantains* | 55 | 53 | 55 |
| Sugar cane | 2,747 | 2,563 | 2,400† |
| Coffee (green) | 47 | 45 | 50† |

* FAO estimate(s).  † Unofficial figure(s).
Source: FAO, *Production Yearbook*.

**LIVESTOCK** ('000 head, year ending September)

|  | 1991 | 1992 | 1993 |
|---|---|---|---|
| Cattle† | 1,600 | 1,640 | 1,645 |
| Pigs* | 570 | 550 | 530 |
| Goats* | 6 | 6 | 6 |
| Horses* | 250 | 250 | 250 |
| Asses* | 8 | 8 | 8 |
| Mules* | 45 | 45 | 45 |

* FAO estimates.  † Unofficial figures.
Poultry (FAO estimates, million): 5 in 1991; 6 in 1992; 6 in 1993.
Source: FAO, *Production Yearbook*.

**LIVESTOCK PRODUCTS** ('000 metric tons)

|  | 1991 | 1992 | 1993 |
|---|---|---|---|
| Beef and veal | 45 | 48 | 48 |
| Pig meat* | 9 | 9 | 10 |
| Poultry meat | 10 | 12 | 14 |
| Cows' milk | 165 | 171 | 182 |
| Butter* | 0.9 | 0.9 | 0.9 |
| Cheese* | 4.7 | 4.9 | 5.2 |
| Hen eggs* | 25.5 | 26.0 | 26.5 |
| Cattle hides* | 7.0 | 7.4 | 7.5 |

* FAO estimates.
Source: FAO, *Production Yearbook*.

# Forestry

**ROUNDWOOD REMOVALS**
(FAO estimates, '000 cubic metres, excluding bark)

|  | 1990 | 1991 | 1992 |
|---|---|---|---|
| Sawlogs, veneer logs and logs for sleepers | 250 | 250 | 250 |
| Other industrial wood* | 50 | 50 | 50 |
| Fuel wood | 3,035 | 3,144 | 3,265 |
| **Total** | 3,335 | 3,444 | 3,565 |

* Assumed to be unchanged since 1975.
Source: FAO, *Yearbook of Forest Products*.

**SAWNWOOD PRODUCTION**
('000 cubic metres, incl. railway sleepers)

|  | 1988* | 1989* | 1990 |
|---|---|---|---|
| Coniferous | 60 | 50 | 34 |
| Broadleaved | 80 | 60 | 46 |
| **Total** | 140 | 110 | 80 |

* FAO estimates.
**1991–92:** Annual production as in 1990 (FAO estimates).
Source: FAO, *Yearbook of Forest Products*.

# Fishing

('000 metric tons, live weight)

|  | 1990 | 1991 | 1992 |
|---|---|---|---|
| Fishes | 1.3 | 2.5 | 2.8 |
| Crustaceans | 1.8 | 3.2 | 3.9 |
| **Total catch** | 3.1 | 5.7 | 6.7 |

Source: FAO, *Yearbook of Fishery Statistics*.

# Mining

('000 metric tons, unless otherwise indicated)

|  | 1989 | 1990 | 1991 |
|---|---|---|---|
| Silver (metric tons)* | 1 | 1 | 1 |
| Gold (kg)* | 1,416 | 1,200 | 1,154 |
| Salt* | 15 | 15 | 15 |
| Gypsum and anhydrite | 7† | 12 | n.a. |

* Data from the US Bureau of Mines.  † Estimate.
Source: UN, *Industrial Statistics Yearbook*.

# Industry

**SELECTED PRODUCTS**
('000 metric tons, unless otherwise indicated)

|  | 1989 | 1990 | 1991‡ |
|---|---|---|---|
| Raw sugar* | 177 | 201 | 225 |
| Cigarettes (million)† | 2,400‡ | 2,400* | 2,400 |
| Motor spirit | 70 | 65 | 60 |
| Kerosene | 22 | 20 | 21 |
| Jet fuel | 15 | 13 | 13 |
| Distillate fuel oils | 120 | 118 | 115 |
| Residual fuel oils | 220 | 215 | 210 |
| Bitumen (asphalt) | 5 | 5 | 5 |
| Liquefied petroleum gas‡ | 18 | 17 | 18 |
| Cement§ | 225 | 140‡ | 140‡ |
| Electric energy (million kWh) | 1,073 | 1,038 | 1,043 |

* Source: FAO.  † Source: US Department of Agriculture.
‡ Estimate(s).
§ Source: UN Economic Commission for Latin America and the Caribbean.
Source: UN, *Industrial Statistics Yearbook*.

# Finance

## CURRENCY AND EXCHANGE RATES

**Monetary Units**
100 centavos = 1 córdoba oro (gold córdoba).

**Sterling and Dollar Equivalents** (31 December 1994)
£1 sterling = 11.127 gold córdobas;
US $1 = 7.112 gold córdobas;
1,000 gold córdobas = £89.87 = $140.61.

**Average Exchange Rate** (gold córdobas per US dollar)
1992   5.00
1993   5.62
1994   6.72

Note: In February 1988 a new córdoba, equivalent to 1,000 of the former units, was introduced, and a uniform exchange rate of US $1 = 10 new córdobas was established. Subsequently, the exchange rate was frequently adjusted. A new currency, the córdoba oro (gold córdoba), was introduced as a unit of account in May 1990 and began to be circulated in August. The value of the gold córdoba was initially fixed at par with the US dollar, but in March 1991 the exchange rate was revised to $1 = 25,000,000 new córdobas (or 5 gold córdobas). On 30 April 1991 the gold córdoba became the sole legal tender.

## BUDGET (million gold córdobas)

| Revenue | 1990 | 1991 | 1992* |
|---|---|---|---|
| Taxation | 205.6 | 1,316.4 | 1,775.5 |
| Income tax | 45.9 | 205.1 | 305.5 |
| Tax on internal transactions | 115.9 | 797.9 | 1,099.5 |
| Import taxes and duties | 32.4 | 266.7 | 364.3 |
| Export taxes and duties | 0.1 | 0.4 | 0.1 |
| Other current revenue | 6.8 | 72.6 | 87.8 |
| Capital revenue | — | 14.7 | 12.6 |
| Transfers | 16.9 | 43.0 | 16.9 |
| Grants | 23.3 | 860.9 | 535.6 |
| **Total** | 252.6 | 2,307.6 | 2,428.4 |

| Expenditure | 1990 | 1991 | 1992* |
|---|---|---|---|
| Current expenditure | 520.9 | 1,742.6 | 2,041.3 |
| Consumption expenditure | 442.7 | 1,168.1 | 1,310.5 |
| Current transfers | 78.1 | 489.7 | 465.0 |
| Internal debt servicing | 0.1 | 0.6 | 0.4 |
| External debt servicing | — | 84.2 | 265.4 |
| Capital expenditure | 24.3 | 260.4 | 567.0 |
| Real investment | 15.5 | 155.9 | 308.2 |
| Capital transfers | 8.8 | 36.9 | 225.2 |
| **Total** | 545.2 | 2,003.0 | 2,608.3 |

* Preliminary.

Source: Banco Central de Nicaragua and Ministerio de Finanzas.

## CENTRAL BANK RESERVES (US $ million at 31 December)*

|  | 1992 | 1993 | 1994 |
|---|---|---|---|
| IMF special drawing rights | 0.08 | 0.04 | 0.01 |
| Foreign exchange | 130.40 | 55.00 | 141.00 |
| **Total** | 130.48 | 55.04 | 141.01 |

* Excluding gold reserves (US $ million at 31 December): 20.06 in 1992; 4.10 in 1993.

Source: IMF, *International Financial Statistics*.

## MONEY SUPPLY (million gold córdobas at 31 December)

|  | 1991 | 1992 | 1993 |
|---|---|---|---|
| Currency outside banks | 401 | 468 | 509 |
| Demand deposits at commercial banks | 324 | 373 | 295 |

Source: IMF, *International Financial Statistics*.

## COST OF LIVING
(Consumer Price Index for Managua. Base: 1988 = 100)

|  | 1990 | 1991 | 1992 |
|---|---|---|---|
| Food | 299,400 | 8,536,400 | 10,487,500 |
| Clothing | 126,800 | 3,813,000 | 4,601,200 |
| Housing (incl. fuel and light) | 245,600 | 8,589,100 | 16,374,500 |
| **All items** (incl. others) | 369,400 | 10,499,800 | 13,917,400 |

Source: ILO, *Year Book of Labour Statistics*.

## NATIONAL ACCOUNTS
(million gold córdobas at current prices)

**Expenditure on the Gross Domestic Product**

|  | 1990 | 1991 | 1992 |
|---|---|---|---|
| Government final consumption expenditure | 508.3 | 1,483.9 | 1,763.4 |
| Private final consumption expenditure | 1,043.3 | 6,164.7 | 8,207.6 |
| Increase in stocks | −13.6 | 124.1 | −0.5 |
| Gross fixed capital formation | 314.9 | 1,328.4 | 1,708.3 |
| **Total domestic expenditure** | 1,852.9 | 9,101.1 | 11,678.8 |
| Exports of goods and services | 390.4 | 1,552.5 | 1,518.0 |
| *Less* Imports of goods and services | 678.9 | 3,713.0 | 4,768.0 |
| **GDP in purchasers' values** | 1,564.4 | 6,940.6 | 8,428.8 |
| **GDP at constant 1980 prices*** | 18,113.2 | 18,049.3 | 18,192.3† |

* Million old córdobas.   † Preliminary.

**Gross Domestic Product by Economic Activity**

|  | 1990 | 1991 | 1992 |
|---|---|---|---|
| Agriculture, hunting, forestry and fishing | 490.7 | 2,093.1 | 2,587.5 |
| Mining and quarrying / Manufacturing | 275.5 | 1,331.3 | 1,530.6 |
| Electricity, gas and water | 17.6 | 78.8 | 97.8 |
| Construction | 40.5 | 160.8 | 205.9 |
| Wholesale and retail trade | 378.4 | 1,699.8 | 1,914.5 |
| Transport and communications | 61.1 | 284.2 | 353.7 |
| Finance and insurance | 44.9 | 196.2 | 236.4 |
| Public administration and defence | 150.5 | 616.2 | 910.9 |
| Other services | 105.2 | 480.2 | 591.5 |
| **Total** | 1,564.4 | 6,940.6 | 8,428.8 |

## BALANCE OF PAYMENTS (US $ million)

|  | 1991 | 1992 | 1993 |
|---|---|---|---|
| Merchandise exports f.o.b. | 368.1 | 223.1 | 267.0 |
| Merchandise imports f.o.b. | −688.0 | −770.8 | −659.4 |
| **Trade balance** | −419.9 | −547.7 | −392.4 |
| Exports of services | 70.2 | 86.2 | 100.2 |
| Imports of services | −136.2 | −148.3 | −156.6 |
| Other income received | 9.7 | 7.5 | 5.4 |
| Other income paid | −373.0 | −502.3 | −434.5 |
| Private unrequited transfers (net) | — | 10.0 | 25.0 |
| Official unrequited transfers (net) | 844.4 | 260.6 | 208.6 |
| **Current balance** | −4.8 | −834.0 | −644.3 |
| Direct investment (net) | — | 15.0 | 38.8 |
| Other capital (net) | −543.6 | −553.3 | −541.6 |
| Net errors and omissions | 84.7 | 60.2 | 128.1 |
| **Overall balance** | −463.7 | −1,312.0 | −1,019.0 |

Source: IMF, *International Financial Statistics*.

NICARAGUA

# External Trade

**PRINCIPAL COMMODITIES** (US $ million)

| Imports c.i.f. | 1990 | 1991 | 1992* |
|---|---|---|---|
| Consumer goods | 158.8 | 223.5 | 303.9 |
| Non-durable | 128.9 | 178.6 | 253.3 |
| Durable | 29.9 | 44.9 | 50.6 |
| Primary materials and intermediate products | 138.5 | 194.3 | 205.9 |
| Agricultural | 35.0 | 45.0 | 17.3 |
| Industrial | 103.5 | 149.3 | 188.6 |
| Mineral fuels and lubricants | 123.0 | 114.5 | 122.0 |
| Petroleum products | 105.4 | 97.6 | 101.9 |
| Non-petroleum products | 17.6 | 16.9 | 20.1 |
| Construction materials | 20.0 | 28.4 | 36.4 |
| Capital goods | 197.2 | 190.6 | 223.3 |
| Industrial | 79.0 | 93.1 | 124.7 |
| Transport | 105.9 | 83.5 | 82.5 |
| **Total** (incl. others) | 637.5 | 751.4 | 892.4 |

| Exports f.o.b. | 1990 | 1991 | 1992* |
|---|---|---|---|
| Coffee | 71.0 | 36.2 | 45.3 |
| Bananas | 27.1 | 28.7 | 10.0 |
| Meat | 56.9 | 37.5 | 40.8 |
| Sugar | 38.6 | 31.3 | 19.1 |
| Cotton | 37.2 | 44.4 | 26.2 |
| Seafood | 8.7 | 12.9 | 15.5 |
| **Total** (incl. others) | 330.5 | 274.9 | 217.5 |

* Preliminary.

Source: Banco Central de Nicaragua.

**PRINCIPAL TRADING PARTNERS** (US $ '000)*

| Imports c.i.f. | 1990 | 1991 | 1992 |
|---|---|---|---|
| Canada | 16,935 | 22,366 | 8,767 |
| Costa Rica | 25,195 | 65,299 | 89,402 |
| Ecuador | 45,531 | 18,652 | 158 |
| El Salvador | 10,859 | 25,168 | 50,318 |
| France | 12,077 | 9,749 | 10,857 |
| Germany | 16,002 | 24,262 | 25,214 |
| Guatemala | 28,993 | 57,560 | 68,946 |
| Honduras | 3,754 | 8,699 | 18,952 |
| Italy | 17,979 | 12,104 | 7,808 |
| Japan | 44,833 | 43,906 | 54,725 |
| Mexico | 16,607 | 14,105 | 27,836 |
| Netherlands | 12,133 | 10,174 | 7,151 |
| Panama | 33,976 | 37,466 | 40,244 |
| Switzerland | 7,180 | 7,363 | 4,833 |
| USSR | 64,218 | 22,942 | — |
| USA | 77,604 | 170,861 | 232,019 |
| Venezuela | 62,159 | 12,016 | 123,889 |
| **Total** (incl. others) | 635,370 | 667,486 | 906,759 |

| Exports f.o.b. | 1990 | 1991 | 1992 |
|---|---|---|---|
| Belgium-Luxembourg | 38,123 | 29,967 | 21,362 |
| Canada | 56,951 | 22,530 | 8,413 |
| Costa Rica | 15,735 | 11,884 | 17,173 |
| Cuba | 7,625 | 2,957 | 3,955 |
| El Salvador | 9,608 | 19,155 | 13,650 |
| Germany | 43,724 | 30,174 | 25,996 |
| Guatemala | 12,949 | 11,435 | 5,294 |
| Honduras | 8,741 | 8,817 | 5,540 |
| Japan | 17,477 | 35,791 | 21,411 |
| Mexico | 20,653 | 12,947 | 13,708 |
| Netherlands | 4,476 | 3,126 | 4,615 |
| Spain | 12,257 | 2,568 | 4,902 |
| USA | 22,399 | 52,390 | 60,108 |
| **Total** (incl. others) | 325,593 | 257,746 | 227,504 |

* Imports by country of provenance; exports by country of final destination.

Source: UN, *International Trade Statistics Yearbook*.

# Transport

**RAILWAYS** (traffic)

| | 1983 | 1984 | 1985* |
|---|---|---|---|
| Passenger-km (million) | 45 | 60 | 66 |
| Freight ton-km (million) | 2 | 5 | 4 |

* Figures are provisional.

Source: UN, *Statistical Yearbook*.

**1991:** 2,100 tons carried; 0.2 million passenger journeys. Source: *Railway Directory*, 1994.

**ROAD TRAFFIC** (motor vehicles in use at 31 December)

| | 1990 | 1991 | 1992 |
|---|---|---|---|
| Cars | 39,823 | 61,385 | 67,158 |
| Buses and coaches | 3,139 | 4,368 | 5,943 |
| Goods vehicles | 30,777 | 50,406 | 63,527 |
| Motorcycles and mopeds | 12,308 | 19,501 | 22,221 |

Source: IRF, *World Road Statistics*.

**INTERNATIONAL SEA-BORNE SHIPPING**
(freight traffic, '000 metric tons)

| | 1988 | 1989 | 1990 |
|---|---|---|---|
| Goods loaded | 328 | 330 | 320 |
| Goods unloaded | 1,603 | 1,664 | 1,629 |

Source: UN, *Monthly Bulletin of Statistics*.

**CIVIL AVIATION** (traffic on scheduled services)

| | 1990 |
|---|---|
| Kilometres flown (million) | 2 |
| Passengers carried ('000) | 130 |
| Passenger-km (million) | 111 |
| Freight ton-km (million) | 4 |

Source: UN, *Statistical Yearbook*.

# Tourism

| | 1990 | 1991 | 1992 |
|---|---|---|---|
| Tourist arrivals ('000) | 106 | 146 | 167 |
| Tourist receipts (US $ million) | 12 | 16 | 21 |

Source: UN, *Statistical Yearbook*.

# NICARAGUA

## Communications Media

|  | 1990 | 1991 | 1992 |
|---|---|---|---|
| Radio receivers ('000 in use) | 962 | 997 | 1,037 |
| Television receivers ('000 in use) | 249 | 249 | 260 |
| Telephones ('000 main lines in use) | 47 | 48 | n.a. |

Daily newspapers: 3 in 1992 (average circulation 90,000 copies).
Non-daily newspapers: 8* in 1988 (average circulation 140,000* copies).
Book production: 41 titles in 1987.

* Estimate.

Source: mainly UNESCO, *Statistical Yearbook*.

## Education

(1992)

|  | Institutions | Teachers | Males | Females | Total |
|---|---|---|---|---|---|
| Pre-primary | 1,152 | 2,102 | 32,445 | 34,282 | 66,727 |
| Primary | 4,571 | 18,901 | 348,655 | 355,199 | 703,854 |
| Secondary |  |  |  |  |  |
| General | n.a. | 4,465 | 83,443 | 94,899 | 178,342 |
| Teacher training | n.a. | 86 | 613 | 1,820 | 2,433 |
| Vocational* | n.a. | 677 | 7,033 | 8,299 | 15,332 |
| Tertiary |  |  |  |  |  |
| University level† | n.a. | 2,058 | 15,380 | 15,103 | 30,483 |
| Distance-learning† | n.a. | 52 | 596 | 278 | 874 |
| Other higher† | n.a. | 20 | 14 | 128 | 142 |

* 1990 figures.   † 1991 figures.

Source: UNESCO, *Statistical Yearbook*.

# Directory

## The Constitution*

Shortly after taking office on 20 July 1979, the Government of National Reconstruction abrogated the 1974 Constitution. On 22 August 1979 the revolutionary junta issued a 'Statute on Rights and Guarantees for the Citizens of Nicaragua', providing for the basic freedoms of the individual, religious freedom and freedom of the press and abolishing the death penalty. The intention of the Statute was formally to re-establish rights which had been violated under the deposed Somoza regime. A fundamental Statute took effect from 20 July 1980 and remained in force until the Council of State drafted a political constitution and proposed an electoral law. A new Constitution was approved by the National Constituent Assembly on 19 November 1986 and promulgated on 9 January 1987. The following are some of the main points of the Constitution:

Nicaragua is an independent, free, sovereign and indivisible state. All Nicaraguans who have reached 16 years of age are full citizens.

### POLITICAL RIGHTS

There shall be absolute equality between men and women. It is the obligation of the State to remove obstacles that impede effective participation of Nicaraguans in the political, economic and social life of the country. Citizens have the right to vote and to be elected at elections and to offer themselves for public office. Citizens may organize or affiliate with political parties, with the objective of participating in, exercising or vying for power.

### SOCIAL RIGHTS

The Nicaraguan people have the right to work, to education and to culture. They have the right to decent, comfortable and safe housing, and to seek accurate information. This right comprises the freedom to seek, receive and disseminate information and ideas, both spoken and written, in graphic or any other form. The mass media are at the service of national interests. No Nicaraguan citizen may disobey the law or prevent others from exercising their rights and fulfilling their duties by invoking religious beliefs or inclinations.

### LABOUR RIGHTS

All have a right to work, and to participate in the management of their enterprises. Equal pay shall be given for equal work. The State shall strive for full and productive employment under conditions that guarantee the fundamental rights of the individual. There shall be an eight-hour working day, weekly rest, vacations, remuneration for national holidays and a bonus payment equivalent to one month's salary, in conformity with the law.

### EDUCATION

Education is an obligatory function of the State. Planning, direction and organization of the secular education system is the responsibility of the State. All Nicaraguans have free and equal access to education. Private education centres may function at all levels.

### LEGISLATIVE POWER

The Asamblea Nacional (National Assembly) exercises Legislative Power through representative popular mandate. The Asamblea Nacional is composed of 92 representatives elected by direct secret vote in regional districts, by means of a system of proportional representation. The number of representatives may be increased in accordance with the general census of the population, in conformity with the law. Representatives shall be elected for a period of six years. The functions of the Asamblea Nacional are to draft and approve laws and decrees; to decree amnesties and pardons; to consider, discuss and approve the General Budget of the Republic; to elect judges to the Supreme Court of Justice and the Supreme Electoral Council; to fill permanent vacancies for the Presidency or Vice-Presidency; and to determine the political and administrative division of the country. The Presidency of the Republic may partially or totally veto a legislative proposal within a period of 15 days following its approval by the Assembly.

### EXECUTIVE POWER

The Executive Power is exercised by the President of the Republic (assisted by the Vice-President), who is the Head of State, Head of Government and Commander-in-Chief of the Defence and Security Forces of the Nation. The election of the President (and Vice-President) is by equal, direct and free universal suffrage in secret ballot. The President shall serve for a period of six years.

### JUDICIAL POWER

The Judiciary consists of the Supreme Court of Justice, Courts of Appeal and other courts of the Republic. The Supreme Court is composed of at least seven judges, elected by the Asamblea Nacional, who shall serve for a term of six years. The functions of the Supreme Court are to organize and direct the administration of justice.

### LOCAL ADMINISTRATION

The country is divided into regions, departments and municipalities for administrative purposes. The municipal governments shall be elected by universal suffrage in secret ballot and will serve a six-year term. The communities of the Atlantic Coast have the right to live and develop in accordance with a social organization which corresponds to their historical and cultural traditions. The State shall implement, by legal means, autonomous governments in the regions inhabited by the communities of the Atlantic Coast, in order that the communities may exercise their rights.

* In February 1995 a comprehensive series of constitutional amendments was approved by the Asamblea Nacional and sub-

mitted to President Chamorro for promulgation within 15 days. However, following Chamorro's refusal to sanction the reforms, on 24 February the legislature released the document for publication, which, according to the Constitution, was sufficient to enact the amendments. Chamorro continued to contest the legitimacy of the legislature's actions until mid-June, when a resolution to the crisis was achieved by the signing of a political accord between the Government and the legislature. Under the terms of the agreement, many of the amendments intended to reduce presidential authority were to be moderated. Legislation defining the interpretation and implementation of the amendments was approved by the Asamblea Nacional in early July, thus enabling the promulgation, by Chamorro, of the amendments, which was expected to occur later that month.

The amendments included reductions in the presidential and legislative terms, from six to five years, the withdrawal of the absolute ban on presidential re-election (although consecutive terms remained prohibited), a consanguinity clause prohibiting close relatives of a serving president from contesting a presidential election, and provision for presidential elections to be conducted in two rounds, should a single candidate fail to secure the necessary 45% of the vote to win outright in the initial round. Measures were also introduced enshrining civilian authority over the depoliticized security forces and amending the title of the armed forces to remove its Sandinista affiliation (it would thenceforth be entitled the Ejército de Nicaragua—Nicaraguan Army). In addition, the number of justices of the Supreme Court was established as 12, and their term of office established as seven years.

## The Government

### HEAD OF STATE

**President:** VIOLETA BARRIOS DE CHAMORRO (took office 25 April 1990).
**Vice-President:** VIRGILIO GODOY REYES.

### CABINET
(June 1995)

**President and Minister of National Defence:** VIOLETA BARRIOS DE CHAMORRO.
**Minister of the Presidency:** Ing. ANTONIO LACAYO OYANGUREN.
**Minister of Government:** SERGIO NARVÁEZ SANTOS.
**Minister of Foreign Affairs:** Ing. ERNESTO LEAL SÁNCHEZ.
**Minister of Finance:** Dr EMILIO A. PEREIRA ALEGRÍA.
**Minister of Economy and Development:** Ing. PABLO PEREIRA GALLARDO.
**Minister of Agriculture and Livestock:** DIONISIO CUADRA KAUT.
**Minister of Construction and Transport:** PABLO VIGIL ICAZA.
**Minister of Labour:** Dr FRANCISCO ROSALES ARGÜELLO.
**Minister of Health:** Lic. MARTHA PALACIOS FERNÁNDEZ.
**Minister of Education:** Dr HUMBERTO BELLI PEREIRA.
**Minister of Foreign Co-operation:** Dr ERWIN J. KRÜGER MALTEZ.
**Minister of Social Action:** Dr WILLIAM BÁEZ SACASA.
**Minister of Tourism:** Lic. FERNANDO GUZMÁN CUADRA.
**Minister of Environment and Natural Resources:** MILTON CALDERA CARDENAL.

### MINISTRIES

**Ministry of Agriculture and Livestock:** Km 8½, Carretera a Masaya, Managua; tel. (2) 97211.
**Ministry of Construction and Transport:** Frente al Estadio Nacional, Managua; tel. (2) 82160; telex 1343; fax (2) 82161.
**Ministry of Economy and Development:** Km 6, Carretera a Masaya, Apdo 2412, Managua; tel. (2) 70176; telex 2410; fax (2) 70095.
**Ministry of Education:** Complejo Cívico Camilo Ortega Saavedra, Managua; tel. (2) 650046.
**Ministry of Environment and Natural Resources:** Km 12½, Carretera Norte, Apdo 5123, Managua; tel. (2) 63-1271; fax (2) 63-1274.
**Ministry of Finance:** Palacio de Héroes y Mártires de la Revolución, Apdo 78, Managua; tel. (2) 27231; telex 1213; fax (2) 27714.
**Ministry of Foreign Affairs:** Detrás de Los Ranchos, Managua; tel. (2) 96563.
**Ministry of Foreign Co-operation:** Apdo 4595, Managua; tel. (2) 61796; telex 1367.
**Ministry of Government:** Apdo 68, Managua; tel. (2) 25014.
**Ministry of Health:** Complejo Cívico Camilo Ortega Saavedra, Managua; tel. (2) 50039.

**Ministry of Labour:** Estadio Nacional, 400m al Norte, Apdo 487, Managua; tel. (2) 26002; fax (2) 82103.
**Ministry of National Defence:** El Chipote, Complejo Germán Pomares, Managua; tel. (2) 27261; telex 1369.
**Ministry of Social Action:** Managua.
**Ministry of Tourism:** Managua.

## President and Legislature

### PRESIDENT

**Election, 25 February 1990**

| Candidate | Votes | % of total |
|---|---|---|
| VIOLETA BARRIOS DE CHAMORRO (UNO) | 777,552 | 54.7 |
| DANIEL ORTEGA SAAVEDRA (FSLN) | 579,886 | 40.8 |
| MOISÉS HASSAN (MUR) | 16,751 | 1.1 |
| ERICK RAMÍREZ (PSC) | 11,136 | 0.7 |
| Others | n.a. | 2.7 |

### ASAMBLEA NACIONAL*
(National Assembly)

**President:** LUIS HUMBERTO GUZMÁN.

**Election, 25 February 1990**

| Party | Seats |
|---|---|
| Unión Nacional Opositora (UNO) | 51 |
| Frente Sandinista de Liberación Nacional (FSLN) | 39 |
| Movimiento de Unidad Revolucionaria (MUR) | 1 |
| Partido Social Cristiano (PSC) | 1 |
| **Total** | **92** |

* Serious political differences within the UNO (which changed its name to the Alianza Política Opositora—APO—in February 1993) led to a series of defections by parties and individuals belonging to the alliance. In late 1992 it lost its majority in the Asamblea Nacional, and by April 1994 the alliance had been reduced to just four parties, represented by as few as 12 deputies.

## Political Organizations

**Acción Nacional Conservadora (ANC):** Costado Oeste SNTV, Managua; tel. (2) 66-8755; Pres. Dr FRANK DUARTE TAPIA.

**Alianza Política Opositora (APO):** formerly Unión Nacional Opositora (UNO), name changed as above February 1993; electoral alliance, emerged from an informal group of 14 parties which, in 1987–88, engaged in national dialogue with the Sandinista Government; by April 1994 reduced to following 4 parties:

**Partido de Acción Nacional (PAN):** Managua; f. 1987; split from PSC; Leader EDUARDO RIVAS.

**Partido Comunista de Nicaragua (PCdeN):** Ciudad Jardín 0-30, Apdo 4231, Managua; tel. (2) 43750; fax (2) 23047; f. 1970; Sec.-Gen. ELI ALTAMIRANO PÉREZ.

**Partido Liberal Independiente (PLI):** Ciudad Jardín, F-29 Frente a Optica Selecta, Managua; tel. (2) 40743; f. 1944; Leader VIRGILIO GODOY REYES; Pres. Dr WILFREDO NAVARRO MOREIRA.

**Partido Nacional Conservador (PNC):** Frente Costado Sur Galería Internacional, Managua; tel. (2) 66-9979; f. 1979; Leader Dr SILVIANO MATAMOROS LACAYO; Pres. ADOLFO CALERO PORTOCARRERO.

**Alianza Popular Conservadora (APC):** Iglesia El Carmen 1½ c. al Lago, Managua; tel. (2) 62-1247; f. 1856 as Partido Conservador de Nicaragua, name changed as above 1989; Pres. FRANCISCO ANZOÁTEGUI LACAYO; Sec.-Gen. MYRIAM ARGÜELLO MORALES.

**Frente Sandinista de Liberación Nacional (FSLN)** (Sandinista National Liberation Front): Costado Oeste Parque El Carmen, Managua; tel. (2) 66-0845; telex 1251; fax (2) 66-1560; f. 1960; led by a 15-member directorate; embraces Izquierda Democrática Sandinista 'orthodox revolutionary' faction, led by DANIEL ORTEGA SAAVEDRA; 120,000 mems; Gen. Sec. DANIEL ORTEGA SAAVEDRA.

**KISAN** (Union of Nicaraguan Coastal Indians): f. 1985 to unify the campaign against the Sandinista Government by Misurasata-SICC, Misura and black creoles; directed by a seven-member committee; Leader ROGER GERMAN.

**Misatán:** f. 1984; pro-Sandinista Indian movement; Leader RUFINO LUCAS WILFRED.

**Movimiento de Acción Popular Marxista-Leninista (MAPML):** Teatro Aguerri, 1 c. Abajo, 2½ c. al Lago, Managua; tel. (2) 23787; Sec.-Gen. ISIDRO TÉLLEZ TORUÑO.

NICARAGUA — *Directory*

**Movimiento Democrático Nicaragüense (MDN):** Casa L-39, Ciudad Jardín Bnd, 50 m al Sur, Managua; tel. (2) 43898; f. 1978; Leader ROBERTO URROZ CASTILLO.

**Movimiento de Renovación Sandinista (MRS):** Managua; f. 1995; former faction of Frente Sandinista de Liberación Nacional; Leader Dr SERGIO RAMÍREZ MERCADO.

**Movimiento de Unidad Revolucionaria (MUR):** Rubenia L-9, Managua; tel. (2) 94663; non-aligned left; Leader MOISÉS HASSAN; Co-ordinator-Gen. FRANCISCO SAMPER BLANCO.

**Partido Acción Nacional (PAN):** Puente La Reynaga, 4 c. Abajo, ½ c. al Lago, Managua; tel. (2) 49-6868; Pres. Dr DUILIO BALTODANO.

**Partido Alianza Democrática Nicaragüense (PADENIC):** Clínica Santa María ½ c. al Lago, Managua; Pres. PEDRO RAFAEL MAYORGA.

**Partido Conservador de Nicaragua (PCN):** Colegio Centroamérica 500 m al Sur, Managua; tel. (2) 67-0484; f. 1992 as result of merger between Partido Conservador Demócrata (PCD) and Partido Socialconservadurismo; Pres. Dr FERNANDO AGÜERO ROCHA.

**Partido Demócrata de Confianza Nacional (PDC):** Iglesia Santa Ana 2 c. Abajo, Managua; tel (2) 41259; Pres. AUGUSTÍN JARQUÍN ANAYA.

**Partido Integracionista de la América Central (PIAC):** Cine Blanco 1 c. Arriba, 2 c. al Lago, Managua; Pres. SERGIO MENDIETA CASTILLO.

**Partido Justicia Nacional (PJN):** Managua; Pres. JORGE DÍAZ CRUZ.

**Partido Liberal Constitucionalista (PLC):** Montoya, 3 c. al Norte, Managua; tel. and fax (2) 66-0328; f. 1968; Pres. Dr ARNOLDO ALEMÁN LACAYO; Sec.-Gen. Dr LEOPOLDO NAVARRO.

**Partido Liberal Independiente de Unidad Nacional (PLIUN):** Munich, 2½ c. Arriba, Managua; tel. (2) 61672; f. 1988; splinter group of PLI; Pres. EDUARDO CORONADO PÉREZ; Sec.-Gen. CARLOS ALONSO.

**Partido Nacional Democrático (PND):** Managua; f. 1994; Leader ALFREDO CÉSAR.

**Partido Neo-Liberal (Pali):** Cine Dorado, 2 c. al Sur, 50 m Arriba, Managua; tel. (2) 66-5166; f. 1986; Pres. Dr RICARDO VEGA GARCÍA.

**Partido Resistencia Nicaragüense (PRN):** Optica Nicaragüense, 100 varas al Lago, Managua; f. 1991; tel. (2) 66-8098; Pres. JUAN ANGEL LÓPEZ ESPINOZA.

**Partido Revolucionario de los Trabajadores (PRT):** Ciudad Jardín, Farmacia de Especialidades ½ c. al Lago, Managua; tel. (2) 41386; Sec.-Gen. BONIFACIO MIRANDA.

**Partido Social Cristiano Nicaragüense (PSCN):** Ciudad Jardín, Pizza María, 1 c. al Lago, Managua; tel. (2) 22026; f. 1957; 42,000 mems; Pres. GERMÁN ALFARO OCAMPO.

**Partido Social Demócrata (PSD):** Frente al Teatro Aguerri, Managua; tel. (2) 28-1277; f. 1979; Pres. ADOLFO JARQUÍN ORTEL; Sec.-Gen. Dr JOSÉ PALLAIS ARANA.

**Partido Socialista Nicaragüense (PSN):** Hospital Militar, 100 m al Norte, 100 m al Oeste, 100 m al Sur, Managua; tel. (2) 66-2321; fax (2) 66-2936; f. 1944; social democratic party; Sec.-Gen. Dr GUSTAVO TABLADA ZELAYA.

**Partido Unidad Nicaragüense Obreros, Campesinos y Profesionales (PUNOCP):** Cine Dario, 1½ al Lago, Managua; Pres. HEBERTO MAYORGA.

**Partido Unionista Centroamericano (PUCA):** Costado Oeste Hotel Intercontinental, 2 c. al Norte, Managua; tel. (2) 27472; f. 1904; Sec.-Gen. BLANCA ROJAS ECHAVERRY.

**Unión Demócrata Cristiana (UDC):** De Iglesia Santa Ana, 2 c. Abajo, Barrio Santa Ana, Apdo 3089, Managua; tel. (2) 66-2576; f. 1976 as Partido Popular Social Cristiano; name officially changed as above December 1993; Pres. Dr LUIS HUMBERTO GUZMÁN; Political Sec. Dr PEDRO ARCEDA PICADO.

## Diplomatic Representation

### EMBASSIES IN NICARAGUA

**Argentina:** Reparto Lomas de Guadalupe, Carretera a Masaya, 1 c. Abajo, 2 c. al Lago y ½ c. Arriba, Apdo 703, Managua; tel. (2) 784824; telex 2321; fax (2) 678406; Ambassador: VÍCTOR FÉLIX REVIOLIO.

**Brazil:** Km 7¾, Carretera Sur, Quinta los Pinos, Apdo 264, Managua; tel. (2) 50035; telex 1237; Ambassador: SERGIO DE QUEIROZ DUARTE.

**Bulgaria:** Reparto Las Colinas, Calle Los Mangos 195, Managua; Ambassador: KIRIL ZLATKOV NIKOLOV.

**Cambodia:** Managua; Ambassador: LONG VISALO.

**Chile:** Km 13.8, Carretera Sur, 200 m a Mano Izquierda, Apdo 1704, Managua; Chargé d'affaires a.i.: EDUARDO VEGA BEZANILLA.

**China, People's Republic:** Managua; Ambassador: HUANG ZHILIANG.

**Colombia:** Reparto Los Robles, Apdo 1062, Managua; tel. (2) 70247; Ambassador: ABELARDO DUARTE.

**Costa Rica:** Centro Comercial Camino de Oriente, Contiguo a AERONICA, Managua; Ambassador: JESÚS MANUEL FERNÁNDEZ.

**Cuba:** Carretera a Masaya, 3a Entrada a las Colinas, Managua; tel. (2) 71182; telex 2107; fax (2) 76-0166; Ambassador: JULIÁN LÓPEZ DÍAZ.

**Czech Republic:** Managua; Ambassador: GUSTAV STOPKA.

**Dominican Republic:** Reparto Las Colinas, Prado Ecuestre 100, con Curva de los Gallos, Apdo 614, Managua; Ambassador: MIGUEL ANGEL DECAMPS.

**Ecuador:** Plaza España, 1½ c. al Oeste, Apdo C-33, Managua; tel. (2) 66-1097; telex 2047; fax (2) 66-8081; Chargé d'affaires: CARLOS LÓPEZ DAMM.

**El Salvador:** Reparto Las Colinas, Avda Las Colinas y Pasaje Los Cerros, Apdo 149, Managua; Chargé d'affaires a.i.: JOAQUÍN MAZA MARTELLI.

**France:** Km 13½, Carretera del Sur, Apdo 1227, Managua; tel. (2) 22-6210; telex 1047; fax 28-1056; Ambassador: GEORGES VAUGIER.

**Germany:** Plaza España, 1½ c. al Lago, Contiguo a la Optica Nicaragüense, Apdo 29, Managua; tel. (2) 66-3917; telex 1070; fax (2) 66-7667; Ambassador: Dr HELMUT SCHÖPS.

**Guatemala:** Km 11½, Carretera a Masaya, Apdo E-1, Managua; tel. (2) 79609; fax (2) 79610; Ambassador BERNA ROLANDO MÉNDEZ MORA.

**Holy See:** Km 10 y 800 m Carretera Sur, Entrada a Quinta Tirrenia, Apdo 506, Managua (Apostolic Nunciature); tel. (2) 65-8052; fax (2) 65-7416; Apostolic Nuncio: Most Rev. PAOLO GIGLIO, Titular Archbishop of Tyndaris.

**Honduras:** Km 7½, Carretera Sur, Reparto Barcelona, Apdo 321, Managua; Ambassador: HERMINIO PINEDA.

**Iran:** Calle Vista Alegre 93, Las Colinas, Managua; Ambassador: (vacant).

**Italy:** Avda del Guerrillero, Estatua Montoya, 1 c. al Lago, Apdo 2092, Managua 4; tel. (2) 66-2961; telex 1437; fax (2) 66-3987; Ambassador: Dr TIBOR HOOR TEMPIS LIVI.

**Japan:** Del Portón del Hospital Militar, 1 c. al Lago y 1½ c. Abajo, Mano Izquierda, Bolonia, Apdo 1789, Managua; tel. (2) 62-3092; telex 1080; fax (2) 62-7393; Ambassador: YOSHIZO KONISHI.

**Libya:** Mansión Teodolinda, 6 c. al Sur, ½ c. Abajo, Managua; Secretary of the People's Bureau: IBRAHIM MOHAMED FARHAT.

**Mexico:** Frente Oficinas Telcor de Altamira, Km 4½ Carretera a Masaya, Apdo 834, Managua; tel. (2) 78-1859; telex 2241; fax (2) 78-2886; Ambassador: EDGARDO FLORES RIVAS.

**Mongolia:** Managua; Ambassador: G. DASHDAAVA.

**Panama:** Reparto San Juan, Calle El Carmen 619, Managua; Ambassador: BALTAZAR AIZPURNA.

**Peru:** Frente a Procuraduría General de Justicia, Bolonia, Apdo 211, Managua; tel. (2) 22376; telex 2100; fax (2) 22381; Ambassador: MANUEL BOZA HECK.

**Russia:** Reparto Las Colinas, Calle Vista Alegre 214, Entre Avda Central y Paseo del Club, Managua; tel. (2) 76-0374; telex 2436; fax (2) 76-0179; Ambassador: YEVGENI M. ASTAKHOV.

**Spain:** Avda Central 13, Las Colinas, Apdo 284, Managua; tel. (2) 74142; telex 2003; fax (2) 67-8153; Ambassador: MIGUEL ANGEL FERNÁNDEZ MAZARAMBROZ.

**Sweden:** De la Sub-Estación de Telcor, Las Palmas, 50 m al Sur, a Mano Derecha, Casa 2601, Apdo 2307, Managua; Ambassador: GÖTE MAGNUSSON.

**United Kingdom:** 1 Plaza Churchill, Reparto Los Robles, Apdo A-169, Managua; tel. (2) 78-0014; fax (2) 78-4085; Ambassador: JOHN CULVER.

**USA:** Km 4½, Carretera Sur, Apdo 327, Managua; tel. (2) 66-6010; Ambassador: HARRY SCHLAUDEMANN.

**Uruguay:** Del Portón del Hospital Militar, 1 c. al Lago, 1½ Abajo, Apdo 3746, Managua; tel. (2) 25542; telex 1348; Ambassador: ALFREDO LAFONE.

**Venezuela:** Edif. Málaga, 2°, Plaza España, Módulo A-13, Apdo 406, Managua; telex 1380; Ambassador: LUIS RAFAEL ZAPATA LUIGI.

**Viet Nam:** Zona Residencial Planetarium, Paseo Saturno, Casa CS 10, esq. Vía Láctea, Managua; Ambassador: LE DUC CANG.

**Yugoslavia:** Apdo 3463, Managua; tel. (2) 72847; Ambassador: DUŠAN TRIFUNOVIĆ.

## Judicial System

**The Supreme Court:** Ciudad Jardín, Managua; tel. (2) 43562; deals with both civil and criminal cases, acts as a Court of Cas-

NICARAGUA

sation, appoints Judges of First Instance, and generally supervises the legal administration of the country.
**President:** Dr ORLANDO TREJOS SOMARRIBA.

## Religion

All religions are tolerated. Almost all of Nicaragua's inhabitants profess Christianity, and the great majority belong to the Roman Catholic Church, which had 4.0m. adherents in 1992 (some 89% of the total population). The Moravian Church predominates on the Caribbean coast.

### CHRISTIANITY
#### The Roman Catholic Church

Nicaragua comprises one archdiocese, six dioceses and the Apostolic Vicariate of Bluefields.

**Bishops' Conference:** Conferencia Episcopal de Nicaragua, Ferretería Lang, Zona 3, Las Piedrecitas, Apdo 2407, Managua; tel. (2) 66-6292; fax (2) 66-8069; f. 1975; Pres. Cardinal MIGUEL OBANDO Y BRAVO, Archbishop of Managua.

**Archbishop of Managua:** Cardinal MIGUEL OBANDO Y BRAVO, Arzobispado, Apdo 3058, Managua; tel. (2) 71174; fax (2) 67-0130.

#### The Anglican Communion

Nicaragua comprises a single missionary diocese of Province IX of the Episcopal Church in the USA.

**Bishop of Nicaragua:** Rt Rev. STURDIE W. DOWNS, Apdo 1207, Managua; tel. (2) 25174.

#### The Baptist Church

**Baptist Convention of Nicaragua:** Apdo 2593, Managua; tel. (2) 25785; fax (2) 24131; f. 1917; 35,000 mems (1988); Pres. Rev. ELÍAS SÁNCHEZ; Gen. Sec. TOMÁS H. TÉLLEZ.

## The Press

### NEWSPAPERS AND PERIODICALS

**Acción:** Managua; official publication of the Partido Social Demócrata.

**Alternativa Liberal:** Managua; f. 1984; official publication of the Partido Liberal Independiente.

**Avance:** Ciudad Jardín 0-30, Apdo 4231, Managua; tel. (2) 43750; f. 1972; weekly publication of the Partido Comunista de Nicaragua; circ. 10,000.

**Barricada:** Camino del Oriente, Apdo 576, Managua; tel. (2) 24291; f. 1979; evening; also publ. in English; Exec. Dir LUMBERTO CAMPBELL; circ. 95,000.

**El Centroamericano:** 4a Calle Norte, Apdo 52, León; f. 1917; evening; independent; Dir R. ABAUNZA SALINAS; circ. 3,500.

**La Crónica:** Managua; f. 1988; weekly; independent; Dir LUIS HUMBERTO GUZMÁN.

**Diario El Pueblo:** Apdo 2346, Managua; tel. (2) 23480; f. 1979; daily; owned by a co-operative; Dir CARLOS CUADRA; circ. 7,000.

**La Gaceta, Diario Oficial:** Avda Central Sur 604, Managua; f. 1912; morning; official.

**La Información:** León; weekly.

**La Nación Nicaragüense:** Camino de Oriente, Managua; weekly.

**Novedades:** Pista P. Joaquín Chamorro, Km 4, Carretera Norte, Apdo 576, Managua; daily; evening.

**Nuevo Diario:** Pista P. Joaquín Chamorro, Km 4, Carretera Norte, Apdo 4591, Managua; f. 1980; daily; independent; Editor XAVIER CHAMORRO CARDENAL; circ. 45,000.

**El Observador:** Apdo 1482, Managua; weekly.

**Paso a Paso:** Managua; weekly; Dir JOAQUÍN MEJÍA.

**Poder Sandinista:** Managua; f. 1980; weekly.

**El Popular:** Managua; monthly; official publication of the Partido Socialista Nicaragüense.

**La Prensa:** Km 4½, Carretera Norte, Apdo 192, Managua; tel. (2) 40139; telex 2051; f. 1926; evening; independent; Dirs VIOLETA BARRIOS DE CHAMORRO, JAIME CHAMORRO; Editor PABLO ANTONIO CUADRA; circ. 75,000 daily.

**Prensa Proletaria:** Managua; fortnightly; official publication of the Movimiento de Acción Popular Marxista-Leninista.

**El Reportero:** Managua; resumed publication Jan. 1988; Editor ARILO MEJÍA.

**Revista del Pensamiento Centroamericano:** Apdo 2108, Managua; quarterly; centre-left; Editor XAVIER ZAVALA CUADRA.

*Directory*

**La Semana Cómica:** Centro Comercial Bello Horizonte, Módulos 7 y 9, Apdo SV-3, Managua; tel. (2) 44909; f. 1980; weekly; Dir RÓGER SÁNCHEZ; circ. 45,000.

**El Socialista:** Managua; fortnightly; official publication of the Partido Revolucionario de los Trabajadores.

### Association

**Unión de Periodistas de Nicaragua (UPN):** Apdo 4006, Managua; Leader LILLY SOTO VÁSQUEZ.

### NEWS AGENCIES

**Agencia Nicaragüense de Noticias (ANN):** Managua; Dir-Gen. ROBERTO GARCÍA.

#### Foreign Bureaux

**Agencia EFE** (Spain): Ciudad Jardín S-22, Apdo 1951, Managua; tel. (2) 24928; Bureau Chief FILADELFO MARTÍNEZ FLORES.

**Agenzia Nazionale Stampa Associata (ANSA)** (Italy): c/o La Prensa, Km 4½, Carretera Norte, Apdo 192, Managua; tel. (2) 40139; telex 2051; Correspondent MARCIO VARGAS.

**Deutsche Presse-Agentur (dpa)** (Germany): Apdo 2095, Managua; tel. (2) 78-1862; telex 1928; fax (2) 78-1863; Correspondent JOSÉ ESTEBAN QUEZADA.

**Informatsionnoye Telegrafnoye Agentstvo Rossii—Telegrafnoye Agentstvo Suverennykh Stran (ITAR—TASS)** (Russia): Col. Los Robles, Casa 17, Managua; Correspondent ALEKSANDR TRUSHIN.

**Inter Press Service (IPS)** (Italy): Residencia El Dorado, Casa 337, Clínica San Rafael, 2½ c. al Lago, Managua; tel. (2) 42933; Correspondent FELIPE JAIME.

**Prensa Latina** (Cuba): De los Semáforos del Portón de Telcor de Villa Fontana, 25 m al Este, 2 c. al Lago, Casa 280, Managua; tel. (2) 72697; telex 2385; Correspondent MARIO MAINADE MARTÍNEZ.

**Reuters** (United Kingdom): Apdo A-150, Managua; tel. (2) 27070; telex 2111; Correspondent M. CAMPBELL.

**United Press International (UPI)** (USA): Reparto Serrano 1166, Managua; tel. (2) 24192; Bureau Chief DOUGLAS TWEEDALE.

**Xinhua (New China) News Agency** (People's Republic of China): De Policlínica Nicaragüense, 80 m al Sur, Apdo 5899, Managua; tel. (2) 62155; telex 1205; Bureau Chief LIU RIUCHANG.

## Publishers

**Academia Nicaragüense de la Lengua:** Calle Central, Reparto Las Colinas, Apdo 2711, Managua; f. 1928; languages; Dir PABLO ANTONIO CUADRA; Sec. JULIO YCAZA TIGERINO.

**Editora de Publicaciones, SA (EDIPSA):** Detrás Edif. Corporación Industrial del Pueblo, Pista de la Resistencia Sur, Managua.

**Editorial Alemana, SA:** Centro Comercial, Módulo B 30, Km 18½, Carretera a Masaya, Apdo E-10, Managua.

**Editorial América, SA:** Ciudad Jardín K-24, Frente al Juzgado, Managua.

**Editorial Artes Gráficas:** Managua.

**Editorial El Socorro:** Cine Aguerri, 1 c. Abajo, 2½ c. al Lago, No 618, Managua.

**Editorial Flórez:** Centro Taller Las Palmas, 75 m al Norte, Managua; Dir JOSÉ MARÍA FLÓREZ MORALES.

**Editorial Impresora Comercial:** Julio C. Orozco L., 9 C.S.E. Entre 27a y 28a Avda, Apdo 10-11, Managua; tel. (2) 42258; art.

**Editorial José Martí:** De donde fue Bunge, 2 c. al Lago, Managua.

**Editorial Lacayo:** 2a Avda Sur Este 507, Managua; religion.

**Editorial Nueva Nicaragua:** Paseo Salvador Allende, Km 3½, Carretera Sur, Apdo 073, Managua; telex 1033; fax (2) 66-6520; f. 1981; Pres. Dr SERGIO RAMÍREZ MERCADO; Dir-Gen. ROBERTO DÍAZ CASTILLO.

**Editorial Rodríguez:** Iglesia Santa Faz, 1½ c. Abajo, B. Costa Rica, Apdo 4702, Managua.

**Editorial San José:** Calle Central Este 607, Managua.

**Editorial Unión:** Avda Central Norte, Managua; travel.

**Editorial Universitaria Centroamérica:** Col. Centroamérica K-752, Managua.

**Editorial Vilma Morales M.:** Academia Militar David Tejada, 2 c. Abajo y ½ c. al Lago, Bello Horizonte K-1-19.

**Librería y Editorial, Universidad Nacional de Nicaragua:** León; tel. (2) 2612; education, history, sciences, law, literature, politics.

## Radio and Television

In 1992, according to UNESCO, there were an estimated 1,037,000 radio receivers and 260,000 television receivers in use.

NICARAGUA

**Dirección de Telecomunicaciones (Telcor):** Apdo 2264, Managua; government supervisory body; Dir ROLANDO RIVAS.

### RADIO

**Radio Católica:** Altamira D'Este 621, 3°, Apdo 2183, Managua; tel. (2) 78-0836; fax (2) 78-2544; f. 1961; controlled by Conferencia Episcopal de Nicaragua; Dir Fr JOSÉ BISMARCK CARBALLO.

**Radio Corporación:** Ciudad Jardín Q-23, Apdo 2442, Managua; tel. (2) 49-0289; Dir JOSÉ CASTILLOS OSEJO.

**Radio Minuto:** Ciudad Jardín, Q-20, Apdo 2442, Managua; tel. (2) 40869; Dir CARLOS GADEA MANTILLA.

**Radio Mundial:** 36 Avda Oeste, Reparto Loma Verde, Apdo 3170, Managua; tel. (2) 66-0402; commercial; Dir MANUEL ARANA VALLE.

**Radio Nicaragua:** Villa Fontana, Contiguo a Telcor, Apdo 4665, Managua; tel. (2) 67-3630; fax (2) 67-1448; f. 1979; government station; Dir-Gen. ADOLFO PASTRÁN ARANCIBIA.

**Radio Noticias:** Colonial Robles 92, 4°, Apdo A-150, Managua; tel. (2) 49-5914; fax (2) 49-6393; Dir AGUSTÍN FUENTES SEQUEIRA.

**Radio Ondas de Luz:** Costado Sur del Hospital Bautista, Apdo 607, Managua; tel. (2) 23140; fax (2) 22755; f. 1959; religious and cultural station; Dir RONALD GONZÁLEZ H.; Gen. Man. JUAN A. RÍOS REYES.

**Radio Reloj:** Ciudad Jardín, Casa I-1, Contiguo a la Iglesia Asunción de María, Apdo 2839, Managua; tel. (2) 24960; Dir FRANCISCO RODRÍGUEZ TÉLLEZ.

**Radio Sandino:** Paseo Tiscapa Este, Contiguo al Restaurante Mirador, Apdo 4776, Managua; tel. (2) 28-1330; telex 1241; fax (2) 62-4052; f. 1977; station controlled by the Frente Sandinista de Liberación Nacional; Dir CONRADO PINEDA AGUILAR.

There are 45 other radio stations.

### TELEVISION

**Sistema Nacional de Televisión (SNTV):** Km 3½, Carretera Sur, Contiguo a Shell, Las Palmas, Apdo 1505, Managua; tel. (2) 66-0879; telex 1226; fax (2) 66-2411; Dir-Gen. MIGUEL SCHIEBEL.

## Finance

(cap. = capital; p.u. = paid up; res = reserves; dep. = deposits; m. = million; amounts in córdobas unless otherwise stated)

### BANKING

All Nicaraguan banks were nationalized in July 1979. Foreign banks operating in the country are no longer permitted to secure local deposits. All foreign exchange transactions must be made through the Banco Central or its agencies. Under a decree issued in May 1985, the establishment of private exchange houses was permitted. In 1990 legislation allowing for the establishment of private banks was enacted.

#### Supervisory Authority

**Superintendencia de Bancos y de Otras Instituciones Financieras:** Edif. 17, 4°, Plaza España, Apdo 788, Managua; tel. (2) 66-8215; fax (2) 66-8301; f. 1991; Superintendent ANGEL NAVARRO DESHON.

#### Central Bank

**Banco Central de Nicaragua:** Carretera Sur, Km 7, Apdos 2252/3, Zona 5, Managua; tel. (2) 65-0500; telex 2460; fax (2) 65-2272; f. 1961; bank of issue and Government fiscal agent; cap. 18.1m., dep. 1,353.5m. (Aug. 1994); Pres. JOSÉ EVENOR TABOADA ARANA; Man., International JOSÉ MÁRQUEZ CEAS.

#### State Banks

**Banco de América (BAMER):** Avda Sandino y 4a Calle Sur Este, Apdo 285, Managua; tel. (2) 26100; telex 1040; f. 1952; nationalized 1979; cap. 42.5m., dep. 288.6m. (Sept. 1982); Exec. Dir Lic. ANTONIO MEDRANO B.; 47 brs.

**Banco Inmobilario (BIN):** Calle Principal, Col. Centroamérica, Apdo 1162, Managua; f. 1980; savings bank and housing funding; cap. 20m., dep. 1,034m.; Exec. Dir ALFREDO BUSTOS LÓPEZ; 19 brs.

**Banco Nacional de Desarrollo (BANADES):** Km 3½, Carretera a Masaya, Apdo 328, Managua; tel. (2) 67-1771; telex 2078; fax (2) 67-4222; f. 1912; cap. and res US $15.8m., dep. $68.2m. (Dec. 1993); Pres. JUAN ALVARO MUNGUIA; Gen. Man. LUIS ANGEL MONTENEGRO ESPINOZA; 64 brs.

**Banco Nicaragüense de Industria y Comercio (BANIC):** Edif. Oscar Pérez Cassar, Km 5½, Carretera a Masaya, Apdo 549, Managua; tel. (2) 67-2730; telex 2456; fax (2) 67-1356; f. 1953; cap. and res US $87,180, dep. $48.3m. (Dec. 1990); Exec. Dir Lic. ANTONIO MEDRANO; 30 brs.

**Banco de Crédito Popular (BCP):** Centro Comercial Nejapa, Apdo 3904, Managua; tel. (2) 66-6614; telex 22238; fax (2) 65-1337; f. 1972 as an autonomous state institution; it specializes in small enterprises, but also provides loans to medium and large enterprises; cap. 51.4m., dep. 143.8m. (Sept. 1982); Exec. Dir JOSÉ ALBERTO NAVARRO RODRÍGUEZ; 19 brs.

#### Private Banks

**Banco de América Central (BAC):** Costado Norte de Lotería Popular, Contiguo a Cámara de Comercio de Nicaragua, Managua; tel. (2) 67-0220; f. 1991; Man. CARLOS MATUS.

**Banco del Campo, SA (BANCAMPO):** Edif. Interplaza, Plaza El Sol, 100 varas Arriba, Apdo 3719, Managua; tel. (2) 78-1236; telex 2002; fax (2) 78-1242; f. 1994; cap. US $2.1m. (Aug. 1994); Man. LUIS MORALES U.

**Banco de Crédito Centroamericano (BANCENTRO):** Edif. BANCENTRO, Km 4½, Carretera a Masaya, Managua; Gen. Man. EDUARDO MONTEALEGRE R.

**Banco Europeo de América Central:** Managua.

**Banco de la Exportación (BANEXPO):** Edif. BANEXPO, Centro Comercial Metrocentro, Managua; tel. (2) 73101; Man. GILBERTO WONG.

**Banco Mercantil, SA (BAMER):** Plaza Banco Mercantil, Managua; tel. (2) 66-8228; telex 1025; fax (2) 66-8024; f. 1991; Pres. HAROLDO J. MONTEALEGRE; Gen. Man. OSCAR MARTÍN AGUADO A.; 6 brs.

**Banco de Préstamos (BANPRES):** Esq. Opuesta, Hotel Intercontinental, Managua; tel. (2) 62-3046; Man. NERVO BERMEO C.

**Banco de la Producción, SA (PANPRO):** Plaza Libertad, Frente a Plaza El Sol, Managua; tel. (2) 78-2508; f. 1991; Man. ARTURO ARANA.

**INTERBANK:** Frente a Lotería Nacional, Managua; tel. (2) 78-5959; Man. JAIME VALDIVIA.

#### Foreign Banks

**Bank of America NT & SA** (USA): Edif. Kodak, Plaza de Compras, Col. Centroamérica, Apdo 2469, Managua; tel. (2) 26561; f. 1964; cap. 10m., dep. 1,140m.; Man. ORLANDO PASOS; 1 br.

**Citibank NA** (USA): Km 3½, Carretera a Masaya, 75 m Arriba, Apdo 3102, Managua; tel. (2) 72124; telex 2009; f. 1967; cap. 10.5m., dep. 33.1m. (Oct. 1980); Man. ENRIQUE ALANIZ D.; 1 br.

**Lloyds Bank (Bank of London and South America) Ltd** (United Kingdom): Plaza de Compras, Col. Centroamérica, Apdo 91, Managua; tel. (2) 74603; telex 2207; f. 1958; cap. 14.6m., dep. 9.5m. (Sept. 1980); Man. ROBERT LOGAN.

### STOCK EXCHANGE

**Bolsa Nacional de Valores:** Edif. Oscar Pérez Cassar, Centro BANIC, Km 5½, Carretera a Masaya, Managua; f. 1994.

### INSURANCE

#### State Company

**Instituto Nicaragüense de Seguros y Reaseguros (INISER):** Centro Comercial Camino de Oriente, Km 6, Carretera a Masaya, Apdo 1147, Managua; tel. (2) 72-2772; telex 2045; fax (2) 67-2121; f. 1979 to assume the activities of all the pre-revolution national private insurance companies; Exec. Pres. CARLOS ARTURO HARDING LACAYO.

#### Foreign Companies

**American Life Insurance Company:** Metrocentro Módulo 7, Apdo 601, Managua; tel. (2) 73356; Admin. Man. DOLORES LEZAMA.

**British American Insurance Co.:** Altamira D'Este 360, Apdo A-56, Managua; Gen. Man. CECIL E. GILL.

**Citizens Standard Life Insurance Co.:** Iglesia El Carmen, 2 c. al Lago, ½ c. Abajo, No 1410, Apdo 3199, Managua; Man. YAGALÍ RIVAS ALEGRÍA.

**Pan American Life Insurance Co.:** Edif. Kodak, Plaza de Compras, Col. Centroamérica, Managua; Man. ALEJANDRO LEIVA CABEZAS.

## Trade and Industry

### CHAMBERS OF COMMERCE

**Cámara de Comercio de Nicaragua:** Frente a Lotería Nacional, Contiguo al Banco de América Central, Apdo 135, Managua; tel. (2) 67-0718; fax (2) 78-0820; f. 1892; 530 mems; Pres. ROBERTO TERÁN B.; Gen. Man. ROGER A. CERDA.

**Cámara de Comercio Americana de Nicaragua:** Transfer UNAN 500 m al Sur, Apdo 2720, Managua; tel. (2) 67-3099; fax (2) 67-3098; f. 1974; Pres. LUCÍA SALVO H.

**Cámara Oficial Española de Comercio de Nicaragua:** Hotel Intercontinental, 2 c. Abajo, 1½ c. al Sur, Casa 1004, Apdo 4103,

# NICARAGUA

Managua; tel. (2) 24044; telex 1396; fax (2) 27916; Pres. RAMÓN HERNÁNDEZ ULLAN.

## INDUSTRIAL AND DEVELOPMENT ORGANIZATIONS

**Asociación Nicaragüense de Productores y Exportadores de Productos No Tradicionales (APPEN):** Del Hotel Intercontinental, 2 c. al Sur y 2 c. Abajo, Bolonia, Managua; tel. (2) 66-5038; fax (2) 66-5039; Pres. SAMUEL MANSELL.

**Cámara de Industria de Nicaragua:** Antiguo Edif. TURNICA, Semáforos de Plaza España, 300 m al Sur, Managua; tel. (2) 66-1891; Pres. ALBERTO CHAMORRO.

**Cámara Nacional de la Mediana y Pequeña Industria (CONAPI):** Plaza 19 de Julio, Frente a la UCA, Apdo 153, Managua; tel. (2) 78-4892; fax (2) 67-0192; Pres. ANTONIO CHÁVEZ JIMÉNEZ.

**Cámara Nicaragüense de la Construcción (CNC):** 2° Callejón, Col. Mántica, Casa 239, Apdo 3016, Managua; tel. (2) 62-2071; f. 1961; construction industry; Pres. Ing. PABLO VIGIL.; Exec. Sec. Lic. FELIPE LAU G.

**Dirección General de Promoción de Exportaciones:** Km 6, Carretera a Masaya, Apdo 8, Managua; tel. (2) 67-0150; fax (2) 67-0095; promotion of non-traditional exports, responsible to Ministry of Economy and Development; Dir-Gen. Lic. ALEJANDRO CARRIÓN M.

**Instituto Nicaragüense de Acueductos y Alcantarillados (INAA):** Km 5, Carretera Sur, Avda Sur Oeste 35, Apdo 3599 y 968, Managua; tel. (2) 66-7873; telex 2144; fax (2) 66-7872; f. 1979; water and sewerage; Dir GUSTAVO MARTÍNEZ MONTOYA.

**Instituto Nicaragüense de Energía (INE):** Ofs Centrales, Pista de la Resistencia, Managua; tel. (2) 67-4380; telex 2344; fax (2) 67-2686; f. 1979; national energy institute, responsible for planning, organization, management, administration, research and development of energy resources; Min.-Dir EMILIO RAPPACCIOLI BALTODANO.

**Instituto Nicaragüense de Fomento Municipal:** Managua; Pres. Ing. SANTIAGO RIVAS LECLAIR.

**Instituto Nicaragüense de Minas (INMINE):** Pista de la Resistencia, Antiguo Centro Comercial El Punto, Contiguo a Migración y Extranjera, Apdo 195, Managua; tel. (2) 65-2073; telex 2146; fax (2) 51043; f. 1979; mines and hydrocarbons; Dir IVAN ORTEGA.

**Instituto Nicaragüense de Reforma Agraria (INRA):** Km 8, Entrada a Sierrita Santo Domingo, Managua; tel. (2) 73210; agrarian reform; Dir BOANERGES MATUS LASSO.

**Instituto Nicaragüense de Seguridad Social y Bienestar (INSSBI):** Apdo 1649, Managua; tel. (2) 49-2981; fax (2) 49-0418; f. 1956; social security and welfare; Pres. Dr SIMEÓN RIZO CASTELLÓN.

**MEDEPESCA:** Km 6½, Carretera Sur, Managua; tel. (2) 67-3490; state fishing agency; Dir Ing. EMILIO OLIVARES.

## STATE TRADING CORPORATIONS

**Empresa Nicaragüense del Algodón (ENAL):** Km 4½, Carretera a Masaya, Apdo 3684, Managua; tel. (2) 67-2751; telex 2216; fax (2) 67-0758; f. 1979; controls cotton trading; Dir JUAN CARRIÓN CALERO.

**Empresa Nicaragüense de Alimentos Básicos (ENABAS):** Salida a Carretera Norte, Apdo 1041, Managua; tel. (2) 23082; telex 1314; fax (2) 26185; f. 1979; controls trading in basic foodstuffs; Dir Lic. IGNACIO VÉLEZ LACAYO.

**Empresa Nicaragüense del Azúcar (ENAZUCAR):** Ministerio de Defensa Nacional, El Chipote, Complejo Germán Pomares, Managua; tel. (2) 27261; telex 1369; f. 1979; controls sugar trading; Dir NOEL CHAMORRO CUADRA.

**Empresa Nicaragüense del Banano (BANANIC):** Edif. Málaga, Plaza España, Apdo 3433, Managua; tel. (2) 678311; telex 2304; fax (2) 73633; f. 1979; controls banana trading; Dir EDUARDO HOLMANN.

**Empresa Nicaragüense del Café (ENCAFE):** Plaza de Compras, Contiguo al Banco de Londres (Lloyds Bank), Col. Centroamérica, Apdo 2482, Managua; tel. (2) 70337; telex 2336; fax (2) 67-2604; f. 1979; controls coffee trading; Dir Dr ARMANDO JARQUÍN SEQUIERA.

**Empresa Nicaragüense de la Carne (ENCAR):** Frente al Edif. Pérez Cassar, Apdo C-11, Managua; tel. (2) 70519; telex 2033; fax (2) 70621; f. 1979; controls trading and export of meat and meat products; Exec. Dir ORLANDO N. BONILLA.

**Empresa Nicaragüense de Insumos Agropecuarios (ENIA):** Distribuidora Vicky, 2 c. Oeste, Apdo C-11, Managua; tel. (2) 71224; telex 2301; f. 1979; agricultural investment goods board; f. 1979; Dir EDUARDO FONSECA FÁBREGAS.

**Empresa Nicaragüense de Productos del Mar (ENMAR):** Frente al Cine Aguerri, Apdo 356, Managua; tel. (2) 23572; telex 1009; f. 1979; controls trading in all seafood products; Dir FRANKLIN MENDIETA MEDINA.

## CO-OPERATIVES

**Cooperativa de Algodoneros de Managua, RL:** Km 3½, Carretera Norte, Apdo 483, Managua; tel. (2) 4515; cotton-growers; Pres. Ing. GUILLERMO LACAYO; Sec. Ing. CARLOS ORTEGA M.

**Cooperativa de Mercadeo de los Artesanos del Calzado:** Managua; tel. (2) 4196; shoemakers and leatherworkers; Dir FÉLIX LECHADO CASTRILLO.

**Empresa Cooperativa de Productores Agropecuarios:** Managua; represents 13,000 members from 48 affiliated co-operatives; Chair. DANIEL NÚÑEZ.

## EMPLOYERS' ORGANIZATIONS

**Asociación de Productores de Café Nicaragüenses:** coffee producers; Pres. Dr NICOLÁS BOLAÑOS.

**Consejo Superior de la Empresa Privada (COSEP):** De Telcor Zacarías Guerra, 1 c. Abajo, Apdo 5430, Managua; tel. (2) 62-2030; fax (2) 62-2041; private businesses; consists of Cámara de Industrias de Nicaragua (CADIN), Unión de Productores Agropecuarios de Nicaragua (UPANIC), Cámara de Comercio, Cámara de la Construcción, Confederación Nacional de Profesionales (CONAPRO), Instituto Nicaragüense de Desarrollo (INDE); mem. of Coordinadora Democrática Nicaragüense; Pres. GILBERTO CUADRA S.; Sec. ORESTES ROMERO ROJAS.

**Instituto Nicaragüense de Desarrollo (INDE):** Ofs de Montoya, 1 c. al Norte, ½ c. al Oeste, Apdo 2598, Managua; tel. (2) 24047; f. 1963; organization of private businessmen; 650 mems; Pres. Ing. GILBERTO CUADRA; Exec. Sec. CARLOS ANTONIO NOGUERA P.

**Unión de Productores Agropecuarios de Nicaragua (UPANIC):** Los Robles, Galería 3 Mundos, 1 c. Abajo, ½ c. al Sur, Casa 300, Apdo 2351, Managua; tel. (2) 78-2586; fax (2) 78-3382; private agriculturalists' association; Pres. GERARDO SALINAS CASTRILLO; Exec. Sec. ROSENDO DÍAZ.

## TRADE UNIONS

**Asociación de Trabajadores del Campo—ATC** (Association of Rural Workers): Apdo A-244, Managua; tel. (2) 23221; f. 1977; Gen. Sec. EDGARDO GARCÍA; 52,000 mems.

**Central de Trabajadores Nicaragüenses—CTN** (Nicaraguan Workers' Congress): Iglesia Santa Ana, 1½ c. al Occidente, Managua; tel. (2) 25981; f. 1962; mem. of Coordinadora Democrática Nicaragüense; Leader CARLOS HUENDES; Sec.-Gen. ANTONIO JARQUÍN.

**Confederación General de Trabajo (Independiente)—CGT(I)** (Independent General Confederation of Labour): Calle 11 de Julio, Managua; f. 1953; Sec.-Gen. CARLOS SALGADO MEMBRENO; 4,843 mems (est.) from six federations with 40 local unions, and six non-federated local unions.

**Confederación de Unificación Sindical—CUS** (Confederation of United Trade Unions): Apdo 4845, Managua; tel. (2) 42039; f. 1972; affiliated to the Inter-American Regional Organization of Workers, etc.; mem. of Coordinadora Democrática Nicaragüense; Leader ALVIN GUTHRIE RIVEZ; Sec. SANTOS TIJERINO.

**Congreso Permanente de los Trabajadores—CPT** (Permanent Workers' Congress): 'umbrella' group for four trade unions, incl. the CTG(I) and CTN.

**Consejo de Acción y Unidad Sindical—CAUS** (Council for Trade Union Action and Unity): Managua; f. 1963; trade union wing of Partido Comunista de Nicaragua.

**Federación de Trabajadores de la Salud—FETSALUD** (Federation of Health Workers): Optica Nicaragüense, 2 c. Arriba ½ c. al Sur, Apdo 1402, Managua; tel. and fax (2) 66-3065; Dir GUSTAVO PORRAS CORTEZ.

**Federación de Trabajadores Nicaragüenses—FTN:** workers' federation; Leader ZACARÍAS HERNÁNDEZ.

**Federación de Transportadores Unidos Nicaragüense—FTUN** (United Transport Workers' Federation of Nicaragua): De donde fue el Vocacional, esq. Este 30 m al Sur, Apdo 945, Managua; f. 1952; Pres. MANUEL SABALLOS; 2,880 mems (est.) from 21 affiliated associations.

**Frente Nacional de Trabajadores—FNT** (National Workers' Front): Calle Colón, Iglesia del Carmen, 1 c. Abajo, 20 m al Sur, Managua; tel. (2) 26484; f. 1979; affiliated to Frente Sandinista de Liberación Nacional; Leader ROBERTO GONZÁLEZ; Gen. Sec. LUCIO JIMÉNEZ.

**Frente Obrero—FO** (Workers' Front): f. 1974; radical Marxist-Leninist trade union.

**Frente de Trabajadores Socialcristiano—FRETRA SC** (Social-Christian Workers' Front): f. 1980; trade-union wing of the Partido Social Cristiano Nicaragüense.

**Solidaridad de Trabajadores Cristianos—STC:** Christian workers; Leader DONALD CASTILLO.

# NICARAGUA

**Unión Nacional de Agricultores y Ganaderos—UNAG** (National Union of Agricultural and Livestock Workers): Reparto Las Palmas, Costado Sur/Oeste del Parque, ½ c. Abajo, Apdo 4526, Managua; tel. (2) 66-2077; fax (2) 66-2433; f. 1981; Pres. Daniel Núñez Rodríguez.

**Unión Nacional de Caficultores de Nicaragua—UNCAFENIC** (National Union of Coffee Growers of Nicaragua): Reparto San Juan, Casa 300, Apdo 3447, Managua; tel. (2) 78-2586; fax (2) 78-2587; Pres. Gerardo Salinas C.

**Unión Nacional Campesina—UNC** (National Union of Rural Workers): f. 1983; affiliated to the Unión Demócrata Cristiana.

**Unión de Productores Agropecuarios de Nicaragua** (Union of Agricultural Producers of Nicaragua): Reparto San Juan, Casa 300, Apdo 2351, Managua; tel. (2) 78-3382; fax (2) 78-2587; Pres. Gerardo Salinas C.

# Transport

## RAILWAYS

**Ferrocarril de Nicaragua:** Plantel Central Casimiro Sotelo, Del Parque San Sebastián, 5 c. al Lago, Apdo 5, Managua; tel. (2) 22-2530; telex 1239; fax (2) 22-2542; f. 1881; government-owned; main line from León via Managua to Granada on Lake Nicaragua (132 km), southern branch line between Masaya and Diriamba (44 km), northern branch line between León and Río Grande (86 km) and Puerto Sandino branch line between Ceiba Mocha and Puerto Sandino (25 km); total length 287 km; a further branch line between León and the Pacific port of Corinto has been inoperative since 1982, owing to hurricane damage; Gen. Man. N. Estrada.

**Ferrocarril del Pacífico de Nicaragua:** Plantel Central Casimiro Sotelo, Del Parque San Sebastián, 5 c. al Lago, Apdo 5, Managua; tel. (2) 22-2530; telex 1239; fax (2) 22-2542; Pacific railway co.

## ROADS

In 1993 there were 15,287 km of roads of which 1,598 km were paved. Of the total only 9,571 km were accessible throughout the entire year. The Pan-American Highway runs for 384 km in Nicaragua and links Managua with the Honduran and Costa Rican frontiers and the Atlantic and Pacific Highways connecting Managua with the coastal regions.

## SHIPPING

Corinto, Puerto Sandino and San Juan del Sur, on the Pacific, and Puerto Cabezas, El Bluff and El Rama on the Caribbean, are the principal ports. Corinto deals with about 60% of trade.

**Administración Portuaria de Corinto:** De Telcor, 1 c. al Oeste, Corinto; tel. (342) 211; f. 1956; port authority at Corinto.

## CIVIL AVIATION

**Aerolíneas Nicaragüenses (AERONICA):** Contiguo Aeropuerto Internacional Augusto C. Sandino, Apdo 6018, Managua; tel. (2) 63-1929; telex 1242; fax (2) 63-1822; f. 1981; domestic services and international services to El Salvador, Costa Rica, Panama, Mexico and USA; Gen. Man. Julio Rocha.

**Nicaragüenses de Aviación (NICA):** Apdo 6018, Managua; tel. (2) 63-1929; fax (2) 63-1822; f. 1992; daily service to Miami, USA; Gen. Dir Mario Medrano.

# Tourism

In 1988 a campaign to attract more tourists to Nicaragua was launched, including a tourist development at Montelimar, which was supported by a US $10m. loan from Italian investors. In 1992 about 167,000 foreigners visited Nicaragua, compared with 55,000 in 1988, and receipts from tourism totalled around $21m.

**Instituto Nicaragüense de Turismo (INTURISMO):** Avda Bolívar Sur, Apdo 122, Managua; tel. (2) 25436; telex 1299; fax (2) 25314; f. 1967; Min. Alvaro Chamorro Mora.

**Asociación Nicaragüense de Agencias de Viajes (ANAVIT):** Apdo 1045, Managua; Pres. Antonio Espino.

**Cámara Nacional de Turismo:** Centro Comercial Plaza España, Managua; tel. (2) 66-5071; Pres. Sergio Escobar F.

# NIGER

## Introductory Survey

### Location, Climate, Language, Religion, Flag, Capital

The Republic of Niger is a land-locked country in western Africa, with Algeria and Libya to the north, Nigeria and Benin to the south, Mali and Burkina Faso to the west, and Chad to the east. The climate is hot and dry, with an average temperature of 29°C (84°F). The official language is French, but numerous indigenous languages, including Hausa (spoken by about one-half of the population), Tuareg, Djerma and Fulani, are also used (the 1991 sovereign National Conference identified 10 'national' languages). More than 85% of the population are Muslims, the most influential Islamic groups being the Tijaniyya, the Senoussi and the Hamallists. Most of the remainder of the population follow traditional beliefs, and there is a small Christian minority. The national flag (proportions 7 by 6) has three equal horizontal stripes, of orange, white and green, with an orange disc in the centre of the white stripe. The capital is Niamey.

### Recent History

Formerly a part of French West Africa, Niger became a self-governing member of the French Community in December 1958 and was granted independence on 3 August 1960. Hamani Diori, leader of the Parti progressiste nigérien, the local section of the Ivorian-dominated Rassemblement démocratique africain, and Prime Minister since December 1958, became Head of State. Following the suppression of Djibo Bakary's left-wing nationalist Union nigérienne démocratique (or Sawaba party) in 1959, Diori was elected President in November 1960, and re-elected in 1965 and 1970. While Diori's one-party Government heavily repressed periodic demonstrations of nationalist sentiment, the President himself gained considerable international prestige as a spokesman for francophone Africa; close links were maintained with France.

The Sahelian drought of 1968–74 was particularly damaging to the Nigerien economy, and, following the discovery of stocks of food supplies at the homes of government ministers, the army took power in a coup in April 1974. Diori was arrested, and Lt-Col (later Maj.-Gen.) Seyni Kountché, the Chief of Staff of the Armed Forces, became President. The new administration, headed by the Conseil militaire suprême (CMS), suspended the Constitution; the legislature was replaced by a consultative Conseil national de développement (CND), and political activity was banned.

The new Government's stated priorities were to eliminate corruption and to foster of economic recovery in the aftermath of the drought. In the interest of national independence, Kountché obtained the withdrawal of French troops and reduced French influence over the exploitation of Niger's deposits of uranium (which France had initiated in 1968). Links were developed with Arab countries, and in February 1977 France and Niger concluded a new bilateral co-operation agreement which, it was claimed, eradicated all traces of French paternalism.

In August 1975 Djibo Bakary (who had lived in exile in Guinea in 1959–74, returning to Niger following the coup) was arrested, together with the Vice-Chairman of the CMS and the head of the national groundnut company, on charges of plotting to seize power. In March 1976 Maj. Moussa Bayere, who had been dismissed from the Government in February, led an abortive coup. He and eight others were later sentenced to death.

In 1977 and 1978, at a time of renewed drought, the Government attempted to broaden the basis of its support, and in March 1978 released a number of political prisoners, including senior members of ex-President Diori's administration. In April 1980 both Diori and Bakary were released from prison, although Diori was placed under house arrest. From late 1977 the proportion of army officers in the Government was progressively reduced, as the unpopular and corrupt administration was gradually replaced. In January 1983 a civilian, Oumarou Mamane, was appointed to the newly-created post of Prime Minister. In October, while Kountché was attending a Franco-African summit meeting in France, ministers loyal to his regime thwarted a coup attempt by officers opposed to the increasing 'civilianization' of the Council of Ministers. Prominent officials who were believed to have instigated the plot fled the country, but several civil servants and two government ministers were arrested on suspicion of complicity. In November Mamane, who in August had been appointed President of the CND (a post which he held until September 1987), was replaced as Prime Minister by Hamid Algabid. In January 1984 Kountché announced the establishment of a special commission to draft a pre-constitutional document, termed a 'national charter'. The recurrence of drought in 1984–85, and the closure (at Nigeria's instigation) of the land border with Nigeria between April 1984 and March 1986, impeded economic adjustment efforts and increased Niger's dependence on external financial assistance.

The draft 'national charter' was approved by an estimated 99.6% of voters in a referendum in June 1987. On 10 November, after a long period of ill health, Kountché died in hospital in France. The CMS, in the hours prior to his death, had issued an announcement designating Col (later Brig.) Ali Saïbou, the army Chief of Staff, as interim Head of State. Saïbou was formally confirmed in the positions of Chairman of the CMS and Head of State on 14 November. Major government changes were announced shortly afterwards. Ex-President Diori was released from house arrest, and an appeal was made to exiled Nigeriens to return to the country. Both Diori and Bakary subsequently met with Saïbou. (Diori died in Morocco in April 1989.)

In December 1987 Saïbou proclaimed a general amnesty for all political prisoners. He also announced proposals for elections to be held to village, local and regional councils and for the establishment of a constitutional committee. The army retained a strong presence in the Government, and Saïbou emphasized that the military would continue to occupy a major role in political life following a return to constitutional rule. In July 1988 Oumarou Mamane was reinstated as Prime Minister. In the same month the CND was given the task of drafting a new constitution. The ban on all political organizations was repealed in August, when Brig. Saïbou announced the formation of a new ruling party, the Mouvement national pour une société de développement (MNSD); however, Saïbou emphasized his opposition to the establishment of a multi-party system. In October four of those who had been implicated in the 1983 coup attempt were sentenced (*in absentia*) to death; 16 others received prison sentences for their part in the plot, and eight defendants were acquitted.

In May 1989 the MNSD congress elected a Conseil supérieur d'orientation nationale (CSON). This body replaced the CMS, and its president (Saïbou) was to be the sole candidate in a presidential election, to be held simultaneously with elections to a proposed legislature (which was to replace the CND). The draft Constitution, which had been adopted by the Council of Ministers in January, was endorsed in a national referendum in September, reportedly receiving the support of 99.3% of those who voted. Elections took place in December, as a result of which Saïbou was confirmed as President, for a seven-year term, by 99.6% of those who voted. At the same time a single list of 93, CSON-approved deputies to the new Assemblée nationale was endorsed by 99.5% of voters. It was subsequently announced that Niger's two remaining political prisoners were to be released, to commemorate Saïbou's inauguration as President of what was designated the Second Republic. An extensive reorganization of the Council of Ministers followed later in the month, as a result of which the post of Prime Minister was abolished.

In February 1990 security forces intervened at a demonstration by students, who had been boycotting classes at the University of Niamey in protest against proposed reforms to the education system and a reduction in the level of graduate recruitment into the civil service. Official reports stated that three students had been killed, and 25 injured, as a result of the police action. Saïbou, who had been abroad at the time of the incident, expressed his regret at the intervention, and announced the appointment of a commission to examine the students' grievances. The dismissal, in March, of the Ministers of the Interior and of Higher Education, Research and Technology, together with the redeployment of the Minister of National Education, indicated Saïbou's desire to appease the students. At the same time a prominent industrialist, Aliou Mahamidou, was assigned to the re-established post of Prime Minister. However, further student action during April prompted the deployment of security forces outside educational establishments, together with the imposition of a ban on all student gatherings and demonstrations. There were renewed disturbances in June. In the same month the trade union federation, the Union des syndicats des travailleurs du Niger (USTN), organized a 48-hour strike, in protest against recently-announced austerity measures (notably the imposition of two-year restrictions on increases in remuneration for public-sector employees). Following a meeting between representatives of the USTN and a CSON *ad hoc* commission, students and trade union leaders who had been detained during June were released from custody, and the USTN agreed to cancel further protests.

In June 1990 the CSON announced that the Constitution was to be amended to facilitate a transition to political pluralism. None the less, industrial unrest persisted. Several strikes took place during August, and the USTN continued to demand the cancellation of elements of the austerity programme, while requesting access to the state-controlled media. A five-day general strike in November halted production of uranium, closed public buildings and disrupted regional and international air links. Participants in the strike were demanding not only a relaxation of the austerity measures, but also a transition to multi-party politics. Later in the month, as further industrial unrest seemed imminent, Saïbou announced that, on the basis of the findings of a constitutional review body, a multi-party political system would be established. It was also announced that less stringent austerity measures would be adopted, in consultation with Niger's external creditors. Interim procedures for the registration of political parties were adopted (the Constitution was amended accordingly in April 1991). It was envisaged that a national conference on political reform would be convened in mid-1991; municipal officers and development advisers would be elected, by universal suffrage, in late 1991, and multi-party legislative elections would take place in early 1992. In the mean time, Saïbou was to remain as President, but his powers were to be reviewed.

All academic institutions were closed in February 1991, following violent demonstrations by students and school pupils in protest against delays in the investigation of the deaths that had occurred during the student unrest of February 1990. In March 1991, during a meeting with Saïbou, opposition leaders demanded that their parties be allowed access to the official media, and that military personnel should withdraw from political life. Shortly afterwards the Chief of Staff of the Armed Forces announced that the armed forces were to distance themselves from the MNSD with immediate effect, prompting the removal of a serving military officer from the post of Minister of the Interior. Later in the month some 2,000 supporters of opposition movements attended a demonstration in Niamey to denounce the MNSD's domination of the reform process and to support demands that opposition groups be accorded access to the official media. However, plans for a general strike were cancelled, following an agreement between the Mahamidou and the USTN regarding austerity measures and access to the media.

In July 1991 Saïbou resigned as Chairman of the MNSD—Nassara (as it had been renamed in March), in order to distance himself from party politics in preparation for the National Conference. The Conference, which was convened (after some delay) in Niamey in late July and attended by about 1,200 delegates (representing, among others, the organs of state and some 24 political organizations, together with professional, women's and students' groups), declared itself sovereign. In August those present voted to suspend the Constitution and to dissolve the legislature and the CND. It was agreed that Saïbou would remain in office as Head of State on an interim basis, and that his powers (by now largely ceremonial) would be exercised under the supervision of the National Conference. State officials, both past and present, were banned from leaving the country, and the Government was deprived of its authority to make financial transactions on behalf of Niger.

Moreover, links with external creditors were effectively severed when delegates voted to suspend adherence to the country's IMF- and World Bank-sponsored programme of economic adjustment. Control of the armed forces and the police was transferred to the Conference, and a special committee was established to examine any abuse of political or economic power that was alleged to have been perpetrated since independence. Although senior members of the armed forces pledged support for the reform process, increasing discontent was rumoured within the military, notably in response to the examination, by the Conference, of the army's suppression of a Tuareg attack on Tchin Tabaraden in May 1990 (see below). In September the Conference appointed a new armed forces Chief and Deputy Chief of Staff and dissolved the Government. In the following month an amnesty was announced for all those who had been implicated in the 1983 coup attempt. Later in October the Conference appointed Amadou Cheiffou (a regional official of the International Civil Aviation Organization) to head a transitional Council of Ministers, which, it was anticipated, would remain in office until early 1993, when elected democratic institutions would be inaugurated. In November 1991, shortly before the conclusion of the National Conference, its President, André Salifou, was designated Chairman of an interim legislative body, the Haut conseil de la République (HCR). The role of the 15-member HCR would be to ensure the transitional Government's implementation of the resolutions adopted by the Conference, to supervise the activities of the Head of State and to oversee the drafting of a new constitution.

Cheiffou's transitional Government (which was dominated by technocrats) immediately introduced austerity measures in the public sector, in an attempt to alleviate the severe financing deficit inherited from the previous administration. Consequent delays in the payment of salaries to civil servants and other state employees were initially accepted with few manifestations of discontent. In February 1992, however, junior-ranking members of the armed forces mutinied, demanding the payment of salary arrears and the release of an army captain who had been detained since October 1991, after having been found responsible by the National Conference for the suppression of the Tchin Tabaraden attack, as well as the dismissal of the Deputy Chief of Staff and other senior members of the armed forces. The troops detained Salifou and the Minister of the Interior, Mohamed Moussa (himself of Tuareg extraction), and took control of the offices of the state broadcasting media in Niamey. Although the rebellion abated when Cheiffou pledged to consider the troops' material demands, troops again took control of the broadcasting media in the following month. The mutiny received little support outside the armed forces, and the USTN and several political parties organized a widely-observed general strike to register their protest against the rebellion. The troops agreed to return to barracks when the Government pledged to give due consideration to all their demands. Later in the month Cheiffou, admitting that the transitional Government had achieved little in its attempts to address the country's principal problems, reorganized the Council of Ministers. Four ministers were dismissed, and Mohamed Moussa was transferred to the Ministry of Trade, Transport and Tourism.

In June 1992 the Government, seemingly motivated by the need urgently to secure external financial assistance (notably to facilitate the payment of salary arrears in the public sector), announced the resumption of diplomatic relations with Taiwan, which had promised credits of some US $50m. (Links had been severed in 1974, following Niger's formal recognition of the People's Republic of China.) However, members of the HCR protested that the transitional authorities had not been empowered by the National Conference to effect such a re-orientation of foreign policy, and the Government was obliged to rescind its earlier announcement. In July, none the less, a vote in the HCR expressing 'no confidence' in Cheiffou was defeated, and the Government announced that diplomatic relations with Taiwan would be re-established. Diplomatic relations with the People's Republic of China were subsequently suspended.

The process of transition to civilian rule, which had been scheduled for completion by the end of January 1993, encountered numerous practical difficulties. A referendum on the new Constitution, which had been scheduled for October 1992, did not in fact take place until 26 December, when the new document was approved by 89.79% of those who voted

(56.58% of the electorate). Elections to the new Assemblée nationale took place, again after considerable delay, on 14 February 1993, and were contested by 12 of the country's 18 legal political parties. Although the MNSD—Nassara won the greatest number of seats (29) in the 83-member assembly, the former ruling party was prevented from resuming power by the rapid formation, in the aftermath of the election, of an alliance of parties that was able to form a parliamentary majority. The Alliance des forces de changement (AFC) grouped six parliamentary parties with a total of 50 seats (and was also supported by three parties that had not secured seats in the legislature), its principal members being the Convention démocratique et sociale—Rahama (CDS—Rahama), which held 22 seats in the legislature, the Parti nigérien pour la démocratie et le socialisme—Tarayya (PNDS—Tarayya), with 13 seats, and the Alliance nigérienne pour la démocratie et le progrès—Zaman Lahiya (ANDP—Zaman Lahiya), with 11 seats. The rate of participation by voters was reported to be somewhat higher than at the time of the constitutional referendum.

The MNSD—Nassara, which denounced opposition tactics in the legislative elections, was similarly frustrated in the elections for the presidency. At the first round, which took place on 27 February 1993, Col (retd) Tandja Mamadou, the leader of the MNSD—Nassara since mid-1991, won the greatest proportion of the votes cast (34.22%). He and his nearest rival, Mahamane Ousmane (the leader of the CDS—Rahama, who took 26.59% of the first-round votes), proceeded to a second round, which eventually took place on 27 March 1993. At the second round Mahamane Ousmane was elected President by 55.42% of those who voted (slightly more than 35% of the electorate): four of the six other candidates at the first round were members of the AFC, and the majority of their supporters had transferred allegiance to Ousmane.

Mahamane Ousmane was inaugurated as President of the Third Republic on 16 April 1993. Shortly beforehand AFC deputies had elected Moumouni Amadou Djermakoye (the leader of the ANDP—Zaman Lahiya and a first-round candidate for the presidency) as the Speaker of the Assemblée nationale. The vote had been boycotted by the MNSD—Nassara and its allies, who protested that Djermakoye's appointment (in accordance with an agreement made by the AFC parties prior to the second round of the presidential election) was in contravention of the procedures outlined in the Constitution, and who later successfully petitioned the Supreme Court to annul his election. Following his inauguration, none the less, Ousmane appointed another first-round presidential candidate, Mahamadou Issoufou of the PNDS—Tarayya, to the post of Prime Minister (again in accordance with a pre-election agreement within the AFC). Issoufou's first Council of Ministers was composed of technocrats whose stated task was to address the country's economic and social crisis. In May AFC deputies (again in the absence of the opposition) reappointed Djermakoye as Speaker of the Assemblée nationale.

Niger's acute economic difficulties persisted during the second half of 1992 and the first months of 1993, with the result that, by the time of the inauguration of the new organs of state, some five months' salary arrears had accumulated. Sporadic industrial action by public sector employees was accompanied by a resurgence of unrest in the education sector. In October 1992 students stormed the office of the Prime Minister, and set fire to official vehicles, in protest at government plans to reduce grants and to introduce competitive entrance procedures for graduates wishing to join the civil service. The announcement, in January 1993, that the University of Niamey was effectively bankrupt precipitated further violent protests, and in March students invaded the treasury building in Niamey, demanding the payment of grant arrears. Shortly afterwards the USTN organized a week-long general strike (with only partial success), in an attempt to secure the payment of outstanding salaries. There was renewed unrest in May, following a decision by the Government to declare the 1992/93 academic year invalid in state secondary schools, owing to the recent disruptions and lack of teaching resources.

During a visit to France in June 1993 Ousmane received pledges of emergency financial assistance from the French Government, as a result of which it was announced that public-sector wages outstanding since April would be paid. However, indications that arrears accumulated under the transitional authorities would be withheld provoked a 48-hour strike by USTN members in July. Shortly afterwards soldiers at Zinder, Tahoua, Agadez and Maradi mutinied over a period of three days, taking local officials hostage and demanding the payment of three months' salary arrears. Calm was restored following intervention by Ousmane and senior members of the military, and the payment of one month's arrears was promised. Rumours that disaffected troops at Zinder had been planning to assassinate Issoufou prompted some 4,000 supporters of the Government to stage a demonstration in Niamey to condemn the mutineers' actions. In August a gathering in Maradi of members of the MNSD—Nassara and its allies, organized to protest against alleged violations of the Constitution by the new regime, was dispersed by the security forces. Although at least eight people were detained in connection with the demonstration, all were released following a court ruling that the arrests had been unauthorized. Further opposition marches to denounce 'unconstitutional' actions by the AFC administration took place in Niamey and elsewhere later in the month.

In accordance with its undertaking to restore a dialogue with the international financial community, with the aim of negotiating new credits and debt-relief measures, the Ousmane administration initiated efforts to curb public expenditure. In September 1993 the USTN organized a 72-hour general strike, following the Government's announcement, despite union objections, of an austerity budget which envisaged a 24% reduction in wages in the public sector, together with the imposition of new taxes and an indefinite suspension of the payment of salary arrears. Further strike action was averted when the Government agreed to suspend implementation of a newly-adopted law restricting the right to strike, and negotiations between the USTN and the Issoufou administration resumed (albeit falteringly). In October the Government and unions reached an understanding whereby public-sector salaries would be reduced by 5%–20%, and employees would forgo three months' wage arrears, in return for which they would be compensated by other financial adjustments.

There was renewed unrest in the education sector from late 1993. The University of Niamey was closed for 10 days in January 1994, following violent clashes when police intervened to prevent students from marching to the Ministry of Education to demand the payment of grant arrears and improved conditions for study. Secondary school pupils in Niamey joined students in demanding the payment of arrears and the reopening of the university, and the arrest (shortly after the resumption of classes) of the Secretary-General of the Union scolaire nigérienne prompted further (peaceful) protests before he was released at the end of the month. Meanwhile, in mid-January Tandja Mamadou was among the leaders of an 8,000-strong demonstration in Niamey, which had been organized to protest against the imposition, in the previous week, of a ban on a demonstration by supporters of the students' movement.

Although the October 1993 agreement between the Government and the USTN ostensibly resulted in a normalization of labour relations for the remainder of the year, the devaluation, in January 1994, of the CFA franc gave rise to further industrial unrest. In response to the devaluation, the Government announced emergency policies to offset the immediate adverse effects of the measure, and in late January the Assemblée nationale (in the absence of opposition deputies, who were boycotting parliamentary sessions) voted to empower Ousmane to issue decrees regarding political, economic and financial affairs without prior reference to the legislature.

University students in Niamey renewed their campaign for the payment of grant arrears in early March 1994, blocking roads and occupying campus buildings. The death of a student in clashes with police precipitated a boycott of classes, as students demanded that those responsible for the death be brought to justice. A government undertaking to pay three months' arrears and to establish a commission to investigate the police actions failed to prevent further violent protests in the capital, where paramilitary forces were deployed since many police officers refused to intervene, in support of colleagues who were implicated in the student's death. Later in the month Niamey was effectively paralysed by a 24-hour general strike, organized by the USTN to protest against the imposition, from mid-March, of the controversial 'right to strike' legislation, and also to demand 30%–50% salary increases to compensate for the devaluation of the national currency. A similar, three-day strike took place in mid-April;

a government announcement of public-sector pay increases of 5%–12% was deemed inadequate, and there was a further 72-hour strike in mid-May.

By the time of the first anniversary of Ousmane's inauguration as President, his administration, already weakened in its attempts at economic adjustment by labour unrest, was challenged by a campaign of civil disobedience, orchestrated by the MNSD—Nassara and its allies, which were demanding representation in the Government proportionate to the percentage of votes won by Mamadou at the second round of presidential voting in 1993. Mamadou was among three opposition leaders who were detained for about five days in mid-April 1994, following an anti-Government demonstration in which one person was killed and about 20 were injured. The arrests prompted further protests, as a result of which about 90 opposition activists were reported to have been detained. The trial of 25 opposition activists, accused of involvement in an unauthorized demonstration and of causing damage to public and private property, took place in mid-May: three defendants were sentenced to two or three years' imprisonment, and banned from residence in Niamey for a further year, while 10 received suspended sentences and the remainder were acquitted. In late May, following a meeting between Ousmane and representatives of the MNSD—Nassara's parliamentary group, the opposition agreed to end its boycott of the Assemblée nationale. In June the Supreme Court ruled that a resolution, adopted by the legislature in April, to revoke the parliamentary immunity of those deputies whose parties were participating in the campaign of civil disobedience had been unconstitutional. Members of the USTN began an indefinite strike in early June, in a renewed attempt to secure their previous demands. At the end of July, however, union leaders agreed temporarily to suspend industrial action, pending attempts to achieve a negotiated settlement with the Government.

The cancellation, by Moumouni Djermankoye, of an extraordinary session of parliament, scheduled for the second half of July 1994, at which a motion expressing 'no confidence' in the Government with regard to its conduct of labour relations was expected to be proposed, prompted the resignation of the assembly's deputy speaker, Jackou Senoussi, from the chairmanship of the CDS—Rahama. In late September the PNDS—Tarayya withdrew from the AFC, and Issoufou resigned as Prime Minister, in protest against what was perceived as the transfer of some of the Prime Minister's powers to the President. Souley Abdoulaye, a member of the CDS—Rahama, who had hitherto been Minister of Trade, Transport and Tourism, was appointed to the premiership. However, his new Government did not command a majority in the Assemblée nationale, and in mid-October a parliamentary motion expressing 'no confidence' in the Abdoulaye administration (proposed by the MNSD—Nassara and the PNDS—Tarayya) was approved by 46 votes to 36. Ousmane responded by dissolving the Assemblée nationale, confirming the Abdoulaye Government in office pending new elections, which were scheduled for late December. (Under the terms of the Constitution the President could also have chosen to designate a Prime Minister from among the new parliamentary majority.)

Ousmane's decision to dissolve the Assemblée nationale provoked criticism from the labour movement, which claimed that the cost of organizing an early general election would be too great, given the country's economic difficulties. From November 1994 the USTN co-ordinated weekly 48-hour strikes, which were reportedly well observed throughout the state sector, in support of its demands for pay increases and the payment of salary arrears, for the cancellation of the 'right to strike' ordinance, and to protest against government privatization plans which would result in the loss of many jobs. Strike action by schoolteachers prevented the commencement of the academic year in Niamey and several other towns.

In late November 1994 it was announced that a lack of funds, together with delays in the compilation of voters' lists and registers of candidates would require the postponement of the elections, which were subsequently rescheduled to take place on 7 January 1995. However, difficulties in producing and distributing voting papers that were acceptable to the national electoral commission necessitated a further postponement of the vote until 12 January, when 774 candidates, including representatives of about 15 political parties, contested the assembly's 83 seats. The official results, published in mid-January and confirmed by the Supreme Court at the end of the month, indicated that the MNSD—Nassara, combining its 29 seats with those of its allies, would be able to form a 43-strong majority group in the Assemblée nationale. While Ousmane's CDS—Rahama increased its representation to 24 seats, the AFC (having lost the support of the PNDS—Tarayya and of the Parti progressiste nigérien—Rassemblement démocratique africain, which withdrew from the alliance shortly before the elections) now held 40 seats, although it appealed unsuccessfully to the Supreme Court to annul the results of elections in seven constituencies where candidates of the MNSD—Nassara and its allies had been elected.

Abdoulaye resigned as Prime Minister in early February 1995. However, there was considerable controversy surrounding the appointment of a new premier, since Ousmane declined to accept the new majority's nominee, Hama Amadou (the Secretary-General of the MNSD—Nassara); he appointed instead another member of that party, Amadou Cissé, stating that the latter, as a former official of the World Bank, would be ideally suited to the essential task of negotiating new funding arrangements with Niger's external creditors. The MNSD—Nassara and its allies denounced the appointment, asserting that they would neither participate in nor co-operate with his administration, and Cissé was expelled from his party. At the same time Issoufou defeated Djermakoye in a vote for the post of Speaker of the Assemblée nationale. In mid-February trade union representatives warned Cissé that their campaign of strike action would continue (employees of the country's two state uranium-mining companies had staged a week-long strike at the end of January, and industrial action continued in many other sectors). Shortly afterwards a parliamentary motion of censure against Cissé was approved by 43 votes to 40, and Ousmane subsequently accepted the majority's nomination of Amadou as the new Prime Minister. Amadou's Government, appointed in late February, included only one member of the AFC: Alitor Mano, of the mainly-Tuareg Union pour la démocratie et le progrès social—Amana (UDPS—Amana), was designated Minister of Agriculture and Livestock. It was announced that benefits and allowances for government officials would be minimized.

In early March 1995 the Government and the USTN reached an agreement for an end to the labour unrest of the previous months. Among the principal provisions of the accord were the cancellation of the 'right to strike' legislation and a commitment to the payment of two months' salary arrears; strikers who had been dismissed as a result of industrial action would be reinstated, and other punitive actions would be withdrawn. Relations between the Amadou Government and Ousmane and his supporters were, however, less conciliatory. In early April Ousmane refused to chair a session of the Council of Ministers, apparently owing to disagreement over the organization of the meeting: in late March the Supreme Court had upheld a complaint by Amadou that the establishment by Ousmane of a cabinet secretariat at the presidency was unconstitutional, deeming that this would impinge upon the responsibilities of the general secretariat of the Government. Later in April AFC deputies began a boycott of the Assemblée nationale, in protest at what they alleged was the Prime Minister's discriminatory attitude against supporters of the President.

Ethnic unrest emerged in 1990, following the return to northern Niger (during the late 1980s) of large numbers of Tuareg nomads, who had migrated to Libya and Algeria in the early 1980s to escape the Sahelian drought. (The 1988 census recorded some 700,000 Tuaregs in Niger—about 10% of the total population.) In early May 1990 Tuaregs attacked the prison and gendarmerie at Tchin Tabaraden. The alleged brutality of the armed forces in quelling the raid (in all, as many as 100 people were later said to have been killed during the attack and its suppression) was to provoke considerable disquiet, both within Niger and internationally. Reports suggested that the incident reflected Tuareg dissatisfaction that promises made by Saïbou following his accession to power, regarding assistance for the rehabilitation of returnees to Niger, had not been fulfilled. In June the Saïbou Government contested allegations that had been made by the human rights organization, Amnesty International, that some 400 Tuaregs had been detained in recent months, and that about 40 nomads had been executed by the security forces. In July the Governments of Algeria, Mali and Niger established a joint commission to monitor the movements of the Tuareg community in the three countries' border region. In September the Heads of State of Algeria, Libya, Mali and Niger met in Algeria, where they agreed measures governing border controls and facilitating the return of refugees to their region of origin. In February 1991, at the time of a visit to Niger by an Amnesty International delegation (at the invitation of the Saïbou administration), an attack on an anti-desertification centre in northern Niger, as a result of which several deaths were reported, was alleged to have been perpetrated by Tuaregs. In April 44 Tuaregs were reported to have been acquitted of involvement in the attack on Tchin Tabaraden.

Although delegates to the 1991 National Conference discussed the Tuareg issue, as a result of which the army officer deemed to have been responsible for the suppression of the Tchin Tabaraden raid was imprisoned (see above), Tuaregs mounted a renewed offensive in October. During the months that followed numerous violent attacks were directed at official targets in the north, and clashes took place between Tuareg rebels and the security forces. Many arrests were reported, while Tuareg groups were known to have kidnapped several armed forces members. In January 1992 the transitional Government intensified security measures in northern Niger. Shortly afterwards the Government formally recognized, for the first time, that there was a rebellion in the country (incidents hitherto had been dismissed as isolated acts of banditry), and acknowledged the existence of a Tuareg movement, the Front de libération de l'Aïr et l'Azaouad (FLAA). In the following month the leader of the FLAA, Rissa Ag Boula, stated that the Tuareg rebels were not seeking to achieve independence, but rather the establishment of a federal system, in which each ethnic group would have its own administrative entity. Prior to his departure from the Ministry of the Interior, in March, Mohamed Moussa initiated a dialogue with representatives of the Tuaregs, and in mid-May a 15-day truce agreement was concluded by the Government and the FLAA, with a view to formal peace negotiations. However, each party alleged violations of the truce accord by the other, and the FLAA resumed its offensive in mid-1992.

In August 1992 the security forces launched a major offensive against the Tuareg rebellion in the north, prompting reports of the imposition of *de facto* martial law in the region. According to official figures, 186 Tuaregs were detained in August and September, both in the north and in Niamey: among those arrested were Mohamed Moussa and the Prefect of Agadez; some detainees were released after a short time, but the issue of the Tuaregs still being detained by the security forces (estimated to number about 180), as well as the 44 members of the Nigerien military being held by militant Tuaregs, was to be a major obstacle to the resumption of dialogue in subsequent months, and, during a brief rebellion at Agadez in September, troops threatened to execute more than 100 Tuareg detainees if the Tuaregs' hostages were not released. Military authority was intensified, following renewed Tuareg attacks, by the appointment, in October, of senior members of the security forces to northern administrative posts. In November, none the less, an *ad hoc* commission that had been appointed by the transitional Government to consider the Tuareg issue recommended a far-reaching programme of decentralization, according legal status and financial authority to local communities.

In December 1992 the Government announced the release from custody of 57 Tuaregs. In January 1993, none the less, five people were killed in a Tuareg attack on an MNSD—Nassara meeting in the northern town of Abala. Although he escaped injury, the principal target of the attack was rumoured to have been Tandja Mamadou (who had been Minister of the Interior at the time of the suppression of the Tchin Tabaraden raid). Although Tuareg attacks and acts of sabotage persisted, later in January 81 Tuaregs, including Mohamed Moussa, were released from detention, and Amadou Cheiffou appointed a Minister of State for National Reconciliation, whose main responsibility would be to seek a solution to the Tuareg issue. In February 30 people were said to have been killed in Tuareg raids in the Tchin Tabaraden region.

In March 1993, following Algerian mediation, Rissa Ag Boula (who was based in Algeria, despite attempts by the Nigerien authorities to secure his extradition) agreed to a unilateral truce for the duration of the campaign for the second round of the presidential election. Shortly afterwards Tuareg representatives in Niamey signed a similar (French-brokered) truce agreement. The election of the new organs of state appeared to offer new prospects for dialogue, and in early April the outgoing transitional Government and the FLAA reached an agreement whereby the truce was extended indefinitely; the remaining Tuareg prisoners were subsequently released from detention, and the rebels released their hostages.

Ousmane and Issoufou identified the resolution of the Tuareg issue as a major priority, and, although sporadic resistance was reported, the truce accord was generally respected. At the beginning of June 1993 it was revealed that representatives of the Nigerien Government and the Tuaregs had for some time been negotiating in France, and on 10 June a formal, three-month truce agreement was signed in Paris. The accord provided for the demilitarization of the north, and envisaged the instigation of negotiations on the Tuaregs' political demands. Financial assistance was promised to facilitate the return of Tuareg refugees (estimated to number about 10,000) from Algeria, and development funds were pledged for northern areas, while a committee was to be established to oversee the implementation of the agreement. However, the Paris accord encountered some opposition among the Tuareg community: a new group, the Armée révolutionnaire de libération du nord-Niger (ARLN, led by Ataher Abdel Moumine), emerged in late June to denounce the truce, and by mid-July a further split in the FLAA was evident between supporters of the truce (led by Mano Dayak, the Tuareg signatory to the agreement), who broke away from the movement to form the Front de libération de Tamoust (FLT), and its detractors (led by Rissa Ag Boula), who stated that they could not support any agreement that contained no specific commitment to discussion of the federalist issue.

In September 1993 the FLT and the Nigerien Government agreed to extend the truce for a further three months. Although the FLAA and the ARLN refused to sign the accord, in the following month they formed, together with the FLT, a joint negotiating body, the Coordination de la résistance armée (CRA), with the aim of presenting a cohesive programme in future dealings with the Nigerien authorities. Efforts were initiated to arrange new talks; however, the absence of Nigerien government negotiators from a scheduled meeting in the Algerian capital in November was followed by the failure of CRA representatives to travel to a meeting in Ouagadougou, Burkina Faso, later in the month. Attacks in December on travellers between Agadez and Zinder were attributed to Tuaregs (the first time for several months that the authorities had blamed disturbances on Tuaregs), and shortly afterwards government forces were reported to have attacked a Tuareg encampment, killing four people, although the Government denied any such offensive.

Unrest continued in January 1994, although discreet mediation efforts continued. In the same month the establishment was reported of a further Tuareg movement, the Front patriotique de libération du Sahara (FPLS, led by Mohamed Anako). In early February the CRA announced its willingness to attend preliminary talks in Ouagadougou, although it declined to sign a new truce agreement with the Nigerien Government. Meeting in Burkina, in mid-February, the CRA and Nigerien officials agreed to full negotiations in Paris in late March, with French, Algerian and Burkinabè mediation. None the less, reports of a Tuareg attack on a uranium installation in the north, and of the harassment of travellers in the north and east, undermined peace efforts in subsequent weeks. Moreover, the CRA's demands for regional autonomy, and for the establishment of quotas for Tuaregs in government, parliament and in the armed forces, received little support in Niamey, where the authorities and parliamentary opposition were prepared to concede the rehabilitation of the north and greater political decentralization. The proposed Paris negotiations did not take place in late March, and a futher round of consultations was postponed indefinitely in mid-April.

Despite an escalation of violence during May 1994 (including clashes, some 200 km to the north of Agadez, between the Nigerien armed forces and a rebel unit of the FPLS, as a result of which as many as 40 deaths were recorded), negotiations resumed in Paris in mid-June. Tentative agreement was reached on the creation of what were termed 'homogeneous' autonomous regions for Niger's ethnic groups, each of which would have its own elected assembly and governor (to be elected by the regional assembly) to function in parallel with the organs of central government. However, there was no agreement regarding the integration of Tuareg fighters into

Niger's armed forces and political and administrative structures.

There was renewed unrest in August and September 1994, including three reported attempts by Tuaregs to disrupt power supplies to uranium mines north of Agadez, which caused considerable damage, as well as a grenade attack on a meeting in Agadez of the UDPS—Amana, as a result of which six people were killed (Tuareg groups accused government forces of responsibility for the assault). At a meeting in Ouagadougou in late September, none the less, the CRA presented Nigerien government negotiators with what it termed a 'comprehensive and final' plan for a restoration of peace. The plan was referred to Ousmane, and formal negotiations resumed, with mediation by the Burkinabè President, Blaise Compaoré, as well as representatives of France and Algeria, in Ouagadougou in early October. A new peace accord was signed on 9 October, which, while emphasizing that Niger was 'unitary and indivisible', also recognized the right of the people to manage their own affairs. Territorial communities were to have their own elected assemblies or councils, to which would be delegated responsibility for the implementation of economic, social and cultural policies at a regional or local level. The Nigerien Government was to take immediate measures to ensure the rehabilitation and development of areas affected by the conflict, and to ensure the elimination of insecurity in the north. Provisions were also to be made to facilitate the return and resettlement of refugees. A renewable three-month truce was to take immediate effect, to be monitored by French and Burkinabè military units. Souley Abdoulaye's interim Government included a minister responsible for decentralization; there was, however, some concern that the new parliamentary majority, led by the MNSD—Nassara, would be less favourable to any policy devolving authority to the Tuareg movement. By the time of the conclusion of the Ouagadougou agreement the number of deaths since the escalation of the Tuareg rebellion in late 1991 was officially put at 150.

In early January 1995 a commission was established to consider the administrative reorganization of the country. Shortly afterwards representatives of the Nigerien Government, the CRA, Algeria, Burkina and France met in Agadez, where they agreed to a three-month renewal of the truce. Mainly-Tuareg groups won five seats at elections to the Assemblée nationale in that month, and the inclusion of a member of the UDPS—Amana in the Government of Hama Amadou dispelled some fears regarding the new administration's commitment to the peace process. Despite occasional reports of incidents apparently involving renegade Tuareg units, observers confirmed general adherence to the truce, and a further round of negotiations was scheduled to take place in Ouagadougou in late March.

The opening of the Ouagadougou talks was, however, briefly delayed by a split in the Tuareg movement. Rissa Ag Boula, who in January 1995 had withdrawn from the CRA (having repeatedly criticized Dayak's negotiating stance), and refused to participate in the decentralization committee, in protest at alleged delays in the implementation of the provisions of the October 1994 agreement, emerged as the leader of the Tuareg delegation (now renamed the Organisation de la résistance armée—ORA) in Ouagadougou: Dayak and the FLT initially remained within the ORA, which was said to accord increased autonomy to each of the six movements now reportedly in existence. In early April 1995 the truce was extended for a further two weeks, and in mid-April it was announced that a lasting peace agreement had been reached. The accord, which essentially confirmed the provisions of the October 1994 agreement, provided for the establishment of a special peace committee, to be overseen by representatives of the three mediating countries, whose task would be to ensure the practical implementation of the accord, including the disarming of combatants and the recovery of armaments. Demobilized rebels were to be integrated into the Nigerien military and public sector, and special military units were to be accorded responsibility for the security of the northern regions; particular emphasis was to be placed on the economic, social and cultural development of the north, and the Government undertook to support the decentralization process. There was to be a general amnesty for all parties involved in the Tuareg rebellion and its suppression, and a day of national reconciliation was to be instituted in memory of the victims of the conflict. The peace agreement, which envisaged the implementation of its provisions within a period of six months, was formally signed by the Nigerien government negotiator, Mai Maigana, and Rissa Ag Boula in Niamey on 24 April 1995. A cease-fire took effect the following day.

There was increasing evidence in late 1994 and early 1995 of ethnic unrest in southern and eastern Niger, especially in the Lake Chad region. Clashes, frequently over grazing rights between settled Toubous and nomadic Peulhs, resulted in numerous deaths, many of which were attributed to the Front démocratique du renouveau—an organization which emerged in October 1994 to demand increased autonomy for south-eastern regions. In November, in compliance with a request by the UN, Niger established a committee whose stated aim was to disarm militias and to combat arms-trafficking: the Agadez and Lake Chad regions were said to be major centres for weapons-trading, with insecurity near the border with Chad being attributed to the presence in Niger, since the overthrow of President Hissène Habré in late 1990, of several thousand (mainly Toubou) Chadian refugees.

## Government

The Constitution of the Third Republic, which was approved in a national referendum in December 1992 and promulgated in January 1993, provides for a civilian, multi-party political system. The President of the Republic, who is Head of State, is elected for five years by universal adult suffrage, and may seek re-election only once. Legislative power is vested in the unicameral Assemblée nationale, whose 83 members are directly elected with a five-year mandate. The President of the Republic appoints the Prime Minister, and, on the latter's recommendation, other government ministers. The Council of Ministers is responsible to parliament.

A reorganization of Niger's administrative structures, with the aim of devolving increased autonomy to local and regional authorities, is in progress.

## Defence

In June 1994 Niger's armed forces totalled 5,300 men (army 5,200; air force 100). Paramilitary forces numbered 5,400 men, comprising the gendarmerie, the republican guard and the national police force. Conscription to the armed forces is selective and lasts for two years. The 1993 budget allocated 9,100m. francs CFA to defence.

## Economic Affairs

In 1993, according to estimates by the World Bank, Niger's gross national product (GNP), measured at average 1991–93 prices, was US $2,313m., equivalent to $270 per head. During 1985–93, it was estimated, GNP per head declined, in real terms, at an average annual rate of 2.1%. Over the same period the population increased by an annual average of 3.2%. Niger's gross domestic product (GDP) declined, in real terms, by an average of 0.7% per year in 1980–92. Real GDP increased by 1.4% in 1993, and by about 4% in 1994.

Agriculture (including hunting, forestry and fishing) contributed 39% of GDP in 1993. About 85.9% of the labour force were employed in the sector in that year. Cowpeas and cotton are cultivated for export. The principal subsistence crops are millet, sorghum, cassava and rice. Niger achieves self-sufficiency in basic foodstuffs in non-drought years: an overall cereals deficit of some 55,000 metric tons was forecast for 1993, but plentiful rains in 1994 ensured a recovery in output. Livestock-rearing is important, especially among the nomadic population: during the 1980s livestock-rearing constituted the second most important source of export revenue, after uranium (although the proportion declined from 14.2% of export earnings in 1985 to 4.9% in 1988). Major anti-desertification and reafforestation programmes are in progress. During 1983–93 agricultural production increased by an annual average of 1.9%.

Industry (including mining, manufacturing, construction and power) contributed 17% of GDP in 1992. Less than 2% of the labour force were employed in industrial activities in 1980. During 1982–91 industrial GDP declined by an annual average of 1.9%.

Mining contributed an estimated 5.2% of GDP in 1990. Niger is among the world's foremost producers of uranium, although the contribution of uranium-mining to the domestic economy is in decline. In 1988 exports of uranium ore accounted for 87.2% of export earnings. Gypsum, coal and cassiterite are also extracted (production of the last has reportedly been at a low level since 1991). Mining of gold and salt, conducted by artisans for some years, is to be developed at an industrial level. There are workable reserves of iron ore, and the existence of deposits of other minerals, including petroleum, calcium phosphates, copper, manganese, lithium, lead, diamonds and tungsten, has been confirmed. The GDP of the mining sector declined by an annual average of 3.4% in 1982–91.

Manufacturing contributed 7% of GDP in 1992. The processing of agricultural products (groundnuts, cereals, cotton and rice) constitutes the principal activity. Some light industries, including a textiles plant, a brewery and a cement works, supply the internal market. Manufacturing GDP increased by an average of 0.6% per year in 1982–91.

The domestic generation of electricity (almost entirely thermal) provides about one-half of Niger's electrical energy requirements, much of the remainder being imported from Nigeria. It is planned to construct a hydroelectric installation and the development of solar and wind power also has considerable potential in Niger. Imports of fuel products accounted for about 20% of the value of merchandise imports in 1992.

In 1993 Niger recorded a visible trade deficit of US $5.7m., while there was a deficit of $29.0m. on the current account of the balance of payments. In 1985 the principal source of imports (27.7%) was France; other major suppliers were the USA, Côte d'Ivoire, Nigeria and the Federal Republic of Germany. France was also the principal market for exports (taking 65.6% of Niger's exports in that year). Other significant purchasers were Nigeria and Japan. Niger's principal exports in 1988 were uranium ore, most of which was purchased, at premium prices, by France (Japan also imports significant quantities of Niger's uranium output), and live animals. The principal imports in that year were machinery and transport equipment, miscellaneous manufactured articles, chemicals, cereals and refined petroleum products.

Excluding grants, Niger recorded a budgetary deficit equivalent to 4.9% of GDP in 1993. Niger's total external debt was US $1,704m. at the end of 1993, of which $1,354m. was long-term public debt. In that year the cost of debt-servicing was equivalent to 31.4% of the value of exports of goods and services. Consumer prices declined by an annual average of 3.6% in 1995–93; however, the average rate of inflation in 1994 (following the devaluation of the CFA franc) was 36.0%. Some 20,926 people were registered as unemployed in 1991.

Niger is a member of numerous regional organizations, including the Economic Community of West African States (ECOWAS, see p. 138), the West African organs of the Franc Zone (see p. 168), the Conseil de l'Entente (see p. 238), the Liptako–Gourma Integrated Development Authority (see p. 239) and the Niger Basin Authority (see p. 240).

The success of the uranium sector in the second half of the 1970s led to a rate of economic growth that could not subsequently be sustained, as the consequences of the decline in international prices for uranium were compounded by Niger's vulnerability to drought, as well as by the constraints imposed by the country's land-locked position, poor infrastructure and high rate of population growth. Development initiatives undertaken during the period of rapid expansion were largely funded by external borrowing, which (despite debt-relief concessions) has contributed to a considerable burden of debt. Upon assuming office, the Ousmane administration acted swiftly to restore a dialogue with the international financial community. However, despite a marked increase in GDP in 1994, the failure to meet targets for increased revenue collection and spending cuts prompted the suspension of IMF funding, and the success of the Government of Hama Amadou in securing new funding will largely depend on its ability to reconcile the demands of the labour movement with the need for rigorous austerity. While the devaluation of the CFA franc, in January 1994, has to some extent benefited the rural economy, promoted domestic production as a substitute for imports and increased the competitiveness of Nigerien uranium (an important new purchase arrangement was concluded with France in late 1994), urban areas have been severely affected by price increases, and the domestic market is too small to provide a major stimulus to the manufacturing sector. The Tuareg rebellion in the north has, since the early 1990s, necessitated increased expenditure on the military, and the outcome of any peace initiatives may depend on the Government's capacity to finance infrastructural projects in remote areas. However, there is optimism among foreign investors regarding the development of the industrial gold-mining sector, which may offer an important new source of government revenue.

### Social Welfare

There is a guaranteed national basic wage. In 1993 Niger had only three national hospitals and five departmental hospitals, while there were 32 maternity units and 40 dispensaries. In the early 1990s there was one physician for every 48,000 inhabitants. Of total projected expenditure by the central Government in the 15 months to the end of December 1990, 12,434m. francs CFA (5.2%) was for health (135m. francs CFA was also allocated to social security and welfare during that period).

### Education

Education is available free of charge, and is officially compulsory for eight years between seven and 15 years of age. Primary education begins at the age of seven and lasts for six years. Secondary education begins at the age of 13 years, and comprises a four-year cycle followed by a further, three-year cycle. Primary enrolment in 1990 included only 25% of children in the appropriate age-group (boys 32%; girls 18%). A basic education project, aiming to improve and to extend access to primary education, was inaugurated in mid-1994. Funding for the project, the cost of which was estimated at US $76m., was to be provided by the International Development Association and the Governments of Niger, Germany and Norway. Enrolment at secondary schools in 1990 included only 6% of the relevant age-group (boys 8%; girls 3%). The University of Niamey was inaugurated in 1973, and the Islamic University of West Africa, at Say (to the south of the capital), was opened in January 1987. Scholarships are also provided for higher education in France and Senegal. Expenditure on education by the central Government in the 15 months to the end of December 1990 was projected at 24,409m. francs CFA, representing 10.3% of total spending. At the time of the 1988 census the adult illiteracy rate averaged 89.1% (males 83.1%; females 94.6%).

### Public Holidays

**1995:** 1 January (New Year's Day), 3 March* (Id al-Fitr, end of Ramadan), 15 April (Anniversary of the 1974 *coup d'état*), 17 April (Easter Monday), 1 May (Labour Day), 10 May* (Id al-Adha, Feast of the Sacrifice), 31 May* (Islamic New Year), 3 August (Independence Day), 9 August* (Mouloud, Birth of the Prophet), 18 December (Republic Day), 25 December (Christmas).

**1996:** 1 January (New Year's Day), 21 February* (Id al-Fitr, end of Ramadan), 8 April (Easter Monday), 15 April (Anniversary of the 1974 *coup d'état*), 29 April* (Id al-Adha, Feast of the Sacrifice), 1 May (Labour Day), 19 May* (Islamic New Year), 28 July* (Mouloud, Birth of the Prophet), 3 August (Independence Day), 18 December (Republic Day), 25 December (Christmas).

* These holidays are dependent on the Islamic lunar calendar and may vary by one or two days from the dates given.

### Weights and Measures

The metric system is in force.

> # Statistical Survey

Source (unless otherwise stated): Direction de la Statistique et de l'Informatique, Ministère des Finances et du Plan, BP 720, Niamey; tel. 72-23-74; telex 5463; fax 73-33-71.

## Area and Population

### AREA, POPULATION AND DENSITY

| | |
|---|---:|
| Area (sq km) | 1,267,000* |
| Population (census results) | |
| 20 November 1977 | |
| Males | 2,514,532 |
| Females | 2,583,895 |
| Total | 5,098,427 |
| 20 May 1988 (provisional) | 7,248,100 |
| Population (official estimate at mid-year) | |
| 1993 | 8,361,000 |
| Density (per sq km) at mid-1993 | 6.6 |

* 489,191 sq miles.

### ETHNIC GROUPS (estimated population at 1 July 1972)*

| | | | |
|---|---:|---|---:|
| Hausa | 2,279,000 | Tuareg, etc | 127,000 |
| Djerma-Songhai | 1,001,000 | Beriberi-Manga | 386,000 |
| Fulani (Peulh) | 450,000 | **Total** | 4,243,000 |

* Provisional figures. Revised total is 4,239,000.

### PRINCIPAL TOWNS (population in 1977)

| | | | |
|---|---:|---|---:|
| Niamey (capital) | 225,314 | Tahoua | 31,265 |
| Zinder | 58,436 | Agadez | 20,475 |
| Maradi | 45,852 | Birni N'Konni | 15,227 |

**1981** (estimates): Niamey 360,000; Zinder 75,000.

### BIRTHS AND DEATHS (UN estimates, annual averages)

| | 1975–80 | 1980–85 | 1985–90 |
|---|---:|---:|---:|
| Birth rate (per 1,000) | 52.2 | 52.0 | 51.7 |
| Death rate (per 1,000) | 23.8 | 22.1 | 20.4 |

**Expectation of life** (UN estimates, years at birth, 1985–90): 44.5 (males 42.9; females 46.1).

Source: UN, *World Population Prospects: The 1992 Revision*.

### ECONOMICALLY ACTIVE POPULATION
(ILO estimates, '000 persons at mid-1980)

| | Males | Females | Total |
|---|---:|---:|---:|
| Agriculture, etc | 1,314 | 1,296 | 2,610 |
| Industry | 45 | 2 | 47 |
| Services | 130 | 78 | 209 |
| **Total labour force** | 1,489 | 1,376 | 2,865 |

Source: ILO, *Economically Active Population Estimates and Projections, 1950-2025*.

**Mid-1993** (estimates in '000): Agriculture, etc. 3,645; Total 4,241 (Source: FAO, *Production Yearbook*).

## Agriculture

### PRINCIPAL CROPS ('000 metric tons)

| | 1991 | 1992 | 1993 |
|---|---:|---:|---:|
| Maize | 1 | 1 | 1* |
| Millet | 1,833 | 1,788 | 1,430* |
| Sorghum | 463 | 387 | 305* |
| Rice (paddy) | 75 | 70† | 72* |
| Sugar cane* | 140 | 140 | 140 |
| Sweet potatoes* | 35 | 35 | 35 |
| Cassava (Manioc)* | 216 | 218 | 220 |
| Onions (dry) | 169 | 170* | 175* |
| Tomatoes | 45 | 45* | 45* |
| Other vegetables | 35 | 36* | 37* |
| Pulses | 441 | 508* | 508* |
| Dates* | 7 | 7 | 7 |
| Other fruit* | 37 | 38 | 39 |
| Groundnuts (in shell) | 46 | 57 | 60* |
| Cottonseed† | 2 | 3 | 2 |
| Cotton (lint)† | 1 | 2 | 1 |
| Tobacco (leaves)* | 1 | 1 | 1 |

* FAO estimate(s).   † Unofficial figure(s).

Source: FAO, *Production Yearbook*.

**Cow-peas** ('000 metric tons): 461.2 in 1991/92; 75.9 in 1992/93; 424.8 in 1993/94 (Source: Banque centrale des états de l'Afrique de l'ouest).

### LIVESTOCK ('000 head, year ending September)

| | 1991 | 1992 | 1993 |
|---|---:|---:|---:|
| Horses* | 82 | 82 | 82 |
| Asses | 449 | 450* | 462* |
| Cattle | 1,790 | 1,800* | 1,800* |
| Camels | 356† | 363† | 370† |
| Pigs* | 38 | 38 | 39 |
| Sheep | 3,253 | 3,400* | 3,505* |
| Goats | 5,214 | 5,400* | 5,407* |

Poultry (million)*: 19 in 1991; 20 in 1992; 21 in 1993.

* FAO estimate(s).   † Unofficial figure.

Source: FAO, *Production Yearbook*.

### LIVESTOCK PRODUCTS (FAO estimates, '000 metric tons)

| | 1991 | 1992 | 1993 |
|---|---:|---:|---:|
| Beef and veal | 34 | 35 | 36 |
| Mutton and lamb | 12 | 12 | 13 |
| Goat meat | 20 | 20 | 20 |
| Pig meat | 1 | 1 | 1 |
| Poultry meat | 22 | 23 | 24 |
| Other meat | 17 | 19 | 20 |
| Cows' milk | 148 | 152 | 161 |
| Sheep's milk | 12 | 12 | 12 |
| Goats' milk | 86 | 87 | 87 |
| Cheese | 11.8 | 12.0 | 12.0 |
| Butter | 4.1 | 4.2 | 4.4 |
| Poultry eggs | 8.7 | 8.8 | 9.0 |
| Cattle hides | 4.3 | 4.3 | 4.3 |
| Sheepskins | 1.5 | 1.5 | 1.5 |
| Goatskins | 3.3 | 3.3 | 3.4 |

Source: FAO, *Production Yearbook*.

# Forestry

**ROUNDWOOD REMOVALS**
(FAO estimates, '000 cubic metres, excluding bark)

|  | 1990 | 1991 | 1992 |
|---|---|---|---|
| Industrial wood | 306 | 316 | 326 |
| Fuel wood | 4,650 | 4,803 | 4,963 |
| **Total** | 4,956 | 5,119 | 5,289 |

Source: FAO, *Yearbook of Forest Products*.

# Fishing

('000 metric tons, live weight)

|  | 1990 | 1991 | 1992 |
|---|---|---|---|
| **Total catch** | 3.4 | 3.2 | 2.1 |

Source: FAO, *Yearbook of Fishery Statistics*.

# Mining

('000 metric tons, unless otherwise indicated)

|  | 1989 | 1990 | 1991 |
|---|---|---|---|
| Salt* | 3 | 3 | 3 |
| Gypsum* | 3† | 3 | 3 |
| Hard coal† | 157 | 158 | 157 |
| Tin (metric tons)‡§ | 63 | 38 | 70 |
| Uranium (metric tons)‡ | 2,962 | 2,831 | 2,777 |

* Data from the US Bureau of Mines.
† Provisional or estimated figure.
‡ Data refer to the metal content of ore.
§ Data from *International Tin Statistics*.

Source: UN, *Industrial Statistics Yearbook*.

**Uranium** (metal content of ore, metric tons): 3,071 in 1992; 2,850 in 1993 (Sources: Société des Mines de l'Aïr; Compagnie Minière d'Akouta).

# Industry

**SELECTED PRODUCTS** ('000 metric tons, unless otherwise indicated)

|  | 1987 | 1988 | 1989 |
|---|---|---|---|
| Salted, dried or smoked fish* | 1.0† | 1.0 | 1.1 |
| Soft drinks ('000 hectolitres) | 105 | 98 | n.a. |
| Woven cotton fabrics (million sq metres)† | 39 | 20 | n.a. |
| Cement‡ | 29 | 40 | 27 |
| Electric energy (million kWh) | 157 | 160 | 163 |

**1990:** Cement ('000 metric tons) 27‡; Electric energy (million kWh) 165.
**1991:** Cement ('000 metric tons) 28‡; Electric Energy (million kWh) 168.

* Data from the FAO.
† Provisional or estimated figures.
‡ Data from the US Bureau of Mines.

Source: UN, *Industrial Statistics Yearbook*.

# Finance

**CURRENCY AND EXCHANGE RATES**

**Monetary Units**
100 centimes = 1 franc de la Communauté financière africaine (CFA).

**French Franc, Sterling and Dollar Equivalents** (31 December 1994)
1 French franc = 100 francs CFA;
£1 sterling = 834.94 francs CFA;
US $1 = 533.68 francs CFA;
1,000 francs CFA = £1.198 = $1.874.

**Average Exchange Rate** (francs CFA per US $)
1992  264.69
1993  283.16
1994  555.20

Note: An exchange rate of 1 French franc = 50 francs CFA, established in 1948, remained in force until January 1994, when the CFA franc was devalued by 50%, with the exchange rate adjusted to 1 French franc = 100 francs CFA.

**BUDGET ESTIMATES** ('000 million francs CFA)

| Revenue | 1991 | 1992 | 1993 |
|---|---|---|---|
| Current revenue | 81.6 | 83.4 | 89.9 |
| Tax receipts | 61.7 | 50.8 | 47.7 |
| Other current revenue | 19.9 | 32.6 | 42.2 |
| Capital receipts | 0.3 | — | — |
| Aid, grants and subsidies | 68.1 | 46.1 | 38.8 |
| Borrowing | 36.2 | 58.9 | 44.7 |
| **Total** | 186.2 | 188.4 | 173.4 |

| Expenditure | 1991 | 1992 | 1993 |
|---|---|---|---|
| Administrative expenditure | 68.9 | 84.7 | 69.6 |
| Investment expenditure | 86.8 | 71.6 | 67.2 |
| Debt-servicing | 30.5 | 32.1 | 37.5 |
| **Total** | 186.2 | 188.4 | 174.3 |

Source: Banque centrale des états de l'Afrique de l'ouest.

**1994** (draft budget, million francs CFA): Recurrent budget balanced at 57,600m.; Investment budget (incl. borrowing) balanced at 108,700m.

**INTERNATIONAL RESERVES** (US $ million at 31 December)

|  | 1991 | 1992 | 1993 |
|---|---|---|---|
| Gold* | 3.9 | 3.8 | 4.1 |
| IMF special drawing rights | 0.4 | — | 0.6 |
| Reserve position in IMF | 12.2 | 11.8 | 11.8 |
| Foreign exchange | 190.1 | 213.2 | 179.7 |
| **Total** | 206.7 | 228.8 | 196.1 |

* Valued at market-related prices.

Source: IMF, *International Financial Statistics*.

**MONEY SUPPLY** ('000 million francs CFA at 31 December)

|  | 1991 | 1992 | 1993 |
|---|---|---|---|
| Currency outside banks | 40.97 | 39.66 | 48.35 |
| Demand deposits at deposit money banks* | 34.71 | 30.51 | 28.83 |
| Checking deposits at post office | 4.25 | 1.51 | 1.92 |
| **Total money** (incl. others)* | 79.93 | 71.70 | 79.52 |

* Excluding the deposits of public enterprises of an administrative or social nature.

Source: IMF, *International Financial Statistics*.

# NIGER

*Statistical Survey*

## COST OF LIVING
(Consumer Price Index for Africans in Niamey; base: 1989 = 100)*

|  | 1991 | 1992 |
|---|---|---|
| Food | 94.2 | 91.6 |
| Clothing | 100.8 | 101.9 |
| **All items** (incl. others) | 96.1 | 94.5 |

* Except rent.

Source: ILO, *Year Book of Labour Statistics*.

## NATIONAL ACCOUNTS (million francs CFA at current prices)
### Expenditure on the Gross Domestic Product

|  | 1988 | 1989 | 1990* |
|---|---|---|---|
| Government final consumption expenditure | 104,994 | 124,420 | 117,567 |
| Private final consumption expenditure | 446,691 | 505,323 | 505,293 |
| Increase in stocks | 53,618 | −506 | 7,992 |
| Gross fixed capital formation | 81,008 | 85,391 | 79,967 |
| **Total domestic expenditure** | 686,311 | 714,628 | 710,819 |
| Exports of goods and services | 140,500 | 129,100 | 114,512 |
| *Less* Imports of goods and services | 148,600 | 151,126 | 142,361 |
| **GDP in purchasers' values** | 678,211 | 692,602 | 682,970 |

* Provisional figures.

### Gross Domestic Product by Economic Activity

|  | 1988 | 1989 | 1990* |
|---|---|---|---|
| Agriculture, hunting, forestry and fishing | 240,164 | 236,903 | 238,095 |
| Mining and quarrying | 44,671 | 43,857 | 34,899 |
| Manufacturing | 40,856 | 43,954 | 44,194 |
| Electricity, gas and water | 15,323 | 17,465 | 12,315 |
| Construction | 16,004 | 14,824 | 17,042 |
| Trade, restaurants and hotels | 130,608 | 130,463 | 137,732 |
| Transport, storage and communications | 31,798 | 28,717 | 27,477 |
| Other marketable services† | 53,837 | 58,106 | 58,815 |
| Non-marketable services | 85,846 | 98,807 | 94,324 |
| **Sub-total** | 659,107 | 673,096 | 664,893 |
| Import duties | 19,104 | 19,506 | 18,077 |
| **GDP in purchasers' values** | 678,211 | 692,602 | 682,970 |

* Provisional figures.
† After deduction of imputed bank service charge.

Source: Banque centrale des états de l'Afrique de l'ouest.

## BALANCE OF PAYMENTS (US $ million)

|  | 1991 | 1992 | 1993 |
|---|---|---|---|
| Merchandise exports f.o.b. | 283.9 | 265.6 | 238.4 |
| Merchandise imports f.o.b. | −273.3 | −266.3 | −244.0 |
| **Trade balance** | 10.6 | −0.8 | −5.7 |
| Exports of services | 57.1 | 52.1 | 49.8 |
| Imports of services | −157.0 | −148.1 | −139.5 |
| Other income received | 1.4 | — | — |
| Other income paid | −38.6 | −37.4 | −36.0 |
| Private unrequited transfers (net) | −37.9 | −39.7 | −33.9 |
| Official unrequited transfers (net) | 157.4 | 129.2 | 136.3 |
| **Current balance** | −7.1 | −44.6 | −29.0 |
| Capital (net) | −22.3 | 12.5 | −25.0 |
| Net errors and omissions | −40.4 | 15.6 | −9.4 |
| **Overall balance** | −69.8 | −16.5 | −63.4 |

Source: IMF, *International Financial Statistics*.

# External Trade

Source: Banque centrale des états de l'Afrique de l'ouest.

## PRINCIPAL COMMODITIES (million francs CFA)

| Imports c.i.f. | 1985* | 1987† | 1988 |
|---|---|---|---|
| **Food and live animals** | 53,826 | 26,510 | 27,957 |
| Food products of animal origin | 3,573 | 1,525 | 4,296 |
| Dairy products | 3,150 | 1,264 | 3,806 |
| Food products of plant origin | 41,419 | 17,120 | 15,334 |
| Cereals | 36,094 | 12,400 | 9,083 |
| Processed foodstuffs | 8,834 | 7,865 | 8,327 |
| Sugar and confectionery | 4,784 | 4,666 | 4,262 |
| **Energy products** | 17,123 | 5,090 | 6,316 |
| Refined petroleum products | 16,944 | 4,943 | 6,163 |
| **Inedible crude materials (except fuels)** | 5,243 | 4,095 | 3,949 |
| **Fats and oils** | 2,993 | 2,990 | 1,157 |
| **Machinery and transport equipment** | 31,695 | 21,265 | 30,684 |
| Non-electrical machinery | 13,660 | 8,071 | 11,179 |
| Electrical machinery | 4,915 | 3,216 | 5,438 |
| Road transport equipment | 12,920 | 9,794 | 13,792 |
| **Other industrial products** | 40,669 | 32,144 | 43,400 |
| Chemicals | 12,500 | 10,682 | 13,993 |
| **Miscellaneous manufactured articles** | 28,169 | 21,462 | 29,407 |
| Cotton yarn and fabrics | 6,482 | 3,591 | 4,176 |
| **Total** (incl. others) | 154,787 | 93,388 | 115,193 |

| Exports f.o.b. | 1985* | 1987† | 1988 |
|---|---|---|---|
| **Food and live animals** | 13,588 | 2,096 | 6,072 |
| Food products of animal origin | 11,207 | 383 | 3,471 |
| Live animals | 10,905 | 372 | 3,463 |
| Food products of plant origin | 2,178 | 1,619 | 2,526 |
| Vegetables | 2,112 | 1,580 | 2,372 |
| **Inedible crude materials (except fuels)** | 76,937 | 87,881 | 76,359 |
| Uranium ore | 74,083 | 85,394 | 74,928 |
| Hides and skins | 2,093 | 312 | 641 |
| **Machinery and transport equipment** | 1,300 | 2,229 | 1,680 |
| **Total** (incl. others) | 93,901 | 93,895 | 85,941 |

* Provisional figures.
† Figures for 1986 are not available.

## PRINCIPAL TRADING PARTNERS (million francs CFA)*

| Imports c.i.f. | 1983 | 1984† | 1985† |
|---|---|---|---|
| Algeria | 1,641 | 985 | 387 |
| Belgium-Luxembourg | 1,430 | 1,557 | 2,152 |
| Brazil | 1,598 | 2,509 | 2,852 |
| Canada | 812 | 1,457 | 3,434 |
| China, People's Republic | 1,229 | 4,468 | 5,003 |
| Côte d'Ivoire | 5,125 | 7,398 | 11,207 |
| France | 40,489 | 34,075 | 42,877 |
| Germany, Federal Republic | 4,468 | 5,487 | 8,551 |
| Italy | 1,200 | 2,158 | 4,073 |
| Japan | 3,613 | 5,239 | 5,842 |
| Netherlands | 1,895 | 2,680 | 2,886 |
| Nigeria | 39,031 | 18,433 | 10,358 |
| Pakistan | 606 | 3,503 | 4,827 |
| Senegal | 1,957 | 1,627 | 1,339 |
| Thailand | 467 | 1,750 | 4,564 |
| United Kingdom | 2,223 | 2,286 | 3,110 |
| USA | 5,633 | 6,140 | 17,666 |
| **Total** (incl. others) | 123,288 | 124,620 | 154,787 |

NIGER

| Exports f.o.b. | 1983 | 1984† | 1985† |
|---|---|---|---|
| Algeria | 201 | 821 | 3,157 |
| Burkina Faso | 333 | 1,888 | 463 |
| Côte d'Ivoire | 311 | 1,130 | 1,599 |
| France | 54,727 | 61,427 | 61,641 |
| Germany, Federal Republic | 5,136 | 7,066 | 71 |
| Italy | 3,547 | 1,180 | 1,084 |
| Japan | 25,942 | 20,894 | 5,676 |
| Mali | 1,142 | 2,063 | 326 |
| Nigeria | 12,608 | 12,618 | 12,859 |
| Spain | 5,913 | 3,900 | 5,474 |
| **Total** (incl. others) | 113,896 | 119,495 | 93,901 |

* Imports by country of production; exports by country of destination.
† Provisional figures.

## Transport

**ROAD TRAFFIC** (vehicles in use at 31 December)

| | 1987* | 1989†‡ | 1990‡ |
|---|---|---|---|
| Cars | 27,254 | 31,342 | 31,427 |
| Buses and coaches | 2,253 | 2,559 | 2,695 |
| Goods vehicles | 5,687 | 5,968 | 6,073 |
| Vans | 14,807 | n.a. | n.a. |
| Tractors, trailers and semi-trailers | 4,696 | 2,144§ | 2,217§ |
| Motor cycles and mopeds | 8,925 | n.a. | n.a. |

* Source: Direction des Transports, Niamey.
† Figures for 1988 are not available.
‡ Source: International Road Federation, *World Road Statistics*.
§ Trailers and semi-trailers only.

**CIVIL AVIATION** (traffic on scheduled services)*

| | 1990 | 1991 | 1992 |
|---|---|---|---|
| Kilometres flown (million) | 2 | 2 | 2 |
| Passengers carried ('000) | 76 | 66 | 66 |
| Passenger-km (million) | 232 | 207 | 201 |
| Total ton-km (million) | 39 | 36 | 34 |

* Including an apportionment of the traffic of Air Afrique.
Source: UN, *Statistical Yearbook*.

## Tourism

| | 1990 | 1991 | 1992 |
|---|---|---|---|
| Tourist arrivals ('000) | 21 | 16 | 13 |
| Tourist receipts (US $ million) | 17 | 16 | 17 |

Source: UN, *Statistical Yearbook*.

## Communications Media

| | 1990 | 1991 | 1992 |
|---|---|---|---|
| Radio receivers ('000 in use) | 460 | 480 | 500 |
| Television receivers ('000 in use) | 35 | 37 | 38 |
| Telephones ('000 in use)* | 13 | 14 | n.a. |
| Daily newspapers | | | |
| Number | 1 | n.a. | 1 |
| Average circulation ('000 copies) | 5 | n.a. | 5 |
| Books published† | | | |
| Titles | n.a. | 5 | n.a. |
| Copies ('000) | n.a. | 11 | n.a. |

* Estimates.   † All first editions.
Sources: UNESCO, *Statistical Yearbook*; UN Economic Commission for Africa, *African Statistical Yearbook*.

## Education

(1990, unless otherwise indicated)

| | Institutions | Teachers | Students Males | Students Females | Students Total |
|---|---|---|---|---|---|
| Pre-primary | 81 | 317 | 6,103 | 5,593 | 11,696 |
| Primary | 2,307 | 8,853 | 235,480 | 133,252 | 368,732 |
| Secondary | | | | | |
| General | n.a. | 2,534 | 52,453 | 21,884 | 74,337 |
| Teacher training | n.a. | 122 | 917 | 661 | 1,578 |
| Vocational | n.a. | 119 | 769 | 74 | 843 |
| University level | n.a. | 341* | 3,831 | 675 | 4,506 |

* 1988 figure.   † 1989 figure.
Source: UNESCO, *Statistical Yearbook*.

# Directory

## The Constitution

The Constitution of the Third Republic of Niger was approved in a national referendum on 26 December 1992, and was promulgated in January 1993.

The Constitution emphasizes the secular nature of Nigerien society.

The President of the Republic is elected, by universal adult suffrage, for a period of five years (renewable only once). The unicameral legislature, the Assemblée nationale, is similarly elected with a five-year mandate. All elections are conducted in the context of a multi-party system.

The President of the Republic, who is Head of State, appoints the Prime Minister, and, on the latter's recommendation, other ministers. The Council of Ministers is responsible to the Assemblée nationale.

The Assemblée nationale appoints a Speaker from among its 83 members. The President of the Republic may dissolve the legislature.

The rights, freedoms and obligations of the individual and of the press, political organizations and other associations are among the principles enshrined in the Constitution. Also guaranteed is the independence of the judiciary.

## The Government

### HEAD OF STATE

**President of the Republic:** MAHAMANE OUSMANE (inaugurated 16 April 1993).

### COUNCIL OF MINISTERS
(June 1995)

**Prime Minister:** HAMA AMADOU.
**Minister of State, in charge of Industrial Development, Trade, Handicrafts and Tourism:** SIDIKI OUMAROU.
**Minister of Foreign Affairs and Co-operation:** MOHAMED BAZOUM.
**Minister of Mines and Energy:** ISSOUFOU ASSOUMANE.
**Minister of Finance and Planning:** ALMOUSTAPHA SOUMAILA.
**Minister of National Defence:** MAHAMANE DOBI.
**Minister of National Education and Spokesperson for the Government:** BOULI ALI DIALLO.
**Minister of Justice:** IBRAHIM BAIDOU.
**Minister of the Interior and Territorial Development:** MOUSSA el Hadj IBRAHIM.
**Minister of Public Health:** AMSTRONG KARNA.
**Minister of Agriculture and Livestock:** ALITOR MANO.
**Minister of Water Resources and the Environment:** SANI BAWA.
**Minister of the Civil Service, Labour and Employment:** ZAHOURI OUSMANE.
**Minister of Equipment and Transport:** AHMOUD OUSMANE.
**Minister of Social Development, Population and Women's Promotion:** AISSATOU DAMBO DODO.
**Minister of Communications, Culture, Youth and Sports:** KAKA AMADOU.
**Minister of Higher Education, Research and Technology:** MOUKE DEJI.

### MINISTRIES

**Office of the President of the Republic:** Palais Présidentiel, Niamey.
**Office of the Prime Minister:** Niamey.
**Ministry of Agriculture and Livestock:** BP 10427, Niamey; tel. 73-31-55.
**Ministry of the Civil Service, Labour and Employment:** Niamey; tel. 72-25-01; telex 5283.
**Ministry of Communications, Culture, Youth and Sports:** Niamey; tel. 72-24-89; telex 5214.
**Ministry of Equipment and Transport:** Niamey; tel. 72-25-01; telex 5283.
**Ministry of Finance and Planning:** BP 720, Niamey; tel. 72-23-74; telex 5463; fax 73-33-71.
**Ministry of Foreign Affairs and Co-operation:** BP 396, Niamey; tel. 72-29-07; telex 5200.
**Ministry of Industrial Development, Trade, Handicrafts and Tourism:** Niamey.
**Ministry of the Interior and Territorial Development:** Niamey; tel. 72-21-76; telex 5214.
**Ministry of Justice:** Niamey; tel. 72-20-94; telex 5214.
**Ministry of Mines and Energy:** BP 11700, Niamey; tel. 73-45-82; telex 5214.
**Ministry of National Defence:** BP 626, Niamey; tel. 72-20-76; telex 5291.
**Ministry of National Education:** Quartier Yantala Haut, BP 11897, Niamey; tel. 72-25-26.
**Ministry of Public Health:** BP 623, Niamey; tel. 72-27-82; telex 5533.
**Ministry of Social Development, Population and Women's Promotion:** Niamey.
**Ministry of Water Resources and the Environment:** Niamey.

## President and Legislature

### PRESIDENT

**Presidential Election, First Ballot, 27 February 1993**

| Candidate | % of votes |
|---|---|
| TANDJA MAMADOU (MNSD—Nassara) | 34.22 |
| MAHAMANE OUSMANE (CDS—Rahama) | 26.59 |
| MAHAMADOU ISSOUFOU (PNDS—Tarayya) | 15.92 |
| MOUMOUNI AMADOU DJERMAKOYE (ANDP—Zaman Lahiya) | 15.24 |
| ILLA KANE (UPDP—Shamuwa) | 2.55 |
| OUMAROU YOUSSOUFOU GARBA (PPN—RDA) | 1.99 |
| KAZELMA OUMAR TAYA (PSDN—Alheri) | 1.82 |
| DJIBO BAKARY (UDFP—Sawaba) | 1.68 |
| **Total** | **100.00** |

**Second Ballot, 27 March 1993**

| Candidate | % of votes |
|---|---|
| MAHAMANE OUSMANE | 55.42 |
| TANDJA MAMADOU | 44.58 |
| **Total** | **100.00** |

### ASSEMBLÉE NATIONALE

**Speaker:** MAHAMADOU ISSOUFOU.

**General Election, 12 January 1995**

| Party | Seats |
|---|---|
| MNSD—Nassara | 29 |
| CDS—Rahama* | 24 |
| PNDS—Tarayya | 12 |
| ANDPS—Zaman Lahiya* | 9 |
| PUND—Salama* | 3 |
| PSDN—Alheri* | 2 |
| UDPS—Amana* | 2 |
| UPDP—Shamuwa | 1 |
| PPN—RDA | 1 |
| **Total** | **83** |

* Denotes organizations participating in the Alliance des forces de changement (see below).

## Political Organizations

There were 20 legalized political parties in early 1995, about 15 of which contested seats at the January legislative elections.

**Alliance des forces de changement (AFC):** f. 1993; alliance of eight parties supporting President Mahamane Ousmane.

**Alliance nigérienne pour la démocratie et le progrès social—Zaman Lahiya (ANDPS—Zaman Lahiya):** Leader MOUMOUNI AMADOU DJERMAKOYE.

**Convention démocratique et social—Rahama (CDS—Rahama):** Chair. MAHAMANE OUSMANE.

**Front démocratique nigérien—Mountounchi (FDN—Mountounchi):** f. 1995 by fmr mems of PPN—RDA; Chair. OUMAROU YOUSSOUFOU EARBA: Sec.-Gen. MOHAMED MUDUR.

**Parti républicain pour les libertés et le progrès au Niger—Nakowa (PRLPN—Nakowa).**

**Parti social-démocrate nigérien—Alheri (PSDN—Alheri):** Leader KAZELMA OUMAR TAYA.

**Parti pour l'unite nationale et le développement—Salama PUND—Salama):** Leader PASCAL MAMADOU.

**Union pour la démocratie et le progrès—Amici (UDP—Amici).**

**Union pour la démocratie et le progrès social—Amana (UDPS—Amana):** Chair. MOHAMED ABDULLAHI.

**Mouvement national pour une société de développement—Nassara (MNSD—Nassara):** f. 1988 as MNSD, name changed in 1991; sole party 1988–90; Chair. Col (retd) TANDJA MAMADOU; Sec.-Gen. HAMA AMADOU.

**Parti nigérien pour la démocratie et le socialisme—Tarayya (PNDS—Tarayya):** mem. of AFC until Sept. 1994; Sec.-Gen. MAHAMADOU ISSOUFOU.

**Parti progressiste nigérien—Rassemblement démocratique africain (PPN—RDA):** associated with the late President Diori; withdrew from AFC prior to January 1995 elections; Chair. DANDIKO DANKOULODO; Sec.-Gen. IDE OUMAROU.

**Union des forces populaires pour la démocratie et le progrès—Sawaba (UFPDP—Sawaba):** Chair. DJIBO BAKARY.

**Union des patriotes démocratiques et progressistes—Shamuwa (UPDP—Shamuwa):** Chair. Prof. ANDRÉ SALIFOU.

## Diplomatic Representation

### EMBASSIES IN NIGER

**Algeria:** ave des Zarmakoye, BP 142, Niamey; tel. 75-30-97; telex 5262; fax 75-32-03; Ambassador: MADJID BOUGUERRA.

**Belgium:** BP 10192, Niamey; tel. 73-34-47; telex 5329; fax 73-37-56; Ambassador: FRANK RECKER.

**Benin:** BP 11544, Niamey; tel. 72-39-19; Ambassador: KOLAWOLÉ IDJI.

**China (Taiwan):** BP 743, Niamey; Ambassador: LIN JYH-HORNG.

**Egypt:** Nouveau Plateau, Niamey; tel. 73-33-55; telex 5245; Ambassador: Dr SOBHY MOHAMED NAFEH.

**France:** BP 10660, Niamey; tel. 72-24-31; telex 5220; Ambassador: JEAN-FRANÇOIS LIONNET.

**Germany:** ave du Général de Gaulle, BP 629, Niamey; tel. 72-25-34; telex 5223; fax 72-39-85; Ambassador: ANGELIKA VÖLKEL.

**Iran:** ave de la Présidence, Niamey; tel. 72-21-98; Chargé d'affaires: FAGHIH ALI ABADI MEHDI.

**Libya:** Rond-point du Grand Hôtel, POB 683, Niamey; tel. 73-47-92; telex 5429; Sec. of People's Cttee: AHMED KHALIFA ERRAJEL.

**Mauritania:** Yantala, BP 12519, Niamey; tel. 72-38-93; Ambassador: MOHAMED EL HOUSSEIN OULD HABIBOU ALLAH.

**Morocco:** ave du Président Lubke, BP 12403, Niamey; tel. 73-40-84; telex 5205; fax 74-14-27; Ambassador: TAHAR NEJJAR.

**Nigeria:** BP 11130, Niamey; tel. 73-24-10; telex 5259; Ambassador: KABIRU AHMED.

**Pakistan:** BP 10426, Niamey; tel. 72-35-84; telex 5268; Chargé d'affaires: IRFAN-UR-REHMAN RAJA.

**Russia:** BP 10153, Niamey; tel. 73-27-40; telex 5539; Ambassador: VITALY Y. LITVINE.

**Saudi Arabia:** Yantala, BP 339, Niamey; tel. 72-32-15; telex 5279; Ambassador: GHASSAN SAID SADEK RACHACH.

**Tunisia:** ave du Général de Gaulle, BP 742, Niamey; tel. 72-26-03; telex 5379; Ambassador: RHIDA TNANI.

**USA:** Yantala, BP 11201, Niamey; tel. 72-26-61; telex 5444; Ambassador: JOHN S. DAVISON.

## Judicial System

**Attorney-General:** SULI ABDOURAHMANE.

**Supreme Court:** Niamey; Pres. MAHAMANE MALLAM AOUMI.

**High Court of Justice:** Niamey; competent to indict the President of the Republic and all other state officials (past and present) in relation to all matters of state except high treason and other crimes against state security; Pres. MOUTARY MAMANE.

**Court of State Security:** Niamey; competent to try cases not within the jurisdiction of the High Court of Justice; incorporates a martial court; Pres. M. MAÏ-MAÏGANA.

**Court of Appeal:** Niamey; court of appeal for judgements of **Criminal** and **Assize Courts** (the latter at Niamey, Maradi, Tahoua and Zinder).

**Courts of First Instance:** located at Niamey (with sub-divisions at Dosso and Tillabéry), Maradi, Tahoua (sub-divisions at Agadez, Arlit and Birni N'Konni) and Diffa (sub-division at Diffa).

**Labour Courts:** function at each Court of the First Instance and sub-division thereof.

## Religion

It is estimated that more than 85% of the population are Muslims, 0.5% are Christians and the remainder follow traditional beliefs.

### ISLAM

The most influential Islamic groups are the Tijaniyya, the Senoussi and the Hamallists.

### CHRISTIANITY

Various Protestant missions maintain 13 centres, with a personnel of 90.

#### The Roman Catholic Church

Niger comprises a single diocese, directly responsible to the Holy See. The diocese participates in the Bishops' Conference of Burkina Faso and Niger (based in Ouagadougou, Burkina Faso). In Niger the Roman Catholic Church has about 19,000 adherents (31 December 1993).

**Bishop of Niamey:** (vacant); Apostolic Admin. Mgr GUY ROMANO, Titular Bishop of Caput Cilla, Evêché, BP 10270, Niamey; tel. 73-30-79; fax 74-10-13.

## The Press

**Amfani:** Niamey; independent.

**Angam:** Niamey; f. 1992; monthly; independent; Dir GRÉMAH BOUKAR.

**Al-Habari:** Niamey; independent.

**Haske:** BP 297, Niamey; tel. 74-18-44; fax 73-20-06; f. 1990; weekly; independent; Dir IBRAHIM CHEIKH DIOP.

**Haske Magazine:** BP 297; tel. 74-18-44; fax 73-20-06; f. 1990; quarterly; independent; Dir IBRAHIM CHEIKH DIOP; circ. 3,000.

**Horizon 2001:** Niamey; f. 1991; monthly; independent; Dir INOUSSA OUSSEÏNI.

**Journal Officiel de la République du Niger:** BP 116, Niamey; tel. 72-39-30; f. 1960; fortnightly; Man. Editor BONKOULA AMINATOU MAYAKI; circ. 800.

**Kakaki:** Niamey; f. 1991; monthly; independent; Dir SIRAJI KANÉ.

**La Marche:** Niamey; f. 1989; monthly; independent; Dir ABDOULAYE MOUSSA MASSALATCHI.

**Nigerama:** Niamey; quarterly; publ. by the Agence Nigérienne de Presse.

**Le Pont Africain:** Niamey; independent; satirical.

**Le Républicain:** Niamey; f. 1991; weekly; independent, pro-Tuareg; Dir MAMANE ABOU.

**Le Sahel:** BP 13182, Niamey; f. 1960; publ. by Office National d'Edition et de Presse; daily; Dir ALI OUSSEÏNI; circ. 5,000.

**Le Sahel Dimanche:** BP 13182, Niamey; publ. by Office National d'Edition et de Presse; weekly; Dir ALI OUSSEÏNI; circ. 3,000.

**La Tribune du Peuple:** Niamey; independent; Man. Editor IBRAHIM HAMIDOU.

### NEWS AGENCIES

**Agence Nigérienne de Presse (ANP):** BP 11158, Niamey; tel. 740809; telex 5497; f. 1987; state-owned; Dir BOUREÏMA MAGAGI.

**Office National d'Edition et de Presse (ONEP):** Niamey; f. 1989; Dir ALI OUSSEÏNI.

## Publisher

### Government Publishing House

**L'Imprimerie Nationale du Niger (INN):** BP 61, Niamey; tel. 73-47-98; telex 5312; f. 1962; Dir E. WOHLRAB.

## Radio and Television

In 1992, according to UNESCO estimates, there were 500,000 radio receivers and 38,000 television receivers in use.

**Office de Radiodiffusion-Télévision du Niger (ORTN):** BP 309, Niamey; tel. 72-31-63; telex 5229; state broadcasting authority; Dir-Gen. MAHAMANE ADAMOU; Tech. Dir (Radio and Television) ZOUDI ISSOUF.

**La Voix du Sahel:** BP 361, Niamey; tel. 72-32-72; fax 72-35-48; f. 1958; govt-controlled radio service; programmes in French, Hausa (Haoussa), Djerma (Zarma), Kanuri, Fulfuldé, Tamajak, Toubou, Gourmantché and Arabic; Dir OMAR TIELLO.

**Télé-Sahel:** BP 309, Niamey; tel. 72-31-53; telex 5229; fax 72-35-48; govt-controlled television service; broadcasts daily; Dir MAMANE MAMADOU.

## Finance

(cap. = capital; res = reserves; m. = million; brs = branches; amounts in francs CFA)

### BANKING

#### Central Bank

**Banque Centrale des Etats de l'Afrique de l'Ouest (BCEAO):** Rond-point de la Poste, BP 487, Niamey; tel. 72-24-91; telex 5218; fax 73-47-43; headquarters in Dakar, Senegal; f. 1955; bank of issue for the seven states of the Union économique et monétaire ouest-africaine (UEMOA), comprising Benin, Burkina Faso, Côte d'Ivoire, Mali, Niger, Senegal and Togo; cap. and res 530.8m. (Sept. 1993); Gov. CHARLES KONAN BANNY; Dir in Niger MAMADOU DIOP; brs at Maradi and Zinder.

#### Commercial Banks

**Bank of Africa-Niger:** Immeuble Sonara II, BP 10973, Niamey; tel. 73-36-20; telex 5321; fax 73-38-18; f. 1994 to acquire assets of Nigeria International Bank Niamey (cap. 1,000m.—Sept. 1993); 35% owned by Bank of Africa-Benin, 30% by African Financial Holding; Chair. JACQUES NIGNON.

**Banque Commerciale du Niger (BCN):** Rond-point Maourey, BP 11363, Niamey; tel. 73-33-31; telex 5292; fax 73-21-63; f. 1978; fmrly Banque Arabe Libyenne-Nigérienne pour le Commerce Extérieur et le Développement; owned by private Nigerien (50%) and Libyan (50%) interests; cap. 5,000m. (Sept. 1993); Chair. and Man. Dir CHEICK MOHAMED METRI.

**Banque Islamique du Niger:** ave de la Mairie, BP 12754, Niamey; tel. 73-57-19; telex 5440; fax 73-48-25; f. 1983; fmrly Banque Masraf Faisal Islami, undergoing restructuring in 1994; owned by Dar al-Maal al-Islami (DMI Trust) and private Nigerien interests; Chair. MAHMOUD EL HELLI; Man. Dir LAMINE MOKTAR.

**BIAO-Niger:** ave de la Mairie, BP 10350, Niamey; tel. 73-31-01; telex 5215; fax 73-35-95; f. 1980; 84% owned by Meridien BIAO SA (Luxembourg); cap. 2,201m. (Sept. 1992); Chair. BOUKAR MOUSSA MAÏNA; Man. Dir JEAN-PIERRE CARPENTIER; 5 brs.

**Nigerian Trust Bank:** Immeuble El Nasr, BP 12792, Niamey; tel. 73-42-87; telex 5456; fax 73-33-03; f. 1992 to acquire assets of the fmr Bank of Credit and Commerce Niger (cap. 600m.—Sept. 1990); owned by Nigeria Trust Fund.

**Société Nigérienne de Banque (SONIBANQUE):** ave de la Mairie, BP 891, Niamey; tel. 73-47-40; telex 5480; fax 73-49-83; f. 1990; 25% owned by Société Tunisienne de Banque; cap. 2,000m. (Sept. 1993); Chair. ALMA OUMAROU; Dir-Gen. CHAKIB SIALA.

#### Development Banks

**Caisse de Prêts aux Collectivités Territoriales (CPCT):** route de Torodi, BP 730, Niamey, tel. 72-34-12; 94% owned by Nigerien local govts; cap. 1,355m. (Sept. 1992); Chair. ASSOUMANE ADAMOU; Man. Dir MAHAMED MOUDDOUR.

**Crédit du Niger:** blvd de la République, BP 213, Niger; tel. 72-27-01; telex 5210; fax 72-23-90; f. 1958; 54% state-owned, 20% owned by Caisse Nationale de Sécurité Sociale; cap. 1,720m. (Sept. 1992); Chair. SANI MAHAMANE; Man. Dir ABOU KANÉ.

**Fonds d'Intervention en Faveur des Petites et Moyennes Entreprises Nigériennes (FIPMEN):** Immeuble Sonara II, BP 252, Niamey; tel. 73-20-98; telex 5569; f. 1990; state-owned; cap. 142m. (Dec. 1991); Chair. AMADOU SALLA HASSANE; Man. Dir IBRAHIM BEIDARI.

#### Savings Bank

**Caisse Nationale d'Epargne (CNE):** BP 11778, Niamey; tel. 73-24-98; total assets 2,437m. (Sept. 1993); Chair. IDI GADO; Man. Dir BACHIR MALLAM MATO.

### INSURANCE

**Agence Nigérienne d'Assurances (ANA):** place de la Mairie, BP 423, Niamey; tel. 72-20-71; telex 5277; f. 1959; cap. 1.5m.; owned by L'Union des Assurances de Paris; Dir JEAN LASCAUD.

**Société Civile Immobilière des Assureurs de Niamey:** BP 423, Niamey; tel. 73-40-71; telex 5277; fax 73-41-85; f. 1962; cap. 14m.; Dir MAMADOU TALATA DOULLA.

**Société Nigérienne d'Assurances et de Réassurances 'Leyma' (SNAR—LEYMA):** ave du Général de Gaulle, BP 426, Niamey; tel. 73-55-26; telex 5202; f. 1973; cap. 345m.; Pres. AMADOU OUSMANE; Dir-Gen. MAMADOU MALAM AOUAMI.

**Union Générale des Assurances du Niger (UGAN):** rue de Kalleye, BP 11935, Niamey; tel. 73-54-06; telex 5277; fax 73-41-85; f. 1985; cap. 500m.; Pres. YVETTE CHASSAGNE; Dir-Gen. MAMADOU TALATA DOULLA; 7 brs.

## Trade and Industry

### DEVELOPMENT ORGANIZATIONS

**Caisse de Stabilisation des Prix des Produits du Niger (CSPPN):** BP 480, Niamey; telex 5286; price control agency for Nigerien goods; Dir IBRAHIM KOUSSOU.

**Mission Française de Coopération:** BP 494, Niamey; tel. 72-20-66; telex 5220; administers bilateral aid from France; Dir JEAN BOULOGNE.

**Office des Eaux du Sous-Sol (OFEDES):** BP 734, Niamey; tel. 73-23-44; telex 5313; govt agency for the maintenance and development of wells and boreholes; Dir ADOU ADAM.

**Office du Lait du Niger (OLANI):** BP 404, Niamey; tel. 73-23-69; telex 5555; f. 1971; govt agency for development and marketing of milk products; Pres. Dr ABDOUA KABO; Dir MAHAMADOU HAROUNA.

**Office National de l'Energie Solaire (ONERSOL):** BP 621, Niamey; tel. 73-45-05; govt agency for research and development, commercial production and exploitation of solar devices; Dir ALBERT WRIGHT.

**Office National des Ressources Minières du Niger (ONAREM):** BP 12716, Niamey; tel. 73-59-26; telex 5300; f. 1976; govt agency for exploration, exploitation and marketing of all minerals; Dir-Gen. OUSMANE GAOURI.

**Office des Produits Vivriers du Niger (OPVN):** BP 474, Niamey; telex 5323; govt agency for developing agricultural and food production; Dir ADAMOU SOUNA.

**Riz du Niger (RINI):** BP 476, Tillabéry, Niamey; tel. 71-13-29; f. 1967; cap. 825m. francs CFA; 27% state-owned; development and marketing of rice; Pres. YAYA MADOUGOU; Dir-Gen. OUSMANE DJIKA.

**Société Nigérienne de Produits Pétroliers (SONIDEP):** BP 11702, Niamey; tel. 73-33-34; telex 5343; f. 1977; govt agency for the distribution and marketing of petroleum products; cap. 1,000m. francs CFA; Man. Dir ADAMOU NAMATA.

### TRADE ORGANIZATIONS

**Centre Nigérien du Commerce Extérieur (CNCE):** place de la Concertation, BP 12480, Niamey; tel. 73-22-88; telex 5434; fax 73-46-68; f. 1984; promotes and co-ordinates all aspects of foreign trade; Dir AÏSSA DIALLO.

**Société Nationale de Commerce et de Production du Niger (COPRO-Niger):** BP 615, Niamey; tel. 73-28-41; telex 5222; fax 73-57-71; f. 1962; monopoly importer of foodstuffs; cap. 1,000m. francs CFA; 47% state-owned; Man. Dir DJIBRILLA HIMA.

### CHAMBERS OF COMMERCE

**Chambre de Commerce, d'Agriculture, d'Industrie et d'Artisanat du Niger:** place de la Concertation, BP 209, Niamey; tel. 73-22-10; telex 5242; f. 1954; comprises 80 full mems and 40 dep. mems; Pres. WAZIN MALLAM AJI; Gen. Sec. MAINA ARI ADJI KIRGAM.

  **Chambre de Commerce, d'Agriculture, d'Industrie et d'Artisanat du Niger, Antenne d'Agadez:** BP 201, Agadez; tel. 44-01-61.

  **Chambre de Commerce, d'Agriculture, d'Industrie et d'Artisanat du Niger, Antenne de Diffa:** BP 91, Diffa; tel. 54-03-92; f. 1988.

  **Chambre de Commerce, d'Agriculture, d'Industrie et d'Artisanat du Niger, Antenne de Maradi:** BP 79, Maradi; tel. 41-03-66.

  **Chambre de Commerce, d'Agriculture, d'Industrie et d'Artisanat du Niger, Antenne de Tahoua:** BP 172, Tahoua; tel. 61-03-84; f. 1984; Sec. ILYESS HABIB.

  **Chambre de Commerce, d'Agriculture, d'Industrie et d'Artisanat du Niger, Antenne de Zinder:** BP 83, Zinder; tel. 51-00-78.

#### EMPLOYERS' ORGANIZATIONS

**Syndicat des Commerçants Importateurs et Exportateurs du Niger (SCIMPEXNI):** BP 535, Niamey; tel. 73-34-66; Pres. ANDRÉ BEAUMONT; Sec.-Gen. C. SALEZ.

**Syndicat National des Petites et Moyennes Entreprises et Industries Nigériennes (SYNAPEMEIN):** BP 11204, Niamey; Pres. El Hadj ALI SOUMANA; Sec.-Gen. BOUBACAR ZEZI.

**Syndicat Patronal des Entreprises et Industries du Niger (SPEIN):** BP 415, Niamey; tel. 73-24-01; telex 5370; fax 73-45-26; f. 1945; Pres. AMADOU OUSMANE.

#### TRADE UNION FEDERATIONS

**Confédération des Syndicats Libres des Travailleurs du Niger (CSLTN):** Niamey; f. 1993; 4 affiliates.

**Union des Syndicats des Travailleurs du Niger (USTN):** Bourse du Travail, BP 388, Niamey; f. 1960; divided into sections for Maradi, Niamey and Zinder; affiliated to the African Trade Union Confed.; 31 affiliates; 200,000 mems; Sec.-Gen. IBRAHIM MAYAKI.

## Transport

#### ROADS

Niger is crossed by highways running from east to west and from north to south, giving access to neighbouring countries. Work on the upgrading of the 428-km Zinder–Agadez road, scheduled to form part of the Trans-Sahara highway, began in 1985.

At 31 December 1990 there were an estimated 11,258 km of classified roads, including 5,971 km of main roads and 2,729 km of secondary roads; about 3,265 km of the total network was paved.

**Société Nationale des Transports Nigériens (SNTN):** BP 135, Niamey; tel. 72-24-55; telex 5338; fax 73-45-26; f. 1961; national road hauliers; cap. 2,500m. francs CFA; 49% state-owned; Dir AMADOU OUSMANE.

#### RAILWAYS

**Organisation Commune Bénin-Niger des Chemins de Fer et des Transports (OCBN):** BP 38, Niamey; tel. 73-27-90; telex 5253; f. 1959; 50% owned by Govt of Niger, 50% by Govt of Benin; manages the Benin-Niger railway project (begun in 1978). There are as yet no railways in Niger.

#### INLAND WATERWAYS

The River Niger is navigable for 300 km within the country. Access to the sea is available by a river route from Gaya, in south-western Niger, to the coast at Port Harcourt, Nigeria, between September and March. Port facilities at Lomé, Togo, are used as a commercial outlet for land-locked Niger, and an agreement providing import facilities at the port of Tema was signed with Ghana in November 1986.

**Niger-Transit (NITRA):** Zone Industrielle, BP 560, Niamey; tel. 73-22-53; telex 5212; fax 73-26-38; f. 1974; 48% owned by SNTN; customs agent, freight-handling, warehousing, etc.; manages Nigerien port facilities at Lomé; Pres. SALEY CHAIBOU; Man. Dir SADE FATIMATA.

**Société Nigérienne des Transports Fluviaux et Maritimes (SNTFM):** Niamey; tel. 73-39-69; telex 5265; river and sea transport; cap. 64.6m. francs CFA; 99% state-owned; Man. Dir BERTRAND DEJEAN.

#### CIVIL AVIATION

There are international airports at Niamey and Agadez, and major domestic airports at Arlit, Diffa, Tahoua and Zinder.

**Air Afrique:** BP 11090, Niamey; tel. 73-30-10; telex 5284; see under Côte d'Ivoire; Dir in Niamey MALLÉ SALL.

**Société Nigérienne des Transports Aériens (SONITA):** Niamey; f. 1991; cap. 50m. francs CFA; owned by private Nigerien (81%) and Cypriot (19%) interests; operates domestic and regional services; Man. Dir ABDOULAYE MAIGA GOUDOUBABA.

**Trans-Niger Aviation:** BP 10454, Niamey; tel. 73-20-21; telex 5250; f. 1989; 38% owned by SNTN, 38% by Société Autonome de Gérance et d'Armement (France); operates domestic and regional services; Man. Dir ABDOU M. GOGE.

## Tourism

Hunting and fishing provide an important attraction for tourists. The Aïr and Ténéré Nature Reserve, covering an area of 77,000 sq km, was established in 1988, and the construction of a tourist village at Boubon (on the river Niger) was announced in 1989. Some 13,000 tourists visited Niger in 1992, compared with 21,000 in 1990. Receipts from tourism in 1992 amounted to US $17m.

**Direction du Tourisme et de l'Hôtellerie:** BP 12130, Niamey; tel. 73-23-85; telex 5249; Dir ALZOUMA MAÏGA.

**Office National du Tourisme (ONT):** ave du Président H. Luebke, BP 612, Niamey; tel. 73-24-47; telex 5467; f. 1977.

**Société Nigérienne d'Hôtellerie (SONHOTEL):** BP 11040, Niamey; tel. 73-23-87; telex 5239; f. 1977; state-owned hotel corpn; cap. 3,500m. francs CFA; Dir-Gen. HABI ABDOU.

# NIGERIA

## Introductory Survey

### Location, Climate, Language, Religion, Flag, Capital

The Federal Republic of Nigeria is a West African coastal state on the shores of the Gulf of Guinea, with Benin to the west, Niger to the north, Chad to the north-east, and Cameroon to the east and south-east. The climate is tropical in the southern coastal areas, with an average annual temperature of 32°C (90°F) and high humidity. It is drier and semi-tropical in the north. Average annual rainfall is more than 2,500mm (98 ins) in parts of the south-east, but in certain areas of the north is as low as 600mm (24 ins). In 1963 the most widely spoken languages were Hausa (20.9%), Yoruba (20.3%), Ibo (16.6%) and Fulani (8.6%). English is the country's official language. In 1963 the principal religious groups were Muslims (47.2%) and Christians (34.5%), while 18% of the total population followed animist beliefs. The national flag (proportions 2 by 1) has three equal vertical stripes, of green, white and green. The capital is Abuja, to which the Federal Government was formally transferred in December 1991; however, many non-government institutions remained in the former capital, Lagos.

### Recent History

The territory of present-day Nigeria, except for the section of former German-controlled Cameroon (see below), was conquered by the United Kingdom, in several stages, during the second half of the 19th century and the first decade of the 20th century. The British dependencies of Northern and Southern Nigeria were merged into a single territory in 1914, administered largely by traditional native rulers, under the supervision of the colonial authorities. In 1947 the United Kingdom introduced a new Nigerian Constitution, establishing a federal system of government, based on three regions: Northern, Western and Eastern. The federal arrangement was an attempt to reconcile religious and regional tensions, and to accommodate Nigeria's diverse ethnic groups, notably the Ibo (in the east), the Yoruba (in the west) and the Hausa and Fulani (in the north). The Northern Region, which was predominantly Muslim, contained about one-half of Nigeria's total population.

In 1954 the federation became self-governing, and the first federal Prime Minister, Alhaji Abubakar Tafawa Balewa (a Muslim northerner), was appointed in August 1957. A constitutional conference, convened in 1958, agreed that Nigeria should become independent in 1960, and elections to an enlarged federal legislature took place in December 1959. The Northern People's Congress (NPC), which was politically dominant in the north, became the single largest party in the new legislature, although lacking an overall majority. Tafawa Balewa (a prominent member of the NPC) continued in office, leading a coalition government of the NPC and the National Council for Nigeria and the Cameroons (NCNC), which attracted most of its support in the Eastern Region.

On 1 October 1960, as scheduled, the Federation of Nigeria achieved independence, initially as a constitutional monarchy. In June 1961 the northern part of the UN Trust Territory of British Cameroons was incorporated into Nigeria's Northern Region as the province of Sardauna, and in August 1963 a fourth region, the Mid-Western Region, was created by dividing the existing Western Region. On 1 October 1963 a revised Constitution was adopted, and the country was renamed the Federal Republic of Nigeria, although it remained a member of the Commonwealth. Dr Nnamdi Azikiwe of the NCNC took office as Nigeria's first President (then a non-executive post).

The first national election after independence, to the federal House of Representatives, took place in December 1964. Widespread electoral malpractice and violence were reported during the election campaign, prompting a boycott of the poll by the main opposition grouping, the United Progressive Grand Alliance (UPGA), a coalition of four parties, dominated by the NCNC (previously renamed the National Convention of Nigerian Citizens). The election resulted in a large majority for the Nigerian National Alliance, a seven-party coalition which was dominated by the NPC and the Nigerian Democratic Party (a recently-formed group that held power in the Western Region). However, the boycott was widely observed in the Eastern Region, necessitating a supplementary election in that region in March 1965, at which the UGPA won every seat.

On 15 January 1966 Tafawa Balewa's civilian Government was overthrown (and the Prime Minister killed) by junior army officers (mainly Ibos from the Eastern Region). Surviving federal ministers transferred power to the Commander-in-Chief of the Army, Maj.-Gen. Johnson Aguiyi-Aronsi (an Ibo), who formed a Supreme Military Council, suspended the Constitution and imposed emergency rule. Following the coup, there were violent anti-Ibo riots in some areas, and many Ibos living outside their native Eastern Region were killed or forced to leave. On 29 July 1966 Aguiyi-Aronsi was killed in a counter-coup by northern troops, and power was transferred to the Chief of Staff of the Army, Lt-Col (later Gen.) Yakubu Gowon, a Christian northerner. Gowon subsequently reintroduced the federal system, which had been suppressed after the January coup.

In early 1967 there was a rapid deterioration in relations between the federal Government and the military Governor of the Eastern Region, Lt-Col Chukwuemeka Odumegwu-Ojukwu, following a dispute between the federal and regional authorities concerning the distribution of petroleum revenues. The increasing tensions in Nigeria's federal structure prompted Gowon to propose the replacement of the four existing regions by 12 states. On 30 May Ojukwu announced the secession of the Eastern Region from the Federation, and proclaimed its independence as the Republic of Biafra. Fighting between the forces of Biafra and the Federal Government began in July; federal forces eventually suppressed the rebellion in December 1969, following Ojukwu's departure into exile, and Biafran forces formally surrendered in January 1970. It was estimated that between 500,000 and 2m. civilians (mainly Ibos) had died in the war, chiefly from starvation, as a result of the Federal Government's economic blockade of Biafra. Meanwhile, the proposed 12-state structure replaced the four federal regions in April 1968.

In October 1970 Gowon announced that military rule would last for a further six years. In October 1974, however, he postponed the restoration of civilian rule indefinitely. Mounting opposition to Gowon culminated in his overthrow by other senior officers in a bloodless coup on 29 July 1975. He was replaced as Head of State by Brig. (later Gen.) Murtala Ramat Muhammed, hitherto Federal Commissioner for Communications. The new regime attracted popular support as a result of its vigorous campaign against waste and corruption, and in October 1975 Muhammed announced a detailed timetable for a transition to civilian rule. In February 1976, however, Muhammed was assassinated during an unsuccessful coup attempt. Power was immediately assumed by Lt-Gen. (later Gen.) Olusegun Obasanjo, the Chief of Staff of the Armed Forces, who promised to fulfil his predecessor's programme for the restoration of civilian rule.

In March 1976 the number of existing states was increased from 12 to 19, and it was announced that a new federal capital was to be constructed near Abuja, in central Nigeria. In September 1978 a new Constitution was promulgated, and the state of emergency, in force since 1966, was ended. At the same time the 12-year ban on political activity was revoked. Elections took place in July 1979 to a new bicameral National Assembly (comprising a Senate and a House of Representatives), and for State Assemblies and State Governors. The National Party of Nigeria (NPN), which included many prominent members of the former NPC and representatives of all the other main political parties in existence before 1966, received the most widespread support in all the elections. The NPN's presidential candidate, Alhaji Shehu Shagari (who had served as an NPC federal minister prior to 1966 and as a federal commissioner in 1970–75), was elected to the new post of executive President in August 1979. He took office on 1 October, whereupon the military regime transferred power to the newly-elected civilian authorities and the new Constitution came into effect.

In 1980–82 a series of riots by Muslim extremists in northern Nigeria were violently suppressed by the armed forces; it was widely believed that increasing economic deprivation was a contributory factor in the unrest. Meanwhile, the new Government introduced an ambitious investment programme, which was dependent on a continuing high level of income from petroleum exports. However, a sharp decline in petroleum prices precipitated an economic crisis in 1982–83, resulting not only in increasing hardship for the majority of Nigerians, but also in widespread corruption.

In August–September 1983 federal, state and local government elections took place. In the presidential election Shagari was returned for a second term of office. The NPN won 13 of the 19 state governorships, and achieved substantial majorities in the Senate and the House of Representatives. Following allegations by the opposition parties of widespread electoral malpractice on the part of the NPN and the Federal Electoral Commission, several contentious results were subsequently reversed.

On 31 December 1983 the civilian Government was deposed in a bloodless military coup, led by Maj.-Gen. Muhammadu Buhari; who had been Federal Commissioner for Petroleum in 1976–78. The Government was replaced by a Supreme Military Council (SMC), headed by Buhari; the National Assembly was dissolved and all political parties were banned. Hundreds of politicians and business executives, including the former President Shagari, were arrested on charges of corruption. Legislation that severely restricted the freedom of the press was introduced, and several journalists were subsequently detained. In July 1985 the Government announced that no schedule for the restoration of civilian rule was planned, and prohibited all debate on the political future of Nigeria.

On 27 August 1985 Buhari's administration was deposed in a bloodless coup, led by Maj.-Gen. (later Gen.) Ibrahim Babangida, the Chief of Staff of the Army and a member of the SMC. A new military administration, the Armed Forces Ruling Council (AFRC), was established, with Babangida as President. The decree on press censorship was revoked, and a number of journalists and other political detainees were released. (Shagari and 17 other former government officials were released in July 1986, having been acquitted of corruption charges.) In October 1985 Babangida declared a state of national economic emergency and assumed extensive interventionist powers over the economy. In December Babangida suspended negotiations with the IMF, a move that received widespread popular support but caused discontent within the army command. On 20 December the AFRC suppressed a coup attempt by disaffected army officers; 10 of the alleged conspirators were later executed.

Babangida announced in January 1986 that the armed forces would transfer power to a civilian government on 1 October 1990. In March 1986 a 'political bureau' was established to collate recommendations for the proposed civilian administration. In February Babangida's announcement that Nigeria had been accepted as a full member of the Organization of the Islamic Conference (OIC, see p. 208) prompted unrest in the non-Muslim sector of the population, reflecting concern at increasing 'Islamization' in Nigeria. In response, Babangida established a national commission to examine the advisability of Nigeria's membership of the OIC. In June 1987, following continued sporadic clashes between Christians and Muslims, the Government established a National Advisory Council for Religious Affairs to examine means of achieving greater religious tolerance in Nigeria.

In July 1987 Babangida announced details of a programme to transfer power to a civilian government by 1992, two years later than originally envisaged. Local government elections, to be contested on a non-party basis, were to take place in late 1987. In 1989 the ban on party politics was to be revoked, and a maximum of two political parties were to be approved to contest state elections in 1990 and further local elections in 1991. In 1991 a national census was to be conducted, prior to legislative and presidential elections, which were scheduled to take place in 1992. In August 1987 the Government established a National Electoral Commission (NEC), to oversee 'fair and free' elections, and in September a Constitutional Review Committee (CRC) was created to examine proposals for a new constitution. In the same month Babangida announced the creation of two new states, Katsina and Akwa Ibom, which increased the total number of states to 21.

In December 1987 local government elections, which were contested by some 15,000 non-party candidates, took place in 301 electoral areas. Following widespread allegations of malpractice, further elections took place in March 1988 in wards where the results had been declared invalid. In May a Constituent Assembly, comprising 450 members elected by local government and 117 members nominated by the AFRC, was inaugurated to prepare a draft constitution, which was to be based on the proposals of the CRC. The progress of the Constituent Assembly was impeded, however, by controversy over the proposed inclusion of Islamic (Shari'a) courts in the new document.

In March 1989 electoral legislation was amended to allow the AFRC to select two official political parties from a list of NEC-recommended associations. In April the Constituent Assembly presented a draft Constitution to Babangida. In May Babangida announced the end of the prohibition on political parties, and the new Constitution was promulgated; the Constitution was scheduled to enter into force on 1 October 1992. Some 35 political parties subsequently emerged, although only 13 parties managed to fulfil the requirements for registration by the stipulated date in July 1989. In September the NEC submitted a list of six political associations to the AFRC; in October, however, it was decided to dissolve all the newly-formed politicial parties, on the grounds that they were too closely associated with discredited former parties. In their place, the AFRC created two new organizations, the Social Democratic Party (SDP) and the National Republican Convention (NRC). The AFRC's actions provoked widespread criticism, and local elections, due to take place in December, were postponed until late 1990. In December 1989, in an extensive government reshuffle, Babangida personally assumed the defence portfolio (thereby gaining greater control over the security forces), in an apparent attempt to pre-empt unrest during the transition to civilian rule.

On 22 April 1990 a coup attempt was staged by junior army officers. The leader of the attempt, Maj. Gideon Orkar, claimed to be acting on behalf of Nigerians in the centre and south of the country, who, he alleged, were under-represented in the Government and armed forces. The attempted coup was suppressed on the same day; numerous casualties were reported, and some 160 members of the armed forces were said to have been arrested. In July Orkar and other alleged conspirators were convicted by a military tribunal on charges of conspiring to commit treason. Following their trial (which provoked international criticism), 69 prisoners, including Orkar, were executed; a further 20 prisoners received custodial sentences.

Following the completion of registration for membership of the SDP and the NRC, the election of party officials for local electoral wards took place in May 1990. In July party executives were elected for each state, and in August the management of the two parties was transferred from government-appointed administrators to these officials. Later in August Babangida implemented extensive changes in the Government: nine ministers were dismissed, and the position of Chief of General Staff, held by Vice-Adm. (later Adm.) Augustus Aikhomu, was replaced by the office of Vice-President (to which Aikhomu was immediately appointed). Babangida subsequently announced that the size of the armed forces was to be substantially reduced. In September, in an attempt to restrict military influence within the Government, three ministers were obliged to retire from the armed forces. Twelve military State Governors were also replaced, and civilian Deputy Governors were appointed to each state, pending gubernatorial elections, scheduled for 1991.

On 8 December 1990 local government elections took place, although only an estimated 20% of registered voters participated. A total of 2,934 candidates representing the SDP were elected as councillors, with a further 232 elected to chair local councils, while 2,558 NRC candidates were elected as councillors, with 208 elected as chairmen. Despite the attempts of the Government to create two parties without regional affiliations, it was reported that the NRC received most support in the north of the country, and the SDP in the south. In January 1991 the Government announced that state subsidies to the NRC and SDP would end in the following September.

In April 1991 demonstrations by Muslims in the northern state of Katsina, in protest at the publication of an article that was considered to be blasphemous, culminated in violence. In the same month some 130 people, mainly Christians, were killed in riots in the northern state of Bauchi, following an announcement that Christians were to slaughter pigs in a local abattoir that was also used by Muslims. It was later reported that some 120 Muslims had been killed by government troops who had been dispatched to the region to suppress the riots.

In June 1991 the NRC and SDP elected 144,950 delegates to contest primary elections, due to take place in August, at which candidates for the gubernatorial and state assembly elections were to be selected. In September, in an apparent attempt to relieve ethnic tensions prior to the elections, nine new states were created, increasing the size of the federation to 30 states. However, violent demonstrations took place in several areas where the Government had ignored demands to create a new state in the region, or where there was discontent concerning the relocation of the state capital. As a result of the ensuing disruption, the Government announced that the primary elections (which had already been postponed from August to September) would take place in October, and would be followed by elections for State Assemblies and State Governors in December. In October demonstrations by Muslims took place in Kano, in the north, in protest against a tour of the state that had been undertaken by a Christian preacher (after the authorities had refused a Muslim leader permission to visit the area). More than 300 people were reported to have been killed in subsequent clashes between Muslims and Christians, which were suppressed by the army.

On 19 October 1991 primary elections took place to select candidates for the forthcoming gubernatorial and state assembly elections. Results were subsequently annulled in nine states, following allegations of electoral malpractice on the part of both the NRC and the SDP; further elections took place in the states concerned in early December. In the gubernatorial and state assembly elections, which took place on 14 December, the NRC gained a majority in 14 State Assemblies, while the SDP won control of 16 State Assemblies. However, candidates representing the NRC were elected as State Governors in 16 of the 30 states, many of which were situated in the south-east of Nigeria, where the SDP had previously received more support. Both the SDP and the NRC disputed the election results in a number of states, on the grounds of electoral malpractice. In February 1992 the election result in the state of Abia was annulled, and the State Governor was removed from office.

On 12 December 1991 the Federal Government was formally transferred from Lagos to Abuja, the new federal capital. In January 1992 Babangida formed a new National Council of Ministers, in which several portfolios were restructured. In the same month the Government announced that elections to a bicameral National Assembly, comprising a 593-member House of Representatives and a 91-member Senate, would take place on 7 November, and would be followed by a presidential election on 5 December. The formal installation of a civilian government (and the implementation of the new Constitution) would thus take place on 2 January 1993, rather than, as previously planned, on 1 October 1992.

In late 1991 fighting erupted in the eastern state of Taruba, apparently as a result of a long-standing land dispute between the Tiv and Jukin ethnic groups. The conflict continued in subsequent months, and by March 1992 between 2,000 and 5,000 people were reported to have been killed. In January demonstrations in Katsina by Islamic fundamentalists, who were demanding the imposition of Shari'a law, were suppressed by the armed forces. In February some 30 people were killed in clashes between the Hausa ethnic group (which was predominantly Muslim) and the Kataf (predominantly Christian).

In March 1992, following discussions between the NEC, the NRC and the SDP, elections to the National Assembly were brought forward to 4 July. Candidates for the legislature were to be selected on 23 May, and primary elections for presidential candidates were to take place between 1 August and 15 September. (The presidential election was still to take place on 5 December.) Later in March legislation that empowered the NEC to disqualify electoral candidates considered to be unsuitable to hold office was introduced. In April a committee, comprising officials from several government ministries, was established to co-ordinate the transfer to civilian rule.

In May 1992 it was reported that several people had been killed during widespread rioting in protest at substantial increases in transport fares (caused by a severe fuel shortage), while a number of demonstrations to demand the Government's resignation were violently suppressed by the armed forces. In the same month some 300 people were reported to have been killed in renewed violence between the Hausa and the Kataf in Kaduna. Shortly afterwards the Government announced that all organizations with religious or ethnic interests were to be prohibited; a National Guard was also to be established, in an attempt to reduce the role of the army in the suppression of riots. Later in May further rioting occurred in Lagos, following the arrest of the Chairman of the Campaign for Democracy (CD—an informal alliance of Nigerian human rights organizations, which had been established in late 1991), Dr Beko Ransome-Kuti, who had accused the Government of deliberately provoking unrest in order to delay the transition to civilian rule. In June Babangida effected an extensive government reorganization, in which the Minister of Finance and Economic Planning, Alhaji Abubakar Alhaji (who had been largely responsible for the adoption of a restrictive structural adjustment programme), was replaced. Later in June several human rights activists, including Ransome-Kuti, were released pending trial (which was later deferred) on charges of conspiring to incite the previous month's riots.

At the elections to the bicameral National Assembly, on 4 July 1992, the SDP secured a majority in both chambers, with 52 seats in the Senate and 314 seats in the House of Representatives, while the NRC won 37 seats in the Senate and 275 seats in the House of Representatives. The formal inauguration of the National Assembly, due to take place on 27 July, was, however, postponed until 5 December, the stipulated date for the presidential election, prompting concern at the AFRC's apparent reluctance to relinquish legislative power.

Voting in primary elections for presidential candidates began on 1 August 1992, but was suspended, owing to widespread electoral irregularities, and initial results were annulled. In early September, in an attempt to reduce corruption, Babangida promulgated legislation that introduced severe penalties for electoral malpractice. Further primary elections took place on 12, 19 and 26 September; however, 10 SDP candidates boycotted the third round, in protest at alleged bias on the part of SDP officials towards certain candidates. In October, shortly before a final round of voting was due to take place, Babangida suspended the primary elections, pending the outcome of an investigation by the NEC into alleged incidents of electoral malpractice. Later that month, following the presentation of a report by the NEC that provided confirmation of malpractice, Babangida announced that the leaders of the NRC and the SDP were to be removed from office and that interim committees would be appointed to assume the administration of the parties until the election of new officials. Several organizations, including the CD, subsequently demanded that the Government pledge to adhere to its programme for the installation of a civilian administration, although 18 of the 30 State Governors indicated that they would be prepared to support a limited delay in order to faciliate the transition to civilian rule.

In November 1992 Babangida announced that the presidential election was to be postponed until 12 June 1993. (The inauguration of the National Assembly was still to take place on 5 December 1992.) On 2 January 1993 (the stipulated date for the completion of the transition to civilian rule) the AFRC was to be replaced by a 14-member ruling National Defence and Security Council (NDSC), and the existing Council of Ministers by a civilian Transitional Council, pending the installation of a civilian government, which was to take place on 27 August 1993. Babangida further announced that the 23 prospective presidential candidates who had contested the discredited primary elections were to be prohibited from political activity during the transitional period: new candidates were to be nominated at a series of party congresses, to be conducted at ward, local government, state and national level. Human rights organizations subsequently claimed that the Government had deliberately extended its tenure in office, and Ransome-Kuti threatened to instigate a campaign of civil disobedience if Babangida failed to relinquish power by January 1993.

On 5 December 1992 Babangida inaugurated the National Assembly. On 2 January 1993 the AFRC and the Council of Ministers were duly dissolved, and the Transitional Council and the NDSC (which comprised the President, Vice-President, the heads of the armed forces and senior members of the Transitional Council) were formally installed. The Chairman of the Transitional Council, Chief Ernest Adegunle Shonekan, was officially designated Head of Government (although supreme power was vested in the NDSC and the President), while Aikhomu retained the post of Vice-President, despite opposition claims that the office had been effectively abolished by the transitional arrangements. Legislation that had been approved by the National Assembly was henceforth to be endorsed by the NDSC, and subsequently by Babangida. In January Ransome-Kuti was temporarily detained in order to pre-empt planned protests at the extension of military rule. In the same month it was reported that some 60 people had been killed in clashes between rival Muslim groups at Funtua, in Katsina. Later in January Babangida promulgated a constitutional amendment that precluded the National Assembly from legislating in certain principal areas, including finance, defence and security, during the transitional period. The Senate boycotted the presentation of the 1993 budget by the NDSC, in protest at the new amendment, and demanded that legislation approved by the National Assembly be directly submitted to the President (without the endorsement of the NDSC) and be promulgated within 30 days. Babangida subsequently initiated discussions with the leading members of the National Assembly, in an attempt to resolve the dispute.

In late January 1993 the NEC announced that it had approved 215 presidential candidates, including the former Chairman of the SDP, Babas Gana Kingibe, and a former Head of Government, Gen. Yakubu Gowon; 71 prospective candidates, including the former Biafran leader, Odumegwu-Ojukwu, were prohibited from contesting the presidential election (without official explanation). In February state government workers staged a national strike in support of demands for wage increases. (The strike was abandoned at the end of February, after State Governors acceded to their demands.) In the same month six people, including two former army officers, were sentenced to death for their involvement in the violence in Kaduna in May 1992.

In accordance with the new programme for the transition to civilian rule, party congresses to select presidential candidates were conducted at ward level on 6 February 1993, at local government level on 20 February, at state level on 6 March, and at national level on 27–29 March; the NRC elected a banker, Alhaji Bashir Othman Tofa, and the SDP a Muslim business executive, Chief Moshood Kastumawo Olawale Abiola, to contest the presidential election. Kingibe and Dr Sylvester Ugoh, a former member of the Shagari administration, were subsequently selected as the respective vice-presidential candidates of the SDP and the NRC. In April the Government promulgated legislation that empowered the NEC to postpone the presidential election indefinitely if such a measure appeared to be necessary. Human rights organizations subsequently claimed that the Government intended to extend military rule after the stipulated date in August. Later in April, however, the NEC indicated that it would not permit further delays that would undermine the schedule for the transition to civilian rule. Shortly afterwards the interim committees of the NRC and SDP transferred power to party officials, who had been elected at the national congresses at the end of March. At the end of April a former business associate of Tofa contested Tofa's presidential candidacy at the High Court, alleging that he had been involved in fraudulent practice. In May, following criticism of Babangida by the former Head of State, Gen. (retd) Olusegun Obasanjo, the Government introduced legislation providing for the death sentence to be imposed on those convicted on charges of sedition.

In June 1993 the Association for a Better Nigeria (ABN), a newly-formed pro-Babangida pressure group, obtained an interim injunction in the Abuja High Court that prohibited the NEC from conducting the presidential election, pending an appeal by the ABN for the extension of military rule until 1997. The NEC, however, announced that the injunction was invalid, and that the election would take place as scheduled. Owing, in part, to confusion caused by the court action, only about 30% of the registered electorate voted in the presidential election, which took place on 12 June. Initial results indicated that Abiola had secured the majority of votes in 11 of 15 states. Shortly afterwards, however, the ABN obtained a further injunction suspending the promulgation of the election results. The court ruling prompted widespread demands that the results be released, and several applications were lodged in an attempt to reverse the injunction. Later in June the CD released election results (which it claimed to be official) indicating that Abiola had secured the majority of votes in 19 states, and Tofa in 11 states; Abiola subsequently proclaimed himself President. Amid increasing tension, the NEC announced that it was to present an application to the Court of Appeal to contest the injunction. Shortly afterwards the Abuja High Court declared the election results to be invalid, on the grounds that the NEC had failed to comply with the ruling that had cancelled the poll.

On 23 June 1993, in what it claimed was an effort to uphold the judicial system, the NDSC annulled the results of the presidential election, suspended the NEC and halted all proceedings pertaining to the election. Babangida subsequently announced that the poll had been marred by widespread irregularities (contradicting reports by international observers that voting had been conducted fairly), but insisted that he remained committed to the transition to civilian rule on 27 August. The SDP and the NRC were to select two new presidential candidates, under the supervision of a reconstituted NEC; prospective candidates would be required to comply with new electoral regulations, which effectively precluded Abiola and Tofa from contesting a further poll. (Abiola, however, continued to claim, with much popular support, that he had been legitimately elected to the presidency.) The annulment of the election attracted international criticism, particularly from the USA and the United Kingdom, which announced the imposition of military sanctions against Nigeria.

In July 1993 a general strike, organized by the CD in support of demands that Abiola be installed as President, culminated in rioting; some 20 people were subsequently killed when security forces violently suppressed the unrest. In the same month Abiola criticized SDP leaders after the party, together with the NRC, accepted a provisional offer by the NDSC to participate in an interim administration. Shortly afterwards the NDSC announced that a new presidential election was to take place on 14 August, in order to fulfil the pledge to transfer power to a civilian government on 27 August. The new electoral schedule was generally viewed with scepticism, while the SDP declared its intention to boycott the poll, on the grounds that it had legitimately won the previous election. Legal proceedings, initiated by Abiola in the Lagos Supreme Court in an attempt to uphold his claim to the presidency, were abandoned after Babangida introduced legislation that prohibited any legal challenges to the annulment of the election. Later in July, following increasing criticism of the Government in the media, the NDSC proscribed five national publishing groups, including Abiola's Concord Press, and ordered the detention of a number of journalists and supporters of democracy.

At the end of July 1993 Babangida announced that an Interim National Government (ING) was to be established, stating that there was insufficient time to permit the scheduled transition to civilian rule on 27 August. A committee, comprising officials of the two parties and senior military officers, headed by Aikhomu, was subsequently established to determine the composition of the ING. Abiola immediately declared his opposition to the proposed administration, and stated his intention of forming a 'parallel government'. (He subsequently fled abroad, following alleged death threats, and attempted to solicit international support for his claim to the presidency.) In August the CD continued its campaign of civil disobedience in protest at the annulment of the election, appealing for a three-day general strike (which was widely observed in the south-west of the country, where Abiola received most popular support). Several prominent members of the CD were arrested, in an attempt to prevent further protests, and additional restrictions were imposed on the press. Later in August Babangida announced his resignation, reportedly as a result of pressure from prominent members of the NDSC, notably the Secretary of Defence, Gen. Sani Abacha. On 27 August a 32-member interim Federal Executive Council, headed by Shonekan, was installed; the new administration, which included several members of the former Transitional Council, was to supervise the organization of local government elections later that year and a presidential election in early 1994, while the transitional period for the return to civilian rule was extended to 31 March 1994. (Shonekan was later designated Head of State and Commander-in-Chief of the Armed Forces.) Supporters of democracy criticized the inclusion in the ING of several members of the now-dissolved NDSC, including Abacha, who was appointed to the new post of Vice-President, and the proposed establishment as organs of government of two predominantly military councils.

At the end of August 1993 the CD staged a further three-day strike, while the Nigerian Labour Congress (NLC) and the National Union of Petroleum and Natural Gas Workers (NUPENG) also announced industrial action in support of the installation of a civilian administration, headed by Abiola. The combined strike action resulted in a severe fuel shortage and the effective suspension of economic activity in the greater part of the country. Following the establishment of the ING, Shonekan pledged his commitment to the democratic process, and, in an effort to restore order, initiated negotiations with the NLC and effected the release of several journalists and prominent members of the CD, including Ransome-Kuti, who had been arrested in July. In early September the NLC and NUPENG provisionally suspended strike action, after the ING agreed to consider their demands.

In September 1993 a series of military appointments, which included the nomination of Lt-Gen. D. O. Diya to the office of Chief of Defence Staff, effectively removed supporters of Babangida from significant posts within the armed forces, thereby strengthening Abacha's position. Diya, who had reportedly opposed the annulment of the presidential election, subsequently declared that military involvement in politics would cease. In the same month Abiola returned to Lagos, amid popular acclaim. Later in September the NRC and SDP agreed to a new timetable whereby local government elections and a presidential election would take place concurrently in February 1994. The CD subsequently announced the resumption of strike action in support of demands for the installation of Abiola as President; an ensuing demonstration by supporters of the CD in Lagos was violently dispersed by security forces, and Ransome-Kuti and other prominent members of the CD were arrested. In October the SDP (which had previously demonstrated limited support for Abiola, as a result of dissension within the party) demanded that he be inaugurated as President, and refused to participate in the new elections. In the same month Shonekan established a committee to investigate the circumstances that had resulted in the annulment of the presidential election.

In late October 1993 members of a hitherto unknown organization, the Movement for the Advancement of Democracy (MAD), hijacked a Nigerian aircraft and issued a number of demands, principally that the ING resign in favour of Abiola; passengers on the aircraft, who were taken hostage, reportedly included high-ranking Nigerian officials. Abiola subsequently denied involvement with the hijackers, and appealed to them to surrender to the authorities. Shortly afterwards the hijackers (who had diverted the aircraft to the Nigerien capital, Niamey) were overpowered by members of the Nigerien security forces, reportedly with the support of French troops. Other members of the MAD were later arrested in Lagos.

In November 1993 the President of the Senate, a strong supporter of Abiola, was removed. Shortly afterwards the Lagos High Court ruled in favour of an application by Abiola, declaring the establishment of the ING to be invalid under the terms of the 1979 Constitution (whereby the President of the Senate was to act as interim Head of State). In the same month the ING dissolved the government councils, prior to local elections, and withdrew state subsidies on petroleum products. The resultant dramatic increase in the price of fuel prompted widespread anti-Government demonstrations, and the NLC announced the resumption of stike action. Meanwhile, the scheduled revision of the electoral register ended in failure, owing to a boycott by supporters of the SDP, and it became apparent that the new schedule for the transition to civilian rule was unviable.

On 17 November 1993, following a meeting with senior military officials, Shonekan announced his resignation as Head of State, and immediately transferred power to Abacha (confirming widespread speculation that the latter had effectively assumed control of the Government following Babangida's resignation). On the following day Abacha dissolved all organs of state and bodies that had been established under the transitional process, replaced the State Governors with military administrators, prohibited political activity (thereby proscribing the NRC and the SDP), and announced the formation of a Provisional Ruling Council (PRC), which was to comprise senior military officials and principal members of a new Federal Executive Council (FEC). He insisted, however, that he intended to relinquish power to a civilian government, and pledged to convene a conference with a mandate to determine the constitutional future of the country. Restrictions on the media were suspended, and the ban that had been imposed on certain publishing groups in July was revoked. Ensuing pro-democracy demonstrations were suppressed by security forces (although protests were generally limited). On 21 November Abacha introduced legislation that formally restored the 1979 Constitution and provided for the establishment of the new government organs. In an apparent attempt to counter domestic and international criticism, several prominent supporters of Abiola, including Kingibe, and four former members of the ING were appointed to the PRC and FEC, which were installed on 24 November. Abacha subsequently removed 17 senior military officers, who were believed to be loyal to Babangida. In the same month discussions between Abacha and Abiola took place, and the NLC agreed to abandon strike action after the Government acted to limit the increase in the price of petroleum products.

In December 1993 increasing controversy was reported regarding the mandate of the proposed constitutional conference, after Abacha stated that the issue of devolution of power in Nigeria would not be considered, while the CD dismissed the conference as an attempt to grant legitimate status to the new administration. Later in December a prominent civil rights lawyer appealed against new legislation that prohibited legal challenges to the decrees promulgated by Abacha in November. In the same month the United Kingdom announced that member nations of the European Union (see p. 143) were to impose further sanctions against Nigeria, including restrictions on the export of armaments. In January 1994 the Government announced the abandonment of economic reforms, which had been initiated in 1986, prompting concern among international financial institutions, and subsequently initiated investigations into the activities of the Central Bank of Nigeria and the Nigerian National Petroleum Corporation. Later in January Abacha established a 19-member National Constitutional Conference Commission to organize the conference. However, several lawyers subsequently contested the mandate of the Commission to determine the composition and agenda of the conference, together with the Government's decision that the recommendations of the conference be submitted for approval by the PRC. In February Gen. (retd) Shehu Musa Yar'Adua, a member of the 1976–1979 regime and a former SDP presidential candidate, was temporarily detained, after criticizing Abacha. Later that month security forces prevented the CD from convening a press conference. In March 1994 the US Government indicated that it would end sanctions against Nigeria if the constitutional conference were to be convened to the satisfaction of the Nigerian people. In April the Government announced a programme for the establishment of a National Constitutional Conference (NCC): some 273 delegates were to be elected in May, while 96 delegates were to be nominated by the Government from a list of eligible citizens submitted by each state. The NCC was to be convened at the end of June, and was to submit recommendations, including a new draft constitution, to the PRC in late October. A further stage in the transitional programme was to commence in mid-January 1995, when the ban on political activity was to end. In May 1994 a new pro-democracy organization, comprising former politicians, retired military officers and human rights activists, the National Democratic Coalition (NADECO), demanded that Abacha relinquish power by the end of that month and urged a boycott of the NCC. Later in May elections took place at ward, and subsequently at local government, level to select the 273 conference delegates; a low level of voter participation was reported. In the same month Ken Saro-Wiwa, a prominent campaigner for the self-determination of the Ogoni ethnic group (in protest at the Government's exploitation of Ogoni territory in Rivers State, which contains significant reserves of petroleum), was arrested in connection with the deaths of four Ogoni traditional leaders during political violence. At the end of May Abiola announced his intention of forming a government of national unity by 12 June (the anniversary of the presidential election). Violent anti-Government protests were reported, following the expiry of the date stipulated by NADECO for the resignation of the military administration.

In early June 1994 two members of the former Senate (including its President) were detained on charges of treason, after the senators reconvened and declared the Government to be illegal. A number of prominent opposition members, including Ransome-Kuti, were also arrested after the CD urged a campaign of civil disobedience, which received the support of NADECO. Following a public gathering, at which Abiola declared himself Head of State and President of a parallel government, a warrant was issued for his arrest on charges of treason; the authorities claimed that he intended to organize an uprising to force the military administration to relinquish power. Later in June security forces arrested Abiola (who had emerged from hiding to attend a rally in Lagos), prompting protests from pro-democracy organizations and from the Governments of the United Kingdom and the USA. Further demonstrations in support of demands for an immediate suspension of military rule and the installation of Abiola as President ensued, while NUPENG threatened to initiate strike action unless the Government agreed to release Abiola. At the initial session of the NCC, which was convened at the end of June, as scheduled, Abacha pledged to relinquish power at a date that would be determined by the conference. (The NCC subsequently established committees to consider issues involved in the transition to civilian rule). In early July the Minister of Justice and Attorney-General, Dr Olu Onagoruwa, was charged with contempt of court, after the Government failed to comply with two orders from the Federal High Court in Lagos to justify the continued detention of Abiola, who had taken legal action challenging his arrest as unconstitutional and in violation of human rights. Shortly afterwards Abiola was arraigned before a special High Court, which had been created by the Government in Abuja, and charged with treason.

In early July 1994 NUPENG initiated strike action in support of demands for Abiola's release and installation as President, and an improvement in government investment in the petroleum industry; the strike was subsequently joined by the senior petroleum workers' union, the Petroleum and Natural Gas Senior Staff Association (PENGASSAN). Government troops distributed fuel in an attempt to ease the resultant national shortage, while it was reported that senior officials of NUPENG and PENGASSAN, including the Secretary-General of NUPENG, Frank Kokori, had been arrested. By mid-July a number of affiliated unions had joined the strike action, resulting in an effective suspension of economic activity in Lagos and other regions in the south-west of the country. However, the national impact of the strike was limited by ethnic and regional divisions; it was reported that unions in northern and eastern regions had failed to join the industrial action. Later in July union officials suspended negotiations with the Government, on the grounds that the authorities had failed to release Kokori from detention. (It subsequently transpired, however, that Kokori had not been held in detention, after he apparently emerged from hiding.) At the end of July it was reported that some 20 people had been killed, when security forces violently suppressed anti-Government demonstrations. In early August the NLC initiated an indefinite general strike in support of NUPENG, but suspended industrial action after two days, following the suppression of further anti-Government protests, in which about five demonstrators were killed. Later in August Abacha dismissed the senior officials of NUPENG and PENGASSAN, and ordered petroleum workers to end strike action. Although some union members failed to comply, the effects of the strike began to decline. In early September the union leaders announced the suspension of strike action, in view of the deterioration of the economy and the resultant widespread hardship. In the same month Abacha promulgated legislation to extend the period of detention without trial to three months, prohibit legal action challenging government decisions, and officially ban three independent newspaper groups. Onagoruwa was subsequently replaced within the Government, after publicly dissociating himself from the new legislation. Later in September Abacha enlarged the PRC from 11 to 25 members, all of whom were senior military officials.

Meanwhile, Abiola's trial was repeatedly adjourned following his legal action, in August 1994, challenging the jurisdiction of the special High Court in Abuja with regard to an offence that had been allegedly committed in Lagos. Despite reports that he was suffering from a medical condition necessitating immediate treatment, Abiola had refused to accept the stipulated conditions for bail requiring him to refrain from political activity. In late September Wole Soyinka, a prominent critic of the Government (who had received the Nobel Prize for Literature in 1986), challenged the legitimacy of the Abacha administration at the Federal High Court in Lagos. (Soyinka was subsequently prevented from leaving the country.) In October 1994 the Federal High Court ruled that Abiola's detention was illegal (following his appeal in June), and awarded him substantial financial compensation. Nevertheless, Abiola remained in detention pending the outcome of his legal action, which had been submitted at the Federal Court of Appeal in Kaduna.

In early October 1994 the Government modified an unofficial increase in the price of petroleum products, following widespread protests. In the same month the NCC adopted constitutional proposals providing for a 'rotational presidency', whereby the office would be held alternately by northerners and southerners; other elective posts, including state governorships, were to be held successively, for a transitional period, by representatives of the territorial districts. In addition, the NCC envisaged a power-sharing arrangement, whereby any political party that secured a minimum of 10% of the seats in the legislature would be guaranteed representation in the Government. Under a proposed transitional timetable, a new constitution was to be adopted by March 1995, the ban on political activity was subsequently to be rescinded, and multi-party elections were to take place at local and national level in 1996, prior to the installation of a new government in January 1997. In October 1994 Abacha replaced the Minister of Finance, who had supported the programme of economic liberalization that had been abandoned by the Government in January. In November the NCC adopted further constitutional recommendations, providing for the creation of three Vice-Presidents and the establishment of a Federal Council of Traditional Rulers, which would function as an advisory body to the Government.

In early November 1994 the Federal Court of Appeal in Kaduna granted Abiola unconditional bail; however, the Government refused to comply with the court order providing for Abiola's release, on the grounds that he was charged with a capital offence. In the same month the human rights organization, Amnesty International, claimed that the Government was responsible for the imprisonment or execution of large numbers of opposition members, and particularly condemned violations of human rights that had allegedly been perpetrated against members of the Ogoni ethnic group in an effort to suppress protests at environmental damage caused by petroleum production in Rivers State. In early December the Federal Court of Appeal in Kaduna rescinded its previous ruling granting Abiola bail, in response to a prosecution appeal for Abiola to be retained in custody in the interests of national security.

In December 1994 the NCC accepted a proposal that the Government relinquish power on 1 January 1996, on the grounds that a prolonged transitional period would result in a further deterioration of the economy; it was agreed that the PRC would draft a new transitional timetable in accordance with the decisions of the conference. In January 1995 Abacha announced the adoption of a new programme of economic reforms, which was designed to secure the approval of the Bretton Woods institutions (see Economic Affairs). In the same month the NCC, which had been scheduled to complete preparations for a draft constitution in October 1994, adjourned until March 1995, prompting increasing concern that its protracted deliberations served to prolong the tenure of the military administration. The trial of Saro-Wiwa and a number of other Ogoni campaigners, on charges of complicity in the murder of the four Ogoni traditional leaders, commenced in mid-January; the defendants were to challenge the legitimacy of the special tribunal, which had been appointed by the Government. In February the Federal Court of Appeal dismissed Abiola's legal action challenging the jurisdiction of the High Court in Abuja.

In February 1995 Abacha dissolved the FEC, after a number of ministers announced their intention of engaging in political activity in the forthcoming transitional period. In March some 150 military officials were arrested, apparently in response to widespread disaffection within the armed forces. The authorities subsequently confirmed reports (which had initially been denied) of a conspiracy to overthrow the Government. (However, opponents of the Abacha administration claimed that the Government had fabricated a coup attempt, with the aim of suppressing dissent within the armed forces.) The Government denied allegations, published in a British newspaper, that about 80 members of the armed forces had been summarily executed. The arrest of the former Head of State, Olusegun Obasanjo, together with other prominent critics of the Government, prompted international protests. In mid-March Abacha appointed a new, 36-member FEC, which included a number of civilians who were believed to support an extended period of military rule.

In April 1995 the NCC endorsed the constitutional proposals that had been approved in late 1994. At the end of that month, however, the conference adopted a motion reversing its previous decision that a civilian government be installed on 1 January 1996, on the grounds that the requisite timetable was untenable. The NCC subsequently undertook the incorporation of the necessary amendments to the constitutional recommendations, which were to be submitted for approval by the Government. Meanwhile, Trans-Africa, a US-based pressure group comprising prominent African-Americans, urged the immediate resignation of the Abacha administration. On 27 June 1995 the NCC formally presented proposals for a draft constitution to Abacha, who rescinded the ban on political activity. The PRC was to approve the constitutional recommendations within a period of three months, following which Abacha was to announce, on 1 October, a programme for transition to civilian rule.

Nigeria has taken a leading role in African affairs and is a prominent member of the Economic Community of West African States (ECOWAS, see p. 138) and other regional organizations. The Nigerian Government has contributed a significant number of troops to the ECOWAS Monitoring Group (ECOMOG, see p. 139), which was deployed in Liberia from August 1990 in response to the conflict between government forces and rebels in that country (see the chapter on Liberia). From October 1992 Nigerian troops under ECOMOG command played a dominant role in a major offensive against rebel forces. Following a peace agreement, which was signed in July 1993, however, the Nigerian Government announced that it was to withdraw its contingent from a restructured ECOMOG force. In early 1995, however, some 6,000 Nigerian troops remained in Liberia. In 1993 Nigerian troops were dispatched to Sierra Leone, in response to a formal request by the Sierra Leonean Government for military assistance to repulse attacks by rebels in that country. In the early 1990s the Nigerian Government also participated in peace-keeping missions that were deployed in several countries, including Angola, Rwanda, Somalia and the former Yugoslavia.

In July 1984 relations between Nigeria and the United Kingdom were adversely affected by the attempted kidnapping, in London, of Umaru Dikko, a political exile and a former minister in the Shagari administration, who was being sought for trial in Nigeria on charges of corruption. The alleged involvement of Nigerian diplomats in the affair resulted in the mutual withdrawal of the two countries' High Commissioners. Full diplomatic relations were restored in February 1986, however, and in March 1988 Nigeria and the United Kingdom resumed annual bilateral talks at ministerial level (which had been suspended since 1984). In mid-1993, however, the United Kingdom, together with other European nations and the USA, imposed sanctions against Nigeria, in response to the suspension of the scheduled transition to civilian rule.

In 1991 the Nigerian Government claimed that Cameroonian security forces had annexed several Nigerian fishing settlements in Cross River State (in south-eastern Nigeria), following a long-standing border dispute, based on a 1913 agreement between Germany and the United Kingdom that ceded the Bakassi peninsula in the Gulf of Guinea (a region of strategic significance) to Cameroon. Subsequent negotiations between Nigerian and Cameroonian officials in an effort to resolve the dispute achieved little progress. In December 1993 some 500 Nigerian troops were dispatched to the region, in response to a number of incidents in which Nigerian nationals had been killed by Cameroonian security forces. Later that month the two nations agreed to establish a joint patrol at the disputed area, and to investigate the cause of the incidents. In February 1994, however, the Nigerian Government increased the number of troops deployed in the region. Later in February the Cameroonian Government announced that it was to submit the dispute for adjudication by the UN, the Organization of African Unity (OAU, see p. 200), and the International Court of Justice, and requested military assistance from France. Subsequent reports of clashes between Cameroonian and Nigerian forces in the region prompted fears of a full-scale conflict between the two nations. In March Cameroon accepted a proposal from the Nigerian Government for bilateral negotiations (without the involvement of international mediators) to resolve the issue. Later that month, however, a proposal by the Nigerian Government that a referendum be conducted in the Bakassi region was rejected by Cameroon. Also in March the OAU issued a resolution urging the withdrawal of troops from the disputed region.

In May 1994 two members of the Nigerian armed forces were killed in further clashes in the Bakassi region. Later that month negotiations between the two countries, with mediation by the Government of Togo, resumed in the Cameroonian capital, Yaoundé. However, a summit meeting to discuss the issue, which was scheduled to take place in July, was postponed, owing to the civil unrest in Nigeria. In September 10 members of the Cameroonian armed forces were killed in further confrontations. Later that year, however, it was announced that the Nigerian and Cameroonian Governments were to continue to co-operate in efforts to achieve a resolution to the dispute.

### Government

On 18 November 1993 a new military Head of State dissolved all existing organs of state and bodies that had been established under the former transitional process to civilian rule, replaced the elected State Governors with military administrators, and prohibited political activity. Supreme executive and legislative power was vested in an 11-member Provisional Ruling Council, comprising senior military officials and principal members of the new cabinet, the Federal Executive Council. On 21 November the Constitution of 1979 (which provided for an executive President, elected for a term of four years, a bicameral National Assembly and elected local government councils) was formally restored.

Nigeria is a federation of 30 states, comprising 589 local government areas, which are divided into electoral wards.

### Defence

In June 1994 the total strength of the armed forces was 76,500 men: the army totalled 62,000 men, the navy 5,000 and the air force 9,500. Military service is voluntary. The defence budget for 1995 was ₦5,344.4m. (equivalent to 12.0% of recurrent federal expenditure).

### Economic Affairs

In 1993, according to estimates by the World Bank, Nigeria's gross national product (GNP), measured at average 1991–93 prices, was US $32,988m., equivalent to $310 per head. During 1985–93, it was estimated, GNP per head increased, in real terms, at an average annual rate of 3.2%, while the population increased by an annual average of 2.9%. Nigeria's gross domestic product (GDP) increased, in real terms, by an annual average of 2.3% during 1980–92.

Agriculture (including hunting, forestry and fishing) contributed 33.5% of GDP in 1993. An estimated 63.7% of the labour force were employed in the sector in that year. The principal cash crops are cocoa (which accounted for 66% of agricultural export earnings in 1982 but only 2.7% of total merchandise exports in 1987), groundnuts, oil palm and rubber. Staple food crops include rice, maize, taro, yams, cassava, sorghum and millet. Some 1,126,000 metric tons of cereals were imported in 1992. Timber production, the raising of livestock (principally goats, sheep, cattle and poultry), and artisanal fisheries are also important. During 1980–92 agricultural GDP increased by an annual average of 3.6%.

Industry (including mining, manufacturing, construction and power) engaged an estimated 6.6% of the employed labour force in 1986, and contributed 42.6% of GDP in 1993. During 1980–92 industrial GDP increased by an annual average of 0.2% (compared with average annual growth of 7.3% in 1970–80).

Mining contributed 35.7% of GDP in 1993, although the sector engaged less than 0.1% of the employed labour force in 1986. The principal mineral is petroleum, of which Nigeria is Africa's leading producer (providing 97.9% of total export earnings in 1992). In addition, Nigeria possesses substantial deposits of natural gas and coal. Tin and iron ore are also mined, while plans were under way in 1989 to exploit deposits of uranium. Mining production declined by 9.2% in 1992, and by 2.6% in 1993.

Manufacturing contributed 5.6% of GDP in 1993, and engaged about 4.3% of the employed labour force in 1986. The principal sectors are food-processing, brewing, petroleum-refining, iron and steel, motor vehicles (using imported components), textiles, cigarettes, footwear, pharmaceuticals, pulp and paper, and cement. Manufacturing GDP declined by an annual average of 1.0% in 1980-90 (compared with an average growth rate of 5.2% per year in 1970-80). However, production increased by 7.6% in 1990, and by 6.1% in 1991. It was estimated that manufacturing GDP increased by only 1.6% in 1994.

Energy is supplied principally by thermal power stations, which are fired by domestically-produced petroleum, natural gas or coal. Fuel wood is widely used for domestic purposes. Imports of fuel products comprised 1.0% of the value of merchandise imports in 1992.

In 1992 Nigeria recorded a visible trade surplus of US $4,611m., and there was a surplus of $2,268m. on the current account of the balance of payments. In 1993 the principal source of imports (16.2%) was Germany; other major suppliers were the United Kingdom, the USA and France. The principal market for exports (45.3%) in that year was the USA; other significant purchasers were Spain, the Netherlands and Italy. The main exports in 1988 were petroleum, cocoa beans and rubber. The principal imports in 1993 were machinery and transport equipment, basic manufactures, chemicals and foodstuffs.

In 1994 there was an estimated budgetary deficit of US $4,000m. (equivalent to about 14% of GDP). Nigeria's external debt totalled $32,531m. at the end of 1993, of which $28,237m. was long-term public debt. In 1992 the cost of servicing a debt of $30,998m. was equivalent to 29.4% of the value of exports of goods and services. The annual rate of inflation averaged 28.7% in 1985-93, the rate being 57.2% in 1993 and an estimated 70% in 1994. An estimated 3.4% of the labour force were unemployed in 1992.

Nigeria is a member of the African Development Bank (see p. 102), of the Economic Community of West African States (ECOWAS, see p. 138), which aims to promote trade and co-operation in West Africa, and of the Organization of the Petroleum Exporting Countries (OPEC, see p. 210).

Nigeria achieved high levels of economic growth in the 1970s. However, the subsequent decline in international prices for petroleum adversely affected the economy, and from 1986 it was necessary to negotiate successive agreements with creditors on the rescheduling of Nigeria's substantial external debt. A long-term structural adjustment programme, imposed by the IMF as a condition of assistance, was undertaken in 1986: it aimed to reduce dependence on imports, to encourage economic diversification, and to promote non-inflationary growth. Further reforms, endorsed by the World Bank in late 1988, included measures to liberalize legislation regulating foreign investment, a privatization programme, and a system for providing a unified exchange rate for the naira, determined by the market. In January 1994 the new military administration announced the abandonment of market reforms, reduced interests rates, and reimposed foreign exchange controls and a fixed exchange rate. In mid-1994 strike action in the petroleum sector (see Recent History) resulted in a severe fuel shortage, disrupted industrial activity and contributed to a dramatic increase in the rate of inflation; by the end of that year the budgetary deficit and external debt arrears had also risen significantly. In January 1995 the Government announced a number of economic reforms under the projected budget for that year, which included the liberalization of foreign exchange controls, the partial removal of restrictions on foreign investment, and improved state control of petroleum export earnings. Despite the creation of an 'autonomous' market for foreign exchange (in which the Central Bank of Nigeria was to be permitted to intervene), the official exchange rate was to be maintained for the public sector, while interest rates were also to remain fixed. The Government envisaged the subsequent adoption of a medium-term economic programme in agreement with the IMF and World Bank, which would entitle Nigeria to concessional debt relief. In April the Bretton Woods institutions declared the implementation of the 1995 budget in the first quarter of the year to be satisfactory, and agreed to engage in discussions with the Government regarding a medium-term programme; however, the conclusion of a debt-rescheduling arrangement remained dependent on sustained economic progress.

### Social Welfare

The National Provident Fund operates a system of benefits for sickness, retirement and old age. A scheme of retirement pensions and other benefits covers government employees. The Basic Health Service Scheme, introduced in 1977, aimed to provide primary health care for the whole population. In 1986 Nigeria had 90,668 hospital beds, and there were 16,003 physicians, 50,946 nurses and 42,423 midwives working in the country. Health and social services were allocated ₦3,335.6m., or 7.5% of total estimated recurrent expenditure, in the 1995 federal budget.

### Education

Education is partly the responsibility of the state governments, although the Federal Government has played an increasingly important role since 1970. Primary education begins at six years of age and lasts for six years. Secondary education begins at 12 years of age and lasts for a further six years, comprising two three-year cycles. Education to junior secondary level (from six to 15 years of age) is free and compulsory. In 1991 total enrolment at primary schools was equivalent to 76% of children in the relevant age-group (85% of boys; 67% of girls), while the comparable ratio for secondary enrolment was only 23% (21% of boys; 26% of girls). In 1993 383,488 students were enrolled in 133 higher education institutions. Education was allocated ₦9,421.2m., or 21.1% of total estimated recurrent expenditure, in the 1995 federal budget. According to UNESCO estimates, the rate of adult illiteracy in 1990 averaged 49.3% (males 37.7%; females 60.5%).

### Public Holidays

**1995:** 1 January (New Year's Day), 3 March* (Id al-Fitr, end of Ramadan), 14–17 April (Easter), 10 May* (Id al-Kabir, Feast of the Sacrifice), 9 August* (Mouloud, Birth of the Prophet), 1 October (National Day), 25–26 December (Christmas).

**1996:** 1 January (New Year's Day), 21 February* (Id al-Fitr, end of Ramadan), 5–8 April (Easter), 29 April* (Id al-Kabir, Feast of the Sacrifice), 28 July* (Mouloud, Birth of the Prophet), 1 October (National Day), 25–26 December (Christmas).

* These holidays are dependent on the Islamic lunar calendar, and may vary by one or two days from the dates given.

### Weights and Measures

The metric system is in force.

# Statistical Survey

Source (unless otherwise stated): Federal Office of Statistics, 7 Okotie-Eboh St, SW Ikoyi, Lagos; tel. (1) 2682935.

## Area and Population

### AREA, POPULATION AND DENSITY

| | |
|---|---:|
| Area (sq km) | 923,768* |
| Population (census results, 28–30 November 1991) | |
|   Males | 44,544,531 |
|   Females | 43,969,970 |
|   Total | 88,514,501 |
| Density (per sq km) at November 1991 | 95.8 |

* 356,669 sq miles.

### STATES (census of November 1991)

| | Population | Capital |
|---|---:|---|
| Abia | 2,297,978 | Umuahia |
| Adamawa | 2,124,049 | Yola |
| Akwa Ibom | 2,359,736 | Uyo |
| Anambra | 2,767,903 | Awka |
| Bauchi | 4,294,413 | Bauchi |
| Benue | 2,780,398 | Makurdi |
| Borno | 2,596,589 | Maiduguri |
| Cross River | 1,865,604 | Calabar |
| Delta | 2,570,181 | Asaba |
| Edo | 2,159,848 | Benin City |
| Enugu | 3,161,295 | Enugu |
| Imo | 2,485,499 | Owerri |
| Jigawa | 2,829,929 | Dutse |
| Kaduna | 3,969,252 | Kaduna |
| Kano | 5,632,040 | Kano |
| Katsina | 3,878,344 | Katsina |
| Kebbi | 2,062,226 | Birnin Kebbi |
| Kogi | 2,099,046 | Lokoja |
| Kwara | 1,566,469 | Ilorin |
| Lagos | 5,685,781 | Ikeja |
| Niger | 2,482,367 | Minna |
| Ogun | 2,338,570 | Abeokuta |
| Ondo | 3,884,485 | Akure |
| Osun | 2,203,016 | Oshogbo |
| Oyo | 3,488,789 | Ibadan |
| Plateau | 3,283,704 | Jos |
| Rivers | 3,983,857 | Port Harcourt |
| Sokoto | 4,392,391 | Sokoto |
| Taraba | 1,480,590 | Jalingo |
| Yobe | 1,411,481 | Damaturu |
| Federal Capital Territory | 378,671 | Abuja |
| **Total** | **88,514,501** | |

### PRINCIPAL TOWNS (estimated population at 1 July 1975)

| | | | | |
|---|---:|---|---:|---|
| Lagos (federal capital)* | 1,060,848 | Ado-Ekiti | 213,000 |
| Ibadan | 847,000 | Kaduna | 202,000 |
| Ogbomosho | 432,000 | Mushin | 197,000 |
| Kano | 399,000 | Maiduguri | 189,000 |
| Oshogbo | 282,000 | Enugu | 187,000 |
| Ilorin | 282,000 | Ede | 182,000 |
| Abeokuta | 253,000 | Aba | 177,000 |
| Port Harcourt | 242,000 | Ife | 176,000 |
| Zaria | 224,000 | Ila | 155,000 |
| Ilesha | 224,000 | Oyo | 152,000 |
| Onitsha | 220,000 | Ikere-Ekiti | 145,000 |
| Iwo | 214,000 | Benin City | 136,000 |

* Federal capital moved to Abuja in December 1991.

### BIRTHS AND DEATHS (UN estimates, annual averages)

| | 1975–80 | 1980–85 | 1985–90 |
|---|---:|---:|---:|
| Birth rate (per 1,000) | 49.0 | 48.8 | 48.5 |
| Death rate (per 1,000) | 18.4 | 17.0 | 15.6 |

**Expectation of life** (UN estimates, years at birth, 1985–90): 50.5 (males 48.8; females 52.2).

Source: UN, *World Population Prospects: The 1992 Revision*.

### ECONOMICALLY ACTIVE POPULATION
(sample survey, '000 persons aged 14 years and over, September 1986)

| | Males | Females | Total |
|---|---:|---:|---:|
| Agriculture, hunting, forestry and fishing | 9,800.6 | 3,458.4 | 13,259.0 |
| Mining and quarrying | 6.8 | — | 6.8 |
| Manufacturing | 806.4 | 457.3 | 1,263.7 |
| Electricity, gas and water | 127.0 | 3.4 | 130.4 |
| Construction | 545.6 | — | 545.6 |
| Trade, restaurants and hotels | 2,676.6 | 4,740.8 | 7,417.4 |
| Transport, storage and communications | 1,094.7 | 17.2 | 1,111.9 |
| Financing, insurance, real estate and business services | 109.8 | 10.3 | 120.1 |
| Community, social and personal services | 3,939.5 | 962.6 | 4,902.1 |
| Activities not adequately defined | 597.1 | 147.8 | 744.9 |
| **Total employed** | 19,704.1 | 9,797.8 | 29,501.9 |
| Unemployed | 809.8 | 453.8 | 1,263.6 |
| **Total labour force** | 20,513.9 | 10,251.6 | 30,765.5 |

Note: Figures are based on a total estimated population of 98,936,800, which may be an overestimate.

Source: ILO, *Year Book of Labour Statistics*.

NIGERIA
*Statistical Survey*

## Agriculture

**PRINCIPAL CROPS** ('000 metric tons)

|  | 1991 | 1992 | 1993 |
|---|---|---|---|
| Wheat* | 60 | 40 | 30 |
| Rice (paddy) | 3,185* | 3,453* | 3,400† |
| Maize† | 1,900 | 1,700 | 2,300 |
| Millet | 3,497 | 3,200† | 3,800† |
| Sorghum | 4,346 | 4,100† | 4,800† |
| Potatoes | 66 | 73 | 75† |
| Sweet potatoes | 35 | 40† | 40† |
| Cassava | 20,000 | 21,320 | 21,000† |
| Yams | 15,603 | 18,500* | 20,000† |
| Taro (Coco yam)† | 1,300 | 1,300 | 1,300 |
| Pulses | 1,559 | 1,575 | 1,650* |
| Soybeans | 153* | 159† | 160† |
| Groundnuts (in shell) | 1,219 | 1,400* | 1,250† |
| Sesame seed | 46* | 49† | 50† |
| Cottonseed† | 200 | 220 | 225 |
| Cotton (lint)† | 90 | 110 | 110 |
| Coconuts | 129* | 135* | 140† |
| Palm kernels | 369 | 385 | 392† |
| Palm oil | 900† | 940 | 965 |
| Tomatoes† | 380 | 390 | 400 |
| Green peppers† | 850 | 880 | 900 |
| Sugar cane† | 1,250 | 1,250 | 1,250 |
| Plantains | 1,314 | 1,454 | 1,400† |
| Other fruit (excluding melons) | 6,250 | 6,350 | 6,450 |
| Cocoa beans* | 110 | 135 | 140 |
| Tobacco (leaves) | 9* | 9† | 10† |
| Natural rubber (dry weight)† | 90 | 110 | 110 |

\* Unofficial figure(s). † FAO estimate(s).

Source: FAO, *Production Yearbook*.

**LIVESTOCK** ('000 head, year ending September)

|  | 1991 | 1992 | 1993 |
|---|---|---|---|
| Cattle | 15,140 | 15,700 | 16,316 |
| Sheep | 13,000 | 13,500 | 14,000* |
| Goats | 23,500 | 24,000 | 24,500* |
| Pigs | 4,263 | 5,328 | 6,660 |
| Horses* | 206 | 205 | 204 |
| Asses* | 960 | 1,000 | 1,000 |
| Camels* | 18 | 18 | 18 |

Poultry (million)*: 120 in 1991; 118 in 1992; 120 in 1993.

\* FAO estimate(s).

Source: FAO, *Production Yearbook*.

**LIVESTOCK PRODUCTS** ('000 metric tons)

|  | 1991 | 1992 | 1993 |
|---|---|---|---|
| Beef and veal | 205 | 210 | 219* |
| Mutton and lamb* | 45 | 48 | 51 |
| Goat meat* | 123 | 126 | 127 |
| Pig meat* | 159 | 199 | 202 |
| Poultry meat* | 165 | 162 | 165 |
| Other meat | 101 | 100 | 100* |
| Edible offals* | 102 | 105 | 109 |
| Cows' milk | 360 | 370 | 380* |
| Butter and ghee* | 8.1 | 8.4 | 8.6 |
| Cheese* | 6.5 | 6.7 | 6.9 |
| Poultry eggs* | 310.0 | 306.0 | 310.0 |
| Cattle hides* | 50.1 | 51.4 | 53.4 |
| Sheepskins* | 8.2 | 8.8 | 9.2 |
| Goatskins* | 19.4 | 19.8 | 20.0 |

\* FAO estimate(s).

Source: FAO, mainly *Production Yearbook*.

## Forestry

**ROUNDWOOD REMOVALS**
(FAO estimates, '000 cubic metres, excluding bark)

|  | 1990 | 1991 | 1992 |
|---|---|---|---|
| Sawlogs, veneer logs and logs for sleepers* | 5,589 | 5,589 | 5,589 |
| Other industrial wood† | 2,279 | 2,279 | 2,279 |
| Fuel wood | 99,864 | 103,113 | 106,421 |
| **Total** | 107,732 | 110,981 | 114,289 |

\* Assumed to be unchanged since 1986.
† Assumed to be unchanged since 1980.

Source: FAO, *Yearbook of Forest Products*.

**SAWNWOOD PRODUCTION**
('000 cubic metres, incl. railway sleepers)

|  | 1989 | 1990 | 1991 |
|---|---|---|---|
| Coniferous (softwood) | 6 | 6 | — |
| Broadleaved (hardwood)* | 2,706 | 2,706 | 2,706 |
| **Total** | 2,712 | 2,712 | 2,706* |

\* FAO estimate(s). Annual production of broadleaved sawnwood is assumed to be unchanged since 1985.

**1992:** Production as in 1991 (FAO estimate).

Source: FAO, *Yearbook of Forest Products*.

## Fishing

('000 metric tons, live weight)

|  | 1990 | 1991 | 1992 |
|---|---|---|---|
| Inland waters | 98.7 | 91.6 | 109.4 |
| Tilapias | 13.9 | 12.0 | 18.6 |
| Upsidedown catfishes | 3.6 | 3.8 | 6.9 |
| Characins | 6.8 | 1.3 | 0.3 |
| Naked catfishes | 7.0 | 7.0 | 3.5 |
| Torpedo-shaped catfishes | 27.5 | 20.0 | 15.0 |
| Other freshwater fishes (incl. unspecified) | 37.8 | 41.7 | 57.1 |
| Nile perch | 2.1 | 5.8 | 7.9 |
| Atlantic Ocean | 217.7 | 175.7 | 209.0 |
| Tonguefishes | 5.3 | 6.6 | 3.1 |
| West African croakers | 15.9 | 17.2 | 17.5 |
| Mullets | 5.3 | 5.9 | 6.3 |
| Threadfins and tasselfishes | 3.4 | 8.7 | 9.9 |
| Sardinellas | 10.3 | 78.4 | 49.2 |
| Bonga shad | 12.9 | 12.9 | 38.2 |
| Sharks, rays, skates, etc. | 8.4 | 7.2 | 8.9 |
| Other marine fishes (incl. unspecified) | 147.7 | 27.6 | 60.9 |
| Southern pink shrimp | 1.9 | 5.0 | 11.9 |
| Other marine crustaceans | 6.7 | 6.2 | 3.1 |
| **Total catch** | 316.3 | 267.2 | 318.4 |

Source: FAO, *Yearbook of Fishery Statistics*.

# NIGERIA

## Mining

('000 metric tons, unless otherwise indicated)

|  | 1989 | 1990 | 1991 |
|---|---|---|---|
| Hard coal* | 85 | 90 | 90 |
| Crude petroleum | 85,510 | 86,029 | 94,314 |
| Natural gas (petajoules) | 169 | 156 | 185 |
| Tin concentrates (metric tons, metal content)† | 316 | 230 | 200 |

* Provisional or estimated figures.
† Data from UNCTAD, *International Tin Statistics* (Geneva).

Source: UN, *Industrial Statistics Yearbook*.

**1992** (metric tons): Crude petroleum 91.6 million; Natural gas 191 petajoules (Source: UN, *Monthly Bulletin of Statistics*).

## Industry

**SELECTED PRODUCTS** ('000 metric tons, unless otherwise indicated)

|  | 1989 | 1990 | 1991 |
|---|---|---|---|
| Raw sugar[1] | 53 | 53 | 59 |
| Cigarettes (metric tons)[2] | 10,000[3] | 10,000 | 10,000 |
| Plywood (cubic metres)[4] | 175,000 | 175,000 | 175,000 |
| Wood pulp[4] | 17 | 7 | 7 |
| Paper and paperboard | 16 | 44[3] | 45[3] |
| Nitrogenous fertilizers (a)[5] | 197.4 | 210.0 | 212.0 |
| Phosphatic fertilizers (b)[5] | 93.5 | 96.1 | 110.6 |
| Jet fuels | 40 | 38 | 40 |
| Motor spirit—petrol | 2,967 | 3,745 | 3,594 |
| Kerosene | 1,537 | 1,941 | 1,899 |
| Distillate fuel oils | 2,393 | 3,019 | 3,029 |
| Residual fuel oils | 2,299 | 2,900 | 2,724 |
| Liquefied petroleum gas[3] | 60 | 55 | 55 |
| Cement[3] | 3,500 | 3,500 | 3,500 |
| Crude steel | 213 | 220 | 200 |
| Tin metal—unwrought (metric tons)[6] | 257 | 320 | n.a. |
| Electric energy (million kWh) | 9,935 | 9,945 | 9,955 |

[1] Source: FAO.
[2] Source: US Department of Agriculture.
[3] Provisional or estimated figure(s).
[4] FAO estimates.
[5] Production in terms of (a) nitrogen or (b) phosphoric acid (Source: FAO, *Quarterly Bulletin of Statistics*).
[6] Data from *International Tin Statistics* (Geneva).

Source: mainly UN, *Industrial Statistics Yearbook*.

## Finance

**CURRENCY AND EXCHANGE RATES**

**Monetary Units**
100 kobo = 1 naira (₦).

**Sterling and Dollar Equivalents** (31 December 1994)
£1 sterling = 34.414 naira;
US $1 = 21.997 naira;
1,000 naira = £29.06 = $45.46.

**Average Exchange Rate** (naira per US $)
1992    17.298
1993    22.065
1994    21.996

## Statistical Survey

**FEDERAL BUDGET ESTIMATES** (₦ million)

| Recurrent Expenditure | 1993 | 1994 | 1995 |
|---|---|---|---|
| Cabinet Office | 4,009.4 | 2,662.1 | 3,381.2 |
| General Staff Headquarters | 709.9 | 364.4 | 420.7 |
| Office of the Head of Service | 80.1 | 82.7 | 95.4 |
| Police | 2,659.7 | 4,299.8 | 4,943.4 |
| Agriculture, water resources and rural development | 1,015.3 | 1,221.7 | 1,465.5 |
| Federal Audit Department | 49.8 | 58.3 | 67.3 |
| Judiciary | 172.8 | 187.8 | 219.9 |
| Communications | 350.1 | 143.9 | 491.6 |
| Defence | 3,085.4 | 4,205.1 | 5,344.4 |
| Education | 6,436.1 | 7,878.1 | 9,421.2 |
| Federal Capital Territory | 57.3 | 68.6 | 79.9 |
| External affairs | 3,124.1 | 3,477.6 | 4,352.8 |
| Finance | 2,129.7 | 2,691.9 | 2,372.2 |
| Industries and technology | 189.9 | 149.6 | 234.8 |
| Information and culture | 606.7 | 886.3 | 1,181.4 |
| Internal affairs | 1,197.5 | 1,742.6 | 2,435.4 |
| Justice | 176.6 | 234.6 | 274.2 |
| Employment, labour and productivity | 303.5 | 298.9 | 330.3 |
| Mines, power and steel | 118.7 | 223.0 | 259.9 |
| Science and technology | 114.4 | 226.2 | 253.4 |
| Social development, youth and sports | 187.0 | 283.1 | 330.4 |
| National Commission for Women | 25.2 | 27.1 | 32.1 |
| Trade | 228.5 | 257.4 | 248.5 |
| Transport and aviation | n.a. | 337.5 | 398.7 |
| Health and social services | 2,331.6 | 2,086.8 | 3,335.6 |
| Works and housing | 1,272.5 | 1,374.2 | 1,679.8 |
| Petroleum and natural resources | 314.0 | 387.5 | 770.5 |
| Contingencies | 250.0 | 250.0 | 250.0 |
| **Total** | 31,195.8 | 36,106.9 | 44,670.5 |

Source: Federal Ministry of Finance, New Secretariat Area II, Garki, Abuja.

**Capital expenditure** (₦ million): 6,741.9 in 1987; 10,593.4 in 1988.

**INTERNATIONAL RESERVES** (US $ million at 31 December)

|  | 1992 | 1993 | 1994 |
|---|---|---|---|
| Gold* | 1 | 1 | 1 |
| Foreign exchange | 967 | 1,372 | 1,386 |
| **Total** | 968 | 1,373 | 1,387 |

* National valuation of gold reserves (687,000 troy ounces in each year).
Source: IMF, *International Financial Statistics*.

**MONEY SUPPLY** (₦ million at 31 December)

|  | 1989 | 1990 | 1991 |
|---|---|---|---|
| Currency outside banks | 12,124 | 14,951 | 23,121 |
| Demand deposits at commercial banks | 9,738 | 15,000 | 20,180 |
| **Total money** (incl. others) | 26,664 | 34,540 | 48,708 |

Source: IMF, *International Financial Statistics*.

**COST OF LIVING**
(Consumer Price Index for rural and urban areas; base: 1986 = 100)

|  | 1991 | 1992 | 1993 |
|---|---|---|---|
| Food | 321.5 | 471.0 | 743.7 |
| **All items** | 296.5 | 428.7 | 673.7 |

Source: ILO, *Year Book of Labour Statistics*.

# NIGERIA

*Statistical Survey*

## NATIONAL ACCOUNTS (₦ million at current prices)

### National Income and Product

|  | 1991 | 1992 | 1993 |
|---|---|---|---|
| Compensation of employees | 46,869 | 59,099 | 74,546 |
| Operating surplus | 258,111 | 468,880 | 599,822 |
| **Domestic factor incomes** | 304,980 | 527,979 | 674,368 |
| Consumption of fixed capital | 15,267 | 16,351 | 17,240 |
| **Gross domestic product (GDP) at factor cost** | 320,247 | 544,330 | 691,608 |
| Indirect taxes | 4,271 | 5,762 | 5,689 |
| Less Subsidies | 508 | 284 | 202 |
| **GDP in purchasers' values** | 324,010 | 549,808 | 697,095 |
| Factor income received from abroad | 2,126 } | −64,405 | −73,211 |
| Less Factor income paid abroad | 26,600 } | | |
| **Gross national product (GNP)** | 299,536 | 485,403 | 623,884 |
| Less Consumption of fixed capital | 15,267 | 16,351 | 17,240 |
| **National income in market prices** | 284,269 | 469,052 | 606,644 |
| Other current transfers from abroad (net) | 7,292 | 12,680 | 17,925 |
| **National disposable income** | 291,561 | 481,732 | 624,569 |

### Expenditure on the Gross Domestic Product

|  | 1991 | 1992 | 1993 |
|---|---|---|---|
| Government final consumption expenditure | 12,690 | 20,430 | 82,050 |
| Private final consumption expenditure | 222,270 | 407,530 | 579,400 |
| Increase in stocks } | 35,620 | 58,940 | 105,200 |
| Gross fixed capital formation } | | | |
| **Total domestic expenditure** | 270,580 | 486,900 | 766,650 |
| Exports of goods and services | 129,691 | 196,904 | 240,250 |
| Less Imports of goods and services | −76,260 | −130,650 | −184,980 |
| **GDP in purchasers' values** | 324,011 | 553,154 | 821,920 |
| **GDP at constant 1990 prices** | 272,962 | 281,089 | 287,488 |

Source: mainly IMF, *International Financial Statistics*.

### Gross Domestic Product by Economic Activity (at factor cost)

|  | 1991 | 1992 | 1993 |
|---|---|---|---|
| Agriculture, hunting, forestry and fishing | 97,464 | 145,225 | 231,833 |
| Mining and quarrying | 120,849 | 255,777 | 246,791 |
| Manufacturing | 18,892 | 26,349 | 38,431 |
| Electricity, gas and water | 1,297 | 1,405 | 1,601 |
| Construction | 4,900 | 6,110 | 8,019 |
| Trade, restaurants and hotels | 42,385 | 63,053 | 102,066 |
| Transport, storage and communications | 6,388 | 9,303 | 15,297 |
| Finance, insurance, real estate and business services | 18,199 | 21,626 | 26,247 |
| Government services | 8,800 | 14,169 | 19,130 |
| Other community, social and personal services | 1,072 | 1,314 | 2,194 |
| **Total** | 320,246 | 544,331 | 691,609 |

## BALANCE OF PAYMENTS (US $ million)

|  | 1990 | 1991 | 1992 |
|---|---|---|---|
| Merchandise exports f.o.b. | 13,585 | 12,254 | 11,791 |
| Merchandise imports f.o.b. | −4,932 | −7,813 | −7,181 |
| **Trade balance** | 8,653 | 4,441 | 4,611 |
| Exports of services | 965 | 886 | 1,053 |
| Imports of services | −1,976 | −2,448 | −1,810 |
| Other income received | 211 | 211 | 156 |
| Other income paid | −2,949 | −2,631 | −2,494 |
| Private unrequited transfers (net) | 1 | 12 | 22 |
| Official unrequited transfers (net) | 84 | 732 | 731 |
| **Current balance** | 4,988 | 1,203 | 2,268 |
| Direct investment (net) | 588 | 712 | 897 |
| Portfolio investment (net) | −197 | −61 | 1,884 |
| Other capital (net) | −4,573 | −3,284 | −10,565 |
| Net errors and omissions | 235 | −92 | −122 |
| **Overall balance** | 1,042 | −1,523 | −5,638 |

Source: IMF, *International Financial Statistics*.

# External Trade

### PRINCIPAL COMMODITIES
(imports by SITC sections, ₦ million)

| Imports c.i.f. | 1991 | 1992 | 1993 |
|---|---|---|---|
| Food and live animals | 7,785.5 | 11,738.4 | 13,912.9 |
| Crude materials (inedible) except fuels | 2,147.7 | 3,578.8 | 4,306.4 |
| Animal and vegetable oil and fats | 715.9 | 1,002.1 | 1,325.0 |
| Chemicals | 15,302.5 | 25,910.4 | 28,322.6 |
| Basic manufactures | 21,029.7 | 32,924.8 | 39,751.1 |
| Machinery and transport equipment | 37,674.5 | 59,837.2 | 70,226.9 |
| Miscellaneous manufactured articles | 4,116.5 | 7,014.4 | 6,293.9 |
| **Total** (incl. others) | 89,488.2 | 143,151.2 | 165,629.4 |

Sources: Central Bank of Nigeria, Lagos, and Federal Office of Statistics.

| Exports f.o.b. | 1985 | 1986 | 1987 |
|---|---|---|---|
| **Food and live animals** | 243.8 | 442.6 | 850.9 |
| Coffee, tea, cocoa and spices | n.a. | n.a. | 805.6 |
| Cocoa | n.a. | n.a. | 796.6 |
| Cocoa beans | 182.1 | 370.7 | 732.0 |
| **Mineral fuels, lubricants, etc.** | 11,335.8 | 8,452.7 | 28,208.6 |
| Petroleum and petroleum products | n.a. | n.a. | 28,208.3 |
| Crude petroleum | 11,275.0 | 8,328.7 | 28,154.0 |
| **Total** (incl. others) | 11,720.8 | 9,047.5 | 29,577.9 |

Source: Federal Office of Statistics, *Nigeria Trade Summary* and *Review of External Trade*.

**1988** (₦ million): Exports f.o.b. 31,193 (Petroleum 28,436).
**1989** (₦ million): Exports f.o.b. 57,791 (Petroleum 55,017).
**1990** (₦ million): Exports f.o.b. 109,886 (Petroleum 106,627).
**1991** (₦ million): Exports f.o.b. 121,534 (Petroleum 116,857).
**1992** (₦ million): Exports f.o.b. 205,613 (Petroleum 201,384).
Source (for 1988–92): IMF, *International Financial Statistics*.

NIGERIA                                                                                                                           *Statistical Survey*

**PRINCIPAL TRADING PARTNERS** (US $ '000)

| Imports c.i.f. | 1989 | 1990 | 1991 |
|---|---|---|---|
| Belgium-Luxembourg | 122,006 | 143,671 | 158,326 |
| Brazil | 106,404 | 175,801 | 177,165 |
| China, People's Republic | 86,591 | 128,230 | 188,484 |
| France | 271,611 | 394,209 | 435,841 |
| Germany | 591,509 | 644,589 | 871,804 |
| Hong Kong | 52,447 | 96,415 | 125,405 |
| India | 45,141 | 67,082 | 84,118 |
| Italy | 185,040 | 193,827 | 294,832 |
| Japan | 231,902 | 257,434 | 397,028 |
| Korea, Republic | 39,543 | 53,977 | 79,887 |
| Netherlands | 132,990 | 207,208 | 296,267 |
| Spain | 44,609 | 59,463 | 58,707 |
| Switzerland | 79,522 | 115,829 | 140,842 |
| United Kingdom | 556,105 | 739,417 | 743,675 |
| USA | 420,123 | 373,963 | 557,858 |
| **Total** (incl. others) | 3,419,079 | 4,317,921 | 5,380,922 |

| Exports f.o.b. | 1989 | 1990 | 1991 |
|---|---|---|---|
| Brazil | 82,307 | 9,423 | 125,102 |
| Canada | 16,275 | 117,584 | 150,205 |
| Côte d'Ivoire | 192,737 | 224,270 | 296,504 |
| France | 349,424 | 292,856 | 305,300 |
| Germany | 335,879 | 591,369 | 412,107 |
| Ghana | 171,746 | 224,694 | 188,981 |
| Italy | 340,367 | 298,146 | 429,276 |
| Netherlands | 651,942 | 933,627 | 472,508 |
| Portugal | 244,797 | 282,531 | 134,292 |
| Spain | 862,201 | 939,451 | 1,106,243 |
| United Kingdom | 142,533 | 298,914 | 147,944 |
| USA | 4,343,233 | 5,551,527 | 3,476,771 |
| **Total** (incl. others) | 8,130,683 | 10,241,646 | 7,681,198 |

Source: UN, *International Trade Statistics Yearbook*.

## Transport

**RAILWAYS** (estimated freight traffic)

|  | 1989 | 1990 | 1991 |
|---|---|---|---|
| Passenger-km (million) | 997 | 453 | n.a. |
| Net ton-km (million) | 1,812 | 1,870 | 1,930 |

Sources: UN Economic Commission for Africa, *African Statistical Yearbook*; UN, *Statistical Yearbook*.

**ROAD TRAFFIC** (estimates, '000 motor vehicles in use)

|  | 1989 | 1990 | 1991 |
|---|---|---|---|
| Passenger cars | 410 | 420 | 425 |
| Commercial vehicles | 45 | 46 | 47 |

Source: UN Economic Commission for Africa, *African Statistical Yearbook*.

**SHIPPING**

**Merchant Fleet** (registered at 30 June)

|  | 1990 | 1991 | 1992 |
|---|---|---|---|
| Displacement ('000 gross tons) | 496 | 493 | 516 |

Source: UN, *Statistical Yearbook*.

**International Sea-borne Freight Traffic** (estimates, '000 metric tons)

|  | 1988 | 1989 | 1990 |
|---|---|---|---|
| Goods loaded | 65,700 | 77,640 | 80,607 |
| Goods unloaded | 9,900 | 10,536 | 10,812 |

Source: UN, *Monthly Bulletin of Statistics*.

**CIVIL AVIATION** (traffic on scheduled services)

|  | 1990 | 1991 | 1992 |
|---|---|---|---|
| Kilometres flown ('000) | 17,000 | 14,000 | 12,000 |
| Passengers carried ('000) | 965 | 930 | 647 |
| Passenger-km (million) | 1,287 | 1,391 | 990 |
| Total ton-km (million) | 143 | 159 | 103 |

Source: UN, *Statistical Yearbook*.

## Tourism

|  | 1990 | 1991 | 1992 |
|---|---|---|---|
| Tourist arrivals ('000) | 190 | 214 | 237 |
| Tourist receipts (US $ million) | 25 | 39 | 29 |

Source: UN, *African Statistical Yearbook*.

## Communications Media

|  | 1990 | 1991 | 1992 |
|---|---|---|---|
| Radio receivers ('000 in use) | 18,700 | 19,350 | 20,000 |
| Television receivers ('000 in use) | 3,500 | 3,650 | 3,800 |
| Telephones ('000 main lines in use)* | 260 | 270 | n.a. |
| Book production (titles†) | n.a. | 1,546 | 1,562 |
| Daily newspapers |  |  |  |
|   Number | 31 | n.a. | 26 |
|   Average circulation ('000 copies)* | 1,700 | n.a. | 1,800 |

* Estimate.
† Including pamphlets (534 in 1992), but excluding university theses.

Sources: UNESCO, *Statistical Yearbook*; UN, *Statistical Yearbook*.

## Education

(1987)

|  | Institutions | Teachers | Students |
|---|---|---|---|
| Primary | 34,240 | 294,783 | 11,276,270 |
| Secondary |  |  |  |
|   General | 5,547 | 122,207 | 2,660,085 |
|   Teacher training | 135 | 4,531 | 108,751 |
|   Technical and vocational | 240 | 5,115 | 89,536 |
| Higher education |  |  |  |
|   Universities | 27 | 11,521 | 160,767 |
|   Polytechnics and colleges of technology and of education | 69 | 3,235 | 58,355 |

**1991/92:** Primary Institutions 36,610, Teachers 384,212, Pupils 14,805,937 (males 8,273,824; females 6,532,113); Secondary Teachers 141,491, Pupils 3,600,620 (males 1,621,575; females 1,979,045); Higher Education Institutions 130 (1992), Teachers 19,601 (1989), Students 376,122 (1992).

Sources: Federal Ministry of Education, Lagos; UNESCO, *Statistical Yearbook*.

**1993:** Primary Institutions 37,812, Pupils 15,911,888; Secondary Institutions 6,162, Pupils 4,150,917; Higher Education Institutions 133, Students 383,488.

Source: Federal Ministry of Education.

# Directory

## The Constitution

On 18 November 1993, following the assumption of power of a new military Head of State, all existing organs of state and bodies that had been established under the former process of transition to civilian rule were dissolved, the elected State Governors were replaced with military administrators, and political activity was prohibited. Supreme executive and legislative power was subsequently vested in an 11-member Provisional Ruling Council (PRC), comprising senior military officials and principal members of the new cabinet, the Federal Executive Council (FEC). The Head of State, who was Commander-in-Chief of the Armed Forces, chaired the PRC and the FEC. On 21 November the Constitution of 1979 (which provided for an executive President, elected for a term of four years, a bicameral National Assembly and elected local government councils) was formally restored. On 27 June 1995 a National Constitutional Conference submitted proposals for a draft constitution for approval by the Government, which rescinded the ban on political activity; a programme for transition to democratic rule was to be announced in October.

The Judiciary comprises the Supreme Court, the Court of Appeal and the Federal High Court at federal level, and High Courts in each state. Judicial appointments below the Supreme Court are made by the Federal Government on the advice of the Advisory Judicial Committee, with the Chief Justice of the Federation as Chairman. Certain states also have a Shari'a Court of Appeal, and others a Customary Court of Appeal, to consider civil cases in Islamic or customary law respectively.

## Federal Government

### HEAD OF STATE

**Head of Government and Commander-in-Chief of the Armed Forces:** Gen. SANI ABACHA (assumed power 17 November 1993).

### PROVISIONAL RULING COUNCIL
(June 1995)

Gen. SANI ABACHA (Chairman)
Lt-Gen. OLADIPO DIYA (Vice-Chairman)
Maj.-Gen. ABDUSALAMI A. ABUBAKAR
Brig.-Gen. ALWALI J. KAZIR
Cdre MIKE AKHIGBE
Air Vice-Marshal JOHN FEMI
Insp.-Gen. Alhaji IBRAHIM COMMASIE
Lt.-Gen. MOHAMED B. HALADU
Rear-Adm. J. O. A. AYINLA
Maj.-Gen. E. U. UNIMNA
Brig.-Gen. AHMED A. ABDULLAHI
Brig.-Gen. P. N. AZIZA
Brig.-Gen. A. T. OLANREWAJU
Brig.-Gen. S. V. L. MALU
Brig.-Gen. ISHAYA R. BAMAIYI
Cdre F. B. PORBENI
Cdre R. O. EYITAYO
Air Cdre N. E. EDUOK
Air Cdre IDI MUSA
Lt-Gen. JEREMIAH T. USENI
Brig.-Gen. T. M. SHELPIDI
Brig.-Gen. I. D. GUMEL
Brig.-Gen. S. I. MOMAH
Capt. A. IKWECHEGH
Air Cdre C. UMENWALIRI

### FEDERAL EXECUTIVE COUNCIL
(June 1995)

**Minister of Justice:** MICHAEL AGBAMUCHE.
**Minister of Agriculture:** Alhaji GAMBO JIMETA.
**Minister of Aviation:** Air Cdre N. EDUOK.
**Minister of Commerce and Tourism:** Rear-Adm I. ARIOLA.
**Minister of Communications:** Maj.-Gen. A. T. OLANREWAJU.
**Minister of Education:** Dr M. T. LIMAN.
**Minister of Finance:** Chief ANTHONY ANI.
**Minister of Federal Capital Territory:** Lt-Gen. J. T. USENI.
**Minister of Foreign Affairs:** Chief TOM IKIMI.
**Minister of Health:** Dr I. C. MADUBUIKE.
**Minister of Industry:** Lt-Gen. MOHAMED B. HALADU.
**Minister of Information:** Dr WALTER OFONAGORO.
**Minister of Internal Affairs:** Alhaji BABAGANA KINGIBE.
**Minister of Labour:** Alhaji UBA AHMED.
**Minister of National Planning:** AYO OGUNLADE.
**Minister of Petroleum Resources:** Chief DAN L. ETETE.
**Minister of Power and Steel:** Alhaji M. B. DALHATU.
**Minister of Science and Technology:** Brig.-Gen. S. I. MOMAH.
**Minister of Solid Minerals Development:** Alhaji KALOMA ALI.
**Minister of Transport:** Maj.-Gen. I. D. GUMEL.
**Minister of Water Resources:** Alhaji ALIYU J. YELWA.
**Minister of Women's Affairs:** JUDITH ATTAH.
**Minister of Works and Housing:** Maj.-Gen. A. K. ADISA.
**Minister of Youth and Sports:** Chief JIM NWOBODO.
**Ministers with Special Duties:** Alhaji WADA NAS, Dr LAZARUS UNAOGU, WOLE OYELESE.
**Minister of State for Agriculture:** Prof. A. ADESINA.
**Minister of State for Education:** IYABO ANISULOWO.
**Minister of State for Finance:** Alhaji ABU GIDADO.
**Minister of State for Federal Capital Territory:** M. C. CLARK.
**Minister of State for Foreign Affairs:** Alhaji A. P. KPAKI.
**Minister of State for Health:** DAVID SADAUKI.
**Minister of State for Petroleum Resources:** Dr KABIRU CHAFE.
**Minister of State for Power and Steel:** Prof. I. HAGHER.
**Minister of State for Works and Housing:** Alhaji ABDULLAHI ADAMU.

### MINISTRIES

**Office of the Head of State:** Abuja.
**Ministry of Agriculture:** Gwagwalada Area, PMB 24, Abuja; tel. (9) 8821080.
**Ministry of Aviation:** Abuja.
**Ministry of Commerce and Tourism:** Federal Secretariat, PMB 88, Garki, Abuja.
**Ministry of Communications:** Headquarters, Lafiaji, Lagos; tel. (1) 2633747.
**Ministry of Education:** PMB 12573, Ahmadu Bello Way, Victoria Island, Lagos; tel. (1) 2616843.
**Ministry of Federal Capital Territory:** Federal Secretariat, Abuja; tel. (9) 2431250.
**Ministry of Finance:** New Secretariat Area II, Garki, Abuja; tel. (9) 2341109.
**Ministry of Foreign Affairs:** Maputo St, PMB 130, Abuja; tel. (9) 5230520.
**Ministry of Health:** New Federal Secretariat Phase II, Ikoyi Rd, Obalende, Lagos; tel. (1) 2684405.
**Ministry of Industry:** Gwagwalada Area, PMB 24, Abuja; tel. (9) 2431250.
**Ministry of Information:** 15 Awolowo Rd, Ikoyi, Lagos; tel. (1) 2610836; telex 22649.
**Ministry of Internal Affairs:** Old Secretariat, Garki, Abuja.
**Ministry of Justice:** New Federal Secretariat, Ikoyi, Lagos; tel. (1) 2684414.
**Ministry of Labour:** Abuja.
**Ministry of National Planning:** Federal Secretariat Phase I, Ikoyi Rd, Ikoyi, Lagos.
**Ministry of Petroleum Resources:** Federal Secretariat, Ikoyi Rd, Ikoyi, Lagos.
**Ministry of Power and Steel:** Federal Secretariat Phase I, Ikoyi Rd, Ikoyi, Lagos.
**Ministry of Science and Technology:** New Federal Secretariat, Ikoyi Rd, Ikoyi, Lagos; tel. (1) 2614250.
**Ministry of Solid Minerals Development:** Abuja.
**Ministry of Transport:** Joseph St, PMB 21038, Ikoyi, Lagos; tel. (1) 2652120; telex 21535.
**Ministry of Water Resources:** Gwagwalada Area, PMB 24, Abuja; tel. (9) 8821080.
**Ministry of Women's Affairs:** Abuja.
**Ministry of Works and Housing:** Tafawa Balewa Sq., Lagos; tel. (1) 2653120.
**Ministry of Youth and Sports:** Abuja.

## Legislature

### NATIONAL ASSEMBLY

The National Assembly, comprising a 91-member Senate and a 593-member House of Representatives, was dissolved by the new military Head of State, Gen. Sani Abacha, on 18 November 1993.

## Political Organizations

On 18 November 1993, following the assumption of power by a new military Head of State, political activity was prohibited, and the two registered political associations (created in 1989 by the former military regime) were proscribed. On 27 June 1995, however, the ban on political activity was rescinded, prior to the adoption of a programme for transition to democratic rule. In mid-1995 the following political pressure groups were active:

**Campaign for Democracy (CD):** f. Nov. 1991; alliance of 25 human rights orgs opposed to the Govt; Chair. Dr BEKO RANSOME-KUTI; Sec.-Gen. SYLVESTER ODION-AKHAINE.

**Eastern Mandate Union:** grouping of politicians and tribal leaders from south-eastern Nigeria; Leader PATRICK DELE COLE.

**Movement for the Survival of the Ogoni People:** supports self-determination for the Ogoni ethnic group; Leader KEN SARO-WIWA.

**National Democratic Alliance:** f. 1993; advocates the continuation of military rule; Leader Chief FRANCIS ARTHUR NZERIBE.

**National Democratic Coalition (NADECO):** grouping of human rights activists, and fmr politicians and mil. officers; supports the installation of Chief Moshood Abiola as Pres.; Sec.-Gen. OYO OPADOKUN.

## Diplomatic Representation

### EMBASSIES AND HIGH COMMISSIONS IN NIGERIA

**Algeria:** 26 Maitama Sule St, SW Ikoyi, POB 7288, Lagos; tel. (1) 2683155; telex 21676; Ambassador: EL-MIHOUB MIHOUBI.

**Angola:** 5 Kasumu Ekomode St, Victoria Island, POB 50437, Lagos; tel. (1) 2611135; Ambassador: B. A. SOZINHO.

**Argentina:** 93 Awolowo Rd, SW Ikoyi, POB 51940, Lagos; tel. (1) 2682797; telex 21403; Ambassador: NICAROHICIO BOSSO.

**Australia:** 2 Ozumba Mbadiwe Ave, Victoria Island, POB 2427, Lagos; tel. (1) 2618875; telex 21219; fax (1) 2618703; High Commissioner: H. BROWN.

**Austria:** Fabac Centre, 3B Ligali Ayorinde Ave, POB 1914, Lagos; tel. (1) 2616081; telex 21463; fax (1) 2617639; Ambassador: Dr WILFRIED ALMOSLECHNER.

**Belgium:** 1A Bank Rd, Ikoyi, POB 149, Lagos; tel. (1) 2603230; telex 21118; fax (1) 2619683; Ambassador: MICHEL CZETWERTYNSKI.

**Benin:** 4 Abudu Smith St, Victoria Island, POB 5705, Lagos; tel. (1) 2614411; telex 21583; Ambassador: PATRICE HOUNGAVOU.

**Brazil:** 257 Kofo Abayomi St, Victoria Island, POB 1931, Lagos; tel. (1) 2610135; telex 23428; fax (1) 2613394; Ambassador: (vacant).

**Bulgaria:** 3 Eleke Crescent, Victoria Island, PMB 4441, Lagos; tel. (1) 2611931; telex 21567; fax (1) 2619879; Ambassador: (vacant).

**Burkina Faso:** 15 Norman Williams St, Ikoyi, Lagos; tel. (1) 2681001; Chargé d'affaires: ADOLPHE T. BENON.

**Cameroon:** 5 Elsie Femi Pearse St, Victoria Island, PMB 2476, Lagos; tel. (1) 2612226; telex 21343; Ambassador: SOUAIBOU HAYATOU.

**Canada:** 4 Idowu Taylor St, Victoria Island, POB 54506, Ikoyi Station, Lagos; tel. (1) 2692195; telex 21275; fax (1) 2692919; High Commissioner: REJEAN FRENETTE.

**Central African Republic:** Plot 137, Ajao Estate, New Airport, Oshodi, Lagos; Ambassador: JEAN-PAUL MOKODOPO.

**Chad:** 2 Goriola St, Victoria Island, PMB 70662, Lagos; tel. (1) 2622590; telex 28882; Ambassador: Dr ISSA HASSAN KHAYAR.

**China, People's Republic:** 19A Taslim Elias Close, Victoria Island, POB 5653, Lagos; tel. (1) 2612586; Ambassador: HU LIPENG.

**Colombia:** 43 Raymond Njoku Rd, POB 2352, Ikoyi, Lagos; Chargé d'affaires: Dr BERNARDO ECHEVERRI.

**Côte d'Ivoire:** 3 Abudu Smith St, Victoria Island, POB 7780, Lagos; tel. (1) 2610936; telex 21120; Ambassador: DÉSIRÉ AMON TANOE.

**Cuba:** Plot 935, Idejo St, Victoria Island, POB 328, Victoria Island, Lagos; tel. (1) 2614836; Ambassador: GIRALDO MAZOLA.

**Czech Republic:** 2 Alhaji Masha Close, Ikoyi, POB 1009, Lagos; tel. (1) 2683207; fax (1) 2683175; Ambassador: EVZEN VACEK.

**Denmark:** 4 Eleke Crescent, Victoria Island, POB 2390, Lagos; tel. (1) 2610841; telex 21349; Ambassador: LARS BLINKENBERG.

**Egypt:** 81 Awolowo Rd, Ikoyi, POB 538, Lagos; tel. (1) 2612922; Ambassador: FUAD YUSUF.

**Equatorial Guinea:** 7 Bank Rd, Ikoyi, POB 4162, Lagos; tel. (1) 2683717; Ambassador: A. S. DOUGAN MALABO.

**Ethiopia:** Plot 97, Ahmadu Bello Rd, Victoria Island, PMB 2488, Lagos; tel. (1) 2613198; telex 21694; fax (1) 2615055; Chargé d'Affaires a.i.: NEGGA BEYENNE.

**Finland:** 13 Eleke Crescent, Victoria Island, POB 4433, Lagos; tel. (1) 2610916; telex 21796; fax (1) 2613158; Ambassador: HEIKKI LATVANEN.

**France:** 1 Queen's Drive, POB 567, Lagos; tel. (1) 2603300; telex 21338; Ambassador: PIERRE GARRIGUE-GUYONNAUD.

**Gabon:** 8 Norman Williams St, POB 5989, Lagos; tel. (1) 2684673; telex 21736; Ambassador: E. AGUEMINYA.

**Gambia:** 162 Awolowo Rd, SW Ikoyi, POB 8037, Lagos; tel. (1) 2681018; High Commissioner: OMAR SECKA.

**Germany:** 15 Eleke Crescent, Victoria Island, POB 728, Lagos; tel. (1) 2611011; telex 21229; Ambassador: (vacant).

**Ghana:** 21–23 King George V Rd, POB 889, Lagos; tel. (1) 2630015; High Commissioner: AARON K. DUAH (acting).

**Greece:** Plot 1644, Oko-Awo Close, Victoria Island, POB 1199, Lagos; tel. (1) 2611412; telex 21747; fax (1) 2614852; Ambassador: HARIS KARABARBOUNIS.

**Guinea:** 8 Abudu Smith St, Victoria Island, POB 2826, Lagos; tel. (1) 2616961; Ambassador: KOMO BEAVOGUI.

**Holy See:** 9 Anifowoshe St, Victoria Island, POB 2470, Lagos (Apostolic Nunciature); tel. (1) 2614441; telex 22455; fax (1) 2618635; Apostolic Pro-Nuncio: Most Rev. CARLO MARIA VIGANÒ, Titular Archbishop of Ulpiana.

**Hungary:** 9 Louis Solomon Close, Victoria Island, POB 3168, Lagos; tel. (1) 2613551; fax (1) 2613717; Ambassador: GÉZA KÓTAI.

**India:** 107 Awolowo Rd, SW Ikoyi, POB 2322, Lagos; tel. (1) 2681297; High Commissioner: KRISHNAN RUGHNATI.

**Indonesia:** 5 Anifowoshe St, Victoria Island, POB 3473, Lagos; tel. (1) 2614601; Ambassador: JOHANNES SUTANTIO.

**Iran:** 1 Alexander Ave, Ikoyi, Lagos; tel. (1) 2681601; telex 22625; Ambassador: BAHMAN TAHERIAN-MOBARAKEH.

**Iraq:** Plot 708A, Adeola Hopewell St, Victoria Island, POB 2859, Lagos; tel. (1) 2610389; Ambassador: A. A. H. AL-SAMMARRAI.

**Ireland:** 34 Kofo Abayomi St, Victoria Island, Lagos; tel. (1) 2615224; telex 21478; Ambassador: DERMOT A. GALLAGHER.

**Israel:** Abuja; Ambassador: MOSHE GILBOA.

**Italy:** 12 Eleke Crescent, Victoria Island, POB 2161, Lagos; tel. (1) 2614066; telex 21202; Ambassador: Dr STEFANO RASTRELLI.

**Jamaica:** Plot 77, Samuel Adedoyin Ave, Victoria Island, POB 75368, Lagos; tel. (1) 2611085; fax (1) 2612100; High Commissioner: DUDLEY THOMPSON.

**Japan:** 24–25 Apese St, Victoria Island, PMB 2111, Lagos; tel. (1) 2614929; telex 21364; fax (1) 2614035; Ambassador: TAKANORI KAZUHARA.

**Kenya:** 53 Queen's Drive, Ikoyi, POB 6464, Lagos; tel. (1) 2682768; telex 21124; High Commissioner: Dr I. E. MALUKI.

**Korea, Democratic People's Republic:** 31 Akin Adesola St, Victoria Island, Lagos; tel. (1) 2610108; Ambassador: CHOE SANG BOM.

**Korea, Republic:** Plot 934, Idejo St, Victoria Island, POB 4668, Lagos; tel. (1) 2615353; telex 21953; Ambassador: CHAI KI-OH.

**Lebanon:** Plot 18, Eleke Crescent, Victoria Island, POB 651, Lagos; tel. (1) 2614511; Ambassador: M. SALAME.

**Liberia:** 3 Idejo St, Plot 162, off Adeola Odeku St, Victoria Island, POB 70841, Lagos; tel. (1) 2618899; telex 23361; Ambassador: Prof. JAMES TAPEH.

**Libya:** 46 Raymond Njoku Rd, SW Ikoyi, Lagos; tel. (1) 2680880; Chargé d'affaires: (vacant).

**Malaysia:** 1 Anifowoshe St, Victoria Island, POB 3729, Lagos; tel. (1) 2619415; High Commissioner: ALFRED KUMARASERI.

**Mauritania:** 1A Karimu Giwa Close, SW Ikoyi, Lagos; tel. (1) 2682971; Ambassador: MOHAMED M. O. WEDDADY.

**Morocco:** Plot 1318, 27 Karimu Katun St, Victoria Island, Lagos; tel. (1) 2611682; telex 21835; Ambassador: SAAD EDDINE TAIEB.

**Namibia:** Victoria Island, PMB 8000, Lagos.

**Netherlands:** 24 Ozumba Mbadiwe Ave, Victoria Island, POB 2426, Lagos; tel. (1) 2613510; telex 21327; Ambassador: L. P. J. MAZAIRAC.

**Niger:** 15 Adeola Odeku St, Victoria Island, PMB 2736, Lagos; tel. (1) 2612300; telex 21434; Ambassador: (vacant).

**Norway:** 3 Anifowoshe St, Victoria Island, PMB 2431, Lagos; tel. (1) 2618467; telex 21429; fax (1) 2618469; Ambassador: FRED H. NOMME.

**Pakistan:** Plot 859, Bishop Aboyade Cole St, Victoria Island, POB 2450, Lagos; tel. (1) 2614129; telex 22758; fax (1) 2614822; High Commissioner: SHAHID M. AMIN.

**Philippines:** Plot 152, No 302, off 3rd Ave, Victoria Island, Lagos; tel. (1) 2614048; telex 23344; Ambassador: MUKHTAR M. MUALLAM.

**Poland:** 10 Idejo St, Victoria Island, POB 410, Lagos; tel. (1) 2614634; telex 21729; Ambassador: KAZIMIERZ GUTKOWSKI.

NIGERIA

**Portugal:** Plot 1677, Olukunle Bakare Close, Victoria Island, Lagos; tel. (1) 2619037; telex 22424; Ambassador: Nuno da Cunha e Tavora Lorena.
**Romania:** Plot 1192, off Olugbosi Close, Victoria Island, POB 72928, Lagos; tel. (1) 2617806; telex 28828; fax (1) 2618249; Chargé d'affaires a.i.: Emil Rapcea.
**Russia:** 5 Eleke Crescent, Victoria Island, POB 2723, Lagos; tel. (1) 2612267; telex 22905; fax (1) 2615022; Ambassador: Lev Parshin.
**Saudi Arabia:** Plot 1412, Victoria Island, POB 2836, Lagos; (1) 2603420; Ambassador: Foud Sadik Mousti.
**Senegal:** 14 Kofo Abayomi Rd, Victoria Island, PMB 2197, Lagos; tel. (1) 2611722; telex 21398; Ambassador: Cherif Y. Diaite.
**Sierra Leone:** 31 Waziri Ibrahim St, Victoria Island, POB 2821, Lagos; tel. (1) 2614666; telex; 21495; High Commissioner: Joseph Blell.
**Slovakia:** POB 1290, Lagos; tel. (1) 2683123; telex 28685; fax (1) 2690423; Ambassador: Anton Hajduk.
**Somalia:** Plot 1270, off Adeola Odeka St, POB 6355, Lagos; tel. (1) 2611283; Ambassador: M. S. Hassan.
**Spain:** 21c Kofo Abayomi Rd, Victoria Island, POB 2738, Lagos; tel. (1) 2615215; telex 22656; fax (1) 2618225; Ambassador Carlos Bárcena Portolés.
**Sudan:** 2b Kofo Abayomi St, Victoria Island, POB 2428, Lagos; tel. (1) 2615889; telex 23500; Ambassador: Ahmed Altigani Saleh.
**Switzerland:** 7 Anifowoshe St, Victoria Island, POB 536, Lagos; tel. (1) 2613918; telex 21597; Ambassador: Anton Greber.
**Syria:** 25 Kofo Abayomi St, Victoria Island, Lagos; tel. (1) 2615860; Chargé d'affaires: Mustafa Haj-Ali.
**Tanzania:** 45 Ademola St, Ikoyi, POB 6417, Lagos; tel. (1) 2613594; High Commissioner: Maj.-Gen. Mirisho Sam Hagai Sarakikya.
**Thailand:** 1 Ruxton Rd, Old Ikoyi, POB 3095, Lagos; tel. (1) 2681337; Ambassador: N. Sathaporn.
**Togo:** 96 Awolowo Rd, SW Ikoyi, POB 1435, Lagos; tel. (1) 2617449; telex 21506; Ambassador: Foli-Agbenozan Tettekpoe.
**Trinidad and Tobago:** 6 Karimu Kotun St, Victoria Island, POB 6392, Lagos; tel. (1) 2614527; telex 21041; fax (1) 2612732; High Commissioner: (vacant).
**Turkey:** 3 Okunola Martins Close, Ikoyi, POB 1758, Lagos; tel. (1) 2683030; Ambassador: Orhan Kulin.
**United Kingdom:** 11 Eleke Crescent, Victoria Island, PMB 12136, Lagos; tel. (1) 2619531; telex 21247; fax (1) 2614021; High Commissioner: J. Thorold Masefield.
**USA:** 2 Eleke Crescent, Victoria Island, Lagos; tel. (1) 2610097; telex 23616; fax (1) 2610257; Ambassador: Walter Carrington.
**Venezuela:** 35b Adetukunbo Ademola St, Victoria Island, POB 3727, Lagos; tel. (1) 2611590; telex 28590; fax (1) 2617350; Ambassador: Alfredo Enrique Vargas.
**Yugoslavia:** 7 Maitama Sule St, SW Ikoyi, PMB 978, Lagos; tel. (1) 2680238; Ambassador: Dr Ilija Janković.
**Zaire:** 23a Kofo Abayomi Rd, Victoria Island, POB 1216, Lagos; tel. (1) 2611799; telex 21365; Ambassador: (vacant).
**Zambia:** 11 Keffi St, SW Ikoyi, PMB 6119, Lagos; High Commissioner: (vacant).
**Zimbabwe:** 6 Kasumu Ekemode St, POB 50247, Victoria Island, Lagos; tel. (1) 2619328; telex 22650; High Commissioner: Isaac L. Nyathi.

# Judicial System

**Supreme Court:** Tafawa Balewa Sq., Lagos; consists of a Chief Justice and up to 15 Justices, appointed by the Armed Forces Ruling Council. It has original jurisdiction in any dispute between the Federation and a State, or between States, and hears appeals from the Federal Court of Appeal.
  **Chief Justice:** Mohammed Bello.
**Federal Court of Appeal:** consists of a President and at least 15 Justices, of whom three must be experts in Islamic law and three experts in Customary law.
**Federal High Court:** consists of a Chief Judge and a number of other judges.
Each State has a **High Court**, consisting of a chief judge and a number of judges, appointed by the federal government. If required, a state may have a **Shari'a Court of Appeal** (dealing with Islamic civil law) and a **Customary Court of Appeal**. In 1986 a **Special Military Tribunal** was established to try former office holders accused of corruption, and a **Special Appeals Tribunal** was established for appeals against rulings of the Special Military Tribunal.

# Religion

## ISLAM

According to the 1963 census, there were more than 26m. Muslims (47.2% of the total population) in Nigeria.
**Spiritual Head:** Alhaji Ibrahim Dasuki, the Sultan of Sokoto.

## CHRISTIANITY

The 1963 census enumerated more than 19m. Christians (34.5% of the total population).

**Christian Council of Nigeria:** 139 Ogunlana Drive, Marina, POB 2838, Lagos; tel. (1) 5836019; f. 1929; 12 full mems and six assoc. mems; Pres. Rev. Luther D. Cishak; Gen. Sec. C. O. Williams.

### The Anglican Communion

Anglicans are adherents of the Church of the Province of Nigeria, comprising 48 dioceses. Nigeria, formerly part of the Province of West Africa, became a separate Province in 1979. The Church had an estimated 10m. members in 1990.

**Archbishop of Nigeria and Bishop of Lagos:** Most Rev. Joseph Adetiloye, Bishopscourt, 29 Marina, POB 13, Lagos; tel. (1) 2635681; fax (1) 2631264.
**Provincial Secretary:** Ven. Samuel B. Akinola, 29 Marina, POB 78, Lagos; tel. (1) 2635681; fax (1) 2631264.

### The Roman Catholic Church

Nigeria comprises nine archdioceses, 38 dioceses and two Catholic Missions, at Bomadi and at Kano. At 31 December 1992 there were an estimated 10.0m. adherents in the country (9.9% of the total population).

**Catholic Bishops' Conference of Nigeria:** 6 Force Rd, POB 951, Lagos; tel. (1) 2635849; telex 28636; (1) fax 2636680; f. 1976; Pres. Most Rev. Dr Albert Obiefuna, Archbishop of Onitsha.
**Catholic Secretariat of Nigeria:** 6 Force Rd, POB 951, Lagos; tel. (1) 2635849; telex 28636; fax (1) 2636680; Sec.-Gen. Rev. Fr Matthew Hassan Kukah.
**Archbishop of Abuja:** Most Rev. John O. Onaiyekan, Archdiocesan Secretariat, Block 64, Area 2, Section II, POB 286, Garki, Abuja; tel. (9) 2341066.
**Archbishop of Benin City:** Most Rev. Patrick E. Ekpu, Archdiocesan Secretariat, POB 35, Benin City, Edo; tel. (52) 243787.
**Archbishop of Calabar:** Most Rev. Brian D. Usanga, Archdiocesan Secretariat, PMB 1044, Calabar, Cross River.
**Archbishop of Ibadan:** Most Rev. Felix Alaba Job, Archdiocesan Secretariat, 8 Latosa Rd, PMB 5057, Ibadan, Osun; tel. (2) 2413544.
**Archbishop of Jos:** Most Rev. Gabriel G. Ganaka, Archdiocesan Secretariat, 20 Joseph Gomwalk Rd, POB 494, Jos, Plateau; tel. (73) 236247.
**Archbishop of Kaduna:** Most Rev. Peter Yariyok Jatau, Archbishop's House, Tafawa Balewa Way, POB 248, Kaduna; tel. (62) 236076.
**Archbishop of Lagos:** Most Rev. Anthony Olubunmi Okogie, Archdiocesan Secretariat, 19 Catholic Mission St, POB 8, Lagos; tel. (1) 2635729.
**Archbishop of Onitsha:** Most Rev. Albert Kanene Obiefuna, Archdiocesan Secretariat, POB 411, Onitsha, Anambra; tel. (46) 210444.
**Archbishop of Owerri:** Most Rev. Anthony J. V. Obinna, Archdiocesan Secretariat, POB 85, Owerri, Imo; tel. (83) 230760.

### Other Christian Churches

**Brethren Church of Nigeria:** c/o Kulp Bible School, POB 1, Mubi, Gongola; f. 1923; 80,000 mems; Gen. Sec. John Boaz Y. Maina.
**Church of the Lord (Aladura):** Anthony Village, Ikorodu Rd, POB 308, Ikeja, Lagos; tel. (1) 4964749; f. 1930; 1.1m. mems; Primate Dr E. O. A. Adejobi.
**Lutheran Church of Christ in Nigeria:** POB 21, Numan, Adamawa; 430,000 mems; Pres. Rt Rev. Dr David L. Windibiziri.
**Lutheran Church of Nigeria:** Obot Idim Ibesikpo, Uyo, Akwa Ibom; tel. (1) 200505; telex 64235; f. 1936; 368,000 mems; Pres. Rev. S. J. Udofia.
**Methodist Church Nigeria:** Wesley House, 21–22 Marina, POB 2011, Lagos; tel. (1) 2631853; 483,500 mems; Patriarch Rev. Sunday Coffie Mbang.
**Nigerian Baptist Convention:** Baptist Bldg, PMB 5113, Ibadan; tel. (2) 412146; 500,000 mems; Pres. Rev. David H. Karo; Gen. Sec. Dr Samuel T. Ola Akande.
**Presbyterian Church of Nigeria:** 26–29 Ehere Rd, Ogbor Hill, POB 2635, Aba, Imo; tel. (82) 222551; f. 1846; 100,000 mems;

# NIGERIA

Moderator Rt Rev. Dr M. O. OGAREKPE; Synod Clerk Rev. E. U. ONWUCHEKWA.

The Salvation Army and the Qua Iboe Church are also active.

## AFRICAN RELIGIONS

The beliefs, rites and practices of the people of Nigeria are very diverse, varying between ethnic groups and between families in the same group. In 1963 about 10m. persons (18% of the total population) were followers of traditional beliefs.

## The Press

### DAILIES

**Abuja Times:** Daily Times of Nigeria Ltd, New Isheri Rd, Agidingbi, PMB 21340, Ikeja, Lagos; tel. (1) 4900850; telex 21333; f. 1992.

**Amana:** Concord House, 42 Concord Way, POB 4483, Ikeja, Lagos; Hausa.

**Daily Champion:** Isolo Industrial Estate, Oshodi-Apapa,Lagos; Editor EMEKA OMEIHE.

**Daily Express:** Commercial Amalgamated Printers, 30 Glover St, Lagos; f. 1938; Editor Alhaji AHMED ALAO (acting); circ. 20,000.

**Daily Sketch:** Sketch Publishing Ltd, Oba Adebimpe Rd, PMB 5067, Ibadan; tel. (2) 414851; telex 31591; f. 1964; govt-owned; Chair. RONKE OKUSANYA; Editor ADEMOLA IDOWU; circ. 64,000.

**Daily Star:** 9 Works Rd, PMB 1139, Enugu; tel. (42) 253561; Editor JOSEF BEL-MOLOKWU.

**Daily Times:** Daily Times of Nigeria Ltd, New Isheri Rd, Agidingbi, PMB 21340, Ikeja, Lagos; tel. (1) 4900850; telex 21333; f. 1925; 60% govt-owned; Editor DAPO ADERINOLA; circ. 400,000.

**The Democrat:** 9 Ahmed Talib Ave, POB 4457, Kaduna South, tel. (62) 231907; f. 1983; Editor ABDULHAMID BABATUNDE; circ. 100,000.

**Evening Times:** Daily Times of Nigeria Ltd, New Isheri Rd, Agidingbi, PMB 21340, Ikeja, Lagos; tel. (1) 4900850; telex 21333; Editor CLEMENT ILOBA; circ. 20,000.

**The Guardian:** Rutam House, Isolo Expressway, Isolo, PMB 1217, Oshodi, Lagos; tel. (1) 524111; telex 23283; f. 1983; banned in 1994; Man. Dir Dr STANLEY MACEBUH; Editor ELUEM E. IZEZE; circ. 80,000.

**Isokan:** Concord House, 42 Concord Way, POB 4483, Ikeja, Lagos; Yoruba.

**National Concord:** Concord House, 42 Concord Way, POB 4483, Ikeja, Lagos; telex 26681; f. 1980; banned in 1994; Editor NSIKAK ESSIEN; circ. 200,000.

**New Nigerian:** Ahmadu Bello Way, POB 254, Kaduna; tel. (62) 201420; telex 71120; f. 1965; govt-owned; Chair. Prof. TEKENA TAMUNO; Editor (vacant); circ. 80,000.

**Nigerian Chronicle:** Cross River State Newspaper Corpn, 17-19 Barracks Rd, POB 1074, Calabar; tel. (87) 224976; telex 65104; f. 1970; Editor OQUA ITU; circ. 70,000.

**Nigerian Herald:** Kwara State Printing and Publishing Corpn, Offa Rd, PMB 1369, Ilorin; tel. (31) 220506; telex 33108; f. 1973; sponsored by Kwara State Govt; Editor DOYIN MAHMOUD; circ. 20,000.

**Nigerian Observer:** The Bendel Newspaper Corpn, 18 Airport Rd, POB 1143, Benin City; tel. (52) 240050; telex 41104; f. 1968; Editor TONY IKEAKANAM; circ. 150,000.

**Nigerian Standard:** 5 Joseph Gomwalk Rd, POB 2112, Jos; telex 33131; f. 1972; govt-owned; Editor SALE ILIYA; circ. 100,000.

**Nigerian Statesman:** Imo Newspapers Ltd, Owerri-Egbu Rd, POB 1095, Owerri; tel. (83) 230099; telex 53207; f. 1978; sponsored by Imo State Govt; Editor EDUBE WADIBIA.

**Nigerian Tide:** Rivers State Newspaper Corpn, 4 Ikwerre Rd, POB 5072, Port Harcourt; telex 61144; f. 1971; Editor AUGUSTINE NJOAGWUANI; circ. 30,000.

**Nigerian Tribune:** African Newspapers of Nigeria Ltd, Imalefalafi St, Oke-Ado, POB 78, Ibadan; tel. (2) 2313410; telex 31186; fax (2) 2317573; f. 1949; Editor FOLU OLAMITI; circ. 109,000.

**The Punch:** Skyway Press, Kudeti St, PMB 21204, Onipetsi, Ikeja; tel. (1) 4963580; f. 1976; banned in 1994; Editor BOLA BOLAWOLE; circ. 150,000.

**Vanguard:** Kirikiri Canal, PMB 1007, Apapa; f. 1984; Editor FRANK AIGBOGUN.

### SUNDAY NEWSPAPERS

**Sunday Chronicle:** Cross River State Newspaper Corpn, PMB 1074, Calabar; f. 1977; Editor-in-Chief ETIM ANIM; circ. 163,000.

**Sunday Concord:** Concord House, 42 Concord Way, POB 4483, Ikeja, Lagos; telex 26681; f. 1980; banned in 1994; Editor DELE ALAKE.

**Sunday Herald:** Kwara State Printing and Publishing Corpn, PMB 1369, Ilorin; tel. (31) 220976; telex 33108; f. 1981; Editor MOLA OLANIYAN.

**Sunday New Nigerian:** Ahmadu Bello Way, POB 254, Kaduna; tel. (62) 201420; telex 71120; Editor (vacant).

**Sunday Observer:** PMB 1334, Bendel Newspapers Corpn, 18 Airport Rd, Benin City; f. 1968; Editor T. O. BORHA; circ. 60,000.

**Sunday Punch:** Kudeti St, PMB 21204, Ikeja; tel. (1) 4964691; telex 91470; fax (1) 4960715; f. 1973; banned in 1994; Man. Editor GODWIN NZEAKAH; Editor DAYO WRIGHT; circ. 150,000.

**Sunday Sketch:** Sketch Publishing Co Ltd, PMB 5067, Ibadan; tel. (2) 414851; f. 1964; govt-owned; Editor OBAFEMI OREDEIN; circ. 125,000.

**Sunday Standard:** Plateau Publishing Co Ltd, 5 Joseph Gornwalic Rd, PMB 2112, Jos; f. 1972; govt-owned; Editor SALE ILIYA.

**Sunday Statesman:** Imo Newspapers Ltd, Owerri-Egbu Rd, PMB 1095, Owerri; tel. (83) 230099; telex 53207; f. 1978; sponsored by Imo State Govt; Editor EDUBE WADIBIA.

**Sunday Sun:** PMB 1025, Okoro House, Factory Lane, off Upper Mission Rd, New Benin.

**Sunday Tide:** 4 Ikwerre Rd, POB 5072, Port Harcourt; telex 61144; f. 1971; Editor AUGUSTINE NJOAGWUANI.

**Sunday Times:** Daily Times of Nigeria Ltd, New Isheri Rd, Agidingbi, PMB 21340, Ikeja, Lagos; tel. (1) 4900850; telex 21333; f. 1953; 60% govt-owned; Editor DUPE AJAYI; circ. 100,000.

**Sunday Tribune:** POB 78, Oke-Ado, Ibadan; tel. (2) 310886; Editor WALE OJO.

**Sunday Vanguard:** PMB 1007, Apapa; Editor DUPE AJAYI.

### WEEKLIES

**Albishir:** Triumph Publishing Co Ltd, Gidan Sa'adu Zungur, PMB 3155, Kano; tel. (64) 260273; telex 77357; f. 1981; Hausa; Editor ADAMU A. KIYAWA; circ. 15,000.

**Business Times:** Daily Times of Nigeria Ltd, New Isheri Rd, Agidingbi, PMB 21340, Ikeja, Lagos; tel. (1) 4900850; telex 21333; f. 1925; 60% govt-owned; Editor GODFREY BAMAWO; circ. 22,000.

**Eleti-Ofe:** 28 Kosoko St, Lagos; f. 1923; English and Yoruba; Editor OLA ONATADE; circ. 30,000.

**Gboungboun:** Sketch Publishing Co Ltd, New Court Rd, PMB 5067, Ibadan; tel. (2) 414851; govt-owned; Yoruba; Editor A. O. ADEBANJO; circ. 80,000.

**The Independent:** Bodija Rd, PMB 5109, Ibadan; f. 1960; English; Roman Catholic; Editor Rev. F. B. CRONIN-COLTSMAN; circ. 13,000.

**Irohin Imole:** 15 Bamgbose St, POB 1495, Lagos; f. 1957; Yoruba; Editor TUNJI ADEOSUN.

**Irohin Yoruba:** 212 Broad St, PMB 2416, Lagos; tel. (1) 410886; f. 1945; Yoruba; Editor S. A. AJIBADE; circ. 85,000.

**Lagos Life:** Guardian Newspapers Ltd, Rutam House, Isolo Expressway, Isolo, PMB 1217, Oshodi, Lagos; f. 1985; Editor BISI OGUNBADEJO; circ. 100,000.

**Lagos Weekend:** Daily Times of Nigeria Ltd, New Isheri Rd, Agidingbi, PMB 21340, Ikeja, Lagos; tel. (1) 4900850; telex 21333; f. 1965; 60% govt-owned; news and pictures; Editor SAM OGWA; circ. 85,000.

**Mid-West This Week:** Arin Associates, 50B New Lagos Rd, Benin City; Editors TONY OKODUWA, PRINCE A. R. NWOKO.

**Newswatch:** 3 Billingsway Rd, Oregun, Lagos; tel. (1) 4960950; telex 27874; fax (1) 4962887; f. 1985; English; Editor-in-Chief RAY EKPU.

**Nigerian Radio/TV Times:** Nigerian Broadcasting Corpn, POB 12504, Ikoyi.

**Sporting Records:** Daily Times of Nigeria Ltd, New Isheri Rd, Agidingbi, PMB 21340, Ikeja, Lagos; tel. (1) 4900850; telex 21333; f. 1961; 60% govt-owned; Editor CYRIL KAPPO; circ. 10,000.

**Times International:** Daily Times of Nigeria Ltd, 3-7 Kakawa St, POB 139, Lagos; f. 1974; Editor Dr HEZY IDOWU; circ. 50,000.

**Truth (The Muslim Weekly):** 45 Idumagbo Ave, POB 418, Lagos; tel. (1) 2668455; telex 21356; f. 1951; Editor S. O. LAWAL.

### ENGLISH LANGUAGE PERIODICALS

**Afriscope:** 29 Salami Saibu St, PMB 1119, Yaba; monthly; African current affairs.

**The Ambassador:** PMB 2011, 1 peru-Remo, Ogun; tel. (39) 620115; quarterly; Roman Catholic; circ. 20,000.

**Benin Review:** Ethiope Publishing Corpn, PMB 1332, Benin City; f. 1974; African art and culture; 2 a year; circ. 50,000.

**Headlines:** Daily Times of Nigeria Ltd, New Isheri Rd, Agidingbi, PMB 21340, Ikeja, Lagos; f. 1973; monthly; Editor ADAMS ALIU; circ. 500,000.

# NIGERIA

**Home Studies:** Daily Times Publications, 3–7 Kakawa St, Lagos; f. 1964; two a month; Editor Dr ELIZABETH E. IKEM; circ. 40,000.

**Insight:** 3 Kakawa St, POB 139, Lagos; quarterly; contemporary issues; Editor SAM AMUKA; circ. 5,000.

**Journal of the Nigerian Medical Association:** 3–7 Kakawa St, POB 139, Apapa; quarterly; Editor Prof. A. O. ADESOLA.

**Lagos Education Review:** Faculty of Education, University of Lagos Akoka, Lagos; tel. (1) 5823593; f. 1978; 2 a year; African education; Editor Prof. M. S. OLAYINKA.

**The Leader:** PMB 1017, Owerri; tel. (83) 230932; fortnightly; Roman Catholic; Editor Rev. KEVIN C. AKAGHA.

**Management in Nigeria:** Plot 22, Idowu Taylor St, Victoria Island, POB 2557, Lagos; tel. (1) 2615105; every 2 months; journal of Nigerian Inst. of Management; Editor DELE QSUNDAHUNSI.

**Marketing in Nigeria:** Alpha Publications, Surulere, POB 1163, Lagos; f. 1977; monthly; Editor B. O. K. NWELIH; circ. 30,000.

**Modern Woman:** 47–49 Salami Saibu St, Marina, POB 2583, Lagos; f. 1964; monthly; Man. Editor TOUN ONABANJO.

**Monthly Life:** West African Book Publishers, POB 3445, Lagos; tel. (1) 4900760; telex 26144; f. 1984; monthly; Editor WOLE OLAOYE; circ. 40,000.

**The New Nation:** 52 Iwaya Rd, Onike, Yaba, Surulere, POB 896, Lagos; tel. (1) 5863629; telex 26517; monthly; news magazine.

**Nigeria Magazine:** Federal Dept of Culture, PMB 12524, Lagos; tel. (1) 5802060; f. 1927; quarterly; travel, cultural, historical and general; Editor B. D. LEMCHI; circ. 5,000.

**Nigerian Businessman's Magazine:** 39 Mabo St, Surulere, Lagos; monthly; Nigerian and overseas commerce.

**Nigerian Journal of Economic and Social Studies:** Nigerian Economic Society, c/o Dept of Economics, University of Ibadan; f. 1959; 3 a year; Editor Prof. S. TOMORI.

**Nigerian Journal of Science:** University of Ibadan, POB 4039, Ibadan; publ. of the Science Asscn of Nigeria; f. 1966; 2 a year; Editor Prof. L. B. KOLAWOLE; circ. 1,000.

**Nigerian Medical Journal:** 3 Kakawa St, POB 139, Lagos; monthly.

**Nigerian Radio/TV Times:** Broadcasting House, POB 12504, Lagos; monthly.

**Nigerian Teacher:** 3 Kakawa St, POB 139, Lagos; quarterly.

**Nigerian Worker:** United Labour Congress, 97 Herbert Macaulay St, Lagos; Editor LAWRENCE BORHA.

**The President:** New Breed Organization Ltd, Plot 14 Western Ave, 1 Rafiu Shitty St, Alaka Estate, Surulere, POB 385, Lagos; tel. (1) 5802690; fax (1) 5831175; fortnightly; management; Chief Editor CHRIS OKOLIE.

**Quality:** Ultimate Publications Ltd, Oregun Rd, Lagos; f. 1987; monthly; Editor BALA DAN MUSA.

**Radio-Vision Times:** Western Nigerian Radio-Vision Service, Television House, POB 1460, Ibadan; monthly; Editor ALTON A. ADEDEJI.

**Savanna:** Ahmadu Bello University Press Ltd, PMB 1094, Zaria; tel. (69) 50054; telex 75241; f. 1972; 2 a year; Editor AUDEE T. GIWA; circ. 1,000.

**Spear:** Daily Times of Nigeria Ltd, New Isheri Rd, Agidingbi, PMB 21340, Ikeja, Lagos; tel. (1) 4900850; f. 1962; monthly; family magazine; Editor COKER ONITA; circ. 10,000.

**Technical and Commercial Message:** Surulere, POB 1163, Lagos; f. 1980; 6 a year; Editor B. O. K. NWELIH; circ. 12,500.

**Today's Challenge:** PMB 2010, Jos; tel. (73) 52230; f. 1951; 6 a year; religious and educational; Editor JACOB SHAIBY TSADO; circ. 15,000.

**Woman's World:** Daily Times of Nigeria Ltd, New Isheri Rd, Agidingbi, PMB 21340, Ikeja, Lagos; monthly; Editor TOYIN JOHNSON; circ. 12,000.

### VERNACULAR PERIODICALS

**Abokiyar Hira:** Albah International Publishers, POB 6177, Bompai, Kano; f. 1987; monthly; Hausa; cultural; Editor BASHARI F. FOUKBAH; circ. 35,000.

**Gaskiya ta fi Kwabo:** Ahmadu Bello Way, POB 254, Kaduna; tel. (62) 201420; telex 71120; f. 1939; 3 a week; Hausa; Editor ABDUL-HASSAN IBRAHIM.

### NEWS AGENCIES

**News Agency of Nigeria (NAN):** c/o National Theatre, Iganmu, PMB 12756, Lagos; tel. (1) 5801290; telex 22648; fax (1) 5450324; f. 1978; Chair. OYEKUNLE OLUWASANMI; Man. Dir Mallam NADA MAIDA.

#### Foreign Bureaux

**Agence France-Presse (AFP):** 26B Keffi St, SW Ikoyi, PMB 2448, Lagos; tel. (1) 2683550; telex 21363; fax (1) 2682752; Bureau Chief GÉRARD VANDENBERGHE.

**Informatsionnoye Telegrafnoye Agentstvo Rossii—Telegrafnoye Agentstvo Suverennykh Stran (ITAR—TASS)** (Russia): 401 St, POB 6465, Victoria Island, Lagos; tel. (1) 617119; Correspondent BORIS VASILIEVICH PILNIKOV.

**Inter Press Service (IPS)** (Italy): c/o News Agency of Nigeria, PMB 12756, Lagos; tel. (1) 5801290; Correspondent REMI OYO.

**Pan-African News Agency (PANA):** c/o News Agency of Nigeria, National Arts Theatre, POB 8715, Marina, Lagos; tel. (1) 5801290; telex 26571; f. 1979.

**Xinhua (New China) News Agency** (People's Republic of China): 161A Adeola Odeku St, Victoria Island, POB 70278, Lagos; tel. (1) 2612464; telex 21541; Bureau Chief ZHAI JINGSHENG.

## Publishers

**Africana-FEP Publishers (Nigeria) Ltd:** Book House, 79 Awka Rd, PMB 1639, Onitsha; tel. (46) 210669; f. 1973; study guides, general science, textbooks; Man. Dir PATRICK C. OMABU.

**Ahmadu Bello University Press:** PMB 1094, Zaria; tel. (69) 50054; telex 75291; f. 1974; history, Africana, social sciences, education, literature and arts; Man. Dir Alhaji SAIBU A. AFEGBUA.

**Albah International Publishers:** 100 Kurawa, Bompai-Kano, POB 6177, Kano City; f. 1978; Africana, Islamic, educational and general, in Hausa; Chair. BASHARI F. ROUKBAH.

**Alliance West African Publishers:** Orindingbin Estate, New Aketan Layout, PMB 1039, Oyo; tel. (85) 230798; f. 1971; educational and general; Man. Dir Chief M. O. OGUNMOLA.

**Aromolaran Publishing Co Ltd:** POB 1800, Ibadan; tel. (2) 715980; telex 34315; f. 1968; educational and general; Man. Dir Dr ADEKUNLE AROMOLARAN.

**Daystar Press:** Daystar House, POB 1261, Ibadan; tel. (2) 8102670; f. 1962; religious and educational; Man. PHILLIP ADELAKUN LADOKUN.

**ECWA Productions Ltd:** PMB 2010, Jos; tel. (73) 52230; telex 81120; f. 1973; religious and educational; Gen. Man. Rev. J. K. BOLARIN.

**Ethiope Publishing Corpn:** Ring Rd, PMB 1332, Benin City; tel. (52) 243036; telex 41110; f. 1970; general fiction and non-fiction, textbooks, reference, science, arts and history; Man. Dir SUNDAY N. OLAYE.

**Evans Brothers (Nigeria Publishers) Ltd:** Jericho Rd, PMB 5164, Ibadan; tel. (2) 417570; telex 31104; fax (2) 410757; f. 1966; general and educational; Chair. Dr S. J. COOKEY; Man. Dir B. O. BOLODEOKU.

**Fourth Dimension Publishing Co Ltd:** Plot 64A, City Layout, PMB 01164, Enugu; tel. (42) 339969; telex 51319; f. 1977; periodicals, fiction, verse, educational and children's; Chair. ARTHUR NWANKWO; Man. Dir V. U. NWANKWO.

**Gbabeks Publishers Ltd:** POB 3538, Kaduna; tel. (62) 217976; f. 1982; educational and technical; Man. Dir TAYO OGUNBEKUN.

**Heinemann Educational Books (Nigeria) Ltd:** 1 Ighodaro Rd, Jericho, PMB 5205, Ibadan; tel. (2) 2412268; telex 31113; fax (2) 2411089; f. 1962; educational, law, medical and general; Chair. AIGBOJE HIGO.

**Heritage Books:** 2–8 Calcutta Crescent, Gate 4, POB 610, Apapa, Lagos; tel. (1) 871333; f. 1971; general; Chair. NAIWU OSAHON.

**Ibadan University Press:** Publishing House, University of Ibadan, PMB 16, IU Post Office, Ibadan; tel. (2) 400550; telex 31128; f. 1951; scholarly, science, law, general and educational; Dir F. A. ADESANOYE.

**Ilesanmi Press Ltd:** Akure Rd, POB 204, Ilesha; tel. 2062; f. 1955; general and educational; Man. Dir G. E. ILESANMI.

**Kolasanya Publishing Enterprise:** 2 Epe Rd, Oke-Owa, PMB 2099, Ijebu-Ode; general and educational; Man. Dir Chief K. OSUNSANYA.

**Literamed Publications Ltd (Lantern Books):** Plot 45, Alausa Bus-stop, Oregun Industrial Estate, Ikeja, PMB 21068, Lagos; tel. (1) 4962512; telex 21068; fax (1) 4972217; general; Man. Dir O. M. LAWAL-SOLARIN.

**Longman Nigeria Ltd:** 52 Oba Akran Ave, PMB 21036, Ikeja, Lagos; tel. (1) 4901150; telex 26639; f. 1961; general and educational; Dir A. O. ECHEBIRI.

**Macmillan Nigeria Publishers Ltd:** Ilupeju Industrial Estate, 4 Industrial Ave, POB 264, Yaba, Lagos; tel. (1) 4962185; f. 1965; educational and general; Exec. Chair. J. O. EMMANUEL; Man. Dir Dr A. I. ADELEKAN.

**Nelson Publishers Ltd:** 8 Ilupeju By-Pass, Ikeja, PMB 21303, Lagos; tel. (1) 4961452; general and educational; Chair. Prof. C. O. TAIWO; Man. Dir. R. O. OGUNBO.

# NIGERIA

**Northern Nigerian Publishing Co Ltd:** Gaskiya Bldg, POB 412, Zaria; tel. (69) 32087; telex 75243; f. 1966; general, educational and vernacular texts; Man. Dir H. HAYAT.

**NPS Educational Publishers Ltd:** Trusthouse, Ring Rd, off Akinyemi Way, POB 62, Ibadan; tel. (2) 316006; telex 31478; f. 1969; academic, scholarly and educational; Chief Exec. T. D. OTESANYA.

**Nwamife Publishers:** 10 Ibiam St, Uwani, POB 430, Enugu; tel. (42) 338254; f. 1971; general and educational; Chair. FELIX C. ADI.

**Obafemi Awolowo University Press Ltd:** Obafemi Awolowo University, Ile-Ife; tel. (36) 230290; f. 1968; educational, scholarly and periodicals; Man. Dir AKIN FATOKUN.

**Obobo Books:** 2–8 Calcutta Crescent, Gate 4, POB 610, Apapa, Lagos; tel. (1) 5871333; f. 1981; children's books; Editorial Dir BAKIN KUNAMA.

**Ogunsanya Press Publishers and Bookstores Ltd:** SW9/1133 Orita Challenge, Idiroko, POB 95, Ibadan; tel. (2) 310924; f. 1970; educational; Man. Dir Chief LUCAS JUSTUS POPO-OLA OGUNSANYA.

**Onibonoje Press and Book Industries (Nigeria) Ltd:** Felele Layout, Challenge, POB 3109, Ibadan; tel. (2) 313956; telex 31657; f. 1958; educational and general; Chair. G. ONIBONOJE; Man. Dir J. O. ONIBONOJE.

**Pilgrim Books Ltd:** New Oluyole Industrial Estate, Ibadan/Lagos Expressway, PMB 5617, Ibadan; tel. (2) 317218; telex 20311; educational and general; Man. Dir JOHN E. LEIGH.

**Spectrum Books Ltd:** Sunshine House, 1 Emmanuel Alayande St, Oluyole Estate, PMB 5612, Ibadan; tel. (2) 2310058; telex 31588; fax (2) 2318502; f. 1978; educational and fiction; Man. Dir JOOP BERKHOUT.

**University of Lagos Press:** University of Lagos, PO Akoka, Yaba, Lagos; tel. (1) 5825048; telex 21210; university textbooks, monographs, lectures and journals; Man. Dir MODUPE F. ADEOGUN (acting).

**University Press Ltd:** Three Crowns Bldg, Eleyele Rd, Jericho, PMB 5095, Ibadan; tel. (2) 411356; telex 31121; fax (2) 412056; f. 1978; associated with Oxford University Press; educational; Man. Dir WAHEED O. OLAJIDE.

**University Publishing Co:** 11 Central School Rd, POB 386, Onitsha; tel. (46) 210013; f. 1959; primary, secondary and university textbooks; Chair. E. O. UGWUEGBULEM.

**Vista Books Ltd:** 59 Awolowo Rd, POB 282, Yaba, Lagos; tel. (1) 2681656; fax (1) 2685679; f. 1991; general fiction and non-fiction, arts, children's and educational; Man. Dir Dr T. C. NWOSU.

**West African Book Publishers Ltd:** Ilupeju Industrial Estate, POB 3445, Lagos; tel. (1) 4900760; telex 26144; f. 1967; textbooks, children's, periodicals and general; Dir Mrs A. O. OBADAGBONYI.

**John West Publications Ltd:** Plot 2, Block A, Acme Rd, Ogba Industrial Estate, PMB 21001, Ikeja, Lagos; tel. (1) 4921010; telex 26446; f. 1964 general; Man. Dir Alhaji L. K. JAKAMDE.

### Government Publishing House

**Government Press:** PMB 2020, Kaduna; tel. 213812.

### PUBLISHERS' ASSOCIATION

**Nigerian Publishers Association:** The Ori-Detu, 1st Floor, Shell Close, Onireke, GPO Box 2541, Ibadan; tel. (2) 411557; telex 31113; f. 1965; Pres. V. NWANKWO.

## Radio and Television

According to UNESCO estimates, there were 20m. radio receivers and 3.8m. television receivers in use in 1992.

### RADIO

**Federal Radio Corporation of Nigeria (FRCN):** Broadcasting House, Ikoyi, PMB 12504, Lagos; tel. (1) 2690301; telex 21484; fax (1) 2690073; f. 1978; controlled by the Fed. Govt and divided into five zones: Lagos (English); Enugu (English, Igbo, Izon, Efik and Tiv); Ibadan (English, Yoruba, Edo, Urhobo and Igala); Kaduna (English, Hausa, Kanuri, Fulfulde and Nupe); Abuja (English, Hausa, Igbo and Yoruba); Dir-Gen. Alhaji ABDURRAHMAN MICIKA.

**Voice of Nigeria (VON):** Broadcasting House, Ikoyi, PMB 40003, Lagos; tel. (1) 2693075; fax (1) 2691944; f. 1990; controlled by the Fed. Govt; external services in English, French, Arabic, Ki-Swahili, Hausa and Fulfulde; Dir-Gen. Mallam YAYA ABUBAKAR.

### TELEVISION

**Nigerian Television Authority (NTA):** Television House, Ahmadu Bello Way, Victoria Island, PMB 12036, Lagos; tel. (1) 2615949; telex 21245; f. 1976; controlled by the Fed. Govt; responsible for all aspects of television broadcasting; Chair. IFEANYINWA NZEAKOR; Dir-Gen. Alhaji MOHAMMED IBRAHIM.

**NTA Aba/Owerri:** PMB 7126, Aba; tel. (83) 220922; Gen. Man. MARTIN A. AKPETI.

**NTA Abeokuta:** PMB 2190, Abeokuta; Gen. Man. H. O. ROBIN.

**NTA Abuja:** Abuja.

**NTA Akure:** PMB 794, Akure; tel. (34) 230351; Gen. Man. JIBOLA DEDENUOLA.

**NTA Bauchi:** PMB 0146, Bauchi; tel. (77) 42748; telex 83270; f. 1976; Man. MUHAMMAD AL-AMIN.

**NTA Benin City:** West Circular Rd, PMB 1117, Benin City; telex 44308; Gen. Man. J. O. N. EZEKOKA.

**NTA Calabar:** 105 Marion Rd, Calabar; telex 65110; Man. E. ETUK.

**NTA Enugu:** Independence Layout, PMB 01530, Enugu, Anambra; tel. (42) 335120; telex 51147; f. 1960; Gen. Man. G. C. MEFO.

**NTA Ibadan:** POB 1460, Ibadan; tel. (2) 713320; telex 31156; Gen. Man. JIBOLA DEDENUOLA.

**NTA Ikeja:** Tejuosho Ave, Surulere.

**NTA Ilorin:** PMB 1453, Ilorin; telex 33118; Gen. Man. D. ALLI.

**NTA Jos:** PMB 2134, Jos; telex 81149; Gen. Man. M. J. BEWELL.

**NTA Kaduna:** POB 1347, Kaduna; tel. (62) 216375; telex 71164; f. 1977; Gen. Man. SAIDU ABUBAKAR.

**NTA Kano:** PMB 3343, Kano; tel. (64) 640072; Gen. Man. BELLO ABUBAKAR.

**NTA Lagos:** Victoria Island, PMB 12005, Lagos; telex 21245; Gen. Man. O. OKUNRINBOYE.

**NTA Maiduguri:** PMB 1487, Maiduguri; telex 82132; Gen. Man. M. M. MAILAFIYA.

**NTA Makurdi:** PMB 2044, Makurdi.

**NTA Minna:** TV House, PMB 79, Minna; tel. (66) 222941; Gen. Man. M. C. DAYLOP.

**NTA Port Harcourt:** PMB 5797, Port Harcourt; Gen. Man. E. T. HALLIDAY.

**NTA Sokoto:** PMB 2351, Sokoto; tel. (60) 232670; telex 73116; f. 1975; Gen. Man. M. B. TUNAU.

**NTA Yola:** PMB 2197, Yola; Gen. Man. M. M. SAIDU.

In July 1993 14 companies were granted licences to operate private television stations.

## Finance

(cap. = capital; p.u. = paid up; res = reserves; dep. = deposits; m. = million; brs = branches; amounts in naira unless otherwise stated)

### BANKING

In early 1995 there were 120 licensed banks operating in Nigeria; however, the Government approved only 68 of these for foreign exchange transactions. It was subsequently announced that the Government planned to resume state control over a number of commercial banks that had been privatized in 1993.

#### Central Bank

**Central Bank of Nigeria:** Tinubu Sq., PMB 12194, Lagos; tel. (1) 2660100; telex 21350; f. 1958; bank of issue; cap. and res 646m., dep. 42,637.3m. (1990); Gov. PAUL AGBAI OGWUMA; 18 brs.

#### Commercial Banks

**Afribank Nigeria Ltd:** 94 Broad St, PMB 12021, Lagos; tel. (1) 2663608; telex 21345; fax (1) 2662793; f. 1969 as International Bank for West Africa Ltd; cap. and res 556.2m. dep. 7,390m. (1993); Man. Dir JOHN EDOZIEN; 123 brs.

**African Continental Bank Ltd:** 148 Broad St, PMB 2466, Lagos; tel. (1) 2664833; f. 1947; cap. and res 24.5m., dep. 1,845.1m. (1989); Chair. Chief J. O. IRUKWU; Man. Dir E. A. EZEKWE; 919 brs.

**African International Bank Ltd:** 42–44 Warehouse Rd, PMB 1040, Apapa, Lagos; tel. (1) 5870389; telex 22377; fax (1) 5877174; f. 1979; cap. and res 190.5m., dep. 1,397.4m. (1990); acquired assets of Bank of Credit and Commerce International (Nigeria) Ltd; Chair. Alhaji MAMMAN DAURA; Man. Dir Alhaji ABDULLAHI MAHMOUD; 47 brs.

**Allied Bank of Nigeria Ltd:** Allied House, 214 Broad St, PMB 12785, Lagos; tel. (1) 2662976; telex 21512; fax (1) 2669602; f. 1962 as Bank of India; cap. and res 80.2m., dep. 2,871.6m. (1992); Chair. B. EHIZUENLEN; Man. Dir Alhaji SHEHU MOHAMMED; 68 brs.

**Bank of the North Ltd:** Ahmadu Bello House, 2 Zaria Rd, POB 211, Kano; tel. (64) 660209; telex 77233; f. 1959; cap. and res 159.3m., dep. 2,748.8m. (1992); Chair. Alhaji ABUBAKAR ZAKI TAMBUWAL; Man. Dir Alhaji YAKUBU SHEHU; 97 brs.

# NIGERIA

**Chartered Bank Ltd:** Plot 1619, Danmole St, POB 73069, Victoria Island, Lagos; tel. (1) 2619250; telex 21155; fax (1) 2615094; cap. and res 107.1m., dep. 1,047.1m. (1992)); Chair. Lt-Gen. (retd) M. I. WUSHISHI; Man. Dir O. OLAGUNDOYE.

**Commercial Bank (Crédit Lyonnais Nigeria) Ltd:** Elephant House, 214 Broad St, PMB 12829, Lagos; tel. (1) 2665594; telex 23157; fax (1) 2665308; f. 1983; cap. p.u. 60m., dep. 1,700m. (1993); Chair. ALLISON A. AYIDA; Man. Dir R. CESSAK; 21 brs.

**Crown Merchant Bank Ltd:** 8 Idowu Taylor St, Victoria Island, Lagos; tel. (1) 2613728; telex 22831; fax (1) 2615545; cap. and res 43.6m., dep. 275.8m. (1991); Man. Dir ORE S. A. ONAKOYA.

**Ecobank Nigeria Ltd:** 2 Ajose Adeogun St, Victoria Island, POB 72688, Lagos; tel. (1) 2612953; telex 21157; fax (1) 216568; cap. p.u. 89m. (Sept. 1993); Man. Dir. DISUN HOLLOWAY.

**Eko International Bank of Nigeria:** cnr Nnamdi Azikiwe and Alli Balogun Sts, PMB 12864, Lagos; tel. (1) 2600350; telex 22902; fax (1) 2665176; cap. 61.2m. (1993), dep. 580.0m. (1991); Chair. J. O. EMANUEL; Man. Dir OLATUNDE FASHINA; 8 brs.

**First Bank of Nigeria Ltd:** Samuel Asabia House, 35 Marina, POB 5216, Lagos; tel. (1) 2665900; telex 28606; fax (1) 2669073; f. 1894 as Bank of British West Africa; cap. and res 1,620m., dep. 24,470m. (1993) Chair. MAHMOUD IBRAHIM ATTA; Man. Dir JOSEPH OLADELE SANUSI; 290 brs.

**FSB International Bank Ltd:** 23 Awolowo Rd, SW Ikoyi, PMB 12521, Lagos; tel. (1) 2690576; telex 23671; fax (1) 2690397; f. 1991 to succeed Federal Savings Bank; Chair. Alhaji A. O. G. OTITI; Man. Dir MOHAMMED HAYATU-DEEN.

**Habib Nigeria Bank Ltd:** 1 Keffi St, POB 54648, Falomo, Ikoyi, Lagos; tel. (1) 2663121; cap p.u. 52.5m. (Dec. 1992), dep. 364.6m. (1989); Chair. Maj.-Gen. (retd) SHEHU MUSA YAR'ADUA; Man. Dir Alhaji FALALU; 65 brs.

**Investment Banking and Trust Co Ltd (IBTC):** Wesley House, 21–22 Marina, PMB 12557, Lagos; tel. (1) 2600200; telex 28747; fax (1) 2634146; cap. and res 379.0m., dep. 1,009.3m. (1993); Chair. DAVID DANKARO; Man. Dir ATEDO A. PETERSIDE.

**Lion Bank of Nigeria:** 34 Ahmadu Bello Way, PMB 2126, Jos, Plateau; tel. (73) 52223; telex 81165; fax (73) 54602; cap. and res 86.9m., dep. 868.0m. (1993); Man. Dir S. P. Y. GANG.

**Nigeria International Bank Ltd (NIB):** Commerce House, 1 Idowu Taylor St, Victoria Island, POB 6391, Lagos; tel. (1) 2662200; telex 23424; fax (1) 2618916; f. 1984; cap. and res 280.6m., dep. 2,741m. (1992); Chair. Chief CHARLES S. SANKEY; Man. Dir NAVEED RIAZ; 12 brs.

**Nigeria Universal Bank Ltd:** Yakubu Gowon Way, POB 1066, Kaduna; tel. (62) 233988; telex 71156; fax (62) 215204; f. 1974; owned by Katsina and Kaduna State Govts; cap. 50m., dep. 447m. (1992); Chair. Alhaji MUHAMMADU HAYATUDDINI; Man. Dir Alhaji USMAN ABUBAKAR; 27 brs.

**Owena Bank (Nigeria) Ltd:** Engineering Close, PMB 1122, Victoria Island, Lagos; tel. (1) 877901; telex 28692; 30% owned by Ondo State Govt; cap. p.u. 60m. (Dec. 1992); Chair. PETER AJAYI; Man. Dir SEGUN AGBETUYI.

**Pan African Bank Ltd:** 31 Azikiwe Rd, PMB 5239, Port Harcourt; tel. (84) 2667045; telex 61157; fax (84) 330616; f. 1971; cap. and res 140.3m., dep. 514.7m. (1991); Chair. W. T. DAMBO; Man. Dir B. A. KONYA; 10 brs.

**People's Bank of Nigeria:** 33 Balogun St, PMB 12914, Lagos; tel. (1) 2664241; fax (1) 2667571; state-owned; cap. p.u. 230m. (Dec. 1991); Chair. Chief E. A. O. OYEYIPO; Man. Dir MARIA O. SOKENU.

**Progress Bank of Nigeria Ltd:** Plot 91, Ikenegbu Layout, POB 1577, Owerri; tel. (83) 23476; telex 53203; f. 1982; controlled by Imo State Govt; cap. and res 48.8m., dep. 873.5m. (1990); Chair. Chief R. E. ODINKEMELU; Man. Dir I. K. UCHE (acting)

**Savannah Bank of Nigeria Ltd:** 62–66 Broad St, POB 2317, Lagos; tel. (1) 2600470; telex 21876; f. 1976; cap. p.u. 34.9m. (March 1991), dep. 1,351.5m. (March 1987); Chair. SIJI SOETAN; Man. Dir Mallam M. A. SHERIFF; 37 brs.

**Société Générale Bank (Nigeria) Ltd:** Sarah House, 13 Martins St, PMB 12741, Lagos; tel. (1) 2661934; telex 23147; fax (1) 2663731; f. 1977; cap. and res 49.0m., dep. 1,501.4m. (1990); Chair. Dr EBENEZER A. IKOMI; Man. Dir ALAN MILTON; 35 brs.

**Tropical Commerical Bank Ltd:** 1 Dr Bala Mohammed Nassarawa, POB 4636, Kano; tel. (64) 627181; telex 77299; fax (64) 644506; 40% state-owned; cap. p.u. 107.6m. (Dec. 1992); Man. Dir Alhaji O. K. DANJUMA.

**Union Bank of Nigeria Ltd:** 40 Marina, PMB 2027, Lagos; tel. (1) 2665439; telex 21222; fax (1) 2663422; f. 1969 as Barclays Bank of Nigeria Ltd; cap. and res 1,217.6m., dep. 22,652.0m. (Sept. 1992); Chair. GREEN ONYEKABA NWANKWO; Man. Dir Alhaji MOHAMMED I. YAHAYA; 241 brs.

**United Bank for Africa (Nigeria) Ltd:** 97–105 Broad St, POB 2406, Lagos; tel. (1) 2667410; telex 21241; fax (1) 2660884; f. 1961; cap. p.u. 100m., dep. 22,227.0m. (March 1993); Chair. SUNDAY V. ADEWUSI; Man. Dir L. E. OKAFOR; 190 brs.

**Universal Trust Bank of Nigeria Ltd:** 4/6 Ajose Adeogun St, Victoria Island, POB 52160, Lagos; tel. (1) 2611192; telex 23445; fax (1) 2610314; f. 1981; cap. p.u. 40m. (1991); Chair. Lt-Gen. T. Y. DANJUMA; Man. Dir KLAUS J. PHILIPPI; 13 brs.

**Wema Bank Ltd:** 27 Nnamdi Azikiwe St, Tinubu, Lagos; tel. (1) 2668105; telex 26554; fax (1) 2669508; f. 1945; cap. and res 142.7m., dep. 1,233.7m. (March 1992); Chair. Dr S. O. OMOBOMI; Man. Dir Chief S. I. ADEGBITE; 66 brs.

## Merchant Banks

**Abacus Merchant Bank Ltd:** Williams House, 8th Floor, 95 Broad St, POB 7908, Lagos; tel. (1) 2660212; telex 21243; cap. and res 24.6m., dep. 312.0m. (1990); Chair. and Man. Dir JULIUS OLAWOLE ADEWUNMI.

**African Banking Consortium (ABC) Merchant Bank (Nigeria) Ltd:** 13 Olosa St, Victoria Island, POB 70647, Lagos; tel. (1) 2616069; telex 23152; fax (1) 2611117; f. 1982; cap. p.u. 40m. (March 1993), dep. 246.4m. (1992); Chair. Chief E. C. IWUANYANWU; Man. Dir C. N. ABARA; 3 brs.

**Century Merchant Bank Ltd:** 11 Burma Rd, PMB 1307, Apapa, Lagos; tel. (1) 2803160; telex 22039; fax (1) 2871603; cap. and res 33.9m., dep. 608.7m. (1991); Chair. Alhaji BASHIR OTHMAN TOFA; Man. Dir CHRIS ENUENWOSU.

**Continental Merchant Bank Nigeria Ltd:** 1 Kingsway Rd, Ikoyi, POB 12035, Lagos; tel. (1) 2690501; telex 21585; fax (1) 2690900; f. 1986; cap. p.u. 43.6m. (Dec. 1992); Chair. Alhaji MOHAMMED SHEKARAU OMAR; Man. Dir Dr CHICHI ASHWE; 3 brs.

**Devcom Merchant Bank Ltd:** 18A Okoawo Close, Victoria Island, Lagos; tel. (1) 2610206; telex 22084; fax (1) 2612615; f. 1989; cap. 18m. (March 1992); Chair. MIKE ADENUGA; Man. Dir ADEREMI LASAKI.

**First City Merchant Bank Ltd:** Primrose Tower, 17A Tinubu St, POB 9117, Lagos; tel. (1) 2665944; telex 22912; fax (1) 2665126; f. 1983; cap. and res 254.3m., dep. 962.3m. (1993); Chair. and CEO OTUNBA M. O. BALOGUN; Dr JONATHAN A. D. LONG.

**First Interstate Merchant Bank (Nigeria) Ltd:** Unity House, 37 Marina, Victoria Island, POB 72295, Lagos; tel. (1) 2667183; telex 23881; fax (1) 2668273; cap. p.u. 40.0m. (March 1992), dep. 801.2m. (1991); Man. Dir O. ODEJIMI (acting).

**ICON Ltd:** ICON House, Plot 999F, cnr Idejo and Danmole Sts, Victoria Island, Lagos; tel. (1) 2660434; f. 1974; cap. p.u. 50.4m. (1991), dep. 1,545.4m. (1990); Chair. Alhaji SAIDU KASSIM; Man. Dir A. A. FEESE; 6 brs.

**Industrial Bank Ltd (Merchant Bankers):** Plot 1637, Adetokunbo Ademola St, Victoria Island, PMB 12637, Lagos; tel. (1) 2622454; telex 22005; fax (1) 619024; cap. p.u. 50.1m. (Dec. 1992); Chair. Dr SAMUEL ADEDOYIN; Man. Dir Chief E. AYO AWODEYI (acting).

**International Merchant Bank (Nigeria) Ltd:** IMB Plaza, 1 Akin Adesola St, Victoria Island, PMB 12028, Lagos; tel. (1) 2612204; telex 28511; fax (1) 615392; f. 1974; affiliate of First National Bank of Chicago (USA); cap. p.u. 36m. (1991), dep. 2,072.9m. (1990); Chair. Gen. M. SHUWA; Man. Dir EDWIN CHINYE; 5 brs.

**Merchant Bank of Africa (Nigeria) Ltd:** St Nicholas House, Catholic Mission St, Falomo, Ikoyi, POB 53611, Lagos; tel. (1) 2601300; telex 23180; fax (1) 2633789; f. 1982; cap. p.u. 28.3m. (1991), dep 465.7m. (1987); Chair. J. T. F. IYALLA; CEO BERNARD O. ANYANWU.

**Merchant Banking Corpn (Nigeria) Ltd:** 16 Keffi St, S W Ikoyi, POB 53289, Lagos; tel. (1) 2690261; telex 22516; fax (1) 2690767; f. 1982; cap. p.u. 40m. (March 1993), dep. 504.4m. (1991); Chair. Dr M. A. MAJEKODUNMI; CEO J. J. AYANDA.

**NAL Merchant Bank:** NAL Towers, 20 Marina, POB 2432, Lagos; tel. (1) 2600420; telex 21505; fax (1) 2633294; f. 1960; cap. and res 602.9m., dep. 1,341.3m. (March 1993); Chair. YAHAYA ABUBAKAR; Man. Dir Dr SHAMSUDEEN USMAN; 4 brs.

**New Africa Merchant Bank Ltd:** 4 Waff Rd, PMB 2340, Kaduna; tel. (62) 235276; telex 71684; fax (62) 217311; cap. and res 59.6m., dep. 457.5m. (1992); Chair. Alhaji UMARU A. MUTALLAB; Man. Dir Mallam UMAR YAHAYA.

**Nigbel Merchant Bank (Nigeria) Ltd:** 77 Awolowo Rd, Ikoyi, POB 52463, Lagos; tel. (1) 2690380; telex 21851; fax (1) 2693256; f. 1987; cap. p.u. 40m. (Dec. 1992), dep. 367.7m. (1991); Chair. Chief N. O. IDOWU; CEO J. M. MARQUEBREUCQ.

**Nigeria-American Merchant Bank Ltd:** Boston House, 10–12 Macarthy St, PMB 12759, Lagos; tel. (1) 2631710; telex 28624; fax (1) 2631712; f. 1979; affiliate of First National Bank of Boston (USA); cap. p.u. 40m. (Dec. 1992), dep. 767.3m. (1991); Chair. Alhaji IBRAHIM DAMCIDA; Man. Dir OSARO ISOKPAN; 3 brs.

**Nigeria-Arab Bank Ltd:** 96–102 Broad St, POB 12807, Lagos; tel. (1) 2661955; telex 21973; f. 1969; cap. and res 38.8m., dep. 1,313.3m. (1991); Chair. Alhaji ABIDU YAZID; Man. Dir A. GUMI; 41 brs.

NIGERIA

**Nigeria Intercontinental Merchant Bank Ltd:** Plot 999c, Intercontinental Plaza, Danmole St, Victoria Island, POB 54434, Lagos; tel. (1) 2636080; telex 28342; fax (1) 2633477; cap. p.u. 101.4m. (Dec. 1992); Chair. RAYMOND C. OBIERI; Man. Dir ERASTUS B. O. AKINGBOLA.

**Nigeria Merchant Bank:** Cowrie House 27–29 Adeyemo Alakija St, PMB 80102, Victoria Island, Lagos; tel. (1) 2620040; telex 23332; fax (1) 2620053; Chair. B. A. EHIZUENLEN; Man. Dir A. O. ADEBO.

**Rims Merchant Bank Ltd:** Kingsway Bldg, Second Floor, 51–52 Merina, POB 73029, Lagos; tel. (1) 2662105; telex 28815; fax (1) 2669947; f. 1988; cap. and res 69.3m., dep. 617.8m. (1992); Chair. Alhaji A. IBRAHIM OFR'SAN; CEO EMMANUEL OCHOLI.

**Stanbic Merchant Bank Nigeria Ltd:** 188 Awolowo Rd, Ikoyi, POB 54746, Lagos; tel. (1) 2690402; telex 23216; fax (1) 2685934; f. 1983 as Grindlays Merchant Bank of Nigeria; cap. p.u. 40m. (Dec. 1992); Chair. Alhaji ISIYAKU RABIU; Man. Dir JOHN N. LEGGETT.

### Development Banks

**Federal Mortgage Bank of Nigeria:** Mamman Kontagora House, 23 Marina St, POB 2078, Lagos; tel. (1) 2647371; telex 21840; f. 1977; loans to individuals and mortgage institutions; cap. p.u. 150m. (1992), dep. 463.8m. (1991); Chair. Alhaji H. B. KOLO; Man. Dir JOHN AKINLEYE; 61 brs.

**Nigerian Agricultural and Co-operative Bank Ltd (NACB):** Hospital Rd, PMB 2155, Kaduna; tel. (62) 201000; telex 71115; fax (62) 210611; f. 1973; for funds to farmers and co-operatives to improve production techniques; cap. p.u. 500m., dep. 4,455.4m. (1992); Chair. Alhaji SULE LAMIDO; Man. Dir Prof. M. B. AJAKAIYE; 38 brs.

**Nigerian Bank for Commerce and Industry (NBCI):** Bankers' House, Plot 19c Adeola Hopewell, Victoria Island, POB 4424, Lagos; tel. (1) 2616194; telex 21917; fax (1) 2614202; f. 1973; govt bank to aid indigenization and development of small and medium-sized enterprises; cap. p.u. 200m. (1990); Administrator UBADIGBO OKONKWO; 19 brs.

**Nigerian Industrial Development Bank Ltd:** NIDB House, 63–71 Broad St, POB 2357, Lagos; tel. (1) 2663495; telex 21701; fax (1) 2667074; f. 1964 to provide medium and long-term finance to industry, manufacturing, non-petroleum mining and tourism; encourages foreign investment in partnership with Nigerians; cap. p.u. 836.9m. (Dec. 1992); Chair. RASHEED GBADAMOSI; Man. Dir Alhaji SAIDU YAYA KASIMU; 5 brs.

### Bankers' Association

**Chartered Institute of Bankers of Nigeria:** 19 Adeola Hopewell St, POB 72273, Victoria Island, Lagos; tel. (1) 2615642; telex 22838; fax (1) 2611306; Chair. JOHNSON O. EKUNDAYO; CEO A. A. ADENUBI.

## STOCK EXCHANGE

**Securities and Exchange Commission (SEC):** Mandilas House, 96–102 Broad St, PMB 12638, Lagos; f. 1979 as govt agency to regulate and develop capital market; responsible for supervision of stock exchange operations; Dir-Gen. GEORGE A. AKAMIOKHOR.

**Nigerian Stock Exchange:** Stock Exchange House, 2–4 Customs St, POB 2457, Lagos; tel. (1) 2660287; telex 23567; fax (1) 2668724; f. 1960; Pres. PASCAL DOZIE; Dir-Gen. HAYFORD ALILE; 6 brs.

## INSURANCE

In December 1994 there were some 134 insurance companies operating in Nigeria. Since 1978 they have been required to reinsure 20% of the sum insured with the Nigeria Reinsurance Corporation.

### Insurance Companies

**African Alliance Insurance Co Ltd:** 112 Broad St, POB 2276, Lagos; tel. (1) 2664300; telex 23461; fax (1) 2660943; life assurance and pensions; Man. Dir OPE OREDUGBA.

**African Insurance Co Ltd:** 134 Nnamdi Azikiwe St, Idumota, POB 274, Lagos; tel. (1) 2661720; f. 1950; all classes except life; Sec. Y. N. MBADIWE; Area Man. N. E. NSA; 4 brs.

**Allco Insurance:** Allco Plaza, Plot PC 12, Afribank St, Victoria Island, POB 2577, Lagos; tel. (1) 2612472; telex 22395; fax (1) 2617433; CEO W. D. MELLO.

**Continental Reinsurance Co Ltd:** 46 Marina, POB 2401, Lagos; tel. (1) 2665350; telex 28426; fax (1) 2665366; CEO E. B. ONIFADE.

**Great Nigeria Insurance Co Ltd:** 47–57 Martins St, POB 2314, Lagos; tel. (1) 2662590; telex 22272; f. 1960; all classes; Man. Dir R. O. ORIMOLOYE.

**Guinea Insurance Co Ltd:** Akuro House, 3rd Floor, 24 Campbell St, POB 1136, Lagos; tel. (1) 2665201; telex 21680; f. 1958; all classes; CEO Alhaji M. A. MUSTAPHA.

*Directory*

**Industrial and General Insurance Co Ltd:** Plot 741, Adeola Hopewell St, POB 52592, Falomo, Lagos; tel. (1) 2613534; fax (1) 614922; CEO REMI OLOWUDE.

**Kapital Insurance Co Ltd:** 15C Murtala Muhammed Way, POB 2044, Kano; tel. (64) 645666; telex 71108; fax (64) 630661; CEO Alhaji M. G. UMAR.

**Law Union and Rock Insurance Co of Nigeria Ltd:** 88–92 Broad St, POB 944, Lagos; tel. (1) 2663526; telex 28427; fax (1) 2664659; fire, accident and marine; 6 brs; Chair. Col S. BELLO; CEO S. O. AKINYEMI.

**Leadway Assurance Co Ltd:** NN 28–29 Constitution Rd, POB 458, Kaduna; tel. (62) 200660; telex 71101; fax (62) 236838; f. 1970; all classes; Chair. Alhaji HASSAN HADEJIA; Man. Dir Chief HASSAN OLU ODUKALE.

**Lion of Africa Insurance Co Ltd:** St Peter's House, 3 Ajele St, POB 2055, Lagos; tel. (1) 2600950; telex 23536; fax (1) 2636111; f. 1952; all classes; Man. Dir G. A. ALEGIEUNO.

**Mercury Assurance Co Ltd:** 17 Martins St, POB 2003, Lagos; tel. (1) 2660216; telex 21952; general; Man. Dir S. N. C. OKONKWO.

**National Insurance Corpn of Nigeria (NICON):** 5 Customs St, POB 1100, Lagos; tel. (1) 2640230; telex 26651; fax (1) 2666556; f. 1969; transferred to private ownership in 1990; all classes; cap. 10m.; Chair. HAMISU BUHARI; Man. Dir Alhaji M. U. A. KARI; 28 brs.

**N.E.M. Insurance Co (Nigeria) Ltd:** 22A Borno Way, Ebute, POB 654, Lagos; tel. (1) 5861920; telex 23287; all classes; Chair. T. J. ONOMIGBO OKPOKO; Man. Dir J. E. UMUKORO.

**Niger Insurance Co Ltd:** 47 Marina, POB 2718, Lagos; tel. (1) 2664452; fax (1) 2662196; all classes; Man. Dir A. K. ONIWINDE; 6 brs.

**Nigeria Reinsurance Corpn:** 46 Marina, PMB 12766, Lagos; tel. (1) 2667049; telex 21092; fax (1) 2668041; all classes of reinsurance; Prof. UKANDI G. DAMACHI; Man. Dir O. OSOKA.

**Nigerian General Insurance Co Ltd:** 1 Nnamdi Azikiwe St, Tirubu Square, POB 2210, Lagos; tel. (1) 2662552; f. 1951; all classes; Chair. Chief J. S. OLAWOYIN; Man. Dir A. F. KILADEJO; 15 brs.

**Phoenix of Nigeria Assurance Co Ltd:** Mandilas House, 96–102 Broad St, POB 2893, Lagos; tel. (1) 2661160; fax (1) 2665069; f. 1964; all classes; cap. 3m.; Chair. Chief JOHN B. MANDILAS; Man. Dir A. A. AKINTUNDE; 5 brs.

**Prestige Assurance Co (Nigeria) Ltd:** 54 Marina, POB 650, Lagos; tel. (1) 2661213; telex 28516; fax (1) 2664110; all classes except life; Chair. Alhaji S. M. ARGUNGU; Man. Dir K. C. MATHEW.

**Royal Exchange Assurance (Nigeria) Group:** New Africa House, 31 Marina, POB 112, Lagos; tel. (1) 2663120; telex 27406; fax (1) 2664431; all classes; Chair. Alhaji MUHTAR BELLO YOLA; Man. Dir JONAH U. IKHIDERO; 6 brs.

**Summit Insurance Co Ltd:** Summit Centre, 9 Bishop Aboyade Cole, Victoria Island, POB 52462, Falomlo, Ikoyi, Lagos; tel. (1) 687476; telex 22652; fax (1) 615850; Man. Dir O. O. LADIPO-AJAYI.

**Sun Insurance Office (Nigeria) Ltd:** Unity House, 37 Marina, POB 2694, Lagos; tel. (1) 2661318; telex 21994; all classes except life; Man. Dir A. T. ADENIJI; 6 brs.

**United Nigeria Insurance Co (UNIC) Ltd:** 53 Marina, POB 588, Lagos; tel. (1) 2663201; telex 22186; fax (1) 2664282; f. 1965; all classes except life; CEO E. O. A. ADETUNJI; 17 brs.

**Unity Life and Fire Insurance Co Ltd:** 25 Nnamdi Azikiwe St, POB 3681, Lagos; tel. (1) 2662517; telex 21657; fax (1) 2662599; all classes; Man. Dir R. A. ODINIGWE.

**Veritas:** NIGUS House, Plot 1412, Victoria Island, Lagos; tel. (1) 2610485; telex 21826; fax (1) 2633688; all classes; Man. Dir SAIDU USMAN.

**West African Provincial Insurance Co:** 27–29 King George V Rd, POB 2103, Lagos; tel. (1) 2636433; telex 21613; fax (1) 2633688; all classes except life; Man. Dir C. O. IDOWU SILVA.

### Insurance Association

**Nigerian Insurance Association:** Nicon House, 1st Floor, 5 Customs St, POB 9551, Lagos; tel. (1) 2640825; f. 1971; Chair. J. U. IKHIDERO.

# Trade and Industry

## CHAMBERS OF COMMERCE

**Nigerian Association of Chambers of Commerce, Industry, Mines and Agriculture:** 15A Ikorodu Rd, Maryland, PMB 12816, Lagos; tel. and fax (1) 4964737; telex 21368; Pres. Chief M. O. ORIGBO; Dir-Gen. L. O. ADEKUNLE.

**Aba Chamber of Commerce and Industry:** UBA Bldg, Ikot Expene Rd/Georges St, POB 1596, Aba; tel. (82) 225148; Pres. Dr S. C. OKOLO.

# NIGERIA

**Abeokuta Chamber of Commerce and Industry:** 29 Kuto Rd, Ishabo, POB 937, Abeokuta; tel. (39) 241230; Pres. Chief S. O. AKINREMI.

**Abuja Chamber of Commerce and Industry:** Wuse, PMB 86, Garki, Abuja; tel. (9) 52341887; Pres. Alhaji ABDULLAHI ADAMU.

**Adamawa Chamber of Commerce and Industry:** c/o Palace Hotel, POB 8, Jimeta, Yola; tel. (75) 255136; Pres. Alhaji ISA HAMMANYERO.

**Akure Chamber of Commerce and Industry:** 57 Oyemekun Rd, Akure; tel. (34) 231051; Pres. GABRIEL AKINJO.

**Awka Chamber of Commerce and Industry:** 220 Enugu Rd, POB 780, Awka; tel. (45) 550105; Pres. Lt-Col (retd) D. ORUGBU.

**Bauchi Chamber of Commerce and Industry:** 96 Maiduguri Rd, POB 911, Bauchi; tel. (77) 42620; telex 83261; f. 1976; Pres. Alhaji MAGAJI MU'AZU.

**Benin Chamber of Commerce, Industry, Mines and Agriculture:** 10 Murtala Muhammed Way, POB 2087, Benin City; tel. (52) 245761; Pres. C. O. EWEKA.

**Benue Chamber of Commerce, Industry, Mines and Agriculture:** 71 Ankpa Qr Rd, PMB 102344, Makurdi; tel. (44) 32573; Chair. Col (retd) R. V. I. ASAM.

**Borno Chamber of Commerce and Industry:** 3 Jos Rd, PMB 1636, Maiduguri; tel. (76) 232942; telex 82112; Pres. Alhaji A. ALI KOTOKO.

**Calabar Chamber of Commerce and Industry:** 45 Akin Rd, POB 76, Calabar; tel. (87) 221558; 92 mems; Pres. Chief TAM OFORIOKUMA.

**Enugu Chamber of Commerce, Industry and Mines:** International Trade Fair Complex, Abakaliki Rd, POB 734, Enugu; tel. (42) 330575; f. 1963; Dir S. C. NWAEKEKE.

**Franco-Nigerian Chamber of Commerce:** Plot 232A, Adeola Odeku St, POB 70001, Victoria Island, Lagos; tel. (1) 2610071; fax (1) 2618825; f. 1985; Chair. OKOYA THOMAS; Pres. J. J. ENGELS.

**Gongola Chamber of Commerce and Industry:** Palace Hotel, POB 8, Jimeta-Yola; tel. (75) 255136; Pres. Alhaji ALIYU IBRAHIM.

**Ibadan Chamber of Commerce and Industry:** Commerce House, Ring Rd, Challenge, PMB 5168, Ibadan; tel. (2) 317223; telex 20311; Pres. JIDE ABIMBOLA.

**Ijebu Chamber of Commerce and Industry:** 51 Ibadan Rd, POB 604, Ijebu Ode; tel. (2) 432880; Pres. DOYIN DEGUN.

**Ikot Ekpene Chamber of Commerce and Industry:** 47 Aba Rd, POB 50, Ikot Ekpene; tel. (85) 400153; Pres. G. U. EKANEM.

**Kaduna Chamber of Commerce, Industry and Agriculture:** 24 Waff Rd, POB 728, Kaduna; tel. (62) 211216; telex 71325; fax (62) 214149; Pres. Alhaji MOHAMMED SANI AMINU.

**Kano Chamber of Commerce, Industry, Mines and Agriculture:** Zoo Rd, POB 10, Kano City, Kano; tel. (64) 667138; Pres. Alhaji AUWALU ILU.

**Katsina Chamber of Commerce and Industry:** 1 Nagogo Rd, POB 92, Katsina; tel. (65) 31014; Pres. ABBA ALI.

**Kwara Chamber of Commerce, Industry, Mines and Agriculture:** 208 Ibrahim Taiwo Rd, POB 1634, Ilorin; tel. (31) 221069; Pres. W. O. ODUDU.

**Lagos Chamber of Commerce and Industry:** Commerce House, 1 Idowu Taylor St, Victoria Island, POB 109, Lagos; tel. (1) 2613898; telex 21368; fax (1) 2610573; f. 1885; 900 mems; Pres. OLUDAYO SONUGA.

**Niger Chamber of Commerce and Industry:** Trade Fair Site, POB 370, Minna; tel. (66) 223153; Pres. Alhaji U. S. NDANUSA.

**Nnewi Chamber of Commerce and Industry:** 31A Nnobi Rd, POB 1471, Nnewi; f. 1987; Pres. Chief C. M. IBETO.

**Oshogbo Chamber of Commerce and Industry:** Obafemi Awolowo Way, Ajegunle, POB 870, Oshogbo, Osun; tel. (35) 231098; Pres. Chief A. A. IBIKUNLE.

**Owerri Chamber of Commerce and Industry:** OCCIMA Secretariat, 123 Okigwe Rd, POB 1640, Owerri; tel. (83) 234849; Pres. Chief BONIFACE N. AMAECHI.

**Oyo Chamber of Commerce and Industry:** POB 67, Oyo; Pres. Chief C. A. OGUNNIYI.

**Plateau State Chambers of Commerce, Industry, Mines and Agriculture:** Shama House, 32 Rwang Pam St, POB 2092, Jos; tel. (73) 53918; telex 81348; f. 1976; Pres. Chief M. E. JACDOMI.

**Port Harcourt Chamber of Commerce, Industry, Mines and Agriculture:** 169 Aba Rd, POB 71, Port Harcourt; tel. (84) 330394; telex 61110; f. 1952; Pres. Chief S. I. ALETE.

**Remo Chamber of Commerce and Industry:** 7 Sho Manager Way, POB 1172, Shagamu; tel. (37) 640962; Pres. Chief S. O. ADEKOYA.

**Sapele Chamber of Commerce and Industry:** 144 New Ogorode Rd, POB 154, Sapele; tel. (54) 42323; Pres. P. O. FUFUYIN.

**Sokoto Chamber of Commerce and Industry:** 12 Racecourse Rd, POB 2234, Sokoto; tel. (60) 231805; Pres. Alhaji ALIYU WAZIRI BODINGA.

**Umahia Chamber of Commerce:** 65 Uwalaka St, POB 86, Umahia; tel. (88) 220055; Pres. Chief S. B. A. ATULOMAH.

**Uyo Chamber of Commerce and Industry:** 141 Abak Rd, POB 2960, Uyo, Akwa Ibom; Pres. Chief DANIEL ITA-EKPOTT.

**Warri Chamber of Commerce and Industry:** Block 1, Edewor Shopping Centre, Warri/Sapele Rd, POB 302, Warri; tel. (53) 233731; Pres. MOSES F. OROGUN.

## TRADE ASSOCIATIONS

**Abeokuta Importers' and Exporters' Association:** c/o Akeweje Bros, Lafenwa, Abeokuta.

**Ijebu Importers' and Exporters' Association:** 16 Ishado St, Ijebu-Ode.

**Nigerian Association of Native Cloth Dealers and Exporters:** 45 Koesch St, Lagos.

**Nigerian Association of Stockfish Importers:** 10 Egerton Rd, Lagos.

**Union of Importers and Exporters:** POB 115, Ibadan; f. 1949; Chair. E. A. SANDA.

## PROFESSIONAL AND EMPLOYERS' ORGANIZATIONS

**Association of Master Bakers, Confectioners and Caterers of Nigeria:** 13–15 Custom St, POB 4, Lagos; f. 1951; 250 mems; Pres. J. ADE TUYO (acting).

**Federation of Building and Civil Engineering Contractors in Nigeria:** Construction House, Plot 6, Adeyemo Alakija St, Professional Centre, Victoria Island, POB 282, Lagos; tel. (1) 2616564; f. 1954; Exec. Sec. T. A. ADEKANMBI.

**Institute of Chartered Accountants of Nigeria:** Plot 16, Professional Layout Centre, Idowu Taylor St, Victoria Island, POB 1580, Lagos; tel. (1) 2622394; fax (1) 610304; f. 1965; CEO and Registrar P. O. OMOREGIE.

**Manufacturers' Association of Nigeria:** Unity House, 12th Floor, 37 Marina, POB 3835, Lagos; tel. (1) 2660755; f. 1971; Pres. HASSAN ADAMU.

**Nigerian Chamber of Mines:** POB 454, Jos; tel. (73) 55003; f. 1950; Pres. A. A. KEHINDE.

**Nigeria Employers' Consultative Association:** Commercial House, 1–11 Commercial Ave, POB 2231, Yaba, Lagos; tel. (1) 5800360; fax (1) 5860309; f. 1957; Pres. Chief J. O. FAGBEMI.

**Nigerian Institute of Architects:** 2 Idowu Taylor St, Victoria Island, POB 278, Lagos; tel. (1) 2617940; f. 1960; Pres. Chief O. O. BALOGUN.

**Nigerian Institute of Building:** 1B Market St, Oyingbo, Ebute-Metta, POB 3191, Marina, Lagos; f. 1970; Pres. S. T. OYEFEKO.

**Nigerian Institution of Estate Surveyors and Valuers:** Flat 2B, Dolphin Scheme, Ikoyi, POB 2325, Lagos; tel. (1) 2685981; Pres. W. O. ODUDU.

**Nigerian Livestock Dealers' Association:** POB 115, Sapele.

**Nigerian Recording Association:** 9 Breadfruit St, POB 950, Lagos.

**Nigerian Society of Engineers:** National Engineering Centre, 1 Engineering Close, Victoria Island, Lagos; tel. (1) 2617315; Pres. IFE AKINTUNDE.

**Pharmaceutical Society of Nigeria:** 4 Tinubu Sq., POB 546, Lagos.

## DEVELOPMENT ORGANIZATIONS

**Anambra State Agricultural Development Corporation:** Garden Ave, PMB 1024, Enugu.

**Anambra-Imo Basin Development Authority:** Chair. SAMUEL C. ELUWA; Gen. Man. WITLY OKONKWO.

**Benin–Owena River Basin Development Authority:** 24 Benin-Sapele Rd, PMB 1381, Obayantor, Benin City; tel. (52) 254415; f. 1976 to conduct irrigation; Gen. Man. Dr G. E. OTEZE.

**Chad Basin Development Authority:** Dikwa Rd, PMB 1130, Maiduguri; tel. (76) 232015; f. 1973; irrigation and agriculture-allied industries; Chair. MOHAMMED ABALI; Gen. Man. Alhaji BUNU S. MUSA.

**Cross River Basin Development Authority:** 32 Target Rd, PMB 1249, Calabar; tel. (87) 223163; f. 1977; Gen. Man. SIXTUS ABETIANBE.

**Cross River State Agricultural Development Corporation:** PMB 1024, Calabar.

**Federal Capital Development Authority:** Abuja; govt agency for design, construction and management of Abuja; Perm. Sec. Alhaji ABUBAKAR KOKO.

**Federal Housing Authority:** Gen. Man. S. P. O. FORTUNE EBIE.

NIGERIA	*Directory*

**Federal Institute of Industrial Research, Oshodi (FIIRO):** Murtala Muhammad Airport, Ikeja, PMB 21023, Lagos; tel. (1) 522905; telex 26006; fax (1) 525880; f. 1956; plans and directs industrial research and provides tech. assistance and information to industry; specializes in foods, minerals, textiles, natural products and industrial intermediates; Dir. Prof. S. A. ODUNFA.

**Gongola State Housing Corpn:** Yola; Chair. DOMINIC M. MAPEO; Gen. Man. DAVID A. GARNVWA.

**Hadejia Jama'are Basin Development Authority:** Bauchi; f. 1976; began building four dams for irrigation and hydroelectric power in 1980; Gen. Man. Alhaji AHMADU RUFAI.

**Imo State Housing Corpn:** Uratta Rd, PMB 1224, Owerri, Imo; tel. (83) 230733; f. 1976; develops housing and industrial estates, grants finance for house purchase and operates a savings scheme; Gen. Man. O. A. KALU.

**Industrial Training Fund:** Federal Secretariat, 8th Floor, PMB 2199, Jos; tel. (73) 55297; telex 81154; f. 1971 to promote and encourage skilled workers in trade and industry; Dir-Gen. Alhaji LAWAL TUDUNWADA.

**Kaduna Industrial and Finance Co Ltd:** Investment House, 27 Ali Akilu Rd, PMB 2230, Kaduna; tel. (62) 217094; telex 20711; fax (62) 215715; f. 1977; development finance institution; Chair. HASSAN A. MU'AZU; CEO JAMILAH S. HAYATUDDINI.

**Kwara State Investment Corpn:** 109–112 Fate Rd, PMB 1344, Ilorin, Kwara; tel. (31) 220510.

**Lagos State Development and Property Corpn:** Ilupeju Industrial Estate, Ikorodu Rd, PMB 1050, Ikeja; POB 907, Lagos; f. 1972; planning and development of Lagos; Gen. Man. G. B. JINADU.

**New Nigerian Development Co Ltd:** 18/19 Ahmadu Bello Way, Ahmed Talib House, PMB 2120, Kaduna; tel. (62) 236250; telex 71108; f. 1968; investment/financial institution owned by the Govts of 11 northern States; 10 subsidiaries, 117 assoc. cos; Chair. Alhaji ABDULLAHI IBRAHIM.

**New Nigeria Development Co (Properties) Ltd:** 18–19 Ahmadu Bello Way, PMB 2040, Kaduna; housing devt agency.

**Niger Delta Basin and Rural Development Authority:** 21 Azikiwe Rd, PMB 5676, Port Harcourt; f. 1976.

**Niger River Basin Development Authority:** f. 1976; Chair. Alhaji HALIRU DANTORO.

**Nigerian Enterprises Promotion Board:** 72 Campbell St, PMB 12553, Lagos; f. 1972 to promote indigenization; Chair. MINSO GADZAMA.

**Nigerian Export Promotion Council:** Kumba St, PMB 133, Garki, Abuja; tel. (9) 5230930; telex 91510; fax (9) 5230931; f. 1976; promotes development and diversification of exports; Dir GEORGE NIYI.

**Nigerian Livestock and Meat Authority:** POB 479, Kaduna; telex 71307.

**Northern Nigeria Investments Ltd:** POB 138, Kaduna; tel. (62) 239654; f. 1959 to identify and invest in industrial and agricultural projects in 16 northern States; cap. p.u. 20m.; Chair. Alhaji ABUBAKAR G. ADAMU.

**Odu'a Investment Co Ltd:** Cocoa House, PMB 5435, Ibadan; tel. (2) 417710; telex 31225; fax (2) 413000; f. 1976; jtly owned by Ogun, Ondo and Oyo States; Man. Dir Alhaji R. S. ARUNA.

**Ogun-Oshun River Basin Development Authority:** f. 1976; Chair. Mrs D. B. A. KUFORIJI; Gen. Man. Dr LEKAN ARE.

**Ogun State Agricultural Credit Corpn:** PMB 2029, Abeokuta; f. 1976.

**Ogun State Housing Corpn:** PMB 2077, Abeokuta; f. 1976; develops housing and industrial estates; grants finance for house purchase and operates a savings plan; Gen. Man. F. O. ABIODUN.

**Ondo State Housing Corpn:** PMB 693, Akure; f. 1976 to develop house-building and industrial estates and to grant mortgages and loans for house purchase; also operates a savings scheme.

**Ondo State Investment Corpn:** PMB 700, Akure; f. 1976 to investigate and promote both agricultural and industrial projects on a commercial basis in the State.

**Oyo State Property Development Corpn:** f. 1976 to develop housing, commercial property and industrial estate and to grant finance for house purchase; also operates a savings scheme.

**Plateau State Housing Corpn:** Jos; plans to build 1,000 housing units a year in addition to another 1,000 units built in the State by the Fed. Govt.

**Plateau State Water Resources Development Board:** Jos; incorporates the fmr Plateau River Basin Devt Authority and Plateau State Water Resources Devt Board.

**Price Intelligence Agency:** c/o Productivity, Prices and Income Board, Lagos; f. 1980; monitors prices.

**Projects Development Agency:** 3 Independence Layout, POB 609, Enugu; f. 1974; promotes the establishment of new industries and develops industrial projects utilizing local raw materials; Dir Dr EZEKWE.

**Rivers State Development Corpn:** Port Harcourt; f. 1970.

**Rivers State Housing Corpn:** 15/17 Emekuku St, PMB 5044, Port Harcourt.

**Rubber Research Institute of Nigeria:** PMB 1049, Benin City; telex 41190; f. 1961; conducts research into the production of rubber and other latex products; Dir Dr E. K. OKAISABOR.

**Sokoto-Rima Basin Development Authority:** f. 1976; Chair. Alhaji MU'AZU LAMIDO.

**Trans Investments Co Ltd:** Bale Oyewole Rd, PMB 5085, Ibadan; tel. (2) 416000; telex 31122; f. 1986; initiates and finances industrial and agricultural schemes; Gen. Man. M. A. ADESIYUN.

**Upper Benue Basin Development Authority:** Chair. Alhaji MOHAMMADU MAI.

### PUBLIC CORPORATIONS

In early 1995 the Government announced plans to lease a number of state-owned enterprises to private operators.

**Ajaokuta Steel Co Ltd:** PMB 1000, Ajaokuta, Kwara; tel. (31) 400450; telex 36390; CEO M. M. INUWA.

**Delta Steel Co Ltd:** Ovwian-Aladja, POB 1220, Warri; tel. (53) 621001; telex 43456; fax (53) 621012; f. 1979; state-owned; operates direct-reduction steel complex with eventual annual capacity of 1m. tons; Chair. Chief TUNJI AROSANYIN; Man. Dir TIM C. EFOBI.

**Gaskiya Corpn Ltd:** Tadun Wada, Zaria; tel. (69) 32201; f. 1938; owned by Kaduna State Govt, New Nigerian Development Co and Jama'atu Nasril Islam; printers; CEO ABDULLAHI HASSAN.

**National Electric Power Authority (NEPA):** 24–25 Marina, PMB 12030, Lagos; tel. (1) 2600640; telex 21212; f. 1972 by merger of the Electricity Corpn of Nigeria and the Niger Dams Authority; a three-year rehabilitation programme, at an estimated cost of US $155m., began in 1990; Man. Dir (vacant).

**National Oil and Chemical Marketing Co:** 38–39 Marina, PMB 2052, Lagos; markets petroleum, petroleum products and chemicals; Chair. Maj.-Gen. USMAN KATSINA; Man. Dir E. O. OKOYE.

**Nigerian Cement Co Ltd (NIGERCEM):** Nkalugu, POB 331, Enugu; tel. (42) 333829; telex 51113; Chair. Dr NNAMDI E. NWAUWA.

**Nigerian Coal Corpn:** PMB 01053, Enugu; tel. (42) 335314; telex 51115; f. 1909; operates four mines; Gen. Man. F. N. UGWU.

**Nigerian Engineering and Construction Co Ltd (NECCO):** Km 14, Badagry Expressway (opp. International Trade Fair Complex), PMB 12684, Lagos; tel. (1) 5880591; telex 21836; building, civil, mechanical and electrical engineers, furniture makers and steel fabricators; Chair. EHIOZE EDIAE.

**Nigerian Liquefied Natural Gas Co:** Lagos; Chair. Alhaji MOHAMMED YUSUFU; Man. Dir THEO OERLEMANS.

**Nigerian Mining Corpn:** Federal Secretariat, 7th Floor, PMB 2154, Jos; f. 1972; exploration, production, processing and marketing of minerals; Chair. (vacant).

**Nigerian National Petroleum Corpn (NNPC):** 7 Kofo Abayomi St, Victoria Island, PMB 12701, Lagos; tel. (1) 2614650; telex 21610; fax (1) 2683784; f. 1977; merged with Nigerian Petroleum Refining Co 1985; reorg. 1988; holding corpn for fed. govt interests in the oil cos; 11 operating subsidiaries; Chair. Secretary of Petroleum and Mineral Resources; Man. Dir (vacant).

**Nigerian National Supply Co Ltd:** 29 Burma Rd, PMB 12662, Apapa, Lagos; state-owned import org.; Chair. Brig. J. I. ONOJA; Gen. Man. Maj. A. DAHIRU.

**Nigerian Petroleum Refining Co Ltd (NPRC):** 21–25 Broad St, Lagos.

### CO-OPERATIVES

There are more than 25,000 co-operative societies in Nigeria.

**Co-operative Federation of Nigeria:** PMB 5533, Ibadan; tel. (2) 711276; telex 31224; fax (2) 711276; Pres. REMI OBISESAN.

**Anambra State Co-operative Federation Ltd:** 213 Agbani Rd, PMB 1488, Enugu; tel. (42) 331157; Pres. C. G. O. NWABUGWU.

**Association of Nigerian Co-operative Exporters Ltd:** New Court Rd, POB 477, Ibadan; f. 1945; producers/exporters of cocoa and other cash crops.

**Co-operative Supply Association Ltd:** Ance Bldg, Jericho, Ibadan; importers and dealers in agricultural chemicals and equipment, fertilizers, building materials, general hardware, grocery and provisions.

**Co-operative Union of Western Nigeria Ltd:** PMB 5101, Jericho Rd, Ibadan.

**Kabba Co-operative Credit and Marketing Union Ltd:** POB 25, Kabba; f. 1953; producers of food and cash crops and retailers of consumer goods; Pres. Alhaji S. O. ONUNDI; Man. H. A. ORISAFUNMI.

NIGERIA                                                                                                                    *Directory*

**Kano State Co-operative Federation Ltd:** 1 Zaria Rd, PMB 3030, Kano; tel. (64) 622182; Pres. G. B. Yako.

**Kwara State Co-operative Federation Ltd:** PMB 1412, Ilorin; operates transport and marketing services in Kwara State; Gen. Man. J. Obaro.

**Lagos State Co-operative Federation Ltd:** 13 Isaacstan Close, Wemco Rd, POB 8632, Ikeja, Lagos; co-operative education and publicity.

**Oyo State Co-operative Federation Ltd:** 3 Olubadan Estate, New Ife Rd, PMB 5101, Ibadan; tel. (2) 710985; Pres. J. A. Aderibigbe.

### TRADE UNIONS
#### Federation

**Nigerian Labour Congress (NLC):** 29 Olajuwon St, off Ojuelegba Rd, Yaba, POB 620, Lagos; tel. (1) 5835582; f. 1978; comprises 42 affiliated industrial unions representing 3.5m. mems (1985); nat. exec. dissolved in Feb. 1988; delegates' conf. in Dec. 1988 returned movement to workers' control; Administrator Asor Bur.

#### Principal Unions

In 1990 a technical committee was created to restructure the existing 42 industrial unions, and ultimately to reduce their number to 20. The principal unions include:

**Agricultural and Allied Workers' Union of Nigeria:** SW8–123A Lagos Bypass, Oke Ado, Ibadan; Gen. Sec. C. O. Farinloye.

**Association of Locomotive Drivers, Firemen, Yard Staff and Allied Workers of Nigeria:** 231 Herbert Macaulay St, Yaba; 3,200 mems; Pres. P. C. Okolo; Sec. Deji Oyeyemi.

**Civil Service Technical Workers' Union of Nigeria:** 9 Aje St, PMB 1064, Yaba, Lagos; tel. (1) 5863722; f. 1941; 7,500 mems; Pres. J. E. Uduagham; Sec.-Gen. S. O. Z. Ejiofoh.

**Ikeja Textile Workers' Union:** 6 Oba Akran Ave, Ikeja; f. 1964; 7,200 mems; Pres. A. L. Oshittu; Sec.-Gen. Rufus Adeyoola.

**Medical and Health Workers' Union of Nigeria:** 2 Jeminatu Braimoh Close, Western Ave, Surulere, POB 563, Lagos; tel. (1) 5832274; Pres. Y. O. Ozigi; Gen. Sec. J. Mbah.

**Ministry of Defence Civil Employees' Union:** 9 Aje St, PMB 1064, Yaba, Lagos; tel. (1) 5863722; 3,600 mems; Pres. J. O. Ogunlesi; Sec. B. N. Obua.

**National Association of Nigerian Nurses and Midwives:** 64B Oduduwa Way, Ikeja, POB 3857, Lagos; tel. (1) 4932173; f. 1978; 7,100 mems; Pres. J. G. Micah; Gen. Sec. M. Olabode.

**National Union of Banks, Insurance and Financial Institutions Employees (NUBIFIE):** 310 Herbert Macaulay St, Yaba, PMB 1139, Lagos; tel. (1) 5863193; f. 1965; 80,000 mems; Pres. J. H. Gimbason; Gen.-Sec. S. A. Ibrahim.

**National Union of Construction and Civil Engineering Workers:** 51 Kano St, Ebute Metta, PMB 1064, Lagos; tel. (1) 5800263; Pres. R. O. Sanyaolu; Gen. Sec. M. O. Faniyi.

**National Union of Electricity and Gas Workers:** 200 Herbert Macaulay St, Ebute Metta, POB 212, Lagos; tel. (1) 5864084; f. 1972; 25,000 mems; Pres. Gen. A. E. Adizua; Gen. Sec. P. T. Kiri-Kalio.

**National Union of Petroleum and Natural Gas Workers (NUPENG):** 2 Jeminatu Braimoh Close, Western Ave, Surulere, POB 7166, Lagos; tel. (1) 5846569; Administrator Dr Ahmed Jalingo.

**National Union of Shop and Distributive Employees:** 64 Olonode St, Yaba, Lagos; tel. (1) 5863536; Pres. L. C. Ogbata; Gen. Sec. E. N. Okongwu.

**Nigeria Union of Construction and Civil Engineering Workers:** 51 Kano St, PMB 1064, Ebute-Metta, Lagos; tel. (1) 5800260; f. 1978; 40,000 mems; Pres R. O. Sanyaolu; Gen. Sec. M. O. Faniyi.

**Nigerian Civil Service Union:** 23 Tokunboh St, POB 862, Lagos; f. 1912; 13,200 mems; Pres. C. Olatunji; Gen. Sec. P. B. Okoro.

**Nigerian Metallic and Non-Metallic Mines Workers' Union:** 95 Enugu St, POB 763, Jos; tel (73) 52401; f. 1948; 13,000 mems; Sec.-Gen. A. Olaniyan.

**Nigerian Textile, Garment and Tailoring Workers' Union:** Textile Worker House, B6–8 Kubi St, Nassarawa Expressway, POB 905, Kaduna South, Kaduna; tel. (62) 214438; f. 1969, reorg. 1978; 47,000 mems; Pres. Aliyu Suleiman; Gen. Sec. A. Oshiomhole.

**Nigerian Union of Agricultural and Allied Workers:** SW8–123A Lagos Bypass, Ibadan; 7,000 mems; Sec.-Gen. C. O. Farinloye.

**Nigerian Union of Journalists:** National Theatre Annex, Iganmu, Lagos; tel. (1) 5833330; 5,200 mems; Pres. Muhammad Sani Zorro; Sec. George Anyakora (acting).

**Nigerian Union of Railwaymen:** 33 Ekololu St, Surulere, Yaba; f. 1950; 5,600 mems; Pres. S. A. Odunuga; Gen. Sec. Chuks Nwajei (acting).

**Nigerian Union of Teachers:** 15 Rosamund St, Surulere, PMB 1044, Yaba; f. 1931; 350,000 mems; Pres. Chief Brendan C. E. Ugwu; Sec.-Gen. Gabriel O. Falade.

**UAC and Associated Companies African Workers' Union:** 81B Simpson St, Ebute-Metta; 8,000 mems; Pres. J. O. Ojewande; Sec. F. N. Kanu.

**Union of Posts and Telecommunications Workers of Nigeria:** 12 Gbaja St, Surulere; 4,100 mems; Pres. J. Shodade; Sec. G. O. Uluocha.

## Transport

### RAILWAYS

There are about 3,505 km of mainly narrow-gauge railways. The two principal lines connect Lagos with Nguru and Port Harcourt with Maiduguri.

**Nigerian Railway Corporation:** Ebute-Metta, Lagos; tel. (1) 5834302; telex 26584; f. 1955; restructured in 1993 into three separate units: Nigerian Railway Track Authority; Nigerian Railways; and Nigerian Railway Engineering Ltd; Man. Dir Joseph Maduekwe.

### ROADS

In 1991 the Nigerian road network totalled some 112,140 km, of which about 30,900 km were principal roads and 19,550 km secondary roads; some 31,500 km were tarred.

**Nigerian Road Federation:** Ministry of Transport and Aviation, Joseph St, PMB 21038, Ikoyi, Lagos; tel. (1) 2652120; telex 21535.

### INLAND WATERWAYS

**Inland Waterways Department:** Ministry of Transport, Joseph St, PMB 21038, Ikoyi, Lagos; tel. (1) 2652120; telex 21535; responsible for all navigable waterways.

### SHIPPING

The principal ports are the Delta Port complex (including Warri, Koko, Burutu and Sapele ports), Port Harcourt and Calabar; other significant ports are situated at Apapa and Tin Can Island, near Lagos. The main petroleum ports are Bonny and Burutu.

**National Maritime Authority:** Lagos; f. 1987; Chair. (vacant).

**Nigeria Shipping Federation:** NPA Commercial Offices, Block 'A', Wharf Rd, POB 107, Apapa, Lagos; f. 1960; Chair. (vacant); Gen. Man. D. B. Adekoya.

**Nigerian Ports Authority:** 26–28 Marina, PMB 12588, Lagos; tel. (1) 2655020; telex 21500; f. 1955; Gen. Man. (vacant).

**Nigerian Green Lines Ltd:** Unity House, 15th Floor, 37 Marina, POB 2288, Lagos; tel. (1) 2663303; telex 21308; 2 vessels totalling 30,751 grt; Chair. Alhaji W. L. Folawiyo.

**Nigerian National Shipping Line Ltd:** Development House, 21 Wharf Rd, POB 326, Apapa, Lagos; tel. (1) 5804240; telex 21253; fax (1) 5870260; f. 1959; govt-owned; cargo and limited fast passenger services between West Africa, the United Kingdom, the Mediterranean, North America and the Far East; CEO and Man. Dir Bob Alfa.

### CIVIL AVIATION

The principal international airports are at Lagos (Murtala Muhammed Airport), Kano, Port Harcourt, Calabar and Abuja. There are also 14 airports for domestic flights. A programme to develop the international airport at Abuja was scheduled for completion by December 1995.

**Nigerian Airports Authority:** Murtala Muhammed Airport, PMB 21607, Ikeja, Lagos; tel. (1) 4900800; telex 26626; Man. Dir Alhaji Ibrahim Mamman.

#### Principal Airlines

**General and Aviation Services (Gas) Air Nigeria:** Plot 5A, Old Domestic Airport, Ikeja, Lagos; tel. (1) 4933510; fax (1) 4962841; domestic and international cargo services; Pres. S. K. S. Olubadewo.

**Kabo Air:** 6775 Ashton Rd, POB 3439, Kano; tel. (64) 639591; telex 77277; fax (64) 645172; f. 1981; domestic services and international charters; Dir SHITU ADAMU.

**Nigeria Airways:** Airways House, Ikeja, PMB 136, Lagos; tel. (1) 4900470; telex 26127; fax (1) 2777675; f. 1958; scheduled domestic and services to Europe, the USA, West Africa and Saudi Arabia; Man. Dir ANDREW AGOM.

**Okada Air:** 17B Sapele Rd, Benin City; tel. (19) 241054; f. 1983; domestic and international charter passenger services, domestic scheduled services; Chair. Chief GABRIEL O. IGBINEDION.

## Tourism

Potential attractions for tourists include fine coastal scenery, dense forests, and the rich diversity of Nigeria's arts. An estimated 237,000 tourists visited Nigeria in 1992, when receipts from tourism amounted to US $29m.

**Nigerian Tourism Development Corporation:** Zone 4, PMB 167, Abuja; tel. (9) 5230418; fax (9) 5230962; Chair. S. A. ALAMATU; Dir Alhaji S. M. JEGA.

# NORWAY

## Introductory Survey

**Location, Climate, Language, Religion, Flag, Capital**

The Kingdom of Norway forms the western part of Scandinavia, in northern Europe. It is bordered to the east by Sweden and, within the Arctic Circle, by Finland and Russia. A long, indented coast faces the Atlantic Ocean. Norway exercises sovereignty over the Svalbard archipelago, Jan Mayen island and the uninhabited dependencies of Bouvetøya and Peter I Øy. Dronning Maud Land, in Antarctica, is also a Norwegian dependency. Norway's climate is temperate on the west coast but colder inland. Average temperatures range from −2°C (28°F) to 8°C (46°F). There are two forms of the Norwegian language, which are officially recognized as equal. About 80% of children in schools use the older form, Bokmål, as their principal language, whereas only 20% use the newer form, Nynorsk (Neo-Norwegian). Lappish is also spoken by the Sámi population in northern Norway. Almost all of the inhabitants profess Christianity: the Evangelical Lutheran Church is the established religion, with about 89% of the population professing adherence in 1994. The civil flag (proportions 11 by 8) has a dark blue cross, bordered with white, on a red background, the upright of the cross being to the left of centre; the state flag (27 by 16) has the same cross, but is in the form of a triple swallow-tail at the fly. The capital is Oslo.

**Recent History**

Norway, formerly linked to the Swedish crown, declared its independence in 1905. The union with Sweden was peacefully dissolved and the Norwegians elected their own monarch, Prince Karl of Denmark, who took the title of King Håkon VII. He reigned for 52 years until his death in 1957, and was succeeded by his son, Olav V. Olav's son, Crown Prince Harald (who had acted as regent since his father suffered a stroke in May 1990), became King Harald V upon Olav's death in January 1991.

During the Second World War Norway was occupied by German forces between 1940 and 1945. Norway abandoned its traditional policy of neutrality after the war, joining NATO in 1949. Norway was also a founder member of the Nordic Council (see p. 187) in 1952 and of the European Free Trade Association (EFTA—see p. 142) in 1960.

The Norwegian Labour Party (Det norske Arbeiderparti) formed the Government from 1935 to 1965, except for the period of German occupation, when a pro-Nazi 'puppet' regime was administered by Vidkun Quisling, and an interlude of one month in 1963. Norway applied for membership of the European Community (EC, now known as the European Union—EU—see p. 143) in 1962, and again in 1967. A general election to the unicameral Parliament (Storting) in September 1965 resulted in a defeat for the Labour Government of Einar Gerhardsen, who had been Prime Minister, with a month's interruption, since 1955. His administration was replaced in October by a non-socialist coalition under Per Borten, leader of the Centre Party (Senterpartiet). In March 1971, however, Borten resigned, following relevations that he had deliberately disclosed confidential details of Norway's negotiations with the EC. He was succeeded by a minority Labour Government, led by Trygve Bratteli. The terms of Norway's entry into the EC were agreed in December 1971, and a preliminary Treaty of Accession was signed in January 1972. In September, however, a consultative referendum on the agreed terms produced a 53.3% majority against entering the EC. The application was withdrawn, and Bratteli resigned in October. A coalition of Liberals (Venstre), the Centre Party and the Christian Democrats' Party (KrF—Kristelig Folkeparti) formed a new minority Government, with Lars Korvald (KrF) as Prime Minister.

Following the general election of September 1973, Bratteli formed another minority Labour Government, dependent on the support of the Socialist Electoral League (from 1975 the Socialist Left Party—SV, Socialistisk Venstreparti). In January 1976 Bratteli was succeeded as Labour Prime Minister by Odvar Nordli. Nordli resigned in February 1981, for reasons of ill health, and was succeeded by Gro Harlem Brundtland, Norway's first female Prime Minister. At the general election in September the Labour Party lost support to centre-right groups.

In October 1981 a minority administration, led by Kåre Willoch, became Norway's first Conservative (Høyre) government since 1928. In June 1983 a coalition of the Conservative Party with the Centre Party and the KrF was formed, with 79 of the 155 parliamentary seats. Kåre Willoch's Government was returned to power, although without an overall majority in the Storting, following the general election in September 1985. The coalition of the Conservative Party, the KrF and the Centre Party received 45.1% of the total votes and won 78 of the 157 seats, but the election showed a swing to the left, with the Labour Party and the SV together winning 77 seats, with a larger share (46.5%) of the votes. The balance of power was held by the right-wing Progress Party (Fremskrittspartiet), which won the two remaining seats in the Storting.

During April 1986 there were labour disputes involving more than 100,000 workers in various sectors of industry, who demanded pay increases and a reduction in working hours. At the end of April the Government presented to the Storting a revised austerity budget for 1986, which, it was hoped, would compensate for a severe fall in government revenue from taxes and levies on petroleum, as the result of a decline in the world price of crude petroleum. The Storting narrowly rejected a proposal to increase taxation on petrol, and Willoch tendered his resignation in early May. The Norwegian Constitution did not permit a general election before the expiry of the Storting's term (due in 1989). Brundtland accepted an invitation by the King to form a minority Labour administration. The new Government devalued the krone by 12%, and a revised budget was approved by the Storting in June.

At the general election in September 1989 both the Labour and Conservative Parties lost support to more radical parties. The SV gained nine seats, to achieve a total of 17 seats in the Storting. The populist right-wing Progress Party increased its representation to 22 seats, despite allegations of racism levelled against it during the election campaign. In the same month the Sámi (Lapps) of northern Norway elected 39 representatives for a new consultative assembly (Sameting), to be based in Karasjok. There was considerable support among the Sámi for a degree of autonomy, in order to protect their traditional way of life.

Brundtland's Government resigned in October 1989, following an agreement made by the Conservatives, the Centre Party and the KrF to form a coalition. The new Government, led by Jan Syse (the Conservative Party leader since January 1988), controlled only 62 seats in the Storting and was dependent upon the support of the Progress Party.

In May 1987 the Government published proposals recommending closer co-operation with the EC. During 1988 some Labour ministers indicated cautious support for submitting a renewed Norwegian application for membership. The Brundtland Government, however, remained reluctant to revive the debate over the issue, following instead a policy of closer economic co-operation with the EC through Norway's membership of EFTA. The Syse administration continued this policy since, although the Conservatives had supported EC membership since 1988, the Centre Party remained strongly opposed to it. In October 1990 the Government announced that the Norwegian krone was to be linked to the European Currency Unit (ECU). Later in that month the coalition collapsed, following disagreement between the Conservative and Centre parties regarding Norwegian demands in the negotiations between EFTA and the EC on the creation of a joint European Economic Area (EEA, see p. 142): the Centre Party refused to approve the proposed relaxation of laws that restricted foreign ownership of property and enterprises in Norway. In November the Labour Party formed another minority Government, led by Brundtland, declaring that it would give priority to reducing unemployment, ensuring a fair distribution of wealth, protecting the environment and improving child care provisions.

During 1991 negotiations between EFTA and the EC to establish the EEA were delayed, in part, because of demands by both sides related to fishing: EFTA sought free access to EC markets for its fish and fish products, while the Community requested that its vessels be allowed to fish in the waters of Norway and Iceland. In October the EC and EFTA agreed on the terms of the EEA treaty, including an agreement that EC countries were to be allowed to take extra quotas of fish from Norwegian waters, while Norwegian fish products were to have increased access to EC markets. The treaty entered into effect on 1 January 1994, following ratification by all of the countries concerned. Many Norwegians remained opposed to membership of the EC, expressing the fear, in particular, that government subsidies which had allowed the survival of remote rural and coastal communities would no longer be permitted if Norway joined the Community. In April 1992 Brundtland declared that she was in favour of applying for EC membership, and that Norway could not afford to remain outside the EC once most of the other Nordic countries had joined. The EEA treaty was ratified by the Storting in October. Brundtland's proposal to apply for EC membership was endorsed by the Labour Party's conference in November, and by the Storting later in the same month (although opinions polls suggested that a majority of Norwegians opposed membership). An application was duly submitted in late November.

In September 1992 there was a reorganization of the State Council, with the principal aim of dealing more effectively with increasing unemployment. In November Brundtland resigned from the leadership of the Labour Party, for personal reasons, and was replaced by the party's Secretary-General, Thorbjørn Jagland. At the general election in September 1993, the Labour Party slightly increased its representation in the Storting, from 63 to 67. The Centre Party (whose electoral campaign had been based on opposition to EC membership) increased its total from 11 seats to 32, thereby becoming the second-largest party in the Storting, while the Conservatives won only 28 seats, compared with 37 at the previous election.

Negotiations on Norway's entry to the EU, as it was now known, were finally concluded in March 1994, when Norway accepted that the EU should assume control of Norwegian fishing grounds in 1998, but should maintain existing Norwegian rules on management and conservation. Additional quotas of fish (as well as those permitted under the EEA agreement—see above) were to be allowed for EU boats fishing in Norwegian waters, while access for Norwegian fish to European markets was to be controlled during a transitional period.

At a national referendum, held on 27–28 November 1994 (shortly after Sweden and Finland had voted to join the EU), 52.4% of voters rejected membership of the EU. The success of the campaign opposing entry to the EU was attributed to several factors: in particular, fears were expressed by farmers that the influx of cheaper agricultural goods from the EU would lead to bankruptcies and unemployment in the agricultural sector, and by workers in the fishing industry that stocks of fish would be severely depleted if EU boats were granted increased access to Norwegian waters. There was also widespread concern that national sovereignty would be compromised by the transfer to the EU of certain executive responsibilities. The campaign in favour of membership had emphasized benefits to industry and trade, and warned that Norway would be unable to influence the development of regional economic, environmental and trade policies if it remained outside the EU. Following the referendum, however, supporters of EU membership conceded the view that the current strength of the economy and Norway's participation in the EEA treaty, together with the security guarantees provided by membership of NATO, had persuaded many voters that Norway would derive little benefit, in the short term, from joining the EU.

In April 1993 the Minister of Foreign Affairs, Thorvald Stoltenberg, agreed to become the UN's negotiator for a political settlement in the former Yugoslavia. During 1993 the Norwegian Government was instrumental in conducting secret negotiations between the Israeli Government and the Palestine Liberation Organization, which led to agreement on Palestinian self-rule in certain areas occupied by Israel. Norway won international acclaim for its role in furthering peace in the Middle East through these negotiations.

Norway declared an exclusive economic zone extending to 200 nautical miles (370 km) from its coastline in 1977, and also unilaterally established a fishery protection zone around its territory of Svalbard. The declaration of an economic zone around Jan Mayen island in 1980 led to agreements with Iceland, in 1980 and 1981, over conflicting claims to fishing and mineral rights. A similar dispute with Denmark, acting for Greenland, was not resolved, and in 1988 Denmark requested arbitration by the International Court of Justice, which gave its judgment on the delimitation of the disputed zones in June 1993 (see under Jan Mayen). Incidents between vessels of the Norwegian coastguard and Icelandic fishing boats, within the economic zone surrounding the Norwegian island of Spitsbergen, occurred in 1994 (see under Svalbard).

Following a moratorium on commercial whaling, adopted by the International Whaling Commission (IWC) with effect from 1985, Norway continued to hunt small numbers of whales for purposes of scientific research, and in 1992 the Norwegian Government declared that it would allow the resumption of commercial hunting of minke whales in 1993, claiming that (according to the findings of the IWC's own scientific commission) this species was plentiful enough to allow whaling on a sustainable basis: the Government argued that many Norwegian coastal communities depended on whaling for their existence. In October 1993 the US Government, although opposed to Norway's resumption of commercial whaling, agreed to delay the imposition of trade sanctions against Norway. In June 1994 the Norwegian Government announced that its quota for minke whales in that year would be 301. In July officers of the Norwegian coastguard boarded two vessels belonging to the environmental protection organization, Greenpeace, which had entered Norwegian waters in order to prevent the whaling. A moratorium on the hunting of seal pups, imposed in 1989, was ended by the Norwegian Government in March 1995, although it was emphasized that the killing of seals would be for strictly scientific purposes. Opponents of sealing, however, voiced their concern that Norway was seeking to resume commercial hunting.

The Norwegian declaration in 1977 of an exclusive economic zone around its coast was countered with a claim by the USSR to a strategic area of 155,000 sq km in the Barents Sea. In 1978 an agreement to establish a 'grey zone', which provided for the joint control of fisheries, was concluded as a temporary measure. The unresolved issue remained a cause of tension. In June 1991, at a meeting in Oslo, the then Soviet President, Mikhail Gorbachev, and Brundtland announced that an agreement on the disputed area had been reached in principle. Environmental issues were also a cause of tension with the USSR. In 1986, following an accident at the nuclear power station at Chernobyl in the USSR, radioactive contamination was found in the reindeer herds of northern Norway, the principal source of income to the Sámi (Lapps). In 1988 damage by 'acid rain' (caused mainly by emissions of sulphur dioxide from industrial plants) to forests, as well as water systems, in northern Norway was attributed to pollution from Soviet industrial centres on the Kola peninsula, east of Norway. Several incidents involving fires on Soviet nuclear-powered submarines during 1989 caused further anxieties about radioactive pollution in northern Norway. The two countries signed a treaty in December of that year providing for the exchange of information concerning such maritime incidents. In 1992 the Russian Government acknowledged that the seas north of Norway had been used by the former Soviet navy for the dumping of nuclear waste, and agreed to co-operate with Norway in locating and testing areas of possible contamination. In January 1993 Norway and the other Nordic countries established a joint council with Russia to promote co-operation in their common border region.

### Government

Norway is a constitutional monarchy. Legislative power is held by the unicameral Parliament (Storting), with 165 members elected for four years by universal adult suffrage, on the basis of proportional representation. For the consideration of legislative proposals, the Storting divides itself into two chambers by choosing one-quarter of its members to form the upper house (Lagting), the remainder forming the lower house (Odelsting). Executive power is nominally held by the monarch but is exercised by the State Council (Council of Ministers), led by the Prime Minister. The Council is appointed by the monarch in accordance with the will of the Storting, to which the Council is responsible. Norway comprises 19 counties (fylker).

## Defence

Norway is a member of NATO, and became an associate member of Western European Union (see p. 221) in November 1992. Every male is liable for national service from the age of 19 to 44 years. At 19 he does 12 months' service in the army or air force, or 15 months in the navy. He is then called back periodically for refresher training. The total strength of the armed forces in June 1994 was 33,500 (including 22,100 conscripts): army 18,000 (14,000 conscripts), navy 6,600 (4,000 conscripts), air force 7,900 (4,100 conscripts), joint services organizations 400, and Home Guard permanent staff 600. There is also a mobilization reserve of 282,000 (army 160,000, navy 21,500, air force 24,900 and Home Guard c. 87,000) and a coastguard of 680. The defence budget estimate for 1994 was 23,000m. kroner.

## Economic Affairs

In 1993, according to estimates by the World Bank, Norway's gross national product (GNP), measured at average 1991–93 prices, was US $113,527m., equivalent to US $26,340 per head. During 1985–93, it was estimated, GNP per head increased, in real terms, at an average annual rate of 0.5%. Over the same period the population increased by an annual average of 0.5%. Norway's gross domestic product (GDP) increased, in real terms, by an annual average of 2.6% in 1980–92, by 2.3% in 1993 and by a projected 4% in 1994.

The contribution of agriculture, forestry and fishing to GDP in 1991 was estimated at 4.5%. In 1993 these sectors engaged 5.5% of the employed labour force. Less than 3% of the land surface is cultivated, and the most important branch of agricultural production is livestock. Fish-farming has been intensively developed by the Government since the early 1970s. The fishing industry provided 6.9% of total export revenue in 1993. During 1980–91 agricultural GDP increased by an annual average of 2.2%.

Industry (including mining, manufacturing, construction, power and public utilities) contributed 34.9% of GDP in 1991, and engaged 22.7% of the employed labour force in 1993. During 1980–91 industrial GDP increased by an annual average of 4.8%.

Mining provided 12.8% of GDP in 1991, but engaged only 1.2% of the employed labour force in 1993. Norway's principal mineral reserves consist of petroleum and natural gas (accounting for 51.3% of total export earnings in 1993). Most of the reserves are located off shore. Norway's other mineral reserves include iron ore, iron pyrites, copper, lead and zinc. Measured in constant prices, the GDP of the mining sector increased at an average rate of 9.4% per year in 1980–91.

Manufacturing contributed 14.4% of GDP in 1991, and employed 14.6% of the working population in 1993. In 1991 the most important branches of manufacturing, measured by gross value of output, were food products (accounting for 21.9% of the total), non-electric machinery (14.2%), metals and metal products (13.4%) and paper products, printing and publishing (12.1%). Other important industries include transport equipment (notably shipbuilding) and chemicals. During 1980–91 manufacturing GDP increased by an annual average of only 0.1% (it rose by 1.2% per year in 1980–87, but declined by 2.0% per year in 1987–91).

Most of Norway's energy requirements are met by hydro-electric power. In 1991 almost 99% of Norway's installed capacity of electric energy was produced by hydroelectric power schemes and in 1993 the export of hydroelectricity began. Norway's substantial reserves of petroleum and natural gas are mainly exploited for sale to foreign markets, since the domestic market is limited. In 1986 agreement was reached to supply natural gas through underwater pipelines from the Troll offshore field (discovered in 1979) to several western European countries. Deliveries were scheduled to begin in 1996, and to total an estimated 50,000m. cu m per year by 2005. Norway possessed estimated total reserves of natural gas of 2,700,000m. cu m in 1994, about one-half of which was located in the Troll field. In 1993 Norway was the world's third largest exporter of petroleum and the sixth largest exporter of natural gas.

Although ship-building has declined since the early 1970s, Norway remains a leading shipping nation. The establishment of the Norwegian International Ship Register in 1987 allowed an expansion of the merchant fleet by more than 300%, in terms of gross tonnage; it totalled 21.0m. grt at the end of 1993.

In 1993 Norway recorded a visible trade surplus of US $8,016m., and there was a surplus on the current account of the balance of payments of $2,453m. In 1993 the European Union (EU, see p. 143) provided 49% of imports and took 67% of exports: Norway's principal trading partners within the EU were the United Kingdom (9% of imports and 25% of exports) and Germany (14% of imports and 13% of exports). Fellow-members of the European Free Trade Association (EFTA, see p. 142), principally Sweden, accounted for 20% of Norway's imports and 13% of exports. There is also significant trade with the USA. In 1993 the principal exports were petroleum and natural gas, transport equipment, non-ferrous metals and fisheries products, and the principal imports were machinery and transport equipment, basic manufactured goods and chemical products.

In the budget for 1994 a deficit of 42,600m. kroner was forecast, compared with a deficit of some 53,900m. kroner in 1993. At the end of 1993 Norway's public debt was US $41,803m., of which 23.9% was foreign debt. During 1985–93 the average annual rate of inflation was 4.9%; consumer prices increased by an average of 2.0% in 1993, and by 1.6% in 1994. In 1993 the average rate of unemployment was 6.0%, declining to an estimated 5.5% in 1994.

In addition to its membership of EFTA, Norway is a member of the European Economic Area (EEA—see p. 142).

Since petroleum and gas were first exported in significant quantities in 1975, the Norwegian economy has become highly dependent on the hydrocarbons sector. The crisis caused by the fall in international prices for these commodities obliged the Government, in 1986, to impose economic austerity measures which, together with increases in both the price and production of petroleum, secured a rapid economic recovery in the late 1980s. In 1991 severe losses in the banking sector forced the Government to take over two of the country's three largest commercial banks, and to acquire a majority shareholding in the third, but in 1993 the principal banks returned to profitability, and a reduction of state holdings began. Expansionary budgets for 1992 and 1993 proposed record deficits, increasing the country's dependence on revenues from petroleum and gas. In December 1992, after a heavy outflow of capital, the krone's link with the European Currency Unit (which had been in force since October 1990) was suspended, thereby effectively devaluing the currency: in January 1993 the Government announced that it would allow the krone to 'float', and in May 1994 it discounted the possibility of the resumption of a linked exchange rate. Petroleum production reached a record average level of more than 2.7m. barrels per day (b/d) in 1994, and was expected to expand further, to more than 3m. b/d by 1996. From the mid-1990s exports of natural gas (amounting to 28,089m. cu m in 1993) were also expected to expand considerably, as a result of the export of gas from the Troll offshore field. The economic security that has been provided by revenue deriving from exports of petroleum and natural gas was regarded as a major factor in the rejection, in a national referendum in 1994, of proposed membership of the EU (see Recent History). Concern was expressed, however, by proponents of EU membership that, despite the predicted increase in natural gas extraction, output of petroleum was expected to decline sharply from 1997, and that Norway should therefore make greater efforts to diversify its economy by stimulating investment in industry.

## Social Welfare

A compulsory National Insurance Scheme covers old age, disability, widows, widowers, children, single parents, sickness, maternity, adoption and rehabilitation. Financed by premiums from those covered, employers' contributions and contributions from the State, the scheme provides a basic pension, irrespective of former income, as well as an additional index-linked pension which is calculated on previous earnings. In 1993 Norway had a total of 22,067 hospital beds, equivalent to one for every 195 inhabitants. In 1994 there were 11,847 active physicians working in the country. Of total current expenditure by the central Government in 1992, an estimated 222,001m. kroner (equivalent to 31.6% of GDP) was social security expenditure.

## Education

Education is compulsory for nine years, between seven and 16 years of age. Elementary education is divided into a six-year lower stage (barneskolen), for children aged seven to 13 years, and a three-year upper stage (ungdomsskolen), beginning at the age of 13. A pupil may then transfer to an upper

## NORWAY

secondary school for a course which may last from one to three years. In 1989 the total enrolment at all primary and secondary schools was equivalent to 98% of the school-age population. Primary enrolment in that year included 98% of children in the appropriate age-group, while the comparable ratio for secondary enrolment was 85% (males 84%; females 86%). As from the 1994/95 academic year, all young people between the ages of 16 and 19 years were to have the statutory right to upper secondary education. Upon completion of a three-year course in general and technical areas of study at an upper secondary school, a pupil may seek admission to one of the four universities or other colleges. A broader system of higher professional education has been organized on a regional basis, including colleges of education and technology. An estimated 30,900m. kroner, some 9% of total current expenditure by the central Government, was allocated to the Ministry of Education, Research and Church Affairs for 1993.

### Public Holidays

**1995:** 1 January (New Year's Day), 13 April (Maundy Thursday), 14 April (Good Friday), 17 April (Easter Monday), 1 May (May Day), 17 May (National Day), 25 May (Ascension Day), 5 June (Whit Monday), 25–26 December (Christmas).
**1996:** 1 January (New Year's Day), 4 April (Maundy Thursday), 5 April (Good Friday), 8 April (Easter Monday), 1 May (May Day), 16 May (Ascension Day), 17 May (National Day), 27 May (Whit Monday), 25–26 December (Christmas).

### Weights and Measures

The metric system is in force.

# Statistical Survey

Sources (unless otherwise stated): Statistics Norway, Skippergt. 15, POB 8131 Dep., 0033 Oslo; tel. 22-86-45-00; fax 22-86-49-73; Nordic Statistical Secretariat (Copenhagen), *Yearbook of Nordic Statistics.*

## Area and Population

### AREA, POPULATION AND DENSITY

| | |
|---|---|
| Area (sq km) | 323,877* |
| Population (census results) | |
| 1 November 1980 | 4,091,132 |
| 3 November 1990 | |
|   Males | 2,099,881 |
|   Females | 2,147,665 |
|   Total | 4,247,546 |
| Population (official estimates at 1 January) | |
| 1992 | 4,274,030 |
| 1993 | 4,299,231 |
| 1994 | 4,324,815 |
| Density (per sq km) at 1 January 1994 | 13.4 |

* 125,050 sq miles.

### COUNTIES (1 January 1994)

| | Area (sq km) | Population* |
|---|---:|---:|
| Østfold | 4,183.4 | 238,712 |
| Akershus | 4,916.5 | 429,595 |
| Oslo | 454.0 | 477,781 |
| Hedmark | 27,388.4 | 187,396 |
| Oppland | 25,259.7 | 183,351 |
| Buskerud | 14,927.3 | 227,102 |
| Vestfold | 2,215.9 | 201,925 |
| Telemark | 15,315.1 | 163,151 |
| Aust-Agder | 9,211.7 | 99,135 |
| Vest-Agder | 7,280.3 | 148,590 |
| Rogaland | 9,140.7 | 350,876 |
| Hordaland | 15,633.8 | 419,885 |
| Sogn og Fjordane | 18,633.5 | 107,563 |
| Møre og Romsdal | 15,104.2 | 239,708 |
| Sør-Trøndelag | 18,831.4 | 255,449 |
| Nord-Trøndelag | 22,463.4 | 127,698 |
| Nordland | 38,327.1 | 240,694 |
| Troms | 25,953.8 | 149,745 |
| Finnmark | 48,637.3 | 76,459 |
| **Total** | 323,877.5 | 4,324,815 |

* Figures are provisional.

### PRINCIPAL TOWNS (population at 1 January 1994)

| | | | |
|---|---:|---|---:|
| Oslo (capital) | 477,781 | Tromsø | 54,503 |
| Bergen | 219,884 | Drammen | 52,401 |
| Trondheim | 142,188 | Skien | 48,290 |
| Stavanger | 102,637 | Sandnes | 47,894 |
| Kristiansand | 67,863 | Sarpsborg | 46,383 |
| Fredrikstad | 64,843 | | |

## BIRTHS, MARRIAGES AND DEATHS

| | Registered live births | | Registered marriages | | Registered deaths* | |
|---|---:|---:|---:|---:|---:|---:|
| | Number | Rate (per 1,000) | Number | Rate (per 1,000) | Number | Rate (per 1,000) |
| 1986 | 52,514 | 12.6 | 20,513 | 4.9 | 43,560 | 10.5 |
| 1987 | 54,027 | 12.9 | 21,081 | 4.9 | 44,959 | 10.7 |
| 1988 | 57,526 | 13.7 | 21,744 | 5.2 | 45,354 | 10.8 |
| 1989 | 59,303 | 14.0 | 20,755 | 4.9 | 45,173 | 10.7 |
| 1990 | 60,939 | 14.4 | 21,926 | 5.2 | 46,021 | 10.9 |
| 1991 | 60,808 | 14.3 | 19,880 | 4.7 | 44,923 | 10.5 |
| 1992 | 60,013 | 14.0 | 19,266 | 4.5 | 44,731 | 10.4 |
| 1993 | 58,152 | 14.0 | 19,464 | 4.5 | 45,013 | 10.5 |

* Including deaths of residents temporarily abroad.

**Expectation of life** (years at birth, 1992): Males 74.16; females 80.34.

### IMMIGRATION AND EMIGRATION

| | 1991 | 1992 | 1993 |
|---|---:|---:|---:|
| Immigrants | 26,283 | 26,743 | 31,711 |
| Emigrants | 18,238 | 16,801 | 18,903 |

### ECONOMICALLY ACTIVE POPULATION
('000 persons aged 16 to 74 years)*

| | 1991 | 1992 | 1993 |
|---|---:|---:|---:|
| Agriculture, hunting, forestry and fishing | 116 | 110 | 111 |
| Mining and quarrying | 21 | 25 | 25 |
| Manufacturing | 294 | 295 | 292 |
| Electricity, gas and water | 21 | 20 | 22 |
| Construction | 130 | 122 | 116 |
| Trade, restaurants and hotels | 354 | 353 | 349 |
| Transport, storage and communications | 162 | 157 | 158 |
| Financing, insurance, real estate and business services | 150 | 153 | 153 |
| Community, social and personal services | 753 | 764 | 775 |
| Activities not adequately defined | 9 | 5 | 3 |
| **Total employed** | 2,010 | 2,004 | 2,004 |
| Unemployed | 116 | 126 | 127 |
| **Total labour force** | 2,126 | 2,130 | 2,131 |
| Males | 1,163 | 1,166 | 1,163 |
| Females | 963 | 964 | 968 |

* Figures are annual averages, based on quarterly sample surveys.

NORWAY

*Statistical Survey*

## Agriculture

**PRINCIPAL CROPS** ('000 metric tons)*

|  | 1991 | 1992 | 1993 |
|---|---|---|---|
| Wheat | 246 | 193 | 360 |
| Rye | 5 | 4 | 13 |
| Barley | 663 | 488 | 631 |
| Oats | 568 | 325 | 380 |
| Potatoes | 415 | 511 | 454 |

* Figures refer to holdings with at least 0.5 ha of agricultural area in use.

**LIVESTOCK** ('000 head)*

|  | 1991 | 1992 | 1993 |
|---|---|---|---|
| Horses | 21 | 21 | 21 |
| Cattle | 974 | 983 | 975 |
| Sheep | n.a. | 2,363 | 2,317 |
| Goats† | 90 | 89 | 89 |
| Pigs | 728 | 766 | 748 |

* Figures refer to holdings with at least 0.5 ha of agricultural area in use.
† Source: FAO, *Production Yearbook* (1993: FAO estimate).

**LIVESTOCK PRODUCTS** ('000 metric tons)

|  | 1991 | 1992 | 1993 |
|---|---|---|---|
| Horse meat | 1 | 1 | 1 |
| Beef and veal | 80 | 85 | 85 |
| Mutton and lamb | 24 | 24 | 25 |
| Pig meat | 85 | 91 | 91 |
| Cows' milk | 1,908 | 1,898 | 1,879 |
| Butter | 20.5 | 19.2 | 18.4 |
| Cheese | 82.0 | 81.3 | 83.5 |
| Hen eggs | 50.3 | 51.4 | 52.7 |

Source: FAO, *Production Yearbook*.

**ROUNDWOOD REMOVALS** ('000 cubic metres, excl. bark)

|  | 1990 | 1991 | 1992* |
|---|---|---|---|
| Sawlogs | 5,322 | 5,699 | 5,699 |
| Pulpwood | 5,364 | 4,436 | 4,037 |
| Fuel wood | 919 | 934 | 934 |
| Other wood | 214 | 214* | 214 |
| **Total** | 11,819 | 11,283 | 10,884 |

* FAO estimate(s).
Source: FAO, *Yearbook of Forest Products*.

**SAWNWOOD PRODUCTION**
('000 cubic metres, incl. railway sleepers)

|  | 1990 | 1991 | 1992 |
|---|---|---|---|
| Coniferous | 2,401 | 2,251* | 2,350 |
| Broadleaved | 12 | 12 | 12* |
| **Total** | 2,413 | 2,263 | 2,362 |

* FAO estimate.
Source: FAO, *Yearbook of Forest Products*.

## Fishing

('000 metric tons, live weight)

|  | 1990 | 1991 | 1992 |
|---|---|---|---|
| Atlantic salmon | 115.3 | 121.5 | 127.1 |
| Atlantic cod | 125.2 | 161.3 | 216.6 |
| Saithe (Coalfish) | 111.9 | 139.3 | 166.9 |
| Norway pout | 142.3 | 120.1 | 162.0 |
| Blue whiting (Poutassou) | 284.3 | 119.2 | 154.6 |
| Sandeels (Sandlances) | 96.2 | 145.4 | 92.7 |
| Atlantic redfishes | 41.2 | 49.5 | 36.9 |
| Capelin | 92.4 | 569.9 | 805.0 |
| Atlantic horse mackerel | 121.8 | 53.1 | 107.4 |
| Atlantic herring | 207.8 | 200.4 | 226.4 |
| Atlantic mackerel | 149.8 | 179.9 | 207.4 |
| Other fishes (incl. unspecified) | 150.2 | 183.6 | 188.4 |
| **Total fish** | 1,701.9 | 2,043.1 | 2,491.5 |
| Northern prawn | 62.7 | 47.8 | 48.8 |
| Other crustaceans | 1.6 | 1.8 | 1.6 |
| Molluscs | 8.6 | 3.2 | 7.2 |
| **Total catch** | 1,711.3 | 2,095.9 | 2,549.1 |
| Inland waters | 0.5 | 0.5 | 0.6 |
| Atlantic Ocean | 1,706.8 | 2,095.4 | 2,536.7 |
| Pacific Ocean | 4.0 | n.a. | 11.8 |

Source: FAO, *Yearbook of Fishery Statistics*.

## Mining

(provisional figures, '000 metric tons, unless otherwise indicated)

|  | 1991 | 1992 | 1993 |
|---|---|---|---|
| Hard coal* | 390 | 449 | 309 |
| Crude petroleum | 93,350 | 106,977 | 114,944 |
| Iron ore† | 2,209 | n.a. | n.a. |
| Iron pyrites (unroasted) | 306 | n.a. | n.a. |
| Copper concentrates (metric tons)† | 17,393 | 39,259 | 37,205 |
| Zinc concentrates (metric tons)† | n.a. | 127 | 129 |
| Natural gas (million cu metres) | 27,278 | 29,419 | 28,089 |

* Production from Norwegian-operated mines in Svalbard (Spitsbergen).
† Figures refer to the metal content of ores and concentrates.

NORWAY

Statistical Survey

## Industry

**SELECTED PRODUCTS**
(provisional figures, '000 metric tons, unless otherwise indicated)

|  | 1991 | 1992 | 1993 |
|---|---|---|---|
| Fish oils | 88.2 | 115.4 | 105.5 |
| Herring meal | 208.2 | 256.8 | 247.4 |
| Margarine | 64.1 | 65.5 | 63.5 |
| Cement | 1,147.3 | 1,241.9 | 1,344.2 |
| Mechanical wood pulp (dry weight) | 1,292.8 | 1,120.0 | 1,362.4 |
| Chemical wood pulp (dry weight) | 815.4 | 789.2 | 751.1 |
| Particle board | 238.9 | 249.9 | 233.3 |
| Wood fibre boards | 71.5 | 83.5 | n.a. |
| Paper and paperboard | 1,786.8 | 1,684.2 | 1,976.7 |
| Wool yarn | 2.6 | 1.5 | 1.6 |
| Woven woollen fabrics | 0.5 | 0.6 | 0.5 |
| Woven cotton fabrics | 1.4 | 1.2 | 0.9 |
| Woven fabrics of discontinuous man-made fibres | 0.3 | 0.4 | 0.3 |
| Ferro-silicon | 377.5 | 376.8 | 399.6 |
| Other ferro-alloys | 483.2 | 468.6 | 525.0 |
| Crude steel | 437.6 | 446.2 | 505.3 |
| Nickel (refined): primary | 58.7 | 55.7 | 56.8 |
| Copper (refined): primary | 38.4 | 39.3 | 37.2 |
| Aluminium (refined): primary | 832.6 | 838.1 | 887.5 |
| Zinc (refined): primary | 124.6 | 127.6 | 129.2 |
| Motor spirit (petrol) | 2,732.7 | 3,304.3 | 3,296.6 |
| Other gasolines | 1,052.5 | 1,140.6 | 971.9 |
| Kerosene | 872.4 | 1,049.5 | 1,096.6 |
| Gas and diesel oils | 6,001.3 | 6,336.9 | 6,503.4 |
| Heavy fuel oil | 1,495.6 | 1,682.9 | 1,611.6 |
| Electricity (million kWh) | 110,950 | 117,506 | 120,001 |

## Finance

**CURRENCY AND EXCHANGE RATES**

**Monetary Units**
100 øre = 1 Norwegian krone (plural: kroner).

**Sterling and Dollar Equivalents** (31 December 1994)
£1 sterling = 10.582 kroner;
US $1 = 6.764 kroner;
1,000 Norwegian kroner = £94.50 = $147.84.

**Average Exchange Rate** (kroner per US $)
1992  6.2145
1993  7.0941
1994  7.0469

**BUDGET ESTIMATES** (million kroner)

| Revenue | 1990 | 1991 | 1992 |
|---|---|---|---|
| Income and property tax | 21,630 | 19,960 | 7,820 |
| Tax and excise on extraction of petroleum | 17,300 | 29,950 | 28,600 |
| Customs and excise | 1,250 | 1,400 | 1,500 |
| Purchase tax | 63,500 | 65,600 | 67,400 |
| Tax on alcohol | 5,647 | 6,159 | 6,313 |
| Tobacco tax | 3,600 | 4,185 | 5,050 |
| **Total** (incl. others) | 298,205 | 356,750 | 353,443 |

| Expenditure | 1992 |
|---|---|
| Ministry of Education, Research and Church Affairs | 26,639.4 |
| Ministry of Health and Social Affairs | 31,081.8 |
| Ministry of Children and Family Affairs | 15,686.2 |
| Ministry of Agriculture | 15,592.4 |
| Ministry of Transport and Communications | 18,568.3 |
| Ministry of Finance | 53,453.8 |
| Ministry of Defence | 22,542.6 |
| State banks | 21,184.5 |
| State petroleum activity | 20,294.0 |
| State Petroleum Fund | 26,201.0 |
| National Insurance | 119,530.2 |
| **Total** (incl. others) | 436,905.0 |

**INTERNATIONAL RESERVES** (US $ million at 31 December)

|  | 1991 | 1992 | 1993 |
|---|---|---|---|
| Gold* | 47.7 | 41.2 | 37.9 |
| IMF special drawing rights | 451.9 | 191.2 | 396.2 |
| Reserve position in IMF | 570.8 | 648.1 | 584.4 |
| Foreign exchange | 12,209.4 | 11,101.0 | 18,641.8 |
| **Total** | 13,279.8 | 11,981.6 | 19,660.3 |

* National valuation.
Source: IMF, *International Financial Statistics*.

**MONEY SUPPLY** ('000 million kroner at 31 December)

|  | 1991 | 1992 | 1993 |
|---|---|---|---|
| Currency outside banks | 31.79 | 32.45 | 35.74 |
| Demand deposits at commercial and savings banks | 206.72 | 234.94 | 245.89 |
| Demand deposits at Post Office | 15.44* | 53.85 | 54.55 |
| **Total money** (incl. others) | 255.80 | 323.33 | 340.12 |

* Estimate.
Source: IMF, *International Financial Statistics*.

**COST OF LIVING** (Consumer Price Index; base: 1979 = 100)

|  | 1992 | 1993 | 1994 |
|---|---|---|---|
| Food | 243 | 240 | 244 |
| Heating | 313 | 322 | n.a. |
| Clothing and footwear | 216 | 221 | 225 |
| Miscellaneous | 260 | 264 | 265 |
| Rent | 246 | 253 | 274 |
| **All items** | 245 | 250 | 254 |

**NATIONAL ACCOUNTS** (million kroner at current prices)
**National Income and Product**

|  | 1991 | 1992 | 1993 |
|---|---|---|---|
| Compensation of employees | 356,381 | 368,476 | 373,161 |
| Operating surplus | 154,996 | 153,242 | 171,899 |
| **Domestic factor incomes** | 511,377 | 521,718 | 545,060 |
| Consumption of fixed capital | 102,462 | 104,190 | 109,021 |
| **Gross domestic product (GDP) at factor cost** | 613,839 | 625,908 | 654,081 |
| Indirect taxes | 115,617 | 121,441 | 128,732 |
| *Less* Subsidies | 42,770 | 44,395 | 49,149 |
| **GDP in purchasers' values** | 686,686 | 702,954 | 733,664 |
| Net factor income from abroad | −17,522 | −22,044 | −22,733 |
| **Gross national product (GNP)** | 669,164 | 680,910 | 710,931 |
| *Less* Consumption of fixed capital | 102,462 | 104,190 | 109,021 |
| **National income in market prices** | 566,701 | 576,720 | 601,909 |
| Other current transfers from abroad (net) | −9,810 | −11,129 | −9,980 |
| **National disposable income** | 556,892 | 565,591 | 591,929 |

**Expenditure on the Gross Domestic Product**

|  | 1991 | 1992 | 1993 |
|---|---|---|---|
| Government final consumption expenditure | 147,478 | 157,220 | 161,779 |
| Private final consumption expenditure | 349,705 | 365,152 | 378,240 |
| Increase in stocks | 2,021 | −5,783 | −17,204 |
| Gross fixed capital formation | 127,053 | 135,246 | 161,046 |
| **Total domestic expenditure** | 626,257 | 651,835 | 683,861 |
| Exports of goods and services | 307,528 | 303,157 | 317,575 |
| *Less* Imports of goods and services | 247,098 | 252,037 | 267,771 |
| **GDP in purchasers' values** | 686,686 | 702,954 | 733,664 |
| **GDP at constant 1990 prices*** | 670,980 | 693,600 | 709,640 |

* Source: IMF, *International Financial Statistics*.

# NORWAY

**Gross Domestic Product by Economic Activity** (at factor cost)

|  | 1989 | 1990 | 1991 |
|---|---|---|---|
| Agriculture, hunting, forestry and fishing | 25,290 | 28,274 | 28,604 |
| Mining and quarrying | 64,073 | 79,715 | 81,469 |
| Manufacturing | 91,094 | 89,869 | 92,126 |
| Electricity, gas and water | 20,762 | 22,352 | 22,775 |
| Construction[1] | 31,634 | 28,460 | 26,170 |
| Trade, restaurants and hotels | 58,323 | 61,867 | 60,849 |
| Transport, storage and communications[2] | 61,730 | 67,124 | 74,341 |
| Financing, insurance, real estate and business services | 93,190 | 97,060 | 101,876 |
| Community, social and personal services[3] | 33,306 | 36,132 | 38,387 |
| Non-market services[3] | 97,631 | 103,800 | 111,491 |
| **Sub-total** | 577,033 | 614,653 | 638,088 |
| *Less* Imputed bank service charge | 25,611 | 25,200 | 24,249 |
| **Total** | 551,420 | 589,453 | 613,839 |

[1] Including the drilling of wells for crude petroleum and natural gas.
[2] Including transportation of petroleum and gas by pipeline.
[3] Government services are included in non-market services.

## BALANCE OF PAYMENTS (US $ million)

|  | 1991 | 1992 | 1993 |
|---|---|---|---|
| Merchandise exports f.o.b. | 34,212 | 35,162 | 31,989 |
| Merchandise imports f.o.b. | −25,516 | −25,860 | −23,974 |
| **Trade balance** | 8,696 | 9,303 | 8,016 |
| Exports of services | 13,214 | 13,521 | 12,687 |
| Imports of services | −12,532 | −14,605 | −13,621 |
| Other income received | 3,657 | 3,161 | 2,570 |
| Other income paid | −6,462 | −6,641 | −5,804 |
| Private unrequited transfers (net) | −338 | −490 | −313 |
| Official unrequited transfers (net) | −1,185 | −1,288 | −1,082 |
| **Current balance** | 5,049 | 2,961 | 2,453 |
| Direct investment (net) | −2,180 | 305 | 1,232 |
| Portfolio investment (net) | −3,107 | 862 | −228 |
| Other capital (net) | −2,294 | −1,542 | 6,052 |
| Net errors and omissions | −219 | −3,442 | −1,659 |
| **Overall balance** | −2,751 | −855 | 7,850 |

Source: IMF, *International Financial Statistics*.

## OFFICIAL ASSISTANCE TO DEVELOPING COUNTRIES
(US $ million)

|  | 1991 | 1992 | 1993 |
|---|---|---|---|
| Bilateral assistance | 734.1 | 810.6 | 658.7 |
| Technical assistance | 109.2 | 137.8 | 98.2 |
| Grants (incl. capital project financing) | 621.1 | 669.8 | 556.8 |
| Loans and credits | 3.8 | 2.9 | 3.7 |
| Multilateral assistance | 443.4 | 462.4 | 355.6 |
| **Total official development assistance** | 1,177.6 | 1,272.9 | 1,014.2 |

# External Trade

Note: Figures include all ships bought and sold but exclude trade in military supplies under defence agreements.

**PRINCIPAL COMMODITIES** (distribution by SITC, US $ million)

| Imports c.i.f.* | 1991 | 1992 | 1993 |
|---|---|---|---|
| **Food and live animals** | 1,313.9 | 1,439.8 | 1,339.3 |
| **Crude materials (inedible) except fuels** | 1,909.1 | 1,794.1 | 1,606.1 |
| Metalliferous ores and metal scrap | 1,214.6 | 1,079.7 | 1,009.7 |
| **Mineral fuels, lubricants, etc.** (incl. electric current) | 1,094.1 | 887.7 | 798.4 |
| Petroleum, petroleum products, etc. | 799.4 | 631.3 | 589.1 |
| **Chemicals and related products** | 2,273.2 | 2,423.6 | 2,280.0 |
| **Basic manufactures** | 4,521.8 | 4,608.5 | 4,110.5 |
| Paper, paperboard and manufactures | 700.9 | 741.1 | 643.2 |
| Textile yarn, fabrics, etc. | 518.1 | 537.8 | 481.0 |
| Iron and steel | 972.2 | 1,171.5 | 1,107.6 |
| **Machinery and transport equipment** | 9,770.2 | 9,844.7 | 9,391.8 |
| Machinery specialized for particular industries | 1,069.7 | 1,108.0 | 930.2 |
| General industrial machinery, equipment and parts | 1,296.6 | 1,382.1 | 1,260.1 |
| Office machines and automatic data-processing equipment | 1,032.6 | 1,100.1 | 1,064.7 |
| Telecommunications and sound equipment | 593.3 | 728.7 | 735.1 |
| Other electrical machinery, apparatus, etc. | 1,315.9 | 1,421.4 | 1,300.6 |
| Road vehicles and parts[1] | 1,258.5 | 1,604.2 | 1,416.4 |
| Other transport equipment[1] | 2,624.1 | 1,897.7 | 2,173.9 |
| **Miscellaneous manufactured articles** | 4,372.0 | 4,795.6 | 4,289.4 |
| Furniture and parts | 467.2 | 492.6 | 427.4 |
| Clothing and accessories (excl. footwear) | 1,243.4 | 1,374.5 | 1,202.6 |
| Professional, scientific and controlling instruments, etc. | 494.6 | 556.3 | 515.0 |
| **Total** (incl. others) | 25,490.9 | 26,075.8 | 24,117.2 |

* Equipment imported directly to the Norwegian sector of the continental shelf is excluded.
[1] Excluding tyres, engines and electrical parts.

| Exports f.o.b. | 1991 | 1992 | 1993 |
|---|---|---|---|
| **Food and live animals** | 2,483.2 | 2,686.6 | 2,512.6 |
| Fish and fish preparations[1] | 2,194.7 | 2,328.5 | 2,214.3 |
| **Crude materials (inedible) except fuels** | 1,007.8 | 1,046.2 | 865.5 |
| **Mineral fuels, lubricants, etc.** | 16,584.9 | 17,468.1 | 16,396.8 |
| Petroleum, petroleum products, etc. | 13,717.6 | 14,796.6 | 13,967.6 |
| Gas (natural and manufactured) | 2,747.3 | 2,547.9 | 2,289.3 |
| **Chemicals and related products** | 2,147.9 | 2,200.4 | 2,024.1 |
| **Basic manufactures** | 5,586.7 | 5,302.0 | 4,791.6 |
| Paper, paperboard and manufactures | 1,060.8 | 940.3 | 893.6 |
| Iron and steel | 900.5 | 916.5 | 837.2 |
| Non-ferrous metals | 2,595.3 | 2,416.2 | 2,116.2 |
| **Machinery and transport equipment** | 5,013.8 | 5,194.8 | 4,152.5 |
| Electrical machinery, apparatus, etc. | 720.7 | 781.6 | 742.0 |
| Transport equipment[2] | 2,623.3 | 2,772.5 | 1,995.6 |
| **Miscellaneous manufactured articles** | 1,074.8 | 1,144.7 | 1,104.7 |
| **Total** (incl. others) | 33,999.4 | 35,165.0 | 31,964.2 |

[1] Including crustaceans and molluscs.
[2] Excluding tyres, engines and electrical parts.

# NORWAY

## PRINCIPAL TRADING PARTNERS (US $ million)

| Imports c.i.f. | 1991 | 1992 | 1993 |
|---|---|---|---|
| Austria | 271.8 | 311.3 | 255.9 |
| Belgium-Luxembourg | 610.6 | 623.4 | 586.7 |
| Canada | 559.4 | 468.7 | 487.2 |
| China, People's Republic | 256.8 | 359.6 | 426.8 |
| Denmark | 1,866.1 | 1,954.4 | 1,791.8 |
| Finland | 802.8 | 922.0 | 789.3 |
| France | 974.3 | 1,059.5 | 1,032.5 |
| Germany | 3,606.2 | 3,762.0 | 3,267.6 |
| Hong Kong | 281.0 | 170.4 | 156.9 |
| Ireland | 235.7 | 239.4 | 270.4 |
| Italy | 857.9 | 876.0 | 833.9 |
| Japan | 1,247.6 | 1,640.5 | 1,930.9 |
| Netherlands | 1,338.5 | 1,028.0 | 987.8 |
| Portugal | 263.2 | 298.0 | 236.0 |
| Spain | 272.4 | 396.7 | 486.3 |
| Sweden | 3,932.1 | 4,023.8 | 3,411.1 |
| Switzerland | 387.1 | 388.6 | 372.4 |
| Taiwan | 226.7 | 265.4 | 227.4 |
| USSR (former) | 361.7 | 385.3 | 345.8* |
| United Kingdom | 2,219.1 | 2,419.9 | 2,206.7 |
| USA | 1,984.1 | 2,225.1 | 1,945.3 |
| **Total** (incl. others) | 25,490.9 | 26,075.8 | 24,117.2 |

* Figure refers to Russia only.

| Exports f.o.b. | 1991 | 1992 | 1993 |
|---|---|---|---|
| Belgium-Luxembourg | 822.3 | 1,008.4 | 733.0 |
| Canada | 904.0 | 914.8 | 741.3 |
| Denmark | 1,914.5 | 1,913.1 | 1,402.5 |
| Finland | 1,024.2 | 898.9 | 815.0 |
| France | 2,551.9 | 2,706.8 | 2,529.0 |
| Germany | 3,760.5 | 4,625.0 | 4,156.8 |
| Ireland | 297.8 | 336.7 | 320.2 |
| Italy | 774.8 | 915.5 | 830.2 |
| Japan | 636.0 | 579.2 | 590.5 |
| Liberia | 615.9 | 495.6 | 273.0 |
| Netherlands | 2,693.0 | 2,510.8 | 2,711.0 |
| Poland | 279.6 | 314.0 | 317.2 |
| Spain | 341.0 | 428.3 | 363.9 |
| Sweden | 3,516.1 | 3,294.9 | 2,783.0 |
| United Kingdom | 9,000.8 | 8,513.6 | 7,857.2 |
| USA | 1,585.6 | 1,782.1 | 1,901.4 |
| **Total** (incl. others) | 33,999.4 | 35,165.0 | 31,964.2 |

## Transport

### STATE RAILWAYS (traffic)

| | 1991 | 1992 | 1993 |
|---|---|---|---|
| Passengers carried ('000) | 33,000 | 33,000 | 38,000 |
| Goods carried ('000 metric tons) | 21,760 | 18,634 | 20,248 |
| Passenger-kilometres (million) | 2,153 | 2,201 | 2,316 |
| Freight ton-kilometres (million) | 2,681 | 2,161 | 2,872 |

### ROAD TRAFFIC (motor vehicles registered at 31 December)

| | 1991 | 1992 | 1993 |
|---|---|---|---|
| Passenger cars (including taxis) | 1,614,623 | 1,619,438 | 1,633,088 |
| Buses | 23,288 | 26,760 | 29,134 |
| Lorries, vans and special vehicles | 311,063 | 314,882 | 323,387 |
| Motor cycles and mopeds | 165,501 | 165,192 | 161,071 |
| **Total** | 2,114,475 | 2,126,272 | 2,146,680 |

## SHIPPING

**Merchant Fleet** (vessels exceeding 100 gross tons, excluding fishing boats, ice-breakers, tugs, etc., at 31 December)

| | 1991 | 1992 | 1993 |
|---|---|---|---|
| Number of vessels | 1,831 | 1,787 | 1,691 |
| Displacement ('000 grt) | 23,297 | 21,982 | 20,965 |

Note: Figures incl. vessels on the Norwegian International Shipping Register (790 vessels in 1993).

**International Sea-borne Shipping*** (freight traffic in '000 metric tons)

| | 1991 | 1992 | 1993 |
|---|---|---|---|
| Goods loaded | 100,372 | 114,265 | 123,548 |
| Goods unloaded | 18,733 | 18,465 | 19,989 |

* Figures exclude transit traffic (other than Swedish iron ore, totalling 12.1m. metric tons in 1987), packing and re-export.

## CIVIL AVIATION (domestic traffic on scheduled services)

| | 1991 | 1992 | 1993 |
|---|---|---|---|
| Kilometres flown ('000) | 49,542 | 51,166 | 50,946 |
| Passengers carried ('000) | 6,583 | 7,059 | 7,516 |
| Passenger-kilometres (million) | 2,853 | 2,903 | 3,169 |
| Cargo, passengers and mail ton-kilometres (million) | 252 | 268 | n.a. |

# Tourism

| | 1991 | 1992 | 1993 |
|---|---|---|---|
| Tourist nights* ('000) | 6,106 | 6,129 | 7,760 |
| Receipts (million kroner) | 10,889 | 14,187 | 13,112 |

* Figures relate to approved hotels, camping sites and other lodging places.

# Communications Media

| | 1991 | 1992 | 1993 |
|---|---|---|---|
| Telephones in use* | 2,198,243 | 2,214,065 | 2,334,836 |
| Television licences | 1,482,000 | 1,495,863 | 1,521,819 |
| Books published (no. of titles) | 3,884 | 4,070 | 4,362 |
| Daily newspapers† | 81 | 84 | 84 |
| Net circulation | 2,521,000 | 2,958,000 | 2,965,000 |

* Telephone subscribers.
† Issued at least four times a week.

# Education

(1992/93)

| | Institutions | Teachers* (Full-time) | Students |
|---|---|---|---|
| Primary (grades 1–9) | 3,332 | 42,767 | 462,569 |
| Secondary and vocational | 582 | 25,576 | 206,020 |
| Special | 232 | 1,913 | 5,250 |
| Teacher-training† | 25 | 1,115 | 19,594 |
| Non-university colleges† | 81 | 2,479 | 63,140 |
| University and equivalent† | 10 | 4,491 | 72,909 |

* Not including teachers at military colleges.
† Public institutions only. Figures are for 1991/92.

Source: Ministry of Education, Research and Church Affairs.

# Directory

## The Constitution

The Constitution was promulgated on 17 May 1814.

According to the Constitution, Norway is a 'free, independent, indivisible, inalienable Kingdom'; its form of government a 'limited and hereditary monarchy'. (In May 1990 the law of succession, which stipulated that a male heir should have precedence in succeeding to the throne, was amended to permit men and women an equal right to the throne. The previous law would still apply to those born before 1990.) The Evangelical Lutheran Church is the established religion of the State.

Executive power is vested in the King, legislative power in the Storting (Parliament), and judicial power in the Judicature.

### EXECUTIVE POWER

The King exercises his power through the Statsråd (State Council). The State Council (the Government) is composed of a Prime Minister and not fewer than seven other Councillors of State, all at least 30 years of age. The business to be dealt with in State Council is prepared by the various executive Ministries, each with a State Councillor at its head. These executive departments conduct the administrative work of the country.

The Government submits the budget estimates and introduces bills in the Storting (Parliament).

Formally, the King appoints the Government, but since the introduction of the parliamentary system in 1884 it is the practice for him to act in accordance with the will of the Storting.

### LEGISLATIVE POWER

The Storting is elected quadrennially by universal suffrage. All Norwegian citizens aged 18 years and over are eligible to vote and every qualified voter who has resided in Norway for at least 10 years is eligible to stand for election. The Storting has 165 members, who elect one-quarter of their own body to constitute the Lagting (upper house); the other three-quarters compose the Odelsting (lower house). All bills must first be introduced in the Odelsting, either by the Government through a State Councillor or by a member of the Odelsting. Should the bill be passed by the Odelsting, it is sent to the Lagting, who may adopt it or return it with amendments. If a bill be passed twice by the Odelsting and rejected on both occasions by the Lagting, it is submitted to the entire Storting and decided by a two-thirds majority. When a bill has thus been passed, it must receive the royal assent in State Council.

Bills for the revision of the Constitution must be introduced in the first, second or third session after a new election. However, only the Storting, after the next election, has power to decide whether the proposed alteration should be adopted. Bills relating to the Constitution are dealt with only by the united Storting. For the adoption of a bill of this nature, a two-thirds majority is required, and the measure becomes law without the royal assent.

The Storting votes all state expenditure and determines state revenue, taxes, customs tariffs and other duties; the Odelsting exercises control over government administration, government appointments and so forth.

The Storting prepares its business through its committees and settles such business, with the exception of bills, in plenum. The State Councillors (Ministers) may attend the Storting, having the right of speech but not of voting.

The Storting determines the duration of each session. It is opened and prorogued by the King each year. The Storting cannot be dissolved either by the King or by its own resolution until the expiry of the quadrennial period for which it has been elected.

Note: In September 1989 the Sámi (Lapps) of northern Norway elected 39 representatives to a new consultative assembly (Sameting). The Sameting is elected quadrennially and is based in the town of Karasjok, in Finnmark.

## The Government

### HEAD OF STATE

King HARALD V (succeeded to the throne 17 January 1991; sworn in 21 January).

### STATE COUNCIL
(June 1995)

**Prime Minister:** GRO HARLEM BRUNDTLAND.
**Minister of Foreign Affairs:** BJØRN TORE GODAL.
**Minister of Finance:** SIGBJØRN JOHNSEN.
**Minister of Defence:** JØRGEN KOSMO.
**Minister of Justice and Police:** GRETE FAREMO.
**Minister of Health:** WERNER CHRISTIE.
**Minister of Social Affairs:** HILL-MARTA SOLBERG.
**Minister of Industry and Energy:** JENS STOLTENBERG.
**Minister of the Environment:** THORBJØRN BERNTSEN.
**Minister of Trade and Shipping:** GRETE KNUDSEN.
**Minister of Fisheries:** JAN HENRY T. OLSEN.
**Minister of Agriculture:** GUNHILD ØYANGEN.
**Minister of Transport and Communications:** KJELL OPSETH.
**Minister of Local Government and Labour:** GUNNAR BERGE.
**Minister of Children and Family Affairs:** GRETE BERGET.
**Minister of Development Co-operation:** KARI NORDHEIM-LARSEN.
**Minister of Education, Research and Church Affairs:** GUDMUND HERNES.
**Minister of Cultural Affairs:** ÅSE KLEVELAND.
**Minister of Government Administration:** NILS O. TOTLAND.

### MINISTRIES

**Office of the Prime Minister:** Akersgt. 42, POB 8001 Dep., 0030 Oslo; tel. 22-34-90-90; telex 21565; fax 22-34-95-00.

**Ministry of Agriculture:** Akersgt. 42, POB 8007 Dep., 0030 Oslo; tel. 22-34-90-90; telex 72969; fax 22-34-95-55.

**Ministry of Children and Family Affairs:** Pløensgt. 8, POB 8036 Dep., 0030 Oslo; tel. 22-34-90-90; fax 22-34-95-15.

**Ministry of Cultural Affairs:** Akersgt. 42, POB 8030 Dep., 0030 Oslo; tel. 22-34-90-90; telex 21428; fax 22-34-95-50.

**Ministry of Defence:** Myntgt. 1, POB 8126 Dep., 0032 Oslo; tel. 22-40-20-00; telex 21605; fax 22-40-23-23.

**Ministry of Education, Research and Church Affairs:** Akersgt. 42, POB 8119 Dep., 0032 Oslo; tel. 22-34-90-90; telex 21428; fax 22-34-95-40.

**Ministry of the Environment:** Myntgt. 2, POB 8013 Dep., 0030 Oslo; tel. 22-34-90-90; telex 21480; fax 22-34-95-60.

**Ministry of Finance:** Akersgt. 42, POB 8008 Dep., 0030 Oslo; tel. 22-34-90-90; telex 21444; fax 22-34-95-05.

**Ministry of Fisheries:** Øvre Slottsgt. 2, POB 8118 Dep., 0032 Oslo; tel. 22-34-90-90; telex 21499; fax 22-34-95-85.

**Ministry of Foreign Affairs:** 7 juni pl. 1, POB 8114 Dep., 0032 Oslo; tel. 22-34-36-00; telex 71004; fax 22-34-95-80; also incl. Ministries of Trade and Shipping and of Development Co-operation.

**Ministry of Government Administration:** Akersgt. 42, POB 8004 Dep., 0030 Oslo; tel. 22-34-90-90; fax 22-34-27-10.

**Ministry of Health and Social Affairs:** Grubbegt. 10, POB 8011 Dep., 0030 Oslo; tel. 22-34-90-90; telex 21428; fax 22-34-95-75.

**Ministry of Industry and Energy:** Pløensgt. 8, POB 8014 Dep., 0030 Oslo; tel. 22-34-90-90; telex 21428; fax 22-34-95-25.

**Ministry of Justice:** Akersgt. 42, POB 8005 Dep., 0030 Oslo; tel. 22-34-90-90; telex 21403; fax 22-34-95-30.

**Ministry of Local Government and Labour:** Møllergt. 43, POB 8112 Dep., 0030 Oslo; tel. 22-34-90-90; telex 21414; fax 22-34-95-45.

**Ministry of Transport and Communications:** Møllergt. 1-3, POB 8010 Dep., 0030 Oslo; tel. 22-34-90-90; telex 21439; fax 22-34-95-70.

## Legislature

### STORTING

**Presidents:** KIRSTI KOLLE GRØNDAHL (DnA), EDVARD GRIMSTAD (SP); Stortinget, Karl Johansgt. 22, 0026 Oslo; tel. 22-31-30-50.

The Storting has 165 members, one-quarter of whom sit as the upper house, the Lagting, and the rest as the lower house, the Odelsting.

**Presidents of the Lagting:** JAN P. SYSE (H), MAGNAR SORTASLØKKEN (SV).

**Presidents of the Odelsting:** GUNNAR SKAUG (DnA), DAG JOSTEIN FJÆRVOLL (KrF).

NORWAY

**General Election, 13 September 1993**

| | Votes | % | Seats |
|---|---|---|---|
| Det norske Arbeiderparti | 908,724 | 36.9 | 67 |
| Senterpartiet | 412,187 | 16.7 | 32 |
| Høyre | 419,373 | 17.0 | 28 |
| Sosialistisk Venstreparti | 194,633 | 7.9 | 13 |
| Kristelig Folkeparti | 193,885 | 7.9 | 13 |
| Fremskrittspartiet | 154,497 | 6.3 | 10 |
| Venstre | 88,985 | 3.6 | 1 |
| Rød Valgallianse | 26,360 | 1.1 | 1 |
| Others | 63,305 | 2.6 | — |
| **Total** | **2,461,949** | **100.0** | **165** |

## Political Organizations

**Fremskrittspartiet (FP)** (Progress Party): POB 8903 Youngstorget, 0028 Oslo; tel. 22-41-07-69; fax 22-42-32-55; f. 1973; formerly Anders Lange's Party; anti-tax; favours privatization, the diminution of the Welfare State and less immigration; Chair. CARL I. HAGEN; Sec.-Gen. GEIR MO.

**Høyre (H)** (Conservative): Stortingsgt. 20, POB 1536 Vika, 0117 Oslo; tel. 22-82-90-00; fax 22-82-90-80; f. 1884; aims to promote economic growth and sound state finances, achieve a property-owning democracy, and to uphold democratic government, social security, private property, private initiative and personal liberty; 100,000 mems; Chair. ANDERS TALLERAAS; Leader JAN PETERSEN; Sec.-Gen. SVEIN GRØNNERN.

**Kristelig Folkeparti (KrF)** (Christian Democratic Party): Øvre Slottsgt. 18–20, POB 478 Sentrum, 0105 Oslo; tel. 22-41-11-80; fax 22-42-32-07; f. 1933; aims to promote a democratic policy based on Christian outlook; Chair. (vacant); Sec. GUNNAR HUSAN.

**Miljøpartiet de Grønne** (Green Environmental Party): POB 2169, 7001 Trondheim; tel. 73-53-09-11; f. 1988.

**Norges Kommunistiske Parti** (Communist Party of Norway): Grønlandsleiret 39, 0135 Oslo; tel. 22-67-33-82; f. 1923; Chair. INGVE IVERSEN; Sec. GUNNAR WAHL.

**Det norske Arbeiderparti (DnA)** (Norwegian Labour Party): POB 8743, Youngstorget, 0028 Oslo; tel. 22-42-91-40; fax 22-42-02-26; f. 1887; social democratic; 115,000 mems; Chair. THORBJØRN JAGLAND; Sec.-Gen. DAG TERJE ANDERSEN.

**Rød Valgallianse** (Red Electoral Alliance): c/o Stortinget, Karl Johansgt. 22, 0026 Oslo; left-wing group; Leader JØRN MAGDAHL.

**Senterpartiet (SP)** (Centre Party): Kristian Augustsgt. 7B, 0130 Oslo; tel. 22-20-67-20; fax 22-20-69-15; f. 1920 as the Bondepartiet (Farmers' Party), name changed 1959; aims at a decentralized society which will secure employment and diversified settlements in all parts of the country; encourages the responsible use of resources and a humane policy of technological development; Chair. ANNE ENGER LAHNSTEIN; Sec.-Gen. STEINAR NESS.

**Sosialistisk Venstreparti (SV)** (Socialist Left Party): Storgt. 45, 0185 Oslo; tel. 22-20-69-79; fax 22-20-09-73; f. 1975 as a fusion of the Socialist People's Party, the Democratic Socialists and other socialist forces united previously in the Socialist Electoral League; advocates non-alignment and socialism independent of international centres, based on workers' control, decentralized powers and ecological principles; Chair. ERIK SOLHEIM.

**Venstre (V)** (Liberal): Møllergt. 16, 0179 Oslo; tel. 22-42-73-20; fax 22-42-43-21; f. 1884; in 1988 reunited with Det Liberale Folkepartiet (Liberal Democratic Party, f. 1972); aims at promoting national and democratic progress on the basis of the present system by gradual economic, social and cultural reforms; Leader ODD EINAR DØRUM; Sec.-Gen. HANS ANTONSEN.

In September 1993 other registered political parties were the **Fedrelandspartiet** (National Party), the **Kristent Konservativt Parti** (Christian Conservative Party) and the **Pensjonistpartiet** (Pensioners' Party).

## Diplomatic Representation

### EMBASSIES IN NORWAY

**Argentina:** Inkognitogt. 10A, 0244 Oslo; tel. 22-55-24-49; telex 19261; fax 22-44-16-41; Ambassador: FEDERICO MIRRÉ.

**Austria:** Thomas Heftyesgt. 19-20, 0244 Oslo; tel. 22-55-23-48; telex 76850; fax 22-55-43-61; Ambassador: Dr HARALD WIESNER.

**Belgium:** Drammensvn 103C, 0244 Oslo; tel. 22-55-22-15; telex 78233; fax 22-44-38-08; Ambassador: FRANS L. CRAENINCKX.

**Brazil:** Sigurd Syrsgt. 4, 0244 Oslo; tel. 22-55-20-29; fax 22-44-39-64; Ambassador: LUIZ ORLANDO C. GÉLIO.

**Bulgaria:** Tidemandsgt. 11, 0244 Oslo; tel. 22-55-40-40; telex 79708; fax 22-55-40-24; Chargé d'affaires: IVAN D. IVANOV.

**Canada:** Oscarsgt. 20, 0244 Oslo; tel. 22-46-69-55; fax 22-69-34-67; Ambassador: ROBERT E. PEDERSEN.

**Chile:** Meltzersgt. 5, 0257 Oslo; tel. 22-44-89-55; telex 77171; fax 22-44-24-21; Ambassador: SERGIO MIMIÇA.

**China, People's Republic:** Tuengen allé 2B, Vinderen, 0244 Oslo; tel. 22-49-38-57; telex 71919; fax 22-92-19-78; Ambassador: ZHU YINGLU.

**Costa Rica:** Bygdøy Allé 93, 0268 Oslo; tel. 22-44-22-51; fax 22-55-57-58; Ambassador: JOSÉ MIGUEL UMANA-GIL.

**Croatia:** Drammensvn 82, 0271 Oslo; tel. 22-44-22-33; fax 22-44-39-00; Chargé d'affaires: IVAN POLJAC.

**Czech Republic:** Fritznersgt. 14, 0244 Oslo; tel. 22-43-00-34; fax 22-55-33-95; Ambassador: TOMÁS PSTROSS.

**Denmark:** Olav Kyrresgt. 7, 0244 Oslo; tel. 22-44-18-46; telex 71275; fax 22-55-46-34; Ambassador: HANS HENRIK BRUUN.

**Egypt:** Drammensvn 90A, 0244 Oslo; tel. 22-20-00-10; telex 78405; fax 22-56-22-68; Ambassador: MAHMOUD AHMED FATHY MUBARAK.

**Estonia:** Frognervn 8, 0244 Oslo; tel. 22-55-39-99; fax 22-55-37-85; Chargé d'affaires: KERSTI NABER.

**Finland:** Thomas Heftyesgt. 1, 0264 Oslo; tel. 22-43-04-00; telex 76755; fax 22-43-06-29; Ambassador: JORMA INKI.

**France:** Drammensvn 69, 0244 Oslo; tel. 22-44-18-20; telex 71280; fax 22-56-32-21; Ambassador: PHILIPPE GUELLUY.

**Germany:** Oscarsgt. 45, 0244 Oslo; tel. 22-55-20-10; telex 71173; fax 22-44-76-72; Ambassador: HARALD HOFMANN.

**Greece:** Nobelsgt. 45, 0244 Oslo; tel. 22-44-27-28; telex 72189; fax 22-56-00-72; Ambassador: MARIA ZOGRAFOU.

**Hungary:** Sophus Liesgt. 3, 0244 Oslo; tel. 22-55-24-18; fax 22-44-76-93; Ambassador: Dr GÁBOR NAGY.

**Iceland:** Stortingsgt. 30, 0161 Oslo; tel. 22-83-34-35; fax 22-83-07-04; Ambassador: EIDUR GUDNASON.

**India:** Niels Juelsgt. 30, 0244 Oslo; tel. 22-55-22-29; telex 78510; fax 22-44-07-20; Ambassador: SHANKAR KUMAR MATHUR.

**Indonesia:** Inkognitogt. 8, 0244 Oslo; tel. 22-44-11-21; telex 72683; fax 22-55-34-44; Ambassador: CATHERINE A. LATUPAPUA.

**Iran:** Drammensvn 88E, 0244 Oslo; tel. 22-55-24-08; fax 22-55-49-19; Ambassador: ABDOLRAHIM GAVAHI.

**Israel:** Drammensvn 82C, 0244 Oslo; tel. 22-44-79-24; fax 22-56-21-83; Ambassador: MICHAEL SHILOH.

**Italy:** Inkognitogt. 7, 0244 Oslo; tel. 22-55-22-33; telex 78870; fax 22-44-34-36; Ambassador: ANTONIO BADINI.

**Japan:** Parkvn 33B, 0244 Oslo; tel. 22-55-10-11; telex 76085; fax 22-44-25-05; Ambassador: MASAKI SEO.

**Korea, Republic:** Inkognitogt. 3, POB 7100 Homansbyen, 0306 Oslo; tel. 22-55-20-18; fax 22-56-14-11; Ambassador: DAE HWA CHOI.

**Mexico:** Drammensvn 108B, 0244 Oslo; tel. 22-43-11-65; fax 22-44-43-52; Ambassador: ANTONIO VILLEGAS.

**Netherlands:** Oscarsgt. 29, 0244 Oslo; tel. 22-60-21-93; telex 71580; fax 22-56-92-00; Ambassador: GERHARD J. VAN HATTUM.

**Pakistan:** Eckersbergsgt. 20, 0244 Oslo; tel. 22-55-54-70; fax 22-55-50-97; Chargé d'affaires: KHIZAR HAYAT KHAN NIAZI.

**Poland:** Olav Kyrres pl. 1, 0244 Oslo; tel. 22-44-86-39; telex 71092; fax 22-44-48-39; Ambassador: LECH SOKÓL.

**Portugal:** Josefinesgt. 37, 0244 Oslo; tel. 22-60-62-25; telex 71200; fax 22-56-43-55; Ambassador: AFONSO DE CASTRO.

**Romania:** Oscarsgt. 51, 0258 Oslo; tel. 22-44-15-12; telex 76844; fax 22-43-16-74; Ambassador: MIHAI CROITORU.

**Russia:** Drammensvn 74, 0271 Oslo; tel. 22-55-32-78; telex 79803; fax 22-55-00-70; Ambassador: ANATOLY F. TISHCHENKO.

**Slovakia:** Thomas Heftyesgt. 32, 0244 Oslo; tel. 22-55-55-90; fax 22-55-50-19; Chargé d'affaires a.i.: MILAN RICHTER.

**South Africa:** Drammensvn 88C, POB 7588 Skillebekk, 0205 Oslo; tel. 22-44-79-10; fax 22-44-39-75; Ambassador: STEPHEN GAWE.

**Spain:** Oscarsgt. 35, 0244 Oslo; tel. 22-44-71-22; telex 76641; fax 22-55-98-22; Ambassador: ALBERTO ESCUDERO.

**Sweden:** Nobelsgt. 16, 0244 Oslo; tel. 22-44-38-15; telex 71300; fax 22-55-15-96; Ambassador: KJELL ANNELING.

**Switzerland:** Bygdøy allé 78, 0244 Oslo; tel. 22-43-05-90; fax 22-44-63-50; Ambassador: GAUDEN VON SALIS.

**Thailand:** Munkedamsvn 59B, 0270 Oslo; tel. 22-83-25-17; telex 79372; fax 22-83-03-84; Ambassador: MONTRI JALICHANDRA.

**Tunisia:** Haakon VII'sgt. 5B, 0161 Oslo; tel. 22-83-19-17; fax 22-83-24-12; Ambassador: RAOUF SAID.

**Turkey:** Halvdan Svartesgt. 5, 0244 Oslo; tel. 22-44-99-20; fax 22-55-62-63; Ambassador: OMÜR ORHUN.

NORWAY                                                                                                          *Directory*

**United Kingdom:** Thomas Heftyesgt. 8, 0244 Oslo; tel. 22-55-24-00; fax 22-55-10-41; Ambassador: Mark Elliott.
**USA:** Drammensvn 18, 0244 Oslo; tel. 22-44-85-50; fax 22-43-07-77; Ambassador: Thomas A. Loftus.
**Venezuela:** Drammensvn 82, POB 7638 Skillebekk, 0205 Oslo; tel. 22-43-06-60; telex 77297; fax 22-43-14-70; Ambassador: Julio César Gil.
**Yugoslavia:** Drammensvn 105, 0244 Oslo; tel. 22-44-81-05; fax 22-55-29-92; Chargé d'affaires a.i.: Dragan Arsenović.

## Judicial System

The judicial system in Norway is organized on three levels. The courts of first instance are the District (Herredsrett) and City (Byrett) Courts. The country is divided into 87 judicial areas, most of which are served by one professional judge and one or two deputies (in the major cities the number of judges ranges from three to 44). The High Court, or Superior Court for Civil and Criminal Cases (Lagmannsrett), consists of six jurisdictions, each with between nine and 29 judges, and two divisions (Appeals and Criminal Divisions). The Supreme Court (Høyesterett) sits in Oslo and decides cases in the last instance. The Court, which is served by 18 judges appointed by the Crown and presided over by a Chief Justice, is competent to try all factual and legal aspects of cases in civil and criminal cause. In criminal cases, however, the competence of the Court is limited to questions concerning the application of the law, the nature of the penalty, and procedural errors of the lower courts.

**Chief Justice of the Supreme Court:** Carsten Smith.
**Presiding Judge of the High Court (Oslo):** Agnes Nygaard Haug.
**Presiding Judge of the High Court (Bergen):** Erik A. Foss.
**Presiding Judge of the High Court (Hamar):** Odd Jarl Pedersen.
**Presiding Judge of the High Court (Skien):** Arne Christiansen.
**Presiding Judge of the High Court (Tromsø):** Gaute Gregusson.
**Presiding Judge of the High Court (Trondheim):** Sverre Dragsten.

### CIVIL COURTS

In each municipality there is a Conciliation Court (Forliksråd) consisting of three lay members elected by the municipal council for four years. With a few exceptions, no case may be taken to a court of justice without a prior attempt at mediation by a Conciliation Court. In addition to mediation, the Conciliation Court has a judicial capacity and is intended to settle minor cases in a simple manner without great expense to the parties involved.

The ordinary lower courts are the District and City Courts, which decide all cases not adjudicated upon by the Conciliation Court, and they also act as courts of appeal from judgments given in the Conciliation Court. The cases are adjudicated by a judge, who sits either alone or with two lay judges.

Judgments delivered in the District and City Courts may be taken, on appeal, to the High Court (Appeals Division) or to the Supreme Court. In the High Court cases are judged by three professional judges, but if requested by one of the parties, lay judges may be summoned.

### CRIMINAL COURTS

The criminal courts are: Examining Courts (Forhørsretten), the District and City Courts, the High Court and the Supreme Court. In the Examining Courts the professional judge presides alone, but in the District and City Courts two lay judges also sit. Cases originating in the lower courts may be retried by the High Court when the question of guilt is at issue (such cases are tried either by two professional judges, and three lay judges with equal votes—meddomsrett, or by three professional judges and a jury of 10 members. For a guilty verdict to be upheld in the latter case, at least seven members of the jury must support the original decision of the lower court. In other cases appeal is directly to the Supreme Court. The maximum penalty permissible under Norwegian law is 21 years of imprisonment.

### OMBUDSMAN

The office of Parliamentary Ombudsman was established in 1962. An Ombudsman is elected by the Storting after every general election for a four-year term (with the possibility of re-election). The Ombudsman is accessible to all citizens, and attempts to ensure against the public administration committing any injustice to the individual citizen. The Ombudsman does not cover private legal affairs, and does not have the right to reverse an official decision, but his pronouncements are normally complied with.

**Stortingets ombudsmann for forvaltningen** (Parliamentary Ombudsman for Public Administration): Arne Fliflet, Møllergt. 4, POB 8028 Dep., 0030 Oslo; tel. 22-42-74-20.

## Religion

### CHRISTIANITY

#### The National Church

**Church of Norway:** Ministry of Education, Research and Church Affairs, POB 8119 Dep., 0032 Oslo; tel. 22-34-90-90; Council of Norwegian Bishoprics, POB 1937 Grønland, 0135 Oslo; tel. 22-19-37-00; the Evangelical Lutheran Church, constituted as the State Church; there are 11 dioceses, 97 archdeaconries, 627 clerical districts and 1,148 parishes. The highest representative body of the Church is the Synod, summoned for the first time in 1984. In 1994 approximately 89% of the population belonged to the State Church.

**Bishop of Oslo:** Andreas Aarflot.
**Bishop of Borg:** Even Fougner.
**Bishop of Hamar:** Rosemarie Köhn.
**Bishop of Tunsberg:** Sigurd Osberg.
**Bishop of Agder:** Halvor Bergan.
**Bishop of Stavanger:** Bjørn Bue.
**Bishop of Bjørgvin:** Ole D. Hagesæther.
**Bishop of Møre:** Odd Bondevik.
**Bishop of Nidaros:** Finn Wagle.
**Bishop of Sør-Hålogaland:** Øystein I. Larsen.
**Bishop of Nord-Hålogaland:** Ola Steinholt.

#### The Roman Catholic Church

For ecclesiastical purposes, Norway comprises the diocese of Oslo and the territorial prelatures of Tromsø and Trondheim. The diocese and the prelatures are directly responsible to the Holy See. At 31 December 1993 there were an estimated 35,278 adherents in Norway.

**Bishops' Conference:** Conferentia Episcopalis Scandiae, Akersvn 5, 0177 Oslo; tel. 22-20-72-26; fax 22-20-48-57; f. 1960 (new statutes approved 1985); Pres. Mgr Paul Verschuren, Bishop of Helsinki; Sec.-Gen. Rt Rev. Gerhard Schwenzer, Bishop of Oslo.
**Bishop of Oslo:** Rt Rev. Gerhard Schwenzer, Katolske Bispedømme, Akersvn 5, 0177 Oslo; tel. 22-20-72-26; fax 22-20-48-57.

#### Other Churches

**Church of England:** St. Edmund's Anglican Church, Mollergt. 30, Oslo; 1,454 mems; Rev. Robert Lewis (Diocese of Gibraltar in Europe).
**Evangelical Lutheran Free Church of Norway:** Kongsvn 82, POB 23, Bekkelagshogda, 1109 Oslo; tel. 22-74-50-90; f. 1877; 20,662 mems; Chair. of Synod Gunnar Engebretsen.
**Norwegian Baptist Union:** Micheletsvei 62, 1320 Stabekk; tel. 67-53-35-90; fax 67-53-92-86; f. 1860; 11,196 mems.
**Pentecostal Movement:** St Olavsgt. 24, 0166 Oslo; tel. 22-11-43-00; fax 22-11-43-43; 44,008 mems.
**United Methodist Church:** POB 2744 St Hanshaugen, 0131 Oslo; tel. 22-56-40-30; fax 22-56-44-48; f. 1856; 14,825 mems (1993).

At the beginning of 1993 there were 15,267 Jehovah's Witnesses in Norway and 6,511 Seventh-day Adventists. There were 7,887 members of the Missionary Alliance.

### OTHER RELIGIONS

At the beginning of 1993 there were 21,685 Muslims in Norway. There was an Orthodox Jewish community numbering 998.

## The Press

The principle of press freedom is safeguarded in the Norwegian Constitution. There is no law specifically dealing with the Press. Editors bear wide responsibility in law for the content of their papers, especially regarding such matters as libel. Although a journalist is legally entitled to conceal his source he may be required to disclose this information under penalty of imprisonment, but such instances are rare. A three-member Council of Conduct gives judgements in cases of complaint against a paper or of disputes between papers. It has no powers of enforcement but its judgements are highly respected. The Press Association has a Code of Ethics aimed at maintaining the standards and reputation of the profession.

The Eastern region is the scene of most press activity. Oslo dailies are especially influential throughout this area, and four of these—*Aftenposten, Verdens Gang, Dagbladet* and *Arbeiderbladet*—have a national readership. Nevertheless, in Norway's other chief cities the large local dailies easily lead in their own districts. In 1993 Norway had 149 newspapers, including 84 dailies, with a total circulation of 3.0m. A few very large papers are responsible for the bulk of this circulation. In 1994 the most popular newspapers were *Verdens Gang* (Oslo), *Aftenposten* (Oslo), *Dagbladet* (Oslo), *Bergens Tidende* (Bergen) and *Adresseavisen* (Trondheim), with a combined circulation of more than 1m. At the beginning of 1994 the principal media holding company was Schibsted A/S, which owned *Aftenposten* and *Verdens Gang* and had substantial holdings in *Adresseavisen* (33.4%), *Stavanger Aftenblad* (30.5%) and several other newspapers. Orkla Media A/S had holdings of 90% or more in eight regional newspapers (and a 50% share in the major magazine publisher Hjemmet Mortensen—see below). The trade-union-owned Norsk Arbeiderpresse is the principal owner of the left-wing press.

In 1994 the weekly magazines with the largest sales were *Se og Hør* (news, television and radio) and the 'family' magazines *Hjemmet*, *Allers* and *Norsk Ukeblad*. The most popular monthly and other magazines included *Illustrert Vitenskap* (science), the sports magazines *Fotball* and *Villmarksliv*, the family magazine *Familien*, and the home and furnishings magazine *Bonytt/Hjem og Fritid*. The principal magazine publishers in 1994 were Hjemmet Mortensen Forlag AS (with 13 titles), A/S Allers Familie-Journal (five titles) and Bonniers Spesialblader AS (eight titles).

## PRINCIPAL NEWSPAPERS

### Ålesund
**Sunnmørsposten:** POB 123, 6001 Ålesund; tel. 70-12-00-00; fax 70-12-98-50; f. 1882; Liberal; Editor Roar Larsen; circ. 36,751.

### Arendal
**Agderposten:** POB 8, 4801 Arendal; tel. 37-00-37-00; fax 37-00-37-17; f. 1874; independent; Editor Thor Bjørn Seland; circ. 25,660.

### Bergen
**Bergens Tidende:** POB 875, 5002 Bergen; tel. 55-21-45-00; telex 42026; fax 55-32-49-44; f. 1868; Editor Hans Erik Matre; circ. 95,455.

**Bergensavisen:** POB 824, 5002 Bergen; tel. 55-32-16-00; fax 55-31-04-86; f. 1927; Labour; Editor Olav Terje Bergo; circ. 27,500.

**Dagen:** POB 76/77, 5002 Bergen; tel. 55-31-17-55; fax 55-31-71-06; f. 1919; religious daily; Editor Finn Jarle Sæle; circ. 12,399.

### Bodø
**Nordlands Framtid:** Storgt. 9, 8002 Bodø; tel. 75-50-50-00; fax 75-50-51-10; f. 1910; Labour; Editor Thor Woje; circ. 21,094.

**Nordlandsposten:** POB 44, 8001 Bodø; tel. (81) 75-52-72-00; fax 75-52-84-60; f. 1862; independent; Editor Iver Hammeren; circ. 17,633.

### Bryne
**Jaerbladet:** POB 23, 4341 Bryne; tel. 51-48-12-22; fax 51-48-37-40; 3 a week; non-political; Editor Jostein Fylling; circ. 12,494.

### Drammen
**Drammens Tidende og Buskeruds Blad:** POB 7033, 3007 Drammen; tel. 32-20-40-00; fax 32-20-43-60; f. 1832 and 1883; Conservative daily; Dir Finn Grundt; Editor Hans Arne Odde; circ. 43,611.

**Fremtiden:** POB 7013, 3007 Drammen; tel. 32-82-35-80; fax 32-82-36-00; f. 1905; Labour; Editor Knut S. Evensen; circ. 17,138.

### Elverum
**Østlendingen, Hamar Dagblad og Østlendingen Solør-Odal:** POB 231, 2401 Elverum; tel. 62-41-01-44; fax 62-41-47-15; f. 1901; Centre; Editor-in-Chief Thor Solberg; Adm. Dir Bjørn Fjellmosveen; circ. 26,650.

### Førde
**Firda:** POB 160, 6801 Førde; tel. 57-82-95-00; fax 57-82-38-18; f. 1918; 5 a week; non-political; Editor-in-Chief Rune Timberlid; circ. 13,270.

### Fredrikstad
**Fredriksstad Blad:** POB 143, 1601 Fredrikstad; tel. 69-31-90-00; fax 69-31-81-01; f. 1889; Conservative; Editor Truls Velgaard; circ. 20,944.

### Gjøvik
**Oppland Arbeiderblad:** POB 24, 2801 Gjøvik; tel. 61-18-93-00; fax 61-17-07-25; f. 1924; daily; Labour; Editor-in-Chief Leif Sveen; circ. 28,155.

### Hamar
**Hamar Arbeiderblad:** POB 263, 2301 Hamar; tel. 62-52-75-40; fax 62-52-69-10; f. 1925; daily; Labour; Editor Magne Bjørnerud; circ. 28,232.

### Harstad
**Harstad Tidende:** POB 85, 9401 Harstad; tel. 77-06-72-22; fax 77-06-74-10; f. 1887; Conservative; Editor Odd R. Olsen; circ. 16,387.

### Haugesund
**Haugesunds Avis:** POB 2024, 5501 Haugesund; tel. 52-72-00-00; fax 52-72-04-44; f. 1895; independent; Chief Editor Kristian Magnus Vikse; circ. 36,730.

### Hønefoss
**Ringerikes Blad:** POB 68, 3501 Hønefoss; tel. 32-12-80-00; fax 32-12-17-74; f. 1845; Conservative; Editor Trond Hjerpseth; circ. 13,835.

### Kongsvinger
**Glåmdalen:** Postuttak 2201 Kongsvinger; tel. 62-81-52-22; fax 62-81-55-19; f. 1926; daily; Labour; Editor Bjørn Taalesen; circ. 22,685.

### Kristiansand
**Faedrelandsvennen:** POB 369, 4601 Kristiansand; tel. 38-01-30-00; fax 38-01-33-33; f. 1875; daily; Liberal independent; Editor Finn Holmer-Hoven; circ. 47,170.

### Kristiansund
**Tidens Krav:** POB 8, 6501 Kristiansund N.; tel. 71-67-00-00; fax 71-67-96-66; f. 1906; Labour; Editor Arve Ødegård; circ. 15,855.

### Larvik
**Østlands-Posten:** POB 2000, 3255 Larvik; tel. 33-18-40-00; fax 33-18-30-95; f. 1881; Liberal independent; Editor Tor R. Jensen; circ. 13,942.

### Lillehammer
**Dagningen:** POB 952, 2601 Lillehammer; tel. 61-25-50-00; fax 61-25-61-29; f. 1924; Labour; Editor Ingar Sletten Kolloen; circ. 12,019.

**Gudbrandsdølen Lillehammer Tilskuer:** POB 70, 2601 Lillehammer; tel. 61-25-80-00; fax 61-26-09-60; f. 1841 and 1894; independent; Editor-in-Chief Asbjørn Ringen; circ. 22,448.

### Lillestrøm
**Akershus/Romerikes Blad:** POB 235, 2001 Lillestrøm; tel. 63-81-90-90; fax 63-81-90-90; fax 63-81-78-88; f. 1913; Labour; Editor-in-Chief Terje Granerud; circ. 39,258.

### Molde
**Romsdals Budstikke:** POB 55, 6401 Molde; tel. 71-25-00-00; fax 71-25-00-14; f. 1843; Conservative independent; Editor Richard Nergaard; circ. 18,604.

### Moss
**Moss Avis:** POB 248/250, 1501 Moss; tel. 69-25-30-40; fax 69-25-56-73; f. 1876; independent; Liberal/Conservative; Editor Svein E. Hildonen; circ. 14,342.

### Oslo
**Aftenposten:** Akersgt. 51, POB 1178 Sentrum, 0107 Oslo; tel. 22-86-30-00; telex 71230; fax 22-42-63-25; f. 1860; Conservative independent; Chief Editor Einar Hanseid; circ. morning 279,965, evening 188,544, Sunday 217,766.

**Akers Avis/Groruddalen Budstikke:** POB 100 Grorudhagen, 0905 Oslo; tel. 22-25-01-89; fax 22-16-01-05; f. 1928; 2 a week; non-political; Editor Hjalmar Kielland; circ. 12,414.

**Arbeiderbladet:** POB 1183 Sentrum, 0107 Oslo; tel. 22-72-60-00; fax 22-64-92-64; f. 1884; Labour; Editor-in-Chief Arvid Jacobsen; circ. 43,528.

**Dagbladet:** POB 1184 Sentrum, 0107 Oslo; tel. 22-31-06-00; telex 71020; fax 22-42-95-48; f. 1869; daily; Chief Editor Bjørn Simensen; circ. 227,796.

**Dagens Naeringsliv:** POB 1182 Sentrum, 0107 Oslo; tel. 22-17-83-00; fax 22-17-62-22; Editor Kare Valebrokk; circ. 52,391.

**Nationen:** Thunes vei 2, 0274 Oslo; tel. 22-44-95-00; fax 22-55-08-08; f. 1918; daily; Centre; Chief Editor Erling Kjekstad; circ. 20,805.

**Verdens Gang:** Akersgt. 55, POB 1185 Sentrum, 0107 Oslo; tel. 22-00-00-00; fax 22-42-67-80; f. 1945; independent; Chief Editor Bernt Olufsen; circ. 386,000.

**Vårt Land:** POB 68 Tveita, 0617 Oslo; tel. 22-75-90-00; fax 22-26-01-05; f. 1945; religious daily; Editor Helge Simonnes; circ. 27,232.

### Sandefjord
**Sandefjords Blad:** POB 2042, 3201 Sandefjord; tel. 33-46-00-00; fax 33-46-29-91; f. 1861; Conservative; Editor Leif M. Flemmen; circ. 15,018.

### Sandvika

**Asker og Baerums Budstikke:** POB 133, 1361 Billingstad; tel. 66-98-09-01; fax 66-98-09-19; f. 1898; 5 a week; Conservative; Editor Andreas Gjølme; circ. 31,720.

### Sarpsborg

**Sarpsborg Arbeiderblad:** POB 87, 1701 Sarpsborg; tel. 69-15-50-00; fax 69-15-55-36; f. 1929; Labour; Editor John Henriksen; circ. 17,731.

### Ski

**Østlandets Blad:** POB 110, 1401 Ski; tel. 64-87-50-60; fax 64-87-60-65; f. 1908; 5 a week; Conservative; Editor Marit Haukom; circ. 18,446.

### Skien

**Telemarks Avisa:** POB 625, 3701 Skien; tel. 35-58-55-00; fax 35-52-82-09; f. 1921; Labour; Editor Jan-Erik Larsen; circ. 20,648.

**Varden:** POB 46, 3701 Skien; tel. 35-54-30-00; fax 35-52-83-23; f. 1874; Conservative; Editor Bjørn Jacobsen; circ. 33,973.

### Stavanger

**Rogalands Avis:** POB 233, 4001 Stavanger; tel. 51-58-50-60; fax 51-58-29-70; f. 1899; Labour; Editor Norulv Øvrebotten; circ. 17,030.

**Stavanger Aftenblad:** POB 229, 4001 Stavanger; tel. 51-50-00-00; telex 33114; fax 51-89-32-23; f. 1893; Chief Editor Thor Bjarne Bore; circ. 72,097.

### Steinkjer

**Trønder-Avisa:** POB 2520, 7701 Steinkjer; tel. 74-16-30-00; fax 74-16-48-77; Centre/Liberal; Editor Johannes Brandtzæg; circ. 23,277.

### Svolvær

**Lofotposten:** POB 85, 8301 Svolvær; tel. 76-07-00-11; fax 76-07-00-09; f. 1896; independent; Chief Editor Brynjar Tollefsen; circ. 12,006.

### Tønsberg

**Tønsbergs Blad:** POB 2003, Postterminalen, 3101 Tønsberg; tel. 33-31-00-00; fax 33-31-00-88; f. 1870; Conservative; Editor-in-Chief Marit Haukom; circ. 32,795.

### Tromsø

**Nordlys:** POB 656, 9001 Tromsø; tel. 77-62-35-00; fax 77-62-35-02; f. 1902; Labour; Editor Ivan Kristoffersen; circ. 32,071.

### Trondheim

**Adresseavisen:** POB 6070, 7003 Trondheim; tel. 72-50-00-00; fax 72-58-06-23; f. 1767; Conservative; Editors Kjell Einar Amdahl, Gunnar Flikke; circ. 90,002.

**Avisa Trondheim:** POB 5440 Lade, 7002 Trondheim; tel. 73-92-11-22; fax 73-92-14-10; Labour; Editor Bjørn Stuevold; circ. 13,648.

## POPULAR PERIODICALS

**Allers:** Persvn 20, POB 250 Økern, 0510 Oslo; tel. 22-63-60-00; telex 71088; fax 22-63-60-98; family weekly; Chief Editor Stig Fossüm; circ. 135,512.

**Bonytt/Hjem og Fritid:** Sørkeldalsvn 10A, POB 5001 Majorstuen, 0301 Oslo; tel. 22-94-10-00; fax 22-36-10-08; home and furnishing; 9 a year; Editor Gerd Storvik; circ. 65,259.

**Facts and Fenomener:** POB 2705 St Hanshaugen, 0131 Oslo; tel. 22-38-28-10; fax 22-37-55-48; previously known as 'Lexicon'; monthly; illustrated general knowledge for young people over 15 years of age; Editor Anker Tiedemann; circ. 30,280.

**Familien:** POB 5001 Majorstuen, 0305 Oslo; tel. 22-94-10-00; telex 76677; fax 22-11-20-69; family fortnightly; Chief Editor Karin Aubert Stenholm; circ. 178,423.

**Foreldre & Barn:** POB 5001 Majorstuen, 0301 Oslo; tel. 22-94-10-00; fax 22-11-30-40; 11 a year; for parents of young children; Editor Edda Espeland; circ. 59,224.

**Henne:** POB 1164 Sentrum, 0107 Oslo; tel. 22-63-60-00; fax 22-63-60-36; women's; Chief Editor Ellen Arnstad; circ. 58,841.

**Hjemmet:** POB 5001 Majorstuen, 0301 Oslo; tel. 22-94-10-00; telex 16677; fax 22-42-32-76; family weekly; Chief Editor Rønnaug Greaker; circ. 267,748.

**Husmorbladet:** Oscarsgt. 43, 0258 Oslo; tel. 22-55-79-07; fax 22-55-82-94; f. 1887; 6 a year; home, environment, culture, cookery; Editor Larz Tvethaug; circ. 22,657.

**Hytteliv:** POB 1161 Sentrum, 0107 Oslo; tel. 22-94-10-00; fax 22-36-10-08; every 6 weeks; for second-home owners; Editor Tore Giljane; circ. 37,500.

**IdéMagasinet:** POB 6754 Rodeløkka, 0503 Oslo; tel. 22-09-75-00; fax 22-09-75-99; Women's; Editor Annichen Large; circ. 45,387.

**I form:** POB 2705 St Hanshaugen, 0131 Oslo; tel. 22-38-28-10; fax 22-37-55-48; monthly; health and fitness; Chief Editor Jens Henneberg; circ. 44,716.

**Illustrert Vitenskap:** POB 2705 St Hanshaugen, 0131 Oslo; tel. 22-38-28-10; fax 22-37-55-48; monthly; popular science; Chief Editor Birgitte Engen; Editor Mona Gravningen Rygh; circ. 82,137.

**KK—Kvinner og Klær:** POB 250 Økern, 0510 Oslo; tel. 22-63-60-00; telex 71088; fax 22-63-61-02; women's weekly; Chief Editor June Trønnes Hanssen; circ. 91,167.

**Mat & Drikke:** POB 250 Økern, 0510 Oslo; tel. 22-63-60-00; fax 22-63-60-36; 7 a year; food and wine; Chief Editor Arnfinn Hanssen; circ. 22,182.

**MOTEjournalen:** POB 5001 Majorstuen, 0301 Oslo; tel. 22-94-10-00; fax 22-94-10-13; Women's; Chief Editor Bent Arnesen; circ. 48,477.

**Norsk Ukeblad:** POB 5001 Majorstuen, 0301 Oslo; tel. 22-96-15-00; fax 22-96-13-81; family weekly; Chief Editor Ola Chr. Nissen; circ. 232,000.

**Det Nye:** POB 5001 Majorstuen, 0301 Oslo; tel. 22-94-10-00; fax 22-11-56-81; young women's monthly; Chief Editor Kristin Ma Berg; circ. 69,399.

**Programbladet:** POB 1180 Sentrum, 0107 Oslo; tel. 22-31-03-10; fax 22-31-04-55; f. 1946; radio and television weekly; Editor Øyvind Risvik; circ. 49,761.

**Romantikk:** POB 148 Kalbakken, 0902 Oslo; tel. 22-25-71-90; fax 22-16-50-59; romantic weekly; Editor Gustav M. Galåsen; circ. 52,000.

**Se og Hør:** POB 1164 Sentrum, 0107 Oslo; tel. 22-41-51-80; telex 71088; fax 22-41-51-70; f. 1978; news weekly (radio and TV); Chief Editors Knut Håvik, Odd J. Nelvik; circ. 371,954.

**Shape-Up:** POB 5001 Majorstuen, 0301 Oslo; tel. 22-94-10-00; fax 22-11-30-40; 11 a year; health and beauty; Editor Eva Sundene Lyngaas; circ. 22,784.

**TOPP:** POB 1164 Sentrum, 0107 Oslo; tel. 22-41-51-80; fax 22-42-49-09; monthly; for young people aged between 10 and 17 years; Editors Odd J. Nelvik, Knut Haavik; circ. 43,337.

**Vi Menn:** POB 5001 Majorstuen, 0301 Oslo; tel. 22-96-15-00; fax 22-96-13-82; men's weekly; Chief Editor Svein E. Hildonen; circ. 124,400.

## SPECIALIST PERIODICALS

**Batmagasinet:** POB 250 Økern, 0510 Oslo; tel. 22-63-60-00; fax 22-63-61-75; 10 a year; boating; Editor Ingvar Johnsen; circ. 28,555.

**Båtnytt:** POB 2705 St Hanshaugen, 0131 Oslo; tel. 22-38-28-10; fax 22-38-40-02; f. 1975; monthly; sailing; Editor Morten Jensen; circ. 12,242.

**Bil:** POB 9247 Vaterland, 0134 Oslo; tel. 22-68-03-13; fax 22-68-20-85; 10 a year; motoring; Editor Kjell-Magne Aalbergsjø; circ. 52,576.

**Bondebladet:** POB 9367 Grønland, 0135 Oslo; tel. 22-05-47-67; fax 22-17-25-05; f. 1974; weekly; farming; Editor Bendik Bendiksen; circ. 96,308.

**Buskap og Avdrått:** POB 4123, 2301 Hamar; tel. (65) 26-028; fax (65) 33-680; f. 1959; quarterly; cattle-farming; Editor Hans André Hals; circ. 32,316.

**Bygge og Bo:** POB 1990 Nordnes, 5024 Bergen; tel. 55-54-74-00; fax 55-54-75-00; construction; circ. 38,910.

**Datatid:** POB 293 Økern, 0511 Oslo; tel. 22-63-60-00; fax 22-63-60-50; f. 1979; computers and information technology (aimed at professional users); monthly; Editor Eirik Rossen; circ. 16,347.

**Elektrikeren:** Youngsgt. 11, 0181 Oslo; tel. 22-03-10-50; fax 22-20-20-70; monthly; electricity and electronics; Editor Nils Waag; circ. 30,371.

**Falken:** POB 154, 1346 Gjettum; tel. 67-54-48-75; fax 67-54-47-96; quarterly; cars; circ. 98,873.

**Finansforum:** POB 9234 Grønland, 0134 Oslo; tel. 22-17-01-40; fax 22-17-06-90; f. 1922; monthly; bank employees and management; Editor Kjersti Aronsen; circ. 30,507.

**Fjell og Vidde:** Stortingsgt. 28, POB 1963 Vika, 0125 Oslo; tel. 22-83-25-50; fax 22-83-24-78; 7 a year; organ of Mountain Touring Asscn; circ. 128,184.

**Fotball:** POB 5001 Majorstuen, 0301 Oslo; tel. 22-96-15-00; fax 22-96-11-02; 8 a year; for football players and spectators; Editor Øyvind Steen Jensen; circ. 95,495.

**Fritidsbåten:** POB 170 Sentrum, 0102 Oslo; tel. 22-33-96-00; fax 22-33-96-10; quarterly; leisure boats; circ. 24,200.

**Gjør det Selv i Hjemmet:** Maridalsvn 139A, 0461 Oslo; tel. 22-38-28-10; fax 22-37-55-48; monthly; for do-it-yourself enthusiasts; Chief Editor Aksel Brinck; circ. 27,259.

NORWAY
*Directory*

**Hagen for alle:** POB 2705 St Hanshaugen, 0131 Oslo; tel. 22-38-28-10; fax 22-37-55-48; monthly; gardening; Editor ULLA HASSELMARK; circ. 24,724.

**Hjelpepleieren:** POB 151 Bryn, 0611 Oslo; tel. 22-64-13-50; fax 22-64-56-02; nursing; 16 a year; circ. 43,113.

**Hundesport:** POB 0163 Bryn, 0611 Oslo; tel. 22-65-60-00; monthly; for dog-owners; circ. 50,000.

**Ingeniør-Nytt:** POB 6754, Rodeløkka, 0503 Oslo; tel. 22-09-75-00; fax 22-09-75-99; weekly; engineering, architecture; circ. 52,010.

**Jakt & Fiske:** POB 94, 1364 Hvalstad; tel. 66-78-38-60; fax 66-90-15-87; monthly; hunting and angling; Editor VIGGO KRISTIANSEN; circ. 79,578.

**Kapital:** Strandvn 5, 1324 Lysaker; tel. 67-58-28-50; fortnightly; business, management; circ. 46,000.

**Kommuniké:** POB 9202, 0134 Oslo; tel. 22-17-33-55; fax 22-17-20-80; f. 1936; 16 a year; organ of Norwegian Confederation of Municipal Employees; Editor AUDUN HOPLAND; circ. 39,071.

**Kontor:** A/S Kobo, POB 14 Røa, 0701 Oslo; tel. 22-52-44-60; fax 22-52-24-80; f. 1977; quarterly; business; Editor THOR O. SANDBERG; circ. 140,000.

**Me'a:** Pir-Senteret, 7005 Trondheim; tel. 73-52-96-80; fax 73-53-47-42; f. 1946; 6 a year; organ of Norwegian Fishermen's Asscn; Editor JON LAURITZEN; circ. 18,960.

**Motor:** POB 494 Sentrum, 0105 Oslo; tel. 22-34-15-60; fax 22-33-21-76; monthly; motoring, travel and leisure; Editor SVEIN OLA HOPE; circ. 445,000.

**Norsk Hagetidend:** POB 9008 Grønland, 0133 Oslo; tel. 22-17-33-60; fax 22-17-23-19; f. 1885; monthly; gardening; Editor KNUT LØNØ; circ. 41,878.

**Norsk Landbruk:** POB 9303 Grønland, 0135 Oslo; tel. 22-17-33-40; fax 22-17-38-81; f. 1882; 22 a year; agriculture, horticulture and forestry; Editor-in-Chief STEIN HOSET; circ. 17,328.

**Norsk Skoleblad:** Rosenkrantzgt. 15, 0160 Oslo; tel. 22-41-58-75; f. 1934; weekly; teachers; Editor KNUT HOVLAND; circ. 64,600.

**Økonomisk Rapport:** POB 493 Sentrum, 0105 Oslo; tel. 22-94-12-00; fax 22-42-48-43; 22 a year; economics; circ. 31,445.

**Skogeieren:** POB 1438 Vika, 0115 Oslo; tel. 22-83-47-00; fax 22-83-40-47; f. 1914; 16 a year; forestry; Editor KÅRE WEDUL; circ. 54,000.

**Skolefokus:** Wergelandsvn 15, 0167 Oslo; tel. 22-03-00-00; fax 22-42-65-87; 22 a year; teaching; circ. 20,154.

**Snø og Ski:** Kongevn 5, 0390 Oslo; tel. 22-92-32-00; fax 22-92-32-50; quarterly; winter and summer sports; Editor WANDA WIDERØE; circ. 42,000.

**Teknisk Ukeblad** (Technology Review Weekly): POB 2476 Solli, 0202 Oslo; tel. 22-94-76-00; fax 22-94-76-01; f. 1854; technology, business, management, marketing and economics journal; Editor-in-Chief ERIK B. OLIMB; circ. 75,000.

**Tidsskriftet Sykepleien:** POB 2633 St Hanshaugen, 0131 Oslo; tel. 22-04-33-04; fax 22-38-35-36; f. 1914; 27 a year; health personnel, nursing; Chief Editor MORTEN E. MATHIESEN; circ. 51,094.

**Utsyn:** Grensen 19, 0159 Oslo; tel. 22-42-91-30; 38 a year; organ of Norsk Luthersk Misjonssamband; circ. 30,000.

**Villmarksliv:** POB 5928 Majorstuen, 0308 Oslo; tel. 22-96-13-87; fax 22-96-13-09; f. 1972; monthly; angling, hunting, photography; Chief Editor DAG KJELSAAS; circ. 95,000.

### NEWS AGENCIES

**Bulls Pressetjeneste A/S:** Ebbelsgt. 3, 0183 Oslo; tel. 22-20-56-01; fax 22-20-49-78; Man. TORMOD WANG.

**Norsk Presse Service A/S** (Norwegian Press Services): Sørkedalsvn 10A, POB 5402 Majorstua, 0304 Oslo; tel. 22-69-16-00; fax 22-69-74-00; f. 1960; Editor-in-Chief PER R. MORTENSEN.

**A/S Norsk Telegrambyrå—NTB** (Norwegian News Agency): Holbergs gt. 1, POB 6817, St Olavs pl., 0130 Oslo; tel. 22-03-44-00; telex 21586; fax 22-03-44-50; f. 1867; Editor-in-Chief THOR VIKSVEEN.

#### Foreign Bureaux

**Agence France-Presse (AFP):** c/o NTB, Holbergsgt. 1, POB 6817 St Olavs pl., 0130 Oslo; tel. 22-03-44-00; telex 21586; fax 22-20-12-29; Correspondent OLE LUDVIG NYMOEN.

**Associated Press (AP)** (USA): Holbergsgt. 1, 0166 Oslo; tel. 22-20-10-30; telex 71019; fax 22-20-52-80; Bureau Chief ERIK A. WOLD.

**Deutsche Presse-Agentur (dpa)** (Germany): Holbergsgt. 1, 0166 Oslo; tel. 22-03-44-00; fax 22-20-12-29; Editor TROND BØRREHAUG HANSEN.

**Informatsionnoye Telegrafnoye Agentstvo Rossii—Telegrafnoye Agentstvo Suverennykh Stran (ITAR—TASS)** (Russia): Fougstadsgt. 9, 0173 Oslo; tel. 08-10-47-22; fax 22-60-70-52; Correspondent IGOR B. PSHENICHNIKOV.

**Inter Press Service (IPS)** (Italy): Holbergsgt. 1, 0166 Oslo; tel. 22-11-50-80; fax 22-11-50-95; Dir PER-ASLAK ERTRESVÅG.

**Reuters Norge A/S:** Rosenkrantz gt. 22, 0160 Oslo; tel. 22-42-50-41; telex 74357; fax 22-42-50-32; Correspondents STELLA BUGGE, ALISTER DOYLE.

**Rossiyskoye Informatsionnoye Agentstvo—Novosti (RIA-Novosti)** (Russia): Thomas Heftyesgt. 4, 0272 Oslo; tel. 22-43-43-72; telex 71791; fax 22-55-65-20; Editor ALEKSANDR GORNOV.

**United Press International (UPI)** (USA): Holbergsgt. 1, 0166 Oslo; tel. 22-03-44-00; fax 22-20-12-29.

### PRESS ASSOCIATIONS

**Norsk Presseforbund** (Norwegian Press Asscn): Prinsensgt. 1, POB 46 Sentrum, 0101 Oslo; tel. 22-41-56-80; fax 22-41-19-80; f. 1910; asscn of newspapermen, editors and journalists; Pres. THOR BJARNE BORE; Sec.-Gen. GUNNAR GRAN.

**Norsk Journalistlag** (Norwegian Union of Journalists): Storgt. 14, 0184 Oslo; tel. 22-17-01-17; fax 22-17-17-82; f. 1946; Sec.-Gen. TORE KRISTIAN ANDERSEN; 5,839 mems.

**Norske Avisers Landsforening** (Norwegian Newspaper Publishers' Asscn): Stortorvet 2, 0155 Oslo; tel. 22-86-12-00; fax 22-86-12-01; Man. Dir ARNE JORGENSEN.

**Den Norske Fagpresses Forening** (Specialized Press Asscn): Rådhusgt. 4, 0151 Oslo; tel. 22-42-43-70; fax 22-33-40-93.

**Ukepressen** (Norwegian Magazine Publishers' Asscn): POB 76, 1343 Eiksmarka; tel. 67-14-81-26; fax 67-14-93-15; Exec. Dir ØYSTEIN PYTTE.

## Publishers

**AD-NOTAM Gyldendal:** Universitetsgt. 14, POB 6730 St Olavs pl., 0130 Oslo; tel. 22-03-43-00; fax 22-03-43-05; f. 1992; university textbooks; Man. Dir FREDRIK NISSEN.

**Alma Mater:** Allègt. 26, POB 4213 Nygårdstangen, 5028 Bergen; tel. 55-31-96-36; fax 55-31-84-68; f. 1985; general, scientific and regional; Publr KNUT LIE.

**Altera Forlag A/S:** POB 2657 St Hanshaugen, 0131 Oslo; tel. 22-56-95-90; fax 22-56-50-88; f. 1983; illustrated children's, art, poetry, international co-productions; Man. Dir KYRIAKOS CHRYSOSTOMIDIS.

**Ansgar Forlag/Atheneum Forlag A/S:** Nesset, 1433 Vinterbro; tel. 64-97-80-00; fax 64-97-80-01; f. 1934; general, fiction, travel, children's, religion; Man. SVENN OTTO BRECHAN.

**Ariel Lydbokforlag:** Fred. Olsensgt. 5, POB 1153 Sentrum, 0107 Oslo; tel. 22-33-57-09; fax 22-41-19-88; audiocassettes; Chief Editors INGER SCHJOLDAGER, MARGARETE WIESE.

**H. Aschehoug & Co (W. Nygaard):** Sehestedsgt. 3, POB 363 Sentrum, 0102 Oslo; tel. 22-40-04-00; fax 22-20-63-95; f. 1872; general non-fiction, fiction, reference, children's, educational, textbooks; Man. Dir WILLIAM NYGÅRD; Asst Man. Dir ERIK HOLST.

**Aventura Forlag A/S:** St Olavs pl., POB 6725, 0130 Oslo; tel. 22-20-47-00; fax 22-20-47-05; f. 1982; fiction, general non-fiction, art books, handbooks, children's; Man. Dir ØIVIND ARNEBERG.

**Bedriftsøkonomens Forlag A/S:** POB 9047 Grønland, 0133 Oslo; tel. 22-17-13-80; fax 22-17-06-00; f. 1946; non-fiction, educational, textbooks; Man. Dir KAI SOLHEIM.

**Bladkompaniet A/S:** Stålfjæra 5, POB 148 Kalbakken, 0902 Oslo; tel. 22-25-71-90; fax 22-16-50-59; f. 1915; general fiction, non-fiction, paperbacks, comics, magazines; Publr CLAUS HUITFELDT; Man. Dir OLE WÅGENES; Editorial Dir FINN ARNESEN.

**Boksenteret A/S:** Rådhusgt. 24, POB 383 Sentrum, 0102 Oslo; tel. 22-42-00-69; fax 22-33-61-70; f. 1985; illustrated, tourism, non-fiction, calendars; Man. Dir ERIK PETTERSEN.

**F. Bruns Bokhandel og Forlag A/S:** Kongensgt. 10, POB 476, 7001 Trondheim; tel. 73-51-00-22; fax 73-50-93-20; f. 1873; local history, technology; Publr FRIDTHJOV BRUN.

**J. W. Cappelens Forlag A/S:** Mariboesgt. 13, POB 350 Sentrum, 0101 Oslo; tel. 22-36-50-00; fax 22-36-50-40; f. 1829; general, educational, popular science, fiction, maps, children's, encyclopaedias; Chair. SIGMUND STRØMME; Man. Dir SINDRE GULDVOG.

**Bonnier Carlsen Forlag A/S:** POB 9153 Grønland, 0134 Oslo; tel. 22-20-49-00; fax 22-20-49-80; f. 1989; children's books; Man. Dir JON DAMMANN.

**N. W. Damm og Søn A/S:** Tordenskioldsgt. 6B, 0055 Oslo; tel. 22-47-11-00; telex 77074; fax 22-47-11-49; f. 1843; children's, reference, handbooks; Man. Dir TOM HARALD JENSSEN.

**Eide Forlag A/S:** POB 4081 Dreggen, 5023 Bergen; tel. 55-32-90-40; fax 55-31-90-18; f. 1945; general, children's, textbooks, fiction, non-fiction; Publr TRINE KOLDERUP FLATEN; Man. Dir ROALD FLATEN.

**Elander Norge A/S:** Brobekkvn 80, POB 1156 Sentrum, 0107 Oslo; tel. 22-63-64-00; fax 22-63-65-94; f. 1844; legislation, magazines, catalogues; Dir BJØRN HAGEN.

**Ex Libris Forlag A/S:** POB 2130, Grünerløkka, 0505 Oslo; tel. 22-38-44-50; fax 22-38-51-60; f. 1982; fiction, non-fiction, children's, calendars; Publr ØYVIND HAGEN; Editor-in-Chief TURID LØVSKAR.

**Fabritius Forlag:** Brobekkvn 80, POB 1156 Sentrum, 0107 Oslo; tel. 22-63-64-00; fax 22-63-65-94; f. 1844; legislation, magazines, catalogues, electronic information services; Dir BJØRN HAGEN.

**Forlaget Fag og Kultur:** Biskop Jens Nilssønsgt. 5A, 0659 Oslo; tel. 22-68-36-30; fax 22-68-06-25; f. 1987; reference; Man. Dir KÅRE BERGLAND.

**Falken Forlag:** Osterhaugsgt. 8, 0183 Oslo; tel. 22-20-86-40; f. 1947; fiction, non-fiction; Man. Dir KIRSTI KRISTIANSEN.

**Fonna Forlag:** POB 6912 St Olavs pl., 0130 Oslo; tel. 22-20-13-03; fax 22-20-12-01; f. 1940; general, fiction; Man. Dir JOHN F. SØRBØ.

**John Grieg Forlag A/S:** Våkleiva 133, POB 84, 5062 Bønes, Bergen; tel. 55-12-12-12; fax 55-12-00-05; f. 1721; children's books, art, education, aquaculture; Publr SVEIN SKOTHEIM.

**Grøndahl og Dreyers Forlag A/S:** Fred. Olsensgt. 5, POB 1153 Sentrum, 0107 Oslo; tel. 22-33-58-50; fax 22-33-52-95; f. 1991, following merger of Grøndahl og Søn Forlag A/S (f. 1812) and Dreyers Forlag A/S (f. 1942); general literature, fiction, art reproductions, nature, cultural history, law; Man. Dir KJELL HJERTØ.

**Gyldendal Norsk Forlag:** POB 6860 St Olavs pl., 0130 Oslo; tel. 22-03-41-00; telex 72880; fax 22-03-41-05; f. 1925; general, non-fiction, fiction, biography, religion, cookery, school and university textbooks, children's, manuals; Man. Dir NILS KÅRE JACOBSEN.

**Hjemmets Bokforlag A/S:** Tordenskildsgt. 6B, POB 1755 Vika, 0122 Oslo; tel. 22-94-15-00; fax 22-36-20-54; f. 1981; international fiction, children's books, encyclopaedias and non-fiction; Man. Dir CATO PRANER; Man. Editor GERHARD ANTHUN.

**Kolibri Forlag A/S:** Huk aveny 2B, POB 33 Bygdøy, 0211 Oslo; tel. 22-43-87-78; fax 22-44-77-40; f. 1982; general non-fiction, cookery, children's, humour, leisure; Publr ELSE LILL BJØNNES.

**Kunnskapsforlaget:** POB 6736 St Olavs pl., 0130 Oslo; tel. 22-03-66-00; fax 22-03-66-05; f. 1975; encyclopaedias, dictionaries; Man. Dir LARS BUCHER-JOHANNESSEN; Editor-in-Chief PETTER HENRIKSEN.

**Libretto Forlag A/S:** Lauritz Sands vn 16B, POB 18, 1343 Eiksmarka; tel. 67-14-98-77; f. 1990; children's, humour and handbooks; Publr TOM THORSTEINSEN.

**Lunde Forlag og Bokhandel A/S:** Grensen 19, 0159 Oslo; tel. 22-42-91-30; telex 74185; fax 22-42-04-91; f. 1905; religious, general, children's; Man. Dir TORSTEIN LINDHJEM.

**Luther Forlag:** Akersgt. 47, POB 6640 St Olavs pl., 0129 Oslo; tel. 22-33-06-08; fax 22-42-10-00; f. 1974; religious, fiction, general; Dir KURT HJEMDAL.

**Ernst G. Mortensen Bokforlag:** Sørkedalsv 10A, POB 5461 Majorstua, 0305 Oslo; tel. 22-96-15-00; fax 22-96-13-09; f. 1941; fiction, non-fiction, children's; Man. Dir RUNAR WARHUS.

**NKI Forlaget:** Hans Burumsvn 30, POB 111, 1341 Bekkestua; tel. 67-58-88-00; fax 67-58-19-02; f. 1972; textbooks for secondary and technical schools and colleges; Publr MARIT ANMARKRUD.

**NKS—Forlaget:** POB 5853 Majorstua, 0308 Oslo; tel. 22-56-85-00; fax 22-56-68-20; f. 1971; educational, textbooks; Publr HALLSTEIN LAUPSA; Editorial Dir REIDAR INDRELID.

**Norsk Bokreidingslag L/L:** POB 2672, 5026 Møhlenpris; tel. 55-99-15-25; f. 1939; fiction, folklore, linguistics, cultural history; Man. JON ASKELAND.

**Det Norske Samlaget:** POB 4672 Sofienberg, 0506 Oslo; tel. 22-68-76-00; fax 22-68-75-02; f. 1868; general literature, fiction, poetry, children's, textbooks; Man. Dir AUDUN HESKESTAD.

**Forlaget Oktober A/S:** Kr. Augustsgt. 11, POB 6848, St Olavs pl., 0130 Oslo; tel. 22-20-77-60; fax 22-20-77-65; f. 1970; fiction, politics, social and cultural books; Publr GEIR BERDAHL.

**Pax Forlag A/S:** Bygdøy allé 9, POB 2336 Solli, 0201 Oslo; tel. 22-55-70-70; fax 22-55-41-83; f. 1964; fiction, non-fiction, feminism, social sciences; Man. Dir BJØRN SMITH-SIMONSEN.

**Sambåndet Forlag:** Søre Bildøy, 5353 Straume; tel. 56-32-09-00; fax 56-32-06-01; f. 1945; religion, children's, fiction; Dir INGAR HJELSET.

**Scandinavian University Press/Universitetsforlaget:** Kolstadgt. 1, POB 2959 Tøyen, 0608 Oslo; tel. 22-57-53-00; fax 22-57-53-53; f. 1950; publishers to the Universities of Oslo, Bergen and Tromsø and various learned societies; school books, university textbooks, specialized journals; Man. Dir TRYGVE RAMBERG.

**Chr. Schibsteds Forlag:** Akersgt. 32, POB 1178 Sentrum, 0107 Oslo; tel. 22-86-30-00; telex 71230; fax 22-42-54-92; f. 1839; reference, biographies, handbooks, hobbies, crafts, children's books, guides, maps; Man. Dir PER DAMSGAARD.

**Skolebokforlaget A/S:** Fred. Olsensgt. 5, 0153 Oslo; tel. 22-33-58-54; fax 22-33-58-05; f. 1979; educational; Man. Dir HANS B. BUTENSCHØN.

**Snøfugl Forlag:** 7084 Melhus; tel. 72-87-00-55; fax 72-87-12-33; f. 1972; fiction, general; Man. ÅSMUND SNØFUGL.

**Solum Forlag A/S:** Hoffsvn 8, POB 140 Skøyen, 0212 Oslo; tel. 22-50-04-00; fax 22-50-14-53; f. 1973; fiction, human sciences, general; Man. Dir KNUT ENDRE SOLUM.

**Stabenfeldt Forlag:** Haugesundsgt. 43, POB 1544 Kjelvene, 4004 Stavanger; tel. 51-52-15-53; telex 30761; fax 51-52-62-17; f. 1920; general fiction, adventure, reference; Man. Dir TOR TJELDFLÅT.

**TANO A/S:** Stortorvet 10, 0155 Oslo; tel. 22-42-55-00; fax 22-42-01-64; f. 1933; professional, educational, general non-fiction, reference; Gen. Man. LAILA STANGE.

**Tiden Norsk Forlag:** POB 8813 Youngsgt., 0028 Oslo; tel. 22-42-95-20; fax 22-42-64-58; f. 1933; general, political, fiction, children's; Man. Dir LIV LYSAKER; Dir PAUL HEDLUND.

**Vett og Viten A/S:** Drammensvn 48, POB 4, 1321 Stabekk; tel. 67-12-50-90; fax 67-12-50-94; f. 1987; medical, technical and engineering textbooks; Publr JAN LIEN.

**Yrkesopplaering ANS:** Kristian IV's gt. 1, POB 6767 St Olavs pl., 0130 Oslo; tel. 22-20-52-30; fax 22-33-68-73; f. 1979; educational, technical; Publr BIRGER MØLBACH.

### PUBLISHERS' ASSOCIATION

**Den norske Forleggerforening** (Norwegian Publishers' Asscn): Øvre Vollgt. 15, 0158 Oslo; tel. 22-42-13-55; fax 22-33-38-30; f. 1895; Chair. TRYGVE RAMBERG; Man. Dir PAUL MARTENS RØTHE; 51 mem. firms.

## Radio and Television

In 1993 the number of radio receivers in use was estimated at some 3.3m.; in the same year there were 1,521,819 television licences.

**Norsk Rikskringkasting (NRK)** (Norwegian Broadcasting Corpn): Bj. Bjørnsons pl. 1, 0340 Oslo; tel. 22-45-90-50; telex 76820; fax 22-45-74-40; autonomous public corpn; Chair. of Govs TRYGVE RAMBERG; Dir.-Gen. EINAR FØRDE; Dir of Radio TOR FUGLEVIK; Dir of Television KENT NILSSEN.

### RADIO

The NRK operates four medium-wave, four short-wave and 46 VHF transmitters, and 1,700 low-power relay stations. There are three national programmes and 18 regional programmes, one of which is in the language of the Sámi (Lappish). There is an international service, Radio Norway International.

A private commercial station (P4), based in Lillehammer, was launched in 1993.

### TELEVISION

There are 45 main transmitters with 2,480 low-power relay stations. Transmissions are obtainable by about 99% of the population.

In the south-east it is possible to receive Swedish TV programmes; Finnish and Russian transmissions can be received in the north, Danish and Swedish programmes on the south coast and British programmes on the south-west coast. There is also a cable television service and satellite television can be received by about 40% of the population.

**TV2:** Bergen; f. 1992; private and commercial television service, with public service obligations.

**TV Norge:** Oslo; private satellite television service.

**TV+:** Oslo; f. 1995; private cable television service; wholly owned by Schibsted AS.

## Finance

Norway's banking system is of comparatively recent date. The central bank, the Bank of Norway, has existed in its present form since 1816; the first savings bank was founded in 1822, and the first commercial bank began operations in 1848. Commercial banking gained impetus during the industrial upsurge in the second half of the 19th century. Foreign-owned banks were permitted to operate in Norway from the beginning of 1985. In 1992/93 there were 20 commercial banks (comprising the major banks, some large regional banks and a number of smaller regional and local banks) and 133 savings banks. There were also 10 publicly-financed government banks.

Until 1991 the two largest banks in Norway, Christiania Bank og Kreditkasse and Den norske Bank, had an extensive network of local offices and branches, and collectively accounted for about two-thirds of the combined total assets of the commercial banks. Substantial losses incurred by the major banks resulted in a crisis in the sector in 1991. Den norske Bank, Christiania Bank and the third largest institution, Fokus Bank, required support from the Government's newly-established Bank Insurance Fund. As a result of the interventions, the State became the owner of Christiania Bank and Fokus Bank and the majority shareholder in Den norske Bank. State intervention was also required in the savings bank sector in October 1991, when the Government Savings Banks' Guarantee Fund provided assistance for Sparebanken Midt-Norge and Sparebanken Rogaland. In 1993 the three principal commercial banks returned to profitability, and reductions in the state shareholdings in Christiania Bank and Den norske Bank were announced in November 1993 and February 1994 respectively. A further reduction was scheduled for 1995.

**Kredittilsynet** (Banking, Insurance and Securities Commission): Østensjøvn 43, POB 100 Bryn, 0611 Oslo; tel. 22-93-98-00; fax 22-63-02-26; finance inspectorate; Pres. BJØRN SKOGSTAD AAMO.

## BANKING

(cap. = capital; dep. = deposits; res = reserves; m. = millions; brs = branches; amounts in kroner).

### Central Bank

**Norges Bank:** Bankplassen 2, POB 1179 Sentrum, 0107 Oslo; tel. 22-31-60-00; telex 71369; fax 22-41-31-05; f. 1816; holds the exclusive right of note issue; cap. and res 46,641.0m., dep. 117,243.7m. (Dec. 1993); Chair. of Supervisory Board P. THYNESS; Gov. TORSTEIN MOLAND; 12 brs.

### Principal Commercial Banks

**Christiania Bank og Kreditkasse:** Middelthunsgt. 17, POB 1166 Sentrum, 0107 Oslo; tel. 22-48-50-00; telex 71043; fax 22-48-47-49; f. 1848; in 1990 absorbed Sunnmørsbanken (f. 1975) and merged with Sørlandsbanken; under state control from 1991 (state holding reduced to 69% from late 1993); subsidiaries include Norske Liv (insurance), Christiania Fonds A/S (securities brokerage) and Christiania Forvaltning A/S (fund management); cap. 3,850m., res 1,000m., dep. 81,144m. (Dec. 1993); Man. Dir BORGER A. LENTH; 150 brs.

**Fokus Bank A/S:** Vestre Rosten 77, 7005 Trondheim; tel. 72-88-20-11; telex 55050; fax 72-88-26-90; f. 1987 by merger of Bøndernes Bank, Buskerudbanken, Forretningsbanken and Vestlandbanken; merged with Tromsbanken in 1990, with Rogalandsbanken in 1991 and with Samvirkebanken in March 1993; state-owned from 1991; cap. 729.7m., res 444.7m., dep. 25,101.4m. (Dec. 1993); Chair. STEIN HOLST ANNEXSTAD; Man. Dir BJARNE BORGERSEN; 69 brs.

**Landsbanken A/S:** Youngsgt. 11, 0181 Oslo; tel. 22-03-10-00; telex 76034; fax 22-03-19-55; f. 1898; cap. 231m., res 59.1m., dep. 7,581.2m. (Dec. 1994); Chair. JAN BALSTAD; Pres. JAN TORE BERG-KNUTSEN; 12 brs.

**Nordlandsbanken A/S:** Storgt. 38, 8002 Bodø; tel. 75-52-15-20; fax 64072; fax 75-52-76-99; f. 1893; cap. 309.8m., res 362.5m., dep. 9,503.2m. (Dec. 1994); Man. Dir TORBJØRN HAUG; 21 brs.

**Den norske Bank A/S:** Stranden 21, POB 1171 Sentrum, 0107 Oslo; tel. 22-48-10-50; telex 78175; fax 22-48-18-70; f. 1990 by merger of Bergen Bank (f. 1975) and Den norske Creditbank (f. 1857); 72% state-owned (proportion to be reduced in 1995); cap. 5,875m., res 2,132m., dep. 114,619m. (Dec. 1993); Man. Dir FINN A. HVISTENDAHL; 150 brs.

**Oslobanken AS:** POB 1368 Vika, 0114 Oslo; tel. 22-94-16-00; telex 79102; fax 22-42-40-04; acquired Norwegian subsidiary of Banque Paribas (France) in 1989; cap. 318.5m., res −91.2m., dep. 4,691m. (Dec. 1991); Pres. ERIK A. LIND.

### Principal Savings Banks

**Sparebanken Hedmark:** POB 203, 2301 Hamar; tel. 62-51-20-00; telex 19423; fax 62-53-29-75; f. 1853; cap. 880.4m., res 15.1m., dep. 7,391.2m. (Dec. 1993); Chair. HELGE NAESS RUSTAD; Man. Dir HARRY KONTERUD; 34 brs.

**Sparebanken Midt-Norge:** Kongensgt. 4, 7005 Trondheim; tel. 73-58-51-11; telex 55177; fax 73-58-64-50; f. 1823; cap. 1,434m., res 358m., dep. 14,807m. (Dec. 1993); Chair. JAN ERIK REINAS; Man. Dir FINN HAUGAN; 77 brs.

**Sparebanken Møre:** Kipervikgt. 4/6, 6002 Ålesund; tel. 70-11-30-00; telex 42193; fax 70-12-99-12; f. 1985; cap. 437.1m., res 11.2m., dep. 7,304.6m. (Dec. 1993); Chair. JOHAN W. GULLIKSEN; Man. Dir KJELL REMVIK; 55 brs.

**Sparebanken NOR (Union Bank of Norway):** Kirkegt. 18, POB 1172 Sentrum, 0107 Oslo; tel. 22-31-90-50; telex 19470; fax 22-42-13-61; f. 1985, as Sparebanken ABC, by merger of Sparebanken Oslo and Union Bank of Norway; merged with four regional savings banks in 1990; cap. 2,288m., res 2,393m., dep. 66,238m. (Dec. 1994); Chair. HANS BØ; Man. Dir KJELL O. KRAN; 180 brs.

**Sparebanken Nord Norge:** Storgt. 65, 9005 Tromsø; tel. 77-62-20-00; telex 64170; fax 77-65-84-08; f. 1989; cap. 731.5m., res 396.2m., dep. 16,599.9m. (Dec. 1993); Pres. KURT MOSBAKK; Man. Dir HANS OLAV KARDE; 110 brs.

**Sparebanken Rogaland:** Loekkevn 51, 4000 Stavanger; tel. 51-50-90-00; telex 33016; fax 51-53-47-55; f. 1839 (as Egersund Sparebank); merger (1976) of 22 savings banks; cap. 831.7m., res 90.3m., dep. 13,385.2m. (Dec. 1993); Chair. REIDAR LUND; Pres. ARNE NORHEIM; 62 brs.

**Sparebanken Sør:** POB 310, 4801 Arendal; tel. 37-02-50-00; fax 37-02-41-50; f. 1825; cap. 549.0m., res 38.8m., dep. 6,525.9m. (Dec. 1994); Chair. TOM F. EVENSEN; Man. Dir HANS A. IVERSEN; 38 brs.

**Sparebanken Vest:** 4 Kaigt., 5016 Bergen; tel. 55-21-70-00; telex 42249; fax 55-21-74-10; f. 1823 as Bergens Sparebank; merger 1982/83 of 25 savings banks; cap. 581m., res 202m., dep. 12,007m. (Dec. 1993); Man. Dir KNUT RAVNÅ; 99 brs.

### Bankers' Organizations

**Den norske Bankforening** (Norwegian Bankers' Asscn): Dronning Maudsgt. 15, POB 1489 Vika, 0116 Oslo; tel. 22-83-31-60; fax 22-83-07-51; f. 1915; Pres. and Chair. FINN A. HVISTENDAHL (Den norske Bank); Man. Dir TROND R. REINERTSEN; 25 mems.

**Sparebankforeningen i Norge** (Savings Banks Asscn): Universitetsgt. 8, POB 6772, 0130 Oslo; tel. 22-11-00-75; fax 22-36-25-33; f. 1914; Pres. KJELL REMVIK (Sparebanken Møre); Man. Dir EINAR FORSBAK; 133 mems.

## STOCK EXCHANGE

**Oslo Børs:** Tollbugt. 2, POB 460 Sentrum, 0105 Oslo; tel. 22-34-17-00; fax 22-41-65-90; f. 1819; Pres. KJELL FRØNSDAL (acting).

## INSURANCE

**Assuranceforeningen Skuld:** Stortingsgt. 18, 0161 Oslo; tel. 22-42-06-40; telex 71091; f. 1897; mutual, shipowners' protection and indemnity; res 948m.; Chair. G. FOSSEN; Man. Dir H. POULSSON.

**Gjensidige Forsikring:** Pilestredet 35, POB 6738 St Olavs pl., 0165 Oslo; tel. 22-48-08-90; telex 19036; f. 1847; merged with Forenede Norge Forsikring and Forenede Skadeforsikring in 1993; Pres. HELGE KVAMME.

**Norske Liv:** Drammensvn 21, POB 2454 Solli, 0202 Oslo; tel. 22-44-39-50; fax 22-55-79-72; f. 1844; mutual life insurance; funds 4,000m.; Chair. H. BJELKE; Man. Dir JOSTEIN SØRVOLL.

**Skibassuranseforeningen Unitas:** POB 1290 Vika, 0253 Oslo; tel. 22-55-34-00; f. 1951; mutual ship insurance; Chair. DAG KLAVENESS; Man. Dir JAN LUNDE.

**Uni Storebrand:** Håkon VII's gt. 10, POB 1380 Vika, 0114 Oslo; tel. 22-31-10-20; f. 1991 by merger of Storebrand (f. 1947) and Uni Forsikring (f. 1984); group includes life, non-life and international reinsurance operations; taken over by govt administrators in June 1992 and new holding co. (Uni Storebrand New) formed, following suspension of payments to creditors; premium income 4,740m. (life), 6,872m. (non-life), 4,702m. (international) (1992); Chair. ERIK KEISERUD; CEO PER TERJE VOLD.

**Vesta Group PLC:** Folke Bernadottesvei 50, 5020 Bergen; tel. 55-17-10-00; telex 42030; fax 55-17-18-99; f. 1884; owned by Skandia (Sweden); includes Skadeforsikringsselskapet Vesta A/S (general insurance), Vesta Liv A/S (life insurance), Vesta Finans A/S (financial services); Chair. JAN EINAR GREVE; Man. Dir JOHAN FR. ODFJELL.

**Vital Insurance:** Folke Bernadottesvei 40, 5020 Bergen; tel. 55-17-80-90; fax 55-17-86-99; f. 1990 by a merger between NKP Forsikring and Hygea; life and pension insurance; premium income 3,314m., total assets 41,802m. (1993); Chair. EGIL GADE GREVE; Pres. BJØRN ELVESTAD.

### INSURANCE ASSOCIATION

**Norges Forsikringsforbund:** Hansteensgt. 2, POB 2473 Solli, 0202 Oslo; tel. 22-04-85-00; fax 22-43-44-56; Man. Dir INGVAR STRØM.

# Trade and Industry

## TRADE COUNCIL AND CHAMBERS OF COMMERCE

**Norwegian Trade Council:** Drammensvn 40, 0243 Oslo; tel. 22-92-63-00; fax 22-92-64-00; f. 1945; promotes Norwegian exports; Man. Dir KJELL-MARTIN FREDERIKSEN.

**Bergen Chamber of Commerce and Industry:** Olav Kyrresgt. 11, 5014 Bergen; tel. 55-32-30-50; fax 55-31-03-97; f. 1915; Pres. ASBJØRN BIRKELAND; Man. Dir HELGE S. DYRNES.

**Oslo Chamber of Commerce:** Drammensvn 30, POB 2874 Solli, 0230 Oslo; tel. 22-55-74-00; fax 22-55-89-53; Man. Dir TORE B. LAURITZSEN.

**Trondhjem Handelsstands Forening:** Dronningensgt. 12, 7011 Trondheim; tel. 73-50-15-75; fax 73-52-02-46; Sec. TORKEL RANUM.

## EMPLOYERS' ASSOCIATIONS

**Næringslivets Hovedorganisasjon (NHO)** (Confederation of Norwegian Business and Industry): Middelthunsgt. 27, POB 5250 Majorstua, 0303 Oslo; tel. 22-96-50-00; telex 71434; fax 22-69-55-93; f. 1989; representative organization for industry, crafts and service industries; Pres. DIDERIK SCHNITLER; Dir-Gen. KARL GLAD; c. 12,000 mems who must also belong to the 27 affiliated national asscns, chief among which are the following:

**Byggeindustriens Landsforening** (Building): POB 11 Blindern, 0314 Oslo; tel. 22-96-55-00; fax 22-46-55-23; Admin. Dir ARNE SKJELLE.

**Fiskerinæringens Landsforening** (Fishing Industry): POB 5471 Majorstua, 0305 Oslo; tel. 22-96-50-18; fax 22-60-15-42; Admin. Dir GEIR ANDREASSEN.

**Flyselskapenes Landsforening** (Airlines): POB 5474 Majorstua, 0305 Oslo; tel. 22-96-50-60; fax 22-56-57-90; Dir TOR SODELAND.

**Grafiske Bedrifter Landsforenings** (Graphic Enterprises): Havnelageret, Langkaia 1, 0150 Oslo; tel. 22-41-21-80; fax 22-33-69-72; Admin. Dir TERJE OVERGÅRD; 340 mems.

**Landsforeningen for Bygg og Anlegg** (General Contractors): POB 128 Blindern, 0314 Oslo; tel. 22-96-55-00; fax 22-69-58-56; Admin. Dir INGE N. DOLVE; 150 mems.

**Møbel-og Innredningsprodusentenes Landsforening** (Furnishings Manufacturers): POB 5391 Majorstua, 0304 Oslo; tel. 22-96-50-50; fax 22-60-75-11; Admin. Dir YRJAR GARSHOL.

**Næringsmiddelindustriens Landsforening** (Food and Drink Industry): POB 5467 Majorstua, 0305 Oslo; tel. 22-96-50-40; fax 22-60-09-93; Admin. Dir GAUTE EGEBERG.

**Norges Bilbransjeforbund** (Motor Car Dealers and Services): Drammensvn 97, POB 7628 Skillebekk, 0205 Oslo; tel. 22-60-12-90; fax 22-56-10-50; f. 1962; Admin. Dir EIRIK HØIEN.

**Norges Elektroentreprenørforbund** (Electrical Contractors Asscn): St Olavsgt. 21B, POB 6794 St Olavs pl., 0130 Oslo; tel. 22-03-30-00; fax 22-36-09-47; Admin. Dir WILHELM A. ANDERSEN.

**Norsk Bryggeri-og Mineralvannindustris Forening** (Breweries and Soft Drink Producers): POB 7087 Homansbyen, 0306 Oslo; tel. 22-46-56-20; fax 22-60-30-04; Man. Dir ODD EINAR FOSS-SKIFTESVIK; 25 mems.

**Norsk Hotell-og Restaurantforbund** (Hotels and Restaurants): POB 5465 Majorstua, Essendrops gt. 6, 0305 Oslo; tel. 22-96-50-80; fax 22-56-96-20; Admin. Dir KJELL B. EINARSEN.

**Norske Avisers Landsforening** (Newspaper Publishers): see under The Press.

**Norske Transportbedrifters Landsforening** (Transport Companies): Sørkedalsvn 6, 0369 Oslo; tel. 22-96-50-20; fax 22-60-50-20; Admin. Dir CHRISTIAN AUBERT.

**Oljeindustriens Landsforening** (Oil Industries): Lervigsvn 32, POB 547, 4001 Stavanger; tel. 51-58-30-00; telex 33108; fax 51-56-21-05; Admin. Dir ARNE FRANCK NIELSEN.

**Oljeserviceselskapenes Landsforening:** Haakon VII's gt. 8, POB 256, 4001 Stavanger; tel. 51-52-90-10; fax 51-52-90-77; Admin. Dir KNUT STAURLAND.

**Prosess- og foredlingsindustriens Landsforening** (Processing and Manufacturing Industries): POB 2724 St Hanshaugen, 0131 Oslo; tel. 22-96-10-00; fax 22-96-10-99; Admin. Dir ARVE THORVIK.

**Rederienes Landsforening** (Coastal Shipping): see under Shipping.

**Servicebedriftenes Landsforening** (Service Industry): Essendropsgt. 6, 0368 Oslo; tel. 22-96-11-30; fax 22-96-11-39; Admin. Dir PETTER FURULAND.

**Skogbrukets Landsforening:** Stortingsgt. 30, POB 1825 Vika, 0123 Oslo; tel. 22-83-22-60; fax 22-83-21-60; Admin. Dir MILJAN ØDEGAARD.

**Teknologibedriftenes Landsforening** (Engineering Industries): POB 7072 Homansbyen, 0306 Oslo; tel. 22-46-58-20; fax 22-46-18-38; f. 1889; Pres. JAN. T. JØRGENSEN; Admin. Dir KARL NYSTERUD; 602 mems with 71,100 employees.

**Teko Landsforening** (Textile, Clothing, Shoe, Leather and Sporting Goods' Industries): Tollbugt. 3, POB 488 Sentrum, 0105 Oslo; tel. 22-42-69-30; fax 22-33-66-17; f. 1989 by merger of several asscns; Chair. HANS STRAND; Admin. Dir OLE A. HANNISDAL; 145 mems.

**Treforedlingsindustriens Bransjeforening (TFB)** (Pulp and Paper): Stensberggt. 27, 0170 Oslo; tel. 22-96-10-00; fax 22-96-10-89; f. 1988; Pres. JAN REINÅS; Admin. Dir ØISTEIN GULBRANDSEN; 40 mems.

**Handels- og Servicenæringens Hovedorganisasjon** (Federation of Commercial and Service Enterprises): Drammensvn 30, POB 2483 Solli, 0202 Oslo; tel. 22-55-82-20; fax 22-55-82-25; f. 1990 by merger of Norges Handelsstands Forbund (f. 1889) and 4 national group organizations; incl. 60 local commercial associations, 34 national branch organizations and the Secretariat of the Norwegian Chamber of Commerce; Pres. TOM WINGEREI; Man. Dir LEIF B. BJØRNSTAD.

**Norges Skogeierforbund** (Forest Owners): Stortingsgt. 30, POB 1438 Vika, 0115 Oslo; tel. 22-83-47-00; fax 22-83-40-47; f. 1913; aims to promote the economic and technical interests of the forest owners, a general forest policy in the interests of private ownership and co-operation between the affiliated associations; Man. Dir EGIL MOLTEBERG; 58,500 mems.

## TRADE UNIONS

**Akademikernes Fellesorganisasjon (AF):** Oslo; f. 1974; Pres. MAGNE SONGVOLL; 230,000 mems in 38 affiliated unions.

**Landsorganisasjonen i Norge (LO)** (Norwegian Confederation of Trade Unions): Folkets Hus, Youngsgt. 11, 0181 Oslo; tel. 22-03-10-50; fax 22-03-17-43; f. 1899; Pres. YNGVE HÅGENSEN; Treasurer SVEIN-ERIK OXHOLM; Int. Sec. JON IVAR NÅLSUND; 770,000 mems in 29 affiliated unions.

All member unions can be contacted by fax at LO, above.

The member unions are:

**Arbeiderpartiets Presseforbund** (Labour Press Union): POB 656, Tromsø; tel. 77-68-11-70; f. 1909; Pres. SVENN A. NIELSEN; 894 mems.

**Fellesforbundet** (United Federation of Trade Unions): Lilletorget 1, 0184 Oslo; tel. 22-17-42-80; fax 22-17-00-44; f. 1988; Pres. KJELL BJØRNDALEN; 153,559 mems.

**Fellesorganisasjonen for barnevernpedagoger, sosionomer og vernepleiere** (Social Educators and Social Workers): POB 4693 Sofienberg, 0506 Oslo; tel. 22-03-11-70; fax 22-03-11-14; f. 1992; Pres. ODDRUN REMVIK; Gen. Sec. KARIN ENDERUD; 11,000 mems.

**Forbundet for Ledelse og Teknikk** (Supervisors and Technical Employees): POB 8976 Youngsgt. 11, 0028 Oslo; tel. 22-03-10-29; fax 22-03-10-17; f. 1951; Pres. MAGNUS MIDTBØ; 16,025 mems.

**Handel og Kontor i Norge:** (Commercial and Office Employees): POB 491 Sentrum, 0105 Oslo; tel. 22-03-11-80; fax 22-03-12-06; f. 1908; Pres. STURE ARNTZEN; 55,607 mems.

**Hotel-og Restaurantarbeiderforbundet** (Hotel and Restaurant Workers): Storgt. 34C, 0182 Oslo; tel. 22-17-65-00; fax 22-20-73-00; f. 1931; Pres. ERLING OEN; 14,761 mems.

**Norges Offisersforbund** (Military Officers): Møllergt. 10, 0179 Oslo; tel. 22-03-10-50; fax 22-03-15-77; f. 1978; Pres. PETER A. MOE; 4,381 mems.

**Norsk Arbeidsmandsforbund** (General Workers): Møllergt. 3, 1079 Oslo; tel. 22-03-10-78; fax 22-03-10-92; f. 1895; Pres. ARNFINN NILSEN; 32,637 mems.

**Norsk Elektriker-og Kraftstasjonsforbund** (Electrical and Power Station Workers): Youngsgt. 11, 0181 Oslo; tel. 22-03-17-80; fax 22-20-20-75; f. 1918; Pres. GUNNAR GRIMNES; 26,479 mems.

**Norsk Fengselstjenestemannsforbund** (Prison Officers): Møllergt. 10, 0179 Oslo; tel. 22-03-15-88; fax 22-42-46-48; f. 1918; Pres. ROAR ØVREBØ; 2,456 mems.

**Norsk Grafisk Forbund** (Graphical Workers): POB 8913 Youngsgt., 0028 Oslo; tel. 22-03-13-00; fax 22-03-13-25; f. 1882; Pres. FINN ERIK THORESEN; 14,267 mems.

**Norsk Jernbaneforbund** (Railway Workers): Møllergt. 10, 0179 Oslo; tel. 22-03-10-50; fax 22-03-13-85; f. 1892; Pres. OVE DALSHEIM; 20,316 mems.

**Norsk Kantor og Organistforbund** (Cantors and Organists): Kvernabekkvn 26A, 5047 Fana; tel. 05-91-66-57; Pres. IVAR MAELAND; 792 mems.

**Norsk Kjemisk Industriarbeiderforbund** (Chemical Workers): Youngsgt. 11, 0181 Oslo; tel. 22-03-13-40; fax 22-03-13-60; f. 1923; Pres. ARTHUR SVENSSON; 32,186 mems.

**Norsk Kommuneforbund** (Municipal Employees): Kristian Augustsgt. 23, 0164 Oslo; tel. 22-36-47-10; fax 22-36-40-25; f. 1920; Pres. JAN DAVIDSEN; 209,257 mems.

**Norsk Lokomotivmannsforbund** (Locomotive Workers): Svingen 2, 0196 Oslo; tel. 22-68-42-50; fax 22-03-10-17; f. 1893; Pres. ØYSTEIN ASLAKSEN; 2,376 mems.

**Norsk Musikerforbund** (Musicians): Youngsgt. 11, 0181 Oslo; tel. 22-03-14-92; fax 22-03-15-77; f. 1911; Pres. TORE NORVIK; 2,299 mems.

**Norsk Næring-og Nytelsesmiddelarbeiderforbund** (Food and Allied Workers): Box 8719, Youngsgt., 0028 Oslo; tel. 22-20-66-75; fax 22-36-47-84; f. 1923; Pres. TORBJØRN DAHL; 35,000 mems.

**Norsk Olje- og Petrokjemisk Fagforbund** (Oil and Petrochemical Workers): POB 1145, 4004 Stavanger; tel. 51-56-79-80; fax 51-56-79-88; f. 1977; Pres. Lars A. Myhre; 10,262 mems.

**Norsk Postforbund** (Postal Workers): Møllergt. 10, 0179 Oslo; tel. 22-33-04-47; fax 22-42-74-86; f. 1901; Pres. Jan Inge Kvistnes; 14,001 mems.

**Norsk Sjømannsforbundet** (Seamen): Grev. Wedels pl. 7, 0151 Oslo; tel. 22-42-18-90; telex 78067; fax 22-33-66-18; f. 1910; Pres. Edvin Ramsvik; 9,356 mems.

**Norsk Tele-og Dataforbundet** (Telecommunications and Data Processing Workers): Møllergt. 10, 0179 Oslo; tel. 22-20-88-15; fax 22-42-17-00; f. 1988 by merger of Norsk Tele Tjeneste Forbund (f. 1930) and Den norske Teleorganisasjon (f. 1901); Pres. Tore Lundberg; 16,044 mems.

**Norsk Tjenestemannslag** (Civil Servants): Møllergt. 10, 0179 Oslo; tel. 22-03-10-50; fax 22-03-15-55; f. 1947; Pres. Jan Werner Hansen; 45,373 mems.

**Norsk Tolkeforbund** (Interpreters): POB 2804 Tøyen, 0608 Oslo; f. 1986; Pres. Hanne Mørk; 64 mems.

**Norsk Transportarbeiderforbund** (Transport Workers): Youngsgt. 11, 0181 Oslo; tel. 22-20-40-55; fax 22-11-35-72; f. 1896; Pres. Walter Kolstad; 15,579 mems.

**Norsk Treindustriarbeiderforbund** (Wood Workers): Henrik Ibsensgt. 7, 0179 Oslo; tel. 22-03-13-90; fax 22-03-13-95; f. 1904; Pres. Anton Solheim; 4,970 mems.

**Den norske Postorganisasjon** (Postal Clerical Workers): Møllergt. 10, 0179 Oslo; tel. 22-03-15-80; f. 1884; Pres. Morten Øye; 15,406 mems.

**Skolenes Landsforbund** (School Employees): Møllergt. 20, 0179 Oslo; tel. 22-03-13-62; fax 22-03-13-83; f. 1982; Pres. Gro Standnes; 3,290 mems.

**Statstjenestemannskartellet** (Government Employees): Møllergt. 10, 0179 Oslo; tel. 22-03-15-78; fax 22-03-15-55; f. 1939; Pres. Terje Moe Gustavsen; 103,804 mems.

**Yrkesorganisasjonenes Sentralforbund (YS):** Oslo; f. 1977; Pres. Eva Bjøreng; 200,000 mems in 18 affiliated unions.

### Co-operative Association

**Norges Kooperative Landsforening** (Co-op Norway): POB 1173 Sentrum, 0107 Oslo; tel. 22-89-95-00; telex 19450; fax 22-41-14-42; f. 1906; Chair. Arnfinn Hofstad; Man. Dir and Gen. Man. Rolf Rønning; 380 local affiliated co-operative societies with 620,000 mems.

### STATE-OWNED ENTERPRISES

**Norsk Forsvarsteknologi (NFT) A/S:** POB 1003, 3601 Kongsberg; tel. 32-73-82-00; fax 32-73-85-86; f. 1814 (fmrly Kongsberg Våpenfabrikk); aerospace, defence systems and maritime systems; Chair. Kjeld Rimberg; Man. Dir Jan T. Jørgensen; 2,100 employees.

**Norsk Hydro a.s.:** Bygdøy allé 2, 0240 Oslo; tel. 22-43-21-00; telex 72948; fax 22-43-27-25; f. 1905; 51% state-owned; large industrial corporation; exploration and production of oil and gas, chemicals, fertilizers, etc.; Chair. Torvild Aakvaag; Pres. Egil Myklebust.

**Hydro Aluminium A/S:** Drammensvn 264, Vakerø, POB 80, 1321 Stabekk; tel. 22-73-81-00; telex 72948; fax 22-43-27-25; f. 1986; owned by Norsk Hydro; produces aluminium and rolled and extruded aluminium products; Pres. Dag Flaa.

**A/S Olivin:** 6146 Åheim; tel. 70-02-49-00; fax 70-02-42-66; f. 1948; 99.99% state-owned; olivine sand, stone, refractory bricks, ballast material; Chair. John M. Kleven; Man. Dir Ola Overlie; Deputy Man. Dir Helge Ove Larsen; 200 employees.

**Raufoss A/S:** 2831 Raufoss; tel. 61-15-20-00; fax 61-15-25-99; manufacture of defence and mechanical products, and vehicle components; Chair. Hans O. Bjøntegaard; Man. Dir Bjarne Gravdahl.

**Statoil (Den norske stats oljeselskap A/S):** 4035 Stavanger; tel. 51-80-80-80; telex 73600; fax 51-80-70-94; f. 1972; production and refining of petroleum and natural gas, manufacture of petrochemicals and plastics (merged petrochemicals divison in 1994 with that of the Finnish state company, Neste Oy); Chair. Helge Kvamme; Pres. Harald Norvik.

# Transport

### RAILWAYS

At 1 January 1993 there were 4,023 km of state railways (standard gauge), of which 2,422 km was electrified.

**Norges Statsbaner (NSB)** (Norwegian State Railways): 0048 Oslo; tel. 22-36-80-00; telex 71168; fax 22-36-71-52; f. 1854 as private line; govt-owned; Man. Dir K. Rambjør.

### ROADS

At 31 December 1993 there were 90,503 km of public roads in Norway, of which 512 km were motorways and 26,406 km were national main roads.

**Vegdirektoratet:** Grensevn 92, 0604 Oslo; tel. 22-63-95-00; fax 22-63-97-68; f. 1864; Dir Olav Søfteland.

### SHIPPING

At the end of 1993 the Norwegian merchant fleet numbered 1,691 vessels, with gross tonnage of 20,965,000 tons (including vessels on the Norwegian International Ship Register, established in July 1987—790 vessels at 1 January 1994).

### Principal Companies

**Actinor Shipping AS:** Rådhusgt. 27, 0158 Oslo; tel. 22-42-78-30; fax 22-42-72-04.

**Bergesen d.y. A/S:** Drammensvn 106, POB 7600 Skillebekk, 0205 Oslo; tel. 22-12-05-05; telex 71172; fax 22-12-05-00; f. 1935; Chair. Petter C. G. Sundt; Man. Dir Morten Sig. Bergesen; tankers, oil-ore vessels, ore-bulk-oil and liquefied gas carriers; 44 vessels, 8.6m. dwt.

**Bergshav AS:** POB 8, 4891 Grimstad; tel. 37-04-42-22; fax 37-04-46-22.

**A/S Billabong:** C. Sundtsgt. 17–19, Grieg Gaarden, POB 781, 5002 Bergen; tel. 55-57-69-50; telex 40576; fax 55-57-69-10; operates a fleet of bulk carriers; 17 vessels, 554,000 dwt.

**Bona Shipping AS:** POB 470 Sentrum, 0105 Oslo; tel. 22-31-00-00; fax 22-31-00-01.

**Bulls Tankrederi A/S:** POB 271, 3236 Sandefjord; tel. 33-46-23-90; fax 33-46-88-31.

**A/S Thor Dahl:** POB 2010, 3201 Sandefjord; tel. 33-46-52-00; fax 33-46-72-00; f. 1887; Owner Thor Christensen; 10 vessels, 1.3m. dwt.

**Farsund Shipping A.S.:** POB 68, 4551 Farsund; tel. 38-39-20-55; fax 38-39-20-77.

**Christian Haaland A/S:** POB 128, 5501 Haugesund; tel. 52-72-30-33; telex 42206; fax 52-72-30-87; 7 vessels, 304,320 dwt.

**Havtor Management A/S:** Kronprinsesse Märthas pl. 1, POB 1374 Vika, 0114 Oslo; tel. 22-41-10-85; telex 71161; fax 22-42-49-14; carriers for liquefied gas, chemicals, ores and other bulk materials; 28 vessels, 1.0m. dwt.

**Leif Høegh & Co A/S:** Wergelandsvn 7, POB 2596 Solli, 0203 Oslo; tel. 22-86-97-00; telex 79350; fax 22-20-14-08; f. 1927; vessels for the transport of containers, liquefied gas, ores and other bulk materials, car and roll-on/roll-off ships and cargo-liners; worldwide services; Chair. Westye Høegh; Pres. Thor J. Guttormsen; 24 vessels, 857,400 dwt.

**Jahre-Wallem Management A/S:** Strandpromenaden 9, 3212 Sandefjord; tel. 33-46-28-01; fax 33-46-70-09.

**Jebsens Thun Management A/S:** POB 4145 Dreggen, 0523 Bergen; tel. 55-31-03-20; telex 42686; fax 55-31-24-21; f. 1929; services in Scandinavia, and to Europe, Far East, Australia, the Americas; Owner Atle Jebsen; 27 vessels, 406,495 dwt.

**Jo Management A/S:** POB 7 Lilleaker, 0216 Oslo; tel. 55-99-87-30; fax 55-99-02-95.

**Torvald Klaveness & Co AS:** POB 183 Skøyen, 0212 Oslo; tel. 22-52-60-00; fax 22-50-67-31; Chair. T. E. Klaveness; Man. Dir Alf Jarbo Andersen; 28 vessels.

**Knutsen OAS Shipping A/S:** POB 158, 5501 Haugesund; tel. 52-71-30-00; telex 42204; fax 52-71-29-45; liner and tanker services; 11 vessels, 610,778 dwt.

**Kvaerner Shipping a.s.:** POB 53 Skøyen, 0212 Oslo; tel. 22-96-71-00; fax 22-96-71-50.

**Einar Lange:** POB 3193 Elisenberg, 0208 Oslo; tel. 22-43-05-50; fax 22-43-04-33; Man. Dir Einar Lange; 5 vessels.

**Lorentzens Rederi Co:** POB 1506 Vika, 0117 Oslo; tel. 22-41-29-49; fax 22-41-58-12.

**A/S J. Ludwig Mowinckels Rederi:** Bradbenken 1, POB 4070 Dreggen, 5023 Bergen; tel. 55-31-80-70; telex 42268; fax 55-32-50-95; f. 1898; tankers and cargo services; Man. Dir Knut J. Meland; 10 vessels, 403,506 dwt.

**Rasmussen Group:** POB 37, 4601 Kristiansand; tel. 38-02-14-90; telex 21843; fax 38-07-03-58; Man. Dir E. Rasmussen; group of cos with shipping and offshore interests; 7 vessels, 822,178 dwt and 4 offshore platforms.

**Red Band A/S:** POB 347 Sentrum, 0101 Oslo; tel. 22-33-84-00; fax 22-33-84-31.

**Smedvig Tankskips Ltd:** POB 110, 4001 Stavanger; tel. 51-50-99-00; fax 51-53-43-96.

**C. H. Sørensen and Sønner A/S:** POB 1684 Myrene, 4801 Arendal; tel. 37-02-58-40; telex 21849; fax 37-02-52-54; tramp services; Dirs H. SORENSEN, B. MARCUSSEN; 11 ships, 1.1m. dwt.

**Det Stavangerske Dampskibsselskab:** POB 40, 4001 Stavanger; tel. 51-51-64-64; fax 51-89-49-60.

**Skibsaksjeselskapet Storli:** POB 25, 5032 Minde; tel. 55-27-00-00; fax 55-28-47-41.

**Tschudi & Eitzen AS:** POB 216, 1324 Lysaker; tel. 67-59-17-00; fax 67-59-15-20; 8 vessels.

**Ugland Group:** POB 128, 4891 Grimstad; tel. 37-04-00-11; telex 21642; fax 37-04-47-22; f. 1930; Owners J. J. UGLAND, A. K. L. UGLAND; Pres. and CEO IVAR LØVALD; group of cos with shipping interests; tankers, car-carriers, dry cargo vessels, offshore construction and service vessels, barges; 49 vessels, 2.2m. dwt.

**Morten Werrings Rederi:** POB 1885 Vika, 0124 Oslo; tel. 22-83-37-58; fax 22-83-37-60; 2 vessels.

**Anders Wilhelmsen & Co AS:** POB 1583 Vika, 0118 Oslo; tel. 22-83-36-70; fax 22-83-68-84; Chair. ARNE WILHELMSEN; Man. Dir ENDRE ORDING SUND; 15 vessels.

**Wilh. Wilhelmsen Ltd A/S:** Olav V's gt. 5, POB 1359 Vika, 0113 Oslo; tel. 22-48-30-30; telex 78900; fax 22-48-30-80; f. 1861; regular fast freight-reefer-mail services between Europe and Australia, New Zealand, USA/Canada/Far East, USA–West Africa, USA—South Africa, Far East–Persian Gulf–Far East; Chief Exec. LEIF T. LØDDESØL; 26 vessels, 1.3m. dwt.

### Shipping Organizations

**Nordisk Skibsrederforening** (Northern Shipowners' Defence Club): Kristinelundvn 22, POB 3033 Elisenberg, 0207 Oslo; tel. 22-55-47-20; telex 76825; fax 22-43-00-35; f. 1889; Pres. FRIDTJOF LORENTZEN; Gen. Man. NICHOLAS HAMBRO.

**Norges Rederiforbund** (Norwegian Shipowners' Asscn): POB 1452 Vika, 0116 Oslo; tel. 22-41-60-80; telex 21561; fax 22-41-50-21; f. 1909; 10 regional asscns; Dir-Gen. ROLF SÆTHER.

  **Arbeidsgiverforening for Skip og Offshorefartøyer** (Norwegian Shipping and Offshore Federation): f. 1940; deals with wages and working conditions for crew on ocean-going and offshore service, drilling and accommodation vessels; Dir-Gen. ROLF SÆTHER.

**Norsk Skipsmeglerforbund** (Norwegian Shipbrokers' Asscn): Fr. Nansens pl. 7, 0160 Oslo; tel. 22-20-14-85; telex 19556; fax 22-42-74-13; f. 1919; Pres. HANS JAKOB GRAM; Gen. Man. GRETE G. NØR; 200 mems.

**Det Norske Veritas:** Veritasvn 1, POB 300, 1322 Høvik; tel. 67-57-99-00; telex 76192; f. 1864; classification and certification of ships, other floating structures and fixed offshore structures, petrochemical installations, marine research and development; stations in over 100 countries throughout the world; Pres. SVEN B. ULLRING; Chair. of the Board WILHELM WILHELMSEN.

**Rederienes Landsforening** (Federation of Norwegian Coastal Shipping): Rådhusgt. 25, POB 1252 Vika, 0111 Oslo; tel. 22-42-41-21; fax 22-42-41-44; Admin. Dir HARALD THOMASSEN.

## CIVIL AVIATION

In 1992 there were 57 scheduled airports in Norway, the principal international airport being Fornebu Airport, Oslo. In 1992 the Storting voted to expand the airport at Gardermøn, some 40 km north of Oslo, to form a new international airport servicing the capital: the project was expected to be completed by 1998.

### Principal Airlines

**Det Norske Luftfartselskap A/S (DNL)** (Norwegian Airlines Ltd): Lufthavn-Fornebu, 1330 Oslo; tel. 67-59-63-99; fax 67-58-08-20; f. 1946; partner in Scandinavian Airlines System (SAS) and SAS Commuter, with Denmark and Sweden (q.v.); Chair. BJØRN EIDEM; Gen. Man. TORSTEIN LJØSTAD.

**Braathens SAFE (Braathens South-American & Far East Airtransport):** Oksenøyvn 3, POB 55 Lufthavn-Fornebu, 1330 Oslo Airport; tel. 67-59-70-00; telex 71595; fax 67-59-13-09; f. 1946; scheduled airline and charter company; domestic routes: all main cities in Norway and Longyearbyen, Svalbard; international routes to London–Gatwick (UK), Newcastle (UK) and Billund (Denmark), and between Tromsø and Murmansk (Russia); Pres. ERIK G. BRAATHEN; Chair. ARVE JOHNSEN.

  **Norwegian Air Shuttle:** Oksenøyvn 10, POB 115 Lufthavn-Fornebu, 1331 Oslo; tel. 67-58-37-77; telex 79950; fax 67-58-32-77; f. 1966, present name since 1993; charter and contract flights; Man. Dir EINAR H. FJELDSTAD.

**Fred. Olsen Flyselskap:** POB 10 Lufthavn-Fornebu, 1330 Oslo; tel. 67-53-09-00; telex 71645; fax 67-12-19-07; f. 1946; owned by Fred. Olsen & Co (transport group); charter cargo services; Gen. Man. FREDERICK HIRSCH.

**Norway Airlines (JA):** POB 88 Lufthavn-Fornebu, 1330 Oslo; tel. 04-69-82-00; fax 04-69-82-23.

**Widerøe's Flyveselskap A/S:** Mustads vei 1, POB 82 Lilleaker, 0216 Oslo; tel. 22-73-65-00; fax 22-73-65-90; f. 1934; scheduled domestic service; Chair. BJØRN EIDEM; Man. Dir BAARD MIKKELSEN.

  **Widerøe Norsk Air:** POB 2047, 3202 Sandefjord; tel. 33-46-90-00; fax 33-47-03-25; f. 1961; acquired by Widerøe in 1989; regional services in Scandinavia; Man. Dir BAARD MIKKELSEN.

# Tourism

Norway is a popular resort for tourists who prefer holidays in rugged, peaceful surroundings. It is also a centre for winter sports. The 1994 Winter Olympics were held at Lillehammer. In 1992 there were 1,122 hotels, providing 118,164 beds. In 1993 receipts from tourism amounted to 13,112m. kroner, compared with 14,187m. kroner in the previous year. In the same year the number of visitors to Norway exceeded 3m.

**NORTRA (Norwegian Tourist Board):** Langkaia 1, POB 499 Sentrum, 0105 Oslo; tel. 22-42-70-44; telex 78582; fax 22-33-69-98; f. 1903; marketing organization, provides information; Gen. Dir TORBJØRN FRØYSNES.

# NORWEGIAN EXTERNAL TERRITORIES

## SVALBARD

### Introductory Survey

**Location and Climate**

The Svalbard archipelago is the northernmost part of the Kingdom of Norway. It lies in the Arctic Sea, 657 km north of mainland Norway, between latitudes 74° and 81°N and longitudes 10° and 35°E, comprising a total area of 62,924 sq km (24,295 sq miles). The group consists of nine principal islands, Spitsbergen (formerly Vestspitsbergen), the main island, Kvitøya, Edgeøya, Barentsøya, Nordaustlandet, Prins Karls Forland, Kong Karls Land, Hopen and Bjørnøya (Bear Island), some 204 km to the south of the main island, together with numerous small islands. Mild Atlantic winds lessen the severity of the Arctic climate, but almost 60% of the land area is covered with glaciers. Average temperatures range from −22°C (−8°F) to 7°C (45°F), and precipitation in the lowlands averages some 200 mm per year.

**History and Government**

The existence of Svalbard has been known since Viking exploration in the 12th century. There were conflicting claims to sovereignty by Britain, the Netherlands and Denmark-Norway in the 17th century, when the area was an important centre for whale hunting, but interest subsequently lapsed until the early years of the 20th century, when coal deposits were discovered. On 9 February 1920 14 nations signed a treaty recognizing Norwegian sovereignty over Svalbard. (In early 1994 a total of 41 states had ratified or acceded to the treaty.) International rights of access and economic exploitation were agreed but use for warlike purposes and the construction of fortifications was expressly forbidden.

Svalbard has been part of the Kingdom of Norway since it was formally incorporated in 1925. The territory is administered by a Sysselmann (Governor), resident at Longyearbyen, on Spitsbergen, which is the administrative centre of the archipelago. The Sysselmann is responsible to the Polar Department of the Ministry of Justice. The Norwegian Polar Institute acts in an advisory capacity to the administration. Svalbard lies within the same judicial jurisdiction as the city of Tromsø.

In accordance with the Svalbard Treaty of 1920, the Norwegian Government prescribed a mining code in 1925, regulating all mineral prospecting and exploitation in the islands and their territorial waters extending to 4 nautical miles (7.4 km). The Mining Code is administered by a Commissioner of Mines. Apart from a small permanent research station established by Poland, only Norway and Russia maintain permanent settlements on Svalbard.

In 1941 the population was evacuated by Allied forces for the duration of the war, and three years later the USSR, to which Svalbard was of considerable strategic interest, unsuccessfully sought Norway's agreement to a revision of the 1920 treaty whereby part of the archipelago would become a Soviet-Norwegian condominium. Russia currently maintains a helicopter station and a mobile radar station adjoining its coal mining settlement at Barentsburg on Spitsbergen. Russia (and, before it, the USSR) has refused to recognise Norway's unilateral declaration of a fisheries protection zone around Svalbard from 1977.

In June 1994 vessels of the Norwegian coastguard severed the nets of Icelandic fishing boats that were alleged to be fishing within the fisheries protection zone. The Icelandic Government subsequently withdrew its boats from the zone; in August, however, Norway claimed that an Icelandic boat had opened fire on a Norwegian coastguard vessel.

Particularly since a Royal Decree of 1971, the Norwegian administration has endeavoured to protect the flora, fauna and environment of Svalbard. The protected areas total some 35,000 sq km, or 56% of the land area.

**Social and Economic Affairs**

The total population in February 1994 was 3,030, of whom 38% were resident in Norwegian settlements and 62% in Russian settlements. There are limited recreational, transport, financial and educational facilities on Svalbard. There is a hospital in Longyearbyen.

During 1994 a total of 212 expeditions visited Svalbard, of which the majority (169) were tourist expeditions.

Coal is the islands' main product. Two Norwegian and two Russian mining camps are in operation. In 1993 about 520,000 metric tons were shipped from mines operated by Russia, and 268,000 tons were shipped from Norwegian mines. The Norwegian state-owned coal company, Store Norske Spitsbergen Kulkompani (SNSK), employed 286 people at 1 January 1994. The company incurred financial losses estimated at 78m. kroner in 1993, and the principal motive for continuing to exploit the coal deposits appeared to be political rather than economic. Until 1989 SNSK operated many local services and provided most of the infrastructure, but in that year these functions were assumed by the state company Svalbard Samfunnsdrift, which employed 118 people at the end of 1994.

Deep drillings for petroleum have been carried out by Norwegian and other companies, but no commercial results have been reported. Svalbard's other mineral resources include reserves of phosphate, asbestos, iron ore, anhydrite, limestone and various sulphides.

For 1995 the Svalbard budget was 73.8m. kroner, of which 56.7m. kroner was a direct subsidy from the Norwegian state budget. Svalbard raises some revenue from the sale of fishing licences.

### Statistical Survey

#### AREA AND POPULATION

**Area** (official estimates, sq km): 62,924 (Spitsbergen 39,368, Bjørnøya 176).
**Population** (February 1994): 3,030 (Russian and Ukrainian 1,880, Norwegian 1,140, Polish 10).
**Density** (1994): 0.05 per sq km.

#### MINING

**Coal Shipments** ('000 metric tons): *Norwegian:* 330 in 1991, 360 in 1992, 268 in 1993. *Soviet/Russian:* 529 in 1990, 439 in 1992, 520 in 1993 (data for 1991 n.a.).

#### FINANCE

Norwegian currency is used (100 øre = 1 Norwegian krone).
**Budget** (million kroner, 1995): Revenue 73.8 (incl. direct grant of 56.7 from central Govt); Estimated expenditure 73.8.

#### TRANSPORT AND TOURISM

**Visitors** (1994): Expeditions 212 (incl. Tourists 169, Scientific investigations 34); participants 940.

### Directory

#### The Government
(June 1995)

##### ADMINISTRATION

**Governor** (Sysselmann): Odd Emil Blomdal.
**Commissioner of Mines:** Johannes Vik.

##### OFFICES

**Office of the Governor:** Kontoret til Sysselmannen på Svalbard, 9170 Longyearbyen, Svalbard; tel. 79-02-31-00; fax 79-02-11-66.
**Ministry of Justice and Police (Polar Department):** Akersgt. 42, POB 8005 Dep., 0030 Oslo; tel. 22-34-90-90; fax 22-34-95-30; responsible for the administration of Svalbard and Jan Mayen, and for the Norwegian 'Antarctic' dependencies.
**Norsk Polarinstitutt, Svalbardkontor** (Norwegian Polar Institute, Svalbard Office): 9170 Longyearbyen, Svalbard; tel. 79-02-26-00; fax 79-02-26-04; f. 1928 (Norwegian Polar Institute, Oslo)

as Norges Svalbard-og Ishavs-undersøkelser; adopted present name and expanded functions in 1948; mapping and research institute; responsible for advising Govt on matters concerning Svalbard, Jan Mayen and the 'Antarctic' dependencies; monitors and investigates environment of the territories; organizes regular Antarctic research expeditions; establishes and maintains aids to navigation in Svalbard waters; Dir Dr OLAV ORHEIM.

**Norsk Polarinstitutts Forskningsstasjon** (Norwegian Polar Institute Research Station): Ny-Ålesund, Svalbard; tel. 79-02-71-15; fax 79-02-70-02; permanent research base in Svalbard.

Svalbard, as an integral part of the Kingdom of Norway, has provision for its Norwegian inhabitants to participate in the national elections. For judicial matters Svalbard lies in the jurisdiction of Tromsø. The state Evangelical Lutheran Church provides religious services.

## Radio and Television

**NRK Svalbard:** 9170 Longyearbyen, Svalbard; part of Norwegian state broadcasting corpn; operates the regional telephone system, as well as the local television and radio service (Svalbard Radio—mainly relays of NRK's national Programme 2); Man. (vacant).

Norway also maintains radio and meteorological stations at Hopen, Isfjord, Ny-Ålesund and Bjørnøya. Satellite communications with the Norwegian mainland were developed in the 1980s.

## Finance

Norwegian currency is used. There are limited banking facilities available.

**Sparebanken Nord-Norge:** 9170 Longyearbyen, Svalbard; tel. 79-02-18-01; fax 79-02-15-90; savings bank.

## Trade and Industry

**Store Norske Spitsbergen Kulkompani A/S:** 9170 Longyearbyen, Svalbard; tel. 79-02-22-00; fax 79-02-18-41; govt-owned co.; operates coal mines; 286 employees; Admin. Dir ATLE FORNES.

**Svalbard Næringsutvikling A/S:** 9170 Longyearbyen, Svalbard; tel. 79-02-21-00; fax 79-02-10-19; state co.; encourages development of industry and trade; Admin. Dir AMUND SOLEND.

**Svalbard Samfunnsdrift A/S:** 9170 Longyearbyen, Svalbard; tel. 79-02-23-00; fax 79-02-12-10; state co.; operates most local services, undertakes infrastructure development; 118 employees; Admin. Dir THOR O. BENDIKSEN.

## Transport

Shipping links operate from June to August, with weekly sailings from Honningsvåg to Longyearbyen and Ny-Ålesund and back via Tromsø. In 1975 an airport was opened near Longyearbyen. SAS and Bråthens SAFE operate services to Tromsø up to five times per week. There are air-strips at Ny-Ålesund and Svea, and a Russian helicopter facility at Barentsburg. Apart from helicopters, and a fixed-wing service between Longyearbyen and Ny-Ålesund, internal traffic is little developed.

### AIRPORT

**Longyearbyen Lufthavn:** Administration Office, Lufthavn, 9170 Longyearbyen, Svalbard; tel. 79-02-38-00; fax 79-02-38-01.

# JAN MAYEN

**Location and Climate**

The lofty volcanic island of Jan Mayen is located in the Arctic Ocean, some 910 km west-north-west of Bodø on the Norwegian mainland, 610 km north-north-east of Iceland and 480 km east of Greenland (Denmark). The island is 53 km in length and has a total area of 380 sq km (147 sq miles). The highest point is the summit of Mt Beerenberg (2,277 m above sea-level). The climate is severe, cold and usually misty.

**History and Government**

The sea north and west of Jan Mayen (which was inhabited by various whalers and hunters for a brief period in the 17th century) has been an important area for sealing by Norwegians since the mid-19th century. Partly to assist their navigation, the Norwegian Meteorological Institute instigated activities on the island in the early 20th century. In 1922 Jan Mayen was declared annexed by the Institute, and on 8 May 1929 Norwegian sovereignty was proclaimed by Royal Decree. The island was made an integral part of the Kingdom of Norway by the Jan Mayen Act of 1930. Jan Mayen is not included in the Svalbard Treaty.

The island has no known exploitable mineral resources and is largely barren. Fishing in the surrounding waters is intermittently productive, and it was once considered that a base for fishing fleets could be established. This is now believed to be unlikely, particularly because of the high cost of building a harbour. In September 1970 there was a violent volcanic eruption, the first since the early 19th century. In the course of the first few days of the eruption a huge glacier melted and millions of cubic metres of ice disappeared as steam. Lava poured into the sea and formed about 3.5 sq km of new land. The island's main use remains as a meteorological, navigational and radio station.

During the Second World War Jan Mayen remained the only part of Norway under Norwegian rule, following the German invasion of the mainland. Despite some conflict, the Norwegian Government and its allies maintained the strategic meteorological station and established a radio-locating station on the island during the war.

In 1946 a new base was established at Nordlaguna, both as a meteorological and a coastal radio station. As a result of a North Atlantic defence co-operation exercise in 1959–60, a long-range navigation (LORAN) network was established, with one base on Jan Mayen. At the same time, it was decided to build an air strip near the new LORAN C base, and in 1962 the personnel of the weather and coastal radio services also moved to the same area.

After negotiations with Iceland in 1980, the Norwegian Government declared an economic zone extending for 200 nautical miles (370 km) around the coast of Jan Mayen. In 1981 a further agreement was made with Iceland, regarding mineral and fishing rights. A dispute with Denmark, acting on behalf of Greenland, concerning the delimitation of maritime economic zones between Greenland and Jan Mayen was referred by Denmark to the International Court of Justice (based in The Hague) in 1988. The Court delivered its judgment in June 1993, deciding that 57% of the disputed area belonged to Norway.

The commanding officer in charge of the LORAN C base is the chief administrative official of the island. The officer is responsible for the 15–25 inhabitants (who usually remain on the island for only one year at a time), and is accountable to the Chief of Police in Bodø, and the Ministry of Justice and Police (as in Svalbard; see above). The LORAN C commander may grant permission for visits of not more than 24 hours. For longer visits, the Bodø Chief of Police or the Ministry must approve the application. Visits are normally allowed only for scientific purposes and only if private provision has been made for transport. There is no public transport or accommodation on Jan Mayen.

**Officer-in-charge:** LORAN C Base, Jan Mayen.

**Chief of Police (Bodø):** Tollbugt. 8, 8000 Bodø, Norway.

For the Ministry of Justice and Police and the Norsk Polarinstitutt (Norwegian Polar Research Institute), see under Svalbard.

# NORWEGIAN DEPENDENCIES

Norway's so-called 'Antarctic' dependencies are all uninhabited and were acquired as a result of Norwegian whaling interests in the region since the 1890s. The three territories are dependencies of the Kingdom of Norway, and are administered by the Polar Department of the Ministry of Justice and Police, with the advice of the Norsk Polarinstitutt (for details, see under Svalbard) and the assistance of the Ministry of the Environment.

## Bouvetøya

Bouvetøya (Bouvet Island) is a volcanic island in the South Atlantic Ocean, some 2,400 km south-west of the Cape of Good Hope (South Africa) and 1,600 km north of Antarctica. The island lies north of the Antarctic Circle (it is not, therefore, encompassed by the terms of the Antarctic Treaty). About 93% of the island's surface is covered by ice. The climate is maritime antarctic, with a mean annual temperature of −1°C and a persistent heavy fog.

Regular landings on the island occurred only as part of Norwegian Antarctic expeditions in the 1920s and 1930s. Bouvetøya was claimed for Norway in 1927, placed under its sovereignty in 1928, and declared a Norwegian dependency in 1930. A Royal Decree of 1971 declared the entire island to be a nature reserve. An automatic weather station was established in 1977, and the island is regularly visited by Norwegian scientific expeditions.

## Dronning Maud Land

Dronning Maud Land (Queen Maud Land) is that sector of the Antarctic continent lying between the longitudes of 20°W (adjoining the British Antarctic Territory to the west) and 45°E (neighbouring the Australian Antarctic Territory). The territory is, in area, several times the size of Norway, and 98% of its surface is covered by ice. The climate is severe, the usual temperature always being below 0°C and, in the winter months of mid-year, falling to −60°C on the coast and −88°C inland. The territory's coast is divided into five named sectors (the exact delimitations of which, and of the territory as a whole, have varied at different periods): Kronprinsesse Märtha Kyst (Crown Princess Märtha Coast), Prinsesse Astrid Kyst, Prinsesse Ragnhild Kyst, Prins Harald Kyst and Kronprins Olav Kyst.

The first Norwegian territorial claims in Antarctica were made in 1929, following many years of Norwegian involvement in the exploration and survey of the continent. Further claims were made in 1931 and 1936–37. These claims were formalized by the Norwegian authorities, and the land placed under their sovereignty, only in 1939. The extent of Dronning Maud Land then received its current limits, between the British and Australian claims. Norway now follows a policy which upholds its claim to sovereignty but supports the pattern of international co-operation, particularly that established under the terms of the Antarctic Treaty (signed in 1959—see p. 366), of which the Kingdom of Norway is an original signatory. There are six wintering stations, staffed by personnel of various nationalities, in Dronning Maud Land.

## Peter I Øy

Peter I Øy (Peter I Island) is located in the Bellingshausen Sea, some 450 km north of Antarctica and more than 1,800 km south-west of Chile, the nearest inhabited territory. It covers an area of some 180 sq km, 95% of which is covered by ice. The island lies within the Antarctic Circle and the area covered by the terms of the Antarctic Treaty. The first recorded landing on the island was not made until 1929, by a Norwegian expedition, which then claimed the island. A Royal Proclamation placed Peter I Øy under Norwegian sovereignty in 1931, and the island was declared a dependency in 1933. Few landings have been made since, but in 1987 the Norsk Polarinstitutt conducted a relatively long survey and established an automatic weather station.

# OMAN

## Introductory Survey

### Location, Climate, Language, Religion, Flag, Capital

The Sultanate of Oman occupies the extreme east and south-east of the Arabian peninsula. It is bordered to the west by the United Arab Emirates (UAE), Saudi Arabia and Yemen. A detached portion of Oman, separated from the rest of the country by UAE territory, lies at the tip of the Musandam peninsula, on the southern shore of the Strait of Hormuz. Oman has a coastline of more than 1,600 km (1,000 miles) on the Indian Ocean, and is separated from Iran by the Gulf of Oman. Oman's frontiers have mostly never been clearly demarcated on the ground, but agreement exists on their general lines. At Muscat the mean annual rainfall is 100 mm and the mean temperature varies between 21°C (70°F) and 35°C (95°F). Rainfall is heavier on the hills of the interior, and the south-western province of Dhofar is the only part of Arabia to benefit from the summer monsoon. The official language is Arabic, although English is also spoken in business circles. The majority of the population are Ibadi Muslims; about one-quarter are Hindus. The national flag (proportions 2 by 1) has three equal horizontal stripes, of white, red and green, with a vertical red stripe at the hoist. In the upper hoist is a representation, in white, of the state emblem, an Omani dagger crossed by two sabres and three links of a chain. The capital is Muscat.

### Recent History

Officially known as Muscat and Oman until 1970, the Sultanate has had a special relationship with the United Kingdom since the 19th century. Full independence was confirmed by a treaty of friendship with the United Kingdom on 20 December 1951, but the armed forces and police still have some British officers. Sultan Said bin Taimur succeeded his father in 1932 and maintained a strictly conservative and isolationist rule until July 1970, when he was overthrown by his son in a bloodless palace coup. The new Sultan, Qaboos bin Said, then began a liberalization of the regime, and increased spending on development.

A 45-member advisory body, the Consultative Assembly (comprising 17 representatives of the Government, 17 representatives of the private sector and 11 regional representatives, all appointed by the Sultan), was created in October 1981, in response to suggestions that Sultan Qaboos was not being made sufficiently aware of public opinion. Its role was to advise on economic and social development. In November 1983 the Assembly's membership was expanded to 55 (including 19 representatives of the Government).

In November 1990 Sultan Qaboos announced that a new Consultative Council (the Majlis al-Shoura), comprising regional representatives, was to replace the Consultative Assembly, to allow 'wider participation' by Omani citizens in national 'responsibilities and tasks'. A selection process was subsequently announced whereby representatives of each of the country's 59 districts (wilayat) would nominate three candidates; the nominations would then be submitted to the Deputy Prime Minister for Legal Affairs, who, with the Sultan's approval, would choose one representative for each district to join the new Majlis. No government official or civil servant would be eligible for election to the new body. The Speaker of the Consultative Council would be appointed by the central Government; however, other executive officers and committee members would be designated by, and from among, the 59 local delegates. Once again, the role of the Majlis was strictly advisory, although government ministers were to be obliged to present annual statements to the assembly and to answer any questions addressed to them. The inaugural session of the Consultative Council (which had been formally established by royal decree in November 1991) was convened in January 1992, when its members were sworn in for a three-year term.

In early December 1991 an extensive cabinet reorganization was implemented and several ministries were amalgamated. Further cabinet changes were announced in May 1992 and January 1994. In June 1994 it was announced that the membership of the Majlis would be increased from 59 to 80, following the expiry of its term in December. Under the new selection process, any district with 30,000 or more inhabitants would be represented in the Majlis by two members, while for each of the remaining regions only one member would be appointed. Women were to be permitted, for the first time, to be nominated as candidates in six regions in and around the capital. In early 1995 two women were appointed to the new Majlis.

In mid-1994 the Omani Government was reported to be employing stringent measures to curb an apparent rise in Islamic militancy in the country. In late August the security forces announced the arrest of more than 200 members of an allegedly foreign-sponsored Islamic organization, most of whom were later released. Among the persons arrested were two junior ministers, university lecturers, students and soldiers. In November several detainees were sentenced to death, having been found guilty of conspiracy to foment sedition; the Sultan subsequently commuted the death sentences to terms of imprisonment.

During the early 1970s relations between Oman and the neighbouring People's Democratic Republic of Yemen (PDRY—united with the Yemen Arab Republic in May 1990) deteriorated, following conflict in Dhofar Province with a guerrilla organization, known from 1974 as the People's Front for the Liberation of Oman, which the PDRY supported. Although a cease-fire was mediated by Saudi Arabia in March 1976, the situation remained tense. Oman's acceptance of US assistance in defence aroused protests from the PDRY in 1981, but mediation by other Gulf states led to a 'normalization' agreement in 1982, and diplomatic relations between Oman and the PDRY were resumed in October 1983. In late 1987 a series of minor clashes between border patrols of the PDRY and Oman took place in Dhofar Province. In October 1988 Oman and the PDRY signed an agreement to increase co-operation in the areas of trade and communication, and in February 1990 the two countries reached an agreement to delineate their common border. An agreement on the demarcation of the border was finally signed in October 1992 and ratified in December of that year.

The Iranian revolution of 1978–79 and the Iran–Iraq War (1980–88) led to increased international awareness of Oman's strategic importance, particularly regarding the Strait of Hormuz, a narrow waterway at the mouth of the Persian (Arabian) Gulf, between Oman and Iran, through which passes, under normal circumstances, about two-thirds of the world's sea-borne trade in crude petroleum. In February 1980 Sultan Qaboos agreed, in principle, to the use by US forces of Masirah Island, off the east coast of Oman, as a military base in an emergency. In June 1980 Oman and the USA signed a defence pact whereby, in exchange for US military and economic aid and a US commitment to Oman's security, Oman would grant the use of port and air base facilities in the Gulf to US forces.

Oman has fostered close co-operation with neighbouring Arab countries. In May 1981 Oman joined with six other Middle Eastern countries to form the Co-operation Council for the Arab States of the Gulf (Gulf Co-operation Council—GCC, see p. 130). Following the conclusion of the Iran–Iraq War, Oman (which, in common with other Arab powers, had tended to condemn Iran's conduct in the region) adopted a more conciliatory policy towards that country. The Iranian Minister of Foreign Affairs visited the Omani capital, Muscat, several times during early 1989, and in March the two countries established an economic co-operation committee. In September 1992 the Governments of Oman and Iran signed an agreement to increase economic co-operation and trade, particularly in the transport and shipping sectors.

In response to the invasion of Kuwait by Iraq in August 1990, Oman, together with the other members of the GCC, gave its support to the deployment of a US-led defensive force in Saudi Arabia. The Omani Government expressed the view that the imposition of economic sanctions would force Iraq to withdraw from Kuwait. In late November there was evidence that Oman had attempted to mediate in the crisis, when the Iraqi Minister of Foreign Affairs, Tareq Aziz, visited Oman (the first official Iraqi visit to a GCC state, other than Kuwait, since the Gulf crisis began). In the aftermath of the Gulf crisis, Sultan Qaboos supported further integration among the GCC member states, and in December 1991, at the annual meeting of GCC Heads of State, he unsuccessfully proposed the creation of a 100,000-strong GCC army. By March 1995, following Iraq's deployment in October 1994 of troops and artillery near the border with Kuwait in what was widely regarded as an attempt to effect the easing of UN economic sanctions imposed in August 1990, Oman's stance on the prolongation of economic restrictions against Iraq appeared ambivalent: Oman and Qatar were, notably, absent from talks held in March 1995 between the US Secretary of State, Warren Christopher, and other members of the GCC on the continuation of sanctions against Iraq.

At the end of January 1992 President Mitterrand of France spent three days in Oman, where he held talks with the Sultan concerning bilateral co-operation, in particular in the sectors of defence, energy and banking. In April the Omani Government reached an agreement with the United Arab Emirates (UAE) to relax restrictions in order to allow nationals to travel between the two countries without a passport. In May the President of the UAE, Sheikh Zayed an-Nahyan, visited Oman for negotiations, as a result of which diplomatic representation between the two countries was raised to ambassadorial level.

In October 1993 Sultan Qaboos visited Yemen, where he pledged US $21m. to finance the construction of a border road between the two countries. In early 1994 Oman supported Jordan in that country's initiative to mediate a settlement to the conflict in Yemen, and in March Sultan Qaboos hosted a meeting in Muscat of the leaders of the two rival Yemeni groups. In October 1993 the Sultanate was elected to be a non-permanent member of the UN Security Council for a two-year term from January 1994, in acknowledgement of its mediatory role in the Middle East.

In April 1994 the Israeli Deputy Minister of Foreign Affairs, Yossi Beilin, participated in talks in Oman. This constituted the first official visit by an Israeli minister to an Arab Gulf state since Israel's declaration of independence in 1948. In late September 1994, moreover, Oman and the other GCC member states announced the partial ending of their economic boycott of Israel. In December the Israeli Prime Minister, Itzhak Rabin, made an official visit to the Sultanate to discuss the Middle East peace process, and in February 1995 it was announced that low-level diplomatic relations were to be established between Oman and Israel with the opening of interests sections, respectively, in Tel-Aviv and Muscat.

### Government

The Sultan appoints, and rules with the advice of, a cabinet. In late 1991 Oman's Consultative Assembly was replaced by a Consultative Council (the Majlis al-Shoura), comprising one representative for each of the country's 59 districts (wilayat) and a government-appointed Speaker. In 1995 the Majlis was expanded to 80 members (one representative from each district with fewer than 30,000 inhabitants, and two each from districts with 30,000 or more inhabitants—see Recent History). Annual meetings are held between the Majlis and members of the Council of Ministers. Each of the wilayat has its own governor (wali).

### Defence

In June 1994 the Omani armed forces numbered 42,900, including about 3,700 expatriate personnel. The army comprised 25,000 men, the navy 4,200, the air force 3,500, and the royal household 6,500. Military service is voluntary. Expenditure on defence and security in the 1994 budget was estimated at RO 612m., equivalent to 30.1% of total expenditure for that year.

### Economic Affairs

In 1993, according to estimates by the World Bank, Oman's gross national product (GNP) measured at average 1991–93 prices, was US $9,631m., equivalent to $5,600 per head. During 1985–93, it was estimated, GNP per head increased, in real terms, at an average rate of 1.2% per year. In the same period the population increased by an annual average of 3.9%. Oman's gross domestic product (GDP), measured at constant prices, increased by an annual average of 8.8% in 1980–91.

According to official figures, real GDP growth was 9.1% in 1992; however, in the following year, it was reported, there was no appreciable growth, and in 1994 real GDP increased by only 0.3%.

Agriculture (including fishing) contributed 3.2% of GDP in 1993, according to provisional figures; it is practised mainly at subsistence level. According to FAO estimates, 37.2% of the labour force were employed in the agricultural sector at mid-1993. The major crops are dates, tomatoes, limes and lucerne (alfalfa). Mangoes, melons, bananas, papaya, coconuts, cucumbers, onions and peppers are also cultivated. The production of frankincense, formerly an important export commodity, is to be revived. Livestock and fishing are also important. During 1980–91 agricultural GDP increased by an annual average of 6.7% in real terms. In 1993, according to provisional official figures, agricultural GDP, in current prices, increased by only 0.1%, compared with the previous year.

Industry (including mining and quarrying, manufacturing, construction and power) employed an estimated 21.8% of the labour force in 1980, and provided 48.3% of GDP in 1993, according to provisional figures. During 1980–91 industrial GDP increased, in real terms, by an annual average of 9.6%.

According to provisional figures, the mining sector contributed 37.7% of GDP in 1993. There were proven petroleum reserves of 5,500m. barrels in mid-1994 when production totalled 800,000 barrels per day. In late 1994, the Government announced that it was to invest US $6,000m. in the crude petroleum production sector during 1995–98, in an attempt to increase petroleum reserves. Exports of Omani crude petroleum provided 77.2% of total export earnings in 1993. Natural gas is also important, and there were proven reserves of 20,000,000m. cu ft (570,588m. cu m) in 1994. Revenue from petroleum and natural gas was expected to contribute 76.7% of total budgetary revenue in 1995. Copper, chromite, marble, gypsum and limestone are also mined. There are deposits of coal and manganese ore, as yet unexploited. During 1980–91 the GDP of the mining sector increased, in real terms, by an annual average of 9.0%. Measured at current prices, mining GDP increased by 13.1% in 1992, but in the following year, according to provisional figures, it declined by 10.7%.

Manufacturing contributed 5.1% of GDP in 1993, according to provisional figures. The most important branches of the sector are petroleum-refining, construction materials, cement production and copper-smelting. During 1980–91 manufacturing GDP increased, in real terms, by an annual average of 20.9%. In 1993, according to provisional figures, manufacturing GDP, in current prices, increased by 21.0%, compared with 1992.

Energy is derived principally from domestic supplies of petroleum. Electricity production by public utilities was 5,833m. kWh in 1993, compared with 5,113m. kWh in 1992. In 1992 the Oman Liquefied Natural Gas Company (OLNGC) was established to co-ordinate a project to construct a US $9,000m. LNG plant to exploit further the country's gas resources and to reduce domestic demand for petroleum. The plant was scheduled to begin production in 1999. In mid-1993 a feasibility study was begun on a project for the construction of a $5,000m. submarine pipeline to transport Omani-produced gas to India.

Services provided 48.5% of GDP (according to provisional figures) in 1993. The GDP of the services sector increased, in real terms, at an average rate of 8.0% per year during 1980–91.

In 1993 Oman recorded a visible trade surplus of US $1,336m., while there was a deficit of $1,069m. on the current account of the balance of payments. In 1993 the principal sources of imports were the United Arab Emirates and Japan (which supplied, respectively, 28.0% and 20.9% of Oman's imports). The most important markets for exports in 1989 were Japan and the Republic of Korea (which took, respectively, 34.6% and 28.8% of exports from Oman). Petroleum is, by far, the principal export; machinery and transport equipment also make a notable contribution to export earnings. The principal imports in 1993 were machinery and transport equipment, basic manufactures and food and live animals.

Oman recorded an overall budgetary deficit of RO 584.5m. in 1992 (equivalent to 13.2% of GDP in that year). The budget deficit for 1995 was forecast at RO 312m. At the end of 1993 Oman's total external debt was US $2,661m., of which $2,319m. was long-term public debt. In 1992 the cost of servicing the external debt (totalling $2,855m. at the end of that year) was equivalent to 9.0% of the total value of exports of goods and services. Annual inflation averaged 2.2% in 1990–93; inflation decreased from 4.6% in 1991 to 0.9% in 1993. There is a labour shortage, offset by the use of immigrant labour (an estimated 350,000 workers in 1992), although there was likely to be a shortage of employment opportunities for young Omani graduates by the mid-1990s.

Oman is a member of the Arab Fund for Economic and Social Development (see p. 237), the Islamic Development Bank (see p. 180) and the Arab Monetary Fund (see p. 237). It was a founder member of the Co-operation Council for the Arab States of the Gulf (the Gulf Co-operation Council, see p. 130). Oman is not a member of the Organization of the Petroleum Exporting Countries (OPEC, see p. 210) nor of the Organization of Arab Petroleum Exporting Countries (see p. 207), but it generally respects OPEC's policies regarding levels of production and prices for petroleum.

Oman's economy expanded considerably in the 1970s, owing to the investment of revenue from petroleum in the country's infrastructure and economic development. Limited petroleum reserves necessitated a series of five-year development plans to diversify the country's economic base, in particular through the expansion of the private sector (including the privatization of certain state assets). Under the fourth Development Plan (1991–95), emphasis was placed on the allocation of investments to less developed districts in Oman, to reduce regional disparities and create employment, in order to pre-empt internal migration. The rapid rate of population growth was partly responsible for a policy of 'Omanizing' the work-force; the Government aimed gradually to reduce its reliance on expatriate labour by offering subsidies to employers recruiting Omani workers. In 1992 a 15-year industrial strategy was adopted, which included the liberalization of credit, the introduction of new regulations simplifying administrative procedures for business executives and the further development of infrastructure. Oman has, in addition, begun to emphasize the development of its reserves of natural gas as an alternative source of revenue to petroleum. In July 1994 the Government initiated a wide-ranging privatization programme to attract private investment for infrastructural projects, and in November a new investment law was introduced to allow foreign nationals to own as much as 100% of 'projects contributing to the development of the national economy', particularly if they pertained to infrastructure.

### Social Welfare

Oman has a free National Health Service, and in 1993 there were 46 hospitals. There were also 86 health centres, 65 preventive health centres, and 24 dispensaries. A total of 4,505 beds were available in hospitals and health centres. In 1993 there were 2,354 physicians working in Oman. In March 1989 it was announced that citizens of other member-states of the Gulf Co-operation Council (see p. 130) would be eligible to receive the same health services as Omani citizens. Of total expenditure by the central Government in 1992, RO 108.5m. (5.7%) was for health services, and a further RO 91.2m. (4.8%) was for social security and welfare.

### Education

Great advances have been made in education since 1970, when Sultan Qaboos came to power. Although education is still not compulsory, it is provided free to Omani citizens from primary to tertiary level, and attendance has greatly increased. Primary education begins at six years of age and lasts for six years. The next level of education, divided into two equal stages (preparatory and secondary), lasts for a further six years. As a proportion of the school-age population, the total enrolment at primary, preparatory and secondary schools increased from 25% (boys 36%; girls 14%) in 1975 to 85% (boys 89%; girls 81%) in 1992. Primary enrolment in 1992 included an estimated 85% of children in the relevant age-group (boys 86%; girls 83%), while preparatory and secondary enrolment was equivalent to 64% of children in the relevant age-group (boys 68%; girls 61%). In 1992/93 the number of institutions in general education (primary, preparatory and secondary) was 857, the number of students 420,056 (boys 220,291; girls 199,765), and the number of teachers 18,325. There were eight teacher-training colleges and 10 vocational institutes, together with institutes of health sciences and banking and four technical institutes. There were also eight Islamic colleges. Oman's first national university, named after Sultan Qaboos, was opened in late 1986, and had 3,504 students (males 1,664; females 1,840) in 1992/93. In 1970 an estimated 80% of Oman's adult population were illiterate; however, government literacy centres for adults (first opened in 1973) have largely redressed this problem. In 1992/93 such centres were attended by 8,906 students (902 males; 8,004 females); more than 200 adult education centres were attended by 20,000 students (10,347 males; 9,653 females). Government expenditure on education in 1992 was RO 209.4m., representing 11.0% of total spending.

### Public Holidays

**1995:** 1 February* (Ramadan begins), 3 March* (Id al-Fitr, end of Ramadan), 10 May* (Id al-Adha, Feast of the Sacrifice), 31 May* (Muharram, Islamic New Year), 9 June* (Ashoura), 9 August* (Mouloud, Birth of the Prophet), 18 November (National Day), 19 November (Birthday of the Sultan), 20 December* (Leilat al-Meiraj, Ascension of the Prophet).

**1996:** 22 January* (Ramadan begins), 21 February* (Id al-Fitr, end of Ramadan), 29 April* (Id al-Adha, Feast of the Sacrifice), 19 May* (Muharram, Islamic New Year), 28 May* (Ashoura), 28 July* (Mouloud, Birth of the Prophet), 18 November (National Day), 19 November (Birthday of the Sultan), 8 December* (Leilat al-Meiraj, Ascension of the Prophet).

* These holidays are dependent on the Islamic lunar calendar and may vary by one or two days from the dates given.

### Weights and Measures

The imperial, metric and local systems are all used, although the metric system was officially adopted in 1974.

# Statistical Survey

*Source (unless otherwise stated): Oman Directorate-General of National Statistics, Development Council, POB 881, Muscat; tel. 698900; telex 5384.*

## Area and Population

### AREA, POPULATION AND DENSITY

| | |
|---|---:|
| Area (sq km) | 212,457* |
| Population (census results) 30 November 1993 Total | 2,017,591† |
| Density (per sq km) at November 1993 | 9.5 |

* 82,030 sq miles. Other sources estimate the area at 300,000 sq km (about 120,000 sq miles).
† Comprising 1,480,531 Omani nationals (males 755,071; females 725,460) and 537,060 non-Omanis.

### POPULATION BY GOVERNORATE (1993 census)

| | | | | |
|---|---:|---|---:|---|
| Al-Batinah | 538,763 | Musandam | 27,669 |
| Al-Dakhiliya | 220,403 | Muscat | 622,506 |
| Al-Dhahira | 169,710 | Al-Sharqiya | 247,551 |
| Dhofar | 174,888 | Al-Wosta | 16,101 |
| | | **Total** | **2,017,591** |

### BIRTHS AND DEATHS (official estimates, Omani nationals only)

| | 1991 | 1992 | 1993 |
|---|---:|---:|---:|
| Birth rate (per 1,000) | 43.9 | 42.2 | 40.3 |
| Death rate (per 1,000) | 7.5 | 7.4 | 7.3 |

**Expectation of life** (official estimates, years at birth, Omani nationals, 1993): 67.1 (males 66.7; females 67.5).

### ECONOMICALLY ACTIVE POPULATION
(ILO estimates, '000 persons at mid-1980)

| | Males | Females | Total |
|---|---:|---:|---:|
| Agriculture, etc. | 135 | 4 | 140 |
| Industry | 55 | 7 | 61 |
| Services | 70 | 9 | 80 |
| **Total labour force** | **260** | **20** | **280** |

Source: ILO, *Economically Active Population Estimates and Projections, 1950–2025.*

**Mid-1993** (estimates in '000): Agriculture, etc. 169; Total 454 (Source: FAO, *Production Yearbook*).

## Agriculture

### PRINCIPAL CROPS (FAO estimates, '000 metric tons)

| | 1991 | 1992 | 1993 |
|---|---:|---:|---:|
| Cereals | 5 | 5 | 5 |
| Potatoes | 5 | 5 | 6 |
| Tomatoes | 30 | 32 | 33 |
| Onions (dry) | 9 | 9 | 9 |
| Other vegetables | 93 | 94 | 95 |
| Watermelons | 27 | 28 | 30 |
| Dates | 125 | 130 | 133 |
| Lemons and limes | 27 | 28 | 29 |
| Mangoes | 9 | 10 | 11 |
| Bananas | 24 | 25 | 26 |
| Tobacco (leaves) | 2 | 2 | 2 |

Source: FAO, *Production Yearbook.*

### LIVESTOCK (FAO estimates, '000 head, year ending September)

| | 1991 | 1992 | 1993 |
|---|---:|---:|---:|
| Asses | 26 | 26 | 26 |
| Cattle | 138 | 140 | 142 |
| Camels | 90 | 92 | 94 |
| Sheep | 143 | 145 | 148 |
| Goats | 725 | 730 | 735 |

Poultry (FAO estimates, million): 3 in 1991; 3 in 1992; 3 in 1993.
Source: FAO, *Production Yearbook.*

### LIVESTOCK PRODUCTS (FAO estimates, '000 metric tons)

| | 1991 | 1992 | 1993 |
|---|---:|---:|---:|
| Beef and veal | 3 | 3 | 3 |
| Mutton and lamb | 12 | 11 | 11 |
| Goat meat | 5 | 5 | 5 |
| Poultry meat | 3 | 3 | 4 |
| Cows' milk | 18 | 18 | 19 |
| Goats' milk | 55 | 60 | 63 |
| Hen eggs | 6.1 | 6.1 | 6.2 |

Source: FAO, *Production Yearbook.*

## Fishing

('000 metric tons, live weight)

| | 1990 | 1991 | 1992 |
|---|---:|---:|---:|
| Fishes | 117.0 | 114.9 | 109.4 |
| Crustaceans and molluscs | 3.2 | 2.9 | 2.9 |
| **Total catch** | **120.2** | **117.8** | **112.3** |

Source: FAO, *Yearbook of Fishery Statistics.*
**1993** ('000 metric tons): Total catch 116.5.

## Mining

| | 1989 | 1990 | 1991 |
|---|---:|---:|---:|
| Crude petroleum ('000 metric tons) | 31,803 | 34,018 | 35,128 |
| Natural gas (petajoules) | 91 | 106 | 104 |

Source: UN, *Industrial Statistics Yearbook.*
**1992:** Crude petroleum 271 million barrels.
**1993:** Crude petroleum 285 million barrels.

OMAN

## Industry

**SELECTED PRODUCTS** ('000 barrels, unless otherwise indicated)

|  | 1991 | 1992 | 1993 |
|---|---|---|---|
| Motor spirit (petrol) | 3,141 | 3,900.9 | 4,227.3 |
| Kerosene | 1,231 | 1,537.0 | 2,325.9 |
| Distillate fuel oils | 3,584 | 4,549.5 | 4,582.1 |
| Bunker fuel | 8,699 | 10,394.6 | 12,070.1 |
| Electric energy (million kWh)* | 4,625 | 5,113 | 5,833 |

* Production by public utilities only. Total production in 1991 was 5,548 million kWh.

Refined copper (metric tons); 12,015 in 1990.

## Finance

**CURRENCY AND EXCHANGE RATES**

**Monetary Units**
1,000 baiza = 1 rial Omani (RO).

**Sterling and Dollar Equivalents** (31 December 1994)
£1 sterling = 601.6 baiza;
US $1 = 384.5 baiza;
100 rials Omani = £166.24 = $260.08.

**Exchange Rate**
Between February 1973 and January 1986 the value of the rial Omani was fixed at US $2.8952 ($1 = 345.4 baiza). In January 1986 the currency was devalued by about 10.2%, with the exchange rate fixed at 1 rial = $2.6008 ($1 = 384.5 baiza).

**BUDGET** (RO million)*

| Revenue† | 1990 | 1991 | 1992 |
|---|---|---|---|
| Taxation on income, profits, etc. | 368.4 | 267.3 | 267.1 |
| Oil companies | 352.1 | 246.4 | 244.3 |
| Import duties | 32.6 | 38.9 | 47.8 |
| Other tax revenue | 19.6 | 21.2 | 19.9 |
| Entrepreneurial and property income | 1,057.4 | 837.0 | 874.3 |
| Petroleum | 998.0 | 777.0 | 808.4 |
| Fees, charges, etc. | 13.9 | 15.3 | 19.7 |
| Other current revenue | 82.5 | 74.5 | 101.6 |
| Capital revenue | 6.3 | 7.2 | 7.7 |
| **Total** | 1,580.7 | 1,261.4 | 1,338.1 |

| Expenditure‡ | 1990 | 1991 | 1992 |
|---|---|---|---|
| General public services | 169.2 | 170.6 | 174.0 |
| Defence | 656.2 | 557.4 | 679.5 |
| Public order and safety | 103.5 | 106.8 | 120.5 |
| Education | 171.0 | 180.1 | 209.4 |
| Health | 74.3 | 85.3 | 108.5 |
| Social security and welfare | 38.0 | 53.0 | 91.2 |
| Housing and community amenities | 107.2 | 153.7 | 156.3 |
| Recreational, cultural and religious affairs | 34.5 | 36.8 | 51.5 |
| Economic affairs and services | 155.3 | 162.0 | 210.9 |
| Fuel and energy | 74.1 | 77.6 | 117.6 |
| Agriculture, forestry and fishing | 31.6 | 38.3 | 39.8 |
| Mining, manufacturing and construction | 2.2 | 1.0 | 2.7 |
| Road transport | 17.9 | 20.7 | 23.0 |
| Other transport and communications | 8.9 | 6.9 | 7.0 |
| Other economic affairs and services | 20.6 | 17.5 | 20.8 |
| Interest payments | 92.4 | 69.4 | 98.5 |
| **Total** | 1,601.6 | 1,575.1 | 1,900.3 |
| Current | 1,431.5 | 1,336.7 | 1,560.0 |
| Capital | 170.1 | 238.4 | 340.3 |

* The data refer to the consolidated accounts of the central Government, including ministries, regional government offices and municipalities.
† Excluding grants received from abroad (RO million): 6.6 in 1990; 23.0 in 1991; 0.9 in 1992.
‡ Excluding lending minus repayment (RO million): 18.5 in 1990; −6.4 in 1991; 23.2 in 1992.

Source: IMF, *Government Finance Statistics Yearbook*.

**1993** (estimates, RO million): Total revenue 1,671.5; Total expenditure 2,111.5.
**1994** (estimates, RO million): Total revenue 1,732.1; Total expenditure 2,033.0.
**1995** (estimates, RO million): Total revenue 1,847.0; Total expenditure 2,159.0.

**INTERNATIONAL RESERVES** (US $ million at 31 December)

|  | 1991 | 1992 | 1993 |
|---|---|---|---|
| Gold* | 68.3 | 68.3 | 68.3 |
| IMF special drawing rights | 22.2 | 4.7 | 6.8 |
| Reserve position in IMF | 32.5 | 54.1 | 52.0 |
| Foreign exchange | 1,608.6 | 1,924.7 | 849.3 |
| **Total** | 1,731.6 | 2,051.8 | 976.4 |

* Valued at RO 90.8 per troy ounce.

Source: IMF, *International Financial Statistics*.

**MONEY SUPPLY** (RO million at 31 December)

|  | 1991 | 1992 | 1993 |
|---|---|---|---|
| Currency outside banks | 215.9 | 226.7 | 232.9 |
| Demand deposits at commercial banks | 189.8 | 206.3 | 218.7 |
| **Total money** | 405.7 | 433.0 | 451.5 |

Source: IMF, *International Financial Statistics*.

**COST OF LIVING** (Consumer Price Index for Muscat; base: 1990 = 100)

|  | 1991 | 1992 | 1993 |
|---|---|---|---|
| Food | 103.1 | 102.4 | 100.8 |
| Fuel, light and water | 96.8 | 97.3 | n.a. |
| Clothing | 102.1 | 98.9 | n.a. |
| Rent | 109.7 | 116.6 | n.a. |
| **All items** (incl. others) | 104.6 | 105.6 | 106.6 |

Source: ILO, *Year Book of Labour Statistics*.

## OMAN

*Statistical Survey*

**NATIONAL ACCOUNTS** (RO million in current prices)

**Expenditure on the Gross Domestic Product**

|  | 1990 | 1991 | 1992 |
|---|---|---|---|
| Government final consumption expenditure | 1,544.9 | 1,394.7 | 1,734.9 |
| Private final consumption expenditure | } 1,080.6 | } 1,485.3 | } 1,476.6 |
| Increase in stocks |  |  |  |
| Gross fixed capital formation | 529.2 | 661.4 | 750.9 |
| **Total domestic expenditure** | 3,154.7 | 3,541.4 | 3,962.4 |
| Exports of goods and services | 2,136.0 | 1,891.0 | 2,154.0 |
| Less Imports of goods and services | 1,240.0 | 1,515.0 | 1,699.0 |
| **GDP in purchasers' values** | 4,050.7 | 3,917.4 | 4,417.4 |

Source: IMF, *International Financial Statistics*.

**Gross Domestic Product by Economic Activity**

|  | 1991 | 1992 | 1993* |
|---|---|---|---|
| Agriculture and livestock† | 93.3 | 92.6 | 96.2 |
| Fishing† | 50.6 | 51.1 | 47.7 |
| Mining and quarrying | 1,669.2 | 1,887.6 | 1,684.9 |
| Crude petroleum | 1,608.7 | 1,820.5 | 1,613.0 |
| Natural gas | 49.7 | 54.6 | 60.6 |
| Manufacturing | 168.3 | 190.2 | 230.1 |
| Electricity, gas and water | 62.7 | 67.5 | 57.4 |
| Construction | 154.5 | 181.3 | 188.1 |
| Trade, restaurants and hotels | 540.6 | 615.9 | 664.8 |
| Transport, storage and communications† | 146.7 | 160.9 | 174.6 |
| Financing, insurance, real estate and business services‡ | 343.5 | 374.1 | 409.0 |
| Government services | 669.5 | 772.5 | 838.9 |
| Public administration and defence | 476.3 | 547.5 | 588.0 |
| Other community, social and personal services | 71.5 | 75.5 | 82.4 |
| **Sub-total** | 3,970.4 | 4,469.2 | 4,474.1 |
| Import duties | 39.4 | 47.8 | 43.6 |
| Less Imputed bank service charge | 92.5 | 95.2 | 98.0 |
| **GDP in purchasers' values** | 3,917.4 | 4,421.8 | 4,419.7 |

* Provisional figures.
† Excluding activities of government enterprises.
‡ Including imputed rents of owner-occupied dwellings.

**BALANCE OF PAYMENTS** (US $ million)

|  | 1991 | 1992 | 1993 |
|---|---|---|---|
| Merchandise exports f.o.b. | 4,871 | 5,555 | 5,365 |
| Merchandise imports f.o.b. | −3,112 | −3,627 | −4,030 |
| **Trade balance** | 1,759 | 1,928 | 1,336 |
| Exports of services | 61 | 13 | 13 |
| Imports of services | −961 | −932 | −896 |
| Other income received | 356 | 328 | 421 |
| Other income paid | −586 | −636 | −632 |
| Private unrequited transfers (net) | −871 | −1,181 | −1,329 |
| Official unrequited transfers (net) | −3 | −16 | 18 |
| **Current balance** | −244 | −496 | −1,069 |
| Direct investment (net) | 149 | 87 | 99 |
| Other capital (net) | 372 | 226 | −49 |
| Net errors and omissions | 253 | 462 | −39 |
| **Overall balance** | 530 | 280 | −1,058 |

Source: IMF, *International Financial Statistics*.

## External Trade

**PRINCIPAL COMMODITIES** (RO million)

| Imports c.i.f. (distribution by SITC) | 1991 | 1992 | 1993 |
|---|---|---|---|
| **Food and live animals** | 171.1 | 180.7 | 187.4 |
| Meat and meat preparations | 25.0 | 25.2 | 27.1 |
| Dairy products and birds' eggs | 30.3 | 31.0 | 33.4 |
| Cereals and cereal preparations | 33.5 | 34.0 | 38.5 |
| Vegetables and fruit | 44.3 | 47.5 | 48.5 |
| **Beverages and tobacco** | 49.4 | 88.4 | 93.7 |
| Tobacco and tobacco manufactures | 36.3 | 71.6 | 75.3 |
| **Crude materials (inedible) except fuels** | 14.2 | 18.7 | 32.5 |
| **Mineral fuels, lubricants, etc.** | 21.1 | 26.7 | 47.3 |
| Petroleum, petroleum products, etc. | 20.6 | 25.5 | 45.2 |
| **Chemicals and related products** | 74.1 | 81.4 | 92.7 |
| **Basic manufactures** | 214.3 | 230.1 | 237.0 |
| Textile yarn, fabrics, etc. | 43.2 | 48.5 | 50.5 |
| Non-metallic mineral manufactures | 23.6 | 29.0 | 34.4 |
| Iron and steel | 68.2 | 62.6 | 59.1 |
| **Machinery and transport equipment** | 514.0 | 633.5 | 683.9 |
| Power-generating machinery and equipment | 51.2 | 36.5 | 36.6 |
| Machinery specialized for particular industries | 105.0 | 83.7 | 102.8 |
| General industrial machinery, equipment and parts | 38.3 | 39.9 | 43.1 |
| Telecommunications and sound equipment | 32.9 | 57.5 | 38.2 |
| Other electrical machinery, apparatus, etc. | 51.6 | 61.6 | 58.7 |
| Road vehicles and parts* | 213.7 | 329.5 | 345.7 |
| Passenger motor cars (excl. buses) | 145.4 | 230.6 | 243.3 |
| **Miscellaneous manufactured articles** | 127.4 | 138.0 | 129.9 |
| **Total** (incl. others) | 1,228.2 | 1,449.2 | 1,581.8 |

* Excluding tyres, engines and electrical parts.

| Exports f.o.b. | 1991 | 1992 | 1993 |
|---|---|---|---|
| Crude petroleum | 1,575.1 | 1,745.8 | 1,594.9 |
| Refined petroleum products | 54.6 | 39.3 | 27.2 |
| Other domestic exports | 79.1 | 96.7 | 122.5 |
| Re-exports | 165.1 | 253.5 | 320.3 |
| **Total** | 1,873.9 | 2,135.3 | 2,064.9 |

**PRINCIPAL TRADING PARTNERS**

| Imports c.i.f. (RO '000) | 1991 | 1992 | 1993 |
|---|---|---|---|
| Australia | 22,996 | 28,801 | 50,828 |
| Bahrain | 7,430 | 10,762 | 27,159 |
| Canada | 2,615 | 5,841 | 15,458 |
| France | 40,261 | 44,715 | 39,245 |
| Germany | 64,170 | 77,133 | 69,788 |
| India | 33,257 | 36,743 | 40,709 |
| Italy | 22,243 | 22,315 | 28,175 |
| Japan | 251,467 | 337,174 | 330,565 |
| Korea, Republic | 12,581 | 19,570 | 29,351 |
| Malaysia | 12,715 | 12,585 | 14,253 |
| Netherlands | 49,273 | 45,501 | 33,712 |
| Pakistan | 12,120 | 9,173 | 15,051 |
| Saudi Arabia | 32,210 | 28,861 | 33,736 |
| Singapore | 16,655 | 9,992 | 11,963 |
| United Arab Emirates | 310,765 | 404,823 | 443,691 |
| United Kingdom | 123,298 | 122,967 | 131,967 |
| USA | 93,766 | 98,815 | 127,587 |
| **Total** (incl. others) | 1,228,083 | 1,449,244 | 1,581,848 |

## OMAN

| Exports f.o.b. (US $ '000) | 1987 | 1988 | 1989 |
|---|---|---|---|
| France | 2,182 | 40,925 | 30,551 |
| India | 132,765 | 36,921 | 5,267 |
| Italy | 137,690 | 5,527 | 5,147 |
| Japan | 1,440,378 | 1,445,166 | 1,361,257 |
| Korea, Republic | 560,611 | 671,817 | 1,132,410 |
| Netherlands | 66,657 | 17,161 | 10,363 |
| Philippines | 54,517 | 81,791 | 163 |
| Saudi Arabia | 18,547 | 18,805 | 39,751 |
| Singapore | 250,373 | 80,028 | 205,237 |
| Thailand | 124,485 | 54,395 | 45,579 |
| United Arab Emirates | 144,084 | 187,047 | 212,690 |
| USA | 207,891 | 51,035 | 109,449 |
| **Total** (incl. others) | 3,776,064 | 3,268,256 | 3,932,767 |

Source (for Exports): UN, *International Trade Statistics Yearbook*.

## Transport

**ROAD TRAFFIC** (vehicles in use at 31 December)

|  | 1991 | 1992 | 1993 |
|---|---|---|---|
| Private cars | 124,884 | 136,960 | 147,199 |
| Taxis | 6,381 | 8,823 | 11,088 |
| Commercial | 78,335 | 81,934 | 85,487 |
| Government | 20,103 | 20,020 | 21,158 |
| Motor-cycles | 4,479 | 4,703 | 4,742 |
| Private hire | 1,528 | 1,954 | 2,577 |
| Diplomatic | 454 | 520 | 592 |
| **Total** | 236,299 | 254,914 | 272,843 |

**INTERNATIONAL SEA-BORNE SHIPPING**
(freight traffic, '000 metric tons)

|  | 1988 | 1989 | 1990 |
|---|---|---|---|
| Goods loaded | 29,230 | 32,576 | 33,843 |
| Goods unloaded | 2,450 | 2,444 | 2,492 |

Source: UN, *Monthly Bulletin of Statistics*.

**CIVIL AVIATION** (traffic on scheduled services)

|  | 1990 | 1991 | 1992 |
|---|---|---|---|
| Kilometres flown (million) | 13 | 12 | 17 |
| Passengers carried ('000) | 853 | 958 | 1,081 |
| Passenger-km (million) | 1,602 | 1,729 | 1,987 |
| Total ton-km (million) | 198 | 216 | 258 |

Note: Figures include an apportionment (one-quarter) of the traffic of Gulf Air, a multinational airline with its headquarters in Bahrain.

Source: UN, *Statistical Yearbook*.

## Communications Media

|  | 1990 | 1991 | 1992 |
|---|---|---|---|
| Radio receivers ('000 in use) | 970 | 1,006 | 1,043 |
| Television receivers ('000 in use) | 1,150 | 1,150 | 1,195 |
| Telephones ('000 main lines in use) | 104 | 120 | n.a. |
| Daily newspapers: |  |  |  |
| Number | 4 | n.a. | 4 |
| Average circulation ('000 copies) | 62 | n.a. | 79 |

**1992:** Book production (excl. pamphlets) 24 titles, 25,000 copies; Non-daily newspapers 5; Other periodicals 15.

Sources: UNESCO, *Statistical Yearbook*; UN, *Statistical Yearbook*.

## Education

(1992)

|  | Insti-tutions | Teachers | Pupils/Students Males | Females | Total |
|---|---|---|---|---|---|
| Government Schools |  |  |  |  |  |
| Pre-primary | 10 | 223 | 2,453 | 1,982 | 4,435 |
| Primary | 416 | 10,839 | 152,343 | 137,568 | 289,911 |
| Secondary | n.a. | 8,537 | 75,324 | 65,437 | 140,761 |

**Higher Education:** 732 teachers, 5,962 students in 1990; 7,322 students in 1991.

Source: UNESCO, *Statistical Yearbook*.

# Statistical Survey, Directory

## The Constitution

Oman has no written constitution. The Sultan has absolute power and legislates by decree. He rules with the assistance of an appointed Council of Ministers, which is permitted to take decisions in his absence. The country has no legislature, but there is a Consultative Council, the Majlis al-Shoura, established in November 1991, whose 80 members are appointed by the Sultan from lists of two or four candidates (depending on the population of the region) nominated by leading figures in each region and are empowered to discuss, and advise on, economic and social affairs.

## The Government

### HEAD OF STATE

**Sultan:** Qaboos bin Said (assumed power on 23 July 1970, after deposing his father).

### COUNCIL OF MINISTERS
(June 1995)

**Prime Minister and Minister of Foreign Affairs, Defence and Finance:** Sultan Qaboos bin Said.

**Deputy Prime Minister for Security and Defence:** Sayed Fahar bin Taimour as-Said.

**Deputy Prime Minister for Cabinet Affairs:** Sayed Fahd bin Mahmoud as-Said.

**Deputy Prime Minister for Financial and Economic Affairs:** Qais bin Abd al-Munim az-Zawawi.

**Special Representative of the Sultan:** Sayed Thuwaini bin Shihab as-Said.

**Special Advisor to the Sultan:** Sayed Hamad bin Hamoud al-Busaidi.

**Minister of Legal Affairs:** Muhammad al-Alawi.

**Minister of Petroleum and Minerals:** Said bin Ahmad bin Said ash-Shanfari.

**Minister of Justice and Awqaf (Religious Endowments) and Islamic Affairs:** Hamoud bin Abdullah al-Harthi.

**Minister of State for Foreign Affairs:** Yousuf bin al-Alawi bin Abdullah.

**Minister of Information:** Abd al-Aziz bin Muhammad ar-Rowas.

**Minister of Electricity and Water:** Sheikh Muhammad bin Ali al-Qutaibi.

**Minister of Posts, Telegraphs and Telephones:** Ahmad bin Sowaidan al-Baluchi.

**Minister of Communications:** SALIM BIN ABDULLAH AL-GHAZALI.
**Minister of Education:** Sayed SAUD BIN IBRAHIM AL-BUSAIDI.
**Minister of Higher Education:** YAHYA BIN MAHFOUZ AL-MANTHARI.
**Minister of Social Affairs and Labour:** AHMAD BIN MUHAMMAD AL-ISA'EE.
**Minister of Housing:** MALEK BIN SULAIMAN AL-MUAMMARI.
**Minister of National Heritage and Culture:** Sayed FAISAL BIN ALI AS-SAID.
**Minister of the Interior:** Sayed BADR BIN SAUD BIN HAREB AL-BUSAIDI.
**Minister of Commerce and Industry:** MAQBOOL BIN ALI BIN SULTAN.
**Minister of Agriculture and Fisheries:** Sheikh MUHAMMAD BIN ABDULLAH BIN ZAHIR AL-HINAI.
**Minister of Water Resources:** HAMID BIN SAID AL-AUFI.
**Minister of Health:** Dr ALI BIN MUHAMMAD BIN MOUSA.
**Minister of Regional Municipalities and of the Environment:** Sheikh AMIR BIN SHUWAIN AL-HOSNI.
**Minister of the Civil Service:** AHMAD BIN ABD AN-NABI MACKI.
**Minister of State for Development Affairs:** MUHAMMAD BIN MUSA AL-YUSUF.
**Governor of Muscat and Minister of State:** Sayed AL-MUTASSIM BIN HAMOUD AL-BUSAIDI.
**Governor of Dhofar and Minister of State:** Sayed MUSSALLAM BIN ALI AL-BOUSAIDI.
**Minister of the Royal Court:** Sayed SAIF BIN HAMAD BIN SAUD.
**Minister of Palace Affairs:** Gen. ALI BIN MAJID AL-MUAMARI.
**Secretary-General to the Council of Ministers:** Sayed HAMOUD BIN FAISAL BIN SAID.
**Speaker of the Consultative Council:** ABDULLAH BIN ALI AL-QATABI.

### MINISTRIES

**Diwan of the Royal Court:** POB 632, Muscat 113; tel. 738711; telex 5016.
**Ministry of Agriculture and Fisheries:** POB 467, Ruwi 113; tel. 696300; telex 3503.
**Ministry of the Civil Service:** POB 3994, Ruwi 112; tel. 696000.
**Ministry of Commerce and Industry:** POB 550, Muscat 113; tel. 799500; telex 3665; fax 794238.
**Ministry of Communications:** POB 684, Muscat 113; tel. 702233; telex 3390; fax 701776.
**Ministry of Defence:** POB 113, Muscat 113; tel. 704096; telex 3228.
**Ministry of Education:** POB 3, Ruwi 113; tel. 775209; telex 3369.
**Ministry of Electricity and Water:** POB 1941, Ruwi 112; tel. 603906; telex 3358; fax 699180.
**Ministry of Financial and Economic Affairs:** POB 896, Muscat 113; tel. 738201; telex 5663; fax 737028.
**Ministry of Foreign Affairs:** POB 252, Muscat 113; tel. 699500; telex 3337.
**Ministry of Health:** POB 393, Muscat 113; tel. 602177; telex 5294.
**Ministry of Housing:** POB 173, Muscat 113; tel. 693333; telex 3694.
**Ministry of Information:** POB 600, Muscat 113; tel. 603222; telex 6265.
**Ministry of the Interior:** POB 3127, Ruwi 113; tel. 602244; telex 5650.
**Ministry of Justice, Awqaf and Islamic Affairs:** POB 354, Ruwi 112; tel. 697699.
**Ministry of National Heritage and Culture:** POB 668, Muscat 113; tel. 602555; telex 5649.
**Ministry of Palace Affairs:** POB 2227, Ruwi 112; tel. 600841.
**Ministry of Petroleum and Minerals:** POB 551, Muscat 113; tel. 603333; telex 5280.
**Ministry of Posts, Telegraphs and Telephones:** POB 338, Ruwi 112; tel. 697888; telex 5625; fax 696817.
**Ministry of Regional Municipalities and of the Environment:** POB 323, Muscat; tel. 696444; telex 5404; fax 602320.
**Ministry of Social Affairs and Labour:** POB 560, Muscat 113; tel. 602444; telex 5002.
**Ministry of Water Resources:** POB 2575, Ruwi 112; tel. 703552.

### MAJLIS AL-SHOURA
(Consultative Council)

In November 1991 Sultan Qaboos issued a decree establishing a Consultative Council, the Majlis al-Shoura (in place of the Consultative Assembly). In early 1995 representation in the Majlis was expanded from 59 to 80 members (one for each region with fewer than 30,000 inhabitants and two for regions with 30,000 or more inhabitants), appointed by the Sultan from lists of two or four candidates (the latter in the larger regions) nominated by elders and prominent personalities in each region. Members serve a three-year term of office. The Majlis is empowered to draft legislation on economic and social matters for acceptance by the appropriate ministry. The Majlis held its inaugural session in January 1992.

**Speaker:** ABDULLAH BIN ALI AL-QATABI.

There are no political parties, and no elections take place, in Oman.

## Diplomatic Representation

### EMBASSIES IN OMAN

**Algeria:** POB 216, Muscat 115; tel. 604169; fax 694419; Ambassador: BRAHIM AISSA.
**Austria:** Moosa Complex Bldg, No 477, 2nd Floor, Way No. 3109, POB 2070, Ruwi 112; tel. 793135; telex 3042; fax 793669; Ambassador: Dr RUDOLF BOGNER.
**Bahrain:** POB 66, Madinat Qaboos, Al-Khuwair; tel. 605075; Chargé d'affaires: AHMED MOHAMED MAHMOUD.
**Bangladesh:** POB 3959, Ruwi 112; tel. 708756; telex 3800; Chargé d'affaires: AHMED SHARFUL AL-HUSSAIN.
**Brunei:** POB 91, Ruwi 112; tel. 603533; Ambassador: Pehin Dato' Haji MAHDINI.
**China, People's Republic:** Madinat Al-Ilam, Way No. 1507, House No. 465, POB 315, Muscat 112; tel. 696782; telex 5114; Ambassador: ZANG SHIXIONG.
**Egypt:** Diplomatic City, Al-Khwair, POB 2252, Ruwi 112; tel. 600411; telex 5438; fax 603626; Ambassador: MAHMOUD HUSSEIN ABD AN-NABY.
**France:** Diplomatic City, Al-Khuwair, POB 208, Muscat 115; tel. 604310; telex 5163; fax 604300; Ambassador: RÉGIS KOETSCHET.
**Germany:** POB 128, Ruwi 112; tel. 702482; telex 3440; fax 705690; Ambassador: KURT MESSER.
**India:** POB 1727, Ruwi 112; tel. 702960; telex 3429; fax 797547; Ambassador: INDRAJIT SINGH RATHORE.
**Iran:** Madinat Qaboos East, Dal, POB 3155, Ruwi 112; tel. 696944; telex 5066; fax 696888; Ambassador: SIAVASH ZARJAR YAGHOUBI.
**Iraq:** Madinat Qaboos, Road D, Villa 2803, Way No. 1737, POB 1848, Ruwi 112; tel. 604178; telex 5110; Ambassador: KHALID ABDULLAH SALEH AS-SAMIRA'I.
**Italy:** Qurum Area, No. 5, Way No. 2411, House No. 842, POB 3727, Muscat 112; tel. 560968; telex 5450; fax 564846; Ambassador: SERGIO EMINA.
**Japan:** Madinat Qaboos West, POB 3511, Ruwi 112; tel. 603464; telex 5087; fax 698720; Ambassador: AKIO IJUIN.
**Jordan:** Diplomatic City, Al-Khuwair, POB 2281, Ruwi 112; tel. 786371; telex 5518; Ambassador: SAMIR AR-RAFAI AL-HAMOUD.
**Korea, Republic:** POB 2220, Ruwi 112; tel. 702322; telex 3132; Ambassador: CHANG SUNG-OK.
**Kuwait:** Diplomatic City, Al-Khuwair, Block No. 13, POB 1798, Ruwi 112; tel. 699626; telex 5746; Ambassador: ABD AL-MOHSIN SALIM AL-HAROON.
**Lebanon:** Al-Harthy Complex, POB 67, Ruwi 118; tel. 695844; Ambassador: Sheikh ADOB ALAMUDDIN.
**Malaysia:** Madinat al-Ilam, Villa No. 1196, Way No. 1518, POB 3939, Ruwi 112; tel. 698329; telex 5565; fax 605031; Ambassador: ZULKIFLI IBRAHIM BIN ABDUL RAHMAN.
**Morocco:** Al-Ensharah Street, Villa No. 197, POB 3125, Ruwi 112; tel. 696152; telex 5560; Ambassador: ALAOUI M'HAMDI MUSTAPHA.
**Netherlands:** O.C. Centre, 7th Floor, POB 3302, Ruwi 112; tel. 705410; telex 3050; fax 799020; Ambassador: CHRISTIAAN C. SANDERS.
**Pakistan:** POB 1302, Ruwi 112; tel. 603439; telex 5451; Ambassador: SULTAN HAYAT KHAN.
**Philippines:** POB 420, Madinat Qaboos 115; tel. 694860; Ambassador: SANCHEZ ALI.
**Qatar:** Al-Mamoura Road, POB 802, Muscat 113; tel. 701802; telex 3460; Ambassador: ABD AR-RAHMAN JASIM AL-MUFTAH.
**Russia:** Shati al-Qurum Way 3032, Surfait Compound, POB 80, Muscat; tel. 602893; telex 5493; fax 602894; Ambassador: ALEKSANDR K. PATSEV.
**Saudi Arabia:** Al-Khuwair, Al-Alaam Area, POB 1411, Ruwi 112; tel. 601744; telex 5406; Ambassador: MOHAMED AL-FAHD AL-ISSA.
**Somalia:** Mumtaz Street, Villa Hassan Jumaa Baker, POB 1767, Ruwi 112; tel. 564412; telex 3253; Ambassador: MUHAMMAD SUBAN NUR.

OMAN — *Directory*

**Sri Lanka:** POB 95, Madinat Qaboos 115; tel. 697841; telex 5158; fax 697336; Ambassador: Mohamed M. Amanul Farouque.

**Sudan:** Diplomatic City, Al-Khuwair, POB 3971, Ruwi 112; tel. 697875; telex 5088; fax 699065; Ambassador: Abbas al-Maatasim Ash-Sheikh.

**Syria:** Madinat Qaboos, Al-Ensharah Street, Villa No. 201, POB 85, Muscat 115; tel. 697904; telex 5029; fax 603895; Chargé d'affaires: Anwar Webbi.

**Thailand:** Villa No. 33–34, Madinat Qaboos East, POB 60, Ruwi 115; tel. 602684; telex 5210; fax 605714; Ambassador: Pensak Charalak.

**Tunisia:** Building 183–185, Al-Ensharah Street, POB 220, Muscat 115; tel. 603486; telex 5252; Ambassador: Fethi Tounsi.

**Turkey:** Bldg. No. 3501, Street No. 3939, Al-Khuwair, South Boshar 239, POB 1511, Mutrah 114; tel. 697050; telex 5571; fax 697053; Ambassador: Emin Gündüz.

**United Arab Emirates:** Diplomatic City, Al-Khuwair, POB 551, Muscat 111; tel. 600988; telex 5299; fax 602584; Ambassador: Hamad Helal Thabit al-Kuwaiti.

**United Kingdom:** POB 300, Muscat 113; tel. 693077; fax 693087; Ambassador: Richard John Sutherland Muir.

**USA:** Diplomatic City, POB 202, Muscat 115; tel. 698989; telex 3785; fax 699771; Ambassador: David Dunford.

**Yemen:** Shati al-Qurum, Area 258, Way No. 2840, Bldg No. 2981, POB 105, Ruwi 115; tel. 604172; telex 5109; fax 605008; Chargé d'affaires: Dr Ameen Mohamed al-Yusufi.

## Judicial System

Jurisdiction is exercised by the Shari'a Courts, applying Islamic law. Local courts are presided over by Qadhis, officers appointed by the Minister of Justice, Awqaf and Islamic Affairs. The Chief Court is at Muscat. Appeals from local courts, including the court in the capital, go to the Court of Appeal at Muscat. In December 1987 a 'flying court' service was established to serve remote communities.

## Religion

### ISLAM

The majority of the population (75%) are Muslims, of whom approximately three-quarters are of the Ibadi sect and about one-quarter are Sunni Muslims.

### HINDUISM

Approximately one-quarter of the population are Hindus.

### CHRISTIANITY

#### The Anglican Communion

Within the Episcopal Church in Jerusalem and the Middle East, Oman forms part of the diocese of Cyprus and the Gulf. In Oman there are inter-denominational churches at Ruwi and Ghala, in Muscat, and at Salalah, and the congregations are entirely expatriate. The Bishop in Cyprus and the Gulf is resident in Cyprus, while the Archdeacon in the Gulf is resident in the United Arab Emirates.

**Chaplaincy:** POB 1982, Ruwi 112; tel. 702372; fax 789943; joint chaplaincy of the Anglican Church and the Reformed Church of America; Chaplain Rev. Martin Weitz.

## The Press

### NEWSPAPERS

**Al-Watan** (The Nation): POB 463, Muscat; tel. 591919; telex 5643; f. 1971; daily; Arabic; Editor-in-Chief Muhammad Sulaiman at-Tai; circ. 23,500.

**Khaleej Times:** POB 6305, Ruwi; tel. 700895; telex 3699.

**Oman Daily Newspaper:** POB 6002, Ruwi 112; tel. 701555; telex tel. 790524; 3638; daily; Arabic; Editor-in-Chief Habib Muhammad Nasib; circ. 15,560.

#### English Language

**Oman Daily Observer:** POB 3002, Ruwi 112; tel. 703055; telex 3638; fax 790524; f. 1981; daily; publ. by Oman Newspaper House; Editor Said bin Khalfan al-Harthi; circ. 22,000.

**Times of Oman:** POB 770, Ruwi 112; tel. 701953; telex 3352; fax 799153; f. 1975; daily; Founder, Propr and Editor-in-Chief Muhammad az-Zedjali; Man. Dir Anis bin Essa az-Zedjali; circ. 18,000.

### PERIODICALS

**Al-Adwaa'** (Lights): POB 580, Muscat; tel. 704353; telex 3376; 2 a month; Arabic; economic, political and social; Editor-in-Chief Habib Muhammad Nasib; circ. 15,600.

**Al-'Akidah** (The Faith): Ruwi; tel. 701000; telex 3399; weekly illustrated magazine; Arabic; Editor Said as-Samhan al-Kathiri; circ. 5,000.

**Al-Ghorfa** (Oman Commerce): POB 1400, Ruwi; tel. 707674; telex 3389; fax 708497; six a year; English and Arabic; business; publ. by Oman Chamber of Commerce and Industry; Editor Yaqoub bin Hamed al-Harthy.

**Al-Markazi** (The Central): POB 1161, Ruwi 112; tel. 702222; telex 3794; f. 1975; bi-monthly magazine; English and Arabic; publ. by Central Bank of Oman.

**Al-Mawared at-Tabeey'iyah** (Natural Resources): POB 551, Muscat; publ. by Ministries of Agriculture and Fisheries and of Petroleum and Minerals; monthly; English and Arabic; Editor Khalid az-Zubaidi.

**Al-Mazari'** (Farms): POB 467, Muscat; weekly journal of the Ministry of Agriculture and Fisheries; Editor Khalid az-Zubaidi.

**An-Nahda** (The Renaissance): POB 979, Muscat; tel. 563104; fax 563106; weekly; illustrated magazine; Arabic; Editor Taleb Said al-Meawaly; circ. 10,000.

**Oman Today:** Apex Publishing, POB 2616, Ruwi 112; tel. 799388; fax 793316; f. 1981; bi-monthly; English; leisure and sports; Editor Brent McCallum.

**Al-Omaniya** (Omani Woman): POB 3303, Ruwi 112; tel. 792700; telex 3758; fax 707765; monthly; Arabic; circ. 11,500.

**Ash-Shurta** (The Police): Muscat; tel. 569216; telex 5377; fax 562341; magazine of Royal Oman Police; Editor Director of Public Relations.

**Al-Usra** (The Family): POB 7440, Mutrah; tel. 794922; telex 3266; fax 795348; f. 1974; weekly; Arabic; socio-economic illustrated family magazine; Chief Editor Sadek Abdowani; circ. 12,585.

**The Commercial:** POB 2002, Muscat; tel. 704022; telex 3189; fax 795885; monthly; Arabic and English; advertising.

**Jund Oman** (Soldiers of Oman): POB 113, Muscat; tel. 613615; telex 5228; fax 613369; monthly; illustrated magazine of the Ministry of Defence; Supervisor: Deputy Prime Minister for Security and Defence.

**Risalat al-Masjed** (The Mosque Message): POB 6066, Muscat; tel. 561178; fax 560607; issued by Diwan of Royal Court Affairs Protocol Dept (Schools and Mosques Section); Editor Jouma bin Muhammad bin Salem al-Wahaibi.

### NEWS AGENCY

**Oman News Agency:** Ministry of Information, POB 3659, Ruwi 112; tel. 696970; telex 5256; Dir-Gen. Muhammad bin Salim al-Marhoon.

## Publishers

**Apex Publishing:** POB 2616, Ruwi; tel. 799388; trade directory and maps, leisure and business magazines and guide books; Man. Dir Saleh M. Talib.

**Arabian Distribution and Publishing Enterprise:** Mutrah; tel. 707079; telex 3085.

**Dar al-Usra:** POB 7440, Mutrah; tel. 712129; telex 5408.

**National Publishing and Advertising LLC:** POB 3112, Ruwi 112; tel. 795373; telex 3352; fax 708445; Man. Dir Anees Essa az-Zedjali.

**Oman Publishing House:** POB 580, Muscat; tel. 704353.

**Ash-Shahmi Publishers and Advertisers:** POB 6112, Ruwi; tel. 703416; telex 3564.

## Radio and Television

In 1992, according to UNESCO estimates, there were 1,043,000 radio receivers and 1.2m. television receivers in use.

### RADIO

**Radio Sultanate of Oman:** Ministry of Information, POB 600, Muscat 113; tel. 603222; telex 3265; fax 601393; f. 1970; transmits in Arabic 20 hours daily, English on FM 15 hours daily; Dir-Gen. Ali bin Abdullah al-Mujeni.

**Radio Salalah:** f. 1970; transmits daily programmes in Arabic and the Dhofari languages; Dir Muhammad bin Ahmad ar-Rowas.

The British Broadcasting Corporation (BBC) has built a powerful medium-wave relay station on Masirah Island. It is used to expand

# OMAN

and improve the reception of the BBC's Arabic, Farsi, Hindi, Pashtu and Urdu services.

## TELEVISION

**Oman Television:** Ministry of Information, POB 600, Muscat; tel. 603222; telex 5454; fax 602381.

A colour television station, built at Qurm, outside Muscat, by the German company Siemens AG, was opened in 1974. A colour television system for Dhofar opened in 1975. Advertising was introduced on local television in August 1987.

# Finance

(cap. = capital; p.u. = paid up; res = reserves; dep. = deposits; m. = million; brs = branches; amounts in rials Omani unless otherwise stated)

## BANKING

At 31 October 1989 there were 24 licensed banks, with a network of 240 branch offices, operating throughout Oman. In 1993 the Central Bank of Oman issued instructions whereby the minimum capital for licensed banks was increased to RO 10m., and incentives were offered to encourage mergers, in an effort to rationalize the domestic banking system.

### Central Bank

**Central Bank of Oman:** POB 1161, Ruwi 112; tel. 702222; telex 3794; fax 702253; f. 1974; cap. 175m., res 213.8m., dep. 308.7m., total assets 1,016.3m. (1992); 100% state-owned; Exec. Pres. HAMOUD SANGOUR HASIM; Deputy Chair. AHMAD BIN ABD AN-NABI MACKI; Pres. Dr ABD AL-WAHAB KHAYATA; 2 brs.

### Commercial Banks

**Bank Muscat Al-Ahli Al-Omani SAOG:** POB 134, Ruwi 112; tel. 703044; telex 3450; fax 707806; f. 1993 by merger; wholly owned by Omani shareholders; cap. 15.0m., res 5.5m., dep. 249.1m., total assets 269.6m. (1993); Chair. Sheikh ZAHER BIN HAMAD AL-HARTHY; Gen. Man. YESHWANT C. DESAI; 14 brs.

**Bank of Oman, Bahrain and Kuwait SAOG (BOBK):** POB 1708, Ruwi 112; tel. 701528; telex 3290; fax 705607; f. 1973; 51% Omaniowned, 49% by Bank of Oman, Bahrain and Kuwait BSC; cap. 15m., res 4.8m., dep. 108.3m., total assets 129.1m. (1994); Chair. MOHSIN HAIDER DARWISH; Gen. Man. IAIN A. MARNOCH; 36 brs.

**Commercial Bank of Oman Ltd SAOG:** POB 1696, Ruwi; tel. 793226; telex 3275; fax 793229; reorg. 1993 (when it absorbed Oman Banking Corporation); 87% Omani-owned, 13% by United Bank Ltd (Pakistan); cap. 11m., res 0.8m., dep. 95.1m., total assets 108.2m. (Dec. 1994); Chair. AMER BIN SHUWAIN AL-HOSNI; Gen. Man. W. S. HARLEY; 25 brs.

**National Bank of Oman Ltd SAOG (NBO):** POB 3751, Ruwi; tel. 708894; telex 3281; fax 707781; f. 1973; 100% Omani-owned; cap. 20m., res 4.4m., dep. 218.1m., total assets 286.6m. (1994); Chair. KHALFAN BIN NASSER AL-WOHAIBI; Gen. Man. AUBYN R. HILL; 50 brs.

**Oman Arab Bank SAO:** POB 2010, Ruwi 112; tel. 700161; telex 3285; fax 797736; f. 1984; purchased Omani European Bank SAOG in 1994; 51% Omani-owned, 49% by Arab Bank (Jordan) Ltd; cap. 10m., res 2.4m., dep. 111.0m., total assets 123.7m. (1993); Chair. AHMED BIN SWAIDAN AL-BALOUSHI; Gen. Man. ABD AL-QADER ASKALAN; 14 brs.

**Oman International Bank SAOG:** POB 1727, Muscat 111; tel. 682500; telex 5406; fax 682800; f. 1984; 100% Omani-owned; cap. 13.5m., res 2.9m., dep. 237.3m., total assets 263.3m. (1993); Chair. Dr OMAR BIN ABD MUNIEM AL-ZAWAWI; CEO JAMES T. M. MCNIE; Gen. Man. YAHYA SAID ABDULLA AL-JABRY; 60 brs.

### Foreign Banks

**ANZ Grindlays Bank PLC** (UK): POB 3550, Ruwi 112; tel. 703013; telex 3393; fax 706911; f. 1969; Man. IAIN B. MCDOUGALL; Dep. Man. MOHD ZAHRAN; 2 brs.

**Bank of Baroda** (India): POB 231, Mutrah 114; tel. 714559; telex 5470; fax 714560; f. 1976; Man. C. B. CHAYYA; 3 brs.

**Bank Dhofar al-Omani al-Fransi SAOC:** POB 1507, Ruwi 112; tel. 790466; telex 3900; fax 797246; f. 1990; cap. 15m., res 0.4m., dep. 72.6m., total assets 96.1m. (1993); acquired 12 branches of former Bank of Credit and Commerce International in 1992; Gen. Man. LUC ROUSSELET; 12 brs.

**Bank Melli Iran:** POB 2643, Ruwi 112; tel. 787189; telex 3295; fax 793017; f. 1974; Gen. Man. ALI JAFFARI LAFTI.

**Bank Saderat Iran:** POB 1269, Ruwi 112; tel. 787189; telex 3146; fax 796478; Man. M. SEFIDARI.

*Directory*

**Banque Banorabe** (France): POB 1608, Ruwi; tel. 703850; telex 3666; fax 707782; f. 1981; fmrly Banque de l'Orient Arabe et d'Outre Mer; Man. WALID AZHARI.

**British Bank of the Middle East** (Channel Islands): POB 240, Ruwi 112; tel. 799929; telex 3110; fax 704241; f. 1948; CEO: IAN W. GILL; 4 brs.

**Citibank NA** (USA): POB 8994, Mutrah; tel. 795705; telex 3444; fax 795724; f. 1975; Vice-Pres. MUHAMMAD ZAHRAN.

**Habib Bank AG-Zürich** (Switzerland): POB 2717, Ruwi 112; tel. 799876; telex 3931; fax 703613; f. 1967; Exec. Vice-Pres. WAZIR MUMTAZ AHMAD; Asst Vice-Pres. MUHAMMAD IQBAL MUMAL; 5 brs.

**Habib Bank Ltd** (incorporated in Pakistan): POB 3538, Ruwi 112; tel. 705272; telex 3305; fax 795283; f. 1972; Sr Vice-Pres. and Gen. Man. S. FAZAL MABOOD; 12 brs.

**National Bank of Abu Dhabi** (UAE): POB 303, Ruwi 113; tel. 798842; telex 3740; fax 794386; f. 1976; Man. DAVID J. RUNDLE.

**Standard Chartered Bank** (UK): POB 2353, Ruwi 112; tel. 703999; telex 3217; fax 796864; f. 1968; Man. A. J. PREBBLE; 4 brs.

### Development Banks

**Oman Bank for Agriculture and Fisheries SAOC:** POB 3077, Ruwi 112; tel. 701761; telex 3046; fax 706473; f. 1981; short-, medium- and long-term finance for all activities in the public sector related to agriculture and fisheries; state-owned; total assets 20.6m. (Dec. 1994); the total value of loans granted to Dec. 1994 was 48.8m.; Chair. Sheikh MUHAMMAD BIN ABDULLAH BIN ZAHER AL-HINAI; Gen. Man. TARIQ BIN ABDULREDHA BIN MUHAMMAD AL-JAMALI; 12 brs.

**Oman Development Bank SAOG:** POB 309, Muscat 113; tel. 738021; telex 5179; fax 738026; f. 1977; short-, medium- and longterm finance for industrial development projects; 54.2% stateowned, 30.5% foreign-owned, 15.3% Omani citizens and companies; total assets 52.5m. (1994); Chair. MUHAMMAD BIN MUSA AL-YOUSUF; Gen. Man. MURTADHA BIN MUHAMMAD FADHIL.

**Oman Housing Bank SAOC:** POB 2555, Ruwi; tel. 704444; telex 3077; fax 704071; f. 1977; medium- and long-term finance for housing development; 100% state-owned; cap. 30m., res 22m., dep. 1.4m; total assets 133m. (1994); Chair. MALIK BIN SULAIMAN BIN SAID AL-MA'MARI; Gen. Man. MAHMOUD BIN MUHAMMAD OMAR BAHRAM; 9 brs.

## STOCK EXCHANGE

**Muscat Securities Market:** POB 3265, Muscat 112; tel. 702607; telex 3220; fax 702691; f. 1990; Dir-Gen. MAHMOUD AL-JARWANI.

## INSURANCE

**Al-Ahlia Insurance Co SAO:** POB 1463, Ruwi; tel. 709331; telex 3518; fax 797151; f. 1985; cap. 2m.; Chair. MOHSIN HAIDER DARWISH; Gen. Man. G. V. RAO.

**Oman National Insurance Co SAOG (ONIC):** POB 5254, Ruwi; tel. 795020; telex 3111; fax 702569; f. 1978; cap. p.u. 2m.; Chair. MUHAMMAD BIN MUSA AL-YUSEF; Gen. Man. MICHAEL J. ADAMS.

**Oman United Insurance Co SAOG:** POB 1522, Ruwi 112; tel. 703990; telex 3652; fax 796327; f. 1985; cap. 2m.; Chair. SAID SALIM BIN NASSIR AL-BUSAIDI; Gen. Man. KHALID MANSOUR HAMED.

# Trade and Industry

**Oman Chamber of Commerce and Industry:** POB 1400, Ruwi 112; tel. 707684; telex 3389; fax 708497; Pres. YAQOUB BIN HAMED AL-HARTHY; 55,000 mems (1992).

## STATE ENTERPRISES

**Oman Cement Co SAO:** POB 560, Ruwi; tel. 626626; telex 5139; fax 626414; f. 1977; development and production of cement; partial privatization commenced in mid-1994; Chair. Dr ALYQDHAN AL-HINAI.

**Oman Flour Mills Co Ltd SAO:** POB 566, Ruwi; tel. 711155; telex 5422; fax 714711; f. 1976; sales US $65m. (1992/93); cap. $10m.; 60% state-owned; produces 6,000 tons per day (t/d) of various flours and 600 t/d of animal feedstuffs; Chair. RASHID BIN SALIM AL-MASROORY; 147 employees.

**Oman Mining Co Ltd LLC:** POB 758, Muscat; tel. 793925; telex 3041; fax 793865; f. 1978; cap. RO 25m.; state-owned; development of copper, gold and chromite mines; Chair. MOHSIN HAIDER DARWISH.

**Oman National Electric Co SAO:** POB 1393, Ruwi; tel. 796353; telex 3328; fax 704420; f. 1978; Chair. HAMOUD BIN SONGOR BIN HASHIM; Gen. Man. M. OSMAN BAIG.

## PETROLEUM

**Petroleum Development Oman LLC (PDO):** POB 81, Muscat; tel. 678111; telex 5212; fax 677106; incorporated in Sultanate of Oman since 1980 by royal decree as limited liability company; 60% owned by Oman Govt, 34% by Shell, 4% by Total-CFP and 2% by Partex; production (1992) averaged 692,000 b/d from 69 fields, linked by a pipeline system to terminal at Mina al-Fahal, near Muscat; Man. Dir H. A. MERLE; 4,500 employees.

**Amoco Oman Petroleum Co:** POB 1690, Ruwi 112; tel. 698402; fax 698408; holds one concession area, totalling 15,000 sq km, in northern Oman. No production recorded to date; Pres. and Man. A. E. ROBINSON.

**BP Middle East:** POB 92, 116 Mina al-Fahal; tel. 561801; telex 5419; fax 561283; CEO MARK M. WARE.

**Elf Petroleum Oman:** POB 353, Ruwi; tel. 694655; fax 694663; concession granted in 1975 for exploration in the onshore region of Butabul; area of 7,000 sq km; converted to a production sharing agreement in October 1976; 48% owned by Elf, 32% by Sumitomo and 20% by Wintershall; present concession area 4,033 sq km (1992) at Butabul; production 6,000 b/d.

**Japex Oman:** POB 543, Ruwi; tel. 602011; telex 5695; fax 602181; f. 1981; operates a concession at Wahibah; 49.6% owned by JNOC, 35.3% by JAPEX and 10.1% by CIECO; present concession area 1,856 sq km (1993) at Wadi Aswad; production 8,000 b/d; Man. K. MAENAMI.

**National Gas Co SAOG:** POB 95, CPO Seeb Airport; tel. Rusail 626073; fax 626307; f. 1979; bottling of liquefied petroleum gas; Gen. Man. P. K. BAGCHI; 83 employees.

**Occidental of Oman Inc.:** POB 2271, Ruwi 112; tel. 603386; telex 5258; fax 603358; fmrly Occidental Petroleum Corpn (Occidental Oman); succeeded Gulf Oman Petroleum as majority shareholders in Suneinah concession in 1983; total area of 9,717 sq km; US $11m. oil stabilization plant completed 1989.

**Oman Liquefied Natural Gas Co (OLNGC):** f. 1992; 51% state-owned; construction and management of 5,000 tons-per-year LNG plant at Bimma, shipping and marketing.

**Oman Refinery Co LLC:** POB 3568, Ruwi 112; tel. 561200; telex 5123; fax 561384; production of light petroleum products; Gen. Man. JAY RODNEY MCINTIRE; 286 employees.

The Government has granted exploration rights over a large area of western and south-western Dhofar to BP, Deminex, AGIP, Hispanoil, Elf/Aquitaine I, the Adolph Lundin Group, Quintana/Gulf and Cluff Oil.

# Transport

**Directorate-General of Roads:** POB 7027, Mutrah; tel. 701577; Dir-Gen. of Roads Sheikh MUHAMMAD BIN HILAL AL-KHALILI.

**Directorate-General of Ports and Public Transport:** POB 684, Muscat; tel. 702044; telex 7390; Dir-Gen. Eng. SALIM BIN HUMAID AL-GHASSANI.

## ROADS

A network of adequate graded roads links all the main centres of population and only a few mountain villages are not accessible by Land Rover. In 1993 there were 5,349 km of asphalt road and 21,000 km of graded roads.

**Oman National Transport Co SAOG:** POB 620, Muscat; tel. 590046; telex 5018; fax 590152; operates local, regional and long-distance bus services from Muscat; Chair. TARIQ BIN MUHAMMAD AMIN AL-MANTHERI; Man. Dir SULEIMAN BIN MUHANA AL-ADAWI.

## SHIPPING

Port Sultan Qaboos, at the entrance to the Persian (Arabian) Gulf, was built in 1974 to provide nine deep-water berths varying in length from 250 to 750 ft (76 to 228 m), with draughts of up to 43 ft (13 m), and three berths for shallow-draught vessels drawing 12 to 16 ft (3.7 to 4.9 m) of water. A total of 12 new berths have been opened and two of the existing berths have been upgraded to a container terminal capable of handling 60 containers per hour. The port also has a 3,000-ton-capacity cold store which belongs to the Oman Fisheries Company. In 1993 1,513 ships visited Port Sultan Qaboos, and 3.0m. tons of cargo were handled. In 1992 work commenced on the upgrading and expansion of Port Sultan Qaboos.

**Port Services Corporation SAOG:** POB 133, Muscat 113; tel. 714001; telex 5233; fax 714007; f. 1976; cap. RO 4.8m.; jointly owned by the Govt of Oman and private shareholders; Chair. SALIM BIN ABDULLAH AL-GHAZALI; Pres. AWAD BIN SALIM ASH-SHANFARI.

The oil terminal at Mina al-Fahal can also accommodate the largest super-tankers on offshore loading buoys. Similar facilities for the import of refined petroleum products exist at Mina al-Fahal. Mina Raysut, near Salalah, has been developed into an all-weather port, and, in addition to container facilities, has four deep-water berths and two shallow berths. During 1992 1,221 ships called at the port. Loading facilities for smaller craft exist at Sohar, Khaboura, Sur, Marbet, Ras al-Had, Kasab, Al-Biaa, Masirah and Salalah.

## CIVIL AVIATION

Domestic and international flights operate from Seeb International Airport. Oman's second international airport, at Salalah, was completed in 1978. In 1993 almost 1.5m. passengers passed through Seeb International Airport. Most towns of any size have small air strips.

**Directorate-General of Civil Aviation:** POB 204, Muscat; tel. 519210; telex 5418; Dir-Gen. Eng. TARIQ BIN MUHAMMAD AL-MANTHERI.

**Gulf Aviation Ltd (Gulf Air):** POB 138, Bahrain; tel. 531166; telex 8255; fax 530385; f. 1950; jointly owned by the Govts of Bahrain, Oman, Qatar and Abu Dhabi (UAE); international services to destinations in Europe, the USA, Africa, the Middle East and the Far East; Chair. YOUSUF AHMAD ASH-SHIRAWI; Pres. and Chief Exec. ALI IBRAHIM AL-MALKI.

**Oman Aviation Services Co SAOG:** POB 1058, Seeb International Airport; tel. 519223; telex 5424; fax 510805; f. 1981; cap. p.u. RO 7m.; 35% of shares owned by Government, 65% by Omani nationals; air-charter, maintenance, handling and catering; operators of Oman's domestic airline; Chair. SALIM BIN ABDULLAH AL-GHAZALI.

# Tourism

Tourism, introduced in 1985, is strictly controlled. Attractions, apart from the capital itself, include Nizwa, ancient capital of the interior, Dhofar and the forts of Nakhl, Rustaq, and Al-Hazm. In 1992 there were 192,000 visitor arrivals in Oman and tourist receipts for that year totalled US $85m.

**Director-General of Tourism:** J. H. SAYYID FATIK.

# PAKISTAN

## Introductory Survey

**Location, Climate, Language, Religion, Flag, Capital**

The Islamic Republic of Pakistan lies in southern Asia, bordered by India to the east and by Afghanistan and Iran to the west. It has a short frontier with the People's Republic of China in the far north-east. The climate is dry and generally hot, with an average annual temperature of 27°C (80°F), except in the mountains, which have very cold winters. Temperatures in Karachi are generally between 13°C (55°F) and 34°C (93°F), with negligible rainfall. The principal languages are Punjabi (the language usually spoken in 48.2% of households in 1981), Pushto (13.1%), Sindhi (11.8%) and Saraiki (9.8%). Urdu (7.6%) is the national language, and English is extensively used. The state religion is Islam, embracing about 97% of the population, the remainder being mainly Hindus or Christians. The national flag (proportions 3 by 2) has a vertical white stripe at the hoist, while the remainder is dark green, with a white crescent moon and a five-pointed star in the centre. The capital is Islamabad.

**Recent History**

Pakistan was created in August 1947 by the partition of the United Kingdom's former Indian Empire into the independent states of India and Pakistan, in response to demands by elements of the Muslim population in the subcontinent for the establishment of a specifically Islamic state. Pakistan originally comprised two distinct regions, East Pakistan and West Pakistan, separated by some 1,600 km (1,000 miles) of Indian territory, and united only by a common religion. Although the majority of the population lived in the smaller part, East Pakistan, political and military power was concentrated in the west, where the Muslim League was the dominant political movement. The leader of the Muslim League, Muhammad Ali Jinnah, popularly known as Quaid-i-Azam ('Great Leader'), became the first Governor-General of Pakistan but died in 1948. The country, formerly a dominion with the British monarch as Head of State, became a republic on 23 March 1956, when Pakistan's first Constitution was promulgated. At the same time Maj.-Gen. Iskander Mirza became Pakistan's first President.

Pakistan came under military rule in early October 1958, when President Mirza abrogated the Constitution, declared martial law, dismissed the national and provincial governments and dissolved all political parties. In late October, however, Gen. (later Field Marshal) Muhammad Ayub Khan, the Martial Law Administrator appointed by Mirza, removed Mirza from office and became President himself. Ayub Khan's autocratic but modernizing regime lasted until March 1969, when he was forced to resign following widespread unrest. Gen. Agha Muhammad Yahya Khan, the Commander-in-Chief of the Army, replaced him, and martial law was reimposed.

In December 1970 the country's first general election was held for a national assembly. Sheikh Mujibur Rahman's Awami League, which advocated autonomy for East Pakistan, won almost all the seats in the east (thus gaining an absolute majority in the National Assembly), while the Pakistan People's Party (PPP), led by Zulfikar Ali Bhutto, won a majority of seats in the west. Following the failure of negotiations to achieve a coalition government of the two parties, on 23 March 1971 East Pakistan declared its independence as the People's Republic of Bangladesh. Civil war immediately broke out, as Pakistani troops clashed with Bengali irregular forces. In December 1971 the Indian army intervened in the conflict to support the Bengalis, and the Pakistani army was forced to withdraw, thus permitting Bangladesh to establish firmly its independence. In the truncated Pakistan that remained in the west, Yahya Khan resigned, military rule was ended, and Bhutto became the new President.

A new Constitution, which came into effect in August 1973, provided for a parliamentary system of government. Bhutto became executive Prime Minister, while Fazal Elahi Chaudry, hitherto Speaker of the National Assembly, became constitutional President. The PPP won an overwhelming majority of seats in elections to the National Assembly in March 1977.

However, the opposition Pakistan National Alliance (PNA) accused the PPP of widespread electoral malpractice and launched a nation-wide campaign of civil disobedience. An estimated 1,000 people died in subsequent clashes between troops and demonstrators, and some 40,000 people were arrested. Armed clashes were also reported between supporters of the PNA and the PPP.

In July 1977 the armed forces intervened in the crisis: Bhutto was deposed in a bloodless military coup and a martial law regime was instituted, with Gen. Mohammad Zia ul-Haq, the Army Chief of Staff, as Chief Martial Law Administrator. President Chaudry remained in office as Head of State. Bhutto was subsequently charged with instigating the murder of a PPP dissident and a member of the dissident's family in 1974. He was sentenced to death in March 1978 and executed in April 1979, after the failure of an appeal to the Supreme Court on his behalf.

In September 1978 President Chaudry resigned and Gen. Zia became President. General elections were postponed several times by the military administration, and in October 1979 Gen. Zia announced an indefinite postponement of the polls. Opposition to the military regime was severely suppressed, particularly after new martial law orders were adopted in May 1980. In March 1981 nine political parties formed an opposition alliance, the Movement for the Restoration of Democracy (MRD), which advocated an end to military rule and a return to a parliamentary system of government. Several opposition politicians were subsequently interned or placed under house arrest. In August 1983 the MRD, led by the PPP, launched a civil disobedience campaign to press for the restoration of parliamentary democracy on the basis of the 1973 Constitution. The campaign enjoyed considerable support in Sindh province, where anti-Government protests resulted in numerous deaths. However, there was limited popular support elsewhere in the country, and the campaign ended in December. Many political leaders and activists, including Benazir Bhutto (daughter of the former President and herself a leading PPP activist), were subsequently imprisoned or went into exile.

Gen. Zia's regime zealously pursued a policy of 'Islamization' of the country's institutions, including the enforcement of Islamic penal codes, and the introduction of Islamic economic principles, such as interest-free banking. In December 1984 an unexpected referendum was held, which sought affirmation of the Islamization process and, indirectly, confirmation in office for a further five years of Gen. Zia. The referendum was boycotted by the MRD, but, according to official figures, 98% of those participating supported the proposal. There were, however, widespread allegations of electoral malpractice.

In February 1985 a general election was held for a national assembly, followed shortly afterwards by elections to four provincial assemblies. The elections were held on a non-party basis, but widespread dissatisfaction with the regime was indicated by the defeat of several of Zia's cabinet ministers and close supporters. The largest two groupings in the new National Assembly were formed by a faction of the Pakistan Muslim League (PML, the successor to the Muslim League), known as the Pagara Group, and former members of the PPP. In late March Gen. Zia appointed Muhammad Khan Junejo, a member of the PML (Pagara Group) as Prime Minister, and an almost entirely civilian Cabinet was formed.

In October 1985 the National Assembly approved changes to the Constitution (the 'Eighth Amendment'), proposed by Gen. Zia, which introduced a powerful executive presidency and indemnified all actions of the military regime during the previous eight years. On 30 December Gen. Zia announced the repeal of martial law and the restoration of the Constitution (as amended in October). The military courts were dissolved, and military personnel were removed from civilian posts, with the exception of Gen. Zia, who remained as President and head of the armed forces. Junejo retained the post of Prime Minister in a new Cabinet. However, the MRD continued to demand the restoration of the unamended 1973 Constitution. In April 1986 its cause was strengthened by the return from exile of Benazir Bhutto, who travelled throughout the country holding political rallies, which attracted thousands of supporters. She demanded the resignation of President Zia and the holding of a free general election, open to all political parties. In May Benazir Bhutto and her mother, Nusrat Bhutto, were elected as Co-Chairwomen of the PPP. In August the Government adopted a less tolerant approach towards the MRD by banning all rallies scheduled for Independence Day and by detaining hundreds of opposition members, including Benazir Bhutto. The arrests provoked violent anti-Government demonstrations in a number of cities.

In late 1986 violent clashes occurred in Karachi, Quetta and Hyderabad, as a result of disputes between rival ethnic groups (primarily between the Pathans, originally from the North-West Frontier Province—NWFP—and Afghanistan, and the Urdu-speaking Muhajirs, who migrated from India when the subcontinent was partitioned in 1947). The violence was most severe in Karachi, where some 170 people were killed in December. The rise of ethnic communalism in Pakistan was reflected in the results of local elections held throughout the country in November 1987. The party of the Muhajirs, the Muhajir Qaumi Movement (MQM), won the majority of seats in Karachi and was also successful in other urban areas of Sindh province. Nation-wide, the government-supported PML won most support, while the PPP won less than 20% of total seats.

In May 1988, in accordance with the authority vested in him through the Eighth Amendment, President Zia dismissed the Prime Minister and his Cabinet, and dissolved the National Assembly and the four provincial assemblies. Zia became head of an interim administration which was to govern until a general election was held. In July Zia announced that the elections to the National Assembly and the provincial assemblies would be held in November. On 17 August 1988, however, President Zia was killed in an air crash in eastern Pakistan. Subsequent speculation that the cause of the crash was sabotage was not officially confirmed. The Chairman of the Senate, Ghulam Ishaq Khan, was appointed acting President, and an emergency National Council (composed of senior military officers, the four provincial governors and four federal ministers) was appointed to take charge of government.

Despite the imposition of a state of emergency after the death of Zia, the general election took place, as scheduled, in November 1988. In the elections to the National Assembly the PPP won 93 of the 207 directly elective seats, and was the only party to secure seats in each of Pakistan's four provinces. The Islamic Democratic Alliance (IDA), a grouping of nine Islamic and right-wing parties (including the PML), gained 54 seats, with the remaining 58 seats (polling in two constituencies was deferred, owing to the deaths of candidates) going to independents and candidates representing seven smaller parties. The PPP did not achieve such a high level of support, however, in the elections to the provincial assemblies, held three days later. The PPP was able to form coalition governments in Sindh and the NWFP, but the IDA took power in Punjab, the most populous province. At the federal level, a coalition Government was formed by the PPP and the MQM, which together had a working majority in the National Assembly (the MQM had 14 seats). Benazir Bhutto, the leader of the PPP, was appointed Prime Minister on 1 December, thus becoming the first female leader of a Muslim country. The state of emergency was repealed on the same day. A new Cabinet was formed, and later in December an electoral college (comprising the Senate, the National Assembly and the four provincial assemblies) elected Ghulam Ishaq Khan as President.

Benazir Bhutto's attempts, in early 1989, to repeal the Eighth Amendment to the Constitution, which severely constrained her powers as Prime Minister, were unsuccessful. Moreover, the fragile coalitions that the PPP had formed in the provincial assemblies soon came under pressure. In late April the coalition Government formed by the PPP and the Awami National Party (ANP) in the NWFP collapsed, following the resignation of five provincial ANP ministers. In May the coalition with the MQM in Sindh province also collapsed, following the resignation of three MQM ministers from the provincial government in the wake of renewed ethnic conflict in the region. In the same month the opposition was strengthened by the formation of an informal parliamentary grouping, the Combined Opposition Party (COP), comprising the IDA, the ANP, the Jamiat-e-Ulema-e-Islam (JUI) and the Pakistan Awami Ittehad. In October the Government suffered its most serious set-back when the MQM withdrew its parliamentary support for the PPP and transferred it to the opposition, claiming that the PPP had failed to honour any of the promises made in the original co-operation agreement between the two parties.

In November 1989 a parliamentary motion of 'no confidence', proposed by the COP against the Government, was narrowly defeated. In January 1990 the COP organized a campaign against the Government, accusing it of corruption, political bribery and mismanagement. Rallies and demonstrations in Sindh province culminated in violence between supporters of the PPP and the MQM; in May about 100 people were killed during violent clashes between police and demonstrators in the region. Calm was temporarily restored by the deployment of army units in Sindh.

By mid-1990 the initial popularity of the PPP Government appeared to have declined considerably: the maintenance of law and order had worsened; no significant new legislation had been introduced; the economic situation was deteriorating; and there were widespread allegations of corruption against high-ranking officials. On 6 August the President, in accordance with his constitutional powers, dissolved the National Assembly, dismissed the Prime Minister and her Cabinet and declared a state of emergency. He also announced that a general election would take place in late October. The President alleged that the ousted Government had violated the Constitution, accusing it of corruption, nepotism and incompetence. Ghulam Mustafa Jatoi, the leader of the COP in the National Assembly, was appointed acting Prime Minister in an interim Government. The four provincial assemblies were also dissolved, and 'caretaker' Chief Ministers appointed. Benazir Bhutto claimed that the dissolution of her administration was illegal and strongly denied the various charges made against her Government. At the end of August several of Benazir Bhutto's former ministers were arrested, and in early September she herself was indicted on more than 10 charges of corruption and abuse of power. In early October Benazir Bhutto's husband was arrested on charges of extortion, kidnapping and financial irregularities.

At the general election, which took place, as scheduled, on 24 October 1990, the IDA doubled its representation in the National Assembly, leaving it only four seats short of an absolute majority, while the People's Democratic Alliance (PDA, an electoral alliance comprising the PPP and three smaller parties) suffered a heavy defeat. Support for the PPP also declined in the provincial elections, where it unexpectedly lost control of its traditional stronghold in Sindh and fared badly elsewhere. Regional and ethnic parties continued to expand their influence, notably the MQM in urban areas of Sindh, and the ANP in the NWFP. On 6 November Mohammad Nawaz Sharif, the leader of the IDA, was elected as the new Prime Minister. He officially ended the three-month-long state of emergency, and appointed a new Cabinet, which included several ministers who had served under President Zia. Sharif promised that one of the Government's major priorities was to establish lasting peace in Sindh, where ethnic conflict and general lawlessness continued. It was alleged, however, that the Government's subsequent campaign of suppression in the province, in response to numerous local murders and kidnappings, was aimed primarily at supporters of the PPP, hundreds of whom were arrested. In January 1991 the IDA won 19 of the 25 by-elections for seats in the National Assembly and the provincial assemblies, and in March won a decisive majority in elections to 42 seats in the Senate.

The Pakistan Government's decision to send 11,000 troops to support the UN-authorized, US-led multinational force deployed in Saudi Arabia in response to the Iraqi invasion of Kuwait in August 1990 (see chapter on Iraq) provoked widespread anti-US and pro-Iraqi protests throughout Pakistan in early 1991. The protests intensified after the multinational force began military action to force Iraq to withdraw from Kuwait, and in March the long-serving Minister of Foreign Affairs, Sahabzada Yaqub Khan (who had consistently advocated amicable relations with the West), was forced to resign.

In May 1991 the National Assembly adopted legislation imposing the incorporation of the Shari'a, the Islamic legal code, in Pakistan's legal system. The Assembly also adopted legislation providing for the Islamization of the educational, economic and judicial systems. Benazir Bhutto criticized the legislation as being extreme and fundamentalist, while the right-wing JUI claimed that the new law's provisions were not stringent enough.

In the latter half of 1991 the Government was accused by the opposition of financial fraud and corruption, following the collapse of about 50 small co-operative banking institutions in Punjab, some of which were owned or controlled by government officials. Sharif's administration was also criticized for failing to contain the ethnic unrest continuing in the provinces of Sindh and Balochistan. Open confrontation between the IDA and the PPP worsened, and in November hundreds of supporters of Benazir Bhutto were arrested in Sindh. The Chief Minister of Sindh claimed that those detained were members of the Al-Zulfikar terrorist group (allegedly a militant wing of the PPP).

In addition to the continuing troubles caused by the opposition, the Prime Minister was faced with a host of problems posed by member parties of the IDA. In March 1992 the National People's Party (NPP), led by Ghulam Mustafa Jatoi, was expelled from the IDA, following the former's transfer of allegiance prior to the election of the new Chief Minister of Sindh. Events in Afghanistan in April also had a significant impact on the political situation in Pakistan. The fundamentalist Jamaat-e-Islami Pakistan (JIP) left the IDA in early May, in protest at the Government's decision to support the new moderate *mujahidin* Government in Kabul. The JIP accused the Government of abandoning the extremist Afghan guerilla leader, Gulbuddin Hekmatyar, and also of failing to effect the full Islamization of Pakistan.

In response to the continuing violence in Sindh, the Government launched 'Operation Clean-up' in May 1992, whereby the army was to apprehend criminals and terrorists, and seize unauthorized weapons. A violent clash between two factions of the MQM (the majority Altaf faction and the small breakaway Haqiqi faction) in Karachi in June provided the armed forces with the opportunity to suppress the extremist elements within the MQM. More than 500 people were arrested; caches of arms were located and seized; and 'torture cells', allegedly operated by the MQM, were discovered. The leader of the MQM(A), Altaf Hussain, accused the Government of attempting to crush the MQM through 'Operation Clean-up'. In protest, 12 of the 15 MQM members in the National Assembly and 24 of the 27 members in the Sindh Assembly resigned their seats. The Government, however, repeatedly gave assurances that the operations were against criminals, and not specifically against the MQM. Benazir Bhutto, on the other hand, insisted upon calling the MQM a terrorist organization, and exploited the informal alliance of the IDA with the MQM to condemn Sharif's Government and demand its resignation (claiming that the 1990 general election result had been manipulated by the IDA).

In mid-November 1992 the PDA intensified its campaign of political agitation and was now supported by the majority of the components of the newly-formed opposition National Democratic Alliance (NDA), including the NPP. The large-scale demonstrations and marches that Benazir Bhutto organized were, however, ruthlessly suppressed by the Government through mass arrests, road-blocks and the imposition of a two-month ban on the holding of public meetings in Islamabad and Rawalpindi and of travel restrictions on the former Prime Minister. By mid-December tension between the Government and opposition had eased considerably, and in January 1993, in an apparently conciliatory move on the part of Sharif's administration, Benazir Bhutto was elected as Chairperson of the National Assembly's Standing Committee on Foreign Affairs. Shortly after Benazir Bhutto had accepted the nomination, her husband was released on bail.

In March 1993 the growing rift between the Prime Minister and the President became more evident when the Government initiated discussions regarding proposed modifications to the Eighth Constitutional Amendment, which afforded the President the power to dismiss the Government and dissolve assemblies, and to appoint judicial and military chiefs. In late March three cabinet ministers resigned in protest at Sharif's nomination as President of the PML (Junejo Group), to succeed Muhammad Khan Junejo (who had died earlier that month), and voiced their support for Ghulam Ishaq Khan in his political struggle with the Prime Minister. In a seemingly final attempt at reconciliation, the Cabinet unanimously decided, in early April, to nominate Ghulam Ishaq Khan as candidate of the PML for the forthcoming presidential election later that year. By mid-April, however, a total of eight ministers had resigned from the Cabinet in protest at Sharif's continued tenure of the premiership. On 18 April the President dissolved the National Assembly and dismissed the Prime Minister and his Cabinet, accusing Sharif of 'maladministration, nepotism and corruption'. The provincial assemblies and governments, however, remained in power, despite demands by the PDA and the NDA for their dissolution. A member of the dissolved National Assembly, Mir Balakh Sher Mazari, was sworn in as acting Prime Minister. At the same time it was announced that elections to the National Assembly would be held on 14 July. In late April a large broadly-based interim Cabinet, including Benazir Bhutto's husband was sworn in. In early May the PML (Junejo Group) split into two factions: one led by Muhammad Nawaz Sharif, the other by Hamid Nasir Chattha, who was supported by the President.

On 26 May 1993, in an historic and unexpected judgment, the Supreme Court ordered that the National Assembly, the Prime Minister and the Cabinet (dismissed in April) should be restored to power immediately, stating that President Khan's order had been unconstitutional. The President agreed to honour the Court's ruling, and the National Assembly and Sharif's Government were reinstated with immediate effect. On the following day Sharif's return to power was consolidated when he won a vote of confidence in the National Assembly. A few days later, however, the political scene was thrown into turmoil following the dissolution, through the machinations of supporters of the President, of the provincial assemblies in Punjab and the NWFP. Finding himself without any real authority in each of the four provinces, Sharif resorted to the drastic measure of imposing federal government's rule on Punjab through a resolution passed by the National Assembly in late June. For its part, the Punjab provincial government refused to obey the federal Government's orders, claiming that they subverted provincial autonomy. The Government asked the Rangers, a federal paramilitary force, to arrange the take-over of the Punjab administration. The army's general headquarters intervened, however, at this point, to pull the Rangers out, claiming that the take-over was unconstitutional since the President had not signed the proclamation imposing direct rule. Meanwhile, an All Parties Conference (APC), including, amongst others, Benazir Bhutto and the Chief Ministers of Punjab and the NWFP, convened in Lahore to pass a resolution, urging the President to dissolve the legislature, dismiss Sharif's Government and hold fresh elections. In early July the Chief of Army Staff, following an emergency meeting of senior army officers, acted as an intermediary in talks between the President and Prime Minister in an attempt to resolve the political crisis. Benazir Bhutto, supported by her APC collaborators, announced a 'long march' on 16 July, with the intention of laying siege to the federal capital and forcing Sharif to resign. Fearing the outbreak of serious violence, the army persuaded Benazir Bhutto to postpone the march, reportedly assuring her that both the President and the Prime Minister would resign and that a general election would be held under a neutral administration. On 18 July, in accordance with an agreement reached under the auspices of the army, both Ghulam Ishaq Khan and Mohommad Nawaz Sharif resigned from their posts, the federal legislature and the provincial assemblies were dissolved, the holding of a general election in October was announced, and neutral administrations were established, at both federal and provincial level. As specified in the Constitution, Ghulam Ishaq Khan was succeeded by the Chairman of the Senate, Wasim Sajjad Jan, who was to hold the presidency for the remaining tenure of the deposed President—i.e. until November. A small, apolitical Cabinet was sworn in, headed by Moeenuddin Ahmad Qureshi, a former Executive Vice-President of the World Bank, as interim Prime Minister.

While in office, Prime Minister Qureshi carried out a number of important political and economic measures: he introduced, for the first time, a tax on agricultural income, in an effort to replenish the greatly depleted foreign-exchange reserves, and he attempted to reduce political corruption involving financial misdeeds and illegal drug-trafficking (politicians linked with either of these two crimes were disqualified from participating in the forthcoming general election).

The general election, held on 6 and 9 October 1993 under military supervision, was widely considered to have been fair, although the turn-out, which some officials estimated to be less than 50%, was disappointing. The polling was closely contested between the PML faction led by Mohammad Nawaz Sharif and the PPP (the MQM boycotted the elections to the National Assembly, claiming systematic intimidation by the army, but took part in the provincial assembly elections a few days later). Neither of the two leading parties, however, won an outright majority in the federal elections and, in the provincial elections, an outright majority was only achieved, by the PPP, in Sindh. Following intensive negotiations with smaller parties and independents in the National Assembly, Benazir Bhutto was elected to head a coalition Government on 19 October. On the following day, a PPP-led coalition assumed control of the provincial administration in Punjab (traditionally a PML stronghold). The provincial governments in the NWFP and in Balochistan were, however, headed by alliances led by the PML (Nawaz Group).

On 13 November 1993 the PPP's candidate, the newly-appointed Minister of Foreign Affairs, Sardar Farooq Ahmad Khan Leghari, was elected the country's President, having secured 274 votes (62% of the total) in the electoral college. The incumbent acting President, Wasim Sajjad Jan, who stood as the candidate of the PML (Nawaz Group), obtained 168 votes (38%). On assuming office, Leghari stated that he intended to end his political ties with the PPP and that he hoped for the repeal or modification of the controversial Eighth Constitutional Amendment in the near future.

In early December 1993 a feud within Benazir Bhutto's immediate family threatened to result in the emergence of a breakaway faction from the ruling party. The Prime Minister's mother, Nusrat Bhutto, challenged her own overthrow as Co-Chairperson of the PPP, claiming that her nomination by her husband in 1977 had been for life. Relations between Benazir Bhutto (who was now sole Chairperson of the PPP) and her mother had become increasingly strained in the latter half of 1993 regarding the future of the Prime Minister's brother, Murtaza Bhutto, who returned to Pakistan from exile in November and who was immediately arrested and imprisoned on charges of insurgency (he was released on bail in June 1994). Nusrat Bhutto allegedly viewed her son, rather than her daughter, as the rightful heir to Zulfikar Ali Bhutto's political legacy.

In late January 1994 the Prime Minister announced the appointment of 11 new cabinet members. In late February the President dismissed the Chief Minister and government in the NWFP, suspended the provincial legislature and imposed governor's rule, following the thwarted introduction of a vote of no confidence against the PML (Nawaz Group)-led coalition by the PPP. The PPP consolidated its hold on federal power in early March by winning the majority of the contested seats in elections to the Senate; however, the ruling party's candidate for the Senate's chairmanship lost to the opposition's nominee. In late April a PPP member was elected as Chief Minister of the newly-revived provincial government in the NWFP; the opposition alliance boycotted the proceedings.

It was reported that at least 20 people were killed in ethnic violence, allegedly instigated by members of the MQM(A), in Karachi in early May 1994. The army was deployed in an attempt to restore order; incidents were also reported in Hyderabad and Sukkur. In June 19 high-ranking members of the MQM(A), including its leader, Altaf Hussain, were each sentenced *in absentia* to 27 years of imprisonment on charges of terrorism.

September 1994 witnessed an upsurge in political unrest when Mohammad Nawaz Sharif organized a nation-wide general strike; in response, the Government arrested hundreds of PML supporters. Relations between the Prime Minister and the leader of the opposition deteriorated in November, when the latter's elderly father, Mian Mohammad Sharif, founder of the Ittefaq group of industries, was arrested on charges of fraud and tax evasion (he was later released on health grounds). In the same month the Government was confronted with a series of uprisings staged by heavily-armed tribesmen in the mountainous regions of Malakand and Swat, demanding the enforcement of Shari'a law. The fundamentalist revolt was suppressed by paramilitary forces (but only after the deaths of several hundred people), and the Shari'a measures were implemented in the tribal areas. By the end of the year, however, the police and paramilitary forces appeared to be losing control of Karachi, which was riven by rapidly escalating ethnic and criminal violence; nearly 170 people were killed in the city in December alone, following the end of the 29-month-old 'Operation Clean-up' and the withdrawal of the army in the previous month. Much of the violence stemmed from the bloody rivalry between the opposing factions of the MQM, whilst other killings were linked to sectarian disputes between Sunni and Shia Muslims. Despite these factors, Pakistani officials primarily accused Indian intelligence agencies of fomenting the unrest and demanded the closure of the Indian consulate in Karachi.

Much controversy, both within Pakistan itself and in the international community, was aroused in February 1995 by the death sentences imposed, under Pakistani Islamic penal code, on a Christian youth and his uncle, who had been convicted of blasphemy. The sentences were later overturned by the High Court in Lahore, but the whole incident served to highlight the increasing persecution of religious minorities in Pakistan. Benazir Bhutto angered the country's Islamic fundamentalists when she said that she was 'shocked and saddened' by the court's initial imposition of the death sentence; in May, however, she assured Muslims that blasphemy would remain a capital offence.

Despite the arrest of large numbers of suspected Islamic militants in early 1995, there was an upsurge in religious violence at the end of February, when 20 Shia Muslims were killed in two mosques in Karachi by suspected Sunni gunmen. This atrocity resulted in a series of retaliatory attacks mounted by both sides.

In foreign relations, Pakistan has traditionally pursued a policy of maintaining close links with Islamic states in the Middle East and Africa and with the People's Republic of China, while continuing to seek aid and assistance from the USA. Pakistan's controversial nuclear programme prompted the USA to terminate development aid in April 1979, but, as a result of the Soviet invasion of Afghanistan in December of that year, military and economic assistance was renewed in 1981. However, increased concern about Pakistan's ability to develop nuclear weapons and Pakistan's refusal to sign the Treaty on the Non-Proliferation of Nuclear Weapons prompted the US Government to suspend military and economic aid again in 1990. In February 1992 the Pakistan Government admitted for the first time that Pakistan had nuclear-weapons capability, but added that it had 'frozen' its nuclear programme at the level of October 1989, when it was still some way off from producing a nuclear device. Relations between Pakistan and the USA were slightly improved following the revival in January 1995 of a bilateral consultative committee (abandoned in 1990), comprising senior defence officials. In March, however, the situation appeared less congenial, when two US consulate employees were shot dead by unidentified gunmen in Karachi. During a 10-day official visit to the USA in April, Prime Minister Benazir Bhutto made little progress in securing the resumption of aid.

Relations with Afghanistan were strained during the 1980s and early 1990s, as rebel Afghan tribesmen (the *mujahidin*) used areas inside Pakistan (notably the city of Peshawar) as bases for their activities. In early 1988 there were an estimated 3.2m. Afghan refugees in Pakistan, most of them in the NWFP. The presence of the refugees prompted cross-border attacks against *mujahidin* bases by Soviet and Afghan government troops. In 1988 Pakistan signed the Geneva Accords on the withdrawal of Soviet troops from Afghanistan, which included agreements on the voluntary repatriation of Afghan refugees from Pakistan. Following the withdrawal of Soviet troops from Afghanistan in 1989, Pakistan maintained its support for the guerrillas' cause, while denying accusations by the Afghan Government that it was taking an active military part in the conflict, or that it was acting as a conduit for arms supplies to the *mujahidin*. The Pakistani Government welcomed the overthrow of the Afghan regime by the guerrillas in April 1992 and supported the interim coalition Government that was formed to administer Afghanistan until the holding of free elections.

Relations with India have dominated Pakistan's foreign policy since the creation of the two states in 1947. Relations deteriorated during the late 1970s and early 1980s, owing to Pakistan's programme to develop nuclear weapons, and as a result of major US arms deliveries to Pakistan. The other major contentious issue between the two states was the disputed region of Kashmir, where, since 1949, a cease-fire line has separated Indian-controlled Kashmir (the state of Jammu and Kashmir) and Pakistani Kashmir, which comprises Azad (Free) Kashmir and the Northern Areas. While Pakistan demanded that the sovereignty of the region be decided in accordance with earlier UN resolutions (which advocated a plebiscite in both parts of the region), India argued that a solution should be reached through bilateral negotiations.

Relations between Pakistan and India reached a crisis in late 1989, when the outlawed Jammu and Kashmir Liberation Front (JKLF) and several other Muslim groups in Indian-controlled Kashmir intensified their campaigns of terrorism, strikes and civil unrest, in support of demands for an independent Kashmir or unification with Pakistan. In response, the Indian Government dispatched troops to Jammu and Kashmir. By early February 1990 it was officially estimated that about 80 people (mostly civilians) had been killed in resulting clashes between troops and protestors. Tension was heightened in early February, after it was reported that three Pakistani civilians had been shot dead by Indian trooops when they attempted to cross the cease-fire line into Indian-controlled Kashmir. The opposition parties in Pakistan organized nationwide strikes, to express their sympathy for the Muslims in Jammu and Kashmir, and urged the Government to adopt more active measures regarding the crisis. In August and September there were reports of heavy skirmishing between Indian and Pakistani troops along the Kashmir border.

In December 1990 discussions were held between the Ministers of External Affairs of Pakistan and India, at which an agreement not to attack each other's nuclear facilities was finalized, but no solution was found to the Kashmir problem. Meanwhile, large concentrations of Indian and Pakistani troops were reported to have been deployed in the border area. Despite further bilateral talks in April 1991, skirmishes between Indian and Pakistani troops along the border in Kashmir continued throughout 1991–94 and into 1995. In February and March 1992 the Pakistani Government deployed thousands of police and paramilitary forces in Azad Kashmir, to prevent planned protest marches (organized by Pakistani members of the JKLF) across the cease-fire line into Indian-controlled Kashmir, thus averting the danger of large-scale confrontation between Indian and Pakistani troops. A number of JKLF supporters were killed in the subsequent clashes between marchers and the Pakistani security troops. High-level talks held in January 1994 between Pakistan and India regarding Kashmir made no progress in resolving the crisis. In February 1995 Benazir Bhutto's Government organized a nation-wide general strike to express solidarity with the independence movement in Jammu and Kashmir and to protest against alleged atrocities carried out by the Indian forces.

Over the years, relations between Pakistan and India have been strained by repeated accusations, made by the latter, that Pakistan has been directly involved in terrorist activity in support of the JKLF in Kashmir and in support of the secessionist Sikhs in the Indian state of Punjab. Such accusations have always been strenuously denied by the Pakistani Government. In March 1993 relations between the two countries reached an extremely low ebb when the Indian Government accused Pakistan of having been involved in bomb explosions in Bombay, which killed more than 300 people. The Pakistan Government closed its consulate in Bombay in March 1994 as a result of deteriorating relations between Pakistan and India.

Pakistan withdrew from the Commonwealth in January 1972, in protest at the United Kingdom's role in the East Pakistan crisis. Pakistan recognized Bangladesh in February 1974, but attempts to rejoin the Commonwealth in the late 1970s and early 1980s were thwarted by India. In January 1989, however, India announced that it would no longer oppose Pakistan's application to rejoin the organization, and in July, during Benazir Bhutto's official visit to the United Kingdom, Pakistan was formally invited to rejoin the Commonwealth, which it did on 1 October 1989.

In early 1992 the Economic Co-operation Organization (ECO, see p. 238), comprising Pakistan, Iran and Turkey, was reactivated, and by the end of the year had been expanded to include Afghanistan and the six central Asian, mainly Muslim, republics of the former USSR; the 'Turkish Republic of Northern Cyprus' joined the ECO in April 1993. Trade delegations from Turkey and the new republics visited Pakistan, and an agreement for the restoration and construction of highways in Afghanistan, to link Pakistan with these republics, was signed. In order to meet the maritime trade requirements of the Muslim republics, the cargo facilities at Karachi Port are being modernized and expanded. In March 1995 Pakistan, the People's Republic of China, Kazakstan and Kyrgyzstan signed a transit trade agreement, restoring Pakistan's overland trade route with Central Asia, through China.

### Government

Following general and provincial elections in February 1985, the 237-member National Assembly and 87-member Senate, the latter elected by the four provincial assemblies, sat jointly as a bicameral Federal Legislature, replacing the *Majlis-i-Shura* (an advisory body, which was established in 1982). The National Assembly, membership of which was later reduced to 217 members, is elected for a five-year term, and the Senate for a six-year term. In March Gen. Zia substantially amended the 1973 Constitution (which had been abeyance since July 1977) to increase the power of the presidency. The Constitution was then revived, with the exception of 28 key provisions relating to treason, subversion, fundamental rights and the jurisdiction of the Supreme Court. In October 1985 the Constitution (Eighth Amendment) Bill was enacted. The new law embodied in the Constitution those amendments which increased the power of the Presidency, and also indemnified all actions of the military regime. In December the enactment of the Political Parties (Amendment) Bill allowed political parties to function, under stringent conditions. In the same month, Gen. Zia repealed martial law and restored the remainder of the Constitution. The process of registering political parties was simplified in September 1988 as a result of amendments made by the Supreme Court.

Pakistan comprises four provinces (each with an appointed Governor and provincial government), the federal capital of Islamabad and federally administered 'tribal areas'.

### Defence

In June 1994 the armed forces totalled 587,000 men: 520,000 in the army, 22,000 in the navy and 45,000 in the air force. Paramilitary forces numbered 275,000 (including a National Guard of 185,000 men). The estimated defence budget for 1994 was 101,900m. rupees. Military service is voluntary.

### Economic Affairs

In 1993, according to estimates by the World Bank, Pakistan's gross national product (GNP), measured at average 1991–93 prices, was US $53,250m., equivalent to $430 per head. During 1985–93, it was estimated, GNP per head increased, in real terms, at an average annual rate of 1.5%. Over the same period, the population rose by an annual average of 3.1%. Pakistan's gross domestic product (GDP) increased, in real terms, by an annual average of 6.1% in 1980–92. GDP grew by 2.3% in the year ending 30 June 1993 and by an estimated 4.0% in 1993/94.

Agriculture (including forestry and fishing) contributed an estimated 26.0% of GDP in the year ending June 1994. About 48.2% of the economically active population were employed in the sector in 1993. The principal cash crops are cotton (textile yarn and fabrics accounted for around 53.6% of export earnings in 1993/94) and rice; wheat, maize and sugar cane are also major crops. Fishing and leather production provide significant export revenues. During 1980–92 agricultural GDP increased by an annual average of 4.5%; it declined by 5.6% in 1992/93 and rose by 2.6% in 1993/94.

Industry (including mining, manufacturing, power and construction) employed 19.8% of the working population in 1989/90, and provided an estimated 25.1% of GDP in 1993/94. During 1980–92 industrial GDP increased by an annual average of 7.3%.

Mining contributed an estimated 0.6% of GDP in 1993/94, and employed 0.1% of the working population in 1989/90. Petroleum and petroleum products are the major mineral exports. Limestone, rock salt, gypsum, silica sand, natural gas and coal are also mined. In addition, Pakistan has reserves of graphite, copper and manganese.

Manufacturing contributed an estimated 17.3% of GDP in 1993/94, and employed about 12.7% of the working population in 1989/90. The most important sectors, measured by gross value of output, are textiles, food products and petroleum refineries. During 1980–92 manufacturing GDP increased by an annual average of 7.4%; in 1992/93 manufacturing output rose by 5.6%.

Energy is derived principally from petroleum and natural gas. It was estimated that domestic production of crude petroleum in April 1991 fulfilled about 41% of national requirements. Imports of petroleum and petroleum products comprised about 16.3% of the cost of total imports in 1993/94. In 1994 Pakistan launched a wide-ranging plan to restructure and privatize its power sector.

In 1993 Pakistan recorded a visible trade deficit of US $2,552m., and there was a deficit of $2,936m. on the current account of the balance of payments. Remittances from Pakistanis working abroad totalled $800m. in 1991; although remittances rose by 7% in 1992/93, the Middle East 'boom' is clearly over and cannot be relied on as a major bolster for the balance of payments. The principal source of imports (15.9%) in 1992/93 was Japan, while the principal market for exports (13.9%) was the USA. Other major trading partners were Germany, the United Kingdom and Saudi Arabia. The principal exports in 1993/94 were textile yarn and fabrics, clothing and accessories, and food and live animals. The principal imports were machinery and transport equipment, mineral fuels and lubricants, and chemicals and related products.

In the financial year ending 30 June 1995 there was a projected budgetary deficit of Rs 186,853.2m. In February 1994 the consortium of aid donors to Pakistan, led by the World Bank, pledged a sum of US $2,500m. for 1994/95. Pakistan's total external debt was $26,050m. at the end of 1993, of which $20,306m. was long-term public debt. The cost of debt-servicing in that year was equivalent to 24.7% of earnings from exports of goods and services. During 1985–93 the average annual rate of inflation was 8.0%. The rate of inflation increased to 9.3% in 1992/93 and had risen to about 15% by early 1995. About 3.1% of the labour force were estimated to be unemployed in 1989/90.

Pakistan is a member of the South Asian Association for Regional Co-operation (SAARC, see p. 241) and of the Asian Development Bank (ADB, see p. 107).

The Pakistan Government launched an extensive economic reform programme in 1988, under which important gains were achieved. The programme included measures to liberalize domestic and external trade, reform the financial sector, and implement a wide-ranging process of privatization. These steps contributed to an increase in the rate of growth of GDP, a rise in export revenue, greater domestic and foreign investment, and a revitalization of the private sector. The country remained vulnerable to natural disasters, however, and in December 1992 the IMF approved a request by Pakistan for emergency assistance of about $262m., following the area's worst floods this century. In mid-1993 the interim Government, headed by Moeenuddin Ahmad Qureshi, introduced stringent fiscal measures, including a rise in the nation-wide sales tax from 12.5% to 15% and an increase in fuel and basic commodity prices, in an attempt to reduce the country's huge fiscal deficit and to lessen Pakistan's dependency on foreign aid and loans. In November of that year the new Government, under Benazir Bhutto, agreed upon a US $1,369m. loan package and three-year austerity plan with the IMF. The new Prime Minister stated that her Government was committed to reducing the persistent budgetary deficit through cutting non-development expenditure and improving the rate of tax recovery (a controversial new tax on landowners was under consideration). By the end of 1994 the Government's economic policies were showing favourable results: the budgetary deficit had decreased from more than 8% of GDP in 1992/93 to 5.8% in 1993/94; foreign exchange reserves had risen to a record $3,000m.; and foreign investment inflows had increased by 20%, compared with the previous year, to reach $693m. in 1993/94 (despite fears about growing violence in Karachi). However, Pakistan's ability to achieve the macroeconomic targets set by the IMF appeared in some doubt, with a third poor cotton harvest, rising inflation and a considerable shortfall in projected public revenues.

### Social Welfare

Social welfare services operate mainly through Development Schemes and Urban Community Projects. Government support is given to voluntary bodies which provide social relief. The National Council of Social Welfare provides care for children, women, delinquents and handicapped people. In 1976 an Old-Age Benefits Scheme, managed by the State Life Insurance Corporation, was inaugurated. In the same year the Government doubled the budget for spending on birth control, and planned the sterilization of 7% of couples by the 1980s. In 1988 Pakistan had 710 hospitals, 57,337 hospital beds, 417 rural health centres (with 3,502 beds), 55,346 registered physicians and 1,757 dentists. Development expenditure on health in 1994/95 was projected at Rs 1,461.1m. (1.6% of the Government's total development spending), and a further Rs 996.2m. (1.1%) was to be allotted to population planning.

### Education

Universal free primary education is a constitutional right, but less than one-half of Pakistan's children actually receive it, and education is not compulsory. Primary education begins at five years of age and lasts for five years. Secondary education, beginning at the age of 10, is divided into two stages, of three and four years respectively. In 1990 the total enrolment at primary and secondary schools was equivalent to 33% of all school-age children (43% of boys; 22% of girls). Primary enrolment in 1990 was equivalent to 46% of children in the relevant age-group (59% of boys; 31% of girls), while the comparable ratio for secondary enrolment was 21% (29% of boys; 13% of girls). In 1993/94 it was estimated that there were 15,532,000 children enrolled at pre-primary and primary schools, and 5,199,000 at middle and secondary schools. All institutions except missions are nationalized. From 1976 agro-technical subjects were introduced into the school curriculum, and 25 trade schools were established in 1976. There are 24 universities. Development expenditure on science and technology and education and training in 1994/95 was projected at Rs 297.8m. (only 0.3% of the Government's total development spending). In 1990, according to estimates by UNESCO, the average rate of adult illiteracy was 65.2% (males 52.7%; females 78.9%).

### Public Holidays

**1995:** 1 February* (Ramadan begins), 3 March* (Id al-Fitr, end of Ramadan), 23 March (Pakistan Day, proclamation of republic in 1956), 14 April† (Good Friday), 17 April† (Easter Monday), 1 May (Labour Day), 10 May* (Id al-Adha, Feast of the Sacrifice), 31 May* (Muharram, Islamic New Year), 9 June* (Ashoura), 9 August* (Eid-i-Milad-un-Nabi, Birth of the Prophet), 14 August (Independence Day), 6 September (Defence of Pakistan Day), 11 September (Anniversary of Death of Quaid-i-Azam), 9 November (Allama Iqbal Day), 25 December (Birthday of Quaid-i-Azam, and Christmas), 26 December† (Boxing Day).

**1996:** 22 January* (Ramadan begins), 21 February* (Id al-Fitr, end of Ramadan), 23 March (Pakistan Day, proclamation of republic in 1956), 5 April† (Good Friday), 8 April† (Easter Monday), 29 April* (Id al-Adha, Feast of the Sacrifice), 1 May (Labour Day), 19 May* (Muharram, Islamic New Year), 28 May* (Ashoura), 28 July* (Eid-i-Milad-un-Nabi, Birth of the Prophet), 14 August (Independence Day), 6 September (Defence of Pakistan Day), 11 September (Anniversary of Death of Quaid-i-Azam), 9 November (Allama Iqbal Day), 25 December (Birthday of Quaid-i-Azam, and Christmas), 26 December† (Boxing Day).

* These holidays are dependent on the Islamic lunar calendar and may vary by one or two days from the dates given.
† Optional holidays for Christians only.

### Weights and Measures

The metric system has been officially introduced. Also in use are imperial and local weights, including:

1 maund = 82.28 lb (37.32 kg).
1 seer = 2.057 lb (933 grams).
1 tola = 180 grains (11.66 grams).

# Statistical Survey

Source (unless otherwise stated): Development Advisory Centre, Karachi; tel. (21) 218129.

## Area and Population

### AREA, POPULATION AND DENSITY*

| | |
|---|---:|
| Area (sq km) | 796,095† |
| Population (census results) | |
| 16 September 1972 | 64,979,732 |
| 1 March 1981 | |
| Males | 44,232,677 |
| Females | 40,020,967 |
| Total | 84,253,644 |
| Population (official estimates at mid-year) | |
| 1991 | 115,520,000 |
| 1992 | 119,107,000 |
| 1993 | 122,802,000 |
| Density (per sq km) at mid-1993 | 154.3 |

* Excluding data for the disputed territory of Jammu and Kashmir. The Pakistani-held parts of this region are known as Azad ('Free') Kashmir, with an area of 11,639 sq km (4,494 sq miles) and a population of 1,980,000 in 1981, and Northern Areas (including Gilgit and Baltistan), with an area of 72,520 sq km (28,000 sq miles) and a population of 562,000 in 1981. Also excluded are Junagardh and Manavadar. The population figures exclude refugees from Afghanistan (estimated to number about 3.8m. in early 1990).

† 307,374 sq miles.

### ADMINISTRATIVE DIVISIONS (population at 1981 census)

| | Area (sq km) | Population |
|---|---:|---:|
| Provinces: | | |
| Balochistan | 347,190 | 4,332,376 |
| North-West Frontier Province | 74,521 | 11,061,328 |
| Punjab | 205,344 | 47,292,441 |
| Sindh | 140,914 | 19,028,666 |
| Federally Administered Tribal Area | 27,220 | 2,198,547 |
| Federal Capital Territory: Islamabad | 906 | 340,286 |
| **Total** | **796,095** | **84,253,644** |

Source: Ministry of Finance, Planning and Development.

### PRINCIPAL CITIES (population at 1981 census)

| | | | | |
|---|---:|---|---:|---|
| Karachi | 5,180,562 | Peshawar | 566,248 | |
| Lahore | 2,952,689 | Sialkot | 302,009 | |
| Faisalabad | | Sargodha | 291,361 | |
| (Lyallpur) | 1,104,209 | Quetta | 285,719 | |
| Rawalpindi | 794,843 | Islamabad | | |
| Hyderabad | 751,529 | (capital) | 204,364 | |
| Multan | 722,070 | Jhang | 195,558 | |
| Gujranwala | 658,753 | Bahawalpur | 180,263 | |

### BIRTHS AND DEATHS (UN estimates, annual averages)

| | 1975-80 | 1980-85 | 1985-90 |
|---|---:|---:|---:|
| Birth rate (per 1,000) | 47.3 | 44.6 | 44.1 |
| Death rate (per 1,000) | 16.0 | 13.7 | 12.2 |

**Expectation of life** (UN estimates, years at birth, 1985–90): 56.5 (males 56.5; females 56.5).

Source: UN, *World Population Prospects: The 1992 Revision*.

### ECONOMICALLY ACTIVE POPULATION (sample surveys, '000 persons aged 10 years and over, excl. armed forces)

| | 1987/88 | 1988/89 | 1989/90 |
|---|---:|---:|---:|
| Agriculture, hunting, forestry and fishing | 14,831 | 15,291 | 15,765 |
| Mining and quarrying | 43 | 45 | 46 |
| Manufacturing | 3,682 | 3,797 | 3,914 |
| Electricity, gas and water | 171 | 176 | 182 |
| Construction | 1,850 | 1,907 | 1,966 |
| Trade, restaurants and hotels | 3,456 | 3,563 | 3,674 |
| Transport, storage and communications | 1,418 | 1,463 | 1,508 |
| Financing, insurance, real estate and business services | 206 | 212 | 219 |
| Community, social and personal services | 3,303 | 3,405 | 3,511 |
| Activities not adequately described | 35 | 36 | 37 |
| **Total employed** | 28,995 | 29,895 | 30,822 |
| Unemployed | 937 | 966 | 996 |
| **Total labour force** | 29,932 | 30,861 | 31,818 |
| Males | 26,523 | 27,346 | 28,194 |
| Females | 3,409 | 3,515 | 3,624 |

Source: ILO, *Year Book of Labour Statistics*.

## Agriculture

### PRINCIPAL CROPS ('000 metric tons)

| | 1991 | 1992 | 1993 |
|---|---:|---:|---:|
| Wheat | 14,565 | 15,684 | 16,157 |
| Rice (paddy) | 4,865 | 4,674 | 5,927 |
| Barley | 142 | 140 | 158 |
| Maize | 1,203 | 1,173 | 1,180 |
| Millet | 139 | 203 | 126 |
| Sorghum | 225 | 238 | 218 |
| Potatoes | 751 | 860 | 933 |
| Other roots and tubers | 6 | 5 | 6 |
| Chick-peas | 531 | 513 | 347 |
| Other pulses | 196 | 198 | 208 |
| Groundnuts (in shell) | 96 | 101 | 105* |
| Sunflower seed | 35 | 39 | 14 |
| Rapeseed | 228 | 220 | 207 |
| Cottonseed | 4,362 | 3,080 | 2,722† |
| Cotton (lint) | 2,181 | 1,540 | 1,361† |
| Green peppers | 101 | 142 | 150* |
| Onions (dry) | 702 | 809 | 854 |
| Garlic | 53 | 63 | 66 |
| Other vegetables (incl. melons) | 2,769 | 2,886 | 3,029 |
| Dates | 293 | 275 | 320* |
| Sugar cane | 35,989 | 38,865 | 38,743 |
| Sugar beet | 319 | 315 | 233 |
| Oranges | 1,141† | 1,160* | 1,200* |
| Other citrus fruits | 493† | 499* | 510* |
| Apples | 295 | 339 | 320* |
| Apricots | 109 | 122 | 112* |
| Mangoes | 776 | 787 | 794 |
| Bananas | 202 | 44 | 215* |
| Tobacco leaves | 75 | 97 | 102 |

* FAO estimate.  † Unofficial figure.

Source: FAO, *Production Yearbook*.

# PAKISTAN

**LIVESTOCK** ('000 head, year ending September)

|  | 1991 | 1992 | 1993 |
|---|---|---|---|
| Cattle | 17,711 | 17,745 | 17,779 |
| Buffaloes | 17,818 | 18,273 | 18,740 |
| Sheep | 26,338 | 26,995 | 27,668 |
| Goats | 36,972 | 38,564 | 40,225 |
| Horses | 363 | 358 | 354 |
| Asses | 3,534 | 3,653 | 3,775 |
| Mules | 73 | 74 | 75 |
| Camels | 1,056 | 1,076 | 1,097 |

Chickens (FAO estimates, million): 75 in 1991; 85 in 1992; 92 in 1993.
Ducks (million): 3 in 1991; 3 in 1992; 3 in 1993.

Source: FAO, *Production Yearbook*.

**LIVESTOCK PRODUCTS** ('000 metric tons)

|  | 1991 | 1992 | 1993 |
|---|---|---|---|
| Beef and veal | 326 | 338 | 350 |
| Buffalo meat | 439 | 465 | 494 |
| Mutton and lamb | 256 | 272 | 288 |
| Goat meat | 409 | 441 | 475 |
| Poultry meat | 159 | 159 | 175 |
| Other meat | 13 | 13 | 14 |
| Cows' milk | 3,653 | 3,788 | 3,928 |
| Buffaloes' milk | 11,256 | 11,884 | 12,546 |
| Sheep's milk | 40 | 42 | 44 |
| Goats' milk | 532 | 566 | 602 |
| Butter and ghee* | 300.0 | 316.7 | 334.4 |
| Hen eggs† | 211.0 | 231.0 | 231.9 |
| Other poultry eggs* | 5.6 | 6.0 | 6.0 |
| Wool: |  |  |  |
| greasy | 48.1 | 49.3 | 50.5 |
| clean† | 28.9 | 29.6 | 30.4 |
| Cattle and buffalo hides* | 114.8 | 120.6 | 123.7 |
| Sheep skins* | 66.9 | 69.9 | 73.0 |
| Goat skins* | 111.0 | 120.2 | 127.6 |

\* FAO estimates.   † Unofficial figures.

Source: FAO, *Production Yearbook*.

## Forestry

**ROUNDWOOD REMOVALS** ('000 cu m, excl. bark)

|  | 1990 | 1991 | 1992 |
|---|---|---|---|
| Sawlogs, veneer logs and logs for sleepers | 2.238 | 2,030 | 1,790 |
| Other industrial wood* | 377 | 388 | 398 |
| Fuel wood* | 23,080 | 23,737 | 24,379 |
| **Total** | 25,695 | 26,155 | 26,567 |

\* FAO estimates.

Source: FAO, *Yearbook of Forest Products*.

**SAWNWOOD PRODUCTION** ('000 cu m, incl. railway sleepers)

|  | 1990 | 1991 | 1992 |
|---|---|---|---|
| Coniferous (softwood) | 312 | 240 | 577 |
| Broadleaved (hardwood) | 1,138 | 1,280 | 926 |
| **Total** | 1,450 | 1,520 | 1,503 |

Source: FAO, *Yearbook of Forest Products*.

## Fishing

('000 metric tons, live weight)

|  | 1990 | 1991 | 1992 |
|---|---|---|---|
| Freshwater fishes | 113.2 | 115.9 | 121.7 |
| Sea catfishes | 14.6 | 27.3 | 27.6 |
| Pike-congers | 1.9 | 7.4 | 8.3 |
| Croakers and drums | 12.3 | 14.4 | 16.6 |
| Mullets | 6.0 | 6.8 | 10.2 |
| Carangids | 15.0 | 17.1 | 18.2 |
| Indian oil sardine | 63.7 | 65.9 | 74.6 |
| Anchovies | 11.7 | 10.3 | 14.5 |
| Clupeoids | 43.8 | 42.1 | 42.1 |
| Narrow-barred Spanish mackerel | 5.9 | 6.3 | 12.1 |
| Skipjack tuna | 7.6 | 7.5 | 8.2 |
| Longtail tuna | 6.1 | 5.0 | 2.8 |
| Yellowfin tuna | 3.2 | 6.5 | 23.4 |
| Requiem sharks | 23.1 | 26.3 | 27.8 |
| Skates and rays | 15.7 | 17.5 | 16.5 |
| Other marine fishes (incl. unspecified) | 100.7 | 101.5 | 95.3 |
| **Total fish** | 446.4 | 476.7 | 519.9 |
| Penaeus shrimps | 27.9 | 32.1 | 26.5 |
| Other crustaceans and molluscs | 4.7 | 6.8 | 6.7 |
| **Total catch** | 479.0 | 515.5 | 553.1 |
| Inland waters | 113.2 | 115.9 | 121.7 |
| Indian Ocean | 365.9 | 399.6 | 431.5 |

Source: FAO, *Yearbook of Fishery Statistics*.

## Mining

(metric tons, unless otherwise indicated, year ending 30 June)

|  | 1991/92 | 1992/93 | 1993/94 |
|---|---|---|---|
| Barytes | 30,000 | 26,337 | 12,000 |
| Chromite | 28,000 | 22,706 | 20,000 |
| Limestone | 8,528,000 | 8,793,000 | 8,995,000 |
| Gypsum | 471,000 | 532,000 | 659,000 |
| Fireclay | n.a. | 132,272 | 116,000 |
| Silica sand | 132,000 | 154,000 | 177,000 |
| Celestite | n.a. | 1,682 | 3,208 |
| Ochres | 1,052 | 1,000 | 805 |
| Rock salt | 833,000 | 895,000 | 895,000 |
| Coal and lignite | 3,073,000 | 3,074,000 | 3,175,000 |
| Crude petroleum ('000 barrels) | 22,400 | 21,884 | 20,900 |
| Natural gas (million cu m) | 15,600 | 16,520 | 18,100 |

Source: State Bank of Pakistan, *Annual Report*.

## Industry

**SELECTED PRODUCTS**
('000 metric tons, unless otherwise indicated, year ending 30 June)

|  | 1991/92 | 1992/93 | 1993/94 |
|---|---|---|---|
| Cotton cloth (million sq m) | 307.8 | 325.4 | 307 |
| Cotton yarn | 1,170.7 | 1,219 | 1,288 |
| Refined sugar | 2,322.5 | 2,397.3 | 2,922 |
| Vegetable ghee | 319 | 725 | 700 |
| Cement | 8,321 | 8,558 | 8,200 |
| Urea | 1,898 | 2,306 | 3,104 |
| Superphosphate | 194 | 205 | 195 |
| Ammonium sulphate | 92.9 | 92.8 | 82 |
| Sulphuric acid | 97.6 | 99.8 | 100 |
| Soda ash | 185.9 | 186.2 | 188 |
| Caustic soda | 82 | 81.3 | 89 |
| Chlorine gas | 6.1 | 5.8 | 6 |
| Cigarettes (million) | 29,673 | 33,300 | 37,500 |

Source: State Bank of Pakistan, *Annual Report*.

# PAKISTAN

## Finance

### CURRENCY AND EXCHANGE RATES

**Monetary Units**
100 paisa = 1 Pakistani rupee.

**Sterling and Dollar Equivalents** (31 December 1994)
£1 sterling = 48.19 rupees;
US $1 = 30.80 rupees;
1,000 Pakistani rupees = £20.75 = $32.47.

**Average Exchange Rate** (rupees per US $)
1992   25.083
1993   28.107
1994   30.567

### CENTRAL GOVERNMENT BUDGET
(estimates, million rupees, year ending 30 June)

| Revenue | 1992/93 | 1993/94* | 1994/95 |
|---|---|---|---|
| Taxes on income | 32,997.0 | 45,000.0 | 53,750.0 |
| Customs duties | 71,375.0 | 68,000.0 | 78,000.0 |
| Excise duties | 44,008.0 | 36,000.0 | 40,430.0 |
| General turnover tax | } 45,328.0 { | 32,100.0 | 39,560.0 |
| Other taxes and surcharges | | 27,113.1 | 28,642.3 |
| Other receipts (non-tax) | 67,292.0 | 83,929.4 | 91,432.0 |
| **Total** | 261,000.0 | 292,142.5 | 331,814.3 |
| Less Transfer to provinces | 64,854.0 | 81,602.8 | 94,201.7 |
| **Net total** | 196,146.0 | 210,539.7 | 237,612.6 |

| Expenditure | 1992/93 | 1993/94* | 1994/95 |
|---|---|---|---|
| Non-development expenditure: | | | |
| Interest on public debt | 93,176.0 | 139,208.2 | 148,113.1 |
| National defence | 82,152.0 | 93,781.3 | 101,849.7 |
| Education and health | 4,065.0 | 4,822.2 | 4,994.3 |
| Other current expenditure on administration | 25,137.0 | 14,432.4 | 15,385.6 |
| Grants to local authorities | 9,236.0 | 10,360.5 | 12,167.5 |
| Subsidies | 5,049.0 | 5,138.2 | 5,432.3 |
| **Total** (incl. others) | 218,815.0 | 385,436.2 | 424,465.8 |

* Revised figures.

### PLANNED DEVELOPMENT EXPENDITURE
(million rupees, year ending 30 June)

| | 1992/93 | 1993/94 | 1994/95 |
|---|---|---|---|
| Sectoral programme: | | | |
| Agriculture (incl. subsidy for fertilizers) | 2,272.1 | 861.5 | 1,134.0 |
| Water | 6,681.6 | 9,705.5 | 11,293.6 |
| Power | 12,689.0 | 12,054.0 | 16,417.6 |
| Industry | 77.3 | 142.7 | 663.3 |
| Fuels | 2,376.1 | 1,804.7 | 2,236.4 |
| Minerals | 720.0 | 1,525.7 | 2,093.7 |
| Transport and communication | 13,456.4 | 17,437.3 | 15,209.9 |
| Physical planning and housing | 562.3 | 1,011.1 | 2,012.7 |
| Science and technology and education and training | 736.4 | 150.5 | 297.8 |
| Social welfare, culture, tourism, sport and manpower and employment | 606.6 | 720.1 | 755.0 |
| Health | 329.4 | 505.9 | 1,461.1 |
| Population planning | 828.9 | 1,100.0 | 996.2 |
| Rural development | 558.1 | 737.5 | 645.9 |
| Mass media | 121.5 | 93.1 | 130.1 |
| Tameer-e-Watan programme | 2,916.0 | 700.0 | 3,000.1 |
| Special grant for Sindh programme | 2,026.0 | 1,500.0 | 2,500.0 |
| Miscellaneous | 2,877.0 | n.a. | n.a. |
| **Total sectoral programme** | 49,834.7 | n.a. | n.a. |
| Annual provincial projects | 15,799.4 | n.a. | n.a. |
| **Total planned development expenditure** | 67,599.7 | 74,757.8 | 90,000.0 |

### STATE BANK RESERVES (US $ million, last Thursday of the year)

| | 1992 | 1993 | 1994 |
|---|---|---|---|
| Gold* | 681 | 692 | 793 |
| IMF special drawing rights | — | 1 | — |
| Foreign exchange | 850 | 1,196 | 2,929 |
| **Total** | 1,531 | 1,889 | 3,722 |

* Revalued annually, in June, on the basis of London market prices.
Source: IMF, *International Financial Statistics*.

### MONEY SUPPLY (million rupees, last Thursday of the year)

| | 1992 | 1993 | 1994 |
|---|---|---|---|
| Currency outside banks | 162,316 | 177,856 | 195,827 |
| Demand deposits at scheduled banks | 203,653 | 191,613 | 235,265 |
| **Total money*** | 371,796 | 378,111 | 435,388 |

* Including also private-sector deposits at the State Bank.
Source: IMF, *International Financial Statistics*.

### COST OF LIVING (Consumer Price Index for industrial, commercial and government employees in 25 cities; base: 1980/81 = 100)

| | 1987/88 | 1988/89 | 1989/90 |
|---|---|---|---|
| Food, beverages and tobacco | 156.84 | 179.04 | 187.05 |
| Clothing and footwear | 169.37 | 183.27 | 197.99 |
| Rent | 133.36 | 137.92 | 147.84 |
| Fuel and lighting | 132.81 | 148.40 | 164.95 |
| **All items** (incl. others) | 151.49 | 167.23 | 177.33 |

**1990/91:** All items 199.78.
**1991/92:** All items 218.99.
**1992/93:** All items 239.26.

### NATIONAL ACCOUNTS
(million rupees at current prices, year ending 30 June)

**National Income and Product**

| | 1990/91 | 1991/92 | 1992/93† |
|---|---|---|---|
| Domestic factor incomes* | 847,734 | 1,005,831 | 1,133,381 |
| Consumption of fixed capital | 60,640 | 71,972 | 84,075 |
| **Gross domestic product at factor cost** | 908,374 | 1,077,803 | 1,217,456 |
| Indirect taxes | 123,437 | 144,815 | 150,192 |
| Less Subsidies | 11,211 | 11,373 | 8,310 |
| **GDP in purchasers' values** | 1,020,600 | 1,211,245 | 1,359,338 |
| Net factor income from abroad | 23,908 | 12,535 | 17,400 |
| **Gross national product** | 1,044,508 | 1,223,780 | 1,376,738 |
| Less Consumption of fixed capital | 60,640 | 71,972 | 84,075 |
| **National income in market prices** | 983,868 | 1,151,808 | 1,292,663 |

* Compensation of employees and the operating surplus of enterprises. The amount is obtained as a residual.
† Figures are provisional.

**Expenditure on the Gross Domestic Product**

| | 1991/92 | 1992/93 | 1993/94 |
|---|---|---|---|
| Government final consumption expenditure | 155,567 | 174,680 | 192,095 |
| Private final consumption expenditure | 850,872 | 968,164 | 1,118,056 |
| Increase in stocks | 18,700 | 21,100 | 24,600 |
| Gross fixed capital formation | 224,302 | 256,644 | 287,261 |
| **Total domestic expenditure** | 1,249,441 | 1,420,588 | 1,622,012 |
| Exports of goods and services | 209,215 | 217,418 | 245,857 |
| Less Imports of goods and services | 247,411 | 296,051 | 313,295 |
| **GDP in purchasers' values** | 1,211,245 | 1,341,955 | 1,554,574 |

# PAKISTAN

## Gross Domestic Product by Economic Activity
(at current factor cost)

|  | 1991/92 | 1992/93 | 1993/94* |
|---|---|---|---|
| Agriculture and livestock | 272,786 | 297,816 | 349,592 |
| Forestry and fishing | 10,130 | 12,576 | 13,614 |
| Mining and quarrying | 7,180 | 7,403 | 8,712 |
| Manufacturing | 187,184 | 207,568 | 241,932 |
| Electricity, gas and water | 37,576 | 38,790 | 45,665 |
| Construction | 43,812 | 42,807 | 55,080 |
| Commerce | 176,766 | 195,532 | 224,255 |
| Transport, storage and communications | 100,155 | 126,883 | 144,870 |
| Banking and insurance | 30,603 | 35,688 | 44,791 |
| Ownership of dwellings | 46,235 | 53,652 | 70,089 |
| Public administration and defence | 85,472 | 94,560 | 105,215 |
| Other services | 79,904 | 92,756 | 109,172 |
| **Total** | 1,077,803 | 1,200,455 | 1,399,374 |

* Figures are provisional.

Source: State Bank of Pakistan, *Annual Report*.

## BALANCE OF PAYMENTS (US $ million)

|  | 1991 | 1992 | 1993 |
|---|---|---|---|
| Merchandise exports f.o.b. | 6,381 | 6,880 | 6,760 |
| Merchandise imports f.o.b. | −8,642 | −9,671 | −9,312 |
| **Trade balance** | −2,262 | −2,790 | −2,552 |
| Exports of services | 1,524 | 1,552 | 1,516 |
| Imports of services | −2,303 | −2,671 | −2,642 |
| Other income received | 73 | 73 | 61 |
| Other income paid | −1,256 | −1,478 | −1,595 |
| Private unrequited transfers (net) | 2,334 | 3,068 | 1,942 |
| Official unrequited transfers (net) | 483 | 377 | 334 |
| **Current balance** | −1,397 | −1,869 | −2,936 |
| Direct investment (net) | 261 | 346 | 348 |
| Portfolio investment (net) | 92 | 370 | 292 |
| Other capital (net) | 538 | 1,840 | 2,309 |
| Net errors and omissions | −78 | 121 | −91 |
| **Overall balance** | −584 | 808 | −78 |

Source: IMF, *International Financial Statistics*.

## FOREIGN AID* (US $ million, year ending 30 June)

|  | Commitments ||| Disbursements |||
|---|---|---|---|---|---|---|
|  | 1991/92 | 1992/93 | 1993/94 | 1991/92 | 1992/93 | 1993/94 |
| Aid to Pakistan Consortium† | 1,824.0 | 1,275.0 | 2,359.0 | 1,772.8 | 1,660.0 | 2,068.0 |
| OPEC/Islamic countries | 12.9 | 15.0 | 42.0 | 19.0 | 18.0 | 40.0 |
| Other sources‡ | 852.5 | 607.0 | 569.0 | 678.2 | 815.0 | 493.0 |
| **Total** | 2,689.4 | 1,897.0 | 2,970.0 | 2,470.9 | 2,493.0 | 2,601.0 |

* Excluding short-term credits of one and less than one year's maturity.
† Including aid committed/disbursed by Consortium members outside Consortium arrangements.
‡ Including relief assistance for Afghan refugees.

# External Trade

Note: Data exclude trade in military goods.

## PRINCIPAL COMMODITIES (million rupees, year ending 30 June)

| Imports c.i.f.* | 1991/92 | 1992/93 | 1993/94 |
|---|---|---|---|
| Food and live animals | 18,010 | 23,067 | 18,128 |
| Wheat and meslin (unmilled) | 8,487 | 12,167 | 7,234 |
| Tea and maté | 4,306 | 5,386 | 5,619 |
| Crude materials (inedible) except fuels | 15,010 | 13,945 | 17,003 |
| Metalliferous ores and metal scrap | 4,684 | 3,603 | 3,654 |
| Mineral fuels, lubricants, etc. | 36,063 | 41,864 | 46,406 |
| Petroleum, petroleum products, etc. | 34,406 | 40,064 | 42,177 |
| Animal and vegetable oils, fats and waxes | 11,491 | 16,668 | 16,667 |
| Fixed vegetable fats and oils | 10,129 | 15,380 | 14,799 |
| Chemicals and related products | 36,493 | 38,781 | 45,065 |
| Organic chemicals | 9,265 | 9,273 | 10,553 |
| Medicinal and pharmaceutical products | 5,184 | 5,980 | 6,992 |
| Manufactured fertilizers | 6,367 | 6,438 | 8,018 |
| Basic manufactures | 23,806 | 22,250 | 25,291 |
| Paper, paperboard and manufactures | 3,935 | 3,583 | 3,755 |
| Iron and steel | 8,076 | 8,206 | 9,862 |
| Machinery and transport equipment | 82,654 | 95,350 | 81,967 |
| Power-generating machinery and equipment | 8,893 | 5,125 | 7,711 |
| Machinery specialized for particular industries | 32,179 | 33,492 | 23,494 |
| General industrial machinery, equipment and parts | 7,407 | 6,983 | 8,174 |
| Telecommunications and sound equipment | 3,946 | 7,671 | 5,752 |
| Other electrical machinery, apparatus, etc. | 7,469 | 6,955 | 8,901 |
| Road vehicles and parts (excl. tyres, engines and electrical parts) | 12,146 | 26,047 | 16,227 |
| Other transport equipment | 8,492 | 6,698 | 8,792 |
| Miscellaneous manufactured articles | 5,960 | 6,364 | 6,333 |
| **Total** (incl. others) | 229,889 | 258,643 | 258,250 |

| Exports f.o.b.† | 1991/92 | 1992/93 | 1993/94 |
|---|---|---|---|
| Food and live animals | 17,211 | 16,821 | 18,538 |
| Fresh, chilled or frozen fish | 2,852 | 4,733 | 4,644 |
| Rice | 10,340 | 8,259 | 7,319 |
| Crude materials (inedible) except fuels | 16,944 | 10,683 | 7,197 |
| Cotton fibres and waste | 14,448 | 8,305 | 4,270 |
| Basic manufactures | 91,066 | 98,428 | 118,716 |
| Leather, leather manufactures and dressed furskins | 6,255 | 6,151 | 7,143 |
| Textile yarn, fabrics, etc. | 83,560 | 91,019 | 110,174 |
| Miscellaneous manufactured articles | 42,087 | 46,833 | 57,336 |
| Clothing and accessories (excl. footwear) | 33,846 | 38,106 | 45,197 |
| **Total** (incl. others) | 171,728 | 177,028 | 205,499 |

* Excluding re-imports (million rupees): 69 in 1991/92.
† Excluding re-exports (million rupees): 1,156 in 1991/92.

Source: State Bank of Pakistan, *Annual Report*.

PAKISTAN
*Statistical Survey*

## PRINCIPAL TRADING PARTNERS
(million rupees, year ending 30 June)

| Imports c.i.f. (excl. re-imports) | 1990/91 | 1991/92 | 1992/93 |
|---|---|---|---|
| Australia | 3,090 | 4,946 | 5,708 |
| Bahrain | 3,947 | 6,028 | 2,707 |
| Belgium | 2,493 | 2,785 | 2,768 |
| Canada | 1,944 | 2,069 | 2,527 |
| China, People's Republic | 8,658 | 9,932 | 10,928 |
| France | 4,949 | 10,883 | 10,774 |
| Germany | 12,429 | 18,276 | 19,354 |
| Indonesia | 1,448 | 2,007 | 2,820 |
| Iran | 4,063 | 3,842 | 4,601 |
| Italy | 5,919 | 9,537 | 8,719 |
| Japan | 22,161 | 32,934 | 41,091 |
| Korea, Republic | 4,778 | 7,625 | 11,566 |
| Kuwait | 1,185 | 2,131 | 8,477 |
| Malaysia | 6,836 | 9,663 | 13,300 |
| Netherlands | 3,061 | 3,719 | 5,154 |
| Qatar | 772 | 2,437 | 2,419 |
| Saudi Arabia | 10,726 | 12,047 | 14,083 |
| Singapore | 5,528 | 3,315 | 4,072 |
| Sweden | 1,651 | 2,009 | 2,857 |
| Switzerland | 4,377 | 6,024 | 5,888 |
| USSR* | 1,257 | 3,553 | 1,317 |
| United Arab Emirates† | 5,065 | 8,017 | 5,388 |
| United Kingdom | 8,435 | 12,533 | 12,414 |
| USA | 20,224 | 24,124 | 24,395 |
| **Total** (incl. others) | 171,114 | 229,889 | 258,643 |

* Russian Federation from December 1991.
† Abu Dhabi and Dubai only.

| Exports f.o.b. (excl. re-exports) | 1990/91 | 1991/92 | 1992/93 |
|---|---|---|---|
| Australia | 1,542 | 2,103 | 2,663 |
| Bangladesh | 2,160 | 3,218 | 2,890 |
| Belgium | 2,380 | 2,398 | 3,001 |
| Canada | 2,323 | 3,293 | 4,020 |
| France | 5,300 | 6,667 | 7,630 |
| Germany | 11,824 | 12,175 | 13,803 |
| Hong Kong | 8,285 | 12,503 | 11,679 |
| India | 933 | 2,814 | 2,175 |
| Indonesia | 706 | 2,129 | 1,608 |
| Iran | 2,190 | 3,576 | 1,130 |
| Italy | 5,200 | 5,482 | 4,520 |
| Japan | 11,448 | 14,226 | 12,109 |
| Korea, Republic | 5,421 | 5,052 | 4,283 |
| Netherlands | 2,753 | 3,707 | 4,679 |
| Saudi Arabia | 4,936 | 7,339 | 8,280 |
| Singapore | 3,093 | 3,067 | 3,542 |
| Sri Lanka | 1,711 | 2,017 | n.a. |
| Sweden | 2,620 | 2,564 | 1,954 |
| Thailand | 1,760 | 2,359 | 1,601 |
| United Arab Emirates* | 4,198 | 7,608 | 10,527 |
| United Kingdom | 10,050 | 11,375 | 12,654 |
| USA | 14,893 | 22,006 | 24,542 |
| **Total** (incl. others) | 138,282 | 171,728 | 177,028 |

* Abu Dhabi and Dubai only.

Source: mainly State Bank of Pakistan, *Annual Report*.

## Transport

### RAILWAYS (year ending 30 June)

| | 1991/92 | 1992/93 | 1993/94 |
|---|---|---|---|
| Passenger journeys ('000) | 73,299 | 58,332 | 61,720 |
| Passenger-km (million) | 18,159 | 16,759 | 16,274 |
| Freight ('000 metric tons) | 7,560 | 7,435 | 8,035 |
| Net freight ton-km (million) | 5,964 | 5,860 | 5,940 |

### ROAD TRAFFIC (registered motor vehicles)

| | 1991 | 1992 | 1993 |
|---|---|---|---|
| Passenger cars | 765,195 | 855,375 | 927,778 |
| Buses and coaches | 89,094 | 94,337 | 96,760 |
| Goods vehicles | 107,171 | 111,323 | 112,053 |
| Motor cycles (incl. rickshaws) | 1,433,575 | 1,534,760 | 1,626,389 |
| Others | 528,878 | 554,663 | 566,908 |
| **Total** | 2,923,913 | 3,150,458 | 3,329,888 |

### SHIPPING
**Merchant Fleet** (displacement at 30 June)

| | 1990 | 1991 | 1992 |
|---|---|---|---|
| **Total** ('000 grt) | 354 | 358 | 380 |

Source: UN, *Statistical Yearbook*.

**International Sea-borne Shipping** (port of Karachi)

| | 1991/92 | 1992/93 | 1993/94 |
|---|---|---|---|
| Vessels ('000 net reg. tons): | | | |
| Entered | 14,576 | 15,096 | 14,798 |
| Cleared | 14,593 | 13,167 | 14,314 |
| Goods ('000 long tons) | | | |
| Loaded | 5,187 | 4,912 | 3,578 |
| Unloaded | 15,266 | 17,257 | 13,042 |

### CIVIL AVIATION
(domestic and international flights, '000, year ending 30 June)

| | 1991/92 | 1992/93 | 1993/94 |
|---|---|---|---|
| Kilometres flown | 66,226 | 68,463 | 68,939 |
| Passenger-km | 10,072,736 | 10,047,804 | 9,228,070 |
| Freight ton-km | 382,845 | 393,595 | 394,534 |
| Mail ton-km | 9,628 | 9,476 | 9,450 |

## Tourism

| | 1992 | 1993 | 1994* |
|---|---|---|---|
| Tourist arrivals | 362,704 | 364,336 | 387,525 |

* Provisional figure.

Receipts from tourism (US $ million): 156.5 in 1990; 119.0 in 1992.

### FOREIGN VISITORS BY COUNTRY OF ORIGIN ('000)

| | 1992 |
|---|---|
| Afghanistan | 17,248 |
| Bangladesh | 7,744 |
| Canada | 7,040 |
| China, People's Republic | 7,040 |
| France | 6,688 |
| Germany | 10,912 |
| India | 76,384 |
| Japan | 9,152 |
| United Kingdom | 84,128 |
| USA | 31,328 |
| **Total** (incl. others) | 362,704 |

## Communications Media

|  | 1990 | 1991 | 1992 |
|---|---|---|---|
| Radio receivers ('000 in use) | 10,650 | 10,980 | 11,300 |
| Television receivers ('000 in use) | 2,080 | 2,205 | 2,300 |
| Daily newspapers | 237 | n.a. | 274 |

Source: UNESCO, *Statistical Yearbook*.

Telephones: ('000 main lines in use): 792 in 1989; 843 in 1990; 1,116 in 1991 (Source: UN, *Statistical Yearbook*).

## Education

(estimates, 1993/94)

|  | Institutions | Teachers | Students |
|---|---|---|---|
| Pre-primary and primary | 156,450 | 383,400 | 15,532,000 |
| Middle | 12,638 | 98,400 | 3,845,000 |
| Secondary | 11,435 | 196,500 | 1,354,000 |
| Higher: |  |  |  |
| Secondary vocational institutes | 712 | 6,850 | 92,000 |
| Arts and science colleges | 680 | 18,690 | 595,000 |
| Professional* | 100 | 4,700 | 77,186 |
| Universities | 24 | 6,258 | 85,635 |

* Including educational colleges.

# Directory

## The Constitution

The Constitution was promulgated on 10 April 1973, and amended on a number of subsequent occasions (see Amendments, below). Several provisions were suspended following the imposition of martial law in 1977. The (amended) Constitution was restored on 30 December 1985.

### GENERAL PROVISIONS

The Preamble upholds the principles of democracy, freedom, equality, tolerance and social justice as enunciated by Islam. The rights of religious and other minorities are guaranteed.

The Islamic Republic of Pakistan consists of four provinces—Balochistan, North-West Frontier Province, Punjab and Sindh—and the tribal areas under federal administration. The provinces are autonomous units.

Fundamental rights are guaranteed and include equality of status (women have equal rights with men), freedom of thought, speech, worship and the press and freedom of assembly and association. No law providing for preventive detention shall be made except to deal with persons acting against the integrity, security or defence of Pakistan. No such law shall authorize the detention of a person for more than one month.

### PRESIDENT

The President is Head of State and acts on the advice of the Prime Minister. He is elected at a joint sitting of the Federal Legislature to serve for a term of five years. He must be a Muslim. The President may be impeached for violating the Constitution or gross misconduct.

### FEDERAL LEGISLATURE

The Federal Legislature consists of the President, a lower and an upper house. The lower house, called the National Assembly, has 207 members elected directly for a term of five years, on the basis of universal suffrage (for adults over the age of 21 years), plus 10 members representing minorities. The upper house, called the Senate, has 87 members who serve for six years, with one-third retiring every two years. Each Provincial Assembly is to elect 19 Senators. The tribal areas are to return eight and the remaining three are to be elected from the Federal Capital Territory by members of the Provincial Assemblies.

There shall be two sessions of the National Assembly and Senate each year, with not more than 120 days between the last sitting of a session and the first sitting of the next session.

The role of the Senate in an overwhelming majority of the subjects shall be merely advisory. Disagreeing with any legislation of the National Assembly, it shall have the right to send it back only once for reconsideration. In case of disagreement in other subjects, the Senate and National Assembly shall sit in a joint session to decide the matter by a simple majority.

### GOVERNMENT

The Constitution provides that bills may originate in either house, except money bills. The latter must originate in the National Assembly and cannot go to the Senate. A bill must be passed by both houses and then approved by the President, who may return the bill and suggest amendments. In this case, after the bill has been reconsidered and passed, with or without amendment, the President must give his assent to it.

### PROVINCIAL GOVERNMENT

In the matter of relations between Federation and Provinces, the Federal Legislature shall have the power to make laws, including laws bearing on extra-territorial affairs, for the whole or any part of Pakistan, while a Provincial Assembly shall be empowered to make laws for that Province or any part of it. Matters in the Federal Legislative List shall be subject to the exclusive authority of the Federal Legislature, while the Federal Legislature and a Provincial Assembly shall have power to legislate with regard to matters referred to in the Concurrent Legislative List. Any matter not referred to in either list may be subject to laws made by a Provincial Assembly alone, and not by the Federal Legislature, although the latter shall have exclusive power to legislate with regard to matters not referred to in either list for those areas in the Federation not included in any Province.

Four provisions seek to ensure the stability of the parliamentary system. First, the Prime Minister shall be elected by the National Assembly and he and the other Ministers shall be responsible to it. Secondly, any resolution calling for the removal of a Prime Minister shall have to name his successor in the same resolution which shall be adopted by not less than two-thirds of the total number of members of the lower house. The requirement of two-thirds majority is to remain in force for 15 years or three electoral terms, whichever is more. Thirdly, the Prime Minister shall have the right to seek dissolution of the legislature at any time even during the pendency of a no-confidence motion. Fourthly, if a no-confidence motion is defeated, such a motion shall not come up before the house for the next six months.

All these provisions for stability shall apply *mutatis mutandis* to the Provincial Assemblies also.

A National Economic Council, to include the Prime Minister and a representative from each province, shall advise the Provincial and Federal Governments.

There shall be a Governor for each Province, appointed by the President, and a Council of Ministers to aid and advise him, with a Chief Minister appointed by the Governor. Each Province has a provincial legislature consisting of the Governor and Provincial Assembly.

The executive authorities of every Province shall be required to ensure that their actions are in compliance with the Federal laws which apply in that Province. The Federation shall be required to consider the interests of each Province in the exercise of its authority in that Province. The Federation shall further be required to afford every Province protection from external aggression and internal disturbance, and to ensure that every Province is governed in accordance with the provisions of the Constitution.

To further safeguard the rights of the smaller provinces, a Council of Common Interests has been created. Comprising the Chief Ministers of the four provinces and four Central Ministers to decide upon specified matters of common interest, the Council is responsible to the Federal Legislature. The constitutional formula gives the net proceeds of excise duty and royalty on gas to the province concerned. The profits on hydroelectric power generated in each province shall go to that province.

## OTHER PROVISIONS

Other provisions include the procedure for elections, the setting up of an Advisory Council of Islamic Ideology and an Islamic Research Institute, and the administration of tribal areas.

## AMENDMENTS

Amendments to the Constitution shall require a two-thirds majority in the National Assembly and endorsement by a simple majority in the Senate.

In 1975 the Constitution (Third Amendment) Bill abolished the provision that a State of Emergency may not be extended beyond six months without the approval of the National Assembly and empowered the Government to detain a person for three months instead of one month.

In July 1977, following the imposition of martial law, several provisions, including all fundamental rights provided for in the Constitution, were suspended.

An amendment of September 1978 provided for separate electoral registers to be drawn up for Muslims and non-Muslims.

In October 1979 a martial law order inserted a clause in the Constitution establishing the supremacy of military courts in trying all offences, criminal and otherwise.

On 26 May 1980, the President issued a Constitution Amendment Order, which amended Article 199, debarring High Courts from making any order relating to the validity of effect of any judgment or sentence passed by a military court or tribunal granting an injunction; from making an order or entering any proceedings in respect of matters under the jurisdiction or cognizance of a military court or tribunal, and from initiating proceedings against the Chief Martial Law Administrator or a Martial Law Administrator.

By another amendment of the Constitution, the Federal Shari'a Court was to replace the Shari'a Benches of the High Courts. The Shari'a Court, on the petition of a citizen or the Government, may decide whether any law or provision of law is contrary to the injunction of Islam as laid down in the Holy Koran and the Sunnah of the Holy Prophet.

In March 1981 the Government promulgated Provisional Constitutional Order 1981, whereby provision is made for the appointment of one or more Vice-Presidents, to be appointed by the Chief Martial Law Administrator, and a Federal Advisory Council (*Majlis-i-Shura*) consisting of persons nominated by the President. All political parties not registered with the Election Commission on 13 September 1979 were to be dissolved and their properties made forfeit to the Federal Council. Any party working against the ideology, sovereignty or security of Pakistan may be dissolved by the President.

The proclamation of July 1977, imposing martial law, and subsequent orders amending the Constitution and further martial law regulations shall not be questioned by any court on any grounds.

All Chief Justices and Judges shall take a new oath of office. New High Court benches for the interior of the provinces shall be set up and retired judges are debarred from holding office in Pakistan for two years. The powers of the High Courts shall be limited for suspending the operation of an order for the detention of any person under any law provided for preventative detention, or release any person on bail, arrested under the same law.

The Advisory Council of Islamic Ideology, which was asked by the Government to suggest procedures for the election and further Islamization of the Constitution, recommended non-party elections, separate electorates, Islamic qualifications for candidates and a federal structure with greater devolution of power by changing the present divisions into provinces.

Under the Wafaqi Mohtasib Order 1982, the President appointed a Wafaqi Mohtasib (Federal Ombudsman) to redress injustice committed by any government agency.

In March 1985 the President, Gen. Zia ul-Haq, promulgated the Revival of the 1973 Constitution Order, which increased the power of the President by amendments such as those establishing a National Security Council, powers to dismiss the Prime Minister, the Cabinet and provincial Chief Ministers, to appoint judicial and military chiefs, and to call elections, and indemnity clauses to ensure the power of the President. The Constitution was then revived with the exception of 28 key provisions relating to treason, subversion, fundamental rights and jurisdiction of the Supreme Court. In October 1985 the Constitution (Eighth Amendment) Bill became law, incorporating most of the provisions of the Revival of the 1973 Constitution Order and indemnifying all actions of the military regime. In December the enactment of the Political Parties (Amendment) Bill allowed political parties to function under stringent conditions (these conditions were eased in 1988). In December Gen. Zia lifted martial law and restored the remainder of the Constitution.

In March 1987 the Constitution (Tenth Amendment) Bill reduced the minimum number of working days of the National Assembly from 160 days to 130 days.

# The Government

## HEAD OF STATE

**President:** Sardar Farooq Ahmad Khan Leghari (took office 14 November 1993).

## CABINET
(June 1995)

A coalition of the Pakistan People's Party (PPP), the Pakistan Muslim League (Junejo Group) and independents.

**Prime Minister and Minister of Finance and Economic Affairs:** Benazir Bhutto (PPP).

**Minister of Foreign Affairs:** Sardar Asif Ahmad Ali (PML–Junejo Group).

**Minister of Defence:** Aftab Shahban Mirani (PPP).

**Minister of the Interior:** Maj.-Gen. (retd) Naseerullah Khan Babar (PPP).

**Minister of Industries and Production:** Brig. (retd) Muhammad Asghar (PML–Junejo Group).

**Financial Adviser with Ministerial Status:** V. A. Jaffery (Independent).

**Minister of Law, Justice and Parliamentary Affairs:** Prof. N. D. Khan (PPP).

**Minister of States, Northern Areas, Frontier Regions and Kashmir Affairs:** Mohammad Afzal Khan (PML—Junejo Group).

**Minister of Petroleum and Natural Resources:** Anwar Saifullah Khan (PML–Junejo Group).

**Minister of Information and Broadcasting:** Khalid Ahmad Khan Kharal (PPP).

**Minister of Education:** Syed Khurshid Ahmad Shah (PML–Junejo Group).

**Minister of Works:** Makhdum Mohammad Amin Fahim (PPP).

**Minister of Food, Agriculture and Livestock:** Nawab Mohammad Yusuf Talpur (PPP).

**Minister of Water and Power:** Malik Ghulam Mustafa Khar (PPP).

**Minister of Commerce:** Chaudhary Ahmad Mukhtar (PPP).

**Minister of Population Welfare:** (vacant)

**Minister without Portfolio:** Pir Aftab Shah Jilani.

**Minister of State for Labour and Manpower:** Ghulam Akbar Lasi (PPP).

## MINISTRIES

**Office of the President:** Constitution Ave, Islamabad; tel. (51) 65971; telex 54058; fax (51) 811390.

**Office of the Prime Minister:** Islamabad; telex 5742.

**Ministry of Commerce:** Block A, Pakistan Secretariat, Islamabad; tel. (51) 825078; telex 5859; fax (51) 825241.

**Ministry of Communications:** Block D, Pakistan Secretariat, Islamabad; tel. (51) 826277; telex 5713.

**Ministry of Culture and Tourism:** College Rd, Shalimar 7/2, Islamabad; tel. (51) 827024; telex 54318; fax (51) 817323.

**Ministry of Defence:** Pakistan Secretariat, No. II, Rawalpindi 46000; tel. (51) 580536; telex 5779; fax (51) 580494.

**Ministry of Education:** Block D, Pakistan Secretariat, Islamabad; tel. (51) 825001.

**Ministry of Finance and Economic Affairs:** Block Q, Pakistan Secretariat, Islamabad; tel. (51) 820928; telex 54202; fax (51) 821941.

**Ministry of Food, Agriculture and Livestock:** Block B, Pakistan Secretariat, Islamabad; tel. (51) 821905; telex 5844; fax (51) 820216.

**Ministry of Foreign Affairs:** Constitution Ave, Islamabad; tel. (51) 812470; telex 5800.

**Ministry of Health, Special Education and Social Welfare:** Block C, Pakistan Secretariat, Islamabad; tel. (51) 824960; telex 54427.

**Ministry of Housing and Works:** Block B, Pakistan Secretariat, Islamabad; tel. (51) 825941.

**Ministry of Industries and Production:** Block A, Pakistan Secretariat, Islamabad; tel. (51) 822164; telex 5774; fax (51) 825130.

**Ministry of Information and Broadcasting:** Block M, Pakistan Secretariat, Islamabad; tel. (51) 821626; telex 5782.

PAKISTAN                                                                                          Directory

**Ministry of the Interior and Narcotics Control:** Block R, Pakistan Secretariat, Islamabad; tel. (51) 820641; telex 54207; fax (51) 818459.

**Ministry of Labour, Manpower and Overseas Pakistanis:** Block B, Pakistan Secretariat, Islamabad; tel. (51) 823686.

**Ministry of Law, Justice and Parliamentary Affairs:** Islamabad; tel. (51) 823397.

**Ministry of Local Government and Rural Development:** Islamabad; tel. (51) 820902; telex 5667; fax (51) 813987.

**Ministry of Petroleum and Natural Resources:** Block A, Pakistan Secretariat, Islamabad; tel. (51) 211220; telex 5862; fax (51) 821770.

**Ministry of Planning and Development:** Block P, Pakistan Secretariat, Islamabad; tel. (51) 829442; telex 5717; fax (51) 822704.

**Ministry of Railways:** Block D, Pakistan Secretariat, Islamabad; tel. (51) 829139; telex 5714.

**Ministry of Religious and Minorities' Affairs:** Plot No. 20, Ramna 6, Islamabad; tel. (51) 827161; telex 54047.

**Ministry of Science and Technology:** Block S, Pakistan Secretariat, Islamabad; tel. (51) 825208; fax (51) 825376.

**Ministry of States, Northern Areas, Frontier Regions and Kashmir Affairs:** Block R, Pakistan Secretariat, Islamabad; tel. (51) 820672; telex 54160; fax (51) 818189.

**Ministry of Water and Power:** Block A, Pakistan Secretariat, Islamabad; tel. (51) 823153; telex 5851; fax (51) 823187.

## Federal Legislature

### SENATE

The Senate comprises 87 members, who are elected by the four provincial legislatures. Its term of office is six years, with one-third of the members relinquishing their seats every two years.

**Chairman:** WASIM SAJJAD JAN.

**Deputy Chairman:** MIR ABDUL JABBAR.

### NATIONAL ASSEMBLY

The 217-member National Assembly is elected for five years. It comprises 207 directly-elected Muslim members and an additional 10 seats reserved for Christians, Hindus and other minorities.

**Speaker:** SYED YUSUF RAZA GILANI.

**Deputy Speaker:** ZAFAR ALI SHAH.

**General Election, 6 October 1993**

|                                               | Seats |
|-----------------------------------------------|-------|
| Pakistan People's Party                       | 86    |
| Pakistan Muslim League (Nawaz Group)          | 73    |
| Pakistan Muslim League (Junejo Group)         | 6     |
| Pakistan Islamic Front                        | 3     |
| Islami Jamhoori Mahaz                         | 3     |
| Pakhtoon Khawa Milli Awami Party              | 3     |
| Awami National Party                          | 3     |
| Muttahida Deeni Mahaz                         | 3     |
| Jamhuri Watan Party                           | 2     |
| Pakhtoonkhwa Qaumi Party                      | 1     |
| Balochistan National Movement (Hai)           | 1     |
| Balochistan National Movement (Mengal)        | 1     |
| National Democratic Alliance                  | 1     |
| National People's Party                       | 1     |
| Independent                                   | 15    |
| **Total\***                                   | 202   |

* Polling was suspended in five constituencies for a variety of reasons, including the death of candidates.

## Provinces

Pakistan comprises the four provinces of Sindh, Balochistan, Punjab and the North-West Frontier Province, plus the federal capital and 'tribal areas' under federal administration.

### GOVERNORS

**Balochistan:** Brig. (retd) ABDUL RAHIM DURRANI.

**North-West Frontier Province:** Maj.-Gen. (retd) KHURSHID ALI KHAN.

**Punjab:** Lt-Gen. (retd) RAJA SAROOP KHAN.

**Sindh:** KAMAL ASGHAR.

### CHIEF MINISTERS

**Balochistan:** Nawab ZULFIQAR ALI MAGSI.

**North-West Frontier Province:** AFTAB AHMAD KHAN SHERPAO.

**Punjab:** Mian MANZOOR AHMED WATTOO.

**Sindh:** SYED ABDULLAH SHAH.

## Political Organizations

**All Pakistan Jammu and Kashmir Conference:** f. 1948; advocates the holding of a free plebiscite in the whole of Kashmir; Pres. Sardar SIKANDAR HAYAT KHAN.

**Awami National Party (ANP)** (People's National Party): Karachi; tel. (21) 534513; telex 23035; f. 1986 by the merger of the National Democratic Party, the Awami Tehrik (People's Movement) and the Mazdoor Kissan (Labourers' and Peasants' Party); federalist and socialist; Pres. AJMAL KHATTAK; Vice-Pres. GHULAM AHMED BILOUR, H. B. NAAREJO.

**Awami Qiyadat Party** (People's Leadership Party): Lahore; f. 1995; Chair. Gen. (retd) ASLAM BEG.

**Balochistan National Alliance:** Quetta; Leader Nawab MOHAMMAD AKBAR BUGTI.

**Balochistan National Movement:** Quetta; Leader ABDUL HAYEE BALUCH.

**Hizbe Jihad:** Leader MURTAZA POOYA.

**Islami Jamhoori Mahaz:** c/o National Assembly, Islamabad.

**Jamiat-e-Ulema-e-Islam (JUI):** f. 1950; advocates adoption of a constitution in accordance with (Sunni) Islamic teachings; Pres. Maulana FAZLUR RAHMAN.

**Jamiat-e-Ulema-e-Pakistan (JUP):** 228A Skindar Rd, Upper Mall, behind International Hotel, Lahore; tel. (42) 874727; f. 1948; advocates progressive (Sunni) Islamic principles; Pres. Maulana SHAH AHMED NOORANI SIDDIQUI; Gen. Sec. Gen. (retd) K. M. AZHAR.

**Muhajir Qaumi Movement (MQM):** Karachi; tel. (21) 689989; fax (21) 689955; f. 1978 as All Pakistan Muhajir Student Organization; name changed 1984; represents the interests of Muslim, Urdu-speaking immigrants in Pakistan; seeks the designation of Muhajir as fifth nationality (after Sindhi, Punjabi, Pathan and Balochi); Leader ALTAF HUSSAIN; Chair. (vacant); Sec.-Gen. Dr IMRAN FAROOQ; c. 1m. mems; split into two factions, the MQM (Altaf) and the smaller MQM (Haqiqi) in 1992.

**Muttahida Deeni Mahaz:** c/o National Assembly, Islamabad.

**National Democratic Alliance (NDA):** Karachi; f. 1992 as an informal alliance of six parties and two independent groups (the latter being led by GHULAM MUSTAFA KHAR and Maulana KAUSER NIAZI); Leader NAWABZADA NASRULLAH KHAN; Sec.-Gen. ABDUL HAFEEZ PIRZADA.

  **Jamhuri Watan Party:** Pres. Nawab AKBAR BUGTI.

  **National People's Party (NPP):** Karachi; f. 1986; advocates a 10-point programme for the restoration of democracy; breakaway faction from PPP; right-wing; Chair. GHULAM MUSTAFA JATOI; Chief Organizer S. M. ZAFAR.

  **Pakistan Democratic Party (PDP):** f. 1969; advocates democratic and Islamic values; Pres. NAWABZADA NASRULLAH KHAN; Sec.-Gen. CHAUDHURY ARSHAD MULTAN.

  **Pakistan National Party:** left-wing; pro-Indian; Pres. BIZEN BEZENJO; Sec.-Gen. ABDUL HAFEEZ PIRZADA.

Other parties belonging to the NDA are the **Awami Jamhuri Party** and the **Mazdoor Kisan Party**.

**Pakhtoon Khawa Milli Awami Party:** Leader SAMAND ACHAKZAI.

**Pakhtoonkhwa Qaumi Party:** c/o National Assembly, Islamabad.

**Pakistan Awami Ittehad (PAI)** (Pakistan People's Alliance): f. 1988.

**Pakistan Islamic Front:** Lahore; f. 1993 as an alliance of Islamic groups; Leader AMIR QAZI HUSSAIN AHMAD.

  **Jamaat-e-Islami Pakistan (JIP):** Mansoorah, Multan Rd, Lahore 54570; tel. (42) 7570124; fax (42) 7832194; f. 1941; seeks the establishment of Islamic (Sunni) order; right-wing; Chair. Amir Qazi HUSSAIN AHMAD; Sec.-Gen. SYED MUNAWAR HASAN.

**Pakistan Khaksar Party:** f. during British rule, dissolved 1947, later revived; upholds Islamic values and advocates universal military training; Pres. MOHAMMAD ASHRAF KHAN.

**Pakistan Muslim League (PML):** Muslim League House, Rawalpindi (Junejo Group); Muslim League House, 33 Agha Khan Rd, Lahore (Fida Group); f. 1906; in 1979 the party split into two factions, the pro-Zia Pagara Group and the Chatta Group (later renamed the Qasim Group, see below); the Pagara Group itself split into two factions when a group of army-supported Zia loyalists, known as the Fida Group, separated from the Junejo Group in August 1988; at the November 1988 general election, however, the Junejo Group and the Fida Group did not present rival candidates; in May 1993 the Junejo Group split into two factions, one led by MOHAMMAD NAWAZ SHARIF, known as the Nawaz Group (Sec.-Gen. SARTAJ AZIZ), and the other by HAMID NASIR CHATTHA, which retained the title of Junejo Group; Pres. (Fida Group) FIDA MOHAMMAD KHAN.

**Pakistan Muslim League (Qasim Group):** f. 1979 as the PML (Chatta Group) one of four factions comprising the Muslim League; Pres. MALIK MOHAMMAD QASIM.

**Pakistan People's Party (PPP):** 70 Clifton, Karachi 75600; tel. (21) 532151; f. 1967; advocates Islamic socialism, democracy and a non-aligned foreign policy; Chair. BENAZIR BHUTTO; Sec.-Gen. Sheikh RAFIQ AHMAD; Sr Vice-Pres. MAKHDOOM MOHAMMED ZAMAN TALIB-UL-MAULA.

**Punjabi Pakhtoon Ittehad (PPI):** f. 1987 to represent the interests of Punjabis and Pakhtoons in Karachi; Pres. MALIK MIR HAZAR KHAN.

**Sindh National Alliance:** Village Sun, Dadu District; f. 1988; nationalist; Chair. (vacant).

**Sipah-i-Sahaba Pakistan (SSP):** Karachi; f. as a breakaway faction of Jamiat-e-Ulema-e-Islam; Sunni extremist; Leader Maulana TARIQ AZAM; Sec.-Gen. HAFIZ AHMED BUKHSH.

**Tehrik-i-Istiqlal:** Abbottabad; Leader Air Marshal (retd) MOHAMMAD ASGHAR KHAN; Sec.-Gen. TASSADDAQ HUSSAIN BALUCH.

**Tehrik-i-Ittehad** (Movement of Unity): f. 1995; Leader Gen. (retd) HAMEED GUL.

**Tehrik-i-Jafria-i-Pakistan (TJP):** f. 1987 as a political party; Shi'a extremist; Leader Allama SAJID ALI NAQVI.

**United National Alliance:** f. 1993 as alliance of five small Sindhi parties.

## Diplomatic Representation

### EMBASSIES AND HIGH COMMISSIONS IN PAKISTAN

**Afghanistan:** 176 Shalimar 7/3, Islamabad; tel. (51) 22566; Ambassador: Sardar MOHAMMAD ROSHAN.

**Algeria:** 20, St 17, F-7/2, POB 1038, Islamabad; tel. (51) 820166; telex 5884; Ambassador: A. S. BEREKSI.

**Argentina:** 20 Hill Rd, F-6/3, POB 1015, Islamabad; tel. (51) 211117; telex 5698; Ambassador: JUAN MARCELO GABASTOU.

**Australia:** University Rd, POB 1046, Islamabad; tel. (51) 214902; telex 5804; fax (51) 214763; High Commissioner: PHILIP KNIGHT.

**Austria:** 13, St 1, Shalimar F-6/3, Islamabad; tel. (51) 820137; telex 5531; Ambassador: Dr FRIEDRICH POSACH.

**Bangladesh:** 24, St 28, F-6/1, Islamabad; tel. (51) 826885; telex 5615; High Commissioner: ANWAR HASHIM.

**Belgium:** 2, St 10, Shalimar F-6/3, Islamabad; tel. (51) 210031; telex 5865; fax (51) 822358; Ambassador: WILFRIED GEENS.

**Brazil:** 194 Atatürk Ave, G-6/3, POB 1053, Islamabad; tel. (51) 822497; telex 5711; Ambassador: ANTÔNIO CARLOS DINIZ DE ANDRADE.

**Bulgaria:** 66 Atatürk Ave, Shalimar G-6/3, Islamabad; Ambassador: GEORGI ILIEV BOZHKOV.

**Canada:** Diplomatic Enclave, Sector G-5, POB 1042, Islamabad; telex 5700; High Commissioner: MARIE A. BEAUCHEMIN.

**Chile:** Islamabad; tel. (51) 821813; telex 54230.

**China, People's Republic:** Ramna 4, Diplomatic Enclave, Islamabad; tel. (51) 826667; Ambassador: ZHOU GANG.

**Cyprus:** Islamabad; High Commissioner: SOTIRIUS ZACKHEOS.

**Czech Republic:** 49, St 27, Shalimar F-6/2, Islamabad; tel. (51) 210195; telex 5705.

**Denmark:** 9, St 90, Ramna 6/3, POB 1118, Islamabad; tel. (51) 214210; telex 5825; fax (51) 823483; Chargé d'affaires a.i.: KURT EBERT.

**Egypt:** 37, 6th Ave, POB 2088, Ramna 6/4, Islamabad; telex 5677; Ambassador: MOHAMMAD SANI HEILA.

**France:** Constitution Ave, Plot 1/6, Diplomatic Enclave, Islamabad; tel. (51) 213981; telex 5819; fax (51) 825389; Ambassador: PIERRE LAFRANCE.

**Germany:** Ramna 5, Diplomatic Enclave, POB 1027, Islamabad; tel. (51) 212412; telex 5871; fax (51) 212911; Ambassador: ALFRED B. VESTRING.

**Greece:** Islamabad; telex 54232; Ambassador: E. N. KARAYA-WINIS.

**Holy See:** Apostolic Nunciature, St 5, Diplomatic Enclave, G-5, POB 1106, Islamabad 44000; tel. (51) 210490; fax (51) 820847; Apostolic Nuncio: Most Rev. RENZO FRATINI, Titular Archbishop of Botriana.

**Hungary:** House No. 12, Margalla Rd, Shalimar 6/3, POB 1103, Islamabad; tel. (51) 211592; Ambassador: ISTVAN VENCZEL.

**India:** G-5, Diplomatic Enclave, Islamabad; tel. (51) 814371; telex 5849; fax (51) 820742; High Commissioner: SATISH CHANDRA.

**Indonesia:** Diplomatic Enclave, Ramna 5/4, POB 1019, Islamabad; tel. (51) 811291; telex 5679; Ambassador: HASSAN ALYDRUS.

**Iran:** 222–238, St. 2, G-5/1, Diplomatic Enclave, Islamabad; tel. (51) 212694; telex 5872; Ambassador: MOHAMMAD MEHDI AKHOUNDZADEH.

**Iraq:** 1, St 15, F-7/2, Islamabad; telex 5868; Ambassador: ADIL AHMAD ZAIDEIN.

**Italy:** 54 Khayaban-e-Margalla, F-6/3, POB 1008, Islamabad; tel. (51) 210791; telex 5861; fax (51) 222986; Ambassador: Dr PIETRO RINALDI.

**Japan:** Plot No. 53-70, Ramna 5/4, Diplomatic Enclave 1, Islamabad 44000; tel. (51) 219721; telex 5805; fax (51) 218073; Ambassador: TAKAO KAWAKAMI.

**Jordan:** 131, St 14, E-7, Islamabad; tel. (51) 821782; telex 5701; Ambassador: FAKHRI ABU TALEB.

**Kazakhstan:** House No. 2, St 4, Sector F-8/3, Islamabad; tel. (51) 262926; fax (51) 262806; Ambassador: AITMUKHAMBETOV TAMAS KALMUKHAMBETOVICH.

**Kenya:** 8, St 88, G-6/3, Islamabad; tel. (51) 811266; telex 5741; High Commissioner: G. W. UKU.

**Korea, Democratic People's Republic:** 9, St 89, Ramna 6/3, Islamabad; tel. (51) 822420; telex 5707; Ambassador: HWANG SAM RIN.

**Korea, Republic:** St 29, Block 13, Diplomatic Enclave-II, POB 1087, Islamabad; tel. (51) 218089; telex 5720; Ambassador: Dr CHANG SOO KO.

**Kuwait:** University Rd, Diplomatic Enclave, Islamabad; tel. (51) 822181; telex 5400; Ambassador: QASIM OMAR AL-YAQOUT.

**Lebanon:** 24, Khayaban-e-Iqbal, Shalimar F-6/3, Islamabad; tel. (51) 821022; telex 5557; Ambassador: WALID A. NASR.

**Libya:** Khayaban-e-Iqbal, 8/3, Islamabad; tel. (51) 821033; telex 5750; Ambassador: MUHAMMAD RASHID AL-MUGHERBI.

**Malaysia:** 224, Shalimar 7/4, Islamabad; tel. (51) 820147; telex 54065; High Commissioner: RASTAM MOHAMMAD ISA.

**Mauritius:** 27, St 26, F-6/2, Islamabad; tel. (51) 823345; telex 54362; High Commissioner: MAHMADE RAFICK ELAHEE.

**Morocco:** 6 Service Rd (South), Sector E-7, Islamabad; tel. (51) 820820; telex 5718; Ambassador: ADIB TAIB.

**Myanmar:** 12/1, St 13, F-7/2, Islamabad; tel. (51) 822460; telex 54282; fax (51) 221210; Ambassador: U PE THEIN TIN.

**Nepal:** H. No. 11, St 84, Atatürk Ave, G-6/4, Islamabad; tel. (51) 210642; telex 54165; fax (51) 217875; Ambassador: MUKUNDA P. DHUNGEL.

**Netherlands:** New PIA Bldg, 2nd Floor, Blue Area, POB 1065, Islamabad; tel. (51) 214336; telex 5877; fax (51) 220947; Ambassador: ALF F. DUYVERMAN.

**Nigeria:** House No. 6, St 22, Sector F-6/2, POB 1075, Islamabad; tel. (51) 212465; telex 5875; fax (51) 824104; High Commissioner: ABDUL RAZAK YUNUSA.

**Norway:** House No. 25, St 19, F-6/2, Islamabad; tel. (51) 211223; telex 5541; fax (51) 223102.

**Oman:** 440 Bazar Rd, Ramna 6/4, Islamabad; tel. (51) 822586; telex 5704; Ambassador: MOHAMMAD YOUSUF SHALWANI.

**Philippines:** 19, St 1, Shalimar 6/3, POB 1052, Islamabad; tel. and fax (51) 820145; telex 56413; Ambassador: NICASIO G. VALDERRAMA.

**Poland:** St 24, G-4, Diplomatic Enclave, POB 1032, Islamabad; tel. (51) 821133; telex 54414; Ambassador: DYONIZY P. BILINSKI.

**Portugal:** 40-A Main Margalla Rd, F-7/2, POB 1067, Islamabad 44000; tel. (51) 213395; telex 5721; fax (51) 221416; Ambassador: Dr GABRIEL MESQUITA DE BRITO.

**Qatar:** 201 Masjid Rd, Shalimar 6/4, Islamabad; tel. (51) 824635; telex 5869; Ambassador: ATIQ MASSER AL-BADER.

**Romania:** 13, St 88, G-6/3, Islamabad; Ambassador: IOSIF CHIVU.

**Russia:** Khayaban-e-Suhrawardy, Diplomatic Enclave, Ramna 4, Islamabad; telex 54241; Ambassador: ALEKSANDR U. ALEKSEYEV.

**Saudi Arabia:** 1, St 4, F-6/3, Islamabad; tel. (51) 820156; telex 54032; Ambassador: YUSEF MOTABBAKANI.

**Singapore:** Islamabad; High Commissioner: TON KENG JIN.

**Somalia:** 15, St 13, F-7/2, Islamabad; tel. (51) 822769; telex 5609; Ambassador: ABDI SALAM HAJI AHMAD LIBAN.

**South Africa:** Islamabad.

**Spain:** St 6, Ramna 5, Diplomatic Enclave, POB 1144, Islamabad; tel. (51) 211070; telex 5803; fax (51) 221927; Ambassador: LORENZO GONZÁLEZ ALONSO.

**Sri Lanka:** 315C, Khayaban-e-Iqbal, F-7/2, Islamabad; tel. (51) 210286; telex 5763; fax (51) 220710; High Commissioner: J. B. NAKKAWDA.

PAKISTAN

**Sudan:** 203, Ramna 6/3, Islamabad; tel. (51) 820171; telex 5617; Ambassador: AHMAD MOHAMMAD ABDULLAH AL-OMERALI.
**Sweden:** 6A, Agha Khan Rd, Markaz Shalimar 6, POB 1100, Islamabad; tel. (51) 822557; telex 5806; Ambassador: GUNNAR HULTNER.
**Switzerland:** St 6, G-5/4, Diplomatic Enclave, POB 1073, Islamabad; tel. (51) 211060; telex 5815; fax (51) 218905; Ambassador: THOMAS H. R. WERNLY.
**Syria:** 30 Hill Rd, Shalimar 6/3, Islamabad; tel. (51) 821077; telex 5619; Ambassador: SAIFI HAMWI.
**Tanzania:** Islamabad; High Commissioner: SADIQ SAHEB ETTABA.
**Thailand:** 4, St 8, Shalimar 8/3, Islamabad; tel. (51) 859130; telex 5527; fax (51) 256730; Ambassador: SUPREE JOTIKAPUKKANA.
**Tunisia:** 187 Main Service Rd, E-7, Islamabad; tel. (51) 213307; telex 5676; fax (51) 7017; Ambassador: JAMELEDDINE GORDAH.
**Turkey:** 58 Atatürk Ave, G-6/3, Islamabad; tel. (51) 210043; Ambassador: CANDAN AZER.
**Turkmenistan:** Islamabad; Ambassador: SAPAR BERDINIYAZOV.
**United Arab Emirates:** Plot No. 1-22, Diplomatic Enclave, Islamabad; tel. (51) 821373; telex 5831; Ambassador: SAEED ALI AL-NOWAIS.
**United Kingdom:** Diplomatic Enclave, Ramna 5, POB 1122, Islamabad; tel. (51) 822131; telex 54122; fax (51) 823439; High Commissioner: Sir CHRISTOPHER MACRAE.
**USA:** Diplomatic Enclave, Ramna 5, POB 1048, Islamabad; tel. (51) 826161; telex 5864; fax (51) 821193; Ambassador: JOHN CAMERON MONJO.
**Yemen:** 16, St 17, F-7/2, POB 1523, Islamabad 44000; tel. (51) 821146; telex 54460; fax (51) 826159; Ambassador: ABDUL MALIK MOHAMMAD WASEA AL-TAYYEB.
**Yugoslavia:** 14, St 87, Ramna 6/3, Islamabad; tel. (51) 821081; Ambassador: (vacant).

## Judicial System

### SUPREME COURT

**Chief Justice:** SAJJAD ALI SHAH.
**Attorney-General:** FAKHRUDDIN G. EBRAHIM.

### Federal Shari'a Court

**Chief Justice:** Mir HAZAR KHAN KHOSO.
**Federal Ombudsman:** Justice USMAN ALI SHAH.

## Religion

### ISLAM

Islam is the state religion. The majority of the population are Sunni Muslims, while about 5% are of the Shi'a sect and only about 0.001% are of the Ahmadi sect.

### CHRISTIANITY

About 2% of the population are Christians.
**National Council of Churches in Pakistan:** 32B Sharah-e-Fatima Jinnah, POB 357, Lahore 54000; tel. (42) 357307; telex 44256; fax (42) 6369745; f. 1949; eight mem. bodies, four associate mems; Exec. Sec. SAMUEL K. GILL.

#### The Roman Catholic Church

For ecclesiastical purposes, Pakistan comprises two archdioceses and four dioceses. At 31 December 1993 there were an estimated 979,519 adherents in the country.
**Bishops' Conference:** Pakistan Episcopal Conference, Sacred Heart Cathedral, 1 Mian Mohammad Shafi Rd, GPOB 909, Lahore 54000; tel. (42) 6366137; fax (42) 6368336; f. 1976; Pres. Most Rev. ARMANDO TRINDADE, Archbishop of Lahore; Sec.-Gen. Rt Rev. ANTHONY LOBO, Bishop of Islamabad-Rawalpindi.
**Archbishop of Karachi:** Most Rev. SIMEON ANTHONY PEREIRA, St Patrick's Cathedral, Shahrah-Iraq, Karachi 74400; tel. (21) 7781532; fax (21) 7783508.
**Archbishop of Lahore:** Most Rev. ARMANDO TRINDADE, Sacred Heart Cathedral, 1 Mian Mohammad Shafi Rd, GPOB 909, Lahore 54000; tel. (42) 6366137; fax (42) 6368336.

#### Protestant Churches

**Church of Pakistan:** Moderator Most Rev. SAMUEL PERVEZ (Bishop of Sialkot), Lal Kothi, Barah Patthar, Sialkot 2; f. 1970 by union of the fmr Anglican Church in Pakistan, the United Methodist Church in Pakistan, the United Church in Pakistan (Scots and English Presbyterians) and the Pakistani Lutheran Church; eight dioceses; c. 700,000 mems (1993); Gen. Sec. S. K. DASS.
**United Presbyterian Church of Pakistan:** POB 395, Rawalpindi; tel. (51) 72503; f. 1961; c. 340,000 mems (June 1989); Moderator Sardar FEROZE KHAN; Sec. Rev. PIYARA LALL.
Other denominations active in the country include the Associated Reformed Presbyterian Church and the Pakistan Salvation Army.

### HINDUISM

Hindus comprise about 1.8% of the population.

### BAHÁ'Í FAITH

**National Spiritual Assembly:** POB 7420, Karachi 74400; tel. (21) 7216429; fax (21) 7215467.

## The Press

In 1988 there were 177 daily newspapers, 368 twice-weeklies and weeklies, 126 fortnightlies, 776 monthlies and 374 quarterlies. The first Urdu-language newspaper, the daily *Urdu Akhbar*, was founded in 1836. After 1947, with the establishment of Pakistan and the introduction of modern equipment, the more influential English-language newspapers, such as *Dawn* and *The Pakistan Times*, were firmly established, while several new Urdu newspapers, for example *Nawa-i-Waqt* and *Daily Jang*, became very popular. The Urdu press comprises almost 800 newspapers, with *Daily Jang*, *Imroze*, *Nawa-i-Waqt*, *Jasarat* and *Mashriq* among the most influential. The daily newspaper with the largest circulation is *Daily Jang*. Although the English-language press reaches only 2% of the population and totals 128 publications, it is influential in political, academic and professional circles. In 1990 the four main press groups in Pakistan were Jang Publications (the *Daily Jang*, *The News*, the *Daily News* and the weekly *Akhbar-e-Jehan*), the Dawn or Herald Group (the *Dawn*, the *Star*, the *Watan* and the monthly *Herald*), the Nawa-i-Waqt Group (the *Nawa-i-Waqt* and the *Nation*), and the National Press Trust (the *Pakistan Times* and the *Mashriq*).

### PRINCIPAL DAILIES

#### Islamabad

**Al-Akhbar:** Al-Akhbar House, Markaz G-8, Islamabad 44870; tel (51) 256006; telex 4642; fax (51) 254499; Urdu; also publ. in Muzaffarabad; Editor-in-Chief ZAHID MALIK.
**The Muslim:** 9 Hameed Chambers, Aabpara, Islamabad; tel. (51) 218924; telex 5656; fax (51) 218928; f. 1979; English; Editor SALAMAT ALI.
**Pakistan Observer:** Al-Akhbar House, Markaz G-8, Islamabad 44870; tel. (51) 256006; telex 4642; fax (51) 254499; f. 1988; English; organ of the IDA; Editor-in-Chief ZAHID MALIK; Editor A. B. S. JAFRI.

#### Karachi

**Aghaz:** 11 Japan Mansion, Preedy St, Sadar, Karachi 74400; tel. (21) 7721688; fax (21) 7722125; f. 1963; evening; Urdu; Editor MOHAMMAD ANWAR FAROOQI; circ. 42,700.
**Amn:** Akhbar Manzil, off I. I. Chundrigar Rd, Karachi 74200; tel. (21) 2634451; fax (21) 2634454; Urdu; Editor AJMAL DEHLVI.
**Business Recorder:** Recorder House, Business Recorder Rd, Karachi 74550; tel. (21) 7210311; telex 20762; fax (21) 7228644; f. 1965; English; Editor M. A. ZUBERI.
**Daily Awam:** HQ Printing House, I. I. Chundrigar Rd, POB 52, Karachi; tel. (21) 2635636; f. 1994; Urdu.
**Daily Beopar:** 118 Bombay Hotel, I. I. Chundrigar Rd, Karachi; tel. (21) 214055; Urdu; Man. Editor TARIQ SAEED.
**Daily Intekhab:** Liaison Office, 3rd Floor, Mashhoor Mahal, Kucha Haji Usman, off I. I. Chundrigar Rd, Karachi; tel. (21) 2631089; fax (21) 7735276; Urdu; also publ. from Hub (Balochistan) and Quetta; Man. Editor SARKAR AHMAD; Publr and Editor ANWAR SAJIDI.
**Daily Jang:** HQ Printing House, I. I. Chundrigar Rd, POB 52, Karachi; tel. (21) 210711; telex 2748; f. 1940; morning; Urdu; also publ. in Quetta, Rawalpindi, Lahore and London; Editor-in-Chief SHAKIL-UR-RAHMAN; combined circ. 750,000.
**Daily Khabar:** A-8 Sheraton Centre, F.B. Area, Karachi; tel. (21) 210059; Urdu; Exec. Editor FAROOQ PARACHA; Editor and Publr SAEED ALI HAMEED.
**Daily Mohasaba:** Imperial Hotel, M.T. Khan Rd, Karachi; tel. (21) 519448; Urdu; Editor TALIB TURABI.
**Daily News:** Printing House, I. I. Chundrigar Rd, Karachi; tel. (21) 210711; telex 2748; f. 1962; evening; English; Editor S. M. FAZAL; circ. 50,000.

# PAKISTAN

**Daily Sindh Sujag:** Campbell St, New Challi, Karachi; tel. (21) 2633242; Sindhi; political; Editor Jabbar Khattak.

**Daily Special:** Ahbab Printers, Beauty House, nr Regal Chowk, Abdullah Haroon Rd, Sadar, Karachi; tel. (21) 7771655; fax (21) 7722776; Urdu; Editor Mohammad al-Tayyab.

**Dawn:** Haroon House, Dr Ziauddin Ahmed Rd, Karachi 4; tel. (21) 520080; telex 23623; f. 1947; English, Gujarati; CEO Khwaja Rahman; Editors Ahmad Ali Khan (English edn), Noor Mohammad (Gujarati edn); circ. 80,000 (English edn).

**Deyanet:** Karachi; tel. (21) 2631333; fax (21) 2631335; Urdu; also publ. in Sukkur and Islamabad.

**Evening Times:** 92 Habib Chambers, nr Civic Centre, Main University Rd, Karachi; tel. (21) 423052; Urdu; Editor Tanvi Kazmi.

**The Finance:** 808 Uni Centre, I. I. Chundrigar Rd, Karachi; tel. (21) 2422560; telex 29088; fax (21) 2422656; English; Chief Editor S. H. Shah.

**Financial Post:** Spencers Bldg, 1st Floor, I. I. Chundrigar Rd, Karachi; tel. (21) 2634831; fax (21) 2635079; f. 1994; English; Editor S. G. M. Badruddin.

**Hilal-e-Pakistan:** Court View Bldg, 2nd Floor, M. A. Jinnah Rd, POB 3737, Karachi 74200; tel. (21) 2624997; fax (21) 2624996; Sindhi; Editor Mohammad Iqbal Dal.

**Hurriyet:** Saifee House, Dr Ziauddin Ahmed Rd, Karachi 74000; tel. (21) 2633988; telex 23623; fax (21) 2633999; Urdu; Chief Editor Farhat H. Rizvi.

**Inqilab:** Grand Hotel Bldg, I. I. Chundrigar Rd, Karachi; tel. (21) 219337; f. 1979; Urdu; Editor S. Majidali; circ. 10,000.

**Jasarat:** Everready Chambers, Mohammad bin Qasim Rd, POB 836, Karachi; tel. (21) 210391; telex 23938; fax (21) 215822; Urdu; Editor Mahmood Ahmad Madani; circ. 50,000.

**Leader:** 191 Altaf Hussain Rd, Karachi 2; tel. (21) 2411515; f. 1958; English; independent; Editor Manzarul Hasan; circ. 11,300.

**Mazdur:** Spencer Bldg, I. I. Chundrigar Rd, Karachi 2; f. 1984; Urdu; Editor Mohammad Anwar bin Abbas.

**Millat:** 191 Altaf Hussain Rd, Karachi 2; tel. (21) 2411514; f. 1946; Gujarati; independent; Editor Inquilab Matri; circ. 22,550.

**New Times:** 122 Bombay Hotel, I. I. Chundrigar Rd, Karachi; tel. (21) 218568; Urdu; Editor Islamullah Khan Shaqi.

**The News International:** I. I. Chundrigar Rd, POB 52, Karachi; tel. (21) 2630611; telex 2748; fax (21) 2638000; f. 1990; English; also publ. from Lahore and Rawalpindi/Islamabad; Editor-in-Chief Mir Shakil Rahman.

**Parliament:** 1013 Qasimabad, Karachi; tel. (21) 422030; f. 1988; English; Chief Editor Farrugh Ahmad Siddiq.

**The Public:** Shaikh Sultan Trust Bldg No. 1, Beaumont Rd, Civil Lines, Karachi; tel. (21) 5687579; f. 1993; Urdu; independent; political; Man. Editor Inquilab Matri; Editor Anwarson Rai.

**Qaumi Akhbar:** Said Mansion, Dr Bilmoria St, off I. I. Chundrigar Rd, Karachi; tel. (21) 211071; f. 1988; Urdu; Editor Ilyas Shakir.

**Roznama Special:** Falak Printing Press, 191 Altaf Hussain Rd, Karachi; tel. (21) 5687522; fax (21) 5687579; Publr and Man. Editor Inquilab Matri; Editor Anwar Sen Roy.

**Savera:** 108 Adam Arcade, Shaheed-e-Millat Rd, Karachi; tel. (21) 419616; Urdu; Editor Rukhsana Saham Mirza.

**Sindh Express:** Mashoor Mahal, 2nd Floor, off I. I. Chundrigar Rd, Karachi; tel. (21) 210430; English; political; Editor and Publr Nasser Brohi.

**Star:** Haroon House, Dr Ziauddin Ahmed Rd, Karachi 4; evening; English; Editor Mohammad Jami.

**The Times of Karachi:** Al-Falah Chambers, 9th Floor, Abdullah Haroon Rd, Karachi; tel. (21) 7727740; evening; English; independent; city news; Editor Mohammad Jami.

**Watan:** Haroon House, Dr Ziauddin Ahmed Rd, Karachi 4; tel. (21) 5683733; f. 1942; Gujarati; Editor M. Ilyas Gadit; circ. 12,000.

## Lahore

**Imroze:** Lahore; tel. (42) 226271; telex 44811; fax (42) 226158; f. 1948; morning; Urdu; Editor Syed Mahmood Jaffer; circ. 50,000 (Lahore), 20,000 (Multan).

**Mahgribi Pakistan:** 20 Beadon Rd, Lahore; tel. (42) 53490; Urdu; also publ. in Bahawalpur and Sukkur; Editor M. Shafaat.

**Mashriq:** 7 Mehmud Ghaznovi Rd, Lahore 54000; tel. (42) 6364421; telex 44345; fax (42) 6367010; f. 1963; Urdu; also publ. in Karachi, Peshawar and Quetta; Exec. Editor Saadet Khyali; circ. 150,000.

**The Nation:** Nipco House, 4 Sharah-e-Fatima Jinnah, POB 1815, Lahore 54000; tel. (42) 304495; telex 44108; fax (42) 6367583; f. 1986; English; Editor Arif Nizami; circ. 36,000.

**Nawa-i-Waqt (Voice of the Time):** 4 Sharah-e-Fatima Jinnah, Lahore 54000; tel. (42) 302050; telex 44870; fax (42) 6367005; f. 1940; English, Urdu; also publ. edns in Karachi, Rawalpindi and Multan; Editor Majid Nizami; combined circ. 400,000.

**Pakistan Daily:** 41 Jail Rd, Lahore; tel. (42) 476301; f. 1990; Urdu; Chief Editor Maqbool Butt.

**Pakistan Times:** Rattan Chand Rd, GPOB 223, Lahore; tel. (42) 7226271; telex 44811; fax (42) 7223766; f. 1947; English; liberal; also publ. in Islamabad; Chief Editor Nasim Ahmad; combined circ. 50,000.

**Tijarat:** 14 Abbot Rd, opp. Nishat Cinema, Lahore; Urdu; Editor Jamil Athar.

**Wifaq:** 6A Waris Rd, Lahore; tel. (42) 302862; Urdu; also publ. in Rawalpindi, Sargodha and Rahimyar Khan; Editor Mostafa Sadiq.

## Rawalpindi

**Daily Jang:** Murree Rd, Rawalpindi; f. 1940; also publ. in Quetta, Karachi and Lahore; Urdu; independent; Editor Mir Javed Rehman; circ. (Rawalpindi) 65,000.

**Daily Wifaq:** 7A C/A, Satellite Town, Rawalpindi; f. 1959; also publ. in Lahore, Sargodha and Rahimyar Khan; Urdu; Editor Mustafa Sadiq.

**The News:** Murree Rd, Rawalpindi; f. 1991; also publ. in Lahore and Karachi; English; independent; Chief Editor Mir Shalilur Rahman; Editor (Rawalpindi) M. Ziauddin.

**Pakistan Times:** Rawalpindi; f. 1947; English; liberal; Chief Editor S. K. Durrani; circ. 10,000.

## Other Towns

**Aftab:** Risala Rd, nr Circular Bldg, Hyderabad; Sindhi; also publ. in Multan; Editor Sheikh Ali Mohammad.

**Al Falah:** Al Falah Bldg, Saddar Rd, Peshawar; f. 1939; Urdu and Pashtu; Editor S. Abdullah Shah.

**Al-Jamiat-e-Sarhad:** Kocha Gilania Chakagali, Karimpura, Peshawar; tel. (521) 212093; f. 1941; Urdu and Pashtu; Propr and Chief Editor S. M. Hassan Gilani.

**Balochistan Times:** Jinnah Rd, Quetta; Editor Syed Fasih Iqbal.

**Daily Awaz:** Cantonment Plaza, Arbab Rd, Sadar, Peshawar; tel. (521) 271195; Urdu; political; Man. Editor Ali Raza Malik.

**Daily Business Report:** Railway Rd, Faisalabad; tel. (41) 642131; fax (41) 621207; Editor Abdul Rashid Ghazi.

**Daily Hewad:** 32 Stadium Rd, Peshawar; tel. (521) 270501; Pashtu; Editor-in-Chief Rehman Shah Afridi.

**Daily Khadim-e-Waten:** B-2, Civil Lines, Hyderabad; Editor Mushataq Ahmad.

**Daily Rehbar:** Jamil Market, Circular Rd, Bahawalpur; tel. (621) 4372; f. 1952; Urdu; Chief Editor Malik Mohammad Hayat; circ. 9,970.

**Daily Sarwan:** 11-EGOR Colony, Hyderabad; tel. (221) 781382; Sindhi; Chief Editor Ghulam Hussain.

**Daily Shabaz:** Nazar Bagh, Grand Trunk Rd, Peshawar; tel. (521) 220188; fax (521) 216483; Urdu; organ of the Awami National Party; Chief Editor Begum Naseem Wali Khan.

**Frontier Post:** 32 Stadium Rd, Peshawar; tel. (521) 79174; telex 52311; fax (521) 76575; f. 1985; English; left-wing; also publ. in Lahore; Editor-in-Chief Rehmat Shah Afridi; Editor Muzaffar Shah Afridi.

**Ibrat:** Hyderabad; tel. (221) 21565; fax (221) 28816; Man. Editor Qazi Asad Abid.

**Jihad:** 15A Islamia Club Bldg, Khyber Bazar, Peshawar; tel. (521) 210522; also publ. in Karachi, Rawalpindi, Islamabad and Lahore; Editor Sharif Farooq.

**Kaleem:** Wallas Rd, POB 88, Sukkur; tel. (71) 22086; Urdu; Editor Shahid Mehr Shamsi.

**Maghribi Pakistan:** Mehran Markaz, Sukkur; Urdu; Editor M. Shafaat.

**Mashriq:** Quetta; Chief Editor Aziz Mazhar.

**Nawai Asma'n:** Mubarak Ali Shah Rd, Hyderabad; tel. and fax (221) 21925; Urdu, Sindhi and Pashtu; Chief Editor Dost Muhammad.

**The News:** Qaumi Printing Press, Peshawar; English; Editor Khurshid Ahmad.

**Punjab News:** Kutchery Bazar, POB 419, Faisalabad; tel. (41) 30151; f. 1968; Chief Editor Pervaiz Pasha; Man. Editor Javaid Himyarite; circ. 20,000.

**Sarhad:** New Gate, Peshawar.

**Sindh Guardian:** Tulsi Das Rd, POB 300, Hyderabad; tel. and fax (221) 21926; telex 22071; English; Chief Editor Dost Muhammad.

**Sindh News:** POB 289, Garikhata, Hyderabad; tel. (221) 25840; Editor Aslam Akber Kazi.

**Sindh Observer:** POB 43, Garikhata, Hyderabad; tel. (221) 27302; English; Editor Aslam Akber Kazi.

# PAKISTAN

**Watan:** 10 Nazar Bagh Flat, Peshawar.
**Zamana:** Jinnah Rd, Quetta; tel. (81) 71217; Urdu; Editor Syed Fasih Iqbal; circ. 5,000.

## SELECTED WEEKLIES

**Aajkal:** Lahore; Urdu; Editor Khaled Ahmed.
**Akhbar-e-Jehan:** Printing House, off I. I. Chundrigar Rd, Karachi; tel. (21) 210710; telex 2748; f. 1967; Urdu; independent; illustrated family magazine; Editor-in-Chief Mir Javed Rahman; circ. 278,000.
**Akhbar-e-Khawateen:** 42-B/6 PECHS, Karachi 29; tel. (21) 431071; telex 25698; f. 1966; women's interests; Editor Shamim Akhtar; circ. 40,000.
**Amal:** Aiwan-e-Abul Kaif Rd, Shah Qabool Colony 1, Namak Mandi, Peshawar; tel. 214520; f. 1958; Urdu, Pashtu and English; Editor-in-Chief F. M. Zafar Kaifi; Exec. Editor Munazima Maab Kaifi.
**Asianews:** 4 Amil St, off Robson Rd, Karachi 1; multilingual news for and about Asians overseas; Man. Editor Ameen Tareen.
**Awam:** Iftikhar Chambers, Altaf Hussain Rd, Karachi 2; f. 1958; Urdu; political; Editor Abdul Rauf Siddiqi; circ. 3,000.
**Badban:** Nai Zindagi Publications, Rana Chambers, Old Anarkali, Lahore; Editor Mujibur Rehman Shami.
**Chatan:** 88 McLeod Rd, Lahore; f. 1948; Urdu; Editor Masud Shorish.
**The Friday Times:** 45 The Mall, Lahore; tel. (42) 7243779; telex 47421; fax (42) 7245097; Editor Najam Sethi.
**Hilal:** Hilal Rd, Rawalpindi; tel. (51) 56134605; f. 1951; Wednesday; Urdu; illustrated armed forces; Editor Mumtaz Iqbal Malik; circ. 80,000.
**Insaf:** P-929, Banni, Rawalpindi; tel. (51) 411038; f. 1955; Editor Mir Abdul Aziz.
**Lahore:** Galaxy Law Chambers, 1st Floor, Room 1, Turner Rd, Lahore 5; f. 1952; Editor Saqib Zeervi; circ. 8,500.
**Mahwar:** D23, Block H, North Nazimabad, Karachi; Editor Shahida Nafis Siddiqi.
**Memaar-i-Nao:** 39 KMC Bldg, Leamarket, Karachi; Urdu; labour magazine; Editor M. M. Mubasir.
**The Muslim World:** 49-B, Block-8, Gulshan-e-Iqbal, Karachi 75300; POB 5030, Karachi 74000; tel. (21) 4960738; telex 2416585; fax (21) 466878; English; current affairs; Editor Khalid Ikramullah Khan.
**Nairang Khayal:** 8 Mohammadi Market, Rawalpindi; f. 1924; Urdu; Chief Editor Sultan Rashk.
**Nigar Weekly:** Victoria Mansion, Abdullah Haroon Rd, Karachi; tel. (21) 510020; Editor Ilyas Rashidi.
**Noor Jehan Weekly:** 32A National Auto Plaza, POB 8833, Karachi 74400; tel and fax (21) 7723946; f. 1948; Urdu; film journal; Editor Khalid Chawla.
**Pakistan and Gulf Economist:** Shafi Court, 2nd Floor, Mereweather Rd, POB 4447, Karachi 4; tel. (21) 551719; telex 25737; f. 1960; English; Editor Akhtar Adil Rizvi; circ. 10,000.
**Pak Kashmir:** Pak Kashmir Office, Soikarno Chowk, Liaquat Rd, Rawalpindi; tel. (51) 74845; f. 1951; Urdu; Editor Muhammed Fayyaz Abbazi.
**Parbat:** Nawabshah; Editor Wahab Siddiqi.
**Parsi Sansar and Loke Sevak:** Marston Rd, Karachi; tel. (21) 7765627; f. 1909; English and Gujarati; Editor Meherji P. Dastur.
**Parwaz:** Madina Office, Bahawalpur; Urdu; Editor Mustaq Ahmed.
**Pictorial:** Jamia Masjid Rd, Rawalpindi; f. 1956; English; Editor Muhammad Safdar.
**Qallandar:** Peshawar; f. 1950; Urdu; Editor M. A. K. Sherwani.
**Quetta Times:** Albert Press, Jinnah Rd, Quetta; f. 1924; English; Editor S. Rustomji; circ. 4,000.
**Shahab-e-Saqib:** Shahab Saqib Rd, Maulana St, Peshawar; f. 1950; Urdu; Editor S. M. Rizvi.
**The Statesman:** 260C, Central C/A, PECHS, Karachi 75400; tel. (21) 435627; f. 1955; English; Editor Mohammad Owais.
**Takbeer:** A-1, 3rd Floor, 'Namco Centre', Campbell St, Karachi 74200; tel. (21) 2626613; fax (21) 2627742; f. 1984; Urdu; Man. Editor (vacant); circ. 70,000.
**Tarjaman-i-Sarhad:** Peshawar; Urdu and Pashtu; Editor Mohammad Shafi Sabir.
**Times of Kashmir:** P-929, Banni, Rawalpindi; tel. (51) 550903; English; Editor Mir Abdul Aziz.
**Ufaq:** 44H, Block No. 2, PECHS, Karachi; tel. (21) 437992; f. 1978; Editor Wahajuddin Chishti; circ. 2,000.

## SELECTED PERIODICALS

**Aalami Digest:** B-1, Momin Sq., Rashid Minhas Rd, Gulshan-e-Iqbal, Karachi; monthly; Urdu; Editor Mrs Zaheda Hina.

**Adabarz:** Misbat Rd, Lahore; monthly; Editor Ibne Wahshi Mahreharvi.
**Afsan Digest:** B-436, Sector 11-A, North Kaveli, Karachi 36; tel. (21) 657074; Urdu; Editor Syed Asim Mahmood.
**Akhbar-e-Watan:** Noor Mohammed Lodge, 444 Dr Ziauddin Ahmed Rd, Karachi; tel. (21) 217231; monthly; Urdu; cricket; Man. Editor Munir Hussain.
**Albalagh:** Darul Uloom, Karachi 14; monthly; Editor Mohammed Taqi Usmani.
**Al-Ma'arif:** Institute of Islamic Culture, Club Rd, Lahore 54000; tel. (42) 6363127; f. 1950; quarterly; Urdu; Dir and Editor-in-Chief Dr Rashid Ahmad Jallandhri.
**Anchal:** 24 Saeed Mansion, I. I. Chundrigar Rd, Karachi; monthly.
**Archi Times:** Ghafoor Chambers, 7th Floor, Abdullah Haroon Rd, Karachi; tel. (21) 7727492; fax (21) 476682; f. 1986; monthly; English; architecture; Editor Mujtaba Hussain.
**Asia Travel News:** 101 Muhammadi House, I. I. Chundrigar Rd, Karachi 74000; tel. (21) 2424837; fax (21) 2420797; fortnightly; travel trade, tourism and hospitality industry; Editor Javed Mushtaq.
**Auto Times:** 5 S. J. Kayani Shaheed Rd, off Garden Rd, Karachi; tel. (21) 713595; fortnightly; English; Editor Muhammad Shahzad.
**Bachoon Ka Risala:** 108–110 Adam Arcade, Shaheed-e-Millat Rd, Karachi; tel. (21) 419616; monthly; Urdu; Editor Rukhsana Seham Mirza.
**Bagh:** 777/18 Federal B Area, POB 485, Karachi; tel. (21) 449662; monthly; Urdu; Editor Rahil Iqbal.
**Bayyenat:** Jamia Uloom-e-Islamia, Binnori Town, Karachi 74800; tel. (21) 4927233; f. 1962; monthly; Urdu; religious and social issues; Editor Maulana Muhammad Yousuf Ludhianvi.
**Beemakar** (Insurer): 85 Press Chambers, I. I. Chundrigar Rd, Karachi; monthly; Urdu; Man. Editor Shamshad Ahmad; Editor A. M. Hashmi.
**Chand:** Nisbet Rd, Lahore; monthly; Editor Pir Jungli.
**Constructor:** 26D, Block 2, PECHS, Karachi 75400; monthly; Editor Gulzar Mohammad.
**The Cricketer:** 1st Floor, Spencer's Bldg, I. I. Chundrigar Rd, POB 3721, Karachi; tel. (21) 215357; fax (21) 2637815; f. 1972; monthly; English; Editor Riaz Ahmed Mansuri.
**Defence Journal:** 16B, 7th Central St, Defence Housing Authority, POB 12234, Karachi 75500; tel. (21) 541911; telex 23625; fax (21) 571710; f. 1975; monthly; English; Editor-in-Chief Brig. (retd) Abdul Rahman Siddiqi; circ. 10,000.
**Dentist:** 70/7, Nazimabad No. 3, Karachi 18; f. 1984; monthly; English and Urdu; Editor Naeemullah Husain.
**Dosheeza:** 108–110 Adam Arcade, Shaheed-e-Millat Rd, Karachi; tel. (21) 4930470; fax (21) 4934369; monthly; Urdu; Editor Rukhsana Seham Mirza.
**Duniya-e-Tibb:** Eveready Chambers, 2nd Floor, Mohd Bin Qasim Rd, off I. I. Chundrigar Rd, POB 1385, Karachi 1; tel. (21) 217354; fax (21) 2637624; f. 1986; monthly; Urdu; modern and Asian medicine; Editor Qutubuddin; circ. 12,000.
**Economic Review:** Al-Masiha, 3rd Floor, 47 Abdullah Haroon Rd, POB 7843, Karachi 74400; tel. (21) 7728434; fax (21) 7727528; f. 1969; monthly; economic, industrial and investment research; Editor Iqbal Haidari.
**Engineering Horizon:** 3/II Shadman Plaza, Shadman Market, Lahore 54000; tel. (42) 7581743; telex 44390; fax (42) 7587422; monthly; English.
**Engineering Review:** 305 Spotlit Chambers, Dr Billimoria St, off Chundrigar Rd, POB 807, Karachi 74200; tel. (21) 2632567; f. 1975; fortnightly; English; circ. 5,000.
**Flyer International:** 187/3-B2, PECHS, POB 8034, Karachi 29; tel. (21) 434310; telex 23988; f. 1966; aviation and tourism; Man. Editor Bashir A. Khan; Editor Semeen Jaffery.
**Hamdard-i-Sehat:** Institute of Health and Tibbi Research, Hamdard Foundation Pakistan, Nazimabad, Karachi 74600; tel. (21) 6616001; telex 24529; fax (21) 6641766; f. 1933; monthly; Urdu; Editor Hakim Mohammed Said; circ. 7,000.
**Hamdard Islamicus:** Hamdard Foundation Pakistan, Nazimabad, Karachi 74600; tel. (21) 6616001; telex 24529; fax (21) 6641766; f. 1978; quarterly; English; Editor Hakim Mohammed Said; circ. 2,000.
**Hamdard Medicus:** Hamdard Foundation Pakistan, Nazimabad, Karachi 74600; tel. (21) 6616001; telex 24529; fax (21) 6641766; f. 1957; quarterly; English; Editor Hakim Mohammed Said; circ. 2,000.
**Hamdard Naunehal:** Hamdard Foundation Pakistan, Nazimabad, Karachi 74600; tel. (21) 6616001; telex 24529; fax (21) 6641766; f. 1952; monthly; Urdu; Editor Masood Ahmad Barakati; circ. 60,000.
**The Herald:** Haroon House, Dr Ziauddin Ahmed Road, Karachi 4; tel. (21) 511519; telex 23623; fax (21) 522157; f. 1970; monthly; English; Editor Sherry Rehman; circ. 15,000.

## PAKISTAN

**Hikayat:** 26 Patiala Ground, Link McLeod Rd, Lahore; monthly; Editor INAYATULLAH.

**Honhar-e-Pakistan:** 56 Aurangzeb Market, Karachi; monthly; Editor MAZHAR YUSAFZAI.

**Hoor:** Hoor St, Nishtar Rd, Lahore; monthly; Editor KHULA RABIA.

**Islami Jumhuria:** Laj Rd, Old Anarkali, Lahore; monthly; Editor NAZIR TARIQ.

**Islamic Studies:** Islamic Research Institute, Faisal Masjid Complex, POB 1035, Islamabad 44000; tel. (51) 850751; telex 54068; fax (51) 853360; f. 1962; quarterly; English, Urdu (Fikro-Nazar) and Arabic (Al Dirasat al-Islamiyyah) edns; Islamic literature, religion, history, geography, language and the arts; Editor Dr ZAFAR ISHAQ ANSARI (acting); circ. 3,000.

**Jamal:** Institute of Islamic Culture, 2 Club Rd, Lahore 3; tel. (42) 363127; f. 1950; annual; English; Dir and Editor-in-Chief MUHAMMAD SUHEYL UMAR.

**Journal of the Pakistan Historical Society:** 30 Dr Moinul Haq Rd, New Karachi Co-operative Housing Society, Karachi 5; f. 1953; quarterly; English; Editor Dr ANSAR ZAHID KHAN.

**Khel-Ke-Duniya:** 6/13 Alyusaf Chamber, POB 340, Karachi; tel. (21) 216888.

**Khwateen Digest:** Urdu Bazar, M. A. Jinnah Rd, Karachi; monthly; Urdu; Editor MAHMUD RIAZ.

**Kiran:** 37 Urdu Bazar, M. A. Jinnah Rd, Karachi; tel. (21) 216606; Editor MAHMUD BABAR FAISAL.

**Medical Variety:** 108–110 Adam Arcade, Shaheed-e-Millat Rd, Karachi; tel. (21) 419616; monthly; English; Editor RUKHSANA SEHAM MIRZA.

**Muslim World Business:** 20 Sasi Arcade, 4th Floor, Main Clifton Rd, POB 10417, Karachi 6; tel. (21) 534870; telex 23258; f. 1989; monthly; English; political and business; Editor-in-Chief MUZAFFAR HASSAN.

**Naey-Ufaq:** 24 Saeed Mansion, I. I. Chundrigar Rd, Karachi; fortnightly.

**NGM Communication:** B-4, Block-9, Gulshan-e-Iqbal, Karachi 75300; quarterly; English; lists newly-released Pakistani publications.

**Pakistan Journal of Applied Economics:** Applied Economics Research Centre, University of Karachi, POB 8403, Karachi 75270; tel. (21) 474749; fax (21) 471634; twice a year; Editor Dr SHAHIDA WIZARAT.

**Pakistan Journal of Scientific and Industrial Research:** Pakistan Council of Scientific and Industrial Research, Scientific Information Centre, 39 Garden Rd, Saddar, Karachi 74400; tel. (21) 7725943; telex 24725; fax (21) 2636704; f. 1958; monthly; English; Exec. Editor Dr JAFAR NAZIR USMANI; circ. 1,000.

**Pakistan Management Review:** Pakistan Institute of Management, Ghulam Faruque Management House, Shahrah Iran, Clifton, Karachi 75600; tel. (21) 531039; f. 1960; quarterly; English; Editor AMJAD HUMAYUN.

**Pakistan Medical Forum:** 15 Nadir House, I. I. Chundrigar Rd, Karachi 2; f. 1966; monthly; English; Man. Editor M. AHSON.

**Pasban:** Faiz Modh Rd, Quetta; fortnightly; Urdu; Editor MOLVI MOHD ABDULLAH.

**Progress:** POB 3942, Karachi 75530; tel. (21) 5681391; telex 29069; fax (21) 5680005; f. 1956; monthly; publ. by Pakistan Petroleum Ltd; Editor and Publr NUSRAT NASARULLAH.

**Qaumi Digest:** 50 Lower Mall, Lahore; tel. (42) 7225143; fax (42) 7233261; monthly; Editor MUJIBUR REHMAN SHAMI.

**Sabrang Digest:** 47–48 Press Chambers, I. I. Chundrigar Rd, Karachi 1; tel. (21) 211961; f. 1970; monthly; Urdu; Editor SHAKEEL ADIL ZADAH; circ. 150,000.

**Sach-Chee Kahaniyan:** 108–110 Adam Arcade, Shaheed-e-Millat Rd, Karachi; tel. (21) 4930470; fax (21) 4934369; monthly; Urdu; Editor RUKHSANA SEHAM MIRZA.

**Sayyarah:** Aiwan-e-Adab, Urdu Bazar, Lahore 54000; tel. (42) 5419508; f. 1962; monthly; Urdu; literary; Chief Editor NAEEM SIDDIQI; Man. Editor HAFEEZ-UR-RAHMAN AHSAN.

**Sayyarah Digest:** 189 Rewaz Garden, Lahore; tel. (42) 57152; monthly; Urdu; Editor AMJAD RAUF KHAN.

**Science Magazine:** Science Book Foundation, Haji Bldg, Hassan Ali Efendi Rd, Karachi; tel. (21) 2625647; monthly; Urdu; Editor QASIM MAHMOOD.

**Seep:** Alam Market, Block No. 16, Federal B Area, Karachi; quarterly; Editor NASIM DURRANI.

**Show Business:** 108–110 Adam Arcade, Shaheed-e-Millat Rd, POB 12540, Karachi; tel. (21) 419616; monthly; Urdu; Editor RUKHSANA SEHAM MIRZA.

**Sindh Quarterly:** 36D Karachi Administrative Co-operative Housing Society, off Shaheed-e-Millat Rd, Karachi 8; tel. (21) 4531988; f. 1973; Editor SAYID GHULAM MUSTAFA SHAH.

**Sports International:** Arshi Market, Firdaus Colony, Nazimabad, Karachi 74600; tel. (21) 622171; f. 1972; fortnightly; Urdu and English; Chief Editor KANWAR ABDUL MAJEED; Editor RAHEEL MAJEED.

**Taj:** Jamia Tajia, St 13, Sector 14/B, Buffer Zone, Karachi 36; POB 18084; monthly; Editor BABA ANWAR SHAH TAJI.

**Talimo Tarbiat:** Ferozsons (Pvt) Ltd, 60 Shahrah-e-Quaid-e-Azam, Lahore 54000; tel. (42) 6301196; telex 44382; fax (42) 6369204; f. 1941; children's monthly; Urdu; Chief Editor A. SALAM; circ. 50,000.

**Textile Today:** Arshi Market, Firdaus Colony, Nazimabad, Karachi 74600; f. 1992; monthly; English; Chief Editor T. A. ABBASI; Exec. Editor KANWAR A. MAJEED.

**Trade Chronicle:** Iftikhar Chambers, Altaf Hussain Rd, POB 5257, Karachi 74000; tel. (21) 218129; telex 20647; fax (21) 2635276; f. 1953; monthly; English; trade, politics, finance and economics; Editor ABDUL RAUF SIDDIQI; circ. 6,000.

**TV Times:** 1st Floor, Spencer's Bldg, I. I. Chundrigar Rd, POB 655, Karachi; tel. (21) 215357; fax (21) 2637815; f. 1987; monthly; English; Editor RIAZ AHMED MANSURI.

**UNESCO Payami:** c/o Allama Iqbal Open University H-8, Islamabad; tel. (51) 854346; monthly; Urdu; Co-ordinating Editor SULEMAN MALIK.

**Universal Message:** D-35, Block-5, Federal 'B' Area, Karachi 75950; tel. (21) 681157; fax (21) 422827; f. 1979; journal of the Islamic Research Acad.; monthly; English; literature, politics, economics, religion; Editor QADIR SHARIF.

**Urdu Digest:** 21-Acre Scheme, Samanabad, Lahore 25; tel. (42) 7589957; telex 44833; fax (42) 7574875; monthly; Urdu; Editor ALTAF HASAN QURESHEE.

**Voice of Islam:** Jamiyatul Falah Bldg, Akber Rd, Saddar, POB 7141, Karachi 74400; tel. (21) 7721394; f. 1952; monthly; Islamic Cultural Centre magazine; English; Editor AKHLAQ AHMED; Man. Editor Prof. SYED LUTFULLAH.

**Wings:** 101 Muhammadi House, I. I. Chundrigar Rd, Karachi 74000; tel. (21) 2412591; fax (21) 2420797; monthly; aviation and defence; English; Editor and Publr JAVED MUSHTAQ.

**Women's Own:** 1st Floor, Spencer's Bldg, I. I. Chundrigar Rd, POB 691, Karachi; tel. (21) 210355; fax (21) 2637815; f. 1987; monthly; English; Editor RIAZ AHMED MANSURI.

**Yaqeen International:** Darut Tasnif, Main Hub River Rd, Mujahidabad, Karachi 75770; tel. (21) 226596; f. 1952; English and Arabic; Islamic organ; Editor Dr HAFIZ MUHAMMAD ADIL.

**Yaran-e-Watan:** 30E Union Plaza, Jinnah Ave (Blue Area), POB 1470, Islamabad 44000; tel. (51) 812456; telex 5694; fax (51) 211613; f. 1982; monthly; Urdu; publ. by the Overseas Pakistanis Foundation; Editor HAROON RASHID.

**Youth World International:** 104/C Central C/A, Tariq Rd, Karachi; tel. (21) 442211; f. 1987; monthly; English; Editor Syed ADIL EBRAHIM.

### NEWS AGENCIES

**Associated Press of Pakistan (APP):** House 1, St 5, F-6/3, POB 1258, Islamabad; tel. (51) 826158; telex 5739; fax (51) 813225; f. 1948; Dir-Gen. M. AFTAB.

**Independent News of Pakistan:** Islamabad; f. 1991; Urdu.

**National News Agency (NNA):** Posh Arcade, Markaz G-9, POB 455, Islamabad; tel. (51) 260082; telex 54705; fax (51) 253560; Chief Editor SOHAIL CHAUDHRY.

**News Network International:** Islamabad; tel. (51) 252566; Editor-in-Chief HAFIZ ABDUL KHALIQ.

**Pakistan Press International (PPI):** Press Centre, Shahrah Kamal Atatürk, POB 541, Karachi; tel. (21) 210368; telex 23868; fax (21) 2631125; f. 1958; Editor FAZAL QURESHI.

**United Press of Pakistan (Pvt) Ltd (UPP):** 1 Victoria Chambers, Haji Abdullah Haroon Rd, Karachi 74400; tel. 5683235; fax (21) 5682694; f. 1949; Man. Dir MAHMUDUL AZIZ; 6 brs.

#### Foreign Bureaux

**Agence France-Presse (AFP):** House 39, St 56, F-6/4, POB 1276, Islamabad; tel. (51) 822485; telex 5783; Chief Rep. HERVÉ CLERC.

**Agenzia Nazionale Stampa Associata (ANSA)** (Italy): House 3, St 55A, Islamabad; tel. (51) 54259; telex 54259; fax (51) 811873; Bureau Chief ABSAR HUSAIN RIZVI.

**Associated Press (AP)** (USA): House 24A, St 10, F-8/3, POB 1010, Islamabad; tel. (51) 852184; telex 5525; Correspondent MOHAMMED AFTAB.

**Deutsche Presse-Agentur (dpa)** (Germany): 40 Nazimuddin Rd, F-6/1, Islamabad; tel. (51) 821925; telex 54259; Correspondent ANWAR MANSURI.

**Inter Press Service (IPS)** (Italy): House 10, St 13, F-8/3, Islamabad; tel. (51) 853356; telex 54169; fax (42) 856430; Correspondent MUSHAHID HUSSAIN.

PAKISTAN

**Reuters** (UK): POB 1219, Karachi 74200; tel. (21) 5685814; telex 20444; fax (21) 5686390; Business Man. (Pakistan and Bangladesh) JAVED FARUQI.

**United Press International (UPI)** (USA); House 39, St 27, F-6/2, Islamabad; tel. (51) 821472; telex 5586; Bureau Chief DENHOLM BARNETSON.

**Xinhua (New China) News Agency** (People's Republic of China): Islamabad; tel. (51) 856614; telex 5592; Chief Correspondent LI JIASHENG.

### PRESS ASSOCIATIONS

**All Pakistan Newspaper Employees Confederation:** Karachi Press Club, M. R. Kayani Rd, Karachi; f. 1976; confed. of all press industry trade unions; Chair. MINHAJ BARNA; Sec.-Gen. HAMEED HAROON.

**All Pakistan Newspapers Society:** 32 Farid Chambers, 3rd Floor, Abdullah Haroon Rd, Karachi 3; f. 1949; Pres. MAJID NIZAMI; Sec.-Gen. HAMEED HAROON.

**Council of Pakistan Newspaper Editors:** c/o United Press of Pakistan, 1 Victoria Chambers, Haji Abdullah Haroon Rd, Karachi 74400; tel. (21) 5682694; telex 23035; fax (21) 7735276; Pres. INQUILAB MATRI; Sec.-Gen. JAMIL ATHER.

**Pakistan Federal Union of Journalists:** Lahore; f. 1950 to secure freedom of the press and better working conditions; Pres. I. H. RASHED; Sec.-Gen. ABDUL HAMEED CHAPPRA.

# Publishers

**Aina-e-Adab:** Chowk Minar, Anarkali, Lahore; tel. (42) 54069; f. 1957; general fiction; Propr ABDUS SALAM.

**Anjuman Tarraqq-i-Urdu Pakistan:** Karachi; tel. (21) 7724023; f. 1903; literature, religion, textbooks, Urdu dictionaries, literary and critical texts; Pres. NORUL HASAN JAFRI; Sec. JAMIL UDDIN AALI.

**Army Education Press:** POB 179, Rawalpindi.

**Camran Publishers:** Jalaluddin Hospital Bldg, Circular Rd, Lahore; f. 1964; general, technical, textbooks; Propr ABDUL HAMID.

**Chronicle Publications:** Iftikhar Chambers, Altaf Hussain Rd, POB 5257, Karachi 74000; tel. (21) 2631587; telex 20647; fax (21) 2635276; f. 1953; reference, directories; Dir ABDUL RAUF SIDDIQI.

**Crescent Publications:** Urdu Bazar, Lahore.

**Economic and Industrial Publishers:** Al-Masiha, 3rd Floor, 47 Abdullah Haroon Rd, POB 7843, Karachi 74400; tel. (21) 7728434; fax (21) 7727582; f. 1965; industrial, economic and investment research.

**Elite Publishers Ltd:** D-118, SITE, Karachi 75700; tel. (21) 297035; telex 23361; fax (21) 295220; f. 1951; Chair. AHMED MIRZA JAMIL.

**Ferozsons (Pvt) Ltd:** 60 Shahrah-e-Quaid-e-Azam, Lahore; tel. (42) 301196; telex 44382; fax (42) 305504; f. 1894; books, periodicals, maps, atlases; Man. Dir A. SALAM; Dir ZAHEER SALAM.

**Frontier Publishing Co:** 22 Urdu Bazar, Lahore; tel. (42) 355262; fax (42) 7247323; academic and general; Execs MUHAMMAD ARIF, MUHAMMAD AMIR, MUHAMMAD ASIM.

**Sh. Ghulam Ali and Sons (Pvt) Ltd:** 14 Lawrence Rd, Lahore 54000; tel. (42) 6361431; telex 44422; fax (42) 6315478; f. 1887; general, religion, technical, textbooks; Dirs NIAZ AHMAD, BASHIR AHMAD.

**Idara Taraqqi-i-Urdu:** S-1/363 Saudabad, Karachi 27; f. 1949; general literature, technical and professional books and magazines; Propr IKRAM AHMED.

**Ilmi Kitab Khana:** Kabeer St, Urdu Bazar, Lahore; tel. (42) 62833; f. 1948; technical, professional, historical and law; Propr Haji SARDAR MOHAMMAD.

**Islamic Book Centre:** 25B Masson Rd, POB 1625, Lahore 54000; tel. (42) 6361803; fax (42) 6360955; religion in Arabic, Urdu and English; Islamic history, text books, dictionaries and reprints; Propr and Man. Dir MUHAMMAD SAJID SAEED.

**Islamic Publications (Pvt) Ltd:** 13E Shahalam Market, Lahore 54000; tel. (42) 7325243; telex 44545; fax (42) 7658674; f. 1959; Islamic literature in Urdu and English; Man. Dir RANA ALLAH DAD KHAN; Gen. Man. ABDUL WAHEED KHAN.

**Jamiyatul Falah Publications:** Jamiyatul Falah Bldg, Akbar Rd, Saddar, POB 7141, Karachi 74400; tel. (21) 7721394; f. 1952; Islamic history and culture; Hon. Sec.-Gen. SHAMSUDDIN KHALID AHMED.

**Kazi Publications:** 121 Zulqarnain Chambers, Ganpat Rd, POB 1845, Lahore; tel. (42) 311359; fax (42) 324003; f. 1978; Islamic literature, religion, law, biographies; Man. MUHAMMAD IKRAM SIDDIQI; Chief Editor MUHAMMAD IQBAL SIDDIQI.

*Directory*

**Lark Publishers:** Urdu Bazar, Karachi 1; f. 1955; general literature, magazines; Propr MAHMOOD RIAZ.

**Lion Art Press (Pvt) Ltd:** 112 Shahrah-e-Quaid-e-Azam, Lahore 54000; tel. (42) 304444; f. 1919; general publs in English; Man. Dir S. A. WAHEED; Dirs KHALID A. SHEIKH, S. A. JAMEEL.

**Maktaba Darut Tasnif:** Hub River Rd, Mujahidabad, Karachi 75770; tel. (21) 226596; f. 1965; Koran and Islamic literature; Dir RIAZ AHMAD.

**Malik Sirajuddin & Sons:** Kashmiri Bazar, POB 2250, Lahore 54000; tel. (42) 7657527; telex 44944; fax (42) 7657490; f. 1905; general, religion, law, textbooks; Man. MALIK ABDUL ROUF.

**Malik Sons:** Karkhana Bazar, Faisalabad.

**Medina Publishing Co:** M. A. Jinnah Rd, Karachi 1; f. 1960; general literature, textbooks; Propr HAKIM MOHAMMAD TAQI.

**Mehtab Co:** Ghazni St, Urdu Bazar, Lahore; tel. (42) 7120071; fax (42) 7353489; f. 1978; Islamic literature; Propr SHAHZAD RIAZ SHEIKH.

**Mohammad Hussain and Sons:** F/1033 Kashmiri Bazar, 17 Urdu Bazar, Lahore 2; tel. (42) 64005; f. 1941; religion, textbooks; Partners MOHAMMAD HUSSAIN, AZHAR ALI SHEIKH, PERVEZ ALI SHEIKH.

**Sh. Muhammad Ashraf:** 7 Aibak Rd, New Anarkali, Lahore 7; tel. (42) 7353171; fax (42) 7353489; f. 1923; books in English on all aspects of Islam; Man. Dir SH. SHAHZAD RIAZ.

**National Book Service:** 22 Urdu Bazar, Lahore; tel. (42) 355262; fax (42) 7247323; academic and general; Execs MUHAMMAD ARIF, MUHAMMAD AMIR, MUHAMMAD ASIM.

**Oxford University Press:** 5 Bangalore Town, Block 7–8, Sharah-e-Faisal, POB 13033, Karachi 75350; tel. (21) 446307; telex 24726; fax (21) 4547640; academic, educational and general; Man. Dir AMEENA SAIYID.

**Pakistan Law House:** Pakistan Chowk, POB 90, Karachi 1; tel. (21) 212455; telex 23259; fax (21) 219762; f. 1950; importers and exporters of legal books and reference books; Man. K. NOORANI.

**Pakistan Publishing House:** Victoria Chambers 2, A. Haroon Rd, Karachi 75400; tel. (21) 5681457; telex 23259; f. 1959; Propr H. NOORANI; Gen. Man. AAMIR HUSSEIN.

**Peco Ltd:** Lahore; f. 1936; Islamic; Man. Dir JAMEEL MAZHAR.

**Pioneer Book House:** 1 Avan Lodge, Bunder Rd, POB 37, Karachi; periodicals, gazettes, maps and reference works in English, Urdu and other regional languages.

**Premier Bookhouse:** Shahin Market, Room 2, Anarkali, Lahore; tel. (42) 64385; academic and reference.

**Publishers International:** Bandukwala Bldg, 4 I. I. Chundrigar Rd, Karachi; f. 1948; reference; Man. Dir KAMALUDDIN AHMAD.

**Publishers United (Pvt) Ltd:** 176 Anarkali, POB 1689, Lahore 54000; tel. (42) 352238; textbooks, technical, reference, oriental literature in English, military and general; Man. Dir Maj. (retd) JAVED AMIN.

**Punjab Religious Books Society:** Anarkali, Lahore 2; tel. (42) 54416; educational, religious, law and general; Gen. Man. A. R. IRSHAD; Sec. NAEEM SHAKIR.

**Reprints Ltd:** 16 Bahadur Shah Market, M. A. Jinnah Rd, Karachi; f. 1983; Pakistani edns of foreign works; Chair. A. D. KHALID; Man. Dir AZIZ KHALID.

**Sindhi Adabi Board** (Sindhi Literary and Publishing Organization): POB 12, Hyderabad; tel. (221) 71276; f. 1951; history, literature, culture of Sindh, in Sindhi, Urdu, English, Persian and Arabic; translations into Sindhi, especially of literature and history; Chair. Dr ABDUL JABBAR JUNEJO; Sec. SHAMSHER AL-HYDERI.

**Taj Co Ltd:** Manghopir Rd, POB 530, Karachi; tel. (21) 294221; telex 24839; f. 1929; religious books; Man. Dir A. H. KHOKHAR.

**Times Press (Pvt) Ltd:** C-18, Al-Hilal Society, off University Rd, Karachi 75290; tel. (21) 410361; telex 29730; fax (21) 4935602; f. 1948; govt printers (security and confidential division), regd publrs of Koran, postal stationery, textbooks and computer stationery; Man. Dir S. M. SHUJAUDDIN.

**Urdu Academy Sind:** 16 Bahadur Shah Market, M. A. Jinnah Rd, Karachi 2; tel. (21) 2634185; f. 1947; brs in Hyderabad and Lahore; reference, general and textbooks; Editor and Man. Dir A. D. KHALID.

**West-Pak Publishing Co (Pvt) Ltd:** 56N, Gulberg-II, Lahore; tel. (42) 877709; f. 1932; govt printers; textbooks and religious books; Chief Exec. S. AHSAN MAHMUD.

### Government Publishing House

**Government Publications:** Federal Publication Branch, Govt of Pakistan, University Rd, Karachi 74800; tel. (21) 411127.

### PUBLISHERS' ASSOCIATION

**Pakistan Publishers' and Booksellers' Association:** YMCA Bldg, Shahrah-e-Quaid-e-Azam, Lahore; Chair. MOHAMMAD AMIN; Sec. ABDUL KHALIQ.

# Radio and Television

In 1992 there were an estimated 11.3m. radio receivers and 2.3m. television receivers in use.

### RADIO

**Pakistan Broadcasting Corporation:** National Broadcasting House, Constitution Ave, Islamabad; tel. (51) 81003317; telex 5816; fax (51) 811861; f. 1947 as Radio Pakistan; home service 323 hrs daily in 20 languages and dialects; external services 30 hrs daily in 15 languages; world service 10 hrs and 45 minutes daily in two languages; 102 news bulletins daily; Chair. HUSSAIN HAQQANI; Man. Dir. QAMAR ALI ABBASI.

National broadcasting network comprises stations located in Abbottabad, Bahawalpur, Chitral, Dera Ismail Khan, Faisalabad, Gilgit, Hyderabad, Islamabad, Karachi, Khaipur Mir, Khuzdar (Balochistan), Lahore, Multan, Peshawar, Quetta, Rawalpindi, Sibi, Skardu and Turbat.

### TELEVISION

**Pakistan Television Corpn Ltd:** Federal TV Complex, Constitution Ave, POB 1221, Islamabad; tel. (51) 810051; telex 5833; f. 1967; daily transmissions from 07.00 to 08.30 and from 16.30 to 23.30; extended transmissions on Fridays; Chair. HUSSAIN HAQQANI; Man. Dir AHMAD HASSAN SHAIKH.

**People's Television Network:** Karachi; tel. (21) 433554; fax (21) 435538; f. 1990; privately-owned; broadcasts 12 hrs daily; programmes include Cable Network News (CNN); Man. Dir TAHIR A. KHAN.

# Finance

(cap. = capital; auth. = authorized; p.u. = paid up; res = reserves; dep. = deposits; m. = million; brs = branches; amounts in rupees unless otherwise stated)

### BANKING

In January 1974 all domestic banks were nationalized. In December 1990 the Government announced that it intended to transfer the five state-owned commercial banks to private ownership. By late 1991 the Muslim Commercial Bank Ltd and the Allied Bank of Pakistan Ltd had been transferred to private ownership. In 1991 the Government granted 10 new private commercial bank licences, the first since banks were nationalized in 1974.

#### Central Bank

**State Bank of Pakistan:** Central Directorate, I. I. Chundrigar Rd, POB 4456, Karachi 2; tel. (21) 2414141; telex 23730; fax (21) 2417865; f. 1948; bank of issue; controls and regulates currency and foreign exchange; cap. p.u. 100m., res 2,650m., dep. 23,270.8m. (June 1993); Gov. Dr MUHAMMAD YAQUB; Dep. Govs Mr SIBGHATULLAH, M. ASHRAF JANJU; 166 brs.

#### Commercial Banks

**Allied Bank of Pakistan Ltd:** 12th–17th Floor, Abbasi Shaheed Rd, off Shahrah-e-Faisal, Karachi 75530; tel. (21) 511031; telex 21746; fax (21) 5680134; f. 1942; cap. p.u. 272.2m., res 309m., dep. 37,120m. (July 1994); transferred to private ownership in 1991; Chair. and Chief Exec. SHAUKAT A. KAZMI; 774 brs in Pakistan and four brs overseas.

**Askari Commercial Bank Ltd:** AWT Plaza, The Mall, POB 1084, Rawalpindi; tel. (51) 586634; telex 54647; fax (51) 563704; f. 1992; cap. 450.0m., res 122.6m., dep. 5,622.0m. (Dec. 1993) Pres. SHAMEEM AHMAD; Chair. Lt-Gen. MOINUDDIN HAIDER; 10 brs.

**Bank Al Habib Ltd:** 126-C Old Bahawalpur Rd, Multan; tel. (61) 44138; telex 42336; fax (61) 44543; f. 1991; cap. 300.0m., res 121.0m., dep. 3,951.1m. (Dec. 1993); Chair. HAMID D. HABIB; Chief Exec. and Man. Dir ABBAS D. HABIB; 10 brs.

**The Bank of Khyber:** State Life Bldg, 24 The Mall, Peshawar; tel. (521) 273456; fax (521) 278146; auth. cap. 1,000m.; Exec. Dir SAJID ALI ABBASI; Man. Dir BASHIR AHMED; 14 brs.

**The Bank of Punjab:** 7 Egerton Rd, POB 2254, Lahore 54000; tel. (42) 6367790; fax (42) 6369662; f. 1989; cap. 362.3m., dep. 6,575.0m. (Feb. 1994); Chair. Dr MOHAMMAD ARIF; 202 brs.

**Bolan Bank Ltd:** 92-514/A Madresa Rd, Quetta; tel. (81) 66562; telex 78310; fax (81) 67595; f. 1991; auth. cap. 600m.; Pres. and Chief Exec. SYED IJAZ HUSSAIN SHAH; 10 brs.

**Habib Bank Ltd:** 11 Habib Bank Plaza, I. I. Chundrigar Rd, Karachi 75650; tel. (21) 219111; telex 20786; fax (21) 2414191; f. 1941; cap. p.u. 2,478m., res 4,224m., dep. 153,431m. (Dec. 1992); state-owned; Pres. YOUNUS DALIA; 1,859 brs in Pakistan and 67 brs overseas.

**Habib Credit and Exchange Bank:** Karachi; f. 1992; subsidiary of Habib Bank Ltd; comprises former brs of Bank of Credit and Commerce International (BCCI); Vice-Pres. RANA ABDUL RASHID.

**Indus Bank Ltd:** F.C. Trust Bldg, Sunehri Masjid Rd, Peshawar; tel. (521) 271639; fax (521) 271072; f. 1992; auth. cap. 500m.; Chair. and Pres. S. KHURSHID SOHAIL; Chief Exec. S. HASAN MUSTAFA; 10 brs.

**Mehran Bank Ltd:** Chapal Plaza, Hasrat Mohani Rd, off I. I. Chundrigar Rd, Karachi 74000; f. 1992; tel. (21) 2427202; telex 29289; fax (21) 2427282; cap. and res 606.0m., dep. 1,583.9m. (Feb. 1994); Chief Exec. TASADDUQ HUSSAIN; 6 brs.

**Muslim Commercial Bank Ltd:** Adamjee House, I. I. Chundrigar Rd, POB 4976, Karachi 74000; tel. (21) 2414091; telex 21750; fax (21) 2413116; f. 1947; cap. 662.5m., res 1,210.2m., dep. 73,553.3m. (Dec. 1993); transferred to private ownership in 1991; Chair. Mian MUHAMMAD MANSHA; Pres. and CEO HUSAIN LAWAI; 1,290 brs in Pakistan and one Overseas Banking Unit Export Processing Zone br. (Karachi).

**National Bank of Pakistan (NBP):** NBP Building, I. I. Chundrigar Rd, POB 4937, Karachi 2; tel. (21) 2416780; telex 23732; fax (21) 2116769; f. 1949; cap. p.u. 1,463.9m., res 3,135.0m., dep. 141,854.8m. (Dec. 1992); state-owned; Pres. SAEED AHMAD QAZI; 1,370 brs in Pakistan and 22 brs overseas.

**Platinum Commercial Bank:** Lahore; Pres. INAM ELAHIE.

**Prime Commercial Bank Ltd:** Library Block, Aiwan-e-Iqbal Complex, Library Block, Egerton Rd, Lahore; tel. (42) 6368725; telex 47721; fax (42) 6369162; f. 1991; cap. 300m., dep. 3,000m. (Dec. 1993); CEO/Dir SAEED I. CHAUDHRY; Chair. HUMAYUN SADIQ; 10 brs.

**Prince Commercial Bank Ltd:** Lahore Stock Exchange Bldg, Khyaban-i-Iqbal, Lahore; tel. (42) 839730; fax (42) 839788; auth. cap. 600m.; Chief Exec. SAEED I. CHAUDHRY; 5 brs.

**Schon Bank Ltd:** Schon Centre, I. I. Chundrigar Rd, Karachi; Pres. BADR-UD-DIN KHAN; Gen. Man. Mr HUSSAINI.

**Soneri Bank Ltd:** 4th Floor, IEP Bldg, 97B/D-1, Gulberg-III, Lahore; tel. (42) 5713101; telex 44447; fax (42) 5713095; f. 1991; cap. 300m., res and retained earnings 117.3m., dep. 2,526m. (July 1994); Chair. BADRUDDIN J. FEERASTA; Gen. Mans M. KARIM NASEERUDDIN, S. FARRUKH HUSSAIN RIZVI; 9 brs.

**Union Bank Ltd:** Central Office, 6 Egerton Rd, Lahore; f. 1991; cap. 450m., res 246.3m., dep. 5,500m. (Dec. 1994); Chair. M. NASIM SAIGOL; 19 brs.

**United Bank Ltd:** State Life Bldg, No 1, I. I. Chundrigar Rd, POB 4306, Karachi 74200; tel. (21) 2417100; telex 20034; fax (21) 2413483; f. 1959; cap. p.u. 1,481.7m., res 2,008m., dep. 87,482.4m. (Dec. 1992); state-owned; Pres. and Chair. AZIZULLAH MEMON; 1,684 brs in Pakistan and 27 brs overseas.

#### Principal Foreign Banks

**ABN—AMRO Bank NV** (Netherlands): Avari Plaza, 242–243 Fatima Jinnah Rd, POB 4096, Karachi 74000; tel. (21) 5687580; telex 21008; fax (21) 5683432; f. 1948; Country Man. SHEHZAD NAQVI; 2 brs.

**American Express Bank Ltd** (USA): Shaheen Commercial Complex, Dr Ziauddin Ahmed Rd, POB 4847, Karachi; tel. (21) 2630343; telex 2610; fax (21) 2631803; f. 1950; Sen. Dir and Country Man. J. DENNIS DUNN; 4 brs.

**ANZ Grindlays Bank PLC** (UK): I. I. Chundrigar Rd, POB 5556, Karachi 74000; tel. (21) 2412671; telex 20055; fax (21) 2414914; offers Islamic banking services; Gen. Man. DENIS ARMSTRONG; 14 brs.

**Bank of America National Trust and Savings Association** (USA): New Jubilee Insurance House, 5th Floor, I. I. Chundrigar Rd, POB 3715, Karachi; tel. (21) 2412520; telex 21081; fax (21) 2415371; f. 1961; Sr Vice-Pres. and Country Man. S. ALI RAZA; Vice-Pres. and Head of Financial Institutions Group HUSSAIN TEJANY; 4 brs.

**Bank of Tokyo Ltd** (Japan): Shaheen Foundation Bldg, 1st Floor, M. R. Kayani Rd, POB 4232, Karachi; tel. (21) 520171; telex 2653; f. 1953; Gen. Man. S. TAKEVEHI; 1 br.

**Banque Indosuez** (France): Muhammadi House, I. I. Chundrigar Rd, POB 6942, Karachi 74000; tel. (21) 2417155; telex 20090; fax (21) 2417503; f. 1973; Gen. Man. MARC DUMETZ; 2 brs.

**Chase Manhattan Bank, NA** (USA): Shaheen Commercial Complex, M. R. Kayani Rd, POB 1161, Karachi; tel. (21) 2633071; telex 25620; fax (21) 2631393; f. 1982; Vice-Pres. RUDOLF VON WATZDORF; 2 brs.

**Citibank, NA** (USA): State Life Bldg, I. I. Chundrigar Rd, POB 4889, Karachi; tel. (21) 2412641; telex 2745; fax (21) 2418993; f. 1961; Gen. Man. SHAUKAT TAREEN; 3 brs.

**Deutsche Bank AG** (Germany): Unitower Bldg, Unicentre Bldg, I. I. Chundrigar Rd, POB 4925, Karachi; tel. (21) 2419611; telex 20453; fax (21) 2416970; f. 1962; Gen. Man. (Pakistan) MOHAMMAD YOUNAS KHAN; 2 brs.

**Doha Bank Ltd** (Qatar): 36/6-2 Lalazar Drive, off Maulvi Tamizuddin Khan Rd, Karachi; tel. (21) 551851; telex 25606; fax (21) 552205; Asst Gen. Man. NOOR E. SHAIKH.

**Emirates Bank International Ltd** (United Arab Emirates): Emirates Bank Bldg, I. I. Chundrigar Rd, POB 831, Karachi; tel. (21) 2416621; telex 25108; fax (21) 2416599; f. 1978; Gen. Man. CLIVE SHEWARD; 9 brs.

**Faysal Islamic Bank of Bahrain E.C.:** Trade Center, 11/13 I. I. Chundrigar Rd, POB 472, Karachi 0221; tel. (21) 218213; telex 25721; fax (21) 2637975; Country Gen. Man. TAYYEB AFZAL; 3 brs.

**Habib Bank AG Zurich (Switzerland):** Hirani Centre, I. I. Chundrigar Rd, Karachi; tel. (21) 2633320; telex 24062; fax (21) 2631419.

**The Hongkong and Shanghai Banking Corpn Ltd** (Hong Kong): Shaheen Commercial Complex, M. R. Kayani Rd, POB 121, Karachi; tel. (21) 2630386; telex 21112; fax (21) 2631526; f. 1982; Man. G. V. JONES; Dep. Man. J. P. HENNESSY; 3 brs.

**Mashreq Bank psc:** Ground and First Floor, Bahria Complex, 24 M.T. Khan Rd, POB 930, Karachi 74000; tel. (21) 5610391; telex 24524; fax (21) 5610830; f. 1978; Country Man. MUBASHAR H. KHOKHAR; 3 brs.

**Middle East Bank Ltd** (United Arab Emirates): Mac Volk Bldg, I. I. Chundrigar Rd, POB 6712, Karachi; tel. (21) 2412986; telex 25129; f. 1978; Gen. Man. KALIM-UR-RAHMAN; 4 brs.

**Pan African Bank Ltd** (Kenya): Al-Falah Court, I. I. Chundrigar Rd, Karachi; tel. (21) 217294; telex 28062; fax (21) 2636534; CEO (Pakistan) Mr HASHIM.

**Rupali Bank Ltd** (Bangladesh): Unitowers, I. I. Chundrigar Rd, POB 6440, Karachi 74000; tel. (21) 2410424; telex 20686; fax (21) 2414322; f. 1976; Country Man. (Pakistan) FASIAR RAHMAN; 1 br.

**Société Générale** (France): 3rd Floor, PNSC Bldg, Maulvi Tamizuddin Khan Rd, POB 6766, Karachi 74000; tel. (21) 5611846; telex 29605; fax (21) 5611672; Gen. Man. CLAUDE DELBOS; Dep. Gen. Man. BERNARD JOURDAN; 1 br.

**Standard Chartered Bank** (UK): I. I. Chundrigar Rd, POB 4896, Karachi 74000; tel. (21) 2416485; telex 2890; fax (21) 2411593; Chief Exec. (Pakistan) FAROOK BENGALI; 4 brs.

### Leasing Banks (Modarabas)

The number of leasing banks (modarabas), which conform to the strictures placed upon the banking system by the Shari'a (the Islamic legal code), rose from four in 1988 to about 60 in 1992. The following are among the most important modarabas in Pakistan.

**Asian Leasing Corporation Ltd:** 85-B Jail Rd, Gulberg, POB 3176, Lahore; tel. (42) 484417; telex 44013; fax (42) 484418.

**Atlas BOT Lease Co Ltd:** Ground Floor, Federation House, Shahrah-e-Firdousi, Main Clifton, Karachi 75600; tel. (21) 570011; telex 2626; fax (21) 5870543; Man. (Accounts and Administration) RAFIQUE UMER.

**B.R.R. Capital Modaraba:** Dean Arcade, Block 8, Kehkeshan, Clifton, Karachi 75600; tel. (21) 572013; telex 24888; fax (21) 5870324.

**Dadabhoy Leasing Ltd:** Ebrahim Estate, D-1, Block 7–8, K.C.H.S.U., Shahrah-e-Faisal, Karachi 75350; tel. (21) 43433; telex 23862.

**English Leasing Ltd:** Room No. 627, Muhammadi House, I. I. Chundrigar Rd, Karachi; tel. (21) 2411910; telex 23662; fax (21) 2417820.

**First Grindlays Modaraba:** Grindlays Services of Pakistan (Pvt) Ltd, ANZ Grindlays Bank Bldg, I. I. Chundrigar Rd, POB 5556, Karachi 74000; tel. (21) 223917; telex 2755; fax (21) 2417197.

**First Habib Bank Modaraba:** 18 Habib Bank Plaza, I. I. Chundrigar Rd, Karachi 74000; tel. (21) 219111; telex 2766; fax (21) 2414191.

**First International Investment Bank Ltd:** 85 Shahrah-e-Quaid-e-Azam, Lahore; tel. (9221) 2639042; fax (9221) 2630678; f. 1990; Chair. Syed BABER ALI; Chief Exec. FREDERICK W. PIECHOCZEK.

**National Development Leasing Corpn Ltd:** NIC Bldg, 10th Floor, Abbasi Shaheed Rd, off Shahrah-e-Faisal, POB 67, Karachi 74400; tel. (21) 519440; telex 20304; fax (21) 5680454; 3 brs.

**Pakistan Industrial and Commercial Leasing Ltd:** Prudential House, Hassan Ali St, off I.I. Chundrigar Rd, POB 1335, Karachi 74200; tel. (21) 210521; telex 23984; fax (21) 2630858; Chief Exec. MOHAMMAD SADIQ SHEIKH.

### Co-operative Banks

In 1976 all existing co-operative banks were dissolved and given the option of becoming a branch of the appropriate Provincial Co-operative Bank, or of reverting to the status of a credit society.

**Federal Bank for Co-operatives:** State Bank Bldg, G-5, POB 1218, Islamabad; tel. (51) 826994; telex 5878; f. 1976; owned jtly by the fed. Govt, the prov. govts and the State Bank of Pakistan; provides credit facilities to each of four prov. co-operative banks and regulates their operations; they in turn provide credit facilities through co-operative socs; supervises policy of prov. co-operative banks and of multi-unit co-operative socs; assists fed. and prov. govts in formulating schemes for development and revitalization of co-operative movement; carries out research on rural credit, etc.; cap. and res. 364m. (1985); Chair. SHAIKH INAMUL HAQ; 4 brs.

### Development Finance Organizations

**Agricultural Development Bank of Pakistan:** 1 Faisal Ave, POB 1400, Islamabad; tel. (51) 824135; telex 5618; fax (51) 812907; f. 1961; provides credit facilities to agriculturists and cottage industrialists in the rural areas and for allied projects; cap. 3,214.3m., res 2,899.1m., dep. 45,857.3m. (June 1993); Chair. KHALID JAVID; 48 regional offices and 334 brs.

**Bankers Equity Ltd:** Finance and Trade Centre, 1st Floor, Shahrah-e-Faisal, Karachi 74400; tel. (21) 520186; telex 24646; fax (21) 5682106; f. 1979 to provide rupee and foreign currency financing for the establishment of large- and medium-scale industrial projects in the private sector; auth. cap. 500m., cap. p.u. 494m. (June 1993); Pres. and Man. Dir AMJAD AZIZ KHAN; 17 brs.

**First Women Bank Ltd:** A-115, 7th Floor, Mehdi Towers, Sindhi Muslim Co-operative Housing Society, Shahrah-e-Faisal, POB 15549, Karachi; tel. (21) 4556093; telex 25837; fax (21) 4556983; f. 1989; cap. p.u. 200m., dep. 1,668m. (Dec. 1994); Pres. AKRAM KHATOON; 31 brs.

**House Building Finance Corpn:** Finance and Trade Centre, Shahrah-e-Faisal, Karachi 74400; tel. (21) 511933; telex 22086; fax (21) 511860; provides loans for the construction and purchase of housing units; Man. Dir. Dr MUHAMMAD ARSHAD MALIK.

**Industrial Development Bank of Pakistan:** State Life Bldg, 2 Wallace Rd, off I. I. Chundrigar Rd, POB 5082, Karachi 74000; tel. (21) 2419160; telex 20722; fax (21) 2411990; f. 1961; provides credit facilities for small and medium-sized industrial enterprises in the private sector; cap. 157.0m. res 624.4m., dep. 13,671.6m. (June 1992); transfer to private ownership pending in 1992; Chair. and Man. Dir KHALID MAHMUD NAGRA; 16 brs.

**Investment Corpn of Pakistan:** NBP Bldg, 5th Floor, I. I. Chundrigar Rd, POB 5410, Karachi 74400; tel. (21) 2415860; telex 20079; fax (21) 2411684; f. 1966 by the Govt to encourage and broaden the base of investments and to develop the capital market; total assets 4,833.0m., cap. p.u. 138.0m., res 231.9m. (June 1993); Chair. M. KHALIL MIAN; Man. Dir MUTIUR RAHMAN; 10 brs.

**National Development Finance Corpn:** 6th Floor, Finance and Trade Centre, Shahrah-e-Faisal, Karachi; tel. (21) 525241; telex 20882; fax (21) 5683923; f. 1973; sanctions loans for industrial development; cap. and res 2,472m., dep. 19,272m. (1995); transfer to private ownership pending in 1992; Man. Dir M. B. ABBASI; 39 brs.

**National Investment (Unit Trust) Ltd:** NBP Bldg, 6th Floor, I. I. Chundrigar Rd, POB 5671, Karachi; tel. (21) 2412056; telex 21476; fax (21) 2430623; f. 1962; mobilizes domestic savings to meet the requirements of growing economic development and enables investors to share in the industrial and economic prosperity of the country; 71,303 Unit holders (1992/93); Man. Dir MUHAMMAD ASSADULLAH SHAIKH.

**Pakistan Industrial Credit and Investment Corpn Ltd (PICIC):** State Life Bldg No. 1, I. I. Chundrigar Rd, POB 5080, Karachi 2; tel. (21) 2414200; telex 2710; fax (21) 213478; f. 1957 as an industrial development bank to provide financial assistance for the establishment of new industries and balancing modernization of those existing in the private sector; in 1979 approved the financing of 22 industrial projects, sanctioning loans equivalent to 350.5m. in foreign currencies; total assets 6,595.8m., cap. p.u. 110.0m., res 772.9m. (Dec. 1986); held 62.9% and 37.3% by local and foreign investors respectively; Chair. K. MARKER; Man. Dir TAHIR ABBAS; 8 brs.

**Pakistan Investment Board (PIB):** Government of Pakistan, Pakistan Secretariat, Block A, Rooms 108 and 109, 1st Floor, Islamabad; tel. (51) 211870; fax (51) 215554; Vice-Chair. SAFDAR ABBAS ZAIDI.

**Pakistan Kuwait Investment Co (Pvt) Ltd:** Tower 'C', 4th Floor, Finance and Trade Centre, Shahrah-e-Faisal, POB 901, Karachi 74200; tel. (21) 513261; telex 21396; fax (21) 5683669; jt venture between the Govt and Kuwait to promote investment in industrial and agro-based enterprises; Man. Dir ADNAN AHMED ALI.

**Pak-Libya Holding Co Ltd:** Finance and Trade Centre, 5th Floor, Tower 'C', Shahrah-e-Faisal, POB 10425, Karachi; tel. (21) 510409; telex 29763; fax (21) 5682389; jt venture between the Govt and Libya to promote industrial investment; Man. Dir SYED ABDUL WASI MOINI.

**Regional Development Finance Corpn:** Ghausia Plaza, 20 Blue Area, Islamabad; tel. (51) 1216453; telex 54000; fax (51) 898974;

# PAKISTAN

promotes industrial investment in the less developed areas of Pakistan; CEO Sikandar Hayat Jamali; more than 10 brs.

**Saudi Pak Industrial and Agricultural Investment Co (Pvt) Ltd:** Quaid-e-Azam Ave, Blue Area, Islamabad; tel. (51) 815001; telex 5663; fax (51) 815005; f. 1981, jtly by Saudi Arabia and Pakistan to make investments in the private sector on a purely commercial basis; cap. p.u. 1,000m.; Gen. Man. and CEO Muhammad Rashid Zahir.

**Small Business Finance Corpn:** NBP Bldg, Ground Floor, Civic Centre, Islamabad 44000; tel. (51) 821639; provides loans for small businesses; Man. Dir Abdul Rashid Mian.

**Youth Investment and Promotion Society:** PIA Bldg, 3rd Floor, Blue Area, Islamabad; tel. (51) 815581; Man. Dir Ashraf M. Khan.

## Bankers' Association

**Pakistan Banks' Association:** National Bank of Pakistan, Head Office Bldg, 2nd Floor, I. I. Chundrigar Rd, POB 4937, Karachi 2; tel. (21) 2416686; telex 2734; fax (21) 2410202; Chair. Inam Elahi; Sec. M. Jameel Sheikh.

## Banking Organizations

**Pakistan Banking Council:** Habib Bank Plaza, I. I. Chundrigar Rd, POB 4204, Karachi; tel. (21) 227121; telex 2751; fax (21) 222232; f. 1973; acts as a co-ordinating body between the nationalized banks and the Ministry of Finance and Economic Affairs; Chair. Muhammad Zaki; Sec. Mir Wasif Ali.

**Pakistan Banking and Finance Service Commission:** 61A Block 7 & 8, Kathiawar Cooperative Housing Society, Jauhar Row, Karachi 75350; tel. (21) 449781; Sec. M. A. Shamsi.

**Pakistan Development Banking Institution:** 4th Floor, Sidco Centre, Strachen Rd, Karachi; tel. (21) 5688229; telex 24852.

## STOCK EXCHANGES

**Islamabad Stock Exchange:** Stock Exchange Bldg, 101E Faz-ul-haq Rd, Blue Area, Islamabad; tel. (51) 215050; telex 54673; fax (51) 215051; f. 1991; 90 mems; Pres. Tariq Iqbal Khan.

**Karachi Stock Exchange (Guarantee) Ltd:** Stock Exchange Bldg, Stock Exchange Rd, Karachi 2; tel. (21) 2413582; telex 20046; fax (21) 2410825; f. 1947; 200 mems, 731 listed cos; Pres. Sirajuddin Cassim; Vice-Pres. Haji Ghani Haji Usman.

**Lahore Stock Exchange (Guarantee) Ltd:** 19 Khayaban-e-Aiwan-e-Iqbal, POB 1315, Lahore 54000; tel. (42) 6368000; telex 44821; fax (42) 6368484; f. 1970; 564 listed cos, 138 mems; Pres. Dr Yasir Mahmood; Sec. Abdul Rauff Butt (acting).

## INSURANCE

In January 1995 legislation came into effect allowing foreign insurance companies to operate in Pakistan.

**Department of Insurance:** Hajra Mansion, 3rd Floor, Zebunnisa St, Saddar, Karachi; tel. (21) 513365; f. 1948; a govt dept attached to the Ministry of Commerce; regulates insurance business; Controller of Insurance A. M. Khalfe; Asst Controller of Insurance M. Abid Hussain.

### Life Insurance

**American Life Insurance Co (Pakistan) Ltd:** POB 8020, Karachi 75400.

**Metropolitan Life Insurance Co:** 410 Qamar House, M. A. Jinnah Rd, Karachi; Chief Exec. Nisar Hussain.

**Postal Life Insurance Organization:** Tibet Centre, M. A. Jinnah Rd, Karachi; tel. (21) 723804; f. 1884; life and group insurance; Gen. Man and CEO Dr Salahuddin Ahmad.

**State Life Insurance Corpn of Pakistan:** State Life Bldg No. 9, Dr Ziauddin Ahmed Rd, POB 5725, Karachi 4; tel. (21) 5683233; telex 21079; fax (21) 5683266; f. 1972; life and group insurance and pension schemes; Chair. M. Zaheer Khan.

### General Insurance

**Adamjee Insurance Co Ltd:** Adamjee House, 6th Floor, I. I. Chundrigar Rd, POB 4850, Karachi 74000; tel. (21) 2412623; telex 25719; fax (21) 2412627; f. 1960; Man. Dir Mohammed Choudhury.

**Alpha Insurance Co Ltd:** State Life Bldg No. 1B, State Life Sq., off I. I. Chundrigar Rd, POB 4359, Karachi 74000; tel. (21) 2416041; telex 24482; fax (21) 2419968; f. 1951; Chair. Iqbal M. Qureshi; Man. Dir V. C. Gonsalves; 9 brs.

**Asia Insurance Co Ltd:** Asia Insurance House, 7 Egerton Rd, Lahore; Chief Exec. Zafar Iqbal Shaikh.

**Central Insurance Co Ltd:** Dawood Centre, POB 3988, Karachi 4; tel. (21) 516001; telex 24358; fax (21) 5680485; Chair. and Man. Dir Ahmed Dawood; Exec. Dir A. Razzak Polani.

**Commercial Union of Pakistan:** 74/1-A, Lalazar, M. T. Khan Rd, Karachi; tel. (21) 5611071; telex 29671; fax (21) 5610805; general and life insurance; 3 brs.

**Co-operative Insurance Society of Pakistan Ltd:** Co-operative Insurance Bldg, POB 147, Shahrah-e-Quaid-e-Azam, Lahore; Gen. Man. Mazhar Ali Khan.

**Crescent Star Insurance Co Ltd:** Nadir House, I. I. Chundrigar Rd, POB 4616, Karachi; tel. (21) 2415521; telex 2848; fax (21) 2415474; Gen. Man. Hamza N. Kapadia.

**East West Insurance Co Ltd:** 410 Qamar House, M. A. Jinnah Rd, Karachi 2; tel. (21) 200461; telex 23264.

**Eastern Federal Union Insurance Co Ltd:** Qamar House, M. A. Jinnah Rd, POB 5055, Karachi 2; f. 1932; Chair. Roshen Ali Bhimjee; Man. Dir Tahir G. Sachek.

**Eastern General Insurance Co Ltd:** 68-D/2, PECHS, Karachi; tel. (21) 4559620; telex 24093; fax (21) 4558554; f. 1955; Chair. and Dir Hussain Aftab; Man. Dir Rehana Hussain.

**Habib Insurance Co Ltd:** State Life Bldg, 6 Habib Sq., M. A. Jinnah Rd, POB 5217, Karachi; tel. (21) 2424038; telex 29341; fax (21) 2424211; f. 1942; Chair. Yusuf A. Habib; Man. Dir Ali Raza D. Habib.

**Heritage Insurance Co Ltd:** 719–726 Muhammadi House, 7th Floor, I. I. Chundrigar Rd, POB 5626, Karachi 74000; tel. (21) 2415670; fax (21) 2430975; f. 1961; Man. Dir Hameed Ullah.

**International General Insurance Co of Pakistan Ltd:** Finaly House, 1st Floor, I. I. Chundrigar Rd, POB 4576, Karachi 2; tel. (21) 236974; telex 20265; fax (21) 2416710; f. 1953; Gen. Man. Basit Hassan Syed.

**Ittefaq General Insurance Co Ltd:** H-16 Murree Rd, Rawalpindi; Chief Exec. Syed Ali Asghar.

**The Muslim Insurance Co Ltd:** 3 Bank Sq., Shahrah-e-Quaid-e-Azam, Lahore; tel. (42) 320542; telex 44504; fax (42) 61003; f. 1934; Chair. Yusuf H. Shirazi.

**National Insurance Corpn:** NIC Bldg, Abbasi Shaheed Rd, Karachi; tel. (21) 524670; telex 25750; govt-owned; Chair. S. T. R. Zaidi.

**National Security Insurance Co Ltd:** M. Ismail Aiwan-i-Science Ferozepur Rd, POB 671, Lahore 54600; tel. (42) 877035; telex 44826; fax (42) 876093; f. 1963; Pres. Mukhtar Ahmed; Sr Vice-Pres. Arshad P. Rana.

**New Jubilee Insurance Co Ltd:** Jubilee Insurance House, I. I. Chundrigar Rd, POB 4795, Karachi; tel. (21) 2416022; telex 23036; f. 1953; Pres. and Man. Dir Masood Noorani.

**Pakistan General Insurance Co Ltd:** Bank Sq., Shahrah-e-Quaid-e-Azam, POB 1364, Lahore; tel. (42) 323569; f. 1948; Chair. Khan Mohammad Arshad Khan; Man. Dir Mazhar Ali Khan.

**Pakistan Guarantee Insurance Co Ltd:** Al-Falah Court, 3rd and 5th Floor, I. I. Chundrigar Rd, POB 5436, Karachi 2; tel. (21) 2636111; telex 29281; fax (21) 2638740; Chief Exec. and Man. Dir Ali Azhar Nasir.

**Pakistan Insurance Corpn:** Pakistan Insurance Bldg, M. A. Jinnah Rd, POB 4777, Karachi 2; telex 2829; f. 1953; all classes of reinsurance except life; majority of shares held by the Govt; Chair. Akhlaq Ahmad.

**The Pakistan Mutual Insurance Co (Guarantee) Ltd:** 17B Shah Alam Market, Lahore; tel. (42) 52543; f. 1946; Chair. Sh. Naseer Ahmed; Gen. Man. Ali Ahmed Khan.

**Pioneer Insurance Co Ltd:** 311–313 Qamar House, M. A. Jinnah Rd, POB 5117, Karachi 3; Man. Dir Abid Zuberi.

**Premier Insurance Co of Pakistan Ltd.:** Wallace Rd, off I. I. Chundrigar Rd, POB 4140, Karachi 74000; tel. (21) 2416331; telex 21630; fax (21) 2416572; f. 1952; Chair. Zahid Bashir; Chief Gen. Man. A. U. Siddiqui.

**Prime Insurance Co Ltd:** Prudential House, Hasan Ali St, off I. I. Chundrigar Rd, Karachi; Man. Dir Sanobar Akhtar Yaqoob.

**Raja Insurance Co of Pakistan Ltd.:** Panorama Centre, 5th Floor, 256 Fatimah Jinnah Rd, POB 10422, Karachi 4; tel. (21) 523056; telex 24208; Chair. Raja Abdul Rahman; Man. Dir Sheikh Humayun Sayeed.

**Reliance Insurance Co Ltd:** 181-A, Sindhi Muslim Co-operative Housing Society, POB 13356, Karachi 2; tel. (21) 4539515; telex 2774; fax (21) 4539412.

**Shalimar General Insurance Co Ltd:** 68-D/2, PECHS, Karachi; tel. (21) 4559620; telex 24093; fax (21) 4558554; f. 1973; Chair. and Dir Hussain Aftab; Man. Dir Andaleeb Aftab.

**Standard Insurance Co Ltd:** Muhammadi House, 9th Floor, I. I. Chundrigar Rd, Karachi; tel. (21) 2416953; telex 20744; fax (21) 2419307; f. 1968; Man. Dir Saeed-ur-Rehman.

**Sterling Insurance Co Ltd:** 26 The Mall, POB 119, Lahore; f. 1949; 250 mems; Man. Dir S. A. Rahim.

PAKISTAN                                                                                                                              *Directory*

**Union Insurance Co of Pakistan Ltd.:** Adamjee House, 9th Floor, I. I. Chundrigar Rd, Karachi; Chair. Mian MOHAMMED HANIF.

**United Insurance Co of Pakistan Ltd:** Valika Chambers, Altaf Husain Rd, Karachi 2; tel. (21) 219591; Chair. CHAUDHARY HABIB-UR-RAHMAN.

**Universal Insurance Co Ltd:** POB 539, Universal Insurance House, 63 Shahrah-e-Quaid-e-Azam, Lahore; tel. (42) 53458; telex 23600; f. 1958; Chair. Lt-Gen. (retd) M. HABIBULLAH KHAN KHATTAK; Chief Exec. MUNIR-UL-HAQ.

### Insurance Associations

**Insurance Association of Pakistan:** Jamshed Katrak Chambers, G. Allana Rd, Machi Miani, POB 4932, Karachi 74000; tel. (21) 204704; fax (21) 205165; f. 1948; mems comprise 53 cos (Pakistani and foreign) transacting general insurance business; issues tariffs and establishes rules for insurance in the country; regional office in Lahore; Chair. MUNIR-UL-HAQ; Sec. K. A. SIDDIQI.

**Pakistan Insurance Institute:** Shafi Court, 2nd Floor, Mereweather Rd, Karachi 4; f. 1951 to encourage insurance education; Chair. MOHAMMAD CHOUDHRY.

## Trade and Industry

### CHAMBERS OF COMMERCE

**The Federation of Pakistan Chambers of Commerce and Industry:** St 28, Block 5, Sharea Ferdousi, Main Clifton, Karachi 6; tel. (21) 532179; telex 25370; fax (21) 570277; f. 1950; 132 mems; Pres. S. M. MUNEER; Sec.-Gen. M. RAFI.

**The Islamic Chamber of Commerce and Industry:** ST-2/A, Block 9, KDA Scheme No. 5, Clifton, POB 3831, Karachi 75600; tel. (21) 5874756; telex 25533; fax (21) 5870765; f. 1979; Pres. SHEIKH ISMAIL ABU DAWOOD; Sec.-Gen. AQEEL AHMAD AL-JASSEM.

**Overseas Investors' Chamber of Commerce and Industry:** Talpur Rd, POB 4833, Karachi; tel. (21) 2410814; telex 2870; fax (21) 2427315; Pres. NIASAR A. MEMON; Sec.-Gen. ZAHID ZAHEER.

### Principal Affiliated Chambers

**Bahawalpur Chamber of Commerce and Industry:** Bahawalpur; Pres. Mian MUHAMMAD ANWAR.

**Faisalabad Chamber of Commerce and Industry:** National Bank Bldg, 2nd Floor, Jail Rd, Faisalabad; tel. (41) 23039; telex 4285; Pres. WASIM AHMAD; Sec. M. D. CHAUDHRY.

**Gujranwala Chamber of Commerce and Industry:** Aiwan-e-Tijarat Rd, POB 96, Gujranwala; tel. (431) 256701; telex 45362; fax (431) 254440; f. 1978; Pres. KH. ZARAR KALEEM; Sec. RAJA ASMATULLAH.

**Hyderabad Chamber of Commerce and Industry:** 526 Shahrah-e-Quaid-e-Azam, POB 99, Cantonment, Hyderabad; tel. (221) 24641; Pres. SETH HIDAYATULLAH WALI BHAI; Sec. A. U. MALIK.

**Islamabad Chamber of Commerce and Industry:** 38 Khayaban-e-Azam, Jinnah Ave, Islamabad; tel. (51) 810490; telex 54570; fax (51) 821874; Pres. KHALID JAVED; Sr Vice-Pres. MUNAWAR MUGHAL.

**Karachi Chamber of Commerce and Industry:** Aiwan-e-Tijarat Rd, off Shahrah-e-Liaquat, POB 4158, Karachi 2; tel. (21) 2416091; telex 23613; f. 1960; 11,705 mems; Pres. AHMAD A. SATTAR; Sec. M. NAZIR ALI.

**Lahore Chamber of Commerce and Industry:** 11 Shahrah-e-Aiwan-e-Tijarat, POB 597, Lahore; tel. (42) 6305538; telex 44833; fax (42) 6368854; f. 1923; 8,000 mems; Pres. BASHIR A. BUKSH; Sec. M. LATIF CHAUDHRY.

**Larkana Chamber of Commerce and Industry:** Larkana, Sindh; Pres. G. HUSSAIN.

**Mirpur Azad Jammu and Kashmir Chamber of Commerce and Industry:** 52, F/1 Jaridan Rd, POB 12, Mirpur; tel. 3034; telex 44704; Pres. Brig. (retd) M. DILAWAR KHAN.

**Mirpur Khas Chamber of Commerce and Industry:** Mirpur Khas, Sindh; Pres. Haji MOHAMMAD AKHTAR.

**Multan Chamber of Commerce and Industry:** Co-operative Bank Bldg, Kutchery Rd, Multan; tel. (61) 40087; telex 42470; fax (61) 43530; Pres. Mian MUGHIS A. SHEIKH; Sec. G. A. BHATTI.

**Quetta Chamber of Commerce and Industry:** Zarghoon Rd, POB 117, Quetta; tel. (81) 821943; telex 821948; fax (81) 821948; f. 1984; Pres. NIAZ MOHAMMAD KHAN; Sec. UMAR HAYAT MALIK.

**Rawalpindi Chamber of Commerce and Industry:** Chamber House, 108 Adamjee Rd, POB 323, Rawalpindi; tel. (51) 566238; telex 5547; fax (51) 586849; f. 1952; Pres. S. M. AZEEM; Sec. MUSHTAQ AHMAD.

**SAARC Chamber of Commerce and Industry:** Federation House, Main Clifton, Karachi 75600; f. 1993; Pres. S. M. ENAM.

**Sarhad Chamber of Commerce and Industry:** Sarhad Chamber House, Chacha Younis Park, G.T. Rd, Peshawar; tel. (521) 215459; telex 52471; fax (521) 217412; f. 1958; 950 mems; Pres. Haji M. AKBAR ZIA; Sec. MUHAMMAD ANWAR.

**Sialkot Chamber of Commerce and Industry:** Shahrah-e-Aiwan-e-Sanat-o-Tijarat, POB 1870, Sialkot 51310; tel. (432) 261881; telex 46314; fax (432) 558835; f. 1982; more than 3,000 mems; Pres. SYED MUKHTAR BOKHARI; Sec. NAWAZ AHMED TOOR.

**Sukkur Chamber of Commerce and Industry:** New Cloth Market, Sukkur; tel. (71) 83938; telex 7726; Pres. KHAN MUNNAWAR KHAN; Sec. MIRZA IQBAL BEG.

### GOVERNMENT-SPONSORED ORGANIZATIONS

**Agricultural Marketing and Storage Ltd:** 27E Ali Plaza, Blue Area, POB 1611, Islamabad; tel. (51) 827407; telex 54118; fax (51) 824607.

**Balochistan Development Authority:** Civil Secretariat, Block 7, Quetta; tel. (81) 71780; created for economic and industrial development of Balochistan; exploration and exploitation of mineral resources; establishment of industries, development of infrastructure, water resources, etc.

**Board of Investment:** Prime Minister's Secretariat, Pak-Saudi Tower, Islamabad; Vice-Chair. SAFDAR ZAIDI; Chief Sec. MOHIB-ULLAH SHAH.

**Capital Development Authority:** Islamabad; tel. (51) 823454.

**Carrier Telephone Industries (Pvt) Ltd:** 1–9/2 Industrial Area, POB 1098, Islamabad; tel. (51) 414855; telex 5581; fax (51) 414859.

**Commission for the Islamization of the Economy:** Government of Pakistan, Finance Division, House No. 7, St 48, F-8/4, Islamabad 44000; tel. (51) 252834; fax (51) 252835; f. 1991; Chair. Dr MUHAMMAD YAQUB; Mem./Sec. ZULFIQAR KHAN.

**Cotton Board:** Dr Abbasi Clinic Bldg, 76 Strachan Rd, Karachi 74200; tel. (21) 215669; fax (21) 5680422; f. 1950; Chair. Mian HABIB-ULLAH; Dep. Sec. Dr MUHAMMAD USMAN.

**Cotton Export Corpn of Pakistan (Pvt) Ltd:** Finance and Trade Centre, Shahrah-e-Faisal, POB 3738, Karachi 74400; tel. (21) 520161; telex 20028; fax (21) 5683968; f. 1973; raw cotton exports in both the public sector and private sector; Chair. SAIYED AHMAD SIDDIQUI; Gen. Man. (Exports) S. S. MOMIN.

**Export Processing Zones Authority (EPZA):** 8th Floor, Finance and Trade Centre, Shahrah-e-Faisal, Karachi 74400; tel. (21) 523524; telex 25692; fax (21) 5686850; Chair. ABRAR H. NAQVI; Dir (Investment Promotion) NURUL AIN H. NADEEM.

**Export Promotion Bureau:** Finance and Trade Centre, Shahrah-e-Faisal, Karachi; tel. (21) 511494; telex 23877; fax (21) 215380; Chair. Mian HABIBULLAH; Vice-Chair. ABU SHAMIM ARIFF.

**Federal Chemical and Ceramics Corpn Ltd:** Ministry of Industries and Production, Government of Pakistan, 12 Ahmad Block, New Garden Town, Lahore; tel. (42) 5834956; fax (42) 5834837; Chair. SAADAT' HUSAIN KHAN.

**Gemstone Corpn of Pakistan Ltd:** 15/C Railway Rd, University Town, Peshawar; tel. (521) 40626; telex 52321; fax (521) 841990; f. 1979; gem exploration, mining, cutting and polishing, jewellery manufacturing and marketing; Man. Dir Dr NASIR ALI BHATTI; Sec. PERVEZ ELAHI MALIK.

**Geological Survey of Pakistan:** Quetta; Dir-Gen. SHAHID NOOR.

**Ghee Corporation of Pakistan Ltd:** LDA Plaza, 5th Floor, Egerton Rd, Lahore; Chair. FAROOQ AYUB.

**Heavy Mechanical Complex:** Taxila; tel. (51) 561681; telex 5607; fax (51) 584168; Man. Dir ZAFAR ALI KHAN.

**Investment Promotion Bureau:** Kandawala Bldg, M. A. Jinnah Rd, Karachi; Dir-Gen. Dr FAZAL MOHAMMAD.

**Karachi Development Authority (KDA):** Civic Centre, Gulshan-e-Iqbal, University Rd, Karachi; tel. (21) 528330; responsible for development of Karachi city; Dir-Gen. ABU SHAMIM ARIF.

**Karachi Electricity Supply Corpn (KESC):** Abdullah Haroon Rd, POB 7197, Karachi; telex 29601; fax (21) 5682408; transfer to private ownership pending in 1994; Chair. and Man. Dir SYED TANZIM HUSSAIN NAQVI.

**Karachi Export Processing Zone (KEPZ):** Landhi Industrial Area Extension, Mehran Highway, POB 17011, Karachi 75150; tel. (21) 211177; telex 25692; fax (21) 7738188; Chair. S. T. R. ZAIDI.

**Karachi Metropolitan Corpn:** M. A. Jinnah Rd, Karachi; Administrator FAHIM ZAMAN.

**Karachi Shipyard and Engineering Works:** West Wharf, Dockyard Rd, POB 4419, Karachi 2; tel. (21) 202761; telex 2706; fax (21) 2415952; f. 1956; building and repairing ships; general engineering; Man. Dir Vice-Adm. SYED IQTIDAR HUSAIN; Man. (Marketing and Public Relations) M. MUZAFFAR RANA.

# PAKISTAN

**Karachi Water and Sewerage Board:** M. R. Kayani Rd, Karachi; Man. Dir Brig. (retd) MANSOOR AHMAD.

**Lahore Development Authority (LDA):** LDA Plaza, Egerton Rd, Lahore.

**National Economic Board:** f. 1979 by the Govt as an advisory body to review and evaluate the state of the economy and to make proposals, especially to further the adoption of the socio-economic principles of Islam; Chair. The Prime Minister.

**National Economic Council:** supreme economic body; the governors and chief ministers of the four provinces and fed. ministers in charge of economic ministries are its mems; sr fed. and prov. officials in the economic field are also associated.

**National Energy Conservation Centre (ENERCON):** Buland Markaz, 33 Blue Area, Islamabad; telex 54128; fax (51) 826212.

**National Engineering Services Pakistan (Pvt) Ltd (NESPAK):** NESPAK House, 1-C, Block-N, Model Town Extension Scheme, POB 1351, Lahore; tel. (42) 5160500; telex 44730; fax (42) 5160509; f. 1973; multidisciplinary consulting company for engineering projects, including irrigation, power stations, roads, town planning, etc.; operates both in Pakistan and abroad; Pres. and Man. Dir IFTIKHAR KHALIL; Vice-Pres. (Business Development and Co-ordination) M. AFZAL ZAFFAR.

**National Fertilizer Corpn of Pakistan (Pvt) Ltd:** Alfalah Bldg, Shahrah-e-Quaid-e-Azam, POB 1730, Lahore; tel. (42) 302904; telex 44726; 6 fertilizer plants; Chair. SAADAT HUSSAIN KHAN.

**National Logistic Cell:** Marketing Cell South Zone, POB 7020, Karachi; tel. (21) 271400; telex 25136; transportation of bulk cargo (e.g. wheat, rice, fertilizer, cement, etc.).

**National Power Construction Corpn (Pvt) Ltd:** 46 Main Gulberg, Lahore 54660; tel. (42) 874714; telex 44825; fax (42) 876227; f. 1974; execution of power projects on turnkey basis, e.g. extra high voltage transmission lines, distribution networks, substations, power generation plants, industrial electrification, external lighting of housing complexes, etc.; Man. Dir MOHAMMAD AJAZ MALIK; Gen. Man. TAUQIR AHMED SHARIFI; project offices in Riyadh and Jeddah (Saudi Arabia).

**Oil and Gas Development Corpn:** Masood Mansion, F-8, Markaz, Islamabad; tel. (51) 853974; telex 5867; fax (51) 858939; f. 1961; plans, promotes, organizes and implements programmes for the exploration and development of petroleum and gas resources, and the production, refining and sale of petroleum and gas; transfer to 49% private ownership pending in 1994; Chair. RIFAT ASKARI; Exec. Dir (Admin.) Maj.-Gen. (retd) S. Z. M. ASKREE.

**Overseas Employment Corpn (Pvt) Ltd:** Red Crescent Bldg, Dr Daud Pota Rd, POB 15541, Karachi; tel. (21) 524794; telex 25475; f. 1976; labour recruitment for foreign countries; Exec. Dir S. A. QARNI.

**Pakdyes and Chemicals Ltd:** Iskanderabad (Daudkhel) Distt. Mianwali; tel. (459) 2434; telex 5845; a project of Federal Chemicals and Ceramics Corpn (Pvt) Ltd; mfrs of all types of direct and acid dyestuffs for cotton, wool and leather.

**Pakistan Atomic Energy Commission (PAEC):** POB 1114, Islamabad; tel. (51) 819030; telex 5725; fax (51) 824908; responsible for harnessing nuclear energy for development of nuclear technology as part of the nuclear power programme; operates KANUPP (POB 3183, nr Paradise Point, Hawksbay Rd, Karachi; tel. (21) 7737401) and is building another nuclear power station at Kundian; establishing research centres, incl. Pakistan Institute of Nuclear Science and Technology (PINSTECH); promoting peaceful use of atomic energy in agriculture, medicine, industry and hydrology; searching for indigenous nuclear mineral deposits; training project personnel; Chair. Dr ISHFAQ AHMAD; Co-ordination Officer SARFRAZ BEG.

**Pakistan Automobile Corpn Ltd (PACO):** 2nd Floor, Finance and Trade Centre, Tower 'B', Shahrah-e-Faisal, POB 4271, Karachi; tel. (21) 525391; telex 2865; fax (21) 525320; f. 1972; Chair. JAVED BURKI.

**Pakistan Engineering Co Ltd:** 6/7 Ganga Ram Trust Bldg, Shahrah-e-Quaid-e-Azam, Lahore 54000; tel. (42) 320255; telex 44750; fax (42) 323108; f. 1950; fmrly Batala Engineering Co Ltd; name changed following nationalization; mfrs pumps, motors, turbines, power looms, concrete mixers, machine tools, bicycles, etc.; Gen. Man. ZAID AKHTAR.

**Pakistan Industrial Development Corpn (PIDC):** PIDC House, Dr Ziauddin Ahmad Rd, Karachi; f. 1962; parastatal body; mfrs of woollen and cotton textiles, carpets, sugar; gas distributors; Chair. (vacant).

**Pakistan Industrial Technical Assistance Centre (PITAC):** Maulana Jalaluddin Roomi Rd (Old Ferozepur Rd), Lahore 54600; tel. (42) 5864171; telex 44448; fax (42) 5862381; f. 1962 by the Govt to provide advanced training to industrial personnel in the fields of metal trades and tool engineering design and related fields; design and production of tools, moulds, jigs, dies, gauges, fixtures, etc.; productivity promotion programmes; Chair. K. B. RIND; Gen. Man. MOHAMMAD ABDUL JABBAR KHAN.

**Pakistan Mineral Development Corpn (Pvt) Ltd:** 13-H/9, P.O. Shaigan, Islamabad; telex 54064; Chair. M. M. KHAN; Man. MOHAMMAD NAWAZ KHAN.

**Pakistan Postal Services Corporation:** G-8/4, Islamabad 44000; tel. (51) 254453; telex 54351; fax (51) 255178.

**Pakistan State Oil Co Ltd:** Dawood Centre, Moulvi Tamizuddin Khan Rd, POB 3983, Karachi 4; tel. (21) 5683570; telex 20024; fax (21) 5680215; f. 1976; import, export, storage, distribution, marketing and blending of all kinds of petroleum products and chemicals; Man. Dir JEHANGIR N. W. ANSARI; Sec. M. A. SAIFIE.

**Pakistan Steel Fabricating Co (Pvt) Ltd:** PSF Administrative Bldg No. 1, POB 9006, Bin Qasim, Karachi 50; tel. (21) 7574663; telex 23804; fax (21) 7732214.

**Pakistan Steel Mills Corpn (Pvt) Ltd:** Bin Qasim, POB 5429, Karachi 75000; tel. (21) 77694141; telex 23804; fax (21) 7731462; f. 1973; iron and steel mfrs; mfrs of coke, coal tar, ammonium sulphate, granulated slag; operates steel mill at Bin Qasim near Karachi, which started production in 1985, with an initial annual capacity of 1.1m. metric tons; annual capacity was to be increased to 1.3m. tons by the end of 1996 and to up to 3.0m. tons by 2000; Chair. SAJJAD HUSSAIN; Sec. SHAH NAWAZ MEHESAR; 21,884 employees.

**Pakistan Telecommunication Corpn:** Ministry of Communications, Block D, Pakistan Secretariat, Islamabad; tel. (51) 824342; fax (51) 210154; Chair. Mian MOHAMMAD JAVED; 12% transferred to private ownership in 1994.

**Pakistan Water and Power Development Authority:** WAPDA House, Shahrah-e-Quaid-e-Azam, Lahore; tel. (42) 6366911; telex 44869; f. 1958 for development of irrigation, water supply and drainage, building of replacement works under the World Bank-sponsored Indo-Pakistan Indus Basin Treaty; flood-control and watershed management; reclamation of waterlogged and saline lands; inland navigation; generation, transmission and distribution of hydroelectric and thermal power; partial transfer to private ownership carried out in 1994; Chair. SHAMS-UL-MULK.

**Peshawar Development Authority (PDA):** State Life Bldg, 34 The Mall, Peshawar.

**Private Power and Infrastructure Board:** 50 Nazimuddin Rd, F-7/4, Islamabad; tel. (51) 222378; telex 5851; fax (51) 217735.

**Privatization Commission:** Experts Advisory Cell Bldg, 5A Constitution Ave, Islamabad; tel. (51) 222245; telex 5746; fax (51) 823076; supervised by Ministry of Finance and Economic Affairs; Chair. SYED NAVEED QAMAR.

**Punjab Seed Corpn:** 4 Lytton Rd, Lahore; tel. (42) 212512; seed trade, crop seed production and marketing.

**Resource Development Corporation (Pvt) Ltd:** Old Baldia House, Ramsay Rd, M. A. Jinnah Rd, Quetta; copper and gold mining projects; Gen. Man. (Commercial) A. Q. BALOCH.

**Rice Export Corpn of Pakistan:** 4th Floor, Block A, Finance and Trade Centre, Shahrah-e-Faisal, POB 457, Karachi; tel. (21) 5170211; telex 23706; fax (21) 511402; f. 1974; procures, mills, cleans, stores, packs and markets standard quality rice for export on monopoly basis; Chair. S. M. ISHAQ.

**Sarhad Development Authority (SDA):** PIA Bldg, Arbab Rd, POB 172, Peshawar; tel. (521) 73076; telex 52305; f. 1972; promotes industrial (particularly mining), commercial development in the North-West Frontier Province; Chair. KHALID AZIZ.

**Sindh Sugar Corpn Ltd:** Shaikh Sultan Trust Bldg, 6th Floor, Beaumont Rd, Karachi 3; Chair. ZAHEER SAJJAD.

**State Cement Corpn of Pakistan (Pvt) Ltd:** PEC Bldg, 97-A/B-D Gulberg III, Lahore; tel. (42) 870341; telex 44636; f. 1973; operates public-sector cement plants; distributes cement; Chair. MALIK AMJAD ALI.

**State Engineering Corpn (Pvt) Ltd:** 2nd Floor, Saeed Plaza, Khayaban-e-Quaid-e-Azam, Blue Area, Islamabad; tel. (51) 819691; telex 54491; fax (51) 819601; f. 1979; Chair. Dr M. AKRAM SHEIKH.

**State Petroleum, Refining and Petro-Chemical Corpn (Pvt) Ltd (PERAC):** Karim Chambers, 4th Floor, Merewether Rd, Karachi; tel. (21) 515071; telex 24546; fax (21) 5680215; Chair. Dr M. H. CHAUDHRY.

**Sui Northern Gas Pipeline Ltd:** 21 Kashmir Rd, Lahore; tel. (42) 304924; telex 44677; fax (42) 368433; f. 1964; transmission and distribution of natural gas; transfer to private ownership pending in 1994.

**Sui Southern Gas Co Ltd:** State Life Bldg No. 2-A, Wallace Rd, POB 318, Karachi 74000; an amalgamation of Southern Gas Co Ltd and Sui Gas Transmission Co Ltd; transfer to private ownership pending in 1994; Chair. KHAN TARIQ HAMID; Sec. S. IFTIKHAR ALI.

**Trading Corpn of Pakistan (Pvt) Ltd:** 4th and 5th Floor, Finance and Trade Centre, Shahrah-e-Faisal, Karachi 75530; tel. (21)

511016; telex 21084; fax (21) 5681389; f. 1967; premier trading house handling bulk import requirements, such as edible oil; exports Pakistani products, such as textiles, food, leather, rice, etc.; Chair. NOORUDDIN AHMAD.

## EMPLOYERS' AND TRADE ASSOCIATIONS

**Employers' Federation of Pakistan:** State Life Bldg No. 2, 2nd Floor, Wallace Rd, off I. I. Chundrigar Rd, POB 4338, Karachi 74000; tel. (21) 2411049; fax (21) 2439347; Pres. ASHRAF WALI MOHAMMAD TABANI; Sec.-Gen. MOHAMMED MUSTAFA SHARIF.

**All Pakistan Bedsheets and Upholstery Manufacturers' Association:** 4th Floor, 204 Naz Chambers, Shahrah-e-Liaquat, Karachi; tel. (21) 2429194; Chair. Mian MOHAMMED ARIF SHAIKH.

**All Pakistan Cloth Exporters' Association:** 30, Ground Floor, Regency Arcade, The Mall, Faisalabad; tel. (41) 615563; telex 43382; fax (41) 617985; Chair. MUKHTAR AHMAD.

**All Pakistan Cloth Merchants' Association:** 64, 4th Floor, Hussain Cloth Market, Dada Chambers, Mereweather Tower, Karachi; tel. (21) 225836; fax (21) 2427483; Chair. ABID CHINOY.

**All Pakistan Cotton Powerlooms' Association:** P-79/3, Montgomery Bazaar, Faisalabad; tel. (41) 612929; telex 43240; fax (41) 28171; Chair. CHAUDRY JAVAID SADIQ.

**All Pakistan Textile Manufacturers' Association:** APTMA House, 44A Lalazar, Moulvi Tamizuddin Khan Rd, POB 5446, Karachi 74000; tel. (21) 552046; telex 25037; fax (21) 551305; Chair. RIAZ TATA; Sec.-Gen. S. M. A. ASHRAF.

**Cigarette Manufacturers' Association of Pakistan:** 202/2–C, Block 2, PECHS, Karachi 75400; tel. (21) 436825; fax (21) 436825.

**Karachi Cotton Association:** The Cotton Exchange, I. I. Chundrigar Rd, Karachi; tel. (21) 2410336; telex 29845; fax (21) 2413035; Chair. ABDUL SATTAR BALAGAMWALA; Sec. FASIHUDDIN.

**Pakistan Art Silk Fabrics and Garments Exporters' Association:** 204 Amber Estate, Shahrah-e-Faisal, Karachi; tel. (21) 443104; telex 23096; fax (21) 4545280; Chair. JAMIL AKHTAR.

**Pakistan Bedwear Exporters' Association:** 12–13 Timber Pond, Keamari Rd, Karachi 75620; tel. (21) 271315; telex 23371; fax (21) 2414251; Chair. SHABBIR AHMED; Sec. M. WASIM ANSARI.

**Pakistan Canvas and Tents Manufacturers' and Exporters' Association:** Room No. W-1, 1st Floor, Dinar Chambers, West Wharf Rd, Karachi; tel. (21) 200303; fax (21) 202647; Chair. RASHEED MOHAMMAD.

**Pakistan Carpet Manufacturers' and Exporters' Association:** Panorama Center, Fatima Jinnah Rd, Karachi 75530; tel. (21) 512189; telex 29240; fax (21) 528649; Chair. IMRAN MALIK; Sec. A. S. HASHMI.

**Pakistan Chemicals and Dyes Merchants' Association:** Chemical-Dye House, Jodia Bazar, Rambharti Rd, Karachi; tel. (21) 227752; telex 24657.

**Pakistan Commercial Towel Exporters' Association:** 207 Uni Plaza, I. I. Chundrigar Rd, POB 6955, Karachi; tel. (21) 2411389; fax (21) 2410135; Chair. JAMIL MAHBOOB MAGOON.

**Pakistan Cotton Fashion Apparel Manufacturers' and Exporters' Association:** Room 5, Amber Court, 2nd Floor, Shaheed-e-Millat Rd, Karachi 75350; tel. (21) 443141; telex 23900; fax (21) 4546711; Chair. JEHANGIR ANWAR.

**Pakistan Cotton Ginners' Association:** 1119–1120 Uni-Plaza, I.I. Chundrigar Rd, Karachi; tel. (21) 231406.

**Pakistan Film Producers' Association:** Regal Cinema Bldg, Shahrah-e-Quaid-e-Azam, Lahore; Chair. A. MAJEED; Sec. MUSHTAQ AHMAD (acting).

**Pakistan Footwear Manufacturers' Association:** 21-KM., Ferozpur Rd, Lahore 53000; tel. (42) 5810928; telex 47428; Chair. IFTIKHAR FIROZ; Sec. NISAR AHMAD CHUGHTAI.

**Pakistan Gloves Manufacturers' and Exporters' Association:** G. H. Jones Bldg, Tajpura, POB 1330, Sialkot; tel. (432) 51847; telex 46482; fax (432) 50182; Chair. M. ANWAR BUTT.

**Pakistan Hardware Merchants' Association:** Mandviwala Bldg, Serai Rd, Karachi 74000; tel. (21) 2420610; telex 24456; fax (21) 2415743; f. 1961; more than 1,500 mems; Central Chair. SAEEDUR RAHMAN; Central Sec. SYED ZAFRUN NABI.

**Pakistan Hosiery Manufacturers' Association:** Amber Estate, 1st Floor, Room Nos 103 and 104, Shahrah-e-Faisal, Karachi; tel. (21) 446138; telex 24082; fax (21) 4532424; Chair. A. G. KAPADIA; Sec. YUNUS BIN AIYOOB.

**Pakistan Iron and Steel Merchants' Association:** 10 Writers' Chambers, 2nd Floor, Dunolly Rd, POB 4827, Karachi 74000; tel. (21) 231264; Pres. MALIK AHMAD HUSSAIN; Gen. Sec. S. S. REHMAN.

**Pakistan Jute Mills Association:** 8 Sasi Town House, Abdullah Haroon Rd, Civil Lines, Karachi 75530; tel. (21) 526986; telex 28880; fax (21) 526463; Chair. AHSAN SALEEM; Exec. Consultant M. Z. CHUGHTAI.

**Pakistan Knitwear and Sweaters Exporters' Association:** Room No. 6, 7th Floor, Textile Plaza, M. A. Jinnah Rd, Karachi; tel. (21) 2411002; telex 25100; fax (21) 2636325; Chair. NASIR HUSSAIN.

**Pakistan Paint Manufacturers' Association:** ST/6A, Block 14, Federal 'B' Area, Karachi 38; tel. (21) 681103; f. 1953; Chair. ABDULLAH ISMAIL; Sec. S. ABDUR RAHMAN.

**Pakistan Plastic Manufacturers' Association:** H-17, Textile Ave, S.I.T.E., Karachi; tel. (21) 2572884; fax (21) 2576928; Pres. USMAN ZAKARIA; Sec. FAYYAZ A. CHAUDHRY.

**Pakistan Readymade Garments Manufacturers' and Exporters' Association:** Shaheen View Bldg, Mezzanine Floor, Plot No. 18A, Block VI, PECHS, Karachi; tel. (21) 449047; fax (21) 440489; Chair. SHAIKH KHURSHEED ANWAR.

**Pakistan Shipowners' Association:** see under Shipping.

**Pakistan Silk and Rayon Mills' Association:** Room Nos 44, 48 and 49, Textile Plaza, 5th Floor, M. A. Jinnah Rd, Karachi 2; tel. (21) 2410288; f. 1974; Chair. M. ASHRAF SHEIKH; Sec. M. H. K. BURNEY.

**Pakistan Small Units Powerlooms' Association:** Room No. 15, Taj Plaza, Kotiwalai Rd, Faisalabad.

**Pakistan Soap Manufacturers' Association:** 148 Sunny Plaza, Hasrat Mohani Rd, Karachi 74200; tel. (21) 210773; Chair. YAQOOB KARIM.

**Pakistan Sports Goods Manufacturers' and Exporters' Association:** Abbot Rd, Sialkot 51310; tel. (432) 87962; fax (432) 561774.

**Pakistan Steel Re-rolling Mills' Association:** Rashid Chambers, 6-Link McLeod Rd, Lahore 54000; tel. (42) 7227136; Chair. HAFIZ MUHAMMAD AKBAR; Sec. Lt-Col (retd) S. H. A. BOKHARI.

**Pakistan Sugar Mills' Association:** Mezzanine Floor, 24D Rashid Plaza, Jinnah Ave, Islamabad; tel. (51) 812111; fax (51) 217738; Chair. ALTAF M. SALEEM; Sec.-Gen. K. ALI QAZILBASH.

**Pakistan Tanners' Association:** Plot No. ST-7, Sector 7A, Korangi Industrial Area, Karachi 74900; tel. (21) 5062077; telex 25133; fax (21) 5060323; Chair. GULZAR FIROZ; Sec. K. M. A. MABUD.

**Pakistan Tea Association:** Mohammed Buksh Bldg, 1st Floor, 23 West Wharf Rd, Karachi; tel. (21) 210415; telex 21471; fax (21) 2415209; Chair. MOHAMMAD HANIF JANOO.

**Pakistan Vanaspati Manufacturers' Association:** 404 Muhammadi House, I. I. Chundrigar Rd, Karachi; tel. (21) 220337.

**Pakistan Wool and Hair Merchants' Association:** 27 Idris Chambers, Talpur Rd, Karachi; Pres. Mian MOHAMMAD SIDDIQ KHAN; Sec. KHALID LATEEF.

**Pakistan Woollen Mills Association:** Republic Motors Bldg, 2nd Floor, Room No. 12, 87 Shahrah-e-Quaid-e-Azam, Lahore 54000; tel. and fax (42) 6306879; telex 44483; Sec. MUHAMMAD YASIN.

**Pakistan Yarn Merchants' Association:** Room Nos 802–4 Business Centre, 8th Floor, Dunolly Rd, Karachi 74000; tel. (21) 2410320; telex 25915; fax (21) 2424896; Chair. MAQSOOD ISMAIL.

**Towel Manufacturers' Association of Pakistan:** Suite Nos 1206, 1212 and 1218, 12th Floor, Kashif Centre, nr Mehran Hotel, Shahrah-e-Faisal, Karachi 75530; tel. (21) 527204; telex 25357; fax (21) 519431; Chair. M. ZAHID.

## TRADE UNIONS

In 1986 trade unions claimed to have almost 1m. members out of an industrial labour force of about 2.5m.

**Pakistan National Federation of Trade Unions (PNFTU):** Solidarity House, ST-37/4, Qasba Township, Manghopir Rd, Karachi 75800; tel. (21) 6658726; telex 26630; f. 1962; 213 affiliated feds; 270,989 mems; Pres. MOHAMMAD SHARIF; Sec.-Gen. RASHID MOHAMMAD.

The principal affiliated federations are:

**All Pakistan Federation of Labour (Durrani Group):** Durrani Labour Hall, Khyber Bazar, Peshawar; tel. (521) 214530; fax (521) 274038; f. 1951; 295 affiliated unions, with 337,000 mems; affiliated to the World Federation of Trade Unions (WFTU); Pres. AURANGZEB DURRANI; Sec.-Gen. SHAH IMROZE ZAFAR.

**All Pakistan Federation of Trade Unions:** Bakhtiar Labour Hall, 28 Nisbat Rd, Lahore; tel. (42) 7229419; telex 44942; fax (42) 7229529; 610,000 mems; Pres. Mian MUHAMMAD MUNIR; Gen. Sec. KHURSHID AHMED.

**Muttahida Labour Federation:** Labour Welfare Society, Block D, Shershah Colony, Karachi 75730; tel. (21) 291576; c. 120,000 mems; Pres. KHAMASH GUL KHATTAK; Sec.-Gen. NABI AHMED.

**Pakistan Central Federation of Trade Unions:** 220 Al-Noor Chambers, M. A. Jinnah Rd, Karachi; tel. (21) 728891.

**Pakistan Railway Employees' Union (PREM):** Cith Railway Station, Karachi; Sec. ABDUL JABBAR QURESHI.

**Pakistan Trade Union Federation:** Khamosh Colony, Karachi; Pres. KANIZ FATIMA; Gen. Sec. SALEEM RAZA.

**Pakistan Transport Workers' Federation:** 110 McLeod Rd, Lahore; 17 unions; 92,512 mems; Pres. MEHBOOB-UL-HAQ; Gen. Sec. CH. UMAR DIN.

## Transport

### RAILWAYS

In June 1994 the Government approved a US $700m., 850-km railway project, which was to link Pakistan with Turkmenistan via Afghanistan.

**Pakistan Railways:** 31 Sheikh Abdul Hamid Bin Bades, Lahore; tel. (42) 6365460; telex 44672; fax (42) 6367673; state-owned; 12,625 km of track and 8,775 route km in 1992; seven divisions (Karachi, Lahore, Multan, Quetta, Rawalpindi, Peshawar and Sukkur); Chair. Syed Naseer Ahmad; Gen. Man. S. Zahoor Ahmad.

### ROADS

The total length of main roads at 30 June 1988 was 58,677 km, while secondary roads totalled 52,560 km. In 1978 the 800-km Karakoram highway was opened, linking Xinjiang Province in the People's Republic of China with Havelian, north of Islamabad. In 1991 plans were announced to construct a 340-km motorway between Islamabad and Lahore. The road, which is due to be completed in mid-1995, will be Pakistan's first inter-city motorway and will constitute the first section of a planned 2,000-km transnational motorway from Peshawar to Karachi.

Government assistance comes from the Road Fund, financed from a share of the excise and customs duty on sales of petrol and from development loans.

**Karachi Transport Corpn:** Annexe-B, 3rd Floor, Civic Centre, Hasan Sq., Gulshan-e-Iqbal, Karachi 74800; Man. Dir Ibrahim Patel; Sec. Karin Bux Siddiqui.

**National Highway Authority:** 27 Mauve Area, G/9–1, POB 1205, Islamabad; tel. (51) 859835; fax (51) 859903; jt venture between Govt and private sector; Chair. Shahid Aziz Siddiqi; Dir-Gen. Mohsin Sheikh.

**Punjab Road Transport Board:** Transport House, 11A Egerton Rd, Lahore.

**Punjab Urban Transport Corpn:** Lahore; Man. Dir Brig. Naeem Khawaja.

**Sindh Urban Transport Corpn:** 3 Modern Housing Society, Dright Rd, Karachi 8; Man. Dir Maj. Mohammad Salahuddin.

### SHIPPING

In 1974 maritime shipping companies were placed under government control. The chief port is Karachi. A second port, Port Mohammad bin Qasim, started partial operation in 1980. A third port, Port Gwadar, is used for the ship-breaking industry. Another port, Port Pasni, which is situated on the Balochistan coast, was completed in 1988. In 1991 the Government amended the 1974 Pakistan Maritime Shipping Act to allow private companies to operate. By mid-1992 31 private companies had been granted licences. In late 1992 the Government announced plans to construct a deep sea port at Port Gwadar.

**Karachi Port Trust (KPT):** POB 4725, Karachi; tel. (21) 201305; telex 2739; fax (21) 2415567; Chair. Vice-Adm. Mohammad Akbar; Sec. Mr Farozuddin.

**Pakistan Shipowners' Association:** Bangalore Town, Main Shahrah-e-Faisal, Karachi; Chair. Masood T. Baghpatee.

**Delta Shipping (Pvt) Ltd:** 1st Floor, Bldg 1-B, State Life Insurance Corpn, Dr Ziauddin Ahmad Rd, Karachi; tel. (21) 2417672.

**National Tanker Co (Pak) (Pvt) Ltd:** 3rd Floor, PNSC Bldg, M. T. Khan Rd, Karachi 74000; tel. (21) 551843; telex 23844; fax (21) 552206; f. 1981 by the Pakistan National Shipping Corpn and the State Petroleum Refining and Petrochemical Corpn Ltd; aims to make Pakistan self-reliant in the transport of crude petroleum and petroleum products; Chair. S. R. Hussain; Gen. Man. Turab Ali Khan.

**Pakistan National Shipping Corpn:** PNSC Bldg, Moulvi Tamizuddin Khan Rd, POB 5350, Karachi 74000; tel. (21) 5611080; telex 21337; fax (21) 5610802; f. 1979 by merger; Chair. Rear Adm. Javaid Ali; Sec. Shireen Ghory.

**The Pan-Islamic Steamship Co Ltd:** Writers' Chambers, Mumtaz Hassan Rd, off I.I. Chundrigar Rd, POB 4855, Karachi 74000; tel. (21) 2412110; telex 20535; fax (21) 2412276; f. 1950; Man. Dir Shahab Khan; Gen. Man. (Commercial) Capt. Anwar Shah.

**Port Qasim Authority (PQA):** Bin Qasim, Karachi 75020; tel. (21) 7737601; telex 2633; fax (21) 7737638; f. 1973; Chair. Syed Mohibullah Shah; Sec. Afsar Din Talpur.

**Tristar Shipping Lines Ltd:** Baghpatee Centre, 4 Bangalore Town, Main Shahrah-e-Faisal, Karachi 75350; tel. (21) 4536933; telex 29680; fax (21) 4536931; privately-owned; Pres. Masood T. Baghpatee.

### CIVIL AVIATION

Karachi, Lahore, Rawalpindi, Peshawar and Quetta have international airports.

In August 1992 the Government ended the air monopoly held by the Pakistan International Airlines Corpn, and opened all domestic air routes to any Pakistan-based company.

**Civil Aviation Authority:** 19 Liaquat Barracks, Karachi; tel. (21) 529681; controls all the civil airports; Man. Dir Air Vice-Marshal Anwar Mahmood Khan.

**Aero-Asia:** 43J, Block 6, PECHS, Karachi; tel. (21) 435980; fax (21) 4550569; Chief Exec. Ashfaq Jan.

**Pakistan International Airlines (PIA):** PIA Bldg, Quaid-e-Azam International Airport, Karachi; tel. (21) 4572011; telex 2832; fax (21) 4572754; f. 1954; merged with Orient Airways in 1955; 58% govt-owned; operates domestic services to 35 destinations and international services to 45 destinations in 40 countries; Chair. Anwar Zahid; Man. Dir Air Vice-Marshal Farooq Umar.

**Raji Airlines:** Raji Hangar, Karachi Airport, Karachi; Chief Exec. Capt. Aijaz Rab.

**Shaheen Air International:** Avari Hotel Bldg, Fatima Jinnah Rd, Karachi; f. 1992; operates domestic services and international services to Europe and the Middle East; Man. Dir Khalid Iqbal; Chief Exec. M. I. Akbar.

## Tourism

The Himalayan hill stations of Pakistan provide magnificent scenery, a fine climate and excellent opportunities for field sports, mountaineering, trekking and winter sports. The archaeological remains and historical buildings are also impressive.

In 1994 Pakistan received an estimated 387,525 foreign visitors and receipts from tourism amounted to around US $119m. in 1992.

**Pakistan Tourism Development Corpn:** House No. 2, St 61, F-7/4, Islamabad 44000; tel. (51) 811001; telex 54356; fax (51) 824173; f. 1970; Chair. Shahzada Mohiuddin; Man. Dir Hamid Ahmad Qureshi.

---

Other affiliated federations include: Pakistan Bank Employees' Federation, Pakistan Insurance Employees' Federation, Automobile, Engineering and Metal Workers' Federation, Pakistan Teachers Organizations' Council, Sarhad WAPDA Employees' Federation, and Balochistan Ittehad Trade Union Federation.

# Related Territories

The status of Jammu and Kashmir has remained unresolved since the 1949 cease-fire agreement, whereby the area was divided into sectors administered by India and Pakistan separately. Pakistan administers Azad (Free) Kashmir and the Northern Areas as *de facto* dependencies, being responsible for foreign affairs, defence, coinage, currency and the implementation of UN resolutions concerning Kashmir.

## AZAD KASHMIR

**Area:** 11,639 sq km (4,494 sq miles).

**Population:** 1,980,000 (1981 census).

**Administration:** Government is based on the Azad Jammu and Kashmir Interim Constitution Act of 1974. There are four administrative districts: Kotli, Mirpur, Muzaffarabad and Poonch.

**Legislative Assembly:** consists of 42 members: 40 directly elected and two women nominated by the other members.

**Azad Jammu and Kashmir Council:** consists of the President of Pakistan as Chairman, the President of Azad Kashmir as Vice-Chairman, five members nominated by the President of Pakistan, six members by the Legislative Assembly, and the Pakistan Minister of States, Northern Areas, Frontier Regions and Kashmir Affairs (ex officio).

**President of Azad Kashmir:** Sardar SIKANDAR HAYAT KHAN.

**Prime Minister:** Sardar ABDUL QAYYUM KHAN.

## NORTHERN AREAS

**Area:** 72,520 sq km (28,000 sq miles).

**Population:** 562,000 (1981 census).

**Administration:** There are three administrative districts: Baltistan, Diamir and Gilgit. The Northern Areas Council consists of 26 members (24 members are elected in a party-based election and two seats are reserved for women), headed by the federal Minister of States, Northern Areas, Frontier Regions and Kashmir Affairs.

# PALAU

## Introductory Survey

### Location, Climate, Language, Religion, Flag, Capital

The Republic of Palau (also known as Belau) consists of more than 200 islands, in a chain about 650 km (400 miles) long, lying about 7,150 km (4,450 miles) south-west of Hawaii and about 1,160 km (720 miles) south of Guam. With the Federated States of Micronesia (q.v.), Palau forms the archipelago of the Caroline Islands. Palau is subject to heavy rainfall, and seasonal variations in rainfall and temperature are generally small. Palauan and English are the official languages. The principal religion is Christianity, much of the population being Roman Catholic. The flag (proportions five by three) features a large golden disc (representing the moon), placed off-centre, towards the hoist, on a light blue background. The provisional capital is Koror, on Koror Island; the Constitution provides for the capital to be established on the as yet undeveloped island of Babeldaob, in Melekeok state.

### Recent History

The Republic of Palau's independence, under the Compact of Free Association, in October 1994 marked the end of the Trust Territory of the Pacific Islands, of which Palau was the final component (for history up to 1965, see chapter on the Marshall Islands). From 1965 there were increasing demands for local autonomy within the Trust Territory. In that year the Congress of Micronesia was formed, and in 1967 a commission was established to examine the future political status of the islands. In 1970 it declared Micronesians' rights to sovereignty over their own lands, self-determination, the right to their own constitution and to revoke any form of free association with the USA. In May 1977, after eight years of negotiations, US President Jimmy Carter announced that his administration intended to adopt measures to terminate the trusteeship agreement by 1981. In the Palau District a referendum in July 1979 approved a proposed local Constitution, which came into effect on 1 January 1981, when the district became the Republic of Palau.

The USA signed the Compact of Free Association with the Republic of Palau in August 1982, and with the Marshall Islands and the Federated States of Micronesia in October. The trusteeship of the islands was due to end after the principle and terms of the Compacts had been approved by the respective peoples and legislatures of the new countries, by the US Congress and by the UN Security Council. Under the Compacts, the four countries (including the Northern Mariana Islands) would be independent of each other and would manage both their internal and foreign affairs separately, while the USA would be responsible for defence and security. In addition, the USA was to allocate some US $3,000m. in aid to the islands.

More than 60% of Palauans voted in February 1983 to support their Compact, but fewer than the required 75% approved changing the Constitution to allow the transit and storage of nuclear materials. In September the Palau Supreme Court ruled that the Compact had effectively been defeated in the plebiscite. A revised Compact, which contained no reference to nuclear issues, was approved by 66% of votes cast in a plebiscite in September 1984. However, the US Government had hoped for a favourable majority of 75% of the votes cast, which would have allowed the terms of the Compact to override the provisions of the Palau Constitution in the event of a conflict between the two.

In June 1985 President Haruo Remeliik of Palau was assassinated: relatives of a rival candidate in the 1984 presidential election, Roman Tmetuchl, were convicted of the murder, but remained at liberty pending an appeal. In August 1987 the Supreme Court of Palau upheld the appeal, citing unreliable evidence as grounds for its ruling. Alfonso Oiterong assumed office as acting President until elections in September 1985, when he was defeated in the presidential contest by Lazarus Salii.

In January 1986 representatives of the Palau and US administrations reached a preliminary agreement on a new Compact, whereby the USA consented to provide US $421m. in economic assistance to the islands. However, the 72% of votes in favour of the new Compact at a referendum in the following month was still less than the 75% required for the constitutional ban on nuclear material to be waived. Both Lazarus Salii, the new President of Palau, and US President Ronald Reagan supported the terms of the Compact, arguing that a simple majority would suffice for its approval, as the USA had guaranteed that it would observe the constitutional ban on nuclear material.

In May 1986 the UN Trusteeship Council endorsed the US administration's request for the termination of the existing trusteeship agreement with the islands. Following this decision, however, a writ was submitted to the Palau High Court, in which it was claimed that approval of the Compact with the USA was unconstitutional because it had failed to obtain the requisite 75% of votes. The High Court ruled in favour of the writ, but the Palau Government appealed against the ruling and in October the Compact was approved by Congress. However, at a new plebiscite in December, only 66% of Palauans voted in favour of the Compact. Therefore, ratification of the Compact remained impossible, and Palau was to continue under the administration of the USA, in accordance with the trusteeship agreement.

In October 1986 the Compact between the Marshall Islands and the USA came into effect, following its approval by the islands' Government, and in November Reagan issued a proclamation formally ending US administration of Micronesia. An Office of Freely Associated State Affairs was established in the USA to conduct that country's relations with the former Trust Territory. Full implementation of the Compacts was dependent on their ratification by the UN.

A fifth plebiscite on Palau's proposed Compact with the USA in June 1987, again failed to secure the 75% vote in favour required by the Constitution. Serious unrest followed when President Salii announced the suspension, without pay, of 70% of the Territory's public employees, as a result of Palau's growing financial crisis. Under alleged physical intimidation by pro-nuclear supporters of the Compact, the House of Representatives agreed to a further referendum in August. In this referendum an amendment to the Constitution was approved, ensuring that a simple majority, rather than one of 75% as previously required, would be needed to approve the Compact. This was duly achieved in a further referendum in the same month. When a writ was entered with the Supreme Court challenging the legality of the decision to allow approval of the Compact by a simple majority of voters, a campaign of arson and bombing followed, and one person was murdered.

In February 1988 a team from the US General Accounting Office, in Washington, travelled to Palau to investigate allegations of corruption and intimidation on the part of the Palau Government. Approval of the Compact by the US Congress was to be delayed until the investigators had announced their findings. However, in April a ruling by the Supreme Court of Palau invalidated the procedure by which the Compact had finally been approved by a simple majority in the previous August. Three government employees, including President Salii's personal assistant, were imprisoned in April, after being found guilty of firing on the home of Santos Olikong, Speaker of Palau's House of Delegates. The attack was widely considered to have been prompted by Olikong's public opposition to the proposed Compact of Free Association.

In August 1988 President Salii, the principal subject of the bribery allegations, apparently committed suicide. The Vice-President, Thomas Remengesau, was sworn in as interim President, pending an election scheduled for November. At the election Ngiratkel Etpison was elected President, with just over 26% of the total votes. Although Etpison advocated the proposed Compact and was supported by the pro-Compact Ta Belau Party, his closest challenger, Roman Tmetuchl, opposed it and was supported by the anti-nuclear Coalition for Open, Honest and Just Government, which had demanded that a special prosecutor from the USA be dispatched to Palau to investigate alleged corruption and violent attacks against opponents of the Compact.

A seventh referendum on the proposed Compact took place in February 1990: only 60% of those voting approved the Compact, again falling short of the required 75%. In July the US Department of the Interior declared its intention to impose stricter controls on the administration of Palau, particularly in financial matters. In the following year the leader of the Council of Chiefs, Ibedul Yutaka Gibbons, initiated proceedings to sue the US Government. His claim centred on demands for compensation for the extensive damage caused to Palau's infrastructure by US forces during the Second World War and the subsequent retardation of the economy, allegedly as a result of the US administration of the islands.

During 1991 the US authorities reopened investigations into the assassination of Remeliik in 1985. In March 1992 the Minister of State, John Ngiraked, his wife, Emerita Kerradel, and Sulial Heinrick (already serving a gaol sentence for another killing) were charged with Remeliik's murder. In March 1993 Ngiraked and Kerradel were found guilty of aiding and abetting the assassination of the President, while Heinrick was acquitted.

Legislative and presidential elections were held in November 1992. The electoral system had been modified earlier in the year to include primary elections for the selection of two presidential candidates. At a secondary election the incumbent Vice-President, Kuniwo Nakamura, narrowly defeated Johnson Toribiong to become President. At the same time as the secondary election a referendum endorsed a proposal that, in future polls, a simple majority be sufficient to approve the adoption of the Compact of Free Association. Some 62% of voters were in favour of the proposal, which was approved in 14 of Palau's 16 states. A further referendum on the proposed Compact took place in November 1993 (following an unsuccessful appeal to the High Court against the result of the previous referendum). Some 64.3% of eligible voters participated in the poll, of whom 68.3% registered a vote in favour of the proposed compact. According to the amended regulations the result gave the Government a mandate to proceed with the adoption of the Compact of Free Association and to appoint a seven-member Transition Committee to administer the islands during the intervening period. However, opposition to the changes remained fierce, and in January 1994 two legal challenges were mounted that questioned the validity of the amendments (claiming that they should have been approved by two-thirds of Palau's legislature) and stated that the Compact's approval had been procured by coercion. The challenges were not successful, however, and on 1 October Palau achieved independence under the Compact of Free Association. At independence celebrations, which were attended by more than 300 foreign dignitaries, President Nakamura appealed to opponents of the Compact to support Palau's new status. He announced that his Government's principal concern was the regeneration of the country's economy, which he aimed to initiate with an economic programme financed by funds from the newly-implemented Compact.

Palau was admitted to the UN in December 1994. In the previous month the islands had established formal diplomatic relations with Japan.

### Government

In October 1994 Palau, the last remaining component of the Trust Territory of the Pacific Islands (a United Nations Trusteeship administered by the USA), achieved independence under the Compact of Free Association. Administrative authority, hitherto exercised by the Assistant Secretary of the Interior (Office of Territorial and International Affairs), was transferred to the Government of Palau (with the USA retaining responsibility for the islands' defence—see below).

A locally-drafted Constitution entered into effect on 1 January 1981, when the islands became known as the Republic of Palau. Under the Constitution, executive authority is vested in the President, elected by direct suffrage for a four-year term. Legislative power is exercised by the Olbiil era Kelulau (Palau National Congress), composed of the elected House of Delegates (comprising one Delegate from each of the 16 states of Palau) and the Senate (currently comprising 14 Senators).

Local governmental units are the municipalities and villages. Elected Magistrates and Councils govern the municipalities. Village government is largely traditional.

### Defence

The USA is responsible for the defence of Palau, according to the Compact of Free Association implemented in October 1994, and has exclusive military access to its waters, as well as the right to operate two military bases on the islands.

### Economic Affairs

Farming and fishing are mainly on a subsistence level, the principal agricultural crops being coconuts, cassava, bananas and sweet potatoes. Fishing licences are sold to foreign fleets, including those of Taiwan, the USA, Japan and the Philippines. The tourist industry, by comparison, is an important source of foreign exchange, although the difficulty of gaining access to the islands, and a lack of suitable facilities, have hindered its development. In 1994 some 44,073 tourists visited the islands (an increase of 34% compared with 1990).

Financial assistance from the USA contributes a large part (estimated at more than 90% in 1990) of the islands' external revenue. Furthermore, upon implementation of the Compact of Free Association with the USA, Palau became eligible for an initial grant of US $141m. and for annual aid of $23m. over a period of 14 years. Palau's gross domestic product (GDP) per head, which was estimated at $5,000 in 1992, is among the highest in the region. However, the islands' economic development has been severely restricted by a lack of investment. There is a persistent budget deficit (totalling some $5m. in 1987), and in early 1989 external debt reached almost $100m. Inflation averaged between 8% and 10% annually in the early 1990s.

In 1991 private Japanese development aid worth some US $150m. was secured, with the aim of beginning the development of Babeldaob island. With the agreement of three state governments and the approval of the national government, a Japanese-dominated consortium was to build an international airport (and operate it for about 30 years to recoup its expenditure) in central Babeldaob and a road system connecting it to Koror. However, the project was not expected to be undertaken until termination of the Trusteeship. In October 1987 Palau signed the Multilateral Fisheries Treaty, concluded by the USA and member states of the South Pacific Forum in April of that year. However, Palau is believed to lose significant amounts of potential revenue through illegal fishing activity. Palauan officials have claimed that US authorities in the region have ignored repeated violations of the islands' waters by Indonesian vessels. In response to this problem, in 1995 the Australian Government agreed to provide a patrol boat by the end of 1996, in order that Palau may monitor its 200-mile economic zone more effectively.

It was hoped that substantial aid payments from the US Government following the implementation of the Compact of Free Association in October 1994 would alleviate the increasingly severe financial crisis in Palau. The Government announced a series of economic measures, which it aimed to introduce with the aid of the newly-released funds. These measures included reducing the size of the public sector (which engaged some 57% of employed Palauans in 1993), incentives to encourage the return of nationals working overseas (principally in the USA and the Northern Mariana Islands) and several projects aimed at encouraging growth in the tourist industry. Plans to establish small-scale industries were envisaged, particularly the manufacture of garments; however, any such projects were expected to rely heavily on imported labour.

### Social Welfare

In 1981 the Trust Territory of the Pacific Islands (including Palau, the Northern Mariana Islands and the Federated States of Micronesia) had nine hospitals, with a total of 629 beds, and there were 55 physicians working in the islands.

### Education

Education is compulsory for children between the ages of six and 14 years. In 1990 there were 22 public elementary schools in Palau, with 2,125 pupils (there were also 369 pupils attending private elementary schools). After eight years of compulsory elementary education, a pupil may enrol in the government-operated high school or one of the five private (church-affiliated) high schools. In 1990 there were 610 students at the government high school, and in 1989 there were 445 at private high schools. The Micronesian Occupational College, based in Palau, provides two-year training programmes.

### Weights and Measures

With certain exceptions, the imperial system is in force. One US cwt equals 100 lb; one long ton equals 2,240 lb; one short ton equals 2,000 lb. A policy of gradual voluntary conversion to the metric system is being undertaken.

# Statistical Survey

### AREA AND POPULATION
**Area:** 508 sq km (196 sq miles); Babeldaob island 409 sq km (158 sq miles).
**Population:** 15,122 at cenus of 1990; 16,000 (official estimate) at mid-1993.
**Density** (1993): 31.5 per sq km (81.6 per sq mile).
**Births and Deaths** (1990): Birth rate 24.5 per 1,000; Death rate 11.0 per 1,000. Source: UN, *Statistical Yearbook for Asia and the Pacific*.
**Expectation of Life** (years at birth, 1989): 61.5 (males 59.6; females 63.3). Source: UN, *Statistical Yearbook of Asia and the Pacific*.

### AGRICULTURE, ETC.
**Fishing** (metric tons, live weight): Total catch 3,894 (FAO estimate) in 1990; 4,068 in 1991; 4,068 (FAO estimate) in 1992. Source: FAO, *Yearbook of Fishery Statistics*.

### FINANCE
**Currency and Exchange Rates:** United States currency is used: 100 cents = 1 United States dollar (US $). *Sterling Equivalents* (31 December 1994): £1 sterling = US $1.5645; US $100 = £63.92.

### EXTERNAL TRADE
**1984** (estimates): Imports US $288.2m. Exports $0.46m. (including trochus, tuna, copra, handicrafts).
(For further statistics, see chapter on the Marshall Islands.)

### TOURISM
**Tourist Arrivals:** 19,383 in 1989; 32,846 in 1990; 44,073 in 1994.

### COMMUNICATIONS MEDIA
**Radio Receivers** (1990): 4,321 in use.
**Television Receivers** (1990): 1,668 in use.

### EDUCATION
**Primary** (1990): 2,125 pupils (369 at private schools); 184 teachers (1980).
**Secondary** (1990): 610 pupils (445 at private schools); 104 teachers (1980).
**Tertiary** (1986): 305 students.

# Directory

## The Constitution

In October 1994 Palau, the last remaining component of the Trust Territory of the Pacific Islands (a United Nations Trusteeship administered by the USA), achieved independence under the Compact of Free Association. Full responsibility for defence lies with the USA, which undertakes to provide regular economic assistance.

From 1986 the three polities of the Commonwealth of the Northern Mariana Islands, the Republic of the Marshall Islands and the Federated States of Micronesia ceased, *de facto*, to be partof the Trust Territory. In December 1990 the United Nations Security Council agreed formally to terminate the Trusteeship Agreement for all the territories except Palau. The agreement with Palau was finally terminated in October 1994.

The islands became known as the Republic of Palau when the locally-drafted Constitution came into effect on 1 January 1981. The Constitution provides for a democratic form of government, with executive authority vested in the directly-elected President and Vice-President. Presidential elections are held every four years. Legislative power is exercised by the Olbiil era Kelulau, the Palau National Congress, which is an elected body consisting of the Senate and the House of Delegates. The Senators represent geographical districts, determined by an independent reapportionment commission every eight years, according to population. There are currently 14 Senators (four from the northern part of Palau, nine from Koror and one from the southern islands). There are 16 Delegates, one elected to represent each of the 16 states of the Republic. The states are: Kayangel, Ngerchelong, Ngaraard, Ngardmau, Ngaremlengui, Ngiwal, Melekeok, Ngchesar, Ngatpang, Aimeliik, Airai, Koror, Peleliu, Angaur, Sonsorol and Tobi. Each state elects its own Governor and legislature.

## The Government

### HEAD OF STATE
**President:** KUNIWO NAKAMURA (took office 1 January 1993).
**Vice-President:** THOMAS REMENGESAU.

### THE CABINET
(June 1995)

**Vice-President and Minister of Justice:** THOMAS REMENGESAU.
**Minister of Administration:** SANDRA PIERANTOZZI.
**Minister of National Resources:** WILHELM RENJILL.
**Minister of Social Services:** NOBUO SWEI.
**Minister of State:** ANDRES UHERBELAU.

### COUNCIL OF CHIEFS
The Constitution provides for an advisory body for the President, comprised of the 16 highest traditional chiefs from the 16 states. They advise on all traditional laws and customs, and any other public matter in which their participation is required.
**Chairman:** Ibedul YUTAKA GIBBONS (Koror).

### GOVERNMENT OFFICES
**Office of the President:** POB 100, Koror, PW 96940; tel. 488-2702; fax 488-1725.
**Department of the Interior, Office of Territorial and International Affairs (OTIA):** OTIA Field Office, POB 6031, Koror, PW 96940; tel. 488-2655; fax 488-2649; Dir J. VICTOR HOBSON, Jr.
All national government offices are based in Koror. Each state has its own administrative headquarters.

## President and Legislature

### PRESIDENT
Election, 4 November 1992

| Candidate | Votes | % |
| --- | --- | --- |
| KUNIWO NAKAMURA | 4,848 | 50.7 |
| JOHNSON TORIBIONG | 4,707 | 49.3 |
| Total | 9,555 | 100.0 |

### OLBIIL ERA KELULAU
(Palau National Congress)
**President of the Senate:** JOSHUA KOSHIBA.
**Speaker of the House of Delegates:** SURANGEL WHIPPS.

## Political Organizations

**Coalition for Open, Honest and Just Government:** c/o Olbiil era Lelulau, Koror, PW 96940; anti-nuclear, opposes the Compact of Free Association.
**Ta Belau Party:** c/o Olbiil era Lelulau, Koror, PW 96940; advocates the Compact of Free Association.

## Diplomatic Representation

### EMBASSY IN PALAU
**USA:** POB 6028, Koror, PW 96940; tel. 488-2920; fax 488-2911; Ambassador: RICHARD G. WATKINS.

## Judicial System

The judicial system of the Republic of Palau consists of the Supreme Court (including Trial and Appellate Divisions), presided over by the Chief Justice, the National Court and the Court of Common Pleas.

**Supreme Court of the Republic of Palau:** POB 248, Koror, PW 96940; tel. 488-2482; fax 488-1597; Chief Justice ARTHUR NGIRAKLSONG.

## Religion

The population is predominantly Christian, mainly Roman Catholic. The Assembly of God, Baptists, Seventh-day Adventists, the Church of Jesus Christ of Latter-day Saints (Mormons), and the Bahá'í and Modignai or Modeknai faiths are also represented.

### CHRISTIANITY
#### The Roman Catholic Church

Palau forms part of the diocese of the Caroline Islands, suffragan to the archdiocese of Agaña (Guam). The Bishop, who is resident in Chuuk, Eastern Caroline Islands (see Federated States of Micronesia), participates in the Catholic Bishops' Conference of the Pacific, based in Suva, Fiji.

### MODIGNAI FAITH

**Modignai Church:** Koror, PW 96940; an indigenous, non-Christian religion; also operates a high school.

## The Press

**Palau Gazette:** POB 100, Koror, PW 96940; tel. 488-2403; fax 488-1662; newsletter publ. by Palau Govt; monthly.

## Radio and Television

There were an estimated 4,321 radio receivers and 1,668 television receivers in use in 1990.

### RADIO

**Palau National Communications Corpn:** POB 279, Koror, PW 96940; tel. 488-2417; telex 8902; fax 488-1432; mem. of the Pacific Islands Broadcasting Asscn; operates station WSZB; broadcasts American, Japanese and Micronesian music; 18 hours a day on weekdays and 16 hours on Sundays; Man. ALBERT SALUSTIANO.

**WSZB Broadcasting Station:** POB 99, Koror, PW 96940; tel. 488-2417; fax 488-1725; Station Man. ALBERT SALUSTIANO.

### TELEVISION

**STV-TV Koror:** POB 2000, Koror, PW 96940; tel. 488-1357; telex 8930; fax 488-1207; broadcasts 12 hours daily; Man. DAVID NOLAN; Technical Man. RAY OMELEN.

**UMDA Cable TV:** Koror, PW 96940; owned by the United Micronesian Development Asscn.

## Finance

(cap. = capital; res = reserves; amounts in US dollars)

### BANKING

**Bank of Guam** (USA): Koror, PW 96940.

**Bank of Hawaii** (USA): POB 340, Koror, PW 96940; tel. 488-2602; telex 8910; fax 488-2427.

**National Development Bank of Palau:** POB 816, Koror, PW 96940; tel. 488-2578; f. 1982; cap. and res 3.1m. (Sept. 1993); Chair. MASAMI ELBELAU.

There are also 22 registered credit unions, with 1,025 members in 1990, but they have been severely affected by the financial crisis in Palau.

### INSURANCE

**NECO Insurance Co:** POB 129, Koror, PW 96940.

**Poltalia National Insurance:** POB 12, Koror, PW 96940; tel. 488-2254; telex 8909.

## Trade and Industry

### CHAMBER OF COMMERCE

**Palau Chamber of Commerce:** Koror, PW 96940; f. 1984; Pres. (vacant).

### CO-OPERATIVES

These include the Palau Fishermen's Co-operative, Palau Boat-builders' Asscn, Palau Handicraft and Woodworkers' Guild. In 1990, of the 13 registered co-operatives, eight were fishermen's co-operatives, three consumers' co-operatives (only two in normal operation) and two farmers' co-operatives (one in normal operation).

## Transport

### ROADS

Macadam and concrete roads are found in the more important islands. Other islands have stone and coral-surfaced roads and tracks. The national government is responsible for 36 km (22 miles) of paved roads and 25 km (15 miles) of coral- and gravel-surfaced roads. Most paved roads are located on Koror and are in a poor state of repair.

### SHIPPING

Most shipping in Palau is government-organized. However, the Micronesia Transport Line operates a service from Sydney (Australia) to Palau. There is one commercial port at Malakal Harbor.

### CIVIL AVIATION

There is an international airport in the south of Babeldaob island, in Airai state, near Koror, and domestic airfields (former Japanese military airstrips) on Angaur and Peleliu. Air Micronesia (Guam) provides the only regular international service. There is one domestic carrier.

**Palau Paradise Air:** Palau Int. Airport, Airai State, Babeldaob, PW 96940; internal services to Peleliu and Angaur.

## Tourism

The tourist industry is becoming increasingly important in Palau, though development is restricted by the limited infrastructure. The islands are particularly rich in their marine environment, and the Government has taken steps to conserve and protect these natural resources. The myriad Rock Islands, now known as the Floating Garden Islands, are a noted reserve in the lagoon to the west of the main group of islands. By 1994 there were an estimated 652 hotel rooms and some 44,073 visitor arrivals.

**Palau Visitors Authority:** POB 256, Koror, PW 96940; tel. 488-2793; fax 488-1453; Man. Dir MARY ANN DELEMEL.

# PANAMA

## Introductory Survey

### Location, Climate, Language, Religion, Flag, Capital

The Republic of Panama is a narrow country situated at the southern end of the isthmus separating North and South America. It is bounded to the west by Costa Rica and to the east by Colombia in South America. The Caribbean Sea is to the north, and the Pacific Ocean to the south. Panama has a tropical maritime climate (warm, humid days and cool nights). There is little seasonal variation in temperatures, which average 23°C–27°C (73°F–81°F) in coastal areas. The rainy season is from April until December. Spanish is the official language. Almost all of the inhabitants profess Christianity, and some 85% are Roman Catholics. The national flag (proportions 3 by 2) is composed of four equal rectangles: on the top row the quarter at the hoist is white, with a five-pointed blue star in the centre, while the quarter in the fly is red; on the bottom row the quarter at the hoist is blue, and the quarter in the fly is white, with a five-pointed red star in the centre. The capital is Panamá (Panama City).

### Recent History

Panama was subject to Spanish rule from the 16th century until 1821, when it became independent as part of Gran Colombia. Panama remained part of Colombia until 1903, when it declared its separate independence with the support of the USA. In that year the USA purchased the concession for construction of the Panama Canal, which was opened in 1914. The 82 km Canal links the Atlantic and Pacific Oceans, and is a major international sea route. Under the terms of the 1903 treaty between Panama and the USA concerning the construction and administration of the Canal, the USA was granted ('in perpetuity') control of a strip of Panamanian territory, known as the Canal Zone, extending for 8 km on either side of the Canal route. The treaty also established Panama as a protectorate of the USA. In exchange for transferring the Canal Zone, Panama was to receive an annuity from the USA. The terms of this treaty and its successors have dominated relations between Panama and the USA since 1903.

The early years of Panama's independence were characterized by frequent changes of government. In 1939 a revised treaty with the USA ended Panama's protectorate status. A new Constitution for Panama was adopted in 1946. Following a period of rapidly changing governments, the 1952 presidential election was won by Col José Antonio Remón, formerly Chief of Police. During his term of office, President Remón negotiated a more favourable treaty with the USA, whereby the annuity payable to Panama was increased. In January 1955, however, before the treaty came into force, Remón was assassinated. He was succeeded by José Ramón Guizado, hitherto the First Vice-President, but, less than two weeks after assuming power, the new President was implicated in the plot to murder his predecessor. Guizado was removed from office and later imprisoned. Remón's Second Vice-President, Ricardo Arias Espinosa, then completed the presidential term, which expired in 1956, when Ernesto de la Guardia was elected President. The next presidential election was won by Roberto Chiari, who held office in 1960–64, and his successor was Marco Aurelio Robles (1964–68). During this period there were frequent public demands for the transfer to Panama of sovereignty over the Canal Zone.

Presidential and legislative elections took place in May 1968. Following a strongly contested campaign, the presidential election was won by Dr Arnulfo Arias Madrid, the candidate supported by the coalition Unión Nacional (which included his own Partido Panameñista). Dr Arias had been President for two previous terms, in 1940–41 and 1949–51, but both terms had ended in his forcible removal from power. He took office for a third term in October 1968 but, after only 11 days, he was deposed by the National Guard (Panama's only military body), led by Col (later Brig.-Gen.) Omar Torrijos Herrera, who accused President Arias of planning to establish a dictatorship. The Asamblea Nacional (National Assembly) was dissolved, and political activity suspended. Political parties were banned in February 1969.

Elections were conducted in August 1972 for a new legislative body, the 505-member Asamblea Nacional de Corregidores (National Assembly of Community Representatives). In October the Asamblea conferred extraordinary powers on Gen. Torrijos as Chief of Government for six years. Considerable agrarian reform was undertaken by the Torrijos administration.

In February 1974 representatives of Panama and the USA concluded an agreement on principles for a new treaty whereby the USA would surrender its jurisdiction over the Canal Zone. Negotiations, however, continued for a further three years. Discontent arising from the Government's handling of the negotiations, combined with deteriorating living standards, culminated in student riots in 1976. Intensified negotiations in 1977 resulted in two new Canal treaties, which were approved by 66% of voters in a referendum, conducted in October. The treaties were conditionally approved by the US Senate in March and April 1978, and became effective from October 1979. Panama assumed control of the former Canal Zone, which was abolished. The Canal was placed under a joint body, the Panama Canal Commission, until the end of 1999. The USA was to retain majority representation on the Commission until 1989. US military forces in Panama (who numbered about 7,100 in 1994), were to remain until the year 2000, and the USA was to be entitled to defend the Canal's neutrality thereafter.

In August 1978 a new Asamblea Nacional de Corregidores was elected. In October the new representatives elected Dr Arístides Royo Sánchez, the Minister of Education since 1973, to be President for a six-year term. Gen. Torrijos resigned as Chief of Government but continued in the post of Commander of the National Guard, and effectively retained power until his death in an air crash in July 1981. President Royo failed to gain the support of the National Guard, and in July 1982 he was forced to resign by Col Rubén Darío Paredes, who had ousted Col Florencio Flores as Commander-in-Chief in March. The Vice-President, Ricardo de la Espriella, was installed as President, and, under the direction of Col Paredes, promoted business interests and pursued a foreign policy more favourable to the USA.

In April 1983 a series of amendments to the Constitution were approved by referendum. However, in spite of new constitutional moves to limit the power of the National Guard, *de facto* power remained with the armed forces, whose position was strengthened by a decision in September to unite all security forces within one organization (subsequently known as the National Defence Forces). In June Col Paredes was succeeded as Commander-in-Chief by Brig. (later Gen.) Manuel Antonio Noriega Morena. In February 1984 Dr Jorge Illueca, hitherto the Vice-President, became Head of State after the sudden resignation of President de la Espriella, who was believed to have been ousted from power by the National Defence Forces.

Elections to the presidency and the legislature (the new 67-member Asamblea Legislativa—Legislative Assembly) took place on 6 May 1984. The principal candidates in the presidential contest were Dr Nicolás Ardito Barletta, a former Minister of Planning and the candidate of the Partido Revolucionario Democrática (PRD), supported by the armed forces, and Dr Arias Madrid, the candidate of the Partido Panameñista Auténtico (PPA) and a long-standing opponent of the armed forces. Despite allegations of extensive electoral fraud, Dr Ardito was eventually declared President-elect, defeating Dr Arias by a narrow margin. Controversy concerning the election results persisted throughout 1984, reinforcing indications of internal instability that had emerged following the elections, and resulting in the polarization of public opinion.

The new Government took office in October 1984, committed to arresting Panama's economic decline. However, as a result of protracted opposition to his economic policies, President Ardito was unable to secure a political base to support his administration, and his position became increasingly isolated. In September 1985 Dr Ardito resigned. Although he claimed that his resignation had been prompted by the deterioration in his relations with the legislature and with the National Defence Forces, there was considerable speculation that he had been forced to resign by Gen. Noriega, to prevent a public scandal over the alleged involvement of the National Defence Forces in the murder of Dr Hugo Spadafora, a former deputy minister under Gen. Torrijos and a leading critic of Gen. Noriega. Dr Ardito was succeeded as President in September by Eric Arturo Delvalle, formerly First Vice-President.

In June 1986 sources in the USA alleged that Gen. Noriega was involved in the trafficking of illegal drugs and weapons and in the transfer of proceeds from these activities through Panamanian banks. In addition, Noriega was implicated in the sale of US national security information and restricted technology to Cuba. There were also renewed allegations of his involvement in the murder of Dr Spadafora and in electoral fraud during the 1984 presidential election. These allegations precipitated strikes and demonstrations, in support of opposition demands for Gen. Noriega's dismissal, which resulted in violent clashes with the National Defence Forces.

Following the outbreak of violence, the US Senate approved a resolution urging the establishment of democracy in Panama, the suspension of Gen. Noriega and the holding of an independent investigation into the allegations against him. The Panamanian Government responded by accusing the USA of interfering in Panamanian affairs, and a wave of anti-US sentiment was unleashed, including an attack on the US embassy by protesters at the beginning of July. Following this incident, the USA suspended economic and military aid to Panama and downgraded its official links with the country. Protests against Gen. Noriega continued throughout the second half of 1987, in an atmosphere of mounting political and economic insecurity. In late 1987 pressure on the Panamanian administration increased, as the investigations by two US Grand Juries into Gen. Noriega's activities yielded further evidence of his involvement in drugs-trafficking and 'laundering' of illicitly-gained funds. Many observers regarded the revelations as part of a concerted campaign by the US administration to oust Noriega: they included statements linking him with Lt-Col Oliver North (a leading figure in the 'Iran-Contra' affair, see Recent History of USA); claims that Gen. Noriega offered to undertake acts of sabotage and assassinations in Nicaragua on behalf of the USA; and testimonies that he had received an estimated US $4,600m. from his drugs-trafficking activities (including allowing the so-called Medellín cartel of cocaine dealers from Colombia to conduct operations from Panama, and to use Panamanian financial institutions to 'launder' their profits).

In February 1988 Gen. Noriega was indicted by both US Grand Juries on charges of drugs smuggling and racketeering. On 25 February President Delvalle dismissed Gen. Noriega from his post, following his refusal to resign voluntarily. However, leading members of the ruling coalition and the National Defence Forces united in support of Gen. Noriega, and on the following day the Asamblea Legislativa voted to remove President Delvalle from office because of his 'failure to abide by the Constitution'. The Minister of Education, Manuel Solís Palma, was appointed acting President. Delvalle refused to accept his dismissal, and the US administration affirmed its support for the ousted President by declining to recognize the new leadership. Delvalle, who went into hiding, became the figurehead of the USA's attempts to remove Gen. Noriega, and in late February, following Delvalle's demand that the US Government should impose an economic boycott on Panama, US courts authorized a 'freeze' on some US $50m. of Panamanian assets held in US banks. This move, coupled with the general strike organized by the Cruzada Civilista Nacional (a broad-based opposition grouping led by the business sector) after Delvalle's dismissal, brought economic chaos to Panama, prompting the closure of all banks for more than two months.

On 16 March 1988 a coup attempt by the chief of police, Col Leónidas Macías, was thwarted by members of the National Defence Forces loyal to Gen. Noriega. However, the coup attempt represented the first indication of opposition to Gen. Noriega from within the armed forces. Subsequently, the Government announced a state of emergency (which was revoked in April) and the suspension of civil rights. Negotiations between Gen. Noriega and a representative of the US administration, during which the USA was reported to have proposed the withdrawal of charges against the General in exchange for his retirement and departure into exile before the elections scheduled for 1989, ended acrimoniously in late March.

During 1988 attempts by the US administration to force greater compliance from Gen. Noriega, through the imposition of several economic sanctions against Panamanian interests, were largely undermined by a succession of inconsistent US policy decisions regarding Panama. The ambiguous nature of the USA's policy on Panama was widely regarded as indicative of the administration's frustration at failing to engineer Gen. Noriega's removal from office.

The election campaign for the presidential, legislative and municipal elections, scheduled for May 1989, was initiated in October 1988. The pro-Government electoral alliance, the Coalición de Liberación Nacional (COLINA), selected a close associate of Gen. Noriega, Carlos Duque Jaén (the leader of the PRD), as its candidate for the presidential contest. The opposition alliance, the Alianza Democrática de Oposición Civilista (ADOC), nominated Guillermo Endara Galimany of the PPA as its presidential candidate. Events during the months preceding the presidential and legislative elections were dominated by accusations of electoral malpractice, and, following the elections (held on 7 May 1989), both ADOC and COLINA claimed victory, despite indications from exit polls and unofficial sources that ADOC had received between 50% and 75% of votes cast. A group of international observers, including the former US President, Jimmy Carter, declared that the election had been conducted fraudulently. A delay in announcing the results of the election was interpreted by the opposition as an attempt by the Government to falsify the outcome. Endara declared himself to be President-elect; in subsequent demonstrations crowds clashed with units of the National Defence Forces, and many members of the opposition, including Endara and other leaders, were savagely beaten. On 10 May the election results were annulled by the Electoral Tribunal, citing US interference. A one-day general strike, advocated by ADOC in opposition to the annulment, attracted only limited support.

Later in May 1989 a delegation of the Organization of American States (OAS—see p. 204) entered into negotiations with ADOC, COLINA and members of the National Defence Forces, but discussions throughout June and July failed to produce an agreement. A declaration was finally drafted by the OAS, urging that a transitional government should be installed by 1 September and that new elections should be conducted as soon as possible. On 31 August Panama's General State Council announced the appointment of a provisional Government and a 41-member Legislative Commission to preserve 'institutional order'. The holding of elections was to be considered within six months, but this was to be largely dependent upon the cessation of US 'hostilities' and the withdrawal of US economic sanctions. On 1 September Francisco Rodríguez, a known associate of Gen. Noriega, and Carlos Ozores Typaldos were inaugurated as President and Vice-President respectively. The USA immediately severed diplomatic relations with Panama and expressed its intention to impose stricter economic sanctions upon the new Government, including a ban on the use of US ports by Panamanian-registered ships (which was implemented later in the year).

In October 1989 an attempted coup, led by middle-ranking officers intending to replace Gen. Noriega at the head of the *de facto* military dictatorship, was suppressed when forces loyal to the General surrounded the insurgents who had captured Gen. Noriega and forced his release. The Government claimed that about 12 rebels had been killed during the fighting, although human rights organizations estimated the death toll at 77, several of whom, it was claimed, had been executed after capture.

In November 1989 the Asamblea Nacional de Corregidores was provisionally re-established. This body, now numbering 510 members, had previously existed between 1972 and 1983, and was intended to fulfil a consultative and (limited) legislative function. Gen. Noriega was elected as its 'national coordinator'. In December relations between the USA and Panama were severely strained, following several incidents in which members of the armed forces from both countries were injured and intimidated in Panama. In that month a resolution adopted by the Asamblea declared Gen. Noriega to be Head of State and 'leader of the struggle for national liberation', and announced that a state of war existed with the USA.

On 20 December 1989 a US military offensive entitled 'Operation Just Cause', involving some 24,000 troops, was launched against Gen. Noriega and the headquarters of the National Defence Forces from US bases within Panama. The objectives of the assault were swiftly brought under US control, although sporadic attacks on US bases by loyalist forces continued for several days, and Gen. Noriega eluded capture long enough to take refuge in the residence of the Papal Nuncio in Panama. On 21 December Endara, who had been installed as Head of State in a ceremony attended by a Panamanian judge at the Fort Clayton US military base only hours before the invasion, was officially inaugurated as President. President Endara declared that the Panamanian judicial system was inadequate to try Gen. Noriega. Following his surrender to US forces in January 1990, Gen. Noriega was immediately transported to the USA and arraigned in Florida on several charges of involvement in drugs-trafficking and 'money-laundering' operations. Gen. Noriega, who claimed the status of a prisoner of war, refused to recognize the right of jurisdiction of a US court. The trial, delayed by legal and procedural complications, finally began in September 1991, and in April 1992 Gen. Noriega was found guilty on eight charges of conspiracy to manufacture and distribute cocaine. In July 1992 Noriega was sentenced to 40 years' imprisonment.

International criticism of the USA's military operation was widespread, despite the administration's citation of the right to self-defence, under Article 51 of the UN Charter, as a legal justification for armed intervention, and US President George Bush's assertion that military action was necessary for the protection of US citizens, the protection of the Panama Canal, support for Panama's 'democratically elected' officials and the pursuit of an indicted criminal. Relations with Latin America in general, and with Cuba, Nicaragua and Peru in particular, were severely strained. Several countries refused to recognize the new Government, at least until all US troops used in the operation had been withdrawn (which occurred by the end of February 1990). In December 1989 the UN General Assembly adopted a resolution deploring the US military intervention as a flagrant violation of international law. According to the US Government, 'Operation Just Cause' resulted in about 500 Panamanian casualties, but a total of at least 1,000 Panamanian deaths was estimated by the Roman Catholic Church and other unofficial sources. Twenty-six US troops were killed, and more than 300 wounded, during the invasion.

In December 1989, following the appointment of a new Cabinet (comprising members of the Movimiento Liberal Republicano Nacionalista—MOLIRENA, the Partido Demócrata Cristiano—PDC, and the Partido Liberal Auténtico—PLA, all part of the ADOC alliance), the Endara administration declared itself to be a 'democratic Government of reconstruction and national reconciliation'. Later in the same month, the Electoral Tribunal revoked its annulment of the elections of May 1989, and announced that ADOC had obtained 62% of the votes cast in the presidential election, according to copies of incomplete results (covering 64% of total votes) that had been held in safe keeping by the Episcopal Conference of the Roman Catholic Church. In February 1990 the composition of the Asamblea Legislativa was announced, based on the same evidence, with 51 seats awarded to ADOC and six to COLINA, while fresh elections were to be held for nine seats which could not be reliably allocated. The National Defence Forces were officially disbanded, and a new 'non-political' Public Force was created.

Although the overthrow of Gen. Noriega immediately released US $375m. in assets that had previously been withheld by the US Government, the new administration inherited serious economic difficulties. The cost of 'Operation Just Cause', in terms of damage and lost revenues alone, was estimated to be at least US $2,000m. Although the Bush administration agreed to provide aid amounting to more than $1,000m., the US Congress was slow to approve the appropriation of funds, and the deteriorating economic situation in Panama was highlighted when President Endara embarked upon a 13-day 'solidarity' fast in March 1990. In April President Bush revoked the economic restrictions that had been imposed two years previously, and in May the US Congress approved the extension to Panama of financial assistance totalling $420m. Of this amount, $130m. was to be used for outstanding debt repayments, while the disbursement of a further substantial tranche was to be dependent upon the successful negotiation of a Mutual Legal Assistance Treaty (MLAT) between the two countries, whereby the US authorities sought to gain greater access to information amassed by Panama City's 'offshore' international finance centre, in order to combat the illegal 'laundering' of money obtained through drugs-related activities. Leading Panamanian bankers denounced the terms of the treaty as being detrimental to the banking sector, and demanded an alternative accord which would guarantee 'judicial sovereignty', suggesting that it was the underlying intention of the US authorities to invoke the treaty in order to curtail tax evasion by US citizens in the region.

In August 1990 the Government announced its 'Strategy of Development and Economic Modernization', which included provisions for the transfer to private ownership of several state-controlled enterprises. The new economic measures encountered vociferous political opposition from the PDC (one of the parties in the ruling coalition), and prompted widespread disaffection among public-sector workers whose jobs were threatened by the short-term divestment programme.

Accusations from public and political opponents that the security forces had not been adequately purged following the removal of Gen. Noriega were seemingly justified by a succession of coup attempts during the early 1990s. Growing public concern at the Government's failure to re-establish adequate civil and economic order in the aftermath of the US removal of Gen. Noriega was reflected in the results of elections held on 27 January 1991 for the nine seats in the Asamblea Legislativa which had not been awarded by the Electoral Tribunal following the elections of May 1989 (see above), together with elections for 170 local officials. Member parties of the former electoral alliance COLINA, which had supported the previous regime, secured five of the contested seats: three were won by the PRD and one each by the Partido Laborista and the Partido Liberal. Parties represented in the governing alliance secured only four seats—two for MOLIRENA and two for the PDC. The failure of President Endara's recently formed Partido Arnulfista (formerly a faction of the PPA) to secure a single seat suggested a lack of popular and political confidence in the President, following recent revelations by investigators of the US Drug Enforcement Agency of Endara's (somewhat tenuous) connection with several Panamanian concerns that were under investigation for alleged participation in drugs-related activities. Serious concern was also expressed at the increasing level of influence exerted by the US Government over the President, particularly when it became known that in July 1990 the Government had accepted US funds to establish, by decree, a 100-strong Council for Public Security, which would maintain close links with the US Central Intelligence Agency.

Long-standing political differences within the Government reached a crisis in mid-March 1991, when the PDC initiated proceedings to impeach President Endara for involving the US armed forces in suppressing an uprising in December 1990 (a technical violation of the 1977 Panama Canal Treaty). Although the proposal was dismissed by the Asamblea Legislativa (since his action had been widely considered to be justifiable at the time of the uprising), President Endara and his supporters strongly criticized leaders of the PDC, accusing them of participating in illegal activities to gather intelligence information and of obtaining armaments in preparation for a coup attempt. The PDC, which had repeatedly expressed reservations concerning aspects of government policy (particularly regarding the economy and judicial procedure), threatened to withdraw from the governing alliance, but were pre-empted by President Endara's decision, taken in early April 1991, to dismiss the five PDC members of his Cabinet, including the First Vice-President, Ricardo Arias Calderón, who had occupied the Government and Justice portfolio. Arias Calderón retained the vice-presidency, however, since he had been elected to the position in May 1989. Endara significantly increased the representation of his own Partido Arnulfista in the Cabinet.

In July 1991 the Asamblea Legislativa approved the terms of the MLAT, following indications in US intelligence documents that drugs-related activities in Panama (and money-laundering in particular) had returned to the levels that had existed prior to the removal of Gen. Noriega. The Panamanian Government's urgent need of direct financial aid (the disbursement of which the USA had made dependent on the MLAT) prompted it to sign the treaty with only minor modifications to the terms of the agreement. In January 1992 it was reported that, as a result of a reduction in US defence expenditure, the US administration was seeking to accelerate the return of US-controlled bases in Panama to the Panamanian authorities, and hoped to transfer five of the remaining 10 bases to the Panamanians by 1995. Mounting public concern that improved economic and military relations with the USA had been achieved at the expense of domestic initiatives to counter worsening social conditions, was exacerbated when a demonstration against unemployment in Colón, in May 1992, ended in violent clashes between local demonstrators and security forces. An official visit to Panama, undertaken by US President George Bush in June, was seriously marred by anti-Government and anti-US protests, prompted by similar concerns.

In October 1991 and February 1992 two further alleged coup attempts were immediately suppressed, and resulted in the detention of several more members of the former National Defence Forces, and the creation, in March 1992, of a presidential police force to be directly responsible to the Head of State. In December 1991 constitutional reforms were approved (subject to ratification) by the Asamblea Legislativa whereby the armed forces were formally abolished (a preliminary constitutional reform to this effect had been approved in June 1991), the autonomy of the Electoral Tribunal was guaranteed, and a post of ombudsman to protect the rights of Panamanian citizens was created. In November 1992, however, the President suffered a serious political reverse, when proposals for more than 50 reforms (including the constitutional abolition of the armed forces and the creation of the post of ombudsman) were rejected by 64% of voters in a referendum organized by the Government in an attempt to consolidate popular support. Opposition groups reiterated demands for the creation of a constituent assembly to draft a new constitution, and stressed popular concerns regarding the future security of the Panama Canal in the absence of an effective Panamanian military force. Following the defeat, at the referendum, of the reform proposals for which he had campaigned, First Vice-President Arias resigned in December. Second Vice-President Guillermo Ford was duly promoted to the office of First Vice-President.

During late 1993 and early 1994 the divergent interests of the constituent parties of the Government were exaggerated by the proximity of presidential and legislative elections scheduled for May 1994. Attempts by the Government to deflect public-sector opposition to a continuing programme of economic adjustment, and widespread criticism of the involvement of the Panamanian Vice-Consul in Barcelona (Spain) in an unauthorized attempt to supply arms, purchased in the Czech Republic, to the war in the Republic of Bosnia and Herzegovina, were complicated by party political manoeuvres within the ruling coalition. In November 1993 Endara reorganized the Cabinet, replacing three ministers who had resigned in preparation for the forthcoming elections, and Julio E. Linares, the Minister of Foreign Affairs, who suffered a fatal heart attack in October. In January 1994 MOLIRENA announced its withdrawal from the ruling alliance in order to support the presidential candidature of Rubén Darío Carles, as part of the Cambio 94 alliance (also comprising the Partido Renovación Civilista—PRC and the Movimiento de Renovación Nacional—Morena), prompting a further reorganization of the Cabinet. The Alianza Democrática was subsequently formed by the President's Partido Arnulfista (in alliance with the Partido Liberal—PL, the Partido Liberal Auténtico—PLA, the Unión Democrática Independiente—UDI and the Partido Nacionalista Popular—PNP), with Mireya Moscoso de Gruber, the widow of former President Arias Madrid, as candidate for the presidency. Indications of a high level of support for Ernesto Pérez Balladares, the presidential candidate of a third electoral alliance, the Pueblo Unido (comprising the PRD, the Partido Liberal Republicano—Libre—and the Partido Laborista—PALA), prompted an opposition move to convince the Supreme Court to interpret the Constitution as providing for a second round of voting between the two most successful candidates in the first round of the presidential contest. However, this initiative was dismissed by the Supreme Court in mid-April 1994.

The presidential poll, conducted on 8 May 1994, resulted in a narrow victory for Pérez Balladares (whose campaign had concentrated on labour issues), with 33.2% of the votes cast, ahead of Moscoso de Gruber, with 29.5%, Rubén Blades (the candidate of the Movimiento Papa Egoró—MPE), with 17.2%, and Carles, with 16.2% of the votes. The failure of the Pueblo Unido alliance to secure a majority in the legislature (the PRD and its supporters won 34 of the seats in the extended, 72-seat Asamblea Legislativa) was reflected in the broad political base of Pérez Balladares' proposed cabinet, announced in May. Post-electoral political manoeuvring resulted in the creation of the Alianza Pueblo Unido y Solidaridad, Pérez Balladares' electoral alliance having secured the additional support of the Partido Solidaridad in the Asamblea. The Alianza gained another seat in the Asamblea (increasing its representation to exactly one-half of the 72 seats) following a repeat election in a district where the results had been annulled after the 8 May poll. It was expected that Rubén Blades' 'non-aligned' MPE (which had gained six seats in the legislature at the recent elections) would fulfil a crucial role in the enactment of future legislation.

In late August the outgoing legislature approved a constitutional amendment which again sought to abolish the armed forces. It seemed unlikely, however, that the amendment would promptly receive the necessary formal endorsement of the new Asamblea, since the PRD continued to express concern that a credible alternative for national defence must first be established.

Pérez Balladares assumed the presidency on 1 September 1994. A new Cabinet, installed on the same day, included former members of the PA and the PDC who had been forced to resign their party membership in order to take up their cabinet posts. (An invitation to participate in a coalition government, issued by the President-Elect in mid-May, had been rejected by the PA.) In his inaugural address, Pérez Balladares described the growth of drugs-related crime, unemployment and poverty as the immediate concerns of his administration, and he announced the initiation of a three-year social programme to address some of these problems.

The acquittal, in September 1993, of seven former soldiers tried for involvement in the brutal murder of Hugo Spadafora (see p. 2391) provoked widespread public outrage. A protest in Panama City was led by the President's wife, Ana Mae Díaz. Manuel Noriega (currently serving a 40-year prison term in the USA) was tried in connection with the affair *in absentia*. In October 1993 Noriega was found guilty and sentenced to 20 years' imprisonment for ordering Spadafora's murder. In March 1994 Noriega was also convicted *in absentia* for the murder, in 1989, of an army major who had led an unsuccessful military coup against him. In October 1994 he was sentenced to a further 20 years' imprisonment for this offence.

In mid-October 1993 President Endara signed a protocol to establish Panama's membership of the Central American Parliament (Parlacen), a regional political forum with its headquarters in Guatemala. Later in the month Endara, together with the five Presidents of the member nations of the Central American Common Market (CACM, see p. 117), signed a protocol to the 1960 General Treaty on Central American Integration, committing Panama to fuller economic integration in the region. However, at a meeting of Central American Presidents, convened in Guácimo (Costa Rica) in August 1994, President-Elect Pérez Balladares (attending as an observer) stated that his administration considered further regional economic integration to be disadvantageous to Panama, owing to the differences between Panama's services-based economy and the reliance on the agricultural sector of the other Central American states.

### Government

Legislative power is vested in the unicameral Asamblea Legislativa (Legislative Assembly), which replaced the Asamblea Nacional de Corregidores (National Assembly of Community Representatives) in 1984 (except for its brief reintroduction in late 1989), with 72 members elected for five years by universal adult suffrage. Executive power is held by the President, also directly elected for a term of five years, assisted by two elected Vice-Presidents and an appointed Cabinet. Panama is divided into nine provinces and three autonomous Indian Reservations. Each province has a governor, appointed by the President.

### Defence

In October 1983 the Legislative Council approved proposals to convert the National Guard into the National Defence Forces, with three branches. In June 1989 the National

Defence Forces numbered 4,400 men: army 3,500, navy 400 and air force 500. There were also paramilitary forces numbering 11,000. In 1990, following the overthrow of Gen. Manuel Noriega, the National Defence Forces were disbanded and a new Public Force (numbering 11,700 men in June 1994), comprising the National Police (11,000 men), the National Air Service (400 men) and the National Maritime Service (an estimated 300 men), was created. The new force was representative of the size of the population, and affiliated to no political party. Defence expenditure for 1994 was forecast at US $85.8m.

### Economic Affairs

In 1993, according to estimates by the World Bank, Panama's gross national product (GNP), measured at average 1991–93 prices, was US $6,621m., equivalent to $2,580 per head. During 1985–93, it was estimated, GNP per head decreased, in real terms, by 0.7% per year. Over the same period the population increased by an annual average of 2.0%. Panama's gross domestic product (GDP) increased, in real terms, by an annual average of 0.9% in 1980–92.

Agriculture (including hunting, forestry and fishing) contributed an estimated 9.9% of GDP in 1993, and an estimated 23.1% of the employed labour force were engaged in agriculture in that year. Rice, maize and beans are cultivated as subsistence crops, while the principal cash crops are bananas (which accounted for an estimated 39.3% of total export earnings in 1993), sugar cane and coffee. Banana production in 1991 was restricted by the adverse effects of an earthquake and drought. Cattle-raising, tropical timber and fisheries (particularly shrimps for export) are also important. During 1980–92 agricultural GDP increased by an annual average of 2.5%.

Industry (including mining, manufacturing, construction and power) contributed an estimated 19.0% of GDP in 1993, and engaged an estimated 16.4% of the employed labour force in 1992. During 1980–92 industrial GDP decreased by an annual average of 2.6%.

Mining contributed an estimated 0.2% of GDP in 1993, and engaged 0.3% of the employed labour force in 1992. Panama has significant deposits of copper and coal. The recent discovery of significant new deposits of copper and molybdenum have encouraged hopes that the value of mineral exports could rival that of bananas by 1998.

Manufacturing contributed an estimated 9.1% of GDP in 1993, and engaged an estimated 9.5% of the employed labour force in 1992. In 1989 the most important sectors, measured by gross value of output, were food-processing, petroleum refining and products (using imported petroleum), beverages, paper and paper products, chemical products, plastic products and clothing. Labour-intensive light assembly operations are conducted in the Colón Free Zone.

An estimated 73% of Panama's total output of electricity was generated by hydroelectric power in 1993.

Panama's economy is dependent upon the services sector, which contributed some 71% of GDP in 1993. The Panama Canal Commission (with some 7,500 employees) contributed about 9% of the country's GDP in 1993. Panama is an important 'offshore' financial centre, and in 1993 the banking sector contributed around 14.9% of GDP. Important contributions to the economy are also made by trade in the Colón Free Zone (which employed some 15,000 workers and contributed about 8.5% of GDP in 1994), and by the registration of merchant ships under a 'flag of convenience' in Panama.

In 1993 Panama recorded a visible trade deficit of US $853m., and there was a surplus of just $2m. on the current account of the balance of payments. In 1992 the principal source of imports (36.2%) was the USA, which was also the principal market for exports (29.4%). Other major trading partners are Japan, Costa Rica, Ecuador, Germany and Venezuela. The principal exports in 1992 were bananas, shrimps, raw sugar, clothing and coffee. The principal imports were mineral products, chemicals and chemical products, electrical and electronic equipment, foodstuffs and transport equipment.

Budget forecasts for 1993 envisaged a deficit of US $367.3m. Panama's external debt at the end of 1993 was $6,802m., of which $3,709m. was long-term public debt. In that year the cost of debt-servicing was equivalent to 9.6% of revenues derived from exports of goods and services. The average annual rate of inflation was 0.7% in 1985–93, and stood at 1.3% in 1994. An estimated 12.5% of the total labour force were unemployed in June 1994.

Panama is a member of the Inter-American Development Bank (see p. 170).

The political problems which developed between Panama and the USA in the late 1980s adversely affected most sectors of the Panamanian economy. The dependence of the Panamanian economy on four main service industries (the Panama Canal, the Colón Free Zone, open-registry shipping and 'offshore' banking) was also fully exploited by US economic sanctions. US military intervention in 1989 was estimated to have cost US $2,000m. in damage and lost revenues alone. In mid-1990 the new Endara administration announced a 'Strategy of Development and Economic Modernization', anticipating the receipt of substantial financial aid promised by the US Government. The plan aimed to create 60,000 new jobs, to transfer state enterprises to the private sector over a two-year period, to relax controls on prices and end the granting of monopolies, and to create a modern free-market economy. The Pérez Balladares administration, which took office in September 1994, outlined a five-year programme of economic modernization based on a reform of the labour code, the dismantling of trade barriers (with a view to becoming a contracting party to the General Agreement on Tariffs and Trade—GATT) and attracting greater foreign investment through renewed commitment to the privatization of major state-owned concerns, including the national ports authority and the state telecommunications company (INTEL). In real terms, GDP growth was 5.4% in 1993 and 4.7% in 1994, and was expected to be 5% in 1995, owing to vigorous trade in the Colón Free Zone and an increase in Canal revenues. Ongoing negotiations to reschedule Panama's estimated US $3,500m. commercial bank debt were expected to resume in May 1995.

### Social Welfare

The social security system provides health and retirement benefits. Both employers and employees contribute to the scheme, which is government-operated. In 1987 it was estimated that Panama had 671 medical centres, 7,798 hospital beds and 2,722 physicians. In that year the national social security system covered 1,422,200 people. Of total budgetary expenditure forecast by the central Government for 1993, an estimated 126.8m. balboas (6.9%) was for health, and a further 6.3m. balboas (0.3%) for social security and labour.

### Education

The education system is divided into elementary, secondary and university schooling, each of six years' duration. Education is free up to university level, and is officially compulsory for six years between six and 15 years of age. Primary education begins at the age of six, and secondary education, which comprises two three-year cycles, at the age of 12. The enrolment at primary schools of children in the relevant age-group was 92% in 1990, and secondary enrolment was 50% in the same year. There are three universities, with regional centres in the provinces. Adult illiteracy in 1990 was estimated at 11.2% (males 10.6%; females 11.7%): one of the lowest rates in Central America. Of total budgetary expenditure forecast by the central Government for 1993, 206.3m. balboas (11.2%) was allocated to education.

### Public Holidays

**1995:** 1 January (New Year's Day), 9 January (National Martyrs' Day), 28 February–1 March (Carnival), 14 April (Good Friday), 1 May (Labour Day), 15 August (Foundation of Panama City; Panama City only)*, 11 October (Revolution Day), 1 November (National Anthem Day)*, 2 November (All Souls' Day), 3 November (Independence from Colombia), 4 November (Flag Day)*, 6 November (for Independence Day; Colón only), 10 November (First Call of Independence), 28 November (Independence from Spain), 8 December (Immaculate Conception, Mothers' Day), 25 December (Christmas).

**1996:** 1 January (New Year's Day), 9 January (National Martyrs' Day), 20–21 February (Carnival), 5 April (Good Friday), 1 May (Labour Day), 15 August (Foundation of Panama City; Panama City only)*, 11 October (Revolution Day), 1 November (National Anthem Day)*, 2 November (All Souls' Day), 3 Nov-

# PANAMA

ember (Independence from Colombia), 4 November (Flag Day)*, 5 November (Independence Day; Colón only)*, 10 November (First Call of Independence), 28 November (Independence from Spain), 8 December (Immaculate Conception, Mothers' Day), 25 December (Christmas).

* Official holiday: banks and government offices closed.

## Weights and Measures

Both the metric and the imperial systems of weights and measures are in use. In 1972 the Government announced the gradual extension of the metric system to replace all other systems.

# Statistical Survey

Sources (unless otherwise stated): Dirección de Estadística y Censo, Contraloría General de la República, Apdo 5213, Panamá 5; tel. 64-3734; Banco Nacional de Panamá, Casa Matriz, Vía España, Apdo 5220, Panamá; tel. 63-5151; telex 2136.

Note: The former Canal Zone was incorporated into Panama on 1 October 1979.

## Area and Population

### AREA, POPULATION AND DENSITY

| | |
|---|---:|
| Area (sq km) | 75,517* |
| Population (census results)† | |
| 11 May 1980 | 1,831,399 |
| 13 May 1990 | |
| Males | 1,178,790 |
| Females | 1,150,539 |
| Total | 2,329,329 |
| Population (official estimates at mid-year) | |
| 1993 | 2,535,000 |
| 1994 | 2,583,000‡ |
| Density (per sq km) at mid-1994 | 34.2‡ |

* 29,157 sq miles.
† Excluding adjustments for underenumeration, estimated to have been 6.4% in 1980.
‡ Provisional figure.

**Principal towns** (population at 1990 census): Panamá (capital) 413,505; David 65,763; Colón 54,654.

### ADMINISTRATIVE DIVISIONS (estimated population at mid-1992)

| Province | Population | Density (per sq km) | Capital (and population) |
|---|---:|---:|---|
| Bocas del Toro | 88,385 | 10.1 | Bocas del Toro (19,953) |
| Chiriquí | 396,842 | 45.9 | David (99,811) |
| Coclé | 177,070 | 35.9 | Penonomé (61,054) |
| Colón* | 222,577 | 30.7 | Colón (137,825) |
| Darién | 45,020 | 2.7 | Chepigana (26,816) |
| Herrera | 108,714 | 46.4 | Chitré (37,914) |
| Los Santos | 82,810 | 21.8 | Las Tablas (21,792) |
| Panamá | 1,168,492 | 98.3 | Panamá (625,150) |
| Veraguas | 224,676 | 20.0 | Santiago (68,010) |

* Includes the Indian Territory of San Blas.

Note: Population figures include the former Canal Zone.

### BIRTHS, MARRIAGES AND DEATHS

| | Registered live births | | Registered marriages | | Registered deaths | |
|---|---:|---:|---:|---:|---:|---:|
| | Number | Rate (per 1,000) | Number | Rate (per 1,000) | Number | Rate (per 1,000) |
| 1985 | 58,038 | 26.6 | 12,430 | 5.7 | 8,991 | 4.1 |
| 1986 | 57,655 | 25.9 | 12,104 | 5.4 | 8,942 | 4.0 |
| 1987 | 57,647 | 25.3 | 11,188 | 5.2 | 9,105 | 4.0 |
| 1988 | 58,459 | 25.2 | 11,060 | 5.0 | 9,382 | 4.0 |
| 1989 | 59,069 | 24.9 | 11,173 | 5.0 | 9,557 | 4.0 |
| 1990 | 59,904 | 24.8 | 12,117 | 5.3 | 9,799 | 4.1 |
| 1991 | 60,080 | 24.4 | 11,714 | 5.0 | 9,683 | 3.9 |
| 1992* | 60,925 | 24.2 | 12,547 | 5.3 | 9,977 | 4.0 |

* Estimates.

**Expectation of life** (UN estimates, years at birth, 1985–90): 72.0 (males 70.1; females 74.1).

### EMPLOYMENT (persons aged 15 years and over, labour force sample surveys at August each year)*

| | 1989 | 1991 | 1992† |
|---|---:|---:|---:|
| Agriculture, hunting, forestry and fishing | 199,578 | 191,830 | 209,099 |
| Mining and quarrying | 278 | 756 | 2,112 |
| Manufacturing | 69,779 | 69,334 | 75,505 |
| Electricity, gas and water | 9,648 | 8,782 | 9,818 |
| Construction | 21,143 | 25,946 | 42,968 |
| Trade, restaurants and hotels | 123,001 | 142,973 | 157,346 |
| Transport, storage and communications | 40,158 | 49,675 | 47,344 |
| Finance, insurance, real estate and business services | 24,903 | 30,032 | 35,619 |
| Community, social and personal services | 196,439 | 196,608 | 210,357 |
| Extraterritorial activities | 1,407 | 3,634 | 3,901 |
| Activities not adequately defined | — | 530 | 1,045 |
| **Total** | **686,334** | **720,100** | **795,114** |
| Males | 473,181 | 495,226 | 560,538 |
| Females | 213,153 | 224,874 | 234,576 |

* Figures exclude indigenous areas, the Canal Zone and permanent residents of collective dwellings.
† Preliminary.

## Agriculture

### PRINCIPAL CROPS ('000 quintales)*

| | 1990/91 | 1991/92 | 1992/93 |
|---|---:|---:|---:|
| Beans | 95.0 | 104.8 | 112.7 |
| Coffee | 240.6 | 253.8 | 226.4 |
| Maize | 2,067.1 | 2,257.9 | 2,321.5 |
| Rice | 4,763.6 | 4,343.6 | 4,377.0 |
| Sugar cane | 28,037.3 | 36,595.9 | 36,311.0 |
| Tobacco | 39.2 | 57.1 | 54.7 |

* Figures are in terms of the old Spanish quintal, equal to 46 kg (101.4 lb).

Bananas ('000 metric tons): 898 in 1990; 850 in 1991; 829 in 1992.

### LIVESTOCK ('000 head)

| | 1990 | 1991 | 1992 |
|---|---:|---:|---:|
| Cattle | 1,388.0 | 1,399.5 | 1,427.2 |
| Pigs | 226.3 | 256.4 | 292.4 |
| Chickens | 6,916.9 | 9,387.1 | 8,376.6 |

### LIVESTOCK PRODUCTS (metric tons, provisional figures)

| | 1990 | 1991 | 1992 |
|---|---:|---:|---:|
| Eggs | 10,725.5 | 11,849.7 | 12,437.5 |
| Milk | 124,066.1 | 139,517.6 | 136,183.8 |

PANAMA  *Statistical Survey*

## Forestry

**ROUNDWOOD REMOVALS** ('000 cubic metres, excluding bark)

|  | 1990 | 1991 | 1992 |
|---|---|---|---|
| Sawlogs, veneer logs and logs for sleepers | 46* | 30 | 58 |
| Other industrial wood* | 60 | 60 | 60 |
| Fuel wood* | 875 | 892 | 910 |
| **Total** | 981 | 982 | 1,028 |

* FAO estimate(s).
Source: FAO, *Yearbook of Forest Products*.

**SAWNWOOD PRODUCTION**
('000 cubic metres, incl. railway sleepers)

|  | 1990 | 1991 | 1992 |
|---|---|---|---|
| **Total** | 48* | 16 | 37 |

* FAO estimate.
Source: FAO, *Yearbook of Forest Products*.

## Fishing

(metric tons, live weight, provisional figures)

|  | 1990 | 1991 | 1992 |
|---|---|---|---|
| Pacific thread herring | 33,018 | 35,857 | 29,769 |
| Central Pacific anchoveta | 54,716 | 65,756 | 63,277 |
| Other marine fishes | 6,460 | 6,289 | 5,023 |
| Spiny lobsters | 315 | 315* | 323 |
| Shrimps and prawns | 6,642 | 10,166 | 7,561 |
| **Total catch** | 101,151 | 118,383 | 105,953 |

* Official estimate.

## Industry

**SELECTED PRODUCTS**
('000 metric tons, unless otherwise indicated)

|  | 1991 | 1992 | 1993* |
|---|---|---|---|
| Salt ('000 quintales)† | n.a. | 571.0 | 409.0 |
| Alcoholic beverages (million litres) | 130.6 | 126.0 | 131.0 |
| Sugar | 122.4 | 150.6 | 146.3 |
| Condensed, evaporated, powdered milk | 22.1 | 21.7 | 22.6 |
| Tomato derivatives (metric tons) | 9.1 | 9.2 | 9.7 |
| Fishmeal | 25.3 | 22.8 | 28.4 |
| Fish oil | 6.4 | 11.2 | 8.0 |
| Cigarettes (million) | 771.4 | 723.7 | 907.3 |
| Electricity (million kWh) | 2,790.0 | 2,902.7 | 3,148.0 |

* Preliminary figures.
† Figures are in terms of the old Spanish quintal, equal to 46 kg (101.4 lb).

## Finance

**CURRENCY AND EXCHANGE RATES**
**Monetary Units**
100 centésimos = 1 balboa (B).

**Sterling and Dollar Equivalents** (31 December 1994)
£1 sterling = 1.5645 balboas;
US $1 = 1.0000 balboas;
100 balboas = £63.92 = $100.00.

**Exchange Rate**
The balboa's value is fixed at par with that of the US dollar.

**BUDGET ESTIMATES** ('000 balboas)

| Revenue | 1991 | 1992 | 1993 |
|---|---|---|---|
| Direct taxes | 236,300 | 305,730 | 387,086 |
| Indirect taxes | 355,192 | 403,161 | 467,008 |
| Income from assets | 32,095 | 41,786 | 35,930 |
| Income from state enterprises | 133,983 | 174,648 | 248,380 |
| Other sources of income | 296,249 | 276,315 | 279,562 |
| Current transfers | 5,097 | 4,062 | 4,336 |
| **Total current revenue** | 1,058,916 | 1,205,702 | 1,422,302 |
| National resources | 7,330 | 36,150 | 82,750 |
| Loans | 268,104 | 182,305 | 284,575 |
| Other capital revenue | 221,805 | 29,632 | 5,129 |
| Surplus from previous years | — | — | 40,179 |
| **Total revenue** | 1,556,155 | 1,453,789 | 1,834,935 |

| Expenditure | 1991 | 1992 | 1993 |
|---|---|---|---|
| National Assembly | 13,165 | 14,291 | 15,760 |
| Inspectorate of Taxes | 18,112 | 18,140 | 21,846 |
| President's Office | 11,488 | 12,584 | 15,238 |
| Home Affairs and Justice | 112,833 | 115,908 | 140,130 |
| Foreign Affairs | 17,409 | 18,966 | 21,105 |
| Treasury | 24,413 | 26,881 | 33,400 |
| Education | 175,247 | 187,458 | 206,332 |
| Public Works | 27,395 | 23,702 | 33,855 |
| Agriculture and Livestock | 22,100 | 21,963 | 24,712 |
| Price Control Office | 1,701 | 1,553 | 1,719 |
| Health | 103,079 | 113,166 | 126,806 |
| Commerce and Industry | 6,816 | 7,026 | 9,090 |
| Labour and Social Security | 5,062 | 5,813 | 6,338 |
| Ministry of Housing | 13,613 | 13,209 | 14,050 |
| Ministry of Planning and Economic Policy | 9,090 | 8,790 | 10,986 |
| Law Courts | 12,328 | 15,608 | 20,231 |
| Public Services | 10,538 | 18,078 | 24,641 |
| Electoral Tribunal | 6,319 | 8,580 | 13,033 |
| External Debt | 288,243 | 153,608 | 195,148 |
| Internal Debt | 190,857 | 184,156 | 228,991 |
| Current Transfers | 200,160 | 278,903 | 333,232 |
| Capital Expenditure | 286,187 | 205,406 | 338,292 |
| **Total expenditure** | 1,556,155 | 1,453,789 | 1,834,935 |

**INTERNATIONAL RESERVES** ('000 balboas)

|  | 1991 | 1992 | 1993 |
|---|---|---|---|
| Gross International Reserves | 4,583,079 | 4,480,777 | 4,411,120 |
| of which: |  |  |  |
| Gold | 476 | 476 | 476 |
| Foreign currency | 160,051 | 131,568 | 305,131 |
| of which: |  |  |  |
| US coin | 3,185 | 1,456 | 1,289 |
| US notes | 156,827 | 130,088 | 129,972 |
| Bank deposits (incl. Canal Zone) | 3,271,156 | 3,361,009 | 3,196,062 |

Note: US treasury notes and coins form the bulk of the currency in circulation in Panama.

**COST OF LIVING**
(Consumer Price Index, Panamá (Panama City). Base: 1987 = 100)

|  | 1991 | 1992 | 1993* |
|---|---|---|---|
| Food and drink | 104.4 | 108.1 | 108.4 |
| Clothing and footwear | 104.1 | 110.5 | 110.8 |
| Rent, fuel and light | 103.3 | 103.3 | 103.8 |
| Household articles | 102.2 | 102.1 | 103.5 |
| Medicines and hygiene products | 96.2 | 100.1 | 102.3 |
| Transport and communications | 99.7 | 99.2 | 98.5 |
| Leisure | 102.9 | 104.0 | 104.3 |
| Miscellaneous | 103.0 | 104.1 | 105.7 |
| **All items** | 102.8 | 104.6 | 105.1 |

* Preliminary figures.

# PANAMA

## Statistical Survey

## NATIONAL ACCOUNTS

**National Income and Product** (million balboas at current prices)

|  | 1990 | 1991 | 1992* |
|---|---|---|---|
| Compensation of employees | 2,288.0 | 2,515.8 | 2,781.9 |
| Operating surplus | 1,865.6 | 2,039.9 | 2,178.7 |
| **Domestic factor incomes** | 4,153.6 | 4,555.7 | 4,960.6 |
| Consumption of fixed capital | 422.1 | 453.9 | 481.1 |
| **Gross domestic product (GDP) at factor cost** | 4,575.7 | 5,009.6 | 5,441.7 |
| Indirect taxes | 443.1 | 496.8 | 569.9 |
| Less Subsidies | 9.4 | 10.0 | 10.5 |
| **GDP in purchasers' values** | 5,009.4 | 5,496.4 | 6,001.1 |
| Factor income received from abroad | 679.6 | 660.3 | 669.9 |
| Less Factor income paid abroad | 933.2 | 905.1 | 728.4 |
| **Gross national product** | 4,755.8 | 5,251.6 | 5,942.6 |
| Less Consumption of fixed capital | 422.1 | 453.9 | 481.1 |
| **National income in market prices** | 4,333.7 | 4,797.7 | 5,461.5 |
| Other current transfers from abroad | 224.9 | 225.5 | 331.0 |
| Less Other current transfers paid abroad | 29.2 | 27.4 | 35.3 |
| **National disposable income** | 4,529.4 | 4,995.8 | 5,757.2 |

* Preliminary.

**Expenditure on the Gross Domestic Product** (million balboas)

|  | 1991 | 1992 | 1993 |
|---|---|---|---|
| Government final consumption expenditure | 958.1 | 1,021.6 | 1,095.8 |
| Private final consumption expenditure | 3,377.3 | 3,593.0 | 3,897.5 |
| Increase in stocks | 68.7 | 102.9 | 35.3 |
| Gross fixed capital formation | 923.9 | 1,270.4 | 1,603.6 |
| **Total domestic expenditure** | 5,328.0 | 5,987.9 | 6,632.2 |
| Exports of goods and services | 2,134.4 | 2,340.5 | 2,429.9 |
| Less Imports of goods and services | 1,966.0 | 2,313.0 | 2,497.2 |
| **GDP in purchasers' values** | 5,496.4 | 6,015.4 | 6,564.9 |
| **GDP at constant 1990 prices** | 5,487.8 | 5,954.7 | 6,276.0 |

**1994** (million balboas): GDP at constant 1990 prices 6,570.9.

Source: IMF, *International Financial Statistics*.

**Gross Domestic Product by Economic Activity**
(million balboas at constant 1970 prices)

|  | 1991 | 1992* | 1993‡ |
|---|---|---|---|
| Agriculture, hunting, forestry and fishing | 220.6 | 234.6 | 238.0 |
| Mining and quarrying | 3.0 | 4.2 | 5.0 |
| Manufacturing | 188.3 | 203.6 | 217.9 |
| Electricity, gas and water | 71.7 | 70.8 | 75.4 |
| Construction | 72.7 | 113.0 | 157.1 |
| Wholesale and retail trade | 241.3 | 260.8 | 278.3 |
| Transport, storage and communications | 535.4 | 579.6 | 597.3 |
| Finance, insurance, real estate and business services | 299.7 | 323.2 | 348.6 |
| Community, social and personal services | 176.6 | 190.3 | 197.2 |
| Government and other services | 274.1 | 285.8 | 280.0 |
| **Sub-total** | 2,083.4 | 2,265.9 | 2,394.8 |
| Import duties | 30.5 | 36.4 | 52.7 |
| Less Imputed bank service charge | 74.5 | 88.2 | 102.4 |
| **GDP in purchasers' values** | 2,039.4 | 2,214.1 | 2,345.1 |

* Preliminary.  ‡ Estimates.

## BALANCE OF PAYMENTS (US $ million)*

|  | 1991 | 1992 | 1993 |
|---|---|---|---|
| Merchandise exports f.o.b. | 4,146 | 5,012 | 5,299 |
| Merchandise imports f.o.b. | −4,961 | −5,892 | −6,152 |
| **Trade balance** | −815 | −880 | −853 |
| Exports of services | 1,322 | 1,385 | 1,407 |
| Imports of services | −412 | −447 | −479 |
| Other income received | 925 | 1,029 | 940 |
| Other income paid | −1,288 | −1,290 | −1,125 |
| Private unrequited transfers (net) | −16 | −27 | −27 |
| Official unrequited transfers (net) | 125 | 146 | 138 |
| **Current balance** | −158 | −84 | 2 |
| Direct investment (net) | −30 | −2 | −41 |
| Portfolio investment (net) | −16 | −149 | −559 |
| Other capital (net) | −783 | −526 | −5 |
| Net errors and omissions | 565 | 444 | 196 |
| **Overall balance** | −422 | −314 | −407 |

* Including the transactions of enterprises operating in the Colón Free Zone.

Source: IMF, *International Financial Statistics*.

# External Trade

**PRINCIPAL COMMODITIES** ('000 balboas)

| Imports c.i.f. | 1991 | 1992 | 1993 |
|---|---|---|---|
| Vegetable products | 55,384 | 72,770 | 66,066 |
| Food products, beverages and tobacco | 96,266 | 109,336 | 118,882 |
| Mineral products | 256,736 | 309,030 | 288,107 |
| Chemicals and chemical products | 203,571 | 217,545 | 242,782 |
| Plastics and synthetic resins | 91,855 | 104,838 | 113,790 |
| Paper and paper products | 94,924 | 116,532 | 118,835 |
| Textiles and textile manufactures | 130,382 | 152,013 | 157,081 |
| Footwear, hats, umbrellas and parasols | n.a. | 40,617 | 44,329 |
| Basic metals and metal manufactures | 126,723 | 155,519 | 160,806 |
| Electrical and electronic equipment | 231,972 | 299,847 | 387,035 |
| Transport equipment | 201,264 | 254,286 | 289,223 |
| Optical, photographic and measuring instruments, clocks and watches | n.a. | 60,236 | 68,814 |
| **Total** (incl. others) | 1,695,646 | 2,018,760 | 2,187,376 |

| Exports f.o.b. | 1991 | 1992 | 1993* |
|---|---|---|---|
| Raw sugar | 24,406 | 19,973 | 21,797 |
| Bananas | 196,461 | 212,521 | 199,528 |
| Coffee | 12,999 | 10,497 | 11,558 |
| Shrimps | 50,447 | 53,994 | 56,965 |
| Clothing | n.a. | 22,096 | 21,435 |
| **Total** (incl. others) | 452,094 | 480,912 | 507,606 |

* Preliminary figures.

**PRINCIPAL TRADING PARTNERS** ('000 balboas)

| Imports | 1990 | 1991 | 1992 |
|---|---|---|---|
| Canada | 11,062 | 24,644 | 15,542 |
| Costa Rica | 43,652 | 46,332 | 54,679 |
| Ecuador | 165,026 | 104,310 | 126,762 |
| Colón Free Zone | 273,516 | 283,502 | 320,013 |
| Germany | 30,172 | 38,165 | 34,477 |
| Guatemala | 28,060 | 23,379 | 25,549 |
| Italy | 10,832 | 12,737 | 15,953 |
| Japan | 74,438 | 114,860 | 165,276 |
| Mexico | 25,401 | 30,789 | 40,597 |
| Sweden | 3,257 | 4,264 | 9,440 |
| Taiwan | 21,830 | 26,725 | 27,531 |
| United Kingdom | 15,026 | 16,647 | 17,113 |
| USA | 502,482 | 599,432 | 730,763 |
| Venezuela | 35,436 | 46,491 | 41,897 |

# PANAMA

*Statistical Survey*

| Exports | 1990 | 1991 | 1992 |
|---|---|---|---|
| Colombia | 3,057 | 3,146 | 2,477 |
| Costa Rica | 29,202 | 26,733 | 30,905 |
| El Salvador | 3,500 | 6,382 | 9,686 |
| Germany | 115,269 | 115,857 | 134,867 |
| Guatemala | 3,370 | 6,390 | 7,594 |
| Italy | 29,986 | 38,679 | 39,942 |
| Nicaragua | 1,507 | 2,989 | 3,119 |
| Puerto Rico | 9,109 | 9,359 | 9,850 |
| USA | 142,559 | 133,073 | 141,288 |
| Venezuela | 1,492 | 2,831 | 3,866 |

## Transport

**RAILWAYS** (traffic on Ferrocarril Nacional de Chiriquí)

|  | 1990 | 1991 | 1992 |
|---|---|---|---|
| Passengers | 77,003 | 117,215 | 87,226 |

**ROAD TRAFFIC** (motor vehicles registered)

|  | 1990 | 1991 | 1992* |
|---|---|---|---|
| Cars | 132,921 | 144,157 | 154,709 |
| Buses | 10,168 | 11,199 | 11,550 |
| Lorries | 35,673 | 41,706 | 47,752 |
| Others | 105 | 120 | 131 |

* Preliminary figures.

### SHIPPING

**Merchant Fleet** (at 30 June)

|  | 1991 | 1992 | 1993 |
|---|---|---|---|
| Number of vessels | 4,953 | 5,424 | 5,564 |
| Displacement ('000 grt) | 44,949 | 52,486 | 57,619 |

Source: Lloyd's Register of Shipping.

**International Sea-borne Freight Traffic** ('000 metric tons)

|  | 1988 | 1989 | 1990 |
|---|---|---|---|
| Goods loaded | 1,382 | 1,420 | 1,432 |
| Goods unloaded | 2,080 | 2,200 | 2,204 |

Source: UN, *Monthly Bulletin of Statistics*.

**Panama Canal Traffic**

|  | 1992 | 1993 | 1994* |
|---|---|---|---|
| Transits | 12,636 | 12,257 | 12,478 |
| Cargo (million long tons) | 159.6 | 158.0 | 168.0 |

* Preliminary figures.

**CIVIL AVIATION** (traffic on scheduled services)

|  | 1990 |
|---|---|
| Kilometres flown (million) | 4 |
| Passengers carried ('000) | 205 |
| Passengers-km (million) | 196 |
| Total ton-km (million) | 27 |

Source: UN, *Statistical Yearbook*.

## Tourism

|  | 1990* | 1991† | 1992† |
|---|---|---|---|
| Number of visitors | 221,677 | 286,835 | 303,428 |
| Total expenditure ('000 balboas) | 115,230 | 146,435 | 159,907 |

* Preliminary figures.   † Estimates.

**1993** (preliminary figure): Number of visitors 327,000.

## Communications Media

|  | 1990 | 1991 | 1992 |
|---|---|---|---|
| Radio receivers ('000 in use) | 540 | 552 | 564 |
| Television receivers ('000 in use) | 400 | 410 | 420 |
| Daily newspapers (number) | 8 | n.a. | 8 |
| Telephones ('000 in use) | 256 | 273 | n.a. |

Sources: UNESCO, *Statistical Yearbook*; UN, *Statistical Yearbook*.

## Education

(1992)

|  | Institutions | Teachers | Pupils |
|---|---|---|---|
| Pre-primary | 835 | 1,452 | 33,248 |
| Primary | 2,712 | 13,987 | 353,154 |
| Secondary | 363 | 10,521 | 201,047 |
| Higher* | 7 | 3,771 | 63,848 |
| Special | 25 | 517 | 6,363 |
| Supplementary | 27 | 222 | 5,201 |

* Including universities.

Source: Ministry of Education.

# Directory

## The Constitution

Under the terms of the amendments to the Constitution, implemented by the adoption of Reform Acts No 1 and No 2 in October 1978, and by the approval by referendum of the Constitutional Act in April 1983, the 67 (later 72) members of the unicameral Asamblea Legislativa (Legislative Assembly) are elected by popular vote every five years. Executive power is exercised by the President of the Republic, who is also elected by popular vote for a term of five years. Two Vice-Presidents are elected by popular vote to assist the President. The President appoints the Cabinet. The armed forces are barred from participating in elections.

## The Government

### HEAD OF STATE

**President:** ERNESTO PÉREZ BALLADARES (took office 1 September 1994).

**First Vice-President:** TOMÁS ALTAMIRANO DUQUE.

**Second Vice-President:** FELIPE ALEJANDRO VIRZI.

### THE CABINET
(June 1995)

**Minister of the Interior and Justice:** RAÚL MONTENEGRO.
**Minister of Foreign Affairs:** RICARDO ALBERTO ARIAS (acting).
**Minister of Public Works:** LUIS ENRIQUE BLANCO.
**Minister of Finance and the Treasury:** OLMEDO MIRANDA.
**Minister of Agricultural Development:** CARLOS ALONSO SOUSA-LENOX.
**Minister of Commerce and Industry:** NITZA DE VILLAREAL.
**Minister of Public Health:** AIDA DE RIVERA.
**Minister of Labour and Social Welfare:** MITCHELL DOENS.
**Minister of Education:** PABLO THALASSINOS.
**Minister of Housing:** FRANCISCO SÁNCHEZ CÁRDENAS.
**Minister of Planning and Economic Policy:** GUILLERMO CHAPMAN.
**Minister of the Presidency:** RAÚL ARANGO.

### MINISTRIES

**Office of the President:** Palacio Presidencial, Valija 50, Panamá 1; tel. 27-4062; telex 2770; fax 27-0076.

**Ministry of Agricultural Development:** Apdo 5390, Panamá 5; tel. 69-3122; telex 2994; fax 69-3706.

**Ministry of Commerce and Industry:** Apdo 9658, Panamá 4; tel. 27-4177; telex 2256; fax 27-5604.

**Ministry of Education:** Apdo 2440, Panamá 3; tel. 62-2645; fax 62-9087.

**Ministry of Finance and the Treasury:** Central Postal Balboa, Ancón, Apdo 5245, Panamá 5; tel. 25-3431; telex 2352; fax 27-2357.

**Ministry of Foreign Affairs:** Panamá 4; tel. 27-0013; telex 2771; fax 27-4725.

**Ministry of Housing:** Apdo 5228, Panamá 5; tel. 62-6470; fax 62-9250.

**Ministry of the Interior and Justice:** Apdo 1628, Panamá 1; tel. 22-8973; telex 2746; fax 62-7877.

**Ministry of Labour and Social Welfare:** Apdo 2441, Panamá 3; tel. 62-1627; telex 3738; fax 63-8125.

**Ministry of Planning and Economic Policy:** Edif. Ooawa, Vía España, Apdo 2694, Panamá 3; tel. 69-2169; telex 3683; fax 69-6822.

**Ministry of the Presidency:** Valija 50, Apdo 2189, Panamá 1; tel. 22-0520; telex 3720; fax 37-4119.

**Ministry of Public Health:** Apdo 2048, Panamá 1; tel. 25-6080; fax 27-5276.

**Ministry of Public Works:** Apdo 1632, Panamá 1; tel. 32-5505; telex 3438; fax 32-5776.

## President and Legislature

### PRESIDENT

**Election, 8 May 1994**

| Candidate | % of votes cast |
|---|---|
| ERNESTO PÉREZ BALLADARES (Pueblo Unido) | 33.2 |
| MIREYA MOSCOSO DE GRUBER (Alianza Democrática) | 29.5 |
| RUBÉN BLADES (MPE) | 17.2 |
| RUBÉN DARÍO CARLES (Cambio 94) | 16.2 |
| EDUARDO VALLARINO (PDC) | 2.0 |
| Others* | 1.9 |
| **Total** | **100.0** |

* Including blank and spoiled votes.

### ASAMBLEA LEGISLATIVA
(Legislative Assembly)

**President:** BALBINA HERRERA (PRD).

**General Election, 8 May 1994**

| Affiliation/Party | Seats |
|---|---|
| Pueblo Unido | |
|   Partido Revolucionario Democrático (PRD) | 31 |
|   Partido Liberal Republicano (Libre) | 1 |
|   Partido Laborista (PALA) | 1 |
| Alianza Democrática | |
|   Partido Arnulfista (PA) | 15 |
|   Partido Liberal Auténtico (PLA) | 4 |
|   Unión Democrática Independiente (UDI) | 1 |
| Cambio 94 | |
|   Movimiento Liberal Republicano Nacionalista (MOLIRENA) | 5 |
|   Partido Renovación Civilista (PRC) | 3 |
|   Movimiento de Renovación Nacional (Morena) | 1 |
| Movimiento Papa Egoró (MPE) | 6 |
| Partido Solidaridad | 2 |
| Partido Liberal Nacional (PLN) | 1 |
| Partido Demócrata Cristiano (PDC) | 1 |
| **Total** | **72** |

## Political Organizations

**Alianza Popular:** Vía Brasil (al lado de Marcorama); formally registered 1992; 27,913 mems (March 1993); Pres. TOMÁS GONZÁLEZ; Sec.-Gen. PUBLIO RODRÍGUEZ.

**Misión de Unidad Nacional (MUN):** Edif. Elga, Vía España y Calle 50 No 3, Apdo 5-4816, Panamá; tel. 69-5670; fax 64-3858; f. 1992; 23,281 mems (March 1993); Pres. JOSÉ MANUEL PAREDES; Sec.-Gen. ERNESTO RIERA.

**Movimiento de Integración Nacional:** Edif. José Esteban (frente al Antiguo Club Millonario, al lado de Restaurante Seoul), Panamá; tel. 69-8489; formally registered 1992; 20,323 mems (March 1993); Pres. Dr ARRIGO GUARDIA; Sec.-Gen. ISAAC RODRÍGUEZ.

**Movimiento Laborista Agrario (MOLA):** Edif. Banco Unión (al lado del Santuario), Panamá; tel. 63-7055; fax 64-5981; formally registered 1993; 1,642 mems (March 1993); Pres. CARLOS ELETA A.

**\*Movimiento Liberal Republicano Nacionalista (MOLIRENA):** Edif. 2-49 (bajando por el Consulado Americano), Calle 40, Apdo 6-5154, Bella Vista, Panamá; tel. 25-1596; fax 25-1177; formally registered 1982; conservative; 33,393 mems (March 1993); Pres. ALFREDO RAMÍREZ; Sec.-Gen. LUIS G. CASCO ARIAS.

**\*Movimiento Papa Egoró (MPE):** Edif. Avon, 3°, Vía España (frente al Rey Kung), Panamá; tel. 69-8003; f. 1991; Pres. FERNANDO MANFREDO; Sec.-Gen. RAÚL ALBERTO LEÍS.

**\*Movimiento de Renovación Nacional (Morena):** Panamá; tel. 36-4930; formally registered 1993; 3,621 mems (March 1993); Pres. PEDRO VALLARINO COX; Sec.-Gen. DEMETRIO DECEREGA.

**Movimiento Social Cristiano (MSC):** Panamá; f. 1994 by dissident members of the PDC; Leader GLORIA MORENO.

**Partido Acción Popular:** c/o Buffette Icaza, González, Ruiz y Alemán (al lado de la Farmacia Arrocha), Vía España (frente al Banco Continental), Panamá; tel. 63-5555; formally registered

# PANAMA

*Directory*

1992; 3,844 mems (March 1993); Pres. JUAN LOMBARDI; Sec.-Gen. JOSÉ ALBERTO DE LA GUARDIA.

**\*Partido Arnulfista (PA):** Avda Perú y Calle 38 Este, No 37-41, (al lads de Casa la Esperanza), Panamá; tel. 27-1267; f. 1990; formed by Arnulfista faction of the Partido Parameñista Auténtico; 112,395 mems (March 1993); Pres. MIREYA MOSCOSO DE GRUBER; Sec.-Gen. CARLOS YOUNG ADAMES.

**Partido Demócrata Cristiano (PDC):** Avda Perú (frente al Parque Porras), Apdo 6322, Panamá 5; tel. 27-3204; telex 3050; fax 27-3944; f. 1960; 19,913 mems (March 1993); Pres. RICARDO ARIAS CALDERÓN; Sec.-Gen. H. L. CAMILO BRENES.

**Partido Laborista (PALA):** Transístmica, Edif. Inversiones Cali (frente al Cementerio de Pueblo Nuevo, entrando por Bandag), Urb. Orillac, Panamá; tel. 61-4174; f. 1982; right-wing; 76,457 mems (March 1993); Pres. Dr CARLOS LÓPEZ GUEVARA; Sec.-Gen. Ing. ARTURO DIEZ P.

**Partido Liberal Auténtico (PLA):** Vía España y Calle 46 (frente a la Clínica Dental Arrocha), Panamá; tel. 27-1041; fax 27-4119; formally registered 1988; 16,846 mems (March 1993); Pres. ARNULFO ESCALONA RIOS; Sec.-Gen. JULIO C. HARRIS.

**Partido Liberal Nacional (PLN):** El Dorado, Apdo 7363, Panamá 6; tel. 64-2026; f. 1979; mem. of Liberal International, and founding mem. of Federación Liberal de Centroamérica y el Caribe (FELICA); 40,645 mems; Pres. Dr ROBERT ALEMÁN; Sec.-Exec. Lic. OSCAR UCROS.

**Partido Liberal Republicano (Libre):** Panamá; tel. 61-4659; formally registered 1993; 8,961 mems (March 1993); Pres. GONZALO TAPIA COLLANTE; Sec.-Gen. CARLOS ORILLAC.

**Partido Nacionalista Popular (PNP):** Edif. de los Juzgados, planta baja, Calle San Miguel, Urb. Obarrio, Panamá; tel. 64-8204; formally registered 1991; 16,831 mems (March 1993); Pres. JORGE FLORES; Sec.-Gen. ALBINO GÓNDOLA VÁSQUEZ.

**Partido Panameñista Doctrinario:** Banco Aliado, 15°, Vía España y Calle Ricardo Arias, Panamá; tel. 69-4644; fax 64-7945; formally registered in 1991; 25,160 mems (March 1993); Pres. JOSÉ SALVADOR MUÑOZ; Sec.-Gen. JULIA SUIRA.

**\*Partido Renovación Civilista (PRC):** Edif. Casa Oceánica, 1°, Of. 4, Avda Aquilino de la Guardia, Panamá; tel. 63-8971; fax 63-8975; formally registered 1992; 30,911 mems (March 1993); Pres. Lic. TOMÁS HERRERA; Sec.-Gen. CARLOS HARRIS.

**\*Partido Revolucionario Democrático (PRD):** Avda 7a Central (frente al Edif. Novey), Apdo 2650, Panamá 9; tel. 25-1050; f. 1979; supports policies of late Gen. Omar Torrijos Herrera; combination of Marxists, Christian Democrats and some business interests; 161,230 mems (March 1993); Pres. GERARDO GONZÁLEZ VERNAZA; Sec.-Gen. ERNESTO PÉREZ BALLADARES.

**Partido Solidaridad:** Edif. Plaza Balboa, Panamá; tel. 63-4097; formally registered 1993; 37,130 mems (March 1993); Pres. SAMUEL LEWIS GALINDO; Sec.-Gen. SIMÓN A. TEJEIRA QUIROS.

**Unión Democrática Independiente (UDI):** c/o Edif. Ejecutivo, 1° alto, Calle Elvira Méndez, Panamá; tel. 63-5466; formally registered 1992; 21,774 mems (March 1993); Pres. JACINTO A. CÁRDENAS M.; Sec.-Gen. ELIDIO GONZÁLEZ.

\* Party that secured 5% or more of the total votes at the May 1994 legislative election, and thereby retained official status.

The following political alliances were formed during 1994 to contest presidential and legislative elections conducted on 8 May 1994:

**Alianza Democrática:** comprising the PA, the PLA, the UDI and the PNP; Presidential Candidate MIREYA MOSCOSO DE GRUBER.

**Cambio 94:** comprising MOLIRENA, the PRC and Morena; Presidential Candidate RUBÉN DARÍO CARLES.

**Concertación Nacional:** comprising the Partido Solidaridad and the MUN; Presidential Candidate LEWIS GALINDO.

**Pueblo Unido:** comprising the PRD, Libre and PALA; Presidential Candidate ERNESTO PÉREZ BALLADARES.

**The Cruzada Civilista Nacional (CCN),** a broad-based opposition movement composed of more than 100 groups, including members of the Roman Catholic Church, civil and professional organizations, and trade unions (leader AURELIO BARRÍA, Jr), is also active. In early 1988 division within the CCN resulted in the formation of a splinter group, the **Movimiento Cívico Popular** (MCP).

The following guerrilla groups are also active:

**M-20 (Movimiento-20):** f. 1990, following the US invasion of Panama; thought to be based in Chiriquí province.

**VPT-20 (Vanguardia Patriótica Torrijista—20 Diciembre):** f. 1993; believed to be linked to Colombian group FARC.

# Diplomatic Representation

## EMBASSIES IN PANAMA

**Argentina:** Edif. del Banco de Iberoamérica, 1°, entre Calles 50 y 53, Apdo 1271, Panamá 1; tel. 64-6561; telex 2679; fax 69-5331; Ambassador: ALEJANDRO TELESFORO MOSQUERA.

**Bolivia:** Edif. Bolivia, Calle 50 No 78, Apdo 8187, Panamá 7; tel. 69-0275; fax 64-3868; Ambassador: JAIME NIÑO DE GUZMÁN Q.

**Brazil:** Edif. El Dorado, 1°, Calle Elvira Méndez y Avda Ricardo Arango, Urb. Campo Alegre, Apdo 4287, Panamá 5; tel. 63-5322; telex 3569; fax 69-6316; Ambassador: MAURO SERGIO COUTO.

**Chile:** Edif. Banco de Boston, 11°, Calle Elvira Méndez y Vía España; Apdo 7341; tel. 23-9748; telex 2969; fax 63-5530; Ambassador: EDUARDO ORMEÑO TOLEDO.

**China (Taiwan):** Torre Banco Unión, 16°, Avda Samuel Lewis, Apdo 7492, Panamá 5; tel. 69-1347; fax 64-9118; Ambassador: KUAN CHING-CHENG.

**Colombia:** Edif. Grobman, 6°, Avda Manuel María Icaza 12, Apdo 4407, Panamá 5; tel. 64-9644; telex 3330; fax 23-1134; Ambassador: ALFONSO ARAÚJO COTES.

**Costa Rica:** Edif. Miraflores, Calle Gerardo Ortega 17, Apdo 8963, Panamá 5; tel. 64-2980; telex 2313; Ambassador: HERBERT WOLF FOURNIER.

**Cuba:** Avda Cuba y Ecuador 33, Apdo 6-2291, El Dorado, Panamá; tel. 27-5277; telex 2788; fax 25-6681; Chargé d'affaires: Lic. MIGUEL MARTÍNEZ RAMIL.

**Dominican Republic:** Edif. Miraflores, 2°, Calle Gerardo Ortega 7, Apdo 6250, Panamá 5; tel. 69-4285; Ambassador: ADOLFO LEVEA POLANCO.

**Ecuador:** Edif. Grobman, 3°, Calle Manuel María Icaza 12, Apdo 8380, Panamá 7; tel. 64-2654; telex 2908; fax 23-0159; Ambassador: GUSTAVO BUCHELI GARCÉS.

**Egypt:** Casa 17323, Avda 5a Norte, Calle 1, El Cangrejo, Apdo 7080, Panamá 5; tel. 63-5020; telex 3572; Ambassador: ABDELRAHMAN A. SALAH.

**El Salvador:** Edif. Citibank, 4°, Of. 408, Vía España 124, Apdo 8016, Panamá 7; tel. 23-3020; telex 3240; fax 64-1433; Ambassador: JOSÉ FERNANDO S. OLIVARES.

**France:** Plaza de Francia 1, Las Bovedas, San Felipe, Apdo 869, Panamá 1; tel. 28-7835; telex 2834; fax 28-7852; Ambassador: ALAIN PALLU DE BEAUPUY.

**Germany:** Edif. Bancomer, Calle 50 y 53, Apdo 4228, Panamá 5; tel. 63-7733; telex 2979; fax 23-6664; Ambassador: VOLKER ANDING.

**Guatemala:** Edif. Versalles, Avda Federico Boyd y Calle 48 de Bella Vista, Apdo 2352, Panamá 9A; tel. 69-3475; fax 23-1922; Ambassador: J. ENRIQUE BETANCOURT F.

**Haiti:** Edif. Dora Luz, 2°, Calle 1, El Cangrejo, Apdo 442, Panamá 9; tel. 69-3443; fax 23-1767; Chargé d'affaires: GEORGES H. BARBEROUSSE.

**Holy See:** Punta Paitilla, Avda Balboa y Via Italia, Apdo 4251, Panamá 5 (Apostolic Nunciature); tel. 69-3138; fax 64-2116; Apostolic Nuncio: Most Rev. BRUNO MUSARÓ, Titular Archbishop of Abari.

**Honduras:** Edif. Tapia, 2°, Of. 202, Calle 31 y Justo Arosemena, Apdo 8704, Panamá 5; tel. 25-8200; fax 25-3283; Ambassador: FRANCISCO SALOMÓN JIMÉNEZ M.

**India:** Edif. Banco Continental, 5°, Vía España 120, Apdo 8400, Panamá 7; tel. 64-3043; telex 2273; fax 64-2855; Ambassador: BAL ANAND.

**Israel:** Edif. Grobman, 5°, Calle Manuel María Icaza 12, Apdo 6357, Panamá 5; tel. 64-8022; fax 64-2706; Ambassador: YAACOV BRAKHA.

**Italy:** Calle 1°, Parque Lefevre 42, Apdo 2369, Panamá 9A; tel. 26-3111; telex 3374; fax 26-3121; Ambassador: GIANMARIO URBINI.

**Jamaica:** Edif. Reprico, Avda Balboa y Calle 26, Panamá 5; tel. 25-4441; Ambassador: EVADUE COYE.

**Japan:** Edif. Don Camilo, planta baja, Calle 50 y Calle 61, Obarrio, Apdo 1411, Panamá 1; tel. 63-6155; telex 2780; fax 63-6019; Ambassador: YOJI SUGIYAMA.

**Korea, Republic:** Edif. Plaza, planta baja, Calle Ricardo Arias y Calle 51E, Campo Alegre, Apdo 8096, Panamá 7; tel. 64-8203; telex 2208; fax 64-8825; Ambassador: SANG-JIN CHOI.

**Libya:** Avda Balboa y Calle 32 (frente al Edif. Atalaya), Apdo 6-894 El Dorado, Panamá; tel. 27-3365; telex 2727; Chargé d'affaires: RAMADAM MOHAMED.

**Mexico:** Edif. Plaza Bancomer, 5°, Calle 50 y Calle 53, Nuevo Campo Alegre, Apdo 8373, Panamá 7; tel. 63-5021; telex 2154; fax 64-2022; Ambassador: JOSÉ IGNACIO GUTIÉRREZ.

**Nicaragua:** Calle 50 y Avda Federico Boyd, Apdo 772, Panamá 1; tel. 23-0981; fax 69-2981; Ambassador: GILBERTO MOLINA.

## PANAMA

**Norway:** Avda Justo Arosemena y Calle 35, Panamá 5; tel. 25-8217; Ambassador: (vacant).
**Peru:** Edif. Dilido, 8°, Calle Manuel María Icaza, Apdo 4516, Panamá 5; tel. 23-1112; telex 2548; fax 69-6809; Ambassador: JUAN MANUEL TIRADO BARRERA.
**Spain:** Calle 53 y Avda Perú (frente a la Plaza Porras), Apdo 1857, Panamá 1; tel. 27-5122; telex 2656; fax 27-4926; Ambassador: MIGUEL ANGEL GARCÍA MINA.
**United Kingdom:** Torre Swiss Bank, 4°, Urb. Marbella, Calle 53, Apdo 889, Panamá 1; tel. 69-0866; fax 23-0730; Ambassador: T. H. MALCOMSON.
**USA:** Avda Balboa y Calle 38, Apdo 6959, Panamá 5; tel. 27-1777; telex 3583; fax 27-1964; Ambassador: (vacant).
**Uruguay:** Edif. Vallarino, 5°, Of. 4, Calle 32 y Avda Justo Arosemena, Apdo 8898, Panamá 5; tel. 25-0049; fax 25-9087; Ambassador: ERNESTO MARTÍNEZ GARIAZZO.
**Venezuela:** Torre Banco Unión, 5°, Avda Samuel Lewis, Apdo 661, Panamá 1; tel. 69-1014; telex 2758; fax 69-1916; Ambassador: LUIS OCHOA TERÁN.

## Judicial System

The judiciary in Panama comprises the following courts and judges: Corte Suprema de Justicia (Supreme Court of Justice), with nine judges appointed for a 10-year term; five Tribunales Superiores de Distrito Judicial (High Courts) with 19 magistrates; 44 Jueces de Circuito (Circuit Judges) and 84 Jueces Municipales (Municipal Judges).

Panama is divided into four judicial districts. The first judicial district covers the provinces of Panamá, Colón, Darién and the region of San Blas and contains two High Courts of Appeals, one dealing with criminal cases, the other dealing with civil cases. In the first functions the first Court of Appeals which deals with civil cases in the provinces of Panamá, Colón, Darién and the region of San Blas, and the second, which deals with criminal cases in the same provinces. The third Court of Appeals, located in Penonomé, in the second judicial district, deals with civil and criminal cases in the provinces of Coclé and Veraguas. The fourth court is based in David and has jurisdiction over the provinces of Chiriquí and Bocas del Toro, in the third judicial district, while the fifth is based in Las Tablas and covers the provinces of Herrera and Los Santos in the fourth judicial district.

**Corte Suprema:** Edif. 236, Ancón, Calle Culebra, Apdo 1770, Panamá 1; tel. 62-9833.
**President of the Supreme Court of Justice:** Dr ARTURO HOYOS.
**Procurator-General:** JOSÉ ANTONIO SOSSA.

## Religion

The Constitution recognizes freedom of worship and the Roman Catholic Church as the religion of the majority of the population.

### CHRISTIANITY

#### The Roman Catholic Church

For ecclesiastical purposes, Panama comprises one archdiocese, five dioceses, the territorial prelature of Bocas del Toro and the Apostolic Vicariate of Darién. At 31 December 1993 there were an estimated 2,046,311 adherents in the country.

**Bishops' Conference:** Conferencia Episcopal de Panamá, Secretariado General, Apdo 87-0033, Panamá 7, tel. 62-6691; fax 23-0042; f. 1980 (statutes approved 1986); Pres. Most Rev. JOSÉ DIMAS CEDEÑO DELGADO, Archbishop of Panamá.
**Archbishop of Panamá:** Most Rev. JOSÉ DIMAS CEDEÑO DELGADO, Arzobispado Metropolitano, Calle 20 y Avda México 24-45, Apdo 386, Panamá 1; tel. 62-7802; fax 62-6691.

#### The Baptist Church

**The Baptist Convention of Panama** (Convención Bautista de Panamá): Apdo 6212, Panamá 5; tel. 64-5585; fax 64-4945; f. 1959; Pres. Rev. EDUARDO HENNINGHAM; Exec. Sec. ESMERALDA DE TUY.

#### The Anglican Communion

Anglicans (Episcopalians) in Panama are adherents of the Episcopal Church in the USA (Province IX).
**Bishop of Panama:** (vacant), Box R, Balboa.

### BAHÁ'Í FAITH

**National Spiritual Assembly of the Bahá'ís:** Apdo 815-0143, Panamá 15; tel. 31-1191; telex 2661; fax 31-6909; mems resident in 531 localities; National Sec. OVIDIO CARRASCO.

## The Press

### DAILIES

**Crítica:** Vía Fernández de Córdoba, Apdo B-4, Panamá 9A; tel. 61-0575; f. 1959; morning; pro-Government; Spanish; circ. 23,000.
**La Estrella de Panamá:** Calle Demetrio H. Brid 7-38, Apdo 159, Panamá; tel. 22-0900; telex 2277; f. 1853; morning; independent; Spanish; Pres. and Dir TOMÁS ALTAMIRANO DUQUE; circ. 17,000.
**El Matutino:** Vía Fernández de Córdoba, Apdo B-4, Panamá 9A; tel. 61-2300; morning; pro-Government; circ. 7,000.
**El Panamá América:** Vía Fernández de Córdoba, Apdo B-4, Panamá 9A; tel. 61-2300; f. 1989; morning; independent; Editor CARLOS A. MENDOZA; circ. 25,000.
**La Prensa:** Avda 11 de Octubre y Calle C. Hato Pintado, Apdo 6-4586, El Dorado, Panamá; tel. 21-7222; telex 3410; fax 21-7328; f. 1980; morning; independent; Spanish; closed by Govt 1988–90; Editor I. ROBERTO EISENMANN, Jr; circ. 45,000.
**La República:** Vía Fernández de Córdoba, Apdo B-4, Panamá 9A; tel. 61-0813; evening; circ. 5,000.
**El Siglo:** Calle 58E, No 12, Apdo W, Panamá 4; tel. 69-3311; fax 69-6954; f. 1985; morning; independent; Spanish; Editor JAIME PADILLA BÉLIZ; circ. 42,000.

### PERIODICALS

**Análisis:** Edif. Señorial, Calle 50, Apdo 8038, Panamá 7; tel. 26-0073; fax 26-3758; monthly; economics and politics; Dir MARIO A. ROGNONI.
**El Camaleón:** Calle 58E, No 12, Apdo W, Panamá 4; tel. 69-3311; fax 69-6954; weekly; satire; Editor JAIME PADILLA BÉLIZ; circ. 80,000.
**Diálogo Social:** Apdo 9A-192, Panamá; tel. 29-1542; fax 61-0215; f. 1967; published by the Centro de Capacitación Social; monthly; religion, economics and current affairs; Pres. CELIA SANJUR; circ. 3,000.
**Estadística Panameña:** Apdo 5213, Panamá 5; tel. 64-3734; fax 69-7294; f. 1941; published by the Contraloría General de la República; statistical survey in series according to subjects; Controller-General: Lic. ARISTIDES ROMERO Jr; Dir of Statistics and Census Lic. MARÍA TERESA S. DE LEÓN.
**FOB Colón Free Zone:** Apdo 6-3287, El Dorado, Panamá; tel. 25-6638; fax 25-0466; annual; bilingual trade directory; circ. 35,000.
**Focus on Panama:** Apdo 6-3287, Panamá; tel. 25-6638; fax 25-0466; f. 1970; 2 a year; visitor's guide; separate English and Spanish editions; Dir KENNETH JONES; circ. 70,000.
**Informativo Industrial:** Apdo 6-4798, El Dorado, Panamá 1; tel. 30-0482; fax 30-0805; monthly; organ of the Sindicato de Industriales de Panamá; Pres. LUIS BARRAZA DE FREITAS.
**Maga:** Calle F No 7, El Cangrejo, Panamá 4; monthly; literature, art and sociology; Dir ENRIQUE JARAMILLO LEVY.
**Sucesos:** Calle 58E, No 12, Apdo W, Panamá 4; tel. 69-3311; fax 69-6854; weekly; circ. 50,000.
**Unidad:** Calle 1a, Apdo 2705, Perejil, Panamá 3; fax 27-3525; f. 1977; fortnightly; publ. of Partido del Pueblo de Panamá; Dir CARLOS F. CHANGMARÍN.

### PRESS ASSOCIATION

**Sindicato de Periodistas de Panamá:** Avda Ecuador y Calle 33, Apdo 2096, Panamá 1; tel. 25-0234; fax 25-0857; f. 1949; Sec.-Gen. a.i. EUCLIDES FUENTES ARROYO.

### FOREIGN NEWS BUREAUX

**Agence-France Presse (AFP):** Panamá; tel. 61-2300; Correspondent ROBERTO R. RODRÍGUEZ.
**Agencia EFE** (Spain): Vía Argentina 60, Apdo 479, Panamá 9A; tel. 23-9020; fax 64-8442; Bureau Chief ANDREU CLARET SERRA.
**Agenzia Nazionale Stampa Associata (ANSA)** (Italy): Edif. Banco de Boston, 17°, Vía España 601, Panamá; tel. 60-6166; telex 3398; Dir LUIS LAMBOGLIA.
**Central News Agency** (Taiwan): Apdo 6-693, El Dorado, Panamá; tel. 23-8837; telex 2024; Correspondent HUANG KWANG CHUN.
**Deutsche Press-Agentur (dpa)** (Germany): Apdo 1550, Panamá; tel. 33-0396; fax 33-5393.
**Informatsionnoye Telegrafnoye Agentstvo Rossii—Telegrafnoye Agentstvo Suverennykh Stran (ITAR—TASS)** (Russia): Apdo 6-1391, El Dorado, Panamá; tel. 69-1993; Bureau Chief ELIDAR ABDULAYEV.
**Inter Press Service (IPS)** (Italy): Apdo 6-3280, Panamá 5; tel. 25-1673; telex 2241; fax 64-7033; Correspondent SILVIO HERNÁNDEZ.

PANAMA — *Directory*

**Prensa Latina** (Cuba): Edif. Doña Luz, Apto 3, Avda Quinta Norte 35, Apdo 6-2799, Panamá; tel. 64-3647; telex 2060; Correspondent RAIMUNDO LÓPEZ MEDINA.

**Rossiyskoye Informatsionnoye Agentstvo—Novosti (RIA—Novosti)** (Russia): Apdo 1190, Panamá 1; tel. 27-4596; Dir RAMIRO OCHOA LÓPEZ.

**United Press International (UPI)** (USA): Altos de Miraflores 4-H, Apdo 393, Panamá 9A; tel. 29-3443; fax 29-3279; Dir TOMÁS A. CUPAS.

**Xinhua (New China) News Agency** (People's Republic of China): Vía Cincuentenario 48, Viña del Mar, Apdo 1467, Panamá 1; tel. 26-4501; telex 2567; Dir HU TAIRAN.

## Publishers

**Editora 'La Estrella de Panamá':** Avda 9a Sur 7-38, Apdo 159, Panamá 1; tel. 22-0900; telex 2277; f. 1853; Dir TOMÁS ALTAMIRANO DUQUE.

**Editora Renovación, SA:** Vía Fernández de Córdoba, Apdo B-4, Panamá 9A; tel. 61-2300; newspapers; government-owned; Exec. Man. ESCOLÁSTICO CALVO.

**Editora Sibauste, SA:** Edif. Panchita c/3, 101 Perejil, Apdo 3375, Panamá 3; tel. 69-0983; Dir ENRIQUE SIBAUSTE BARRÍA.

**Editorial Litográfica, SA (Edilito):** Vía España entre Calles 95 y 96 (al lado de Orange Crush), Apdo 810014, Panamá 10; tel. 24-3087; Pres. EDUARDO ÁVILES C.

**Editorial Universitaria:** Vía José de Fábrega, Panamá; tel. 64-2087; f. 1969; history, geography, law, sciences, literature; Dir CARLOS MANUEL GASTEAZORO.

**Focus Publications:** Apdo 6-3287, El Dorado, Panamá; tel. 25-6638; fax 25-0466; f. 1970; guides, trade directories and yearbooks.

**Fondo Educativo Interamericano:** Edif. Eastern, 6°, Avda Federico Boyd 10 y Calle 51, Apdo 6-3099, El Dorado, Panamá; tel. 69-1511; telex 2481; educational and reference; Dir ALICIA CHAVARRÍA.

**Industrial Gráfica, SA:** Vía España entre Calles 95 y 96 (al lado de Orange Crush), Apdo 810014, Panamá 10; tel. 24-3994; Pres. EDUARDO ÁVILES C.

**Publicaciones Panameñas, SA:** Edif. YASA, 2°, Of. 1, Urb. Obarrio, Calle 59, Apdo 9-103, Panamá 9; tel. 63-5190; Dir EMPERATRIZ S. DE CÁRDENAS.

**Publicar Centroamericana, SA:** Edif. Banco de Boston, 7°, Via España 200 y Cl. Elvira Mendez, Apdo 4919, Panamá 5; tel. 23-9655; telex 2111; fax 69-1964.

### Government Publishing House

**Editorial Mariano Arosemena:** Instituto Nacional de Cultura, Apdo 662, Panamá 1; tel. 22-3233; f. 1974; literature, anthropology, social sciences, archaeology; Dir ESTHER URIETA DE REAL.

## Radio and Television

In 1992, according to UNESCO estimates, there were approximately 564,000 radio receivers in use, and 420,000 television receivers in use.

**Dirección Nacional de Medios de Comunicación Social:** Avda 7a Central y Calle 3a, Apdo 1628, Panamá 1; tel. 62-3197; telex 2746; fax 62-9495; Dir Ing. OCTAVIO CHANG.

### RADIO

In March 1990 the Government approved the creation of the National State Radio Broadcasting Directorate, which was to be a department of the Ministry of the Presidency.

**Asociación Panameña de Radiodifusión:** Apdo 7387, Estafeta de Paitilla, Panamá; tel. 63-5252; fax 26-4396; Pres. FERNANDO ELETA CASSANOVA.

In 1990 there were 59 AM (Medium Wave) stations, and in 1984 there were 43 FM stations. Most stations are commercial.

### TELEVISION

**Corporación Panameña de Radiodifusión, SA (Canal 4):** Edif. Chesterfield, Avda 11 y Calle 28, Apdo 1795, Panamá 1; tel. 25-0160; telex 2622; f. 1960; commercial; Gen. Man. JAIME DE LA GUARDIA.

**Fundación para la Educación en la Televisión (FETV):** Calle 51 y Calle Manuel María Icaza, Edif. Proconsa, 3°, Apdo 6-7295, El Dorado, Panamá; tel. 64-6555; fax 23-5966; f. 1992; Dir MANUEL BLANQUER.

**Panavisión del Istmo, SA (Canal 5):** Torre Plaza Regency, Vía España, Apdo 6-2605, El Dorado, Panamá 8; tel. 69-6816; telex 3347; f. 1983; Dir ALFONSO DE LA ESPRIELLA.

**RPC Televisión:** Apdo 1795, Panamá 1.

**Sistema de Televisión Educativa (Canal 11):** Universidad de Panamá, Estafeta Universitaria, Calle José de Fábrega, Panamá; tel. 69-3755; f. 1978; educational and cultural; Dir-Gen. I. VELÁSQUEZ DE CORTES.

**Southern Command Network—SCN (Canal 8):** Edif. 209, Fuerte Clayton, Apdo 919, Panamá; tel. 87-5567; f. 1943; Dir Col CHARLES B. SIMONS.

**Telemetro (Canal 13):** Apdo 8-116, Calle 50, No. 6, Panamá 8; tel. 69-2122; telex 2609; f. 1961; commercial; Man. BOLÍVAR MÁRQUEZ III.

**Televisora Nacional, SA:** Apdo 6-3092, El Dorado, Panamá; tel. 36-2222; fax 36-2987; Dir-Gen. Lic. ALEJANDRO AYALA V.

## Finance

(cap. = capital; res = reserves; dep. = deposits; m. = million; amounts in balboas, unless otherwise stated)

### BANKING

In December 1993 a total of 106 banks operated in Panama, including 60 with general licence, 28 with international licence, and 18 representative offices.

**Comisión Bancaria Nacional** (National Banking Commission): Cond. Plaza Internacional, Torre B planta baja, Vía España, Apdo 1686, Panamá 1; tel. 23-2844; fax 23-2864; f. 1970 to license and control banking activities within and from Panamanian territory; 7 full mems incl. 2 ministers, Gen. Man. of Banco Nacional de Panamá and 3 representatives of private banking; Exec. Dir ERNESTO A. BOYD S.

#### National Bank

**Banco Nacional de Panamá:** Casa Matriz, Vía España, Apdo 5220, Panamá 5; tel. 63-5151; telex 2136; fax 69-2529; f. 1904; government-owned; cap. 150m., res 39.8m., dep. 2,174.7m. (Dec. 1994); Pres. ALFREDO ALEMÁN; Gen. Man. JOSÉ ANTONIO DE LA OSSA; 49 brs.

#### Development Banks

**Banco de Desarrollo Agropecuario—BDA:** Avda de los Mártires, Apdo 5282, Panamá 5; tel. 62-0266; fax 62-1713; f. 1973; government-sponsored agricultural and livestock credit organization; Pres. Minister of Agricultural Development; Gen. Man. JAIME ADAMES.

**Banco Hipotecario Nacional:** Edif. Peña Prieta, Avda Balboa y Calle 40 Bella Vista, Apdo 222, Panamá 1; tel. 27-0055; fax 25-4190; f. 1973; government-sponsored; finances national housing projects and regulates national savings system; Pres. Minister of Housing; Gen. Man. LUIS SÁNCHEZ ALMENGOR.

#### Savings Banks

**Banco General, SA:** Calle 34 Este y Avda Cuba, Apdo 4592, Panamá 5; tel. 27-3200; telex 2733; fax 27-3427; f. 1955; cap. 60.0m., dep. 744.6m., total assets 867.9m. (Dec. 1993); Chair. and CEO FEDERICO HUMBERT, Jr; Exec. Vice-Pres. and Gen. Man. RAÚL ALEMÁN Z.; 19 brs.

**Banco Panameño de la Vivienda:** Avda Chile y Calle 41, Apdo 8639, Panamá 5; tel. 27-4020; telex 3391; fax 27-5433; f. 1981; cap. and res 3.2m., dep. 30.7m., total assets 45.1m. (Dec. 1987); Gen. Man. MARIO L. FÁBREGA AROSEMENA; 3 brs.

**Banco Provincial, SA:** Avda Rodolfo Chiari, Apdo 122, Aguadulce; tel. 97-5010; fax 97-6433; f. 1987; cap. US $2.5m., dep. US $18.6m. (Dec. 1994); Gen. Man. J. PEDRO M. BARRAGÁN.

**Caja de Ahorros:** Vía España y Calle Thais de Pons, Apdo 1740, Panamá 1; tel. 63-6233; telex 2417; f. 1934; government-owned; cap. and res 10.1m., dep. 310.7m., total assets 359.6m. (1987); Chair. RAMÓN MORALES; Gen. Man. CARLOS GARCÍA DE PAREDES; 34 brs.

**Primer Banco de Ahorros, SA:** Avda Justo Arosemena y Calle 32, Apdo 7322, Panamá 5; tel. 27-2225; telex 2766; fax 27-4037; f. 1963; cap. and res 29.2m., dep. 249.1m., total assets 259.9m. (Dec. 1987); Gen. Man. JOAQUÍN DE LA GUARDIA; 15 brs.

#### Domestic Private Banks

**Banco Agro-Industrial y Comercial de Panamá, SA (BANAICO):** Edif. Cond. Bella Vista, planta baja, Avda Balboa 41-45, Apdo 4312, Panamá 5; tel. 27-1111; telex 2457; fax 25-9769; f. 1978; cap. 4.4m., res 1.6m., dep. 114.8m. (Dec. 1992); Gen. Man. GONZALO GONZÁLEZ O.

**Banco Comercial de Panamá (BANCOMER):** Plaza Bancomer, Avda Nicanor de Obarrio (Calle 50), Apdo 7659, Panamá 5; tel. 63-6800; telex 2439; fax 63-8033; f. 1979; cap. US $5.0m., res US $12.7m., dep. US $291.8m., total assets US $320.3m. (Dec. 1993); Pres. and Gen. Man. EMANUEL-GONZÁLEZ REVILLA; 5 brs.

**Banco Continental de Panamá, SA:** Vía España 120, Apdo 135, Panamá 9A; tel. 63-5955; telex 3201; fax 64-3359; f. 1972; cap. and res 9.4m., dep. 126.7m., total assets 136.8m. (Dec. 1987); Pres. ROBERTO MOTTA; Gen. Man. PAUL SMITH ALEGRE; 2 brs.

**Banco Disa, SA:** Calles Ricardo Arias y 51 Este, Apdo 7201, Panamá 5; tel. 63-5933; telex 3713; fax 64-1084; f. 1986; Gen. Man. JOAQUÍN J. VALLARINO, Jr.

**Banco Internacional de Panamá (BIPAN):** Complejo Plaza Marbella, Avda Aquilino de la Guardia y Calles 47 y 48, Apdo 11181, Panamá 6; tel. 63-9000; telex 3238; fax 63-9514; f. 1973; cap. US $18.8m., dep. US $172m., total assets US $211m. (Dec. 1993); Gen. Man. RENÉ A. DÍAZ; 3 brs.

**Banco del Istmo, SA:** Avda Nicanor de Obarrio (Calle 50) y Calle 54, Apdo 6-3823, El Dorado, Panamá; tel. 69-5555; telex 2146; fax 69-5168; f. 1984; cap. US $8.0m., res US $1.9m., dep. US $87.7m. (Dec. 1988); Gen. Man. ALBERTO VALLARINO; 12 brs.

**Banco Panamericano, SA (PANABANK):** Edif. Panabank, Casa Matriz, Calle 50, Apdo 1828, Panamá 1; tel. 63-9266; telex 3173; fax 64-5357; f. 1983; cap. and res 3.2m., dep. 42.5m., total assets 46.0m. (June 1991); Exec. Vice-Pres. GUIDO J. MARTINELLI, Jr.

**Banco de Santa Cruz de la Sierra (Panamá), SA:** Calle Samuel Lewis, Torre Banco Unión, 11°, Apdo 6-4416, El Dorado, Panamá; tel. 63-8477; telex 2613; fax 63-8404; f. 1980; cap. 3.0m., res 1.1m., dep. 74.5m. (Dec. 1994); Chair. JUAN MANUEL PARADA P.

**Banco Transatlántico, SA:** Calles Ricardo Arias y Manuel María Icaza, Apdo 7655, Panamá 5; tel. 69-2318; telex 3458; fax 69-4948; f. 1979; cap. and res 3.5m., dep. 31.9m., total assets 34.6m. (Dec. 1987); Gen. Man. RAÚL DE MENA; 2brs.

**Multi Credit Bank Inc:** Edif. Prosperidad, planta baja, Vía España 127, Apdo 8210, Panamá 7; tel. 69-0188; telex 3357; fax 64-4014; f. 1990; cap. and res 15.5m., dep. 137.6m. (Dec. 1994); Gen. Man. PEDRO OLIVA.

**Republic National Bank Inc.:** Calle 51 entre Avda Federico Boyd y Calle 47 (Colombia), Apdo 8962, Panamá 5; tel. 64-7777; telex 3243; fax 63-4722; f. 1969; cap. 4.0m., res 0.8m., dep. 30.0m. (Dec. 1987); Gen. Man. LUIS E. GUIZADO.

### Domestic Private Bank with International Licence

**Towerbank International Inc.:** Edif. Tower Plaza, Calle 50 y Ricardo Arias, Panamá; tel. 69-6900; telex 3733; fax 69-1536; f. 1971; dep. US $170.3m., total assets US $223.6m. (Dec. 1993); Pres. SAM KARDONSKI; Gen. Man. GYSBERTUS ANTONIUS DE WOLF; 1 br.

### Foreign Banks
Principal Foreign Banks with General Licence

**ABN AMRO Bank, NV** (Netherlands): Calle Manuel María Icaza 4, Apdo 10147, Panamá 4; tel. 63-6200; telex 2644; fax 69-0526; Gen. Man. ANDRÉ F. S. VAN DER MEULEN.

**American Express International Banking Corpn** (USA): Calle Manuel María Icaza 14, Panamá 4; tel. 63-5522; telex 6481; fax 69-1081; f. 1971; cap. and res 236.4m., dep. 2,317.4m., total assets 2,057.7m. (Dec. 1987); Gen. Man. INDURSEN GIDWANI.

**Banco Bilbao Vizcaya (PANAMA) SA** (Spain): Calle 51 y Aquilino de la Guardia, Apdo 3-392, Panamá 3; tel. 63-6922; telex 2340; fax 63-6483; f. 1982; cap. 10.0m., res 21.5m., dep. 154.0m. (Dec. 1993); Gen. Man. PAULINO GARCÍA TORAÑO MARTÍNEZ.

**Banco de Bogotá, SA** (Colombia): Centro Comercial Plaza Paitilla, Avda Balboa y Vía Italia, Apdo 8653, Panamá 5; tel. 64-6000; telex 2072; fax 63-8037; f. 1967; cap. 16.0m., dep. 264.6m., total assets 310.1m. (Dec. 1994); merged with Banco del Comercio, SA (Colombia) in 1994; Gen. Man. ANDREW L. CLARKSON.

**Banco do Brasil, SA:** Edif. Interseco, planta baja, Calle Elvira Méndez 10, Apdo 87-1123, Panamá 7; tel. 63-6566; telex 2767; fax 69-9867; f. 1973; cap. and res 52.3m., dep. 1,248.1m., total assets 1,320.2m. (Dec. 1993); Gen. Man. CELSO DE MEDEIROS DRUMMOND; 1 br.

**Banco Cafetero, SA** (Colombia): Avda Manuel María Icaza y Calle 52 Este 18, Apdo 384/Z9A, Panamá 9A; tel. 64-6777; telex 2512; fax 63-6115; f. 1966; cap. 24.5m., res 2.3m., dep. US $366.5m., (Dec. 1993); President GILBERTO GÓMEZ ARANGO; Gen. Man. ALVARO NARANJA SALAZAR; 2 brs.

**Banco Central, SA** (Spain): Edif. Banco Central, Avda Samuel Lewis y Calle Gerardo Ortega, Apdo 88-381, Panamá 8; tel. 63-9044; telex 3190; fax 69-5824; Gen. Man. JOSÉ ALONSO SÁNCHEZ.

**Banco Comercial Antioqueño, SA** (Colombia): Calle 52 y Elvira Méndez, Apdo 1630, Panamá 1; tel. 63-6577; fax 63-6865; Gen. Man. J. ANCIZAR MUÑOZ ECHEVERRÍA.

**Banco de Colombia, SA:** Edif. Hatillo, Avda Cuba y Calle 36, Apdo 4213, Panamá 5; tel. 27-3633; telex 2140; fax 27-0434; f. 1964; cap. and res 25.1m., dep. 123.6m., total assets 132.8m. (Dec. 1987); Gen. Man. JOSÉ A. LLINAS B.

**Banco del Comercio, SA** (Colombia): Calle Aquilino de la Guardia 48-49, Apdo 4599, Panamá 5; tel. 63-5655; telex 2086; fax 63-6063; f. 1967; cap. and res 5.2m., dep. 29.5m., total assets 40.6m. (Dec. 1987); Gen. Man. JUAN ANTONIO NIÑO.

**Banco Consolidado, SA** (Venezuela): Calle Manuel María Icaza 19, Urban. Campo Alegre, Apdo 4489, Panamá 5; tel. 69-5300; telex 2853; fax 69-6344; f. 1980; cap. US $8.5m., res US $1.1m., dep. US $134.2m. (Dec. 1993); Gen. Man. IGNACIO FÁBREGA O.

**Banco do Estado de São Paulo, SA** (Brazil): Apdo 8332, Panamá 7; tel. 63-5152; cap. 5.4m., dep. 392.2m. (Dec. 1986); total assets 369.6m. (Dec. 1985); Gen. Man. WILSON FERRAZ DE CAMPOS.

**Banco Exterior, SA** (Spain): Avda Balboa esq. Calles 42 y 43, Apdo 8673, Panamá 5; tel. 27-1122; telex 2991; fax 27-3663; f. 1966; cap. 10.6m., res 0.7m., dep. 249.5m., total assets 273.2m. (Dec. 1992); Pres. IÑIGO DE LA SOTA GALDÉZ; Gen. Man. ANTONIO DÍAZ SUFFO; 8 brs.

**Banco Ganadero, SA** (Colombia): Calles Manuel María Icaza y 51 Este, El Dorado, Apdo 6-3567, Panamá; tel. 63-7933; telex 2036; fax 63-8985; f. 1980; cap. US $19.5m., res. US $8.5m., dep. US $117.0m. (Nov. 1993); Gen. Man. ABEL MERCADO.

**Banco de Iberoamérica, SA** (Spain): Avda Nicanor de Obarrio (Calle 50) y Calle 53, Apdo 6553, Panamá 5; tel. 63-5366; telex 2972; fax 69-1616; f. 1975; cap. 18m., res 5.0m., dep. 207.7m., total assets 253.0m. (Dec. 1993); Gen. Man. JUAN MANUEL LIMA BAUTISTA; 4 brs.

**Banco Industrial Colombiano de Panamá, SA** (Colombia): Calle Manuel María Icaza 11, Apdo 8593, Panamá 5; tel. 63-6955; telex 2731; fax 69-1138; f. 1973; cap. 4.0m., res 2.6m., dep. 161.4m. (Dec. 1992); Gen. Man. JORGE DURÁN OSPINA.

**Banco Latinamericano de Exportaciones (BLADEX)** (Multinational): Casa Matriz, Calle 50 y Aquilino de la Guardia, Apdo 6-1497, El Dorado, Panamá 5; tel. 63-6766; telex 2240; fax 69-6333; f. 1979; groups together 269 Latin American commercial and central banks and 28 international banks, the International Finance Corpn (affiliate of World Bank) and some 3,000 New York Stock Exchange shareholders; cap. US $369.4m., dep. US $1,472.8m., total assets US $4,022.5m. (Dec. 1994); Gen. Man. and CEO JOSÉ CASTAÑEDA.

**Banco de Occidente (Panamá), SA** (Colombia): Edif. Lizak, Calle 50 y Aquilino de la Guardia, Apdo 6-7430, El Dorado, Panamá; tel. 63-8144; telex 3420; fax 69-3261; Pres. MAURICIO CABRERA GALVIZ.

**Banco del Pacífico, SA** (Ecuador): Edif. Banco del Pacífico, Aquilino de la Guardia y Calle 52, Apdo 6-3100, El Dorado, Panamá; tel. 63-5833; telex 2824; fax 63-7481; f. 1980; cap. US $6.0m., res US $4.5m., dep. US $205.3m. (Dec. 1993); Pres. LUIS A. SANTAMARÍA.

**Banco Popular Dominicano (Panama), SA** (Dominican Republic): Edif. Banco Iberoamérica, 3rd Floor, Calle 50 y Calle 53, Apdo 5404, Panamá 9; tel. 69-4166; telex 2061; fax 69-1309; f. 1983; cap. 2.0m., res 0.8m., dep. 51.6m. (Dec. 1993); Pres. RAFAEL A. RODRÍGUEZ.

**Banco Real, SA** (Brazil): Calle Manuel María Icaza 16, Apdo 7048, Panamá 5; tel. 69-1444; telex 2924; fax 69-1716; f. 1975; cap. and res 48.7m., dep. 224.6m., total assets 245.2m. (Dec. 1993); Gen. Man. ROBSON MARZANO LOPES DE ARAUJO; 1 br.

**Banco Santander Panamá, SA** (Spain): Cond. Plaza Internacional, planta baja, Vía España y Calle 55, Apdo 484, Panamá 9A; tel. 63-6262; telex 2996; fax 63-7553; f. 1967 as Banco de Santander y Panamá; name changed in 1987; cap. 10.8m., res 0.31m., dep. 58.1m., total assets 72.0m. (Dec. 1988); Pres. EMILIO BOTIN-SANZ DE SAUTUOLA; Vice-Pres. and Gen. Man. MANUEL J. BARREDO M.; 2 brs.

**Banco Unión, SACA** (Venezuela): Torre Banco Unión, 1°, Avda Samuel Lewis, Apdo 'A', Panamá 5; tel. 64-9133; telex 2569; fax 63-9985; f. 1974; cap. and res 15.6m., dep. 177.1m. (Dec. 1993); Gen. Man. MARÍA M. DE MÉNDEZ; 1 br.

**Bank Leumi Le-Israel, BM** (Israel): Edif. Grobman, planta baja, Calle Manuel María Icaza, Apdo 6-4518, El Dorado, Panamá; tel. 63-9377; telex 2936; fax 69-2674; Gen. Man. ALBERT BITTON; 2 brs.

**Bank of Boston** (USA): Vía España 122, Apdo 5368, Panamá 5; tel. 64-2244; telex 3232; fax 64-7402; f. 1973; fmrly The First National Bank of Boston; cap. and res 3.7m., dep. 80.6m., total assets 79.2m. (Dec. 1987); Gen. Man. LUIS A. NAVARRO; 2 brs.

**Bank of Nova Scotia** (Canada): Calle Manuel María Icaza, Apdo 7327, Panamá 5; tel. 63-6255; telex 3266; fax 63-8636; Gen. Man. MARCELA GONZÁLEZ D.

**The Bank of Tokyo Ltd** (Japan): Vía España y Calle Aquilino de la Guardia, Apdo 1313, Panamá 1; tel. 63-6777; telex 2159; fax 63-5269; f. 1973; cap. and res 7.0m., dep. 963.0m., total assets 989m. (Mar. 1994); Gen. Man. KAZUTOSHI HOSHINO.

**Banque Nationale de Paris (Panama), SA** (France): Edif. Omanco, Vía España 200, Apdo 1774, Panamá 1; tel. 63-6900; telex 2681; fax 63-6970; f. 1948; incorporates Banco Fiduciario de Panamá; cap. 6.6m., res 4.2m., dep. 154.1m., total assets 222.0m. (Dec. 1993); Pres. ARISTIDES ROMERO; Gen. Man. DENIS MADAULE; 3 brs.

**Banque Sudameris** (Multinational): Avda Balboa y Calle 41, Apdo 1846, Panamá 9A; tel. 27-2777; fax 27-5828; Gen. Man. PAUL PINELLI; 2 brs.

**The Chase Manhattan Bank, NA** (USA): Plaza Chase, Calle 47 y Avda Aquilino de la Guardia; Apdo 9A-76, Panamá 9A; tel. 63-5855; telex 2067; fax 63-6009; f. 1915; cap. 15.5m., dep. 689.7m., total assets 735.9m. (Dec. 1994); Gen. Man. OLEGARIO BARRELIER; 10 brs.

**Citibank NA** (USA): Vía España 124, Apdo 555, Panamá 9A; tel. 63-8377; telex 2129; fax 69-4171; f. 1904; cap. and res 8.0m., dep. 236.0m., total assets 259.8m. (Dec. 1988); Gen. Man. EDUARDO URRIOLA; 10 brs.

**The Dai Ichi Kangyo Bank, SA** (Japan): Edif. Plaza Internacional, Vía España, Apdo 2637, Panamá 9A; tel. 69-6111; telex 2030; fax 69-6815; f. 1979; cap. and res 2.0m., dep. 216.1m., total assets 218.4m. (Sept. 1991); Gen. Man. TOSHIO SAHARA.

**Grupo Dresdner Bank** (Germany): Torre Banco Germánico, Calle 50 y Calle 55 Este, Apdo 5400, Panamá 5; tel. 63-5055; telex 2420; fax 69-1877; f. 1971; affiliated to Dresdner Bank AG; cap. 5.0m., dep. 1,131.4m., total assets 1,186.1m. (Dec. 1992); Gen. Man. PETER NAEHR.

**Hongkong and Shanghai Banking Corpn Ltd** (Hong Kong): Torre Banco Unión, planta baja, Avda Samuel Lewis, Panamá; tel. 69-6200; telex 2284; fax 69-5577; Gen. Man. JOSEPH L. SALTERIO, Jr; 2 brs.

**The International Commerical Bank of China** (Taiwan): Edif. ICBC, Avda Nicanor de Obarrio, Apdo 4453, Panamá 5; tel. 63-8108; telex 2294; fax 63-8392; Gen. Man. TAI-HSIUNG LEE.

**Korea Exchange Bank** (Republic of Korea): Avda Balboa y Calle 42, Apdo 8358, Panamá 7; tel. 27-3211; telex 2189; fax 27-3900; Gen. Man. YOUNG-BU BAEK.

**Lloyds Bank PlC** (United Kingdom): Calles Aquilino de la Guardia y 48, Apdo 8522, Panamá 5; tel. 63-6277; fax 64-7931; Gen. Man. JORGE E. FRANCKE; 3 brs.

**The Mitsui Taiyo Kobe Bank Ltd** (Japan): Avda Ricardo Arango y Calle 53 Este, Urb. Obarrio, Apdo 8-028, Panamá 8; tel. 23-8802; telex 3322; f. 1980; cap. 2.1m., dep. 175.3m. (Mar. 1987); total assets 264.4m. (Dec. 1987); Gen. Man. EDUARDO FERRER; 1 br.

**The Sanwa Bank Ltd** (Japan): Edif. Vallarino, planta baja, Calle Elvira Méndez y Calle 52, Apdo 6-2494, Panamá; tel. 64-6633; telex 2503; fax 64-0269; f. 1980; cap. and res. 11.2m., dep. 147.5m., total assets 1,469.3m. (Dec. 1987); Gen. Man. JUAN CARLOS ROSAS; 1 br.

**State Bank of India** (India): Avda Federico Boyd y Calle 51 No 10, Apdo 6-4526, El Dorado, Panamá; tel. 63-6866; telex 2442; fax 69-6780; Gen. Man. S. C. PATHAK.

**Swiss Bank Corporation (Overseas), SA:** Torre Swiss Bank, Calle 53 Este Marbella, Apdo 61, Panamá 9A; tel. 63-7181; telex 3166; fax 69-5995; f. 1968; cap. US $6m., dep. US $1,153.4m., total assets US $1,186.1m. (Dec. 1994); Pres. ERNST BALSIGER.

### Principal Foreign Banks with International Licence

**Arlabank International, EC** (Bahrain): Edif. Vallarino, 6°, Calle Elvira Méndez y Calle 52, Apdo 6-8082, Panamá; tel. 64-9802; telex 3372; fax 69-4989; Man. JAIME MARÍA LUZULA.

**Banco Alemán Platina, SA:** Edif. BAP, Avda Federico Boyd y Avda 4A, A Sur, Apdo 6180, Panamá 5; tel. 23-8005; telex 2090; fax 69-0910; f. 1965; as Banco Alemán-Panameño, current name adopted in 1993; cap. US $6.0m., res US $15.5m., dep. US $205.8m. (Aug. 1993); Pres. FRANK BÜRSING.

**Banco de la Nación Argentina:** Avda Federico Boyd y Calle 51, Apdo 6-3298, El Dorado, Panamá; tel. 69-4666; telex 2996; fax 69-6719; f. 1977; cap. and res 183.1m., dep. 1,015.2m. (Dec. 1984); total assets 3,314.7m. (Dec. 1985); Gen. Man. OLGA DE SOLIS.

**Banco de la Provincia de Buenos Aires** (Argentina): Edif. Banco Exterior, 22°, Avda Balboa, entre Calles 42 y 43, Apdo 6-4592, El Dorado, Panamá; tel. 27-2167; telex 6444; fax 25-0431; f. 1982; total assets 1,755.1m. (Dec. 1990); Gen. Man. JUAN CARLOS STURLESI.

**Crédit Lyonnais** (France): Edif. Interseco, 7°, Calle Elvira Méndez 10, Apdo 1778, Panamá 9A; tel. 63-6522; telex 2231; fax 63-5904; f. 1978; cap. and res 1.3m., dep. 1,212.7m. (Dec. 1984); total assets 1,041.9m. (Dec. 1985); Gen. Man. PIERRE LEBRETON.

**Mitsubishi Trust and Banking Corpn** (Japan): Torre Swiss Bank, Calle 53, Apdo 61, Panamá 9A; tel. 63-7181; fax 69-5991; f. 1981; cap. and res 10.4m., dep. 646.5m. (Dec. 1984); total assets 622.8m. (Dec. 1985); Gen. Man. HANS-JORG BOSCH.

### Banking Association

**Asociación Bancaria de Panamá (ABP):** Torre Banco Unión, 15°, Avda Samuel Lewis, Apdo 4554, Panamá 5; tel. 63-7044; fax 63-7783; f. 1962; 77 mems; Pres. PAULINO GARCÍA-TORAÑO M.; Vice-Pres. RAÚL DE MENA.

### STOCK EXCHANGE

**Bolsa de Valores de Panamá:** Edif. Vallarino, planta baja, Calle Elvira Méndez y Calle 52, Panamá; tel. 69-1966; fax 69-2457; f. 1960; Gen. Man. ROBERTO BRANES P.

### INSURANCE

**Administración de Seguros, SA:** Edif. ASSA, Avda Nicanor de Obarrio (Calle 50), Apdo 5371, Panamá 5; tel. 69-0444; telex 2742; fax 63-9234; Pres. VICENTE PASCUAL; Man. CARLOS A. RABAT MALLOL.

**Aseguradora Mundial, SA:** Edif. Aseguradora Mundial, Avda Balboa y Calle 41, Apdo 8911, Panamá 5; tel. 27-4444; telex 2591; fax 25-8176; general; f. 1937; Man. ORLANDO SÁNCHEZ AVILÉS.

**ASSA Cía de Seguros, SA:** Edif. ASSA, Avda Nicanor de Obarrio (Calle 50), Apdo 5371, Panamá 5; tel. 69-0444; telex 2742; fax 63-9234; f. 1981; Pres. LORENZO ROMAGOSA; Man. CARLOS A. RABAT MALLOL.

**Cía Colonial de Seguros de Panamá, SA:** Edif. Bank of America, 12°, Calle 50, Panamá 5; tel. 69-3222; telex 2974; fax 64-7977; Man. JOSÉ ROGELIO ARIAS III.

**Cía General de Seguros, SA:** Edif. ASSA, Avda Nicanor de Obarrio (Calle 50), Apdo 5371, Panamá 5; tel. 69-0444; telex 2742; fax 63-9234; Pres. RAMÓN M. ARIAS C.; Man. CARLOS A. RABAT MALLOL.

**Cía Internacional de Seguros, SA:** Avda Cuba y Calles 35 y 36, Apdo 1036, Panamá 1; tel. 27-4000; telex 2635; f. 1910; Pres. ARTURO MULLER A.; Gen. Man. ROMEO CORONADO G.

**Cía Nacional de Seguros, SA:** Calle 47 y Aquilino de la Guardia, Plaza Marbella, Apdo 5303, Panamá 5; tel. 63-8222; fax 69-6568; f. 1957; Pres. GABRIEL J. DE LA GUARDIA; Gen. Man. RAÚL MORRICE.

**Cía Panameña de Seguros, SA:** Edif. ASSA, Avda Nicanor de Obarrio (Calle 50), Apdo 3065, Panamá 3; tel. 69-0444; telex 2742; fax 63-9234; f. 1948; Pres. LORENZO ROMAGOSA; Man. CARLOS A. RABAT MALLOL.

**Cía de Seguros Chagres, SA:** Edif. Chagres, Avda 4a Sur No 62, Apdo 6-1599, El Dorado, Panamá; tel. 67-7433; telex 2449; fax 63-9106; Man. RAÚL NOVEY.

**La Seguridad de Panamá, Cía de Seguros SA:** Edif. Lizak, Calle 50 esq. Aquilino de la Guardia, Apdo 718, Panamá 1; telex 2091; Man. COURTNEY STEMPEL.

**LARSA Latin American Reinsurance Co Inc.:** Apdo 810, Panamá 1; tel. 63-5866; telex 2641; fax 63-5713; Pres. LAURENCIO JAÉN O.

## Trade and Industry

**Colón Free Zone (CFZ):** Avda Roosevelt, Apdo 1118, Colón; tel. 45-1035; telex 8677; f. 1948 to manufacture, import, handle and re-export all types of merchandise; some 786 companies were established by 1976. Well-known international banks operate in the CFZ, where there are also customs, postal and telegraph services. In 1993 the value of imports was 4,493m. balboas. Re-exports amounted to 5,115m. balboas. The main exporters to the CFZ are Japan, the USA, Hong Kong, Taiwan, the Republic of Korea, Colombia, France, Italy and the United Kingdom. The main importers from the CFZ are Brazil, Venezuela, Mexico, Ecuador, the Netherlands Dependencies, Bolivia, the USA, Chile, Argentina and Colombia. In view of the rapid expansion in turnover of the Zone in recent years, the total area of 138.2 ha was to be extended to 485.3 ha. The expansion was expected to result in an increase of 68% in the movement of goods. Gen. Man. JAIME FORD.

### CHAMBER OF COMMERCE

**Cámara de Comercio, Industrias y Agricultura de Panamá:** Avda Cuba y Ecuador 33A, Apdo 74, Panamá 1; tel. 27-1233; fax 27-4186; f. 1915; Pres. RICARDO J. DURÁN; Exec. Dir Ing. JOSÉ RAMÓN VARELA; 1,300 mems.

### INDUSTRIAL ORGANIZATIONS

**Cámara Oficial Española de Comercio:** Calle 33 este, Apdo 1857, Panamá 1; tel. 25-1487; telex 3471; Pres. EDELMIRO GARCÍA VILLA VERDE; Sec.-Gen. ATILIANO ALFONSO MARTÍNEZ.

**Cámara Panameña de la Construcción:** Calle Aquilino de la Guardia No 19, Apdo 6793, Panamá 5; tel. 64-2255; fax 64-2384; represents interests of construction sector; Pres. Ing. JOSÉ F. JELENSZKY.

**Codemín:** Edif. Banco Nacional, 1a Torre, 12°, Vía España, Panamá; tel. 63-7475; state mining organization; Dir JAIME ROQUEBERT.

**Consejo Nacional de Inversiones (CNI):** Edif. Banco Nacional de Panamá, Apdo 2350, Panamá; tel. 64-7211; telex 3499; f. 1982; national investment council; promotes private local and foreign investments; Exec. Dir Lic. JULIO E. SOSA.

**Corporación Azucarera La Victoria:** Calle II Juegos Centroamericanos, Apdo 1228, Panamá 1; tel. 33-3833; telex 2601; state sugar corporation; scheduled for transfer to private ownership in 1994; Dir Prof. ALEJANDRO VERNAZA.

**Corporación para el Desarrollo Integral del Bayano:** Avda Balboa, al lado de la estación del tren, Estafeta El Dorado, Panamá 2; tel. 32-6160; f. 1978; state agriculture, forestry and cattle-breeding corporation; Dir Ing. JOSÉ MARÍA CHAVERRI.

**Corporación Financiera Nacional—COFINA:** Apdo 6-2191, Estafeta El Dorado, Panamá; telex 2583; f. 1976 to develop state and private undertakings in productive sectors; Dir Lic. PEDRO SOTOMAYOR.

**Dirección General de Industrias:** Edif. de la Lotería, 19°, Apdo 9658, Panamá 4; tel. 27-4403; government body which undertakes feasibility studies, analyses and promotion; Dir-Gen. LUCÍA DE FERGUSON; National Dir of Business Development ULPIANO PRADO.

**Instituto Panameño de Comercio Exterior (IPCE):** Edif. Banco Exterior, Torre Chica, 3° y 4°, Apdo 55-2359, Paitilla, Panamá; tel. 25-7244; fax 25-2193; f. 1984; foreign trade organization; Exec. Dir ROY A. RIVERA.

**Instituto de Recursos Hidráulicos y Electrificación (IRHE):** Edif. Poli, Avda Justo Arosemena y 26 Este, Apdo 5285, Panamá 5; tel. 62-6272; telex 2158; state organization responsible for the national public electricity supply; scheduled for partial privatization in 1992; Dir-Gen. BENJAMÍN COLAMARCO.

**Sindicato de Industriales de Panamá:** Vía Ricardo J. Alfaro, Entrada Urb. Sara Sotillo, Apdo 6-4798, Estafeta El Dorado, Panamá; tel. 30-0169; fax 30-0805; f. 1945; represents and promotes activities of industrial sector; Pres. LUIS BARRAZA DE FREITAS.

### EMPLOYERS' ORGANIZATIONS

**Asociación Panameña de Ejecutivos de Empresas (APEDE):** Edif. APEDE, Calle 42 Bella Vista y Avda Balboa, Apdo 1331, Panamá 1; tel. 27-3511; fax 27-1872; Pres. RICARDO E. ORTEGA C.

**Consejo Nacional de la Empresa Privada (CONEP):** Calle 41, Bella Vista, Apdo 1276, Panamá 1; tel. 25-5306; telex 2434; fax 25-2663; Pres. DARÍO SELLES.

**Consejo Nacional para el Desarrollo de la Pequeña Empresa:** Ministry of Commerce and Industry, Apdo 9658, Panamá 4; tel. 27-3559; telex 3197; fax 27-3927; f. 1983; advisory and consultative board to the Ministry of Commerce and Industry.

### TRADE UNIONS

In 1981 the Labour Code which had been promulgated in 1977 was amended, establishing the right to strike and increasing compensation for dismissal. Collective bargaining is permitted and employers must pay workers' salaries during the whole period of a legal strike.

**Central Istmeña de Trabajadores—CIT** (Isthmian Labour Confederation): Vía España 16, Of. 1, Apdo 6308, Panamá 5; tel. 64-0509; f. 1971; Sec.-Gen. JULIO CÉSAR PINZÓN.

**Confederación de Trabajadores de la República de Panamá—CTRP** (Confederation of Workers of the Republic of Panama): Calle 31 entre Avdas México y Justo Arosemena 3-50, Apdo 8929, Panamá 5; tel. 25-0293; fax 25-0259; f. 1956; admitted to ICFTU/ORIT; Sec.-Gen. ANIANO PINZÓN REAL; 62,000 mems from 13 affiliated groups.

**Consejo Nacional de Trabajadores Organizados—CONATO** (National Council of Organized Labour): Panamá; tel. 27-0409; Co-ordinators EDUARDO RÍOS, MARTÍN GONZÁLEZ; 150,000 mems.

**Federación Nacional de Asociaciones de Empleados Públicos—FENASEP** (National Federation of Associations of Public Employees): Panamá; Pres. HÉCTOR ALEMÁN.

A number of unions exist without affiliation to a national centre.

# Transport

### RAILWAYS

In early 1989 the Panama Railroad announced details of a joint project with the Autoridad Portuaria Nacional (see section on Shipping) to renovate the national railway system.

**Chiriquí Land Co:** Apdo 6-2637, Estafeta El Dorado, Panamá; tel. 78-8240; telex 2292; operates two lines which run in Costa Rica: the Northern Line (Almirante, Bocas del Toro) with 243 km and the Southern Line (Puerto Armuelles, Chiriquí) with 133 km; purchased by the Government in 1978; Gen. Man. G. C. FORSYTH.

**Ferrocarril Nacional de Chiriquí:** Apdo 12B, David City, Chiriquí; tel. 75-4241; fax 75-4105; 126 km linking Puerto Armuelles and David City; Gen. Man. M. ALVARENGA.

**Ferrocarril de Panamá:** Apdo 2023, Estafeta de Balboa; tel. 32-6086; fax 32-5343; government-owned and operated mainly as a tourist attraction and for cargo transport; operates 76 km; Dir-Gen. J. E. MORALES Q.

### ROADS

In 1992 there were 10,103 km of roads, of which 793 km were highways. The two most important highways are the Pan-American Highway and the Boyd-Roosevelt or Trans-Isthmian, linking Panamá (Panama City) and Colón. The Pan-American Highway to Mexico City runs for 545 km in Panama. There is a highway to San José, Costa Rica.

### SHIPPING

The Panama Canal opened in 1914. In 1984 more than 4% of all the world's seaborne trade passed through the waterway. It is 82 km long, and ships take an average of eight hours to complete a transit. In 1994 an estimated 12,478 transits were recorded. The Canal can accommodate ships with a maximum draught of 12 m and beams of up to approximately 32.3 m (106 ft) and lengths of up to about 290 m (950 ft), roughly equivalent to ships with a maximum capacity of 65,000–70,000 dwt. Improvements to the Canal increased the transit capacity to 42 vessels per day. Almost 70% of all traffic through the Canal either originates from, or is destined for, the USA. Japan is the second most regular user of the Canal, and in 1986 Japan, the USA and Panama established a commission to consider the future of the Canal. The commission's report, published in early 1994, concluded that no major development work would be necessary before 2010. Terminal ports are Balboa, on the Pacific Ocean, and Cristóbal, on the Caribbean Sea. A ferry service between Colón and Cartagena (Colombia) was inaugurated in December 1994.

**Autoridad Portuaria Nacional:** Apdo 8062, Panamá 7; tel. 69-3921; telex 2765; fax 69-6992; national port authority; Gen. Dir Dr HUGO TORRIJOS.

**Dirección General Consular y de Naves:** Ministerio de Hacienda y Tesoro, Apdo 5245, Panamá 5; tel. 27-1166; telex 2537; fax 27-2716; government-controlled general consular and shipping directorate; Dir-Gen. ABRAHAM SOFER B.

**Panama Canal Commission:** Balboa Heights, Panamá; tel. 52-3165; telex 3034; fax 52-2122; in October 1979 the Panama Canal Commission, a US Government agency, was established to perform the mission, previously accomplished by the Panama Canal Company, of managing, operating and maintaining the Panama Canal. The Commission will operate the Canal until 31 December 1999, when the waterway will be ceded to the Government of Panama. The supervisory board of the Commission consists of five US and four Panamanian citizens. Until 31 December 1989 the Administrator was a US citizen and, from 1 January 1990, until 31 December 1999, the Administrator will be a Panamanian citizen; Administrator GILBERTO GUARDIA FÁBREGA.

**Autoridad del Canal de Panamá (ACP):** Panamá; f. 1994; semi-autonomous body established to supervise the conservation, modernization and maintenance of the Canal, after 1999.

**Autoridad de la Región Interoceánica (ARI):** Panamá; f. 1993; govt body created to administer the land and property of the former Canal Zone following their transfer from US to Panamanian control, after 1999; legislation approved in early 1995 transferred control of the ARI to the President of the Republic; Dir Dr NICOLÁS ARDITO BARLETTA.

**Panama City Port Authority and Foreign Trade Zone 65:** Apdo 15095, Panamá, FL 32406, USA; Dir RUDY ETHEREDGE.

There are deep-water ports at Balboa and Cristóbal (including general cargo ships, containers, shipyards, industrial facilities); Coco Solo (general cargo and containers); Bahía Las Minas (general bulk and containers); Vacamonte (main port for fishing industry); Puerto Armuelles and Almirante (bananas); Aguadulce and Pedregal (export of crude sugar and molasses, transport of fertilizers and chemical products); and Charco Azul and Chiriquí Grande (crude oil).

The Panamanian merchant fleet was the largest in the world in June 1993, with an aggregate displacement of 57.6m. gross tons and numbering 5,564 vessels.

### CIVIL AVIATION

Tocumen (formerly Omar Torrijos) international airport was inaugurated in June 1978. The Marcos A. Gelabert airport at Paitilla handles some domestic and private services.

**Aerolíneas Pacífico Atlántico, SA (Aeroperlas):** Apdo 6-3596, El Dorado, Panamá; tel. 23-5300; telex 2870; fax 23-0606; operates scheduled domestic flights; fmrly state-owned, transferred to private ownership in 1987; Pres. RAÚL ESPINOSA; Gen. Man. RAÚL ARIAS DE LA GUARDIA.

**Compañía Panameña de Aviación, SA (COPA):** Avda Justo Arosemena 230 y Calle 39, Apdo 1572, Panamá 1; tel. 27-2522; telex 2893; fax 27-1952; f. 1944; scheduled passenger and cargo services from Panamá (Panama City) to Colombia, Central America, the Caribbean and the USA; Chair. and Pres. ALBERTO MOTTA C.; Gen. Man. PEDRO O. HEILBRON.

**Dirección de Aeronaútica Civil:** Apdo 7615, Panamá 7; tel. 27-0211; telex 2618; directorate for civil aviation; Dir Capt. ZÓSIMO GUARDIA VARELA.

**Panama Air International, SA:** Avda Justo Arosemena y Calle 34, Panamá 5; tel. 27-2371, telex 2665; fax 27-2281; f. 1967; fmrly state-owned (as Air Panama International), transferred to private ownership in Dec. 1991; services from Panamá (Panama City) to destinations throughout the Americas; Pres. JOAQUÍN J. VALLARINO.

A new airline, Panavia, was established in 1994, while Trans Canal Airways, was expected to begin scheduled passenger and cargo services to Miami (USA) in July 1995.

# Tourism

Panama's attractions include Panamá (Panama City), the ruins of Portobelo and 800 sandy tropical islands, including the resort of Contadora, one of the Pearl Islands in the Gulf of Panama, and the San Blas Islands, lying off the Atlantic coast. The number of foreign visitors to Panama declined from 370,369 in 1982 to 200,436 in 1989, partly as a result of internal and regional instability. By 1992 the number of visitors had increased to an estimated 303,428 and income from tourism an estimated US $159.9m.; the estimated number of visitors increased to 327,000 in 1993.

**Instituto Panameño de Turismo (IPAT):** Centro de Convenciones ATLAPA, Vía Israel, Apdo 4421, Panamá 5; tel. 26-7000; telex 3359; fax 26-3483; f. 1960; Dir-Gen. ANEL E. BÉLIZ.

**Asociación Panameña de Agencias de Viajes y Turismo (APAVIT):** Apdo 55-1000 Paitilla, Panamá 3; tel. 23-5263; fax 23-0175; Pres. MICHELLE DE GUIZADO.

# PAPUA NEW GUINEA

## Introductory Survey

### Location, Climate, Language, Religion, Flag, Capital

The Independent State of Papua New Guinea lies east of Indonesia and north of the north-eastern extremity of Australia. It comprises the eastern section of the island of New Guinea (the western section of which is Irian Jaya, part of Indonesia) and about 600 smaller islands, including the Bismarck Archipelago (mainly New Britain, New Ireland and Manus) and the northern part of the Solomon Islands (mainly Bougainville and Buka). The climate is hot and humid throughout the year, with an average maximum temperature of 33°C (91°F) and an average minimum of 22°C (72°F). Rainfall is heavy on the coast but lower inland: the annual average varies from about 1,000 mm (40 ins) to 6,350 mm (250 ins). There are an estimated 742 native languages, but Pidgin and, to a lesser extent, standard English are also spoken, and, together with Motu, are the official languages in Parliament. More than 90% of the population profess Christianity. The national flag (proportions 4 by 3) is divided diagonally from the upper hoist to the lower fly: the upper portion displays a golden bird of paradise in silhouette on a red ground, while the lower portion has five white five-pointed stars, in the form of the Southern Cross constellation, on a black ground. The capital is Port Moresby.

### Recent History

Papua New Guinea was formed by the merger of the Territory of Papua, under Australian rule from 1906, with the Trust Territory of New Guinea, a former German possession which Australia administered from 1914, first under a military Government, then under a League of Nations mandate, established in 1921, and later under a trusteeship agreement with the UN. During the Second World War, parts of both territories were occupied by Japanese forces from 1942 to 1945.

A joint administration for the two territories was established by Australia in July 1949. The union was named the Territory of Papua and New Guinea. A Legislative Council was established in November 1951 and was replaced by a House of Assembly, with an elected indigenous majority, in June 1964. The territory was renamed Papua New Guinea in July 1971. It achieved internal self-government in December 1973 and full independence on 16 September 1975, when the House of Assembly became the National Parliament.

Michael Somare, who from 1972 served as Chief Minister in an interim coalition government, became Prime Minister on independence. He remained in office until 1980, despite widespread allegations of inefficiency in government ministries and of discrimination against the Highland provinces. The first elections since independence were held in June and July 1977, and Somare's Pangu (Papua New Guinea Unity) Pati formed a governing coalition, first with the People's Progress Party (PPP) and later with the United Party (UP).

In March 1980 the Government lost a vote of confidence, the fourth in 15 months, and Sir Julius Chan, the leader of the PPP and a former Deputy Prime Minister, succeeded to the premiership. Somare became Prime Minister again in August 1982, following a general election in June. In 1983, in spite of a general policy of decentralization, the Somare Government effected a constitutional change to provide the central authorities with greater control of the provincial governments as a means of preventing abuse of their powers. As a result, Somare was able to suspend the Enga provincial government in February 1984, and two others later in the year, for financial mismanagement. Between 1983 and March 1991 a total of nine provincial governments were suspended by the central Government for alleged maladministration.

In March 1985 the Deputy Prime Minister, Paias Wingti, resigned his position and his membership of the Pangu Pati, in order to challenge Somare for the premiership. A motion expressing 'no confidence' in Somare's Government was introduced in Parliament by Chan, who nominated Wingti as alternative Prime Minister. Somare quickly formed a coalition, comprising the ruling Pangu Pati, the National Party (NP) and the Melanesian Alliance (MA), and the 'no confidence' motion was defeated. Fourteen members of Parliament who had supported the motion were expelled from the Pangu Pati, and subsequently formed a new political party, the People's Democratic Movement (PDM), under the leadership of Wingti, who was replaced as Deputy Prime Minister by Father John Momis, the leader of the MA.

In August 1985 the NP, led by Iambakey Okuk, withdrew from Somare's coalition Government, and in November Chan presented another motion of 'no confidence', criticizing Somare's handling of the economy. Somare was defeated by 58 votes to 51, and Wingti took office as Prime Minister of a new five-party coalition Government (comprising the PDM, the PPP, the NP, the UP and the MA), with Chan as Deputy Prime Minister.

At the mid-1987 general election to the National Parliament, polling took place in 106 of the 109 constituencies (having been postponed in three). Somare's Pangu Pati won 26 seats and Wingti's PDM obtained 18. However, by forming a coalition with minor parties, Wingti succeeded in securing a parliamentary majority of three and was re-elected Prime Minister. In July 1988 Wingti was defeated in a 'no confidence' motion, proposed by Rabbie Namaliu, who had replaced Somare as leader of the Pangu Pati. As a result, Namaliu took office as Prime Minister and announced a new coalition Government, comprising members of the Pangu Pati and five minor parties: the People's Action Party (PAP), the MA, the NP, the League for National Advancement (LNA) and the Papua Party. An amendment to the Constitution, whereby a motion expressing 'no confidence' in the Prime Minister could not be proposed until he or she had completed 30 months in office, was approved by the National Executive Council (cabinet), subject to adoption by the legislature, in October. In August Ted Diro, the leader of the PAP, was acquitted on a charge of perjury by the Supreme Court (having been accused in 1987 of illegally appropriating funds for his party, after which he resigned from the Government). In early 1989 the leader of the NP, Michael Mel, withdrew his support for Namaliu's Government. A motion of 'no confidence' in the Government, presented in March 1989, was to be debated when Parliament resumed in July: the motion was withdrawn in July, however, following the murder of the Minister of Communications, Malipu Balakau, and in view of the continuing unrest on the island of Bougainville (see below).

In April 1988 landowners on the island of Bougainville submitted compensation claims amounting to K10,000m., for land mined by the Australian-owned Bougainville Copper Ltd since 1972. When no payment was forthcoming, acts of sabotage were perpetrated in November and December of that year by the Bougainville Revolutionary Army (BRA), led by Francis Ona, a former mine surveyor and landowner, and the mine was obliged to suspend operations for an initial period of six days. However, when repairs had been completed, the mine's owners refused to resume operations for fear of further attack, and Namaliu was forced to deploy members of the security forces in the area. Production at the mine recommenced in December, but, after further violence in January 1989, a curfew was imposed. In early 1989 it was announced that, in an attempt to appease landowners, their share of mining royalties was to be increased from 5% to 20%.

The BRA's demands increasingly favoured secession from Papua New Guinea for Bougainville (and for North Solomons Province), together with the closure of the mine until their demands for compensation and secession had been met. In May 1989, as the violent campaign on the island intensified, the mine was forced once more to suspend production, and in June the Papua New Guinea Government declared a state of emergency on Bougainville, sending 2,000 security personnel to the island. In September a minister in the provincial government, who had been negotiating an agreement with Bougainville land-owners to provide them with $A300m. in compensation, was shot dead. The signing of the accord, due to take place the following day, was postponed indefinitely. Diro, who had been reinstated in the Government in May, as Minister of State with responsibility for overseeing the Bougainville crisis, responded by offering a reward for the capture or killing of Ona and seven of his deputies, including the BRA's military commander, Sam Kauona.

The Government's difficulties were further compounded in September 1989 by sustained rioting in the city of Lae, in Morobe Province, where rival groups claimed control of local administration. The provincial government was suspended and a curfew was introduced. In October the Government rejected demands by environmentalists for the closure of the Ok Tedi gold and copper mine, whose operators planned to dispose of mine waste directly into the Fly River. In December the owners of the Bougainville mine announced plans to make redundant 2,000 of the remaining 2,300 staff in January 1990.

The escalation of violence on Bougainville led the Australian Government to announce plans to send in military forces to evacuate its nationals trapped on the island, and to withdraw the remaining 300 personnel of Bougainville Copper Ltd. Criticism of the Government's failure to resolve the dispute, the rising death toll among the security forces, rebels and civilians and a worsening economic crisis, which was aggravated by the conflict, led the Government to negotiate a cease-fire with the BRA, with effect from the beginning of March 1990. The Government undertook to withdraw its security forces and to release 80 detainees. The island came under the control of the BRA in mid-March, after the sudden departure of the security forces. The premature withdrawal of the troops was seen as an attempt by Paul Tohian, the police commissioner who had been in charge of the state of emergency on Bougainville, to disrupt the peace process, and was followed by an apparent abortive coup, allegedly led by Tohian, who was summarily dismissed from his post.

In late March 1990 the Government imposed an economic blockade on Bougainville; this was intensified in May, when banking, telecommunications and public services on the island were suspended. On 17 May the BRA, apparently in response to the Government's implementation of economic sanctions, proclaimed Bougainville's independence, renaming the island the Republic of Bougainville. The unilateral declaration of independence, made by Ona, who also proclaimed himself interim President, was immediately dismissed by Namaliu as unconstitutional and invalid. On 29 July negotiations between the BRA and the Government finally began on board a New Zealand naval vessel, *Endeavour*, and lasted eight days. In the resulting 'Endeavour Accord', the BRA representatives, faced with the threat of renewed military action by government forces on Bougainville, agreed to defer implementation of the May declaration of independence and to hold further discussions on the political status of the island. The Government agreed to end the blockade, and to restore essential services to the island. However, despite assurances from Namaliu that no security forces would be sent to the island, the first two ships that left for Bougainville with supplies were found to be carrying 70 soldiers and 30 police, intending to disembark on the island of Buka, north of Bougainville. The BRA accused the Government of violating the accord, and a week later the security forces and the two ships, together with the supplies, withdrew. In mid-September the Government sent armed troops to take control of Buka, stating that this was in response to a petition for help from Buka islanders. In ensuing clashes between the BRA and the armed forces on Buka, 23 people were reported to have been killed.

In January 1991 further negotiations took place between representatives of the Papua New Guinea Government and of Bougainville, in Honiara, the capital of Solomon Islands. Later in the month the former Premier of the North Solomons Province (which includes Bougainville), Joseph Kabui, and the Minister for Foreign Affairs, Sir Michael Somare (as he had become), signed the 'Honiara Accord'. The agreement stated that the Papua New Guinea Government would not station its security forces on Bougainville if the islanders agreed to disband the BRA and to surrender all prisoners and weapons to a multinational peace-keeping force. The Bougainville secessionists were guaranteed immunity from prosecution. The agreement, however, made no provision for any change in the political status of Bougainville, and by early March it appeared to have failed. Namaliu urged that the agreement be upheld, while Diro (who had been appointed Deputy Prime Minister and Minister for Public Service in April 1990) advocated the resumption of a military attack on Bougainville. The Minister for Justice, Bernard Narokobi, resigned from the Government's negotiating team, reportedly frustrated at delays in restoring essential services to Bougainville. Somare also indicated that he would resign unless a new round of peace talks were held with the BRA. In April Diro was suspended from office, after being charged with misconduct.

According to official estimates, about 200 people died in the conflict between 1988 and early 1991. However, Australian diplomatic sources estimated that 3,000 people died as a result of the economic blockade.

Government troops launched a further attack on Bougainville in April 1991, and it was subsequently reported that the rebel resistance on the island was subsiding. In June Col Leo Nuia was dismissed from his post as commander of the defence forces on Bougainville, after admitting that his troops had committed atrocities during fighting on the island in February 1990. Further allegations of human rights abuses and summary executions of BRA members and sympathizers by government troops prompted Namaliu to announce plans for an independent inquiry into the claims.

In November 1991 it was reported that 34 BRA members were killed and six defence personnel were injured, following renewed violence on Bougainville and Buka. The Government responded to the renewed hostilities by announcing that more troops would be sent to the area and by cancelling the passports of 11 prominent BRA activists. In January 1992 the situation deteriorated further when, in an attempt to force the Government to end its economic blockade of the island, the BRA intercepted and set fire to a supply ship, and held its crew hostage. As a result, all shipping and air services to Bougainville were suspended.

In October 1992 government troops began a major offensive against rebel-held areas of Bougainville and, later in the month, announced that they had taken control of the main town, Arawa. The BRA, however, denied the claim and began a campaign of arson against government offices and public buildings in Arawa. Violence on the island intensified in early 1993, and further casualties were reported. In April the BRA proposed a cease-fire, in order that an investigative mission to the island might be conducted by the International Commission of Jurists; however, this was rejected by the Government. In the same month BRA rebels and the island's chiefs agreed to form a 13-member committee aimed at facilitating discussion between the two sides, and offered to meet government representatives on neutral ground for negotiations. Continued violence, however, hampered any attempts to resolve the conflict, and allegations of atrocities and violations of human rights by both sides were widely reported (most significantly in a report published by the human rights organization, Amnesty International, in November 1993).

In June 1994 talks were held in Honiara betweeen government representatives and secessionists, which led to an agreement to reconvene for further negotiations later in the year. The apparently positive outcome of the meeting was confirmed when Wingti made an official visit to Bougainville in the following month. Another significant development was the recapture by government forces in August of the Panguna copper mine, which had been under BRA control since 1990. Negotiations in Honiara were resumed, and on 3 September 1994 the new Prime Minister, Chan (see below), and Kauona signed a cease-fire agreement, which came into effect six days later. Under the terms of the agreement, a regional peace-keeping force, composed of troops from Fiji, Vanuatu and Tonga, was deployed in October (with the Governments of Australia and New Zealand in a supervisory role) and the economic blockade of Bougainville was lifted. In the following month Chan and a group of non-BRA Bougainville leaders signed the Charter of Mirigini, which provided for the establishment of a transitional Bougainville government. The BRA declared its opposition to the proposed authority, reiterating its goal of outright secession, and by the end of December it was reported that several people had been killed in renewed violence. Air links to the island were suspended in February 1995, following an attack on a commercial aircraft by BRA rebels which resulted in the death of a passenger. None the less, in April, 27 members of the 32-member transitional administration were sworn in at a ceremony on Buka Island, attended by the Prime Minister and several foreign dignitaries. Theodore Miriong, a former legal advisor to Ona, was elected Premier of the authority. However, the three seats reserved for the BRA leaders, Ona, Kauona and Kabui, remained vacant, as the rebels urged their supporters to reject the new administration and to continue the violent campaign for independence.

Apart from the continued unrest on Bougainville, the principal cause for concern in Papua New Guinea's domestic affairs during the 1980s and early 1990s was the increase in serious crime. When the National Parliament reconvened in May 1991 it approved a programme of severe measures to combat crime, including the introduction of the death penalty and the tattooing of the foreheads of convicted criminals.

In late September 1991 a leadership tribunal found Diro guilty of 81 charges of misconduct in office. However, the Governor-General, Sir Serei Eri, refused to ratify the tribunal's decision and reinstated Diro as Deputy Prime Minister, despite recommendations that he be dismissed. A constitutional crisis subsequently arose, during which a government envoy was sent to the United Kingdom to request that the monarch dismiss Eri. However, on 1 October the resignation of the Governor-General was announced; this was followed shortly afterwards by that of Diro. Akoka Doi was subsequently appointed Deputy Prime Minister.

In early 1992 the Government continued to be troubled by allegations of corruption and misconduct. In April Tony Ila, the Minister for Labour and Employment, was convicted on 43 charges, which included the acceptance of substantial payments (allegedly in order not to support a motion of 'no confidence' in the Government). As a result of the trial, Namaliu, the Minister for Finance, Paul Pora, and four former ministers were charged with the misuse of public funds in June 1993, but were acquitted.

The general election campaign began amid serious fighting among the various political factions, which led to rioting, in April 1992, by some 10,000 supporters of rival candidates. The PAP, in particular, provoked criticism from the Pangu Pati for the revival of its nationalist slogan used in the 1970s: 'Papua for the Papuans'. At the election, held on 13-27 June, a total of 59 members of the legislature (including 15 ministers) lost their seats. Some controversy arose when Namaliu, who was expected to be defeated, retained his seat by a narrow majority, following an unexplained power-cut during the counting of votes. However, the final result gave the Pangu Pati 22 seats, while the PDM secured 15. Independent candidates were most successful, winning a total of 31 seats.

On 17 July 1992 Paias Wingti was elected Prime Minister by the National Parliament, defeating Namaliu by a single vote. Wingti formed a coalition of PDM, PPP and LNA members, as well as several independents. The new Government announced that its immediate objectives were rural development and the introduction of measures to combat corruption in the business and public sectors. As part of this anticorruption policy, Wingti suspended six provincial governments for financial mismanagement in October, and threatened to abolish the entire local government system. Five provinces subsequently warned that they would secede from the rest of the country, in protest at the proposals. In April 1994, however, the leaders of the five provinces in question agreed to proceed with negotiations for a form of regional autonomy, and undertook not to pursue outright secession.

From early 1993 a resurgence of tribal violence, mainly in the Enga province, resulted in the deaths of more than 100 people. During one incident in mid-1993 an entire village was burnt down by police officers who had been called to quell a tribal fight, in which one of their colleagues had been killed. In response to such incidents, together with a continued increase in violent crime throughout the country (in spite of the severe measures introduced in May 1991), the National Parliament approved a new internal security act in May 1993. The legislation provided the Government with greatly increased powers, which permitted the introduction of a system of national registration, the restriction of freedom of movement within the country and the erection of permanently-policed gates on all major routes into the capital, Port Moresby. Most significantly, the legal system was to be changed so that defendants accused of serious crimes would be required to prove their innocence, rather than be proved guilty. The measures attracted criticism from the opposition, whose leader, Jack Genia, described them as oppressive. Genia, however, died, following a sudden illness, in July, and was replaced as leader of the Pangu Pati by Chris Haiveta. In May 1994 the Supreme Court nullified six of the 26 sections of the act (most of which concerned the extension of police powers), denouncing them as unconstitutional.

In September 1993 Paias Wingti announced his resignation to Parliament. The Speaker immediately requested nominations, and Wingti was re-elected unopposed with 59 of the 109 votes. According to the Constitution (as amended in July 1991), a motion of 'no confidence' in the Prime Minister could not be presented for at least 18 months, and Wingti claimed that his action had been necessary in order to secure a period of political stability for the country. Opposition members, however, described the events as an abuse of the democratic process, and several thousand demonstrators gathered in the capital to demand the resignation of the Prime Minister. In December the National Court rejected a constitutional challenge from the opposition to Wingti's re-election. However, in August 1994 the Supreme Court declared Wingti's re-election in September 1993 invalid. Wingti did not contest the ensuing parliamentary vote for a new Prime Minister, in which Chan defeated the Speaker, Bill Skate, by 66 votes to 32. Namaliu was elected to the position of Speaker, while Haiveta succeeded Chan as Deputy Prime Minister. Chan announced that his administration's priorities would include more stringent controls on government expenditure and a reduction in the country's consistently large budget deficit.

In September 1994 a state of emergency was declared following major volcanic eruptions and earthquakes around Rabaul in East New Britain Province. Some 100,000 inhabitants were evacuated from the area, during what the Government described as the country's worst recorded natural disaster. A programme of rehabilitation for the area announced in early 1995 was expected to cost some K100m.

In January 1995, during provincial elections in the Western Highlands, widespread fighting was reported and several people were killed in clashes between supporters of rival candidates. In a further attempt by the Government to control the prevalence of violent confrontations such as these, and of violent crime in general, it was announced that police numbers were to be increased by 20% over the next three years.

The abolition of the provincial government system, as proposed by Wingti, was rejected by Chan's Government. However, there was still considerable support among the opposition for the proposed changes, and, as a result, it was decided that Parliament would vote on a series of motions to amend the Constitution accordingly; the first of these was approved in March 1995.

In 1984 more than 9,000 refugees crossed into Papua New Guinea from the Indonesian province of Irian Jaya, as a consequence of operations by the Indonesian army against Melanesian rebels of the pro-independence Organisasi Papua Merdeka (Free Papua Movement—OPM). For many years relations between Papua New Guinea and Indonesia had been strained by the conflict in Irian Jaya, not least because the independence movement drew sympathy from many among the largely Melanesian population of Papua New Guinea. A new border treaty was signed in October 1984, and attempts were made to repatriate the refugees, based on assurances by the Indonesian Government that there would be no reprisals against those who returned. In October 1985 representatives of the Papua New Guinea and Indonesian Governments signed a treaty providing for the settlement of disputes by consultation, arbitration and 'other peaceful means'. The treaty, however, provoked strong criticism among opposition politicians in Papua New Guinea, who claimed that it effectively precluded the censure of any violation of human rights in Irian Jaya. In 1988 the Government condemned the incursions by Indonesian soldiers into Papua New Guinea, in search of OPM members, as a breach of bilateral accords, and affirmed that Papua New Guinea would not support Indonesia in its attempt to suppress the OPM. Following a further round of discussions in July 1989, however, it was announced that Papua New Guinea would establish a consulate in the capital of Irian Jaya, Jayapura, and that an Indonesian consulate would be opened in the border town of Vanimo. (The Indonesian consulate was finally established in October 1992.) A Status of Forces Agreement, signed by both sides in January 1992, aimed to improve security co-operation between Papua New Guinea and Indonesian forces; meanwhile, large numbers of refugees moved into Papua New Guinea's Western Province as fighting continued between government troops and rebels in Irian Jaya. During an official visit to Indonesia in February 1993, Wingti was warned by that country's President that the border dispute must be resolved if relations between the two countries were to remain constructive. However, in late 1993 the opposition alleged that the Government had attempted to suppress numerous reports concerning the murder of some 13 Papua New Guineans by Indonesian troops in the Western Province in October, in order to maintain good relations with Indonesia.

Following reports of incursions by Papua New Guinea fishermen into Solomon Islands' territorial waters, an agreement was concluded in 1989 on a maritime boundary between the two countries. In early 1990, however, relations deteriorated because of the Bougainville crisis, with the Solomon Islands Government alleging that Papua New Guinea patrol boats were obstructing the traditional crossing between Bougainville Island and the Shortland Islands (in Solomon Islands), and the Papua New Guinea Government accusing the Solomon Islands Government of harbouring members of the BRA and providing them with supplies. In March 1992 Papua New Guinea forces made two incursions into Solomon Islands territory to destroy a fuel storage depot believed to be supplying the BRA. The Solomon Islands Government protested vehemently against the raids, which were denied by the Papua New Guinea authorities before a formal apology was offered. Relations seemed to improve in 1993 when, in April, an agreement was signed permitting military personnel from the two countries to cross the maritime boundary by up to 30 km in pursuit of suspects. As a further gesture of co-operation, the Solomon Islands Government agreed to close the BRA office in Honiara.

After the 1987 election Wingti announced that Papua New Guinea had applied to join the Non-aligned Movement (see p. 249), and was to pursue a policy of establishing closer diplomatic relations with countries outside the Pacific region. In March 1988 Papua New Guinea signed an agreement with Vanuatu and Solomon Islands to form the 'Melanesian Spearhead Group', dedicated to the preservation of Melanesian cultural traditions and to achieving independence for the French Overseas Territory of New Caledonia. In 1989 Papua New Guinea increased its links with South-East Asia, signing a Treaty of Amity and Co-operation with the Association of South East Asian Nations (ASEAN—see p. 109) and entering into negotiations with Malaysia over the creation of a Port Moresby Stock Exchange (subsequently scheduled to open in April 1996).

In October 1993 Papua New Guinea signed an agreement with a Russian consortium and an Australian company permitting the establishment of a 'spaceport' in New Ireland Province. The facility was expected to begin launching commercial rockets in 1997.

## Government

Executive power is vested in the British monarch, represented locally by the Governor-General, who is appointed on the recommendation of the Prime Minister and acts on the advice of the National Executive Council (the Cabinet), led by the Prime Minister. Legislative power is vested in the unicameral National Parliament, with 109 members elected by universal adult suffrage for a term of five years. The Cabinet is responsible to Parliament. Local government represents more than 90% of the population through more than 160 councils. For administrative purposes, Papua New Guinea comprises the National Capital District (with its own governing body) and 19 provincial governments. However, plans to reform the provincial government system were under consideration from late 1992.

## Defence

In June 1994 Papua New Guinea's national Defence Force numbered 3,800, comprising an army of 3,200, a navy of 500 and an air force of 100. In addition, 100 Australian troops (including 75 advisers) were stationed in the country. The paramilitary border patrol police numbered 4,600 in 1991. Military service is voluntary. Budget estimates for 1993 allocated K54.4m. to defence (equivalent to 3.7% of total expenditure by the central Government).

## Economic Affairs

In 1993, according to estimates by the World Bank, Papua New Guinea's gross national product (GNP), measured at average 1991–93 prices, was US $4,637m., equivalent to US $1,120 per head. During 1985–93, it was estimated, GNP per head increased, in real terms, at an average annual rate of 1.1%. Over the same period the population increased by an annual average of 2.3%. Papua New Guinea's gross domestic product (GDP) increased, in real terms, by an annual average of 2.3% in 1980–92. Real GDP increased by an estimated 14.4% in 1993.

Agriculture (including hunting, forestry and fishing) contributed an estimated 26% of GDP in 1993, and engaged some 64% of the labour force in that year. The principal cash crops are coffee (which accounted for about 4.2% of export earnings in 1992), cocoa, coconuts (for the production of copra), pineapples, palm oil, rubber and tea. Roots and tubers, vegetables, bananas and melons are also grown as food crops. Rice farming was introduced in 1990 as an alternative crop in five provinces. Livestock, poultry and fishing are also important, and shark oil became a significant export in the early 1990s. The sale of fishing licences to foreign fleets provides a substantial source of revenue. Exports of wood (mostly unprocessed) provided 9.1% of export earnings in 1992. There is serious concern about the environmental damage caused by extensive logging activity in the country, much of which is illegal. Plans to implement more stringent regulations were postponed following intense opposition from Malaysian-owned logging companies in early 1994, despite a report, compiled by the Papua New Guinea National Research Institute, indicating that the current rate of logging was three times the sustainable yield of the country's forests. It was subsequently announced that exports of logs were to be reduced by 10% annually from 1995. During 1980–92 agricultural GDP increased by an annual average of 1.7%, and output from the sector increased by a further 4.8% in 1993 and by an estimated 7.2% in 1994.

Industry (including mining, manufacturing, construction and power) contributed an estimated 38% of GDP in 1992. During 1980–92 industrial GDP increased by an annual average of 3.3%.

Mining and quarrying employed 0.6% of the working population in 1980, and contributed an estimated 15.2% of GDP in 1991. Copper (which accounted for about 31.9% of export earnings in 1992), gold and silver are the major mineral exports. Papua New Guinea also has substantial reserves of natural gas and petroleum, and deposits of chromite, cobalt, nickel and quartz. Production of petroleum began, at a rate of about 150,000 barrels per day (b/d), in 1992. In early 1994 plans were approved for the construction of two oil refineries in Port Moresby and Kopi, which would process some 50,000 b/d. Following the discovery of large gold deposits at several sites during the 1980s (including the largest known deposit outside South Africa), gold production was expected to rise to 90–130 metric tons per year by the mid-1990s (compared with 44 tons in 1986 and 66 tons in 1992), making Papua New Guinea the third biggest gold producer in the world. Gold provided 36.7% of total export earnings in 1992.

Manufacturing contributed 9% of GDP in 1992, and employed 1.9% of the working population in 1980. Measured by the value of output, the principal branches of manufacturing are food products, beverages, tobacco, wood products, metal products, machinery and transport equipment. A tuna cannery, which was to create 1,500 jobs and to earn some K65m. annually in exports, was established in Madang in 1992, and a mackerel cannery in Lae was opened in early 1995. A further two canneries were to be constructed in that year. A cement plant in Lae began commercial production in late 1993. During 1980–92 manufacturing GDP increased by an annual average of 0.1%, but in 1993 grew by more than 9%.

Energy is derived principally from hydroelectric power. The sugar industry also provides the raw material for the production of ethyl alcohol (ethanol) as an alternative fuel. Imports of mineral fuels comprised 8% of the value of total imports in 1992.

A five-year tourism development plan, announced in 1989, aimed to increase the number of visitors to Papua New Guinea from the 48,910 who visited in that year to 60,000 per year. However, political instability and reports of widespread crime have had a detrimental effect on the industry, with the total number of visitors falling to 40,533 in 1992, and by an estimated 50% further in the following year.

In 1993 Papua New Guinea recorded a visible trade surplus of US $1,369.9m., and a surplus of US $546.2m. on the current account of the balance of payments. In 1990 the principal source of imports (46.1%) was Australia; other major suppliers were Japan, the USA and Singapore. In 1992 Japan was the principal market for non-gold exports (33.5%); other major markets were Germany, South Korea, Australia the United Kingdom and Singapore. The principal exports in 1992 were gold, copper ore and concentrates and timber. The principal imports in 1990 were machinery and transport equipment,

# PAPUA NEW GUINEA

basic manufactures, food and live animals, miscellaneous manufactured articles, chemicals and mineral fuels.

In 1994 there was a projected budgetary deficit of K242.8m. Papua New Guinea receives grants for budgetary aid from Australia (expected to be equivalent to about 16% of budgetary revenue in 1990). Papua New Guinea's external debt was US $3,168m. at the end of 1993, of which $1,516m. was long-term public debt. In that year the cost of debt-servicing was equivalent to 31.6% of exports of goods and services. The annual rate of inflation averaged 5.2% in 1985–93; consumer prices increased by an average of 5.0% in 1993.

Papua New Guinea is a member of the Asian Development Bank (see p. 107), the South Pacific Commission (see p. 215), the South Pacific Forum (see p. 217), the International Cocoa Organization (see p. 235) and the International Coffee Organization (see p. 235).

During the 1980s and early 1990s Papua New Guinea remained dependent on aid from Australia and other international donors for its economic development, and it was estimated that at least 70% of the population were within the subsistence sector of the economy. The country's difficult terrain and lack of infrastructure, the limited domestic market and a shortage of skilled workers all impeded industrial development, and an increase in migration from rural areas to urban centres led to a rise in unemployment. Civil unrest on Bougainville adversely affected the economy. The indefinite closure of the Bougainville copper mine since 1989 and the high cost of the security operations there (see Recent History) coincided with a period of low prices for Papua New Guinea's key agricultural commodities. This development led the Government, in late 1992, to establish a five-year price support scheme for producers of cash crops. After declining steadily in the late 1980s, GDP increased by some 9% in both 1991 and 1992, owing largely to the success of the new Porgera gold mine. Growth of more than 14% in 1993 was largely attributed to an increase in petroleum production at the Kutubu oilfield. However, the country's economy continued to be troubled by a persistent budget deficit, and, in an attempt to reduce this, the Chan Government announced a programme of strict economic measures in September 1994. These included the devaluation of the kina by 12% against the US dollar, a 'freeze' on government spending until the end of 1994 and a moratorium on wage increases until the end of 1995. In its 1995 budget the Government agreed to a further programme of economic reforms recommended by the World Bank, in return for structural adjustment assistance worth US $215m.

Growing ethnic and environmental problems, widespread crime and concern over foreign exploitation, however, continued to threaten Papua New Guinea's prospects for long-term economic success.

## Social Welfare

In 1989 Papua New Guinea had 492 hospitals and health centres, with a total of 15,335 beds, and in that year there were 361 physicians and 3,241 nurses working in the country. Of total estimated expenditure by the central Government in the budget for 1993, K128.13m. (8.6%) was for health and K10.99m. (0.7%) was for social security and welfare. Christian missions also provide medical and health services, with government assistance.

## Education

Education is not compulsory. Primary education, available at community schools, begins at seven years of age and lasts for six years. Secondary education, beginning at the age of 13, lasts for up to six years (comprising two cycles, the first of four years, the second two). Originally, schooling was free, but in recent years fees and charges for equipment have been introduced. In 1992 the total enrolment at primary schools was equivalent to 73% of children in the relevant age-group (78% of boys; 66% of girls). In the same year total secondary enrolment was equivalent to 13% of children in the relevant age-group (boys 15%; girls 10%). Tertiary education is provided by the University of Papua New Guinea and the University of Technology. There are also teacher training colleges and higher institutions which cater for specific professional training. In 1990, according to estimates by UNESCO, adult illiteracy averaged 48.0% (males 35.1%; females 62.2%). Budget estimates for 1993 allocated K251.14m. to education (representing 16.9% of total expenditure by the central Government).

## Public Holidays

**1995:** 1 January (New Year's Day), 14–17 April (Easter), 15 June (Queen's Official Birthday), 23 July (Remembrance Day), 16 September (Independence Day and Constitution Day), 25 December (Christmas Day), 26 December (Boxing Day).

**1996:** 1 January (New Year's Day), 5–8 April (Easter), 17 June (Queen's Official Birthday), 23 July (Remembrance Day), 16 September (Independence Day and Constitution Day), 25 December (Christmas Day), 26 December (Boxing Day).

## Weights and Measures

The metric system is in force.

# Statistical Survey

Source (unless otherwise stated): Papua New Guinea National Statistical Office, Post Office, Wards Strip, Waigani; tel. 271705; telex 22144.

## Area and Population

### AREA, POPULATION AND DENSITY

| | |
|---|---:|
| Area (sq km) | 462,840* |
| Population (census results) | |
| 22 September 1980 | |
| Males | 1,575,672 |
| Females | 1,435,055 |
| Total | 3,010,727 |
| July 1990 (provisional) | 3,607,954 |
| Population (official estimates at mid-year) | |
| 1991 | 3,772,000 |
| 1992 | 3,847,000 |
| 1993 | 3,922,000 |
| Density (per sq km) at mid-1993 | 8.5 |

* 178,704 sq miles.

Administrative Capital: Port Moresby, with an estimated population of 173,500 in 1990.

**BIRTHS AND DEATHS** (1987 estimates)

Live births 122,240 (birth rate 35.1 per 1,000); Deaths 42,540 (death rate 12.2 per 1,000).

**Expectation of life** (UN estimates, years at birth, 1985–90): 53.9 (males 53.2; females 54.7) (Source: UN, *World Population Prospects: The 1992 Revision*).

# PAPUA NEW GUINEA

### ECONOMICALLY ACTIVE POPULATION*
(estimates based on 1980 census results)

| | |
|---|---:|
| Agriculture, hunting, forestry and fishing† | 564,500 |
| Mining and quarrying | 4,300 |
| Manufacturing | 14,000 |
| Electricity, gas and water | 2,800 |
| Construction | 21,600 |
| Trade, restaurants and hotels | 25,100 |
| Transport, storage and communications | 17,400 |
| Financing, insurance, real estate and business services | 4,500 |
| Community, social and personal services | 77,100 |
| Others (incl. activities not stated or not adequately described) | 1,500 |
| **Total labour force†** | **732,800** |

\* Figures refer to citizens of Papua New Guinea only.

† Excluding persons solely engaged in subsistence agriculture, hunting, forestry and fishing.

**Mid-1993** (estimates in '000): Agriculture, etc. 1,241; Total 1,941 (Source: FAO, *Production Yearbook*).

## Agriculture

### PRINCIPAL CROPS ('000 metric tons)

| | 1991 | 1992 | 1993 |
|---|---:|---:|---:|
| Maize* | 2 | 2 | 2 |
| Sorghum* | 1 | 1 | 1 |
| Sweet potatoes* | 470 | 475 | 480 |
| Cassava (Manioc)* | 112 | 113 | 113 |
| Yams* | 215 | 220 | 220 |
| Taro (Coco yam)* | 215 | 217 | 218 |
| Other roots and tubers* | 255 | 257 | 260 |
| Pulses* | 2 | 2 | 2 |
| Groundnuts (in shell)* | 1 | 1 | 1 |
| Coconuts | 618† | 794† | 790* |
| Copra | 87 | 117 | 120 |
| Palm kernels† | 50 | 57 | 61 |
| Vegetables and melons* | 363 | 370 | 376 |
| Sugar cane | 310* | 350* | 340† |
| Pineapples* | 12 | 13 | 13 |
| Bananas* | 1,200 | 1,250 | 1,280 |
| Coffee (green) | 58† | 50 | 64 |
| Cocoa beans† | 34 | 41 | 37 |
| Tea* | 9 | 9 | 9 |
| Natural rubber (dry weight)† | 3† | 3† | 3* |

\* FAO estimate(s).   † Unofficial figure(s).

Source: FAO, *Production Yearbook*.

### LIVESTOCK (FAO estimates, '000 head, year ending September)

| | 1991 | 1992 | 1993 |
|---|---:|---:|---:|
| Horses | 2 | 2 | 2 |
| Cattle | 105 | 105 | 105 |
| Pigs | 1,000 | 1,010 | 1,022 |
| Sheep | 4 | 4 | 4 |
| Goats | 2 | 2 | 2 |

Poultry (FAO estimates, million): 3 in 1991; 3 in 1992; 3 in 1993.

Source: FAO, *Production Yearbook*.

### LIVESTOCK PRODUCTS (FAO estimates, '000 metric tons)

| | 1991 | 1992 | 1993 |
|---|---:|---:|---:|
| Beef and veal | 2 | 2 | 2 |
| Pig meat | 27 | 28 | 28 |
| Other meat | 22 | 22 | 23 |
| Poultry eggs | 3.0 | 3.3 | 3.5 |

Source: FAO, *Production Yearbook*.

## Forestry

### ROUNDWOOD REMOVALS ('000 cubic metres, excluding bark)

| | 1985 | 1986* | 1987* |
|---|---:|---:|---:|
| Sawlogs, veneer logs and logs for sleepers | 1,878 | 2,141 | 2,480 |
| Pulpwood* | 218 | 218 | 218 |
| Fuel wood* | 5,533 | 5,533 | 5,533 |
| **Total** | **7,629** | **7,892** | **8,231** |

\* FAO estimates.

**1988 and 1989:** Annual output as in 1987 (FAO estimate).

**1990, 1991 and 1992** ('000 cubic metres): Total annual output 8,188 (pulpwood 175).

Source: FAO, *Yearbook of Forest Products*.

### SAWNWOOD PRODUCTION
('000 cubic metres, including railway sleepers)

| | 1983* | 1984* | 1985† |
|---|---:|---:|---:|
| Coniferous (soft wood) | 46 | 46 | 43 |
| Broadleaved (hard wood) | 78 | 78 | 74 |
| **Total** | **124** | **124** | **117** |

\* FAO estimates.   † Unofficial estimates.

**1986–92:** Annual production as in 1985 (unofficial estimates).

Source: FAO, *Yearbook of Forest Products*.

## Fishing

(FAO estimates, '000 metric tons, live weight)

| | 1990 | 1991 | 1992 |
|---|---:|---:|---:|
| Inland waters | 14.6 | 13.3 | 13.5 |
| Pacific Ocean | 12.0 | 12.0 | 12.2 |
| **Total catch** | **26.6** | **25.3** | **25.7** |

Source: FAO, *Yearbook of Fishery Statistics*.

## Mining

| | 1989 | 1990 | 1991 |
|---|---:|---:|---:|
| Copper ore ('000 metric tons)* | 204.0 | 170.2† | 204.5 |
| Silver (metric tons) | 92 | 130 | 125 |
| Gold (kg) | 27,538‡ | 31,035 | 60,780 |

\* Figures refer to metal content of ore.

† Source: Metallgesellschaft Aktiengesellschaft, Frankfurt am Main, Germany.

‡ Estimate.

## Industry

### SELECTED PRODUCTS

| | 1989 | 1990 | 1991 |
|---|---:|---:|---:|
| Palm oil ('000 metric tons)*† | 130 | 114 | 114 |
| Electric energy (million kWh) | 1,775 | 1,790 | 1,790 |
| Raw Sugar ('000 metric tons)† | 31 | 38 | 43 |

\* Estimates.   † Source: FAO.

Source: UN, *Industrial Statistics Yearbook*.

**Beer:** 46,804,000 litres in 1989.

# PAPUA NEW GUINEA

# Finance

## CURRENCY AND EXCHANGE RATES

**Monetary Units**
100 toea = 1 kina (K).

**Sterling and Dollar Equivalents** (31 December 1994)
£1 sterling = 1.844 kina;
US $1 = 1.179 kina;
100 kina = £54.23 = $84.85.

**Average Exchange Rate** (US $ per kina)
1992  1.0367
1993  1.0221
1994  0.9950

Note: The foregoing information refers to the mid-point exchange rate of the central bank. In October 1994 it was announced that the kina would be allowed to 'float' on foreign exchange markets.

## BUDGET (million kina)*

| Revenue† | 1991 | 1992‡ | 1993§ |
|---|---|---|---|
| Taxation | 639.4 | 771.3 | 669.2 |
| Taxes on income, profits, etc. | 313.2 | 419.5 | 314.3 |
| Individual | 222.1 | 260.7 | 209.3 |
| Corporate | 90.0 | 156.1 | 103.0 |
| Domestic taxes on goods and services | 98.7 | 108.8 | 115.4 |
| Excises | 79.2 | 93.0 | 93.9 |
| Taxes on international trade and transactions | 208.1 | 224.1 | 218.7 |
| Import duties | 189.5 | 198.0 | 197.4 |
| Other current revenue | 261.4 | 158.5 | 455.2 |
| Entrepreneurial and property income | 104.3 | 85.0 | 81.8 |
| From non-financial public enterprises and public financial institutions | 67.8 | 64.5 | 50.0 |
| Capital revenue | 0.7 | 0.9 | 0.8 |
| **Total** | **901.5** | **930.6** | **1,125.2** |

| Expenditure‖ | 1991 | 1992‡ | 1993§ |
|---|---|---|---|
| General public services | 94.9 | 136.2 | 110.7 |
| Defence | 50.1 | 56.5 | 54.4 |
| Public order and safety | 117.0 | 114.8 | 129.9 |
| Education | 221.0 | 200.4 | 251.1 |
| Health | 109.3 | 106.4 | 128.1 |
| Social security and welfare | 12.1 | 10.0 | 11.0 |
| Housing and community amenities | 5.8 | 8.3 | 12.2 |
| Recreational, cultural and religious affairs and services | 21.8 | 21.4 | 21.7 |
| Economic affairs and services | 298.5 | 288.5 | 346.5 |
| Fuel and energy | 34.7 | 34.0 | 43.3 |
| Agriculture, forestry, fishing and hunting | 75.8 | 91.5 | 112.4 |
| Transport and communications | 108.4 | 96.0 | 111.9 |
| Other purposes | 343.2 | 395.3 | 416.4 |
| Transfers to other levels of government | n.a. | n.a. | 91.6 |
| Interest payments and debt-servicing | n.a. | n.a. | 144.3 |
| **Total** | **1,273.6** | **1,337.8** | **1,482.0** |
| Current | 1,076.7 | 1,211.5 | 1,258.0 |
| Capital | 196.8 | 126.3 | 224.0 |

* Figures refer to the operations of the General Budget and of central government units with individual budgets. Data for 1993 exclude the accounts of certain government agencies.
† Excluding grants received from abroad (million kina): 311.7 in 1991; 196.3 in 1992; 197.5 in 1993.
‡ Figures are provisional.
§ Estimates.
‖ Excluding lending minus repayments (million kina): 7.6 in 1991; 7.7 in 1992; 3.6 in 1993.

Source: IMF, *Government Finance Statistics Yearbook*.

**1994** (estimates, K million): Revenue 1,390.7; Expenditure 1,633.5.

## INTERNATIONAL RESERVES (US $ million at 31 December)

|  | 1992 | 1993 | 1994 |
|---|---|---|---|
| Gold (national valuation) | 11.09 | 11.09 | 11.09 |
| IMF special drawing rights | 0.14 | 0.05 | 0.11 |
| Reserve position in IMF | 0.06 | 0.07 | 0.08 |
| Foreign exchange | 238.39 | 141.34 | 95.88 |
| **Total** | **249.67** | **152.54** | **107.16** |

Source: IMF, *International Financial Statistics*.

## MONEY SUPPLY (million kina at 31 December)

|  | 1991 | 1992 | 1993 |
|---|---|---|---|
| Currency outside banks | 137.36 | 141.17 | 160.70 |
| Demand deposits at deposit money banks | 275.03 | 293.10 | 368.17 |
| **Total money** (incl. others) | **417.16** | **437.42** | **530.34** |

Source: IMF, *International Financial Statistics*.

## COST OF LIVING (Consumer Price Index; base: 1980 = 100)

|  | 1991 | 1992 | 1993 |
|---|---|---|---|
| Food | 178.2 | 184.0 | 188.4 |
| Clothing | 144.5 | 153.2 | 157.3 |
| Rent, fuel and light | 124.5 | 126.7 | 131.0 |
| **All items** (incl. others) | **188.3** | **196.4** | **206.1** |

Source: ILO, *Year Book of Labour Statistics*.

## NATIONAL ACCOUNTS (million kina at current prices)

**National Income and Product**

|  | 1989 | 1990 | 1991 |
|---|---|---|---|
| Compensation of employees | 1,268.5 | 1,262.4 | 1,348.7 |
| Operating surplus | 1,115.6 | 1,144.6 | 1,455.8 |
| **Domestic factor incomes** | **2,384.1** | **2,407.0** | **2,804.5** |
| Consumption of fixed capital* | 315.5 | 339.4 | 416.8 |
| **Gross domestic product (GDP) at factor cost** | **2,699.6** | **2,746.4** | **3,221.3** |
| Indirect taxes | 347.6 | 331.6 | 386.1 |
| *Less* Subsidies | 1.6 | 2.0 | 2.0 |
| **GDP in purchasers' values** | **3,045.7** | **3,076.1** | **3,605.5** |
| Net factor income from abroad | −115.0 | −117.9 | −117.9 |
| **Gross national product** | **2,930.7** | **2,958.2** | **3,487.6** |
| *Less* Consumption of fixed capital* | 315.5 | 339.4 | 416.8 |
| **National income in market prices** | **2,615.2** | **2,618.8** | **3,070.8** |

* Excluding producers of government-owned houses and hostels.

Source: UN, *National Accounts Statistics*.

**Expenditure on the Gross Domestic Product**

|  | 1989 | 1990 | 1991 |
|---|---|---|---|
| Government final consumption expenditure | 744.9 | 763.9 | 808.1 |
| Private final consumption expenditure | 1,962.0 | 1,816.3 | 2,165.9 |
| Increase in stocks | −83.4 | −21.0 | −22.0 |
| Gross fixed capital formation | 790.7 | 772.9 | 1,010.1 |
| **Total domestic expenditure** | **3,414.2** | **3,332.1** | **3,962.1** |
| Exports of goods and services | 1,238.0 | 1,249.7 | 1,523.9 |
| *Less* Imports of goods and services | 1,606.5 | 1,505.7 | 1,880.5 |
| **GDP in purchasers' values** | **3,045.7** | **3,076.1** | **3,605.5** |
| **GDP at constant 1983 prices** | **2,423.4** | **2,350.8** | **2,574.8** |

Source: UN, *National Accounts Statistics*.

# PAPUA NEW GUINEA

### Gross Domestic Product by Economic Activity

|  | 1989 | 1990 | 1991 |
|---|---|---|---|
| Agriculture, hunting, forestry and fishing | 856.3 | 891.2 | 936.5 |
| Mining and quarrying | 352.7 | 452.2 | 612.9 |
| Manufacturing | 336.9 | 275.8 | 345.1 |
| Electricity, gas and water | 49.0 | 52.3 | 59.2 |
| Construction | 161.3 | 155.1 | 224.0 |
| Wholesale and retail trade | 328.2 | 296.8 | 358.5 |
| Transport, storage and communications | 163.5 | 190.9 | 243.0 |
| Finance, insurance, real estate and business services | 172.9 | 130.8 | 147.6 |
| Public administration | 543.4 | 551.3 | 588.7 |
| **Sub-total** | 2,964.2 | 2,996.4 | 3,515.0 |
| Adjustments | 81.5 | 79.7 | 90.5 |
| **GDP in purchasers' values** | 3,045.7 | 3,076.1 | 3,605.5 |

Source: UN, *National Accounts Statistics*.

### BALANCE OF PAYMENTS (US $ million)

|  | 1991 | 1992 | 1993 |
|---|---|---|---|
| Merchandise exports f.o.b. | 1,482.6 | 1,950.9 | 2,504.7 |
| Merchandise imports f.o.b. | −1,403.8 | −1,321.7 | −1,134.8 |
| **Trade balance** | 78.8 | 629.2 | 1,369.9 |
| Exports of services | 303.5 | 349.9 | 315.0 |
| Imports of services | −542.5 | −687.8 | −808.5 |
| Other income received | 70.6 | 39.2 | 23.4 |
| Other income paid | −320.5 | −425.8 | −396.3 |
| Private unrequited transfers (net) | −64.1 | −62.6 | −129.8 |
| Official unrequited transfers (net) | 323.6 | 255.0 | 172.7 |
| **Current balance** | −150.6 | 97.0 | 546.2 |
| Direct investment (net) | 202.8 | 290.9 | 0.6 |
| Other capital (net) | −140.0 | −442.6 | −658.0 |
| Net errors and omissions | 2.2 | −17.5 | 29.1 |
| **Overall balance** | −85.5 | −72.2 | −82.0 |

Source: IMF, *International Financial Statistics*.

# External Trade

### PRINCIPAL COMMODITIES (distribution by SITC, US $ '000)*

| Imports f.o.b. | 1988 | 1989 | 1990 |
|---|---|---|---|
| **Food and live animals** | 211,667 | 225,285 | 206,032 |
| Meat and preparations | 44,726 | 48,880 | 43,864 |
| Fish and preparations | 43,690 | 40,349 | 36,198 |
| Cereals and preparations | 58,119 | 70,518 | 64,955 |
| Rice | 37,379 | 42,876 | 41,013 |
| **Mineral fuels, etc.** | 113,424 | 74,484 | 83,810 |
| Petroleum and petroleum products | 112,952 | 73,965 | 83,066 |
| Petroleum products, refined | 112,319 | 73,513 | 82,768 |
| Gas oils | 48,084 | 35,443 | 45,848 |
| **Chemicals and related products** | 97,606 | 92,071 | 86,130 |
| **Basic manufactures** | 241,190 | 297,377 | 237,345 |
| Rubber manufactures | 33,376 | 34,525 | 27,936 |
| Iron and steel | 49,752 | 76,603 | 52,682 |
| Other metal manufactures | 84,240 | 102,050 | 81,639 |
| **Machinery and transport equipment** | 533,122 | 712,213 | 472,195 |
| Power-generating machinery and equipment | 49,508 | 58,370 | 37,964 |
| Machinery specialized for particular industries | 135,182 | 166,017 | 101,576 |
| Civil engineering and contractors' plant and equipment and parts thereof | 93,621 | 102,368 | 74,146 |
| Construction and mining machinery | 52,476 | 76,472 | 37,854 |
| General industrial machinery and equipment | 66,648 | 86,349 | 64,630 |
| Electrical machinery, apparatus and appliances, etc. | 53,947 | 60,358 | 58,325 |

### PRINCIPAL COMMODITIES (distribution by SITC, US $ '000)*

| Imports f.o.b. — *continued* | 1988 | 1989 | 1990 |
|---|---|---|---|
| Road vehicles | 115,931 | 150,513 | 98,492 |
| Passenger cars | 26,019 | 37,899 | 34,824 |
| Lorries and goods vehicles | 59,230 | 77,031 | 43,275 |
| Aircraft and associated equipment, and parts thereof | 46,357 | 116,163 | 64,411 |
| **Miscellaneous manufactured articles** | 116,629 | 131,300 | 105,466 |
| **Total** (incl. others) | 1,347,072 | 1,576,451 | 1,233,088 |

| Exports f.o.b. | 1990 | 1991 | 1992 |
|---|---|---|---|
| **Food and live animals** | 168,152 | 140,887 | 133,903 |
| Coffee, tea, cocoa, spices and manufactures thereof | 150,282 | 121,537 | 113,367 |
| Coffee and substitutes | 108,531 | 80,082 | 70,558 |
| Cocoa | 34,178 | 36,746 | 35,695 |
| Cocoa beans, raw or roasted | 34,178 | 36,740 | 35,695 |
| **Crude materials (inedible) except fuels** | 691,905 | 711,242 | 716,526 |
| Cork and wood | 90,040 | 101,576 | 154,583 |
| Metalliferous ores and metal scrap | 583,578 | 595,865 | 541,809 |
| Copper ores and concentrates | 582,653 | 595,032 | 541,188 |
| **Animal and vegetable oils, fats and waxes** | 43,718 | 61,294 | 88,628 |
| Palm oil | 28,468 | 47,286 | 58,661 |
| **Machinery and transport equipment** | 72,218 | 135,562 | 102,886 |
| Aircraft and associated equipment, and parts thereof | 21,203 | 96,387 | 38,811 |
| **Non-monetary gold (excl. ores and concentrates)** | 233,135 | 533,054 | 623,067 |
| **Total** (incl. others) | 1,261,730 | 1,641,763 | 1,698,897 |

* Figures include migrants' and travellers' dutiable effects, but exclude military equipment and some parcel post.

Source: UN, *International Trade Statistics Yearbook*.

**Total Imports** (million kina): 1,336.5 in 1991; 1,275.0 in 1992.

**1993** (million kina): Imports f.o.b. 1,110.4; Exports f.o.b. 2,429.3.

### PRINCIPAL TRADING PARTNERS (US $'000)

| Imports f.o.b. (excl. gold) | 1988 | 1989 | 1990 |
|---|---|---|---|
| Australia | 587,774 | 625,426 | 567,901 |
| Canada | 14,445 | 34,023 | 23,714 |
| China, People's Repub. | 29,837 | 31,259 | 25,016 |
| France (incl. Monaco) | 8,821 | 56,056 | 13,992 |
| Germany, Fed. Repub. | 27,603 | 22,991 | 16,326 |
| Hong Kong | 26,502 | 33,815 | 19,691 |
| Japan | 240,271 | 236,663 | 160,453 |
| Korea, Repub. | 17,574 | 16,212 | 11,318 |
| Netherlands | 14,407 | 21,235 | 4,902 |
| New Zealand | 50,021 | 49,534 | 40,805 |
| Singapore | 79,641 | 106,213 | 105,686 |
| USSR | 8 | 117 | 13,636 |
| United Kingdom | 41,308 | 45,067 | 29,022 |
| USA | 139,835 | 205,658 | 119,553 |
| **Total** (incl. others) | 1,347,072 | 1,576,451 | 1,233,088 |

PAPUA NEW GUINEA

| Exports f.o.b. (excl. gold) | 1990 | 1991 | 1992 |
|---|---|---|---|
| Australia | 102,797 | 77,727 | 74,683 |
| Bulgaria | — | 37,791 | 18 |
| Finland | 35,801 | 32,956 | 40,934 |
| Germany* | 201,225 | 147,322 | 163,940 |
| Japan | 351,422 | 361,678 | 360,034 |
| Korea, Repub. | 124,939 | 147,761 | 133,823 |
| Netherlands | 8,145 | 8,418 | 25,634 |
| New Zealand | 11,616 | 27,447 | 5,294 |
| Philippines | 53,677 | 69,521 | 47,231 |
| Singapore | 18,499 | 34,293 | 62,410 |
| USSR | — | 14,983 | — |
| United Kingdom | 54,165 | 65,706 | 72,917 |
| USA | 30,069 | 36,109 | 36,004 |
| **Total** (incl. others) | 1,028,595 | 1,106,709 | 1,075,830 |

* Figures refer to exports to the united Germany.
Source: UN, *International Trade Statistics Yearbook*.

## Transport

**ROAD TRAFFIC** (licensed vehicles)

|  | 1986 | 1987 | 1988 |
|---|---|---|---|
| Cars and station wagons | 16,5764 | 17,121 | 17,532 |
| Commercial vehicles | 26,989 | 26,061 | 29,021 |
| Motor cycles | 1,246 | 1,232 | 1,204 |
| Tractors | 1,287 | 1,313 | 1,414 |

**SHIPPING** (international sea-borne freight traffic)

|  | 1988 | 1989 | 1990 |
|---|---|---|---|
| Cargo unloaded ('000 metric tons) | 1,834 | 1,845 | 1,784 |
| Cargo loaded ('000 metric tons) | 2,331 | 2,452 | 2,463 |

Source: UN, *Monthly Bulletin of Statistics*.

**CIVIL AVIATION** (traffic on scheduled services)

|  | 1990 | 1991 | 1992 |
|---|---|---|---|
| Kilometres flown (million) | 17 | 17 | 17 |
| Passengers carried ('000) | 931 | 911 | 954 |
| Passenger-km (million) | 681 | 676 | 699 |
| Total ton-km (million) | 77 | 77 | 82 |

Source: UN, *Statistical Yearbook*.

## Tourism

**FOREIGN TOURIST ARRIVALS**

| Country of Origin | 1988 | 1989 | 1990 |
|---|---|---|---|
| Australia | 20,345 | 24,839 | 18,845 |
| Japan | 2,184 | 1,924 | 1,830 |
| New Zealand | 1,823 | 2,462 | 1,882 |
| United Kingdom | 2,211 | 2,243 | 3,101 |
| USA | 4,480 | 4,984 | 4,332 |
| **Total** (incl. others) | 40,529 | 48,910 | 40,747 |

**Total tourist arrivals:** 37,366 in 1991; 40,533 in 1992.

## Communications Media

**Radio Receivers** (1992): 298,000 in use.

**Television Receivers** (1992): 10,000 in use.

**Telephones** (main lines, 1991): 34,000 in use.

**Daily Newspapers** (1992): 2 (combined circulation 64,000 copies per issue).

Sources: UNESCO, *Statistical Yearbook*; UN, *Statistical Yearbook*.

## Education

**Pre-primary** (1992): 856 pupils (males 445; females 411).

**Primary** (1992): 2,821 schools; 14,117 teachers; 443,552 pupils (males 245,832; females 197,720).

**Secondary** (1992): 3,293 teachers; 69,596 pupils (males 42,785; females 28,811).

**Tertiary** (1986): 902 teachers; 6,397 pupils (males 4,832; females 1,565).

Source: UNESCO, *Statistical Yearbook*.

# Directory

## The Constitution

The present Constitution came into effect on 16 September 1975, when Papua New Guinea became independent. The main provisions of the Constitution are summarized below:

### PREAMBLE

The national goals of the Independent State of Papua New Guinea are: integral human development, equality and participation in the development of the country, national sovereignty and self-reliance, conservation of natural resources and the environment and development primarily through the use of Papua New Guinean forms of social, political and economic organization.

### BASIC HUMAN RIGHTS

All people are entitled to the fundamental rights and freedoms of the individual whatever their race, tribe, place of origin, political opinion, colour, creed or sex. The individual's rights include the right to freedom, life and the protection of the law, freedom from inhuman treatment, forced labour, arbitrary search and entry, freedom of conscience, thought, religion, expression, assembly, association and employment, and the right to privacy. Papua New Guinea citizens also have the following special rights: the right to vote and stand for public office, the right to freedom of information and of movement, protection from unjust deprivation of property and equality before the law.

### THE NATION

Papua New Guinea is a sovereign, independent state. There is a National Capital District which shall be the seat of government.

The Constitution provides for various classes of citizenship. The age of majority is 19 years.

### HEAD OF STATE

Her Majesty the Queen of Great Britain and Northern Ireland is Queen and Head of State of Papua New Guinea. The Head of State appoints and dismisses the Prime Minister on the proposal of the National Parliament and other ministers on the proposal of the Prime Minister. The Governor-General and Chief Justice are

# PAPUA NEW GUINEA

appointed and dismissed on the proposal of the National Executive Council. All the privileges, powers, functions, duties and responsibilities of the Head of State may be exercised or performed through the Governor-General.

### Governor-General

The Governor-General must be a citizen who is qualified to be a member of Parliament or who is a mature person of good standing who enjoys the respect of the community. No one is eligible for appointment more than once unless Parliament approves by a two-thirds majority. No one is eligible for a third term. The Governor-General is appointed by the Head of State on the proposal of the National Executive Council in accordance with the decision of Parliament by simple majority vote. He may be dismissed by the Head of State on the proposal of the National Executive Council in accordance with a decision of the Council or of an absolute majority of Parliament. The normal term of office is six years. In the case of temporary or permanent absence, dismissal or suspension he may be replaced temporarily by the Speaker of the National Parliament until such time as a new Governor-General is appointed.

## THE GOVERNMENT

The Government comprises the National Parliament, the National Executive and the National Judicial System.

### National Parliament

The National Parliament, or the House of Assembly, is a single-chamber legislature of members elected from single-member open or provincial electorates. The National Parliament has 109 members elected by universal adult suffrage. The normal term of office is five years. There is a Speaker and a Deputy Speaker, who must be members of Parliament and must be elected to these posts by Parliament. They cannot serve as government ministers concurrently.

### National Executive

The National Executive comprises the Head of State and the National Executive Council. The Prime Minister, who presides over the National Executive Council, is appointed and dismissed by the Head of State on the proposal of Parliament. The other ministers, of whom there shall be not fewer than six nor more than a quarter of the number of members of the Parliament, are appointed and dismissed by the Head of State on the proposal of the Prime Minister. The National Executive Council consists of all the ministers, including the Prime Minister, and is responsible for the executive government of Papua New Guinea.

### National Judicial System

The National Judicial System comprises the Supreme Court, the National Court, Local Courts and Village Courts. The judiciary is independent.

The Supreme Court consists of the Chief Justice, the Deputy Chief Justice and the other judges of the National Court. It is the final court of appeal. The Chief Justice is appointed and dismissed by the Head of State on the proposal of the National Executive Council after consultation with the minister responsible for justice. The Deputy Chief Justice and the other judges are appointed by the Judicial and Legal Services Commission. The National Court consists of the Chief Justice, the Deputy Chief Justice and no fewer than four nor more than six other judges.

The Constitution also makes provision for the establishment of the Magisterial Service and the establishment of the posts of Public Prosecutor and the Public Solicitor.

## THE STATE SERVICES

The Constitution establishes the following State Services which, with the exception of the Defence Force, are subject to ultimate civilian control.

### National Public Service

The Public Service is managed by the Department of Personnel Management which is headed by a Secretary, who is appointed by the National Executive Council on a four-year contract.

### Police Force

The Police Force is subject to the control of the National Executive Council through a minister and its function is to preserve peace and good order and to maintain and enforce the law.

### Papua New Guinea Defence Force

The Defence Force is subject to the superintendence and control of the National Executive Council through the Minister of Defence. The functions of the Defence Force are to defend Papua New Guinea, to provide assistance to civilian authorities in a civil disaster, in the restoration of public order or during a period of declared national emergency.

The fourth State Service is the Parliamentary Service.

The Constitution also includes sections on Public Finance, the office of the Auditor-General, the Public Accounts Commission and the declaration of a State of National Emergency.

# The Government

**Head of State:** HM Queen Elizabeth II.

**Governor-General:** Sir Wiwa Korowi (appointed 11 November 1991).

### NATIONAL EXECUTIVE COUNCIL
(June 1995)

A coalition of the People's Democratic Movement (PDM), People's Progress Party (PPP), League for National Advancement (LNA) and several independents.

**Prime Minister and Minister for Foreign Affairs and Trade:** Sir Julius Chan.

**Deputy Prime Minister and Minister for Finance and Planning:** Chris Haiveta.

**Minister for Agriculture and Livestock:** Bernard Narokobi.

**Minister for Fisheries and Marine Resources:** Titus Philomen.

**Minister for Energy Development:** (vacant).

**Minister for Forests:** (vacant).

**Minister for Housing:** Dick Mune.

**Minister for Provincial Affairs and Village Development:** Castan Maibawa.

**Minister for Transport:** Andrew Baing.

**Minister for Lands and Physical Planning:** Sir Albert Kipalan.

**Minister for Justice and Attorney-General:** Robert Timo Nagele.

**Minister for Education and Culture:** Joseph Onguglo.

**Minister for Defence:** Mathias Ijape.

**Minister for Public Service:** Bart Philemon.

**Minister for Police:** Paul Mambei.

**Minister for Communications:** John Momis.

**Minister for Works:** Peter Yama.

**Minister for Environment and Conservation:** Perry Zeipi.

**Minister for Mining and Petroleum:** John Giheno.

**Minister for Health:** Peter Barter.

**Minister for Labour and Employment:** Jerry Nalau.

**Minister for Tourism and Civil Aviation:** Paul Pora.

**Minister for Home Affairs:** Nakikus Konga.

**Minister for Commerce and Industry:** David Mai.

**Minister for Correctional Services:** Syvanius Siembo.

**Minister for Higher Education, Science and Technology:** Moi Avei.

**Minister for State Affairs and Administrative Services:** Paul Tohian.

**Senior Minister Assisting the Prime Minister:** Arnold Marsipal.

### MINISTRIES

**Prime Minister's Office:** POB 6605, Boroko; tel. 276715; telex 22388; fax 276629.

**Department of Agriculture and Livestock:** POB 417, Konedobu; tel. 213002; telex 22143; fax 211337.

**Department of State for Bougainville:** Central Government Offices, Kumul Ave, Post Office, Wards Strip, Waigani; tel. 276634; fax 276513.

**Department of Commerce and Industry:** Central Government Offices, Kumul Ave, Post Office, Wards Strip, Waigani; tel. 271115; fax 271750.

**Department of Communications:** National Parliament, Waigani, POB 1279, Boroko; tel. 276681; telex 22237; fax 252298.

**Department of Correctional Services and Liquor Licensing:** POB 6889, Boroko; tel. 214917; telex 23433; fax 217686.

**Department of Defence:** Free Mail Bag, Boroko; tel. 242270; telex 22170; fax 256117.

**Department of Education:** PSA Haus, Boroko; tel. 272340; telex 22193; fax 254648.

**Department of Energy Development:** Central Government Offices, Kumul Ave, Post Office, Wards Strip, Waigani.

**Department of Environment and Conservation:** Central Government Offices, Kumul Ave, Post Office, Wards Strip, Waigani; tel. 271692; fax 271900.

**Department of Finance and Planning:** POB 710, Waigani; tel. 288000; telex 22218; fax 288141.
**Department of Fisheries and Marine Resources:** POB 165, Konedobu; tel. 271799; telex 22392; fax 213696.
**Department of Foreign Affairs and Trade:** Central Government Offices, Kumul Ave, Post Office, Wards Strip, Waigani; tel. 271311; telex 22136; fax 254467.
**Department of Forests:** POB 5055, Boroko; tel. 277800; telex 22360; fax 254433.
**Department of Health:** POB 3991, Boroko; tel. 248600; telex 22151; fax 250826.
**Department of Higher Education, Science and Technology:** POB 352, Konedobu; tel. 214011; telex 22211; fax 213701.
**Department of Home Affairs:** Maori Kiki Bldg, 2nd Floor, POB 7354, Boroko; tel. 254967; telex 22151; fax 213821.
**Department of Housing:** POB 1550, Boroko; tel. 247200; fax 259918.
**Department of Justice and Attorney-General:** Central Government Offices, Kumul Ave, Post Office, Wards Strip, Waigani; tel. 276521; telex 22127; fax 259265.
**Department of Labour and Employment:** POB 5644, Boroko; tel. 272262; telex 22375; fax 257092.
**Department of Lands and Physical Planning:** POB 5665, Boroko; tel. 277344; telex 22106; fax 213709.
**Department of Mining and Petroleum:** Konedobu.
**Department of Police:** POB 85, Konedobu; tel. 226183; telex 22113; fax 226113.
**Department of Provincial Affairs and Village Development:** Central Government Offices, Kumul Ave, Post Office, Wards Strip, Waigani; tel. 271787; telex 22141; fax 211623.
**Department of Public Service:** Wards Strip, Waigani; tel. 271901; fax 271226.
**Department of State:** Haus To Makala, 5th Floor, Post Office, Wards Strip, Waigani; tel. 276758; telex 23402; fax 214861.
**Department of Tourism and Civil Aviation:** Central Government Offices, Kumul Ave, Post Office, Wards Strip, Waigani.
**Department of Transport:** POB 457, Konedobu; tel. 211866; telex 22203; fax 217310.
**Department of Works:** POB 1108, Boroko; tel. 241123; telex 23267; fax 241182.

## Legislature

### NATIONAL PARLIAMENT

The unicameral legislature has 109 elective seats: 89 representing open constituencies and 20 representing provincial constituencies. There is constitutional provision for up to three nominated members.

**Speaker:** RABBIE NAMALIU.

**General Election, 13–27 June 1992**

| Party | Seats |
| --- | --- |
| Pangu Pati | 22 |
| People's Democratic Movement | 15 |
| People's Action Party | 13 |
| People's Progress Party | 10 |
| Melanesian Alliance | 9 |
| League for National Advancement | 5 |
| National Party | 2 |
| Melanesian United Front | 1 |
| Independents | 31 |
| **Total** | 108* |

* The election in one constituency was postponed, owing to the death of a candidate.

## Political Organizations

**Bougainville Revolutionary Army (BRA):** demands independence for island of Bougainville; Leaders FRANCIS ONA, SAM KAUONA.
**League for National Advancement (LNA):** POB 6101, Boroko; f. 1986; Leader KARL STACK.
**Melanesian Alliance (MA):** POB 3828, Port Moresby; tel. 277635; telex 23326; f. 1978; socialist; Chair. Fr JOHN MOMIS; Gen. Sec. FABIAN WAU KAWA.
**Melanesian United Front:** Boroko; f. 1988; fmrly Morobe Independent Group; Leader UTULA SAMANA.
**National Party (NP):** Private Bag, Boroko, f. 1979; fmrly People's United Front; Leader MICHAEL MEL.
**Pangu (Papua New Guinea Unity) Pati:** POB 289, Waigani; tel. 277628; fax 277611; f. 1967; urban and rural-based; Leader CHRIS HAIVETA.
**People's Action Party (PAP):** POB 3043, Boroko; tel. 251343; f. 1985; Leader AKOKA DOI.
**People's Democratic Movement (PDM):** POB 972, Boroko; f. 1985; Leader PAIAS WINGTI.
**People's Progress Party (PPP):** POB 6030, Boroko; f. 1970; Leader Sir JULIUS CHAN; Nat. Chair. Sir ZIBANG ZURENUOC.

## Diplomatic Representation

### EMBASSIES AND HIGH COMMISSIONS IN PAPUA NEW GUINEA

**Australia:** POB 129, Hohola; tel. 259333; fax 259183; High Commissioner: BILL FARMER.
**China, People's Republic:** POB 1351, Boroko; tel. 259836; telex 23073; fax 258247; Ambassador: YUAN ZUDE.
**France:** Pacific View Apts, 9th Floor, Pruth St, Korobosea, POB 1155, Port Moresby, tel. 253740; telex 22186; fax 250861; Ambassador: CLAUDE MAYNOT.
**Germany:** Pacific View Apts, 2nd Floor, Pruth St, Korobosea, POB 3631, Boroko; tel. 252971; telex 23037; fax 251029; Chargé d'affaires: KLAUS SOERING.
**Holy See:** POB 98, Port Moresby; tel. 256021; fax 252844; Apostolic Nuncio: Most Rev. RAMIRO MOLINER INGLÉS, Titular Archbishop of Sarda.
**Indonesia:** POB 7165, Boroko; tel. 253116; fax 250535; Ambassador: BAGUS SUMITRO.
**Japan:** ANG House, Hunter St, POB 1040, Port Moresby; tel. 211800; telex 22215; fax 214868; Ambassador: TADASHI MASUI.
**Korea, Republic:** POB 381, Port Moresby; tel. 254755; fax 259996; Ambassador: SUK-GON LEE.
**Malaysia:** POB 1400, Port Moresby; tel. 252076; telex 23240; High Commissioner: V. YOOGALINGAM.
**New Zealand:** Embassy Drive, POB 1051, Waigani; tel. 259444; fax 250565; High Commissioner: JOHN CLARKE.
**Philippines:** POB 5916, Boroko; tel. 256577; telex 23012; Ambassador: RODOLFO L. DIAZ.
**United Kingdom:** Kiroki St, Waigani, POB 4778, Boroko; tel. 251677; fax 253547; High Commissioner: BRIAN B. LOW.
**USA:** Douglas St, POB 1492, Port Moresby; tel. 211455; fax 213423; Ambassador: RICHARD W. TEARE.

## Judicial System

The Supreme Court is the highest judicial authority in the country, and deals with all matters involving the interpretation of the Constitution, and with appeals from the National Court. The National Court has unlimited jurisdiction in both civil and criminal matters. All National Court Judges (except acting Judges) are Judges of the Supreme Court. District Courts are responsible for civil cases involving compensation, for some indictable offences and for the more serious summary offences, while Local Courts deal with minor offences and with such matters as custody of children under the provision of Custom. There are also Children's Courts, which judge cases involving minors. Appeal from the District, Local and Children's Courts lies to the National Court. District and Local Land Courts deal with disputes relating to Customary land, and Warden's Courts with civil cases relating to mining. In addition, there are other courts with responsibility for determining ownership of government land and for assessing the right of Customary landowners to compensation. Village Courts, which are presided over by Magistrates with no formal legal qualification, are responsible for all Customary matters not dealt with by other courts.

**Supreme Court of Papua New Guinea:** POB 7018, Boroko; tel. 245700; fax 234492; Chief Justice Sir ARNOLD K. AMET; Dep. Chief Justice Sir MARI KAPI.

## Religion

The belief in magic or sorcery is widespread, even among the significant proportion of the population that has adopted Christianity (nominally 93% in 1966). Pantheism also survives. There are many missionary societies.

# PAPUA NEW GUINEA

## CHRISTIANITY

**Melanesian Council of Churches:** POB 1015, Boroko; tel. 256410; f. 1965; seven mem. churches; Chair. Rev. JIM BAITEL; Gen. Sec. Fr WALTER ATAEMBO.

### The Anglican Communion

Formerly part of the Province of Queensland within the Church of England in Australia (now the Anglican Church of Australia), Papua New Guinea became an independent Province in February 1977. The Anglican Church of Papua New Guinea comprises five dioceses.

**Archbishop of Papua New Guinea and Bishop of the New Guinea Islands:** Most Rev. BEVAN MEREDITH, POB 159, Rabaul, East New Britain Province; tel. 922237; fax. 922239.

**General Secretary:** PETER SHEPHERD, POB 673, Lae, Morobe Province; fax 421852.

### The Roman Catholic Church

For ecclesiastical purposes, Papua New Guinea comprises four archdioceses and 14 dioceses. At 31 December 1993 there were 1,227,517 adherents, representing 31.3% of the total population.

**Catholic Bishops' Conference of Papua New Guinea and Solomon Islands:** POB 398, Waigani; tel. 259577; fax 232551; f. 1959; Pres. Rt Rev. BRIAN BARNES, Bishop of Aitape.

**Archbishop of Madang:** Most Rev. BENEDICT TO VARPIN, Archbishop's Residence, POB 750, Madang; tel. 822599; fax 822596.

**Archbishop of Mount Hagen:** Most Rev. MICHAEL MEIER, Archbishop's Office, POB 54, Mount Hagen; tel. 521285; fax 522128.

**Archbishop of Port Moresby:** Most Rev. Sir PETER KURONGKU, Archbishop's House, POB 1032, Boroko; tel. 251192; fax 256731.

**Archbishop of Rabaul:** Most Rev. KARL HESSE, Archbishop's House, POB 357, Kokopo, East New Britain Province; tel. 928369; fax 928404.

### Other Christian Churches

**Baptist Union of Papua New Guinea Inc:** POB 705, Mount Hagen; tel. 521030; fax 522832; f. 1976; Gen. Supt MARTIN WAYNE.

**Evangelical Lutheran Church of Papua New Guinea:** Bishop Rt Rev. Sir GETAKE GAM; POB 80, Lae; tel. 423711; telex 42577; fax 421056; f. 1956; Sec. KURIA GOMIA; 558,522 mems.

**Gutnius Lutheran Church of Papua New Guinea:** Bishop Rev. DAVID P. PISO, POB 72, Wabag, Enga Province; tel. 571054; fax 571192; f. 1948; Gen. Sec. RICHARD R. MOSES; 102,000 mems.

**Papua New Guinea Union Mission of the Seventh-day Adventist Church:** POB 86, Lae; tel. 421488; fax 421873; Pres. Pastor YORI HIBO; Sec. Pastor G. C. PORTER; 200,000 adherents.

**The United Church in Papua New Guinea and Solomon Islands:** POB 1401, Port Moresby; tel. 211744; fax 214930; f. 1968 by union of the Methodist Church in Melanesia, the Papua Ekalesia and United Church, Port Moresby; Moderator Rev. EDEA KIDU; 700,000 mems.

## BAHÁ'Í FAITH

**National Spiritual Assembly:** Private Mail Bag, Boroko; tel. 250286; fax 250286.

# The Press

There are numerous newspapers and magazines published by government departments, statutory organizations, missions, sporting organizations, local government councils and provincial governments. They are variously in English, Tok Pisin (Pidgin), Motu and vernacular languages.

**Ailans Nius:** POB 1239, Rabaul; weekly.

**Arawa Bulletin:** POB 86, Arawa, North Solomons Province; tel. 951028; fax 952402; f. 1972; weekly; Man. Editor C. J. KABLEAN ALBON; circ. 4,500.

**Education Gazette:** Dept of Education, PSA Haus, POB 446, Waigani; tel. 272413; telex 22193; fax 254648; quarterly; Editor OLIVER A. TAPUA; circ. 8,000.

**Foreign Affairs Review:** Dept of Foreign Affairs, Central Government Offices, Kumul Ave, Post Office, Wards Strip, Waigani; tel. 271401; telex 22136; fax 254886.

**Hailans Nius:** Mount Hagen; weekly.

**Hiri:** National Information Service, POB 1424, Port Moresby; tel. 200196; fax 214254; monthly; English, Motu and Tok Pisin; development information; publ. by the Government; Editor KONIO SENEKA.

**The National:** POB 6817, Boroko, Port Moresby; tel. 246888; fax 246767; f. 1993; daily; publ. by Pacific Star Pty Ltd; Editor FRANK SENGE KOLMA; circ. 20,000.

**New Nation:** POB 1982, Boroko; tel. 252500; telex 22213; f. 1977; 10 a year; English; young adults' magazine; Publr KEVIN WALCOT; Editor CLAIRE SWALE; circ. 60,000.

**Niugini Nius:** POB 3019, Boroko; tel. 252177; telex 23370; daily.

**Lae Nius:** POB 759, Lae; 2 a week.

**Pacific Star:** Port Moresby; f. 1993; Deputy Editor FRANK SENGE.

**Papua New Guinea Business:** POB 1982, Boroko; tel. 252500; fax 252579; monthly; English; Editor FAY DUEGA; circ. 12,000.

**Papua New Guinea Journal of Agriculture, Forestry and Fisheries:** Dept of Agriculture and Livestock, POB 417, Konedobu; tel. 258191; fax 230279; Man. Editor Prof. RAY KUMAR; Editor JONES HIASO.

**Papua New Guinea Post-Courier:** POB 85, Port Moresby; tel. 212577; f. 1969; daily; English; independent; Gen. Man. DON KENNEDY; Editor LUKE SELA; circ. 30,484.

**Papua New Guinea Today:** National Information Services, POB 1424, Port Moresby; tel. 213188; fax 214254; quarterly; development issues.

**Rugby League News:** POB 1982, Boroko; tel. 252500; telex 22213; fax 252579; weekly; Publr ANNA SOLOMON; Editor BARBARA TOMI; circ. 7,000.

**The Saturday Independent:** POB 1982, Boroko; tel. 252500; fax 252579; f. 1995 as replacement for the Times of Papua New Guinea; weekly; English; Publr and Editor ANNA SOLOMON.

**Wantok:** POB 1982, Boroko; tel. 252500; fax 252579; f. 1970; weekly in New Guinea Pidgin; mainly rural readership; Publr ANNA SOLOMON; Editor LEO WAFIWA; circ. 15,000.

**Weekend Sport:** POB 1982, Boroko; tel. 252500; telex 22213; weekly; English; Publr KEVIN WALCOT; Editor JAMES KILA; circ. 8,000.

# Publishers

**Gordon and Gotch (PNG) Pty Ltd:** POB 107, Boroko; tel. 254855; fax 250950; f. 1970; general non-fiction; Gen. Man. CHRISTOPHER CHIN.

**Scripture Union of Papua New Guinea:** POB 280, University NCD, Boroko; tel. 253987; f. 1966; religious; Chair. KUMA AUA.

**Word Publishing Co Pty Ltd:** POB 1982, Boroko; tel. 252500; fax 252579; f. 1979; 55% owned by the Catholic Church, 45% by Evangelical Lutheran, Anglican and United Churches; Gen. Man. IAN FRY; Publr ANNA SOLOMON.

# Radio and Television

In 1992, according to UNESCO estimates, there were 298,000 radio receivers and 10,001 television receivers in use.

**EM TV:** POB 443, Boroko; tel. 257322; fax 254450; f. 1988; operated by Media Niugini Pty Ltd; CEO JOHN TAYLOR.

**Kalang Service (FM):** private radio company established by National Broadcasting Commission; Chair. CAROLUS KETSIMUR.

**Media Niugini Pty Ltd:** POB 443, Boroko; tel. 257322; fax 254450; f. 1985; owned by Nine Network Australia; CEO JOHN TAYLOR.

**National Broadcasting Commission of Papua New Guinea:** POB 1359, Boroko; tel. 255233; telex 22112; f. 1973; broadcasting in English, Melanesian, Pidgin, Motu and 30 vernacular languages; Chair. Sir ALKAN TOLOLO; Programme Dir C. APELIS.

# Finance

(cap. = capital; res = reserves; dep. = deposits; m. = million; brs = branches; amounts in kina unless otherwise stated)

## BANKING

### Central Bank

**Bank of Papua New Guinea:** Douglas St, POB 121, Port Moresby; tel. 212999; telex 22128; fax 211617; f. 1973; bank of issue since 1975; cap. 15.0m., res 181.1m., dep. 296.5m. (Dec. 1992); Gov. and Chair. KOIARI TARATA.

### Commercial Banks

**Australia and New Zealand Banking Group (PNG) Limited:** Defens Haus, 2nd Floor, Cnr of Champion Parade and Hunter St, POB 1152, Port Moresby; tel. 223333; telex 22178; fax 223253; f. 1976; cap. 5.0m., dep. 259.0m. (Sept. 1994); Chair. P. S. WILSON; Man. Dir R. G. JONES; 8 brs.

**Bank of South Pacific Ltd:** Douglas St, POB 173, Port Moresby; tel. 212444; telex 22166; fax 217302; f. 1974; acquired from National Australia Bank Ltd by Papua New Guinea consortium (National Investment Holdings) in 1993; cap. 2.3m., res 5.5m., dep.

154.7m. (Dec. 1993); Chair. NOREO BEANGKE; Man. Dir N. R. SMITH; 8 brs.

**Indosuez Niugini Bank Ltd:** Burns House, Champion Parade, POB 1390, Port Moresby; tel. 213533; telex 23274; fax 213115; f. 1983; cap. 3.0m., res 0.5m., dep. 49.1m. (Dec. 1994); Chair. PIERRE LESTANG; Man. Dir JEAN-PHILIPPE AUDUBERT; 2 brs.

**MBF Finance:** Port Moresby; f. 1989.

**Maybank (PNG) Ltd:** Port Moresby; f. 1995.

**Niugini-Lloyds International Bank Ltd:** POB 336, Port Moresby; tel. 213111; telex 23257; fax 213141; f. 1983; 49% owned by Lloyds Bank PLC (UK), 35% state-owned; cap. 3.0m., dep. 55.1m. (Dec. 1989); Chair. B. J. HANSON; Gen. Man. MARTIN R. SLOUGH; 3 brs.

**Papua New Guinea Banking Corporation:** Cnr of Douglas and Musgrave Sts, POB 78, Port Moresby; tel. 211999; telex 22160; fax 211683; f. 1974; cap. 11.3m., res 35.1m., dep. 680.4m. (Dec. 1992); Chair. ROGER PALME; Man. Dir HENRY FABILA; 21 brs.

**Westpac Bank—PNG—Ltd:** Mogoru Motu Bldg, 5th Floor, Champion Parade, POB 706, Port Moresby; tel. 220800; telex 23243; fax 213367; f. 1910 as Bank of New South Wales, present name since 1982; 90% owned by Westpac Banking Corpn, Australia; cap. 5.3m., res 7.4m., dep. 368.5m. (Sept. 1994); Chair. BRUCE ALEXANDER; Man. Dir ARTHUR L. ROBERTSON; 22 brs.

### Development Bank

**Rural Development Bank of Papua New Guinea:** POB 6310, Boroko; tel. 247500; telex 22295; fax 259817; f. 1967; cap. 32.6m., res –19.9m. (Dec. 1991); statutory govt agency; Chair. Sir FREDERICK REIHER; Man. Dir SHEM PAKE.

### Savings and Loan Societies

**Registry of Savings and Loan Societies:** Banking Supervision Dept, POB 121, Port Moresby; tel. 227200; telex 22128; fax 211617; 124 savings and loan societies (1993); 110,657 mems; total funds 108.2m., loans outstanding 71.3m., investments 15.6m. (Dec. 1993).

## STOCK EXCHANGE

The Port Moresby Stock Exchange was due to open in April 1996.

## INSURANCE

**Niugini Insurance Corporation Ltd:** POB 331, Port Moresby; tel. 214077; fax 217898; f. 1978; 20% govt-owned; Gen. Man. GRAHAM WOOLEY.

**Pan Asia Pacific Assurance (PNG) Pty Ltd (PAPA):** Port Moresby; f. 1993; Chair. BENIAS SABUMEI.

There are branches of several Australian and United Kingdom insurance companies in Port Moresby, Rabaul, Lae and Kieta.

# Trade and Industry

## INDUSTRIAL AND DEVELOPMENT ORGANIZATIONS

**Bougainville Copper Ltd:** Mogoru Motu Bldg, 1st Floor, Champion Parade, Port Moresby; tel. 212044; fax 213634; 53% owned by CRA Ltd (Australia), 19% state-owned; Chair. MARK RAYNER; Sec. B. P. BARTHOLOMAEUS.

**Cocoa Board of Papua New Guinea:** POB 532, Rabaul; tel. 921354; telex 92935; fax 921794; f. 1974.

**Coffee Industry Corpn Ltd:** POB 137, Goroka; tel. 721266; telex 72647; fax 721431; CEO RON GANARAFO.

**Commonwealth Development Corpn:** POB 907, Port Moresby; tel. 212944; fax 212867.

**Copra Marketing Board of Papua New Guinea:** Port Moresby; telex 22135; markets all copra in Papua New Guinea; consists of a chair. and mems representing producers; Chair. Sir JOHN GUISE; Gen. Man. JOE BAE.

**Forest Industries Council:** POB 1829, Port Moresby; tel. 256399; telex 22226; fax 212911; Exec. Dir PETER J. EDDOWES (acting).

**Higaturu Oil Palms Pty Ltd:** POB 28, Popondetta; tel. 297177; telex 29188; fax 297137; f. 1976; jtly owned by the Commonwealth Development Corpn (UK) and the Papua New Guinea Govt; major producer of palm oil and cocoa.

**Investment Corporation of Papua New Guinea:** Hunter St, POB 155, Port Moresby; tel. 212855; telex 22354; fax 211240; f. 1971 as govt body to support local enterprise and to purchase shares in foreign businesses operating in Papua New Guinea; transferred to private ownership in late 1993.

**Investment Promotion Authority (IPA):** POB 5053, Boroko; tel. 217311; fax 212819; f. 1992, following reorganization of National Investment and Development Authority; a statutory body responsible for the promotion, supervision and regulation of foreign investment; the first contact point for foreign investors for advice on project proposals and approvals of applications for registration to conduct business in the country; contributes to planning for investment and recommends priority areas for investment to the Govt; also co-ordinates investment proposals; Man. Dir AIVU R. TAUVASA.

**Mineral Resources Development Company:** Dir BOB NEEDHAM.

**National Contractors' Association:** Port Moresby; formed by construction companies for the promotion of education, training and professional conduct in the construction industry; Pres. ROY THORPE.

**National Investment Holdings Corpn Pty Ltd (NIH):** Port Moresby; Chair. ALFRED DANIEL.

**New Britain Palm Oil Development Ltd:** Kimbe, West New Britain; tel. 935177; fax 935285; f. 1967; jtly owned by the Govt and Harrisons and Crosfield (London); major producer of palm oil and coffee and supplier of high quality oil palm seed; Man. Dir N.M. THOMPSON.

**Niugini Produce Marketing Pty Ltd:** POB 1811, Lae; telex 42409; f. 1982; govt-owned; handles distribution of fruit and vegetables throughout the country.

**Papua New Guinea Cocoa and Coconut Institute:** Port Moresby; Chair. VALENTINE KAMBORI.

**Papua New Guinea Forest Authority:** Port Moresby; Man. Dir JEAN KEKEDO.

**Papua New Guinea Holdings Corpn:** POB 131, Port Moresby; fax 217545; f. 1992; responsible for managing govt privatization programme; Chair. MICHAEL MEL; Man. Dir PETER STEELE.

**Papua New Guinea Log Carriers Asscn:** f. 1993.

**Pita Lus National Silk Institute:** Kagamuga, Mount Hagen; f. 1978; govt silk-producing project.

## CHAMBERS OF COMMERCE

**Papua New Guinea Chamber of Commerce and Industry:** POB 1621, Port Moresby; tel. 213057; fax 214203; Pres. STAN JOYCE.

**Papua New Guinea Chamber of Manufacturers:** Port Moresby; Pres. WAYNE GOLDING.

**Papua New Guinea Chamber of Mines and Petroleum:** POB 1032, Port Moresby; tel. 212988; fax 217107; Exec. Dir GREG ANDERSON; Pres. MARK PUCKETT.

**Port Moresby Chamber of Commerce and Industry:** POB 1764, Port Moresby; tel. 213077; fax 214203; Pres. HENRY KILA.

**Lae Chamber of Commerce and Industry:** POB 265, Lae.

## TRADE UNIONS

The Industrial Organizations Ordinance requires all industrial organizations that consist of no fewer than 20 employees or four employers to register. In 1977 there were 56 registered industrial organizations, including a general employee group registered as a workers' association in each province and also unions covering a specific industry or profession.

**Papua New Guinea Trade Union Congress:** POB 4729, Boroko; tel. 256041; 30 affiliates, 60,000 mems; Pres. JOHN DUMIT; Gen. Sec. JOHN PASKA.

The following are among the major trade unions:

**Bougainville Mining Workers' Union:** POB 777, Panguna; tel. 958272; Pres. MATHEW TUKAN; Gen. Sec. ALFRED ELISHA TAGORNOM.

**Central Province Building and Construction Industry Workers' Union:** POB 265, Port Moresby.

**Central Province Transport Drivers' and Workers' Union:** POB 265, Port Moresby.

**Employers' Federation of Papua New Guinea:** POB 490, Port Moresby; tel. 214772; fax 214070; f. 1963; Pres. W. D. COPLAND; Gen. Sec. G. J. HOGG; 170 mems.

**Journalists' Association (PNG):** POB 85, Port Moresby; tel. 212577; fax 212721; f. 1989; Pres. FRANK SENGE KOLMA; Vice-Pres. SORARIBA NASH.

**National Federation of Timber Workers:** Madang; f. 1993; Gen. Sec. a.i. MATHIAS KENUANGI.

**Papua New Guinea Teachers' Association:** POB 6546, Boroko; tel. 260711; fax 260941; f. 1971; Pres. TAINA DAI; Gen. Sec. MOSES TAIAN; 13,924 mems.

**Papua New Guinea Waterside Workers' and Seamen's Union:** Port Moresby; f. 1979; an amalgamation of four unions; Sec. AUGUSTINE WAVIKI.

**Police Association of Papua New Guinea:** POB 903, Port Moresby; tel. 214172; f. 1964; Pres. A. AVIAISA; Gen. Sec. (vacant); 4,596 mems.

**Port Moresby Council of Trade Unions:** POB 265, Boroko; Gen. Sec. JOHN KOSI.

# PAPUA NEW GUINEA

**Port Moresby Miscellaneous Workers' Union:** POB 265, Boroko.
**Printing and Kindred Industries Union:** Port Moresby.
**Public Employees Association:** POB 965, Boroko; tel. 252955; fax 252186; f. 1974; 28,000 mems; Pres. NAPOLEON LIOSI; Gen. Sec. JACK N. KUTAL.

## Transport

### ROADS

In 1986 there were 19,736 km of roads in Papua New Guinea, of which 4,865 km were classified as highways or trunk roads. Work was in progress in 1985 to construct a transnational highway linking Port Moresby with the Highlands and the north coast, and in 1993 the Government announced that it was to upgrade roads in Port Moresby at a cost of K20m. over five years. In 1995 the Australian Government announced that it was to donate $A155m. over five years for major road-building projects.

### SHIPPING

Papua New Guinea has 16 major ports and a coastal fleet of about 300 vessels.

**Port Authority of Kieta:** POB 149, Kieta, North Solomons Province; tel. 956066; telex 95905; fax 956255; Port Man. AUGUSTINE PAKUNDU.
**Port Authority of Lae:** POB 563, Lae; tel. 422477; telex 42414; fax 422543; Port Man. N. PAIMAT.
**Port Authority of Madang:** POB 273, Madang; tel. 822352; fax 823097; Port Man. AUGUSTINE PAKUNDU.
**Port Authority of Port Moresby:** POB 671, Port Moresby; tel. 211400; telex 22243; Gen. Man. T. AMAO.
**Port Authority of Rabaul:** POB 592, Rabaul; tel. 921227; telex 92918; fax 921367; Port Man. AUGUSTINE PAKUNDU.

#### Shipping Companies

**Century Group of Companies:** NIC House, 3rd Floor, Champion Parade, POB 1403, Port Moresby; tel. 229275; telex 22116; fax 229251; joint venture between Burns Philp (PNG) Ltd and P & O (Australia); Man. Capt. ANIL SINGH.
**Consort Express Line Pty Ltd:** Port Moresby; operates services between Cairns (Australia) and Papua New Guinea; Gen. Man. PETER KYAM.
**New Guinea Australia Line Pty Ltd:** POB 145, Port Moresby; tel. 212377; telex 22139; fax 214879; f. 1970; operates regular container services between Australia, Papua New Guinea, Vanuatu, Tuvalu and Solomon Islands; Chair. (vacant); Gen. Man. GEOFFREY CUNDLE.
**Pacific Tankships:** Rabaul; f. 1990; bulk delivery of oil and fuel; Chair. JOE TAUVASA; Man. Dir JOHN O'CONNOR.
**Papua New Guinea Shipping Corporation Pty Ltd:** POB 634, Port Moresby; tel. 220290; telex 22198; fax 212815; f. 1977; owned by Steamships Trading Co Ltd; provides a container/break-bulk service to Australia, Pacific islands and Japan; Exec. Dir Capt. DUNCAN M. TELFER.
**Papua Shipping and Stevedoring Co:** operates a shipping service, stevedoring and the delivery of cargo between Papua New Guinea, the Pacific region and other overseas ports.
**South Sea Lines Proprietary Ltd:** POB 1908, Lae; tel. 423602; operates four vessels.
**Sullivans:** POB 2181, Lae.
**Western Tug & Barge Co P/L:** POB 175, Port Moresby; tel. 212099; telex 22116; fax 217950; shipowning arm of Century Group of Companies; operates 12 vessels.

Shipping companies operating container/break bulk services to Papua New Guinea include NGAL/PNGL/CONPAC consortium (every nine days from Australia and Solomon Islands); Niugini Express Lines (two a month); Karlander New Guinea Line (monthly) from Australia; Angel Line, operated by Sofrana-Unilines (Australia) Pty (every three weeks from Melbourne and Sydney); Bank Line, which operates 28-day services from the United Kingdom and Continent via Pacific Islands and returning via Mediterranean; China Navigation Co, which operates a monthly service from the Philippines, Hong Kong, Taiwan and Singapore to several Pacific islands; Sofrana-Unilines, which connects Papua New Guinea with Solomon Islands, Australia and New Zealand; Pacific Forum Lines, monthly from New Zealand via Fiji; NYK Line and Mitsui-OSK operate a 20-day service from Japan; Daiwa Line operates a monthly service from Australia and Pacific Islands.

### CIVIL AVIATION

There is an international airport at Port Moresby and over 400 other airports and airstrips throughout the country. In 1988 it was announced that a new international airport was to be built by the early 1990s, at a cost of nearly K40m. Work to upgrade the country's air traffic control systems began in 1993.

**Air Niugini:** POB 7186, Boroko; tel. 273200; telex 22225; fax 273482; f. 1973; govt-owned national airline; operates scheduled domestic cargo and passenger services within Papua New Guinea and international services to Australia, Indonesia, Solomon Islands, Philippines, Singapore, Japan and Hong Kong; Chair. Sir MEKERE MORAUTA; Gen. Man. DIETER SEEFELD.

## Tourism

Despite Papua New Guinea's spectacular scenery and abundant wildlife, tourism makes only a small contribution to the economy. In 1991 the industry earned K43m. There were 40,533 visitor arrivals in 1992.

**Tourism Promotion Authority:** POB 7144, Boroko; tel. 272521; fax 259119; Man. Dir MALI VOI; Investment Man. Dr P. K. BASU.

# PARAGUAY

## Introductory Survey

### Location, Climate, Language, Religion, Flag, Capital

The Republic of Paraguay is a land-locked country in central South America. It is bordered by Bolivia to the north, by Brazil to the east, and by Argentina to the south and west. The climate is sub-tropical. Temperatures range from an average maximum of 34.3°C (93.7°F) in January to an average minimum of 14°C (51°F) in June. The official language is Spanish, but the majority of the population speak Guaraní, an indigenous Indian language. Almost all of the inhabitants profess Christianity, and about 90% adhere to the Roman Catholic Church, the country's established religion. There is a small Protestant minority. The national flag (proportions 5 by 3) has three equal horizontal stripes, of red, white and blue. It is the only national flag with a different design on each side, having a varying emblem in the centre of the white stripe: the obverse side bears the state emblem (a white disc with a red ring bearing the words 'República del Paraguay', in yellow capitals, framing a blue disc with the five-pointed 'May Star', in yellow, surrounded by a wreath, in green), while the reverse side carries the seal of the Treasury (a white disc with a red ribbon bearing the words 'Paz y Justicia' in yellow capitals above a lion supporting a staff, surmounted by the red 'Cap of Liberty'). The capital is Asunción.

### Recent History

Paraguay, ruled by Spain from the 16th century, achieved independence in 1811. In 1865 Paraguay was involved in a disastrous war against Brazil, Argentina and Uruguay (the Triple Alliance), resulting in the loss of more than one-half of its population. Paraguay also suffered heavy losses in the Chaco Wars of 1928–30 and 1932–35 against Bolivia, but won a large part of the disputed territory when the boundary was fixed in 1938. General Higinio Morínigo established an authoritarian regime in 1940, but the return of a number of political exiles in 1947 precipitated a civil war in which supporters of the right-wing Asociación Nacional Republicana (Partido Colorado) defeated the Liberals and the Partido Revolucionario Febrerista, leading to the overthrow of Gen. Morínigo in June 1948. A period of great instability ensued. In May 1954 Gen. Alfredo Stroessner Mattiauda, the Army Commander-in-Chief, assumed power in a military coup. He nominated himself for the presidency, as the Colorado candidate, and was elected unopposed in July to complete the term of office of his predecessor, Federico Chávez. In 1955 Stroessner assumed extensive powers, and established a state of siege. Regular purges of the Partido Colorado membership, together with the mutual co-operation of the ruling party, the armed forces and the business community, enabled Stroessner to become the longest-serving dictator in Latin America: he was re-elected President, by large majorities, at five-yearly elections in 1958–88.

In February 1978 President Stroessner revoked the state of siege in all areas except Asunción. The assassination of the former Nicaraguan dictator, Gen. Anastasio Somoza Debayle, in Asunción in September 1980, however, caused President Stroessner to doubt the security of his own position, and the state of siege was reimposed throughout the country; harassment of leaders of the political opposition and of peasant and labour groups continued. The leader of the Partido Demócrata Cristiano, Luis Alfonso Resck, was arrested and expelled from the country in June 1981, and Domingo Laíno, leader of the Partido Liberal Radical Auténtico (PLRA), was deported in December 1982. After Ronald Reagan took office as President of the USA in 1981, Paraguay encountered less pressure from the US Government to curb abuses of human rights, and the use of torture against detainees reportedly became widespread once more. It was estimated at this time that more than 60% of all Paraguayans resided outside the country.

Beginning in 1982 the advanced age of many of the members of the Council of Ministers, combined with economic policies that alienated the private sector, resulted in increasing political discord. Government employment was conditional on membership of the Partido Colorado. Most opposition parties boycotted the presidential and legislative elections of February 1983. This enabled Stroessner to obtain more than 90% of the votes cast at the presidential election, and in August he formally took office for a further five-year term. In May 1983 the Government instigated a campaign of repression against students and trade unionists. There was, however, some hope of a moderation in government policy when, in January 1984, Gen. Stroessner granted an amnesty to politicians in exile, with the notable exception of Luis Alfonso Resck and Domingo Laíno. It was believed that the President had been prompted into adopting a more conciliatory line in order to arrest the decline in his popularity, following the victory (in October 1983) of Dr Raúl Alfonsín in Argentina's presidential election and the general agitation within Paraguay for an improvement in human rights. In February 1984 opposition parties organized demonstrations in Asunción for the first time in 30 years.

During the 1980s the question of the eventual succession to President Stroessner became of increasing concern, prompting more open discussion of the future of the country. In the second half of 1984 the Partido Colorado was reported to be divided into two factions over the issue. The 'Militantes' sought an eighth presidential term for Gen. Stroessner, and supported his son, Gustavo, as an eventual successor. By contrast, the 'Tradicionalistas' believed that the continuation of rule by the Partido Colorado would be most effectively secured if Gen. Stroessner were to retire in 1988, after seven terms in office, making way for a civilian leader. A third faction, the 'Eticos', emerged in 1985 to oppose a further presidential term for Stroessner.

In January 1986 the US Ambassador to Paraguay held discussions with leaders of a grouping of opposition parties, formed in 1978, known as the Acuerdo Nacional, thereby granting some measure of recognition to opposition groups excluded from the political process. Subsequently, the US ambassador was repeatedly threatened with expulsion by the Paraguayan authorities for criticizing press censorship and for maintaining contact with opposition groups. In June the US Government protested at an attack by police on Domingo Laíno, as he attempted (for the fifth time since his expulsion in 1982) to re-enter the country. In early April 1987 Stroessner announced that the state of siege was to be ended, since extraordinary security powers were no longer necessary to maintain peace. (Later in the month Laíno was finally allowed to return to Paraguay.) However, the state of siege was subsequently replaced by a new penal code, and the suppression of civil liberties and of political activity continued; during 1987 several gatherings by opposition parties were violently dispersed by the police, and in August the only remaining opposition newspaper, the weekly *El Pueblo*, was banned.

Stroessner was nominated as the presidential candidate of the Partido Colorado for the February 1988 presidential election. The poll (which took place simultaneously with legislative elections) was also contested by two other candidates, Luis María Vega of the Partido Liberal Radical and Carlos Ferreira Ibarra of the Partido Liberal. The level of participation in the election was reported to be 92.6% of eligible voters, and it was announced that Gen. Stroessner had received 88.6% of the votes cast. However, opposition leaders (who had urged voters to boycott the elections) complained of electoral malpractice, and denounced Stroessner's re-election as fraudulent.

In May 1988 Pope John Paul II visited Paraguay; during the visit he met opposition representatives. Following the Pope's departure the Government imposed strict curbs on opposition activities. However, demonstrations against the Stroessner regime continued. In August 50,000 people attended a demonstration in Asunción to protest against the Government's harassment of the Roman Catholic Church, and in November marches to commemorate the 40th anniversary of the UN General Assembly's adoption of the Universal Declaration of Human Rights were dispersed by the police.

On 3 February 1989 Gen. Stroessner was overthrown in a coup, led by Gen. Andrés Rodríguez, the second-in-command of the armed forces. The official number of fatalities was 17; however, independent observers claimed that as many as 300 people died in the coup. Stroessner was allowed to leave for exile in Brazil, as Gen. Rodríguez assumed the presidency (in a provisional capacity) and appointed a new Council of Ministers. The interim President pledged to respect human rights, to strengthen links with neighbouring countries and to improve relations with the Church. It was announced that presidential and legislative elections, open to all political parties except the Partido Comunista Paraguayo (PCP), would take place on 1 May, and Gen. Rodríguez confirmed that he would be the presidential candidate of the Partido Colorado. A request by opposition groups that polling be postponed in order to allow them more time to organize their campaigns was denied. Following his formal nomination as the presidential candidate of the Partido Colorado, Rodríguez gave assurances that, if elected, he would relinquish power to a civilian successor in 1993, and promised constitutional reforms. On 1 May Gen. Rodríguez was confirmed as President, receiving 74.2% of the votes cast; his closest rival, Domingo Laíno, secured 19.6% of the votes. The Partido Colorado, having won 72.8% of the votes in the congressional election, automatically took two-thirds of the seats in both the Chamber of Deputies and the Senate (48 and 24, respectively). The most successful opposition party was the PLRA, which obtained 19 seats in the Chamber of Deputies and 10 in the Senate. Despite widespread allegations of electoral fraud, all parties agreed to respect the results.

Following the overthrow of Gen. Stroessner, many of Paraguay's landless families (estimated to number 300,000) began to occupy privately-owned land. In June 1989 President Rodríguez convened a meeting of prominent politicians to discuss the issue of agrarian reform. Evictions of those illegally occupying land ensued: the Government maintained that reforms could not be implemented unless existing property laws were first respected. Later in June a demonstration by landless peasants to protest against the evictions was ended by force. However, the occupation by peasants of privately-owned land continued during 1990, as did evictions by the security forces. Many peasants were detained, often without charge, and it was alleged that some were tortured or otherwise ill-treated while in detention.

In July 1989 the Chamber of Deputies ratified the San José Pact on Human Rights, adopted by the Organization of American States (OAS—see p. 204) in 1978. In August 1989 Congress initiated judicial proceedings against former government officials for violations of human rights. In December the Secretary-General of the PCP, Ananías Maidana (who had been expelled from Paraguay in 1978), returned to the country: the repeal, in August 1989, of laws that had provided a basis for political repression under the Stroessner regime had allowed for the formal legalization of the PCP. Despite the progress made towards greater official respect for human rights in Paraguay, in November 1990 Rodríguez vetoed congressional proposals for the establishment of a legislative commission to investigate alleged violations of human rights.

Divisions within the Partido Colorado became evident at its annual convention in December 1989, when the 'Tradicionalistas' attempted to elect new party officials drawn exclusively from their own membership. The newly-emerged 'Democrático' faction, led by Blás Riquelme (then a vice-president of the party), succeeded in obtaining a judicial annulment of all decisions of the convention. The political crisis led to the resignation of the entire Council of Ministers. However, President Rodríguez subsequently re-elected all but one of the outgoing ministers to their former posts. In February 1990 a new electoral code was adopted, banning party affiliation for serving members of the armed forces and the police and reforming procedures for the election of party officials. In March the 'Tradicionalista' President of the Partido Colorado resigned. In July the then acting President of the party, Dr Luis María Argaña, was dismissed from his post as Minister of Foreign Affairs, after having publicly vowed that the Partido Colorado would never relinquish power and would retain control by whatever means possible.

Paraguay's first direct municipal elections took place in late May 1991, overseen by representatives of three international organizations, including the OAS. Although the Partido Colorado secured control of a majority of municipalities, the important post of mayor of Asunción was won by a relatively unknown candidate, Carlos Filizzola, the representative of a new centre-left coalition, Asunción Para Todos (APT). Defeat in the capital precipitated mutual recriminations within the increasingly fragmented Partido Colorado, and, shortly after Filizzola's election, the ruling party's youth wing, Juventud Colorada, organized a demonstration to demand the resignation of the 'Tradicionalista' Argaña from the party presidency.

In August 1991 the Congreso Nacional (National Congress) approved proposals for a complete revision of the 1967 Constitution. Elections for a National Constituent Assembly, the function of which would be to draft a new document, were scheduled for 1 December 1991. In anticipation of the elections, President Rodríguez and military leaders made concerted efforts to forge unity within the Partido Colorado, with the result that the party's three main factions, the 'Renovadores', the 'Democráticos' and the 'Autónomos' were persuaded to present a single list of candidates, under the title 'Tradicionalistas', to represent the ruling party in the elections to the Constituent Assembly. In the elections, the Partido Colorado secured 55.1% of the votes cast, thus winning an overwhelming majority of the Assembly's 198 seats. The PLRA took 27.0% of the votes, while Constitución Para Todos, formed in the aftermath of APT's success in the municipal elections, took 11.0% of the votes. The new body was convened in January 1992.

In November 1991 new legislation, drafted by President Rodríguez in co-operation with military leaders, was approved by the Congreso Nacional. The law appeared to guarantee the autonomy of the armed forces, and the definition of the role of the military was expanded to include responsibility, at the request of the Head of State, for civil defence and internal order. Moreover, no restrictions were placed on political activities by serving members of the armed forces (seemingly in contradiction of the February 1990 electoral code). Provision was also made for the President to delegate the functions of Commander-in-Chief of the Armed Forces to a senior military officer (with the Head of State retaining only ceremonial powers as the military commander). Opposition parties protested that, should the new legislation be entrenched in the new Constitution, the armed forces would remain a 'parallel' political force following the transition to civilian rule.

On 20 June 1992 the new Constitution was promulgated before the Constituent Assembly, despite the absence of Rodríguez, senior army commanders and members of the Supreme Court. The presidential boycott resulted from a dispute between Rodríguez and the Constituent Assembly, which indicated further divisions within the ruling Partido Colorado. The dispute concerned a 'transitory clause' introduced by the Assembly, extending a ban on the re-election of the President to include the current term of office. In order for the clause to be approved, a faction of the Partido Colorado, led by Argaña (himself an aspiring presidential candidate), sided with the opposition deputies, thus ensuring that Rodríguez would be unable to contest the presidency in the forthcoming election. Rodríguez, who had already stated that he would not be a candidate in the election, denounced the Assembly for doubting his assurance, and delayed signing the new Constitution until 22 June. As a consequence of the rift within the Partido Colorado, Argaña resigned as party President.

Under the new Constitution, the President and the Vice-President (a newly created post) were to be elected by a simple majority of voters. The Constituent Assembly had ostensibly disregarded the military legislation, approved in November 1991, by confirming the President as Commander-in-Chief of the Armed Forces and excluding officers on active duty from participating directly in politics. Other significant changes in the Constitution included the abolition of the death penalty, the expansion of the Supreme Court from five to nine members, and the granting of the right to form a trade union and to strike to public-sector employees (excluding the armed forces and police).

In early August 1992, in what was regarded as a major advance in the democratization of the party, the members of the Partido Colorado were afforded the opportunity, for the first time, to elect directly the party president and the entire membership of the central committee. Blás Riquelme was appointed President of the party.

An intensification, towards the end of 1992, of the antagonism dividing the Partido Colorado seriously threatened to jeopardize the party's prospects of retaining power at the forthcoming elections. An internal election in late December to select the party's presidential candidate was declared to have been won by Argaña, the candidate of the far-right. However, the candidate believed to be favoured by Rodríguez, Juan Carlos Wasmosy, refused to recognize the result, claiming that the vote had been fraudulent. An electoral tribunal failed to resolve the issue, and, following intense pressure and alleged death threats by both factions, several members of the tribunal resigned. Party leaders organized an extraordinary national convention in mid-February 1993, at which a new electoral tribunal was to be chosen. Wasmosy was eventually confirmed as the winner of the December election and therefore as presidential candidate of the Partido Colorado. The decision was denounced by Argaña, whose faction threatened to resign *en masse* from the party.

At the presidential and legislative elections, which took place on 9 May 1993, Juan Carlos Wasmosy was elected President with 39.91% of the votes cast, ahead of Domingo Laíno (32.13%) and Guillermo Caballero Vargas of Encuentro Nacional (EN) (23.24%). However, in the legislative elections the Partido Colorado failed to gain a majority in either the Chamber of Deputies or the Senate. In a further reverse for Wasmosy, the faction of the Partido Colorado led by Argaña, the Movimiento de Reconciliación Colorada (MCR), negotiated with the PLRA and the EN to exclude supporters of the President-elect from appointment to important posts in the Congreso Nacional (with the support of the MCR, the overall opposition strength stood at 35 of a total of 45 seats in the Senate and 64 of the 80 seats in the Chamber of Deputies, sufficient to approve legislation affecting the Constitution).

Wasmosy was inaugurated as President on 15 August 1993. Concern was expressed by the opposition at the composition of the recently-named Council of Ministers, many of whom had served in the administrations of Rodríguez and Stroessner. Despite Wasmosy's apparent desire to restrict the influence of the military (notably appointing a civilian to the post of Minister of National Defence), the designation of Gen. Lino César Oviedo Silva as Commander of the Army provoked further criticism; immediately prior to the elections, Oviedo had publicly stated that the army would not accept an opposition victory.

In early September 1993 the legislature voted to repeal a law on the reorganization of the military which had been adopted immediately before expiry of the mandate of the previous Congress in July. The law was regarded by the opposition as an attempt to curtail the constitutional powers of the President of the Republic as Commander-in-Chief of the Armed Forces and to increase those of the military by creating the new position of Commander of the Armed Forces. In mid-September, in an attempt to forge an agreement with the opposition to facilitate the implementation of a coherent economic and legislative programme, the Government held discussions with the PLRA and two parties without representation in the legislature. However, the signing of a 'governability pact' with the opposition was suspended in early October, following a violent demonstration outside the Congress building by supporters of the Partido Colorado. The demonstrators were protesting against draft legislation to exclude serving members of the armed forces and the police from holding membership of any political party. (The bill enlarged on the provisions of the August 1992 Constitution, which had been interpreted as a ban only on new applications for membership.) Despite the violence of the demonstration (during which several members of the Congreso Nacional were assaulted), the police failed to intervene, prompting opposition criticism which led to the dismissal of the national police chief. (Subsequent to a protracted debate, legislation was finally approved in May 1994 providing for the temporary suspension of members of the security forces from party membership until retirement from service. Following the enactment of the legislation, both the Partido Colorado and the military high command initiated proceedings contesting the legislation on constitutional grounds.) In mid-December 1993 Wasmosy dismissed the Minister of Foreign Affairs, Diógenes Martínez, following a disagreement regarding the administration of the Itaipú hydroelectric complex (operated jointly with Brazil).

A preliminary agreement on a 'governability pact' was signed in mid-October 1993, and this, in turn, facilitated an agreement between the Government and the legislature towards resolving the controversial question of judicial reform. Under the latter agreement, the two sides were to appoint members of the Supreme Court and the Supreme Electoral Tribunal by consensus. (The new members of the Supreme Court, enlarged from five to nine justices in accordance with the 1992 Constitution, were eventually elected in April 1995). In early January 1993 Blás Riquelme resigned as President of the Partido Colorado, following disagreements with Wasmosy, specifically with regard to the Government's implementation of a programme of price increases for public utilities, to which Riquelme was opposed. He was replaced by Eugenio Sanabria Cantero. In the same month serious agricultural unrest erupted in several departments of the country, as groups of peasants, who were demanding an equitable distribution of land and an increase in the minimum price paid for cotton (Paraguay's principal export), blocked roads and took illegal possession of land. The demonstrators were forcibly dispersed by the police, but, as the protests escalated, Wasmosy threatened to deploy the army. In late February labour confederations staged a protest march in Asunción in support of the peasants' demands. Despite concessions by Wasmosy (including the replacement of senior officials in the Instituto de Bienestar Social, the agency in charge of land settlement), the protests continued, abating only when Wasmosy agreed to conduct direct discussions with peasant leaders. However, the talks proved inconclusive, and in mid-March some 10,000 peasants marched to the capital to demand immediate solutions to the country's rural problems. Demands were also made for the dismissal of the Minister of Agriculture and Livestock, Raúl Torres Segovia, who was forced to resign at the end of the month. In early May labour confederations organized a one-day general strike, in support of demands for a 40% increase in wages, a halt to plans for the transfer to private ownership of state enterprises and the suspension of Paraguay's involvement in Mercosur (see below).

In September 1994 Wasmosy announced a reorganization of the military high command, including the removal of the commanders of the air force and the navy and the head of the armed forces joint chiefs of staff, and the retirement of several senior officers. The measures, which were widely recognized to have strengthened the position of Gen. Oviedo, were reported to be the cause of serious tensions within the armed forces and between the military high command and the presidency. In November Wasmosy ordered three officers, including two of those removed from high military office in the September reshuffle, to be placed under military arrest on the grounds that, by publicly alleging that Wasmosy had attained the presidency by means of electoral fraud, the officers had cast doubt on his legitimacy as head of state and Commander-in-Chief of the Armed Forces, and, in doing so, had breached the military code. The allegations of fraud referred to the disputed Colorado internal elections held in December 1992 to select a candidate for the forthcoming presidential election; the officers maintained that Gen. Oviedo had used his influence to manipulate the election results in Wasmosy's favour. In the light of this statement Argaña, who had lost the candidacy to Wasmosy, subsequently submitted a formal request to the Chamber of Deputies for impeachment proceedings to be initiated against Wasmosy, although the request was denied.

In October 1994 concern at widespread corruption in Paraguay was heightened following the assassination, in Asunción, of the Executive Secretary of the National Anti-Narcotics Secretariat, Gen. Ramón Rosa Rodríguez. The killing was believed to have been perpetrated by a member of his own staff, Capt. Juan Ruiz Díaz. In an informal statement Wasmosy linked the assassination to the activities of a domestic network of drugs-traffickers, but dismissed any connection with international drugs cartels.

In early 1995 speculation concerning unrest in the armed forces reached such a level that Wasmosy was forced to issue a public statement discounting the possibility of a military coup. In February Wasmosy announced a further minor reorganization of the military high command. Plans for a one-day general strike, to be organized in May by the country's principal labour organizations, were abandoned following negotiations with the Government which resulted in the granting of an increase of 15% in the minimum wage. In May 1995, following an investigation into corruption at the Central Bank, the Minister of the Interior, Carlos Podestá, was granted leave of absence by the President in order to defend himself against allegations of involvement in the affair. In the following month the President of the Central Bank, Jacinto Estigarribia, resigned.

In March 1991 the Presidents and Ministers of Foreign Affairs of Argentina, Brazil, Uruguay and Paraguay met in Asunción to sign a formal agreement creating a common market of the 'Southern Cone' countries, the Mercado Común del Sur (Mercosur, see p. 240). The agreement allowed for the dismantling of trade barriers between the four countries, and entered full operation in 1995.

**Government**

Under the 1992 Constitution, legislative power is held by the bicameral Congreso Nacional (National Congress), whose members serve for five years. The Senate has 45 members, and the Chamber of Deputies 80 members. Elections to the legislature are by universal adult suffrage. Executive power is held by the President, directly elected for a single term of five years at the same time as the legislature. The President of the Republic governs with the assistance of a Vice-President and an appointed Council of Ministers. Paraguay is divided into 17 departments, each administered by an elected governor.

**Defence**

The armed forces totalled 16,500 men (including 10,800 conscripts) in June 1994. There was an army of 12,500 men and an air force of 1,000. The navy, which operates on the rivers, had 3,000 men, including 500 marines. There were 8,000 men in the paramilitary police force. Military service, which is compulsory, lasts for 12 months in the army and for two years in the navy. The defence budget for 1994 totalled 151,000m. guaraníes.

**Economic Affairs**

In 1993, according to estimates by the World Bank, Paraguay's gross national product (GNP), measured at average 1991–93 prices, was US $6,995m., equivalent to $1,500 per head. During 1985–93, it was estimated, GNP per head increased, in real terms, by an average of 1.3% per year. Over the same period the population increased by an annual average of 2.9%. Paraguay's gross domestic product (GDP) increased, in real terms, by an annual average of 2.8% in 1980–92, by 4.1% in 1993, and by an estimated 3.7% in 1994.

Agriculture (including forestry and fishing) contributed 24.5% of GDP in 1993. In that year 41.5% of the working population were employed in the sector. The principal cash crops are oil-seeds (principally soya beans), which accounted for 30.8% of total export revenue in 1993, and cotton (22.7%). Other significant crops are sugar cane, cassava, maize and wheat. Timber and wood manufactures provided 8.8% of export revenues in 1993. The raising of livestock (particularly cattle and pigs) is also important. Meat accounted for 6.5% of export earnings in 1993. During 1980–92 agricultural GDP increased by an annual average of 3.4%.

Industry (including mining, manufacturing, construction and power) contributed 26.2% of GDP and employed 22.5% of the working population in 1993. During 1980–92 industrial GDP increased by an annual average of only 0.4% (compared with average annual growth of 11.2% in 1970–80).

Paraguay has almost no commercially exploited mineral resources, and the mining sector employed only 0.2% of the labour force in 1993. However, foreign companies have been involved in exploration for petroleum deposits.

Manufacturing contributed 16.5% of GDP and employed 11.0% of the working population in 1993. In 1987 the production of food, beverages and tobacco (measured in terms of value added) comprised 51% of total manufacturing output. The other principal sectors were wood and wood products; textiles (chiefly cotton), clothing and leather; chemicals (including petroleum, coal, rubber and plastic products); non-metallic mineral products; paper, printing and publishing; and metal products and machinery. During 1980–92 manufacturing GDP increased by an annual average of 2.2%.

Energy is derived principally from hydroelectric power. Imports of petroleum and petroleum products comprised 10.0% of the value of total imports in 1993. Ethyl alcohol (ethanol), derived from sugar cane, is widely used as a component of vehicle fuel.

In 1993 Paraguay recorded a visible trade deficit of US $1,018.6m., and there was a deficit of $603.0m. on the current account of the balance of payments. In that year the principal source of imports (23.0%) was Brazil; other major suppliers were Argentina, the USA and Japan. Brazil was also the principal market for exports (29.7%) in 1993; other notable purchasers were the Netherlands, Argentina and the USA. The principal exports in 1993 were oil-seeds (principally soya beans), raw cotton and wood and wood manufactures. The principal imports were machinery, transport equipment, mineral fuels, electrical appliances and beverages and tobacco.

In 1993 there was an overall deficit on the General Budget of 18,831m. guaraníes (equivalent to 0.2% of GDP). Paraguay's total external debt was US $1,599m. at the end of 1993, of which $1,283m. was long-term public debt. In that year the cost of debt-servicing was equivalent to 14.8% of the total value of exports of goods and services. The average annual rate of inflation was 24.8% in 1985–93; consumer prices increased by an average of 18.3% in 1993. Some 9.0% of the labour force were unemployed in 1993.

Paraguay is a member of the Inter-American Development Bank (see p. 170), of the Latin American Integration Association (ALADI, see p. 181), of the Latin American Economic System (SELA, see p. 239) and of the Mercado Común del Sur (Mercosur, see p. 240).

While pledging to continue policies of economic liberalization initiated by the previous administration, the Government of Juan Carlos Wasmosy, inaugurated in August 1993, announced a series of economic adjustment measures, with a view to achieving sustained economic growth. Among its main priorities was to be the reduction of the inherited public deficit (estimated at some 1,400,000m. guaraníes in mid-1993), principally by means of budgetary controls and a rationalization of the public sector. The need was also acknowledged to reduce the balance-of-payments deficit and to restore international reserves. A reform of the taxation system and of the banking sector was envisaged, as was the management of interest rates so as to encourage national savings and medium- and long-term investment. By fostering monetary restraint, it was also aimed to curtail inflation. Measures were also to be undertaken to expedite the privatization of unprofitable state enterprises, while incentives were to be offered to stimulate investment by domestic and foreign interests in both existing and new enterprises. The diversification and modernization of the agricultural sector was to be promoted, as was the improved use of indigenous, renewable energy resources. It was hoped, moreover, that the installation of civilian organs of state would result in an improvement in relations with the international financial community, and the new Government swiftly entered into negotiations with the IMF and the World Bank, with the aim of negotiating new credits and thereby facilitating a rescheduling of external debt. Plans were under way in 1995 to develop the country's main waterways, as part of a regional project to create a fully integrated and navigable waterways network. The project, which was expected to take some 12 years to complete, would link Argentina, Bolivia, Brazil, Paraguay and Uruguay, and was expected significantly to reduce transport costs in the region.

**Social Welfare**

In 1975 Paraguay had 143 hospital establishments, with a total of 3,816 beds, and in 1984 there were 2,453 physicians working in the country. The welfare of Paraguay's indigenous Indians is the responsibility of the National Indian Institute (INDI). Of total expenditure by the central Government's General Budget in 1990, 25,981m. guaraníes (4.3%) was for health, and a further 70,822m. guaraníes (11.8%) for social security and welfare. In addition, extrabudgetary funds disburse large amounts (33,022m. guaraníes in 1987) on social security.

**Education**

Education is, where possible, compulsory for six years, to be undertaken between seven and 13 years of age, but there are insufficient schools, particularly in the remote parts of the country. Primary education begins at the age of seven and lasts for six years. Secondary education, beginning at 13 years of age, lasts for a further six years, comprising two cycles of three years each. In 1992 98% of children in the relevant age-group were enrolled at primary schools (males 99%; females 97%), while secondary enrolment included 28% of children in the relevant age-group (males 28%; females 29%). There is one state and one Roman Catholic university in Asunción. According to estimates by UNESCO, the rate of adult illiteracy averaged 9.9% (males 7.9%; females 11.9%) in 1990. Expenditure on education by the ministry responsible for education

## PARAGUAY

was 154,328m. guaraníes (10.3% of total government expenditure) in 1991.

### Public Holidays

**1995:** 1 January (New Year's Day), 3 February (San Blás, Patron Saint of Paraguay), 1 March (Heroes' Day), 13 April (Maundy Thursday), 14 April (Good Friday), 1 May (Labour Day), 14–15 May (Independence Day celebrations), 25 May (Ascension Day), 12 June (Peace of Chaco), 15 June (Corpus Christi), 15 August (Founding of Asunción), 25 August (Constitution Day), 29 September (Battle of Boquerón), 12 October (Day of the Race, anniversary of the discovery of America), 1 November (All Saints' Day), 8 December (Immaculate Conception), 25 December (Christmas Day).

**1996:** 1 January (New Year's Day), 3 February (San Blás, Patron Saint of Paraguay), 1 March (Heroes' Day), 4 April (Maundy Thursday), 5 April (Good Friday), 1 May (Labour Day), 14–15 May (Independence Day celebrations), 16 May (Ascension Day), 6 June (Corpus Christi), 12 June (Peace of Chaco), 15 August (Founding of Asunción), 25 August (Constitution Day), 29 September (Battle of Boquerón), 12 October (Day of the Race, anniversary of the discovery of America), 1 November (All Saints' Day), 8 December (Immaculate Conception), 25 December (Christmas Day).

### Weights and Measures

The metric system is in force.

## Statistical Survey

Sources (unless otherwise stated): Dirección General de Estadística y Censos, Humaitá 473, Asunción; tel. (21) 47900; Banco Central del Paraguay, Avda Pablo VI y Avda Sargento Marecos, Asunción; tel. (21) 60-8019; telex 46000; fax (21) 60-8150; Secretaría Técnica de Planificación, Presidencia de la República, Iturbe y Eligio Ayala, Asunción.

## Area and Population

### AREA, POPULATION AND DENSITY

| | |
|---|---:|
| Area (sq km) | 406,752* |
| Population (census results)† | |
| 11 July 1982 | |
| Total | 3,029,830 |
| 26 August 1992 (provisional) | |
| Males | 2,069,673 |
| Females | 2,053,877 |
| Total | 4,123,550 |
| Population (official estimates at mid-year)‡ | |
| 1991 | 4,397,306 |
| 1992 | 4,519,328 |
| 1993 | 4,642,624 |
| Density (per sq km) at mid-1993 | 11.4 |

* 157,048 sq miles.
† Excluding adjustments for underenumeration.
‡ Not revised to take account of the 1992 census results.

### PRINCIPAL TOWNS (population at 1982 census)

| | | | |
|---|---:|---|---:|
| Asunción (capital) | 454,881 | Ciudad del Este* | 62,328 |
| San Lorenzo | 74,552 | Coronel Oviedo | 60,757 |
| Lambaré | 67,168 | Pedro Juan Caballero | 50,808 |
| Fernando de la Mora | 66,597 | Concepción | 49,978 |
| Caaguazú | 66,111 | Encarnación | 48,006 |

* Formerly Puerto Presidente Stroessner.

### BIRTHS, MARRIAGES AND DEATHS

| | Estimated live births | | Registered marriages* | | Estimated deaths | |
|---|---:|---:|---:|---:|---:|---:|
| | Number | Rate (per 1,000) | Number | Rate (per 1,000) | Number | Rate (per 1,000) |
| 1983 | 121,500 | 35.3 | 13,394 | 3.9 | 23,800 | 6.7 |
| 1984 | 124,500 | 35.2 | 16,354 | 4.6 | 24,400 | 6.7 |
| 1985 | 127,500 | 35.2 | 18,370 | 5.0 | 25,000 | 6.7 |
| 1986 | 130,500 | 35.1 | 16,050 | 4.2 | 25,600 | 6.6 |
| 1987 | 133,500 | 35.0 | 17,741 | 4.5 | 26,200 | 6.6 |
| 1988 | 136,500 | 34.9 | 15,659 | 3.9 | 26,800 | 6.5 |
| 1989 | 143,400 | 34.5 | 12,627 | 3.0 | 27,400 | 6.5 |
| 1990 | 142,500 | 34.1 | 7,708 | 1.8 | 28,000 | 6.5 |

* Source: *Anuario Estadístico del Paraguay*.

**Expectation of life** (UN estimates, years at birth, 1985–90): 66.9 (males 64.8; females 69.1) (Source: UN, *World Population Prospects: The 1992 Revision*).

### ECONOMICALLY ACTIVE POPULATION

| | 1991 | 1992 | 1993 |
|---|---:|---:|---:|
| Agriculture, hunting, forestry and fishing | 606,717 | 607,100 | 631,688 |
| Mining and quarrying | 3,267 | 3,417 | 3,379 |
| Manufacturing | 165,540 | 165,927 | 167,869 |
| Electricity, gas and water | 4,900 | 5,095 | 5,377 |
| Construction | 132,467 | 154,002 | 166,214 |
| Transport, storage and communications | 51,345 | 53,058 | 55,415 |
| Trade, restaurants and hotels } Financing, insurance, real estate and business services | 198,599 | 199,530 | 205,504 |
| Community, social and personal services | 206,799 | 210,798 | 212,897 |
| Activities not adequately defined | 65,468 | 69,211 | 73,036 |
| **Total employed** | 1,435,102 | 1,468,138 | 1,521,380 |
| Unemployed | 148,372 | 159,276 | 150,428 |
| **Total labour force** | 1,583,474 | 1,627,414 | 1,671,808 |

PARAGUAY

## Agriculture

**PRINCIPAL CROPS** ('000 metric tons)

|  | 1991 | 1992 | 1993 |
|---|---|---|---|
| Wheat | 259.3 | 328.4 | 425.4 |
| Rice (paddy) | 43.2 | 54.0 | 78.1 |
| Maize | 401.3 | 449.7 | 439.1 |
| Sorghum | 14.3 | 25.8 | 19.9 |
| Sweet potatoes | 84.2 | 84.5 | 98.9 |
| Cassava (Manioc) | 1,292.5 | 1,295.7 | 1,328.0 |
| Kidney beans | 47.1 | 41.0 | 46.1 |
| Soybeans (Soya beans) | 1,032.7 | 1,617.9 | 1,793.5 |
| Groundnuts | 34.0 | 38.9 | 40.2 |
| Seed cotton | 631.7 | 391.4 | 420.8 |
| Tomatoes | 42.1 | 42.9 | 44.2 |
| Avocados | 15.4 | 15.0 | 14.7 |
| Watermelons | 112.4 | 113.3 | 114.5 |
| Sugar cane | 3,521.4 | 3,485.3 | 3,514.3 |
| Oranges | 176.6 | 177.2 | 178.7 |
| Tangerines | 25.1 | 25.3 | 26.2 |
| Grapefruit and pomelo | 73.2 | 74.0 | 74.2 |
| Mangoes | 35.4 | 35.9 | 36.6 |
| Pineapples | 33.5 | 39.8 | 42.9 |
| Grapes | 10.5 | 10.6 | 10.6 |
| Bananas | 84.6 | 89.3 | 89.9 |
| Pumpkins and gourds | 82.6 | 84.4 | 86.1 |
| Spurge | 17.7 | 14.1 | 16.2 |
| Tung nuts | 45.9 | 46.3 | 46.3 |
| Maté | 62.6 | 63.0 | 64.2 |
| Mint | 51.4 | 52.4 | 52.5 |
| Bitter orange (leaves) | 180.3 | 189.4 | 189.5 |

**LIVESTOCK** ('000 head, year ending September)

|  | 1991 | 1992 | 1993* |
|---|---|---|---|
| Cattle | 7,627 | 7,886 | 8,074 |
| Horses | 320 | 327 | 330 |
| Pigs | 2,580 | 2,700* | 2,915 |
| Sheep | 357 | 365 | 371 |
| Goats | 102 | 115 | 117 |

Poultry (million): 11 in 1991; 12 in 1992; 12 in 1993.

* FAO estimate(s).

Source: FAO, *Production Yearbook*.

**LIVESTOCK PRODUCTS** ('000 metric tons)

|  | 1991 | 1992 | 1993 |
|---|---|---|---|
| Beef and veal | 167* | 171* | 180† |
| Pig meat† | 150 | 162 | 167 |
| Poultry meat† | 18 | 20 | 21 |
| Cows' milk | 240 | 240† | 250† |
| Hen eggs | 35.8 | 36.0† | 36.8† |
| Cattle hides† | 26.0 | 26.6 | 28.0 |

* Unofficial figure.   † FAO estimate(s).

Source: FAO, *Production Yearbook*.

## Forestry

**ROUNDWOOD REMOVALS**
(FAO estimates, '000 cubic metres, excluding bark)

|  | 1990 | 1991 | 1992 |
|---|---|---|---|
| Sawlogs, veneer logs and logs for sleepers | 2,692 | 2,692 | 2,692 |
| Other industrial wood | 414 | 414 | 414 |
| Fuel wood | 5,324 | 5,360 | 5,396 |
| **Total** | 8,430 | 8,466 | 8,502 |

Source: FAO, *Yearbook of Forest Products*.

*Statistical Survey*

**SAWNWOOD PRODUCTION**
('000 cubic metres, including railway sleepers)

|  | 1990 | 1991 | 1992 |
|---|---|---|---|
| **Total** | 228 | 313 | 313* |

* FAO estimate.

Source: FAO, *Yearbook of Forest Products*.

## Fishing

('000 metric tons, live weight)

|  | 1990 | 1991 | 1992 |
|---|---|---|---|
| **Total catch** | 12.5 | 13.0 | 18.0 |

Source: FAO, *Yearbook of Fishery Statistics*.

## Industry

**SELECTED PRODUCTS**
(metric tons, unless otherwise indicated)

|  | 1990 | 1991 | 1992 |
|---|---|---|---|
| Soya bean oil (refined) | 15,517 | 22,886 | 82,357 |
| Alcohol (100%) | 21,220 | 36,913 | 27,953 |
| Fuel alcohol | 2,604 | 3,575 | 4,561 |
| Sugar (refined) | 103,705 | 135,845 | 133,417 |
| Portland Cement | 343,661 | 340,737 | 475,758 |
| Beer | 107,583 | 113,933 | 114,144 |
| Electricity (million kWh) | 27,228 | 29,400 | 27,136 |
| Cotton thread | 442 | 570 | 576 |
| Cotton fabrics ('000 metres) | 14,648 | 18,967 | 19,170 |

## Finance

**CURRENCY AND EXCHANGE RATES**

**Monetary Units**
  100 céntimos = 1 guaraní (G).

**Sterling and Dollar Equivalents** (31 December 1994)
  £1 sterling = 3,035.1 guaraníes;
  US $1 = 1,940.0 guaraníes;
  10,000 guaraníes = £3.295 = $5.155.

**Average Exchange Rate** (guaraníes per US dollar)
  1992   1,500.3
  1993   1,744.3
  1994   1,911.5

# PARAGUAY

## Statistical Survey

### BUDGET (million guaraníes)*

| Revenue† | 1988 | 1989 | 1990 |
|---|---|---|---|
| Taxation | 281,734‡ | 409,608 | 584,272 |
| Taxes on income, profits, etc. | 41,464 | 57,155 | 73,726 |
| Social security contributions | 42,410 | n.a. | n.a. |
| Taxes on payroll or work force | 4,393 | 5,754 | 7,332 |
| Taxes on property | 27,449 | 54,955 | 73,589 |
| Sales taxes | 26,823 | 36,433 | 50,489 |
| Excises | 52,131 | 67,335 | 99,398 |
| Other domestic taxes on goods and services | 2,818 | 6,302 | 4,970 |
| Import duties | 33,526 | 59,422 | 111,577 |
| Exchange taxes | 3,374 | 51,166 | 46,247 |
| Other taxes on international trade and transactions | 891 | 1,072 | 1,523 |
| Stamp taxes | 39,903 | 54,100 | 76,274 |
| Entrepreneurial and property income | 19,731 | 73,857 | 145,857 |
| Administrative fees and charges, non-industrial and incidental sales | 6,465 | 11,501 | 15,063 |
| Other current revenue | 13,865 | 27,927 | 47,040 |
| Capital revenue | 182 | 428 | 425 |
| **Total** | 321,977 | 523,321 | 792,657 |

| Expenditure§ | 1987 | 1989 | 1990 |
|---|---|---|---|
| General public services | 48,155 | 71,469 | 131,775 |
| Defence | 23,310 | 57,340 | 79,883 |
| Education | 25,586 | 51,341 | 76,106 |
| Health | 6,675 | 18,498 | 25,981 |
| Social security and welfare | 54,103 | 55,801 | 70,822 |
| Housing and community amenities | 5,900 | 4,287 | 18,329 |
| Recreational, cultural and religious affairs and services | 331 | 390 | 494 |
| Economic affairs and services | 21,251 | 61,763 | 76,919 |
| Fuel and energy | — | 7,818 | 18,215 |
| Agriculture, forestry, fishing and hunting | 2,698 | 3,417 | 7,833 |
| Mining, manufacturing and construction | 697 | 73 | 194 |
| Transport and communications | 13,125 | 47,031 | 44,664 |
| Interest on public debt | 20,016 | 41,186 | 60,686 |
| Other purposes (incl. unclassified) | 19,333 | 52,026 | 59,878 |
| **Total** | 224,660 | 414,101 | 600,873 |
| Current | 179,430 | 364,424 | 497,614 |
| Capital | 45,230 | 49,677 | 103,259 |

**1988** (million guaraníes): Expenditure 285,959 (current 218,725; capital 67,234), excluding net lending (11,422).

* Figures for 1987 and 1988 refer to the consolidated accounts of the central Government, including social security funds. Figures for 1989 and 1990 refer to the General Budget only, excluding social security funds and other government units with their own budgets.
† Excluding grants received (million guaraníes): 601 in 1988; 1,724 in 1989; 1,066 in 1990.
‡ After adjusting for tax advances and taxes receivable (6,552 million guaraníes).
§ Excluding net lending (million guaraníes): 7,798 in 1987; 14,248 in 1989; 2,191 in 1990.

Source: IMF, *Government Finance Statistics Yearbook*.

**1991** (General Budget, million guaraníes): *Revenue:* Taxation 734,712; Other current revenue 231,686; Capital revenue and grants 8,088; Total 974,486. *Expenditure:* Current expenditure 479,402; Capital expenditure 130,604; Total 610,006.

**1992** (General Budget, million guaraníes): *Revenue:* Taxation 848,802; Other current revenue 454,637; Capital revenue and grants 9,260; Total 1,312,699. *Expenditure:* Current expenditure 1,110,444; Capital expenditure 211,755; Total 1,322,199.

**1993** (General Budget, million guaraníes): *Revenue:* Taxation 1,018,664; Other current revenue 500,631; Capital revenue and grants 26,489; Total 1,545,784. *Expenditure:* Current expenditure 1,334,434; Capital expenditure 230,181; Total 1,564,615.

### CENTRAL BANK RESERVES
(US $ million at 31 December)

| | 1992 | 1993 | 1994 |
|---|---|---|---|
| Gold* | 11.60 | 13.70 | 13.40 |
| IMF special drawing rights | 85.42 | 89.39 | 98.73 |
| Reserve position in IMF | 23.29 | 22.63 | 21.20 |
| Foreign exchange | 452.82 | 519.16 | 896.20 |
| **Total** | 573.13 | 644.88 | 1,029.53 |

* National valuation of gold reserves (35,000 troy ounces in each year), based on market-related prices.

Source: IMF, *International Financial Statistics*.

### MONEY SUPPLY ('000 million guaraníes at 31 December)

| | 1991 | 1992 | 1993 |
|---|---|---|---|
| Currency outside banks | 379.92 | 531.26 | 635.77 |
| Demand deposits at commercial banks | 288.88 | 306.57 | 367.48 |
| **Total money** (incl. others) | 738.91 | 905.03 | 1,054.01 |

Source: IMF, *International Financial Statistics*.

### COST OF LIVING
(Consumer Price Index for Asunción; base: 1980 = 100)

| | 1991 | 1992 | 1993 |
|---|---|---|---|
| Food | 1,025.5 | 1,178.0 | 1,381.4 |
| Housing (incl. fuel and light) | 621.6 | 712.7 | 844.2 |
| Clothing | 966.4 | 1,072.0 | 1,205.2 |
| **All items** (incl. others) | 888.2 | 1,022.5 | 1,209.2 |

Source: ILO, *Year Book of Labour Statistics*.

### NATIONAL ACCOUNTS (million guaraníes at current prices)
**National Income and Product**

| | 1991 | 1992 | 1993 |
|---|---|---|---|
| Compensation of employees | 2,108,985 | 2,872,829 | 3,583,408 |
| Operating surplus* | 5,021,669 | 5,371,694 | 6,663,317 |
| **Domestic factor incomes** | 7,130,654 | 8,244,523 | 10,246,725 |
| Consumption of fixed capital | 690,261 | 769,094 | 930,669 |
| **Gross domestic product (GDP) at factor cost** | 7,820,915 | 9,013,617 | 11,177,394 |
| Indirect taxes | 459,969 | 657,380 | 814,515 |
| *Less* Subsidies | 112 | 159 | 190 |
| **GDP in purchasers' values** | 8,280,772 | 9,670,838 | 11,991,719 |
| Factor income received from abroad | 290,088 | 453,450 | 531,794 |
| *Less* Factor income paid abroad | 175,298 | 431,400 | 488,796 |
| **Gross national product** | 8,395,562 | 9,692,888 | 12,034,717 |
| *Less* Consumption of fixed capital | 690,261 | 769,094 | 930,669 |
| **National income in market prices** | 7,705,301 | 8,923,794 | 11,104,048 |

* Obtained as a residual.

**Expenditure on the Gross Domestic Product**

| | 1991 | 1992 | 1993 |
|---|---|---|---|
| Government final consumption expenditure | 546,531 | 629,069 | 801,908 |
| Private final consumption expenditure* | 6,483,234 | 7,611,722 | 9,119,267 |
| Increase in stocks† | 93,913 | 97,621 | 109,550 |
| Gross fixed capital formation | 1,961,821 | 2,117,426 | 2,642,052 |
| **Total domestic expenditure** | 9,085,499 | 10,455,838 | 12,672,777 |
| Exports of goods and services | 2,045,845 | 2,092,500 | 2,792,687 |
| *Less* Imports of goods and services | 2,850,572 | 2,877,500 | 3,473,745 |
| **GDP in purchasers' values** | 8,280,772 | 9,670,838 | 11,991,719 |
| **GDP at constant 1982 prices** | 950,208 | 967,312 | 1,007,377 |

* Obtained as a residual.   † Figures refer to livestock only.

# PARAGUAY

## Gross Domestic Product by Economic Activity

|  | 1991 | 1992 | 1993 |
|---|---|---|---|
| Agriculture, hunting and fishing | 1,969,735 | 2,107,976 | 2,613,621 |
| Forestry and logging | 229,592 | 261,068 | 325,862 |
| Mining and quarrying | 30,092 | 36,368 | 44,161 |
| Manufacturing | 1,405,345 | 1,643,211 | 1,979,450 |
| Electricity, gas and water | 235,850 | 301,697 | 407,135 |
| Construction | 451,879 | 558,926 | 709,513 |
| Trade, finance and insurance | 2,487,440 | 2,929,879 | 3,646,338 |
| Transport, storage and communications | 326,024 | 384,728 | 470,236 |
| Owner-occupied dwellings | 158,585 | 203,645 | 250,481 |
| Public administration and defence | 274,011 | 402,796 | 507,650 |
| Other services (incl. restaurants and hotels) | 712,219 | 840,544 | 1,037,272 |
| **Total** | 8,280,772 | 9,670,838 | 11,991,719 |

## BALANCE OF PAYMENTS (US $ million)

|  | 1991 | 1992 | 1993 |
|---|---|---|---|
| Merchandise exports f.o.b. | 1,120.8 | 1,081.5 | 1,653.0 |
| Merchandise imports f.o.b. | −1,867.6 | −1,950.6 | −2,671.6 |
| **Trade balance** | −746.8 | −869.1 | −1,018.6 |
| Exports of services | 903.6 | 825.6 | 1,018.7 |
| Imports of services | −546.9 | −541.8 | −608.8 |
| Other income received | 108.6 | 129.6 | 90.5 |
| Other income paid | −114.9 | −178.3 | −126.8 |
| Private unrequited transfers (net) | 6.7 | 2.7 | 4.6 |
| Official unrequited transfers (net) | 65.6 | 31.2 | 37.4 |
| **Current balance** | −324.1 | −600.1 | −603.0 |
| Direct investment (net) | 83.5 | 136.6 | 111.0 |
| Other capital (net) | 131.5 | 55.4 | 198.2 |
| Net errors and omissions | 472.0 | 457.7 | 483.2 |
| **Overall balance** | 362.9 | 49.6 | 189.4 |

Source: IMF, *International Financial Statistics*.

# External Trade

## PRINCIPAL COMMODITIES (US $'000)

| Imports c.i.f. | 1991 | 1992 | 1993 |
|---|---|---|---|
| Foodstuffs | 38,428 | 58,298 | 66,446 |
| Beverages and tobacco | 111,440 | 111,724 | 112,160 |
|   Beverages | 65,210 | 64,697 | 62,996 |
|   Cigarettes | 42,695 | 44,316 | 44,687 |
| Mineral fuels and lubricants | 129,735 | 144,995 | 147,243 |
|   Gas oil | 44,155 | 59,384 | 68,617 |
|   Crude petroleum | 46,893 | 39,406 | 30,794 |
| Paper, cardboard and manufactures | 26,486 | 30,163 | 37,736 |
| Chemical and pharmaceutical products | 79,358 | 84,184 | 100,188 |
| Transport equipment | 153,051 | 175,325 | 206,743 |
|   Buses and lorries | 36,396 | 56,272 | 65,016 |
|   Cars, jeeps and light trucks | 56,223 | 66,204 | 72,747 |
| Textiles | 32,320 | 26,828 | 44,355 |
| Iron and iron manufactures | 48,307 | 47,255 | 53,441 |
| Machinery, equipment and engines | 426,936 | 268,976 | 339,439 |
|   Boilers, steam engines and tractors | 29,941 | 22,313 | 32,037 |
|   Extractors | 27,424 | 33,850 | 29,541 |
|   Electrical appliances | 32,450 | 98,800 | 119,694 |
| **Total (incl. others)** | 1,275,387 | 1,237,148 | 1,477,540 |

| Exports f.o.b. | 1991 | 1992 | 1993 |
|---|---|---|---|
| Wood and wood manufactures | 44,374 | 53,328 | 63,839 |
| Meat products | 55,199 | 47,496 | 47,082 |
| Cattle hides | 28,269 | 37,454 | 53,880 |
| Oil-seeds | 157,125 | 137,221 | 223,689 |
| Cotton lint | 318,912 | 209,415 | 164,909 |
| Essential oils | 19,418 | 14,729 | 8,151 |
| Oil cake | 31,344 | 54,438 | 30,088 |
| **Total (incl. others)** | 737,096 | 656,555 | 725,217 |

## PRINCIPAL TRADING PARTNERS
(countries of first and last consignments, US $'000)

| Imports c.i.f. | 1991 | 1992 | 1993 |
|---|---|---|---|
| Argentina | 152,329 | 200,655 | 211,056 |
| Brazil | 234,256 | 263,243 | 340,412 |
| France | 20,592 | 21,697 | 21,394 |
| Germany | 54,413 | 50,844 | 52,864 |
| Hong Kong | 42,979 | 17,185 | 18,824 |
| Italy | 31,086 | 25,584 | 18,984 |
| Japan | 164,607 | 141,457 | 170,660 |
| Korea, Republic | 59,972 | 46,695 | 57,780 |
| Netherlands | 7,046 | 9,387 | 19,427 |
| Taiwan | 79,362 | 57,348 | 91,090 |
| United Kingdom | 56,588 | 56,324 | 52,188 |
| USA | 185,529 | 169,342 | 203,416 |
| Uruguay | 10,297 | 11,114 | 19,271 |
| **Total (incl. others)** | 1,275,387 | 1,237,148 | 1,477,540 |

| Exports f.o.b. | 1991 | 1992 | 1993 |
|---|---|---|---|
| Argentina | 45,050 | 64,149 | 64,943 |
| Belgium | 7,524 | 8,285 | 2,077 |
| Brazil | 203,082 | 171,447 | 215,123 |
| France | 11,226 | 14,063 | 11,557 |
| Germany | 36,222 | 20,330 | 6,481 |
| Italy | 39,324 | 22,487 | 17,103 |
| Netherlands | 109,601 | 138,879 | 189,254 |
| Spain | 13,201 | 7,453 | 5,209 |
| Switzerland | 35,175 | 8,751 | 25,982 |
| United Kingdom | 3,803 | 5,337 | 13,965 |
| USA | 34,220 | 34,404 | 52,861 |
| Uruguay | 11,319 | 10,804 | 7,211 |
| **Total (incl. others)** | 737,096 | 656,555 | 725,218 |

# Transport

## RAILWAYS (traffic)

|  | 1988 | 1989 | 1990 |
|---|---|---|---|
| Passengers carried | 178,159 | 196,019 | 125,685 |
| Freight (metric tons) | 200,213 | 164,980 | 289,099 |

## ROAD TRAFFIC (vehicles in use)

|  | 1988 | 1989 | 1990 |
|---|---|---|---|
| Cars | 60,246 | 108,001 | 117,067 |
| Buses | 2,734 | 3,151 | 3,375 |
| Lorries | 1,863 | n.a. | n.a. |
| Vans | 22,327 | 41,264 | 45,660 |
| Jeeps | 978 | 2,268 | 2,278 |
| Motor cycles | 16,025 | n.a. | n.a. |

PARAGUAY

**CIVIL AVIATION** (traffic on scheduled services)

|  | 1990 | 1991 | 1992 |
|---|---|---|---|
| Kilometres flown (million) | 6 | 9 | 9 |
| Passengers carried ('000) | 273 | 309 | 314 |
| Passenger-km (million) | 591 | 1,073 | 1,141 |
| Total ton-km (million) | 58 | 102 | 125 |

Source: UN, *Statistical Yearbook*.

## Tourism

|  | 1990 | 1991 | 1992 |
|---|---|---|---|
| Tourist arrivals ('000) | 280 | 361 | 334 |
| Tourist receipts (US $ million) | 112 | 165 | 153 |

Source: UN, *Statistical Yearbook*.

## Communications Media

|  | 1990 | 1991 | 1992 |
|---|---|---|---|
| Radio receivers ('000 in use) | 730 | 750 | 775 |
| Television receivers ('000 in use) | 250 | 220 | 370 |
| Telephones ('000 main lines in use) | 112 | 120 | n.a. |

Daily newspapers: 5 in 1992 (average circulation 168,000 copies).

Sources: UNESCO, *Statistical Yearbook*; UN, *Statistical Yearbook*.

## Education

(1992)

|  | Institutions | Teachers | Males | Females | Total |
|---|---|---|---|---|---|
| Pre-primary | 76 | 2,255 | 20,128 | 20,273 | 40,401 |
| Primary | 4,807 | 32,732 | 387,407 | 361,929 | 749,336 |
| Secondary |  |  |  |  |  |
| General | } 801* | 12,218† { | n.a. | n.a. | 176,547 |
| Vocational |  |  | n.a. | n.a. | 16,228 |
| Tertiary |  |  |  |  |  |
| University level‡ | n.a. | n.a. | 15,829 | 13,618 | 29,447 |
| Other higher‡ | n.a. | n.a. | n.a. | n.a. | 3,437 |

* 1990 Ministry of Education figure.
† 1991 figure.
‡ 1990 figures.

Source: mainly UNESCO, *Statistical Yearbook*.

# Directory

## The Constitution

A new Constitution for the Republic of Paraguay came into force on 22 June 1992, replacing the Constitution of 25 August 1967.

### FUNDAMENTAL RIGHTS, DUTIES AND FREEDOMS

Paraguay is an independent republic whose form of government is representative democracy. The powers accorded to the legislature, executive and judiciary are exercised in a system of independence, equilibrium, co-ordination and reciprocal control. Sovereignty resides in the people, who exercise it through universal, free, direct, equal and secret vote. All citizens over 18 years of age and resident in the national territory are entitled to vote.

All citizens are equal before the law and have freedom of conscience, travel, residence, expression, and the right to privacy. The freedom of the press if guaranteed. The freedom of religion and ideology is guaranteed. Relations between the State and the Catholic Church are based on independence, co-operation and autonomy. All citizens have the right to assemble and demonstrate peacefully. All public- and private-sector workers, with the exception of the Armed Forces and the police, have the right to form a trade union and to strike. All citizens have the right to associate freely in political parties or movements.

The rights of the indigenous peoples to preserve and develop their ethnic identity in their respective habitat are guaranteed.

### LEGISLATURE

The legislature (National Congress) comprises the Senate and the Chamber of Deputies. The Senate is composed of 45 members, the Chamber of Deputies of 80 members, elected directly by the people. Legislation concerning national defence and international agreements may be initiated in the Senate. Departmental and municipal legislation may be initiated in the Chamber of Deputies. Both chambers of Congress are elected for a period of five years.

### GOVERNMENT

Executive power is exercised by the President of the Republic. The President and the Vice-President are elected jointly and directly by the people, by a simple majority of votes, for a period of five years. They may not be elected for a second term. The President and the Vice-President govern with the assistance of an appointed Council of Ministers. The President participates in the formulation of legislation and enacts it. The President is empowered to veto legislation sanctioned by Congress, to nominate or remove ministers, to direct the foreign relations of the Republic, and to convene extraordinary sessions of Congress. The President is Commander-in-Chief of the Armed Forces.

### JUDICIARY

Judicial power is exercised by the Supreme Court of Justice and by the tribunals. The Supreme Court is composed of nine members who are appointed on the proposal of the Consejo de la Magistratura, and has the power to declare legislation unconstitutional.

## The Government

### HEAD OF STATE

**President:** Ing. JUAN CARLOS WASMOSY (took office 15 August 1993).
**Vice-President:** Dr ANGEL ROBERTO SEIFART.

### COUNCIL OF MINISTERS
(June 1995)

**Minister of the Interior:** CARLOS PODESTÁ*.
**Minister of Foreign Affairs:** Dr LUIS MARÍA RAMÍREZ BOETTNER.
**Minister of Finance:** ORLANDO BAREIRO.
**Minister of Industry and Commerce:** Dr UBALDO SCAVONE.
**Minister of Public Works and Communications:** Ing. CARLOS FACETTI.
**Minister of National Defence:** HUGO ESTIGARRIBIA ELIZECHE.
**Minister of Public Health and Social Welfare:** ANDRÉS VIDOVICH MORALES.
**Minister of Justice and Labour:** JUAN MANUEL MORALES.

PARAGUAY

**Minister of Agriculture and Livestock:** ARSENIO VASCONCELLOS PORTAS.
**Minister of Education and Culture:** Dr CÉSAR NICANOR DUARTE FRUTOS.
* In May 1995 the Minister of the Interior was granted leave of absence by the President in order to defend himself against allegations of involvement in financial corruption.

### MINISTRIES

**Ministry of Agriculture and Livestock:** Presidente Franco 472, Asunción; tel. (21) 44-9614; telex 324; fax (21) 49-7965.
**Ministry of Education and Culture:** Chile, Humaitá y Piribebuy, Asunción; tel. (21) 44-3078; telex 290; fax (21) 44-3919.
**Ministry of Finance:** Chile 128 esq. Palmas, Asunción; tel. (21) 44-0010; telex 917; fax (21) 44-8283.
**Ministry of Foreign Affairs:** Juan E. O'Leary y Presidente Franco, Asunción; tel. (21) 49-4593; telex 111; fax (21) 49-3910.
**Ministry of Industry and Commerce:** Avda España 323, Asunción; tel. (21) 20-4638; fax (21) 21-3529.
**Ministry of the Interior:** Estrella y Montevideo, Asunción; tel. (21) 49-3661; telex 153; fax (21) 44-8446.
**Ministry of Justice and Labour:** G. R. de Francia y Estados Unidos, Asunción; tel. (21) 49-3515; fax (21) 20-8469.
**Ministry of National Defence:** Avda Mariscal López y Vice-Presidente Sánchez, Asunción; tel. (21) 20-4771; telex 762; fax (21) 21-1583.
**Ministry of Public Health and Social Welfare:** Avda Pettirossi y Brasil, Asunción; tel. (21) 20-7328; telex 609; fax (21) 20-6700.
**Ministry of Public Works and Communications:** Oliva y Alberdi, Asunción; tel. (21) 44-4411; telex 162; fax (21) 44-4421.

## President and Legislature

### PRESIDENT
**Election, 9 May 1993**

| Candidate | % of votes |
| --- | --- |
| JUAN CARLOS WASMOSY (Partido Colorado) | 39.91 |
| Dr DOMINGO LAÍNO (Partido Liberal Radical Auténtico) | 32.13 |
| GUILLERMO CABALLERO VARGAS (Encuentro Nacional) | 23.24 |

### CONGRESO NACIONAL
**President of Senate:** EVELIO FERNÁNDEZ ARÉVALOS (PLRA).
**President of Chamber of Deputies:** FRANCISCO JOSÉ DE VARGAS (PLRA).
**General election, 9 May 1993**

| | Seats | |
| --- | --- | --- |
| Party | Chamber of Deputies | Senate |
| Partido Colorado | 38 | 20 |
| Partido Liberal Radical Auténtico | 33 | 17 |
| Encuentro Nacional | 9 | 8 |
| **Total** | **80** | **45** |

## Political Organizations

**Asociación Nacional Republicana—Partido Colorado** (National Republican Party): Asunción; f. 19th century, ruling party since 1940; 947,430 mems (1991); Pres. EUGENIO SANABRIA CANTERO.
**Asunción Para Todos (APT):** Asunción; f. 1991 to contest municipal elections; also campaigned nationally; Leader Dr CARLOS FILIZZOLA.
**Encuentro Nacional (EN):** Asunción; coalition comprising factions of PRF, PDC, APT and a dissident faction of the Partido Colorado formed to contest presidential and legislative elections of May 1993; Leader GUILLERMO CABALLERO VARGAS.
**Partido Comunista Paraguayo (PCP):** Asunción; f. 1928; banned 1928–46, 1947–89; Sec.-Gen. ANANÍAS MAIDANA.
**Partido de los Trabajadores (PT):** Asunción; f. 1989; Socialist.
**Partido Demócrata Cristiano (PDC):** Colón 871, Casilla 1318, Asunción; telex 5213; f. 1960; 20,500 mems; Pres. Prof. Dr JERÓNIMO IRALA BURGOS; Vice-Pres Dr JOSÉ M. BONÍN, JUAN C. DESCALZO BUONGERMINI; Gen. Sec. Dr LUIS M. ANDRADA NOGUÉS.
**Partido Humanista (PH):** Asunción.

**Partido Liberal Radical Auténtico (PLRA):** Asunción; f. 1978; centre party; Leaders Dr DOMINGO LAÍNO, JUAN MANUEL BENÍTEZ FLORENTÍN (Pres.), JUAN CARLOS ZALDÍVAR, HERMES RAFAEL SAQUIER, MIGUEL ANGEL MARTÍNEZ YARYEF; Sec.-Gen. MIGUEL ABDÓN SAGUIER.
**Partido Revolucionario Febrerista (PRF):** Casa del Pueblo, Manduvira 552, Asunción; tel. (21) 94041; f. 1951; social democratic party; affiliated to the Socialist International; Pres. EÚCLIDES ACEVEDO; Gen. Sec. NILS CANDIA-GINI.

## Diplomatic Representation

### EMBASSIES IN PARAGUAY

**Argentina:** Avda Mariscal López 2029, Asunción; tel. (21) 20-0034; telex 127; Ambassador: RAÚL A. J. QUIJANO.
**Belgium:** Edif. Parapití, 5°, Juan E. O'Leary 509 casi Estrella, Apdo 503, Asunción; tel. (21) 44075; Chargé d'affaires: DESIRÉE ORENS.
**Bolivia:** Eligio Ayala 2002, esq. General Bruguez, Asunción; tel. (21) 22662; Ambassador: Dr RAÚL BOTELHO GONZÁLVEZ.
**Brazil:** 25 de Mayo y General Aquino, Asunción; tel. (21) 20-0031; telex 148; Ambassador: SOARES CARBONAR.
**Chile:** Guido Spano 1687, Calle Juan B. Motta, Asunción; tel. (21) 66-0344; telex 163; Ambassador: JORGE F. O'RYAN BALBONTIN.
**China (Taiwan):** Avda Mariscal López 1043, Asunción; tel. (21) 22371; telex 702; Ambassador: Gen. WANG SHENG.
**Colombia:** Avda Mariscal López 2240, Asunción; tel. (21) 62162; Ambassador: MIGUEL ANTONIO GÓMEZ PADILLA.
**Costa Rica:** San José 447, Casilla 1936, Asunción; tel. and fax (21) 21-3535; Chargé d'affaires a.i.: Dr JORGE E. VALERIO HERNÁNDEZ.
**Ecuador:** Edif. Inter-Express, 9°, Of. 901, Herrera 195 esq. Yegros, Asunción; tel. (21) 46150; telex 5160; Ambassador: JORGE LASSO.
**El Salvador:** Edif. Líder W, 11°, Estrella 692 y Juan E. O'Leary, Apdo 115, Asunción; tel. (21) 95503; Ambassador: (vacant).
**France:** España 893, Calle Pucheu, Casilla 97, Asunción; tel. (21) 21-2439; telex 137; fax (21) 21-1690; Ambassador: RICHARD NARICH.
**Germany:** Avda Venezuela 241, Casilla 471, Asunción; tel. (21) 21-4009; telex 22068; fax (21) 21-2863; Ambassador: JOACHIM KAUSCH.
**Holy See:** Calle Ciudad del Vaticano, entre 25 de Mayo y Caballero, Casilla 83, Asunción (Apostolic Nunciature); tel. (21) 20-0750; fax (21) 21-2590; Apostolic Nuncio: Most Rev. JOSÉ SEBASTIÁN LABOA, Titular Archbishop of Zaraï.
**Israel:** Edif. San Rafael, 8°, Yegras 437, Asunción; tel. (21) 49-5097; fax (21) 49-6355; Ambassador: YOAV BAR-ON.
**Italy:** Avda Mariscal López 1104, esq. Mayor Bullo, Asunción; tel. (21) 22029; telex 22104; (21) 21-2630; Ambassador: ANTONIO CAVATERRA.
**Japan:** Avda Mariscal López 2364, Casilla 1957, Asunción; tel. (21) 60-4616; telex 131; fax (21) 60-6901; Ambassador: NAKASONE GORO.
**Korea, Republic:** Avda Mariscal López 486, Casilla 1303, Asunción; tel. (21) 20-6069; telex 201; Ambassador: KWON YOUNG-SOON.
**Mexico:** Edif. Parapití, 5°, Estrella y Juan E. O'Leary, Asunción; tel. (21) 44-4421; telex 213; fax (21) 44-1877; Ambassador: FRANCISCO CORREA VILLALOBOS.
**Panama:** Edif. Betón I, 11B°, Calle Eduardo Víctor Haedo 179, Asunción; tel. (21) 44-5545; telex 5147; fax (21) 44-6192; Chargé d'affaires: AUGUSTO LUIS VILLARREAL.
**Peru:** Avda Mariscal López 648, Asunción; tel. (21) 20-0949; Ambassador; JORGE PÉREZ-GARREAUD.
**South Africa:** Edif. Sudameris, 4°, Independencia Nacional y Cerro Corá, Asunción; tel. (21) 44331; telex 325; Ambassador: LEN M. BRAUD.
**Spain:** Yegros 437, Asunción; tel. (21) 90686; telex 473; Ambassador: EDUARDO CERRO GODINHO.
**Switzerland:** Edif. Parapití, 4°, Juan E. O'Leary 409 y Estrella, Asunción; tel. (21) 48022; Chargé d'affaires: L. ATTENBACH.
**United Kingdom:** Presidente Franco 706, Casilla 404, Asunción; tel. (21) 44-4472; telex 44023; fax (21) 44-6385; Ambassador: GRAHAM PIRNIE (designate).
**USA:** Avda Mariscal López 1776, Casilla 402, Asunción; tel. (21) 21-3715; telex 203; fax (21) 21-3728; Ambassador: ROBERT SERVICE.
**Uruguay:** 25 de Mayo 1894 esq. General Aquino, Asunción; tel. (21) 25391; telex 22096; fax (21) 23970; Ambassador: CARLOS VILLAR RIVERO.
**Venezuela:** Edif. Delime II, 1°, Juan E. O'Leary esq. Eduardo Víctor Haedo, Apdo 94, Asunción; tel. (21) 44242; telex 353; Ambassador: SANTIAGO OCHOA ANTICH.

## Judicial System

**The Supreme Court:** Palacio de Justicia, Asunción; tel. (21) 84383; telex 290; composed of nine judges appointed on the proposal of the Consejo de la Magistratura.

PARAGUAY

**President:** Dr José Alberto Correa.

Under the Supreme Court are the Courts of Appeal, the Tribunal of Jurors and Judges of First Instance, the Judges of Arbitration, the Magistrates (Jueces de Instrucción), and the Justices of the Peace.

## Religion

Some 91% of the population belong to the Roman Catholic Church, the established religion, although all sects are tolerated.

### CHRISTIANITY

#### The Roman Catholic Church

For ecclesiastical purposes, Paraguay comprises one archdiocese, ten dioceses and two Apostolic Vicariates. In 1993 there were an estimated 4.4m. adherents in the country.

**Bishops' Conference:** Conferencia Episcopal Paraguaya, Calle Alberdi 782, Casilla 1436, Asunción; tel. (21) 49-0920; fax (21) 49-5115; f. 1977 (statutes approved 1984); Pres. Rt Rev. Oscar Páez Garcete, Bishop of Alto Paraná.

**Archbishop of Asunción:** Most Rev. Felipe Santiago Benítez Avalos, Arzobispado, Independencia Nacional y Coronel Bogado 130, Casilla 654, Asunción; tel. (21) 44-4150; fax (21) 44-7510.

#### The Anglican Communion

Paraguay constitutes a single diocese of the Iglesia Anglicana del Cono Sur de América (Anglican Church of the Southern Cone of America). The Presiding Bishop of the Church is the Bishop of Chile.

**Bishop of Paraguay:** Rt. Rev. John Ellison, Iglesia Anglicana, Casilla 1124, Asunción; tel. (21) 20-0933; fax (21) 21-4328.

#### The Baptist Church

**Baptist Evangelical Convention of Paraguay:** Casilla 1194, Asunción; tel. (21) 27110; Exec. Sec. Lic. Rafael Altamirano.

### BAHÁ'Í FAITH

**National Spiritual Assembly of the Bahá'ís of Paraguay:** Eligio Ayala 1456, Apdo 742, Asunción; tel. (21) 25747; telex 25505; fax (21) 55-3403; Sec. Mirna Llamosas de Riquelme.

## The Press

### DAILIES

**ABC Color:** Yegros 745, Asunción; tel. (21) 49-1160; telex 44076; fax (21) 49-3059; f. 1967; independent; circ. 75,000; Propr Aldo Zuccolillo.

**El Diario Noticias:** Avda Artigas y Avda Brasilia, Casilla 3017, Asunción; tel. (21) 29-2721; telex 22922; fax (21) 29-2840; f. 1984; independent; Dir Néstor López Moreira; circ. 55,000.

**Hoy:** Avda Mariscal López 2948, Asunción; tel. (21) 60-3401; telex 46013; fax (21) 60-3400; f. 1977; Dir Hugo Oscar Aranda; circ. 40,000.

**Patria:** Tacuari 443, Asunción; tel. (21) 92011; f. 1946; Colorado Party; Dir Juan Ramón Chávez; circ. 8,000.

**Ultima Hora:** Benjamín Constant 658, Asunción; tel. (21) 49-6261; fax (21) 44-7071; f. 1973; independent; Dir Demetrio Rojas; circ. 45,000.

### PERIODICALS

**Acción:** Casilla 1072, Asunción; tel. (21) 33-3962; monthly; Dir Bartomeu Melià.

**La Opinión:** Boggiani esq. Luis Alberto de Herrera; tel. (21) 50-7501; fax (21) 50-2297; weekly; Dir Francisco Laws; Editor Bernardo Neri.

**Tiempo 14:** Mariscal Estiggaribia 4187, Asunción; tel. (21) 60-4308; fax (21) 60-9394; weekly; Dir Humberto Rubín; Editor Alberto Peralta.

### FOREIGN NEWS BUREAUX

**Agencia EFE** (Spain): Calle Paí Pérez 690, Asunción; tel. (21) 23719; Bureau Chief Francisco Figueroa.

**Agenzia Nazionale Stampa Associata (ANSA)** (Italy): Edif. Interexpress, 4°, Of. 403, Luis Alberto de Herrera 195, Asunción; tel. (21) 44-9286; telex 386; fax (21) 44-2986; Agent Víctor E. Carugati.

**Associated Press (AP)** (USA): Calle Caballero 742, Casilla 264, Asunción; tel. (21) 46424; Correspondent (vacant).

**Deutsche Presse-Agentur (dpa)** (Germany): Edif. Ypacarai, 3°, Of. 31, Alberdi 733, Asunción; tel. (21) 49-5451; fax (21) 44-8116; Correspondent Carlos R. Talavera.

*Directory*

**Inter Press Service (IPS)** (Italy): Edif. Segesa, 3°, Of. 5, Oliva 393 y Alberdi, Asunción; tel. and fax (21) 44-6350; Legal Rep. Clara Rosa Gagliardone.

**United Press International (UPI)** (USA): Azara 1098, Asunción; tel. (21) 21-2710; Correspondent José Galeano.

TELAM (Argentina) is also represented in Paraguay.

## Publishers

**La Colmena, SA:** Asunción; tel. (21) 20-0428; Dir Daumas Ladouce.

**Ediciones Diálogo:** Calle Brasil 1391, Asunción; tel. (21) 20-0428; f. 1957; fine arts, literature, poetry, criticism; Man. Miguel Angel Fernández.

**Ediciones Nizza:** Eligio Ayala 1073, Casilla 2596, Asunción; tel. (21) 47160; medicine; Pres. Dr José Ferreira Martínez.

**Editorial Comuneros:** Cerro Corá 289, Casilla 930, Asunción; tel. (21) 44-6176; f. 1963; social history, poetry, literature, law; Man. Ricardo Rolón.

**R. P. Ediciones:** Eduardo Víctor Haedo 427, Asunción; tel. (21) 49-8040; Man. Rafael Peroni.

### ASSOCIATION

**Cámara Paraguaya del Libro:** Eduardo Víctor Haedo 184 esq. Nuestra Señora de la Asunción, Casilla 1705, Asunción; tel. (21) 47053; f. 1968; Pres. Lic. Nidia Vera Radice; Sec. Gail Joule.

## Radio and Television

In 1992, according to UNESCO, there were an estimated 775,000 radio receivers and 370,000 television receivers in use.

### RADIO

**Administración Nacional de Telecomunicaciones (Antelco):** Presidencia del Consejo, 4°, Alberdi y General Díaz, Casilla 84, Asunción; tel. (21) 44-2005; fax (21) 44-4100; f. 1926; Pres. of Bd Col (retd) Miguel H. Gini E.

#### Government Station

**Radio Nacional del Paraguay:** Montevideo y Estrella, Asunción; tel. (21) 44-1542; medium- and short-wave and FM; Dir Filemón Argüello.

#### Commercial Stations

There are some 60 commercial stations, including:

**Radio Asunción:** Avda Artigas y Capitán Lombardo, Asunción; tel. (21) 29-0618; Dir Miguel G. Fernández.

**Radio Cáritas:** Kubitschek y Azara, Casilla 1313, Asunción; tel. (21) 21-3570; fax (21) 20-4161; f. 1936; station of the Franciscan order; medium-wave; Pres. Most Rev. Felipe Santiago Benítez Avalos (Archbishop of Asunción); Dir Cristóbal López.

**Radio Chaco Boreal:** Avda Mariscal López 2948, Asunción; tel. (21) 66-2616; Dir-Gen. Humberto Domínguez Dibb.

**Radio Concepción:** Coronel Panchito López 241, entre Schreiber y Colombia, Casilla 78, Concepción; tel. (31) 2318; fax (31) 2254; f. 1963; medium-wave; Dir Sergio E. Dacak.

**Radio Encarnación:** General Artigas 724, Encarnación; tel. (71) 2261; commercial but owned by Antelco; medium- and short-wave; Dir Ramón Giménez B.

**Radio Guairá:** Alejo García y Presidente Franco, Villarica; tel. (541) 2385; fax (541) 2130; f. 1950; medium-, long- and short-wave; Dir Lídice Rodríguez de Traversi.

**Radio Guaraní:** Avda José F. Bogado y Batallón 40, Asunción; tel. (21) 24313; medium- and short-wave; Dir Esteban Cáceres Almada.

**Radio Ñandutí:** Choferes del Chaco 1194, esq. Mariscal Estigarribia, Casilla 1179, Asunción; tel. (21) 60-4308; fax (21) 60-6074; f. 1962; Dirs Humberto Rubín, Gloria Rubín.

**Radio Paraguay:** Avda General Santos y 18 de Julio, Asunción; tel. (21) 34591; medium-wave and FM; Dir Roque A. Fleitas T.

**Radio Primero de Marzo:** Avda General Santos y Felicidad, Asunción; tel. (21) 31992; Dirs Juan Angel Napout, Alcides Riveros.

### TELEVISION

**Teledifusora Paraguaya—Canal 13:** Estudio 8 esq. 2 y 3 Lámbare, Casilla 247, Asunción; tel. (21) 44-3093; telex 5109; f. 1981; Gen. Man. Nicolás Bo.

**Televisión Cerro Corá—Canal 9:** Avda Carlos A. López 572, Asunción; tel. (21) 84222; telex 370; fax (21) 49-8911; commercial; Dir Alcides Riveros.

PARAGUAY

**Televisora del Este:** San Pedro, Calle Pilar, Area 5, Ciudad del Este; commercial; tel. (61) 8859; Dir Lic. JALIL SAFUAN; Gen. Man. A. VILLALBA V.

**Televisión Itapua:** Avda Gen. Irrazábal y 25 de Mayo, Barrio Ipvu, Encarnación; tel. (71) 4450; commercial; Dir Lic. JALIL SAFUAN; Station Man. JORGE MATEO GRANADA.

# Finance

(cap. = capital; res = reserves; dep. = deposits;
m. = million; amounts in guaraníes)

## BANKING

**Superintendencia de Bancos:** Edif. Banco Central del Paraguay, Avda Pablo VI y Avda Sargento Marecos, Asunción; tel. (21) 60-8011; telex 134; fax (21) 60-8149; Superintendent AGUSTÍN SILVERA ORUE.

### Central Bank

**Banco Central del Paraguay:** Avda Pablo VI y Avda Sargento Marecos, Asunción; tel. (21) 60-8019; telex 46000; fax (21) 60-8150; f. 1952; cap. and res 19,300m. (June 1985); Pres. (vacant); Gen. Man. CARLOS AQUINO BENÍTEZ.

### Development Banks

**Banco de Desarrollo del Paraguay, SA (COMDESA):** Eduardo Víctor Haedo 195, Casilla 1531, Asunción; tel. (21) 44-8222; telex 44177; fax (21) 44-4885; f. 1970; cap. 3,000m., res 1,009m., dep. 36,052.7m. (Dec. 1992); Pres. EVELIO GONZÁLEZ PÉREZ; Gen. Man. ROBERTO GÓMEZ VAESKEN.

**Banco de Inversiones del Paraguay, SA (BIP):** Palma y Nuestra Señora de la Asunción, Casilla 702, Asunción; tel. (21) 44-9550; telex 44236; fax (21) 44-3749; cap. 3,637.7m., dep. 57,070.8m. (Dec. 1992); Pres. Dr RUBÉN HUG DE BELMONT; Vice-Pres. Dr IGNACIO ALFONSI.

**Banco Nacional de Fomento:** Independencia Nacional y Cerro Corá, Casilla 134, Asunción; tel. (21) 44-3762; telex 130; fax (21) 44-6053; f. 1961 to take over the deposit and private banking activities of the Banco del Paraguay; cap. and res 31,368,999m., dep. 39,500,815m. (Dec. 1988); Pres. JULIO M. REJIS SANGUINA; 52 brs.

**Banco Paraguayo Oriental de Inversión y de Fomento SA:** Azara 197 y Yegros, Casilla 1496, Asunción; tel. (21) 44-4212; telex 44381; fax (21) 44-6820; f. 1988; cap. 3,000m., res 907.1m., dep. 103,429.3m. (Dec. 1993) Pres. CHAN WAI FU; Gen. Man. NELSON MÉNDEZ MORINIGO.

**Banco Union SA de Inversión y Fomento (BUSAIF):** Calles España y Brasil, Apdo 2973, Asunción; tel. (21) 21-1471; telex 22134; fax (21) 21-2587; Pres. Dr ERNESTO ROTELA P.; Gen. Man. Dr RAÚL CASSIGNOL.

**Crédito Agrícola de Habilitación:** Caríos y Primera, Asunción; Pres. Ing. Agr. CANCIO URBIETA E.

**Fondo Ganadero:** Avda Artigas 1921, Asunción; tel. (21) 29-4361; fax (21) 44-6922; Pres. GUILLERMO SERRATTI G.

### Commercial Banks

**Banco Comercial Paraguayo, SA (BANCOPAR):** Avda Mariscal López 780, Casilla 2350, Asunción; tel. (21) 20-7251; telex 22123; fax (21) 20-7259; f. 1981; cap. 12,814m., res 1,306m., dep. 95,674m. (Dec. 1993); Pres. Dr RAÚL I. CODAS RIBAROLA; Gen. Man. JOSÉ A. BRUNETTI V.; 6 brs.

**Banco Continental, SA:** Estrella 621, Casilla 2260, Asunción; tel. (21) 44-6801; telex 44167; fax (21) 44-2001; f. 1980; Pres. Dr OSCAR PÉREZ URIBE; Man. Dir PEDRO D. MIRAGLIO.

**Banco Corporación SA:** Eduardo Víctor Haedo 103 esq. Independencia Nacional, Casilla 317, Asunción; tel. (21) 44-9388; telex 44187; fax (21) 49-3772; f. 1987; Pres. MIGUEL A. LARREINEGABE LESME; Gen. Man. Dr NELSON MENDOZA.

**Banco Finamérica SA:** Chile y Oliva, Casilla 1321, Asunción; tel. (21) 49-1021; telex 44389; fax (21) 44-5604; f. 1988; Pres. Dr GUILLERMO HEISECKE VELÁZQUEZ; Gen. Man. ENRIQUE FERNÁNDEZ ROMAY.

**Banco General SA:** Chile y Eduardo Víctor Haedo, Asunción; tel. (21) 49-1682; telex 44371; fax (21) 49-6822; f. 1987; cap. 9,952.0m., res 1,455.1m., dep. 158,495.2m. (Dec. 1993); Pres. (vacant).

**Banco Nacional de Trabajadores (BNT):** 15 de Agosto 629, Casilla 1822, Asunción; tel. (21) 49-2214; telex 44072; fax (21) 44-8327; f. 1973 to make credit available to workers and to encourage savings; cap. 22,670m., dep. 89,337m. (Feb. 1994); Pres. Dr EDGAR CATALDI CASAL RIBEIRO; Man. MARÍA EDELIRA L. DE ACOSTA.

**Banco Unión, SA:** Avda Mariscal López 3333 esq. Dr Weiss, Casilla 726, Asunción; tel. (21) 60-6450; telex 46063; fax (21) 60-7743; f. 1978; cap. 29,966.5m., res 10,954.4m., dep. 238,265.7m. (Dec. 1994); Dir ALBA CAVINA DE LLANO; Gen. Man. ISMAEL ARANDA COSTAS; 20 brs.

*Directory*

**Interbanco, SA:** Oliva 349 y Chile, Casilla 392, Asunción; tel. (21) 49-4992; telex 44121; fax (21) 44-8587; f. 1978; cap. 4,718.6m., res 2,054.7m., dep. 146,317.1m. (Dec. 1992); Pres. JOSÉ CARLOS PESANHA LIMA; Gen. Man. SERGIO ROBERTO SOUZA TAVARES.

### Foreign Banks

**Banco Alemán Paraguayo SA:** (Germany): Estrella 505, Casilla 1426, Asunción; tel. (21) 49-0166; telex 44030; Pres. JUAN PEIRANO; Gen. Man. Lic. RICARDO CASTILLO FRACCHIA.

**Banco de Asunción, SA:** Palma esq. 14 de Mayo, Asunción; tel. (21) 49-3191; telex 42020; fax (21) 49-3190; f. 1964; major shareholder Banco Central Hispano (Spain); cap. 1,617m., dep. 15,399m., res 501m. (Dec. 1985); Pres. LUIS CORONEL DE PALMA; Gen. Man. JOSÉ ALONSO SÁNCHEZ; 2 brs.

**Banco do Brasil, SA:** Oliva y Nuestra Señora de la Asunción, Casilla 667, Asunción; tel. (21) 44-5802; telex 136; fax (21) 44-8761; f. 1941; Gen. Man. ANISIO RESENDE DE SOUZA.

**Banco Central Hispano** (Spain): Palma esq. 14 de Mayo, Asunción; tel. (21) 49-3191; telex 132; fax (21) 49-3190.

**Banco do Estado de São Paulo (BANESPA)** (Brazil): Independencia Nacional esq. Fulgencio R. Moreno, Casilla 2211, Asunción; tel. (21) 44-8698; telex 44108; fax (21) 49-4985; Gen. Man. ERIMAR DA COSTA LEITE.

**Banco Exterior, SA** (Spain): Yegros 435 y 25 de Mayo, Casilla 824, Asunción; tel. (21) 44-8650; telex 44018; fax (21) 44-8103; f. 1961; cap. 1,126m., res 1,931m., dep. 30,455m. (Dec. 1987); Pres. INIGO DE LA SOTA; Gen. Man. ANÍBAL QUEVEDO ORTIZ.

**Banco Holandés Unido** (Netherlands): Independencia Nacional y Eduardo Víctor Haedo, Apdo 1180, Asunción; tel. (21) 49-1744; telex 140; Man. PIETER C. VAN DIJK.

**Banco de la Nación Argentina:** Chile y Palma, Asunción; tel. (21) 44-7433; telex 44221; fax (21) 44-4365; f. 1942; Man. EDUARDO V. FERNÁNDEZ; 3 brs.

**Banco del Paraná, SA:** 25 de Mayo y Yegros, Casilla 2298, Asunción; tel. (21) 44-6691; telex 44388; fax (21) 44-7309; f. 1981; cap. 3,208.9m., res 644.7m., dep. 40,364.6m. (Dec. 1991); Pres. HEITOR WALLACE DE MELLO E SILVA; Dir and Gen. Man. Dr JOSÉ STEGANI; 4 brs.

**Banco Real de Paraguay:** Alberdi esq. Estrella, Asunción; tel. (21) 49-3171; telex 44063; fax (21) 44-3664; Pres. CELIO TUNHOLI; Man. ALEXANDRE SCHU.

**Banco Sudameris Paraguay, SA:** Independencia Nacional y Cerro Corá, Casilla 1433, Asunción; tel. (21) 44-4172; telex 44015; fax (21) 44-8670; f. 1961; savings and commercial bank; subsidiary of Banque Sudameris; cap. 9,825m., res 7,487m., dep. 151,610m. (Dec. 1994); Pres. Dr JOSÉ ANTONIO MORENO RUFFINELLI; Man. GIUSEPPE DI FRANCESCO; 5 brs.

**Citibank NA** (USA): Chile y Estrella 345, Asunción; tel. (21) 44-8948; telex 44082; fax (21) 44-4612; Vice-Pres. and Gen. Man. GUSTAVO MARIN.

**Lloyds Bank PLC** (United Kingdom): Palma esq. Juan E. O'Leary, Apdo 696, Asunción; tel. (21) 49-1090; telex 44336; fax (21) 44-3569; f. 1920; Man. J. SCOTT DONALD.

### Banking Associations

**Asociación de Bancos Privados del Paraguay:** Edif. Parapití, 3°, Of. 323/5, Estrella esq. Juan E. O'Leary, Asunción; tel. (21) 49-1450; mems: Paraguayan banks and foreign banks with brs in Asunción; Pres. SERGIO ROBERTO SOUZA TAVARES.

**Cámara de Bancos Paraguayos:** 25 de Mayo esq. 22 de Setiembre, Asunción; tel. (21) 22-2373; Pres. MIGUEL ANGEL LARREINEGABE.

## STOCK EXCHANGE

**Bolsa de Valores y Productos de Asunción SA:** Estrella 540, Asunción; tel. (21) 44-2445; fax (21) 44-2446; f. 1992; Pres. ROLANDO PENNER.

## INSURANCE

**La Agrícola SA de Seguros Generales y Reaseguros:** Mariscal Estigarribia 1173, Constitución, Casilla 1349, Asunción; tel. (21) 21-3746; telex 726; fax (21) 21-3685; f. 1982; general; Pres. Dr VICENTE OSVALDO BERGUES; Gen. Man. CARLOS ALBERTO LEVI SOSA.

**Aseguradora Paraguaya, SA:** República de Israel 309, esq. Rio de Janeiro, Casilla 277, Asunción; tel. (21) 21-5086; fax (21) 22217; f. 1976; life and risk; Pres. GERARDO TORCIDA CONEJERO.

**Atalaya SA de Seguros Generales:** Independencia Nacional 565, 1°, esq. Azara y Cerro Corá, Asunción; tel. (21) 49-2811; telex 173; fax (21) 49-6966; f. 1964; general; Pres. HEINZ GERARDO DOLL; Gen. Man. CECILIO BEJARANO Z.

**Central SA de Seguros:** Edif. Beton, 1° y 2°, Eduardo Víctor Haedo 179, Independencia Nacional, Casilla 1802, Asunción; tel. (21) 49-4654; telex 44028; fax (21) 49-4655; f. 1976; general; Pres. MIGUEL JACOBO VILLASANTI; Gen. Man. Dr FÉLIX AVEIRO.

PARAGUAY — *Directory*

**Cigna Worldwide Insurance Company:** Humaitá 937 y Montevideo, Casilla 730, Asunción; tel. (21) 44-5595; telex 383; fax (21) 49-5209; f. 1989; general; Gen. Man. Dra Teresa Ma G. B. de Romero Pereira.

**El Comercio Paraguayo SA Cía de Seguros Generales:** Alberdi 453 y Oliva, Asunción; tel. (21) 49-2324; fax (21) 49-3562; f. 1947; life and risk; Dir Dr Braulio Oscar Elizeche.

**La Consolidada SA de Seguros y Reaseguros:** Chile 719 y Eduardo Víctor Haedo, Casilla 1182, Asunción; tel. (21) 49-1980; telex 44210; fax (21) 44-5795; f. 1961; life and risk; Pres. Dr Juan de Jesús Bibolini; Gen. Man. Lic. Jorge Patricio Ferreira Ferreira.

**La Continental Paraguaya SA de Seguros y Reaseguros:** Chile 680 y Eduardo Víctor Haedo, 3°, Asunción; tel. (21) 44-6210; telex 166; fax (21) 44-6210; f. 1986; life and risk; Pres. Guillermo Heisecke Velázquez; Man. Jorge A. Lloret.

**La Independencia de Seguros y Reaseguros, SA:** Edif. Parapatí, 1°, Juan E. O'Leary 409 esq. Estrella, Casilla 980, Asunción; tel. (21) 44-7021; fax (21) 44-8996; f. 1965; general; Pres. Severiano Ramón Jiménez; Gen. Man. Juan Francisco Franco López.

**Intercontinental SA de Seguros y Reaseguros:** Iturbe 1047, Teniente Fariña, Altos, Asunción; tel. (21) 49-2348; fax (21) 49-1227; f. 1978; Pres. Dr Miguel Angel Chávez B.

**Mundo SA Seguros Generales y Reaseguros:** Estrella 917 y Montevideo, Asunción; tel. (21) 49-2787; fax (21) 44-5486; f. 1970; life and risk; Pres. Juan Martín Villalba de los Rios; Gen.-Man. Blás Marcial Cabral Barrios.

**Nanawa SA de Seguros y Reaseguros:** Edif. Nanawa, Oliva 756, Casilla 2003, Asunción; tel. (21) 49-4961; telex 44151; fax (21) 44-9673; f. 1975; Pres. Roberto Salomón; Gen. Man. José Luis Cuevas.

**Ñane Reta SA de Seguros y Reaseguros:** Paí Pérez 617, Azara, Casilla 1658, Asunción; tel. (21) 44-9745; fax (21) 44-7042; f. 1980; Pres. Werner Bäertschi; Gen. Man. Carlos Molina Laterra.

**La Paraguaya SA de Seguros:** Edif. La Paraguaya, 3°, Estrella 625 y 15 de Agosto, Casilla 375, Asunción; tel. (21) 49-1367; fax (21) 44-8235; f. 1905; life and risk; Pres. Dr Oscar Pérez Uribe; Gen. Man. Dr Manuel Nogués Zubizarreta.

**Patria SA de Seguros y Reaseguros:** Edif. San Rafael, 9°, Yegros 437 esq. 25 de Mayo, Casilla 2735, Asunción; tel. (21) 44-5389; telex 44123; fax (21) 44-8230; f. 1968; general; Pres. Rolf Dieter Kemper; Exec. Dir Dr Marcos Pereira R.

**La Previsora SA de Seguros Generales:** Edif. Banco do Brasil, 7°, Nuestra Señora de la Asunción 540 y Oliva, Casilla 976, Asunción; tel. (21) 49-2442; fax (21) 49-4791; f. 1964; general; Pres. Rubén Odilio Domecq M.; Man. Jorge Enrique Domecq F.

**Real Paraguaya de Seguros, SA:** Edif. Banco Real, 1°, Estrella esq. Alberdi, Casilla 1442, Asunción; tel. (21) 49-3171; telex 240; fax (21) 49-8129; f. 1974; general; Chair. Celio Tunholi; Man. Dir José Carlos Utwari.

**Rumbos SA de Seguros:** Estrella 851, Ayolas, Casilla 1017, Asunción; tel. (21) 44-9488; telex 44313; fax (21) 44-9492; f. 1960; general; Pres. Dr Antonio Soljancic; Man. Dir Roberto Gómez Verlangieri.

**La Rural del Paraguay SA Paraguaya de Seguros:** 15 de Agosto 608 esq. General Díaz, Casilla 21, Asunción; tel. (21) 49-1917; fax (21) 44-1592; f. 1920; general; Pres. Dr José Federico Gómez; Gen. Man. Eduardo Barrios Perini.

**Seguros Chaco SA de Seguros y Reaseguros:** Mariscal Estigarribia 982, Casilla 3248, Asunción; tel. (21) 44-7118; fax (21) 44-9551; f. 1977; general; Pres. Emilio Velilla Laconich; Exec. Dir Alberto R. Zarza Taboada.

**Seguros Generales, SA (SEGESA):** Edif. SEGESA, 1°, Oliva 393 esq. Alberdi, Casilla 802, Asunción; tel. (21) 49-1362; telex 44191; fax (21) 49-1360; f. 1956; life and risk; Pres. César Avalos.

**Universo de Seguros y Reaseguros, SA:** Edif. de la Encarnación, 9°, 14 de Mayo esq. General Díaz, Casilla 788, Asunción; tel. (21) 44-8530; fax (21) 44-7278; f. 1979; Pres. Daniel Cerezuela Sánchez.

**Yacyretá SA de Seguros y Reaseguros:** Padre Juan Pucheu 556, Avda España, Casilla 2487, Asunción; tel. (21) 20-8407; telex 5193; fax (21) 21-3108; f. 1980; Pres. Dr Ernesto Rotela Prieto; Gen. Man. Benito Giménez Caballero.

### Insurance Association

**Asociación Paraguaya de Cías de Seguros:** 15 de Agosto esq. Lugano, Casilla 1435, Asunción; tel. (21) 44-6474; fax (21) 44-4343; f. 1963; Pres. Juan Carlos Delgadillo Echague; Sec. Lic. Guillermo Gross Brown.

## Trade and Industry

### STATE PROPERTY AGENCY

**Consejo de Privatización:** Edif. Ybaga, 10°, Presidente Franco 173, Asunción; fax (21) 44-9157; responsible for the privatization of state-owned enterprises; Exec. Dir José María Espínola.

### CHAMBER OF COMMERCE

**Cámara y Bolsa de Comercio:** Estrella 540, Asunción; tel. (21) 49-3321; fax (21) 44-0817; f. 1898; Pres. Nicolás González Oddone; Gen. Man. Dr Ricardo Franco L.

### INDUSTRIAL AND DEVELOPMENT ORGANIZATIONS

**Secretaría Técnica de Planificación de la Presidencia de la República:** Edif. AYFRA, 3°, Presidente Franco esq. Ayolas, Asunción; tel. (21) 44-8074; fax (21) 44-6493; govt body responsible for overall economic and social planning; Exec. Sec. Ing. Raúl Cubas Grau; Sec.-Gen. Dr Carlos González.

**Aceros del Paraguay (ACEPAR):** Asunción; national steel company, scheduled for privatization in 1994; Pres. Julián Aguero de León; Sec.-Gen. Jacinto Santa María.

**Administración Nacional de Electricidad (ANDE):** Avda España 1268, Asunción; tel. (21) 22713; telex 22072; fax (21) 21-2371; f. 1949; national electricity board; Pres. Miguel Fulgencio Rodríguez Romero.

**Administración Paraguaya de Alcoholes (APAL):** Asunción; state-owned distillery, scheduled for privatization in 1994.

**Consejo Nacional de Coordinación Económica:** Presidencia de la República, Paraguayo Independiente y Juan E. O'Leary, Asunción; responsible for overall economic policy; Sec. Fulvio Monges Ocampos.

**Consejo Nacional de Desarrollo Industrial** (National Council for Industrial Development): Asunción; national planning institution.

**Consejo Nacional para las Exportaciones:** Asunción; f. 1986; founded to eradicate irregular trading practices; Dir Minister of Industry and Commerce.

**Corporación de Obras Sanitarias:** José Berges 516, entre Brasil y San José, Asunción; tel. (21) 25001; telex 172; fax 21-2624; responsible for public water supply, sewage disposal and drainage.

**Federación de la Producción, Industria y Comercio (FEPRINCO):** Palma 751 y 15 de Agosto, Asunción; tel. (21) 46638; organization of private sector business executives; Pres. Alirio Ugarte Díaz.

**Instituto Nacional del Indígena (INDI):** Don Bosco 745, Asunción; tel. (21) 497137; fax (21) 447154; f. 1981; responsible for welfare of Indian population; Pres. Valentín Gamarra.

**Instituto de Bienestar Rural (IBR):** Tacuary 276, Asunción; tel. (21) 43930; responsible for rural welfare and colonization; Pres. Hugo Halley Merlo.

**Instituto Nacional de Tecnología y Normalización (INTN)** (National Institute of Technology and Standardization): Avda General Artigas y General Roa, Casilla 967, Asunción; tel. (21) 29-0160; telex 306; national standards institute.

**Instituto de Previsión Social:** Constitución y Luis Alberto de Herrera, Casilla 437, Asunción; tel. (21) 23141; telex 848; f. 1943; responsible for employees' welfare and health insurance scheme.

**Petróleos Paraguayos (PETROPAR):** Oliva 299, 4°, Casilla 571, Asunción; tel. (21) 49-5117; telex 44274; fax (21) 49-6232; f. 1981; national petroleum company; Pres. Dr Emilio Ramírez Russo.

**ProParaguay:** Padre Cardozo 469, Asunción; tel. (21) 20-8276; fax (21) 20-0425; f. 1991; responsible for promoting investment in Paraguay and the export of national products; Gen. Dir Ing. Francisco Gutierrez Campos.

**Siderurgia Paraguaya (SIDEPAR):** Azara 197, 6°, esq. Yegros, Asunción; tel. (21) 95963; telex 287; f. 1974; state steel company; Pres. (vacant); Man. Gen. Rolando González Murdoch.

**Unión Industrial Paraguaya (UIP):** Cerro Corá 1038, Casilla 782, Asunción; tel. (21) 21-2556; fax 21-3360; f. 1936; organization of business entrepreneurs; Pres. Dr Arturo Jara Avelli.

### TRADE UNIONS

**Central Nacional de Trabajadores (CNT):** Piribebuy 1078, Asunción; tel. (21) 44-4084; fax (21) 49-2154.

**Central de Trabajadores del Estado Paraguayo:** Asunción.

**Central Unica de Trabajadores (CUT):** Asunción; f. 1989; Pres. Víctor Báez Mosqueira; Sec.-Gen. Jorge Alvarenga.

**Confederación Paraguaya de Trabajadores—CPT** (Confederation of Paraguayan Workers): Yegros 1309-1333 y Simón Bolívar, Asunción; tel. (21) 72434; f. 1951; Sec.-Gen. Julio Etcheverry Espinola; 43,500 mems from 189 affiliated groups.

## Transport

### RAILWAYS

**Ferrocarril Central del Paraguay:** Asunción; state railway company, scheduled for privatization in 1994.

# PARAGUAY

**Ferrocarril Presidente Carlos Antonio López:** México 145, Casilla 453, Asunción; tel. (21) 44-3273; fax (21) 44-7848; f. 1854, state-owned since 1961; 441 km open; service to Encarnación and Buenos Aires (1,510 km) three times a week; Pres. P. BERGANZA: Sec.-Gen. J. DANIEL G.

## ROADS

In 1983 there were 11,320 km of roads, of which 2,094 km were paved. The Pan-American Highway runs for over 700 km in Paraguay and the Trans-Chaco Highway extends from Asunción to Bolivia.

## SHIPPING

**Administración Nacional de Navegación y Puertos (ANNP)** (National Shipping and Ports Administration): Colón e Isabel la Católica, Asunción; tel. and fax (21) 49-2196; f. 1965; responsible for ports services and maintaining navigable channels in rivers and for improving navigation on the Rivers Paraguay and Paraná; Pres. EUGENIO SANABRIA CANTERO.

### Inland Waterways

**Flota Mercante del Estado (FLOMERES):** Estrella 672-686, Casilla 454, Asunción; tel. (21) 44-7409; telex 159; fax (21) 44-6010; state-owned; boats and barges up to 1,000 tons displacement on Paraguay and Paraná rivers; cold storage ships for use Asunción–Buenos Aires–Montevideo; Pres. Capt. ANÍBAL GINO PERTILE R.

### Ocean Shipping

**Compañía Paraguaya de Navegación de Ultramar, SA:** Chile 668, entre General Díaz y Eduardo Víctor Haedo, Casilla 77, Asunción; tel. (21) 49-2137; telex 44012; fax (21) 44-5013; f. 1963 to operate between Asunción, USA and European ports; 2 vessels; Exec. Pres. JUAN BOSCH B.

**Flota Mercante del Estado:** Estrella 672-686, Casilla 454, Asunción; tel. (21) 44-7409; telex 159; fax (21) 44-6010; state-owned; Pres. Capt. ANÍBAL GINO PERTILE R.

## CIVIL AVIATION

The major international airport, Aeropuerto Silvio Pettirossi is situated 15 km from Asunción. A second airport, Aeropuerto Guaraní, 30 km from the Brazilian border, was inaugurated in August 1993.

### National Airline

**Líneas Aéreas Paraguayas (LAP):** Oliva 455–467, Asunción; tel. (21) 91041; telex 5230; fax (21) 96484; f. 1962; services to destinations within South America and to Europe; 80% owned by SAETA (Ecuador); Chair. Gen. GERALDO JOHANSEN ROUX; Pres. Gen. RAÚL F. CALVERT.

# Tourism

Tourism is undeveloped, but, with recent improvements in the infrastructure, efforts are being made to promote the sector. Tourist arrivals in Paraguay in 1992 totalled 334,000. In the same year tourist receipts were US $153m.

**Dirección General de Turismo:** Ministerio de Obras Públicas y Comunicaciones, Palma 468, Asunción; tel. (21) 44-1530; telex 162; fax (21) 49-1230; f. 1940; Pres. and Dir-Gen. Dr DERLIS RUBÉN ESTECHE VÁSQUEZ.

# PERU

## Introductory Survey

### Location, Climate, Language, Religion, Flag, Capital

The Republic of Peru lies in western South America, bordered by Ecuador and Colombia to the north, by Brazil and Bolivia to the east, and by Chile to the south. Peru has a coastline of more than 2,300 km (1,400 miles) on the Pacific Ocean. The climate varies with altitude, average temperatures being about 11°C (20°F) lower in the Andes mountains than in the coastal plain. The rainy season is between October and April, with heavy rainfall in the tropical forests. Temperatures in Lima are usually between 13°C (55°F) and 28°C (82°F). The three official languages are Spanish, Quechua and Aymará. Almost all of the inhabitants profess Christianity, and the great majority are adherents of the Roman Catholic Church. The civil flag (proportions 3 by 2) has three equal vertical stripes, of red, white and red. The state flag is identical, but for the addition of the national coat of arms (a shield divided into three unequal segments: red, with a golden cornucopia spilling coins of yellow and white at the base, blue, with a yellow vicuña in the dexter chief, and white, with a green tree in the sinister chief; all surmounted by a green wreath, and framed by branches of palm and laurel, tied at the bottom with a red and white ribbon) in the centre of the white stripe. The capital is Lima.

### Recent History

There have been human settlements in Peru for more than 10,500 years. The last of the indigenous Indians' ruling civilizations, the Inca empire, was ended when Spanish colonists arrived in the early 16th century, attracted by the legendary mineral wealth of the region. Since independence from Spain, declared in 1821, and finally achieved in 1824, Peruvian politics have been characterized by alternating periods of civilian administration and military dictatorship.

In the early 1920s opposition to the dictatorial regime of President Augusto Bernardino Leguía resulted in the creation of the Alianza Popular Revolucionaria Americana (APRA—also known as the Partido Aprista Peruano), Peru's oldest political party to command mass support. The party, founded as a nationalist revolutionary movement, was formally established in Peru in 1930, when President Leguía was deposed and the party's founder (and its leader for more than 50 years), Dr Víctor Raúl Haya de la Torre, returned from enforced exile in Mexico. A long-standing tradition of hostility developed between APRA and the armed forces, and the party was banned in 1931–45, and again in 1948–56.

During 1945–63 political power shifted regularly between the armed forces and elected government. In 1948 Dr José Luis Bustamante y Rivera was deposed by Gen. Manuel Odría, following a right-wing military rebellion. Odría established a military junta which governed until 1950, when the General was elected unopposed to the Presidency, and subsequently appointed a cabinet composed of military officers and civilians. In 1956 Odría was succeeded by Dr Manuel Prado y Ugartache (who had been President in 1939–45). An inconclusive presidential election in 1962 precipitated military intervention, and power was assumed by Gen. Ricardo Pérez Godoy, at the head of a military junta. In March 1963, however, Pérez was supplanted by his second-in-command, Gen. Nicolás Lindley López.

Fernando Belaúnde Terry, the joint candidate of his own Acción Popular (AP) party and the Partido Demócrata Cristiano, emerged as the successful contestant at presidential elections conducted (together with a congressional poll) in June 1963, and was inaugurated as President in the following month. An increase in internal disturbances in predominantly Indian areas was attributed to communist subversion, and resulted in the temporary suspension of constitutional guarantees in 1965–66 and an intensive military campaign of counter-insurgency. Although the Belaúnde administration successfully promoted agrarian reform, lack of congressional support for the Government contributed to a succession of ministerial crises which, together with continuing internal unrest, prompted renewed military intervention in October 1968, when Gen. Juan Velasco Alvarado assumed the Presidency, dissolved Congress and appointed a military cabinet.

Despite the re-emergence of internal disturbances and dissension within the armed forces, provoked by the introduction of radical reforms and austerity measures, Velasco retained power until August 1975, when he was overthrown and replaced by Gen. Francisco Morales Bermúdez. In July 1977 President Morales announced plans for the restoration of civilian rule. Accordingly, a national election was conducted in June 1978 to select the members of a constituent assembly, which was to draft a new constitution in preparation for presidential and congressional elections. In the election, APRA emerged as the largest party, and in July the assembly elected the 83-year-old Dr Haya de la Torre to be its President. The new Constitution, adopted in July 1979, provided for elections by universal adult suffrage, and extended the franchise to the sizeable illiterate population.

At the presidential and congressional elections, which took place in May 1980, the presidential contest was won decisively by Belaúnde. At the same time the AP won an outright majority in the Cámara de Diputados and also secured the greatest representation in the Senado. The new organs of state were inaugurated in July, when the new Constitution became fully effective.

While Belaúnde sought to liberalize the economy and to reverse many of the agrarian and industrial reforms implemented under Velasco, much of his term of office was dominated by the increasing threat to internal stability posed by the emergence, in the early 1980s, of the Maoist terrorist group, the Sendero Luminoso (SL, Shining Path). The situation deteriorated following the uncompromising response of the armed forces to terrorist activity in a designated emergency zone, which extended to 13 provinces (primarily in the departments of Ayacucho, Huancavelica and Apurímac) by mid-1984, and a dramatic increase in violent deaths and violations of human rights was reported.

At elections on 14 April 1985 Alan García Pérez (the candidate for APRA) received 45.7% of the total votes in the presidential poll, while APRA secured a majority in both houses of the legislature. García's victory was ensured in May, prior to a second round of voting, when his closest opponent, Dr Alfonso Barrantes Lingán (of the left-wing Izquierda Unida coalition), withdrew his candidature. At his inauguration in July, President García announced that his Government's priorities would be to eradicate internal terrorism and to arrest Peru's severe economic decline. In September García announced the formation of a Peace Commission to investigate acts of terrorism and to uphold human rights. In January 1986, however, the Commission resigned, complaining that it lacked adequate political influence. By July a successor Commission had also resigned, in protest at the Government's approval of military intervention to restore order in three prisons where mutinies were staged in June, when it became known that some 250 prisoners (principally members of SL) had been killed in the course of the operation.

Despite APRA successes at municipal elections in 1986, widespread opposition to the Government's economic programme was manifested in a succession of well-supported general strikes in 1987 and 1988. Plans for the nationalization of Peru's banks and private financial and insurance institutions, announced by President García in July 1987, encountered considerable opposition from the banking community, and prompted the creation of Libertad, a 'freedom movement' expressing opposition to the plans (which were subsequently modified), which was established under the leadership of the author, Mario Vargas Llosa. The authority of the García administration was further undermined by persistent rumours of military unrest, allegations of links between members of the Government and the right-wing paramilitary 'death squad', the Comando Rodrigo Franco, and by the continuing terrorist activities of SL and a resurgence of activity by the Movimiento Revolucionario Tupac Amarú (MRTA) guerrilla group, in north-east Peru.

Despite the capture of leading members of both groups in 1988 and 1989, violent attacks by SL and (to a lesser extent) by the MRTA against political and industrial targets and rural self-defence groups (or 'rondas campesinas') had reached an unprecedented level in 1989 during the campaign for local government elections, and persisted into 1990, intensified by the proximity of the presidential and legislative elections scheduled for 8 April. Figures released by the Senado's Human Rights Commission in 1990 noted that 3,198 people were killed in political violence in 1989. In 1989 the human rights organization, Amnesty International, criticized the Peruvian Government's methods of combating political violence, claiming that an estimated 3,000 people had 'disappeared' while in police custody since 1982, while a further 3,000 had been executed by the national security forces.

General elections took place on 8 April 1990, despite the attempts of SL to disrupt the elections with another 'armed strike' and a campaign of bombing and looting. In the presidential election Mario Vargas Llosa, the candidate of the centre-right FREDEMO alliance (established in early 1988 by the AP, Libertad and the Partido Popular Cristiano), obtained the largest percentage of the total votes cast, narrowly defeating a hitherto little-known agronomist, Alberto Fujimori, the candidate of the Cambio 90 group of independents. As the April election failed to produce a candidate with the required absolute majority for an outright win, a second round of voting, contested by the first- and second-placed candidates, was conducted on 10 June. Fujimori, whose campaign had advocated 'hard work, honesty and technology', emerged as the successful candidate with some 57% of the votes cast in the second round, having attracted late support from left-wing parties and from APRA. Following his inauguration, on 28 July 1990, Fujimori announced the composition of a new centre-left Council of Ministers, with Juan Carlos Hurtado Miller, a member of the AP, as Prime Minister and Minister of Economy and Finance. Fujimori identified two immediate aims as being the eradication of corruption at a senior level, and the reduction of inflation.

The Government's proposals for economic readjustment, announced in early August 1990, were widely interpreted as a betrayal of promises made during the electoral campaign that economic restructuring could be achieved without severe austerity programmes. The Government abolished subsidies for consumers, thereby introducing increases in prices of more than 3,000% for petrol and of between 300% and 600% for basic foods. Plans for the abolition of monopolies and for other structural reforms, including a significant divestment programme in the state sector and the simplification of the taxation system, were announced later in the year. By December, despite suggestions that the economic policies pursued by the Government had plunged the country into recession, Fujimori had impressed international financial organizations sufficiently to enter into negotiations for a 'bridging' loan of US $2,000m. and to persuade a group of international banks to suspend a $2,000m. lawsuit initiated against the Peruvian Government in May 1990 for the recovery of debts.

In February 1991 Hurtado announced his resignation from the Council of Ministers, following several weeks of internal dispute regarding the efficacy of anti-inflationary economic measures. The former Minister of Labour, Carlos Torres y Torres Lara, was appointed Prime Minister and Minister of Foreign Affairs, while the finance and economy portfolio was assumed by a right-wing economist, Carlos Boloña Behr. New measures, announced by Boloña in March 1991, sought further to liberalize the economy, by reducing import tariffs and removing all non-tariff restrictions on imports of consumer goods. In April new banking legislation was introduced (former President García's controversial bank nationalization law having been formally repealed by the Congreso in December 1990), whereby government restrictions on financial institutions and on the participation of foreign banks in the sector were relaxed.

Despite the success of the Government's programme of economic austerity, liberalization and divestment in securing Peru's return to the international financial community, economic policy continued to provoke widespread domestic opposition and industrial unrest. In November 1991, despite mounting public and congressional dissent, Fujimori took advantage of a 150-day period of emergency legislative powers (granted to him in June in order that the economic and security problems which threatened to undermine national stability might swiftly be addressed) to issue a series of economic decrees that represented a continuation of policies which had been initiated with the deregulation of the docks and maritime, air and public transport, and concerned the elimination of state monopolies of telecommunications, postal networks and railways, the opening to private investment of the power sector, the privatization of schools and a reform of the health and social security services. The unexpected resignation of Torres at the end of October, in reponse to criticism of his handling of renewed border tension with Ecuador (see below), resulted in the assumption of the premiership by the Minister of Labour, Alfonso de los Heros Pérez Albela.

The increasing divergence of interests of President Fujimori and the Congreso (which had expressed considerable disaffection with the President's reliance upon emergency legislative powers and his attempts to govern by decree) was exacerbated, in early January 1992, by congressional approval of the draft budget for 1992, which Fujimori had opposed on the grounds that it contained provisions for excessive expenditure. On 5 April Fujimori announced the immediate suspension of the 1979 Constitution and the dissolution of the Congreso, pending a comprehensive restructuring of the legislature. The President maintained that the reform of the Congreso was essential in order to eradicate 'corruption and inefficiency' and to enable him to implement a programme of 'pacification' of the nation through the resolution of problems posed by terrorism and drugs-trafficking, and fully to implement free-market economic policies. Fujimori also criticized the inefficiency of the judicial system, and announced that the judiciary would be reformed to create an 'honest and efficient administration of justice'. The constitutional coup (or 'autogolpe') was implemented, without recorded casualties, with the full co-operation and support of the armed forces. Troops cordoned off the parliament and other official buildings, radio stations were occupied and permitted to broadcast only military communiqués, political opposition leaders, trade union leaders and the Presidents of both houses of the Congreso were placed under temporary house arrest, and armoured vehicles were deployed in the capital, Lima. Fujimori stated that plans for reform of the legislature would be submitted to a referendum at a future date. In the interim the country would be governed by an Emergency and National Reconstruction Government, in accordance with a draft 'basic law' whereby legislative power would be exercised by the President, with the approval of the Council of Ministers. On the following day Prime Minister Alfonso de los Heros resigned, in protest against Fujimori's actions; the majority of the Council of Ministers, however, elected to remain in office. Members of the dissolved parliament declared Fujimori to be incapable of continuing in office, and, later in the month, attempted to establish Máximo San Román, the First Vice-President, as the 'head of the constitutional government', with an alternative council of ministers; however, this was undermined by a lack of domestic and international support.

While Fujimori's actions prompted outrage from politicians, judges, intellectuals and the media, popular reaction to the 'autogolpe' was more subdued, and the Peruvian population resisted exhortations from the political opposition and the media (who were freed from censorship on 9 April) to exercise their (1979) constitutional right to take up arms in defence of democracy. Bolstered by demonstrations of public support for his actions, Fujimori proceeded to dismiss 13 of Peru's 28 Supreme Court judges, whom he accused of corruption, and attempted to undermine support for political opponents with the continued detention of prominent opposition party figures.

A tentative timetable for return to constitutional government (to be enacted over a 12- to 18-month period) that had been announced by the Minister of Foreign Affairs, Augusto Blacker Miller, in the aftermath of the coup, had not received presidential endorsement and did little to alleviate mounting international pressure upon the Government to take immediate steps to return to full democracy. A meeting of the Organization of American States (OAS, see p. 204), convened in the US capital in mid-April and attended by Blacker, approved a motion deploring the actions of President Fujimori, and voted to dispatch an OAS mission, headed by Secretary-General João Soares, to attempt to effect a reconciliation between the legislature and the executive. The failure of the OAS to impose sanctions upon Peru was largely attributed to Blacker's diplomatic assurances to the OAS that the suspension of democracy was both necessary and temporary.

On 21 April 1992 Fujimori defined a more comprehensive timetable for the restoration of democracy, with congressional elections to be conducted in February 1993. It was subsequently announced that Blacker and the Minister of Industry, Commerce, Tourism and Integration, Victor Joy Way, were to resign. Jorge Chávez, the President of the Central Bank, was also removed from office, as were 134 judges. Twelve provisional members of the Supreme Court were later appointed.

The threat posed to Fujimori's programme of radical reform by economic constraints, resulting from the suspension of international financial aid to Peru, prompted the President to present a revised timetable for a return to democracy in late May 1992, and in early June Fujimori confirmed that national elections would be conducted in October to a unicameral constituent congress, the function of which would be to draft a new constitution (to be submitted for approval in a national referendum at a later date). In order to guard against party political manoeuvring, those elected to the interim body would be ineligible for further congressional office for the duration of two subsequent full congressional terms. The President also announced that, pending approval of a new document, the 1979 Constitution would be reinstated without certain articles that might 'impede the progress of the Government'.

In June 1992 Prime Minister de la Puente invited opposition parties to participate, individually, in a National Dialogue for Peace and Development, which was inaugurated at the end of the month and which sought to identify, through discussions with the political opposition and with the public, important issues for future consideration by the Congreso Constituyente Democrático (CCD). Elections to the CCD, conducted on 22 November and attended by an invited observer mission from the OAS, were a qualified success for pro-Government parties. An electoral coalition of Cambio 90 and the Nueva Mayoría (a new independent party, comprising many former cabinet ministers), headed by Fujimori's former Minister of Energy and Mines, Jaime Yashiyama Tanaka (who was subsequently elected President of the CCD), secured 44 of the 80 congressional seats. The only significant opposition party not to boycott the elections, the Partido Popular Cristiano, took eight seats. At the inaugural meeting of the CCD, in December, Tanaka identified its immediate aims as the restoration of the autonomy of the judiciary, the eradication of terrorism, the generation of employment and of favourable conditions for foreign investment, and the projection of an enhanced national image abroad. In January 1993, having formally reinstated the 1979 Constitution, the CCD confirmed Fujimori as constitutional Head of State.

The resignation of the Minister of Economy and Finance, Carlos Boloña Behr, in January 1993, following a disagreement with Fujimori arising from the President's efforts to attract increased popular support through the temporary relaxation of economic restrictions, prompted a reallocation of ministerial posts later in the month. Following the resignation of de la Puente's Government in July, Alfonso Bustamente y Bustamente (hitherto Minister of Industry, Commerce, Tourism and Integration) was appointed Prime Minister in August.

The final text of the draft Constitution, which enhanced presidential powers and provided for the establishment of a unicameral legislature, was approved by the CCD in September 1993: the Congreso declared that the document had been formulated with the aim of alleviating the country's economic difficulties and of combating terrorism. A national referendum on the new Constitution was scheduled for 31 October—the first occasion on which such popular consultation had been sought in Peru. Among the text's most controversial articles were the introduction of the death penalty for convicted terrorists and a provision permitting a President of the Republic to be re-elected for a successive five-year term of office. Demonstrations (several of which were dispersed by riot police) took place in September and October, mostly involving students and trade union activists, to protest against the document. Opposition politicians, who claimed that the new Constitution vested excessive power in the executive and removed certain rights of parliament, formed a committee to campaign for a rejection of the document in the referendum. However, the results of the plebiscite, which was monitored by OAS representatives, revealed a small majority of public support for the Constitution, which was approved by an overall 52.2% of the votes cast. Support for the new text was strongest in Lima, while voters in more than one-half of the country's 25 provinces rejected its provisions. Opposition members of the CCD boycotted the ceremony at which the Constitution was promulgated on 29 December, in order to register their disapproval of the new charter.

In April 1993 members of the army staged a demonstration in Lima, in support of the Commander of the Army and President of the Joint Command of the Armed Forces, Gen. Nicolas de Bari Hermoza Rios, following accusations by opposition members of the CCD of the involvement of paramilitary forces in the 'disappearance' of a professor and nine students (suspected of being supporters of SL) from the Enrique Guzmán y Valle University at La Cantuta, to the east of Lima, in July 1992. In May 1993 Fujimori rejected allegations, made by a senior army officer, Gen. Rodolfo Robles Espinoza, that violations of human rights (referring specifically to the La Cantuta 'disappearances') had been perpetrated by the army with the full knowledge of Hermoza and also of Capt. Vladimiro Montesimos, the presidential security adviser. (Robles was subsequently discharged from the army and fled to Argentina.) Following confirmation that bodies discovered in July and November were those of the La Cantuta 'activists', civil proceedings were initiated in mid-December against 11 army officers who were accused of involvement in their kidnap and murder. In February 1994, however, considerable controversy was caused when new legislation was promulgated allowing the Supreme Court to rule that the case be transferred to a military court. This judicial manoeuvring provoked outrage among opposition parties and independent legal and humanitarian groups, as well as a formal protest from the US Government at what it regarded as a breach of the autonomy of the judiciary. Moreover, Alfonso Bustamente, dissociating himself from the process, resigned as Prime Minister—he was replaced by the Minister of Foreign Affairs, Efraín Goldemberg Schreiber, in the ensuing government reorganization. Later in February, after a brief trial at the Supreme Council of Military Justice, nine officers received prison sentences of between one and 20 years for their part in the La Cantuta murders. The conduct and outcome of the proceedings prompted protests both within Peru and internationally.

Domestic politics during 1994 were dominated by the approaching presidential and legislative elections, scheduled to be held in April 1995. A much-publicized dispute between the President and his wife, Susana Higuchi de Fujimori, was intensified in August when new legislation was approved banning members of the presidential family from standing for office. Having criticized her husband's administration, made allegations of corruption within the Government and of human rights violations by the armed forces, and subsequently been deposed of her position as First Lady, Sra Higuchi announced her intention to contest the presidential election, and gathered support for her candidacy through the formation of a new political movement, Armonía Siglo XXI (21st-Century Harmony). However, her candidature was disallowed by the Electoral Board in October, on the grounds that there were insufficient signatures in support of her movement. In all, 14 candidates were approved to contest the election. A reorganization of the Council of Ministers was undertaken in October, following the resignation of four ministers who announced their intention of standing as candidates in the legislative elections. In early 1995, despite the proximity of the elections, there was little political campaigning, owing to Peru's border conflict with Ecuador (see below). Opposition parties refrained from criticizing Fujimori, in the interest of maintaining national unity, which served to heighten media speculation that the conflict was manufactured to augment support for the President within the country.

In the presidential election, conducted on 9 April 1995, Fujimori, despite being the leading candidate, secured an unexpected outright victory over his closest opponent, Javier Pérez de Cuéllar (the former UN Secretary-General and the candidate of the Unión por el Perú—UPP), obtaining 64.42% of the total votes. In the concurrent legislative elections, Fujimori's coalition movement, Cambio 90-Nueva Mayoría (C90-NM), also secured a majority in the unicameral Congreso, winning 67 out of 120 seats. (The UPP won 17 seats and APRA eight.) The election results were criticized as fraudulent by opposition candidates and groupings, owing to the discovery of several thousand pre-marked election papers in a C90-NM local office prior to the elections; however, a team of OAS observers who monitored the elections confirmed the validity of the results.

Despite suggestions in 1990 that internal divisions were threatening to undermine the strength of SL, the transfer of political power in July appeared to intensify guerrilla activity. Assassination attempts and bomb attacks against government and military targets, strategic power installations, commercial enterprises and rural defence groups continued in the early 1990s. While a state of emergency continued to extend to some 50% of the population, the efforts of the armed forces to restore public order were hampered by improvements in the training and equipping of guerrilla forces, and were undermined by increasingly low morale within the ranks themselves, together with the erosion of public confidence in national security.

In June 1991 Fujimori was granted emergency legislative powers for 150 days in which to draft resolution proposals to address the national problems of economic and industrial instability (see above), drugs-trafficking and guerrilla activity. Accordingly, among more than 120 decrees issued by the President in November were emergency security provisions which sought to increase the powers of the armed forces, who were to be granted absolute access to prisons and universities (considered to be popular SL recruitment sites), and the right to override civilian authority in the expropriation of property and financial resources. Heavy penalties were to be imposed on those failing to comply with comprehensive censorship. The decrees prompted immediate condemnation from the political left and the trade unions.

Widespread concern was expressed that the suspension of the articles of the Constitution and the enforced dissolution of the Congreso (see above), effected by Fujimori in April 1992 (partly in response to continuing congressional opposition to his efforts to expand the role of the armed forces), would facilitate the assumption, by the security forces, of a greater degree of autonomy and of unprecedented rights of civil intervention. While the guerrilla response to the 'constitutional coup' was predictably violent (four people were killed and more than 20 were injured in a massive bomb attack on a Lima police station), Fujimori stressed his commitment to the eradication of terrorist violence by the end of his term of office in 1995.

During 1992 the Government enjoyed unprecedented success in its campaign to curtail internal terrorism, with the rearrest, in June, of Víctor Polay Campos, the supposed leader of the MRTA (who had escaped from detention in 1990) and, most significantly, with the capture, in September 1992, of Abimael Guzmán Reynoso, SL's founder and leader, together with 20 prominent SL members. In accordance with new anti-terrorist legislation, decreed by President Fujimori in July, Guzmán was tried by a military court, where he was found guilty of treason and sentenced to life imprisonment. SL, however, remained highly active, and in early 1993 was held responsible for the assassination of 20 candidates campaigning in local elections. A three-day 'armed strike' by the organization in May resulted in a stoppage by public transport workers in several cities, who feared that they might be the target of attacks. In August SL guerrillas killed at least 55 people, and mutilated children, in attacks on rural communities of Amazon Indians. A similar incident in the following month confirmed suspicions that the targets of such attacks were villages that had formed self-defence militia units. Despite the violence, and persistent terrorist acts in central Lima throughout 1993, the Government claimed continued success in combating subversive groups. In October Guzmán made several appeals to the Government, which were publicized by Fujimori prior to the constitutional referendum in order to promote his anti-terrorist measures, to commence a dialogue for peace and urged his organization to co-operate. In January 1994 the Government reported a split in the SL command between those supporting Guzmán's calls for peace and a faction advocating a continuation of the armed struggle. By the end of 1993, meanwhile, the MRTA was widely believed to be near collapse, owing to the arrests of many high-ranking activists and the surrender, in October, of a substantial number of its remaining members. The Government pursued its offensive against terrorist organizations during 1994, and publicized the detention of leading members of SL, the MRTA and the dissident SL Sendero Rojo faction. In early August the CCD approved the termination of the 'repentance' law, part of the Government's anti-terrorist legislation under which activists surrendering to the authorities frequently received a reduced or commuted sentence in return for co-operation or information, with effect from 1 November 1994. By that date an estimated total of 5,108 terrorists had surrendered under the terms of the law since its introduction in May 1992, of whom 3,485 had done so in 1994.

An anti-drugs programme, entitled 'Operation Snowcap', was relaunched by the Peruvian and US Governments in September 1989. In April 1990 it was announced that élite US forces were to be stationed in the Upper Huallaga river valley for the purpose of training Peruvian units in combating guerrillas and drugs-trafficking forces. In July 1991 a new joint initiative to combat the production and distribution of illicit drugs was finalized. Under the terms of the agreement, Peru was to receive US $34.9m. in military aid (to be concentrated in the Upper Huallaga region) and $60m. to be used for initiatives such as crop substitution in order to stabilize the economy. Critics of the agreement expressed concern that US interventionist ambitions were being encouraged by a clause that linked anti-guerrilla activity to efforts to counter drugs-traffickers. However, mounting international criticism of continuing abuses of human rights in Peru prompted the US Congress to suspend the disbursement of funding for the programme. In April 1992, following Fujimori's suspension of constitutional government, the US Government announced its intention to withhold disbursements of all non-humanitarian aid to Peru and to withdraw its élite forces from the Huallaga valley region. In January 1994 the Peruvian authorities stated that the US Government had, on humanitarian grounds, refused to disburse economic aid to Peru totalling some $105m. during 1993. In 1994 the US contribution to combat drugs-trafficking was reportedly reduced to $6m., while the Peruvian Government allocated some $300m. to counter the problem.

In February 1990, in Cartagena, Colombia, the Presidents of Peru, Colombia, Bolivia and the USA signed the Cartagena Declaration, pledging their Governments to intensify efforts to combat the consumption, production and trafficking of illegal drugs.

In Caracas, in May 1991, the presidents of the five South American nations comprising the Andean Group formalized their commitment to the full implementation of an Andean free-trade area by the end of 1995, to be achieved by a gradual reduction in tariffs and other trade barriers. In April 1994 Peru, which had suspended its membership of the organization in 1992, was readmitted as a full member of the Group, although it was to participate solely as an observer in the negotiations to establish a common external tariff.

The long-standing border dispute with Ecuador over the Cordillera del Cóndor erupted into a war in January 1981. A cease-fire was declared a few days later, under the auspices of the guarantors of the Rio de Janeiro Protocol of 1942, which had awarded the area, affording access to the Amazon river basin, to Peru. The border was eventually reopened in April 1981. Further skirmishes occurred in the border zone in January 1982 and again in January 1983. Renewed tension in the border zone in October 1991 had been defused by the end of the month after both sides withdrew troops from a potential confrontation and requested international arbitration in the dispute. The leaders of the two countries met to discuss the dispute, for the first time, during the 'summit' meeting of the Group of Rio in Colombia in December. In January 1992, in an address to the Ecuadorean Congress, Fujimori reiterated his proposal that a settlement should be concluded whereby navigation rights on the northern Peruvian Amazon would be guaranteed for Ecuador, and whereby the territorial boundaries would be decided in the context of the Rio de Janeiro Protocol. However, the Protocol has never been recognized by Ecuador, and, despite mutual efforts to achieve a constructive dialogue, the matter has continued to be a source of tension between the two countries. In early January 1995 a confrontation between Peruvian and Ecuadorean troops increased tensions along the disputed border in the Cordillera del Cóndor. Later that month serious fighting broke out, with each country accusing the other of initiating air and mortar attacks and of territorial violations. The dispute rapidly escalated, in spite of efforts on the part of the international community to mediate between the conflicting parties. Peru organized a large-scale movement of troops towards the border with Ecuador. In early February representatives of both countries, meeting under the auspices of the Rio de Janeiro Protocol guarantors (Argentina, Brazil, Chile and the USA), in Rio de Janeiro, Brazil, approved a provisional cease-fire. However, negotiations subsequently collapsed, owing to Ecuadorean concerns that the agreement would restrict its access to the Amazon River. Further negotiations secured an agreement which included the intention to commence bilateral talks to find a lasting solution to the dispute. Following the announcement of a unilateral cease-fire by Peru, both countries signed the Itamaraty Peace Declaration (so-called after the Palácio do Itamaraty in Brasília, the office of the Brazilian Ministry of Foreign Affairs) on 17 February. A few days later there were reports that the cease-fire had been violated by ongoing clashes around the Cenepa River valley. At the end of February Efraín Goldemberg and the Ecuadorean Minister of Foreign Affairs, meeting in Uruguay, signed the Montevideo Declaration, which reaffirmed the principles of the Itamaraty agreement, including the presence of international observers, and provided for the withdrawal of troops to assigned observation posts on either side of the border. Further breaches of the cease-fire were reported by both countries in late March; however, the initial separation of forces, conducted under the supervision of observers from the guarantor countries, was completed by early April. The complete withdrawal of forces from the disputed border area was achieved by mid-May. However, reports of further armed clashes prompted requests from both countries for an extension of the observer mission. At the end of May Fujimori accepted a proposal by the guarantor countries concerning the establishment of a demilitarized zone in the disputed Cenepa River region.

In January 1992 the presidents of Peru and Bolivia concluded an agreement whereby Bolivia would be granted access to the Pacific Ocean via the Peruvian port of Ilo (which would be jointly developed as a free zone). In return, Bolivia agreed to help facilitate Peruvian access to the Atlantic Ocean (through Brazil) by way of the Bolivian town of Puerto Suárez.

## Government

A new Constitution, that had been drafted by the Congreso Constituyente Democrático, was approved by a national referendum on 31 October 1993 and promulgated on 29 December. Under the Constitution, executive power is vested in the President, who is elected for a five-year term by universal adult suffrage and is eligible for re-election for a successive term of office. Two Vice-Presidents are also elected. The President governs with the assistance of an appointed Council of Ministers. Legislative power is vested in a single-chamber Congreso, consisting of 120 members, elected for five years by a single national list system. For administrative purposes, Peru comprises 25 departmental capital councils, 155 provincial councils and 1,586 district councils.

## Defence

Military service is selective and lasts for two years. In June 1994 the armed forces numbered 115,000 men (including an estimated 65,500 conscripts): an army of 75,000, a navy of 25,000 and an air force of 15,000. There are paramilitary police forces numbering 60,000 men. Defence and domestic security expenditure for 1994 was estimated at 1,646m. new soles.

## Economic Affairs

In 1993, according to estimates by the World Bank, Peru's gross national product (GNP), measured at average 1991–93 prices, was US $34,030m., equivalent to $1,490 per head. During 1985–93, it was estimated, GNP per head decreased, in real terms, at an average annual rate of 3.5%. Over the same period the population increased by an annual average of 2.1%. Peru's gross domestic product (GDP) decreased, in real terms, by an annual average of 0.6% in 1980–92. Real GDP declined by 2.4% in 1992 (owing largely to the effects of drought), but increased by an estimated 6.5% in 1993 and by 12.9% in 1994.

Agriculture (including fishing) contributed an estimated 6.6% of GDP in 1991. In 1992 some 33.0% of the total working population were employed in agriculture (including forestry and fishing). Rice, maize and potatoes are the principal food crops. Some 2,015,000 metric tons of cereals were imported in 1992. The principal cash crop is coffee (which accounted for an estimated 2.0% of total export earnings in 1992). Peru is the world's leading producer of coca, and the cultivation of this shrub, for the production of the illicit drug cocaine, reportedly generated revenue of US $1,000m. per year in the early 1990s. Revenue from the export of coca is believed to exceed revenue from legal exports. Fishing, particularly for the South American pilchard and the anchoveta, provides another important source of revenue. Fishmeal accounted for an estimated 12.6% of total export earnings in 1992. During 1980–92 agricultural GDP increased by an annual average of 1.7%.

Industry (including mining, manufacturing and construction) provided 36.6% of GDP in 1991, and the sector (including power) employed 16.9% of the working population in 1992. During 1980–92 industrial GDP decreased by an annual average of 0.5%.

Mining contributed 2.5% of GDP in 1991, and the mining sector employed 2.5% of the working population in 1992. Copper (which accounted for 23.1% of total export earnings in 1992), zinc, gold, petroleum and its derivatives, lead and silver are the major mineral exports. Export revenue from the mining sector amounted to an estimated US $1,800m. in 1994.

Manufacturing contributed an estimated 25.1% of GDP in 1991, and employed 10.4% of the working population in 1992. In 1988 the principal branches of manufacturing, measured by gross value of output, were food-processing (17.3%, excluding fish products), textiles and clothing, petroleum refineries, chemicals, machinery and transport equipment, metals and beverages. During 1980–92 manufacturing GDP decreased by an annual average of 0.7%.

Energy is derived principally from domestic supplies of petroleum and hydroelectric power, although an estimated 75% of the population were without electricity in the late 1980s. In 1992 industry was severely affected by a shortage of energy, as a result of drought in the highlands region (which reduced output from hydroelectric plants). In 1994 the Government initiated an extensive programme to develop the country's energy sector. A loan of US $177.7m., which was received from the Japanese Government in March 1995, was to be used to build new hydroelectric plants, and to repair existing power transmission facilities. Imports of fuel products comprised 11% of the value of merchandise imports in 1992.

In 1993 Peru recorded a visible trade deficit of US $580m. and there was a deficit of $1,800m. on the current account of the balance of payments. In 1991 the principal source of imports (25.7%) was the USA, which was also the principal market for exports (23.1%) in 1990. Other major trading partners were Japan, Colombia, Brazil, Argentina, the People's Republic of China and the United Kingdom. The principal exports in 1992 were metals (particularly copper, zinc and gold), fishmeal and petroleum and its derivatives. The principal imports in the same year were basic foodstuffs (particularly cereals).

In 1992 there was an estimated budgetary deficit of 927m. new soles, equivalent to 1.8% of GDP. Peru's external debt at the end of 1993 was US $20,328m., of which $16,123m. was long-term public debt. In that year the cost of debt-servicing was equivalent to 63.7% of exports of goods and services. The annual rate of inflation averaged 100.8% in 1990–94; annual inflation, which had averaged 409.5% in 1991, was 23.7% in 1994. An estimated 8.9% of the labour force in the capital, Lima, were unemployed in 1994. An estimated 50% of the total population were unemployed, or underemployed, in that year.

Peru is a member of the Andean Group (see p. 104), the Inter-American Development Bank (see p. 170) and the Latin American Integration Association (see p. 181), all of which encourage regional economic development, and of the Group of Rio (formerly the Group of Eight, see p. 247), which attempts to reduce regional indebtedness.

During the early 1990s the Fujimori administration undertook a major reform of the economy, achieving considerable success in restoring international reserves and in reducing the rate of inflation. By the implementation of economic liberalization measures and the repayment of arrears, relations were generally improved with the international financial community. In March 1993 the IMF approved a three-year (1993–96) credit of SDR 1,018m. With this support, the Government aimed to consolidate gains already made, envisaging real average GDP growth of 3.5% per year and annual inflation of less than 10% by the end of the period. Reforms of the taxation and banking systems were to be pursued, and the privatization of state concerns was to continue. (The 1993 Constitution guarantees equal conditions for foreign and international investors, and defines the State's role as being to invest resources only in strategic sectors of the economy.) Funding also ensued from the World Bank, and in May the 'Paris Club' of official creditors agreed to a rescheduling of some US $3,100m. of debt. Fujimori's re-election in April 1995 ensured the continuation of his economic reform programme, with renewed efforts to consolidate economic growth, to attract foreign investment (in particular by proceeding with privatization plans) and to promote exports. The fishing and minerals sectors represent the strongest potential growth sectors, the latter having attracted a record number of prospective applications from foreign investors in 1994, largely as a result of the decline in terrorist activity. The Government has pledged to increase investment in education and welfare projects in order to compensate for the social costs of the economic reform programme (notably large-scale job losses resulting from attempts to rationalize the public sector) and to alleviate the conditions of extreme poverty in which large sections of the population continue to live.

### Social Welfare

Social insurance is compulsory, and benefits cover sickness, disability and old age. There are separate systems for wage-earners and salaried employees. Labour legislation guarantees conditions of employment. A new social security pension law, introduced in 1974, established a single unified scheme for all employees. An emergency health care plan, implemented in 1981, included the inauguration of a nutrition fund to help young and expectant mothers, and the construction of 100 health centres in rural areas and shanty towns. The central Government proposed to spend 1,018m. new soles on health (6.3% of the total budget) in 1994. The Seguro Social del Perú (social security system) has its own budget, and there are also 106 public welfare agencies. In 1977 Peru had 437 hospital establishments, with a total of 29,934 beds, and in 1984 there were 18,200 physicians working in the country.

### Education

Reforms that were introduced after the 1968 revolution have instituted a three-level educational system. The first is for children up to six years of age in either nurseries or kindergartens. The second level, basic education, is free and, where possible, compulsory between six and 12 years of age. Primary education lasts for six years. Secondary education, beginning at the age of 12, is divided into two stages, of two and three years respectively. In 1988 some 95% of children in the relevant age-group were enrolled at primary schools, and in 1989 secondary enrolment included 42% of the appropriate age-group. Higher education includes the pre-university and university levels. There are 27 national and 19 private (two Roman Catholic) universities. There is also provision for adult literacy programmes and bilingual education. Under the new Constitution, adopted in 1993, the principle of free university education was abolished. In the 1994 budget, the Government allocated 2,608m. new soles for the education sector (16.1% of total expenditure). In 1972 adult illiteracy averaged 27.5% (males 16.7%; females 38.2%), but in rural areas the rate was 51.1%. By 1990, according to estimates by UNESCO, the rate had declined to 14.9% (males 8.5%; females 21.3%).

### Public Holidays

**1995:** 1 January (New Year's Day), 13 April (Maundy Thursday), 14 April (Good Friday), 1 May (Labour Day), 24 June (Day of the Peasant, half-day only), 29 June (St Peter and St Paul), 28–29 July (Independence), 30 August (St Rose of Lima), 1 November (All Saints' Day), 8 December (Immaculate Conception), 25 December (Christmas Day).

**1996:** 1 January (New Year's Day), 4 April (Maundy Thursday), 5 April (Good Friday), 1 May (Labour Day), 24 June (Day of the Peasant, half-day only), 29 June (St Peter and St Paul), 28–29 July (Independence), 30 August (St Rose of Lima), 1 November (All Saints' Day), 8 December (Immaculate Conception), 25 December (Christmas Day).

### Weights and Measures

The metric system is in force.

# Statistical Survey

Sources (unless otherwise stated): Banco Central de Reserva del Perú, Jirón Miró Quesada 441, Lima 1; tel. (14) 276250; telex 20169; Instituto Nacional de Estadística.

## Area and Population

### AREA, POPULATION AND DENSITY

| | |
|---|---:|
| Area (sq km) | |
|   Land | 1,280,000 |
|   Inland water | 5,216 |
|   Total | 1,285,216* |
| Population (census results)† | |
|   4 June 1972 | 13,538,208 |
|   12 July 1981 | |
|     Males | 8,456,957 |
|     Females | 8,548,253 |
|     Total | 17,005,210 |
| Population (official estimates at mid-year) | |
|   1990 | 21,550,322 |
|   1991 | 21,998,261 |
|   1992 | 22,453,861 |
| Density (per sq km) at mid-1992 | 17.5 |

\* 496,225 sq miles.

† Excluding adjustment for underenumeration, estimated at 3.9% in 1972 and 4.1% in 1981. The adjusted total for 1972 was 14,121,564, including an estimate of 39,800 for Indian jungle inhabitants.

### PRINCIPAL TOWNS
(estimated population of towns and urban environs at mid-1990)

| | | | | |
|---|---:|---|---|---:|
| Lima (capital) | 6,414,500* | | Huancayo | 207,600 |
| Arequipa | 634,500 | | Huánuco | 169,150‡ |
| Trujillo | 532,000 | | Sullana | 154,800 |
| Callao | 515,200† | | Pucallpa | 153,000 |
| Chiclayo | 426,300 | | Ica | 152,300 |
| Piura | 324,500 | | Tacna | 150,200 |
| Chimbote | 296,600 | | Santa | 145,500§ |
| Cuzco | 275,000 | | Juliaca | 134,200 |
| Iquitos | 269,500 | | Ayacucho | 101,600 |

\* Metropolitan area (Gran Lima) only.

† Estimated population of town, excluding urban environs, at mid-1985.

‡ Population at 1981 census.

§ Estimated population of town, excluding urban environs, at mid-1988.

Source: mainly UN, *Demographic Yearbook*.

PERU  
*Statistical Survey*

## BIRTHS AND DEATHS*
(excluding Indian jungle population)

| | Live births Number | Rate (per 1,000) | Deaths Number | Rate (per 1,000) |
|---|---|---|---|---|
| 1983 | 689,000 | 36.8 | 199,000 | 10.6 |
| 1984 | 698,000 | 36.4 | 198,000 | 10.3 |
| 1985 | 699,000 | 36.0 | 196,000 | 10.1 |
| 1986 | 714,000 | 35.3 | 196,000 | 9.7 |
| 1987 | 721,000 | 34.8 | 194,000 | 9.4 |
| 1988 | 727,000 | 34.2 | 192,000 | 9.0 |
| 1989 | 730,000 | 33.5 | 189,000 | 8.7 |
| 1990 | 734,000 | 32.9 | 186,000† | 8.3† |

* Data are tabulated by year of registration rather than by year of occurrence. Registration is incomplete but the figures include an upward adjustment for under-registration.
† Provisional.

**1992:** Live births 651,500, Rate (per 1,000) 29.0; Deaths 170,070, Rate (per 1,000) 7.6.

**Expectation of life** (excluding Indian jungle population, years at birth, 1990): males 62.93; females 66.58 (Source: UN, *Demographic Yearbook*).

## ECONOMICALLY ACTIVE POPULATION
('000 persons)

| | 1990 | 1991 | 1992 |
|---|---|---|---|
| Agriculture, hunting, forestry and fishing | 2,575 | 2,604 | 2,658 |
| Mining and quarrying | 181 | 190 | 198 |
| Manufacturing | 792 | 816 | 840 |
| Electricity, gas and water | 23 | 24 | 25 |
| Construction | 280 | 288 | 300 |
| Business services | 1,176 | 1,235 | 1,297 |
| Transport | 332 | 345 | 355 |
| Financial services | 181 | 187 | 192 |
| Other services | 2,036 | 2,118 | 2,199 |
| **Total** | **7,576** | **7,807** | **8,064** |

# Agriculture

## PRINCIPAL CROPS ('000 metric tons)

| | 1991 | 1992 | 1993 |
|---|---|---|---|
| Wheat | 127 | 73 | 108 |
| Rice (paddy) | 814 | 829 | 950 |
| Barley | 117 | 69 | 50* |
| Maize | 660 | 520 | 785 |
| Potatoes | 1,451 | 998 | 1,475 |
| Sweet potatoes | 140 | 126 | 175* |
| Cassava | 406 | 386 | 290* |
| Seed cotton | 176 | 108 | 94 |
| Palm oil† | 23.1 | 25.0 | 25.0 |
| Tomatoes | 76 | 86 | 85* |
| Pumpkins, squash and gourds* | 65 | 65 | 65 |
| Onions (dry) | 125 | 115 | 115* |
| Sugar cane* | 6,500 | 5,500 | 5,000 |
| Oranges | 174 | 184 | 184* |
| Lemons and limes | 224 | 203 | 205* |
| Avocados | 44 | 44* | 44* |
| Mangoes | 68 | 66 | 56* |
| Pineapples | 76 | 76* | 77* |
| Plantains | 809 | 699 | 710 |
| Coffee (green) | 83 | 87 | 86 |
| Cocoa (beans) | 15 | 15* | 15* |
| Tea (made) | 2 | 2* | 2* |

* FAO estimate(s).   † Unofficial figures.
Source: FAO, *Production Yearbook*.

## LIVESTOCK ('000 head, year ending September)

| | 1991 | 1992 | 1993 |
|---|---|---|---|
| Horses* | 660 | 665 | 665 |
| Mules* | 222 | 224 | 224 |
| Asses* | 500 | 520 | 520 |
| Cattle | 4,042 | 3,972 | 3,950 |
| Pigs | 2,417 | 2,396 | 2,400 |
| Sheep | 12,226 | 11,912 | 11,915 |
| Goats | 1,747 | 1,776 | 1,780 |

Poultry (million): 67 in 1991; 63 in 1992; 60 in 1993.
* FAO estimate(s).
Source: FAO, *Production Yearbook*.

## LIVESTOCK PRODUCTS ('000 metric tons)

| | 1991 | 1992 | 1993 |
|---|---|---|---|
| Beef and veal | 109 | 111 | 105 |
| Mutton and lamb | 19 | 19 | 19 |
| Goat meat | 9 | 9 | 9 |
| Pig meat* | 84 | 88 | 91 |
| Poultry meat | 292 | 320 | 303 |
| Other meat | 37 | 38 | 35 |
| Cows' milk | 786 | 768 | 795 |
| Goats' milk† | 19 | 19 | 19 |
| Cheese† | 18.9 | 20.0 | 20.0 |
| Poultry eggs | 117.0 | 106.7 | 107.0 |
| Wool: | | | |
| greasy | 9.8 | 9.6 | 9.5 |
| clean* | 4.9 | 4.8 | 4.8 |
| Cattle hides† | 15.7 | 14.1 | 13.8 |
| Sheepskins† | 6.6 | 7.0 | 7.0 |

* Unofficial estimates.   † FAO estimates.
Source: FAO, *Production Yearbook*.

# Forestry

## ROUNDWOOD REMOVALS
('000 cubic metres, excluding bark)

| | 1990 | 1991 | 1992 |
|---|---|---|---|
| Sawlogs, veneer logs and logs for sleepers | 1,056 | 920 | 920 |
| Pulpwood* | 5 | 5 | 5 |
| Other industrial wood* | 88 | 88 | 88 |
| Fuel wood | 6,590 | 6,813 | 6,813 |
| **Total** | **7,739** | **7,826** | **7,826** |

* FAO estimates (annual output assumed to be unchanged since 1982).
Source: FAO, *Yearbook of Forest Products*.

## SAWNWOOD PRODUCTION
('000 cubic metres, including railway sleepers)

| | 1990 | 1991 | 1992* |
|---|---|---|---|
| Coniferous (softwood) | 5 | 5 | 5 |
| Broadleaved (hardwood) | 494 | 481 | 481 |
| **Total** | **499** | **486** | **486** |

* FAO estimates.
Source: FAO, *Yearbook of Forest Products*.

PERU                                                                                                          *Statistical Survey*

## Fishing

('000 metric tons, live weight)

|  | 1990 | 1991 | 1992 |
|---|---|---|---|
| Chilean jack mackerel | 191.1 | 136.3 | 96.4 |
| South American pilchard (sardine) | 3,265.3 | 3,398.4 | 2,296.5 |
| Anchoveta (Peruvian anchovy) | 2,926.4 | 3,081.0 | 4,163.7 |
| Other fishes (incl. unspecified) | 425.3 | 219.4 | 197.6 |
| **Total fish** | 6,808.1 | 6,835.1 | 6,754.1 |
| Other aquatic animals | 67.0 | 114.3 | 88.6 |
| **Total catch*** | 6,875.1 | 6,949.4 | 6,842.7 |
| Inland waters | 31.3 | 30.0 | 29.5 |
| Pacific Ocean | 6,843.8 | 6,919.4 | 6,813.2 |

* Excluding aquatic plants ('000 metric tons): 0.3 in 1990; 0.1 in 1991; 0.3 in 1992.

Source: FAO, *Yearbook of Fishery Statistics*.

## Mining*

|  | 1988 | 1989 | 1990 |
|---|---|---|---|
| Crude petroleum ('000 barrels) | 51,717 | 47,597 | 47,050 |
| Natural gas ('000 terajoules)† | 24 | 20 | 20 |
| Coal ('000 metric tons)†‡ | 160 | 145 | 145 |
| Copper ('000 metric tons) | 316 | 368 | 323 |
| Lead ('000 metric tons) | 161 | 203 | 210 |
| Zinc ('000 metric tons) | 499 | 621 | 598 |
| Tin (metric tons)† | 4,181 | 5,082 | 5,134 |
| Iron ore ('000 metric tons) | 2,838 | 2,954 | 2,181 |
| Tungsten (metric tons)† | 825 | 1,228 | 1,372 |
| Molybdenum (metric tons)† | 4,000 | 5,000 | 2,000 |
| Silver (metric tons) | 1,650 | 1,932 | 1,928 |
| Gold (kilograms)† | 9,720 | 9,898 | 6,850 |

* Figures for metallic minerals refer to metal content only.
† Source: UN, *Industrial Statistics Yearbook*.
‡ Estimates.

**1991** ('000 metric tons, unless otherwise indicated): Crude petroleum ('000 barrels) 41,898; Copper 382; Lead 200; Zinc 628; Iron ore 2,347; Silver (metric tons) 1,769.

**1992** ('000 metric tons, unless otherwise indicated): Crude petroleum ('000 barrels) 42,298; Copper 369; Lead 194; Zinc 603; Iron ore 1,849; Silver (metric tons) 1,572.

Source: Ministry of Energy and Mines.

## Industry

**SELECTED PRODUCTS**
('000 metric tons, unless otherwise indicated)

|  | 1989 | 1990 | 1991 |
|---|---|---|---|
| Canned fish | 57.5 | 39.6 | 24.8 |
| Prepared animal feeds | 580 | 494 | 543 |
| Wheat flour | 893 | 479 | 599 |
| Raw sugar | 607 | 590 | 562 |
| Beer ('000 hectolitres) | 5,548 | 5,844 | 6,711 |
| Cigarettes (million) | 2,439 | 2,673 | 2,695 |
| Rubber tyres ('000) | 710 | 745 | 682 |
| Motor spirit (petrol) | 1,184 | 1,101 | n.a. |
| Kerosene | 843 | 741 | n.a. |
| Distillate fuel oils | 1,162 | 1,174 | n.a. |
| Residual fuel oils | 3,450 | 3,552 | n.a. |
| Cement | 2,105 | 2,185 | 2,103 |
| Crude steel | 265 | 168 | 225 |
| Copper (refined) | 220.1 | 181.5 | 244.5 |
| Lead (refined) | 68.8 | 69.8 | 74.5 |
| Zinc (refined) | 137.1 | 121.7 | 154.3 |
| Electric energy (million kWh) | 13,358 | 13,817 | 14,503 |

## Finance

**CURRENCY AND EXCHANGE RATES**

**Monetary Units**
100 céntimos = 1 nuevo sol (new sol).

**Sterling and Dollar Equivalents** (31 December 1994)
£1 sterling = 3.411 new soles;
US $1 = 2.180 new soles;
100 new soles = £29.32 = $45.87.

**Average Exchange Rate** (new soles per US $)
1992  1.2458
1993  1.9883
1994  2.1950

Note: On 1 February 1985 Peru replaced its former currency, the sol, by the inti, valued at 1,000 soles. A new currency, the nuevo sol (equivalent to 1m. intis), was introduced in July 1991.

**BUDGET** ('000 new soles)

| Revenue | 1990 | 1991 | 1992* |
|---|---|---|---|
| Taxes on earnings | 37,071 | 249,584 | 749,090 |
| Income tax | 36,631 | 242,818 | 744,329 |
| Other taxes | 440 | 6,766 | 4,761 |
| Wealth taxes | 48,107 | 177,162 | 201,276 |
| Import duties | 62,667 | 293,488 | 549,367 |
| Export duties | 2,031 | 1,452 | 0 |
| Taxes on production and consumption | 325,656 | 1,846,189 | 3,304,448 |
| Goods and services | 95,046 | 649,317 | 1,457,913 |
| Mineral fuel receipts | 150,645 | 781,482 | 1,099,781 |
| Others | 79,965 | 415,390 | 746,754 |
| Other tax revenue | 127,181 | 243,857 | 170,002 |
| Adjustment of tax revenue to cash basis | −31,005 | −78,044 | −71,214 |
| Other current revenue | 25,789 | 275,078 | 857,254 |
| **Total** | 597,497 | 3,008,766 | 5,760,223 |

* Figures are preliminary.

| Expenditure | 1990 | 1991 | 1992* |
|---|---|---|---|
| Current expenditure | 744,117 | 3,016,767 | 5,490,771 |
| Remuneration | 151,012 | 683,776 | 1,375,276 |
| Goods and services | 51,075 | 209,745 | 418,849 |
| Transfers | 187,151 | 779,788 | 1,593,025 |
| Public institutions | 13,222 | 11,674 | 47,436 |
| Local government, public institutions and public welfare agencies | 33,945 | 257,815 | 444,188 |
| Pensions and others | 139,984 | 510,299 | 1,101,401 |
| Interest | 225,120 | 864,842 | 1,102,567 |
| Internal debt | 78,840 | 205,345 | 102,377 |
| External debt | 146,280 | 659,497 | 1,000,190 |
| Defence and domestic security | 129,759 | 478,616 | 1,001,054 |
| Capital expenditure | 87,831 | 478,874 | 1,273,752 |
| Gross capital formation | 77,769 | 400,653 | 766,334 |
| Transfers | 9,883 | 63,669 | 434,832 |
| Non-financial public companies | 3,679 | 3,693 | 38,913 |
| Financial public companies | 263 | 0 | 0 |
| Local government, public institutions and public welfare agencies | 5,941 | 59,976 | 395,919 |
| Other capital expenditure | 179 | 14,552 | 72,586 |
| **Total** | 831,948 | 3,495,641 | 6,764,523 |

* Figures are preliminary.

**INTERNATIONAL RESERVES**
(US $ million at 31 December)

|  | 1991 | 1992 | 1993 |
|---|---|---|---|
| Gold* | 556.5 | 515.6 | 434.0 |
| IMF special drawing rights | — | — | 0.9 |
| Foreign exchange | 2,443.0 | 2,849.0 | 3,407.0 |
| **Total** | 2,999.5 | 3,364.6 | 3,841.9 |

* National valuation.

Source: IMF, *International Financial Statistics*.

# PERU

## Statistical Survey

### MONEY SUPPLY (million new soles at 31 December)

|  | 1990 | 1991 | 1992 |
|---|---|---|---|
| Currency outside banks | 273 | 643 | 1,101 |
| Demand deposits at commercial and development banks | 275 | 656 | 1,298 |
| **Total money** (incl. others) | 708 | 1,608 | 2,884 |

Source: IMF, *International Financial Statistics*.

### COST OF LIVING
(Consumer Price Index, Lima metropolitan area; base: 1990 = 100)

|  | 1991 | 1992 | 1993 |
|---|---|---|---|
| Food | 448.2 | 769.9 | n.a. |
| All items | 509.5 | 884.2 | 1,313.7 |

Source: ILO, *Year Book of Labour Statistics*.

### NATIONAL ACCOUNTS
**National Income and Product**
('000 new soles at current prices)

|  | 1989 | 1990 | 1991 |
|---|---|---|---|
| Compensation of employees | 31,356 | 1,719,943 | 5,533,638 |
| Operating surplus | 70,543 | 4,407,995 | 25,106,377 |
| **Domestic factor incomes** | 101,899 | 6,127,938 | 30,640,015 |
| Consumption of fixed capital | 7,818 | 431,058 | 2,180,329 |
| **Gross domestic product (GDP) at factor cost** | 109,717 | 6,558,996 | 32,820,344 |
| Indirect taxes | 6,495 | 517,980 | 2,359,192 |
| Less Subsidies | 1,097 | 35,976 | 27,829 |
| **GDP in purchasers' values** | 115,115 | 7,041,000 | 35,151,707 |
| Factor income received from abroad | 881 | 35,086 | −751,738 |
| Less Factor income paid abroad | 2,498 | 212,567 |  |
| **Gross national product** | 113,498 | 6,863,519 | 34,399,969 |
| Less Consumption of fixed capital | 7,818 | 431,058 | 2,180,328 |
| **National income in market prices** | 105,680 | 6,432,461 | 32,219,641 |
| Other current transfers from abroad | 835 | 47,317 | 174,731 |
| Less Other current transfers paid abroad | 55 | 834 |  |
| **National disposable income** | 106,460 | 6,478,944 | 32,394,372 |

Source: UN, *National Accounts Statistics*.

### Expenditure on the Gross Domestic Product
(million new soles at current prices)

|  | 1991 | 1992 | 1993 |
|---|---|---|---|
| Government final consumption expenditure | 1,803 | 3,481 | 5,321 |
| Private final consumption expenditure | 26,216 | 41,795 | 63,788 |
| Increase in stocks | 739 | 680 | 1,446 |
| Gross fixed capital formation | 4,711 | 8,036 | 13,648 |
| **Total domestic expenditure** | 33,469 | 53,992 | 84,203 |
| Exports of goods and services | 3,201 | 5,389 | 8,628 |
| Less Imports of goods and services | 3,811 | 6,983 | 11,189 |
| **GDP in purchasers' values** | 32,857 | 52,398 | 81,641 |
| **GDP at constant 1990 prices** | 6,598 | 6,443 | 6,858 |

Source: IMF, *International Financial Statistics*.

### Gross Domestic Product by Economic Activity
('000 new soles at current prices)

|  | 1989 | 1990 | 1991 |
|---|---|---|---|
| Agriculture, hunting, forestry and fishing | 9,256 | 476,633 | 2,323,413 |
| Mining and quarrying | 3,212 | 191,241 | 847,737 |
| Manufacturing | 29,090 | 1,939,762 | 8,782,634 |
| Electricity, gas and water | 404 | 40,185 | 201,532 |
| Construction | 8,948 | 533,512 | 3,012,457 |
| Trade, restaurants and hotels | 21,963 | 1,315,720 | 6,584,540 |
| Transport, storage and communications | 5,706 | 338,626 | 2,086,149 |
| Finance, insurance, real estate, etc. | 15,081 | 1,018,692 | 6,179,769 |
| Community, social and personal services | 10,263 | 677,046 | 3,472,164 |
| Government services | 9,579 | 468,630 | 959,763 |
| Other producers | 1,738 | 119,239 | 598,710 |
| **Sub-total** | 115,239 | 7,119,286 | 35,048,868 |
| Less Imputed bank service charge | 1,340 | 145,452 | 207,578 |
| Import duties | 1,215 | 67,166 | 310,417 |
| **GDP in purchasers' values** | 115,115 | 7,041,000 | 35,151,707 |

Source: UN, *National Accounts Statistics*.

### BALANCE OF PAYMENTS (US $ million)

|  | 1991 | 1992 | 1993 |
|---|---|---|---|
| Merchandise exports f.o.b. | 3,330 | 3,485 | 3,463 |
| Merchandise imports f.o.b. | −3,495 | −4,050 | −4,043 |
| **Trade balance** | −165 | −565 | −580 |
| Exports of services | 877 | 846 | 892 |
| Imports of services | −1,329 | −1,514 | −1,548 |
| Other income received | 117 | 137 | 153 |
| Other income paid | −1,149 | −1,047 | −1,134 |
| Unrequited transfers (net) | 318 | 433 | 417 |
| **Current balance** | −1,331 | −1,710 | −1,800 |
| Direct investment (net) | −7 | 127 | 349 |
| Portfolio investment (net) | — | — | 222 |
| Other capital (net) | −959 | −190 | −355 |
| Net errors and omissions | 1,618 | 1,347 | 1,037 |
| **Overall balance** | −679 | −426 | −547 |

Source: IMF, *International Financial Statistics*.

## External Trade

### PRINCIPAL COMMODITIES (US $ million)

| Imports | 1990 | 1991* | 1992* |
|---|---|---|---|
| Consumer goods | 339 | 638 | 841 |
| Wheat | 141 | 92 | 104 |
| Maize and sorghum | 59 | 59 | 82 |
| Rice | 83 | 75 | 77 |
| Capital goods | 886 | 934 | 1,120 |
| **Total** (incl. others) | 2,891 | 3,494 | 4,051 |

| Exports | 1990 | 1991* | 1992* |
|---|---|---|---|
| Fishmeal | 336 | 467 | 440 |
| Coffee | 98 | 119 | 69 |
| Copper | 700 | 738 | 806 |
| Gold | 9 | 137 | 215 |
| Silver | 79 | 68 | 78 |
| Lead | 185 | 162 | 161 |
| Zinc | 416 | 324 | 335 |
| Petroleum and derivatives | 258 | 169 | 196 |
| **Total** (incl. others) | 3,231 | 3,329 | 3,484 |

* Figures are preliminary.

# PERU

## PRINCIPAL TRADING PARTNERS (US $ million)

| Imports f.o.b. | 1989 | 1990 | 1991 |
|---|---|---|---|
| Argentina | 164.4 | 231.9 | 206.6 |
| Belgium-Luxembourg | 43.8 | 45.2 | 28.1 |
| Brazil | 124.6 | 168.1 | 166.5 |
| Canada | 34.8 | 44.3 | 64.9 |
| Chile | 44.4 | 88.5 | 85.7 |
| Colombia | 75.6 | 101.3 | 212.2 |
| Ecuador | 103.6 | 138.5 | 134.7 |
| France (incl. Monaco) | 34.1 | 32.1 | 35.1 |
| Germany | 119.5 | 173.0 | 167.2 |
| Italy | 63.0 | 79.2 | 110.9 |
| Japan | 86.7 | 90.5 | 173.2 |
| Mexico | 48.3 | 99.4 | 85.1 |
| Panama | 13.2 | 12.8 | 31.7 |
| Spain | 24.4 | 31.7 | 27.7 |
| Sweden | 38.4 | 58.1 | 55.5 |
| Switzerland-Liechtenstein | 33.8 | 51.8 | 39.5 |
| United Kingdom | 55.3 | 49.9 | 52.6 |
| USA | 621.4 | 743.6 | 723.4 |
| Venezuela | 36.2 | 56.4 | 99.2 |
| **Total** (incl. others) | 2,008.6 | 2,634.0 | 2,813.4 |

| Exports f.o.b. | 1988 | 1989 | 1990 |
|---|---|---|---|
| Belgium-Luxembourg | 123.8 | 116.9 | 151.5 |
| Bolivia | 5.4 | 13.0 | 34.3 |
| Brazil | 62.2 | 102.3 | 105.8 |
| Chile | 30.0 | 59.3 | 56.8 |
| China, People's Republic | 111.5 | 71.8 | 55.5 |
| Colombia | 60.8 | 76.6 | 94.1 |
| France (incl. Monaco) | 39.2 | 29.6 | 56.0 |
| Germany | 138.5 | 207.4 | 252.9 |
| Italy | 118.8 | 116.3 | 273.4 |
| Japan | 270.0 | 301.2 | 420.1 |
| Korea, Republic | 16.0 | 33.8 | 65.3 |
| Mexico | 20.3 | 53.2 | 39.8 |
| Netherlands | 91.1 | 88.3 | 109.6 |
| Spain | 46.7 | 32.8 | 40.5 |
| USSR | 25.4 | 120.1 | 63.3 |
| United Kingdom | 244.4 | 125.7 | 149.1 |
| USA | 599.3 | 730.4 | 764.1 |
| Venezuela | 71.6 | 37.4 | 57.6 |
| Yugoslavia | 26.2 | 29.5 | 48.2 |
| **Total** (incl. others) | 2,506.5 | 2,757.8 | 3,312.8 |

Source: UN, *International Trade Statistics Yearbook*.

## Transport

### RAILWAYS (traffic)

|  | 1989 | 1990 | 1991 |
|---|---|---|---|
| Passenger-km (million) | 659 | 469 | 320 |
| Freight ton-km (million) | 929 | 894 | 827 |

Source: UN, *Statistical Yearbook*.

### ROAD TRAFFIC ('000 motor vehicles in use)

|  | 1989 | 1990 | 1991 |
|---|---|---|---|
| Passenger cars | 372.8 | 368.2 | 379.1 |
| Commercial vehicles | 239.5 | 237.4 | 244.9 |

Source: UN, *Statistical Yearbook*.

### SHIPPING
**Merchant Fleet** (vessels registered at 30 June)

|  | 1990 | 1991 | 1992 |
|---|---|---|---|
| Total displacement ('000 grt) | 617 | 605 | 433 |

Source: UN, *Statistical Yearbook*.

### International Sea-Borne Shipping
(freight traffic, '000 metric tons)

|  | 1988 | 1989 | 1990 |
|---|---|---|---|
| Goods loaded | 8,851 | 9,402 | 10,197 |
| Goods unloaded | 5,020 | 5,059 | 5,077 |

Source: UN, *Monthly Bulletin of Statistics*.

### CIVIL AVIATION (traffic on scheduled services)

|  | 1990 | 1991 | 1992 |
|---|---|---|---|
| Kilometres flown (million) | 20 | 19 | 19 |
| Passengers carried ('000) | 1,816 | 1,491 | 1,330 |
| Passenger-km (million) | 2,025 | 1,759 | 1,526 |
| Total ton-km (million) | 216 | 184 | 178 |

Source: UN, *Statistical Yearbook*.

## Tourism

|  | 1990 | 1991 | 1992 |
|---|---|---|---|
| Tourist arrivals | 316,973 | 232,012 | 216,534 |
| Receipts (US $ million) | 259 | 252 | 237 |

Source: UN, *Statistical Yearbook*.

## Communications Media

|  | 1990 | 1991 | 1992 |
|---|---|---|---|
| Radio receivers ('000 in use) | 5,450 | 5,570 | 5,700 |
| Television receivers ('000 in use) | 2,080 | 2,150 | 2,200 |
| Telephones ('000 in use) | 769 | n.a. | n.a. |
| Daily newspapers |  |  |  |
|   Number | 66 | n.a. | 59 |
|   Estimated average circulation ('000 copies) | 1,700 | n.a. | 1,590 |

Book production: 1,063 titles in 1991.

Sources: UNESCO, *Statistical Yearbook*; UN, *Statistical Yearbook*.

## Education

(1991)

|  | Institutions* | Teachers | Pupils |
|---|---|---|---|
| Nursery | 9,649 | 25,319 | 874,433 |
| Primary | 28,860 | 139,284 | 4,080,184 |
| Secondary | 6,462 | 97,715 | 2,018,766 |
| Higher | 447 | 15,642 | 275,525 |
| University | 46 | 28,901 | 475,706 |
| Special | 367 | 2,578 | 22,192 |
| Occupational | 1,157 | 9,255 | 309,313 |

* Figures refer to 1990.

Source: Ministerio de Educación.

**1992**: Primary teachers 135,502, pupils 3,853,098; Secondary teachers 87,624, pupils 1,703,997; University teachers 30,098, students 510,911 (Source: UNESCO, *Statistical Yearbook*).

# Directory

## The Constitution

In 1993 the Congreso Constituyente Democrático (CCD) began drafting a new constitution to replace the 1979 Constitution. The CCD approved the final document in September 1993, and the Constitution was endorsed by a popular national referendum that was conducted on 31 October. The Constitution was promulgated on 29 December 1993.

### THE EXECUTIVE POWER

Executive power is vested in the President, who is elected for a five-year term of office by universal adult suffrage; this mandate is renewable once. The successful presidential candidate must obtain at least 50% of the votes cast, and a second round of voting is held if necessary. Two Vice-Presidents are elected in simultaneous rounds of voting. The President is competent to initiate and submit draft bills, to review laws drafted by the legislature (Congreso) and, if delegated by the Congreso, to enact laws. The President is empowered to appoint ambassadors and senior military officials without congressional ratification, and retains the right to dissolve parliament if two or more ministers have been censured or have received a vote of 'no confidence' by the Congreso. In certain circumstances the President may, in accordance with the Council of Ministers, declare a state of emergency for a period of 60 days, during which individual constitutional rights are suspended and the armed forces may assume control of civil order. The President appoints the Council of Ministers.

### THE LEGISLATIVE POWER

Legislative power is vested in a single-chamber Congreso (removing the distinction in the 1979 Constitution of an upper and lower house) consisting of 120 members. The members of the Congreso are elected for a four-year term by universal adult suffrage from national party lists. The Congreso is responsible for approving the budget, for endorsing loans and international treaties and for drafting and approving bills. It may conduct investigations into matters of public concern, and question and censure the Council of Ministers and its individual members. Members of the Congreso elect a Standing Committee, to consist of not more than 25% of the total number of members (representation being proportional to the different political groupings in the legislature), which is empowered to make certain official appointments, approve credit loans and transfers relating to the budget during a parliamentary recess, and conduct other business as delegated by parliament.

### THE ELECTORAL SYSTEM

All citizens of more than 18 years of age, including illiterate persons, are eligible to vote. Voting in elections is compulsory for all citizens until they reach 70 years of age, when it becomes optional.

### THE JUDICIAL POWER

Judicial power is vested in the Supreme Court of Justice and other tribunals. The Constitution provides for the establishment of a National Council of the Judiciary, consisting of nine independently-elected members, which is empowered to appoint judges to the Supreme Court. An independent Constitutional Court, comprising seven members elected by the Congreso for a five-year term, may interpret the Constitution and declare legislation and acts of government to be unconstitutional.

The death penalty may be applied by the Judiciary in cases of terrorism or of treason (the latter in times of war).

Under the Constitution, a People's Counsel is elected by the Congreso with a five-year mandate which authorizes the Counsel to defend the constitutional and fundamental rights of the individual. The Counsel may draft laws and present evidence to the legislature.

According to the Constitution, the State promotes economic and social development, particularly in the areas of employment, health, education, security, public services and infrastructure. The State recognizes a plurality of economic ownership and activity, supports free competition, and promotes the growth of small businesses. Private initiative is permitted within the framework of a social market economy. The State also guarantees the free exchange of foreign currency.

## The Government

### HEAD OF STATE

**President:** ALBERTO FUJIMORI (sworn in 28 July 1990; re-elected 9 April 1995).
**First Vice-President:** RICARDO MÁRQUEZ FLORES.
**Second Vice-President:** CÉSAR PAREDES CANTO.

### COUNCIL OF MINISTERS
(June 1995)

**Prime Minister and Minister of Foreign Affairs:** EFRAÍN GOLDEMBERG SCHREIBER.
**Minister of the Interior:** Gen. JUAN BRIONES DÁVILA.
**Minister of Energy and Mines:** AMADO YATACO.
**Minister of Economy and Finance:** JORGE CAMET DICKMAN.
**Minister of Public Education:** DANTE CÓRDOVA.
**Minister of Labour and Social Promotion:** AUGUSTO ANTONIOLLI VÁSQUEZ.
**Minister of Industry, Tourism, Integration and International Trade Negotiations:** LILIANA CANALE.
**Minister of Transport, Communications, Housing and Construction:** JUAN CASTILLO MEZA.
**Minister of Health:** EDUARDO YONG MOTTA.
**Minister of Agriculture:** ABSALÓN VÁSQUEZ VILLANUEVA.
**Minister of Fisheries:** JAIME AGUSTÍN SOBERO TAIRA.
**Minister of Justice:** Dr FERNANDO VEGA SANTA GADEA.
**Minister of Defence:** Gen. VÍCTOR MALCA VILLANUEVA.
**Minister of the Presidency:** MANUEL VARA OCHOA.
**Comptroller-General:** MARÍA HERMINIA DRAGO CORREA.
**President of Joint Command of the Armed Forces:** Gen. ARNALDO VELARDE RAMÍREZ (Air Force).

### MINISTRIES

**Prime Minister's Office:** Ucayali 363, Lima; tel. (14) 273860; telex 20467; fax (14) 323266.
**Ministry of Agriculture and Food:** Avda Salaverry s/n, Edif. Ministerio de Trabajo, Lima; tel. (14) 324040; telex 25835; fax (14) 320990.
**Ministry of Defence:** Avda Arequipa 291, Lima 1; tel (14) 324040; telex 25835; fax (14) 320990.
**Ministry of Economy and Finance:** Jirón Junín 319, Lima; tel. (14) 289550; telex 20187; fax (14) 328495.
**Ministry of Energy and Mines:** Avda Las Artes s/n, San Borja, Apdo 2600, Lima 100; tel. (14) 750065; telex 25731; fax (14) 750689.
**Ministry of Fisheries:** Avda Javier Prado Este 2465, San Luis, Lima; tel. (14) 362630; telex 21058; fax (14) 704101.
**Ministry of Foreign Affairs:** Ucayali 363, Lima; tel. (14) 273860; telex 20467; fax (14) 323266.
**Ministry of Health:** Cuadra Avda Salaverry 8, Jesús María, Lima 11; tel. (14) 326242; fax (14) 313671.
**Ministry of Industry, Tourism, Integration and International Trade Negotiations:** Calle 1 Oeste, Corpac, San Isidro, Lima 27; tel. (14) 400436; telex 20194; fax (14) 415388.
**Ministry of the Interior:** Plaza 30 de Agosto 150, San Isidro, Lima; tel. (14) 411913; telex 21697; fax (14) 415128.
**Ministry of Justice:** Edif. del Banco Continental, 7°, Esq. de la Avda Emancipación y Jirón Lampa, Lima; tel. (14) 278181.
**Ministry of Labour and of Social Promotion:** Avda Salaverry s/n, Jesús María, Lima; tel. (14) 322510.
**Ministry of the Presidency:** Centro Cívico, 4°, Avda Garcilaso de la Vega 1351, Lima 1; tel. (14) 320298.
**Ministry of Public Education:** Instituto Nacional de Cultura, Jirón Ancash 390, Apdo 5247, Lima; tel. (14) 275680; telex 25803; fax (14) 330230.
**Ministry of Transport, Communications, Housing and Construction:** Avda 28 de Julio 800, Lima; tel. (14) 333790; telex 25511; fax (14) 333402.

## President and Legislature

### PRESIDENT
**Election, 9 April 1995**

| Candidate | % of votes cast |
| --- | --- |
| ALBERTO FUJIMORI (C90-NM) | 64.42 |
| JAVIER PÉREZ DE CUÉLLAR (UPP) | 21.81 |
| MERCEDES CABANILLAS (APRA) | 4.11 |
| ALEJANDRO TOLEDOA (Code—País Posible) | 3.24 |
| RICARDO BELMONT (MOC) | 2.58 |
| Other candidates | 3.84 |
| **Total** | **100.0** |

### CONGRESO*
**General Election, 9 April 1995**

| Political parties | Seats |
| --- | --- |
| Cambio 90-Nueva Mayoría (C90-NM) | 67 |
| Unión por el Perú (UPP) | 17 |
| Alianza Popular Revolucionaria Americana (APRA) | 8 |
| Frente Independiente Moralizador | 6 |
| Coordinación Democrática—Perú País Posible (Code—País Posible) | 5 |
| Acción Popular (AP) | 4 |
| Renovación | 3 |
| Partido Popular Cristiano (PPC) | 3 |
| Izquierda Unida (IU) | 2 |
| Movimiento Obras Cívicas (MOC) | 2 |
| Frente Popular Agrícola | 1 |
| Movimiento Independiente Agrario | 1 |
| Movimiento Peru al 2000 | 1 |
| **Total** | **120** |

* Elections for the President and Vice-President of the Congreso were to be held after members of the new legislature formally took office on 28 July 1995.

## Political Organizations

**Acción Popular (AP):** Paseo Colón 218, Lima 1; tel. (14) 404907; f. 1956; 1.2m. mems; pro-USA; liberal; Leader Arq. FERNANDO BELAÚNDE TERRY; Sec.-Gen. RAÚL DÍEZ CANSECO.

**Alianza Popular Revolucionaria Americana (APRA):** Avda Alfonso Ugarte 1012, Lima 5; tel. (14) 313909; telex 25801; f. in Mexico 1924, in Peru 1930 as Partido Aprista Peruano (PAP); legalized 1945; democratic left-wing party; Leader ARMANDO VILLANEUVA DEL CAMPO; Sec.-Gen. AGUSTÍN MANTILLA; 700,000 mems.

**Cambio 90 (C90):** Lima; group of independents formed to contest the 1990 elections, entered into coalition with Nueva Mayoría (see below) in 1992 to contest elections to the CCD, local elections in 1993 and the presidential and congressional elections in 1995; Leader ALBERTO FUJIMORI; Sec. PABLO CORREA.

**Confluencia Socialista:** Lima; f. 1991; left-wing alliance comprising:
  **Acción Política Socialista (APS).**
  **Movimiento de Acción Socialista (MAS).**
  **Movimiento No Partidarizado (MNP).**
  **Partido Mariateguista Revolucionario (PMR).**

**Coordinación Democrática—Perú País Posible (Code—País Posible):** Lima; f. 1992 by dissident APRA members; Leader JOSÉ BARBA CABALLERO.

**Izquierda Nacionalista:** Lima; f. 1984; left-wing party; Leader PEDRO REYNALDO CÁCERES VELÁSQUEZ.

**Izquierda Socialista:** Lima; coalition of left-wing groups which broke away from Izquierda Unida before the elections of April 1990; Leader Dr ALFONSO BARRANTES LINGÁN.

**Unidad Democrática Popular (UDP):** Plaza 2 de Mayo 46, Lima 1; tel. (14) 230309; f. 1978; extreme left-wing; Leader Dr ALFONSO BARRANTES LINGÁN.

**Izquierda Unida (IU)** (Unified Left): Avda Grau 184, Lima 23; tel. (14) 278340; f. 1980; Leader GUSTAVO MOHOME; left-wing alliance comprising:
  **Frente Nacional de Trabajadores y Campesinos (FNTC/FRENATRACA):** Avda Colonial 105, Lima 1; tel. (14) 272868; f. 1968; left-wing party; Pres. Dr RÓGER CÁCERES VELÁSQUEZ; Sec.-Gen. Dr EDMUNDO HUANQUI MEDINA.

**Partido Comunista Peruano (PCP):** Jirón Lampa 774, Lima 1; f. 1928; Pres. JORGE DEL PRADO.

**Unión de Izquierda Revolucionaria (UNIR)** (Union of the Revolutionary Left): Jirón Puno 258, Apdo 1165, Lima 1; tel. (14) 274072; f. 1979; Chair. Senator ROLANDO BREÑA PANTOJA; Gen. Sec. JORGE HURTADO POZO.

**Movimiento de Bases Hayistas (MBH):** Pasaje Velarde 180, Lima; f. 1982; faction of APRA, which supports fundamental policies of APRA's founder, Dr Víctor Raúl Haya de la Torre; Leader Dr ANDRÉS TOWNSEND EZCURRA.

**Nueva Mayoría:** Lima; f. 1992; group of independents, including former cabinet ministers, formed coalition with Cambio 90 in 1992 in order to contest elections to the CCD, and local elections in 1993; Leader JAIME YOSHIYAMA TANAKA.

**Partido Aprista Peruano (PAP):** see entry for APRA.

**Partido Demócrata Cristiano (PDC):** Avda España 321, Lima 1; tel. (14) 238042; telex 25491; f. 1956; 95,000 mems; Chair. CARLOS BLANCAS BUSTAMANTE.

**Partido Liberal (PL):** Lima; f. 1987; right-wing; formerly Libertad movement; Sec.-Gen. MIGUEL CRUCHAGA.

**Partido Obrero Revolucionario Marxista-Partido Socialista de los Trabajadores (PORM-PST):** Jirón Apurimac 465, Lima 1; tel. (14) 280443; PORM f. 1971; PST f. 1974; unified 1982; Trotskyist; Leaders Senator RICARDO NAPURÍ, ENRIQUE FERNÁNDEZ CHACÓN.

**Partido Popular Cristiano (PPC):** Avda Alfonso Ugarte 1484, Lima; tel. (14) 238723; fax (14) 236582; f. 1966; splinter group of Partido Demócrata Cristiano; 120,000 mems; Pres. Dr LUIS BEDOYA REYES; Sec.-Gen. LOURDES FLORES.

**Partido Revolucionario de los Trabajadores (PRT):** Plaza 2 de Mayo 38, Apdo 2449, Lima 100; f. 1978; Trotskyist; Leader HUGO BLANCO; 5,000 mems.

**Partido Socialista del Perú (PSP):** Jirón Azángaro 105, Lima 1; f. 1930; left-wing; Leader Dr MARÍA CABREDO DE CASTILLO.

**Renovación:** Lima; f. 1992; Leader RAFAEL REY REY.

**Unión Nacional Odriísta (UNO):** right-wing; Leader FERNANDO NORIEGA.

**Unión por el Perú (UPP):** independent movement; f. 1995 to contest presidential and legislative elections; Leader JAVIER PÉREZ DE CUÉLLAR.

Other parties include the Marxist Acción Socialista Revolucionaria (ASR), Partido Comunista del Perú—Bandera Roja, Movimiento de Izquierda Revolucionaria (MIR), Vanguardia Revolucionaria, the right-wing Movimiento Democrático Peruano (MDP), Frente Obrero, Campesino Estudiantil y Popular (FOCEP), Partido Comunista Revolucionario (PCR), Partido Integración Nacional (PADIN), Partido Socialista Revolucionario (PSR), Partido Unificado Mariateguista (PUM), Frente de Liberación Nacional (FLN), Movimiento de Izquierda Revolucionaria (MIR-Perú), Partido Comunista del Perú—Patria Roja, Movimiento de Solidaridad y Democracia, Movimiento Libertad, Partido Unificado, Frente Independiente Moralizador (FIM), Movimiento Democrático de Izquierda (MDI), Movimiento Obras Cívicas (MOC), Movimiento Independiente Agrario, Movimiento Perú al 2000 and Frente Popular Agrícola.

### Guerrilla groups

**Sendero Luminoso** (Shining Path): f. 1970; began armed struggle 1980; splinter group of PCP; based in Ayacucho; advocates the policies of the late Mao Zedong and his radical followers, including the 'Gang of Four' in the People's Republic of China; founder Dr ABIMAEL GUZMÁN REYNOSO (alias Commdr GONZALO—arrested September 1992); Current leaders MARGIE CLAVO PERALTA (arrested March 1995), PEDRO QUINTEROS AYLLON (alias Comrade Luis).

  **Sendero Rojo** (Red Path): dissident faction of Sendero Luminoso opposed to leadership of Abimael Guzmán; Leader: OSCAR RAMÍREZ DURAND.

**Comando Rodrigo Franco:** f. 1988; right-wing paramilitary organization.

**Comandos Revolucionarios del Pueblo (CRP):** f. 1985; left-wing.

**Comité Comunista Unificado Marxista-Leninista (CCUML):** comprises: splinter group of Patria Roja (Leader JERÓNIMO PASACHE), MIR-El Militante (Marxist-Leninist faction of PSR), and Vanguardia-Revolucionaria-Proletario Campesino (Leader JULIO MEZZICH).

**Ejército de Liberación Nacional:** f. 1962; Marxist-Leninist; Leader JUAN PABLO CHANG NAVARRO; 15 mems.

**Frente Anti-imperialista de Liberación (FAL):** f. 1992; leftwing; Leader RODRIGO FONSECA.

**Movimiento Revolucionario Tupac Amarú (MRTA):** f. 1984; began negotiations with the Government to end its armed struggle in September 1990; Leader VÍCTOR POLAY CAMPOS (alias Commdr

# PERU

Rolando—arrested Feb. 1989; escaped in 1990; rearrested 1992); Provisional Leader Lucero Cumpa Miranda (arrested in May 1993).

**Núcleos Marxista-Leninistas:** f. 1974; splinter group of Bandera Roja; based in Chimbote.

**Puka Llakta** (Red Fatherland): active in Mantaro, La Oroya and Cerro de Pasco.

**Victoria Navarro:** offshoot of MIR-Perú; based in Chosica.

**Victoriano Esparraga Cumbi:** offshoot of MIR-Perú; based in Piura, Cajamarca and La Libertad; 60 mems.

## Diplomatic Representation

### EMBASSIES IN PERU

**Angola:** Lima; Ambassador: (vacant).

**Argentina:** Avda Arequipa 1155, 7°, Lima; tel. (14) 729920; telex 25246; Ambassador: Anselmo Marini.

**Austria:** Avda Central 643, 5°, Lima 27; tel. (14) 420503; telex 21128; fax (14) 428851; Ambassador: Artur Schuschnigg.

**Belgium:** Avda Angamos 392, Lima 18; tel. (14) 463335; telex 20182; Ambassador: Willy Tilemans.

**Bolivia:** Los Castaños 235, San Isidro, Lima 27; tel. (14) 413836; telex 20275; fax (14) 402298; Ambassador: Jorge Gumucio Granier.

**Brazil:** Avda Comandante Espinar 181, Miraflores, Lima; tel. (14) 462635; telex 20205; Ambassador: Raul Fernando Belford Roxo Leite Ribeiro.

**Bulgaria:** Jirón Paul Harris 289, San Isidro, Lima; tel. (14) 221145; telex 25276; Ambassador: (vacant).

**Canada:** Federico Gerdes 130, Miraflores, Apdo 1212, Lima; tel. (14) 444015; telex 25323; fax (14) 444347; Ambassador: Anne Charles.

**Chile:** Avda Javier Prado Oeste 790, San Isidro, Lima; tel. (14) 403300; telex 20181; Ambassador: Alfonso Rivero.

**China, People's Republic:** Jirón José Granda 150, San Isidro, Lima; tel. (14) 400782; telex 25283; Ambassador: Chen Jiuchang.

**Colombia:** Natalio Sánchez 125, 4°, Lima 1; tel. (14) 338922; fax (14) 339630; Ambassador: Rafael Ariza Andrade.

**Costa Rica:** Camino Real 159, Of. 500, San Isidro, Lima; tel. (14) 409982; Ambassador: Tomás Soley Soler.

**Cuba:** Coronel Portillo 110, San Isidro, Lima; tel. (14) 227128; telex 25644; Ambassador: Luis Karakadze Berrayarza.

**Czech Republic:** Baltazar La Torre 398, San Isidro, Lima; tel. (14) 408765; fax (14) 424164; Chargé d'affaires: Dr Lubomír Hladík.

**Dominican Republic:** Apdo 14-0335, Lima 14; tel. (14) 339837; fax (14) 332856; Ambassador: José Ramón Díaz Valdepares.

**Ecuador:** Las Palmeras 356 y Javier Prado Oeste, San Isidro, Lima; tel. (14) 409991; telex 25706; Ambassador: Miguel Antonio Vasco Vasco.

**Egypt:** Avda Jorge Basadre 1470, San Isidro, Lima; tel. (14) 402642; telex 25589; Ambassador: Sameer Abdel Salam.

**El Salvador:** Los Cedros 421-A, San Isidro, Lima; tel. (14) 222497; Ambassador: Roberto Arturo Castrillo Hidalgo.

**Finland:** Edif. El Plateado, 7°, Los Eucaliptos 291, San Isidro, Apdo 4501, Lima 100; tel. (14) 703750; telex 25436; Ambassador: Esko Lipponen.

**France:** Avda Coronel Portillo 302, San Isidro, Lima; tel. (14) 238616; telex 25658; Ambassador: Camille Rohou.

**Germany:** Avda Arequipa 4202, Miraflores, Apdo 0504, Lima 18; tel. (14) 457033; telex 20039; fax (14) 462348; Ambassador: Franz Freiherr von Mentzingen.

**Guatemala:** Calle Uno 314, Urbanización Corpac, San Isidro, Lima 27; tel. and fax (14) 408335; Ambassador: Edgar Arturo López Calvo.

**Haiti:** Avda Orrantia 910, San Isidro, Lima; tel. (14) 223362; Ambassador: Antoine Bernard.

**Holy See:** Avda Salaverry 6a cuadra, Apdo 397, Lima 100 (Apostolic Nunciature); tel. (14) 319436; telex 25751; fax (14) 323236; Apostolic Nuncio: Most Rev. Fortunato Baldelli, Titular Archbishop of Bevagna.

**Honduras:** Thomas Edison 215, San Isidro, Lima 27; tel. (14) 408881; telex 21383; Ambassador: Dr Carlos Martínez Castillo.

**Hungary:** Avda Jorge Basadre 1580, San Isidro, Lima; tel. (14) 429648; telex 25413; fax (14) 419806; Ambassador: János Tóth.

**India:** Avda Salaverry 3006, San Isidro, Lima 27; tel. (14) 621840; telex 25515; fax (14) 610374; Ambassador: Dilip Lahiri.

**Israel:** Natalio Sánchez 125, 6°, Santa Beatriz, Lima; tel. (14) 334431; fax (14) 338925; Ambassador: Yuval Metser.

**Italy:** Avda Gregorio Escobedo 298, Apdo 0490, Lima 11; tel. (14) 632727; telex 25460; fax (14) 635317; Ambassador: Giulio C. Vinci Gigliucci.

**Japan:** Avda San Felipe 356, Apdo 3708; Jesús María, Lima; tel. (14) 614041; telex 25533; fax (14) 630302; Ambassador: Nobuo Nishizaki.

**Korea, Democratic People's Republic:** Lima; Ambassador: Kim Kyong-Ho.

**Korea, Republic:** Avda Principal 190, 7°, Lima 13; tel. (14) 704201; telex 25539; Ambassador: Kim Jae-Hoon.

**Mexico:** Avda Santa Cruz 330, San Isidro, Lima; tel. (14) 405465; telex 25417; Ambassador: Manuel Martínez del Sobral.

**Morocco:** Nicolás de Rivera 890, San Isidro, Lima; tel. (14) 417393; telex 21520; Ambassador: Mohamed ben Moufti.

**Netherlands:** Avda Principal 190, 4°, Urb. Santa Catalina, La Victoria, Lima; tel. (14) 761069; telex 20212; fax (14) 756536; Ambassador: J. A. Walkate.

**New Zealand:** Avda Salaverry 3006, San Isidro, Apdo 5587, Lima 100; tel. (14) 621840; telex 20254; fax (14) 610374; Ambassador: Barry H. Brooks.

**Nicaragua:** Calle Hipólito Unanue 1560, Lince, Lima; tel. (14) 710585; telex 25659; Ambassador: Mauricio Cuadra Schulz.

**Paraguay:** Avda del Rosario 415, San Isidro, Lima; tel. (14) 418134; fax (14) 400318; Ambassador: Dr Julio Peña.

**Philippines:** José del Llano Zapata, Miraflores, Lima 18; tel. (14) 416318; fax (14) 420432; Ambassador: Romeo A. Arguelles.

**Poland:** Avda Salaverry 1978, Jesús María, Lima; tel. (14) 713920; telex 25548; Ambassador: Dr Jarosław Spyra.

**Portugal:** Avda Central 643, 4°, Lima 27; tel. (14) 409905; telex 25734; fax (14) 429655; Ambassador: Dr José Sarmento.

**Romania:** Avda Orrantia 690, San Isidro, Lima; tel. (14) 409396; telex 25624; Ambassador: Ion Ciucu.

**Russia:** Avda Salaverry 3424, San Isidro, Lima; tel. (14) 611775; telex 25608; fax (14) 617326; Ambassador: Viktor A. Tkachenko.

**Saudi Arabia:** Lima; Ambassador: (vacant).

**Slovakia:** Avda Angamos 1626, San Isidro, Lima; tel. (14) 418272; fax (14) 410160; Chargé d'affaires: Dr Pavol Sípka.

**Spain:** Jorge Basadre 498, San Isidro, Lima; tel. (14) 705600; telex 21575; fax (14) 410084; Ambassador: Fernando González-Camino.

**Sweden:** Centro Camino Real, Torre El Pilar, 9°, Avda Camino Real, San Isidro, Apdo 2068, Lima 100; tel. (14) 213400; telex 20245; fax (14) 429547; Ambassador: Lars Schönander.

**Switzerland:** Avda Salaverry 3240, Apdo 378, Lima 100; tel. (14)624090; telex 20020; fax (14) 626577; Ambassador: Sylvia Pauli.

**United Kingdom:** Edif. El Pacífico Washington, 12°, Plaza Washington, esq. Avda Arequipa, Apdo 854, Lima 100; tel. (14) 334738; fax (14) 334735; Ambassador: John Illman.

**USA:** Avda Inca Garcilaso de la Vega 1400, Apdo 1995, Lima 100; tel. (14) 338000; fax (14) 316682; Ambassador: Alvin P. Adams.

**Uruguay:** Avda Larco 1913, Dptos 201-202, Miraflores, Lima; tel. (14) 462047; Ambassador: Dr Luis Zerbino.

**Yugoslavia:** Carlos Porras Osores 360, San Isidro, Apdo 0392, Lima 18; tel. (14) 404754; Ambassador: Ladislav Varga.

## Judicial System

The Supreme Court consists of a President and 17 members. There are also Higher Courts and Courts of First Instance in provincial capitals.

### SUPREME COURT

**Corte Suprema:** Palacio de Justicia, 2°, Avda Paseo de la República, Lima 1; tel. (14) 284457.

**President:** Luis Eduardo Serpa Segura.

**Attorney-General:** Blanca Nelida Colan Maguino.

## Religion

### CHRISTIANITY

#### The Roman Catholic Church

For ecclesiastical purposes, Peru comprises seven archdioceses, 15 dioceses, 11 territorial prelatures and eight Apostolic Vicariates. At 31 December 1993 there were an estimated 10.6m. adherents of the Roman Catholic Church representing 93% of the country's population.

**Bishops' Conference:** Conferencia Episcopal Peruana, Rio de Janeiro 488, Apdo 310, Lima 100; tel. (14) 631010; fax (14)

PERU                                                                                                              Directory

636125; f. 1981 (statutes approved 1987, revised 1992); Pres. Cardinal Augusto Vargas Alzamora, Archbishop of Lima.

**Archbishop of Arequipa:** Fernando Vargas Ruiz de Somocurcio, Arzobispado, Moral San Francisco 118, Apdo 149, Arequipa; tel. (54) 215248; fax (54) 242721.

**Archbishop of Ayacucho or Huamanga:** (vacant), Arzobispado, Jirón 28 de Julio 140, Apdo 30, Ayacucho; tel. (64) 912367.

**Archbishop of Cuzco:** Alcides Mendoza Castro, Arzobispado, Hatun Rumiyoc 414, Apdo 148, Cuzco; tel. (84) 225211; fax (84) 222781.

**Archbishop of Huancayo:** (vacant), Arzobispado, Jirón Puno 430, Apdo 245, Huancayo; tel. (64) 234952; fax (64) 239189.

**Archbishop of Lima:** Cardinal Augusto Vargas Alzamora, Arzobispado, Plaza de Armas, Apdo 1512, Lima 100; tel. (14) 275980; fax (14) 271967.

**Archbishop of Piura:** Oscar Rolando Cantuarias Pastor, Arzobispado, Libertad 1105, Apdo 197, Piura; tel. and fax (74) 327561.

**Archbishop of Trujillo:** Manuel Prado Pérez-Rosas, Arzobispado, Jirón Mariscal de Orbegoso 451, Apdo 42, Trujillo; tel. (44) 231474; fax (44) 231473.

### The Anglican Communion

The Iglesia Anglicana del Cono Sur de América (Anglican Church of the Southern Cone of America), formally inaugurated in April 1983, comprises six dioceses, including Peru (with Bolivia). The Presiding Bishop of the Church is the Bishop of Chile.

**Bishop of Peru:** (vacant), Miraflores, Apdo 18-1032, Lima 18; tel. (14) 449622; fax (14) 453044.

### The Methodist Church

There are an estimated 4,200 adherents of the Iglesia Metodista del Perú.

**President:** Bishop Juan E. Hollemweguer N., Apdo 1386, Lima 100; tel. (14) 245970; telex 20339.

### Other Protestant Churches

Among the most popular are the Asamblea de Dios, the Iglesia Evangélica del Perú, the Iglesia del Nazareno, the Alianza Cristiana y Misionera, and the Iglesia de Dios del Perú.

### BAHÁ'Í FAITH

**National Spiritual Assembly of the Bahá'ís of Peru:** Horacio Urteaga 827, Jesús María, Apdo 11-0209, Lima 11; tel. (14) 316077; fax (14) 333005; mems resident in 1,888 localities.

# The Press

### DAILIES

#### Lima

**El Comercio:** Empresa Editora 'El Comercio', SA, Jirón Antonio Miró Quesada 300, Lima; tel. (14) 287620; telex 20115; fax (14) 310810; f. 1839; morning; Dirs Aurelio Miró Quesada, Alejandro Miró Quesada Garland; circ. 150,000 weekdays, 220,000 Sundays.

**Expreso:** Ica 646, Lima 1; tel. (14) 287470; telex 25307; fax (14) 318314; f. 1961; morning; conservative; Editor Manuel D'Ornellas; circ. 120,000.

**Extra:** Ica 646, Lima; tel. (14) 287470; telex 25307; f. 1964; evening edition of *Expreso*; Dir Guillermo Córtez Núñez; circ. 80,000.

**Ojo:** Avda Garcilaso de la Vega, Lima 27; f. 1968; morning; Dir Fernando Viaña Villa; circ. 180,000.

**El Peruano** (Diario Oficial): Quilca 556, Apdo 303, Lima; f. 1825; morning; official State Gazette; Dir Jesús Mimbela Pérez; circ. 75,000.

**La República:** Jirón Camaná 320, Lima 1; f. 1982; left-wing; Dir Carlos Maraví Gutarra; circ. 110,000.

**La Tercera:** Jirón Andahuaylas 1472, Apdo 928, Lima; evening; Dir Augusto Tamayo Vargas; circ. 25,000.

#### Arequipa

**Correo:** Calle Bolívar 204, Arequipa; tel. (54) 235150; telex 51229; Dir José Antonio Puyó Perry; circ. 70,000.

**El Pueblo:** Sucre 208, Apdo 35, Arequipa; f. 1905; morning; independent; Dir Pedro Morales Blondet; circ. 70,000.

#### Chiclayo

**El Ciclón:** Calle Balta 910, 3°, Chiclayo; Dir Ricardo Cervera Niño; circ. 50,000.

**La Industria:** Tacna 610, Chiclayo; tel. (54) 238021; fax (54) 227678; f. 1952; Dir José Ramirez Ruiz; circ. 80,000.

#### Cuzco

**El Comercio:** Apdo 70, Cuzco; f. 1896; evening; independent; Dir Abel Ramos Perea; circ. 60,000.

**El Sol:** Mesón de la Estrella 172, Cuzco; f. 1901; morning; Dir Claudio Zúñiga; circ. 5,000.

#### Huacho

**El Imparcial:** Avda Grau 203, Huacho; f. 1891; tel. (34) 324410; evening; Dir Adan Manrique Romero; circ. 5,000.

**La Verdad:** Jirón Colón 130, Apdo 61, Huacho; f. 1930; popular; Dir José M. Carbajal Manrique; circ. 3,500.

#### Huancayo

**Correo:** Jirón Cuzco 337, Huancayo; evening; Dir Carlos Ordoñez Berrospi.

**La Opinión Popular:** Huancas 251, Huancayo; tel. (64) 231149; f. 1922; Dir Bernabé Suárez Osorio.

#### Ica

**La Opinión:** Avda Los Maestros 801, Apdo 186, Ica; tel. (34) 235571; f. 1922; evening; independent; Dir Gonzalo Tueros Ramírez.

**La Voz de Ica:** Castrovirreyna 193, Ica; f. 1918; evening; tel. (34) 232112; Dir Atilio Nieri Boggiano; circ. 4,500.

#### Iquitos

**El Eco:** Jirón Lima 100-108, Apdo 170, Iquitos; f. 1924; evening; independent; Dir F. Reátegui; circ. 6,000.

**El Oriente:** Morona 153, Apdo 161, Iquitos; f. 1905; evening; Editor P. Salazar; circ. 7,000.

#### Pacasmayo

**Ultimas Noticias:** 2 de Mayo 27-29, Pacasmayo; f. 1913; evening; independent; Dir Alberto Ballena Sánchez; circ. 3,000.

#### Piura

**Correo:** Jirón Ica 782, Piura; Dir Mario Castro Arenas; circ. 12,000.

**Ecos y Noticias:** Libertad 902 y Ayacucho 307, Apdo 110, Piura; f. 1934; evening; independent; Man. Dir José del C. Rivera; circ. 4,000.

**El Tiempo:** Ayacucho 751, Piura; tel. (74) 323671; f. 1916; morning; independent; Dir Víctor M. Helguero Checa; circ. 30,000.

#### Puno

**Los Andes:** Jirón Lima 775, Apdo 110, Puno; tel. 352142; f. 1928; morning; Dir Dr Samuel Frisancho Pineda; circ. 5,100.

#### Tacna

**Correo:** Jirón Hipólito Unanue 605, Tacna; Dir Mario Castro Arenas; circ. 8,000.

#### Trujillo

**La Industria:** Gamarra 443, Trujillo; f. 1895; morning; independent; Editor Daniel Gardillo; circ. 8,000.

**La Nación:** Francisco Pizarro 511, Apdo 33, Trujillo; f. 1931; morning; democratic, independent; Dir José Luis Humberto; circ. 7,000.

### PERIODICALS AND REVIEWS

#### Lima

**Alerta Agrario:** Avda Salaverry 818, Lima 11; tel. (14) 336610; fax (14) 331744; f. 1987 by Centro Peruano de Estudios Sociales; monthly review of rural problems; Dir Bertha Consiglieri; circ. 100,000.

**Amautá:** Jirón Lampa 1115, Of. 605, Lima; fortnightly; Dir Florentino Gómez Valerio; circ. 10,000.

**The Andean Report:** Pasaje Los Pinos 156, Of. B6, Miraflores, Apdo 531, Lima; tel. (14) 472552; fax (14) 467888; f. 1975; weekly newletter; economics, trade and commerce; English; Publisher Eleanor Griffis de Zúñiga; circ. 1,000.

**Caretas:** Camaná 615, Of. 308, Lima; tel. (14) 287520; weekly; current affairs; Editor Enrique Zileri Gibson; circ. 90,000.

**Debate:** Apdo 671, Lima 100; tel. (14) 467070; fax (14) 455946; f. 1980; every 2 months; Editor Augusto Alvarez-Rodrich.

**Debate Agrario:** Avda Salaverry 818, Lima 11; tel. (14) 336610; fax (14) 331744; f. 1987 by Centro Peruano de Estudios Sociales; every 4 months; rural issues; Dir Fernando Eguren L.

**Hora del Hombre:** Apdo 2378, Lima 1; tel. (14) 220208; f. 1943; monthly; cultural and political journal; illustrated; Dir Jorge Falcón.

**Industria Peruana:** Los Laureles 365, San Isidro, Apdo 632, Lima 27; f. 1896; monthly publication of the Sociedad de Industrias; Editor Rolando Celi Burneo.

**Lima Times:** Pasaje Los Pinos 156, Of. B 6, Miraflores, Apdo 531, Lima 100; tel. (14) 469120; fax (14) 467888; f. 1975; monthly; travel, cultural events, general news on Peru; English; Editor Kristin Keenan de Cueto; circ. 10,000.

**Monos y Monadas:** Camaná 615, Of. 104, Lima; f. 1981; fortnightly; satirical; Editor Nicolás Yerovi; circ. 17,000.

**Oiga:** Pedro Venturo 353, Urb. Aurora, Miraflores, Lima; tel. (14) 475851; weekly; right-wing; Dir Francisco Igartua; circ. 60,000.

**Ondas:** Apdo 3758, Lima; f. 1959; monthly cultural review; Dir José Alejandro Valencia-Arenas; circ. 5,000.

**Orbita:** Avda Pershing 290, Of. 301, Magdalena Nueva, Lima; weekly; Dir Luz Chávez Mendoza; circ. 10,000.

**Perú Económico:** Apdo 671, Lima 100, tel. (14) 467070; fax (14) 455946; f. 1978; monthly; Editor Augusto Alvarez-Rodrich.

**Quehacer:** León de la Fuente 110, Magdalena del Mar, Lima 17; tel. (14) 627193; fax (14) 617309; f. 1979; fortnightly; supported by Desco research and development agency; circ. 5,000.

**Runa:** Apdo 5247, Lima; f. 1977; monthly; review of the Instituto Nacional de Cultura; Dir Mario Razzeto; circ. 10,000.

**Semana Económica:** Apdo 671, Lima 100; tel. (14) 455237; fax (14) 455946; f. 1985; weekly; Editor Augusto Alvarez-Rodrich.

**Unidad:** Jirón Lampa 271, Of. 703, Lima; tel. (14) 270355; weekly; Communist; Dir Gustavo Esteves Ostolaza; circ. 20,000.

**Vecino:** Avda Petit Thouars 1944, Of. 15, Lima 14; tel. (14) 706787; telex 25950; f. 1981; fortnightly; supported by Yunta research and urban publishing institute; Dirs Patricia Córdova, Mario Zolezzi; circ. 5,000.

### NEWS AGENCIES
#### Government News Agency

**Agencia de Noticias Andina:** Jirón de la Unión 264, Lima; tel. (14) 282595; telex 25804.

#### Foreign Bureaux

**Agence France-Presse (AFP):** Huancavelica 279, Apdo 2959, Lima 1101; tel. (14) 279419; telex 25347; Bureau Chief Daniel Sire.

**Agencia EFE** (Spain): Manuel González Olaechea 207, San Isidro, Lima; tel. (14) 412094; telex 25313; fax (14) 412422; Bureau Chief Francisco Rubio Figueroa.

**Agenzia Nazionale Stampa Associata (ANSA)** (Italy): Avda Gen. Córdoba 2594, Lince, Lima 14; tel. (14) 225130; telex 25313; fax (14) 229087; Correspondent Alberto Ku-King Maturana.

**Associated Press (AP)** (USA): Jirón Cailloma 377, Apdo 119, Lima; tel. (14) 277775; telex 5245; Bureau Chief Monte Hayes.

**Deutsche Presse-agentur (dpa)** (Germany): Schell 343, Of. 707, Miraflores, Apdo 1362, Lima 18; tel. (14) 441437; telex 25884; fax (14) 443775; Bureau Chief Gonzalo Ruiz Tovar.

**Informatsionnoye Telegrafnoye Agentstvo Rossii—Telegrafnoye Agentstvo Suverennykh Stran (ITAR—TASS)** (Russia): Aurelio Miró Quezada 576, San Isidro, Apdo 1402, Lima; Chief Vitaly Globa.

**Inter Press Service (IPS)** (Italy): Daniel Olaechea y Olaechea 285, Lima 11; tel. (14) 623958; fax (14) 631021; Correspondent Abraham Lama.

**Prensa Latina** (Cuba): Edif. Astoria, Of. 303, Avda Tacna 482, Apdo 5567, Lima; tel. (14) 233908; telex 20091; Correspondent Luis Manuel Arce Isaac.

**Reuters** (United Kingdom): Avda Paseo de la República 3505, 4°, San Isidro, Lima 27; tel. (14) 410507; telex 21112; fax (14) 418992; Man. Eduardo Hilgert.

**United Press International (UPI) Inc.** (USA): Avda La Paz 374A, 2°, Miraflores, Lima 18; tel. (14) 445095; Correspondent Vidal Silva Navarrete; Dir Man. Hubert Cam Valencia.

**Xinhua (New China) News Agency** (People's Republic of China): Parque Javier Prado 181, San Isidro, Lima; tel. (14) 403463; telex 25283; Bureau Chief Wang Shubo.

#### PRESS ASSOCIATIONS

**Asociación Nacional de Periodistas del Perú:** Jirón Huancavélica 320, Apdo 2079, Lima 1; tel. (14) 270687; fax (14) 278493; f. 1928; 3,500 mems; Pres. Roberto Mejía Alarcón; Sec.-Gen. Roberto Mejía Alarcón.

**Federación de Periodistas del Perú (FPP):** Avda Abancay 173, Lima; tel. (14) 284373; f. 1950; Pres. Alberto Delgado Oré; Sec.-Gen. Jorge Paredes Cabada.

## Publishers

**Librerías ABC, SA:** Avda Paseo de la República 3440, Local B-32, Lima 27; tel. (14) 422900; fax (14) 422901; f. 1956; history, Peruvian art and archaeology; Man. Dir Herbert H. Moll.

**Editorial Amarú:** Jr. Canta 651, Lima 13; f. 1981; Dir Carlos Matta.

**Colección Artes y Tesoros del Perú:** Calle Centenario 156, Urbanización Las Laderas de Melgarejo, La Molina, Lima; f. 1971; founded by Banco de Crédito.

**Ediciones Ave:** Yauli 1440, Chacra Ríos Norte, Lima; Man. Augusto Villanueva P.

**Biblioteca Nacional del Perú:** Avda Abancay 4a c., Apdo 2335, Lima 1; tel. (14) 4287690; fax (14) 4277331; f. 1821; general non-fiction, directories; Dir Martha Fernández de Lopez.

**Asociación Editorial Bruño:** Avda Arica 751, Apt. 05-144, Breña, Lima; tel. (14) 244134; fax (14) 322246; f. 1950; educational; Man. Dir Máximo Sagredo Sagredo.

**Editorial Colegio Militar Leoncio Prado:** Avda Costanera 1541, La Perla, Callao; f. 1946; textbooks and official publications; Man. Oscar Morales Quina.

**Editorial D.E.S.A.:** General Varela 1577, Breña, Lima; f. 1955; textbooks and official publications; Man. Enrique Miranda.

**Editorial Desarrollo, SA:** Ica 242, 1°, Apdo 3824, Lima; tel. and fax (14) 286628; f. 1965; business administration, accounting, auditing, industrial engineering, English textbooks, dictionaries, and technical reference; Dir Luis Sosa Núñez.

**Fundación del Banco Continental para el Fomento de la Educación y la Cultura (EDUBANCO):** Avda República de Panamá 3055, San Isidro, Apdo 4687, Lima 27; tel. (14) 217222; fax (14) 419729; f. 1973; Pres. Luis Hidalgo Viacava; Man. Enrique Alvarez-Calderón.

**Editorial Horizonte:** N. de Piérola 995, Apdo 2118, Lima 1; tel. (14) 279364; fax (14) 274341; f. 1968; social sciences, literature etc.; Man. Humberto Damonte.

**Industrial Gráfica, SA:** Chavín 45, Breña, Lima; f. 1981; Pres. Francisco Soto M.

**INIDE:** Van de Velde 160, Urb. San Borja, Lima; f. 1981; owned by National Research and Development Institute; educational books; Editor-in-Chief Ana Ayala.

**Editorial Labrusa, SA:** Los Frutales Avda 670-Ate, Lima; tel. (14) 358443; fax (14) 372925; f. 1988; literature, educational, cultural; Gen. Man. Adrián Reuilla Calvo; Man. Federico Díaz Tineo.

**Ediciones Médicas Peruanas, SA:** Avda Angamos Oeste 371, Of. 405, Miraflores, Apdo 6150, Lima 18; f. 1965; medical; Man. Alberto Lozano Reyes.

**Editorial Milla Batres, SA:** Avda Pardo 764, Of. 13, Miraflores, Lima; tel. (14) 467396; fax (14) 759487; f. 1963; history, literature, art, archaeology, linguistics and encyclopaedias on Peru; Dir-Gen. Carlos Milla Batres.

**Editorial Navarrete SRL-Industria del Offset:** Manuel Tellería 1842, Apdo 4173, Lima; tel. (14) 319040; telex 25103; fax (14) 230991; Man. Luis Navarrete Lechuga.

**Pablo Villanueva Ediciones:** Yauli 1440, Chacra Ríos Norte, Lima; f. 1938; literature, history, law etc.; Man. Augusto Villanueva Pacheco.

**Editorial Salesiana:** Avda Brasil 218, Apdo 0071, Lima 5; tel. (14) 235225; f. 1918; religious and general textbooks; Man. Dir Dr Francesco Vacarello.

**Librería San Pablo:** Jirón Callao esq. Camaná, Lima; f. 1981; religious texts.

**Sociedad Bíblica Peruana, AC:** Avda Petit Thouars 991, Apdo 448, Lima 100; tel. (14) 335815; fax (14) 336389; f. 1821; Christian literature and bibles; Gen. Sec. Pedro Arana-Quiroz.

**Librería Studium, SA:** Plaza Francia 1164, Lima; tel. (14) 326278; fax (14) 325354; f. 1936; textbooks and general culture; Man. Dir Eduardo Rizo Patrón Recavarren.

**Editorial Universo, SA:** Avda Nicolás Arriola 2285, Urb. Apolo, La Victoria, Apdo 241, Lima; f. 1967; literature, technical, educational; Pres. Clemente Aquino; Gen. Man. Ing. José A. Aquino Benavides.

**Universidad Católica:** Fondo Editorial, Avda Universitaria, 18c., San Miguel, Lima; tel. (14) 626390; fax (14) 611785; Man. Dir José E. Aguero González.

**Universidad Nacional Mayor de San Marcos:** Oficina General de Editorial, Avda República de Chile 295, 5°, Of. 508, Lima; tel. (14) 319689; f. 1850; textbooks, education; Man. Dir Jorge Campos Rey de Castro.

#### Association

**Cámara Peruana del Libro:** Jirón Washington 1206, Of. 507–508, Apdo 0253, Lima 1; tel. (14) 249695; fax (14) 325694; f. 1946;

170 mems; Pres. Julio César Flores Rodríguez; Exec. Dir Guillermo Skinner G.

## Radio and Television

There are around 300 radio stations in Peru. In 1992, according to UNESCO, an estimated 5.7m. radio receivers and an estimated 2.2m. television receivers were in use.

**Asociación de Radiodifusoras del Perú (ARP):** Manuel Corpancho 208, Lima 1; Pres. Genaro Delgado Parker.

**Dirección General de Telecomunicaciones:** Avda 28 de Julio 800, 2°, Lima 1; tel. (14) 330752; telex 25584; Dir-Gen. Ing. Raúl Gómez Sáenz.

**Empresa de Cine, Radio y Televisión Peruana, SA (RTP):** Avda José Gálvez 1040, Santa Beatriz, Lima; tel. (14) 715570; telex 25029; part of the Sistema Nacional de Comunicación Social (SINACOMS); operates 29 radio stations and 27 television channels; Exec. Pres. Carlos Lecca Arrieta.

### RADIO
#### Government Station

**Radio Nacional del Perú:** Avda Petit Thouars 447, Santa Beatriz, Lima; f. 1937; stations at Lima, Ayacucho, Chiclayo, Cajamarca, Chimbote, Piura, Huánuco, Huaraz, Ica, Jauja, Huancayo, Moquegua, La Oroya, Mollendo, Puerto Maldonado, Trujillo, Tarma, Talara, Tumbes, Iquitos, Puno and Tacna; 5 medium-wave and 12 short-wave transmitters.

There are two other government stations and eight cultural stations.

#### Principal Commercial Stations

**Radio América:** Montero Rosas 1099, Santa Beatriz, Lima 1; f. 1943; Dir-Gen. Karen Crousillat.

**Radio El Sol:** Avda Uruguay 355, 7°, Lima; tel. (14) 260107; Man. Emilio García Lara.

**Radio Panamericana:** Mariano Carranza 126, Santa Beatriz, Lima 1; tel. (14) 710040; f. 1953; Dir-Gen. Mauricio Alcantará.

### TELEVISION
#### Government Station

**Ministerio de Educación Pública:** Instituto Nacional de Cultura, Jirón Ancash 390, Apdo 5247, Lima; tel. (14) 275680; telex 25803; daily cultural programmes; Dir Pedro Gjurinovic Canevaro.

#### Commercial Stations

**Andina de Televisión:** Avda Arequipa 3570, San Isidro, Lima; tel. (14) 426666; f. 1983; Dir Julio Vera Abad.

**Compañía Latinoamericana de Radiodifusión—Canal 2 TV:** Avda san Felipe 968, Jesús María, Lima 11; f. 1983; tel. (14) 707272; telex 25795; fax (14) 712688; Dir Baruch Ivcher; Gen. Man. Julio Sotelo Casanova.

**Compañía Peruana de Radiodifusión, SA (América Televisión—Canal 4):** Montero Rosas 1099, Santa Beatriz, Lima; tel. (14) 728985; telex 20217; fax (14) 719582; f. 1958; 12 relay stations; Pres. Nicanor González Urrutia.

**Panamericana de Televisión, SA—Canal 5:** Avda Arequipa 1110, 5°, Lima 1; tel. (14) 718920; telex 25670; 93 relay stations; Pres. Manuel Delgado Parker; Gen. Man. Eduardo Bruce.

**Universal de Televisión:** Roma 160, Miraflores, Lima 18; f. 1981; tel. (14) 471169; fax (14) 465038; Exec. Pres. José Luis Banchero Hanza.

## Finance

In April 1991 a new banking law was introduced, which relaxed state control of the financial sector and reopened the sector to foreign banks (which had been excluded from the sector by a nationalization law promulgated in 1987).

### BANKING

(cap. = capital;  res = reserves;  dep. = deposits;  m. = million; amounts in new soles, unless otherwise stated)

**Superintendencia de Banca y Seguros:** Jirón Huancavelica 140, Lima 1; tel. (14) 288210; telex 25807; fax (14) 319800; f. 1931; Superintendent Luis Cortavarría Checkley.

#### Central Bank

**Banco Central de Reserva del Perú:** Jirón Antonio Miró Quesada 441, Lima 1; tel. (14) 276250; telex 20169; f. 1922; refounded 1931; cap. and res 50m., dep. 10,270.2m. (Nov. 1993); Pres. Germán Suárez Chávez; Gen. Man. Javier de la Rocha Marie; 7 brs.

#### Other Government Banks

**Banco Central Hipotecario del Perú:** Carabaya 421, Apdo 1005, Lima; tel. (14) 273845; telex 25826; fax (14) 319729; f. 1929; Pres. Ausejo Roncagliolo Carlos; 63 brs.

**Banco de la Nación:** Avda Nicolás de Piérola 1065, Lima 1; Apdo 1835, Lima 100; tel. (14) 4261133; telex 20003; fax (14) 4268099; f. 1966; cap. 595.2m., res 208.8m., dep. 3,798.1m., total assets 4,620.0m. (Sept. 1993); conducts all commercial banking operations of official government agencies; Pres. Alfredo Jalilie Awapara; Gen. Man. José Luis Miguel de Priego Palomino; 417 brs.

**Corporación Financiera de Desarrollo (COFIDE):** Augusto Tamayo 160, San Isidro, Lima 27; tel. (14) 422550; telex 21516; fax (14) 423374; f. 1971; Pres. Manuel Vásquez Perales; Gen. Man. Mauro Chávez Sandoval; 11 brs.

#### Development Banks

**Banco Agrario del Perú:** Jirón Junín 319, Apdo 2683, Lima 1; tel. (14) 276140; telex 25467; fax (14) 271335; f. 1933; cap. and res 2,121.5, dep. 7,413.6 (July 1988); loans to farmers for agricultural development; Pres. Alfredo García Llosa; Vice-Pres. César Fuentes Barriga; 26 brs.

**Banco de Desarrollo (BANDESCO):** Jirón Camaná 700, Apdo 5056, Lima 1; tel. (14) 277665; telex 20437; fax (14) 329742; f. 1980; cap. 24.5m., dep. 89.7m., total assets 128.2m. (Dec. 1993); Pres. and Chair. Tony Chen Kang; Gen. Man. Humberto Meneses Arancibia; 23 brs.

**Banco Industrial del Perú:** Jirón Lampa 535–545, Apdo 1230, Lima 1; tel. (14) 288080; telex 25482; fax (14) 282213; f. 1936; cap. 54,862, res 6.0m., dep. 12.7m., total assets 503.6m. (Dec. 1990); Pres. Reynaldo Susano Lucero; Gen. Man. Mario Vizcarra Villavicencio; 34 brs.

**Banco Latino (BCOLATIN):** Paseo de la República 3505, Lima 27; tel. (14) 416090; telex 25531; fax (14) 414076; f. 1982; cap. 33.3m., res 10.7m., dep. 484.8m. (June 1993); Pres. Dr. Jorge Picasso Salinas; Gen. Man. Julio Pflucker Arenaza; 51 brs.

**Banco de la Vivienda del Perú:** Jirón Camaná 616, Apdo 5425, Lima 100; tel. (14) 276655; telex 20077; f. 1962; cap. and res 10,926.7, dep. 2,989.9 (July 1988); Pres. Ramón Arrospide Mejía; Man. Víctor Castro Muñoz; 5 brs.

#### Commercial Banks

**Banco de Comercio:** Jirón Lampa 560, Apdo 4195, Lima; tel. (14) 289400; telex 25604; fax (14) 328454; f. 1967; formerly Banco Peruano de Comercio y Construcción; cap. 13.7m., res 0.9m., dep. 112.6m. (Dec. 1992); Pres. and Chair. Germán Flórez García-Rada; Gen. Man. César Salinas Castro; 25 brs.

**Banco Continental:** Avda República de Panamá 3050-3065, San Isidro, Apdo 3849, Lima 27; tel. (14) 727565; telex 21281; fax (14) 419495; f. 1951; merged with Bancó Amazónico and Banco Nor-Perú Continorte 1992; 60% shares acquired by Banco Bilbao Vizcaya in April 1995; cap. 169.0m., res 48.0m., dep. 1,785.2m., total assets 2,227.8m. (Dec. 1993); Pres. Luis Hidalgo; Gen. Man. Alberto Salazar; 17 brs.

**Banco de Crédito del Perú:** Calle Centenario 156, Apdo 12-067, Lima 12; tel. (14) 373838; f. 1889; cap. 371.6m., res 127.0m., total assets 7,094.3m. (Dec. 1994); designated a private self-managing institution by the Govt in March 1988; Pres. Dionisio Romero Seminario; Gen. Man. Raimundo Morales Dasso; 204 brs.

**Banco Exterior de los Andes y de España (EXTEBANDES):** Avda Enrique Canaval y Moreyra 454, Lima 27; tel. (14) 422121; telex 25773; f. 1982; cap. and res US \$53.0m., dep. US \$371.9m. (Dec. 1987); Pres. Rosario Orellana Yépez; Regional Gen. Man. Henry Barclay Rey de Castro; 3 brs.

**Banco de Lima:** Esq. Carabaya y Puno, Apdo 3181, Lima 1; tel. (14) 329002; telex 25266; fax (14) 332505; f. 1952; cap. 30.7m., res 5.5m., dep. 490.7m. (Dec. 1993); Pres. Carlos Palacios Rey; Gen. Man. Claude Mahieux; 37 brs.

**Banco Mercantil del Perú:** Jirón Ricardo Rivera Navarrete 641, San Isidro, Apdo 5926, Lima 27; tel. (14) 428000; telex 21245; fax (14) 425277; f. 1984; cap. 22.0m., dep. 247.2m. (Dec. 1993); Pres. Salvador Majluf; Gen. Man. Giovanni Castoldi Castillo; 4 brs.

**Banco Popular del Perú:** Jirón Haullaga 380, Apdo 143, Lima 1; tel. (14) 277686; telex 20033; fax (14) 320370; f. 1899; state-controlled, scheduled for transfer to private ownership; cap. 165,047, res 5,546,134, dep. 102,001,447, total assets 108,507,064 (Dec. 1990); Pres. Roberto Carrión Pollit; Gen. Man. Rodolfo Abram Calaverino; 202 brs.

**Banco del Progreso (Probank):** Avda Javier Prado Este 595, San Isidro, Lima 27; tel. (14) 212800; telex 21594; fax (1) 411058; f. 1980; cap. 16.9m., dep. 133.9m., (Dec. 1993); Pres. Salomón Lerner Ghitis; Gen. Man. David Ellenbogen Schauer.

**Banco Sudamericano:** Avda Camino Real 815, San Isidro, Lima 27; tel. (14) 417850; telex 21471; fax (14) 411169; f. 1981; cap.

20.0m., dep. 206.3m., total assets 250.1m. (Dec. 1994); Pres. Roberto Calda Cavanna; Gen. Man. Ricardo Wenzel Ferrada.

**Banco Wiese Ltdo:** Jirón Cuzco 245, Apdo 1235, Lima 100; tel. (14) 283400; telex 25509; fax (14) 330266; f. 1943; cap. 57.9m., dep. 2,321.5m., total assets 2,728.0m. (Dec. 1993); taken over by Govt in Oct. 1987; returned to private ownership in Oct. 1988; Pres. and Chair. Dr Guillermo Wiese de Osma; Dir and Gen. Man. Víctor Miró Quesada Gatjens; 6 brs.

**INTERBANC (Banco Internacional del Perú):** Jirón de la Unión 600, Apdo 148, Lima 100; tel. (14) 334200; telex 20214; fax (14) 273203; f. 1897; commercial bank; cap. 69.9m., dep. 914.9m., total assets 1,062.8m. (Dec. 1993); Pres. Ernesto Mitsumatsu; Gen. Man. Raúl Iraola; 88 brs.

### Provincial Banks

**Banco Regional del Norte:** Esq. Libertad e Ica 723, Apdo 131, Piura; tel. (74) 325992; telex 41052; fax (74) 332742; f. 1960; cap. and res US $9.6m., dep. US $67.6m. (Dec. 1992); Pres. Juan Arturo Atkins Morales; CEO Francisco González García; 10 brs.

**Banco del Sur del Perú:** Calle Moral 101, Arequipa; tel. (54) 215728; telex 51096; fax (54) 215630; f. 1962; cap. 31.4m., res 12.2m., dep. 332.7m. (Dec. 1993); Pres. Ing. Alfonso Bustamante y Bustamante; Gen. Man. Eugenio Bertini Vinci; 24 brs.

### Savings Bank

**Caja de Ahorros de Lima:** Jirón Augusto N. Wiese 638, Apdo 297, Lima 100; tel. (14) 276663; telex 25836; f. 1868; cap. and res 114.5m., dep. 942.0m. (Dec. 1986); Pres. Ricardo La Puente Robles; Gen. Man. Ing. David Ellenbogen Schauer; 5 brs.

### Foreign Banks

**Banco Arabe Latinoamericano (ARLABANK):** Calle Juan de Arona 830, San Isidro, Apdo 10070, Lima 100; tel. (14) 413150; telex 25138; fax (14) 414277; f. 1977; Chair. César Rodríguez Batile; Gen. Man. Fernando Accame Feijoo.

**Citibank NA** (USA): Torre Real, Avda Camino Real 456, 5°, Lima 27; tel. (14) 214000; telex 21227; fax (14) 409044; f. 1920; cap. US $7,910m., res $272m., dep. 67,347m. (Dec. 1994); Vice-Pres. Rafael Venegas; 1 br.

### Banking Association

**Asociación de Bancos del Perú:** Jirón Antonio Miró Quesada 247, Of. 409, Lima 1; tel. (14) 288850; fax (14) 333665; f. 1929; refounded 1967; Pres. Dr Jorge Picasso Salinas; Gen. Man. María Lucrecia Vivanco de French.

### STOCK EXCHANGE

**Bolsa de Valores de Lima:** Pasaje Acuña 191, Lima 1; tel. (14) 327939; fax (14) 337650; f. 1860; Exec. Pres. José Carlos Luque Otero; Gen. Man. José Antonio Almenara Battifora.

### INSURANCE

#### Lima

**América Terrestre y Marítima, SA, Cía de Seguros Generales—América de Seguros:** Jirón Sinchi Roca 2728, Apdo 5803, Lince, Lima 100; tel. (14) 703510; telex 25026; fax (14) 418730; f. 1954; Pres. Rogerio Marcondes de Carvalho; Gen. Man. Luis Salcedo Marsano.

**Cía de Seguros Atlas:** Jirón Antonio Miró Quesada 191, Apdo 1751, Lima 100; tel. (14) 275820; telex 20228; fax (14) 279912; f. 1896; Pres. Ing. Juan B. Isola Cambana; Gen. Man. Miguel Olavarría Novoa.

**Cía de Seguros Cóndor:** Miguel Dasso 274, San Isidro, Lima; tel. (14) 726265; fax (14) 427550; f. 1980; Pres. Gonzalo de la Puente y Lavalle; Gen. Man. Marino Costa Bauer.

**Cía de Seguros La Fénix Peruana:** Avda Cte Espinar 689, Miraflores, Apdo 1356, Lima 100; tel. (14) 479070; telex 25425; fax (14) 455840; f. 1927; Pres. Alfredo Ferreyros Gaffron; Gen. Man. Carlos Ortega Wiesse.

**Cía de Seguros La Nacional:** Esq. Avda La Fontana con La Molina, Apdo 275, Lima 1; tel. (14) 369100; telex 20117; fax (14) 369258; f. 1904; Pres. Ing. Roberto Calda Cavanna; Gen. Man. Renzo Calda Giurato.

**Cía de Seguros y Reaseguros Peruano Suiza, SA:** Edif. Peruano Suiza, 8°, Jirón Camaná 370, Apdo 2395, Lima 100; tel. (14) 275110; telex 25050; fax (14) 273066; f. 1948; Pres. Dionisio Romero Seminario; Gen. Man. Dr Miguel Pérez Muñoz.

**Generali Perú, Cía de Seguros:** Jirón Antonio Miró Quesada 191, Lima; tel. (14) 277349; telex 20228; fax (14) 322698; f. 1942; Pres. Piero Sacchi Checcuci; Gen. Man. Giancarlo Landotti Speroni.

**El Pacífico, Cía de Seguros y Reaseguros:** Avda Arequipa 660, Apdo 595, Lima 100; tel. (14) 333626; telex 25817; fax (14) 333388; f. 1943; Pres. José Antonio Onrubia Romero; Gen. Man. Arturo Rodrigo Santistevan.

**Panamericana Cía de Seguros y Reaseguros:** Jirón Augusto Tamayo 180, San Isidro, Lima; tel. (14) 715070; telex 25879; fax (14) 703769; f. 1958; Pres. Juan Banchero Rossi; Gen. Man. Rodolfo Gordillo Tordoya.

**Popular y Porvenir, Cía de Seguros:** Avda Cuzco 177, Apdos 220–237, Lima 1; tel. (14) 276220; fax (14) 285570; f. 1904; Pres. Augusto Miyagusuku Miagui; Gen. Man. Victor Rendón Valencia.

**La Positiva Seguros y Reaseguros SA:** Esq., Javier Prado Este y Francisco Masías, Apdo 1456, Lima 27; tel. (14) 426250; fax (14) 401124; f. 1937; Pres. Ing. Juan Manuel Peña Roca; Gen. Man. Jaime S. Pérez Rodríguez.

**La Real, Cía de Seguros Generales, SA:** Avda Angamos 1269, Miraflores, Lima; tel. (14) 414502; telex 25782; fax (14) 422374; f. 1980; Pres. César Vilchez Vivanco Cahuas Bonino; Gen. Man. José Antonio León Roca.

**Reaseguradora Peruana, SA:** Chinchón 890, San Isidro, Apdo 3672, Lima 100; tel. (14) 425065; telex 21168; fax (14) 417959; f. 1965; state-controlled; Pres. Rafael Villegas Cerro; Gen. Man. Ernesto Becerra Mejía.

**Rimac Internacional, Cía de Seguros:** Las Begonias 475, 3°, San Isidro, Apdo 245, Lima; 100; tel. (14) 222780; fax (14) 210590; f. 1896; Pres. Ing. Pedro Brescia Cafferata; Gen. Man. Alex Fort Brescia.

**SECREX, Cía de Seguro de Crédito y Garantías:** Avda Angamos Oeste 1234, Miraflores, Apdo 0511, Lima 100; tel. (14) 424033; telex 20388; fax (14) 425328; f. 1980; Pres. Carlos Ortega Wiesse; Gen. Man. Juan A. Giannoni.

**El Sol, Cía de Seguros Generales:** Avda 28 de Julio 873, Miraflores, Apdo 323, Lima 100; tel. (14) 444515; telex 20368; fax (14) 468456; f. 1950; Pres. Italo Calda Cavanna; Gen. Man. Renzo Caldag.

**La Vitalicia, Cía de Seguros:** Avda Ricardo Rivera Navarrete 791, San Isidro, Apdo 5597, Lima 27; tel. (14) 422424; telex 20368; fax (14) 422766; f. 1950; Pres. Benjamín Perelman Zelter; Gen. Man. Aristides González Vigil.

#### Insurance Association

**Asociación Peruana de Empresas de Seguros (APESEG):** Arias Araguez 146, Miraflores, Apdo 1684, Lima 100; tel. (14) 442294; telex 25392; fax (14) 468538; f. 1904; Pres. Guillermo Carrillo Flecha; Gen. Man. Manuel Portugal Mariátegui.

## Trade and Industry

### CHAMBERS OF COMMERCE

**Confederación de Cámaras de Comercio y Producción del Perú (CONFECAMARAS):** Avda Gregorio Escobedo 398, Lima 11; tel. (14) 633434; fax (14) 632820; f. 1970; Pres. Dr Guillermo Arguedas Schiantarelli; Man. Dr Pedro A. Flores Polo; 60 mems.

**Cámara de Comercio de Lima** (Lima Chamber of Commerce): Avda Gregorio Escobedo 398, Lima 11; tel. (14) 633434; fax (14) 632820; f. 1888; Pres. Juan Musso Torres; Gen. Man. Dr Pedro A. Flores Polo; 3,000 mems.

There are also Chambers of Commerce in Arequipa, Cuzco, Callao and many other cities.

### DEVELOPMENT ORGANIZATIONS

**Asociación de Dirigentes de Ventas y Mercadotecnia del Perú (ADV—PERU):** Avda Belén 158, Apdo 1280, Lima 27; tel. (14) 419988; fax (14) 410303; f. 1958; Pres. Franco Carabelli Pace; Gen. Man. Stefan Arie Singer; 1,500 mems.

**Asociación de Exportadores (ADEX):** Las Palmeras 375, Apdo 1806, Lima 27; tel. (14) 400693; telex 25272; fax (14) 216510; f. 1969; Pres. Ing. Juan Pendavis P.; Gen. Man. Julio Alvarado; 780 mems.

**Comisión Nacional de Desarrollo Regional** (National Regional Development Commission): Lima; f. 1975 to promote economic and social development in the eleven administrative regions; Pres. the Prime Minister.

**Consejo Nacional de Conciliación Agraria (CNCA):** Lima; f. 1988; acts as mediator between the Government and producers in agricultural sector; Pres. Minister of Agriculture.

**Consejo Nacional de Desarrollo—CONADE:** Avda Agusto Tamayo 160, Lima 27; national development council; Chair. José Palomino.

**Instituto de Comercio Exterior—ICE:** Bernardo Monteagudo 210, Apdo 110133, Lima 1; tel. (14) 617094; telex 25301; fax (14) 617396; f. 1986; responsible for supervision and promotion of foreign trade; Pres. (vacant).

PERU — *Directory*

**Instituto Nacional de Planificación:** Calle Siete 229, Rinconada Baja, La Molina, Apdo 2027, Lima 1; tel. (14) 358141; f. 1962; national planning institute; Dir JAVIER TANTALEÁN ARBULÚ.

**Instituto Peruano de Energía Nuclear (IPEN):** Avda Canadá 1470, San Borja, Apdo 1687, Lima 41; tel. (14) 724349; f. 1975; to promote, co-ordinate, advise and represent the development of nuclear energy and its applications in Peru; the first experimental 10-MW reactor at Huarangal was inaugurated, in December 1988, following delays resulting from budgetary difficulties; Exec. Dir CONRADO SEMINARIO ARCE.

**Proinversión:** Lima; f. 1981; agency to supervise public investment projects; Pres. ROBERTO DAÑINO; Exec. Dir DRAGO KISIC.

**Sociedad Nacional de Industrias (SNI)** (National Industrial Association): Los Laureles 365, San Isidro, Apdo 632, Lima 27; tel. (14) 408700; fax (14) 422573; f. 1896; comprises permanent commissions covering various aspects of industry including labour, integration, fairs and exhibitions, industrial promotion; its Small Industry Committee groups over 2,000 small enterprises; Pres. Ing. ROBERTO NESTA; Gen. Man. Ing. BRUNO TOMATIS; 90 dirs (reps of firms); 2,500 mems; 60 sectorial committees.

### STATE CORPORATIONS

**Centromín, SA (Empresa Minera del Centro del Perú):** Edif. Solgas, Avda Javier Prado Este 2175, San Borja, Apdo 2412, Lima 41; tel. (14) 761010; telex 21238; fax (14) 769908; f. 1974; mining corporation; undergoing transfer to private ownership; Pres. HERNÁN BARRETO BOGGIO; Gen. Man. GUILLERMO GUANILO MOYA; 11,527 employees (Dec. 1993).

**Corpac (Corporación Peruana de Aeropuertos y Aviación Comercial, SA):** Aeropuerto Internacional Jorge Chávez, Avda Elmer Faucett, Lima; tel. (14) 529570; telex 26055; commercial aviation; Pres. Maj-Gen. ALFREDO ARROSUEÑO GOYENECHEA; Gen. Man. Col-Gen. CARLOS MAS ORTUZ.

**Electroperú:** Centro Cívico, Paseo de la República 144, Lima 1; tel. (14) 310664; telex 25680; scheduled to be transferred to private ownership; electricity; Exec. Pres. Ing. EDUARDO CAILLAUX ANGULO; Gen. Man. HUMBERTO ZELAYA SOTOMAYOR.

**Enci (Empresa Nacional de Comercialización de Insumos):** Galerías San Felipe 111, Cuadra 7, Avda Gregorio Escobedo, Apdo 1834, Lima 11; tel. (14) 632122; telex 20030; fax (14) 626242; f. 1974; controls the import, export and national distribution of agricultural and basic food products; Gen. Man. LUZMILA KAMISATO NAKA.

**Epsep (Empresa Peruana de Servicios Pesqueros):** Lima; tel. (14) 362630; telex 25498; edible fish; Pres. ANTONIO HUDTWALCKER TEXEIRA; Gen. Man. ANTONIO ROMANO THANTAWATAE.

**Minero Perú (Empresa Minera del Perú):** Bernardo Monteagudo 222, Apdo 4332, Lima 17; tel. (14) 620740; telex 25598; fax (14) 627049; f. 1970; state-owned mining company; undergoing transfer to private ownership in 1993–94; Pres. Ing. CARLOS PHILLIPS JARAMILLO; Gen. Man. Ing. HUGO CORAZAO ALZAMORA; 632 employees (in 1988).

**Minpeco, SA (Empresa Comercializadora de Productos Mineros):** Jirón Scipión Llona 350, Miraflores, Apdo 0274, Lima 18; tel. (14) 473561; telex 20360; fax (14) 402840; f. 1974 as the state mining marketing agency to be responsible for the sale of traditional and non-traditional mining products; in 1981 Minpeco lost its monopoly; Chair. Lic. FERMÍN BUSTAMENTE MOSCOSO; Gen. Man. MARIO MESIA.

**PescaPerú (Empresa Nacional Pesquera SA):** Avda Petit Thoars 119-115, Apdo 4682, Lima 1; tel. (14) 320454; telex 25601; fax (14) 311259; f. 1973; took over Epchap in 1979; fishmeal and fishoil production and export; scheduled for transfer to private ownership; Pres. JUAN REBAZA CARPIO.

**Petroperú (Empresa de Petróleos del Perú):** Paseo de la República 3361, San Isidro, Apdo 3126/1081, Lima 27; tel. (14) 414402; telex 20303; fax (14) 425416; f. 1969; petroleum; scheduled for transfer to private ownership by 1995; Pres. ALBERTO BRUCE; Gen. Man. Ing. MIGUEL CELI RIVERA.

**Petróleos del Mar (Petromar):** Lima; f. 1986, following the nationalization of the US company, Belco Petroleum; state petroleum prospecting company; Pres. ALBERTO VERA LA ROSA.

**Siderperú (Empresa Siderúrgica del Perú):** Avda Tacna 543, 9°–12°, Of. 121, Lima 1; tel. (14) 283450; telex 20270; fax (14) 276156; f. 1958; iron and steel; scheduled for transfer to private ownership; Pres. (vacant); Gen. Man. Dr ANTONIO MARTÍNEZ GONZÁLES.

Other state corporations include **Enapu** (Ports—see under Transport), the **Empresa Nacional del Tabaco—Enata** (Tobacco), **Endepalma** (Palm products), **Fertiperú** (Fertilizers), and **Tintaya** (Mining).

### EMPLOYERS' ASSOCIATIONS

**Asociación Automotriz del Perú:** Dos de Mayo 299, Apdo 1248, Lima 27; tel. (14) 404119; telex 25257; fax (14) 428865; f. 1926; association of importers of motor cars and accessories; 360 mems; Pres. CÉSAR RATTO BERNUY; Gen. Man. CÉSAR MARTÍN BARREDA.

**Asociación de Ganaderos del Perú** (Association of Stock Farmers of Peru): Pumacahua 877, 3°, Jesús María, Lima; f. 1915; Gen. Man. Ing. MIGUEL J. FORT.

**Comité de Minería de la Cámara de Comercio e Industria de Arequipa:** Apdo 508, Arequipa; mining association; Pres. F. CH. WILLFORT.

**Confederación Nacional de Instituciones Empresariales Privadas—CONFIEP** (Confederation of Private Businesses): Pres. ARTURO WOODMAN.

**Instituto Peruano del Café:** f. 1965; representatives of Government and industrial coffee growers.

**Sociedad Nacional de Minería y Petróleo:** Las Flores 346, Lima; tel. (14) 704260; fax (14) 704245; f. 1940; Pres. ROQUE BENAVIDES; Vice-Pres. WALTER SOLOGUREN; Gen. Man. CARLOS DIEZ CANSECO; mine owners' association; 70 mems.

**Sociedad Nacional de Pesquería (SNP):** Lima; f. 1976; private sector fishing interests; Pres. JAVIER REATEGUI ROSSELLO.

### TRADE UNIONS

The right to strike was restored in the Constitution of July 1979. In 1982 the Government recognized the right of public employees to form trade unions.

**Central Unica de Trabajadores Peruanos (CUTP):** Lima; f. 1992; comprises:

**Central de Trabajadores de la Revolución Peruana (CTRP):** Lima.

**Confederación General de Trabajadores del Perú (CGTP):** Plaza 2 de Mayo 4, Lima; tel. (14) 231707; f. 1968; Pres. VALENTÍN PACHO QUISPE; Sec.-Gen. TEÓDULO HERNÁNDEZ VALLE.

**Confederación Nacional de Trabajadores (CNT):** Avda San Martín 787, Lima; tel. (14) 631173; affiliated to the PPC; 12,000 mems (est.); Sec.-Gen. ANTONIO GALLARDO EGOAVIL.

**Confederación de Trabajadores Peruanos (CTP):** Lima; affiliated to APRA; Gen. Sec. JULIO CRUZADO EZCURRA.

**Confederación Intersectorial de Trabajadores Estatales (CITE)** (Union of Public Sector Workers): Jirón Callao 326, Apdo 2178, Lima; tel. (14) 245525; f. 1978; Leader CÉSAR PASSALACQUA PEREYRA; Sec.-Gen. RAÚL CABALLERO VARGAS; 600,000 mems.

**Federación de Empleados Bancarios (FEB)** (Union of Bank Employees): Leader ANTONIO ZÚÑIGA; Sec.-Gen. AUGUSTO GARCÍA DUQUE.

**Federación Nacional de Trabajadores Mineros, Metalúrgicos y Siderúrgicos—FNTMMS** (Federation of Peruvian Mineworkers): Lima; Pres. VÍCTOR TAIPE; Vice-Pres. LEONARDO RAMÍREZ; 70,000 mems.

**Movimiento de Trabajadores y Obreros de Clase (MTOC):** Lima.

**Sindicato Unico de Trabajadores de Educación del Perú—SUTEP** (Union of Peruvian Teachers): Lima; fax (14) 762792; Sec.-Gen. JOSÉ RAMOS.

Independent unions, representing an estimated 37% of trade unionists, include: Comité para la Coordinación Clasista y la Unificación Sindical, Confederación de Campesinos Peruanos (CCP—Sec.-Gen. ANDRÉS LUNA VARGAS), Confederación Nacional Agraria (Pres. FELIPE HUMÁN YAYAHUANCA).

**Confederación Nacional de Comunidades Industriales (CONACI):** Lima; co-ordinates worker participation in industrial management and profit-sharing.

The following agricultural organizations exist:

**Consejo Unitario Nacional Agrario (CUNA):** f. 1983; represents 36 farmers' and peasants' organizations, including:

**Confederación Campesina del Perú (CCP):** radical left-wing; Pres. ANDRÉS LUNA VARGAS; Sec. HUGO BLANCO (arrested Feb. 1989).

**Organización Nacional Agraria (ONA):** organization of dairy farmers and cattle-breeders.

# Transport

### RAILWAYS

In the early 1990s there were some 3,500 km of track. A programme to develop a national railway network (Sistema Nacional Ferroviario) was begun in the early 1980s, aimed at increasing the length of track to about 5,000 km initially. The Government also plans to electrify the railway system and extend the Central and Southern Railways.

**Ministerio de Transportes, Comunicaciones, Vivienda y Construcción:** Avda 28 de Julio 800, Lima; tel. (14) 245088; telex 25511.

# PERU

**Empresa Nacional de Ferrocarriles del Perú, SA (Enafer-Perú):** Ancash 207, Apdo 1379, Lima; tel. (14) 289440; telex 25068; f. 1972; nationalized; 1,672 km open; Pres. M. J. ZARIQUEY PANIZO; Gen. Man. J. NICHOLSON ROMANA; operates the following lines:

**Ferrocarril del Centro del Perú** (Central Railway of Peru): Ancash 201, Apdo 301, Lima; tel. (14) 276620; 511 km open; Man. DAVID SAN ROMÁN B.

**Ferrocarril del Sur del Perú ENAFER, SA** (Southern Railway): Avda Tacna y Arica 200, Apdo 194, Arequipa; tel. (54) 215350; telex 51071; 1,099 km open; also operates steamship service on Lake Titicaca; Man. L. QUIJADA MIRANDA.

**Tacna–Arica Ferrocarril** (Tacna–Arica Railway): Avda Aldarracín 484, Tacna; 62 km open.

**Empresa Minera del Centro del Perú SA—División Ferrocarriles (Centromín-Perú SA)** (fmrly Cerro de Pasco Railway): Edif. Solgas, Avda Javier Prado Este 2175, San Borja, Apdo 2412, Lima 41; tel. (14) 761010; telex 21238; fax (14) 769757; 212.2 km; Pres. HERNÁN BARRETO; Gen. Man. GUILLERMO GUANILO.

**Ferrocarril Pimentel** (Pimentel Railway): Pimentel, Chiclayo, Apdo 310; 56 km open; owned by Empresa Nacional de Puertos; cargo services only; Pres. R. MONTENEGRO; Man. LUIS DE LA PIEDRA ALVIZURI.

### Private Railways

**Ferrocarril Ilo–Toquepala–Cuajone:** Apdo 2640, Lima; 219 km open, incl. five tunnels totalling 27 km; owned by the Southern Peru Copper Corporation for transporting copper supplies and concentrates only; Supt. RUSSEL D. ALLEY; Gen. Foreman T. L. CHAPMAN.

**Ferrocarril Supe–Barranca–Alpas:** Barranca; 40 km open; Dirs CARLOS GARCÍA GASTAÑETA, LUIS G. MIRANDA.

## ROADS

In 1987 there were 69,942 km of roads in Peru, of which 7,459 km were asphalted and more than 13,538 km surfaced. The most important highways are: the Pan-American Highway (2,495 km), which runs southward from the Ecuadorean border along the coast to Lima; Camino del Inca Highway (3,193 km) from Piura to Puno; Marginal de la Selva (1,688 km) from Cajamarca to Madre de Dios; and the Trans-Andean Highway (834 km), which runs from Lima to Pucallpa on the River Ucayali via Oroya, Cerro de Pasco and Tingo María.

## SHIPPING

Most trade is through the port of Callao but there are 17 deepwater ports, mainly in northern Peru (including Salaverry, Pacasmayo and Paita) and in the south (including the iron ore port of San Juan). There are river ports at Iquitos, Pucallpa and Yurimaguas, aimed at improving communications between Lima and Iquitos, and a further port is under construction at Puerto Maldonado.

**Empresa Nacional de Puertos, SA (Enapu):** Terminal Marítimo del Callao, Edif. Administrativo, 3°, Apdo 260, Callao; tel. (14) 299210; telex 26010; fax (14) 656415; f. 1970; government agency administering all coastal, river and lake ports; Pres. G. B. Z. BALLÓN; Chair. Ing. MIGUEL ÁNGEL ROJAS VIVERO.

**Asociación Marítima del Perú:** Avda Javier Prado Este 897, Of. 33, San Isidro, Apdo 3520, Lima 27; tel. and fax (14) 221904; f. 1957; association of 20 international and Peruvian shipping companies; Pres. LUIS FELIPE VILLENA GUTIÉRREZ.

**Consorcio Naviero Peruano SA:** Avda Central 643, San Isidro, Apdo 929, Lima 1; tel. (14) 215800; telex 25369; fax (14) 425136; f. 1959.

**Naviera Amazónica Peruana, SA:** Avda San Borja Norte 761, San Borja, Lima 41; tel. (14) 752033; telex 21072; fax (14) 759680; Pres. L. ALZAMORA; Exec. Dir OSCAR UBILLUZ.

**Naviera Humboldt, SA:** Edif. Pacífico–Washington, 9°, Natalio Sánchez 125, Apdo 3639, Lima 1; tel. (14) 334005; telex 20281; fax (14) 337151; f. 1970; cargo services; Pres. AUGUSTO BEDOYA CAMERE; Man. Dir LUIS FREIRE R.

**Naviera Santa, SA:** Avda José Pardo 182, 8°, Miraflores, Apdo 86, Lima; tel. (14) 450584; telex 20161; fax (14) 469268; Gen. Man. ROBERTO L. RIVEROS.

**Naviera Universal, SA:** Las Oropendolas 265, San Isidro, Apdo 10307, Lima 100; tel. (14) 757020; telex 21358; fax (14) 755233; Chair. HERBERT C. BUERGER.

**Petroleos del Perú (PETROPERU):** Paseo de la República 3361, San Isidro, Apdo 1081, Lima; tel. (14) 411919; telex 21064; Pres. JUAN F. C. RASSELET.

A number of foreign lines call at Peruvian ports.

## CIVIL AVIATION

Of Peru's 310 airports, the major international airport is Jorge Chávez Airport near Lima. Other important international airports are Coronel Francisco Secada Vignetta Airport, near Iquitos, Velasco Astete Airport, near Cuzco, and Rodríguez Ballón Airport, near Arequipa.

### Domestic Airlines

**Aeroperú:** Avda José Pardo 601, Miraflores, Lima 18; tel. (14) 478900; telex 21382; fax (14) 443974; f. 1973 as the national airline, partially 'privatized', in 1981; 47% share sold to Aero-México (Mexico) in 1993; operates internal services and international routes to Central and South America and the USA; Pres. ROBERTO ABUSADA; Gen. Man. ALEJANDRO GÓMEZ MONTOY.

**Aeronaves del Perú, SA:** Jirón José Cálvez 711, Lima 18; tel. (14) 476488; telex 21213; fax (14) 479558; f. 1965; scheduled cargo services and charter flights between Lima and major Central and South American destinations, and the USA (Miami); Pres. ALFREDO ZANATTI.

**Compañía de Aviación Faucett:** Aeropuerto Jorge Chávez, Apdo 1429, Lima; tel. (14) 643424; telex 25225; fax (14) 641114; f. 1928; scheduled internal passenger services, cargo and passenger services to Miami via Panama City and Iquitos and passenger and cargo charters; Pres. ROBERTO LEIGH.

# Tourism

Tourism is centred on Lima, with its Spanish colonial architecture, and Cuzco, with its pre-Inca and Inca civilization, notably the 'lost city' of Machu Picchu. Lake Titicaca, lying at an altitude of 3,850 m above sea-level, and the Amazon jungle region to the north-east also form popular resorts, and tourist authorities plan to develop fishing, trekking and mountaineering holidays. In the early 1990s efforts to develop the sector were adversely affected, owing to concerns about guerrilla violence in the country. In 1992 Peru received 216,534 visitors, a decline of 40% from the number of tourists in 1988. Receipts from tourism amounted to US $237m. in 1992.

## PRINCIPAL TOURIST ORGANIZATIONS

**Viceministerio de Turismo:** Ministerio de Industria, Comercio, Turismo e Integración, Calle 1 Oeste, Corpac, San Isidro, Lima 27; tel. (14) 402129; telex 20194.

**Fondo de Promoción Turística (FOPTUR):** Calle Uno, 14°, Urbanización Corpac, San Isidro, Lima; fax (14) 429280; f. 1979; Pres. JUAN LIRA; Gen. Man. JUAN MANUEL ECHEVERRÍA.

# THE PHILIPPINES

## Introductory Survey

### Location, Climate, Language, Religion, Flag, Capital

The Republic of the Philippines lies in the western Pacific Ocean, east of mainland South-East Asia. The island of Kalimantan (Borneo) is to the south-west, and New Guinea to the south-east. The principal islands of the Philippine archipelago are Luzon, in the north, and Mindanao, in the south. Between these two (which together account for 66% of the country's area) lie the 7,000 islands of the Visayas. The climate is maritime and tropical. It is generally hot and humid, except in the mountains. There is abundant rainfall, and the islands are frequently in the path of typhoons. At the 1990 census there were 988 languages; the most frequently used were Tagalog (by 27.9% of the population), Cebuano (24.3%), Ilocano (9.8%), Hiligaynon (Ilongo—9.3%) and Bicol (5.8%). Filipino, based on Tagalog, is the native national language. English is widely spoken, and Spanish is used in some communities. In 1991 94.2% of the population were Christians (84.1% Roman Catholics, 6.2% belonged to the Philippine Independent Church (Aglipayan) and 3.9% were Protestants). In 1990 an estimated 4.6% of the population were Muslims. The national flag (proportions 2 by 1) has two equal horizontal stripes, of blue and red, with a white triangle, enclosing a gold 'Sun of Liberty' (with eight rays) and three five-pointed gold stars (one in each corner), at the hoist. The capital is Manila, on the island of Luzon.

### Recent History

The Philippines became a Spanish colony in the 16th century. During the Spanish–American War, the independence of the Philippines was declared on 12 June 1898 by Gen. Emilio Aguinaldo, leader of the revolutionary movement, with the support of the USA. Under the Treaty of Paris, signed in December 1898, Spain ceded the islands to the USA. A new Constitution, ratified by plebiscite in May 1935, gave the Philippines internal self-government and provided for independence after 10 years. During the Second World War the islands were occupied by Japanese forces from 1942, but, after Japan's surrender in 1945, US rule was restored. The Philippines became an independent republic on 4 July 1946, with Manuel Roxas as its first President. A succession of Presidents, effectively constrained by US economic interests and the Filipino land-owning class, did little to help the peasant majority or to curb disorder and political violence.

At elections in November 1965 the incumbent President, Diosdado Macapagal of the Liberal Party, was defeated by Ferdinand Marcos of the Nacionalista Party (NP). Rapid development of the economy and infrastructure followed. President Marcos was re-elected in 1969. His second term was marked by civil unrest and economic difficulties. During the early 1970s there was also an increase in guerrilla activity, by the New People's Army (NPA), the armed wing of the outlawed (Maoist) Communist Party of the Philippines (CPP), in the north of the country, and by the Moro National Liberation Front (MNLF), a Muslim separatist movement, in the south.

In September 1972, before completing the (then) maximum of two four-year terms of office, President Marcos declared martial law in order to deal with subversive activity and to introduce drastic reforms. The bicameral Congress was suspended, opposition leaders were arrested, the private armies of the landed oligarchs were disbanded, stringent press censorship was introduced, and Marcos began to rule by decree. In November a new Constitution was approved by a constitutional convention, and in January 1973 it was ratified by Marcos. It provided for a unicameral National Assembly and a Constitutional President, with executive power held by a Prime Minister, to be elected by the legislature. Transitional provisions gave the incumbent President the combined authority of the presidency (under the 1935 Constitution) and the premiership, without any fixed term of office. Under martial law, the definitive provisions of the new Constitution remained in abeyance.

A referendum in July 1973 approved Marcos's continuation in office beyond his elected term. Referendums in February 1975 and October 1976 approved the continuation of martial law and the adoption of constitutional amendments, including a provision for the formation of an interim assembly. In December 1977 a fourth referendum approved the extension of Marcos's presidential term.

Criticism of Marcos became more widespread after November 1977, when a sentence of death was imposed by a military tribunal on the principal opposition leader, Benigno Aquino, Jr (a former senator and Secretary-General of the Liberal Party, who had been detained since 1972), for alleged murder, subversion and the possession of firearms. Marcos allowed a stay of execution, and conceded some relaxation of martial law in 1977. Elections to the interim National Assembly took place in April 1978. Opposition parties were allowed to participate, but the pro-Government Kilusang Bagong Lipunan (KBL—New Society Movement), founded in 1978 by Marcos and former members of the NP, won 151 of the Assembly's 165 elective seats. The Assembly was inaugurated in June, when Marcos was also confirmed as Prime Minister. Martial law remained in force, and Marcos retained the power to legislate by decree. Local elections, the first to be held in eight years, took place in January 1980, resulting in decisive victories for the KBL. In May Aquino was released from prison to undergo medical treatment in the USA, where he renewed his opposition to Marcos's regime.

In January 1981 martial law was ended, although Marcos retained most of his former powers. A referendum in April approved constitutional amendments that permitted Marcos to renew his mandate by direct popular vote and to nominate a separate Prime Minister. In June, amid allegations of electoral malpractice, Marcos was re-elected President for a six-year term. In April 1982 the United Nationalist Democratic Organization (UNIDO), an alliance of opposition groups, formed an official coalition: it included Lakas ng Bayan (the People's Power Movement, founded by Aquino in 1978) and the Pilipino Democratic Party (PDP), which merged to form PDP-Laban in 1983.

In August 1983 Aquino, returning from exile in the USA, was shot dead on arrival at Manila airport. Rolando Galman, the alleged communist assassin, was killed immediately by military guards. A commission of inquiry, nominated by the Government, concluded that Aquino's murder had been a military conspiracy. The Supreme Court announced in December 1985, however, that the evidence submitted to the commission was inadmissible, acquitted the 26 military personnel who had been accused of conspiring to murder Aquino and upheld the Government's assertion that the assassin was Galman.

Aquino's death proved to be a turning-point in Philippine politics, uniting the opposition in its criticism of Marcos. At elections to the National Assembly in May 1984, public participation was high, and, after numerous accusations by the opposition of electoral fraud and corruption by Marcos, the opposition won 59 of the 183 elective seats, compared with 14 in 1978.

In November 1985, in response to US pressure (and after continued appeals for domestic reform), Marcos announced that a presidential election would be held in February 1986, 18 months earlier than scheduled. Corazon Aquino, the widow of Benigno Aquino, was chosen as the UNIDO presidential candidate, in spite of her lack of political experience. More than 100 people were killed in violence during the election campaign. Vote-counting was conducted by the government-controlled National Commission on Elections (Comelec) and by the independent National Citizens' Movement for Free Elections (Namfrel). Allegations of large-scale electoral fraud and irregularities, apparently perpetrated by supporters of Marcos, were substantiated by numerous international observers. On 16 February 1986 the National Assembly declared Marcos the winner of the presidential election, with 10.8m. votes, compared with 9.3m. for Aquino, according to figures from Comelec. According to Namfrel figures (based on 69% of the total votes), Aquino was in the lead. Marcos immediately announced the resignation of the Cabinet, and declared his intention to establish a council of presidential advisers. Aquino rejected an offer to participate in the council, and launched a campaign of non-violent pressure on the Government, including a boycott of many organizations connected with the Marcos family.

On 22 February 1986 Lt-Gen. (later Gen.) Fidel Ramos, the acting Chief of Staff of the Armed Forces, and Juan Enrile, the Minister of National Defense, along with about 300 troops, established a rebel headquarters in the Ministry of National Defense in Manila (later moving to the police headquarters), stating that they no longer accepted Marcos's authority and asserting that Aquino was the rightful President. Attempts by forces loyal to Marcos to attack the rebels were foiled by large unarmed crowds which gathered to protect them. Troops supporting Ramos subsequently secured control of the government broadcasting station, with little bloodshed. On 25 February rival ceremonies were held, at which both Marcos and Aquino were sworn in as President. Later the same day, however, under pressure from the USA, Marcos finally agreed to withdraw, and left the Philippines for Hawaii.

President Aquino received worldwide recognition, including that of the US Government, upon her inauguration. She appointed her Vice-President, Salvador Laurel (the President of UNIDO), to be Prime Minister and Minister of Foreign Affairs, while Enrile retained the post of Minister of National Defense. Ramos was appointed Chief of Staff of the Armed Forces. At the end of February 1986 Aquino ordered the controversial release of all political prisoners, including communist leaders. In March the Government announced the restoration of habeas corpus, the abolition of press censorship and the suspension of local government elections (scheduled for May). The Government also secured the resignation of all Justices of the Supreme Court, as well as the resignation of Comelec members. On 25 March Aquino announced that the 1973 Constitution was to be replaced by an interim document, providing for the immediate abolition of the National Assembly and for the inauguration of a provisional government, with the President being granted emergency powers. The post of Prime Minister was temporarily abolished, and in May a commission was appointed to draft a new constitution.

During 1986 and 1987 the Aquino Government struggled to maintain control over the army (which was divided into reformist and pro-Marcos factions) while, at the same time, appeasing left-wing labour movements and endeavouring to bring to an end the 17-year insurgency by the NPA and the 14-year war of secession in Mindanao by Muslim separatists. These problems were compounded by dissension within the Government regarding major policies and by the near-bankruptcy of the country's economy.

In March 1986 military leaders pledged their loyalty to Aquino as President and Commander-in-Chief of the Armed Forces. The Government then began to implement a programme of military reform, in accordance with the demands of officers of the Rebolusyonaryong Alyansang Makabayan (RAM—Nationalist Revolutionary Alliance—also known as the Reform the Armed Forces Movement), who had supported the February revolution. In September the Supreme Court ordered the retrial of the members of the military who had earlier been acquitted of the murder of Benigno Aquino. In September 1990, following a trial lasting more than three years, a special court convicted 16 members of the armed forces of the murder of both Aquino and Galman; a further 20 defendants were acquitted.

In July 1986 an abortive coup took place in Manila, led by Arturo Tolentino, a former Minister of Foreign Affairs and Marcos's vice-presidential candidate, and a group of 300 pro-Marcos troops. One of the principal reasons for military dissatisfaction was the new Government's conciliatory attitude towards communist insurgents. In June the Government had attempted to bring guerrilla activity by the NPA (estimated to number 25,000–30,000 members at that time) to an end, announcing that formal negotiations for a cease-fire agreement would begin with representatives of the National Democratic Front (NDF—a left-wing group that included the CPP and the NPA). In October, however, increasing pressure from Enrile and the RAM prompted Aquino to threaten the insurgents with open warfare if a solution were not reached by the end of November. In late November a group of army officers attempted to gain control of several military camps and to replace Aquino with Nicanor Yniguez, a former Speaker of the National Assembly. The rebellion was quelled by Ramos and troops loyal to Aquino; Enrile was dismissed from the Cabinet, and replaced by his deputy, Gen. Rafael Ileto. In January 1987 there was a further coup attempt by 500 disaffected troops, who seized control of military camps and a broadcasting station; an attempt by Marcos to return to the Philippines was thwarted by US officials, and the two-day rebellion was crushed by pro-Aquino forces.

In February 1987 a new Constitution was approved by 76% of voters in a national plebiscite. The new Constitution gave Aquino a mandate to rule until 30 June 1992, and established an executive presidency (see Government, below). All members of the armed forces swore an oath of allegiance to the new Constitution. An order followed disbanding all 'fraternal organizations' (such as the RAM) within the armed forces, because they 'encouraged divisiveness'. Elections to the bicameral Congress of the Philippines took place on 11 May 1987 (as provided for in the new Constitution), at which more than 83% of the electorate participated. Aquino's Lakas ng Bayan coalition secured 180 of the 200 elective seats in the House of Representatives and 22 of the 24 seats in the Senate.

In August 1987 Ramos and troops loyal to Aquino averted a serious coup attempt, when rebel officers (led by Col Gregorio Honasan, an officer closely associated with Enrile) occupied the army headquarters, and captured a radio and television station. In the intense fighting that ensued in Manila and Cebu, 53 people were killed. Honasan and his supporters fled the following day, successfully evading capture by government forces until December. (Honasan, however, escaped from detention in April 1988.)

In late January 1988 Ileto resigned from the Cabinet, and was replaced as Secretary of National Defense by Ramos (who was, in turn, succeeded as Chief of Staff of the Armed Forces by Gen. Renato de Villa). Shortly afterwards the Government announced an intensification of its campaign against communist rebels. In March 1988 the General Secretary of the CPP, Rafael Baylosis, and the commander of the NPA, Romulo Kintanar, were captured by the armed forces. (Kintanar escaped in November.)

In June 1988 members of pro-Government parties, comprising a faction of PDP-Laban and Lakas ng Bansa, formed a grouping named Laban ng Demokratikong Pilipino (LDP). In September the Speaker of the House of Representatives, Ramon Mitra, was elected President of the new alliance. Laurel formally dissociated himself from Aquino in August, and announced the formation, under his leadership, of the Union for National Action (UNA), a broadly-based opposition front.

In October 1988 Marcos and his wife, Imelda, were indicted in the USA and charged with the illegal transfer into the country of some US $100m. that had allegedly been obtained by embezzlement and racketeering. Marcos was said to be too ill to attend the proceedings. In November thousands of civilian supporters of Marcos entered Manila and distributed leaflets demanding a military rebellion to overthrow Aquino, before being dispersed by the armed forces. In February 1989 Laurel visited Marcos in hospital in Hawaii, and began to campaign for Marcos to be permitted to return to the Philippines. In May Marcos's NP was revived, with Laurel as President and Enrile as Secretary-General.

In September 1989 the Philippine Government began the first of 35 planned civil suits against Marcos *in absentia*, following charges of corruption filed in Manila in July 1987. After Marcos's death in Hawaii at the end of September 1989, the opposition, particularly Laurel, aligned themselves with Marcos loyalists to exert pressure on Aquino to allow Marcos a funeral in the Philippines. In October the Supreme Court upheld (by a narrow majority) its previous ruling prohibiting the return of Marcos's body, in response to a petition, submitted by the former President's supporters, asking the court to overrule the ban. The trial of Imelda Marcos, on charges of fraud and of the illegal transfer of stolen funds into the USA, began in New York in April 1990; she was acquitted of all charges in July.

In December 1989 an abortive coup was staged by members of two elite military units, in collusion with the now illicit RAM and officers loyal to Marcos. At Aquino's request units of the US Air Force were mobilized to deter further aerial attacks by the rebels. Aquino subsequently addressed a rally of 100,000 supporters, during which she accused Laurel and Enrile (who were both included in an eight-member provisional junta named by the rebels) of involvement in the coup attempt.

In February 1990 Enrile was arrested on charges of 'rebellion complexed with murder' and of harbouring the reputed rebel leader, Honasan. He was subsequently released on bail pending a court ruling on the validity of the former charge. In June the Supreme Court ordered the charge of 'rebellion complexed with murder' against Enrile and 22 other alleged rebels to be amended to 'simple rebellion' or 'illegal possession of firearms'. The court ruled that the original charge had been removed by Aquino from the statute book in 1986 by a presidential decree.

In July 1990 an earthquake in the north, with its epicentre in Baguio City, affected Central and Northern Luzon and killed about 1,600 people. In response to the earthquake, the NPA unilaterally declared a cease-fire in Manila, Mountain Province, Baguio City, Benguit and Nueva Viscaya. Aquino, however, ordered that military action against the communist rebels should continue. In August right-wing dissident soldiers bombed the Department of Trade and Industry in Manila. There followed a series of bombings of businesses that were owned by US interests or associated with the Aquino Government, and that had been accused of corruption. At the end of August Aquino expressed willingness to hold discussions with both dissident troops and communist rebels, in an effort to achieve a general reconciliation. Opposition leaders, including Enrile, were also invited to attend. In early September Aquino suspended offensives against the NPA in Manila and in northern areas affected by the earthquake. However, in late September the NPA ended the truce and threatened to intensify the insurgency. The dissident members of the armed forces also continued their campaign to destabilize the Government: between mid-August and the beginning of October about 40 incendiary devices were planted (allegedly by members of the armed forces) in and around Manila.

In December 1990 a military court sentenced 81 members of the armed forces to prison terms of up to 32 years for their part in the rebellion of August 1987. In April 1991 Aquino disregarded traditional considerations of seniority and appointed Maj.-Gen. (later Gen.) Lisandro Abadio, hitherto the Chief of Staff of the Army, as Chief of Staff of the Armed Forces. In early 1991 the NPA conducted a successful campaign, killing 563 members of the armed forces between January and April, and maintaining an active presence in 55 of the 73 provinces. In July, however, government troops captured the NPA's most important base, Camp Venus, in Sagada, Mountain Province. In July and August government forces seized 13 senior NPA members, including Kintanar.

In July 1991 Ramos resigned as Secretary of National Defense in order to contest the presidential election (scheduled for 1992); he was replaced in the Government by de Villa. Ramos had joined the ruling LDP in April to compete with Ramon Mitra for the party's nomination for the presidential election. Later in 1991 Aquino announced that Imelda Marcos and her family would be permitted to return to the Philippines to stand trial on charges of fraud and tax evasion. Following several postponements Imelda Marcos eventually arrived in Manila in November; she was brought to trial on seven charges of tax evasion in December.

In January 1992 Aquino endorsed the presidential candidacy of Ramos, thus ending speculation that, despite her constant denials, she might seek re-election. Aquino's support for Ramos threatened to divide the LDP, which, in November 1991, had selected Mitra as its presidential candidate. Ramos, whose candidature elicited much support from the commercial sector, initially conceded defeat, but subsequently resigned from the LDP and formed the Partido Lakas Tao (People Power Party—PPP). Aquino's support for Ramos, a Protestant, was contrary to the preference of the Roman Catholic Church, which had hitherto been a close ally of Aquino and had played an important role in the overthrow of President Marcos in 1986. Cardinal Jaime Sin, the Catholic Archbishop of Manila, later endorsed Mitra's candidacy and criticized Ramos's involvement (as Chief of Staff of the Armed Forces) in the Marcos regime. Shortly after Aquino's endorsement Ramos discarded the PPP and registered a new party, EDSA-LDP, with the support of 25 former LDP members of Congress. (EDSA was the popular acronym for the Epifanio de los Santos Avenue, the main site of the February 1986 uprising.) The party, which formed an informal electoral alliance with the National Union of Christian Democrats (Lakas-NUCD), subsequently altered its title to Lakas ng EDSA.

In November 1991 the NP divided into three factions, following Laurel's expulsion of Enrile and Eduardo Cojuangco (Aquino's estranged cousin), his two rivals for the party nomination in the presidential election, for allegedly infringing party rules. In February 1992 Enrile withdrew as a candidate for the presidency and gave the support of his faction of the NP to Mitra, in exchange for places in the LDP's list of candidates for the legislative and local elections. Later in February Comelec adopted a resolution authorizing the candidacies of only eight of the 78 presidential nominees: Mitra; Cojuangco (whose wing of the NP had been renamed the Nationalist People's Coalition—NPC); Ramos; Imelda Marcos, whose candidacy was supported by what remained of the KBL; Laurel, supported by his faction of the NP; Miriam Defensor Santiago, a former Secretary of Agrarian Reform, supported by the People's Reform Party (PRP); Jovita Salonga, leader of the Liberal Party; and Joseph Estrada, a former film actor and senator, who later withdrew his presidential candidacy in order to contest the election as a vice-presidential candidate, supporting Cojuangco.

In February 1992 the human rights organization, Amnesty International, published a report accusing the Aquino administration of acquiescence in violations of human rights by the armed forces. The report, which followed previous documents critical of the Aquino Government, alleged that 550 extra-judicial killings had taken place during 1988–91. The armed forces refuted the report's findings, and accused Amnesty International of ignoring rebel atrocities.

On 11 May 1992 elections took place to select the President, Vice-President, 24 senators, 200 members of the House of Representatives and 17,014 local officials. More than 100 people were killed in outbreaks of violence during the pre-election period. Owing to the protracted vote-counting procedure, the result of the presidential election was not proclaimed by Congress until 22 June. Ramos was elected to the presidency, with 23.6% of the votes cast; his closest rivals were Santiago (with 19.7%) and Cojuangco (18.2%). The election was relatively free and fair, and Santiago's allegations of electoral fraud remained largely unsubstantiated. The success of Ramos and the high level of support for Santiago (whose electoral campaign had emphasized the need to eradicate corruption) was widely regarded as a rejection of traditional patronage party politics, since neither candidate was supported by a large-scale party organization. In the legislative elections, however, the LDP (the only party that had local bases in every province) won 16 of the 24 seats in the Senate and 89 of the 200 elective seats in the House of Representatives.

Following his inauguration on 30 June 1992, Ramos formed a new administration that included six members of the outgoing Government, among them de Villa, who remained Secretary of National Defense, and many senior business executives. Despite his party's poor representation in Congress, Ramos managed to gain the support of Cojuangco's NPC, the Liberal Party and 55 defectors (now known as Laban) from the LDP, to form a 'rainbow coalition', comprising 145 of the 200 elected members of the House of Representatives. The Senate remained nominally under the control of the LDP, but Ramos ensured that he maintained good relations with individual senators. The Senate's support for the new regime was demonstrated in January 1993, when Edgardo Angara, an LDP senator regarded as sympathetic to Ramas, replaced Neptali Gonzales (also of the LDP) as President of the Senate.

In July 1992 Ramos formed the Presidential Anti-Crime Commission (PACC), headed by Estrada, to combat organized crime in the Philippines. A principal concern of the PACC was the alarming increase in abduction, mainly of wealthy ethnic Chinese Filipinos, for ransom, owing to its detrimental effect on investment. It emerged that members of the Philippine National Police (PNP) were largely responsible for the abductions, and in August the Chief of Police resigned. In April 1993, following a complete review of the PNP, Ramos ordered the discharge of hundreds of personnel, including 63 of the 194 senior officers. There was also a serious decline in public respect for the judiciary, following allegations that seven Supreme Court judges were accepting bribes from drugs-dealers and other criminal syndicates. The Chief Justice, Andres Narvas, ordered an extensive internal inquiry into charges of corruption in the Supreme Court. In February Congress adopted legislation (which was signed into law in December) to reinstate the death penalty, which had been banned under the 1987 Constitution with a provision for its reintroduction under extreme circumstances. In July 1993 Ramos established a 60-day period during which the security forces were to disarm the 560 private armies in the Philippines, which were controlled mostly by provincial politicians and wealthy landowners. The deadline for the dissolution of the private militias was subsequently extended until the end of November, although by this date little progress had been made.

In August 1992 Ramos gave permission (which had been denied by Aquino) for the remains of Ferdinand Marcos to be brought from Hawaii to the Philippines for a private burial in his native province of Ilocos Norte. After considerable delay, in September 1993 Marcos's remains were returned to the Philippines, and a funeral service was conducted in Ilocos Norte, attended by only a few thousand supporters. Later that month Imelda Marcos was convicted of corruption and sentenced to 18 years' imprisonment; she declared her intention to appeal against the conviction. She was acquitted of two other charges but was banned from holding public office. In February 1994 a district court in Honolulu, Hawaii awarded US $1,200m. in punitive damages to 10,000 Filipinos tortured under President Marcos's administration, following a court ruling in October 1992 that victims of abuses of human rights under the Marcos regime could sue his estate for compensation. Imelda Marcos announced that she would appeal against the decision. Further charges of embezzlement were filed against her in April and June 1994.

On assuming power, Ramos undertook to give priority to the restoration of order by persuading mutinous right-wing soldiers, communist insurgents and Muslim separatists to abandon their armed struggle. In July 1992 two communist leaders, including Baylosis, were conditionally released, and Ramos submitted to Congress an amnesty proclamation for about 4,500 members of the NPA, the MNLF and renegade former members of the armed forces who had already applied for amnesty. In August the National Unification Commission (NUC) was formed to consult rebel groups and formulate a viable amnesty programme. Later that month Ramos ordered the temporary release from prison of more communist leaders, including Kintanar and the NDF Spokesman, Saturnino Ocampo, and also of 16 rebel soldiers. In the same month the Government began discussions with exiled representatives of the NDF in the Netherlands.

In September 1992 Ramos repealed anti-subversion legislation, in place since 1957, that proscribed the CPP. However, the exiled leadership of the NDF issued a statement to the effect that the CPP would continue its armed struggle, although there was a widening division within the CPP over the issue of co-operation with the NUC. Jose Maria Sison, a founder member of the CPP who had been based in the Netherlands since his release from prison in 1986, resumed the party chairmanship in April 1992. The party's command structure was thrown into disarray, as his election to the leadership was not recognized by all party members. In December Sison, who adopted an intransigent stance towards the Government's peace moves and who initiated a (largely ignored) purge in the CPP of those members who had deviated from Maoist orthodoxy, accused his opponents, including Kintanar, of collusion with the Ramos administration. Also in December the amnesty programme was expanded to include political prisoners who had been convicted on criminal charges.

In July 1993 the CPP's influential Manila-Rizal regional committee publicly broke away from the CPP Central Committee led by Sison. This followed the reported dissolution five months earlier by Sison of the region's leading committee and its armed unit, the Alex Boncayao Brigade, accused of factionalism and military excesses. The Manila-Rizal organization, which comprised about 40% of CPP members, was subsequently joined by the CPP regional committee of the Visayas. In August the division in the CPP caused the collapse of several national left-wing organizations, including the independent trade union, Kilusang Mayo Uno. In the same month the Government and the NDF, still under the control of Sison, agreed that the second round of discussions should take place in Viet Nam. In October four communist leaders, including Kintanar and Arturo Tabara, the Secretary-General of the Central Philippine Command of the NPA, were expelled from the CPP and the NPA for refusing to recognize the authority of Sison. (In January 1994 four regional communist leaders, including Tabara, were arrested.) In December 1993 Sison accepted an earlier government offer of travel documents valid for six months to enable him to attend the proposed negotiations in Viet Nam, but continued to delay the commencement of discussions. In January 1994 Sison requested that a second round of preliminary talks be held in the Netherlands prior to negotiations in Viet Nam. In early May the then General Secretary of the CPP, Wilma Tiamzon, was arrested with four other suspected dissidents. Tiamzon was detained in a hospital for two weeks, while receiving medical treatment, before being released (following discussions with Ramos) on humanitarian grounds. Fileman Lagman, reputedly the commander of the Alex Boncayao Brigade and head of the CPP's Manila committee, was arrested in Quezon City later in the month, but was released on bail in June. Negotiations resumed between the Government and the NPA in the Netherlands in October, but later collapsed, owing to the failure of the two sides to agree terms for the granting of immunity. It was subsequently agreed to resume talks in Belgium in June 1995.

In September 1992 seven military renegades, including Honasan, were granted passes of safe conduct to enable peace talks to proceed. In December the seven fugitives emerged from hiding to sign a preliminary agreement to take part in talks with the Government. Discussions between the NUC and representatives of the RAM and the Young Officers' Union (YOU—a progressive offshoot of the RAM, which was alleged to have played an important role in the December 1989 coup attempt) began in January 1993, were suspended (owing to disagreement), resumed in February and were subsequently suspended again. In early 1993 left- and right-wing rebels formed an unlikely alliance to promote peace negotiations, styling themselves the Warriors for Peace. Members of the movement included Kintanar and Ocampo of the CPP and Brig.-Gen. Edgardo Abenino of the RAM and the YOU. In February 1994 Abenino announced that peace negotiations with the RAM and the YOU would continue to be suspended, pending the release of six military detainees. The following month Ramos proclaimed a general amnesty for all rebels and for members of the security forces charged with offences committed during counter-insurgency operations, as recommended by the NUC in a report submitted to Ramos in July 1993; the amnesty did not, however, include persons convicted of torture, arson, massacre, rape and robbery. The RAM rejected the amnesty on the grounds that it failed to address the causes of the rebellion, while Ocampo dismissed the proclamation as being biased against the communist rebels. The RAM sought a resumption of peace talks in December 1994.

In January 1994 an increase in petroleum prices took effect following a levy imposed by Ramos in September 1993, which had initially been charged to the Oil Price Stabilization Fund. The Philippine Left, a group of autonomous socialist organizations led by elements of the CPP, organized a popular campaign in protest at price increases, the Trade Union Congress of the Philippines threatened a general strike, and the Alex Boncayao Brigade initiated bomb attacks on the country's three leading petroleum companies. At the end of February Ramos rescinded the levy, and established a committee to study alternative methods of raising government revenue. In May legislation was enacted amending the system of value-added tax (VAT) in order to offset the losses in revenue arising from the withdrawal of the levy on petroleum prices. However, popular opposition to the extended VAT gathered momentum during June, and Ramos's attempts to diminish dissent by granting certain exemptions fuelled the public perception that the legislation was flawed. Opposition parties organized broadly-based coalitions to oppose the law, while senators who initially supported the bill began to advocate its abrogation. At the end of June the Supreme Court issued an injunction on the legislation, preventing its implementation at the beginning of July, pending rulings on legal challenges that the legislation and its enactment violated the Constitution. In August the Supreme Court ruled that the VAT legislation was constitutional; however, it could not be implemented pending the outcome of an appeal against the ruling by opposition groupings.

In July 1994 the majority leader of the House of Representatives, Ronald Zamora, defected from the Lakas-NUCD to the NPC; shortly afterwards he and 19 other members of the NPC resigned from the ruling coalition. In August an electoral alliance (Lakas-Laban) was agreed between the Lakas-NUCD coalition and the LDP, which allowed for a common list of candidates at elections, due in 1995, for 12 senatorial seats, as well as for the elective seats in the House of Representatives and provincial governorships and other local government posts.

In January 1995 Pope John Paul II visited the Philippines; an estimated 4m. people attended a mass held in Manila. Prior to his arrival the Government claimed to have uncovered an assassination plot by Muslim extremists, one of whom was allegedly implicated in the bombing of the World Trade Center in New York in 1993.

During January 1995 the Marcos estate was ordered by the Honolulu district court to pay a total of some US $774m. to more than 9,000 Filipinos who had suffered torture under the regime of Ferdinand Marcos; of the total, $7.3m. was awarded in respect of individual actions taken by 21 victims, the remainder being awarded collectively. At the end of January the Philippine Supreme Court restored a 'freeze' on the assets of more than 530 companies controlled by associates of Marcos, which had been revoked on technical grounds by a lower court in 1991. In March 1995 Imelda Marcos announced that she would seek election to the House of Representatives. Comelec disqualified her candidacy, ruling that she failed to fulfil residency criteria; however, she appealed to the Supreme Court to overturn the disqualification, and was allowed to contest the election pending the outcome of her appeal. Marcos's son, Ferdinand 'Bong-Bong' Marcos II, contested (unsuccessfully) a seat in the Senate.

In the six weeks of campaigning for the elections an estimated 80 people were reported to have been killed. The elections, on 8 May 1995, were generally believed to have been conducted in a free and fair manner, although Comelec subsequently began investigations into alleged electoral malpractice in three contested senate seats. During the campaign Ramos declared that the elections would signify a referendum on his three years as President, and stressed the economic successes that had been achieved during 1994. Some 80% of all eligible voters were estimated to have participated in the elections. Ramos claimed victory for his electoral alliance before voting had been completed, and announced that he had secured an overwhelming mandate to continue his policies of reform. In June candidates of the Lakas-Laban electoral alliance were declared to have won nine of the 12 contested seats in the Senate; the PRP won two seats, and the NPC one. The coalition was also expected to have won an estimated 90% of the 204 elective seats in the House of Representatives, and more than 80% of the provincial governorships. By mid-July the official results of the elections to the House of Representatives had yet to be announced, pending the outcome of various legal challenges.

During 1986 the Aquino Government conducted negotiations to seek a solution to the conflict with Muslim separatists in the south. A cease-fire was established with the MNLF in September, following an announcement by the Government that it would grant legal and judicial autonomy to four predominantly Muslim provinces in Mindanao. Further talks ensued, under the auspices of the Organization of the Islamic Conference (OIC—see p. 208), and on 5 January 1987 the MNLF signed an agreement to relinquish demands for complete independence in Mindanao, and to accept autonomy. In February 1988 however, the MNLF resumed its offensive against the Government, which had attempted to prevent the MNLF from gaining membership of the OIC (which would imply that the MNLF was regarded as representing an independent state). The 1987 Constitution granted eventual autonomy to Muslim provinces in Mindanao, which had been promised by President Marcos in 1976. In November 1989 a plebiscite was held, in the country's 13 southern provinces and nine cities in Mindanao, on proposed legislation that envisaged the autonomy of these provinces and cities, with direct elections to a unicameral legislature in each province; this contrasted with the MNLF's demand for autonomy in 23 provinces, to be granted without a referendum. Four provinces (Lanao del Sur, Maguindanao, Tawi-Tawi and Sulu) voted in favour of the government proposal, and formed the autonomous region of Muslim Mindanao.

In February 1990 the candidate favoured by Aquino, Zacaria Candao (formerly the legal representative of the MNLF), was elected to the governorship of Muslim Mindanao. In October the autonomous regional government was granted limited executive powers. The MNLF boycotted the election, on the grounds that the provisions for autonomy were more limited than those reached with Marcos in 1976. Under Ramos's programme of reconciliation, the MNLF participated in discussions with the NUC. In October 1992 the leader of the MNLF, Nur Misuari, agreed to return to the Philippines from exile in Libya to facilitate negotiations. In January 1993 talks were suspended, and violence in Mindanao escalated prior to the impending elections for the region's Governor and Assembly. At the elections, which took place on 25 March, a former ambassador, Lininding Pangandaman, won 72% of the votes cast in the gubernatorial contest, with the unofficial support of Ramos; 81% of the electorate voted. The local branch of the Lakas-NUCD won nine of the 21 legislative seats.

In April 1993 exploratory discussions in Jakarta, Indonesia, between Nur Misuari and representatives of the Philippine Government led to an agreement on the resumption of formal peace talks under the auspices of the OIC. Further exploratory talks took place in Saudi Arabia in June, prior to the first formal negotiations in October in Jakarta, where the MNLF demanded the creation of an autonomous Islamic state in the south, as agreed in 1976. In November the two sides signed a memorandum of understanding and an interim cease-fire was agreed. In response to the progress of the negotiations further violence occurred in the south, including an assault on a Roman Catholic cathedral in Davao City followed by retaliatory attacks on three mosques by Christian extremists. In January 1994 the terms of the cease-fire were agreed, stipulating that both government and rebel forces should remain in place and refrain from provocative action. Nur Misuari subsequently gave an assurance that MNLF demands for a transitional government in Mindanao would not affect the terms of office of the officials of the exisiting autonomous region of Muslim Mindanao, which expired in 1996. The second round of formal peace negotiations between the Government and the MNLF took place in Jakarta in April 1994.

In early June 1994 the Government undertook a major offensive against Abu Sayyaf, a Muslim secessionist group held responsible for numerous attacks, principally on the islands of Jolo and Basilan, to the south of Mindanao. In retaliation for the capture by the armed forces of its base on Jolo, the group took a number of Christians hostage on Basilan, killing 15. All but one of the remaining 21 hostages were released in mid-June, following the apparent payment of a ransom and the intercession of the MNLF. Later in June government troops captured the group's main headquarters in Basilan. In early August it was reported that Abu Sayyaf's leader had been killed; the group's remaining hostage was released, and the authorities announced that Abu Sayyaf had been 'eliminated'. In April 1995, however, the group was believed to be responsible for an attack by an estimated 200 guerrillas on the town of Ipil, in Mindanao, as a result of which as many as 100 people were killed. Some of the assailants were also believed to be part of a splinter group of the MNLF, the Islamic Command Council. Some 14 hostages were reportedly killed as the army pursued the rebels in their retreat from Ipil. Despite the attack, Ramos pledged to continue negotiations with the MNLF, which condemned the guerrilla's actions. In early September 1994 a further round of talks with the MNLF took place in Jakarta, at which agreement was reached, *inter alia*, regarding the establishment by an MNLF government of a bank and the issue of treasury bills (in co-operation with the country's Central Bank). However, the question of the integration of former MNLF fighters into the armed forces remained unresolved. Negotiations between the Government and the MNLF proceeded in Mindanao in January 1995, at the end of which it was announced that the Government had agreed to the establishment of a provisional MNLF government in Mindanao, subject to approval by Congress and the holding of a referendum. In December 1994 clashes took place in North Cotabato between government forces and the Moro Islamic Liberation Front (MILF), a rival independentist organization which refused to co-operate in the peace process; in late January 1995 it was announced that representatives of the military and the MILF had signed a truce.

Under an agreement signed in June 1983 between the Philippine and US Governments, the continued use by US forces of Subic Bay naval base and Clark air base (both on Luzon island) until 1989 was permitted, confirming the Philippines' sovereignty over the base areas and providing for military and economic assistance worth US $900m. Under a further agreement, signed in October 1988, the USA was to provide $962m. in assistance; prior approval was required from the Philippine Government for storing nuclear weapons on the bases, but nuclear-armed vessels and aircraft in transit were under no obligation to declare the presence of nuclear weapons. The 1987 Constitution stated, however, that foreign military bases would not be allowed in the country after 1991, except under the provisions of a treaty approved by a two-thirds' majority in the Senate and ratified by voters in a referendum.

Popular resentment towards the USA increased in early 1990, despite the US intervention in the coup attempt in December 1989 (see above). Exploratory talks were held in May 1990 to investigate the possibility of negotiating a new agreement on the bases, which would take effect in 1991. During the discussions the Philippine Government served formal notice of the termination of the previous agreement on military bases, to take effect in September 1991. Negotiations extended over 14 months, with disagreements arising primarily from the USA's refusal to consent to elevated Philippine requests for compensation. The eruption of Mt Pinatubo in June 1991, which devastated Clark Air Base, adversely affected the Philippines' negotiating position, however, facilitating an accord. Despite widespread popular support for the US installations, the Senate, led by the Liberal Party and PDP-Laban, rejected the terms of a new treaty, agreed in August, by 12 votes to 11. The Government, however, rescinded the formal notice on termination of the previous lease, effectively extending the lease for another year. At the end of November the US military formally transferred management of the Clark Air Base to the Philippines. In late December negotiations for an extended withdrawal period from Subic Bay naval base collapsed, owing principally to the USA's unwillingness to depart from its policy of refusing to confirm or deny the presence of nuclear weapons (prohibited from the Philippines under the 1987 Constitution) on board naval vessels. The Philippine Government served notice that US forces were to leave Subic Bay by the end of 1992. US personnel duly withdrew from Subic Naval Bay at the end of September, and from the Cubi Point Naval Air Station towards the end of November. In early November the two countries had agreed that US warships, aircraft and troops would continue to have access to military installations in the Philippines. The base area was subsequently transformed into an industrial zone, under the auspices of the newly-created Subic Bay Metropolitan Authority.

In November 1994 the Philippine Government rejected draft proposals (presented by President Bill Clinton of the USA during a visit to the Philippines earlier in the month) intended to facilitate access for US naval vessels to ports in the Philippines. The Secretary of National Defense, de Villa, stated that signature of an accord (regarded by the US authorities as routine), which had been scheduled for mid-December, would be delayed until certain 'ambiguous and objectionable' provisions had been revised.

Following his inauguration, President Ramos visited Brunei, Thailand, Malaysia, Singapore and Japan, demonstrating an increasing interest in regional relations. The Philippines' commitment to the Association of South East Asian Nations (ASEAN, see p. 109) also intensified. Relations with Malaysia were slightly strained, owing to the Philippines' claim to the Malaysian state of Sabah, dating from 1962, before Sabah joined the Federation of Malaysia. Sabah was ruled by the Sultan of Sulu, in the southern Philippines, until 1878, when it was leased to what was to become the British North Borneo Company. The Malaysian Government continues to pay a nominal rent to the Sultan. Attempts by both Marcos and Aquino to abandon the claim were thwarted by the Senate. In August 1993 the Philippine and Malaysian ministers responsible for foreign affairs signed a memorandum creating a commission to address bilateral issues including the Philippines' claim to Sabah.

A crisis in relations with Singapore was precipitated in March 1995 by the hanging in that country of a Filipino woman who had been convicted of two murders. In protest, the Philippine Government postponed an impending visit by the Singaporean Prime Minister, and withdrew its Ambassador to Singapore (prompting the withdrawal for consultations of the Singaporean Ambassador to Manila). Joint naval exercises, planned for June, were cancelled by the Philippines. There was public outrage in the Philippines at both the perceived intransigence of the Singaporean Government in response to international appeals for clemency, and at the apparent inability of the Philippine Government to protect its nationals' interests abroad. A commission established by Ramos to investigate the affair concluded in early April that the woman had been 'mistakenly blamed' for the murders, and accused the Singaporean authorities of extracting a confession by torture. Several public officials, including the Philippine Ambassador to Singapore, were suspended from office, in accordance with the recommendations of the commission. In mid-April Roberto Romulo resigned as Secretary of Foreign Affairs, and, shortly before the elections, Ramos accepted the resignation of the Secretary of Labor and Employment, Maria Nieves Confessor. In April the Alex Boncayao Brigade claimed responsibility for an attack on an office of Singapore Airlines in Makati.

Diplomatic relations were established with the People's Republic of China in 1975, at which time the Philippine Government recognized Taiwan as an 'inalienable' part of the People's Republic. Conflicting claims to the Spratly Islands, in the South China Sea, were, however, a source of tension between the Philippines and the People's Republic of China. (The islands are also claimed by Viet Nam, Brunei, Malaysia and Taiwan.) In February 1989 Chinese and Philippine warships exchanged gunfire in the vicinity of the Spratly Islands, although it was later declared that the incident occurred as a result of 'confusion over rules of engagement'. Negotiations over the sovereignty of the Spratly Islands took place in January 1990, July 1991 and mid-1992; all parties agreed to reach a settlement by peaceful means and to develop jointly the area's natural resources. In December 1993 the Philippines and Malaysia agreed to co-operate on fishing rights for the disputed Spratly Islands in the area not claimed by the other four countries. Following a visit to Viet Nam (the first official visit by a Philippine Head of State to that country), Ramos appealed for the six countries with claims to the Spratly Islands to remove all armed forces from the area.

In May 1994 the People's Republic of China made an official protest after the Philippine Goverment granted a permit to a US company to explore for petroleum off Palawan, in an area including part of the disputed territory of the Spratly Islands. In February 1995 the Philippine Government formally protested when it was revealed that Chinese armed forces had occupied a reef claimed to be within Philippine waters. In subsequent weeks the Philippines announced its intention to reinforce its military presence in the Spratly Islands, and to mark its territories in the disputed area. Bilateral negotiations took place in the Chinese capital, Beijing in late March, in an attempt to resolve the issue; although the discussions ended without formal agreement, both countries expressed their desire to hold further negotiations. However, tensions in the disputed region were exacerbated during March by the arrest, by the Philippine naval forces, of more than 60 Chinese fishermen, as well as the seizure of vessels and the destruction of territorial markings allegedly deployed by the People's Republic of China.

In March 1994 an East ASEAN Growth Area (EAGA), encompassing the southern Philippines, the Malaysian states of Sabah and Sarawak, Brunei and the Indonesian islands of Celebes (Sulawesi) and the Moluccas (Maluku), was formally established. However, the inaugural EAGA conference, which was scheduled to be held in Davao in May, was postponed, owing to the refusal of the Indonesian representatives to attend, in protest at a private conference (convened in Manila in late May) to discuss alleged abuses of human rights in the Indonesian-held territory of East Timor.

## Government

The Constitution, which was approved by a national referendum on 2 February 1987, provides for a bicameral Congress, comprising a Senate, with 24 members directly elected by universal suffrage (initially for a five-year term, thereafter to be extended to six years, with one-half of the membership being elected every three years), and a House of Representatives (with a three-year mandate), with a maximum of 250 members, 204 of whom are directly elected: a further 50 may be appointed by the President from minority groups. Elections are supervised by a Commission on Elections, which registers political parties.

The President is Head of State, Chief Executive of the Republic and Commander-in-Chief of the Armed Forces. The President is elected by the people for a six-year term, and is not eligible for re-election. The President cannot prevent the enactment of legislative proposals if they are approved by a two-thirds' majority vote in Congress. The President may declare martial law in times of national emergency, but Congress is empowered to revoke such actions at any time, by a majority vote of its members. The President appoints a Cabinet and other officials, with the approval of the Commission on Appointments (drawn from members of both chambers of Congress).

Local government is by Barangays (citizens' assemblies), and autonomy is granted to any region where its introduction is endorsed in a referendum.

### Defence

The total strength of the active armed forces in June 1994 was 106,500, comprising an army of 68,000, a navy of approximately 23,000 and an air force of 15,500. There were also reserve forces of 131,000. Paramilitary forces included the Citizens Armed Forces Geographical Units, which comprised about 60,000 men. Under the 1995 budget defence was allocated an estimated 26,100m. pesos. Legislation enacted in February 1995 allocated about US $2,000m. for the purchase of modern weaponry (mainly to upgrade the navy) over a 15-year period.

### Economic Affairs

In 1993, according to estimates by the World Bank, the Philippines' gross national product (GNP), measured at average 1991–93 prices, was US $54,609m., equivalent to $830 per head. During 1985–93, it was estimated, GNP per head increased by an annual average of 1.6%, in real terms. Over the same period the population increased by 2.3% per year. The Philippines' gross domestic product (GDP) increased, in real terms, by an annual average of 1.2% in 1980–92. GDP growth was 2.1% in 1993, and 4.3% in 1994.

Agriculture (including forestry and fishing) contributed some 22% of GDP in 1993, and engaged 45.8% of the employed labour force in that year. Rice, maize and cassava are the main subsistence crops. The principal crops cultivated for export are coconuts, sugar cane, bananas and pineapples. Livestock (chiefly pigs, buffaloes, goats and poultry) and fisheries are important. Exports of logs, an important source of foreign exchange, were suspended in 1986, owing to the effects of deforestation. In 1989 exports of sawnwood were banned in an attempt to increase the value of forestry-related exports through encouraging the manufacture of wood products. Deforestation continues at a high rate, however, owing to illegal logging and to 'slash-and-burn' farming techniques. During 1980–92 agricultural GDP increased by an annual average of 1.0%.

Industry (including mining, manufacturing, construction and power) contributed 33% of GDP in 1992, and engaged an estimated 15.5% of the employed labour force in 1993. During 1980–92 industrial GDP declined by an annual average of 0.2%.

Mining contributed 1.4% of GDP in 1991, and engaged 0.5% of the employed labour force in 1993. Copper is the Philippines' leading mineral product; reserves of copper ore were estimated at 3,691m. tons in 1989. Gold, silver, chromium, nickel and coal are also extracted. Commercial production of crude petroleum began in 1979. A substantial natural gas field and petroleum reservoir, off the island of Palawan, has proven recoverable reserves of 100m. barrels of crude petroleum and an estimated 54,000m.–100,000m. cu m of gas. It was expected that production from the deposits would begin in 2001.

Manufacturing contributed 24% of GDP in 1992, and engaged 10.0% of the employed labour force in 1993. Based on the value of output, the principal branches of manufacturing are food products, petroleum refineries, chemical products, electrical machinery (mainly telecommunications equipment), beverages, metals and metal products and textiles. During 1980–92 manufacturing GDP increased by an annual average of 0.7%.

Energy is derived principally from oil-fired thermal plants (relying chiefly on imported petroleum), which provide more than one-half of the total power supply. Hydroelectric power and coal account for most of the remainder of electrical energy requirements. Geothermal sources provided generating capacity of approximately 1,044 MW in 1994. There are frequent and prolonged losses of power, owing to a severe shortage of capacity. In 1994, however, 11 new plants, with a total capacity of 1,074 MW, became operational. In 1994 imports of mineral fuels accounted for 9.5% of the value of total merchandise imports.

Remittances from Filipino workers abroad, which totalled US $2,100m. in 1993, constitute the Government's principal source of foreign exchange. Tourism, although periodically affected by political unrest, remains a significant sector of the economy. In 1992 approximately 1,170,000 tourists visited the Philippines and revenue from tourism was estimated at $1,674m.

In 1993 the Philippines recorded a visible trade deficit of US $6,222m. and there was a deficit of $3,289m. on the current account of the balance of payments. In 1994 the trade deficit was an estimated $7,800m. In 1994 the principal source of imports (accounting for 24.1% of the total) was Japan; other significant suppliers were the USA, Singapore, Taiwan, the Republic of Korea and Hong Kong. The USA was the principal market for exports (36.8%); other major purchasers were Japan and Singapore. The principal imports in 1994 were machinery and transport equipment, basic manufactures, chemical products, mineral fuels and food and live animals. The principal exports were electronic products (notably semiconductors and microcircuits), garments and agricultural products (particularly fruit and seafoods).

In 1994 there was an overall budgetary surplus of 18,114m. pesos (equivalent to 1.1% of GDP). The Philippines' external debt totalled US $35,269m. at the end of 1993, of which $27,471m. was long-term public debt. In that year the cost of servicing the debt was equivalent to 24.9% of the value of exports of goods and services. The annual rate of inflation averaged 9.2% in 1985–93; consumer prices increased by an average of 7.6% in 1993 and 9.1% in 1994. The rate of unemployment averaged 8.9% of the labour force in 1993.

The Philippines is a member of the Asian Development Bank (see p. 107), the Association of South East Asian Nations (ASEAN, see p. 109) and the Colombo Plan (see p. 238). In January 1993 the establishment of the ASEAN Free Trade Area, which was to be implemented over 15 years, commenced.

The Philippines' economy has been adversely affected by several factors: the burden of servicing the large external debt, incurred mainly by the Marcos regime; natural disasters; an acute shortage of electric power; and a substantial budget deficit. In the late 1980s the Aquino Government initiated a privatization programme, which served to reduce debt and encourage private investment. Austerity measures were implemented, including reductions in government spending, the depreciation of the peso, the abolition of subsidies on domestic petroleum prices and the liberalization of laws on foreign investment. In September 1992 the Ramos administration ended restrictions on the transfer of foreign currency in the Philippines, with the aim of attracting overseas capital. In 1994 economic performance improved, prompted, initially, by a dramatic improvement in electricity supply to domestic and industrial consumers (in April 1993 Ramos had been granted emergency powers to combat the electricity shortage). In June 1994 the IMF approved a three-year funding arrangement valued at some US $684m. This was followed in July by a rescheduling by official creditors of debts totalling $469m., which, in turn, was expected to facilitate the granting of new credits. In May 1994 legislation was enacted allowing for the establishment in the Philippines of as many as 10 new foreign banks, as part of its continuing policy of liberalizing the economy and encouraging foreign investment, and the introduction of a new mining code in early 1995 allowed for 100% ownership by foreign companies of mining projects and removed restrictions on profits allowed to foreign partners in joint ventures. The success of the governing alliance in the elections held in May 1995 was interpreted as a popular endorsement of Ramos's economic policies (despite the unpopularity of attempts to increase petroleum prices and extend value-added tax during 1994—see Recent History). Proposed reforms in 1995 included a rationalization of the civil service and the introduction of an enforceable tax collection system to help increase government revenue (it was estimated in 1994 that only 1.6m. workers out of a total labour force of 27.5m. paid any taxes).

### Social Welfare

Government social insurance provides cover for retirement and compensation for dependants in cases of loss of life. Employed persons contribute to the scheme from their wages. Public health services, such as inoculation and vaccination, are provided free in the State Dispensaries. In 1989 the Philippines had 1,750 hospitals (of which 33% were government hospitals and 67% were privately administered), with a total of 90,146 beds. In 1989 there were an estimated 54,000 physicians. A total of 10,971m. pesos (3.8% of total expenditure) was allo-

# THE PHILIPPINES

cated to health in the 1992 budget. A major decentralization of the Philippine health service was under way in 1995. In June of that year a new senate bill was expected to be approved that would provide for universal medical cover through the creation of a National Health Insurance Corporation (NHIC).

## Education

Elementary education, beginning at seven years of age and lasting for six years, is officially compulsory, and is provided free of charge at public (government-administered) schools. Secondary education begins at the age of 13 and lasts for up to four years: there is a common general curriculum for all students in the first two years, and more varied curricula in the third and fourth years, leading to either college or technical vocational courses. In 1992 96% of all children in the relevant age-group were enrolled at primary schools, while the comparable ratio for secondary enrolment was 58%. Instruction is in both English and Filipino. There were 55 universities and more than 1,000 colleges in 1992. Among the population aged 15 and over, the average illiteracy rate at the time of the 1990 census was estimated at 6.4% (males 6.0%, females 6.8%). The 1995 budget allocated 52,300m. pesos (13.7% of total expenditure) to education.

## Public Holidays

**1995:** 1 January (New Year's Day), 25 February (Freedom Day, anniversary of the People's Revolution), 13 April (Maundy Thursday), 14 April (Good Friday), 1 May (Labour Day), 6 May (Araw ng Kagitingan), 12 June (Independence Day, anniversary of 1898 declaration), 27 August (National Heroes' Day), 11 September (Barangay Day), 21 September (National Thanksgiving Day), 1 November (All Saints' Day), 30 November (Bonifacio Day), 25 December (Christmas Day), 30 December (Rizal Day), 31 December (Last Day of the Year).

**1996:** 1 January (New Year's Day), 25 February (Freedom Day, anniversary of the People's Revolution), 4 April (Maundy Thursday), 5 April (Good Friday), 1 May (Labour Day), 6 May (Araw ng Kagitingan), 12 June (Independence Day, anniversary of 1898 declaration), 27 August (National Heroes' Day), 11 September (Barangay Day), 21 September (National Thanksgiving Day), 1 November (All Saints' Day), 30 November (Bonifacio Day), 25 December (Christmas Day), 30 December (Rizal Day), 31 December (Last Day of the Year).

## Weights and Measures

The metric system is in force.

# Statistical Survey

Source (unless otherwise stated): National Census and Statistics Office, National Economic and Development Authority, Solicarel 1, Magsaysay Blvd, cnr Ampil St, POB 779, Metro Manila; tel. (2) 613645; fax (2) 610794.

## Area and Population

### AREA, POPULATION AND DENSITY

Area of islands (sq km)
| | |
|---|---|
| Luzon | 104,688 |
| Mindanao | 94,630 |
| Samar | 13,080 |
| Negros | 12,710 |
| Palawan | 11,785 |
| Panay | 11,515 |
| Mindoro | 9,735 |
| Leyte | 7,214 |
| Cebu | 4,422 |
| Bohol | 3,865 |
| Masbate | 3,269 |
| Others | 23,087 |
| Total | 300,000* |

Population (census results)
1 May 1980
| | |
|---|---|
| Males | 24,128,755 |
| Females | 23,969,705 |
| Total | 48,098,460 |
| 1 May 1990 | 60,703,206 |

Population (official estimates at mid-year)†
| | |
|---|---|
| 1990 | 61,480,000 |
| 1991 | 62,868,000 |
| 1992 | 64,259,000 |

Density (per sq km) at 1 May 1990 . . . . 202.3

* 115,831 sq miles.
† Not adjusted to take account of the 1990 census results.

### PRINCIPAL TOWNS (population at 1990 census)

| | | | |
|---|---|---|---|
| Manila (capital)* | 1,601,234 | Iloilo City | 309,505 |
| Quezon City* | 1,669,776 | Angeles City | 236,686 |
| Davao City | 849,947 | Butuan City | 227,829 |
| Caloocan City* | 763,415 | Iligan City | 226,568 |
| Cebu City | 610,417 | Olongapo City | 193,327 |
| Zamboanga City | 442,345 | Batangas City | 184,970 |
| Pasay City* | 368,366 | Cabanatuan City | 173,065 |
| Bacolod City | 364,180 | San Pablo City | 161,630 |
| Cagayan de Oro City | 339,598 | Cadiz City | 119,772 |

* Part of Metropolitan Manila.

### BIRTHS, MARRIAGES AND DEATHS*

| | Registered live births | | Registered marriages | | Registered deaths | |
|---|---|---|---|---|---|---|
| | Number | Rate (per 1,000) | Number | Rate (per 1,000) | Number | Rate (per 1,000) |
| 1983 | 1,506,356 | 28.9 | 351,663 | 6.8 | 327,260 | 6.3 |
| 1984 | 1,478,205 | 27.7 | 380,171 | 7.2 | 313,359 | 5.9 |
| 1985 | 1,437,154 | 26.3 | 378,550 | 6.9 | 334,663 | 6.1 |
| 1986 | 1,493,995 | 26.7 | 389,482 | 7.0 | 326,749 | 5.8 |
| 1987 | 1,582,469 | 27.6 | 400,760 | 7.0 | 335,254 | 5.8 |
| 1988 | 1,565,372 | 26.7 | 393,514 | 6.7 | 325,098 | 5.5 |
| 1989 | 1,565,254 | 26.0 | 375,657 | 6.3 | 325,622 | 5.4 |
| 1990 | 1,631,069 | 26.9 | 422,041 | 7.0 | 373,890 | 5.2 |

* Registration is incomplete. According to UN estimates, the average annual rates were: births 35.6 per 1,000 in 1980–85, 33.2 per 1,000 in 1985–90; deaths 8.5 per 1,000 in 1980–85, 7.7 per 1,000 in 1985–90.

**Expectation of life** (UN estimates, years at birth, 1992): Males 63.0; Females 66.8 (Source: UN, *Statistical Yearbook for Asia and the Pacific*).

# THE PHILIPPINES

## ECONOMICALLY ACTIVE POPULATION*
('000 persons aged 15 years and over, October)

|  | 1991 | 1992 | 1993 |
|---|---|---|---|
| Agriculture, hunting, forestry and fishing | 10,403 | 10,867 | 11,194 |
| Mining and quarrying | 150 | 146 | 130 |
| Manufacturing | 2,391 | 2,535 | 2,455 |
| Electricity, gas and water | 99 | 84 | 106 |
| Construction | 1,046 | 1,055 | 1,102 |
| Wholesale and retail trade | 3,172 | 3,325 | 3,415 |
| Transport, storage and communication | 1,143 | 1,217 | 1,359 |
| Financing, insurance, real estate and business services | 451 | 445 | 496 |
| Community, social and personal services (incl. restaurants and hotels) | 4,116 | 4,202 | 4,174 |
| Activities not adequately defined | 9 | 23 | 13 |
| **Total employed** | 22,979 | 23,898 | 24,443 |
| Unemployed | 2,267 | 2,224 | 2,379 |
| **Total labour force** | 25,246 | 26,122 | 26,822 |
| Males | 15,932 | 16,402 | 16,852 |
| Females | 9,314 | 9,721 | 9,970 |

* Figures refer to civilians only and are based on annual household surveys (excluding institutional households).

# Agriculture

## PRINCIPAL CROPS ('000 metric tons)

|  | 1991 | 1992 | 1993 |
|---|---|---|---|
| Rice (paddy) | 9,673 | 9,129 | 9,434* |
| Maize | 4,655 | 4,619* | 4,798* |
| Potatoes | 65 | 66 | 70† |
| Sweet potatoes | 662 | 677 | 650† |
| Cassava (Manioc) | 1,816 | 1,798 | 1,800† |
| Yams† | 28 | 29 | 29 |
| Taro† | 110 | 112 | 110 |
| Pulses† | 37 | 37 | 37 |
| Groundnuts (in shell) | 31 | 34 | 37† |
| Castor beans | 6 | 7‡ | 7‡ |
| Coconuts | 8,923 | 9,013 | 9,300† |
| Copra | 1,883 | 1,890‡ | 1,844‡ |
| Vegetables (incl. melons) | 4,248 | 4,342 | 4,430† |
| Sugar cane† | 25,380 | 29,400 | 2,778† |
| Mangoes | 307 | 330 | 350† |
| Pineapples | 1,117 | 1,135 | 1,200† |
| Bananas and plantains | 2,951 | 3,005 | 3,100† |
| Soybeans‡ | 12 | 12 | 13 |
| Abaca (Manila hemp)* | 85 | n.a. | n.a. |
| Garlic | 12 | 12 | 11 |
| Coffee (green) | 133 | 128 | 111† |
| Cocoa beans | 10 | 10 | 7‡ |
| Tobacco (leaves) | 85 | 117 | 107‡ |
| Natural rubber | 181 | 173 | 170† |

* Source: Bureau of Agricultural Statistics, Quezon City.
† FAO estimate(s).
‡ Unofficial figure(s).

Source (unless otherwise indicated): FAO, *Production Yearbook*.

## LIVESTOCK ('000 head, year ending 30 June)

|  | 1991 | 1992 | 1993 |
|---|---|---|---|
| Cattle | 1,680 | 1,729 | 1,781 |
| Pigs | 8,006 | 8,022 | 7,954 |
| Buffaloes | 2,647 | 2,577 | 2,561 |
| Horses* | 200 | 200 | 210 |
| Goats | 2,102 | 2,240 | 2,562 |
| Sheep* | 30 | 30 | 30 |

Chickens (million): 65 in 1991; 64 in 1992; 65 in 1993.
Ducks (million): 8 in 1991; 9 in 1992; 8 in 1993.

* FAO estimates.

Source: FAO, *Production Yearbook*.

## LIVESTOCK PRODUCTS ('000 metric tons)

|  | 1991 | 1992 | 1993 |
|---|---|---|---|
| Beef and veal* | 86 | 86 | 81 |
| Buffalo meat* | 44 | 43 | 45 |
| Pig meat | 691 | 710* | 712* |
| Poultry meat | 288 | 311 | 330 |
| Cows' milk† | 14 | 14 | 14 |
| Buffalo milk† | 16 | 16 | 15 |
| Hen eggs† | 267.0 | 256.0 | 264.0 |
| Other poultry eggs† | 54.0 | 55.0 | 55.0 |
| Cattle and buffalo hides† | 14.6 | 15.1 | 13.6 |

* Unofficial figure(s). † FAO estimates.

Source: FAO, *Production Yearbook*.

# Forestry

## ROUNDWOOD REMOVALS ('000 cu metres, excluding bark)

|  | 1990 | 1991 | 1992 |
|---|---|---|---|
| Sawlogs, veneer logs and logs for sleepers | 2,156 | 1,561 | 619 |
| Pulpwood | 335 | 349 | 382 |
| Other industrial wood* | 2,503 | 2,559 | 2,613 |
| Fuel wood | 33,448 | 34,213 | 35,038 |
| **Total** | 38,442 | 38,682 | 38,652 |

* FAO estimate(s).

Source: FAO, *Yearbook of Forest Products*.

## SAWNWOOD PRODUCTION
('000 cu metres, including railway sleepers)

|  | 1990 | 1991 | 1992 |
|---|---|---|---|
| **Total** | 841 | 726 | 452 |

Source: FAO, *Yearbook of Forest Products*.

# Fishing

('000 metric tons, live weight)

|  | 1990 | 1991 | 1992 |
|---|---|---|---|
| Tilapias | 97.4 | 96.3 | 110.6 |
| Milkfish | 213.8 | 237.1 | 174.5 |
| Threadfin-breams | 44.1 | 45.6 | 31.2 |
| Ponyfishes (Slipmouths) | 69.4 | 70.0 | 60.0 |
| Scads (Decapterus) | 250.3 | 278.2 | 297.9 |
| Sardinellas | 156.7 | 158.6 | 204.9 |
| 'Stolephorus' anchovies | 107.0 | 100.9 | 84.7 |
| Frigate and bullet tunas | 88.8 | 93.2 | 125.7 |
| Kawakawa | 43.8 | 47.9 | 31.9 |
| Skipjack tuna | 99.7 | 102.4 | 83.2 |
| Yellowfin tuna | 81.1 | 95.6 | 45.0 |
| Indian mackerel | 66.4 | 62.5 | 63.2 |
| Other fishes | 551.3 | 581.9 | 538.9 |
| **Total fish** | 1,869.8 | 1,970.3 | 1,851.6 |
| Crustaceans | 112.0 | 112.9 | 180.6 |
| Freshwater molluscs | 149.8 | 151.5 | 149.1 |
| Marine molluscs | 73.0 | 73.5 | 86.8 |
| Other aquatic animals | 4.1 | 3.7 | 3.8 |
| **Total catch** | 2,208.8 | 2,311.8 | 2,271.9 |
| Inland waters | 585.8 | 612.4 | 581.0 |
| Pacific Ocean | 1,623.1 | 1,699.4 | 1,690.9 |

Source: FAO, *Yearbook of Fishery Statistics*.

THE PHILIPPINES

## Mining

('000 metric tons, unless otherwise indicated)

|  | 1988 | 1989 | 1990 |
|---|---|---|---|
| Coal | 1,336 | 1,345 | 1,247 |
| Iron ore: gross weight | n.a. | 7 | 6 |
| Chromium ore (dry)* | 119 | 220 | 218 |
| Copper ore† | 216 | 192 | 180 |
| Manganese ore† | 2 | 3 | 15 |
| Zinc concentrates† | 1.4 | 1.2 | 0.1 |
| Salt (refined) | 492.1 | 488.7 | 490.0 |
| Phosphate rock | n.a. | 34 | 41 |
| Nickel ore† | 10.3 | 15.4 | 15.8 |
| Gold (metric tons)† | 30 | 30 | 25 |
| Silver (metric tons)† | 55 | 51 | 47 |

**1991** (metric tons)†: Gold 26; Silver 39.

\* Figures refer to metallurgical ore and refractory ore.
† Figures refer to the metal content of ores and concentrates.

**Crude petroleum** ('000 metric tons): 245 in 1990; 165 in 1991; 418 in 1992 (Source: UN, *Industrial Commodity Statistics Yearbook*.)

## Industry

### SELECTED PRODUCTS
('000 metric tons, unless otherwise indicated)

|  | 1989 | 1990 | 1991 |
|---|---|---|---|
| Wheat flour | 746 | n.a. | n.a. |
| Raw sugar* | 1,645 | 1,810 | 1,780 |
| Cigarettes (million)[1]† | 69,700 | 71,500 | 70,710 |
| Cotton yarn—pure[2] | 38.4 | n.a. | n.a. |
| Woven cotton fabrics (million metres)‡ | 449.0 | n.a. | n.a. |
| Plywood ('000 cubic metres)[3] | 344 | 414 | 312 |
| Mechanical wood pulp[3] | 50 | 50‡ | 39 |
| Chemical wood pulp[3] | 103 | 103‡ | 113 |
| Paper and paperboard[3] | 239 | 245 | 395 |
| Nitrogenous fertilizers(a)[4] | 127.0 | 120.8‡ | 143.2 |
| Phosphate fertilizers(b)[4] | 191.0 | 199.4 | 191.9 |
| Jet fuels | 569 | 441 | 445 |
| Motor spirit—petrol | 1,482 | 1,678 | 1,396 |
| Naphthas | 285 | 226 | 387 |
| Kerosene | 440 | 502 | 425 |
| Distillate fuel oils | 2,878 | 3,282 | 3,341 |
| Residual fuel oils | 3,347 | 3,992 | 3,645 |
| Lubricating oils | 85 | 0 | 120 |
| Liquefied petroleum gas | 195 | 232 | 239 |
| Rubber tyres ('000)[5] | 2,016‡ | 2,208 | n.a. |
| Cement | 3,624 | 6,360 | 4,499‡ |
| Smelter (unrefined) copper‡§ | 105.0 | 110.0 | 105.0 |
| Passenger motor cars ('000)[6] | 27 | 34 | n.a. |
| Electric energy (million kWh) | 25,573 | 26,327 | 22,484 |
| Manufactured gas (terajoules) | 202 | 210 | 190‡ |

\* Data from the FAO.
† Data from the US Department of Agriculture.
‡ Estimate(s).
§ Data from the US Bureau of Mines.
[1] Twelve months ending 30 June of the year stated.
[2] Excluding yarn made from waste.
[3] Source: FAO, *Yearbook of Forest Products*.
[4] Production in terms of (a) nitrogen or (b) phosphoric acid. Source: FAO, *Quarterly Bulletin of Statistics*.
[5] Tyres for road motor vehicles only.
[6] Vehicles assembled from imported parts.

Source: mainly UN, *Industrial Statistics Yearbook*.

## Finance

### CURRENCY AND EXCHANGE RATES

**Monetary Units**
100 centavos = 1 Philippine peso.

**Sterling and Dollar Equivalents** (31 December 1994)
£1 sterling = 38.20 pesos;
US $1 = 24.42 pesos;
1,000 Philippine pesos = £26.18 = $40.95.

**Average Exchange Rate** (pesos per US $)
1992   25.512
1993   27.120
1994   26.417

### BUDGET (million pesos)

| Revenue* | 1990 | 1991 | 1992 |
|---|---|---|---|
| Current revenue | 174,164 | 213,423 | 238,692 |
| Tax revenue | 151,700 | 182,275 | 208,705 |
| Taxes on income, profits and capital gains | 49,366 | 60,775 | 69,978 |
| Individual | 15,673 | 20,843 | 23,105 |
| Corporate | 19,301 | 25,133 | 30,645 |
| Taxes on property | 1,030 | 525 | 453 |
| Domestic taxes on goods and services | 53,616 | 55,173 | 62,602 |
| General sales tax | 13,079 | 14,951 | 18,113 |
| Excise duties | 28,036 | 24,542 | 27,522 |
| Taxes on specific services | 6,208 | 7,967 | 8,276 |
| Taxes on international trade and transactions | 43,702 | 60,729 | 68,538 |
| Import duties | 43,085 | 60,155 | 67,841 |
| Other taxes | 3,986 | 5,073 | 7,134 |
| Stamp taxes | 3,544 | 4,837 | 6,419 |
| Other current revenue | 22,464 | 31,148 | 29,987 |
| Entrepreneurial and property income | 13,585 | 17,340 | 19,152 |
| Administrative fees and charges, non-industrial and incidental sales | 6,437 | 8,196 | 6,890 |
| Fines and forfeits | 2 | 1 | 2 |
| Others | 2,440 | 5,611 | 3,943 |
| Capital revenue | 4,182 | 4,175 | 1,878 |
| Sales of fixed capital assets | 4,181 | 4,119 | 1,877 |
| **Total** | 178,346 | 217,598 | 240,570 |

# THE PHILIPPINES

| Expenditure† | 1990 | 1991 | 1992 |
|---|---|---|---|
| General public services | 18,426 | 21,221 | 25,868 |
| Defence | 23,321 | 26,010 | 26,321 |
| Public order and safety | 3,324 | 4,567 | 5,066 |
| Education | 35,741 | 38,643 | 39,917 |
| Pre-primary, primary and secondary | 26,893 | 28,982 | 29,928 |
| Tertiary | 5,554 | 5,669 | 5,778 |
| Health | 8,623 | 10,158 | 10,971 |
| Hospitals | 5,087 | 5,892 | 6,323 |
| Social security and welfare | 3,452 | 5,885 | 7,022 |
| Housing and community amenities | 1,356 | 3,035 | 4,535 |
| Recreational, cultural and religious affairs and services | 930 | 1,514 | 2,707 |
| Economic affairs and services | 49,836 | 59,158 | 71,249 |
| Fuel and energy | 6,698 | 7,009 | 8,515 |
| Agriculture, forestry, fishing and hunting | 14,331 | 17,508 | 21,627 |
| Mining and mineral resources, manufacturing and construction | 2,919 | 3,223 | 4,748 |
| Transport and communications | 19,473 | 24,293 | 28,390 |
| Road transport | 12,959 | 15,713 | 18,015 |
| Other economic affairs and services | 6,415 | 7,125 | 7,969 |
| Other purposes | 75,825 | 81,628 | 95,427 |
| **Sub-total** | 220,834 | 251,819 | 289,083 |
| Adjustment to cash basis | −2,738 | −4,683 | −30,403 |
| **Total** | 218,096 | 247,136 | 258,680 |

* Excluding grants received (million pesos): 2,556 in 1990; 3,189 in 1991; 2,144 in 1992.
† Including domestic lending minus repayments (million pesos): 6,912 in 1990; 7,666 in 1991; −6,949 in 1992.

Source: IMF, *Government Finance Statistics Yearbook*.

## INTERNATIONAL RESERVES (US $ million at 31 December)

| | 1992 | 1993 | 1994 |
|---|---|---|---|
| Gold* | 935 | 1,245 | 1,104 |
| IMF special drawing rights | 1 | 10 | 24 |
| Reserve position in IMF | 120 | 120 | 127 |
| Foreign exchange | 4,283 | 4,546 | 5,866 |
| **Total** | 5,338 | 5,921 | 7,121 |

* Valued at market-related prices.
Source: IMF, *International Financial Statistics*.

## MONEY SUPPLY (million pesos at 31 December)*

| | 1991 | 1992 | 1993 |
|---|---|---|---|
| Currency outside banks | 69,390 | 74,300 | 84,080 |
| Demand deposits at commercial banks | 31,980 | 34,720 | 49,100 |
| **Total money** (incl. others) | 107,690 | 117,540 | 143,710 |

* Figures are rounded to the nearest 10 million pesos.
Source: IMF, *International Financial Statistics*.

## COST OF LIVING (Consumer Price Index; base: 1988 = 100)

| | 1990 | 1991 | 1992 |
|---|---|---|---|
| Food, alcoholic beverages and tobacco | 127.6 | 147.2 | 157.3 |
| Clothing | 120.3 | 140.6 | 155.7 |
| Housing and repair | 132.8 | 159.6 | 187.6 |
| Fuel, light and water | 136.0 | 173.3 | 183.1 |
| Services | 129.3 | 171.4 | 183.6 |
| Miscellaneous | 120.5 | 140.0 | 158.8 |
| **All items** | 128.1 | 152.0 | 165.6 |

## NATIONAL ACCOUNTS
### National Income and Product
(million pesos at current prices)

| | 1989 | 1990 | 1991 |
|---|---|---|---|
| Compensation of employees | 324,386 | 363,078 | 427,035 |
| Operating surplus | 452,977 | 537,688 | 600,993 |
| **Domestic factor incomes** | 777,363 | 900,766 | 1,028,028 |
| Consumption of fixed capital | 72,001 | 82,249 | 101,782 |
| **Gross domestic product (GDP) at factor cost** | 849,364 | 983,015 | 1,129,810 |
| Indirect taxes | 82,705 | 101,185 | 122,473 |
| Less Subsidies | 6,208 | 13,300 | 8,246 |
| **GDP in purchasers' values** | 925,161* | 1,070,900 | 1,244,037 |
| Factor income from abroad | 38,938 | 50,846 | 70,071 |
| Less Factor income paid abroad | 50,256 | 45,536 | 52,454 |
| **Gross national product (GNP)** | 913,843 | 1,076,210 | 1,261,654 |
| Less Consumption of fixed capital | 72,001 | 82,249 | 101,782 |
| **National income in market prices** | 841,842 | 993,961 | 1,159,872 |
| Other current transfers from abroad | 18,047 | 17,458 | 23,000 |
| Less Other current transfers paid abroad | 9,155 | 15,773 | 16,388 |
| **National disposable income** | 850,734 | 995,646 | 1,166,484 |

* Including adjustments.
Source: UN, *National Accounts Statistics*.

### Expenditure on the Gross Domestic Product
('000 million pesos at current prices)

| | 1992 | 1993 | 1994 |
|---|---|---|---|
| Government final consumption expenditure | 130.5 | 149.1 | 168.3 |
| Private final consumption expenditure | 1,019.2 | 1,122.5 | 1,258.8 |
| Increase in stocks | 5.6 | 3.1 | 8.3 |
| Gross fixed capital formation | 282.8 | 358.4 | 418.2 |
| Statistical discrepancy | −20.3 | −27.9 | −33.7 |
| **Total domestic expenditure** | 1,417.8 | 1,605.2 | 1,819.9 |
| Exports of goods and services | 393.7 | 462.4 | 583.3 |
| Less Imports of goods and services | 459.9 | 592.6 | 715.6 |
| **GDP in purchasers' values** | 1,351.6 | 1,475.0 | 1,687.6 |
| **GDP at constant 1990 prices** | 1,074.6 | 1,097.6 | 1,144.6 |

Source: IMF, *International Financial Statistics*.

### Gross Domestic Product by Economic Activity
(million pesos at current prices)

| | 1989 | 1990 | 1991 |
|---|---|---|---|
| Agriculture, hunting, forestry and fishing | 210,009 | 235,956 | 263,201 |
| Mining and quarrying | 15,446 | 16,659 | 17,504 |
| Manufacturing | 233,192 | 267,485 | 315,938 |
| Electricity, gas and water | 21,748 | 24,299 | 30,625 |
| Construction | 57,281 | 64,903 | 62,083 |
| Wholesale and retail trade, restaurants and hotels | 142,159 | 160,594 | 189,508 |
| Transport, storage and communication | 43,840 | 54,345 | 73,909 |
| Finance, insurance, real estate and business services | 95,623 | 114,709 | 134,862 |
| Community social and personal services | 43,437 | 52,605 | 63,756 |
| Government services | 60,272 | 77,031 | 89,880 |
| Other services | 2,154 | 2,314 | 2,771 |
| **Total** | 925,161 | 1,070,900 | 1,244,037 |

Source: UN, *National Accounts Statistics*.

# THE PHILIPPINES

## BALANCE OF PAYMENTS (US $ million)

|  | 1991 | 1992 | 1993 |
|---|---:|---:|---:|
| Merchandise exports f.o.b. | 8,840 | 9,824 | 11,375 |
| Merchandise imports f.o.b. | −12,051 | −14,519 | −17,597 |
| **Trade balance** | −3,211 | −4,695 | −6,222 |
| Exports of services | 3,654 | 4,742 | 4,673 |
| Imports of services | −1,748 | −2,253 | −3,030 |
| Other income received | 1,969 | 2,755 | 2,855 |
| Other income paid | −2,525 | −2,365 | −2,264 |
| Private unrequited transfers (net) | 473 | 473 | 398 |
| Official unrequited transfers (net) | 354 | 344 | 301 |
| **Current balance** | −1,034 | −999 | −3,289 |
| Direct investment (net) | 544 | 228 | 763 |
| Portfolio investment (net) | 110 | 40 | −164 |
| Other capital (net) | 2,273 | 2,940 | 2,687 |
| Net errors and omissions | −138 | −520 | 292 |
| **Overall balance** | 1,755 | 1,689 | 289 |

Source: IMF, *International Financial Statistics*.

# External Trade

## PRINCIPAL COMMODITIES
(distribution by SITC, US $ million)

| Imports c.i.f. | 1992 | 1993 | 1994 |
|---|---:|---:|---:|
| **Food and live animals** | 1,114.8 | 1,267.8 | 1,506.1 |
| Dairy products and birds' eggs | 267.1 | 272.9 | 332.7 |
| Cereals and cereal preparations | 350.6 | 400.1 | 462.8 |
| Wheat and meslin (unmilled) | 271.8 | 297.8 | 368.9 |
| **Crude materials (inedible) except fuels** | 679.8 | 775.5 | 977.5 |
| **Mineral fuels, lubricants, etc.** | 2,158.8 | 2,162.0 | 2,160.5 |
| Petroleum and petroleum products | 2,005.3 | 1,947.2 | 1,936.7 |
| Crude petroleum oils, etc. | 1,684.0 | 1,366.3 | 1,350.6 |
| Refined petroleum products | 288.8 | 544.2 | 561.7 |
| **Chemicals and related products** | 1,618.4 | 1,812.8 | 2,190.8 |
| Organic chemicals | 328.0 | 343.4 | 384.6 |
| Artificial resins, plastic materials, etc. | 336.2 | 393.4 | 501.4 |
| Polymerization and copolymerization products | 273.2 | 309.6 | 390.6 |
| **Basic manufactures** | 2,330.6 | 2,813.6 | 3,142.6 |
| Textile yarn, fabrics, etc. | 667.8 | 740.0 | 821.9 |
| Iron and steel | 756.1 | 921.1 | 970.2 |
| Ingots and other primary forms | 237.7 | 301.4 | 375.6 |
| **Machinery and transport equipment** | 4,421.6 | 6,144.5 | 7,585.1 |
| Power-generating machinery and equipment | 397.2 | 815.5 | 886.4 |
| Machinery specialized for particular industries | 608.6 | 656.6 | 925.4 |
| General industrial machinery, equipment and parts | 436.0 | 605.2 | 727.0 |
| Office machines and automatic data-processing equipment | 378.1 | 280.6 | 341.9 |
| Telecommunications and sound equipment | 447.1 | 613.1 | 895.3 |
| Other electrical machinery, apparatus, etc. | 1,115.5 | 1,419.3 | 1,805.3 |
| Thermionic valves, tubes, etc. | 548.1 | 671.0 | 929.1 |
| Road vehicles and parts (excl. tyres, engines and electrical parts) | 632.5 | 911.4 | 1,097.0 |
| Passenger motor cars (excl. buses) | 291.6 | 402.9 | 541.0 |
| Aircraft, associated equipment and parts | 281.8 | 621.2 | 140.7 |
| **Miscellaneous manufactured articles** | 454.2 | 622.8 | 775.7 |
| **Total** (incl. others) | 15,464.4 | 18,768.1 | 22,638.0 |

| Exports f.o.b. | 1992 | 1993 | 1994 |
|---|---:|---:|---:|
| **Food and live animals** | 1,132.4 | 1,329.4 | 1,332.7 |
| Fish, crustaceans and molluscs | 392.2 | 476.6 | 532.5 |
| Crustaceans and molluscs (fresh, chilled, frozen or salted) | 258.4 | 282.2 | 310.3 |
| Vegetables and fruit | 503.8 | 600.3 | 571.7 |
| Fresh or dried fruit and nuts (excl. oil nuts) | 307.8 | 370.1 | 348.1 |
| Bananas | 157.8 | 226.1 | 215.3 |
| **Crude materials (inedible) except fuels** | 492.1 | 387.7 | 411.0 |
| Metalliferous ores and metal scrap | 318.6 | 200.3 | 226.7 |
| **Mineral fuels, lubricants, etc.** | 238.0 | 228.8 | 215.5 |
| **Animal and vegetable oils, fats and waxes** | 495.2 | 370.2 | 490.7 |
| Fixed vegetable oils and fats | 482.8 | 358.8 | 475.8 |
| Coconut (copra) oil | 481.2 | 357.6 | 475.2 |
| **Chemicals and related products** | 268.2 | 261.6 | 305.9 |
| **Basic manufactures** | 682.4 | 756.5 | 874.0 |
| Non-ferrous metals | 236.7 | 284.4 | 297.8 |
| Copper | 222.1 | 273.3 | 286.3 |
| Copper (unwrought) | 217.4 | 264.4 | 269.9 |
| **Machinery and transport equipment** | 1,646.5 | 2,099.0 | 2,906.6 |
| Office machines and automatic data-processing equipment | 193.9 | 214.6 | 232.9 |
| Telecommunications and sound equipment | 408.5 | 506.0 | 681.2 |
| Other electrical machinery, apparatus, etc. | 949.7 | 1,229.6 | 1,756.6 |
| Equipment for distributing electricity | 268.1 | 310.0 | 450.8 |
| Insulated wire, cable, etc. | 267.9 | 303.0 | 442.6 |
| Thermionic valves, tubes, etc. | 569.7 | 786.0 | 1,100.0 |
| Diodes, transistors, etc. | 182.5 | 197.7 | 263.8 |
| Electronic microcircuits | 374.5 | 575.0 | 798.8 |
| **Miscellaneous manufactured articles** | 1,657.3 | 1,772.4 | 1,982.3 |
| Furniture and parts thereof | 181.2 | 203.1 | 240.0 |
| Clothing and accessories (excl. footwear) | 850.8 | 834.6 | 896.7 |
| Knitted or crocheted outer garments and accessories (excl. gloves, stockings, etc.), non-elastic | 275.8 | n.a. | n.a. |
| Knitted or crocheted undergarments (incl. foundation garments of non-knitted fabrics) | 226.4 | n.a. | n.a. |
| **Total** (incl. others) | 9,726.3 | 11,209.9 | 13,482.9 |

## PRINCIPAL TRADING PARTNERS (US $ million)

| Imports c.i.f | 1992 | 1993 | 1994 |
|---|---:|---:|---:|
| Australia | 457.8 | 531.6 | 639.0 |
| Brazil | 211.3 | 235.4 | 282.2 |
| Canada | 218.2 | 167.0 | 154.6 |
| China, People's Republic | 201.2 | 201.9 | 332.8 |
| France (incl. Monaco) | 225.3 | 215.4 | 258.0 |
| Germany | 699.3 | 647.2 | 797.5 |
| Hong Kong | 744.9 | 913.8 | 1,164.8 |
| Indonesia | 196.4 | 368.1 | 399.1 |
| Iran | 173.7 | 72.5 | 71.2 |
| Japan | 3,281.8 | 4,276.0 | 5,458.9 |
| Korea, Republic | 737.3 | 943.7 | 1,172.4 |
| Kuwait | 86.8 | 202.3 | 86.8 |
| Malaysia | 410.0 | 350.3 | 441.2 |
| Netherlands | 192.3 | 249.0 | 294.9 |
| Saudi Arabia | 921.4 | 796.5 | 994.3 |
| Singapore | 573.0 | 1,016.1 | 1,494.3 |
| Taiwan | 996.8 | 1,071.6 | 1,280.9 |
| Thailand | 145.8 | 189.5 | 212.2 |
| United Arab Emirates | 276.4 | 272.2 | 230.2 |
| United Kingdom | 313.9 | 393.4 | 106.3 |
| USA | 2,821.4 | 3,743.8 | 4,179.5 |
| **Total** (incl. others) | 15,464.9 | 18,772.7 | 22,638.0 |

| Exports f.o.b. | 1992 | 1993 | 1994 |
|---|---|---|---|
| Australia | 112.6 | 114.4 | 139.8 |
| Belgium-Luxembourg | 76.8 | 94.1 | 97.2 |
| Canada | 159.8 | 194.1 | 195.8 |
| China, People's Republic | 113.9 | 173.9 | 164.5 |
| France (incl. Monaco) | 178.9 | 208.9 | 185.0 |
| Germany | 520.8 | 586.0 | 665.3 |
| Hong Kong | 462.8 | 548.2 | 651.4 |
| Italy | 99.5 | 85.5 | 90.5 |
| Japan | 1,745.0 | 1,817.4 | 2,024.1 |
| Korea, Republic | 175.8 | 221.0 | 292.1 |
| Malaysia | 127.8 | 159.0 | 216.9 |
| Netherlands | 406.3 | 361.8 | 516.1 |
| Singapore | 252.3 | 379.4 | 708.5 |
| Taiwan | 286.8 | 346.1 | 452.8 |
| Thailand | 98.4 | 168.7 | 363.8 |
| United Arab Emirates | 110.5 | 149.7 | 130.2 |
| United Kingdom | 436.4 | 540.5 | 638.6 |
| USA | 3,843.3 | 4,230.7 | 4,965.9 |
| **Total** (incl. others) | 9,789.6 | 11,374.8 | 13,482.9 |

## Transport

**RAILWAYS** (traffic)

| | 1990 | 1992* | 1993 |
|---|---|---|---|
| Passengers ('000) | 928 | 467 | 402 |
| Passenger-km (million) | 271 | 121 | 102 |
| Freight ('000 metric tons) | 32 | 5 | 18 |
| Freight ton-km (million) | 7 | 731 | n.a. |

* Figures for 1991 are unavailable.

Source: Philippine National Railways.

**ROAD TRAFFIC** (registered motor vehicles at 31 December)

| | 1991 | 1992 | 1993 |
|---|---|---|---|
| Motor cars | 456,606 | 483,622 | 531,240 |
| Commercial vehicles* | 670,848 | 744,190 | 834,168 |
| Trucks and trailers | 157,095 | 166,986 | 187,449 |
| Buses | 20,690 | 25,827 | 24,603 |
| Motor cycles | 410,127 | 458,938 | 547,655 |

* Including jeepneys.

Source: Land Transportation Commission.

**SHIPPING**

**Merchant Fleet** (at 30 June)

| | 1991 | 1992 | 1993 |
|---|---|---|---|
| Number of vessels | 1,465 | 1,521 | 1,469 |
| Displacement (grt) | 8,625,561 | 8,470,441 | 8,466,171 |

Source: Lloyd's Register of Shipping.

**International Sea-borne Shipping** (freight traffic)

| | 1990 | 1991 | 1992 |
|---|---|---|---|
| Vessels ('000 net registered tons) | | | |
| Entered | 40,041 | 44,249 | 44,815 |
| Cleared | 45,596 | 44,300 | 44,810 |
| Goods ('000 metric tons) | | | |
| Loaded | 14,122 | 15,786 | 14,122 |
| Unloaded | 31,662 | 31,150 | 34,868 |

**CIVIL AVIATION** (total scheduled services, '000)

| | 1989* | 1990* | 1991 |
|---|---|---|---|
| Kilometres flown | 59,150 | 57,986 | 55,630 |
| Passengers carried | 5,912 | 5,665 | 5,412 |
| Passenger-km | 10,592,931 | 10,518,467 | 10,115,424 |
| Freight carried (kg) | 113,897 | 111,163 | 105,836 |
| Total ton-km | 1,381,451 | 1,360,203 | 1,258,561 |

* Source: Philippine Airlines.

## Tourism

| | 1990 | 1991 | 1992 |
|---|---|---|---|
| Number of visitors | 1,024,520 | 951,365 | 1,167,917 |
| Estimated spending (US $'000) | 1,306,000 | 1,281 | 1,674 |

Source: Department of Tourism.

## Communications Media

| | 1990 | 1991 | 1992 |
|---|---|---|---|
| Radio receivers ('000 in use) | 8,600 | 8,810 | 9,030 |
| Television receivers ('000 in use) | 3,000 | 2,800 | 2,900 |
| Telephones ('000 main lines in use) | 610 | 648 | n.a. |
| Book production (titles) | 1,112 | 825* | n.a. |
| Daily newspapers (number) | 47 | n.a. | 43 |
| Non-daily newspapers (number) | 306 | n.a. | n.a. |
| Periodicals (number) | 1,570 | n.a. | n.a. |

* Including 62 pamphlets.

Sources: UNESCO, *Statistical Yearbook*; UN, *Statistical Yearbook*.

## Education

(1990/91)

| | Institutions | Teachers | Pupils |
|---|---|---|---|
| Pre-elementary | 4,201 | 9,644 | 397,364 |
| Elementary schools | 34,081 | 311,013 | 10,427,077 |
| Secondary schools | 5,550 | 122,688 | 4,033,597 |
| Post-secondary, non-degree, non-technical and vocational schools | 1,262 | 13,265 | 361,736 |
| Higher education | 809 | 56,880 | 1,347,750 |

Source: Department of Education, Culture and Sports.

**Primary** (1992/93): 34,570 institutions; 294,485 teachers (public education only); 10,679,748 pupils.

**Secondary** (1992/93): 89,063 teachers (public education only); 4,421,649 pupils.

**Higher education** (1991/92): 1,656,815 students (males 681,565; females 975,250).

Source: UNESCO, *Statistical Yearbook*.

# Directory

## The Constitution

A new Constitution for the Republic of the Philippines was ratified by national referendum on 2 February 1987. Its principal provisions are summarized below:

### BASIC PRINCIPLES

Sovereignty resides in the people, and all government authority emanates from them; war is renounced as an instrument of national policy; civilian authority is supreme over military authority.

The State undertakes to pursue an independent foreign policy, governed by considerations of the national interest; the Republic of the Philippines adopts and pursues a policy of freedom from nuclear weapons in its territory.

Other provisions guarantee social justice and full respect for human rights; honesty and integrity in the public service; the autonomy of local governments; and the protection of the family unit. Education, the arts, sport, private enterprise and agrarian and urban reforms are also promoted. The rights of workers, women, youth, the urban poor and minority indigenous communities are emphasized.

### BILL OF RIGHTS

The individual is guaranteed the right to life, liberty and property, under the law; freedom of abode and travel, freedom of worship, freedom of speech, of the press and of petition to the Government are guaranteed, as well as the right of access to official information on matters of public concern, the right to form trade unions, the right to assemble in public gatherings, and free access to the courts.

The Constitution upholds the right of habeas corpus and prohibits the intimidation, detention, torture or secret confinement of apprehended persons.

### SUFFRAGE

Suffrage is granted to all citizens over 18 years of age, who have resided for at least one year previously in the Republic of the Philippines, and for at least six months in their voting district. Voting is by secret ballot.

### LEGISLATURE

Legislative power is vested in the bicameral Congress of the Philippines, consisting of the Senate and the House of Representatives, with a total of 278 members. All members shall make a disclosure of their financial and business interests upon assumption of office, and no member may hold any other office. Provision is made for voters to propose laws, or reject any act or law passed by Congress, through referenda.

The Senate shall be composed of 24 members; Senators are directly elected for six years by national vote, and must be natural-born citizens, at least 35 years of age, literate and registered voters in their district. They must be resident in the Philippines for at least two years prior to election, and no Senator shall serve for more than two consecutive terms. One-half of the membership of the Senate shall be elected every three years. No treaty or international agreement may be considered valid without the approval, by voting, of at least two-thirds of members.

A maximum of 250 Representatives may sit in the House of Representatives. Its members may serve no more than three consecutive three-year terms. Representatives must be natural-born citizens, literate, and at least 25 years of age. A total of 204 representatives may be directly elected by district; they must be registered voters in their district, and resident there for at least one year prior to election. In addition, 50 representatives (or 20% of the total) shall be appointed by the President from lists of nominees proposed by indigenous, but non-religious, minority groups (such as the urban poor, peasantry, women and youth), for three consecutive terms following the ratification of the Constitution.

The Senate and the House of Representatives shall each have an Electoral Tribunal which shall be the sole judge of contests relating to the election of members of Congress. Each Tribunal shall have nine members, three of whom must be Justices of the Supreme Court, appointed by the Chief Justice. The remaining six members shall be members of the Senate or of the House of Representatives, as appropriate, and shall be selected from the political parties represented therein, on a proportional basis.

### THE COMMISSION ON APPOINTMENTS

The President must submit nominations of heads of executive departments, ambassadors and senior officers in the armed forces to the Commission on Appointments, which shall decide on the appointment by majority vote of its members. The President of the Senate shall act as ex-officio Chairman; the Commission shall consist of 12 Senators and 12 members of the House of Representatives, elected from the political parties represented therein, on the basis of proportional representation.

### THE EXECUTIVE

Executive power is vested in the President of the Philippines. Presidents are limited to one six-year term of office, and Vice-Presidents to two successive six-year terms. Candidates for both posts are elected by direct universal suffrage. They must be natural-born citizens, literate, at least 40 years of age, registered voters and resident in the Philippines for at least 10 years prior to election.

The President is Head of State and Chief Executive of the Republic. Bills (legislative proposals) that have been approved by Congress shall be signed by the President; if the President vetoes the bill, it may become law when two-thirds of members in Congress approve it.

The President shall nominate and, with the consent of the Commission on Appointments, appoint ambassadors, officers of the armed forces and heads of executive departments.

The President is Commander-in-Chief of the armed forces and may suspend the writ of habeas corpus or place the Republic under martial law for a period not exceeding 60 days when, in the President's opinion, the public safety demands it. Congress may revoke either action by a majority vote.

The Vice-President may be a member of the Cabinet; in the event of the death or resignation of the President, the Vice-President shall become President and serve the unexpired term of the previous President.

### THE JUDICIARY

The Supreme Court is composed of a Chief Justice and 14 Associate Justices, and may sit *en banc* or in divisions comprising three, five or seven members. Justices of the Supreme Court are appointed by the President, with the consent of the Commission on Appointments, for a term of four years. They must be citizens of the Republic, at least 40 years of age, of proven integrity, and must have been judges of the lower courts, or engaged in the practice of law in the Philippines, for at least 15 years.

The Supreme Court, sitting *en banc*, is the sole judge of disputes relating to presidential and vice-presidential elections.

### THE CONSTITUTIONAL COMMISSIONS

These are the Civil Service Commission and the Commission on Audit, each of which has a Chairman and two other Commissioners, appointed by the President (with the approval of the Commission on Appointments) to a seven-year term; and the Commission on Elections, which enforces and administers all laws pertaining to elections and political parties. The Commission on Elections has seven members, appointed by the President (and approved by the Commission on Appointments) for a seven-year term. The Commission on Elections may sit *en banc* or in two divisions.

### LOCAL GOVERNMENT

The Republic of the Philippines shall be divided into provinces, cities, municipalities and barangays. The Congress of the Philippines shall enact a local government code providing for decentralization. A region may become autonomous, subject to approval by a majority vote of the electorate of that region, in a referendum. Defence and security in such areas will remain the responsibility of the national Government.

### ACCOUNTABILITY OF PUBLIC OFFICERS

All public officers, including the President, Vice-President and members of Congress and the Constitutional Commissions, may be removed from office if impeached for, or convicted of, violation of the Constitution, corruption, treason, bribery or betrayal of public trust.

Cases of impeachment must be initiated solely by the House of Representatives, and tried solely by the Senate. A person shall be convicted by a vote of at least two-thirds of the Senate, and will then be dismissed from office and dealt with according to the law.

### SOCIAL JUSTICE AND HUMAN RIGHTS

The Congress of the Philippines shall give priority to considerations of human dignity, the equality of the people and an equitable distribution of wealth. The Commission on Human Rights shall investigate allegations of violations of human rights, shall protect human rights through legal measures, and shall monitor the Government's compliance with international treaty obligations. It may advise Congress on measures to promote human rights.

## AMENDMENTS OR REVISIONS

Proposals for amendment or revision of the Constitution may be made by:
 i) Congress (upon a vote of three-quarters of members);
 ii) A Constitutional Convention (convened by a vote of two-thirds of members of Congress);
 iii) The people, through petitions (signed by at least 12% of the total number of registered voters).

The proposed amendments or revisions shall then be submitted to a national plebiscite, and shall be valid when ratified by a majority of the votes cast.

## MILITARY BASES

Foreign military bases, troops or facilities shall not be allowed in the Republic of the Philippines following the expiry, in 1991, of the Agreement between the Republic and the USA; except under the provisions of a treaty approved by the Senate, and, when required by Congress, ratified by the voters in a national referendum.

# The Government

### HEAD OF STATE

**President:** Gen. Fidel V. Ramos (inaugurated 30 June 1992).
**Vice-President:** Joseph E. Estrada.

### THE CABINET
(July 1995)

**Secretary of Foreign Affairs:** Domingo Siazon.
**Secretary of Finance:** Roberto de Ocampo.
**Secretary of Justice:** Teofisto T. Guingona, Jr.
**Secretary of Agriculture:** Roberto S. Sebastian.
**Secretary of Public Works and Highways:** Gregorio R. Vigilar.
**Secretary of Education, Culture and Sports:** Ricardo T. Gloria.
**Secretary of National Defense:** Gen. Renato S. de Villa.
**Secretary of Health:** Jaime Galvez-Tan.
**Secretary of Labor and Employment:** Jose Brillantes.
**Secretary of Trade and Industry:** Rizalino S. Navarro.
**Secretary of Agrarian Reform:** Ernesto D. Garilao.
**Secretary of the Interior and Local Government:** Rafael M. Alunan.
**Secretary of Tourism:** Eduardo Pilapil (acting).
**Secretary of the Environment and Natural Resources:** Victor O. Ramos.
**Secretary of Transportation and Communications:** Jesus B. Garcia.
**Secretary of Social Welfare and Development:** Corazon Alma G. de Leon.
**Secretary of the Budget and Management:** Salvador M. Enriquez, Jr.
**Secretary of Science and Technology:** William Padolina.
**Director-General of the National Economic Development Authority (NEDA):** Cielito F. Habito.
**Secretary of Energy:** Francisco Viray.

### Officials with Cabinet Rank

**Executive Secretary:** Ruben Torres.
**Presidential Legal Counsel:** Antonio T. Carpio.
**Presidential Adviser on Rural Development:** Daniel Lacson.
**Presidential Adviser on Economic Affairs:** Emilio Osmena.
**Director-General, National Security Council and Presidential Security Adviser:** Jose T. Almonte.
**Press Secretary and Presidential Spokesperson:** Hector Villanueva.
**Chairman of Muslim Affairs:** Dimasangkay Pundato.
**Head of the Presidential Commission on Good Government:** Magtanggol Gunigundo.
**Head of the Presidential Anti-Crime Commission:** Joseph E. Estrada.
**Head of the Bureau of Customs:** Guillermo L. Parayno, Jr.
**Head of the Bureau of Internal Revenue:** Liwayway V. Chato.
**Solicitor-General:** Raul Goco.

### MINISTRIES

**Office of the President:** Presidential Guest House, Malacañang Palace Compound, J. P. Laurel St, San Miguel, Metro Manila; tel. (2) 5212301; telex 40213; fax (2) 7421641.
**Department of Agrarian Reform:** Elliptical Rd, Diliman, Quezon City, Metro Manila; tel. (2) 997031; fax (2) 973968.
**Department of Agriculture:** Elliptical Rd, Diliman, Quezon City, Metro Manila; tel. (2) 997011; telex 27726; fax (2) 978183.
**Department of the Budget and Management:** Administration Bldg, Malacañang, Metro Manila; tel. (2) 483475; fax (2) 5301174.
**Department of Education, Culture and Sports:** University of Life Bldg, Meralco Ave, Pasig, 1600 Metro Manila; tel. (2) 6321361; fax (2) 6321371.
**Department of Energy:** Philippine National Petroleum Center, Merritt Rd, Fort Bonifacio, Makati, Metro Manila; tel. (2) 857051; fax (2) 851021.
**Department of the Environment and Natural Resources:** DENR Bldg, Visayas Ave, Diliman, Quezon City, Metro Manila; tel. (2) 976671.
**Department of Finance:** DOF Bldg, Valencia Circle, Ermita, Metro Manila; tel. (2) 595262; fax (2) 5219495.
**Department of Foreign Affairs:** 2330 Roxas Blvd, Pasay City, Metro Manila; tel. (2) 8344000; fax (2) 8320683.
**Department of Health:** San Lazaro Compound, Rizal Ave, Santa Cruz, Metro Manila; tel. (2) 7116080; fax (2) 7116055.
**Department of the Interior and Local Government:** PNCC Complex, Epifanio de los Santos Ave, cnr Reliance St, Mandaluyong, Metro Manila; tel. (2) 6318777; fax (2) 6318814.
**Department of Justice:** Padre Faura St, Ermita, Metro Manila; tel. (2) 5213721.
**Department of Labor and Employment:** DOLE Bldg, Gen. Luna St, cnr San José St, Intramuros, 1002 Metro Manila; tel. (2) 5300144; telex 40386; fax (2) 472857.
**Department of National Defense:** Camp Aguinaldo, Quezon City, Metro Manila; tel. (2) 7219031; telex 22471.
**Department of Public Works and Highways:** DPWH Bldg, Bonifacio Drive, Port Area, Metro Manila; tel. (2) 482011; telex 2335; fax (2) 401683.
**Department of Science and Technology:** Gen. Santos Ave, Bicutan, Taguig, Metro Manila; tel. (2) 8238939; fax (2) 8238937.
**Department of Social Welfare and Development:** Constitution Hills, Quezon City, Metro Manila; tel. (2) 9317916; fax (2) 7416939.
**Department of Tourism:** DOT Bldg, T. M. Kalaw St, Agrifina Circle, Rizal Park, POB 3451, Metro Manila; tel. (2) 599031; fax (2) 501751.
**Department of Trade and Industry:** Trade and Industry Bldg, 361 Gil J. Puyat Ave Ext., POB 2303, Makati, 3117 Metro Manila; tel. (2) 8185701; telex 14830; fax (2) 856487.
**Department of Transportation and Communications:** Philcomcen Bldg, Ortigas Ave, Pasig, Metro Manila: tel. (2) 7213781; fax (2) 6329985.
**National Economic Development Authority (NEDA—Department of Economic Planning):** NEDA Bldg, Amber Ave, Pasig, Metro Manila; tel. (2) 6310945; telex 29058; fax (2) 6313747.
**Philippine Information Agency (Office of the Press Secretary):** Visayas Ave, Diliman, Quezon City, Metro Manila; tel. (2) 9227477; Dir-Gen. Honesto M. Isleta.

# President and Legislature

### PRESIDENT

**Election, 11 May 1992**

| Candidate | Votes | % of votes |
|---|---|---|
| Gen. Fidel Ramos (Lakas-NUCD) | 5,342,521 | 23.6 |
| Miriam Defensor Santiago (PRP) | 4,468,173 | 19.7 |
| Eduardo Cojuangco (Nationalist People's Coalition) | 4,116,376 | 18.2 |
| Ramon Mitra (LDP) | 3,316,661 | 14.6 |
| Imelda Marcos (KBL) | 2,338,294 | 10.3 |
| Jovito Salonga (Liberal Party) | 2,302,124 | 10.2 |
| Salvador Laurel (Nacionalista Party) | 770,046 | 3.4 |

## THE CONGRESS OF THE PHILIPPINES
### Senate
**President of the Senate:** EDGARDO ANGARA (LDP).

**Elections, 11 May 1992 and 8 May 1995**

| | Seats |
|---|---|
| Lakas-Laban: | |
|   Laban ng Demokratikong Pilipino (LDP) | 15 |
|   Lakas ng EDSA-National Union of Christian Democrats (Lakas-NUCD) | 6 |
| People's Reform Party (PRP) | 2 |
| Nationalist People's Coalition (NPC) | 1 |
| **Total** | **24** |

Note: Elections for one-half of the members of the Senate took place on 8 May 1995. The overall composition of the Senate following these elections is represented above.

### House of Representatives
**Speaker of the House:** JOSE DE VENECIA (Lakas-NUCD).

**General Election, 11 May 1992**

| | Seats |
|---|---|
| Laban ng Demokratikong Pilipino (LDP) | 89 |
| Nationalist People's Coalition (NPC) | 42 |
| Lakas ng EDSA-National Union of Christian Democrats (Lakas-NUCD) | 33 |
| Liberal Party/PDP-Laban | 15 |
| Nacionalista Party | 7 |
| Kilusang Bagong Lipunan (KBL) | 3 |
| Others | 11 |
| **Total*** | **200** |

* A maximum of 50 further representatives may be appointed by the President from lists of nominees submitted by minority and cause-orientated groups.

Note: A general election to the House of Representatives took place on 8 May 1995. Official results had not been published by mid-July, owing to unresolved legal challenges.

## Autonomous Region
### MUSLIM MINDANAO

Muslim Mindanao comprises the provinces of Lanao del Sur, Maguindanao, Tawi-Tawi and Sulu. The region was granted autonomy in November 1989. Elections took place in February 1990, and the formal transfer of limited executive powers took place in October 1990. At elections on 25 March 1993 the Strength-National Union of Christian Democrats won nine of the 21 legislative seats.

**Governor:** LININDING PANGANDAMAN (elected 25 March 1993).

**Vice-Governor:** NABIL TAN.

**Assembly Speaker:** (vacant).

## Political Organizations

**Bandila:** Metro Manila; f. 1985; small pro-Aquino centrist group.

**Kababaihan Para Sa Inang Bayan** (Women for the Mother Country): Metro Manila; f. 1986; the first all-women's political party in the Philippines and Asia; militant group; Chair. TARHATA LUCMAN.

**Kilusang Bagong Lipunan (KBL)** (New Society Movement): Metro Manila; f. 1978 by Pres. Marcos and fmr mems of the Nacionalista Party; Sec.-Gen. VICENTE MELLORA.

**Laban:** Metro Manila; f. 1992; comprises defectors from the LDP who joined Gen. Ramos's 'rainbow coalition'.

**Laban ng Demokratikong Pilipino (LDP)** (Fight of Democratic Filipinos): Metro Manila; f. 1987, reorg. 1988 as an alliance of Lakas ng Bansa and a conservative faction of the PDP-Laban Party; formed electoral alliance (Lakas-Laban) with Lakas-NUCD in Aug. 1994; Pres. EDGARDO ANGARA; Sec.-Gen. JOSE COJUANGCO.

**Lakas ng Bansa** (Strength of the Nation): Metro Manila; f. 1987; pro-Aquino; part of LDP group; Pres. NEPTALI GONZALES.

**Lakas ng EDSA** (Power of EDSA)-**National Union of Christian Democrats (Lakas-NUCD):** Metro Manila; f. 1992 as alliance to support the presidential candidacy of Gen. FIDEL V. RAMOS; formed electoral alliance (Lakas-Laban) with the LDP in Aug. 1994; Sec.-Gen. JOSE DE VENECIA.

**Liberal Party:** Metro Manila; f. 1946; represents centre-liberal opinion of the fmr Nacionalista Party, which split in 1946; Leader JOVITO SALONGA.

**Mindanao Alliance:** Cagayan de Oro, Mindanao; f. 1978; advocates the economic development of Mindanao and the protection of civil and human rights; Leader HOMOBONO ADAZA.

**Nacionalista Party*:** Metro Manila; Pres. SALVADOR LAUREL.

**Nacionalista Party*:** Metro Manila; tel. (2) 854418; fax (2) 865602; JUAN PONCE ENRILE is the dominant force behind this wing; Pres. ARTURO TOLENTINO; Sec.-Gen. RENE ESPINA.

**Nationalist People's Coalition (NPC)*:** Metro Manila; f. 1991; Leader ERNESTO MACEDA; Pres. ISIDRO RODRIGUEZ.

**Partido Demokratiko Sosyalista ng Pilipinas—Philippine Democratic Socialist Party (PDSP):** Metro Manila; f. 1981 by mems of the Batasang Pambansa allied to the Nacionalista (Roy faction), Pusyon Visaya and Mindanao Alliance parties; Leader NORBERTO GONZALES.

**Partido Komunista ng Pilipinas (PKP)** (Communist Party of the Philippines): f. 1930; pro-Soviet; Pres. FELICISIMO MACAPAGAL; Sec.-Gen. MERLIN MAGALLONA.

**Partido Nacionalista ng Pilipinas (PNP)** (Philippine Nationalist Party): Metro Manila; f. 1986 by fmr mems of KBL; Leader BLAS F. OPLE.

**Partido ng Bayan** (New People's Alliance): f. May 1986 by JOSE MARIA SISON (imprisoned in 1977–86), the head of the Communist Party of the Philippines (CPP); militant left-wing nationalist group; Chair. FIDEL AGCAOLI; Sec.-Gen. SONIA P. SOTTO.

**Partido ng Masang Pilipino (PMP):** Metro Manila; Leader JOSEPH E. ESTRADA.

**PDP-Laban Party:** Metro Manila; f. February 1983 following merger of Pilipino Democratic Party (f. 1982 by fmr mems of the Mindanao Alliance) and Laban (Lakas ng Bayan—People's Power Movement, f. 1978 and led by Benigno S. Aquino, Jr, until his assassination in August 1983); centrist; c. 110,000 mems; formally dissolved in Sept. 1988, following the formation of the LDP, but a faction continued to function as a political movement; Chair. AQUILINO PIMENTEL; Pres. JUANITO FERRER; Sec.-Gen. AUGUSTO SANCHEZ.

**People's Reform Party (PRP):** f. 1991 by MIRIAM DEFENSOR SANTIAGO to support her candidacy in the 1992 presidential election.

**Pusyon Visaya Party:** f. 1978; won 13 seats in the Visayas region of the central Philippines in 1978 elections; split into two factions in 1981; Pres. and Sec.-Gen. VALENTINO LEGASPI.

* The Nacionalista Party was founded in 1907, but subsequently split into various factions. It became effectively defunct after Ferdinand Marcos formed the Kilusang Bagong Lipunan in 1978, was revived in 1989 and split into three wings in 1991, under Salvador Laurel, Juan Ponce Enrile and Eduardo Cojuangco (whose faction was renamed the Nationalist People's Coalition).

The following organizations are in conflict with the Government:

**Abu Sayyaf** (Bearer of the Sword): Mindanao; radical Islamic group seeking the establishment of an Islamic state in Mindanao; severely weakened by attacks by govt forces in 1994; est. strength 150–600; Leader ABDURAJAK ABUBAKAR JANJALANI.

**Alex Boncayao Brigade:** communist urban guerrilla group, fmrly linked to CPP; Leader FILEMAN LAGMAN.

**Mindanao Independence Movement:** Mindanao; claims a membership of 1m.; Leader REUBEN CANOY.

**Moro Islamic Liberation Front (MILF):** based mainly in Lanao del Sur; comprises a faction that broke away from the MNLF in 1978; its armed wing, the Bangsa Moro Islamic Armed Forces, has an estimated strength of 40,000; Chair. HASHIM SALAMAT; Vice-Chair. Haji MURAD.

**Moro National Liberation Front (MNLF):** seeks autonomy for Muslim communities in Mindanao and other islands in the southern Philippines; its armed wing, the Bangsa Moro Army, comprises an est. 10,000; Chair. and Pres. of Cen. Cttee NUR MISUARI. The MNLF includes:

**Bangsa Moro National Liberation Front (BMNLF):** includes the Bangsa Moro Islamic Party faction; est. strength 11,000; Leader DIMAS PUNDATO.

**National Democratic Front (NDF):** a left-wing alliance of 14 mem. groups; Chair. MANUEL ROMERO; Spokesman SATURNINO OCAMPO. The NDF includes:

**Communist Party of the Philippines (CPP):** f. 1968; a breakaway faction of the PKP; legalized Sept. 1992; in July 1993 the Metro Manila-Rizal regional committee, controlling 40% of total CPP membership (est. 15,000 in 1994), split from the Central Committee; Chair. JOSE MARIA SISON; Gen. Sec. BENITO TIAMZON.

THE PHILIPPINES                                                                                                    *Directory*

**New People's Army (NPA):** f. 1969 as the military wing of the CPP; based in central Luzon, but operates throughout the Philippines; est. strength 2,500; C-in-C SOTERO LLAMAS.

## Diplomatic Representation

### EMBASSIES IN THE PHILIPPINES

**Argentina:** ACT Tower, 6th Floor, 135 Sen. Gil J. Puyat Ave, Salcedo Village, Makati, Metro Manila; tel. (2) 8108301; Ambassador: JOSÉ GARCÍA GHIRELLI.

**Australia:** Doña Salustiana Dee Ty Bldg, Ground-5th Floors, 104 Paseo de Roxas, cnr Perea St, Makati, 1200 Metro Manila; tel. (2) 8177911; telex 63744; fax (2) 8173603; Ambassador: RICHARD SMITH.

**Austria:** Prince Bldg, 4th Floor, 117 Rada St, Legaspi Village, Makati, 1200 Metro Manila; tel. (2) 8179191; telex 23452; fax (2) 8134238; Ambassador: Dr HEIDE KELLER.

**Bangladesh:** UniversalRe Bldg, 2nd Floor, 106 Paseo de Roxas, Legaspi Village, Makati, Metro Manila; tel. (2) 8175001; Ambassador: MOHAMMAD ABU HENA.

**Belgium:** Don Jacinto Bldg, 6th Floor, cnr de la Rosa and Salcedo Sts, Legaspi Village, POB 2165, Makati, 1251 Metro Manila; tel. (2) 8926571; telex 23099; fax (2) 8172566; Ambassador: JOHAN BALLEGEER.

**Brazil:** RCI Bldg, 6th Floor, 105 Rada St, Legaspi Village, POB 1587, Makati, 1255 Metro Manila; tel. (2) 8928181; telex 63639; fax (2) 8182622; Ambassador: ANTÔNIO CARLOS COELHO DA ROCHA.

**Brunei:** Bank of the Philippine Islands Bldg, 11th Floor, Ayala Ave, cnr Paseo de Roxas, Makati, Metro Manila; tel. (2) 8162836; Ambassador: Pengiran MUSTAPHA BIN Pengiran METASSAN.

**Bulgaria:** 1212 Tamarind Rd, Dasmariñas Village, Makati, Metro Manila; tel. (2) 8181321; telex 64489; Chargé d'affaires: GEORGI MLADENOV.

**Canada:** Allied Bank Center, 9th Floor, 6754 Ayala Ave, Makati, Metro Manila; tel. (2) 8108861; telex 63676; fax (2) 8108839; Ambassador: STEPHEN HEENEY.

**Chile:** Doña Salustiana Dee Ty Bldg, 6th Floor, 104 Paseo de Roxas, Legaspi Village, Makati, Metro Manila; tel. (2) 8103149; telex 66568; fax (2) 8150795; Ambassador: PATRICIO RODRÍGUEZ.

**China, People's Republic:** 4896 Pasay Rd, Dasmariñas Village, Makati, Metro Manila; tel. (2) 853148; Ambassador: GUAN DEMING.

**Colombia:** Aurora Tower, 18th Floor, Araneta Center, Quezon City, Metro Manila; tel. (2) 9212701; telex 40219; Ambassador: RAMIRO ZAMBRANO CÁRDENAS.

**Cuba:** Heart Tower Condominium, 11th Floor, 108 Valero St, Salcedo Village, Makati, Metro Manila; tel. (2) 8171192; telex 63609; fax (2) 8164094; Chargé d'affaires: TERESITA FERNÁNDEZ DÍAZ.

**Denmark:** Doña Salustiana Dee Ty Bldg, 6th Floor, 104 Paseo de Roxas, Legaspi Village, Makati, 3120 Metro Manila; POB 7707, 1300 Metro Manila; tel. (2) 8940086; telex 23066; fax (2) 8175729; Chargé d'affaires: MOGENS JENSEN.

**Egypt:** 2229 Paraiso cnr Banyan St, Dasmariñas Village, Makati, Metro Manila; tel. (2) 8920396; telex 45190; fax (2) 8170885; Ambassador: Dr ABBAS RUSHDY EL-AMMARY.

**Finland:** Bank of the Philippine Islands Bldg, 14th Floor, Ayala Ave, cnr Paseo de Roxas, Makati, Metro Manila; tel. (2) 8162105; telex 22694; fax (2) 8151401; Chargé d'affaires: JUHA KUUSI.

**France:** Pacific Star Bldg, 16th Floor, Makati Ave, cnr Sen. Gil J. Puyat Ave, Makati, Metro Manila; tel. (2) 8101981; telex 63864; fax (2) 8175047; Ambassador: OLIVIER GAUSSOT.

**Germany:** Solidbank Bldg, 6th Floor, 777 Paseo de Roxas, Makati, 1226 Metro Manila; tel. (2) 8924906; telex 22655; fax (2) 8104703; Ambassador: Dr KARL-FRIEDRICH GANSÄUER.

**Holy See:** 2140 Taft Ave, POB 3604, 1099 Metro Manila (Apostolic Nunciature); tel. (2) 5210306; fax (2) 5211235; Apostolic Nuncio: Most Rev. GIAN VINCENZO MORENI, Titular Archbishop of Turris in Mauretania.

**India:** 2190 Paraiso St, Dasmariñas Village, Makati, Metro Manila; tel. (2) 872445; telex 63595; Ambassador: SHYMALA B. COWSIK.

**Indonesia:** Indonesian Embassy Bldg, Salcedo St, Legaspi Village, Makati, Metro Manila; tel. (2) 855061; Ambassador: HASSAN WIRAYUDA.

**Iran:** Don Jacinto Bldg, 4th Floor, cnr Salcedo and de la Rosa Sts, Legaspi Village, Makati, Metro Manila; tel. (2) 871561; telex 63711; Chargé d'affaires: SEYED KAMAL SADJJADI.

**Iraq:** 1368 Caballero St, Dasmariñas Village, Makati, Metro Manila; tel. (2) 856715; telex 45265; Ambassador: ALI M. SUMAIDA.

**Israel:** Philippine Savings Bank Bldg, 5th Floor, 6813 Ayala Ave, Makati, Metro Manila; tel. (2) 8925329; telex 22448; fax (2) 8190561; Ambassador: AMOS SHETIBEL.

**Italy:** Zeta Bldg, 6th Floor, 191 Salcedo St, Legaspi Village, Makati, Metro Manila; tel. (2) 8924531; telex 64142; fax (2) 8171436; Ambassador: ALESSANDRO SERAFINI.

**Japan:** LC Bldg, 375 Sen. Gil Puyat Ave, Makati, Metro Manila; tel. (2) 8189011; telex 22171; fax (2) 8176562; Ambassador: TOSHIFUMI MATSUDA.

**Jordan:** Golden Rock Bldg, 3rd Floor, Suite 502, 168 Salcedo St, Legaspi Village, Makati, Metro Manila; tel. (2) 8177494; Ambassador: HASAN ZIYADEH.

**Korea, Republic:** ALPAP 1 Bldg, 3rd Floor, 140 Alfaro St, Salcedo Village, Makati, Metro Manila; tel. (2) 8175705; telex 22157; fax (2) 8175845; Ambassador: CHANG SOO LEE.

**Libya:** 4928 Pasay Rd, Dasmariñas Village, Makati, Metro Manila; tel. (2) 8173461; Ambassador: SALEM ADEM.

**Malaysia:** 107 Tordesillas St, Salcedo Village, Makati, Metro Manila; POB 1967, Makati, 1299 Metro Manila; tel. (2) 8174581; telex 52758; fax (2) 8163158; Ambassador: Emam MOHAMMED HANIFF.

**Mexico:** 814 Pasay Rd, San Lorenzo Village, Makati, Metro Manila; tel. (2) 857323; telex 23459; Ambassador: JOSÉ HÉCTOR M. IBARRA.

**Myanmar:** Basic Petroleum Bldg, 4th Floor, 104 Carlos Palanca Jr St, Legaspi Village, Makati, Metro Manila; tel. (2) 8172373; telex 66017; fax (2) 8175895; Ambassador: U BO NI.

**Netherlands:** King's Court Bldg, 9th Floor, 2129 Pasong Tamo, POB 2448, Makati, 1264 Metro Manila; tel. (2) 8125981; telex 63551; fax (2) 8154579; Ambassador: ERIC T. J. T. KWINT.

**New Zealand:** Gammon Centre, 3rd Floor, 126 Alfaro St, Salcedo Village, POB 3228, Makati, Metro Manila; tel. (2) 8180916; fax (2) 8164457; Ambassador: COLIN BELL.

**Nigeria:** 2211 Paraiso St, Dasmariñas Village, Makati, 3117 Metro Manila; POB 3174 Makati, 1271 Metro Manila; tel. (2) 8173836; telex 64638; fax (2) 8152005; Chargé d'affaires a.i.: S. I. AJEWOLE.

**Norway:** 69 Paseo de Roxas, Urdaneta Village, Makati, Metro Manila; tel. (2) 8939686; telex 63964; fax (2) 8183330; Ambassador: ØYVIND RISENG.

**Pakistan:** Alexander House, 6th Floor, 132 Amorsolo St, Legaspi Village, Makati, Metro Manila; tel. (2) 8172776; telex 64219; Ambassador: AFZAL QADIR.

**Panama:** Victoria Bldg, 5th Floor, 429 United Nations Ave, Ermita, Metro Manila; tel. (2) 5211233; telex 66420; Ambassador: AURELIO CHU-YI.

**Papua New Guinea:** 2280 Magnolia St, Dasmariñas Village, Makati, Metro Manila; tel. (2) 8108456; telex 22692; fax (2) 8171080; Ambassador: STEPHEN N. IGO.

**Peru:** FM Lopez Bldg, cnr Legaspi and Herrera Sts, Legaspi Village, Makati, Metro Manila; tel. (2) 8188209; telex 22304; Ambassador: JULIO BALBUENA LÓPEZ ALFARO.

**Romania:** 1216 Acacia Rd, Dasmariñas Village, Makati, Metro Manila; tel. (2) 8109491; telex 45460; Chargé d'affaires: VALERIU SIMION.

**Russia:** 1245 Acacia Rd, Dasmariñas Village, Makati, Metro Manila; tel. (2) 8109614; telex 63709; fax (2) 8109614; Ambassador: VITALY B. KOUTCHOUK.

**Saudi Arabia:** Insular Life Bldg, 8th Floor, 6781 Ayala Ave, Makati, Metro Manila; tel. (2) 8173371; telex 45043; Ambassador: FAUD MUHAMMAD HASSAN FAKI.

**Singapore:** ODC International Plaza Bldg, 6th Floor, 219 Salcedo St, Legaspi Village, Makati, Metro Manila; tel. (2) 894596; telex 63631; Ambassador: AZIZ MAHMOOD.

**Spain:** ACT Tower, 135 Sen. Gil J. Puyat Ave, 5th Floor, Metro Manila; tel. (2) 8183561; telex 45892; Ambassador: FRANCISCO JAVIER CONDE DE SARO.

**Sweden:** PCI Bank Tower, 16th Floor, Makati Ave, Makati, Metro Manila; POB 2322, Makati, 1263 Metro Manila; tel. (2) 8191951; telex 22029; fax (2) 8153002; Ambassador: CRISTOFER GYLLENSTIERNA.

**Switzerland:** Solidbank Bldg, 18th Floor, 777 Paseo de Roxas, POB 2068, Makati, 1260 Metro Manila; tel. (2) 8190202; telex 22339; fax (2) 8150381; Ambassador: H. P. STRAUCH.

**Thailand:** 107 Rada St, Legaspi Village, Makati, 1229 Metro Manila; tel. (2) 8154220; telex 62288; fax (2) 8154221; Ambassador: SORAYOUTH PROMPOJ.

**Turkey:** Paraiso St, Dasmariñas Village, Makati, Metro Manila; tel. (2) 8171550; Ambassador: ERHAN YIGITBASIOGLU.

**United Arab Emirates:** Renaissance Bldg, 2nd Floor, Sakedo St, Legaspi Village, Makati, Metro Manila; tel. (2) 8173906; Ambassador: HASSAN MOHAMMED OBAID AL-SUWAIDI.

**United Kingdom:** Locsin Bldg, 15th–17th Floors, 6752 Ayala Ave, cnr Makati Ave, Makati, 1226 Metro Manila; tel. (2) 8167116; telex 63282; fax (2) 8197206; Ambassador: ADRIAN THORPE.

**USA:** 1201 Roxas Blvd, Metro Manila; tel. (2) 5217116; telex 27366; Ambassador: JOHN NEGROPONTE.

THE PHILIPPINES                                                                                                                         *Directory*

**Venezuela:** Sterling Centre, Esteban St, cnr Dela Rosa St, Legaspi Village, Makati, Metro Manila; tel. (2) 8179118; Ambassador: TIBISAY URDANETA.

**Viet Nam:** 554 Vito Cruz, Malate, Metro Manila; tel. (2) 500364; Ambassador: LUU DINH VE.

**Yugoslavia:** 2157 Paraiso St, Dasmariñas Village, Makati, Metro Manila; tel. (2) 879701; telex 63933; Ambassador: ZORAN ANDRIĆ.

## Judicial System

The February 1987 Constitution provides for the establishment of a Supreme Court comprising a Chief Justice and 14 Associate Justices; the Court may sit *en banc*, or in divisions of three, five or seven members. Justices of the Supreme Court are appointed by the President from a list of a minimum of three nominees prepared by a Judicial and Bar Council. Other courts comprise the Court of Appeals, Regional Trial Courts, Metropolitan Trial Courts, Municipal Courts in Cities, Municipal Courts and Municipal Circuit Trial Courts. There is also a special court for trying cases of corruption (the Sandiganbayan). The Office of the Ombudsman (Tanodbayan) investigates complaints concerning the actions of public officials.

**Chief Justice:** RICARDO FRANCISCO.

**Court of Appeals:** Consists of a Presiding Justice and 50 Associate Justices.

**Presiding Justice:** RODOLFO A. NOCON.

Islamic Shari'a courts were established in the southern Philippines in July 1985 under a presidential decree of February 1977. They are presided over by three district magistrates and six circuit judges.

## Religion

In 1991 94.2% of the population were Christians: 84.1% were Roman Catholics, 6.2% belonged to the Philippine Independent Church (Aglipayan) and 3.9% were Protestants. In 1993 an estimated 83.5% of the population were Roman Catholics. There is an Islamic community, and an estimated 43,000 Buddhists. Animists and persons professing no religion number approximately 400,000.

### CHRISTIANITY

**Sangguniang Pambansa ng mga Simbahan sa Pilipinas** (National Council of Churches in the Philippines): POB 1767, Metro Manila; tel. (2) 998636; fax (2) 967076; f. 1963; 10 mem. churches, seven assoc. mems; Gen. Sec. Dr FELICIANO CARIÑO.

#### The Roman Catholic Church

For ecclesiastical purposes, the Philippines comprises 16 archdioceses, 50 dioceses, six territorial prelatures and seven apostolic vicariates.

**Catholic Bishops' Conference of the Philippines (CBCP):** 470 General Luna St, POB 3601, 1099 Metro Manila; tel. (2) 477759; fax (2) 409704; f. 1945 (statutes approved 1988); Pres. Most Rev. CARMELO DOMINADOR F. MORELOS, Archbishop of Zamboanga.

**Archbishop of Caceres:** Most Rev. LEONARDO Z. LEGASPI, Archbishop's House, Elias Angeles St, POB 28, 4400 Naga City; tel. (21) 738483; fax (21) 739098.

**Archbishop of Cagayan de Oro:** Most Rev. JESUS B. TUQUIB, Archbishop's Residence, POB 113, 9000 Cagayan de Oro City; tel. (8822) 722375.

**Archbishop of Capiz:** Most Rev. ONESIMO C. GORDONCILLO, Chancery, Chancery Office, POB 44, 5800 Roxas City; tel. (33) 211053.

**Archbishop of Cebu:** HE Cardinal RICARDO J. VIDAL, Chancery, Cardinal Rosales Pastoral Center, corner P. Gomez and P. Burgos Sts, POB 52, 6000 Cebu City; tel. (32) 213382; fax (32) 54458.

**Archbishop of Cotabato:** Most Rev. PHILIP FRANCIS SMITH, Archbishop's Residence, Sinsuat Ave, POB 186, 9600 Cotabato City; tel. (82) 212918; fax (82) 211446.

**Archbishop of Davao:** Most Rev. ANTONIO LLOREN MABUTAS, Archbishop's Residence, Fr. Torres St, POB 80418, 8000 Davao City; tel. (82) 75992.

**Archbishop of Jaro:** Most Rev. ALBERTO J. PIAMONTE, Archbishop's House, Jaro, 5000 Iloilo City; tel. (33) 72575.

**Archbishop of Lingayen-Dagupan:** Most Rev. OSCAR V. CRUZ, Archbishop's House, 2400 Dagupan City; tel. (75) 2716; fax (75) 5221878.

**Archbishop of Lipa:** Most Rev. GAUDENCIO B. ROSALES, Archbishop's House, St Lorenzo Ruiz St, Lipa City, 4217 Batangas; tel. (43) 562573.

**Archbishop of Manila:** HE Cardinal JAIME L. SIN, Arzobispado, 121 Arzobispo St, Intramuros, POB 132, 1099 Metro Manila; tel. (2) 5317034; fax (2) 5322567.

**Archbishop of Nueva Segovia:** Most Rev. ORLANDO B. QUEVEDO, Archbishop's House, Vigan, 2700 Ilocos Sur; tel. (77) 7222018; fax (77) 7222019.

**Archbishop of Ozamis:** Most Rev. JESUS A. DOSADO, Archbishop's House, POB 2670, 7200 Ozamis City; tel. (65) 20127.

**Archbishop of Palo:** Most Rev. PEDRO R. DEAN, Archdiocesan Chancery, cnr Pedrosa Ave and San Jose St, POB 173, Tacloban City, 6500 Leyte; tel. (323) 2408.

**Archbishop of San Fernando (Pampanga):** Most Rev. PACIANO B. ANICETO, Chancery House, San José, San Fernando, 2000 Pampanga; tel. (45) 9612819.

**Archbishop of Tuguegarao:** Most Rev. DIOSDADO A. TALAMAYAN, Archbishop's House, Tuguegarao, 3500 Cagayan; tel. (0822) 4461663.

**Archbishop of Zamboanga:** Most Rev. CARMELO DOMINADOR F. MORELOS, Sacred Heart Center, POB 1, Justice R. T. Lim blvd, 7000 Zamboanga City; tel. (62) 9911329.

#### Other Christian Churches

**Convention of Philippine Baptist Churches:** POB 263, 5000 Iloilo City; tel. (33) 73874; fax (33) 74995; f. 1935; Gen. Sec. Rev. Dr NATHANIEL M. FABULA; Pres. Dr DOMINGO J. DIEL, Jr.

**Episcopal Church in the Philippines:** 275 E. Rodriguez Sr Ave, Quezon City, Metro Manila; POB 10321, Quezon City, 1112 Metro Manila; tel. (2) 7215061; fax (2) 7211923; five dioceses; Prime Bishop Most Rev. NARCISO V. TICOBAY.

**Iglesia Evangélica Metodista en las Islas Filipinas** (Evangelical Methodist Church in the Philippines): 1240 Gen. Luna St, Ermita, Metro Manila; tel. (2) 504183; fax (2) 5219164; f. 1909; 120,000 mems (1985); Gen. Supt Bishop GEORGE F. CASTRO.

**Iglesia Filipina Independiente** (Philippine Independent Church): 1500 Taft Ave, Ermita, 1000 Metro Manila; tel. (2) 598634; fax (2) 5213932; f. 1902; 35 dioceses; 5.5m. mems; Obispo Maximo (Supreme Bishop) Most Rev. ALBERTO B. RAMENTO; Gen. Sec. Most Rev. ADMIRADOR A. FEDERIS.

**Iglesia ni Cristo:** Central Ave, Diliman, Quezon City, 1107 Metro Manila; tel. (2) 980611; fax (2) 9225749; f. 1914; 2m. mems; Exec. Minister Brother ERAÑO G. MANALO.

**Lutheran Church:** 4461 Old Santa Mesa, Sampaloc, Metro Manila; tel. (2) 605041; f. 1946; Pres. Dr THOMAS P. BATONG, POB 507, Manila 2800; telex 27854.

**Union Church of Manila:** cnr Rodriguez and Legaspi Sts, Legaspi Village, POB 1386, Makati, 1253 Metro Manila; tel. (2) 8921631; fax (2) 8180362; Senior Pastor CHARLIE R. PRIDMORE.

**United Church of Christ in the Philippines:** 877 Epifanio de los Santos Ave, West Triangle, Quezon City, Metro Manila; tel. (2) 9240219; fax (2) 9240207; f. 1948; 500,000 mems; Gen. Sec. Rev. ERME R. CAMBA, Bishop.

Among other denominations active in the Philippines are the Iglesia Evangélica Unida de Cristo and the United Methodist Church.

### ISLAM

Some 14 different ethnic groups profess the Islamic faith in the Philippines, and Muslims comprised 4.6% of the total population at the census of 1990. Mindanao and the Sulu and Tawi-Tawi archipelago, in the southern Philippines, are predominantly Muslim provinces, but there are 10 other such provinces, each with its own Imam, or Muslim religious leader. More than 500,000 Muslims live in the north of the country (mostly in, or near to, Manila).

**Confederation of Muslim Organizations of the Philippines (CMOP):** Metro Manila; Nat. Chair. JAMIL DIANALAN.

### BAHÁ'Í FAITH

**National Spiritual Assembly:** POB 4323, 1099 Metro Manila; tel. (2) 500404; fax (2) 505918; mems resident in 7,344 localities; Chair. Dr ROLANDO MADDELA; Sec. FE SAMANIEGO.

## The Press

The Office of the President implements government policies on information and the media. Freedom of the press and freedom of speech are guaranteed under the 1987 Constitution.

### METRO MANILA
#### Dailies

**Abante:** Metro Manila; tel. (2) 984416; fax (2) 998404; morning; Filipino and English; Editor TONY P. TABBAD; circ. 100,000.

THE PHILIPPINES

**Abante Tonite:** Metro Manila; tel. (2) 984416; fax (2) 998404; afternoon; Filipino and English; Man. Editor NICOLAS QUIJANO; circ. 200,000.

**Ang Pilipino Ngayon:** 202 Railroad St, cnr 13th St, Port Area, Metro Manila; tel. (2) 401871; fax (2) 5224998; Filipino; Publr and Editor JOSE M. BUHAIN; circ. 286,452.

**Balita:** Liwayway Bldg, 2249 Pasong Tamo, Makati, Metro Manila; tel. (2) 888671; f. 1972; morning; Filipino; Editor MARCELO S. LAGMAY; circ. 181,415.

**Bongga:** 371A Bonifacio Drive, Port Area, Metro Manila; tel. (2) 401719; fax (2) 496948; Filipino; Man. Editor DANNY VIBAS; circ. 120,000.

**Evening Star:** Philippines Today Inc, 13th and Railroad Sts, Port Area, Metro Manila; tel. (2) 401871; Editor-in-Chief LUIS D. BELTRAN.

**Headline:** Vista Cinema Bldg, 2nd Floor, Recto Ave, Metro Manila; tel. (2) 478661; fax (2) 478668; f. 1988; English and Filipino; Publr JUAN P. DAYANG; circ. 105,000.

**The Journal:** Journal Bldg, 19th St, cnr Railroad St, Port Area, Metro Manila; tel. (2) 487511; English; Publr and Editor-in-Chief MANUEL C. VILLA REAL, Jr.

**Malaya:** CC Castro Bldg, 38 Timog Ave, Quezon City, Metro Manila; tel. (2) 983271; fax (2) 998404; f. 1983; English; Editor JOY C. DE LOS REYES; circ. 120,000.

**Manila Bulletin:** Bulletin Publishing Corpn, cnr Muralla and Recoletos Sts, Intramuros, POB 769, Metro Manila; tel. (2) 473621; telex 40240; f. 1972; English; Publr EMILIO YAP; Editor BEN RODRIGUEZ; circ. 260,000.

**Manila Chronicle:** Manila Chronicle Publishing Corpn, 371 Bonifacio Drive, Port Area, Metro Manila; tel. (2) 478261; telex 29037; fax (2) 481085; f. 1986; Editor-in-Chief AMANDO DORONILA; circ. 162,000.

**Manila Evening Post:** Oriental Media Inc, 20th St, Port Area, Metro Manila; tel. (2) 481234; telex 2510; f. 1975; afternoon; English; Editor KERIMA P. TUVERA; circ. 90,000.

**Manila Times:** 30 Pioneer St, cnr EDSA, Mandaluyong, Metro Manila; tel. (2) 6318971; telex 2573; fax (2) 6317788; f. 1945; morning; English; Editor-in-Chief FREDERICK K. AGCAOILI.

**News Herald:** Times Journal Bldg, Railroad St, cnr 19th and 20th Sts, Port Area, Metro Manila; tel. (2) 487511; English; Editor AUGUSTO VILLANUEVA; circ. 175,000.

**Observer:** Times Journal Bldg, Railroad St, cnr 19th and 20th Sts, Port Area, Metro Manila; tel. (2) 487511; f. 1986; English and Filipino; Editor YEN MAKABENTA; circ. 60,000.

**People Tonight:** Times Journal Bldg, Railroad St, cnr 19th and 20th Sts, Port Area, Metro Manila; tel. (2) 487511; f. 1978; English and Filipino; Editor ALFREDO M. MARQUEZ; circ. 500,000.

**People's Journal:** Times Journal Bldg, Railroad St, cnr 19th and 20th Sts, Port Area, Metro Manila; tel. (2) 487511; fax (2) 486872; English and Filipino; Editor LOURDES G. GUTIERREZ; circ. 383,200.

**Philippine Daily Globe:** Nova Communications Inc, 2nd Floor, Rudgen Bldg, 17 Shaw Blvd, Metro Manila; tel. (2) 6730191; Editor-in-Chief YEN MAKABENTA; circ. 40,000.

**Philippine Daily Inquirer:** YIC Bldg, 1006 Romualdez St, cnr U.N. Ave, Ermita, Metro Manila; tel. (2) 508061; fax (2) 5361466; f. Dec. 1985; English; Chair. MARIXI R. PRIETO; Editor LETICIA J. MAGSANOC; circ. 285,000.

**Philippine Herald-Tribune:** Metro Manila; tel. (2) 406078; f. 1987; Christian-orientated; Pres. AMADA VALINO.

**Philippine Star:** Philippines Today Inc, 13th and Railroad Sts, Port Area, Metro Manila; tel. (2) 401871; fax (2) 5224998; f. 1986; Chair. of Editorial Board MAXIMO V. SOLIVEN; circ. 225,000.

**Taliba:** Times Journal Bldg, Railroad St, cnr 19th and 20th Sts, Port Area, Metro Manila; tel. (2) 487526; Filipino; Editor BEN ESQUIVEL; circ. 100,000.

**Tempo:** Bulletin Publishing Corpn, Recoletos St, cnr Muralla St, Intramuros, Metro Manila; tel. (2) 493563; telex 40240; fax (2) 499050; f. 1982; English and Filipino; Editor AUGUSTO P. SANTA ANA; circ. 250,000.

**Today:** Metro Manila; f. 1993; Editor-in-Chief TEODORO L. LOCSIN, Jr.

**United Daily News:** 812–818 Benavides St, Binondo, Metro Manila; tel. (2) 219806; f. 1973; Chinese and English; Editor CHUA KEE; circ. 27,653.

### Selected Periodicals
#### Weeklies

**Bannawag:** Liwayway Bldg, 2249 Pasong Tamo, Makati, Metro Manila; tel. (2) 8193101; f. 1934; Ilocano; Editor DIONISIO S. BULONG; circ. 80,000.

**Bisaya:** Liwayway Bldg, 2249 Pasong Tamo, Makati, Metro Manila; tel. (2) 888671; f. 1934; Cebu-Visayan; Editor TIBURCIO BAGUIO; circ. 90,000.

**Focus Philippines:** 200 Second St, Port Area, Metro Manila; f. 1972; English; general interest; Editor KERIMA P. TUVERA; circ. 70,000.

**Jingle TV Guide:** 158 P. Tuazon Blvd, cnr 7th Ave, Quezon City, Metro Manila; tel. (2) 709211; English; Editor NERISSA MATA; circ. 110,000.

**Liwayway:** Liwayway Bldg, 2249 Pasong Tamo, Makati, Metro Manila; tel. (2) 888671; fax (2) 8175167; f. 1922; Filipino; Editor RODOLFO SALANDANAN; circ. 159,000.

**National Midweek:** 43 Roces Ave, 1103 Quezon City, Metro Manila; English; Editor LUIS V. TEODORO.

**Panorama:** Recoletos St, Intramuros, Metro Manila; tel. (2) 471551; telex 40240; fax (2) 499050; f. 1968; English; Editor Dr MARCELINO A. FORONDA; circ. 280,000.

**Philippine Starweek:** 202 13th St, cnr Railroad St, Port Area, Metro Manila; tel. (2) 401871; fax (2) 5224998; English; Publr MAXIMO V. SOLIVEN; circ. 202,000.

**The Rizal Chronicle:** Metro Manila; tel. (2) 6822115; f. 1959; Wed.; Editor J. JESS. D. CABRERA; circ. 10,000.

**Weekend:** Bonifacio Drive, Port Area, Metro Manila; Man. Editor NEAL CRUZ.

**Woman's Home Companion:** 70 18th Ave, Murphy, Quezon City, Metro Manila; tel. (2) 7216603; f. 1972; Wed.; English; Editor DORIS TRINIDAD; circ. 98,752.

**Women's Journal:** Chronicle Bldg, Meralco Ave, Tektite Rd, Pasig, Metro Manila; English; Editor LUISA H. A. LINSANGAN; circ. 80,000.

#### Monthlies

**Asia Mining:** Metro Manila; tel. (2) 874348; English; Editor ERNESTO O. RODRIGUEZ; circ. 16,851.

**Farming Today:** Quezon City, Metro Manila; f. 1974; English; Editor BERNARDITA AZURIN QUIMPO; circ. 20,000.

**National Observer:** 407 Leyba Bldg, Dasmariñas, Metro Manila.

### SELECTED REGIONAL PUBLICATIONS
#### Bicol Region

**Naga Times:** 801 Ojeda IV, Naga City; f. 1959; weekly; English; Editor RAMON S. TOLARAM; circ. 5,000.

**Sorsogon Today:** 2886 Burgos St, POB 20, 4700 Sorsogon; tel. (32) 6125; fax (32) 3369202; f. 1977; weekly; Publr and CEO MARCOS E. PARAS, Jr; circ. 2,400.

#### Cagayan Valley

**Cagayan Star:** Arellano St, Tuguegarao; Sunday.

**The Valley Times:** Daang Maharlika, San Felipe, Ilagan, Isabela; f. 1962; weekly; English; Editor AUREA A. DE LA CRUZ; circ. 5,000.

#### Central Luzon

**Palihan:** Diversion Rd, cnr Sanciangco St, Cabanatuan City; f. 1966; weekly; Filipino; Editor and Publr NONOY M. JARLEGO; circ. 5,000.

**The Tribune:** Maharlika Highway, 2301 Cabanatuan City; f. 1960; weekly; English and Filipino; Editor and Publr ORLANDO M. JARLEGO; circ. 8,000.

#### Ilocos Region

**Baguio Midland Courier:** 16 Kisad Rd, POB 50, Baguio City; English and Ilocano; Editor SINAI C. HAMADA.

#### Mindanao

**Mindanao Star:** 44 Kolambagohan-Capistrano St, Cagayan de Oro City; weekly; Editor ROMULFO SABAMAL.

**Pagadian Times:** Pagadian City, 7824 Zamboanga del Sur; tel. 586; f. 1969; weekly; English; Publr PEDE G. LU; Editor JACINTO LUMBAY; circ. 2,500.

**The Voice of Islam:** Davao City; tel. (82) 81368; f. 1973; monthly; English and Arabic; official Islamic news journal; Editor and Publr NASHIR MUHAMMAD AL'RASHID AL HAJJ.

**Zamboanga Times:** Campaner St, Zamboanga City; three a week; Man. RENE FERNANDEZ.

#### Southern Tagalog

**Bayanihan Weekly News:** Bayanihan Publishing Co, Santa Cruz, Laguna; tel. (645) 1001; f. 1966; Mon.; Filipino and English; Editor ARTHUR A. VALENOVA; circ. 1,000.

**The Quezon Times:** 220 Quezon Ave, Lucena City; English; Editor VEN ZOLETA.

#### Visayas

**The Aklan Reporter:** 1227 Rizal St, Kalibo, Aklan; tel. (33) 3181; f. 1971; weekly; English and Aklanon; Editor ROMAN A. DE LA CRUZ; circ. 2,000.

THE PHILIPPINES                                                                                                                              *Directory*

**Ang Bagong Kasanag:** Bonifacio Drive, Iloilo City; Publr MARIANO M. DIOLOSA; Editor DOUGLAS K. MONTERO.

**Bohol Chronicle:** 56 B. Inting St, Tagbilaran City, Bohol; tel. (32) 3100; f. 1954; weekly; English and Cebuano; Editor and Publr ZOILO DEJARESCO; circ. 4,000.

**The Kapawa News:** 10 Jose Abad Santos St, POB 365, 6100 Bacolod City; tel. (34) 21073; fax (34) 27017; f. 1966; weekly; Sat.; Hiligaynon and English; Editor NATALIO V. SITJAR; circ. 15,000.

**The Visayan Tribune:** 826 Iznart St, Iloilo City; tel. (33) 75760; f. 1959; weekly; Tue.; English; Editor HERBERT L. VEGO; circ. 10,000.

**The Weekly Negros Gazette:** Broce St, San Carlos City, 6033 Negros Occidental; f. 1956; weekly; Editor NESTORIO L. LAYUMAS, Sr; circ. 5,000.

**Weekly Scope:** 28 Rosario St, Bacolod City; Man. AURELIO SERVANDO, Jr.

### NEWS AGENCIES

**Philippines News Agency:** Metro Manila; tel. (2) 976661; telex 63465; f. 1973; Gen. Man. JOSE PAVIA; Man. Editor GENE N. RAMOS.

#### Foreign Bureaux

**Agence France-Presse (AFP):** VIP Bldg, 3rd Floor, 1140 Roxas Blvd, POB 1019, Ermita, Metro Manila; tel. (2) 5214205; telex 63267; fax (2) 5220185; Bureau Chief DAVID BOTBOL.

**Agencia EFE** (Spain): 47 Juan Luna St, San Lorenzo Village, Makati, Metro Manila; tel. (2) 8171128; telex 64929; fax (2) 8171135; Bureau Chief JOSÉ R. RODRIGUEZ.

**Agenzia Nazionale Stampa Associata (ANSA)** (Italy): Block 5, Lot 5, Northridge Park Subdivision, Santa Monica, Quezon City; tel. (2) 5212051; fax (2) 5212074; Correspondent MARTIN B. ABBUGAO, Jr.

**Associated Press (AP)** (USA): POB 7263, Airmail Distribution Center, Pasay City, 1300, Metro Manila; tel. (2) 5212430; telex 27571; Bureau Chief ROBERT REID.

**Deutsche Presse Agentur (dpa)** (Germany): Physicians Tower Bldg, 533 United Nations Ave, 1000 Ermita, Metro Manila; tel. (2) 591321; telex 23476; Representative NIKOLAUS PREDE.

**Inter Press Service (IPS)** (Italy): Amberland Plaza, Room 510, J. Vargas Ave, Ortigas Complex Pasig, 1600 Metro Manila; tel. (2) 6353421; fax (2) 6353660; Correspondent JOHANNA SON.

**Jiji Tsushin-sha (Jiji Press)** (Japan): Legaspi Tower, Suite 21, 3rd Floor, 2600 Roxas Blvd, Metro Manila; tel. (2) 521472; telex 40389; fax (2) 5211474; Correspondent TSUTOMU MATSUNAGA.

**Kyodo News Service** (Japan): Manila Hilton Hotel, Room 275, United Nations Ave, Ermita, Metro Manila; tel. (2) 591363; Correspondent KAZUYOSHI NISHIKURA.

**Reuters** (UK): L.V. Locsin Bldg, 10th Floor, Ayala Ave, cnr Makati Ave, Makati, 1226 Metro Manila; tel. (2) 8109636; telex 63982; fax (2) 8176267; Bureau Chief MALCOLM DAVIDSON.

**United Press International (UPI)** (USA): Manila Pavilion Hotel, Room 526C, United Nations Ave, Ermita, 1000 Metro Manila; tel. (2) 5212051; fax (2) 5212074; Bureau Chief MICHAEL DI CICCO.

**Xinhua (New China) News Agency** (People's Republic of China): 2008 Roxas Blvd, POB 2959, Metro Manila; tel. (2) 500974; telex 27477; Chief Correspondent ZHAI SHUYAO.

### PRESS ASSOCIATION

**National Press Club of the Philippines:** Magallanes Drive, Intramuros, Metro Manila; tel. (2) 494242; f. 1952; Pres. ANTONIO NIEVA; Vice-Pres. RECAH TRINIDAD; 942 mems.

## Publishers

**Abiva Publishing House Inc:** 851 Gregorio Araneta Ave, Quezon City, 1113 Metro Manila; tel. (2) 7120248; fax (2) 7320308; f. 1937; reference and textbooks; Pres. LUIS Q. ABIVA, Jr.

**Ateneo de Manila University Press:** POB 154, 1099 Metro Manila; tel. (2) 9244495; fax (2) 9244690; f. 1972; literary, textbooks, humanities, social sciences, reference books on the Philippines; Dir ESTHER M. PACHECO.

**Bookman Publishing House:** 373 Quezon Ave, Quezon City, Metro Manila; tel. (2) 7124818; fax (2) 7124860; f. 1945; textbooks, reference, educational; Pres. CEFERINO M. PICACHE.

**Capitol Publishing House Inc:** 54 Don Alejandro Roces Ave, Quezon City, 1103 Metro Manila; f. 1947; tel. (2) 997061; fax (2) 990535; Gen. Man. NICOLAS B. FAZON.

**R. M. Garcia Publishing House:** POB 1860, 1090 Metro Manila; tel. (2) 321578; f. 1951; textbooks, historical and religious; Pres. and Gen. Man. ROLANDO M. GARCIA.

**Heritage Publishing House:** 33 4th Ave, cnr Main Ave, Cubao, Quezon City, POB 3667, Metro Manila; tel. (2) 7220468; fax (2) 7221484; art, anthropology, history, political science; Pres. MARIO R. ALCANTARA; Man. Dir RICARDO S. SANCHEZ.

**The Lawyers' Co-operative Publishing Co. Inc:** 1071 R. del Pan St, Makati, 1206 Metro Manila; tel. (2) 596463; fax (2) 5220638; f. 1908; law and educational; Pres. ELSA K. ELMA.

**Liwayway Publishing Inc:** 2249 Pasong Tamo, Makati, Metro Manila; tel. (2) 8193101; fax (2) 8175167; magazines and newspapers.

**Macar Enterprises:** Rizal St, Kalibo, 5501 Aklan; tel. (33) 3181; fiction and non-fiction, poetry, history, theology, juvenalia; publrs of 'The Aklan Reporter'; Publr and Editor ROMAN A. DE LA CRUZ.

**G. Miranda & Sons:** 844 North Reyes St, Metro Manila; tel. (2) 7414938; textbooks, comics, reprints; Pres. ELOISA D. MIRANDA.

**Mutual Books Inc:** 429 Shaw Blvd, Mandaluyong, Metro Manila; tel. (2) 796050; fax (2) 7213056; f. 1959; textbooks on accounting, management and economics, computers and secretarial; Pres. ALFREDO S. NICDAO, Jr.

**Phoenix Publishing House Inc:** 927 Quezon Ave, Quezon City, 1104 Metro Manila; tel. (2) 9243329; fax (2) 9213788; f. 1958; sciences, languages, religion, literature, history; Pres. JESUS ERNESTO SIBAL.

**Regal Publishing Co:** 1729 J. P. Laurel St, San Miguel, 2804 Metro Manila; tel. (2) 7410660; f. 1958; Philippine literature; Man. Dir CORINNA BENIPAYO MOJICA.

**Reyes Publishing Inc:** Mariwasa Bldg, 4th Floor, 717 Aurora Blvd, Quezon City, 1112 Metro Manila; tel. (2) 783976; telex 63740; f. 1964; art, history and culture; Man. PAOLO REYES.

**Sinag-Tala Publishers Inc:** Regina Bldg, 4th Floor, 100 Aguirre St, cnr Trasierra St, Legaspi Village, Makati, 1200 Metro Manila; tel. (2) 8192563; fax (2) 8192681; f. 1969; educational textbooks; business, professional and religious books; Man. Dir LUIS A. USON.

**University of the Philippines Press:** U. P. Campus, Diliman, Quezon City, 1101 Metro Manila; tel. (2) 992558; literature, philosophy, religion, fiction, art, anthropology, business, science, educational; Dir REYNALDO GUIOGUIO (acting).

**Vibal Publishing House Inc:** Gregorio Araneta Ave, cnr Maria Clara St, Talayan, Quezon City, Metro Manila; tel. (2) 7122722; telex 40404; pre-school, elementary, high school, college textbooks, reference.

### PUBLISHERS' ASSOCIATIONS

**Philippine Educational Publishers' Asscn:** 927 Quezon Ave, Quezon City, 1104 Metro Manila; tel. (2) 9243271; fax (2) 9213788; Pres. JESUS ERNESTO SIBAL; Vice-Pres. DOMINADOR BUHAIN.

**Publishers' Association of the Philippines Inc:** Gammon Center, Alfaro St, Salcedo Village, Makati, Metro Manila; f. 1974; mems comprise all newspaper, magazine and book publrs in the Philippines; Pres. KERIMA P. TUVERA; Exec. Dir ROBERTO M. MENDOZA.

## Radio and Television

In 1992, according to UNESCO, there were an estimated 9.0m. radio receivers and 2.9m. television receivers in use.

**National Telecommunications Commission (NTC):** Vibal Bldg, Epifanio de los Santos Ave, cnr Times St, Quezon City, Metro Manila; tel. (2) 981160; telex 63912; f. 1979; supervises and controls all private and public telecommunications services; Commr SIMEON KINTANAR.

### RADIO

There are about 270 broadcasting radio stations (commercial and non-commercial). The following are the principal operating networks:

**Banahaw Broadcasting Corpn:** Capitol Hills, Diliman, Quezon City, 3005 Metro Manila; tel. (2) 961109; telex 63886; 14 stations; Gen. Man. VICTORINO VIANZON.

**Far East Broadcasting Co Inc:** POB 1, Valenzuela, 0560 Metro Manila; tel. (2) 2921152; fax (2) 359490; f. 1948; 18 stations; operates a classical music station, eight domestic stations and an overseas service in 64 languages throughout Asia; Man. Dir CARLOS L. PENA; Pres. BILL TARTER.

**Manila Broadcasting Co:** FJE Bldg, 4th Floor, 105 Esteban St, Legaspi Village, Makati, Metro Manila; tel. (2) 882234; f. 1946; 10 stations; Pres. FRED J. ELIZALDE, Sr; Gen. Man. EDUARDO L. MONTILLA.

**Nation Broadcasting Corpn:** NBC Tower, Epifanio de los Santos Ave, Guadelupe, Makati, 1200 Metro Manila; tel. (2) 8195673; fax (2) 8197234; f. 1963; 31 stations; Pres. ABELARDO L. YABUT, Sr.

# THE PHILIPPINES

**Newsounds Broadcasting Network Inc:** Florete Bldg, Ground Floor, 2406 Nobel, cnr Edison St, Makati, 3117 Metro Manila; tel. (2) 899990; 10 stations; Gen. Man. E. BILLONES.

**Philippines Broadcasting Service (PBS):** Bureau of Broadcast Services, Office of the Press Sec., Philippine Information Agency Bldg, 4th Floor, Visayas Ave, Quezon City, Metro Manila; tel. (2) 9242607; fax (2) 9242745; Philippine overseas service (Radyo Pilipinas), Bureau of Broadcasts, Office of Media Affairs.

**Philippine Federation of Catholic Broadcasters:** 2307 Pedro Gil, Santa Ana, POB 3169, Metro Manila; tel. (2) 5221873; fax (2) 5218125; 43 radio stations and three TV channels; Pres. Father FRANCIS LUCAS.

**Radio Philippines Network:** Broadcast City, Capitol Hills, Diliman, Quezon City, Metro Manila; tel. (2) 977661; telex 63886; fax (2) 984322; f. 1969; seven TV stations, 14 radio stations; Pres. WILLIAM M. ESPOSO; Gen. Man. FELIPE G. MEDINA.

**Radio Veritas Asia:** Philippine Radio Educational and Information Center, POB 939, Metro Manila; tel. (2) 907476; telex 64220; fax (2) 907436; Catholic short-wave station, broadcasts in 14 languages; Pres. and Chair. Cardinal JAIME SIN; Gen. Man. ERLINDA G. SO.

**Republic Broadcasting System Inc:** Epifanio de los Santos Ave, Diliman, Quezon City, Metro Manila; tel. (2) 997021; telex 63467; fax (2) 8163042; f. 1950; Chair. FELIPE J. GOZON; Pres. and CEO MENARDO R. JIMENEZ.

## TELEVISION

There are five major television networks operating in the country with 19 carrier and seven relay stations. In January 1992 Congress approved legislation providing for the creation of a public television network, the People's Television Network (PTV4). The following are the principal operating television networks:

**ABS-CBN Broadcasting Corpn:** Mother Ignacia Ave, Quezon City, Metro Manila; telex 27344; fax (2) 9215888; Chair. EUGENIO LOPEZ, Jr; Gen. Man. FEDERICO GARCIA.

**Banahaw Broadcasting Corpn:** Capitol Hills, Quezon City, 3005 Metro Manila; tel. (2) 961109; telex 63886; Gen. Man. VICTORINO VIANZON.

**GMA Rainbow Satellite** (Republic Broadcasting System): RBS Bldg, Epifanio de los Santos Ave, Diliman, Quezon City, 1103 Metro Manila; tel. (2) 997021; telex 63467; fax (2) 9242430; f. 1950; transmits nationwide through 38 TV stations; Chair. FELIPE L. GOZON; Pres. and CEO MENARDO JIMENEZ.

**Inter-Island Broadcasting Corpn:** Broadcast City Complex, Capitol Hills, Diliman, Quezon City, Metro Manila; tel. (2) 976137; fax (2) 968556; 19 stations; Gen. Man. RUBEN V. NOÑER.

**Maharlika Broadcasting System:** Media Center, Sgt. Esguerra Ave, Quezon City, 3005 Metro Manila; tel. (2) 9220880; telex 42220; jtly operated by the Bureau of Broadcasts and the National Media Production Center; Dir ANTONIO BARRIERO.

**Radio Philippines Network, Inc:** Broadcast City, Capitol Hills, Diliman, Quezon City, Metro Manila; tel. (2) 977661; telex 63886; 7 primary TV stations, 14 relay stations; Pres. WILLIAM M. ESPOSO; Gen. Man. FELIPE G. MEDINA; Asst Gen. Man. (Programmes) CASEY FRANCISCO.

## ASSOCIATION

**Kapisanan ng mga Brodkaster sa Pilipinas (KBP)** (Association of Broadcasters in the Philippines): LTA Bldg, 6th Floor, 118 Perea St, Legaspi Village, Makati, Metro Manila; tel. (2) 8151990; fax (2) 8151989; Chair. ANDRE S. KAHN; Pres. JOSE E. ESCANER, Jr.

# Finance

(cap. = capital; dep. = deposits; m. = million; brs = branches; amounts in pesos)

## BANKING

Legislation enacted in June 1993 provided for the establishment of a new monetary authority, the Bangko Sentral ng Pilipinas, to replace the Central Bank of the Philippines. The Government was thus able to restructure the Central Bank's debt (308,000m. pesos).

In May 1994 legislation was promulgated providing for the establishment in the Philippines of up to 10 new foreign bank branches over the following five years (although at least 70% of the banking system's total resources were to be owned by Philippine entities). Prior to this legislation only four foreign banks (which had been in operation when the law restricting the industry to locally-owned banks was enacted in 1948) were permitted to operate.

### Central Bank

**Bangko Sentral ng Pilipinas** (Central Bank of the Philippines): A. Mabini St, cnr Vito Cruz St, Malate, 1004 Metro Manila; tel. (2) 507051; telex 27550; fax (2) 5215224; f. 1993; cap. 50m. (1993); Gov. GABRIEL SINGSON.

### Government Banks

**Philippine National Bank (PHILNABANK):** PNB Bldg, 257 Escolta St, POB 1844, 1099 Metro Manila; tel. (2) 402051; telex 40179; fax (2) 496091; f. 1916; 57% state-owned, sale of part of govt holding scheduled for 1995; cap. 7,651m., dep. 94,902m. (Dec. 1993); Chair. DANIEL L. LACSON, Jr; Pres. ARSENIO BARTOLOME III; 311 brs.

See also under Development Banks.

### Principal Commercial Banks

**Al-Amanah Islamic Investment Bank:** Metro Manila; f. 1990; auth. cap. 1,000m.

**Allied Banking Corpn:** Allied Bank Centre, 6754 Ayala Ave, Makati, Metro Manila; tel. (2) 8187961; telex 45567; fax (2) 8160921; f. 1977; cap. 495m., dep. 24,074m. (Dec. 1992); Chair. LUCIO C. TAN; Pres. ROMEO Y. CO; 113 brs.

**Associated Bank:** 411 Quintin Paredes St, Binondo, Metro Manila; tel. (2) 476061; telex 0341; f. 1965; cap. 177m., dep. 2,129m. (1987); Chair. LEONARDO K. TY; Pres. JESUS P. ESTANISLAO; 32 brs.

**Bank of Commerce:** Boston Bank Center, 6764 Ayala Ave, Makati, Metro Manila; tel. (2) 8174906; telex 64622; fax (2) 8172426; f. 1983; fmrly Boston Bank of the Philippines; cap. 764m., dep. 3,682m. (Dec. 1993); Pres. ROBERTO D. ANONAS; Chair. JOSELIN G. FRAGADA; 36 brs.

**Bank of the Philippine Islands:** Ayala Ave, cnr Paseo de Roxas, POB 1827, Makati, Metro Manila; tel. (2) 8185541; telex 63673; fax (2) 8159434; f. 1851; cap. 1,750m., dep. 66,695m. (Dec. 1993); Pres. XAVIER P. LOINAZ; Chair. JAIME ZOBEL; 301 brs.

**BPI Family Bank:** Paseo de Roxas, cnr de la Rosa St, Makati, Metro Manila; tel. (2) 8177936; telex 23519; fax (2) 8158499; f. 1985; controlled by Bank of the Philippine Islands; cap. 1,637m., dep. 12,865m. (Dec. 1992); Chair. JAIME ZOBEL DE AYALA; Pres. AURELIO R. MONTINOLA III; 137 brs.

**China Banking Corpn:** cnr Paseo de Roxas and Villar Sts, Makati, 1200 Metro Manila; tel. (2) 8177981; telex 63298; fax (2) 8153169; f. 1920; cap. 2,943m., dep. 14,491m. (Dec. 1993); Chair. GILBERT U. DEE; Pres. and CEO PETER S. DEE; 64 brs.

**CityTrust Banking Corpn:** Citytrust Bldg, 379 Sen. Gil J. Puyat Ave, Makati, Metro Manila; tel. (2) 8180411; telex 45666; fax (2) 8152595; f. 1961; cap. 702m., dep. 10,122m. (1993); Pres. JOSE R. FACUNDO; Chair. HENRY A. BRIMO; 49 brs.

**Equitable Banking Corpn:** 262 Juan Luna St, Binondo 1006, Metro Manila; tel. (2) 2427101; fax (2) 2416164; f. 1950; cap. 1,508.7m., dep. 19,065.0m. (June 1994); Chair. GEORGE L. GO; Pres. WILFRIDO C. TECSON; 57 brs.

**Far East Bank and Trust Co:** FEBTC Bldg, Muralla St, Intramuros, POB 1411, 2801 Metro Manila; tel. (2) 401020; telex 20221; f. 1960; cap. 2,000m., dep. 40,625m. (Dec. 1993); Chair. RAMON V. DEL ROSARIO, Snr; Pres. and CEO OCTAVIO V. ESPIRITU; 163 brs.

**International Corporate Bank:** InterBank Bldg, 111 Paseo de Roxas, cnr Legaspi St, Makati, 3117 Metro Manila; tel. (2) 8186511; telex 64233; fax (2) 8154442; f. 1977; acquired by private investors, incl. the American Express Corpn, in 1987; cap. 1,553.7m., dep. 7,611.7m. (1992); Chair. ARTHUR N. AGUILAR; Pres. JOVENCIO F. CINCO; 52 brs.

**Metropolitan Bank and Trust Co:** Metrobank Plaza, Sen. Gil J. Puyat Ave, Makati, Metro Manila; tel. (2) 8103311; telex 63555; fax (2) 8176248; f. 1962; cap. 8,509m., dep. 80,399m. (December 1994); Chair. GEORGE S. K. TY; Pres. ANTONIO S. ABACAN, Jr; 262 brs.

**Philippine Banking Corpn (Philbank):** 6797 Ayala Ave, cnr Herrera St, Makati, Metro Manila; tel. (2) 8170901; telex 63764; fax (2) 8170892; f. 1935 as Square Deal Inc.; present name adopted 1957; cap. 1,000m., dep. 4,284.8m. (1992); Chair. SIY YAP CHUA; Pres. and CEO NORBERTO C. NAZARENO; 60 brs.

**Philippine Commercial International Bank:** 1 PCI Bank Towers, Makati Ave, cnr H. V. de la Costa St, Makati, Metro Manila; tel. (2) 8171021; telex 63265; fax (2) 8183946; f. 1938; cap. 5,500m., dep. 27,250m. (Dec. 1992); Chair. EUGENIO LOPEZ, Jr; Pres. RAFAEL B. BUENAVENTURA; 262 brs.

**Philtrust Bank (Philippine Trust Co):** Philtrust Bank Bldg, United Nations Ave, cnr San Marcelino St, Metro Manila; tel. (2) 573961; telex 40359; fax (2) 5217309; f. 1916; cap. 1,000m., dep. 7,009.8m. (Dec. 1993); Pres. JAIME C. LAYA; Chair. EMILIO T. YAP; 27 brs.

**Pilipinas Bank:** ACT Tower, 135 Sen. Gil J. Puyat Ave, Makati, Metro Manila; tel. (2) 8191931; telex 63737; fax (2) 8153140; cap.

# THE PHILIPPINES

890m., dep. 3,127m.; Chair. WILLIAM S. TIOSIC; Pres. and CEO CARLOS A. PEDROSA; 35 brs.

**PNB Republic Bank:** Legaspi Towers 300, Roxas Blvd, cnr Vito Cruz, Metro Manila; tel. (2) 573851; telex 64146; fax (2) 5218513; f. 1953; cap. 89.9m., dep. 1,892m. (Dec. 1991); acquired by the Philippine National Bank in 1992; Chair. CATALINO MACARAIG; Pres. FLORIDO P. CASUELA; 60 brs.

**Prudential Bank & Trust Co:** Prudential Bank Bldg, Ayala Ave, Makati, Metro Manila; tel. (2) 8178981; fax (2) 8175146; f. 1952; cap. 1,559m., dep. 10,399m. (Dec. 1992); Chair. AUGUSTO A. SANTOS; Pres. JOSE L. SANTOS; 71 brs.

**Rizal Commercial Banking Corpn:** RCBC Commercial Banking Corpn, POB 1005 MCC/ADC 7575, 333 Sen. Gil J. Puyat Ave Ext., Makati, Metro Manila; tel. (2) 8193061; telex 63547; fax (2) 8190458; f. 1960; cap. 399m., dep. 27,699m. (Dec. 1993); Chair. ALFONSO T. YUCHENGCO; Gen. Man. MARCELO A. MIRASOL, Jr; 44 brs.

**Security Bank and Trust Co:** SBTC Bldg, 6778 Ayala Ave, Makati, Metro Manila; tel. (2) 8187677; telex 22465; fax (2) 8164213; f. 1951; cap. 956m., dep. 11,795m. (Dec. 1993); Pres. PETER B. FAVILA; Chair. FREDERICK Y. DY; 82 brs.

**Solidbank Corpn:** Solidbank Bldg, cnr Juan Luna and Dasmariñas Sts, Binondo, Metro Manila; tel. (2) 2428601; telex 27467; fax (2) 2421964; f. 1963; fmrly Consolidated Bank & Trust Co; 40% owned by the Bank of Nova Scotia (Canada); cap. 409m., dep. 12,473m. (Dec. 1993); Chair. JOSE P. MADRIGAL; Pres. DEOGRACIAS N. VISTAN; 71 brs.

**Traders Royal Bank:** TRB Tower, Roxas Blvd, Pasay City, Metro Manila; tel. (2) 8312821; telex 63254; fax (2) 8312494; f. 1963; cap. 284.3m., dep. 5,970m. (December 1994); Chair. ROBERTO S. BENEDICTO; Pres. ANDRES L. AFRICA; 52 brs.

**Union Bank of the Philippines:** SSS Makati Bldg, Ayala Ave, Makati, Metro Manila; tel. (2) 8920011; telex 66589; fax (2) 8186058; f. 1982; cap. 1,417m., dep. 10,778m. (Dec. 1993); Chair. JUSTO A. ORTIZ; Pres. ARMAND F. BRAUN, Jr; 120 brs.

**United Coconut Planters Bank:** UCPB Bldg, Makati Ave, Makati, Metro Manila; tel. (2) 8188361; telex 23068; fax (2) 8186863; f. 1963; cap. 6,049m., dep. 27,566m. (Dec. 1993); Chair. TIRSO D. ANTIPORDA, Jr; Pres. GLORIA C. CARREON; 139 brs.

### Rural Banks

Small private banks have been established with the encouragement and assistance (both financial and technical) of the Government in order to promote and expand the rural economy. Conceived mainly to stimulate the productive capacities of small farmers, merchants and industrialists in rural areas, and to combat usury, their principal objectives are to place within easy reach and access of the people credit facilities on reasonable terms and, in co-operation with other agencies of the Government, to provide advice on business and farm management and the proper use of credit for production and marketing purposes. The nation's rural banking system consisted of 1,145 units in June 1985.

### Development Banks

**Development Bank of the Philippines:** POB 1996, Makati Central PO, Makati, 1200 Metro Manila; tel. (2) 8189511; telex 22197; fax (2) 8172097; f. 1946 as the Rehabilitation Finance Corpn; govt-owned; provides long-term loans for agricultural and industrial developments; cap. 5,000m., dep. 10,110m. (1994); Chair. ALFREDO C. ANTONIO; 61 brs.

**Land Bank of the Philippines:** LBP Bldg, 319 Sen. Gil J. Puyat Ave, Makati, Metro Manila; tel. (2) 8189411; telex 22679; fax (2) 8433155; f. 1963; provides financial support in all phases of the Govt's agrarian reform programme; cap. 1,800m., dep. 57,766m. (1993); Chair. RAMON DEL ROSARIO; Pres. JESLI A. LAPUS; 128 brs.

**Philippine Amanah Bank:** La Purisima St, Plaza Pershing, Zamboanga City; f. 1974; operates on Islamic banking principles; promotes the socio-economic development of Mindanao; cap. 50m., dep. 144m. (1981); Chair. CESAR C. ZALAMEA; Pres. MICHAEL O. MASTURA; 8 brs.

### Foreign Banks

**Bank of America NT & SA** (USA): BA–Lepanto Bldg, 8747 Paseo de Roxas, POB 1767, 1257 Makati, Metro Manila; tel. (2) 8155000; telex 22245; fax (2) 8155895; f. 1946; cap. 8,195m., dep. 1,503m. (Dec. 1987); Vice-Pres. and Country Man. GILBERT ANTHONY TRAVERS.

**Citibank NA** (USA): Citibank Center Bldg, 8741 Paseo de Roxas, Makati, Metro Manila; tel. (2) 8157000; telex 22557; fax (2) 8157703; f. 1902; cap. 6,714m., dep. 3,642m. (1983); Country Corporate Officer WILLIAM FERGUSON; 3 brs.

**Hongkong and Shanghai Banking Corpn** (Hong Kong): Royal Match Bldg, 6780 Ayala Ave, Makati, Metro Manila; tel. (2) 8145200; telex 22361; fax (2) 8171953; dep. 3,396m. (1992); CEO D. H. HODGKINSON; 1 br.

*Directory*

**Standard Chartered Bank** (Hong Kong): 7901 Makati Ave, Makati, Metro Manila; tel. (2) 850961; telex 22434; fax (2) 8153084; f. 1872; cap. 1,487m., dep. 1,363m. (1989); Man. WILLIAM MOORE; 3 brs.

### Major 'Offshore' Banks

**American Express Bank Ltd** (USA): 6750 Ayala Ave, 11th Floor, Makati, Metro Manila; tel. (2) 8186731; telex 45340; fax (2) 8172589; f. 1977; Senior Dir and Country Man. VICENTE L. CHUA.

**Bank of Boston** (USA): Pacific Star Bldg, Ground Floor, Sen. Gil J. Puyat, cnr Makati Ave, Makati, Metro Manila; tel. (2) 8170456; telex 66453; fax (2) 8186802; Vice-Pres. and Gen. Man. BENJAMIN SEVILLA.

**The Bank of California, NA** (USA): Ace Bldg, 8th Floor, Rada cnr De La Rosa St, Legaspi Village, Makati, Metro Manila; tel. (2) 863056; telex 45556; f. 1977; Vice-Pres. and Gen. Man. BENITO A. GONZALES, Jr.

**Bank of Nova Scotia** (Canada): Solidbank Bldg, 9th Floor, 777 Paseo de Roxas, Makati, 1200 Metro Manila; tel. (2) 8179751; fax (2) 8178796; f. 1977; Man. M. S. (CORITO) SEVILLA.

**Bank of Tokyo Ltd** (Japan): Ayala Bldg, 5th Floor, Ayala Ave, Makati, Metro Manila; tel. (2) 8921976; telex 22182; fax (2) 8160413; f. 1977; Gen. Man. SUSUMU NAKAICHI.

**Bankers Trust Co** (USA): Pacific Star Bldg, 12th Floor, Sen. Gil Puyat Ave, Makati, Metro Manila; tel. (2) 8190231; telex 63603; Vice-Pres. and Gen. Man. JOSE ISIDRO N. CAMACHO.

**Banque Indosuez** (France): Corinthian Plaza, Ground Floor, 122 Paseo de Roxas, Legaspi Village, 1229 Makati, Metro Manila; tel. (2) 8104291; telex 63644; fax (2) 8187247; f. 1977; Gen. Man. PHILIPPE CHAVANON.

**Banque Nationale de Paris** (France): PCIB Tower II, 14th Floor, Makati Ave, Makati, Metro Manila; tel. (2) 8158821; telex 63707; fax (2) 8179237; f. 1977; Vice-Pres. and Country Man. J. DESMOND ORMSBY.

**Barclays Bank PLC** (United Kingdom): Dolmar Gold Tower Bldg, 4th Floor, 107 Alvarado St, Legaspi Village, Makati, Metro Manila; POB 2976, MCPO, Makati, Metro Manila; tel. (2) 8159291; telex 63768; fax (2) 8162526; f. 1977; Man. A. S. ANDERSON

**Chase Manhattan Bank, NA** (USA): Filinvest Financial Centre Bldg, 18th Floor, Paseo de Roxas, Makati, Metro Manila; tel. (2) 8189851; f. 1977; Vice-Pres. and Man. G. ROBERT HESS.

**Chemical Bank** (USA): Corinthian Plaza, 121 Paseo de Roxas, Legaspi Village, Makati, Metro Manila; tel. (2) 8159901; telex 63497; fax (2) 8190866; Vice-Pres. ARMINCAR B. BOSSI.

**Crédit Lyonnais** (France): Pacific Star Bldg, 14th Floor, Makati Ave, Makati, Metro Manila; POB 1859 MCC, 3117 Makati, Metro Manila; tel. (2) 8171616; telex 66418; fax (2) 8177145; f. 1981; Man. JEAN MICHEL GIOVANNETTI.

**Deutsche Bank (Asia)** (Germany): Filinvest Financial Centre Bldg, 17th Floor, 8753 Paseo de Roxas, 1274 Makati, POB 2286, Metro Manila; tel. (2) 8172961; telex 22583; fax (2) 8172861; f. 1977 (as European Asian Bank); Man. SANTIAGO S. CUA, Jr.

**First Interstate Bank of California** (USA): Metrobank Plaza, 12th Floor, Sen. Gil J. Puyat Ave Ext., Makati, POB 2093 Metro Manila; tel. (2) 8159241; telex 63741; fax (2) 8103554; f. 1977; Vice-Pres. and Gen. Man. SCOTT STEVENSON.

**First National Bank of Chicago** (USA): Solidbank Bldg, 17th Floor, 777 Paseo de Roxas, Makati, Metro Manila; tel. (2) 8183511; Asst Vice-Pres. and Gen. Man. JUERG H. VONTOBEL.

**International Bank of Singapore:** Corinthian Plaza, 7th Floor, Paseo de Roxas, Makati, Metro Manila; tel. (2) 8179951; telex 64073; fax (2) 8173285; f. 1977; Man. WILLIAM ANG CHOON WEE.

**Korea Exchange Bank** (Republic of Korea): Metrobank Plaza, 19th Floor, Sen. Gil J. Puyat Ave Ext., Makati, Metro Manila; tel. (2) 8172178; telex 23495; fax (2) 8180074; Gen. Man. KYUNG-SIK KOH.

**Security Pacific National Bank** (USA): Metrobank Plaza, 11th Floor, Sen. Gil J. Puyat Ave Ext., Makati, Metro Manila; tel. (2) 853891; f. 1977; Gen. Man. J. B. GREENHALGH.

**Société Générale** (France): Corinthian Plaza, Ground Floor, Paseo de Roxas, Makati, Metro Manila; tel. (2) 856061; telex 64047; f. 1980; Gen. Man. MICHEL SEVIN-ALLOUET.

**Wells Fargo Bank, NA** (USA): Metro Manila; tel. (2) 8173228; Asst Vice-Pres. and Gen. Man. SYLVIA JALANDONI.

### Banking Association

**Bankers Association of the Philippines:** Sagittarius Cond. Bldg, 11th Floor, H. de la Costa St, Salcedo Village, Makati, Metro Manila; tel. (2) 8122870; fax (2) 8103860; Exec. Dir LEONILO CORONEL.

## STOCK EXCHANGES

**Securities and Exchange Commission:** SEC Bldg, Epifanio de los Santos Ave, Greenhills, Mandaluyong, Metro Manila; tel. (2) 780931; fax (2) 7220990; Chair. ROSARIO N. LOPEZ.

# THE PHILIPPINES

**Manila International Futures Exchange:** Producers' Bank Bldg, 7th Floor, Paseo de Roxas, Makati, Metro Manila; tel. (2) 8127776; fax (2) 8185529; f. 1986; trades in sugar, soybeans, copra, coffee and foreign currencies; Exec. Man. PATRICK POON.

**Metropolitan Stock Exchange:** SEC Bldg, Epifanio de los Santos Ave, Greenhills, Mandaluyong, Metro Manila; f. 1974; Pres. TEOFILO REYES, Jr; 34 mems.

**Philippine Stock Exchange:** Philippine Stock Exchange Centre, Tektite Tower I, Exchange Rd, Ortigas Centre, Pasig, Metro Manila; f. 1994, following the merger of the Manila and Makati Stock Exchanges; under the merger plan, the two rival trading floors continue to operate, but a single set of indices is in place; Pres. EDUARDO DE LOS ANGELES.

**Makati Stock Exchange, Inc:** Makati Stock Exchange Bldg, Ayala Ave, Makati, Metro Manila; tel. (2) 7210286; telex 29010; fax (2) 7219238; f. 1963; 92 mems; Chair. EDUARDO C. LIM; Pres. JUAN B. FRANCISCO.

**Manila Stock Exchange:** Philippine Stock Exchange Centre, Tektite Tower Bldg, 12th Floor, Ortigas Center, Pasig, Metro Manila; tel. (2) 6345037; telex 40503; fax (2) 6346901; f. 1927; 90 mems; Chair. ROBERT COYIUTO, Jr; Acting Pres. VICTOR SAYITIPEK.

## INSURANCE

### Principal Domestic Companies

**Blue Cross Insurance Inc:** Philippine Bank of Communication Bldg, 7th Floor, Ayala Ave, Makati, Metro Manila; tel. (2) 8150836; telex 64981; fax 8179398; f. 1949; Pres. HILARIO O. OBALDO.

**Central Surety & Insurance Co:** UniversalRe Bldg, 2nd Floor, 106 Paseo de Roxas St, Legaspi Village, Makati, 1200 Metro Manila; tel. (2) 8174931; telex 45396; fax (2) 8170006; f. 1945; bonds, fire, marine, casualty, motor car; Pres. CONSTANCIO T. CASTAÑEDA, Jr.

**Commonwealth Insurance Co:** Manila Bank Bldg, 4th Floor, Ayala Ave, Makati, Metro Manila; tel. (2) 8187626; fax (2) 8160369; f. 1935; Chair. SENEN P. VALERO.

**Co-operative Insurance System of the Philippines:** 80 Malakas St, Diliman, Quezon City, Metro Manila; tel. (2) 9240471; Chair. RUPERTO A. VILLANOY; Gen. Man. ARTURO J. JIMENEZ.

**Domestic Insurance Co of the Philippines:** Domestic Insurance Bldg, Bonifacio Drive, Port Area, Manila; tel. (2) 472161; telex 66752; fax (2) 8162938; f. 1946; cap. 10m.; Pres. JULIAN J. CRUZ; Man. Dir MAR S. LOPEZ.

**Dominion Insurance Corpn:** Zeta II Annex Bldg, 6th Floor, 191 Salcedo St, Legaspi Village, Makati, Metro Manila; tel. (2) 875751; fax (2) 8183630; f. 1960; fire, marine, motor car, accident, worker compensation, bonds; Pres. JUAN DOMINO.

**Empire Insurance Co:** Prudential Life Bldg, 2nd–3rd Floors, 843 Arnaiz Ave, Legaspi Village, Makati, 1229 Metro Manila; tel. (2) 8159561; fax (2) 8152599; f. 1949; fire, bonds, marine, accident, motor car, extraneous perils; Chair. and Pres. SERGIO CORPUS.

**Equitable Insurance Corpn:** Equitable Bank Bldg, 4th Floor, 262 Juan Luna St, Binondo, POB 2104, Metro Manila; tel. (2) 2430291; fax (2) 2415768; f. 1950; fire, marine, casualty, motor car, bonds; Pres. MELECIO C. MALLILLIN; Vice-Pres. ELMA R. BONDAD.

**FGU Insurance Corpn:** BPI Bldg, 16th–18th Floors, Ayala Ave, Makati, 1226 Metro Manila; tel. (2) 8170971; (2) 8179806; f. 1963; cap. 16.8m. (1993); Chair. JAIME ZOBEL DE AYALA; Pres. FIDEL M. ALFONSO.

**Filipinas Life Assurance Co:** Filipinas Life Bldg, 6786 Ayala Ave, Makati, Metro Manila; tel. (2) 8160511; f. 1933; cap. 80m. (1983); Pres. ISAGANI DE CASTRO.

**First National Surety & Assurance Co Inc:** Metro Manila; tel. (2) 478271; f. 1950; general; Pres. DANIEL L. MERCADO, Sr.

**Insular Life Assurance Co Ltd:** Insular Life Bldg, 6781 Ayala Ave, cnr Paseo de Roxas, Makati, POB 71, Metro Manila; tel. (2) 8173051; fax (2) 8184646; f. 1910; members' equity 3,600m. (Dec. 1990); Chair. JOSE Y. FERIA; Pres. and CEO VICENTE R. AYLLON.

**Makati Insurance Co Inc:** Builders Centre Bldg, 4th Floor, 170 Salcedo St, Legaspi Village, Makati, Metro Manila; tel. (2) 8159236; telex 64120; fax (2) 8183320; f. 1965; non-life; Pres. WILFRIDO V. VERGARA; Chair. OCTAVIO V. ESPIRITU.

**Malayan Insurance Co Inc:** Yuchengco Tower, 4th Floor, 500 Quintin Paredes St, POB 3389, 1099 Metro Manila; tel. (2) 2428888; telex 27277; fax (2) 2422222; f. 1949; cap. 50.8m. (1993); insurance and bonds; Pres. HELEN Y. DEE.

**Manila Surety & Fidelity Co Inc:** 66 P. Florentino, Quezon City, Metro Manila; tel. (2) 7122251; f. 1945; Pres. Dr ELISA V. PEÑA; Vice-Pres. MA. LOURDES V. PEÑA.

**Mercantile Insurance Co, Inc:** Mercantile Insurance Bldg, cnr Gen. Luna and Beaterio Sts, Intramuros, Metro Manila; tel. (2) 493791; cap. 35m. (1983); Pres. EDMUNDO F. UNSON, Jr.

*Directory*

**Metropolitan Insurance Co:** Oledan Bldg, 131 Ayala Ave, Makati, Metro Manila; tel. (2) 8108151; telex 22459; f. 1933; non-life; Pres. JOSÉ M. PERIQUET, Jr; Vice-Pres. ISAGANI J. LIZARONDO.

**National Life Insurance Co of the Philippines:** National Life Insurance Bldg, 6762 Ayala Ave, Makati, Metro Manila; tel. (2) 8100251; fax (2) 8178718; f. 1933; Pres. BENJAMIN L. DE LEON; Sr Vice-Pres. JOSE L. BURGOS.

**National Reinsurance Corpn of the Philippines:** Cacho-Gonzales Bldg, 4th Floor, 101 Aguirre St, cnr Trasierra St, Legaspi Village, Makati, Metro Manila; tel. (2) 8928501; telex 64130; fax (2) 8153003; f. 1978; Pres. FIDEL ALFONSO; Chair. CESAR R. ALINA.

**Paramount Insurance Corpn:** Sage House, 15th Floor, 110 Herrera St, Makati, Metro Manila; tel. (2) 8127956; fax (2) 8133043; f. 1950; fire, marine, casualty, motor car; Pres. PATRICK L. GO; Chair. DANIEL C. GO.

**People's Trans-East Asia Insurance Corpn:** Mercantile Insurance Bldg, 2nd Floor, cnr Gen. Luna and Beaterio Sts, Intramuros, Metro Manila; Pres. and Gen. Man. EDMUNDO L. UNSON, Jr.

**Philippine American General Insurance Co Inc:** AIU-philamgen-Philhome Bldg, Dela Rosa, cnr Alvarado St, Legaspi Village, Makati, Metro Manila; tel. (2) 8178726; telex 12328; f. 1939; cap. 184m. (1983); non-life; Pres. RODRIGO DE LOS REYES; Chair. M. CAMPOS.

**Philippine Prudential Life Insurance Co Inc:** Philippine Prudential Life Bldg, 633 Gen. Luna St, Intramuros, Metro Manila; tel. (2) 478271; f. 1963; life, health and accident; Pres. D. L. MERCADO.

**Pioneer Insurance and Surety Corpn:** Pioneer House-Makati, 108 Paseo de Roxas, Makati, Metro Manila; tel. (2) 8179071; telex 45495; fax (2) 8171461; f. 1954; cap. 100m. (1994); Pres. and CEO DAVID C. COYUKIAT.

**Reinsurance Co of the Orient Inc:** Eurasia Bldg, Makati, Metro Manila; tel. (2) 868021; f. 1956; all classes; Pres. LUIS PANLILIO.

**Rico General Insurance Corpn:** Union Bank Bldg, Ground Floor, 843 Pasay Rd, Makati, Metro Manila; tel. (2) 8162752; f. 1964; Chair. Justice ESPERANZA P. ALVENDIA; Pres. LUIS D. PANLILIO.

**Rizal Surety and Insurance Co:** Prudential Life Bldg, 2nd–3rd Floors, 843 Arnaiz Ave, Legaspi Village, Makati, Metro Manila; tel. (2) 8159561; fax (2) 8152599; f. 1939; fire, bond, marine, motor car, accident, extraneous perils; Chair. and Pres. SERGIO CORPUS.

**Standard Insurance Co Inc:** Stanisco Towers, 5th Floor, 999 Pedro Gil St, cnr F. Agoncillo St, Metro Manila; tel. (2) 509006; fax (2) 5223230; f. 1958; Pres. and Chair. LOURDES T. ECHAUZ.

**Tabacalera Insurance Co Inc:** Tabacalera Bldg, 2nd Floor, 900 North Romualdez St, Paco, Metro Manila; tel. (2) 508026; telex 63638; fax (2) 5216273; f. 1937; Chair. JOSÉ MA MENDIETA; Pres. THELMA S. DOS PUEBLOS.

**Universal Reinsurance Corpn:** Ayala Life Bldg, 9th Floor, 6786 Ayala Ave, Makati, Metro Manila; tel. (2) 8178556; telex 45240; fax (2) 8173745; f. 1949; life and non-life; Chair. JAIME ZOBEL DE AYALA; Pres. MANUEL Q. BENGSON.

**World-Wide Insurance & Surety Co Inc:** Cardinal Bldg, 4th Floor, 999 Pedro Gil St, cnr F. Agoncillo St, Metro Manila; tel. (2) 593290; f. 1950; affiliated with Standard-Cardinal Life Insurance Companies; fire, marine, motor car, accident, workmen's compensation, loans, mortgages, bonds, aviation; Pres. EDUARDO T. ECHAUZ.

# Trade and Industry

## CHAMBERS OF COMMERCE AND INDUSTRY

**American Chamber of Commerce of the Philippines:** Corinthian Plaza, 2nd Floor, Paseo de Roxas, Makati, Metro Manila; tel. (2) 8187917; Pres. WILLIAM TIFFANY.

**Chamber of Agriculture and Natural Resources of the Philippines:** Quezon City, Metro Manila; tel. (2) 856296; Pres. ALFREDO MONTELIBANO.

**Chamber of International Trade:** Metro Manila; Pres. RAMON P. TAMBUNTING.

**Chinese Chamber of Commerce of the Philippines:** Federation Centre Bldg, 6th Floor, Muelle de Binondo, Binondo, Manila; tel. (2) 2419201.

**European Chamber of Commerce of the Philippines:** King's Court II Bldg, 5th Floor, 2129 Don Chino Roces Ave, Makati, Metro Manila; tel. (2) 8112234; telex 66045; fax (2) 8152688; f. 1978; 800 mems; Pres. DAVID H. HODGKINSON; Exec. Vice-Pres. HENRY J. SCHUMACHER.

**Federation of Filipino-Chinese Chambers of Commerce and Industry Inc:** Federation Center, 6th Floor, Muelle de Binondo St, POB 23, Metro Manila; tel. (2) 2419201; fax (2) 2422361; Pres. JIMMY T. TANG; Sec-Gen. GUILLERMO M. DE JOYA.

**Japanese Chamber of Commerce of the Philippines:** Jaycem Bldg, 6th Floor, 104 Rada St, Legaspi Village, Makati, Metro Manila.

THE PHILIPPINES  *Directory*

**Philippine Chamber of Coal Mines (Philcoal):** Rm 1007, Princeville Condominium, S. Laurel St, cnr Shaw Blvd, 1552 Mandaluyong City; tel. and fax (2) 5315513; Exec. Dir BERTRAND GONZALES.

**Philippine Chamber of Commerce and Industry:** PICC Secretariat Bldg, Ground Floor, CCP Complex, Roxas Blvd, Pasay City; tel. (2) 8338891; telex 62042; fax (2) 8338895; f. 1977; Pres. JOSE LUIS YULO, Jr; Dir-Gen. EMMANUEL T. VELASCO.

## STATE CORPORATIONS

**National Power Corpn (NAPOCOR):** Agham Rd, East Triangle, Diliman, Quezon City, Metro Manila; tel. (2) 9213541; f. 1936; state-owned corpn supplying electric and hydroelectric power throughout the country; scheduled for privatization in 1995; Pres. GUIDO ALFREDO DELGADO.

**National Steel Corpn:** 377 Sen. Gil J. Puyat Ave Ext., Makati, Metro Manila; tel. (2) 8162036; telex 22524; fax (2) 8152036; f. 1974; steel mfrs; 65% scheduled for privatization in mid-1995; Chair. LUIS M. MIRASOL; Pres. ROLANDO S. NARCISO.

**Philippine Cement Corpn (Philcemcor):** Cocho-Gonzales Bldg, Makati, Metro Manila.

**Philippine International Trading Corpn (PITC):** Philippines International Centre, 116 Tordesillas St, Salcedo Village, Makati, 1227 Metro Manila; POB 2253, 1056 Metro Manila; tel. (2) 8189801; telex 63745; fax (2) 8190562; f. 1973; state trading company to conduct international marketing of general merchandise, industrial and construction goods, raw materials, semi-finished and finished goods, and bulk trade of agri-based products; also provides financing, bonded warehousing, shipping, cargo and customs services; Pres. JOSE LUIS U. YULO, Jr.

**Philippine National Construction Corpn (PNCC):** PNCC Bldg, Epifanio de los Santos Ave, cnr Reliance St, Mandaluyong, Metro Manila; tel. (2) 7216584; telex 64148; 80% govt-owned; construction; design engineering; steel and concrete products, heavy machinery; sales 474.93m. pesos (1987); Chair. EDGARDO B. ESPIRITU; Pres. EDUARDO B. OLAGUER.

**Philippine National Oil Co:** PNOC Bldg, 7901 Makati Ave, Makati, Metro Manila; tel. (2) 859061; telex 22259; fax (2) 8121070; f. 1973; state-owned energy development agency mandated to ensure stable and sufficient supply of oil products and to develop domestic energy resources; Chair. RAUL MANGLAPUS; Pres. and CEO MONICA V. JACOB.

**Wenagro Industrial Corpn:** 92 Mindanao Ave, Quezon City, Metro Manila; producer and exporter of Philippine products; took over Philippine Exporters Trading Corpn (PETCOR) in 1980; Man. Dir FRANCISCO C. WENCESLAO.

## DEVELOPMENT ORGANIZATIONS

**Bases Conversion Development Authority:** responsible for the conversion of former military bases to civilian use; Chair. VICTOR LIM.

**Export Processing Zone Authority:** Legaspi Tower, 4th Floor, Roxas Blvd, Metro Manila; tel. (2) 5210585; telex 2525; operates four Export Processing Zones, in Bataan, Cebu, Baguio City and Cavite.

**National Development Co (NDC):** Producers Bank Bldg, 371 Sen. Gil J. Puyat Ave, Makati, Metro Manila; tel. (2) 8183284; telex 14823; fax (2) 8154472; f. 1919; govt-owned corpn engaged in the organization, financing and management of subsidiaries and corpns incl. commercial, industrial, mining, agricultural and other enterprises assisting national economic development, incl. jt industrial ventures with other ASEAN countries; Chair. RIZALINO S. NAVARRO; Gen. Man. ARTHUR N. AGUILAR.

**Private Development Corpn of the Philippines (PDCP):** Bankers' Centre, 6764 Ayala Ave, POB 757, Makati, Metro Manila; tel. (2) 8100231; telex 22080; fax (2) 8195376; f. 1963 with World Bank assistance; medium- and long-term loans; provides small business term loans, equity investment and guarantees, funds mobilization, underwriting and private placements, external funds management, insurance brokerage; business consultancy services; cap. and res 2,300m. pesos (1989); in 1991 PDCP extended financial assistance amounting to 503.7m. pesos for 861 projects; Chair. LUIS V. Z. SISON; Pres. CARLOS C. TORRES.

**Subic Bay Metropolitan Authority:** Leader RICHARD GORDON.

## GOVERNMENT AGENCIES

**Asset Privatization Trust:** BA-Lepanto Bldg, 8747 Paseo de Roxas, Makati, Metro Manila; tel. (2) 8159201; fax (2) 8184591; f. 1986 to handle the privatization of govt assets.

**Philippine Coconut Administration:** Elliptical Rd, Diliman, Quezon City, Metro Manila; POB 3386, Metro Manila; tel. (2) 994501; telex 42016; fax (2) 9216173; f. 1972; Administrator VIRGILIO M. DAVID.

## EMPLOYERS' ASSOCIATIONS

**Employers' Confederation of the Philippines (ECOP):** ECC Bldg, 4th Floor, 355 Sen. Gil J. Puyat Ave, Makati, Metro Manila; tel. (2) 8163813; telex 27181; fax (2) 858576; f. 1975; Pres. ANCHETA K. TAN; Dir-Gen. VICENTE LEOGARDO, Jr.

**Filipino Shipowners' Association:** Magsaysay Bldg, Room 512, 520 T. M. Kalaw St, Ermita, Metro Manila; tel. (2) 598662; telex 27830; fax (2) 503164; f. 1950; 35 mems; Pres. CARLOS C. SALINAS; Exec. Sec. AUGUSTO ARREZA, Jr.

**Philippine Cigar and Cigarette Manufacturers' Association:** Heritage Condominium Bldg, Metro Manila; Pres. RALPH NUBLA.

**Philippine Coconut Producers' Federation, Inc:** Lorenzo Bldg, 2nd–3rd Floors, cnr Taft Ave and Vito Cruz, Metro Manila; Pres. MARIA CLARA L. LOBREGAT.

**Philippine Sugar Millers' Association Inc:** Pacific Bank Bldg, Room 1402, 14th Floor, 6776 Ayala Ave, Makati, Metro Manila; tel. (2) 8151279; fax (2) 8101291; f. 1922; 18 mems; Pres. JOSE M. T. ZABALETA; Exec. Dir ENRICO G. DAYANGHIRANG.

**Textile Mills Association of the Philippines, Inc (TMAP):** Alexander House, 132 Amorsolo St, Legaspi Village, Makati, Metro Manila; tel. (2) 8186601; fax (2) 8183107; f. 1956; 23 mems; Pres. HERMENEGILDO C. ZAYCO.

**Textile Producers' Association of the Philippines, Inc:** Downtown Center Bldg, Room 513, 516 Quintin Paredes St, Binondo, Metro Manila; tel. (2) 5301043; Pres. GO CUN UY; Exec. Sec. ROBERT L. TAN.

## TRADE UNION FEDERATIONS

In 1988 a total of 3,127 trade unions, representing c. 4.93m. members, were registered with the Department of Labor and Employment.

In 1986 the Government established the Labor Advisory Consultation Committee (LACC) to facilitate communication between the Government and the powerful labour movement in the Philippines. The LACC granted unions direct recognition and access to the Government, which, under the Marcos regime, had been available only to the Trade Union Congress of the Philippines (KMP-TUCP). The KMP-TUCP refused to join the Committee.

In May 1994 a new trade union alliance, the Caucus for Labor Unity, was established; its members included the KMP-TUCP and three groups that had dissociated themselves from the former Kilusang Mayo Uno.

**Katipunang Manggagawang Pilipino (KMP-TUCP)** (Trade Union Congress of the Philippines): TUCP Training Center Bldg, TUCP/PGEA Compound, Masaya St, cnr Maharlika St, Diliman, Quezon City, Metro Manila; tel. (2) 9215236; telex 2362; fax (2) 9219758; f. 1975; 1.5m. mems; Pres. DEMOCRITO T. MENDOZA; Gen. Sec. ERNESTO F. HERRERA; 50 affiliates:

**Alyansang Likha ng mga Anak ng Bayan (ALAB):** David Bldg, Room 3A, 11 Shaw Blvd, Mandaluyong, Metro Manila; tel. (2) 704011; Pres. OSCAR B. SILVESTRE.

**Associated Labor Unions (ALU—TUCP):** PGEA Compound, Elliptical Rd, Diliman, Quezon City, 1101 Metro Manila; tel. (2) 9222575; telex 2362; fax (2) 9223199; f. 1954; 350,000 mems; Pres. DEMOCRITO T. MENDOZA.

**Associated Labor Union for Metalworkers (ALU—METAL):** National Labour Centre, Elliptical Rd, Diliman, Quezon City, 1101 Metro Manila; tel. (2) 9222575; telex 2362; fax (2) 9223199; 29,700 mems; Pres. CECILIO T. SENO.

**Associated Labor Union for Textile Workers (ALU—TEXTILE):** PGEA Compound, Elliptical Rd, Diliman, Quezon City, 1101 Metro Manila; tel. (2) 9222575; telex 2362; fax (2) 9223199; 41,400 mems; Pres. RICARDO I. PATALINJUG.

**Associated Labor Unions (ALU—TRANSPORT):** Philbanking Bldg, 2nd Floor, Quirino Ave, Paranaque, Metro Manila; tel. (2) 8323524; 49,500 mems; Pres. MARIO S. SANTOS.

**Associated Professional, Supervisory, Office and Technical Employees Union (APSOTEU):** National Labour Centre, Elliptical Rd, Diliman, Quezon City, 1101 Metro Manila; tel. (2) 9222575; fax (2) 9223199; Pres. CECILIO T. SENO.

**Association of Independent Unions of the Philippines:** Vila Bldg, Mezzanine Floor, Epifanio de los Santos Ave, Cubao, Quezon City, Metro Manila; tel. (2) 9224652; Pres. EMMANUEL S. DURANTE.

**Association of Leyte Teachers' Organizations (ALTO):** 246 Veteranos St, Tacloban City, Leyte; 13,000 mems; Pres. AGRIPINA SAUCELO.

**Association of Trade Unions (ATU):** Antwel Bldg, Room 1, 2nd Floor, Santa Ana, Port Area, Davao City; tel. (35) 72394; 2,997 mems; Pres. JORGE ALEGARBES.

**Confederation of Filipino Workers (CFW):** Pasay City; tel. 592827; 50,000 mems; Pres. EFREN ARANZAMENDEZ.

THE PHILIPPINES                                                                                                                    Directory

**Confederation of Labor and Allied Social Services (CLASS):** Don Santiago Bldg, TUCP Suite 414, 1344 Taft Ave, Ermita, Metro Manila; tel. (2) 540415; f. 1979; 4,579 mems; Pres. LEONARDO AGTING.

**Farmers' Growers Organization (FGO):** UPRIIS-NIS-IDD Office, Cabanatuan City, Nuera Ecija; Pres. TEODORO ANTONIO.

**Federación Obrera de la Industria Tabaquera y Otros Trabajadores de Filipinas (FOITAF):** Diamond Bldg, Room 306, 156 Libertad St, Pasay City; tel. (2) 856238; 25,000 mems; Pres. JOSE T. MAGHARI.

**Federated Union of Energy Leaders—General Allied Services (FUEL—GAS):** Phoenix Bldg, Room 703, Recoletos St, Intramuros, Metro Manila; tel. (2) 495404; Pres. JESUS B. DIAMONON.

**Federation of Agrarian and Industrial Toiling Hands (FAITH):** Kalayaan, cnr Masigla St, Diliman, Quezon City, Metro Manila; tel. (2) 9225244; 220,000 mems; Pres. RAYMUNDO YUMUL.

**Federation of Consumers' Co-operatives in Negros Oriental (FEDCON):** Bandera Bldg, Cervantes St, Dumaguete City; tel. (32) 2048; Chair. MEDARDO VILLALON.

**Federation of Filipino Civilian Employees Association (FFCEA):** 14 Murphy St, Pagasa, Olongapo City; tel. (2) 2222373; 21,560 mems; Pres. ROBERTO FLORES.

**Federation of Unions of Rizal (FUR):** Perpetual Savings Bank Bldg, 3rd Floor, Quirino Ave, Paranaque, Metro Manila; tel. (2) 8320110; 10,853 mems; Officer-in-Charge EDUARDO ASUNCION.

**Government Employees' Association for Reforms (GEAR):** 246 Veteranos St, Tacloban City, Leyte; tel. (2) 9222575; 10,000 mems; Pres. AARON REDUBLA.

**Grand Labor Union (GLU):** 14 3rd St, St Ignatius Village, Quezon City, Metro Manila; tel. (2) 784326; Pres. CHITA GUEVARRA ROCHESTER.

**Lakas sa Industriya ng Kapatirang Haligi ng Alyansa (LIKHA):** PCI Bank Bldg, Plaza Santa Cruz, Santa Cruz, Metro Manila; tel. (2) 404907; Pres. DOLORA C. SALIGAO.

**Leyte Organization of Associated Drivers (LOAD):** 25 Kaibaan St, Tacloban City, Leyte; 8,000 mems; Pres. VICENTE VELOSO.

**Manggagawa ng Komunikasyon sa Pilipinas (MKP):** 22 Libertad St, Mandaluyong, Metro Manila; tel. (2) 5310786; fax (2) 5310701; f. 1951; 13,500 mems (1992); Pres. MANOLITO PARAN; Gen. Sec. VIRGILIO VARGAS TULAY.

**National Association of Free Trade Unions (NAFTU):** Butuan City; tel. (8822) 3620941; 7,385 mems; Pres. JAIME RINCAL.

**National Congress of Unions in the Sugar Industry of the Philippines (NACUSIP):** Matrinco Bldg, Room 36, 2178 Pasong Tamo, Makati, Metro Manila; tel. (2) 8128209; 32 affiliated unions and 57,424 mems; Nat. Pres. ZOILO V. DELA CRUZ, Jr.

**National Labor Unions (NLU):** 3199 Magsaysay Blvd, Santa Mesa, Metro Manila; tel. (2) 614265; Pres. EULOGIO R. LERUM.

**National Mines and Allied Workers' Union (NAMAWU):** Isabel Bldg, Suite 202-210, España, Metro Manila; tel. (2) 7310711; 13,233 mems; Pres. ROBERTO A. PADILLA.

**National Union of Bank Employees (NUBE):** Dona Consolacion Bldg, Room 310, Gen. Santos Ave, Cubao, Quezon City, Metro Manila; tel. (2) 9225656; 7,500 mems; Pres. JOSE UMALI, Jr.

**North Harbor Labor Federation (NHLF):** 1106–1108 Marcos Rd, Pier 6, North Harbor, Tondo, Metro Manila; tel. (2) 267895; 4,525 mems; Pres. FRANCISCO YLADE.

**Pambansang Kilusan ng Paggagawa (KILUSAN):** PGEA Compound, Elliptical Rd, Diliman, Quezon City, 1101 Metro Manila; tel. (2) 994651; 13,093 mems; Pres. AVELINO VALERIO; Sec.-Gen. IGMIDIO T. GANAGANA.

**Philippine Agricultural, Commercial and Industrial Workers' Union (PACIWU):** Matrinco Bldg, Room 36, 2178 Pasong Tamo, Makati, Metro Manila; tel. (2) 8128209; Pres. ZOILO V. DELA CRUZ, Jr.

**Philippine Association of Free Labor Unions (PAFLU—September Convention):** Insurance Center Bldg, Room 309, 633 Gen. Luna St, Intramuros, Metro Manila; tel. (2) 5219827; 18,990 mems; Pres. ISRAEL BOCOBO.

**Philippine Communications, Electronics and Electricity Workers' Federation (PCWF):** PGEA Compound, Elliptical Rd, Diliman, Quezon City, 1101 Metro Manila; Pres. HENRY I. SANTOS.

**Philippine Federation of Labor (PFL):** FEMII Bldg, 5th Floor, Aduana St, Intramuros, Metro Manila; tel. (2) 494152; fax (2) 475056; 8,869 mems; Pres. ALEJANDRO VILLAVIZA.

**Philippine Federation of Teachers' Organizations (PFTO):** BSP Bldg, Room 112, Concepcion St, Ermita, Metro Manila; tel. (2) 495746; Pres. FEDERICO D. RICAFORT.

**Philippine Government Employees' Association (PGEA):** PGEA Compound, Elliptical Rd, Diliman, Quezon City, Metro Manila; tel. (2) 9230383; f. 1945; 15,000 mems; Pres. ESPERANZA OCAMPO.

**Philippine Integrated Industries Labor Union (PIILU):** Mendoza Bldg, Room 319, 3rd Floor, Pilar St, Zamboanga City; tel. (991) 2299; f. 1973; Pres. JOSE J. SUAN.

**Philippine Labor Federation (PLF):** PLF Bldg, R. Palma St, Cebu City 6000; tel. (991) 2299; 15,462 mems; Pres. CRISPIN GASTARDO.

**Philippine Seafarers' Union (PSU):** PGEA Compound, Elliptical Rd, Diliman, Quezon City, Metro Manila; tel. (2) 9222575; fax (2) 9223199; 10,000 mems; Pres. DEMOCRITO T. MENDOZA; Gen. Sec. ERNESTO F. HERRERA.

**Philippine Technical, Clerical, Commercial Employees Association (PTCCEA):** 41 Sicoba St, Santa Mesa Heights, Quezon City, Metro Manila; tel. (2) 7319008; 15,893 mems; Pres. RICARDO MANALAD.

**Philippine Transport and General Workers' Organization (PTGWO—D):** Cecilleville Bldg, 3rd Floor, Quezon Ave, Quezon City, Metro Manila; tel. (2) 9244929; f. 1953; 33,400 mems; Pres. ANDRES L. DINGLASAN, Jr.

**Port and General Workers' Federation (PGWF):** Capilitan Engineering Corpn Bldg, 206 Zaragoza St, Tondo, Manila; tel. 208959; Pres. FRANKLIN D. BUTCON.

**Public Sector Labor Integrative Center (PSLINK):** TUCP-PGEA Compound, 1101 Diliman, Quezon City, Metro Manila; tel. (2) 961573; 35,108 mems; Gen. Sec. ANNIE GERON.

**Samahang Manggagawang Pilipino (SMP)** (National Alliance of Teachers and Office Workers): Fersal Condominium II, Room 33, 130 Kalayaan Ave, Quezon City, 1104 Metro Manila; tel. and fax (2) 9242299; Pres. ADELISA RAYMUNDO.

**Solidarity Trade Conference for Progress:** Rizal Ave, Dipolog City; tel. (8822) 2209; Pres. NICOLAS E. SABANDAL.

**Unión de Obreros Estivadores de Filipinas (UOEF):** 681 Sevilla St, Binondo, Metro Manila; tel. (2) 8280862; 8,267 mems; Pres. ENRICO ANTONI.

**United Lumber and General Workers of the Philippines (ULGWP):** LAWA-AN Bldg, C. M. Recto St, Davao City; Pres. GODOFREDO PACENO.

**United Sugar Farmers' Organization (USFO):** SPCMA Annex Bldg, 3rd Floor, 1 Luzuriaga St, Bacolod City; Pres. BERNARDO M. REMO.

**Western Agusan Workers' Union:** M. H. del Pilar St, Nasipit, Agusan del Norte; f. 1948; Pres. JORGE T. JIMENEA.

**Workers' Alliance Trade Unions (WATU):** DELTA Bldg, 3rd Floor, Delta Ave, Quezon City, Metro Manila; tel. (2) 574606; fax (2) 586841; f. 1978; 25,000 mems; Pres. TEMISTOCLES DEJON.

### INDEPENDENT LABOUR FEDERATIONS

The following organizations are not affiliated to the KMP-TUCP:

**Associated Marine Officers and Seamen's Union of the Philippines (AMOSUP):** Seaman's Centre, cnr Cabildo and Sta Potenciana Sts, Intramuros, Metro Manila; tel. (2) 495415; telex 40256; f. 1960; 23 affiliated unions with 15,000 mems; Pres. GREGORIO S. OCA.

**Federation of Free Workers (FFW):** FFW Bldg, 1943 Taft Ave, Malate, Metro Manila; tel. (2) 571511; fax (2) 5218335; f. 1950; affiliated to the Brotherhood of Asian Trade Unionists and the World Confed. of Labour; 300 affiliated local unions and 400,000 mems; Pres. JUAN C. TAN; Nat. Vice-Pres. RAMON J. JABAR.

**Kilusang Magbubukid ng Pilipinas (KMP—Movement of Philippine Farmers):** Metro Manila; militant organization opposed to govt programme for land reform; 750,000 mems; Sec.-Gen. RAFAEL MARIANO.

**Lakas ng Manggagawa Labor Center:** 14 Ortigas St, cnr Yachengco Sts, BF Homes, Paranaque, Metro Manila; tel. (2) 8010974; a grouping of 'independent' local unions; Chair. 'BOY' ARRANJUEZ.

**National Confederation of Labor:** Metro Manila; f. 1994 by fmr mems of Kilusang Mayo Uno.

**Philippine Social Security Labor Union (PSSLU):** Carmen Bldg, Suite 309, Ronquillo St, Quiapo, Metro Manila; f. 1954; Nat. Pres. ANTONIO B. DIAZ; Nat. Sec. OFELIA C. ALAVERA.

**Trade Unions of the Philippines and Allied Services (TUPAS):** Med-dis Bldg, Suites 203–204, Solana St, cnr Real St, Intramuros, Metro Manila; tel. (2) 493449; affiliated to the World Fed. of Trade Unions; 280 affiliated unions and 75,000 mems; Nat. Pres. DIOSCORO O. NUÑEZ; Sec.-Gen. VLADIMIR R. TUPAZ.

# Transport

### RAILWAYS

The railway network is confined mainly to the islands of Luzon and Panay. In 1989 there were 805 km of track.

THE PHILIPPINES — *Directory*

**Light Rail Transit Authority (Metrorail):** Adm. Bldg, LRTA Cpd, Aurora Blvd, Pasay City, Metro Manila; tel. (2) 8320423; telex 64614; fax (2) 8316449; managed by Light Rail Transit Authority (LRTA) and operated by Metro Transit Org. (METRO), a subsidiary of LRTA; electrically-driven mass transit system; Line 1 (14 km, Baclaran to Manila to Monumento) began commercial operations in Dec. 1984; Line 2 (11.7 km, Manila to Quezon City) was scheduled to be operational in 1998; engineering design of the Line 1 capacity expansion and Line 2 construction projects started in November 1994 and was expected to be finished by early 1996.

**Philippine National Railways:** Management Center, Torres Bugallon St, Kaloocan City, Metro Manila; tel. (2) 3620824; fax (2) 3620824; f. 1887; govt-owned; the northern line runs from Manila to Meycauayan, Bulacan and the southern line from Manila to Polangui, Albay; Chair. JESUS B. GARCIA Jr; Gen. Man. JOSE B. DADO.

**Phividec Railways:** Iloilo City, Panay; tel. (6333) 74806; fmrly Philippine Railway Co; Chair. R. S. BENEDICTO.

### ROADS

In 1992 there were 160,633 km of roads in the Philippines, of which about 14% were paved with concrete or asphalt. Bus services provided the most widely-used form of inland transport.

**Department of Public Works and Highways:** Bonifacio Drive, Port Area, Metro Manila; tel. (2) 479311.

**Philippine Motor Association:** 683 Aurora Blvd, Quezon City, Metro Manila; tel. (2) 7215761; fax (2) 785878; f. 1931; Pres. CONRADO R. AYUYAO; Vice-Pres. CARLOS D. ARGUELLES.

### SHIPPING

In 1991 there were 626 public ports (including 19 base ports and 58 terminal ports) and 559 private ports. The eight major ports are Manila, Cebu, Iloilo, Cagayan de Oro, Zamboanga, General Santos, Polloc and Davao.

**Pangasiwaan ng Daungan ng Pilipinas (Philippine Ports Authority):** Marsman Bldg, 22 Muelle de Francisco St, South Harbour, Metro Manila; tel. (2) 479204; telex 40404; fax (2) 486237; f. 1977; supervises all national, municipal and private ports; Gen. Man. ROGELIO A. DAYAN.

#### Domestic Lines

**Aboitiz Shipping Corpn:** 110 Legaspi Bldg, Legaspi Village, Makati, Metro Manila; tel. (2) 208332; fax (2) 8184814; Pres. ENDIKA M. ABOITIZ; Chair. JON RAMON ABOITIZ.

**Albar Shipping and Trading Corpn:** 2649 Molave St, United Parañaque 1, Parañaque, Metro Manila; tel. (2) 8232391; telex 45238; fax (2) 8233046; Chair. and Pres. AKIRA S. KATO; Gen. Man. RUFO C. ZARATE.

**Candano Shipping Lines, Inc:** Victoria Bldg, 6th Floor, 429 United Nations Ave, Ermita, Metro Manila; tel. (2) 503306; inter-island chartering, cargo shipping; Pres. and Gen. Man. JOSE CANDANO.

**Carlos A. Gothong Lines, Inc:** Quezon Blvd, Reclamation Area, POB 152, Cebu City; tel. (32) 211181; fax (32) 212265; Exec. Vice-Pres. BOB D. GOTHONG.

**Delsan Transport Lines Inc:** 992 M. Naval St, Navotas, Metro Manila; tel. (2) 235051; Pres. VICENTE A. SANDOVAL; Gen. Man. CARLOS A. BUENAFE.

**Eastern Shipping Lines, Inc:** ESL Bldg, 54 Anda Circle, Port Area, POB 4253, 2803 Metro Manila; tel. (2) 401081; telex 63238; fax (2) 489708; f. 1957; services to Japan; brs in Tokyo, Yokohama, Kobe and Osaka; Pres. JAMES L. CHIONGBIAN; Exec. Vice-Pres. ERWIN L. CHIONGBIAN.

**Loadstar Shipping Co Inc:** Loadstar Bldg, 1294 Romualdez St, Paco, 1007 Metro Manila; tel. (2) 598071; telex 40064; fax (2) 5218061; Pres. and Gen. Man. TEODORO G. BERNARDINO.

**Lorenzo Shipping Corpn;** Pier 10, North Harbour, Tondo, Metro Manila; tel. (2) 2861228; fax (2) 2860838; Chair. JOSE GO, Sr; Pres. RAMON C. GARCIA; Exec. Vice-Pres. JOSE GO, Jr.

**Luzteveco (Luzon Stevedoring Corpn):** Tacoma and 2nd Sts, Port Area, POB 582, Metro Manila; tel. (2) 7420261; telex 40261; f. 1909; two brs; freight-forwarding, air cargo, world-wide shipping, broking, stevedoring, salvage, chartering and oil drilling support services; Pres. JOVINO G. LORENZO; Vice-Pres. RODOLFO B. SANTIAGO.

**National Shipping Corpn of the Philippines:** Knights of Rizal Bldg, Bonifacio Drive, Port Area, Metro Manila; tel. (2) 473631; telex 40931; fax (2) 5300169; services to Hong Kong, Taiwan, Korea, USA; Pres. TONY CHOW.

**Negros Navigation Co Inc:** Negros Navigation Bldg, 849 Pasay Rd, Makati, Metro Manila; tel. (2) 864921; telex 22307; Chair. CARLOS LEDESMA; Man. Dir DANIEL L. LACSON.

**Philippine National Oil Co (PNOC) Tankers Corpn:** PNOC Bldg, 7901 Makati Ave, POB 1031 MCC, Makati, Metro Manila; tel. (2) 859061; telex 22666; fax (2) 574781; Chair. MONICA V. JACOB, Jr; Pres. MANUEL A. ESTRELLA.

**Philippine Pacific Ocean Lines:** Delgado Bldg, Bonifacio Drive, Port Area, POB 184, Metro Manila; tel. (2) 478541; telex 7227633; Vice-Pres. C. P. CARANDANG.

**Philippine President Lines, Inc:** PPL Bldg, 1000–1046 United Nations Ave, Metro Manila; tel. (2) 509011; telex 27719; trading world-wide; Chair. EMILIO T. YAP, Jr; Pres. ENRIQUE C. YAP.

**Sulpicio Lines, Inc:** 1st St, Reclamation Area, POB 137, Cebu; tel. (32) 73839; telex 24605; Pres. ENRIQUE S. GO; Exec. Vice-Pres. EUSEBIO S. GO.

**Sweet Lines Inc:** Pier 6, North Harbour, Metro Manila; tel. (2) 274469; telex 2397; fax (2) 205534; f. 1937; Pres. EDUARDO R. LOPINGCO; Exec. Vice-Pres. SONNY R. LOPINGCO.

**Transocean Transport Corpn:** Magsaysay Bldg, 8th Floor, 520 T. M. Kalaw St, Ermita, Metro Manila; tel. (2) 506611; telex 40560; Pres. and Gen. Man. MIGUEL A. MAGSAYSAY; Vice-Pres. EDUARDO U. MANESE.

**United Philippine Lines, Inc:** UPL Bldg, Santa Clara St, Intramuros, POB 127, Metro Manila; tel. (2) 498961; telex 63288; services world-wide; Exec. Vice-Pres. and Gen. Man. FERNANDO V. LISING.

**William Lines, Inc:** 1508 Rizal Ave Extension, Caloocan City, Metro Manila; tel. (2) 3610764; telex 48031; f. 1949; passenger and cargo inter-island services; Pres. V. S. CHIONGBIAN; Chair. W. L. CHIONGBIAN.

### CIVIL AVIATION

In 1993 there were 84 airports in the Philippines. In addition to the international airports at Manila and Mactan (Cebu), there are four alternative international airports: Laoag City, Ilocos Norte; Davao City; Zamboanga City; Puerto Princesa City. Construction of a new international airport at the former Clark US Air Base was scheduled to begin in 1998. Philippine Airlines maintains domestic and international air services.

**Bureau of Air Transportation:** Manila International Airport, Pasay City, Metro Manila; tel. (2) 8323047; implements govt policies for the development and operation of a safe and efficient aviation network; Dir VICTORINO G. PALPAL-LATOC.

**Grand International Airways:** Manila International Airport, Pasay City, Metro Manila; operates domestic routes to Cebu and Davao and plans to operate international routes by the end of 1995; Pres. REBECCA PANLILIO.

**Philippine Airlines Inc (PAL):** PAL Bldg, Legaspi St, Legaspi Village, Makati, POB 954, Metro Manila; tel. (2) 8180111; fax (2) 8178689; f. 1941; in Jan. 1992 67% of PAL was transferred to the private sector; operates domestic, regional and international services to destinations in the Far East, Australasia, the Middle East, Europe and the USA; Chair. LUCIO TAN; Pres. JOSE ANTONIO GARCIA.

## Tourism

Tourism, although adversely affected periodically by political unrest, remains an important sector of the economy. In 1992 1.17m. visitors spent an estimated US $1,674m., an increase of 20.9% compared with 1991. In 1993 arrivals increased by 19%, to 1.39m., and in 1994 arrivals exceeded 1.5m., according to official estimates.

**Philippine Convention and Visitors' Corpn:** Legaspi Towers, 4th Floor, 300 Roxas Blvd, Metro Manila; tel. (2) 575031; telex 40604; fax (2) 5216165; Chair. VICENTE J. CARLOS; Exec. Dir DANIEL G. CORPUZ.

**Tourism Council of the Philippines:** Manila; Pres. ERMIN GARCIA Jr.

# POLAND

## Introductory Survey

### Location, Climate, Language, Religion, Flag, Capital

The Republic of Poland (until December 1989 the Polish People's Republic) is situated in Eastern Europe, bounded to the north by the Baltic Sea and an enclave of the Russian Federation, to the north-east by Lithuania, to the east by Belarus, to the south-east by Ukraine, to the west by Germany and to the south by the Czech Republic and Slovakia. The climate is temperate in the west but continental in the east. Poland has short summers and cold, snowy winters. Temperatures in Warsaw are generally between −6°C (21°F) and 24°C (75°F). Most of the inhabitants profess Christianity: more than 90% are adherents of the Roman Catholic Church, but there are numerous other denominations, the largest being the Polish Autocephalous Orthodox Church. The official language is Polish, spoken by almost all of the population, and there is a small German-speaking community. The national flag (proportions 8 by 5) has two equal horizontal stripes, of white and red. The capital is Warsaw (Warszawa).

### Recent History

Poland, partitioned since the 18th century, was declared an independent republic on 11 November 1918, at the end of the First World War. The country was ruled by a military regime from 1926 until 1939. In that year Poland was invaded by both Germany and the USSR and partitioned between the two powers. After Germany declared war on the USSR, in June 1941, its forces occupied the whole of Poland until being expelled by Soviet troops in March 1945.

At the end of the Second World War, a pro-communist 'Polish Committee of National Liberation', established under Soviet auspices in July 1944, was transformed into a Provisional Government. Under the Potsdam Agreement, signed by the major Allied powers in 1945, the former German territories lying east of the rivers Oder and Neisse (which now comprise one-third of Poland's total area) came under Polish sovereignty, while Poland's frontier with the USSR was also shifted westward. These border changes were accompanied by a major resettlement of the population in the affected areas.

Non-communist political groups suffered severe intimidation during national elections in January 1947, and the communist-led 'democratic bloc' claimed an overwhelming victory. A People's Republic was established in February, with the Polish Workers' Party (PWP), led by Władysław Gomułka, as the dominant group. Gomułka's reluctance to implement certain aspects of Soviet economic policies, notably the collectivization of agriculture, led to his dismissal as First Secretary of the PWP in 1948. In December 1948 the PWP merged with the Polish Socialist Party to form the Polish United Workers' Party (Polska Zjednoczona Partia Robotnicza—PZPR). Two other parties, the United Peasants' Party (Zjednoczone Stronnictwo Ludowe—ZSL) and the Democratic Party (Stronnictwo Demokratyczne—SD), were permitted to remain in existence, but were closely controlled by the PZPR, and Poland effectively became a one-party state.

The PZPR's strict control over public life eased slightly following the death of Stalin, the Soviet leader, in 1953. In 1956 food shortages prompted demonstrations by industrial workers, which were suppressed by security forces. In the ensuing political crisis, Gomułka was returned to office, despite the opposition of the Soviet leadership. A period of stability and some liberalization followed, and in 1964–70 some limited economic reforms were implemented, although these failed to effect major improvements in the standard of living. In December 1970 a sharp rise in food prices led to strikes and demonstrations in the Baltic port of Gdańsk and in other cities. Many demonstrators were killed or injured in clashes with the police and army, and Gomułka was forced to resign as First Secretary of the PZPR. He was succeeded by Edward Gierek (hitherto the party leader in Katowice region). Gierek attempted to introduce economic reforms and raise living standards during the 1970s, but with little success. There were further strikes and protests in 1976, forcing the postponement of planned price rises.

In July 1980 the introduction of higher prices for meat prompted strikes in factories near the capital, Warsaw, and soon labour unrest spread throughout the country. In addition to their economic claims, shipyard employees in the Baltic ports, notably at Gdańsk, demanded the right to form free trade unions. Following negotiations with the Government, permission was finally granted to establish several self-governing trade unions, under the guidance of Solidarity (Solidarność), the organization involved in the Gdańsk strike, which was led by a local worker, Lech Wałęsa.

In September 1980, as mass labour unrest continued, Gierek was replaced as First Secretary of the PZPR by Stanisław Kania, a member of the party's Politburo. Under the growing influence of Solidarity (which claimed an estimated 10m. members in 1981), strikes continued throughout the country, and in February Józef Pińkowski resigned as Chairman of the Council of Ministers. He was succeeded by Gen. Wojciech Jaruzelski, who had been Minister of Defence (a post that he retained) since 1968. In May 1981 the Rural Solidarity movement was formally recognized, thereby ending a protracted dispute betwen the Government and Poland's 3.5m. private farmers. Despite further concessions to Solidarity by the Government, the crisis continued, forcing Kania's resignation in October: he was succeeded by Jaruzelski, who thus held the leading posts in both the PZPR and the Government.

On 13 December 1981 martial law was imposed throughout Poland. A Military Council of National Salvation, led by Jaruzelski, was established to govern the country; all trade union activity was suspended, and Wałęsa and other Solidarity leaders were detained. Violent clashes between workers and security forces followed, and thousands of protesters were arrested. Sporadic disturbances continued in 1982, particularly in response to legislation (introduced in October) abolishing all trade unions. In November, however, Wałęsa was released, and in December martial law was suspended and some other prisoners were freed. During the 12 months of martial law 10,000 prisoners had been detained, and at least 15 demonstrators had been killed. In July 1983 martial law was formally ended, the Military Council of National Salvation was dissolved, and an amnesty was declared for most political prisoners and underground activists. In October Wałęsa was awarded the Nobel Peace Prize.

In July 1984, to mark the 40th anniversary of the Polish communist regime, a wide-ranging amnesty was announced, under which some 35,000 detainees were released. In August US sanctions (imposed following the declaration of martial law in December 1981) were relaxed. However, the murder, in October 1984, of Father Jerzy Popiełuszko, a well-known pro-Solidarity Roman Catholic priest, provoked renewed unrest. In February 1985 four officers from the Ministry of Internal Affairs were found guilty of the murder, and received long prison sentences. (The case was subsequently reopened, and the trial of two generals, accused of directing the murder, began in April 1992. In August 1994, however, both officers were acquitted of the charges against them.)

Legislative elections (postponed from March 1984) took place in October 1985. New regulations gave voters a choice of two candidates for 410 of the Sejm's 460 seats, the remaining 50 deputies being elected unopposed on a national list. Solidarity appealed to voters to boycott the polls, and subsequently disputed the Government's claim that 79% of the electorate had participated. In November Jaruzelski resigned as Chairman of the Council of Ministers, in order to become President of the Council of State (Head of State). His former post was taken by Prof. Zbigniew Messner (hitherto a Deputy Chairman of the Council of Ministers), who pledged to continue the policies of his predecessor.

At the 10th Party Congress of the PZPR, in June 1986, the incoming 230-member Central Committee (which included 175 new members) re-elected Jaruzelski as First Secretary. In December, in an effort to increase popular support for the regime, Jaruzelski established a 56-member Consultative Council, which was attached to the Council of State and comprised mainly non-PZPR members, including a number of independent Roman Catholic activists and former members of Solidarity. Nevertheless, public discontent became more evident in 1987. Supporters of Solidarity attempted to disrupt the official May Day celebrations in several cities, and in June there were violent clashes between the police and protesters during the third visit of Pope John Paul II to his homeland.

In October 1987 the Government announced plans for economic and political reforms, which were submitted for approval by the electorate in a national referendum in November. The leadership of Solidarity advocated a boycott of the plebiscite, and the Government failed to achieve the requisite support of 51% of the total electorate, and was forced to modify its proposals. However, the Government proceeded to impose significant price rises in February 1988, and in April and May of that year widespread demonstrations and strikes were organized to demand compensatory wage increases. Official May Day celebrations were again disrupted by Solidarity supporters. In Gdańsk a strike at the Lenin Shipyard, in support of Solidarity's campaign for legal status, was eventually abandoned, after the authorities used force to end a similar protest at the Nowa Huta steelworks. In August a strike by coalworkers, also in support of Solidarity, rapidly spread to other sectors, leading to the most serious industrial unrest since 1981. In an effort to resolve the crisis, the Government offered to negotiate with the leadership of Solidarity, and, in response to appeals by Wałęsa, the strikers returned to work.

In September 1988 the Messner Government resigned, owing to its lack of popular support and its failure to implement economic reforms. Dr Mieczysław Rakowski, who had served as Deputy Chairman in 1981–85, was appointed Chairman of a new Council of Ministers, which included several non-PZPR members and younger, reformist politicians. However, the new administration failed to commence proposed 'round-table' talks, scheduled for mid-October among representatives of the Government, Solidarity and other groups. Moreover, the Government's announcement that the Lenin Shipyard in Gdańsk was to be closed, ostensibly for economic reasons, provoked further strike action, despite Wałęsa's appeals to trade-union activists to remain at work.

In early 1989 the Government finally agreed to negotiate on the restoration of legal status to Solidarity and on other political issues. In February the 'round-table' talks began, and by early April the participants had reached agreement on the main questions: Solidarity was to regain its legal status, and elections were to be held to a new, bicameral legislature, the National Assembly (Zgromadzenie Narodowe). Solidarity and other non-communist groups were to be permitted to contest all the seats in a new upper chamber, the Senat, which would have a limited right of veto over the lower chamber, the Sejm. However, just 35% of the seats in the Sejm were to be subject to free elections, the remainder being contested only by candidates of the PZPR and its associate organizations. A new post of executive President was also to be introduced. The necessary amendments to the Constitution were duly approved by the Sejm, and in mid-April Solidarity was formally legalized. In May the Roman Catholic Church was also accorded legal status.

Elections to the new legislature took place, in two stages, on 4 and 8 July 1989, with 62% of eligible voters participating in the first round, but only 25% in the second. The Solidarity Citizen's Committee, the electoral wing of the trade union movement, achieved a decisive victory in the elections to the Senat, securing 99 of the 100 seats (the remaining seat being won by an independent candidate). In the elections to the 460-member Sejm, Solidarity secured all the 161 seats that it was permitted to contest, while the other 299 seats were divided between the PZPR (173 seats), its allied parties—the ZSL (76) and the SD (27)—and members of Roman Catholic organizations (23).

In July 1989 the new legislature narrowly elected Jaruzelski, unopposed, to the post of executive President. He was replaced as First Secretary of the PZPR by Mieczysław Rakowski. In early August Lt-Gen. Czesław Kiszczak (hitherto Minister of Internal Affairs) was elected Chairman of the Council of Ministers by the Sejm, but was unable to form a government, owing to opposition from the ZSL and the SD. President Jaruzelski therefore accepted Wałęsa's proposal of a coalition between Solidarity, the SD and the ZSL. The appointment of Tadeusz Mazowiecki, a respected newspaper editor and moderate member of Solidarity, as Chairman of the Council of Ministers, was approved by the Sejm on 24 August, thus ending almost 45 years of exclusive communist rule in Poland. An administration mainly comprising Solidarity members was formed in September, although, in accordance with a previous agreement, the internal affairs and defence portfolios were granted to the PZPR, and that party's members were also granted two other ministerial posts.

The new Government immediately began a programme of radical political and economic reforms, which emphasized the creation of democratic institutions and the introduction of a market economy. In December 1989 the National Assembly voted to rename the country the Republic of Poland, and the national symbols of pre-communist Poland were reintroduced. In January 1990 Leszek Balcerowicz, the radical Minister of Finance, announced a programme of major economic reforms. The plan aimed to free all prices by removing government subsidies, while restraining wages to limit inflation. In addition, exports were to be encouraged by introducing limited convertibility of the złoty, and subsidies would also be withdrawn from state-owned enterprises. Meanwhile, at its 11th Party Congress, also in January, the PZPR was dissolved, to allow the establishment of a new left-wing party, Social Democracy of the Republic of Poland (Socjaldemokracja Rzeczypospolitej Polskiej—SRP).

The local elections of May 1990 were the first fully free elections in Poland for more than 50 years. Candidates of the Solidarity Citizens' Committee won more than 41% of the seats, being particularly successful in the major cities. Nominally independent candidates secured 38% of the seats. Only 42% of the electorate, however, participated, indicating an apparent disenchantment with the Government's austere economic policies.

In mid-1990 internal divisions within Solidarity, which had developed as a result of disagreements regarding the pace of reform and over the future direction of the movement, became increasingly evident. Tension had developed between Wałęsa, who advocated an acceleration of economic reform and 'privatization', and Mazowiecki, who favoured a more cautious approach. The rift was confirmed in July, when a number of prominent Solidarity activists founded the Citizens' Movement-Democratic Action (Ruch Obywatelski-Akcja Demokratyczna—ROAD), with the aim of supporting Mazowiecki's Government. This new organization presented a direct challenge to the Centre Alliance (Porozumienie Centrum), which had been formed in May by supporters of Wałęsa.

In September 1990 President Jaruzelski agreed to resign, prior to the expiry of his six-year term of office, to permit direct presidential elections to take place. The first ballot, which was held on 25 November, was contested by six candidates, of which the strongest contenders were expected to be Wałęsa and Mazowiecki. However, Mazowiecki suffered a humiliating defeat, receiving fewer votes than both Wałęsa and a previously unknown émigré business executive, Stanisław Tymiński. Since no candidate had secured the requisite 50% of the vote, Wałęsa and Tymiński contested a second round of voting, on 9 December, which Wałęsa won overwhelmingly, with 74.3% of the votes cast. Wałęsa resigned the chairmanship of Solidarity (he was replaced in February 1991 by Marian Krzaklewski), and in late December 1990 was inaugurated as the country's President for a five-year term. Jan Krzysztof Bielecki, a radical economist, became Prime Minister (Mazowiecki had resigned from office following his defeat in the elections), after the President's first nominee, Jan Olszewski, had failed to form a government. A new Council of Ministers, in which only two ministers (one of whom was Leszek Balcerowicz) retained their posts from the outgoing administration, took office in January 1991.

President Wałęsa suffered an early reverse in March 1991, when the Sejm refused to endorse his proposal for the dissolution of the lower chamber and the holding of fully democratic elections in May, voting instead for polling later in the year. At the end of May public discontent at the Government's stringent economic policies resulted in a nation-wide day of strikes and demonstrations, organized by Solidarity. In August, owing to disputes over the course of economic policy, the Council of Ministers tendered its resignation, but it was rejected by the Sejm. In mid-September, as economic conditions worsened and the Sejm continued to delay economic legislation, a proposed law to give the Government special powers to rule by decree narrowly failed to secure the requisite two-thirds' majority in the Sejm.

Elections to the Sejm and the Senat took place on 27 October 1991, with only 43.2% of the electorate participating. A total of 29 parties won representation in the Sejm, but none acquired a decisive mandate. The party with the largest number of deputies (62) was the Democratic Union (Unia Demokratyczne—UD), formed in May 1991 by the merger of ROAD and two other organizations, and led by Tadeusz Mazowiecki. The Democratic Left Alliance (Sojusz Lewicy Demokratycznej—SLD), an electoral coalition of the SRP and the All Poland Trade Unions Alliance (Ogólnopolskie Porozumienie Związków Zawodowych), won 60 seats. In the Senat the UD was also the largest single party, with 21 seats, while Solidarity was represented by 11 senators.

Although the UD had the largest single representation in the new legislature, President Wałęsa nominated Jan Olszewski of the Centre Alliance as Prime Minister. However, following criticism of his economic programme by the President and the withdrawal of two parties from the coalition negotiations, Olszewski submitted his resignation. It was rejected by the Sejm, which proceeded to approve a new centre-right Council of Ministers, now incorporating members of the Centre Alliance, the pro-Solidarity Peasant Alliance and the Christian National Union (Zjednoczenie Chrześcijańsko-Narodowe—ZChN).

In February 1992, shortly before the Government's formal presentation of its economic programme, the Minister of Finance, Karol Lutkowski, unexpectedly resigned. He was replaced by Andrzej Olechowski, who, in turn, resigned in May, following a vote in the Sejm which authorized retrospective wage increases to public-sector workers and increased state pensions, thus jeopardizing the Government's commitment to budgetary restraint (and therefore the support of the IMF for the programme of economic reform). Meanwhile, relations between the President and the Prime Minister worsened, as Wałęsa reiterated his desire for greater powers in order to address perceived problems of 'stagnation and chaos', urging that the Constitution be amended to create a stronger presidency, based broadly on the French model.

In early June 1992, following controversy regarding government attempts to expose alleged communist conspirators, the Sejm approved a motion of 'no confidence' in the Government. Waldemar Pawlak, the leader of the Polish Peasant Party (Polskie Stronnictwo Ludowe—PSL), succeeded Jan Olszewski as Prime Minister, but he resigned in early July, having failed to form a government. Hanna Suchocka of the UD was proposed as Prime Minister, and her appointment was approved by the Sejm in mid-July. Suchocka proceeded to form a seven-party coalition, dominated by the UD and the ZChN.

The new Government was immediately challenged when 40,000 workers at a copper plant in Legnica went on strike in late July 1992, supported by several transport and power workers' unions. However, the strike ended after one month, without the strikers' demands for higher wages having been satisfied. Further industrial action followed in December, when miners in Silesia withdrew their labour in protest at government plans to restructure the coal industry, as a result of which the number of workers in the sector was expected to be almost halved.

In December 1992 an interim Constitution, known as the 'Small Constitution', entered into effect. The document defined the competences of the President, the Government and the legislature, and the balance of power between these bodies, and was to remain in force while a comprehensive revision of the 1952 Constitution (begun in November 1992) was in progress. In March 1993 the Government's programme of reforms suffered a further reverse when the Sejm rejected a 'mass privatization' plan, which was to have entailed the transfer of some 600 state enterprises to private ownership. Despite this decision, new government proposals for the divestment of the state sector were approved by the Sejm in late April and by the Senat in early May. Nevertheless, a motion of 'no confidence', proposed by the Solidarity group as a result of continuing opposition dissatisfaction with government economic and social policies (and prompted by the failure of negotiations between the Government and striking teachers and health-care workers), was approved in the Sejm by a margin of one vote in late May. Wałęsa, however, refused to accept the resignation of Suchocka; instead, he dissolved the Sejm, scheduling new elections to both houses of parliament for 19 September 1993.

Amendments to the electoral code were adopted in late May 1993, with the principal aim of reducing the number of political parties represented in parliament and thereby ensuring greater political stability. The principal reform was a new stipulation that a party (with the exception of organizations representing national minorities) must secure at least 5% of the total votes cast (8% in the case of an electoral alliance) in order to gain parliamentary representation. The general election, in September, resulted in an overwhelming victory for parties of the left: the SLD and the PSL, both dominated by former communists and their allies, won, respectively, 171 and 132 seats in the Sejm, and 37 and 36 seats in the Senat. Under the new electoral law, the two parties, which together won 35.8% of the total votes in the elections to the Sejm, secured more than 65% of the seats in that chamber. The UD took 74 seats in the Sejm (with 10.6% of the votes cast) and returned four senators, while Solidarity won 10 seats in the Senat (although none in the Sejm). Wałęsa's Non-Party Bloc for Reform (Bezpartyjny Bloc Wspierania Reform), established in June in an attempt to consolidate support for the President in parliament, won 16 seats in the Sejm (with 5.4% of the votes cast) and two seats in the Senat. The Centre Alliance and the ZChN notably failed to win representation in either chamber. In all, almost 35% of the votes cast in elections to the Sejm were for parties that received less than 5% of the total votes, and therefore secured no representation; the rate of participation by voters was 52.1%. The success of the left, and the defeat of the centre and right—the extent of which had not been anticipated—was largely attributed to dissatisfaction among voters at the adverse consequences of economic reforms.

Following protracted negotiations, in late October 1993 the President of the PSL, Waldemar Pawlak, formed a coalition Government, comprising eight representatives of his party, five from the SLD, one member of the Union of Labour (Unia Pracy) and independent ministers. Pawlak expressed his Government's support for a continuation of market-orientated reforms, but pledged new measures to alleviate the adverse social effects of such policies.

In late January 1994 Pawlak dismissed the (SLD) Deputy Minister of Finance, Stefan Kawalek, who had been responsible for the transfer to private ownership, in late 1993, of Bank Śląski SA w Katowicach, which was believed by critics of the Government to have been severely undervalued at the time of its sale. Kawalek's dismissal prompted the resignation, in early February 1994, of the Deputy Prime Minister and Minister of Finance, Marek Borowski (also of the SLD), who protested that his authority had been undermined, and that the coalition agreement had been violated, by the Prime Minister's unilateral action. In April Wałęsa, who had recently rejected a nomination for the post of Minister of Finance, threatened to dissolve parliament in response to a proposal, made by PSL-SLD deputies, for an amendment to the Small Constitution whereby the Sejm, and not the Head of State, would be ultimately responsible for ratifying government appointments. Wałęsa eventually nominated Prof. Grzegorz Kołodko as Deputy Prime Minister and Minister of Finance in late April.

Labour unrest re-emerged in early February 1994, when at least 20,000 people took part in a demonstration in Warsaw, organized by Solidarity, to demand increased government investment in the public sector and improved measures to combat unemployment. In the following month Solidarity began a nation-wide programme of strike action, intended to affect different sectors of the economy in rotation. Negotiations between the Government and Solidarity began later in the month, but stoppages intensified in early May. However, in mid-May Solidarity abandoned plans for a general strike, and coal-miners returned to work after being granted pay increases.

Only some 30% of eligible voters participated in local elections in June 1994. The SLD largely retained its dominant position in urban areas, but there was also a rise in support for right-wing parties. The elections had little impact on national politics, which continued to be dominated by confrontation between the right-wing President and the left-wing governing coalition. In October Wałęsa demanded the resignation of the Minister of National Defence, Adm. Piotr Kolodziejczyk, claiming that he was failing to implement military reforms.

In early November Pawlak acceded to Wałęsa's demand, but for the next two months the President and the Government proved unable to agree on a successor to Kolodziejczyk. In January 1995 further controversy was caused by Wałęsa's refusal to endorse legislation raising rates of personal income tax. Wałęsa urged the population not to pay the increased rates, but his actions were ruled unconstitutional by the Constitutional Tribunal, and he was forced to approved the legislation.

In early February 1995 relations between the Government and the President deteriorated sharply, when Wałęsa demanded the resignation of Pawlak, and threatened to dissolve parliament if the Prime Minister was not replaced. In response, the Sejm voted to begin impeachment proceedings against the President should he attempt to dissolve the legislature. Further conflict was avoided by the resignation of Pawlak, a decision supported by the SLD members of the coalition, dissatisfied at the domination of the coalition by the smaller PSL (of which Pawlak was President). In early March Józef Oleksy, a member of the SLD and hitherto Marshal (Speaker) of the Sejm, took office as Prime Minister, and Wałęsa rescinded his threat to dissolve the legislature. Oleksy formed a new Government, comprising members of the SLD, the PSL and independents.

In foreign affairs, Poland's formal links with other eastern European states, through its membership of the Warsaw Pact and the Council for Mutual Economic Assistance, were ended in 1991 upon the dissolution of these two organizations. Close relations were retained with the Czech Republic, Hungary and Slovakia through the structure of the Visegrad Group, and with other countries of the region belonging to the Council of Baltic Sea States (see p. 238). In 1991–92 Poland established diplomatic relations with the former republics of the USSR, developing particularly strong links with Ukraine. However, relations with neighbouring Lithuania were initially strained by concerns regarding the status of the Polish minority in that country. Relations improved in 1993–94, and in April 1994 Poland and Lithuania signed a treaty of friendship and co-operation, in which both countries renounced any claims on each other's territory. All former Soviet combat troops had been withdrawn from Poland by November 1992, and the last remaining (non-combat) Russian military presence was withdrawn in September 1994.

The prospect of a united Germany initially gave rise to much disquiet in Poland, where it was feared that the country's existing (post-1945) borders might not be respected by the new German state. However, in November 1990 Poland and Germany signed a border treaty, confirming the post-war frontier. In June 1991 the two countries also signed a treaty of 'good neighbourliness and friendly co-operation'.

In December 1991 Poland signed an association agreement with the European Community (known as the European Union—EU—see p. 143, from November 1993), as part of its continuing effort to integrate more closely with western European institutions; the agreement became fully effective from February 1994. In April 1994 Poland made a formal application for membership of the EU, and successive administrations reiterated the aim of full accession to the EU by 2000. Poland joined the Council of Europe (see p. 134) in November 1991.

Following the disintegration of the communist bloc and its institutions, Poland, in common with the other eastern European countries, regarded membership of NATO as a major priority in guaranteeing regional security. In late January 1994, while expressing disappointment that no clear timetable had been established for full NATO membership, Poland announced that it was to join that organization's newly-formulated 'partnership for peace' programme (see p. 192). A defence co-operation agreement was duly signed by Poland and NATO in March. In May Poland was granted associate partnership status in Western European Union (WEU—see p. 221).

### Government

A 'Small Constitution', which came into force in December 1992, was to define the powers of, and relationship between, the Head of State, the Government and parliament, pending the completion of a full revision of the existing Constitution. Under the 1952 Constitution, as amended since 1989, legislative power is vested in the bicameral National Assembly, which is elected for a four-year term, subject to dissolution, and comprises the 100-member Senate (upper chamber) and the 460-member Sejm (lower chamber and former unicameral legislature). The Senat reviews the laws adopted by the Sejm and may propose their rejection. All 100 senators are elected by a majority vote on a provincial basis. Each province is represented by two senators, with the exception of Warsaw and Katowice, which elect three delegates. In the Sejm, however, deputies are elected under a complex system of proportional representation: 391 members are chosen from lists for multi-seat electoral districts, the remaining 69 deputies being elected from national lists. Executive power is vested in the President of the Republic, who is directly elected (a second ballot being held if necessary), for a five-year term, and may be re-elected only once. The President governs with the assistance of an appointed Cabinet, led by a Prime Minister. The Cabinet is responsible for its activities to the Sejm, and to the President between sessions of the Sejm.

The country is divided into 49 provinces (voivodships), each administered by an appointed governor. Under reforms introduced in 1990, complete autonomy was granted to the directly-elected local councils.

### Defence

In June 1994 the strength of the armed forces was estimated to be 283,600 (including 160,000 conscripts): army 185,900, air force 78,700 and navy 19,000. Paramilitary forces included border guards and police prevention units. Military service normally lasts for 18 months. In 1988 legislation permitting conscientious objectors to perform an alternative community service was enacted. The estimated defence budget for 1993 totalled 33,090,200m. złotys (6.6% of budgetary spending).

### Economic Affairs

In 1993, according to estimates by the World Bank, Poland's gross national product (GNP), measured at average 1991–93 prices, was US $87,315m., equivalent to $2,270 per head. Between 1985 and 1993, it was estimated, GNP per head decreased, in real terms, by an annual average of 1.8%. Over the same period the population increased at an average annual rate of 0.4%. Poland's gross domestic product (GDP) grew, in real terms, by an average annual rate of 0.6% in 1980–92. Real GDP increased by about 4.0% in 1993 and by some 5.5% in 1994.

Agriculture (including forestry and inland fishing) contributed 7.3% of GDP in 1993. In the previous year the sector engaged 24.8% of the employed labour force. The principal crops are potatoes, sugar beets, wheat, rye and barley. Livestock production is important to the domestic food supply. During 1982–93 agricultural output increased at an average rate of 1.2% annually. In 1994 crop production was severely affected by drought, and agricultural output decreased by an estimated 10%, compared with the previous year.

Industry (including mining, manufacturing, sea fishing, power and construction) accounted for 41.7% of GDP in 1993. In 1992 the sector engaged 31.9% of the employed labour force. Industrial production (including sea fishing but excluding construction) increased at an average rate of 1.1% per year during 1980–89; output declined by 24.2% in 1990 and by 11.9% in 1991. However, industrial production recovered in 1992–93, and increased by an estimated 15.0% in 1994, a rise largely attributed to improved productivity resulting from the 'privatization' of state-owned industries.

In 1991 the mining industry employed 2.9% of the civilian labour force. The mineral industry is an important source of foreign exchange earnings, exports of hard coal, alone, accounting for 6.9% of total export earnings in 1993. Poland is a significant producer of copper, silver and sulphur; there are also considerable reserves of natural gas. Mining output increased by an annual average of 0.6% in 1980–89, but declined by 26.4% in 1990; in 1993 hard-coal output was estimated to represent only 60% of production levels in the 1980s.

The manufacturing sector employed 24.7% of the civilian labour force in 1990. Measured by the value of output, the principal branches of manufacturing in 1991 were machinery and transport equipment, food products, metals and metal products, chemicals, beverages and tobacco, textiles and clothing, and petroleum refining. During 1980–91 manufacturing output declined by an annual average of 3.2%.

Energy is derived principally from coal, which in the late 1980s satisfied about 80% of the country's total energy requirements. Imports of fuels and power accounted for 12.6%

of total import costs in 1993. Financial difficulties have delayed Poland's nuclear energy programme.

In 1993 Poland recorded a visible trade deficit of US $3,505m., and there was a deficit of $5,788m. on the current account of the balance of payments. The principal source of imports in 1993 was Germany (28.0%); other major suppliers were Italy, Russia and the United Kingdom. Germany was also the principal market for exports in 1993; other notable purchasers were the Netherlands, Italy and Russia. The principal exports in 1993 were electro-engineering products (notably transport equipment), textiles, metallurgical products, chemicals, fuels and power (especially hard coal), food products, clothing and leather products, wood and paper products and unprocessed agricultural products. The principal imports in that year were electro-engineering products, chemicals, fuels and power (notably crude petroleum and natural gas), textiles and food products.

In 1994 Poland recorded a budgetary deficit equivalent to 2.4% of GDP (significantly below the 'ceiling' of 3.6% that had been stipulated by the IMF as a prerequisite for continued assistance). Poland's external debt totalled US $45,306m. at the end of 1993, of which $41,426m. was long-term public debt. In that year the cost of servicing the foreign debt was equivalent to 10.6% of revenue from exports of goods and services. In 1985–93 the annual rate of inflation averaged 92.0%. Although the rate reached a record 1,266% in February 1990, inflation declined to 36.9% in 1993 and to 32.2% in 1994. By the end of 1994 some 16.0% of the labour force were unemployed, a slight decrease from 16.4% at the end of 1993.

Poland is a member, as a 'Country of Operations', of the European Bank for Reconstruction and Development (EBRD, see p. 140), and signed an association agreement with the European Community (subsequently the European Union) in December 1991, which became fully effective from February 1994. In November 1993 a free-trade agreement concluded with the European Free Trade Association (see p. 142) came into force.

Beginning in 1989, and with assistance from the international financial community (including the IMF, the World Bank and, from 1991, the EBRD), Poland undertook an ambitious, market-orientated programme of economic reform, which was pursued, to varying effect, by successive administrations during the early 1990s. By the end of 1992 Poland had achieved a marginal recovery in GDP growth (which accelerated significantly during 1993–94), as well as a notable reduction in the rate of inflation. Measures to strengthen Poland's external trading position and to maintain the value of the złoty at a realistic level achieved some success, and the divestment of state-owned enterprises, the progress of which had hitherto been faltering, was accelerated from mid-1993, following parliamentary approval of a 'mass privatization' programme. The main element of the programme—the privatization of some 450 large state-owned enterprises—was expected to be implemented in 1995. A reduction in the budget deficit was also achieved, assisted by increased revenue from taxation (including from newly-imposed value-added tax). Poland's foreign debt—identified as a serious impediment to growth at the beginning of the 1990s—was significantly alleviated by concessions from the 'Paris Club' of official creditors, which facilitated a two-stage (April 1991 and April 1994), 50% reduction in public debt, and by an effective reduction, of 42.5%, of private debt, agreed by the 'London Club' of commercial creditors in March 1994. By such concessions, it was anticipated that Poland would attract additional foreign investment. None the less, the high rate of unemployment, and other social problems attributed to the economic transformation, caused concern, although the private sector, which was expected to enjoy sustained growth in the mid-1990s, was seen as an important source of new employment, while there was also optimism for renewed growth in hitherto loss-making state sectors.

### Social Welfare

The Polish social welfare system is controlled by the Ministries of Health and of Labour and Social Policy. Locally the system is administered by the Health and Social Welfare Departments of the Presidiums of the National Councils. Medical care is provided free for all workers and rural population. Radical reforms of the health insurance scheme have been under consideration since 1989. The 1993 budget allocated 71,321,400m. (old) złotys to health care (representing 14.2% of total expenditure by the central Government) and 137,064,800m. złotys (27.3%) to social welfare and social insurance. At the end of 1993 there were 85,367 physicians and 16,951 dental surgeons in practice. There were 214,786 general hospital beds. A total of 698 general hospitals were in operation. The Polish Red Cross organizes and undertakes the care of the sick at home and general home assistance to those who are incapacitated through ill health, etc. Alimony is assured by law to single mothers. Welfare benefits are available to the unemployed. Pensions are organized and managed by the Union of Pensioners, Invalids and Retired Persons.

### Education

Education is free and compulsory for eight years between the ages of seven and 14 years. Before the age of seven, children may attend crèches (żłobki) and kindergartens (przedszkola). In 1993/94 42.7% of children between the ages of three and six years attended kindergarten, and 94.4% of six-year olds attended pre-school educational establishments. Basic schooling begins at seven years of age with the eight-year school (szkoła podstawowa). Curricula are uniform throughout Poland. In 1993/94 there were 985 private schools, administered under state supervision. In 1989 the Roman Catholic Church was granted the right to operate its own schools. Secondary education is provided free of charge to candidates who are successful in the entrance examination, and in 1992 about 96% of pupils continued their studies. Of these, 57.7% attended vocational and technical schools (technika zawodowe), or basic vocational schools (zasadnicze szkoły). The latter provide three-year courses consisting of three days' theoretical and three days' practical training per week, and in addition some general education is given. Vocational technical schools provide five-year courses of general education and vocational training, and can lead to qualifications for entering higher educational establishments. Children who leave the eight-year school to continue with their education enter general secondary schools (licea ogólnokształcące), where four-year courses lead to college or university entrance. In 1993/94 there were 140 higher educational establishments in Poland, including 11 universities and 20 technical universities. Expenditure from the government budget on education and the care of children for 1993 was 51,748,200m. (old) złotys (10.3% of total budgetary expenditure), while 12,696,100m. złotys (2.5%) were allocated to higher education.

### Public Holidays

**1995:** 1 January (New Year's Day), 17 April (Easter Monday), 1 May (Labour Day), 3 May (Polish National Day, Proclamation of 1791 Constitution), 9 May (Victory Day), 15 June (Corpus Christi), 15 August (Assumption), 1 November (All Saints' Day), 11 November (Independence Day), 25–26 December (Christmas).

**1996:** 1 January (New Year's Day), 8 April (Easter Monday), 1 May (Labour Day), 3 May (Polish National Day, Proclamation of 1791 Constitution), 9 May (Victory Day), 6 June (Corpus Christi), 15 August (Assumption), 1 November (All Saints' Day), 11 November (Independence Day), 25–26 December (Christmas).

### Weights and Measures

The metric system is in force.

# Statistical Survey

Source (unless otherwise indicated): Główny Urząd Statystyczny (Central Statistical Office), 00-925 Warsaw, Al. Niepodległości 208; tel. (2) 6252215; telex 814581; fax (2) 6251525.

## Area and Population

### AREA, POPULATION AND DENSITY

| Area (sq km) | |
|---|---|
| Land | 304,465 |
| Inland water | 8,220 |
| Total | 312,685* |

| Population (census results)† | |
|---|---|
| 7 December 1978 | 35,061,450 |
| 6 December 1988 | |
| Males | 18,464,373 |
| Females | 19,414,268 |
| Total | 37,878,641 |

| Population (official estimates at 31 December)† | |
|---|---|
| 1991 | 38,309,226 |
| 1992 | 38,418,108 |
| 1993 | 38,504,707 |
| Density (per sq km) at 31 December 1993 | 123.1 |

* 120,728 sq miles.
† Figures exclude civilian aliens within the country and include civilian nationals temporarily outside the country.

### VOIVODSHIPS (estimated population at 31 December 1993)

| | Area (sq km) | Total ('000) | Density (per sq km) | Capital* ('000) |
|---|---|---|---|---|
| Warszawskie | 3,788 | 2,412.7 | 637 | 1,642.7 |
| Bialskopodlaskie | 5,348 | 309.0 | 58 | 55.6 |
| Białostockie | 10,055 | 699.2 | 70 | 276.1 |
| Bielskie | 3,704 | 911.5 | 246 | 181.0 |
| Bydgoskie | 10,349 | 1,126.5 | 109 | 384.8 |
| Chełmskie | 3,866 | 249.6 | 65 | 68.6 |
| Ciechanowskie | 6,362 | 434.8 | 68 | 45.9 |
| Częstochowskie | 6,182 | 781.8 | 126 | 259.9 |
| Elbląskie | 6,103 | 488.3 | 80 | 127.8 |
| Gdańskie | 7,394 | 1,444.8 | 195 | 463.1 |
| Gorzowskie | 8,484 | 507.9 | 60 | 125.0 |
| Jeleniogórskie | 4,379 | 522.8 | 119 | 93.2 |
| Kaliskie | 6,512 | 719.6 | 111 | 106.7 |
| Katowickie | 6,650 | 3,954.3 | 595 | 359.4 |
| Kieleckie | 9,211 | 1,135.5 | 123 | 214.1 |
| Konińskie | 5,139 | 477.2 | 93 | 82.1 |
| Koszalińskie | 8,470 | 517.1 | 61 | 111.1 |
| Krakowskie | 3,254 | 1,235.4 | 380 | 745.1 |
| Krośnieńskie | 5,702 | 503.7 | 88 | 49.5 |
| Legnickie | 4,037 | 521.5 | 129 | 107.1 |
| Leszczyńskie | 4,154 | 394.2 | 95 | 60.4 |
| Lubelskie | 6,792 | 1,023.8 | 151 | 351.6 |
| Łomżyńskie | 6,684 | 352.9 | 53 | 62.3 |
| Łódzkie | 1,523 | 1,126.1 | 739 | 833.7 |
| Nowosądeckie | 5,576 | 721.3 | 129 | 81.2 |
| Olsztyńskie | 12,327 | 765.9 | 62 | 166.2 |
| Opolskie | 8,535 | 1,026.7 | 120 | 130.0 |
| Ostrołęckie | 6,498 | 405.5 | 62 | 53.3 |
| Pilskie | 8,205 | 489.7 | 60 | 75.2 |
| Piotrkowskie | 6,266 | 644.8 | 103 | 81.4 |
| Płockie | 5,117 | 521.0 | 102 | 125.9 |
| Poznańskie | 8,151 | 1,346.6 | 165 | 582.8 |
| Przemyskie | 4,437 | 412.6 | 93 | 68.6 |
| Radomskie | 7,294 | 761.1 | 104 | 231.6 |
| Rzeszowskie | 4,397 | 739.6 | 168 | 158.5 |
| Siedleckie | 8,499 | 659.4 | 78 | 73.6 |
| Sieradzkie | 4,869 | 411.9 | 85 | 44.3 |
| Skierniewickie | 3,960 | 423.2 | 107 | 47.6 |
| Słupskie | 7,453 | 423.2 | 57 | 102.4 |
| Suwalskie | 10,490 | 482.0 | 46 | 64.9 |
| Szczecińskie | 9,982 | 984.9 | 99 | 417.7 |
| Tarnobrzeskie | 6,283 | 607.8 | 97 | 50.4 |
| Tarnowskie | 4,151 | 687.1 | 166 | 122.2 |
| Toruńskie | 5,348 | 667.5 | 125 | 203.1 |
| Wałbrzyskie | 4,168 | 741.6 | 178 | 140.3 |
| Włocławskie | 4,402 | 433.9 | 99 | 122.9 |
| Wrocławskie | 6,287 | 1,134.3 | 180 | 642.3 |
| Zamojskie | 6,980 | 493.4 | 71 | 65.4 |
| Zielonogórskie | 8,868 | 669.5 | 75 | 115.6 |
| **Total** | 312,685 | 38,504.7 | 123 | — |

* Each Voivodship is named after the town from which it is administered.

### PRINCIPAL TOWNS (estimated population at 31 December 1993)

| | | | |
|---|---|---|---|
| Warszawa (Warsaw) | 1,642,694 | Ruda Śląska | 167,971 |
| Łódź | 833,698 | Olsztyn | 166,142 |
| Kraków (Cracow) | 745,101 | Rzeszów | 158,510 |
| Wrocław | 642,332 | Rybnik | 143,793 |
| Poznań | 582,813 | Wałbrzych | 140,294 |
| Gdańsk | 463,058 | Tychy | 136,754 |
| Szczecin | 417,747 | Dąbrowa Górnicza | 132,784 |
| Bydgoszcz | 384,830 | Opole | 129,978 |
| Katowice | 359,408 | Elbląg | 127,828 |
| Lublin | 351,646 | Chorzów | 127,049 |
| Białystok | 276,045 | Płock | 125,894 |
| Częstochowa | 259,864 | Gorzów Wielkopolski | 124,998 |
| Gdynia | 250,590 | Włocławek | 122,882 |
| Sosnowiec | 250,398 | Tarnów | 122,219 |
| Radom | 231,626 | Zielona Góra | 115,557 |
| Bytom | 229,605 | Koszalin | 111,140 |
| Gliwice | 214,494 | Legnica | 107,108 |
| Kielce | 214,086 | Kalisz | 106,680 |
| Zabrze | 203,950 | Grudziądz | 103,733 |
| Toruń | 203,147 | Jastrzębie Zdrój | 103,629 |
| Bielsko-Biała | 180,953 | Słupsk | 102,449 |

### BIRTHS, MARRIAGES AND DEATHS

| | Registered live births | | Registered marriages | | Registered deaths | |
|---|---|---|---|---|---|---|
| | Number | Rate (per 1,000) | Number | Rate (per 1,000) | Number | Rate (per 1,000) |
| 1986 | 634,748 | 17.0 | 257,887 | 6.9 | 376,316 | 10.1 |
| 1987 | 605,492 | 16.1 | 252,819 | 6.7 | 378,365 | 10.1 |
| 1988 | 587,741 | 15.5 | 246,791 | 6.5 | 370,821 | 9.8 |
| 1989 | 562,530 | 14.8 | 255,643 | 6.7 | 381,173 | 10.0 |
| 1990 | 545,817 | 14.3 | 255,369 | 6.7 | 388,440 | 10.2 |
| 1991 | 545,954 | 14.3 | 233,206 | 6.1 | 403,951 | 10.6 |
| 1992 | 513,616 | 13.4 | 217,240 | 5.7 | 393,131 | 10.2 |
| 1993 | 492,925 | 12.8 | 207,674 | 5.4 | 390,874 | 10.2 |

**Expectation of life** (years at birth, 1993): males 67.4; females 76.0.

### IMMIGRATION AND EMIGRATION*

| | 1991 | 1992 | 1993 |
|---|---|---|---|
| Immigrants | 5,040 | 6,512 | 5,924 |
| Emigrants | 20,977 | 18,115 | 21,376 |

* Figures refer to immigrants arriving for permanent residence in Poland and emigrants leaving for permanent residence abroad.

# POLAND

*Statistical Survey*

**ECONOMICALLY ACTIVE POPULATION** (sample survey, '000 persons aged 15 years and over, November 1992)

|  | Males | Females | Total |
|---|---|---|---|
| Agriculture, hunting, forestry and fishing | 2,071 | 1,687 | 3,758 |
| Mining and quarrying | | | |
| Manufacturing | 2,539 | 1,288 | 3,827 |
| Electricity, gas and water | | | |
| Construction | 868 | 128 | 995 |
| Trade, restaurants and hotels | 671 | 965 | 1,636 |
| Transport, storage and communications | 590 | 241 | 831 |
| Financing, insurance, real estate and business services | 43 | 161 | 204 |
| Community, social and personal services | 1,526 | 2,357 | 3,884 |
| **Total employed** | 8,308 | 6,827 | 15,135 |
| Unemployed | 1,172 | 1,221 | 2,394 |
| **Total labour force** | 9,481 | 8,048 | 17,529 |

Source: ILO, *Year Book of Labour Statistics*.

**November 1993** (sample survey, '000 persons aged 15 years and over, excluding armed forces): Total employed 14,772 (males 8,093, females 6,679); Unemployed 2,595 (males 1,276, females 1,319); Total labour force 17,367 (males 9,369, females 7,998).

**November 1994** (sample survey, '000 persons aged 15 years and over): Total employed 14,747 (males 8,070, females 6,677).

**CIVILIAN LABOUR FORCE EMPLOYED** ('000 persons)

|  | 1989 | 1990 | 1991 |
|---|---|---|---|
| Agriculture, hunting, forestry and fishing | 4,729.5 | 4,597.0 | 4,415.2 |
| Mining and quarrying | 614.7 | 607.9 | 480.8 |
| Manufacturing | 4,680.6 | 4,335.9 | 4,026.9 |
| Electricity, gas and water | 195.1 | 148.7 | 147.2 |
| Construction | 1,432.3 | 1,320.9 | 1,203.8 |
| Trade, restaurants and hotels | 1,787.0 | 1,652.9 | 1,750.5 |
| Transport, storage and communications | 1,303.2 | 1,127.2 | 999.7 |
| Financing, insurance, real estate and business services | 395.4 | 337.8 | 341.7 |
| Community, social and personal services | 3,066.6 | 3,084.3 | 3,099.3 |
| Activities not adequately defined | 233.6 | 339.5 | 95.2 |
| **Total** | 18,438.0 | 17,552.1 | 16,560.3 |

Source: ILO, *Year Book of Labour Statistics*.

# Agriculture

**PRINCIPAL CROPS** ('000 metric tons)

|  | 1991 | 1992 | 1993 |
|---|---|---|---|
| Wheat | 9,270 | 7,368 | 8,243 |
| Barley | 4,257 | 2,819 | 3,255 |
| Maize | 340 | 206 | 290 |
| Rye | 5,900 | 3,981 | 4,992 |
| Oats | 1,873 | 1,229 | 1,493 |
| Buckwheat and millet | 39 | 36 | 50 |
| Triticale (wheat-rye hybrid) | 2,449 | 1,711 | 1,894 |
| Mixed grain | 3,683 | 2,612 | 3,200 |
| Potatoes | 29,038 | 23,388 | 36,270 |
| Dry beans | 133 | 98 | 107 |
| Other pulses | 547 | 500 | 532 |
| Rapeseed | 1,043 | 758 | 594 |
| Cabbages | 1,848 | 1,286 | 1,954 |
| Tomatoes | 450 | 404 | 363 |
| Cauliflowers | 254 | 198 | 256 |
| Cucumbers and gherkins | 463 | 395 | 377 |
| Onions (dry) | 670 | 539 | 724 |
| Carrots | 842 | 672 | 931 |
| Beets | 533 | 449 | 594 |
| Other vegetables and melons* | 1,062 | 880 | 938 |
| Sugar beets | 11,412 | 11,052 | 15,621 |
| Apples | 1,145 | 1,569 | 1,842 |
| Pears | 53 | 67 | 89 |
| Plums | 67 | 98 | 99 |
| Cherries (incl. sour) | 96 | 145 | 179 |
| Strawberries | 262.6 | 204.5 | 200.0 |
| Raspberries | 31.7 | 28.1 | 32.5 |
| Currants | 169.2 | 213.4 | 195.7 |
| Gooseberries | 41 | 45 | 47 |
| Tobacco (leaves) | 57 | 45 | 36 |

* Including all vegetables grown under glass ('000 metric tons): 282 in 1991; 265 in 1992; 263 in 1993.

Source: partly FAO, *Production Yearbook*.

**LIVESTOCK** ('000 head in June)

|  | 1991 | 1992 | 1993 |
|---|---|---|---|
| Horses | 939 | 900 | 841 |
| Cattle | 8,844 | 8,221 | 7,643 |
| Pigs | 21,868 | 22,086 | 18,860 |
| Sheep | 3,234 | 1,870 | 1,268 |
| Chickens* | 50,202 | 45,623 | 44,292 |
| Ducks* | 7,412 | 7,298 | 7,275 |
| Geese* | 1,021 | 912 | 867 |
| Turkeys* | 808 | 847 | 896 |

* At 31 December.

**LIVESTOCK PRODUCTS** ('000 metric tons)

|  | 1991 | 1992 | 1993 |
|---|---|---|---|
| Beef and veal | 663 | 544 | 484* |
| Mutton and lamb | 33 | 23 | 13* |
| Pig meat | 1,947 | 2,036 | 1,995* |
| Horse meat | 4 | 4 | 4† |
| Poultry meat | 333 | 322 | 305 |
| Other meat | 22 | 21 | 22 |
| Edible offals | 185 | 169 | 154† |
| Cows' milk | 14,442 | 13,153 | 12,680* |
| Sheep's milk | 6 | 4 | 4† |
| Cheese | 294.4 | 288.3 | 293.4 |
| Butter | 220* | 180 | 165* |
| Poultry eggs | 361.8 | 340.0 | 344.7* |
| Honey | 14.1 | 12.9 | 12.9† |
| Wool: | | | |
| greasy | 10.7 | 6.6 | 4.5† |
| scoured | 6.4 | 4.0 | 2.7† |
| Cattle hides† | 69 | 57 | 50 |
| Sheepskins† | 5.7 | 3.9 | 1.6 |

* Unofficial figure.   † FAO estimate(s).

Source: FAO, mainly *Production Yearbook*.

POLAND  *Statistical Survey*

## Forestry

**ROUNDWOOD REMOVALS** ('000 cubic metric metres, excluding bark)

|  | 1990 | 1991 | 1992 |
|---|---|---|---|
| Sawlogs, veneer logs and logs for sleepers | 8,673 | 7,886 | 9,126 |
| Pulpwood | 4,740 | 4,324 | 6,016 |
| Other industrial wood | 2,136 | 2,123 | 2,123* |
| Fuel wood | 2,224 | 2,848 | 3,213 |
| **Total** | 17,773 | 17,181 | 20,478 |

* FAO estimate.
Source: FAO, *Yearbook of Forest Products*.
**1993** ('000 cubic metres): Pulpwood 6,296.

**SAWNWOOD PRODUCTION**
('000 cubic metres, including railway sleepers)

|  | 1990 | 1991 | 1992 |
|---|---|---|---|
| Coniferous (softwood) | 3,399 | 2,644 | 2,503 |
| Broadleaved (hardwood) | 730 | 561 | 454 |
| **Total** | 4,129 | 3,205 | 2,957 |

Source: FAO, *Yearbook of Forest Products*.

## Fishing

('000 metric tons, live weight)

|  | 1990 | 1991 | 1992 |
|---|---|---|---|
| Common carp | 22.0 | 25.0 | 25.0 |
| Atlantic cod | 28.8 | 25.8 | 13.3 |
| Alaska (Walleye) pollack | 223.5 | 230.6 | 297.7 |
| Southern blue whiting | 50.6 | 24.8 | 15.2 |
| Atlantic herring | 60.9 | 46.0 | 52.9 |
| European sprat | 14.3 | 23.2 | 30.1 |
| Other fishes (incl. unspecified) | 40.1 | 39.3 | 36.7 |
| **Total fish** | 440.1 | 414.6 | 470.9 |
| Antarctic krill | 1.3 | 9.6 | 8.6 |
| Squids | 31.6 | 33.2 | 26.2 |
| **Total catch** | 473.0 | 457.4 | 505.7 |
| Inland waters | 45.0 | 48.0 | 51.0 |
| Atlantic Ocean | 200.8 | 172.9 | 156.1 |
| Pacific Ocean | 227.2 | 236.5 | 298.7 |

Source: FAO, *Yearbook of Fishery Statistics*.
**1993** ('000 metric tons): Freshwater fishing 34; Sea fishing 360.

## Mining

('000 metric tons, unless otherwise indicated)

|  | 1991 | 1992 | 1993 |
|---|---|---|---|
| Hard coal | 140,376 | 131,531 | 130,479 |
| Lignite | 69,406 | 66,852 | 68,105 |
| Crude petroleum | 158 | 199 | 235 |
| Salt (unrefined) | 3,840 | 3,887 | 3,817 |
| Native sulphur (per 100%) | 3,935 | 2,917 | 1,893 |
| Copper ore (metric tons)[1,2] | 381,700 | 332,000 | 382,500 |
| Lead ore (metric tons)[1,2,3] | 47,300 | 51,000 | 49,000 |
| Magnesite—crude (metric tons)[1] | 8,100 | n.a. | n.a. |
| Silver (metric tons)[2] | 899 | 798 | n.a. |
| Zinc ore (metric tons)[1,2,3] | 144,700 | n.a. | n.a. |
| Natural gas (million cu metres) | 4,132 | 4,019 | 4,949 |

[1] Source: UN, *Industrial Statistics Yearbook* and *Monthly Bulletin of Statistics*.
[2] Figures refer to the metal content of ores.
[3] Estimated by Metallgesellschaft Aktiengesellschaft, Frankfurt am Main.

## Industry

**SELECTED PRODUCTS** (metric tons, unless otherwise indicated)

|  | 1991 | 1992 | 1993 |
|---|---|---|---|
| Sausages and smoked meat | 676,000 | 669,000 | 676,000 |
| Refined sugar ('000 metric tons) | 1,636 | 1,468 | 1,982 |
| Margarine | 194,000 | 234,000 | 276,000 |
| Wine and mead ('000 hectolitres) | 2,970 | 2,290 | 2,470 |
| Beer ('000 hectolitres) | 13,633 | 14,100 | 12,600 |
| Cigarettes (million) | 90,400 | 86,600 | 99,700 |
| Cotton yarn[1] | 73,200 | 84,400 | 94,300 |
| Woven cotton fabrics ('000 metres)[2] | 286,200 | 239,000 | 229,000 |
| Flax and hemp yarn[1] | 9,500 | 9,600 | 9,400 |
| Linen and hemp fabrics ('000 metres)[2] | 26,600 | 20,300 | 18,800 |
| Wool yarn[1] | 37,400 | 33,800 | 35,800 |
| Woven woollen fabrics ('000 metres)[2] | 44,323 | 32,900 | 31,800 |
| Cellulosic continuous filaments | 8,100 | n.a. | n.a. |
| Cellulosic staple and tow | 25,500 | 22,000 | 23,500 |
| Leather footwear ('000 pairs) | 28,538 | 22,800 | 20,900 |
| Mechanical wood pulp | 84,200 | 83,700 | 77,300 |
| Chemical wood pulp | 509,000 | 567,000 | 597,000 |
| Newsprint ('000 metric tons) | 64.2 | 60.8 | 46.2 |
| Other paper ('000 metric tons) | 885 | 970 | 1,024 |
| Paperboard | 111,000 | 116,000 | 114,000 |
| Synthetic rubber | 79,500 | 88,900 | 75,100 |
| Rubber tyres ('000)[3] | 4,516 | 5,607 | 6,479 |
| Ethyl alcohol ('000 hectolitres) | 1,766 | n.a. | n.a. |
| Sulphuric acid—100% ('000 metric tons) | 1,088 | 1,244 | 1,145 |
| Nitric acid—100% ('000 metric tons) | 1,438 | 1,388 | 1,608 |
| Caustic soda—96% | 324,000 | 326,000 | 296,000 |
| Soda ash—98% | 962,000 | 929,000 | 815,000 |
| Nitrogenous fertilizers (a) ('000 metric tons)[4] | 1,148 | 1,167 | 1,224 |
| Phosphate fertilizers (b) ('000 metric tons)[4] | 253 | 329 | 282 |
| Plastics and synthetic resins | 596,000 | 650,000 | 671,000 |
| Motor spirit—Petrol ('000 metric tons)[5] | 3,307 | 4,091 | 4,547 |
| Distillate fuel oils ('000 metric tons) | 3,694 | 4,333 | 4,920 |
| Residual fuel oils ('000 metric tons) | 2,655 | 2,578 | 2,728 |
| Coke-oven coke ('000 metric tons) | 11,316 | 11,036 | 10,275 |
| Gas coke ('000 metric tons) | 55 | 27 | 7 |
| Cement ('000 metric tons) | 12,012 | 11,908 | 12,200 |
| Pig-iron ('000 metric tons)[6] | 6,515 | 6,498 | 6,298 |
| Crude steel ('000 metric tons) | 10,432 | 9,866 | 9,939 |
| Rolled steel products ('000 metric tons) | 8,036 | 7,550 | 7,632 |
| Aluminium—unwrought[7] | 45,793 | 43,628 | 46,942 |
| Refined copper—unwrought | 378,479 | 387,010 | 404,170 |
| Refined lead—unwrought | 50,800 | 53,700 | 62,300 |
| Zinc—unwrought[7] | 126,067 | 134,594 | 149,107 |
| Radio receivers ('000) | 589 | 334 | 329 |
| Television receivers ('000) | 438 | 652 | 855 |
| Merchant ships launched (gross reg. tons) | 219,000 | 341,000 | 385,000 |
| Passenger motor cars (number) | 168,791 | 218,808 | 335,175 |
| Lorries (number) | 21,625 | 19,850 | 20,193 |
| Domestic washing machines (number) | 336,000 | 363,000 | 402,000 |

POLAND

*Statistical Survey*

| — continued | 1991 | 1992 | 1993 |
|---|---|---|---|
| Domestic refrigerators (number) | 553,000 | 500,000 | 588,000 |
| Construction: dwellings completed (number) | 136,790 | 132,969 | 94,449 |
| Electric energy (million kWh) | 134,715 | 132,750 | 133,863 |
| Manufactured gas: from gasworks (million cu metres) | 27.3 | 21.4 | 14.0 |
| from cokeries (million cu metres) | 4,702 | 4,563 | 4,077 |

[1] Pure and mixed yarns. Cotton includes tyre cord yarn.
[2] Pure and mixed fabrics, after undergoing finishing processes. Cotton and wool include substitutes.
[3] Tyres for passenger motor cars and commercial vehicles, including inner tubes and tyres for animal-drawn road vehicles, and tyres for non-agricultural machines and equipment.
[4] Fertilizer production is measured in terms of (*a*) nitrogen or (*b*) phosphoric acid. Phosphate fertilizers include ground rock phosphate.
[5] Including synthetic products.
[6] Including blast-furnace ferro-alloys.
[7] Figures refer to both primary and secondary metal. Zinc production includes zinc dust and remelted zinc.

# Finance

**CURRENCY AND EXCHANGE RATES**
**Monetary Units**
100 groszy (singular: grosz) = 1 złoty.

**Sterling and Dollar Equivalents** (31 December 1994)
£1 sterling = 38,130 złotys;
US $1 = 24,372 złotys;
100,000 złotys = £2.623 = $4.103.

**Average Exchange Rate** (złotys per US dollar)
1992  13,626
1993  18,115
1994  22,723

Note: On 1 January 1995 Poland introduced a new złoty, equivalent to 10,000 of the former units. Figures in this Survey are still in terms of old złotys.

**STATE BUDGET** ('000 million old złotys)

| Revenue | 1991 | 1992 | 1993 |
|---|---|---|---|
| Domestic revenue | 210,780.7 | 312,615.1 | 458,950.3 |
| Taxation | 163,173.4 | 246,154.8 | 369,621.4 |
| Turnover tax | 61,195.7 | 103,099.1 | 94,094.8 |
| Value-added tax | — | — | 51,290.8 |
| Excises | — | — | 31,203.2 |
| Taxes on earnings | 53,761.4 | 122,880.9 | 181,995.5 |
| Tax on salary increases | 27,098.2 | 16,988.3 | 9,986.7 |
| Other current revenue | 45,897.9 | 61,615.9 | 81,525.2 |
| Customs duties | 17,050.2 | 26,773.8 | 43,832.3 |
| Receipts from privatization | 1,709.4 | 4,844.4 | 7,803.7 |
| External revenue | 104.4 | 160.3 | 57.6 |
| **Total** | 210,885.1 | 312,775.4 | 459,007.9 |

| Expenditure | 1991 | 1992 | 1993 |
|---|---|---|---|
| Science | 6,128.6 | 7,404.4 | 8,928.1 |
| Education and care of children | 28,128.4 | 39,695.4 | 51,748.2 |
| Higher education | 6,649.7 | 10,109.9 | 12,696.1 |
| Health care | 38,854.1 | 56,734.4 | 71,321.4 |
| Social welfare | 13,290.4 | 26,395.2 | 32,857.5 |
| State administration | 7,043.7 | 10,222.3 | 16,009.8 |
| Public safety | 8,493.2 | 14,344.8 | 20,437.5 |
| Finance | 20,259.1 | 54,941.2 | 74,862.7 |
| Social insurance | 36,393.9 | 73,453.1 | 104,207.3 |
| National defence | 18,071.2 | 25,364.8 | 33,090.2 |
| Subsidies | 22,025.1 | 19,839.9 | 19,564.9 |
| **Total** (incl. others) | 241,857.7 | 381,890.2 | 502,428.3 |
| Current | 225,069.6 | 362,388.6 | 477,651.5 |
| Capital | 16,788.1 | 19,501.6 | 24,776.8 |

**INTERNATIONAL RESERVES** (US $ million at 31 December)

| | 1992 | 1993 | 1994 |
|---|---|---|---|
| Gold* | 189.0 | 189.0 | 189.0 |
| IMF special drawing rights | 1.1 | 0.7 | 1.5 |
| Reserve positition in IMF | 106.1 | 105.9 | 112.6 |
| Foreign exchange | 3,992.0 | 3,985.3 | 5,727.7 |
| **Total** | 4,288.1 | 4,280.9 | 6,030.8 |

* National valuation (US $400 per troy ounce).
Source: National Bank of Poland.

**MONEY SUPPLY** ('000 million old złotys at 31 December)

| | 1992 | 1993 | 1994 |
|---|---|---|---|
| Currency outside banks | 77,984 | 99,824 | 122,738 |
| Demand deposits at commercial banks | 70,957 | 96,536 | 151,755 |
| **Total money** (incl. others) | 149,627 | 196,460 | 274,501 |

Source: IMF, National Bank of Poland.

**COST OF LIVING** (Consumer Price Index; base: 1980 = 100)

| | 1991 | 1992 | 1993 |
|---|---|---|---|
| Food | 37,727 | 51,611 | 68,384 |
| Fuel and light | 85,135 | 165,332 | 243,039 |
| Clothing | 25,961 | 36,294 | 49,214 |
| Rent | 74,332 | 118,634 | 158,020 |
| **All items** (incl. others) | 38,082 | 54,458 | 73,681 |

Source: ILO, *Year Book of Labour Statistics*.

**NATIONAL ACCOUNTS** ('000 million old złotys at current prices)
**Expenditure on the Gross Domestic Product**

| | 1991 | 1992 | 1993 |
|---|---|---|---|
| Government final consumption expenditure | 183,327 | 247,888 | 318,338 |
| Private final consumption expenditure | 480,009 | 709,553 | 982,000 |
| Increase in stocks | 3,279 | -18,597 | -5,202 |
| Gross fixed capital formation | 157,748 | 192,966 | 247,485 |
| **Total domestic expenditure** | 824,363 | 1,131,811 | 1,542,621 |
| Exports of goods and services | 190,257 | 272,418 | 357,326 |
| *Less* Imports of goods and services | 205,791 | 254,787 | 342,147 |
| **GDP in purchasers' values** | 808,829 | 1,149,442 | 1,557,800 |
| **GDP at constant 1990 prices** | 521,206 | 534,889 | 555,159 |

**Gross Domestic Product by Economic Activity**

| | 1992 | 1993 |
|---|---|---|
| Industry* | 395,670 | 509,361 |
| Construction | 82,527 | 91,743 |
| Agriculture | 73,397 | 98,617 |
| Forestry | 5,746 | 6,689 |
| Transport | 41,204 | 53,739 |
| Communications | 19,649 | 27,508 |
| Trade | 143,644 | 220,101 |
| Other activities of the material sphere | 38,141 | 31,801 |
| Community services | 24,159 | 30,314 |
| Other non-material services | 301,059 | 373,263 |
| **Sub-total** | 1,125,196 | 1,443,136 |
| Import duties | 46,836 | 70,343 |
| Value-added tax | — | 51,291 |
| *Less* Imputed bank service charge | 22,590 | 6,970 |
| **GDP in purchasers' values** | 1,149,442 | 1,557,800 |

* Principally manufacturing, mining, sea fishing, electricity, gas and water.

## POLAND

### BALANCE OF PAYMENTS (US $ million)

|  | 1991 | 1992 | 1993 |
|---|---|---|---|
| Merchandise exports f.o.b. | 14,393 | 13,929 | 13,582 |
| Merchandise imports f.o.b. | −15,104 | −14,060 | −17,087 |
| **Trade balance** | **−711** | **−131** | **−3,505** |
| Exports of services | 3,687 | 4,773 | 4,201 |
| Imports of services | −2,994 | −4,045 | −3,631 |
| Other income received | 573 | 728 | 579 |
| Other income paid | −3,469 | −4,895 | −4,192 |
| Private unrequited transfers (net) | 723 | 213 | 621 |
| Official unrequited transfers (net) | 45 | 253 | 139 |
| **Current balance** | **−2,146** | **−3,104** | **−5,788** |
| Direct investment (net) | 298 | 665 | 1,697 |
| Other capital (net) | −4,481 | −1,710 | 644 |
| Net errors and omissions | −767 | −148 | −106 |
| **Overall balance** | **−7,096** | **−4,297** | **−3,553** |

Source: IMF, *International Financial Statistics*.

## External Trade

### PRINCIPAL COMMODITIES ('000 million old złotys)

| Imports c.i.f. | 1991 | 1992 | 1993 |
|---|---|---|---|
| **Fuels and power** | 31,182.2 | 36,979.1 | 42,796.3 |
| Crude petroleum and natural gas | 24,401.5 | 29,038.2 | 34,879.0 |
| Petroleum products and synthetic liquid fuels | 6,452.7 | 7,585.0 | 7,439.8 |
| **Products of metallurgical industry** | 7,088.3 | 9,933.0 | 15,760.2 |
| **Electro-engineering products** | 62,292.1 | 78,201.3 | 116,975.7 |
| Metal products | 4,983.0 | 8,594.5 | 13,677.0 |
| Machinery and equipment for textile industry and food-manufacturing | 4,497.8 | 5,305.2 | 6,194.3 |
| Precision instruments and apparatus | 9,488.0 | 14,809.2 | 22,768.0 |
| Transport equipment | 13,194.8 | 9,455.7 | 16,717.2 |
| Electric and electrical engineering products | 14,137.0 | 14,762.6 | 23,260.0 |
| **Chemical products** | 20,973.5 | 38,359.8 | 59,552.7 |
| Organic chemicals | 2,937.0 | 6,439.3 | 10,006.3 |
| Pharmaceutical products | 4,703.8 | 7,186.7 | 11,938.3 |
| Articles of synthetic plastic | 3,167.2 | 6,087.8 | 11,004.4 |
| **Non-metallic mineral products** | 2,912.4 | 4,994.9 | 7,091.5 |
| **Products of wood and paper industry** | 7,837.0 | 8,988.4 | 12,082.9 |
| Paper and paper products | 3,023.5 | 5,556.6 | 8,988.4 |
| **Textiles, clothing and leather products** | 10,182.6 | 9,843.9 | 34,029.8 |
| Cotton textile products | 2,296.6 | 2,218.5 | 7,944.7 |
| **Products of food industry** | 17,489.7 | 18,738.9 | 26,023.5 |
| **Agricultural products (unprocessed)** | 5,152.8 | 7,872.5 | 14,192.9 |
| **Total** (incl. others) | 166,743.8 | 219,950.3 | 340,183.1 |

| Exports f.o.b. | 1991 | 1992 | 1993 |
|---|---|---|---|
| **Fuels and power** | 16,803.8 | 18,990.1 | 24,536.8 |
| Hard coal | 9,797.3 | 12,526.1 | 17,697.5 |
| **Products of metallurgical industry** | 25,128.7 | 30,172.3 | 37,589.0 |
| Rolled iron and steel products | 8,648.0 | 7,308.9 | 12,837.9 |
| Non-ferrous metals | 8,963.3 | 11,167.6 | 14,509.7 |
| **Electro-engineering products** | 35,338.5 | 43,659.4 | 66,492.5 |
| Metal products | 5,687.1 | 8,911.6 | 12,402.9 |
| Transport equipment | 8,849.1 | 14,365.2 | 27,529.6 |
| Road motor vehicles | 1,623.8 | 5,565.9 | 11,954.5 |
| Ships and boats | 4,460.5 | 6,279.3 | 12,227.0 |
| **Chemical products** | 18,273.0 | 21,800.0 | 25,182.9 |
| Organic chemicals | 3,453.9 | 5,185.2 | 5,988.5 |
| **Non-metallic mineral products** | 5,383.6 | 5,683.2 | 8,412.3 |

| Exports f.o.b. — *continued* | 1991 | 1992 | 1993 |
|---|---|---|---|
| **Products of wood and paper industry** | 10,316.6 | 13,704.5 | 21,316.5 |
| Wood products | 8,946.1 | 11,464.3 | 18,233.8 |
| Furniture and joinery | 3,788.0 | 5,403.5 | 10,344.3 |
| **Textiles, clothing and leather products** | 9,639.2 | 15,261.4 | 39,437.0 |
| Knitted goods and hosiery | 1,382.1 | 2,672.4 | 5,156.3 |
| Clothing | 4,468.1 | 6,925.8 | 25,326.3 |
| Textile clothing | 3,170.1 | 5,761.1 | 22,222.1 |
| **Products of food industry** | 15,762.3 | 17,614.5 | 23,350.5 |
| Dairy produce | 2,898.8 | 3,611.9 | 4,717.6 |
| Preparations of fruit, vegetables and mushrooms | 3,048.2 | 4,683.9 | 6,196.3 |
| **Construction** | 7,549.8 | — | — |
| **Agricultural products (unprocessed)** | 10,362.6 | 9,667.6 | 7,801.7 |
| Field crops | 4,350.6 | 4,515.2 | 1,474.5 |
| Products of animal husbandry | 4,094.5 | 3,296.3 | 3,407.8 |
| Livestock, poultry and insects | 4,031.6 | 3,111.9 | 3,143.6 |
| **Total** (incl. others) | 157,715.9 | 179,687.1 | 257,568.4 |

**1994** ('000 million old złotys): Total imports c.i.f. 486,300; Total exports f.o.b. 387,670 (Source: IMF, *International Financial Statistics*).

### PRINCIPAL TRADING PARTNERS ('000 million old złotys)*

| Imports c.i.f. | 1991† | 1992 | 1993 |
|---|---|---|---|
| Austria | 10,335.9 | 9,870 | 11,035 |
| Belarus | n.a. | 2,256 | 2,034 |
| Belgium | 4,376.7 | 5,394 | 7,722 |
| China, People's Republic | 454.6 | 2,224 | 4,094 |
| Czech Republic | n.a. | n.a. | 6,329 |
| Czechoslovakia | 5,487.4 | 6,941 | — |
| Denmark | 3,486.5 | 4,644 | 8,255 |
| Finland | 1,738.7 | 5,189 | 6,870 |
| France | 5,951.7 | 9,804 | 14,439 |
| Germany | 43,596.8 | 52,582 | 95,297 |
| Iran | 4,461.1 | 5,451 | 5,397 |
| Italy | 7,323.3 | 15,236 | 26,462 |
| Japan | 2,650.8 | 4,615 | 5,944 |
| Netherlands | 8,115.4 | 10,386 | 15,866 |
| Norway | 2,642.9 | 4,883 | 6,436 |
| Russia | n.a. | 18,702 | 23,098 |
| Spain | 1,537.1 | 2,640 | 4,566 |
| Sweden | 2,901.4 | 4,206 | 7,680 |
| Switzerland | 5,649.7 | 4,084 | 5,703 |
| USSR | 23,193.1 | — | — |
| United Kingdom | 6,531.1 | 14,732 | 19,662 |
| USA | 3,716.7 | 7,473 | 17,413 |
| **Total** (incl. others) | 164,259.3 | 219,950 | 340,183 |

| Exports f.o.b. | 1991 | 1992 | 1993 |
|---|---|---|---|
| Austria | 7,162.4 | 5,748 | 6,159 |
| Belarus | n.a. | 2,166 | 1,860 |
| Belgium | 3,163.9 | 4,760 | 6,654 |
| China, People's Republic | 426.7 | 687 | 2,894 |
| Czech Republic | n.a. | n.a. | 6,217 |
| Czechoslovakia | 7,284.2 | 6,854 | — |
| Denmark | 3,657.5 | 4,511 | 7,635 |
| Finland | 2,312.3 | 3,550 | 3,623 |
| France | 5,969.7 | 6,552 | 10,753 |
| Germany | 46,427.9 | 56,488 | 93,507 |
| Hungary | 1,161.6 | 2,333 | 3,178 |
| Italy | 6,466.5 | 9,980 | 13,427 |
| Netherlands | 8,172.4 | 10,752 | 15,145 |
| Norway | 955.2 | 2,123 | 1,401 |
| Russia | n.a. | 9,925 | 11,923 |
| Slovakia | n.a. | n.a. | 2,995 |
| Sweden | 4,146.9 | 4,474 | 5,644 |
| Switzerland | 7,031.8 | 2,475 | 3,298 |
| USSR | 17,311.7 | — | — |
| United Kingdom | 11,210.8 | 7,704 | 11,086 |
| USA | 3,923.9 | 4,149 | 7,539 |
| Yugoslavia (former) | 2,153.6 | n.a. | n.a. |
| **Total** (incl. others) | 157,715.9 | 179,687 | 257,568 |

* Imports by country of purchase; exports by country of sale.
† Imports f.o.b.

POLAND

*Statistical Survey*

## Transport

**POLISH STATE RAILWAYS** (traffic)

|  | 1991 | 1992 | 1993 |
|---|---|---|---|
| Paying passengers ('000 journeys) | 651,991 | 549,302 | 541,089* |
| Freight ('000 metric tons) | 227,797 | 201,663 | 214,212 |
| Passenger-kilometres (million) | 40,115 | 32,571 | 30,865* |
| Freight ton-kilometres (million) | 65,146 | 57,763 | 64,359 |

* Including passengers travelling free of charge.

**ROAD TRAFFIC** (motor vehicles registered at 31 December)

|  | 1991 | 1992 | 1993 |
|---|---|---|---|
| Passenger cars | 6,112,171 | 6,504,716 | 6,770,557 |
| Goods vehicles* | 1,151,000 | 1,212,058 | 1,235,200 |
| Buses and coaches | 86,951 | 86,258 | 86,154 |
| Motorcycles and scooters | 1,235,640 | 1,134,366 | 1,067,634 |

* Including non-agricultural tractors.

**INLAND WATERWAYS** (traffic)

|  | 1991 | 1992 | 1993 |
|---|---|---|---|
| Passengers carried ('000) | 975 | 667 | 606 |
| Freight ('000 metric tons) | 7,828 | 7,875 | 8,720 |
| Passenger-kilometres (million) | 21 | 15 | 13 |
| Freight ton-kilometres (million) | 737 | 750 | 661 |

**MERCHANT SHIPPING FLEET** (at 30 June)

|  | 1991 | 1992 | 1993 |
|---|---|---|---|
| Number of vessels | 673 | 635 | 591 |
| Displacement ('000 gross registered tons) | 3,348 | 3,109 | 2,646 |

Source: Lloyd's Register of Shipping.

**SEA TRANSPORT** (Polish merchant ships only)

|  | 1991 | 1992 | 1993 |
|---|---|---|---|
| Passengers carried ('000) | 573 | 680 | 630 |
| Freight ('000 metric tons) | 27,563 | 26,953 | 23,869 |
| Passenger-kilometres (million) | 195 | 214 | 189 |
| Freight ton-kilometres (million) | 202,281 | 193,086 | 155,092 |

**INTERNATIONAL SEA-BORNE SHIPPING AT POLISH PORTS**

|  | 1991 | 1992 | 1993 |
|---|---|---|---|
| Vessels entered ('000 net reg. tons) | 26,795 | 30,229 | 32,344 |
| Passengers (number): |  |  |  |
| Arrivals | 270,185 | 281,498 | 310,677 |
| Departures | 255,505 | 319,139 | 322,458 |
| Cargo* ('000 metric tons): |  |  |  |
| Loaded† | 26,899 | 28,868 | n.a. |
| Unloaded† | 13,877 | 16,774 | n.a. |

* Including ships' bunkers.   † Including transhipments.

**CIVIL AVIATION**

**Polish Airlines—'LOT'** (scheduled and non-scheduled flights)

|  | 1991 | 1992 | 1993 |
|---|---|---|---|
| Passengers carried ('000) | 1,208 | 1,254.3 | 1,405.3 |
| Passenger-kilometres (million) | 3,589 | 3,577.3 | 3,653.4 |
| Cargo (metric tons) | 11,000 | 12,674 | 15,017 |
| Cargo ton-kilometres ('000) | 45,000 | 51,900 | 54,919 |

Source: Ministry of Transport and Maritime Economy.

## Tourism

**FOREIGN TOURIST ARRIVALS** ('000, including visitors in transit)

| Country of Residence | 1991 | 1992 | 1993 |
|---|---|---|---|
| Belarus | n.a. | n.a. | 1,660.6 |
| Czech Republic | n.a. | n.a. | 5,625.1 |
| Czechoslovakia | 6,101.9 | 8,257.6 | — |
| Germany | 20,885.4 | 30,687.7 | 42,574.0 |
| Lithuania | n.a. | n.a. | 1,343.8 |
| Russia | n.a. | n.a. | 1,546.8 |
| Slovakia | n.a. | n.a. | 2,418.2 |
| Ukraine | n.a. | n.a. | 2,301.6 |
| USSR (former) | 7,545.5 | 7,788.8 | n.a. |
| **Total** (incl. others) | 36,845.8 | 49,015.0 | 60,951.2 |

## Communications Media

|  | 1991 | 1992 | 1993 |
|---|---|---|---|
| Radio licences ('000)* | 10,783 | 10,917 | 10,900 |
| Television licences ('000)* | 9,809 | 10,043 | 10,111 |
| Telephones ('000 main lines in use)* | 3,565 | 3,938 | 4,416 |
| Book production†: |  |  |  |
| Titles | 10,688 | 10,727 | 9,788 |
| Copies ('000) | 125,509 | 125,821 | 102,533 |
| Daily newspapers: |  |  |  |
| Number | 68 | 72 | 71 |
| Average circulation ('000 copies) | 5,258 | 6,085 | 6,381 |
| Non-daily newspapers: |  |  |  |
| Number | 54 | 57 | 53 |
| Average circulation ('000 copies) | 1,604 | 1,856 | 1,710 |
| Other periodicals: |  |  |  |
| Number | 2,968 | 2,950 | 3,139 |
| Average circulation ('000 copies) | 48,710 | 54,703 | 56,440 |

* At 31 December.
† Including pamphlets (1,776 titles and 18,318,000 copies in 1991; 1,555 titles and 18,406,000 copies in 1992; 1,290 titles and 9,737,000 copies in 1993).

## Education

(1993/94)

|  | Institutions | Teachers ('000) | Students ('000) |
|---|---|---|---|
| Pre-primary | 21,055 | 74.6 | 979.1 |
| Primary | 16,621 | 310.8 | 5,178.1 |
| Secondary (General) | 1,561 | 29.5 | 601.9 |
| Technical, art and vocational | 9,655 | 85.6 | 1,801.8 |
| Higher | 140 | 65.3 | 584.0 |

# Directory

## The Constitution

The Constitution that had been adopted on 22 July 1952 was amended in 1989, to incorporate reforms such as the establishment of an upper legislative chamber, and again in 1990, to permit the holding of direct presidential elections. In April 1992 the procedural law for the drafting of a new constitution was approved by the Sejm. In December 1992 an interim 'Small Constitution' came into force, designed principally to regulate relations between the legislative and executive authorities, pending a full revision of the Constitution, which was initiated in November 1992. The following is a summary of the provisions of the amended 1952 Constitution:

### STATE AUTHORITIES

The Sejm consists of 460 deputies, elected for a four-year term, subject to dissolution. Its prerogatives include the adoption of laws; the adoption of the national socio-economic plans and state financial plans; the appointment and recall of the Chairman of the Council of Ministers (at the motion of the President); the appointment and recall of the members of the Council of Ministers (at the motion of the Chairman presented in conjunction with the President or on the Chairman's own initiative); the appointment of the Civil Rights Ombudsman (with consent of the Senate); the adoption of a resolution concerning a state of war; the expression of consent for prolongation (at most for three months) of a state of emergency imposed by the President (consent for such a decision must also be given by the Senate). The Speaker (Marshal) of the Sejm acts in the capacity of President if this office is vacant.

The Senate is made up of 100 members. Its term coincides with that of the Sejm, subject to dissolution. The Senate reviews the laws adopted by the Sejm; it may proffer its comments and proposals on these laws or even propose their rejection in full. The Senate can be overridden by the Sejm by a qualified majority of two-thirds. Its also reviews drafts of national socio-economic plans and financial plans of the State. It has the right of legislative initiative.

The National Assembly is the combined Sejm and Senate. It should be convened by the Sejm Speaker (Marshal) within two months of elections to the Sejm and the Senate. The National Assembly may be convened in order to declare the permanent incapacity of the President to serve his office and to consider impeaching the President in the Tribunal of State.

The President of the Republic of Poland is the highest representative of the Polish State in domestic and international relations. He is to monitor observance of the Constitution, safeguard the sovereignty and security of the State, inviolability of its territory and observance of political and military alliances entered into by the State. Any Pole aged over 35 years with full electoral rights may stand as a presidential candidate, a minimum of 100,000 signatures being required to secure nomination. The President is directly elected for a five-year term and may be re-elected only once. The President's duties include the calling of elections to the Sejm, Senate and local councils; heading the armed forces; proposing a motion in the Sejm for the appointment or recall of the Chairman of the Council of Ministers; (when necessary) imposing martial law on a segment or the entire territory of the country if such is dictated by defence considerations or an outside threat to state security (the President may announce a partial or general mobilization for the same reasons); (when necessary) introducing a state of emergency on a segment or the entire territory of the country when there is a threat to the domestic security of the State or in case of a natural disaster; the President may introduce it for a period not longer than three months and prolong it (with the consent of the Sejm and the Senate) for another three months.

The Council of Ministers is the supreme executive and managing agency of state authority, serving functions typical of the executive branch and carrying out the decisions adopted by the Sejm. It is appointed by the Sejm which may recall the entire Council of Ministers or its individual members. The Council is responsible to the Sejm and reports to it on its activities. In periods between Sejm terms, this function towards the Council is served by the President. The Council of Ministers co-ordinates actions of the entire state administration.

### CONSTITUTIONAL TRIBUNAL AND TRIBUNAL OF STATE

The Constitutional Tribunal pronounces judgment on the consistence with the Constitution of laws and other normative acts issued by the supreme and central state organs. Its decisions are binding. Members of the Tribunal are independent and are subject only to the Constitution.

The Tribunal of State pronounces judgment on the responsibility of persons holding high state positions for violation of the Constitution and laws; it can also pass judgment on penal responsibility of those persons for offences committed in connection with the positions which they have held. Its head is the first president of the Supreme Court. Judges of the Tribunal are independent and subject only to the law.

### LOCAL ORGANS OF STATE ADMINISTRATION

Poland comprises 49 voivodships, a government-appointed official supervising state administration in each area. The members of each provincial assembly are elected by local councils. Local councils are directly elected and are completely autonomous, territorial self-government being the basic form of the organization of public life in the rural community.

### COURTS AND PUBLIC PROSECUTOR'S OFFICE

The administration of justice is carried out by the Supreme Court, the Supreme Administrative Court, General Courts and Courts Martial. The Supreme Court is the highest judicial organ, and is to be appointed by the Sejm for an unlimited term.

### FUNDAMENTAL RIGHTS AND DUTIES OF CITIZENS

The Republic of Poland strengthens and extends the rights and liberties of citizens. Citizens have equal rights, irrespective of sex, origin, education, occupation, nationality, race, religion, descent or social status. Citizens have the right to work and the right to rest; the right to health protection, and the right to education. Women are guaranteed equal rights with men. Freedom of conscience is guaranteed. The Church is separated from the State. Citizens are guaranteed freedom of speech, of the press, of meetings etc.; the right to unite in public organizations; and the inviolability of the person and of the home.

### PRINCIPLES OF ELECTORAL LAW

Election to the Sejm and Senate, and to People's Councils, is universal, equal, direct and carried out by secret ballot. At the age of 18 every citizen has the right to vote, and is eligible for election to People's Councils; at the age of 21 every citizen is eligible for election to the Sejm and Senate. Candidates to the Sejm and Senate are nominated by political and social organizations uniting citizens of town and country.

### COAT-OF-ARMS, COLOURS AND CAPITAL OF THE REPUBLIC OF POLAND

The coat-of-arms of the Republic of Poland is a white eagle with a golden crown on the head, and with golden beak and claws, on a red field. The National Anthem is the *Mazurka Dabrowskiego*. The capital of the Republic of Poland is Warsaw.

## The Government

### HEAD OF STATE

**President:** LECH WAŁĘSA (sworn in 22 December 1990).

### CABINET
(June 1995)

The Government is a coalition of the Democratic Left Alliance (Sojusz Lewicy Demokratycznej—SLD), the Polish Peasant Party (Polskie Stronnictwo Ludowe—PSL) and independents.

**Prime Minister:** JÓZEF OLEKSY (SLD).

**Deputy Prime Minister and Minister of Finance:** Prof. GRZEGORZ KOŁODKO (SLD).

**Deputy Prime Minister and Head of Scientific Research Committee:** ALEKSANDER ŁUCZAK (PSL).

**Deputy Prime Minister and Minister of Agriculture:** ROMAN JAGIELIŃSKI (PSL).

**Minister-Head of the Office of the Cabinet:** MAREK BOROWSKI (SLD).

**Minister of Foreign Affairs:** WŁADYSŁAW BARTOSZEWSKI (independent).

**Minister of Internal Affairs:** ANDRZEJ MILCZANOWSKI (independent).

**Minister of National Defence:** ZBIGNIEW OKOŃSKI (independent).

POLAND                                                                                                           Directory

**Minister-Head of the Central Planning Office:** MIROSŁAW PIETREWICZ (PSL).
**Minister of Justice:** JERZY JASKIERNIA (independent).
**Minister of Foreign Economic Relations:** JACEK BUCHACZ (PSL).
**Minister of Transport and Maritime Economy:** BOGUSŁAW LIBERADZKI (independent).
**Minister of Environmental Protection, Natural Resources and Forestry:** STANISŁAW ŻELICHOWSKI (PSL).
**Minister of Labour and Social Policy:** LESZEK MILLER (SLD).
**Minister of Culture:** KAZIMIERZ DEJMAK (PSL).
**Minister of Health:** RYSZARD JACEK ŻOCHOWSKI (SLD).
**Minister of Industry and Trade:** KLEMENS ŚCIERSKI (independent).
**Minister of Regional Planning and Construction:** BARBARA BLIDA (SLD).
**Minister of Communication:** ANDRZEJ ZIELIŃSKI (independent).
**Minister of Ownership Transformation (Privatization):** WIESŁAW KACZMAREK (SLD).
**Minister of National Education:** RYSZARD CZARNY (independent).

### MINISTRIES

**Central Planning Office:** 00-507 Warsaw, Pl. Trzech Krzyży 5; tel. (2) 6935000; telex 814698.
**Office of the Prime Minister:** 00-567 Warsaw, Al. Ujazdowskie 1/3.
**Ministry of Agriculture:** 00-930 Warsaw, ul. Wspólna 30; tel. (22) 296127; telex 814597; fax (22) 212326.
**Ministry of Communication:** 00-940 Warsaw, pl. Małachowskiego 2; tel. (22) 267366; telex 813001; fax (22) 267366.
**Ministry of Culture:** 00-071 Warsaw, ul. Krakowskie Przedmieście 15/17; tel. (22) 267331; fax (22) 267533.
**Ministry of Environmental Protection, Natural Resources and Forestry:** 00-067 Warsaw, ul. Wawelska 52/54; tel. (22) 253355; telex 812816; fax (22) 253355.
**Ministry of Finance:** 00-916 Warsaw, ul. Świętokrzyska 12; tel. (22) 265595; telex 815592; fax (22) 266352.
**Ministry of Foreign Affairs:** 00-580 Warsaw, Al. Szucha 23; tel. (2) 6239000; fax (2) 6257652.
**Ministry of Foreign Economic Relations:** 00-950 Warsaw, Pl. Trzech Krzyży 5; tel. (2) 6935000; telex 814501; fax (22) 286808.
**Ministry of Health:** 00-923 Warsaw, ul. Miodowa 15; tel. (22) 312144; telex 817441; fax (2) 6359245.
**Ministry of Industry and Trade:** 00-926 Warsaw, ul. Wspólna 4; tel. (22) 210351; telex 814261; fax (22) 295043.
**Ministry of Internal Affairs:** 00-904 Warsaw, ul. Rakowiecka 2B; tel. (22) 210251; telex 813681.
**Ministry of Justice:** 00-950 Warsaw, Al. Ujazdowskie 11; tel. (2) 6284431; telex 813891; fax (22) 281692.
**Ministry of Labour and Social Policy:** 00-513 Warsaw, ul. Nowogrodzka 1/3/5; tel. (2) 6289041; telex 814710; fax (22) 296750.
**Ministry of National Defence:** 00-909 Warsaw, Któlewska 1; tel. and fax (22) 260586.
**Ministry of National Education:** 00-918 Warsaw, Al. Szucha 25; tel. (22) 297241; telex 813523; fax (2) 6288561.
**Ministry of Ownership Transformation (Privatization):** 00-522 Warsaw, ul. Krucza 36; tel. (2) 6280281; fax (22) 213361.
**Ministry of Regional Planning and Construction:** 00-926 Warsaw, ul. Wspólna 2; tel. (22) 212725; telex 814411; fax (2) 6284030.
**Ministry of Transport and Maritime Economy:** 00-928 Warsaw, ul. Chałubińskiego 4/6; tel. (22) 215676; telex 813614; fax (22) 219968.

## President and Legislature

### PRESIDENT
**Elections, 25 November and 9 December 1990**

|  | First ballot | Second ballot |  |
|---|---|---|---|
| LECH WAŁĘSA | 6,569,889 | 10,622,696 | (74.25%) |
| STANISŁAW TYMIŃSKI | 3,797,605 | 3,683,098 | (25.75%) |
| TADEUSZ MAZOWIECKI | 2,973,264 | — |  |
| WŁODZIMIERZ CIMOSZEWICZ | 1,514,025 | — |  |
| ROMAN BARTOSZCZE | 1,176,175 | — |  |
| LESZEK MOCZULSKI | 411,516 | — |  |

### ZGROMADZENIE NARODOWE
(National Assembly)

#### Senat (Senate)
**Marshal:** ADAM STRUZIK.

**Election, 19 September 1993**

| Parties and alliances | Votes ('000) | % of votes | Seats |
|---|---|---|---|
| Democratic Left Alliance* | 2,593.0 | 34.3 | 37 |
| Polish Peasant Party | 1,956.0 | 25.9 | 36 |
| Solidarity | 1,004.1 | 13.3 | 10 |
| Democratic Union† | 607.6 | 8.0 | 4 |
| Non-Party Bloc for Reform | 557.2 | 7.4 | 2 |
| Union of Labour | 163.8 | 2.2 | 2 |
| Liberal Democratic Congress† | 117.8 | 1.6 | 1 |
| Socio-Cultural Associations of the German Minority‡ | 69.6 | 0.9 | 1 |
| Others | 485.0 | 6.4 | 7 |
| **Total** | **7,554.1** | **100.0** | **100** |

* An electoral coalition of Social Democracy of the Republic of Poland and the All Poland Trade Unions Alliance.
† Merged in 1994 to form the Freedom Union.
‡ Including the German Minority of Lower Silesia and the Socio-Cultural Association of Germans of Upper Silesia.

#### Sejm
**Marshal:** JÓZEF ZYCH.
**Deputy Marshal:** OLGA KRZYZANOWSKA.

**Election, 19 September 1993**

| Parties and alliances | Votes ('000) | % of votes | Seats |
|---|---|---|---|
| Democratic Left Alliance* | 2,815.2 | 20.4 | 171 |
| Polish Peasant Party | 2,124.4 | 15.4 | 132 |
| Democratic Union† | 1,461.0 | 10.6 | 74 |
| Union of Labour | 1,005.0 | 7.3 | 41 |
| Catholic Electoral Committee 'Homeland'§ | 878.4 | 6.4 | — |
| Confederation for an Independent Poland | 795.5 | 5.8 | 22 |
| Non-Party Bloc for Reform | 746.7 | 5.4 | 16 |
| Solidarity | 676.3 | 4.9 | — |
| Centre Alliance | 610.0 | 4.4 | — |
| Liberal Democratic Congress† | 550.6 | 4.0 | — |
| Socio-Cultural Associations of the German Minority‡ | 84.2 | 0.6 | 3 |
| Others | 2,048.9 | 14.8 | 1 |
| **Total** | **13,796.2** | **100.0** | **460** |

*, † and ‡ See footnotes to Senat.
§ Did not gain representation in the Sejm, having gained less than 8% of the votes cast (the minimum share required for electoral alliances; parties, excluding those representing national minorities, needed to gain at least 5% of the total votes in order to be represented).

## Political Organizations

Under the 1990 law, political parties are not obliged to file for registration, but by 1 May 1992 a total of 135 parties had been registered.

**Centre Alliance** (Porozumienie Centrum): 02-927 Warsaw, ul. Zawojska 47; tel. (22) 6428289; fax (22) 6426987; f. 1990 by supporters of Lech Wałęsa; Christian democratic party; main component of Centre Citizens' Alliance, coalition formed to contest 1991 elections; supports market economy based on private ownership; 10,000 mems; Chair. JAROSŁAW KACZYŃSKI.

**Christian Democratic Party** (Pracy Chrześcijanska Demokracja—PChD): Warsaw; f. 1991; right-wing; Chair. PAWEŁ LACZKOWSKI.

**Christian Democratic Labour Party** (Chrześcijanska Demokracja Stronnictwo Pracy—ChDSP): 00-585 Warsaw, ul. Bagatela 10, m. 7; tel. (22) 291611; fax (2) 6252095; f. 1937, reactivated 1989, merged with Christian Democracy group in 1994; 2,750 mems; Chair. TOMASZ JACKOWSKI; Gen. Sec. ZBIGNIEW JECZMYK.

**Christian National Union** (Zjednoczenie Chrześcijańsko-Narodowe—ZChN): 00-853 Warsaw, ul. Twarda 28; f. 1989; about 10,000 mems; Pres. RYSZARD CZARNECKI; Vice-Pres. STEFAN NIESIOŁOWSKI.

POLAND

**Confederation for an Independent Poland** (Konfederacja Polski Niepodległej—KPN): 00-920 Warsaw, ul. Nowy Świat 18/20; tel. (22) 261043; fax (22) 261400; f. 1979; centre-right; Chair. LESZEK MOCZULSKI.

**Democratic Left Alliance** (Sojusz Lewicy Demokratycznej—SLD): Warsaw; f. 1991; Leader ALEKSANDER KWAŚNIEWSKI; electoral coalition of Social Democracy of the Republic of Poland and the All Poland Trade Unions Alliance:

**Social Democracy of the Republic of Poland** (Socjaldemokracja Rzeczypospolitej Polskiej—SRP): 00-419 Warsaw, ul. Rozbrat 44A; tel. (22) 6210341; telex 825581; fax (22) 6216657; f. 1990 to replace Polish United Workers' Party (Polska Zjednoczona Partia Robotnicza—PZPR; f. 1948), which held power until 1989; over 60,000 mems (May 1995); Chair. ALEKSANDER KWAŚNIEWSKI; Gen. Sec. JERZY SZMAJDZIŃSKI.

**All Poland Trade Unions Alliance** (Ogólnopolskie Porozumienie Związków Zawodowych—OPZZ): see section on Trade and Industry (Trade Unions).

**Democratic Party** (Stronnictwo Demokratyczne—SD): 00-021 Warsaw, ul. Chmielna 9; tel. (22) 261001; telex 812502; f. 1939; 80,000 mems (1991); Chair. ZBIGNIEW ADAMCZYK.

**Freedom Union** (Unia Wolności—UW): 00-024 Warsaw, Al. Jerozolimskie 30; tel. (22) 275047; fax (22) 277851; f. 1994 by merger of Democratic Union (Unia Demokratyczna—UD) and the Liberal Democratic Congress (Kongres Liberalno-Demokratyczny—KLD); Leader LESZEK BALCEROWICZ; Dep. Leader DONALD TUSK.

**German Minority of Lower Silesia** (Mniejszość Niemiecka Śląska Opolskiego): Leader HENRYK KRÓL.

**Movement for the Republic of Poland (RdR):** Chair. STANISŁAW WĘGŁOWSKI.

**Non-Party Bloc for Reform** (Bezpartyjny Blok Wspierania Reform—BBWR): Warsaw; f. 1993 by Lech Wałęsa; Leader ANDRZEJ OLECHOWSKI; Chair. Prof. ZBIGNIEW RELIGA.

**Party X:** 02-017 Warsaw, Al. Jerozolimskie 119A, m. 29; tel. (22) 6214917; f. 1991; advocates free-market economy, expansion of industry and agriculture, gradual elimination of unemployment and universal access to education, culture and health; 9,000 mems; Leader STANISŁAW TYMIŃSKI.

**Peasant Christian Party** (Polskie Stronnictwo Ludowe—Chrześcijańskie): 00-020 Warsaw, ul. Chmielna 24, m. 1; tel. (22) 262614; f. 1989; fmrly Polish Peasant Party—Solidarity; 20,000 mems; Leader JÓZEF ŚLISZ.

**Polish Beer-Lovers' Party:** Warsaw; f. 1991 by LESZEK BUBEL; contested legislative elections with support of business executives; subsequently split into 'Large Beer' (now Polish Economic Programme, see below) and 'Small Beer'.

**Polish Economic Programme** (Polski Program Gospodarczy—PPG): Warsaw; f. following split in Polish Beer Lovers' Party; Leader TOMASZ BANKOWSKI.

**Polish Peasant Party** (Polskie Stronnictwo Ludowe—PSL): 00-131 Warsaw, ul. Grzybowska 4; tel. (22) 200251; telex 814367; f. 1990 to replace United Peasant Party (Zjednoczone Stronnictwo Ludowe; f. 1949) and Polish Peasant Party—Rebirth (Polskie Stronnictwo Ludowe—Odrodzenie; f. 1989); stresses development of agriculture and food-processing; 200,000 mems; Pres. WALDEMAR PAWLAK; Leader GABRIEL JANOWSKI.

**Polish Socialist Party** (Polska Partia Socjalistyczna—PPS): 00-325 Warsaw, ul. Krakowskie Przedmieście 6; tel. (22) 262054; fax (22) 266908; f. 1892, re-established 1987; 5,000 mems; Chair. PIOTR IKONOWICZ; Chair. Cen. Exec. Cttee ANDRZEJ LIPSKI.

**Socio-Cultural Association of Germans of Upper Silesia** (Towarzystwo Społeczno-Kulturalne Niemców Województwa Katowickiego): Katowice.

**Solidarity** (Solidarność): c/o The Sejm, Warsaw; the electoral wing of the trade-union movement (see section on trade unions); Chair. MARIAN KRZAKLEWSKI.

**Union of Labour** (Unia Pracy—UP): Warsaw; f. 1993; Leader RYSZARD BUGAJ.

## Diplomatic Representation

### EMBASSIES IN POLAND

**Afghanistan:** 02-053 Warsaw, ul. Reja 4; tel. (22) 251648; Ambassador: AZIZULLAH KARZI.

**Albania:** 00-789 Warsaw, Słoneczna 15; tel. (22) 498516; Ambassador: SUZANA FAJA.

**Algeria:** 03-932 Warsaw, ul. Dąbrowiecka 21; tel. (22) 175855; telex 817019.

**Argentina:** 03-928 Warsaw, ul. Jana Styki 17/19; tel. (2) 6176028; telex 812412; fax (2) 6177162; Ambassador: NICOLÁS A. E. GARCÍA PINTO.

**Australia:** 03-903 Warsaw, Estońska 3/5; tel. (2) 6176081; telex 813032; fax (2) 6176756; Ambassador: JONATHAN THWAITES.

**Austria:** 00-748 Warsaw, ul. Gagarina 34; tel. (22) 410081; telex 813629; fax (22) 410085; Ambassador: GERHARD WAGNER.

**Bangladesh:** 02-516 Warsaw, Rejtana 15, m. 20/21; tel. (22) 497610; telex 816409; Ambassador: KHAIRUL ANAM.

**Belarus:** 03-978 Warsaw, ul. Ateńska 67; tel. (2) 6173212; fax (2) 6178441; Ambassador: GEORGI TARAZEVICH.

**Belgium:** 00-095 Warsaw, Senatorska 34; tel. (22) 270233; telex 813340; fax (22) 355711; Ambassador: FRANÇOIS RONSE.

**Brazil:** 03-931 Warsaw, Poselska 11, Saska Kepa; tel. (2) 6174800; telex 813748; fax (2) 6178689; Ambassador: LUIZ VILLARINHO PEDROSO.

**Bulgaria:** 00-540 Warsaw, Al. Ujazdowskie 33/35; tel. (22) 294071; Ambassador: YANI MILCHAKOV.

**Canada:** 00-481 Warsaw, Matejki 1/5; tel. (22) 298051; fax (22) 296457; Ambassador: ANNE LEAHY.

**Chile:** 02-932 Warsaw, ul. Morszyńska 71B; tel. (2) 6428155; telex 814542; fax (22) 409041; Ambassador: MAXIMO LIRA ALCAYAGA.

**China, People's Republic:** 00-203 Warsaw, Bonifraterska 1; tel. (22) 313836; telex 813589; fax (22) 409041; Ambassador: LIU YANSHUN.

**Colombia:** 03-936 Warsaw, Zwycięzców 29; tel. (2) 6177157; telex 816496; fax (2) 6176684; Ambassador: CARLOS BULA CAMACHO.

**Costa Rica:** 02-516 Warsaw, ul. Starościńska 1, m. 17; tel. (22) 481478; Ambassador: (vacant).

**Cuba:** 03-932 Warsaw, ul. Katowicka 22; tel. (22) 178428; telex 813588; Ambassador: ANA MARÍA ROVIRA INGIDUA.

**Czech Republic:** 00-555 Warsaw, Koszykowa 18; tel. (2) 6287221; fax (22) 298045; Ambassador: MARKÉTA FIALKOVÁ.

**Denmark:** 02-517 Warsaw, ul. Rakowiecka 19; tel. (2) 490056; telex 813387; fax (22) 494485; Ambassador: NIELS PETER GEORG HELSKOV.

**Egypt:** 03-972 Warsaw, ul. Alzacka 18; tel. (22) 176973; telex 813605; Ambassador: MOHAMED MAHMOUD SOLIMAN.

**Finland:** 00-559 Warsaw, Chopina 4/8; tel. (22) 294091; telex 814286; fax (22) 216010; Ambassador: JYRKI AIMONEN.

**France:** 00-477 Warsaw, Piękna 1; tel. (2) 6288401; telex 825580; fax (22) 291239; Ambassador: ALAIN BRY.

**Germany:** 03-932 Warsaw, Dąbrowiecka 30; tel. (2) 6173011; telex 813455; fax (2) 6173582; Ambassador: Dr JOHANNES BAUCH.

**Greece:** 01-640 Warsaw, Jana Paska 21; tel. (2) 3334889; telex 813692; fax (22) 331735; Ambassador: GEORGE ALEXANDROPOULOS.

**Holy See:** 00-580 Warsaw, Al. J. Ch. Szucha 12, POB 163 (Apostolic Nunciature); tel. (2) 6288488; telex 816550; fax (2) 6284556; Apostolic Nuncio: Most Rev. JÓZEF KOWALCZYK, Titular Archbishop of Heraclea.

**Hungary:** 00-559 Warsaw, Chopina 2; tel. (2) 6284451; telex 814672; fax (22) 218561; Ambassador: ÁKOS ENGELMAYER.

**India:** 02-516 Warsaw, Rejtana 15; tel. (22) 495800; telex 814891; fax (22) 496705; Ambassador: JAGANNATH DODDAMANI.

**Indonesia:** 00-950 Warsaw, Wąchocka 9, POB 33; tel. (22) 172935; telex 813680; Ambassador: ABDUL SALAM GANI.

**Iran:** 03-928 Warsaw, Królowej Aldony 22; tel. (22) 174293; telex 813823; fax (22) 178452; Ambassador: MOHAMMAD REZA ASTANEH.

**Iraq:** 03-932 Warsaw, Dąbrowiecka 9A; tel. (2) 6175773; telex 813918; fax (2) 6177065; Ambassador: MOHAMMED RIFAT ALI M. AL-ANI.

**Ireland:** 02-614 Warsaw, ul. Lenartowicza 18; tel. (22) 446440; telex 812305; fax (22) 480211; Ambassador: RICHARD ANTHONY O'BRIEN.

**Israel:** 02-078 Warsaw, Krzywickiego 24; tel. (22) 250028; telex 817660; fax (22) 251607; Ambassador: GERSHON ZOHAR.

**Italy:** 00-055 Warsaw, Plac Dąbrowskiego 6; tel. (22) 263471; telex 813742; fax (22) 278507; Ambassador: VINCENZO MANNO.

**Japan:** 02-548 Warsaw, ul. Grążny 11; tel. (22) 498781; fax (22) 498494; Ambassador: NAGAO HYODO.

**Korea, Democratic People's Republic:** 00-728 Warsaw, ul. Bobrowiecka 1A; tel. (22) 405813; telex 812707; Ambassador: (vacant).

**Korea, Republic:** 02-611 Warsaw, ul. Ignacego Krasickiego 25; tel. (2) 4833337; telex 817069; Ambassador: WOONG CHOI.

**Laos:** 02-516 Warsaw, Rejtana 15, m. 26; tel. (22) 484786; telex 812847; fax (22) 497122; Ambassador: KYDENG THAMMAVONG.

**Libya:** 03-934 Warsaw, Krynicza 2; tel. (22) 174822; telex 825508; fax (22) 175091; Chargé d'affaires: MOHAMED M. MATMATI.

**Lithuania:** 00-580 Warsaw, ul. J. Ch. Szucha 5; tel. (2) 6253368; fax (2) 6253440; Ambassador: DAINIUS JUNEVIČIUS.

# POLAND

**Malaysia:** 03-902 Warsaw, ul. Gruzińska 3; tel. (22) 174413; telex 825368; fax (22) 177920; Ambassador: ABDUL RAHMAN BIN ABDUL RAHIM.

**Mexico:** 02-516 Warsaw, Starościńska 1B, m. 4/5; tel. (22) 495250; telex 814629; fax (22) 487617; Ambassador: JOSÉ LUIS VALLARTA MARRÓN.

**Mongolia:** 02-516 Warsaw, ul. Rejtina 15; tel. (2) 487920; telex 814399; fax (2) 484264; Ambassador: BUDSÜREN TÜMEN.

**Morocco:** 02-516 Warsaw, Starościńska 1, m. 11/12; tel. (22) 496341; telex 813740; Ambassador: ABDELMAJID ALEM.

**Netherlands:** 00-791 Warsaw, ul. Chocimska 6; tel. (22) 492351; telex 813666; fax (22) 488345; Ambassador: S. I. H. GOSSES.

**Nigeria:** 00-791 Warsaw, Chocimska 18; tel. (22) 486944; telex 814675; fax (22) 485379; Chargé d'affaires a.i.: ONUORAH OBODOZIE.

**Norway:** 00-559 Warsaw, Chopina 2A; tel. (22) 214231; telex 813738; fax (2) 6280938; Ambassador: ARNT RINDAL.

**Pakistan:** 02-516 Warsaw, Starościńska 1, m. 1/2; tel. (22) 494808; telex 816063; Ambassador: S. M. INAAMULLAH.

**Peru:** 02-516 Warsaw, Starościńska 1, m. 3; tel. (22) 494485; telex 814320; Ambassador: CORD DAMMERT.

**Philippines:** 00-484 Warsaw, ul. Górnośląska 22, m. 5; tel. (22) 219523; Chargé d'affaires: CHARLIE PACAÑA MANANGAN.

**Portugal:** 03-910 Warsaw, Dąbrowiecka 19; tel. and fax (22) 176021; telex 815509; Ambassador: RUI FERNANDO MEIRA FERREIRA.

**Romania:** 00-559 Warsaw, Chopina 10; tel. (2) 6283156; telex 813420; Ambassador: IOAN GRIGORESCU.

**Russia:** 00-761 Warsaw, Belwederska 49; tel. (22) 213453; fax (2) 213794; Ambassador: YURY KACHLEV.

**Slovakia:** 00-581 Warsaw, ul. Litewska 6; tel. (2) 6284051; telex 813585; fax (2) 6284055; Ambassador: MARIÁN SERVÁTKA.

**Spain:** 00-459 Warsaw, Myśliwiecka 4; tel. (2) 6224250; telex 814515; fax (2) 6225408; Ambassador: FERNANDO RIQUELME.

**Sweden:** 00-585 Warsaw, ul. Bagatela 3; tel. (2) 6289700; telex 813457; fax (22) 495243; Ambassador: KARL VILHELM WÖHLER.

**Switzerland:** 00-540 Warsaw, Ujazdowskie 27; tel. (2) 6280481; telex 813528; fax (2) 210548; Ambassador: J. RICHARD GAECHTER.

**Syria:** 02-536 Warsaw, Narbutta 19A; tel. (22) 491454; telex 825465; Ambassador: AHMAD SAKER.

**Thailand:** 02-516 Warsaw, Starościńska 1B, m. 2/3; tel. (22) 494730; telex 825392; fax (22) 492630; Ambassador: SURIYA ROGHANABUDDHI.

**Tunisia:** 00-459 Warsaw, Myśliwiecka 14; tel. (2) 6286330; telex 812827; fax (22) 216298; Ambassador: HOUCINE LONGO.

**Turkey:** 02-622 Warsaw, Malczewskiego 32; tel. (22) 443201; fax (22) 443737; Ambassador: KORKMAZ HAKTANIR.

**Ukraine:** Warsaw, ul. Szucha 7; tel. (2) 6250127; fax (2) 6253230; Ambassador: PETRO D. SARDACHUK.

**United Kingdom:** 00-556 Warsaw, Al. Róz 1; tel. (2) 6281001; telex 813694; fax (22) 217161; Ambassador: MICHAEL LLEWELLYN SMITH.

**USA:** 00-540 Warsaw, Al. Ujazdowskie 29/31; tel. (2) 6283041; telex 813304; fax (2) 6257290; Ambassador: NICHOLAS A. REY.

**Uruguay:** 02-516 Warsaw, Rejtana 15, m. 12; tel. (22) 495040; telex 814647; Chargé d'affaires a.i.: MARINÉS BENAVIDES.

**Venezuela:** 02-516 Warsaw, Rejtana 15, m. 10/11; tel. (22) 494227; telex 812788; fax (22) 496746; Ambassador: GUILLERMO HERRERA HURTADO.

**Viet Nam:** 02-589 Warsaw, ul. Kazimierzowska 14; tel. (22) 446723; Ambassador: DAO THITAM.

**Yemen:** 02-686 Warsaw, ul. Olimpijska 11; tel. (22) 440234; fax (22) 446129; Ambassador: MANSOOR ABDUL GALIL ABDUL RAB.

**Yugoslavia:** 00-540 Warsaw, Al. Ujazdowskie 23/25; tel. (2) 6285161; fax (22) 297173; Chargé d'affaires a.i.: VLADIMIR STANIMIROVIĆ.

**Zaire:** Warsaw; tel. (2) 6422369; telex 816015; Ambassador: (vacant).

## Judicial System

### SUPREME COURT

**The Supreme Court:** 00-951 Warsaw, ul. Ogrodowa 6; tel. (2) 6203975; telex 817989; fax (2) 6203714; the highest judicial organ; exercises supervision over the decision-making of all other courts; its functions include: the examination of appeals made against final decisions of other courts and bodies; the adoption of resolutions aimed at providing interpretation of legal provisions that give rise to doubts. Justices of the Supreme Court are appointed by the President of the Republic on motions of the National Council of Judiciary and serve until the age of retirement (life tenure). The First President of the Supreme Court is appointed (and dismissed) from among the Supreme Court Justices by the Sejm on the motion of the President of the Republic. The other presidents of the Supreme Court are appointed by the President of the Republic.

**First President:** Prof. Dr hab. ADAM STRZEMBOSZ.

### OTHER COURTS

**The Supreme Administrative Court** examines, in one procedure, complaints concerning the legality of administrative decisions; it is vested exclusively with the powers of court of cassation.

## Religion

### CHRISTIANITY

#### The Roman Catholic Church

The Roman Catholic Church was granted full legal status in May 1989, when three laws regulating aspects of relations between the Church and the State were approved by the Sejm. The legislation guaranteed freedom of worship, and permitted the Church to administer its own affairs. The Church was also granted access to the media, and allowed to operate its own schools, hospitals and other charitable organizations.

For ecclesiastical purposes, Poland comprises 14 archdioceses and 25 dioceses (including one for the Catholics of the Byzantine-Ukrainian Rite and one Military Ordinariate). In 1993 an estimated 35m. people (some 91% of the population) were adherents of the Roman Catholic Church.

**Bishops' Conference:** Konferencja Episkopatu Polski, 01-015 Warsaw, Skwer Kardynała Stefana Wyszyńskiego 6; tel. (22) 389251; telex 816550; fax (22) 380967; f. 1969 (statutes approved 1987); Pres. Cardinal JÓZEF GLEMP, Archbishop of Warsaw.

*Latin Rite*

**Archbishop of Warsaw and Primate of Poland:** Cardinal JÓZEF GLEMP, Sekretariat Prymasa Polski, 00-246 Warsaw, ul. Miodowa 17/19; tel. (22) 312157; telex 817000; fax (2) 6358745.

**Archbishop of Białystok:** Most Rev. STANISŁAW SZYMECKI, 15-087 Białystok, pl. Jana Pawła II 1; tel. (85) 416473; telex 853161; fax (85) 416473.

**Archbishop of Częstochowa:** Most Rev. STANISŁAW NOWAK, 42-200 Częstochowa, Al. Najśw. Maryi Panny 54; tel. (34) 243375; telex 37611; fax (34) 651182.

**Archbishop of Gdańsk:** Most Rev. TADEUSZ GOCŁOWSKI, 80-330 Gdańsk, ul. Cystersów 15; tel. (58) 522808; telex 512182; fax (58) 520051.

**Archbishop of Gniezno:** Most Rev. HENRYK MUSZYŃSKI, 62-200 Gniezno, ul. Kanclerza Jana Łaskiego 7; tel. (66) 262102; telex 414655; fax (66) 261285.

**Archbishop of Katowice:** Most Rev. DAMIAN ZIMOŃ, 40-027 Katowice, ul. Francuska 47; tel. (3) 1554673; telex 315749; fax (32) 512160.

**Archbishop of Kraków:** Cardinal FRANCISZEK MACHARSKI, 31-004 Kraków, ul. Franciszkańska 3; tel. (12) 211533; telex 322700; fax (12) 215012.

**Archbishop of Łódź:** Most Rev. WŁADYSŁAW ZIÓŁEK, 93-423 Łódź, ul. Rudzka 55/57; tel. (42) 844343; telex 884707; fax (42) 361696.

**Archbishop of Lublin:** Most Rev. BOLESŁAW PYLAK, 20-105 Lublin, ul. Kard. S. Wyszyńskiego 2; tel. (81) 23468; telex 643599; fax (81) 28194.

**Archbishop of Olsztyn (Warmia):** Most Rev. EDMUND PISZCZ, 10-025 Olsztyn, ul. Staszica 5A; tel. (89) 272291; telex 522857.

**Archbishop of Poznań:** Most Rev. JERZY STROBA, 61-109 Poznań, ul. Mieszka I 1; tel. (61) 528556; telex 414220; fax (61) 526797.

**Archbishop of Przemyśl:** Most Rev. JÓZEF MICHALIK, 37-700 Przemyśl, Pl. Katedralny 4; tel. (10) 786694; fax (10) 782674.

**Archbishop of Szczecin-Kamień:** Most Rev. MARIAN PRZYKUCKI, 71-423 Szczecin, ul. Piotra Skargi 30; tel. (91) 225157; telex 425530; fax (91) 220238.

**Archbishop of Wrocław:** Cardinal HENRYK ROMAN GULBINOWICZ, 50-328 Wrocław, ul. Katedralna 11; tel. (71) 224214; telex 712261; fax (71) 222340.

*Byzantine-Ukrainian Rite*

**Bishop of Przemyśl, Sanok and Sanik:** Rt Rev. JAN MARTYNIAK, 37-700 Przemyśl, ul. Fryderyka Chopina 8; tel. (10) 783523.

#### Old Catholic Churches

**Mariavite Catholic Church** (Kościół Katolicki Mariawitów): Felicjanów, 09-470 Bodzanów, k. Płocka; tel. Bodzanów 10; f. 1893; 3,007 mems (1995); Archbishop JÓZEF M. RAFAEL WOJCIECHOWSKI.

POLAND — *Directory*

**Old Catholic Mariavite Church** (Starokatolicki Kościół Mariawitów): 09-400 Płock, ul. Wieczorka 27; f. 1907; 25,250 mems (1992); Chief Bishop STANISŁAW KOWALSKI.

**Polish Catholic Church in Poland** (Kościół Polskokatolicki w R.P.): 00-464 Warsaw, ul. Szwolèzerów 4; tel. (22) 413743; f. 1920; 52,400 mems (1995); Prime Bishop Most Rev. TADEUSZ R. MAJEWSKI.

### The Orthodox Church

**Polish Autocephalous Orthodox Church** (Polski Autokefaliczny Kościół Prawosławny): 03-402 Warsaw, Al. Solidarności 52; tel. (22) 190886; 870,600 mems (1989); Archbishop of Warsaw and Metropolitan of All Poland BAZYLI (WŁODZIMIERZ DOROSZKIEWICZ); Archbishop of Białystok and Gdańsk SAWA (MICHAŁ HRYCUNIAK); Archbishop of Łódź and Poznań SZYMON (SZYMON ROMAŃCZUK); Bishop of Przemyśl and Nowy Sącz ADAM (ALEKSANDER DUBEC); Bishop of Wrocław and Szczecin JEREMIASZ (JAN ANCHIMIUK); Bishop of Lublin and Chełm ABEL (ANDRZEJ POPŁAWSKI).

### Protestant Churches

In 1993 there were some 85,000 Protestants in Poland.

**Baptist Union of Poland** (Polski Kościół Chrześcijan Baptystów): 00-865 Warsaw, ul. Waliców 25; tel. and fax (22) 242783; f. 1858; 3,335 baptized mems; Pres. Rev. KONSTANTY WIAZOWSKI; Gen. Sec. RYSZARD GUTKOWSKI.

**Evangelical Augsburg Church in Poland** (Kościół Ewangelicko-Augsburski): 00-246 Warsaw, ul. Miodowa 21; tel. (22) 315187; fax (22) 312348; 90,000 mems (1994); Bishop and Pres. of Consistory JAN SZAREK.

**Evangelical-Reformed Church** (Kościół Ewangelicko-Reformowany): 00-145 Warsaw, Al. Solidarności 76A; tel. (22) 314522; fax (22) 310827; f. 16th century; 4,500 mems (1992); Bishop ZDZISŁAW TRANDA; Pres. of the Consistory Prof. JAROSŁAW SWIDERSKI.

**Pentecostal Church** (Kościół Zielonoświątkowy): 00-825 Warsaw, Sienna 68/70; tel. (22) 248575; fax (22) 204073; f. 1910; 14,500 mems (1992); Pres. MICHAŁ HYDZIK.

**Seventh-day Adventist Church in Poland** (Kościół Adwentystów Dnia Siódmego): 00-366 Warsaw, ul. Foksal 8; tel. (22) 277611; telex 812359; fax (22) 278619; f. 1921; 10,024 mems, 81 preachers (1995); Pres. WŁADYSŁAW POLOK; Sec. ROMAN R. CHALUPKA.

**United Methodist Church** (Kościół Ewangelicko-Metodystyczny): 00-561 Warsaw, ul. Mokotowska 12; tel. and fax (2) 6285328; f. 1921; 5,000 mems; Gen. Supt Rev. EDWARD PUŚLECKI.

There are also several other small Protestant churches, including the Church of Christ, the Church of Evangelical Christians, the Evangelical Christian Church and the Jehovah's Witnesses.

### ISLAM

In 1989 there were about 4,000 Muslims of Tartar origin in Białystok Province (eastern Poland), and smaller communities in Warsaw, Gdańsk and elsewhere.

**Religious Union of Muslims in Poland** (Muzułmański Związek Religijny): 15-426 Białystok, Rynek Kosciuszki 26, m. 2; tel. (85) 414970; Chair. STEFAN MUCHARSKI.

### JUDAISM

**Union of Jewish Communities in Poland** (Związek Gmin Wyznaniowych Zydowskich w Rzeczypospolitej Polskiej): 00-950 Warsaw, ul. Twarda 6; tel. (22) 204324; 14 synagogues and about 2,500 registered Jews; Pres. PAWEŁ WILDSTEIN.

## The Press

Legislation to permit the formal abolition of censorship and to guarantee freedom of expression was approved in April 1990. In 1993 there were 71 daily newspapers in Poland, with a total circulation of 6,381,000. In the same year there were 3,139 periodicals, with a combined circulation of 56.4m. copies.

### PRINCIPAL DAILIES

#### Białystok

**Gazeta Współczesna**: 15-950 Białystok, POB 193, ul. Suraska 1; tel. (85) 23241; f. 1951; Editor ADAM JERZY SOCHA; circ. 35,000.

#### Bydgoszcz

**Gazeta Pomorska**: 85-011 Bydgoszcz, ul. Śniadeckich 1; tel. (52) 221928; telex 056-2386; fax (52) 221542; f. 1948; local independent newspaper for the provinces of Bydgoszcz, Toruń and Włocławek; Editor MACIEJ KAMIŃSKI; circ. 100,000 (weekdays), 300,000 (weekends).

**Ilustrowany Kurier Polski**: 85-950 Bydgoszcz, ul. Marshala Focha 20; tel. (52) 225501; telex 056-2387; f. 1945; regional; Editor-in-Chief MAREK FAŚCISZEWSKI; circ. 40,000.

#### Gdańsk

**Dziennik Bałtycki**: 80-886 Gdańsk, Targ Drzewny 3/7; tel. and fax (58) 313560; f. 1945; non-party; Editor JAN JAKUBOWSKI; circ. 80,000.

**Głos Wybrzeża**: 80-886 Gdańsk, ul. Targ Drzewny 3/7; tel. (58) 311572; f. 1991; Editor-in-Chief ZBIGNIEW ZUKOWSKI; circ. 50,000.

#### Katowice

**Dziennik Zachodni**: 40-925 Katowice, ul. Młyńska 1; tel. (3) 1539984; telex 0315455; fax (3) 1538196; f. 1945; non-party; Chief Editor MACIEJ WOJCIECHOWSKI; circ. 100,000.

**Trybuna Śląska**: 40-098 Katowice, ul. Młyńska 1; tel. (32) 537703; telex 0312432; fax (32) 537997; f. 1945; fmrly Trybuna Robotnicza; independent; Editor TADEUSZ BIEDZKI; circ. 180,000 (weekdays), 800,000 (weekends).

#### Kielce

**Słowo Ludu** (Word of the People): 25-953 Kielce 12, Targowa 18; tel. (41) 42480; fax (41) 46979; f. 1949; independent; Editor KRZYSZTOF FALKIEWICZ; circ. 50,000 (weekdays), 130,000 (weekends).

#### Koszalin

**Głos Pomorza** (Voice of Pomerania): 75-604 Koszalin, ul. Zwycięstwa 137/139; tel. (94) 22693; f. 1952; Editor-in-Chief WIESŁAW WISNIEWSKI; circ. 60,000 (weekdays), 130,000 (weekends).

#### Kraków

**Czas Krakowski**: 31-015 Kraków, ul. Pijarska 9; tel. (12) 225355; telex 0322717; fax (12) 217502; f. 1848, reactivated 1990; independent; Editor JAN POLKOWSKI; circ. 150,000 (weekdays), 260,000 (weekends).

**Echo Krakowa**: 31-072 Kraków, ul. Wielopole 1; tel. (12) 224678; f. 1946; independent; evening; Editor WITOLD GRZYBOWSKI; circ. 60,000 (weekdays), 90,000 (weekends).

**Gazeta Krakowska**: 31-072 Kraków, ul. Wielopole 1; tel. (12) 220985; telex 0325785; fax (12) 221563; f. 1949; Editor-in-Chief JERZY SADECKI; circ. 60,000 (weekdays), 150,000 (weekends).

#### Łódź

**Dziennik Łódzki**: 90-113 Łódź, ul. Sienkiewicza 315; tel. (42) 364585; telex 886138; fax (42) 322832; f. 1945; non-party; Editor MACIEJ ROSALAK; circ. 65,000 (weekdays), 130,000 (weekends).

**Głos Poranny**: 90-113 Łódź, ul. Sienkiewicza 3/5; tel. (42) 366785; f. 1945; fmrly Głos Robotniczy; Editor GUSTAW ROMANOWSKI; circ. 52,000 (weekdays), 118,000 (weekends).

#### Lublin

**Dziennik Lubelski**: 20-601 Lublin, ul. Zana 38C; tel. (81) 558000; f. 1990; fmrly Sztandar Ludu; Editor ALOJZY LESZEK GZELLA; circ. 45,000 (weekdays), 210,000 (weekends).

**Kurier Lubelski**: 20-950 Lublin, ul. Armii Wojska Polskiego 5; tel. (81) 26634; fax (81) 26835; f. 1830; independent; evening; Editor WŁODZIMIERZ WÓJCIKOWSKI; circ. 40,000 (weekdays), 100,000 (weekends).

#### Olsztyn

**Gazeta Olsztyńska** (Olsztyn Gazette): 10-417 Olsztyn, ul. Towarowa 2; tel. (889) 330277; telex 0526371; fax (889) 332691; f. 1886, renamed 1970; independent; Editor-in-Chief TOMASZ ŚRUTKOWSKI; circ. 45,000 (weekdays), 90,000 (weekends).

#### Opole

**Trybuna Opolska**: 45-086 Opole, ul. Powstańców Śląskich 9; tel. (77) 37407; telex 732131; fax (77) 33737; f. 1952; independent; Editor MARIAN SZCZUREK; circ. 80,000.

#### Poznań

**Gazeta Poznańska**: 60-782 Poznań, ul. Grunwaldzka 19; tel. (61) 665568; f. 1991; independent; Editor PRZEMYSŁAW NOWICKI; circ. 80,000 (weekdays), 320,000 (weekends).

**Głos Wielkopolski**: 60-959 Poznań, ul. Grunwaldzka 19; tel. (61) 45409; telex 0413410; f. 1945; independent; Editor MAREK PRZYBYLSKI; circ. 110,000 (weekdays), 160,000 (weekends).

#### Rzeszów

**Gazeta Codzienna 'Nowiny'**: 35-959 Rzeszów, ul. Unii Lubelskiej 3; tel. (17) 628471; telex 0632220; fax (17) 628836; f. 1949; evening; Editor JAN MUSIAŁ; circ. 100,000.

#### Szczecin

**Głos Szczeciński** (Voice of Szczecin): 70-952 Szczecin 2, Pl. Hołdu Pruskiego 8; tel. (91) 341306; telex 0422242; fax (91) 345472; f. 1947; Editor-in-Chief ANDRZEJ PALMIRSKI; circ. 60,000 (weekdays), 180,000 (weekends).

# POLAND

## Warsaw

**Express Wieczorny:** 02-017 Warsaw, Al. Jerozolimskie 125/127; tel. (2) 6285231; telex 825466; fax (2) 6284929; f. 1946; non-party; evening; Editor ANDRZEJ URBAŃSKI; circ. 140,000 (weekdays), 400,000 (weekends).

**Gazeta Wyborcza:** 00-732 Warsaw, ul. Czerska 8/10; tel. (22) 415513; telex 825703; fax (22) 416920; f. 1989; non-party; national edn and 18 local edns; weekend edn: Gazeta Świateczna; special supplements; Editor-in-Chief ADAM MICHNIK; circ. 460,000 (daily); 770,000 (weekends).

**Kurier Polski:** 00-018 Warsaw, ul. Zgoda 11; tel. (22) 278081; telex 814725; fax (22) 270552; f. 1729; Editor ANDRZEJ NIERYCHŁO; circ. 150,000 (weekdays), 190,000 (weekends).

**Polska Zbrojna:** 00-950 Warsaw, ul. Grzybowska 77; tel. (22) 204293; telex 813664; fax (22) 202127; f. 1943; fmrly Zolnierz Wolności, name changed 1990; Editor JERZY ŚLASKI; circ. 50,000.

**Przegląd Sportowy:** 02-017 Warsaw, Al. Jerozolimskie 125/127, POB 181; tel. (2) 6289116; telex 814731; fax (22) 218697; f. 1921; Editor MACIEJ POLKOWSKI; circ. 110,000.

**Rzeczpospolita** (The Republic): 02-015 Warsaw, Pl. Starynkiewicza 7; tel. (2) 6280493; telex 817131; fax (2) 6280588; f. 1982; Editor-in-Chief DARIUSZ FIKUS; circ. 250,000.

**Słowo—Dziennik Katolicki:** 00-551 Warsaw, ul. Mokotowska 43; tel. (22) 297767; telex 814434; f. 1993; fmrly Słowo Powszechne, organ of the 'Pax' Catholic Association; Editor JERZY MARCHLEWSKI; circ. 150,000.

**Sztandar Młodych:** 00-687 Warsaw, ul. Wspólna 61; tel. (2) 6287661; telex 814767; fax (2) 6282049; f. 1950; Editor JERZY DOMAŃSKI; circ. 110,000 (weekdays), 500,000 (weekends).

**Trybuna:** 00-835 Warsaw, Miedziania 11; tel. (2) 6253015; telex 816301; fax (22) 204100; f. 1991; fmrly Trybuna Ludu; organ of Social Democracy of the Republic of Poland; Editor DARIUSZ SZYMCZYCHA; circ. 120,000 (weekdays), 250,000 (weekends).

**Zycie Warszawy** (Warsaw Life): 00-575 Warsaw, Al. Armii Ludowej 3/5; tel. (2) 6256990; telex 814507; fax (22) 252829; f. 1944; independent; Editor TOMASZ WOLEK; circ. 250,000 (weekdays), 460,000 (weekends).

## Wrocław

**Gazeta Robotnicza:** 50-010 Wrocław, ul. Podwale 62; tel. (71) 35756; telex 712665; fax (71) 35756; f. 1948; Editor ANDRZEJ BUŁAT; circ. 30,000 (weekdays), 315,000 (weekends).

## Zielona Góra

**Gazeta Lubuska:** 65-042 Zielona Góra, POB 120, Al. Niepodległości 25; tel. (68) 70955; telex 0432262; fax (68) 3707; f. 1952; independent; Editor MIROSŁAW RATAJ; circ. 100,000 (weekdays), 200,000 (weekends).

## PERIODICALS

**Fantastyka:** 00-640 Warsaw, ul. Mokotowska 5/6; tel. (22) 253475; f. 1982; monthly; science fiction and fantasy; Editor MACIEJ PAROWSKI; circ. 100,000.

**Filipinka:** 00-236 Warsaw, Świętojerska 5/7; tel. (22) 312221; f. 1957; fortnightly; illustrated for teenage girls; Editor HANNA JAWOROWSKA-BŁOŃSKA; circ. 125,600.

**Film:** 02-595 Warsaw, Puławska 61; tel. (22) 455325; fax (22) 454651; f. 1946; monthly; illustrated magazine; Editor-in-Chief LECH KURPIEWSKI; circ. 105,000.

**Forum:** 00-678 Warsaw, ul. Śniadeckich 10; tel. (22) 256150; f. 1965; weekly; survey of foreign press; political, social, cultural and economics; Editor-in-Chief BOHDAN HERBICH; circ. 33,000.

**Gazeta Bankowa:** 00-696 Warsaw, Pankiewicza 3; tel. (2) 6287272; fax (2) 6212653; f. 1988; weekly; business and finance; Editor ANDRZEJ WRÓBLEWSKI; circ. 40,000.

**Głos Nauczycielski** (Teachers' Voice): 00-389 Warsaw, ul. Smulikowskiego 6/8; tel. (22) 276630; fax (22) 276630; f. 1917; weekly; organ of the Polish Teachers' Union; Editor WOJCIECH SIERAKOWSKI; circ. 40,000.

**Gromada-Rolnik Polski:** 00-375 Warsaw, ul. Smolna 12; tel. (22) 278815; telex 814741; fax 278815; f. 1951; 3 a week; agricultural; Editor ZBIGNIEW LUBAK; circ. 281,800.

**IMT Światowid:** 00-695 Warsaw, ul. Nowogrodzka 49; tel. (22) 215762; fax (22) 212376; f. 1955; monthly; illustrated tourist magazine; Editor BEATA TALLAR; circ. 50,000.

**Karuzela** (The Merry-Go-Round): 90-113 Łódź, ul. Sienkiewicza 3/5; tel. (42) 339083; f. 1956; satirical; Editor HALINA SIBIŃSKA; circ. 60,000.

**Kobieta i Zycie** (Women and Life): 00-564 Warsaw, ul. Koszykowa 6A; tel. and fax (2) 6287811; f. 1946; weekly; women's; Editor ZOFIA KAMIŃSKA; circ. 400,000.

**Literatura:** 00-562 Warsaw, Koszykowa 6A; tel. (22) 214856; f. 1972; monthly; literary; Editor JACEK SYSKI; circ. 40,000.

**Morze:** 00-023 Warsaw, ul. Widok 10; tel. and fax (22) 273551; f. 1924; illustrated monthly; maritime affairs; Editor-in-Chief JANUSZ WOLNIEWICZ; circ. 50,000.

**Nie:** 00-789 Warsaw, ul. Słoneczna 25; tel. (22) 484420; fax (22) 497258; f. 1990; satirical weekly; Editor JERZY URBAN; circ. 730,000.

**Nie z tej Ziemi** (Not from that World): 00-840 Warsaw, Wronia 23; tel. (22) 241485; fax (22) 241481; f. 1990; monthly; para-science, ghost stories, etc.; Editor TADEUSZ LACHOWICZ; circ. 150,000.

**Nowa Fantastyka:** 00-640 Warsaw, ul. Mokotowska 5/6; tel. (22) 253475; fax (22) 252089; f. 1982; monthly; science fiction and fantasy; Editor MACIEJ PAROWSKI; circ. 80,000.

**Nowa Wieś:** 00-480 Warsaw, ul. Wiejska 17; tel. and fax (2) 6284583; f. 1948; weekly; peasant illustrated magazine; Editor KAZIMIERZ DŁUGOSZ; circ. 60,000.

**Panorama:** 40-082 Katowice, Sobieskiego 11; tel. (3) 1538595; fax (3) 1538374; f. 1960; weekly; socio-cultural magazine; Editor ADAM JAZWIECKI; circ. 150,000.

**Państwo i Prawo** (State and Law): 00-490 Warsaw, ul. Wiejska 12; tel. (2) 6288296; f. 1946; monthly organ of the Polish Academy of Sciences; Editor Dr LESZEK KUBICKI; circ. 3,000.

**Polityka** (Politics): 00-182 Warsaw, ul. Dubois 9; tel. (2) 6353091; telex 812546; fax (2) 6351797; f. 1956; weekly; political, economic, cultural; Editor JAN BIJAK; circ. 350,000.

**Poradnik Gospodarski:** 60-837 Poznań, ul. A. Mickiewicza 33; tel. (61) 476001; fax (61) 411881; f. 1889; monthly; agriculture; Editor-in-Chief WAWRZYNIEC TRAWIŃSKI; circ. 10,000.

**Prawo i Zycie** (Law and Life): 00-028 Warsaw, ul. Bracka 20A; tel. (22) 272466; fax (22) 267585; f. 1956; weekly; legal and social; Editor ROMAN KRUSZEWSKI; circ. 85,000.

**Przegląd Tygodniowy:** 00-950 Warsaw, POB 992, ul. Bracka 22; tel. (22) 271899; telex 816400; fax (22) 279128; f. 1981; weekly; political, economic, social, historical, cultural, scientific and artistic; Editor-in-Chief ANDRZEJ NIERYCHŁO; circ. 130,000.

**Przekrój:** 31-012 Kraków, ul. Reformacka 3; tel. (12) 221833; telex 0322733; fax (12) 214929; f. 1945; weekly; illustrated; Editor-in-Chief MIECZYSŁAW CZUMA; circ. 190,000.

**Przyjaciółka** (The Friend): 00-490 Warsaw, ul. Wiejska 16; tel. (2) 6280583; fax (2) 6285866; f. 1948; weekly; women's magazine; Editor EWA ŁUSZCZUK; circ. 1,300,000.

**Res Publica Nowa:** 00-950 Warsaw 1, POB 856, ul. Smolna 12; tel. (22) 263047; fax (22) 262329; f. 1987; monthly; political and cultural; Editor MARCIN KRÓL; circ. 5,000.

**Sport:** 40-082 Katowice, Sobieskiego 11, POB 339; tel. (3) 1539995; fax (3) 1537138; f. 1945; 5 a week; Editor ADAM BARTECZKO; circ. 135,000.

**Sportowiec** (Sportsman): 00-543 Warsaw, ul. Mokotowska 40; tel. (22) 216208; f. 1949; weekly; Chief Editor LECH UFEL; circ. 70,000.

**Spotkania:** 01-756 Warsaw, ul. Przasnyska 6; tel. (22) 399022; telex 817403; fax (22) 241423; f. 1990; weekly; illustrated; political, social, economic, cultural and scientific magazine; Editor MACIEJ IŁOWIECKI; circ. 80,000.

**Sprawy Międzynarodowe** (International Affairs): 00-950 Warsaw, ul. Warecka 1A; tel. (22) 263026; fax (22) 274738; f. 1948; quarterly; published by the Polski Instytut Spraw Międzynarodowych; Editor HENRYK SZLAJFER; circ. 1,200.

**Szpilki:** 00-490 Warsaw, Pl. Trzech Krzyży 16A; tel. (2) 6280429; f. 1935; weekly; illustrated satirical; Editor JACEK JANCZARSKI; circ. 100,000.

**Teatr:** 03-902 Warsaw, ul. Jakubowska 14; tel. (2) 6175594; f. 1945; monthly; illustrated; theatrical life; Editor ANDRZEJ WANET; circ. 4,500.

**Twoje Dziecko:** 02-548 Warsaw, ul. Grążyny 13; tel. (22) 452742; fax (22) 454216; f. 1951; monthly; women's magazine concerning children's affairs; Editor-in-Chief EWA SZPERLICH; circ. 150,000.

**Tygodnik Solidarność:** 00-950 Warsaw, POB P-6, ul. Czackiego 15/17; tel. (22) 273303; telex 816992; fax (22) 264451; f. 1981, reactivated 1989; weekly; Editor ANDRZEJ GELBREG; circ. 60,000.

**The Warsaw Voice:** 00-950 Warsaw, POB 28; tel. (22) 375138; fax (22) 371995; f. 1988; weekly; economic, political, social, cultural and economic; in English for foreigners; Editor ANDRZEJ JONAS; Gen. Dir JULIUSZ KŁOSOWSKI; circ. 15,000.

**Zielony Sztandar** (Green Banner): 00-950 Warsaw, ul. Grzybowska 4; tel. (22) 207554; fax (22) 207557; f. 1931; weekly; main organ of the Polish Peasant Party; Editor PAWEŁ POPIAK; circ. 100,000.

**Zołnierz Polski:** 00-800 Warsaw, ul. Grzybowska 77; tel. (22) 204286; fax (22) 202127; f. 1945; monthly; illustrated magazine primarily about the armed forces; Editor IRENEUSZ CZYŻEWSKI; circ. 40,000.

POLAND

*Zycie Gospodarcze:* 00-490 Warsaw, ul. Wiejska 12; tel. (2) 6280628; fax (2) 6288392; f. 1945; weekly; economic; Editor Karol Szwarc; circ. 35,700.

### NEWS AGENCIES

**Polska Agencja Prasowa—PAP** (Polish Press Agency): 00-950 Warsaw, Al. Jerozolimskie 7; tel. (2) 6280001; telex 812509; fax (2) 6218518; f. 1944; brs in 28 Polish towns and 22 foreign capitals; 274 journalist and photojournalist mems; information is transmitted abroad in English only; Pres. Włodzimierz Gogołek; Dir-Gen. Jerzy Wysokiński.

**Polska Agencja Informacyjna** (Polish Information Agency): 00-585 Warsaw, ul. Bagatela 12; tel. (2) 6250822; fax (2) 6284651; f. 1967; multi-lingual books, magazines, bulletins and news, television films, feature and photo services on Polish culture, foreign policy and economics; press centre for foreign journalists and publishers; advertising and promotional services; Editor-in-Chief Zbigniew Domarańczyk.

#### Foreign Bureaux

**Allgemeiner Deutscher Nachrichtendienst (ADN)** (Germany): 00-116 Warsaw, ul. Świętokrzyska 36, m. 61; tel. (22) 201152; fax (22) 201015; Chief Correspondent Jörg Schreiber.

**Agence France-Presse (AFP):** 00-672 Warsaw, ul. Piękna 68, p. 305; tel. (22) 298444; telex 813620; fax (2) 6216747; Correspondent Michel Viatteau.

**Agencia EFE** (Spain): 00-656 Warsaw, Śniadeckich 18, Lokal 16; tel. (2) 6282567; telex 7849; fax (22) 215989; Bureau Chief Jorge Ruiz Lardizabal.

**Agenzia Nazionale Stampa Associata (ANSA)** (Italy): 00-672 Warsaw, ul. Piękna 68, p. 301; tel. (22) 298413; telex 813724; fax (22) 299843; Bureau Chief Maurizio Salvi.

**Associated Press (AP)** (USA): 00-433 Warsaw, ul. Profesorska 4; tel. (2) 6287231; telex 813440; fax (22) 295240; Correspondent Paul Alexander.

**Bulgarska Telegrafna Agentsia (BTA)** (Bulgaria): 00-019 Warsaw, Kniewskiego 9, m. 14; tel. (22) 278059; telex 813720; Correspondent Weselin Jankow.

**Česká tisková kancelář (ČTK)** (Czech Republic): 03-946 Warsaw, ul. Brazylioska 14A, m. 31; tel. (2) 6728780; telex 813746; fax (2) 6728780; Correspondent Petr Starý.

**Deutsche-Presse Agentur (dpa)** (Germany): 03-908 Warsaw, ul. Saska 7A; tel. (22) 171058; telex 813374; Correspondent Renata Marsch-Potocka.

**Informatsionnoye Telegrafnoye Agentstvo Rossii—Telegrafnoye Agentstvo Suverennykh Stran (ITAR—TASS)** (Russia): 00-582 Warsaw, Al. 1 Armii Vojska Polskego 2/4, m. 33; tel. (22) 292192; fax (22) 296131; Correspondent Aleksandr L. Potemkin.

**Inter Press Service (IPS)** (Italy): 00-116 Warsaw, ul. Jana Pawła II 23, m. 133; tel. (22) 243982; fax (22) 205508; Correspondent Iwona Dmochowska-Knothe.

**Kyodo News Service** (Japan): 00-655 Warsaw, ul. Waryńskiego 9 m. 56; tel. and fax (22) 298416; telex 816997; Chief Susumu Sakata.

**Magyar Távirati Iroda (MTI)** (Hungary): 02-954 Warsaw, ul. Jakuba Kubickiego 19/22, m. 21; tel. (22) 420089; telex 8144460; Correspondent János Barabás.

**Reuters** (United Kingdom): 00-695 Warsaw, ul. Nowogrodzka 47A, IV Floor; tel. (2) 6256303; telex 813821; fax (2) 6257501; Correspondent Anthony Barker.

**Rossiyskoye Informatsionnoye Agentstvo—Novosti (RIA—Novosti)** (Russia): 00-582 Warsaw, Al. Szucha 5; tel. (2) 6283092; telex 813555; 6 Correspondents.

**Tlačová agentúra Slovenskej republiky (TASR)** (Slovakia): 03-535 Warsaw, ul. Goscieradowska 2, m. 21; tel. and fax (2) 6780399; Correspondent Igor Rabatin.

**United Press International (UPI)** (USA): 00-672 Warsaw, ul. Piękna 68, p. 306; tel. (2) 6280704; telex 813417; Chief Correspondent Patricia Koza.

**Xinhua (New China) News Agency** (People's Republic of China): 00-203 Warsaw, ul. Bonifraterska 1; tel. (22) 313876; telex 813357; Correspondents Tang Deqiao, Dong Fusheng, Schao Jin.

### PRESS ASSOCIATION

**Stowarzyszenie Dziennikarzy Polskich—SDP** (Polish Journalists' Association): 00-366 Warsaw, ul. Foksal 3/5; tel. and fax (22) 278720; f. 1951, dissolved 1982, legal status restored 1989; 1,700 mems; Acting Pres. Andrzej Sawicki.

## Publishers

A total of 9,788 titles (books and pamphlets) were published in 1993.

**AGPOL** (Foreign Trade Publicity and Publishing Enterprise): 00-957 Warsaw, ul. Kierbedzia 4, POB 7; tel. (22) 416061; telex 813364; fax (22) 405607; f. 1956; foreign trade publicity services for Polish firms, export-import of goods and services; Man. Dir Tadeusz Polanowski.

**Instytut Prasy i Wydawnictw 'Novum' Unii Chrześcijansko-Społecznej:** 00-580 Warsaw, ul. I. Armii Wojska Polskiego 3; tel. (22) 213413; telex 816721; religious books; Dir Krzysztof Bielecki.

**Instytut Wydawniczy Pax** (Pax Publishing Institute): 00-390 Warsaw, Wybrzeże Kościnszkowskie 21A; tel. (2) 6253398; fax (2) 6253398; f. 1949; theology, philosophy, religion, history, literature; Editor-in-Chief Amelia Szafrańska.

**Instytut Wydawniczy Związków Zawodowych** (Trade Unions' Publishing Institute): 00-950 Warsaw, ul. Spasowskiego 1/3; tel. (22) 279011; f. 1950; social, economic, scientific, cultural, labour safety and trade union literature and fiction; Dir and Editor-in-Chief Stanisław Grześniak.

**Krajowa Agencja Wydawnicza—KAW** (National Publishing Agency—KAW): 00-950 Warsaw, ul. Wilcza 46; tel. (2) 6286481; telex 813487; fax (22) 296007; f. 1974; publishes children's and youths' fiction, history, art, popular reference books, postcards, posters and calendars, and audio records, cassettes and compact discs; Dir and Editor-in-Chief Jan Wysokiński.

**Księgarnia św. Wojciecha** (St Adalbert Printing and Publishing Co): 60-967 Poznań, Pl. Wolności 1; tel. (61) 529186; telex 0414220; f. 1895; textbooks and Catholic publications; Dir Rev. Bolesław Jurga; Editor-in-Chief Bozysław Walczak.

**Ludowa Spółdzielnia Wydawnicza** (People's Publishing Co-operative): 00-131 Warsaw, ul. Grzybowska 4/8; tel. (2) 6205718; fax (2) 6207277; f. 1949; fiction and popular science; Chair. and Editor-in-Chief Krzysztof Rajewski.

**Niezależna Oficyna Wydawnicza NOWA** (Independent Publishing House NOWA): 00-251 Warsaw, ul. Miodowa 10; tel. (2) 6359994; belles-lettres, memoirs, essays, recent history, politics; Pres. Grzegorz Boguta; Editor-in-Chief Mirosław Kowalski.

**Oficyna Literacka:** 30-112 Kraków, ul. Smoleńsk 38, m. 12; tel. (12) 218472; f. 1982 clandestinely, 1990 officially; belles-lettres, poetry, including débuts, essays; Editor-in-Chief Henryk Karkosza.

**Oficyna Wydawnicza Volumen:** 02-942 Warsaw, ul. Konstancińska 3A, m. 59; tel. and fax (22) 264221; f. 1984 (working clandestinely as WERS), 1989 officially; science, popular history, anthropology and socio-political sciences; Dir Adam Borowski.

**Pallottinum—Wydawnictwo Stowarzyszenia Apostolstwa Katolickiego:** 60-959 Poznań, Al. Przybyszewskiego 30, POB 23; tel. (61) 675233; fax (61) 675238; f. 1947; religious books; Dir Mgr Stefan Dusza.

**Państwowe Wydawnictwo Ekonomiczne** (State Publishing House for Economic Literature): 00-098 Warsaw, ul. Niecała 4A; tel. (22) 275567; f. 1949; economics books and magazines; Dir and Editor-in-Chief Alicja Rutkowska.

**Państwowe Wydawnictwo Rolnicze i Leśne** (State Agricultural and Forestry Publishers): 00-950 Warsaw, Al. Jerozolimskie 28; tel. and fax (22) 276338; f. 1947; for professional publications on agriculture and forestry; Dir and Editor-in-Chief Jolanta Kuczyńska.

**Państwowy Instytut Wydawniczy** (State Publishing Institute): 00-950 Warsaw, POB 377, ul. Foksal 17; tel. (22) 260201; fax (22) 261536; f. 1946; Polish and foreign classical and contemporary literature, fiction, literary criticism, biographies, performing arts, culture, history, popular science and fine arts; Dir Andrzej Gruszecki; Editor-in-Chief Alojzy Kołodziej.

**Polska Oficyna Wydawnicza BGW** (Polish Publishing House BGW): 02-001 Warsaw, Al. Jerozolimskie 91; tel. (2) 6217680; fax (2) 6284652; telex 817-965; f. 1990; encyclopaedias, compendia of knowledge, books for children; Pres. Roman Górski.

**Polskie Przedsiębiorstwo Wydawnictw Kartograficznych im. Eugeniusza Romera** (Romer Polish Cartographical Publishing House Co): 00-410 Warsaw, ul. Solec 18; tel. (2) 6283251; fax (2) 6280236; f. 1951; maps, atlases, travel guides, books on geodesy and cartography, and a quarterly review; Dir Alina Meljon.

**Polskie Wydawnictwo Muzyczne** (PWM—Edition): 31-111 Kraków, Al. Krasińskiego 11A; tel. (12) 227328; telex 813370; fax (12) 220174; f. 1945; music and books on music; Dir Jan Bętkowski.

**Spółdzielnia Wydawnicza Czytelnik** (Reader Co-operative Publishing House): 00-490 Warsaw, ul. Wiejska 12A; tel. (2) 6281441; fax (2) 6283178; f. 1944; general, especially fiction and contemporary Polish literature; Chair. Włodzimierz Michalak; Editor-in-Chief Henryk Chłystowski.

**Wydawnictwa Artystyczne i Filmowe** (Art and Film Publications): 02-595 Warsaw, ul. Puławska 61; tel. (22) 455301; fax (22) 455584; f. 1959; theatre, cinema, photography and art publications and reprints; Man. Dir Janusz Fogler.

POLAND
*Directory*

**Wydawnictwa Komunikacji i Łączności** (Transport and Communications Publishing House): 02-546 Warsaw, ul. Kazimierzowska 52; tel. and fax (22) 492322; telex 812736; f. 1949; technical books on motorization, electronics, radio engineering, television and telecommunications, road, rail and air transport; Dir Jerzy Kozłowski; Editor-in-Chief Bogumił Zieliński.

**Wydawnictwa Naukowo-Techniczne** (Scientific-Technical Publishers): 00-950 Warsaw, ul. Mazowiecka 2/4, POB 359; tel. (22) 267271; fax (22) 268293; f. 1949; scientific and technical books on mathematics, physics, chemistry, foodstuffs industry, electrical and electronic engineering, computer science, automation, mechanical engineering, light industry; technological encyclopaedias and dictionaries; Gen. Man. Dr Aniela Topulos.

**Wydawnictwa Normalizacyjne Alfa** (Standardization Publishing House): 00-950 Warsaw, ul. Nowogrodzka 22; tel. (22) 216751; telex 812374; f. 1956; standards, catalogues and reference books on standardization, periodicals; popular science for children, science fiction, household directories; Dir and Editor-in-Chief Jerzy Wysokiński.

**Wydawnictwa Polskiej Agencji Ekologicznej** (Polish Ecological Publishing House): 00-975 Warsaw, ul. Rakowiecka 4; tel. (22) 494927; fax (22) 495081; f. 1953; geology; Dir Jerzy Chodkowski.

**Wydawnictwa Szkolne i Pedagogiczne—WSiP** (Polish Educational Publishers): 00-950 Warsaw, POB 480, Pl. Dąbrowskiego 8; tel. (22) 268382; telex 816132; fax (22) 279280; f. 1945; school textbooks and popular science books, scientific literature for teachers, visual teaching aids, periodicals for teachers and youth; Man. Dir Andrzej Chrzanowski.

**Wydawnictwo Adamski i Bieliński:** 00-420 Warsaw, ul. Szara 10A, rms 302/303; tel. and fax (22) 294930; telex 825970.

**Wydawnictwo Arkady:** 00-959 Warsaw, ul. Dobra 28, POB 137; tel. (22) 269316; fax (22) 274194; f. 1957; publications on building, town planning, architecture and art; Dir and Pres. Janina Krysiak.

**Wydawnictwo Bellona:** 00-873 Warsaw, ul. Grzybowska 77; tel. (22) 204291; f. 1947; fiction, history and military; Dir Col Józef Skrzypiec.

**Wydawnictwo Czasopism i Książek Technicznych Sigma NOT, Spółka z o.o.** (Sigma Publishers of Technical Periodicals and Books, Ltd): 00-950 Warsaw, ul. Biała 4, POB 1004; tel. (22) 203118; telex 814550; fax (22) 203116; f. 1949; popular and specialized periodicals and books on general technical subjects; Dir and Editor-in-Chief Dr Andrzej Kusyk.

**Wydawnictwo Interpress** (Interpress Publishers): 04-028 Warsaw, Al. Stanów Zjednoczonych 53; tel. (22) 134669; telex 816170; fax (22) 134924; Poland past and present, handbooks, monographs, guide-books, albums; publishing co-operation and printing services; Editor-in-Chief Bohdan Gawroński.

**Wydawnictwo 'iskry' Spółka z o. o.** (Iskry Publishing House Ltd): 00-375 Warsaw, ul. Smolna 11/13; tel. (22) 279415; fax (22) 279415; f. 1952; travel, Polish and foreign fiction, science fiction, essays, popular science, history, memoirs; Dir and Editor-in-Chief Dr Wiesław Uchański.

**Wydawnictwo Lekarskie PZWL** (Medical Publishers Ltd): 00-238 Warsaw, ul. Długa 38/40; tel. (22) 312161; fax (22) 310054; f. 1945; medical literature and manuals, lexicons, encyclopaedias; Pres. Maria Dziak.

**Wydawnictwo Literackie** (Literary Publishing House): 31-147 Kraków, ul. Długa 1; tel. (12) 224644; fax (12) 225423; f. 1953; works of literature and belles-lettres; Dir Janusz Adamczyk.

**Wydawnictwo Łódzkie:** 90-447 Łódź, ul. Piotrkowska 171/173; tel. (42) 360331; fax (42) 368524; f. 1957; contemporary and classical Polish literature, juvenile literature, memoirs, essays, translations, popular science; Dir and Editor-in-Chief Ireneusz Rezner.

**Wydawnictwo Lubelskie** (Lublin Publishing House): 20-022 Lublin, ul. Okopowa 7; tel. (81) 27344; f. 1957; social and political literature, memoires, essays, fiction, poetry, translations from Ukrainian literature; Dir and Editor-in-Chief Ireneusz Caban.

**Wydawnictwo Morskie** (Maritime Publishing House): 80-835 Gdańsk, ul. Szeroka 38/40; tel. (58) 311031; f. 1951; popular science, humanities, maritime economy, belles-lettres, encyclopaedias, dictionaries, children's books; Dir and Editor-in-Chief Joanna Konopacka (acting).

**Wydawnictwo Nasza Księgarnia Spólka z o.o.** (Publishing House Nasza Księgarnia Ltd): 00-389 Warsaw, ul. Smulikowskiego 4; tel. (22) 263648; fax (22) 263646; f. 1921; books and periodicals for children and educational publications; Pres. Mirosław Tokarczyk.

**Wydawnictwo Naukowe PWN, Sp. z o. o.** (Polish Scientific Publishers Ltd): 00-251 Warsaw, ul. Miodowa 10; tel. (22) 312738; fax (22) 267163; f. 1951; publications and journals on all sciences, encyclopaedias, university textbooks, dictionaries; Dir Grzegorz Boguta; Editor-in-Chief Jan Kofman.

**Wydawnictwo Ossolineum** (Ossolineum Publishing House): 50-106 Wrocław, Rynek 9; tel. (71) 38625; telex 712771; fax (71) 448103; f. 1817; humanities and sciences; Dir Edward Malak; Editor-in-Chief Janusz Sowiński.

**Wydawnictwo Prawnicze** (Legal Publishing House): 02-520 Warsaw, ul. Wiśniowa 50; tel. (22) 494705; fax (22) 499410; f. 1952; Dir and Editor-in-Chief Dr Jerzy Kowalski.

**Wydawnictwo Śląsk Sp. z o.o.** (Silesia Publishing House Ltd): 40-161 Katowice, Al. W. Korfantego 51; tel. (32) 580756; fax (32) 583229; f. 1954; belles-lettres, social, popular science, children's books and regional literature; Pres. Tadeusz Sierny.

**Wydawnictwo Spółdzielcze:** 00-013 Warsaw, ul. Jasna 1; tel. (22) 271524; telex 813622; books, periodicals, information bulletins, catalogues, albums; Dir Sylwester Komarnicki.

**Wydawnictwo Sport i Turystyka** (State Sport and Tourism Publishers): 00-021 Warsaw, ul. Chmielna 7/9; tel. (22) 271303; telex 816578; fax (22) 274250; f. 1953; publications in the field of tourism, sports, popular topography, and artistic albums; Dir and Editor-in-Chief Kataryna Balicka.

**Wydawnictwo Spotkania:** 00-867 Warsaw, ul. Chłodna 29; tel. (22) 241615; fax (22) 207092; f. 1976 (outside Poland), f. 1990 (officially in Poland); memoirs, books on history, including military history, albums, postcards, cassettes, weekly *Spotkania*; Propr Piotr Jegliński.

**Wydawnictwo Wiedza Powszechna** (Popular Knowledge): 00-054 Warsaw, ul. Jasna 26; tel. (22) 269592; fax (22) 268594; f. 1952; popular scientific books, Polish and foreign language dictionaries, teach-yourself handbooks, foreign language textbooks, encyclopaedias and lexicons; Dir Józef Chlabicz.

**Zakład Wydawnictw Statystycznych** (Statistical Publishing Establishment): 00-925 Warsaw, Al. Niepodległości 208; tel. (22) 251455; telex 814581; fax (22) 259545; f. 1971; statistics and theory of statistics, periodicals; Dir Andrzej Stasiun.

**Zakłady Wydawnicze, Produkcyjne i Handlowe Epoka:** 00-950 Warsaw, ul. Zgoda 11, POB 393; tel. (22) 272495; fax (22) 277042; f. 1957; newspapers, periodicals, political and social publs of Democratic Party; Pres. Adam Karas.

**Znak Społeczny Instytut Wydawniczy** (Znak Social Publishing Institute): 30-105 Kraków, ul. Kościuszki 37; tel. (12) 219776; telex 0325707; fax (12) 219814; f. 1959; religion, philosophy, belles-lettres, essays, history; CEO Henryk Woźniakowski; Editor-in-Chief Jerzy Illg.

### PUBLISHERS' ASSOCIATION

**Polskie Towarzystwo Wydawców Książek** (Polish Society of Book Editors): 00-048 Warsaw, ul. Mazowiecka 2/4; tel. (22) 260735; f. 1926; Chair. Andrzej Karpowicz; 1,000 mems.

### WRITERS' ORGANIZATION

**Agencja Autorska** (Authors' Agency): 00-950 Warsaw, ul. Hipoteczna 2; tel. (22) 278396; telex 812470; f. 1964; represents Polish writers, composers, graphic artists and photographers; publishes monographs on contemporary Polish writers, and periodicals; places foreign books with Polish publishing houses; Dir Ewa Michalska; Pres. Antoni Marianowicz.

## Radio and Television

In 1993 there were 10.9m. radio and 10.1m. television subscribers. Legislation passed by the National Assembly in December 1992 brought to an end the state monopoly over broadcasting. In January 1994 Poland's first national commercial television licence was awarded to PolSat, a Polish satellite television company.

**National Council for Radio and Television:** Warsaw; f. 1993; regulatory body; Chair. (vacant).

### RADIO

**Polskie Radio** (Polish Radio): 00-950 Warsaw, ul. Woronicza 17; tel. (22) 478100; telex 814825; fax (22) 430141; Pres. Janusz Zaorski; Dir of International Relations Hanna Dąbrowska.

**Home Service:** there are four national channels broadcasting 80 hours per day; one long-wave transmitter (600 kW) broadcasting on 225 kHz; 14 medium-wave transmitters and 18 relay stations; 98 VHF transmitters covering all four programmes and 17 local programmes; Head of Radio Jan Marek Owsiński.

**Foreign Service:** Seven transmitters broadcast on 10 frequencies on short-wave, one transmitter broadcasting on medium-wave. Beamed programmes in Polish, English, Esperanto, German, Russian, Belarusian, Ukrainian, Lithuanian and Czech.

### TELEVISION

There are two national public channels, one broadcasting for 22 hours, the other for 16 hours per day via 84 transmitters and 134 relay stations, and one national private channel, broadcasting for 18 hours per day. Moreover, there is one satellite channel of Polish Television, TV Polonia, broadcasting for 16 hours per day. In addition to the various local programmes for Gdańsk, Katowice, Szczecin, Wrocław (seven hours per day) and Lublin (four hours per day), there are regional programmes for Bydgoszcz, Kraków, Łódź, Poznań, Rzeszów and Warsaw (three hours per day). Poland's first private (commercial) TV station began operating in Wrocław in early 1990. Broadcasting is regulated by the Broadcasting Bill, enacted in 1993.

**Telewizja Polska** (Polish Television): 00-950 Warsaw, ul. Woronicza 17, POB 211; tel. (22) 478501; telex 825331; fax (22) 435779; f. 1952; Chair. WIESŁAW WALENDZIAK; Man. Dir BARBARA BORYS-DAMIECKA.

**PolSat**: Warsaw; f. 1992; Polish satellite company, awarded Poland's first national, private television licence in 1994; Propr ZYGMUNT SOLORZ.

# Finance

(cap. = capital; res = reserves; dep. = deposits; m. = million; amounts in old złotys; brs = branches)

### BANKING

A major restructuring of the Polish banking system began in 1987, numerous new banks subsequently being established. The Banking Law of January 1989 allowed the involvement of foreigners in Polish banking. In accordance with Poland's association agreement with the EU, foreign banks will be permitted to operate freely in the country from 1997.

All figures given below are in terms of old złotys: on 1 January 1995 a new złoty, equivalent to 10,000 old złotys, was introduced.

### National Bank

**Narodowy Bank Polski** (National Bank of Poland): 00-919 Warsaw, ul. Świętokrzyska 11/21, POB 1011; tel. (2) 6200321; telex 814681; fax (22) 263932; f. 1945; state central bank; 49 brs throughout Poland; by early 1993 nine independent regional banks (since 1991 joint-stock companies), two state banks, three foreign banks and 84 commercial banks (joint-stock companies, including eight with foreign capital) had been granted licences by the National Bank; Pres. HANNA GRONKIEWICZ-WALTZ; First Deputy Pres. WITOLD KOZIŃSKI.

### Other Banks

**Bank-Agrobank SA**: 04-398 Warsaw 44, ul. Minska 25, POB 2; tel. (22) 102930; telex 816883; fax (22) 103355; f. 1989; Pres. ALEKSY MISIEJUK; 15 brs.

**Bank Depozytowo-Kredytowy w Lublinie SA** (Deposit and Credit Bank in Lublin): 20-954 Lublin, ul. Lubomelska 1/3, POB 184; tel. (81) 21712; telex 643515; fax (81) 713153; f. 1989; cap. 291,000m., res 1,635,259m., dep. 11,403,290m. (Dec. 1993); Pres. WŁODZIMIERZ KOSACKI.

**Bank Energetyki SA**: 26-600 Radom, ul. Zeromskiego 75; tel. (48) 455271; telex 0672469; fax (48) 455120; f. 1990; fmrly Bank Ziemi Radomskiej; Pres. LOUIS MONTMORY.

**Bank Gdański**: 80-958 Gdańsk, ul. Targ Drzewny 1, POB 436; tel. (58) 379222; telex 0512896; fax (58) 379618; f. 1989; due to be privatized in 1995; cap. 490,300m., dep. 14,070,863m. (Dec. 1992); Pres. EDMUND TOLWIŃSKI; 48 brs.

**Bank Gospodarki Żywnościowej** (Bank of Food Economy): 00-131 Warsaw, ul. Grzybowska 4; tel. (22) 257206; telex 825198; fax (22) 206112; f. 1975; finances agriculture, forestry and food processing; cap. 267,200m., res 3,509,600m., dep. 39,802,400m. (Dec. 1992); Chair. KAZIMIERZ OLESIAK; 102 brs.

**Bank Gospodarstwa Krajowego** (National Economy Bank): 00-800 Warsaw, ul. Grzybowska 80/82, POB 57; tel. (2) 6586894; telex 813232; fax (22) 204602; f. 1924; cap. 100,146m., res 32,745m., dep. 628,452m. (Dec. 1993); Pres. DANUTA CHMIELEWSKA.

**Bank Handlowo-Kredytowy SA**: 40-163 Katowice, Plac Gwarków 1, POB 189; tel. (32) 592542; telex 315792; fax (32) 582410; f. 1990; Pres. FRANCISZEK SOBCZAK; 4 brs.

**Bank Handlowy w Warszawie SA**: 00-950 Warsaw, ul. Chałubińskiego 8, POB 129; tel. (22) 303000; telex 814811; fax (22) 300113; f. 1870; authorized foreign exchange bank; cap. 2,600,000m., res 9,861,343m., dep. 42,995,753m. (Dec. 1993); Pres. CEZARY STYPULKOWSKI; 28 brs.

**Bank Inicjatyw Gospodarczych BIG SA** (Bank of Economic Initiatives): 00-950 Warsaw, Al. Jerozolimskie 44, POB 97; tel. (22) 272391; telex 814869; fax (22) 271330; f. 1989; 63.4% private cap.; cap. 164,129m., res 356,872m., dep. 9,815,835m. (Sept. 1993); Chair. BOGUSŁAW KOTT; 9 brs.

**Bank Polska Kasa Opieki SA (Pekao)**: 00-950 Warsaw, ul. Grzybowska 53/57, POB 1008; tel. (2) 6560000; telex 816582; fax (2) 6560004; f. 1929; joint-stock savings bank; domestic and foreign business; specializes in trade and project finance; cap. 400,000m., res 3,511,000m., dep. 119,354,000m. (Dec. 1993); Chair. MARIAN KANTON; 80 brs.

**Bank Przemysłowo-Handlowy SA** (Industrial and Commercial Bank): 30-527 Kraków, Na Zjeździe 11; tel. (12) 223333; telex 0326426; fax (12) 216914; f. 1989; privatized in 1995; cap. 518,000m., res 3,316,696m., dep. 23,992,925m. (Dec. 1993); Pres. JANUSZ QUANDT; 56 brs.

**Bank Rozwoju Eksportu SA** (Export Development Bank SA): 00-950 Warsaw, POB 728, Plac Bankowy 2; tel. (2) 6355926; telex 817118; fax (2) 39120160; f. 1986; privatized in 1993; provides credit for ventures that promote export growth; cap. 400,000m., res 444,345m., dep. 4,031,499m. (Dec. 1992); Pres. KRZYSZTOF SZWARC; 10 brs.

**Bank Rozwoju Rolnictwa SA (Rolbank)**: 61-773 Poznań, ul. Stary Rynek 85/86; tel. (61) 521800; telex 412049; fax (61) 525194; f. 1990; commercial bank; cap. 156,164m., res 21,370m., dep. 1,795,953m.; Pres. JERZY MAŁECKI; 21 brs.

**Bank Rozwoju Rzemiosła, Handlu i Przemysłu Market SA**: 61-773 Poznań, Stary Rynek 73/74, POB 72; tel. (61) 528231; telex 0413375; fax (61) 528237; Pres. ERYK WOJCIECHOWSKI.

**Bank Śląski SA w Katowicach**: 40-950 Katowice, ul. Warszawska 14, POB 137; tel. (3) 1537281; telex 312727; fax (3) 1537364; f. 1989; commercial bank; privatized in 1993; cap. 926,000m., res 1,661,004m., dep. 26,397,366m. (Dec. 1993); Pres. BRUNO BARTKIEWICZ; 58 brs.

**Bank Staropoloski SA w Pozanniu**: 60-967 Poznań, ul. Nowowiejskiego 5; tel. (61) 522568; telex 424782; fax (61) 522568; f. 1990; commercial bank; cap. 102,149m., dep. 823,280m. (Dec. 1992); Pres. JULIUSZ BARSZCZEWSKI.

**Bank Wschodnio-Europejski SA** (East European Bank): 00-953 Warsaw, ul. Mysia 3; tel. (2) 6255565; telex 815059; fax (2) 6256505; f. 1990 as Bank Turystyki SA; commercial bank for tourism industry; privatized and renamed in 1993; cap. and res 69,927m., dep. 246,908m. (Dec. 1992); Pres. ANDRZEJ OLECHOWSKI; 4 brs.

**Bank Zachódni Spółka Akcyjna** (Western Bank): 50-950 Wrocław, ul. Ofiar Oświęcimskich 41/43, POB 1109; tel. (71) 445411; telex 712837; fax (71) 32883; f. 1989; cap. 512,000m., res 2,137,801m., dep. 16,081,827m. (Dec. 1993); Pres. TADEUSZ GŁUSZCZUK.

**Bydgoski Bank Budownictwa SA**: 85-065 Bydgoszcz, ul. Chodkiewicza 15; tel. (52) 212661; telex 563178; fax (52) 212009; f. 1990; savings bank; cap. 51,741m., res 8,853m., dep. 370,650m. (Dec. 1992); Pres. BOGUSŁAW SALAMOŃSKI; 7 brs.

**Bydgoski Bank Komunalny SA**: 85-097 Bydgoszcz, ul. Jagiellońska 34; tel. (52) 229061; telex 562838; fax (52) 211902; f. 1989; commercial bank; cap. 24,000m., res 60,250m., dep. 970,290m. (Dec. 1993); Pres. JACEK PRZYWIECZERSKI; 10 brs.

**Polski Bank Rozwoju SA** (Polish Development Bank SA): 00-680 Warsaw, ul. Zurawia 47/49; tel. (2) 6300402; telex 812698; fax (2) 6300403; f. 1990; cap. 1,372,451m., res 437,484m., dep. 3,895,501m. (Dec. 1993); Pres. WOJCIECH KOSTRZEWA.

**Pomorski Bank Kredytowy SA** (Pomeranian Credit Bank): 70-952 Szczecin, Pl. Żołnierza Polskiego 16, POB 613; tel. (91) 334769; telex 422239; fax (91) 533114; f. 1989; cap. 354,000m., res 902,126m., dep. 14,706,840m. (Dec. 1993); Chair. WŁADYSŁAW JERMAKOWICZ; 57 brs.

**Powszechna Kasa Oszczędności—Bank Państwowy** (State Savings Bank): 00-950 Warsaw, Nowy Świat 6/12, POB 639; tel. (2) 6354000; telex 816829; fax (2) 6355851; f. 1919; cap. 3,740,000m., (1993); Pres. ANDRZEJ TOPIŃSKI; 854 brs and sub-brs.

**Powszechny Bank Gospodarczy w Łodzi** (Universal Economic Bank in Łódź): 90-950 Łódź, Al. Piłsudskiego 12, POB 12; tel. (42) 361470; telex 885411; fax (42) 367772; f. 1989; cap. 331,500m., res 631,960m., dep. 25,619,808m. (Dec. 1993); Pres. ANDRZEJ SZUKALSKI; 33 brs.

**Powszechny Bank Kredytowy SA w Warszawie** (Warsaw Credit Bank): 00-400 Warsaw, Nowy Świat 6/12; tel. (22) 299348; telex 815027; fax (22) 296988; f. 1989; cap. and res 2,625,411m., dep. 20,876,342m. (Dec. 1992); Chair. of Bd BARBARA ZAMBRZYCKA; 47 brs.

**Prosper-Bank SA w Krakowie**: 30-960 Kraków, ul. Solskiego 43; tel. (12) 225872; telex 0325403; f. 1990; Pres. ADAM KAWALEC.

**Warszawski Bank Zachodni SA**: 00-973 Warsaw 37, Al. Jerozolimskie 91, POB 57; tel. and fax (2) 6255248; Pres. WOJCIECH MIERNIK.

**Wielkopolski Bank Kredytowy SA w Poznaniu** (Credit Bank in Poznań): 60-967 Poznań 9, Pl. Wolności 15, POB 516; tel. (61) 542900; telex 0414501; fax (61) 521113; f. 1989; privatized in 1993; cap. 640,000m., res 553,312m., dep. 16,879,338m. (Dec. 1993); Pres. FRANCISZEK POŚPIECH; 48 brs.

POLAND — *Directory*

#### Foreign Banks

By the early 1990s many foreign banks, including Banque Nationale de Paris, Société Générale (France), Deutsche Bank AG, Dresdner Bank AG (Germany), Banca Commerciale Italiana (Italy) and Citibank NA (USA) had opened representative offices in Poland. The Bank Amerykański w Polsce SA (American Bank in Poland) was established in late 1989 with US and Polish capital.

### STOCK EXCHANGES

The stock-exchange service was re-established in April 1991. The Warsaw securities exchange reopened in July of that year.

**Warsaw Stock Exchange:** 00-400 Warsaw, Nowy Świat 6/12; tel. (2) 6283232; fax (2) 6281754; opened for trading in 1991; Pres. WIESŁAW ROZŁUCKI.

### INSURANCE

In 1994 there were some 30 insurance companies operating in Poland, but the market was dominated by Polish National Insurance (Państwowy Zakład Ubezpieczeń—PZU), which had 68% of property insurance business, and Warta Insurance and Reinsurance, which specialized in vehicle insurance, and foreign business. PZU's subsidiary, PZU Life, was the largest life insurance company.

**Państwowy Zakład Ubezpieczeń—PZU** (Polish National Insurance): 00-916 Warsaw, ul. Traugutta 5; tel. (22) 269115; telex 814487; fax (22) 269743; f. 1803; company dealing in property and other types of insurance; Pres. ROMAN FULNECZEK; 400 brs.

**Towarzystwo Ubezpieczeń i Reasekuracji Warta SA** (Warta Insurance and Reinsurance Co Ltd): 00-697 Warsaw, Al. Jerozolimskie 65/79; tel. (22) 272625; telex 817026; fax (22) 300336; f. 1920; marine, air, motor, fire, illness, luggage and credit; deals with all foreign business; Pres. ANDRZEJ WOJTYŃSKI; 13 brs; representatives in London and New York.

## Trade and Industry

### STATE PROPERTY AGENCY

**General Privatization Programme:** c/o Department of National Investment Funds, Ministry of Ownership Transformation (Privatization), 00-522 Warsaw, ul. Krucza 36; tel. (2) 292587; fax (2) 297129; responsible for the divestment of various state-owned enterprises.

### CHAMBERS OF COMMERCE

**Krajowa Izba Gospodarcza** (Polish Chamber of Commerce): Head Office, 00-074 Warsaw, Trębacka 4, POB 361; tel. (22) 260221; telex 814361; fax (22) 274673; f. 1990; Pres. ANDRZEJ ARENDARSKI; Chair. KAZIMIERZ PAZGAN; 150 mems.

**Izba Przemysłowo-Handlowa Inwestorów Zagranicznych** (Chamber of Industry and Trade for Foreign Investors): 00-071 Warsaw, ul. Krakowski Przedmieście 47/51; telex 817105; fax (2) 268593.

### TRADE UNIONS

**All Poland Trade Unions Alliance** (Ogólnopolskie Porozumienie Związków Zawodowych—OPZZ): 00-924 Warsaw, Kopernika 36/40; tel. (22) 267106; telex 813834; fax (22) 265102; f. 1984; 4.5m. mems (1994); Chair. EWA SPYCHALSKA.

**Independent Self-governing Trade Union Solidarity National Commission** (NSZZ Solidarność Komisja Krajowa): 80-855 Gdańsk, Wały Piastowskie 24; tel. (58) 316722; telex 513170; fax (58) 316722; f. 1980; outlawed 1981–89; 2.5m. mems; Chair. MARIAN KRZAKLEWSKI.

**Rural (Private Farmers') Solidarity:** Leader PIOTR BAUMGART.

### TRADE FAIRS

**Poznań International Fair Ltd:** 60-734 Poznań, ul. Głogowska 14; tel. (61) 692592; telex 413251; fax (61) 665827; f. 1921; international fair of investment goods in June and 24 other fairs (one in Katowice); 15,000 exhibitors, 1m. visitors annually; Pres. STANISŁAW LASKOWSKI.

## Transport

### RAILWAYS

At the end of 1993 there were 24,926 km of railway lines making up the state network, of which 11,482 km were electrified and 1,614 km were narrow gauge. Substantial modernization, with assistance from the World Bank and other sources, was planned for the 1990s.

**Polish State Railways** (Polskie Koleje Państwowe—PKP): 00-928 Warsaw, ul. Chałubińskiego 4; tel. (22) 244400; telex 816651; fax (22) 212705; f. 1842; Dir-Gen. ALEKSANDER JANISZEWSKI.

### ROADS

In December 1993 there were 368,364 km of roads, of which 257 km were motorways, 45,376 km were national roads and 128,528 km were provincial roads.

**PKS/Państwowa Komunikacja Samochodowa** (Polish Motor Communications): 00-973 Warsaw, ul. Grójecka 17; tel. (22) 220011; telex 816598; f. 1945; state enterprise organizing inland road transport for passengers and goods. Bus routes cover a total of 121,000 km; passengers carried 2,553,968 (1989); freight 7,650m. ton-kilometres (1989).

**Pekaes Auto-Transport SA:** 01-204 Warsaw, ul. Siedmiogrodzka 1/3; tel. (2) 3222519; telex 817419; fax (22) 321092; f. 1958; road transport of goods to all European and Middle Eastern countries.

### INLAND WATERWAYS

Poland has 6,850 km of waterways, of which 3,997 km were navigable in 1989. The main rivers are the Wisła (Vistula, 1,047 km), Odra (Oder, 742 km in Poland), Bug (587 km in Poland), Warta (808 km), San, Narew, Noteć, Pilica, Wieprz and Dunajec. There are some 5,000 lakes, the largest being the Śniardwy, Mamry, Łebsko, Dąbie and Miedwie. In addition, there is a network of canals (approximately 1,215 km).

About 606,000 passengers and 8,720,000 tons of freight were carried on inland water transport in 1993.

**Zjednoczenie Żeglugi Śródlądowej** (United Inland Navigation and River Shipyards): 50-149 Wrocław 2, Wita Stwosza 28; includes five inland navigation enterprises and eight inland shipyards.

### SHIPPING

Poland has three large harbours on the Baltic Sea: Gdynia, Gdańsk and Szczecin. The Polish merchant fleet had 591 ships in June 1993, with a total displacement of 2,646,000 grt.

Principal shipping companies:

**Polskie Linie Oceaniczne—PLO** (Polish Ocean Lines): 81-364 Gdynia, ul. 10 Lutego 24, POB 265; tel. (58) 201901; telex 054231; fax (58) 278480; f. 1951; 16 ships totalling 163,474 dwt and serving all five continents; Dir-Gen. HENRYK DĄBROWSKI; Exec. Dir ANDRZEJ WALENCIAK.

**Polska Żegluga Morska—PZM** (Polish Steamship Co): 70-419 Szczecin, Plac Rodła 8; tel. (91) 533958; telex 422136; fax (91) 344346; f. 1951; world-wide tramping; fleet of 118 vessels totalling 3,008,775 dwt (Dec. 1991); Chair. and Dir-Gen. JANUSZ LEMBAS.

**Przedsiębiorstwo Połowów Dalekomorskich i Usług Rybackich Gryf:** 70-952 Szczecin, Port Rybacki, ul. Władysława IV 1; tel. (91) 533772; telex 0425491; fax (91) 47989; f. 1957; deep-sea fishing and fish-processing; Man. Dir PIOTR JASNOWSKI.

### CIVIL AVIATION

Okęcie international airport is situated near Warsaw. A city terminal was completed in October 1989 under a joint-venture scheme with Austrian and US interests. There are also international airports at Kraków and Gdańsk. Domestic flights serve Gdańsk, Goleniow, Katowice, Kraków, Poznań, Rzeszów, Szczecin, Warsaw and Wrocław.

**Polskie Linie Lotnicze—LOT** (Polish Airlines—LOT): 00-697 Warsaw, Al. Jerozolimskie 65/79; tel. (2) 6283443; telex 813552; fax (22) 305860; f. 1929; domestic services and international services to the Middle East, Africa, Asia, Canada, USA, and throughout Europe; Pres. JAN LITWIŃSKI.

## Tourism

The Polish Tourist and Country-Lovers' Society is responsible for tourism and maintains about 420 branches across the country. The Society runs about 250 hotels, hostels and campsites. Poland is rich in historic cities, such as Gdańsk, Wrocław, Kraków and Warsaw. There are 30 health and climatic resorts, while the mountains, forests and rivers provide splendid scenery and excellent facilities for touring and sporting holidays. In 1994 Poland was visited by some 74m. foreign tourists, 64% of whom were from Germany. Numerous projects to improve Poland's tourist infrastructure were under way in the mid-1990s.

**Polish Tourist and Country-Lovers' Society** (Polskie Towarzystwo Turystyczno-Krajoznawcze): 00-075 Warsaw, ul. Senatorska 11; tel. (22) 265735; telex 812441; fax (22) 262505; f. 1950; Chair. ADAM CHYŻEWSKI; the Society has about 250 tourist accommodation establishments; 138,000 mems (1995).

**Orbis SA:** 00-028 Warsaw, str. Bracka 16; tel. (22) 260271; telex 814757; fax (22) 273301; f. 1923; national tourist enterprise; Gen. Man. JACEK WRÓBEL; 162 branch offices and 54 tourist hotels.

# PORTUGAL

## Introductory Survey

**Location, Climate, Language, Religion, Flag, Capital**

The mainland portion of the Portuguese Republic lies in western Europe, on the Atlantic side of the Iberian peninsula, bordered by Spain to the north and east. The country also includes two archipelagos in the Atlantic Ocean, the Azores and the Madeira Islands. The climate is mild and temperate, with an average annual temperature of 16°C (61°F). In the interior the weather is drier and hotter. Almost all of the inhabitants speak Portuguese and are Christians of the Roman Catholic Church. The national flag (proportions 3 by 2) has two vertical stripes, of green and red, the green occupying two-fifths of the total area; superimposed on the stripes (half on the green, half on the red) is the state coat of arms: a white shield, containing five small blue shields (each bearing five white roundels) in the form of an upright cross, with a red border containing seven yellow castles, all superimposed on a yellow armillary sphere. The capital is Lisbon (Lisboa).

**Recent History**

The monarchy that had ruled Portugal from the 11th century was overthrown in 1910, when the King was deposed in a bloodless revolution, and a republic was proclaimed. A period of great instability ensued until a military coup installed the regime of the Estado Novo (New State) in 1926. Dr António de Oliveira Salazar became Minister of Finance in 1928 and Prime Minister in 1932, establishing a right-wing dictatorial regime, influenced by Italian Fascism. A new Constitution, establishing a corporate state, was adopted in 1933. Only one political party was authorized, and suffrage was limited. Portugal remained neutral during the Second World War. The Government strove to achieve international acceptance, but Portugal was not admitted to the UN until 1955. Unlike the other European colonial powers, Portugal insisted on maintaining its overseas possessions, regarding them as 'inalienable'. In 1961 Portuguese enclaves in India were successfully invaded by Indian forces, and in the same year a rebellion against Portuguese rule began in Angola. Similar rebellions followed, in Portuguese Guinea (1963) and Mozambique (1964), and protracted guerrilla warfare ensued in the three African provinces. Salazar remained in power until illness forced his retirement in September 1968. He was succeeded by Dr Marcello Caetano, who had been Deputy Prime Minister in 1955–58. Caetano pursued slightly more liberal policies. Opposition parties were legalized for elections to the National Assembly in October 1969, but the União Nacional, the government party, won all 130 seats. Immediately after the elections, the opposition groups were outlawed again. The government party, renamed Acção Nacional Popular in February 1970, also won every seat at the next elections to the Assembly, in October 1973, following the withdrawal of all opposition candidates.

The drain on Portugal's economy by the long wars against nationalist forces in the overseas provinces contributed to the overthrow of Caetano in the bloodless coup of 25 April 1974, initiated by the Movimento das Forças Armadas (MFA), a group of young army officers. Gen. António Ribeiro de Spínola, head of the Junta of National Salvation which had then assumed power, became President in May and promised liberal reforms. In July Brig.-Gen. Vasco dos Santos Gonçalves replaced Prof. Adelino da Palma Carlos as Prime Minister. The new Government recognized the right of Portugal's overseas territories to self-determination. The independence of Guinea-Bissau (formerly Portuguese Guinea), proclaimed in September 1973, was recognized by Portugal in September 1974. The remaining African territories were all granted independence in 1975. Portugal also withdrew from Portuguese (East) Timor in 1975.

Following a split between the Junta's right and left wings, President Spínola resigned in September 1974 and was replaced by Gen. Francisco da Costa Gomes. An abortive counter-coup by high-ranking officers in March 1975 resulted in a swing to the left. All existing organs of the MFA were dissolved, a Supreme Revolutionary Council (SRC) was created, and six of the political parties agreed that it would stay in power for five years. On 25 April, the first anniversary of the overthrow of the Caetano regime, a general election was held for a Constituent Assembly. Of the 12 parties contesting the election, the Partido Socialista (PS) obtained the largest share of the votes and won 116 of the Assembly's 250 seats. Disputes between Socialists and Communists, however, provoked withdrawals from the new coalition Government, and Gen. Vasco Gonçalves was dismissed. Admiral José Pinheiro de Azevedo became Prime Minister in August. In September the provisional Government resigned and a new Government of 'united action' was formed, including members of the armed forces, the PS, the Partido Popular Democrático (PPD) and the Partido Comunista Português (PCP). In November the Government suspended its activities, owing to a lack of support from the armed forces. An abortive leftist military coup resulted from the political turmoil. Changes took place within the SRC, and in December the armed forces announced a plan to reduce its political power.

A new Constitution, committing Portugal to make a transition to socialism, took effect on 25 April 1976. The SRC was renamed the Council of the Revolution, becoming a consultative body, headed by the President, with powers to delay legislation and the right of veto in military matters. At the general election for the new Assembly of the Republic, the PS won 107 of the Assembly's 263 seats. In June the Army Chief of Staff, Gen. António Ramalho Eanes, a non-party candidate supported by the PS, the PPD and the Centro Democrático Social (CDS), was elected President. He took office in July, when a minority Socialist Government was formed under Dr Mário Lopes Soares, who had been Minister of Foreign Affairs in 1974–75. The Government resigned in December 1977, but the President again invited Dr Soares to take office as Prime Minister. A new PS-CDS coalition was established in January 1978, but it collapsed after only six months. A new Government was formed in November under Prof. Carlos Mota Pinto, but he resigned in July 1979.

President Eanes appointed Dr Maria de Lourdes Pintasilgo to head a provisional Government. In September 1979 the President dissolved the Assembly of the Republic and announced that an early general election would be held in December. The centre-right alliance, Aliança Democrática (AD), which included the Partido Social Democrata (PSD, formerly the PPD) and the CDS, won 128 of the 250 seats in the Assembly. Dr Francisco Sá Carneiro, leader of the PSD, was appointed Prime Minister. At the general election held in October 1980, as scheduled in the Constitution, the AD increased its majority of seats in the Assembly from six to 18. In December 1980 Dr Sá Carneiro was killed in an air crash. The presidential election took place as planned, however, and President Eanes won a clear victory over five rival candidates, receiving 56.4% of the valid votes. Dr Francisco Pinto Balsemão, co-founder of the PSD, was appointed Prime Minister. In March 1981 the offices of President of the Republic and Chief of Staff of the Armed Forces were formally separated.

In August 1982 the Assembly of the Republic approved the final draft of the new Constitution, which abolished the Council of the Revolution and reduced the powers of the President, thus completing the transition to full civilian government. Following divisions within the PSD, and losses at local elections in December 1982, Dr Balsemão resigned as Prime Minister. The Deputy Prime Minister and leader of the CDS, Prof. Diogo Freitas do Amaral, announced his resignation from all party and political posts. President Eanes dissolved the Assembly, and announced that a premature general election would be held. In February 1983 Dr Balsemão was replaced as leader of the PSD by Prof. Carlos Mota Pinto. At the general election, held in April, the PS, led by the former Prime Minister, Dr Mário Soares, won 101 of the Assembly's 250 seats. Dr Soares succeeded in forming a coalition Government with the PSD (the AD having been dissolved), which took office in June.

In November 1983 there was an open disagreement between President Eanes and the Prime Minister when, on the latter's recommendation, the President was obliged to dismiss the Chief of Staff of the Army. In April 1984 tension between the trade unions and the Government increased, following an unauthorized demonstration by unpaid employees of state industries, which resulted in hundreds of arrests. Following an increase in urban terrorism, for which the radical left-wing group, Forças Populares de 25 Abril (FP-25), claimed responsibility, controversial legislation proposing the establishment of a security intelligence agency, was introduced in the Assembly of the Republic in June 1984. The arrest of more than 40 terrorist suspects, including Lt-Col Otelo Saraiva de Carvalho, the former revolutionary commander, coincided with the introduction of the legislation. Further guerrilla suspects were arrested subsequently.

In January 1985 relations between the President and the Prime Minister were further strained, following the President's New Year message, in which he was critical of the Government's performance. In February Prof. Carlos Mota Pinto resigned as leader of the PSD, and subsequently as Deputy Prime Minister and Minister of Defence, following his failure to secure adequate support from within his party, and was replaced by Rui Machete, the Minister of Justice. A government reshuffle then took place. In May Machete was replaced as PSD leader by Prof. Aníbal Cavaco Silva, a former Minister of Finance.

In June 1985, on the day after Portugal signed its treaty of accession to the EC, the PS-PSD coalition disintegrated, following disagreements over labour and agricultural reforms. Dr Mário Soares resigned as Prime Minister, and President Eanes was obliged to call another premature general election for October, at which the PSD won 88 of the 250 seats in the Assembly of the Republic, while the PS won 57 seats and the Partido Renovador Democrático (PRD, a new party founded in early 1985 by supporters of President Eanes) won 45 seats. Prof. Aníbal Cavaco Silva was able to form a minority government acceptable to President Eanes.

In January 1986 four candidates contested the presidential election. As no candidate achieved the requisite 50% majority, a second round of voting was held in February: having secured the support of all the leftist parties, Dr Mário Soares, the former Prime Minister, narrowly defeated Prof. Diogo Freitas do Amaral, former leader of the CDS, to become Portugal's first civilian President for 60 years, taking office in March.

The Government of Cavaco Silva hoped to embark on a reformist programme but, owing to its lack of a majority, encountered difficulties in securing the adoption of legislation by the Assembly of the Republic. The Government suffered its first defeat in April 1986, on proposals for the budget. In June, following the legislature's rejection of his proposals to amend the labour laws (adopted following the revolution of 1974), in order to permit the dismissal of surplus workers, Cavaco Silva survived a vote of 'no confidence'. In July proposed revisions to the agrarian reform law were rejected. President Soares made use of his right of veto for the first time in September 1986, when he refused to approve legislation to revise the autonomy statute of the Azores.

In April 1987 Cavaco Silva resigned, following his defeat in a motion of censure, presented by the PRD and supported by the PS and the PCP. President Soares dissolved the Assembly of the Republic, prior to the holding of an early general election in July. The election resulted in a decisive victory for the PSD, which secured 148 of the 250 seats in the Assembly of the Republic and thus became the first party since 1974 to win an absolute majority. The PS won 60 seats, and the Coligação Democrático Unitária (CDU, a new left-wing coalition comprising mainly the PCP) won 31 seats. The PRD suffered a serious reverse, winning only seven seats, compared with 45 at the 1985 election, and Gen. Eanes announced his resignation from the presidency of the party shortly afterwards.

Upon his return to the office of Prime Minister, Prof. Cavaco Silva appointed Eurico de Melo to the new post of Deputy Prime Minister, and made several other changes to the Council of Ministers. Cavaco Silva announced a programme of radical economic reform, with emphasis on the importance of free enterprise. The gradual partial privatization of state industries was to continue (full privatization being subject to a revision of the 1976 Constitution), and fundamental changes in the sectors of agriculture, education and the media were proposed. The most controversial aspect of the programme, however, was the Government's renewed attempt to reform the restrictive labour laws.

In early 1988 industrial unrest, particularly in the public-transport sector, began to increase, and in March an estimated 1.5m. workers, fearing for the security of their jobs, took part in a 24-hour general strike to protest against the Government's proposed legislation. Nevertheless, in April the labour laws were approved by the Assembly of the Republic. The Government suffered a set-back in the following month, however, when the Constitutional Court ruled that the new legislation violated the Constitution. Nevertheless, the Government's proposals for agrarian and fiscal reforms, adopted by the Assembly of the Republic in July, were approved by the Constitutional Court in August. In October the PSD and the opposition PS reached agreement on proposed constitutional revisions. Marxist elements were to be removed from the Constitution (thereby permitting the Government's full privatization programme to proceed), subject to approval by the requisite two-thirds majority of the Assembly of the Republic. Having gained this approval, and also the agreement of President Soares, the constitutional amendments entered into force in August 1989.

In late 1988 the Secretary-General of the PS, Vítor Constâncio, unexpectedly resigned, and in January 1989 he was replaced by Jorge Sampaio. The PCP also continued to fall into disarray. Disagreements over policy led to expulsions from the Central Committee of the party. In January 1990 the PCP expelled a leading advocate of reform, and in March declared its intention to remain a Marxist-Leninist party. In February the President of the PRD resigned.

Opposition to the new labour legislation was renewed in January 1989, when 10,000 demonstrators took part in a protest in Lisbon. The legislation was approved by President Soares in February. Labour unrest continued. A strike by public-service workers in December 1988 was repeated in June 1989. Further strike action by transport workers continued throughout 1989. The country's doctors and bank employees also went on strike, all demanding wage increases sufficient to offset the level of inflation.

At elections to the European Parliament in June 1989, the PSD succeeded in retaining most of its seats. The Portuguese Greens won their first seat in Strasbourg. In October the Government survived a motion of censure, presented by the PS, which was highly critical of the Government's 'lack of ethics'. The opposition party's accusations related to two scandals earlier in the year involving the Minister of Finance, who was alleged to have evaded property-transfer tax, and the Minister of Health, who was suspected of irregularities regarding hospital contracts. At municipal elections, held in December, the PSD suffered a further reverse when the PS, supported by the PCP and the Greens, took control of Lisbon, Jorge Sampaio (the PS Secretary-General) becoming Mayor of the capital. The PSD also lost other major cities.

In January 1990 the Deputy Prime Minister and Minister of Defence, Eurico de Melo, was reported to have resigned shortly before Cavaco Silva's announcement of a government reshuffle. A new Deputy Prime Minister was not appointed. Other changes included the replacement of the Ministers of Finance and of Health, both accused of misconduct during 1989. A new Ministry of the Environment was established. In April 1990 the sudden resignation of the Minister of Public Works, Transport and Communications followed the election of an opponent as PSD Secretary-General.

In February 1990 a financial scandal relating to the Government of the Portuguese overseas territory of Macau threatened to jeopardize relations between the Prime Minister and the socialist President. It was alleged that Carlos Melancia, the socialist Governor of Macau, had accepted 50m. escudos from a German company which hoped to secure a consultancy contract for the construction of an airport in Macau. The integrity of President Soares was therefore called into question. In September Carlos Melancia was served with a summons in connection with the alleged bribery. Although he denied any involvement in the affair, the Governor of Macau resigned. Melancia was acquitted in August 1993, but in February 1994 it was announced that he was to be retried. (See p. 2526.)

In October 1990 President Soares confirmed his intention to seek a renewal of his mandate at the forthcoming presidential election. The campaign was dominated by the Macau scandal. Nevertheless, at the election, held on 13 January 1991 and contested by four candidates, Soares secured an outright victory. Supported by both the PS and the PSD, the incumbent President received more than 70% of the votes cast. Basílio Horta of the CDS won 14%, Carlos Carvalhas of the PCP received 13% and Carlos Marques of the extreme left-wing won less than 3%. The level of abstention was 38%.

Legislative elections were held on 6 October 1991. The PSD, which had based its campaign largely on its record of sustained economic growth and on the prospect of continued political stability, renewed its absolute majority, winning 135 of the 230 seats in the Assembly of the Republic. The PS secured 72 seats, the CDU 17 and the CDS five. An abstention rate of 34% was recorded. A new Government was appointed in late October, the most notable change being the replacement of the Minister of Finance.

Following the electorate's clear endorsement of the PSD's policies, Prof. Diogo Freitas do Amaral resigned from the leadership of the CDS (a post to which he had returned in 1988), not being succeeded until March 1992, upon the appointment of Manuel Monteiro. In February the Secretary-General of the PS, Jorge Sampaio, was replaced by António Gutteres.

In March 1992 the Minister of Education was obliged to resign, following large-scale student protests against the university entrance examination system. The demonstrations had attracted widespread public support. There was renewed unrest in late 1992, when public-service workers went on strike in support of claims for pay increases. In November a two-day strike by doctors, protesting against the Government's proposals to transfer some health services to the private sector, took place.

During 1992 tension between President Soares and Cavaco Silva became more evident, owing to the President's increasingly frequent use of his power of veto in order to obstruct the passage of legislation. In May President Soares vetoed a government decree drastically to reduce the strength of the armed forces. Although this particular decision was subsequently reversed, at a PSD congress in November the Prime Minister was highly critical of the President's use of the veto and of his repeated recourse to the Constitutional Court.

In November 1992 José Manuel Durão Barroso replaced João de Deus Pinheiro as Minister of Foreign Affairs, upon the latter's appointment as EC Commissioner. In early 1993 the Government was embarrassed by accusations of corruption. It was alleged that EC funds, destined for various projects in Portugal, had gone astray. The Minister of Finance, Jorge Braga de Macedo, was among those under investigation.

During 1993 the apparent shortcomings of the country's health service attracted much public attention. In June the Minister of the Environment and Natural Resources was obliged to resign, following protests over an offensive remark he had made regarding renal dialysis patients who had died in Evora as a result of the excessive level of aluminium in the hospital's water supply. The Minister of Health was among those replaced in a government reorganization in December 1993. Furthermore, in January 1994 a former Secretary of State for Health received a seven-year prison sentence, having been found guilty of corruption charges relating to the awarding of hospital contracts in 1986–87.

Relations between the Head of State and the Prime Minister were strained once again in August 1993 when, upon the President's exercise of his right of veto, an extraordinary session of the Assembly of the Republic was convened to discuss controversial legislation entailing severe restrictions on the statutory right of refugees to asylum in Portugal. The law was adopted in modified form. In the same month the implementation of a government decree reducing the minimum legal age of employment to 14 years provoked strong criticism, particularly from the trade unions.

In October 1993 there were violent scenes at Lisbon airport when employees of TAP—Air Portugal, incensed by the carrier's proposals to 'freeze' wages and to implement 2,500 redundancies, clashed with riot police. In the following month student demonstrators, protesting against an increase in university fees, were involved in similar disturbances outside the Assembly of the Republic. In November the human rights organization, Amnesty International, expressed concern at the numerous allegations of torture and mistreatment of detainees by Portuguese police and prison officers.

In December 1993 Cavaco Silva effected a ministerial reorganization. Changes included the replacement of the Minister of Finance. Local elections were held in the same month. The opposition PS secured 36% of the votes, while the PSD received 34%. The PS retained control of Lisbon and Porto. The PCP, with 13% of the votes, maintained its position, particularly in southern Portugal.

In early 1994 strike action by public-service workers was renewed, to protest against the Government's plans to restrict forthcoming pay increases to 2.5%. In May the head of the country's intelligence service and the organization's regional director in Madeira were dismissed, following the discovery of an electronic surveillance device in the office of the Attorney General (who had been investigating allegations of corruption among government officials) and the revelation of other illegal activities. At elections to the European Parliament in June 1994, the PS won 10 of the country's 25 seats in Strasbourg, while the PSD won nine seats. The level of voter participation, however, was only 35.7%, the lowest percentage recorded for any election since the restoration of democracy in 1975. Also in June Miguel Beleza, the governor of the central bank, was obliged to resign, following differences with the Government over monetary policy. The independence of the central bank was called into question upon Beleza's replacement by António de Sousa, hitherto the Secretary of State for Finance and a close associate of the Prime Minister. In the same month the Government was further embarrassed by the resignation of António Pinto Cardoso, a junior minister for Employment and Training, as a result of allegations of his involvement in the reported misuse of European Social Fund resources. President Soares exercised his right of veto once again in August 1994, when he returned to the Assembly of the Republic three items of legislation, two of which related to proposed restrictions on the freedom of information. In October the Government survived a vote of 'no confidence' in the legislature.

In January 1995 Cavaco Silva announced his intention to resign as leader of the PSD. At the party congress in the following month, despite his implication in recent scandals relating to the servicing of Indonesian and Angolan military aircraft in contravention of embargoes (see below) and consequent opposition demands for his resignation, Joaquim Fernando Nogueira, Minister of Defence, narrowly defeated his principal rival, José Manuel Durão Barroso, Minister of Foreign Affairs, in the contest for the leadership. Cavaco Silva undertook to remain as Prime Minister pending the forthcoming legislative elections, scheduled to be held by October 1995. Presidential elections were to take place in early 1996, upon the expiry of Soares's second term of office. In March 1995 Fernando Nogueira resigned as Minister of Defence, following the President's veto of the former's proposed appointment as Deputy Prime Minister.

Meanwhile, terrorist attacks by FP-25 and other groups had continued, targets including both Portuguese and foreign business interests, NATO installations and the US Embassy in Lisbon. In July 1985 the trial of more than 70 alleged members of FP-25 (including Lt-Col Saraiva de Carvalho) opened, but was adjourned, owing to the fatal shooting of a key prosecution witness. In September 1985, 10 of the defendants escaped from prison, but the trial later resumed and in October 1986 former President Eanes testified in favour of Lt-Col Saraiva de Carvalho. Terrorist attacks continued, and it was alleged that FP-25 was receiving financial support from Libya. Upon the conclusion of the trial of the FP-25 suspects in May 1987, Lt-Col Saraiva de Carvalho was found guilty of subversion and sentenced to 15 years' imprisonment (subsequently increased to 18 years). Almost 50 other defendants also received prison sentences. In May 1989, when the Supreme Court ruled that irregularities had occurred at his trial, Lt-Col Saraiva de Carvalho was released (along with 28 others convicted on similar charges), pending a decision on a fresh hearing. In February 1990 he renounced the armed struggle and requested an amnesty. In December, however, the Supreme Court confirmed his conviction and ordered his imprisonment. New charges were brought against him in October 1992. In July 1986 two people were killed in a series of explosions, for which responsibility was claimed by a hitherto unknown group, Organização Revolucionária Armada. Anti-terrorist legislation was strengthened, but in September a number of bombs exploded around Algarve holiday resorts.

Relations with Spain improved in the late 1980s. In December 1987 President Soares made a successful six-day official visit to Spain, and in May 1989 King Juan Carlos became the first Spanish monarch to address the Portuguese

Assembly of the Republic, during a four-day visit. Regular 'summit' meetings between Cavaco Silva and Felipe González, the Spanish Prime Minister, took place subsequently. Both Portugal and Spain were admitted to Western European Union (see p. 221) in November 1988.

Negotiations with the People's Republic of China on the question of the Portuguese overseas territory of Macau (see p. 2525) began in June 1986, and in April 1987 Portugal and China signed an agreement whereby Portugal would transfer the administration of Macau to China in December 1999. Prior to that date, full Portuguese passports were to be available to certain Macau residents. In August 1989 China gave Portugal an assurance that it would honour the agreement to maintain the territory's capitalist system after 1999. The Chinese Premier paid an official visit to Lisbon in February 1992, as did President Jiang Zemin in November 1993. During visits to China and Macau in April 1994, the Portuguese Prime Minister expressed confidence in the future of the territory.

The former Portuguese territory of East Timor was unilaterally annexed by Indonesia in 1976. UN-sponsored negotiations between Portugal and Indonesia began in 1983. Portugal refused to attend the EC-ASEAN meeting of foreign ministers, held in Jakarta in October 1986. In September 1987 the Portuguese Government indicated its desire for an early diplomatic solution to the problem. Portugal submitted an official protest to the UN in late 1988, when President Suharto of Indonesia paid a visit to East Timor. In 1992 Portugal attempted to obstruct EC plans for greater co-operation with ASEAN. Under UN auspices, talks between Portugal and Indonesia on the East Timor issue were resumed in December 1992, but ended without agreement. In June 1993 the Portuguese President awarded a freedom prize to the East Timor resistance leader, Xanana Gusmão, following the latter's sentencing to life imprisonment by a court in Dili (see p. 1516). Nevertheless, discussions between Portugal and Indonesia continued intermittently. In July 1994 the Portuguese Government condemned an assault by Indonesian security forces on a student protest in East Timor, in which about 20 demonstrators were reportedly injured, and urged a strong international response. In November Portugal granted political asylum to 29 East Timorese student activists, who had taken refuge in the US embassy in Jakarta. In January 1995 Portugal and Indonesia agreed to the holding of discussions, under UN auspices, between the factions of East Timor. In the same month the Portuguese Government was embarrassed by allegations that it had authorized the servicing of Indonesian military helicopters, in violation of its embargo against Indonesia.

Portugal's relations with Australia were strained by the latter's plans to exploit petroleum fields off the coast of East Timor, which Portugal claimed to be a violation of international law. In December 1989, upon the signing of a prospecting agreement between Australia and Indonesia, Portugal withdrew its ambassador from Canberra in protest. In February 1991 Portugal instituted proceedings against Australia at the International Court of Justice. Following hearings in early 1995, the Court commenced its consideration of the case.

In early 1988 Portugal announced that it was to review the terms of the 1983-91 agreement permitting the continued US use of the Portuguese air base at Lajes in the Azores, in return for US economic and military aid. On a visit to the USA in February 1988, the Portuguese Prime Minister expressed his disappointment at the decline in the level of US aid since 1983, but nevertheless stated that he did not intend to reduce the facilities at Lajes. In February 1989 the USA agreed to increase its level of compensation for its use of the base. In January 1990, on a visit to Washington, Cavaco Silva reiterated his desire to negotiate a new treaty with the USA. Discussions on the renewal of the treaty began in January 1991.

In 1988 Portugal expressed its willingness to assist in the reconstruction of the economy of Angola, a former Portuguese overseas possession. Portugal played a significant role in the Angolan peace process. Several meetings between representatives of the Angolan Government and the rebel UNITA were held in Lisbon, culminating in the signing of a peace accord in mid-1991. In January 1993, following the resumption of hostilities, President Soares issued an appeal for peace. In June UNITA rejected Portugal's status as an observer in the peace process, and in September, shortly before the UN's imposition of sanctions on UNITA, President Soares refused to meet a delegation of the movement in Lisbon. In May 1994 a UNITA spokesman welcomed the possibility of further Portuguese mediation. A new peace agreement was signed in November 1994. In early 1995, however, the neutrality of the Portuguese Government was undermined by allegations that it had given technical assistance to the Government of Angola.

Portugal was also active in the quest for peace in Mozambique. Relations with Mozambique, however, deteriorated in March 1989, when a Mozambican diplomat was expelled from Portugal, following his implication in the assassination, in Lisbon in April 1988, of a Mozambican resistance leader. Nevertheless, in April 1990 President Chissano of Mozambique paid an official visit to Portugal. In January 1992 Portugal received a formal invitation to attend the peace talks as an observer, and in October a peace treaty was signed in Italy.

### Government

A new Constitution, envisaging the construction of a socialist society in Portugal, was promulgated in 1976, and revised in 1982. Further revisions, which included the removal of Marxist elements, were approved by the Assembly of the Republic in 1989. The organs of sovereignty are the President, the Assembly of the Republic and the Government. The President, elected by popular vote for a five-year term, appoints the Prime Minister and, on the latter's proposal, other members of the Government, principally the Council of Ministers. The Council of State is a consultative body. The unicameral Assembly has 230 members (reduced from 250 at the 1991 election), including four representing Portuguese abroad, elected by universal adult suffrage for four years (subject to dissolution). The overseas territory of Macau (see p. 2525) is governed by special statute, and the Azores and Madeira (integral parts of the Portuguese Republic) were granted autonomy in 1976.

### Defence

Compulsory military service lasts from four to eight months in the army and from four to 18 months in the navy and air force. Conscientious objectors are allowed to perform an alternative community service. Portugal is a member of NATO and of Western European Union. In June 1994 the total strength of the armed forces was 50,700 (including 17,600 conscripts), comprising: army 27,200, navy 12,500 (including 1,850 marines) and air force 11,000. The paramilitary National Republican Guard, the Public Security Police and the Border Security Guard totalled 20,900, 20,000 and 8,900 respectively. In mid-1994 a total of 1,155 US troops were stationed in Portugal, mainly at the air force base at Lajes in the Azores. Defence expenditure for 1994 was budgeted at 258,500m. escudos.

### Economic Affairs

In 1993, according to estimates by the World Bank, Portugal's overall gross national product (GNP), measured at average 1991-93 prices, was US $77,749m., equivalent to $7,890 per head. Between 1985 and 1993, it was estimated, GNP per head increased, in real terms, at an average rate of 4.7% per year. Over the same period, the population declined by an average rate of 0.6% per year. The average annual increase in overall gross domestic product (GDP), in real terms, was 2.9% during 1980-92.

Agriculture (including forestry and fishing) contributed an estimated 4.7% of GDP at constant prices in 1992. The sector employed 11.6% of the working population in 1993. The principal crops are wheat, maize, potatoes, tomatoes and grapes. In 1994 it was announced that much wheat and maize was to be replaced by the more profitable sugar beet. The production of wine, particularly port, is significant. Agricultural GDP increased at an average annual rate of 6.1% in 1985-88 and by 12.5% in 1989, but fell by 1.7% in 1990, by 0.5% in 1991 and by 1.0% in 1992, when production was affected by drought. The fishing industry is important, the sardine catch, at 83,347 metric tons in 1992, being by far the largest.

Industry (comprising mining, manufacturing, construction and power) contributed an estimated 36.1% of GDP at constant prices in 1992. In 1993 the sector employed 32.7% of the working population. During 1985-89 industrial production increased at an average annual rate of 5.4%. Output rose by 9.6% in 1990, remained stagnant in 1991, and declined by 2.9% in 1992 and by 4.0% in 1993. An increase in production of 1.7% was forecast for 1994.

The mining and quarrying industry makes a minimal contribution to GDP, employing 0.4% of the working population in

1993. Limestone, granite, marble, copper pyrites, gold and uranium are the most significant products.

Manufacturing and mining (excluding energy production) provided 25.4% of GDP at constant prices in 1992, and manufacturing employed 23.4% of the working population in 1993. The textile and clothing industry is the most important branch of manufacturing, clothing alone accounting for an estimated 18.3% of total export earnings in 1994. Other significant manufactured products include footwear, paper pulp, cork items, chemicals, electrical appliances and ceramics. Manufacturing output rose by 4.6% per year in 1985–89. The value of production increased by 5.3% in 1990, compared with the previous year, but declined by 0.5% in 1991 and by 2.5% in 1992.

Energy is derived mainly from imported petroleum and from hydroelectric power. In 1993 imports of petroleum and its products accounted for an estimated 7.3% of total import costs.

Services provided 59.2% of GDP at constant prices in 1992, and employed 55.7% of the working population in 1993. Between 1985 and 1990 the GDP of the services sector increased, in real terms, at an average rate of 5.4% per year. The tourism industry remained a significant source of foreign-exchange earnings in 1994, when receipts totalled an estimated 634,406m. escudos, equivalent to 8% of GDP. Emigrants' remittances are also important to the Portuguese economy, reaching an estimated US $4,492m. in 1991.

In 1993 Portugal recorded a visible trade deficit of US $6,886m., but a surplus of $947m. on the current account of the balance of payments. Most of Portugal's trade is with other members of the EU. In 1993 Spain, Germany and France supplied an estimated 17.8%, 15.0% and 12.7%, respectively, of total imports. The principal export markets were Germany (which purchased 19.6% of the total), France (15.1%) and Spain (14.4%). In 1994 the main exports were clothing, textiles, footwear, pulp and waste paper, wood and cork manufactures, electrical equipment, chemicals and petroleum and its products. The principal imports were foodstuffs, textile yarn, chemicals, petroleum and its products and transport equipment.

The 1995 budget envisaged a deficit of 731,600m. escudos, equivalent to 5.8% of GDP (compared with an estimated 6.4% in 1994). Portugal's total external debt at the end of 1993 was US $36,942m., of which $25,173m. was long-term public debt. The cost of servicing the debt in 1992 was equivalent to 18.4% of revenue from exports of goods and services. In 1985–93 the annual rate of inflation averaged 10.4%. The average rate of inflation (excluding rent) in 1994 was 5.2%. The level of unemployment rose from 5.5% of the labour force in 1993 to 6.8% in 1994.

Portugal became a member of the EC (now EU, see p. 143) in January 1986. The Maastricht Treaty on European Union (see p. 149) was ratified by the Portuguese legislature in December 1992. The European Regional Development Fund committed ECU 1,296.5m. towards projects in Portugal in 1993. In April 1992 Portugal joined the exchange rate mechanism of the EMS (see p. 160). Portugal is also a member of the OECD (see p. 194).

In preparation for European economic and monetary union, the Portuguese Government remained committed to its programme of austerity and its objective of convergence with other EU countries. The escudo was devalued by 6.5% in May 1993 and by 3.5% in March 1995. The 1994–99 regional development plan, which was to be partly funded by the EU and the European Investment Bank, envisaged expenditure of 6,580,000m. escudos. In October 1993, as the economy entered recession, the Government was obliged to announce a supplementary budget. The 1994 and 1995 budgets aimed to encourage foreign investment, which had begun to decline sharply, and to promote recovery. Other difficulties facing the Government included structural weaknesses, particularly in the agricultural sector, and the need for greater efficiency and competitiveness. The programme of privatization of state-owned companies (many of which had incurred heavy financial losses) was initiated in 1989. Revenue from this source in 1994 totalled almost 200,000m. escudos, close to the Government's target. Plans to promote the role of the small investor were announced in April 1994. GDP contracted by 1.0% in 1993. A growth rate of 1.5% was recorded in 1994, and expansion of 3.2% envisaged for 1995.

### Social Welfare

The State is obliged to provide a social security system and full health facilities. In August 1990 the Assembly of the Republic approved a new law on basic health. Private practices are allowed to coexist. In 1993 Portugal had 38,654 hospital beds, and there were 28,769 physicians working in the country. Family allowances, old-age and veterans' pensions, pensions for the handicapped and the statutory minimum wage are increased annually, under the Ministry of Employment and Social Security. In 1989 a new unemployment insurance scheme was introduced. Unemployment benefit is not universally available. About 69% of those unemployed were receiving state allowances in 1993. Sickness and maternity benefits are also available. The 1993 state budget allocated 10.5% of total expenditure to health services.

### Education

Formal education at all levels is provided at both public and private institutions. Pre-school education, for three- to six-year olds, is not compulsory and is available free of charge in public nursery schools. Basic education is compulsory for nine years, between the ages of six and 15, and is provided free of charge in public schools. It is divided into three cycles: the first lasts for four years, the second for two years and the third for three years. Students over 14 years of age attend supplementary courses (day and evening classes). Secondary education, which is not compulsory, lasts for three years. The final year of secondary education (the 12th school year) has two branches: pre-university and pre-vocational. Technical-vocational and vocational courses may follow the ninth year of schooling. The technical-vocational courses last for three years, corresponding to the 10th–12th years of schooling. The vocational courses consist of one year of schooling and six months of vocational training. Special education aims to promote the integration of handicapped children into normal classes. In 1991 the total enrolment in basic and secondary education was equivalent to 99% of the school-age population (males 91%; females 107%). Enrolment in basic education (primary and preparatory) in that year included 100% of children in the age-group six to 11 years.

Access to higher education is subject to a quota system, fixed every year for every subject and school. Candidates must hold a secondary-school-leaving certificate and apply for enrolment in a national competitive examination. Higher education is also open to certain adults over 25 years of age who do not have the required academic qualifications. Higher education comprises two systems: education provided in universities, grouping several faculties, departments, institutes or schools, which award the following academic degrees: the licenciatura, after four to six years of study, the mestrado, after one or two years of study and the presentation and discussion of research work, and the doutoramento (doctorate); the second system is provided in regional polytechnic institutes, grouping technical, management, educational and fine arts schools, which offer three-year courses leading to the bacharel, and specialized studies leading to a diploma after one to two years. Non-formal education and special classes include vocational training, adult education, literacy and basic education and cultural and scientific improvement and updating. Between 1970 and 1985 the adult illiteracy rate declined from 29.0% to 16.0%, standing at an estimated 15.0% (males 11.2%; females 18.5%) in 1990. Expenditure on education by the central Government in 1990 was about 426,600m. escudos (11.9% of total spending).

### Public Holidays

**1995:** 1 January (New Year's Day), 28 February (Carnival Day), 14 April (Good Friday), 25 April (Liberty Day), 1 May (Labour Day), 10 June (Portugal Day), 13 June (St Anthony—Lisbon only), 15 June (Corpus Christi), 24 June (St John the Baptist—Porto only), 15 August (Assumption), 5 October (Proclamation of the Republic), 1 November (All Saints' Day), 1 December (Restoration of Independence), 8 December (Immaculate Conception), 25 December (Christmas Day).

**1996:** 1 January (New Year's Day), 20 February (Carnival Day), 5 April (Good Friday), 25 April (Liberty Day), 1 May (Labour Day), 6 June (Corpus Christi), 10 June (Portugal Day), 13 June (St Anthony—Lisbon only), 24 June (St John the Baptist—Porto only), 15 August (Assumption), 5 October (Proclamation of the Republic), 1 November (All Saints' Day), 1 December (Restoration of Independence), 8 December (Immaculate Conception), 25 December (Christmas Day).

### Weights and Measures

The metric system is in force.

PORTUGAL

# Statistical Survey

Source (unless otherwise stated): Instituto Nacional de Estatística (INE), Av. de António José de Almeida 5, 1078 Lisbon Codex; tel. (1) 8470050; telex 63738; fax (1) 7951507.

## Area and Population

### AREA, POPULATION AND DENSITY

| | |
|---|---:|
| Area (sq km) | |
|   Land | 91,831 |
|   Inland water | 439 |
|   Total | 92,270* |
| Population (census results) | |
|   16 March 1981 | 9,833,014 |
|   15 April 1991 (provisional) | |
|     Males | 4,754,700 |
|     Females | 5,107,900 |
|     Total | 9,862,700 |
| Population (official estimates at 31 December) | |
|   1991 | 9,855,400 |
|   1992 | 9,859,600 |
|   1993 (provisional) | 9,868,000 |
| Density (per sq km) at 31 December 1993 | 106.9 |

* 35,626 sq miles.

### ADMINISTRATIVE DIVISIONS
(estimated population at 31 December 1992)

| | Area (sq km)* | Population ('000) | Density (per sq km) |
|---|---:|---:|---:|
| Continental Portugal: Districts | 88,790 | 9,368.0 | 105.5 |
| Aveiro | 2,800 | 658.4 | 235.2 |
| Beja | 10,223 | 166.5 | 16.3 |
| Braga | 2,695 | 754.7 | 280.0 |
| Bragança | 6,597 | 154.7 | 23.4 |
| Castelo Branco | 6,616 | 211.8 | 32.0 |
| Coímbra | 3,971 | 425.4 | 107.1 |
| Évora | 7,396 | 172.4 | 23.4 |
| Faro | 4,986 | 342.0 | 68.6 |
| Guarda | 5,540 | 185.4 | 33.5 |
| Leiria | 3,508 | 426.2 | 121.3 |
| Lisbon | 2,758 | 2,048.0 | 742.6 |
| Portalegre | 6,064 | 132.4 | 21.8 |
| Porto | 2,341 | 1,652.0 | 705.5 |
| Santarém | 6,707 | 441.9 | 66.0 |
| Setúbal | 5,064 | 716.2 | 141.4 |
| Viana do Castelo | 2,210 | 248.3 | 112.3 |
| Vila Real | 4,305 | 233.1 | 54.1 |
| Viseu | 5,009 | 398.8 | 79.6 |
| Autonomous Regions: | | | |
| The Azores | 2,247 | 237.8 | 105.8 |
| Madeira | 794 | 253.8 | 319.6 |
| **Total** (Metropolitan Portugal) | 91,831 | 9,859.6 | 107.4 |

* Excluding river estuaries (439 sq km).

### PRINCIPAL TOWNS (population at 1991 census)

| | | | |
|---|---:|---|---:|
| Lisboa (Lisbon, the capital) | 681,063 | Matosinhos | 152,067 |
| Porto (Oporto) | 309,485 | Coímbra | 147,722 |
| Vila Nova de Gaia | 247,499 | Braga | 144,290 |
| Amadora | 176,137 | Funchal | 126,889 |
| Cascais | 155,437 | Seixal | 115,204 |
| Almada | 153,189 | Setúbal | 103,241 |

### BIRTHS, MARRIAGES AND DEATHS

| | Registered live births | | Registered marriages | | Registered deaths | |
|---|---:|---:|---:|---:|---:|---:|
| | Number | Rate (per 1,000) | Number | Rate (per 1,000) | Number | Rate (per 1,000) |
| 1985 | 130,492 | 13.2 | 68,461 | 6.9 | 97,339 | 9.8 |
| 1986 | 126,748 | 12.8 | 69,271 | 7.0 | 95,828 | 9.7 |
| 1987 | 123,218 | 12.4 | 71,656 | 7.2 | 95,423 | 9.6 |
| 1988 | 122,121 | 12.3 | 71,098 | 7.2 | 98,236 | 9.9 |
| 1989 | 118,560 | 12.0 | 73,195 | 7.4 | 96,220 | 9.7 |
| 1990 | 116,383 | 11.8 | 71,654 | 7.3 | 103,115 | 10.4 |
| 1991 | 116,415 | 11.8 | 71,808 | 7.3 | 104,361 | 10.6 |
| 1992 | 115,018 | 11.7 | 69,887 | 7.1 | 101,161 | 10.3 |

**1993** (rates per 1,000): Births 10.2; Deaths 10.6 (Source: UN, *Monthly Bulletin of Statistics*).

**Expectation of life** (years at birth, 1992): Males 70.83; females 78.16.

### ECONOMICALLY ACTIVE POPULATION
(ISIC Major Divisions, '000 persons aged 14 years and over)

| | 1991* | 1992 | 1993 |
|---|---:|---:|---:|
| Agriculture, hunting, forestry and fishing | 847.9 | 522.3 | 515.6 |
| Mining and quarrying | 30.7 | 22.4 | 19.7 |
| Manufacturing | 1,158.0 | 1,073.0 | 1,042.5 |
| Electricity, gas and water | 48.8 | 33.6 | 32.1 |
| Construction | 392.1 | 370.5 | 365.3 |
| Trade, restaurants and hotels | 778.8 | 897.8 | 867.2 |
| Transport, storage and communications | 232.5 | 219.6 | 207.9 |
| Financing, insurance, real estate and business services | 217.4 | 286.4 | 300.0 |
| Community, social and personal services* | 1,150.0 | 1,117.5 | 1,107.3 |
| Activities not adequately defined | 1.4 | — | — |
| **Total employed**† | 4,857.4 | 4,543.1 | 4,457.6 |
| Unemployed | 207.5‡ | 194.1 | 257.5 |
| **Total labour force** | 5,064.9 | 4,737.2 | 4,715.0 |
| Males | 2,841.9 | 2,639.4 | 2,606.0 |
| Females | 2,223.1 | 2,097.8 | 2,109.1 |

* Persons aged 12 years and over.

† Including regular members of the armed forces (31,200 in 1992; 33,680 in 1993), but excluding persons on compulsory military service (35,446 in 1993).

‡ Persons aged 10 years and over.

Source: ILO, *Year Book of Labour Statistics*.

PORTUGAL                                                                                                                          *Statistical Survey*

## Agriculture

**PRINCIPAL CROPS** ('000 metric tons)

|  | 1991 | 1992 | 1993 |
|---|---|---|---|
| Wheat | 618 | 301 | 367 |
| Rice (paddy) | 170 | 110 | 85 |
| Barley | 124 | 54 | 70 |
| Maize | 656 | 628 | 586 |
| Rye | 80 | 70 | 59 |
| Oats | 79 | 45 | 61 |
| Potatoes | 1,370 | 1,593 | 1,352 |
| Sweet potatoes* | 28 | 25 | 22 |
| Dry beans | 37 | 24 | 35* |
| Olives | 271 | 444 | 153 |
| Cabbages | 145† | 145* | 145* |
| Tomatoes | 915 | 700 | 718† |
| Onions (dry) | 57† | 57* | 57* |
| Garlic* | 1 | 1 | 1 |
| Carrots | 83† | 83* | 83* |
| Grapes | 1,470 | 1,125 | 1,300* |
| Sugar beets | 17 | 19† | 32† |
| Apples | 260 | 277 | 220 |
| Pears | 94 | 100 | 83 |
| Peaches and nectarines | 95 | 108 | 85 |
| Oranges | 162 | 168 | 144 |
| Bananas | 40 | 45* | 45* |

* FAO estimate(s).   † Unofficial figure.

Source: FAO, *Production Yearbook*.

**LIVESTOCK** ('000 head, year ending September)

|  | 1991 | 1992 | 1993 |
|---|---|---|---|
| Horses* | 26 | 25 | 25 |
| Mules* | 80 | 80 | 80 |
| Asses* | 170 | 170 | 170 |
| Cattle† | 1,375 | 1,416 | 1,345 |
| Pigs | 2,664 | 2,564 | 2,547 |
| Sheep† | 5,673 | 5,640 | 5,601 |
| Goats | 857 | 862 | 858 |

* FAO estimates.   † Unofficial figures.

Chickens (FAO estimates, million): 19 in 1991; 22 in 1992; 22 in 1993.
Turkeys (FAO estimates, million): 6 in 1991; 5 in 1992; 5 in 1993.

Source: FAO, *Statistical Yearbook*.

**LIVESTOCK PRODUCTS** ('000 metric tons)

|  | 1991 | 1992 | 1993 |
|---|---|---|---|
| Beef and veal | 128 | 124 | 115 |
| Mutton and lamb | 27 | 24 | 25* |
| Goat meat | 3 | 3 | 3* |
| Pig meat | 263 | 265 | 285 |
| Poultry meat | 150 | 150 | 151 |
| Edible offals* | 43 | 46 | 43 |
| Cows' milk | 1,550 | 1,531 | 1,467 |
| Sheep's milk | 93 | 97 | 90* |
| Goats' milk | 44 | 45 | 44* |
| Cheese | 64.1 | 65.1 | 57.5 |
| Butter | 16.0 | 16.6 | 16.1 |
| Hen eggs | 98.8 | 88.8 | 83.4 |
| Wool: |  |  |  |
|   greasy | 8.9 | 8.8 | 7.6 |
|   clean | 3.6 | 3.6 | 3.0 |
| Cattle hides* | 14.2 | 13.9 | 13.0 |
| Sheepskins* | 4.9 | 4.7 | 4.7 |

* FAO estimate(s).

Sources: FAO, *Production Yearbook* and *Quarterly Bulletin of Statistics*.

## Forestry

**ROUNDWOOD REMOVALS** ('000 cubic metres, excluding bark)

|  | 1990 | 1991 | 1992* |
|---|---|---|---|
| Sawlogs, veneer logs and logs for sleepers | 4,880 | 3,910 | 3,910 |
| Pulpwood | 5,765 | 6,339 | 6,339 |
| Other industrial wood | 60* | 60* | 60 |
| Fuel wood | 598 | 598* | 598 |
| **Total** | 11,303 | 10,907 | 10,907 |

* FAO estimate(s).

Source: FAO, *Yearbook of Forest Products*.

**SAWNWOOD PRODUCTION**
('000 cubic metres, including railway sleepers)

|  | 1990 | 1991 | 1992 |
|---|---|---|---|
| Coniferous (softwood) | 1,750 | 1,350 | 1,220 |
| Broadleaved (hard wood) | 340* | 320 | 240 |
| **Total** | 2,090 | 1,670 | 1,460 |

* FAO estimate.

Source: FAO, *Yearbook of Forest Products*.

## Fishing

(metric tons, live weight*)

|  | 1990 | 1991 | 1992 |
|---|---|---|---|
| Greenland halibut | 11,170 | 13,961 | 10,539 |
| Atlantic cod | 15,653 | 14,147 | 7,117 |
| Pouting | 3,050 | 3,477 | 4,315 |
| Blue whiting (Poutassou) | 2,864 | 2,984 | 2,173 |
| European hake | 3,736 | 3,713 | 4,746 |
| Atlantic redfishes | 18,641 | 12,329 | 7,557 |
| Atlantic horse mackerel | 21,639 | 21,000 | 24,442 |
| Other jack and horse mackerels | 1,865 | 1,170 | 2,382 |
| European pilchard (sardine) | 93,538 | 87,224 | 83,347 |
| Skipjack tuna | 3,918 | 8,044 | 7,471 |
| Bigeye tuna | 5,954 | 5,578 | 5,504 |
| Silver scabbardfish | 4,569 | 6,158 | 8,318 |
| Black scabbardfish | 6,865 | 6,656 | 6,919 |
| Chub mackerel | 10,346 | 11,335 | 9,926 |
| Atlantic mackerel | 3,819 | 2,632 | 3,576 |
| Skates | 15,170 | 24,728 | 8,611 |
| Other fishes (incl. unspecified) | 72,979 | 70,056 | 63,015 |
| **Total fish** | 295,776 | 295,192 | 260,048 |
| Crustaceans | 2,149 | 1,411 | 1,322 |
| Grooved carpet shell | 5,242 | 9,923 | 15,070 |
| Squids | 7,344 | 5,696 | 3,939 |
| Octopuses | 7,030 | 7,551 | 9,652 |
| Other molluscs | 4,469 | 4,970 | 5,253 |
| Echinoderms | 1 | — | — |
| **Total catch** | 322,011 | 324,743 | 295,284 |
| Inland waters | 2,567 | 2,570 | 2,570 |
| Atlantic Ocean | 319,444 | 321,895 | 292,394 |
| Mediterranean and Black Sea | — | 278 | 320 |

* Figures exclude aquatic plants (metric tons): 4,833 in 1990; 5,000 (FAO estimate) in 1991; 5,000 (FAO estimate) in 1992. Also excluded are aquatic mammals.

Source: FAO, *Yearbook of Fishery Statistics*.

## Mining

('000 metric tons, unless otherwise indicated)

|  | 1989 | 1990 | 1991 |
|---|---|---|---|
| Hard coal | 258 | 281 | 270 |
| Copper-bearing ores (metric tons)*† | 103,700 | 159,700 | 157,300 |
| Tin-bearing ores (metric tons)* | 64 | 1,404 | 3,100 |
| Tungsten-bearing ores (metric tons)*. | 1,381 | 1,405 | 1,400 |
| Uranium-bearing ores (metric tons)*. | 137 | 111 | 28 |
| Gold-bearing ores (kg)* | 295‡ | 350 | 360 |
| Marble ('000 cu m) | 278 | n.a. | n.a. |
| Granite, porphyry, sandstone, etc. | 6,410 | n.a. | n.a. |
| Limestone flux and calcareous stone | 16,595 | 14,000 | n.a. |
| Clay | 2,226 | n.a. | n.a. |
| Iron pyrites (unroasted) | 166 | 144 | n.a. |
| Salt (unrefined) | 733 | 726 | 653 |
| Gypsum (crude) | 300‡ | 300 | 300 |

* Figures refer to the metal content of ores.
† Figures exclude copper sediments obtained from copper-bearing pyrites.
‡ Provisional.

Source: mainly UN, *Industrial Statistics Yearbook*.

## Industry

**SELECTED PRODUCTS**
('000 metric tons, unless otherwise indicated)

|  | 1989 | 1990 | 1991 |
|---|---|---|---|
| Frozen fish | 39.4 | 30.7 | 24.8 |
| Tinned fish | 43.3 | 37.4 | 40.2 |
| Margarine and other prepared fats | 69.7 | 67.9 | 53.0 |
| Olive oil (crude) | 44 | 26 | 40 |
| Flour | 599 | 541 | 487 |
| Refined sugar | 394 | 335 | 441 |
| Prepared animal feeds | 3,212 | 3,039 | 3,028 |
| Distilled alcoholic beverages ('000 hectolitres) | 55 | 85 | 73 |
| Wine ('000 hectolitres) | 8,450* | 10,970 | 9,910 |
| Beer ('000 hectolitres) | 6,874 | 6,582 | 6,309 |
| Cigarettes (metric tons) | 15,424 | 16,090 | 16,545 |
| Wool yarn (pure and mixed) | 13.8 | 13.2 | 13.1 |
| Cotton yarn (pure and mixed) | 158.4 | 147.5 | 313.4 |
| Woven cotton fabrics | 79 | 73 | 71 |
| Woven woollen fabrics | 11.3 | 10.0 | 10.2 |
| Knitted fabrics | 61.4 | 63.0 | 58.1 |
| Footwear, excl. rubber ('000 pairs) | 40,315 | 72,734 | 70,437* |
| Wood pulp (sulphate and soda) | 1,362 | 1,331 | 1,487 |
| Sulphuric acid | 289 | 174 | n.a. |
| Caustic soda (Sodium hydroxide) | 90 | 81 | 77 |
| Soda ash (Sodium carbonate) | 269 | 273 | 320 |
| Nitrogenous fertilizers† | 159 | 154 | 126 |
| Jet fuels | 704 | 891 | 773 |
| Motor spirit (petrol) | 1,533 | 1,704 | 1,623 |
| Naphthas | 776 | 811 | 691 |
| Distillate fuel oils | 2,856 | 2,984 | 2,345 |
| Residual fuel oils | 3,639 | 3,816 | 3,438 |
| Liquefied petroleum gas | 355 | 357 | 312 |
| Coke | 261 | 230 | 240 |
| Gas from cokeries (terajoules) | 2,190 | 2,200* | 2,244 |
| Tyres for road motor vehicles ('000) | 4,292 | 2,967 | 2,180 |
| Rubber footwear ('000 pairs) | 495 | 867 | 125 |
| Household ware of porcelain or china (metric tons) | 16,506 | 15,430 | 15,832 |
| Household ware of other ceramic materials (metric tons) | 53,121 | 33,371 | 56,056 |
| Clay building bricks | 3,829 | 3,509 | 3,316 |
| Cement | 6,673 | 7,049 | 7,342 |
| Pig iron | 377 | 346 | 300 |
| Crude steel for castings | 300* | 300* | n.a. |
| Refrigerators for household use ('000) | 376 | 381 | 529 |
| Television receivers ('000) | 304 | 329 | 318 |

| — continued | 1989 | 1990 | 1991 |
|---|---|---|---|
| Radio receivers ('000) | 1,071 | 1,435 | 1,522 |
| Passenger motor cars ('000)‡ | 77 | 78 | 81 |
| Lorries (number)‡ | 61,996 | 57,949 | 53,309 |
| Electric energy (million kWh) | 25,547 | 28,499 | 29,870 |
| Gas from gas works (terajoules) | 2,698 | 2,700* | 2,891 |

* Estimated or provisional output.
† Figures refer to the nitrogen content of production in the 12 months ending 30 June of the year stated.
‡ Vehicles assembled from imported parts.

Source: mainly UN, *Industrial Statistics Yearbook*.

## Finance

**CURRENCY AND EXCHANGE RATES**

**Monetary Units**
100 centavos = 1 Portuguese escudo (1,000 escudos are known as one *conto*).

**Sterling and Dollar Equivalents** (31 December 1994)
£1 sterling = 249.1 escudos;
US $1 = 159.2 escudos;
1,000 Portuguese escudos = £4.015 = $6.281.

**Average Exchange Rate** (escudos per US dollar)
1992   135.00
1993   160.80
1994   165.99

**BUDGET** ('000 million escudos)*

| Revenue† | 1988 | 1989 | 1990 |
|---|---|---|---|
| Taxation | 1,937.9 | 2,346.0 | 2,795.3 |
| Taxes on incomes, profits and capital gains | 411.7 | 605.0 | 719.5 |
| Social security contributions | 560.1 | 658.4 | 832.2 |
| Domestic taxes on goods and services | 805.6 | 943.3 | 1,074.7 |
| General sales, turnover or value-added taxes | 407.1 | 486.4 | 559.1 |
| Excises | 308.2 | 345.1 | 400.4 |
| Surtax on petroleum products, etc. | 0.3 | 3.4 | 0.7 |
| Taxes on international trade and transactions | 77.4 | 63.7 | 71.3 |
| Import duties | 77.0 | 63.7 | 71.3 |
| Other current revenue | 114.3 | 139.7 | 250.6 |
| Entrepreneurial and property income | 70.2 | 92.2 | 141.9 |
| Capital revenue | 2.0 | 4.0 | 19.2 |
| **Sub-total** | 2,054.2 | 2,489.7 | 3,065.1 |
| Adjustment to total revenue | −23.7 | 60.1 | 2.4 |
| **Total revenue** | 2,030.5 | 2,549.8 | 3,067.5 |

**PORTUGAL**                                                                                                              *Statistical Survey*

| Expenditure‡ | 1988 | 1989 | 1990 |
|---|---|---|---|
| General public services | 171.2 | 234.9 | 296.8 |
| Defence | 146.7 | 168.8 | 188.0 |
| Education | 274.9 | 345.0 | 426.6 |
| Health | 225.3 | 217.8 | 286.3 |
| Social security and welfare | 641.1 | 795.0 | 972.9 |
| Housing and community amenities | 28.0 | 22.6 | 27.3 |
| Recreational, cultural and religious affairs | 22.4 | 24.5 | 27.4 |
| Economic affairs and services | 272.3 | 326.4 | 374.1 |
| Other expenditures | 671.9 | 770.5 | 989.9 |
| **Sub-total** | 2,453.8 | 2,905.5 | 3,589.3 |
| Current | 2,241.7 | 2,637.0 | 3,296.8 |
| Capital | 212.1 | 268.5 | 292.6 |
| Adjustment to total expenditure | 39.2 | −32.2 | −21.6 |
| **Total expenditure** | 2,492.9 | 2,873.3 | 3,567.8 |

\* Figures refer to the consolidated accounts of the central Government.
† Excluding grants received ('000 million escudos): 105.9 (current 93.8, capital 12.1) in 1988; 126.0 (current 115.3, capital 10.7) in 1989; 144.5 (current 111.4, capital 33.1) in 1990.
‡ Excluding lending minus repayments ('000 million escudos): 166.5 in 1988; −28.0 in 1989; −93.1 in 1990.
Source: IMF, *Government Finance Statistics Yearbook*.

**INTERNATIONAL RESERVES** (US $ million at 31 December)

|  | 1992 | 1993 | 1994 |
|---|---|---|---|
| Gold* | 5,188 | 5,189 | 5,185 |
| IMF special drawing rights | 46 | 58 | 71 |
| Reserve position in IMF | 314 | 301 | 337 |
| Foreign exchange | 18,769 | 15,481 | 15,164† |
| **Total** | 24,317 | 21,029 | 20,757† |

\* Valued at $323 per troy ounce.
† Excluding the Treasury's reserves of foreign exchange ($ million): 25 in 1992; 39 in 1993.
Source: IMF, *International Financial Statistics*.

**MONEY SUPPLY** ('000 million escudos at 31 December)

|  | 1992 | 1993 | 1994 |
|---|---|---|---|
| Currency outside banks | 708.2 | 752.9 | 796.3 |
| Demand deposits at commercial and savings banks | 2,613.8 | 2,908.7 | 3,115.3 |
| **Total money** (incl. others) | 3,416.4 | 3,774.5 | 3,949.1 |

Source: IMF, *International Financial Statistics*.

**COST OF LIVING**
(Consumer Price Index for Continental Portugal; base: 1991 = 100)

|  | 1992 | 1993 |
|---|---|---|
| Foodstuffs and beverages | 107.1 | 110.03 |
| Clothing and footwear | 111.9 | 119.68 |
| Housing expenditure | 115.7 | 126.70 |
| Home comforts | 109.6 | 117.23 |
| Health | 115.5 | 130.08 |
| Transport and communication | 109.7 | 121.77 |
| Education, culture and recreation | 109.5 | 119.42 |
| Tobacco, etc. | 119.1 | 132.75 |
| Other goods and services | 108.6 | 122.99 |
| **Total** | 109.5 | 116.91 |

**NATIONAL ACCOUNTS**
(million escudos at current prices)

**Composition of the Gross National Product**
(provisional)

|  | 1990 | 1991 | 1992 |
|---|---|---|---|
| Compensation of employees | 4,652,530 | 5,394,865 | 6,204,095 |
| Operating surplus | } 3,842,075 | 4,543,216 | 5,191,498 |
| Consumption of fixed capital |  |  |  |
| **Gross domestic product (GDP) at factor cost** | 8,494,605 | 9,938,081 | 11,395,593 |
| Indirect taxes | 1,384,945 | 1,603,604 | 1,892,300 |
| *Less* Subsidies | 167,936 | 227,654 | 310,700 |
| **GDP in purchasers' values** | 9,711,614 | 11,314,031 | 12,977,193 |
| Factor income from abroad | 190,889 | 221,052 | 299,333 |
| *Less* Factor income paid abroad | 240,304 | 232,543 | 219,902 |
| **Gross national product (GNP)** | 9,662,199 | 11,302,540 | 13,056,624 |

**Expenditure on the Gross Domestic Product**
(provisional)

|  | 1990 | 1991 | 1992 |
|---|---|---|---|
| Government final consumption expenditure | } 8,041,751 | 9,476,187 | 10,781,697 |
| Private final consumption expenditure |  |  |  |
| Increase in stocks | 141,592 | 121,646 | 140,744 |
| Gross fixed capital formation | 2,681,270 | 3,066,485 | 3,516,873 |
| **Total domestic expenditure** | 10,864,613 | 12,664,318 | 14,439,314 |
| Exports of goods and services | 2,635,271 | 2,679,056 | 2,829,269 |
| *Less* Imports of goods and services | 3,788,270 | 4,029,343 | 4,291,390 |
| **GDP in purchasers' values** | 9,711,614 | 11,314,031 | 12,977,193 |

**Gross Domestic Product by Economic Activity***

|  | 1988 | 1989† | 1990† |
|---|---|---|---|
| Agriculture, hunting, forestry and fishing | 365,145 | 441,014 | 490,787 |
| Mining and quarrying | } 1,707,316 | 2,055,923 | 2,373,090 |
| Manufacturing |  |  |  |
| Electricity, gas and water | 211,218 | 209,762 | 261,311 |
| Construction | 368,504 | 452,708 | 585,382 |
| Trade, restaurants and hotels | 1,185,020 | 1,397,819 | 1,681,487 |
| Transport, storage and communications | 361,260 | 412,995 | 462,412 |
| Finance, insurance and real estate | 685,497 | 841,636 | 1,112,586 |
| Other commercial services | 201,854 | 242,524 | 294,756 |
| Government services | } 759,704 | 926,340 | 1,156,989 |
| Other non-commercial services |  |  |  |
| **Sub-total** | 5,845,518 | 6,980,721 | 8,418,800 |
| Import duties | 117,081 | 124,671 | 146,439 |
| Value-added tax | 422,738 | 497,167 | 570,058 |
| *Less* Imputed bank service charge | 382,586 | 472,299 | 627,863 |
| **GDP in purchasers' values** | 6,002,751 | 7,130,260 | 8,507,434 |

\* Data refer to continental Portugal only, excluding the Autonomous Regions of the Azores and Madeira.
† Figures are provisional. The revised totals (in '000 million escudos) are: 7,177.2 in 1989; 8,560.6 in 1990 (Source: IMF, *International Financial Statistics*).

# PORTUGAL

## BALANCE OF PAYMENTS (US $ million)

|  | 1991 | 1992 | 1993 |
|---|---|---|---|
| Merchandise exports f.o.b. | 16,231 | 18,195 | 15,444 |
| Merchandise imports f.o.b. | −24,079 | −27,735 | −22,330 |
| **Trade balance** | −7,848 | −9,540 | −6,886 |
| Exports of services | 5,375 | 5,638 | 6,663 |
| Imports of services | −4,305 | −4,656 | −5,494 |
| Other income received | 1,565 | 2,080 | 2,479 |
| Other income paid | −1,479 | −1,532 | −2,530 |
| Private unrequited transfers (net) | 4,593 | 4,794 | 3,842 |
| Official unrequited transfers (net) | 1,381 | 3,032 | 2,874 |
| **Current balance** | −716 | −184 | 947 |
| Direct investment (net) | 1,985 | 1,186 | 1,136 |
| Portfolio investment (net) | 1,895 | −3,064 | −530 |
| Other capital (net) | 656 | 928 | −4,229 |
| Net errors and omissions | 1,893 | 978 | −171 |
| **Overall balance** | 5,713 | −156 | −2,847 |

Source: IMF, *International Financial Statistics*.

# External Trade

## PRINCIPAL COMMODITIES
(distribution by SITC, million escudos)

| Imports c.i.f. | 1992 | 1993 | 1994 |
|---|---|---|---|
| **Food and live animals** | 418,561 | 432,006 | 510,202 |
| Fish, crustaceans, molluscs and preparations | 99,638 | 98,790 | 114,117 |
| Cereals and cereal preparations | 92,358 | 95,311 | 100,371 |
| Vegetables and fruit | 59,307 | 69,319 | 82,592 |
| **Crude materials (inedible) except fuels** | 177,106 | 158,770 | 202,089 |
| **Mineral fuels, lubricants, etc.** | 327,964 | 339,779 | 378,224 |
| Petroleum, petroleum products, etc. | 283,709 | 288,877 | 323,338 |
| **Chemicals and related products** | 369,851 | 357,906 | 434,202 |
| Organic chemicals | 66,773 | 65,300 | 83,874 |
| **Basic manufactures** | 754,823 | 679,803 | 817,571 |
| Paper, paperboard etc. | 75,589 | 71,490 | 80,032 |
| Textile yarn, fabrics, etc. | 261,825 | 225,948 | 260,348 |
| **Machinery and transport equipment** | 1,553,429 | 1,382,820 | 1,510,846 |
| Machinery specialized for particular industries | 170,583 | 135,316 | 130,276 |
| General industrial machinery, equipment and parts | 175,540 | 141,914 | 132,788 |
| Office machines and automatic data-processing equipment | 107,952 | 95,182 | 99,469 |
| Telecommunications and sound equipment | 137,474 | 125,379 | 124,758 |
| Other electrical machinery, apparatus, etc. | 216,120 | 212,880 | 263,233 |
| Road vehicles and parts (excl. tyres, engines and electrical parts) | 622,406 | 554,627 | 578,170 |
| Passenger motor cars (excl. buses) | 321,992 | 301,648 | 309,041 |
| **Miscellaneous manufactured articles** | 427,037 | 420,145 | 430,459 |
| Clothing and accessories (excl. footwear) | 109,013 | 109,632 | 114,704 |
| **Total** (incl. others) | 4,087,577 | 3,882,777 | 4,403,637 |

| Exports f.o.b. | 1992 | 1993 | 1994 |
|---|---|---|---|
| **Food and live animals** | 95,807 | 88,063 | 108,176 |
| **Beverages and tobacco** | 78,523 | 73,601 | 81,610 |
| Beverages | 77,015 | 72,453 | 80,430 |
| Alcoholic beverages | 75,468 | 71,122 | 78,582 |
| Wine (incl. grape must) | 67,951 | 65,052 | 70,464 |
| **Crude materials (inedible) except fuels** | 161,976 | 138,417 | 175,262 |
| Pulp and waste paper | 73,710 | 58,163 | 84,140 |
| **Mineral fuels, lubricants, etc.** | 72,864 | 81,454 | 116,013 |
| Petroleum, petroleum products, etc. | 72,162 | 81,371 | 114,342 |
| **Chemicals and related products** | 105,074 | 106,695 | 143,585 |
| **Basic manufactures** | 559,814 | 577,908 | 694,073 |
| Cork and wood manufactures (excl. furniture) | 109,383 | 107,922 | 129,663 |
| Cork manufactures | 76,382 | 77,099 | 90,035 |
| Textile yarn, fabrics, etc. | 193,913 | 191,685 | 214,999 |
| Non-metallic mineral manufactures | 113,346 | 117,207 | 142,203 |
| **Machinery and transport equipment** | 534,935 | 522,780 | 614,525 |
| Telecommunications and sound equipment | 66,626 | 68,603 | 90,292 |
| Other electrical machinery, apparatus, etc. | 168,094 | 176,913 | 213,001 |
| Road vehicles and parts (excl. tyres, engines and electrical parts) | 159,148 | 132,265 | 152,493 |
| **Miscellaneous manufactured articles** | 853,605 | 844,643 | 931,353 |
| Clothing and accessories (excl. footwear) | 537,534 | 500,576 | 529,681 |
| Women's and girls' clothing of non-knitted textile fabrics* | 70,514 | 56,020 | 60,110 |
| Women's and girls' clothing of knitted textile fabrics* | 49,685 | 46,081 | 47,138 |
| Footwear | 215,172 | 237,772 | 277,552 |
| **Total** (incl. others) | 2,475,202 | 2,474,401 | 2,900,380 |

* Excluding babies' clothing, pullovers, singlets, elasticated garments, swimwear, ski suits and track suits.

## PRINCIPAL TRADING PARTNERS (million escudos)

| Imports c.i.f. | 1991 | 1992 | 1993 |
|---|---|---|---|
| Algeria | 37,029 | 28,729 | 51,873 |
| Belgium-Luxembourg | 153,935 | 154,902 | 146,937 |
| Brazil | 54,143 | 48,529 | 53,982 |
| France | 454,801 | 525,547 | 493,842 |
| Germany | 570,479 | 615,235 | 583,328 |
| Italy | 390,557 | 418,649 | 336,854 |
| Japan | 110,598 | 125,092 | 125,329 |
| Netherlands | 232,195 | 280,166 | 191,121 |
| Nigeria | 46,058 | 53,869 | 55,164 |
| Norway | 44,373 | 58,153 | 53,459 |
| Spain | 602,572 | 677,809 | 692,892 |
| Sweden | 52,628 | 51,987 | 75,829 |
| Switzerland | 68,655 | 68,947 | 46,630 |
| United Kingdom | 285,418 | 292,211 | 287,473 |
| USA | 129,691 | 123,634 | 123,020 |
| **Total** (incl. others) | 3,811,076 | 4,087,577 | 3,882,777 |

PORTUGAL

| Exports f.o.b. | 1991 | 1992 | 1993 |
|---|---|---|---|
| Angola | 79,066 | 110,581 | 55,685 |
| Austria | 28,089 | 27,426 | 28,842 |
| Belgium-Luxembourg | 75,725 | 80,911 | 87,038 |
| Denmark | 49,961 | 53,709 | 52,983 |
| Finland | 35,158 | 30,259 | 24,551 |
| France | 337,859 | 351,859 | 374,502 |
| Germany | 450,040 | 473,860 | 483,887 |
| Italy | 93,872 | 95,348 | 74,114 |
| Netherlands | 134,899 | 134,976 | 128,808 |
| Norway | 28,701 | 28,221 | 25,587 |
| Spain | 351,347 | 366,963 | 355,608 |
| Sweden | 88,107 | 83,972 | 63,625 |
| Switzerland | 46,456 | 44,975 | 51,459 |
| United Kingdom | 254,244 | 275,110 | 281,050 |
| USA | 89,678 | 86,265 | 107,760 |
| **Total** (incl. others) | 2,354,083 | 2,475,202 | 2,474,401 |

# Transport

**RAILWAYS** (traffic)

|  | 1990 | 1991 | 1992 |
|---|---|---|---|
| Passenger journeys ('000) | 225,882 | 223,631 | 224,621 |
| Passenger-kilometres (million) | 5,664 | 5,692 | 5,694 |
| Freight ('000 metric tons) | 6,683 | 7,724 | 7,441 |
| Freight ton-kilometres (million) | 1,588 | 1,784 | 1,767 |

**ROAD TRAFFIC**
(motor vehicles registered at 31 December)

|  | 1990 | 1991 | 1992 |
|---|---|---|---|
| Cars and vans | 3,380,810 | 3,671,166 | 4,028,843 |
| Motorcycles | 134,594 | 144,979 | 162,232 |
| Tractors | 197,178 | 205,568 | 213,453 |
| Light and heavy goods vehicles | 781,191 | 847,403 | 927,591 |

**SHIPPING**

|  | 1990 | 1991 | 1992 |
|---|---|---|---|
| Merchant fleet (gross registered tons) | 809,284 | 753,244 | 1,084,335 |
| Vessels entered ('000 gross registered tons) | 83,231 | 81,629 | 87,378 |
| Goods loaded ('000 metric tons) | 18,343 | 14,848 | 16,611 |
| Goods unloaded ('000 metric tons) | 39,267 | 35,938 | 40,225 |

**CIVIL AVIATION** (TAP and SATA only, '000)

|  | 1990 | 1991 | 1992 |
|---|---|---|---|
| Kilometres flown | 56,288 | 59,548 | 66,373 |
| Passenger-kilometres (million) | 6,881 | 7,072 | 7,721 |
| Freight ton-kilometres | 166,994 | 163,081 | 116,847 |
| Mail ton-kilometres | 12,287 | 12,715 | 14,078 |

# Tourism

**FOREIGN VISITOR ARRIVALS***

| Country of Origin | 1991 | 1992 | 1993 |
|---|---|---|---|
| Belgium | 198,434 | 207,272 | 196,554 |
| Brazil | 114,053 | 106,080 | 85,142 |
| Canada | 69,299 | 73,955 | 71,230 |
| Denmark | 112,220 | 119,587 | 108,751 |
| France | 711,493 | 682,064 | 590,711 |
| Germany | 851,858 | 877,456 | 794,734 |
| Italy | 290,971 | 281,913 | 265,263 |
| Netherlands | 360,452 | 365,756 | 369,014 |
| Spain | 14,583,216 | 15,553,444 | 15,776,374 |
| Sweden | 114,315 | 108,417 | 93,361 |
| Switzerland | 79,890 | 72,534 | 82,582 |
| United Kingdom | 1,307,312 | 1,433,228 | 1,368,356 |
| USA | 178,133 | 220,452 | 207,651 |
| **Total** (incl. others) | 19,641,329 | 20,733,893 | 20,579,333 |

* Including excursionists. Visitors staying at least one night in Portugal (excluding Portuguese nationals resident abroad) totalled 8,656,956 in 1991 and 8,884,143 in 1992.

Source: Direcção-Geral do Turismo, Lisbon.

# Communications Media

|  | 1991 | 1992 | 1993 |
|---|---|---|---|
| Telephones | 2,851,361 | n.a. | 2,236,411 |
| Television receivers | n.a. | n.a. | 2,970,892 |
| Books published (number of titles) | 6,430 | 6,511 | 7,673 |
| Daily newspapers (number of titles) | 29 | 25 | 27 |
| Daily newspapers (total circulation) | 155,397,332 | 160,412,547 | 155,721,778 |

**1992:** Radio receivers in use: 2,260,000 (Source: UNESCO, *Statistical Yearbook*).
**1994:** Telephones: 2,328,926; Television receivers: 3,007,472.

# Education

(1991/92)

|  | Institutions | Teachers | Students |
|---|---|---|---|
| Pre-primary | 5,010 | 12,774* | 175,122 |
| Primary and preparatory | 12,422 | 71,105* | 989,295 |
| Secondary: |  |  |  |
| General | n.a. | n.a. | 822,516 |
| Vocational | n.a. | n.a. | 69,034 |
| Higher | 232 | n.a. | 190,954 |

* Source: UNESCO, *Statistical Yearbook*.

# Directory

## The Constitution

The Constitution of the Portuguese Republic was promulgated on 2 April 1976, and came into force on 25 April. It was revised in 1982, when ideological elements were reduced and the Council of the Revolution was abolished; in 1989, to permit economic reforms and a greater role for the private sector; and in 1992, prior to the ratification of the Treaty on European Union (the Maastricht Treaty). The following is a summary of the Constitution's main provisions:

### FUNDAMENTAL PRINCIPLES

Portugal is a sovereign Republic based on the dignity of the individual and the will of the people, which strives to create a just, caring and free society and to realize economic, social and cultural democracy. It comprises the territory defined by history on the European continent and the archipelagos of the Azores and Madeira. The Azores and Madeira shall constitute autonomous regions.

The fundamental duties of the State include the following: to safeguard national independence; to guarantee fundamental rights and freedoms; to defend political democracy and to encourage citizens' participation in the solving of national problems; and to promote the welfare, quality of life and equality of the people.

### FUNDAMENTAL RIGHTS AND DUTIES

All citizens are equal before the law. Rights, freedoms and safeguards are upheld by the State and include the following: the right to life; of *habeas corpus*; to the inviolability of the home and of correspondence; to freedom of expression and of conscience; to freedom of movement, emigration and of assembly. Freedom of the press is guaranteed.

Rights and duties of citizens include the following: the right and the duty to work; the right to vote (at 18 years of age); the right to form and participate in political associations and parties; the freedom to form trade unions and the right to strike; the right to set up co-operatives; the right to private property; the right to social security and medical services; the duty of the State and of society to protect the family and the disabled; the right to education, culture and sport; consumer rights.

### ECONOMIC ORGANIZATION

The economic and social organization of Portugal shall be based on the subordination of economic power to political power, the co-existence of the public, private, co-operative and social sectors of ownership, and the collectivization of the means of production and land, in accordance with the public interest, as well as natural resources; and on the democratic planning of the economy, and democratic intervention by the workers. Enterprises nationalized after 25 April 1974 may be reprivatized. The aims of economic and social development plans include the promotion of economic growth, the harmonious development of sectors and regions, the fair individual and regional distribution of the national product and the defence of the environment and of the quality of life of the Portuguese people. The consultative Economic and Social Council participates in the formulation of development plans. It comprises representatives of the Government, workers' organizations, economic enterprises and representatives of autonomous regions and local organizations.

The aims of agrarian policy are to improve the situation of farm workers and to increase agricultural production and productivity. *Latifúndios* (large estates) will be adjusted in size, and property which has been expropriated, with compensation, shall be handed over to small farmers or co-operatives for exploitation. *Minifúndios* (small estates) will be adjusted in size, through the granting of incentives to integrate or divide. The aims of commercial policy include the development and diversification of foreign economic relations. The aims of industrial policy include an increase in production in the context of modernization and adjustment, greater competition, the support of small and medium enterprises and the support of industrial and technological innovation. The financial and fiscal system aims at encouraging savings and achieving the equal distribution of wealth and incomes. The State Budget shall be supervised by the Accounts Court and the Assembly of the Republic. Economic policy includes the stimulation of competition, the protection of consumers and the combating of speculative activities and restrictive trade practices.

### POLITICAL ORGANIZATION

Political power shall lie with the people. The organs of sovereignty shall be: the President of the Republic, the Assembly of the Republic, the Government and the Courts. Direct, secret and regular elections shall be held. No-one shall hold political office for life.

### PRESIDENT OF THE REPUBLIC

The President of the Republic shall represent the Republic. The President guarantees national independence, the unity of the state, and the proper working of democratic institutions. The President shall be elected by direct and secret universal adult suffrage. The candidate who obtains more than half the valid votes will be elected President. The President shall hold office for five years. The President may not be re-elected for a third consecutive term of office.

The duties of the President include the following: to preside over the Council of State; to set dates for elections; to convene extraordinary sessions of the Assembly of the Republic; to dissolve the Assembly of the Republic; to appoint and dismiss the Prime Minister; to appoint and dismiss the members of the Government at the proposal of the Prime Minister; to promulgate laws; to veto laws; to apply to the Constitutional Court; to nominate ambassadors, upon the proposal of the Government; to accredit diplomatic representatives; to ratify international treaties, after they have been duly approved.

### COUNCIL OF STATE

The Council of State is the political consultative organ of the President of the Republic. It is presided over by the President of the Republic and comprises the President of the Assembly of the Republic, the Prime Minister, the President of the Constitutional Court, the Superintendent of Justice, the Presidents of the Regional Governments, certain former Presidents of the Republic, five citizens nominated by the President of the Republic and five citizens elected by the Assembly of the Republic.

### ASSEMBLY OF THE REPUBLIC

The Assembly represents all Portuguese citizens, and shall have a minimum of 230 and a maximum of 235 members, elected under a system of proportional representation by the electoral constituencies. The duties of the Assembly include the following: to present and approve amendments to the Constitution and to approve the political and administrative statutes of the Autonomous Regions and the Statute of the territory of Macau; to enact legislation; to confer legislative authority on the Government; to approve plans and the Budget; to approve international conventions and treaties; to propose to the President of the Republic that questions of national interest be submitted to referendum; to supervise the fulfilment of the Constitution and laws. The Assembly supports the participation of Portugal in the process of building the European Union. Each legislative period shall last four years. The legislative session shall run from 15 October to 15 June each year.

### GOVERNMENT

The Government formulates the general policy of the country and is the highest organ of public administration. It shall comprise the Prime Minister, Ministers, Secretaries and Under-Secretaries of State and may include one or more Deputy Prime Ministers. The Prime Minister is appointed and dismissed by the President. Other members of the Government are appointed by the President at the proposal of the Prime Minister. The Government shall be responsible to the President and the Assembly. The Government's programme shall be presented to the Assembly for scrutiny within 10 days of the appointment of the Prime Minister.

### JUDICIARY

The courts are independent organs of sovereignty with competence to administer justice. There shall be Courts of First Instance (District Courts), Courts of Second Instance (Courts of Appeal), the Supreme Administrative Court and the Supreme Court of Justice, in addition to the Constitutional Court. There shall also be military courts and an Accounts Court. There may be maritime courts and courts of arbitration.

The jury shall comprise the judges of the plenary court and the jurors. People's judges may be created. It is the duty of the Ministério Público to represent the State. Its highest organ is the Procuradoria-Geral which is presided over by the Procurador-Geral, who is appointed and dismissed by the President of the Republic.

## AUTONOMOUS REGIONS

The special political and administrative arrangements for the archipelagos of the Azores and Madeira shall be based on their geographical, economic and social conditions and on the historic aspirations of the people to autonomy. The sovereignty of the Republic is represented in each of the Autonomous Regions by a Minister of the Republic.

The organs of government in the Autonomous Regions (which are subject to dissolution by the President of the Republic) are: the Regional Legislative Assembly, elected by direct and secret universal adult suffrage, and the Regional Government which shall be politically responsible to the Regional Legislative Assembly. Its Chairman is appointed by the Minister of the Republic. The Minister shall appoint or dismiss members of the Regional Government on the proposal of its Chairman.

## LOCAL GOVERNMENT

The local authorities shall be territorial bodies corporate with representative organs serving the particular interests of the local population. The local authorities on the mainland shall be the parishes, municipal authorities and administrative regions. The Autonomous Regions of the Azores and Madeira shall comprise parishes and municipal authorities.

## PUBLIC ADMINISTRATIVE AUTHORITIES

The public administrative authorities shall seek to promote the public interest whilst respecting the legal interests and rights of all citizens. Citizens shall have the right to be informed of, and to have redress against, the public administrative authorities when the matter directly concerns them.

## ARMED FORCES

The President of the Republic is Supreme Commander-in-Chief of the Armed Forces, and appoints and dismisses the Chiefs of Staff. The defence forces shall safeguard national independence and territorial integrity. Military service shall be compulsory. The right to conscientious objection is recognized.

## SAFEGUARDS AND REVISION OF THE CONSTITUTION

Changes in the Constitution shall be approved by a majority of two-thirds of the members of the Assembly present, provided that the number of such members exceeds an absolute majority of the members entitled to vote. Constitutional revisions must comply with the independence, unity and secularism of the State; the rights, freedoms and safeguards of citizens; universal, direct and secret suffrage and the system of proportional representation, etc.

The Statute of the territory of Macau, promulgated on 17 February 1976, shall continue in force as long as the territory remains under Portuguese administration. Portugal shall remain bound by its responsibility to promote and safeguard the right to self-determination and independence of East Timor.

# The Government

## HEAD OF STATE

**President:** Dr MÁRIO ALBERTO NOBRE LOPES SOARES (took office 9 March 1986, re-elected 13 January 1991, mandate expires January 1996).

### COUNCIL OF MINISTERS
(June 1995)

**Prime Minister:** Prof. ANÍBAL CAVACO SILVA.
**Minister of Defence:** FIGUEIREDO LOPES.
**Minister of State (Parliamentary Affairs):** Dr LUÍS MARQUES MENDES.
**Minister of Home Affairs:** Dr MANUEL DIAS LOUREIRO.
**Minister of Finance:** Dr EDUARDO DE ALMEIDA CATROGA.
**Minister of Planning and Territorial Administration:** Prof. LUÍS VALENTE DE OLIVEIRA.
**Minister of Justice:** Dr ALVARO JOSÉ BRILHANTE LABORINHO LÚCIO.
**Minister of Foreign Affairs:** JOSÉ MANUEL DURÃO BARROSO.
**Minister of Agriculture and the Sea:** ANTÓNIO DUARTE SILVA.
**Minister of Industry and Energy:** Eng. LUÍS FERNANDO DE MIRA AMARAL.
**Minister of Education:** Dra MARIA MANUELA DIAS FERREIRA LEITE.
**Minister of Public Works, Transport and Communications:** Eng. JOAQUIM MARTINS FERREIRA DO AMARAL.
**Minister of Health:** Dr ADALBERTO PAULO DA FONSECA MENDO.
**Minister of Employment and Social Security:** Eng. JOSÉ BERNARDO VELOSO FALCÃO E CUNHA.
**Minister of Trade and Tourism:** Eng. FERNANDO MANUEL BARBOSA FARIA DE OLIVEIRA.
**Minister of the Environment and Natural Resources:** TERESA PATRICIO GOUVEIA.

### MINISTRIES

**Office of the President:** Presidência da República, Palácio de Belém, 1300 Lisbon; tel. (1) 3637141; telex 16733; fax (1) 3636603.
**Office of the Prime Minister:** Presidência do Conselho de Ministros, Rua da Imprensa 8, 1300 Lisbon; telex 12176.
**Ministry of Agriculture:** Praça do Comércio, 1100 Lisbon; tel. (1) 3464878; telex 44516; fax (1) 3472291.
**Ministry of Defence:** Av. Ilha de Madeira, 1400 Lisbon; tel. (1) 3010001.
**Ministry of Education:** Av. 5 de Outubro 107, 1051 Lisbon Codex; tel. (1) 778793; telex 18428.
**Ministry of Employment and Social Security:** Praça de Londres, 1000 Lisbon; tel. (1) 544560; telex 63425.
**Ministry of the Environment and Natural Resources:** Av. D. Carlos I 126-6°, 1200 Lisbon.
**Ministry of Finance:** Rua da Alfândega, 1100 Lisbon; tel. (1) 877555; telex 12143.
**Ministry of Foreign Affairs:** Largo do Rilvas, 1354 Lisbon Codex; tel. (1) 601028; telex 12276.
**Ministry of Health:** Av. João Crisóstomo 9, 1093 Lisbon Codex; tel. (1) 544560; telex 15655; fax (1) 522861.
**Ministry of Home Affairs:** Praça do Comércio, 1100 Lisbon; tel. (1) 3464521; telex 16765; fax (1) 3468031.
**Ministry of Industry and Energy:** Rua da Horta Seca 15, 1200 Lisbon; tel. (1) 3463091; telex 62660; fax (1) 3475901.
**Ministry of Justice:** Praça do Comércio, 1194 Lisbon Codex; tel. (1) 3474780; telex 42998; fax (1) 3467692.
**Ministry of Planning and Territorial Administration:** Praça do Comércio, 1100 Lisbon; tel. (1) 3420734; telex 12566; fax (1) 3464539.
**Ministry of Parliamentary Affairs:** Estrada das Laranjeiras 195, 1600 Lisbon; tel. (1) 7265375; telex 62189; fax (1) 7264136.
**Ministry of Public Works, Transport and Communications:** Praça do Comércio, 1100 Lisbon; tel. (1) 879541; telex 13461.
**Ministry of the Sea:** Av. Brasília, 1600 Lisbon.
**Ministry of Trade and Tourism:** Av. da República 79, 1600 Lisbon; tel. (1) 730412; telex 13455.

### COUNCIL OF STATE

The Council of State is a consultative body, presided over by the President of the Republic (see The Constitution).

# President and Legislature

## PRESIDENT

**Election, 13 January 1991**

| Candidate | Votes | % |
|---|---|---|
| MÁRIO ALBERTO NOBRE LOPES SOARES | 3,459,521 | 70.35 |
| BASÍLIO ADOLFO MENDONÇA HORTA DA FRANCA | 696,379 | 14.16 |
| CARLOS ALBERTO DO VALE GOMES CARVALHAS | 635,373 | 12.92 |
| CARLOS MANUEL MARQUES DA SILVA | 126,581 | 2.57 |

## ASSEMBLÉIA DA REPÚBLICA

**President:** Prof. ANTÓNIO BARBOSA DE MELO.

**General Election, 6 October 1991**

| Party | % of votes | Seats |
|---|---|---|
| Partido Social Democrata (PSD) | 50.60 | 135 |
| Partido Socialista (PS) | 29.13 | 72 |
| Coligação Democrático Unitária (CDU)* | 8.80 | 17 |
| Centro Democrático Social (CDS)† | 4.43 | 5 |
| Partido de Solidariedade Nacional (PSN) | 1.68 | 1 |
| Others | 5.36 | — |
| Total | 100.00 | 230 |

* Electoral coalition of the Partido Comunista Português and minor left-wing parties.
† Now Partido Popular.

Note: The next legislative elections were to be held on October 1995, the presidential election being scheduled for early 1996.

PORTUGAL                                                                                                                                                     *Directory*

## Political Organizations

**Partido Comunista Português—PCP** (Portuguese Communist Party): Rua Soeiro Pereira Gomes 1, 1699 Lisbon Codex; tel. (1) 7936272; fax (1) 7969126; f. 1921, legalized 1974; theoretical foundation is Marxism-Leninism; aims are the defence and consolidation of the democratic regime and the revolutionary achievements, and ultimately the building of a socialist society in Portugal; 163,506 mems (1992); Sec.-Gen. CARLOS CARVALHAS; Pres. of Nat. Council Dr ALVARO BARREIRINHAS CUNHAL.

**Partido Popular—PP** (Popular Party): Largo Adelino Amaro da Costa 5, 1196 Lisbon Codex; tel. (1) 8869735; telex 14337; fax (1) 8860454; f. 1974; fmrly Centro Democrático Social; centre-right; mem. of International Democratic Union; supports social market economy and reduction of public sector intervention in the economy; defended revision of 1976 Constitution; Pres. MANUEL MONTEIRO.

**Partido Popular Monárquico—PPM** (People's Monarchist Party): Lisbon; tel. (1) 366587; f. 1974; environmentalist party, opposed to nuclear power; advocates preservation of Portugal's cultural identity and restoration of the monarchy.

**Partido Renovador Democrático—PRD** (Democratic Renewal Party): Travessa do Fala Só 9, 1200 Lisbon; tel. (1) 323997; telex 14439; f. 1985; centre-left; 8,000 mems.

**Partido Social Democrata—PSD** (Social Democratic Party): Rua de São Caetano 9, 1296 Lisbon Codex; tel. (1) 3952140; telex 135288; fax (1) 3976967; f. 1974; fmrly Partido Popular Democrático—PPD; aims to promote private enterprise, taking into account the welfare of the community; supports EU membership; 130,000 mems; Leader Dr JOAQUIM FERNANDO NOGUEIRA; Sec.-Gen. EDUARDO AZEVEDO SOARES.

**Partido Socialista—PS** (Socialist Party): Largo do Rato 2, 1200 Lisbon; tel. (1) 690404; fax (1) 693845; f. 1973 from former Acção Socialista Portuguesa (Portuguese Socialist Action); affiliate of the Socialist International and Party of European Socialists; advocates a society of greater social justice and co-operation between public, private and co-operative sectors, while respecting public liberties and the will of the majority attained through free elections; 100,000 mems; Pres. ALMEIDA SANTOS; Sec.-Gen. Eng. ANTÓNIO GUTERRES.

**Partido Socialista Revolucionário—PSR** (Revolutionary Socialist Party): Rua Palma 268, Lisbon; tel. (1) 864643; f. 1978 through merger of two Trotskyist groups.

**Partido de Solidariedade Nacional—PSN** (National Solidarity Party): c/o Assembléia da República, Lisbon; f. 1991; upholds interests of senior citizens; 20,000 mems; Pres. MANUEL SÉRGIO.

**União Democrática Popular—UDP** (People's Democratic Union): Lisbon; tel. (1) 689413; f. 1974; Maoist; comprises various political groups of the revolutionary left; Leader MÁRIO TOMÉ.

**Os Verdes** (The Greens): ecological party; Leader MARIA SANTOS.

## Diplomatic Representation

### EMBASSIES IN PORTUGAL

**Algeria:** Rua Duarte Pacheco Pereira 58, 1400 Lisbon; tel. (1) 3016356; fax (1) 3010393; Ambassador: M'HAMED ACHACHE.
**Angola:** Av. da República 68, 1000 Lisbon; tel. (1) 7961830; telex 43407; fax (1) 7971238; Ambassador: RUI ALBERTO VIEIRA DIAS MINGAS.
**Argentina:** Av. João Crisóstomo 8 r/c Esq., 1000 Lisbon; tel. (1) 7977311; telex 13611; fax (1) 7974702; Ambassador: DANIEL OLMOS.
**Austria:** Av. Infante Santo 43-4°, 1350 Lisbon; tel. (1) 3958220; telex 16768; fax (1) 3958224; Ambassador: Dr ALFRED MISSONG.
**Belgium:** Praça Marquês de Pombal 14-6°, 1250 Lisbon Codex; tel. (1) 549263; telex 12860; fax (1) 3561556; Ambassador: JEAN COENE.
**Brazil:** Quinta das Mil Flores, Estrada das Laranjeiras 144, 1600 Lisbon; tel. (1) 7267777; telex 61736; fax (1) 7267623; Ambassador: ITAMAR CANTIERO FRANCO (designate).
**Bulgaria:** Rua do Sacramento à Lapa 31, 1200 Lisbon; tel. (1) 3976364; fax (1) 3976361; Ambassador: VLADIMIR IVANOV FILIPOV.
**Canada:** Av. da Liberdade 144–156, 4°, 1200 Lisbon; tel. (1) 3474892; telex 12377; fax (1) 3476466; Ambassador: PATRICIA MARSDEN-DOLE.
**Cape Verde:** Av. do Restelo 33, 1400 Lisbon; tel. (1) 3015271; telex 13765; fax (1) 3015308; Ambassador: JOSÉ LUÍS JESUS.
**Chile:** Av. Miguel Bombarda 5-1°, 1000 Lisbon; tel. (1) 528054; telex 18805; fax (1) 3150909; Ambassador: EMILIO FILIPPI.
**China, People's Republic:** Rua de São Caetano 2, 1200 Lisbon; tel. (1) 3961882; telex 14762; fax (1) 3975632; Ambassador: WEI DONG.
**Colombia:** Praça José Fontana 10-5° Dto, 1000 Lisbon; tel. (1) 3557096; fax (1) 3528665; Ambassador: OSCAR BOTERO RESTREPO.
**Costa Rica:** Av. Columbano Bordalo Pinheiro 93-6°, 1000 Lisbon; tel. (1) 7264295; Ambassador: (vacant).
**Cuba:** Rua Pero da Covilhã 14 (Restelo), 1400 Lisbon; tel. (1) 3015317; telex 12167; fax (1) 3011895; Ambassador: GERMÁN BLANCO PUJOL.
**Czech Republic:** Pero de Alenquer 14, 1400 Lisbon; tel. (1) 3010487; fax (1) 3010629; Ambassador: MARTIN STROPNICKÝ.
**Denmark:** Rua Castilho 14-C-3°, 1296 Lisbon Codex; tel. (1) 545099; telex 18302; fax (1) 570124; Ambassador: MOGENS ISAKSEN.
**Egypt:** Av. D. Vasco da Gama 8, 1400 Lisbon; tel. (1) 3018301; telex 18394; fax (1) 3017909; Ambassador: WAHID FAWZY.
**Finland:** Rua Miguel Lupi 12-5°, 1200 Lisbon; tel. (1) 607551; telex 13582; fax (1) 604758; Ambassador: DIETER VITZTHUM.
**France:** Rua de Santos-o-Velho 5, 1293 Lisbon Codex; tel. (1) 608121; telex 12367; fax (1) 3978327; Ambassador: ALAIN GRENIER.
**Germany:** Campo Mártires da Pátria 38, 1100 Lisbon; tel. (1) 8810210; telex 12559; fax (1) 8853846; Ambassador: Dr WALTER NEUER.
**Greece:** Rua do Alto do Duque 13, 1400 Lisbon; tel. (1) 3016991; telex 18832; fax (1) 3011205; Ambassador: MICHEL-AKIS PAPAGEORGIOU.
**Guinea-Bissau:** Rua de Alcolena 17–17A, 1400 Lisbon; tel. (1) 3015371; telex 14326; fax (1) 3017040; Ambassador: ADELINO MANO QUETA.
**Holy See:** Av. Luís Bivar 18, 1050 Lisbon; tel. (1) 3157186; fax (1) 3538075; Apostolic Nuncio: Most Rev. EDOARDO ROVIDA, Titular Archbishop of Taormina.
**Hungary:** Calçada de Santo Amaro 85, 1300 Lisbon; tel. (1) 3645928; telex 13385; fax (1) 3632314; Ambassador: Dr ANDRÁS GULYÁS.
**India:** Rua Pero da Covilhã 16, 1400 Lisbon; tel. (1) 3017291; telex 62670; fax (1) 3016576; Ambassador: SURENDRA K. ARORA.
**Iran:** Rua do Alto do Duque 49, 1400 Lisbon; tel. (1) 3011560; fax (1) 3010777; Ambassador: ABOLFAZI RAHNAMA.
**Iraq:** Rua da Arriaga à Lapa 9, 1200 Lisbon; tel. (1) 607112; telex 14042; Ambassador: (vacant).
**Ireland:** Rua da Imprensa à Estrela 1-4°, 1200 Lisbon; tel. (1) 3961569; fax (1) 3977363; Ambassador: EAMONN RYAN.
**Israel:** Rua António Enes 16-4°, 1000 Lisbon; tel. (1) 570251; telex 12223; fax (1) 3528545; Ambassador: BENJAMIN ORON.
**Italy:** Largo Conde de Pombeiro 6, 1198 Lisbon; tel. (1) 546144; telex 12336; Ambassador: LUDOVICO ORTONO.
**Japan:** Rua Mouzinho da Silveira 11, 1200 Lisbon; tel. (1) 3523485; telex 12378; fax (1) 3534802; Ambassador: KATSUHIRO ICHIOKA.
**Korea, Republic:** Edif. Presidente, Av. Miguel Bombarda 36-7°, 1000 Lisbon; tel. (1) 7937200; telex 13457; fax (1) 7977176; Ambassador: SOON KYU CHUN.
**Libya:** Av. das Descobertas 24, 1400 Lisbon; tel. (1) 3016301; telex 43131; fax (1) 3012378; Head of People's Bureau: MOHAMED MAHMOND EL KHOJA.
**Luxembourg:** Rua das Janelas Verdes 43, 1200 Lisbon; tel. (1) 3962781; fax (1) 601410; Ambassador: PAUL FABER.
**Mexico:** Rua Castilho 50-4° Esq., 1250 Lisbon; tel. (1) 3862683; telex 12822; fax (1) 3860563; Chargé d'affaires, a.i.: Dr JORGE LUIS OLIVÁREZ NOVALES.
**Morocco:** Rua Borges Carneiro 32-1°, 1200 Lisbon; tel. (1) 3979193; telex 62197; fax (1) 3970309; Ambassador: AZIZ MEKOUAR.
**Mozambique:** Av. de Berna 7, 1000 Lisbon; tel. (1) 7971994; telex 13641; fax (1) 7932720; Ambassador: ESPERANÇA ALFREDO SAMUEL MACHAVELA.
**Netherlands:** Av. Infante Santo 43-5°, 1350 Lisbon; tel. (1) 3961163; telex 12126; fax (1) 3966436; Ambassador: P. C. NIEMAN.
**Nigeria:** Rua Fernão Mendes Pinto 50 (Restelo), 1400 Lisbon; tel. (1) 3016189; telex 18418; fax (1) 3018152; Ambassador: OLUFEMI O. GEORGE.
**Norway:** Av. D. Vasco da Gama 1, 1400 Lisbon; tel. (1) 3015344; telex 16505; fax (1) 3016158; Ambassador: HÅKON WEXELSEN FREIHOW.
**Pakistan:** Av. da República 20-1°, 1000 Lisbon; tel. (1) 3538446; telex 64699; fax (1) 3158805; Ambassador: TARIQ KHAN AFRIDI.
**Panama:** Rua Pedro de Sintra 15, 1400 Lisbon; tel. (1) 3019046; fax (1) 3019063; Chargé d'affaires: ELIDA G. DE PAREDES AUED.
**Peru:** Rua Castilho 50-4° Dto, 1200 Lisbon; tel. (1) 3861552; telex 64000; fax (1) 3860005; Ambassador: JOSÉ EMILIO ROMERO C.
**Poland:** Av. das Descobertas 2, 1400 Lisbon; tel. (1) 3012350; fax (1) 3010202; Ambassador: JANUSZ RYMWID-MICKIEWICZ.

**Romania:** Rua de São Caetano 5, 1200 Lisbon; tel. (1) 3960866; telex 13377; fax (1) 3960984; Ambassador: Mihu Miron Biji.

**Russia:** Rua Visconde de Santarém 59, 1000 Lisbon; tel. (1) 8462424; telex 60233; fax (1) 8463008; Ambassador: Alexandr Smirnov.

**São Tomé and Príncipe:** Rua da Junqueira 2, 1300 Lisbon; tel. (1) 3638242; fax (1) 3644803; Ambassador: Orlando Bonfim Dias da Graça.

**Slovakia:** Av. Fontes Pereira de Melo 19-7° Dto, 1000 Lisbon; tel. (1) 549890; telex 13406; fax (1) 3520892; Ambassador: Peter Zsoldós.

**South Africa:** Av. Luís Bivar 10, 1097 Lisbon Codex; tel. (1) 3535041; telex 12894; fax (1) 3535713; Ambassador: Pieter Swanepoel.

**Spain:** Rua do Salitre 1, 1296 Lisbon; tel. (1) 3472381; telex 12505; fax (1) 3472384; Ambassador: Raúl Morodo.

**Sweden:** Rua Miguel Lupi 12-2°, 1200 Lisbon; tel. (1) 3955224; telex 12554; fax (1) 3965688; Ambassador: Kerstin Asp-Johnsson.

**Switzerland:** Travessa do Patrocínio 1, 1399 Lisbon Codex; tel. (1) 3973121; telex 12893; fax (1) 3977187; Ambassador: Eric R. Lang.

**Thailand:** Rua de Alcolena 12A, 1400 Lisbon; tel. (1) 3014848; fax (1) 3018181; Ambassador: Surapong Jayanama.

**Turkey:** Av. das Descobertas 22, 1400 Lisbon; tel. (1) 3014275; telex 13392; fax (1) 3017934; Ambassador: Gündoğdu Can.

**United Kingdom:** Rua de São Bernardo 33, 1200 Lisbon Codex; tel. (1) 3961191; fax (1) 3976768; Ambassador: Roger Westbrook.

**USA:** Av. das Forças Armadas (Sete Rios), 1600 Lisbon Codex; tel. (1) 7266600; telex 12528; fax (1) 7269109; Ambassador: Elizabeth Frawley Bagley.

**Uruguay:** Rua Sampaio e Pina 16-2°, 1070 Lisbon: tel. (1) 3889265; telex 14591; fax (1) 3889245; Chargé d'affaires: Rolando Visconti.

**Venezuela:** Av. Duque de Loulé 47-4°, 1000 Lisbon; tel. (1) 573803; telex 18402; fax (1) 3527421; Ambassador: Arturo Hernández-Grisanti.

**Yugoslavia:** Av. das Descobertas 12, 1400 Lisbon; tel. (1) 3015311; telex 18352; fax (1) 3015313; Chargé d'affaires: Vladimir Vilotijević.

**Zaire:** Av. Fontes Pereira de Melo 31-7°, 1000 Lisbon; tel. (1) 3533438; telex 18438; fax (1) 3533438; Ambassador: Mbia Magubu Mazobande.

# Judicial System

For civil and penal cases, the Portuguese Republic is divided into 221 comarcas, or judicial districts. The principle of *habeas corpus* is recognized, and persons illegally detained may appeal to the Supreme Court.

Judges are appointed for life and are irremovable. Conditions of appointment, service, dismissal, pension and transfer are governed by law. Practising judges may not hold any other office, whether public or private, except a non-remunerated position in teaching or research in the legal field. The Conselho Superior da Magistratura controls their appointment, transfer and promotion and the exercise of disciplinary action.

The jury system was reintroduced in 1976, although it operates only at the request of the prosecutor or defendant.

### PUBLIC PROSECUTION

The State is represented in the courts by the Public Prosecution, whose highest organ is the Procuradoria-Geral da República (Attorney General's Office).

**Procurador-Geral:** Dr José Narciso da Cunha Rodrigues.

### SUPREME COURT

**Supremo Tribunal de Justiça:** Praça do Comércio, 1100 Lisbon; tel. (1) 3475536; the highest organ of the judicial system; has jurisdiction over Metropolitan Portugal, The Azores and Madeira; it consists of a president and 50 judges.

**President:** Joaquim de Carvalho.

### COURTS OF SECOND INSTANCE

There are four Courts of Second Instance (or Courts of Appeal); that in Lisbon consists of a president and 73 judges; in Porto, of a president and 56 judges; in Coímbra, of a president and 30 judges; and in Évora, of a president and 25 judges.

### COURTS OF FIRST INSTANCE

For the purposes of Courts of First Instance, Portuguese territory is divided into judicial districts, judicial circuits and comarcas. In each comarca there are courts of general competence; courts of specialized competence, specific competence or of combined competence may also exist. The newly-established Circuit Courts, of general, specialized or specific competence, exercise jurisdiction over their respective areas. The Maritime Courts are courts of first instance, of specialized competence, pending the establishment of a court in Lisbon.

### SPECIAL COURTS

These have exclusive jurisdiction in certain matters, i.e. military courts for military crimes, an Accounts Court to judge the public accounts and administrative and revenue courts.

### CONSTITUTIONAL COURT

**Tribunal Constitucional:** Rua do Século 111, Lisbon; tel. (1) 360024; rules on matters of constitutionality according to the terms of the Constitution of the Portuguese Republic; exercises jurisdiction over all Portuguese territory; consists of 13 judges.

**President:** Prof. José Manuel Moreira Cardoso da Costa.

### SUPREME ADMINISTRATIVE COURT

**Supremo Tribunal Administrativo:** Rua S. Pedro de Alcântara 75, Lisbon; tel. (1) 3467797; highest organ of the administrative system; has jurisdiction over metropolitan Portugal, the Azores and Madeira; consists of 38 judges.

**President:** Dr Luciano Patrão.

# Religion

There is freedom of religion in Portugal. The dominant Christian denomination is Roman Catholicism, but a number of Protestant churches have been established.

### CHRISTIANITY

**Conselho Português de Igrejas Cristãs—COPIC** (Portuguese Council of Christian Churches): Rua da Lapa 9, Sala 1, 2°, 3080 Figueira da Foz; tel. (33) 28279; fax (33) 22603; f. 1971; three mem. churches, two observers; Gen. Sec. Rev. Manuel Pedro Cardoso.

### The Roman Catholic Church

For ecclesiastical purposes, Portugal comprises 20 dioceses, grouped into three metropolitan sees (the patriarchate of Lisbon and the archdioceses of Braga and Évora). At 31 December 1992 about 90% of the Portuguese population were adherents of the Roman Catholic Church.

**Bishops' Conference:** Conferência Episcopal Portuguesa, Campo dos Mártires da Pátria 43-1° Esq., 1100 Lisbon; tel. (1) 8852123; fax (1) 8850559; f. 1932; Pres. Rt Rev. João Alves, Bishop of Coímbra.

**Patriarch of Lisbon:** Cardinal António Ribeiro, Campo dos Mártires da Pátria 45, 1198 Lisbon Codex; tel. (1) 8853665.

**Archbishop of Braga:** Most Rev. Eurico Dias Nogueira, Cúria Arquiepiscopal, Rua de Santa Margarida 181, 4719 Braga Codex; tel. (53) 613281; fax (53) 612006.

**Archbishop of Évora:** Most Rev. Maurílio Jorge Quintal de Gouveia, Cúria Arquiepiscopal, Rua D. Augusto Eduardo Nunes 2, 7000 Évora; tel. (66) 22186; fax (66) 28545.

### The Anglican Communion

**Church of England:** Rua Henrique Lopes de Mendonça 253-4° Dto, Hab. 42, 4100 Porto; tel. (2) 6177772; Auxiliary Bishop of Gibraltar (Diocese of Gibraltar in Europe) Rt Rev. Daniel de Pina Cabral.

**Igreja Lusitana Católica Apostólica Evangélica** (Lusitanian Catholic Apostolic Evangelical Church): Rua 1° de Maio 54-2°, 4400 Vila Nova de Gaia; tel. (2) 304018; fax (2) 302016; f. 1880; Bishop Rt Rev. Fernando Luz Soares.

### Other Christian Churches

**Assembleia de Deus** (Assembly of God): Rua Neves Ferreira 13-3°, 1170 Lisbon; tel. (1) 8142040; Pastors José Neves, Dinis Rodrigues.

**Associação de Igrejas Baptistas Portuguesas** (Asscn of Portuguese Baptist Churches): Rua da Escola, 18 Maceira, 2715 Pero Pinheiro; tel. (1) 9271150; f. 1955; Pres. Rev. João S. Regueiras.

**Convenção Baptista Portuguesa** (Portuguese Baptist Convention): Lisbon; tel. (1) 8143424; Gen. Sec. Dr José P. Sousa; Pres. Rev. Daniel Machado.

**Igreja Evangélica Alemã de Lisboa** (German Evangelical Church in Lisbon): Av. Columbano Bordalo Pinheiro 48, 1000 Lisbon; tel. (1) 7260976; Pastor Rev. Kurt Hermann.

**Igreja Evangélica Metodista Portuguesa** (Portuguese Evangelical Methodist Church): Praça Coronel Pacheco 23, 4050 Porto; tel. (2) 2007410; fax (2) 2086961; Rev. Ireneu da Silva Cunha.

PORTUGAL
*Directory*

**Igreja Evangélica Presbiteriana de Portugal** (Evangelical Presbyterian Church of Portugal): Rua Tomás da Anunciação, 56–1° Dto, 1300 Lisbon; tel. (1) 674959; fax (1) 3956326; f. 1952; Pres. Rev. João S. Neto.

### ISLAM
Muslims number an estimated 15,000.

### JUDAISM
There are Jewish communities in Lisbon and Porto, estimated to total 2,000.

## The Press

Under the 1976 Constitution, the freedom of the press is guaranteed. Legislation to return seven state-owned newspapers to private ownership was approved in early 1988. The reprivatization of the press was completed in 1991. In 1993 27 daily newspapers were published.

### PRINCIPAL DAILIES

#### Aveiro
**Diário de Aveiro:** Av. Dr Lourenço Peixinho 15-5° A, 3800 Aveiro; tel. (34) 24601; telex 37489; fax (34) 22635; f. 1985; morning; Dir Adriano Callé Lucas; circ. 4,500.

#### Braga
**Correio do Minho:** Palácio de Exposições e Desportos, Apdo 290, 4703 Braga Codex; tel. (53) 74087; telex 32337; morning; Dir Rui Madeira; circ. 1,573.

**Diário do Minho:** Rua de Santa Margarida 4A, 4709 Braga Codex; tel. (53) 613414; telex 32340; fax (53) 215466; f. 1919; morning; Dir Padre Domingos da Silva Araújo; circ. 4,000.

#### Coímbra
**Diário de Coímbra:** Rua da Sofia 179 ou Estrada de Eiras, 3000 Coímbra; tel. (39) 25461; telex 52147; fax (39) 492128; f. 1930; morning; *Domingo* publ. on Sun. (f. 1974; circ. 8,000); Dir Eng. Adriano Mário da Cunha Lucas; circ. 9,000.

#### Évora
**Diário do Sul:** Travessa de Santo André 8, 7001 Évora Codex, Apdo 37; tel. (66) 23144; fax (66) 741252; f. 1969; morning; Dir Manuel Madeira Piçarra; circ. 6,500.

**Notícias d'Évora:** Rua do Raimundo 41–43, 7002 Évora Codex; tel. (66) 22348; f. 1900; morning; Dir Rosa Souto Armas; circ. 3,000.

#### Leiria
**Diário de Leiria:** Av. Heróis de Angola 76-3°-C, 2400 Leiria; tel. (44) 33881; telex 65264; fax (44) 812498; f. 1987; morning; Dir Adriano Callé Lucas; circ. 3,500.

#### Lisbon
**A Bola:** Travessa da Queimada 23, r/c E. 2° D., 1294 Lisbon Codex; tel. (1) 3463981; telex 12880; fax (1) 3464503; f. 1945; sport; Dir Carlos Miranda; Editors Vítor Serpa, Joaquim Rita; circ. 180,000.

**A Capital:** Travessa do Poço da Cidade 26, 1124 Lisbon Codex; tel. (1) 3465908; telex 12386; fax (1) 3463497; f. 1968; evening; Dir José Sarabando; circ. 40,000.

**Correio da Manhã:** Rua Mouzinho da Silveira 27, 1200 Lisbon; tel. (1) 527636; telex 42439; fax (1) 3533726; f. 1979; morning; independent; Pres. and Dir-Gen. Dr Vítor Direito; circ. 85,000.

**Diário de Notícias:** Av. da Liberdade 266, 1200 Lisbon; tel. (1) 561151; telex 12379; fax (1) 536627; f. 1864; morning; Dir Dinis de Abreu; Editor-in-Chief Fernando Pires; circ. 58,898.

**Jornal de O Dia:** Praceta da Tabaqueira Lote A 5°, Porta B, Matinha, 1900 Lisbon; tel. (1) 8583421; telex 15558; fax (1) 8584421; f. 1975 as *O Dia*; morning; right-wing; Dir Adelino Alves.

**Público:** Rua Amilcar Cabral, Lote 1, Quinta do Lambert, 1700 Lisbon; tel. (1) 7599135; telex 65205; fax (1) 7587638; f. 1990; morning; Dir Vincente Jorge Silva; circ. 75,000.

#### Porto
**Record:** Travessa dos Inglesinhos 3-1°, 1200 Lisbon; tel. (1) 3475675; telex 42451; fax (1) 3476279; f. 1949; sport; Dir Rui Cartaxana; Editor-in-Chief João Marcelino; circ. 132,000.

**O Comércio do Porto:** Rua Fernandes Tomás 352, 7°, 4000 Porto; tel. (2) 563571; telex 25108; fax (2) 569859; f. 1854; morning; Dir Alberto Carvalho; circ. 30,295.

**Jornal de Notícias:** Rua Gonçalo Cristóvão 195, 4052 Porto Codex; tel. (2) 2096171; telex 22122; fax (2) 2002861; f. 1888; morning; Dir Frederico Martins Mendes; circ. 90,000.

**O Primeiro de Janeiro:** Rua de Santa Catarina 339, 1°, 4000 Porto; tel. (2) 5101095; telex 22124; fax (2) 2005723; f. 1868; independent; morning; Dir José Manuel Barroso; circ. 50,000.

#### Madeira
(Funchal)

**Diário de Notícias:** Rua da Alfândega 8, 9000 Funchal; tel. (91) 220031; telex 72161; fax (91) 228912; f. 1876; morning; independent; Dir José Bettencourt da Câmara; circ. 15,413.

**Jornal da Madeira:** Rua Dr Fernão de Ornelas 35 r/c, 9000 Funchal; tel. (91) 20014; telex 72114; fax (91) 31897; f. 1927; morning; Catholic; Dir Canon Manuel Tomé Teixeira Velosa; circ. 8,000.

#### The Azores
**Açoriano Oriental:** Rua Dr Bruno Tavares Carreiro 36, 9500 Ponta Delgada; tel. (96) 629700; telex 82175; fax (96) 629018; f. 1835; morning; Dir Gustavo Moura; circ. 6,000.

**O Correio da Horta:** Rua Ernesto Rebelo 5, 9900 Horta; tel. (92) 22821; f. 1930; evening; Dir Francisco Gomes; circ. 1,020.

**Correio dos Açores:** Rua da Misericórdia 42, 9500 Ponta Delgada; tel. (96) 24218; telex 82286; f. 1920; morning; Dir Jorge do Nascimento Cabral; circ. 3,800.

**Diário dos Açores:** Rua Diário dos Açores 11, 9500 Ponta Delgada; tel. (96) 24355; fax (96) 24355; f. 1870; morning; Dir Maria Isabel Carreiro M. Costa; circ. 2,380.

**Diário Insular:** Rua das Minhas Terras 17–21, 9700 Angra do Heroísmo; tel. (95) 22173; telex 82281; f. 1946; morning; Dir José Lourenço; circ. 2,240.

**O Telégrafo:** Rua Conselheiro Medeiros 30, 9902 Horta; tel. (92) 22245; fax (92) 22245; f. 1893; morning; Dir Ruben Rodrigues; circ. 2,500.

**A União:** Rua Padre António Cordeiro 9–17, 9700 Angra do Heroísmo; tel. (95) 24030; f. 1893; morning; Dir Padre Manuel Coelho de Sousa; circ. 1,500.

### PRINCIPAL PERIODICALS

In 1990 an estimated total of 937 periodicals were published in Portugal. Among the more widely known are:

**Activa:** Largo da Lagoa 15c, 2795 Linda-a-Velha; tel. (1) 4143078; fax (1) 4107050; f. 1991; monthly; for women.

**Africa Hoje:** Rua Joaquim António de Aguiar 45-5° Esq., 1000 Lisbon; tel. (1) 557175; telex 42487; fax (1) 3557667; f. 1985; monthly; African affairs; circ. 30,000.

**Anglo-Portuguese News:** Apdo 113, 2765 Estoril, Lisbon; tel. (1) 4661455; fax (1) 4660358; f. 1937; every Thursday; English language newspaper; Publr and Editor Nigel Batley; circ. 30,000.

**Autosport:** Av. Infante D. Henrique 334, 1800 Lisbon; tel. (1) 8510152; fax (1) 8518990; weekly; motoring; Dir Rui Freire; circ. 30,000.

**Avante:** Rua Soeiro Pereira Gomes, 1699 Lisbon; tel. (1) 769725; weekly; organ of the Communist Party; Dir Carlos Brito.

**Brotéria—Revista de Cultura:** Rua Maestro António Taborda 14, 1200 Lisbon; tel. (1) 3961660; fax (1) 3956629; f. 1926; monthly; review of culture; Dir Luís Archer.

**Casa e Decoração:** Av. Alvares Cabral 84, 10D, 1000 Lisbon; tel. (1) 3877926; fax (1) 3877926; f. 1981; 10 a year; home and interior decoration; circ. 35,000.

**Casa & Jardim:** Rua da Misericórdia 137, S/L Esq., 1200 Lisbon; tel. (1) 3472127; fax (1) 3421490; f. 1978; monthly; home, interior design, fine arts and gardening; Dir Eduardo Fortunato de Almeida; circ. 20,000.

**Colóquio/Artes:** Av. de Berna 45, 1000 Lisbon; tel. (1) 7935131; telex 63768; fax (1) 7935139; f. 1971; 4 a year; arts; Dir Dr José Augusto França; circ. 4,000.

**Colóquio/Letras:** Av. de Berna 56-3°, 1093 Lisbon Codex; tel. (1) 7935131; telex 63768; fax (1) 7935139; f. 1971; 4 a year; literary; Dir Dr David Mourão Ferreira; circ. 3,600.

**Correio da Madeira:** Rua do Carmo 19-3° Dto, 9000 Funchal; tel. (91) 20738; f. 1987; weekly newspaper; Dir José Campos; circ. 5,000.

**Cosmopolitan:** Largo da Lagoa 15c, 2795 Linda-a-Velha; tel. (1) 4143078; f. 1992; monthly; women's magazine.

**O Diabo:** Rua Alexandre Herculano 7-5° Esq., 1100 Lisbon; tel. (1) 572367; telex 64331; fax (1) 570263; f. 1976; weekly newspaper; Dir Vera Lagoa; circ. 46,000.

**Eles e Elas:** Rua de São Bento 311, 3° Esq., 1200 Lisbon; tel. (1) 3961771; fax (1) 605688; f. 1983; monthly; social events; Dir Maria da Luz de Bragança.

**Elle:** Rua Filipe Folque 40-1°, 1000 Lisbon; tel. (1) 736878; f. 1988; monthly; women's magazine; Dir Maria Teresa Coelho; circ. 40,000.

PORTUGAL
*Directory*

**Expresso:** Rua Duque de Palmela 37-3° Dto, 1296 Lisbon Codex; tel. (1) 3526141; telex 16583; fax (1) 543858; weekly newspaper; Dir José António Paula Saraiva; circ. 160,000.
**Gazeta dos Desportos:** Rua Poço dos Negros 163-1°, 1200 Lisbon; tel. (1) 609523; telex 42479; 3 a week; sport; Dir Joaquim Queirós.
**Guia—Revista Prática:** Av. Almirante Gago Coutinho 113, 1700 Lisbon; tel. (1) 8474410; fax (1) 8474425; weekly women's magazine; fashion and housekeeping; Editor Rui Mendonça; Editor-in-Chief Maria Elvira Bento; circ. 80,000.
**O Independente:** Rua Actor Taborda 27-1°, 1000 Lisbon; tel. (1) 3526306; fax (1) 3531766; f. 1988; weekly; Propr SOCI; Dir Paulo Portas; circ. 103,500.
**JL—Jornal de Letras, Artes e Ideias:** Av. da Liberdade 232-r/c Dto, 1200 Lisbon; tel. (1) 574520; telex 18386; weekly; Dir José Carlos de Vasconcelos; Editor Manuel Beca Murias; circ. 80,000.
**Manchete:** Rua de São Bento 311, 3° Esq., 1250 Lisbon; tel. (1) 3961771; fax (1) 605688; f. 1992; monthly; national and international current and social events; Dir Maria da Luz de Bragança.
**Maria:** Av. Miguel Bombarda 33, 2745 Queluz; tel. 4364401; fax 4365001; f. 1977; weekly; women's magazine; Dir Jacques Rodrigues; Editor-in-Chief Paula Rodrigues; 392,000.
**Marie Claire:** Rua Mouzinho da Silveira 27, 1200 Lisbon; tel. (1) 527547; fax (1) 527943; f. 1989; women's magazine; Dir Inês Pedrosa; circ. 50,000.
**Máxima:** Rua Vítor Cordon 37-3°, 1200 Lisbon; tel. (1) 3423136; f. 1989; women's magazine; Dir Margarida Maraute; circ. 45,000.
**Moda e Moda:** Rua Braamcamp 12, r/c Dto, 1250 Lisbon; tel. (1) 3862426; 5 a year; fashion; Dir Marionela Gusmão; circ. 20,000.
**Mulher Moderna:** Av. Miguel Bombarda 33, 2745 Queluz; tel. 4364401; fax 4365001; f. 1988; weekly; women's magazine; Dir Jacques Rodrigues; Editor-in-Chief Paula Rodrigues; circ. 60,000.
**O Mundo Agrícola:** Rua da Rosa 257-2° Esq., 1200 Lisbon; tel. (1) 3460964; telex 62784; fax (1) 3460944; monthly; agriculture; Dir A. Morais da Silva.
**Nova Gente:** Av. Miguel Bombarda 33, 2745 Queluz; tel. 4364388; fax 4365001; f. 1979; weekly; popular; Dir Jacques Rodrigues; Editor-in-Chief António Simões; circ. 200,000
**Portugal Socialista:** Largo do Rato 2, 1200 Lisbon; tel. (1) 3464375; telex 13390; f. 1967; quarterly; organ of the Socialist Party; Dir António Reis; circ. 5,000.
**Portugal Turismo Actualidade:** Rua Joaquim António de Aguiar 45-5° Esq., 1000 Lisbon; tel. (1) 557175; telex 42487; fax (1) 557667; f. 1980; monthly; tourism; circ. 40,000.
**Povo Livre:** Rua S. Caetano 9, 1200 Lisbon; tel. (1) 3952140; fax (1) 3976967; weekly; organ of the Social Democratic Party; Dir José Pacheco Pereira.
**A Revista:** Rua de São Bento 311, 3° Esq., 1250 Lisbon; tel. (1) 3961771; fax (1) 605688; f. 1990; 2 a year; national and international current events; Dir Maria da Luz de Bragança.
**Revista ACP:** Av. Barbosa du Bocage 23-2° Esq., 1000 Lisbon; tel. (1) 7930211; fax (1) 7934026; f. 1908; monthly; motoring and tourism; Propr Automóvel Club de Portugal; Editor José Macedo e Cunha; circ. 190,000.
**Revista Exame:** Largo da Lagoa 15c, 2795 Linda-a-Velha; tel. (1) 4143078; fax (1) 4107050; monthly; finance; circ. 21,000.
**Revista Negócios:** Rua do Norte 14-2°, 1200 Lisbon; monthly; business and finance; tel. (1) 3471259; telex 42644; circ. 10,000.
**Segredos de Cozinha:** Av. Miguel Bombarda 33, 2745 Queluz; tel. 4364388; fax 4365001; f. 1986; weekly; cookery; Dir Jacques Rodrigues; Editor-in-Chief Paula Rodrigues; circ. 40,000.
**Selecções do Reader's Digest:** Rua D. Francisco Manuel de Melo 21, 1070 Lisbon; tel. (1) 3810000; telex 12410; fax (1) 3859203; monthly magazine; Dir Margarida Sarda; circ. 293,670.
**Semanário:** Av. 24 de Julho 6, 1200 Lisbon; tel. (1) 604003; telex 64150; fax (1) 609270; weekly newspaper; Dir Dr João Amaral; circ. 55,000.
**Semanário Económico:** Rua de Santa Marta 47-2° Dto, 1100 Lisbon; tel. (1) 3558525; telex 61780; fax (1) 558515; weekly; economic newspaper; Dir Nicolau Santos; circ. 20,000.
**Sete:** Av. da Liberdade 190-2° Dto, 1298 Lisbon Codex; tel. (1) 766062; telex 18386; weekly; general interest; Dir Cáceres Monteiro; circ. 54,300.
**Tal & Qual:** Rua Rodrigo da Fonseca 60-4° Dto, 1200 Lisbon; tel. (1) 3862090; telex 65936; fax (1) 3866446; weekly; popular newspaper; Dir José Rocha Vieira; circ. 87,000.
**TV Guia:** Av. Almirante Gago Coutinho 113, 1700 Lisbon; tel. (1) 8474410; fax (1) 8474425; weekly; TV programmes and general features; Dir Rui Mendonça; circ. 257,000.
**TV 7 Dias:** Av. Miguel Bombarda 33, 2745 Queluz; tel. 4364401; fax 4365001; f. 1985; weekly; television magazine; Dir Jacques Rodrigues; Editor-in-Chief António Simões; circ. 100,000.

**Vida Económica:** Rua Gonçalo Cristovão 111-5°, 4000 Porto; tel. (2) 2003661; fax (2) 318098; weekly; financial; Dir João Peixoto de Sousa; Editor-in-Chief João Luís de Sousa.
**Visão:** Av. da Liberdade 232 r/c Dto, 1298 Lisbon Codex; tel. (1) 574520; telex 18386; fax (1) 540575; weekly magazine; Dir Cáceres Monteiro; circ. 55,000.

### NEWS AGENCIES

**Agência Europeia de Imprensa, Lda (AEI):** Calçada da Rosa 6, 1100 Lisbon; tel. (1) 8883715; fax (1) 875725; Man. Dir Dr Alexandre Cordeiro; Gen. Dir António Pena.
**Agência Lusa de Informação:** Rua Dr João Couto, Lote C, 1500 Lisbon; tel. (1) 7144099; telex 12539; fax (1) 7145443; f. 1987; Pres. Fernando Rodrigues Rocha.
**Agência de Representações Dias da Silva, Lda (ADS):** Av. Almirante Reis 82-6° Dto, 1100 Lisbon; tel. (1) 8123217; fax (1) 8154542; f. 1964; pictorial news, features, photographic reports, news, comic strips, literary material, etc.; Dir Júlio Calderon Dias da Silva.

### Foreign Bureaux

**Agence France-Presse (AFP):** Rua Rosa Araújo 34-3°, 1200 Lisbon; tel. (1) 3556504; telex 18582; fax (1) 3520866; Dir Michèle Houx.
**Agencia EFE** (Spain): Largo da Rosa 5–7, Lisbon 1100; tel. (1) 875712; telex 18512; Dir Miguel Higueras Cleries.
**Agenzia Nazionale Stampa Associata (ANSA)** (Italy): Praça da Alegria 58-3° G, 1200 Lisbon; tel. (1) 3421409; telex 12391; Dir Riccardo Carucci.
**Associated Press (AP)** (USA): Praça da Alegria 58-3°A, 1250 Lisbon; tel. (1) 3470967; telex 12530; fax (1) 3471257; Admin. Dir Emma E. A. Gilbert.
**Deutsche Presse-Agentur (dpa)** (Germany): Praça da Alegria 58-5b, 1200 Lisbon; tel. (1) 3469837; Bureau Chief Artur Margalho.
**Inter Press Service (IPS)** (Italy): Av. Visconde de Valmor 354-4° Dto, 1000 Lisbon; tel. (1) 7933276; telex 64598; fax (1) 7939909; Correspondent Mario Dujisin.
**Prensa Latina** (Cuba): Av. Duque de Avila 66-7°, Lisbon; tel. (1) 537470; telex 16788; Correspondent Luis Lazo Carranca.
**Reuters** (UK): Edif. Miroir, Rua Camilo Castelo Branco 42–44, 1°, 1000 Lisbon; tel. (1) 3538254; telex 62829; fax (1) 3150036; Chief Correspondent Robert Powell.
**Rossiyskoye Informatsionnoye Agentstvo—Novosti (RIA—Novosti)** (Russia): Praça Andrade Caminha 3, 1700 Lisbon; tel. and fax (1) 8463295; Dir A. Zditovetski.
**United Press International (UPI)** (USA): Praça da Alegria 58, 5C, Lisbon 1200; tel. (1) 372616; telex 12524; Dir Alexander Sloop.
**Xinhua (New China) News Agency** (People's Republic of China): Rua Gonçalo Velho Cabral 11a, Restelo, Lisbon 3; tel. (1) 615783; telex 14305; Chief Correspondent Xiao Ziaoquan.

ČTK (Czech Republic) is also represented in Portugal.

### PRESS ASSOCIATIONS

**Associação da Imprensa Diária** (Association of the Daily Press): Rua de Artilharia Um 69-2°, 1297 Lisbon Codex; tel. (1) 657584; fax (1) 3873541; f. 1976; 27 mems; Pres. António Freitas Cruz; Sec. Jorge Moura.
**Associação da Imprensa Não-Diária—AIND** (Association of the Non-Daily Press): Rua Gomes Freire 183-4° Esq., 1199 Lisbon Codex; tel. (1) 3555092; fax (1) 522191; f. 1961; Pres. Dr Henrique Granadeiro; Sec.-Gen. Joana Ramada Curto.

# Publishers

**Assírio & Alvim:** Rua Passos Manuel 67b, 1150 Lisbon; tel. (1) 3555580; fax (1) 3152935; f. 1972; sociology, history, economics, poetry, literature, photography, anthropology.
**Ática SA:** Av. 25 de Abril 205-A, Pontinha, 1675 Lisbon; tel. (1) 4796026; f. 1935; poetry, literature, essays, theatre, history, philosophy; CEOs Vasco Silva, José Rodrigues.
**Brasília Editora:** Rua José Falcão 173, 4050 Porto; tel. (2) 315854; f. 1961; literature, history, general; Dirs Dr J. Carvalho Branco, Dra Zulmira Carvalho Branco, Isabel Carvalho Branco.
**Coímbra Editora, Lda:** Rua Ferreira Borges 77, Apdo 101, 3002 Coímbra Codex; tel. (39) 23372; fax (39) 37531; f. 1920; law, education, linguistics; Man. Dr João Carlos A. Oliveira Salgado.
**Contexto Editora, Lda:** Rua da Rosa 105-2° Dto, 1200 Lisbon; tel. (1) 3479769; fax (1) 3479770; fiction, poetry, children's literature; Dir Manuel de Brito.

PORTUGAL

**Difusão Cultural—Sociedade Editorial e Livreira, Lda:** Rua Luís de Freitas Branco 3 A-B, 1600 Lisbon; tel. (1) 7599373; telex 60380; fax (1) 7594418; f. 1986; literature, history, economics, philosophy, children's books, educational; Man. EDUARDO MARTINS SOARES.

**Distri Editora—Grupo Electroliber:** Rua Prof. Reinaldo dos Santos 50-A, 1500 Lisbon; tel. (1) 789918; telex 16588; f. 1977; fiction, poetry, essays, educational; Man. Dir PEDRO RICARDO ANSCHEL DE VASCONCELOS.

**Edições Afrontamento, Lda:** Rua de Costa Cabral 859, 4200 Porto; tel. (2) 529271; fax (2) 591777; f. 1963; fiction, poetry, cinema, children's books, history, sociology, philosophy, economics, politics, etc.; Dirs MARCELA TORRES, A. FLEMING, J. SOUSA RIBEIRO.

**Edições Asa:** Rua dos Mártires da Liberdade 77, 4004 Porto Codex; tel. (2) 2002279; telex 26833; f. 1951; schoolbooks, children's books, educational equipment; Gen. Man AMÉRICO A. AREAL.

**Edições Cosmos:** Rua da Emenda 111-1°, 1200 Lisbon; tel. (1) 3468201; fax (1) 3478255; f. 1938; paperback classics; new collections of history, human sciences, sociology and law; Dir M. MÁRIO REIS.

**Edições Paulistas:** Rua Dom Pedro de Cristo 10, 1700 Lisbon; tel. (1) 805273; fax (1) 808009; religion, theology, psychology, etc.; Dir ADÉRITO LOURENÇO LOURO.

**Edições Rolim, Lda:** Apdo 3079, 1032 Lisbon Codex; tel. (1) 553375; f. 1976; fiction, history, politics, law; Man. Dir MARIA ROLIM RAMOS.

**Edições João Sá da Costa, Lda:** Av. do Brasil 118-3° Esq., 1700 Lisbon; tel. (1) 800428; telex 43534; fax (1) 3534194; f. 1984; linguistics, poetry, dictionaries, geography, history, reference books; Man. Dirs IDALINA SÁ DA COSTA, JOÃO SÁ DA COSTA.

**Edições 70, Lda:** Rua Luciano Cordeiro 123-2°, Esq., 1050 Lisbon; tel. (1) 3158752; fax (1) 3158429; f. 1970; history, linguistics, anthropology, philosophy, psychology, education, art, architecture, science, reference books; Dir JOAQUIM JOSÉ SOARES DA COSTA.

**Editora A Educação Nacional, Lda:** Rua do Almada 125, 4000 Porto; tel. (2) 20423; school textbooks and review, *Educação Nacional*.

**Editora McGraw-Hill de Portugal, Lda:** Av. Almirante Reis 59-6°, 1100 Lisbon; tel. (1) 3154984; fax (1) 3521975; scientific and technical.

**Editora Pergaminho, Lda:** Rua Tierno Galvan, Torre 3, Sala 607, 1000 Lisbon; tel. (1) 652441; fax (1) 687543; f. 1990; cinema, music, humour, fiction; Dir MÁRIO MENDES DE MOURA.

**Editora Portugalmundo, Lda:** Rua Heliodoro Salgado 50-A, 1100 Lisbon; tel. (1) 8155351; fax (1) 3556726; children's books, poetry, law; Dir Dra MARIA JOSÉ PALMELA PINTO.

**Editora Replicação, Lda:** Av. Infante Santo 343, r/c Esq., 1350 Lisbon; tel. (1) 3977058; fax (1) 3969808; f. 1982; textbooks, children's books, dictionaries, language materials; Dir JOSÉ CARLOS ANAIA CRISTO.

**Editora Ulisseia, Lda:** Av. Visconde de Valmor 47, 1° Dto., 1000 Lisbon; tel. (1) 7934300; fax (1) 3562139; classical literature and translations, history, politics, economics; Dir F. GUEDES.

**Editorial Avante, SA:** Av. Almirante Reis 90-7°A, 1150 Lisbon; tel. (1) 8153511; fax (1) 8153495; fiction, politics, history, philosophy, economics; Dir FRANCISCO MELO.

**Editorial Confluência:** Calçada do Combro 99, Apdo 2620, 1116 Lisbon Codex; tel. (1) 3471709; fax (1) 3426921; f. 1945; dictionaries; Man. EDUARDO LOUREIRO DE MOURA.

**Editorial Estampa, Lda:** Rua da Escola do Exército 9, r/c Dto, 1100 Lisbon; tel. (1) 3555663; fax (1) 521911; politics, sociology, economics, occult, fiction, sport, history; Dir ANTÓNIO CARLOS MANSO PINHEIRO.

**Editorial Futura:** Rua Gen. Morais Sarmento 9, C/V Esq., 1500 Lisbon; tel. (1) 7155848; general.

**Editorial Inquérito, Lda:** Estrada Lisboa–Sintra, Km 14, Edif. CETOP, Apdo 33, 2726 Mem Martins; tel. (1) 9170096; telex 42255; fax (1) 9170130; f. 1938; sciences, politics, literature, history, etc.; Man. FRANCISCO LYON DE CASTRO.

**Editorial Minerva:** Rua Luz Soriano 31–33-1°, 1200 Lisbon; tel. (1) 322535; f. 1927; literature, politics, children's; Man. JOÃO DOMINGUES.

**Editorial Notícias:** Rua da Cruz da Carreira 4B, 1100 Lisbon; tel. (1) 3522490; telex 64381; fax (1) 3522066; children's books, fiction, linguistics, education, law books, education, dictionaries, ethnology.

**Editorial Presença, Lda:** Rua Augusto Gil 35-A, 1000 Lisbon; tel. (1) 7934191; fax (1) 7977560; f. 1960; social sciences, fiction, history, computer books, business, leisure, health, children's books, etc.; Dir FRANCISCO ESPADINHA.

**Editorial Verbo SA:** Rua Carlos Testa 1, 1050 Lisbon; tel. (1) 3562131; fax (1) 3562139; f. 1959; encyclopaedias, dictionaries, reference, history, general science, textbooks, education and children's books; Dir FERNANDO GUEDES.

**Empresa Literária Fluminense, Lda:** Av. Almirante Gago Coutinho 59A, 1700 Lisbon; tel. (1) 8486192; fax (1) 806344; textbooks, dictionaries; Gen. Man. ANTÓNIO NOBRE.

**Europress—Editores e Distribuidores de Publicações, Lda:** Praceta da República, Loja a Póvoa de Santo Adrião, 2675 Odivelas; f. 1982; tel. (1) 9387317; fax (1) 9377560; academic, children's, law, poetry, health, novels, history, etc.; Man. ANTÓNIO BENTO VINTÉM.

**Gradiva—Publicações, Lda:** Rua Almeida e Sousa 21-r/c Esq., 1350 Lisbon; tel. (1) 3974067; fax (1) 3953471; f. 1981; philosophy, education, history, fiction, science, children's books; Man. Dir GUILHERME VALENTE.

**Guimarães Editores Lda:** Rua da Misericórdia 68–70, 1200 Lisbon; tel. (1) 3462436; fax (1) 3432601; literature, philosophy, history, etc.

**Ibis Editores:** Av. D. Vasco da Gama 30, 1300 Lisbon; tel. (1) 3018387; history, literature, anthology, ethnography, poetry, photography, etc.; Dirs MARINA TAVARES DIAS, JOÃO PAULO CAXARIA.

**Impala, Sociedade Editorial, Lda:** Av. Miguel Bombarda 33, 2745 Queluz; tel. (1) 4364388; telex 16088; fax (1) 4365001; magazines and children's books; Dir JACQUES RODRIGUES.

**Imprensa Nacional—Casa de Moeda:** Rua D. Francisco Manuel de Melo 5, 1000 Lisbon; tel. (1) 3873002; telex 15328; fax (1) 7978632; Portuguese literature, arts, philosophy, history, geography, sociology, economics, encyclopedias, dictionaries; Man. Dir Dr AMÉRICO FARINHA DE CARVALHO.

**Lello & Irmão:** Rua das Carmelitas 144, 4000 Porto; tel. (2) 2002037; fax (2) 318511; fiction, poetry, history, children's books, graphic art; Man. JOSÉ MANUEL BERNARDES PEREIRA LELLO.

**Lidel—Edições Técnicas, Lda:** Rua D. Estefânia 183 r/c Dto, 1096 Lisbon Codex; tel. (1) 3151218; fax (1) 577827; f. 1963; Portuguese as a foreign language, management, technology, computer science; Man. Dir Eng. FREDERICO CARLOS DA SILVA ANNES.

**Livraria Bertrand, SA:** Rua Anchieta 31-1°, 1200 Lisbon; tel. (1) 3420081; fax (1) 3468286; literature, arts, humanities, educational; Man. DAVID DUARTE.

**Livraria Civilização:** Américo Fraga Lamares & Ca, Lda, Rua Alberto Aires de Gouveia 27, 4000 Porto; tel. (2) 2002286; fax (2) 2012382; f. 1920; social sciences, politics, economics, history, art, fiction, children's; Man. Dir MOURA BESSA.

**Livraria Clássica Editora:** Praça dos Restauradores 17, 1298 Lisbon Codex; tel. (1) 321229; telex 18570; fiction, agronomics, linguistics, economics, etc.; Dir FRANCISCO PAULO.

**Livraria Editora Figueirinhas, Lda:** Rua do Almada 47, 4000 Porto; tel. (2) 325300; fax (2) 325907; f. 1898; literature, school textbooks; Dir FRANCISCO GOMES PIMENTA.

**Livraria Multinova:** Av. Santa Joana Princesa 12-E, 1700 Lisbon; tel. (1) 8483365; fax (1) 8483436; f. 1970; schoolbooks, general, religion, Brazilian works; Dir CARLOS SANTOS.

**Livraria Sá da Costa Editora:** Rua Garrett 100–102, 1200 Lisbon; tel. (1) 360721; telex 15574; literature, history, philosophy sociology, politics, etc.; Dir MANUEL SÁ DA COSTA.

**Livros do Brasil, SA:** Rua dos Caetanos 22, 1200 Lisbon; tel. (1) 3462621; fax (1) 3428487; f. 1944; literature, history, politics, pedagogy and science; Dir ANTÓNIO DE SOUZA-PINTO.

**Livros Horizonte, Lda:** Rua das Chagas 17-1°, Apdo 2818, 1121 Lisbon Codex; tel. (1) 3466917; fax (1) 3426921; f. 1953; art, pedagogy, history; Chair. ROGÉRIO MENDES DE MOURA.

**Joaquim Machado, Lda-Livraria Almedina:** Arco de Almedina 15, 3049 Coímbra Codex; tel. (39) 26980; fax (39) 22507; law, education; Dir JOAQUIM MACHADO.

**Mosaico Editores Lda:** Calçada dos Mestres 1-6° Dto, 1000 Lisbon; tel. (1) 3881902; f. 1986; Dir JOÃO PAULO ARAGÃO.

**Plátano Editora, SARL:** Av. de Berna 31-2°, Esq., 1093 Lisbon Codex; tel. (1) 7979278; fax (1) 7979277; f. 1972; literature, educational, technical, dictionaries, etc.; Dir FRANCISCO PRATA GINJA.

**Porto Editora, Lda:** Rua da Restauração 365, 4099 Porto Codex; tel. (2) 6062813; telex 27205; fax (2) 6062072; f. 1944; general literature, school books, dictionaries, children's books; Dirs VASCO TEIXEIRA, JOSÉ ANTÓNIO TEIXEIRA, ROSÁLIA TEIXEIRA.

**Publicações Alfa, SA:** Rua Luís Pastor de Macedo 1B, 1700 Lisbon; tel. (1) 7587320; telex 43063; fax (1) 7587258.

**Publicações Europa-América, Lda:** Estrada Lisboa/Sintra Km 14, Apdo 8, 2726 Mem Martins; tel. 9211461; telex 42255; fax 9217846; f. 1945; fiction, current affairs, economics, reference, history, technical, children's; Dir FRANCISCO LYON DE CASTRO.

**Publicações Dom Quixote:** Rua Luciano Cordeiro 116-2°, 1098 Lisbon Codex; tel. (1) 3158079; fax (1) 574595; f. 1965; general fiction, poetry, history, philosophy, psychology, politics, didactics

# PORTUGAL

*Directory*

and sociology; university text books; children's books; Dir NELSON DE MATOS.

**Quimera Editores Lda:** Rua Nova da Trindade 15A, 1200 Lisbon; tel. (1) 3429882; fax (1) 3431180; f. 1987; literature, art, history, photography, etc.; Dirs JOSÉ ALFARO, LUÍS VEIGA.

**Rês—Editora, Lda:** Praça Marquês de Pombal 78, 4000 Porto; tel. (2) 484174; economics, philosophy, law, sociology; Dir REINALDO DE CARVALHO.

**João Romano Torres & Cia Lda:** Rua Marcos Portugal 20-A, 1200 Lisbon; tel. (1) 601244; f. 1885; fiction; Dir FRANCISCO NORONHA E ANDRADE.

**Texto Editora, Lda:** Alto da Bela Vista, Casal de Vale Mourão, 2735 Cacém; tel. (1) 4261001; fax (1) 4261532; f. 1977; school textbooks, management, pedagogy, health, beauty, recipes, children's books; Man. Dirs MANUEL JOSÉ DO ESPÍRITO SANTO FERRÃO, ANA MARIA MORGADO M. VALE FONTES DE MELO.

**Vulgus Editora, Lda:** Qta Galiza 8 r/c Esq., 2765 Estoril; tel. (1) 4689072; fax (1) 4571306; f. 1982; school textbooks, linguistics, psychology, law, education; Man. Dir FERNANDO MONTEIRO.

### PUBLISHERS' ASSOCIATION

**Associação Portuguesa de Editores e Livreiros:** Av. dos Estados Unidos da América 97-6°Esq., 1700 Lisbon; tel. (1) 8489136; fax (1) 8489377; f. 1939; Pres. ANTÓNIO LUÍS DE SOUZA PINTO; Sec.-Gen. JORGE SÁ BORGES; Man. JOSÉ NARCISO VIEIRA.

## Radio and Television

In 1992 there were 2.3m. licensed radio receivers in use. In 1994 the number of licensed television receivers in use was 3,007,472.

### RADIO

**RDP—Radiodifusão Portuguesa, SA:** Av. Eng. Duarte Pacheco 6, 1000 Lisbon; tel. (1) 3871109; telex 64774; fax (1) 3871402; f. 1975 after the nationalization of nine radio stations and their merger with the existing national broadcasting company; Pres. Dr ARLINDO DE CARVALHO.

Domestic Services: **Antena 1** (tel. (1) 3860181; fax (1) 3966992; Dir PEDRO CASTELO) broadcasts 24 hours daily on medium-wave and FM; **Antena 2** (tel. (1) 3860181; fax (1) 3978057; Dir JOSÉ MANUEL NUNES) broadcasts classical music 24 hours daily on FM; **Antena 3** (tel (1) 3871109; fax (1) 3878038; Dir JAIME FERNANDES) broadcasts 24 hours daily on FM.

**RDP/International—Radio Portugal:** Rua de São Marçal 1, 1200 Lisbon; tel. (1) 3475065; telex 43247; fax (1) 3474475; programmes in Portuguese to Europe, North America, South America, India and Timor; in English, French and Italian to Europe, in English to the USA and Canada, India, the Middle East and Africa; also in French to Africa; Dir JAIME MARQUES DE ALMEIDA.

Regional Centres:

**RDP/Açores:** Rua Dr Aristides Moreira da Mota 33, 9500 Ponta Delgada, São Miguel, Azores; tel. (96) 22045; telex 82139; fax (96) 629379; Dir CARLOS MELO TAVARES.

**RDP/Madeira:** Rua Tenente Coronel Sarmento 15, 9000 Funchal, Madeira; tel. (91) 229155; telex 72111; fax (91) 230753; one medium-wave transmitter on 1,332 kHz and one FM transmitter on 94.1 mHz; Dir JOÃO AFONSO DE ALMEIDA.

Regional Delegations:

**RDP/Norte** (Northern Zone): Rua Cândido dos Reis 74-1°, 4099 Porto Codex; tel. (2) 320163; telex 22449; fax (2) 2009078; Dir Dr DIALINO ESTEVES.

**RDP/Centro** (Central Zone): Rua Dr José Alberto dos Reis, 3049 Coímbra Codex; tel. (39) 404010; telex 52280; fax (39) 724253; Dir DOMINGOS GRILO.

**RDP/Sul** (Southern Zone): Campo da Sra da Saúde, 8000 Faro; tel. (89) 805971; fax (89) 802192; Dir JORGE AMORIM.

#### Private Stations
#### National Station

**Rádio Renascença (RR):** Rua Capelo 5, 1294 Lisbon Codex; tel. (1) 3475270; fax (1) 3422658; f. 1938; Roman Catholic station; broadcasts 24 hrs a day on FM1 network and on medium-wave network/FM2 network/shortwave to Europe (9,680 kHz, 9,575 kHz); Man. FERNANDO MAGALHÃES CRESPO.

#### Regional and Local Stations

**Clube Asas do Atlântico:** Aeroporto de Santa Maria, 9580 Vila do Porto, Santa Maria, Azores; tel. 86182; fax 86459; f. 1946; one medium-wave transmitter on 191 metres, 1566 kHz and one FM transmitter on 103.2 MHz; Pres. ADRIANO FERREIRA.

**Correio da Manhã—Rádio:** Rua Tierno Galvan, Torre 3, Amoreiras, 7°, Sala 706, 1200 Lisbon; tel. (1) 658385; telex 65905; fax (1) 659963; regional station (southern zone); commenced transmissions Dec. 1990; broadcasts 24 hours daily on FM stereo 104.3 MHz; Dir RUI PÊGO.

**Estação Rádio da Madeira:** CP 450, Pico dos Barcelos, Funchal, Madeira; tel. (91) 64395; f. 1948; AM 1485, 1kW; FM 96.0, 300W; broadcasts daily from 06.00 to 01.00 in Portuguese; also broadcasts in Danish, English, French and German; Dir MARIA TERESA SARDINHA.

**Posto Emissor de Radiodifusão do Funchal:** Rua Ponte de S. Lázaro 3, 9000 Funchal, Madeira; tel. (91) 227249; telex 72519; fax (91) 221797; two medium-wave transmitters on 196.2 metres 1530 kHz and on 196.2 metres 1017 kHz, and one FM transmitter in stereo on 92 MHz; Dir MARIA FRANCISCA TERESA CLODE.

**Rádio Altitude:** Rua Batalha Reis, 6300 Guarda; tel. 212232; fax 221492; f. 1949; broadcasts 24 hours daily; 1584 kHz medium wave and 90.9 MHz FM stereo; Dir HELDER SEQUEIRA.

**Radio Press:** Rua das Merçes 58/62, 4200 Porto; tel. (2) 4102348; telex 28979; fax (2) 493150; regional station (northern zone); commenced transmissions Dec. 1990; broadcasts 24 hours daily on FM stereo 105.3 MHz; Dir Dr MANUEL PINTO TEIXEIRA.

At October 1991 a total of 313 local stations were operating in Portugal (including the Azores and Madeira).

### TELEVISION

In early 1990 it was announced that RTP's monopoly on TV broadcasting was to end. Two new private stations were awarded licences in February 1992.

**Televisão Portuguesa, SA:** Av. 5 de Outubro 197, Apdo 2934, 1000 Lisbon; tel. (1) 7931774; telex 14527; fax (1) 7931758; f. 1956; nationalized in 1975; became limited co (with state capital) in May 1991; studios in Lisbon, Porto, Ponta Delgada and Funchal; Chair. ANTÓNIO FREITAS CRUZ.

Regional Delegations:

**RTP—Porto:** Rua Conceição Fernandes, Apdo 174, 4402 Vila Nova de Gaia Codex; tel. (2) 712975; fax (2) 7123744.

**RTP—Madeira:** Rua das Maravilhas 42, 9000 Funchal; tel. (91) 742874; telex 72478; fax (91) 742343; Dir ARMINDO ABREU.

**RTP—Azores:** Rua Ernesto Canto 19, 9500 Ponta Delgada, São Miguel; tel. (96) 22036; fax (96) 22093.

The Televisão Portuguesa network serves 94.95% of the population of Portugal on Canal 1 (VHF) and 72.7% on TV-2, its second channel (UHF).

#### Private Stations

**Sociedade Independente de Comunicação (SIC):** Estrada da Outurela, Carnaxide, 2795 Linda-a-Velha; tel. 4173138; fax 4173119; commenced transmissions 1992; Head FRANCISCO PINTO BALSEMÃO; Dir of Programmes EMÍDIO RANGEL.

**Televisão Independente (TVI-4):** Edif. Berna, Rua Marquês de Tomar, 1000 Lisbon; tel. (1) 7940641; fax (1) 7941242; commenced transmissions 1993; sponsored by Roman Catholic Church; Head Bishop JOSÉ POLICARPO; Dir of Programmes RIBEIRO E CASTRO.

#### Cable Television

In early 1995 there were 14 cable companies operating throughout Portugal, including Madeira and the Azores.

**Cabo TV Portugal, SA:** Rua Soeiro Pereira Gomes 7, Escritório 13, 1600 Lisbon; fax (1) 7959237; invited tenders for distribution system in late 1993.

## Finance

(cap. = capital; res = reserves; dep. = deposits; m. = million; brs = branches; amounts in escudos)

### BANKING

In 1974–75 nearly all banks were nationalized and management boards were appointed by the Government. There was a fundamental change of policy in mid-1983, when new legislation permitted competition from the private sector, and enabled a limited number of foreign banks to open branches. Under the Decree Law of February 1984 relating to private initiative in the banking sector, 10 new banks were authorized, four of which were Portuguese. In 1986 the União de Bancos Portugueses was the first of the nationalized commercial banks to become a limited liability company with public capital. All others followed suit in subsequent years. The process of transferring public banks to the private sector began in 1989.

#### Central Bank

**Banco de Portugal:** Rua do Ouro 27, 1100 Lisbon; tel. (1) 3462931; telex 16554; fax (1) 3465890; f. 1846, reorganized 1931 with the

# PORTUGAL

sole right to issue notes; nationalized Sept. 1974; cap. 200m., dep. 2,212,150m. (Dec. 1993); chief br. Porto, with 22 others including Madeira and Azores; Gov. ANTÓNIO DE SOUSA.

### Domestic Banks

**Banco Borges e Irmão, SA:** POB 4033, 4001 Porto Codex; tel. (2) 324517; telex 26899; fax (2) 310546; f. 1884; nationalized 1975; became limited liability co with state majority holding in Jan. 1989; cap. 20,000m., res 44,977m., dep. 617,551m. (Dec. 1993); Pres. Dr MIGUEL JOSÉ RIBEIRO CADILHE; 150 brs, incl. 10 in France.

**Banco Comercial dos Açores:** POB 1379, 9503 Ponta Delgada, Azores Codex; tel. (96) 629070; telex 82111; fax (96) 25304; f. 1912; fmrly Banco Micaelense; cap. 8,000m., res 376m., dep. 86,823m. (Dec. 1993); Pres. Dr ALVARO CORDEIRO DAMASO; 29 brs.

**Banco Comercial de Macau, SA:** Av. da Boavista 757, 4100 Porto; tel. (2) 6005579; telex 26050; fax (2) 6005596; f. 1974; cap. 8,750m., res 3,944m., dep. 869,192m. (Dec. 1993); Chair. Dr M. C. CARVALHO FERNANDES; 43 brs, incl. 13 in Macau.

**Banco Comercial Português (BCP):** Rua Júlio Dinis 705–719, 4000 Porto; tel. (2) 6091101; telex 64713; fax (2) 699512; f. 1985; cap. 109,686m., res 56,340m., dep. 1,574,722m. (Dec. 1993); Pres. Eng. JORGE JARDIM GONÇALVES; 311 brs.

**Banco de Comércio e Indústria (BCI):** Av. da Boavista 3383, Apdo 1108, 4100 Porto; tel. (2) 6105542; telex 28606; fax (2) 6106004; f. 1985; cap. 31,116m., res 10,113m., dep. 278,837m. (Dec. 1993); Pres. RICARDO ALONSO CLAVEL; 106 brs.

**Banco Espírito Santo e Comercial de Lisboa:** Av. da Liberdade 195, 1200 Lisbon; tel. (1) 3158331; telex 12191; fax (1) 3532931; f. 1987 by merger; transfer to private sector completed in Feb. 1992; cap. and res 160,654m., dep. 1,308,057m. (Dec. 1993); Pres. RICARDO SILVA SALGADO; 262 brs.

**Banco Essi:** Rua Tierno Galvan, Torre 3 (Amoreiras) 4°, 1050 Lisbon; tel. (1) 3870137; fax (1) 3888259; merchant bank; Pres. Dr MANUEL ANTÓNIO RIBEIRO SERZEDELO DE ALMEIDA.

**Banco Finantia:** Rua General Firmino Miguel 5-1°, 1600 Lisbon; tel. (1) 7267540; fax (1) 7265310; f. 1992; investment bank; cap. 8,187m., res 2,202m., dep. 68,090m. (Dec. 1992); Pres. ANTÓNIO MANUEL AFONSO GUERREIRO.

**Banco de Fomento e Exterior, SA:** Av. Casal Ribeiro 59, 1000 Lisbon; tel. (1) 3562021; telex 64752; fax (1) 534925; f. 1959; fmrly Banco de Fomento Nacional; cap. 80m., res 16,900m., dep. 306,000m. (Dec. 1994); Pres. Dr MIGUEL JOSÉ RIBEIRO CADILHE; 41 brs.

**Banco Fonsecas e Burnay:** Rua do Comércio 132, Apdo 2231, 1106 Lisbon Codex; tel. (1) 874081; telex 44085; fax (1) 3467308; f. 1967 by merger; transfer to private sector completed in 1992; cap. and res 51,199m. (Dec. 1994); Pres. Dr ARTUR SANTOS SILVA; 162 brs.

**Banco Internacional de Crédito (BIC), SARL:** Av. Fontes Pereira de Melo 27, 1050 Lisbon; tel. (1) 3157135; telex 62353; fax (1) 526165; f. 1986; cap. 11,600m., res 3,868m., dep. 178,556m. (Dec. 1993); Pres. Dr JOSÉ MANUEL FERREIRA NETO; 21 brs.

**Banco Internacional do Funchal:** Rua de João Tavira 30, 9000 Funchal, Madeira; tel. (91) 222162; fax (91) 224822; f. 1988; cap. 17,500m., res 11,384m., dep. 234,330m. (Dec. 1993); Pres. Dr JOSÉ MANUEL CASTRO ROCHA.

**Banco Mello, SA:** Rua Alexandre Herculano 50-5°, 1296 Lisbon Codex; tel. (1) 3155000; telex 65952; fax (1) 3155904; f. 1969; fmrly Sociedade Financeira Portuguesa—Banco de Investimento; cap. 9,000m., res 3,714m., dep. 78,635m. (Dec. 1992); Pres. Dr FRANCISCO JOSÉ QUEIROZ DE BARROS DE LACERDA.

**Banco Nacional de Crédito Imobiliário (BNC):** Rua do Comércio 85, 1101 Lisbon Codex; tel. (1) 3479570; telex 42561; fax (1) 3479510; f. 1991; mortgage institution; cap. 10,000m., res 300m., dep. 53,048m. (Dec. 1993); Pres. Dr ALBERTO ALVES DE OLIVEIRA PINTO; 12 brs.

**Banco Nacional Ultramarino:** Av. 5 de Outubro 175, POB 2419, 1111 Lisbon Codex; tel. (1) 7930112; telex 13305; fax (1) 7937835; f. 1864; cap. 49,200m., res −11,721m., dep. 920,849m. (Dec. 1993); Pres. Dr CARLOS MANUEL TAVARES DA SILVA; 179 brs, incl. 3 in Madeira, 2 in the Azores, 9 in Macau and 2 in London.

**Banco Pinto e Sotto Mayor:** Av. F. Pereira de Melo 7, 1050 Lisbon Codex; tel. (1) 542978; telex 12516; fax (1) 542020; f. 1914; cap. 30,500m., res 29,100m., dep. 1,240,900m. (Dec. 1993); Pres. LUÍS DE MELO CHAMPALIMAUD; 241 brs in Portugal, 22 in France.

**Banco Português do Atlântico (BPA), SA:** Praça D. João I, 4001 Porto Codex; tel. (2) 323971; telex 22720; fax (2) 2005175; f. 1919; 51% privatized in Dec. 1992; cap. 100,000m., res 68,472m., dep. 2,964,032m. (Dec. 1993); Pres. Dr JOÃO DOS SANTOS OLIVEIRA; 254 brs, incl. 14 abroad.

**Banco Português de Investimento (BPI), SA:** Rua Tenente Valadim 284, 4100 Porto; tel. (2) 699951; telex 26887; fax (2) 698787; f. 1984 from Sociedade Portuguesa de Investimentos, SARL; cap. 36,448m., res 18,979m. (Dec. 1994); br. in Lisbon; Pres. Dr ARTUR SANTOS SILVA.

**Banco Totta e Açores (BTA), SA:** Rua do Ouro 88, 1100 Lisbon; tel. (1) 3469421; telex 44762; fax (1) 3462386; f. 1970 by merger; 49% privatized in 1989; fully privatized in 1990; cap. 55,000m., res 62,256m., dep. 1,797,498m. (Dec. 1993); Pres. and CEO Dr ALÍPIO PEREIRA DIAS; 266 brs.

**Caixa Central de Crédito Agrícola Mútuo:** Rua Pascoal de Melo 49, 1000 Lisbon; tel. (1) 3559719; telex 64943; fax (1) 3154607; f. 1984; co-operative bank; cap. 5,567m., res 795m., dep. 104,227m. (Dec. 1992); Pres. Dr JOSÉ ALBERTO TAVARES MOREIRA.

**Caixa Económica Montepio Geral:** Rua do Ouro 219/241, 1100 Lisbon; tel. (1) 3476361; telex 14273; fax (1) 3462004; f. 1844; cap. 5,700m., res 11,760m., dep. 211.0m. (1991); Pres. Dr ANTÓNIO DE SEIXAS DA COSTA LEAL; 55 brs.

**Caixa Geral de Depósitos:** Av. João XXI 63, 1000 Lisbon; tel. (1) 7953000; telex 15438; fax (1) 7905051; f. 1876; grants credit for agriculture, industry, building, housing, energy, trade and tourism; dep. 4,016,584m. (Dec. 1993); CEO Dr EMÍLIO RUI VILAR; 499 brs.

**Crédito Predial Português:** Campo Pequeno 81, 1000 Lisbon; tel. (1) 7968140; telex 62533; fax (1) 733017; f. 1864 to further building development for industrial, commercial and residential purposes; cap. 25,000m., res 2,666m., dep. 533,888m. (Dec. 1993); Pres. and CEO Dr ALÍPIO PEREIRA DIAS; 136 brs.

**União de Bancos Portugueses SA:** Praça D. João I 80, Apdo 4011, 4001 Porto Codex; tel. (2) 2000961; telex 24398; fax (2) 2007043; f. 1978 by merger; cap. 30,000m., dep. 538,323m. (1994); Pres. Dr MANUEL CARLOS CARVALHO FERNANDES; 174 brs.

### Foreign Banks

**ABN-AMRO Bank NV:** Rua Mouzhinho da Silveira 12, 1250 Lisbon; tel. (1) 3521572; telex 64540; fax (1) 3521577; Dir-Gen. Dr JAN C. PANMAN.

**Banco Bilbao Vizcaya, SA** (Spain): Av. da Liberdade 222, 1250 Lisbon; tel. (1) 311720; telex 62633; fax (1) 3117500; Man. Dir JOSÉ LUÍS JOLÓ MARÍN.

**Banco do Brasil:** Praça Marquês de Pombal 16, 1250 Lisbon; tel. (1) 3521640; telex 12117; fax (1) 523180; Gen. Man. Dr WOLNEY BONFIM FERREIRA.

**Banco Chemical (Portugal), SA** (USA): Rua Barata Salgueiro 33, 1250 Lisbon; tel. (1) 3523000; telex 64146; fax (1) 691302; f. 1985; Man. Dir Dr CARLOS RODRIGUES.

**Banco Exterior de España, SA:** Rua Castilho 39, 1250 Lisbon; tel. (1) 3862027; telex 66299; fax (1) 3863208; Dir-Gen. AMADOR MANUEL VILLAR SANTOS.

**Banco Itaú Europa, SA** (Brazil): Rua Tierno Galvan, Torre 3-11°, 1070 Lisbon; tel. (1) 3870061; telex 60476; fax (1) 3887258; Pres. ROBERTO SETUBAL.

**Bank of Tokyo Ltd:** Rua Castilho 165-2°, 1200 Lisbon; tel. (1) 692104; telex 43673; fax (1) 692363; Man. Dir MIKIHIKO OHIRA.

**Banque Nationale de Paris** (France): Av. da Liberdade 38, 1200 Lisbon; tel. (1) 3465704; telex 12960; fax (1) 3462769; f. 1985; Dir-Gen. FRANÇOIS FALQUE PIERROTIN.

**Barclays Bank PLC** (UK): Av. da República 50-2°, 1000 Lisbon; tel. (1) 7935020; telex 42838; fax (1) 7979610; f. 1987; Gen. Man. Dr ALMERINDO MARQUES.

**Citibank Portugal, SA** (USA): Rua Barata Salgueiro 30-4°, 1250 Lisbon; tel. (1) 3116300; telex 15316; fax (1) 3116399; f. 1985; Pres. Dr DAVID KYLE.

**Crédit Lyonnais Portugal:** Rua Camilo Castelo Branco 46, 1250 Lisbon; tel. (1) 3509000; telex 64205; fax (1) 524317; Pres. JACQUES SAINT GEORGES.

**Deutsche Bank de Investimento:** Rua Castilho 20, 1250 Lisbon; tel. (1) 3111200; fax (1) 3526265; Pres. RUI LEÃO MARTINHO.

**Generale Bank** (Belgium): Rua Alexandre Herculano 50-6°, 1250 Lisbon; tel. (1) 571122; telex 42996; fax (1) 3526936; f. 1986; Pres. JACQUES WALA.

### Banking Association

**Associação Portuguesa de Bancos (APB):** Av. da República 35-5°, 1050 Lisbon; tel. (1) 579804; fax (1) 579533; Pres. Dr JOÃO SALGUEIRO; Sec.-Gen. Dr JOÃO MENDES RODRIGUES.

### STOCK EXCHANGES

**Associação da Bolsa de Valores de Lisboa:** Edif. da Bolsa, Rua Soeiro Pereira Gomes, 1600 Lisbon; tel. (1) 7909904; fax (1) 7952021; f. 1769; Pres. TAVARES MOREIRA; CEO JOSÉ CARLOS PESTANA TEIXEIRA.

**Bolsa de Valores do Porto:** Palácio da Bolsa, Rua Ferreira Borges, 4050 Porto; tel. (2) 2026231; fax (2) 316859; f. 1891; CEO MANUEL ALVES MONTEIRO.

PORTUGAL   *Directory*

### Regulatory Authority

**Commissão do Mercado de Valores Mobiliários (CMVM):** Av. Fontes Pereira de Melo 21, 1050 Lisbon; tel. (1) 3503000; fax (1) 3537077; f. 1991; independent securities exchange commission; Pres. Alvaro Dâmaso.

### INSURANCE

The Portuguese insurance market is developing in accordance with EU regulations and practices. By the end of 1994 all but one of the public companies had been transferred to the private sector. Total premiums amounted to 628,430m. escudos in 1994, life assurance premiums having increased by 31% and non-life by 14%, compared with the previous year.

### Supervisory Authority

**Instituto de Seguros de Portugal (ISP):** Av. de Berna 19, 1094 Lisbon Codex; tel. (1) 7938542; telex 66362; fax (1) 7954191; f. 1982; office in Porto; Pres. Dr José Monteiro Fernandes Braz.

### Representative Bodies

**Associação das Empresas Gestoras de Fundos de Pensões (AEGFP):** Rua da Misericórdia 76, 1200 Lisbon; tel. (1) 3210147; fax (1) 3210299; pension funds; Pres. Dr José Manuel Vaz S. Mendinhos; Sec.-Gen. Dr Francisco J. de Medeiros Cordeiro.

**Associação Nacional dos Corretores de Seguros (ANCOSE):** Av. Almirante Reis 13-6°E, 1000 Lisbon; tel. (1) 523950; fax (1) 523950; f. 1983; Pres. José Guilherme Formozinho Sanches.

**Associação Portuguesa de Seguradores (APS):** Av. José Malhoa, Lote 1674-5°, 1070 Lisbon; tel. (1) 7268123; fax (1) 7261951; f. 1982; Pres. Ruy Octávio Matos de Carvalho.

**Associação Portuguesa dos Produtores Profissionais de Seguros (APROSE):** Rua Gonçalo Cristóvão 116-1° Esq., 4000 Porto; tel. (2) 2003000; telex 20646; fax (2) 383937; f. 1976; Pres. Olimpio de Magalhães Pinto.

### Principal Companies

**Aliança Seguradora, SA:** Rua Gonçalo Sampaio 39/55, 4100 Porto; tel. (2) 6081100; telex 22396; fax (2) 6001092; f. 1980 from merger of five companies; non-life; cap. 6,000m. (Dec. 1992); 49% privatized in 1989; full privatization completed in 1991; Pres. Dr Carlos Sousa e Brito.

**Aliança UAP, Companhia de Seguros de Vida, SA:** Praça Marquês de Pombal 14, 1200 Lisbon; tel. (1) 3562771; telex 13724; fax (1) 3556827; life and pension funds; cap. 2,000m. (Dec. 1992); Chair. Dr Carlos Sousa e Brito.

**Bonança Vida, Companhia de Seguros, SA:** Rua do Ouro 100, 1100 Lisbon; tel. (1) 3469241; telex 12776; fax (1) 3478538; f. 1808; life and pension funds; 60% privatized in 1991; cap. 1,500m. (Dec. 1992); Pres. Dr Armando Francisco da Silva Almeida.

**BPA, Seguros de Vida, SA:** Rua Costa Cabral 797/799, 4200 Porto; tel. (2) 5504286; fax (2) 5504405; f. 1991; life; cap. 1,800m. (Dec. 1992); Chair. Dr Fernando Soares da Silva.

**Companhia de Seguros Açoreana, SA:** Largo da Matriz 45/52, Apdo 186, 9500 Ponta Delgada, S. Miguel, Azores; tel. (96) 629021; telex 82279; fax (96) 629101; f. 1892; life and non-life; cap. 1,500m. (Dec. 1992); Pres. João Vasco Paiva.

**Companhia de Seguros Bonança, SA:** Apdo 9876, 1900 Lisbon; tel. (1) 7216000; telex 12776; fax (1) 7216161; non-life; cap. 6,000m. (Dec. 1992); Chair. Dr Manuel Carlos de Carvalho Fernandes.

**Companhia de Seguros Fidelidade, SA:** Largo do Corpo Santo 13, 1014 Lisbon Codex; tel. (1) 3460321; telex 18823; fax (1) 3472208; f. 1980 from merger of four companies; life, non-life and pension funds; cap. 12,500m. (Dec. 1992); Pres. Dr Alvaro João Duarte Pinto Correia.

**Companhia de Seguros Garantia, SA:** Rua Gonçalo Sampaio 39/55, 4100 Porto; tel. (2) 6081000; telex 23642; fax (2) 6001092; f. 1853; non-life; cap. 558m.; Pres. Manuel Nogueira Lobo de Alarcão e Silva.

**Companhia de Seguros Império, SA:** Rua Garrett 62, 1200 Lisbon; tel. (1) 3462921; fax (1) 3463927; f. 1942; all branches of insurance and reinsurance; transferred to private sector, 1992; cap. 25,000m.; Pres. Dr Vasco Maria Guimarães José de Mello.

**Companhia de Seguros Metrópole, SA:** Rua Barata Salgueiro 41, Edif. Zurich, 1200 Lisbon; tel. (1) 3561161; telex 15688; fax (1) 3561024; f. 1918; non-life; cap. 2,000m. (Dec. 1992); Pres. Dr Nuno Maria Serra Soares da Fonseca.

**Companhia de Seguros Mundial—Confiança, SA:** Largo do Chiado 8, 1200 Lisbon; tel. (1) 3401500; telex 15065; fax (1) 3401650; f. 1980; all branches of insurance and reinsurance; privatization pending, 1992; cap. 10,000m. (Dec. 1992); Pres. Luis de Melo Champalimaud.

**Companhia de Seguros Tranquilidade, SA:** Av. da Liberdade 242, 1250 Lisbon; tel. (1) 3561181; telex 12164; fax (1) 573836; f. 1871; life, non-life, pension funds and reinsurance; cap. 19,000m. (Dec. 1992); 100% privatized in 1990; Pres. Dr Luís Frederico Redondo Lopes.

**Companhia Europeia de Seguros, SA:** Av. Fontes Pereira de Melo 6, 1000 Lisbon; tel. (1) 3563887; telex 12701; fax (1) 3554452; f. 1922; life and non-life; cap. 3,150m. (Dec. 1992); Pres. Dr António Carvalho Nunes da Mota.

**Cosec—Companhia de Seguros de Créditos, SA:** Av. da República 58, 1094 Lisbon; tel. (1) 760131; telex 12885; fax (1) 7934614; f. 1969; domestic and export credit insurance; bond insurance; cap. 1,500m.; Pres. Dr António Jorge Ferreira Filipe.

**Gan Portugal Vida, Companhia de Seguros, SA:** Av. de Berna 26-A, 1000 Lisbon; tel. (1) 7954240; telex 14102; fax (1) 7954269; life and pension funds; cap. 1,500m. (Dec. 1992); Chair. Dr Jean Jacques Bonnaud.

**Global—Companhia de Seguros, SA:** Av. Duque de Avila 171, 1000 Lisbon; tel. (1) 3554239; telex 64537; fax (1) 3554021; non-life; cap. 3,250m. (Dec. 1992); Pres. Dr Diamantino Pereira Marques.

**Lusitânia—Companhia de Seguros, SA:** Av. Duarte Pacheco, Torre 2-12°, Amoreiras, 1000 Lisbon; tel. (1) 3811500; telex 62066; fax (1) 3885023; cap. 3,850m.; Pres. Dr António da Costa Leal.

**Lusitânia Vida, Companhia de Seguros, SA:** Av. Duarte Pacheco, Torre 2-12°, Amoreiras, 1000 Lisbon; tel. (1) 3889023; telex 62066; fax (1) 3889025; f. 1987; life insurance and pension funds; cap. 1,800m.; Pres. Luís António Burnay Pinto de Carvalho Daün e Lorena.

**Oceanica, Companhia de Seguros, SA:** Rua do Ferragial 33-3°, 1200 Lisbon; tel. (1) 365623; telex 12879; fax (1) 3474512; f. 1936; personal accident, marine, workers' compensation; cap. 1,540m.; Pres. Dr José Santos Batista.

**Ocidental—Companhia Portuguesa de Seguros, SA/Ocidental—Companhia Portuguesa de Seguros de Vida, SA/Occidental Holding SGPS:** Av. República 26, 1000 Lisbon; tel. (1) 3161000; fax (1) 3531172; cap. 2,500m./2,500m./20,200m.; Pres. Eng. João Luís Ramalho de Carvalho Talone.

**Portugal Previdente—Companhia de Seguros, SA:** Rua Andrade Corvo 19, 1098 Lisbon; tel. (1) 3522911; telex 18362; fax (1) 576224; f. 1907; cap. 3,000m.; Chair. D. Bernardo de Sousa Holstein Beck.

**Real—Companhia de Seguros, SA:** Rua Marechal Saldanha 604, 4100 Porto; tel. (2) 6170153; telex 20083; fax (2) 6189426; f. 1988; cap. 3,000m. (Dec. 1992); life, non-life and reinsurance; Pres. Dr José Manuel Dias da Fonseca.

**A Social—Companhia Portuguesa de Seguros, SA:** Rua Braamcamp 11, 1297 Lisbon; tel. (1) 3522210; telex 16453; fax (1) 3561465; f. 1927; life and non-life; cap. 3,000m. (Dec. 1992); Pres. Dr Artur Luís Alves Conde.

**Sociedade Portuguesa de Seguros SA:** Av. da Liberdade 259, 1250 Lisbon; tel. (1) 3524045; telex 13055; fax (1) 521738; f. 1900; life, non-life and pension funds; cap. 3,000m. (Dec. 1992); Pres. Andre Charles Marie Renaudin; Gen. Man. Dra Maria do Carmo Portela Herédia Vieira da Fonseca.

**O Trabalho—Companhia Portuguesa de Seguros, SA:** Rua Engenheiro Vieira da Silva 12, 1000 Lisbon; tel. (1) 3537174; telex 18838; fax (1) 545377; f. 1921; non-life; cap. 1,800m. (Dec. 1992); Pres. Dr Artur dos Santos Ferreira Nobre.

**UAP Portugal, Companhia de Seguros, SA:** Praça Marquês de Pombal 14, 1298 Lisbon Codex; tel. (1) 3506100; telex 13724; fax (1) 3571783; non-life; cap. 350m. (Dec. 1992); Pres. Michelle Ebstein Genin.

**Victoria, Companhia de Seguros de Vida, SA:** Av. A. A. Aguiar 148, 1000 Lisbon; tel. (1) 3874301; fax (1) 3874047; life and pension funds; cap. 1,500m. (Dec. 1992); Chair. Gert Schlosser.

### Mutual Companies

**Mútua dos Armadores da Pesca do Arrasto:** Av. António Augusto de Aguiar 7-1°, 1000 Lisbon; tel. (1) 561051; telex 16095; fax (1) 561058; f. 1942; personal accident, marine and workers' compensation; cap. 750m.; Pres. C. J. Gouveia Mourisca.

**Mútua dos Pescadores (Sociedade Mútua de Seguros):** Av. Torre de Belém 29, 1400 Lisbon; tel. (1) 3017375; fax (1) 3016489; f. 1942; privately owned; insurance and reinsurance; cap. 1,000m.

### Foreign Companies

In 1994 two mutual companies and 49 companies with head offices outside Portugal were in operation in the country. Their branches took 9% of all Portuguese premiums in 1994.

# Trade and Industry

**CHAMBERS OF COMMERCE AND TRADE ORGANIZATIONS**

**Associação Comercial e Industrial do Funchal (ACIF)/Câmara de Comércio e Indústria da Madeira (CCIM):** Av. Arriaga 41,

PORTUGAL

9000 Funchal; tel. (91) 230137; telex 72293; fax (91) 222005; f. 1836; Pres. MIGUEL SANTA CLARA.

**Associação Comercial de Lisboa/Câmara de Comérico e Indústria Portuguesa:** Palácio do Comércio, Rua das Portas de Santo Antão 89, 1194 Lisbon Codex; tel. (1) 3427179; telex 13441; fax (1) 3424304; f. 1834; Pres. Eng. VASCO PINTO BASTO; Gen. Sec. ANTÓNIO MONICA; 2,100 mems.

**Associação Comercial do Porto/Câmara de Comércio e Indústria do Porto:** Palácio da Bolsa, Rua Ferreira Borges, 4000 Porto; tel. (2) 2011448; telex 22159; fax (2) 2084760; f. 1834; Pres. VIRGÍLIO FOLHADELA; 700 mems.

**Associação dos Comerciantes e Industriais de Bebidas Espirituosas e Vinhos (ACIBEV):** Largo do Carmo 15-1°, 1200 Lisbon; tel. (1) 3462318; telex 42737; fax (1) 3427517; spirit and wine traders and manufacturers; Pres. LUÍS GONZAGA MORAIS CARDOSO.

**Associação dos Industriais e Exportadores de Cortiça do Norte:** Av. Comendador Henrique Amorim, Sta Maria de Lamas, 4535 Lourosa; tel. (2) 7642176; telex 24410; fax (2) 7649768; asscn of cork manufacturers and exporters; Pres. AMÉRICO AMORIM.

**Associação dos Industriais e Exportadores de Cortiça:** Av. Duque d'Avila 169-2° Esq., 1000 Lisbon; tel. (1) 3521173; fax (1) 570878; national asscn of cork manufacturers and exporters; Pres. EDMUNDO PEREIRA.

**Associação Nacional de Comerciantes e Industriais de Produtos Alimentares (ANCIPA):** Largo S. Sebastião da Pedreira 31, 1000 Lisbon; tel. (1) 3528803; telex 15669; national asscn of food products manufacturers and traders; Pres. LUÍS MATOS PIRES.

**Associação Portuguesa dos Exportadores de Têxteis:** Rua Campo Alegre 276, 1° Dto, 4100 Porto; tel. (2) 6002106; fax (2) 6065870; textile exporters' asscn; Pres. MADATH ALY JAMAL.

**Câmara de Comércio e Indústria dos Açores (CCIA):** Rua Ernesto do Canto 13/15, 9500 Ponta Delgada, Azores; tel. (96) 22427; fax (96) 24268; f. 1979; Pres. JOSÉ MANUEL MONTEIRO DA SILVA.

**Confederação do Comércio Português (CCP):** Rua dos Correeiros 79, 1° andar, 1100 Lisbon; tel. (1) 3477430; telex 14829; fax (1) 3478638; f. 1977; Pres. VASCO SOUSA DA GAMA; Gen. Sec. JOSÉ ANTÓNIO CORTEZ; mems 143 trade asscns.

**ICEP—Investimentos, Comércio e Turismo de Portugal:** Av. 5 de Outubro 101, 1016 Lisbon Codex; tel. (1) 7930103; telex 16498; fax (1) 7935028; f. 1982; promotes Portuguese exports of goods and services, foreign direct investment in Portugal, Portuguese investment abroad and tourism; Pres. Prof. Dr MIGUEL ATHAYDE MARQUES.

### INDUSTRIAL ORGANIZATIONS

**Associação Industrial Portuguesa (AIP):** Praça das Indústrias, Apdo 3200, 1304 Lisbon Codex; tel. (1) 3601000; fax (1) 3635808; f. 1837; Pres. Dr JORGE ROCHA DE MATOS; 3,500 mems.

**Associação Industrial Portuense:** Leça da Palmeira, 4450 Matosinhos; tel. (2) 9981500; telex 25492; fax (2) 9964213; f. 1849; represents industry in Northern Portugal in all sectors; organizes trade fairs and exhibitions; Pres. Eng. ANGELO LUDGERO MARQUES; 2,000 mems.

**Associação Nacional das Indústrias Têxteis Algodeiras e Fibras (ANITAF):** Rua Gonçalo Cristovão 96, 1°, 4000 Porto; tel. (2) 317961; fax (2) 310343; cotton textile and fibres manufacturers' asscn; Pres. Eng. ALBERTO JOSÉ COSTA.

**Associação Nacional das Indústrias de Vestuário e Confecção (ANIVEC):** Av. da Boavista 3.523-7°, 4100 Porto; tel. (2) 6100050; telex 23843; fax (2) 6100049; clothing manufacturers' asscn; Pres. ALEXANDRE PINHEIRO; Vice-Pres. JORGE DE LEMOS DA COSTA.

**Associação Portuguesa de Cerâmica:** Rua Artilharia Um 104, 2° Andar, CP 1070, 1000 Lisbon; tel. (1) 3875262; fax (1) 3852986; ceramics asscn; Pres. JOSÉ FILIPE NOBRE GUEDES; Gen. Sec. (vacant).

**Associação Portuguesa dos Industriais de Calçado, Componentes, e Artigos de Pele e seus Sucedâneos (APICCAPS):** Rua Alves Redol 372, Apdo 2257, 4204 Porto Codex; tel. (2) 5506776; fax (2) 524997; footwear and leather goods manufacturers' asscn; Pres. BASÍLIO DE OLIVEIRA.

**Confederação dos Agricultores de Portugal (CAP):** Calçada Ribeiro dos Santos 19 r/c, 1200 Lisbon; tel. (1) 3974063; telex 43025; fax (1) 3977309; farmers' confederation; Pres. RAÚL MIGUEL ROSADO FERNANDES.

**Confederação da Indústria Portuguesa (CIP):** Av. 5 de Outubro 35-1°, 1000 Lisbon; tel. (1) 547454; telex 13564; fax (1) 545094; f. 1974; represents employers; Pres. Dr PEDRO FERRAZ DA COSTA; over 35,000 mems.

**Gabinete Portex:** Rua Rainha D. Estefânia 246, 35/36, 4100 Porto; tel. (2) 6068758; telex 26037; fax (2) 600058; textile manufacturers; Pres. ALEXANDRE PINHEIRO; Gen. Sec. Dr JOSÉ LUÍS SOARES BARBOSA.

*Directory*

### DEVELOPMENT ORGANIZATIONS

**Centro para o Desenvolvimento e Inovação Tecnológicos (CEDINTEC):** Rua de São Domingos à Lapa 117-2° Dto, 1200 Lisbon; tel. (1) 3955302; fax (1) 3961203; f. 1982; supports the creation of technological infrastructures; Pres. Eng. JOÃO PEDRO DE SALDANHA VERSCHNEIDER GONÇALVES.

**Gabinete de Estudos e Planeamento:** Av. Conselheiro Fernando de Sousa 11, 12° a 15°, 1092 Lisbon Codex; tel. (1) 3879186; telex 13567; fax (1) 658685; planning and research board (Ministry of Industry and Energy); Dir Eng. ALBERTO MORENO.

**Instituto de Apoio às Pequenas e Médias Empresas e ao Investimento (IAPMEI):** Rua Rodrigo da Fonseca 73, 1297 Lisbon Codex; tel. (1) 3864333; fax (1) 3563161; financial and technical aid to small and medium-sized enterprises; Pres. Dr JOSÉ RAMALHO DE ALMEIDA.

**Instituto para a Cooperação Económica (ICE):** Av. da Liberdade 192-2°, 1200 Lisbon; tel. (1) 549311; fax (1) 527897; an official body for economic co-operation; Pres. FERNANDO D'OLIVEIRA NEVES.

**Instituto Financeiro de Apoio ao Desenvolvimento da Agricultura e Pescas (IFADAP):** Av. João Crisóstomo 11, 1000 Lisbon; tel. (1) 3558337; telex 64138; fax (1) 3525925; provides loans for agriculture and fisheries; Chair. IVO PINHO.

**Instituto de Investimento e Privatizações dos Açores (IIPA):** Praça 5 de Outubro 12, Ponta Delgada, Azores; tel. (96) 24146; telex 82407; fax (96) 25349; supervises all investment projects and privatization in the Azores; Pres. JOÃO BERNARDO RODRIGUES.

**Instituto Nacional de Engenharia e Tecnologia Industrial (INETI):** Estrada do Paço do Lumiar, 1699 Lisbon Codex; tel. (1) 7165181; telex 42486; fax (1) 7160901; f. 1977; industrial and technological research (Ministry of Industry and Energy); Pres. Prof. Dr MANUEL JOSÉ BARATA MARQUES.

**Instituto Português de Qualidade (IPQ):** Rua C à Av. dos Três Vales, 2825 Monte da Caparica; tel. (1) 2948100; fax (1) 2948101; manages and develops the Portuguese Quality System (SPQ); Pres. CÂNDIDO DOS SANTOS.

**Instituto do Vinho do Porto:** Rua Ferreira Borges, 4000 Porto; tel. (2) 2006522; telex 25337; fax (2) 2080465; an official body dealing with quality control and the promotion of port wine; also gives technical advice to exporters; Pres. Prof. Dr FERNANDO BIANCHI DE AGUIAR.

**Sociadade de Desenvolvimento da Madeira (SDM):** Rua Imperatriz D. Amélia, POB 4164, 9052 Funchal Codex, Madeira; tel. (91) 225466; telex 72271; fax (91) 228950; responsible for the management of the Madeira offshore zone; Chair. Dr FRANCISCO COSTA.

**Sociedade de Desenvolvimento da Zona Franca Mariense SA (ZOFRAMA):** Av. Infante D. Henrique, Edifício Sol Mar-10 EF, 9500 Ponta Delgada, Azores; tel. (96) 25573; fax (96) 25530; responsible for management of the Santa Maria dos Açores offshore zone; Pres. ARMINDO RODRIGO VIEIRA LEITE.

**Sociedade Nacional de Empreendimentos e Desenvolvimento Económico:** Av. Fontes Pereira de Melo 35–19A, 1000 Lisbon; tel. (1) 549043; telex 13530; fax (1) 523099; private consultancy co in economy and management; Pres. Dr ALFREDO GONZALEZ ESTEVES BELO.

### LABOUR ORGANIZATIONS

**Confederação Geral dos Trabalhadores Portugueses-Intersindical Nacional (CGTP-IN):** Rua Victor Cordon 1–2° e 3°, 1200 Lisbon; tel. (1) 3472181; telex 13672; fax (1) 3472189; f. 1970; reorganized 1974; 877,000 mems.

**União Geral dos Trabalhadores de Portugal (UGTP):** Rua de Buenos Aires 11, 1200 Lisbon; tel. (1) 3976503; fax (1) 3974612; f. 1978; pro-socialist; 942,325 mems; Pres. JOSÉ PEREIRA LOPES; Gen. Sec. JOÃO PROENÇA.

# Transport

### RAILWAYS

In 1992 the total length of track operated by the nationalized railway was 3,588 km, of which 464 km were electrified. Mining companies operate 48.5 km of private railways.

**Caminhos de Ferro Portugueses, EP (CP):** Calçada do Duque 20, 1294 Lisbon Codex; tel. (1) 3463181; telex 13334; fax (1) 3476524; f. 1856, nationalized in 1975; incorporated Sociedade Estoril Caminhos de Ferro from Cais do Sodré to Cascais in 1977; Pres. ANTÓNIO BRITO DA SILVA.

**Metropolitano de Lisboa, EP (ML):** Av. Fontes Pereira de Melo 28, 1050 Lisbon; tel. (1) 3558457; fax (1) 574908; opened 1959; operates the 19-km underground system; Pres. Eng. JOSÉ MANUEL CONSIGLIERI PEDROSO.

PORTUGAL                                                                                                                    *Directory*

### ROADS

The country is divided into 18 road districts and 4 regions: North, Centre, Lisbon and South. At the end of 1989 there were 70,176 km of roads in continental Portugal, of which 9,071 km were national roads and 259 km were motorway. In December 1993 national roads totalled 9,069 km and motorways 519 km. A motorway between Lisbon and Setúbal was opened in 1979. The final section of the 295-km motorway between Lisbon and Porto opened in 1991.

**Junta Autónoma de Estradas (JAE):** Praça da Portagem, 2800 Almada; tel. (1) 2956040; fax (1) 2951997; f. 1927; responsible, under Ministry of Public Works, Transport and Communications, for planning, construction, improvement and maintenance of national road network and bridges; Pres. Eng. José Luís Catela Rangel de Lima.

**Rodoviária Nacional Investimentos e Participações (RNIP), SA:** Av. Columbano Bordalo Pinheiro 86, 1093 Lisbon Codex; tel. (1) 7267123; telex 15028; fax (1) 7267299; f. 1975 by incorporating the nationalized transportation enterprises; national bus co; passenger and goods transport; reorganized 1991 upon privatization; Pres. António Brito da Silva.

### SHIPPING

The principal Portuguese ports are Lisbon, Leixões (Porto), Setúbal and Funchal (Madeira), and the Viana do Castelo port is being developed. The ports of Portimão (Algarve) and the Azores regularly receive international cruise liners.

#### Principal Shipping Companies

**Portline—Transportes Marítimos Internacionais, SA:** Rua Actor António Silva 7–11°, 1600 Lisbon; tel. (1) 7584553; telex 62052; fax (1) 7586748; f. 1984; marine transport; Pres. Georg Scheder-Bieschin.

**Soponata—Sociedade Portuguesa de Navios Tanques, SA:** Rua Barata Salgueiro 33-5°, 1250 Lisbon; tel. (1) 3538644; telex 61129; fax (1) 3538789; f. 1947; oil tankers; Pres. Dr José Luís de Almeida Fernandes.

**Transinsular—Transportes Marítimos Insulares, SA:** Av. Santos Dumont 57-8°, 1000 Lisbon; tel. (1) 7934123; telex 62027; fax (1) 7978152; f. 1984; goods transport to international destinations and Madeira and the Azores; CEO Dr João Fernando do Amaral Carvalho.

### CIVIL AVIATION

There are international airports at Lisbon, Porto, Faro (Algarve), Funchal (Madeira), Santa Maria (Azores) and São Miguel (Azores).

**TAP—Air Portugal, SA:** Aeroporto de Lisboa, Apdo 50194, 1704 Lisbon Codex; tel. (1) 8415000; telex 12231; fax (1) 8415881; f. 1945; international services to Europe, Africa, Middle East, North and South America; Chair. of Board Eng. Fernando Augusto dos Santos Martins.

**Air Columbus, SA:** Rua do Surdo 38-2°, Esq., 9000 Funchal, Madeira; tel. and fax (91) 233980; telex 25082; charter services within Europe and to USA.

**LAR Transregional—Linhas Aéreas Regionais, SA:** Rua C, Edif. 70, Aeroporto de Lisboa, 1700 Lisbon; tel. (1) 8487162; telex 63505; fax (1) 899552; f. 1985 to replace TAP—Regional; operates domestic services and flights to mainland Spain, Canary Islands, France and Italy; licensed to operate scheduled flights Sept. 1989; Pres. Dr Armando Afonso Moreira; CEO Capt. Rogélio Palma Rodrigues.

**Portugália — Companhia Portuguesa de Transportes Aéreos, SA:** Av. Almirante Gago Coutinho 88, 1700 Lisbon; tel. (1) 8486693; telex 64090; fax (1) 8494862; f. 1989; scheduled services linking Lisbon, Porto and Faro; charter service to Funchal; scheduled services to Spain, Italy, Belgium and Germany; international charter flights also available; Pres. João Ribeiro da Fonseca.

**SATA—Air Açores (Serviço Açoreano de Transportes Aéreos, EP):** Av. Infante D. Henrique, 9500 Ponta Delgada, San Miguel, Azores; tel. (96) 25067; telex 82276; fax (96) 24695; f. 1947; owned by the regional government of the Azores; inter-island services in the Azores; Pres. and CEO Dra Berta Cabral.

#### TRANSPORT ASSOCIATION

**Federação Portuguesa dos Transportes:** Rua Viriato 5-1°, 1000 Lisbon; tel. (1) 577562; telex 18862; fax (1) 574104; Pres. Eng. José Carlos Gonçalves Viana.

## Tourism

Portugal is popular with visitors because of its mild and clement weather. Apart from Lisbon and the Algarve on the mainland. Madeira and the Azores are much favoured as winter resorts. Earnings from tourism reached an estimated 634,406m. escudos in 1994. In 1993 the number of foreign visitors exceeded 20.5m., compared with 7.0m. in 1980. At July 1994 there were 203,241 hotel beds.

**Secretaria de Estado do Turismo:** Palácio Foz, Praça dos Restauradores, 1200 Lisbon; tel. (1) 3463580; telex 12562; fax (1) 3470473; Sec. of State Alexandre Carlos Vieira de Mello Costa Relvas.

**Direcção-Geral do Turismo:** Av. António Augusto de Aguiar 86, Apdo 1929, 1004 Lisbon Codex; tel. (1) 575086; telex 13408; fax (1) 556917; Dir-Gen. Enga Paulina Dália Verde Martins Morais Rosa.

**Investimentos, Comércio e Turismo de Portugal (ICEP):** Tourism Information Dept: Av. Conde de Valbom 30-4°, 1016 Lisbon Codex; tel. (1) 3525810; fax (1) 3525779; Exec. Vice-Pres. responsible for Tourism Eng. Luís Correia da Silva.

**Fundo de Turismo:** Av. António Augusto de Aguiar 122-10°, 1050 Lisbon; tel. (1) 3526237; fax (1) 524221; Pres. José Manuel Castelão Costa.

**Instituto Nacional de Formação Turística:** Rua Engenheiro Arantes e Oliveira 7, 1900 Lisbon; tel. (1) 8473071; telex 65740; fax (1) 8498879; Dir-Gen. Manuel Coelho da Silva.

# PORTUGUESE OVERSEAS TERRITORY

## MACAU

## Introductory Survey

**Location, Climate, Language, Religion, Capital**

Macau comprises the peninsula of Macau, an enclave on the mainland of southern China, and two nearby islands, Taipa, which is linked to the mainland by two bridges, and Coloane, which is connected to Taipa by a causeway. The territory lies opposite Hong Kong on the western side of the mouth of the Xijiang (Sikiang) river. The climate is subtropical. There are two official languages, Portuguese and Chinese (Cantonese being the principal dialect). English is also widely spoken, speakers of English outnumbering Portuguese-speakers. The predominant religions are Roman Catholicism, Chinese Buddhism, Daoism and Confucianism. The capital, the city of Macau, is situated on the peninsula.

**Recent History**

Established by the Portuguese in 1557 as a trading post with China, Macau became a Portuguese Overseas Province in 1951.

After the military coup in Portugal in April 1974, Col José Garcia Leandro was appointed Governor of the province. A new statute, promulgated in February 1976, redefined Macau as a 'Special Territory' under Portuguese jurisdiction, but with a great measure of administrative and economic independence (see Government, below). Proposals to enlarge the Legislative Assembly from 17 to 21 members, thus giving the Chinese population an increased role in the administration of Macau, were abandoned when they did not receive the approval of the Government of the People's Republic of China in March 1980. Upon the establishment of diplomatic relations between China and Portugal in February 1979, it appeared that Macau would remain under Portuguese administration.

In February 1979 Col Leandro was replaced as Governor by Gen. Nuno de Melo Egídio, deputy chief of staff of Portugal's armed forces. In June 1981 Gen. Egídio was, in turn, replaced by Commodore (later Rear-Adm.) Vasco Almeida e Costa, a Portuguese former minister and naval commander. Following a constitutional dispute in March 1984 over the Governor's plans for electoral reform (extending the franchise to the ethnic Chinese majority), the Legislative Assembly was dissolved. Elections for a new Assembly were held in August, at which the Chinese majority were allowed to vote for the first time, regardless of their length of residence in the territory. Four of the six directly-elected seats were won by the Electoral Union, a coalition of pro-Beijing and conservative Macanese (lusophone Eurasian) groups, while the six indirectly-elected members, all Chinese, were returned unopposed. The Governor appointed four government officials and a Chinese business executive to complete the Assembly, which was then for the first time dominated by ethnic Chinese deputies.

In January 1986 Governor Almeida e Costa resigned. In May he was replaced by Joaquim Pinto Machado, who had hitherto been a professor of medicine. Pinto Machado's appointment represented a break in the tradition of military governors for Macau, but his political inexperience placed him at a disadvantage. In May 1987 he resigned, citing 'reasons of institutional dignity' (apparently referring to the problem of corruption in the Macau administration). He was replaced in August by Carlos Melancia, a former Socialist deputy in the Portuguese legislature, who had held ministerial posts in several Portuguese governments.

In May 1985, meanwhile, President Eanes visited Beijing and Macau, and it was announced that the Portuguese and Chinese Governments would negotiate the future of Macau during 1986. It was expected that an eventual transfer of administration in Macau would be based on an accord similar to the agreement between China and the United Kingdom concerning Hong Kong, although Portugal's acceptance of China's sovereignty greatly simplified the issue. The first round of negotiations took place in June 1986 in Beijing. On 13 April 1987, following the conclusion of the fourth round of negotiations, a joint declaration was formally signed in Beijing by the Portuguese and Chinese Governments, during an official visit to China by the Prime Minister of Portugal. According to the agreement (which was formally ratified in January 1988), Macau was to become a 'special administrative region' (SAR) of the People's Republic (to be known as Macau, China) on 20 December 1999. Macau was thus to have the same status as that agreed (with effect from 1997) for Hong Kong, and was to enjoy autonomy in most matters except defence and foreign policy. A Joint Sino-Portuguese Liaison Group, established to oversee the transfer of power, held its inaugural meeting in Lisbon in April 1988. After 1999 a Chief Executive for Macau was to be appointed by the Chinese Government, following 'elections or consultations to be held in Macau', and the territory's legislature was to contain 'a majority of elected members'. The inhabitants of Macau were to become citizens of the People's Republic of China, and the Chinese Government refused to allow the possibility of dual Sino-Portuguese citizenship, although Macau residents in possession of Portuguese passports were apparently to be permitted to retain them for travel purposes. The agreement guaranteed a 50-year period during which Macau would be permitted to retain its free capitalist economy, and to be financially independent of China.

In August 1988 the establishment of a Macau Basic Law Drafting Committee was announced by the Chinese Government. Comprising 30 Chinese members and 19 representatives from Macau, the Committee was to draft a law determining the territory's future constitutional status within the People's Republic of China.

Elections to the Legislative Assembly were held in October 1988. Low participation (fewer than 30% of the electorate) was recorded, and a 'liberal' grouping secured three of the seats reserved for directly-elected candidates, while the Electoral Union won the other three.

In January 1989 it was announced that Portuguese passports were to be issued to about 100,000 ethnic Chinese inhabitants, born in Macau before October 1981, and it was anticipated that as many as a further 100,000 would be granted before 1999. Unlike their counterparts in the neighbouring British dependent territory of Hong Kong, therefore, these Macau residents (but not all) were to be granted the full rights of a citizen of the European Community (EC, now European Union—EU). In February 1989 President Mário Soares of Portugal visited Macau, in order to discuss the transfer of the territory's administration to China.

Following the violent suppression of the pro-democracy movement in China in June 1989, as many as 100,000 residents of Macau participated in demonstrations in the enclave to protest against the Chinese Government's action. The events in the People's Republic caused great concern in Macau, and it was feared that many residents would wish to leave the territory prior to 1999. In August 1989, however, China assured Portugal that it would honour the agreement to maintain the capitalist system of the territory after 1999.

In March 1990 the implementation of a programme to grant permanent registration to parents of 4,200 Chinese residents, the latter having already secured the right of abode in Macau, developed into chaos when other illegal immigrants demanded a similar concession. The authorities decided to declare a general amnesty, but were unprepared for the numbers of illegal residents who rushed to take advantage of the scheme, thereby revealing the true extent of previous immigration from China. In the ensuing stampede by 50,000 illegal immigrants, desperate to obtain residency rights, about 200 persons were injured and 1,500 arrested. Border security was increased, in an effort to prevent any further illegal immigration from China. Following the pandemonium, 200 members of the security forces staged a demonstration in support of demands for higher wages. The Governor dismissed the chief-of-staff of the security forces and his deputy.

In late March 1990 the Legislative Assembly approved the final draft of the territory's revised Organic Law. The Law was approved by the Portuguese Assembly of the Republic in mid-April, and granted Macau greater administrative, economic, financial and legislative autonomy, in advance of 1999. The powers of the Governor and of the Legislative Assembly, where six additional seats were to be created, were therefore increased. The post of military commander of the security forces was abolished, responsibility for the territory's security being assumed by a civilian Under-Secretary.

In June 1990 the Under-Secretary for Justice, Dr Manuel Magalhães e Silva, resigned, owing to differences of opinion on the issues of Macau's political structure and Sino-Portuguese relations. In the same month, while on a visit to Lisbon for consultations with the President and Prime Minister, Carlos Melancia rebuked the Chinese authorities for attempting to interfere in the internal affairs of Macau. This unprecedented reproach followed criticism of the Governor's compromising attitude towards the People's Republic of China.

Meanwhile, in February 1990, Carlos Melancia had been implicated in a financial scandal. It was alleged that the Governor had accepted 50m. escudos from a Federal German company which hoped to be awarded a consultancy contract for the construction of the new airport in Macau. In September Melancia was served with a summons in connection with the alleged bribery. Although he denied any involvement in the affair, the Governor resigned, and was replaced on an acting basis by the Under-Secretary for Economic Affairs, Dr Francisco Murteira Nabo. In September 1991 it was announced that Melancia and five others were to stand trial on charges of corruption. Melancia's trial opened in April 1993. At its conclusion in August the former Governor was acquitted on the grounds of insufficient evidence. In February 1994, however, it was announced that Melancia was to be retried, owing to irregularities in his defence case.

The ability of Portugal to maintain a stable administration in the territory had once again been called into question. Many observers believed that the enclave was being adversely affected by the political situation in Lisbon, as differences between the socialist President and centre-right Prime Minister were being reflected in rivalries between officials in Macau. In an attempt to restore confidence, therefore, President Soares visited the territory in November 1990. In January 1991, upon his re-election as Head of State, the President appointed Gen. Vasco Rocha Vieira (who had served as the territory's Chief of Staff in 1973/74 and as Under-Secretary for Public Works and Transport in 1974/75) to be the new Governor of Macau. In March 1991 the Legislative Assembly was expanded from 17 to 23 members. All seven Under-Secretaries were replaced in May.

Following his arrival in Macau, Gen. Rocha Vieira announced that China would be consulted on all future developments in the territory. The 10th meeting of the Sino-Portuguese Liaison Group took place in Beijing in April 1991. Topics under regular discussion included the participation of Macau in international organizations, progress towards an increase in the number of local officials employed in the civil service (hitherto dominated by Portuguese and Macanese personnel) and the status of the Chinese language. The progress of the working group on the translation of local laws from Portuguese into Chinese was also examined, a particular problem being the lack of suitably-qualified bilingual legal personnel. It was agreed that Portuguese was to remain an official language after 1999. The two sides also reached agreement on the exchange of identity cards for those Macau residents who would require them in 1999. Regular meetings of the Liaison Group continued.

In July 1991 the Macau Draft Basic Law was published by the authorities of the People's Republic of China. Confidence in the territory's future was enhanced by China's apparent flexibility on a number of issues. Unlike the Hong Kong Basic Law, that of Macau did not impose restrictions on holders of foreign passports assuming senior posts in the territory's administration after 1999, the only exception being the future Chief Executive. Furthermore, the draft contained no provision for the stationing of troops from China in Macau after the territory's return to Chinese administration.

In November 1991 the Governor of Macau visited the People's Republic of China, where it was confirmed that the 'one country, two systems' policy would operate in Macau from 1999. Following a visit to Portugal by the Chinese Premier in February 1992, the Governor of Macau stated that the territory was to retain 'great autonomy' after 1999. In March 1993 the final draft of the Basic Law of the Macau SAR was ratified by the National People's Congress in Beijing, which also approved the design of the future SAR's flag. The adoption of the legislation was welcomed by the Governor of Macau, who reiterated his desire for a smooth transfer of power in 1999. The Chief Executive of the SAR was to be selected by an electoral college, comprising 300 local representatives. Candidates for the post would require nomination by no fewer than 50 members of the college. The SAR's first Legislative Council was to comprise 23 members, of whom eight would be directly elected. Its term of office would expire in October 2001, when it would be expanded to 27 members, of whom 10 would be directly elected.

Meanwhile, elections to the Legislative Assembly were held in September 1992. The level of participation was higher than on previous occasions, with 59% of the registered electorate (albeit only 13.5% of the population) attending the polls. Fifty candidates contested the eight directly-elective seats, four of which were won by members of the main pro-Beijing parties, the União Promotora para o Progresso and the União para o Desenvolvimento.

Relations between Portugal and China remained cordial. In June 1993 the two countries reached agreement on all outstanding issues regarding the construction of the territory's airport and the future use of Chinese air space. Furthermore, Macau was to be permitted to negotiate air traffic agreements with other countries. In October, upon the conclusion of a three-day visit to Macau, President Soares expressed optimism regarding the territory's smooth transition to Chinese administration. In November President Jiang Zemin of China was warmly received in Lisbon, where he had discussions with both the Portuguese President and Prime Minister. In February 1994 the Chinese Minister of Communications visited Macau to discuss with the Governor the progress of the airport project.

In April 1994, during a visit to China, the Portuguese Prime Minister received an assurance that Chinese nationality would not be imposed on Macanese people of Portuguese descent, who would be able to retain their Portuguese passports. Speaking in Macau itself, the Prime Minister expressed confidence in the territory's future. Regarding the issue as increasingly one of foreign policy, he stated his desire to transfer jurisdiction over Macau from the Presidency of the Republic to the Government, despite the necessity for a constitutional amendment.

In July 1994 a group of local journalists dispatched a letter, alleging intimidation and persecution in Macau, to President Soares, urging him to intervene to defend the territory's press freedom. The journalists' appeal followed an incident involving the director of the daily *Gazeta Macaense*, who had been obliged to pay 300,000 escudos for reproducing an article from *Semanário*, a Lisbon weekly newspaper, and now faced trial. The territory's press had been critical of the Macau Supreme Court's decision to extradite ethnic Chinese to the mainland (despite the absence of any extradition treaty) to face criminal charges and the possibility of a death sentence.

Gen. Rocha Vieira embarked upon a second visit to China in August 1994. The Governor of Macau had discussions with the Chinese Minister of Foreign Affairs, who declared Sino-Portuguese relations to be sound but, as a result of a gaffe relating to the delegation's distribution to the press of a biography of Premier Li Peng containing uncomplimentary remarks, stressed the need for vigilance.

The draft of the new penal code for Macau did not incorporate the death penalty. In January 1995, during a visit to Portugal, Vice-Premier Zhu Rongji of China confirmed that the People's Republic would not impose the death penalty in Macau after 1999, regarding the question as a matter for the authorities of the future SAR.

On another visit to the territory in April 1995, President Soares emphasized the need for Macau to assert its identity, and stressed the importance of three issues: the modification of the territory's legislation; the rights of the individual; and the preservation of the Portuguese language. Travelling on to Beijing, accompanied by Gen. Rocha Vieira, the Portuguese President had successful discussions with his Chinese counterpart on various matters relating to the transition.

## Government

Macau is a Special Territory of Portugal. Executive power (except in foreign affairs, which are the responsibility of the President of Portugal) is vested in the Governor, who is appointed by the President of Portugal, after consultation with the Legislative Assembly of Macau. The Governor is assisted by as many as seven Under-Secretaries, to whom executive powers are delegated, and who are appointed by the

Portuguese President. The Governor presides over a Superior Council of Security, responsible for the security of the territory, and a Consultative Council. The Legislative Assembly comprises 23 deputies with a mandate of four years. Seven deputies are appointed by the Governor from among residents of recognized reputation, eight are elected by direct and universal suffrage and eight are elected by indirect suffrage.

**Defence**

The Forças de Segurança de Macau are under the direct control of the Governor, and consist of the Public Security Police, the Maritime and Fiscal Police and the fire brigade, totalling 3,000 members in 1990. There were 150 officers from the armed forces of Portugal. By 1999 senior posts were to be filled by local officers.

**Economic Affairs**

In 1993, according to official estimates, Macau's gross domestic product (GDP), measured at current prices, was 46,481m. patacas (about US $5,830m.), equivalent to 119,500 patacas (US $15,000) per head. During 1985–89 the territory's GDP increased, in real terms, at an average annual rate of 8.1%. Compared with the previous year, real GDP grew by 12% in 1992, by 5% in 1993 and by 4% in 1994. Between 1985 and 1993 the population increased at an average annual rate of 3.2%.

Agriculture is of minor importance. In 1989 only 0.6% of the economically active population were employed in agriculture and fishing. The main crops are rice and vegetables. Cattle, buffaloes and pigs are reared.

Industry (including manufacturing, construction and public utilities) employed 35.4% of the economically active population in 1993. Mining is negligible. The most important manufacturing industry is the production of textiles and garments. Other industries include toys, footwear, furniture, electronics and optical articles.

Macau possesses few natural resources. The territory receives part of its water supply from the People's Republic of China. In 1984 China also began to supply electricity to Macau. It was envisaged that Macau would eventually receive 70% of its power requirements from the People's Republic. In 1989 more than 90% of the territory's electricity was domestically produced. Imports of fuels and lubricants accounted for 4.7% of total import costs in 1994.

Tourism makes a substantial contribution to the territory's economy, receipts totalling US $1,982m. in 1993. In 1991 the tourism industry employed an estimated 12% of the economically active population. The tourism sector contributed an estimated 37% of GDP in 1991. The number of visitor arrivals totalled 7.8m. in 1994. In 1993 the number of visitors from the People's Republic of China increased rapidly, but declined in 1994, following the mainland authorities' imposition of stricter exit regulations. The Government's gambling and betting revenues rose from 3,600m. patacas in 1992 to 4,200m. in 1993, when they accounted for about 34% of the territory's total budget revenue. The construction industry continued to show strong growth in the early 1990s. Construction of several large hotels commenced during 1990. Other projects include a shopping centre and a 2,000m.-patacas complex, incorporating Macau's largest casino and office building. Offshore banking legislation was introduced in 1987. It was hoped that the territory would develop as an international financial centre. The Financial System Act, which took effect in September 1993, aimed to improve the reputation of Macau's banks by curbing the unauthorized acceptance of deposits.

In 1994 Macau recorded a trade deficit of 2,071.2m. patacas, compared with a surplus of 1,295.1m. patacas in 1990. The principal sources of imports in 1994 were Hong Kong (which supplied 30.4% of the total), the People's Republic of China (18.8%) and Japan (12.8%). The principal market for exports was the USA (which purchased 37.2%), followed by the People's Republic of China, Hong Kong, Germany and France. The main exports were textiles and garments (which accounted for 73.5% of the total), toys and electronic equipment. The principal imports were raw materials for industry and consumer goods. After 1999 Macau was to retain its status as a free port, and was to remain a separate customs territory.

A budget surplus of 1,782.4m. patacas was recorded in 1993. The average annual rate of inflation between 1985 and 1993 was 9.5%, declining from 6.7% in 1993 to 6.3% in 1994. There is a shortage of labour in Macau, although the territory is able to hire workers from the People's Republic of China.

In 1991 Macau became a party to the UN's General Agreement on Tariffs and Trade (GATT, now the World Trade Organization, see p. 64) and an associate member of the Economic and Social Commission for Asia and the Pacific (ESCAP, see p. 27). In June 1992 Macau and the European Community (now the European Union) signed a five-year trade and economic co-operation agreement, granting mutual preferential treatment on tariffs and other commercial matters.

Macau's development has been hindered by the territory's lack of infrastructure. However, the opening of an airport, scheduled for 1995/96, will not only enhance Macau's role as a point of entry to the People's Republic of China but also afford the enclave access to international transport networks. Attempts to diversify the economy, in order to reduce dependence on the textile industry and tourism, have been impeded by the labour shortage and by the lack of suitable building land. In 1988 regulations governing the entry of foreign workers were relaxed. A major land reclamation programme was also under way. A large industrial estate on reclaimed land near the site of the new airport was under construction. The completion of the Nam Van Lakes project, scheduled for 1999, would enlarge the territory's peninsular area by 20%. Details of this land-reclamation project, which was to cost US $1,400m., were announced in July 1993 by a prominent entrepreneur, following the scheme's approval by the People's Republic of China. Co-operation between Macau and the neighbouring Chinese Special Economic Zone of Zhuhai is mainly in the form of joint ventures. The violent suppression of the pro-democracy movement in China in June 1989, however, gave rise to fears for the future of Macau. As in Hong Kong, many skilled personnel were expected to leave the territory before its return to Chinese administration, in 1999. In August 1994 the availability of stipends to public servants willing to serve in Macau beyond 1999 was announced. The Macau Government Economic Committee, chaired by the Governor, was established in February 1994.

**Social Welfare**

In addition to the network of health centres, Macau has two major hospitals (one public and one private). In 1992 there were 570 physicians and 784 nurses working in the territory. Hospital beds totalled 969 (392 persons per bed). The elderly have access to free medicines. Certain others receive subsidized medicines. In 1990 the sum of 390m. patacas, or 12% of the territory's total budget, was allocated to the health sector.

**Education**

Education is officially compulsory for five years, to be undertaken between six and 12 years of age. In 1990, however, only 89.7% of children aged six to 11 were reported to be receiving education, while only 58.2% of those aged 12 to 14 were attending school. A system of free education for six years was introduced in 1990/91, and extended to nine years in 1994/95. Primary education begins at the age of six and lasts for five years. Secondary education, beginning at 11 years of age, lasts for up to five years. In 1992/93 a total of 21,432 pupils were enrolled in pre-primary schools, 40,037 in primary schools and 19,461 in secondary schools, most of whom attended schools at which the medium of instruction was Chinese (Cantonese), the remainder attending Anglo-Chinese, Luso-Chinese and Portuguese schools. In the same year 6,803 students were enrolled at institutes of higher education. The 1991 budget allocated 410m. patacas to education. The University of Macau was inaugurated, as the University of East Asia, in 1981 (passing from private to government control in 1988), and had 2,091 full-time and 68 part-time students in 1993. The languages of instruction are primarily English, Cantonese and Portuguese. In 1989/90 about 20% of students were from overseas, mainly Chinese from South-East Asia.

**Public Holidays**

**1995:** 1 January (New Year), 31 January–2 February (Chinese Lunar New Year), 5 April (Ching Ming), 14–16 April (Easter), 25 April (anniversary of the Portuguese Revolution), 1 May (Labour Day), 2 June (Dragon Boat Festival), 10 June (Camões Day and Portuguese Communities Day), 24 June (St John the Baptist, Patron Saint of Macau), 10 September (day following Chinese Mid-Autumn Festival), 1 October (National Day of the People's Republic of China), 5 October (Portuguese Republic Day), 1 November (Festival of Ancestors—Chung Yeung), 2 November (All Souls' Day), 1 December (Restoration of Portuguese Independence, 1640), 8 December (Immaculate

# PORTUGUESE OVERSEAS TERRITORY
*Macau*

Conception), 22 December (Winter Solstice), 24–25 December (Christmas).
**1996** (provisional): 1 January (New Year), 19–21 February (Chinese Lunar New Year), 5 April (Ching Ming), 5–7 April (Easter), 25 April (anniversary of the Portuguese Revolution), 1 May (Labour Day), 10 June (Camões Day and Portuguese Communities Day), 20 June (Dragon Boat Festival), 24 June (St John the Baptist, Patron Saint of Macau), 28 September (day following Chinese Mid-Autumn Festival), 1 October (National Day of the People's Republic of China), 5 October (Portuguese Republic Day), 20 October (Festival of Ancestors—Chung Yeung), 2 November (All Souls' Day), 1 December (Restoration of Portuguese Independence, 1640), 8 December (Immaculate Conception), 22 December (Winter Solstice), 24–25 December (Christmas).

**Weights and Measures**
The metric system is in force.

# Statistical Survey

Source (unless otherwise indicated): Serviços de Estatística e Censos, Rua Inácio Baptista 4D, CP 3022, Macau; tel. 550935; fax 307825.

## AREA AND POPULATION

**Area** (1993): 19.30 sq km (7.43 sq miles).
**Population:** 355,693 (males 172,492, females 183,201) at census of 30 August 1991; 101,245 inhabitants were of Portuguese nationality; 395,304 at 31 December 1993 (estimate).
**Density:** 20,482 per sq km (31 December 1993).
**Births, Marriages and Deaths** (1994): Registered live births 6,115 (birth rate 16.1 per 1,000 in 1993); Registered marriages 2,742 (marriage rate 8.7 per 1,000 in 1993); Registered deaths 1,330 (death rate 3.9 per 1,000 in 1993). Note: Data for births cover only events recorded by the Health Service.
**Expectation of Life** (years at birth, 1992): males 70.1; females 75.7. Source: UN, *Statistical Yearbook for Asia and the Pacific*.
**Economically Active Population** (1993): Manufacturing 42,849; Electricity, gas and water 696; Construction and Public Works 17,128; Trade, restaurants and hotels 44,511; Transport and communications 10,453; Finance, insurance and services 9,209; Personal and social services 45,473; Others 1,033; Total 171,352.

## AGRICULTURE, ETC.

**Meat Production** (1994, metric tons, slaughter weight): Buffaloes 1,521.3, Pigs 10,553.8.
**Fishing** ('000 metric tons, live weight): Total catch 2.8 in 1992; 1.9 in 1993; 1.9 in 1994.

## INDUSTRY

**Production** (1993): Wine 424,866 litres; Knitwear 18.8m. units; Footwear 2.3m. pairs; Clothing 165.3m. units; Furniture 41,896 units; Explosives and pyrotechnic products 762.9 metric tons; Optical articles 289,120 units; Electric energy (1994) 1,159.1m. kWh.

## FINANCE

**Currency and Exchange Rates:** 100 avos = 1 pataca. *Sterling and Dollar Equivalents* (31 December 1994): £1 sterling = 12.485 patacas; US $1 = 7.970 patacas; 1,000 patacas = £80.09 = $125.47.
**Budget** (million patacas, 1993): *Total revenue:* 12,225.3 (direct taxes 5,503.8; indirect taxes 753.3; others 5,968.2). *Total expenditure:* 10,442.9
**Money Supply** (million patacas at 31 December): *Total money:* 20,987.9 in 1992; 20,602.8 in 1993; 18,809.5 in 1994.
**Cost of Living** (Consumer Price Index; base: October 1988/September 1989 = 100): 127.4 in 1992; 135.9 in 1993; 144.4 in 1994.
**Gross Domestic Product** (million patacas at current prices): 32,118.2 in 1991; 40,259.0 in 1992; 46,481.4 in 1993.

## EXTERNAL TRADE

**Principal Commodities** (million patacas): *Imports (1994):* Foodstuffs, beverages and tobacco 1,943.0, Raw materials 9,089.5, Fuels and lubricants 793.4, Capital goods 2,242.7, Other consumer goods 2,856.5, Total 16,925.1. *Exports (1994):* Textiles and garments 10,918.2, Radios, television sets, etc. 565.6, Toys 728.3, Total (incl. others) 14,853.9.
**Principal Trading Partners** (million patacas): *Imports (1994):* China, People's Republic 3,186.4, EU 2,452.3 (France 502.7, Germany 389.2), Hong Kong 5,136.8, Japan 2,164.6, USA 1,156.5, Total (incl. others) 16,925.1. *Exports (1994):* China, People's Republic 1,887.3, EU 4,669.9 (France 1,066.4, Germany 1,528.4), Hong Kong 1,660.2, Japan 140.5, USA 5,522.2, Total (incl. others) 14,853.9.

## TRANSPORT

**Road Traffic** (motor vehicles in use, Dec. 1994): Light vehicles 36,596, Heavy vehicles 3,683, Motor cycles 26,419.
**Shipping** (international sea-borne freight traffic, '000 metric tons, 1990): Goods loaded 755; Goods unloaded 3,935. Source: UN, *Monthly Bulletin of Statistics*.

## COMMUNICATIONS MEDIA

**Radio receivers** (1992): 135,000 in use.
**Television receivers** (1992): 34,000 in use.
Source: UNESCO, *Statistical Yearbook*.
**Daily newspapers** (1994): 12.
**Telephones** (Dec. 1994): 170,021 in use.

## TOURISM

**Arrivals** (from Hong Kong by sea, '000): 6,219.4 in 1992 (total arrivals 7,699.2); 5,987.6 in 1993 (total arrivals 7,829.3); 5,958.8 in 1994 (total arrivals 7,833.8).

## EDUCATION
(1992/93)

**Kindergarten:** 66 schools, 734 teachers, 21,432 pupils.
**Primary:** 72 schools, 1,476 teachers, 40,037 pupils.
**Secondary:** 36 schools, 1,024 teachers, 19,461 pupils.
**Teacher-Training:** 2 institutes, 13 teachers, 353 students.
**Nurse-Training:** 2 institutes, 76 teachers, 115 students.
**Higher:** 9 institutes, 512 teachers, 6,803 students.
Note: Figures for schools and teachers refer to all those for which the category is applicable. Some schools and teachers provide education at more than one level.

PORTUGUESE OVERSEAS TERRITORY                                                                                            *Macau*

# Directory

## The Constitution

The Constitution of Macau is embodied in an organic statute of Portugal, promulgated on 17 February 1976 and revised in 1990.

Macau, comprising the town of Nome de Deus de Macau (God's Name of Macau) and the Taipa and Coloane islands, has administrative, economic, financial and legislative autonomy.

The sovereign organs of Portugal are represented in the territory by the Governor. In foreign relations and international agreements or conventions, Macau is represented by the President of Portugal who may delegate to the Governor if the matters concern the territory only.

The judicial power is independent.

### THE GOVERNOR

Executive authority is vested in the Governor, who is appointed (after consultation with the local population, through the Legislative Assembly) and dismissed by the President of Portugal, to whom he is responsible politically. He has a rank similar to that of a Minister of Government in Portugal. The Governor is assisted by a maximum of seven Under-Secretaries.

### THE UNDER-SECRETARIES

The Under-Secretaries, up to seven in number, are appointed by the President of Portugal on the Governor's advice. Each has a rank similar to a Secretary of State of Government in Portugal.

They exercise the executive powers that have been delegated by the Governor.

### THE SUPERIOR COUNCIL OF SECURITY

The Superior Council of Security works in conjunction with the Governor, who presides over it. It includes the Under-Secretaries. Its duties are to settle and to co-ordinate directives relating to the security of the territory.

### THE LEGISLATIVE ASSEMBLY

The Legislative Assembly comprises 23 deputies with a mandate of four years. Seven deputies are appointed by the Governor from among residents of recognized reputation, eight are elected by direct and universal suffrage and eight are elected by indirect suffrage.

The President of Portugal can dissolve the Assembly in the public interest on the Governor's recommendation.

### THE CONSULTATIVE COUNCIL

The Consultative Council is presided over by the Governor. Five members are appointed by the Governor and five are elected for a four-year term (two elected by the members of the administrative bodies and from among them, one by organizations representing moral, cultural and welfare interests, and two by associations with economic interests); there are three statutory members (the Under-Secretary for the Civil Administration Services, the Attorney of the Republic and the Chief of Finance Services); and two members nominated by the Governor.

### JUDICIAL SYSTEM

See below.

### FINANCE

Macau draws up its own budget, which is annual and unitary.

Money issue is guaranteed through the Monetary Authority of Macau (which replaced the Issuing Institute of Macau in 1989), while the Government's banker of the territory remains the Banco Nacional Ultramarino.

The annual public accounts of the territory must be submitted to the judgment of the Administrative Law Court.

Note: For details of the joint Sino-Portuguese declaration, providing for the return of Macau to Chinese administration in 1999, see p. 2525.

## The Government

(June 1995)

**Governor:** Gen. VASCO JOAQUIM ROCHA VIEIRA (sworn in 23 April 1991).

**Under-Secretary for Economy and Finance:** VÍTOR MANUEL DE SILVA RODRIGUES PESSOA.

**Under-Secretary for Transport and Public Works:** JOSÉ MANUEL MACHADO.

**Under-Secretary for Public Security (Police, Marine, Customs, Immigration and Fire Brigade):** Brig. HENRIQUE MANUEL LAJES RIBEIRO.

**Under-Secretary for Justice:** ANTÓNIO MANUEL MACEDO DE ALMEIDA.

**Under-Secretary for Communication, Tourism and Culture:** Dr ANTÓNIO MANUEL SALAVESSA DA COSTA.

**Under-Secretary for Administration, Education and Youth:** Dr JORGE HAGEDORN RANGEL.

**Under-Secretary for Health and Social Affairs:** ANA MARIA SIQUEIRA BASTO PEREZ.

The Under-Secretaries are appointed by the President of Portugal on the Governor's advice. There is a Consultative Committee of ex-officio and nominated members representing the Chinese community.

**Office of the Governor:** Government Palace, Rua da Praia Grande, Macau; tel. 565555; telex 88201; fax 972746.

## Legislature

### LEGISLATIVE ASSEMBLY

Following the revision of Macau's Organic Law in 1990, the Assembly comprises 23 members: seven appointed by the Governor, eight elected directly and eight indirectly. Members serve for four years. The Assembly chooses its President from among its members, by secret vote. The most recent elections were held in September 1992, pro-Beijing candidates of the União Promotora para o Progresso and of the União para o Desenvolvimento winning four (two each) of the eight directly-elective seats. The Associação de Novo Macau Democrático, Unidade para o Futuro de Macau, Solidariedade Laboral and Associação de Amizade each won one seat.

**President:** ANABELA RITCHIE.

## Political Organizations

There are no formal political parties, but a number of civic associations exist. Those contesting the 1992 Legislative Assembly elections included the pro-Beijing União Promotora para o Progresso (UNIPRO), União para o Desenvolvimento (UPD), Associação de Novo Macau Democrático (ANMD), Unidade para o Futuro de Macau (UNIF), Solidariedade Laboral (LABOR), Associação de Amizade (AMI), União Eleitoral (UNE), Três Unidos (TÚ) and Associação pela Democracia e Bem-Estar Social de Macau (ADBM).

## Judicial System

The judicial system was administered directly from Portugal until 1993, when formal autonomy was granted to the territory's judiciary.

**President of the Supreme Court:** AMARO FARINHA RIBEIRAS.

## Religion

The majority of the Chinese residents profess Buddhism, and there are numerous Chinese places of worship, Daoism and Confucianism also being widely practised.

### CHRISTIANITY

#### The Roman Catholic Church

Macau forms a single diocese, directly responsible to the Holy See. At 31 December 1994 there were 22,129 adherents in the territory.

**Bishop of Macau:** Rt Rev. DOMINGOS LAM KA TSEUNG, Paço Episcopal, Largo da Sé s/n, POB 324; tel. 3975229; fax 309861.

#### The Anglican Communion

Macau forms part of the Anglican diocese of Hong Kong (q.v.).

## The Press

A new Press Law, prescribing journalists' rights and obligations, was enacted in August 1990.

### PORTUGUESE LANGUAGE

**Boletim Oficial:** Rua da Imprensa Nacional, CP 33; tel. 573822; telex 88540; fax 596802; f. 1838; govt weekly; Dir Dr EDUARDO RIBEIRO.

**O Clarim:** Rua Central 26-A; tel. 573860; fax 307867; f. 1948; weekly; Editor Albino Bento Pais; circ. 1,500.

**Comércio de Macau:** Rua da Praia Grande 9, Edif. Hang Chong 4D; tel. 310428; fax 310423; weekly; Dir Carlos Borges; circ. 1,500.

**Expresso do Oriente:** Rua do Chunambeiro 6–8, Edif. Keng Fai, 60c; tel. 566395; weekly.

**O Futuro de Macau:** Av. da Amizade, Edif. Nam Fong, Bloco 1–6F; tel. 705238; fax 705242; daily; circ. 1,500.

**Gazeta Macaense:** Rua de Santa Clara, Edif. Ribeiro 5, 7F; tel. 573318; fax 338245; f. 1962; daily; Dir Paulo Reis; circ. 1,700.

**Jornal de Macau:** Calçada do Tronco Velho 6, POB 945; tel. 329270; fax 572277; f. 1982; daily; Editor João Fernandes; circ. 2,000.

**Jornal Novo:** Rua da Praia Grande 33, G/F; tel. 381278; telex 88508; fax 337305; daily; Editor José Rocha Dinis; circ. 1,500.

**Macau Hoje:** Rua do Chunambeiro 6–8, 6D; tel. 314467; fax 566379; daily; Dir Meira Burguete; circ. 1,000.

**Ponto Final:** Rua da Praia Grande, Edif. Si Toi 17°, Sala 1703; tel. 339566; fax 339563; Dir Luís Ortet; circ. 1,500.

**Semanário Desportivo:** Rua Henrique de Macedo 5, 2 Bl. 5; tel. 383039; fax 316083; weekly; sport; Dir Fong Sio Lon; Editor-in-Chief Fong Lin Lam; circ. 2,000.

**Tribuna de Macau:** Rua da Praia Grande 33, G/F; tel. 381278; telex 88508; fax 337305; f. 1982; weekly; Editor José Rocha Dinis; circ. 3,000.

### CHINESE LANGUAGE

**Cheng Pou:** Rua da Sé 12, R/C Bl. B; tel. 307586; fax 573662; daily; Dir Kong Su Kan; Editor-in-Chief Cheng Pui; circ. 4,000.

**Cheong Ian Chao Pou:** Av. Almeida Ribeiro 140-1; tel. 922469; fax 920234; weekly; Dir Leong Iao Meng; circ. 2,000.

**Gazeta:** weekly Chinese edn of Gazeta Macaense—see above; circ. 1,500.

**Hou Kong Tribuna:** Est. Dna Maria II, Edif. Duplo Dragão 1F; tel. 333336; fax 317262; weekly; Exec. Dir Kuan Wei Lam; Editor-in-Chief Lau Su Cheng; circ. 8,000.

**Jornal Hou Hoi:** Istmo Ferreira do Amaral s/n, Bl. 1, 12M, Edif. Hoi Nam Garden; tel. 435797; fax 361782; weekly; Dir Iao Sao Wa; circ. 3,000.

**Jornal Son Pou:** Rua da Casa Forte 4, R/C; tel. 561557; fax 566575; weekly; Dir Chao Chong Peng; circ. 6,000.

**Ou Mun Iat Pou** (Macau Daily News): Rua Pedro Nolasco da Silva 37; tel. 371688; fax 331998; f. 1958; daily; Dir Lei Seng Chun; Editor-in-Chief Lei Pang Chu; circ. 88,000.

**Seng Pou** (Star): Travessa da Caldeira 9; tel. 84023; fax 388192; f. 1963; daily; Dir Kok Kam Seng; Editor-in-Chief Tou Man Kam; circ. 5,000.

**Si Man Pou** (Jornal do Cidadão): Rua dos Mercadores 45–3; tel. 355031; fax 355080; f. 1944; daily; Dir Kung Man; Editor Lei Foc Lon; circ. 8,000.

**Tai Chung Pou:** Rua dos Mercadores 126; tel. 578378; fax 510317; f. 1933; daily; Dir Choi Hak Meng; Editor-in-Chief Sou Kim Keong; circ. 13,000.

**Today Macau Journal:** Pátio da Barca 12; tel. 385985; fax 334399; daily; Dir Lam Vo Yee; circ. 4,000.

**Va Kio Pou:** Rua da Alfândega 7–9; tel. 345888; fax 580638; f. 1937; daily; Dir Chiu U Nang; Editor-in-Chief Lui Vai Leng; circ. 30,000.

### REGIONAL AND FOREIGN NEWS AGENCIES

**Agence France-Presse (AFP):** CTT Bldg, Av. Alfonso Henriques, CP 145; tel. 560111; fax 511233; Correspondent Lucia Marquis.

**Agência Noticiosa Lusa:** Rua de São Domingos 1, S/L; tel. 511231; fax 511233; Dir Paulo Ramalheira.

**Agência Noticiosa Luso-Chinesa:** Rua Luís Gonzaga Gomes s/n, 15°, Bl. 4, Edif. San On Garden; tel. 567242; telex 88416; fax 558998; Correspondent Si Sio Tang.

**Associated Press (AP)** (USA): CP 221; tel. 361204; fax 343220; Correspondent Adam Lee.

**Xinhua (New China) News Agency** (People's Republic of China): Rua da Praia Grande 65-A; tel. 84255; fax 346120; Dir Wang Qiren.

### PRESS ASSOCIATION

**Associação dos Jornalistas de Macau:** Travessa do Auto Novo 301–303; tel. 75245; Pres. Chiu U Nang.

## Radio and Television

In 1990 there were an estimated 125,000 radio receivers and 35,000 television receivers in use. Macau is within transmission range of the Hong Kong television stations.

**Rádio Comercial Vila Verde:** Rua Francisco Xavier Pereira 133H, 13°; tel. 573355; fax 311668; private radio station; programmes in Chinese; Man. Kok Hoi.

**Teledifusão de Macau, SARL (TDM):** Rua Francisco Xavier Pereira 157-A, CP 446; tel. 335888 (Radio), 519188 (TV); telex 88309; fax 520208; privately-owned; two radio channels: **Radio Macau** (Av. Dr Rodrigo Rodrigues, Edif. Nam Kwong, 7° andar; fax 343220) in Portuguese, broadcasting 24 hours per day, and **Ou Mun Tin Toi** in Chinese, 24 hours per day; also 7.5 hours per day of TV broadcasting in Chinese, 5 hours in Portuguese on **TDM** and **TDM 2° Canal**; Chair. Stanley Ho; Exec. Vice-Chair. Dr Maria do Carmo Figueiredo.

## Finance

(cap. = capital; res = reserves; dep. = deposits; m. = million; brs = branches; amounts in patacas unless otherwise indicated)

### BANKING

Macau has no foreign-exchange controls. The Financial System Act, aiming to improve the reputation of the territory's banks and to comply with international standards, took effect in September 1993.

#### Issuing Authority

**Autoridade Monetária e Cambial de Macau—AMCM** (Monetary and Foreign Exchange Authority of Macau): POB 3017; tel. 325416; fax 325433; f. 1989, to replace the Instituto Emissor de Macau; govt-owned; Pres. Dr José Carlos Rodrigues Nunes.

#### Banks of Issue

**Banco Nacional Ultramarino, SA:** Av. Almeida Ribeiro 2, CP 465; tel. 376644; telex 88202; fax 355653; f. 1864, est. in Macau 1902; Head Office in Lisbon; agent of Macau Government; Gen. Man. Alberto Soares.

**Bank of China:** Bank of China Bldg, Av. Dr Mário Soares; tel. 781828; telex 88231; fax 781833; f. 1950 as Nan Tung Bank, name changed 1987; authorized to issue banknotes from Oct. 1995; Gen. Man. Wang Zhenjun.

#### Other Commercial Banks

**Banco Comercial de Macau, SA:** Rua da Praia Grande 22; tel. 569622; telex 88463; fax 580967; f. 1974; Head Office in Porto; cap. 8,750m. escudos, dep. 206,429m. escudos (Dec. 1993); Chair. Dr M. C. Carvalho Fernandes.

**Banco Delta Asia, SARL:** Av. Conselheiro Ferreira de Almeida 79; tel. 559898; telex 88243; fax 570068; f. 1935; fmrly Banco Hang Sang; cap. 80.0m., res 41.2m., dep. 1,512.1m. (Dec. 1993); Chair. Stanley Au; Gen. Man. Albert Mak.

**Banco Seng Heng, SARL:** Av. da Praia Grande 351; tel. 555222; fax 570758; f. 1972; cap. 150m., dep. 5,493m. (Dec. 1994); Gen. Man. Alex Li; 5 brs.

**Banco Tai Fung, SARL:** Tai Fung Bank Bldg, Av. Almeida Ribeiro 32; tel. 322323; telex 88212; fax 570737; f. 1971; cap. 375m., dep. 9,613m. (Dec. 1994); Chair. Fung Ka York; Gen. Man. Edmund H. W. Ho; 16 brs.

**Banco Totta e Açores, SA** (Portugal): 57 Rua da Praia Grande, 21st Floor, POB 912; tel. 573299; telex 88517; fax 563852; f. 1843; est. in Macau 1982; Gen. Man. Dr João Figueiredo.

**Banco Weng Hang, SARL:** Av. Almeida Ribeiro 21; tel. 335678; telex 88225; fax 576527; f. 1973; cap. 120m., dep. 2,524m. (Dec. 1993); Chair. Tsang Wing-Hong; Gen. Man. and Dir Tam Man Kuen; 8 brs.

**Guangdong Development Bank:** Rua da Praia Grande 35A; tel. 323628; fax 323668; Gen. Man. Li Ro-hong.

**Luso International Banking Ltd:** Av. Dr Mário Soares 47; tel. 378977; telex 88220; fax 578517; f. 1974; cap. 151.5m., res 36.3m., dep. 2,606.8m. (Dec. 1993); Chair. Eugene Ho; Gen. Man. Ip Kai Ming; 13 brs.

#### Foreign Banks

**Bank of America (Macau) Ltd:** Av. Almeida Ribeiro 2F–2G, CP 165; tel. 568821; fax 570386; f. 1937; fmrly Security Pacific Asian Bank (Banco de Cantão); cap. 36m., dep. 381m. (Dec. 1993); Man. Alfred Lau.

**Banque Nationale de Paris** (France): Rua da Praia Grande 25; tel. 562777; telex 88299; fax 560626; f. 1979; Gen. Man. Kenneth Chan.

**Citibank NA** (USA): Rua da Praia Grande 31B-C; tel. 378188; telex 88384; fax 578451; Man. Alex Li.

**Deutsche Bank AG** (Germany): 7/F Nam Wah Commercial Bldg, 1L–1LB Av. Almeida Ribeiro; tel. 378440; telex 88550; fax 304939; Man. Sammy Wong.

**Hongkong and Shanghai Banking Corporation Ltd** (Hong Kong): Rua da Praia Grande 73–75, CP 476; tel. 553669; telex 88205; fax 216469; f. 1972; CEO Tony Frazer.

**Overseas Trust Bank Limited** (Hong Kong): Rua de Santa Clara 5–7E, Edif. Ribeiro, Loja C e D; tel. 329338; telex 88217; fax 323711; Man. Edmund Kwok.

**Standard Chartered Bank** (UK): 16F–17F Edif. Centro Comercial Central, 60–64 Av. Infante D. Henrique; tel. 378271; telex 88518; fax 594134; f. 1982; Man. Ken Y. L. Au.

### Offshore Banks

Offshore banking legislation was implemented in 1987.

**Banco Comercial Português** (Portugal): Av. Dr Mário Soares s/n, Bank of China Bldg, 21st Floor; tel. 786769; fax 786772; Gen. Man. Dr Rui M. M. Semedo.

**Banco Português do Atlântico** (Portugal): Rua da Praia Grande 26, 6th Floor; tel. 84999; telex 88532; fax 595817; f. 1981; Gen. Man. Dr José Morgado.

### Banking Association

**Associação de Bancos de Macau—ABM** (The Macau Association of Banks): Rua da Praia Grande 69A, Edif. 'Finanças', 15/F; tel. 511921; fax 346049; Chair. Edmund Ho Hau-wah.

### INSURANCE

**AIA Co (Bermuda):** Centro Comercial da Praia Grande, 26/F; tel. 5999111; fax 335940; Rep. Jack Li.

**Asia Insurance Co Ltd:** Rm 1103, Luso International Bank Bldg, Av. da Amizade 11; tel. 563166; fax 570438; Rep. S. T. Chan.

**Carlingford Insurance Co Ltd:** Rm 1404, Si Toi Commercial Centre; tel. 373604; fax 373607; Rep. Johnny Ho.

**China Insurance Co Ltd:** Centro Comercial de Praia Grande, 10/F; tel. 378499; telex 88488; fax 570919; Rep. Jiang Ji Dong.

**China Life Insurance Co Ltd:** Centro Comercial de Praia Grande, 24/F; tel. 558918; fax 559348; Rep. Bai Yuanqin.

**Commercial Union Ass. Co Ltd:** Av. Dr Mário Soares s/n, Bank of China Bldg, 18F-A; tel. 787333; fax 786525; Rep. Victor Wu.

**Companhia de Seguros de Macau, SARL:** Centro Comercial de Praia Grande 57, 18/F; tel. 555078; telex 88373; fax 551074; Gen. Man. Alberto Estima de Oliveira.

**Crown Life Insurance Co:** 37 Rua da Praia Grande, 8/F, Block B, Nam Yue Commercial Centre; tel. 570828; fax 570844; Rep. Steven Siu.

**Forex Insurance Co Ltd:** Av. da Praia Grande 51, Edif. Keng Ou, 13° D, tel. 337036; telex 88243; fax 337037; Rep. Eric Sung.

**Insurance Co of North America:** Rm 806–7, Tai Fung Bank Bldg, Av. Almeida Ribeiro; tel. 557191; fax 570188; Rep. James Ho.

**Lombard General Insurance Ltd:** 1L-1LB, Av. Almeida Ribeiro, Edif. Comercial Nam Wah, Rm 601; tel. 573286; fax 556460; Rep. Juliana Io Iok Pok.

**Luen Fung Hang Insurance Co Ltd:** Av. Dr Mário Soares s/n, Bank of China Bldg, 25F-B; tel. 781265; fax 786969; Rep. Si Chi Hok.

**Min Xin Insurance Co Ltd:** Luso International Bank Bldg, 27/F, Rm 2704, Av. da Amizade 11; tel. 305684; fax 305600; Rep. Ming Fai Cheng.

**National Mutual Ins. Co (Bermuda) Ltd:** Commercial Union Ass. Bldg, Rua de Xang Hai 175; tel. 781188; fax 780022; Rep. Trevor Chan.

**QBE Insurance (International) Ltd:** Rm 2003, Luso International Bank Bldg, Rua Dr Pedro José Lobo 11; tel. 567214; fax 580948; Rep. Sally Siu.

**Sumitomo Marine and Fire Insurance Co, Ltd:** Rm 802, Tai Fung Bank Bldg, Av. Almeida Ribeiro 32; tel. 385917; fax 596667; Rep. Carmen Pang.

**Taikoo Royal Insurance Co Ltd:** 15/F, Edif. Banco Comercial de Macau, Rua da Praia Grande 20–22; tel. 577322; fax 577216; Rep. Donald Smith.

**The Wing On Fire & Marine Insurance Co Ltd:** Centro Comercial de Praia Grande, 11/F; tel. 550233; fax 333710; Rep. Hazel Ao.

### Insurers' Association

**Macau Insurers' Association:** Rua da Praia Grande, Edif. 'Finanças', 15F; tel. 511923; fax 337531; Pres. Si Chi Hok.

## Trade and Industry

**Euro-Info Centre Macau:** Av. Dr Rodrigo Rodrigues 223–225, Edif. Nam Kwong, 13° andar F; tel. 713338; fax 713339; promotes trade with EU; Dir Vítor Rosário.

**ICEP:** Av. da Amizade, Edif. Nam Fong, 6° B; tel. 707460; fax 707461; Dir Joaquim Mendonça Moreira.

**Instituto de Promocão do Comércio e do Investimento de Macau** (Macau Trade and Investment Promotion Institute): Luso International Bank Bldg, 7th–8th Floors, Rua Dr Pedro José Lobo 1–3; Investment Promotion: tel. 340090; telex 88413; fax 712659; Export Promotion: tel. 378221; telex 88413; fax 590309; Pres. João Domingos.

**Macau Business Centre:** POB 138, Edif. Ribeiro, Loja D; est. through private initiative.

**World Trade Centre:** Rua de Pequim 183, Edif. Marina Plaza, 5° andar A-B; tel. 565225; telex 88831; fax 563398; f. 1995; Man. Dir António Leça.

### CHAMBER OF COMMERCE

**Associação Comercial de Macau:** Rua de Xangai 175, Edif. ACM, 5° andar; tel. 576833; telex 88229; fax 594513; Pres. Ma Man Kei.

### INDUSTRIAL ASSOCIATIONS

**Associação dos Construtores Civis** (Macau Association of Building Development Cos): Rua do Campo 9–11, 6th Floor A; tel. 573226; fax 345710; Pres. Chui Tak Kei.

**Associação dos Exportadores e Importadores de Macau:** Av. Infante D. Henrique 60–64, 3rd Floor, Centro Comercial 'Central';, tel. 375859; fax 512174; Pres. Vítor Ng.

**Associação dos Industriais de Tecelagem e Fiação de Lã de Macau** (Macau Weaving and Spinning of Wool Manufacturers' Asscn): Av. da Amizade 57–67B, Edif. Kam Wa Kok, 6th Floor A; tel. 553378; fax 511105; Pres. Wong Shoo Kee.

**Associação Industrial de Macau:** Edif. AIM, 17th Floor, Rua Dr Pedro José Lobo 32–36, CP 70; tel. 574125; fax 578305; f. 1959; Pres. Peter Pan.

### TRADE UNIONS

**Macau Federation of Trade Unions:** Rua Ribeira do Patane 2; tel. 576231; fax 553110; Pres. Tong Seng Chun.

## Transport

### RAILWAYS

There are no railways in Macau. A plan to connect Macau with Guangzhou (People's Republic of China) is under consideration.

### ROADS

In 1988 there were 97 km of roads. The peninsula of Macau is linked to the islands of Taipa and Coloane by two bridges (the first being a 2.5-km bridge) and by a 2.2-km causeway respectively. In conjunction with the construction of an airport on Taipa (see below), a new 4.4-km four-lane bridge to the mainland was opened in April 1994. A new road linking Macau with Zhuhai, Guangzhou and Shenzhen, near Hong Kong, was also under construction. The Macau–Guangzhou section was scheduled for completion in 1996.

### SHIPPING

There are representatives of shipping agencies for international lines in Macau. There are passenger and cargo services to the People's Republic of China. Jetfoils and ferries operate a regular service during daylight between Macau and Hong Kong; a jetfoil night service was introduced in 1980. These services carried 14.0m. passengers between Macau and Hong Kong in 1992. A new terminal, handling high-speed ferries, jetfoils and catamarans, opened in late 1993. The new port of Kao-ho, on the island of Coloane, entered into service in 1991.

**Hong Kong Macau Hydrofoil Co Ltd:** Terminal Marítimo de Macau, Piso 2, Sala 2.011B, Av. Amizade Porto Exterior; tel. 726266; fax 726277.

**STDM Shipping Dept:** Terminal Marítimo do Porto Exterior, Av. da Amizade; tel. 726111; fax 726234; Gen. Man. Alan Ho; Exec. Man. Capt. Augusto Lizardo.

### Association

**Associação de Agências de Navegação e Congêneres de Macau:** Av. Horta e Costa 7D-E, CP 6133; tel. 528207; fax 302667; Pres. Vong Kok Seng.

### Port Authority

**Capitania dos Portos de Macau:** Quartel dos Mouros; tel. 559922; fax 511986.

### CIVIL AVIATION

In August 1987 plans were approved for the construction of an international airport, on reclaimed land near the island of Taipa, and work began in 1989. The revised cost of the project was an estimated 7,300m. patacas. The airport was scheduled to be completed by mid-1995 and to be operational by early 1996. In its first year of operation, the airport was expected to handle 2.2m. passengers and 80,000 tons of cargo. A new airline, Air Macau, was formally established in 1994. A helicopter service between Hong Kong and Macau, which commenced in 1990, transported a total of 23,964 passengers in 1992.

**AACM—Macau Civil Aviation Authority:** Rua Dr Pedro José Lobo 1–3, Luso International Bank Bldg, 26th Floor; tel. 511213; fax 338089; Pres. JOSÉ ERNESTO DA COSTA QUEIROZ.

**Concessionária do Aeroporto de Macau—CAM (Sociedade do Aeroporto Internacional de Macau):** Bank of China Bldg, 29th Floor, Av. Dr Mário Soares; tel. 785448; fax 785465; f. 1989; franchise co for design, construction and operation of airport; Chair. Prof. ANTÓNIO DIOGO PINTO.

**Air Macau:** f. 1994; 51% controlled by the Civil Aviation Administration of China (CAAC).

## Tourism

Tourism is now a major industry, a substantial portion of the Government's revenue being derived from the territory's casinos. The other attractions are the cultural heritage, dog-racing, horse-racing, and annual events such as Chinese New Year (January/February), the Macau Arts Festival (February/March), Dragon Boat Festival (June), the Macau International Fireworks Festival (September/October) and the Macau Grand Prix for racing cars and motorcycles (November). Hotel capacity was expected to increase from 7,700 rooms in late 1993 to 10,000 by 1995. In 1994 total tourist arrivals reached 7.8m., of whom almost 6.0m. were arrivals from Hong Kong by sea.

**Macau Government Tourist Office (MGTO):** Direcção dos Serviços de Turismo, Largo do Senado 9, Edif. Ritz, CP 3006; tel. 375156; telex 88338; fax 510104; Dir Eng. JOÃO MANUEL COSTA ANTUNES.

**Associação das Agencias de Turismo de Macau:** Rua de Nagasaki ZAPE, Edif. Xin Hua, 10° andar; tel. 700888; fax 706611; Chair. LEI KUAI.

**Gabinete de Comunicação Social** (Government Information Services): Rua de S. Domingos 1, CP 706; tel. 332886; fax 355426; Dir AFONSO CAMÕES.

**Sociedade de Turismo e Diversões de Macau (STDM), SARL:** Macau; tel. 566065; fax 371981; operates nine casinos, five hotels, tour companies, helicopter and jetfoil services from Hong Kong, etc.; Chair. STANLEY HO.

# QATAR

## Introductory Survey

### Location, Climate, Language, Religion, Flag, Capital

The State of Qatar occupies a peninsula, projecting northwards from the Arabian mainland, on the west coast of the Persian (Arabian) Gulf. It is bordered, to the south, by Saudi Arabia and the United Arab Emirates. The archipelago of Bahrain lies to the north-west. On the opposite side of the Gulf lies Iran. The climate is exceptionally hot in the summer, when temperatures may reach 49°C (120°F), with high humidity on the coast; conditions are relatively mild in the winter. Rainfall is negligible. The official language is Arabic, although English is also spoken in business and official circles. Almost all of the inhabitants are adherents of Islam. Native Qataris, who form less than one-third of the total population, belong mainly to the strictly orthodox Wahhabi sect of Sunni Muslims. The national flag (proportions 28 by 11) is maroon, with a broad vertical white stripe at the hoist, the two colours being separated by a serrated line. The capital is Doha.

### Recent History

Qatar was formerly dominated by the Khalifa family of Bahrain. The peninsula became part of Turkey's Ottoman Empire in 1872, but Turkish forces evacuated Qatar at the beginning of the First World War. The United Kingdom recognized Sheikh Abdullah ath-Thani as Ruler of Qatar, and in 1916 made a treaty with him, providing British protection against aggression in return for supervision of Qatar's external affairs. A 1934 treaty extended fuller British protection to Qatar.

In October 1960 Sheikh Ali ath-Thani, who had been Ruler of Qatar since 1949, abdicated in favour of his son, Sheikh Ahmad ath-Thani. In 1968 the British Government announced its intention to withdraw British forces from the Persian (Arabian) Gulf area by 1971. As a result, Qatar attempted to associate itself with Bahrain and Trucial Oman (now the United Arab Emirates) in a proposed federation. In April 1970 Sheikh Ahmad announced a provisional Constitution for Qatar, providing for a partially-elected Consultative Assembly; however, effective power remained in the monarch's hands. In May the Deputy Ruler, Sheikh Khalifa ath-Thani (a cousin of Sheikh Ahmad), was appointed Prime Minister. After the failure of attempts to agree terms for union with neighbouring Gulf countries, Qatar became fully independent on 1 September 1971, whereupon the Ruler took the title of Amir. The 1916 treaty was replaced by a new treaty of friendship with the United Kingdom.

In February 1972 a bloodless coup in support of Sheikh Khalifa, the Crown Prince and Prime Minister, deposed the Amir. Claiming support from the royal family and the armed forces, Sheikh Khalifa proclaimed himself Amir, while retaining the premiership. He subsequently adopted a policy of wide-ranging social and economic reform, and the previous extravagance and privileges of the royal family were curbed. In accordance with the 1970 Constitution, the Amir appointed an Advisory Council in April 1972 to complement the ministerial Government. The Council was expanded from 20 to 30 members in December 1975 and to 35 members in November 1988. Its term was extended for four years in May 1978, and for further terms of four years in 1982, 1986, 1990 and 1994.

In January 1992 a petition was presented to the Amir in which 50 prominent Qataris demanded the establishment of a consultative assembly that would have legislative authority. The signatories alleged abuse of power in Qatar, and appealed for the reform of the economy and of the education system. They further appealed specifically for the repeal of a law which prevented men with non-Qatari wives from bringing their children into the country.

On 27 June 1995 the Deputy Amir, Heir Apparent, Minister of Defence and Commander-in-Chief of the Armed Forces, Maj.-Gen. Sheikh Hamad bin Khalifa ath-Thani, deposed the Amir in a bloodless coup. Sheikh Hamad proclaimed himself Amir, claiming the support of the royal family and the Qatari people. Sheikh Khalifa, who was in Switzerland at the time of the coup, immediately denounced his son's actions, and vowed to return to Qatar. Although Sheikh Khalifa had effectively granted Sheikh Hamad control of the emirate's affairs in 1992 (with the exception of the treasury), a power struggle was reported to have emerged between the two in the months preceding the coup: Sheikh Khalifa was particularly opposed to his son's notably independent foreign policy (which had led to the strengthening of relations with both Iran and Iraq, and with Israel, thereby jeopardizing relations with Saudi Arabia and the other Gulf states), and had attempted to regain influence in policy decisions. Sheikh Hamad, none the less, reputedly enjoyed widespread support both nationally and internationally, owing to his implementation of domestic reforms (including the rationalization of the armed forces, the reduction of the privileges of members of the royal family and senior officials, and the employment of Qataris in positions previously occupied by foreign nationals), which were perceived to have contributed to the stability of the emirate at a time when social unrest and Islamic fundamentalism were emerging in the region. The United Kingdom and the USA quickly recognized the new Amir; Saudi Arabia endorsed the regime shortly afterwards. In mid-July Sheikh Hamad reorganized the Council of Ministers and appointed himself Prime Minister, while retaining the posts of Minister of Defence and Commander-in-Chief of the Armed Forces.

In early 1981 Qatar joined the newly-established Co-operation Council for the Arab States of the Gulf (generally known as the Gulf Co-operation Council—GCC, see p. 130), which aims to improve economic co-operation in the region. Co-operation in defence is also a priority for Qatar, whose own defences are relatively weak. In June 1992 Qatar followed Kuwait and Bahrain in signing a defence pact with the USA. In mid-1993 Qatar and the United Kingdom signed a memorandum of understanding on defence, and defence procurement agreements were subsequently signed with the United Kingdom and France. In March 1995 Qatar signed an agreement with the USA, in which the USA was given permission to preposition military equipment in the emirate.

In April 1986 Qatari military forces raided the island of Fasht ad-Dibal, which had been artificially constructed on a coral reef (submerged at high tide), situated midway between Bahrain and Qatar; both countries claimed sovereignty over the island. During the raid Qatar seized 29 foreign workers who were constructing a Bahraini coastguard station on the island. Officials of the GCC met representatives from both states in an attempt to reconcile them and to avoid a split within the Council, and in May the workers were released and the two Governments agreed to destroy the island. Other areas of dispute between the two countries are Zubara, in mainland Qatar, and the area of the Hawar islands, which is believed to contain reserves of petroleum and natural gas. In July 1991 Qatar instituted proceedings at the International Court of Justice (ICJ) regarding the issue of the Hawar islands (in 1939 a British judgement had awarded sovereignty of the islands to Bahrain), the shoals of Dibal and Qit'at Jaradah (over which the British had recognized Bahrain's 'sovereign rights' in 1947), together with the delimitation of the maritime border between Qatar and Bahrain. In September 1991 Qatar protested that a Bahraini gunboat had opened fire on a Qatari vessel in Qatar's territorial waters (a claim that was refuted by Bahrain). Bahrain's insistence that the two countries seek joint recourse to the ICJ was rejected by Qatar, and the matter was further confused in April 1992, when the Government of Qatar issued a decree redefining its maritime borders to include territorial waters claimed by Bahrain. It was also reported that Bahrain had attempted to widen the issue to include its claim to the area around Zubara. In February 1994 a hearing of the ICJ opened in The Hague, the Netherlands, with the aim of determining whether the court had jurisdiction to give a ruling on the dispute. In July the ICJ requested that Qatar and Bahrain resubmit their dispute by 30 November, either jointly or separately. However, the two countries failed to reach agreement on presenting the dispute to the Court, and at the end of November Qatar submitted a unilateral request to continue its case through the ICJ. In February

1995, while the ICJ declared that it would have authority to adjudicate in the dispute (despite Bahrain's refusal to accept the principle of an ICJ ruling), Saudi Arabia also proposed to act as mediator between the two countries. Sheikh Hamad, then Deputy Amir and Heir Apparent, subsequently indicated that Qatar would be willing to withdraw the case from the ICJ if Saudi arbitration proved successful.

Qatar consistently supported Iraq during the Iran–Iraq war (1980–88). In August 1990, however, Qatar was among the Arab states that condemned Iraq's forcible annexation of Kuwait. In late August it was announced that Qatar would allow the deployment of foreign forces on its territory, as part of the multinational attempt to bring about an Iraqi withdrawal from Kuwait. US, Canadian, French and Egyptian military aircraft and personnel were subsequently deployed in Qatar. Units of the Qatari armed forces later participated in the military operation to liberate Kuwait in January–February 1991. Qatar resumed tentative contact with Iraq in 1993, and in February 1994, following the screening on Qatari television of reports depicting the severe economic hardships in Iraq as a result of UN economic sanctions (imposed in August 1990), Kuwait temporarily recalled its Ambassador from Qatar in protest at the apparent *rapprochement* of Qatar and Iraq. In March 1995, during the first official visit to the country by a senior Iraqi official since the Gulf War, the Iraqi Minister of Foreign Affairs, Muhammad Saeed as-Sahaf, attended a meeting with his Qatari counterpart, Sheikh Hamad bin Jaber ath-Thani, to discuss the furtherance of bilateral relations. At a press conference at the end of the visit, the Qatari minister indicated Qatar's determination to pursue a foreign policy independent from that of its GCC neighbours when he announced his country's support for the ending of UN sanctions against Iraq. In 1994 Qatar also strengthened its relations with Iran in the areas of defence and economic co-operation, and with Jordan in cultural, political and commercial matters.

In September 1992 tension arose with Saudi Arabia (with which Qatar has generally enjoyed close links) when Qatar accused Saudi forces of attacking the Qatari border post of al-Khofous, killing two border guards and capturing a third in the process. In protest, in October Qatar suspended a 1965 border agreement with Saudi Arabia (which had never been fully ratified) and temporarily withdrew its 200-strong contingent from the Saudi-based GCC 'Peninsula Shield' force (at the time stationed in Kuwait). The Saudi Government denied the involvement of its armed forces, claiming that the incident had been caused by fighting between rival Bedouin tribes within Saudi territory. In October it was reported that relations between the two countries had improved as a result of mediation by Kuwait, and the Qatari hostage was released; Qatar nevertheless registered its disaffection by not attending meetings of GCC ministers which took place in Abu Dhabi and Kuwait in November. In December, however, after mediation by President Hosni Mubarak of Egypt, Sheikh Khalifa and King Fahd of Saudi Arabia signed an agreement whereby a committee was to be established formally to demarcate the border between the two states by the end of 1993. Qatar subsequently resumed attendance of GCC sessions. By mid-1995, however, the border between Qatar and Saudi Arabia had yet to be officially demarcated. In November 1994 Qatar boycotted a meeting in Saudi Arabia of GCC ministers of the interior, in protest at what it alleged to have been armed incidents on the border with Saudi Arabia in March and October, during one of which a Qatari citizen was reported to have been wounded by Saudi border guards.

In January 1994 Qatar was reported to have commenced discussions with Israel regarding the supply of natural gas to that country, in apparent disregard for the Arab economic boycott of Israel. Following pressure from its GCC allies, Qatar subsequently announced that the proposed sale would depend on a feasibility study and on Israel's withdrawal from all Arab territories occupied in 1967. In late September, however, Qatar, along with the other GCC states, revoked aspects of the economic boycott of Israel. In early November the Israeli Deputy Minister of Foreign Affairs, Yossi Beilin, made an official visit to Qatar, and in December negotiations were reported to be in progress on the establishment of an Israeli interests office in Doha.

### Government

Qatar is an absolute monarchy, with full powers vested in the Amir as Head of State. A provisional Constitution took effect in 1970. Executive power is exercised by the Council of Ministers, which is appointed by the Head of State, who is also Prime Minister. An Advisory Council was formed in April 1972, with 20 nominated members, and was expanded to 30 members in December 1975 and to 35 members in November 1988. The Advisory Council's constitutional entitlements include the power to debate legislation drafted by the Council of Ministers before ratification and promulgation. It also has the power to request ministerial statements on matters of general and specific policy, including the draft budget. Qatar has no legislature or political parties.

### Defence

In June 1994 the armed forces comprised 10,100 men: an army of 8,500, a navy of 800 (including Marine Police) and an air force of 800. Estimated defence expenditure for 1994 was QR 1,100m.

### Economic Affairs

In 1993, according to estimates by the World Bank, Qatar's gross national product (GNP), measured at average 1991–93 prices, was US $7,871m., equivalent to $15,140 per head. During 1985–93, it was estimated, GNP per head declined, in real terms, at an annual average rate of 0.7% per year. This decrease was partly attributable to a high rate of population growth, which averaged 5.3% per year over the same period (caused mainly by an influx of immigrant labour). Non-Qataris account for more than 70% of the total population. Qatar's gross domestic product (GDP) declined, in real terms, at an average rate of 4.1% per year in 1980–85, but increased by an annual average of 1.0% in 1985–89. Real GDP reportedly decreased by 9.3% in 1991; however, it increased by 5.0% in 1992, before declining again by 2.0% and 1.0% in 1993 and 1994, respectively.

Agriculture (including fishing) contributed an estimated 1.0% of GDP in 1993, and employed 3.1% of the economically active population at March 1986. All agricultural land is owned by the Government. The principal crops are cereals, vegetables and dates. Qatar is self-sufficient in winter vegetables and nearly self-sufficient in summer vegetables. Some vegetables are exported to other Gulf countries. Official figures, released in early 1990, indicated that 60% of milk, 80% of fish and 8% of cereal requirements were produced domestically. Livestock-rearing is also important. Agricultural GDP increased by an annual average of 4.8% in 1980–85, and by 1.6% per year in 1985–89.

Industry (including mining, manufacturing, construction and power) contributed an estimated 49.8% of GDP in 1993, and employed 32.2% of the economically active population at March 1986. Industrial GDP decreased by an annual average of 6.7% in 1980–85; no further decline was registered over the period 1985–89.

The petroleum sector contributed 32.4% of GDP in 1993, and mining and quarrying employed 2.4% of the economically active population at March 1986. Petroleum is currently the major mineral export, but proven recoverable crude petroleum reserves in January 1994 were only 3,700m. barrels (sufficient to maintain production for just less than 21 years at 1993 levels). In late 1993 Qatar accepted a new production quota within the Organization of the Petroleum Exporting Countries (OPEC, see p. 210) of 378,000 barrels per day (b/d); production averaged about 390,000 b/d in 1994, slightly above the OPEC quota. Several types of petroleum products are produced, including light gas oil, fuel oil, and gasoline. There are two oil refineries. There are proven gas reserves of 6,428,000m. cu m, at January 1992, in the North Field, the world's largest gas reserve not associated with petroleum. Extraction of gas from the North Field began in September 1991, initially at a rate of some 22.67m. cu m per day (mainly for domestic consumption).

Non-petroleum manufacturing contributed an estimated 11.2% of GDP in 1993, and employed 6.9% of the economically active population at March 1986. In 1991 the major sectors of manufacturing as a whole (measured by gross value of output) were petroleum-refining (32.3% of the total), industrial chemicals (31.8%), and iron and steel (13.0%). Other important activities include the production of flour, cement, concrete, plastics and paint.

Petroleum was the principal source of energy until the early 1990s, but was to be replaced by gas following the inauguration of the North Field. Solar energy is being developed in conjunction with desalination. Exports of crude petroleum accounted for 70% of total exports in 1992.

In 1993 Qatar recorded a trade surplus of QR 4,931m., but there was a deficit of QR 1,809m. on the current account of the balance of payments. In 1993 the principal source of imports (16.4%) was Japan; other important suppliers in that year were the USA and the United Kingdom. In 1989 Japan took 19% of Qatar's exports. The principal export is petroleum. Among the principal imports in 1993 were machinery and transport equipment, basic manufactures, food and live animals, miscellaneous manufactured articles and chemicals.

Budget estimates for 1995/96 envisaged a deficit of QR 3,531m., compared with an estimated deficit of QR 3,471m. in the previous financial year. Qatar's total external debt was estimated at US $619m. in 1987. The annual rate of inflation averaged 3.6% in 1986–91; consumer prices increased by an annual average of 3.1% in 1992, but decreased by an average of 0.9% in 1993. The Qatari economy is dependent on immigrant workers, owing to a shortage of indigenous labour.

Other than its membership of OPEC, Qatar is a member of the Organization of Arab Petroleum Exporting Countries (OAPEC, see p. 207), the Arab Fund for Economic and Social Development (AFESD, see p. 237), the Arab Monetary Fund (see p. 237) and the Islamic Development Bank (see p. 180). In April 1994 Qatar became a contracting party to the General Agreement on Tariffs and Trade (see p. 64—to be superseded by the World Trade Organization).

The Qatari economy is based on the production and export of petroleum, although it seems certain that the production and export of natural gas will eclipse the petroleum sector within the next decade. In 1986 the collapse in world prices for crude petroleum led to economic recession in Qatar, but by 1988 prices had revived, and trading conditions in the region improved following the cease-fire in the Iran–Iraq war in August. The development of the North Field gas project is of prime importance to the future of the economy, which, despite efforts at diversification, will remain dependent on the hydrocarbons sector for the foreseeable future. Government policy for the 1990s aimed to develop energy-intensive heavy industries using gas, to encourage the participation of private enterprise in industries hitherto controlled by the State, and to direct private-sector investment into new small and medium-sized industries. In mid-1994 the Government announced a 10% reduction in total expenditure in the 1994/95 budget, following a decrease in revenue from petroleum caused by declining international prices for that commodity. The Government was also reported to be considering the introduction of treasury bonds to finance future budget deficits.

### Social Welfare

Free health services are provided to all residents, whether Qatari or non-Qatari, and fixed monthly allowances are paid to widows, divorcees, orphans and the elderly. In 1993 Qatar had three government hospitals, with a total of 1,103 beds, and there were 784 physicians working in official medical services. The Hamad General Hospital has 582 beds. In 1993 there were 24 health centres and four out-patient clinics. There is a hospital for women, offering 272 beds. The 1995/96 budget allocated QR 280m. to social services and health (2.2% of total government expenditure).

### Education

A state education system was introduced in 1956. Education is free at all levels, although not compulsory. Primary education begins at six years of age and lasts for six years. The next level of education, beginning at the age of 12, is divided into two cycles of three years (preparatory and secondary). In 1992 the equivalent of 95% of children in the relevant age-group (boys 98%; girls 91%) were enrolled at primary schools, while the comparable ratio for secondary enrolment was equivalent to 88% (boys 86%; girls 91%). In the academic year 1993/94 there were 7,351 students and a teaching staff of 636 at the University of Qatar. The 1995/96 budget allocated QR 85m. to education and youth welfare. The average rate of adult illiteracy in 1986 was 24.3% (males 23.2%; females 27.5%).

### Public Holidays

**1995:** 1 February* (Ramadan begins), 22 February (Anniversary of the Amir's Accession), 3 March* (Id al-Fitr, end of Ramadan), 10 May* (Id al-Adha, Feast of the Sacrifice), 31 May* (Islamic New Year), 3 September (National Day), 20 December* (Leilat al-Meiraj, Ascension of the Prophet).

**1996:** 22 January* (Ramadan begins), 21 February* (Id al-Fitr, end of Ramadan), 22 February (Anniversary of the Amir's Accession), 29 April* (Id al-Adha, Feast of the Sacrifice), 19 May* (Islamic New Year), 3 September (National Day), 8 December* (Leilat al-Meiraj, Ascension of the Prophet).

\* These holidays are dependent on the Islamic lunar calendar and may differ by one or two days from the dates given.

### Weights and Measures

The metric system has been adopted legally, but imperial measures are still used.

# Statistical Survey

Source (unless otherwise stated): Press and Publications Dept, Ministry of Information, POB 5147, Doha; telex 4552.

### AREA AND POPULATION

**Area:** 11,437 sq km (4,416 sq miles).

**Population:** 369,079 (males 247,852; females 121,227) at census of 16 March 1986; 559,208 (official estimate) at mid-1993.

**Density:** 48.9 per sq km (mid-1993).

**Principal Towns** (population at March 1986): Doha (capital) 217,294; Rayyan 91,996; Wakrah 23,682; Umm Salal 11,161.

**Births, Marriages and Deaths** (1993): Registered live births 10,822 (birth rate 19.4 per 1,000); Registered marriages 1,570 (marriage rate 2.8 per 1,000); Registered deaths 913 (death rate 1.6 per 1,000).

**Expectation of Life** (UN estimates, years at birth, 1985–90): 68.6 (males 66.9; females 71.8). Source: UN, *World Population Prospects: The 1992 Revision.*

**Economically Active Population** (persons aged 15 years and over, March 1986): Agriculture and fishing 6,283; Mining and quarrying 4,807; Manufacturing 13,914; Electricity, gas and water 5,266; Building and construction 40,523; Trade, restaurants and hotels 21,964; Transport and communications 7,357; Finance, insurance and real estate 3,157; Social and community services 96,466; Activities not adequately defined 501; Total employed 200,238. **Mid-1993** (estimate): Total labour force 233,000 (Source: FAO, *Production Yearbook*).

### AGRICULTURE, ETC.

**Principal Crops** ('000 metric tons, 1993): Cereals 5.4; Vegetables 36.9; Dates 10.7; Other fruit 1.0.

**Livestock** ('000 head, 1993): Horses 1.3; Cattle 11.7; Camels 42.9; Sheep 165.5; Goats 142.3; Deer 4.4; Chickens 3.1.

**Livestock Products** ('000 metric tons, 1993): Beef and veal 2.6; Poultry meat 3.7; Milk and dairy products 29.9; Hen eggs 3.3.

**Fishing** (metric tons, live weight, 1993): Total catch 6,994.

### MINING

**Production** ('000 metric tons, unless otherwise indicated, 1991): Crude petroleum 18,831; Natural gas (petajoules) 339; Natural gasolene 180 (estimate). Source: UN, *Industrial Statistics Yearbook.*

### INDUSTRY

**Production** ('000 metric tons, unless otherwise indicated, 1990): Wheat flour 112; Nitrogenous fertilizers (nitrogen content) 761 (official figure); Jet fuels 427 (1991); Motor spirit (petrol) 399 (1991); Distillate fuel oils 702 (1991); Residual fuel oils 943 (1991); Liquefied petroleum gas 1,360 (estimate, 1991); Cement 354 (official figure, 1992); Steel bars 588 (1992); Electric energy 5,525 million kWh (official figure, 1993). Source: mainly UN, *Industrial Statistics Yearbook.*

## FINANCE

**Currency and Exchange Rates:** 100 dirhams = 1 Qatar riyal (QR). *Sterling and Dollar Equivalents* (31 December 1994): £1 sterling = 5.695 riyals; US $1 = 3.640 riyals; 100 Qatar riyals = £17.56 = $27.47. *Exchange Rate:* Since June 1980 the rate has been fixed at US $1 = QR 3.64.

**Budget** (QR million, year ending 31 March): 1991/92: *Revenue:* 10,369; *Expenditure:* 11,773; 1992/93 (estimates): *Revenue* 12,250; *Expenditure* 12,866; 1993/94 (estimates): *Revenue* 10,865; *Expenditure* 13,291; 1994/95 (estimates): *Revenue* 8,359; *Expenditure* 11,830; 1995/96 (estimates): *Revenue* 9,204; *Expenditure* 12,735.

**International Reserves** (US $ million at 31 December 1993): Gold 41.5; IMF special drawing rights 25.6; Reserve position in IMF 46.4; Foreign exchange 621.7; Total 735.2. Source: IMF, *International Financial Statistics*.

**Money Supply** (QR million at 31 December 1993): Currency outside banks 1,337.2; Demand deposits at commercial banks 2,805.4; Total money 4,142.6.

**Cost of Living** (Consumer Price Index for Doha; base: 1988 = 100): 111.1 in 1991; 114.5 in 1992; 113.5 in 1993.

**Expenditure on the Gross Domestic Product** (estimates, QR million at current prices, 1993): Government final consumption expenditure 9,350; Private final consumption expenditure 8,623; Increase in stocks 450; Gross fixed capital formation 5,100; *Total domestic expenditure* 23,523; Exports of goods and services 12,030; *Less* Imports of goods and services 9,370; *GDP in purchasers' values* 26,183.

**Gross Domestic Product by Economic Activity** (preliminary estimates, QR million at current prices, 1993): Agriculture and fishing 273; Petroleum sector 8,480; Non-petroleum manufacturing 2,930; Electricity and water 350; Construction 1,290; Trade, restaurants and hotels 1,790; Transport and communications 880; Finance, insurance, real estate and business services 3,185; Other services 7,005; Total 26,183.

**Balance of Payments** (estimates, QR million, 1993): Exports f.o.b. 11,813; Imports c.i.f. −6,882; Trade balance 4,931; Services, private and official transfers (net) −6,740; Current balance −1,809; Capital (net) −161; Overall balance −1,970.

## EXTERNAL TRADE

**Imports c.i.f.** (QR million): 6,261 in 1991; 7,336 in 1992; 6,882 in 1993.

**Exports f.o.b.** (QR million): 11,684 in 1991; 13,980 in 1992; 11,813 in 1993.

**Principal Commodities** (distribution by SITC, QR million, 1993): *Imports c.i.f.:* Food and live animals 884.8; Crude materials (inedible) except fuels 174.7; Chemicals and related products 538.8; Basic manufactures 1,321.6; Machinery and transport equipment 2,915.2; Miscellaneous manufactured articles 881.6; Total (incl. others) 6,882.1.

**Principal Trading Partners** (QR million): *Imports* (1993): Australia 138.7; France 235.7; Germany 549.2; India 196.2; Italy 311.3; Japan 1,129.6; Republic of Korea 131.6; Netherlands 167.0; Saudi Arabia 366.0; United Arab Emirates 495.2; United Kingdom 708.2; USA 801.4; Total (incl. others) 6,882.1. *Exports* (petroleum only, 1983): France 708.0; Federal Republic of Germany 403.0; Italy 806.0; Japan 5,119.7; Spain 620.9; Total (incl. others) 10,893.

## TRANSPORT

**Road Traffic** (licensed vehicles, 1993): Government 5,169; Private 130,570; Public Transport 58,765; Heavy vehicles 4,197; Taxis 1,574; Motorcycles 2,851; Trailers 1,939; General transport 787; Total 205,852.

**Shipping** (international sea-borne freight traffic, '000 metric tons, 1990): *Goods loaded:* 18,145; *Goods unloaded:* 2,588. Source: UN, *Monthly Bulletin of Statistics*; (shipping fleet, '000 gross registered tons, mid-1992): 125. Source: UN, *Statistical Yearbook*.

**Civil Aviation** (scheduled services 1992): Kilometres flown 16 million; Passengers carried 981,000; Passenger-km 1,922 million; Total ton-km 252 million. Figures include an apportionment (one-quarter) of the traffic of Gulf Air, a multinational airline with its headquarters in Bahrain. Source: UN, *Statistical Yearbook*.

## TOURISM

**Tourist arrivals** (1992): 141,000. Source: UN, *Statistical Yearbook*.

**Hotel beds** (1993): 2,366.

## COMMUNICATIONS MEDIA

**Radio Receivers** (1992): 201,000 in use*.
**Television Receivers** (1992): 205,000 in use*.
**Telephones** (1993): 110,300 lines in use.
**Daily Newspapers** (1993): 4.
**Non-daily Newspapers** (1993): 1.
**Book Titles Published** (1992): 372*.

* Source: UNESCO, *Statistical Yearbook*.

## EDUCATION

**Pre-primary** (1992): 57 schools; 348 teachers; 5,905 pupils.
**Primary** (1992): 160 schools; 4,917 teachers; 49,059 pupils.
**Secondary** (1992): 5,016 teachers (general 4,888, vocational 128); 35,013 pupils (general 34,231, vocational 782).
**University** (1993/94): 636 teaching staff; 7,351 students.
Source: mainly UNESCO, *Statistical Yearbook*.

# Directory

## The Constitution

A provisional Constitution was adopted on 2 April 1970. Executive power is vested in the Amir, as Head of State, and exercised by the Council of Ministers, appointed by the Head of State, who is also Prime Minister. The Amir is assisted by the appointed Advisory Council of 20 members (increased to 30 in December 1975 and to 35 in November 1988), whose term was extended for six years in May 1975, for a further four years in May 1978, and for further terms of four years in 1982, 1986, 1990 and 1994. All fundamental democratic rights are guaranteed. In December 1975 the Advisory Council was granted power to summon individual ministers to answer questions on legislation before promulgation. Previously the Advisory Council was restricted to debating draft bills and regulations before framing recommendations to the Council of Ministers.

## The Government

### HEAD OF STATE

**Amir:** Maj.-Gen. Sheikh HAMAD BIN KHALIFA ATH-THANI (assumed power 27 June 1995).

### COUNCIL OF MINISTERS
(July 1995)

**Prime Minister, Minister of Defence and Commander-in-Chief of the Armed Forces:** Maj.-Gen. Sheikh HAMAD BIN KHALIFA ATH-THANI.

**Deputy Prime Minister and Minister of the Interior:** Sheikh ABDULLAH BIN KHALIFA ATH-THANI.

**Minister of State for Amiri Diwan (Royal Court) Affairs:** Sheikh HAMAD BIN SUHAIM ATH-THANI.

**Minister of Foreign Affairs:** Sheikh HAMAD BIN JASIM BIN JABER ATH-THANI.

**Minister of Finance, Economy and Trade:** Sheikh MUHAMMAD BIN KHALIFA ATH-THANI.

**Minister of State:** Sheikh AHMAD BIN SAIF ATH-THANI.

**Minister of State for Defence Affairs and Deputy Commander-in-Chief of the Armed Forces:** Sheikh HAMAD BIN ABDULLAH ATH-THANI.

**Minister of Awqaf (Religious Endowments) and Islamic Affairs:** Sheikh ABDULLAH BIN KHALID ATH-THANI.

**Minister of Municipal Affairs and Agriculture:** Sheikh AHMAD BIN HAMAD ATH-THANI.

**Minister of State for Council of Ministers Affairs:** Sheikh MUHAMMAD BIN KHALID ATH-THANI.

QATAR

**Minister of Communication and Transport:** ABDULLAH BIN SALEH AL-MANEI.
**Minister of Education:** ABD AL-AZIZ ABDULLAH TURKI.
**Minister of Electricity and Water:** AHMAD MUHAMMAD ALI AS-SUBAY'I.
**Minister of Energy and Industry:** ABDULLAH BIN HAMAD AL-ATTIYA.
**Minister of Information and Culture:** Dr HAMAD ABD AL-AZIZ HAMAD AL-KUWARI.
**Minister of Health:** ALI SAID AL-KHAYARIN.
**Minister of Justice:** Dr NAJIB MUHAMMAD AN-NUAIMI.
**Minister of State for Foreign Affairs:** AHMAD ABDULLAH AL-MAHMOUD.

### MINISTRIES

**Ministry of Amiri Diwan Affairs:** POB 923, Doha; tel. 468333; telex 4297; fax 412617.
**Ministry of Awqaf (Religious Endowments) and Islamic Affairs:** POB 232, Doha; tel. 466222; fax 327383.
**Ministry of Communication and Transport:** POB 3416, Doha; tel. 464000; telex 4800; fax 835888.
**Ministry of Defence:** Qatar Armed Forces, POB 37, Doha; tel. 404111; telex 4245.
**Ministry of Education:** POB 80, Doha; tel. 413444; telex 4316; fax 351780.
**Ministry of Electricity and Water:** POB 41, Doha; tel. 326622; telex 4478; fax 420048.
**Ministry of Energy and Industry:** POB 2599, Doha; tel. 832121; telex 4323.
**Ministry of Finance, Economy and Trade:** POB 83, Doha; tel. 434888; telex 4315; fax 413617.
**Ministry of Foreign Affairs:** POB 250, Doha; tel. 415000; telex 4577; fax 426279.
**Ministry of Information and Culture:** POB 1836, Doha; tel. 831333; telex 4229; fax 831518.
**Ministry of the Interior:** POB 920, Doha; tel. 330000; telex 4383.
**Ministry of Justice:** POB 917 (Dept of Legal Affairs), Doha; tel. 427444; telex 4238; fax 832868.
**Ministry of Labour, Social Affairs and Housing:** POB 201, Doha; tel. 321934; telex 4227; fax 432929.
**Ministry of Municipal Affairs and Agriculture:** POB 2727, Doha; tel. 413535; telex 4476; fax 413233.
**Ministry of Public Health:** POB 42, Doha; tel. 441555; telex 4261; fax 429565.

### ADVISORY COUNCIL

The Advisory Council was established in April 1972, with 20 nominated members. It was expanded to 30 members in December 1975, and to 35 members in November 1988.

**Speaker:** ALI BIN KHALIFA AL-HITMI.

## Diplomatic Representation

### EMBASSIES IN QATAR

**Algeria:** POB 2494, Doha; tel. 662900; telex 4604; fax 663658; Ambassador: HADEF BOUTHALDJA.
**Bangladesh:** POB 2080, Doha; tel. 671927; telex 5102; fax 671190; Ambassador: Dr IFTEKHAR AHMED CHOUDHURY.
**China, People's Republic:** POB 17200, Doha; tel. 824200; telex 5120; fax 873959; Ambassador: TAN SHENGCHENG.
**Egypt:** POB 2899, Doha; tel. 832555; telex 4321; fax 832196; Ambassador: MOSTAFA MAHMOUD HUSSEIN.
**France:** POB 2669, Doha; tel. 832281; telex 4280; fax 832254; Ambassador: HENRI DENIAUD.
**Germany:** POB 3064, Doha; tel. 671100; telex 4528; fax 670011; Ambassador: KLAUS SCHRÖDER.
**India:** POB 2788, Doha; tel. 672021; telex 4646; fax 670448; Ambassador: K. P. FABIAN.
**Iran:** POB 1633, Doha; tel. 835300; telex 4251; fax 831665; Ambassador: SEYED BAGHER SAKHAIE.
**Iraq:** POB 1526, Doha; tel. 662244; telex 4296; Ambassador: ANWAR SABRI ADL AR-RAZZAQ.
**Italy:** POB 4188, Doha; tel. 436842; telex 5133; fax 446466; Ambassador: MARIO BONDIOLI-OSIO.
**Japan:** POB 2208, Doha; tel. 831224; telex 4339; fax 832178; Ambassador: KOICHI KIMURA.

**Jordan:** POB 2366, Doha; tel. 832202; telex 4192; fax 832173; Ambassador: TRAD EL-FAYEZ.
**Korea, Republic:** POB 3727, Doha; tel. 832238; telex 4105; fax 833264; Ambassador: NAM JOON CHOI.
**Kuwait:** POB 1177, Doha; tel. 832111; telex 4113; fax 832042; Ambassador: MUHAMMAD AHMAD AL-MIGRIN AR-ROUMI.
**Lebanon:** POB 2411, Doha; tel. 444468; telex 4404; fax 324817; Chargé d'affaires: ZOUHER AL-CHOKER.
**Mauritania:** POB 3132, Doha; tel. 670458; telex 4379; fax 670455; Ambassador: OUTHMAN OULD SHEIKH AHMED ABU AL-MAALY.
**Morocco:** POB 3242, Doha; tel. 831885; telex 4473; fax 833416; Ambassador: ABBES BERRADA SOUNNI.
**Oman:** POB 3766, Doha; tel. 670744; telex 4341; fax 670747; Ambassador: SAID BIN ALI BIN SALIM AL-KALBANI.
**Pakistan:** POB 334, Doha; tel. 832525; fax 832227; Ambassador: Mir MUHAMMED NASEER MENGAL.
**Philippines:** POB 24900, Doha; tel. 831585; fax 831595; Ambassador: ANTONIO B. MAGIBAY.
**Romania:** POB 22511, Doha; tel. 426740; fax 444348; Ambassador: AUREL TURBACEANU.
**Russia:** POB 15404, Doha; tel. 417417; Ambassador: IGOR VELIKHOV.
**Saudi Arabia:** POB 1255, Doha; tel. 427144; telex 4483; fax 883049; Ambassador: ABD AR-RAHMAN ASH-SHUBAILI.
**Somalia:** POB 1948, Doha; tel. 832200; telex 4275; Ambassador: SHARIF MUHAMMAD OMAR.
**Sudan:** POB 2999, Doha; tel. 423007; telex 4707; fax 351366; Ambassador: LIAQUAT MAHMOOD.
**Syria:** POB 1257, Doha; tel. 421873; telex 4447; fax 442167; Chargé d'affaires: ALCHAYCHE TERKAWI.
**Tunisia:** POB 2707, Doha; tel. 832645; telex 4422; fax 832649; Ambassador: M. HEDI DRISSI.
**Turkey:** POB 1977, Doha; tel. 835553; telex 4406; fax 835206; Ambassador: SELCUK TARLAN.
**United Arab Emirates:** POB 3099, Doha; tel. 822833; fax 822837; Ambassador: MUHAMMAD SULTAN EL-ZA'ABI.
**United Kingdom:** POB 3, Doha; tel. 421991; fax 438692; Ambassador: PATRICK FRANCIS MICHAEL WOGAN.
**USA:** POB 2399, Doha; tel. 864701; fax 861669; Ambassador: KENTON KEITH.
**Yemen:** POB 3318, Doha; tel. 432555; telex 5130; fax 429400; Ambassador: ABD AL-WAHAB NASSER JAHAF.

## Judicial System

Justice is administered by five courts (Higher Criminal, Lower Criminal, Commercial and Civil, Labour and the Court of Appeal) on the basis of codified laws. In addition the *Shari'a* Court decides on all issues regarding the personal affairs of Muslims, specific offences where the defendant is Muslim, and civil disputes where the parties elect to have them adjudicated upon, by recourse to Islamic Law of the Holy Quran and the Prophet's Sunna or tradition. Non-Muslims are invariably tried by a court operating codified law. Independence of the judiciary is guaranteed by the provisional Constitution.

**Presidency of Shari'a Courts and Islamic Affairs:** POB 232, Doha; tel. 452222; telex 5115; Pres. Sheikh ABDUL BIN SAID AL-MAHMOUD.

**Chief Justice:** AL-FATEH AWOUDA.

## Religion

The indigenous population are Muslims of the Sunni sect, most being of the strict Wahhabi persuasion.

## The Press

**Al-Ahd** (The Pledge): POB 2531, Doha; tel. 601506; telex 4920; fax 671388; f. 1974; weekly magazine; Arabic; political; publ. by al-Ahd Est. for Journalism, Printing and Publications Ltd; Editor-in-Chief KHALIFA AL-HUSSAINI; circ. 15,000.
**Akhbar al-Usbou'** (News of the Week): POB 4896, Doha; tel. 445561; telex 4234; fax 433778; f. 1986; weekly magazine; Arabic; socio-political; publ. by Ali bin Ali Printing and Publishing Est.; Editor-in-Chief ADEL ALI BIN ALI; circ. 15,000.
**Al-'Arab** (The Arabs): POB 633, Doha; tel. 325874; telex 4497; fax 429424; f. 1972; daily; Arabic; publ. by Dar al-Ouroba Printing and Publishing; Editor-in-Chief KHALID NAAMA; circ. 20,000.

# QATAR

**Ad-Dawri** (The Tournament): POB 310, Doha; tel. 447039; fax 447039; f. 1978; weekly; Arabic; sport; publ. by Abdullah Hamad al-Atiyah and Ptnrs; Editor-in-Chief Sheikh RASHID BIN OWAIDA ATH-THANI; circ. 2,000.

**Gulf Times:** POB 2888, Doha; tel. 350478; telex 4600; fax 350474; f. 1978; daily and weekly editions; English; political; publ. by Gulf Publishing and Printing Org.; Editor-in-Chief ABD AR-RAHMAN SAIF AL-MADHADI; circ. 15,000 (daily).

**Al-Jawhara** (The Jewel): POB 2531, Doha; tel. 423526; telex 4920; fax 671388; f. 1977; monthly; Arabic; women's magazine; publ. by al-Ahd Est. for Journalism, Printing and Publications Ltd; Editor-in-Chief ABDULLAH YOUSUF AL-HUSSAINI; circ. 5,000.

**Al-Mash'al** (The Torch): Qatar General Petroleum Corporation, POB 3212, Doha; tel. 491491; telex 4343; fax 831125; f. 1977; 2 a month; Arabic and English; Editor-in-Chief FAISAL A. AS-SUWAIDI; circ. 3,000.

**Al-Murshid** (The Guide): POB 8545, Doha; tel. 429920; telex 4420; fax 447793; f. 1983; bi-monthly; Arabic and English; tourist and commercial information; publ. by Dallah Advertising Agency; Editor-in-Chief RASHID MUHAMMAD AN-NOAIMI; circ. 15,000.

**Nada** (A Gathering): POB 4896, Doha; tel. 445564; telex 4234; fax 433778; f. 1991; weekly; social and entertainment; published by Akhbar al-Usbou'; Editor-in-Chief ADEL ALI BIN ALI.

**Al-Ouroba** (Arabism): POB 633, Doha; tel. 325874; telex 4497; fax 429424; f. 1970; weekly; political; publ. by Dar al-Ouroba Press and Publishing; Editor-in-Chief YOUCEF NAAMA; circ. 12,000.

**Qatar Lil Inshaa** (Qatar Construction): POB 2203, Doha; tel. 424988; telex 4877; fax 432961; f. 1989; publ. by Almaha Trade and Construction Co; Gen. Man. MUHAMMAD H. AL-MIJBER; circ. 10,000.

**Ar-Rayah** (The Banner): POB 3464, Doha; tel. 466555; telex 4600; fax 350476; f. 1979; daily and weekly editions; Arabic; political; publ. by Gulf Publishing and Printing Org.; Editor AHMAD ALI; circ. 25,000.

**Ash-Sharq** (The Orient): POB 3488, Doha; tel. 662444; telex 5103; fax 662450; f. 1985; daily; Arabic; political; publ. by Dar Ash-Sharq Printing, Publishing and Distribution House; Gen. Supervisor NASSER AL-OTHMAN; circ. 40,000.

**At-Tarbiya** (Education): POB 9865, Doha; tel. 861412; telex 4672; fax 820911; f. 1971; quarterly; publ. by Qatar National Commission for Education, Culture and Science; Editor-in-Chief FAHD J. H. ATH-THANI; circ. 2,500.

**This is Qatar and What's On:** POB 3272, Doha; tel. 413813; telex 4787; fax 413814; f. 1978; quarterly; English; tourist and information; publ. by Oryx Publishing and Advertising Co (Qatar); Editor-in-Chief ALWALEED Y. AL-DARNISH; circ. 10,000.

### NEWS AGENCY

**Qatar News Agency (QNA):** POB 3299, Doha; tel. 450450; telex 4394; fax 439362; f. 1975; Dir and Editor-in-Chief AHMAD JASSIM AL-HUMAR.

## Publishers

There are more than 25 publishing houses in Qatar.

**Qatar National Printing Press:** POB 355, Doha; tel. 448452; telex 4072; Propr KHALED BIN NASSER AS-SUWAIDI; Dir ABD AL-KARIM DIB.

## Radio and Television

In 1992, according to UNESCO, an estimated 201,000 radio receivers and 205,000 television receivers were in use.

### RADIO

**Qatar Broadcasting Service (QBS):** POB 3939, Doha; tel. 894444; telex 4597; fax 822888; f. 1968; government service transmitting in Arabic, English, French and Urdu; Dir MUBARAK JAHAM AL-KUWARI.

### TELEVISION

**Qatar Television Service:** POB 1944, Doha; tel. 894444; telex 4040; fax 874170; f. 1970; 200 kW transmitters began transmissions throughout the Gulf in 1972. Colour transmissions began in 1974. There are eight channels. Dir SA'AD MUHAMMAD AL-RUMAIHI; Asst. Dir ABD AL-WAHAB MUHAMMAD AL-MUTAWA'A.

## Finance

(cap. = capital; res = reserves; dep. = deposits; m. = million; brs = branches; amounts in Qatar riyals unless otherwise stated)

### BANKING

#### Central Bank

**Qatar Central Bank:** POB 1234, Doha; tel. 456456; telex 4335; fax 413650; f. 1966 as Qatar and Dubai Currency Board; became Qatar Monetary Agency in 1973; renamed Qatar Central Bank in 1993; cap. 50m., res 133.6m., currency in circulation 1,495m. (1994); Gov. ABDULLAH BIN KHALID AL-ATTIYA; Dep. Gov. Sheikh ABDULLAH BIN SAID ABD AL-AZIZ ATH-THANI.

#### Commercial Banks

**Al-Ahli Bank of Qatar QSC:** POB 2309, Doha; tel. 326611; telex 4884; fax 444652; f. 1984; cap. 60m., res 37.1m., dep. 902.1m., total assets 1,015m. (1991); Chair. Sheikh MUHAMMAD BIN HAMAD ATH-THANI; Gen. Man. TAHA S. OMAR; 3 brs.

**Commercial Bank of Qatar QSC:** Grand Hamad Ave, POB 3232, Doha; tel. 490222; telex 4351; fax 438182; f. 1975; cap. 105.5m., res 147.1m., dep. 1,728.5m., total assets 2,282.7m. (1994); owned 20% by board of directors and 80% by Qatari citizens; Chair. Sheikh ALI BIN JABER ATH-THANI; Gen. Man. T. P. NUNAN; 7 brs.

**Doha Bank Ltd:** POB 3818, Doha; tel. 435444; telex 4534; fax 416631; f. 1979; cap. 78.7m., res 179.3m., dep. 2,332.6m., total assets 2,849.4m. (1993); Chair. ALI BIN SAUD BIN ABD AL-AZIZ ATH-THANI; Gen. Man. MAQBOOL H. KHALFAN; 11 brs.

**Qatar International Islamic Bank:** POB 664, Doha; tel. 436776; telex 4161; fax 444101; f. 1990; cap. 100m. (1993); 2 brs.

**Qatar Islamic Bank SAQ:** POB 559, Doha; tel. 409409; telex 5177; fax 412700; f. 1983; cap. 50m., res 10.8m., dep. 666.1m., total assets 766.2m. (Dec. 1993); Chair. Sheikh ABD AR-RAHMAN BIN ABDULLAH AL-MAHMOUD; Man. Dir KHALID BIN AHMAD AS-SUWAIDI; 4 brs.

**Qatar National Bank SAQ:** POB 1002, Doha; tel. 407407; telex 4212; fax 413753; f. 1965; owned 50% by Government of Qatar and 50% by Qatari nationals; cap. 354.4m., res 1,664.7m., dep. 13,173.3m., total assets 15,268.5m. (1993); Chair. Minister of Finance, Economy and Trade; Man. Dir ABDALLA A. AL-KHATER; 18 brs in Qatar and 4 brs abroad.

#### Foreign Banks

**ANZ Grindlays Bank PLC** (UK): POB 2001, Rayyan Rd, Doha; tel. 418222; telex 4209; fax 428077; f. 1956; total assets 706.3m. (1989); Gen. Man. F. J. GAMBLE.

**Arab Bank PLC** (Jordan): POB 172, Doha; tel. 437979; telex 4202; fax 410774; f. 1957; total assets 958m. (31 Dec. 1989); Regional Man. GHASSAN BUNDAKJI; Dep. Man. SAAD AD-DIN ELAYAN; 2 brs.

**Bank Saderat Iran:** POB 2256, Doha; tel. 414646; telex 4225; fax 430121; f. 1970; Man. M. TAFAZOLI MEHRJERDI.

**Banque Paribas** (France): POB 2636, Doha; tel. 433844; telex 4268; fax 410861; f. 1973; Gen. Man. PIERRE IMHOF.

**British Bank of the Middle East:** POB 57, Doha; tel. 423124; telex 4204; fax 416353; f. 1954; total assets 3,100m. (1994); Gen. Man. J. P. PASCOE; 2 brs.

**Al-Fardan Exchange and Finance Co.:** POB 339, Doha; tel. 426544; telex 4283; fax 417468.

**Mashreq Bank PSC** (UAE): POB 173, Doha; tel. 413213; telex 4235; fax 413880; f. 1971; Gen. Man. ADEL GAAFAR; 40 brs.

**Standard Chartered PLC** (UK): POB 29, Doha; tel. 414252; telex 4217; fax 413739; f. 1950; total assets 428.6m. (1991); Gen. Man. A. R. PARRY.

**United Bank Ltd** (Pakistan): POB 242, Doha; tel. 320216; telex 4222; fax 424600; f. 1970; Gen. Man. and Vice-Pres. RAI MANSOOR AHMAD KHAN.

### INSURANCE

**Al-Khaleej Insurance Co of Qatar (SAQ):** POB 4555, Doha; tel. 414151; telex 4692; fax 430530; f. 1978; authorized and cap. 12m. (1994); all classes except life; Chair. ABDULLAH BIN MUHAMMAD JABER ATH-THANI; Gen. Man. MUHAMMAD NOOR AL-OBAIDLY.

**Qatar General Insurance and Reinsurance Co SAQ:** POB 4500, Doha; tel. 417800; telex 4742; fax 437302; f. 1979; cap. 15m. (1993); all classes; Chair. Sheikh ALI BIN SAUD ATH-THANI; Gen. Man. GHAZI ABU NAHL.

**Qatar Insurance Co SAQ:** POB 666, Doha; tel. 490490; telex 4216; fax 831569; f. 1964; cap. 90m. (1994); all classes; the Government has a majority share; Chair. Sheikh KHALID BIN MUHAMMAD ALI ATH-THANI; Gen. Man. KHALIFA A. AS-SUBAY'I; br in Dubai.

# Trade and Industry

## CHAMBER OF COMMERCE

**Qatar Chamber of Commerce and Industry:** POB 402, Doha; tel. 425131; telex 4078; fax 447905; f. 1963; 17 mems appointed by decree; Pres. Sheikh Hamad bin Jassem bin Mohammed ath-Thani; Dir-Gen. Dr Majid Abdullah al-Malki.

## DEVELOPMENT ORGANIZATION

**Department of Industrial Development:** POB 2599, Doha; tel. 832121; telex 4323; fax 832024; government-owned; conducts research, development and supervision of new industrial projects; Dir-Gen. Majid Abdullah al-Malki.

## STATE ENTERPRISES

**Qatar General Petroleum Corporation (QGPC):** POB 3212, Doha; tel. 491491; telex 4343; fax 831125; f. 1974; cap. QR 5,000m.; the State of Qatar's interest in companies active in petroleum and related industries has passed to the Corporation. In line with OPEC policy, the Government agreed a participation agreement with the Qatar Petroleum Company and Shell Company of Qatar in 1974 to secure Qatar's interest and obtained a 60% interest in both. In late 1976, under two separate agreements, the Government secured a 100% interest in both companies. The Qatar Petroleum Producing Authority (QPPA) was established in 1976 as a subsidiary, wholly owned by the Corporation, to undertake all operations previously conducted by the two companies. In February 1980 the QPPA was merged with the Corporation.

Qatar General Petroleum Corporation wholly or partly owns: National Oil Distribution Co (NODCO), Qatar Fertilizer Co Ltd (QAFCO), Qatar Liquefied Gas Co (QATARGAS), Qatar Petrochemical Co Ltd (QAPCO), Ras Laffan LNG Co, Compagnie Pétrochimique du Nord (COPENOR), Arab Maritime Petroleum Transport Co Ltd, Arab Petroleum Pipelines Co (SUMED), Arab Shipbuilding and Repair Yard Co (ASRY), Arab Petroleum Services Co and Arab Petroleum Investments Corpn (APICORP); Chair. Minister of Energy and Industry; Vice-Chair. Dr Jaber Abd al-Hadi al-Marri.

**National Oil Distribution Co (NODCO):** POB 50033, Umm Said; tel. 776555; telex 4324; fax 771232; operates two refineries with a capacity of 62,000 b/d; responsible for the nationwide distribution of petroleum products; wholly owned by QGPC; Gen. Man. Mahmoud H. al-Hifnawi.

**Qatar Fertilizer Co (QAFCO) SAQ:** POB 50001, Umm Said; tel. 779779; telex 4215; fax 770347; produced 785,000 tons of ammonia and 858,000 tons of urea in 1994; QGPC has a 75% share, Norsk Hydro holds the remaining 25%; Chair. Abdullah H. Salatt; Gen. Man. Faisal M. as-Suwaidi.

**Qatar Liquefied Gas Co (QATARGAS):** POB 22666, Doha; tel. 327121; telex 4500; fax 327144; f. 1984 to develop North Dome field of unassociated gas; cap. QR 500m.; QGPC has a 65% share; Mobil and Total—Cie Française des Pétroles hold 10% each; the Marubeni Corpn and Mitsui and Co of Japan hold 7.5% each; Chair. Minister of Energy and Industry.

**QGPC (Onshore Operations):** Doha; tel. 343287; telex 4253; fax 444554; produces and exports crude petroleum from the Dukhan oilfield and processes and exports natural gas liquids from the onshore and offshore oilfields in Qatar; also responsible for the internal distribution of fuel gas and support services; 182.6m. US barrels of condensate, 223,384 metric tons of butane and 362,180 tons of propane produced in 1987; Man. Dir Jaber al-Marri; Dep. Exec. Man. Ajlan Ali al-Kuwari.

**QGPC (Offshore Operations):** POB 47, Doha; tel. 402000; telex 4201; fax 402584; state-owned organization for offshore oil/gas exploration and production; (now merged with QGPC) average production in 1990 was 188,000 b/d, total approximately 68.7m. barrels; Man. Dir Jaber A. al-Marri; Exec. Man. Muhammad Saud ad-Dolaimi.

**Qatar Petrochemicals Co (QAPCO) SAQ:** POB 756, Doha; tel. 321105; telex 4361; fax 324700; f. 1974; QGPC has an 80% share; 10% is held by ELF-ATOCHEM (France); the remaining 10% is held by ENICHEM (Italy); total assets QR 2,600m.; operation of petrochemical plant at Umm Said (tel. 777111; telex 4871); produced 357,500 tons of ethylene, 185,900 tons of low-density polyethylene, and 62,300 tons of solid sulphur in 1994; Gen. Man. Hamad Rashid al-Mohannadi.

**Qatar Electricity and Water Co (QEWC):** POB 22046, Doha; tel. 410161; fax 326176; f. 1990; manages state-owned utilities.

**Qatar Flour Mills Co SAQ:** POB 1444, Doha; tel. 770452; telex 4285; f. 1968; produced 26,200 metric tons of wheat flour in 1987; Chair. Sheikh Ahmad bin Abdullah ath-Thani; Gen. Man. Ghazi Abd al-Halim as-Salimi.

**Qatar General Poultry Establishment:** POB 3606, Doha; tel. 740042; telex 4348; produces between 1m. and 2.5m. broiler chickens, and between 10m. and 25m. eggs, per year; Dir Ismail Faiti al-Ismail.

**Qatar Steel Co (QASCO):** POB 50090, Steel Mill, Umm Said; tel. 778778; telex 4606; fax 771424; the plant was completed in 1978, and produced 600,000 tons of concrete reinforcing steel bars in 1993; the Government owns a 70% share, with Kobe Steel (20%) and Tokyo Boeki (10%); Chair. Ahmad Muhammad Ali as-Subay'i; Man. Dir Nasser Muhammad al-Mansouri.

**Qatar National Cement Co SAQ:** POB 1333, Doha; tel. 350805; telex 4337; fax 417846; f. 1965; produced 266,393 tons of ordinary Portland cement and 100,174 tons of sulphate-resisting cement in 1991; Chair. Khalifa Abdullah as-Subay'i; Gen. Man. Saeed M. al-Kuwari.

# Transport

## ROADS

In 1991 there were some 1,191 km (740 miles) of surfaced road linking Doha and the petroleum centres of Dukhan and Umm Said with the northern end of the peninsula. A 105-km (65-mile) road from Doha to Salwa was completed in 1970, and joins one leading from Al Hufuf in Saudi Arabia, giving Qatar land access to the Mediterranean. A 418-km (260-mile) highway, built in conjunction with Abu Dhabi, links both states with the Gulf network.

## SHIPPING

Doha Port has four berths of 9.14 m depth and five berths of 7.5 m depth. Total length of berths is 1,699 m. At Umm Said Harbour the Northern Deep Water Wharves consist of a deep-water quay 730 m long with a dredged depth alongside of 15.5 m, and a quay 570 m long with a dredged depth alongside of 13.0 m. The General Cargo Wharves consist of a quay 400 m long with a dredged depth alongside of 10.0 m. The Southern Deep Water Wharves consist of a deep water quay 508 m long with a dredged depth alongside of 13.0 m. Cold storage facilities exist for cargo of up to 500 tons. The North Field gas project has increased the demand for shipping facilities. In 1991 QGPC invested US $800m. in a new industrial port at Ras Laffan. In mid-1993 a major upgrading and expansion of Doha port, at an estimated cost of $150m., was announced.

**Department of Ports, Maritime Affairs and Land Transport:** POB 313, Doha; tel. 457457; telex 4378; fax 413563; Dir of Ports G. A. Genkeer.

**Qatar National Navigation and Transport Co Ltd (QNNTC):** West Bay, Al-Tameen St, POB 153, Doha; tel. 468666; telex 4206; fax 468777; f. 1957; 100%-owned by Qatari nationals; sole shipping agents, stevedoring, chandlers, forwarding, shipowning, repair, construction, etc.; Chief Exec. Abd al-Aziz H. Salatt.

## CIVIL AVIATION

Doha International Airport is equipped to receive all types of aircraft. In 1993 the total number of passengers using the existing airport, excluding those in transit, was 1,406,552. In 1991 it was announced that a new international airport was to be built in Doha, at a cost of QR 1,000m. Construction of the airport was expected to commence in 1994, and completion was scheduled for 1997. The new airport would have the capacity to handle 2m. passengers per year.

**Department of Civil Aviation:** POB 3000, Doha; tel. 426262; telex 4306; fax 429070; Dir of Civil Aviation Abd al-Aziz an-Noaimi.

**Doha International Airport:** POB 3000, Doha; tel. 351550; telex 4306; fax 429070; Airport Man. Mohd al-Muhannadi.

**Gulf Air Co Ltd:** POB 3394, Doha; tel. 455455; telex 5150; fax 449955; jointly owned by the Governments of Bahrain, Oman, Qatar and Abu Dhabi (see Oman—Civil Aviation).

**Gulf Helicopters:** POB 811, Doha; tel. 433991; telex 4353; fax 411004; f. 1974; owned by Gulf Air Co GSC; Chair. Abdullah bin Hamad al-Attiya.

**Qatar Air:** Doha; tel. 430707; telex 4444; fax 352433; services throughout the Middle East; CEO Sheikh Hamad bin Ali Jaber ath-Thani.

# ROMANIA

## Introductory Survey

**Location, Climate, Language, Religion, Flag, Capital**

Romania (formerly the Socialist Republic of Romania) lies in south-eastern Europe, bounded to the north and east by Ukraine, to the north-east by Moldova, to the north-west by Hungary, to the south-west by Yugoslavia (Serbia) and to the south by Bulgaria. The south-east coast is washed by the Black Sea. Romania has hot summers and cold winters, with a moderate rainfall. The average summer temperature is 23°C (73°F) and the winter average is −3°C (27°F). The official language is Romanian, a Romance language, although minority groups speak Hungarian (Magyar), German and other languages. Most of the inhabitants profess Christianity, and about 83% of believers are adherents of the Romanian Orthodox Church. The national flag (proportions 5 by 3) consists of three equal vertical stripes, of blue, yellow and red. The capital is Bucharest (Bucureşti).

**Recent History**

Formerly part of Turkey's Ottoman Empire, Romania became an independent kingdom in 1881. During the dictatorship of the Fascist 'Iron Guard' movement, Romania entered the Second World War as an ally of Nazi Germany. Soviet forces entered Romania in 1944, when the pro-German regime was overthown. Under Soviet pressure, King Michael accepted the appointment of a communist-led coalition Government in March 1945. At elections in November 1946 a communist-dominated bloc claimed 89% of the votes cast, but the results were widely believed to have been fraudulent. In 1947 the small Romanian Communist Party (RCP), led since 1945 by Gheorghe Gheorghiu-Dej, merged with the Social Democratic Party to become the Romanian Workers' Party (RWP). King Michael was forced to abdicate on 30 December 1947, when the Romanian People's Republic was proclaimed.

In 1948 the republic's first Constitution was adopted, and in the same year the nationalization of the main industrial and financial institutions was begun. In 1949 private landholdings were expropriated and amalgamated into state and collective farms. The implementation of Soviet-style economic policies was accompanied by numerous arrests of non-communists and the establishment of full political control by the RWP.

In 1952, following a purge of the RWP membership, a new Constitution, closer to the Soviet model, was adopted. Gheorghiu-Dej, the First Secretary of the RWP, became Romania's unchallenged leader and proceeded to implement large-scale plans for the industrialization of the country, despite the Soviet leadership's preference for Romania to remain as a supplier of agricultural goods. Gheorghiu-Dej died in 1965; he was succeeded as First Secretary of the RWP by Nicolae Ceauşescu, a Secretary of the RWP Central Committee since 1954. In June 1965 the RWP again became the RCP, while Ceauşescu's post of First Secretary was restyled General Secretary. A new Constitution, adopted in August of that year, changed the country's name to the Socialist Republic of Romania.

Ceauşescu continued his predecessor's relatively independent foreign policy, criticizing the invasion of Czechoslovakia by Warsaw Pact troops in 1968, and establishing links with Western states and institutions. However, the use of foreign loans for investment in Romania's industry and infrastructure led to serious indebtedness, and by the early 1980s the country was experiencing severe economic problems. In order to strengthen his own position as the economic situation deteriorated, Ceauşescu (who had become President of the Republic in 1974) implemented frequent personnel changes in the RCP leadership and the Government. In March 1980 the President's wife, Elena Ceauşescu, became a First Deputy Chairman of the Council of Ministers, and numerous other family members held government and party posts.

At the 13th RCP Congress, held in November 1984, Ceauşescu was re-elected General Secretary of the ruling party for a further five-year term. Legislative elections were held in March 1985, when 2.27% of the total number of voters (99.99% of the electorate were claimed to have participated) were reported to have voted against the candidates approved by the RCP. The Grand National Assembly re-elected Ceauşescu as President of Romania, and a new Council of Ministers was appointed. Numerous reorganizations of the Council of Ministers were carried out in 1985. In October of that year the long-running production difficulties of the country's energy sector culminated in an unprecedented crisis and a declaration of a state of emergency in the electric power industry. As a result, several ministers and senior officials were dismissed. A further major reshuffle of the Council of Ministers took place in August 1986.

Shortages of fuel and power led to strict energy rationing in early 1987. The situation was exacerbated by adverse weather conditions, and signs of public discontent became evident. Anti-Government leaflets were reported to be in circulation, and a number of strikes, to protest against food shortages and delays in the payment of wages, took place in provincial factories. In March certain vital factories and mines were reportedly placed under military supervision to forestall the threat of further labour unrest. In November thousands of people, led by workers from a tractor factory, marched through the city of Braşov to protest against the decline in living standards and in working conditions, and stormed the local RCP headquarters. Hundreds of arrests were made when the demonstration was broken up by the authorities. Similar protests were reported from Timişoara and other cities in December. At a national conference of the RCP in mid-December, President Ceauşescu announced improvements in food supplies and increases in wages, but continued to oppose any reform of the system. To mark his 70th birthday in January 1988, Ceauşescu granted an amnesty for certain prisoners.

In March 1988 President Ceauşescu announced details of a controversial rural urbanization programme. The plan entailed the demolition of up to 8,000 villages, located mainly in Transylvania, and the resettlement of their residents (mostly ethnic Hungarians) in multi-storey housing complexes, which were to form part of new 'agro-industrial centres'. The plan attracted increasing internal and international criticism, but Ceauşescu rejected accusations that the policy involved the destruction of a traditional way of life, maintaining that the programme would raise living standards and ensure social equality.

During 1988 and 1989 Romania became increasingly isolated from the international community, largely owing to its rural urbanization programme and continuing abuses of human rights. On a visit to Bucharest in May 1987 Mikhail Gorbachev, the Soviet leader, had emphasized the desirability of economic and political reforms, a view reiterated during Ceauşescu's visit to the USSR in October 1988. Furthermore, Romania continued to obstruct progress at the Vienna Conference on Security and Co-operation in Europe (begun in November 1986); on adoption of the final document by the Conference in January 1989, Romania declared that it did not consider itself bound by certain provisions relating to human rights, considering them to constitute the right of interference in a country's internal affairs. By early 1989 relations with countries of the European Community (EC, now European Union — EU — see p. 143) had deteriorated to such an extent that the Ambassadors of France and the Federal Republic of Germany were recalled from Bucharest.

There were also signs of increasing criticism of the regime within Romania. In March 1989, in an open letter to President Ceauşescu, six retired RCP officials criticized the leader's policies, accusing him of disregard for the Constitution and of mismanagement of the economy. The signatories were particularly critical of the rural urbanization programme. It was subsequently reported that the authors of the letter had been detained. Ceauşescu continued to criticize the reforms taking place elsewhere in Eastern Europe, and in November, at the 14th Congress of the RCP, he was re-elected as the party's General Secretary for a further five-year term.

In mid-December 1989 there was unrest in Timişoara, following the authorities' eviction of Father László Tőkes, an outspoken Protestant clergyman, from his church. Supporters of the pastor, an ethnic Hungarian who had repeatedly criticized the Government's policies, marched through the town to demonstrate their opposition to his eviction. A further protest, at which there was considerable criticism of the regime, was attended by thousands of local residents. Security forces opened fire on the crowd, reportedly killing several hundred. Protests were reported from other Romanian towns, and the country's borders were closed.

On 21 December 1989 President Ceauşescu attended a mass rally in Bucharest, intended to demonstrate popular support for the President. Instead, his address was interrupted by hostile chanting, in an unprecedented display of opposition to the leader. Anti-Government demonstrations followed later in the day, leading to clashes between protesters and members of the Securitate, the secret police force, during which many civilians were killed. The disturbances quickly spread to other parts of the country, and on the following day Ceauşescu declared a state of emergency. As the uprising gathered momentum, soldiers of the regular army declared their support for the protesters. When demonstrators forced their way into the RCP Central Committee headquarters, Nicolae and Elena Ceauşescu escaped by helicopter from the roof of the building. The revolutionaries seized control of the radio and television stations, where an opposition National Salvation Front (NSF) was formed. Ceauşescu and his wife were captured near Târgovişte, and on 25 December, after a summary trial, were executed by firing squad. However, fierce fighting continued in Bucharest and elsewhere for several days, mainly between Securitate forces and regular soldiers.

An 11-member Executive Bureau was elected from among the 145 members of the NSF, and a provisional Government, comprising liberal communists, intellectuals and members of the armed forces, was established. Ion Iliescu, a former Secretary of the RCP Central Committee, became interim President, while Petre Roman, an academic, was appointed Prime Minister. The new Government immediately decreed an end to the RCP's constitutional monopoly of power and cancelled the rural urbanization programme. The RCP was banned (in 1990 it was replaced by the Socialist Labour Party—SLP). Free elections were announced for 1990, and the country was renamed simply Romania. By early January 1990 the army had restored order, and the Securitate was abolished. It was initially feared that many thousands had died during the revolution, but the final official death toll was given as 689.

The trials of many of Ceauşescu's former associates began in January 1990, special military tribunals having been established for the purpose. In early February four senior RCP officials were found guilty of responsibility for the shootings in Timişoara and Bucharest and were sentenced to life imprisonment. Numerous other former government and RCP members faced similar and related charges. In September Nicu Ceauşescu (Ceauşescu's son), who was alleged to have ordered security forces to open fire on demonstrators in Sibiu in December 1989, initially received a 20-year prison sentence, but was released in November 1992 on the grounds of ill health. In March 1991 Gen. Iulian Vlad, the former head of the Securitate, was sentenced to three-and-a-half years in prison, and subsequently received further sentences, bringing the total to 12 years of imprisonment; in January 1994, however, he was provisionally released (as part of a general amnesty), having served only four years of his sentence. In December 1991 eight former associates of President Ceauşescu were sentenced to prison terms of up to 25 years for their part in the shootings in Timişoara in December 1989.

Despite the widespread jubilation that followed the downfall of Ceauşescu, the NSF did not enjoy total public support. Many citizens believed that the Front's leadership was too closely connected with the Ceauşescu regime, and were particularly critical of the NSF's control of the media. Furthermore, the NSF's announcement, in early January 1990, that it was to contest the forthcoming elections, to be held on 20 May 1990, and its reversal of a decision to abolish the RCP, increased fears that members of the RCP were attempting to regain power. In late January Doina Cornea, a veteran dissident, and Dumitru Mazilu, the interim First Deputy President, resigned from the NSF, further undermining the Front's credibility.

As discontent with the NSF grew, clashes occurred between supporters and opponents of the Front. In late January 1990 the offices of two prominent opposition parties, the National Liberal Party (NLP) and the National Peasants' Party, were attacked by NSF supporters. Student demonstrators demanded that the NSF be replaced by a neutral body, pending the elections. In early February, after negotiations among representatives of 29 political parties, the NSF agreed to share power with the opposition in a 180-member Provisional National Unity Council (PNUC). Each of the political parties represented in the negotiations was allocated three seats on the Council. The PNUC was subsequently expanded to 253 members to permit representation by other political parties. Nevertheless, NSF members and supporters occupied 111 seats in the Council. The PNUC elected a 21-member Executive Bureau, with Ion Iliescu as its President.

Despite the establishment of the PNUC, opposition to the NSF continued to increase, particularly in the armed forces, members of which demanded the resignation of the Ministers of National Defence and of the Interior, both of whom were considered to be too closely associated with the previous regime. In response to their demands, in mid-February 1990 Gen. Nicolae Militaru was replaced as Minister of National Defence by Col-Gen. Victor Stanculescu, hitherto Minister of the National Economy. Two days later, however, thousands of anti-Government demonstrators demanded the resignation of President Iliescu, and some 250 protesters forcibly entered the NSF headquarters. Numerous demonstrators were arrested and 38 were tried, some of them receiving short prison sentences.

As the elections approached, massive anti-communist demonstrations continued on a daily basis, with University Square in the centre of Bucharest occupied by protesters demanding the resignation of the interim President and his Government. The election campaign became increasingly acrimonious, and there were widespread accusations of systematic intimidation and harassment of the NSF's opponents. At the presidential and legislative elections, held on 20 May 1990, the NSF achieved an overwhelming victory. Allegations of irregularities, however, were confirmed by international observers. According to official figures, Ion Iliescu won 85.07% of the valid votes cast in the presidential poll. In the elections to the bicameral legislature, the NSF won 65% of the votes cast, securing 263 of the 387 seats in the Chamber of Deputies and 91 of the 119 seats in the Senate.

Unrest continued after the elections, and in mid-June 1990, after seven weeks of occupation, the protest in University Square was forcibly broken up by the police, numerous arrests being made. The brutal treatment of the demonstrators provoked renewed clashes, in which the armed forces opened fire on rioters. In an attempt to disperse the protesters, following an appeal for support by President Iliescu, some 7,000 miners and other workers from the Jiu Valley were transported to the capital, where they swiftly seized control of the streets, attacking those suspected of being opponents of the Government. The disturbances resulted in several deaths and hundreds of people injured; more than 1,000 people were detained. The scenes of violence in Bucharest provoked severe international criticism. Following President Iliescu's inauguration, in late June, Petre Roman was reappointed Prime Minister, and a new Council of Ministers was formed, in which nearly all the members of the previous administration were replaced.

In August 1990 there were further anti-Government demonstrations in Bucharest, and large protests, mainly concerned with the deteriorating economic situation, also occurred in Braşov. In the months that followed, as popular disillusionment appeared to increase, widespread strike action was reported. In October, in response to continuing economic problems, Petre Roman announced extensive economic reforms, including the transfer of state enterprises to the private sector and the removal of price controls. However, the implementation of price increases in early November led to demonstrations in Bucharest against the economic reforms, including a protest march by some 100,000 people, organized by the Civic Alliance, a newly-founded opposition grouping. In late December workers in Timişoara, demanding the resignation of the President and the Government, initiated a general strike. As a result of such protests, which continued into 1991, the Government was obliged to modify its economic programme.

In February 1991 a strike by railway workers, in support of a demand for increased pay, caused serious disruption to the economy. Nevertheless, the Government proceeded with its economic programme, allowing further large price rises in early April. At the end of April Roman carried out an extensive reshuffle of the Council of Ministers, in which three portfolios were allocated to opposition politicians. In June, however, negotiations between the NSF and opposition parties regarding the possibility of forming a coalition government ended in failure.

In September 1991 miners in the Jiu Valley, who by now were opposed to President Iliescu, went on strike in support of demands for pay increases, a 'freeze' on prices and the resignation of the Government. Thousands of miners travelled to Bucharest, where violent clashes, this time between the miners and the security forces, again ensued. The miners attacked government offices and ransacked the parliament building. Four people were killed and hundreds injured during the violence, as a result of which Petre Roman and the Council of Ministers were obliged to resign. The outgoing Prime Minister was replaced by Theodor Stolojan, a former Minister of Finance. In October Stolojan succeeded in forming a coalition Government, comprising members of the NSF, the NLP, the Agrarian Democratic Party of Romania (ADPR) and the Romanian Ecological Movement.

A new Constitution, enshrining a multi-party system, a free-market economy and guarantees of the respect of human rights, was approved by the legislature in November 1991. In the following month it was endorsed by the electorate in a referendum. Local elections took place in several stages between February and April 1992. The results confirmed the decline in support for the NSF. Many seats were won by members of the centre-right Democratic Convention of Romania (DCR) Alliance, a newly-formed alliance of 18 parties and organizations opposed to the NSF, including the Christian Democratic National Peasants' Party and the Party of the Civic Alliance. Disputes within the NSF finally led to a formal rift in the movement; in March 1992, following the confirmation of Petre Roman as the President of the NSF, it divided into two factions, with supporters of President Iliescu founding the NSF—22 December, which in late April was registered as the Democratic National Salvation Front (DNSF), a moderate left-wing party which favoured only limited reforms.

Against a background of renewed labour unrest, legislative and presidential elections took place on 27 September 1992. The DNSF gained 117 of the 328 elective seats in the Chamber of Deputies and 49 of the 143 seats in the Senate, making it the largest party in the new Parliament. Its closest rival was the DCR Alliance, which gained 82 seats in the Chamber of Deputies and 34 in the Senate. The NSF secured only 43 and 18 seats, respectively. The DCR appealed unsuccessfully for a recount, after it was was revealed that some 15% of the votes cast had been declared invalid. In the presidential election, the first round produced no outright winner. The two leading candidates, Ion Iliescu, the incumbent, and Emil Constantinescu, representing the DCR, therefore proceeded to a second round of voting on 11 October, which was won by Iliescu, with 61.43% of the votes cast. In early November, following protracted negotiations, Nicolae Văcăroiu, an economist with no professed party affiliation (he had been a junior minister in the outgoing administration), formed a Government that included equal numbers of DNSF members and independents.

In mid-February 1993 thousands of people staged a demonstration in Bucharest to protest against rising prices, low wages and unemployment. In the following month, however, a parliamentary motion presented by the centrist opposition expressing 'no confidence' in the Government's economic programme was defeated. The abolition of price subsidies for many basic commodities and services, with effect from the beginning of May, precipitated renewed labour unrest. A threat of strike action by public-sector employees in early May obliged the Government to increase the minimum wage in the sector by about 75%; later in the month workers in the steel industry withdrew their labour, demanding wage increases commensurate with the level of price rises. Anti-Government strikes and demonstrations calling for wage increases spread across the country. In mid-1993, however, the implementation of further measures aimed at liberalizing the monetary system led to the largest price increases in Romania since 1989.

The position of the Văcăroiu Government remained precarious throughout 1993. In the course of the year the opposition attempted four times to bring down the Government through parliamentary motions of 'no confidence', all of which were defeated. In addition, two political scandals were uncovered in mid-1993. In June the Government was accused of being involved in an allegedly corrupt shipping deal, in which a majority share in Romania's state-owned merchant shipping company, Petromin, was sold to a Greek company. Prime Minister Văcăroiu and President Iliescu denied any involvement in the affair. In the following month three high-ranking government officials, including the Deputy Prime Minister and Minister of Finance, Florin Georgescu, were implicated in another corruption scandal. The third motion of 'no confidence' presented against the Government in 1993 was introduced by the opposition in late October in protest at Văcăroiu's appointment of four new ministers, in August of that year, without parliamentary approval. (The reshuffle of the Council of Ministers had followed the resignation from office of the Deputy Prime Minister and Chairman of the Council for Economic Co-ordination, Strategy and Reform, Misu Negritoiu, one of the Government's principal economic reformers.) In the mean time, the ruling party, the DNSF, had changed its name to the Party of Social Democracy of Romania (PSDR) in July and absorbed three other left-wing parties, confirming its position as Romania's principal party of the left. In May, in an apparently similar attempt to distance itself from the events of 1989–90, Petre Roman's NSF had renamed itself the Democratic Party—National Salvation Front (DP—NSF).

By late 1993 both the opposition and large numbers of the general public were increasing their demands for a new government, as Văcăroiu's administration appeared increasingly unstable. In November a protest march in Bucharest, demanding rapid economic reforms, was the largest public demonstration in the country since the overthrow of the Ceauşescu regime. In mid-December the Government survived the fourth vote of 'no confidence', presented in protest against the lack of progress in the economic reform programme, by only 13 votes. At the end of the month the PSDR began inter-party discussions concerning the possibility of the formation of a new, coalition government.

The Government again defeated a vote of 'no confidence' by only a few votes in January 1994. In February renewed industrial unrest led to the holding of a general strike (on 28 February and 1 March). Meanwhile, Văcăroiu appeared to be considering establishing a coalition with the PSDR's parliamentary allies: the extreme nationalist Romanian National Unity Party (RNUP) and the Greater Romania Party, as well as two parties dominated by former communists, the ADPR and the SLP. However, all four parties threatened to withdraw their support for the PSDR in the Parliament unless they were granted portfolios in a new coalition, and ultimately the inter-party talks proved inconclusive. The relatively minor government reshuffle that was carried out in March continued the pattern of single-party (PSDR) rule supplemented by independent technocrats (although later in the year two members of the RNUP were appointed to the Council of Ministers). In April the ADPR withdrew its parliamentary support for the Government, and in June the same party proposed a fresh vote of 'no confidence' in the Council of Ministers (which it survived). In the same month the DCR Alliance initiated impeachment proceedings against Iliescu; the move was prompted by statements made by the President in May, in which he had appealed to local authorities not to implement court decisions restoring to former owners property nationalized during the communist period. In early July, however, the Constitutional Court unanimously ruled against the implementation of impeachment proceedings; this ruling was endorsed (by a considerable margin) at a joint session of the Chamber of Deputies and the Senate on 7 July.

In May 1994 the RCP was re-registered by a Bucharest court; in the following month, however, the Supreme Court reversed this decision, and the party remained banned.

Romania experienced frequent occurrences of ethnic unrest after the fall of Ceauşescu. In 1991 there were organized attacks on Gypsy (Roma) communities throughout Romania, resulting in the emigration of many Gypsies to Germany. In September 1992 Germany repatriated 43,000 Romanian refugees, more than one-half of whom were Gypsies, to Romania, having agreed to provide a grant of DM30m. to finance their resettlement. Repatriations continued in 1993–94, during which time the incidence of physical attacks against Gypsies in Romania was reported to have increased.

In the late 1980s Romania's relations with Hungary became increasingly strained by the question of the ethnic and cultural rights of Romania's large Hungarian minority (numbering an estimated 1.7m.), many of whom wished to leave Romania and resettle in Hungary. The commencement of Ceaușescu's rural urbanization programme (see above) further exacerbated the deterioration in relations between the two countries. Following the overthrow of Ceaușescu in December 1989, ethnic Hungarians attempted to increase their cultural and linguistic autonomy in Transylvania. However, in March 1990, demonstrations by ethnic Hungarians demanding such rights were attacked by Romanian nationalists in Târgu Mureș. Tanks and troops were deployed to quell the unrest, in which several people were killed, and a state of emergency was declared in the town. In mid-1992 there was renewed tension when the mayor of Cluj-Napoca, Gheorghe Funar (later head of the right-wing RNUP), ordered the removal of Hungarian-language street signs in the city, and ethnic Hungarian prefects in Covasna and Harghita were subsequently replaced by ethnic Romanians. The Government attempted to calm the situation by appointing 'parallel' prefects of ethnic Hungarian background, but further controversy was caused by the removal in September of the only ethnic Hungarian State Secretary in the Government. In June 1993 talks between government representatives and leaders of the ethnic Hungarian community led to an agreement, signed in mid-July, on Hungarian minority rights, guaranteeing, among other clauses, bilingual street signs in areas with Hungarian populations of at least 30% and the training of Hungarian-speaking schoolteachers. In early 1994, however, discrimination against ethnic Hungarians was continuing to be openly pursued in many parts of Romania. There was hope for an improvement in relations between Romania and Hungary in June, when the Hungarian Prime Minister-designate, Gyula Horn, appealed for an 'historic reconciliation' with Romania; in the following month, however, ethnic tensions flared up again in Cluj-Napoca. In early August the ethnic Hungarian leader, Béla Markó, demanded that the Hungarian-Romanian state treaty (currently being negotiated) enshrine a 'special status' for ethnic Hungarians in Romania. Markó's proposals included the equal status of the Hungarian and Romanian languages in predominantly Hungarian-populated areas and greater control for the minority over educational and cultural affairs. In February 1995 Government and ethnic Hungarian representatives agreed to maintain inter-ethnic dialogue. Negotiations on the Hungarian-Romanian treaty continued in mid-1995.

Measures taken to combat a rise in xenophobia in Romania culminated in mid-1993 in a demand made by President Iliescu for action to be taken against right-wing extremist groups and anti-Semitism in the media. Iliescu also urged the Prosecutor-General to commence judicial proceedings against the publishers of a Romanian-language edition of *Mein Kampf*, written by Adolf Hitler, the leader of Nazi Germany (1933–45). However, such anti-racist measures appeared undermined in August 1994, when two extreme right-wing politicians (members of the RNUP) were appointed to cabinet posts.

Although Romania joined the Soviet-dominated Council for Mutual Economic Assistance (CMEA) in 1949, and the Warsaw Pact in 1955, from the early 1960s the Romanian leadership gradually adopted a more independent role in international affairs, refusing to endorse certain aspects of Soviet foreign policy. However, President Ceaușescu's resistance to reform left Romania isolated in the international community, and, even after his overthrow in 1989, Romania's relations with other countries only slowly improved. President Mitterrand of France visited Romania in April 1991, and in April 1992 Romania and Germany signed a treaty of friendship and co-operation. Relations with other EC countries took longer to develop, but an association agreement with the EC was signed in February 1993; in early 1995 Romania announced its intention to apply for full membership of the EU (as it had now become). Romania applied for membership of the Council of Europe in May 1993, but was initially rejected, owing to its poor record concerning civil liberties. In October, however, Romania was admitted to the Council of Europe; Hungary abstained from voting. The human rights issue continued to tarnish Romania's image, however, and in early 1994 it was announced that the Council of Europe was to conduct an inquiry into civil liberties in Romania.

Diplomatic relations with the former Soviet republic of Moldova (where a majority of the population are ethnic Romanians and much of which formed part of Romania until 1940) were established in August 1991, and some political groups began advocating the unification of the two states. The Romanian leadership opposed unification, but encouraged the development of closer cultural and economic ties with Moldova. In mid-1992 Romania was reported to be supplying armaments to the Moldovans for use in the conflict between ethnic Romanian Moldovans and ethnic Slavs in the Transdnestr region (see chapter on Moldova). The support of the Russian military in Moldova for the secessionist movement in the self-proclaimed republic of Transdnestr damaged relations between Romania and Russia. In March 1994 a plebiscite was held in Moldova on the question of reunification with Romania; more than 95% of those who took part in the referendum voted for an independent state, effectively signalling the demise of the pro-unification movement.

Attempts by the Romanian authorities to enforce the UN embargo on Yugoslavia (Serbia and Montenegro), by preventing the passage of vessels to or from that country via the Danube, encountered fierce opposition from the Yugoslav authorities, notably threats of petroleum spillages if tankers were not permitted to pass. In January 1993 Yugoslavia impounded 22 Romanian ships in retaliation for the detention of 40 Yugoslav vessels by Romania, and in February 12 Yugoslav tugboats blockaded the Danube. The Romanian Government displayed a somewhat ambiguous attitude towards Yugoslavia following these incidents. Romania reiterated its commitment to upholding the UN embargo in February 1993, but proceeded to sign a treaty with Yugoslavia on bilateral political relations in April 1994.

In June 1992 Romania, together with 10 other countries (including six of the former Soviet republics), established the Black Sea Economic Co-operation Group (see p. 238), which aimed to encourage regional trade and co-operation in developing transport and infrastructure; the creation of a regional investment bank was also envisaged. In December Romania signed a free trade accord with the European Free Trade Association (see p. 142). In May 1994 Romania was granted associate partnership status of Western European Union (WEU—see p. 221).

**Government**

Under the 1991 Constitution (drafted to replace that of 1965), legislative power is vested in the bicameral Parliament, comprising the 341-seat Chamber of Deputies (lower house) and the 143-seat Senate (upper house). Parliament is elected by universal adult suffrage on the basis of proportional representation for a term of four years. Executive power is vested in the President of the Republic, who may serve a maximum of two four-year terms and who is directly elected by universal adult suffrage. The President appoints the Prime Minister, who in turn appoints the Council of Ministers.

For administrative purposes, Romania comprises 40 administrative divisions (counties) and the municipality of Bucharest.

**Defence**

Romania was a member of the Warsaw Pact until the organization's dissolution in 1991 (Romania, however, did not participate in military exercises, nor did it allow Pact troops on its soil). In January 1994 Romania became the first former Warsaw Pact state to join NATO's 'Partnership for Peace' programme (see p. 192). Military service is compulsory and lasts for 12 months in the army and air force, and for 18 months in the navy. In June 1994 active forces totalled an estimated 230,500 (including 125,000 conscripts), comprising: army 160,500, navy 19,000 and air force 27,400, as well as 15,300 staff of the Ministry of National Defence and 8,300 personnel in centrally-controlled units. There were also 23,800 border guards, a gendarmerie of 10,000 and a Security Guard of 38,300 (all of which are under the control of the Ministry of the Interior). According to provisional figures, the 1993 budget allocated 419,578m. lei to defence.

**Economic Affairs**

In 1993, according to estimates by the World Bank, Romania's gross national product (GNP), measured at average 1991–93 prices, totalled US $25,427m., equivalent to $1,120 per head. Between 1985 and 1993, it was estimated, GNP per head decreased, in real terms, at an average rate of 6.5% annually. Over the same period there was no discernable increase or decrease in Romania's population. It was estimated that the country's gross domestic product (GDP) increased by 1% in 1993, following four years of negative growth which had culminated in a decrease of 13.5% in 1992.

Agriculture contributed 18.0% of GDP in 1992, and employed 35.9% of the economically active population in the following year. The principal crops are maize, wheat, potatoes, sugar beet, barley, grapes and apples. Wine production plays a significant role in Romanian agriculture. Forestry, the cropping of reeds (used as a raw material in the paper and cellulose industry) and the breeding of fish are also significant activities. In mid-1992 a severe drought critically affected agricultural output, which declined by some 18.8% in that year; the sector had recovered by 1993, however, when it registered an increase in output of 16.6%. Under the Government's decollectivization programme, 46% of agricultural land had been returned to its original owners and their heirs by early 1994. By early 1995 some 80% of Romania's farmlands had been privatized.

In 1992 industry (including mining, manufacturing, construction, power and water) accounted for 46.8% of GDP. The industrial sector employed 35.8% of the civilian labour force in 1993. Industrial production decreased by 21.8% in 1992; however, in 1993 it rose by 0.5%, and in 1994 it was reported to have increased by 3.3%.

The mining sector employed some 2.6% of the civilian labour force in 1993. Brown coal, hard coal, bauxite, copper, lead, zinc, salt and iron ore are mined. Onshore production of crude petroleum continued to decline in the late 1980s. By 1990, however, seven offshore platforms were operating in the Romanian sector of the Black Sea, accounting for more than 10% of annual hydrocarbon production. Methane gas is also extracted.

Manufacturing (which employed some 25.9% of the civilian labour force in 1993) is based mainly on the metallurgical, mechanical engineering, chemical and timber-processing industries. However, many industries (particularly iron and steel) have been hampered by shortages of electricity and raw materials. Manufacturing output increased by an annual average of 3.3% in 1980–89, but declined by 18.7% in 1990. Production continued to decline in 1991–93.

Energy is derived mainly from petroleum, gas and coal. A number of hydroelectric power stations are also in operation. Imports of mineral fuels and oils comprised some 26.4% of the value of merchandise imports in 1993. The first unit of Romania's first nuclear power station was expected to become operational by late 1995.

In 1993 Romania recorded a visible trade deficit of US $1,128m., while there was a deficit of $1,162m. on the current account of the balance of payments. In that year the principal source of imports was Germany, which provided 15.9% of the total. Russia was also a major supplier, accounting for 12.1% of total imports, as were Iran (9.8%) and Italy (9.3%). The main market for exports in that year was Germany, which purchased 14.4%, followed by Italy (8.3%), China (8.1%) and Turkey (5.7%). In 1993 the principal imports were mineral products, machinery and mechanical appliances, and textiles. Machinery and transport equipment, textiles, and iron and steel were among the country's major exports.

The draft state budget for 1995 envisaged expenditure of 16,616,000m. lei and revenue of 14,684,000m., giving a deficit of 1,932,000m. lei. Romania's total external public debt at the end of 1993 was US $4,456m., of which $2,080m. was long-term public debt. In that year the cost of debt-servicing was equivalent to 6.2% of revenue from exports of goods and services. Following the implementation of a price liberalization programme, the annual rate of inflation averaged 232.5% in 1991–93; consumer prices increased by an annual average of 256.1% in 1993, but the rate slowed to 136.8% in 1994. The rate of unemployment was estimated at 10.5% of the labour force in May 1995.

Romania was a member of the CMEA until its dissolution in 1991. Romania is a member (as a 'Country of Operations') of the European Bank for Reconstruction and Development (EBRD, see p. 140). In February 1993 Romania signed an association agreement with the European Union (EU, see p. 143), and a free-trade agreement with the European Free Trade Association (EFTA, see p. 142) came into effect in May 1993.

Following the overthrow of President Ceauşescu in 1989, a complete restructuring of Romania's economy was planned, with emphasis on the role of market forces and private ownership. The National Agency for Privatization was established August 1990; by late 1994 the private sector contributed some 31% of GDP and 41% of total employment. Sharp devaluations of the leu against convertible currencies were effected from 1990, and in November 1991 a unified exchange rate was introduced, internal convertibility being established. During 1992 a programme of reductions in price subsidies was begun. However, Romania's style of government meant that foreign businesses were initially reluctant to invest in the country, although by 1993 the situation had begun to improve, with an increase of 42.6% in foreign investment, compared with the previous year. In March 1993 the Government announced a four-year economic reform programme which was to be implemented in conjunction with a US $700m. IMF stand-by agreement. The programme included the progressive elimination of price subsidies for staple goods and services, the removal of controls on interest and exchange rates, a trade liberalization programme, accelerated privatization and a reduction in inflation. The reforms were also intended to revive foreign companies' interest in Romania through the offer of significant tax incentives to large investors. The opening of a Romanian stock market, in June 1995, was expected to provide the mechanism necessary to attract foreign capital. By mid-1994 the Government's adherence to the four-year reform programme appeared to have greatly improved Romania's economic situation, although, owing to the necessary austerity measures, it had also led to widespread domestic unrest (see Recent History). There had been a sharp decline in inflation, free-floating exchange rates had been established, and a rise in exports was helping to increase reserves. Romania now possesses certain economic advantages which, when combined, mean that real growth is possible in the medium term. Agriculture and tourism are two sectors that hold particular potential. The prospects of economic recovery in Romania are, however, heavily dependent on the continuation of monetary discipline, the acceleration of reforms and clear exchange-rate policies.

**Social Welfare**

Romania has a comprehensive state insurance scheme, premiums being paid by enterprises and institutions on behalf of their wage-earners. A new law on unemployment allowance was adopted in January 1991. In addition, funds are allotted to sickness benefits, children's allowances, pensions and the provision of health resorts. There were 215,796 hospital beds and 41,813 doctors and 6,717 dentists in practice in 1990. The 1995 state budget allocated 2,490,500m. lei to health (an increase of 49.7% from 1994). Following the revolution of December 1989, international attention was focused on the orphanages containing large numbers of unwanted and neglected children (contraception and abortion having been prohibited during the Ceauşescu years), many of whom were found to be suffering from AIDS, hepatitis and other serious illnesses. Owing to persistent shortages of foodstuffs, many Romanians were believed to be suffering from malnutrition. In 1992 Romania had one of the highest infant mortality rates in Europe (23.4 per 1,000 live births). In 1991 the World Bank approved loans of US $180m. and $150m. towards the reconstruction and improvement of Romania's health service.

**Education**

Children under the age of six years may attend crèches (creşe), and kindergartens (grădiniţe de copii). In 1991 75% of pre-school age children were attending kindergarten. Between the ages of six and 16 years children are obliged to attend the general education school (şcoală de cultură generală de zece ani). The general secondary school (liceul), for which there is an entrance examination, provides a specialized education suitable for entering college or university. There are also specialized secondary schools, where the emphasis is on industrial, agricultural and teacher training, and art schools, which correspond to secondary schools but cover several years of general education. Vocational secondary schools (şcoli profesionale de ucenici) train pupils for a particular career. Tuition in minority languages, particularly Hungarian and German, is available. There are 63 higher educational institutes, with a total enrolment, in 1993/94, of 250,087 students. The 1993 state budget allotted 605,562m. lei to education (14.7% of central government expenditure in that year). Following the downfall of President Ceauşescu in December 1989, the education system was reorganized, including the elimination of ideological training. In March 1995 it was announced that Romania was to receive US $33m. from the European Union for the modernization of its educational system.

# ROMANIA

## Public Holidays

**1995:** 1–2 January (New Year), 14 April (Good Friday), 17 April (Easter Monday), 1–2 May (International Labour Day), 1 December (National Day), 25 December (Christmas).

**1996:** 1–2 January (New Year), 15 April (Good Friday), 8 April (Easter Monday), 1–2 May (International Labour Day), 1 December (National Day), 25 December (Christmas).

## Weights and Measures

The metric system is in force.

# Statistical Survey

Source (unless otherwise indicated): Comisia Natională de Statistică (National Statistics Commission), Bucharest, Str. Stavropoleos 6; tel. (1) 158200; telex 111153.

## Area and Population

### AREA, POPULATION AND DENSITY

| | |
|---|---:|
| Area (sq km) | |
| Land | 229,077 |
| Inland water | 8,423 |
| Total | 237,500* |
| Population (census results) | |
| 5 January 1977 | 21,559,910 |
| 7 January 1992† | |
| Males | 11,182,290 |
| Females | 11,578,159 |
| Total | 22,760,449 |
| Population (official estimates at mid-year) | |
| 1993 | 22,755,000 |
| 1994 | 22,736,000 |
| Density (per sq km) at mid-1994 | 95.7 |

* 91,699 sq miles.
† Figures are provisional. The revised total is 22,810,035.

### ADMINISTRATIVE DIVISIONS (at 1992 census)

| | Area (sq km) | Population ('000)* | Density (per sq km) | Administrative capital (with population) |
|---|---:|---:|---:|---|
| Alba | 6,231 | 414 | 66.5 | Alba Iulia (71,254) |
| Arad | 7,652 | 487 | 63.7 | Arad (190,088) |
| Argeş | 6,801 | 681 | 100.1 | Piteşti (179,479) |
| Bacău | 6,606 | 736 | 111.4 | Bacău (204,495) |
| Bihor | 7,535 | 634 | 84.2 | Oradea (220,848) |
| Bistriţa-Năsăud | 5,305 | 327 | 61.7 | Bistriţa (87,793) |
| Botoşani | 4,965 | 459 | 92.4 | Botoşani (126,204) |
| Brăila | 4,724 | 392 | 83.0 | Brăila (234,706) |
| Braşov | 5,351 | 643 | 120.1 | Braşov (323,835) |
| Buzău | 6,072 | 516 | 85.0 | Buzău (148,247) |
| Călăraşi | 5,074 | 339 | 66.8 | Călăraşi (76,886) |
| Caraş-Severin | 8,503 | 376 | 44.2 | Reşiţa (96,798) |
| Cluj | 6,650 | 735 | 110.5 | Cluj-Napoca (328,008) |
| Constanţa | 7,055 | 748 | 106.0 | Constanţa (350,476) |
| Covasna | 3,705 | 233 | 62.8 | Sfântu Gheorghe (68,070) |
| Dâmboviţa | 4,036 | 560 | 138.7 | Târgovişte (97,876) |
| Dolj | 7,413 | 761 | 102.7 | Craiova (303,520) |
| Galaţi | 4,425 | 640 | 144.6 | Galaţi (325,788) |
| Giurgiu | 3,511 | 313 | 89.2 | Giurgiu (74,236) |
| Gorj | 5,641 | 400 | 70.9 | Târgu Jiu (98,267) |
| Harghita | 6,610 | 348 | 52.6 | Miercurea-Ciuc (46,029) |
| Hunedoara | 7,016 | 548 | 78.1 | Deva (78,366) |
| Ialomiţa | 4,449 | 304 | 68.3 | Slobozia (55,614) |
| Iaşi | 5,469 | 807 | 147.5 | Iaşi (342,994) |
| Maramureş | 6,215 | 539 | 86.7 | Baia Mare (148,815) |
| Mehedinţi | 4,900 | 332 | 67.8 | Drobeta-Turnu-Severin (115,526) |
| Mureş | 6,696 | 607 | 90.7 | Târgu Mureş (163,625) |

| —continued | Area (sq km) | Population ('000)* | Density (per sq km) | Administrative capital (with population) |
|---|---:|---:|---:|---|
| Neamţ | 5,890 | 578 | 98.1 | Piatra-Neamţ (123,175) |
| Olt | 5,507 | 521 | 94.6 | Slatina (85,336) |
| Prahova | 4,694 | 873 | 186.0 | Ploieşti (252,073) |
| Sălaj | 3,850 | 266 | 69.2 | Zalău (68,322) |
| Satu Mare | 4,405 | 400 | 90.8 | Satu Mare (131,859) |
| Sibiu | 5,422 | 453 | 83.5 | Sibiu (169,696) |
| Suceava | 8,555 | 701 | 81.9 | Suceava (114,355) |
| Teleorman | 5,760 | 482 | 83.7 | Alexandria (58,582) |
| Timiş | 8,692 | 700 | 80.6 | Timişoara (334,278) |
| Tulcea | 8,430 | 270 | 32.1 | Tulcea (97,500) |
| Vâlcea | 5,705 | 436 | 76.5 | Râmnicu Vâlcea (113,356) |
| Vaslui | 5,297 | 458 | 86.4 | Vaslui (80,151) |
| Vrancea | 4,863 | 393 | 80.7 | Focşani (101,296) |
| Bucharest Municipality | 1,820 | 2,351 | 1,291.7 | Bucharest (2,064,474) |
| **Total** | 237,500 | 22,760 | 95.8 | |

* Provisional.

### PRINCIPAL TOWNS
(estimated population at 1 July 1993)

| | | | | |
|---|---:|---|---:|
| Bucureşti (Bucharest, the capital) | 2,066,723 | Sibiu | 168,619 |
| | | Târgu Mureş | 165,502 |
| Constanţa | 348,985 | Baia Mare | 150,018 |
| Iaşi | 337,643 | Buzău | 149,032 |
| Timişoara | 325,359 | Satu Mare | 131,386 |
| Galaţi | 324,234 | Botoşani | 127,337 |
| Braşov | 324,104 | Piatra-Neamţ | 125,157 |
| Cluj-Napoca | 321,850 | Drobeta-Turnu-Severin | 118,086 |
| Craiova | 303,033 | Suceava | 116,232 |
| Ploieşti | 254,304 | Râmnicu-Vâlcea | 114,165 |
| Brăila | 236,344 | Focşani | 101,414 |
| Oradea | 221,559 | Târgovişte | 98,752 |
| Bacău | 206,995 | Tulcea | 97,255 |
| Arad | 188,609 | Reşiţa | 97,029 |
| Piteşti | 182,931 | Târgu Jiu | 96,978 |

# ROMANIA

## BIRTHS, MARRIAGES AND DEATHS

|      | Registered live births Number | Rate (per 1,000) | Registered marriages Number | Rate (per 1,000) | Registered deaths Number | Rate (per 1,000) |
|------|---------|------|---------|-----|---------|------|
| 1986 | 376,896 | 16.5 | 167,254 | 7.3 | 242,330 | 10.6 |
| 1987 | 383,199 | 16.7 | 168,079 | 7.3 | 254,286 | 11.1 |
| 1988 | 380,043 | 16.5 | 172,527 | 7.5 | 253,370 | 11.0 |
| 1989 | 369,544 | 16.0 | 177,943 | 7.7 | 247,306 | 10.7 |
| 1990 | 314,746 | 13.6 | 192,652 | 8.3 | 247,086 | 10.6 |
| 1991 | 275,275 | 11.9 | 183,388 | 7.9 | 251,760 | 10.9 |
| 1992 | 260,393 | 11.4 | 174,593 | 7.7 | 263,855 | 11.6 |
| 1993 | 249,994 | 11.0 | 161,595 | 7.1 | 263,323 | 11.6 |

**Expectation of life** (years at birth, 1989–91): Males 66.59; Females 73.05 (Source: UN, *Demographic Yearbook*).

## CIVILIAN LABOUR FORCE EMPLOYED ('000 persons at 31 December)

|  | 1991* | 1992 | 1993 |
|---|---|---|---|
| Agriculture, forestry and hunting | 3,205 | 3,443 | 3,614 |
| Mining and quarrying | 277 | 272 | 259 |
| Manufacturing | 3,372 | 2,865 | 2,606 |
| Electricity, gas and water | 154 | 164 | 165 |
| Construction | 501 | 579 | 574 |
| Trade, restaurants and hotels | 912 | 929 | 716 |
| Transport, storage and communications | 689 | 649 | 592 |
| Finance, insurance, real estate and business services | 465 | 498 | 483 |
| Public administration, defence and compulsory social security | 99 | 113 | 117 |
| Education | 426 | 432 | 432 |
| Health and social welfare | 311 | 306 | 308 |
| Other activities | 374 | 208 | 196 |
| **Total** | **10,786** | **10,458** | **10,062** |

* Employment in state and co-operative sectors only.

# Agriculture

**PRINCIPAL CROPS** ('000 metric tons)

|  | 1991 | 1992 | 1993 |
|---|---|---|---|
| Wheat | 5,473 | 3,206 | 5,314 |
| Rice (paddy) | 31 | 39 | 37 |
| Barley | 2,951 | 1,678 | 1,553 |
| Maize | 10,497 | 6,828 | 7,988 |
| Rye | 86 | 21 | 40 |
| Oats | 258 | 508 | 554 |
| Potatoes | 1,873 | 2,602 | 3,709 |
| Dry beans | 46 | 41 | 48 |
| Dry peas | 32 | 33 | 36 |
| Soybeans (Soya beans) | 179 | 126 | 95 |
| Sunflower seed | 612 | 774 | 696 |
| Linseed | 23 | 18 | 28 |
| Cabbages | 617 | 676 | 854 |
| Tomatoes | 693 | 831 | 799 |
| Pumpkins, squash and gourds | 134* | 200* | 360† |
| Cucumbers and gherkins | 62 | 99 | 111 |
| Green peppers | 167 | 182 | 176 |
| Onions (dry) | 219 | 339 | 344 |
| Garlic | 32 | 44 | 49 |
| Green beans | 40* | 35 | 47 |
| Green peas | 55 | 45 | 29 |
| Other vegetables | 331 | 381 | 464 |
| Melons and watermelons | 741 | 623 | 601 |
| Grapes | 849 | 905 | 1,339 |
| Sugar beet | 4,703 | 2,897 | 1,776 |
| Apples | 505 | 541 | 1,097 |
| Pears | 58 | 63 | 109 |
| Peaches | 44 | 37 | 50 |
| Plums | 419 | 347 | 704 |
| Apricots | 26 | 41 | 42 |
| Cherries (incl. sour) | 60 | 73 | 106 |
| Strawberries | 13.8 | 12.8 | 7.3 |
| Other fruits | 37 | 46 | 51 |
| Walnuts | 18.0 | 21.8 | 32.6 |
| Tobacco (leaves) | 14 | 8 | 11 |

* Unofficial figure.   † FAO estimate.
Source: mainly FAO, *Production Yearbook*.

**LIVESTOCK** ('000 head at 1 January)

|  | 1992 | 1993 | 1994 |
|---|---|---|---|
| Horses | 749 | 721 | 751 |
| Cattle | 4,355 | 3,683 | 3,597 |
| Pigs | 10,954 | 9,852 | 9,262 |
| Sheep | 13,879 | 12,079 | 11,499 |
| Goats | 954 | 805 | 776 |
| Chickens | 106,032 | 87,725 | 76,532 |

Buffaloes ('000 head): 170 in 1992 (Source: FAO, *Production Yearbook*).

**LIVESTOCK PRODUCTS** ('000 metric tons)

|  | 1991 | 1992 | 1993 |
|---|---|---|---|
| Beef and veal | 380 | 300 | 250* |
| Mutton and lamb | 90 | 96 | 90* |
| Goat meat* | 7 | 6 | 5 |
| Pig meat | 834 | 789 | 804* |
| Poultry meat | 380 | 337 | 100† |
| Cows' milk | 3,619 | 3,463 | 2,900* |
| Sheep's milk | 442 | 398 | 390* |
| Cheese | 80.7 | 57.6 | 51.8 |
| Butter | 22.7 | 20.5 | 13.7 |
| Hen eggs | 343 | 290 | 300* |
| Other poultry eggs | 22 | 23 | 22* |
| Honey | 8.3 | 10.4 | 10.0* |
| Wool: |  |  |  |
| greasy | 32.5 | 28.0 | 34.0* |
| clean | 19.2 | 18.9* | 24.0* |
| Cattle and buffalo hides (fresh)* | 60.3 | 48.5 | 40.4 |
| Sheepskins (fresh)* | 15.6 | 16.6 | 15.6 |

* FAO estimate(s).   † Unofficial figure.
Source: FAO, *Production Yearbook*.

ROMANIA

## Forestry

**ROUNDWOOD REMOVALS** ('000 cubic metres, excluding bark)

|  | 1990 | 1991 | 1992* |
|---|---|---|---|
| Sawlogs, veneer logs and logs for sleepers | 5,164 | 4,640 | 4,640 |
| Pulpwood | 2,947 | 3,021 | 3,021 |
| Other industrial wood | 2,614 | 3,300 | 3,300 |
| Fuel wood | 2,579 | 2,696 | 2,696 |
| **Total** | 13,304 | 13,657 | 13,657 |

* FAO estimates.
Source: FAO, *Yearbook of Forest Products*.

**SAWNWOOD PRODUCTION**
('000 cubic metres, including railway sleepers)

|  | 1990 | 1991 | 1992 |
|---|---|---|---|
| Coniferous (softwood) | 1,357 | 1,019 | 960 |
| Broadleaved (hardwood) | 1,554 | 1,214 | 1,600 |
| **Total** | 2,911 | 2,233 | 2,560 |

Source: FAO, *Yearbook of Forest Products*.

## Fishing

('000 metric tons, live weight)

|  | 1991 | 1992 | 1993 |
|---|---|---|---|
| Common carp | 13.4 | 9.4 | 7.0 |
| Goldfish | 4.2 | 5.7 | 6.0 |
| Silver carp | 13.9 | 11.9 | 10.0 |
| Bighead carp | 7.3 | 6.9 | 5.4 |
| Other freshwater fishes | 8.6 | 6.1 | 5.0 |
| Cape horse mackerel | 7.2 | — | — |
| Other jack and horse mackerels | 8.8 | 17.0 | 16.7 |
| False scad | 5.5 | 10.0 | 12.5 |
| Round sardinella | 14.4 | 18.6 | 6.9 |
| Madeiran sardinella | 5.7 | 7.3 | 4.2 |
| European pilchard (sardine) | 16.8 | 19.9 | 8.8 |
| Chub mackerel | 6.0 | 5.8 | 3.0 |
| Other fishes | 16.0 | 6.3 | 9.8 |
| **Total catch** | 127.7 | 124.9 | 95.3 |
| Inland waters | 48.2 | 40.5 | 34.5 |
| Mediterranean and Black Sea | 6.3 | 1.2 | 3.7 |
| Atlantic Ocean | 73.2 | 83.2 | 57.0 |

Source: FAO, *Yearbook of Fishery Statistics*.

## Mining

('000 metric tons, unless otherwise indicated)

|  | 1991 | 1992 | 1993 |
|---|---|---|---|
| Hard coal | 3,836 | 4,098 | 4,228 |
| Brown coal | 28,578 | 34,272 | 35,523 |
| Crude petroleum | 6,791 | 6,615 | 6,676 |
| Iron ore* | 1,461 | 1,229 | 855 |
| Bauxite | 200 | 175 | 186 |
| Copper concentrates† | 26.4 | 24.7 | 25.3 |
| Lead concentrates† | 16.2 | 16.7 | 16.9 |
| Zinc concentrates† | 26.3 | 25.8 | 28.0 |
| Salt (unrefined) | 3,255 | 2,556 | 2,186 |
| Natural gas (million cu metres) | 24,807 | 22,138 | 21,317 |

* Figures refer to gross weight. The estimated iron content (in '000 metric tons) was: 290 in 1991; 247 in 1992.
† Figures refer to the metal content of concentrates.
**1994** ('000 metric tons): Crude petroleum 6,693; Bauxite 184; Copper 25.5; Lead 21.4; Zinc 33.2 (Source: UN, *Monthly Bulletin of Statistics*).

## Industry

**SELECTED PRODUCTS**
('000 metric tons, unless otherwise indicated)

|  | 1991 | 1992 | 1993 |
|---|---|---|---|
| Refined sugar | 348 | 290 | 185 |
| Margarine | 26.5 | 19.8 | 25.0 |
| Wine ('000 hectolitres) | 5,008 | 4,707 | 4,625 |
| Beer ('000 hectolitres) | 9,803 | 10,014 | 9,929 |
| Tobacco products | 26 | 26 | 23 |
| Cotton yarn—pure and mixed | 92 | 65 | 63 |
| Cotton fabrics—pure and mixed (million sq metres) | 437 | 289 | 271 |
| Woollen yarn—pure and mixed | 49 | 40 | 44 |
| Woollen fabrics—pure and mixed (million sq metres) | 100 | 69 | 68 |
| Silk fabrics—pure and mixed (million sq metres)* | 98 | 81 | 74 |
| Flax and hemp yarn—pure and mixed | 22 | 15 | 9 |
| Linen, hemp and jute fabrics—pure and mixed (million sq metres) | 76 | 42 | 25 |
| Chemical filaments and fibres | 142 | 113 | 101 |
| Footwear (million pairs) | 68 | 44 | 45 |
| Chemical wood pulp | 259 | 182 | 159 |
| Paper and paperboard | 380 | 310 | 285 |
| Synthetic rubber | 55 | 36 | 30 |
| Rubber tyres ('000) | 4,363 | 3,247 | 3,929 |
| Sulphuric acid | 745 | 572 | 527 |
| Caustic soda (sodium hydroxide) | 461 | 372 | 330 |
| Soda ash (sodium carbonate) | 471 | 452 | 371 |
| Nitrogenous fertilizers (a)† | 824 | 1,086 | 1,001 |
| Phosphatic fertilizers (b)† | 216 | 260 | 246 |
| Insecticides, fungicides, etc. | 17 | 17 | 20 |
| Plastics and resins | 350 | 272 | 259 |
| Motor spirit (petrol) | 3,122 | 2,923 | 3,078 |
| Kerosene and white spirit | 407 | 385 | 394 |
| Distillate fuel oils | 3,895 | 3,693 | 3,731 |
| Residual fuel oils | 4,969 | 3,855 | 3,707 |
| Lubricating oils | 273 | 265 | 230 |
| Petroleum bitumen (asphalt) | 379 | 367 | 319 |
| Liquefied petroleum gas | 224 | 228 | 239 |
| Coke | 2,608 | 2,902 | 7,405 |
| Cement | 7,405 | 6,946 | 6,864 |
| Unworked glass (million sq metres) | 46 | 44 | 46 |
| Pig-iron | 4,525 | 3,111 | 3,189 |
| Crude steel | 7,130 | 5,376 | 5,446 |
| Aluminium—unwrought | 167 | 120 | 117 |
| Refined copper—unwrought | 26 | 27 | 25 |
| Radio receivers ('000) | 435 | 83 | 80 |
| Television receivers ('000) | 389 | 318 | 431 |
| Merchant ships launched ('000 deadweight tons) | 264 | 273 | 250 |
| Passenger motor cars ('000) | 74 | 64 | 82 |
| Motor tractors, lorries and dump trucks (number) | 7,592 | 4,456 | 4,433 |
| Tractors ('000) | 22 | 21 | 26 |
| Sewing machines ('000) | 30 | 25 | 32 |
| Combine harvester-threshers (number) | 1,274 | 584 | 375 |
| Domestic refrigerators ('000) | 389 | 402 | 435 |
| Domestic washing machines ('000) | 188 | 159 | 166 |
| Domestic cookers ('000) | 526 | 440 | 452 |
| Electric energy (million kWh) | 56,912 | 54,195 | 55,476 |

* Including fabrics of artificial silk.
† Production in terms of (a) nitrogen or (b) phosphoric acid.

# ROMANIA

## Finance

### CURRENCY AND EXCHANGE RATES

**Monetary Units**
100 bani (singular: ban) = 1 Romanian leu (plural: lei).

**Sterling and Dollar Equivalents** (31 December 1994)
£1 sterling = 2,764.5 lei;
US $1 = 1,767.0 lei;
10,000 Romanian lei = £3.617 = $5.659.

**Average Exchange Rate** (lei per US $)
1992    307.95
1993    760.05
1994  1,655.09

### STATE BUDGET (million lei)*

| Revenue | 1991 | 1992 | 1993† |
|---|---|---|---|
| Taxation | 479,395 | 1,291,839 | 3,654,410 |
| Direct taxes | 278,887 | 789,383 | 1,880,475 |
| Tax on profits | 104,865 | 315,679 | 750,339 |
| Tax on wages | 172,170 | 457,709 | 1,093,154‡ |
| Indirect taxes | 200,508 | 502,456 | 1,773,935 |
| Turnover tax and excises | 182,478 | 418,520 | 743,905 |
| Value-added tax | — | — | 726,007 |
| Customs duties | 16,584 | 78,857 | 269,321 |
| Other current revenue | 11,233 | 50,796 | 132,909 |
| Capital revenue | 6,150 | 21,249 | 5,033 |
| **Total** | 496,778 | 1,363,884 | 3,792,352 |

| Expenditure | 1991 | 1992 | 1993† |
|---|---|---|---|
| Social and cultural services | 187,057 | 474,815 | 1,264,704 |
| Education | 77,807 | 209,261 | 605,562 |
| Health | 62,110 | 152,991 | 365,123 |
| Allowances, etc., for children | 31,460 | 57,573 | 160,920 |
| Pensions, etc., for war invalids, orphans and war widows | 6,675 | 31,307 | 92,053 |
| National defence | 78,256 | 195,709 | 419,578 |
| Public order | 19,661 | 58,101 | 219,840 |
| State administration | 15,444 | 48,945 | 173,436 |
| Economic affairs | 189,360 | 654,056 | 1,507,755 |
| Industry (incl. energy) | 96,930 | 326,668 | 709,054 |
| Agriculture, forestry, waters and environment | 35,822 | 217,151 | 515,943 |
| Transport and communications | 32,384 | 62,562 | 182,229 |
| Transfers to other budgets | 41,410 | 169,632 | 328,240 |
| Interest on public debt | — | 6,500 | 130,797 |
| **Total** (incl. others) | 537,874 | 1,626,908 | 4,128,779 |

* Excluding the accounts of central government units with individual budgets (including social security funds). The consolidated operations of the central Government (in '000 million lei) were: Revenue 822.8 in 1991, 2,200.5 in 1992; Expenditure 780.0 in 1991, 2,406.0 (excluding net lending 76.7) in 1992 (Source: IMF, *International Financial Statistics*).
† Figures are provisional.
‡ Including an adjustment relating to local budgets.

### INTERNATIONAL RESERVES (US $ million at 31 December)

|  | 1992 | 1993 | 1994 |
|---|---|---|---|
| IMF special drawing rights | 11 | 2 | 56 |
| Foreign exchange | 815 | 994 | 2,031 |
| **Total** (excl. gold) | 826 | 995 | 2,086 |

Source: IMF, *International Financial Statistics*.

### MONEY SUPPLY ('000 million lei at 31 December)

|  | 1992 | 1993 | 1994 |
|---|---|---|---|
| Currency outside banks | 411.7 | 1,048.1 | 2,200.6 |
| Demand deposits at deposit money banks | 599.8 | 1,138.2 | 2,691.8 |
| **Total money** | 1,011.5 | 2,186.3 | 4,892.4 |

Source: IMF, *International Financial Statistics*.

### COST OF LIVING (Consumer Price Index; base: 1991 = 100)

|  | 1992 | 1993 |
|---|---|---|
| Food | 337 | 1,174 |
| Fuel and light | 358 | 1,966 |
| Clothing | 270 | 977 |
| Rent | 100 | 137 |
| **All items** (incl. others) | 310 | 1,105 |

Source: ILO, *Year Book of Labour Statistics*.

### NATIONAL ACCOUNTS ('000 million lei at current prices)

**Expenditure on the Gross Domestic Product**

|  | 1991 | 1992 | 1993 |
|---|---|---|---|
| Government final consumption expenditure | 128.1 | 362.4 | 14,756.0 |
| Private final consumption expenditure | 1,544.4 | 4,221.5 | |
| Increase in stocks | 301.1 | 968.7 | 2,647.3 |
| Gross fixed capital formation | 317.0 | 888.6 | 2,521.4 |
| **Total domestic expenditure** | 2,290.5 | 6,441.1 | 19,924.7 |
| Exports of goods and services | 388.0 | 1,623.3 | 4,282.0 |
| *Less* Imports of goods and services | 474.6 | 2,082.1 | 5,371.5 |
| **GDP in purchasers' values** | 2,203.9 | 5,982.3 | 18,835.2 |
| **GDP at constant 1990 prices** | 747.2 | 646.0 | n.a. |

Source: IMF, *International Financial Statistics*.

**Gross Domestic Product by Economic Activity**

|  | 1990 | 1991 | 1992 |
|---|---|---|---|
| Agriculture, hunting, forestry and fishing | 155.2 | 412.2 | 1,130.2 |
| Mining and quarrying | | | |
| Manufacturing | 435.1 | 952.5 | 2,673.9 |
| Electricity, gas and water | | | |
| Construction | 46.0 | 104.4 | 261.0 |
| Trade, restaurants and hotels | 58.0 | 310.5 | 790.0 |
| Transport, storage and communications | 54.4 | 138.4 | 382.5 |
| Finance, insurance, real estate and business services | 23.2 | 57.8 | 311.7 |
| Government services | 63.6 | 179.4 | 465.7 |
| Other community, social and personal services | 21.9 | 53.1 | 151.9 |
| Other producers | 20.4 | 37.8 | 105.0 |
| **Sub-total** | 877.8 | 2,246.1 | 6,271.9 |
| *Less* Imputed bank service charge | 19.9 | 47.2 | 289.6 |
| **GDP in purchasers' values** | 857.9 | 2,198.9 | 5,982.3 |

Source: UN, *National Accounts Statistics*.

### BALANCE OF PAYMENTS (US $ million)

|  | 1991 | 1992 | 1993 |
|---|---|---|---|
| Merchandise exports f.o.b. | 4,266 | 4,364 | 4,892 |
| Merchandise imports f.o.b. | −5,372 | −5,558 | −6,020 |
| **Trade balance** | −1,106 | −1,194 | −1,128 |
| Exports of services | 680 | 659 | 799 |
| Imports of services | −819 | −946 | −910 |
| Other income received | 104 | 54 | 63 |
| Other income paid | −89 | −144 | −208 |
| Private unrequited transfers (net) | 20 | 19 | 103 |
| Official unrequited transfers (net) | 198 | 46 | 119 |
| **Current balance** | −1,012 | −1,506 | −1,162 |
| Direct investment (net) | 37 | 73 | 87 |
| Portfolio investment (net) | — | — | −73 |
| Other capital (net) | 283 | 1,307 | 955 |
| Net errors and omissions | 15 | −12 | 139 |
| **Overall balance** | −677 | −138 | −54 |

Source: IMF, *International Financial Statistics*.

# ROMANIA

## External Trade

### PRINCIPAL COMMODITIES (million lei)

| Imports c.i.f. | 1991 | 1992 | 1993 |
|---|---|---|---|
| Vegetable products | 29,557 | 137,471 | 360,553 |
| Prepared foodstuffs; beverages, spirits and vinegar; tobacco and manufactured substitutes | 28,805 | 141,621 | 312,054 |
| Mineral products | 210,277 | 649,597 | 1,500,230 |
|   Mineral fuels and oils, etc. | 183,932 | 595,365 | 1,345,144 |
| Products of chemical or allied industries | 32,865 | 132,002 | 380,111 |
|   Organic chemicals and products | 8,697 | 44,406 | 102,821 |
| Plastics, rubber and articles thereof | 6,110 | 57,624 | 153,253 |
| Textiles and textile articles | 19,689 | 180,034 | 505,862 |
|   Discontinuous synthetic and artificial fibres | 1,018 | 41,765 | 111,958 |
| Base metals and articles thereof | 19,420 | 87,171 | 208,909 |
| Machinery and mechanical appliances; electrical equipment; sound and television apparatus | 67,081 | 292,862 | 889,132 |
|   Nuclear reactors, boilers, machinery and mechanical appliances | 44,535 | 190,607 | 595,179 |
|   Electrical machinery and appliances; sound and television apparatus | 22,546 | 102,255 | 293,953 |
| Vehicles, aircraft, vessels and associated transport equipment | 11,405 | 94,119 | 239,376 |
|   Passenger motor cars, tractors and other road vehicles | 9,603 | 48,671 | 97,089 |
| **Total** (incl. others) | 463,932 | 2,005,396 | 5,087,390 |

| Exports f.o.b. | 1991 | 1992 | 1993 |
|---|---|---|---|
| Live animals and animal products | 11,853 | 59,130 | 134,733 |
| Mineral products | 49,693 | 183,151 | 430,014 |
|   Mineral fuels and oils, etc. | 42,781 | 157,420 | 361,928 |
| Products of chemical or allied industries | 22,857 | 134,944 | 260,671 |
|   Inorganic chemicals and products | 4,792 | 28,131 | 44,837 |
|   Fertilizers | 11,556 | 67,683 | 128,468 |
| Wood, cork and articles thereof; wood charcoal; manufactures of straw, esparto, etc. | 9,203 | 49,564 | 143,451 |
|   Wood, charcoal and articles of wood | 7,983 | 44,464 | 134,885 |
| Textiles and textile articles | 32,342 | 145,907 | 608,634 |
|   Knitted or crocheted clothing and accessories | 6,594 | 26,939 | 105,693 |
|   Non-knitted clothing and accessories | 16,144 | 66,800 | 382,821 |
| Footwear, headgear, umbrellas, walking-sticks, whips, etc.; prepared feathers; artificial flowers; articles of human hair | 6,954 | 23,287 | 127,924 |
|   Footwear and parts | 6,806 | 22,110 | 123,855 |
| Articles of stone, plaster, cement, asbestos, mica, etc.; ceramic products; glass and glassware | 6,013 | 28,248 | 73,910 |
| Base metals and articles thereof | 50,792 | 235,496 | 716,079 |
|   Iron and steel | 27,747 | 140,196 | 502,631 |
|   Manufactures of iron and steel | 11,428 | 44,094 | 110,778 |
|   Aluminium and articles thereof | 10,160 | 43,550 | 77,079 |
| Machinery and mechanical appliances; electrical equipment; sound and television apparatus | 55,392 | 162,779 | 345,520 |
|   Nuclear reactors, boilers, machinery and mechanical appliances | 48,192 | 139,083 | 263,822 |
|   Electrical machinery and appliances; sound and television apparatus | 7,200 | 23,696 | 81,698 |
| Vehicles, aircraft, vessels and associated transport equipment | 39,373 | 151,494 | 304,792 |
|   Vehicles and equipment for railways, etc. | 13,304 | 39,008 | 62,307 |
|   Passenger motor cars, tractors and other road vehicles | 17,053 | 75,897 | 194,161 |
|   Vessels and equipment for maritime and river navigation | 7,629 | 34,015 | 34,483 |
| Furniture, bed linen, etc.; lighting devices | 32,040 | 115,074 | 294,648 |
| **Total** (incl. others) | 341,594 | 1,397,899 | 3,775,942 |

### PRINCIPAL TRADING PARTNERS (million lei)

| Imports c.i.f. | 1991 | 1992 | 1993 |
|---|---|---|---|
| Austria | 14,889 | 61,189 | 127,846 |
| Belgium | 4,103 | 22,822 | 62,362 |
| Bulgaria | 5,243 | 28,612 | 52,984 |
| China, People's Republic | 12,358 | 23,573 | 70,257 |
| Czechoslovakia (former) | 7,943 | 25,214 | 45,284* |
| Egypt | 25,864 | 51,417 | 66,913 |
| France | 17,776 | 152,017 | 385,931 |
| Germany | 47,334 | 264,727 | 806,444 |
| Greece | 7,266 | 23,961 | 51,207 |
| Hungary | 9,858 | 57,144 | 126,743 |
| Iran | 36,809 | 149,470 | 500,583 |
| Israel | 2,071 | 15,033 | 64,071 |
| Italy | 16,727 | 156,078 | 473,200 |
| Japan | 5,771 | 24,330 | 48,044 |
| Libya | 9,592 | 23,038 | 15,746 |
| Moldova | 1,619 | 38,589 | 65,625 |
| Netherlands | 7,687 | 48,600 | 118,372 |
| Russia | 82,746 | 255,776 | 618,043 |
| Saudi Arabia | 26,416 | 31,451 | 18,000 |
| Switzerland | 10,350 | 40,251 | 101,465 |
| Turkey | 10,651 | 56,526 | 114,673 |
| Ukraine | 280 | 47,449 | 105,335 |
| United Kingdom | 11,835 | 60,122 | 125,999 |
| USA | 14,757 | 71,219 | 304,189 |
| **Total** (incl. others) | 463,932 | 2,005,396 | 5,087,390 |

* Czech Republic 26,058; Slovakia 19,226.

ROMANIA

| Exports f.o.b. | 1991 | 1992 | 1993 |
|---|---|---|---|
| Austria | 8,377 | 33,543 | 57,976 |
| Belgium | 3,783 | 15,625 | 59,091 |
| Bulgaria | 4,828 | 37,193 | 81,714 |
| China, People's Republic | 11,179 | 63,672 | 307,306 |
| Egypt | 5,547 | 24,821 | 78,673 |
| France | 13,718 | 54,880 | 168,782 |
| Germany | 37,085 | 153,549 | 543,025 |
| Greece | 4,206 | 37,018 | 67,447 |
| Hungary | 6,573 | 25,944 | 88,333 |
| Iran | 4,115 | 38,741 | 54,811 |
| Israel | 2,290 | 9,813 | 44,449 |
| Italy | 20,973 | 84,961 | 312,688 |
| Japan | 7,920 | 19,193 | 39,703 |
| Lebanon | 6,582 | 34,847 | 36,290 |
| Moldova | 1,069 | 22,980 | 77,913 |
| Netherlands | 18,096 | 35,198 | 146,256 |
| Nigeria | 3,491 | 4,127 | 53,117 |
| Poland | 7,104 | 16,934 | 16,330 |
| Russia | 77,583 | 132,799 | 170,478 |
| Singapore | 750 | 12,688 | 42,698 |
| Switzerland | 5,352 | 20,975 | 93,432 |
| Syria | 4,558 | 34,438 | 107,456 |
| Turkey | 12,247 | 70,216 | 215,476 |
| Ukraine | — | 33,468 | 79,928 |
| United Kingdom | 12,756 | 50,482 | 136,487 |
| USA | 10,012 | 26,754 | 53,987 |
| **Total** (incl. others) | 341,594 | 1,397,899 | 3,775,942 |

## Transport

### RAILWAYS (traffic)

| | 1991 | 1992 | 1993 |
|---|---|---|---|
| Passenger journeys (million) | 362.6 | 323.8 | 225.4 |
| Passenger-km (million) | 25,429 | 24,269 | 19,402 |
| Freight transported (million metric tons) | 146.3 | 111.4 | 99.0 |
| Freight ton-km (million) | 37,853 | 28,170 | 25,170 |

**1994:** Passenger-km 18,312 million; Freight ton-km 24,704 million.

### ROAD TRAFFIC

| | 1991 | 1992 | 1993 |
|---|---|---|---|
| Passenger journeys (million)* | 760.0 | 677.7 | 506.1 |
| Passenger-km (million)* | 20,639 | 25,341 | 19,817 |
| Freight transported (million metric tons) | 986.2 | 707.5 | 574.5 |
| Freight ton-km (million) | 20,390 | 15,271 | 14,534 |

* Public transport.

### INLAND WATERWAYS (traffic)

| | 1991 | 1992 | 1993 |
|---|---|---|---|
| Passenger journeys ('000) | 1,361 | 1,124 | 868 |
| Passenger-km (million) | 33 | 26 | 25 |
| Freight transported ('000 metric tons) | 8,249 | 6,198 | 7,074 |
| Freight ton-km (million) | 2,030 | 1,890 | 1,592 |

**1994:** Passenger-km 25 million; Freight ton-km 1,586 million.

### SEA-BORNE SHIPPING (traffic)

| | 1991 | 1992 | 1993 |
|---|---|---|---|
| Freight transported ('000 metric tons) | 22,316 | 14,133 | 6,918 |
| Freight ton-km (million) | 108,089 | 62,076 | 38,175 |

### CIVIL AVIATION (traffic)

| | 1991 | 1992 | 1993 |
|---|---|---|---|
| Passenger journeys ('000) | 1,712 | 1,714 | 1,717 |
| Passenger-km (million) | 2,694 | 2,732 | 2,698 |
| Freight transported ('000 metric tons) | 13* | 47 | 35 |
| Freight ton-km (million) | 26* | 136 | 108 |

* Excluding transport by aircraft leased to some foreign agencies.

## Tourism

**FOREIGN TOURIST ARRIVALS** ('000)

| Country of origin | 1992 | 1993 | 1994 |
|---|---|---|---|
| Bulgaria | 1,058 | 845 | 1,022 |
| Czech Republic | — | 108 | 121 |
| France | n.a. | 51 | 40 |
| Germany | 214 | 214 | 203 |
| Greece | 48 | 62 | n.a. |
| Hungary | 856 | 631 | 628 |
| Italy | 78 | 99 | 93 |
| Poland | 170 | 139 | 119 |
| Slovakia | — | 43 | n.a. |
| Turkey | 222 | 468 | n.a. |
| USSR (former) | 2,319 | 1,110 | 1,091 |
| Yugoslavia (former) | 845 | 995 | 634 |
| **Total** (incl. others) | 6,401 | 5,786 | 5,898 |

## Communications Media

| | 1990 | 1991 | 1992 |
|---|---|---|---|
| Radio receivers ('000 in use) | n.a. | 4,620 | 4,640 |
| Television receivers ('000 in use) | n.a. | 4,560 | 4,580 |
| Telephones ('000 main lines in use) | 2,366 | 2,443 | n.a. |
| Book production (incl. pamphlets): | | | |
| Titles | 2,178 | 2,914 | 3,662 |
| Copies ('000) | 52,477 | 57,272 | 66,598 |
| Daily newspapers | 65 | 83 | 102 |
| Other periodicals | 1,379 | 1,253 | 1,103 |

**1993:** Daily newspapers 100; Other periodicals 987.

Sources: partly UNESCO, *Statistical Yearbook*; UN, *Statistical Yearbook*.

## Education

(1993/94)

| | Institutions | Pupils | Teachers |
|---|---|---|---|
| Kindergartens | 12,715 | 712,136 | 37,303 |
| Primary and gymnasium schools | 13,945 | 2,533,491 | 164,780 |
| Secondary schools | 1,277 | 722,421 | 59,488 |
| Vocational schools | 739 | 300,413 | 6,222 |
| Specialized technical schools | 861 | 66,955 | 1,976 |
| Higher schools | 63 | 250,087 | 19,130 |

# Directory

## The Constitution

Following its assumption of power in December 1989, the National Salvation Front decreed radical changes to the Constitution of 1965. The name of the country was changed from the 'Socialist Republic of Romania' to 'Romania'. The leading role of a single political party was abolished, a democratic and pluralist system of government being established.

The combined chambers of the legislature elected in May 1990, working as a constituent assembly, drafted a new Constitution (based on the Constitution of France's Fifth Republic), which was approved in a national referendum on 8 December 1991.

Under the 1991 Constitution political power in Romania belongs to the people and is exercised according to the principles of democracy, freedom and human dignity, of inviolability and inalienability of basic human rights. Romania is governed on the basis of a multi-party democratic system and of the separation of the legal, executive and judicial powers. Romania's legislature, consisting of the Chamber of Deputies (the lower house, with 341 seats, of which 13 are reserved for various ethnic minorities) and the Senate (the upper house, with 143 seats), and Romania's President are elected by universal, free, direct and secret vote, the President serving a maximum of two terms. The term of office of the legislature and of the President is four years. Citizens have the right to vote at the age of 18, and may be elected at the age of 21 to the Chamber of Deputies and at the age of 30 to the Senate, with no upper age limit. Those ineligible for election include former members of the Securitate (the secret police of President Ceauşescu) and other former officials guilty of repression and abuses. Independent candidates are eligible for election to the Chamber of Deputies and to the Senate if supported by at least 251 electors and to the Presidency if supported by 100,000 electors. Once elected, the President may not remain a member of any political party. The President appoints the Prime Minister, who in turn appoints the Council of Ministers

## The Government

### HEAD OF STATE

**President:** ION ILIESCU (assumed power as President of the National Salvation Front 26 December 1989, confirmed as President of Provisional National Unity Council 13 February 1990; elected by direct popular vote 20 May 1990, re-elected 11 October 1992).

### COUNCIL OF MINISTERS
(June 1995)

Composed of independents (Ind.) and members of the Party of Social Democracy of Romania (PSDR) and the Romanian National Unity Party (RNUP).

**Prime Minister:** NICOLAE VĂCĂROIU (Ind.).
**Deputy Prime Minister and Chairman of the Council for Economic Co-ordination, Strategy and Reform:** MIRCEA DUMITRU COŞEA (Ind.).
**Deputy Prime Minister and Minister of Employment and Social Protection:** DAN MIRCEA POPESCU (PSDR).
**Deputy Prime Minister and Minister of Finance:** FLORIN GEORGESCU (Ind.).
**Deputy Prime Minister and Minister of Foreign Affairs:** TEODOR VIOREL MELEŞCANU (Ind.).
**Minister of Justice:** IOSIF GAVRIL CHIUZBAIAN (Ind.).
**Minister of National Defence:** Lt-Gen. GHEORGHE TINCA (PSDR).
**Minister of the Interior:** DORU-IOAN TĂRĂCILĂ (PSDR).
**Minister of Industry:** DUMITRU POPESCU (PSDR).
**Minister of Agriculture and Food:** VALERIU TABĂRĂ (RNUP).
**Minister of Transport:** AUREL NOVAC (Ind.).
**Minister of Communications:** ADRIAN TURICU (RNUP).
**Minister of Commerce:** PETRU CRIŞAN (Ind.).
**Minister of Tourism:** DAN MATEI AGATHON (PSDR).
**Minister of Public Works and Land Improvement:** MARIN CRISTEA (PSDR).
**Minister of Waters, Forestry and Environmental Protection:** AUREL CONSTANTIN ILIE (Ind.).
**Minister of Education:** LIVIU MAIOR (PSDR).
**Minister of Research and Technology:** DORU DUMITRU PALADE (Ind.).
**Minister of Health:** Prof. IULIAN MINCU (PSDR).
**Minister of Culture:** VIOREL MĂRGINEAN (Ind.).
**Minister of Youth and Sports:** ALEXANDRU MIRONOV (PSDR).
**Minister for Relations with Parliament:** VALER DORNEANU (Ind.).

### MINISTRIES

**Office of the Prime Minister:** 71201 Bucharest, Piaţa Victoriei 1; tel. (1) 143400; telex 11057; fax (1) 592018.
**Ministry of Agriculture and Food:** 70433 Bucharest, Bd. Carol I 24; tel. (1) 154412; telex 11217; fax (1) 130322.
**Ministry of Commerce:** 70663 Bucharest, Str. Apolodor 17; tel. (1) 141141; telex 10564; fax (1) 3122342.
**Ministry of Communications:** 70060 Bucharest, Bd. Libertăţii 14; tel. (1) 401100; telex 11372; fax (1) 401742.
**Ministry of Culture:** 71341 Bucharest, Piaţa Presei Libere 1; tel. (1) 170906; fax (1) 594781.
**Ministry of Education:** 70749 Bucharest, Str. Berthelot 30; tel. (1) 144588; telex 11637; fax (1) 157736.
**Ministry of Employment and Social Protection:** 70119 Bucharest 1, Str. Demetru I. Dobrescu 2–4; tel. (1) 6156563; fax (1) 6156563.
**Ministry of Finance:** 70663 Bucharest, Str. Apolodor 17; tel. (1) 311784; telex 11239; fax (1) 121630.
**Ministry of Foreign Affairs:** 71274 Bucharest, Al. Modrogan 14; tel. (1) 334060; telex 11220; fax (1) 127589.
**Ministry of Health:** 70109 Bucharest, Str. Ministerului 1–3; tel. (1) 6141526; telex 11982; fax (1) 3124883.
**Ministry of Industry:** 71101 Bucharest, Calea Victoriei 152; tel. (1) 503168; telex 11109; fax (1) 503029.
**Ministry of the Interior:** 70622 Bucharest, Str. Mihai Voda 6; tel. (1) 6151108; fax (1) 3113555.
**Ministry of Justice:** 70602 Bucharest, Bd. M. Kogălniceanu 33; tel. (1) 148623; telex 11964; fax (1) 131219.
**Ministry of National Defence:** 77303 Bucharest, Intrarea Drumul Taberei 9; tel. (1) 6315553; fax (1) 7450238.
**Ministry of Public Works and Land Improvement:** 70663 Bucharest, Str. Apolodor 17; tel. (1) 141690; telex 11727; fax (1) 121130.
**Ministry for Relations with Parliament:** Bucharest.
**Ministry of Research and Technology:** Bucharest.
**Ministry of Tourism:** 70663 Bucharest, Str. Apolodor 17; tel. (1) 6310554; telex 11278; fax (1) 3120481.
**Ministry of Transport:** 77113 Bucharest, Bd. Dinicu Golescu 38; tel. (1) 6387886; telex 11372; fax (1) 3120984.
**Ministry of Waters, Forestry and Environmental Protection:** 70005 Bucharest, Bd. Libertăţii 12; tel. (1) 7816394; telex 11457; fax (1) 3124227.
**Ministry of Youth and Sports:** 70139 Bucharest, Str. Vasile Conta 16; tel. (1) 3120160; telex 11180; fax (1) 3120161.
**Council for Economic Co-ordination, Strategy and Reform:** Bucharest.

## President

**Presidential Election, 27 September and 11 October 1992**

| Candidates | First ballot votes cast Number | % | Second ballot votes cast % |
|---|---|---|---|
| ION ILIESCU (DNSF) | 5,633,456 | 47.34 | 61.43 |
| EMIL CONSTANTINESCU (DCR) | 3,717,006 | 31.24 | 38.57 |
| GHEORGHE FUNAR (RNUP) | 1,294,388 | 10.88 | — |
| CAIUS DRAGOMIR (NSF) | 564,655 | 4.75 | — |
| ION MANZATU (RP) | 362,485 | 3.05 | — |
| MIRCEA DRUC (Independent) | 326,866 | 2.75 | — |
| **Total** | 11,898,856 | 100.00 | 100.00 |

In addition, a total of 554,948 invalid votes were cast in the first ballot.

## Legislature

### PARLIAMENT

**Chairman of the Chamber of Deputies:** ADRIAN NĂSTASE (PSDR).
**Chairman of the Senate:** OLIVIU GHERMAN (PSDR).

# ROMANIA

## General Election, 27 September 1992

|  | Seats | |
| --- | ---: | ---: |
|  | Chamber of Deputies | Senate |
| Democratic National Salvation Front (DNSF)* | 117 | 49 |
| Democratic Convention of Romania (DCR) Alliance | 82 | 34 |
| Christian Democratic National Peasants' Party | 42 | 21 |
| Party of the Civic Alliance | 13 | 7 |
| National Liberal Party—Democratic Convention† | 2 | 4 |
| National Liberal Party—Youth Wing† | 11 | 1 |
| Romanian Social Democratic Party‡ | 10 | 1 |
| Romanian Ecological Party | 4 | — |
| National Salvation Front (NSF)§ | 43 | 18 |
| Romanian National Unity Party (RNUP) | 30 | 14 |
| Hungarian Democratic Union of Romania (HDUR) | 27 | 12 |
| Greater Romania Party (România Mare) | 16 | 6 |
| Socialist Labour Party (SLP) | 13 | 5 |
| Agrarian Democratic Party of Romania (ADPR) | — | 5 |
| **Total** | 328‖ | 143 |

\* Name changed to Party of Social Democracy of Romania (PSDR) in 1993.
† United in 1993 to form the Liberal Party 1993.
‡ Absorbed into the PSDR in 1993.
§ Name changed to Democratic Party—National Salvation Front (NSF) in 1993.
‖ In addition, a total of 13 seats were reserved in the Chamber of Deputies for ethnic minorities, giving an overall total of 341 seats.

## Political Organizations

Following the downfall of President Ceauşescu in December 1989, numerous political parties were formed or re-established in preparation for the holding of free elections. By April 1990 more than 80 parties had been registered by the Bucharest Municipal Court, and by the time of the September 1992 general election there were 91 registered political parties. The financing of political parties from abroad is not permitted.

**Agrarian Democratic Party of Romania (ADPR) (Partidul Democrat Agrar din România):** Bucharest, Al. Alexandru 45; tel. (1) 336672; f. 1990; supported by agricultural workers; advocates defence of the Romanian villagers' way of life; 172,000 mems; Pres. VICTOR SURDU.

**Christian Democratic National Peasants' Party (Partidul Naţional Ţărănesc-Creştin şi Democrat):** 70433 Bucharest, Bd. Carol 34; tel. (1) 147819; fax (1) 154533; f. 1990 by merger of centre-right Christian Democratic Party and traditional National Peasant Party (f. 1869, banned 1947, revived Dec. 1989; original party re-established in Aug. 1990 by separate group); supports pluralist democracy and the restoration of peasant property; 615,000 mems; Pres. CORNELIU COPOSU.

**Civic Alliance (Alianţa Civică):** Bucharest; f. 1990 as alliance of opposition groupings outside legislature; voted, in July 1991, to create a parallel political party, the Party of the Civic Alliance (see below); Chair. ANA BLANDIANA.

**Democratic Convention of Romania (DCR) Alliance:** 70001 Bucharest, Splaiul Unirii 5, ap. 1, sect. 3; tel. (1) 3124014; fax 3124041; f. 1992; alliance of 18 centre-right parties and other organizations (see Legislature, above); Pres. EMIL CONSTANTINESCU.

**Democratic Party—National Salvation Front (NSF):** 70024 Bucharest, Al. Modrogan 1; tel. (1) 2121421; fax (1) 2121332; f. Dec. 1989, as National Salvation Front, changed name in May 1993; centre-left; advocates a modern and social-democratic Romania, with a free-market economy, freedom of press and of religion, and respect for the rights and freedoms of national minorities; Pres. PETRE ROMAN.

**Greater Romania Party (România Mare):** Bucharest; nationalist; Chair. CORNELIU VADIM TUDOR.

**Hungarian Democratic Union of Romania (HDUR) (Uniunea Democrată Maghiară din România):** Bucharest, str. Herăstrău 13; tel. (1) 3214935; fax (1) 2121675; f. 1990; supports the rights of Hungarians in Romania; Hon. Pres. LÁSZLÓ TŐKES; Pres. BÉLA MARKÓ.

**Liberal Monarchist Party of Romania (Partidul Liberal Monarhist din România):** Bucharest, Bd. George Coşbuc 1; tel. (1) 6134940; f. 1990; advocates the restoration of the monarchy; Pres. DAN CERNOVODEANU.

**Liberal Party 1993:** Bucharest; f. 1993 by merger of the National Liberal Party—Democratic Convention and the National Liberal Party—Youth Wing; later joined by faction of the Party of the Civic Alliance; Pres. DINU PATRICIU.

**Liberal Union 'Bratianu' (Uniunea Liberală 'Bratianu'):** Bucharest, Calea Victoriei 95–97, Sector 1; tel. (1) 6594487; fax (1) 3120808; f. 1990 following split in National Liberal Party; Pres. ION I. BRATIANU.

**National Liberal Party (Partidul Naţional Liberal):** Bucharest, Bd. Bălcescu 21; tel. (1) 6143235; fax (1) 6157638; f. 1869, banned 1947; merged with Socialist Liberal Party in 1990; advocates separation of powers in the State, restoration of democracy, freedom of expression and religion, observance of the equal rights of all minorities, the abolition of collectivization and nationalization in agriculture, the gradual privatization of enterprises, trade union freedom and the right to strike; Pres. MIRCEA IONESCU-QUINTUS.

**Party of the Civic Alliance (PCA) (Partidul Alianţei Civice):** 73311 Bucharest, Bd. Matiunilor Unite 5, block 110; tel. (1) 615310; f. 1991; set up by Civic Alliance to contest elections; Pres. NICOLAE MANOLESCU.

**Party of Social Democracy of Romania (PSDR):** Bucharest, Str. Filioara 3, Sector 2; tel. (1) 611777; f. 1992 (as National Salvation Front—22 December, later known as the Democratic National Salvation Front) by supporters of Ion Iliescu, following split in the National Salvation Front (f. 1989); renamed as above in July 1993; social-democratic party; merged with the Democratic Co-operationist Party, the Republican Party and the Romanian Social Democratic Party in July 1993; Pres. OLIVIU GHERMAN; Exec. Pres. ADRIAN NĂSTASE.

**Romanian Ecological Movement (Mişcarea Ecologistă din România):** Bucharest, Al. Alexandru Phillippide 11; tel. (1) 6142943; f. 1990; advocates protection of the environment and the pursuit of democratic pacifist and humanist values; Chair. TOMA GEORGE MAIORESCU.

**Romanian Ecological Party (Partidul Ecologist Român):** Bucharest, Bd. George Coşbuc 1, block P58; tel. (1) 6312350; supports protection of the environment; Chair. OTTO WEBER.

**Romanian National Unity Party (RNUP) (Partidul Unităţii Naţionale Române):** 4300 Târgu Mureş, Str. Bolyai F30; tel. (65) 433619; f. 1990; political wing of the nationalist Romanian movement, Vatra Românească; Leader GHEORGHE FUNAR.

**Socialist Labour Party (SLP) (Partidul Socialist al Muncii):** Bucharest, Str. Olari 12; tel. (1) 6351375; f. 1990 by Romanian Communist Party members and left-wing Democratic Labour Party; Chair. ILIE VERDEŢ.

**Traditional Social Democratic Party of Romania (Partidul Social Democrat Traditional din România):** Bucharest 2, Str. Aron Florian 1; tel. (1) 2110479; f. 1991 by merger of Traditional Social Democratic Party and National Democratic Party; supports the Party of Social Democracy of Romania; centre-left; Pres. EUGEN BRÂNZAN; Sec.-Gen. BOGDAN PASCU.

## Diplomatic Representation

### EMBASSIES IN ROMANIA

**Albania:** Bucharest, Str. Ştefan Gheorghiu 4; Ambassador: FRAN ZEF CUKAJ.

**Algeria:** Bucharest, Bd. Ana Ipătescu 29; tel. (1) 2115150; telex 10448; fax (1) 2115695; Ambassador: MOHAMED CHÉRIR.

**Argentina:** Bucharest, Str. Drobeta 11; tel. (1) 2117290; telex 11412; fax (1) 2101412; Ambassador: LILA SUBIRAN DE VIANA.

**Austria:** 70254 Bucharest, Str. Dumbrava Roşie 7; tel. (1) 2109377; telex 11333; fax (1) 2100885; Ambassador: PAUL ULLMANN.

**Bangladesh:** Bucharest, Bd. Kiseleff 55; tel. (1) 171544; telex 10197; Chargé d'affaires a.i.: MOHAMMED HASIB AZIZ.

**Belgium:** 79359 Bucharest, Bd. Dacia 58; tel. (1) 3122968; telex 11482; fax (1) 3122903; Ambassador: IGNACE VAN STEENBERGE.

**Brazil:** 71248 Bucharest, Str. Praga 11; tel. (1) 129823; telex 11307; fax (1) 127549; Ambassador: ADOLPHO CORRÊA DE SÁ E BENEVIDES.

**Bulgaria:** Bucharest, Str. Rabat 5; tel. (1) 2122150; fax (1) 3127654; Ambassador: MIRCHO IVANOV.

**Canada:** 71118 Bucharest, Str. N. Iorga 36; tel. (1) 3128345; telex 10690; fax (1) 3120366; Ambassador: MURRAY FAIRWEATHER.

**Chile:** Bucharest, Bd. Ana Ipătescu 8; tel. (1) 115691; telex 11197; Ambassador: SERGIO MIMICA BEZMALINOVIC.

**China, People's Republic:** Bucharest, Şos. Nordului 2; tel. (1) 6331925; telex 11316; fax (1) 3127523; Ambassador: LU QIUTIAN.

**Colombia:** Bucharest, Str. Polonă 35, ap. 3; tel. (1) 2115106; telex 10498; fax (1) 2100155; Ambassador: César Pardo Villalba.

**Congo:** Bucharest, Str. Armeneasca 35; tel. (1) 3128296; Ambassador: (vacant).

**Costa Rica:** Bucharest, Str. Lt. Gheorghe Manu 3–5, et. 1, ap. 10; tel. (1) 592008; telex 11939; Ambassador: Jorge Hasbum Pacheco.

**Cuba:** Bucharest, Str. Cámpina 46–48; tel. and fax (1) 6655769; telex 11305; Ambassador: Eulogio Rodríguez Millares.

**Czech Republic:** Bucharest 3, Str. Ion Ghica 11; tel. (1) 6159142; fax (1) 3122539; Ambassador: Jaromír Kvapil.

**Denmark:** 73102 Bucharest, Str. Dr Burhelea 3; tel. (1) 3120352; telex 11325; fax (1) 3120358; Ambassador: Ulrik Helweg-Larsen.

**Ecuador:** Bucharest, Str. Polonă 35, ap. 1; tel. (1) 110503; telex 10836; Chargé d'affaires: Rafael Veintimilla C.

**Egypt:** Bucharest, Bd. Dacia 21; tel. (1) 110138; telex 11549; Ambassador: Saad Abou el-Kheir.

**Finland:** Bucharest, Str. Atena 2 bis; tel. (1) 335440; telex 11293; fax (1) 3127505; Ambassador: Timo Koponen.

**France:** Bucharest, Str. Biserica Amzei 13–15; tel. (1) 3120217; telex 11320; fax (1) 3120200; Ambassador: Bernard Boyer.

**Germany:** 71272 Bucharest, Str. Rabat 21; tel. (1) 2122580; telex 10834; fax (1) 3129846; Ambassador: Dr Anton Rossbach.

**Greece:** Bucharest, Str. Orlando 6; tel. (1) 503988; telex 11321; Ambassador: Giorgios Linardos.

**Guinea:** Bucharest, Str. Bocşa 4; tel. (1) 111893; telex 10255; Ambassador: Abel Niouma Sandouno.

**Holy See:** 70749 Bucharest, Str. Pictor C. Stahi 5–7 (Apostolic Nunciature); tel. (1) 6139490; fax (1) 3120316; Apostolic Nuncio: Most Rev. Janusz Bolonek, Titular Archbishop of Madaurus.

**Hungary:** Bucharest, Str. J. L. Calderon 63; tel. (1) 146621; telex 11323; fax (1) 142846; Ambassador: Ernö Rudas.

**India:** 71274 Bucharest, Str. Uruguay 11; tel. (1) 2228715; telex 11619; fax (1) 2232681; Ambassador: Mani Lal Tripathi.

**Indonesia:** Bucharest, Orlando 10; tel. (1) 507720; telex 11258; Ambassador: Lamtiur Andaliah Panggabean.

**Iran:** Bucharest, Bd. Ana Ipătescu 39; tel. (1) 334471; telex 11507; Ambassador: Abdoul Rasoul Mohager Hegeazi.

**Iraq:** Bucharest, Str. Polonă 8; tel. (1) 110835; Ambassador: Sultan Ibrahim Shuja.

**Israel:** 73102 Bucharest, Str. Dr Burghelea 5; tel. (1) 3113465; telex 11685; fax (1) 120431; Ambassador: Avshalom Megiddon.

**Italy:** Bucharest, Str. Henri Coanda 7–9; tel. (1) 6507090; telex 11602; fax (1) 3120422; Ambassador: Giuseppe de Michelis di Slonghello.

**Japan:** Bucharest, Str. Polonă 4, Sector 1; tel. (1) 3120790; telex 11322; fax (1) 3120272; Ambassador: Yoshiki Sugiura.

**Jordan:** Bucharest, Str. Dumbrava Roşie 1; tel. (1) 2104705; telex 11477; fax (1) 210320; Ambassador: Fawaz Abu-Tayeh.

**Korea, Democratic People's Republic:** Bucharest, Şos. Nordului 6; tel. (1) 331926; Ambassador: Kim Yu Sun.

**Korea, Republic:** 70412 Bucharest, Calea Victoriei 2; tel. (1) 137941; Ambassador: Yi Hyun-Hong.

**Lebanon:** Bucharest, Str. Atena 28; tel. (1) 3120301; telex 11645; fax (1) 3127534; Ambassador: Emile Bedran.

**Liberia:** Bucharest, Str. Mihai Eminescu 82–88; tel. (1) 6193029; Chargé d'affaires: G. Marcus Kelley.

**Libya:** Bucharest, Bd. Ana Ipătescu 15; tel. (1) 6507105; telex 10290; fax (1) 3120232; Chargé d'affaires: Abdula F. Yala.

**Malaysia:** Bucharest, Bd. Dacia 30; tel. (1) 113801; Ambassador: Zainuddin bin Abdul Rahman.

**Mauritania:** Bucharest, Str. Duiliu Zamfirescu 7; tel. (1) 592305; telex 10595; Ambassador: Kane Cheikh Mohamed Fadhel.

**Moldova:** Bucharest, Al. Alexandru 40, Sector 1; tel. and fax (1) 3129790; telex 10910; Ambassador: Grigore Eremei.

**Mongolia:** Bucharest, Str. Făgăraş 6; tel. (1) 6387370; telex 11504; fax (1) 3121325; Chargé d'affaires a.i.: Tündevdorjïn Zalaa-Ul.

**Morocco:** Bucharest, Bd. Dacia 25; tel. (1) 192945; telex 11687; Ambassador: Mohamed Halim.

**Netherlands:** 71271 Bucharest, Str. Atena 18; tel. (1) 2122242; telex 11474; fax (1) 3127620; Ambassador: Monique P. A. Frank.

**Nigeria:** Bucharest, Str. Orlando 9; tel. (1) 6504050; telex 10478; Ambassador: Dr L. E. Okogwu.

**Pakistan:** Bucharest, Str. Barbu Delavrancea 22; tel. (1) 6177402; Ambassador: Nawabzada Mehboob Ali Khan.

**Peru:** Bucharest, Str. Paris 45a; tel. (1) 331124; telex 11566; Ambassador: Guillermo Gerdau O'Connor.

**Philippines:** Bucharest, Vasile Conta 12; tel. (1) 3120083; fax: (1) 3123479; Ambassador: Alicia C. Palacios.

**Poland:** Bucharest, Al. Alexandru 23; tel. (1) 2122330; telex 11302; fax (1) 3129832; Ambassador: Bogumił Luft.

**Russia:** Bucharest, Şos. Kiseleff 6; tel. (1) 170120; Ambassador: Yevgeny Ostrovenko.

**Slovakia:** Bucharest 2, Str. Otetari 3; tel. (1) 3123352; telex 11548; fax (1) 6150338; Ambassador: Milan Resutík.

**Spain:** Bucharest, Str. Tirana 1; tel. (1) 335730; telex 11508; Ambassador: Antonio Núñez García-Sauco.

**Sudan:** Bucharest, Bd. Dacia 35; tel. (1) 118352; telex 10855; Ambassador: Lawrence Mode Tombe.

**Sweden:** Bucharest, Str. Sofia 5; tel. (1) 173184; telex 11313; Ambassador: Nils G. Rosenberg.

**Switzerland:** 70152 Bucharest 1, Str. Pitar Moş 12; tel. (1) 2100299; telex 11579; fax (1) 2100324; Ambassador: Jean-Pierre Vettovaglia.

**Syria:** Bucharest, Bd. Ana Ipătescu 50; tel. (1) 503195; telex 10061; Ambassador: Hicham Kahaleh.

**Thailand:** Bucharest, Str. Mihai Eminescu 44–48; tel. (1) 2101338; telex 10247; fax (1) 2102600; Ambassador: Dr Suphasin Jayanama.

**Tunisia:** Bucharest, Aurel Vlaicu 13; tel. (1) 2100319; telex 11829; fax (1) 2100318; Chargé d'affaires: Abdeljaoued Mezoughi.

**Turkey:** Bucharest, Calea Dorobanţilor 72; tel. (1) 193625; Ambassador: Tugay Ulucevik.

**Ukraine:** Bucharest, Rabat Str. 1; tel. (1) 124547; fax (1) 124514; Ambassador: Leontiy I. Sandulyak.

**United Kingdom:** 70154 Bucharest, Str. Jules Michelet 24; tel. (1) 3120303; telex 11295; fax (1) 3120229; Ambassador: Andrew P. F. Bache.

**USA:** Bucharest, Str. Tudor Arghezi 7–9; tel. (1) 214042; telex 11416; fax (1) 2100395; Ambassador: Alfred H. Moses.

**Uruguay:** Bucharest, Str. Polonă 35; tel. (1) 2118212; telex 10475; fax (1) 2100348; Ambassador: Gastón Sciarra.

**Venezuela:** Bucharest, Str. Pictor Mirea 18, Sector 1; tel. (1) 6185874; telex 10470; fax (1) 2224311; Ambassador: Gustavo Garaicoechea.

**Viet Nam:** Bucharest, Str. Gr. Alexandrescu 86; tel. (1) 116120; telex 11604; Ambassador: Nguyen Trong Lieu.

**Yugoslavia:** Bucharest, Calea Dorobanţilor 34; tel. (1) 2119871; telex 92535; fax (1) 191752; Ambassador: Dr Desimir Jevtić.

**Zaire:** Bucharest, Al. Alexandru 41; tel. (1) 795717; telex 11503; Ambassador: Musungayi Nkuembe Mampuya.

## Judicial System

### SUPREME COURT

The Supreme Court of Justice, which was reorganized under Law 56 of 9 July 1993, exercises control over the judicial activity of all courts. It ensures the correct and uniform application of the law. The members of the Supreme Court are appointed by the President of Romania at the proposal of the Superior Council of Magistrates.

**President:** Dr Gheorghe Uglean; 70503 Bucharest, Calea Rahovei 2–4; tel. (1) 6133736; telex 11165; fax (1) 3125893.

### COUNTY COURTS AND LOCAL COURTS

The judicial organization of courts at the county and local levels was established by Law 92 of 4 August 1992. In each of the 40 counties of Romania there is a county court and between three and six local courts. The county courts also form 15 circuits of appeal courts, where appeals against sentences passed by local courts are heard, which are generally considered courts of first instance. There is also a right of appeal from the appeal courts to the Supreme Court. In both county courts and local courts the judges are professional magistrates.

### MILITARY COURTS

Military courts were reorganized through Law 54 of 9 July 1993. Generally they judge contraventions of the law by service personnel at one of the two military courts in the country. These are the Territorial Military Court, with a right of appeal to the Appeal Military Court. There is also a military department within the Supreme Court which judges appeals in some special cases. The judges are professional lawyers and career officers.

### GENERAL PROSECUTING MAGISTRACY

The General Prosecuting Magistracy functions under Law 92 of 4 August 1992. There are prosecuting magistracies operating through each court, under the authority of the Minister of Justice.

**Prosecutor-General:** Vasile Manea-Drăgulin; tel. (1) 812727.

ROMANIA  *Directory*

## Religion

In Romania there are 15 religious denominations and more than 120 religious associations recognized by the State. About 83% of believers belong to the Romanian Orthodox Church.

**State Secretariat for Religious Affairs:** 70136 Bucharest, Str. Snagov 40; tel. (1) 6112125; f. 1990; Minister Sec. of State: Prof. GHEORGHE VLĂDUȚESCU.

### CHRISTIANITY
#### The Romanian Orthodox Church

The Romanian Orthodox Church is the major religious organization in Romania (with more than 19m. believers) and is organized as an autocephalous patriarchate, being led by the Holy Synod, headed by a patriarch. The Patriarchate consists of five metropolitanates, nine archbishoprics and 10 bishoprics.

**Holy Synod:** 70666 Bucharest, Str. Antim 29; tel. (1) 6313413; fax (1) 3120873; Sec. TEOFAN SINAITUL.

**Patriarhia Română/(Romanian Patriarchate):** 70526 Bucharest 4, Str. Patriarhiei 2; tel. (1) 6156772; fax (1) 3128056.

**Patriarch, Metropolitan of Muntênia and Dobrogea and Archbishop of Bucharest:** TEOCTIST ARĂPAȘU.

**Metropolitan of Banat and Archbishop of Timișoara and Caransebeș:** Dr NICOLAE CORNEANU (resident in Timișoara).

**Metropolitan of Moldova and Bukovina and Archbishop of Iași:** Dr DANIEL CIOBOTEA (resident in Iași).

**Metropolitan of Oltenia and Archbishop of Craiova:** Dr NESTOR VORNICESCU (resident in Craiova).

**Metropolitan of Transylvania, Crișana and Maramureș and Archbishop of Sibiu:** Dr ANTONIE PLĂMĂDEALĂ (resident in Sibiu).

**Archbishop of Suceava and Rădăuti:** PIMEN ZAINEA (resident in Suceava).

**Archbishop of Târgoviște:** Dr VASILE COSTIN (resident in Târgoviște).

**Archbishop of Tomis:** LUCIAN FLOREA (resident in Galați).

**Archbishop of Vad, Feleac and Cluj:** BARTOLOMEU ANANIA (resident in Cluj-Napoca).

#### The Roman Catholic Church

Catholics in Romania include adherents of the Armenian, Latin and Romanian (Byzantine) Rites.

*Latin Rite*

There are two archdioceses and four dioceses. At 31 December 1993 there were 1,265,835 adherents of the Latin Rite (about 6% of the total population).

**Archbishop of Alba Iulia:** Most Rev. GYÖRGY-MIKLÓS JACUBINYI, 2500 Alba Iulia, Str. Mihai Viteazul 21; tel. (58) 811689; fax (58) 811454.

**Archbishop of Bucharest:** Most Rev. IOAN ROBU, 70749 Bucharest, Str. Nuferilor 19; tel. (1) 6133936; fax (1) 3121207.

*Romanian Rite*

There is one metropolitan and four dioceses. At 31 December 1993 there were 2,005,385 adherents of the Romanian Rite (some 9% of the population).

**Metropolitan of the Romanian Uniate Church and Archbishop of Făgăraș and Alba Iulia:** Most Rev. LUCIAN MUREȘAN, 3175 Blaj, Str. P. P. Aron 2; tel. (58) 712057; fax (58) 710855.

#### Protestant Churches

**Baptist Union of Romania:** 78152 Bucharest 1, Bd. N. Titulescu 56/A; tel. (1) 6173705; 1,300 churches; Pres. Rev. VASILE AL. TALOȘ.

**Evangelical Church of the Augsburg Confession:** 2400 Sibiu, Str. General Magheru 4; tel. and fax (69) 217864; Gen. Sec. HANS-GERALD BINDER; tel. (69) 433680; telex 69200; fax (69) 433680; founded in the 16th century, comprises some 21,000 mems, mainly of German nationality; Bishop of Sibiu Dr CHRISTOPH KLEIN; Gen. Sec. HANS-GERALD BINDER.

**Reformed (Calvinist) Church:** 700,000 mems; two bishoprics:

**Bishop of Cluj-Napoca:** Dr KÁLMÁN CSIHA, 3400 Cluj-Napoca, Str. I. C. Brătianu 51; tel. (64) 117472; fax (64) 195104.

**Bishop of Oradea:** LÁSZLÓ TÖKES, 3700 Oradea, Str. Craiovei 1; tel. (991) 31710.

**Synodo-Presbyterian Evangelical-Lutheran Church:** 3400 Cluj-Napoca, Bd. 21 Decembrie 1; tel. (64) 116614; fax (64) 193897; comprises about 25,000 mems of Hungarian, 4,000 mems of Slovak and 200 mems of Romanian nationality; Superintendent ÁRPÁD MÓZES.

**Unitarian Church:** 3400 Cluj-Napoca, Bd. 22 Decembrie 9; tel. (64) 15927; fax (64) 15927; f. 1568; comprises about 75,000 mems of Hungarian nationality; Bishop LAJOS KOVÁCS.

#### Other Christian Churches

**Armenian-Gregorian Church:** 70334 Bucharest, Str. Armenească 9; tel. (1) 6140208; fax (1) 3121083; 5,000 mems.; Archbishop TIRAIR MARTICHIAN.

**Old-Rite Christian Church:** 6100 Brăila, Str. Zidari 1; 50,000 mems. of Russian nationality; Metropolitan TIMON GAVRILA.

**Open Brethren Church:** Head: MELITON LAZAROVICI.

**Pentecostal Church:** Bucharest, Str. Carol Davila 81; tel. (1) 6384425; 350,000 mems; Pres. Rev. RIVIS TIPEI PAVEL.

**Seventh-day Adventist Church:** Bucharest, Str. Plantelor 12; tel. (1) 3129253; fax (1) 3129255; 63,500 mems; Pres. of the Union Rev. NELU DUMITRESCU.

**Union of Brethren Assemblies:** 72461 Bucharest, Andronache 60A; tel. and fax (1) 2407865; f. 1925; Pres. Dr SILVIU CIOATĂ.

### ISLAM

The Muslim Community comprises some 55,000 members of Turkish-Tatar nationality.

**Grand Mufti:** OSMAN NEGEAT, 8700 Constanța, Bd. Tomis 41.

### JUDAISM

In 1994 there were about 14,000 Jews, organized in 70 communities, in Romania.

**Federation of Jewish Communities:** 70478 Bucharest, Str. Sf. Vinieri 9–11; tel. (1) 6132538; telex 10798; fax (1) 3120869; Chief Rabbi (vacant); Pres. Prof. Dr NICOLAE CAJAL.

## The Press

The Romanian press is highly regionalized, with newspapers and periodicals appearing in all of the administrative districts. In 1993 there were a total of 1,087 newspapers and periodicals in circulation in Romania, including 100 daily newspapers. Some 106 newspapers and periodicals are published in the languages of co-inhabiting nationalities in Romania, including Hungarian, German, Serbian, Ukrainian, Armenian and Yiddish. The Ministry of Culture relinquished control of the press in June 1990.

The publications listed below are in Romanian, unless otherwise indicated.

### PRINCIPAL NEWSPAPERS

**Academia Catavencu** (Dubious Academy): Bucharest, Str. Virtutii 3, ap. 23; tel. (1) 4209454; fax (1) 6103894; f. 1992; weekly; satirical; Editors SORIN VULPE, LIVIO MINAIU, MIRCEA TOMA; circ. 85,000.

**Adevărul** (Truth): 71341 Bucharest, Piața Presei Libere 1; tel. (1) 6182030; telex 11342; fax (1) 175540; f. 1989; daily except Sun.; independent; Editor-in-Chief DUMITRU TINU; circ. 137,627.

**Alianța Civică** (Civic Alliance): 71102 Bucharest, Calea Victoriei 133-135, Sc. A, et. 3; tel. and fax (1) 595909; f. 1991; daily; organ of the Civic Alliance.

**Allgemeine Deutsche Zeitung für Rumänien:** 79777 Bucharest, Piața Presei Libere 1; tel. (1) 2228537; fax (1) 2223319; f. 1949; fmrly *Neuer Weg*; daily except Sun. and Mon.; political, economic, social and cultural news; in German; Editor-in-Chief EMMERICH REICHRATH; circ. 10,000.

**Azi** (Today): 70101 Bucharest, Calea Victoriei 39A; tel. (1) 3121574; telex 11054; fax (1) 3120128; f. 1990; daily; independent; Editor-in-Chief OCTAVIAN ȘTIREANU.

**Cotidianul** (The Daily): 77103 Bucharest, Calea Plevnei 114; tel. (1) 6377795; fax (1) 6377892; f. 1991; daily except Sun.; Founder ION RAȚIU; Editor DOINA BÂSCĂ.

**Cronica Română:** Bucharest; daily; circ. 29,000.

**Curierul Național** (National Messenger): 70109 Bucharest, Ministerului 2-4; tel. (1) 3121299; fax (1) 3121300; f. 1990; daily; Dir-Gen. VALENTIN PAUNESCU; Editor-in-Chief MARIUS PETREAN; circ. 55,000.

**Dreptatea** (Justice): 71102 Bucharest, Calea Victoriei 133–135, et. 2; tel. (1) 504125; f. 1990; daily evening newspaper published by Christian Democratic National Peasants' Party; Dir PAUL LĂZĂRESCU.

**Evenimentul Zilei** (Event of the Day): Bucharest, Piața Presei Libere 1; tel. (1) 6172094; fax (1) 3128381; f. 1992; tabloid daily; Editor-in-Chief ION CRISTOIU; circ. 450,000.

**Gazeta Sporturilor** (Sports Gazette): 79778 Bucharest 2, Str. Vasile Conta 16; tel. (1) 6116033; fax (1) 6113459; f. 1924; daily except Sun.; independent; Editor-in-Chief CONSTANTIN MACOVEI; circ. 150,000.

**Informatia Zilei:** 70711 Bucharest, Str. Brezoianu 23-25, Sector 1; tel. (1) 3120383; telex 10169; fax (1) 3120393; f. 1953; Editor-in-Chief OCTAVIAN ANDRONIC.

**Libertatea** (Freedom): 70711 Bucharest, Str. Brezoianu 23–25; tel. (1) 3120383; telex 10169; fax (1) 3120393; f. 1989; daily except Sun.; morning paper; Man. OCTAVIAN ANDRONIC; circ. 75,000.

**Ora** (Hour): 71102 Bucharest, Calea Victoriei 133-135; tel. (1) 6596239; fax (1) 6502698; f. 1992; independent; Dir NICOLAE CRISTACHE; circ. 25,517.

**România Liberă** (Free Romania): 71341 Bucharest, Piaţa Presei Libere 1; tel. (1) 61776010; telex 11179; fax (1) 174205; f. 1943; daily except Sun.; independent; Editor-in-Chief MIHAI CREANGĂ; circ. 100,000.

**Romániai Magyar Szó** (Hungarian Word from Romania): 79776 Bucharest, Piaţa Presei Libere 1; tel. (1) 6180302; fax (1) 6181562; f. 1947; daily except Sun. and Mon.; in Hungarian; Editor-in-Chief JÁNOS GYARMATH.

**Tineretul Liber** (Free Youth): 71341 Bucharest, Piaţa Presei Libere 1; tel. (1) 176736; fax (1) 177876; f. 1989; daily except Sun. and Mon.; Editor-in-Chief STEFAN MITROI.

**Viitorul Românesc** (Future of Romania): 71102 Bucharest, Calea Victoriei 133–135, et. 5; tel. (1) 596239; fax (1) 117938; f. 1991; daily; Dir VLADIMIR SIMON.

### DISTRICT NEWSPAPERS

#### Alba

**Ardealul:** 2500 Alba Iulia, Piaţa Iuliu Maniu 29; tel. (58) 13026; f. 1990; daily; Editor-in-Chief IOAN MAIER.

**Unirea** (The Union): 2500 Alba Iulia, Str. Decebal 27; tel. (58) 11420; f. 1990; independent; daily except Mon.; Editor-in-Chief HORIA SANDU; circ. 32,000.

#### Arad

**Adevărul** (The Truth): 2900 Arad, Bd. Revoluţiei 81; tel. (57) 13302; fax (57) 16854; f. 1990; independent; daily; Editor-in-Chief DUMITRU TOMA.

**Jelen Tükör** (Present Mirror): 2900 Arad, Bd. Revoluţiei 81; tel. (57) 12414; telex 76373; f. 1989; fmrly Vörös Lobogó; daily except Sun. and Mon.; independent; in Hungarian; Editor-in-Chief LAJOS NOTAROS; circ. 8,000.

#### Argeş

**Argeşul Liber** (Free Argeş): Piteşti, Str. Dija 7A; tel. (76) 30490; f. 1990; independent; daily; Editor-in-Chief MARIN MANOLACHE.

#### Bacău

**Deşteptărea** (The Awakening): 5500 Bacău, Str. Vasile Alecsandri 63; tel. (34) 111272; telex 21205; fax (34) 124794; f. 1989; Man. CORNEL GALBEN; Editor-in-Chief IOAN ENACHE; circ. 50,000.

**Glasul Moldovei** (Voice of Moldova): 5500 Bacău, Str. Nicolae Bălcescu 1; tel. (34) 126789; f. 1990; socio-political and cultural; weekly; Dir VASILE MIHĂILESCU.

**Moldova:** 5500 Bacău, Str. Eliberării 7; tel. (34) 134752; f. 1990; opinion weekly; Editor-in-Chief VIOREL SAVIN.

**Moldova Sport:** 5500 Bacău, Str. Vasile Alecsandri 63; tel. (34) 111272; telex 21205; fax (34) 124794; f. 1990; weekly; Man. CORNEL GALBEN; Editor-in-Chief IOAN ENACHE; circ. 20,000.

#### Bihor

**Bihari Napló:** 3700 Oradea, Str. Stadionului 25; tel. (59) 112727; fax (59) 115450; f. 1990; daily except Mon.; in Hungarian; Editor-in-Chief LÁSZLÓ SZŰCS; circ. 25,000.

**Crişana:** 3700 Oradea, Str. Romană 3; tel. (59) 117421; f. 1946; daily except Mon.; Editor-in-Chief IOAN CREŢU.

**Erdélyi Napló** (Chronicle of Ardeal): 3700 Oradea, Stadionului 25; tel. (59) 117158; fax (59) 117126; f. 1990; in Hungarian; weekly; Editor-in-Chief ISTVÁN STANIK.

#### Bistriţa-Năsăud

**Răsunetul** (Sound): 4400 Bistriţa, Str. Bistricioarei 6; tel. (90) 11684; f. 1990; journal of the National Salvation Front, Bistriţa-Năsăud County; Editor-in-Chief VASILE TABĂRĂ.

#### Botoşani

**Gazeta de Botoşani:** 6800 Botoşani, Bd. Mihai Eminescu 91; tel. (40) 851106; f. 1990; fmrly *Clopotul*; 33; daily; Editor-in-Chief GHEORGHE ZANEA.

#### Brăila

**Libertatea** (Freedom): 6100 Brăila, Piaţa Independenţei 1; tel. (94) 635946; f. 1989; independent daily; Editor-in-Chief RODICA CANĂ.

#### Braşov

**Brassói Lapok** (Braşov Gazette): 2200 Braşov, Str. M. Sadoveanu 3; tel. and fax (68) 150675; telex 61224; f. 1849; weekly; in Hungarian; Editor-in-Chief LAJOS GELLERT.

**Gazeta de Transilvania:** 2200 Braşov, Str. M. Sadoveanu 3; tel. (68) 42029; telex 61224; fax (68) 52927; f. 1838, ceased publication 1946, re-established 1989; daily except Mon.; independent; Editor-in-Chief EDUARD HUIDAN.

**Karpatenrundschau** (Carpathian Panorama): 2200 Braşov, Str. M. Sadoveanu 3; tel. and fax (68) 154044; f. 1968; weekly; in German; Editor-in-Chief DIETER DROTLEFF; circ. 2,000.

#### Buzău

**Opinia** (Opinion): 5100 Buzău, Str. Chiristigii 3; tel. (40) 12764; f. 1969; independent; daily; Editor-in-Chief CORNELIU ŞTEFAN.

#### Călăraşi

**Pământul** (Free Earth): 8500 Călăraşi, Str. Bucureşti 187; tel. (911) 15840; fax (911) 313630; f. 1990; socio-political; weekly; Editor-in-Chief GHEORGHE FRANGULEA.

#### Caraş-Severin

**Timpul** (The Times): 1700 Reşiţa, Piaţa Republicii 7; tel. (40) 412739; telex 74235; fax (40) 416709; f. 1990; independent daily; Editor-in-Chief GHEORGHE JURMA.

#### Cluj

**Adevărul de Cluj** (Truth of Cluj): 3400 Cluj-Napoca, Str. Napoca 16; tel. (64) 111032; f. 1990; daily; independent; Editor-in-Chief ILIE CĂLIAN; circ. 200,000.

**Atlas-Clusium** (Atlas Free Cluj): 3400 Cluj-Napoca, Piaţa Unirii 1; tel. (64) 116940; f. 1990; weekly; independent; Gen. Man. VALENTIN TAŞCU.

**Mesagerul transilvan** (Transylvanian Messenger): 3400 Cluj-Napoca, Blvd. 22 Decembrie 58; tel. (64) 16416; daily; independent; Editor-in-Chief ION ISTRATE; circ. 250,000.

**Nu** (No): 3400 Cluj-Napoca, Calea Motilor 18; tel. and fax (95) 195269; f. 1990; weekly; opinion and culture for youth; Editor-in-Chief LIVIU MAN.

**Szabadság** (Freedom): 3400 Cluj-Napoca, Str. Napoca 16, POB 340; tel. (64) 118985; telex 31447; fax (64) 197206; f. 1989; daily except Sun. and Mon.; in Hungarian; Editor-in-Chief ZOLTÁN TIBORI SZABÓ; circ. 30,000.

#### Constanţa

**Cuget Liber** (Free Thinking): 8700 Constanţa, Bd. I. C. Brătianu 5; tel. (41) 65605; telex 14385; fax (41) 665606; f. 1990; independent; daily; Dir ARCADI STRAHILEVICI.

#### Covasna

**Cuvântul nou** (New Word): 4000 Sfântu Gheorghe, Str. Pieţei 8; tel. (40) 2311388; f. 1968; new series 1990; daily except Mon.; Editor-in-Chief DUMITRU MĂNOLĂCHESCU.

**Háromszék** (Three Chairs): 4000 Sfântu Gheorghe, Str. Pieţei 8A; tel. (40) 2311504; fax (40) 311135; f. 1989; socio-political; daily; in Hungarian; Editor-in-Chief LAJOS MAGYARI.

#### Dâmboviţa

**Dâmboviţa:** 0200 Târgovişte, Str. Unirii 32; f. 1990; independent; daily; Editor-in-Chief ALEXANDRU ILIE.

#### Dolj

**Cuvântul Libertăţii** (Word of Liberty): 1100 Craiova, Str. Lyon 8; tel. (51) 2457; fax (51) 4141; f. 1989; daily except Sun.; Editor-in-Chief DAN LUPESCU; circ. 40,000.

#### Galaţi

**Viaţa Noua** (New Life): 6200 Galaţi, Str. Domnească 48; tel. (93) 414620; f. 1990; independent; daily; Dir RADU MACOVEI.

#### Giurgiu

**Cuvântul Liber** (Free Word): 8375 Giurgiu, Str. 1 Dec. 1918 60A; tel. (912) 21227; f. 1990; weekly; Editor-in-Chief ION GAGHII; circ. 10,000.

#### Gorj

**Gorjanul:** 1400 Târgu Jiu, Str. Constantin Brâncuşi 15; tel. (929) 17464; telex 45203; f. 1990; socio-political; daily; Editor-in-Chief NICOLAE BRÎNZAN.

#### Harghita

**Adevărul Harghitei** (Truth of Harghita): 4100 Miercurea-Ciuc, Str. Leticeni 45; tel. (58) 13019; f. 1990; independent; daily; Editor-in-Chief MIHAI GROZA.

ROMANIA                                                                                                                                      *Directory*

**Új Sport** (New Sport): 4100 Miercurea-Ciuc; tel. (958) 15940; telex 67228; fax (58) 152514; independent sports; daily; in Hungarian; Editor-in-Chief PÉTER LÁSZLÓ.

### Hunedoara
**Cuvântul Liber** (Free Word): 2700 Deva, Str. 1 Decembrie 35; tel. (56) 11275; fax (56) 18061; f. 1949; daily except Mon.; Editor-in-Chief NICOLAE TÎRCOB; circ. 25,000.

### Ialomiţa
**Tribuna Ialomiţei** (Ialomiţa Tribune): 8400 Slobozia, Str. Dobrogeanu-Gherea 2; f. 1969; weekly; Editor-in-Chief TITUS NIŢU.
**Evenimentul:** 6600 Iaşi, Str. Ştefan cel mare 4; tel. (32) 12023; fax (32) 12025; Editor-in-Chief CONSTANTIN PALADUTA.

### Iaşi
**Evenimentul:** 6600 Iaşi, Str. Ştefan cel Mare 4; tel. (32) 12023; fax (32) 12025; Editor-in-Chief CONSTANTIN PALADUTA.
**Monitorul:** 6600 Iaşi, Str. Smirdan 5; tel. (32) 271271; fax (32) 270415; daily; Editor-in-Chief DAN RADU; circ. 40,000.
**Opinia** (Opinion): 6600 Iaşi, Str. Vasile Alecsandri 8; tel. (32) 452105; f. 1990; social, political and cultural; daily; Editor-in-Chief VÂSILE FILIP.
**Opinia Studenţească** (Students' Opinion): 6600 Iaşi, Bd. Copou 18; tel. (32) 145610; f. 1990; independent; weekly; Editor-in-Chief DANIEL CONDURACHE; circ. 15,000.

### Maramureş
**Graiul Maramureşului** (Voice of Maramureş): 4800 Baia Mare, Bd. Bucureşti 25; tel. (99) 431035; telex 33221; fax (99) 430870; f. 1989; independent; daily; Editor-in-Chief AUGUSTIN COZMUŢA.
**Bányavidéki Új Szó** (Miner's New Word): 4800 Baia Mare, Bd. Bucureşti 25; tel. (99) 432585; f. 1989; weekly; in Hungarian; Editor-in-Chief GYÖRGY CSOMA.

### Mehedinţi
**Datina** (Tradition): 1500 Drobeta-Turnu-Severin, Str. Traïan 89; tel. (978) 119950; f. 1990; independent; daily; Editor-in-Chief GHEORGHE BUREŢEA.

### Mureş
**Cuvântul Liber** (Free Word): 4300 Târgu Mureş, Str. Gh. Doja 9; tel. (65) 36636; f. 1990; independent; daily; Editor-in-Chief LAZĂR LADARIU.
**Népújság** (People's Journal): 4300 Târgu Mureş, Str. Gh. Doja 9; tel. (65) 166780; fax (65) 168854; f. 1990; daily; in Hungarian; Editor-in-Chief JÁNOS MAKKAI.

### Neamţ
**Ceahlăul:** 5600 Piatra-Neamţ, Al. Tiparului 14; tel. and fax (33) 625282; f. 1989; daily; Editor-in-Chief VIOREL TUDOSE; circ. 20,000.

### Olt
**Glasul Adevărului** (Voice of the Truth): 0500 Slatina, Str. Filimon Sîrbu 5; tel. (44) 22131; f. 1990.

### Prahova
**Curierul de Prahova** (Courier of Prahova): 2000 Ploieşti, Bd. Republicii 2; tel. (97) 143192; weekly; Editor-in-Chief IOAN POPESCU.
**Prahova:** 2000 Ploieşti, Bd. Republicii 2; tel. (97) 145691; f. 1990; independent; daily; Editor-in-Chief OCTAVIAN GÎLĂ.

### Sălaj
**Graiul Sălajului** (Voice of Sălaj): 4700 Zalău, Piaţa Unirii 7; tel. (99) 614120; f. 1990; daily; Editor-in-Chief IOAN LUPA.
**Szilágyaság** (Word from Sălaj): 4700 Zalău, Piaţa Libertăţii 9, POB 68; tel. (99) 633736; f. 1990; organ of Hungarian Democratic Union of Romania; weekly; Editor-in-Chief JÁNOS KUI.

### Satu Mare
**Ardealul:** 3900 Satu Mare, Bd. Republicii 24; tel. (99) 730661; f. 1990; organ of Christian Democratic National Peasants' Party; weekly; Dir NAE ANTONESCU.
**Szatmári Hirlap** (Satu Mare Journal): 3900 Satu Mare, Calea Traian 1; f. 1968; daily except Mon.; in Hungarian; Editor-in-Chief STEFAN IOSIF STHAL.

### Sibiu
**Dimineaţa** (Morning): 2400 Sibiu, Str. Samuel Brukenthal 2; tel. (92) 418103; f. 1990; independent socio-cultural; daily; Editor-in-Chief TRAIAN SUCIUI.
**Tribuna:** Sibiu, Str. Dr Ratiu 7; tel. (92) 413833; telex 69247; fax (92) 412026; f. 1884; daily; independent; Editor-in-Chief OCTAVIAN RUSU; circ. 40,000.

### Suceava
**Crai nou:** 5800 Suceava, Str. Ştefan cel Mare 36; tel. (987) 14723; f. 1990; daily; Editor-in-Chief ION PARANICI.

### Teleorman
**Teleormanul Liber** (Free Teleorman): 0700 Alexandria, Str. Dunării 178; tel. (913) 11950; f. 1990; daily; Editor-in-Chief GHEORGHE FILIP.

### Timiş
**Gazeta de Timişoara** (Timişoara Gazette): 1900 Timişoara, C P 1127; f. 1990; independent opinion and news; weekly; Dir PREDA MARIA IRINA.
**Neue Banater Zeitung:** 1900 Timişoara, Bd. Revoluţiei din Decembrie 1989 8; tel. (96) 115586; fax (96) 115586; f. 1957; daily except Sun. and Mon.; in German; Editor-in-Chief GERHARD BINDER; circ. 5,000.
**Timişoara:** 1900 Timişoara, Str. Proclamatia de la Timişoara 5; tel. and fax (96) 190120; f. 1990; daily; Dir GEORGE SERBAN; Editor-in-Chief IOSIF COSTINAS.

### Tulcea
**Delta** (The Delta): 8800 Tulcea, Str. Spitalului 4; tel. (915) 12406; telex 52235; f. 1885; new series 1990; daily except Mon.; Editor-in-Chief NECULAI AMIHULESEI.

### Vâlcea
**Curierul de Vâlcea** (Courier of Vâlcea): 1000 Râmnicu Vâlcea, Calea lui Traian 127; tel. (94) 712326; fax (94) 718265; f. 1990; independent; daily except Mon.; commerce; Editor-in-Chief GHEORGHE SEMPREANU.

### Vaslui
**Adevărul** (Truth): 6500 Vaslui, Str. Ştefan cel Mare 79; tel. (983) 12203; social-cultural publication; twice weekly; f. 1990; Editor-in-Chief TEODOR PRAXIU.

### Vrancea
**Milcovul Liber** (Free Milcov): 5300 Focşani, Bd. Unirii 18; tel. (939) 14579; f. 1989; weekly; Editor-in-Chief IONEL NISTOR.

## PRINCIPAL PERIODICALS
### Bucharest
**22:** 70179 Bucharest, Calea Victoriei 120; tel. (1) 141776; fax (1) 141525; f. 1990; weekly; published by the Group for Social Dialogue; Editor-in-Chief GABRIELA ADAMEŞTEANU; circ. 12,000.
**Agricultura României** (Agriculture of Romania): 71341 Bucharest, Piaţa Presei Libere 1; tel. (1) 176020; f. 1974; weekly; published by the Ministry of Agriculture and Food; Editor-in-Chief LUCIAN ROŞCA.
**A Hét** (The Week): 79776 Bucharest, Piaţa Presei Libere 1; tel. (1) 6184939; f. 1970; weekly; in Hungarian; social, cultural, scientific and ecological review; Editor-in-Chief GÁLFALVI ZSOLT.
**Albina** (The Bee): 71341 Bucharest, Piaţa Presei Libere 1; tel. (1) 6173487; f. 1897; monthly; social and cultural review; Editor-in-Chief VLADIMIR PANĂ.
**Anticipaţia:** 79781 Bucharest, Piaţa Presei Libere 1; tel. (1) 6175833; fax (1) 2228494; f. 1990; monthly; science-fiction literature; Editor-in-Chief PAVELESCU MIHAI-DAN.
**Arhitectura** (Architecture): 70109 Bucharest, Str. Academiei 18-20; f. 1906; published twice a year in 6 issues; review of the Union of Romanian Architects; Editor AUGUSTIN IOAN.
**Armata României** (The Armed Forces of Romania): Bucharest, Str. General Cristescu 5; tel. (1) 6133393; fax (1) 6159456; f. 1859; weekly; published by Ministry of National Defence; Editor-in-Chief GHEORGE VĂDUVA.
**Arta (Art):** Bucharest 13, POB 13-80; tel. (1) 6131380; fax (1) 3121008; f. 1953; 6 a year; visual arts and media magazine; Editor-in-Chief CĂLIN DAN.
**Biserica Ortodoxă Română** (The Romanian Orthodox Church): 70526 Bucharest, Intrarea Patriarhiei 9; tel. (1) 234449; f. 1822; monthly; official bulletin of the Romanian Patriarchate; Editor Rev. DUMITRU SOARE.
**Bucuria Copiilor—Luminiţa** (Children's Happiness—The Little Light): 71341 Bucharest, Piaţa Presei Libere 1; tel. (1) 176010; telex 11272; f. 1949; monthly; Editor-in-Chief DUMITRU DOBRICĂ; circ. 50,000.
**Business Club:** 70711 Bucharest, Str. Brezoianu 23-25, Sector 1; tel. (1) 3120383; telex 10169; fax (1) 3120393; f. 1990; quarterly; Editor-in-Chief OCTAVIAN ANDRONIC; circ. 5,000.
**Cimboro** (Friend): 71341 Bucharest, Piaţa Presei Libere 1; tel. (1) 176010; f. 1922; monthly; in Hungarian; for children; Editor-in-Chief GABRIELLA CSIRE.

**Contemporanul—Ideea Europeană:** 71341 Bucharest, Piaţa Presei Libere 1; tel. (1) 177316; f. 1881; weekly; cultural, political and scientific review, published by the Ministry of Culture; Dir NICOLAE BREBAN.

**Curierul Comercial** (Commercial Messenger): 71341 Bucharest, Piaţa Presei Libere 1; tel. (1) 181387; f. 1898, re-established Dec. 1989; weekly trade journal; Editor-in-Chief SILVIU SORIN TRUSCĂ.

**Curierul Românesc:** 71273 Bucharest, Al. Alexandru 38; tel. (1) 2120510; fax (1) 3127559; f. Dec. 1989 to replace Tribuna României; monthly; cultural and social; published by the Romanian Cultural Foundation; circulated internationally; Pres. AUGUSTIN BUZURA; circ. 10,000.

**Cuvântul** (The Word): 70112 Bucharest, Bd. N. Balcescu 23A; tel. (1) 6157813; fax (1) 3110516; opinion; weekly; f. 1990; Editor-in-Chief MIRCEA ŢICUDEAN; circ. 50,000.

**Democratia** (Democracy): 70101 Bucharest, Calea Victoriei 39A; tel. (1) 130190; f. 1990; independent periodical; Editor-in-Chief EUGEN FLORESCU.

**Expres:** 71102 Bucharest, Calea Victoriei 135; tel. (1) 503041; fax (1) 507994; f. 1990; independent; weekly; Editor-in-Chief ILIE ŞERBĂNESCU.

**Expres Magazin:** 71341 Bucharest 1, Piaţa Libere 1; tel. (1) 6173523; fax (1) 3128381; independent; weekly; Editor-in-Chief ION CRISTOIU; circ. 98,000.

**Falvak Népe** (Peasants): 71341 Bucharest, Piaţa Presei Libere 1; tel. (1) 185292; f. 1945, new series 1990; weekly; in Hungarian; Editor-in-Chief FERENCZ L. IMRE.

**Fapta** (The Deed): Bucharest; tel. (1) 331577; f. 1990; weekly; Editor-in-Chief PETRU ŞTEŢ.

**Femeia** (Woman): 71341 Bucharest, Piaţa Presei Libere 1; f. 1948; monthly; published by National Women's Council; Editor-in-Chief CONSTANŢA NICULESCU.

**Filatelia:** 70100 Bucharest, POB 1-870; tel. (1) 6131007; f. 1950; monthly; published by Philatelists' Federation; Editor-in-Chief AURELIAN DÂRNU.

**Flacăra** (The Flame): 71341 Bucharest 1, Piaţa Presei Libere 1; tel. (1) 6174763; fax (1) 3128289; f. 1911; weekly; Editor-in-Chief LIVIU TIMBUS; circ. 50,000.

**Fotbal** (Football): 79778 Bucharest, Vasile Conta 16; tel. (1) 2111288; fax (1) 2100153; f. 1966; weekly; independent; Editor-in-Chief LAURENTIU DUMITRESCU; circ. 55,000.

**Gazeta cooperaţiei:** 71341 Bucharest, Piaţa Presei Libere 1; tel. (1) 176020; weekly; published by Centrocoop; Editor-in-Chief GHEORGHE ANGELESCU.

**Ifi Fórum** (Youth Forum): POB 95, 4100 Miercurea-Cluc; tel. (1) 968-16940; fax (1) 92-162614; f. 1990; organ of Hungarian youth in Romania; weekly; in Hungarian; Editor-in-Chief ISTVÁN FERENCZES.

**Közoktatás** (Public Education): 71341 Bucharest 33, Piaţa Presei Libere 1, Corpul Central, Etajul 9, camera 902; tel. (1) 2228539; fax (1) 2223363; f. 1957, known as Tanügyi Újság until 1989; monthly; published by Ministry of Education; in Hungarian; Editor LÁSZLÓ GERGELY; circ. 3,000.

**Luceafărul** (The Morning Star): 71102 Bucharest, Calea Victoriei 133; tel. (1) 596760; f. 1958; weekly; published by the Writers' Union; Dir LAURENTIU ULICI.

**Lumea Azi** (The World Today): 71341 Bucharest, Piaţa Presei Libere 1; tel. (1) 185081; telex 11272; f. 1963; weekly; independent review of international affairs; Dir MAGDALENA BOIANGIU; circ. 20,000.

**Lupta CFR** (Romanian Railway Workers' Struggle): 77113 Bucharest, Bd. Dinicu Golescu 38; telex 10876; f. 1932; weekly; Editor-in-Chief IONEL CHIRU.

**Magazin istoric** (Historical Magazine): 70100 Bucharest, Str. Ministerului 2; tel. (1) 6159091; fax (1) 63127668; f. 1967; monthly; review of historical culture; Chief Editor CRISTIAN POPIŞTEANU.

**Manuscriptum:** Bucharest, Str. Fundaţiei 4; tel. (1) 6502096; telex 10376; f. 1970; quarterly; published by the Ministry of Culture; Editor-in-Chief PETRU CRETIA; circ. 2,000.

**Modelism—International:** 71341 Bucharest, Piaţa Presei Libere 1, POB 33-126; quarterly; hobbies; Editor-in-Chief Dr CRISTIAN CRĂCIUNOIU; circ. 60,000.

**Neamul Românesc (Serie Nouă)** (The Romanian Nation—New Series): 6600 Iaşi, Str. Anastasi Panu 60; f. 1990; independent periodical of opinion, information, science and culture; Editor-in-Chief DUMITRU POPA.

**Noul Cinema:** 71341 Bucharest, Piaţa Presei Libere 1; fax (1) 3127668; f. 1963 as 'Cinema'; monthly; Editor-in-Chief ADINA DARIAN; circ. 90,000.

**Novîi vik** (New Age): 71341 Bucharest, Piaţa Presei Libere 1; f. 1949; fortnightly; social, political and cultural journal for the Ukrainian population; Editor-in-Chief ION COLESNIC.

**Panoramic Radio-TV:** 70747 Bucharest, Str. Gral Berthelot 60–62; tel. (1) 1593050; fax (1) 156992; weekly; circ. 207,000.

**PC World Romania:** 72231 Bucharest, Calea Floreasca 167, Rm 604; tel. (1) 2121980; fax (1) 3127612; monthly; computing magazine; Editor-in-Chief ION DIAMANDI.

**Pentru patrie** (For the Motherland): 70622 Bucharest, Sector 5, Str. Mihai Vodă 17; tel. (1) 143795; telex 88810; f. 1949; monthly; illustrated; published by Ministry of the Interior; Editor-in-Chief OLIMPIAN UNGHEREA.

**Psihologia:** 79781 Bucharest, Piaţa Presei Libere 1; tel. (1) 6175833; fax (1) 2228494; f. 1991; bi-monthly; psychology; Editor-in-Chief ADINA CHELCEA.

**Rebus:** 71341 Bucharest 1, Piaţa Presei Libere 1; tel. (1) 6175969; fax (1) 3128289; f. 1931; monthly; Editor-in-Chief ALEXANDRU PĂSĂRIN; circ. 300,000.

**Revista Cultului Mozaic** (Review of the Mosaic Creed): 70478 Bucharest, Popa Rusu 24; tel. (1) 118080; telex 10798; fax (1) 130911; f. 1956; fortnightly; English, Romanian, Hebrew and Yiddish; published by Federation of Jewish Communities; Pres. (vacant).

**Revista Română de Statistică** (Romanian Review of Statistics): 70542 Bucharest, Bd. Libertăţii 16; tel. (1) 7816744; fax (1) 3124873; f. 1952; monthly; organ of the National Statistics Commission; Editor-in-Chief NICOLAE GÂRCEAG.

**România apicolă** (Apicultural Romania): 70231 Bucharest, Str. I. Fuçík 17; tel. (1) 137877; telex 11205; f. 1926; monthly; review of apiculture published by the Beekeepers' Association; Editor ELISEI TARŢA.

**România Literară** (Literary Romania): 71102 Bucharest, Calea Victoriei 133; tel. (1) 506286; fax (1) 6503369; f. 1968 as successor to Gazeta Literară; weekly; literary, artistic and political magazine; published by the Fundation România Literară (Writers' Union); Editor-in-Chief ALEX ŞTEFĂNESCU.

**România Mare** (Greater Romania): 70101 Bucharest, Calea Victoriei 39A; tel. (1) 6156093; fax (1) 3125396; f. 1990; weekly; independent nationalist; Editor-in-Chief CORNELIU VADIM TUDOR; circ. 90,000.

**România pitorească** (Picturesque Romania): 70148 Bucharest, Str. Gabriel Péri 8; tel. (1) 597474; telex 11724; f. 1972; monthly; published by the Ministry of Commerce; Editor-in-Chief ANDA RAICU.

**Romanian Foreign Trade:** 79502 Bucharest, Chamber of Commerce and Industry, Bd. Nicolae Bălcescu 22; f. 1952; quarterly; in English, French, German, Russian and Spanish.

**Romanian Insight:** 79502 Bucharest, Chamber of Commerce and Industry, Bd. Nicolae Bălcescu 22; tel. (1) 6132379; telex 11374; fax (1) 3122091; f. 1952; in English; Editor CONSTANTIN GOLIAT; circ. 5,000.

**Romanian Panorama:** 71341 Bucharest, Piaţa Presei Libere 1, Corp B, POB 33-38; tel. (1) 6173836; fax (1) 3110526; f. 1955; monthly; in Chinese, English, French, German, Russian and Spanish; economy, politics, social questions, science, history, culture, sport, etc.; published by the Foreign Languages Press Group; Dir NICOLAE ŞARAMBEI; circ. 166,000.

**Romanian Review:** 71341 Bucharest, Piaţa Presei Libere 1; tel. (1) 6173836; fax (1) 3110526; f. 1946; monthly; in English, French, German and Russian; literature, the arts, history, philosophy, sociology, etc.; published by Foreign Languages Press Group; Editor-in-Chief VALENTIN F. MIHAESCU; circ. 51,000.

**Satul Românesc** (Romanian Village): 71341 Bucharest, Piaţa Presei Libere 1; tel. (1) 170304; weekly; pub. by Federation of Agricultural Cos of Romania; Editor-in-Chief TITU CONSTANTIN.

**Sănătatea** (Health): 70172 Bucharest, Str. Biserica Amzei 29; tel. (1) 506233; f. 1952; monthly; published by the National Council of the Red Cross; Editor-in-Chief GHEORGHE M. GEORGE.

**Secolul 20** (20th Century): 71102 Bucharest, Calea Victoriei 115; f. 1961; monthly; published by the Writers' Union; Editor-in-Chief DAN HÃULICĂ.

**Start 2001:** 71341 Bucharest, Piaţa Presei Libere 1; tel. (1) 181361; f. 1990; monthly review; Editor-in-Chief IOAN VOICU.

**Ştiinţă şi Tehnică** (Science and Technology): 79781 Bucharest, Piaţa Presei Libere 1; tel. (1) 6175833; fax (1) 2228494; f. 1949; monthly; Editor-in-Chief VOICHITA DOMANEANTU.

**Studentimea Democrata:** 77119 Bucharest, Str. Ştefan Furtună 140; tel. (1) 157086; f. 1990; independent students' weekly.

**Tehnium:** 79784 Bucharest, Piaţa Presei Libere 1; tel. (1) 2223374; f. 1970; monthly; hobbies; Editor-in-Chief Ing. ILIE MIHÃESCU; circ. 100,000.

**Telecom Romania:** 72231 Bucharest, Calea Floreasca 167, Rm 604; tel. (1) 2121980; bi-monthly; networking and telecommunications; Editor-in-Chief MIHAELA GORODCOV.

# ROMANIA

**Totusi iubirea:** 70184 Bucharest, Str. Dionisie Lupu 84; tel. (1) 115533; f. 1990; culture and civilization; weekly; Dir ADRIAN PĂUNESCU.

**Tribuna economică** (Economic Tribune): 70159 Bucharest, Bd. Magheru 28–30; tel. (1) 6595158; fax (1) 6592192; f. 1886; weekly; Editor-in-Chief BOGDAN PADURE; circ. 50,000.

**Tribuna învăţământului** (Education's Tribune): 71341 Bucharest, Piaţa Presei Libere 1; tel. (1) 2225115; fax (1) 2223363; f. 1990; weekly; guide to schools and colleges; Editor-in-Chief DUMITRU MIRCEA RECEANU; circ. 30,000.

**Universul cărtii:** 71341 Bucharest, Piaţa Presei Libere 1; tel. (1) 176010; 173306; f. 1991; monthly; published by Ministry of Culture; Editor-in-Chief PAUL DUGNEANU.

**Urzica** (Stinging Nettle): 79751 Bucharest, Str. Brezoianu 23–25, Sector 1; f. 1949; monthly; humour and satire; Editor-in-Chief TUDOR POPESCU.

**Viaţa** (Life): Bucharest; tel. and fax (1) 135617; f. 1990 to replace *Săptămîna culturală a capitalei*; weekly socio-cultural review; Editor-in-Chief FLORIN BOLOLOI.

**Viaţa Armatei** (Army Life): 70764 Bucharest, Str. Gen. Cristescu 5, Sector 1; tel. (1) 6142012; telex 11995; fax (1) 6159456; f. 1947; fmrly *Viaţa Militară*; monthly illustrated review of the Ministry of National Defence; Editor-in-Chief ION JIANU.

**Viaţa Românească** (Romanian Life): Bucharest; tel. (1) 142512; monthly; published by Writers' Union; Editor-in-Chief CEZAR BALTAG.

**Vânătorul şi Pescarul Român** (The Romanian Hunter and Angler): 70344 Bucharest, Calea Moşilor 128; tel. (1) 6136698; fax (1) 6136804; f. 1948; monthly review; published by the General Association of Hunters and Anglers; Editor-in-Chief GABRIEL CHEROIU.

**Volk und Kultur:** Bucharest; tel. (1) 176010; monthly; in German; published by Ministry of Culture; Editor-in-Chief ANNA BRETZ.

**Zig-Zag Magazin:** 70602 Bucharest, Bd. Iancu de Hunedoara 66; tel. (1) 8600833; fax (1) 312036; f. 1990; independent; weekly; Editor-in-Chief MARIAN PETCU.

### Bacău

**Ateneu** (Atheneum): 5500 Bacău, Str. V. Alecsandri 7; tel. (34) 112497; f. 1964; monthly; cultural review; Editor-in-Chief SERGIU ADAM.

### Braşov

**Astra:** 2200 Braşov, Str. M. Sadoveanu 3; tel. (68) 143179; f. 1966; monthly; literature, art, culture, philosophy; Editor-in-Chief VASILE GOGEA.

### Cluj-Napoca

**Családi Tükör** (Family Mirror): Cluj-Napoca, Str. Napoca 16; tel. (64) 111734; f. 1945; fmrly *Dolgozó Nő*; monthly; in Hungarian; Editor-in-Chief Dr MAGDA KOVÁCS; circ. 40,000.

**Helikon:** 3400 Cluj-Napoca, Str. Eroilor 2; tel. (64) 112420; weekly; organ of the Writers' Union; in Hungarian; Editor-in-Chief ISTVÁN SZILÁGYI.

**Korunk** (Our Time): 3400 Cluj-Napoca, Str. Iasilor 14; tel. (64) 194836; f. 1926; monthly; social review; in Hungarian; Editor-in-Chief LAJOS KÁNTOR.

**Napsugár** (Sun Ray): 3400 Cluj-Napoca, Piaţa Păcii 1–3, POB 137; tel. (64) 111184; fax (64) 157295; f. 1957; monthly illustrated literary magazine for children aged 7–10 years; in Hungarian; Editor-in-Chief EMESE ZSIGMOND; circ. 22,000.

**Steaua** (Star): 3400 Cluj-Napoca, Piaţa Libertăţii 1; tel. (64) 115852; f. 1949; monthly review of the Writers' Union; Editor-in-Chief AUREL RĂU; circ. 2,000.

**Szivárvány** (Rainbow): 3400 Cluj-Napoca, Piaţa Păcii 1–3, POB 137; tel. (64) 111184; fax (64) 157295; f. 1979; monthly illustrated literary magazine for children aged 3–6 years; in Hungarian; Editor-in-Chief EMESE ZSIGMOND; circ. 23,000.

**Tribuna:** 3400 Cluj-Napoca, Str. Universităţii 1; tel. (64) 117548; f. 1884; weekly; cultural review; Editor-in-Chief AUGUSTIN BUZURA.

### Constanţa

**Tomis:** 8700 Constanţa, Str. J. Lahovari 87; tel. (41) 611172; f. 1966; monthly review; Chief Editor CONSTANTIN NOVAC.

### Craiova

**Ramuri** (Branches): 1100 Craiova, bis Str. Săvineşti 3 bis; tel. (51) 414414; fax (51) 417385; f. 1905; monthly; review of culture; Editor-in-Chief GABRIEL CHIFU.

### Iaşi

**Convorbiri Literare** (Literary Conversations): 6600 Iaşi, Str. Dimitrov 1; tel. (32) 116242; f. 1867, new series 1972; weekly; review of literature; published by the Writers' Union, Iaşi branch; Editor-in-Chief AL DOBRESCU.

**Cronica:** 6600 Iaşi, Str. Vasile Alecsandri 8; tel. (32) 146433; f. 1966; weekly; political, social and cultural review; Editor-in-Chief IOAN HOLBAN; circ. 8,000.

### Oradea

**Familia** (Family): 3700 Oradea, Str. Romană 3; tel. (59) 1114129; f. 1865, new series 1965); monthly; social and cultural review; Editor-in-Chief IOAN MOLDOVAN; circ. 2,000.

### Piteşti

**Calende:** 0300 Piteşti, Bd. Republicii Bl. G 1, et. 2; tel. (97) 633592; f. 1966, known as *Argeş* until 1991; monthly; literary review; Editor-in-Chief NICOLAE OPREA.

### Sibiu

**Transilvania:** 2400 Sibiu, Str. Dr I Raţiu 2; tel. (69) 413377; f. 1868; 2 issues quarterly; political, social and cultural; Editor-in-Chief ION MIRCEA.

**Tribuna Sporturilor:** 2400 Sibiu, Str. George Coşbuc 38; tel. (69) 412810; telex 69247; fax (69) 412026; f. 1990; weekly; sports magazine; Editor-in-Chief MIRCEA BIŢU.

### Timişoara

**Orizont** (Horizon): 1900 Timişoara, Piaţa Sf. Gheorghe 3; tel. and fax (61) 133376; f. 1949; weekly; review of the Writers' Union (Timişoara branch); Editor-in-Chief MIRCEA MIHAIES.

### Târgu Mureş

**Erdélyi Figyelö** (Transylvanian Observer): 4300 Târgu-Mures, Str. Primăriei 1; tel. (65) 26780; f. 1958; fmrly *Új Élet*; fortnightly; illustrated magazine; in Hungarian; Editor-in-Chief JÓZSEF WELEMAN.

**Látó** (Visionary): 4300 Târgu Mureş, Str. Primăriei 1; tel. (65) 26610; f. 1953; fmrly *Igaz Szó*; monthly; in Hungarian; literature; Editor-in-Chief BÉLA MARKÓ; circ. 2,500.

**Vatra** (Home): 4300 Târgu Mureş, Str. Primăriei 1; tel. (65) 164139; fax (65) 165008; f. 1894, 1971; monthly; review of literature, arts, sociology; published by the Writers' Union of Romania, Mureş branch; Editor-in-Chief CORNEL MORARU.

## NEWS AGENCIES

**ROMPRES** (National News Agency): 71341 Bucharest, Piaţa Presei Libere 1; tel. (1) 6182878; telex 11272; fax (1) 6170487; f. 1949; fmrly Agerpres; co-operates with, and provides news and photo services to, 64 overseas news agencies; daily news released in English, French, Russian and Spanish; publs news and feature bulletins in English, French, Russian and Spanish; Dir-Gen. NEAGU UDROIU.

**Nord-Est Press:** 6600 Iaşi, Str. Smirdan 5; tel. and fax (32) 144776; independent regional news agency for north-east Romania; Editor MONA DIRTU.

### Foreign Bureaux

**Agence France-Presse (AFP):** Bucharest; tel. (1) 2100261; telex 10848; Correspondent FRANÇOISE MICHEL.

**Agenzia Nazionale Stampa Associata (ANSA)** (Italy): 70185 Bucharest, Bd. Dacia 9A, ap. 6; tel. and fax (1) 6335325; telex 11642; f. 1970; Chief Correspondent GIAN MARCO VENIER.

**Allgemeiner Deutscher Nachrichtendienst (ADN)** (Germany): Bucharest; tel. (1) 111214; telex 11327; Correspondent MICHAEL HUBE.

**Bulgarska Telegrafna Agentsia (BTA)** (Bulgaria): Bucharest, Str. Mihai Eminescu 124, Inter B et 5 ap. 12; tel. (1) 191880; telex 11484; Correspondent PETYO PETKOV.

**Deutsche Presse-Agentur (dpa)** (Germany): Bucharest, Bul. Jancu Hunedoara 66 (fost Ilie Pintelie), ap. 45 et 4; tel. (1) 121481; fax (1) 123079; Correspondent JOACHIM SONNENBERG.

**Informatsionnoye Telegrafnoye Agentstvo Rossii—Telegrafnoye Agentstvo Suverennykh Stran (ITAR—TASS)** (Russia): Bucharest, Str. Armeneasca 41; tel. (1) 2106050; fax 2107490; Correspondent NIKOLAY N. MOROZOV.

**Magyar Távirati Iroda (MTI)** (Hungary): 72238 Bucharest, Al. Alexandru 10, ap. 1; tel. (1) 3127745; telex 11211; Correspondent DÉNES BARACS.

**Novinska Agencija Tanjug** (Yugoslavia): Bucharest, Str. Drobeta 4–10; tel. (1) 116208; telex 11304; Correspondent PETAR TOMICI.

**Polska Agencja Prasowa (PAP)** (Poland): Bucharest; tel. (1) 206870; telex 11298; Correspondent STANISŁAW WOJNAROWICZ.

**Rossiyskoye Informatsionnoye Agentstvo—Novosti (RIA-Novosti)** (Russia): Bucharest; tel. (1) 795648; telex 11300; Correspondent VYACHESLAV SAMOSHIN.

ROMANIA

**Xinhua (New China) News Agency** (People's Republic of China): Bucharest, Şos. Nordului 2; tel. (1) 331927; telex 11308; Correspondent ZHANG HANWEN.

### PRESS ASSOCIATIONS

**Societatea Ziariştilor din România—Federaţia Sindicatelor din Întreaga Presă** (Society of Romanian Journalists—Federation of All Press Unions): Bucharest, Piaţa Presei Libere 1; tel. (1) 6171591; fax (1) 3128266; f. 1990; affiliated to International Organization of Journalists and to International Federation of Journalists; Pres. MIOARA VERGU IORDACHE; 1,600 mems.

The **Union of Professional Journalists** (Pres. ŞTEFAN MITROI) was established in 1990, as was the **Democratic Journalists' Union** (Pres. P. M. BACANU).

## Publishers

In 1992 some 3,622 book titles (66.6m. copies) were published.

**Editura Academiei Române** (Publishing House of the Romanian Academy): 76117 Bucharest, Calea 13 Septembrie 13; tel. (1) 6317400; f. 1948; important books and periodicals on original scientific work, 96 periodicals in Romanian and foreign languages; Dir CONSTANTIN BUSUIOCEANU.

**Editura Albatros:** 71341 Bucharest, Piaţa Presei Libere 1, Of. 33; tel. (1) 6180448; f. 1971; Editor-in-Chief GEORGETA DIMISIANO.

**Editura Artemis** (Artemis Publishing House): 71341 Bucharest, Piaţa Presei Libere 1; tel. (1) 6181699; f. 1991; fine arts, fiction, children's literature, history; Dir MANUELA CORAVU.

**Editura Cartea Românească** (Publishing House of The Romanian Book): 79721 Bucharest, Str. Gral Berthelot 41; tel. (1) 149352; f. 1969; Romanian contemporary literature; Dir MARGARETA BEDROSIAN.

**Editura Ceres:** 79722 Bucharest, Piaţa Presei Libere 1; tel. (1) 180174; f. 1953; books on agriculture and forestry; Dir Eng. ECATERINA MOŞU.

**Editura Ion Creangă** (Ion Creangă Publishing House): 71341 Bucharest, Piaţa Presei Libere 1; tel. (1) 2223254; fax (1) 2231112; f. 1969; children's books; Dir DANIELA CRĂSNARU.

**Editura Dacia** (Dacia Publishing House): 3400 Cluj-Napoca, Str. Emil Isac 23; tel. and fax (64) 198912; telex 31347; f. 1969; classical and contemporary literature, art books, literary, philosophical and scientific books in Romanian, Hungarian and German; Dir VASILE IGNA.

**Editura Didactică şi Pedagogică** (Educational Publishing House): 79724 Bucharest, Str. Spiru Haret 12; tel. (1) 3122885; telex 011352; f. 1951; school, university, technical and vocational textbooks; pedagogic literature and methodology; teaching materials; Dir Dr CONSTANTIN FLORICEL.

**Editura Enciclopedică** (Encyclopaedic Publishing House): 71341 Bucharest, Piaţa Presei Libere 1; tel. (1) 2223322; f. 1968, merged with Scientific Publishing House, as Editura Ştiinţifică şi Enciclopedică, 1974–90; encyclopaedias, dictionaries, bibliographies, chronologies and reference books; popular and informational literature; provides photographs and encyclopaedic and statistical data about Romania for publishing houses abroad; Dir MARCEL POPA.

**Editura Humanitas** (Humanitas Publishing House): 79734 Bucharest, Piaţa Presei Libere 1; tel. (1) 2228546; fax (1) 2228252; f. 1990; philosophy, religion, political and social sciences, economics, history, fiction; Dir GABRIEL LIICEANU.

**Editura Junimea** (Junimea Publishing House): 6600 Iaşi, O. P. 1, POB 28; tel. (32) 117290; f. 1969; Romanian literature, art books, translations, scientific and technical books; Dir ANDI ANDRIEŞ.

**Editura Kriterion** (Kriterion Publishing House): 71341 Bucharest, Piaţa Presei Libere 1; tel. (1) 6174060; fax (1) 6182430; f. 1969; classical and contemporary literature, reference books in science and art in Hungarian, German, Romanian, Russian, Serbian, Slovak, Tatar, Turkish, Ukrainian and Yiddish; translations in Romanian, Hungarian and German; Dir GYULA H. SZABÓ.

**Editura Litera** (The Letter Publishing House): 71341 Bucharest, Piaţa Presei Libere 1; tel. (1) 182471; 1969; original literature; Dir VIORICA OANCEA.

**Editura Medicală** (Medical Publishing House): 79728 Bucharest, Str. Smîrdan 5; tel. (1) 6143252; fax (1) 3124879; f. 1954; medical literature; Dir Prof. AL. C. OPROIU.

**Editura Meridiane** (Meridiane Publishing House): 71341 Bucharest, Piaţa Presei Libere 1; tel. (1) 2223393; f. 1952; fine arts, theatre, cinema, architecture; art history, theory and criticism; picture art books, monographs, postcards; Editor-in-Chief CORNEL BISTRICEANU.

**Editura Mihai Eminescu** (Mihai Eminescu Publishing House): 71341 Bucharest, Piaţa Presei Libere 1; tel. (1) 177380; f. 1969; contemporary original literary works and translations of world literature; Dir EUGEN NEGRICI.

**Editura Militară** (Military Publishing House): 70764 Bucharest, Str. General Cristescu 3–5; tel. (1) 6133601; fax (1) 6159456; f. 1950; military history, theory, science, technics and medicine, and fiction; Dir ALEXANDRU MIHALCEA.

**Editura Minerva** (Minerva Publishing House): 71341 Bucharest, Piaţa Presei Libere 1; tel. (1) 6184464; f. 1969; Romanian classical literature, world literature, original literary works, literary criticism and history; Dir ZIGU ORNEA.

**Editura Muzicală** (Musical Publishing House): 70718 Bucharest, Str. Poiana Narciselor 6; tel. (1) 138743; f. 1957; books on music, musicology and musical scores; Dir VLAD ULPIU.

**Editura pentru Turism** (Tourism Publishing House): 70161 Bucharest, Bd. Gh. Magheru 7, Sector 1; tel. (1) 6145160; telex 11270; f. 1990; tourism; Dir VICTOR CRĂCIUN.

**Editura Porto-Franco** (Porto-France Publishing House): 6200 Galati, Bd. George Coşbuc 223A; tel. (93) 27602; f. 1990; literary and scientific books, translations; Dir RADU DORIN MIHĂESCU.

**Editura Presa Libera** (Free Press Publishing House): 71341 Bucharest, Piaţa Presei Libere 1; f. 1954; newspapers, magazines; Dir (vacant).

**Editura Scrisul Românesc** (Romanian Writing Publishing House): 1100 Craiova, Str. Mihai Viteazul 4; tel. (41) 13763; f. 1972; socio-political, technical, scientific and literary works; Dir MARIN SORESCU.

**Editura Sport-Turism** (Sport-Tourism Publishing House): 79736 Bucharest, Str. Vasile Conta 16; tel. (1) 107480; f. 1968; sport, tourism, monographs, translations, postcards, children's books; Dir MIHAI CAZIMIR.

**Editura Ştiinţifică** (Scientific Publishing House): 71341 Bucharest, Piaţa Presei Libere 1; tel. and fax (1) 2223330; f. 1990; fmrly Editura Ştiinţifică şi Enciclopedică; language dictionaries, bibliographies, monographs, chronologies, reference books, popular and informational literature; Dir DINU GRAMA.

**Editura Tehnică** (Technical Publishing House): 71341 Bucharest, Piaţa Presei Libere 1; tel. (1) 2223321; fax (1) 2223776; f. 1950; technical and scientific books, technical dictionaries; Gen. Man. Dr Eng. IOAN GANEA.

**Editura Univers:** 71341 Bucharest, Piaţa Presei Libere 1; tel. (1) 2226629; fax (1) 2225652; f. 1961; translations from world literature, criticism, essays; Dir MIRCEA MARTIN.

**Editura de Vest** (West Publishing House): 1900 Timişoara, Piaţa Sfântul Gheorghe 2; tel. (61) 18218; fax (1) 14212; f. 1972 as Editura Facla; socio-political, technical, scientific and literary works in Romanian, Hungarian, German and Serbian; Dir VASILE POPOVICI.

**Întreprinderea de Stat pentru Imprimate şi Administrarea Publicaţiilor** (State Enterprise for Printed Matter and Periodicals): 71341 Bucharest, Piaţa Presei Libere 1; f. 1951; general publications; Dir NICOLAE BAZAC.

**Tribuna Press and Publishing House:** 2400 Sibiu, Str. George Coşbuc 38; tel. (24) 12810; telex 69247; fax (24) 12026; f. 1991; Dir EMIL DAVID.

### PUBLISHERS' ASSOCIATIONS

**Cultura Nationala:** 79715 Bucharest, Piaţa Presei Libere 1; tel. (1) 6181255; state organization attached to Ministry of Culture; administration, production and distribution of literary magazines and books of national interest; organization of imports and exports.

**Societatii Patronilor de Edituri din România:** Braşov, Bd dul 15 Noeimbrei 3; tel. (68) 114876; fax (68) 150394; f. 1993; 50 mems; Pres. DANIEL DRAGAN.

### WRITERS' UNION

**Uniunea Scriitorilor din România** (Romanian Writers' Union): Bucharest, Calea Victoriei 133; tel. (1) 6507245; telex 11796; fax (1) 3129634; f. 1949; Pres. MIRCEA DINESCU.

## Radio and Television

In 1992 there were 4.6m. radio receivers and 4.6m. television receivers in use. Romania's first regional TV station (at Timişoara) was registered in December 1989. Romania's first satellite TV channel, Tele 7 ABC, was launched in 1994.

**Radioteleviziunea Română** (Romanian Radio and Television): Bucharest, Calea Dorobanţilor 191, POB 63–1200; tel. (1) 331092; telex 10182; fax (1) 337544; Pres. Prof. Dr RĂZVAN THEODORESCU.

### RADIO

**Societatea Română de Radiodifuziune:** Bucharest, Str. Gral Berthelot 60–62, POB 63–1200; tel. (1) 6503055; telex 11252;

fax (1) 3121057; f. 1928; 39 transmitters on medium-wave, 69 transmitters on VHF; First, Second and Third Programme, plus two local programmes; foreign broadcasts on one medium-wave and eight short-wave transmitters in Arabic, English, French, German, Greek, Hungarian, Italian, Farsi, Portuguese, Romanian, Russian, Serbian, Spanish, Turkish and Ukrainian; Sec.-Gen. CRISTINEL POPA.

**Radio 'Nord-Est':** 6600 Iaşi, Bd. Copou 3; tel. (32) 211570; fax (32) 146363; f. 1992; independent; Dir ALEXANDRU LAZESCU; Man. Dir RADU OLTEANU.

### TELEVISION

**Televiziunea Română—Telecentrul Bucureşti** (Romanian Television—Bucharest TV Centre): Bucharest, Calea Dorobanţilor 191, POB 63-1200; tel. (1) 6334710; telex 11251; fax (1) 6337544; 39 transmitters; daily transmissions; Dir-Gen. DUMITRU POPA.

**Channel 2 TV Română:** Bucharest; f. 1992 as a jt venture; 80% owned by Atlantic Television Ltd (UK-Canada), 20% by Radioteleviziunea Română; independent commercial channel; to braodcast six hours of programmes daily; Man. Dir ROBIN EDWARDS.

## Finance

(cap. = capital; res = reserves; dep. = deposits; m. = million; amounts in lei; brs = brs)

### BANKING
#### Central Bank

**Banca Naţională** (National Bank of Romania): 70421 Bucharest, Str. Lipscani 25; tel. (1) 6140262; telex 11136; fax (1) 6415055; f. 1880; until 1948 was the Banca Natională a României; from 1948–65 was the Banca Republicii Populare Române; central bank and bank of issue; manages monetary policy; supervises commercial banks and credit business; res 31,751.5m., dep. 5,115,177.5m. (Dec. 1993); Gov. MUGUR ISĂRESCU; 141 brs.

#### Other Banks

**Banca Agricolă SC** (Agriculture Bank): 70006 Bucharest, Str. Smîrdan 3; tel. (1) 144260; telex 11622; fax (1) 120340; f. 1968; fmrly Banca pentru Agricultură şi Industrie Alimentară, present name since 1990; cap. 29,000m. (May 1993), res 1,145m., dep. 365,029m. (Dec. 1991); state-owned; Pres. GHEORGHE BĂRBULESCU; 41 brs.

**Banca Comerciala Română SA** (Romanian Commercial Bank): 70348 Bucharest, Bd. Republicii 14; tel. and fax (1) 6142166; telex 10893; f. 1990; commercial banking services for domestic and foreign customers; subscribed cap. 30,000m., res 1,682m., dep. 686,109m. (Dec. 1992); Pres. ION GHICA; 200 brs and agencies.

**Banca Română de Comerț Exterior SA** (Romanian Bank for Foreign Trade—RBFT): 70012 Bucharest, Calea Victoriei 22–24; tel. (1) 6149190; telex 11235; fax (1) 6141598; f. 1968, reorganized 1991; joint-stock company; cap. 61,900m. (1994), res 11,800m.(1993), dep. 110,000m. (1993); 69.1% state-owned; Pres. RĂZVAN TEMEŞAN; 15 brs.

**Banca Română Pentru Dezvoltare** (Romanian Bank for Development): 70016 Bucharest 3, Str. Doamnei 4; tel. (1) 6133200; telex 11238; fax (1) 6158750; f. 1990 to replace Investment Bank (f. 1948); financial and banking services and operations to all economic units, public enterprises and individuals for investment, production and commercial activities, etc.; cap. 14,000m. (Dec. 1992); state-owned; Pres. and CEO MARIAN CRISAN; 171 brs.

**Bankcoop SA** (The Cooperative Credit Bank): 70418 Bucharest, Str. Ion Ghica 13; tel. (1) 3120035; telex 11202; fax (1) 3120037; f. 1990; cap. 2,500m., res 32,781m., dep. 174,753m. (Dec. 1993); Pres. ALEXANDRU DINULESCU; 41 brs.

**Bank for Small Industry and Free Enterprise—Mindbank:** Bucharest, 46–48 Calea Plevnei; tel. (1) 6130788; telex 10228; fax (1) 3120031; f. 1990; cap. 5,356m., res 6,213m., dep. 34,524m. (Dec. 1994); privately-owned; Chair. IOAN PRUNDUS; 7 brs.

**Casa de Economii şi Consemnaţiuni—CEC** (Savings and Consignation Bank): Bucharest, Calea Victoriei 13; tel. (1) 6154810; telex 11466; fax (1) 3123159; f. 1864; handles private savings and loans for the inter-banking market; cap. and res. 48,579m., dep. 1,267,296m. (Dec. 1994); state-owned; Pres. EMIL ACHIM BADIU; 42 brs.

Other private banks founded since 1990 include the Banca Comerciala Ion Tiriac SA, Bankost, Creditbank, the Romanian Bank and the Export Import Bank (initial cap. 20,000m. lei).

### BANKING ASSOCIATION

**Romanian Banking Association:** Bucharest; Chair. DAN PASCARIU.

### INSURANCE

**Asigurarea Românească SA (Asirom):** 70406 Bucharest 3, Str. Smîrdan 5; tel. (1) 3125020; telex 11269; fax (1) 3124819; f. 1991; all types of insurance, including life insurance; Gen. Man. GHEORGHE PARASCHIV; 41 brs.

**Insurance and Reinsurance Company SA (Aatra):** 79118 Bucharest, Str. Smîrdan 5; tel. (1) 150986; telex 11209; fax (1) 139306; all types of insurance, including commercial insurance; Gen. Man. EMIL BOLDUŞ.

## Trade and Industry

### STATE PROPERTY AGENCIES

**National Agency for Privatization:** Bucharest; Pres. (vacant).

**State Ownership Fund:** Bucharest; responsible for the sale of shareholdings totalling 70% in about 6,000 state-owned enterprises; Chair. EMIL DIMA.

### INVESTMENT ORGANIZATION

**Romanian Development Agency:** Bucharest; promotes foreign investment in Romanian industry; Pres. (vacant).

### CHAMBER OF COMMERCE AND INDUSTRY

There are chambers of commerce throughout Romania.

**Chamber of Commerce and Industry of Romania:** 79502 Bucharest, Bd. Nicolae Bălcescu 22; tel. (1) 6154703; telex 11374; fax (1) 3122091; f. 1868; non-governmental organization; Pres. AUREL GHIBUTIU.

### CO-OPERATIVE ORGANIZATIONS

**Federaţia agricultorilor privatizaţi din România** (Romanian Private Farmers' Federation): 70111 Bucharest, Bd. Nicolae Bălcescu 17–19, Sector 1; tel. (1) 6131619; fax (1) 6133043; f. 1991; represents 4,000 farming co-operatives and 41 district unions; Pres. GHEORGHE PREDILA.

**Uniunea centrală a cooperativelor de consum şi de credit—Centrocoop** (Central Union of Consumer and Credit Co-operatives): Bucharest, Str. Brezoianu 31; tel. (1) 6144800; telex 11591; fax (1) 6142991; f. 1950; 2,500 producer and 850 credit co-operatives were affiliated to the Central Union in 1992; represents 10m. members.

**Uniunea centrală a cooperativelor meşteşugăreşti—UCECOM** (Central Union of Handicrafts Co-operatives): Bucharest, Calea Plevnei 46; tel. (1) 151810; Chair. Ing. DUMITRU DĂNGĂ.

### TRADE UNIONS

The regulations governing trade unions were liberalized in early 1990. The Uniunea Generală a Sindicatelor din România (UGSR) was dissolved. Several new trade union organizations have since been established.

**Alianţa Confederativă Intersindicală 15 Noiembrie:** 2200 Braşov, Str. Michael Weiss 13; tel. and fax (68) 151936; f. 1991; 120,000 mems; Pres. ADRIAN LAHARIA.

**Blocul Naţional Sindical:** Bucharest; f. 1991; 500,000 mems; Chair. MATEI BRĂTIANU.

**Cartelul Alfa:** f. 1990; 1.1m. mems; Leader BOGDAN HOSSU.

**Confederaţia COSIN:** f. 1990; 10,000 mems.

**Confederaţia Fides:** 180,000 mems; Leader CĂTĂLIN CROITORU.

**Confederaţia Hercules:** Bucharest; f. 1990; transport workers.

**Confederaţia Naţională a Sindicatelor Libere din România—Frăţia** (CNSLR-Frăţia—National Free Trade Union Confederation of Romania): 70109 Bucharest, Str. Ministerului 1–3; tel. (1) 3125292; telex 10844; fax (1) 3123598; f. 1990, merged with Confederaţia Naţională a Sindicatelor Libere Frăţia in 1993; 2.6m. mems (1994); 49 professional or branch federations, in all sectors of the economy, and 41 territorial leagues; Pres PAVEL TODORAN; Exec. Pres. MIRON MITREA.

**Confederation of Democratic Trade Unions of Romania:** Bucharest; f. 1994; 34 branch federations; 640,000 mems; Pres. VICTOR CIORBEA.

Other organizations include Infratirea, the Justice and Brotherhood Union and the Convention of Non-Affiliated Trade Unions of Romania.

### TRADE FAIRS

**Romexpo SA (Fairs and Exhibitions Co):** 71331 Bucharest, Bd. Mărăşti 65–67, POB 32-3; tel. (1) 6181160; telex 11108; fax (1) 6183724; f. 1970; Gen. Dir GEORG COJOCARU.

ROMANIA

## Transport

### RAILWAYS

In 1994 there were 11,374 km of track, of which 3,866 km were electrified lines.

**Societatea Nationale a Căilor Ferate Române—SNCFR** (Romanian Railways): 77113 Bucharest 1, Bd. Dinicu Golescu 38; tel. (1) 6386550; telex 115531; fax (1) 3123205; f. 1880; Pres. Nicolae Ionescu.

### Metropolitan Transport

The Bucharest underground railway network, sections of which were opened between 1979 and 1989, totals 60 km in length.

**Regia de Éxploatare a Metroului București:** 79917 Bucharest 1, Bd. Dinicu Golescu 38; tel. (1) 6387515; telex 11665; fax (1) 3125149; f. 1977; Gen. Man. Octavian Udriste.

### ROADS

At the end of 1994 there were 72,829 km of roads, of which 113 km were motorways, 14,683 km national roads and 58,146 km secondary roads. Under the 1991–2005 road development programme, more than 3,000 km of motorways were to be built and 4,000 km of existing roads were to be modernized.

**Administrația Națională a Drumurilor—AND** (National Administration of Roads): Ministerul Transporturilor, Bucharest 1, Bd. Dinicu Golescu 38; tel. (1) 6387886; telex 10835; fax (1) 3120984; Dir-Gen. Dr Ing. Danila Bucsa.

### INLAND AND OCEAN SHIPPING

Navigation on the River Danube is open to shipping of all nations. The Danube–Black Sea Canal was officially opened to traffic in May 1984, and has an annual handling capacity of 80m. metric tons. Work on the 85-km Danube–Bucharest Canal was abandoned in early 1990. The first joint Romanian-Yugoslav Iron Gates (Porțile de Fier) power and navigation system on the Danube was completed in 1972, and Iron Gates-2 opened to navigation in December 1984. Romania's principal seaports are Constanța (on the Black Sea), Tulcea, Galați, Brăila and Giurgiu (on the Danube).

In June 1992 Romania's merchant fleet had 439 vessels, with a total displacement of 3,266,168 grt.

**NAVROM** (Romanian Shipping Co): 8700 Constanța; tel. (41) 615821; telex 14217; fax (41) 618413; organizes sea transport; operates routes to most parts of the world; Gen. Man. Manea Ghiocel.

**Petromin SA:** Constanța; operates merchant fleet of 92 ships and tankers totalling 4.6m. gross registered tons.

**Romline:** 8700 Constanța, Gate 2 Hostel; tel. (41) 617285; telex 14327; fax (41) 615647; f. 1990; merchant shipping company.

### CIVIL AVIATION

There are international airports at Bucharest-Baneasa, Bucharest-Otopeni, M. Kogălniceanu-Constanța, Timișoara and Arad.

**Transporturile Aeriene Române—TAROM** (Romanian Air Transport): 71557 Bucharest, Otopeni Airport; tel. (1) 6333137; telex 11181; fax (1) 3129767; f. 1954; services to 42 countries throughout Europe, the Middle East, Africa, Asia and the USA and extensive internal flights; Dir-Gen. Nicolae Brutaru.

**Liniile Aeriene Române—LAR:** 70733 Bucharest, Calea Știrbei Vodă 2–4; tel. (1) 6153276; telex 10069; fax (1) 3120148; f. 1975 by TAROM to operate passenger charter services; re-established as independent airline in 1990; Man. Dir Dorin Ivașcu.

## Tourism

The Carpathian mountains, the Danube delta and the Black Sea resorts (Mamaia, Eforie, Mangalia and others) are the principal attractions. In 1994 there were 5.9m. tourist arrivals.

**Arcadia Tour Ltd:** Bucharest, Bd. Nicolae Titulescu 1; tel. (1) 3126789; fax (1) 3126794; Gen. Man. Enea Giurchescu.

**Litoral SA:** 8741 Mamaia-Constanța, Hotel București; tel. (18) 31152; telex 14377; fax (18) 31276; f. 1970; Gen. Man. Corneliu Culețu.

**ONT Carpați SA** (Carpați National Travel Agency): 70161 Bucharest, Bd. Magheru 7; tel. (1) 6145160; telex 11270; fax (1) 6151084; f. 1936; Gen. Man. Mihai Voicu.

**S. C. Postăvural—Tourism Co:** 2200 Brașov, Str. Mureșenilor 12; tel. (68) 142754; fax (68) 150496; f. 1990; fmrly National Tourist Office; promotes tourism in Brașov; Gen. Man. Mladin George.

# THE RUSSIAN FEDERATION

## Introductory Survey

**Location, Climate, Language, Religion, Flag, Capital**

The Russian Federation, or Russia (until 25 December 1991 officially known as the Russian Soviet Federative Socialist Republic—RSFSR), constituted the major part of the USSR, providing some 76% of its area and some 51% of its population in 1990. It is bounded by Norway, Finland, Estonia and Latvia to the north-west and by Belarus and Ukraine to the west. The southern borders of European Russia are with the Black Sea, Georgia, Azerbaijan, the Caspian Sea and Kazakhstan. The Siberian and Far Eastern regions have southern frontiers with the People's Republic of China, Mongolia and the Democratic People's Republic of Korea. The eastern coastline is on the Sea of Japan, the Sea of Okhotsk, the Pacific Ocean and the Barents Sea. The northern coastline is on the Arctic Ocean. The region around Kaliningrad (formerly Königsberg in East Prussia), on the Baltic Sea, became part of the Russian Federation in 1945. It is separated from the rest of the Russian Federation by Lithuania and Belarus. It borders Poland to the south, Lithuania to the north and east and has a coastline on the Baltic Sea. The climate of Russia is extremely varied, ranging from extreme Arctic conditions in northern areas and much of Siberia to generally temperate weather in the south. The average temperature in Moscow in July is 19°C (66°F); the average for January is -9°C (15°F). Average annual precipitation in the capital is 575 mm. The official language is Russian, but a large number of other languages are in daily use. Religious adherence is varied, with many religions closely connected with particular ethnic groups. Christianity is the major religion, mostly adhered to by ethnic Russians and other Slavs. The Russian Orthodox Church is the largest denomination. The main concentrations of adherents of Islam are among Volga Tatars, Chuvash and Bashkirs, and the peoples of the northern Caucasus, including the Chechen, Ingush, Ossetians, Kabardinians and the peoples of Daghestan. Buddhism is the main religion of the Buryats, the Tuvans and the Kalmyks. The large pre-1917 Jewish population has been depleted by war and emigration, but there remain some 656,000 Jews in the Russian Federation. The national flag (approximate proportions 2 by 1) consists of three equal horizontal stripes of white, blue and red. The capital is Moscow.

**Recent History**

By the end of the 19th century the Russian Empire extended throughout vast territories in Eastern Europe, and included most of northern and central Asia, a result of the territorial expansionism of the Romanov dynasty, which had ruled Russia since 1613. Despite the attempts of Tsar Alexander II (1855–81) to introduce liberal reforms, until 1905 the Empire remained an autocracy, under the personal rule of Tsar Nicholas II (1894–1917).

Growing dissatisfaction in urban areas with economic conditions, combined with the shock of defeats in the Russo–Japanese War (1904–05), culminated in street demonstrations against the regime in early 1905. The brutal repression of a demonstration in January, and the final capitulation of Russia in the war with Japan forced the Tsar to issue a manifesto in October 1905, which promised respect for civil liberties and the introduction of some constitutional order in Russia.

The attempt at reforms which followed, under Prime Ministers Sergei Witte (1905–06) and Petr Stolypin (1906–11), did not effect the transformations necessary to placate the increasingly restive workers and peasants. In 1917 strikes and demonstrations took place in the capital, Petrograd (the new name for St Petersburg since 1914). In February the Tsar was forced to abdicate, and a provisional Government, composed mainly of liberal landowners, took power. However, most real power lay with the Petrograd and other soviets (councils), which were composed largely of workers and soldiers, and were attracted to socialist ideas.

The inability of the Provisional Government, first under Prince Lvov and then under the moderate socialist Aleksandr Kerensky, to fulfil the expectations of the peasants with regard to land reform, or to effect a withdrawal from the First World War, allowed more extreme groups, such as the Bolshevik faction of the Russian Social Democratic Labour Party (RSDLP), led by Vladimir Ulyanov (Lenin), to develop support among disaffected soldiers and workers. On 7 November 1917 (25 October, Old Style) the Bolsheviks, who had come to dominate the Petrograd Soviet, seized power in the capital, with minimal use of force. On the same day, the Russian Soviet Federative Socialist Republic (RSFSR or Russian Federation) was proclaimed.

Initially, the Russian Federation was presented as the territorial successor to the Russian Empire, but the Bolsheviks also claimed that they would respect the self-determination of the Empire's many nations. Poland, Finland and the Baltic States (Estonia, Latvia and Lithuania) achieved independence, but other independent states which had been established in 1917–18 were forced, by military means, to declare themselves Soviet Republics. These were proclaimed as 'independent' socialist republics, in alliance with the Russian Federation, but the laws, Constitution and Government of the Russian Federation were supreme in all the republics. This recentralization of Russian power, with the Russian Federation controlling all but the newly-independent Baltic territories, was recognized as politically damaging by the Bolsheviks. Thus, in 1922 the Russian Federation joined the Belarusian (Byelorussian), Ukrainian and Transcaucasian republics as constitutionally equal partners in a Union of Soviet Socialist Republics (USSR), and institutions of the RSFSR were reformed as institutions of the new Union. The USSR, or Soviet Union, eventually came to number 15 constituent Soviet Socialist Republics (SSR).

The Russian Federation, in common with the other republics, experienced considerable hardship as a result of the collectivization campaign of the early 1930s and the widespread repression under Iosif Jugashvili (Stalin), who established a brutal dictatorship after the death of Lenin in 1924. The centralized Five-Year Plans, introduced in the late 1920s to effect the rapid industrialization of the USSR, concentrated on the Russian Federation, but with considerable investment directed towards the previously neglected eastern regions. This relocation of the industrial 'heartland' of Russia was reinforced by the removal of strategic industries from the west of the republic to the Ural regions during the Second World War or 'Great Patriotic War' (1941–1945). Under the Nazi-Soviet Treaty of Non-Aggression (the 'Molotov-Ribbentrop Pact') of August 1939, the USSR had been able to annex the Baltic States as well as other territories. Victory over Germany and Japan in the Second World War led to further territorial gains for the Russian Federation itself. In the west it gained part of East Prussia around Königsberg (now Kaliningrad) from Germany, a small amount of territory from Estonia and those parts of Finland that had been annexed during the Soviet-Finnish War (1939–40). In the east it gained the strategically important Kurile Islands from Japan. In addition, the nominally independent Republic of Tuva, situated between the USSR and Mongolia, was annexed in 1944, and subsequently became an autonomous republic within the Russian Federation. The present territorial extent of the Russian Federation was achieved in 1954, when Crimea was ceded to the Ukrainian SSR.

Shortly after the death of Stalin, in March 1953, Nikita Khrushchev took over the post of First Secretary of the Communist Party of the Soviet Union (CPSU—as the Communist Party had been renamed in 1952), and gradually assumed predominance in the Soviet leadership over his main rivals, Georgy Malenkov and Vyacheslav Molotov. The most brutal aspects of the Stalinist regime were ended under Khrushchev, and thousands of prisoners were released. The process of cautious liberalization was accelerated in 1956 when, for the first time, Khrushchev admitted that large-scale repressions had occurred under Stalin. However, Khrushchev's attempts to reform the Soviet bureaucracy, his erratic plans for economic reform and his conduct of international relations led to his overthrow in 1964. He was replaced as First Secretary (later General Secretary) of the CPSU by Leonid Brezhnev, who remained in power until 1982. During the 1970s relations with the West, which had been severely strained since the early 1950s, experienced a considerable *détente*, but further *rapprochement* was ended by the Soviet invasion of Afghanistan in 1979. Meanwhile, throughout the 1970s Soviet economic performance gradually worsened, and widespread corruption and inefficiency were evident. Brezhnev's successor as CPSU General Secretary, Yuri Andropov (1982–84), began a major anti-corruption policy and made some cautious attempts at economic reform. He was succeeded upon his death (in February 1984) by Konstantin Chernenko, a former close ally of Brezhnev, who achieved little before his death in March 1985.

Chernenko's successor as General Secretary was Mikhail Gorbachev, the youngest member of the Politburo. During 1986 and 1987 Gorbachev replaced a large number of leading state and CPSU officials, and appointed several reformist politicians to the Politburo. Meanwhile, a policy of *glasnost* (openness), which provided a greater degree of freedom for the mass media, permitted freer discussion of previously censored aspects of Russian and Soviet history, as well as more critical views concerning contemporary politics. It also allowed the overt development of different strains of Russian nationalism, which, although previously evident, had not been permitted open form. Right-wing groups such as Pamyat (Memory), while stressing their concern for the preservation of Russian culture, represented extreme chauvinistic views, and were accused of perpetrating attacks on non-Russians and especially Jews.

In November 1987 the supporters of *perestroika* (restructuring), as Gorbachev's programme of cautious political and economic reform came to be known, seemed to have suffered a reverse with the dismissal from the Politburo of Boris Yeltsin (a former CPSU Secretary in Sverdlovsk, who advocated accelerated and more radical reform), after he severely criticized senior members of the leadership for what he claimed was their opposition to reform. In June 1988, at the first Extraordinary Party Conference since 1941, Gorbachev announced plans for comprehensive changes in the political system, with the introduction of a two-tier legislature, elected largely by competitive elections. In the elections to the USSR Congress of People's Deputies, held in March 1989, many conservative candidates were defeated by reformist politicians, including Boris Yeltsin, who won an overwhelming victory in the Moscow constituency. In May 1989, when the Congress was convened in Moscow, it elected Gorbachev to the new post of executive President of the USSR.

The position of the Russian Federation within the Soviet federal system was paradoxical. It was clearly the predominant union republic, both economically and politically, and ethnic Russians dominated the Soviet élite. However, this prominence within the USSR meant that Russia developed few institutions of its own. Thus, all republics had an academy of sciences, cultural institutions, trade unions, and above all communist parties, except the Russian Federation. This asymmetry in the federal system continued until the beginning of the 1990s.

The initial stage in the process of achieving Russian sovereignty from all-Union institutions was the election of the RSFSR Congress of People's Deputies in March 1990 by largely free and competitive elections. The Congress, consisting of 1,068 deputies, convened in May, and narrowly elected Boris Yeltsin as Chairman of the Supreme Soviet (the permanent working body of the Congress). This was the highest state post in the RSFSR, and a position from which Yeltsin could effectively challenge the authority of President Gorbachev and the all-Union institutions which he represented. Ruslan Khasbulatov, a little-known Chechen economist, was elected as First Deputy Chairman. Finally, the Congress elected the necessary 252 deputies to serve in the Supreme Soviet.

On 12 June 1990 the Congress adopted a declaration of sovereignty, which asserted that the RSFSR was a sovereign republic, that the laws of the RSFSR had primacy over all-Union legislation, and that the RSFSR authorities had full sovereignty over the natural resources of the republic. This led to increased conflict with the all-Union Government and President, but the process of creating republican institutions continued. In September 1989 the all-Union Government had outlined plans for the creation of new political and economic structures for the Russian Federation, and in December the CPSU announced the establishment of a Central Committee Russian Bureau. In mid-1990 the Russian Communist Party (RCP) was established, led by Ivan Polozkov, a conservative communist opposed to Yeltsin. The institutions that Russia had lacked, including a trade union organization, a journalists' union, an academy of sciences and national cultural organizations, began to be established. In 1991 a radio and television broadcasting network, controlled by the Russian Government (and largely supportive of Boris Yeltsin in its political stance) began broadcasting, and the all-Union Committee of State Security (KGB) permitted the establishment of a republican branch of the KGB, under the jurisdiction of the RSFSR.

Although these were all important developments in the process of creating a Russian sovereign state, Yeltsin himself had little power to effect the policies which he announced. Thus in March 1991, when a referendum was held in most republics of the USSR to determine whether a restructured USSR should be retained, voters in the RSFSR also approved an additional question on the introduction of a Russian presidency. Direct presidential elections took place in June, and were won overwhelmingly by Yeltsin and his Vice-President, Aleksandr Rutskoy, with 57.3% of the votes cast. Nikolai Ryzhkov, the former Soviet Prime Minister, was his nearest challenger, with 16.9% of the votes, while the extreme right-wing candidate, Vladimir Zhirinovsky, achieved an unexpectedly high level of support (8%). Direct election as President gave Yeltsin a sufficient popular mandate to challenge the jurisdiction of President Gorbachev and the all-Union authorities. Yeltsin announced a new reform programme, including a reorganization of the system of government and the beginnings of economic adjustment, aimed at creating the basis for a market economy in Russia within 500 days. He remained committed, none the less, to a restructured Soviet federation, agreeing to sign a proposed new union treaty which aimed to provide the union republics with extensive autonomy.

On 19 August 1991, one day before the union treaty was due to be signed, a self-proclaimed State Committee for the State of Emergency (SCSE), composed of the Vice-President and other leading officials, seized power in Moscow. Within three days, however, the attempted coup collapsed, partly owing to the opposition of Yeltsin. The failure of the coup further enhanced Yeltsin's power, both as a result of his role in opposing the *putsch* and owing to the subsequent virtual collapse of all-Union institutions. The CPSU and the RCP were suspended, and Yeltsin asserted his control over all-Union bodies, dismissing the head of the all-Union television and radio company and appointing Russian Federation ministers to head central economic ministries and institutions. Although some of these decrees were later annulled, the power of the centre was sharply diminished.

In late October 1991, at the fifth RSFSR Congress of People's Deputies, Yeltsin announced a programme of radical economic reforms. In early November a new Government was announced, with Yeltsin himself taking the office of Prime Minister, while Gennady Burbulis was appointed First Deputy Prime Minister, and Yegor Gaidar, a leading free-market economist, was appointed Deputy Prime Minister and Minister of Finance. Also in early November Yeltsin announced that the CPSU and the RCP were banned, and their property was transferred to the State. The fifth Congress granted Yeltsin special powers for a period of one year, including the right to issue decrees with the same force as legislation adopted by the legislature, the right to appoint the leaders of local administrations and presidential representatives to ensure that presidential decrees were enforced, and the right to appoint government ministers without the approval of parliament. At the same Congress Ruslan Khasbulatov was elected Yeltsin's successor as Chairman of the Supreme Soviet (he had failed to achieve the necessary majority in July).

Yeltsin's approach to the establishment of the new all-Union structures in the aftermath of the coup was initially ambiguous. He agreed to the creation of an economic community, which was founded by eight republics on 18 October 1991, and seemed to favour the 'Union of Sovereign States' proposed by President Gorbachev to replace the USSR. Following the reorganization of the Government in November, however, opposition to the creation of any new federation increased. Burbulis and his allies in the new Government were reported to be strongly opposed to any new all-Union structure, and were apparently influential in the proposal for the creation of a Commonwealth of Independent States (CIS, see p. 126), which was agreed between the leaders of Belarus, Ukraine and Russia on 8 December. At the same time the three leaders announced that the 1922 Union Treaty, which had established the USSR, was annulled and the USSR had ceased to exist. Within days a further eight republics had expressed their intention to join the CIS, which was to be merely a co-ordinating organization rather than a new state. The Alma-Ata Declaration of 21 December (see p. 127) formally established a commonwealth of 11 states, leaving, of the former Soviet republics, only Georgia and the three Baltic States outside the new body. On 25 December President Gorbachev resigned as the last President of the USSR. On the same day the Russian Supreme Soviet formally changed the name of the RSFSR to the Russian Federation.

On 2 January 1992, as part of the new Russian Government's economic reform programme, state controls on the prices of most goods were ended, resulting in substantial price increases. The policy was strongly criticized by many politicians, including Vice-President Aleksandr Rutskoy. Several thousand people were reported to have attended protests in Moscow to condemn the price rises. There were further demonstrations in Moscow in early February, organized both by supporters and opponents of Yeltsin.

Opposition to the Government's economic policies was evident at the sixth Congress of People's Deputies, held in Moscow in early April 1992. Following criticism of its economic reform programme at the Congress, the Government offered its resignation, but the offer was rejected by Yeltsin. An attempt by the Congress to deprive Yeltsin of some of the powers granted to him in November 1991 was unsuccessful, but many deputies asserted the right of the Congress to exercise greater control over economic policies. Yeltsin strongly criticized the Congress for failing to support legislation necessary for the introduction of a market economy, and was subsequently reported as having stated that the Congress would have to be dissolved.

On 15 June 1992 Yeltsin appointed Yegor Gaidar (since May joint First Deputy Prime Minister) as acting Prime Minister. The appointment of Gaidar was widely regarded as an important victory for advocates of radical economic reform. Also in June the Supreme Soviet adopted legislation permitting large-scale 'privatization', and a presidential decree introduced (for the first time) bankruptcy regulations. A new political alliance, Civic Union, which described itself as a 'constructive opposition', was established in late June. The organization depended largely on the support of industrial managers, but was also joined by Vice-President Rutskoy and the Democratic Party of Russia, which had previously supported the Government. Although in principle it supported the transition to a market economy, Civic Union advocated a far slower pace of reform, in order to prevent economic collapse and to counteract the increasing level of poverty in the country. More extreme opposition was evidenced by some 15,000 neo-communist and nationalist demonstrators, who for almost two weeks in mid-June organized anti-government protests at the television centre in Moscow, until being dispersed by security forces.

Controversy regarding economic policy continued in July 1992, with the resignation of the Chairman of the Central Bank, Georgy Matyukhin, who had been severely criticized by the Government for his liberal monetary policies. He was replaced by Viktor Gerashchenko, a former Chairman of the USSR State Bank. In September negotiations took place in Cheboksary (Chuvash Republic) between Yeltsin, Ruslan Khasbulatov and the heads of Russia's republics and regions, in an attempt to achieve a solution to the continuing constitutional dispute. Yeltsin announced that legislative bodies at all levels would serve their remaining terms of office, thus repudiating his alleged threats to dissolve the Congress of People's Deputies prematurely.

In late October 1992 Yeltsin issued a decree banning the National Salvation Front (NSF), which united a number of extreme nationalist and communist groups. (This decree was subsequently declared illegal by the Constitutional Court, which, however, permitted the outlawing of groups seeking to incite the overthrow of the state or ethnic and social unrest.) At the same time a further presidential decree ordered the disbandment of the Directorate for the Protection of the Supreme Bodies of Power and Government, an armed formation of some 5,000 men that was reported to be under the personal command of Ruslan Khasbulatov. On 30 November the Constitutional Court announced its verdict in the cases regarding the legality of Yeltsin's ban on the CPSU and the RCP of November 1991, a case which had been in progress since July 1992. Although the Court upheld the dissolution of the national structures of the CPSU and RCP and the decision to confiscate communist party property which belonged to the state, it decreed that a ban on local party branches was unlawful. The decision was widely viewed as a compromise between the President and communist groups, which immediately announced that they would attempt to establish a new communist party. A successor to the RCP, the Communist Party of the Russian Federation (CPRF), emerged in early 1993.

In early December 1992, at the seventh Congress of People's Deputies, Yegor Gaidar, acting Prime Minister since June, was rejected by the Congress, and Yeltsin was forced to appoint a new Prime Minister, Viktor Chernomyrdin, who had a more conservative reputation with regard to economic reform. Further threats of conflict between the executive and legislature were temporarily defused by a compromise agreement between Yeltsin and Khasbulatov, which envisaged that a draft constitution would be voted on in a referendum in April 1993, while all constitutional amendments adopted at the Congress (which aimed to limit the powers of the President) would be suspended, and Yeltsin's special powers to rule by decree, which were due to expire in December, would be retained until the time of the referendum.

The appointment of Chernomyrdin as Prime Minister led to expectation that there would be significant changes in the personnel of the Government. However, when the new cabinet was announced in late December most ministers in the outgoing Government retained their portfolios. Moreover, Boris Federov, a liberal economist (hitherto Russian representative at the World Bank), was appointed as Deputy Prime Minister with responsibility for the economy. Shortly after his appointment Chernomyrdin announced a plan to stabilize prices by limiting the levels of profits which producers could achieve, but in January 1993 the scheme was deemed 'unworkable' and was abandoned, after strong opposition from Federov.

In February 1993 negotiations between Yeltsin and Khasbulatov failed to achieve a settlement of the constitutional dispute. At the eighth Congress of People's Deputies, which took place in Moscow in mid-March, the Congress voted to annul the constitutional compromise adopted at the seventh Congress, thus depriving Yeltsin of the special powers granted him in November 1991. The Congress also rejected the proposed referendum on the respective roles of the president and legislature. In response, on 20 March 1993 President Yeltsin announced that he intended to rule by decree until 25 April, when the referendum would take place, and that, although neither the Supreme Soviet nor the Congress would be suspended, their decisions would have no legal force in the interim period. Yeltsin's announcement was severely criticized by the Supreme Soviet and by Vice-President Rutskoy, and the Constitutional Court declared it to be unconstitutional. At an extraordinary session of the Congress of People's Deputies, delegates failed narrowly to initiate impeachment proceedings against Yeltsin, but imposed their own set of four questions for consideration at the forthcoming referendum, which appeared to reduce the likelihood that Yeltsin would achieve a high level of popular support.

The referendum took place, as scheduled, on 25 April 1993. Despite expectations of a low level of participation, 65.7% of the electorate voted. The first question (on confidence in Yeltsin as the President of the Russian Federation) received a positive response from 57.4% of voters, while an unexpectedly high proportion (53.7%) also responded positively to the second question, which asked for approval of Yeltsin's socio-economic policies. Support for early presidential elections (the subject of the third question) was relatively low (49.1%), but there was much greater enthusiasm for early elections to the Congress of People's Deputies (70.6%). Yeltsin gained most support in the large cities, particularly in Yekaterinburg (where 85.7% endorsed the first question) and Moscow (75.1%). Support for the President in rural areas and among non-Russians tended to be much lower, with only 2% of voters in Ingushetia and just 15% in Daghestan expressing confidence in him.

Despite the vote of confidence in Yeltsin in the April referendum, the President's position nevertheless remained precarious in mid-1993. On 1 May neo-communist and nationalist forces staged a demonstration of protest against Yeltsin in Moscow, which ended in violent clashes and the death of a police officer. By this time the ideological confrontation between Yeltsin and his Vice-President, Aleksandr Rutskoy, had widened to the extent that Rutskoy was divested of all his official responsibilities by Yeltsin (although nominally he remained Vice-President). Rutskoy in turn made repeated allegations of widespread corruption within Yeltsin's administration.

At the same time there was renewed disagreement between Yeltsin and his opponents in the Congress of People's Deputies over the drafting of the new Constitution to define the structures and direction of Russian politics. Yeltsin's draft, presented in late April, envisaged a strong presidency with a weakened role for the parliament, while that drafted by the Supreme Soviet effectively proposed an exact reversal of these functions. In order to exclude the Congress of People's Deputies from the constitutional process, Yeltsin decreed a special convention to be held in June, an action that was denounced by Khasbulatov. The Constitutional Conference comprised delegates from all the major political and social organizations, as well as from all but one of the country's 89 republics and regions (only Chechnya was not represented). In July the conference approved a compromise draft, based largely on the President's version but also incorporating parts of the 'parliamentary' draft. The document provided for a presidential system with a bicameral parliament, the Federal Assembly, comprising a lower chamber (State Duma) and an upper chamber (Federation Council), the latter composed of two representatives from each republic and region. The Government would be subordinate to both the President and the legislature. However, the draft did not win the approval of the Congress of People's Deputies; there was also opposition to it by some of the republics and regions.

The long-standing impasse between Yeltsin's administration and the legislature evolved into violent confrontation in early October 1993. On 21 September Yeltsin had suspended both the Congress of People's Deputies and the Supreme Soviet, stating that their efforts to frustrate his economic and constitutional reforms had severely undermined the state and would, if unchecked, lead to its disintegration. Yeltsin also announced that elections would be held to a new bicameral Federal Assembly (as envisaged in the draft Constitution) in early December. His actions were denounced as a 'coup' by Rutskoy, who was declared President by the Supreme Soviet, following its dismissal of Yeltsin. Rutskoy's appointment was confirmed at an emergency sitting of the Congress of People's Deputies, which also voted to impeach Yeltsin. Rival demonstrations were held in Moscow in support of both Yeltsin and his adversaries. On 27 September the parliament building (known as the White House) was surrounded by government troops; some 180 deputies, including Rutskoy and Khasbulatov, remained inside the building, with armed supporters. Despite attempts by the Constitutional Court and the Patriarch of the Russian Orthodox Church, Aleksey II, to mediate, the deputies remained defiant of the Government's ultimatum of 4 October to leave the White House. On 3 October armed conflict erupted between supporters of the rebels and forces loyal to Yeltsin, as the former attempted to seize control of the Ostankino television station and other strategic buildings. Yeltsin declared a state of emergency in Moscow (which remained in force for the following two weeks). On 4 October army tanks bombarded the parliament building, effecting the surrender of the rebels. The leaders of the rebellion were imprisoned (Rutskoy having been officially dismissed as Vice-President on 3 October), and charges of inciting 'mass disorder' were subsequently brought against them. According to official figures, some 170 people were estimated to have been killed in the fighting. However, unofficial sources claimed that several hundred people had been killed in the conflict.

In the immediate aftermath of the rebellion, Yeltsin moved to consolidate his position, temporarily strengthening government control of the media (several opposition newspapers were not permitted to appear for a short period, while others were banned altogether), and suspending several parties that either supported or participated in the rebellion. However, in mid-October 1993 the NSF, the CPRF and Rutskoy's own party, the People's Party of Free Russia (subsequently renamed the Russian Social Democratic People's Party), among others, were relegalized. Yeltsin announced that early presidential elections, provisionally scheduled for mid-1994, would not take place, and that he would fulfil his mandate (due to expire in June 1996). Yeltsin also sought to accelerate the drafting of the Constitution. The new version that the Constitutional Conference finalized in early November 1993 was submitted for approval in a national referendum on 12 December, when legislative elections were held simultaneously. It was reported that 54.8% of the registered electorate participated in the plebiscite, of whom 58.4% endorsed the draft. The Constitution guaranteed broad powers for the President and a much diminished role for the legislature (the Federal Assembly). It differed from earlier drafts in deleting any reference to the sovereignty of Russia's constituent republics and divesting them of the right of secession.

An estimated 53% of the electorate participated in the election of the Federal Assembly, held concurrently with the referendum. Of the 450 members of the State Duma (lower chamber), 225 were elected by proportional representation on the basis of party lists, while the remaining 225 were to be elected in single-member constituencies. (In fact only 219 of the latter were elected, owing to boycotts in Chechnya and one electoral district of Tatarstan, while the results in the four remaining constituencies of Tatarstan were declared invalid. However, in March 1994 Tatarstan's five deputies were successfully elected, bringing the total number of single-member-constituency seats to 224.) A total of 13 parties and blocs, as well as independents, contested the election to the Duma (eight parties or blocs were refused registration). It was estimated that only a small minority of deputies of the former Congress of People's Deputies stood for re-election.

No single party or bloc won a decisive majority of seats in the Duma. However, the result of the poll demonstrated an unexpectedly high level of support for extreme right-wing or anti-reformist elements, alarming the reformists in Russia as well as foreign governments. The ultra-nationalist Liberal Democratic Party (LDP) of Vladimir Zhirinovsky won the largest share (22.8%) of the votes cast according to party lists, although few individual candidates were elected in the single-member constituencies. Nevertheless, the LDP gained a total of 64 seats in the Duma, the largest obtained by any single party or alliance. Pro-communist parties also performed well: the CPRF gained 48 seats, while the Agrarian Party and Women of Russia won 33 and 23 seats, respectively. Civic Union failed to gain representation in the Duma. Russia's Choice (an alliance of pro-reform groups, led by Yegor Gaidar, which had been formed in the previous month and which was partly drawn from members of the Government and of Yeltsin's senior staff) performed less well than had been expected; it gained only 15.4% of the party votes, thus winning 40 seats, although it gained the largest number of single-member constituency seats (18), obtaining a total of 58 seats in the Duma. However, with the ensuing realignment of independents (130 of whom were elected) and parties into parliamentary factions, Russia's Choice reportedly emerged as the strongest grouping in the Duma (76 seats in January 1994). New Regional Policy, comprising 65 centrist independents, formed the second largest faction, followed by the LDP faction (63 seats, although this total subsequently declined, owing to defections from the faction). The election was monitored by approximately 1,000 foreign observers, who declared it largely free and democratic.

A total of 178 deputies were to be elected to the Federation Council, two from each of Russia's 89 republics and regions. However, voting was not held in the separatist territories of Tatarstan and Chechnya nor in Chelyabinsk region, and in two other districts only one deputy was elected. As a consequence, only 170 of the Council's seats were filled. (However, by May 1994 this total had increased to 176, with only the deputies from Chechnya remaining to be elected.) The majority of the Council's deputies were republican or regional leaders, few of whom held party affiliations. However, supporters of Yeltsin were believed to outnumber the communist and nationalist opposition.

A new, smaller Government, reported to be more conservative than its predecessor, was appointed gradually in late January 1994. Many of the most prominent figures in the outgoing Council of Ministers were retained, including Viktor Chernomyrdin (Chairman, or Prime Minister), Pavel Grachev (Minister of Defence), Andrey Kozyrev (Foreign Affairs) and Viktor Yerin (Internal Affairs). However, two leading reformers tendered their resignations: Boris Federov as Deputy Prime Minister and Minister of Finance, and Yegor

Gaidar as First Deputy Prime Minister and Minister of the Economy (posts he had held only since September 1993). Nevertheless, Yeltsin declared his commitment to furthering the process of democratic and economic reform. It was, however, thought likely that the distribution of seats in the State Duma—with combined opposition forces reportedly outnumbering the reformists—would produce further obstacles to Yeltsin's objectives. Indeed, in February 1994 the Russia's Choice faction in the lower chamber was unable to prevent a majority vote in favour of granting amnesties for Rutskoy, Khasbulatov and the other leaders of the parliamentary rebellion, as well as for the leaders of the SCSE attempted coup of August 1991 and for organizers of the violent demonstration in May 1993. However, following the amnesties there was widespread discussion of a treaty of public accord, as proposed by the Chairman (speaker) of the State Duma, Ivan Rybkin, in order to effect some sort of consensus among Russia's various parties, factions and movements. In late April the treaty was signed by all the major parties (excluding the CPRF and the Agrarian Party), as well as by representatives of most of the Russian republics and regions, more than 200 public organizations, and representatives of industrial, agricultural, banking and business associations.

The signature of the treaty of public accord introduced a short period of stability in Russian politics. However, in October 1994 a sudden fall in the value of the rouble by some 25% (relative to the US dollar) prompted the resignation or dismissal of several ministers, including the Chairman of the Central Bank, Viktor Gerashchenko. Despite the monetary crisis, the Government survived a vote of 'no confidence' held in the State Duma in late October. In a subsequent government reshuffle, in November, the reformist Anatoly Chubais (hitherto Deputy Chairman and Chairman of the State Committee for State Property Management—responsible for the privatization programme) was promoted to the post of First Deputy Chairman, but other appointments seemed to provide evidence of growing opposition within the leadership to further economic reforms. Chubais was replaced as head of the privatization programme by Vladimir Polevanov, who immediately threatened to renationalize some privatized enterprises. However, he was dismissed in January 1995, and an economic reformist, Sergey Belyayev, was subsequently appointed to the post.

There was growing evidence in late 1994 of the increasing influence of anti-liberal elements within the presidential administration. In late November the Security Council (which was increasingly seen as the major policy-making body in Russia) agreed to intervene militarily in the separatist Republic of Chechnya (see below). There was particular criticism in the media of the prominent role of Gen. Korzhakov, head of the Presidential Security Service and a leading adviser to President Yeltsin, whose forces raided the headquarters of the Most-Bank (a major source of finance for democratic political groups) in early December, and who was accused of conducting a political vendetta against Yury Luzhkov, the democratic Mayor of Moscow. The military campaign in Chechnya was strongly criticized by liberal elements in the media, and by many political groups, including Russia's Choice (which had reconstituted itself as a political party, Russia's Democratic Choice Party, RDCP) and the CPRF, and it served to deepen the political differences between President Yeltsin and his erstwhile democratic allies.

Despite the opposition of democratic political groups and much of the media to the war in Chechnya, there was only limited public protest against the intervention. However, the conflict further damaged the political position and popularity of President Yeltsin, already seriously undermined by the deteriorating state of the economy and persistent rumours as to his state of physical and mental health. Moreover, Yeltsin was confronted with an enormous rise in organized crime throughout the country, especially in the cities, where a multitude of 'mafia'-style criminal groups had proliferated. In 1994–95 there were frequent murders of leading businessmen, politicians and journalists, the most prominent being the killing, in March 1995, of Vladislav Listyev, a popular broadcaster and the newly-appointed head of Public Russian Television. In May 1995, in an attempt to recover political support, President Yeltsin endorsed the creation of two new political parties. The more conservative of the two formations, Our Home is Russia, was to be led by the Prime Minister, Viktor Chernomyrdin, while a more left-wing version was to be led by Ivan Rybkin, the Chairman of the Duma. The creation of the parties was widely seen as an attempt by Yeltsin to achieve a loyal legislature after parliamentary elections, due to be held in December 1995.

President Yeltsin's credibility was further undermined by the crisis in Budennovsk in June 1995 (see below). Four leading members of Yeltsin's administration were widely criticized for their alleged mismanagement of the crisis, and on 21 June the State Duma overwhelmingly approved a motion expressing 'no confidence' in the Government. As a result, Yeltsin was forced to dismiss the Minister of Internal Affairs, Viktor Yerin, the Deputy Chairman and Minister of Nationalities and Regional Policy, Nikolay Yegorov, and the Director of the Federal Security Service (the successor body to the KGB), Sergey Stepashin. However, Gen. Pavel Grachev, the Minister of Defence, whose resignation had also been demanded by the Duma, remained in office. A second vote of confidence (as required by the Constitution) failed to secure the necessary majority.

During 1990 and 1991 the Russian Federation faced similar problems to the USSR as a whole in attempting to satisfy the aspirations of its many nationalities for self-determination. Autonomous territories within the Russian Federation adopted declarations of sovereignty and attempted to exert greater influence over local affairs. In some regions, notably Tatarstan and Chechen-Ingushetia, there was considerable support for secession from the Russian Federation. Other nationalities, notably the Karachai and the Ingush, whose separate autonomous territories had been abolished after the Second World War and incorporated into other autonomous formations, began campaigns for the restoration of separate territories. Germans in the Russian Federation campaigned for the restoration of the Volga Autonomous Republic, which had been an autonomous territory for ethnic Germans until the Second World War. However, the Russian Federation largely avoided the violent ethnic conflicts which broke out in many other republics of the former USSR following its disintegration. In March 1992 18 of the 20 autonomous republics within Russia signed a federation treaty. The two dissenters, both oil-producing regions, were Tatarstan, which had voted for self-rule earlier in the month and Chechen-Ingushetia, which had declared independence from Russia in November 1991 (as the Republic of Chechnya). The new treaty gave the regions, which were autonomous in name only under Soviet rule, greater authority, including control of natural resources and formal borders. It also allowed them to conduct their own foreign trade. In February 1994 Tatarstan signed an agreement with the Russian Government, allowing Tatarstan a considerable measure of sovereignty.

In March 1992, in response to the declaration of independence by Chechnya, the Ingush inhabitants of the former Chechen-Ingushetia demanded the establishment of a separate Ingush republic within the Russian Federation. The formation of the new republic was formalized by the Russian Supreme Soviet in June. In addition to Ingush territories within Chechen-Ingushetia, many Ingush activists claimed territories in neighbouring North Ossetia, which had formed part of the Ingush autonomous republic prior to the Second World War. However, their claims to the territories (the eastern regions of North Ossetia and part of the North Ossetian capital of Vladikavkaz) were strongly opposed by the North Ossetian authorities.

In October 1992 violent conflict broke out in Prigorodny rayon in North Ossetia, a region inhabited mainly by Ingush. In late October the Russian Security Council (which had been established in May) agreed to deploy 3,000 special security forces in the region and to introduce state of emergency in North Ossetia and Ingushetia. By mid-November more than 300 people had died in the conflict and some 50,000 Ingush had been forced to flee to Ingushetia.

In late 1993 the situation in Chechnya deteriorated into armed hostilities, as opponents of the Chechen leader, Gen. Jokhar Dudayev, clashed with his forces. Chechnya boycotted the Russian general election and referendum of December 1993; the situation in the region in that month was described as 'close to civil war'. In May 1994 Dudayev survived an assassination attempt, in which, however, two of his ministers were killed. There was a further attempt to overthrow the Dudayev regime in August by opposition forces, widely believed to be aided by the Russian security services, but the attack was defeated by troops loyal to Dudayev. A further offensive in November was also defeated.

In late November 1994, following the latest failure of the opposition to overthrow Dudayev, the Russian Security Council finalized plans for military intervention by Russian troops in Chechnya. In early December Russian troops entered Chechnya from neighbouring territories, with the stated aim of introducing constitutional rule in the republic. Despite opposition, by late December Russian troops had taken control of much of the lowland area of northern Chechnya, where support for Dudayev (a member of a clan from the mountainous south) was weakest. Dudayev's forces, estimated to number some 15,000 irregular troops, were concentrated in the Chechen capital, Grozny. In late December Russian troops reached Grozny, and launched an assault on the city, following heavy bombardment from the air. Initially, Russian troops sustained significant casualties in battles with Chechen rebels. However, the Russian forces gradually took control of the city, seizing the presidential palace, the headquarters of Dudayev's forces, in late January 1995. Grozny suffered severe devastation during the assault, and there were reported to be thousands of civilian casualties.

Conflict continued in early 1995 as Russian forces attempted to capture smaller towns, to which Chechen forces had retreated. By early April, according to official sources, some 1,500 Russian troops had been killed in the fighting, with a further 4,500 wounded. Official Russian sources estimated Chechen losses to be approximately 7,000, while Russian human rights groups estimated that 25,000 civilians had been killed in the conflict. By May Russian troops claimed to have gained control of some two-thirds of the republic's territory and to have captured all the main towns. However, resistance by Chechen rebels continued, from their bases in the southern mountain region. A two-week cease-fire (declared by President Yeltsin in early May to coincide with the arrival of Western leaders in Moscow for celebrations marking the 50th anniversary of the end of the Second World War in Europe) was only partially observed by Russian troops. In mid-June Russian forces claimed to have captured the last important stronghold of the Chechen rebels.

On 14 June 1995 some 70 Chechen gunmen stormed the city of Budennovsk in southern Russia (some 200 km from the border with Chechnya), where, after street battles with local security forces, they took hostage more than 1,000 people (including 400 medical personnel) in the city hospital. The rebels demanded that the Russian Government initiate talks with Dudayev on the immediate halting of Russian military intervention in Chechnya and the withdrawal of Russian troops; they threatened to kill all the hostages if their demands were not satisfied. Following the failure of attempts by Russian army units to free the hostages, negotiations were conducted by telephone between the rebel leader, Shamil Basayev, and Prime Minister Chernomyrdin. By this time, it was reported, approximately 100 people had been killed in the violence. As a result of the talks, the rebels began to release hostages gradually, while a cease-fire entered into force in Chechnya. With most of the hostages freed, the rebels were permitted to return to Chechnya; however, they took with them some 150 volunteer hostages as a security guarantee (these were released as soon as the convoy reached Chechen territory). As agreed, a Russian government delegation travelled to Grozny, and peace talks with the Chechen leadership began in late June.

Following the dissolution of the USSR in December 1991, the Russian Federation was widely recognized as the successor to the USSR in the international community, and was granted the USSR's permanent seat on the UN Security Council. Relations with the West, which had already improved considerably under Gorbachev, were further improved by the Russian leadership in 1992, partly prompted by the need for significant western economic assistance. In January 1993 President Yeltsin and US President Bush signed the second Strategic Arms Reduction Treaty, which envisaged a reduction in the strategic nuclear weapons of both powers to about one-third of their current level. In 1994–95 Russia's relations with the USA and western European countries were severely strained by disagreements over the proposed enlargement of NATO to include some eastern European countries (see below). Increasing criticism by western countries of Russia's military intervention in Chechnya also damaged relations, as did policy disagreements concerning the conflict in Bosnia and Herzegovina.

Relations with Japan were complicated by a continuing dispute over the status of the Kurile Islands, which had become part of the USSR at the end of the Second World War. Japan reiterated its long-standing demand that four of the islands be returned to Japanese sovereignty, and delayed any significant aid contributions until Russia admitted the validity of the Japanese claim. President Yeltsin visited Japan in October 1993, when significant progress was reported to have been made towards a full normalization of relations, although the territorial dispute remained unresolved. Relations with other Asian countries, including the People's Republic of China, the Republic of Korea and India, improved significantly in 1992–93.

In the early 1990s Russia's most immediate foreign policy problems were with the other former Soviet republics. Relations with Ukraine were damaged by a dispute over the division of the former Soviet Black Sea Fleet, and by the status of Crimea, which some Russian nationalists demanded be returned to Russia. There were also difficulties concerning economic issues and the status of nuclear weapons on Ukrainian territory (see chapter on Ukraine). Relations with Estonia, Latvia and Lithuania were initially hampered by ostensible Russian unwillingness to effect a rapid withdrawal of former Soviet troops (now under Russian jurisdiction) from those republics. However, all Russian troops had been withdrawn from the three states by the end of August 1994. Nevertheless, relations with Estonia and Latvia continued to be strained, as a result of Russian criticism of allegedly discriminatory policies towards ethnic Russian minorities in those countries.

While the withdrawal of Russian (former Soviet) troops from Poland, Germany and other parts of central and eastern Europe was largely completed by 1994, there were indications that the Russian Federation was intent on re-establishing its political and military influence in the so-called 'near-abroad', or republics of the former USSR, especially those areas involved in civil or ethnic conflicts, or republics with large ethnic Russian populations. Russian troops were deployed in Tajikistan to support the Tajik Government against rebel forces, and to control the Tajik–Afghan border (see chapter on Tajikistan). There were also allegations that the Russian Government provided active military support for the separatist movements in Moldova and Georgia. Both sides in the Armenian–Azerbaijani conflict over sovereignty of Nagorny Karabakh claimed that their respective adversary had received military support from Russia.

There were also indications that the Russian Federation was eager to reclaim the role that the former USSR had played in international politics. In February 1994 Russia was instrumental in persuading Bosnian Serb forces to withdraw their artillery from around Sarajevo, thus temporarily bringing to an end the bombardment of the city and averting the threat of NATO air strikes. Russia also contributed peace-keeping forces to the UN personnel in Bosnia and Herzegovina. However, in 1995 the Russian leadership became increasingly critical of UN policy towards the former Yugoslavia, and it continued to develop stronger relations with its traditional ally in the region, Serbia. Despite its increasing assertiveness in international affairs, the Russian Federation showed concern at what it perceived as NATO expansionism in eastern Europe and some republics of the former USSR. In June 1994, however, after several months' hesitation, Russia formally joined NATO's 'partnership for peace' programme of military co-operation with former 'eastern bloc' states (see p. 192), which had already been joined by some 20 countries. Over the next 12 months, however, Russia repeatedly refused to sign any more detailed programme of co-operation with NATO. Nevertheless, in late May 1995 Russia and NATO agreed a plan to implement wide-ranging military and security co-operation within the 'partnership for peace' programme.

### Government

Under the Constitution of December 1993, the Russian Federation is a democratic, federative, multi-ethnic republic, in which state power is divided between the legislature, executive and judiciary, which are independent of one another. The President of the Russian Federation is Head of State and Commander-in-Chief of the Armed Forces, but also holds broad executive powers. The President is elected for a term of four years by universal direct suffrage. The President

# THE RUSSIAN FEDERATION

*Introductory Survey*

appoints the Chairman (Prime Minister) of the Government, which also includes Deputy Chairmen and Federal Ministers. Supreme legislative power is vested in the bicameral Federal Assembly, which is elected by universal direct suffrage for a period of four years. The Assembly's upper chamber is the 178-member Federation Council, which comprises two representatives from each of the country's federal territorial units; its lower chamber is the 450-member State Duma.

According to the Federation Treaty, approved in March 1992, the Russian Federation comprises 20 republics (16 of which were autonomous republics under the previous system, and four of which were autonomous oblasts—regions), one autonomous oblast, 49 administrative oblasts and six krais (provinces). There are also ten autonomous okrugs (districts), under the jurisdiction of the oblast or krai within which they are situated. A further republic, the Ingush Republic, was created in June 1992. The cities of Moscow and St Petersburg have special administrative status.

## Defence

In May 1992 the Russian Federation established its own armed forces, on the basis of former Soviet forces on the territory of the Russian Federation and former Soviet forces outside its territory not subordinate to other former republics of the USSR. In June 1994 the total Russian armed forces numbered some 1,714,000 (including some 950,000 conscripts and 150,000 staff of the Ministry of Defence). Naval forces comprised some 295,000 men (including an estimated 180,000 conscripts), the air forces some 170,000 (including 85,000 conscripts), while ground forces numbered some 780,000 personnel (including approximately 450,000 conscripts). There were a further 280,000 paramilitary troops, including 100,000 border troops. Conscription is compulsory for males over the age of 18 years, and lasts for two years. However, the rate of conscription evasion is reported to be extremely high. Projected budget expenditure on defence for 1995 was 48,577,007m. roubles (or some 19.6% of total expenditure).

Following the dissolution of the USSR in December 1991 and the establishment of the Commonwealth of Independent States (CIS), member states of the CIS concluded a series of agreements on military co-operation and the co-ordination of armed forces. However, in 1992–93 opposition to the idea of joint CIS forces increased, as individual republics began the formation of their own national armies. None the less, in early 1995 Russian troops remained on the territory of the majority of CIS republics.

## Economic Affairs

In 1993, according to estimates by the World Bank, Russia's gross national product (GNP), measured at average 1991–93 prices, was US $348,413m., equivalent to $2,350 per head. Between 1985 and 1993, it was estimated, GNP per head decreased, in real terms, at an average annual rate of 5.0%. Over the same period the population increased by an annual average of 0.4%. Gross domestic product (GDP) decreased, in real terms, by 18.5% in 1992, in comparison with 1991. Real GDP declined by a further 12% in 1993 and by 15% in 1994.

Agriculture and forestry (excluding fishing) contributed 15.6% of net material product (NMP) in 1991. Some 15.4% of the employed labour force were engaged in the agricultural sector in the following year. Principal agricultural products are grain, potatoes and livestock. In 1990 the Russian Government began a programme to encourage the development of private farming, to replace the inefficient state and collective farms. By mid-1994 280,000 private farms (mainly small-scale) had been established, although more than 90% of the country's agriculture continued to be practised by state and collective farms. Annual agricultural production increased slightly in 1986–90, but declined by 5% in 1991, by 8% in 1992, by 4% in 1993 and by 9% in 1994.

Industry (including mining, manufacturing, construction and power) contributed 59.8% of NMP in 1991. In the following year the industrial sector employed 38.6% of the total labour force. Gross industrial output decreased by 18.0% in 1992, by 16.2% in 1993 and by a further 20.9% in 1994. Russia's industrial stagnation was attributed, in large part, to a decrease in demand for military equipment.

Mining and quarrying employed some 1.7% of the total labour force in 1992. Russia has considerable reserves of energy-bearing minerals, including large deposits of petroleum, coal, natural gas and peat. The level of extraction of all fuels declined in 1992: petroleum (including gas condensate) by 14%; natural gas by 0.4%; and coal by 5%. The decline in petroleum production is largely attributable to the exhaustion of existing fields and the lack of development of new deposits, many of which are in highly inaccessible areas of Siberia. Other minerals exploited include copper, iron ore, lead, phosphate rock, nickel, manganese, gold and diamonds. Annual production in the mining sector decreased progressively in the early 1990s: by 4% in 1991, by 11% in 1992, by 15% in 1993, and by 14% in the first six months of 1994.

In 1992 manufacturing provided some 26% of employment. Production in the sector decreased, in real terms, by 8% in 1991, by 19% in 1992, by 16% in 1993, and by 30% in the first six months of 1994.

Electric energy is derived from oil-, gas- and coal-fired power stations, nuclear power stations and hydroelectric installations. Despite fears concerning the safety of nuclear power stations in Russia, there are no plans to decommission any plants in the near future. In 1993 Russia's 29 nuclear reactors supplied 12.5% of total electricity generation. In 1993 total production of electric energy totalled 956,600m. kWh, a decline of 5% in comparison with 1992. The decrease in production corresponded to a fall in demand, owing to the decline in industrial production.

The services sector expanded rapidly in the early 1990s: in 1993 it contributed 42.2% of overall GDP (compared with 32.4% in 1990), and in 1994 the proportion was reported to have risen to some 50%. In 1994 the volume of services provided by banks, insurance companies, other financial organizations and real estate agents was estimated to have increased by more than 30%, compared with 1993.

The value of Russian exports to countries outside the former USSR amounted to US $48,027m. in 1994, while imports were valued at $28,196m., resulting in a trade surplus of $19,831m. Trade declined sharply with former members of the Council for Mutual Economic Assistance, as a result of a transfer to payments in freely convertible currencies and at world prices. The share of the former communist bloc countries in total Russian trade turnover declined from 24% in 1991 to 17% in 1992 and to 14% in 1993. In 1994 Russia's principal trading partner outside the former USSR was Germany (accounting for 13% of total Russian trade turnover), followed by the USA (7.3%), the United Kingdom (6.4%), Italy (5.7%) and the People's Republic of China (5.0%). In the same year exports to former communist countries declined by 19.5%, while imports from them declined by 2.5%. The principal exports in 1994 were fuels and energy (comprising 44.7% of Russia's total exports), followed by ferrous and non-ferrous metals and derivatives (20.2%), chemical products (7.6%), machinery and transport equipment (5.3%) and timber and paper products (4.3%). The principal imports in 1994 were machinery and transport equipment (accounting for 34.0% of total imports), followed by foodstuffs (29.2%), chemical products (10.7%), textiles, clothing and footwear (6.8%) and metals (3.5%).

According to official statistics, the budget deficit at the end of 1993 was estimated to be 17,000,000m. roubles, equivalent to about 10.5% of GDP. The budget for 1995 projected a deficit of as much as 73,183,700m. roubles (equivalent to approximately 8% of GDP). Russia's external debt was US $83,089m. at the end of 1993, of which $72,769m. was long-term public debt. Consumer prices rose by an average of 1,353% in 1992, although the annual rate of inflation declined to an average of 896% in 1993 and to 294% in 1994. In May 1995 some 2,040,000 people were registered as unemployed (2.4% of the labour force); however, this estimate did not take into account 'hidden' unemployment.

In June 1992 Russia became a member of the World Bank, and in July of that year it formally joined the IMF. Russia is also a member (as a 'Country of Operations') of the European Bank for Reconstruction and Development (EBRD, see p. 140). In June 1994 Russia signed an agreement of partnership and co-operation with the European Union.

Russia suffered severe economic problems in 1991–92 in attempting to effect a transition from a centrally-planned economy to a market-orientated system. The economic reforms initiated by Yegor Gaidar in January 1992 aimed to liberalize most prices, drastically to reduce central government expenditure in order to attain financial stability, and to achieve lasting structural changes by means of the transfer to private ownership of state enterprises. Considerable progress was made in liberalizing prices (at the cost of high inflation), and in October mass 'privatization' was inaugurated, initially by means of a voucher system. By late 1994 the private sector reportedly accounted for some 62% of GDP. Although in 1994 overall GDP declined for the fifth consecutive year, there were indications in the final quarter of the year that industrial production had begun to revive. Moreover, the annual rate of inflation, although still high, was substantially reduced. In its economic programme for 1993–95 the Government intended to tighten fiscal and monetary policy, to curb inflation further, and to integrate Russia more fully into the world economy. The Government also sought to counter the alarming increase in organized crime, which was not only detrimental to the national economy but also a potential deterrent to foreign investment in the country.

**Social Welfare**

The Russian Federation provides a basic social security and health system for all its citizens. Until 1990, when a Social Insurance Fund was established, all benefit payments were financed from the general budget. The Social Insurance Fund is financed by employers on behalf of their workers, and is administered by the Federation of Independent Trade Unions of the Russian Federation. It provides payments for loss of earnings owing to ill-health, as well as maternity benefit (which is payable for up to 18 weeks).

Old-age pensions are provided for women over the age of 55 years and men over the age of 60, if they have worked for the qualifying period of at least 20 years (women) or 25 years (men). Some categories of worker may receive pensions on completion of the qualifying period. Since 1991 pensions have been provided from a Pension Fund (financed largely by employer contributions, but also including contributions from workers, and with a budgetary transfer to pay for family benefits). Citizens who have worked less than five years of the qualifying period may receive a social pension, which amounts to two-thirds of the minimum pension. Disability benefits are also payable from the Pension Fund. Family benefits include a child-care allowance for all children under six years old. In April 1991 a further allowance was introduced for children between the ages of six and 16.

Unemployment benefit was introduced in 1991, when a Federal Employment Fund was established (financed by employer contributions and government funds). Benefit is paid to those who have been out of work for more than three months (for the first three months the previous employer is obliged to continue paying the ex-employee's salary). Benefit is normally payable for a maximum of 12 months.

A basic health service is provided for all citizens. All health care was formerly financed directly by the State, but in 1993 a health insurance scheme was introduced, with payment by employers rather than by the State. In 1991 there were 47 physicians, 123 auxiliary staff and 137 hospital beds per 10,000 of the population. Projected budgetary expenditure on health care for 1995 was 4,293,631m. roubles (some 1.7% of total expenditure), while projected expenditure on social welfare was 4,470,853m. roubles (1.8% of the total).

During the early 1990s wages in the health sector fell, in real terms, and there was a severe shortage of medical supplies. As in most other former Soviet republics production of medicines in Russia effectively collapsed as most newly-privatized pharmaceutical companies became unprofitable. The difficulties experienced by the health-care system were reflected in a serious deterioration in the health of the population. In the early 1990s the number of cases of typhoid, diphtheria and dysentery rose significantly. The reasons cited for this increase were unsatisfactory environmental conditions, a decline in immunity, a shortage of vitamins and medicine, and insufficient innoculations. In November 1993, according to official figures, some 35% of children in Russia were suffering from chronic illnesses and only 14% of children were healthy. In the period 1990–95 average life expectancy for males decreased from 64 to 58 years. Foreign aid programmes existed at this time, but they were insufficient to compensate for the severe problems in the health-care system.

**Education**

Education is compulsory for all children between the ages of seven and 17 years, for a period of 10 years. State education is generally provided free of charge, although in 1992 some higher education establishments began charging tuition fees. Students in higher education receive a small stipend from the State. The level of education in the Russian Federation is relatively high, with 27 graduates per 10,000 of the population in 1991. At the beginning of the 1988/89 academic year 98.2% of pupils in general education day-schools were taught in the Russian language. However, there were 10 other languages in use in secondary education, including Tatar (0.5%), Yakut (0.3%), Chuvash (0.2%) and Bashkir (0.2%). In the 1992/93 academic year total enrolment in secondary education (including teacher training and vocational schools) was 9.4m., while 2.6m. students were enrolled in higher educational establishments. Projected budgetary expenditure on education for 1995 was 8,998,200m. roubles (representing 3.6% of total expenditure).

All educational institutions were state-owned under Soviet rule, but a wide range of private schools and colleges were introduced in the early 1990s. In 1992 there were some 300 non-state schools, with more than 20,000 pupils, and 40 non-state higher education institutions. In the early 1990s there were extensive changes to the curriculum in all branches of the education system, including an end to the study of politically-inspired subjects, a new approach to the study of Soviet and Russian history, and the introduction of study of previously banned literary works.

**Public Holidays**

**1995:** 1 January (New Year's Day), 7 January (Christmas), 8 March (International Women's Day), 24 April (Orthodox Easter), 1–2 May (Spring and Labour Day), 9 May (Victory Day), 12 June (Russian Independence Day), 22 August (National Flag Day), 7 November (Anniversary of the October Revolution).

**1996:** 1 January (New Year's Day), 7 January (Christmas), 8 March (International Women's Day), 15 April (Orthodox Easter), 1–2 May (Spring and Labour Day), 9 May (Victory Day), 12 June (Russian Independence Day), 22 August (National Flag Day), 7 November (Anniversary of the October Revolution).

**Weights and Measures**

The metric system is in force.

# Statistical Survey

Sources (unless otherwise indicated): State Committee of Statistics of the USSR; State Committee for Statistics of the Russian Federation, 103616 Moscow, Maly Cherkassky per. 2/6; tel. (095) 921-47-68; fax (095) 921-39-65; IMF, *Russian Federation, Economic Review*; World Bank, *Statistical Handbook: States of the Former USSR*.

## Area and Population

### AREA, POPULATION AND DENSITY

| | |
|---|---:|
| Area (sq km) | 17,075,400* |
| Population (census results)† | |
| 17 January 1979 | 137,409,921 |
| 12 January 1989 | |
|    Males | 68,713,869 |
|    Females | 78,308,000 |
|    Total | 147,021,869 |
| Population (official estimate at 1 January) | |
| 1993 | 148,673,000 |
| 1994 (provisional) | 148,300,000 |
| 1995 (provisional) | 148,200,000 |
| Density (per sq km) at 1 January 1995 | 8.7 |

* 6,592,850 sq miles.

† Figures refer to *de jure* population. The *de facto* total at the 1989 census was 147,400,537.

### REPUBLICS WITHIN THE FEDERATION
(census of 12 January 1989)

| Republic | Area (sq km) | Population ('000) | Capital (with population, '000) |
|---|---:|---:|---|
| Adygheya* | 7,600 | 432 | Maikop (149) |
| Altay* | 92,600 | 192 | Gorno-Altaysk (40‡) |
| Bashkortostan | 143,600 | 3,952 | Ufa (1,083) |
| Buryatia | 351,300 | 1,042 | Ulan-Ude (353) |
| Chechen Republic-Ichkeria† | n.a. | n.a. | Grozny (401) |
| Chuvashia | 18,300 | 1,336 | Cheboksary (420) |
| Daghestan | 50,300 | 1,792 | Makhachkala (315) |
| Ingushetia† | n.a. | n.a. | Nazran (n.a.) |
| Kabardin-Balkaria | 12,500 | 760 | Nalchik (235) |
| Kalmykia | 75,900 | 322 | Elista (120) |
| Karachay-Cherkessia* | 14,100 | 418 | Cherkessk (113) |
| Karelia | 172,400 | 792 | Petrozavodsk (270) |
| Khakassia | 61,900 | 569 | Abakan (153) |
| Komi | 415,900 | 1,263 | Syktyvkar (233) |
| Mari-El | 23,300 | 750 | Yoshkar-Ola (242) |
| Mordovia | 26,200 | 964 | Saransk (312) |
| North Ossetia | 8,000 | 634 | Vladikavkaz (300) |
| Sakha (Yakutia) | 3,103,200 | 1,081 | Yakutsk (187) |
| Tatarstan | 68,000 | 3,640 | Kazan (1,094) |
| Tyva | 170,500 | 309 | Kyzyl (n.a.) |
| Udmurt Republic | 42,100 | 1,609 | Izhevsk (635) |

* Under the terms of the 1992 Federation Treaty, these former autonomous oblasts (regions) were granted the status of republic.

† Until 1992 the territories of the Republic of Chechnya and the Ingush Republic were combined in the Chechen-Ingush autonomous republic (area 19,300 sq km; population 1,277,000 at 1989 census).

‡ At 1 January 1976.

### PRINCIPAL TOWNS
(estimated population at 1 January 1992)

| | | | |
|---|---:|---|---:|
| Moskva (Moscow, the capital) | 8,746,700 | Naberezhnye Chelny* | 514,400 |
| Sankt Peterburg (St Petersburg)* | 4,436,700 | Astrakhan | 512,200 |
| | | Tomsk | 504,700 |
| Novosibirsk | 1,441,900 | Tyumen | 496,200 |
| Nizhny Novgorod* | 1,440,600 | Viyatka* | 492,500 |
| Yekaterinburg* | 1,370,700 | Ivanovo | 480,400 |
| Samara* | 1,239,200 | Murmansk | 468,300 |
| Omsk | 1,168,600 | Bryansk | 460,500 |
| Chelyabinsk | 1,143,000 | Lipetsk | 463,600 |
| Kazan | 1,104,000 | Tver* | 455,600 |
| Perm | 1,098,600 | Magnitogorsk | 441,200 |
| Ufa | 1,097,200 | Cheboksary | 438,900 |
| Rostov-na-Donu | 1,027,100 | Nizhny Tagil | 437,400 |
| Volgograd | 1,006,100 | Kursk | 435,200 |
| Krasnoyarsk | 925,000 | Arkhangelsk | 413,600 |
| Saratov | 909,300 | Kaliningrad | 410,700 |
| Voronezh | 902,200 | Grozny | 387,500 |
| Tolyatti | 665,700 | Chita | 376,500 |
| Simbirsk* | 656,400 | Ulan-Ude | 366,000 |
| Izhevsk* | 650,700 | Kurgan | 365,100 |
| Vladivostok | 647,800 | Vladimir | 356,100 |
| Irkutsk | 637,000 | Smolensk | 351,600 |
| Yaroslavl | 636,900 | Kaluga | 346,800 |
| Krasnodar | 634,500 | Orel | 346,600 |
| Khabarovsk | 614,600 | Sochi | 344,200 |
| Barnaul | 606,200 | Makhachkala | 339,300 |
| Novokuznetsk | 600,200 | Stavropol | 331,800 |
| Orenburg | 556,500 | Vladikavkaz* | 324,700 |
| Penza | 552,300 | Saransk | 322,000 |
| Tula | 541,400 | Komsomolsk-na-Amure | 318,600 |
| Ryazan | 528,500 | Cherepovets | 317,100 |
| Kemerovo | 520,600 | Belgorod | 314,200 |
| | | Tambov | 310,600 |

* Some towns that were renamed during the Soviet period have reverted to their former names: St Petersburg (Leningrad); Nizhny Novgorod (Gorky); Yekaterinburg (Sverdlovsk); Samara (Kuybyshev); Simbirsk (Ulyanovsk); Izhevsk (Ustinov); Naberezhnye Chelny (Brezhnev); Viyatka (Kirov); Tver (Kalinin); Vladikavkaz (Ordzhonikidze).

Source: UN, *Demographic Yearbook*.

### BIRTHS, MARRIAGES AND DEATHS

| | Registered live births | | Registered marriages | | Registered deaths | |
|---|---:|---:|---:|---:|---:|---:|
| | Number | Rate (per 1,000) | Number | Rate (per 1,000) | Number | Rate (per 1,000) |
| 1987 | 2,499,974 | 17.1 | 1,442,622 | 9.9 | 1,531,585 | 10.5 |
| 1988 | 2,348,494 | 16.0 | 1,397,445 | 9.5 | 1,569,112 | 10.7 |
| 1989 | 2,160,559 | 14.6 | 1,384,307 | 9.4 | 1,583,743 | 10.7 |
| 1990 | 1,988,858 | 13.4 | 1,319,928 | 8.9 | 1,655,993 | 11.2 |
| 1991 | 1,794,626 | 12.1 | 1,277,232 | 8.6 | 1,690,657 | 11.4 |

**Expectation of life** (years at birth, 1991): Males 63.5; females 74.3.

Source: UN, *Demographic Yearbook*.

**1992:** Registered live births 1,587,644 (birth rate 10.7 per 1,000); Registered deaths 1,807,441 (death rate 12.2 per 1,000).

**1993:** Registered live births 1,378,983 (birth rate 9.4 per 1,000); Registered deaths 2,129,339 (death rate 14.5 per 1,000).

Source: UN, *Population and Vital Statistics Report*.

# THE RUSSIAN FEDERATION

## Statistical Survey

**EMPLOYMENT** (annual averages, '000 employees)

|  | 1990 | 1991 | 1992 |
|---|---|---|---|
| Agriculture, hunting, forestry and fishing | 10,499.1 | 10,485.9 | 11,078.9 |
| Mining and quarrying | 1,235.9 | 1,256.7 | 1,252.8 |
| Manufacturing | 20,181.9 | 19,812.1 | 18,682.8 |
| Electricity, gas and water | 595.1 | 612.3 | 669.3 |
| Construction | 8,168.1 | 7,632.2 | 7,246.6 |
| Trade, restaurants and hotels | 5,085.8 | 4,942.2 | 4,914.2 |
| Transport, storage and communications | 5,818.2 | 5,750.0 | 5,631.8 |
| Financing, insurance, real estate and business services | 401.6 | 439.6 | 493.6 |
| Community, social and personal services | 19,607.1 | 19,519.6 | 18,641.8 |
| Activities not adequately defined | 3,731.9 | 3,397.2 | 3,459.3 |
| **Total** | 75,324.7 | 73,847.8 | 72,071.1 |

**1989 census** ('000 persons aged 15 years and over): Total labour force 77,283 (males 39,767; females 37,516).

Source: ILO, *Year Book of Labour Statistics*.

## Agriculture

**PRINCIPAL CROPS** ('000 metric tons)

|  | 1991 | 1992 | 1993 |
|---|---|---|---|
| Wheat | 38,899 | 46,167 | 42,480* |
| Rice (paddy) | 773 | 754 | 686* |
| Barley | 22,174 | 26,989 | 26,628* |
| Maize | 1,969 | 2,135 | 2,447* |
| Rye | 10,639 | 13,887 | 9,150* |
| Oats | 10,372 | 11,241 | 11,539* |
| Millet | 1,041 | 1,535 | 1,124* |
| Potatoes | 34,329 | 38,224 | 38,000 |
| Dry peas | 2,093 | 2,607 | 3,360* |
| Soybeans | 622 | 505 | 550* |
| Sunflower seed | 2,896 | 3,110 | 2,800 |
| Cabbages |  | 4,844* | 4,772* |
| Tomatoes |  | 1,450* | 1,250* |
| Onions (dry) | 10,426 | 559* | 640* |
| Carrots |  | 1,313* | 1,270* |
| Other vegetables |  | 296* | 304* |
| Watermelons† | 2,100 | 714 | 650 |
| Grapes | 543 | 529 | 500† |
| Apples |  | 1,830* | 1,700† |
| Plums | 2,204 | 266* | 272† |
| Other fruits and berries |  | 433* | 384† |
| Sugar beets | 24,280 | 25,548 | 25,500 |

* Unofficial figure.  † FAO estimate(s). Figures for watermelons include melons, pumpkins and squash.

Source: FAO, *Production Yearbook*.

**LIVESTOCK**
('000 head at 1 January, unless otherwise indicated)

|  | 1991 | 1992 | 1993 |
|---|---|---|---|
| Horses | 2,618 | 2,590 | 2,556 |
| Cattle | 57,043 | 54,677 | 52,226 |
| Pigs | 38,314 | 35,384 | 31,520 |
| Sheep | 55,200 | 52,195 | 48,183 |
| Goats | 2,953 | 3,060 | 3,186 |
| Chickens (million) | 634* | 628* | 625† |
| Turkeys (million) | 26* | 24* | 24† |

* Unofficial figure.  † FAO estimate.

Source: mainly FAO, *Production Yearbook*.

**LIVESTOCK PRODUCTS** ('000 metric tons)

|  | 1991 | 1992 | 1993 |
|---|---|---|---|
| Beef and veal | 3,989 | 3,500 | 3,400* |
| Mutton and lamb | 342 | 280† | 270† |
| Pig meat | 3,190 | 2,700 | 2,550* |
| Poultry meat | 1,751 | 1,577* | 1,420* |
| Cows' milk | 51,890 | 46,930 | 42,600* |
| Cheese | n.a. | 300* | 280* |
| Butter | 729 | 746 | 700* |
| Hen eggs* | 2,623* | 2,370* | 2,128† |
| Wool: |  |  |  |
| greasy | 204.5 | 179.0 | 180.0† |
| scoured | 122.7 | 107.4 | 108.0† |
| Cattle and buffalo hides | n.a. | 320† | 315† |

* Unofficial figure.  † FAO estimate.

Source: FAO, *Production Yearbook*.

## Fishing*

('000 metric tons, live weight)

|  | 1991 | 1992 |
|---|---|---|
| Common carp | 91.7 | 53.4 |
| Other cyprinids | 87.0 | 63.0 |
| Pink (humpback) salmon | 217.7 | 86.9 |
| Azov tyulka | 122.1 | 111.9 |
| Atlantic cod | 122.6 | 182.9 |
| Pacific cod | 106.5 | 154.3 |
| Alaska pollack | 2,495.8 | 2,340.7 |
| Blue whiting | 147.5 | 159.4 |
| Capelin | 346.6 | 425.6 |
| Pacific saury | 49.9 | 50.2 |
| Chilean jack mackerel | 419.7 | 31.4 |
| Other jack and horse mackerels | 333.6 | 276.9 |
| Pacific herring | 98.3 | 109.3 |
| Round sardinella | 65.4 | 65.6 |
| Japanese pilchard | 655.8 | 165.3 |
| European pilchard (sardine) | 262.6 | 144.6 |
| **Total fish** (incl. others) | 6,640.7 | 5,243.7 |
| King crabs | 39.8 | 38.8 |
| Antarctic krill | 32.6 | 151.7 |
| Other crustaceans | 27.7 | 23.5 |
| Squids | 144.2 | 137.8 |
| Other molluscs | 3.5 | 9.7 |
| Sea-urchins | 5.8 | 5.9 |
| **Total catch** | 6,894.2 | 5,611.2 |
| Inland waters | 440.5 | 378.0 |
| Mediterranean and Black Sea | 15.8 | 14.2 |
| Atlantic Ocean | 1,771.5 | 1,855.5 |
| Indian Ocean | 9.8 | 18.8 |
| Pacific Ocean | 4,656.5 | 3,344.7 |

* Figures exclude seaweeds and other aquatic plants ('000 metric tons): 61.2 in 1991; 29.7 in 1992.

Source: FAO, *Yearbook of Fishery Statistics*.

## Mining

('000 metric tons, unless otherwise indicated)

|  | 1991 | 1992 | 1993 |
|---|---|---|---|
| Crude petroleum* | 462,300 | 399,337 | 353,500 |
| Coal† | 353,300 | 337,300 | 305,300 |
| Natural gas (million cu m) | 643,400 | 641,000 | 618,500 |

* Including gas condensates.
† Figures refer to gross weight. Excluding waste, output in 1992 (in '000 metric tons) was: Hard coal 193,470; Brown coal (incl. lignite) 123,596 (Source: UN, *Industrial Commodity Statistics Yearbook*).

# THE RUSSIAN FEDERATION

## Industry

### SELECTED PRODUCTS
('000 metric tons, unless otherwise indicated)

|  | 1991 | 1992 | 1993 |
|---|---|---|---|
| Margarine | 627 | n.a. | n.a. |
| Vegetable oil | 1,165 | 994 | 1,137 |
| Flour | 20,497* | 20,400 | 17,200 |
| Granulated sugar | 2,052 | 2,248 | 2,506 |
| Cigarettes (million) | 144,000* | n.a. | n.a. |
| Cotton fabrics (million sq. metres) | 5,295 | 3,292 | 2,324 |
| Woollen fabrics (million sq. metres) | 386 | 276 | 206 |
| Leather footwear ('000 pairs) | 334,422* | n.a. | n.a. |
| Paper | 4,765 | 3,604 | 2,882 |
| Paperboard | 2,619 | 2,157 | 1,613 |
| Caustic soda (sodium hydroxide) | 2,042 | 1,836 | 1,423 |
| Motor spirit (petrol) | 38,800 | 35,289* | 30,200 |
| Distillate fuel oils | 72,200 | 65,131* | 57,200 |
| Residual fuel oils | 97,100 | 89,262* | 82,300 |
| Cement | 77,463* | 61,700 | 52,200 |
| Crude steel | 77,100* | n.a. | n.a. |
| Tractors ('000) | 178 | 137 | 89 |
| Domestic refrigerators and freezers ('000) | 3,710 | 3,184 | 3,485 |
| Domestic washing machines ('000) | 5,541 | 4,289 | 3,863 |
| Television receivers ('000) | 4,439 | 3,672 | 3,975 |
| Radio receivers ('000) | 5,537 | 4,015 | 2,870 |
| Passenger motor cars ('000) | 1,030 | 963 | 956 |
| Cameras: photographic ('000) | 1,965* | n.a. | n.a. |
| Watches ('000) | 61,553* | n.a. | n.a. |
| Electric energy (million kWh) | 1,068,200 | 1,008,450* | 956,600 |

* Figure from UN, *Industrial Commodity Statistics Yearbook*.

## Finance

### CURRENCY AND EXCHANGE RATES

**Monetary Units**
100 kopeks = 1 rubl (ruble or rouble).

**Sterling and Dollar Equivalents** (31 December 1994)
£1 sterling = 5,006 roubles;
US $1 = 3,200 roubles;
10,000 roubles = £1.997 = $3.125.

**Average Exchange Rate** (roubles per US dollar)
1989   0.6274
1990   0.5856
1991   0.5819

Note: The figures for average exchange rates refer to official rates for the Soviet rouble. However, a multiple exchange rate system was in operation, with separate non-commercial and tourist rates. A commercial exchange rate was introduced on 1 November 1990, replacing the official rate for most transactions. The commercial rate (roubles per US dollar) was: 1.692 at 31 December 1990; 1.671 at 31 December 1991. Between November 1989 and April 1991 the tourist exchange rate valued the rouble at one-tenth of the official rate. In April 1991 this rate, renamed the 'special rate', was set at $1 = 27.6 roubles. It was subsequently adjusted. The average market exchange rate in 1991 was $1 = 31.2 roubles. Following the dissolution of the USSR in December 1991, Russia and several other former Soviet republics retained the rouble as their monetary unit. The average interbank market rate for Russian roubles per US dollar was 222 in 1992 and 933 in 1993.

### BUDGET (million roubles)

|  | 1992* | 1994† | 1995† |
|---|---|---|---|
| Revenue | 5,231,700 | 120,700,000 | 175,160,600 |
| Expenditure | 7,884,200 | 182,200,000 | 248,344,300 |
| Culture and social welfare | 1,383,100 | 11,400,000 | 12,082,550 |
| National defence | 855,300 | 37,120,000 | 48,577,007 |
| State administration | 105,900 | 3,800,000 | 3,896,040 |

* Actual.   † Forecasts.

### MONEY SUPPLY (million roubles at 31 December)

|  | 1991 | 1992 | 1993 |
|---|---|---|---|
| Currency outside banks | 167,000 | 1,678,000 | 13,277,000 |

### COST OF LIVING
(Consumer price index; base: 1991 = 100)

|  | 1992 | 1993 |
|---|---|---|
| Food | 1,690 | 16,750 |
| All items | 1,629 | 15,869 |

Source: ILO, *Year Book of Labour Statistics*.

### NATIONAL ACCOUNTS (million roubles at current prices)
**Net Material Product by Economic Activity**

|  | 1989 | 1990 | 1991 |
|---|---|---|---|
| Agriculture and forestry | 77,984 | 89,002 | 146,989 |
| Industry | 183,597 | 187,729 | 451,141 |
| Construction | 53,549 | 56,620 | 112,133 |
| Transport and communications | 24,061 | 30,621 | 52,597 |
| Other material activities | 73,474 | 80,593 | 179,119 |
| **Total** | 412,665 | 444,565 | 941,979 |

### BALANCE OF PAYMENTS
**External Transactions** (US $ million)*

|  | 1991 | 1992 | 1993 |
|---|---|---|---|
| Merchandise exports f.o.b. | 53,200 | 41,600 | 46,300 |
| Merchandise imports f.o.b. | -44,500 | -37,200 | -34,300 |
| **Trade balance** | 8,700 | 4,400 | 11,900 |
| Services (net) | -2,400 | -5,500 | -5,300 |
| Income (net) | -2,200 | -4,600 | -4,300 |
| Unrequited transfers (net) | 1,600 | 3,000 | 2,800 |
| **Current balance** | 5,700 | -2,700 | 5,100 |
| Capital (net) | 2,000 | -4,200 | -12,900 |
| Net errors and omissions | -1,800 | -6,400 | -6,500 |
| **Overall balance** | 5,900 | -13,300 | -14,400 |

* Excluding transactions with other (former) Soviet republics (see below).

**Inter-republican Transactions** (US $ million): *1992:* Merchandise exports f.o.b. 10,800; Merchandise imports f.o.b. -9,300; Trade balance 1,500; Net services and capital (incl. errors and omissions) 3,100; Overall balance 4,600. *1993:* Merchandise exports f.o.b. 15,400; Merchandise imports f.o.b. -10,400; Trade balance 5,000; Services and other income (net) -1,500; Current balance 3,600; Capital (net) -7,700; Net errors and omissions 1,300; Overall balance -2,900.

Source: partly IMF, *International Financial Statistics: Supplement on Countries of the Former Soviet Union*.

THE RUSSIAN FEDERATION

*Statistical Survey*

# External Trade

**PRINCIPAL COMMODITIES** (US $ million)*

| Imports | 1992 | 1993 |
|---|---|---|
| Machinery and equipment | 13,290 | 9,912 |
|   Equipment for the petroleum and nuclear industries | 6,512 | 4,560 |
|   Electrical machinery | 2,525 | 1,685 |
|   Railway equipment | 1,063 | 396 |
|   Road vehicles | 1,728 | 1,784 |
| Mineral and metal products | 1,046 | 729 |
| Chemical products | 3,431 | 1,621 |
|   Pharmaceuticals | 926 | 308 |
| Products of light industries | 4,094 | 4,382 |
|   Knitwear | 655 | 833 |
|   Textile clothing | 901 | 1,183 |
|   Leather footwear | 1,269 | 1,096 |
| Food products | 10,019 | 5,546 |
|   Sugar | 1,236 | 1,240 |
|   Cereals | 3,644 | 1,578 |
| **Sub-total** (incl. others) | 35,300 | 23,750 |
| Humanitarian aid | 1,900 | 950 |
| Adjustments† | n.a. | 9,600 |
| **Total** | 37,200 | 34,300 |

| Exports | 1992 | 1993 |
|---|---|---|
| Energy products | 21,124 | 19,892 |
|   Crude petroleum | 8,539 | 8,378 |
|   Petroleum products | 4,269 | 3,507 |
|   Natural gas | 7,522 | 7,598 |
| Machinery and equipment | 5,975 | 5,471 |
|   Equipment for the petroleum and nuclear industries | 1,255 | 1,149 |
|   Railway equipment | 120 | 1,313 |
|   Road vehicles | 1,793 | 109 |
| Mineral and metal products | 5,696 | 10,297 |
|   Iron and steel | 1,542 | 3,964 |
|   Diamonds | 801 | 1,081 |
|   Gold | — | 967 |
|   Aluminium | 1,259 | 1,934 |
| Chemical products | 2,598 | 2,735 |
|   Fertilizers | 1,117 | 848 |
| Products of light industries / Food products | 2,642 | 3,691 |
|   Fish | 767 | 1,374 |
| **Sub-total** (incl. others) | 41,600 | 42,900 |
| Adjustments† | n.a. | 3,400 |
| **Total** | 41,600 | 46,300 |

\* Excluding transactions with other former Soviet republics (see below).
† Adjustments made to official trade data on the basis of information from partner countries.

**Inter-republican Trade** ('000 million roubles)

| | 1991 | 1992 | 1993 |
|---|---|---|---|
| **Total imports** | 116 | 1,849 | 9,722 |
| **Total exports** | 135 | 2,147 | 14,385 |
|   Petroleum and petroleum products | 12 | 405 | 2,683 |
|   Natural gas | 5 | 196 | 2,702 |

**PRINCIPAL TRADING PARTNERS** (US $ million)*

| Imports† | 1992 | Exports | 1992 |
|---|---|---|---|
| Austria | 991 | Austria | 657 |
| Bulgaria | 584 | Belgium | 884 |
| Canada | 1,076 | Bulgaria | 1,165 |
| China, People's Republic | 1,670 | China, People's Republic | 2,737 |
| Cuba | 632 | Czechoslovakia | 2,598 |
| Czechoslovakia | 1,020 | Finland | 1,564 |
| Finland | 1,223 | France | 1,967 |
| France | 1,286 | Germany | 5,873 |
| Germany | 6,725 | Hungary | 1,506 |
| Hungary | 1,089 | India | 568 |
| India | 822 | Italy | 2,951 |
| Italy | 3,052 | Japan | 1,569 |
| Japan | 1,680 | Netherlands | 2,277 |
| Korea, Republic | 753 | Poland | 1,649 |
| Netherlands | 368 | Romania | 605 |
| Poland | 1,230 | Spain | 526 |
| Romania | 431 | Sweden | 653 |
| Spain | 420 | Switzerland | 857 |
| Sweden | 652 | Turkey | 649 |
| Switzerland | 480 | United Kingdom | 2,287 |
| Turkey | 383 | USA | 694 |
| United Kingdom | 562 | Yugoslavia (former) | 1,032 |
| USA | 2,884 | | |
| Yugoslavia (former) | 843 | | |
| **Total** (incl. others) | 34,981 | **Total** (incl. others) | 39,967 |

\* Excluding transactions with other former Soviet republics (see below).
† Excluding humanitarian aid.

**Inter-republican Trade** (million roubles)

| | 1990 Imports | 1990 Exports |
|---|---|---|
| Armenia | 1,851 | 1,777 |
| Azerbaijan | 3,705 | 2,242 |
| Belarus | 9,938 | 9,295 |
| Estonia | 1,816 | 1,863 |
| Georgia | 3,558 | 2,700 |
| Kazakhstan | 4,276 | 9,074 |
| Kyrgyzstan | 897 | 1,539 |
| Latvia | 2,513 | 2,470 |
| Lithuania | 2,707 | 3,688 |
| Moldova | 3,489 | 2,461 |
| Tajikistan | 1,168 | 1,497 |
| Turkmenistan | 1,276 | 1,275 |
| Ukraine | 25,249 | 28,892 |
| Uzbekistan | 4,840 | 5,937 |
| **Total** | 67,283 | 74,710 |

# Transport

**RAILWAYS** (traffic)

| | 1992 | 1993 | 1994 |
|---|---|---|---|
| Passenger-km (million) | 253,200 | n.a. | 227,100 |
| Freight ton-km (million) | 1,967,100 | n.a. | 1,195,500 |

Source: UN, *Monthly Bulletin of Statistics*.

**INTERNATIONAL SEA-BORNE SHIPPING**
(freight traffic '000 metric tons)

| | 1992 |
|---|---|
| Goods loaded | 27,672 |
| Goods unloaded | 7,320 |

Source: UN, *Monthly Bulletin of Statistics*.

# THE RUSSIAN FEDERATION

## CIVIL AVIATION (traffic on scheduled services)

|  | 1991 | 1992 |
|---|---|---|
| Kilometres flown (million) | 143 | 134 |
| Passengers carried ('000) | 128,274 | 62,174 |
| Passenger-km (million) | 224,648 | 116,139 |
| Total ton-km (million) | 22,953 | 12,085 |

Source: UN, *Statistical Yearbook*.

## Communications Media

|  | 1991 | 1992 |
|---|---|---|
| Radio receivers ('000 in use) | n.a. | 48,500 |
| Television receivers ('000 in use) | n.a. | 54,850 |
| Book production: |  |  |
| Titles | 34,050 | 28,716 |
| Copies (million) | 1,630 | 1,313 |
| Daily newspapers: |  |  |
| Number | n.a. | 339 |
| Average circulation ('000) | n.a. | 57,367 |
| Non-daily newspapers: |  |  |
| Number | n.a. | 4,498 |
| Average circulation ('000) | n.a. | 86,677 |

Source: UNESCO, *Statistical Yearbook*.

**Telephones** ('000 main lines in use): 19,300 in 1989; 20,700 in 1990; 22,296 in 1991 (Source: UN, *Statistical Yearbook*).

## Education

(1992/93)

|  | Teachers | Students |
|---|---|---|
| Pre-primary | 905,232 | 7,236,425 |
| Primary |  | 11,872,357 |
| Secondary: | 1,384,000 |  |
| General |  | 7,772,208 |
| Teacher training | n.a. | 77,753 |
| Vocational | n.a. | 1,593,366 |
| Higher | 247,000 | 2,638,000 |

**Schools:** 81,999 pre-primary in 1992/93.
Source: UNESCO, *Statistical Yearbook*.

# Directory

## The Constitution

The current Constitution of the Russian Federation came into force on 12 December 1993, following its approval by a majority of participants in a nation-wide plebiscite. It replaced the Constitution originally passed on 12 April 1978 but amended many times after 1990.

### THE PRINCIPLES OF THE CONSTITUTIONAL SYSTEM

Chapter One of Section One declares that the Russian Federation (Russia) is a democratic, federative, law-based state with a republican form of Government. Its multi-ethnic people bear its sovereignty and are the sole source of authority. State power in the Russian Federation is divided between the legislative, executive and judicial branches, which are independent of one another. Ideological pluralism and a multi-party political system are recognized. The Russian Federation is a secular state and all religious associations are equal before the law. All laws are made public and in accordance with universally acknowledged principles and with international law.

### HUMAN AND CIVIL RIGHTS AND FREEDOMS

Chapter Two states that the basic human rights and freedoms of the Russian citizen are guaranteed regardless of sex, race, nationality or religion. It declares the right to life and to freedom and personal inviolability. The principles of freedom of movement, freedom of expression and freedom of conscience are upheld. Censorship is prohibited. Citizens are guaranteed the right to vote and stand in state and local elections and to participate in referendums. Individuals are to have equal access to state employment, and the establishment of trade unions and public associations is permitted. The Constitution commits the State to protection of motherhood and childhood and to granting social security, state pensions and social benefits. Each person has the right to housing. Health care and education are free of charge. Basic general education is compulsory. Citizens are guaranteed the right to receive qualified legal assistance. Payment of statutory taxes and levies is obligatory, as is military service.

### THE ORGANIZATION OF THE FEDERATION

Chapter Three names the 89 members (federal territorial units) of the Russian Federation. Russian is declared the state language, but all peoples of the Russian Federation are guaranteed the right to preserve their native tongue. The state flag, emblem and anthem of the Russian Federation are to be established by a federal constitutional law. The Constitution defines the separate roles of the authority of the Russian Federation, as distinct from that of the joint authority of the Russian Federation and the members of the Russian Federation. It also establishes the relationship between federal laws, federal constitutional laws and the laws and other normative legal acts of the subjects of the Russian Federation. The powers of the federal executive bodies and the executive bodies of the members of the Russian Federation are defined.

### THE PRESIDENT OF THE RUSSIAN FEDERATION

Chapter Four describes the powers and responsibilities of the Head of State, the President of the Russian Federation. The President is elected to office for a term of four years by universal, direct suffrage. The same individual may be elected to the office of President for no more than two consecutive terms. The President may appoint the Chairman of the Government (Prime Minister) of the Russian Federation, with the approval of the State Duma, and may dismiss the Deputy Chairmen and the federal ministers from office. The President is entitled to chair sessions of the Government. The President's responsibilities include scheduling referendums and elections to the State Duma, dissolving the State Duma, submitting legislative proposals to the State Duma and promulgating federal laws. The President is responsible for the foreign policy of the Russian Federation. The President is Commander-in-Chief of the Armed Forces and may introduce martial law or a state of emergency under certain conditions.

If the President is unable to carry out the presidential duties, these will be assumed by the Chairman of the Government. The Acting President, however, will not possess the full powers of the President, such as the right to dissolve the State Duma or order a referendum. The President may only be removed from office by the Federation Council on the grounds of a serious accusation by the State Duma.

### THE FEDERAL ASSEMBLY

Chapter Five concerns the Federal Assembly, which is the highest representative and legislative body in the Russian Federation. It consists of two chambers: the Federation Council (upper chamber) and the State Duma (lower chamber). The Federation Council comprises two representatives from each member of the Russian Federation, one from its representative and one from its executive body (178 deputies in total). The State Duma is composed of 450 deputies. The State Duma is elected for a term of four years. The procedures for forming the Federation Council and for electing the State Duma are to be determined by federal legislation. The deputies of the Russian Federation must be over 21 years of age and may not hold government office or any other paid job. (Section Two of the Constitution states that the State Duma and the Federation Council of the first convocation are to be elected for a term of two years and that a deputy of the State Duma of first convocation may concurrently be a member of the Government.) The Federal Assembly is a permanently working body.

Both chambers of the Federal Assembly may elect their Chairman and Deputy Chairmen, who preside over parliamentary sessions and supervise the observance of their regulations. Each chamber adopts its code of procedure. The powers of the Federation Council include the approval of the President's decrees on martial law and a state of emergency, the scheduling of presidential elections and the impeachment of the President. The State Duma has the power to approve the President's nominee to the office of Chairman of the Government. Both chambers of the Federal Assembly adopt resolutions by a majority vote of the total number of members. All federal and federal constitutional laws are adopted by the State Duma and submitted for approval first to the Federation Council and then to the President. If the Federation Council or the President reject proposed legislation it is submitted for repeat consideration to one or both chambers of the Federal Assembly.

The State Duma may be dissolved by the President if it rejects all three candidates to the office of Chairman of the Government or adopts a second vote of 'no confidence' in the Government. However, it may not be dissolved during a period of martial law or a state of emergency or in the case of charges being lodged against the President. A newly elected State Duma should be convened no later than four months after dissolution of the previous parliament.

### THE GOVERNMENT OF THE RUSSIAN FEDERATION

The executive authority of the Russian Federation is vested in the Government, which is comprised of the Chairman, the Deputy Chairmen and federal ministers. The Chairman is appointed by the President and his nomination approved by the State Duma. If the State Duma rejects three candidates to the office of Chairman, the President will appoint the Chairman, dissolve the State Duma and order new elections. The Government's responsibilities are to submit the federal budget to the State Duma and to supervise its execution, to guarantee the implementation of a uniform state policy, to carry out foreign policy and to ensure the country's defence and state security. Its duties also include the maintenance of law and order.

Regulations for the activity of the Government are to be determined by a federal constitutional law. The Government can adopt resolutions and directives, which may be vetoed by the President. The Government must submit its resignation to a newly elected President of the Russian Federation, which the President may accept or reject. A vote of 'no confidence' in the Government may be adopted by the State Duma. The President can reject this decision or demand the Government's resignation. If the State Duma adopts a second vote of 'no confidence' within three months, the President will announce the Government's resignation or dissolve the State Duma.

### JUDICIAL POWER

Justice is administered by means of constitutional, civil, administrative and criminal judicial proceedings. Judges in the Russian Federation must be aged 25 or over, have a higher legal education and have a record of work in the legal profession of no less than five years. Judges are independent, irremovable and inviolable. Proceedings in judicial courts are open. No criminal case shall be considered in the absence of a defendant. Judicial proceedings may be conducted with the participation of a jury.

The Constitutional Court comprises 19 judges. The Court decides cases regarding the compliance of federal laws and enactments, the constitutions, statutes, laws and other enactments of the members of the Russian Federation, state treaties and international treaties which have not yet come into force. The Constitutional Court settles disputes about competence among state bodies. Enactments or their individual provisions which have been judged unconstitutional by the Court are invalid. At the request of the Federation Council, the Court will pronounce its judgment on bringing an accusation against the President of the Russian Federation.

The Supreme Court is the highest judicial authority on civil, criminal, administrative and other cases within the jurisdiction of the common plea courts. The Supreme Arbitration Court is the highest authority in settling economic and other disputes within the jurisdiction of the courts of arbitration.

The judges of the three higher courts are appointed by the Federation Council on the recommendation of the President. Judges of other federal courts are appointed by the President.

The Prosecutor's Office is a single centralized system. The Prosecutor-General is appointed and dismissed by the Federation Council on the recommendation of the President. All other prosecutors are appointed by the Prosecutor-General.

### LOCAL SELF-GOVERNMENT

Chapter Eight provides for the exercise of local self-government through referendums, elections and through elected and other bodies. The responsibilities of local self-government bodies include: independently managing municipal property; forming, approving and executing the local budget; establishing local taxes and levies; and maintaining law and order.

### CONSTITUTIONAL AMENDMENTS AND REVISION OF THE CONSTITUTION

Chapter Nine states that no provision contained in Chapters One, Two and Nine of the Constitution is to be reviewed by the Federal Assembly, while amendments to the remaining Chapters may be passed in accordance with the procedure for a federal constitutional law. If a proposal for a review of the provisions of Chapters One, Two and Nine wins a three-fifths majority in both chambers, a Constitutional Assembly will be convened.

### CONCLUDING AND TRANSITIONAL PROVISIONS

Section Two states that the Constitution came into force on the day of the nation-wide vote, 12 December 1993. Should the provisions of a federal treaty contravene those of the Constitution, the constitutional provisions will apply. All laws and other legal acts enforced before the Constitution came into effect will remain valid unless they fail to comply with the Constitution. The President of the Russian Federation will carry out the presidential duties established by the Constitution until the expiry of his term of office. The Council of Ministers will acquire the rights, duties and responsibility of the Government of the Russian Federation established by the Constitution and henceforth be named the Government of the Russian Federation. The courts will administer justice in accordance with their powers established by the Constitution and retain their powers until the expiry of their term.

The Federation Council and the State Duma of first convocation will both be elected for a term of two years. A deputy of the State Duma of first convocation may also be a member of the Government. Deputies to the Federation Council of first convocation will carry out their duties on a part-time basis.

# The Government

### HEAD OF STATE

**President of the Russian Federation:** Boris N. Yeltsin (elected President 12 June 1991).

### THE GOVERNMENT
(July 1995)

**Chairman:** Viktor S. Chernomyrdin.

**First Deputy Chairman:** Oleg N. Soskovets, Anatoly B. Chubais.

# THE RUSSIAN FEDERATION

**Deputy Chairmen:** ALEKSANDR K. ZAVERYUKHA, YURY F. YAROV, SERGEY M. SHAKHRAY, ALEKSEY BOLSHAKOV, VITALY N. IGNATENKO.

**Deputy Chairman and Minister of Foreign Economic Relations:** OLEG D. DAVYDOV.

**Minister of Agriculture and Food:** ALEKSANDR G. NASARCHUK.

**Minister of Civil Defence, Emergencies and Natural Disasters:** SERGEY K. SHOYGU.

**Minister of Communications:** VLADIMIR B. BULGAK.

**Minister of Culture:** YEVGENY YU. SIDOROV.

**Minister of Defence:** Gen. PAVEL S. GRACHEV.

**Minister of Economics:** YEVGENY G. YASIN.

**Minister of Education:** YEVGENY V. TKACHENKO.

**Minister of Environmental Protection and Natural Resources:** VIKTOR I. DANILOV-DANILYAN.

**Minister of Finance:** VLADIMIR G. PANSKOV.

**Minister of Foreign Affairs:** ANDREY V. KOZYREV.

**Minister of Fuel and Power Engineering:** YURY K. SHAFRANIK.

**Minister of Health and the Medical Industry:** EDUARD A. NECHAYEV.

**Minister of Internal Affairs:** Col-Gen. ANATOLY KULIKOV.

**Minister of Justice:** VALENTIN KOVALEV.

**Minister of Labour:** GENNADY G. MELIKYAN.

**Minister of Nationalities and Regional Policy:** VYACHESLAV MIKHAILOV.

**Minister of Nuclear Energy:** VIKTOR N. MIKHAILOV.

**Minister of Railways:** GENNADY M. FADEYEV.

**Minister of Science and Technical Policy:** BORIS G. SALTYKOV.

**Minister of Social Welfare of the Population:** LYUDMILA BEZLEPKINA.

**Minister of Transport:** VITALY B. YEFIMOV.

**Minister without portfolio:** NIKOLAY I. TRAVKIN.

### Chairmen of Principal State Committees

**Chairman of the State Committee for Anti-Monopoly Policy and Support for New Economic Structures:** LEONID A. BOCHIN.

**Chairman of the State Committee for Architecture and Construction:** YEFIM V. BASIN.

**Chairman of the State Committee for State Property Management:** SERGEY BELYAYEV.

The Chairman of the Central Bank of the Russian Federation (TATYANA PARAMONOVA, acting) is *ex officio* a member of the Russian Federation Government.

### MINISTRIES

**Office of the Government:** Moscow, Krasnopresenskaya 2; tel. (095) 925-35-81; fax (095) 205-42-19.

**Ministry of Agriculture and Food:** 107139 Moscow, Orlikov per. 1/11; tel. (095) 207-42-43; telex 411258; fax (095) 288-95-80.

**Ministry of Civil Defence, Emergencies and Natural Disasters:** 103012 Moscow, Teatralny pr. 3; tel. (095) 926-35-82; telex 412327; fax (095) 924-84-10.

**Ministry of Communications:** 103375 Moscow, ul. Tverskaya 7; tel. (095) 292-10-75; fax (095) 201-69-37.

**Ministry of Culture:** 103693 Moscow, Kitaysky proyezd 7; tel. (095) 220-45-00; fax (095) 925-11-95.

**Ministry of Defence:** 103160 Moscow, ul. Myasnitskaya 37; tel. (095) 296-89-00.

**Ministry of Economics:** 103009 Moscow, ul. Okhotny ryad 1; tel. (095) 292-91-39.

**Ministry of Education:** 101856 Moscow, Chistoprudny bul. 6; tel. (095) 924-84-68; fax (095) 924-69-89.

**Ministry of Environmental Protection and Natural Resources:** 123812 Moscow, Bolshaya Gruzinskaya ul. 4/6; tel. (095) 254-76-83; fax (095) 254-82-83.

**Ministry of Finance:** 103097 Moscow, ul. Ilyinka 9; tel. (095) 206-21-71; fax (095) 924-69-89.

**Ministry of Foreign Affairs:** 121200 Moscow, Smolenskaya-Sennaya pl. 32/34; tel. (095) 244-34-48; fax (095) 924-32-32.

**Ministry of Foreign Economic Relations:** Moscow, Ovchinnikovskaya nab. 18/1; tel. (095) 220-13-50; fax (095) 244-39-81.

**Ministry of Fuel and Power Engineering:** 103074 Moscow, Kitaysky proyezd 7; tel. (095) 220-55-00; fax (095) 220-56-56.

**Ministry of Health and the Medical Industry:** 101431 Moscow, Rakhmanovsky per. 3; tel. (095) 923-84-06; telex 411407; fax (095) 292-41-53.

**Ministry of Internal Affairs:** 117049 Moscow, Zhitnaya ul. 19; tel. (095) 239-65-00; fax (095) 293-59-98.

**Ministry of Justice:** 101434 Moscow, ul. Yermolovoy 10A; tel. (095) 209-60-55; fax (095) 209-60-98.

**Ministry of Labour:** 103706 Moscow, Birzhevaya pl. 1; tel. (095) 928-06-83; fax (095) 230-24-07.

**Ministry of Nationalities and Regional Policy:** 117292 Moscow, ul. Ivana Babushkina 16; tel. (095) 125-21-50.

**Ministry of Nuclear Energy:** 101000 Moscow, ul. B. Ordynka 24/26; tel. (095) 239-49-08; fax (095) 230-24-20.

**Ministry of Railways:** Moscow, Novobasmannaya ul. 2; tel. (095) 262-10-02; telex 411832.

**Ministry of Science and Technical Policy:** 103905 Moscow, ul. Tverskaya 11; tel. (095) 229-11-92; telex 411241; fax (095) 230-28-23.

**Ministry of Social Welfare of the Population:** 103715 Moscow, Slavyanskaya pl. 4, kor. 1; tel. (095) 220-93-10; fax (095) 924-36-90.

**Ministry of Transport:** 101433 Moscow, Sadovo-Samotechnaya ul. 10; tel. (095) 200-08-03.

### State Committees

**State Committee for Anti-Monopoly Policy and Support for New Economic Structures:** 117947 Moscow, pr. Vernadskogo 41; tel. (095) 434-27-47.

**State Committee for Architecture and Construction:** 103828 Moscow, Georgiyevsky per. 2; tel. (095) 292-17-77; fax (095) 292-43-01.

**State Committee for Industrial Policy:** Moscow, 1-ya Tverskaya-Yamskaya ul. 1; tel. (095) 209-82-22; fax (095) 200-5284.

**State Committee for State Property Management:** 103685 Moscow, Nikolsky per. 9; tel. (095) 206-15-25; fax (095) 923-88-77.

## President and Legislature

### PRESIDENT

**Election, 12 June 1991**

| Candidate | Votes | % of total |
|---|---|---|
| BORIS N. YELTSIN | 45,552,041 | 57.30 |
| NIKOLAI RYZHKOV | 13,395,335 | 16.85 |
| VLADIMIR ZHIRINOVSKY | 6,211,007 | 7.81 |
| AMAN-GELDY TULEYEV | 5,417,464 | 6.81 |
| VADIM BAKATIN | 2,719,757 | 3.42 |
| ALBERT MAKASHOV | 11,136 | 0.7 |

### FEDERAL ASSEMBLY

The Federal Assembly is a bicameral legislative body, comprising the Federation Council and the State Duma. Elections to the Federal Assembly were held on 12 December 1993. There were no elections in some constituencies or, in others, an insufficient number of electors participated to validate the ballot. Further rounds of voting took place at subsequent dates.

### Federation Council

The Federation Council is the upper chamber of the Federal Assembly. It comprises a maximum of 178 deputies, two from each of the constituent members (federal territorial units) of the Russian Federation. By May 1994 176 of the Council's deputies had been elected (with only Chechnya unrepresented).

**Chairman:** VLADIMIR SHUMEYKO.

**Deputy Chairmen:** RAMAZAN ABDULATIPOV, VALERYAN VIKTOROV.

### State Duma

The State Duma is the 450-seat lower chamber of the Federal Assembly. Members of the State Duma are elected for a term of four years. By March 1994 449 of the Duma's deputies had been elected.

**Chairman:** IVAN RYBKIN.

**First Deputy Chairman:** MIKHAIL MITYUKOV.

**Deputy Chairmen:** ALEVTINA FEDULOVA, ALEKSANDR VENGEROVSKY.

# THE RUSSIAN FEDERATION

## General Election, 12 December 1993

| Parties and blocs | Party lists % of vote | Party lists Seats | Single-member constituency seats | Total seats* |
|---|---|---|---|---|
| Liberal Democratic Party | 22.79 | 59 | 5 | 64 |
| Russia's Choice | 15.38 | 40 | 18 | 58 |
| Communist Party of the Russian Federation | 12.35 | 32 | 16 | 48 |
| Agrarian Party | 7.90 | 21 | 12 | 33 |
| Women of Russia | 8.10 | 21 | 2 | 23 |
| Yavlinsky–Boldyrev–Lukin (Yabloko) | 7.83 | 20 | 2 | 22 |
| Party of Russian Unity and Accord | 6.76 | 18 | 1 | 19 |
| Democratic Party of Russia | 5.50 | 14 | 1 | 15 |
| Democratic Russia Movement | } 13.39 | — | 5 | 5 |
| Russian Movement for Democratic Reforms | | | 4 | 4 |
| Others | | | 153† | 153 |
| Total | 100.00 | 225 | 219‡ | 444‡ |

\* In mid-January 1994, according to Western estimates, the parliamentary factions in the State Duma were as follows: Russia's Choice (76 seats); New Regional Policy (centrist faction comprising independents—65); Liberal Democratic Party (63); Agrarian Party (55); Communist Party of the Russian Federation (45); Party of Russian Unity and Accord (30); Yavlinsky–Boldyrev–Lukin (Yabloko—25); Women of Russia (23); Democratic Party of Russia (15). In early 1995 a new faction, Stability, attracted members from Russia's Choice, Yabloko and other groupings.

† Including 130 members without party affiliations.

‡ Totals exclude one deputy from Chechnya and one from the Naberezhnye Chelny district of Tatarstan, where the election was boycotted, and four deputies from the remaining constituencies of Tatarstan (where fewer than 25% of registered voters took part, thereby invalidating the poll). However, in March 1994, in fresh elections in Tatarstan, the five deputies were successfully elected to the State Duma, bringing its total membership to 449.

## Political Organizations

In 1995 a large number of new political parties and movements was formed, in anticipation of the parliamentary elections due in December of that year. In March 1995 there were 63 legally registered nation-wide political parties. There were also many regional political organizations.

**Agrarian Party:** Moscow; f. 1993; opposes the dissolution of state and collective farms and supports their workers; Leader MIKHAIL LAPSHIN.

**Civic Union:** Moscow, ul. Shabolovka 8; f. 1992; Chair. ARKADY VOLSKY; centrist coalition including:

    **All-Russian Union for Renewal:** Moscow; advocates gradual economic reform, combined with a strong industrial policy; Co-Chair. ALEKSANDR VLADISLAVLEV, IGOR SMIRNOV.

**Communist Party of the Russian Federation:** Moscow; tel. (095) 206-87-51; fax (095) 206-87-51; f. 1993; claims succession to the Russian Communist Party which was banned in 1991; Chair. of Central Cttee GENNADY ZYUGANOV; c. 500,000 mems.

**Congress of Russian Communities:** Moscow; f. 1995; alliance of nationalist and conservative groups; Leaders YURY SKOKOV, DMITRY ROGOZIN, Lt-Gen. ALEKSANDR LEBED.

**Democratic Party of Russia:** Moscow, ul. Shabolovka 8; tel. (095) 237-09-22; f. 1990; liberal-conservative; Chair. SERGEY GLAZYEV.

**Derzhava** (Power): Moscow; f. 1994; alliance of right-wing parties; affiliated groups include National Republican Party, Russian Christian-Democratic Movement, Soyuz, State Renaissance Party, Social Democratic People's Party; Leader ALEKSANDR RUTSKOY.

**Forward, Russia!:** Moscow; f. 1995 on basis of 12 December Liberal Democratic Union; democratic party; Leader BORIS FEDEROV.

**Liberal Democratic Party:** Moscow; tel. (095) 923-63-70; right-wing nationalist; Leader VLADIMIR ZHIRINOVSKY.

**Majority Party:** Moscow; f. 1994; conservative; Chair. VYACHESLAV GRECHNEV; 150,000 mems.

**New Names:** Moscow; f. 1993; fmrly Russia's Future—New Names; formed as electoral bloc by the Free Russia youth movement; advocates ideas of nonconfrontational policy and national statehood; Chair. OLEG SOKOLOV.

**Our Home is Russia:** Moscow; f. 1995; conservative, pro-Government; Leader VIKTOR CHERNOMYRDIN.

**Party of Economic Freedom:** Moscow, Novaya pl. 3/4; tel. (095) 262-36-19; fax (095) 924-78-62; f. 1992; advocates economic liberalism, but supports Civic Union on some policies; Co-Chair. KONSTANTIN BOROVOY, SERGEY FEDEROV; 100,000 mems.

**Party of Russian Unity and Accord:** Moscow; f. 1993; democratic bloc; Leader SERGEY SHAKHRAY.

**Russian All-People's Union:** Moscow; f. as party 1994; right-wing, nationalist; Leader SERGEY BABURIN.

**Russian Christian-Democratic Movement:** Moscow; f. 1990; alliance of groups advocating application of Christian principles to society; conservative-nationalist; Chair. of Political Cttee VIKTOR AKSYUCHITS; c. 6,000 mems.

**Russia's Democratic Choice Party:** Moscow; tel. (095) 290-23-09; f. 1993 as a democratic electoral bloc, Russia's Choice; reconstituted as a political party in 1994; Leader YEGOR GAIDAR; the following are mems or affiliates:

    **Democratic Russia Movement:** 109180 Moscow, 36 Starometny per.; tel. (095) 233-00-23; f. 1990; alliance of democratic parties; Co-Chair. GLEB YAKUNIN, LEV PONOMAREV; c. 150,000 mems.

    **Free Democratic Party of Russia:** 198255 St Petersburg, pr. Veteranov 55, kv. 94; tel. (0812) 356-84-27; f. 1990 as a result of a split in the Democratic Party of Russia; radical democratic party; Co-Chair. MARINA SALYE, LEV PONOMAREV, IGOR SOSHNIKOV; c. 1,000 mems.

    **Free Labour Party:** 109193 Moscow, ul. Petra Romanova 18/2/8; tel. (095) 277-67-02; f. 1990; party of business people and professionals; advocates economic liberalism; Chair. of Political Cttee IGOR KOROVIKOV; c. 1,500 mems.

    **Peasants' Party of Russia:** 119619 Moscow, ul. Narfominskaya 2-192; tel. (095) 189-89-51; f. 1990; advocates agricultural reform, and the return of collectivized land to individual farmers; Chair. YURY CHERNENKO; c. 1,500 mems.

    **Republican Party of the Russian Federation:** 109044 Moscow, 11/31-6 Siminovsky val; tel. (095) 298-13-49; f. 1990 by former members of the Democratic Platform in the CPSU; advocates a mixed economy, defence of sovereignty of Russia; mem. of Liberal Union; Chair. VLADIMIR LYSENKO; c. 7,000 mems.

**Social Democratic Party of the Russian Federation:** 109044 Moscow, POB 35; tel. and fax (095) 201-49-26; f. 1990; advocates democratic society, social partnership between employers and trade unions, and observation of human rights; Chair. ANATOLY GOLOV; Sec. ALEKSANDR GORBUNOV; 4,500 mems.

**Women of Russia:** Moscow, ul. Nemirovich Danchenko 6; tel. (095) 209-77-08; fax (095) 200-02-74; Leader ALEVTINA FEDULOVA.

**Yavlinsky–Boldyrev–Lukin (Yabloko):** Moscow; f. 1993; democratic-centrist; Leaders: GRIGORY YAVLINSKY, YURY BOLDYREV, VLADIMIR LUKIN.

## Diplomatic Representation

### EMBASSIES IN RUSSIA

**Afghanistan:** Moscow, Sverchkov per. 3/2; tel. (095) 928-50-44; telex 413270; fax (095) 924-04-78; Ambassador: ABDUL WAHAB ASSEFI.

**Albania:** Moscow, ul. Mytnaya 3, kv. 25; tel. (095) 230-78-75; telex 414506; fax (095) 230-76-35; Ambassador: ARBEN CICI.

**Algeria:** Moscow, Krapivinsky per. 1A; tel. (095) 200-66-42; telex 413273; fax (095) 200-22-25; Ambassador: H. BOURKI.

**Angola:** ul. Olof Palme 6; tel. (095) 143-63-24; telex 413402; Ambassador: LOUIS DOUKUI PAULO DE CASTRO.

**Argentina:** Moscow, ul. Sadovo-Triumfalnaya 4/10; tel. (095) 299-03-67; telex 413259; fax (095) 200-42-18; Ambassador: ARNOLDO MANUEL LISTRE.

**Armenia:** Moscow, Armyansky per. 2; tel. (095) 924-12-69; fax (095) 923-09-85; Ambassador: YURY I. MKRTUMYAN.

**Australia:** Moscow, Kropotkinsky per. 13; tel. (095) 956-61-70; telex 413474; fax (095) 956-60-70; Ambassador: CAVAN O. HOGUE.

**Austria:** Moscow, Starokonyushenny per. 1; tel. (095) 201-73-79; telex 413398; fax (095) 230-23-65; Ambassador: FRIEDRICH BAUER.

**Azerbaijan:** Moscow, Leontiyevsky per. 16; tel. (095) 229-16-49; telex 412470; fax (095) 202-50-72; Ambassador: RAMIZ G. RIZAYEV.

**Bahrain:** Moscow, ul. B. Ordynka 18; tel. (095) 230-00-13; fax (095) 230-24-01; Ambassador: Dr SALMAN AL-SOFFAR.

**Bangladesh:** Moscow, Zemledelchesky per. 6; tel. (095) 246-79-00; telex 413196; fax (095) 248-31-85; Ambassador: Maj.-Gen. AMSA AMIN.

**Belarus:** 101000 Moscow, ul. Maroseyka 17/6; tel. (095) 924-70-31; fax (095) 928-64-03; Ambassador: VIKTOR DANILENKO.

# THE RUSSIAN FEDERATION

**Belgium:** Moscow, ul. Malaya Molchanovka 7; tel. (095) 291-60-27; telex 413471; fax (095) 291-60-05; Ambassador: Baron THIERRY DE GRUBEN.
**Benin:** Moscow, Uspensky per. 4A; tel. (095) 299-23-60; telex 413645; fax (095) 200-02-26; Ambassador: JULES ANTOINE LALEYE.
**Bolivia:** Moscow, Lopukhinsky per. 5; tel. (095) 201-25-08; telex 413356; Ambassador: RAMIRO VELASCO ROMERO.
**Brazil:** Moscow, ul. B. Nikitskaya 54; tel. (095) 290-40-22; telex 413476; fax (095) 200-12-85; Ambassador: SEBASTIÃO DO REGO BARROS NETTO.
**Bulgaria:** Moscow, ul. Mosfilmovskaya 66; tel. (095) 143-90-22; Ambassador: KHRISTO MILADINOV.
**Burkina Faso:** 129090 Moscow, Meshchanskaya ul. 17; tel. (095) 971-37-49; telex 413284; fax (095) 200-22-77; Ambassador JEAN-BAPTISTE ILBOUDO.
**Burundi:** Moscow, Uspensky per. 7; tel. (095) 299-72-00; telex 413316; Ambassador: EMMANUEL GAHUNGU.
**Cambodia:** Moscow, Starokonyushenny per. 16; tel. (095) 201-47-36; telex 413261; fax (095) 201-76-68; Ambassador: SEK SETHA.
**Cameroon:** Moscow, ul. Povarskaya 40; tel. (095) 290-65-49; telex 413445; Ambassador: ANDRÉ NGONGANG OUANDJI.
**Canada:** Moscow, Starokonyushenny per. 23; tel. (095) 956-66-66; telex 413401; fax (095) 241-44-00; Ambassador: JEREMY KINSMAN.
**Cape Verde:** Moscow, Rublevskoye shosse 26; tel. (095) 415-45-03; telex 413929; Chargé d'affaires a.i.: JÚLIO CESAR FREIRE DE MOURAIS.
**Central African Republic:** 117571 Moscow, ul. 26-Bakinskikh-Kommissarov 9, kv. 124–125; tel. (095) 434-45-20; telex 413737; Ambassador: CLAUDE BERNARD BELOUM.
**Chad:** Moscow, Rublevskoye shosse 26, kor. 1, kv. 20–21; tel. (095) 415-41-39; telex 413623; Ambassador: AL-HABBO MAHAMAT SALEH.
**Chile:** 111395 Moscow, ul. Yunosti 11; tel. (095) 373-9176; telex 413751; fax (095) 373-77-25; Ambassador: JAMES HOLGER.
**China, People's Republic:** Moscow, Leninskiye Gory, ul. Druzhby 6; tel. (095) 143-15-40; telex 413981; Ambassador: WANG JINQING.
**Colombia:** Moscow, ul. Burdenko 20; tel. (095) 248-30-42; telex 413206; fax (095) 248-30-25; Ambassador: GONZALO BULA HOYOS.
**Congo:** Moscow, Kropotkinsky per. 12; tel. (095) 246-02-34; telex 413487; Ambassador: ALPHONSE NGANGA-MUNGWA.
**Costa Rica:** Moscow, Rublevskoye shosse 26, kv. 23–25; tel. and fax (095) 415-40-42; telex 413963; Ambassador: ARTURO ROBLES ARIAS.
**Côte d'Ivoire:** Moscow, Korobeinikov per. 14/9; tel. (095) 201-24-00; telex 413091; fax (095) 200-12-92; Ambassador: DIEUDONNÉ ESSIENNE.
**Croatia:** Moscow, Krasnopresnenskaya nab. 12; tel. (095) 253-12-53; fax (095) 253-12-70; Ambassador: NIKO BEZMALINOVIĆ.
**Cuba:** Moscow, ul. Spiridonovka 28; tel. (095) 290-28-82; Ambassador: ROGELIO MONTENEGRO GUASP.
**Cyprus:** 121069 Moscow, ul. Nikitskaya 51; tel. (095) 290-21-54; telex 413477; fax (095) 200-12-54; Ambassador: ANTONIS VAKIS.
**Czech Republic:** Moscow, ul. Yuliusa Fuchika 12/14; tel. (095) 251-05-40; Ambassador: RUDOLF SLÁNSKÝ.
**Denmark:** Moscow, Prechistensky per. (Ostrovskogo) 9; tel. (095) 201-78-60; telex 413378; fax (095) 201-53-57; Ambassador: HENRIK RÉE IVERSEN.
**Ecuador:** Moscow, Gorokhovsky per. 12; tel. (095) 261-55-44; telex 413174; fax (095) 267-70-79; Ambassador: JUAN SALAZAR SANCISI.
**Egypt:** Moscow, Skatertny per. 25; tel. (095) 291-32-09; telex 413276; fax (095) 291-46-09; Ambassador: NABIL EL-ORABI.
**Equatorial Guinea:** Moscow, Kutuzovsky pr. 7/4, kor. 5, kv. 37; tel. (095) 243-96-11; Ambassador: POLICARPO MENSUY MBA.
**Estonia:** Moscow, M. Kislovsky per. 5; tel. (095) 290-50-13; fax (095) 202-38-30; Ambassador: MART HELME.
**Ethiopia:** Moscow, Orlovo-Davydovsky per. 6; tel. (095) 230-20-36; telex 413980; Ambassador: Dr KASSA G. HIWOT.
**Finland:** Moscow, Kropotkinsky per. 15/17; tel. (095) 246-40-27; telex 413405; fax (095) 230-27-21; Ambassador: ARTO MANSALA.
**France:** Moscow, ul. Bolshaya Yakimanka 45/47; tel. (095) 236-00-03; telex 413290; fax (095) 230-21-69; Ambassador: PIERRE MOREL.
**Gabon:** Moscow, ul. Vesnina 16; tel. (095) 241-00-80; telex 413245; fax (095) 244-06-94; Ambassador: MARCEL ONDONGUI-BONNARD.
**Georgia:** Moscow, ul. Paliashvili 6; tel. (095) 291-21-36; Ambassador: VAZHA LORTKIPANIDZE.
**Germany:** 119285 Moscow, Mosfilmovskaya ul. 56; tel. (095) 956-10-80; telex 413411; fax (095) 938-23-54; Ambassador: OTTO VON DER GABLNETZ.
**Ghana:** Moscow, Skatertny per. 14; tel. (095) 202-18-70; telex 413475; Ambassador: JOHN EWUNTOMAH BAWAH.

**Greece:** Moscow, Leontiyevsky per. 4; tel. (095) 290-22-74; telex 413472; fax (095) 200-12-52; Ambassador: KYRIAKOS RODOUSAKIS.
**Guinea:** Moscow, Pomerantsev per. 6; tel. (095) 201-36-01; telex 413404; Ambassador: CHÉRIF DIALLO.
**Guinea-Bissau:** Moscow, ul. Bolshaya Ordynka 35; tel: (095) 231-79-28; telex 413055; Ambassador: CHÉRIF TURÉ.
**Holy See:** 117049 Moscow, ul. Mytnaya 3, kv. 30 (Apostolic Nunciature); tel. (095) 230-29-94; fax (095) 230-20-40; Apostolic Nuncio: Most Rev. JOHN BUKOVSKY, Titular Archbishop of Tabalta.
**Hungary:** Moscow, ul. Mosfilmovskaya 62; tel. (095) 143-86-11; telex 414428; fax (095) 143-46-25; Ambassador: GYÖRGY NANOVFSKY.
**Iceland:** Moscow, ul. Mosfilmovskaya 54; tel. (095) 956-76-05; telex 413181; fax (095) 956-76-12; Ambassador: GUNNAR GUNNARSSON.
**India:** Moscow, ul. Vorontsovo Polye 6–8; tel. (095) 917-08-20; telex 413409; fax (095) 975-23-37; Ambassador: RANENDRA SEN.
**Indonesia:** Moscow, ul. Novokuznetskaya 12; tel. (095) 231-95-50; telex 413444; fax (095) 230-64-31; Ambassador: RACHMAT WITOELAR.
**Iran:** 109028 Moscow, Pokrovsky bul. 7; tel. (095) 227-57-88; telex 413493; Ambassador: MEHDI SAFARI.
**Iraq:** Moscow, Pogodinskaya ul. 12; tel. (095) 246-55-06; telex 413184; fax (095) 230-29-22; Ambassador: HASAN FAHMI JUMAH.
**Ireland:** Moscow, Grokholsky per. 5; tel. (095) 288-41-01; telex 413204; Ambassador: PATRICK MCCABE.
**Israel:** Moscow, ul. Bolshaya Ordynka 56; tel. (095) 230-67-00; fax (095) 238-13-46; Ambassador: (vacant).
**Italy:** Moscow, ul. Vesnina 5; tel. (095) 241-15-33; telex 413453; fax (095) 253-92-89; Ambassador: FEDERICO DI ROBERTO.
**Jamaica:** Moscow, Korovy val 7, kv. 70–71; tel. (095) 237-23-20; telex 413358; fax (095) 230-21-02; Chargé d'affaires a.i.: PAUL A. ROBOTHAM.
**Japan:** Moscow, Kalashny per. 12; tel. (095) 291-85-00; telex 413141; fax (095) 200-12-40; Ambassador: KOJI WATANABE.
**Jordan:** Moscow, Mamonovsky per. 3; tel. (095) 299-95-64; telex 413447; fax (095) 299-43-54; Ambassador: Dr KHALDOUN AHMAD AL-DHAHIR.
**Kazakhstan:** Moscow, Chistoprudny bul. 3A; tel. (095) 208-98-52; Ambassador: TAIR A. MANSUROV.
**Kenya:** Moscow, ul. Bolshaya Ordynka 70; tel. (095) 237-47-02; telex 413495; fax (095) 230-23-40; Ambassador: D. I. KATHAMBANA.
**Korea, Democratic People's Republic:** Moscow, ul. Mosfilmovskaya 72; tel. (095) 143-62-49; telex 413272; Ambassador: SON SONG PIL.
**Korea, Republic:** 119121 Moscow, ul. Spiridonovka 14; tel. (095) 956-14-74; telex 413718; fax (095) 202-83-97; Ambassador: KIM SOK-KYU.
**Kuwait:** Moscow, ul. Mosfilmovskaya 44; tel. (095) 147-44-41; telex 413353; fax (095) 956-60-32; Ambassador: FAWZI AL-JASEM.
**Kyrgyzstan:** Moscow, ul. Bolshaya Ordynka 64; tel. (095) 237-48-82; fax (095) 237-44-52; Ambassador: AKMATBEK NANAYEV.
**Laos:** Moscow, M. Nikitskaya 18; tel. (095) 290-25-60; telex 413101; Ambassador: SOUKTHAVONE KEOLA.
**Latvia:** Moscow, ul. Chaplygina 3; tel. (095) 925-27-07; fax (095) 925-92-95; Ambassador: JĀNIS PĒTERS.
**Lebanon:** Moscow, Sadovo-Samotechnaya ul. 14; tel. (095) 200-00-22; telex 413120; fax (095) 200-32-22; Ambassador: SELIM TADMOURY.
**Libya:** Moscow, ul. Mosfilmovskaya 38; tel. (095) 143-03-54; telex 413443; fax (095) 143-76-44; Secretary (Ambassador): MOHAMED HOSNI SHABAN.
**Lithuania:** Moscow, Borisoglebsky per. 10; tel. (095) 291-16-98; fax (095) 202-35-16; Ambassador: ROMUALDAS KOZYROVIČIUS.
**Luxembourg:** 119034 Moscow, Khrushchevsky per. 3; tel. (095) 202-53-81; telex 413131; fax (095) 200-52-43; Ambassador: JEAN HOSTERT.
**Macedonia, former Yugoslav republic:** Moscow, ul. Dmitriya Ulyanova 16, kor. 2, kv. 510; tel. (095) 124-33-57; fax (095) 124-33-59; Ambassador: GANE TODOROVSKI.
**Madagascar:** Moscow, Kursovoy per. 5; tel. (095) 290-02-14; telex 413370; Ambassador: SIMON RABOARA RABE.
**Malaysia:** Moscow, ul. Mosfilmovskaya 50; tel. (095) 147-15-14; telex 413478; fax (095) 147-15-26; Ambassador: MOHAMED HARON.
**Mali:** Moscow, Novokuznetskaya ul. 11; tel. (095) 231-06-55; telex 413396; Ambassador: Dr ABDOULAYE CHARLES DANIOKO.
**Malta:** Moscow, Korovy val 7, kv. 219; tel. (095) 237-19-39; fax (095) 237-21-58; Ambassador: GEORGE SALIBA.
**Mauritania:** Moscow, ul. Bolshaya Ordynka 66; tel. (095) 237-37-92; telex 413439; Ambassador: ALY GUELADIO KAMARA.

**Mexico:** Moscow, B. Levshinsky per. 4; tel. (095) 201-25-53; telex 413125; fax (095) 230-20-42; Chargé d'affaires a.i.: JUAN PABLO-DUCH.

**Moldova:** Moscow, Kuznetsky most 18; tel. (095) 928-54-05; fax (095) 924-95-90; Ambassador: VALERIU PASAT.

**Mongolia:** Moscow, Borisoglebsky per. 11; tel. (095) 290-30-61; fax (095) 291-61-71; Ambassador: (vacant).

**Morocco:** Moscow, ul. Donskaya 18/7 per. Ostrovskogo 8; tel. and fax (095) 952-10-06; telex 413446; Ambassador: ABDESELAM ZENINED.

**Mozambique:** Moscow, ul. Gilyarovskogo 20; tel. (095) 284-40-07; telex 413369; Ambassador: JOSÉ RUI MOTA DO AMARAL.

**Myanmar:** Moscow, ul. Nikitskaya 41; tel. (095) 291-05-34; telex 413403; fax (095) 956-31-86; Ambassador: U KHIN MAUNG SOE.

**Namibia:** Moscow, Kazachny per. 7; tel. (095) 230-01-13; telex 413827; fax (095) 230-22-74; Ambassador: NICKY P. NASHANDI.

**Nepal:** Moscow, 2-Neopalimovsky per. 14/7; tel. (095) 244-02-15; telex 413292; Ambassador: KUMAR P. GYAWALI.

**Netherlands:** Moscow, Kalashny per. 6; tel. (095) 291-29-99; telex 413442; fax (095) 200-52-64; Ambassador: Baron GODERT W. DE VOS VAN STEENWIJK.

**New Zealand:** 121069 Moscow, ul. Povarskaya 44; tel. (095) 956-35-79; fax (095) 956-35-83; Ambassador: RICHARD WOODS.

**Nicaragua:** Moscow, Mosfilmovskaya ul. 50, kor. 1; tel. (095) 938-27-01; telex 413264; Ambassador: ADOLFO JOSÉ EVERTSZ VÉLEZ.

**Niger:** Moscow, Kursovoy per. 7/31; tel. (095) 290-01-01; telex 413180; fax (095) 200-42-51; Ambassador: (vacant).

**Nigeria:** Moscow, ul. M. Nikitskaya 13; tel. (095) 290-37-83; telex 413489; fax (095) 290-37-87; Ambassador: JIBRIN D. CHINADE.

**Norway:** Moscow, ul. Povarskaya 7; tel. (095) 290-38-72; telex 413488; fax (095) 200-12-21; Ambassador: PER TRESSELT.

**Oman:** Moscow, per. Obukha 6; tel. (095) 928-56-30; telex 411432; fax (095) 975-21-74; Ambassador: DAWOOD HAMDAN AL-HAMDAN.

**Pakistan:** Moscow, Sadovo-Kudrinskaya ul. 17; tel. (095) 254-97-91; telex 413194; Ambassador: TANVIR AHMED KHAN.

**Panama:** Moscow, ul. Mosfilmovskaya 50; tel. and fax (095) 143-06-31; Ambassador: FLAVIO GABRIEL MÉNDEZ ALTAMIRANO.

**Peru:** Moscow, Smolensky bul. 22/14, kv. 15; tel. (095) 248-77-38; telex 413400; fax (095) 230-20-00; Ambassador: Dr ARMANDO LECAROS DE COSSÍO.

**Philippines:** Moscow, Karmanitsky per. 6; tel. (095) 241-38-70; telex 413156; fax (095) 956-60-87; Ambassador: SAMUEL T. RAMEL.

**Poland:** Moscow, ul. Klimashkina 4; tel. (095) 255-00-17; telex 414362; fax (095) 254-22-86; Ambassador: STANISŁAW CIOSEK.

**Portugal:** Moscow, Botanichesky per. 1; tel. (095) 230-24-35; telex 413221; fax (095) 230-26-51; Ambassador: JOSÉ MANUEL DE VILLAS-BOAS.

**Qatar:** Moscow, Korovy val 7, kv. 197–198; tel. (095) 230-15-77; telex 413728; fax (095) 230-22-40; Ambassador: FAHD AL-KHATER.

**Romania:** Moscow, ul. Mosfilmovskaya 64; tel. (095) 143-04-24; telex 414355; fax (095) 143-04-49; Ambassador: CONSTANTIN GÎRBEA.

**Rwanda:** Moscow, ul. Bolshaya Ordynka 72; tel. (095) 237-32-22; telex 413213; Ambassador: ANASTASE NTEZILYAYO.

**Saudi Arabia:** Moscow, 3-Neopalimovsky per. 3; tel. (095) 245-23-10; fax (095) 246-94-71; Ambassador: ABDUL-AZIZ MOHEDDIN KHOJAH.

**Senegal:** Moscow, ul. Donskaya 12; tel. (095) 236-20-40; telex 413438; Ambassador: ABSA CLAUDE DIALLO.

**Sierra Leone:** Moscow, ul. Paliashvili 4; tel. (095) 203-62-00; telex 413461; Ambassador: OLU WILLIAM HARDING.

**Singapore:** Moscow, per. Voyevodina 5; tel. (095) 241-37-02; telex 413128; fax (095) 230-29-37; Ambassador: BILAHARI KAUSIKAN.

**Slovakia:** Moscow, ul. Yuliusa Fuchika 17–19; tel. (095) 250-56-09; telex 414480; fax (095) 973-20-81; Ambassador: ROMAN PALDAN.

**Slovenia:** Moscow, Gruzinsky per. 3, kv. 41-42; tel. (095) 254-35-31; fax (095) 254-72-23; Ambassador: S. I. GERZINA.

**Somalia:** Moscow, Spasopeskovskaya pl. 8; tel. (095) 241-96-24; telex 413164; Chargé d'affaires a.i.: MAYE MAO DERE.

**South Africa:** 113054 Moscow, B. Strochenovsky per. 22/25; tel. (095) 230-68-69; fax (095) 230-68-65; Ambassador: Dr GERRIT C. OLIVIER.

**Spain:** Moscow, ul. B. Nikitskaya 50/8; tel. (095) 202-21-61; telex 413220; fax (095) 200-12-30; Ambassador: EUGENIO BREGOLAT OBIOLS.

**Sri Lanka:** Moscow, ul. Shchepkina 24; tel. (095) 288-16-51; telex 413140; Ambassador: NISSANKA PARAKRAMA WIJEYERATNE.

**Sudan:** Moscow, ul. Povarskaya 9; tel. (095) 290-39-93; telex 413448; Ambassador: ANDREW MAKUR THOU.

**Sweden:** Moscow, ul. Mosfilmovskaya 60; tel. (095) 956-12-00; telex 413410; fax (095) 956-12-02; Ambassador: SVEN HIRDMAN.

**Switzerland:** Moscow, per. Ogorodnopi Slobody 2/5; tel. (095) 925-53-22; telex 413418; fax (095) 200-17-28; Ambassador: JOHANN BUCHER.

**Syria:** Moscow, Mansurovsky per. 4; tel. (095) 203-15-21; telex 413145; Ambassador: Dr GHASSAN RUSLAN.

**Tajikistan:** 121069 Moscow, Skatertny per. 19; tel. (095) 290-61-02; fax (095) 290-06-09; Ambassador: RAMAZAN Z. MIRZOYEV.

**Tanzania:** Moscow, ul. Pyatnitskaya 33; tel. (095) 231-81-46; telex 413352; fax (095) 230-29-68; Ambassador: JAMES L. KATEKA.

**Thailand:** Moscow, Eropkinsky per. 3; tel. (095) 201-48-93; telex 413309; Ambassador: SUCHITRA HIRANPRUECK.

**Togo:** 103001 Moscow, Granatny per. 1; tel. (095) 290-65-99; telex 413967; fax (095) 200-12-50; Ambassador: CHARLES DJABABOU NANA.

**Tunisia:** Moscow, ul. M. Nikitskaya 28/1; tel. (095) 291-28-58; telex 413449; Ambassador: AHMED KHALED.

**Turkey:** Moscow, 7-Rostovsky per. 12; tel. (095) 245-67-34; fax (095) 245-65-02; Ambassador: AYHAN KAMEL.

**Turkmenistan:** Moscow, per. Aksakova 22; tel. (095) 291-66-36; fax (095) 291-09-35; Ambassador: NIYAZ NURKLICHEV.

**Uganda:** Moscow, Mamonovsky per. Sadovskikh 5; tel. (095) 299-83-97; telex 413473; fax (095) 200-42-00; Ambassador: FELIX OKOBOI.

**Ukraine:** 103009 Moscow, Leontiyevsky per. 18; tel. (095) 229-10-79; fax (095) 229-64-44; Ambassador: VLADIMIR FEDEROV.

**United Arab Emirates:** Moscow, Olof Palme ul. 4; tel. (095) 147-62-86; telex 413547; fax (095) 938-21-37; Ambassador: NASSER SALMAN AL-ABOODI.

**United Kingdom:** Moscow, Sofiyskaya nab. 14; tel. (095) 956-72-00; telex 413341; fax (095) 956-74-20; Ambassador: Sir ANDREW WOOD (designate).

**USA:** 121099 Moscow, Novinsky bul. 19/23; tel. (095) 252-24-51; telex 413160; fax (095) 255-97-66; Ambassador: THOMAS R. PICKERING.

**Uruguay:** 117330 Moscow, Lomonosovsky pr. 38; tel. (095) 143-04-01; telex 413238; fax (095) 938-20-45; Ambassador: PEDRO DONDO.

**Uzbekistan:** Moscow, Pogorelsky per. 12; tel. (095) 230-00-76; fax (095) 238-89-18; Ambassador: SHAMANSUR SHAKHALILOV.

**Venezuela:** Moscow, B. Karetny per. 13–15; tel. (095) 299-96-21; telex 413119; fax (095) 200-02-48; Ambassador: RAFAEL LEÓN MORALES.

**Viet Nam:** Moscow, Bolshaya Pirogovskaya ul. 13; tel. (095) 247-02-12; Ambassador: HO HUAN NGHIEM.

**Yemen:** Moscow, 2-Neopalimovsky per. 6; tel. (095) 246-15-31; telex 413214; Ambassador: ALI ABDULLA AL-BUGERY.

**Yugoslavia:** Moscow, ul. Mosfilmovskaya 46; tel. (095) 147-41-06; telex 414423; fax (095) 147-41-04; Chargé d'affaires a.i.: MILAN ROCEN.

**Zaire:** Moscow, Prechistensky per. 12; tel. (095) 201-76-64; telex 413479; fax (095) 201-79-48; Ambassador: MITIMA K. MURAIRI.

**Zambia:** Moscow, pr. Mira 52A; tel. (095) 288-50-01; telex 413462; Ambassador: NCHIMUNYA JOHN SIKAULU.

**Zimbabwe:** Moscow, Serpov per. 6; tel. (095) 248-43-67; telex 413029; fax (095) 230-24-97; Ambassador: (vacant).

# Judicial System

In January 1995 a new code of civil law came into effect. It included new rules on commercial and financial operations, and on ownership issues. The Constitutional Court rules on the conformity of government policies with the Constitution. It was suspended in October 1993, following its condemnation of President Yeltsin's dissolution of the legislature, but was reinstated, with a new membership of 19 judges, in April 1995. The Supreme Arbitration Court rules on disputes between commercial bodies. The Supreme Court overseas all criminal and civil law, and is the final court of appeal from lower courts.

**Constitutional Court of the Russian Federation:** 103132 Moscow, ul. Ilyinka 21; tel. (095) 206-18-39; fax (095) 206-17-86; f. 1991; Chair. VLADIMIR A. TUMANOV.

**Supreme Arbitration Court of the Russian Federation:** 101000 Moscow, ul. Griboyedova 12; tel. (095) 208-11-19; fax (095) 208-11-62; f. 1993; Chair. VENIAMIN F. YAKOVLEV.

**Supreme Court of the Russian Federation:** 103289 Moscow, ul. Ilyinka 7/3; tel. (095) 924-23-47; fax (095) 202-71-18; Chair. VYACHESLAV M. LEBEDEV.

**Office of the Prosecutor-General:** 103793 Moscow, K-9, ul. Bolshaya Dmitrovskaya 15A; tel. (095) 292-88-69; fax (095) 292-88-48; Prosecutor-General ALEKSEY N. ILYUSHENKO (acting).

THE RUSSIAN FEDERATION

## Religion

The majority of the population of the Russian Federation are adherents of Christianity, but there are significant Islamic, Buddhist and Jewish minorities.

### CHRISTIANITY
#### The Russian Orthodox Church

The Russian Orthodox Church is the dominant religious organization in the Russian Federation, with an estimated 35m. adherents. In 1994 there were 4,566 registered Orthodox groups in Russia. In May 1991 the Russian Orthodox Church announced plans to begin building 542 churches throughout Russia. In 1988–92 more than 2,000 churches were returned to religious use. The Church's jurisdiction is challenged by the Russian Orthodox Church Abroad, which was established in the Soviet period and rejects the hierarchy of the Moscow Patriarchate.

**Moscow Patriarchate:** 113191 Moscow, Danilov Monastery, Danilovsky val 22; tel. (095) 954-04-54; fax (095) 230-26-19; Patriarch ALEKSY II.

#### The Roman Catholic Church

At 31 December 1993 there were an estimated 300,000 Roman Catholics in European Russia and 122,000 in Siberia.

**Apostolic Administrator of European Russia:** Most Rev. TADEUSZ KONDRUSIEWICZ (Titular Archbishop of Hippo Diarrhytus), 101000 Moscow, ul. Malaya Lubyanka 12; tel. (095) 925-20-34; fax (095) 261-67-14.

**Apostolic Administrator of Siberia:** Rt Rev. JOSEPH WERTH (Titular Bishop of Bulna), 630000 Novosibirsk, Marinnaya ul. 19, kv. 163; tel. (3832) 21-61-09; fax (3832) 21-88-06.

#### Protestant Churches

**Euro-Asiatic Federation of the Unions of Evangelical Christians-Baptists:** Moscow, Trekhsvyatitelny per. 3; tel. (095) 227-39-90; fax (095) 975-23-67; Pres. GRIGORY KOMENDANT; Gen. Sec. V. MITSKEVICH.

#### Other Christian Churches

**Armenian Apostolic Church:** Moscow, ul. Sergeya Makeyeva 10; tel. (095) 255-50-19.

**Old Believers** (The Old Faith): Moscow, Rogozhsky pos. 29; tel. (095) 361-51-92; divided into three branches: the Belokrinitsky Concord (under the Metropolitan of Moscow and All-Russia), the Bespopovtsy Concord and the Beglopopovtsy Concord; Metropolitan of Moscow and All-Russia: Bishop ALIMPI.

### ISLAM

Most Muslims in the Russian Federation are adherents of the Sunni sect. Muslims in the Russian Federation come under the spiritual jurisdiction of the Muslim Board of European Russia and Siberia and the Muslim Board of the North Caucasus.

### JUDAISM

Although many Jews emigrated from the USSR in the 1970s and 1980s, there is still a significant Jewish population (656,000 in late 1993) in the Russian Federation, particularly in the larger cities. There are a small number of Jews in the Jewish Autonomous Oblast, in the Far East of the Russian Federation. There is an Orthodox Jewish Seminary (yeshiva) in Moscow. In the Jewish Autonomous Oblast the teaching of Yiddish has begun in schools and institutes.

**Chief Rabbi of Moscow:** PINCHAS GOLDSCHMIDT.

### BUDDHISM

Buddhism (established as an official religion in Russia since 1741) is most widespread in the Republic of Buryatia, where the Central Spiritual Department of Buddhists of Russia has its seat, the Republics of Kalmykia and Tyva and in some districts of the Irkutsk and Chita Oblasts. There are also newly established communities in Moscow and St Petersburg. Before 1917 there were more than 40 datsans (monasteries) in Buryatia, but by 1990 only two of these remained in use.

**Chairman of the Central Spiritual Department of Buddhists:** (vacant).

## The Press

In 1992 there were 4,837 officially-registered newspaper titles published in the Russian Federation, of which 222 were national newspapers. There were also 3,681 periodicals, including 3,389 in Russian. Owing to the economic situation, almost all newspapers and periodicals suffered a sharp decrease in circulation in 1992 and 1993. Despite losing over 25m. subscribers, *Argumenty i Fakty* remained the best-selling Russian weekly newspaper in 1995, while *Izvestiya, Komosomolskaya Pravda* and *Trud* were the most popular dailies.

**Russian Federation Press Committee:** 101409 Moscow, Strastnoy bul. 5; tel. (095) 229-33-53; fax (095) 200-22-81; f. 1993 to replace the Ministry of Press and Information and the Federal Information Centre of Russia; central organ of federal executive power; Chair. SERGEY P. GRYZUNOV.

### PRINCIPAL NEWSPAPERS
#### Moscow

**Argumenty i Fakty** (Arguments and Facts): 101000 Moscow, ul. Myasnitskaya 42; tel. (095) 923-23-82; telex 114769; fax (095) 200-22-52; f. 1978; weekly; Editor VLADISLAV A. STARKOV; circ. 4,340,000 (1995).

**Glasnost** (Openness): 103132 Moscow, Novaya pl. 14; tel. (095) 231-47-78; weekly; publ. by Pressa Publishing House; left-wing; Editor-in-Chief YU. P. IZYUMOV; circ. 40,000 (1995).

**Izvestiya** (News): 103791 Moscow, ul. Tverskaya 18/1; tel. (095) 209-91-00; telex 411121; fax (095) 230-23-03; f. 1917; fmrly organ of the Presidium of the Supreme Soviet of the USSR; independent; Editor I. GOLEMBIOVSKY; circ. 814,000.

**Komsomolskaya Pravda** (Komsomol Pravda): 125865 Moscow, ul. Pravdy 24; tel. (095) 257-21-39; telex 111551; fax (095) 200-22-93; f. 1925; fmrly organ of the Leninist Young Communist League (Komsomol); independent; Editor V. SIMONOV; circ. 1,500,000 (1995).

**Krasnaya Zvezda** (Red Star): 123826 Moscow, Khoroshevskoye shosse 38; tel. (095) 941-21-58; fax (095) 941-40-57; f. 1924; organ of the Ministry of Defence; Editor V. L. CHUPAKHIN; circ. 122,000 (1995).

**Krestiyanskaya Rossiya** (Peasant Russia): 123022 Moscow, ul. 1905 goda 7; tel. (095) 259-47-98; fax (095) 259-93-37; weekly; f. 1906; Editor-in-Chief KONSTANTIN LYSENKO; circ. 90,000 (1995).

**Kuranty** (Chimes): 103009 Moscow, ul. Stankevicha 12; tel. (095) 203-06-10; fax (095) 292-55-15; f. 1991; 5 a week; Editor-in-Chief ANATOLY PANKOV; circ. 135,000 (1995).

**Moskovskaya Pravda** (Moscow Pravda): 123846 Moscow, ul. 1905 goda 7; tel. (095) 259-82-33; fax (095) 259-63-60; f. 1918; fmrly organ of the Moscow city committee of the CPSU and the Moscow City Soviet; 5 a week; independent; Editor SH. S. MULADZHANOV; circ. 431,000 (1995).

**Moskovsky Komsomolets** (Member of the Leninist Young Communist League of Moscow): 123848 Moscow, ul. 1905 goda 7; tel. (095) 259-50-36; fax (095) 259-43-58; f. 1919; 6 a week; independent; Editor-in-Chief PAVEL GUSEV; circ. 1,000,000 (1995).

**Novaya Ezhednevnaya Gazeta** (New Daily Newspaper): 125015 Moscow, Novodmitrovskaya ul. 5A; tel. (095) 285-89-27; f. 1993; 5 a week; Editor VLADIMIR LEPEKHIN; circ. 135,000 (1995).

**Obshchaya Gazeta** (General Newspaper): 121151 Moscow, Kutuzovsky pr. 22; tel. (095) 915-22-88; fax (095) 915-51-71; f. 1991; weekly; Editor-in-Chief YEGOR YAKOVLEV; circ. 100,000 (1995).

**Pravda** (Truth): 125867 Moscow, ul. Pravdy 24; tel. (095) 257-37-86; telex 411209; fax (095) 200-22-91; f. 1912; fmrly organ of the Cen. Cttee of the CPSU; independent; left-wing; Editor-in-Chief ALEKSANDR ILYIN; circ. 210,000 (1995).

**Rabochaya Tribuna** (Workers' Tribune): 125880 Moscow, ul. Pravdy 24; tel. (095) 257-27-51; telex 114040; fax (095) 973-20-02; f. 1969; fmrly organ of the Cen. Cttee of the CPSU; organ of the Federation of Independent Trade Unions of the Russian Federation and the Russian Union of Industrialists and Businessmen; Editor-in-Chief ANATOLY YURKOV; circ. 175,000 (1995).

**Rossiskaya Gazeta** (Russian Newspaper): 125881 Moscow, ul. Pravdy 24; tel. (095) 257-22-52; fax (095) 973-22-56; f. 1990; organ of the Russian Government; 5 a week; Editor-in-Chief N. POLEYAEVA; circ. 555,000 (1995).

**Rossiiskiye Vesti** (Russian News): 103379 Moscow, ul. Bolshaya Sadovaya 8, podyezd 4; tel. (095) 209-98-22; fax (095) 209-98-20; f. 1991; 5 a week; organ of the Presidential administration; Editor-in-Chief VALERY KUCHER; circ. 150,000 (1995).

**Rossiya** (Russia): 125865 Moscow, ul. Pravdy 24; tel. (095) 257-24-91; independent; weekly; Editor-in-Chief ALEKSANDR DROZDOV; circ. 81,500 (1995).

**Segodnya** (Today): 125865 Moscow, ul. Pravdy 24; tel. (095) 250-63-43; 5 a week; independent; Editor DMITRY V. OSTALSKY; circ. 100,000 (1995).

**Selskaya Zhizn** (Country Life): 125869 Moscow, ul. Pravdy 24; tel. (095) 257-29-63; fax (095) 257-20-00; f. 1918; 3 a week; fmrly organ of the Cen. Cttee of the CPSU; independent; Editor-in-Chief ALEKSANDR P. KHARLAMOV; circ. 221,500 (1995).

**Sovetskaya Rossiya** (Soviet Russia): 125868 Moscow, ul. Pravdy 24; tel. (095) 257-28-84; fax (095) 200-22-90; f. 1956; fmrly organ of the Cen. Cttee of the CPSU and the Russian Federation Supreme Soviet and Council of Ministers; 5 a week; independent; Editor V. CHIKIN; circ. 250,000 (1995).

**Trud** (Labour): 103792 Moscow, Nastasyinsky per. 4; tel. (095) 292-49-47; fax (095) 200-01-24; f. 1921; 6 a week; independent trade union newspaper; Editor ALEKSANDR S. POTAPOV; circ. 1,501,700 (1995).

**Vechernyaya Moskva** (Moscow Evening): 123846 Moscow, ul. 1905 goda 7; tel. (095) 259-05-26; fax (095) 253-95-75; f. 1923; independent; Chief Editor A. LISIN; Chief Exec. F. POSPELOU; circ. 360,000 (1995).

### St Petersburg

**Chas Pik** (Rush Hour): 191040 St Petersburg, Nevsky pr. 81; tel. (812) 279-25-65; fax (812) 277-13-40; f. 1990; weekly; Editor-in-Chief NATALIYA CHAPLINA; circ. 45,000 (1994).

**Sankt-Peterburgskiye Vedomosti** (St Petersburg News): 191023 St Petersburg, Fontanka 59; tel. (812) 314-71-76; f. 1918; fmrly *Leningradskaya Pravda* (Leningrad Truth); organ of the St Petersburg Mayoralty; Editor O. KUZIN; circ. 240,000 (1994).

**Vecherny Peterburg** (St Petersburg Evening): St Petersburg, Fontanka 59; tel. (812) 311-88-75; fax (812) 314-31-05; f. 1946; organ of the St Petersburg City Council; Editor V. MAYOROV; circ. 88,000 (1994).

## PRINCIPAL PERIODICALS
### Agriculture, Forestry, etc.

**Agrokhimiya** (Agricultural Chemistry): Moscow, Podsosensky per. 21; f. 1964; monthly; publ. by the Nauka (Science) Publishing House; journal of the Russian Academy of Sciences; results of theoretical and experimental research work; Editor N. N. MELNIKOV; circ. 5,900.

**Doklady Rossiiskoy Akademii Selskokhozaistvennykh Nauk** (Reports of the Russian Academy of Agricultural Sciences): 117218 Moscow, ul. Krzhizhanovsky 15; tel. (095) 207-76-60; f. 1936; 6 a year; the latest issues in agriculture; Editor-in-Chief N. S. MARKOVA; circ. 1,000.

**Ekonomika Selskokhozyaistvennykh i Pererabatyvayushchikh Predpriyatiyakh** (Economics of Agricultural and Processing Enterprises): 107807 Moscow, Sadovaya-Spasskaya ul. 18; tel. (095) 207-15-80; f. 1926; monthly; publ. by Kolos Publishing House and Ministry of Agriculture and Food; Editor V. A. ORLOV; circ. 25,970.

**Lesnaya Promyshlennost** (Forest Industry): 125047 Moscow, Bokzal pl. 3; tel. (095) 250-46-23; f. 1926; 3 a week; fmrly organ of the USSR State Committee for Forestry and the Cen. Cttee of the Timber, Paper and Wood Workers' Union of the USSR; Editor V. A. ALEKSEYEV; circ. 250,000.

**Mekhanizatsiya i Elektrifikatsiya Selskogo Khozyaistva** (Mechanization and Electrification of Agriculture): 107807 Moscow, Sadovaya-Spasskaya ul. 18; f. 1930; monthly; Editor I. E. CHESNOKOV; circ. 27,890.

**Mezhdunarodny Selsko-Khozhiaistveny Zhurnal** (International Agricultural Journal): 107807 Moscow, Sadovaya-Spasskaya ul. 18; tel. (095) 207-16-56; monthly.

**Molochnoye i Myasnoye Skotovodstvo** (Dairy and Meat Cattle Breeding): Moscow, Sadovaya-Spasskaya ul. 18; tel. (095) 207-21-20; f. 1956; 6 a year; Editor V. V. KORGENEVSKY; circ. 39,800.

**Selskokhozyaistvennaya Biologiya** (Agricultural Biology): 117218 Moscow, ul. Krzhizhanovsky 15; tel. (095) 921-93-88; f. 1966; 6 a year; publ. by the Russian Academy of Agricultural Sciences; Editor E. M. BORISOVA; circ. 1,000.

**Svinovodstvo** (Pig Breeding): Moscow, Sadovaya-Spasskaya ul. 18; f. 1930; 6 a year; Editor K. D. BAYEV; circ. 37,830.

**Tekhnika v Selskom Khozyaistve** (Agricultural Technology): 107807 Moscow, Sadovaya-Spasskaya ul. 18; tel. (095) 207-37-62; fax (095) 207-28-70; f. 1941; 6 a year; journal of the Ministry of Agriculture and Food Production and the Russian Academy of Agricultural Sciences; Editor-in-Chief PETR S. POPOV; circ. 4,000.

**Vestnik Selskokhozyaistvennoy Nauki** (Agrarian Science Bulletin): Moscow, Sadovaya-Spasskaya ul. 18; tel. (095) 207-18-37; f. 1956; every 2 months; produced by the Kolos Publishing House; Editor-in-Chief V. B. ZILBERQUIT; circ. 2,000.

**Veterinariya** (Veterinary Science): Moscow, Sadovaya-Spasskaya ul. 18; tel. (095) 207-10-60; fax (095) 207-28-70; f. 1924; monthly; Editor V. A. GARKAVTSEV; circ. 9,000.

**Zashchita Rastenii** (Plant Protection): 107807 Moscow, Sadovaya-Spasskaya ul. 18; tel. (095) 207-21-30; f. 1932; monthly; Editor V. E. SAVZDARG; circ. 22,000.

**Zemledeliye** (Farming): Moscow, Sadovaya-Spasskaya ul. 18; f. 1939; monthly; Editor V. IVANOV; circ. 53,000.

**Zhivotnovodstvo** (Cattle Breeding): Moscow, Sadovaya-Spasskaya ul. 18; f. 1928; monthly; Editor A. T. MYSIK; circ. 106,870.

### For Children

**Koster** (Campfire): 193024 St Petersburg, Mytninskaya ul. 1/20; tel. (0812) 274-15-72; telex 321584; f. 1936; monthly; fmrly journal of the Union of Pioneer Organizations (Federation of Children's Organizations) of the USSR; fiction, poetry, sport, reports and popular science; for 10–14 years; Editor-in-Chief O. A. TSAKUNOV; circ. 35,000 (1995).

**Murzilka**: 125015 Moscow, Novodmitrovskaya ul. 5A; tel. (095) 285-18-81; f. 1924; monthly; publ. by the Molodaya Gvardiya (Young Guard) Publishing House; fmrly journal of the Union of Pioneer Organizations (Federation of Children's Organizations) of the USSR; illustrated; for first grades of school; Editor T. ANDROSENKO; circ. 500,000 (1995).

**Pioner** (Pioneer): 101459 Moscow, Bumazhny proyezd 14; tel. (095) 257-34-27; f. 1924; monthly; fmrly journal of the Cen. Cttee of the Leninist Young Communist League; fiction; illustrated: for children of fourth–eighth grades; Editor A. S. MOROZ; circ. 32,400 (1995).

**Pionerskaya Pravda** (Pioneer Pravda): 101502 Moscow, Sushchevskaya ul. 21; tel. (095) 972-22-38; f. 1925; 3 a week; fmrly organ of the Union of Pioneer Organizations (Federation of Children's Organizations) of the USSR; Editor O. I. GREKOVA; circ. 88,500 (1995).

**Veselye Kartinki** (Merry Pictures): 125015 Moscow, Novodmitrovskaya ul. 5A; tel. (095) 285-80-90; f. 1956; monthly; publ. by the Molodaya Gvardiya (Young Guard) Publishing House; humorous; for pre-school and first grades; Editor R. A. VARSHAMOV; circ. 500,000.

**Yuny Naturalist** (Young Naturalist): Moscow, Novodmitrovskaya ul. 5A; f. 1928; monthly; publ. by the Molodaya Gvardiya (Young Guard) Publishing House; fmrly journal of the Union of Pioneer Organizations (Federation of Children's Organizations) of the USSR; popular science for children of fourth–10th grades who are interested in biology; Editor B. CHAKSHAGIN; circ. 69,000 (1994).

**Yuny Tekhnik** (Young Technologist): 125015 Moscow, Novodmitrovskaya ul. 5A; tel. (095) 285-80-81; f. 1956; monthly; publ. by the Molodaya Gvardiya (Young Guard) Publishing House; popular science for schoolchildren; Editor BORIS CHEREMISINOV; circ. 50,700 (1994).

### Culture and Arts

**7 Dnei** (7 Days): 129090 Moscow, Vtoroy Troitsky per. 4; tel. (095) 915-33-55; f. 1967; television listings magazine; Editor I. E. PETROVSKAYA; circ. 160,000 (1995).

**Avrora** (Aurora): 191065 St Petersburg, ul. Millionaya 4; tel. (095) 312-13-23; fax (095) 312-59-76; f. 1969; monthly; journal of the Russian Union of Writers; fiction; Editor-in-Chief E. SHEVELYOV; circ. 1,090,000.

**Biblioteka 'V Pomoshch Khudozhestvennoy Samodeyatelnosti'** (Amateur Art): Moscow; f. 1945; 2 a month; publ. by the Sovetskaya Rossiya (Soviet Russia) Publishing House; songs, plays and articles by leading actors; Editor N. M. SERGOVANTSEV; circ. 72,000.

**Dekorativnoye Iskusstvo** (Decorative Art): 103009 Moscow, ul. Tverskaya 9; tel. (095) 229-19-10; fax (095) 229-27-60; f. 1957; monthly; all aspects of contemporary visual art; illustrated; Editor A. KURKCHY; circ. 5,000 (1995).

**Ekran** (Screen Magazine): Moscow, ul. Chasovaya 5B; tel. (095) 152-79-37; fax (095) 152-97-91; f. 1925; 8 a year; publ. by the Pressa Publishing House; Russian and foreign cinema; Editor B. V. PINSKY; circ. 40,000 (1995).

**Film** (Film): 103009 Moscow, B. Gnezdnikovsky per. 9; tel. (095) 229-06-43; telex 411143; fax (095) 200-12-56; f. 1957; monthly; Russian, English, French, German and Spanish; illustrated; Russian and foreign films; Editor VALERY S. KICHIN; circ. 130,000.

**Foto** (Photography): Moscow, ul. Malaya Lubyanka 16; tel. (095) 924-93-05; fax (095) 925-10-07; f. 1926; 6 a year; journal of the Union of Journalists of Russia; Editor G. M. CHUDAKOV; circ. 20,000.

**Iskusstvo** (Art): Moscow, Vorotnikovsky per. 11; f. 1933; monthly; publ. by the Iskusstvo (Art) Publishing House; journal of the Union of Artists of Russia and the Russian Academy of Arts; fine arts; Editor V. ZIMENKO; circ. 18,500.

**Iskusstvo Kino** (Cinema Art): 125319 Moscow, Usievicha 9; tel. (095) 151-56-51; telex 411939; fax (095) 151-02-72; f. 1931; monthly; journal of the Russian Film-makers' Union; Editor DANIIL DONDUREY; circ. 10,000 (1995).

**Knizhnoye Obozreniye** (Book Review): 129272 Moscow, Sushchevsky val 64; tel. (095) 281-62-66; fax (095) 281-62-66; f. 1966;

# THE RUSSIAN FEDERATION

weekly; summaries of newly published books; Editor E. S. Averin; circ. 50,100 (1995).

**Kultura (Culture):** 101484 Moscow, ul. Novoslobodskaya 73; tel. (095) 214-60-31; f. 1929; fmrly *Sovetskaya Kultura* (Soviet Culture); weekly; Editor A. A. Belyayev; circ. 35,000 (1995).

**Kultura i Zhizn** (Culture and Life): 103674 Moscow, proyezd Sapunova 13–15; tel. (095) 921-35-60; f. 1957; monthly; Russian, English, French, Spanish and German; publ. by the Society for Cultural and Friendly Relations with Foreign Countries; Editor Ado Kukanov; circ. 16,300 (1994).

**Literaturnaya Gazeta** (Literary Newspaper): 103654 Moscow, Kostyansky per. 13; tel. (095) 200-24-17; telex 411294; fax (095) 200-02-38; f. 1830; publ. restored 1929; weekly; independent; fmrly organ of the USSR Writers' Union; Editor-in-Chief Arkady Udaltsov; circ. 325,000 (1995).

**Literaturnaya Rossiya** (Literary Russia): 103662 Moscow, Tsvetnoy bul. 30; tel. (095) 200-41-58; fax (095) 200-27-55; f. 1958; weekly; essays, verse, literary criticism, political reviews; Editor Ernst I. Safonov.

**Moskva** (Moscow): 121918 Moscow, Arbat 20; tel. (095) 291-71-10; f. 1957; monthly; journal of the Russian Federation Union of Writers and its Moscow branch; fiction; Editor-in-Chief Mikhail N. Alekseyev; circ. 20,000 (1995).

**Muzykalnaya Akademiya** (Musical Academy): 103009 Moscow, ul. Ogareva 13; tel. (095) 229-81-66; f. 1933; fmrly *Sovetskaya Muzyka* (Soviet Music); quarterly; publ. by the Kompozitor (Composer) Publishing House; journal of the Union of Composers of the Russian Federation and the Ministry of Culture; Editor Yu. S. Korev; circ. 2,000 (1994).

**Muzykalnaya Zhizn** (Musical Life): 103006 Moscow, Sadovaya-Triumfalnaya ul. 14–12; tel. (095) 209-75-24; f. 1957; fortnightly; publ. by the Kompozitor (Composer) Publishing House; journal of the Union of Composers of the Russian Federation and the Ministry of Culture; development of music; Editor J. Platek; circ. 12,700 (1995).

**Neva** (The River Neva): 191186 St Petersburg, Nevsky pr. 3; tel. (812) 312-65-37; fax (812) 311-61-18; f. 1955; monthly; journal of the St Petersburg Writers' Organization; fiction, poetry, literary criticism; Editor B. Nikolsky; circ. 30,000 (1995).

**Oktyabr** (October): Moscow, ul. Pravdy 11; tel. (095) 214-62-05; fax (095) 214-50-29; f. 1924; monthly; published by the Pressa Publishing House; independent literary journal; new fiction and essays by Russian and foreign writers; Editor A. A. Ananiyev; circ. 35,000 (1995).

**Teatr** (Theatre): 121069 Moscow, ul. Gertsena 49; tel. (095) 291-57-88; monthly; publ. by the Izvestiya (News) Publishing House; journal of the Theatrical Workers' Union and the Russian Federation Union of Writers; new plays by Russian and foreign playwrights; Editor A. Shub; circ. 50,000.

### Economics, Finance

**Dengi i Kredit** (Money and Credit): 103016 Moscow, Neglinnaya ul. 12; tel. (095) 925-45-03; f. 1927; monthly; publ. by the Finansy i statistika (Finances and Statistics) Publishing House; all aspects of banking and money circulation; Editor Y. G. Dmitriev; circ. 29,190.

**Ekonomika i Matematicheskiye Metody** (Economics and Mathematical Methods): 117418 Moscow, ul. Krasikova 32; tel. (095) 332-46-39; fax (095) 310-70-15; f. 1965; 4 a year; publ. by the Nauka (Science) Publishing House; journal of the Institute of Economics and Mathematics and the Institute of Market Problems; theoretical and methodological problems of economics, econometrics; Editor V. L. Makarov; circ. 1,570.

**Ekonomika i Zhizn** (Economics and Life): 101462 Moscow, Bumazhny proyezd 14; tel. (095) 250-57-93; fax (095) 212-30-93; f. 1918; weekly; fmrly *Ekonomicheskaya gazeta*; news and information about the economy and business; Editor Yuri Yakutin; circ. 1,100,000 (1995).

**Finansy** (Finances): 103050 Moscow, ul. Tverskaya 22b; tel. (095) 299-43-33; fax (095) 299-93-06; f. 1991; monthly; publ. by the Finansy (Finances) Publishing House; fmrly journal of the Ministry of Finance; theory and information on finances; compiling and execution of the state budget, insurance, lending, taxation etc.; Editor Yu. M. Artemov; circ. 25,280.

**Kommersant:** Moscow, Khoroshovskoye Shosse 41; tel. (095) 941-09-00; f. 1989; independent; economics, business and politics; Editor Mikhail Rogozhnikov; circ. 103,000 (1995).

**Mir Daidzhest Pressi** (Business World Press Digest): 191180 St Petersburg, POB 55; f. 1989; 8 a year; publ. by St Petersburg branch of Union of Journalists; all aspects of finance; Editors Yan Strugach, Sergei Grachev.

**Mirovaya Ekonomika i Mezhdunarodniye Otnosheniya** (World Economy and International Relations): Moscow, Profsoyuznaya ul. 23; tel. (095) 128-08-83; telex 411687; fax (095) 31-07-27; f. 1957; monthly; publ. by the Nauka (Science) Publishing House; journal of the Institute of the World Economy and International Relations of the Russian Academy of Sciences; problems of theory and practice of world socio-economic development, international policies, international economic co-operation, economic and political situation in different countries of the world, etc.; Editor Prof. G. G. Diligensky; circ. 5,058 (1994).

**Rossiisky Ekonomichesky Zhurnal** (Russian Economic Journal): 109542 Moscow, Ryazansky pr. 99; tel. (095) 377-25-56; f. 1958; monthly; fmrly *Ekonomicheskiye Nauki* (Economic Sciences); theory and practice of economics and economic reform; Editor A. Yu. Melentev; circ. 17,500.

**Voprosy Ekonomiki** (Problems of Economics): 117218 Moscow, ul. Krasikova 27; tel. (095) 129-04-44; fax (095) 124-52-28; f. 1929; monthly; journal of the Institute of Economics of the Russian Academy of Sciences; theoretical problems of economic develoment, market relations, social aspects of transition to a market economy, international economics, etc.; Editor L. Abalkin; circ. 10,800.

### Education

**Pedagogika** (Pedagogics): 119034 Moscow, Smolensky bul. 4; tel. (095) 248-51-49; f. 1937; monthly; publ. by Academy of Pedagogical Sciences; Chief Editor G. N. Filonov; circ. 46,500.

**Professionalno-tekhnicheskoye Obrazovaniye** (Vocational and Technical Education): 125319 Moscow, ul. Chernyakhovskogo 9; tel. (095) 152-75-41; f. 1941; monthly; Editor-in-Chief Vladimir G. Chernykh; circ. 35,000 (1991).

**Rodnoy Yazyk** (The Mother Tongue): 121819 Moscow, Trubnikovsky per. 19; f. 1993; 6 a year; Editor M. I. Isayev; circ. 2,000.

**Semya** (Family): Moscow; f. 1988; weekly; fmrly publ. by Soviet Children's Fund; Editor-in-Chief Sergey A. Abramov; circ. 500,000 (1995).

**Semya i Shkola** (Family and School): 129278 Moscow, ul. Pavla Korchagina 7; tel. (095) 283-80-09; f. 1871; monthly; Editor V. F. Smirnov; circ. 60,000.

**Shkola i Proizvodstvo** (School and Production): 103051 Moscow, Tsvetnoy bul. 2; tel. (095) 246-65-91; f. 1957; 6 a year; publ. by the Shkola (School) Publishing House; Editor Yu. Ye. Rives-Korobkov; circ. 205,000.

**Uchitelskaya Gazeta** (Teachers' Gazette): 103012 Moscow, Vetoshny proyezd 13/15; tel. (095) 928-82-53; f. 1924; weekly; independent pedagogical newspaper; distributed throughout the CIS; Editor P. Polozhevetz; circ. 200,000 (1995).

**Vestnik Vysshey Shkoly** (Higher Schools' Review): 103031 Moscow, ul. Rozhdestvenka 11; tel. (095) 924-73-43; f. 1940; monthly; Editor O. V. Dolzhenko; circ. 17,000.

**Vospitaniye Shkolnikov** (The Upbringing of Schoolchildren): Moscow, Lefortovsky per. 8; f. 1966; 6 a year; publ. by Pedagogika (Pedagogics) Publishing House; Editor L. V. Kuznetsova; circ. 733,230.

### International Affairs

**Ekho Planety** (Echo of the Planet): 103009 Moscow, Tverskoy bul. 10–12; tel. (095) 202-69-96; fax (095) 229-06-37; f. 1988; weekly; publ. by ITAR—TASS; international affairs, economic, social and cultural; Editor-in-Chief Valentin Vasilets; circ. 50,000 (1995).

**Mezhdunarodnaya Zhizn** (International Life): 103064 Moscow, Gorokhovsky per. 14; tel. (095) 265-37-81; f. 1954; monthly; Russian, English and French; publ. by the Pressa Publishing House; problems of foreign policy and diplomacy of Russia and other countries; Editor B. D. Pyadyshev; circ. 71,620.

**Novoye Vremya** (New Times): 103782 Moscow, pl. Pushkina 5; tel. (095) 229-88-72; telex 411164; fax (095) 200-41-92; f. 1943; weekly; Russian, English, French, German, Spanish, Portuguese, Italian, Polish, Greek and Czech; publ. by the Moskovskaya Pravda Publishing House; foreign and Russian affairs; Editor A. Pumpyansky; circ. 25,000 (1995).

**Za Rubezhom** (Abroad): 125865 Moscow, ul. Pravdy 24; tel. (095) 257-23-87; telex 411421; fax (095) 200-22-96; f. 1960; weekly; publ. by the Pressa Publishing House; review of foreign press; Editor-in-Chief S. Morozov; circ. 650,000.

### Language, Literature

**Filologicheskiye Nauki** (Philological Sciences): Moscow, Okhotny ryad 18; f. 1958; 6 a year; publ. by the Vysshaya Shkola (Higher School) Publishing House; reports of institutions of higher learning on the most important problems of literary studies and linguistics; Editor P. A. Nikolayev; circ. 2,960.

**Lepta** (Mite): 121248 Moscow, Kutuzovsky pr. 1/7; tel. (095) 243-38-78; fax (095) 243-03-66; f. 1931; fmrly *Sovetskaya Literatura*

# THE RUSSIAN FEDERATION

(Soviet Literature); monthly; English and Russian; novels, short stories, verses, poems, literary criticism, non-fiction and topical articles; Editor ALEKSEY BARKHATOV; circ. 50,000.

**Russkaya Literatura** (Russian Literature): 199164 St Petersburg, nab. Makarova 4; f. 1958; quarterly; journal of the Institute of Russian Literature of the Russian Academy of Sciences; development of Russian literature from its appearance up to the present day; Editor V. V. SKATOV; circ. 13,149.

**Russkaya Rech** (Russian Speech): Moscow, ul. Volkhonka 18/2; f. 1967; 6 a year; publ. by the Nauka (Science) Publishing House; journal of the Institute of Russian Language of the Academy of Sciences; popular; history of the development of the literary Russian language; Editor V. P. VOMPENSKY; circ. 7,300.

**Russky Yazyk za Rubezhom** (The Russian Language Abroad): 117485 Moscow, ul. Volgina 6; tel. (095) 336-66-47; f. 1967; 6 a year; publ. by the Russky Yazyk (Russian Language) Publishing House; journal of the Pushkin Institute of the Russian Language; current problems of methodology of teaching the Russian language to foreigners; Editor A. V. ABRAMOVICH; circ. 44,300.

**Voprosy Literatury** (Questions of Literature): 103009 Moscow, Bolshoy Gnezdnikovsky per. 10; tel. (095) 229-49-77; f. 1957; 6 a year; joint edition of the Institute of World Literature of the Academy of Sciences and the Literary Thought Foundation; theory and history of modern literature and aesthetics; Editor L. I. LAZAREV; circ. 10,000.

**Voprosy Yazykoznaniya** (Questions of Linguistics): 121019 Moscow, Volkhonka 18/2; tel. (095) 201-74-42; f. 1952; 6 a year; publ. by the Nauka (Science) Publishing House; journal of the Department of Literature and Language of the Russian Academy of Sciences; actual problems of general linguistics on the basis of different languages; Editor N. I. TOLSTOY; circ. 2,800.

### Leisure, Physical Culture and Sport

**Filateliya** (Philately): 121069 Moscow, Khlebny per. 8; f. 1966; monthly; journal of the Publishing and Trading Centre 'Marka'; Editor-in-Chief ZH. G. BEKHTEREV; circ. 4,600.

**Fizkultura i Sport** (Physical Culture and Sport): Moscow, Kalyayevskaya ul. 27; f. 1922; monthly; publ. by the Beta-print Publishing House; fmrly journal of the USSR State Committee for Physical Culture and Sport; activities and development of Russian sport; Editor A. CHAIKOVSKY; circ. 717,000.

**Mir Puteshestvy** (World of Travels): 107078 Moscow, Bolshoi Kharitonyevsky per. 14; tel. (095) 923-64-23; telex 230-27-84; f. 1929, fmrly *Turist*; journal of the Sputnik tourist company; monthly; publ. by the Profizdat (Trade Union Literature) Publishing House; articles, photo-essays, information, recommendations about routes and hotels for tourists, natural, cultural and historical places of interest; Editor BORIS V. MOSKVIN; circ. 10,000.

**Shakhmatny Vestnik** (Chess Herald): 121019 Moscow, POB 10, Gogolevsky bul. 14; tel. (095) 291-87-70; f. 1921; fmrly *Shakhmaty v SSSR* (Chess in the USSR); monthly; publ. by the Beta-print Publishing House; journal of the Russian Chess Federation and International Chess Players' Union; Editor Y. AVERBAKH; circ. 15,000.

**Sportivnye Igry** (Sports): 101421 Moscow, Kalyayevskaya ul. 27; tel. (095) 258-06-56; fax (095) 200-12-17; f. 1955; monthly; publ. by the Fizkultura i Sport (Physical Culture and Sport) Publishing House; fmrly journal of the USSR State Committee for Physical Culture and Sport; Editor D. L. RYZHKOV; circ. 160,000.

**Sport, Rossiya i Mir** (Sport, Russia and the World): 103772 Moscow, ul. Moskvina 8; tel. (095) 229-14-19; f. 1963; monthly; Russian, English, Spanish, and Hindi; publ. by Voskresenye Publishing Corporation; illustrated; Editor A. POLITKOVSKY.

**Teoriya i Praktika Fizicheskoy Kultury** (Theory and Practice of Physical Culture): Moscow, Kalyayevskaya ul. 27; f. 1925; monthly; publ. by the Fizkultura i Sport (Physical Culture and Sport) Publishing House; fmrly journal of the USSR State Committee for Physical Culture and Sport; Editor A. V. SEDOV; circ. 16,200.

### Politics and Military Affairs

**Ekspress-Khronika** (Express-Chronicle): 111399 Moscow, POB 5; tel. (095) 264-97-91; fax (095) 264-57-42; f. 1987; weekly; independent chronicle of events throughout the former USSR; also an edition in English; Editor ALEKSANDR PODRABINEK.

**Moskovskiye Novosti** (Moscow News): 103829 Moscow, ul. Tverskaya 16/2; tel. (095) 209-19-84; fax (095) 209-17-28; f. 1930; weekly in English. 2 a week in Russian; independent; Editor-in-Chief VIKTOR LOSHAK; circ. 250,000.

**Politicheskoye Obrazovaniye** (Political Education): Moscow, ul. Pravdy 24; f. 1957; monthly; publ. by the Pressa Publishing House; fmrly journal of the Cen. Cttee of the CPSU; Editor N. Y. KLEPACH; circ. 1,862,000.

*Directory*

**Rossiyskaya Federatsiya**: Moscow, Staraya pl. 4; f. 1994; journal of the Russian Govt.

**Svobodnaya Mysl** (Free Thought): 119875 Moscow, ul. Marksa i Engelsa 5; tel. (095) 291-60-67; f. 1924; fmrly *Kommunist* (Communist), the theoretical journal of the Cen. Cttee of the CPSU; 18 a year; problems of political theory, philosophy, economy, etc.; Editor-in-Chief N. B. BIKKENIN; circ. 995,000.

### Popular, Fiction and General

**Druzhba Narodov** (Friendship of Peoples): 121827 Moscow, ul. Vorovskogo 52; tel. (095) 291-62-27; f. 1939; monthly; publ. by the Izvestiya (News) Publishing House; independent; prose, poetry and literary criticism; Editor A. RUDENKO-DESNYAK; circ. 250,000.

**Inostrannaya Literatura** (Foreign Literature): Moscow, Pyatnitskaya ul. 41; tel. (095) 233-51-47; fax (095) 230-23-03; f. 1955; monthly; publ. by the Izvestiya (News) Publishing House; independent; Russian translations of modern foreign authors; Editor-in-Chief VLADIMIR LAKSHIN; circ. 200,000.

**Moskva** (Moscow): Moscow, ul. Arbat 20; f. 1957; monthly; publ. by the Khudozhestvennaya Literatura (Fiction) Publishing House; Editor M. N. ALEKSEYEV; circ. 760,000.

**Nash Sovremennik** (Our Contemporary): Moscow, Tsvetnoy bul. 30; f. 1933; monthly; publ. by the Literaturnaya Gazeta (Literary Gazette) Publishing House; Editor STANISLAV KUNAYEV; circ. 270,000.

**Novy Mir** (New World): 103806 Moscow, Maly Putinkovsky per. 1/2; tel. (095) 200-08-29; fax (095) 200-09-34; f. 1925; monthly; publ. by the Izvestiya (News) Publishing House; new fiction and essays; Editor SERGEY P. ZALYGIN; circ. 25,800.

**Ogonek** (Beacon): 101456 Moscow, Bumazhny per. 14; tel. (095) 257-36-69; fax (095) 943-00-70; f. 1923; weekly; independent; popular illustrated; Editor LEV GUSHCHIN; circ. 1,500,000.

**Rodina** (Motherland): 103132 Moscow, Vozdvizhenka 4/7; f. 1989; monthly; popular historical; illustrated; Editor V. DOLMATOV; circ. 100,000 (1994).

**Roman-Gazeta** (Novels): Moscow, Novo-Basmannaya ul. 19; tel. 261-49-29; f. 1927; fortnightly; contemporary fiction including translations into Russian; Editor V. GANICHEV; circ. 100,000.

**Stolitsa** (Capital): 101425 Moscow, ul. Petrovka 22; tel. (095) 928-23-49; telex 413739; fax (095) 921-29-85; f. 1990; weekly; general; Editor ANDREY MALGIN; circ. 100,000.

**Vokrug Sveta** (Around the World): 125015 Moscow, Novodmitrovskaya ul. 5A; tel. (095) 285-88-83; fax (095) 972-05-72; f. 1861; monthly, including the supplement *Iskatel* (Seeker) in alternate issues and the book supplement *Library of Vokrug Sveta*; publ. by Vokrug Sveta joint stock co; geographical, travel, adventure and science fiction, detective stories; illustrated; Editor A. A. POLESHCHUK; circ. 210,000.

**Voskreseniye** (Resurrection): 103772 Moscow, ul. Moskvina 8; tel. (095) 229-14-19; fax (095) 229-74-14; f. 1930; monthly; Russian, English, French, German, Spanish; publ. by the New Russia Publishing Corporation; illustrated; Editor A. N. MISHARIN.

**Zakon** (Law): 103798 Moscow, Pushkinskaya pl. 5; tel. (095) 299-74-55; f. 1991; publ. by the Izvestiya printing house; publishes legislation relating to business and commerce; legal issues for businessmen; Editor YURY FEOFANOV.

**Znamya** (Banner): Moscow, ul. Nikolskaya 8/1; f. 1931; monthly; independent; novels, poetry, essays; Editor-in-Chief SERGEY CHUPRININ; circ. 64,400.

**Zvezda** (Star): St Petersburg, Mokhovaya 20; tel. (812) 272-89-48; f. 1924; monthly; publ. by the Zvezda Publishing House; journal of the Russian Federation Union of Writers; novels, short stories, poetry and literary criticism; Editors A. YA. ARZHEV, I. A. GORDIN; circ. 43,000.

### Popular Scientific

**HF Magazine**: 103045 Moscow, Selivertsov per. 10; tel. (095) 292-65-11; f. 1992; 6 a year; supplement to *Radio*; Chief Editor B. G. STEPANOV; circ. 5,000.

**Meditsinskaya Gazeta** (Medical Gazette): 129010 Moscow, Sukharevskaya pl. 1/2; tel. (095) 208-86-95; f. 1938; 2 a week; organ of the Union of Medical Workers of Russia; Editor K. V. SHEGLOV; circ. 1,430,000.

**Modelist-Konstruktor** (Modelling-Designing): 125015 Moscow, ul. Novodmitrovskaya 5A; tel. (095) 285-17-04; f. 1962; monthly; publ. by the Molodaya Gvardiya (Young Guard) Publishing House; designs and descriptions of technical models; Editor A. RAGUZIN; circ. 60,000.

**Nauka i Religiya** (Science and Religion): 109004 Moscow, Ulyanovskaya 43; f. 1959; monthly; Editor V. F. PRAVOTVOROV; circ. 480,000.

**Nauka i Zhizn** (Science and Life): 101877 Moscow, ul. Myasnitskaya 24; tel. (095) 923-21-22; fax (095) 200-22-59; f. 1934; monthly; publ. by the Pressa Publishing House; popular; recent developments in all branches of science and technology; Chief Editor I. K. LAGOVSKY; circ. 130,000.

**Priroda** (Nature): 117069 Moscow, Maronovsky per. 26; tel. (095) 238-26-33; f. 1912; monthly; publ. by the Nauka (Science) Publishing House; journal of the Presidium of the Academy of Sciences; popular; natural sciences; Editor A. F. ANDREYEV; circ. 25,000.

**Radio**: 103045 Moscow, Seliverstov per. 10; tel. (095) 207-68-89; fax (095) 208-13-11; f. 1924; monthly; audio, video, communications, practical electronics, computers; Editor A. V. GOROKHOVSKY; circ. 87,000.

**Tekhnika-Molodezhi** (Engineering—For Youth): 125015 Moscow, Novodmitrovskaya ul. 5A; tel. (095) 285-89-81; fax (095) 285-16-87; f. 1933; monthly; popular; engineering and science; Editor A. N. PEREVOZCHIKOV; circ. 115,000.

**Vrach** (Physician): 119435 Moscow, ul. Pogodinskaya 7; tel. (095) 248-57-27; fax (095) 248-02-14; f. 1990; monthly; medical, scientific and socio-political; illustrated; Editor-in-Chief MIKHAIL A. PALTSEV; circ. 100,000.

**Zdorovye** (Health): Moscow, Bumazhny per. 24; f. 1955; monthly; publ. by the Pressa Publishing House; publ. by the Ministry of Health; popular scientific; medicine and hygiene; Editor M. D. PIRADOVA; circ. 16,800,000.

**Zemlya i Vselennaya** (Earth and Universe): Moscow, Maronovsky per. 26; tel. (095) 238-42-32; f. 1965; 6 a year; publ. by the Nauka (Science) Publishing House; joint edition of the Academy of Sciences and the Society of Astronomy and Geodesy; popular; current hypotheses of the origin and development of the earth and universe; astronomy, geophysics and space research; Editor V. K. ABALAKIN; circ. 7,500.

**Znaniye—Sila** (Knowledge is Strength): 113114 Moscow, Kozhevnicheskaya ul. 19; tel. (095) 235-89-35; f. 1926; monthly; publ. by the Znaniye (Knowledge) Publishing House; general scientific; Editor G. A. ZELENKO; circ. 350,000.

### The Press, Printing and Bibliography

**Bibliografiya** (Bibliography): 129272 Moscow, Sushchevsky val 64; tel. (095) 284-57-65; f. 1929; 6 a year; publ. by the Knizhnaya Palata (Book Chamber) Publishing House; theoretical, practical and historical aspects of bibliography; Editor G. A. ALEKSEEVA; circ. 5,000.

**Knizhnaya Letopis** (Book Chronicle): 127018 Moscow, Oktyabrskaya ul. 4; tel. (095) 288-92-01; f. 1907; weekly; publ. by the Knizhnaya palata (Book Chamber) Publishing House; registration of all books published in the CIS, with description of books; Editors V. N. TYURICHEVA, G. N. DMITRIYENKO; circ. 1,600.

**Notnaya Letopis** (Chronicle of Music): 127018 Moscow, Oktyabrskaya ul. 4; tel. (095) 288-92-38; f. 1931; monthly; publ. by the Knizhnaya palata (Book Chamber) Publishing House; registration of issues of music in the CIS; Editors N. A. ROSTOVSKAYA, G. N. DMITRIYENKO; circ. 776.

**Poligrafiya** (Printing): 129272 Moscow, Sushchevsky val 64; tel. (095) 281-74-81; fax (095) 288-97-66; f. 1924; 6 a year; equipment and technology of the printing industry; Dir N. N. KONDRATIYEVA; circ. 10,000.

**Slovo** (Word): 129272 Moscow, Sushchevsky val 64; tel. (095) 281-50-98; f. 1936; monthly; fmrly *V Mire Knig* (in the World of Books); publ. by the Knizhnaya Palata (Book Chamber) Publishing House; reviews of new books, theoretical problems of literature, historical and religious; Editor A. V. LARIONOV; circ. 10,000.

**Zhurnalist** (Journalist): 101453 Moscow, Bumazhny proyezd 14; tel. (095) 257-30-58; fax (095) 257-35-89; f. 1920; monthly; journal of the Confederation of Journalists' Unions; problems of professionalism, journalistic ethics and the life of journalists; Editor D. S. AVRAAMOV; circ. 10,000.

### Religion

**Bratsky Vestnik** (Herald of the Brethren): 109028 Moscow, Maly Vuzovsky per. 3; tel. (095) 916-08-68; fax (095) 916-39-90; f. 1945; 6 a year; organ of the Euro-Asiatic Federation of the Unions of Evangelical Christians-Baptists; Chief Editor G. I. KOMENDANT; circ. 10,000 (1995).

**Pravoslavnaya Beseda** (Orthodox Discussion): Moscow; f. 1991; publ. by the Orthodox Brotherhood.

**Zhurnal Moskovskoy Patriarkhii** (Journal of the Moscow Patriarchate): 119435 Moscow, Pogodinskaya 20; tel. (095) 246-98-48 (Russian), (095) 245-14-41 (English); fax (095) 230-27-35; f. 1931; monthly; publ. by the Patriarchate in Russian and English; Editor Metropolitan PITIRIM (K. V. NECHAEV); circ. 40,000.

### Satirical

**Krokodil** (Crocodile): 101455 Moscow, Bumazhny proyezd 14; tel. (095) 250-10-86; f. 1922; 3 a month; publ. by the Pressa Publishing House; Editor A. S. PYANOV; circ. 2,200,000.

### Trade, Trade Unions, Labour and Social Security

**Chelovek i Trud** (Man and Labour): 103062 Moscow, Lyalin per. 14; tel. (095) 297-29-67; monthly; employment issues and problems of unemployment; Editor-in-Chief G. L. PODVOYSKY; circ. 40,000.

**Profsoyuzy** (Trade Unions): 101000 Moscow, ul. Myasnitskaya 13; tel. (095) 921-36-73; f. 1917; monthly; fmrly publ. by the General Confederation of Trade Unions of the USSR; Editor M. P. MUDROV; circ. 50,000.

**Sotsialnoye Obespecheniye** (Social Security): Moscow, ul. Shabolovka 14; f. 1926; monthly; journal of the Ministry of Social Welfare of the Population; Editor L. S. MALANCHEV.

**Torgovlya** (Trade): Moscow, Berezhkovskaya nab. 6; tel. (095) 240-48-37; f. 1927; monthly; fmrly *Sovetskaya Torgovlya*; Editor M. M. LYSOV; circ. 50,000.

**Vneshnyaya Torgovlya** (Foreign Trade): 121108 Moscow, ul. Minskaya 11; tel. (095) 145-68-94; fax (095) 145-51-92; f. 1921; monthly; Russian and English; fmrly organ of the Ministry of Foreign Economic Relations; Editor-in-Chief V. N. DUSHENKIN; circ. 25,000.

### Transport and Communication

**Avtomatika, Telemekhanika i Svyaz** (Automation, Telemechanics and Communication): Moscow, Krasnovorotsky proyezd 3B; f. 1923; monthly; publ. by the Transport Publishing House; fmrly journal of the USSR Ministry of Railway Transport; utilization of new equipment in rail transport; Editor L. P. SLOBODYANYUK; circ. 27,780.

**Grazhdanskaya Aviyatsiya** (Civil Aviation): Moscow; f. 1931; monthly; journal of the Union of Civil Aviation Workers; development of air transport; utilization of aviation in construction, agriculture and forestry; Editor A. M. TROSHIN.

**Radiotekhnika** (Radio Engineering): Moscow, Kuznetsky most 20; f. 1937; monthly; publ. by the Svyaz (Communication) Publishing House; journal of the A. S. Popov Scientific and Technical Society of Radio Engineering, Electronics and Electrical Communication; theoretical and technical problems of radio engineering; Editor A. L. MIKAELYAN.

**Radiotekhnika i Elektronika** (Radio Engineering and Electronics): Moscow, Mokhovaya ul. 11; tel. (095) 203-47-89; f. 1956; monthly; journal of the Russian Academy of Sciences; theory of radio engineering; Editor N. D. DEVYATKOV; circ. 8,098.

**Vestnik Svyazi** (Herald of Communication): Moscow, ul. Kazakova 8A; tel. (095) 261-05-55; f. 1917; monthly; publ. by the IRIAS Agency; mechanization and automation of production; Editor E. B. KONSTANTINOV; circ. 9,000.

### For Women

**Krestyanka** (Peasant Woman): 101460 Moscow, Bumazhny per. 14; tel. (095) 257-39-39; fax (095) 257-39-63; f. 1922; monthly; publ. by the Krestyanka Publishing House; popular; Editor A. V. KOUPRIYANOVA; circ. 600,000 (1995).

**Mir Zhenshchiny** (Woman's World): 125267 Moscow, Miusskaya pl. 6; tel. (095) 250-15-56; f. 1945; monthly; fmrly *Zhenshchina* (Woman); Russian, Chinese, English, French, German, Hindi, Hungarian, Japanese, Korean, Bengali, Arabic, Spanish, Portuguese, Finnish and Vietnamese; fmrly publ. by the Soviet Women's Committee and the General Confederation of Trade Unions; popular; illustrated; Editor-in-Chief V. I. FEDOTOVA; circ. 105,000 (1995).

**Moda i Mir** (Fashion and the World): 103031 Moscow, Kuznetsky most 7/9; tel. (095) 921-73-93; annually; Editor (vacant); circ. 250,000.

**Modeli Sezona** (Models of the Season): 103031 Moscow, Kuznetsky most 7/9; tel. (095) 921-73-93; f. 1957; 4 a year; Editor-in-Chief N. A. KASATKINA; circ. 150,000.

**Rabotnitsa** (Working Woman): 101460 Moscow, Bumazhny per. 14; f. 1914; monthly; publ. by the Pressa Publishing House; popular; Editor Z. P. KRYLOVA; circ. 20,500,000.

**Zhurnal Mod** (Fashion Journal): 103031 Moscow, Kuznetsky most 7/9; tel. (095) 921-73-93; f. 1945; 4 a year; Editor-in-Chief N. A. KASATKINA; circ. 250,000.

### Youth

**Molodaya Gvardiya** (Young Guard): 125015 Moscow, Novodmitrovskaya ul. 5A; tel. (095) 285-88-58; f. 1922; monthly; publ. by the Molodaya Gvardiya (Young Guard) Publishing House; fiction, criticism, popular science; Editor A. IVANOV; circ. 640,000.

**Perspektivy** (Perspectives): 125015 Moscow, Novodmitrovskaya ul. 5A; tel. (095) 285-88-05; telex 411261; fax (095) 972-05-82; f. 1918; monthly; publ. by the Molodaya Gvardiya (Young Guard) Publishing House; fmrly *Molodoy Kommunist* (Young Communist), the journal of the Cen. Cttee of the Leninist Young Communist League; Editor Z. G. APRESYAN; circ. 630,000.

# THE RUSSIAN FEDERATION

**Rovesnik** (Contemporary): 125015 Moscow, Novodmitrovskaya ul. 5A; tel. (095) 285-89-20; fax (095) 285-88-44; f. 1962; publ. by the Molodaya Gvardiya (Young Guard) Publishing House; fmrly journal of the Cen. Cttee of the Leninist Young Communist League and the Publishing-Printing Unit of Molodaya Gvardiya; popular illustrated monthly of fiction, music, cinema, sport and other aspects of youth culture; Editor I. A. TCHERNYSHKOV; circ. 240,000.

**Selskaya Molodezh** (Rural Youth): Moscow, Novodmitrovskaya ul. 5A; tel. (095) 285-80-04; fax (095) 285-08-30; f. 1925; monthly; publ. by the Molodaya Gvardiya (Young Guard) Publishing House; fmrly journal of the Cen. Cttee of the Leninist Young Communist League; popular illustrated, fiction, verses, problems of rural youth; Editor A. SHEVELEV; circ. 26,000.

**Smena** (Rising Generation): 101457 Moscow, Bumazhny proyezd 14; tel. (095) 212-15-07; fax (095) 250-59-28; f. 1924; monthly; publ. by the Pressa Publishing House; popular illustrated, short stories, essays and problems of youth; Editor-in-Chief M. G. KIZILOV; circ. 98,000.

**Yunost** (Youth): Moscow, ul. Tverskaya 32/1; f. 1955; monthly; publ. by the Pressa Publishing House; journal of the Russian Federation Union of Writers; novels, short stories, essays and poems by beginners; Editor A. DEMENTEV; circ. 3,300,000.

## NEWS AGENCIES

**Informatsionnoye Telegrafnoye Agentstvo Rossii—Telegrafnoye Agentstvo Suverennykh Stran (ITAR—TASS)** (Information Telegraphic Agency of Russia—Telegraphic Agency of the Sovereign Countries): Moscow, Tverskoy bul. 10; tel. (095) 229-79-25; telex 411186; fax (095) 203-31-80; f. 1925; state information agency; Dir-Gen. VITALY N. IGNATENKO.

**Interfax:** 103006 Moscow, 1-aya Tverskaya-Yamskaya ul. 2; tel. (095) 250-92-03; telex 612176; fax (095) 250-89-94; f. 1989; independent news agency; Pres. M. KOMISSAR.

**Postfactum:** Moscow, ul. 1905 goda 7; tel. (095) 259-03-25; telex 412415; fax (095) 259-20-14; f. 1987; independent news agency; Pres. GLEB O. PAVLOVSKY; Chief Exec. KIRILL V. TANAYEV.

**Rossiyskoye Informatsionnoye Agentstvo—Novosti (RIA—Novosti)** (Russian Information Agency—Novosti Press Agency): 103786 Moscow, Zubovsky bul. 4; tel. (095) 201-50-60; telex 411102; fax (095) 201-45-46; f. 1961; collaborates by arrangement with foreign press and publishing organizations in 110 countries of the world; Chair. VLADIMIR MARKOV.

### Foreign Bureaux

**Agence France-Presse (AFP):** Moscow, Sadovo-Samotechnaya ul. 12/24, kv. 67–68; tel. (095) 200-12-44; telex 413321; fax (095) 200-19-46; Dir BERNARD ESTRADE.

**Agencia EFE** (Spain): 103051 Moscow, Sadovo-Samotechnaya ul. 12/24, kv. 23; tel. (095) 200-15-32; telex 413114; fax (095) 200-02-19; Bureau Chief SILVIA ODORIZ GONZÁLEZ.

**Agenzia Nazionale Stampa Associata (ANSA)** (Italy): 121248 Moscow, Kutuzovsky pr. 9, kv. 12–14; tel. (095) 230-27-54; telex 413451; fax (095) 243-06-37; Bureau Chief ALESSANDRO PARONE.

**Anatolian News Agency** (Turkey): Moscow, Rublevskoe shosse 26, kor. 1, kv. 279; tel. (095) 415-44-19; telex 413641; fax (095) 415-29-34; Correspondent REMZI ONER OZKAN.

**Associated Press (AP)** (USA): Moscow, Kutuzovsky pr. 7/4, kor. 5, kv. 33; tel. (095) 243-51-53; telex 413422; fax (095) 230-2845; Bureau Chief BARRY RENFREW.

**Baltic News Service** (News Agency of Estonia, Latvia and Lithuania): Moscow, Kalashny per. 8; tel. (095) 202-38-05; fax (095) 202-75-05; Bureau Chief GEORGE SHABAD.

**Bulgarska Telegrafna Agentsia (BTA)** (Bulgaria): Moscow, Kutuzovsky pr. 9, kor. 2, kv. 64–65; tel. (095) 243-65-80; telex 414494; Correspondent NACHO HALACHEV.

**Česká tisková kancelář (ČTK)** (Czech Republic): 125047 Moscow, 3-ya Tverskaya-Yamskaya ul. 31/35, kor. 5, kv. 96; tel. (095) 251-71-63; telex 414463; fax (095) 258-76-07; Correspondent VÁCLAV FRANK.

**Dan News Agency** (Argentina): Moscow, pl. Vosstaniya 1, kv. 371; tel. (095) 255-47-21; telex 413361; Correspondent ILDA RANDI.

**Deutsche Presse-Agentur (dpa)** (Germany): Moscow, Kutuzovsky pr. 7/4, kv. 210; tel. (095) 243-97-90; telex 413122; fax (095) 230-25-43; Correspondent Dr FRANZ SMETS.

**Excelsior** (Mexico): 123056 Moscow, Bolshoy Gruzinsky per. 3, kv. 266; tel. (095) 250-41-65; telex 413013; Correspondent MIGUEL ANGEL BARBERENA.

**Interpress** (Poland): 121248 Moscow, Kutuzovsky pr. 7/4, kor. 6, kv. 63; tel. (095) 243-75-23; telex 414376; Bureau Chief TOMAS PIVOVARUN.

**Iraqi News Agency:** Moscow, ul. Pogodinskaya 12; tel. (095) 316-99-75; telex 413484; Correspondent AHMED SAKRAN KDEP.

**Islamic Republic News Agency (IRNA)** (Iran): Moscow, Rublevskoye shosse 36, kor. 2, kv. 264; tel. (095) 415-43-62; telex 413715; fax (095) 415-42-88; Bureau Chief JAMSHID SHAFIEI.

**Jiji Tsushin-sha (Jiji Press)** (Japan): Moscow, Sadovaya-Samotechnaya ul. 12/24, kv. 21; tel. (095) 200-10-17; telex 413137; fax (095) 200-02-31; Bureau Chief MASAO OMURO.

**Korea Central News Agency** (Democratic People's Republic of Korea): Moscow, ul. Mosfilmovskaya 72; tel. (095) 143-90-71; Bureau Chief CHAN KON SOB.

**Kuwait News Agency (KUNA):** Moscow, Korovy val 7, kv. 52; tel. (095) 237-49-32; telex 413463; fax (095) 230-25-10; Correspondent ADIB AL-SAYYED.

**Kyodo News Service** (Japan): 121059 Moscow, B. Dorogomilovskaya 12; tel. (095) 956-60-22; fax (095) 956-60-26; Bureau Chief HIROYASU YAMAZAKI.

**Magyar Távirati Iroda (MTI)** (Hungary): Moscow, Bolshaya Spasskaya ul. 12, kv. 46; tel. (095) 280-04-21; telex 414419; fax (095) 280-04-21; Bureau Chief LORANT KOTI.

**Middle East News Agency (MENA)** (Egypt): Moscow, Sokolnichesky val 24, kor. 2, kv. 176; tel. (095) 264-82-76; fax (095) 288-95-27; Correspondent Dr MAMDOUH MUSTAFA.

**Mongol Tsahilgaan Medeeniy Agentlag (Montsame)** (Mongolia): Moscow, ul. Gilyarovskogo 8, kv. 81–82; tel. (095) 284-48-14; fax (095) 229-98-83; Bureau Chief CH. TUMENDELGER.

**News Agency of Nigeria (NAN)** (Nigeria): Moscow, Leninsky pr. 148, kv. 231; tel (095) 434-73-07; telex 413914; Correspondent VICTOR A. UDOM.

**News Agencies of Sweden, Norway, Denmark and Finland:** Moscow, Kutuzovsky pr. 7/4, 196; tel. (095) 243-06-74; fax (095) 956-60-50; Correspondent ANDERS RHODINER.

**Novinska Agencija Tanjug** (Yugoslavia): Moscow, pr. Mira 74, kv. 124; tel. (095) 971-01-77; Bureau Chief GEORGE MILOCEVIĆ.

**Polska Agencja Prasowa (PAP)** (Poland): Moscow, Leninsky pr. 45, kv. 411; tel. and fax (095) 135-11-06; telex 414367; Bureau Chief ZDZISŁAW RACZYŃSKI.

**Prensa Latina** (Cuba): 103031 Moscow, ul. Petrovka 15, kv. 22; tel. (095) 208-10-51; telex 414476; fax (095) 921-76-98; Chief Correspondent LUIS ENRIQUE GONZÁLEZ.

**Press Trust of India:** 129041 Moscow, Bolshaya Pereyaslavskaya ul. 7, kv. 133–134; tel. (095) 280-27-49; telex 413319; fax (095) 230-65-39; Correspondent NANDAN KRISHNAN.

**Reuters** (United Kingdom): 125167 Moscow, Leningradsky pr. 37, kor. 9; tel. (095) 241-01-27; telex 413342; fax (095) 213-92-20; Chief Representative MICHAEL SCHUBAKOFF.

**Rompres** (Romania): Moscow, Kutuzovsky pr. 14, kv. 21; tel. (095) 243-87-96; Bureau Chief NICOLAE CRETU.

**Syrian Arab News Agency (SANA):** Moscow, Kutuzovsky pr. 7/4, kv. 184–185; tel. (095) 243-13-00; fax (095) 243-75-12; Dir FAHED KAMNAKESH.

**Tlačová agentúra Slovenskej republiky (TASR)** (Slovakia): Moscow, ul. Yuliusa Fuchika 17–19; tel. and fax (095) 250-24-89; Correspondent ELENA POVAŽANOVÁ.

**United Press International (UPI)** (USA): Moscow, Kutuzovsky pr. 7/4, kv. 67; tel. (095) 243-68-29; telex 413424; Bureau Chief JEFF BERLINER.

**Viet Nam News Agency (VNA):** Moscow, Leninsky pr. 45, kv. 326–327; tel. (095) 135-11-08; telex 414490; fax (095) 137-38-67; Bureau Chief KIEU XUAN SON.

**Xinhua (New China) News Agency** (People's Republic of China): Moscow, ul. Druzhby 6, kor. 4, kv. 118; tel. (095) 143-15-64; telex 413983; fax (095) 938-20-07; Chief Correspondent WAN CHENGCAI.

**Yonhap (United) News Agency** (Republic of Korea): Moscow, Tverskoy bul. 10, Rm 425; tel. (095) 290-65-75; Correspondent LEE BYUNG-RO.

## PRESS ASSOCIATIONS

**All-Russian Association of Publishers and Newspapers:** Moscow; f. 1993; Dir-Gen. IVAN LAPTEV.

**Confederation of Journalists' Unions:** 119021 Moscow, Zubovsky bul. 4; tel. (095) 201-77-70; telex 411421; fax (095) 200-42-37; f. 1991; fmrly Union of Journalists of the USSR; Chair. EDUARD SAGALAYEV.

# Publishers

Following the failure of the coup attempt in the USSR in 1991, all publishing houses affiliated to the Communist Party of the Soviet Union (CPSU) were transferred to the jurisdiction of the Russian Federation Government. Many were subsequently transferred to private ownership.

**Avrora** (Aurora): 191065 St Petersburg, Nevsky pr. 7/9; tel. (812) 312-37-53; fax (812) 312-54-60; f. 1969; fine arts; published in foreign languages; Dir Zenobius Spetchinsky.

**Bolshaya Rossiyskaya Entsiklopediya** (The Great Encyclopedia of Russia): 109817 Moscow, Pokrovsky bul. 8; tel. (095) 297-74-83; fax (095) 227-56-24; f. 1925; universal and special encyclopedias; Dir V. G. Panov.

**Detskaya Entsiklopediya:** 107042 Moscow, Bakuninskaya ul. 55; tel. (095) 269-52-76; f. 1933; science fiction, literature, poetry, biographical and historical novels.

**Detskaya Literatura** (Children's Literature): Moscow, Maly Cherkassky per. 1; tel. (095) 928-08-03; f. 1933; State Publishing House of Children's Literature (other than school books); Dir T. M. Shatunova.

**Ekologiya** (Ecology): 101000 Moscow, ul. Myasnitskaya 40A; tel. (095) 928-78-60; fmrly *Lesnaya Promyshlennost* (Forest Industry); publications about environmental protection, forestry, wood and paper products, nature conservation; Dir P. P. Tizengauzen.

**Ekonomika** (Economy): 121864 Moscow, Berezhkovskaya nab. 6; tel. (095) 240-48-77; fax (095) 240-58-18; f. 1963; various aspects of economics, management and marketing; Dir G. I. Mazin.

**Energoatomizdat:** 113114 Moscow, Shluzovaya nab. 10; tel. (095) 925-99-93; f. 1981; different kinds of energy, nuclear science and technology; Dir A. P. Aleshkin.

**Finansy i Statistika** (Finances and Statistics): 101000 Moscow, ul. Chernishevskogo 7; tel. (095) 925-47-08; f. 1924; banking, taxation, accountancy, etc.; Dir A. N. Zvonova.

**Fizkultura i Sport** (Physical Culture and Sport): 101421 Moscow, Dolgoroukovskaya ul. 27; tel. (095) 258-26-90; fax (095) 200-12-17; f. 1923; books and periodicals relating to all forms of sport, chess and draughts, etc.; Dir V. L. Shteinbakh; Editor-in-Chief V. I. Vinokurov.

**Iskusstvo** (Art): 103009 Moscow, Sobinovsky per. 3; tel. (095) 203-58-72; f. 1938; fine arts, architecture, cinema, photography, television and radio, theatre; Dir O. A. Makarov.

**Izdatelstvo Novosti** (Novosti Publishers): 107082 Moscow, Bolshaya Pochtovaya ul. 7; tel. (095) 265-63-35; telex 412474; fax (095) 975-20-65; f. 1964; fmrly *Izdatelstvo Agenstva Pechati Novosti* (Novosti Press Agency Publishing House); politics, economics, fiction, translated literature; Dir Aleksandr Yeidinov.

**Izobrazitelnoye Iskusstvo** (Fine Art): Moscow, Sushchevsky val 64; tel. (095) 281-65-48; reproductions of pictures, pictorial art, books on art, albums, calendars, postcards; Dir V. S. Kuzyakov.

**Izvestiya** (News): 103798 Moscow, Pushkinskaya pl. 5; tel. (095) 209-91-00; publishes the newspaper *Izvestiya* (News) with weekly supplement *Nedelya* (Week), and other publications and journals; Dir Y. I. Balanenko.

**Khimiya** (Chemistry): Moscow B-76, ul. Strominka 21, kor. 2; tel. (095) 268-29-76; f. 1963; chemistry and the chemical industry; Dir Boris S. Krasnopevtsev.

**Khudozhestvennaya Literatura** (Fiction): Moscow, Novo-Basmannaya ul. 19; tel. (095) 261-88-65; telex 412162; fax (095) 261-83-00; fiction and works of literary criticism, history of literature, etc.; Dir G. A. Andjaparidze.

**Khudozhnik** (Artist): 125319 Moscow, ul. Chernyakhovskogo 4; tel. (095) 151-25-02; f. 1969; art reproduction, art history and criticism; Dir V. V. Goryainov.

**Kniga and Business Ltd:** 125047 Moscow, ul. 1-Tverskaya-Yamskaya 22; tel. (095) 251-60-03; fax (095) 250-04-89; fiction, biographies, history, commerce, general; Dir Viktor N. Adamov.

**Kolos:** 107807 Moscow, Sadovaya-Spasskaya ul. 18; tel. (095) 207-29-92; fax (095) 207-28-70; f. 1918; all aspects of agricultural production; Dir Anatoly M. Ulyanov.

**Kompozitor** (Composer): 103006 Moscow, Sadovaya-Triumfalnaya ul. 12-14; tel. (095) 209-23-84; f. 1957; established by the Union of Composers of the USSR; music and music criticism; Dir Y. Y. Belayev.

**Legprombytizdat** (Light Industry and Consumer Services Literature): 113035 Moscow, 1 Kadashevsky per. 12; tel. (095) 233-09-47; f. 1932; scientific and technical publishing house on light industry (clothing, footwear, sewing, etc., welfare services, domestic science); Dir S. R. Ashitkov.

**Malysh** (Little One): 121352 Moscow, Davydkovskaya ul. 5; tel. (095) 443-06-54; fax (095) 443-06-55; f. 1958; books, booklets and posters for children aged between 3–10 years; Dir V. A. Rybin.

**Mashinostroyeniye** (Machine Building): 107076 Moscow, Stromynsky per. 4; tel. (095) 268-38-58; fax (095) 269-48-97; f. 1931; books and journals on mechanical engineering, aerospace technology, computers; Dir Maksim A. Kovalevsky.

**Meditsina** (Medicine): 101000 Moscow, Petroverigsky per. 6/8; tel. (095) 928-86-48; telex 412282; fax (095) 928-60-03; f. 1918; imprint of Association for Medical Literature; books and journals on medicine and health; Dir A. M. Stochik.

**Metallurgiya** (Metallurgy): 119034 Moscow, 2 Obydensky per. 14; tel. (095) 202-55-32; f. 1939; metallurgical literature; Dir A. G. Belikov.

**Mezhdunarodnye Otnosheniya** (International Relations): 107078 Moscow, Sadovaya-Spasskaya ul. 20; tel. (095) 207-67-93; fax (095) 200-22-04; f. 1957; international relations, economics and politics of foreign countries, foreign trade, international law, foreign language textbooks and dictionaries, translations and publications for UN and other international organizations; Dir B. P. Likhachev.

**Mir** (Peace): 129820 Moscow, Pervy Rizhsky per. 2; tel. (095) 286-17-83; fax (095) 288-95-22; f. 1946; Russian translations of foreign scientific, technical and science fiction books; translations of Russian books on science and technology into foreign languages; Dir G. B. Kurganov.

**Molodaya Gvardiya** (Young Guard): 103030 Moscow, Sushchevskaya ul. 21; tel. (095) 972-05-46; telex 411261; fax (095) 972-05-82; f. 1922; fmrly publishing and printing combine of the Leninist Young Communist League; joint-stock co; books and magazines, newspaper for children and for adolescents; Gen. Dir V. F. Yurkin.

**Moscow University Press:** 103009 Moscow, ul. Gertsena 5/7; tel. (095) 229-50-91; telex 411483; f. 1756; more than 200 titles of scientific, educational and reference literature annually, 19 scientific journals; Dir N. S. Timofeyev.

**Moskovsky Rabochy** (Moscow Worker): 101854 Moscow, Chistoprudny bul. 8; tel. (095) 921-07-35; f. 1922; publishing house of the Moscow city and regional soviets; all types of work, including fiction; Dir D. V. Yevdokimov.

**Muzyka** (Music): 103031 Moscow, Neglinnaya ul. 14; tel. (095) 923-04-97; fax (095) 200-52-48; f. 1861; sheet music, music scores and related literature; Dir Leonid S. Sidelnikov.

**Mysl** (Idea): Moscow, Leninsky pr. 15; tel. (095) 234-07-22; f. 1964; science, popular science, economics, philosophy, demography, history, geography; Dir V. M. Vodolagin.

**Nauka** (Science): 117864 Moscow, Profsoyuznaya ul. 90; tel. (095) 336-02-66; telex 411612; fax (095) 420-22-20; f. 1964; publishing house of the Academy of Sciences; general and social science, mathematics, physics, chemistry, biology, earth sciences, oriental studies, books in foreign languages, university textbooks, scientific journals, translation, typesetting and printing services; Dir-Gen. V. Vasiliyev.

**Nedra** (Natural Resources): 125047 Moscow, Tverskaya zastava 3; tel. (095) 250-52-55; fax (095) 250-27-72; f. 1963; geology, natural resources, mining and coal industry, petroleum and gas industry; Dir Yu. B. Kupriyanov.

**Pedagogika Press** (Pedagogics Press): 119034 Moscow, Smolensky bul. 4; tel. (095) 246-59-69; fax (095) 246-59-69; f. 1969; scientific and popular books on pedagogics, didactics, psychology, developmental physiology; young people's encyclopaedia, dictionaries; Dir I. Kolesnikova.

**Planeta** (Planet): Moscow, ul. Petrovka 8/11; tel. (095) 923-04-70; telex 411733; fax (095) 200-52-46; f. 1969; postcards, calendars, guidebooks, brochures, illustrated books; co-editions with foreign partners; Dir V. G. Seredin.

**Pressa:** 125865 Moscow, ul. Pravdy 24; tel. (095) 257-46-21; fax (095) 200-22-95; f. 1934 as Pravda (Truth) Publishing House; publishes booklets, books and many newspapers and periodicals; Dir V. P. Leontev.

**Profizdat** (Trade Union Literature): 101000 Moscow, ul. Myasnitskaya 13; tel. (095) 924-57-40; fax (095) 975-23-29; f. 1930; publishing house of the CIS Labour Union Federation; economic, legal and other matters; Dir Aleksandr Gavrilov.

**Progress** (Progress): 119847 Moscow, Zubovsky bul. 17; tel. (095) 246-90-32; telex 411800; fax (095) 246-07-56; f. 1931; translations of Russian language books into foreign languages and of foreign language books into Russian; political and scientific, fiction, literature for children and youth, training and reference books; Dir A. K. Avelichev.

**Prosveshcheniye** (Education): 127521 Moscow, POB 24; tel. (095) 289-14-05; fax (095) 200-42-66; f. 1969; textbooks; Dir D. D. Zuev.

**Radio i Svyaz** (Radio and Communication): 101000 Moscow, ul. Myasnitskaya 40; tel. (095) 258-53-51; telex 411665; f. 1981; radio engineering, electronics, communications, computer science; Dir Ye. N. Salnikov; Editor-in-Chief I. K. Kalugin.

**Raduga** (Rainbow): 121839 Moscow, Sivtsev Vrazhek 43; tel. (095) 241-68-15; telex 411826; fax (095) 241-63-53; f. 1982; translations of Russian fiction into foreign languages and of foreign authors into Russian; Dir Nina S. Litvinets.

**Respublika** (Republic): Moscow, Miusskaya pl. 7, A-47; tel. (095) 251-45-94; fax (095) 200-22-54; f. 1918; fmrly *Politizdat* (Political

# THE RUSSIAN FEDERATION

Publishing House); books on politics, human rights, philosophy, history, economics, religion, fiction, children's literature; Dir A. P. POLYAKOV.

**Russkaya Kniga** (Russian Book): 123557 Moscow, Tishinsky per. 38; tel. (095) 205-33-77; fax (095) 205-34-27; f. 1957 as Sovetskaya Rossiya; fiction, politics, history, social sciences, health, do-it-yourself, children's; Dir M. F. NENASHEV.

**Russky Yazyk** (Russian Language): 103012 Moscow, Staropansky per. 1/5; tel. (095) 928-37-55; telex 411603; fax (095) 928-89-06; f. 1974; textbooks, reference, dictionaries; Dir V. I. NAZAROV.

**Sovremenny Pisatel** (Contemporary Writer): 121069 Moscow, ul. Povarskaya 11; tel. (095) 202-50-51; f. 1934; fiction and literary criticism, history, biography; publ. house of the International Confederation of Writers' Unions and the Union of Russian Writers; Dir A. N. ZHUKOV.

**Stroyizdat** (Construction Literature): 101442 Moscow, Kalyayevskaya ul. 23A; tel. (095) 251-69-67; f. 1932; building, architecture, environmental protection, fire protection and building materials; Dir V. A. KASATKIN.

**Sudostroyeniye** (Shipbuilding): 191186 St Petersburg, ul. Malaya Morskaya 8; tel. (0812) 312-44-79; fax (0812) 312-08-21; f. 1940; shipbuilding, ship design, navigation, marine research, underwater exploration; Dir and Editor-in-Chief A. A. ANDREYEV.

**Transport** (Transport): 107174 Moscow, Basmanny tupik 6A; tel. (095) 262-67-73; f. 1923; publishes works on all forms of transport; Dir V. P. TITOV.

**Vneshtorgizdat** (The Foreign Trade Economic Printing and Publishing Association): 125047 Moscow, ul. Fadeyev 1; tel. (095) 250-51-62; telex 411238; fax (095) 253-97-94; f. 1925; publishes foreign technical material translated into Russian, and information on export goods, import and export firms, joint ventures; in several foreign languages; Dir-Gen. V. I. PROKOPOV.

**Voyenizdat** (Military Publishing House): Moscow K-160, Voyennoye Izdatelstvo; tel. (095) 195-45-95; military theory and history, general fiction; Dir YURY I. STADNIUK.

**Vysshaya Shkola** (Higher School): Moscow, Neglinnaya ul. 29/14; tel. (095) 200-04-56; fax (095) 973-21-80; f. 1939; textbooks for higher-education institutions; Dir M. I. KISELEV.

**Yuridicheskaya Literatura** (Law Literature): 121069 Moscow, ul. Kachalova 14; tel. (095) 202-83-84; fax (095) 973-21-80; f. 1917; law subjects; official publishers of enactments of the Russian President and Govt; Dir I. A. BUNIN.

**Znaniye** (Knowledge): 101835 Moscow, proyezd Serova 4; tel. (095) 928-15-31; f. 1951; popular books and brochures on politics and science; Dir V. K. BELYAKOV.

## Radio and Television

In December 1993 the Federal Television and Radio Broadcasting Service was established to replace the Ministry of Press and Information and the Federal Information Service of Russia. Its function was to co-ordinate the activity of national and regional state television and broadcasting organizations. In 1995 there was extensive reorganization of Russian broadcasting. A new organization, Public Russian Television (PRT), was formed to take over the broadcasting responsibilities of the Ostankino Russian State Television and Radio Broadcasting Company. Ostankino retained responsibility for several radio stations, including Mayak, Radio-1, Orfey and Yunost. PRT broadcasts Channel 1, which is received throughout Russia and many parts of the CIS. All-Russian State Television broadcasts Channel 2 ('Rossiya'), which reaches some 92% of the Russian population. It also broadcasts an educational channel ('Russian Universities'). In addition to the two nation-wide television channels, there are local channels in Moscow and St Petersburg, and the Independent Television (Nezavisimoe televidenie—NTV) channel is broadcast in most of central Russia. In the regions part of Channel 2's programming is devoted to local affairs, with broadcasts in minority languages in the national republics.

**Federal Television and Radio Broadcasting Service of Russia:** 113326 Moscow, Pyatnitskaya ul. 25; tel. (095) 217-98-38; fax (095) 215-93-56; Chair. VALENTIN V. LAZUTKIN.

**All-Russian State Television and Radio Broadcasting Company** (Vserossiyskaya Gosudarstvennaya Teleradiokompaniya): 125124 Moscow, ul. Yamskogo Polya 5-ya 19/21; tel. (095) 251-40-50; telex 411252; fax (095) 214-47-67; f. 1991; broadcasts 'Rossiya' channel; Chair. OLEG POPTSOV.

**Public Russian Television:** (Obshchestvennoe Rossiiskoe Televidenie—ORT): 127000 Moscow, ul. Akademika Koroleva 12; f. 1995; broadcasts Russia's main television channel; Dir-Gen. SERGEY BLAGOVOLIN.

**Voice of Russia** (Golos Rossii): 113326 Moscow; tel. (095) 233-78-01; telex 411137; fax (095) 230-28-28; fmrly Radio Moscow International; international broadcasts in 30 languages; Man. Dir ARMEN OGANESYAN.

## Finance

(cap. = capital; dep. = deposits; res = reserves; m. = million; brs = branches; amounts in roubles, unless otherwise stated)

### BANKING

The structure of the banking system in the Russian Federation was legally defined by the Law on Co-operatives, which was passed in 1988 and allowed the establishment of commercial banks, and the 1990 Laws on Central Banking and Banking Activity. The five Soviet sectoral banks (Sberbank, Vneshtorgbank, Promstroibank, Agroprombank and Zhilsotsbank) were reorganized according to the 1990 Laws. Zhilsotsbank was closed in mid-1991. In early 1995 there were some 2,500 private banks operating in Russia.

**Central Bank of the Russian Federation:** 103016 Moscow, ul. Neglinnaya 12; tel. (095) 237-30-65; telex 411283; fax (095) 921-64-65; Chair. TATYANA PARAMONOVA (acting).

**Rosvneshtorgbank** (Bank for Foreign Trade of the Russian Federation): 103031 Moscow, Kuznetsky most 16; tel. (095) 204-64-42; telex 412362; fax (095) 956-37-27; Chair. YURY V. POLETAYEV.

### Major Commercial and Co-operative Banks

**Agroprombank—Agricultural Bank:** 103780 Moscow, ul. Neglinnaya 12; tel. (095) 928-85-07; fax (095) 921-76-46; f. 1987; reorganized as joint-stock co. in 1990; cap. and res 40,281m., dep. 3,927,660m. (Jan. 1994); Chair. YURY V. TRUSHIN; 1,160 brs.

**Alfa-Bank:** 107078 Moscow, ul. Mashy Poryvayevoy 11; tel. (095) 207-00-59; telex 412089; fax (095) 207-61-36; f. 1990; cap. 4,508m., dep. 236,848m. (Dec. 1993); Chair. A. N. RAPPOPORT.

**Bank Vozrozhdeniye:** 103699 Moscow, Khrustalny per. 1; tel. (095) 230-28-73; telex 412735; fax (095) 230-25-72; f. 1991; public joint stock co; cap. and res 45,829m., dep. 374,136m. (Dec. 1994); Chair. DMITRY L. ORLOV.

**Conversbank Ltd:** 109017 Moscow, ul. Bolshaya Ordynka 24/26; tel. (095) 239-20-28; telex 911591; fax (095) 233-25-40; f. 1989; all principal banking operations; cap. 200m., dep. 77,694m., res 4,272.8m. (Jan. 1993); Chair. NIKOLAY G. PISEMSKY; 11 brs.

**Credo Bank:** 103009 Moscow, Leontievsky per. 10; tel. (095) 229-23-33; telex 412308; fax (095) 925-80-74; f. 1989; cap. 28,339.4m., dep 892,818m., res 48,272m. (July 1994); Pres. YURY AGAPOV; 24 brs.

**Ekonombank:** 410753 Saratov, ul. Radishcheva 28; tel. (095) 24-06-13; telex 241124; fax (095) 26-61-98; f. 1990; cap. 630.7m., dep. 1,339.2m., res 501.7m. (Dec. 1992); Chair. ALEKSANDR V. SUSLOV.

**Elektrobank:** 103074 Moscow, Kitaysky proezd 7; tel. (095) 229-22-79; telex 412072; fax (095) 262-78-12; f. 1990; provides finance for power industry; cap. 1,500m., dep. 122,273m., res 150,849 (Jan. 1994); Chair. VIKTOR V. MUZHITSKIKH; 19 brs.

**Imperial Bank:** 113035 Moscow, ul. Osipenko 63/7; tel. (095) 237-76-41; telex 412093; fax (095) 237-77-17; f. 1990; reorganized as joint stock bank 1992; cap. 776m., dep. 663,832m., res 10,201m. (Jan. 1994); Pres. REM I. VYAKHIREV.

**Inkombank:** 117420 Moscow, ul. Nametkina 14, kor. 1; tel. (095) 332-06-99; telex 412345; fax (095) 331-88-33; f. 1991; cap. and res 175,760m., dep. 1,212,126m. (Jan. 1994); Pres. VLADIMIR P. GROSHEV; 20 brs.

**International Moscow Bank:** 103009 Moscow, ul. Pushkinskaya 5/6; tel. (095) 292-96-32; telex 412284; fax (095) 975-22-14; f. 1989 and opened for operations 1990; joint venture between Banca Commerciale Italiana (12%), Bayerische Vereinsbank (12%), Creditanstalt-Bankverein (12%), Credit Lyonnais (12%), Kansallis-Osake-Pankii (12%) and three former credit banks of the USSR banking system, Vneshekonombank (20%), Promstroibank (10%) and Sberbank (10%); specializing in the financing of joint ventures, investments and projects of domestic and foreign customers and international trade deals; cap. 275m., dep. 2,557,669m., res 99,485m. (Dec. 1993); Chair. OTTO K. FINSTERWALDER.

**Kuzbassprombank:** Kemerovo, Ostrovskogo 12; tel. (3842) 26-62-43; telex 215122; fax (3842) 26-84-84; f. 1922; commercial and joint stock bank; cap. 3,000m., dep. 234,116m., res 24,905m. (Jan 1994); Pres. NIKOLAY N. ZHURAVLEV; 22 brs.

**Menatep:** 101000 Moscow, Kolpachny per. 4; tel. (095) 235-90-03; telex 412323; fax (095) 923--59-31; public joint-stock co.; cap. 9,703m., dep. 776,111m., res 11,771m. (Jan. 1994); Pres. PLATON L. LEBEDEV; 17 brs.

**Mezhcombank—InterBranch Commercial Bank:** 125319 Moscow, Dmitrovsky per. 3/4; tel. (095) 152-70-83; telex 612642; fax (095) 155-72-33; f. 1990; cap. 24,400m., dep. 1,701,683m., res 186,411m. (Dec. 1994); Chair. of Bd SERGEY K. OVSIANNIKOV.

# THE RUSSIAN FEDERATION

**Mosbusinessbank:** 103780 Moscow, Kuznetsky most 15; tel. (095) 924-30-38; telex 412362; fax (095) 924-04-90; f. 1990; public joint-stock co.; cap. 1,796m., dep. 1,460,873m., res 102,284m.; Pres. VIKTOR BUKATO; 40 brs.

**Moskovsky Industrialny Bank** (Moscow Industrial Bank): 117419 Moscow, Ordzhonikidze 5; tel. (095) 952-74-08; telex 613055; fax (095) 952-77-94; f. 1990; cap. 20,000m., dep. 1,570,700m., res 303,600m. (Jan. 1995); Pres. F. A. PLESKANOVSKY; 28 brs.

**Most-Bank:** 121205 Moscow, Novy Arbat 36; tel. (095) 203-25-52; telex 613085; fax (095) 203-29-76; f. 1991; cap. 18,250m., dep. 468,990m., res 5,075m. (Dec. 1993); Pres. VLADIMIR A. GUSINSKY; 4 brs.

**National Credit Bank:** 103009 Moscow, ul. Ogarova 9/2; tel. (095) 229-12-64; telex 911067; fax (095) 229-13-94; f. 1990; cap. 29,834m., dep. 222,132m., res 605m. (Jan. 1994); Chair. OLEG BOIKO; 4 brs.

**Permkombank:** 614000 Perm, ul. Sovetskaya 6; tel. (3422) 32-48-46; telex 614215; fax (3422) 32-72-02; f. 1989; cap. 7,000m., dep. 154,057m., res 10,713m. (Jan. 1994); Chair. ANATOLY V. FEDYANIN; 19 brs.

**Petroagroprombank—Joint Stock Commercial Agro-industrial Bank of St Petersburg:** 191186 St Petersburg, nab. kan. Griboyedova 13; tel. (812) 315-44-92; telex 121205; fax (812) 314-83-42; cap. 900m., dep. 46,956m., res 34,279m. (Jan. 1994); Pres. YURY V. TRUSOV; 23 brs.

**Promstroibank:** 103867 Moscow, Tverskoy bul. 13; tel. (095) 229-22-92; telex 411943; fax (095) 200-65-07; f. 1922; cap. 6,000m., dep. 1,009,440m., res 89,591m. (Dec. 1993); Chair. YAKOV N. DUBENETSKY; 70 brs.

**Rodina Bank:** 123812 Moscow, ul. B. Gruzinskaya 4/6; tel. (095) 252-52-62; telex 613712; fax (095) 254-09-47; f. 1990; cap. 444.6m., dep. 5,407.8m., res 644.1m. (Jan. 1994); Pres. KONSTANTIN A. FOKIN.

**Rossiisky Kredit:** 121002 Moscow, Smolensky bul. 26/9; tel. (095) 248-08-11; telex 412012; fax (095) 248-08-11; f. 1990; cap. 67,247m., dep. 1,020,278m., res 18,996m. (Jan. 1994); Pres. BIDZINA G. IVANISHVILI; 34 brs.

**Sberbank—Savings Bank of the Russian Federation:** 103473 Moscow, ul. Seleznevskaya 40; tel. (095) 281-84-67; telex 412487; fax (095) 281-93-33; f. 1842 as a deposit taking institution, reorganized as a joint-stock commercial bank in 1991; cap. 594,517m., dep. 4,723,029m., res 8,344m. (Jan. 1994); Pres. of Council VIKTOR V. GERASHCHENKO; Chair. OLEG V. YASHIN; 79 brs.

**Stolichny Joint-Stock Commercial Bank:** 113095 Moscow, ul. Pyatnitskaya 70; tel. (095) 233-39-16; telex 411913; fax (095) 956-39-27; f. 1989; provides finance for small manufacturing companies; cap. 25,000m.; Pres. ALEKSANDR P. SMOLENSKY.

**TverUniversal Bank:** 170000 Tver, Voldarsky 34; tel. (08222) 312-43; telex 171215; fax (08222) 261-20; f. 1990; cap. 3,000m., dep. 240,019m., res 8,716m. (Jan. 1994); Pres. ALEKSANDRA KOZYREVA; 21 brs.

**Unikombank:** 103701 Moscow, Khrustalny per. 1; tel. (095) 284-16-40; telex 612443; fax (095) 286-73-14; f. 1990; cap. 12,000m., dep. 229,062m., res 189,640m. (Jan. 1995); Pres. IGOR V. ANTONOV; 70 brs.

### Association

**Association of Russian Banks:** 103379 Moscow, B. Sadovaya ul., stroeniye 2, dom 4; tel. (095) 209-10-37; unites some 900 private banks; Chair. YE. YEGOROV.

### INSURANCE

**Gosstrakh** (State Insurance): Moscow, Nastasinsky per. 3, kor. 2; tel. (095) 299-29-42; fax (095) 200-42-02.

**Ingosstrakh Insurance Co. Ltd:** 113805 Moscow, Pyatnitskaya ul. 12; tel. (095) 231-16-77; telex 411144; fax (095) 230-25-18; f. 1947; undertakes all kinds of insurance and reinsurance; Chair. VLADIMIR P. KRUGLIAK.

**Insurance Company of the Russian Federation:** Moscow, ul. Petrovka 20/21; tel. (095) 200-29-95; fax (095) 200-50-41.

### STOCK EXCHANGES

**Moscow International Stock Exchange:** 103045 Moscow, Prosvirin per. 4; tel. (095) 923-33-39; fax (095) 923-33-39; f. 1990; Pres. ANDREY ZAKHAROV.

**Siberian Stock Exchange:** 630104 Novosibirsk, ul. Frunze 5; tel. (3832) 21-60-67; fax (3832) 21-06-90; f. 1991; Pres. ALEKSANDR V. NOVIKOV.

### COMMODITY EXCHANGES

**Asiatic Commodity Exchange:** 670000 Ulan-Ude, Sovetskaya ul. 23, kom. 37; tel. (30122) 2-26-81; fax (30122) 2-26-81; f. 1991; Chair. ANDREY FIRSOV.

**Commodity and Raw Materials Exchange 'Konversia':** 140056 Moscow region, Dzerzhinsk, ul. Sovetskaya 6; tel. (095) 551-01-88; fax (095) 175-24-94; f. 1991; Gen. Dir VADIM KRASNOV.

**Khabarovsk Commodity Exchange (KHCE):** 680037 Khabarovsk, ul. Karla Marksa 66; tel. (4212) 33-65-60; fax (4212) 33-65-60; f. 1991; Pres. YEVGENY V. PANASENKO.

**Komi Commodity Exchange (KOCE):** 167610 Syktyvkar, Komi Republic, Oktiabrsky pr. 16; tel. (82122) 2-32-86; fax (82122) 3-84-43; f. 1991; Pres. PETR S. LUCHENKOV.

**Kuzbass Commodity and Raw Materials Exchange (KECME):** 650090 Kemerogo, Novgradskaya ul. 19; tel. (3842) 23-45-40; fax (3842) 23-49-56; f. 1991; Gen. Man. FEDOR MASENKOV.

**Kuznetsk Commodity and Raw Materials Exchange (KCME):** 650079 Novokuznetsk, ul. Nevskogo 2; tel. (3843) 42-15-29; fax (3843) 42-22-75; f. 1991; Gen. Man. YURY POLYAKOV.

**Moscow Commodity Exchange (MCE):** 129223 Moscow, pr. Mira, Russian Exhibition Centre, Pavilion 69 (4); tel. (095) 187-83-07; fax (095) 187-99-82; f. 1990; organization of exchange trading (cash, stock and futures market); Pres. and Chair. of Bd YURY MILIUKOV.

**Moscow Exchange of Building Materials (ALISA):** 117334 Moscow, Leninsky pr. 45; tel. (095) 137-00-06; fax (095) 137-67-23; f. 1990; Chair. of Exchange Cttee GERMAN STERLIGOV.

**Petrozavodsk Commodity Exchange (PCE):** 185028 Petrozavodsk, ul. Krasnaya 31; tel. 7-80-57; fax 7-80-57; f. 1991; Gen. Man. VALERY SAKHAROV.

**Russian Commodity and Raw Materials Exchange (RCME):** 101000 Moscow, ul. Myasnitskaya 26; tel. (095) 262-80-80; fax (095) 262-57-57; f. 1990; Pres. and Chief. Man. ALEKSEY VLASOV.

**Russian Commodity Exchange of the Agro-Industrial Complex** (ROSAGROBIRZHA): Moscow, Volokolamskoye shosse 11; tel. (095) 209-52-25; f. 1990; Chairman of Exchange Committee: ALEKSANDR VASILIYEV.

**St Petersburg Commodity and Stock Exchange (CSE St Petersburg):** 199026 St Petersburg, 26-aya liniya v.o. 15; tel. (812) 355-68-67; fax (812) 355-68-63; f. 1990; Pres. and CEO VIKTOR NIKOLAYEV.

**Surgut Commodity and Raw Materials Exchange (SCME):** 626400 Surgut, ul. 30 Lyet Pobedy 32; tel. (34561) 2-05-69; telex 412547; f. 1991.

**Tyumen Commodity and Stock Exchange (TCE):** 625016 Tyumen, ul. Melnikayte 106; tel. (3452) 24-48-30; f. 1991; Pres. SERGEY DENISOV; 5 brs.

**Udmurt Commodity Universal Exchange (UCUE):** 426074 Izhevsk, ul. Sovetskaya 107; tel. (3412) 69-64-87; f. 1991; Pres. YURY UTEKHIN.

**Yekaterinburg Commodity Exchange (UCE):** 620012 Yekterinburg, pr. Kosmonavtov 23; tel. (3432) 34-43-01; fax (3432) 51-53-64; f. 1991; Chair. of Exchange Cttee KONSTANTIN ZHUZHLOV.

## Trade and Industry

### STATE PROPERTY AGENCY

**Russian Federal Property Fund:** Moscow; Chair. FIRYAT TABEYEV.

### CHAMBER OF COMMERCE

**Chamber of Commerce and Industry of the Russian Federation:** 103684 Moscow, ul. Ilyinka 6; tel. (095) 923-43-23; telex 411126; fax (095) 230-24-55; f. 1991; Pres. STANISLAV A. SMIRNOV.

### TRADE UNIONS

Until 1990 trade unions were united in the All-Union Central Council of Trade Unions (ACCTU), which operated strictly under the control of the Communist Party of the Soviet Union. During the late 1980s, however, several informal, independent labour movements were established by workers dissatisfied with the official organizations. Prominent among the new movements was the Independent Trade Union of Miners (ITUM), formed by striking miners in 1989. In 1990, in response to the growing independent labour movement, several branch unions of the ACCTU established the Federation of Independent Trade Unions of the Russian Federation (FITUR), which took control of part of the property and other assets of the ACCTU. The ACCTU was itself reformed as the General Confederation of Trade Unions of the USSR, which was in turn renamed the CIS Labour Federation in 1992. In November of that year, in an attempt to challenge the influence of the FITUR, the ITUM and several other independent trade unions established a consultative council to co-ordinate their activities.

**CIS Labour Union Federation:** 117119 Moscow, Leninsky pr. 42; tel. (095) 938-70-00; telex 411010; fax (095) 938-21-55; f. 1990; fmrly the General Confederation of Trade Unions of the USSR;

## THE RUSSIAN FEDERATION

co-ordinating body for trade unions in CIS member states; Pres. VLADIMIR I. SHCHERBAKOV.

**Federation of Independent Trade Unions of the Russian Federation** (FITUR): 117119 Moscow, Leninsky pr. 42; tel. (095) 938-83-13; telex 111265; fax (095) 137-06-94; f. 1990; Chair. MIKHAIL SHMAKOV; unites 38 branch unions (with c. 50m. members), including:

**Aircraft Engineering Workers' Union:** 117119 Moscow, Leninsky pr. 42; tel. (095) 930-81-06; fax (095) 930-97-84; f. 1934; Pres. A. F. BREUSOV.

**All-Russian Committee 'Electrounion':** 117119 Moscow, Leninsky pr. 42; tel. (095) 938-83-78; telex 411010; fax (095) 930-98-62; f. 1990; electrical workers; Pres. VALERY P. KUZICHEV.

**Automobile, Tractor and Farm Machinery Industries Workers' Union:** 117119 Moscow, Leninsky pr. 42; Pres. A. P. KASHIRIN.

**Automobile Transport and Road Workers' Unions Federation of Russia:** 117218 Moscow, ul. Krzhizhanovskogo 20/30, kv. 5; tel. (095) 125-13-31; fax (095) 125-09-74; f. 1990; Pres. VICTOR I. MOKHNACHEV.

**Civil Aviation Workers' Union:** Moscow V-218, ul. Krzhizhanovskogo 20/30, kor. 5; Pres. A. G. GRIDIN.

**Coal Mining Industry Workers' Union:** Moscow, Zemlyanoy val 64, kor. 1; Pres. M. A. SREBNY.

**Construction and Building Materials Industry Workers' Union of Russia:** 117119 Moscow, Leninsky pr. 42; tel. (095) 930-81-74; fax (095) 952-55-47; f. 1991; Pres. BORIS A. SOSHENKO.

**Educational and Scientific Workers' Union:** 117119 Moscow, Leninsky pr. 42; tel. (095) 930-87-77; fax (095) 930-68-15; f. 1990; Pres. V. YAKOVLEV.

**Engineering and Instrument-Making Industries Workers' Union:** 117119 Moscow, Leninsky pr. 42; tel. (095) 930-85-25; fax (095) 930-80-25; Pres. ANATOLY Y. RYBAKOV.

**Federation of the Agroindustrial Unions of the CIS:** 117119 Moscow, Leninsky pr. 42; tel. (095) 938-75-95; f. 1919, merged with Food Workers' Union in 1986; Pres. M. B. RYZHIKOV; 37m. mems.

**Federation of Communication Workers' Unions of the CIS:** 117119 Moscow, Leninsky pr. 42; tel. (095) 930-84-58; fax (095) 938-21-63; f. 1905; Pres. ANATOLY NAZEYKIN.

**Federation of Cultural Workers' Unions:** 109004 Moscow, Zemlyanoy val 64, kor. 1; tel. (095) 297-86-12; fax (095) 925-85-17; Pres. I. A. NAUMENKO.

**Federation of Timber and Related Industries Workers' Unions of the CIS:** 117119 Moscow, Leninsky pr. 42; tel. (095) 938-82-02; fax (095) 938-82-04; Pres. VIKTOR P. KARNIUSHIN.

**Geological Survey Workers' Union:** 117119 Moscow, Leninsky pr. 42; Pres. M. GOUBKIN.

**Health Workers' Union:** 117119 Moscow, Leninsky pr. 42; tel. (095) 938-77-62; fax (095) 938-81-34; f. 1990; Chair. M. M. KUZMENKO.

**Heavy Engineering Workers' Union:** 117119 Moscow, Leninsky pr. 42; Pres. N. I. ZINOVIYEV.

**Independent Trade Union of Railwaymen and Transport Construction Workers:** 107217 Moscow, Sadovo-Spasskaya ul. 21; tel. (095) 262-58-73; Pres. I. A. SHINKEVICH.

**International Trade Union Alliance of Municipal, Local Industry and Communal Services Workers and Allied Trades:** 117119 Moscow, Leninsky pr. 42; tel. (095) 938-85-12; f. 1991 to replace the Local Industries and Public Services Workers' Union Federation; Pres. Y. Y. ABRAMOV.

**International Trade Union Federation of State and Public Employees:** 117119 Moscow, Leninsky pr. 42; tel. (095) 938-80-53; telex 411010; fax (095) 938-21-55; f. 1918; Pres. I. L. GREBENSHIKOV.

**Moscow Federation of Trade Unions:** Moscow; largest regional branch of FITUR; Chair. MIKHAIL V. SHMAKOV; 6m. mems.

**Oil, Gas and Construction Workers' Union:** 117119 Moscow, Leninsky pr. 42; tel. (095) 930-11-24; fax (095) 939-87-63; f. 1990; Pres. LEV A. MIRONOV.

**Radio and Electronics Industry Workers' Union:** Moscow, Pervy Golutvinsky per. 3; Pres. V. N. TUZOV.

**Russian Chemical and Allied Industries Workers' Unions of the CIS:** 117119 Moscow, Leninsky pr. 42, corp. 3; tel. (095) 938-70-62; fax (095) 938-2155; Pres. VALERY STANIN.

**Russian Fishing Industry Workers' Union:** 117119 Moscow, Leninsky pr. 42; tel. (095) 938-77-82; fax (095) 930-77-31; f. 1986; Pres. V. A. ZYRIANOV.

**Sea and River Workers' Union:** 109004 Moscow, Zemlyanoy val 64, kor. 1; tel. (095) 227-29-96; Pres. K. YU. MATSKYAVICHYUS.

**Shipbuilding Workers' Union:** 117119 Moscow, Leninsky pr. 42; Pres. A. G. BURIMOVICH.

**State Trade and Consumer Co-operative Workers' Union:** 117119 Moscow, Leninsky pr. 42; Pres. G. N. ZAMYTSKAYA.

**Textile and Light Industry Workers' Union of Russia:** 117119 Moscow, Leninsky pr. 42; tel. (095) 938-78-24; fax (095) 930-69-93; f. 1990; Pres. T. I. SOSNINA.

### Independent Trade Unions

**Federation Union of Air Traffic Controllers:** Moscow; Chair. ALFRED MALINOVKSY.

**Independent Trade Union of Miners:** Moscow; f. 1989 in opposition to the official coal-miners' union; Chair. ALEKSANDR SERGEYEV; 50,000 mems.

**Metallurgical Industry Workers' Union:** Moscow; Pushkinskaya ul. 5/6; left the FITUR in 1992 to form independent organization; Pres. BORIS MISNIK.

**Russian Union of Sailors:** Moscow; Pres. V. NEKRASOV.

**Russian Union of Locomotive Workers:** Moscow; Chair. V. KUROCHIN.

**Russian Union of Dock Workers:** Moscow; Chair. V. VASILYEV.

# Transport

### RAILWAYS

In 1993 the total length of railway track in use was 87,079 km, of which 37,365 km were electrified. The railway network is of great importance in the Russian Federation, owing to the poor road system and relatively few private vehicles. The Trans-Siberian Railway provides the main route connecting European Russia with Siberia and the Far East.

**Russian Railways:** 107174 Moscow, ul. Novobasmannaya 2; tel. (095) 262-16-28; fax (095) 262-65-61; comprises 17 of the 32 regional divisions of the former Soviet Railways (SZD); in 1992 these were reorganized into 19 operating divisions; Gen. Mans A. SEDENKO, V. N. SHATAYEV.

### ROADS

At 31 December 1990 the total length of roads was 879,100 km, of which 652,500 km were hard-surfaced. The road network is of most importance in European Russia; in Siberia and the Far East there are few roads, and they are often impassable in winter. At the beginning of 1994 the World Bank granted Russia a loan of US $300m. to finance the construction of 10,000 km of roads to the west of the Urals.

### SHIPPING

The seaports of the Russian Federation provide access to the Pacific Ocean, in the east, the Baltic Sea and the Atlantic Ocean, in the west, and the Black Sea, in the south. Major eastern ports are at Vladivostok, Nakhodka, Vostochny, Magadan and Petropavlovsk. In the west St Petersburg and Kaliningrad provide access to the Baltic Sea, and the northern ports of Murmansk and Archangelsk have access to the Atlantic Ocean, via the Barents Sea. Novorossiysk and Sochi are the principal Russian ports on the Black Sea.

#### Principal Shipowning Companies

**Baltic Shipping Company:** 198035 St Petersburg, Mezhevoy kanal 5; tel. (812) 251-07-42; telex 121501; fax (812) 186-85-44; freight and passenger services; Pres. Capt. ARNOLD P. RUSIN.

**Far Eastern Shipping Company:** 690019 Vladivostok, ul. Aleutskaya 15; tel. (4232) 22-19-06; telex 213115; Pres. VIKTOR M. MISKOV.

**Kamchatka Shipping Company:** 683600 Petropavlovsk-Kamchatsky, ul. Radiosvyazi 65; tel. (41522) 2-22-63; telex 244112; fax (41522) 2-19-60; f. 1949; freight services; Pres. NIKOLAY M. ZABLOTSKY.

**Murmansk Shipping Company:** 183636 Murmansk, ul. Kominterna 15; tel. (8152) 55-23-93; telex 126113; fax (8152) 1-04-95; f. 1939; shipping and icebreaking services; Gen. Dir Capt. NIKOLAI MATYUSHENKO.

**Northern Shipping Company:** 163061 Arkhangelsk, nab. Sev. Dviny 36; tel. (81822) 3-59-63; telex 242111; fax (81822) 3-83-10; f. 1870; Pres. A. N. GAGARIN.

**Novorossiysk Shipping Company:** 353900 Novorossiysk, ul. Svobody 1; tel. (86134) 5-33-09; telex 279113; fax (86134) 140-12-56; Chair. and Gen. Dir LEONID I. LOZA.

**Primorsk Shipping Company:** 692904 Primorsky Krai, Nakhodka 4, Administrativny Gorodok; tel. (42366) 4-44-29; telex 213812; fax (42366) 4-29-95; f. 1972, reorganized as joint-stock co 1992; tanker shipowner; Pres. A. D. KIRILICHEV.

**Sakhalin Shipping Company:** 694620 Sakhalin, Kholmsk, ul. Pobedy 16; tel. 2-29-20; telex 412613; fax 2-39-61; Pres. Yakub Zh. Alegedpinov.

**White Sea and Onega Shipping Company:** 185640 Petrozavodsk, ul. Rigachina 7; tel. 6-13-08; telex 121591; fax 5-77-17; Gen. Dir Oleg S. Bachinsky.

### CIVIL AVIATION

Until 1991 Aeroflot was the only airline operating on domestic routes in the former USSR. In 1992–94 some 300 different airlines emerged on the basis of Aeroflot's former regional directorates. Several small private airlines were also established. In 1995 it was announced that Aeroflot would become a joint-stock company, although the Government planned to retain a majority of shares.

**Aeroflot—Russian International Airlines:** 125167 Moscow, Leningradsky pr. 37; tel. (095) 155-66-48; telex 411967; fax (095) 155-66-47; f. 1923 as Dobrolet, restyled Aeroflot in 1932; air services in the former USSR; international flights, covering about 250,000 km, serve 120 destinations in 102 countries in Europe, Africa, Asia and the Americas; Dir-Gen. Vladimir Tikhonov.

## Tourism

**Intourist:** 103009 Moscow, ul. Mokhovaya 13; tel. (095) 292-22-60; telex 411211; fax (095) 203-52-67; f. 1929; branches throughout Russia and in other countries; Pres. Anatoly Yarochkin.

**Intourist Holdings:** 103031 Moscow, ul. Petrovka 14; tel. (095) 925-95-62; fax (095) 200-45-04; f. 1992; travel and tourism investment co; owns a tour-operating subsidiary; publishing; intermediary services in trade and commerce; Chair. Igor Konovalov.

# RWANDA

## Introductory Survey

### Location, Climate, Language, Religion, Flag, Capital

The Rwandan Republic is a land-locked country in eastern central Africa, just south of the Equator, bounded by Zaire to the west, by Uganda to the north, by Tanzania to the east and by Burundi to the south. The climate is tropical, although tempered by altitude. It is hot and humid in the lowlands, but cooler in the highlands. The average annual rainfall is 785 mm (31 in). The main rainy season is from February to May. The population is composed of three ethnic groups: the Hutu (85%), the Tutsi (14%) and the Twa (1%). French and Kinyarwanda, the native language, are both in official use, and Kiswahili is widely spoken. About one-half of the population adhere to animist beliefs. Most of the remainder are Christians, mainly Roman Catholics. There are Protestant and Muslim minorities. The national flag (proportions 3 by 2) has three equal vertical stripes, of red (at the hoist), yellow and green (at the fly), with a black letter R in the centre of the yellow stripe. The capital is Kigali.

### Recent History

Rwanda, with the neighbouring state of Burundi, became part of German East Africa in 1899. In 1916 it was occupied by Belgian forces from the Congo (now Zaire). From 1920 Rwanda was part of Ruanda-Urundi, administered by Belgium under a League of Nations mandate and later as a UN Trust Territory. Dissension between the majority Hutu tribe and their former overlords, the Tutsi, has existed for many years, and in 1959 led to a rebellion and the proclamation of a state of emergency. In September 1961 it was decided by referendum to abolish the monarchy and to establish a republic. Internal autonomy was granted in 1961 and full independence followed on 1 July 1962. Serious tribal strife erupted in December 1963, and large-scale massacres (estimated at 20,000 deaths) were perpetrated by the Hutu against the Tutsi. During 1964–65 large numbers of displaced Rwandans were resettled in neighbouring countries. In 1969 Grégoire Kayibanda, the new Republic's first President, was re-elected, and all 47 seats in the legislature were retained by the governing party, the Mouvement démocratique républicain (MDR), also known as the Parti de l'émancipation du peuple Hutu (Parmehutu).

Tension between Hutu and Tutsi escalated again at the end of 1972 and continued throughout February 1973. In July the Minister of Defence and head of the National Guard, Maj.-Gen. Juvénal Habyarimana, led a bloodless coup against President Kayibanda, proclaimed the Second Republic and established a military administration. In August a new Council of Ministers, with Habyarimana as President, was formed. The normal legislative processes were suspended, and all political activity was banned until July 1975, when a new ruling party, the Mouvement révolutionnaire national pour le développement (MRND), was formed. Its establishment was preceded by an extensive government reorganization in which several military ministers were replaced by civilians. The first national congress of the MRND was held in January 1976.

A national referendum in December 1978 approved a new Constitution aimed at returning the country to democratically-elected government (in accordance with an undertaking made by Habyarimana in 1973 to end the military regime within five years). An unsuccessful coup attempt took place in April 1980, and elections were held to the legislature, the Conseil national de développement (CND), in December 1981. In December 1983 Habyarimana was re-elected President. Elections to the CND in the same month were followed by a government reshuffle in January 1984. Habyarimana, a native of the northern town of Gisenyi, fostered the predominance of northern elements in the government and administration, and by 1985 it appeared that regional rivalries would displace Hutu–Tutsi strife as the prime focus of political competition.

A presidential election was held in December 1988, at which Habyarimana was re-elected President (unopposed) for a third term of office, securing 99.98% of the votes cast. In the same month elections to the CND were conducted, followed by a government reshuffle in January 1989, in which six new ministers were appointed.

In July 1990 President Habyarimana declared that, in recognition of the need for political reform, a national charter would be drafted before July 1992 which would provide for the establishment of a multi-party system. Also in July 1990 a minor government reshuffle was effected. In September the Commission nationale de synthèse was established to compile recommendations for the draft charter. In February 1991 Habyarimana implemented a government reshuffle which included the appointment of six new ministers and the creation of two new ministerial posts.

In April 1991, following the CND's revision of the Commission's proposals for constitutional reform, the provisions of the draft Constitution were made known at an extraordinary congress of the MRND, at which a new party name (the Mouvement républicain national pour la démocratie et le développement—MRNDD) was formally adopted. On 10 June 1991 the reforms were promulgated by the President.

The new provisions of the Constitution sought to establish a greater division of the responsibilities of the executive, the legislature and the judiciary. The tenure of the President was to be limited to a maximum of two consecutive five-year terms; the duties and authority of the President, in the instance of his absence or of his inability to fulfil his functions, would be carried out by the head of the legislature (and not, as previously, by the Secretary-General of the MRNDD); a new post of Prime Minister was to be created; and civil servants were to be awarded the right to strike. (However, concern was expressed that the new terms of the Constitution contained no reference to an electoral timetable). A new law to regulate the formation of political parties was adopted simultaneously. Parties were to be non-tribal, independent and headquartered in Kigali, and members of the security forces and the judiciary would be banned from political activity. By the end of July the MRNDD and the revived MDR had been recognized as legal political parties. (By June 1992 15 parties were known to have been registered with the Ministry of the Interior and Communal Development.)

In October 1991 Sylvestre Nsanzimana, hitherto Minister of Justice, was appointed Prime Minister, and in December he announced the composition of a two-party transitional Government. All but two of the portfolios in the new Government, formed in co-operation with the Parti démocratique chrétien (PDC), were, in fact, allocated to members of the MRNDD. In November 1991 and January 1992 major opposition parties, which had been excluded from participation in the transitional Government for having insisted that the Prime Minister be chosen from a party other than the MRNDD, organized anti-Government demonstrations, demanding the removal of the Prime Minister and the convening of a national conference (as detailed in the new provisions of the Constitution).

A series of negotiations between the Government and the four major opposition parties was initiated in February 1992, and in April the MRNDD, the MDR, the Parti social-démocrate (PSD), the Parti libéral (PL) and the Parti socialiste rwandais (PSR) signed a protocol agreement for the installation of a new transitional government, with Dismas Nsengiyaremye of the MDR as Prime Minister. Habyarimana announced that multi-party elections would be conducted within one year of the installation of the new Government. The composition of the new Government was announced in mid-April; the Council of Ministers comprised representatives of those parties that had signed the protocol agreement, with the exception of the PSR, and also included one member of the PDC.

In late April 1992, in accordance with the provisions of the amended Constitution prohibiting the participation of the armed forces in political activity, Habyarimana resigned his military title and functions. In November Stanislaus Mbonampeka resigned the justice portfolio, attributing his decision to a lack of co-operation from national security departments. At the end of March 1993 President Habyarimana resigned as leader of the MRNDD in order to attend more fully to presidential duties.

Relations with neighbouring Uganda were frequently strained during the 1980s, owing mainly to the presence of an estimated 250,000 Rwandan refugees in Uganda, most of whom were members of Rwanda's Tutsi minority (and their descendants) who had fled their homeland following successive outbreaks of persecution by the Hutu regime in 1959, 1963 and 1973. An appreciable improvement in relations between the two countries was achieved through increased diplomatic activity in the late 1980s. However, this was undermined when, in early October 1990, rebel forces, based in Uganda, invaded northern Rwanda, occupying several towns. The 4,000-strong rebel army, known as the Front patriotique rwandais (FPR) or *Inkotanyi*, was composed mainly of Rwandan Tutsi refugees, including its leader, Maj.-Gen. Fred Rwigyema, a deputy commander in Uganda's armed forces, the National Resistance Army (NRA) and formerly Ugandan Deputy Minister of Defence. The FPR's avowed aim was the overthrow of the Habyarimana regime and the repatriation of all Rwandan refugees. The Rwandan Government accused the Ugandan leadership of supporting the rebel forces (many of whom had served in the NRA), although this accusation was strenuously denied. With the assistance of French, Belgian and Zairean troops, the Rwandan army succeeded in repelling the FPR before it could reach Kigali. According to government reports, hundreds of rebels were killed. In late October the Government declared a cease-fire, although hostilities continued in northern Rwanda. In early November it was reported that Rwigyema had been killed by his second-in-command during the early stages of the invasion, following conflict within the FPR. Further incursions into Rwanda by the FPR occurred in December 1990 and in January and February 1991, but were repulsed by the Rwandan armed forces. A conference on the issue of the Rwandan refugees was convened in Tanzania in mid-February 1991. In an attempt to end the civil war, the Rwandan Government offered a general amnesty for all Tutsi refugees residing abroad and, in the event of a cease-fire, for FPR members. In late March, following high-level discussions in Zaire, the Government and the FPR agreed to observe a cease-fire, but in April it was reported that attacks by the FPR continued.

Negotiations to reach a peace settlement, conducted under the aegis of the Organization of African Unity (OAU) in early September 1991 in Zaire (and attended by President Habyarimana, the Presidents of Burundi, Zaire and Nigeria, the Prime Minister of Tanzania and the Ugandan Minister of Foreign Affairs), resulted in a unanimous commitment to the immediate implementation of a new cease-fire. Several days later the Rwandan Minister of Foreign Affairs announced the Government's readiness to enter into an unconditional dialogue with the FPR. Following the first round of direct negotiations between the two sides, with the personal mediation of President Mobutu of Zaire, both sides expressed their willingness to abide by the terms of the newly-amended cease-fire agreement. By mid-November, however, the terms of the cease-fire had been breached on numerous occasions.

Renewed dialogue was initiated between the new transitional Government and FPR representatives in May 1992, and formal discussions were conducted in Paris during June. Further negotiations, in Arusha, Tanzania, in July, resulted in an agreement on the implementation of a new cease-fire, to be effective from the end of July, and the creation of an OAU-sponsored military observer group (GOM), to comprise representatives from both sides, together with officers drawn from the armed forces of Nigeria, Senegal, Zimbabwe and Mali. However, subsequent negotiations in Tanzania, during August, September and October, failed to resolve outstanding problems concerning the creation of a 'neutral zone' between the Rwandan armed forces and the FPR (to be enforced by the GOM), the incorporation of the FPR in a future combined Rwandan national force, the repatriation of refugees, and the demands of the FPR for full participation in a transitional government and legislature. In January 1993 a preliminary agreement on the last of these issues was immediately rejected by the MRNDD leadership, and by the President, prompting violent political and ethnic clashes. Boniface Ngulinzaira, the Minister of Foreign Affairs and Co-operation (and an MDR member), was subsequently replaced as leader of the Government's peace delegation by the Minister of National Defence, James Gasana, of the MRNDD.

A resurgence in violence followed the breakdown of negotiations in early February 1993, resulting in the deaths of hundreds on both sides. An estimated 1m. civilians fled southwards and to neighbouring Uganda and Tanzania, in order to escape the fighting, as the FPR advanced as far as Ruhengeri and seemed, for a time, poised to occupy Kigali. The actions of the FPR were denounced by Belgium, France and the USA. French reinforcements were dispatched to join a small French military contingent, stationed in Kigali since October 1990 in order to protect French nationals. Meanwhile, the Commander of the 50-member GOM declared that it had inadequate manpower and resources to contain the FPR front line, and was to request an additional 400 troops from the OAU.

In late February 1993 the Government accepted FPR terms for a cease-fire, in return for an end to attacks against FPR positions and on Tutsi communities, and the withdrawal of foreign troops. Although fighting continued with fluctuating intensity, fresh peace negotiations were convened in March, in Arusha. In late March the French Government began to withdraw French troops to the Central African Republic.

Negotiations conducted during April 1993 failed to produce a solution to the crucial issue of the structure of a future single armed Rwandan force. In the same month the five participating parties in the ruling coalition agreed to a three-month extension of the Government's mandate, in order to facilitate the successful conclusion of a peace accord. Significant progress was made during fresh talks between the Government and the FPR in the northern town of Kinihira, during May, when a timetable for the demobilization of 19,000-strong security forces was agreed. Later in the month further consensus was reached on the creation of a 'neutral zone'. In June agreement was concluded on a protocol for the repatriation of all Rwandan refugees resident in Uganda, Tanzania and Zaire, including recommendations that compensation should be made available to those forced into exile more than 12 years ago. In late June the UN Security Council approved the creation of the UN Observer Mission Uganda-Rwanda (UNOMUR), comprising 81 military observers and 24 officials, to be deployed on the Ugandan side of the border for an initial period of six months, in order to ensure that no military supply line might be maintained for the FPR.

In July 1993, in the context of the improved likelihood of a prompt resolution of the conflict, President Habyarimana met with delegates from the five political parties represented in the Government and sought a further extension of the mandate of the coalition Government. However, the Prime Minister's insistence that the FPR should be represented in any newly-mandated government exacerbated existing divisions within the MDR, prompting Habyarimana to conclude the agreement with a conciliatory group of MDR dissidents, including the education minister, Agathe Uwilingiyimana, who was elected to the premiership. Several changes to the Council of Ministers were subsequently effected in order to fill positions vacated by disaffected MDR members. The outgoing Prime Minister, Dismas Nsengiyaremye, accused Habyarimana of having deliberately jeopardized the peace accord with the FPR, and of having committed procedural malpractice in the selection of Uwilingiyimana as his successor.

In late July 1993 the new Prime Minister reported that she had been abducted by MDR members, who had attempted to force her to resign the premiership. Meanwhile, a communiqué from MDR officials loyal to former Prime Minister Nsengiyaremye announced that Uwilingiyimana, together with three MDR ministers and party President Faustin Twagiramungu, had been expelled from the MDR.

On 4 August 1993 a peace accord was formally signed by President Habyarimana and Col Alex Kanyarengwe of the FPR, in Arusha, Tanzania. A new transitional government, to be headed by a mutually-approved Prime Minister (later identified as Faustin Twagiramungu), would be installed by 10 September. Multi-party general elections would be conducted after a 22-month period during which the FPR would join the political mainstream and participate in a transitional government and national assembly. In mid-August the curfew in Kigali was ended, and military road-blocks were removed from all but three northern prefectures. By the end of the month, however, the Prime Minister was forced to make a national appeal for calm, following reports of renewed outbreaks of violence in Kigali and Butare. Failure to establish a transitional government and legislature by 10 September was attributed by the Government and the FPR to the increasingly precarious national security situation, and both sides urged the prompt dispatch of a neutral UN force to facilitate the implementation of the accord. Meanwhile, relations between the Government and the FPR deteriorated, following the rebels' assertion that the Government had infringed the terms of the accord by attempting to dismantle and reorganize those government departments assigned to the FPR under the terms of the peace agreement.

On 5 October 1993 the UN Security Council adopted Resolution 872, endorsing the recommendation of the UN Secretary-General for the creation of UN Assistance Mission to Rwanda (UNAMIR), to be deployed in Rwanda for an initial period of six months, with a mandate to monitor observance of the cease-fire, to contribute to the security of the capital and to facilitate the repatriation of refugees. UNAMIR, which was to incorporate UNOMUR and GOM, was formally inaugurated on 1 November, and was expected to comprise some 2,500 personnel when fully operational. (Resolution 928, approved by the Security Council in June 1994, provided for the termination of UNOMUR on 21 September 1994.) In early December 1993, in compliance with the stipulations of the Arusha accord, the French Government announced the withdrawal of its military contingent in Kigali, and in mid-December the UN Secretary-General's Special Representative in Rwanda, Jacques-Roger Booh-Booh, declared that the UN was satisfied that conditions had been sufficiently fulfilled to allow for the inauguration of the transitional institutions by the end of the month.

In late December 1993 a 600-strong FPR battalion was escorted to the capital by UNAMIR officials (as detailed in the Arusha accord), in order to ensure the safety of FPR representatives selected to participate in the transitional government and legislature. However, dissension within a number of political parties had obstructed the satisfactory nomination of representatives to the transitional institutions, forcing a further postponement of their inauguration. On 5 January 1994 Juvénal Habyarimana was invested as President of a transitional government, for a 22-month period, under the terms of the Arusha accord. (Habyarimana's previous term of office, in accordance with the Constitution, had expired on 19 December 1993.) The inauguration of the transitional government and legislature, scheduled for the same day, was again postponed when several important participants, notably representatives of the FPR, the MDR, the PSD and the PDC, and the President of the Constitutional Court, failed to attend. While government spokesmen identified the need to resolve internal differences within the MDR and the PL as the crucial expedient for the implementation of the new government and legislature, a joint statement, issued by the PSD, the PDC and factions of the MDR and the PL, accused the President of having abused the authority afforded his office by the Arusha accord by interfering in the selection of prospective ministers and deputies. This charge was reiterated by the FPR in late February, when it rejected a list of proposed future gubernatorial and legislative representatives (tentatively agreed following several days of discussions between the President, the Prime Minister and the five participating parties of the current administration) as having been compiled as the result of a campaign of intimidation and manipulation by the President in order to secure the participation of his own supporters, and thereby prolong his political influence. The FPR insisted that a definitive list of each party's representatives in the future transitional institutions had been approved by the Constitutional Court in January. In March the Prime Minister designate, Faustin Twagiramungu, declared that he had fulfilled his consultative role as outlined in the Arusha accord, and announced the composition of a transitional government, in an attempt to accelerate the installation of the transitional bodies. However, political opposition to the proposed Council of Ministers persisted, and President Habyarimana insisted that the list of proposed legislative deputies, newly presented by Agathe Uwilingiyimana, should be modified to include representatives of additional political parties, including the reactionary Coalition pour la défense de la république (CDR—whose participation was vociferously opposed by the FPR, owing to its alleged failure to subscribe to the code of ethics that governed the behaviour of political parties and which proscribed policies advocating tribal discrimination), prompting a further postponement of the establishment of a transitional administration.

Meanwhile political frustration had erupted into violence in late February 1994, with the murder of the Minister of Public Works and Energy, Félicien Gatabazi of the PSD, who had actively pursued the peace accord and the transitional administration. Hours later, the CDR leader, Martin Bucyana, was killed, in apparent retaliation, by an angry mob of PSD supporters, provoking a series of violent confrontations resulting in some 30–40 deaths.

In early April 1994 the UN Security Council (which in February had warned that the UN presence in Rwanda might be withdrawn if no further progress was swiftly made in the implementation of the Arusha accord) agreed to extend UNAMIR's mandate for four months, pending a review of progress made in implementing the accord, to be conducted after six weeks.

On 6 April 1994 the President's aircraft, returning from a regional summit meeting in Dar es Salaam, Tanzania, was fired upon, above Kigali airport, and exploded on landing, killing all 10 passengers, including President Habyarimana. The President of Burundi, Cyprien Ntaryamira, two Burundian cabinet ministers, the Chief of Staff of the Rwandan armed forces, and a senior diplomat were among the other victims. In Kigali the presidential guard immediately initiated a brutal campaign of retributive violence against political opponents of the late President, although it remained unclear who had been responsible for the attack on the aircraft, and UNAMIR officials attempting to investigate the site of the crash were obstructed by the presidential guard. As politicians and civilians fled the capital, the horror of the political assassinations was compounded by attacks on the clergy, UNAMIR personnel (10 Belgian troops were reportedly persuaded to disarm before being executed) and members of the Tutsi tribe. Hutu civilians were forced, under pain of death, to murder their Tutsi neighbours, and the mobilization of the *interahamwe*, or unofficial militias (allegedly affiliated to the MRNDD and the CDR), apparently committed to the massacre of Government opponents and Tutsi civilians, was encouraged by the presidential guard (with support from some factions of the armed forces) and by inflammatory broadcasts from Radio-Télévision Libre des Mille Collines in Kigali. The Prime Minister, Agathe Uwilingiyimana, the President of the Constitutional Court, the Ministers of Labour and Social Affairs and of Information, and the Chairman of the PSD were among the prominent politicians murdered, or pronounced missing and presumed dead, within hours of the death of President Habyarimana.

On 8 April 1994 the Speaker of the CND, Dr Théodore Sindikubwabo, announced that he had assumed the office of interim President of the Republic, in accordance with the provisions of the 1991 Constitution. The five remaining participating political parties and factions of the Government selected a new Prime Minister, Jean Kambanda, and a new Council of Ministers (drawn largely from the MRNDD) from among their ranks. The legitimacy of the new administration was immediately challenged by the FPR, who claimed that the constitutional right of succession to the Presidency of the Speaker of the CND had been superseded by Habyarimana's inauguration, in January, as President under the terms of the Arusha accord. (However, Félicien Ngango, who had been nominated to lead the transitional national assembly, and therefore to succeed the President in the event of his untimely death, had been an early victim of the presidential guard's campaign of political 'cleansing'.) The legal status of the Government (which promptly removed to the town of Gitarama to escape escalating violence in the capital) was subsequently rejected by factions of the PL and the MDR (led by Faustin Twagiramungu), and by the PDC and the PSD (who in May announced their alliance as the Forces démocratiques pour le changement).

In mid-April 1994 the FPR announced its intention to resume an armed offensive from its northern stronghold, in order to relieve its beleaguered battalion in Kigali, to restore order to the capital and to halt the massacre of civilians. Grenade attacks and mortar fire intensified in the capital, prompting the UN to mediate a fragile 60-hour cease-fire, during which small evacuation forces from several countries escorted foreign nationals out of Rwanda. Belgium's UNAMIR contingent of more than 400 troops was also withdrawn, having encountered increasing hostility as a result of persistent rumours that Belgian elements had been involved in the attack on President Habyarimana's aircraft, and were providing logistical support to the FPR (accusations which were formally levelled by the Rwandan Ambassador to Zaire later in the month), which were emphatically denied by the Belgian Government.

In late April 1994 members of the Government embarked upon a diplomatic offensive throughout Europe and Africa, seeking to enhance the credibility of the Government through international recognition of its legal status. However, this initiative achieved only limited success (notably in France, Egypt and Togo), and the FPR's continued refusal to enter into dialogue with the 'illegal' administration (preferring to negotiate with representatives of the military high command) proved a major obstacle to attempts, undertaken by the UN and the Presidents of Tanzania and Zaire, to sponsor a new cease-fire agreement in late April and early May.

As the violent political crusade unleashed by the presidential guard and the *interahamwe* (described by the human rights organization, Amnesty International, as a carefully trained militia numbering some 30,000) gathered national momentum, the militia's indentification of all members of the Tutsi tribe as political opponents of the State promoted tribal polarization, resulting in an effective pogrom. Reports of mass Tutsi graves and unprovoked attacks on fleeing Tutsi refugees, and on those seeking refuge in schools, hospitals and churches, provoked unqualified international condemnation and outrage, and promises were made of financial and logistical aid for an estimated 2m. displaced Rwandans (some 250,000 had fled across the border to Tanzania in a 24-hour period in late April 1994) who were threatened by famine and disease in makeshift camps. By late May attempts to assess the full scale of the humanitarian catastrophe in Rwanda were complicated by unverified reports that the FPR (who claimed to control more than one-half of the country) was perpetrating retaliatory atrocities against Hutu civilians. However, unofficial estimates indicated that 200,000–500,000 Rwandans had been killed since early April.

On 21 April 1994, in the context of the deteriorating security situation in Kigali, and the refusal of the Rwandan armed forces to agree to the neutral policing of the capital's airport (subsequently secured by the FPR), the UN Security Council resolved to reduce significantly its representation in Rwanda to 270 personnel, a move which attracted criticism from the Government, the FPR, international relief organizations and the international community in general. However, on 16 May, following intense international pressure and the disclosure of the vast scale of the humanitarian crisis in the region, the UN Security Council approved Resolution 917, providing for the eventual deployment of some 5,500 UN troops with a revised mandate, including the policing of Kigali's airport (in order to safeguard the arrival of vital relief supplies) and the protection of refugees in designated 'safe areas'. Full deployment of the force, however, was to be delayed pending a comprehensive assessment of the most effective positioning of the troops, owing largely to the reservations of the USA, which had favoured the dispatch of a smaller mission to police 'protective zones' for refugees along the country's borders. In late May the UN Secretary-General criticized the failure of the UN member nations to respond to his invitation to participate in the enlarged force (only Ghana, Ethiopia and Senegal had agreed to provide small contingents). Further UN-sponsored attempts to negotiate a cease-fire failed in late May and early June, and the FPR made significant territorial gains in southern Rwanda, forcing the Government to flee Gitarama and seek refuge in the western town of Kibuye.

In early June 1994 the UN Security Council adopted Resolution 925, whereby the mandate of the revised UN mission in Rwanda (UNAMIR II) was extended until December 1994. However, the UN Secretary-General continued to encounter considerable difficulty in securing equipment and armaments requested by those African countries which had agreed to participate. By mid-June the emergence of confirmed reports of retributive murders committed by FPR members (including the massacres, in two separate incidents in early June, of 22 clergymen, among them the Roman Catholic Archbishop of Kigali) and the collapse of a fragile truce (negotiated at a summit meeting of the OAU in Tunis, Tunisia) prompted the French Government to announce its willingness to lead an armed police action, endorsed by the UN, in Rwanda. Although the French Government insisted that the French military presence (expected to total 2,000 troops) would maintain strict political neutrality, and operate, from the border regions, in a purely humanitarian capacity pending the arrival of a multinational UN force, the FPR was vehemently opposed to its deployment, citing the French administration's maintenance of high-level contacts with representatives of the self-proclaimed Rwandan Government as an indication of political bias. While the UN Secretary-General welcomed the French initiative, and tacit endorsement of the project was contained in Resolution 929, approved by the Security Council in late June, the OAU expressed serious reservations regarding the appropriateness of the action. On 23 June a first contingent of 150 French marine commandos launched 'Operation Turquoise', entering the western town of Cyangugu, in preparation for a large-scale operation to protect refugees in the area. By mid-July the French had successfully relieved several beleaguered Tutsi communities, and had established a temporary 'safe haven' for the displaced population in the south-west, through which a massive exodus of Hutu refugees began to flow, prompted by reports (disseminated by supporters of the defeated interim government) that the advancing FPR forces were seeking violent retribution against the Hutu. An estimated 1m. Rwandans sought refuge in the Zairean border town of Goma, while a similar number attempted to cross the border elsewhere in the south-west. The FPR had swiftly secured all major cities and strategic territorial positions, but had halted its advance several kilometres from the boundaries of the French-controlled neutral zone, requesting the apprehension and return for trial of those responsible for the recent atrocities. (At the end of June the first report of the UN's Special Rapporteur on Human Rights in Rwanda—appointed in May— confirmed that as many as 500,000 Rwandans had been killed since April, and urged the establishment of an international tribunal to investigate allegations of genocide; in early July the UN announced the creation of a commission of inquiry for this purpose.)

On 19 July 1994 Pasteur Bizimungu, a Hutu, was inaugurated as President for a five-year term. On the same day the FPR announced the composition of a new Government of National Unity, to be headed by Faustin Twagiramungu as Prime Minister. The majority of cabinet posts were assigned to FPR members (including the FPR military chief Maj.-Gen. Paul Kagame, who became Minister of Defence and also assumed the newly-created post of Vice-President), while the remainder were divided among the MDR, the PL, the PSD and the PDC. The new administration urged all refugees to return to Rwanda, and issued assurances that civilian Hutus could return safely to their homes. The Prime Minister identified the immediate aims of the administration as the restoration of peace and democracy, the reactivation of the economy and the repatriation of refugees. Identity cards bearing details of ethnic origin were to be abolished forthwith. The new Government declared its intention to honour the terms of the Arusha accord within the context of an extended period of transition. However, the MRNDD and the CDR were to be excluded from participation in government.

The FPR victory and the new administration were promptly recognized by the French Government, which urged the new Rwandan Government to assume responsibility for relief operations. In return, Twagiramungu was reported to have expressed his appreciation of the humanitarian and stabilizing nature of the French operation. The French Government announced its intention to begin a reduction in personnel by the end of July 1994, with a view to complete withdrawal by the end of August. In mid-July France began to equip a force of 500 troops drawn from Senegal, the Congo, Chad, Niger and Guinea-Bissau, to assist the French contingent and facilitate the eventual transfer of responsiblity to a UN force.

Meanwhile, conditions in refugee camps in Zaire had continued to deteriorate, as hunger and cholera became more widespread. By the end of July 1994, despite an intensification of international relief efforts in the region, at least 2,000 refugees were dying each day, adding to a refugee camp death toll already in excess of 20,000. In response to a UN plea for some US $434m. to address the refugee crisis, the US President, Bill Clinton, pledged $185m. in aid and announced a relief programme which included the establishment of an airlift centre in Uganda and the provision of uncontaminated water. Later in the month it was reported that the new Rwandan Government had granted permission for the USA to establish a relief programme headquarters in Kigali. As many as 2,000 US troops were expected to carry out humanitarian missions in Rwanda and eastern Zaire. Also in July, the British Government approved the deployment of a British military contingent in the border region, to help relief efforts. However, non-governmental relief agencies were highly critical of the inadequate and tardy nature of the international response to the crisis. In late July President Bizimungu met with the Presidents of Zaire and Tanzania, and concluded agreements on the disarmament and gradual repatriation of refugees.

Amid persistent rumours that the Rwandan armed forces were attempting to regroup and rearm in Zaire in preparation for a counter-offensive strike against the FPR, the exiled former Government continued to seek recognition as the legitimate Rwandan administration and urged the international community to oversee the establishment in Rwanda of political institutions based on broad consensus and the organization of general elections within one year. However, the claims of the former Government were seriously undermined by the European Union's recognition of the new Rwandan Government of National Unity in mid-September 1994.

On 20 August 1994 the UN initiated the deployment of some 2,500 UNAMIR II forces, largely drawn from Ghana and Ethiopia, in the security zone (which was redesignated 'zone four'). The following day French troops began to withdraw from the area (the final contingent departed on 20 September), prompting hundreds of thousands of internally displaced Hutu refugees within the zone to move to Zairean border areas. The Zairean Government announced the immediate closure of the border crossing at Bukavu and the regulation of refugee arrivals at other border posts, expressing concern that the country had inadequate resources to sustain another refugee camp on the scale of that at Goma. An estimated 500,000 refugees remained at camps in the former security zone at the end of August, as the first Rwandan government officials were assigned to customs and immigration and army recruitment duties in the region.

In early August the Prime Minister, Faustin Twagiramungu, declared the country bankrupt, accusing the former Government of having fled to Zaire with all Rwanda's exchange reserves. (New banknotes were subsequently printed in order to invalidate the former currency.) Twagiramungu stressed that economic recovery could only be achieved following the return to their farms and workplaces of the country's displaced population. The Government suffered a further financial setback in October, when the Minister of Foreign Affairs and Co-operation, Jean-Marie Ndagijimana, was reported to have absconded, while abroad, with government funds for diplomatic missions abroad totalling US $187,000. A replacement minister, Anastase Gasana, was named in December.

In November 1994 a multi-party protocol of understanding was concluded, providing for a number of amendments to the terms of the August 1993 Arusha accord relating to the establishment of a transitional legislature. The most notable of the new provisions was the exclusion from the legislative process of members of those parties implicated in alleged acts of genocide during 1994. A 70-member National Transitional Assembly was formally inaugurated on 12 December, with a composition including five representatives of the armed forces and one member of the national police force. On 5 May 1995 the new legislature announced its adoption of a new Constitution based on selected articles of the 1991 Constitution, the terms of the August 1993 Arusha accord, the FPR's victory declaration of July 1994 and the November multi-party protocol of understanding.

In late 1994 Hutu refugees within Rwanda and in neighbouring countries were continuing to resist the exhortations of the UN and the new Rwandan administration to return to their homes, despite the deteriorating security situation in many camps which had forced the withdrawal of a number of relief agencies. Hutu militia were reported to have assumed control of several camps, notably Katale in Zaire and Benaco in Tanzania, where it was reported that a state of near lawlessness existed. Reports also emerged that Hutu civilians intending to return to their homes were subjected to violent intimidation by the militia. It was further alleged that male Hutu refugees were being forced to undergo military training in preparation for a renewed military conflict. In early November the UN Secretary-General appealed to the international community for contributions to a 12,000-strong force to police the refugee camps. By late January 1995, however, the UN had abandoned attempts to raise the force, having failed to secure a commitment from any of 60 petitioned nations for the provision of equipment or personnel for such a mission. A compromise agreement was subsequently concluded with Zairean troops for the supervision of camps in Zaire. At the end of November 1994 the UNAMIR II mandate was extended for a further six months, and in June 1995, at the request of the Rwandan Government, the strength of the force was reduced from 5,586 to 2,330 personnel (to be further reduced by September), and the six-month mandate was again renewed.

The reluctance of many refugees to return to their homes was also attributed to persistent allegations that the Tutsi-dominated FPR armed forces (the Armée patriotique rwandaise—APR) were conducting a systematic campaign of reprisal attacks against returning Hutu civilians. In an address to the UN General Assembly in early October 1994, President Bizimungu refuted these allegations, presented by investigating officers of the UN High Commissioner for Refugees, and insisted that the Government should not be held responsible for what a UN inquiry, conducted earlier in the month, had concluded were frequent but individual acts of retaliation. In late August Bizimungu had announced the execution of two FPR members, following their court martial for involvement in violent acts of reprisal. It was reported that some 50–70 FPR members were awaiting trial for similar offences. In February 1995 the UN Security Council adopted Resolution 977, whereby Arusha was designated the venue for the International Criminal Tribunal for Rwanda. The six-member Tribunal, to be headed by a Senegalese lawyer, Laity Kama, was inaugurated in late June for a four-year term. It was reported that the Tribunal intended to investigate allegations made against some 400 individuals (many of them resident outside of Rwanda) of direct involvement in the planning and execution of a series of crimes against humanity perpetrated in Rwanda during 1994. At a national level, preliminary hearings against an estimated 35,000 Rwandan nationals, imprisoned in Kigali on similar charges, were initiated in early 1995 but were immediately suspended owing to lack of resources.

International scepticism regarding the Government's programme of refugee repatriation increased in early 1995, following a series of uncompromising initiatives to encourage the return of internally displaced Rwandans (including the interruption of food supplies to refugee camps), culminating in the forcible closure of the camps through military intervention. An attempt to dismantle the Kibeho camp in southern Rwanda, in late April, provoked widespread international condemnation after APR troops opened fire on refugees amid confusion arising from the actions of some hostile elements within the camp and a sudden attempt by large numbers of anxious refugees to break the military cordon. While the Government stated that the number of fatalities (many as a result of suffocation) from the ensuing panic was 338, independent witnesses estimated as many as 5,000 deaths. The report of an international inquiry into the incident, published in mid-May, concluded that the massacre had not been premeditated but that the armed forces had employed excessive force in its response to the situation. The commission also estimated the number of fatalities to be far in excess of the official total. In June 1995, according to official government estimates, there were about 2m. externally displaced Rwandans, largely concentrated in Zaire, Tanzania and Burundi. Of the 1.3m. refugee to have returned to the country since the FPR victory some 700,000 were displaced before the events of April 1994.

In 1985 Rwanda and Burundi signed an accord of co-operation covering political, economic, commercial, technical, scientific, social and cultural affairs. However, in recent years bilateral relations have been undermined frequently by the problems arising from a regular flow of large numbers of refugees between the two countries as a result of ethnic and political violence.

In 1976 Rwanda, with Burundi and Zaire, established a regional grouping, the Economic Community of the Great Lakes Countries (Communauté économique des pays des Grands Lacs—CEPGL). In January 1989 the Presidents of Rwanda, Burundi and Zaire agreed to form a joint commission, within the framework of the CEPGL, to guarantee the security of the three countries.

## Government

Executive power is exercised by the President (Head of State), assisted by an appointed Council of Ministers. Legislative power is held by the President in conjunction with the 70-member Transitional National Assembly. The country is divided into 11 prefectures and subdivided into 145 communes or municipalities, each administered by a governor, who is appointed by the President and assisted by an elected council of local inhabitants.

**Defence**

All armed services form part of the army. In June 1993 the total strength of the army was 5,200 (including 200 air force personnel), and paramilitary forces totalled 1,200 men. Following the victory of the Front patriotique rwandais (FPR) over the Rwandan armed forces in July 1994, responsibility for national defence was assumed by the FPR's military wing, the Armée patriotique rwandaise (APR). Defence expenditure for 1991 was 13,184.2m. Rwanda francs, equivalent to 33.8% of total government expenditure.

**Economic Affairs**

In 1993, according to estimates by the World Bank, Rwanda's gross national product (GNP), measured at average 1991–93 prices, was US $1,499m., equivalent to $200 per head. During 1985–93, it was estimated, GNP per head decreased, in real terms, at an average annual rate of 3.5%. Over the same period, the population increased by an annual average of 2.9%. Rwanda's gross domestic product (GDP) increased, in real terms, by an annual average of 0.3% in 1980–92.

Agriculture (including forestry and fishing) contributed an estimated 41% of GDP in 1992. An estimated 91% of the labour force were employed in the sector (mainly at subsistence level) in 1993. The principal food crops are plantains, sweet potatoes, cassava and dry beans. The principal cash crops are coffee (which provided 60.2% of total export earnings in 1991), tea and pyrethrum. Goats and cattle are the principal livestock. During 1980–92 agricultural GDP declined by an annual average of 0.3%.

Industry (including mining, manufacturing, power and construction) employed about 3% of the working population in 1989, and provided 21.5% of GDP in the same year. During 1980–92 industrial GDP increased by an annual average of 1.0%.

Mining and quarrying contributed only 0.4% of GDP in 1989, and the sector employed 0.1% of the labour force in that year. Cassiterite (a tin-bearing ore) is Rwanda's principal mineral resource. There are also reserves of wolframite (a tungsten-bearing ore), gold, columbo-tantalite and beryl, and work has begun on the exploitation of natural gas reserves beneath Lake Kivu, which are believed to be among the largest in the world.

Manufacturing employed only 1.4% of the labour force in 1989, but provided 13.5% of GDP in that year. Based on the value of output, the principal branches of manufacturing in 1986 were beverages and tobacco (37.8% of the total), food products, chemical, petroleum, rubber and plastic products, and metals, metal products, machinery, etc. During 1980–92 manufacturing GDP increased by 1.6% per year.

Electrical energy is derived almost entirely from hydroelectric power. In 1990 Rwanda imported 54% of its electricity, but was expected to be in a position to export, following the completion of the Ruzizi-II plant (a joint venture with Burundi and Zaire). Imports of mineral fuels comprised 12.8% of the total value of imports in 1991.

In 1992 Rwanda recorded a visible trade deficit of US $171.9m., and there was a deficit of $84.6m. on the current account of the balance of payments. Rwanda's principal trading partners are Kenya, the Belgo-Luxembourg Economic Union and other countries of the European Union (EU), Japan and the USA. The principal exports in 1991 were coffee and tea. Imports comprised consumer goods (including food, clothing, mineral fuels and lubricants), semi-manufactures (including construction materials) and capital goods (including transport equipment, machinery and tools).

For 1993 a budgetary deficit of 19,590m. Rwanda francs was envisaged. The development budget for 1990 was set at 14,320m. Rwanda francs, of which about 60% was to come from external sources. At the end of 1993 Rwanda's external debt totalled US $910.1m., of which $835.8m. was long-term public debt. The cost of debt-servicing in 1993 was equivalent to 5.0% of the value of exports of goods and services. In 1985–93 the average annual rate of inflation was 6.4%; consumer prices increased by an average of 12.4% in 1993.

Rwanda is a member of the Organization for the Management and Development of the Kagera River Basin (see p. 240), and, with Burundi and Zaire, is a founding member of the Economic Community of the Great Lakes Countries (see p. 238). In November 1993 Rwanda was among members of the Preferential Trade Area for Eastern and Southern African States (see p. 240) to sign a treaty providing for the establishment of a Common Market for Eastern and Southern Afica.

Rwanda's economic development is hampered by its high level of population density (the highest in continental Africa), as well as by its remoteness from the sea. As a result, Rwanda has traditionally relied heavily on foreign aid, particularly from the EU and its individual member states. In recent years agricultural production in many areas of Rwanda has diminished, owing to erosion and over-intensive farming methods. Attempts to increase the yield of small farm plots have included a recent initiative to cultivate climbing beans. In late 1993 the International Development Association approved a loan of US $15m. to help finance agricultural research projects and the transformation of existing research institutes in Rwanda. It was envisaged that the full implementation of the research development programme would generate an annual increase in the sector's growth of some 4%. A World Bank initiative to restock Rwanda's seed bank was announced in December 1994. The invasion of northern Rwanda by rebel forces in October 1990 (and the subsequent sustained hostilities) proved a major obstacle to the establishment of economic stability. Rwanda's economic prospects were further undermined by the unprecedented scale of political chaos and attendant violence resulting from the violent death of President Habyarimana in April 1994. The success of attempts by any future administration to address the economic repercussions of the humanitarian catastrophe represented by the massacre of an estimated 200,000–500,000 civilians, the flight to neighbouring countries or displacement within Rwanda of some 2m. refugees, and considerable damage to the country's communications infrastructure, seemed likely to be wholly dependent upon the financial response of the international aid community. Although commitments to the provision of substantial levels of financial assistance were made by the World Bank, the USA and the EU in late 1994 and early 1995, these fell well short of the US $1,400m. requested from the UN by the Rwandan authorities for the purposes of reconstruction, and disbursement of these amounts was expected to be declared dependent on the Government's observance of human rights, following the Kibeho refugee camp massacre in April 1995 (see Recent History).

**Social Welfare**

State schemes cover family allowances, accidents and pensions. All wage-earners must take part in the Social Security Scheme. The Government-assisted Native Welfare Fund provides community centres and medical services. Religious missions also provide socio-medical services. Of total expenditure by the central Government in 1991, 1,285m. Rwanda francs (3.3%) was for health. In 1981 Rwanda had 232 hospital establishments, with a total of 7,882 beds, and in 1983 there were 163 physicians working in the country. In November 1993 the Belgian Government announced financial support amounting to 326.5m. Rwanda francs for health projects in Rwanda.

**Education**

Primary education, beginning at seven years of age and lasting for seven years, is officially compulsory. Secondary education, which is not compulsory, begins at the age of 15 and lasts for a further six years. Schools are administered by the state and by Christian missions. In 1990 enrolment at primary schools included an estimated 72% of children in the relevant age-group, but the comparable ratio for secondary enrolment was only 8%. In 1978, according to estimates by UNESCO, the average rate of adult illiteracy was 61.8% (males 49.2%; females 73.4%). Rwanda has a university, with campuses at Butare and Ruhengeri, and several other institutions of higher education, but some students attend universities abroad, particularly in Belgium, France or Germany. In 1989/90 an estimated 3,389 students were receiving higher education. In 1991 an estimated 17.1% of total government expenditure was allocated to education.

**Public Holidays**

**1995:** 1 January (New Year), 28 January (Democracy Day), 17 April (Easter Monday), 1 May (Labour Day), 25 May (Ascension Day), 5 June (Whit Monday), 1 July (National Holiday, anniversary of independence), 15 August (Assumption), 25 September (Kamarampaka Day, anniversary of 1961 refer-

RWANDA

endum), 26 October (Armed Forces Day), 1 November (All Saints' Day), 25 December (Christmas).
**1996:** 1 January (New Year), 28 January (Democracy Day), 8 April (Easter Monday), 1 May (Labour Day), 16 May (Ascension Day), 27 May (Whit Monday), 1 July (National Holiday, anniversary of independence), 15 August (Assumption), 25 September (Kamarampaka Day, anniversary of 1961 referendum), 26 October (Armed Forces Day), 1 November (All Saints' Day), 25 December (Christmas).

**Weights and Measures**
The metric system is in force.

# Statistical Survey

Source (unless otherwise stated): Office rwandais d'information, BP 83, Kigali; tel. 5665.

## Area and Population

### AREA, POPULATION AND DENSITY

| | |
|---|---:|
| Area (sq km) | 26,338* |
| Population (census results) | |
| 15–16 August 1978 | 4,830,984 |
| 15 August 1991† | |
| Males | 3,487,189 |
| Females | 3,677,805 |
| Total | 7,164,994 |
| Density (per sq km) at 1991 census | 272.0 |

* 10,169 sq miles.   † Provisional results, revised total 7,142,755.

### POPULATION BY PREFECTURE (1990)*

| | |
|---|---:|
| Butare | 762,735 |
| Byumba | 782,230 |
| Cyangugu | 514,279 |
| Gikongoro | 466,576 |
| Gisenyi | 734,690 |
| Gitarama | 851,288 |
| Kibungo | 651,887 |
| Kibuye | 471,066 |
| Kigali | 913,481 |
| Kigali-Ville | 232,733 |
| Ruhengeri | 767,531 |
| **Total** | 7,148,496 |

* Provisional.

### PRINCIPAL TOWNS (population at 1978 census)

| | | | |
|---|---:|---|---:|
| Kigali (capital) | 117,749 | Ruhengeri | 16,025 |
| Butare | 21,691 | Gisenyi | 12,436 |

### BIRTHS AND DEATHS (UN estimates, annual averages)

| | 1975–80 | 1980–85 | 1985–90 |
|---|---:|---:|---:|
| Birth rate (per 1,000) | 52.8 | 52.2 | 52.1 |
| Death rate (per 1,000) | 20.2 | 18.8 | 18.0 |

Source: UN, *World Population Prospects: The 1992 Revision*.

**Expectation of life** (census results, years at birth, 1978): males 45.1; females 47.7.

### ECONOMICALLY ACTIVE POPULATION
(persons aged 14 years and over, official estimates at January 1989)

| | Males | Females | Total |
|---|---:|---:|---:|
| Agriculture, hunting, forestry and fishing | 1,219,586 | 1,612,972 | 2,832,558 |
| Mining and quarrying | 4,652 | 40 | 4,692 |
| Manufacturing | 32,605 | 12,483 | 45,088 |
| Electricity, gas and water | 2,445 | 116 | 2,561 |
| Construction | 37,674 | 563 | 38,237 |
| Trade, restaurants and hotels | 61,169 | 18,857 | 80,026 |
| Transport, storage and communications | 6,796 | 536 | 7,332 |
| Financing, insurance, real estate and business services | 2,202 | 926 | 3,128 |
| Community, social and personal services | 89,484 | 30,537 | 120,021 |
| Activities not adequately defined | 5,392 | 4,021 | 9,413 |
| **Total employed** | 1,462,005 | 1,681,051 | 3,143,056 |

Source: ILO, *Year Book of Labour Statistics*.

**Mid-1993** (estimates, '000 persons): Agriculture, etc. 3,348; Total labour force 3,690 (Source: FAO, *Production Yearbook*).

## Agriculture

### PRINCIPAL CROPS ('000 metric tons)

| | 1991 | 1992 | 1993 |
|---|---:|---:|---:|
| Maize | 104* | 109 | 70† |
| Sorghum | 205* | 154 | 109 |
| Potatoes† | 280 | 280 | 260 |
| Sweet potatoes† | 850 | 770 | 700 |
| Cassava (Manioc)† | 450 | 400 | 350 |
| Yams† | 4 | 5 | 5 |
| Taro (Coco yam)† | 40 | 60 | 62 |
| Dry beans† | 210 | 200 | 190 |
| Dry peas† | 16 | 18 | 18 |
| Groundnuts (in shell)† | 10 | 12 | 12 |
| Plantains† | 2,800 | 2,900 | 2,700 |
| Coffee (green)* | 29 | 38 | 31 |
| Tea (made) | 13 | 14 | 14 |

* Unofficial figure(s).   † FAO estimate(s).
Source: FAO, *Production Yearbook*.

### LIVESTOCK (FAO estimates, '000 head)

| | 1991 | 1992 | 1993 |
|---|---:|---:|---:|
| Cattle | 600 | 610 | 610 |
| Pigs | 120 | 130 | 130 |
| Sheep | 390 | 395 | 402 |
| Goats | 1,090 | 1,100 | 1,119 |

Source: FAO, *Production Yearbook*.

# RWANDA

**LIVESTOCK PRODUCTS** (FAO estimates, '000 metric tons)

|  | 1991 | 1992 | 1993 |
|---|---|---|---|
| Beef and veal | 14 | 14 | 14 |
| Goat meat | 4 | 4 | 4 |
| Other meat | 13 | 13 | 14 |
| Cows' milk | 88 | 89 | 91 |
| Goats' milk | 14 | 14 | 14 |
| Poultry eggs | 1.9 | 1.9 | 2.0 |
| Cattle hides | 2.0 | 2.0 | 2.0 |

Source: FAO, *Production Yearbook*.

## Forestry

**ROUNDWOOD REMOVALS** ('000 cubic metres, excluding bark)

|  | 1990 | 1991 | 1992 |
|---|---|---|---|
| Sawlogs, veneer logs and logs for sleepers | 20 | 20 | 60 |
| Other industrial wood* | 208 | 208 | 208 |
| Fuel wood | 5,353 | 5,392 | 5,392* |
| **Total** | 5,581 | 5,620 | 5,660 |

* FAO estimate(s).

Source: FAO, *Yearbook of Forest Products*.

**SAWNWOOD PRODUCTION**
('000 cubic metres, including railway sleepers)

|  | 1990 | 1991 | 1992 |
|---|---|---|---|
| Total | 8 | 8 | 36 |

Source: FAO, *Yearbook of Forest Products*.

## Fishing

('000 metric tons, live weight)

|  | 1990 | 1991 | 1992 |
|---|---|---|---|
| **Total catch** (freshwater fishes) | 2.5 | 3.6 | 3.7 |

Source: FAO, *Yearbook of Fishery Statistics*.

## Mining*

(metric tons, unless otherwise indicated)

|  | 1989 | 1990 | 1991 |
|---|---|---|---|
| Tin concentrates† | 700 | 700 | 730 |
| Tungsten concentrates | 22 | 156 | 175 |
| Gold ore (kilograms) | 732‡ | 700 | 700 |

* Figures refer to the metal content of ores and concentrates.
† Source: Metallgesellschaft AG (Frankfurt).
‡ Source: US Bureau of Mines.

Source: UN, *Industrial Statistics Yearbook*.

Natural gas: about 1 million cubic metres per year.

## Industry

**SELECTED PRODUCTS**

|  | 1989 | 1990 | 1991 |
|---|---|---|---|
| Beer ('000 hectolitres) | 717 | 592 | 915 |
| Soft drinks ('000 hectolitres) | 161 | 130 | 101 |
| Cigarettes (million) | 552 | 290 | 331 |
| Footwear ('000 pairs) | 32 | 22 | 24 |
| Soap ('000 metric tons) | 9 | 10 | 9 |
| Cement ('000 metric tons) | 67 | 60 | 57 |
| Radio receivers ('000) | 8 | 6 | 2 |
| Electric energy (million kWh) | 105 | 78 | 81 |

## Finance

**CURRENCY AND EXCHANGE RATES**

**Monetary Units**
100 centimes = 1 franc rwandais (Rwanda franc).

**Sterling and Dollar Equivalents** (28 February 1994)
£1 sterling = 214.36 Rwanda francs;
US $1 = 144.24 Rwanda francs;
1,000 Rwanda francs = £4.665 = $6.933.

**Average Exchange Rate** (Rwanda francs per US $)
1991   125.14
1992   133.35
1993   144.25

Note: Since September 1983 the currency has been linked to the IMF special drawing right (SDR). Until November 1990 the mid-point exchange rate was SDR 1 = 102.71 Rwanda francs. In November 1990 a new rate of SDR 1 = 171.18 Rwanda francs was established. This remained in effect until June 1992, when the rate was adjusted to SDR 1 = 201.39 Rwanda francs.

**BUDGET** (provisional, million Rwanda francs)

| Revenue* | 1990 | 1991 | 1992 |
|---|---|---|---|
| Tax revenue | 20,310 | 23,349 | 25,274 |
| Taxes on income, profits, etc. | 4,056 | 3,602 | 4,487 |
| Social security contributions | 1,560 | 1,193 | 684 |
| Taxes on property | 107 | 15 | 80 |
| Domestic taxes on goods and services | 7,851 | 9,316 | 9,973 |
| Taxes on international trade and transactions | 5,945 | 8,278 | 8,920 |
| Other current revenue | 2,834 | 2,707 | 3,449 |
| **Total revenue** | 23,144 | 26,506 | 28,723 |

| Expenditure† | 1990 | 1991 | 1992 |
|---|---|---|---|
| Current expenditure‡ | 27,034 | 29,864 | 40,670 |
| Expenditure on goods and services | 21,312 | 26,483 | 35,593 |
| Wages and salaries | 11,773 | 13,390 | 14,545 |
| Interest payments | 2,131 | 4,292 | 4,800 |
| Subsidies and other current transfers | 6,632 | 2,898 | 4,504 |
| Capital expenditure | 13,402 | 17,794 | 14,198 |
| **Total expenditure** | 40,436 | 47,658 | 54,868 |

* Excluding grants received (million Rwandan francs): 5,871 in 1990; 13,682 in 1991; 10,796 in 1992.
† Excluding net lending (million Rwanda francs): −141 in 1990; −369 in 1991; −315 in 1992.
‡ After adjustment for changes in outstanding arrears (million Rwanda francs): −3,041 in 1990; −3,809 in 1991; −4,227 in 1992.

**1993** (estimates, million Rwanda francs): Total revenue 29,597, excluding grants (19,171); total expenditure 68,742, excluding net lending (−384).

Source: IMF, *Government Finance Statistics Yearbook*.

# RWANDA

## Statistical Survey

**NATIONAL BANK RESERVES** (US $ million at 31 December)

|  | 1992 | 1993 | 1994 |
|---|---|---|---|
| IMF special drawing rights | 3.34 | 2.90 | 2.55 |
| Reserve position in IMF | 14.30 | 13.45 | 14.29 |
| Foreign exchange | 61.08 | 31.11 | n.a. |
| **Total** | 78.72 | 47.46 | n.a. |

Source: IMF, *International Financial Statistics*.

**MONEY SUPPLY** (million Rwanda francs at 31 December)

|  | 1991 | 1992 | 1993 |
|---|---|---|---|
| Currency outside banks | 8,822 | 10,321 | 11,522 |
| Demand deposits at deposit money banks | 8,587 | 11,571 | 12,876 |
| **Total money** (incl. others) | 18,145 | 22,631 | 25,041 |

Source: IMF, *International Financial Statistics*.

**COST OF LIVING**
(Consumer Price Index for Kigali; base: 1981 = 100)

|  | 1989 | 1990 | 1991 |
|---|---|---|---|
| Food | 176.1 | 185.0 | 210.2 |
| Fuel and light | 70.1 | 72.2 | 82.4 |
| Clothing | 136.2 | 137.0 | 165.5 |
| Rent | 91.7 | 98.6 | 98.7 |
| **All items** (incl. others) | 137.8 | 143.6 | 171.8 |

**1992:** Food 225.0; All items 188.1.
**1993:** All items 211.4.

Source: ILO, *Year Book of Labour Statistics*.

**NATIONAL ACCOUNTS**
(million Rwanda francs at current prices*)
**National Income and Product**

|  | 1987 | 1988 | 1989 |
|---|---|---|---|
| Compensation of employees | 42,530 | 45,050 | 46,970 |
| Operating surplus | 102,920 | 105,310 | 116,250 |
| **Domestic factor incomes** | 145,450 | 150,360 | 163,220 |
| Consumption of fixed capital | 11,080 | 12,360 | 14,540 |
| **Gross domestic product (GDP) at factor cost** | 156,530 | 162,720 | 177,760 |
| Indirect taxes | 14,910 | 15,460 | 12,460 |
| *Less* Subsidies | — | 250 | |
| **GDP in purchasers' values** | 171,440 | 177,930 | 190,220 |
| Factor income from abroad | 800 | 690 | 750 |
| *Less* Factor income paid abroad | 3,540 | 4,260 | 2,980 |
| **Gross national product (GNP)** | 168,700 | 174,360 | 187,990 |
| *Less* Consumption of fixed capital | 11,080 | 12,360 | 14,540 |
| **National income in market prices** | 157,620 | 162,000 | 173,450 |
| Other current transfers from abroad | 6,290 | 7,120 | 6,470 |
| *Less* Other current transfers paid abroad | 2,010 | 1,950 | 1,810 |
| **National disposable income** | 161,900 | 167,170 | 178,110 |

**Expenditure on the Gross Domestic Product**

|  | 1989 | 1990 | 1991 |
|---|---|---|---|
| Government final consumption expenditure | 24,460 | 33,100 | 46,000 |
| Private final consumption expenditure | 156,940 | 159,900 | 174,900 |
| Increase in stocks | 140 | −1,800 | −3,200 |
| Gross fixed capital formation | 25,280 | 23,900 | 25,400 |
| **Total domestic expenditure** | 206,820 | 215,100 | 243,100 |
| Exports of goods and services | 15,610 | 14,900 | 20,800 |
| *Less* Imports of goods and services | 32,210 | 37,100 | 50,900 |
| **GDP in purchasers' values** | 190,220 | 192,900 | 212,900 |

**Gross Domestic Product by Economic Activity**

|  | 1987 | 1988 | 1989 |
|---|---|---|---|
| Agriculture, hunting, forestry and fishing | 65,350 | 67,440 | 75,690 |
| Mining and quarrying | 340 | 360 | 790 |
| Manufacturing | 25,040 | 24,980 | 24,930 |
| Electricity, gas and water | 1,020 | 1,170 | 950 |
| Construction | 11,940 | 12,230 | 12,880 |
| Trade, restaurants and hotels | 23,620 | 22,660 | 24,400 |
| Transport, storage and communications | 11,900 | 12,640 | 12,930 |
| Finance, insurance, real estate, etc. | 12,940 | 14,560 | 16,050 |
| Community, social and personal services | 14,610 | 15,660 | 15,760 |
| **Sub-total** | 166,760 | 171,700 | 184,380 |
| Import duties | 4,680 | 6,240 | 5,840 |
| **GDP in purchasers' values** | 171,440 | 177,940 | 190,220 |

* Figures are rounded to the nearest 10 million francs.

Source: UN, *National Accounts Statistics*.

**1990:** GDP 193,900 million francs.
**1991:** GDP 212,800 million francs.
**1992:** GDP 217,300 million francs.

(Source: IMF, *International Financial Statistics*.)

**BALANCE OF PAYMENTS** (US $ million)

|  | 1990 | 1991 | 1992 |
|---|---|---|---|
| Merchandise exports f.o.b. | 102.6 | 95.6 | 68.5 |
| Merchandise imports f.o.b. | −227.7 | −228.1 | −240.4 |
| **Trade balance** | −125.1 | −132.5 | −171.9 |
| Exports of services | 42.2 | 43.0 | 31.4 |
| Imports of services | −130.9 | −111.5 | −114.6 |
| Other income received | 4.4 | 3.5 | 4.7 |
| Other income paid | −21.1 | −17.3 | −17.4 |
| Private unrequited transfers (net) | 5.8 | 20.9 | 22.1 |
| Official unrequited transfers (net) | 115.8 | 159.8 | 161.1 |
| **Current balance** | −108.8 | −34.1 | −84.6 |
| Direct investment (net) | 7.7 | 4.6 | 2.2 |
| Portfolio investment (net) | −0.3 | −0.1 | — |
| Other capital (net) | 48.3 | 94.6 | 60.2 |
| Net errors and omissions | 30.3 | 0.2 | 18.2 |
| **Overall balance** | −22.9 | 65.2 | −4.0 |

Source: IMF, *International Financial Statistics*.

# External Trade

**PRINCIPAL COMMODITIES** (million Rwanda francs)

| Imports c.i.f. | 1989 | 1990 | 1991 |
|---|---|---|---|
| Consumer goods | 7,610.7 | n.a. | 10,819.7 |
| Food | 2,323.8 | 2,673.0 | 4,366.9 |
| Clothing | 1,143.4 | 554.0 | 915.9 |
| Mineral fuels and lubricants | 3,850.5 | 3,689.2 | 4,913.1 |
| Capital goods | 6,909.9 | 4,826.2 | 6,725.8 |
| Transport equipment | 1,832.5 | 901.8 | 1,322.2 |
| Machinery and tools | 3,969.5 | 2,496.0 | 4,260.6 |
| Semi-manufactures | 8,329.3 | 7,999.0 | 16,015.9 |
| Construction materials | 1,570.0 | 1,316.1 | 1,486.5 |
| **Total** (incl. others) | 26,700.4 | 23,057.4 | 38,474.5 |

| Exports f.o.b. | 1989 | 1990 | 1991 |
|---|---|---|---|
| Coffee (green) | 4,691.0 | 5,424.5 | 7,209.8 |
| Tea | 1,557.3 | 1,736.8 | 2,796.6 |
| Tin ores and concentrates | 381.2 | 294.5 | 319.7 |
| Pyrethrum | 151.4 | 160.2 | 279.3 |
| Quinquina | 60.6 | 29.9 | 24.1 |
| **Total** (incl. others) | 8,376.6 | 8,478.0 | 11,971.2 |

Sources: Banque Nationale du Rwanda; Ministère des Finances et de l'Economie, Kigali.

# RWANDA

**PRINCIPAL TRADING PARTNERS** (million Rwanda francs)

| Imports | 1989 | 1990 | 1991 |
|---|---|---|---|
| Belgium-Luxembourg | 5,020.0 | 4,468.7 | 6,588.9 |
| Burundi | 149.2 | 102.8 | 259.1 |
| France | 1,899.2 | 1,782.4 | 2,616.3 |
| Germany, Federal Republic | 2,189.8 | 2,540.4 | 2,324.9 |
| Italy | 866.3 | 584.9 | 1,088.9 |
| Japan | 3,177.3 | n.a. | n.a. |
| Kenya | 3,907.1 | 3,818.4 | 5,153.0 |
| Netherlands | 790.7 | 837.2 | 1,043.3 |
| Uganda | 145.9 | 257.0 | 3.6 |
| United Kingdom | 556.2 | 527.0 | 808.3 |
| USA | 236.5 | 168.9 | 402.8 |
| Zaire | 303.6 | 190.8 | 266.9 |
| **Total** (incl. others) | 26,700.4 | 23,057.3 | 38,474.5 |

| Exports | 1989 | 1990 | 1991 |
|---|---|---|---|
| Belgium-Luxembourg | 1,610.8 | 1,158.4 | 1,412.7 |
| Burundi | 15.0 | 23.7 | 120.1 |
| France | 313.4 | 54.7 | 137.7 |
| Germany, Federal Republic | 1,515.9 | 1,822.8 | 2,552.7 |
| Italy | 299.8 | 190.9 | 199.6 |
| Kenya | 20.4 | 14.3 | 4.3 |
| Netherlands | 945.4 | 1,083.4 | 2,246.9 |
| Uganda | 133.8 | 64.2 | 22.0 |
| United Kingdom | 546.4 | 708.1 | 767.2 |
| USA | 427.9 | 448.1 | 689.1 |
| Zaire | 45.1 | 27.7 | 37.7 |
| **Total** (incl. others) | 8,376.6 | 8,478.2 | 11,971.2 |

Source: Banque Nationale du Rwanda, Kigali.

## Transport

**ROAD TRAFFIC** (motor vehicles in use at 31 December)

| | 1989 | 1990 | 1991 |
|---|---|---|---|
| Motor cycles and scooters | 8,202 | 8,054 | 8,207 |
| Passenger cars | 8,135 | 9,255 | 10,217 |
| Other vehicles | 11,692 | 9,150 | 8,670 |
| **Total** | 28,029 | 26,459 | 27,094 |

Source: Banque Nationale du Rwanda, Kigali.

**CIVIL AVIATION** (traffic)

| | 1989 | 1990 | 1991 |
|---|---|---|---|
| Freight loaded (metric tons) | 5,281 | 3,094 | 2,674 |
| Freight unloaded (metric tons) | 7,456 | 3,814 | 4,794 |
| Passenger arrivals ('000) | 44 | 39 | 29 |
| Passenger departures ('000) | 46 | 42 | 30 |

Source: Banque Nationale du Rwanda, Kigali.

## Tourism

| | 1990 | 1991 | 1992 |
|---|---|---|---|
| Tourist arrivals ('000) | 16 | 3 | 5 |
| Tourist receipts (US $ million) | 10 | 4 | 4 |

Source: UN, *Statistical Yearbook*.

## Communications Media

| | 1990 | 1991 | 1992 |
|---|---|---|---|
| Radio receivers ('000 in use) | 450 | 467 | 485 |
| Telephones ('000 main lines) | 10 | 11 | n.a. |
| Daily newspapers (number) | 1 | n.a. | 1 |

Source: mainly UNESCO, *Statistical Yearbook*.

## Education

(1991/92, unless otherwise indicated)

| | Insti- tutions | Teachers | Males | Females | Total |
|---|---|---|---|---|---|
| Primary | 1,710 | 18,937 | 556,731 | 548,171 | 1,104,902 |
| Secondary | n.a. | 3,413 | 52,882 | 41,704 | 94,586 |
| Tertiary* | n.a. | 646 | 2,750 | 639 | 3,389 |

* Figures are for 1989/90.

Source: UNESCO, *Statistical Yearbook*.

# Directory

## The Constitution

On 10 June 1991 presidential assent was granted to a series of amendments to the Constitution in force since 19 December 1978. The document, as amended, provided, *inter alia*, for a multi-party political system, the separation of the functions of the executive, judiciary and legislature, the limitation of presidential tenure to no more than two consecutive five-year terms of office, the establishment of the office of Prime Minister, freedom of the press, and the right of workers to withdraw their labour. On 5 May 1995 the Transitional National Assembly announced its adoption of a new Constitution based on selected articles of the 1991 Constitution, the August 1993 Arusha peace accord, the FPR victory declaration of July 1994 and the multi-party protocol of understanding concluded in November 1994 (see Recent History).

## The Government

### HEAD OF STATE

**President:** PASTEUR BIZIMUNGU (took office 19 July 1994).
**Vice-President:** Maj.-Gen. PAUL KAGAME.

### COUNCIL OF MINISTERS
(June 1995)

A coalition council of national unity, comprising the Mouvement démocratique républicain (MDR), the Front patriotique rwandais (FPR), the Parti social-démocrate (PSD), the Parti libéral (PL), and the Parti démocratique chrétien (PDC).

**Prime Minister:** FAUSTIN TWAGIRAMUNGU (MDR).

**Deputy Prime Minister and Minister of the Civil Service:** Col ALEXIS KANYARENGWE (FPR).

**Vice-President and Minister of National Defence:** Maj.-Gen. PAUL KAGAME (FPR).

**Minister of the Interior and Communal Development:** SETH SENDASHONGA (FPR).

**Minister of Foreign Affairs and Co-operation:** ANASTASE GASANA.

**Minister of Planning:** JEAN-BERCHMANS BIRARA (Independent).

**Minister of Transport and Communications:** IMMACULÉE KAYUMBA (FPR).

**Minister of Agriculture and Livestock:** AUGUSTIN IYAMUREMYE (PSD).

RWANDA

**Minister of Primary and Secondary Education:** Pierre Célestin Rwigema (MDR).
**Minister of Higher Education and Scientific Research:** Joseph Nsengimana (PL).
**Minister of Finance:** Marc Rugenera (PSD).
**Minister of Youth and Associated Movements:** Patrick Mazimpaka (FPR).
**Minister of Information:** Jean-Baptiste Nduwingoma (MDR).
**Minister of Justice:** Alphonse-Marie Nkubito (MDR).
**Minister of Health:** Col Joseph Karemera (FPR).
**Minister of Labour and Social Affairs:** Pie Mugabo (PL).
**Minister of Public Works and Energy:** Charles Ntakirutinka (PSD).
**Minister of Environment and Tourism:** Jean-Nepomucène Nayinzira (PDC).
**Minister of Commerce, Industry, and Artisan's Affairs:** Prosper Higiro (PL).
**Minister of Women's Affairs and the Family:** Aloysia Inyumba (FPR).
**Minister of State with Responsibility for Reconstruction, Refugees, Displaced Persons and Army Demobilization:** Jacques Bihozagara (FPR).

### MINISTRIES

**Office of the President:** BP 15, Kigali; tel. 75432; telex 517.
**Ministry of Agriculture and Livestock:** BP 621, Kigali; tel. 75324.
**Ministry of the Civil Service:** BP 403, Kigali; tel. 86578.
**Ministry of Commerce, Industry and Artisan's Affairs:** BP 476, Kigali; tel. 73875.
**Ministry of Environment and Tourism:** BP 2378, Kigali; tel. 77415; fax 74834.
**Ministry of Finance:** BP 158, Kigali; tel. 75410; telex 502.
**Ministry of Foreign Affairs and Co-operation:** BP 179, Kigali; tel. 75257.
**Ministry of Health:** BP 84, Kigali; tel. 76681.
**Ministry of Higher Education and Scientific Research:** BP 624, Kigali; tel. 85422.
**Ministry of the Interior and Communal Development:** BP 446, Kigali; tel. 86708.
**Ministry of Justice:** BP 160, Kigali; tel. 866626.
**Ministry of Labour and Social Affairs:** BP 790, Kigali; tel. 73481.
**Ministry of Planning:** BP 46, Kigali; tel. 75513.
**Ministry of Primary and Secondary Education:** BP 622, Kigali; tel. 85422.
**Ministry of Public Works and Energy:** BP 24, Kigali; tel. 86649.
**Ministry of Transport and Communications:** BP 720, Kigali; tel. 72424.
**Ministry of Youth and Associated Movements:** BP 1044, Kigali; tel. 75861; telex 22502.

## Legislature

In November 1994 a multi-party protocol of understanding was concluded providing for a number of amendments to the terms of the August 1993 Arusha peace accord relating to the establishment of a transitional legislature. The most notable of the new provisions was the exclusion from all legislature processes of members of those parties implicated in alleged acts of genocide during 1994. A 70-member Transitional National Assembly was formally inaugurated on 12 December 1994.

**Speaker of the Transitional National Assembly:** Juvénal Nkusi.

## Political Organizations

Legislation authorizing the formation of political parties was promulgated in June 1991.

**Coalition pour la défense de la république (CDR):** Kigali; f. 1992; uncompromising Hutu support; unofficial militia known as *impuza mugambi*; participation in transitional government and legislature proscribed by FPR-led administration during 1994; Leader (vacant).
**Front patriotique rwandais (FPR):** f. 1990, also known as *Inkotanyi*; comprises mainly Tutsi exiles, but claims multi-ethnic support; began armed invasion of Rwanda from Uganda in Oct. 1990; took control of Rwanda in July 1994, following renewed offensive; Chair. Col Alex Kanyarengwe; Sec.-Gen. Dr Théogène Rudasingwa.
**Mouvement démocratique républicain (MDR):** Kigali; banned 1973–91; fmrly also known as Parti de l'émancipation du peuple Hutu (Parmehutu), dominant party 1962–73; split into two factions in late 1993 early 1994: pro-MRNDD faction led by Froduald Karamira, with mainly Hutu support; anti-MRNDD faction led by Faustin Twagiramungu, with multi-ethnic support.
**Mouvement républicain national pour la démocratie et le développement (MRNDD):** BP 1055, Kigali; f. 1975 as the Mouvement révolutionnaire nationale pour le développement (MRND); sole legal party until 1991; adopted current name in April 1991; draws support from uncompromising Hutu groups; Chair. Mathieu Ngirumpatse; large unofficial militia (*interahamwe*) led by Robert Kadjuga; participation in transitional government and legislature proscribed by FPR-led administration during 1994.
**Parti démocrate chrétien (PDC):** BP 2348, Kigali; tel. 76542; fax 72237; f. 1990; Leader Jean Nepomucène Nayinzira.
**Parti démocratique islamique (PDI):** Kigali; f. 1992.
**Parti démocratique rwandais (Pader):** Kigali; f. 1992; cen. cttee of four mems; Sec. Jean Ntagungira.
**Parti écologiste (Peco):** Kigali; f. 1992.
**Parti libéral (PL):** BP 1304, Kigali; tel. 77916; fax 77838; f. 1991; split into two factions in late 1993–early 1994: pro-MRNDD faction led by Justin Mugenzi and Agnès Ntambyariro; anti-MRNDD faction led by Prosper Higiro, Joseph Musengimana and Esdra Kayiranga.
**Parti progressiste de la jeunesse rwandaise (PPJR):** Kigali; f. 1991; political motto of 'patriotism, peace and progress'; Leader André Hakizimana.
**Parti républicain rwandais (Parerwa):** Kigali; f. 1992; Leader Augustin Mutamba.
**Parti social-démocrate (PSD):** Kigali; f. 1991 by a breakaway faction of the MRND; Pres. (vacant).
**Parti socialiste rwandais (PSR):** Kigali; f. 1991; workers' rights.
**Rassemblement travailliste pour la démocratie (RTD):** BP 1894, Kigali; tel. 75622; fax 76574; f. 1991; Leader Emmanuel Nizeyimana.
**Union démocratique du peuple rwandais (UDPR):** Kigali; f. 1992; Pres. Vincent Gwabukwisi; Vice-Pres. Sylvestre Hubi.
**Union du peuple rwandais (UPR):** Brussels, Belgium; f. 1990; Hutu-led; Pres. Silas Majyambere; Sec.-Gen. Emmanuel Twagilimana.

## Diplomatic Representation

Note: Many diplomatic missions closed in April 1994, when diplomatic personnel were withdrawn, owing to the escalation of civil disorder.

### EMBASSIES IN RWANDA

**Algeria:** Kigali; tel. 85831; Ambassador: Mohamed Laala.
**Belgium:** rue Nyarugence, BP 81, Kigali; tel. 75554; fax 73995; Ambassador: Frank de Coninck.
**Burundi:** rue de Ntaruka, BP 714, Kigali; tel. 75010; telex 536; Ambassador: Salvator Ntihabose.
**Canada:** rue Akagera, BP 1177, Kigali; tel. 73210; fax 72719; Ambassador: Lucie Edwards.
**China, People's Republic:** ave Député Kayuku, BP 1345, Kigali; tel. 75415; Ambassador: Huang Shejiao.
**Egypt:** BP 1069, Kigali; tel. 82686; telex 22585; fax 82686; Ambassador: Sameh Samy Darwish.
**France:** 40 ave Député Kamuzinzi, BP 53, Kigali; tel. 75225; telex 522; Ambassador: Jacques Courbin.
**Germany:** 8 rue de Bugarama, BP 355, Kigali; tel. 75222; telex 22520; fax 77267; Ambassador: Dieter Hölscher.
**Holy See:** 49 ave Paul VI, BP 261, Kigali (Apostolic Nunciature); tel. 75293; fax 75181; Apostolic Nuncio: (vacant).
**Kenya:** BP 1215, Kigali; tel. 82774; telex 22598; Ambassador: Peter Kihara Mathanjuki.
**Libya:** BP 1152, Kigali; tel. 76470; telex 549; Secretary of the People's Bureau: Moustapha Masand El-Ghailushi.
**Russia:** ave de l'Armée, BP 40, Kigali; tel. 75286; telex 22661; Ambassador: (vacant).
**Uganda:** BP 656, Kigali; tel. 76495; telex 22521; fax 73551; Ambassador: (vacant).
**USA:** blvd de la Révolution, BP 28, Kigali; tel. 75601; fax 72128; Ambassador: David P. Rawson.
**Zaire:** 504 rue Longue, BP 169, Kigali; tel. 75289; Ambassador: Kabala Kiseke Seka.

RWANDA                                                                                                          *Directory*

## Judicial System

The judicial system comprises a Council of State with administrative jurisdiction, a Court of Cassation, a Constitutional Court consisting of the Court of Cassation and the Council of State sitting jointly, a Court of Accounts responsible for examining all public accounts, and courts of appeal, courts of first instance and provincial courts.

**President of the Constitutional Court:** (vacant).
**State Prosecutor:** (vacant).

## Religion

### AFRICAN RELIGIONS

About one-half of the population hold traditional beliefs.

### CHRISTIANITY

#### The Roman Catholic Church

Rwanda comprises one archdiocese and eight dioceses. At 31 December 1993 there were an estimated 3,526,388 adherents in the country, representing around 48% of the total population.

**Bishops' Conference:** Conférence Episcopale du Rwanda, BP 357, Kigali; tel. 75439; telex 566; f. 1980; Pres. (vacant).

**Archbishop of Kigali:** (vacant), Archevêché, BP 715, Kigali; tel. 75769; fax 76371.

#### The Anglican Communion

The Church of the Province of Rwanda, inaugurated in 1992, has eight dioceses.

**Archbishop of Rwanda and Bishop of Shyira:** Most Rev. AUGUSTIN NSHAMIHIGO, BP 15, Vunga, Via Ruhengeri; fax 46383.

**Provincial Secretary:** Rt Rev. JONATHAN RUHUMULIZA (Assistant Bishop of Kigali), BP 2487, Kigali; fax 82172.

#### Other Protestant Churches

**Eglise Baptiste:** Nyantanga, BP 59, Butare; Pres. Rev. DAVID BAZIGA; Gen. Sec. ELEAZAR ZIHERAMBERE.

There are about 250,000 other Protestants, including a substantial minority of Seventh-day Adventists.

### BAHÁ'Í FAITH

**National Spiritual Assembly:** BP 652, Kigali; tel. 75982.

### ISLAM

There is a small Islamic community.

## The Press

**Bulletin Agricole du Rwanda:** OCIR-Café, BP 104, Kigali-Gikondo; telex 13; quarterly; in French; Pres. of Editorial Bd Dr AUGUSTIN NZINDUKIYIMANA; circ. 800.

**Coopérative Trafipro Umunyamalyango:** BP 302, Kigali; monthly; trade journal; in French and Kinyarwanda.

**Dialogue:** BP 572, Kigali; tel. 74178; f. 1967; every 2 months; Christian issues; circ. 2,000.

**Etudes Rwandaises:** Université Nationale du Rwanda, Rectorat, BP 56, Butare; tel. 30302; telex 605; f. 1977; quarterly; pure and applied science, literature, human sciences; in French; Pres. of Editorial Bd CHARLES NTAKIRUTINKA; circ. 1,000.

**Hobe:** BP 761, Kigali; f. 1955; monthly; for children; in Kinyarwanda; Dir ANDRÉ SIBOMANA; circ. 95,000.

**Imvaho:** Office Rwandais d'Information, BP 83, Kigali; tel. 75724; telex 557; f. 1960; weekly; in Kinyarwanda; circ. 51,000.

**Journal Officiel:** President's Office, BP 15, Kigali; tel. 75324; telex 517; f. 1979; fortnightly; govt publication in French.

**Kinyamateka:** 5 blvd de l'OUA, BP 761, Kigali; tel. 76164; f. 1933; fortnightly; economics; Editorial Dir ANDRÉ SIBOMANA; circ. 11,000.

**Nouvelles du Rwanda:** Université Nationale du Rwanda, BP 117, Butare; every 2 months.

**La Relève:** Office Rwandais d'Information, BP 83, Kigali; tel. 75665; telex 557; f. 1976; monthly; politics, economics, culture; in French; Dir CHRISTOPHE MFIZI; circ. 1,700.

**Revue Medicale Rwandaise:** Ministry of Health, BP 83, Kigali; tel. 76681; f. 1968; quarterly; in French.

**Revue Pédagogique:** Ministry of Primary and Secondary Education, BP 622, Kigali; tel. 85697; telex 5697; quarterly; in French.

**Umuhinzi-Mworozi:** OCIR-Thé, BP 104, Kigali; f. 1975; monthly; circ. 1,500.

**Urunana:** Grand Séminaire de Nyakibanda, BP 85, Butare; tel. 30792; f. 1967; 3 a year; religious; Editor-in-Chief ACHILLE BAWE.

### PRESS AGENCIES

**Agence Rwandaise de Presse (ARP):** 27 ave du Commerce, BP 83, Kigali; tel. 75735; telex 557; f. 1975.

#### Foreign Bureau

**Agence France-Presse (AFP):** BP 83, Kigali; tel. 72997; telex 557; Correspondent MARIE-GORETTI UWIBAMBE ORINFOR.

## Publishers

**Implico:** BP 721, Kigali; tel. 73771.

**Imprimerie de Kabgayi:** BP 66, Gitarama; tel. 62252; fax 62345; f. 1932.

**Imprimerie de Kigali, SARL:** place du 5 juillet, BP 956, Kigali; tel. 85795; fax 84047; f. 1980; Dir THÉONESTE NSENGIMANA.

**Imprimerie URWEGO:** BP 762, Kigali; tel. 86027; Dir JEAN NSENGIYUNVA.

**Pallotti-Presse:** BP 863, Kigali; tel. 74084.

**Printer Set:** BP 184, Kigali; tel. 74116; fax 74121; f. 1984.

### Government Publishing Houses

**Imprimerie Nationale du Rwanda:** BP 351, Kigali; tel. 75350; f. 1967; Dir JUVÉNAL NDISANZE.

**Régie de l'Imprimerie Scolaire:** BP 1347, Kigali; tel. 85695; fax 85695; f. 1985; Dir STANISLAS SINIBAGIWE.

## Radio and Television

In 1992, according to UNESCO estimates, there were 485,000 radio receivers in use.

**Radiodiffusion de la République Rwandaise:** BP 83, Kigali; tel. 75665; telex 22557; fax 76185; f. 1961; state-controlled; daily broadcasts in Kinyarwanda, Swahili, French and English; Chief of Programmes FRODUALD NTAWULIKURA; Dir of Information FERDINAND NAHIMANA.

**Deutsche Welle Relay Station Africa:** Kigali; daily broadcasts in German, English, French, Hausa, Swahili, Portuguese and Amharic.

A privately-controlled station, Radio-Télévision Libre des Mille Collines (RTLM), broadcast pro-MRNDD and pro-CDR transmissions from Kigali (and subsequently from Gisenyi) during 1993 and 1994. Radio Muhabura, the official station of the FPR, broadcast to Rwanda in Kinyarwanda from 1991 until July 1994. A humanitarian station, Radio Amaharo, based in Brussels, Belgium, began broadcasting (in Kinyarwanda) to Rwanda and neighbouring countries where Rwandan refugees were sheltering, from transmitters in Gabon and Ethiopia, in August 1994.

## Finance

(cap. = capital; res = reserves; dep. = deposits; m. = million; brs = branches; amounts in Rwanda francs)

### BANKING

#### Central Bank

**Banque Nationale du Rwanda:** BP 531, Kigali; tel. 75249; telex 508; fax 72551; f. 1964; bank of issue; cap. and res 7,491m. (1994); Gov. GÉRARD NIYITEGEKA.

#### Commercial Banks

**Banque Commerciale du Rwanda, SA:** BP 354, Kigali; tel. 75591; telex 22505; fax 73395; f. 1963; 44.5% state-owned; cap. 12,895.0m. (Dec. 1992); Pres. CÔME BIZIMUNGU; Dir-Gen. CLAVER MVUYEKURE; 13 brs.

**Banque Continentale Africaine (Rwanda), SA (BACAR):** 20 blvd de la Révolution, BP 331, Kigali; tel. 74456; telex 22544; fax 73486; f. 1983; 51% owned by Banque Continentale du Luxembourg; cap. 200m., total assets 4,573.7m. (Dec. 1992); Pres. NASIR ABID; Dir-Gen. PASTEUR MUSABE.

**Banque de Kigali, SA:** 63 ave du Commerce, BP 175, Kigali; tel. 76931; telex 22514; fax 73461; f. 1966; cap. 300.0m., total assets 9,574.6m. (Dec. 1991); Pres. JEAN DAMASCÈNE HATEGEKIMANA; Dir-Gen. EDOUARD BOVY; 9 brs.

RWANDA — *Directory*

### Development Banks

**Banque Rwandaise de Développement, SA (BRD):** BP 1341, Kigali; tel. 73557; telex 22563; fax 73569; f. 1967; 47% state-owned; cap. and res 2,152.1m., total assets 4,492.2m. (Dec. 1993); Pres. DONAT HAKIZIMANA; Dir-Gen. DOMINIQUE MUNYANGOGA.

**Union des Banques Populaires du Rwanda (Banki z'Abaturage mu Rwanda):** BP 1348, Kigali; tel. 73559; telex 584; fax 73579; f. 1975; cap. 136.1m., dep. 4,919.9m. (Dec. 1993); Pres. (vacant); Gen. Man. (vacant); 145 brs.

### Savings Bank

**Caisse d'Epargne du Rwanda:** BP 146, Kigali; tel. 75928; telex 22553; f. 1963; 100% state-owned; cap. 162.0m., dep. 2,127m. (Dec. 1992); Chair. Dr DONAT HAKIZIMANA; Dir-Gen. DOMINIQUE MUNYANGOGA; 16 brs.

### INSURANCE

**Société Nationale d'Assurances du Rwanda (SONARWA):** BP 1035, Kigali; tel. 72101; telex 540; fax 72052; f. 1975; cap. 500m.; Dir-Gen. SIMÉON NTEZIRAYO.

**Société Rwandaise d'Assurances, SA (SORAS):** BP 924, Kigali; tel. 73716; fax 73362; f. 1984; cap. 201m.; Dir-Gen. (Admin.) CHARLES MHORANYI.

## Trade and Industry

### CHAMBER OF COMMERCE

**Chambre de Commerce et d'Industrie du Rwanda:** BP 319, Kigali; tel. 83537; telex 22662; fax 83532; f. 1982; co-ordinates commerce and industry on national scale; Pres. BONIFACE RUCAGU; Sec.-Gen. THOMAS KIGUFI.

### ASSOCIATION

**Association des Industriels du Rwanda:** BP 39, Kigali; tel. and fax 75430; Sec. JEAN DE DIEU HABINEZA.

### DEVELOPMENT ORGANIZATIONS

**Coopérative de Promotion de l'Industrie Minière et Artisanale au Rwanda (COOPIMAR):** BP 1139, Kigali; tel. 82127; fax 72128; Dir JEAN MBURANUMWE.

**Electrogaz:** Kigali; state water, electricity and gas concern.

**Institut de Recherches Scientifiques et Technologiques (IRST):** BP 227, Butare; tel. 30396; fax 30939; Dir-Gen. FRANÇOIS GASENGAYIRE.

**Institut des Sciences Agronomiques du Rwanda (ISAR):** BP 138, Butare; tel. 30642; fax 30644; for the development of subsistence and export agriculture; Dir ANDRÉ NDEREYEHE; 6 centres.

**Office des Cultures Industrielles du Rwanda-Café (OCIR-Café):** BP 104, Kigali; tel. 75004; telex 22513; fax 73992; f. 1978; development of coffee and other new agronomic industries; operates a coffee stabilization fund; Dir SYLVESTRE MUNYANEZA.

**Office des Cultures Industrielles du Rwanda-Thé (OCIR-Thé):** BP 1344, Kigali; tel. 72416; telex 22582; fax 73943; development and marketing of tea; Dir MICHEL BAGARAGAZA.

**Office National pour le Développement de la Commercialisation des Produits Vivriers et des Produits Animaux (OPROVIA):** BP 953, Kigali; tel. 82946; fax 82945; Dir INNOCENT BUTARE.

**Office du Pyrèthre du Rwanda (OPYRWA):** BP 79, Ruhengeri; tel. 46306; telex 22606; fax 46364; f. 1978; development of pyrethrum; Dir JOSEPH NTAMFURAYINDA.

**Office de la Valorisation Industrielle des Bananes du Rwanda (OVIBAR):** BP 1002, Kigali; tel. 85857; Dir GASPARD NZABAMWITA.

**Régie des Mines du Rwanda (REDEMI):** BP 2195, Kigali; tel. 73632; f. 1988; state org. for mining tin, tantalum and tungsten (replacing Société des Mines du Rwanda, bankrupt in 1985 after closure of mines, owing to decline in world prices); Man. Dir JEAN BOSCO M. BICAMUMPAKA.

**Régie Sucrière de Kibuye:** Kigali; sugar manufacture and distribution.

**Rwandatel:** Kigali; telecommunications.

**Rwandex:** Kigali; exports of tea and coffee.

### TRADE UNIONS

**Centrale d'Education et de Coopération des Travailleurs pour le Développement/Alliance Coopérative au Rwanda (CECOTRAD/ACORWA):** BP 295, Kigali; f. 1984 to succeed the Conféd. Syndicale des Travailleurs du Rwanda (COSTRAR); Pres. ELIE KATABARWA.

**Centrale Syndicale des Travailleurs du Rwanda:** BP 1645, Kigali; tel. 84012; Sec.-Gen. MELCHIOR KANYAMIRWA.

## Transport

### RAILWAYS

There are no railways in Rwanda although plans exist for the eventual construction of a line passing through Uganda, Rwanda and Burundi, to connect with the Kigoma–Dar es Salaam line in Tanzania. Rwanda is linked by road to the Tanzanian railways system.

### ROADS

In 1990 there were 13,173 km of roads, of which 5,200 km were main roads. Around 954 km of roads were paved in 1993 and it was hoped that the total length of paved roads would increase to 1,085 km by 1995. There are international road links with Uganda, Tanzania, Burundi and Zaire. Armed conflict between internal factions during 1994 has resulted in considerable damage to the road network, including the destruction of several important bridges.

**Office National des Transports en Commun (ONATRACOM):** BP 720, Kigali; tel. 75064; Dir (vacant).

### INLAND WATERWAYS

There are services on Lake Kivu between Cyangugu, Gisenyi and Kibuye, including two vessels operated by ONATRACOM.

### CIVIL AVIATION

The Kanombe international airport at Kigali can process up to 500,000 passengers annually. There is a second international airport at Kamembe, near the border with Zaire. There are airfields at Butare, Gabiro, Ruhengeri and Gisenyi, servicing internal flights.

**Air Rwanda (Société Nationale des Transports Aériens du Rwanda):** BP 808, Kigali; tel. 75492; telex 554; fax 72462; f. 1975; operates domestic passenger and cargo services and international cargo flights within Africa to Bujumbura (Burundi), Goma (Zaire), Entebbe (Uganda), Tanzania, Kenya and to Ostend (Belgium); Gen. Man. JORAM MUSHIMIYIMANA.

## Tourism

Attractions for tourists include national parks, Lake Kivu and fine mountain scenery. In 1992 there were an estimated 5,000 foreign visitors to Rwanda. Total receipts from tourism were estimated at US $5m. in that year. In recent years the sector has been adversely effected by an increase in violence, arising from border insecurity, and political and tribal conflicts within Rwanda.

**Ministry of Environment and Tourism:** BP 2378, Kigali; tel. 77415; fax 74834.

**Office rwandais du tourisme et des parcs nationaux (ORTPN):** BP 905, Kigali; tel. 76514; fax 76512; f. 1973; the status and structure of ORTPN were under review in 1993.

# SAINT CHRISTOPHER* AND NEVIS

## Introductory Survey

**Location, Climate, Language, Religion, Flag, Capital**

The Federation of Saint Christopher and Nevis is situated at the northern end of the Leeward Islands chain of the West Indies, with Saba and St Eustatius (both in the Netherlands Antilles) to the north-west, Barbuda to the north-east and Antigua to the south-east. Nevis lies about 3 km (2 miles) to the south-east of Saint Christopher, separated by a narrow strait. The tropical heat, varying between 17°C (62°F) and 33°C (92°F), is tempered by constant sea winds, and annual rainfall averages 1,400 mm (55 ins) on Saint Christopher and 1,220 mm (48 ins) on Nevis. English is the official language. The majority of the population are Christians of the Anglican Communion, and other Christian denominations are represented. The national flag (proportions 3 by 2) comprises two triangles, one of green (with its base at the hoist and its apex in the upper fly) and the other of red (with its base in the fly and its apex in the lower hoist), separated by a broad, yellow-edged black diagonal stripe (from the lower hoist to the upper fly) bearing two five-pointed white stars. The capital is Basseterre, on Saint Christopher.

**Recent History**

Saint Christopher, settled in 1623, was Britain's first colony in the West Indies. The French settled part of the island a year later, and conflict over possession continued until 1783, when, after fierce battles, Saint Christopher was ceded to Britain under the Treaty of Versailles. Nevis was settled by the British in 1628 and, although it came under both French and Spanish attacks in the 17th and 18th centuries, remained one of the most prosperous of the Antilles until the middle of the 19th century. The island of Anguilla was first joined to the territory in 1816. The St Kitts-Nevis-Anguilla Labour Party, formed in 1932, campaigned for independence for the islands. In 1958 Saint Christopher-Nevis-Anguilla became a member of the West Indies Federation, remaining so until the Federation's dissolution in 1962. A new Constitution, granted to each of the British territories in the Leeward Islands in 1960, provided for government through an Administrator and an enlarged Legislative Council.

After an abortive attempt to form a smaller East Caribbean Federation, five of the colonies involved became Associated States in an arrangement which gave them full internal autonomy, while the United Kingdom retained responsibility for defence and foreign relations. Saint Christopher-Nevis-Anguilla attained Associated Statehood in February 1967. The Legislative Council was replaced by the House of Assembly, the Administrator became Governor, and the Chief Minister, Robert Bradshaw, leader of the Labour Party, became the state's first Premier. Three months later Anguilla rebelled against government from Saint Christopher, and in 1971 reverted to being a *de facto* British dependency (see chapter on Anguilla), although this was strongly opposed by the Saint Christopher administration. Anguilla was formally separated from the other islands in December 1980.

General elections in 1971 returned Robert Bradshaw to the premiership, with the Labour Party gaining seven of the nine elective seats in the House of Assembly. The two seats for Nevis were secured by the People's Action Movement (PAM) and the Nevis Reformation Party (NRP), formed in 1970, which advocated the separation of Nevis from Saint Christopher. In the 1975 elections the Labour Party again won seven seats, while the NRP took both the Nevis seats. Bradshaw died in May 1978 and was succeeded as Premier by Paul Southwell, hitherto Deputy Premier (and a former Chief Minister). Southwell pledged to lead the country towards independence; however, he died in May 1979, and was replaced by the party's leader, Lee L. Moore (hitherto the Attorney-General).

In February 1980 the Labour Party was removed from government for the first time in nearly 30 years: the Labour Party secured four seats in the legislative elections, while the PAM took three and the NRP retained the two Nevis seats. Although the Labour Party had won 58% of the popular vote, a PAM/NRP coalition Government was formed under Dr Kennedy A. Simmonds, leader of the PAM. The change of government led to the suspension of a timetable for independence, which had been scheduled for June 1980. In 1982 proposals for a greater degree of autonomy for Nevis and for independence for the whole state were approved by the House of Assembly, although the Labour Party opposed the plans, arguing that the coalition Government did not have a mandate for its independence policy. Disagreements concerning the content of the proposed independence Constitution led to civil disturbances, with outbreaks of arson in 1982 and industrial unrest in 1983. Nevertheless, Saint Christopher and Nevis became an independent state, under a federal Constitution, on 19 September 1983. The Labour Party boycotted most of the celebrations, condemning the special provisions for Nevis in the Constitution (see below) as giving the island a powerful role in government that was disproportionate to its size and population. Elections to the Nevis Island Assembly were held in August, at which the NRP, led by Simeon Daniel, won all five elective seats. Upon independence Saint Christopher and Nevis became a full member of the Commonwealth (see p. 119).

Early elections to an enlarged National Assembly (now with 11 elective seats) took place in June 1984, at which the ruling PAM/NRP coalition was returned to power. The Labour Party took only two seats on Saint Christopher, and did not contest the three Nevis seats, which were won by the NRP. The PAM, which won a clear majority of the popular vote on Saint Christopher, secured six seats, while the NRP no longer held the balance of power in the National Assembly.

At an election to the Nevis Island Assembly in December 1987, the NRP retained four seats and the Concerned Citizens' Movement (CCM) secured one. At the general election of March 1989, however, the CCM took one of the three Nevis seats from the NRP, receiving 37% of the votes cast on that island. The PAM retained its six seats, and the Labour Party its two, but the number of votes was more narrowly divided. (Lee L. Moore, who had lost his seat at the 1984 elections, again failed to win a seat, and subsequently resigned as leader of the Labour Party, to be replaced by Denzil Douglas.) The electoral success of the coalition Government under the leadership of Simmonds was attributed to its economic policies, and was achieved despite persistent rumours of drugs-trafficking on the islands (allegations made in 1986 and 1987 indicated official connivance). In 1989 the authorities initiated a campaign to curb the cultivation of, and trade in, the illicit drug marijuana (hemp). Industrial unrest occurred during 1990, when the Simmonds administration refused to accede to demands from agricultural workers for a 10% increase in remuneration, and instead arranged to recruit 1,000 workers from Saint Vincent and the Grenadines to harvest the annual sugar crop.

At an election to the Nevis Island Assembly in June 1992, the CCM gained a majority, securing three seats, while the NRP retained two. The leader of the CCM, Vance Amory, became Premier. Three days after swearing in the new Assembly, the Deputy Governor-General (the Governor-General's representative on Nevis), Weston Parris, was found dead at sea in suspicious circumstances.

At a general election on 29 November 1993 neither the PAM nor the Labour Party managed to secure a majority in the National Assembly; both parties won four seats. On Nevis the CCM secured two seats and the NRP took the remaining seat. Following the refusal of Amory to form a coalition government with either the PAM or the Labour Party, the Governor-General, Sir Clement Arrindell, invited Simmonds to form a minority Government with the support of the NRP. Douglas protested against the decision and appealed for a general strike to support his demands that a further general election take place by mid-February 1994. Demonstrations by Labour Party supporters led to serious disturbances when security forces attempted to disperse the protesters. On 2 December

---

* While this island is officially called Saint Christopher as part of the state, the name is usually abbreviated to St Kitts.

the Governor-General declared a 21-day state of emergency, and, as a precautionary measure, a contingent of the Regional Security System (a security network comprising police, coastguards and army units that was formed by independent East Caribbean states in 1982) was dispatched from Barbados to support the local security forces. The units were withdrawn a week later, and the state of emergency was ended on 14 December. In early December Simmonds withdrew from negotiations with Douglas, although an initial agreement to hold a further general election had been reached, owing to Douglas's premature public revelations of the agreement.

In late January 1994 the opening session of the National Assembly was boycotted by Labour Party members in protest at the appointment of the minority Government and in support of demands for a general election. The boycott remained in force in late February when the National Assembly reconvened for the presentation of the annual budget. Demonstrations by Labour Party supporters during both parliamentary sessions resulted in further confrontations with the security forces.

An escalation in violent crime in late 1994 prompted renewed concern that drugs-trafficking operations were being conducted on the islands. In October six people were charged in connection with the murder, in Basseterre, of the head of the Saint Christopher special investigations police unit, Jude Matthew, who had been conducting an investigation into the disappearances of William Herbert, the country's Permanent Representative to the UN (who resigned as Ambassador to the USA in 1987, following allegations of his involvement in the laundering of funds obtained through illegal drugs-related activities), who had failed to return from a fishing trip in June, and Vincent Morris, a son of the Deputy Prime Minister (Sidney Morris), who had disappeared with a female companion earlier in October. Preliminary investigations suggested that these events were connected to the discovery, at the same time as the couple's disappearance, of a large consignment of cocaine on the north coast of Saint Christopher. The investigation provoked a political crisis in mid-November, when Deputy Prime Minister Morris resigned his post, following the arrest of two other sons on charges related to drugs and firearms offences. The prompt release, on bail, of both men, provoked considerable outrage among long-term remand prisoners at Basseterre gaol. Subsequent rioting resulted in considerable fire damage to prison buildings and the escape of a number of prisoners. However, the security crisis was promptly resolved, and all but one of the former inmates were returned to police custody on the following day, after the deployment on the island of a number of members of both the Barbados Defence Force and Caribbean Regional Security System. Police investigations into the disappearance of Vincent Morris were at the same time intensified, following the discovery of the burnt wreck of a vehicle previously used by Morris, which contained the burnt remains of two bodies.

A 'forum for national unity' was convened on 22 November 1994, at which representatives of all political parties, church organizations and tourism, trade, labour and law associations agreed to seek closer political co-operation in the months preceding the organization of a general election (to be conducted before 15 November 1995—three years in advance of the next required poll—and to be monitored by a Commonwealth observer mission), in order to halt the advance of drugs-related crime and the attendant erosion of local- and foreign-investor confidence in the islands. The post of Deputy Prime Minister was assumed by the Minister of Agriculture, Lands, Housing and Development, Hugh Heyliger, who also assumed Morris's Education, Youth and Community Affairs portfolio. Simmonds took personal responsibility for Morris's Communications, Works and Public Utilities portfolio.

General elections, conducted in early July, were won by the Labour Party. However, full results of the poll were not immediately available.

Saint Christopher and Nevis is a member of the Caribbean Community and Common Market (CARICOM, see p. 114) and of the Organisation of Eastern Caribbean States (OECS, see p. 116). During 1987 and 1988 regional discussions were held on the issue of political unity in the East Caribbean. Saint Christopher and Nevis expressed interest in political unity only if the proposed merger included its Leeward Island neighbours and the Virgin Islands, where an estimated 10,000 Kittitians and Nevisians reside. From January 1990 the OECS agreed to relax restrictions on travel between member states. Nevertheless, following expressions of reluctance by Antigua and Barbuda and Montserrat, Saint Christopher and Nevis abandoned plans to participate in any future political union of OECS member states.

In February 1989 Venezuela upgraded its diplomatic relations with Saint Christopher and Nevis to resident ambassadorial level, and in April 1991 the two countries announced plans for an accord governing commercial and political co-operation. In 1992 diplomatic relations at non-resident ambassadorial level were established with Guatemala, Malaysia and Nicaragua.

### Government

Saint Christopher and Nevis is a constitutional monarchy. Executive power is vested in the British monarch, as Head of State, and is exercised locally by the monarch's personal representative, the Governor-General, who acts in accordance with the advice of the Cabinet. Legislative power is vested in Parliament, comprising the monarch and the National Assembly. The National Assembly is composed of the Speaker, three (or, if a nominated member is Attorney-General, four) nominated members, known as Senators (two appointed on the advice of the Premier and one appointed on the advice of the Leader of the Opposition), and 11 elected members (Representatives), who are chosen from single-member constituencies for up to five years by universal adult suffrage. The Cabinet comprises the Prime Minister, who must be able to command the support of the majority of the members of the National Assembly, the Attorney-General (*ex officio*) and four other ministers. The Prime Minister and the Cabinet are responsible to Parliament.

The Nevis Island legislature comprises the Nevis Island Assembly and the Nevis Island Administration, headed by the British monarch, represented on the island by the Deputy Governor-General. It operates similarly to the Saint Christopher and Nevis legislature but has power to secede from the Federation, subject to certain restrictions (see Constitution below).

### Defence

The small army was disbanded by the Government in 1981, and its duties were absorbed by the Volunteer Defence Force and a special tactical unit of the police. St Christopher and Nevis participates in the US-sponsored Regional Security System, comprising police, coastguards and army units, which was established by independent East Caribbean states in 1982. Budgetary expenditure on defence in 1987 was approximately EC $80,000.

### Economic Affairs

In 1993, according to estimates by the World Bank, Saint Christopher and Nevis's gross national product (GNP), measured at average 1991–93 prices, was US $185m., equivalent to US $4,470 per head. During 1985–93, it was estimated, GNP per head increased, in real terms, at an average annual rate of 5.2%. Over the same period the population declined by an annual average of 0.4%. In 1992 Saint Christopher and Nevis's gross domestic product (GDP) increased, in real terms, by an estimated 4.5%, compared with the figure for the previous year. A similar increase in GDP was predicted for 1993, and a growth rate of 3% was forecast for 1994.

Agricultural production increased by 7.7% in 1993 and the sector (including forestry and fishing) contributed 6.1% of GDP in 1992 (according to the Eastern Caribbean Central Bank). Some 29.6% of the working population were employed in the agriculture sector in 1984. The principal cash crop is sugar cane. In 1989 output of processed sugar cane declined to its lowest level since 1975, owing to adverse climatic conditions (most notably 'Hurricane Hugo' in September 1989), and to labour difficulties; none the less, sugar and sugar products accounted for 40.1% of total export earnings in 1989. In 1992, following a severe drought, output declined by 8.9%. However, in 1993 output recovered to 219,586 metric tons; an increase of 9.9% compared with 1992. Diversification in agriculture, the principal productive sector of the economy, has been encouraged, and other important crops include yams, sweet potatoes and bananas. The cultivation of rice and coffee was being developed in the 1980s. The principal crops on Nevis are coconuts and sea-island cotton. Fishing is an increasingly important commercial activity.

Industry (including mining, manufacturing, construction and public utilities) employed 24.3% of the working population in 1984, and provided 27.0% of GDP in 1989. The mining and quarrying sector accounted for only 0.3% of GDP in 1989, and activity is mainly connected with the construction industry, which contributed 13.5% of GDP in 1991. Manufacturing provided 14.7% of GDP in 1989, and employed 14.7% of the working population in 1984. Apart from the sugar industry (the production of raw sugar and ethyl alcohol), the principal manufactured products are garments, electrical components, beer and other beverages. The islands are dependent upon imports of petroleum (4.9% of total imports in 1988) for their energy requirements.

Tourism is a major contributor to the economy, accounting for 9.1% of GDP in 1991. Some 12.6% of the employed population were engaged in tourism-related activities, according to an employment survey published in April 1995. A development plan, which aimed to double earnings from the sector over four years, was announced in mid-1991.

In 1993 Saint Christopher and Nevis recorded a visible trade deficit of EC $169.4m. (equivalent to 38.2% of GDP) and a deficit of EC $68.6m. on the current account of the balance of payments. In 1988 the principal source of imports was the USA (47.4% of the total value of imports), which was also the principal market for exports (62.4%). In the same year the United Kingdom provided 18.1% of imports and purchased 21.9% of exports. Trade with other Caribbean states, notably Trinidad and Tobago and Saint Vincent and the Grenadines, is also important. The sugar industry is the country's leading exporter, and the principal imports are foodstuffs (15.5% of the total in 1988) and basic manufactures. Exports of sugar increased by 2.2%, to EC $36.5m., in 1993.

Preliminary figures for the 1993 financial year (January–December) indicate that the central Government of Saint Christopher and Nevis recorded a budgetary deficit of EC $9.3m., compared with a deficit of EC $5.0m. in 1992. A budgetary surplus of EC $1.5m. was projected for the 1995 financial year. The country's total external debt was estimated to be US $42.6m. at the end of 1993, of which US $39.5m. was long-term public debt. In 1992 the cost of debt servicing was equivalent to 2.3% of the value of exports of goods and services. The annual rate of inflation averaged 2.5% in 1985–92. Some 4.3% of the labour force were estimated to be unemployed, according to the results of an employment survey published in April 1995. There is, however, a recurring problem of labour shortages in the agricultural sector (notably the sugar industry and the construction industry), and the rate of unemployment is mitigated by mass emigration, particularly from Nevis (remittances from abroad provide an important source of revenue, estimated to be worth one-half of the total earnings from domestic exports in the late 1980s).

Saint Christopher and Nevis is a member of the Caribbean Community and Common Market (CARICOM, see p. 114), which aims to stimulate regional economic development, in particular by encouraging trade between member states, and of the Organisation of Eastern Caribbean States (OECS, see p. 116). The Eastern Caribbean Central Bank is based in Basseterre.

The economy of Saint Christopher and Nevis is traditionally based on agriculture, predominantly the cultivation and processing of sugar cane. In the 1980s, however, the agricultural sector attempted to reduce dependence on sugar cane through diversification. The development of light manufacturing also helped to broaden the islands' economic base, but in the 1980s the most rapidly developing industry was tourism. In 1993 the Government introduced further plans to increase investment in the islands' infrastructure, particularly in areas relating to the tourist industry, and in that year borrowing of EC $200m. was authorized by the Legislature for development projects. In October 1993 the islands were declared ineligible for further concessionary loan financing by the World Bank, owing to improved economic conditions. (Future loans were to be repaid at commercial rates.) In the 1994 budget certain taxes were increased, but small businesses were exempted from corporation and trade tax. In a further attempt to encourage the tourism sector, small hotels were excused from paying accommodation tax in the low season.

### Social Welfare

In 1987 Saint Christopher and Nevis had four hospitals, with a total of 258 beds, and 22 health centres, and in 1989 there was one physician for every 1,920 inhabitants. Of total budgetary expenditure by the central Government in 1987, about EC $10.0m. (12.4%) was for health services, and a further EC $7.6m. (9.4%) for social security and welfare.

### Education

Education is compulsory for 12/13 years between five and 17/18 years of age. Primary education begins at the age of five, and lasts for seven years. Secondary education, from the age of 12, comprises a first cycle of either four or five years, followed by a second cycle of two years. Budgetary expenditure on education at the first and second levels by the central Government in 1991 was approximately EC $12.0m. (11.6% of total spending). In 1980 the average rate of adult literacy was 97.3%.

### Public Holidays

**1995:** 1 January (New Year's Day—Carnival), 14 April (Good Friday), 17 April (Easter Monday), 1 May (Labour Day), 3 June (Queen's Official Birthday), 5 June (Whit Monday), 7 August (August Monday), 19 September (Independence Day), 14 November (Prince of Wales' Birthday), 25–26 December (Christmas), 31 December (Carnival).

**1996:** 1 January (New Year's Day—Carnival), 5 April (Good Friday), 8 April (Easter Monday), 1 May (Labour Day), 27 May (Whit Monday), 4 June (Queen's Official Birthday), 5 August (August Monday), 19 September (Independence Day), 14 November (Prince of Wales' Birthday), 25–26 December (Christmas), 31 December (Carnival).

### Weights and Measures

The imperial system is used.

# Statistical Survey

Source (unless otherwise stated): OECS Economic Affairs Secretariat, *Statistical Digest*.

## AREA AND POPULATION

**Area** (sq km): 261.6 (St Christopher 168.4, Nevis 93.2).

**Population**: 43,309 (males 20,840; females 22,469) at census of 12 May 1980; 44,000 (official estimate for mid-1988).

**Density** (mid-1988): 168.2 per sq km.

**Principal Town** (estimated population, 1980): Basseterre (capital) 14,161.

**Births and Deaths** (1989): Registered live births 989 (birth rate 22.3 per 1,000); Registered deaths 484 (death rate 10.9 per 1,000). Source: UN, *Demographic Yearbook*.

**Expectation of life** (years at birth, 1988) males 65.87; females 70.98. Source: UN, *Demographic Yearbook*.

**Employment** (ISIC Major Divisions, official estimates, '000 persons, 1984): Agriculture, hunting, forestry and fishing 4.38; Manufacturing 2.17; Electricity, gas and water 1.03; Construction 0.40; Trade, restaurants and hotels 0.94; Transport, storage and communications 0.45; Finance, insurance, real estate and business services 0.28; Community, social and personal services 4.70; *Total* 14.80 (males 8.92, females 5.88). Source: ILO, *Year Book of Labour Statistics*.

## AGRICULTURE, ETC.

**Principal Crops** (FAO estimates, '000 metric tons, 1993): Sugar cane 200; Coconuts 2; Fruit and vegetables 3; Roots and tubers 1. Source: FAO, *Production Yearbook*.

**Livestock** (FAO estimates, '000 head, year ending September 1993): Cattle 5; Pigs 2; Sheep 14; Goats 10. Source: FAO, *Production Yearbook*.

**Fishing** (FAO estimates, metric tons, live weight): Total catch 1,720 in 1990; 1,750 in 1991; 1,700 in 1992. Source: FAO, *Yearbook of Fishery Statistics*.

## INDUSTRY

**Production** (1993): Raw sugar 21,228 metric tons.

## FINANCE

**Currency and Exchange Rates**: 100 cents = 1 East Caribbean dollar (EC $). *Sterling and US Dollar Equivalents* (31 December 1994): £1 sterling = EC $4.224; US $1 = EC $2.700; EC $100 = £23.67 = US $37.04. *Exchange Rate*: Fixed at US $1 = $2.70 since July 1976.

**Budget** (preliminary results, EC $ million, 1993): *Revenue*: Revenue from taxation 88.1 (of which, Taxes on international trade and transactions 49.1); Other current revenue 33.4; Capital revenue 2.1; Foreign grants 1.0; Total 124.6. *Expenditure*: Personal emoluments 48.4; Goods and services 44.6; Public debt charges 12.8; Transfers 6.8; Capital expenditure 21.3; Total 133.9. Source: Eastern Caribbean Central Bank, *Report and Statement of Accounts*.

**International Reserves** (US $ million at 31 December 1993): Reserve position in IMF 0.02; Foreign exchange 29.40; Total 29.42. Source: IMF, *International Financial Statistics*.

**Money Supply** (EC $ million at 31 December 1993): Currency outside banks 28.08; Demand deposits at deposit money banks 47.83; Total money 75.92. Source: IMF, *International Financial Statistics*.

**Cost of Living** (consumer price index; base: 1990 = 100): 107.2 in 1992; 109.1 in 1993; 112.0 in 1994. Source: IMF, *International Financial Statistics*.

**Gross Domestic Product by Economic Activity** (EC $ million at current factor cost, 1989): Agriculture, hunting, forestry and fishing 27.70; Mining and quarrying 1.08; Manufacturing 47.38; Electricity, gas and water 2.85; Construction 35.81; Trade, restaurants and hotels 62.25; Transport, storage and communications 43.51; Finance, insurance, real estate and business services 35.70; Government services 54.49; Other community, social and personal services 11.42; Sub-total 322.19; *Less* Imputed bank service charge 19.92; Total 302.27. Source: UN, *National Accounts Statistics*.

**Balance of Payments** (preliminary figures, EC $ million, 1993): Merchandise exports f.o.b. 76.0; Merchandise imports f.o.b. −245.3; *Trade balance* −169.4; Travel 175.7; Other services −105.9; Transfers (net) 30.8; *Current balance* −68.6; Capital account 76.4; *Overall balance* 7.8. Source: Eastern Caribbean Central Bank, *Annual Report*.

## EXTERNAL TRADE

**Principal Commodities** (US $ million, 1988): *Imports c.i.f.*: Food and live animals 14.5; Mineral fuels, lubricants, etc. 5.1; Chemicals 7.0; Basic manufactures 18.9; Machinery and transport equipment 29.9; Miscellaneous manufactured articles 12.2; Total (incl. others) 93.3. *Exports f.o.b.*: Food and live animals 10.2 (Sugar, sugar preparations and honey 8.8); Beverages 1.1; Machinery and transport equipment 9.4; Miscellaneous manufactured articles 5.7 (Clothing 5.4); Total (incl. others) 27.4. Source: UN, *International Trade Statistics Yearbook*.

**Imports f.o.b.** (EC $ million): 262.0 in 1991; 233.7 in 1992; 245.3 in 1993 (preliminary figure).

**Exports f.o.b.** (EC $ million): 79.0 in 1991; 77.4 in 1992; 76.0 in 1993 (preliminary figure).

**Principal Trading Partners** (US $ million, 1988): *Imports*: Barbados 2.6; Canada 3.9; Japan 3.6; Republic of Korea 1.1; Netherlands Antilles 1.9; Saint Vincent and the Grenadines 2.0; Trinidad and Tobago 6.1; United Kingdom 16.9; USA 44.2; Total (incl. others) 93.3. *Exports*: Anguilla 0.4; Antigua and Barbuda 0.6; Trinidad and Tobago 1.2; United Kingdom 6.0; USA 17.1; Total (incl. others) 27.4. Source: UN, *International Trade Statistics Yearbook*.

## TRANSPORT

**Road Traffic** (registered motor vehicles): 5,797 in 1985; 6,106 in 1986; 6,565 in 1987.

**Shipping**: *Arrivals* (1987): 595. *International Freight Traffic* ('000 metric tons, 1990): Goods loaded 24; Goods unloaded 36. Source: UN, *Monthly Bulletin of Statistics*.

**Civil Aviation** (aircraft arrivals): 14,200 in 1985; 15,300 in 1986; 15,700 in 1987.

## TOURISM

**Visitor Arrivals**: 109,730 in 1990; 135,737 (82,903 by air, 52,834 cruise-ship passengers) in 1991; 163,670 (89,719 by air, 73,951 cruise-ship passengers) in 1992.

## COMMUNICATIONS MEDIA

**Non-Daily Newspapers** (1992): Titles 2; Circulation 6,000.

**Periodicals** (1992): Titles 9; Circulation 43,000.

**Radio Receivers** ('000 in use, 1992): 27.

**Television Receivers** ('000 in use, 1992): 9.

**Telephones** ('000 in use, 1986): 3.8.

Sources: UNESCO, *Statistical Yearbook*; UN, *Statistical Yearbook*.

## EDUCATION

**Pre-primary** (1992): 56 schools (1991); 116 teachers; 1,706 pupils.

**Primary** (1991): 32 schools; 350 teachers; 7,236 pupils.

**Secondary** (1991): 6 schools (1988, public education only); 294 teachers; 4,396 pupils.

**Tertiary** (1992): 2 institutions (1987); 51 teachers; 394 students.

Source: UNESCO, *Statistical Yearbook*.

# Directory

## The Constitution

The Constitution of the Federation of Saint Christopher and Nevis took effect from 19 September 1983, when the territory achieved independence. Its main provisions are summarized below:

### FUNDAMENTAL RIGHTS AND FREEDOMS

Regardless of race, place of origin, political opinion, colour, creed or sex, but subject to respect for the rights and freedoms of others and for the public interest, every person in Saint Christopher and Nevis is entitled to the rights of life, liberty, security of person, equality before the law and the protection of the law. Freedom of conscience, of expression, of assembly and association is guaranteed, and the inviolability of personal privacy, family life and property is maintained. Protection is afforded from slavery, forced labour, torture and inhuman treatment.

### THE GOVERNOR-GENERAL

The Governor-General is appointed by the British monarch, whom the Governor-General represents locally. The Governor-General must be a citizen of Saint Christopher and Nevis, and must appoint a Deputy Governor-General, in accordance with the wishes of the Premier of Nevis, to represent the Governor-General on that island.

### PARLIAMENT

Parliament consists of the British monarch, represented by the Governor-General, and the National Assembly, which includes a Speaker, three (or, if a nominated member is Attorney-General, four) nominated members (Senators) and 11 elected members (Representatives). Senators are appointed by the Governor-General; one on the advice of the Leader of the Opposition, and the other two in accordance with the wishes of the Prime Minister. The Representatives are elected by universal suffrage, one from each of the 11 single-member constituencies.

Every citizen over the age of 18 years is eligible to vote. Parliament may alter any of the provisions of the Constitution.

### THE EXECUTIVE

Executive authority is vested in the British monarch, as Head of State, and is exercised on the monarch's behalf by the Governor-General, either directly or through subordinate officers. The Governor-General appoints as Prime Minister that Representative who, in the Governor-General's opinion, appears to be best able to command the support of the majority of the Representatives. Other ministerial appointments are made by the Governor-General, in consultation with the Prime Minister, from among the members of the National Assembly. The Governor-General may remove the Prime Minister from office if a resolution of 'no confidence' in the Government is passed by the National Assembly and if the Prime Minister does not resign within three days or advise the Governor-General to dissolve Parliament.

The Cabinet consists of the Prime Minister and other Ministers. When the office of Attorney-General is a public office, the Attorney-General shall, by virtue of holding that office, be a member of the Cabinet in addition to the other Ministers. The Governor-General appoints as Leader of the Opposition in the National Assembly that Representative who, in the Governor-General's opinion, appears to be best able to command the support of the majority of the Representatives who do not support the Government.

### CITIZENSHIP

All persons born in Saint Christopher and Nevis before independence who, immediately before independence, were citizens of the United Kingdom and Colonies automatically become citizens of Saint Christopher and Nevis. All persons born in Saint Christopher and Nevis after independence automatically acquire citizenship, as do those born outside Saint Christopher and Nevis after independence to a parent possessing citizenship. There are provisions for the acquisition of citizenship by those to whom it is not automatically granted.

### THE ISLAND OF NEVIS

There is a Legislature for the island of Nevis which consists of the British monarch, represented by the Governor-General, and the Nevis Island Assembly. The Assembly consists of three nominated members (one appointed by the Governor-General in accordance with the advice of the Leader of the Opposition in the Assembly, and two appointed by the Governor-General in accordance with the advice of the Premier) and such number of elected members as corresponds directly with the number of electoral districts on the island.

There is a Nevis Island Administration, consisting of a premier and two other members who are appointed by the Governor-General. The Governor-General appoints the Premier as the person who, in the Governor-General's opinion, is best able to command the support of the majority of the elected members of the Assembly. The other members of the Administration are appointed by the Governor-General, acting in accordance with the wishes of the Premier. The Administration has exclusive responsibility for administration within the island of Nevis, in accordance with the provisions of any relevant laws.

The Nevis Island Legislature may provide that the island of Nevis is to cease to belong to the Federation of Saint Christopher and Nevis, in which case this Constitution would cease to have effect in the island of Nevis. Provisions for the possible secession of the island contain the following requirements: that the island must give full and detailed proposals for the future Constitution of the island of Nevis, which must be laid before the Assembly for a period of at least six months prior to the proposed date of secession; that a two-thirds majority has been gained in a referendum which is to be held after the Assembly has passed the motion.

## The Government

**Head of State:** HM Queen Elizabeth II.

**Governor-General:** Sir Clement Arrindell (took office 19 September 1983).

**Deputy Governor-General:** Eustace John.

### CABINET
(June 1995)

**Prime Minister and Minister of Finance, of Home Affairs, of Foreign Affairs and of Communications, Works and Public Utilities:** Dr Kennedy Alphonse Simmonds.

**Deputy Prime Minister, Minister of Agriculture, Lands, Housing and Development, Education, Youth and Community Affairs:** Hugh C. Heyliger.

**Minister of Tourism, Trade and Industry:** Joseph Parry.

**Minister of Health, Labour and Women's Affairs:** Constance V. Mitcham.

**Attorney-General:** S. W. Tapley Seaton.

### MINISTRIES

**Office of the Governor-General:** Government House, Basseterre; tel. 465-2315.

**Government Headquarters:** Church St, POB 186, Basseterre; tel. 465-2521; telex 6820.

**Ministry of Agriculture, Lands, Housing and Development:** Church St, POB 186, Basseterre; tel. 465-2220.

**Ministry of Communications, Works and Public Utilities:** Church St, POB 186, Basseterre; tel. 465-2521; telex 6820.

**Ministry of Education, Youth and Community Affairs:** Cayon St, POB 333, Basseterre; tel. 465-2521; fax 465-9069.

**Ministry of Finance:** Church St, POB 186, Basseterre; tel. 465-2612.

**Ministry of Foreign Affairs:** Church St, POB 186, Basseterre; tel. 465-2521; telex 6820.

**Ministry of Home Affairs:** Church St, POB 186, Basseterre; tel. 465-2521; telex 6820.

**Ministry of Health, Labour and Women's Affairs:** Church St, POB 186, Basseterre; tel. 465-2521; telex 6820.

**Ministry of Natural Resources and the Environment:** Church St, POB 186, Basseterre; tel. 465-2521; telex 6820.

**Ministry of Tourism, Trade and Industry:** Church St, POB 186, Basseterre; tel. 465-2302; fax 465-8794.

### NEVIS ISLAND ADMINISTRATION

**Premier:** Vance Amory.

There are also two appointed members.

**Administrative Centre:** Charlestown, Nevis; tel. 469-5521.

SAINT CHRISTOPHER AND NEVIS                                                                                                    *Directory*

## Legislature

### NATIONAL ASSEMBLY*
**Speaker:** IVAN BUCHANAN.
Elected members: 11. Nominated members: 3.

**Election, 29 November 1993** (preliminary results)

| Party | Votes Cast | Seats |
| --- | --- | --- |
| Labour Party . . . . | 8,405 | 4 |
| People's Action Movement . . | 6,449 | 4 |
| Concerned Citizens' Movement | 2,100 | 2 |
| Nevis Reformation Party . . | 1,641 | 1 |
| United People's Party . . . | 650 | — |

* General elections, conducted in early July, were won by the Labour Party. Full results were not available.

### NEVIS ISLAND ASSEMBLY
Elected members: 5. Nominated members: 3.
Elections to the Nevis Island Assembly took place in June 1992. The Concerned Citizens' Movement took three seats, and the Nevis Reformation Party retained two seats.

## Political Organizations

**Concerned Citizens' Movement (CCM):** Charlestown, Nevis; alliance of four parties; Leader VANCE AMORY.

**Labour Party (Workers' League):** Masses House, Church St, POB 239, Basseterre; tel. 465-2229; f. 1932; socialist party; Chair. HERBERT WYCLIFFE-MORTON; Leader DENZIL DOUGLAS.

**Nevis Reformation Party (NRP):** POB 480, Charlestown, Nevis; f. 1970; campaigns for secession for Nevis from St Christopher; Leader JOSEPH PARRY; Sec. LEVI MORTON.

**People's Action Movement (PAM):** Basseterre; f. 1965; Leader Dr KENNEDY ALPHONSE SIMMONDS.

**People's Democratic Party (PDP):** Nevis; Leader THEODORE HOBSON.

**Progressive Liberal Party:** Basseterre; f. 1988; Leader JAMES SUTTON.

**United National Movement (UNM):** Charlestown, Nevis; Leader EUGENE WALWYN.

**United People's Party (UPP):** Basseterre; f. 1993; Leader MICHAEL POWELL.

## Diplomatic Representation

### EMBASSIES IN SAINT CHRISTOPHER AND NEVIS

**China (Taiwan):** Chinese Embassy, Taylor's Range, Basseterre; tel. 465-2421; Chargé d'affaires: CHARLES TSAI.

**Venezuela:** Delisle St, POB 435, Basseterre; tel. 465-2073; telex 6839; fax 465-5452; Ambassador: LISAN STREDEL.

Diplomatic relations with other countries are maintained at consular level, or with ambassadors and high commissioners resident in other countries of the region.

## Judicial System

Justice is administered by the Eastern Caribbean Supreme Court, based in Saint Lucia and consisting of a Court of Appeal and a High Court. One of the nine puisne judges of the High Court is responsible for Saint Christopher and Nevis and presides over the Court of Summary Jurisdiction. The Magistrates' Courts deal with summary offences and civil offences involving sums of not more than EC $5,000.

**Puisne Judge:** VELMA HYLTON.
**Magistrates' Office:** Losack Rd, Basseterre; tel. 465-2926.

## Religion

### CHRISTIANITY
**St Kitts Christian Council:** Basseterre; Chair. Rev. HAROLD GILL.
**St Kitts Evangelical Association:** Basseterre.

### The Anglican Communion
Anglicans in Saint Christopher and Nevis are adherents of the Church in the Province of the West Indies. The islands form part of the diocese of the North Eastern Caribbean and Aruba. The Bishop, who is also Archbishop of the Province, is resident in St John's, Antigua.

### The Roman Catholic Church
The diocese of Saint John's-Basseterre, suffragan to the archdiocese of Castries (Saint Lucia), includes Anguilla, Antigua and Barbuda, the British Virgin Islands, Montserrat and Saint Christopher and Nevis. At 31 December 1993 the diocese contained an estimated 14,827 adherents. The Bishop participates in the Antilles Episcopal Conference (currently based in Port of Spain, Trinidad and Tobago).

**Bishop of Saint John's-Basseterre:** Rt Rev. DONALD JAMES REECE (resident in St John's, Antigua).

### Other Churches
There are also communities of Methodists, Moravians, Seventh-day Adventists, Baptists, Pilgrim Holiness, the Church of God, Apostolic Faith and Plymouth Brethren.

## The Press

**The Democrat:** Cayon St, POB 30, Basseterre; tel. 465-2091; f. 1948; weekly on Saturdays; organ of PAM; Dir Capt. J. L. WIGLEY; Editor FITZROY P. JONES; circ. 3,000.

**The Labour Spokesman:** Masses House, Church St, POB 239, Basseterre; tel. 465-2229; fax 465-5519; f. 1957; Wednesdays and Saturdays; organ of St Kitts-Nevis Trades and Labour Union; Editor DAVID BYRON; Man. WALFORD GUMBS; circ. 6,000.

### FOREIGN NEWS AGENCIES

**Inter Press Service (IPS)** (Italy): Fort Lands, Basseterre; tel. 465-0465; Correspondent VON SOUTHWELL.

**United Press International (UPI)** (USA): Basseterre; tel. 465-3242; Correspondent BERTRAM GILLFILLIAN.

## Radio and Television

In 1992, according to UNESCO, there were an estimated 27,000 radio receivers and 9,000 television receivers in use.

**Radio Paradise:** POB 423, Charlestown, Nevis; tel. 469-1994; owned by US co (POB A, Santa Ana, CA 92711); religious; Dir R. A. MAYER.

**Trinity Broadcasting Ltd:** Ramsbury Site, Nevis; tel. 469-5425.

**ZIZ Radio and Television:** Springfield, POB 331, Basseterre; tel. 465-2621; telex 6820; fax 465-5624; f. 1961; television from 1972; commercial; govt-owned; Gen. Man. CLAUDETTE MANCHESTER.

## Finance

### BANKING
#### Central Bank
**Eastern Caribbean Central Bank (ECCB):** Headquarters Bldg, Cnr Church and Central Sts, POB 89, Basseterre; tel. 465-2537; telex 6828; fax 465-1051; f. 1965 as East Caribbean Currency Authority; expanded responsibilities and changed name 1983; responsible for issue of currency in Anguilla, Antigua and Barbuda, Dominica, Grenada, Montserrat, Saint Christopher and Nevis, Saint Lucia and Saint Vincent and the Grenadines; total assets EC $887.5m. (March 1994); Gov. K. DWIGHT VENNER.

#### Local Banks
**Bank of Nevis Ltd:** Main St, POB 450, Charlestown, Nevis; tel. 469-5564; telex 6862; fax 469-5798.

**Nevis Co-operative Banking Co Ltd:** Chapel St, POB 60, Charlestown, Nevis; tel. 469-5277; fax 469-1493; f. 1955; Man. Dir I. WALWYN.

**St Kitts-Nevis-Anguilla National Bank Ltd:** Central St, POB 343, Basseterre; tel. 465-2204; telex 6826; fax 465-1050 (Saint Christopher), 469-0194 (Nevis); majority govt-owned; total assets EC $326m. (1994); Chair. WILLIAM LIBURD; Gen. Man. E. PISTANA; br. on Nevis.

#### Foreign Banks
**Bank of Nova Scotia:** Fort St, POB 433, Basseterre; tel. 465-4141; telex 6882; fax 465-8600; Man. J. H. CALDWELL.

**Barclays Bank PLC** (UK): POB 42, Basseterre; tel. 465-2449; telex 6823; fax 465-1041; Man. L. F. VASQUEZ; POB 502, Chapel St, Charlestown, Nevis; tel. 469-5309; fax 465-5106; Man. N. VIDAL.

**Royal Bank of Canada:** POB 91, Basseterre; tel. 465-2389; telex 6856; Man. JOHN A. FERGUSON.

# SAINT CHRISTOPHER AND NEVIS

### Development Bank
**St Kitts-Nevis Development Bank:** Church St, Basseterre; tel. 465-4041; fax 465-4016; f. 1981; Man. AUCKLAND HECTOR.

### INSURANCE
Several foreign companies have offices in Saint Christopher and Nevis.

**National Caribbean Insurance Co Ltd:** Bay Rd, POB 374, Basseterre; tel. 465-2694; fax 465-3659.

## Trade and Industry

### CHAMBER OF COMMERCE
**St Kitts-Nevis Chamber of Industry and Commerce:** South Sq. St, POB 332, Basseterre; tel. 465-2980; telex 6822; fax 465-4490; incorporated 1949; 115 mems; Pres. SAM FRANKS; Exec. Dir ALEXIS KNIGHT.

### DEVELOPMENT CORPORATIONS AND STATE AUTHORITIES
**Central Marketing Corpn (CEMACO):** Pond's Pasture, Basseterre; tel. 465-2326; Man. MAXWELL GRIFFIN.

**Frigate Bay Development Corporation:** POB 315, Basseterre; tel. 465-8339; fax 465-4463; promotes tourist and residential developments.

**Investment Promotion Agency:** Investment Promotion Division, Ministry of Trade and Industry, Church St, POB 186, Basseterre; tel. 465-4106; fax 465-1778; f. 1987.

**St Kitts Sugar Manufacturing Corpn:** St Kitts Sugar Factory, POB 96, Basseterre; tel. 465-8099; merged with National Agricultural Corpn in 1986; plans for a transfer to the private sector announced in December 1993; Man. Dir DESMOND MALLALIEU.

**Social Security Board:** POB 79, Bay Rd, Basseterre; tel. 465-2535; fax 465-5051; f. 1977; Dir ROBERT E. MANNING.

### EMPLOYERS' ASSOCIATIONS
**Nevis Cotton Growers' Association Ltd:** Charlestown, Nevis; Pres. IVOR STEVENS.

**St Kitts-Nevis Manufacturers' Association:** POB 392, Basseterre; tel. 465-6626.

**Small Business Association:** Anthony Evelyn Bldg, Ponds Industrial Estate, POB 286, Basseterre; tel. 465-1430; fax 465-5623; Pres. KEITH MORTON.

### TRADE UNIONS
**St Kitts-Nevis Trades and Labour Union:** Masses House, Church St, POB 239, Basseterre; tel. 465-2229; fax 465-5519; f. 1940; affiliated to Caribbean Maritime and Aviation Council, Caribbean Congress of Labour, International Federation of Plantation, Agricultural and Allied Workers and International Confederation of Free Trade Unions; associated with Labour Party; Pres. LEE L. MOORE; Gen. Sec. JOS N. FRANCE; about 2,000 mems.

**United Workers' Union (UWU):** Market St, Basseterre; tel. 465-4130; associated with People's Action Movement.

## Transport

### RAILWAYS
There are 58 km (36 miles) of narrow-gauge light railway on Saint Christopher, serving the sugar plantations. A major renovation of the railway was to be undertaken during 1993.

**St Kitts Sugar Railway:** St Kitts Sugar Manufacturing Corpn, POB 96, Basseterre; tel. 465-8099; telex 6812; fax 465-1049; Man. Dir DESMOND MALLALIEU.

### ROADS
There are 300 km (186 miles) of road in Saint Christopher and Nevis, of which approximately 124 km (77 miles) are tarred.

### SHIPPING
The Government maintains a commercial motor boat service between the islands, and numerous shipping lines call at the islands. A deep-water port was opened at Basseterre in 1981. In May 1995 an agreement was concluded with the Kuwait Fund for Arab Development for the construction of a cargo and cruise ship port at Charlestown, Nevis.

**St Kitts Air and Sea Ports Authority:** Administration Bldg, Deep Water Port, Bird Rock, Basseterre; tel. 465-8121; fax 465-8124; f. 1993 combining St Kitts Port Authority and Airports Authority; Gen. Man. SIDNEY OSBORNE; Airport Man. EDWARD HUGHES; Sea Port Man. CARL BRAZIER-CLARKE.

### CIVIL AVIATION
Golden Rock International Airport, 4 km (2½ miles) from Basseterre, is equipped to handle jet aircraft and is served by scheduled links with most Caribbean destinations, and with the USA. Saint Christopher and Nevis is a shareholder in the regional airline, LIAT (see chapter on Antigua and Barbuda). Newcastle Airfield, 11 km (7 miles) from Charlestown, Nevis, has regular scheduled services to St Kitts and other islands in the region.

**St Kitts Air and Sea Ports Authority:** (see above).

## Tourism

The introduction of regular air services to Miami and New York has opened up the islands as a tourist destination. Visitors are attracted by the excellent beaches on Saint Christopher and the spectacular mountain scenery of Nevis, the historical Brimstone Hill Fort on Saint Christopher and the islands' associations with Lord Nelson and Alexander Hamilton. In 1992 there were 163,670 visitors, (an increase of some 21% compared with the total for 1992), of whom 73,951 were cruise-ship passengers. In 1990 there were 1,186 hotel rooms on the islands.

**St Kitts-Nevis Tourist Board:** Treasury Pier, POB 132, Basseterre; tel. 465-4040; fax 465-8794; Main St, Nevis; Chair. COLIN PEREIRA.

**St Kitts-Nevis Hotel Association:** POB 438, Basseterre; tel. 465-5304; fax 465-7746; f. 1972; Pres. GLENN KNORR; Exec. Dir VAL HENRY.

# SAINT LUCIA

## Introductory Survey

### Location, Climate, Language, Religion, Flag, Capital

Saint Lucia is in the Windward Islands group of the West Indies, lying 40 km (25 miles) to the south of Martinique and 32 km (20 miles) to the north-east of Saint Vincent, in the Caribbean Sea. The island is volcanic, with spectacular mountain scenery. The average annual temperature is 26°C (79°F), with a dry season from January to April, followed by a rainy season from May to August. The average annual rainfall is 1,500 mm (60 ins) in the low-lying areas, and 3,500 mm (138 ins) in the mountains. The official language is English, although a large proportion of the population speak a French-based patois. Almost all of the island's inhabitants profess Christianity, and 77% are adherents of the Roman Catholic Church. The national flag (proportions 2 by 1) is blue, bearing in its centre a white-edged black triangle partly covered by a gold triangle rising from a common base. The capital is Castries.

### Recent History

British settlers made an unsuccessful attempt to colonize the island (originally inhabited by a Carib people) in 1605. A further British party arrived in 1638 but were killed by the indigenous Carib population. France claimed sovereignty in 1642, and battles between French and Caribs continued until 1660, when a peace treaty was signed. Control of Saint Lucia was transferred 14 times before it became a British colony in 1814, ceded by the French under the Treaty of Paris. It remained under British rule for the next 165 years.

Representative government was introduced in 1924. The colony was a member of the Windward Islands, under a federal system, until December 1959. It joined the newly-formed West Indies Federation in January 1958, and remained a member until the Federation's dissolution in May 1962. From January 1960 Saint Lucia, in common with other British territories in the Windward Islands, was given a new Constitution, with its own Administrator and an enlarged Legislative Council.

In 1951 the first elections under adult suffrage were won by the St Lucia Labour Party (SLP), which retained power until 1964, when John Compton, of the newly-formed conservative United Workers' Party (UWP), became Chief Minister. In March 1967 Saint Lucia became one of the West Indies Associated States, gaining full autonomy in internal affairs, with the United Kingdom retaining responsibility for defence and foreign relations only. The Legislative Council was replaced by a House of Assembly, the Administrator was designated Governor, and the Chief Minister became Premier. The UWP retained power until 1979.

In 1975 the Associated States agreed that they would seek independence individually. After three years of negotiations, Saint Lucia became independent on 22 February 1979, remaining within the Commonwealth. Compton became the country's first Prime Minister.

A general election in July 1979 returned the SLP to government with a clear majority, and its leader, Allan Louisy, succeeded Compton as Prime Minister. In February 1980 a new Governor-General, Boswell Williams, was appointed. This led to disputes within the Government and contributed to a split in the SLP. Louisy's resignation was demanded by 12 SLP members of the House of Assembly, who favoured his replacement by George Odlum, the Deputy Prime Minister. The controversy continued until April 1981, when Odlum and three other SLP members of the House voted with the opposition against the Government's budget, and Louisy was forced to resign. In May Winston Cenac, the Attorney-General in the Louisy Government, took office as Prime Minister, with a parliamentary majority of one. (Odlum and two other SLP members had broken away to form the Progressive Labour Party—PLP.) Cenac upheld his declared intention not to call fresh elections, despite large demonstrations in Castries throughout May and June demanding a change of government. In July the Cenac administration succeeded in obtaining legislative approval for its budget proposals, and in September it defeated by one vote a motion of 'no confidence', introduced jointly by UWP and PLP members of the House, who accused the Government of political and economic mismanagement. In January 1982 a government proposal to alter legislation regarding the expenses of members of Parliament produced widespread accusations of corruption and provoked a series of strikes. Demands for the Government's resignation increased from all sectors of the community, culminating in a general strike. Cenac resigned, and an all-party interim administration was formed, under the deputy leader of the PLP, Michael Pilgrim, pending a general election that was scheduled for May. At the election the UWP was returned to power, obtaining 56% of the votes cast and winning 14 of the 17 seats in the House of Assembly. John Compton was therefore re-elected Prime Minister, and stated that his immediate objective was the restoration of economic growth. In December Sir Allen Lewis was reappointed Governor-General, following the dismissal of Boswell Williams because of his previous close association with the SLP.

In 1984 the opposition parties, which had been in disarray after their 1982 defeat, began to reorganize in order to present a more effective opposition to the UWP Government. Proposals, made by Odlum in 1985 and 1986, for an alliance between the PLP and the SLP were rejected by the SLP. At a general election for the 17-member House of Assembly on 6 April 1987, the UWP secured nine seats and the SLP eight. A further election took place on 30 April, in the hope of a more decisive result. As before, the UWP obtained about 53% of the votes, and the distribution of seats remained unchanged. In June the UWP's majority in the House was increased to three seats, when Cenac defected to the party from the SLP. He was subsequently appointed Minister of Foreign Affairs.

In late October 1988 the Government introduced legislation whereby it assumed control of the important banana industry for one year. Subsequently, the 1988 annual convention of the Saint Lucia Banana Growers' Association (SLBGA) was cancelled, and the Government dismissed the association's board of directors. The opposition parties alleged that the Government's actions reflected the fact that prominent supporters of the ruling UWP were the SLBGA's principal debtors. Government control was extended until July 1990, despite continued protests which included demonstrations by banana producers and the SLP.

Legislation against the trade in illicit drugs was enacted in November 1988, following an inquiry into police corruption and inefficacy. The inquiry also resulted in the dismissal of the police Commissioner and two other senior officers. In October 1990 the Government announced the creation of a special force to combat drugs-trafficking, and plans to intensify co-operation with Saint Vincent and Martinique, aimed at preventing smugglers from travelling between the islands, were also defined.

At a general election on 27 April 1992 the UWP won 56.3% of the votes cast and secured 11 seats, while the SLP, with 43.5% of the votes, took the remaining six. The SLP attributed its defeat largely to the fact that the Government had redefined constituency boundaries prior to the election (a move which had caused considerable animosity between the two parties). The claims were dismissed by the Compton Government, which asserted that the changes were necessary owing to population movement. In July 1992 the Minister of Health and Local Government, Stephenson King, announced an inquiry into allegations of corruption and mismanagement in Castries City Council. King stated that the Government was considering the reintroduction of local government elections (abolished in the 1970s), as a result of the claims.

In early October 1993 a three-day strike was organized by a newly-formed pressure group, the Banana Salvation Committee (BSC), in support of demands for an increase in the minimum price paid to local producers for bananas and for the dismissal of the board of directors of the SLBGA. Access to the ports was obstructed during the strike, and resultant losses to the economy were estimated to be in excess of EC $2m. Confrontations between the security forces and

2611

demonstrators resulted in two deaths. The Government subsequently appointed a committee to review the prices paid by the SLBGA and devise a new administrative structure for the banana industry. In accordance with the recommendations of the committee, the Government implemented price increases and dismissed the board of directors of the SLBGA, who were replaced by an interim board, which included representatives of the BSC. In January 1994 the Government announced that the SLBGA was to be placed into receivership; in March a strike was organized by the BSC in protest at the decision. In December 1994 and February 1995 the BSC organized further strikes by banana farmers in support of demands for the convention of an extraordinary meeting of the SLBGA (to discuss recent negotiations between the Government and Geest—the multinational concern responsible for the marketing of the island's fruit) and an inquiry into the deaths of two demonstrators during strike action organized in October 1993 (see above). The Government responded by propelling an amendment to the criminal code, restricting the right to strike, through all the necessary parliamentary procedures during March 1995, a move which was immediately challenged by the opposition SLP and by the Industrial Solidarity Pact (ISP) of six trade union organizations, which threatened to organize nation-wide protests against the enactment of the proposed legislation. Opposition to the Government intensified following allegations, made in April, that the administration had been involved in the misappropriation for electoral funding of some US $100,000 in UN contributions. The Minister of State with Responsibility for Financial Services and the National Development Corporation, Rufus Bousquet (who claimed to have been an unwitting recipient of the funds), was dismissed in early May, following his public questioning of the appropriateness of the Government's continuing in office, pending investigation of the affair. The inauguration of a commission of inquiry into the allegations was postponed later in the month, owing to a judicial review.

On 10 September 1994 four islanders were killed, and structural damage (including the destruction of some 60%–70% of the island's banana crop) estimated to total some EC $50m. was sustained, following the passage over the island of Tropical Storm Debbie. Financial contributions towards reconstruction efforts were subsequently pledged by the Organization of American States, the European Union (EU) and regional agricultural compensation bodies.

As a member of the Caribbean Community and Common Market (CARICOM, see p. 114), Saint Lucia was able to secure limited protection for some of its products when the organization removed its internal trade barriers in October 1988. The country's most important export market, however, is the United Kingdom, which receives most of the banana crop under the terms of the Lomé Convention (see p. 165). In July 1993 new regulations came into effect governing the level of imports of bananas by the European Community (now EU). The regulations were introduced to protect traditional producers covered by the Lomé Convention from competition from the expanding Latin American producers. At the instigation of the Latin American producers consecutive dispute panels were appointed by GATT to rule on whether the EU's actions contravened GATT rules. Although the dispute panels ruled in favour of the Latin American producers, the rulings were not enforceable. In October 1994 the US Government announced its intention to investigate illegal discrimination by the EU against US-based banana-marketing companies. In the same month the EU granted an increase in its Latin American banana import quota in order to allow the Windward Islands to fulfill their EU import allocations through re-exports, following the severe storm damage sustained by plantations on the islands in September 1994. Negotiations between the EU and the USA were scheduled to continue in mid-1995, in an attempt to reach agreement on a mutually-acceptable banana-marketing regime.

The country is also a member of the Organisation of Eastern Caribbean States (OECS, see p. 116), and, since May 1987, has been a prominent advocate of the creation of a unitary East Caribbean state. In 1988 however, Antigua and Barbuda expressed its opposition to political union, thereby discouraging any participation by Montserrat or Saint Christopher and Nevis. Therefore, in November the four English-speaking Windward Islands countries (Saint Lucia, Dominica, Grenada and Saint Vincent and the Grenadines) announced plans to proceed independently towards a more limited union. In late 1990 the leaders of the four countries established a new body, the Regional Constituent Assembly. Following a series of discussions, the Assembly issued its final report in late 1992, in which it stated that the four countries were committed to the establishment of economic and political union under a federal system.

### Government

Saint Lucia is a constitutional monarchy. Executive power is vested in the British monarch, as Head of State, and is exercisable by the Governor-General, who represents the monarchy and is appointed on the advice of the Prime Minister. Legislative power is vested in Parliament, comprising the monarch, the 17-member House of Assembly, elected from single-member constituencies for up to five years by universal adult suffrage, and the Senate, composed of 11 members appointed by the Governor-General, including six appointed on the advice of the Prime Minister and three on the advice of the Leader of the Opposition. Government is effectively by the Cabinet. The Governor-General appoints the Prime Minister and, on the latter's recommendation, the other Ministers. The Prime Minister must have majority support in the House, to which the Cabinet is responsible.

### Defence

The Royal Saint Lucia Police Force, which numbers about 300 men, includes a Special Service Unit for purposes of defence. Saint Lucia participates in the US-sponsored Regional Security System, comprising police, coastguards and army units, which was established by independent East Caribbean states in 1982. There is also a patrol vessel for coastguard duties.

### Economic Affairs

In 1993, according to estimates by the World Bank, Saint Lucia's gross national product (GNP), measured at average 1991–93 prices, was US $480m., equivalent to $3,040 per head. During 1985–93, it was estimated, GNP per head increased, in real terms, at an average annual rate of 4.3%. Over the same period the population increased by an annual average of 1.8%. Saint Lucia's gross domestic product (GDP) increased, in real terms, by 1.6% in 1991, by 6.6% in 1992 and by an estimated 3.1% in 1993.

Agriculture (including forestry and fishing) contributed 11% of GDP in 1993 and, it has been estimated, employs some 30% of the labour force. Bananas are the principal cash crop, and in 1991 accounted for 54.7% of the value of merchandise earnings. Other important crops include coconuts, mangoes, citrus fruit, cocoa and spices. During 1993 value added by the sector contracted by some 6% compared with the previous year, owing largely to drought and the effect of low prices on banana production. Commercial fishing is being developed.

Industry (including mining, manufacturing, public utilities and construction) contributed 19.7% of GDP in 1987. Mining and quarrying are not important economic activities. In 1992 manufacturing accounted for 7.4% of GDP, and in 1989 employed some 20% of the labour force. Output increased in the late 1980s, but declined by 9% in 1991 before recovering slightly, with an increase of 2.6%, in 1992. An estimated increase of 4.2% in the value added by the sector was recorded in 1993. The principal manufacturing industries, which have been encouraged by the establishment of 'free zones', include the processing of agricultural products, the assembly of electronic components and the production of garments, plastics, paper and packaging (associated with banana production), beer, rum and other beverages.

Energy is traditionally derived from imported hydrocarbon fuels (6.8% of total imports in 1992). There is a petroleum transhipment terminal on the island. In 1988, however, a geothermal energy development project, at Soufrière, succeeded in tapping a reservoir of high-pressure steam, estimated to have a generating capacity of 5 MW of electri city. A new electricity-generating plant was inaugurated in late 1990.

Tourism is the most important of the service industries, accounting for one-half of all receipts of foreign exchange in the late 1980s. In 1992 tourist arrivals increased by 7.4%, to 342,440, while revenue from tourism totalled EC $561.2m., an increase of 20.3% compared with the previous year. Some 348,500 tourists visited in 1993.

In 1993 Saint Lucia recorded a visible trade deficit of EC $427.3m., and a deficit of EC $119.0m. on the current account of the balance of payments. The principal source of

# SAINT LUCIA

imports in 1992 was the USA (33.8% of the total), which also received 21.4% of exports. The principal market for exports is the United Kingdom, which received 51.4% of total exports in 1992. Within the Caribbean Community and Common Market (CARICOM, see p. 114) whose member states accounted for 17.0% of imports and 16.8% of exports in 1992, the principal trading partner is Trinidad and Tobago. Bananas, sent mainly to the United Kingdom, are the principal export commodity, accounting for US $50.7m. in revenues in 1993. The principal imports are foodstuffs, basic manufactures, machinery and transport equipment.

In the financial year ending 31 March 1994 there was an overall budgetary deficit of EC $24.8m. Saint Lucia's total external debt at the end of 1993 was US $101.2m., of which US $96.8m. was long-term public debt. In 1992 the cost of debt servicing was equivalent to 3.5% of the value of exports of goods and services. The annual rate of inflation averaged 3.8% in 1985–93. In 1991 the rate of unemployment was estimated to be 16.7%.

Saint Lucia is a member of CARICOM, which aims to encourage regional development, particularly by increasing trade between member states, and of the Organisation of Eastern Caribbean States (OECS, see p. 116).

Saint Lucia has been a strong advocate of closer political and economic integration within the Caribbean region. It has been argued that a larger political unit in the region could better maintain improvements in social and economic conditions. The Governments of the Windward Islands have focused particularly on the banana industry as an area where greater co-operation between their countries would enhance productivity and profitability. Meanwhile, Saint Lucia has developed a diversified and fairly prosperous economy, although in the early 1990s its performance remained dominated by the agricultural sector, particularly bananas. Other crops are being encouraged for export (the cultivation of cashew nuts began in 1989, with Brazilian aid) and domestic consumption. The fishing industry was also expected to benefit from a major Japanese project undertaken in 1993. Investment in the island's infrastructure has benefited all the main sectors of the economy, but particularly manufacturing and tourism, which were fundamental to increased employment in the 1980s. Tourism was regarded as the sector with the greatest growth potential in the 1990s. New deep-water container port facilities completed at Vieux Fort in mid-1993 provided the potential for St Lucia to become a major transhipment centre.

### Social Welfare

There were four hospitals on Saint Lucia in 1993, with a total of 435 beds: the main hospital and a hospital for psychiatric patients are in Castries. There were also 33 health centres and a drugs and alcohol rehabilitation centre. Saint Lucia had 64 practising physicians in 1992, and 256 nurses. In February 1991 the Government inaugurated a National Population Unit to conduct a two-year public education programme aimed at further reducing the island's birth rate.

### Education

Education is compulsory for 10 years between five and 15 years of age. Primary education begins at the age of five and lasts for seven years. Secondary education, beginning at 12 years of age, lasts for five years, comprising a first cycle of three years and a second cycle of two years. Free education is provided in more than 90 government-assisted schools. Facilities for industrial, technical and teacher training are available at an educational complex at Morne Fortune, which also houses an extra-mural branch of the University of the West Indies. Public expenditure on education in 1986 was EC $38.4m.

### Public Holidays

**1995:** 1–2 January (New Year), 6–7 February (Carnival), 22 February (Independence Day), 14 April (Good Friday), 17 April (Easter Monday), 1 May (Labour Day), 3 June (Queen's Official Birthday), 5 June (Whit Monday), 15 June (Corpus Christi), 7 August (August Bank Holiday), 2 October (Thanksgiving Day), 13 December (Saint Lucia Day), 25–26 December (Christmas).

**1996:** 1–2 January (New Year), 5–6 February (Carnival), 22 February (Independence Day), 5 April (Good Friday), 8 April (Easter Monday), 1 May (Labour Day), 27 May (Whit Monday), 4 June (Queen's Official Birthday), 6 June (Corpus Christi), 1 August (August Bank Holiday), 3 October (Thanksgiving Day), 13 December (Saint Lucia Day), 25–26 December (Christmas).

### Weights and Measures

The imperial system is in use.

# Statistical Survey

Sources (unless otherwise stated): Ministry of Foreign Affairs, New Government Bldgs, John Compton Highway, Castries; tel. 452-1178; telex 6394; Government Information Service, Brazil St, Castries; tel. 452-3016; fax 453-1614; OECS Economic Affairs Secretariat, *Statistical Digest*.

### AREA AND POPULATION

**Area:** 616.3 sq km (238 sq miles).

**Population:** 120,300 (males 56,818; females 63,482) at census of 12 May 1980; 135,685 at census of 12 May 1991.

**Density** (census of 1991): 220.2 per sq km.

**Principal Towns:** Castries (capital), population 51,994 at census of 1991; 53,883 in 1992 (official estimate); other towns Vieux Fort, Soufrière and Gros Islet.

**Births and Deaths** (1992, provisional): Registered live births 3,624 (birth rate 26.5 per 1,000); Registered deaths 874 (death rate 6.4 per 1,000).

**Expectation of life** (years at birth, 1992) males 69.3; females 74.0.

**Economically Active Population** (1980 census): 49,451 (males 22,152; females 27,299).

### AGRICULTURE, ETC

**Principal Crops** (FAO estimates, '000 metric tons, 1993): Roots and tubers 11 (Yams 4); Bananas 160; Mangoes 26; Other fruit 7; Coconuts 37. Source: FAO, *Production Yearbook*.

**Livestock** (FAO estimates, '000 head, year ending September 1993): Horses, mules and asses 3; Cattle 12; Pigs 13; Sheep 16; Goats 12. Source: FAO, *Production Yearbook*.

**Livestock Products** (FAO estimates, '000 metric tons, 1993): Meat 2; Cows' milk 1. Source: FAO, *Production Yearbook*.

**Fishing** (metric tons, live weight): Total catch 903 in 1990; 909 in 1991 (estimate); 989 in 1992. Source: FAO, *Yearbook of Fishery Statistics*.

### INDUSTRY

**Production:** Non-alcoholic beverages 1,191,000 gallons (1986); Electric energy 107 million kWh (1992, Source: UN, *Industrial Statistics Yearbook*); Copra 3,914 metric tons (1991); Coconut oil (raw) 909,780 gallons (1990); Rum 7,000 hectolitres (1991, Source: UN, *Industrial Statistics Yearbook*).

### FINANCE

**Currency and Exchange Rates:** 100 cents = 1 East Caribbean dollar (EC $). *Sterling and US Dollar Equivalents* (31 December 1994): £1 sterling = EC $4.224; US $1 = EC $2.700; EC $100 = £23.67 = US $37.04. *Exchange Rate:* Fixed at US $1 = EC $2.70 since July 1976.

**Budget** (EC $ million, preliminary figures, year ending 31 March 1994): *Revenue:* Taxation 307.6 (Taxes on income 80.1, Taxes on goods and services 38.0, Taxes on international trade and transactions 187.9); Other current revenue 38.5; Capital revenue 0.1; Grants 31.9; Total 378.1. *Expenditure:* Wages and salaries 130.9; Interest payments 10.8; Goods and services 53.6; Transfers 55.6; Capital expenditure and net lending 152.0; Total 402.9. Source: Eastern Caribbean Central Bank, *Report and Statement of Accounts*.

**International Reserves** (US $ million at 31 December 1993): IMF special drawing rights 1.84; Foreign exchange 58.10; Total 59.94. Source: IMF, *International Financial Statistics*.

**Money Supply** (EC $ million at 31 December 1993): Currency outside banks 67.88; Demand deposits at deposit money banks 157.78; Total money (incl. others) 226.02. Source: IMF, *International Financial Statistics*.

**Cost of Living** (Consumer price index; base: 1990 = 100): 105.7 in 1991; 111.1 in 1992; 112.0 in 1993. Source: IMF, *International Financial Statistics*.

**Gross Domestic Product by Economic Activity** (EC $ million at current factor cost, 1987): Agriculture, hunting, forestry and fishing 64.1; Mining and quarrying 2.7; Manufacturing 35.0; Electricity, gas and water 18.5; Construction 36.1; Trade, restaurants and hotels 104.4; Transport, storage and communications 42.7; Finance, insurance and real estate 46.0; Government services 98.4; Other services 20.7; Sub-total 468.6; *Less* Imputed bank service charge 23.1; Total 445.5. Source: UN, *National Accounts Statistics*.

**Balance of Payments** (EC $ million, preliminary figures, 1993): Merchandise exports f.o.b. 285.8; Merchandise imports f.o.b. −713.2; *Trade balance* −427.3; Travel 428.2; Other services −191.5; Transfers (net) 71.6. *Current balance* −119.0; Capital account 131.0; *Overall balance* 12.0. Source: Eastern Caribbean Central Bank, *Report and Statement of Accounts*.

### EXTERNAL TRADE

**Principal Commodities** (US $ '000, 1992): *Imports c.i.f.*: Food and live animals 61,424; Beverages and tobacco 10,545; Crude materials excluding fuels 10,011; Mineral fuels, etc 21,321; Animal and vegetable fats and oils 1,080; Chemicals and related products 31,301; Basic manufactures 69,718; Machinery and transport equipment 66,745; Miscellaneous manufactured articles 40,835; Total (incl. others) 313,135. *Exports f.o.b.*: Food and live animals 70,317; Beverages and tobacco 6,747; Crude materials excluding fuels 618; Animal and vegetable oils and fats 3,227; Chemicals and related products 437; Basic manufactures 6,918; Machinery and transport equipment 4,284; Miscellaneous manufactured articles 21,288; Other goods 8,950; Total 122,787. Source: UN, *International Trade Statistics Yearbook*.

**Total Trade** (EC $ million): *Imports f.o.b.*: 705.8 in 1991; 731.3 in 1992; 713.2 in 1993. *Exports f.o.b.*: 297.8 in 1991; 331.5 in 1992; 285.8 in 1993. Source: Eastern Caribbean Central Bank, *Report and Statement of Accounts*.

**Principal Trading Partners** (US $'000, 1992): *Imports c.i.f.*: Barbados 8,510; Canada 10,146; France 9,460; Japan 19,374; Saint Vincent and the Grenadines 6,893; Trinidad and Tobago 28,695; United Kingdom 43,038; USA 105,935; Total (incl. others) 313,135. *Exports f.o.b.*: Antigua and Barbuda 1,670; Barbados 4,214; Dominica 5,005; Grenada 1,861; Italy 7,690; Jamaica 2,154; Saint Vincent and the Grenadines 1,748; Trinidad and Tobago 2,354; United Kingdom 63,097; USA 26,268; Total (incl. others) 122,787. Source UN, *International Trade Statistics Yearbook*.

### TRANSPORT

**Road Traffic** (registered motor vehicles, 1990): 12,759 (Passenger cars 6,524).

**Shipping:** *Arrivals:* Visitors 4,686 (1987); Vessels 2,063 (1990). *International Freight Traffic* ('000 metric tons, 1990): Goods loaded 150; Goods unloaded 234. Sources: UN, *Monthly Bulletin of Statistics*; UN, *Statistical Yearbook*.

**Civil Aviation** (aircraft arrivals): 12,764 in 1988; 14,595 in 1989; 15,872 in 1990.

### TOURISM

**Tourist Arrivals:** 318,763 in 1991; 342,440 (stop-over visitors 177,508) in 1992; 348,500 in 1993.

### COMMUNICATIONS MEDIA

**Daily Newspapers** (1986): 1 daily (circ. 8,000).
**Non-Daily Newspapers** (1990): 3 (circ. 18,000).
**Radio Receivers** (1992): 104,000 in use.
**Television Receivers** (1992): 26,000 in use.
**Telephones** (1992): 26,000 in use.

Sources: as above, and UNESCO, *Statistical Yearbook*.

### EDUCATION

**Pre-primary** (1991): 125 schools; 318 teachers; 5,300 pupils.
**Primary** (1992/93): 84 schools; 1,137 teachers (1989); 32,204 pupils.
**General Secondary** (1992/93): 14 schools; 376 teachers (1989/90, public education only); 7,612 pupils.
**Tertiary** (1992/93): 1,125 students (incl. technical 269, teacher-training 135).

Source: as above, and UNESCO, *Statistical Yearbook*.

# Directory

## The Constitution

The Constitution came into force at the independence of Saint Lucia on 22 February 1979. Its main provisions are summarized below:

### FUNDAMENTAL RIGHTS AND FREEDOMS

Regardless of race, place of origin, political opinion, colour, creed or sex but subject to respect for the rights and freedoms of others and for the public interest, every person in Saint Lucia is entitled to the rights of life, liberty, security of the person, equality before the law and the protection of the law. Freedom of conscience, of expression, of assembly and association is guaranteed and the inviolability of personal privacy, family life and property is maintained. Protection is afforded from slavery, forced labour, torture and inhuman treatment.

### THE GOVERNOR-GENERAL

The British monarch, as Head of State, is represented in Saint Lucia by the Governor-General.

### PARLIAMENT

Parliament consists of the British monarch, represented by the Governor-General, the 11-member Senate and the House of Assembly, composed of 17 elected Representatives. Senators are appointed by the Governor-General: six on the advice of the Prime Minister, three on the advice of the Leader of the Opposition and two acting on his own deliberate judgement. The life of Parliament is five years.

Each constituency returns one Representative to the House who is directly elected in accordance with the Constitution.

At a time when the office of Attorney-General is a public office, the Attorney-General is an *ex-officio* member of the House.

Every citizen over the age of 21 is eligible to vote.

Parliament may alter any of the provisions of the Constitution.

### THE EXECUTIVE

Executive authority is vested in the British monarch and exercisable by the Governor-General. The Governor-General appoints as Prime Minister that member of the House who, in the Governor-General's view, is best able to command the support of the majority of the members of the House, and other Ministers on the advice of the Prime Minister. The Governor-General may remove the Prime Minister from office if the House approves a resolution expressing no confidence in the Government, and if the Prime Minister does not resign within three days or advise the Governor-General to dissolve Parliament.

The Cabinet consists of the Prime Minister and other Ministers, and the Attorney-General as an *ex-officio* member at a time when the office of Attorney-General is a public office.

The Leader of the Opposition is appointed by the Governor-General as that member of the House who, in the Governor-General's view, is best able to command the support of a majority of members of the house who do not support the Government.

### CITIZENSHIP

All persons born in Saint Lucia before independence who immediately prior to independence were citizens of the United Kingdom and Colonies automatically become citizens of Saint Lucia. All persons born in Saint Lucia after independence automatically acquire Saint Lucian citizenship, as do those born outside Saint Lucia after independence to a parent possessing Saint Lucian citizenship. Provision is made for the acquisition of citizenship by those to whom it is not automatically granted.

SAINT LUCIA

# The Government

**Head of State:** HM Queen ELIZABETH II.
**Governor-General:** Sir STANISLAUS A. JAMES (took office in an acting capacity 10 October 1988, confirmed in the post 22 February 1992).

## CABINET
(June 1995)

**Prime Minister, Minister of Finance and of Planning and Development:** JOHN G. M. COMPTON.
**Deputy Prime Minister, Minister of Home Affairs, of Foreign Affairs and of Trade and Industry:** W. GEORGE MALLET.
**Minister of Health, Information and Broadcasting:** STEPHENSON KING.
**Minister of Education, Culture and Labour:** LOUIS GEORGE.
**Minister of Tourism, Public Utilities, Civil Aviation and National Mobilization:** ROMANUS LANSIQUOT.
**Minister of Community Development, Youth, Sports, Social Affairs, Local Government and Co-operatives:** DESMOND BRATHWAITE.
**Minister of Agriculture, Lands, Fisheries and Forestry:** IRA D'AUVERGNE.
**Attorney-General and Minister of Legal Affairs and Women's Affairs:** LORRAINE WILLIAMS.
**Minister of Communications, Works, and Transport:** GREGORY AVRIL.
**Minister of State in the Prime Minister's Office with responsibility for Financial Services and the National Development Corporation:** (vacant).
**Minister of State in the Prime Minister's Office, with responsibility for Housing, Urban Development and Renewal:** MICHAEL PILGRIM.
**Minister of State in the Prime Minister's Office with responsibility for Trade and Industry:** EDWARD INNOCENT.

## MINISTRIES

**Office of the Prime Minister:** Castries; tel. 452-3980; telex 6243; fax 453-7352.
**Ministry of Agriculture, Lands, Fisheries and Forestry:** The Waterfront, Castries; tel. 452-2526; fax 453-6314.
**Ministry of Communications, Works and Transport:** Micoud St, Castries; tel. 452-2429; telex 6394; fax 453-2769.
**Ministry of Community Development, Youth, Sports, Social Affairs, Local Government and Co-operatives:** 4th Floor, New Government Bldgs, John Compton Highway, Castries; tel. 452-3276; fax 452-3276.
**Ministry of Education, Culture and Labour:** Laborie St, Castries; tel. 452-2476; telex 6394; fax 453-2299.
**Ministry of Finance:** Old Government Bldgs, Laborie St, Castries; tel. 452-5315; telex 6223; fax 453-1648.
**Ministry for Foreign Affairs:** New Government Bldgs, John Compton Highway, Castries; tel. 452-1178; telex 6394.
**Ministry of Health, Information and Broadcasting:** Chaussee Rd, Castries; tel. 452-2827.
**Ministry of Home Affairs:** Castries.
**Ministry of Legal Affairs and Women's Affairs:** Old Government Bldgs, Laborie St, Castries.
**Ministry of Planning and Development:** Castries; tel. 452-2611; telex 6243; fax 452-2506.
**Ministry of Tourism, Public Utilities, Civil Aviation and National Mobilization:** NIS Bldg, John Compton Highway, Castries; tel. 451-6849; fax 451-7414.
**Ministry of Trade and Industry:** 4th Floor, Block B, NIS Bldg, John Compton Highway, Castries.

# Legislature

## PARLIAMENT
### Senate
The Senate has nine nominated members and two independent members.
**President:** NEVILLE CENAC.

### House of Assembly
**Speaker:** WILFRED ST CLAIR DANIEL.
**Clerk:** DORIS BAILEY.

Election, 27 April 1992

| Party | Seats |
| --- | --- |
| United Workers' Party | 11 |
| Saint Lucia Labour Party | 6 |
| **Total** | **17** |

# Political Organizations

**Progressive Labour Party (PLP):** 19 St Louis St, Castries; tel. 452-2203; f. 1981 as a result of a split within the SLP; socialist party; Chair. and Leader GEORGE ODLUM.
**Saint Lucia Labour Party (SLP):** POB 64, Castries; tel. 23927; telex 6338; f. 1946; socialist party; Leader JULIAN R. HUNTE; Chair. THOMAS WALCOTT.
**United Workers' Party (UWP):** 1 Riverside Rd, Castries; tel. 452-3438; f. 1964; right-wing party; Leader JOHN G. M. COMPTON.

# Diplomatic Representation

### EMBASSIES AND HIGH COMMISSION IN SAINT LUCIA
**China (Taiwan):** Chinese Embassy, Castries; tel. 450-0643.
**France:** Vigie, Castries; tel. 452-2462; telex 6359; fax 452-7899; Ambassador: JEAN-PAUL SCHRICKE.
**United Kingdom:** Colombus Square, POB 227, Castries; tel. 452-2484; telex 6314; fax 453-1543; (High Commissioner resident in Barbados); Resident Acting High Commissioner: M. W. GROWCOTT.
**Venezuela:** Vigie, Castries; tel. 452-4033; telex 6347; Ambassador: AMINTA GUACARÁN.

# Judicial System

## SUPREME COURT
**Eastern Caribbean Supreme Court:** Waterfront, Government Bldgs, Castries; tel. 452-2574. The West Indies Associated States Supreme Court was established in 1967 and was known as the Supreme Court of Grenada and the West Indies Associated States from 1974 until 1979, when it became the Eastern Caribbean Supreme Court. Its jurisdiction extends to Anguilla, Antigua and Barbuda, the British Virgin Islands, Dominica, Grenada (which rejoined in 1991), Montserrat, Saint Christopher and Nevis, Saint Lucia and Saint Vincent and the Grenadines. It is composed of the High Court of Justice and the Court of Appeal. The High Court is composed of the Chief Justice and nine Puisne Judges. The Court of Appeal is presided over by the Chief Justice and includes two other Justices of Appeal. Jurisdiction of the High Court includes fundamental rights and freedoms, membership of the parliaments, and matters concerning the interpretation of constitutions. Appeals from the Court of Appeal lie to the Judicial Committee of the Privy Council, based in the United Kingdom.
**Chief Justice:** Judge VINCENT F. FLOISSAC.

# Religion

## CHRISTIANITY
### The Roman Catholic Church
Saint Lucia forms a single archdiocese. The Archbishop participates in (and is currently President of) the Antilles Episcopal Conference (currently based in Port of Spain, Trinidad and Tobago). At 31 December 1993 there were an estimated 105,356 adherents, equivalent to some 77% of the population.
**Archbishop of Castries:** KELVIN EDWARD FELIX, Archbishop's House, POB 267, Castries; tel. 452-2416; fax 452-3697.

### The Anglican Communion
Anglicans in Saint Lucia are adherents of the Church in the Province of the West Indies, comprising eight dioceses. The Archbishop of the West Indies is the Bishop of the North Eastern Caribbean and Aruba. Saint Lucia forms part of the diocese of the Windward Islands (the Bishop is resident in Kingstown, Saint Vincent).

### Other Christian Churches
**Seventh-day Adventist Church:** St Louis St, Castries; tel. 452-4408; Pastor A. J. LEWIS.
**Trinity Evangelical Lutheran Church:** Gablewoods, POB GM 858, Castries; tel. 450-1484; Pastor J. JAEGER.

SAINT LUCIA
*Directory*

Baptist, Methodist, Pentecostal and other churches are also represented in Saint Lucia.

## The Press

**The Catholic Chronicle:** POB 778, Castries; f. 1957; monthly; Editor Rev. PATRICK A. B. ANTHONY; circ. 3,000.

**The Crusader:** 19 St Louis St, Castries; tel. 452-2203; f. 1934; weekly; Editor GEORGE ODLUM; circ. 4,000.

**The Mirror:** Castries; f. 1994; weekly; Editor GUY ELLIS.

**The Vanguard:** Hospital Rd, POB 690, Castries; fortnightly; Editor ANDREW SEALY; circ. 2,000.

**The Voice of St Lucia:** Odessa Bldg, Darling Rd, POB 104, Castries; tel. 452-2490; fax 453-1453; f. 1885; 3 a week; Editor (vacant); circ. 5,000.

### FOREIGN NEWS AGENCIES

**Inter Press Service (IPS)** (Italy): Hospital Rd, Castries; tel. 452-2770; Correspondent EARL BOUSQUET.

**United Press International (UPI)** (USA): Castries; tel. 452-3556; Correspondent ERNIE SEON.

## Publishers

**Caribbean Publishing Co Ltd:** American Drywall Bldg, Vide Boutielle Highway, POB 104, Castries; tel. 452-3188; telex 6353; fax 452-3181; f. 1978; publishes telephone directories and magazines.

**Star Publishing Co:** John Compton Highway, POB 1146, Castries; tel. 452-3558; fax 453-1616.

**Voice Publishing Co Ltd:** Darling Rd, POB 104, Castries; tel. 452-2590; fax 453-1453.

## Radio and Television

In 1992, according to UNESCO, there were an estimated 104,000 radio receivers and some 26,000 television receivers in use.

### RADIO

**Radio Caribbean International:** Mongiraud St, POB 121, Castries; tel. 452-2636; telex 6240; fax 452-2637; operates Radio Caraïbes; English and Creole services; broadcasts 24 hrs; Pres. H. COQUERELLE; Station Man. WINSTON FOSTER.

**Radio Koulibwi:** POB 20, Marchand PO, Castries.

**Saint Lucia Broadcasting Corporation:** Morne Fortune, POB 660, Castries; tel. 452-2337; fax 453-1568; govt-owned; Man. KEITH WEEKES.

**Radio Saint Lucia (RSL):** Morne Fortune, POB 660, Castries; tel. 452-2337; fax 453-1568; English and Creole services; Chair. VAUGHN LOUIS FERNAND; Man. KEITH WEEKES.

### TELEVISION

**Cablevision:** George Gordon Bldg, Bridge St, POB 111, Castries; tel. 452-3301; telex 6362; fax 453-2544.

**Daher Broadcasting Service:** Vigie, POB 1623, Castries; tel. 452-4055; fax 452-3544; Man. Dir LINDA DAHER.

**Helen Television System (HTS):** National Television Service of St Lucia, POB 621, Castries; tel. 452-2693; telex 6254; fax 454-1737; f. 1967; commercial station; Man. Dir LINFORD FEVRIERE; Prog. Dir VALERIE ALBERT.

## Finance

(cap. = capital; m. = million; br. = branch)

### BANKING

The Eastern Caribbean Central Bank (see p. 116), based in Saint Christopher, is the central issuing and monetary authority for Saint Lucia.

#### Local Banks

**National Commercial Bank of Saint Lucia:** John Compton Highway, POB 1031, Castries; tel. 452-2103; fax 453-1604; f. 1981; cap. US $0.4m.; Man. MCDONALD DIXON; 4 brs.

**Saint Lucia Co-operative Bank Ltd:** 21 Bridge St, POB 168, Castries; tel. 452-2881; fax 453-1630; incorporated 1937; commercial bank; auth. cap. EC $5,000,000; Pres. FERREL CHARLES; Man. Dir ALNITA SIMMONS; 3 brs.

There is also a Government Savings Bank.

#### Development Bank

**Saint Lucia Development Bank:** John Compton Highway, POB 368, Castries; tel. 452-3561; fax 453-6720; f. 1981; merged with former Agricultural and Industrial Development Bank; provides credit for agriculture, industry, tourism, housing and workforce training; Man. Dir DANIEL GIRARD.

#### Foreign Banks

**Bank of Nova Scotia Ltd** (Canada): 6 William Peter Blvd, POB 301, Castries; tel. 452-2292; telex 6385; fax 453-1051; Man. ROBERT HAINES; 3 brs.

**Barclays Bank PLC** (United Kingdom): Bridge St, POB 335, Castries; tel. 452-3306; telex 6348; fax 452-6860; Man. GEOFFREY HART; 4 brs.

**Canadian Imperial Bank of Commerce:** William Peter Blvd, POB 350, Castries; tel. 452-3751; telex 6352; fax 452-3735; Man. F. D. ROCK; 2 brs.

**Royal Bank of Canada:** William Peter Blvd, POB 280, Castries; tel. 452-2245; telex 6309; fax 452-7855; Man. JOHN MILLER.

### INSURANCE

There were 25 insurance companies operating in Saint Lucia in 1990. Local companies include the following:

**Ennia General Insurance Co Ltd:** 18 Micoud St, POB 544, Castries; tel. 452-3892.

**First National Insurance Co Ltd:** Cnr Brazil St and Chaussee Rd, POB 547, Castries; tel. 452-2871; fax 452-7117.

**Saint Lucia Insurances Ltd:** Micoud St, POB 1084, Castries; tel. 452-3240; fax 452-2240.

## Trade and Industry

### CHAMBER OF COMMERCE

**Saint Lucia Chamber of Commerce, Industry and Agriculture:** Micoud St, POB 482, Castries; tel. 452-3165; fax 453-6907; f. 1884; 125 mems; Pres. INGRID SKERRET.

### DEVELOPMENT CORPORATIONS

**National Development Corporation (NDC):** 27 Brazil St, POB 495, Castries; tel 452-3614; fax 452-1841; f. 1971 to promote the economic development of Saint Lucia; owns and manages four industrial estates; br. in New York, USA; Chair. LESLIE R. CLARKE; Gen. Man. CROMWELL R. GOODRIDGE.

### EMPLOYERS' ASSOCIATIONS

**Saint Lucia Agriculturists' Association Ltd:** Mongiraud St, POB 153, Castries; tel. 452-2494; Chair. and Man. Dir C. ALCINDOR; Sec. R. RAVENEAU.

**Saint Lucia Banana Growers' Association:** 7 Manoel St, POB 197, Castries; tel. 452-2251; fax 452-7334; f. 1953, became statutory corporation 1967; placed into receivership in Feb. 1994 pending the reorganization of the banana industry; 8,000 mems.

**Saint Lucia Coconut Growers' Association Ltd:** Manoel St, POB 259, Castries; tel. 452-2360; fax 453-1499; Chair. JOHANNES LEONCE; Man. N. E. EDMUNDS.

**Saint Lucia Employers' Federation:** Linmore's Bldg, Coral St, Castries; tel. 452-2190.

**Saint Lucia Fish Marketing Corpn:** Castries; tel. 452-1341; fax 451-7073.

**Saint Lucia Industrial and Small Business Association:** 2nd Floor, Ivy Crick Memorial Bldg, POB 312, Castries; tel. 453-1392; Pres. LEO CLARKE; Exec. Dir Dr URBAN SERAPHINE.

**Saint Lucia Marketing Board:** Conway, POB 441, Castries; tel. 452-3214; fax 453-1424; Chair. DAVID DEMAQUE; Man. MICHAEL WILLIAMS.

**Windward Islands Banana Development and Exporting Co (Wibdeco):** Castries; f. 1994 in succession to the Windward Islands Banana Growers' Association (WINBAN); regional organization dealing with banana development and marketing; jointly owned by the Windward governments and island banana associations; Chair. BERNARD YANKEY.

### TRADE UNIONS

**Farmers' and Farm Workers' Union:** St Louis St, Castries; Pres. Senator FRANCES MICHEL; Sec. CATHERINE BURT; 3,500 mems.

**National Workers' Union:** POB 713, Castries; tel. 452-3664; telex 6227; affiliated to World Federation of Trade Unions; Pres. TYRONE MAYNARD; Sec. GEORGE GODDARD; 6,000 mems.

**Saint Lucia Civil Service Association:** POB 244, Castries; tel. 452-3903; f. 1951; Pres. MARTIN SATNEY; Gen. Sec. HENRY CHARLES.

# SAINT LUCIA

**Saint Lucia Nurses' Association:** POB 819, Castries; tel. 452-1403; fax 453-0960; f. 1947; Pres. Lilia Harracksingh; Gen. Sec. Esther Felix.

**Saint Lucia Seamen, Waterfront and General Workers' Trade Union:** Reclamation Grounds, POB 166, Castries; tel. 452-2277; f. 1945; affiliated to International Confederation of Free Trade Unions (ICFTU) and Caribbean Congress of Labour; Pres. Hilford Deterville; Sec. Crescentia Phillips; 2,500 mems.

**Saint Lucia Teachers' Union:** POB 821, Castries; tel. 452-4469; f. 1934; Pres. Julian Delouney; Sec.-Gen. Gilroy Satney.

**Saint Lucia Workers' Union:** Reclamation Grounds, Conway, Castries; tel. 452-2620; f. 1939; affiliated to ICFTU; Pres. George Louis; Sec. Titus Francis; 1,000 mems.

**Vieux Fort General and Dock Workers' Union:** New Dock St, POB 224, Vieux Fort; tel. 454-6193; f. 1954; Pres. Fitzroy Alexander; 550 mems.

### CO-OPERATIVE SOCIETIES

There are 39 co-operative societies.

## Transport

### RAILWAYS

There are no railways in Saint Lucia.

### ROADS

There is a total of approximately 970 km (600 miles) of roads, of which 790 km (490 miles) are main roads and the remainder principally feeder roads. The main highway passes through every town and village on the island. Internal transport is handled by private concerns.

### SHIPPING

The ports at Castries and Vieux Fort have been fully mechanized. Castries has six berths with a total length of 2,470 ft (753 metres). Two additional cruise-ship berths are planned for the Pointe Seraphine cruise-ship terminal. A project to upgrade the port at Vieux Fort to a full deep-water container port was completed in mid-1993. The port of Soufrière has a deep-water anchorage, but no alongside berth for ocean-going vessels. There is a petroleum transhipment terminal at Cul de Sac Bay. During 1992 and 1993 a total of 750 cruise ships, carrying 319,305 passengers, called at Saint Lucia. Regular services are provided by a number of shipping lines, including ferry services to neighbouring islands.

**Saint Lucia Air and Sea Ports Authority:** Micoud St, POB 651, Castries; tel. 452-2893; fax 452-2062; Gen. Man. Gregory St Helene.

### CIVIL AVIATION

There are two airports in use: Hewanorra International (formerly Beane Field near Vieux Fort), 64 km (40 miles) from Castries, which is equipped to handle large jet aircraft; and Vigie, in Castries, which is capable of handling medium-range jets. In May 1993 new facilities at Hewanorra, including a new departure terminal, were opened. Saint Lucia is served by scheduled flights to the USA, Europe and most destinations in the Caribbean. The country is a shareholder in the regional airline LIAT (see chapter on Antigua and Barbuda).

**Saint Lucia Air and Sea Ports Authority:** (see above).

**Air Antilles:** Laborie St, POB 1065, Castries; f. 1985; designated as national carrier of Grenada in 1987; flights to destinations in the Caribbean, the United Kingdom and North America; charter co.

**Caribbean Air Transport:** POB 253, Castries; telex 6393; f. 1975 as Saint Lucia Airways; local shuttle service, charter flights.

**Eagle Air Services Ltd:** Vigie Airport, POB 838, Castries; tel. 452-1900; fax 452-9683; charter flights; Man. Dir Capt. Ewart F. Hinkson.

**Helenair Corpn Ltd:** Vigie Airport, POB 253, Castries; tel. 452-7196; fax 452-1958; f. 1987; charter flights.

## Tourism

Saint Lucia possesses spectacular mountain scenery, a tropical climate and sandy beaches. Historical sites, rich birdlife and the sulphur baths at Soufrière are other attractions. In 1993 Saint Lucia received an estimated 348,500 visitors. The USA is the principal market (almost 29% of total arrivals in 1993), followed by the United Kingdom (25%). There were an estimated 3,200 hotel rooms in 1993.

**Saint Lucia Tourist Board:** Pointe Seraphine, POB 221, Castries; tel. 452-5968; fax 453-1121; 4 brs overseas; Chair. Stephen McNamara; Dir Agnes Francis.

**Saint Lucia Hotel and Tourism Association:** POB 545, Castries; tel. 452-5978; fax 452-7967; f. 1962; Pres. Richard Michelin; Exec. Vice Pres. Darrell Theobalds.

# SAINT VINCENT AND THE GRENADINES

## Introductory Survey

### Location, Climate, Language, Religion, Flag, Capital

Saint Vincent and the Grenadines is situated in the Windward Islands group, approximately 160 km (100 miles) west of Barbados, in the West Indies. The nearest neighbouring countries are Saint Lucia, some 34 km (21 miles) to the north-east, and Grenada, to the south. As well as the main volcanic island of Saint Vincent, the state includes the 32 smaller islands and cayes known as the Saint Vincent Grenadines, the northerly part of an island chain stretching between Saint Vincent and Grenada. The principal islands in that part of the group are Bequia, Canouan, Mustique, Mayreau, Isle D'Quatre and Union Island. The climate is tropical, with average temperatures of between 18°C and 32°C (64°F–90°F). Annual rainfall ranges from 1,500 mm (60 ins) in the extreme south to 3,750 mm (150 ins) in the mountainous interior of the main island. English is the official language. Most of the inhabitants profess Christianity and are adherents of the Anglican, Methodist or Roman Catholic Churches. The national flag (proportions 3 by 2) has three unequal vertical stripes, of blue, yellow and green, with three lozenges in green, in a 'V' formation, superimposed on the broad central yellow stripe. The capital is Kingstown, on the island of Saint Vincent.

### Recent History

The islands were first settled by an Arawak people, who were subsequently conquered by the Caribs. The arrival of shipwrecked and escaped African slaves resulted in the increase of a so-called 'Black Carib' population, some of whose descendants still remain. Under the collective name of Saint Vincent, and despite the opposition of the French and the indigenous population, the islands finally became a British possession during the 18th century. With other nearby British territories, St Vincent was administered by the Governor of the Windward Islands, under a federal system, until December 1959. The first elections under universal adult suffrage took place in 1951. The islands participated in the West Indies Federation from its foundation in January 1958 until its dissolution in May 1962. From January 1960, St Vincent, in common with the other Windward Islands, had a new Constitution, with its own Administrator and an enlarged Legislative Council.

After the failure of negotiations to form a smaller East Caribbean Federation, most of the British colonies in the Leeward and Windward Islands became Associated States, with full internal self-government, in 1967. This change of status was delayed in St Vincent because of local political differences. At controversial elections to the Legislative Council in 1966, the ruling People's Political Party (PPP) was returned with a majority of only one seat. Further elections took place in May 1967, when the Saint Vincent Labour Party (SVLP) secured six of the nine seats in the Council. Milton Cato, leader of the SVLP, became Chief Minister, in succession to Ebenezer Joshua of the PPP. On 27 October 1969, despite objections from the PPP, St Vincent became an Associated State, with the United Kingdom retaining responsibility for defence and foreign relations only. The Legislative Council was renamed the House of Assembly, the Administrator was designated Governor, and the Chief Minister became Premier.

Elections were held in April 1972 for an enlarged, 13-seat House of Assembly. The PPP and the SVLP each obtained six seats, while the remaining one was secured by James Mitchell (formerly a minister in the SVLP Government), who stood as an independent. The PPP agreed to form a Government with Mitchell as Premier and Joshua as Deputy Premier and Minister of Finance. In September 1974 Joshua resigned after policy disagreements with the Premier. A motion expressing 'no confidence' in Mitchell's Government was approved, and the House was dissolved. In the ensuing elections, which took place in December, the PPP and SVLP campaigned in a 'unity agreement'. The SVLP secured 10 of the 13 seats, and the PPP two. (Mitchell was again elected as an independent.) Cato became Premier again, at the head of a coalition with the PPP, and committed his Government to attaining full independence from the United Kingdom.

After a constitutional conference in September 1978, the colony became fully independent, within the Commonwealth, as Saint Vincent and the Grenadines, on 27 October 1979. The Governor became Governor-General, while Cato took office as the country's first Prime Minister.

Cato's position was reinforced in the general election of December 1979, when the SVLP obtained 11 of the 13 elective seats in the 19-member House of Assembly. Attempts by the other parties to form a united opposition to the Government repeatedly failed. In 1982 the leader of the United People's Movement (UPM), Dr Ralph Gonsalves, resigned in protest against what he alleged to be Marxist tendencies within the UPM, and founded a new party, the Movement for National Unity (MNU). In June 1984 Cato announced an early general election, hoping to take advantage of divisions within the opposition in order to secure his return to power. However, the repercussions of scandals surrounding the Cato Government, and the economic and taxation policies of the SVLP, helped to produce an unexpected victory for the centrist New Democratic Party (NDP) at the election in July. The NDP (formed in 1975 by James Mitchell) won nine of the 13 elective seats in the House of Assembly, and Mitchell became Prime Minister. Five SVLP ministers lost their seats. Cato subsequently retired from politics, and, in the ensuing by-election, the NDP gained another seat. Hudson Tannis (the Deputy Prime Minister until the 1984 election) replaced Cato as leader of the SVLP in January 1985, but was killed in an aircraft accident in August 1986; he was succeeded as party leader by Vincent Beache.

Despite considerable controversy during 1987 regarding what was considered in some quarters to be excessive government influence over the media, the NDP obtained more than 66% of the valid votes cast, and won all 15 elective seats in the newly-enlarged House of Assembly, at a general election in May 1989. Mitchell remained as Prime Minister and formed a new Cabinet.

In mid-1991 the SVLP and the MNU demanded the resignation of the Government, following its decision to prohibit public access to the log of a Saint Vincentian ship suspected of being used for drugs-trafficking. Meanwhile, in the continued absence of a united parliamentary opposition, an organization, the People's Parliament, was formed, and, in late 1992, established itself as a political pressure group, with the aim of voicing popular dissatisfaction with government policy.

In May 1993 the Minister of Health, Burton Williams, was demoted to the post of Minister in the Prime Minister's Office, following his mishandling of a dispute concerning private medical practice. Mitchell was obliged to acknowledge a lack of public confidence in the health system. In January 1994 Williams resigned from his new post and criticized Mitchell's leadership. In that month a minor reorganization of the Cabinet was implemented.

At a general election on 21 February 1994 the NDP secured its third consecutive term of office, obtaining 12 seats in the House of Assembly. An electoral alliance formed by the SVLP and the MNU and headed by the former SVLP leader, Vincent Beache, won the three remaining elective seats. The Cabinet remained largely unchanged, although Mitchell introduced the position of Deputy Prime Minister for the first time since taking office, to which he appointed the Attorney-General and Minister of Justice, Information and Ecclesiastical Affairs, Parnell R. Campbell. Beache was confirmed as the official Leader of the Opposition, and in September 1994 the MNU and the SVLP announced their formal merger as the United Labour Party (ULP).

Opposition charges that the Government had failed to address problems presented by a marked decline in banana production, a crisis in the health and education sectors and persistent allegations that drugs-related activities were being conducted on the islands culminated in the defeat, by 10 votes to three, of a motion of 'no confidence' in the Government, brought by the opposition in August 1994. The execution, by hanging, of three convicted murderers in February 1995 provoked outrage from international human rights organizations, who expressed concern that the sentences had been implemented with a suspicious degree of alacrity and secrecy.

Saint Vincent and the Grenadines is a member of the Caribbean Community and Common Market (CARICOM, see p. 114), of the Organisation of Eastern Caribbean States (OECS, see p. 116) and is a signatory of the Lomé Convention (see p. 165). During the late 1980s Mitchell's Government was one of the principal advocates of East Caribbean unity, claiming that only a unitary state could develop a strong and indigenous economy for the island countries of the region. Moreover, the country played a major role in the decision, in 1988, by the Prime Ministers of the four English-speaking Windward Islands countries (St Vincent and the Grenadines, Dominica, Grenada and Saint Lucia) to proceed with plans towards a more limited union, following the reluctance of other OECS members to pursue such a project. In late 1990 the leaders of the four countries accordingly created a new body, the Regional Constituent Assembly. Following a series of discussions, the Assembly issued its final report in late 1992, in which it stated that the four countries were committed to the establishment of economic and political union under a federal system.

In July 1993 new regulations came into effect governing the level of imports of bananas by the European Community (now the European Union—EU). The regulations were introduced to protect traditional producers covered by the Lomé Convention from competition from the expanding Latin American producers. At the instigation of the Latin American producers consecutive dispute panels were appointed by GATT to rule on whether the EU's actions contravened GATT rules. Although the dispute panels ruled in favour of the Latin American producers, the rulings were not enforceable. In October 1994 the US Government announced its intention to investigate illegal discrimination by the EU against US-based banana-marketing companies. In the same month the EU granted an increase in its Latin American banana import quota in order to allow the Windward Islands to fulfill their EU import allocations through re-exports, following the severe storm damage sustained by plantations on the islands in September 1994. Negotiations between the EU and the USA were scheduled to continue in mid-1995, in an attempt to reach agreement on a mutually-acceptable banana-marketing regime.

Relations with Venezuela developed in 1988, and in February 1989 that country upgraded its relations with Saint Vincent and the Grenadines to resident ambassador status. In mid-1992 the islands established diplomatic relations with Cuba.

### Government

Saint Vincent and the Grenadines is a constitutional monarchy. Executive power is vested in the British monarch, as Head of State, and is exercisable by the Governor-General, who represents the British monarch locally and who is appointed on the advice of the Prime Minister. Legislative power is vested in Parliament, comprising the Governor-General the House of Assembly (composed of 21 members: six nominated Senators and 15 Representatives, elected for up to five years by universal adult suffrage). Senators are appointed by the Governor-General: four on the advice of the Prime Minister and two on the advice of the Leader of the Opposition. Government is effectively by the Cabinet. The Governor-General appoints the Prime Minister and, on the latter's recommendation, selects the other Ministers. The Prime Minister must be able to command the support of the majority of the House, to which the Cabinet is responsible.

### Defence

Saint Vincent and the Grenadines participates in the US-sponsored Regional Security System, comprising police, coastguards and army units, which was established by independent East Caribbean states in 1982. Since 1984, however, the paramilitary Special Service Unit has had strictly limited deployment. Government expenditure on defence in the financial year 1989/90 was EC $8.7m. (5.6% of total expenditure).

### Economic Affairs

In 1993, according to estimates by the World Bank, Saint Vincent and the Grenadines' gross national product (GNP), measured at average 1991–93 prices, was US $233m., equivalent to $2,130 per head. During 1985–93, it was estimated, GNP per head increased, in real terms, at an average annual rate of 4.6% per year. Over the same period the population increased by an annual average of 0.9%. Saint Vincent and the Grenadines' gross domestic product (GDP) increased, in real terms, by an average annual rate of 6.8% between 1984 and 1990, by 3.1% in 1991, and by 4.8% in 1992. Preliminary estimates suggest that growth slowed to just 1.3% for 1993.

Agriculture (including forestry and fishing) contributed 17.9% of GDP in 1990. The sector employed 25.7% of the working population, according to the census of 1980, and agricultural products earned 79.5% of total export revenue in 1990. The principal cash crop is bananas, which contributed 57.3% of the value of merchandise exports in 1990. Despite some decline in production, Saint Vincent and the Grenadines remains the world's leading producer of arrowroot starch, production levels of which increased in 1991 by 50.6% compared with 1990. Other important crops are vegetables, plantains, coconuts, tobacco and spices. Forestry development is strictly controlled. Fishing is increasingly important, mainly for the domestic market. Agricultural production increased steadily in the 1980s, but declined by 9.4% in 1991 before recovering in 1992, only to decline again (by some 11%) in 1993, largely owing to reduced banana production arising from uncertainty regarding the future of the export market.

Industry (including mining, manufacturing, electricity, water and construction) employed 16.8% of the labour force in 1980, and provided 22.0% of GDP in 1990. Mining and quarrying activity is negligible. The manufacturing sector accounted for 8.2% of GDP in 1990, but in 1980 it employed only 5.1% of the working population (although employment in the sector subsequently increased). Apart from a garment industry and the assembling of electrical components, the most important activities involve the processing of agricultural products, including flour-milling, brewing, rum distillation, and processing dairy products. The manufacture of tennis racquets, which earned 11.2% of merchandise exports in 1988, ceased entirely in 1990. Manufacturing output declined by 16.0% in 1990 but, after a year without discernible growth in 1991, increased by 2.0% in 1992, only to decline by 4.0% during 1993, owing to weak market demand.

Energy is derived principally from the use of hydrocarbon fuels (mineral fuels accounted for 6.1% of total imports in 1990). There is, however, an important hydroelectric plant in Cumberland.

Tourism is an important service industry, but is smaller in scale than in most other Caribbean islands, contributing less than 5% of GDP in 1989. Although the numbers of stop-over and cruise-ship visitors increased in the 1980s and early 1990s, the most important contributors to the sector are still the yacht-based arrivals (4,659 in 1991) and wealthy visitors who own property in the islands. Tourist activity remains concentrated in the Grenadines and caters for the luxury market. However, growth in the hotels and restaurants sector (estimated at 6.4% in 1993) is expected to continue. There is a small 'offshore' financial sector.

In 1993 Saint Vincent and the Grenadines recorded a visible trade deficit of EC $133.0m., while there was a deficit of EC $68.9m. on the current account of the balance of payments. The principal source of imports is the USA (36.0% of the total in 1990). Other important suppliers in that year were the United Kingdom and Trinidad and Tobago. The United Kingdom is the principal market for exports (almost 57.0% of total exports in 1990). Other important markets in that year were the USA, Trinidad and Tobago, and other Eastern Caribbean states. The principal exports are bananas and other agricultural produce, while the principal imports are manufactured items. Revenue from the export of bananas declined from EC $99m. in 1993 to just EC $58m. in 1994. The cost of imports was equivalent to 85.9% of GDP in 1990.

In the financial year ending 31 December 1993 there was an overall budgetary deficit of EC $18.6m. Saint Vincent and the Grenadines' total external debt was US $86.2m. at the end of 1993, of which US $62.4m. was long-term public debt. In 1992 the cost of debt-servicing was equivalent to 3.5% of the value of exports of goods and services. The average annual rate of inflation was 3.5% in 1985–93. At the 1991 census 20.0% of the labour force were unemployed.

Saint Vincent and the Grenadines is a member of the Caribbean Community and Common Market (CARICOM, see p. 114),

# SAINT VINCENT AND THE GRENADINES

which seeks to encourage regional development, particularly by increasing trade between member states, and the Organisation of Eastern Caribbean States (OECS, see p. 116).

Agriculture is the dominating sector of the economy and, although the introduction of other crops has reduced dependence on the vulnerable banana harvest, performance is significantly affected by weather conditions (in 1991, for example, drought impeded agricultural production) or occasional volcanic activity (as in 1979). Nevertheless, from 1984 government policy encouraged an increase in agricultural production, with emphasis on the cultivation of food crops for domestic consumption. In 1993 a coastal fisheries development project received substantial financial support from Japan. In the 1994 budget income tax reductions of about EC $4m. were introduced as part of a tax reform programme. The Government announced its intention to eliminate a 3% export tax on bananas, beginning with a reduction of 1% in January 1994. Later that year the Government announced its intention to restructure the banana industry, with the assistance of the European Union, at a cost of EC $96m. Budget proposals, announced in December 1994, anticipated GDP growth of 4%, proceeding from an increase in tourist receipts and a recovery in banana production (following adverse weather conditions during 1994).

## Social Welfare

In 1989 there were four hospitals and 35 government-run clinics and dispensaries located throughout the islands, with some 500 hospital beds, of which 207 are in the Central General Hospital. There was one physician for every 2,700 inhabitants in Saint Vincent and the Grenadines in 1989. Budgetary expenditure by the central Government in the financial year 1989/90 included EC $23.5m. (15.1% of total expenditure) for health, and in 1989/90 EC $3.5m. (2.3%) was for social security and welfare.

## Education

Free primary education, beginning at five years of age and lasting for seven years, is available to all children in government schools, although it is not compulsory and attendance is low. There are 60 government, and several private, primary schools. Secondary education, beginning at 12 years of age, comprises a first cycle of five years and a second, two-year cycle. However, government facilities at this level are limited, with only one girls' high school and one co-educational school. Otherwise, secondary education is provided in schools administered by religious organizations, with government assistance. There are also a number of junior secondary schools. There is one teacher-training college and one technical college. In 1983 the average rate of adult literacy was about 85%. Expenditure on education by the central Government in 1989/90 was EC $28.1m. (18.1% of total expenditure).

## Public Holidays

**1995:** 1 January (New Year's Day), 22 January (Saint Vincent and the Grenadines Day), 14 April (Good Friday), 17 April (Easter Monday), 1 May (Labour Day), 5 June (Whit Monday), 3 July (CARICOM Day), 4 July (Carnival), 7 August (Emancipation Day), 27 October (National Day), 25–26 December (Christmas).

**1996:** 1 January (New Year's Day), 22 January (Saint Vincent and the Grenadines Day), 5 April (Good Friday), 8 April (Easter Monday), 1 May (Labour Day), 27 May (Whit Monday), 1 July (CARICOM Day), 2 July (Carnival), 5 August (Emancipation Day), 27 October (National Day), 25–26 December (Christmas).

## Weights and Measures

The imperial system is used.

# Statistical Survey

Sources (unless otherwise stated): Statistical Office, Ministry of Finance and Planning, Kingstown; OECS Economic Affairs Secretariat, *Statistical Digest.*

## AREA, POPULATION AND DENSITY

**Area:** 389.3 sq km (150.3 sq miles). The island of Saint Vincent covers 344 sq km (133 sq miles).

**Population:** 97,845 (males 47,409; females 50,436) at census of 12 May 1980; 107,598 (males 53,977; females 53,621) at census of 12 May 1991; 109,000 (official estimate for mid-1992).

**Density** (1991): 276.4 per sq km.

**Principal Town:** Kingstown (capital), population 15,670 (at census of 1991).

**Births and Deaths** (registrations, 1991): Live births 2,591 (birth rate 24.1 per 1,000); Deaths 654 (death rate 6.1 per 1,000).

**Economically Active Population** (persons aged 15 years and over, 1980 census): Agriculture, hunting, forestry and fishing 8,928; Mining and quarrying 108; Manufacturing 1,781; Electricity, gas and water 402; Construction 3,549; Trade, restaurants and hotels 2,566; Transport, storage and communications 1,882; Financing, insurance, real estate and business services 351; Community, social and personal services 7,579; Activities not adequately defined 7,593; Total labour force 34,739 (males 22,193; females 12,546).

**1991** (census results): Total labour force 41,682 (males 26,734; females 14,948). Source: ILO, *Year Book of Labour Statistics.*

## AGRICULTURE, ETC.

**Principal Crops** (metric tons, 1990): Nutmeg and mace 111, Arrowroot starch 56, Ginger 834, Taro (Dasheen, Eddo) 5,240, Tannias 577.

**1993** (FAO estimates, '000 metric tons): Bananas 83, Plantains 3, Sweet potatoes 4, Cassava 3 (1991), Yams 2, Sugar cane 44, Coconuts 23. Source: FAO *Production Yearbook.*

**Livestock** (FAO estimates, '000 head, year ending September 1993): Asses 2, Cattle 6, Pigs 9, Sheep 12, Goats 6. Source: FAO, *Production Yearbook.*

**Livestock Products** (FAO estimates; '000 metric tons, 1993): Meat 1, Cows' milk 1, Hen eggs 0.6. Source: FAO, *Production Yearbook.*

**Fishing** (metric tons, live weight): Total catch 8,830 in 1990; 7,994 in 1990; 2,188 in 1992. Source: FAO, *Yearbook of Fishery Statistics.*

## INDUSTRY

**Selected Products:** Rum 4,000 hectolitres (1992); Electric energy 51 million kWh (1992). Source: UN, *Industrial Statistics Yearbook.*

## FINANCE

**Currency and Exchange Rates:** 100 cents = 1 East Caribbean dollar (EC $). *Sterling and US Dollar Equivalents* (31 December 1994): £1 sterling = EC $4.224; US $1 = EC $2.700; EC $100 = £23.67 = US $37.04. *Exchange rate:* Fixed at US $1 = EC $2.70 since July 1976.

**Budget** (EC $ million, preliminary figures, year ending 31 December 1993): *Revenue:* Revenue from taxation 141.8 (of which, Taxes on international trade and transactions 75.9); Other current revenue 33.9; Foreign grants 1.3; Total 177.0. *Expenditure:* Personal emoluments 81.5; Goods and services and transfers 39.1; Interest payments 7.4; Other 21.8; Capital expenditure 45.8; Total 195.6. Source: Eastern Caribbean Central Bank, *Report and Statement of Accounts.*

**International Reserves** (US $ million at 31 December 1993): IMF special drawing rights 0.12; Reserve position in IMF 0.69; Foreign exchange 30.50; Total 31.31. Source: IMF, *International Financial Statistics.*

**Money Supply** (EC $ million at 31 December 1993): Currency outside banks 28.22; Demand deposits at deposit money banks 62.86; Total money (incl. others) 91.10. Source: IMF, *International Financial Statistics.*

**Cost of Living** (Consumer Price Index; base: 1990 = 100): 109.1 in 1992; 113.8 in 1993; 114.3 in 1994.

**Gross Domestic Product by Economic Activity** (EC $ million at current prices, 1990): Agriculture, hunting, forestry and fishing 83.89; Mining and quarrying 1.22; Manufacturing 38.51; Electricity and water 21.56; Construction 42.28; Wholesale and retail trade 51.70; Hotels and restaurants 10.10; Transport 63.56; Com-

SAINT VINCENT AND THE GRENADINES — *Statistical Survey, Directory*

munications 30.02; Banks and insurance 37.14; Real estate and housing 12.01; Government services 69.63; Other community, social and personal services 8.25; Sub-total 469.88; *Less* Imputed bank service charge 26.19; GDP at factor cost 443.69.

**Balance of Payments** (EC $ million, preliminary figures, 1993): Merchandise exports f.o.b. 175.0; Merchandise imports f.o.b. −308.0; *Trade balance* −133.0; Services (net) 25.6; Other income (net) −18.1; Transfers (net) 56.6; *Current balance* −68.9; Capital account 63.4. *Overall balance* −5.5. Source: Eastern Caribbean Central Bank, *Report and Statement of Accounts*.

### EXTERNAL TRADE

**Principal Commodities** (EC $'000, 1990): *Imports:* Food and live animals 79,756 (Wheat 16,082); Beverages and tobacco 7,529; Crude materials (inedible) except fuels 13,282; Mineral fuels, lubricants, etc. 22,395; Chemicals 40,284; Basic manufactures 87,685; Machinery and transport equipment 79,828; Miscellaneous manufactured articles 36,050 (Clothing 10,771); Total (incl. others) 367,409. *Exports:* Food and live animals 166,992 (Bananas 120,283, Flour 19,466, Tubers 9,865); Basic manufactures 16,778; Machinery and transport equipment 2,356; Miscellaneous manufactured articles 18,554; Total (incl. others) 210,000.

**Total Trade** (EC $ million): *Imports f.o.b.:* 323.2 in 1991; 320.3 in 1992; 308.0 in 1993. *Exports f.o.b.:* 181.6 in 1991; 209.3 in 1992; 175.0 in 1993. Source: Eastern Caribbean Central Bank, *Report and Statement of Accounts*.

**Principal Trading Partners** (EC $'000, 1990): *Imports:* Barbados 14,968; Canada 14,252; Japan 12,197; Trinidad and Tobago 46,009; United Kingdom 64,896; USA 132,222; Total (incl. others) 367,409. *Exports:* Antigua and Barbuda 7,868; Barbados 5,441; Saint Lucia 13,861; Trinidad and Tobago 26,959; United Kingdom 119,616; USA 17,433; Total (incl. others) 210,000.

### TRANSPORT

**Road Traffic** ('000 registered motor vehicles): 8.4 in 1985; 8.9 in 1987; 9.8 (Passenger cars 4.5, Commercial vehicles 3.6, Motor cycles 1.2) in 1989. *1990* ('000 in use): Passenger cars 5.3, Commercial vehicles 2.8 (Source, UN, *Statistical Yearbook*).

**Shipping:** *Arrivals:* Visitors 2,571 (1987); Vessels 1,016 (1991). *International Freight Traffic* (estimates, '000 metric tons, 1991): Goods loaded 80; Goods unloaded 140. *Merchant Fleet* (total displacement, vessels registered at 30 June): 4,698,000 grt in 1992. (Source: Lloyd's Register of Shipping.)

**Civil Aviation** (visitor arrivals): 34,887 in 1986; 45,990 in 1987; 51,608 in 1989.

### TOURISM

**Visitor Arrivals:** 173,292 in 1991; 155,203 (63,420 cruise-ship passengers) in 1992; 163,120 in 1993.

**Hotel Rooms:** 1,164 in 1993.

### COMMUNICATIONS MEDIA

**Newspapers** (1988): 2 (none daily); average circ. 11,000.
**Radio Receivers** (1992): 76,000 in use.
**Television Receivers** (1992): 16,000 in use.
**Telephones** (1991 estimate): 15,000 main lines in use.
Sources: UNESCO, *Statistical Yearbook*; UN, *Statistical Yearbook*.

### EDUCATION

**Pre-primary** (1990): 77 schools; 180 teachers; 2,492 pupils. Source: UNESCO, *Statistical Yearbook*.
**Primary** (1991/92): 60 schools; 1,215 teachers; 24,134 pupils.
**Secondary** (1991/92): 21 schools; 408 teachers; 7,124 pupils.
**Teacher-Training College** (1991/92): 1 institution; 143 students.
**Technical College** (1991/92): 1 institution; 194 full-time students.

# Directory

## The Constitution

The Constitution came into force at the independence of Saint Vincent and the Grenadines on 27 October 1979. The following is a summary of its main provisions:

### FUNDAMENTAL RIGHTS AND FREEDOMS

Regardless of race, place of origin, political opinion, colour, creed or sex, but subject to respect for the rights and freedoms of others and for the public interest, every person in Saint Vincent and the Grenadines is entitled to the rights of life, liberty, security of the person and the protection of the law. Freedom of conscience, of expression, of assembly and association is guaranteed and the inviolability of a person's home and other property is maintained. Protection is afforded from slavery, forced labour, torture and inhuman treatment.

### THE GOVERNOR-GENERAL

The British Monarch is represented in Saint Vincent and the Grenadines by the Governor-General.

### PARLIAMENT

Parliament consists of the British monarch, represented by the Governor-General, and the House of Assembly, comprising 15 elected Representatives (increased from 13 under the provisions of an amendment approved in 1986) and six Senators. Senators are appointed by the Governor-General—four on the advice of the Prime Minister and two on the advice of the Leader of the Opposition. The life of Parliament is five years. Each constituency returns one Representative to the House who is directly elected in accordance with the Constitution. At a time when the office of Attorney-General is a public office, the Attorney-General is an *ex-officio* member of the House. Every citizen over the age of 18 is eligible to vote. Parliament may alter any of the provisions of the Constitution.

### THE EXECUTIVE

Executive authority is vested in the British monarch and is exercisable by the Governor-General. The Governor-General appoints as Prime Minister that member of the House who, in the Governor-General's view, is the best able to command the support of the majority of the members of the House, and selects other Ministers on the advice of the Prime Minister. The Governor-General may remove the Prime Minister from office if a resolution of no confidence in the Government is passed by the House and the Prime Minister does not either resign within three days or advise the Governor-General to dissolve Parliament.

The Cabinet consists of the Prime Minister and other Ministers and the Attorney-General as an *ex-officio* member at a time when the office of Attorney-General is a public office. The Leader of the Opposition is appointed by the Governor-General as that member of the House who, in the Governor-General's view, is best able to command the support of a majority of members of the House who do not support the Government.

### CITIZENSHIP

All persons born in Saint Vincent and the Grenadines before independence who, immediately prior to independence, were citizens of the United Kingdom and Colonies automatically become citizens of Saint Vincent and the Grenadines. All persons born outside the country after independence to a parent possessing citizenship of Saint Vincent and the Grenadines automatically acquire citizenship, as do those born in the country after independence. Provision is made for the acquisition of citizenship by those to whom it would not automatically be granted.

## The Government

**Head of State:** HM Queen ELIZABETH II.
**Governor-General:** Sir DAVID JACK (took office 20 September 1989).

### CABINET
(June 1995)

**Prime Minister and Minister of Finance and Planning:** Sir JAMES F. MITCHELL.

**Deputy Prime Minister, Attorney-General and Minister of Justice, Information and Ecclesiastical Affairs:** PARNELL R. CAMPBELL.

**Minister of Agriculture, Industry and Labour:** ALLAN CRUICKSHANK.

# SAINT VINCENT AND THE GRENADINES

**Minister of Education, Culture, Youth and Women's Affairs:** JOHN A. HORNE.
**Minister of Housing, Community Development and Local Government:** LOUIS JONES.
**Minister of Health and the Environment:** YVONNE FRANCIS GIBSON.
**Minister of Communications and Works:** JEREMIAH SCOTT.
**Minister of Foreign Affairs and Tourism:** ALPIAN ALLEN.
**Minister of Trade and Consumer Affairs:** BERNARD WYLLIE.
**Minister of State in the Ministry of Communications and Works:** STEPHANIE BROWNE.
**Minister of State in the Office of the Prime Minister** (responsible for Grenadines Affairs): MONTY ROBERTS.
**Minister without Portfolio:** JONATHAN PETERS.

### MINISTRIES

**Office of the Prime Minister:** Kingstown; tel. 456-1703.
All other Ministries are also in Kingstown; tel. 456-1111.

## Legislature

### HOUSE OF ASSEMBLY

**Speaker:** MONTY MAULE.
**Senators:** 6.
**Elected Members:** 15.
**Clerk:** THERESA ADAMS.

**Election, 21 February 1994**

| Party | Votes | % | Seats |
|---|---|---|---|
| New Democratic Party (NDP) | 25,650 | 54.47 | 12 |
| Saint Vincent Labour Party (SVLP)/ Movement for National Unity (MNU) | 20,587 | 43.72 | 3 |
| Independents | 512 | 1.09 | — |
| Total* | 47,091 | 100.00 | 15 |

* Includes 342 spoiled votes (0.73%).

## Political Organizations

**New Democratic Party (NDP):** POB 1300, Kingstown; f. 1975; democratic party supporting political unity in the Caribbean, social development and free enterprise; Pres. Sir JAMES MITCHELL; Sec.-Gen. STUART NANTON; 7,000 mems.
**United Labour Party (ULP):** Kingstown; f. 1994 by merger of Movement for National Unity (MNU) and the Saint Vincent Labour Party (SVLP); moderate, social-democratic party; Leader VINCENT IAN BEACHE; Dep. Leader RALPH E. GONSALVES.
**United People's Movement (UPM):** Paul's Ave, POB 519, Kingstown; tel. 456-1391; f. 1979; formed as electoral alliance; consolidated as socialist party in 1980; Leader OSCAR ALLEN.

## Diplomatic Representation

### EMBASSIES AND HIGH COMMISSION IN SAINT VINCENT AND THE GRENADINES

**China (Taiwan):** Chinese Embassy, Murray's Rd, POB 878, Kingstown; tel. 456-2431; telex 7596 (Ambassador resident in the Dominican Republic).
**United Kingdom:** Granby St, POB 132, Kingstown; tel. 457-1701; telex 7516; fax 456-2750; (High Commissioner resident in Barbados); Resident Acting High Commissioner ALEXANDER FERGUSON.
**Venezuela:** Granby St, POB 852, Kingstown; tel. 456-1374; telex 7580; fax 457-1934; Ambassador: MIRIAM FEIL.

## Judicial System

Justice is administered by the Eastern Caribbean Supreme Court, based in Saint Lucia and consisting of a Court of Appeal and a High Court. A puisne judge is resident in Saint Vincent. There are four Magistrates, one of whom acts as the Registrar of the Supreme Court.

**Puisne Judge:** MONICA JOSEPH.
**Registrar of the Supreme Court:** PAULA DAVID.
**Magistrates:** M. MALCOLM, O. JACK, BRUCE LYLE.

## Religion

### CHRISTIANITY

**Saint Vincent Christian Council:** Melville St, POB 445, Kingstown; tel. 456-1408; f. 1969; four mem. churches; Chair. Mgr RENISON HOWELL.

#### The Anglican Communion

Anglicans in Saint Vincent and the Grenadines are adherents of the Church in the Province of the West Indies, comprising eight dioceses. The Archbishop of the West Indies is the Bishop of the North Eastern Caribbean and Aruba, and is resident in Antigua. The diocese of the Windward Islands includes Grenada, Saint Lucia and Saint Vincent and the Grenadines.

**Bishop of the Windward Islands:** Rt Rev. SEHON GOODRIDGE, Bishop's House, POB 128, Kingstown; tel. 456-1895.

#### The Roman Catholic Church

Saint Vincent and the Grenadines comprises a single diocese (formed when the diocese of Bridgetown-Kingstown was divided in October 1989), which is suffragan to the archdiocese of Port of Castries (Saint Lucia). The Bishop participates in the Antilles Episcopal Conference, currently based in Port of Spain, Trinidad and Tobago. At 31 December 1993 there were an estimated 10,000 adherents in the diocese, comprising about 9.4% of the population.

**Bishop of Kingstown:** Rt Rev. ROBERT RIVAS, Bishop's Office, POB 862, Edinboro, Kingstown; tel. 456-2427; fax 457-1903.

#### Other Christian Churches

The Methodists, Seventh-day Adventists, Baptists and other denominations also have places of worship.

### BAHÁ'Í FAITH

**National Spiritual Assembly:** POB 1043, Kingstown; tel. 456-4717.

## The Press

### PERIODICALS

**Government Bulletin:** Government Information Service, Kingstown; tel. 456-1600; periodically; circ. 300.
**Government Gazette:** POB 12, Kingstown; f. 1868; Government Printer ADOLPHUS MILLER; circ. 492.
**The Independent Weekly:** 85 Sharpe St, Kingstown; tel. 457-2866; Man. Editor CONLEY ROSE.
**Justice:** POB 519, Kingstown; weekly; organ of the United People's Movement; Editor RENWICK ROSE.
**The New Times:** POB 1300, Kingstown; f. 1984; Thursdays; organ of the New Democratic Party.
**The News:** Grenville St, POB 1078, Kingstown; tel. 456-2942; fax 456-2941.
**The Star:** POB 854, Kingstown; fortnightly; organ of the Saint Vincent Labour Party.
**The Vincentian:** Paul's Ave, POB 592, Kingstown; tel. 456-1123; f. 1919; weekly; owned by the Vincentian Publishing Co; Man. Dir EGERTON M. RICHARDS; Editor-in-Chief ESLEE CARBERRY; circ. 5,500.

## Publisher

**The Vincentian Publishing Co:** Paul's Ave, POB 592, Kingstown; tel. 456-1123; Man. Dir EGERTON M. RICHARDS.

## Radio and Television

In 1992, according to UNESCO, there were an estimated 76,000 radio receivers and 16,000 television receivers in use.

**National Broadcasting Corporation of Saint Vincent and the Grenadines:** Richmond Hill, POB 705, Kingstown; tel. 456-1078; fax 456-1015; govt-owned; Chair. ST CLAIR LEACOCK; controls:

**Radio 705:** POB 705, Kingstown; tel. 457-1111; telex 7473; fax 456-2749; commercial; broadcasts BBC World Service (United Kingdom) and local programmes; Man. BERNARD JOHN; Prog. Man. P. BARBOUR.

**SVG Television:** Dorsetshire Hill, POB 617, Kingstown; tel. 456-1078; fax 456-1015; broadcasts US and local programmes; Chief Engineer R. P. MACLEISH.

Television services from Barbados can be received in parts of the islands.

# Finance

(cap. = capital; res = reserves; dep. = deposits; m. = million; br. = branch)

### BANKING

The Eastern Caribbean Central Bank (see p. 116), based in Saint Christopher, is the central issuing and monetary authority for Saint Vincent and the Grenadines.

#### Principal Banks

**Caribbean Banking Corporation Ltd:** 81 South River Rd, POB 118, Kingstown; tel. 456-1501; telex 7540; fax 456-2141; f. 1985; cap. EC $7.9m., res $1.0m., dep. $89.4m. (July 1992); Gen. Man. FRANCIS V. BOWMAN; Chair. PETER JULY.

**First Saint Vincent Bank Ltd:** Granby St, Kingstown; tel. 456-1873; fax 457-2675; f. 1988; fmrly Saint Vincent Agricultural Credit and Loan Bank; Man. Dir R. B. RUSSELL.

**National Commercial Bank of Saint Vincent:** cnr of Halifax and Egmont Sts, POB 880, Kingstown; tel. 457-1844; telex 7522; fax 457-2612; f. 1977; govt-owned; cap. EC $16.2m., dep. $20.2m. (June 1992); Chair. RICHARD JOACHIM; Man. BEVERLY BRISBANE; 6 brs.

**Owens Bank Ltd:** Blue Caribbean Bldg, Bay St, POB 178, Kingstown; tel. 457-1230; telex 7592; fax 457-2610; f. 1926.

#### Foreign Banks

**Bank of Nova Scotia:** 108 Halifax St, POB 237, Kingstown; tel. 457-1601; telex 7546; fax 457-2623; Man. TIM J. AUGUSTINE.

**Barclays Bank:** Halifax St, POB 604, Kingstown; tel. 456-1706; telex 7520; fax 456-2985; Man. IVAN B. BROWNE; 5 brs.

**Canadian Imperial Bank of Commerce:** POB 212, Kingstown; tel. 457-1587; telex 7532; fax 457-2873; Man. W. G. LYONS.

### INSURANCE

A number of foreign insurance companies have offices in Kingstown.
Local companies include the following:

**Metrocint General Insurance Co Ltd:** St Georges Place, POB 692, Kingstown; tel. 457-2821.

**Saint Hill Insurance Co Ltd:** 93 Upper Bay St, Kingstown; tel. 457-1227; fax 456-2374.

**Saint Vincent Insurances Ltd:** Halifax St, POB 210, Kingstown; tel. 456-1733; telex 7548; fax 456-2225.

# Trade and Industry

### CHAMBER OF COMMERCE

**Saint Vincent and the Grenadines Chamber of Industry and Commerce (Inc):** Halifax St, POB 134, Kingstown; tel. 457-1464; fax 456-2944; f. 1925; Pres. FRANKLIN YOUNG; Exec. Dir LEROY ROSE.

### DEVELOPMENT ORGANIZATION

**Saint Vincent Development Corporation (Devco):** Granby St, POB 841, Kingstown; tel. 457-1358; fax 457-2838; f. 1970; finances industry, agriculture, fisheries, tourism; Chair. SAMUEL GOODLUCK; Man. CLAUDE M. LEACH.

### EMPLOYERS' ASSOCIATIONS

**Saint Vincent Arrowroot Industry Association:** Kingstown; tel. 457-1511; f. 1930; producers, manufacturers and sellers; 186 mems; Chair. GEORGE O. WALKER.

**Saint Vincent Banana Growers' Association:** Sharpe St, POB 10, Kingstown; tel. 457-1605; fax 456-2585; f. 1955; over 7,000 mems; Chair. LESLINE BEST; Man. SIMEON GREENE.

**Saint Vincent Employers' Federation:** POB 348, Kingstown; tel. 456-1269; Dir J. CLEMENT NOEL.

### TRADE UNIONS

**Commercial, Technical and Allied Workers' Union (CTAWU):** Lower Middle St, POB 245, Kingstown; tel. 456-1525; f. 1962; affiliated to CCL, ICFTU and other international workers' organizations; Pres. ALICE MANDEVILLE; Gen. Sec. LLOYD SMALL; 2,500 mems.

**National Workers' Movement:** Grenville St, POB 1290, Kingstown; tel. 457-1950; fax 457-1823; Gen. Sec. NOEL C. JACKSON.

**Public Services Union of Saint Vincent and the Grenadines:** McKies Hill, POB 875, Kingstown; tel. 457-1801; f. 1943; Pres. CARETHIA TURRENTINE; Exec. Sec. ROBERT I. SAMUEL; 738 mems.

**Saint Vincent Union of Teachers:** POB 304, Kingstown; tel. 457-1062; f. 1952; members of Caribbean Union of Teachers affiliated to FISE; Pres. TYRONE BURKE; 1,175 mems.

### CO-OPERATIVE AND MARKETING ORGANIZATIONS

There are 26 Agricultural Credit Societies, which receive loans from the Government, and five Registered Co-operative Societies.

**Saint Vincent Marketing Corporation:** Kingstown; tel. 457-1603; fax 456-2673.

# Transport

### ROADS

There are 1,109 km (689 miles) of roads, of which 346 km (215 miles) are all-weather, 378 km (235 miles) rough motorable and 386 km (240 miles) tracks and byways.

### SHIPPING

The deep-water harbour at Kingstown can accommodate two ocean-going vessels and about five motor vessels. There are regular motor-vessel services between the Grenadines and Saint Vincent. A weekly service to the United Kingdom is operated by Geest Industries, the major banana purchaser. Numerous shipping lines also call at Kingstown harbour. Exports are flown to Barbados to link up with international shipping lines. In early 1993 work began on a marina and shipyard complex at Otley Hall, Kingstown. Work was due to begin in 1994 on a container port at Campden Park, near Kingstown.

**Saint Vincent Port Authority:** Kingstown; tel. 456-2732; fax 456-2732.

### CIVIL AVIATION

There is a civilian airport at Arnos Vale, situated about 3 km (2 miles) south-east of Kingstown, served by Air Martinique, as well as the regional airline LIAT (see chapter on Antigua and Barbuda), in which Saint Vincent and the Grenadines is a shareholder. Projects to upgrade the airports on the islands of Bequia and Union were completed in 1992. The islands of Mustique and Canouan have landing strips for light aircraft only.

**Mustique Airways:** POB 1232, Arnos Vale; tel. 458-4380; telex 7542; fax 456-4586; charter flights.

**Saint Vincent Airways:** POB 39, Blue Lagoon; tel. 456-5610; telex 7500; fax 458-4697; charter flights.

# Tourism

The island chain of the Grenadines is the country's main tourist asset. There are superior yachting facilities, but the lack of major air links with countries outside the region has resulted in a relatively slow development for tourism. In 1993 Saint Vincent and the Grenadines received 163,120 tourists (including almost 70,000 cruise-ship passengers). Revenue from tourism totalled US $52.7m. in 1992.

**Department of Tourism:** POB 834, Kingstown; tel. 457-1502; telex 7531; fax 456-2610; Dir ANDREAS WICKHAM.

**Saint Vincent and the Grenadines Hotel Association:** Kingstown; tel. 457-1072.

# SAN MARINO

## Introductory Survey

### Location, Climate, Language, Religion, Flag, Capital

The Republic of San Marino lies in southern Europe. The country is situated on the slopes of Mount Titano, in the Apennines, within the central Italian region of Emilia-Romagna. San Marino has cool winters and warm summers, with temperatures generally between −2°C (28°F) and 30°C (86°F). Average annual rainfall totals 880 mm (35 ins). The language is Italian. Almost all of the inhabitants profess Christianity, and the state religion is Roman Catholicism. The civil flag (proportions 4 by 3) has two equal horizontal stripes, of white and light blue. The state flag has, in addition, the national coat of arms (a shield, framed by a yellow cartouche, bearing three green mountains—each with a white tower, surmounted by a stylized ostrich feather, at the summit—the shield being surmounted by a bejewelled crown and framed by branches of laurel and oak, and surmounting a white ribbon bearing, in black, the word 'libertas') in the centre. The capital is San Marino.

### History

San Marino, which evolved as a city-state in the early Middle Ages, is the sole survivor of the numerous independent states that existed in Italy prior to its unification in the 19th century. An initial treaty of friendship and co-operation with Italy was signed in 1862. It was renewed in March 1939 and revised in September 1971. San Marino has evolved a multi-party political system.

From 1945 to 1957 San Marino was ruled by a left-wing coalition of the Partito Comunista Sammarinese (PCS) (Communists) and the Partito Socialista Sammarinese (PSS) (Socialists). Defections from the PCS in 1957 led to a bloodless revolution, after which a coalition of the Partito Democratico Cristiano Sammarinese (PDCS) (Christian Democrats) and the Partito di Democrazia Socialista (PDS) (Social Democrats) came to power.

This coalition survived until January 1973, when an internal dispute between the two ruling parties over economic policy led to the resignation of the Government. In March 1973 a new Government was formed by an alliance between the PDCS and the PSS. The PSS withdrew from the coalition in November 1975, bringing down the Government. The Captains-Regent took over the administration until March 1976, when a new coalition between the PDCS and the PSS was formed. This Government collapsed in late 1977 but continued in an interim capacity until a new administration was formed. Attempts by the PCS to form a government were frustrated by the lack of a clear majority in the unicameral legislature, the Great and General Council.

Eventually the Council agreed to a dissolution and elections were held in May 1978, when the PDCS gained 26 of the 60 seats. However, they were still unable to form an administration and the three left-wing parties, the PCS, PSS and the Partito Socialista Unitario (PSU), which together held 31 seats, agreed to form a coalition Government led by the PCS. San Marino thus reverted to the left-wing administration of 20 years before and became the only Western European country with a communist-led government. Before the elections of May 1983, the PDCS made accusations of financial mismanagement against the Government, but they failed to increase their share of the vote. A left-wing coalition of the PCS, PSS and PSU again formed the administration.

In 1982 the judiciary reversed an existing law and gave women who were born in San Marino the right to keep their citizenship if they married a foreign citizen. In 1984 legislation was approved to allow citizenship for foreign nationals who had been resident in San Marino for 30 years.

In July 1986 a six-week political crisis, resulting from a financial scandal which allegedly involved several Socialists, led to the formation of a new coalition Government, the first to be composed of the PDCS and the PCS. At the general election of May 1988, the PDCS and the PCS obtained 27 and 18 seats, respectively. In June the two parties agreed to form a coalition Government comprising six Christian Democrats and four Communists. In March 1990 the PCS was renamed the Partito Democratico Progressista (PDP). In March 1992 the PDCS accepted the formation of a coalition Government with the PSS. The PDCS had decided that it no longer wished to maintain an alliance with the PDP because the arrangement was considered to be outdated, in view of the demise of communism in Europe.

At the general election of 30 May 1993 the PDCS and the PSS obtained 26 and 14 seats, respectively. The election was regarded as a defeat for the PDP, which secured only 11 seats, and was also notable for the success of three recently-formed parties, the Alleanza Popolare, the Movimento Democratico and the Rifondazione Comunista, in gaining a number of seats. In June the PDCS and the PSS agreed to form a coalition Government, comprising six Christian Democrats and four Socialists.

In November 1988 San Marino became the 22nd member state of the Council of Europe (see p. 134). In March 1992 San Marino became a member of the UN.

### Government

San Marino is divided into nine 'Castles' corresponding to the original parishes of the republic. Each 'Castle' is governed by a Castle-Captain, who holds office for two years, and an Auxiliary Council, which holds office for five years.

Legislative power is vested in the unicameral Great and General Council, with 60 members elected by universal adult suffrage, under a system of proportional representation, for five years (subject to dissolution). Women have had the right to vote since 1960, and to stand for election to the Council since 1973. The Council elects two of its members to act jointly as Captains-Regent (Capitani Reggenti), with the functions of Head of State and Government, for six months at a time (ending in March and September). Executive power is held by the Congress of State, with 10 members elected by the Council for the duration of its term. The Congress, presided over by the Captains-Regent, has three Secretaries of State and seven Ministers of State.

### Defence

There are combined Voluntary Military Forces. There is no obligatory military service but citizens between 16 and 55 years may be enlisted, in certain circumstances, to defend the state.

### Economic Affairs

There are no available figures for the gross national product (GNP) of San Marino, but, according to World Bank estimates, GNP per head was at least US $8,626 in 1993. Gross domestic product per head, measured at current prices, was $7,001 in 1985.

Agriculture (including forestry and fishing) employed 2.1% of the working population in 1993. The principal crops are wheat, barley, maize, olives and grapes. Dairy farming is also important. Olive oil and wine are produced for export.

Industry (manufacturing and construction) employed 41.6% of the working population in 1993.

Stone-quarrying is the only mining activity in San Marino, and is an important export industry.

Manufacturing employed 33.2% of the working population in 1993. The most important branches are the production of cement, synthetic rubber, leather, textiles and ceramics.

Energy is derived principally from gas (more than 75%). San Marino is dependent on the Italian state energy companies for much of its energy requirements.

Tourism is the main source of income, contributing about 60% of government revenue. In 1994 San Marino received 3,104,231 visitors, of whom 381,200 stayed at least one night in the country. The sale of postage stamps, mainly to foreign collectors, provides 10% of annual revenue. Commerce with Italy, conducted under free-trade agreements, is also important.

Data concerning imports and exports are included in those of Italy, with which San Marino maintains a customs union.

# SAN MARINO

The principal source of imports is Italy, upon which the country is dependent for its supply of raw materials. The major exports are wine, woollen goods, furniture, ceramics, building stone and artisan- and hand-made goods.

The 1995 budget envisaged expenditure and revenue balancing at 521,000m. lire. San Marino receives a subsidy from the Italian Government, amounting to about 9,000m. lire annually, in exchange for the Republic's acceptance of Italian rules concerning exchange controls and the renunciation of customs duties. The cost of living increased by 5.3% in 1993. In December 1993 4.1% of the total labour force were unemployed. Nearly 13,000 San Marinesi are resident abroad, mostly in Italy, but also in the USA and France. The high rate of emigration combines with a decreasing birth rate to produce only small annual rises in the Republic's population.

Traditionally, the economy of San Marino was based on agriculture, forestry and stone-quarrying, but these industries have declined in importance during the second half of the 20th century. The economy is dependent on the tourist industry. The expansion of light industries, based on imported materials from Italy, has been encouraged in order to reduce the country's dependence on revenue from tourism. The manufacture of rubber, leather, footwear and textile products and cement and ceramics increased considerably in the early 1990s. A development plan, introduced in the late 1980s, aimed to diversify the economy further and to promote co-operation between private capital and public resources. In September 1992 San Marino became the 173rd member of the IMF, with an initial quota of approximately US $9m.

## Education

Education is compulsory for eight years between the ages of six and 16 years. Primary education begins at six years of age and lasts for five years. Secondary education begins at the age of 11 and may last for up to eight years: a first cycle of three years and a second of five years. In 1987 the illiteracy rate among the population aged 10 years and over was only 1.6% (males 1.2%; females 2.1%). Government expenditure on education was 26,067m. lire in 1991.

## Public Holidays

**1995:** 1 January (New Year's Day), 6 January (Epiphany), 5 February (Liberation Day and St Agatha's Day), 25 March (Anniversary of the Arengo), 1 April (Investiture of the new Captains-Regent), 17 April (Easter Monday), 1 May (Labour Day), 15 June (Corpus Christi), 28 July (Fall of Fascism), 15 August (Assumption of the Virgin), 3 September (San Marino Day and Republic Day), 1 October (Investiture of the new Captains-Regent), 1 November (All Saints' Day), 2 November (Commemoration of the Dead), 8 December (Immaculate Conception), 25 December (Christmas), 26 December (St Stephen's Day).

**1996:** 1 January (New Year's Day), 6 January (Epiphany), 5 February (Liberation Day and St Agatha's Day), 25 March (Anniversary of the Arengo), 1 April (Investiture of the new Captains-Regent), 8 April (Easter Monday), 1 May (Labour Day), 6 June (Corpus Christi), 28 July (Fall of Fascism), 15 August (Assumption of the Virgin), 3 September (San Marino Day and Republic Day), 1 October (Investiture of the new Captains-Regent), 1 November (All Saints' Day), 2 November (Commemoration of the Dead), 8 December (Immaculate Conception), 25 December (Christmas), 26 December (St Stephen's Day).

## Weights and Measures

The metric system is in force.

# Statistical Survey

## AREA AND POPULATION

**Area:** 60.5 sq km (23.4 sq miles).

**Population:** 19,149 (males 9,654; females 9,495) at census of 30 November 1976; 24,335 (males 11,918; females 12,417) in January 1994.

**Density** (January 1994): 402 per sq km.

**Capital:** San Marino (estimated population 4,385 at 31 December 1994).

**Births and Deaths** (registrations, 1993): Live births 244 (birth rate 10.1 per 1,000); Deaths 145 (death rate 6.0 per 1,000).

**Expectation of Life** (official estimates, years at birth, 1977–86): males 73.16; females 79.12. Source: UN, *Demographic Yearbook*.

**Economically Active Population** (official estimates, persons aged 14 years and over, 1993): Agriculture, hunting, forestry and fishing 294; Manufacturing 4,739; Construction 1,195; Wholesale and retail trade, restaurants and hotels 2,499; Transport, storage and communications 278; Finance, insurance, real estate and business services 390; Community, social and personal services 4,863; Total employed 14,258; Unemployed 616 (males 177; females 439); Total labour force 14,874 (males 8,808; females 6,066).

## FINANCE

**Currency and Exchange Rates:** Italian currency: 100 centèsimi = 1 lira (plural: lire). *Sterling and Dollar Equivalents* (31 December 1994): £1 sterling = 2,538.0 lire; US $1 = 1,622.25 lire; 10,000 lire = £3.940 = $6.164. *Average Exchange Rates* (lire per US $): 1,232.4 in 1992; 1,573.7 in 1993; 1,612.4 in 1994.

**Budget** (estimates, million lire, 1995): Revenue 521,000; Expenditure 521,000.

**Cost of Living** (Consumer Price Index; base: 1980 = 100): 269.7 in 1991; 288.8 in 1992; 304.1 in 1993. Source: UN, *Monthly Bulletin of Statistics*.

## EXTERNAL TRADE

Data concerning imports and exports are included in those of Italy, with which San Marino maintains a customs union.

## TOURISM

**Visitor arrivals** (incl. excursionists): 3,208,290 in 1992; 3,072,030 in 1993; 3,104,231 in 1994.

**Tourist arrivals** ('000, staying at least one night): 515 in 1992; 462 in 1993; 381 in 1994. Source: UN, *Statistical Yearbook*.

## COMMUNICATIONS MEDIA

(1992)

Radio receivers: 9,000 licensed.

**Television receivers:** 7,500 licensed.

**Telephones:** 22,300 in use.

## EDUCATION

(1993)

**Pre-primary:** 15 schools, 102 teachers, 811 pupils.

**Primary:** 14 schools, 219 teachers, 1,166 pupils.

**Secondary:** 3 schools, 133 teachers, 772 pupils.

There is also a higher secondary school (lyceum), a technical institute, and vocational training schools: total pupils 274; total teachers 44.

SAN MARINO

# Directory

## The Government
(June 1995)

### HEADS OF STATE
**Captains-Regent:** SETTIMIO LONFERNINI, MARINO BOLLINI (April–September 1995).

### CONGRESS OF STATE
A coalition of Christian Democrats (PDCS) and Socialists (PSS).
**Secretary of State for Foreign and Political Affairs:** GABRIELE GATTI (PDCS).
**Secretary of State for Finance, Budget, Planning and Information:** CLELIO GALASSI (PDCS).
**Secretary of State for Home Affairs:** ANTONIO LAZZARO VOLPINARI (PSS).
**Minister of State for Industry and Handicrafts:** FIORENZO STOLFI (PSS).
**Minister of State for Territory, Environment and Agriculture:** EMMA ROSSI (PSS).
**Minister of State for Commerce and relations with the Castle Boards:** OTTAVIANO ROSSI (PDCS).
**Minister of State for Health and Social Security:** SANTE CANDUCCI (PDCS).
**Minister of State for Education, Culture, University and Justice:** PIER MARINO MENICUCCI (PDCS).
**Minister of State for Labour and Co-operation:** CLAUDIO PODESCHI (PDCS).
**Minister of State for Transport, Communications, Tourism and Sport:** AUGUSTO CASALI (PSS).

### MINISTRIES
**Secretariat of State for Foreign and Political Affairs:** Palazzo Begni, San Marino; tel. 882209; fax 992018.
**Secretariat of State for Home Affairs:** Palazzo Giovagnoli, Via della Capannaccia, San Marino; tel. 882283; fax 882197.
**Secretariat of State for Finance, Budget, Planning and Information:** Palazzo Begni, 47031 San Marino; tel. 882242; fax 882244.

## Legislature
### CONSIGLIO GRANDE E GENERALE
(Great and General Council)

**Election, 30 May 1993**

| Party | Seats |
| --- | --- |
| PDCS | 26 |
| PSS | 14 |
| PDP | 11 |
| AP | 4 |
| MD | 3 |
| RC | 2 |

## Political Organizations

**Partito Democratico Cristiano Sammarinese (PDCS)** (San Marino Christian Democrat Party): Via delle Scalette 6, 47031 San Marino; tel. 991193; fax 992694; f. 1948; Sec.-Gen. CESARE ANTONIO GASPERONI; 3,000 mems.

**Partito Democratico Progressista (PDP)** (Democratic Progressive Party): Via Sentier Rosso 1, San Marino; tel. 991199; f. 1941 as the Partito Comunista Sammarinese; adopted present name March 1990; closely linked to Italy's Partito Democratico della Sinistra (formerly the Italian Communist Party); Sec.-Gen. STEFANO MACINA; 1,200 mems.

**Partito Socialista Sammarinese (PSS)** (San Marino Socialist Party): Via G. Ordelaffi 46, San Marino; tel. 902016; fax 906438; in 1990 merged with Partito Socialista Unitario (f. 1975); Sec.-Gen. MAURIZIO RATTINI.

Recently-formed parties that enjoyed success in the 1993 legislative elections included the **Alleanza Popolare (AP)**, the **Movimento Democratico (MD)** and the **Rifondazione Comunista (RC)**.

## Diplomatic Representation
### EMBASSY IN SAN MARINO
**Italy:** Via del Voltone 55, 47031, San Marino; tel. 991271; telex 550889; Ambassador: GIOVANNI FERRARI.

## Judicial System
The administration of justice is entrusted to foreign judges, with the exception of the Justice of the Peace, who must be of San Marino nationality, and who judges minor civil suits. The major legislative institutions are as follows:
**Law Commissioner** (Commissario della Legge): deals with civil and criminal cases where the sentence does not exceed three years' imprisonment.
**Criminal Judge of the Primary Court of Claims:** deals with criminal cases which are above the competence of the Law Commissioner.
**Court of Appeal:** two judges, who deal with civil and criminal proceedings.
**Council of Twelve** (Consiglio dei XII): has authority as a Supreme Court of Appeal, for civil proceedings only.

## Religion
### CHRISTIANITY
**The Roman Catholic Church**

Roman Catholicism is the official state religion of San Marino. The Republic forms part of the diocese of San Marino–Montefeltro (comprising mainly Italian territory), suffragan to the archdiocese of Ravenna-Cervia.

**Bishop of San Marino–Montefeltro:** Rt Rev. MARIANO DE NICOLÒ (also Bishop of Rimini), Curia Vescovile, 61016 Pennabilli, Italy; tel. (0541) 928415; fax 928766.

## The Press
There are three daily newspapers and several periodicals, mainly published by the political organizations.
**Corriere di San Marino:** San Marino; daily.
**Il Quotidiano Sammarinese:** San Marino; daily.
**Sì–San Marino Italia:** San Marino; daily.
**Notizia:** San Marino; organ of the Department of External Affairs; periodical.
**Il nuovo Titano:** San Marino; organ of the PSS; periodical; circ. 1,300.
**Progresso:** San Marino; organ of the PDP; periodical.
**San Marino:** San Marino; organ of the PDCS; periodical.

## Publishers
**AIEP Editore:** Via G. Giacomini 97, San Marino; tel. 992590; fax 990398; f. 1986; book publishing; Man. MORGANTI GIUSEPPE MARIA.
**Edinter Editore Internazionali:** Via Ca'Giello 6, San Marino; tel. and fax 991672; newspapers; Dir GORACCI MONICA.
**Edizioni del Titano:** Via 1e P. Franciosi 214, San Marino; tel. and fax 991932; f. 1991; book publishing; Man. Dir DORDONI GIANNI.

## Radio and Television
In 1987 a 1939 co-operation agreement with Italy, preventing San Marino from operating its own broadcasting services, was abrogated, and a joint venture between San Marino and the Italian state-owned radio and television corporation, Radiotelevisione Italiana, (RAI—TV), was established in order to operate an independent broadcasting station for 15 years. RAI (see chapter on Italy) broadcasts a daily information bulletin about the Republic under the title 'Notizie di San Marino'. San Marino RTV, established in 1991, began broadcasting in mid-1993. There is one private radio station.

**San Marino RTV (Radiotelevisione):** viale Kennedy 13, 47031 San Marino; tel. 882000; fax 882060; f. 1991; Chair. Dott. SERGIO ZAVOLI.

**Radio Titano:** Via delle Carrare 35, Frazione Murata, 47031 San Marino; tel. 997251; Dir P. FAETANINI.

# Finance

(cap. = capital; res = reserves; dep. = deposits; m. = million; brs = branches; amounts in Italian lire)

### BANKING

**Banca Agricola Commerciale della Repubblica di San Marino SA:** Via Oddone Scarito 13, Borgo Maggiore, 47031 San Marino; tel. 903271; telex 471; f. 1920; cap. 40m., res 400m., dep. 21,300m. (Dec. 1985); Pres. LINO ALBERTINI; Dir PIER PAOLO FABBRI; 5 brs.

**Cassa di Risparmio della Repubblica di San Marino:** Piazzetta del Titano 2, 47031 San Marino; tel. 991011; telex 337; fax 991657; f. 1882; cap. 102m., dep. 802m. (Dec. 1990); Pres. Dott. GILBERTO GHIOTTI; Dir MARIO FANTINI; 12 brs.

**Cassa Rurale di Depositi e Prestiti di Faetano:** Strada La Croce, 47031 Faetano; tel. 996015; Pres. SERGIO ZANOTTI; Dir. MARCELLO MALPELI; 4 brs.

**Credito Industriale Sammarinese:** Piazza Bertoldi 8, Serravalle; tel. 900368; fax 901513; Pres. CEOLA ANTONIO; Dir-Gen. ALBERTO FARINA.

### INSURANCE

Several major Italian insurance companies have agencies in San Marino.

# Trade and Industry

### TRADE UNIONS

**Centrale Sindacale Unitaria:** Via Napoleone Bonaparte 75, San Marino.

**Confederazione Democratica dei Lavoratori Sammarinesi:** Via Napoleone Bonaparte 75, 47031 San Marino; tel. and fax 992178; f. 1957; affiliated to ICFTU; Sec.-Gen. MARCO BECCARI; 1,800 mems.

**Confederazione Sammarinese del Lavoro (CSdL):** Via Napoleone Bonaparte 75, San Marino; tel. 992007; fax 992333; f. 1943; Sec.-Gen. GIOVANNI GHIOTTI; 2,500 mems.

# Transport

The capital, San Marino, is connected with Borgo Maggiore, about 1.5 km away, by funicular. There is also a bus service, and a highway down to the Italian coast at Rimini, about 12 km away. San Marino has an estimated 220 km of good roads. The nearest airport to the Republic is at Rimini. There are no frontier or customs formalities.

**Azienda Autonoma di Stato per i Servizi Pubblici (AASS):** Via A. de Superchio 16, Cailungo, 47031 San Marino; tel. 903903; fax 902312; f. 1981; autonomous state service company; numerous responsibilities include public transport and funicular railway; Pres. RENZO GIARDI; Dir-Gen. Ing. MARINO MAIANI.

# Tourism

The mild climate attracts many visitors to San Marino each year. The contrasting scenery and well-preserved medieval architecture are also attractions. There are facilities for shooting, fishing and various other recreations. In 1994 San Marino received 3,104,231 visitors, of whom 381,200 stayed at least one night in the country. In 1995 there were 26 hotels and 57 restaurants.

**Ufficio di Stato per il Turismo** (State Tourist Board): Contrada Omagnano 20, 47031 San Marino; tel. 882400; telex 282; fax 882575; Dir EDITH TAMAGNINI.

# SÃO TOMÉ AND PRÍNCIPE

## Introductory Survey

**Location, Climate, Language, Religion, Flag, Capital**

The Democratic Republic of São Tomé and Príncipe lies in the Gulf of Guinea, off the west coast of Africa. There are two main islands, São Tomé and Príncipe, and the country also includes the rocky islets of Caroço, Pedras and Tinhosas, off Príncipe, and Rôlas, off São Tomé. The climate is warm and humid, with average temperatures ranging between 22°C (72°F) and 30°C (86°F). The rainy season extends from October to May, and average annual rainfall varies from 500 mm (20 ins) in the southern highlands to 1,000 mm (39 ins) in the northern lowlands. Portuguese is the official language, and native dialects are widely spoken. Almost all of the inhabitants profess Christianity, and the overwhelming majority are adherents of the Roman Catholic Church. The national flag (proportions 2 by 1) has three horizontal stripes, of green, yellow (one-half of the depth) and green, with a red triangle at the hoist and two five-pointed black stars on the yellow stripe. The capital is the town of São Tomé, on São Tomé island.

**Recent History**

A former Portuguese colony, São Tomé and Príncipe became an overseas province of Portugal in 1951 and received local autonomy in 1973. A nationalist group, the Comissão de Libertação de São Tomé e Príncipe, was formed in 1960 and became the Movimento de Libertação de São Tomé e Príncipe (MLSTP) in 1972, under the leadership of Dr Manuel Pinto da Costa. Based in Libreville, Gabon, the MLSTP was recognized by the Organization of African Unity (see p. 200) in 1973.

Following the military coup in Portugal in April 1974, the Portuguese Government recognized the right of the islands to independence, although negotiations did not take place until November. Portugal then recognized the MLSTP as the sole representative of the people, and it was agreed that the islands should become independent. On 12 July 1975 independence was achieved, with Dr da Costa as the country's first President and Miguel Trovoada (regarded as one of the 'moderates' of the MLSTP) as Prime Minister. In December 1975 a legislative Assembléia Popular Nacional (National People's Assembly) was elected.

In March 1978 the Prime Minister stated that an attempted coup by foreign mercenaries, supervised from Gabon by Carlos Alberto Monteiro Dias da Graça, the exiled former Minister of Health, and supported by opponents of agrarian reform, had been suppressed. Angolan troops were called in to support the Government, and in March 1979 the alleged conspirators were sentenced to terms of imprisonment. President da Costa took over the post of Prime Minister, and Trovoada was arrested in September and charged with complicity in the coup attempt. He was released and allowed to go into exile in 1981. Another alleged coup attempt was forestalled in November 1980. There were riots on Príncipe in December 1981, following food shortages and the reported distribution of pamphlets advocating that island's independence.

In March 1986 two opposition groups based outside the country, the União Democrática Independente de São Tomé e Príncipe and the more radical Frente de Resistência Nacional de São Tomé e Príncipe (FRNSTP), founded by da Graça, announced that they had formed a coalition, the Coalizão Democrática de Oposição, and demanded the holding of democratic elections. In April a fishing vessel containing 76 São Tomé citizens, claiming to be members of the FRNSTP, arrived at Walvis Bay, then a South African enclave within Namibia, reportedly requesting military aid from South Africa against the São Tomé Government. The FRNSTP leadership, however, stated that the refugees had been expelled from the organization. In May da Graça resigned as President of the FRNSTP and expressed his willingness to co-operate with the Government, while demanding the removal of Angolan and Cuban troops from São Tomé. In May 1987 the South African Government denied reports that refugees from São Tomé were receiving military training for a coup attempt against the São Tomé Government.

Worsening economic conditions, following a severe drought in 1982, prompted the Government to review the country's close ties with communist bloc regimes and its consequent isolation from major Western aid sources. In late 1984 da Costa declared São Tomé and Príncipe to be 'non-aligned', and in early 1985 the Ministers of Foreign Affairs and of Planning, both of whom had supported close co-operation with the USSR, were dismissed, and their portfolios assumed by the President. The number of Angolan, Cuban and Soviet military personnel was reduced, and the responsibilities of Eastern bloc advisers in government departments were substantially curtailed. In late 1986 da Costa visited Western Europe and the USA to seek support for his country's economic recovery plans. However, in January 1987 the Minister of Planning and Commerce, who had been largely responsible for the programme (which involved considerable lessening of state controls), was dismissed, and the Minister of Foreign Affairs and Co-operation, who had also been prominent in negotiations with donor agencies, was deprived of the foreign affairs portfolio.

In October 1987 the Central Committee of the MLSTP announced major constitutional reforms, including the election by universal adult suffrage of the President of the Republic and of members of the Assembléia Popular Nacional. The amended Constitution also allowed 'independent' candidates to contest legislative elections, although the President of the MLSTP, chosen by the MLSTP Congress from two candidates proposed by the central committee, would continue to be the sole candidate for the presidency of the Republic. The MLSTP Central Committee also envisaged the restoration of the post of Prime Minister (abolished in 1979), and questioned the role of the MLSTP as the sole authorized party in the country. In January 1988 the legislature approved a constitutional amendment providing for the re-establishment of the premiership, and President da Costa appointed Celestino Rochas da Costa, until then the Minister of Education, Labour and Social Security, as Prime Minister. Rochas da Costa formed a new Council of Ministers appointing da Graça as Minister of Foreign Affairs.

On 8 March 1988 armed men landed on São Tomé island and attempted to seize the police headquarters outside the capital. Security forces killed two of the men and captured the others. The attack was led by Afonso dos Santos, the leader of a dissident faction of the FRNSTP, who apparently intended to depose President da Costa and assume the presidency. The FRNSTP leadership condemned the attempted coup and denied the Government's claim that the group was responsible for the venture. In September 1989 Afonso dos Santos was sentenced to 22 years' imprisonment, while 38 other defendants were also given custodial sentences.

In October 1989 the Central Committee of the MLSTP examined proposals for new party statutes and for a new constitution. In December a national conference of the MLSTP adopted more radical recommendations for political reform, which were submitted to the party's leadership in early 1990. In March 1990 the draft Constitution was approved by a joint meeting of the Assembléia Popular Nacional and the MLSTP Central Committee, subject to endorsement by referendum. The draft Constitution provided for the establishment of a multi-party system, limited the duration of the President's tenure of office to two five-year terms, and permitted independent candidates to participate in legislative elections.

In April 1990 dos Santos and his accomplices in the March 1988 coup attempt were granted an amnesty by presidential decree. In May 1990 Trovoada returned from exile to São Tomé to contest the presidential election (originally scheduled for July, but later postponed). On 22 August, in a national referendum, 90.7% of participating voters (72% of the electorate) endorsed the new Constitution. In September new legislation on the formation of political parties came into effect.

Delegates to the MLSTP Congress in October 1990 voted to replace da Costa as party President by appointing da Graça to the newly-created post of Secretary-General of the MLSTP.

In addition, the party's name was amended to the Movimento de Libertação de São Tomé e Príncipe—Partido Social Democrata (MLSTP—PSD). In November da Graça resigned the foreign affairs portfolio. In the same month impatience at successive postponements of the legislative and presidential elections resulted in public demonstrations. Several thousands took part in a demonstration led by the newly-registered opposition parties, notably the Partido de Convergência Democrática—Grupo de Reflexão (PCD—GR), whose Secretary-General, Daniel Lima dos Santos Daio, was a former Minister of National Defence and had left the MLSTP in 1982. The protesters claimed that the extended period of transition to a multi-party system was creating a climate of instability. A series of strikes in important sectors threatened economic activity in late 1990 and early 1991. Workers, including those in the vital cocoa-producing sector, went on strike in support of demands for salary increases and improvements in working conditions.

On 20 January 1991 elections to the new Assembléia Nacional resulted in defeat for the MLSTP—PSD, which secured only 30.5% of the votes cast and 21 seats in the 55-member legislature. The PCD—GR obtained 54% of the votes and 33 seats in the legislature. The Partido Democrático de São Tomé e Príncipe—Coligação Democrático da Oposição (PDSTP—CODO), with 5% of the votes, took the remaining seat.

In February 1991 a transitional Government, headed by Daio, was installed, pending the presidential election, to be held in March. Also in February President da Costa announced that he would be retiring from politics and would not be contesting the forthcoming election. The MLSTP—PSD did not present an alternative candidate. In late February two of the three remaining presidential candidates withdrew from the election. Miguel Trovoada, who stood as an independent candidate (with the support of the PCD—GR), was thus the sole contender, and on 3 March he was elected President, receiving the support of 81% of those who voted. He took office on 3 April. The transitional Government resigned in mid-April, and was reappointed shortly afterwards.

In April 1992 more than 1,000 people joined a demonstration, which had been organized outside the presidential palace by opponents of the PCD—GR, to demand the resignation of the Daio Government. Widespread popular dissatisfaction had been precipitated by the imposition, since the second half of 1991, of stringent austerity measures that had been stipulated by the IMF and the World Bank as preconditions for economic assistance. The measures, including a 40% depreciation in the value of the currency and a substantial increase in petroleum prices, had contributed to a marked decline in the islanders' living standards. Some 7,000 people were reported to have attended a further demonstration later in April 1992. The protesters demanded that President Trovoada dismiss the Government, and strike action was threatened should he fail to do so. On the following day Trovoada dismissed the Daio administration. Daio had previously publicly blamed the President for the country's economic plight and attendant political unrest, and had called into question the extent of the presidential powers accorded by the Constitution. While affirming his support for the economic adjustment efforts that had been instituted by Daio, Trovoada criticized the lack of an effective dialogue between the Government and the presidency. The PCD—GR, which protested that Trovoada's action constituted an 'institutional coup', was invited to designate a new Prime Minister, and in May Norberto Costa Alegre (the Minister of Economy and Finance in the outgoing administration, who was said to have been instrumental in the negotiation of the recent structural adjustment measures with the country's external creditors) was chosen to replace Daio as Prime Minister. A new Government was named shortly afterwards, in which Arlindo Carvalho, hitherto Secretary of State with responsibility for Finance, assumed the economy and finance portfolio (his nomination to this ministry was said to have been a precondition of Alegre's acceptance of the post of Prime Minister).

In August 1992 there were violent clashes between the police and members of the armed forces, following the forced entry into a police station in the capital of about 40 members of the armed forces, who were attempting to secure the release of two of their colleagues who were being detained there. The conflict followed mounting tensions between the two forces, which observers attributed to a lack of definition as to their respective roles in the country, and to discontent within the military at its impending reorganization (see Defence, below).

On 6 December 1992, in the first local elections to be held since independence, the PCD—GR suffered a considerable reverse, failing to secure control of any of the seven districts. Conversely, the opposition MLSTP—PSD gained control of five districts.

In February 1993 Daio resigned as Secretary-General of the ruling PCD—GR, and in April was replaced by the more moderate João do Sacramento Bonfim. Expectation among opposition parties that the appointment of Bonfim would facilitate political dialogue, and even lead to the formation of a government of national unity, proved unfounded; in November four opposition parties issued a communiqué accusing the Government of authoritarianism and incompetence, and, in turn, were accused of fomenting instability.

In April 1994 the Assembléia Nacional adopted legislation, drafted by the MLSTP—PSD, reinforcing the rights of the parliamentary opposition. Under the provisions of the law, all opposition parties represented in the legislature were to be consulted on major political issues, including defence, foreign policy and the budget. In the same month the Assembléia Nacional began discussion of a draft bill providing for a degree of autonomy for the island of Príncipe. The proposals under consideration included provision for the creation of a five-member regional council, to operate under the authority of the Minister-Delegate for the Region of Príncipe. The introduction of the draft bill was prompted by concern, expressed by inhabitants of Príncipe, that the island had been neglected by the central administration. (Following ratification of the legislation, elections to the five-member regional council were held in March 1995.)

Relations between the Government and the Presidency began to deteriorate in 1994, and in April Trovoada publicly dissociated himself from government policy. Political tension increased in June when the PCD—GR accused Trovoada of systematic obstruction of the government programme. In that month opposition parties petitioned the President to dismiss the Government, conduct early legislative elections and appoint foreign auditors to investigate the management of public finances during the three years that the PCD—GR had been in government.

On 2 July 1994 Trovoada dismissed the Alegre administration, citing 'institutional conflict' as justification for the decision, following a dispute concerning the control of the budget. The Government had insisted that it was responsible for management of the budget and accountable only to parliament. Trovoada maintained that this was indicative of the Government's attempts to reduce the extent of presidential jurisdiction and of its intention, moreover, to replace the semi-presidential system of government enshrined in the Constitution with a legislative regime. On 4 July Trovoada appointed Evaristo do Espírito Santo de Carvalho (the Minister of Defence and Security in the outgoing administration) as Prime Minister. The PCD—GR, which refused to participate in an administration formed on presidential initiative, announced its unmitigated opposition to the new Government and subsequently expelled Carvalho from the party. An interim, eight-member Government, comprising principally technocrats and senior civil servants, was appointed on 8 July. On 10 July, in an attempt to end the prevailing political crisis, Trovoada dissolved the Assembléia Nacional, thus preventing the PCD—GR from using its parliamentary majority to declare the new Government unconstitutional, and announced a fresh legislative election to be held on 2 October.

The legislative election resulted in victory for the MLSTP—PSD, which secured 27 seats, one short of an absolute majority. The PCD—GR and Acção Democrática Independente each obtained 14 seats. The level of voter participation, which was as low as 40%, was believed to reflect the disillusionment of the electorate at the failure of democracy immediately to realize their expectations of a transformation of the country's social and economic prospects. In late October 1994 da Graça was appointed Prime Minister. Despite his efforts to involve opposition parties in a government of national unity, the Council of Ministers subsequently appointed was dominated by members of the MLSTP—PSD.

In mid-October 1994 employees in the banking sector began an indefinite strike, in support of demands that compensation be paid to those made redundant since the rationalization of the sector began in 1992; the bank workers' trade union had also initiated legal proceedings in support of the demands. In December da Graça dismissed a number of senior civil servants, including the administrative heads of all public enterprises, and announced that more objective criteria would be introduced for future appointments. Among those dismissed was the Governor of the Central Bank, Adelino Santiago Castelo David, who was accused of misappropriation of funds.

In early February 1995 the Government appealed for international aid to mitigate the effects of the imminent return of some 6,000–7,000 Santomeans from Gabon, from where all illegal immigrants were to be expelled that month. In mid-February the Government announced that a general salary increase, of 64%–90%, for public- and private-sector employees would be introduced at the end of the month, in an effort to assuage increasing social tension caused by the constantly rising cost of living. Later that month, with the aim of securing the release of suspended funds from the World Bank, the Government announced the introduction of austerity measures, including a 25% increase in fuel prices, the dismissal of some 300 civil servants, and an increase in interest rates.

São Tomé and Príncipe has important trade links with the nearby mainland states of Gabon, Cameroon and Equatorial Guinea. It also maintains cordial relations with the other former Portuguese African colonies and with Portugal. In July 1988 Rochas da Costa made an official visit to Portugal, and in November the Portuguese Prime Minister made a reciprocal visit to São Tomé and Príncipe (the first such visit since the attainment of independence by the former colony): a number of agreements on Portuguese aid were signed on both occasions. President da Costa's visit to Portugal in September 1989 strengthened co-operative links between the two countries. Since 1989 São Tomé has played an active role in encouraging Angolan peace initiatives.

### Government

Under the 1990 Constitution legislative power is vested in the Assembléia Nacional, which comprises 55 members, elected by universal adult suffrage for a term of four years. No limit is placed on the number of political parties permitted to operate. Executive power is vested in the President of the Republic, who is Head of State, and who governs with the assistance of an appointed council of ministers, led by the Prime Minister. The President is elected by universal suffrage for a term of five years. The President's tenure of office is limited to two successive terms. The Prime Minister, who is appointed by the President, is, in theory, nominated by the deputies of the Assembléia Nacional.

### Defence

In 1992 a reorganization was initiated of the islands' armed forces (estimated to comprise some 900 men) and the police into two separate police forces, one for public order and another for criminal investigation.

### Economic Affairs

In 1993, according to estimates by the World Bank, São Tomé and Príncipe's gross national product (GNP), measured at average 1991–93 prices, was US $41m., equivalent to $330 per head. During 1985–93, it was estimated, GNP per head declined, in real terms, at an average rate of 1.8% per year. Over the same period the population increased by an annual average of 2.4%. According to estimates by the World Bank, São Tomé's gross domestic product (GDP) declined, in real terms, by an annual average of 2.4% in 1980–85, but increased by 7.7% in 1985–93.

Agriculture (including forestry and fishing) contributed 27.7% of GDP in 1993. About 39.9% of the working population were employed in the sector in 1991. The principal cash crop is cocoa, which accounted for about 78% of export earnings in 1993. Secondary cash crops include coconuts, coffee and palm oil and kernels. Owing to the concentration of agriculture on export commodities, by the mid-1980s São Tomé and Príncipe was estimated to be importing 90% of its food requirements. With the development of smallholder agriculture, which was introduced in the late 1980s, imports of food had fallen to an estimated 45% of consumption by 1992. Fishing is also a significant activity. The sale of fishing licences to foreign fleets is an important source of income. Agricultural GDP decreased by an annual average of 4.7% in 1982–91.

Industry (including manufacturing, construction and power) contributed 13.6% of GDP in 1993, and employed 13.6% of the working population in 1991. Industrial GDP decreased by an average of 0.5% per year in 1982–91.

Mining and manufacturing together employed 5.6% of the working population in 1981. The mining sector is negligible. The manufacturing sector consists solely of small processing factories, producing soap, soft drinks, textiles and beer; the sector accounted for 1.7% of GDP in 1988. Manufacturing GDP increased by an average of 1.3% per year in 1982–91.

In 1994 São Tomé and Príncipe projected a trade deficit of US $16.7m., and a deficit of $16.1m. on the current account of the balance of payments. In 1992 the principal source of imports (40.3%) was Portugal, and the principal market for exports (62.4%) was the Netherlands. Other major trading partners were Spain and Angola. The principal export in 1993 was cocoa. The principal imports in that year were capital goods, foodstuffs and mineral fuels.

In 1992 there was a budgetary deficit of 1,661.5m. dobras. São Tomé's total external debt was US $254.0m. at the end of 1993, of which $225.8m. was long-term public debt. In that year the cost of debt-servicing was equivalent to 21.8% of the total value of exports of goods and services. Consumer prices increased by an average of 37.6% in 1992, and by 27.3% in 1993.

São Tomé and Príncipe is a member of the African Development Bank (ADB, see p. 102) and of the Communauté économique des états de l'Afrique centrale (see p. 238), which promotes economic co-operation between member states.

São Tomé and Príncipe's economy is dominated by cocoa production, and is therefore vulnerable to adverse weather conditions and to fluctuations in international prices for cocoa. Efforts at economic adjustment in the second half of the 1980s included measures to foster private enterprise and to liberalize foreign and wholesale trade; foreign management was introduced to rehabilitate the cocoa plantations, and a restructuring of the public investment programme was undertaken. In the early 1990s financing was secured from the World Bank for the diversification of agriculture through the transfer of publicly-owned estates to private ownership and the promotion of farming by smallholders: some 20,000 ha of land was to be transferred to smallholders between 1993 and 1998. In mid-1991 the Government adopted an economic adjustment programme in co-operation with the IMF and the ADB. Subsequent measures, including a devaluation of the currency, increases in petroleum and electricity prices and the privatization of non-agricultural state enterprises, succeeded in narrowing the country's fiscal deficit. However, the continued implementation of such measures in subsequent years resulted in a constantly increasing cost of living and in concomitant popular discontent. In 1993 the tourism sector was identified as one of the principal areas for future development, although considerable improvements to the country's infrastructure would be an essential prerequisite to any such development. In late 1994 the new da Graça administration expressed its intention to create a free trade zone, transforming the country into an entrepôt for foreign trade and a centre for services, including 'offshore' banking.

### Social Welfare

In 1992 São Tomé and Príncipe had eight hospitals, five health centres and 23 medical stations, with a total of 556 beds. In that year there were 66 physicians working in the country.

### Education

Primary education is officially compulsory for a period of four years between seven and 14 years of age. Secondary education lasts for a further seven years, comprising a first cycle of four years and a second cycle of three years. In 1989 the country had 64 primary schools, with a total enrolment of 19,822 pupils. There are three secondary schools and a technical school on São Tomé, staffed mainly by foreign teachers. In 1991 the average rate of adult illiteracy was 75% (males 83%; females 68%). Expenditure on education by the central Government in 1986 was 100.2m. dobras, equivalent to 18.8% of total government expenditure.

### Weights and Measures

The metric system is in force.

# Statistical Survey

Source (unless otherwise stated): Banco Central de São Tomé e Príncipe, Praça da Independência, CP 13, São Tomé; tel. 22901; Direcção de Estatística, São Tomé.

## AREA AND POPULATION

**Area:** 1,001 sq km (386.5 sq miles).

**Population:** 96,611 (males 48,031; females 48,580) at census of 15 August 1981; 117,504 (males 57,577; females 59,927) at census of 4 August 1991; 122,000 at mid-1993 (official estimate).

**Density** (mid-1993): 121.9 per sq km.

**Births and Deaths** (1992): Registered live births 5,153 (birth rate 43.0 per 1,000); Registered deaths 1,011.

**Expectation of Life** (years at birth, 1992): 67.0.

**Economically Active Population** (1991 census): Agriculture, hunting, forestry and fishing 13,592; Industry 1,510; Electricity, gas and water 269; Public works and civil construction 2,866; Trade, restaurants and hotels 4,451; Financing, insurance, real estate and business services 176; Transport, storage and communications 2,186; Education 1,650; Health 1,133; Public administraion 2,809; Other services 2,369; Other activities 1,057; Total employed 34,068 (males 22,758, females 11,310); Unemployed 15,148; Total labour force 49,216.

## AGRICULTURE, ETC.

**Principal Crops** ('000 metric tons, 1993): Bananas 3.0 (FAO estimate); Bread-fruit 1.5 (1992); Cabbages 2.0 (1992); Cassava 5.0 (FAO estimate); Cocoa 4.7 (1994); Coconuts 36.0 (FAO estimate); Maize 1.0 (FAO estimate); Matabala (Taro) 6.0 (1992); Palm kernels 0.3 (FAO estimate); Tomatoes 4.0 (1992). Source: partly FAO, *Production Yearbook*.

**Livestock** (FAO estimates, '000 head, year ending September 1993): Cattle 4; Sheep 2; Goats 4; Pigs 3. Source: FAO, *Production Yearbook*.

**Livestock Products** (estimates, metric tons unless otherwise indicated, 1994): Beef 7.0; Pork 30.0; Mutton and goat meat 26.0; Poultry meat 115.0; Eggs 1.5 (million); Milk 1.5 ('000 litres). Source: Direcção de Planeamento Agrícola.

**Forestry** ('000 cubic metres): Roundwood removals 9 in 1989; 1990–92 annual production as in 1989 (FAO estimates). Source: FAO, *Yearbook of Forest Products*.

**Fishing** ('000 metric tons, live weight): Total catch 3.6 in 1990; 3.5 in 1991 (FAO estimate); 3.6 in 1992 (FAO estimate). Source: FAO, *Yearbook of Fishery Statistics*.

## INDUSTRY

**Production** (metric tons, unless otherwise indicated, 1992): Frozen fish 400 (UN estimate, 1989); Bread and biscuits 3,000; Soap 400; Copra 679; Beer (litres) 2,475,300; Palm oil (litres) 1,261,000; Electric energy (million kWh) 18.1. Source: partly UN, *Industrial Statistics Yearbook*.

## FINANCE

**Currency and Exchange Rates:** 100 cêntimos = 1 dobra (Db). *Sterling and Dollar Equivalents* (31 December 1994): £1 sterling = 1,854.4 dobras; US $1 = 1,185.3 dobras; 10,000 dobras = £5.393 = $8.437. *Average Exchange Rate* (dobras per US $): 143.3 in 1990; 201.8 in 1991; 320.4 in 1992.

**Budget** (million dobras, 1992): Revenue 1,945.7; Total Expenditure 3,607.2.

**Cost of Living** (Consumer Price Index; base: 1990 = 100): 119.4 in 1991; 164.3 in 1992; 209.2 in 1993.

**Gross Domestic Product by Economic Activity** (estimates, million dobras at current prices, 1993): Agriculture, forestry and fishing 4,663; Manufacturing, electricity, gas and water 1,326; Construction 970; Trade and transport 4,642; Public administration 3,870; Other services 1,366; *Total* 16,837.

**Balance of Payments** (projections, US $ million, 1994): Merchandise exports f.o.b. 7.1; Merchandise imports f.o.b. −23.8; *Trade balance* −16.7; Services (net) −15.1; Transfers (net) 15.8; *Current balance* −16.1; Long-term capital (net) 7.3; *Overall balance* −8.8.

## EXTERNAL TRADE

**Principal Commodities** (US $ million, 1993): *Imports c.i.f.*: Food and live animals 6.6 (of which donations 3.0); Petroleum and petroleum products 3.1; Capital goods 9.0; Total (incl. others) 28.1. *Exports f.o.b.*: Cocoa 3.9; Total (incl. others) 5.0.

**Principal Trading Partners** (US $ '000, 1992): *Imports:* Angola 2,800; Belgium 1,000; China, People's Republic 1,000; France 2,000; Gabon 2,000; Italy 2,000; Japan 1,000; Netherlands 500; Portugal 12,400; Spain 3,000; Total (incl. others) 30,800. *Exports:* Netherlands 3,415.6; Portugal 72.1; Total (incl. others) 5,472.2.

## TRANSPORT

**Road Traffic** (registered vehicles, 1992): Light vehicles 4,581, Heavy vehicles 561; Motor cycles 815; Tractors 299.

**International Sea-borne Shipping** (estimated freight traffic, metric tons, 1992): Goods loaded 16,000; Goods unloaded 45,000.

**Civil Aviation** (traffic on scheduled services, 1990): Passengers carried ('000) 22; Passenger-km (million) 8; Total ton-km (million) 1. Source: UN, *Statistical Yearbook*. (1992) Passengers carried 29,975; Freight 297,422 metric tons.

## COMMUNICATIONS MEDIA

**Radio receivers** (1992): 33,000 in use. Source: UNESCO, *Statistical Yearbook*.

**Non-daily newspapers and periodicals** (1994): Titles 6; Estimated average circulation 1,000 copies.

**Telephones** (1992): 2,267 lines in use.

## EDUCATION

**Pre-primary** (1989): 13 schools; 116 teachers; 3,446 pupils (males 1,702; females 1,744).

**Primary** (1989): 64 schools; 559 teachers; 19,822 pupils (males 10,428; females 9,394).

**General Secondary** (1989): 318 teachers; 7,446 pupils (males 3,992; females 3,454).

**Teacher Training:** 10 teachers (1983); 188 students (males 74; females 114) (1987).

**Vocational Secondary** (1989): 18 teachers; 101 students (males 68; females 33).

Source: UNESCO, *Statistical Yearbook*.

# Directory

## The Constitution

The Constitution came into force on 10 September 1990 as the result of a national referendum, in which 72% of the electorate voted in favour of a draft that had been introduced by the Central Committee of the Movimento de Libertação de São Tomé e Príncipe and approved in March 1990 by the Assembléia Popular Nacional. The following is a summary of its main provisions:

The Democratic Republic of São Tomé and Príncipe is a sovereign, independent, unitary and democratic state. There shall be complete separation between Church and State. Sovereignty resides in the people, who exercise it through universal, direct and secret vote, according to the terms of the Constitution.

Legislative power is vested in the Assembléia Nacional, which comprises 55 members elected by universal adult suffrage. The Assembléia Nacional is elected for four years and meets in ordinary session twice a year. It may meet in extraordinary session on the proposal of the President, the Council of Ministers or of two-thirds of its members. The Assembléia Nacional elects its own President. In the period between ordinary sessions of the Assembléia Nacional its functions are assumed by a permanent commission elected from among its members.

Executive power is vested in the President of the Republic, who is elected for a period of five years by universal adult suffrage. The President's tenure of office is limited to two successive terms. He is the Supreme Commander of the Armed Forces and is accountable to the Assembléia Nacional. In the case of the President's death, permanent incapacity or resignation, his functions shall be assumed by the President of the Assembléia Nacional until a new president is elected.

The Government is the executive and administrative organ of State. The Prime Minister is the Head of Government and is appointed by the President. Other ministers are appointed by the President on the proposal of the Prime Minister. The Government is responsible to the President and the Assembléia Nacional.

Judicial power is exercised by the Supreme Court and all other competent tribunals and courts. The Supreme Court is the supreme judicial authority, and is accountable only to the Assembléia Nacional. Its members are appointed by the Assembléia Nacional. The right to a defence is guaranteed.

The Constitution may be revised only by the Assembléia Nacional on the proposal of at least three-quarters of its members. Any amendment must be approved by a two-thirds majority of the Assembléia Nacional.

## The Government

### HEAD OF STATE

**President and Commander-in-Chief of the Armed Forces:** MIGUEL DOS ANJOS DA CUNHA LISBOA TROVOADA (took office 3 April 1991).

### COUNCIL OF MINISTERS
(June 1995)

**Prime Minister:** Dr CARLOS ALBERTO MONTEIRO DIAS DA GRAÇA.
**Deputy Prime Minister:** ARMINDO VAZ D'ALMEIDA.
**Minister of Foreign Affairs and Co-operation:** GUILHERME POSSER DA COSTA.
**Minister of Defence and Internal Order:** ALBERTO PAULINO.
**Minister of Economic Affairs:** JOAQUIM RAFAEL BRANCO.
**Minister of Planning and Finance:** CARLOS QUARESMA BATISTA DE SOUSA.
**Minister of Justice, Public Administration, Employment and Social Security:** MANUEL VAZ AFONSO FERNANDES.
**Minister of Social Equipment and Environment:** ALCINO MARTINHO DE BARROS PINTO.
**Minister of Education, Youth and Sport:** GUILHERME OCTAVIANO VIEGAS DOS RAMOS.
**Minister of Health:** FERNANDO DA CONCEIÇÃO SILVEIRA.
**Minister-Delegate for the Region of Príncipe:** ZEFERINO VAZ DOS SANTOS DOS PRAZERES

There are three secretaries of state.

### MINISTRIES

**Office of the Prime Minister:** CP 302, São Tomé; tel. 22890; telex 267; fax 21670.
**Ministry of Agriculture:** CP 47, São Tomé; tel. 22714.
**Ministry of Defence and Internal Order:** São Tomé; tel. 21092.
**Ministry of Economic Affairs:** CP 168, São Tomé; tel. 22372; fax 22182.
**Ministry of Education, Youth and Sport:** CP 41, São Tomé; tel. 21398.
**Ministry of Foreign Affairs and Co-operation:** CP 111, São Tomé; tel. 21166; telex 211; fax 22597.
**Ministry of Health:** CP 23, São Tomé; tel. 22722.
**Ministry of Information:** CP 112, São Tomé; tel. 21538; telex 217.
**Ministry of Justice and Public Administration:** São Tomé; tel. 23263; fax 22256.
**Ministry of Planning and Finance:** São Tomé; tel. 21083; fax 22790.
**Ministry of Social Equipment and Environment:** CP 130, São Tomé; tel. 22648; telex 242.

## Legislature

### ASSEMBLÉIA NACIONAL

**General Election, 2 October 1994**

|  | Seats |
| --- | --- |
| Movimento de Libertação de São Tomé e Príncipe— Partido Social Democrata | 27 |
| Acção Democrática Independente | 14 |
| Partido de Convergência Democrática—Grupo de Reflexão | 14 |
| **Total** | **55** |

## Political Organizations

**Acção Democrática Independente (ADI):** São Tomé; f. 1992; Leader CARLOS AGOSTINHO DAS NEVES.

**Aliança Popular (AP):** São Tomé; f. 1993; Leader CARLOS ESPÍRITO SANTO.

**Frente Democrata Cristã—Partido Social da Unidade (FDC—PSU):** São Tomé; f. 1990; Leader DANIEL POSSER DA COSTA.

**Movimento de Libertação de São Tomé e Príncipe—Partido Social Democrata (MLSTP—PSD):** São Tomé; f. 1972 as MLSTP, adopted present name in 1990; sole legal party 1972–90; Sec.-Gen. CARLOS ALBERTO MONTEIRO DIAS DA GRAÇA.

**Partido de Convergência Democrática—Grupo de Reflexão (PCD—GR):** São Tomé; f. 1987 by a breakaway faction of the MLSTP; Chair. LEONEL MÁRIO D'ALVA; Sec.-Gen. JOÃO DO SACRAMENTO BONFIM.

**Partido Democrático de São Tomé e Príncipe—Coligação Democrática da Oposição (PDSTP—CODO):** São Tomé; f. 1990; Leader VIRGILIO CARVALHO.

## Diplomatic Representation

### EMBASSIES IN SÃO TOMÉ AND PRÍNCIPE

**Angola:** Avda Kwame Nkrumah 45, São Tomé; tel. 22206; telex 227; Ambassador: ANDRÉ MIRANDA.

**China, People's Republic:** Avda Kwame Nkrumah, São Tomé; tel. 21323; Ambassador: WANG CHANGAN.

**Gabon:** Avda das Nações Unidas 4, CP 157, São Tomé; tel. 21043; telex 222; Ambassador: JEAN BAPTISTE MBATCHI.

**Portugal:** Avda Marginal de 12 de Julho, CP 173, São Tomé; tel. 22470; telex 261; fax 21190; Ambassador: ANTÓNIO FRANCO.

## Judicial System

Judicial power is exercised by the Supreme Court of Justice and the Courts of Primary Instance. The Supreme Court is the ultimate judicial authority.

**President of the Supreme Court:** JOSÉ PAQUETE.

# SÃO TOMÉ AND PRÍNCIPE

## Religion

More than 90% of the population are Christians, almost all of whom are Roman Catholics.

### CHRISTIANITY
#### The Roman Catholic Church

São Tomé and Príncipe comprises a single diocese, directly responsible to the Holy See. At 31 December 1993 there were an estimated 95,700 adherents in the country, representing about 80% of the population. The bishop participates in the Episcopal Conference of Angola and São Tomé (based in Luanda, Angola).

**Bishop of São Tomé e Príncipe:** Rt Rev. ABÍLIO RODAS DE SOUSA RIBAS, Centro Diocesano, CP 104, São Tomé; tel. 21408; telex 213; fax 21365.

## The Press

**Diário da República:** Cooperativa de Artes Gráficas, CP 28, São Tomé; tel. 22661; f. 1836; government gazette; weekly; Dir NELSON MENDES.

**O Independente:** São Tomé; tel. 22675; f. 1994; Dir CARLOS BORBOLETA.

**Notícias:** Rua 3 de Fevereiro, CP 112, São Tomé; tel. 22087; f. 1991; Dir. MANUEL BARROS.

**Nova República:** CP 523, São Tomé; tel. 22788; f. 1992; Dir. RAFAEL BRANCO.

**O País Hoje:** CP 455, São Tomé; f. 1993; Dir. SÃO DEUS LIMA.

**O Parvo:** CP 535, São Tomé; tel. 21031; f. 1994; Editor ARMINDO CARDOSO.

### NEWS AGENCY

**STP-Press:** c/o Rádio Nacional de São Tomé e Príncipe, Avda Marginal de 12 de Julho, CP 44, São Tomé; tel. 21342; telex 217; f. 1985; operated by the radio station in asscn with the Angolan news agency, ANGOP.

## Radio and Television

In 1992 there were an estimated 33,000 radio receivers in use. Portuguese technical and financial assistance in the establishment of a television service was announced in May 1989. Transmissions commenced in 1992, and currently broadcasts six days per week. The creation of the Companhia Santomense de Telecomunicações (CST), agreed in 1989 between a Portuguese company, Radio Marconi, and the Government of São Tomé, was to allow increased telecommunications links and television reception via satellite.

**Rádio Nacional de São Tomé e Príncipe:** Avda Marginal de 12 de Julho, CP 44, São Tomé; tel. 23293; f. 1958; state-controlled; home service in Portuguese and Creole; Dir ADELINO LUCAS.

**Televisão de São Tomé e Príncipe (TVS):** Bairro Quinta de Santo António, São Tomé; tel. 21493; fax 21942; state-controlled; Dir CARLOS TEIXEIRA D'ALVA.

## Finance

### BANKING

**Banco Central de São Tomé e Príncipe (BCSTP):** Praça da Independência, CP 13, São Tomé; tel. 22901; f. 1992 following reconstruction of banking system, assuming central banking functions of fmr Banco Nacional de São Tomé e Príncipe; bank of issue; Gov. CARLOS QUARESMA BAPTISTA DA SOUSA (acting).

**Banco Internacional de São Tomé e Príncipe (BISTP):** Praça da Independência, CP 536, São Tomé; tel. 21436; telex 293; fax 22427; f. 1993; international commercial bank; Pres. of Admin. Bd TEOTÓNIO ANGELO D'ALVA TORRES.

**Caixa Nacional de Poupança e Crédito (CNPC):** Rua Soldado Paulo Ferreira, CP 390, São Tomé; tel. and fax 21811; f. 1980 as Caixa Popular de São Tomé e Príncipe; restructured 1993 and renamed as above; savings; loans for housing; Co-ordinator ADELINO IZIDRO (acting).

There is also a post office savings institution.

### INSURANCE

**Caixa de Previdência dos Funcionários Públicos:** São Tomé; insurance fund for civil servants.

**Empresa Nacional de Seguros e Resseguros 'A Compensadora':** Rua Viriato Cruz, CP 190, São Tomé; tel. 22907; f. 1980; privatization pending.

## Trade and Industry

### CHAMBER OF COMMERCE

**Câmara do Comércio da Indústria e Agricultura:** Rua de Moçambique, São Tomé; tel. 22793; Pres. FRADIQUE BANDEIRA MELO DE MENEZES.

### TRADE UNIONS

**Organizacão Nacional de Trabalhadores de São Tomé e Príncipe (ONTSTP):** Rua Cabo Verde, São Tomé; Sec.-Gen. ARTURO PINHO.

**União Geral dos Trabalhadores de São Tomé e Príncipe (UGSTP):** Avda Kwame Nkrumah, São Tomé; tel. 22443; Sec.-Gen. COSME BONFIM AFONSO RITA.

## Transport

### RAILWAYS

There are no railways in São Tomé and Príncipe.

### ROADS

In 1994 there were 380 km of roads, of which 250 km were asphalted.

### CIVIL AVIATION

The principal airport is at São Tomé. In 1986 the African Development Bank agreed to provide most of the finance for a US $16m. project for the improvement of São Tomé airport: the runway extension plan was completed in September 1992, and a new administrative building and control tower were completed later that year.

**Air São Tomé e Príncipe:** Avda Marginal de 12 de Julho, CP 45, São Tomé; tel. 21976; fax 21375; f. 1993 to replace Equatorial Airlines of São Tomé and Príncipe; owned by Govt of São Tomé (35%), TAP-Air Portugal, SA (40%), Golfe International Air Service (France) (24%) and Mistral Voyages (France) (1%); operates domestic service between the islands of São Tomé and Príncipe and international flights to Libreville (Gabon).

## Tourism

The islands benefit from spectacular mountain scenery, unpeopled beaches and unique species of wildlife and flora. Although still largely undeveloped, tourism is currently the sector of the islands' economy attracting the highest level of foreign investment. However, the high level of rainfall during most of the year limits the duration of the tourist season, and the expense of reaching the islands by air is also an inhibiting factor. The first modern tourist hotel was completed in 1986. In 1994 there were 11 hotels, with a total of 200 beds.

# SAUDI ARABIA

## Introductory Survey

### Location, Climate, Language, Religion, Flag, Capital

The Kingdom of Saudi Arabia occupies about four-fifths of the Arabian peninsula, in south-western Asia. It is bordered by Jordan, Iraq and Kuwait to the north, by Yemen to the south, by Oman to the south and east, and by Qatar and the United Arab Emirates to the north-east. Saudi Arabia has a long western coastline on the Red Sea, facing Egypt, Sudan and Ethiopia, and a shorter coastline (between Kuwait and Qatar) on the Persian (Arabian) Gulf, with the Bahrain archipelago just off shore and Iran on the opposite coast. Much of the country is arid desert, and some places are without rain for years. In summer average temperatures in coastal regions range from 38°C to 49°C (100°F–120°F), and humidity is high. Temperatures sometimes reach 54°C (129°F) in the interior. Winters are mild, except in the mountains. Annual rainfall averages between 100 mm (4 ins) and 200 mm (8 ins) in the north, but is even lower in the south. The official language is Arabic, which is spoken by almost all of the population. Except for the expatriate community (estimated to represent some 27% of the total population at the time of the 1992 census), virtually all of the inhabitants are adherents of Islam, the official religion, which originated in Arabia. About 85% of the population are Sunni Muslims, and most of the indigenous inhabitants belong to the strictly orthodox Wahhabi sect. About 15% of the population are Shi'a Muslims, principally in the east of the country. The national flag (proportions 3 by 2) is green and bears, in white, in the upper hoist, an Arabic inscription ('There is no God but Allah and Muhammad is the prophet of Allah') above a white sabre. The royal capital is Riyadh and the administrative capital is Jeddah.

### Recent History

The whole of the Arabian peninsula became part of Turkey's Ottoman Empire in the 16th century. Under the suzerainty of the Ottoman Sultan, the local tribal rulers enjoyed varying degrees of autonomy. The Wahhabi movement, dedicated to the reform of Islam, was launched in the Najd (Nejd) region of central Arabia in the 18th century. A Wahhabi kingdom, ruled by the House of Sa'ud from its capital at Riyadh, quickly expanded into the Hejaz region on the west coast of Arabia. This first Saudi kingdom reached its zenith in c. 1800 but subsequently declined. In 1890 the rival Rashidi family seized control of Riyadh. In 1901 a member of the deposed Sa'udi family, Abd al-Aziz ibn Abd ar-Rahman, set out from Kuwait, where he had been living in exile, to regain the family's former domains. In 1902, with only about 200 followers, Abd al-Aziz captured Riyadh, expelled the Rashidi dynasty and proclaimed himself ruler of Najd. In subsequent years he recovered and consolidated the outlying provinces of the kingdom, defeating Turkish attempts to subjugate him. Having restored the House of Sa'ud as a ruling dynasty, Abd al-Aziz became known as Ibn Sa'ud. In order to strengthen his position, he instituted the formation of Wahhabi colonies, known as Ikhwan ('Brethren'), throughout the territory under his control.

During the First World War, in which Turkey was allied with Germany, the Arabs under Ottoman rule rebelled. In 1915 the United Kingdom signed a treaty of friendship with Ibn Sa'ud, who was then master of central Arabia, securing his co-operation against Turkey. Relations subsequently deteriorated as a result of the British Government's decision to support Hussein ibn Ali, who proclaimed himself King of the Hejaz in 1916, as its principal ally in Arabia. Hussein was also Sharif of Mecca (the holiest city of Islam), which had been governed since the 11th century by his Hashimi (Hashemite) family, rivals of the House of Sa'ud. The rivalry was exacerbated by the post-war decision to nominate Hashemites to the thrones of Iraq and Transjordan (later renamed Jordan). At the end of the war, following Turkey's defeat, the Ottoman Empire was dissolved. Continuing his conquests, Ibn Sa'ud successfully campaigned against the rulers of four Arabian states (the Hejaz, Asir, Hayil and Jauf) between 1919 and 1925. In September 1924 his forces captured Mecca, forcing Hussein to abdicate, and in 1925 they overran the whole of the Hejaz. In January 1926 Ibn Sa'ud was proclaimed King of the Hejaz and Sultan of Najd. On 23 September 1932 the dual monarchy ended when the two areas were merged as the unified Kingdom of Saudi Arabia.

Exploration for petroleum, the basis of Saudi Arabia's modern prosperity, began in 1933, and commercially exploitable deposits were discovered in the Eastern Province in 1938. Saudi Arabia remained neutral during most of the Second World War but declared war on Germany and Japan in February 1945. After the war, the exploitation of the kingdom's huge reserves of petroleum was begun on a large scale. A consortium of US companies pioneered exploration, establishing close ties between Saudi Arabia and the USA. Saudi Arabia's growing income from petroleum royalties was used to develop and modernize the country's infrastructure and services.

Ibn Sa'ud opposed the creation of the State of Israel in 1948, and a small Saudi Arabian force took part in the first Arab–Israeli war. Generally acknowledged as an outstanding leader and the creator of modern Arabia, Ibn Sa'ud remained in power until his death in November 1953. All subsequent rulers of Saudi Arabia have been sons of Ibn Sa'ud. The kingdom has remained an absolute monarchy, and despite its great wealth, a traditional Islamic society. The King is the supreme religious leader as well as the Head of State, and governs by royal decree. In foreign affairs, Saudi Arabia has historically allied itself with the USA and other Western countries.

Ibn Sa'ud's immediate successor was Sa'ud ibn Abd al-Aziz, hitherto the Crown Prince, who had been appointed Prime Minister in October 1953. Another of the late King's sons, Faisal ibn Abd al-Aziz, replaced Sa'ud as Crown Prince and Prime Minister. In March 1958, bowing to pressure from the royal family, King Sa'ud conferred on Crown Prince Faisal full powers over foreign, internal and economic affairs. In December 1960 the Crown Prince resigned as Prime Minister, and King Sa'ud assumed the premiership. Faisal resumed office in October 1962, following the revolution in the neighbouring Yemen Arab Republic (YAR). The ensuing civil war in the YAR, in which Saudi Arabia supplied military equipment to the royalist forces of the deposed Imam, strained Saudi relations with the United Arab Republic (Egypt), whose troops supported the victorious republicans.

In March 1964 King Sa'ud relinquished power to Crown Prince Faisal, and in November was forced by the royal family to abdicate in his favour. The new King Faisal retained the post of Prime Minister, and appointed his half-brother, Khalid ibn Abd al-Aziz, to be Crown Prince in March 1965. In the Six-Day War of June 1967, Saudi Arabian forces collaborated with Iraqi and Jordanian troops in action against Israel. As a result of the Arab–Israeli war of October 1973, Saudi Arabia led a movement by Arab petroleum producers to exert pressure on Western countries by reducing supplies of crude oil.

In March 1975 King Faisal was assassinated by one of his nephews, and was immediately succeeded by Crown Prince Khalid. The new King Khalid also became Prime Minister, and appointed his brother, Fahd ibn Abd al-Aziz (Minister of the Interior since 1962), as Crown Prince and First Deputy Prime Minister.

The religious fervour that swept through the Middle East in the wake of the Iranian Revolution affected Saudi Arabia in November 1979, when an armed group of about 250 Sunni Muslim extremists attacked and occupied the Grand Mosque in Mecca, the most important centre of pilgrimage for Muslims. In a simultaneous but unrelated incident, there was a riot by members of the Shi'ite Muslim community in the Eastern Province. In response to the discontent revealed by these disturbances, Crown Prince Fahd announced in January 1980 that a consultative assembly would be formed to act as an advisory body. (The construction of an assembly building was completed in Riyadh in the late 1980s, but it was not until December 1993 that the assembly was inaugurated—see below.)

# SAUDI ARABIA

*Introductory Survey*

King Khalid died in June 1982 and was succeeded by Crown Prince Fahd, who, following precedent, became Prime Minister and appointed a half-brother, Abdullah ibn Abd al-Aziz (Commander of the National Guard since 1962), to be Crown Prince and First Deputy Prime Minister.

As a result of its position as the world's leading exporter of petroleum, Saudi Arabia is a dominant member of the Organization of the Petroleum Exporting Countries (see p. 210) and one of the most influential countries in the Arab world. In May 1981 the kingdom joined five neighbouring states in establishing the Co-operation Council for the Arab States of the Gulf (more generally known as the Gulf Co-operation Council—GCC, see p. 130). In August Crown Prince Fahd announced an eight-point plan for the settlement of the Arab–Israeli conflict. His proposals, by implication, recognized Israel as a legitimate state. At a summit conference of Arab states in September 1982, the so-called 'Fahd Plan' formed the basis of an agreed proposal for the achievement of peace in the Middle East, and during 1983 Saudi Arabia sponsored repeated diplomatic initiatives within the region.

During 1984 a series of attacks on Saudi Arabian oil tankers in the Gulf by warring Iraqi and Iranian aircraft led to urgent commissioning of improved defence systems from the USA. In August the *Hajj* (annual pilgrimage to Mecca) was disrupted by demonstrating Iranian pilgrims, and a plot by armed Libyans to occupy the Grand Mosque in Mecca was thwarted. In 1984–86 Saudi Arabia concluded agreements with France, Brazil, the United Kingdom and the USA for the purchase of armaments and for military training facilities. In October 1985 it was announced that the GCC states had established a 'rapid deployment force', following the ratification of a joint defence strategy.

After the outbreak of the Iran–Iraq War in September 1980, Saudi Arabia consistently provided Iraq with financial support. In May 1985 the Iranian-based al-Jihad group claimed responsibility for two bomb explosions in Riyadh, causing increased hostility between Saudi Arabia and Iran. In July 1987 relations between the two countries deteriorated further following clashes between Iranian pilgrims and Saudi security forces during the *Hajj*, in which 402 people, including 275 Iranians, were killed. Mass demonstrations took place in Teheran, where the Saudi Arabian embassy was sacked, and Iranian leaders vowed to avenge the pilgrims' deaths by overthrowing the Saudi ruling family.

At an extraordinary meeting of the League of Arab States (the Arab League, see p. 182), held in Jordan in November 1987, delegates unanimously condemned Iran for its prolongation of the Iran–Iraq War, and at a GCC meeting in Riyadh, held in the following month, the six member states urged the UN Security Council to enforce its resolution (No. 598) that ordered Iran and Iraq to observe a cease-fire in the war. Also in November 1987 Saudi Arabia resumed full diplomatic relations with Egypt, following a decision taken by the Arab League that permitted member states to restore relations with Egypt at their own discretion. Relations had been severed in 1979, following the signing of the peace treaty between Egypt and Israel.

In March 1988 the Government announced its intention temporarily to limit the number of pilgrims from abroad during the *Hajj* season by allocating national quotas. In April Saudi Arabia severed diplomatic relations with Iran, which subsequently refused to send pilgrims on that year's *Hajj*.

Also in March 1988 the disclosure that Saudi Arabia had taken delivery of an unspecified number of medium-range missiles from the People's Republic of China provoked threats by Israel of a pre-emptive military strike. The USA subsequently warned Israel against such action, but in April it was reported that King Fahd had made an unprecedented request for the replacement of the US Ambassador to Saudi Arabia, following his delivery of an official complaint from the USA concerning the purchase of the missiles. In July, after the US Congress had refused to sanction an agreement to supply military equipment to Saudi Arabia, the Government signed an agreement with the United Kingdom, valued at a record US $20,000m., for the supply of military aircraft and minesweepers and for assistance in the construction of two airbases. Through this agreement the United Kingdom became Saudi Arabia's main supplier of military equipment, a position previously held by the USA.

In October 1988 four Saudi Arabian Shi'a Muslims, convicted of perpetrating acts of sabotage at a petrochemicals plant and of collaborating with Iran, were executed. King Fahd subsequently decreed that the kingdom's official media should halt criticism of Iran, in an attempt to demonstrate the sincerity of Saudi Arabia's intention to improve relations between the two countries. In March 1989 King Fahd signed a pact of non-aggression with Iraq, a development apparently designed to ease concerns among conservative Arab Gulf states about the political ambitions of President Saddam Hussain of Iraq following the Iran–Iraq War.

Iran boycotted the *Hajj* for the second time in July 1989, owing to Saudi Arabia's refusal to abandon the quota system restricting the number of pilgrims. Two explosions, which killed one pilgrim and wounded 16 during the *Hajj* that year, widened the rift between the two countries. In September 16 Kuwaiti Shi'ite Muslims, who had allegedly planned the explosions, were executed in Saudi Arabia; 10 of those executed were of Iranian origin. In February 1990 three Saudi Arabian diplomats were assassinated in Thailand, apparently by Shi'a fundamentalists linked to Iran. In July Saudi Arabia was criticized by some Islamic countries, including Iran, when 1,426 pilgrims attending the *Hajj* in Mecca were killed in a stampede in a pedestrian tunnel. Iran had again boycotted the *Hajj*. In May 1994 an estimated 270 pilgrims were killed in a similar incident at the *Hajj* (a total of 829 deaths was recorded at that year's pilgrimage).

Saudi Arabia's concern about its capacity to defend itself, and its fear of Iraqi expansionism, were substantiated in August 1990, when Iraq invaded and annexed Kuwait and proceeded to deploy armed forces along the Kuwaiti–Saudi Arabian border. (For details of events leading to the Iraqi invasion, see the chapter on Kuwait.) Following consultations with the US Government, King Fahd requested that US forces be deployed in Saudi Arabia, as part of a multinational force, in order to deter an attack on the country by Iraq. The dispatch of US combat troops and aircraft to Saudi Arabia signified the beginning of 'Operation Desert Shield' for the defence of Saudi Arabia, in accordance with Article 51 of the UN Charter. In September it was reported that Saudi Arabia planned to double the size of its armed forces, and to purchase more than US $20,000m.-worth of advanced military technology from the USA. However, the value of the sale was reduced substantially following objections by Israel and by pro-Israeli members of the US Congress. Also in September diplomatic relations between Saudi Arabia and the USSR, which had been severed more than 50 years previously, were restored, following the USSR's condemnation of Iraqi aggression and expressions of Soviet support for UN efforts to liberate Kuwait.

By early January 1991 some 30 countries had contributed ground troops, aircraft and warships to the US-led multinational force based in Saudi Arabia and the Gulf region. The entire Saudi Arabian armed forces (numbering about 67,500 men) were mobilized in defence of the country. In mid-January, following the failure of international diplomacy to secure Iraq's withdrawal from Kuwait, the multinational force launched a military campaign ('Operation Desert Storm') to liberate Kuwait. As part of its response to the aerial bombardment which began the campaign, Iraq launched 35 *Scud* missiles against targets in Saudi Arabia and Israel. However, fighting on Saudi Arabian territory was confined to a few minor incidents. In early February Iraq formally severed diplomatic relations with Saudi Arabia.

Kuwait was liberated and a cease-fire was declared between Iraq and the multinational force in late February 1991. In March the Ministers of Foreign Affairs of the members of the GCC met their Syrian and Egyptian counterparts in Damascus, Syria, in order to discuss regional security issues. The formation of an Arab peace-keeping force, comprising mainly Egyptian and Syrian troops, was subsequently announced. In May, however, following the endorsement by the GCC member states of US proposals for an increased Western military presence in the Gulf region, Egypt announced its decision to withdraw all of its forces from the Gulf region, casting doubt on the future of joint Arab regional security arrangements. Diplomatic relations between Saudi Arabia and Iran were re-established in March, and it was agreed that 110,000 Iranian pilgrims would be permitted to attend the *Hajj* later that year, in accordance with the quota system.

In February and May 1991 two petitions, presented to King Fahd, appealed for more extensive Islamization in areas as diverse as the armed forces, the press and all administrative and educational systems. In June the Government's Higher

Judicial Council issued a statement warning the signatories of the consequences of issuing any further criticism of the King.

In September 1991 it was revealed that 37,000 of the 541,000 troops who had been deployed in Saudi Arabia during the Gulf crisis remained in the country in a non-military capacity. Islamic fundamentalists in the kingdom were opposed to a formal defence agreement with the USA, but later in September President George Bush of the USA announced that he was authorizing the sale of 72 F-15 aircraft to Saudi Arabia.

In January 1992 there were widespread reports that fundamentalist dissent had been suppressed in the previous two months. It was also reported that the Minister of Justice had ordered the deposition of Sheikh Abd al-Ubaykan, the head of Riyadh's main court, who had criticized government policies and opposed the deployment of US troops in Saudi Arabia and the convening of a Middle East peace conference (begun in October 1991).

In March 1992 King Fahd announced by royal decree the imminent creation of a Consultative Council. The 60 members of this council were to be selected by the King every four years, and to have an advisory, rather than legislative, function. Two further decrees, issued at the same time, provided for the establishment of regional authorities, and a 'basic law of government', equivalent to a written constitution. However, in a subsequent interview the King made it clear that, in his view, Western-style democracy was not suited to the Gulf region and that Islam favoured 'the consultative system and openness between a ruler and his subjects', rather than free elections. In September Sheikh Muhammad al-Jubair, hitherto Minister of Justice, was appointed Chairman of the Consultative Council. In November a major reorganization of the 18-member Council of Ulema (Saudi Arabia's most senior Islamic authority) was instigated by royal decree. Among 10 new members appointed by the King was the new Minister of Justice, Abdullah ibn Muhammad ash-Sheikh. In December King Fahd warned the religious community not to use public platforms to discuss secular matters. He also denounced the spread of Islamic fundamentalism, and referred to attempts by 'foreign currents' to de-stabilize the country. The Consultative Council (Majlis ash-Shoura) was inaugurated by King Fahd at the end of December 1993.

In September 1992 the Government sent a memorandum to the Government of Yemen, in an attempt to expedite demarcation of the Saudi-Yemeni border. Sporadic negotiations, through the medium of a joint border commission, subsequently took place. Also in September Qatar accused a Saudi force of attacking a Qatari border post, killing two border guards and capturing a third. As a result, Qatar suspended a 1965 border agreement with Saudi Arabia, which had never been fully ratified. The Saudi Government claimed that the incident had been caused by fighting between rival Bedouin tribes within Saudi territory. In October it was reported that relations between the two countries had improved, following Kuwaiti mediation, but Qatar nevertheless registered its disaffection by not attending GCC meetings at ministerial level, held in the United Arab Emirates and Kuwait in November. In December, however, following mediation by President Hosni Mubarak of Egypt, the Qatari Amir, Sheikh Khalifa, signed an agreement in Medina with King Fahd to establish a committee, the function of which was to be to demarcate the disputed border by the end of 1994. In late November 1994 Qatar boycotted a GCC ministerial session in Riyadh, in protest at alleged armed incidents on the Saudi-Qatari border earlier in that year (in one of which, it was claimed, a Qatari citizen had been wounded by Saudi border guards); the Saudi Government, however, refuted the allegations. By mid-1995 the border had yet to be officially demarcated.

In March 1993 the leaders of eight Afghan *mujahidin* factions travelled to Mecca, at the instigation of King Fahd, in order to discuss their differences. The leaders subsequently ratified the Islamabad Afghanistan peace accord, which aimed at achieving a peaceful settlement in the region, and which was also signed by King Fahd and the Pakistani Prime Minister, Nawaz Sharif, as co-guarantors.

In May 1993 the Saudi authorities disbanded the recently-formed Committee for the Defence of Legitimate Rights (CDLR), established by a group of six prominent Islamic scholars and lawyers. The six founders of the committee were also dismissed from their positions, and their spokesman, Muhammad al-Masari, arrested, in an action that was taken, according to an official source, 'in the light of the dictates of the public interest'. In April 1994 it was reported that members of the CDLR, including al-Masari (who had recently been released from custody), had relocated their organization to the United Kingdom. In October 1993 it was reported that an accommodation had been reached between the Saudi authorities and an opposition Shi'a organization, the Reform Movement, whereby members of that organization undertook to cease 'dissident' activities, in return for permission to return to Saudi Arabia and for the release of a number of Shi'a Muslims held in detention there.

During 1994 the Saudi Government was the subject of a series of accusations of corruption and malpractice, made by foreign journalists and Saudi citizens residing abroad. In June Muhammad al-Khiweli, a high-ranking diplomat at the Saudi mission to the UN headquarters in New York, sought political asylum in the USA, accusing the Saudi Government of human rights violations, terrorism and corruption. In the same month another Saudi diplomat residing in the USA, Ahmad az-Zahrani, levelled similar accusations against the Government and sought asylum in the United Kingdom. The defections caused embarrassment to the US and British Governments, which appeared averse to jeopardizing commercial and political ties with Saudi Arabia. In August, none the less, al-Khiweli was granted asylum in the USA. Meanwhile, az-Zahrani was denied political asylum in the United Kingdom, and in November the British authorities announced their intention to deport him. (In February 1995, however, al-Masari successfully appealed against the deportation order.)

In September 1994 the CDLR was among organizations to report the arrest of more than 1,000 people, including clerics and academics, most of whom had attended a demonstration in Buraidah, 300 km to the north-west of Riyadh, to protest at the arrest of two religious leaders who had allegedly been agitating for the stricter enforcement of Shari'a (Islamic) law. The Government subsequently confirmed that 110 arrests had been made, but in mid-October announced that 130 of the 157 people arrested in September had since been released. In early October the King approved the creation of a Higher Council for Islamic Affairs, under the chairmanship of Prince Sultan ibn Abd al-Aziz, the Second Deputy Prime Minister and Minister of Defence and Civil Aviation, in what was widely interpreted as a measure to limit the influence of militant clerics and to diminish the authority of the powerful Council of Ulema. In April 1995 the human rights organization, Amnesty International, expressed concern at the sharp increase in the number of public executions in Saudi Arabia: by late April some 96 executions had taken place, compared with 53 during the whole of 1994 and 85 in 1993. The increase in executions coincided with the Government's strict enforcement of the Saudi residency law, which resulted in the expulsion or voluntary repatriation of more than 100,000 illegal immigrants between December 1994 and February 1995.

In January 1994 the Chairman of the Palestine Liberation Organization (PLO), Yasser Arafat, visited Riyadh to discuss the Middle East peace settlement with King Fahd. This meeting represented a significant *rapprochement* between Saudi Arabia and the PLO in the wake of the 1990-91 Gulf crisis. In January 1995 King Fahd held a meeting in Mecca with Yasser Arafat, and in April Saudi Arabia became the first Arab country to recognize passports issued by the Palestine National Authority for Palestinians in Gaza and Jericho.

In May 1994 the Saudi Government appealed to both sides in the conflict in neighbouring Yemen to cease hostilities (for further details, see the chapter on Yemen); however, it became apparent that the Government's allegiance lay with the secessionists, and, following their defeat in July, tensions between the two countries increased. In early December Yemen accused Saudi Arabia of encroaching on its territory by erecting monitoring posts and constructing roads on Yemeni territory. Relations deteriorated further in January 1995, when the two countries failed to renew the 1934 Ta'if agreement (renewable every 20 years), which delineated their *de facto* frontier. Following military clashes between the two sides, and intense mediation by Syria, a joint statement was issued in mid-January 1995, in which Saudi Arabia and Yemen undertook to halt all military activity in the border area; it was subsequently agreed to pursue the demarcation of the disputed border area by a joint committee. In late February the Saudi and Yemeni Governments signed a memorandum of understanding that reaffirmed their commitment to the legitimacy of the Ta'if agreement and provided for the establishment of

# SAUDI ARABIA

*Introductory Survey*

several joint committees to delineate the land and sea borders. In mid-March, shortly after the Saudi Council of Ministers approved the memorandum of understanding, the joint Saudi-Yemeni military committee, also established by the memorandum, held its first meeting in Riyadh.

In April 1995 Libyan pilgrims were permitted by the UN to fly to Saudi Arabia for that year's *Hajj*. In March it was announced that quotas for Israeli Muslims wishing to participate in the *Hajj* were to be ended.

In September 1994 Saudi Arabia, in common with the other GCC members, agreed to a partial removal of the economic boycott of Israel. In November Saudi Arabia and Russia signed an agreement governing trade, investment and economic co-operation.

## Government

Saudi Arabia is an absolute monarchy, with no legislature or political parties. Constitutionally, the King rules in accordance with the *Shari'a*, the sacred law of Islam. He appoints and leads a Council of Ministers, which serves as the instrument of royal authority in both legislative and executive matters. Decisions of the Council are reached by majority vote, but require royal sanction. A Consultative Council (Majlis ash-Shoura) was officially inaugurated in December 1993.

## Defence

In June 1994 the active armed forces totalled 104,000 men: army 70,000, air force 18,000, navy 12,000 (including 1,500 marines); there were also air defence forces numbering 4,000. Military service is voluntary. In addition, there is a National Guard with 57,000 active personnel and 20,000 tribal levies. The allocation for defence and security in the budget for 1994 was 53,549m. Saudi riyals, equivalent to 33.5% of total expenditure for that year.

## Economic Affairs

In 1992, according to estimates by the World Bank, Saudi Arabia's gross national product (GNP) per head, measured at average 1990–92 prices, was US $7,780. During 1985–93, it was estimated, GNP per head declined, in real terms, at an average rate of 0.9% per year. In the same period the population increased by an annual average of 4.4%. Saudi Arabia's gross domestic product (GDP) increased, in real terms, by an annual average of 0.4% in 1980–92. GDP increased by 0.6%, in real terms, in 1994.

Agriculture (including forestry and fishing) contributed an estimated 6.4% of GDP in 1992, and employed an estimated 36.6% of the working population at mid-1993. The principal crop is wheat. From the late 1980s a large wheat surplus was exported. Barley, sorghum, millet, tomatoes, dates and watermelons are also significant crops. Saudi Arabia is self-sufficient in many dairy products, and in eggs and broiler chickens. In 1988 agricultural exports accounted for about 40% of non-oil exports. Agricultural GDP increased by an estimated annual average of 14.0% in 1980–92.

Industry (including mining, manufacturing, construction and power) employed only about 14% of the labour force in 1980, but provided an estimated 51.1% of GDP in 1992. During 1980–92 industrial GDP declined by an annual average of 2.9%.

Mining and quarrying contributed an estimated 35.2% of GDP in 1992. The sector is dominated by petroleum and natural gas, which provided an estimated 34.8% of GDP in that year. Saudi Arabia is the third largest petroleum producer in the world. The production of petroleum and petroleum products is the most important industry in Saudi Arabia, providing 92.0% of total export revenue in 1992. In early 1994 Saudi Arabia's proven recoverable reserves of petroleum were 261,200m. barrels, equivalent to about one-quarter of the world's proven oil reserves. Crude petroleum production averaged 8.1m. barrels per day (b/d) in 1994, and sustainable production capacity of 10m. b/d (achieved in late 1994) was to be maintained for 1995. Saudi Arabia's production quota at this time, as a member of the Organization of the Petroleum Exporting Countries (OPEC, see p. 210), was 8m. b/d. Gas reserves, mostly associated with petroleum, totalled 5,170,000m. cu m at January 1992. There are also unassociated gas reserves, as yet unexploited. Other minerals produced are limestone, gypsum, marble, clay and salt, while there are substantial deposits of gold and other metals. The GDP of the mining sector increased by an annual average of 10.5% in 1985–92.

Manufacturing contributed an estimated 7.0% of GDP in 1992, when the most important product was refined petroleum. Manufacturing GDP increased by an annual average of 8.1% in 1980–92.

Electrical energy is generated by thermal power stations, using Saudi Arabia's own petroleum resources. The contribution to GDP by the electricity, water and gas sector grew by an estimated 3.7% in 1993.

In 1993 Saudi Arabia recorded a visible trade surplus of US $19,020m., but there was a deficit of $14,218m. on the current account of the balance of payments. In 1992 the principal source of imports (22.5%) was the USA; other important suppliers were Japan, the United Kingdom and Germany. The USA was also the principal market for exports (22.9%) in 1991; other major markets were Japan, the Netherlands, the Republic of Korea and Singapore. The dominant exports are crude and refined petroleum, and petrochemicals. The principal imports in 1992 were machinery and transport equipment, food, beverages and tobacco, chemicals and chemical products, base metals and metal manufactures and textiles and clothing.

Following a series of budgetary deficits, the provisional budget for 1995 forecast a reduction of 6% in the level of expenditure, to SR150,000m. Revenue was expected to reach SR135,000m. in that year, leaving a budgetary deficit of SR15,000m. The cost of living increased by an annual average of 0.6% in 1985–93; inflation declined from 0.8% in 1993 to 0.6% in 1994. There is a labour shortage in Saudi Arabia, and long-term unemployment has been negligible.

In addition to its membership of OPEC, Saudi Arabia is a member of the Islamic Development Bank (see p. 180), and the Organization of Arab Petroleum Exporting Countries (OAPEC, see p. 207). Saudi Arabia is the major aid donor in the region, disbursing loans to developing countries through the Arab Fund for Economic and Social Development (AFESD, see p. 237), the Arab Bank for Economic Development in Africa (BADEA, see p. 183) and other organizations.

Saudi Arabia's prosperity is based on exploitation of its petroleum reserves; however, the decline in the price of petroleum in the early 1990s, and consequent budgetary deficits, led the Government to consider alternative sources of income. Future priorities for the development of the economy include the continued increase of petroleum production capacity, the expansion of refining capacity, and a policy of industrial expansion, in particular of the petrochemicals sector. The Government's 1995–2000 economic plan envisages the privatization of a number of state interests (including the national airline, Saudia, and the telecommunications and health sectors), the reduction of direct and indirect state subsidies, the development and diversification of the manufacturing industry, and the increase in private-sector activity, particularly in infrastructure projects. In January 1995 the Government doubled the domestic price of petroleum and electricity, which, following an anticipated subsequent decline in domestic consumption and wastage, would allow for an increase in their more lucrative export. The price of telephone calls, water usage and domestic flights was also raised, as was the cost of visas for overseas workers (expected both to augment revenue and contain the number of foreign nationals working in Saudi Arabia). The 1995 budget maintained a high level of defence spending, which accounted for 33.0% of total expenditure in that year.

## Social Welfare

Revenues from the petroleum industry have enabled the Saudi Arabian Government to provide free medicine and medical care for all citizens and foreign residents. The number of hospitals increased from 75 in 1971 to 267 in 1994, when there was a total of more than 36,000 hospital beds, and almost 100,000 medical and para-medical personnel. In early 1991 there were four hospital beds for every 1,000 inhabitants, a ratio similar to that in the USA. In 1994 there were 1,668 health centres. The King Faisal Medical City, on the outskirts of Riyadh, is claimed to be the most technically advanced unit in the world. In 1994 the budget allocation for expenditure on health and social services was estimated at SR11,259m., equivalent to 7.0% of total government expenditure.

## Education

According to estimates by UNESCO, adult illiteracy declined from 97.5% in 1962 to 37.6% (males 26.9%; females 51.9%)

in 1990. Elementary, secondary and higher education are available free of charge, but education is not compulsory. Primary education begins at six years of age and lasts for six years. From the age of 12 there are three years of intermediate education, followed by three years of secondary schooling. Enrolment of children in the primary age-group increased from 32% in 1970 to 64% (boys 68%; girls 59%) in 1992. Over the same period enrolment at intermediate and secondary schools rose from 9% to 36% (boys 39%; girls 32%). The proportion of females enrolled in Saudi Arabian schools increased from 25% of the total number of pupils in 1970 to 46.4% in 1991. In the 1991/92 academic year 143,476 students were enrolled in higher education. Tertiary institutions in that year included 68 university colleges and 17 colleges exclusively for women. Government expenditure on education in 1995 was provisionally estimated at SR26,987m., equivalent to 18.0% of total expenditure.

### Public Holidays

**1995:** 3 March (Id al-Fitr, end of Ramadan), 10 May and subsequent five days (Id al-Adha, Feast of the Sacrifice), 31 May (Muharram, Islamic New Year), 9 June (Ashoura), 9 August (Mouloud, Birth of the Prophet), 20 December (Leilat al-Meiraj, Ascension of the Prophet).

**1996:** 21 February (Id al-Fitr, end of Ramadan), 29 April and subsequent five days (Id al-Adha, Feast of the Sacrifice), 19 May (Muharram, Islamic New Year), 28 May (Ashoura), 28 July (Mouloud, Birth of the Prophet), 8 December (Leilat al-Meiraj, Ascension of the Prophet).

These holidays are dependent on the Islamic lunar calendar and may vary by one or two days from the dates given.

### Weights and Measures

The metric system is in force.

# Statistical Survey

Sources (unless otherwise indicated): Kingdom of Saudi Arabia, *Statistical Yearbook*; Saudi Arabian Monetary Agency, *Annual Report* and *Statistical Summary*.

## Area and Population

### AREA, POPULATION AND DENSITY

| | |
|---|---|
| Area (sq km) | 2,240,000* |
| Population (census results) | |
| 9–14 September 1974 | 7,012,642 |
| 27 September 1992 | 16,929,294† |
| Density (per sq km) at 1992 census | 7.6† |

* 864,869 sq miles.
† Preliminary.

### SAUDI ARABIA-IRAQ NEUTRAL ZONE

The Najdi (Saudi Arabian) frontier with Iraq was defined in the Treaty of Mohammara in May 1922. Later a Neutral Zone of 7,044 sq km was established adjacent to the western tip of the Kuwait frontier. No military or permanent buildings were to be erected in the zone and the nomads of both countries were to have unimpeded access to its pastures and wells. A further agreement concerning the administration of this zone was signed between Iraq and Saudi Arabia in May 1938. In July 1975 Iraq and Saudi Arabia signed an agreement providing for an equal division of the diamond-shaped zone between the two countries, with the border following a straight line through the zone.

### SAUDI ARABIA-KUWAIT NEUTRAL ZONE

A Convention signed at Uqair in December 1922 fixed the Najdi (Saudi Arabian) boundary with Kuwait. The Convention also established a Neutral Zone of 5,770 sq km immediately to the south of Kuwait in which Saudi Arabia and Kuwait held equal rights. The final agreement on this matter was signed in 1963. Since 1966 the Neutral Zone, or Partitioned Zone as it is sometimes known, has been divided between the two countries and each administers its own half, in practice as an integral part of the State. However, the petroleum deposits in the Zone remain undivided and production from the onshore oil concessions in the Zone is shared equally between the two states' concessionaires (Aminoil and Getty).

### PRINCIPAL TOWNS (population at 1974 census)

| | | | |
|---|---|---|---|
| Riyadh (royal capital) | 666,840 | Hufuf | 101,271 |
| Jeddah (administrative capital) | 561,104 | Tabouk | 74,825 |
| | | Buraidah | 69,940 |
| Makkah (Mecca) | 366,801 | Al-Mobarraz | 54,325 |
| At-Ta'if | 204,857 | Khamis-Mushait | 49,581 |
| Al-Madinah (Medina) | 198,186 | Al-Khobar | 48,817 |
| Dammam | 127,844 | Najran | 47,501 |
| | | Ha'il (Hayil) | 40,502 |

### BIRTHS AND DEATHS (UN estimates, annual averages)

| | 1975–80 | 1980–85 | 1985–90 |
|---|---|---|---|
| Birth rate (per 1,000) | 45.9 | 43.2 | 42.1 |
| Death rate (per 1,000) | 10.7 | 9.0 | 7.6 |

**Expectation of life** (UN estimates years at birth, 1985–90): 60.7 (males 59.1; females 62.5).

Source: UN, *World Population Prospects: The 1992 Revision*.

### ECONOMICALLY ACTIVE POPULATION
(ILO estimates, '000 persons at mid-1980)

| | Males | Females | Total |
|---|---|---|---|
| Agriculture, etc. | 1,289 | 43 | 1,333 |
| Industry | 387 | 9 | 395 |
| Services | 903 | 121 | 1,023 |
| **Total labour force** | 2,579 | 172 | 2,751 |

Source: ILO, *Economically Active Population Estimates and Projections, 1950–2025*.

**Mid-1993** (estimates in '000): Agriculture, etc. 1,877; Total 5,126 (Source: FAO, *Production Yearbook*).

SAUDI ARABIA

## Agriculture

**PRINCIPAL CROPS** ('000 metric tons)

|  | 1991 | 1992 | 1993 |
|---|---|---|---|
| Wheat | 3,934 | 4,070 | 3,600† |
| Barley | 394 | 406 | 1,100† |
| Millet | 10 | 11 | 11* |
| Sorghum | 161 | 176 | 180* |
| Potatoes | 78 | 87 | 87* |
| Pulses* | 7 | 7 | 8 |
| Sesame seed | 3 | 4 | 4* |
| Tomatoes* | 470 | 480 | 490 |
| Pumpkins, squash and gourds | 61 | 64 | 65* |
| Cucumbers and gherkins | 97 | 100 | 100* |
| Aubergines (Eggplants) | 75 | 72* | 75* |
| Onions (dry) | 11 | 10 | 10* |
| Carrots | 23 | 24 | 24* |
| Other vegetables* | 935 | 1,063 | 1,141 |
| Watermelons | 413 | 418 | 420* |
| Melons | 144 | 146 | 145* |
| Grapes | 110 | 116 | 120* |
| Dates | 544 | 555 | 560* |
| Citrus fruit | 32 | 34 | 35* |
| Other fruits | 191 | 217 | 218* |

* FAO estimate(s).   † Unofficial figure.

Source: FAO, *Production Yearbook*.

**LIVESTOCK** ('000 head, year ending September)

|  | 1991 | 1992 | 1993* |
|---|---|---|---|
| Cattle | 200 | 204 | 210 |
| Sheep | 6,847 | 7,046 | 7,100 |
| Goats | 3,337 | 3,350 | 3,400 |
| Asses* | 103 | 102 | 100 |
| Camels | 412 | 417 | 420 |

Poultry (million)*: 80 in 1991; 83 in 1992; 86 in 1993.

* FAO estimates.

Source: FAO, *Production Yearbook*.

**LIVESTOCK PRODUCTS** ('000 metric tons)

|  | 1991 | 1992 | 1993 |
|---|---|---|---|
| Beef and veal† | 27 | 28 | 28 |
| Mutton and lamb | 56† | 63* | 63* |
| Goat meat | 23† | 23* | 23* |
| Poultry meat | 285 | 304 | 319† |
| Other meat | 42 | 41 | 42 |
| Cows' milk | 275 | 300 | 303* |
| Sheep's milk* | 40 | 40 | 39 |
| Goats' milk* | 54 | 55 | 56 |
| Poultry eggs | 112.8 | 112.4 | 112.8* |
| Wool: greasy* | 6.1 | 6.0 | 5.9 |
| clean* | 3.3 | 3.3 | 3.3 |
| Cattle hides (fresh)* | 3.9 | 4.0 | 4.0 |
| Sheepskins (fresh)* | 9.6 | 10.7 | 10.7 |
| Goatskins (fresh)* | 4.0 | 4.1 | 4.1 |

* FAO estimate(s).   † Unofficial figure(s).

Source: FAO, *Production Yearbook*.

## Fishing

(metric tons, live weight)

|  | 1990 | 1991 | 1992 |
|---|---|---|---|
| Fishes | 41,189* | 40,152 | 39,877* |
| Crustaceans and molluscs | 5,238* | 3,089 | 4,131* |
| **Total catch** | 46,427 | 43,241 | 44,008 |
| Inland waters | 1,427 | 1,982 | 1,706 |
| Indian Ocean and adjacent seas | 45,000 | 41,259 | 42,302 |

* FAO estimate.

Source: FAO, *Yearbook of Fishery Statistics*.

## Mining

('000 metric tons, unless otherwise indicated)

|  | 1989 | 1990 | 1991 |
|---|---|---|---|
| Crude petroleum* | 252,433 | 320,375 | 404,506 |
| Natural gasoline* | 3,879 | 4,517 | 6,651† |
| Natural gas (petajoules) | 1,042 | 1,288 | 1,452 |
| Gypsum (crude) | 375† | 375 | 375 |

* Including 50% of the total output of the Neutral or Partitioned Zone, shared with Kuwait.
† Estimated production.

Source: UN, *Industrial Statistics Yearbook*.

**1992:** Crude petroleum 416.4 million metric tons; Natural gas 1,342.6 petajoules (Source: UN, *Monthly Bulletin of Statistics*).

## Industry

**SELECTED PRODUCTS** ('000 metric tons, unless otherwise indicated)

|  | 1989 | 1990 | 1991 |
|---|---|---|---|
| Nitrogenous fertilizers (a)* | 428 | 584 | 658 |
| Phosphatic fertilizers (b)* | n.a. | 27 | 200 |
| Jet fuel | 2,345 | 2,450 | 2,560 |
| Motor spirit (petrol) | 9,938 | 10,709 | 10,910 |
| Naphtha | 4,537 | 4,650 | 4,900 |
| Kerosene | 3,853 | 3,900 | 4,100 |
| Distillate fuel oils | 20,149 | 21,714 | 22,500 |
| Residual fuel oils | 22,406 | 24,146 | 25,500 |
| Lubricating oils | 410 | 400 | 510 |
| Petroleum bitumen (asphalt) | 877 | 900 | 920 |
| Liquefied petroleum gas: |  |  |  |
| from natural gas plants | 9,690 | 12,699 | 15,000† |
| from petroleum refineries† | 720 | 890 | 910 |
| Cement† | 9,500 | 10,000 | 12,002 |
| Crude steel‡ | 1,810† | 1,833 | n.a. |
| Electric energy (million kWh)§ | 47,446 | 46,666 | 47,710 |

* Production in terms of (a) nitrogen or (b) phosphoric acid. Data are from the FAO's *Quarterly Bulletin of Statistics*.
† Provisional or estimated figure(s).
‡ Data from the US Bureau of Mines.
§ Including 50% of the total output of the Neutral Zone.

Source: mainly UN, *Industrial Statistics Yearbook*.

**1992** ('000 metric tons): Nitrogenous fertilizers 661.7; Phosphatic fertilizers 172.2; Motor spirit 10,442; Kerosene and jet fuel 7,234; Distillate fuel oils 22,027; Residual fuel oils 25,932 (Sources: FAO, *Quarterly Bulletin of Statistics*; UN, *Monthly Bulletin of Statistics*).

## Finance

**CURRENCY AND EXCHANGE RATES**

**Monetary Units**
100 halalah = 20 qurush = 1 Saudi riyal (SR).

**Sterling and Dollar Equivalents** (31 December 1994)
£1 sterling = 5.859 riyals;
US $1 = 3.745 riyals;
100 Saudi riyals = £17.068 = $26.702.

**Exchange Rate**
Since June 1986 the official mid-point rate has been fixed at US $1 = 3.745 riyals.

# SAUDI ARABIA

*Statistical Survey*

## BUDGET ALLOCATIONS (million riyals)

| | 1992 | 1993 | 1994 |
|---|---|---|---|
| Defence and security | 57,601 | 61,692 | 53,549 |
| Transport and communications | 8,452 | 8,197 | 6,855 |
| Education | 31,855 | 32,121 | 29,226 |
| Municipal services | 5,922 | 6,121 | 5,224 |
| Economic resources | 4,615 | 5,063 | 4,284 |
| Health and social services | 13,534 | 13,626 | 11,259 |
| Infrastructure | 2,090 | 2,078 | 1,580 |
| Local subsidies | 7,107 | 9,167 | 6,970 |
| Residual allocations | 49,824 | 58,885 | 41,053 |
| **Total expenditure** | 181,000 | 196,950 | 160,000 |
| **Total revenue** | 151,000 | 169,150 | 160,000 |

**1995** (estimates, million riyals): Total revenue 135,000; Total expenditure 150,000.

## INTERNATIONAL RESERVES (US $ million in December each year)

| | 1992 | 1993 | 1994 |
|---|---|---|---|
| Gold* | 221 | 221 | 235 |
| IMF special drawing rights | 278 | 553 | 607 |
| Reserve position in IMF | 1,096 | 1,193 | 882 |
| Foreign exchange | 4,561 | 5,682 | 5,888 |
| **Total** | 6,156 | 7,649 | 7,613 |

* Valued at SDR 35 per troy ounce.

Source: IMF, *International Financial Statistics*.

## MONEY SUPPLY (million riyals in December)

| | 1991 | 1992 | 1993 |
|---|---|---|---|
| Currency outside banks | 44,620.1 | 43,769.6 | 42,622.8 |
| Demand deposits at commercial banks | 75,850.3 | 84,160.0 | 82,268.3 |
| **Total money** | 120,470.5 | 127,929.6 | 124,891.1 |

## COST OF LIVING (consumer price index for all cities; base: 1988 = 100)

| | 1991 | 1992 | 1993 |
|---|---|---|---|
| Food, drink and tobacco | 111.9 | 116.0 | 117.5 |
| Housing | 102.1 | 103.4 | 108.5 |
| Textiles and clothing | 98.0 | 99.2 | 98.3 |
| House furnishing | 101.4 | 102.2 | 101.1 |
| Medical care | 100.2 | 101.9 | 101.9 |
| Transport and communications | 126.8 | 111.6 | 107.8 |
| Entertainment and education | 102.8 | 105.0 | 105.1 |
| **All items** (incl. others) | 107.8 | 107.4 | 108.3 |

## NATIONAL ACCOUNTS (million riyals at current prices)

### Expenditure on the Gross Domestic Product

| | 1990 | 1991 | 1992* |
|---|---|---|---|
| Government final consumption expenditure | 120,126 | 165,000 | 148,965 |
| Private final consumption expenditure | 155,874 | 168,751 | 183,919 |
| Increase in stocks | 2,751 | 7,340 | 8,945 |
| Gross fixed capital formation | 73,803 | 86,510 | 98,975 |
| **Total domestic expenditure** | 352,554 | 427,601 | 440,804 |
| Exports of goods and services | 181,132 | 197,278 | 196,098 |
| *Less* Imports of goods and services | 141,693 | 182,842 | 181,770 |
| **GDP in purchasers' values** | 391,993 | 442,037 | 455,132 |
| **GDP at constant 1970 prices** | 56,243 | 61,700 | 63,484 |

* Estimates.

### Gross Domestic Product by Economic Activity

| | 1990* | 1991† | 1992† |
|---|---|---|---|
| Agriculture, forestry and fishing | 25,143 | 26,902 | 28,929 |
| Mining and quarrying: | | | |
|   Crude petroleum and natural gas | 139,277 | 149,575 | 157,024 |
|   Other | 1,812 | 1,866 | 1,936 |
| Manufacturing: | | | |
|   Petroleum refining | 9,922 | 10,655 | 10,847 |
|   Other | 17,404 | 19,144 | 20,867 |
| Electricity, gas and water | 780 | 811 | 701 |
| Construction | 34,099 | 36,486 | 39,222 |
| Trade, restaurants and hotels | 27,382 | 29,751 | 31,387 |
| Transport, storage and communications | 24,738 | 26,953 | 28,840 |
| Finance, insurance, real estate and business services: | | | |
|   Ownership of dwellings | 6,314 | 6,692 | 6,893 |
|   Other | 17,848 | 18,331 | 18,881 |
| Government services | 72,616 | 90,240 | 93,124 |
| Other community, social and personal services | 11,985 | 12,185 | 12,429 |
| **Sub-total** | 389,320 | 429,591 | 451,080 |
| Import duties | 7,000 | 7,000 | 7,500 |
| *Less* Imputed bank service charge | 4,326 | 4,672 | 5,046 |
| **GDP in purchasers' values** | 391,994 | 431,919 | 453,534 |

* Revised estimates. † Preliminary estimates.

Source: Central Department of Statistics, Ministry of Finance and National Economy.

## BALANCE OF PAYMENTS (US $ million)

| | 1991 | 1992 | 1993 |
|---|---|---|---|
| Merchandise exports f.o.b. | 47,623 | 47,049 | 44,918 |
| Merchandise imports f.o.b. | −25,968 | −30,248 | −25,897 |
| **Trade balance** | 21,656 | 16,801 | 19,020 |
| Exports of services | 3,028 | 3,477 | 3,526 |
| Imports of services | −38,804 | −31,782 | −24,311 |
| Other income received | 8,700 | 7,378 | 6,154 |
| Other income paid | −1,933 | −1,944 | −1,951 |
| Private unrequited transfers (net) | −13,746 | −13,397 | −15,717 |
| Official unrequited transfers (net) | −6,489 | −1,501 | −940 |
| **Current balance** | −27,589 | −20,967 | −14,218 |
| Direct investment (net) | 160 | −79 | −79 |
| Portfolio investment (net) | 470 | −3,646 | 8,448 |
| Other capital (net) | 27,008 | 19,028 | 7,345 |
| **Overall balance** | 49 | −5,664 | 1,496 |

Source: IMF, *International Financial Statistics*.

# External Trade

**PRINCIPAL COMMODITIES** (million riyals)

| Imports c.i.f. | 1990 | 1991 | 1992 |
|---|---|---|---|
| Live animals and animal products | 4,838 | 5,613 | 3,770 |
| Vegetable products | 3,880 | 3,653 | 6,484 |
| Prepared foodstuffs, beverages, spirits, vinegar and tobacco | 3,639 | 4,446 | 2,419 |
| Products of chemical and allied industries | 7,232 | 8,065 | 8,397 |
| Artificial resins, plastic materials, rubber, etc. | 3,518 | 4,213 | 3,967 |
| Textiles and textile articles | 7,947 | 9,169 | 9,838 |
| Pearls, precious stones, etc. | 6,213 | 5,531 | 5,910 |
| Base metals and articles of base metal | 7,830 | 9,931 | 11,179 |
| Machinery (incl. electric) and parts | 14,777 | 21,115 | 26,285 |
| Transport equipment and parts thereof | 18,471 | 22,868 | 29,910 |
| Scientific instruments, photographic equipment, watches, musical instruments, recorders, etc. | 2,836 | 3,072 | 3,422 |
| **Total** (incl. others) | 90,282 | 108,924 | 124,537 |

| Exports (excl. re-exports) | 1988 | 1989 | 1990* |
|---|---|---|---|
| Mineral products | 75,987 | 90,840 | 150,873 |
| Crude petroleum | 55,055 | 70,624 | 123,281 |
| Refined petroleum products | 20,613 | 19,612 | 27,002 |
| Products of chemical and allied industries | 6,333 | 5,616 | 5,720 |
| Artificial resins, plastic materials, rubber, etc. | 3,813 | 4,160 | 3,819 |
| **Total** (incl. others) | 88,896 | 103,892 | 166,339 |

* Including re-exports, totalling 2,414 million riyals.

**1991** (million riyals): Crude petroleum 139,830; Refined petroleum products 23,660; Total (incl. others) 178,974 (of which re-exports 2,297).
**1992** (preliminary estimates, million riyals): Crude petroleum 139,075; Refined petroleum products 23,316; Total (incl. others) 176,473 (of which re-exports 1,545).

**PRINCIPAL TRADING PARTNERS** (million riyals)

| Imports c.i.f. | 1990 | 1991 | 1992 |
|---|---|---|---|
| Australia | 1,081 | 1,047 | 761 |
| Belgium | 1,558 | 2,044 | 2,285 |
| Brazil | 943 | 1,434 | 1,308 |
| China, People's Republic | 1,668 | 2,345 | 2,645 |
| France | 3,573 | 4,366 | 5,997 |
| Germany | 6,645 | 8,520 | 9,247 |
| India | 1,027 | 1,097 | 1,538 |
| Indonesia | 793 | 1,154 | 1,310 |
| Italy | 4,180 | 5,028 | 6,176 |
| Japan | 13,815 | 14,915 | 17,590 |
| Korea, Republic | 2,960 | 3,220 | 3,329 |
| Netherlands | 2,036 | 2,101 | 1,974 |
| Spain | 984 | 1,385 | 1,448 |
| Sweden | 1,169 | 1,433 | 1,556 |
| Switzerland | 5,929 | 5,282 | 5,694 |
| Taiwan | 1,969 | 2,128 | 2,093 |
| Thailand | 1,021 | 1,182 | 1,223 |
| Turkey | 1,116 | 1,316 | 1,344 |
| United Kingdom | 10,182 | 12,267 | 13,410 |
| USA | 15,066 | 22,003 | 28,064 |
| **Total** (incl. others) | 90,282 | 108,924 | 124,537 |

| Exports (incl. re-exports)* | 1989 | 1990 | 1991 |
|---|---|---|---|
| Australia | 1,151 | 1,166 | 1,677 |
| Bahrain | 4,777 | 6,564 | 5,836 |
| Brazil | 2,452 | 5,482 | 4,933 |
| Egypt | 528 | 2,423 | 3,048 |
| France | 5,549 | 7,917 | 8,203 |
| India | 2,571 | 4,115 | 4,103 |
| Indonesia | 439 | 621 | 2,301 |
| Italy | 4,305 | 5,978 | 7,675 |
| Japan | 18,545 | 31,559 | 28,689 |
| Korea, Republic | 2,100 | 6,254 | 9,938 |
| Kuwait | 1,096 | 746 | 2,501 |
| Netherlands | 4,746 | 7,857 | 10,802 |
| Pakistan | 1,157 | 1,682 | 1,774 |
| Philippines | 660 | 2,215 | 2,016 |
| Singapore | 6,352 | 8,917 | 9,094 |
| Spain | 1,827 | 2,181 | 3,563 |
| Taiwan | 4,069 | 5,634 | 4,968 |
| Turkey | 787 | 2,838 | 5,235 |
| United Arab Emirates | 1,868 | 3,010 | 3,193 |
| United Kingdom | 1,620 | 2,664 | 3,525 |
| USA | 27,437 | 39,890 | 40,969 |
| **Total** (incl. others) | 106,241 | 166,339 | 178,974 |

* Figures for individual countries exclude bunker fuel, totalling (in million riyals): 271 in 1989; 449 in 1990; 490 in 1991.

# Transport

**RAILWAYS** (traffic)

| | 1990 | 1991 | 1992 |
|---|---|---|---|
| Passenger journeys ('000) | 421.6 | 414.3 | 416.7 |
| Freight carried ('000 metric tons) | n.a. | 1,845.4 | 2,093.3 |

**ROAD TRAFFIC** (motor vehicles in use at 31 December)

| | 1989 | 1990 | 1991 |
|---|---|---|---|
| Passenger cars | 2,550,465 | 2,664,028 | 2,762,132 |
| Buses and coaches | 50,856 | 52,136 | 54,089 |
| Goods vehicles | 2,153,297 | 2,220,658 | 2,286,541 |
| **Total** | 4,754,618 | 4,936,822 | 5,103,205 |

Source: IRF, *World Road Statistics*.

**SHIPPING**

**Merchant Fleet**
(displacement, '000 grt, vessels registered at 30 June)

| | 1990 | 1991 | 1992 |
|---|---|---|---|
| Oil tankers | 928 | 561 | 265 |
| **Total** (incl. others) | 1,683 | 1,321 | 1,016 |

Source: UN, *Statistical Yearbook*.

**International Sea-borne Freight Traffic** ('000 metric tons*)

| | 1988 | 1989 | 1990 |
|---|---|---|---|
| Goods loaded | 161,666 | 165,989 | 214,070 |
| Goods unloaded | 42,546 | 42,470 | 46,437 |

* Including Saudi Arabia's share of traffic in the Neutral or Partitioned Zone.

Source: UN, *Monthly Bulletin of Statistics*.

SAUDI ARABIA

**CIVIL AVIATION** (traffic on scheduled services)

|  | 1990 | 1991 | 1992 |
|---|---|---|---|
| Kilometres flown ('000) | 103,000 | 87,000 | 106,000 |
| Passengers carried ('000) | 10,311 | 9,409 | 11,155 |
| Passenger-kilometres (million) | 16,068 | 14,881 | 17,563 |
| Total ton-km ('000) | 2,089 | 1,848 | 2,283 |

Source: UN, *Statistical Yearbook*.

## Tourism

**PILGRIMS TO MECCA FROM ABROAD***

| Country of Origin | 1984/85 | 1985/86 | 1986/87 |
|---|---|---|---|
| Egypt | 130,872 | 98,606 | 97,216 |
| India | 33,691 | 39,344 | 40,854 |
| Indonesia | 41,965 | 59,172 | 57,519 |
| Iran | 152,227 | 152,149 | 157,395 |
| Iraq | 33,856 | 14,551 | 29,522 |
| Pakistan | 87,889 | 92,305 | 93,013 |
| Turkey | 41,693 | 54,624 | 96,711 |
| Yemen Arab Republic | 41,121 | 43,512 | 61,416 |
| **Total** (incl. others) | 851,761 | 856,718 | 960,386 |

**Total pilgrims:** 762,755 in 1987/88; 774,560 in 1988/89.

* Figures relate to Islamic lunar years. The equivalent dates in the Gregorian calendar are: 26 September 1984 to 14 September 1985; 15 September 1985 to 4 September 1986; 5 September 1986 to 24 August 1987; 25 August 1987 to 12 August 1988; 13 August 1988 to 1 August 1989.

**1993/94:** more than 2m. pilgrims.

## Communications Media

|  | 1990 | 1991 | 1992 |
|---|---|---|---|
| Radio receivers ('000 in use) | 4,500 | 4,670 | 4,840 |
| Television receivers ('000 in use) | 4,000 | 4,100 | 4,260 |
| Telephones ('000 main lines in use) | 1,234 | 1,296 | n.a. |
| Daily newspapers | 12 | n.a. | 13* |
| Non-daily newspapers | 6 | n.a. | n.a. |

* Combined average circulation 729,000 copies.

Sources: UNESCO, *Statistical Yearbook*; UN, *Statistical Yearbook*.

## Education

(1992)

|  | Institutions | Teachers | Students |
|---|---|---|---|
| Pre-primary | 806 | 5,098 | 81,464 |
| Primary | 10,228 | 141,930 | 2,025,948 |
| Secondary: |  |  |  |
|   General* | n.a. | 89,171 | 1,033,521 |
|   Teacher training | n.a. | 911 | 13,884 |
|   Vocational | n.a. | 2,893 | 25,956 |
| Higher: |  |  |  |
|   University and equivalent† | n.a. | 10,116 | 135,780 |
|   Other† | n.a. | 1,566 | 27,908 |

* Including education at the intermediate level.
† Figures refer to 1991.

Source: UNESCO, *Statistical Yearbook*.

# Directory

## The Constitution

An eight-man committee under the Chairmanship of Prince Nayef, Minister of the Interior, was formed in March 1980 to prepare a 200-article basic 'system of rule', based entirely on Islamic principles. Plans, for which King Fahd pledged his support, were also to be made for the establishment of a consultative council. In March 1992 royal decrees were issued that provided for the introduction of a basic law of government and for the creation of a Consultative Council (Majlis ash-Shoura—comprising 60 members and a chairman), to be appointed by the King for a term of four years.

Meanwhile Saudi Arabia is an absolute monarchy, with no legislature or political parties. The King rules in accordance with the *Shari'a*, the sacred law of Islam. He appoints and leads the Council of Ministers, which serves as the instrument of royal authority in both legislative and executive matters. The term of office of the Council of Ministers, and that of each of its members, is fixed at four years. The King is also assisted by advisory councils, nominated or approved by him.

The organs of local government are the General Municipal Councils and the tribal and village councils. A General Municipal Council is established in the towns of Mecca, Medina and Jeddah. Its members are proposed by the inhabitants and must be approved by the King. Functioning concurrently with each General Municipal Council is a General Administration Committee, which investigates ways and means of executing resolutions passed by the Council. Every village and tribe has a council composed of the sheikh, who presides, his legal advisers and two other prominent personages. These councils have power to enforce regulations. A system of provincial government was announced in late 1993 by royal decree. The decree defined the nature of government for 13 newly-created regions, as well as the rights and responsibilities of their governors, and appointed councils of prominent citizens for each region to monitor development and advise the government. Each council is to meet four times a year under the chairmanship of a governor, who will be an emir with ministerial rank. A royal decree, issued in April 1994, further divided the 13 regions into 103 governorates.

## The Government

### HEAD OF STATE

King FAHD IBN ABD AL-AZIZ AS-SA'UD (acceded to the throne 13 June 1982).

**Crown Prince:** ABDULLAH IBN ABD AL-AZIZ AS-SA'UD.

### COUNCIL OF MINISTERS
(June 1995)

**Prime Minister:** King FAHD IBN ABD AL-AZIZ AS-SA'UD.

**First Deputy Prime Minister and Commander of the National Guard:** Crown Prince ABDULLAH IBN ABD AL-AZIZ AS-SA'UD.

**Second Deputy Prime Minister and Minister of Defence and Civil Aviation:** Prince SULTAN IBN ABD AL-AZIZ AS-SA'UD.

**Deputy Ministers of Defence and Civil Aviation (with Ministerial rank):** Gen. OTHMAN AL-HUMAID, Prince ABD AR-RAHMAN IBN ABD AL-AZIZ.

**Minister of Public Works and Housing:** Prince MUTAIB IBN ABD AL-AZIZ.

**Minister of the Interior:** Prince NAYEF IBN ABD AL-AZIZ AS-SA'UD.

**Minister of Foreign Affairs:** Prince SA'UD AL-FAISAL.

**Minister of Petroleum and Mineral Resources:** Sheikh HISHAM MOHI AD-DIN NAZER.

**Minister of Labour and Social Affairs:** MUHAMMAD AL-ALI AL-FAYEZ.

**Minister of Education and Acting Minister of Agriculture and Water:** Dr ABD AL-AZIZ AL-ABDULLAH AL-KHUWAITER.

**Minister of Higher Education:** KHALID IBN MUHAMMAD AL-ANGARI.

**Minister of Communications:** Sheikh HUSSEIN IBRAHIM AL-MANSOURI.

**Minister of Finance and National Economy:** Sheikh MUHAMMAD ALI ABA AL-KHAIL.

# SAUDI ARABIA

**Minister of Planning:** ABD AL-WAHAB AS-SALIM AL-ATTAR.
**Minister of Information:** ALI HASSAN ASH-SHAER.
**Minister of Industry and Electricity:** ABD AL-AZIZ AZ-ZAMIL.
**Minister of Commerce:** Dr SULAIMAN ABD AL-AZIZ AS-SULAIM.
**Minister of Justice:** Dr ABDULLAH IBN MUHAMMAD ASH-SHEIKH.
**Minister of Pilgrimage (Hajj) Affairs:** MAHMOUD IBN MUHAMMAD SAFAR.
**Minister of Municipal and Rural Affairs:** MUHAMMAD IBN ABD AL-AZIZ IBN ABDULLAH IBN HASSAN ASH-SHEIKH.
**Minister of Awqaf (Religious Endowments), Dawa, Mosques and Guidance Affairs:** ABDULLAH IBN ABD AL-MOHSEN AT-TURKI.
**Minister of Health:** FAISAL IBN ABD AL-AZIZ AL-HEJAILAN.
**Minister of Posts, Telegraphs and Telecommunications:** Dr ALAWI DARWISH KAYYAL.
**Ministers of State:** Sheikh MUHAMMAD IBRAHIM MASOUD, OMAR ABD AL-QADER FAQIH, ABD AL-WAHAB ABD AL-WASI, Sheikh ABD AL-AZIZ IBN BAZ (General Mufti).

## MINISTRIES

Most ministries have regional offices in Jeddah.

**Council of Ministers:** Murabba, Riyadh 11121; tel. (1) 488-2444; telex 6655766.
**Ministry of Agriculture and Water:** Airport Rd, Riyadh 11195; tel. (1) 401-6666; telex 40690; fax (1) 404-4592.
**Ministry of Commerce:** POB 1774, Airport Rd, Riyadh 11162; tel. (1) 401-2222; telex 401057; fax (1) 403-8421.
**Ministry of Communications:** Airport Rd, Riyadh 11178; tel. (1) 404-3000; telex 401616; fax (1) 403-5743.
**Ministry of Defence and Civil Aviation:** POB 26731, Airport Rd, Riyadh 11496; tel. (1) 478-9000; telex 4055500.
**Ministry of Education:** POB 3734, Airport Rd, Riyadh 11481; tel. (1) 411-5777; telex 402650; fax (1) 411-2051.
**Ministry of Finance and National Economy:** Airport Rd, Riyadh 11177; tel. (1) 405-0000; telex 401021.
**Ministry of Foreign Affairs:** Nasseriya St, Riyadh 11124; tel. (1) 405-5000; telex 405000.
**Ministry of Health:** Airport Rd, Riyadh 11176; tel. (1) 401-5555; telex 404020; fax (1) 402-9876.
**Ministry of Higher Education:** King Faisal Hospital St, Riyadh 11153; tel. (1) 441-9849; telex 401481; fax (1) 441-9004.
**Ministry of Industry and Electricity:** POB 5729, Omar bin al-Khatab St, Riyadh 11432; tel. (1) 477-666; telex 401154.
**Ministry of Information:** POB 570, Nasseriya St, Riyadh 11161; tel. (1) 406-8888; telex 401461; fax (1) 404-4192.
**Ministry of the Interior:** POB 2833, Airport Rd, Riyadh 11134; tel. (1) 401-1111; telex 404416.
**Ministry of Justice:** Riyadh 11137; tel. (1) 405-7777; telex 405-9443.
**Ministry of Labour and Social Affairs:** Omar bin al-Khatab St, Riyadh 11157; tel. (1) 477-8888; telex 401043; fax (1) 478-9175.
**Ministry of Municipal and Rural Affairs:** Nasseriya St, Riyadh 11136; tel. (1) 441-8888; telex 404018; fax (1) 441-7368.
**Ministry of Petroleum and Mineral Resources:** POB 247, Ma'ather St, Riyadh 11191; tel. (1) 478-7777; telex 400997; fax (1) 478-0552.
**Ministry of Pilgrimage (Hajj) Affairs:** Omar bin al-Khatab St, Riyadh 11183; tel. (1) 404-3003; telex 400189.
**Ministry of Planning:** POB 358, University St, Riyadh 11182; tel. (1) 401-3333; telex 402851; fax (1) 404-9300.
**Ministry of Posts, Telegraphs and Telecommunications:** Sharia al-Ma'azer, Intercontinental Rd, Riyadh 11112; tel. (1) 463-4444; telex 400200.
**Ministry of Public Works and Housing:** POB 56095, Ma'ather St, Riyadh 11554; tel. (1) 407-3618; telex 400415.

## MAJLIS ASH-SHOURA
(Consultative Council)

In March 1992 King Fahd issued a decree to establish a Consultative Council of 60 members, whose powers include the right to summon and question ministers. The composition of the Council was announced by King Fahd in August 1993, and it was officially inaugurated in December of that year. Each member is to serve for four years.

**Chairman:** Sheikh MUHAMMAD IBN IBRAHIM AL-JUBAIR.

# Diplomatic Representation

## EMBASSIES IN SAUDI ARABIA

**Afghanistan:** Tariq al-Madina, Kilo No. 3, Jeddah; tel. (2) 53142.
**Algeria:** POB 94388, Riyadh 11693; tel. (1) 488-7616; telex 402828; Ambassador: ABD AL-KARIM GHARIB.
**Argentina:** POB 94369, Riyadh 11693; tel. (1) 465-2600; telex 405988; fax (1) 465-1632; Ambassador: JULIO URIBURU FRENCH.
**Australia:** POB 94400, Riyadh 11693; tel. (1) 488-7788; fax (1) 488-7973; Ambassador: WARWICK WEEMAES.
**Austria:** POB 94373, Riyadh 11693; tel. (1) 477-7445; telex 406333; fax (1) 476-6791; Ambassador: Dr MARIUS CALLIGARIS.
**Bahrain:** POB 94371, Riyadh 11693; tel. (1) 488-0044; telex 407055; Ambassador: ISSA MUHAMMAD AL-KHALIFA.
**Bangladesh:** POB 94395, Riyadh 11693; tel. (1) 465-5300; telex 406133; Ambassador: Maj.-Gen. QUAZI GOLAM DASTGIR.
**Belgium:** POB 94396, Riyadh 11693; tel. (1) 488-2888; telex 406344; fax (1) 488-2033; Ambassador: PIETER BERGHS.
**Brazil:** POB 94348, Riyadh 11693; tel. (1) 488-0018; telex 406711; fax (1) 488-1073; Ambassador: SÉRGIO M. THOMPSON-FLORES.
**Burkina Faso:** POB 94300, Riyadh 11693; tel. (1) 454-6168; telex 403844; Ambassador: HAROUNA KOUFLA.
**Burundi:** POB 94355, Riyadh 11693; tel. (1) 464-1155; telex 406477; fax (1) 465-9997; Ambassador: JACQUES HAKIZIMANA.
**Cameroon:** POB 94336, Riyadh 11693; tel. (1) 488-0022; telex 408866; fax (1) 488-1463; Ambassador: MOHAMADOU LABARANG.
**Canada:** POB 94321, Riyadh 11693; tel. (1) 488-2288; telex 404893; fax (1) 488-0137; Ambassador: ALLAN N. LEAVER.
**Chad:** POB 94374, Riyadh 11693; tel. (1) 465-7702; telex 406366; Ambassador: al-Hajji DJIME TOUGOU.
**China, People's Republic:** Riyadh; Ambassador: ZHENG DAYONG.
**Denmark:** POB 94398, Riyadh 11693; tel. (1) 488-0101; telex 404672; fax (1) 488-1366; Ambassador: POUL HOINESS.
**Djibouti:** POB 94340, Riyadh 11693; tel. (1) 454-3182; telex 406544; Ambassador: IDRISS AHMAD CHIRWA.
**Egypt:** POB 94333, Riyadh 11693; tel. (1) 465-2800; Ambassador: FATHY AL-SHAZLY.
**Ethiopia:** POB 94341, Riyadh 11693; tel. (1) 479-0904; telex 406633; fax (1) 478-2461; Ambassador: MOGUES HABTEMARIAM.
**Finland:** POB 94363, Riyadh 11693; tel. (1) 488-1515; fax (1) 488-2520; Ambassador: ANTERO VIERTIÖ.
**France:** POB 94367, Riyadh 11693; tel. (1) 488-1255; telex 406967; fax (1) 488-2882; Ambassador: HUBERT FORQUENOT DE LA FORTELLE.
**Gabon:** POB 94325, Riyadh 11693; tel. (1) 456-3323; telex 406766; fax (1) 456-4068; Ambassador: MOHAMED MAURICE LEFLEM.
**Gambia:** POB 94322, Riyadh 11693; tel. (1) 454-9156; telex 406767; Ambassador: BABA DRAMMAH.
**Germany:** POB 94001, Riyadh 11693; tel. 488-0700; fax (1) 488-0660; telex 402297; Ambassador: Dr RUDOLF RAPKE.
**Ghana:** POB 94339, Riyadh 11693; tel. and fax (1) 454-5122; telex 406599; Ambassador: ABUKARI SUMANI.
**Greece:** POB 94375, Riyadh 11693; tel. (1) 465-5026; telex 406322; Ambassador: PAUL APOSTOLIDES.
**Guinea:** POB 94326, Riyadh 11693; tel. (1) 231-0631; telex 404944; Ambassador: el-Hadj MAMADOU S. SYLLA.
**India:** POB 94387, Riyadh 11693; tel. (1) 477-7006; telex 406077; fax (1) 477-8627; Ambassador: ISHRAT AZIZ.
**Indonesia:** POB 94343, Riyadh 11693; tel. (1) 488-9127; telex 406577; Ambassador: H. A. KUNAEFI.
**Iran:** POB 94394, Riyadh 11693; tel. (1) 482-6111; telex 406066; Ambassador: ABD AL-LATIF AL-MEIMANI.
**Ireland:** POB 94349, Riyadh 11693; tel. (1) 488-2300; telex 406877; fax (1) 488-0927; Ambassador: MICHAEL COLLINS.
**Italy:** POB 94389, Riyadh 11693; tel. (1) 488-1212; telex 406188; fax 488-0590; Ambassador: MARIO SCIALOJA.
**Japan:** POB 4095, Riyadh 11491; tel. (1) 488-1100; telex 405866; fax (1) 488-0189; Ambassador: MINOURO TAMBA.
**Jordan:** POB 7455, Riyadh 11693; tel. (1) 454-3192; telex 406955; Ambassador: HANI KHALIFAH.
**Kenya:** POB 94358, Riyadh 11693; tel. (1) 488-2484; telex 406055; Ambassador: ALI MUHAMMAD ABDI.
**Korea, Republic:** POB 94399, Riyadh 11693; tel. (1) 488-2211; telex 406922; fax (1) 488-1317; Ambassador: JOONG-BAE NA.
**Kuwait:** POB 2166, Riyadh 11451; tel. (1) 488-3401; telex 401301; Ambassador: ABD AR-RAHMAN AHMAD AL-BAKR.

**Lebanon:** POB 94350, Riyadh 11693; tel. (1) 465-1000; telex 406533; fax (1) 462-6774; Ambassador: ZOUHEIR HAMDAN.
**Libya:** POB 94365, Riyadh 11693; tel. (1) 454-4511; telex 406399; Ambassador: MILOUD RAMADAN ERIBI.
**Malaysia:** POB 94335, Riyadh 11693; tel. (1) 488-7100; telex 406822; Ambassador: Datuk Haji MOKHTAR BIN Haji AHMAD.
**Mali:** POB 94331, Riyadh 11693; tel. (1) 465-8900; telex 406733; Ambassador: SEICKO SOUMANO.
**Mauritania:** POB 94354, Riyadh 11693; tel. (1) 465-6313; telex 406466; Ambassador: BABA OULD MUHAMMAD ABDULLAH.
**Mexico:** POB 94391, Riyadh 11693; tel. (1) 476-1200; fax (1) 478-1900; Ambassador: RICARDO VILLANUEVA.
**Morocco:** POB 94392, Riyadh 11693; tel.(1) 465-4900; telex 406155; Ambassador: HASSAN ABOUYOUB.
**Nepal:** POB 94384, Riyadh 11693; tel. (1) 403-6433; telex 406288; fax (1) 403-6488; Ambassador: NARAYAN S. THAPA.
**Netherlands:** POB 94307, Riyadh 11693; tel. (1) 488-0011; telex 403820; fax (1) 488-0544; Ambassador: G. MEIHUIZEN.
**New Zealand:** POB 94397, Riyadh 11693; tel. (1) 488-7988; telex 405878; fax (1) 488-7912; Ambassador: GRAEME AMMUNDSEN.
**Niger:** POB 94334, Riyadh 11693; tel. (1) 464-3116; telex 406722; Ambassador: ABDOULAYE MOUMOUNI DJERNAKOYE.
**Nigeria:** POB 94386, Riyadh 11693; tel. (1) 482-3024; telex 406177; fax (1) 482-4134; Ambassador: Prof. SHEHU AHMAD S. GALADANCI.
**Norway:** POB 94380, Riyadh 11693; tel. (1) 488-1904; telex 406311; fax (1) 488-0854; Ambassador: PAUL MOE.
**Oman:** POB 94381, Riyadh 11693; tel. (1) 465-0010; telex 206277; Ambassador: HAMAD H. AL-MO'AMARY.
**Pakistan:** POB 6891, Riyadh 11452; tel. (1) 476-7266; telex 406500; Ambassador: WALIULLA KHAN KHAISHGI.
**Philippines:** POB 94366, Riyadh 11693; tel. (1) 454-0777; telex 406377; Ambassador: Dr MAUYAG MUHAMMAD TAMANO.
**Portugal:** POB 94328, Riyadh 11693; tel. (1) 464-4853; telex 404477; Ambassador: JOSÉ MANUEL WADDINGTON MATOS PARREIRA.
**Qatar:** POB 94353, Riyadh 11461; tel. (1) 482-5544; telex 405755; Ambassador: M. ALI AL-ANSARI.
**Russia:** Riyadh; fax (1) 481-1890; Ambassador: GENNADY TARASSOV.
**Rwanda:** POB 94383, Riyadh 11693; tel. (1) 454-0808; telex 406199; fax (1) 456-1769; Ambassador: SIMON INSONERE.
**Senegal:** POB 94352, Riyadh 11693; tel. (1) 454-2144; telex 406565; Ambassador: Alhaji AMADOU THIAM.
**Sierra Leone:** POB 94329, Riyadh 11693; tel. (1) 463-3149; telex 406744; fax (1) 464-3892; Ambassador: UMARU WURIE.
**Singapore:** POB 94378, Riyadh 11693; tel. (1) 465-7007; telex 406211; Chargé d'affaires a.i.: RAM CHANDRA NAIR.
**Somalia:** POB 94372, Riyadh 11693; tel. (1) 454-0111; Ambassador: ABD AR-RAHMAN A. HUSSEIN.
**Spain:** POB 94347, Riyadh 11693; tel. (1) 488-0606; telex 406788; Ambassador: JOSÉ LUIS XIFRA DE OCERIN.
**Sri Lanka:** POB 94360, Riyadh 11693; tel. (1) 463-4200; telex 405688; fax (1) 465-0897; Ambassador: ABD AL-CADER MARKAR.
**Sudan:** POB 94337, Riyadh 11693; tel. (1) 488-7728; Ambassador: OMER YOUSIF BIRIDO.
**Sweden:** POB 94382, Riyadh 11693; tel. (1) 488-3100; telex 406266; fax (1) 488-0604; Ambassador: STEEN HOWÜ-CHRISTENSEN.
**Switzerland:** POB 9265, Riyadh 11413; tel. (1) 488-1291; telex 406055; Ambassador: MAURICE JEAN RENAUD.
**Syria:** POB 94323, Riyadh 11693; tel. (1) 465-3800; telex 406677; Ambassador: MUHAMMAD KHALID AT-TALL.
**Tanzania:** POB 94320, Riyadh 11693; tel. 454-2839; telex 406811; fax (1) 454-9660; Ambassador: Prof. A. A. SHAREEF.
**Thailand:** POB 94359, Riyadh 11693; tel. (1) 482-6002; telex 406433; Ambassador: THONGTERM KOMOLSUK.
**Tunisia:** POB 94368, Riyadh 11693; tel. (1) 465-4585; telex 406464; Ambassador: KACEM BOUSNINA.
**Turkey:** POB 94390, Riyadh 11693; tel. (1) 488-0101; telex 407633; Ambassador: TÜRKEKUL KURTTEKIN.
**Uganda:** POB 94344, Riyadh 11693; tel. (1) 454-4910; telex 406588; fax (1) 454-9260; Ambassador: al-Haj Prof. BADRU DDUNGU KATEREGGA.
**United Arab Emirates:** POB 94385, Riyadh 11693; tel. (1) 482-6803; telex 406222; Ambassador: ISSA K. AL-HURAIMIL.
**United Kingdom:** POB 94351, Riyadh 11693; tel. (1) 488-0077; telex 406488; fax (1) 488-2373; Ambassador: DAVID ALWYN GORE-BOOTH.
**USA:** POB 94309, Riyadh 11693; tel. (1) 488-3800; telex 406866; fax (1) 488-3278; Ambasdsador: RAYMOND MABUS.
**Uruguay:** POB 94346, Riyadh 11693; tel. (1) 462-0739; telex 406611; fax (1) 462-0638; Ambassador: CARLOS A. CLULOW.
**Venezuela:** POB 94364, Riyadh 11693; tel. (1) 476-7867; telex 405599; fax (1) 476-8200; Ambassador: NORMAN PINO.
**Yemen:** POB 94356, Riyadh 11693; tel. (1) 488-1757; Ambassador: Dr MUHAMMAD AHMAD AL-KABAB.

## Judicial System

Judges are independent and governed by the rules of Islamic *Shari'a*. The following courts operate:

**Supreme Council of Justice:** consists of 11 members and supervises work of the courts; reviews legal questions referred to it by the Minister of Justice and expresses opinions on judicial questions; reviews sentences of death, cutting and stoning; Chair. Sheikh SALIH AL-LIHAYDAN.

**Court of Cassation:** consists of Chief Justice and an adequate number of judges; includes department for penal suits, department for personal status and department for other suits.

**General (Public) Courts:** consist of one or more judges; sentences are issued by a single judge, with the exception of death, stoning and cutting, which require the decision of three judges.

**Summary Courts:** consist of one or more judges; sentences are issued by a single judge.

**Specialized Courts:** Article 26 of the judicial system stipulates that the setting up of specialized courts is permissible by Royal Decree on a proposal from the Supreme Council of Justice.

## Religion

### ISLAM

Arabia is the centre of the Islamic faith, and Saudi Arabia includes the holy cities of Mecca and Medina. Except in the Eastern Province, where a large number of people follow Shi'a rites, the majority of the population are Sunni Muslims, and most of the indigenous inhabitants belong to the strictly orthodox Wahhabi sect. The Wahhabis originated in the 18th century but first became unified and influential under Abd al-Aziz (Ibn Sa'ud), who became the first King of Saudi Arabia. They are now the keepers of the holy places and control the pilgrimage to Mecca. In 1986 King Fahd adopted the title of Custodian of the Two Holy Mosques. The country's most senior Islamic authority is the Council of Ulema.

**Mecca:** Birthplace of the Prophet Muhammad, seat of the Great Mosque and Shrine of Ka'ba, visited by 993,000 Muslims in the Islamic year 1413 (1992/93).

**Medina:** Burial place of Muhammad, second sacred city of Islam.

### CHRISTIANITY

#### The Roman Catholic Church

**Apostolic Vicariate of Arabia:** POB 54, Abu Dhabi, United Arab Emirates; responsible for a territory comprising most of the Arabian peninsula (including Bahrain, Oman, Qatar, Saudi Arabia, the United Arab Emirates and Yemen), containing an estimated 750,000 Roman Catholics at 31 December 1993; Vicar Apostolic GIOVANNI BERNARDO GREMOLI, Titular Bishop of Masuccaba.

#### The Anglican Communion

Within the Episcopal Church in Jerusalem and the Middle East, Saudi Arabia forms part of the diocese of Cyprus and the Gulf. The Anglican congregations in the country are entirely expatriate. The Bishop in Cyprus and the Gulf is resident in Cyprus, while the Archdeacon in the Gulf is resident in the United Arab Emirates.

#### Other Denominations

The Greek Orthodox Church is also represented.

## The Press

Since 1964 most newspapers and periodicals have been published by press organizations, administered by boards of directors with full autonomous powers, in accordance with the provisions of the Press Law. These organizations, which took over from small private firms, are privately owned by groups of individuals experienced in newspaper publishing and administration (see Publishers).

There are also a number of popular periodicals published by the Government and by the Saudi Arabian Oil Co, and distributed

# SAUDI ARABIA

free of charge. The press is subject to no legal restriction affecting freedom of expression or the coverage of news.

## DAILIES

**Arab News:** POB 4556, Jeddah 21412; tel. (2) 669-1888; telex 604397; fax (2) 667-1650; f. 1975; English; publ. by Saudi Research and Marketing Co; Editor-in-Chief KHALED A. AL-MAEENA; circ. 110,000.

**Al-Bilad** (The Country): POB 6340, Jeddah 21442; f. 1934; Arabic; publ. by Al-Bilad Publishing Org.; Editor-in-Chief Dr ABD AL-MAJID ASH-SHUBUKSHI; circ. 30,000.

**Al-Iktesadia:** Jeddah; f. 1992; Arabic; economic and financial; Editor-in-Chief MOHAMMAD AT-TUNISI.

**Al-Jazirah** (The Peninsula): POB 354, Riyadh 11411; tel. (1) 441-9999; telex 401479; fax (1) 441-3826; Arabic; Dir-Gen. SALEH ABD AL-AZIZ AS-SALEM; Editor-in-Chief MUHAMMAD BIN NASSIR BIN ABBAS; circ. 90,030.

**Al-Madina al-Munawara** (Medina—The Enlightened City): POB 807, Jeddah; tel. (2) 688-0344; telex 601356; f. 1937; Arabic; publ. by Al-Madina Press Est; Editor OSMAN HAFEZ; circ. 46,370.

**An-Nadwah** (The Council): Jarwal Sheikh Sayed Halabi Bldg, Mecca; tel. (2) 542-7868; telex 401205; f. 1958; Arabic; publ. by Mecca Printing and Information Establishment; Editors HAMED MUTAWI'E, SALEH MUHAMMAD JAMAL; circ. 35,000.

**Okaz:** POB 1508, Jeddah 21412; tel. (2) 672-2630; telex 401360; f. 1960; Arabic; Editor-in-Chief HASHIM ABDU HASHIM; circ. 95,000.

**Ar-Riyadh:** POB 851, Riyadh; tel. (1) 442-0000; telex 401664; fax (1) 441-7580; f. 1965; Arabic; publ. by Al-Yamama Press Establishment; Editor TURKI A. AS-SUDARI; circ. 150,000 (Sat.–Thurs.), 90,000 (Friday).

**Saudi Gazette:** POB 5576, Jeddah 21432; tel. (2) 676-1852; telex 600920; fax (2) 672-7621; f. 1976; English; economic and financial; publ. by Okaz Org.; Dir-Gen. MUHAMMAD AL-HASSOUN; Editor-in-Chief RIDAH MUHAMMAD LARRY; circ. 22,102.

**Al-Yaum** (Today): POB 565, Dammam; tel. (3) 843-3334; telex 801109; fax (3) 843-3337; f. 1965; Editor SULTAN AL-BAZIE; circ. 50,000.

## WEEKLIES

**Arabian Sun:** POB 5000, Dhahran 31311; tel. (3) 874-3856; fax (3) 873-8490; f. 1945; English; publ. by Saudi Aramco, Dhahran.

**Ad-Da'wa** (The Call): POB 626, Islamic University, Sharia Ibn Khaldun, Riyadh; f. 1965; Arabic.

**Al-Muslimoon** (The Muslims): POB 4556, Jeddah 21412; tel. (2) 669-1888; telex 604397; Arabic; cultural and religious affairs; publ. by Saudi Research and Marketing Co.

**News from Saudi Arabia:** Ministry of Information, Jeddah; f. 1961; English; domestic affairs; Editor IZZAT MUFTI.

**Rabitat al-'Alam al-Islami** (The Journal of the Muslim World League): POB 538, Mecca; tel. and fax (2) 544-1622; telex 60009; monthly in both Arabic and English; Editors ABDULLAH A. ADH-DHARI (Arabic), HAMID HASSAN AR-RADDADI (English).

**Saudi Arabia Business Week:** POB 2894, Riyadh; English; trade and commerce.

**Saudi Business:** POB 4556, Jeddah 21412; tel. (2) 669-1888; telex 40570; f. 1975; English; publ. by Saudi Research and Marketing Co; Editor-in-Chief Dr TALAL K. HAFIZ; circ. 27,300.

**Saudi Economic Survey:** POB 1989, Jeddah 21441; tel. (2) 651-4952; fax (2) 651-4952; f. 1967; English; a weekly review of Saudi Arabian economic and business activity; Publr S. A. ASHOOR; Man. Editor ABD AL-HAKIM GHAITH; circ. 3,000.

**Sayidati** (My Lady): POB 5455, Jeddah; telex 401205; Arabic; women's magazine; publ. by Saudi Research and Marketing Co.

**Al-Yamama:** Al-Yamama Press Establishment, POB 851, Riyadh; telex 401664; f. 1952; Dir AHMAD AL-HOSHAM; circ. 35,000.

## OTHER PERIODICALS

**Ahlan Wasahlan** (Welcome): POB 8013, Jeddah 21482; tel. (2) 686-2349; telex 601007; fax (2) 686-2006; monthly; flight journal of Saudi Arabian Airlines; Gen. Man. and Editor-in-Chief YARUB A. BALKHAIR; circ. 150,000.

**Arabia:** POB 4288, Jeddah; telex 402687; publ. by Islamic Press Agency.

**Al-'Arab** (The Arabs): POB 137, Hamad al-Jasser St, Riyadh 11411; tel. and fax (1) 462-1223; f. 1967; every 2 months; history and geography of the Arabian Peninsula; Editor HAMAD AL-JASSER.

**Al-Faysal:** POB 3, Al-Orouba St, Solaymaniyah, Riyadh; tel. (1) 465-3027; telex 402600; f. 1976; Arabic; Editor-in-Chief ALAWY TAHA AS-SAFY.

**Hajj:** Ministry of Pilgrimage Affairs and Awqaf, Omar bin al-Khatab St, Riyadh 11183; tel. (1) 402-2200; telex 401603; f. 1947; Arabic and English; general interest; Editor MUHAMMAD SAID AL-AMONDI.

**Al-Leqa'** (The Meeting): POB 812, Riyadh; monthly; Editor IBRAHIM AL-ULAI AL-MAIMAN.

**Al-Manhal** (The Spring): POB 2925, Jeddah; tel. (2) 643-2124; fax (2) 642-8853; f. 1937; monthly; Arabic; cultural, literary, political and scientific; Editor NABIH ABD AL-QUDOUS ANSARI.

**Majallat al-Iqtisad wal-Idara** (Journal of Economics and Administration): Research and Development Center, King Abd al-Aziz University, POB 1540, Jeddah; monthly; Chief Editor Dr MUHAMMAD M. N. QUOTAH.

**Saudi Review:** POB 4288, Jeddah 21491; tel. (2) 651-7442; telex 601845; fax (2) 653-0693; f. 1966; English; monthly; newsletter from Saudi newspapers and broadcasting service; publ. by International Communications Co; Chief Editor MUHAMMAD SALAHUDDIN; circ. 5,000.

**Ash-Sharkiah-Elle** (Oriental Elle): POB 6, Riyadh; telex 40112; monthly; Arabic; women's magazine; Editor SAMIRA M. KHASHAGGI.

**As-Soqoor** (Falcons): POB 2973, Riyadh 11461; tel. (1) 476-6566; f. 1978; 2 a year; air-force journal; cultural activities; Editor HAMAD A. AS-SALEH.

**At-Tadhamon al-Islami** (Islamic Solidarity): Ministry of Pilgrimage (Hajj) Affairs and Awqaf, Omar bin al-Khatab St, Riyadh 11183; monthly; Editor Dr MUSTAFA ABD AL-WAHID.

**At-Tijarah** (Commerce): POB 1264, Jeddah; f. 1960; monthly; for businessmen; publ. by Jeddah Chamber of Commerce and Industry; Chair. Sheikh ISMAIL ABU DAUD; Gen. Man. ABDULLAH S. DAHLAN; circ. 8,000.

**At-Tijarah as-Sina'iya** (Industrial Trade): POB 596, Riyadh; Arabic; Editor FAHAD AL-FRAYAN.

## NEWS AGENCIES

**Islamic Press Agency:** POB 4288, Jeddah; telex 402687.

**Saudi Press Agency:** c/o Ministry of Information, POB 570, Nasseriya St, Riyadh 11161; tel. (1) 402-3065; telex 401074; f. 1970; Dir-Gen. ABDULLAH HILAIL.

# Publishers

**Al-Bilad Publishing Organization:** POB 6340, As-Sahafa St, Jeddah 21442; tel. (2) 671-1000; telex 601205; publishes *Al-Bilad* and *Iqra'a*; Dir-Gen. AMIN ABDULLAH AL-QARQOURI.

**Dar al-Yaum Press, Printing and Publishing Ltd:** POB 565, Dammam; tel. (3) 833-1906; telex 801109; f. 1964; publishes *Al-Yaum*; Dir-Gen. MANSOUR M. AL-HASSAN.

**Al-Jazirah Organization for Press, Printing and Publishing:** POB 354, Riyadh 11411; tel. (1) 402-5555; telex 401479; fax (1) 441-3826; f. 1964; 34 mems; publishes *Al-Jazirah* and *Al-Masaeyah* (both dailies); Dir-Gen. SALEH ABD AL-AZIZ AS-SALEM; Editor-in-Chief MUHAMMAD BIN NASSIR BIN ABBAS.

**Al-Madina Press Establishment:** POB 807, Jeddah; tel. (2) 688-0344; telex 601356; f. 1937; publishes *Al-Madina al-Munawara*; Admin. Man. A. S. AL-GHAMDI; Gen. Man. AHMAD SALAH JAMJOOM.

**International Publications Agency (IPA):** POB 70, Dhahran Airport; tel. (3) 895-4921; telex 671229; publishes material of local interest; Man. SAID SALAH.

**Mecca Printing and Information Establishment:** Jarwal Sheikh Sayed Halabi Bldg, Mecca; tel. (2) 574-8150; telex 640039; publishes *An-Nadwah* daily newspaper; Man. Dir ABBAS A. ZOWAWI.

**Okaz Organization for Press and Publication:** POB 5941, Jeddah; tel. (2) 660-0789; telex 402645; publishes *Okaz*, *Saudi Gazette* and *Child*; Man. Dir ALI H. SHOBOKSHI.

**Saudi Publishing and Distributing House:** Al-Jouhara Bldg, South Block, Bughdadia, Medina Road, POB 2043, Jeddah 21451; tel. (2) 642-4043; telex 601845; fax (2) 643-2821; publishers, importers and distributors of English and Arabic books; Chair. MUHAMMAD SALAHUDDIN.

**Saudi Research and Publishing Co:** POB 4556, Jeddah 21412; tel. (2) 669-1888; telex 604397; publishes *Arab News*, *Asharq al-Awsat*, *Al-Majalla*, *Al-Muslimoon* and *Sayidati*; Dirs-Gen. HISHAM ALI HAFEZ, MUHAMMAD ALI HAFEZ.

**Al-Yamamah Press Establishment:** POB 25848, Riyadh 11476; tel. (1) 442-0000; telex 401664; fax (1) 441-7580; publishes *Ar-Riyadh* and *Al-Yamamah*; Dir-Gen. FAHED AL-ORAIFY.

# Radio and Television

In 1992, according to UNESCO, there were an estimated 4.8m. radio receivers and 4.3m. television receivers in use.

# SAUDI ARABIA

## RADIO

**Saudi Arabian Broadcasting Service:** c/o Ministry of Information, POB 60059, Riyadh; tel. (1) 401-4440; telex 401149; fax (1) 403-8177; 24 medium- and short-wave stations, including Jeddah, Riyadh, Dammam and Abha, broadcast programmes in Arabic and English; 23 FM stations; overseas service in Bengali, English, Farsi, French, Hausa, Indonesian, Somali, Swahili, Turkestani, Turkish and Urdu; Dir-Gen. KHALID H. GHOUTH.

**Saudi Aramco FM Radio:** Bldg 3030 LIP, Dhahran; tel. (3) 876-1845; telex 801120; fax (3) 876-1608; f. 1957; private station broadcasting music and programmes in English for the entertainment of employees of Saudi Aramco; Man. A. A. AL-ARFAJ.

## TELEVISION

**Saudi Arabian Government Television Service:** POB 570, Riyadh 11421; tel. (1) 401-4440; telex 401030; fax (1) 404-4192; began transmission 1965; 112 stations, incl. six main stations at Riyadh, Jeddah, Medina, Dammam, Qassim, Abha, transmit programmes in Arabic and English; Dir-Gen. A. RAHMAN YAHMOOR (Channel 1).

**Saudi Arabian Government Television Service Channel 2:** POB 7959, Riyadh 11472; tel. (1) 442-8400; telex 401030; fax (1) 403-3826; began transmission 1983; Dir-Gen. ABD AL-AZIZ S. ABU ANNAJA.

**Dhahran HZ-22 TV, Channel 3 TV:** Bldg 3030 LIP, Dhahran; tel. (3) 876-4634; telex 801120; fax (3) 876-1608; non-commercial private co; started 1957, since 1969 English language film-chain operation only; Man. (Media Productions and Operations) A. A. AL-ARFAJ.

# Finance

(cap. = capital; res = reserves; dep. = deposits; m. = million; brs = branches; amounts in Saudi riyals unless otherwise stated)

## BANKING

In 1990 the Saudi Arabian banking system consisted of: the Saudi Arabian Monetary Agency, as central note-issuing and regulatory body; 12 commercial banks (three national and nine foreign banks); and five specialist banks. There is a policy of 'Saudiization' of the foreign banks.

### Central Bank

**Saudi Arabian Monetary Agency (SAMA):** POB 2992, Riyadh 11169; tel. (1) 463-3000; telex 404400 (English), 401466 (Arabic); f. 1952; functions include stabilization of currency, administration of monetary reserves, regulation of banking and issue of notes and coins; cap. and res 24,457m., dep. 177,408m., total assets 275,192m. (Dec. 1992); Gov. Sheikh HAMAD SA'UD AS-SAYARI; 10 brs.

### National Banks

**National Commercial Bank (NCB):** POB 3555, King Abd al-Aziz St, Jeddah 21481; tel. (2) 644-6644; telex 605571; f. 1954; cap. 6,000m., res 952.3m., dep. 51,274m. (Dec. 1993); Gen. Man. Sheikh SALIM AHMAD IBN MAHFOUZ; 240 brs, incl. international representative offices.

**Riyad Bank Ltd:** POB 22622, King Abd al-Aziz St, Riyadh 11416; tel. (1) 401-3030; telex 407490; fax (1) 404-1255; f. 1957; cap. 2,000m., res 4,000m., dep. 41,628m., total assets 50,022m. (Dec. 1992); Chair. Sheikh ISMAIL ABU DAUD; Gen. Man. Sheikh SULAIMAN AL-MANDEEL; 177 brs.

**United Saudi Commercial Bank (USCB):** POB 25895, Riyadh 11476; tel. (1) 478-4200; telex 405461; fax (1) 478-3197; f. 1983; jointly owned by Saudi nationals (80%), Bank Melli Iran (10%) and United Bank Ltd (10%); cap. 500m., res 889.9m., dep. 5,586.1m., total assets 10,378.2m. (Dec. 1994); Man. Dir MAHER G. AL-AUJAN; 16 brs.

### Specialist Banks

**Arab Investment Co SAA (TAIC):** POB 4009, Riyadh 11491; tel. (1) 476-0601; telex 401011; fax (1) 476-0514; f. 1974 by 15 Arab countries for investment and banking; cap. US $300m., total assets US $931.5m. (1994); Chair. Dr AHMAD ABDULLAH AL-MALIK, Dir-Gen. Dr SALIH AL-HUMAIDAN; 4 brs throughout Middle East.

**Ar-Rajhi Banking and Investment Corporation (ARABIC):** POB 28, Riyadh 11411; tel. (1) 405-4244; telex 406317; fax (1) 403-2969; f. 1988; fmrly Ar-Rajhi Co for Currency Exchange and Commerce; operates according to Islamic financial principles; 44% owned by Ar-Rajhi family; cap. 1,500m., total assets 28,598m. (1993); Chair. Sheikh SALEH IBN ABD AL-AZIZ AR-RAJHI; Man. Dir Sheikh SULAIMAN IBN ABD AL-AZIZ AR-RAJHI; 316 brs.

**Saudi Arabian Agricultural Bank (SAAB):** POB 11126, Riyadh; tel. (1) 402-2361; telex 201184; f. 1963; cap. 10,000m. (1982); Controller-Gen. ABDULLAH SAAD AL-MENGASH; Gen. Man. ABD AL-AZIZ MUHAMMAD AL-MANQUR; 71 brs.

**Saudi Credit Bank:** POB 3401, Riyadh 11471; tel. (1) 402-9128; f. 1973; provides interest-free loans for specific purposes to Saudi citizens of moderate means; Chair. SAID BIN SAIED; Dir-Gen. MUHAMMAD AD-DRIES.

**Saudi Investment Bank (SAIB):** POB 3533, Riyadh 11481; tel. (1) 477-8433; telex 401170; fax (1) 477-6781; f. 1976; provides a comprehensive range of traditional and specialized banking services to business and individuals; foreign shareholders, incl. Chase Manhattan Bank, Industrial Bank of Japan and J. Henry Schroder Wagg & Co Ltd, have provided 25% of cap.; cap. 180m., res 248m., dep. 6,169.8m., total assets 6,598.2m. (Dec 1994); Chair. Dr ABD AL-AZIZ O'HALI; Gen. Man. SAUD AS-SALEH; 10 brs.

### Banks with Foreign Interests

**Al-Bank as-Saudi al-Fransi** (Saudi French Bank): POB 56006, Riyadh 11554; tel. (1) 404-2222; telex 407666; fax (1) 404-2311; f. 1977; Saudi Arabian nationals have 68.9% participation, Banque Indosuez has 31.1%; cap. 900m., res 1,430m., dep. 23,035.8m., total assets 25,469.4m. (Dec. 1993); Chair. IBRAHIM A. AL-TOUQ; Man. Dir HENRI GUILLEMIN; 59 brs.

**Arab National Bank (ANB):** POB 56921, Riyadh 11564; tel. (1) 402-9000; telex 402660; fax (1) 402-7747; f. 1980; fmrly Arab Bank Ltd, Jordan, but Saudi public acquired 60% participation; cap. 1,200m., res 1,200m., dep. 18,946m., total assets 32,407m. (Dec. 1993); Chair. Sheikh RASHID AR-RASHID; Man. Dir ELIE EL-HADJ; 123 brs.

**Bank al-Jazira:** POB 6277, Jeddah 21442; tel. (2) 651-8070; telex 601574; fax (2) 653-2478; 94.17% Saudi-owned; cap. 600m., dep. 1,540.9m., total assets 4,965.0m. (Dec. 1994); Chair. ABD AL-AZIZ MUHAMMAD AL ABDULKADER; Gen. Man. MISHARI I. AL-MISHARI; 12 brs.

**Saudi American Bank (SAMBA):** POB 833, Riyadh 11421; tel. and fax (1) 477-4770; telex 400195; 60% owned by Saudi nationals; cap. 2,400m., res 1,233m. dep. 31,625m., total assets 43,605m. (Dec. 1994); Chair. ABD AL-AZIZ IBN HAMAD AL-GOSAIBI; Man. Dir JAMES J. COLLINS; 43 brs.

**Saudi British Bank:** POB 9084, Riyadh 11413; tel. (1) 405-0677; telex 402349; fax (1) 405-0660; a joint-stock co f. in 1978, when Saudi citizens acquired a 60% interest in the British Bank of the Middle East; cap. 1,000m., res 1,591.6m., dep. 16,971.9m., total assets 27,109.1m. (Dec. 1994); Chair. Sheikh ABDULLAH MUHAMMAD AL-HUGAIL; Man. Dir RONDELL LEE SHAW; 59 brs.

**Saudi Cairo Bank:** POB 11222, Jeddah 21453; tel. and fax (2) 660-8820; telex 600205; f. 1979; fmrly Banque du Caire; Saudi shareholders have 55% participation; cap. 1,200m., res 389m., dep. 12,909m., total assets 15,552m. (Dec. 1993); Chair. Sheikh WAHIB IBN ZAGR; Gen. Man. EL-REFAI KAMAL EISA; 69 brs.

**Saudi Hollandi Bank** (Saudi Dutch Bank): POB 1467, Riyadh 11431; tel. (1) 401-0288; telex 401488; fax (1) 403-1104; a joint-stock co f. in 1977 to take over the activities of Algemene Bank Nederland NV in Saudi Arabia; ABN AMRO Bank (Netherlands) has 40%, Saudi citizens have 60% participation; cap. 210m., res 962m., dep. 13,928m., total assets 15,101m. (Dec. 1993); Chair. Sheikh SULAIMAN A. R. AS-SUHAIMI; Man. Dir SHELDON E. BOEGE; 39 brs.

### INSURANCE COMPANIES

In 1990 there were 38 insurance companies based in Saudi Arabia.

**Al-Alamiya Insurance Co Ltd (E.C.):** POB 2374, Jeddah 21451; tel. (2) 671-8851; telex 606456; fax (2) 671-1377; managed by Sun Alliance, London; total assets US $25.0m. (1994); Chair. Sheikh WAHIB S. BINZAGIR; Man. Dir C. ROBERT BRADSHAW.

**Arabia CIGNA Insurance Co Ltd (E.C.):** POB 276, Dammam 31411; tel. (3) 832-4441; telex 801259; fax (3) 834-9389; f. 1976 as Pan Arabian Insurance Co; cap. US $1m.; Chair. Sheikh ABD AL-KARIM AL-KHERELJI; Man. Dir TAJUDDIN HASSAN.

**Gulf Union Insurance Co:** POB 5719, Damman 31432; tel. (3) 833-3802; telex 802458; fax (3) 833-3517; f. 1982; primarily non-life insurance; cap. US $20m.; Chair. SAAD MUHAMMAD AL-MOAJIL; Gen. Man. PERCY A. SEQUEIRA.

**Independent Insurance Co of Saudi Arabia Ltd:** POB 1178, Jeddah 21431; tel. (2) 651-7732; telex 601580; fax (2) 651-1968; f. 1977; all classes of insurance; cap. US $1m.; Pres. KHALID TAHER.

**National Company for Co-operative Insurance (NCCI):** POB 86959, Riyadh 11632; tel. (1) 482-6969; telex 406828; fax (1) 488-1719; f. 1985 by royal decree; owned by three government agencies; auth. cap. SR500m.; Chair. AHMED ABD AL-LATIF; Man. Dir and Gen. Man. MOUSA AR-RUBAIAN; 7 brs.

**Red Sea Insurance (Saudi Arabia) E.C. Group:** POB 5627, Jeddah 21432; tel. (2) 660-3538; telex 601228; fax (2) 665-5418; f. 1974; insurance, development, and reinsurance; cap. US $27.5m.; Chair. SALEH SALIM BIN MAHFOUZ; Man. Dir KHALDOUN B. BARAKAT.

# SAUDI ARABIA

**Saudi Arabian Insurance Co Ltd:** POB 58073, Riyadh 11594; tel. (1) 479-3311; telex 407017; fax (1) 477-2376; f. 1979; all classes of insurance; cap. 4m. Bahraini dinars; Chair. Prince FAHD IBN KHALID IBN ABDULLAH AS-SA'UD.

**Saudi Continental Insurance Co:** POB 2940, Riyadh; tel. (1) 476-6903; telex 406325; fax (1) 476-9310; f. 1983; all classes of insurance; cap. US $3m.; Chair. OMAR A. AGGAD; Gen. Man. J. A. MCROBBIE.

**Saudi National Insurance Co EC:** POB 5832, Jeddah 21432; tel. and fax (2) 660-6200; telex 601791.

**Saudi United Insurance Co Ltd:** POB 933, Al-Khobar 31952; tel. (3) 894-9090; telex 871335; fax (3) 894-9428; f. 1976; all classes of insurance and reinsurance except life; cap. US $5m.; majority shareholding held by Ahmad Hamad al-Gosaibi & Bros; Chair. and Man. Dir Sheikh ABD AL-AZIZ HAMAD AL-GOSAIBI; Dir and Gen. Man. AHMAD MUHAMMAD SABBAGH 6 brs.

**U.C.A. Insurance Co (E.C.):** POB 5019, Jeddah 21422; tel. (2) 653-0068; telex 601906; fax (2) 651-1936; f. 1974 as United Commercial Agencies Ltd; all classes of insurance; cap. US $4m.; Chair. JACQUES G. SACY; Dir and Gen. Man. MACHAAL A. KARAM.

**Al-Yamanah Insurance Co Ltd:** POB 41522, Riyadh 11531; tel. (1) 477-4498; telex 400818; fax (1) 477-4497; f. 1979; all classes of insurance; cap. 15m.; Chair. ABDULLAH AHMAD AL-GOREER; Man. Dir FAYED MAHMOUD ASH-SHIHABI.

## Trade and Industry

### DEVELOPMENT

**Arab Petroleum Investments Corpn:** POB 448, Dhahran Airport 31932; tel. (3) 864-7400; telex 870068; fax (3) 894-5076; f. 1975; affiliated to the Organization of Arab Petroleum Exporting Countries (see p. 207); specializes in financing petroleum and petrochemical projects and related industries in the Arab world and in other developing countries; shareholders: Kuwait, Saudi Arabia and the United Arab Emirates (17% each), Libya (15%), Iraq and Qatar (10% each), Algeria (5%), Bahrain, Egypt and Syria (3% each); cap. US $400m. (1992); Chair. ABDULLAH A. AZ-ZAID; Gen. Man. Dr NUREDDIN FARRAG.

**General Investment Fund** (Public Investment Fund): c/o Ministry of Finance and National Economy, Airport Rd, Riyadh 11177; tel. (1) 405-0000; telex 401021; f. 1970; provides government's share of capital to mixed capital cos; 100% state-owned; cap. 1,000m.; Chair. Minister of Finance and National Economy; Sec.-Gen. SULEIMAN MANDIL.

**National Agricultural Development Co (NADEC):** POB 2557, Riyadh 11461; tel. (1) 404-0000; telex 403681; fax (1) 405-5522; f. 1981; interests include a dairy farm, 39,760 ha for cultivation of wheat, barley, forage and vegetables and processing of dates; the government has a 20% share; chief agency for agricultural development; cap. 400m.; Chair. Minister of Agriculture and Water.

**National Industrialization Co (NIC):** f. 1984 to develop private investment in industry; cap. 600m.; 86% of cap. owned by Saudi nationals (1985); Chair. MAHSOUN BAHJAT JALAL.

**Royal Commission for Jubail and Yanbu:** POB 5964, Riyadh 11432; tel. (1) 479-4445; telex 401386 (English), 404560 (Arabic); f. 1975 to create the basic infrastructure for new industrial cities at Jubail and Yanbu; Chair. Prince ABDULLAH IBN FAISAL IBN TURKI AL-ABDULLAH AS-SA'UD; Dir-Gen. for Jubail AHMAD AL-MUBARAK, for Yanbu ABD AR-RAZAG A. ALGAIN.

**Saudi Consulting House (SCH):** POB 1267, Riyadh 11431; tel. (1) 448-4533; telex 404380; fax (1) 448-1234; f. 1979; engineering, economic, industrial and management consultants; Chair. ABD AL-AZIZ AZ-ZAMIL (Minister of Industry and Electricity); Dir-Gen. MUHAMMAD ALI AL-MUSALLAM.

**Saudi Fund for Development (SFD):** POB 1887, Riyadh 11441; tel. (1) 464-0292; telex 401145; fax (1) 464-7450; f. 1974 to help finance projects in developing countries; cap. 31,000m. (1991); had financed 320 projects by 1992; total commitments amounted to 25,814m.; Chair. Minister of Finance and National Economy; Vice-Chair. and Man. Dir MUHAMMAD A. AS-SUGAIR.

**Saudi Industrial Development Fund (SIDF):** POB 4143, Riyadh 11149; tel. (1) 477-4002; telex 401065; fax (1) 479-0165; f. 1974; supports and promotes industrial and electrical development in the private sector, providing long-term interest-free loans to industry; also offers marketing, technical, financial and administrative advice; cap. 7,000m. (1992); Chair. Dr AHMED AL-MALEK; Dir-Gen. SALEH ABDULLAH AN-NAIM.

### CHAMBERS OF COMMERCE

**Council of Saudi Chambers of Commerce and Industry:** POB 16683, Riyadh 11474; tel. (1) 405-3200; telex 405808; fax (1) 402-4747; comprises one delegate from each of the 19 chambers of commerce in the Kingdom; Chair. Sheikh ABD AR-RAHMAN AL-JERAISY; Sec.-Gen. ABDALLAH T. DABBAGH.

**Abha Chamber of Commerce and Industry:** POB 722, Abha; tel. (7) 227-1818; telex 905001; fax (7) 227-1919; Pres. ABDULLAH SAFEED ABU MELHA; Sec.-Gen. HAMDI ALI AL-MALKI.

**Al-Ahsa Chamber of Commerce and Industry:** POB 1519, Horuf 31982; tel. (3) 582-0458; telex 861230; fax (3) 587-5274; Pres. ABD AL-AZIZ SULAIMAN AL-AFALIQ; Sec.-Gen. SAAD ABD AR-RAHMAN AL-IBRAHIM.

**Ar'ar Chamber of Commerce and Industry:** POB 440, Ar'ar; tel. (4) 662-6544; telex 812058; fax (4) 662-4581; Pres. SALIH YAHYA AL-AS'AF; Sec.-Gen. MATAB MOZIL AS-SARRAH.

**Al-Baha Chamber of Commerce and Industry:** POB 311, al-Baha; tel. (7) 725-4116; telex 731048; fax (7) 727-0308; ; Pres. AHMED WANNAN AL-GHAMDI; Sec.-Gen. YAHYA AZ-ZAHRANI.

**Eastern Province Chamber of Commerce and Industry:** POB 719, Dammam 31421; tel. (3) 857-1111; telex 801086; fax (3) 857-0607; f. 1952; Chair. HAMAD AZ-ZAMIL; Sec.-Gen. HAMDAN M. AS-SORAIHY.

**Federation of Gulf Co-operation Council Chambers (FGCCC):** POB 2198, Dammam 31451; tel. (3) 826-5943; fax (3) 826-6794; Pres. HASSAN A. AN-NOMAN; Sec.-Gen. MUHAMMAD A. AL-MULLA.

**Ha'il Chamber of Commerce and Industry:** POB 1291, Ha'il; tel. (6) 532-1060; telex 311086; fax (6) 533-1366; Pres. SAAD AD-DAKHIL ALLAH AS-SAID; Sec.-Gen. KHADDAM AS-SALIH AL-FAYEZ.

**Islamic Chamber of Commerce and Industry:** Riyadh; tel. (1) 532-3190; telex 25533; Chair. Sheikh ISMAIL ABU DAUD; Sec.-Gen. ELION WATT.

**Jeddah Chamber of Commerce and Industry:** POB 1264, Jeddah 21431; tel. (2) 651-5111; telex 601069; fax (2) 651-7373; f. 1950; Chair. Sheikh ISMAIL ABU DAWOOD; Sec.-Gen. Dr ABDULLAH SADIQ DAHLAN.

**Al-Jizan Chamber of Commerce and Industry:** POB 201, al-Jizan; tel. (7) 322-3763; telex 911065; fax (7) 322-3507; Pres. ABDO HASSAN HAKAMI; Sec.-Gen. YAHYA Y. ASH-SHARIF.

**Al-Jouf Chamber of Commerce and Industry:** POB 585, al-Jouf; tel. (4) 624-9060; telex 821065; fax (4) 624-0108; Pres. MA'ASHI DUKAN AL-ATTIYEH; Sec.-Gen. AHMAD KHALIFA AL-MUSALLAM.

**Al-Majma' Chamber of Commerce and Industry:** POB 165, al-Majma' 11952; tel. (6) 432-0268; telex 447020; fax (6) 432-2655; Pres. FAHD MUHAMMAD AR-RABIAH; Sec.-Gen. ABDULLAH IBRAHIM AL-JAAWAN.

**Mecca Chamber of Commerce and Industry:** POB 1086, Mecca; tel. (2) 534-3838; telex 540011; fax (2) 534-2904; f. 1945; Pres. ABD AR-RAHMAN A. FAKIEH; Sec.-Gen. NABIL M. S. QUTUB.

**Medina Chamber of Commerce and Industry:** POB 443, Airport Rd, Medina; tel. (4) 822-5190; telex 570009; fax (4) 826-8965; Sec.-Gen. TARRIEF HUSSAINHASHIM.

**Najran Chamber of Commerce and Industry:** POB 1138, Najran; tel. (7) 522-2216; telex 921066; fax (7) 522-3926; Pres. FAISAL HASSAN ABU SAAQ; Sec.-Gen. MAKHFOOR ABDULLAH AL-BISHER.

**Qassim Chamber of Commerce and Industry:** POB 444, Buraydah, Qassim; tel. (6) 381-4000; telex 301060; fax (6) 381-4528; Pres. ABD AR-REHMAN AL-MUSHAIKEH; Sec.-Gen. ABDALLAH AL-YEHYA ASH-SHARIDA.

**Al-Qurayat Chamber of Commerce and Industry:** POB 416, Al-Qurayat; tel. (4) 642-3034; fax (4) 642-3172; Pres. OTHMAN ABDULLAH AL-YOUSEF; Sec.-Gen. JAMAL ALI AL-GHAMDI.

**Riyadh Chamber of Commerce and Industry:** POB 596, Riyadh 11421; tel. (1) 404-0044; telex 401054; fax (1) 402-1103; f. 1961; acts as arbitrator in business disputes, information centre; Chair. ABD AR-RAHMAN AL-JERAISY; Sec.-Gen. Sheikh SALEH ABDULLAH AT-TOAIMI; 23,000 mems.

**Tabouk Chamber of Commerce and Industry:** POB 567, Tabouk; tel. (4) 422-2736; telex 681173; fax (4) 422-7387; Pres. ABDULAZIZ M. OWADEH; Sec.-Gen. AWADH AL-BALAWI.

**Ta'if Chamber of Commerce and Industry:** POB 1005, Ta'if; tel. (2) 746-4624; telex 751009; fax (2) 738-0040; Pres. IBRAHIM ABDULLAH KAMAL; Sec.-Gen. Eng. YOUSUF MUHAMMAD ASH-SHAFI.

**Union of Arabian Chambers of Commerce and Industry:** POB 112837, Riyadh; tel. (1) 814269; telex 20347; Chair. BADR ED-DIN SHALLAH; Sec.-Gen. BURHAN AD-DAJANI.

**Yanbu Chamber of Commerce and Industry:** POB 58, Yanbu; tel. (4) 322-4257; telex 661036; fax (4) 322-6800; f. 1979; produces quarterly magazine; 2,500 members; Pres. Dr TALAL ALI ASH-SHAIR; Sec.-Gen. MUHAMMAD ABDULLAH AL-OMAR.

### PETROLEUM

**Saudi Arabian Oil Co (Saudi Aramco):** POB 5000, Dhahran 31311; tel. (3) 877-0110; telex 801220; fax (3) 873-8190; f. 1933;

# SAUDI ARABIA

previously known as Arabian-American Oil Co (Aramco); in 1993 incorporated the Saudi Arabian Marketing and Refining Co (SAMAREC, f. 1988) by merger of operations; holds the principal working concessions in Saudi Arabia; Pres. and CEO ALI NAIMI; Exec. Vice-Pres. S. AL-HUSSEINI.

**Arabian Drilling Co:** POB 708, Dammam 31421; tel. (3) 857-6060; telex 871212; fax (3) 857-7114; f. 1964; PETROMIN shareholding 51%, remainder French private cap.; undertakes contract drilling for oil (on shore and off shore), minerals and water both inside and outside Saudi Arabia; Chair. SULEIMAN J. AL-HERBISH; Man. Dir SULEIMAN M. AL-AMRY.

**Arabian Geophysical and Surveying Co (ARGAS):** POB 2109, Jeddah 21451; tel. (2) 671-0087; telex 601786; fax (2) 6726352; f. 1966, with the General Petroleum and Mineral Organization (PETROMIN) having a shareholding of 51%; remainder provided by Cie Générale de Géophysique; geophysical exploration for petroleum, other minerals and ground water, as well as all types of land, airborne and marine surveys; Man. Dir SULTAN J. SHAWLI; Tech. Dir ROBERT GALIN.

**Arabian Marine Petroleum Co (MARINCO):** POB 50, Dhahran Airport 31932; tel. (3) 891-3831; telex 870047; f. 1968; SAMAREC shareholding 51%, remainder held by McDermott Co of New Orleans, USA; undertakes marine construction work (pipelines, rigs, sea terminals, etc.); Chair. ALI I. AR-RUBAISHI.

**Jeddah Oil Refinery Co (JORC):** POB 1604, Jeddah 21441; tel. (2) 636-7411; telex 601150; f. 1967; SAMAREC shareholding 75%, remainder held by Saudi Arabian Refining Co (SARCO); the refinery at Jeddah, Japanese-built, has a capacity of 90,525 b/d; total production 30.7m. barrels (1990); responsible for distribution in the Western Province; Chair. MANSOUR A. AS-SUHAIMI; Man. Dir MATOUQ H. JANNAH.

**Petromin—Jet:** POB 7550, Jeddah 21472; tel. (2) 685-7592; telex 603402; f. 1979 as a subsidiary of the General Petroleum and Mineral Organization (PETROMIN); became wholly-owned by SAMAREC; supplies petroleum products, in particular jet fuel, to King Abd al-Aziz International Airport; Chair. and Exec. Asst ABDULLAH O. ATTAS (acting).

**Petromin Lube Oil Blending and Grease Manufacturing Plant (SAUDI LUBE):** POB 10382, Jubail 31961; tel. (3) 341-1209; telex 832168; f. 1987; wholly-owned by PETROLUBE; production and marketing of lubricants and grease, capacity 1m. barrels lubricants and 4,000 tons grease per year; Man. Dirs BADDAH S. AS-SEBAI'E (Finance and Trade), ABD AR-RAHMAN M. AL-CABBANI.

**Petromin Lubricating Oil Co (PETROLUBE):** POB 1432, Jeddah 21431; tel. (2) 661-3333; telex 606175; fax (2) 661-3322; f. 1968; PETROMIN took a 71% share, Mobil Oil Investment owns 29%; for the processing, manufacture, marketing and distribution of lubricating oils and other related products; production 199m. litres (1988); cap. 110m.; Chair., Pres. and CEO AHMAD AL-MUHAMMAD AL-KHEREIJI.

**Petromin Lubricating Oil Refining Co (LUBEREF):** POB 5518, Jeddah 21432; tel. (2) 636-7411; telex 602781; fax (2) 636-6932; f. 1975; owned 70% by PETROMIN and 30% by Mobil; production 1,889,000 barrels (1992); Chair. and Exec. Man. Dir BAKR A. KHOJA.

**Petromin Marketing (PETMARK):** POB 5250, Jeddah 21422; tel. (2) 667-6233; telex 870009; fax (2) 669-4081; f. 1967; wholly-owned by SAMAREC; operates the installations and facilities for the distribution of petroleum products in the Eastern, Central, Southern and Northern provinces of Saudi Arabia; Pres. and CEO HUSSEIN A. LINJAWI.

**Petromin Mobil Yanbu Refinery:** POB 30078, Yanbu; tel. (4) 396-4000; telex 662325; fax (4) 396-0942; f. 1984; operated by SAMAREC and Mobil, capacity 300,000 b/d; Man. Dir ALI TAHER AD-DABBAGH.

**Petromin Riyadh Refinery (PRR):** POB 3946, Riyadh 11199; tel. (1) 498-0995; telex 401015; f. 1974; wholly-owned by SAMAREC; production capacity 120,000 b/d; total production 43.6m. barrels (1990); Exec. Man. Dir ANWAD A. AL-NAQQAR.

**Petromin Services Department (PETROSERVE):** POB 2329, Jeddah 21451; tel. (2) 636-6309; telex 601867; f. 1968; operates all types of services in medical care, social and sports activities, telecommunications, computers, housing, security and training; Pres. HUSSEIN A. LINJAWI.

**Petromin-Shell Refinery Co:** POB 10088, Jubail 31961; tel. (3) 357-2000; telex 832060; operated by SAMAREC and Shell; capacity 250,000 b/d; exports began in 1985; Chair. Dr FAISAL BASHIR.

**Petromin Yanbu Refinery:** POB 30021, Yanbu; tel. (4) 321-8402; telex 662337; fax (4) 396-2756; f. 1983, with an initial capacity of 170,000 b/d; production 60m. barrels (1990); Exec. Dir YAHYA A. AZ-ZAID; Vice-Pres. AWDAH A. AL-AHMADI.

**Vela International Marine Ltd (VELA):** T-1010, Tower Building, Dhahran; tel. (3) 875-3445; fax (3) 873-2039; Pres. D. A. F. AL-UTAIBI.

**Saudi Basic Industries Corpn (SABIC):** POB 5101, Riyadh 11422; tel. (1) 401-2033; telex 401177; fax (1) 401-3831; f. 1976; to foster the petrochemical industry and other hydrocarbon-based industries through joint ventures with foreign partners, and to market their products; cap. 10,000m.; 30% of shares sold to Saudi and other GCC nationals in 1984; production 20.7m. tons (1994); total assets 37,160m. (1993); Chair. Minister of Industry and Electricity; Vice-Chair. and Man. Dir IBRAHIM BIN SALAMAH.

Projects include:

**Al-Jubail Fertilizer Co (Samad):** POB 10046, Jubail 31961; tel. (3) 341-6488; telex 832024; fax (3) 341-7122; f. 1979; capacity of 620,000 tons per year of urea; jt venture with Taiwan Fertilizer Co; Pres. AHMAD A. AL-AHMAD.

**Al-Jubail Petrochemical Co (Kemya):** POB 10084, Jubail 31961; tel. (3) 357-6000; telex 832058; f. 1980; began production of linear low-density polyethylene in 1984, of high-density polyethylene in 1985, and of high alfa olefins in 1986, capacity of 330,000 tons per year of polyethylene; jt venture with Exxon Corpn, (USA) and SABIC; Pres. KHALIL I. AL-GANNAS; Exec. Vice-Pres. CLAY LEWIS.

**Arabian Petrochemical Co (Petrokemya):** POB 10002, Jubail 31961; tel. (3) 358-7000; telex 832053; fax (3) 358-4480; produced 1.2m. tons of ethylene, 135,000 tons of polystyrene, 100,000 tons of butene-1; 300,000 tons of propylene, 100,000 tons of butadiene and 70,000 tons of benzene in 1993; wholly-owned subsidiary of SABIC; owns 50% interest in ethylene glycol plant producing 203,000 tons per year of monoethylene glycol, 21,700 tons per year of diethylene glycol and 1,300 tons per year of triethylene glycol; Chair. IBRAHIM A. IBN SALAMAH; Pres. NABIL A. MANSOURI.

**Eastern Petrochemical Co (Sharq):** POB 10035, Jubail 31961; tel. (3) 357-5000; telex 832037; fax (3) 358-0383; f. 1981 to produce linear low-density polyethylene, ethylene glycol; total capacity 330,000 tons of ethylene glycol and 140,000 tons of polyethylene per year; a SABIC joint venture; Pres. AHMAD M. AN-NEKHILAN.

**Jeddah Steel Rolling Co (Sulb):** POB 1826, Jeddah 21441; tel. (2) 636-7462; telex 602127; fax (2) 636-8161; f. 1967; capacity of 150,000 tons per year of reinforcing steel bars; cap. 62.4m.; Chair. YOUSSEF M. ALIREZA.

**National Industrial Gases Co (Gas):** POB 10110, Jubail; tel. (3) 358-1993; telex 832082; fax (3) 358-5542; total capacity of 876,000 tons of oxygen and 492,750 tons of nitrogen per year; jt venture with Saudi private sector; Dir-Gen. SAAD H. AL-GHURAIRI.

**National Methanol Co (Ibn Sina):** POB 10003, Jubail 31961; tel. (3) 340-5500; telex 832033; fax (3) 340-5506; began commercial production of chemical-grade methanol in November 1984; capacity 1m. tons per year; began commercial production of methyl-tertiary-butyl ether (MTBE) in May 1994; capacity 700,000 tons per year; jt venture of SABIC, Hoechst-Celanese Corpn (USA) and Panhandle Eastern Corpn (USA); Pres. K. S. RAWAF.

**National Plastics Co (Ibn Hayyan):** POB 10002, Jubail; tel. (3) 358-7000; telex 832053; fax (3) 358-4480; produces 300,000 tons per year of vinylchloride monomer and 200,000 tons per year of polyvinylchloride; jt venture with Lucky Group (Republic of Korea), SABIC and three other cos; Pres. IBRAHIM S. ASH-SHEWEIR.

**Saudi Arabian Fertilizer Co (SAFCO):** POB 553, Dammam 31421; tel. (3) 857-5011; telex 870117; fax (3) 857-4311; produced 353,744 tons of urea, 225,735 tons of ammonia, 98,535 tons of sulphuric acid and 20,240 tons of melamine in 1993; owned 41% by SABIC, 10% by its staff and 49% by private Saudi investors; Pres. HUSSEIN EID AL-JUBEIHI.

**Saudi-European Petrochemical Co (Ibn Zahr):** POB 10330, Jubail 31961; tel. (3) 341-5060; telex 832517; f. 1985; annual capacity 500,000 tons of methyl-tertiary-butyl ether (MTBE); SABIC has a 70% share, Ecofuel, Nesté Corpn and APICORP each have 10%; Pres. ABD AR-RAHMAN A. AL-GARAWI.

**Saudi Iron and Steel Co (Hadeed):** POB 10053, Madinat al-Jubail as-Sinaiyah 31961; tel. (3) 357-1100; telex 832022; fax (3) 358-7385; f. 1979; produced 1.8m. tons of steel reinforcing rods and bars in 1992; Pres. SAMI A. AS-SUWAIGH.

**Saudi Methanol Co (ar-Razi):** POB 10065, Jubail Industrial City 31961; tel. (3) 357-7838; telex 832023; fax (3) 358-5552; f. 1979; capacity of 1,280,000 tons per year of chemical-grade methanol; total methanol exports in 1992 were 1,338,000 tons; jt venture with a consortium of Japanese cos; cap. 259m.; Pres. ABD AL-AZIZ I. ALAUDAH; Exec. Vice-Pres. T. SEKI.

**Saudi Petrochemical Co (Sadaf):** POB 10025, Jubail Industrial City 31961; tel. (3) 357-3000; telex 832032; fax (3) 357-3142;

# SAUDI ARABIA

f. 1980; to produce ethylene, ethylene dichloride, styrene, crude industrial ethanol and caustic soda; total capacity of 2,490,000 tons per year; Shell (Pecten) has a 50% share; Pres. A. A. AL-ASSAF.

**Saudi Yanbu Petrochemical Co (Yanpet):** POB 3033, Madinat Yanbu as-Sinaiyah; tel. (4) 396-5000; telex 662359; f. 1980; to produce 820,000 tons per year of ethylene, 600,000 tons per year of high-density polyethylene and 340,000 tons per year of ethylene glycol; total capacity 1,692,200 tons per year by 1990; Mobil and SABIC each have a 50% share; Pres. ALI AL-KHURAIMI; Exec. Vice-Pres. P. J. FOLEY.

### Foreign Concessionaires

**Arabian Oil Co Ltd (AOC):** POB 50584, Riyadh 11533 (Head Office in Japan); f. 1958; holds concession (2,200 sq km at Dec. 1987) for offshore exploitation of Saudi Arabia's half-interest in the Kuwait-Saudi Arabia Neutral Zone; Chair. HIROMICHI EGUCHI; Pres. KEIICHI KONAGA.

**Saudi Arabian Texaco Inc:** POB 363, Riyadh; tel. (1) 462-7274; fax (1) 464-1992; also office in Kuwait; f. 1928; fmrly Getty Oil Co; holds concession (5,200 sq km at Dec. 1987) for exploitation of Saudi Arabia's half-interest in the Saudi Arabia-Kuwait Neutral Zone.

### TRADE UNIONS

Trade unions are illegal in Saudi Arabia.

# Transport

### RAILWAYS

Saudi Arabia has the only rail system in the Arabian peninsula. The Saudi Government Railroad comprises 719 km of single and 157 km of double track. In addition, the total length of spur lines and sidings is 348 km. The main line, which was opened in 1951, is 578 km in length; it connects Dammam port, on the Gulf coast, with Riyadh, and passes Dhahran, Abqaiq, Hufuf, Harad and al-Kharj. A 310-km line, linking Hufuf and Riyadh, was inaugurated in May 1985. A total of 416,700 passengers travelled by rail in the Kingdom in 1992.

**Saudi Railways Organization:** POB 36, Dammam 31241; tel. (3) 871-3001; telex 801050; fax (3) 871-2293; an independent entity with a Board of Dirs headed by the Minister of Communications; Pres. FAISAL M. ASH-SHEHAIL.

### ROADS

Asphalted roads link Jeddah to Mecca, Jeddah to Medina, Medina to Yanbu, Ta'if to Mecca, Riyadh to al-Kharj, and Dammam to Hufuf as well as the principal communities and certain outlying points in Aramco's area of operations. During the 1980s the construction of other roads was undertaken, including one extending from Riyadh to Medina. The trans-Arabian highway, linking Dammam, Riyadh, Ta'if, Mecca and Jeddah, was completed in 1967. A causeway linking Saudi Arabia with Bahrain was opened in November 1986. A 317-km highway linking Riyadh to Qassim was completed in the late 1980s. At the end of 1992 there were 151,532 km of roads, of which 21,746 km were main roads (including motorways) and 18,776 km were secondary roads. In 1992 there were about 60 road-building projects in progress in the Kingdom. Metalled roads link all the main population centres. At the end of 1991 there were 5.1m. road motor vehicles registered in Saudi Arabia.

**Saudi Public Transport Co (SAPTCO):** POB 10667, Riyadh; tel. (1) 454-5000; telex 402414; fax (1) 454-2100; f. 1979; operates a public bus service throughout the country and to neighbouring countries; the Government holds a 30% share; Chair. Dr NASIR AS-SALOOM; CEO Dr ABD AL-AZIZ AL-OHALY.

**National Transport Company of Saudi Arabia:** Queen's Bldg, POB 7280, Jeddah 21462; tel. (2) 643-4561; telex 401235; specializes in inward clearance, freight forwarding, general and heavy road haulage, re-export, charter air freight and exhibitions; Man. Dir A. D. BLACKSTOCK; Operations Man. I. CROXSON.

### SHIPPING

The commercial ports of Jeddah, Dammam, Yanbu and Gizan, the King Fahd Industrial Ports of Jubail and Yanbu, and the oil port of Ras Tanura, as well as a number of minor ports, are under the exclusive management of the Ports Authority. In 1991/92 the total cargo handled by Saudi Arabian ports, excluding crude petroleum, was 74.6m. metric tons, compared with 68.2m. tons in 1990/91.

*Jeddah* is the principal commercial port and the main point of entry for pilgrims bound for Mecca. It has berths for general cargo, container traffic, 'roll on, roll off' (ro-ro) traffic, livestock and bulk grain shipments, with draughts ranging from 8 m to 14 m. The port also has a 200-ton floating crane, cold storage facilities and a fully-equipped ship-repair yard. In 1991/92 a total of 3,857 vessels called at Jeddah Islamic Port, and 16.1m. tons of cargo were handled.

*Dammam* is the second largest commercial port and has general cargo, container, ro-ro, dangerous cargo and bulk grain berths. Draughts at this port range from 9 m to 14 m. It has a 200-ton floating crane and a fully equipped ship repair yard. In 1991/92 a total of 1,820 vessels called at King Abd al-Aziz Port in Dammam, and 9.9m. tons of cargo were handled.

*Jubail* has one commercial and one industrial port. The commercial port has general cargo, bulk grain and container berths with ro-ro facilities, and a floating crane. Draughts at this port range from 12 m to 14 m. In 1991/92 a total of 105 vessels called at Jubail Commercial Port, and 1.1m. tons of cargo were handled. The industrial port has bulk cargo, refined and petrochemical and ro-ro berths, and an open sea tanker terminal suitable for vessels up to 300,000 dwt. Draughts range from 6 m to 30 m. In 1991/92 King Fahd Industrial Port in Jubail handled 21.9m. tons of cargo, of which 19.3m. tons were exported.

*Yanbu*, which comprises one commercial and one industrial port, is Saudi Arabia's nearest major port to Europe and North America, and is the focal point of the most rapidly growing area, in the west of Saudi Arabia. The commercial port has general cargo, ro-ro and bulk grain berths, with draughts ranging from 10 m to 12 m. It also has a floating crane, and is equipped to handle minor ship repairs. In 1991/92 a total of 51 vessels called at Yanbu Commercial Port, and 1.2m. tons of cargo were handled. The industrial port has berths for general cargo, containers, 'roll on-roll off' traffic, bulk cargo, crude petroleum, refined and petrochemical products and natural gas liquids, and a tanker terminal on the open sea. In 1991/92 a total of 902 vessels called at King Fahd Industrial Port in Yanbu; the port handled 24.0m. tons of cargo, of which 23.5m. tons were exported.

*Gizan* is the main port for the southern part of the country. It has general cargo, ro-ro, bulk grain and container berths, with draughts ranging from 8 m to 12 m. It also has a 200-ton floating crane. In 1991/92 a total of 100 vessels called at Gizan Port, and 324,407m. tons of cargo were handled.

In addition to these major ports, there are a number of minor ports suitable only for small craft, including Khuraiba, Haql, Dhiba, al-Wajh, Umlujj, Rabigh, al-Lith, Qunfoudah, Farasan and al-Qahma on the Red Sea coast and al-Khobar, Qatif, Uqair, Darin and Ras al-Khafji on the Gulf coast. Ras Mishab, on the Gulf coast, is operated by the Ministry of Defence and Civil Aviation.

**Arabian Marine Operating Co Ltd:** POB 5449, Al-Jawhara Bldg, Bagh da Dieh, Jeddah 21422; tel. (2) 642-9408; telex 601083; Chair. Prince ABDULLAH AL-FAISAL AS-SA'UD; Gen. Man. C. HAKIM.

**Arabian Petroleum Supply Co Ltd:** POB 1408, Quarantina Rd, Jeddah 21431; tel. (2) 637-1120; telex 602613; fax (2) 636-2366; Gen. Man. V. C. CAMINITI.

**Nashar Saudi Lines:** POB 6697, Jeddah; tel. (2) 642-3600; telex 601156; owners of livestock carriers trading in Arabian Gulf, Red Sea, Mediterranean and Black Sea.

**National Shipping Co of Saudi Arabia (NSCSA):** POB 8931, Riyadh 11492; tel. (1) 478-5454; telex 405624; fax (1) 477-8036; f. 1979; regular container, ro-ro and general cargo service from USA to the Middle East, South-East Asia and Far East; capacity 16,684 20-ft equivalent units (1995); Chair. SALEH A. AL-NAIM; Chief Exec. MUHAMMAD SULAIMAN AL-JARBOU.

**Saudi International Petroleum Carriers Ltd (SIPCA):** POB 5572, Riyadh 11432; tel. (1) 465-9077; telex 401709; Chair. OMAR AGGAD.

**Saudi Lines:** POB 66, Jeddah; regular cargo and passenger services between Red Sea and Indian Ocean ports; Pres. M. A. BAKHASHAB PASHA; Man. Dir A. M. BAKHASHAB.

**Saudi Shipping and Maritime Services Co Ltd:** POB 7522, Jeddah 21472; tel. (2) 644-0577; telex 601845; fax (2) 644-0932; Chair. Prince SA'UD IBN NAYEF IBN ABD AL-AZIZ; Man. Dir Capt. MUSTAFA T. AWARA.

**Seaports Authority (SEAPA):** POB 5162, Riyadh 11188; tel. (1) 405-0005; telex 401783; fax (1) 402-7394; f. 1976; Pres. and Chair. Dr FAYEZ IBN IBRAHIM BADR; Vice-Chair. and Dir-Gen. MUHAMMAD IBN ABD AL-KARIM BAKR.

**Shipping Corpn of Saudi Arabia Ltd:** POB 1691, 2nd Floor, National Marketing Group Bldg, 8 Malik Khalid St, Jeddah 21441; tel. (2) 647-1137; telex 601078; fax (2) 647-8222; Pres. and Man. Dir ABD AL-AZIZ AHMAD ARAB.

### CIVIL AVIATION

King Abdulaziz International Airport, which was opened in 1981, has three terminals, one of which is specifically designed to cope with the needs of the many thousands of pilgrims who visit Mecca and Medina each year. King Khalid International Airport, at Riyadh, opened in 1983 with four terminals. It handled 7.9m. passengers in 1993. A third major airport, King Fahd International Airport, (with an initial handling capacity of 5.2m. passengers per year), opened in the Eastern Province in 1993. Expansion of 21 domestic airports began in 1984. Saudia, the Kingdom's national airline, carried 20.9m. passengers in 1993. There is a total of 25 commercial airports in the kingdom.

**Presidency of Civil Aviation (PCA):** POB 887, Jeddah 21421; tel. (2) 640-5000; telex 601093; fax (2) 640-1477; Pres. Dr ALI ABD AR-RAHMAN AL-KHALAF.

**Saudia—Saudi Arabian Airlines:** POB 620, Saudia Bldg, Jeddah 21231; tel. (2) 686-0000; telex 601007; fax (2) 686-4552; f. 1945 and began operations in 1947; in 1993 Saudia carried 12.3m. passengers, its fleet numbering 111 aircraft; regular services to 25 domestic and 54 international destinations; regular international services worldwide; Chair. Prince SULTAN IBN ABD AL-AZIZ; Dir-Gen. KHALID IBN ABDULLAH IBN BAKR; Exec. Vice-Pres. (operations) ADNAN AL-DABBAGH.

## Tourism

All devout Muslims try to make at least one visit to the holy cities of Medina, the burial place of Muhammad, and Mecca, his birthplace. In 1993/94 more than 2m. pilgrims visited Saudi Arabia. In 1988 there were 246 hotels in the kingdom, with a total of 22,298 rooms.

**Saudi Hotels and Resort Areas Co (SHARACO):** POB 5500, Riyadh 11422; tel. (1) 465-7177; telex 400366; fax (1) 465-7172; f. 1975; Saudi Government has 40% interest; cap. SR500m.; Chair. Dr SOLIMAN AL-HUMAYYED; Dir-Gen. ABD AL-AZIZ AL-AMBAR.

**National Tourism Co:** f. 1992.

# SENEGAL

## Introductory Survey

### Location, Climate, Language, Religion, Flag, Capital

The Republic of Senegal lies on the west coast of Africa, bordered to the north by Mauritania, to the east by Mali, and to the south by Guinea and Guinea-Bissau. In the southern part of the country The Gambia forms a narrow enclave extending some 320 km (200 miles) inland. The climate is tropical, with a long dry season followed by a short wet season—from June to September in the north, and from June to October in the south. Average annual temperatures range from 22°C (72°F) to 28°C (82°F). French is the official language, but the three main language groups, with their principal languages, are: Senegalo-Guinean (Wolof, Serer and Diola), Mandé (Bambara and Sarakolé) and Peulh (Toucouleur and Peul). About 90% of the population are Muslims and some 6% Christians, mostly Roman Catholics. The remainder follow traditional beliefs. The national flag (proportions 3 by 2) has three equal vertical stripes, of green, yellow and red, with a five-pointed green star in the centre of the yellow stripe. The capital is Dakar.

### Recent History

In November 1958, after 300 years as a French colony, Senegal became a self-governing member of the French Community. The formation in April 1959 of the Mali Federation, linking Senegal with Soudan (later the Republic of Mali), was not successful, and the entity had only two months of independence before being dissolved when Senegal seceded, to become a separate independent state, on 20 August 1960. The Republic of Senegal was proclaimed on 5 September, with Léopold Sédar Senghor, leader of the Union progressiste sénégalaise (UPS), as the country's first President. Relations with France remain close.

In late 1962, following the discovery of a coup attempt led by the Prime Minister, Mamadou Dia, President Senghor assumed the premiership himself. (Dia was subsequently sentenced to life imprisonment.) Following a decisive win for the UPS at elections to the Assemblée nationale in 1963, other political parties were gradually absorbed into it or outlawed, so that by 1966 a one-party state was in existence. In 1970 the office of Prime Minister was re-created and assigned to a young but experienced provincial administrator, Abdou Diouf, who in 1976 was made Senghor's constitutional successor. In 1973 Senghor, the sole candidate, was re-elected as President.

Senghor, who promised a gradual return to multi-party democracy, freed all political prisoners (including Dia and his accomplices in the 1962 coup plot) in 1974, and amended the Constitution in March 1976 to allow three parties to contest elections. In December the UPS was renamed the Parti socialiste (PS), which became the 'democratic socialist' party provided for in the Constitution. The Parti démocratique sénégalais (PDS) was recognized as the 'liberal democratic' party, and the Parti africain de l'indépendance was accepted as the 'Marxist-Leninist' faction. The first nation-wide elections under the three-party system took place in February 1978. The PS won 83 of the 100 seats in the legislature, the remainder being won by the PDS. In the concurrent presidential election, Senghor overwhelmingly defeated the leader of the PDS, Abdoulaye Wade.

Senghor retired in December 1980, and was succeeded as President by Diouf in January 1981. An amnesty was declared for political dissidents, and the Constitution was amended to allow the existence of more than four political parties (a fourth party, the right-wing Mouvement républicain sénégalais, had been legalized in December 1978—it had ceased to exist by the early 1990s). Elections in February 1983 brought overwhelming victory for Diouf, who received 83.5% of the presidential vote (compared with 14.8% for his nearest rival, Wade), and for the PS, which won 111 of the 120 seats in the legislature. The PDS won eight seats, and the Rassemblement national démocratique one. Disputing the results, the Government's opponents boycotted the Assemblée nationale, although most had taken their seats by the end of the year.

In April Diouf had assumed greater powers for his own office by abolishing the post of Prime Minister.

In July 1985 the PDS and four other opposition parties formed an alliance, but the union was declared unconstitutional by Diouf. Sixteen prominent opposition politicians, including Wade and the leader of the Ligue démocratique—Mouvement pour le parti du travail (LD—MPT), Abdoulaye Bathily, were subsequently arrested and detained for a week, accused of 'unauthorized demonstration'. The PDS suffered a crisis in October, when three of its eight representatives in the Assemblée nationale left the party, and was further weakened in June 1986, when its deputy leader resigned from both the PDS and the legislature. A faction of the PDS was registered as a new political party, the Parti Démocratique Sénégalais—Rénovation (PDS—R), in August 1987, exacerbating the fragmentation of the opposition.

When preliminary results of the February 1988 presidential and legislative elections indicated overwhelming victories for both Diouf and the PS, opposition parties alleged fraud on the part of the ruling party, and rioting broke out in the Dakar region. A state of emergency was announced, and public gatherings were banned, educational establishments closed and a night-time curfew imposed in the capital. Wade and Amath Dansokho, the leader of the Marxist-Leninist Parti de l'indépendance et du travail, were arrested, together with other opposition members. The official results of the presidential election, announced in March, showed that Diouf had obtained 73.2% of the votes cast; of the other three candidates, Wade obtained 25.8% of the votes. The PS won 103 seats in the legislature, and the PDS the remaining 17. (Primary schools and the University were formally reopened in March, and curfew hours were reduced: the curfew was ended in April, although the state of emergency remained in force until May.) Wade, Dansokho and other opposition activists were tried in April on charges of incitement to violence and attacks on the internal security of the State; Dansokho and five others were subsequently acquitted, but in May Wade received a one-year suspended prison sentence. Later in the month, however, Diouf announced an amnesty for all those who had been condemned in the aftermath of the elections, as well as for 320 Casamance separatists (see below). Subsequent attempts to establish an effective dialogue between the Government and the opposition failed. In March 1989, none the less, Diouf announced the establishment of an executive committee within the PS to initiate the reform of the electoral system, the formulation of a 'National Democratic Charter', and to consider the status of the opposition. In the following month changes were announced to the electoral code, involving measures that were said to ensure the legitimate registration of the electorate; a system of proportional representation (within administrative departments) was to be introduced for legislative elections, and access to the state-owned media was to be granted to opposition parties. However, the opposition stated that the nature of the reforms would, in fact, enhance the influence of the PS, to the detriment of other political organizations. The changes were approved in October by PS representatives in the Assemblée nationale (PDS deputies had begun a boycott of legislative sessions in mid-1989, in protest against what they alleged to be unsatisfactory coverage by the media of parliamentary debates). The legislature also approved the 'National Democratic Charter', which provided for the dissolution of any political party that did not abide by the Constitution, or by the principles of democracy, or that received susbsidies from abroad.

Secondary school pupils (who had been boycotting classes since October 1987) and university students failed to return to classes after the 1988 elections, and the 1987/88 academic year was declared invalid by the Government. In October 1988 a programme for the rehabilitation of the national education system was announced, and in November the Diouf Government agreed to students' demands for improved welfare provisions, and gave assurances regarding the autonomy of Dakar's Cheikh Anta Diop University. The 1988/89 academic year was, nevertheless, disrupted by a three-month strike by academic staff in early 1989, and by continuing protests by students concerning academic and welfare issues. In April two senior army officers were forced into retirement, while Gen. Joseph Louis Tavares da Souza (until June 1988 the Chief of the General Staff of the Armed Forces), was removed from his post as the Senegalese Ambassador to the Federal Republic of Germany, as a result of investigations into a coup plot that was alleged to have been formulated in the aftermath of the February 1988 elections.

In February 1990 Wade returned to Senegal after an absence of more than six months. PDS supporters, who had gathered to welcome him, were dispersed by the security forces. Although Wade stated that he no longer disputed Diouf's victory in the February 1988 elections, he demanded that, in view of the deteriorating economic and social conditions in Senegal, the electorate be allowed to choose new leaders. A series of days of action and protests were subsequently organized by the opposition parties; several participants were detained following intervention by the security forces.

In March 1990 Diouf announced an extensive reorganization of the Government, as a result of which the membership of the Council of Ministers was reduced (in accordance with a policy of retrenchment in the public sector, as recommended by Senegal's external creditors). Among the most significant changes was the dismissal of Jean Collin, who had been prominent since the time of French colonial rule, from the post of Minister of State and Secretary-General of the Presidency of the Republic. (Members of the opposition had recently criticized Collin's close links with France and the USSR, and his allegedly excessive influence over Diouf.) In April Collin also relinquished senior posts within the PS; he was appointed special adviser to President Eyadéma of Togo in early 1991, and died in France in October 1993.

In May 1990 the Government announced that changes affording the opposition greater access to the state-owned media would be effected. In November, however, a delegation that was scheduled to meet representatives of the Diouf administration to discuss the issue staged a demonstration in protest against what it alleged was a restrictive policy governing the official media. Security forces intervened to disperse the demonstrators, and several party leaders were briefly detained. The opposition organized a boycott of municipal and rural elections in November, claiming that the modified electoral code permitted widespread electoral malpractice. Unrest re-emerged in the education sector in early 1991, when 17 students were arrested following action at the Cheikh Anta Diop University in support of a boycott of classes by secondary school pupils: it was alleged that the Diouf Government had reneged on concessions agreed as a result of earlier protests.

In March 1991 the legislature approved several amendments to the Constitution, notably the restoration of the post of Prime Minister. It was also agreed that opposition parties would, henceforth, be allowed to participate in government. In April Habib Thiam (who had been premier at the time of the abolition of the post, in April 1983) was restored as Prime Minister. Thiam subsequently appointed a new Government, including four representatives of the PDS (Wade was designated Minister of State, while Ousmane Ngom, the parliamentary leader of the PDS, was appointed Minister of Labour and Professional Training) and Amath Dansokho, who became Minister of Town Planning and Housing.

In May 1991 it was announced that a national commission was to be established to consider the further reform of Senegal's electoral code. Following consultations with most political parties, the commission submitted its recommendations to Diouf in late August, and in the following month the Assemblée nationale adopted a series of amendments to the electoral code, as defined in the Constitution. Among the most important changes were those affecting the procedure by which the President was elected. Presidential elections would henceforth take place, in two rounds if necessary (under the new regulations, the President would have to be elected by at least one-quarter of registered voters, and by an absolute majority of the votes cast), every seven years. Furthermore, elections to the presidency would no longer coincide with legislative elections, which would continue to take place at five-yearly intervals. Moreover, restrictions were for the first time imposed on the renewal of the presidential mandate: the President would be limited to two terms of office. The amendments also included the lowering of the age of eligibility to vote from 21 to 18 years of age. The opposition criticized the Government's intention to hold the 1993 presidential and legislative elections three months apart, stating that few parties would be able to finance two separate electoral campaigns. A major reform of the organs of the judiciary was implemented in May 1992, as a result of which the Supreme Court was abolished and its functions assumed by three new bodies: a Constitutional Court, a Council of State and a Court of Higher Appeal (Cour de Cassation).

In January 1992 security forces clashed with students who were attempting to stage a demonstration in Dakar. The students had been boycotting classes at the Cheikh Anta Diop University since late 1991, in support of their demands for improved educational facilities. The strike ended in February 1992, when the Government agreed to several of the students' demands, including the appointment of more academic staff and increases in the level of grants.

In October 1992 Wade (who had already declared his intention to contest the 1993 presidential election) and his three PDS colleagues resigned from the Council of Ministers, protesting that they had been excluded from the governmental process. Prior to the election Wade alleged that the PS retained privileged access to the state-owned media (contrary to earlier agreements between the Government and the opposition) and that the Government was acting to hinder the registration of voters.

The presidential election, which took place on 21 February 1993, was contested by eight candidates. Despite some irregularities, voting was reported to be well ordered in most areas; serious incidents did, however, occur in the Casamance region (see below). The opposition denounced preliminary results, which indicated that, although Wade had enjoyed considerable success in Dakar and in the nearby manufacturing centre of Thiès, Diouf had won a clear majority of the overall votes. The process of determining the official outcome of the election encountered considerable delay, owing to disagreements within the electoral commission (a body comprising a presiding magistrate and representatives of the candidates at the election). Difficulties in proclaiming the results prompted the resignation of the President of the Constitutional Council in early March, and it was not until 13 March that the Council was able to announce that Diouf had been re-elected with 58.4% of the votes cast (51.6% of the electorate had voted); Wade secured 32.0% of the votes. Diouf subsequently announced that the electoral code was to be modified, with the aim of avoiding similar delays in the announcement of future election results.

Elections to the Assemblée nationale took place on 9 May 1993. It was announced that the electoral commission would be required to submit the results to the Constitutional Council within five days, and on 14 May the commission duly announced that the PS had won 84 of the legislature's 120 seats. The PDS took 27 seats, the remainder being divided between three other parties and one electoral alliance. Participation by voters was only 40.7%. Shortly after the announcement of the results the Vice-President of the Constitutional Council, Babacar Seye, was assassinated, and, although an organization styling itself the 'Armée du peuple' claimed responsibility, Wade and three other PDS leaders were detained for three days in connection with the murder. The PDS denounced what it alleged to be a plot to discredit the party, and Wade, following his release, suggested that attempts to implicate him in the assassination may have been orchestrated by persons who sought to prevent any accord between himself and Diouf. The official results of the elections were confirmed by the Constitutional Council on 24 May.

Wade and the PDS were excluded from the new Government, which was formed by Habib Thiam in June 1993. Dansokho, who had supported Diouf's presidential campaign, retained his portfolio, while Abdoulaye Bathily (himself a candidate for the presidency, and whose LD—MPT had won three seats in the legislature) was appointed to the Ministry of the Environment and Nature Conservation. Other new appointments included Papa Ousmane Sakho, hitherto the national director of the Banque centrale des états de l'Afrique de l'ouest, as Minister of the Economy, Finance and Planning, and Serigne Diop, the leader of the PDS—R, to the Ministry of Employment, Labour and Professional Training.

In July 1993 there were clashes in Dakar when security forces intervened to disperse a violent demonstration that had been organized to demand the release of a PDS deputy, Mody

Sy (detained in the second half of May, together with Samuel Sarr—a close associate of Wade—and two others, in connection with Seye's murder), who, it was alleged, had been tortured while in custody. Six members of the Assemblée nationale (representatives of the PDS and the LD—MPT) were briefly detained in connection with the incident. Severe labour unrest arose in August, when the Government, citing the need to reduce the budget deficit in order to secure vital economic support from external creditors, announced wide-ranging austerity measures. As well as modifications to the tax code and a 'rationalization' of the diplomatic corps, it was proposed that Diouf's salary and allowances would be halved, that the salaries of government ministers and members of the legislature would be reduced by 25% (and their allowances by 50%), and that wages throughout the public sector would be reduced by 15%; employees in the private sector, meanwhile, would be required to forfeit one day's pay per month. The emergency plan was duly adopted by the Assemblée nationale. However, trade unions and opposition parties denounced, in particular, the reduction in public-sector salaries, and, following the failure of attempts to reach a compromise, the PS-affiliated Confédération nationale des travailleurs sénégalais (CNTS) organized a 24-hour general strike in September. Diouf subsequently announced the postponement, by one week, of the imposition of the unpopular measures, pending further negotiations between the Government and trade unions. However, talks again failed, as the Government refused to accede to union demands that the prices of staple foods be lowered to compensate for losses in income. Two 72-hour general strikes (denounced as illegal by the Government, which threatened to withdraw the right to strike, as guaranteed under the Constitution) were organized, with only partial success, by the CNTS and other workers' confederations in October.

Relations between the Diouf administration and parties outside the government coalition, which formed a Coordination des forces démocratiques (CFD), deteriorated further in the second half of 1993. In October Wade was charged with complicity in the assassination of Seye; Wade's wife and a PDS deputy were also charged with 'complicity in a breach of state security'. None was detained, although Mody Sy, Sarr and three others remained in custody in connection with the murder. Later in the month a PDS motion expressing 'no confidence' in the Thiam Gvernment was defeated in the Assemblée nationale. The PDS subsequently announced that it was to boycott parliamentary sessions, in protest against what it considered to be biased coverage by the state-owned media of the vote.

In November 1993 Ngom and Landing Savané, the leader of And Jëf—Parti africain pour la démocratie et le socialisme (AJ—PADS), were among those detained following a protest in Dakar to demand the cancellation of the Government's austerity plan. The action coincided with a demonstration, at which arrests were also made, to appeal for the release of Moustapha Sy, the leader of an Islamic youth movement, Dahira Moustarchidine wal Moustarchidate, who had recently been arrested after having criticized the Government (and who had also reportedly claimed to know the circumstances and authors of Seye's assassination). Ngom, Savané and some 87 others were convicted of participating in an unauthorized demonstration, and received six-month suspended prison sentences. In January 1994 Moustapha Sy was sentenced to one year's imprisonment.

Following the devaluation of the CFA franc, in January 1994, emergency measures (among them the cancellation of the previous year's wage reductions) were adopted to offset the immediate adverse effects of the loss in value of the national currency. However, the opposition held Diouf (who, despite having previously denied that any devaluation would be imposed, was widely regarded as a principal architect of the policy) responsible for resultant hardship. A demonstration in Dakar in mid-February, organized by the CFD to denounce the devaluation, degenerated into serious rioting throughout the capital, as a result of which eight people (including six police officers) were killed. Dahira Moustarchidine wal Moustarchidate, which was identified by the authorities as being implicated in much of the violence, was banned in the aftermath of the disturbances, and the Government stated that it regarded the CFD (which the authorities stressed was an unauthorized organization) as responsible for the unrest. Wade, Savané and more than 70 others were subsequently detained and charged with attacks on state security. Opposition activists alleged that some of the accused had been tortured while in custody (as a result of which one detainee had died), and Wade and Savané instigated a hunger strike, in support of their demands for access to proper legal procedures (they were not formally charged until mid-March).

In late May 1994 charges against Wade and his opposition associates (including Mody Sy and Samuel Sarr) in connection with the murder of Seye were dismissed on the grounds of insufficient evidence. Wade and Savané, awaiting trial in connection with the post-devaluation violence, were not released from custody. Sarr and Mody Sy, who remained in detention pending the outcome of an appeal by the state prosecution against their release, staged a hunger strike in late June, and were subsequently released on bail. Similarly, Wade, Savané and four others, who had also begun a hunger strike, were provisionally released in early July. Legal proceedings against them and 140 others implicated in the February riots were dismissed later in July, again on the grounds of insufficient evidence (a ruling that was confirmed at an appeal hearing at the end of August). In late September 24 alleged members of Dahira Moustarchidine wal Moustarchidate received prison sentences of between six months and two years for their part in the violence. Meanwhile, in mid-September Moustapha Sy had been granted a presidential pardon and released from custody. The trial of the four alleged assassins of Seye began in late September: in early October three of the accused were convicted and sentenced to between 18 and 20 years' imprisonment, with hard labour, while the fourth defendant was acquitted of involvement in the murder.

In August 1994 the 1993/94 academic year was declared invalid for students at the Cheikh Anta Diop University, following almost three months of disruption by students who were protesting against proposed reforms to the higher education system.

In early September 1994 the PDS and AJ—PADS joined with the Mouvement pour le socialisme et l'unité to form Bokk Sopi Senegal (Uniting to Change Senegal). In subsequent months both the Government and opposition expressed their desire to restore a national consensus. Diouf indicated his preparedness to accept other influences within government; in January 1995 he and Wade held their first private meeting since the latter's departure from the Council of Ministers in 1992, and in late February 1995 Wade was formally invited to rejoin the Government. Thiam named a new Council of Ministers in mid-March: Wade was designated Minister of State at the Presidency, while four other PDS members, including Ngom (as Minister of Public Health and Social Action), were also appointed to the new administration. Djibo Ka, a long-serving government member who recently, as Minister of the Interior, had been associated with the legal proceedings against Wade and other opposition leaders, left the Government.

Long-standing resentment against the Government of Senegal in the southern province of Casamance (which is virtually cut off from the rest of the country by the enclave of The Gambia) was more formally embodied from the early 1980s by the emergence of the separatist Mouvement des forces démocratiques de la Casamance (MFDC), which was periodically involved in clashes with the authorities in the south, who attempted to suppress the activities of the movement. Supporters of separatism initiated a new offensive from April 1990: ambushes and raids, most of which were perpetrated on administrative targets in the Casamance region, took place during 1990 and early 1991. Tensions escalated when the Senegalese Government dispatched military reinforcements to the region, and in September 1990 a military governor was appointed for Casamance. The human rights organization, Amnesty International, expressed concern in several reports regarding events in Casamance; the Government promised to investigate reports of the abuse of human rights, and subsequently refuted Amnesty International's allegations. By April 1991 at least 100 people were said to have been killed as a result of violence in the region, while more than 300 Casamançais had been transported to Dakar, where they were awaiting trial for sedition. Among those being detained, it was reported, was the President of the MFDC, Abbé Augustin Diamacouné Senghor. Meanwhile, in late 1990 reports suggested that some 1,600 Senegalese had taken refuge in Guinea-Bissau, after having fled southern Senegal to escape clashes between the Senegalese armed forces and the MFDC. In April 1991 the Thiam Government alleged that an attack by separatists in the Casamance region had been perpetrated by a

2653

faction of the MFDC that refused to recognize a truce negotiated by the leaders of the MFDC in co-operation with the Senegalese authorities. The announcement, in May, of the imminent release of more than 340 detainees (including Diamacouné Senghor) who had been arrested in connection with unrest in Casamance facilitated the conclusion, shortly afterwards in Guinea-Bissau, of a cease-fire agreement by representatives of the Senegalese Government and of the MFDC. In June the region's military Governor was replaced by a civilian, as part of the demilitarization of Casamance that had been envisaged in the May accord. An amnesty was approved by the Assemblée nationale later in June, to the benefit of some 400 Casamançais, including those whose release had been announced in the previous month (as well as for others, among them Gen. Tavares da Souza, who had been implicated in the unrest that had followed the February 1988 elections). A period of calm ensued. In December 1991, however, a PS deputy and a local village chief were assassinated in the region of Ziguinchor (the provincial capital); MFDC leaders denied involvement in the killings). At the same time it was reported that more than 400 residents of the region had fled to The Gambia, fearing a further MFDC offensive.

In January 1992 a peace commission (the Comité de gestion de la paix en Casamance), comprising government representatives and members of the MFDC, was established, with mediation by Guinea-Bissau. At the end of the same month, none the less, more than 100 people fled to The Gambia, following a brutal attack, allegedly perpetrated by Casamance separatists, on their village. A resurgence of violence in Casamance during July and August prompted the Government to redeploy armed forces in the region. This, in turn, exacerbated tensions, and gave rise to MFDC protests that the 'remilitarization' of Casamance was in contravention of the cease-fire agreement. The death of a police-officer, in late July, was followed in early August by a violent clash near Ziguinchor, in which, according to official figures, 50 separatist rebels and two members of the armed forces were killed. Contradictory statements made by leaders of the MFDC, regarding their commitment to the truce accord, evidenced a split within the movement. The so-called 'Front nord' and the MFDC Vice-President, Sidi Badji, appealed to the rebels to lay down their arms; meanwhile the 'Front sud', based in areas of dense forest near the border with Guinea-Bissau, and led by Diamacouné Senghor (himself now based in Guinea-Bissau), appeared determined to continue the armed struggle. Negotiations between representatives of the Senegalese Government and the MFDC achieved little, and in October 32 people (most of whom were seasonal fishermen from other regions of Senegal) were killed when separatist rebels attacked a fishing village near the Cap-Skirring tourist resort, causing local residents and tourists to flee the region. A further attack on a fishing village in the same area in November resulted in at least seven deaths. Following the deaths of two Senegalese soldiers in December, the army instigated a major security operation, launching air attacks on supposed rebel bases along the border with Guinea-Bissau (see below).

Indications in advance of the 1993 presidential and legislative elections that MFDC rebels would seek to prevent voting in Casamance prompted Diouf to begin his electoral campaign in the province. His visit, in January, proceeded amid strict security measures, following the recent deaths of seven aid workers in Casamance. About 30 people were reported to have been killed in rebel attacks on voters on the day of the presidential election. Army reinforcements were dispatched to Casamance in March (raising the total number of armed forces personnel in the region to as many as 5,000), following further clashes between the security forces and rebels.

Abbé Diamacouné Senghor returned to Ziguinchor in March 1993, having seemingly been expelled from Guinea-Bissau. Violence persisted, but in April Diamacouné Senghor reportedly appealed for a cease-fire, and expressed a willingness to negotiate with the Senegalese Government. Ten days later, none the less, at least 100 rebels and three members of the armed forces were reportedly killed in a clash near the border with Guinea-Bissau. In late April the Senegalese authorities confirmed their willingness to observe a truce, stating that the security forces would henceforth act only in a defensive capacity, and gave assurances regarding the continuation of negotiations and the resumption of economic initiatives in Casamance. A period of relative calm followed, although in June it was reported that 20 suspected members of the MFDC had been killed by security forces. In July a cease-fire agreement was signed in Ziguinchor by the Senegalese Government and, on behalf of the MFDC, Diamacouné Senghor. The accord envisaged the release of Casamançais prisoners, and made provision for the return of those who had fled the region. Guinea-Bissau was to act as a guarantor of the agreement, and the Government of France was to be asked to submit an historical arbitration regarding the Casamance issue. (The Senegalese authorities had consistently refuted MFDC assertions that documents from the colonial era indicated that France favoured independence for Casamance.) Shortly afterwards a soldier was killed in a skirmish involving separatist rebels and members of the armed forces. None the less, 256 Casamançais were released from detention in the second half of July, in accordance with the Ziguinchor accord. At the time of the conclusion of the new cease-fire agreement the total number of casualties in the conflict was uncertain, since the Senegalese authorities had not disclosed details of military operations in Casamance for some months. However, various sources estimated that, in the year preceding the new accord, between 500 and 1,000 people had been killed, and many hundreds injured, while humanitarian organizations estimated that 25,000–30,000 people had been displaced by the unrest, fleeing to The Gambia or Guinea-Bissau, or to other regions of Senegal. Although there were sporadic reports of clashes in Casamance during the remainder of 1993, as a result of which at least five deaths were recorded, the cease-fire was generally observed. In December France issued its judgment that Casamance had not existed as an autonomous territory prior to the colonial period, and that independence for the region had been neither demanded nor considered at the time of decolonization.

Casamance was widely regarded as being among the regions of Senegal that benefited most from the devaluation of the CFA franc at the beginning of 1994; tourists returned to the region, and the fishing sector flourished, while several donor-sponsored development initiatives were undertaken with the aim of enhancing the region's economic potential. From early 1995, however, renewed violence in the south, near the border with Guinea-Bissau, indicated a re-emergence of divisions between the northern and southern factions of the MFDC. Rebels in the south were reportedly frustrated at the slow progress of the dialogue between the MFDC and the authorities, and accused the Senegalese armed forces, by their military operations in the south, of violating the provisions of the 1993 cease-fire accord. At least 20 soldiers were reported to have been killed in military operations in southern Casamance between January and May 1995, and there were believed to have been heavy casualties among the rebels; the deaths were also reported of a Muslim elder in Ziguinchor, in early April, and of a sub-prefect of the region, who was found dead, with three others, in early May. A major military operation was instigated following the disappearance, in early April, of four French tourists in the Basse-Casamance region. More than 1,000 élite troops were deployed in southern Casamance, and were assisted in their search by French reconnaissance aircraft; although by mid-June they had failed to locate the missing tourists, the aim of the operation appeared increasingly to be to dislodge MFDC dissidents from the border region. Strong resistance was encountered, but rebel strongholds in the south were captured by the armed forces. Both the northern and southern factions of the MFDC denied any involvement in the apparent kidnap of the tourists, and Diamacouné Senghor accused the Senegalese army of responsibility for the disappearances. The MFDC leader was placed under house arrest in Ziguinchor in late April, and four of his close associates were taken into custody.

Beginning in 1989 Senegal's regional relations underwent a period of considerable strain. The deaths in April of that year of two Senegalese farmers, following a disagreement with Mauritanian livestock-breeders regarding land rights in the border region between the two countries, precipitated a crisis that was fuelled by long-standing ethnic and economic rivalries. Mauritanian nationals residing in Senegal were attacked, and their businesses looted (the retail trade in Senegal had hitherto been dominated by the estimated 300,000 mainly light-skinned Mauritanians resident in that country), while Senegalese nationals in Mauritania, who were said to number 30,000, suffered similar aggression. Estimates of the number of casualties varied, but it was believed that by early May several hundred people, mostly Senegalese, had been killed.

Operations to repatriate nationals of both countries were conducted, with international assistance, and mediation attempts were initiated, notably by the Organization of African Unity (OAU, see p. 200). However, although both Senegal and Mauritania expressed their commitment to the principle of a negotiated settlement to the dispute, Senegal's insistence on the inviolability of the border that had been defined at the time of French colonial rule, and Mauritania's demand that its nationals be compensated for property lost in Senegal, remained among the greatest impediments to a solution. The two countries suspended diplomatic relations in August. Further outbreaks of violence were reported in late 1989, when black Mauritanians who had been expelled to Senegal from Mauritania crossed into their former homeland (assisted, the Government of Mauritania alleged, by the Senegalese armed forces) to recover their property. In early 1990 attempts at mediation by the OAU were thwarted by military engagements in the disputed border region, as a result of which several deaths were reported, and by the stipulation by the Governments of both countries of preconditions to the restoration of diplomatic relations. In October of that year the Senegalese authorities alleged that Casamançais rebels had procured weapons from Iraq, with the assistance of both Mauritania and The Gambia. Hopes of a *rapprochement* were further undermined in late 1990, when Mauritania accused Senegal of complicity in an alleged plot against the Taya administration (the Senegalese authorities denied any involvement). In January and February 1991 incidents were reported in which Mauritanian naval vessels had opened fire on Senegalese fishing boats, apparently in Senegal's territorial waters, and in March several deaths resulted from a military engagement, on Senegalese territory, between the two countries' armed forces, following an incursion by Senegalese troops into Mauritania. Further diplomatic initiatives culminated, in July, in a meeting in Guinea-Bissau of the ministers responsible for foreign affairs of Senegal and Mauritania, at which they agreed in principle to the reopening of the joint border and to a resumption of diplomatic relations. (However, the issues of the demarcation of the border and of the fate of Mauritanian refugees in Senegal were not discussed.) Bilateral contacts continued, and diplomatic links, at ambassadorial level, were finally restored in April 1992. The process of reopening the border began in May. None the less, the contentious issues that had hitherto impeded the normalization of relations (notably the question of border demarcation and the status of Mauritanian refugees in Senegal) remained to be resolved. Further tensions were reported in September 1993, when the Mauritanian authorities announced that Senegalese nationals would henceforth be required to fulfil certain criteria, including currency exchange formalities, before being allowed to remain in (or enter) Mauritania. In December 1994, however, the Governments of Senegal and Mauritania agreed new co-operation measures, including efforts to facilitate the free movement of goods and people between the two countries, and in early 1995 it was reported that diplomatic initiatives were in progress with a view to the repatriation of some 70,000 black Mauritanians from Senegal. In January of that year, moreover, the Governments of Senegal, Mauritania and Mali undertook to co-operate in resolving joint border issues and in combating extremism, arms-smuggling and drugs-trafficking.

Senegal's relations with Guinea-Bissau deteriorated in late July 1989, following a ruling in favour of Senegal, by an international arbitration panel, regarding the sovereignty of a maritime zone that is believed to contain valuable reserves of petroleum and stocks of fish. In August the Government of Guinea-Bissau referred the matter to the International Court of Justice (ICJ). Moreover, Guinea-Bissau accused Senegal of violating its airspace and maritime borders during April 1990, while the Diouf Government alleged that members of the MFDC were being allowed to train in Guinea-Bissau. Meetings between representatives of the two countries culminated in the conclusion, in May, of an accord under the terms of which each country undertook to refrain from harbouring organizations hostile to the other, to maintain troops at a 'reasonable' distance from the border (skirmishes involving troops from Senegal and Guinea-Bissau had occurred earlier in the same month) and to promote more frequent bilateral contact. In March 1991 President Vieira of Guinea-Bissau stated that his country would not tolerate the use of its territory by Casamançais whose aim was to destabilize the Senegalese Government. In November the ICJ ruled that the delimitation of the maritime border, as agreed by the French and Portuguese colonial powers in April 1960, remained valid, thereby confirming Senegal's sovereignty over the disputed zone. Senegal and Guinea-Bissau signed a treaty recognizing this judgment in February 1993.

Although Guinea-Bissau (together with France) played an important role in the formulation of the 1991 cease-fire agreement between the Senegalese Government and the MFDC, relations were again strained in late 1992. In December an offensive by the Senegalese armed forces against MFDC strongholds close to the border with Guinea-Bissau (some reports suggested that MFDC bases within Guinea-Bissau had been targeted) resulted in the deaths of two nationals of that country. The Vieira Government formally protested at Senegalese violations of Guinea-Bissau's airspace, and reiterated that, as a guarantor of the 1991 accord, it was not assisting the rebels. Although Senegal apologized for the incident, a further violation was reported in January 1993. None the less, Guinea-Bissau was again active in efforts to bring about the new cease-fire agreement between the Senegalese Government and the MFDC in mid-1993, and in October of that year the two countries signed a major 20-year agreement regarding the joint exploitation and management of fishing and petroleum resources in their maritime zones.

Renewed operations by the Senegalese military against MFDC rebels in southern Casamance, from early 1995, again affected relations with Guinea-Bissau. In early March Diouf visited Guinea-Bissau to discuss joint security issues and to apologize for two attacks, perpetrated by the Senegalese armed forces, on villages in Guinea-Bissau during February. In April Guinea-Bissau temporarily deployed as many as 500 troops near the border with Senegal, as part of attempts to locate the four missing French tourists: the Government of Guinea-Bissau subsequently announced that it was satisfied that the tourists were not on its territory, and reiterated that it was not harbouring separatists (although reports persisted of sightings of the French nationals, apparently with MFDC members, in Guinea-Bissau). In May, following the withdrawal of its troops from the border region, Guinea-Bissau pledged assistance in the establishment of an enduring settlement between the Senegalese authorities and the MFDC.

In November 1980 Senegalese troops were sent to The Gambia, in accordance with a mutual assistance accord, to protect the Government of that country from an alleged threat by Libyan-backed forces. Following an attempted coup against the Gambian Government in July 1981, Senegalese troops again intervened in The Gambia, and in August plans to merge the two countries were announced. The confederation of Senegambia thus came into being on 1 February 1982. Agreements on co-ordination of foreign policy, communications, defence and security were subsequently concluded, and negotiations on economic and monetary union were initiated. However, the Senegalese authorities were critical of The Gambia's apparent reluctance to complete the process of confederation. In August 1989 Diouf announced the withdrawal of Senegalese troops from The Gambia, in protest at a request by President Jawara of that country that The Gambia be accorded more power within the confederal agreement (and also, it was widely believed, in response to Senegal's continuing dispute with Mauritania). Later in the same month Diouf stated that, in view of The Gambia's reluctance to proceed towards full political and economic integration with Senegal, the functions of the nominal confederation should be suspended, and the two countries should endeavour to formulate more attainable co-operation accords. The confederation was dissolved in September. The Jawara Government subsequently accused Senegal of imposing restrictions governing customs duties and travel that were unfavourable to Gambian interests, and of preventing supplies of important commodities from entering The Gambia via Senegal. Relations between the two countries remained tense during 1990, and in October of that year the Diouf Government accused the Gambian authorities of allowing members of the MFDC to train in, and mount offensives from, The Gambia. In January 1991, none the less, the two countries signed a bilateral treaty of friendship and co-operation. In July Diouf visited The Gambia for the first time since the dissolution of the Senegambia confederation, and in December Jawara attended a summit meeting in Dakar of the Organization of the Islamic Conference. However, Senegal's abrupt, unilateral decision to close the Senegalese–Gambian border in September 1993, apparently to reduce smuggling between the two countries, again strained relations, although negotiations subsequently took place between representatives of Senegal and The Gambia in an attempt to minimize the adverse effects of the closure on The Gambia's regional trading links. Following the *coup d'état* in The Gambia in July 1994, Jawara was initially granted asylum in Senegal; in subsequent months, however, the Diouf Government appeared to forge cordial relations with the new Gambian regime of Capt. Yaya Jammeh, and Senegal's failure openly to condemn the suspension of constitutional rule in The Gambia was believed to have influenced the generally muted regional response to Jawara's overthrow.

In January 1993 it was announced that Senegal was to withdraw its contingent, estimated to number about 1,500 men, from the Monitoring Group (ECOMOG) of the Economic Community of West African States (ECOWAS, see p. 138) in Liberia. Senegal had committed troops to Liberia in September 1991, but was rumoured to have been increasingly dissatisfied with the conduct of ECOMOG operations (for further details, see the chapter on Liberia). The decision to withdraw from ECOMOG was said to have been necessitated by domestic security imperatives, given the forthcoming presidential and legislative elections and the escalation of violence in Casamance. None the less, Senegal confirmed that it would continue to co-operate with ECOWAS in initiatives to secure an enduring peace settlement in Liberia. In May 1994 Senegal announced that it would commit army personnel to an enlarged UN force in Rwanda, and in June Senegalese troops joined the French-led 'Operation Turquoise' (see the Recent History of Rwanda).

## Government

Under the terms of the Constitution of 1963, as subsequently amended, executive power is held by the President, who is directly elected for a maximum of two seven-year terms. Legislative power rests with the unicameral Assemblée nationale, with 120 members elected for five years by universal adult suffrage. The President appoints the Prime Minister, who, in consultation with the President, appoints the Council of Ministers. Senegal comprises 10 regions, each with an appointed governor, an elected local assembly and a separate budget.

## Defence

In June 1994 Senegal's active armed forces totalled 13,350 men: army 12,000 (mostly conscripts), navy 700, air force 650. There was also a 4,000-strong gendarmerie. Military service is by selective conscription and lasts for two years. France and the USA provide technical and material aid, and in June 1994 there were 1,500 French troops stationed in Senegal. The 1993 budget allocated an estimated 33,528m. francs CFA to the Ministry of Defence (representing 7.0% of total expenditure by the central Government).

## Economic Affairs

In 1993, according to estimates by the World Bank, Senegal's gross national product (GNP), measured at average 1991–93 prices, was US $5,867m., equivalent to $730 per head. During 1985–93, it was estimated, GNP per head declined, in real terms, at an average annual rate of 0.3%. Over the same period the population increased by an annual average of 3.0%. Senegal's gross domestic product (GDP) increased, in real terms, by an average of 3.0% per year in 1980–92. Real GDP declined by 2.0% in 1993.

According to World Bank estimates, agriculture (including forestry and fishing) contributed about 19% of GDP in 1993. Some 77.7% of the labour force were engaged in the sector in that year. The principal cash crops are groundnuts (exports of groundnuts, groundnut oil and cake accounted for 22.3% of export earnings in 1990) and cotton. Groundnuts, millet, sorghum, maize, rice and vegetables are produced for domestic consumption. The Government aims to achieve self-sufficiency in basic foodstuffs by 2000: some 585,000 tons of cereals (predominantly rice) were imported in 1992. The fishing sector makes an important contribution to both the domestic food supply and export revenue: fish and fish products had become Senegal's principal export commodity by the mid-1980s, and provided 27.6% of export earnings in 1990; the sale of fishing licences to the European Union is an important source of revenue. During 1980–92 agricultural GDP increased by an annual average of 2.7%.

The World Bank estimates that industry (including mining, manufacturing, construction and power) contributed 19% of GDP in 1992. About 6.2% of the labour force were employed in the industrial sector in 1980. During 1980–92 industrial GDP increased by an annual average of 3.8%.

According to the UN Economic Commission for Africa, mining contributed 2.0% of GDP in 1991. The principal activity is the extraction of calcium phosphates (aluminium phosphates are also present). Deposits of salt, fuller's earth (attapulgite) and natural gas are also exploited, and there is considerable potential for the development (scheduled for the mid-1990s) of gold reserves. The eventual extraction of iron ore and peat is also envisaged. Offshore deposits of petroleum are also known to exist. The GDP of the mining sector increased by an annual average of 9.4% in 1982–91.

The manufacturing sector, according to World Bank estimates, contributed 13% of GDP in 1992. The most important sectors are food-processing (notably fish, groundnuts and sugar), chemicals and textiles. Imported petroleum is refined at Dakar. Manufacturing GDP increased by an annual average of 5.1% in 1980–92.

Electrical energy is almost wholly derived from thermal installations. A solar-powered plant was inaugurated in 1988. The Manantali hydroelectric installation (constructed under the auspices of the Organisation pour la Mise en Valeur du Fleuve Sénégal—OMVS) was formally inaugurated in late 1992, and was due to supply Senegal with power from 1999. Imports of fuel products comprised 16% of the value of merchandise imports in 1992.

Tourism is a major source of foreign exchange. In 1990 the tourism sector contributed almost 3% of GDP; about 4,500 people were directly employed in the sector at that time. However, the Senegalese tourist industry suffered a decline from the late 1980s, owing notably to the border dispute with Mauritania and the unrest in the Casamance region.

In 1993 Senegal recorded a visible trade deficit of US $382.8m., while there was a deficit of $304.8m. on the current account of the balance of payments. In 1990 the principal source of imports (32.9%) was France; other major suppliers were Nigeria, Italy and the USA. France was also the principal market for exports (taking 34.9% of the total) in that year; India, Mali and Italy were also important purchasers of Senegalese exports. The principal exports in 1990 were fresh and processed fish, groundnuts and related products, chemicals, calcium phosphates and related products and refined petroleum products. The principal imports in that year were food and live animals (most notably cereals), machinery and transport equipment, basic manufactures, mineral fuels and chemicals products.

Senegal's overall budgetary deficit in 1993 was equivalent to 3.9% of GDP. Total external debt was US $3,768m. at the end of 1993, of which $3,011m. was long-term public debt. In that year the cost of debt-servicing was equivalent to 9.0% of the value of exports of goods and services. In 1985–93 consumer prices declined by an annual average of 0.2%. Prices declined by 0.6% in 1993, but, following the devaluation of the CFA franc (see below), increased by 32.3% in 1994. An estimated 20% of the labour force were unemployed in the late 1980s; some 11,970 people were registered as unemployed in Dakar in 1992.

Senegal is a member of the Economic Community of West African States (ECOWAS, see p. 138), of the West African organs of the Franc Zone (see p. 168), of the African Groundnut Council (see p. 234), of the Gambia River Basin Development Organization (OMVG, see p. 239), and of the OMVS (see p. 240).

Although Senegal is classified by the World Bank as a lower-middle-income country, the attainment of sustained economic growth has been impeded by the country's dependence on revenue from a narrow export base, and by its consequent vulnerability to fluctuations in international prices for commodities such as groundnuts and phosphates. The further development and diversification of agriculture is imperative, given the high rate of population growth. Recent (donor-funded) economic adjustment efforts have sought to enhance the profitability of the public sector, while fostering private enterprise and implementing stringent fiscal and monetary policies. The Government's aims, following the 50% devaluation, in January 1994, of the CFA franc, included average annual GDP growth of some 4.7% in 1995–97. Funded by organizations including the IMF and the World Bank, policies of economic liberalization were to be pursued, and monopolies dismantled (notably in the agricultural sector). The currency devaluation was of considerable benefit to the tourism and fishing sectors, and also increased the competitiveness of exports of groundnuts and cotton; the rate of inflation in 1994 was within its IMF target, and was forecast to return to pre-devaluation levels in 1996. However, the decline in revenue from sources such as import duties, as well as a lack of confidence among potential investors, jeopardized government revenue targets. Moreover, concern was expressed that overfishing by foreign fleets was depleting Senegal's fish stocks and undermining the traditional sector, while it was feared that renewed insecurity in Casamance in the first half of 1995 might again deter tourists.

### Social Welfare

Social services include a state medical service and certain family and maternity benefits for workers. In 1986 there were 16 hospitals and 112 health centres, with a total of 4,813 beds. In that year there were 298 physicians, 26 dentists, 58 pharmacists and 416 midwives working in the country. Of total budgeted expenditure by the central Government in 1993, 11,851m. francs CFA (2.5%) was allocated to the Ministry of Health and Social Development.

### Education

Primary education, which usually begins at seven years of age and lasts for six years, is officially compulsory. In 1991 some 48% of children in the relevant age-group were enrolled at primary schools (girls 41%; boys 55%). In early 1993 the International Development Association announced funding of US $40m., in support of a project that aims to increase by 7% the level of primary enrolment for both sexes by 1998. Secondary education usually begins at the age of 13, and comprises a first cycle of four years and a further cycle of three years. In 1991 secondary enrolment was equivalent to only 17% of children in the relevant age-group (girls 12%; boys 22%). Since 1981 the reading and writing of national languages has been actively promoted. The 1988 census recorded a rate of adult illiteracy of 73.1% (males 63.1%; females 82.1%). In accordance with the policy of 'negritude', the Université Cheikh Anta Diop, at Dakar, specializes in local studies. The Université Gaston-Berger, at Saint-Louis, was established in 1990. Some 14,000 students attended university-level institutions in the early 1990s. Budget estimates for 1993 allocated 63,843m. francs CFA to the Ministry of National Education (representing 13.3% of total expenditure by the central Government).

### Public Holidays

**1995:** 1 January (New Year's Day), 3 March* (Korité, end of Ramadan), 4 April (National Day), 14 April (Good Friday), 17 April (Easter Monday), 1 May (Labour Day), 10 May* (Tabaski, Feast of the Sacrifice), 25 May (Ascension Day), 5 June (Whit Monday), 14 July (Day of Association), 9 August* (Mouloud, Birth of the Prophet), 15 August (Assumption), 1 November (All Saints' Day), 25 December (Christmas).

**1996:** 1 January (New Year's Day), 21 February* (Korité, end of Ramadan), 4 April (National Day), 5 April (Good Friday), 8 April (Easter Monday), 29 April* (Tabaski, Feast of the Sacrifice), 1 May (Labour Day), 12 May (Ascension Day), 27 May (Whit Monday), 14 July (Day of Association), 28 July* (Mouloud, Birth of the Prophet), 15 August (Assumption), 1 November (All Saints' Day), 25 December (Christmas).

* These holidays are determined by the Islamic lunar calendar and may vary by one or two days from the dates given.

### Weights and Measures

The metric system is in force.

# Statistical Survey

Source (unless otherwise stated): Direction de la Statistique, Ministère l'Economie, des Finances et du Plan, rue René Ndiaye, BP 4017, Dakar; tel. 21-06-99; telex 3203; fax 22-41-95.

## Area and Population

**AREA, POPULATION AND DENSITY**

| | |
|---|---:|
| Area (sq km) | 196,722* |
| Population (census results) | |
| 16 April 1976 | 5,085,388† |
| 27 May 1988 | |
| Males | 3,353,599 |
| Females | 3,543,209 |
| Total | 6,896,808 |
| Population (official estimate at mid-year) | |
| 1993 | 8,152,000 |
| Density (per sq km) at mid-1993 | 41.4 |

* 75,955 sq miles.

† Figure refers to the *de jure* population. The *de facto* population at the 1976 census was 4,907,507.

**REGIONS** (population at 1976 census)

| | Area (sq km) | Population | Density (per sq km) | Capital | Estimated population |
|---|---:|---:|---:|---|---:|
| Cap-Vert* | 550 | 984,660 | 1,790.3 | Dakar | 800,000 |
| Casamance | 28,350 | 736,527 | 26.0 | Ziguinchor | 73,000 |
| Diourbel | } 33,547 | 425,113 | } 25.1 | Diourbel | 51,000 |
| Louga | | 417,137 | | Louga | n.a. |
| Fleuve† | 44,127 | 528,473 | 12.0 | Saint-Louis | 88,000 |
| Sénégal Oriental‡ | 59,602 | 286,148 | 4.8 | Tambacounda | n.a. |
| Sine Saloum | 23,945 | 1,007,736 | 42.1 | Kaolack | 106,000 |
| Thiès | 6,601 | 698,994 | 105.9 | Thiès | 117,000 |
| **Total** | 196,722 | 5,085,388 | 25.9 | | |

* Renamed Dakar in 1984.
† Renamed Saint-Louis in 1984.
‡ Renamed Tambacounda in 1984.

Note: In July 1984 Casamance region was divided into Ziguinchor and Kolda regions; Sine Saloum region was divided into Kaolack and Fatick regions.

Source: mainly Société Africaine d'Edition, *Le Sénégal en chiffres*.

**Principal Towns** (estimated population, 1979): Dakar (capital) 850,000; Thiès 120,000; Kaolack 110,000 (Source: *L'Afrique Noire Politique et Economique, 1983.*)

**PRINCIPAL ETHNIC GROUPS**

1960 census: Wolof 709,000, Fulani 324,000, Serer 306,000, Toucouleur 248,000, Diola 115,000.

SENEGAL  
*Statistical Survey*

**BIRTHS AND DEATHS** (UN estimates, annual averages)

|  | 1975–80 | 1980–85 | 1985–90 |
|---|---|---|---|
| Birth rate (per 1,000) | 49.3 | 47.2 | 45.5 |
| Death rate (per 1,000) | 21.7 | 19.4 | 17.7 |

**Expectation of life** (UN estimates, years at birth, 1985–90): 47.3 (males 46.3; females 48.3).

Source: UN, *World Population Prospects: The 1992 Revision*.

**ECONOMICALLY ACTIVE POPULATION**
(ILO estimates, '000 persons at mid-1980)

|  | Males | Females | Total |
|---|---|---|---|
| Agriculture, etc. | 1,148 | 980 | 2,128 |
| Industry | 140 | 25 | 165 |
| Services | 263 | 84 | 347 |
| **Total labour force** | 1,551 | 1,090 | 2,641 |

Source: ILO, *Economically Active Population Estimates and Projections, 1950–2025*.

**Mid-1993** (estimates in '000): Agriculture, etc. 2,613; Total 3,362 (Source: FAO, *Production Yearbook*).

## Agriculture

**PRINCIPAL CROPS** ('000 metric tons)

|  | 1991 | 1992 | 1993 |
|---|---|---|---|
| Rice (paddy) | 170 | 177 | 189 |
| Maize | 103 | 115 | 125 |
| Millet and sorghum | 671 | 563 | 755 |
| Potatoes* | 13 | 13 | 14 |
| Cassava (Manioc) | 25 | 46 | 43 |
| Pulses | 17 | 9 | 44 |
| Groundnuts (in shell) | 724 | 578 | 628 |
| Cottonseed* | 30 | 30 | 28 |
| Cotton (lint) | 20 | 19 | 20† |
| Palm kernels* | 6.2 | 6.2 | 6.3 |
| Tomatoes | 56 | 57 | 62* |
| Dry onions | 38 | 31 | 32* |
| Other vegetables | 48 | 49 | 48* |
| Mangoes | 54 | 57 | 58* |
| Oranges | 26 | 24 | 24* |
| Bananas | 5 | 5 | 5* |
| Other fruit | 24 | 24 | 24* |
| Coconuts* | 5 | 5 | 5 |
| Sugar cane | 808 | 837 | 850* |

* FAO estimate(s).  † Unofficial figure.

Source: FAO, *Production Yearbook*.

**LIVESTOCK** ('000 head, year ending September)

|  | 1991 | 1992 | 1993 |
|---|---|---|---|
| Cattle | 2,687 | 2,700* | 2,750* |
| Sheep† | 3,800 | 4,200 | 4,400 |
| Goats† | 2,831 | 3,064 | 3,118 |
| Pigs* | 300 | 310 | 320 |
| Horses | 453 | 431 | 498 |
| Asses | 328 | 362 | 364 |
| Camels* | 15 | 15 | 15 |

* FAO estimate(s).  † Unofficial figures.

Poultry (million) 24 in 1991; 28 in 1992; 34 in 1993.

Source: FAO, *Production Yearbook*.

**LIVESTOCK PRODUCTS** (FAO estimates, '000 metric tons)

|  | 1991 | 1992 | 1993 |
|---|---|---|---|
| Beef and veal | 44 | 44 | 45 |
| Mutton and lamb | 13 | 14 | 15 |
| Goat meat | 12 | 13 | 13 |
| Pig meat | 7 | 7 | 7 |
| Horse meat | 6 | 5 | 6 |
| Poultry meat | 38 | 43 | 52 |
| Other meat | 5 | 7 | 6 |
| Cows' milk | 100 | 101 | 103 |
| Sheep's milk | 16 | 17 | 17 |
| Goats' milk | 13 | 14 | 14 |
| Poultry eggs | 18.4 | 22.4 | 27.0 |
| Cattle hides | 8.7 | 8.8 | 9.0 |
| Sheepskins | 2.8 | 3.0 | 3.1 |
| Goatskins | 2.5 | 2.8 | 2.8 |

Source: FAO, *Production Yearbook*.

## Forestry

**ROUNDWOOD REMOVALS**
('000 cubic metres, excluding bark)

|  | 1990 | 1991 | 1992 |
|---|---|---|---|
| Sawlogs, veneer logs and logs for sleepers | 40 | 40 | 40 |
| Other industrial wood* | 598 | 615 | 632 |
| Fuel wood | 4,264 | 4,273 | 4,236 |
| **Total** | 4,902 | 4,928 | 4,908 |

* FAO estimates.

Source: FAO, *Yearbook of Forest Products*.

## Fishing*

('000 metric tons, live weight)

|  | 1990 | 1991 | 1992† |
|---|---|---|---|
| Freshwater fishes | 18.5 | 19.1 | 26.3 |
| Flatfishes | 4.3 | 8.4 | 8.4 |
| Sea catfishes | 8.0 | 4.1 | 4.1 |
| Grunts, sweetlips, etc. | 9.3 | 8.5 | 8.5 |
| West African croakers | 7.4 | 4.9 | 4.9 |
| Dentex, seabreams, etc. | 8.1 | 8.9 | 8.9 |
| Mullets | 3.9 | 6.3 | 6.3 |
| Lesser African threadfin | 6.2 | 2.9 | 2.9 |
| Sardinellas | 140.0‡ | 160.0‡ | 160.0 |
| Bonga shad | 12.7 | 11.5 | 11.5 |
| Other marine fishes (incl. unspecified) | 57.2 | 54.1 | 54.1 |
| **Total fish** | 275.6 | 289.0 | 296.2 |
| Cuttlefishes and bobtail squids | 4.6 | 7.8 | 7.8 |
| Octopuses | 8.6 | 12.4 | 12.4 |
| Other crustaceans and molluscs | 9.0 | 10.5 | 10.5 |
| **Total catch** | 297.9 | 319.7 | 326.9 |

* Figures cover the artisanal Senegalese fishery, the industrial Senegalese tuna fishery, the industrial Senegalese and French trawler fishery, and the industrial Senegalese sardine fishery.
† FAO estimates.
‡ Estimated catch.

Source: FAO, *Yearbook of Fishery Statistics*.

SENEGAL

## Mining

('000 metric tons)

|  | 1989 | 1990 | 1991 |
|---|---|---|---|
| Natural phosphates | 2,273 | 2,147 | n.a. |
| Fuller's earth (attapulgite)* | 99 | 100 | 115 |
| Salt (unrefined) | 100 | 100 | 100 |

* Data from the US Bureau of Mines.

Source: UN, *Industrial Statistics Yearbook*.

## Industry

**SELECTED PRODUCTS**
('000 metric tons, unless otherwise indicated)

|  | 1989 | 1990 | 1991 |
|---|---|---|---|
| Frozen fish (metric tons)* | 72,400 | 78,800 | n.a. |
| Tinned fish (metric tons) | 200 | 200 | n.a. |
| Salted, dried or smoked fish (metric tons)* | 16,800 | 25,000 | n.a. |
| Palm oil*† | 6 | 6 | 6 |
| Raw sugar* | 79 | 87 | 90 |
| Cigarettes (million) | 3,350 | 3,350 | 3,350 |
| Cotton yarn (metric tons) | 600† | n.a. | n.a. |
| Footwear—excl. rubber ('000 pairs) | 600 | 600 | n.a. |
| Nitrogenous fertilizers‡ | 12.0† | 14.4 | 15.7 |
| Phosphate fertilizers‡ | 35.0† | 27.5 | 50.0† |
| Jet fuel | 91 | 92 | 90 |
| Motor spirit—petrol | 115 | 117 | 118 |
| Kerosene | 14 | 14 | 15 |
| Distillate fuel oils | 215 | 165 | 170 |
| Residual fuel oils | 210 | 212 | 210 |
| Lubricating oils | 3 | 3 | 3 |
| Liquefied petroleum gas† | 2 | 2 | 3 |
| Cement† | 380 | 380 | 499 |
| Electric energy (million kWh) | 697 | 734 | 756 |

* Data from the FAO.
† Provisional or estimated figure(s).
‡ Figures for fertilizers are in terms of nitrogen or phosphoric acid, and relate to output during the 12 months ending 30 June of the year stated.

Source: mainly UN, *Industrial Statistics Yearbook*.

## Finance

**CURRENCY AND EXCHANGE RATE**

**Monetary Units**
100 centimes = 1 franc de la Communauté financière africaine (CFA).

**French Franc, Sterling and Dollar Equivalents**
(31 December 1994)
1 French franc = 100 francs CFA;
£1 sterling = 834.94 francs CFA;
US $1 = 533.68 francs CFA;
1,000 francs CFA = £1.198 = $1.874.

**Average Exchange Rate** (francs CFA per US $)
1992  264.69
1993  283.16
1994  555.20

Note: An exchange rate of 1 French franc = 50 francs CFA, established in 1948, remained in force until January 1994, when the CFA franc was devalued by 50%, with the exchange rate adjusted to 1 French franc = 100 francs CFA.

**BUDGET**
(estimates, million francs CFA, year ending 30 June)

| Revenue* | 1988 | 1989 | 1990 |
|---|---|---|---|
| Fiscal receipts | 209,496 | 217,966 | 215,100 |
| Taxes on income and profits | 51,170 | 52,500 | 53,400 |
| Corporate and business taxes | 51,000 | 52,000 | 53,000 |
| Taxes on goods and services | 65,526 | 69,866 | 69,000 |
| Turnover taxes | 51,500 | 54,000 | 53,000 |
| Consumption taxes | 8,026 | 9,216 | 9,200 |
| Taxes on use of goods or on permission to use goods or to perform activities | 5,800 | 6,500 | 6,500 |
| Taxes on international trade and transactions | 89,600 | 92,100 | 88,700 |
| Import duties | 89,000 | 91,500 | 88,000 |
| Other current receipts | 36,063 | 48,847 | 55,314 |
| Property income | 5,610 | 11,860 | 9,860 |
| Aid, grants and subsidies | 33,291 | 24,934 | 43,839 |
| **Total** | 278,850 | 291,747 | 314,253 |

| Expenditure | 1988 | 1989 | 1990 |
|---|---|---|---|
| General public services | 60,087 | 73,563 | 80,924 |
| Defence | 28,967 | 30,293 | 30,685 |
| Public order and security | 23,673 | 22,225 | 22,709 |
| Education | 48,037 | 51,576 | 55,954 |
| Public health | 11,030 | 10,867 | 11,868 |
| Social security and welfare | 2,769 | 2,860 | 2,897 |
| Housing and community services | 2,323 | 2,325 | 2,144 |
| Other community and social services | 3,786 | 3,715 | 3,849 |
| Economic services | 111,385 | 101,254 | 113,489 |
| Agriculture, hunting, forestry and fishing | 57,980 | 60,688 | 70,705 |
| Mining, manufacturing and power | 11,870 | 7,212 | 16,242 |
| Transport and communications | 26,406 | 31,539 | 24,731 |
| Other economic services | 15,129 | 1,815 | 1,811 |
| Debt-servicing | 115,200 | 128,300 | 113,700 |
| Other purposes | 48,510 | 61,646 | 68,636 |
| **Total** | 455,767 | 488,624 | 506,855 |

* Revenue excludes net borrowing: 176,917m. francs CFA in 1988; 196,877m. francs CFA in 1989; 192,602 in 1990.

Source: Banque centrale des états de l'Afrique de l'ouest.

**1990/91** (estimates, million francs CFA): Administrative revenue 226,000; Administrative expenditure 221,800; Investment and capital budget balanced at 169,200.
**1991/92** (estimates, million francs CFA, 1 July 1991–31 December 1992): Budget balanced at 660,900.
**1993** (estimates, million francs CFA): Budget balanced at 479,600 (excluding net borrowing: 171,500).
**1994** (estimates, million francs CFA): Budget balanced at 518,600.

**INTERNATIONAL RESERVES** (US $ million at 31 December)

|  | 1992 | 1993 | 1994 |
|---|---|---|---|
| Gold* | 10.1 | 10.8 | 10.8 |
| IMF special drawing rights | — | 0.4 | 1.1 |
| Reserve position in IMF | 1.4 | 1.5 | 1.7 |
| Foreign exchange | 10.9 | 1.5 | 173.3 |
| **Total** | 22.5 | 14.2 | 186.9 |

* Valued at market-related prices.

Source: IMF, *International Financial Statistics*.

**MONEY SUPPLY** ('000 million francs CFA at 31 December)

|  | 1992 | 1993 | 1994 |
|---|---|---|---|
| Currency outside banks | 107.18 | 93.03 | 146.58 |
| Demand deposits at deposit money banks | 106.63 | 101.43 | 155.35 |
| Checking deposits at post office | 3.40 | 2.96 | — |
| **Total money** (incl. others) | 217.39 | 197.75 | 302.38 |

Source: IMF, *International Financial Statistics*.

## SENEGAL

### COST OF LIVING
(Consumer price index, Dakar. Base: 1980 = 100)

|  | 1990 | 1991 | 1992 |
|---|---|---|---|
| Food | 163.0 | 157.9 | 156.3 |
| Fuel and light | 190.4 | 195.9 | 192.8 |
| Clothing | 193.5 | 196.3 | 197.6 |
| Rent* | 177.3 | 175.3 | 173.4 |
| **All items** (incl. others) | 176.5 | 173.4 | 173.4 |

* Including expenditure on the maintenance and repair of dwellings.

**1993:** Food 153.6; All items 172.2.

Source: International Labour Office, *Year Book of Labour Statistics*.

### NATIONAL ACCOUNTS
(million francs CFA at current prices)

**Expenditure on the Gross Domestic Product***

|  | 1989 | 1990 | 1991 |
|---|---|---|---|
| Government final consumption expenditure | 238,800 | 226,030 | 248,300 |
| Private final consumption expenditure | 1,108,650 | 1,123,360 | 1,079,670 |
| Increase in stocks | 3,030 | 2,880 | 1,000 |
| Gross fixed capital formation | 234,560 | 224,390 | 225,190 |
| **Total domestic expenditure** | 1,585,040 | 1,576,660 | 1,554,160 |
| Exports of goods and services | 360,040 | 403,140 | 489,770 |
| *Less* Imports of goods and services | 453,080 | 457,800 | 444,070 |
| **GDP in purchasers' values** | 1,492,000 | 1,522,000 | 1,599,850 |
| **GDP at constant 1980 prices** | 787,000 | 794,900 | 815,580 |

* Figures are rounded to the nearest 10m. francs CFA.

**Gross Domestic Product by Economic Activity***

|  | 1989 | 1990 | 1991 |
|---|---|---|---|
| Agriculture, hunting, forestry and fishing | 255,090 | 257,890 | 272,320 |
| Mining and quarrying | 16,330 | 24,240 | 26,780 |
| Manufacturing | 239,360 | 242,190 | 256,590 |
| Electricity, gas and water | 23,590 | 24,270 | 25,820 |
| Construction | 96,020 | 98,870 | 105,690 |
| Trade, restaurants and hotels | 185,450 | 188,260 | 198,610 |
| Transport, storage and communications | 112,940 | 113,390 | 119,900 |
| Finance, insurance, real estate, etc. | 52,420 | 53,360 | 56,720 |
| Government services | 176,410 | 179,230 | 184,400 |
| Other services | 82,180 | 83,100 | 88,090 |
| **GDP at factor cost** | 1,239,780 | 1,264,790 | 1,334,920 |
| Indirect taxes *less* subsidies | 252,220 | 257,210 | 264,930 |
| **GDP in purchasers' values** | 1,492,000 | 1,522,000 | 1,599,850 |

* Figures are rounded to the nearest 10m. francs CFA.

Source: UN Economic Commission for Africa: *African Statistical Yearbook*.

### BALANCE OF PAYMENTS (US $ million)

|  | 1991 | 1992 | 1993 |
|---|---|---|---|
| Merchandise exports f.o.b. | 824.2 | 831.9 | 722.6 |
| Merchandise imports f.o.b. | −1,114.1 | −1,200.3 | −1,105.4 |
| **Trade balance** | −290.0 | −368.4 | −382.8 |
| Exports of services | 560.4 | 592.4 | 563.6 |
| Imports of services | −573.2 | −606.6 | −574.6 |
| Other income received | 24.1 | 26.1 | 24.7 |
| Other income paid | −220.1 | −228.3 | −215.8 |
| Private unrequited transfers (net) | 28.4 | 36.6 | 40.3 |
| Official unrequited transfers (net) | 265.1 | 279.9 | 239.8 |
| **Current balance** | −205.2 | −268.2 | −304.8 |
| Capital (net) | 51.0 | 79.0 | 42.2 |
| Net errors and omissions | −26.2 | 82.6 | 114.8 |
| **Overall balance** | −180.4 | −106.7 | −147.8 |

Source: IMF, *International Financial Statistics*.

## External Trade

### PRINCIPAL COMMODITIES
(distribution by SITC, US $ million)

| Imports c.i.f. | 1988 | 1989 | 1990 |
|---|---|---|---|
| **Food and live animals** | 173.7 | 342.7 | 403.0 |
| Dairy products and birds' eggs | 37.5 | 42.9 | 46.5 |
| Milk and cream | n.a. | 35.4 | 38.1 |
| Fish, crustaceans and molluscs | n.a. | 37.0 | 47.4 |
| Fresh, chilled or frozen fish | n.a. | 35.3 | 43.2 |
| Cereals and cereal preparations | 95.0 | 156.5 | 180.5 |
| Wheat and meslin (unmilled) | 15.8 | 39.6 | 75.7 |
| Rice | 77.1 | 106.9 | 92.4 |
| Semi-milled or milled rice | n.a. | 102.5 | 92.4 |
| Vegetables and fruit | 23.9 | 27.5 | 30.0 |
| Sugar, sugar preparations and honey | 2.7 | 9.3 | 36.5 |
| Sugar and honey | 2.7 | 8.4 | 35.1 |
| Refined sugars (solid) | 0.6 | 7.5 | 33.9 |
| Coffee, tea, cocoa and spices | 10.0 | 32.9 | 30.2 |
| **Crude materials (inedible) except fuels** | n.a. | 41.4 | 59.2 |
| Crude fertilizers and crude minerals | n.a. | 22.0 | 30.3 |
| **Mineral fuels, lubricants, etc.** | 144.4 | 361.0 | 258.7 |
| Petroleum, petroleum products, etc. | 144.4 | 353.1 | 248.6 |
| Crude petroleum oils, etc. | n.a. | 211.2 | 130.5 |
| Refined petroleum products | 58.0 | 139.8 | 113.7 |
| Motor spirit (gasoline) and other light oils | 6.7 | 35.8 | 21.8 |
| Gas oils (distillate fuels) | 17.2 | 35.9 | 52.3 |
| **Animal and vegetable oils, fats and waxes** | 16.7 | 19.4 | 33.2 |
| **Chemicals and related products** | 126.1 | 147.5 | 157.6 |
| Medicinal and pharmaceutical products | 34.9 | 41.4 | 46.0 |
| Medicaments (incl. veterinary) | n.a. | 38.0 | 42.9 |
| Artificial resins, plastic materials, etc. | 33.1 | 25.7 | 32.4 |
| **Basic manufactures** | 182.7 | 218.6 | 259.8 |
| Paper, paperboard, etc. | 35.2 | 33.7 | 39.0 |
| Textile yarn, fabrics, etc. | 41.0 | 42.0 | 45.5 |
| Iron and steel | 35.6 | 49.1 | 64.9 |
| **Machinery and transport equipment** | 245.9 | 310.4 | 344.5 |
| Power-generating machinery and equipment | 9.5 | 29.8 | 34.8 |
| Machinery specialized for particular industries | 40.7 | 37.5 | 50.1 |
| General industrial machinery, equipment and parts | 104.5 | 51.7 | 66.6 |
| Electrical machinery, apparatus, etc. | n.a. | 56.3 | 62.7 |
| Road vehicles and parts (excl. tyres, engines and electrical parts) | 91.1 | 107.0 | 102.3 |
| Passenger motor cars (excl. buses) | 37.4 | 50.0 | 46.4 |
| **Miscellaneous manufactured articles** | 15.4 | 63.2 | 75.1 |
| **Total** (incl. others) | 1,079.5 | 1,534.0 | 1,620.4 |

# SENEGAL

| Exports f.o.b. | 1988 | 1989 | 1990 |
|---|---|---|---|
| **Food and live animals** | 209.7 | 271.3 | 270.6 |
| Fish, crustaceans and molluscs | 154.0 | 208.1 | 216.0 |
| Fresh, chilled or frozen fish | 49.8 | 57.5 | 86.9 |
| Fresh, chilled, frozen, salted or dried crustaceans and molluscs | 54.7 | 49.5 | 34.7 |
| Prepared or preserved fish, crustaceans and molluscs | 49.5 | 97.4 | 90.7 |
| Fish (incl. caviar) | n.a. | 51.4 | 60.0 |
| Crustaceans and molluscs | n.a. | 46.1 | 30.7 |
| Feeding stuff for animals (excl. unmilled cereals) | 41.2 | 40.6 | 36.9 |
| Oil-cake, etc. | 41.2 | 39.1 | 35.4 |
| Groundnut cake | 41.2 | 34.7 | 34.2 |
| **Crude materials (inedible) except fuels** | 88.5 | 106.7 | 105.8 |
| Crude fertilizers and crude minerals | 72.4 | 74.8 | 70.1 |
| Crude fertilizers | 72.4 | 63.9 | 57.0 |
| Natural calcium phosphates, etc. | 72.4 | 63.9 | 57.0 |
| **Minerals fuels, lubricants, etc.** | 65.0 | 84.5 | 96.8 |
| Petroleum, petroleum products, etc. | 65.0 | 84.4 | 96.7 |
| Refined petroleum products | 65.0 | 84.3 | 96.4 |
| Motor spirit (gasoline) and other light oils | n.a. | 29.8 | 47.7 |
| Spirit-type jet fuel | n.a. | 24.9 | 42.0 |
| Gas oils (distillate fuels) | n.a. | 33.3 | 30.7 |
| **Animal and vegetable oils, fats and waxes** | n.a. | 103.3 | 130.1 |
| Fixed vegetable oils and fats | n.a. | 103.0 | 130.1 |
| Groundnut (peanut) oil | n.a. | 102.8 | 130.0 |
| **Chemicals and related products** | n.a. | 97.5 | 116.7 |
| Inorganic chemicals | n.a. | 55.7 | 73.6 |
| Inorganic chemical elements, oxides and halogen salts | n.a. | 55.5 | 73.4 |
| Inorganic acids and oxygen compounds of non-metals | n.a. | 55.1 | 73.1 |
| Phosphorus pentoxide and phosphoric acids | n.a. | 54.9 | 73.0 |
| Manufactured fertilizers | 4.0 | 24.2 | 28.6 |
| **Basic manufactures** | 6.5 | 35.9 | 29.0 |
| **Machinery and transport equipment** | n.a. | 28.2 | 18.5 |
| **Total** (incl. others) | 591.1 | 750.9 | 782.6 |

Source: UN, *International Trade Statistics Yearbook*.

## PRINCIPAL TRADING PARTNERS (US $ million)*

| Imports c.i.f. | 1988 | 1989 | 1990 |
|---|---|---|---|
| Angola | n.a. | 25.6 | 0.9 |
| Belgium-Luxembourg | 23.9 | 32.6 | 44.5 |
| Brazil | 6.5 | 20.4 | 18.2 |
| Canada | n.a. | 19.8 | 17.3 |
| China, People's Repub. | 23.7 | 33.2 | 37.2 |
| Côte d'Ivoire | 61.3 | 67.4 | 72.3 |
| France (incl. Monaco) | 340.2 | 438.2 | 533.7 |
| Gabon | 22.2 | 118.0 | 43.6 |
| Germany | 42.0 | 43.6 | 57.8 |
| Italy | 42.3 | 76.1 | 104.9 |
| Japan | 45.5 | 57.0 | 58.5 |
| Netherlands | 28.7 | 46.1 | 49.7 |
| Netherlands Antilles | n.a. | 2.9 | 18.0 |
| Nigeria | 46.8 | 124.1 | 121.9 |
| Pakistan | 36.9 | 38.1 | 24.6 |
| Spain | 51.2 | 68.9 | 67.7 |
| Thailand | n.a. | 37.6 | 47.6 |
| United Kingdom | 25.2 | 24.5 | 27.2 |
| USA | 69.1 | 90.2 | 86.0 |
| Viet Nam | n.a. | 9.9 | 15.5 |
| **Total** (incl. others) | 1,079.5 | 1,534.0 | 1,620.4 |

| Exports f.o.b. | 1988 | 1989 | 1990 |
|---|---|---|---|
| Cameroon | 11.2 | 18.5 | 19.8 |
| Côte d'Ivoire | 19.1 | 20.8 | 21.8 |
| France (incl. Monaco) | 222.4 | 250.8 | 272.8 |
| Gambia | 4.3 | 9.1 | 6.9 |
| Germany | 6.2 | 7.9 | 6.3 |
| Greece | 7.6 | 7.2 | 6.0 |
| Guinea | 6.3 | 16.5 | 15.3 |
| India | n.a. | 69.5 | 83.3 |
| Iran | n.a. | n.a. | 13.9 |
| Italy | 24.5 | 46.9 | 54.9 |
| Japan | 10.4 | 28.4 | 15.6 |
| Mali | 24.2 | 49.2 | 55.7 |
| Mauritania | 18.1 | 11.3 | 0.2 |
| Netherlands | 24.4 | 22.4 | 41.3 |
| Philippines | n.a. | 16.1 | 14.3 |
| Spain | 22.3 | 30.0 | 22.8 |
| Togo | 1.6 | 8.5 | 5.1 |
| United Kingdom | 11.9 | 4.1 | 3.6 |
| **Total** (incl. others) | 591.1 | 750.9 | 782.6 |

* Imports by country of production; exports by country of last consignment.

Source: UN, *International Trade Statistics Yearbook*.

# Transport

**RAILWAYS** (estimated traffic)

|  | 1989 | 1990 | 1991 |
|---|---|---|---|
| Passenger-km (million) | 163 | 169 | 174 |
| Freight ton-km (million) | 565 | 580 | 610 |

Source: UN Economic Commission for Africa, *African Statistical Yearbook*.

**ROAD TRAFFIC** (estimates, '000 motor vehicles in use)

|  | 1989 | 1990 | 1991 |
|---|---|---|---|
| Passenger cars | 65 | 66 | 67 |
| Commercial vehicles | 37 | 38 | 38 |

Source: UN Economic Commission for Africa, *African Statistical Yearbook*.

**SHIPPING**
Merchant fleet (vessels registered at 30 June)

|  | 1990 | 1991 | 1992 |
|---|---|---|---|
| **Total displacement** ('000 grt) | 52 | 55 | 58 |

Source: UN, *Statistical Yearbook*.

**International Sea-Borne Shipping**
(freight traffic at Dakar, '000 metric tons)

|  | 1989 | 1990 | 1991 |
|---|---|---|---|
| Goods loaded | 2,801 | 2,868 | 2,591 |
| Goods unloaded | 2,350 | 2,204 | 2,477 |

Source: Banque centrale des états de l'Afrique de l'ouest.

**CIVIL AVIATION** (traffic on scheduled services)*

|  | 1990 | 1991 | 1992 |
|---|---|---|---|
| Km flown (million) | 3 | 3 | 3 |
| Passengers carried ('000) | 148 | 138 | 138 |
| Passenger-km (million) | 253 | 229 | 222 |
| Total ton-km (million) | 41 | 37 | 36 |

* Including an apportionment of the traffic of Air Afrique.

Source: UN, *Statistical Yearbook*.

## Tourism

**FOREIGN TOURIST ARRIVALS**

| Country of Origin | 1989 | 1990 | 1991 |
|---|---|---|---|
| Benelux | 7,363 | 5,908 | 5,474 |
| Canada | 2,809 | 1,866 | 1,858 |
| France | 155,839 | 147,524 | 132,254 |
| Germany, Federal Republic | 13,661 | 13,736 | 13,106* |
| Italy | 11,322 | 12,786 | 16,280 |
| Spain | 2,339 | 2,161 | 1,762 |
| Switzerland | 4,085 | 4,545 | 4,315 |
| United Kingdom | 3,064 | 3,457 | 3,533 |
| USA | 9,452 | 8,736 | 6,220 |
| **Total** (incl. others) | 259,096 | 245,881 | 233,512 |

* The figure for 1991 is for the united Germany.

**1992:** Total foreign tourist arrivals 245,581.

Source: Ministère du Tourisme et des Transports aériens, Dakar.

## Communications Media

|  | 1990 | 1991 | 1992 |
|---|---|---|---|
| Radio receivers ('000 in use) | 830 | 860 | 890 |
| Television receivers ('000 in use) | 265 | 273 | 282 |
| Daily newspapers |  |  |  |
| Number | 3 | n.a. | 1 |
| Average circulation ('000 copies) | 50 | n.a. | 50 |

Book production (1983): 42 titles (first editions, excluding pamphlets); 169,000 copies.

Source: UNESCO, *Statistical Yearbook*.

**Telephones** ('000 in use): 55 in 1993 (Source: Société Nationale des Télécommunications du Sénégal, Dakar).

## Education

(1991, unless otherwise indicated)

|  | Institutions | Teachers | Students Males | Females | Total |
|---|---|---|---|---|---|
| Pre-primary | 173 | 714 | 8,818 | 8,614 | 17,432 |
| Primary | 2,434 | 12,307 | 418,143 | 307,353 | 725,496 |
| Secondary |  |  |  |  |  |
| General | n.a. | 5,374* | 119,629 | 63,442 | 183,071 |
| Teacher training | n.a. | 80† | 616 | 173 | 789 |
| Vocational | n.a. | 179*† | 5,032 | 2,539 | 7,571 |
| Tertiary | n.a. | 949 | 16,300 | 5,262 | 21,562 |

* Public education only.
† 1989 figure.

University level (1989): Teachers 810; Students 16,764 (males 13,082; females 3,682).

Source: UNESCO, *Statistical Yearbook*.

# Directory

## The Constitution

The Constitution of the Republic of Senegal was promulgated on 7 March 1963. It has since been amended, with the most recent amendments being effected in May 1992. The main provisions are summarized below:

### PREAMBLE

Affirms the Rights of Man, liberty of the person and religious freedom. National sovereignty belongs to the people who exercise it through their representatives or by means of referendums. There is universal, equal and secret suffrage for adults of 18 years of age and above. French is the official language.

### THE PRESIDENT

The President of the Republic is elected by direct universal suffrage for a seven-year term and may seek re-election only once. The President holds executive power and, as Commander of the Armed Forces, is responsible for national defence. The President of the Republic appoints the Prime Minister. He may, after consultation with the President of the Assemblée nationale, with the Prime Minister and with the appropriate organ of the judiciary, submit any draft law to referendum. In circumstances where the security of the State is in grave and immediate danger, he can assume emergency powers and rule by decree. The President of the Republic can be impeached only on a charge of high treason or by a secret ballot of the Assemblée nationale carrying a three-fifths' majority.

### THE PRIME MINISTER

The Prime Minister is appointed by the President of the Republic, and, in turn, appoints the Council of Ministers in consultation with the President.

### THE LEGISLATURE

Legislative power is vested in the Assemblée nationale, which is elected by universal direct suffrage for a five-year term. The Assembly discusses and votes legislation and submits it to the President of the Republic for promulgation. The President can direct the Assembly to give a second reading to the bill, in which case it may be made law only by a three-fifths' majority. The President of the Republic can also call upon the Constitutional Court to declare whether any draft law is constitutional and acceptable. Legislation may be initiated by either the President of the Republic or the Assemblée nationale. Should the Presidency fall vacant, the President of the legislature is automatic successor to the Head of State. A motion expressing 'no confidence' in the Government can be considered if it has been endorsed by one-tenth of the members of the Assembly.

### LOCAL GOVERNMENT

Senegal is divided into 10 regions, each having a governor and an elected local assembly.

### POLITICAL PARTIES

There is no limit to the number of political parties.

### AMENDMENTS

The President of the Republic and Deputies to the Assemblée nationale may propose amendments to the Constitution. Draft

SENEGAL

amendments are adopted by a three-fifths majority vote of the Assemblée nationale. Failing this, they are submitted to referendum.

## The Government

### HEAD OF STATE

**President:** ABDOU DIOUF (took office 1 January 1981; elected President on 27 February 1983, re-elected 28 February 1988 and 21 February 1993).

### COUNCIL OF MINISTERS
(June 1995)

A coalition of the Parti socialiste sénégalais (PS); Parti démocratique sénégalais (PDS); Parti de l'indépendance et du travail (PIT); Parti démocratique sénégalais—Rénovation (PDS—R); Ligue démocratique—Mouvement pour le parti du travail (LD—MPT).

**President of the Republic and Head of Government:** ABDOU DIOUF (PS).
**Prime Minister:** HABIB THIAM (PS).
**Minister of State at the Presidency:** Me ABDOULAYE WADE (PDS).
**Minister of State, Minister of Foreign Affairs and Senegalese Abroad:** MOUSTAPHA NIASSE (PS).
**Minister of State, Minister of Agriculture:** ROBERT SAGNA (PS).
**Minister of State, Minister of Presidential Services and Affairs:** OUSMANE TANOR DIENG (PS).
**Minister of Justice and Keeper of the Seals:** JACQUES BAUDIN (PS).
**Minister of the Interior:** ABDOURAHMANE SOW.
**Minister of the Armed Forces:** CHEIKH HAMIDOU KANE.
**Minister of the Economy, Finance and Planning:** PAPA OUSMANE SAKHO (no party affiliation).
**Minister of the Environment and Nature Conservation:** ABDOULAYE BATHILY (LD—MPT).
**Minister of Housing and Town Planning:** AMATH DANSOKHO (PIT).
**Minister of Public Health and Social Action:** OUSMANE NGOM (PDS).
**Minister of National Education:** ANDRÉ SONKO (PS).
**Minister of Energy, Mines and Industry:** MAGUED DIOUF.
**Minister of Modernization of the State:** NENE BABACAR MBAYE.
**Minister of Culture:** ABDOULAYE ELIMANE KANE (PS).
**Minister of Communications:** SERIGNE DIOP (PDS—R).
**Minister of Labour and Employment:** ASSANE DIOP (PS).
**Minister of Women's, Children's and Family Affairs:** AMINATA MBENGUE (PS).
**Minister of Equipment and Land Transport:** LANDING SANE (PS).
**Minister of Trade, Crafts and Industrialization:** IDRISSA SECK (PDS).
**Minister of Youth and Sports:** OUSMANE PAYE (no party affiliation).
**Minister of Fisheries and Maritime Transport:** ALASSANE DIALY.
**Minister of Tourism and Air Transport:** TIJANE SYLLA (PS).
**Minister of Water Resources:** MAMADOU FAYE (no party affiliation).
**Minister of Scientific Research and Technology:** MARIE-LOUISE COREA (PS).
**Minister of Towns:** DAOUR CISSÉ (no party affiliation).

There are, in addition, nine ministers-delegate.

### MINISTRIES

**Office of the President:** ave Roume, BP 168, Dakar; tel. 23-10-88; telex 258.
**Ministry of Agriculture and Water Resources:** Immeuble Administratif, Dakar; tel. 23-10-88; telex 3151.
**Ministry of the Armed Forces:** BP 176, Dakar; tel. 23-10-88; telex 482.
**Ministry of Communications:** 58 blvd de la République, Dakar; tel. 23-10-65; fax 21-41-04.
**Ministry of Culture:** Immeuble Administratif, Dakar; tel. 23-10-88; telex 482.
**Ministry of the Economy, Finance and Planning:** rue René Ndiaye, BP 4017, Dakar; tel. 21-06-99; telex 3203; fax 22-41-95.
**Ministry of Employment, Labour and Professional Training:** BP 403, Dakar; tel. 23-10-88; telex 482.

**Ministry of Energy, Mines and Industry and of Trade, Crafts and Industrialization:** 122 bis ave André Peytavin, BP 4037, Dakar; tel. 22-99-94; telex 61149; fax 22-55-94.
**Ministry of the Environment and Nature Conservation:** Dakar.
**Ministry of Equipment, of Land and Maritime Transport and Fisheries:** Immeuble Communal, blvd du Général de Gaulle, Dakar; tel. 21-42-01; telex 3151.
**Ministry of Foreign Affairs and Senegalese Abroad:** place de l'Indépendance, Dakar; tel. 21-62-84; telex 482.
**Ministry of Housing and Town Planning:** ave André Peytavin, BP 4028, Dakar; tel. 23-91-27; fax 22-56-01.
**Ministry of the Interior:** Rond-point de la République, Dakar; tel. 21-41-51; telex 3351.
**Ministry of Justice:** BP 784, Dakar; tel. 23-10-88; telex 482.
**Ministry of Modernization of the State:** Dakar.
**Ministry of National Education:** rues Calmette et René Ndiaye, BP 4025, Dakar; tel. 22-12-28; fax 21-89-30.
**Ministry of Public Health and Social Action:** Immeuble Administratif, Dakar; tel. 23-10-88; telex 482.
**Ministry of Tourism and Air Transport:** 23 rue Calmette, BP 4049, Dakar; tel. 23-65-02; fax 22-94-13.
**Ministry of Women's, Children's and Family Affairs:** Dakar.
**Ministry of Youth and Sports:** ave Abdoulaye Fadiga, Dakar.

## President and Legislature

### PRESIDENT

**Presidential Election, 21 February 1993**

|  | Votes | % of votes |
|---|---|---|
| ABDOU DIOUF (PS) | 757,311 | 58.40 |
| ABDOULAYE WADE (PDS) | 415,295 | 32.03 |
| LANDING SAVANÉ (AJ—PADS) | 37,787 | 2.91 |
| ABDOULAYE BATHILY (LD—MPT) | 31,279 | 2.41 |
| IBA DER THIAM (CDP) | 20,840 | 1.61 |
| MADIOR DOUF (RND) | 12,635 | 0.97 |
| MAMADOU LÔ (Independent) | 11,058 | 0.85 |
| BABACAR NIANG (PLP) | 10,450 | 0.81 |
| **Total** | **1,296,655** | **100.00** |

### ASSEMBLÉE NATIONALE

**President:** CHEIKH ABDOUL KHADRE CISSOKHO.

**General Election, 9 May 1993**

| Party | Votes | % of votes | Seats |
|---|---|---|---|
| PS | 602,171 | 56.56 | 84 |
| PDS | 321,585 | 30.21 | 27 |
| Japoo* | 52,189 | 4.90 | 3 |
| LD—MPT | 43,950 | 4.13 | 3 |
| PIT | 32,348 | 3.04 | 2 |
| UDS—R | 12,339 | 1.16 | 1 |
| **Total** | **1,064,582** | **100.00** | **120** |

* An electoral alliance of AJ—PADS, the CDP and the RND, as well as independent candidates.

## Advisory Council

**Conseil Economique et Social:** 25 ave Pasteur, BP6100, Dakar; tel. 23-59-35; f. 1964; Pres. BABACAR NDOYE.

## Political Organizations

**And Jëf—Parti africain pour la démocratie et le socialisme (AJ—PADS):** BP 12025, Dakar; tel. 22-54-63; f. 1991 by merger of And Jëf—Mouvement révolutionnaire pour la démocratie nouvelle, Organisation socialiste des travailleurs and Union pour la démocratie populaire; progressive reformist; Sec.-Gen. LANDING SAVANÉ.

**Convention des démocrates et des patriotes (CDP):** 96 rue 7, Bopp, Dakar; f. 1992; Sec.-Gen. Prof. IBA DER THIAM.

**Ligue démocratique—Mouvement pour le parti du travail (LD—MPT):** BP 10172, Dakar Liberté; tel. 22-67-06; regd 1981; Marxist-Leninist; Sec.-Gen. ABDOULAYE BATHILY.

**Mouvement pour le socialisme et l'unité (MSU):** Villa no 54, rue 4, Bopp, Dakar; f. 1981 as Mouvement démocratique populaire; socialist; Sec.-Gen. MAMADOU DIA.

**Parti africain des écologistes—Sénégal (PAES):** Ecole Normale Germaine Legoff, Dakar; Sec.-Gen. ABOUBACRY DIA.

**Parti africain de l'indépendance (PAI):** BP 820, Dakar; f. 1957, reorg. 1976; Marxist; Sec.-Gen. MAJHEMOUTH DIOP.

**Parti africain pour l'indépendance des masses (Pai—M):** 440, Cité Abdou Diouf Guédiawaye, Dakar; tel. 34-75-90; f. 1982; social-democratic; Sec.-Gen. ALY NIANE.

**Parti démocratique sénégalais (PDS):** 5 blvd Dial Diop, Dakar; f. 1974; liberal-democratic; Sec.-Gen. Me ABDOULAYE WADE.

**Parti démocratique sénégalais—Rénovation (PDS—R):** 343 Gibraltar II, Dakar; regd 1987; breakaway group from PDS; Sec.-Gen. SERIGNE DIOP.

**Parti de l'indépendance et du travail (PIT):** BP 5612, Dakar Fann; regd 1981; Marxist-Leninist; Sec.-Gen. AMATH DANSOKHO.

**Parti pour la libération du peuple (PLP):** 4025 Sicap Amitié II, Dakar; f. 1983 by RND dissidents; neutralist and anti-imperialist; Sec.-Gen. Me BABACAR NIANG; Asst Sec.-Gen. ABDOULAYE KANE.

**Parti populaire sénégalais (PPS):** Clinique Khadim Diourbel, Dakar; regd 1981; populist; Sec.-Gen. Dr OUMAR WANE.

**Parti socialiste sénégalais (PS):** Maison du Parti, ave Cheikh Amadou Bamba, Rocade Fann, Bel Air, BP 12010, Dakar; f. 1958 as Union progressiste sénégalaise, reorg. under present name 1978; democratic socialist; Sec.-Gen. ABDOU DIOUF; Political Sec. DJIBO KA.

**Rassemblement national démocratique (RND):** Villa no 29, Cité des Professeurs, Fann Résidence, Dakar; f. 1976, legalized 1981; progressive; Sec.-Gen. MADIOR DIOUF.

**Union démocratique sénégalaise—Rénovation (UDS—R):** Villa no 273, Ouagou Niayes, Dakar; f. 1985 by PDS dissidents; nationalist-progressive; Sec.-Gen. MAMADOU PURITAIN FALL.

An outlawed separatist group, the **Mouvement des forces démocratiques de la Casamance (MFDC)**, is active in the southern province of Casamance.

## Diplomatic Representation

### EMBASSIES IN SENEGAL

**Algeria:** 5 rue Mermoz, BP 3233, Dakar; tel. 22-35-09; telex 61173; Ambassador: TEDJINI SALANANDJI.

**Argentina:** 34-36 blvd de la République, BP 3343, Dakar; tel. 21-51-71; telex 51457; Ambassador: HÉCTOR TEJERINA.

**Austria:** 24 blvd DJILY MBAYE, BP 3247, Dakar; tel. 22-38-86; telex 51611; fax 21-03-09; Ambassador: Dr PETER LEITENBAUER.

**Bangladesh:** Immeuble Kébé, Appts 11–12, 7e étage, ave André Peytavin, BP 403, Dakar; tel. 21-68-81; telex 51298; Ambassador: M. D. MANIRUZZAMAN MIAH.

**Belgium:** route de la Petite Corniche-Est, BP 524, Dakar; tel. 22-47-20; telex 51265; fax 21-63-45; Ambassador: JACQUES-BENOÎT FOBE.

**Brazil:** Immeuble Résidence Excellence, 2e étage, 4 ave Roume, BP 136, Dakar; tel. 23-25-92; fax 23-71-81; Ambassador: JORGE SALTARELLI, Jr.

**Cameroon:** 157–9 rue Joseph Gomis, BP 4165, Dakar; tel. 21-33-96; telex 21429; Ambassador: EMMANUEL MBONJO EJANGUE.

**Canada:** Immeuble Daniel Sorano, 45 blvd de la République, BP 3373, Dakar; tel. 23-92-90; telex 51632; fax 23-87-49; Ambassador: JACQUES BILODEAU.

**Cape Verde:** Immeuble El Fahd, BP 2319, Dakar; tel. 21-18-73; telex 61128; Ambassador: VÍCTOR AFONSO GONÇALVES FIDALGO.

**China, People's Republic:** rue Projetée, Fann Résidence, BP 342, Dakar; tel. 22-14-67; Ambassador: CANG YOUHENG.

**Congo:** Mermoz Pyrotechnie, BP 5243, Dakar; tel. 24-83-98; Ambassador: CHRISTIAN GILBERT BEMBET.

**Côte d'Ivoire:** 2 ave Albert Sarraut, BP 359, Dakar; tel. 21-01-63; telex 61170; Ambassador: JULES HIÉ NÉA.

**Czech Republic:** rue Aimé Césaire, Fann Résidence, BP 3253, Dakar; tel. 24-65-26; fax 24-14-06; Ambassador: LADISLAV SKEŘÍK.

**Egypt:** Immeuble Daniel Sorano, 45 blvd de la République, BP 474, Dakar; tel. 21-24-75; fax 21-89-93; Ambassador: MOHAMED ABDEL-RAHMAN DIAB.

**Ethiopia:** BP 379, Dakar; tel. 21-75-73; telex 51413; Ambassador: SAHLE-WORK ZEWDE.

**France:** 1 rue Amadou Assane Ndoye, BP 4035, Dakar; tel. 23-91-81; telex 51597; fax 22-18-05; Ambassador: RENÉ ALA.

**Gabon:** Villa no 7606 Mermoz, BP 436, Dakar; tel. 24-09-95; fax 25-98-26; Ambassador: SIMON OMBEGUE.

**Gambia:** 11 rue de Thiong, BP 3248, Dakar; tel. 21-44-76; telex 51617; Ambassador: El Hadj ABDOULIE SULAYMAN MBOOB.

**Germany:** 20 ave Pasteur, BP 2100, Dakar; tel. 23-48-84; telex 21686; fax 22-52-99; Ambassador: Dr THOMAS FISCHER-DIESKAU.

**Guinea:** km 4.5, route de Ouakam, BP 7123, Dakar; tel. 21-86-06; telex 3242; Ambassador: HERVÉ VINCENT BANGOURA.

**Guinea-Bissau:** Point E, rue 6, BP 2319, Dakar; tel. 21-59-22; telex 243; Ambassador: PIO GOMES CORREIA.

**Holy See:** rue Aimé Césaire, angle Corniche-Ouest, Fann Résidence, BP 5076, Dakar; tel. 24-26-74; fax 24-19-31; Apostolic Nuncio: Mgr ANTONIO MARIA VEGLIÒ, Titular Archbishop of Aeclanum.

**India:** 5 ave Carde, BP 398, Dakar; tel. 22-58-75; telex 51514; fax 22-35-85; Ambassador: VIDYA BHUSHAN SONI.

**Indonesia:** 126 ave Cheikh Anta Diop, x ave Bourguiba, BP 5859, Dakar; tel. 25-73-16; telex 21644; Ambassador: UTOJO YAMTOMO.

**Italy:** rue Alpha Hachamiyou Tall, BP 348, Dakar; tel. 22-00-76; fax 21-75-80; Ambassador: GUIDO RIZZO VENCI.

**Japan:** Immeuble Electra II, rue Malan, BP 3140, Dakar; tel. 23-91-41; telex 51677; fax 23-73-51; Ambassador: TAKESHI NAKAMURA.

**Korea, Democratic People's Republic:** rue Aimé Césaire, Fann Résidence, BP 3156, Dakar; tel. 23-09-99; Ambassador: KIM GI CHAN.

**Korea, Republic:** Immeuble Fayçal, BP 3338, Dakar; tel. 22-58-22; telex 51242; Ambassador: SEUNG HO.

**Kuwait:** blvd Martin Luther King, Dakar; tel. 24-17-23; telex 3327; Ambassador: KHALAF ABBAS KHALAF.

**Lebanon:** 18 blvd de la République, BP 234, Dakar; tel. 22-09-20; telex 3190; Ambassador: NAJI ABDOU ASSI.

**Mali:** 46 blvd de la République, BP 478, Dakar; tel. 23-48-93; telex 51429; Ambassador: MOHAMED ALI BATHILY.

**Mauritania:** Corniche Ouest, Fann Résidence, BP 2019, Dakar; tel. 25-98-07; fax 25-72-64; Ambassador: MALIFOND OULD DADDAH.

**Morocco:** ave Cheikh Anta Diop, BP 490, Dakar; tel. 24-69-27; telex 51567; fax 25-70-21; Ambassador: MOHAMED HALIM.

**Netherlands:** 37 rue Kléber, BP 3262, Dakar; tel. 23-94-83; telex 51610; fax 21-70-84; Ambassador: GERARD J. H. C. KRAMER.

**Nigeria:** Point E, rue 1 x Fa, BP 3129, Dakar; tel. 21-69-22; telex 51404; Ambassador: Alhaji ABUBAKAR MUHAMMADU SANI YARIMA.

**Pakistan:** 10 ave Borgnis Desbordes, BP 2635, Dakar; tel. 21-20-31; Ambassador: RASHEED AHMED.

**Poland:** 7627 route de la Pologne, BP 343, Dakar; tel. 24-23-54; telex 51245; fax 23-05-26; Chargé d'affaires a.i.: JANUSZ MROWIEC.

**Portugal:** 5 ave Carde, BP 281, Dakar; tel. 23-58-22; telex 61134; fax 23-50-96; Ambassador: FERNANDO PINTO DOS SANTOS.

**Romania:** Point E, blvd de l'Est x rue 4, Dakar; tel. and fax 25-19-13; telex 61115; Chargé d'affaires a.i.: IONEL ILIE.

**Russia:** ave Jean-Jaurès, angle rue Carnot, BP 3180, Dakar; tel. 22-48-21; telex 21432; Ambassador: VALERY N. LIPNYAKOV.

**Saudi Arabia:** 33 rue Kléber, BP 3109, Dakar; tel. 22-23-67; telex 51294; Ambassador: ABDULLAH A. ALTOBAISHI.

**Spain:** 45 blvd de la République, BP 2091, Dakar; tel. 21-11-78; telex 51451; Ambassador: MIGUEL ANGEL GARCÍA MINA ORAA.

**Switzerland:** rue René Ndiaye, BP 1772, Dakar; tel. 22-58-48; telex 51411; Ambassador: WALTER GYGER.

**Syria:** Point E, rue 1 x blvd de l'Est, BP 498, Dakar; tel. 21-62-77; telex 62102; Chargé d'affaires a.i.: HILAL AL-RAHEB.

**Thailand:** Fann Résidence, 10 rue Léon Gontran Damas, BP 3721, Dakar; tel. 24-30-76; telex 61279; Ambassador: NARONK KHEMAYODHIN.

**Tunisia:** rue El Hadj Seydou Nourou Tall, BP 3127, Dakar; tel. 23-47-47; telex 54564; fax 23-72-04; Ambassador: ALI HACHANI.

**Turkey:** ave des Ambassadeurs, Fann Résidence, BP 6060, Etoile, Dakar; tel. 24-58-11; telex 51472; fax 25-69-77; Ambassador: MEHMET GORKAY.

**United Kingdom:** 20 rue du Dr Guillet, BP 6025, Dakar; tel. 23-73-92; telex 21690; fax 23-27-66; Ambassador: ALAN EDWIN FURNESS.

**USA:** ave Jean XXIII, BP 49, Dakar; tel. 23-42-96; telex 21793; fax 22-29-91; Ambassador: MARK JOHNSON.

**Zaire:** 16 rue Léo Frobénius, Fann Résidence, BP 2251, Dakar; tel. 25-19-79; telex 21661; Ambassador: KALENGA WA BELABELA.

**Zimbabwe:** km 5.5, route de Ouakam, BP 2762, Dakar; tel. 23-03-25; telex 3231; Ambassador: CHIMBIDZAYI EZEKIEL SANYANGARE.

## Judicial System

Unter the terms of a revision of the judicial system, implemented in May 1992, the principal organs of the judiciary are as follows:

SENEGAL

**Conseil Constitutionnel:** Pres. YOUSSOUPHA NDIAYE.
**Conseil d'Etat:** Pres. LOUIS PREIRA DE CARVALHO; Sec.-Gen. DOUDOU NDIR.
**Cour de Cassation:** Pres. (vacant); Procurator-Gen. SEYDOU BA; Sec.-Gen. MOUSTAPHA TOURÉ.
**Cour d'Appel:** Pres. ANDRÉSIA VAZ; Procurator-Gen. PAPA BOUGOUMA DIENE.

# Religion

About 90% of the population are Muslims, while about 6% are Christians, mainly Roman Catholics, and 4% follow traditional beliefs.

### ISLAM

There are four main Islamic brotherhoods: the Mourides, the Tidjanes, the Layennes and the Qadiriyas.
**Grand Imam:** El Hadj MAODO SYLLA.
**Association pour la coopération islamique (ACIS):** Dakar; f. 1988; Pres. Dr THIERNAO KÂ.
**National Association of Imams:** Dakar; f. 1984; Pres. El Hadj MAODO SYLLA.

### CHRISTIANITY

#### The Roman Catholic Church

Senegal comprises one archdiocese and five dioceses. At 31 December 1993 adherents of the Roman Catholic Church comprised about 4.9% of the total population.
**Bishops' Conference:** Conférence des Evêques du Sénégal, de la Mauritanie, du Cap Vert et de Guinée-Bissau, BP 941, Dakar; f. 1973; Pres. Rt Rev. THÉODORE-ADRIEN SARR, Bishop of Kaolack.
**Archbishop of Dakar:** Cardinal HYACINTHE THIANDOUM, Archevêché, ave Jean XXIII, BP 1908, Dakar; tel. 23-69-18.

#### The Anglican Communion

The Anglican diocese of The Gambia, part of the Church of the Province of West Africa, includes Senegal and Cape Verde. The Bishop is resident in Banjul, The Gambia.

#### Other Denominations

**Eglise Protestante Sénégalaise:** rue Wagare Diouf, BP 847, Dakar; tel. 21-55-64; telex 3310; f. 1862; Pastor Rev. KANGURDIE MAME.

### BAHÁ'Í FAITH

**National Spiritual Assembly:** BP 1662, Dakar; tel. 24-23-59; registered 1975; mems resident in 340 localities.

# The Press

### NEWSPAPERS

**Réveil de l'Afrique Noire:** Dakar; f. 1986; daily; Dir MAM LESS DIA.
**Le Soleil:** Société sénégalaise de presse et de publications, route du Service géographique, BP 92, Dakar; tel. 32-46-92; telex 51431; fax 32-03-81; f. 1970; daily; publ. by Parti socialiste sénégalais; Man. Dir ALIOUNE DRAME; circ. 45,000.
**Sud au Quotidien:** Immeuble Fahd, BP 4130, Dakar; tel. 22-53-93; fax 22-52-90; daily; fmrly Sud Hebdo; Editor ABDOULAYE NDIAGA SYLLA; circ. 30,000.
**Wal Fadjiri** (The Dawn): Dakar; Islamic daily; circ. 15,000.

### PERIODICALS

**Afrique Economique:** Dakar; f. 1975; monthly; Editor ASSANE SECK; circ. 10,000.
**Afrique Médicale:** 10 rue Abdou Karim Bourgi, BP 1826, Dakar; tel. 23-48-80; telex 1300; fax 22-56-30; f. 1960; monthly; review of tropical medicine; Editor JOËL DECUPPER; circ. 7,000.
**Afrique Nouvelle:** 9 rue Paul Holle, BP 283, Dakar; tel. 22-51-22; telex 1403; f. 1947; weekly; development issues; Roman Catholic; Dir RENÉ ODOUN; circ. 15,000.
**Amina:** BP 2120, Dakar; monthly; women's magazine.
**Bingo:** 17 rue Huart, BP 176, Dakar; f. 1952; monthly; illustrated; Editor E. SOELLE; circ. 110,750.
**Le Cafard Libéré:** 10 rue Tolbiac x autoroute, 3e étage, Dakar; tel. 22-84-43; f. 1987; weekly; satirical; Editor LAYE BAMBA DIALLO; circ. 10,000.
**Combat pour le Socialisme:** Dakar; f. 1987; politics; circ. 10,000.

*Directory*

**Construire l'Afrique:** BP 3770, Dakar; tel. 23-07-90; fax 24-19-61; f. 1985; six a year; African business; Dir and Chief Editor CHEIKH-OUSMANE DIALLO.
**Le Démocrate:** 10 rue de Thiong, Dakar; f. 1974; monthly; publ. by Parti démocratique sénégalais.
**Ethiopique:** BP 260, Dakar; f. 1974; monthly; publ. by Parti démocratique sénégalais.
**Fippu:** Dakar; f. 1987; quarterly; feminist; Dir FATOUMATA SOW.
**Journal Officiel de la République du Sénégal:** Rufisque; f. 1856; weekly; govt journal.
**La Lutte:** BP 820, Dakar; f. 1977; quarterly; publ. by Parti africain de l'indépendance; Editor BARA GOUDIABY; circ. 1,000.
**Momsareew:** BP 820, Dakar; f. 1958; monthly; publ. by Parti africain de l'indépendance; Editor-in-Chief MALAMINE BADJI; circ. 2,000.
**L'Observateur Africain:** Dakar; Dir ALIOUNE DIOP.
**Le Politicien:** Dakar; f. 1977; fortnightly; satirical; Editor MAM LESS DIA.
**Promotion:** Dakar; Dir BOUBACAR DIOP.
**Le Rénovateur:** BP 12172, Dakar; monthly; publ. by Parti démocratique sénégalais—Rénovation.
**République:** Dakar; f. 1989; weekly; independent; current affairs.
**Sénégal d'Aujourd'hui:** 58 blvd de la République, BP 4027, Dakar; monthly; publ. by Ministry of Culture; circ. 5,000.
**Sopi** (Change): Dakar; f. 1988; weekly; publ. by Parti démocratique sénégalais; Dir of Publishing JOSEPH NDONG (arrested March 1994).
**Souka-Magazine:** 10 rue Amadou Assane Ndoye, BP 260, Senegal; tel. 22-15-80; telex 21450; fax 22-36-04; f. 1989; monthly; circ. 20,000.
**L'Unité Africaine:** BP 22010, Dakar; f. 1974; monthly; publ. by Parti socialiste sénégalais.
**Xareli** (Struggle): BP 12136, Dakar; tel. 22-54-63; fortnightly; publ. by And Jëf—Parti africain pour la démocratie et le socialisme; circ. 7,000.

### NEWS AGENCIES

**Agence de Presse Sénégalaise:** 72 blvd de la République, BP 117, Dakar; tel. 21-14-27; telex 51520; f. 1959; govt-controlled; Dir AMADOU DIENG.
**Pan-African News Agency (PANA):** BP 4056, Dakar; tel. 22-61-20; telex 3307; f. 1979, restructured 1992–93; news service to 38 African countries; Co-ordinator-Gen. BABACAR FALL.

#### Foreign Bureaux

**Agence France-Presse (AFP):** Immeuble Maginot, 7e étage, BP 363, Dakar; tel. 23-21-92; telex 51564; fax 22-16-07; Dir FRANÇOIS-XAVIER HARISPE.
**Agenzia Nazionale Stampa Associata (ANSA)** (Italy): Dakar; tel. 22-11-97; telex 61338; Correspondent ALIOUNE TOURÉ DIA.
**Wikalat al-Maghreb al Arabi** (Morocco): 15 rue Galandou Diouf, 4e étage, Dakar; tel. 21-97-13; Dir MOHAMED KHAYATE.
**Xinhua (New China) News Agency** (People's Republic of China): Villa 1, 2 route de la Pyrotechnie, Stele Mernoz, BP 426, Dakar; tel. 23-05-38; telex 283; Chief Correspondent ZHOU WEIBO.

IPS (Italy), ITAR—TASS (Russia), Reuters (UK) and UPI (USA) are also represented in Dakar.

# Publishers

**Africa Editions:** BP 1826, Dakar; tel. 23-48-80; telex 1300; fax 22-56-30; f. 1958; general, reference; Man. Dir JOËL DECUPPER.
**Agence de Distribution de Presse:** km 2.5, blvd du Centenaire de la Commune de Dakar, BP 374, Dakar; tel. 32-02-78; fax 32-49-15; f. 1943; general, reference; Man. Dir THIERRY SABOURET.
**Altervision:** BP 3770, Dakar; tel. 23-07-90; fax 24-19-61; f. 1985; business; Dir-Gen. CHEIKH-OUSMANE DIALLO.
**Editions Juridiques Africaines (EDJA):** 164 ave du Président Lamine Guèye, BP 2875, Dakar; tel. 22-25-49; fax 22-24-83; f. 1986; law.
**Editions des Trois Fleuves:** blvd de l'Est, angle Cheikh Anta Diop, BP 123, Dakar; tel. 23-09-23; fax 25-59-37; f. 1972; general non-fiction; luxury edns; Man. Dir BERTRAND DE BOISTEL.
**Enda:** 4–5 rue Kléber, BP 3370, Dakar; tel. 22-42-29; telex 51456; third-world environment and development.
**Grande imprimerie africaine:** 9 rue Amadou Assane Ndoye, BP 51, Dakar; tel. 22-14-08; fax 22-39-27; f. 1917; law, administration; Man. Dir Cheikh ALIMA TOURÉ.

**Institut fondamental d'Afrique noire (IFAN):** BP 206, Dakar; scientific and humanistic studies of black Africa.

**Librairie Clairafrique:** 2 rue El Hadji Mbaye Guèye, BP 2005, Dakar; tel. 22-21-69; fax 21-84-09; f. 1951; politics, law, sociology, anthropology, literature, economics, development, religion, school books.

**Nouvelles éditions africaines du Sénégal (NEAS):** 10 rue Amadou Assane Ndoye, BP 260, Dakar; tel. 22-15-80; fax 22-36-04; f. 1972; general; Man. Dir DOUDOU NDIAYE.

**Société africaine d'édition:** 16 bis rue de Thiong, BP 1877, Dakar; tel. 21-79-77; f. 1961; African politics and economics; Man. Dir PIERRE BIARNES.

**Société d'édition 'Afrique Nouvelle':** 9 rue Paul Holle, BP 283, Dakar; tel. 22-38-25; telex 1403; f. 1947; information, statistics and analyses of African affairs; Man. Dir ATHANASE NDONG.

**Société nationale de Presse, d'édition et de publicité (SONA-PRESS):** Dakar; f. 1972; Pres. OBEYE DIOP.

**Sud-Communication:** Dakar; operated by a journalists' cooperative; periodicals.

### Government Publishing House

**Société sénégalaise de presse et de publications (SSPP):** route du Service géographique, BP 92, Dakar; tel. 32-46-92; telex 51431; fax 32-03-81; f. 1970; 62% govt-owned; Pres. and Man. Dir ALIOUNE DRAME.

## Radio and Television

In 1992, according to estimates by UNESCO, there were an estimated 890,000 radio receivers and 282,000 television receivers in use.

**Société Nationale de Radiodiffusion Télévision Sénégalaise (RTS):** BP 1765, Dakar; tel. 21-78-01; telex 21818; fax 22-34-90; fmrly Office de Radiodiffusion-Télévision du Sénégal; state broadcasting co; Man. Dir GUILA THIAM; Dir (Radio) IBRAHIM SANE; Dir (Television) BABACAR DIAGNE.

### RADIO

There are two RTS radio networks, broadcasting in French, Portuguese, Arabic, English and six vernacular languages from Saint-Louis, Ziguinchor, Tambacounda and Kaolack.

**FM 92:** Dakar; broadcasts commenced 1991; jt venture by RTS and Radio France International (RFI); 24 hours daily of FM broadcasts to Dakar (RFI 18 hours, RTS six hours).

**FM 94/Dakar FM:** Dakar; broadcasts commenced 1990; eight hours of local broadcasts daily.

### Commercial Station

**Sud FM:** Dakar; f. 1994, broadcasts began 1995; operated by Sud-Communication; Man. Dir CHERIF ELVALIDE SEYE.

Broadcasts by Africa No. 1, the Gabonese-based radio station, are received in Dakar.

### TELEVISION

There are 10-kW transmitters at Dakar, Thiès, Ziguinchor, Tambacounda and Louga. Following an agreement with France in 1989, Senegal was to receive direct transmissions from that country.

**Canal Horizons Sénégal:** Dakar; f. 1990, broadcasts commenced 1991; private coded channel; 18.8% owned by RTS and Société Nationale des Télécommunications du Sénégal, 15% by Canal Horizons (France); Man. Dir JACQUES BARBIER DE CROZES.

**TV5 Afrique:** Dakar; broadcasts commenced 1992; operated by the French-based TV5 to transmit programmes by satellite to francophone Africa; Chair. PATRICK IMHAUS.

### SUPERVISORY AUTHORITY

**Haut Conseil de la Radio Télévision:** Dakar; f. 1991; Pres. BABACAR KEBE.

## Finance

(cap. = capital; res = reserves; m. = million; brs = branches; amounts in francs CFA)

### BANKING

#### Central Bank

**Banque Centrale des Etats de l'Afrique de l'Ouest (BCEAO):** ave Abdoulaye Fadiga, BP 3108, Dakar; tel. 23-16-15; telex 21815; fax 23-93-35; National headquarters: blvd du Général de Gaulle, angle Triangle Sud, BP 3159, Dakar; tel. 23-53-84; telex 21839; fax 23-57-57; central bank of issue for mems of the Union économique et monétaire ouest africaine (UEMOA), comprising Benin, Burkina Faso, Côte d'Ivoire, Mali, Niger, Senegal and Togo; f. 1962; cap. and res 530,826m. (Sept. 1993); Gov. CHARLES KONAN BANNY; Dir in Senegal SEYNI NDIAYE (acting); domestic brs at Kaolack and Ziguinchor.

#### Commercial Banks

**Banque Internationale pour le Commerce et l'Industrie du Sénégal (BICIS):** 2 ave Roume, BP 392, Dakar; tel. 23-10-33; telex 21642; fax 23-37-07; f. 1962; 28% owned by Société Financière pour les Pays d'Outre-Mer, 25% state-owned, 22% owned by Banque Nationale de Paris; cap. 3,500m. (Sept. 1993); Pres. and Man. Dir CLAUDE RUFFIN; 4 brs.

**Compagnie Bancaire de l'Afrique Occidentale (CBAO):** 1 place de l'Indépendance, BP 129, Dakar; tel. 23-10-00; telex 21663; fax 23-20-05; f. 1980; fmrly BIAO-Sénégal; 90% privately owned; cap. 2,200m. (Sept. 1992); Pres. JEAN-CLAUDE MIMRAN; Dir-Gen. ABDOUL MBAYE; 10 brs.

**Crédit Lyonnais Sénégal (CLS):** blvd Djily Mbaye, angle rue Huart, BP 56, Dakar; tel. 23-10-08; telex 21622; fax 23-84-30; f. 1989; 95% owned by Crédit Lyonnais (France); cap. 2,000m. (Sept. 1992); Pres. BERNARD NORMAND; Dir-Gen. RENÉ BERARDENGO; 1 br.

**Crédit National du Sénégal (CNS):** 7 ave Roume, BP 319, Dakar; tel. 23-34-86; telex 61283; fax 23-72-92; f. 1990 by merger; 90% state-owned; cap. 2,500m. (Feb. 1990); Pres. ALIA DIÈNE DRAME.

**Société Générale de Banques au Sénégal SA (SGBS):** 19 ave Roume, BP 323, Dakar; tel. 23-10-60; telex 21801; fax 23-90-36; f. 1962; 38.2% owned by private Senegalese interests, 37.9% by Société Générale (France); cap. 4,312m. (Sept. 1993); Chair. IDRISSA SEYDI; Man. Dir GUY POUPET; 3 brs.

#### Development Banks

**Banque de l'Habitat du Sénégal (BHS):** blvd du Général de Gaulle, BP 229, Dakar; tel. 23-10-04; telex 61275; fax 23-80-43; f. 1979; cap. 1,650m. (Sept. 1992); Pres. GOUNKA DIOUF; Man. Dir AMADOU BASSIROU DIA; 1 br.

**Banque Sénégalo-Tunisienne (BST):** 57 ave Georges Pompidou, BP 4111, Dakar; tel. 23-62-30; telex 61169; fax 23-82-38; f. 1986; cap. 1,100m. (Sept. 1991); Pres. ABOUBAKRY KANE; Dir-Gen. TAOUFIK BAAZIZ.

**Caisse Nationale de Crédit Agricole du Sénégal (CNCAS):** 45 ave Albert Sarrault, BP 3890, Dakar; tel. 22-23-90; telex 61345; fax 21-26-06; f. 1984; 23.9% state-owned; cap. 2,300m. (Sept. 1992); Man. Dir SOMCIDINE DIENG; 4 brs.

#### Banking Association

**Association Professionnelle des Banques et des Etablissements Financiers du Sénégal (APBEF):** c/o SGBS, 19 ave Roume, BP 323, Dakar; Pres. LOUIS FRANCESCHINI.

### INSURANCE

**Assurances Générales Sénégalaises (AGS):** 43 ave Albert Sarraut, BP 225, Dakar; tel. 23-49-94; telex 51647; fax 23-37-01; f. 1977; cap. 2,990m.; Man. Dir A. SOW.

**Compagnie d'Assurances-Vie et de Capitalisation (La Nationale d'Assurances-Vie):** 7 blvd de la République, BP 3853, Dakar; tel. 22-11-81; telex 51251; fax 21-28-20; f. 1982; cap. 80m.; Pres. MOUSSA DIOUF; Man. Dir BASSIROU DIOP.

**Compagnie Sénégalaise d'Assurances et de Réassurances (CSAR):** 5 place de l'Indépendance, BP 182, Dakar; tel. 23-27-76; telex 61125; fax 23-46-72; f. 1972; cap. 945m.; 49.8% state-owned; Pres. MOUSTAPHA CISSÉ; Man. Dir MAMADOU ABBAS BA.

**SA Capillon V-Assurances:** 5 ave Roume, BP 425, Dakar; tel. 22-90-26; telex 684; f. 1951; cap. 10m.; Pres. and Man. Dir GILLES DE MONTALEMBERT.

**La Sécurité Sénégalaise (ASS):** Gare Routière, BP 2623, Dakar; tel. 23-75-95; telex 3207; f. 1984; cap. 100m.; Pres. LOBATT FALL; Man. Dir MBACKE SENE.

**Société Africaine d'Assurances:** ave Roume, angle Victor Hugo, BP 508, Dakar; tel. 23-64-75; fax 23-44-72; f. 1945; cap. 9m.; Dir CLAUDE GERMAIN.

**Société Inter-Africane de Courtage de Réassurances (SIACRE):** 41 rue C, Fann Résidence, BP 3135, Dakar; tel. 23-04-84; telex 61244; f. 1977; cap. 50m.; Dir M. BABO.

**Société Nationale d'Assurances Mutuelles (SONAM):** 6 ave Roume, BP 210, Dakar; tel. 23-10-03; telex 51571; fax 20-70-25; f. 1973; cap. 1,464m.; Pres. ABDOULAYE FOFANA; Man. Dir DIOULDÉ NIANE.

**Société Sénégalaise de Courtage et d'Assurances (SOSECODA):** 16 ave Roume, BP 9, Dakar; tel. 23-54-81; telex 51436;

SENEGAL

fax 21-54-62; f. 1963; cap. 10m.; 55% owned by SONAM; Man. Dir A. Aziz Ndaw.

**Société Sénégalaise de Réassurances SA (SENRE):** 6 ave Roume x Carnot, BP 386, Dakar; tel. 22-80-89; telex 61144; fax 21-56-52; cap. 600m.

### Insurance Association

**Syndicat Professionel des Agents Généraux d'Assurances du Sénégal:** 43 ave Albert Sarraut, BP 1766, Dakar; Pres. Urbain Alexandre Diagne; Sec. Jean-Pierre Cairo.

## Trade and Industry

### DEVELOPMENT AND MARKETING ORGANIZATIONS

**Caisse Française de Développement (CFD):** 15 ave Mandéla, BP 475, Dakar; tel. 23-11-88; telex 51653; fax 23-40-10; f. 1941 as Caisse Centrale de Coopération Economique, name changed 1992; Dir in Senegal Jean-Claude Bredeloux.

**Mission Française de Coopération:** BP 2014, Dakar; telex 3103; administers bilateral aid from France; Dir François Chappellet.

**Société de Développement Agricole et Industriel (SODAGRI):** Immeuble Fondation King Fahd, 9e étage, blvd Djily Mbaye x Macodou Ndiaye, BP 222, Dakar; tel. 21-04-26; fax 22-54-06; cap. 120m. francs CFA; agricultural and industrial projects; Pres. and Man. Dir Amadou Tidiane Wane.

**Société de Développement des Fibres Textiles (SODE–FITEX):** km 4.5, blvd du Centenaire de la Commune de Dakar, BP 3216, Dakar; tel. 32-47-80; telex 280; f. 1974; 70% state-owned; responsible for planning and development of cotton industry; cap. 750m. francs CFA; Dir-Gen. Falilou Mbacke.

**Société de Développement et de Vulgarisation Agricole (SODEVA):** 92 rue Moussé Diop, BP 3234, Dakar; tel. 23-16-78; telex 51638; fax 21-01-53; f. 1968; cap. 100m. francs CFA; 55% state-owned; development of intensive farming methods and diversified livestock breeding; Dir-Gen. Papa Ousmane Diallo.

**Société d'Exploitation des Ressources Animales du Sénégal (SERAS):** km 2.5, blvd du Centenaire de la Commune de Dakar, BP 14, Dakar; tel. 32-31-78; telex 51256; fax 32-06-90; f. 1962; cap. 619.2m. francs CFA; 28.5% state-owned; livestock development; Dir Dr Mamadou Faye; Man. Dir Macodou Seye.

**Société Nationale d'Aménagement et d'Exploitation des Terres du Delta du Fleuve Sénégal et des Vallées du Fleuve Sénégal et de la Falémé (SAED):** route de Khor, BP 74, Saint-Louis; tel. 61-15-33; telex 75124; fax 61-14-63; f. 1965; cap. 2,500m. francs CFA; state-owned; controls the agricultural development of 30,000 ha around the Senegal river delta; Pres. and Man. Dir Sidy Moctar Keita.

**Société Nationale de Commercialisation des Oléagineux du Sénégal (SONACOS):** Immeuble SONACOS, 32–36 rue du Dr Calmette, BP 639, Dakar; tel. 23-10-52; telex 51418; fax 23-88-05; f. 1975; cap. 4,800m. francs CFA; 80% state-owned; restructured 1994; marketing of groundnuts and groundnut products; Pres. and Man. Dir Abdoulaye Diop.

**Société Nationale d'Etudes et de Promotion Industrielle (SONEPI):** derrière Résidence Seydou Nourou Tall, ave Bourguiba Prolongée, BP 100, Dakar; tel. 25-21-30; telex 61178; fax 24-65-65; f. 1969; cap. 150m. francs CFA; 28% state-owned; promotion of small and medium-sized enterprises; Chair. and Man. Dir Hady Mamadou Ly.

**Société Nationale d'Exploitation des Eaux du Sénégal (SONEES):** 97 ave André Peytavin, BP 400, Dakar; tel. 21-28-65; telex 61137; f. 1972; cap. 3,927m. francs CFA; 97% state-owned; restructuring and privatization of certain services announced 1995; waterworks and supplies; Pres. Abdoul Magib Seck; Man. Dir Abdoulaye Bouna Fall.

**Société Nouvelle des Etudes de Développement en Afrique (SONED—AFRIQUE):** Immeuble SONACOS, 32–36 rue Calmette, BP 2084, Dakar; tel. 23-94-57; telex 51464; fax 23-42-31; f. 1974; cap. 98m. francs CFA; 61% state-owned; Pres. El Hadj Ibrahima Ndao; Man. Dir Rudolph Kern.

### CHAMBERS OF COMMERCE

**Chambre de Commerce, d'Industrie et d'Agriculture de la Région de Dakar:** 1 place de l'Indépendance, BP 118, Dakar; tel. 23-71-89; telex 61112; fax 23-93-63; f. 1888; Pres. Mamadou Lamine Niang; Sec.-Gen. Mbaye Ndiaye.

**Chambre de Commerce, d'Industrie et d'Artisanat de la Région de Diourbel:** BP 7, Diourbel; tel. 71-12-03; Pres. Cheikh Mamadou Ndiongue; Sec.-Gen. Alioune Diop.

**Chambre de Commerce de la Région de Fatick:** BP 66, Fatick; tel. 49-51-27; Sec.-Gen. Seydou Nourou Ly.

**Chambre de Commerce et d'Industrie de la Région du Kaolack:** BP 203, Kaolack; tel. 41-20-52; telex 7474; Pres. Idrissa Guèye; Sec.-Gen. Aroha Traoré.

**Chambre de Commerce d'Industrie et d'Agriculture de la Région de Kolda:** BP 23; Kolda; tel. 96-12-30; fax 96-10-68; Sec.-Gen. Yaya Camara.

**Chambre de Commerce de la Région de Louga:** BP 26, Louga; tel. 67-11-14; Pres. El Hadj Amadou Bamba Sourang; Sec.-Gen. Souleymane N'Diaye.

**Chambre de Commerce, d'Industrie et d'Agriculture de la Région de Saint-Louis:** rue Bisson Nord, BP 19, Saint-Louis; tel. 61-10-88; f. 1879; Pres. El Hadj Momar Sourang; Sec.-Gen. Massamba Diop.

**Chambre de Commerce, d'Industrie et d'Agriculture de la Région de Tambacounda:** BP 127, Tambacounda; tel. 81-10-14; Pres. Djiby Cissé; Sec.-Gen. Tenguella Ba.

**Chambre de Commerce, d'Industrie et d'Agriculture de la Région de Thiès:** ave Lamine-Guèye, BP 3020, Thiès; tel. 51-10-02; f. 1883; 38 mems; Pres. El Hadj Alioune Palla M'Baye; Sec.-Gen. Abdoul Khadre Camara.

**Chambre de Commerce, d'Industrie et d'Artisanat de la Région de Ziguinchor:** BP 26, Ziguinchor; tel. 91-13-10; f. 1908; Pres. Youssouf Seydi; Sec.-Gen. Mamadi Diatta.

### PRINCIPAL EMPLOYERS' ASSOCIATIONS

**Conseil National du Patronat du Sénégal (CNP):** BP 3537, Dakar; tel. 22-61-01; Pres. Amadou Moctar Sow; Sec.-Gen. Cheikh Seck.

**Groupement Professionnel de l'Industrie du Pétrole du Sénégal (GPP):** blvd du Centenaire de la Commune de Dakar, BP 479, Dakar; tel. 23-10-80; telex 21838; fax 32-90-65; Pres. Mercier Ythier; Sec.-Gen. Ousmane Sow.

**Syndicat des Commerçants Importateurs, Prestataires de Services et Exportateurs de la République du Sénégal (SCIMPEX):** 2 rue Parent x ave Abdoulaye Fadiga, BP 806, Dakar; tel. and fax 21-36-62; f. 1943; Pres. Jacques Conti; Sec.-Gen. Maurice Sarr.

**Syndicat Patronal de l'Ouest Africain des Petites et Moyennes Entreprises et des Petites et Moyennes Industries:** 41 blvd Djily Mbaye, BP 3255, Dakar; tel. 21-35-10; f. 1937; Pres. Babacar Seye; Sec. Mamadou Makhtar Diagne.

**Syndicat Professionnel des Entrepreneurs de Bâtiments et de Travaux Publics du Sénégal:** ave Abdoulaye Fadiga, BP 593, Dakar; tel. 23-43-73; telex 3167; f. 1930; 130 mems; Pres. Christian Virmaud.

**Syndicat Professionnel des Industries du Sénégal (SPIDS):** ave Abdoulaye Fadiga x Thann, BP 593, Dakar; tel. 23-43-73; fax 22-08-84; f. 1944; 110 mems; Pres. Donald Baron; Sec. Gen. Philippe Barry.

### TRADE UNIONS

**Confédération Nationale des Travailleurs Sénégalais (CNTS):** 15 rue Escarfait, BP 937, Dakar; f. 1969; affiliated to Parti socialiste sénégalais; exec. cttee of 47 mems; Sec.-Gen. Madia Diop; 120,000 mems.

**Confédération des Syndicats Autonomes (CSA):** Dakar.

**Union Démocratique des Travailleurs du Sénégal (UDTS):** Dakar.

**Union Nationale des Commerçants et Industriels du Sénégal (UNCIS):** Dakar.

**Union Nationale des Syndicats Autonomes du Sénégal (UNSAS):** Dakar; Sec.-Gen. Mademba Sock.

### TRADE FAIR

**Foire Internationale de Dakar:** Centre International du Commerce Extérieur du Senegal, route de l'Aéroport, BP 8166, Dakar-Yoff; tel. 20-12-02; telex 31512; fax 35-07-12; f. 1986; Man. Dir Ibrahima Diagne.

## Transport

### RAILWAYS

There are 1,225 km of main line including 70 km of double track. One line runs from Dakar north to Saint-Louis (262 km), and the main line runs to Bamako (Mali). All the locomotives are diesel-driven. The rehabilitation and expansion of the railway network is proceeding.

**Société Nationale des Chemins de Fer du Sénégal (SNCFS):** BP 175, Cité Ballabey, Thiès; tel. 51-10-13; telex 77129; fax 51-13-93; state-owned; Pres. Alieu Diene Drame; Man. Dir Mbaye Diouf.

## ROADS

In 1990 there were 13,850 km of roads, of which 3,900 km were surfaced. Work on a 160-km road between Dialakoto and Kédougou, the construction of which (at a cost of some US $45m.) was to be financed by regional donor organizations, began in October 1991. The road was to form part of an eventual transcontinental highway linking Cairo with the Atlantic coast, via N'Djamena (Chad), Bamako (Mali) and Dakar.

## INLAND WATERWAYS

Senegal has three navigable rivers: the Senegal, navigable for three months of the year as far as Kayes (Mali), for six months as far as Kaédi (Mauritania) and all year as far as Rosso and Podor, and the Saloun and Casamance. Senegal is a member of the Organisation de mise en valeur du fleuve Gambie and of the Organisation pour la mise en valeur du fleuve Sénégal both based in Dakar. These organizations aim to develop navigational facilities, irrigation and hydroelectric power in the basins of the Gambia and Senegal Rivers respectively.

## SHIPPING

The port of Dakar is the second largest in west Africa, after Abidjan (Côte d'Ivoire), and the largest deep sea port in the region, serving Senegal, Mauritania, The Gambia and (by rail) Mali. It handled a total of 5.1m. metric tons of international freight in 1994. The extension of the container terminal was completed in 1993, and the port also has extensive facilities for fishing vessels and fish processing.

**Société nationale de Port Autonome de Dakar (PAD):** 21 blvd de la Libération, BP 3195, Dakar; tel. 23-45-45; telex 21404; fax 23-36-06; f. 1865; state-operated port authority; Pres. El Hadj MALICK SY; Man. Dir M. NDIAYE.

**Compagnie Sénégalaise de Navigation Maritime (COSENAM):** rue le Dantec, angle Huart, BP 683, Dakar; tel. 21-57-66; telex 61301; fax 21-08-95; f. 1979; 26.1% state-owned, 65.9% owned by private Senegalese interests, 8.0% by private French, German and Belgian interests; river and ocean freight transport; Pres. ABDOURAHIM AGNE; Man. Dir SIMON BOISSY.

**SDV:** 8–10 allée Robert Delmas, BP 164, Dakar; tel. 23-56-82; telex 21652; fax 21-45-47; f. 1936; fmrly Union Sénégalaise d'Industries Maritimes; shipping agents, warehousing; Pres. GASTON GUILLABERT.

**Société pour le Développement de l'Infrastructure de Chantiers Maritimes du Port de Dakar (DAKAR-MARINE):** blvd de l'Arsenal, BP 438, Dakar; tel. 23-36-88; telex 61104; fax 23-83-99; f. 1981; privately-controlled; operates facilities for the repair and maintenance of supertankers and other large vessels; Man. YORO KANTE.

**SOCOPAO-Sénégal:** 47 ave Albert Sarraut, BP 233, Dakar; tel. 23-10-01; telex 21496; fax 23-56-14; f. 1926; warehousing, shipping agents, sea and air freight transport; Man. Dir GILLES CUCHE.

## CIVIL AVIATION

The international airport is Dakar-Yoff. There are other major airports at Saint-Louis, Ziguinchor and Tambacounda, in addition to about 12 smaller airfields. Facilities at Ziguinchor and Cap-Skirring were being upgraded during the mid-1990s, with the aim of improving direct access to the Casamance region.

**African West Air:** 19 bis rue Robert Brun, Dakar; tel. 22-45-38; fax 22-46-10; f. 1993; services to western Europe and Brazil; Man. Dir J. P. PIEDADE.

**Air Afrique:** place da l'indépendance; BP 3132, Dakar; tel. 39-42-00; fax 23-89-37; see under Côte d'Ivoire; Dir at Dakar MAHAMAT BABA ABATCHA.

**Air Sénégal—Société Nationale des Transports Aériens du Sénégal:** BP 8010, Dakar-Yoff, Dakar; tel. 20-09-13; telex 31513; fax 20-00-33; f. 1971; 50% state-owned, 40% owned by Air Afrique; domestic and international services; Gen. Man. ABDOULAYE NDIAYE.

# Tourism

Senegal's attractions for tourists include six national parks and its fine beaches. The island of Gorée, near Dakar, is of considerable historic interest as a former centre for the slave-trade. Some 245,581 tourists (of whom 52.4% were from France) visited Senegal in 1992. In that year receipts from tourism totalled about 39,200m. francs CFA. However, income from tourism was expected to have declined to an estimated 27,000m. francs CFA in 1993, owing largely to the suspension of tourist activity in the Casamance region in that year. The tourism sector recovered strongly in 1994, owing, in large part, to the devaluation of the national currency in January of that year: some 346,000 tourists were estimated to have visited Senegal in 1994. Renewed insecurity in Casamance in the first half of 1995 prompted fears that tourists would again be deterred from visiting the country. There were 188 hotels, with a total of 14,947 beds, in 1992.

**Ministry of Tourism and Air Transport:** 23 rue Calmette, BP 4049, Dakar; tel. 23-65-02; fax 22-94-13.

# SEYCHELLES

## Introductory Survey

**Location, Climate, Language, Religion, Flag, Capital**

The Republic of Seychelles comprises more than 100 islands, widely scattered over the western Indian Ocean. Apart from the Seychelles archipelago, the country contains several other island groups, the southernmost being about 210 km (130 miles) north of Madagascar. The climate is tropical, with small seasonal variations in temperature and rainfall. The average temperature in Victoria is nearly 27°C (80°F) and average annual rainfall 236 cm (93 ins). In 1981 Creole, spoken by virtually all Seychellois, was made the official language, replacing English and French. Almost all of the inhabitants are Christians, of whom more than 90% belong to the Roman Catholic Church. The national flag (proportions 2 by 1) has three horizontal stripes: a broad red band separated from a narrower dark green band by an undulating white band. The capital is Victoria, on the island of Mahé.

**Recent History**

Seychelles was uninhabited until annexed by France in the 18th century. It was ceded to the United Kingdom in 1814 and administered as a dependency of Mauritius until 1903, when it became a Crown Colony.

Several political parties were formed in the 1960s, of which the most important were the Seychelles Democratic Party (SDP), led by James (later Sir James) Mancham, and the Seychelles People's United Party (SPUP), led by Albert René. A ministerial system of government was introduced in 1970, with the SDP holding a majority of seats in the Legislative Council, and with Mancham as Chief Minister. The SPUP, supported by the Organization of African Unity, demanded immediate independence for Seychelles, while Mancham favoured integration of the colony within the United Kingdom. An independence Constitution was eventually agreed in January 1976; Seychelles thereby became a sovereign republic, within the Commonwealth, on 29 June, under a coalition Government with Mancham as President and René as Prime Minister. Under the independence agreement, the United Kingdom returned to Seychelles the islands of Aldabra, Farquhar and Desroches, detached in 1965 to form part of the British Indian Ocean Territory (q.v.) and subsequently leased to the USA. In 1982 the Aldabra group, which (including its lagoon) represents about one-third of Seychelles' total area, was designated by UNESCO as a world heritage site.

On 4–5 June 1977 the SPUP staged an armed coup while Mancham was absent from the islands. René was declared President, the National Assembly was dissolved and the Constitution suspended, although it was reintroduced in amended form in July. René assumed power to rule by decree. In May 1978 the SPUP was renamed the Seychelles People's Progressive Front (SPPF). A new Constitution, proclaimed in March 1979, established a one-party state. In June elections for a new National Assembly were held. René was the sole candidate in the concurrent presidential election and was re-elected for a second five-year term of office in June 1984. Following the election, Dr Maxime Ferrari, hitherto Minister of Planning and External Relations, resigned from the Government and subsequently left the islands. General elections for the National Assembly took place in 1983 and 1987.

Opponents of René's socialist Government made a number of attempts to overthrow the SPPF regime, with the use of foreign-backed mercenaries. Tanzania undertook to provide defence support after the second of these coup attempts in November 1979. The most serious assault took place in November 1981, when 44 mercenaries, mainly South Africans, flew to join insurgents already on the islands. When the rebellion was suppressed most of the mercenaries escaped to South Africa, where several of their number were later tried and imprisoned. In August 1982 there was a mutiny by a small group of Seychellois soldiers, in which nine people died, but this was later stated to have been directed against certain army officers and not President René. Further plots were discovered in October 1982 and November 1983: both were believed to have been organized by the same Seychellois exiles who had planned the 1981 attempt, and the plot discovered in October 1982 was again alleged to involve foreign mercenaries. In November 1985 Gerard Hoareau, a former government official and leader of an exiled opposition group, was shot dead in the United Kingdom. The incident formed one of a series of attacks on, and disappearances of, anti-René figures. In September 1986 it was reported that the Minister of Youth and Defence, Col Ogilvy Berlouis, had been asked to resign, together with three senior army officers, following an unsuccessful attempted coup for which Berlouis was blamed. In the same month President René reorganized the Council of Ministers, assuming the post of Minister of Defence himself, and several ministries were restructured.

In July 1987 a plot against the Seychelles Government was discovered by police in the United Kingdom, along with details of a plan to abduct leading members of the then-outlawed African National Congress of South Africa (ANC), who were based in London. Four men were subsequently accused of conspiracy to kidnap the ANC members, but the charges were later withdrawn, on the grounds of insufficient evidence.

In June 1989 President René, again as sole candidate, was elected for a third term of office, the maximum period permitted under the 1979 Constitution. Following the election, René appointed four new members to the Council of Ministers. President René, while retaining responsibility for defence, also assumed the post of Minister of Industry but relinquished the portfolios of Planning, External Affairs, Finance and Tourism.

Until the early 1990s exiled opposition to President René remained split among a number of small groups based principally in London. In July 1991 five of these parties, including the Rassemblement du Peuple Seychellois pour la Démocratie, founded by Dr Maxime Ferrari, established a coalition, the United Democratic Movement (UDM), under Ferrari's leadership, while ex-President Mancham rallied his supporters in a 'Crusade for Democracy'.

During 1991 President René came under increasing pressure from France and the United Kingdom, the islands' principal aid-donors, to return Seychelles to a democratic political system. Internally, open opposition to the SPPF was fostered by the newly-formed Parti Seselwa, or Parti Seychellois (PS), led by an Anglican clergyman, Wavel Ramkalawan, and which included Maxime Ferrari's son, Jean-François, among its members. In August Maxime Ferrari returned from exile to organize support for the UDM, and in November President René invited all political dissidents to return to the islands. In the following month the Minister of Tourism and Transport, Jacques Hodoul, left the Government; he subsequently formed the Seychelles Movement for Democracy.

In December 1991 the SPPF agreed to surrender the party's monopoly of power. It was announced that, from January 1992, political groups numbering at least 100 members would be granted official registration, and that multi-party elections would take place in July for a constituent assembly, whose proposals for constitutional reform would be submitted to a national referendum, with a view to holding multi-party parliamentary elections before the end of 1992. In April ex-President Mancham returned from exile to lead the New Democratic Party (NDP). At the July elections for the 20-seat constitutional commission, the SPPF won 58.4% of the votes, while the NDP received 33.7%. The PS, which took 4.4% of the votes, was the only other political party to obtain representation on the commission.

The commission, which comprised 11 representatives from the SPPF, eight from the NDP (now renamed the Democratic Party—DP) and one from the PS, completed its deliberations in October 1992. In September, however, the DP withdrew its delegation, on the grounds that the SPPF had allegedly refused to permit a full debate of reform proposals. It also expressed objections that the commission's meetings had been closed to the public and news media. Following publication of the draft Constitution, the DP focused its opposition on proposed voting arrangements for a new National Assembly, whose members were to be elected on a basis of one-half by direct vote and one-half by proportional representation. The latter formula was to reflect the percentage of votes obtained by the successful candidate in presidential elections, and was intended to ensure that the President's party would secure a legislative majority. Other sections of the proposed Constitution, relating to social issues, were strongly opposed by the Roman Catholic Church, to which more than 90% of the islanders belong.

The draft Constitution, which required the approval of at least 60% of voters, was endorsed by only 53.7% and opposed by 44.6% at a referendum held in November 1992. A second constitutional commission, whose meetings were opened to the public, began work in January 1993 on proposals for submission to a further referendum. In April President René reshuffled the Government, relinquishing the defence portfolio.

In May 1993 the second commission unanimously agreed on a new draft Constitution, in which a compromise plan was reached on the electoral formula for a new National Assembly. With the joint endorsement of René and Mancham, the draft document was submitted to a national referendum in June, at which voters approved the constitutional plan by 73.9% to 24.0%. Opponents of the new constitutional arrangements comprised the PS, the Seychelles National Movement (SNM) and the National Alliance Party (NAP). At the presidential and legislative elections that followed in July, René received 59.5% of the vote, against 36.7% for Mancham and 3.8% for Philippe Boullé, the United Opposition candidate representing the PS, the Seychelles Christian Democrat Party (SCDP), the SNM and the NAP. In the legislative elections, the SPPF secured 21 of the 22 seats elected by direct vote, and the DP one seat. Of the 11 additional seats allocated on a proportional basis, the SPPF received a further seven seats, the DP three seats and the PS one seat. Immediately following the elections, President René, whose decisive victory was widely attributed to his promise of increased expenditure on social programmes, implemented an extensive reshuffle of the Council of Ministers.

Following the 1993 elections, however, the Government began to promote a gradual transition from socialism to free-market policies, aimed at maximizing the country's potential as an 'offshore' financial and business centre. State-owned port facilities were transferred to private ownership in 1994, when plans were also announced for the creation of a duty-free International Trade Zone to provide transhipment facilities. Arrangements were proceeding during 1995 for the privatization of government activities in tourism, agriculture and tuna-processing. The economic liberalization, accompanied by diminished levels of aid and the consequent pressure to reduce budgetary deficits, led the Government to announce, in February 1995, that some state-funded welfare services were to be reduced.

Seychelles has traditionally followed a policy of non-alignment in international affairs, and supports movements for the creation of a 'zone of peace' in the Indian Ocean area. Until 1983 all naval warships wishing to dock at Seychelles had to provide a guarantee that they were not carrying nuclear weapons. The United Kingdom and US Governments refused to agree to this condition, and their respective naval fleets were therefore effectively banned from using Seychelles port facilities. This requirement was withdrawn in September 1983, although Seychelles continued, in theory, to refuse entry to ships carrying nuclear weapons. In 1986 Seychelles and the USA renegotiated an agreement, signed in 1976 and renewed in 1981, which allowed the USA to maintain a satellite-tracking station on Mahé. The future of this installation, however, was under review by the US Government in 1995, as part of cost-reduction measures in its defence expenditure. Since the late 1980s Seychelles has expanded the scope of its formal diplomatic contacts. Relations have been established with the Comoros and with Mauritius, and agreements have been made with the latter for co-operation in health and economic development matters. In 1989 diplomatic relations were established with Morocco, Madagascar and Côte d'Ivoire, and in 1990 with Kenya. During 1992 formal relations were established with Israel and South Africa.

### Government

Under the 1993 Constitution, executive power is vested in the President, who is Head of State and Commander-in-Chief of the Armed Forces. The President, who is elected by direct popular vote, appoints and leads the Council of Ministers, which acts in an advisory capacity to him. The President also appoints the holders of certain public offices and the judiciary. The President may hold office for a maximum period of three five-year terms. The legislature is the unicameral National Assembly, with 33 members: 22 directly elected for five years and 11 allocated on a proportional basis.

### Defence

At June 1994 the army numbered 800 men. Paramilitary forces comprised a 1,000-strong national guard and a coastguard of about 300. Defence expenditure was budgeted at SR82.2m. in 1993.

### Economic Affairs

In 1993, according to estimates by the World Bank, Seychelles' gross national product (GNP), measured at average 1991–93 prices, was US $444m., equivalent to $6,370 per head. During 1985–93, it was estimated, GNP per head increased, in real terms, at an average rate of 4.0% per year. Over the same period the population increased by an annual average of 0.9%. Seychelles' gross domestic product (GDP) increased, in real terms, by an annual average of 4.6% in 1985–93. Real GDP declined by 2.9% in 1991, but rose by 2.0% in 1992 and by 3.9% in 1993.

Agriculture (including hunting, forestry and fishing) contributed an estimated 4.1% of GDP in 1993, and engaged 9.9% of the employed labour force in 1989. Much of Seychelles' production of coconuts is exported in the form of copra. Other cash crops include cinnamon bark, tea, patchouli, vanilla and limes. Tea, sweet potatoes, cassava, yams, sugar cane, bananas, eggs and poultry meat are produced for local consumption. However, imports of food and live animals constituted 16.9% of the value of total imports in 1991. Fishing became increasingly important in the 1980s, and exports of fish and fish preparations contributed 32.4% of the value of total exports in 1991. Licence fees from foreign fishing vessels, allowed to operate in Seychelles' waters, contribute significantly to foreign exchange. Agricultural GDP increased, in real terms, by an estimated annual average of 0.4% in 1985–93. However, it declined by 6.7% in 1992 and by 1.8% in 1993.

Industry (including mining, manufacturing, construction and power) contributed 18.9% of GDP in 1993, and employed 18.7% of the working population in 1989. In real terms, industrial GDP expanded at an average rate of 5.2% per year during 1985–93, with growth of 11.4% in 1993. Manufacturing and mining together provided 11.2% of GDP in 1993, and the combined GDP of these two sectors increased by an annual average of 7.0% in 1985–93, with growth reaching 12.4% in 1993.

The mining sector is small; the sole mineral export is guano (of which 6,000 metric tons was exported in 1990). There are deposits of natural gas, and during the 1980s concessions were sold to several foreign companies, allowing exploration for petroleum. Exploratory drilling was to commence in late 1995. A survey of offshore ocean areas, initiated in 1980, revealed the presence of nodules, containing deposits of various metals, on the sea-bed. The possibility of renewed commercial exploitation of Seychelles' granite reserves is under investigation.

Measured by the value of output, the principal branches of manufacturing in 1984 were food, beverages and tobacco (73% of the total), paper, metals, chemicals, and wood products. Apart from a tuna-canning plant (opened in 1987), the manufacturing sector consists mainly of small-scale activities, including boat-building, printing and furniture-making.

Energy is derived principally from oil-fired power stations. In 1991 mineral fuels accounted for 21.9% of the value of total imports. (However, the vast majority of fuel imports are re-exported—exports of refined petroleum products contributed 60.6% of total export earnings in that year.)

Services engaged 71.3% of the employed labour force in 1989, and provided 76.9% of GDP in 1993. The GDP of the service sectors increased, in real terms, at an average rate of 4.8% in 1985–93. In 1990 tourism generated 17% of GDP and about 60% of total earnings from exports of goods and services. Tourist arrivals totalled an estimated 107,500 in 1994, when income from that source amounted to SR 538m. The majority of visitors are from western Europe, notably from the United Kingdom, France and Italy.

In 1992 the Seychelles recorded a visible trade deficit of US $143.3m. In the same year there was a deficit of $1.7m. on the current account of the balance of payments. The principal source of imports (16.2%) in 1991 was Bahrain (Seychelles'

# SEYCHELLES

*Introductory Survey, Statistical Survey*

main source of petroleum supplies in that year): other important suppliers were the Southern African Customs Union (Botswana, Lesotho, Namibia, South Africa and Swaziland), Singapore, the United Kingdom, France and Japan. The principal markets for exports in 1991 were the United Kingdom (18.9%) and France (9.0%). The principal exports in 1991 were fish and fish preparations and refined petroleum products. Seychelles' major imports were machinery and transport equipment, refined petroleum products, basic manufactures, food and live animals, miscellaneous manufactured articles and chemicals and related products.

In the budget for 1989 there was a deficit of SR 119.8m. (equivalent to 7.0% of GDP). Seychelles' total external debt was US $163.2m. at the end of 1993, of which $138.1m. was long-term public debt. In that year the cost of debt-servicing was equivalent to 6.5% of the value of exports of goods and services. The annual rate of inflation averaged 2.1% in 1985–93; consumer prices increased by an average of 1.3% in 1993 and by 1.9% in 1994. Some 8.3% of the labour force were registered as unemployed in 1993.

Seychelles is a member of the African Development Bank (see p. 102), of the Preferential Trade Area for Eastern and Southern African States (PTA, see p. 240) and of the Indian Ocean Commission (see p. 239), which aims to promote co-operation in the region. Seychelles has acceded to the PTA treaty providing for the establishment of a Common Market for Eastern and Southern Africa, which took effect in December 1994.

Since the early 1970s tourism has been the mainstay of the Seychelles economy. However, this sector has been affected at various times by political instability and attendant interruptions of foreign air services, and its vulnerability to these factors was made particularly apparent by the Gulf war in 1991. Development of agriculture is impeded by the lack of cultivable land. Income from fisheries expanded greatly after the commissioning of a tuna-canning plant in 1987 and the establishment of a prawn farm in the early 1990s. Manufacturing growth is inhibited, however, by the lack of natural resources, although since 1988 the Government has offered incentives for new manufacturing enterprises. A five-year Development Plan (1990–94) sought to attract foreign investment. Measures were being implemented in 1995 to develop Seychelles as an 'offshore' financial services centre, and to establish the islands as a centre for transhipment and air freight in the Indian Ocean area. Legislation was also being promoted to establish an export-processing zone, and to expedite the transfer to private-sector ownership of state interests in hotels and fishing. However, in the absence of significant debt-relief concessions, the cost of servicing the external debt will remain a major impediment to balanced growth.

### Social Welfare

Almost all medical care is provided by the State. In 1984 there were 16 permanent and three temporary clinics and five hospitals. A new, 250-bed general hospital has since been constructed, and in 1990 there were 421 hospital beds. In that year there were 48 physicians, 10 dentists, three pharmacists and 282 nurses. There is government welfare provision for children and mothers in need, and for workers' insurance against injury or death. In 1979 an old-age pension scheme was introduced. Unemployment benefit is provided in exchange for manual work. In the budget for 1995, health services were allotted SR 93m., or about 9.7% of total expenditure.

### Education

In 1979 free and compulsory primary education was introduced for children between six and 15 years of age, and in 1980 the Government initiated a programme of educational reform, based on the British comprehensive system. In 1991 a two-year National Youth Training Scheme, which catered for the secondary education of most children between 15 and 17 years of age, was to be reduced to 12 months. In the same year the duration of primary education was reduced from nine to six years, while that of general secondary education was increased from two to five years (of which the first three years are compulsory), beginning at 12 years of age. Pre-primary and special education facilities are also available. Seychelles Polytechnic, inaugurated in 1982, had 1,428 students in 1993. Several students study abroad, principally in the United Kingdom. In 1990 the average rate of adult illiteracy was estimated at 15%. In the budget for 1995, education was allocated SR 135m., or about 14.1% of total expenditure.

### Public Holidays

**1995:** 1 January (New Year), 14–15 April (Easter), 1 May (Labour Day), 5 June (Liberation Day, anniversary of 1977 coup), 15 June (Corpus Christi), 29 June (Independence Day), 15 August (Assumption), 1 November (All Saints' Day), 8 December (Immaculate Conception), 25 December (Christmas Day).

**1996:** 1 January (New Year's Day), 5–6 April (Easter), 1 May (Labour Day), 5 June (Liberation Day, anniversary of 1977 coup), 6 June (Corpus Christi), 29 June (Independence Day), 15 August (Assumption), 1 November (All Saints' Day), 8 December (Immaculate Conception), 25 December (Christmas Day).

### Weights and Measures

The imperial system is being replaced by the metric system.

# Statistical Survey

Source (unless otherwise stated): Department of Information and Telecommunications, Union Vale, POB 321, Victoria; tel. 224220; telex 2320.

### AREA AND POPULATION

**Area:** 454 sq km (175.3 sq miles), incl. Aldabra lagoon (145 sq km).

**Population:** 61,898 at census of 1 August 1977; 68,598 (males 34,125, females 34,473) at census of 17 August 1987; 72,000 (official estimate) at mid-1993.

**Density** (mid-1993): 158.6 per sq km.

**Principal Town:** Victoria (capital), population 24,324 (incl. suburbs) at the 1987 census.

**Births and Deaths** (registered in 1993): Live births 1,689 (birth rate 23.4 per 1,000); Deaths 597 (death rate 8.3 per 1,000). Source: UN, *Population and Vital Statistics Report*.

**Expectation of Life** (years at birth, 1981–85): Males 65.26; Females 74.05. Source: UN, *Demographic Yearbook*.

**Economically Active Population:** 1981–82 (persons aged 12 years and over): Employed 18,835 (males 12,228, females 6,607); Unemployed 9,527 (males 2,097, females 7,430); Total labour force 28,362. June 1989 (persons aged 15 years and over): Total labour force 29,494 (males 16,964, females 12,530).

**Employment** (1989): Agriculture, hunting, forestry and fishing 2,212; Manufacturing, electricity and water 2,537; Construction, mining and quarrying 1,651; Trade, restaurants and hotels 4,419; Transport, storage and communications 3,141; Financing, insurance, real estate and business services 705; Public administration (incl. activities not adequately defined) 3,106; Other community, social and personal services 4,567; Total 22,338. Figures exclude self-employed persons, unpaid family workers and employees in private domestic services. Source: ILO, *Year Book of Labour Statistics*.

### AGRICULTURE, ETC.

**Principal Crops** (metric tons, 1993): Coconuts 6,000*; Copra 1,000*; Bananas 2,000*; Tea (green leaf) 117†; Cinnamon bark (exports) 243‡. (*FAO estimate. †1985 figure. ‡1989 figure.) Source: mainly FAO, *Production Yearbook*.

**Livestock** (FAO estimates, '000 head, year ending September 1993): Cattle 2; Pigs 18; Goats 5. Source: FAO, *Production Yearbook*.

**Livestock Products** (FAO estimates, metric tons): Meat 2,000; Hen eggs 1,520; Other poultry eggs 12. Source: FAO, *Production Yearbook*.

# SEYCHELLES

*Statistical Survey*

**Fishing** (metric tons, live weight): Total catch 5,382 in 1990; 7,990 in 1991; 6,632 (FAO estimate) in 1992. Source: FAO, *Yearbook of Fishery Statistics*.

## MINING AND INDUSTRY

**Mining** (1990): Guano 6,000 metric tons (exports). Source: UN Economic Commission for Africa, *African Statistical Yearbook*.

**Industrial Production** (1991, unless otherwise indicated): Frozen fish 1,500 metric tons (1990); Tinned fish 3,600 metric tons; Beer 59,000 hectolitres; Soft drinks 56,000 hectolitres; Cigarettes 69 million; Electric energy 102 million kWh. Source: UN, *Industrial Statistics Yearbook*.

## FINANCE

**Currency and Exchange Rates:** 100 cents = 1 Seychelles rupee (SR). *Sterling and Dollar Equivalents* (31 December 1994): £1 sterling = 7.775 rupees; US $1 = 4.9695 rupees; 100 Seychelles rupees = £12.86 = $20.12. *Average Exchange Rate* (Seychelles rupees per US $): 5.1220 in 1992; 5.1815 in 1993; 5.0559 in 1994. Note: Since November 1979 the value of the Seychelles rupee has been linked to the IMF's special drawing right (SDR). Since March 1981 the mid-point exchange rate has been SDR 1 = 7.2345 rupees.

**Budget** (SR million, 1989): *Revenue:* Taxation 770.8 (Taxes on income, etc. 145.1, Social security contributions 137.7, Import duties 436.9); Other current revenue 191.5; Capital revenue 0.8; Total 963.1, excl. grants received (26.4). *Expenditure:* Current 799.9 (Wages and salaries 230.2, Other purchases of goods and services 240.8, Interest payments 147.3, Subsidies 88.1, Other current transfers 93.5); Capital 177.6; Total 977.5, excl. net lending (131.8). Note: Figures represent the consolidated accounts of the central Government, covering the operations of the Recurrent and Capital Budgets and of the Social Security Fund. Source: IMF, *Government Finance Statistics Yearbook*.

**International Reserves** (US $ million at 31 December 1993): IMF special drawing rights 0.02; Reserve position in IMF 1.10; Foreign exchange 34.46; Total 35.58. Source: IMF, *International Financial Statistics*.

**Money Supply** (SR million at 31 December 1994): Currency outside banks 141.6; Demand deposits at commercial banks 184.4; Total money (incl. others) 326.6. Source: IMF, *International Financial Statistics*.

**Cost of Living** (Consumer Price Index; base: 1990 = 100): 105.3 in 1992; 106.7 in 1993; 108.7 in 1994. Source: IMF, *International Financial Statistics*.

**Expenditure on the Gross Domestic Product** (SR million at current prices, 1992): Government final consumption expenditure 674.6; Private final consumption expenditure 1,124.7; Increase in stocks 6.0; Gross fixed capital formation 465.2; *Total domestic expenditure* 2,270.4; Exports of goods and services 1,016.9; *Less* Imports of goods and services 1,066.2; *GDP in purchasers' values* 2,221.1. Source: IMF, *International Financial Statistics*.

**Gross Domestic Product by Economic Activity** (SR million at current prices, 1991): Agriculture, hunting, forestry and fishing 86; Mining and manufacturing 181; Electricity, gas and water 35; Construction 94; Trade, restaurants and hotels 195; Transport, storage and communications 301; Finance, insurance, real estate and business services 334; Government services 250; Other services 36; *GDP at factor cost* 1,511; Indirect taxes, *less* subsidies 301; *GDP in purchasers' values* 1,812. Source: UN Economic Commission for Africa, *African Statistical Yearbook*.

**Balance of Payments** (US $ million, 1992): Merchandise exports f.o.b. 19.6, Merchandise imports f.o.b. −162.9, *Trade balance* −143.3; Exports of services 247.0, Imports of services −112.6, Other income received 4.8, Other income paid −18.6, Private unrequited transfers (net) −2.8, Official unrequited transfers (net) 23.8, *Current balance* −1.7; Direct investment (net) 18.6, Other capital (net) −6.2, Net errors and omissions −6.9, Overall balance 3.9. Source: IMF, *International Financial Statistics*.

## EXTERNAL TRADE

**Principal Commodities** (US $ '000, 1991): *Imports c.i.f.:* Food and live animals 29,206 (Dairy products and birds' eggs 3,784, Fish and fish preparations 5,325, Cereals and cereal preparations 7,769, Vegetables and fruit 5,239); Beverages and tobacco 3,795; Mineral fuels, lubricants, etc. 37,714 (Refined petroleum products 36,988); Chemicals and related products 10,417 (Essential oils, perfume materials and cleansing preparations 3,949); Basic manufactures 29,223 (Paper, paperboard, etc. 3,989, Iron and steel 3,562); Machinery and transport equipment 39,833 (Machinery specialized for particular industries 5,769, Telecommunications and sound equipment 7,283, Road vehicles 4,750); Miscellaneous manufactured articles 17,712; Total (incl. others) 172,474. *Exports f.o.b.:* Fish and fish preparations 15,806; Refined petroleum products 29,529; Machinery and transport equipment 1,952; Total (incl. others) 48,712. Source: UN, *International Trade Statistics Yearbook*.

**Principal Trading Partners** (US $ '000, 1991): *Imports c.i.f.:* Bahrain 27,927; France 15,184; Germany 5,479; Italy 4,256; Japan 9,050; Malaysia 6,938; Netherlands 3,484; Singapore 19,998; Southern African Customs Union* 22,343; Thailand 3,611; United Kingdom 19,875; USA 4,238; Total (incl. others) 172,458. *Exports f.o.b.:* France 4,379; Réunion 2,267; United Kingdom 9,207; Total (incl. others) 48,712. * Comprising Botswana, Lesotho, Namibia, South Africa, Swaziland. Source: UN, *International Trade Statistics Yearbook*.

## TRANSPORT AND TOURISM

**Road Traffic** (motor vehicles in use, 1989): Passenger cars 4,072; Commercial vehicles 1,105; Buses 216; Motor cycles 102.

**Shipping** (sea-borne freight traffic, 1990): Vessels entered 953; Freight ('000 metric tons): Loaded 11.2; Unloaded 347.7.

**Civil Aviation** (traffic on scheduled services, 1992): Kilometres flown 3 million; Passengers carried 181,000; Passenger-km 321 million; Total ton-km 42 million. Source: UN, *Statistical Yearbook*.

**Tourism:** (1994): Foreign visitor arrivals 107,500; Gross receipts SR 538m.

## COMMUNICATIONS MEDIA

**Radio Receivers** (1992): 34,000 in use. Source: UNESCO, *Statistical Yearbook*.

**Television Receivers** (1992): 6,000 in use. Source: UNESCO, *Statistical Yearbook*.

**Telephones** (1990): 8,000 main lines in use. Source: UN, *Statistical Yearbook*.

**Book Production** (1980): 33 titles (2 books, 31 pamphlets).

**Daily Newspapers** (1992): 1 (average circulation 3,000 copies). Source: UNESCO, *Statistical Yearbook*.

**Non-daily Newspapers** (1988): 4 (estimated average circulation 9,000 copies). Source: UNESCO, *Statistical Yearbook*.

## EDUCATION

**Pre-Primary** (1993): 34 schools; 159 teachers; 3,125 pupils.

**Primary** (1993): 26 schools; 548 teachers; 9,873 pupils.

**Secondary** (1993):.
  **General:** 576 teachers; 7,683 pupils.
  **Teacher training:** 27 teachers; 290 pupils.
  **Vocational:** 132 teachers; 1,138 pupils.

**Special Education** (1990): 1 school, 78 pupils.

Source (for education): mainly UNESCO, *Statistical Yearbook*.

# Directory

## The Constitution

The independence Constitution of 1976 was suspended after the coup in June 1977 but reintroduced in July with important modifications. A successor Constitution, which entered into force in March 1979 was superseded by a new Constitution, approved by national referendum on 18 June 1993.

The President is elected by popular vote simultaneously with elections for the National Assembly. The President fulfils the functions of Head of State and Commander-in-Chief of the armed forces and may hold office for a maximum period of three consecutive five-year terms. The Assembly consists of 33 seats, of which 22 are directly elected and 11 are allocated on a proportional basis. The Council of Ministers is appointed by the President and acts in an advisory capacity to him.

## The Government

### HEAD OF STATE

**President:** FRANCE ALBERT RENÉ (assumed power 5 June 1977; elected President 26 June 1979, re-elected 18 June 1984, 12 June 1989 and 23 July 1993).

### COUNCIL OF MINISTERS
(June 1995)

**President:** FRANCE ALBERT RENÉ.

**Minister of Finance, Information and Defence:** JAMES MICHEL.

**Minister of Administration and Manpower:** JOSEPH BELMONT.

**Minister of Foreign Affairs, Planning and Environment:** DANIELLE DE ST JORRE.

**Minister of Industry:** RALPH ADAM.

**Minister of Local Government, Youth and Sports:** SYLVETTE FRICHOT.

**Minister of Health:** JAQUELIN DUGASSE.

**Minister of Tourism and Transport:** SIMONE DE COMARMOND.

**Minister of Employment and Social Affairs:** WILLIAM HERMINIE.

**Minister of Education and Culture:** PATRICK PILLAY.

**Minister of Community Development:** DOLOR ERNESTA.

**Minister of Agriculture and Marine Resources:** ESMÉ JUMEAU.

### MINISTRIES

**Office of the President:** State House, Victoria; tel. 224391.

**Ministry of Administration and Manpower:** National House, POB 56, Victoria; tel. 224041; telex 2333; fax 224936.

**Ministry of Agriculture and Marine Resources:** Independence House, POB 166, Victoria; tel. 225333; telex 2418; fax 225245.

**Ministry of Community Development:** Independence House, Independence Ave, POB 199, Victoria; tel. 224030; telex 2312.

**Ministry of Education and Culture:** POB 48, Mont Fleuri; tel. 224777; telex 2365; fax 224859.

**Ministry of Employment and Social Services:** Unity House, POB 190, Victoria; tel. 222321; telex 2352; fax 221880.

**Ministry of Finance and Information:** Central Bank Bldg, POB 313, Victoria; tel. 225252; telex 2363; fax 225265.

**Ministry of Foreign Affairs, Planning and Environment:** POB 656, Mont Fleuri; tel. 224688; telex 2260; fax 224845.

**Ministry of Health:** POB 52, Botanical Gardens, Mahé; tel. 224400; telex 2302; fax 224792.

**Ministry of Local Government, Youth and Sports:** POB 731, Victoria; tel. 225477; telex 2240; fax 225262.

**Ministry of Tourism and Transport:** Independence House, Independence Ave, POB 92, Victoria; tel. 225333; telex 2275; fax 225131.

## President and Legislature

### PRESIDENT

**Election, 23 July 1993**

| Candidate | Votes | % of total |
|---|---|---|
| FRANCE ALBERT RENÉ (SPPF) | 25,627 | 59.5 |
| JAMES MANCHAM (DP) | 15,815 | 36.7 |
| PHILIPPE BOULLÉ (United Opposition*) | 1,631 | 3.8 |

* An electoral coalition comprising the Parti Seychellois, the Seychelles Christian Democrat Party, the National Alliance Party and the Seychelles National Movement.

### NATIONAL ASSEMBLY

**Speaker:** FRANCIS MACGREGOR.

**Election, 23 July 1993**

| Party | Number of votes | % of votes | Seats* |
|---|---|---|---|
| Seychelles People's Progressive Front | 24,642 | 57.5 | 28 |
| Democratic Party | 14,062 | 32.8 | 4 |
| United Opposition | 4,163 | 9.7 | 1 |

* The Assembly consists of 33 seats, of which 22 seats are directly elected and 11 seats are allocated on a proportional basis to parties obtaining at least 9% of total votes cast.

## Political Organizations

A ban on political activity by parties other than the Seychelles People's Progressive Front, which had operated since 1978, was suspended in December 1991, and formally terminated following the constitutional referendum held in June 1993. The official registration of active political organizations, affording them corporate status, was proceeding in mid-1995.

**Democratic Party (DP):** POB 109, Victoria; tel. 224916; fax 224302; f. 1992; successor to the Seychelles Democratic Party (governing party 1970–77); Leader Sir JAMES MANCHAM; Sec.-Gen. DANIEL BELLE.

**\*National Alliance Party:** 210 Victoria House, POB 673, Victoria; tel. 225562; fax 225626; f. 1992; Leader PHILIPPE BOULLÉ.

**\*Parti Seychellois/Parti Seselwa:** Victoria; Leader Rev. WAVEL RAMKALAWAN.

**\*Seychelles Christian Democrat Party/Rassemblement du Peuple Seychellois pour la Démocratie:** Victoria; f. 1990; Leaders Dr MAXIME FERRARI, ANDRÉ UZICE.

**Seychelles Liberal Party:** Victoria; f. 1992; Leader OGILVY BERLOUIS.

**Seychelles Movement for Democracy:** f. 1992; Leader JACQUES HODOUL.

**\*Seychelles National Movement:** Victoria; f. 1992; Leaders EDMOND CAMILLE, ROBERT FRICHOT.

**Seychelles Nationalist Party:** Victoria; f. 1992; Leader PHILIP REVERE.

**Seychelles People's Progressive Front (SPPF):** POB 91, Victoria; tel. 224030; telex 2226; fmrly the Seychelles People's United Party; renamed in 1978; sole legal party 1978–91; socialist; Sec.-Gen. JAMES MICHEL.

* Member of the United Opposition coalition that contested the July 1993 presidential and legislative elections.

## Diplomatic Representation

### EMBASSIES AND HIGH COMMISSIONS IN SEYCHELLES

**China, People's Republic:** POB 680, St Louis; tel. 266588; Ambassador: ZHANG DAXUN.

**Cuba:** Bel Eau; tel. 224094; telex 2354; Ambassador: (vacant).

**France:** Arpent Vert, POB 478, Victoria; tel. 224523; telex 2238; fax 225248; Ambassador: PIERRE VIAUX (designate).

SEYCHELLES  *Directory*

**India:** Le Chantier, Victoria; tel. 224489; telex 2349; fax 224810; High Commissioner: Pranab Mukhopadhyay.
**Netherlands:** POB 372, Victoria; tel. 261200; telex 2344; fax 261221.
**Russia:** Le Niol, POB 632, Victoria; tel. 221590; telex 2392; fax 224653; Ambassador: Sergei Borisovich Kisselev.
**South Africa:** Victoria.
**United Kingdom:** Victoria House, POB 161, Victoria; tel. 225225; telex 2269; fax 225127; High Commissioner: Peter A. B. Thomson.
**USA:** Victoria House, POB 251, Victoria; tel. 225256; fax 225189; Ambassador: Carl Burton Stokes.

## Judicial System

There are three Courts, the Court of Appeal, the Supreme Court and the Magistrates' Courts. The Court of Appeal hears appeals from the Supreme Court in both civil and criminal cases. The Supreme Court is also a Court of Appeal from the Magistrates' Courts as well as having jursidiction at first instance. The Constitutional Court, which forms part of the Supreme Court, determines matters of a constitutional nature, and considers cases bearing on civil liberties. The judicial system also includes an industrial court and a rent tribunal.

**Chief Justice:** V. Alleear.
**President of the Court of Appeal:** Harry Goburdhun.
**Justices of Appeal:** Annel Silungwe, Emmanuel Ayoola, Louis Venchard; Mahomed Ali Adam.
**Puisne Judges:** A. Perera, C. A. Amerasinghe, S. J. Bwana.

## Religion

Almost all of the inhabitants are Christians, of whom more than 90% are Roman Catholics and about 8% Anglicans.

### CHRISTIANITY

#### The Anglican Communion

The Church of the Province of the Indian Ocean comprises five dioceses: three in Madagascar, one in Mauritius and one in Seychelles.

**Bishop of Seychelles (also Archbishop of the Province of the Indian Ocean):** Most Rev. French Kitchener Chang-Him, POB 44, Victoria; tel. 224242; fax 224296.

#### The Roman Catholic Church

Seychelles comprises a single diocese, directly responsible to the Holy See. At 31 December 1993 there were an estimated 65,645 adherents in the country, representing 90.3% of the total population.

**Bishop of Port Victoria:** Rt Rev. Xavier Baronnet, Bishop's House, Olivier Maradan St, POB 43, Victoria; tel. 322152; fax 324045.

## The Press

**L'Echo des Iles:** POB 138, Victoria; fortnightly; French, Creole and English; Roman Catholic; Editor P. Symphorien; circ. 2,800.
**The People:** POB 91, Victoria; monthly; Creole, French and English; organ of the SPPF; circ. 1,000.
**Regar:** Victoria; political weekly.
**The Seychelles Nation:** Information, Culture and Sports Division, POB 321, Victoria; tel. 224161; telex 2320; fax 221006; Mon. to Sat.; govt publ.; English, French and Creole; Chief Editor René Morrell; circ. 3,500.
**Seychelles Today:** Seychelles Agence de Presse, Information Division, POB 321, Victoria; tel. 224161; telex 2322; fax 221006; monthly; circ. 4,000.
**Seychelles Weekend Nation:** Information, Culture and Sports Division, POB 321, Victoria; tel. 224161; telex 2322; fax 221006; Sat.; English, French and Creole; Chief Editor René Morrell; circ. 3,800.
**Seychellois:** POB 32, Victoria; f. 1928; publ. by Seychelles Farmers Asscn; quarterly; circ. 1,800.

### NEWS AGENCY

**Seychelles Agence de Presse (SAP):** Victoria Rd, POB 321, Victoria; tel. 224161; telex 2320; fax 226006.

## Radio and Television

In 1992, according to UNESCO, there were 34,000 radio receivers and 6,000 television receivers in use.

**Seychelles Broadcasting Corporation (SBC):** Hermitage, POB 321, Victoria; tel. 224161; telex 2315; fax 225641; f. 1983 as Radio-Television Seychelles; reorg. as independent corpn in 1992; programmes in Creole, English and French; Man. Dir Ibrahim Afif.

### RADIO

**FEBA Radio (Far East Broadcasting Association):** POB 234, Mahé; tel. 224449; fax 225171; Christian programmes; Dir Stewart Pepper.
**SBC Radio:** Union Vale, POB 321, Victoria; tel. 224161; telex 2315; fax 224515; f. 1941; programmes in Creole, English and French; Programme Man. (Radio) Marguerite Hermitte.

### TELEVISION

**SBC TV:** Hermitage, POB 321, Mahé; tel. 224161; telex 2315; fax 225641; f. 1983; programmes in Creole, English and French; Programme Man. (Television) Jean-Claude Matombe.

## Finance

(cap. = capital; res = reserves; dep. = deposits; m. = million; brs = branches; amounts in Seychelles rupees)

### BANKING

#### Central Bank

**Central Bank of Seychelles (CBS):** Independence Ave, POB 701, Victoria; tel. 225200; telex 2301; fax 224958; f. 1983; bank of issue; cap. and res 11m., dep. 300.8m. (Dec. 1993); Chair. Aboo Aumeeruddy.

#### National Banks

**Development Bank of Seychelles:** Independence Ave, POB 217, Victoria; tel. 224471; telex 2348; fax 224274; f. 1978; 55% state-owned; cap. and res 62.7m., total assets 175m. (1994); Chair. Antonio Lucas; Man. Dir A. G. Yakub.
**Seychelles International Mercantile Banking Corporation Ltd (Nouvobanq):** Victoria House, State House Ave, POB 241, Victoria; 2tel. 225011; telex 2253; fax 224670; f. 1991; 78% state-owned, 22% by Standard Chartered Bank (UK); cap. and res 62.4m., dep. 318.7m. (Dec. 1993); Chair. Norman Weber; Pres. Ahmad Saeed; 1 br.
**Seychelles Savings Bank Ltd:** Kingsgate House, POB 531, Victoria; tel. 225251; telex 2416; fax 224713; f. 1902; state-owned; term deposits, savings and current accounts; cap. and res 7.8m. (Dec. 1992); Man. Dir Roger Toussaint; 4 brs.

#### Foreign Banks

**Bank of Baroda** (India): Albert St, POB 124, Victoria; tel. 323038; telex 2241; fax 324057; f. 1978; Sr Man. A. K. Arora.
**Banque Française Commerciale–Océan Indien** (France): POB 122, Victoria; tel. 323096; telex 2261; fax 322676; f. 1978; Man. Henri Allain D'Offay; 3 brs.
**Barclays Bank** (United Kingdom): Independence Ave, POB 167, Victoria; tel. 224101; telex 2225; fax 224678; f. 1959; Man. M. P. Landon; 3 brs and 5 agencies.
**Habib Bank Ltd** (Pakistan): Frances Rachel St, POB 702, Victoria; tel. 224371; telex 2242; fax 225614; f. 1976; Man. Javed Iqbal Sheikh.

### INSURANCE

**State Assurance Corporation of Seychelles (SACOS):** Pirate's Arms Bldg, POB 636, Victoria; tel. 225000; telex 2331; fax 224495; f. 1980; all classes of insurance; Exec. Chair. Antonio Lucas.

### STOCK EXCHANGE

A Stock Exchange was to be established in Victoria in 1995.

## Trade and Industry

### CHAMBER OF COMMERCE

**Seychelles Chamber of Commerce and Industry:** 38 Premier Bldg, POB 443, Victoria; tel. 223812; Chair. Mickey Mason.

### DEVELOPMENT CORPORATION

**International Business Authority:** Victoria; f. 1995 to supervise registration of companies, transhipment and 'offshore' banking in international free trade zone covering area of 23 ha near Mahé international airport; Man. Dir Conrad Benoiton.

### TRADING ORGANIZATIONS

**Seychelles Agricultural Development Co Ltd (SADECO):** POB 172, Victoria; tel. 276618; f. 1980; Gen. Man. Leslie Préa (acting).

**Seychelles Industrial Development Corporation:** POB 537, Victoria; tel. 224941; telex 2415; fax 225121.

**Seychelles Marketing Board (SMB):** Oceangate House, POB 516, Victoria; tel. 224444; telex 2368; f. 1984; state trading org. for food production and processing, fisheries development and toiletries; transfer to private sector of agro-industries subsidiaries announced in 1992; Chair. France Albert René; Man. Jacques Garcin.

**Seychelles National Oil Co:** POB 230, Victoria; tel. 225182; fax 225177; Man. Dir Eddie Belle.

**Seychelles Timber Co (SEYTIM):** Grand Anse, Mahé; tel. 278343; telex 2368; logging, timber sales, joinery and furniture; operates sawmill at Grande Anse.

### TRADE UNION

**National Workers' Union:** Maison du Peuple, Latanier Rd, POB 154, Victoria; tel. 224030; f. 1978 to amalgamate all existing trade unions; affiliated to the Seychelles People's Progressive Front; 25,200 mems; Chair. Olivier Charles; Sec. Michael A. Memee.

## Transport

### RAILWAYS

There are no railways in Seychelles.

### ROADS

In 1988 there were 269 km of roads, of which 187 km were tarmac roads. On Mahé there are 138 km of tarmac roads, and 43 km of earth roads. Praslin has about 24 km of tarmac roads and 28 km of earth roads. La Digue has 5 km of surfaced and 11 km of unsurfaced roads.

### SHIPPING

Ferry and private licensed schooner services connect Victoria and the islands of Praslin and La Digue.

**Port and Marine Services Division, Ministry of Tourism and Transport:** POB 47, Victoria; tel. 224701; fax 224004; Dir-Gen. (Port of Victoria) Sam Andrade.

**Allied Agency:** Victoria; shipping agents.

**CSD Trading:** Premier Bldg, Victoria.

**Hunt, Deltel and Co Ltd:** Victoria House, POB 14, Victoria; tel. 225352; telex 2249; fax 225367.

**Mahé Shipping Co Ltd:** Shipping House, POB 336, Victoria; tel. 322100; telex 2216; fax 322978; agents for Royal Fleet Auxiliary, US Navy, P & O, Nedlloyd Lines and numerous other shipping cos; Chair. Capt. G. C. C. Adam.

**Harry Savy & Co.:** Victoria; shipping agents.

**Seychelles Shipping Line:** Victoria; f. 1994 to operate a freight service between Seychelles and Durban, South Africa; 90% owned by Tern Shipping Co of South Africa, 10% by Seychelles Govt; Man. Dir Ted Keeley.

**The Union Lighterage Co Ltd:** POB 38, Victoria; tel. 224624; telex 2425; fax 224734; f. 1929; reorg. as four separate cos in 1994; stevedoring, shipping, clearing and forwarding agents; Man. Dir Guy D'Unienville.

### CIVIL AVIATION

**Air Seychelles:** Victoria House, POB 386, Victoria; tel. 225300; telex 2289; fax 225159; f. 1979; operates scheduled internal flights from Mahé to Praslin and charter services to Frégate, Bird, Desroches and Denis Islands; international services to Europe and South Africa; Chair. and CEO Fredy Karkaria.

## Tourism

Seychelles enjoys an equable climate, and is renowned for its fine beaches and attractive scenery. There are more than 500 varieties of flora and many rare species of birds. Most tourist activity is concentrated on Mahé, Praslin and La Digue. It is government policy that the development of tourism should not blight the environment, and strict laws govern the construction of hotels. At the end of 1990 there were some 3,500 hotel beds. Receipts from tourism totalled an estimated SR 538m. in 1994, when there were an estimated 107,500 tourist and business arrivals; most visitors (almost 82% in 1994) are from western Europe.

**Compagnie Seychelloise de Promotion Hotelière Ltd:** POB 683, Victoria; tel. 224694; telex 2407; fax 225291; promotes govt-owned hotels.

**Seychelles Tourist Board:** Independence House, POB 92, Victoria; tel. 225333; telex 2275; parastatal body; Dir-Gen. Monica Chetty.

# SIERRA LEONE

## Introductory Survey

### Location, Climate, Language, Religion, Flag, Capital

The Republic of Sierra Leone lies on the west coast of Africa, with Guinea to the north and east, and Liberia to the south. The climate is hot and humid, with an average annual temperature of 27°C (80°F). The rainy season lasts from May to October. The average annual rainfall is about 3,436 mm (13.5 ins). English is the official language, while Krio (Creole), Mende, Limba and Temne are also widely spoken. The majority of the population follow animist beliefs, but there are significant numbers of Islamic and Christian adherents. The national flag (proportions 3 by 2) has three equal horizontal stripes, of green, white and blue. The capital is Freetown.

### Recent History

Sierra Leone was formerly a British colony and protectorate. A new Constitution, which provided for universal adult suffrage, was introduced in 1951. In that year the Sierra Leone People's Party (SLPP) won the majority of votes in elections. The leader of the SLPP, Dr (later Sir) Milton Margai, became Chief Minister in 1953 and Prime Minister in 1958. On 27 April 1961 Sierra Leone achieved independence as a constitutional monarchy within the Commonwealth. The SLPP retained its majority at elections in May 1962. Margai died in April 1964 and was succeeded as Prime Minister by his half-brother, Dr (later Sir) Albert Margai, previously the Minister of Finance.

Following disputed elections in March 1967, the army assumed control and established a ruling body, the National Reformation Council. The Governor-General was subsequently forced to leave the country. In December a commission of inquiry announced that the All-People's Congress (APC) had won the elections in March. In April 1968 a further coup was staged by army officers, and power was subsequently transferred to a civilian Government, under Dr Siaka Stevens, the leader of the APC, who was elected as Prime Minister later that month. In April 1971 a republican Constitution was introduced and Dr Stevens became executive President.

The 1972 by-elections and the general election in May 1973 were not contested by the SLPP, and subsequently no official opposition party held seats in the House of Representatives. In 1976 Stevens, the sole candidate, was unanimously re-elected to the presidency for a second five-year term of office. In May 1977 the APC won the majority of votes in legislative elections, which were contested by the SLPP; however, outbreaks of violence and allegations of corruption and intimidation were reported. The APC reiterated demands for a one-party state, and in July the House of Representatives ruled that the SLPP was no longer the official opposition party, on the grounds that it was incapable of undertaking government administration. A new Constitution, which provided for a one-party system, was promulgated in May 1978, approved in a national referendum and adopted by the House of Representatives in June. The APC thus became the sole legitimate political organization. Stevens was inaugurated as President for a seven-year term on 14 June 1978. He subsequently released political detainees and allocated ministerial posts to several former SLPP members (who had joined the APC).

The Government faced increasing opposition in 1981, following a scandal involving government officials and several cabinet ministers in the misappropriation of public funds. In August a state of emergency was declared, in an attempt to suppress a general strike that had been organized in protest at food shortages resulting from an increase in the price of commodities. Stevens temporarily assumed the additional post of Minister of Finance in December, following a second financial scandal implicating senior civil servants. Legislative elections took place in May 1982, amid serious outbreaks of violence. In May 1983 a disputed election result provoked inter-tribal clashes in the Pujehun district, and in November troops were sent to the area to restore order. Civil unrest, which was prompted by increasing economic hardship, continued in 1984 and 1985.

In April 1985 Stevens, who was believed to be about 80 years of age, announced that (contrary to earlier indications) he would not seek re-election to the presidency upon the expiry, in June, of his existing mandate. The House of Representatives subsequently approved a constitutional amendment extending Stevens' current term of office for six months, to allow time for registration of voters and the nomination of a presidential candidate. In June the House of Representatives approved a further constitutional amendment providing for a presidential council (rather than, as hitherto stipulated, the First Vice-President) to govern the country in the event of the President's absence, resignation or death. At a conference of the APC in August 1985, Maj.-Gen. Joseph Momoh, a cabinet minister and the Commander of the Army, was the sole candidate for the leadership of the party and for the presidential nomination. In the national presidential election in October, Momoh received 99% of the votes cast, and was inaugurated as President on 28 November. Although retaining his military status, Momoh appointed a civilian Cabinet, which included several members of the previous administration. Elections to the House of Representatives took place in May 1986. In June Momoh appointed a new, enlarged Cabinet. In December Momoh released 27 political prisoners, including 12 who had been implicated in a coup attempt in 1974.

Following his appointment to the presidency, Momoh's popularity declined, owing to his administration's failure to improve the serious economic situation. In March 1987 the Government announced that it had suppressed an attempted coup; more than 60 people were subsequently arrested, including the First Vice-President, Francis Minah. Shortly afterwards, Momoh effected a government reorganization. In October, following a five-month trial, Minah and 15 other defendants were sentenced to death for plotting to assassinate Momoh and to overthrow the Government, and two defendants received custodial sentences for misprision of treason. In October 1989 Minah and five others were executed, despite international appeals for clemency, and a campaign on behalf of the six men by the human rights organization, Amnesty International.

In 1987 Momoh initiated a campaign against financial malpractices in the public sector. During 1987 and 1988 a minister, two deputy ministers and a number of other senior officials in the civil service and the Bank of Sierra Leone were charged with fraud and financial malpractice. In November 1987, following a series of strikes by workers in the public sector, which were provoked by the Government's inability to pay salaries (owing to a shortage of currency), Momoh declared a state of emergency in the economy, and announced measures to prevent hoarding of currency and essential goods. Corruption was redefined as a criminal offence, and people accused of any crime could be tried *in absentia*. Severe penalties were introduced for the publication of 'defamatory' articles in newspapers; private mail could be inspected, and a censor was subsequently appointed by the Government. In March 1988 a 12-month extension of the economic emergency regulations was approved by the House of Representatives.

In November 1988 an extensive government reorganization was effected, in which, among other changes, the two Vice-Presidents lost their ministerial portfolios, and their posts became purely ceremonial. At a conference of the APC, which took place in January 1989, Momoh was re-elected unopposed as Secretary-General of the APC. An official code of conduct for political leaders and public servants was also adopted during the conference. In August the House of Representatives adopted legislation requiring public servants who intended to participate in forthcoming legislative elections (due to take place in 1991), to leave their employment no later than May 1990. In December 1989 the Minister of Finance was replaced, following allegations of irregular conduct at the Finance Ministry.

In mid-August 1990, at a session of the Central Committee of the APC, Momoh (who had hitherto made clear his opposition to the establishment of a multi-party political system) conceded the necessity of electoral reforms, and announced an extensive review of the Constitution. The Central Committee adopted a number of constitutional amendments that relaxed restrictions on prospective electoral candidates in public service, who would be required henceforth to leave employment only six months prior to participation in elections. In addition, the Central Committee proposed that the number of Vice-Presidents be reduced from two to one, and that a deputy leader of the APC be elected, who would also stand as the vice-presidential candidate in presidential elections. Momoh subsequently appointed a 30-member committee, the National Constitutional Review Commission, to revise the one-party Constitution. In January 1991, however, the Government announced that legislative elections, scheduled for May that year, were to be conducted under the provisions of the one-party Constitution.

In March 1991 the National Constitutional Review Commission submitted a draft Constitution, which provided for a multi-party system, for consideration by the Government. The new Constitution stipulated that the President was to be elected by a majority of votes cast nationally and at least 25% of the votes cast in more than one-half of the electoral districts. The maximum duration of the President's tenure of office was to be limited to two five-year terms. The President was to appoint the Cabinet, which was to include one Vice-President, rather than two. Legislative power was to be vested in a bicameral parliament, elected by universal adult suffrage for a term of five years. Members of the parliament were not permitted concurrently to hold ministerial portfolios. The Government subsequently accepted the majority of the Commission's recommendations. The proposed formation of an upper legislative chamber was, however, rejected; instead, the Government approved the establishment of a 22-member advisory body, to be known as the State Advisory Council, which was to comprise 12 Paramount Chiefs (one from each district) and 10 members appointed by the President. In early June the Government presented the draft Constitution to the House of Representatives, and announced that the parliamentary term, which was due to end that month, was to be extended for a further year, owing to the disruption caused by the conflict between government forces and Liberian rebels in the south of the country (see below). Legislative elections were to be postponed until May 1992 to allow time for the transition to a multi-party system.

In mid-July 1991 the Minister of Social Affairs, Rural Development and Youth, Musa Kabia, resigned, following disputes within the APC over the new Constitution. Ten members of the House of Representatives, including Kabia, were later suspended from the APC for alleged activities contrary to the interests of the party (but were reinstated in September). In early August the House of Representatives formally approved the new Constitution, subject to endorsement by a national referendum. At the national referendum, which was conducted between 23 and 30 August, the new Constitution was approved by 60% of voters, with 75% of the electorate participating. On 3 September the Government formally adopted the new Constitution (although the Constitution of 1978 also remained officially in force). In the same month six newly-created political associations formed an alliance, known as the United Front of Political Movements (UNIFOM), which subsequently demanded that the forthcoming elections be monitored by international observers, and that the incumbent Government be dissolved and an interim administration established. On 23 September, following the resignation of the First Vice-President and Second Vice-President from both the APC and the Government, Momoh announced the formation of a new 18-member Cabinet, which retained only seven members of the previous Government. Later that month legislation that formally permitted the formation of political associations was introduced; several organizations, including the APC, were subsequently granted legal recognition. In December, following discussions between Momoh and leaders of the other registered political parties, the opposition movements pledged to co-operate in the establishment of a multi-party system.

In January 1992 *New Breed*, the official newspaper of the National Democratic Party (NDP), published the alleged records of a secret meeting between leaders of the APC and the security forces, which indicated that the APC intended to prolong the conflict in the south in order to delay the installation of a multi-party system. The Chairman of the NDP, Dr Alusine Fofanah, and the editor of *New Breed*, George Khoyama, were subsequently charged with criminal libel.

On 29 April 1992 members of the armed forces, led by a five-member military junta known as the Patriotic Officers and Soldiers of the Sierra Leonean Armed Forces, seized a radio station in Freetown and broadcast demands that arrears in salary be paid and conditions in the armed forces be improved. The rebel troops later occupied the presidential offices, and the leader of the military junta, Capt. Valentine E. M. Strasser, announced that the Government had been overthrown; some 12 people were reported to have been killed in subsequent incidents of violence in Freetown. Momoh appealed for assistance to the Guinean Government, which dispatched troops to Freetown to guard him. On 30 April he fled to Guinea, and Strasser announced the establishment of a governing council, to be known as the National Provisional Ruling Council (NPRC). Strasser affirmed the NPRC's commitment to the introduction of a multi-party system, and pledged to end the conflict in the country. On the same day the Constitutions of 1991 and 1978 were suspended, the House of Representatives was dissolved, a state of emergency, which included a curfew, was imposed, and the country's air, sea and land borders were temporarily closed. A demonstration by some 700 students in support of the coup subsequently took place. On 1 May the NPRC (which was principally composed of military officers), chaired by Strasser, was formed. Shortly afterwards, a new 19-member Cabinet, which included a number of members of the NPRC, was appointed, and the Commander of the Armed Forces and the head of the security forces were replaced. On 4 May a proclamation retroactively provided for the establishment of the NPRC (which was to comprise a maximum of 30 members, including a Chairman and a Vice-Chairman), the dissolution of the House of Representatives and the suspension of all political activity. Later in May it was reported that some 55 people, including members of the former administration, had been detained. On 6 May Strasser was inaugurated as Head of State. Later that month the Government established three commissions of inquiry to investigate alleged malpractice on the part of former members of the Momoh administration.

In June 1992 security forces arrested three British nationals, alleged to be mercenaries, who were suspected of planning a coup attempt; the detainees subsequently claimed that they had visited Freetown in order to warn the authorities of a conspiracy to overthrow the Government by an opposition movement based in France. In early July Strasser replaced three members of the NPRC in the Cabinet with civilians, and removed all civilian cabinet ministers from the NPRC. Later that month he announced extensive structural changes, which were designed to reduce the direct involvement of the NPRC in government administration: the NPRC was officially designated the Supreme Council of State, while the Cabinet was reconstituted as the Council of Secretaries (headed by the Chief Secretary of State), which was to be responsible for government administration, subject to the authority of the NPRC. The three members of the NPRC who had been removed from the Cabinet earlier that month were appointed Principal Liaison Officers, with responsibility for the supervision of government administration in a number of ministries (henceforth known as departments). The Secretary of State in the Office of the Chairman, John Benjamin, subsequently became the Chief Secretary of State. In the same month the Government introduced legislation that imposed severe restrictions on the media.

In September 1992 the Deputy Chairman of the NPRC, Capt. Solomon A. J. Musa, temporarily assumed the office of Head of State during a visit by Strasser to the USA to obtain medical treatment for injuries sustained in military operations against rebels in the south of the country. In that month Musa suspended a number of senior army officers and members of the security forces. In early October a minor reorganization of the Council of Secretaries was effected. In November some 30 people, who were alleged to be supporters of Momoh, were arrested by the security forces and charged with involvement in subversive activities. In early December Strasser announced a reorganization of the Council of Secretaries, in which the two remaining members of the Momoh administration, the Secretary of State for Foreign Affairs, and the Secretary of State for Finance, Development and Economic Planning (who had resigned in November, following dissension over the Government's implementation of economic policies), were replaced. In the same month Musa became Chief Secretary of State. Later in December, in an apparent attempt to regain public support, the Government established a 19-member National Advisory Council, comprising representatives of various non-governmental organizations, which was to draft a programme for transition to civilian rule.

At the end of December 1992 the Government announced that the security forces had suppressed a coup attempt by a group known as the Anti-Corruption Revolutionary Movement (which included former members of the army and security forces), who attacked Strasser's official residence. Shortly afterwards, nine of those accused of involvement in the attempted coup were convicted by a special military tribunal, and, together with 17 prisoners who had been convicted in November on charges of treason, were summarily executed. Human rights organizations subsequently contested the Government's statement that a coup attempt had been staged, while lawyers condemned the establishment of the special tribunal earlier in December. In January 1993 the United Kingdom announced the suspension of economic aid to Sierra Leone in protest at the executions; however, a number of demonstrations in support of the NPRC subsequently took place. Later that month, in an apparent response to criticism from foreign governments, several former members of the Momoh administration, who had been detained in May 1992, were released. In mid-January, however, the Government imposed further press restrictions: all newspapers were required to reapply for registration, which was subject to the fulfilment of certain criteria regarding finance and personnel. In the same month the behaviour of Musa, who was reported to have assaulted a journalist and ordered his summary detention, prompted widespread concern.

In February 1993 the commissions of inquiry that had been established in May 1992 promulgated reports that provided evidence of corruption on the part of former members of the Momoh administration. In March 1993 the European Parliament adopted a resolution demanding that the Government submit records of the trials of those executed in December 1992, abrogate press restrictions, release prisoners detained without trial, and present a programme for the transition to civilian rule. Later that month a group of Sierra Leoneans based in Guinea, who were alleged to be supporters of Momoh, were accused of conspiring to import armaments from Ukraine to overthrow the Government. In late April Strasser announced that a programme providing for a transition to civilian rule within a period of three years was to be adopted; in addition, all political prisoners were to be released, press restrictions would be relaxed, and the function of special military tribunals (which had attracted widespread criticism, following the conviction and execution of a number of alleged conspirators in December 1992) was to be reviewed. In a government reorganization in July 1993, Musa was replaced as Deputy Chairman of the NPRC and Chief Secretary of State by Capt. Julius Maada Bio, ostensibly on the grounds that false allegations against him had proved detrimental to the stability of the administration. Musa (who was widely believed to be responsible for the repressive measures undertaken by the Government) took refuge in the Nigerian high commission in Freetown, amid widespread speculation regarding his dismissal, and subsequently emigrated to the United Kingdom. Also in July a number of political prisoners were released. In August, however, Amnesty International accused the Government of detaining more than 170 civilians, including a number of children, on suspicion of involvement with the rebel insurrection. In September the Government appropriated assets of several former politicians, including Momoh, following reports from the commissions of inquiry that had investigated their activities. In October a former minister in the Stevens administration, Dr Abbas Bundu, was appointed Secretary of State for Foreign Affairs and International Co-operation. In November the Government claimed to have pre-empted a coup attempt, after four British citizens, alleged to be mercenaries, were arrested in Freetown. (In January 1994 the four detainees, who were accused of conspiring with Musa and other disaffected Sierra Leonean nationals to overthrow the Government, were placed on trial on charges of treason.)

At the end of November 1993 Strasser announced the details of a two-year transitional programme, which provided for the installation of a civilian government by January 1996: the National Advisory Council was to promulgate constitutional proposals in December 1993, and, in conjunction with a committee of legal experts, was to produce a draft constitution by June 1994, which was to be submitted for approval in a national referendum in May 1995; a national commission was to be established to instruct the population about the new constitution; district council elections (which were to be contested by candidates without political affiliations) were scheduled for November 1994; the registration of political parties was to take place in June 1995, prior to a presidential election in November and legislative elections in December of that year. In December, in accordance with the transitional programme, a five-member Interim National Electoral Commission, chaired by Dr James Jonah (the Assistant Secretary-General of the UN, in charge of Political Affairs), was established to organize the registration of voters and the demarcation of constituency boundaries, in preparation for the forthcoming local government elections. In the same month the National Advisory Council submitted several constitutional proposals (which included a number of similar provisions to the 1991 Constitution), stipulating that: executive power was to be vested in the President, who was to be required to consult with the Cabinet (except in the event of a national emergency), and was to be restricted to a tenure of two four-year terms of office; only Sierra Leonean nationals of more than 40 years of age were to qualify to contest a presidential election (thereby precluding Strasser and the majority of NPRC members, on the grounds of age); the President was to be elected by a minimum of 50% of votes cast nationally, and at least by 25% of the votes cast in each of the four provinces; the legislature was to comprise a House of Representatives, which was to be elected by universal adult suffrage for a term of five years, and a 30-member upper chamber, the Senate, which was to include a number of regional representatives and five presidential nominees; members of the House of Representatives were not to be permitted to hold ministerial portfolios concurrently.

At the end of December 1993 the Government ended the state of emergency that had been imposed in April 1992 (although additional security measures remained in force). In March 1994 the authorities introduced further legislation regulating the registration of newspapers, which effectively prevented a number of independent publications from renewing their licence. In April 13 senior members of the armed forces were dismissed, following criticism of the Government's failure to end the civil conflict, and rumours of complicity between military officers and the rebels. In May several senior members of the former administration were arrested, after failing to provide compensation for funds that they had allegedly misappropriated. In August Strasser reconstituted the Council of Secretaries. In a further government reorganization in September, the three regional Secretaries of State were replaced. Later that month the Attorney-General and Secretary of State for Judicial Affairs, Franklyn Kargbo, resigned in protest at the death sentence imposed on an elderly military official, who had been convicted by military tribunal on charges of collaborating with the rebels; Kargbo fled into exile, and was subsequently granted political asylum in the United Kingdom.

In October 1994 a draft Constitution was submitted to the NPRC. In early November the four British citizens who had been detained on charges of involvement in a conspiracy to overthrow the Government were released, after the new Attorney-General requested that their trial be abandoned. Later that month, in accordance with the transitional programme, a five-member National Commission for Civil Education was established to inform the public regarding the principles of the new Constitution. However, an increase in rebel activity (see below) prevented the organization of district council elections, which had been scheduled to take place later that month, and was expected to impede the further implementation of the transitional programme.

In January 1995 Strasser reorganized the Council of Secretaries. In March Musa was apparently ordered to retire from the armed forces, after Strasser rejected his proposal for the installation of a transitional civilian government. Later that month the Council of Secretaries was reorganized to allow principal military officials in the Government to assume active functions within the armed forces (following the advance of rebel forces towards Freetown); Lt-Col Akim Gibril became Chief Secretary of State, replacing Maada Bio, who was appointed Chief of Defence Staff. The Government claimed that the higher proportion of civilians within the reconstituted Council of Secretaries reflected the commitment of the NPRC to the transitional process. At the end of April, on the anniversary of the NPRC's assumption of power, Strasser formally rescinded the ban on political activity and announced that a National Consultative Conference was to be convened to discuss the transitional process; he further indicated that elections were to take place by the end of that year, prior to the installation of a civilian government in January 1996, in accordance with the provisions of the transitional programme.

Sierra Leone's foreign policy has been traditionally non-aligned. In November 1985 the Liberian Head of State, Samuel Doe, accused Sierra Leone of direct involvement in an attempted coup in Liberia, and closed the border between the two countries. In August 1986 the border was reopened, and in September Sierra Leone, Liberia and Guinea signed an agreement on non-aggression and security co-operation. In 1988 relations with Liberia again deteriorated, following the expulsion and alleged ill treatment of Sierra Leonean citizens in July. In September, however, a summit meeting between the heads of state of the two nations, together with those of Nigeria and Togo, took place, and the four leaders issued a declaration reaffirming their commitment to the objectives of the Economic Community of West African States (ECOWAS, see p. 138).

Following the outbreak of civil conflict in Liberia in December 1989 (see chapter on Liberia), an estimated 125,000 Liberians took refuge in Sierra Leone. The Sierra Leonean Government contributed troops to the ECOWAS Monitoring Group that was dispatched to Liberia in August 1990 (ECOMOG, see p. 139). In November of that year Charles Taylor, the leader of the principal Liberian rebel faction, the National Patriotic Front of Liberia (NPFL), threatened to attack Freetown International Airport (alleged to be a base for ECOMOG offensives against rebel strongholds). In early April, following repeated border incursions by members of the NPFL, which resulted in the deaths of several Sierra Leoneans, government forces entered Liberian territory and launched a retaliatory attack against NPFL bases. By the end of that month, however, NPFL forces had advanced 150 km within Sierra Leone. The Momoh Government alleged that the rebel offensive had been instigated by Charles Taylor, in an attempt to force Sierra Leone's withdrawal from ECOMOG, and also accused the Government of Burkina Faso of actively assisting the rebels. It was reported, however, that members of a Sierra Leonean resistance movement, known as the Revolutionary United Front (RUF), led by Foday Sankoh, had joined the NPFL in attacks against government forces. In mid-1991 Sierra Leonean forces, with the assistance of military units from Nigeria and Guinea, initiated a counter-offensive against the rebels, and succeeded in recapturing several towns in the east and south of the country. Government forces were also assisted by some 1,200 Liberian troops, who had fled to Sierra Leone in September 1990, in fighting against the rebels, while a number of countries, including the United Kingdom and the USA, provided logistical support to Sierra Leone.

In September 1991 former supporters of the Liberian President, Samuel Doe, grouped in the United Liberation Movement of Liberia for Democracy (ULIMO), initiated attacks from Sierra Leone against NPFL forces in north-western Liberia. The Sierra Leonean Government denied allegations by Taylor that Sierra Leonean troops were involved in the offensive. The Liberian Interim President, Amos Sawyer, subsequently met Momoh in Freetown to discuss the conflict. In October clashes between ULIMO and the NPFL continued near Mano River Bridge on the border with Liberia. Following protracted negotiations between the Liberian Interim Government and the NPFL, a summit meeting in Yamoussoukro, Côte d'Ivoire, at the end of October resulted in a peace agreement, whereby all Liberian forces would be withdrawn from Sierra Leone, and a demilitarized zone, under the control of ECOMOG, would be created along the border between the two countries. In December, however, Momoh claimed that, contrary to the terms of the peace agreement, the NPFL had continued its offensive in Sierra Leone; it was reported that the NPFL had regained control of several villages near the border with Liberia. In January 1992 discussions took place in the Liberian capital, Monrovia, under the auspices of ECOWAS, between members of the Sierra Leonean Government and leaders of the Liberian factions, in an attempt to resolve the conflict. Sierra Leone reiterated claims that the conditions of the peace agreement had not been implemented, while the NPFL objected to Sierra Leone's participation in ECOMOG. It was agreed that delegations from the two countries would meet regularly to discuss the conflict. In May ECOMOG began to deploy troops along the border between Sierra Leone and Liberia, despite continued hostilities between ULIMO and NPFL forces in the area. (The establishment of the demilitarized zone was, however, later abandoned.) In the same month the RUF rejected appeals by the NPRC to end the civil conflict, and demanded that all foreign troops be withdrawn from Sierra Leone as a precondition for the cessation of hostilities.

In August 1992 government forces, with the assistance of Guinean troops, initiated an offensive against rebel positions near the border with Liberia and succeeded in recapturing a number of villages; in subsequent months, however, territorial gains on both sides were constantly reversed. In early 1993 the RUF became militarily disadvantagd by the reduction of logistical support from the NPFL, after ULIMO gained control of the greater part of western Liberia (see chapter on Liberia); by April it was reported that only Kailahun District in the extreme east of Sierra Leone, near the border with Liberia, and Pujehun District in the south of the country remained under the control of rebel forces.

In July 1993 government units, with the assistance of ULIMO, initiated an offensive against members of the RUF in north-western Liberia. Later that year government forces advanced within Kailahun District, regaining control of the principal town of Kailahun in September, and a number of other towns, including Koindu, 250 km east of Freetown, in November. Several towns in Pujehun District were also recaptured by government troops in November. At the end of that month Strasser extended an offer of amnesty to members of the RUF who agreed to cease hostilities; in December, however, despite the Government's declaration of a unilateral cease-fire, the RUF launched repeated attacks in Kailahun District. In January 1994 the Government claimed that it had regained control of further rebel bases in Pujehun District and the principal industrial town of Kenema near the border with Liberia. It was reported, however, that some 100 civilians had been killed in attacks by the RUF in the region of Bo, to the south-east of Freetown. Later that year fighting in the south and east of Sierra Leone intensified, and in April it was reported that the RUF, which had been joined by disaffected members of the armed forces, had initiated attacks in the north of the country. In addition, it was reported that another rebel movement, the National Front for the Restoration of Democracy, had emerged, and was launching attacks from Guinea.

In May 1994 it was reported that government troops had destroyed an important rebel base in the Northern Province. In July Israeli-trained government units assisted in the recapture of two principal towns in eastern Sierra Leone, following a military co-operation accord between the Governments of Sierra Leone and Israel. In the same month a National Security Council, chaired by Strasser, was established to co-ordinate the operations of the armed forces. Later in July, however, it was reported that the RUF had effectively besieged Kenema, after launching a series of attacks in the surrounding area. In August government troops initiated counter-offensives against rebel positions in the region of Kenema, following reports that the RUF were exploiting diamond reserves in the area in order to finance their activities.

Later in 1994 reports emerged of an increase in rebel activity, with widespread looting and killing by unidentified armed groups, prompting speculation regarding the cohesion of both the RUF and the armed forces. In October the Government announced that a newly-established organization, the Sierra Leonean Initiative for Peace, had assisted the RUF in military operations against government forces. In early November the RUF seized two British members of the non-governmental organization, Voluntary Service Overseas, following an attack against the northern town of Kabala. Strasser subsequently proposed that the Government and the rebels negotiate to resolve the conflict; however, the RUF rejected the conditions stipulated by the authorities, which included the imposition of an immediate cease-fire and the release of the two British prisoners. Sankoh (who continued to lead the RUF) insisted that the United Kingdom suspend military assistance to the NPRC as a precondition for the release of the two hostages; he further demanded that the British authorities recognize the RUF as a political organization and provide the rebels with armaments and medical supplies. However, the British Government denied the claims of the rebels that the Strasser administration received armaments from the United

# SIERRA LEONE

Kingdom. In December it was announced that discussions were to take place between representatives of the Government and the rebels near Mano River Bridge; however, the meeting proved to be abortive.

In January 1995 the RUF gained control of the mining installations owned by the Sierra Leone Ore and Metal Company (SIEROMCO) and Sierra Rutile Ltd, and seized a number of employees of the two enterprises, including eight foreign nationals. Later in January seven Roman Catholic nuns (who were Italian and Brazilian nationals), together with a number of Sierra Leonean citizens, were abducted, following an attack by the RUF against the north-western town of Kambia. In the same month the RUF threatened to kill the British hostages if the Sierra Leonean authorities executed an officer, who had been convicted by military tribunal of collaborating with the rebels. In early February Sankoh indicated that the RUF was prepared to negotiate with the Government, and invited the International Committee of the Red Cross (ICRC, see p. 177) to mediate in the discussions. Later that month, however, the RUF rejected appeals by the UN and the Organization of African Unity (OAU, see p. 200) that peace negotiations be initiated, and demanded that all troops that had been dispatched by foreign Governments to assist the Strasser administration be withdrawn as a precondition to discussions. In mid-February government forces (which had succeeded in recapturing the mining installations owned by Sierra Rutile) launched an offensive against a principal rebel base in the Kangari region, east of Freetown. Meanwhile, continued atrocities perpetrated against civilians were increasingly attributed to 'sobels', disaffected members of the armed forces who engaged in acts of looting, banditry and indiscriminate killing. By mid-February some 900,000 civilians had been displaced as a result of the increase in the civil conflict, of which about 185,000 had fled to Guinea and 90,000 to Liberia.

In February 1995 the military administration (which had ordered the total mobilization of the armed forces to repulse rebel attacks) engaged 58 Gurkha mercenaries, who had previously served in the British army, prompting further concern regarding the safety of the British hostages in Sierra Leone. In March government forces regained control of the mining installations owned by SIEROMCO and the principal town of Moyamba, 100km south-east of Freetown (which had been captured by the RUF earlier that month). Later that month the rebels released the seven nuns who had been abducted in January. Despite the successful counter-offensives by government forces, by April it was reported that the RUF had advanced towards Freetown and had initiated a series of attacks against towns in the vicinity (including Songo, which was situated only 35km east of Freetown), apparently prior to besieging the capital. The Guinean administration announced that it was to dispatch an additional 300 troops to assist government forces in repulsing the rebel advances. Later in April the 10 remaining foreign nationals who had been seized by the RUF, together with six Sierra Leoneans, were released to the ICRC. (It was reported, however, that the rebels continued to hold a number of Sierra Leonean civilians as hostages.) At the end of April the RUF rejected an unconditional offer by Strasser to initiate peace negotiations.

## Government

Following a military coup on 29 April 1992, the Constitutions of 1978 and 1991 were suspended, the House of Representatives was dissolved, all political activity was prohibited, and a governing body, known as the National Provisional Ruling Council (NPRC), was established. In July the NPRC was designated the Supreme Council of State, and the Cabinet was reconstituted as the Council of Secretaries (headed by the Chief Secretary of State). The Council of Secretaries was to be responsible for government administration, subject to the authority of the NPRC. Three members of the NPRC were appointed Principal Liaison Officers, and were to supervise administration in a number of departments (which replaced the existing ministries). In 1993 the Government announced the adoption of a transitional programme, which provided for the installation of a civilian government by January 1996, following multi-party presidential and legislative elections. In April 1995 the Government rescinded the ban on political activity, and announced that elections were to take place by the end of that year as scheduled, despite widespread civil conflict (see Recent History).

The country is divided into four regions: the Northern, Eastern and Southern Provinces, and the Western Area, which comprise 12 districts. There are 147 chiefdoms, each controlled by a Paramount Chief and a Council of Elders, known as the Tribal Authority.

## Defence

In June 1994 the Republic of Sierra Leone Military Forces comprised an army of 6,000 men and a navy of 150. In that year some 800 Nigerian troops were based in Sierra Leone to support government forces in repulsing attacks by a rebel faction, the Revolutionary United Front (which was estimated to number 1,000); the Sierra Leonean authorities also received military assistance from Guinea (which contributed 800 troops in early 1995) and Israel. The defence budget for 1993 was estimated at Le 7,700m.

## Economic Affairs

In 1993, according to estimates by the World Bank, Sierra Leone's gross national product (GNP), measured at average 1991–93 prices, was US $647m., equivalent to $140 per head. During 1985–93, it was estimated, GNP per head declined, in real terms, at an average annual rate of 0.6%. Over the same period the population increased by an annual average rate of 2.6%. Sierra Leone's gross domestic product (GDP) increased, in real terms, by an annual average of 1.3% in 1980–92.

Agriculture (including forestry and fishing) contributed an estimated 43.2% of GDP in 1993/94. In 1993 the sector employed 60.0% of the working population. The principal cash crops are coffee (which accounted for 2.3% of total export earnings in 1994) and cocoa beans. Staple food crops include cassava, rice and bananas. Cattle, sheep and poultry are the principal livestock. Agricultural GDP increased by an annual average of 2.3% during 1980–92.

Industry (including mining, manufacturing, construction and power) contributed an estimated 21.0% of GDP in 1993/94, and employed an estimated 16.7% of the working population in 1988/89. During 1980–92 industrial GDP declined by an annual average of 1.3%.

Mining and quarrying contributed an estimated 7.4% of GDP in 1993/94. The principal mineral exports are rutile (titanium dioxide—which accounted for 47.8% of export earnings in 1994), diamonds, bauxite and gold. The production of iron ore, previously an important mineral export, was suspended in 1985. The exploitation of further deposits of diamond-bearing kimberlite commenced in 1991.

Manufacturing contributed an estimated 11.3% of GDP in 1993/94. The manufacturing sector consists mainly of the production of palm oil and other agro-based industries, textiles and furniture-making. During 1980–92 the real GDP of the manufacturing sector declined by an annual average of 4.6%.

Energy is derived principally from oil-fired thermal power stations. However, a project to reduce the country's dependence on fuel imports, by developing hydroelectric resources, was initiated in early 1990. The use of solar energy for domestic purposes was also introduced in 1990. Imports of mineral fuels comprised 18.5% of the value of total imports in 1994.

In 1991 Sierra Leone recorded a visible trade surplus of US $11.2m., and there was a surplus of $10.7m. on the current account of the balance of payments. In 1985 the principal source of imports (14.2%) was the United Kingdom; other major suppliers were the Federal Republic of Germany, the People's Republic of China and the USA. In 1993 the principal market for exports was the USA (taking 32.3% of the total); other significant purchasers were the United Kingdom and Germany. The principal exports in 1994 were rutile, diamonds, bauxite, cocoa beans and coffee. The principal imports in that year were foodstuffs and livestock, mineral fuels, machinery and transport equipment and basic manufactures.

In the financial year ending 30 June 1993 there was a budgetary deficit of Le 17,099m. (equivalent to 4.3% of GDP). Sierra Leone's external debt totalled US $1,388m. at the end of 1993, of which $728m. was long-term public debt. In that year the cost of debt-servicing was equivalent to 11.9% of the total value of exports of goods and services. The annual rate of inflation averaged 76.2% in 1985–93; however, consumer prices increased by an average of only 22.2% in 1993 and 24.2% in 1994. An estimated 50% of the labour force were unemployed in early 1990.

Sierra Leone is a member of the African Development Bank (see p. 102), of ECOWAS (see p. 138) and of the Mano River Union (see p. 239), which aims to promote economic co-operation with Guinea and Liberia.

# SIERRA LEONE

In the late 1980s, in response to a deterioration in the economy (resulting from the rapid increase, in the 1970s, of international petroleum prices), the Government implemented an economic adjustment programme, based on IMF recommendations. However, economic reforms were subsequently suspended, following the IMF's withdrawal of financial support (owing to the Government's continued failure to control debt arrears). From 1991 the conflict in principal economic areas in the south of the country (see Recent History) caused severe disruption in the agricultural and mining sectors, and resulted in a substantial increase in government expenditure. A two-year economic adjustment programme, which was introduced in April 1992 under the aegis of the IMF, envisaged the adoption of stricter monetary controls, the development of a foreign exchange market, and the continuation of structural reforms, which included the transfer of a number of state-owned enterprises to the private sector. In March 1994 the IMF declared Sierra Leone to be eligible to receive new credits, following its payment of accumulated debt arrears, and subsequently approved loans under a three-year Enhanced Structural Adjustment Facility. In July official bilateral creditors agreed to reschedule debt arrears in recognition of the Government's recovery efforts. At the end of that year the Government's success in containing budgetary expenditure and improving tax administration had resulted in a decline in the fiscal deficit. By early 1995, however, increasing rebel activity, which affected the greater part of the country (see Recent History), had effectively suspended mining operations (apart from illicit trade), and prompted a withdrawal of foreign investment, thereby undermining the Government's principal sources of fiscal revenue.

## Social Welfare

Sierra Leone's medical services are insufficient to provide basic health care for the population. In 1980–85, according to UN estimates, the country had the world's highest death rate and the lowest life expectancy, averaging only 39 years at birth. In the same period, it was estimated, the infant mortality rate was among the highest in the world: for every 1,000 live births, there were 166 deaths of children less than one year of age. In 1984 there were 262 physicians and 2,568 nurses (including midwives) working in the country. In 1988 there were 53 hospitals and 237 health centres. The Government provides community development centres, youth clubs and maternity welfare centres. Of total budgetary expenditure by the central Government in the financial year 1990/91, Le 768.9m. (3.2%) was for health. Missions and voluntary organizations make an important contribution to the provision of medical and other social services.

## Education

Primary education in Sierra Leone begins at six years of age and lasts for six years. Secondary education, beginning at the age of 12, lasts for a further six years, comprising two three-year cycles. In 1987 tuition fees for government-owned primary and secondary schools were abolished. In 1990 primary enrolment was equivalent to 48% of children in the appropriate age-group (boys 56%; girls 39%), while the comparable ratio for secondary enrolment was 16% (boys 21%; girls 12%). Budgetary expenditure on education by the central Government in 1988 was Le 420.2m. (18.1% of total spending). In 1990, according to UNESCO estimates, adult illiteracy averaged 79.3% (males 69.3%; females 88.7%).

## Public Holidays

**1995:** 1 January (New Year's Day), 3 March* (Id al-Fitr, end of Ramadan), 14–17 April (Easter), 27 April (Independence Day), 10 May* (Id al-Adha, Feast of the Sacrifice), 9 August* (Mouloud, Birth of the Prophet), 25–26 December (Christmas and Boxing Day).

**1996:** 1 January (New Year's Day), 21 February* (Id al-Fitr, end of Ramadan), 5–8 April (Easter), 27 April (Independence Day), 29 April* (Id al-Adha, Feast of the Sacrifice), 28 July* (Mouloud, Birth of the Prophet), 25–26 December (Christmas and Boxing Day).

* Islamic religious holidays, dependent on the lunar calendar, may vary by one or two days from the dates given.

## Weights and Measures

The metric system is in force.

# Statistical Survey

Source (unless otherwise stated): Bank of Sierra Leone, POB 30, Siaka Stevens St, Freetown; tel. (22) 226501; telex 3232; fax (22) 224764.

## Area and Population

### AREA, POPULATION AND DENSITY

| | |
|---|---|
| Area (sq km) | 71,740* |
| Population (census results)† | |
| 8 December 1974 | 2,735,159 |
| 14 December 1985 | |
| Males | 1,746,055 |
| Females | 1,769,757 |
| Total | 3,515,812 |
| Population (UN estimates at mid-year)‡ | |
| 1990 | 4,151,000 |
| 1991 | 4,261,000 |
| 1992 | 4,376,000 |
| Density (per sq km) at mid-1992 | 61.0 |

* 27,699 sq miles.
† Excluding adjustment for underenumeration, estimated to have been 10% in 1974. The adjusted total for 1974 (based on a provisional total of 2,729,479 enumerated) is 3,002,426, and that for 1985 is 3,700,000 (estimate).
‡ Source: UN, *World Population Prospects: The 1992 Revision*.

### PRINCIPAL TOWNS (population at 1985 census)

| | | | | |
|---|---|---|---|---|
| Freetown (capital) | 384,499 | Kenema | | 52,473 |
| Koindu | 82,474 | Makeni | | 49,474 |
| Bo | 59,768 | | | |

### BIRTHS AND DEATHS (UN estimates, annual averages)

| | 1975–80 | 1980-85 | 1985–90 |
|---|---|---|---|
| Birth rate (per 1,000) | 48.6 | 48.4 | 48.2 |
| Death rate (per 1,000) | 27.1 | 25.2 | 23.4 |

**Expectation of life** (UN estimates, years at birth, 1985–90): 41.0 (males 39.4; females 42.6).

Source: UN, *World Population Prospects: The 1992 Revision*.

### ECONOMICALLY ACTIVE POPULATION
(sample survey, '000 persons, 1988/89)

| | Males | Females | Total |
|---|---|---|---|
| Agriculture, etc. | 551.2 | 673.3 | 1,224.5 |
| Industry | 235.9 | 98.9 | 334.8 |
| Services | 198.4 | 223.0 | 421.4 |
| **Total** | 985.5 | 995.2 | 1,980.7 |

**Mid-1993** (estimates in '000): Agriculture, etc. 910; Total 1,518 (Source: FAO, *Production Yearbook*).

# SIERRA LEONE

## Agriculture

**PRINCIPAL CROPS** ('000 metric tons)

|  | 1991 | 1992 | 1993 |
|---|---|---|---|
| Maize | 11 | 11* | 12* |
| Millet | 22 | 24* | 26* |
| Sorghum | 22 | 22* | 24* |
| Rice (paddy) | 544 | 411 | 486* |
| Sweet potatoes | 15 | 11* | 12* |
| Cassava (Manioc)* | 90 | 92 | 97 |
| Taro (Coco yam) | 3 | 3† | 3† |
| Tomatoes† | 23 | 23 | 23 |
| Dry broad beans | 1 | 1† | 1† |
| Citrus fruit† | 77 | 77 | 75 |
| Mangoes† | 6 | 6 | 6 |
| Palm kernels | 30 | 35† | 35† |
| Palm oil | 51 | 60† | 50† |
| Groundnuts (in shell) | 21 | 20† | 21† |
| Coconuts | 3 | 3 | 3† |
| Coffee (green) | 26 | 29* | 36* |
| Cocoa beans | 24 | 24† | 24† |

* Unofficial figure(s).   † FAO estimate(s).

Source: FAO, *Production Yearbook*.

**1994** ('000 metric tons): Maize 13; Millet 25; Rice (paddy) 486; Sweet potatoes 17; Cassava (Manioc) 106; Taro (Coco yam) 3 (FAO estimate); Palm kernels 10.8; Palm oil 48; Groundnuts (in shell) 24. Source: Department of Agriculture and Forestry, Freetown.

**LIVESTOCK** ('000 head, year ending September)

|  | 1991 | 1992* | 1993* |
|---|---|---|---|
| Cattle | 333 | 333 | 333 |
| Pigs* | 50 | 50 | 50 |
| Sheep | 274 | 275 | 278 |
| Goats | 151 | 152 | 153 |

Poultry (million): 6 in 1991; 6* in 1992; 6* in 1993.

* FAO estimate(s).

Source: FAO, *Production Yearbook*.

**LIVESTOCK PRODUCTS** (FAO estimates, '000 metric tons)

|  | 1991 | 1992 | 1993 |
|---|---|---|---|
| Beef and veal | 5 | 5 | 5 |
| Poultry meat | 9 | 9 | 9 |
| Other meat | 5 | 5 | 5 |
| Cows' milk | 17 | 17 | 17 |
| Poultry eggs | 6.9 | 6.9 | 6.9 |

Source: FAO, *Production Yearbook*.

## Forestry

**ROUNDWOOD REMOVALS** ('000 cubic metres, excl. bark)

|  | 1990 | 1991 | 1992 |
|---|---|---|---|
| Sawlogs, veneer logs and logs for sleepers | 18 | 2 | — |
| Other industrial wood*† | 120 | 120 | 120 |
| Fuel wood* | 2,948 | 3,025 | 3,105 |
| **Total** | 3,086 | 3,147 | 3,225* |

* FAO estimate(s).
† Assumed to be unchanged since 1980.

Source: FAO, *Yearbook of Forest Products*.

**SAWNWOOD PRODUCTION**
('000 cubic metres, incl. railway sleepers)

|  | 1990 | 1991 | 1992 |
|---|---|---|---|
| Total | 11 | 9 | 9* |

* FAO estimate.

Source: FAO, *Yearbook of Forest Products*.

## Fishing

('000 metric tons, live weight)

|  | 1990* | 1991 | 1992 |
|---|---|---|---|
| Freshwater fishes | 15.0 | 13.0* | 16.0* |
| Sardinellas | 6.4 | 7.9 | 7.8 |
| Bonga shad | 20.0 | 22.4 | 22.1 |
| Other marine fishes (incl. unspecified) | 6.7 | 6.4* | 7.7* |
| Crustaceans and molluscs | 3.8 | 1.7* | 2.6* |
| **Total catch** | 51.8 | 51.4 | 56.2 |

* FAO estimate(s).

Source: FAO, *Yearbook of Fishery Statistics*.

## Mining

('000 metric tons, unless otherwise indicated)

|  | 1992 | 1993 | 1994 |
|---|---|---|---|
| Bauxite | 1,257 | 1,165 | 729 |
| Ilmenite | 60 | 64 | 54 |
| Rutile concentrates | 149 | 150 | 144 |
| Diamonds ('000 metric carats) | 312 | 157 | 197* |
| Salt ('000 bags) | 155 | 360 | 166 |

* Shipments.

## Industry

**SELECTED PRODUCTS** ('000 metric tons, unless otherwise indicated)

|  | 1989 | 1990 | 1991 |
|---|---|---|---|
| Beer ('000 hectolitres) | 43 | 59 | 48 |
| Cigarettes (million) | 1,200 | 1,200 | 1,200 |
| Jet fuels | 14 | 15 | 15 |
| Motor spirit (petrol) | 35 | 35 | 13 |
| Kerosene | 20 | 18 | 20 |
| Distillate fuel oils | 101 | 103 | 33 |
| Residual fuel oils | 88 | 88 | 90 |
| Electric energy (million kWh) | 222 | 224 | 230 |

Source: mainly UN, *Industrial Statistics Yearbook*.

**1992** ('000 metric tons, unless otherwise indicated): Beer ('000 hectolitres) 36; Cigarettes (million) 531; Motor spirit (petrol) 1.7; Kerosene 1.7; Distillate fuel oils 7.4.
**1993**: Beer ('000 cartons) 627.5; Cigarettes (million) 513.
**1994**: Beer ('000 cartons) 370; Cigarettes (million) 344.

## Finance

**CURRENCY AND EXCHANGE RATES**

**Monetary Units**
  100 cents = 1 leone (Le).

**Sterling and Dollar Equivalents** (31 December 1994)
  £1 sterling = 959.05 leones;
  US $1 = 613.01 leones;
  1,000 leones = £1.043 = $1.631.

**Average Exchange Rate** (leones per US $)
  1992   499.44
  1993   567.46
  1994   586.74

# SIERRA LEONE

**BUDGET** (Le million, year ending 30 June)

| Revenue | 1991/92 | 1992/93 | 1993/94 |
| --- | --- | --- | --- |
| Direct taxes | 8,275 | 13,195 | 14,900 |
| Import duties | 12,333 | 18,792 | 26,608 |
| Excise duties | 8,470 | 12,463 | 16,275 |
| Other sources* | 6,306 | 9,844 | 9,632 |
| **Total** | 35,384 | 54,294 | 67,415 |

* Including licences, duties, fees and receipts for departmental services, receipts from posts and telecommunications royalties, and revenue from government lands, contributions from government corporations and companies, interest and loan repayments, etc.

| Expenditure | 1987/88 | 1989/90 | 1990/91 |
| --- | --- | --- | --- |
| Education and social welfare | 424.5 | 1,310.0 | 2,775.1 |
| Health | 143.3 | 412.7 | 768.9 |
| General administration | 371.9 | 1,131.1 | 2,847.3 |
| Transport and communications | 12.3 | 82.1 | 334.6 |
| Police and justice | 88.8 | 370.3 | 916.4 |
| Defence | 156.1 | 860.6 | 1,876.0 |
| Agriculture and natural resources | 124.7 | 239.5 | 652.9 |
| Tourism and cultural affairs | 1.8 | 28.0 | 46.3 |
| Pensions and gratuities | 36.9 | 169.6 | 270.3 |
| Trade and industry | 2.5 | 79.5 | 94.5 |
| Construction and development | 190.9 | 426.9 | 400.3 |
| Housing and country planning | 4.7 | 70.2 | 124.7 |
| Other current expenditure | 1,678.5 | 1,809.7 | 6,552.1 |
| Public debt charges | 723.9 | 1,704.3 | 6,058.7 |
| **Total** | 3,960.8 | 8,694.5 | 23,718.1 |

**Total expenditure** (Le million, year ending 30 June): 61,845 in 1991/92; 82,126 in 1992/93; 97,705 in 1993/94.

**CENTRAL BANK RESERVES** (US $ million at 31 December)

| | 1992 | 1993 | 1994 |
| --- | --- | --- | --- |
| IMF special drawing rights | 1.7 | 3.8 | 9.0 |
| Foreign exchange | 18.9 | 28.9 | 40.6 |
| **Total** | 20.6 | 32.8 | 49.7 |

Source: IMF, *International Financial Statistics*.

**MONEY SUPPLY** (Le million at 31 December)

| | 1992 | 1993 | 1994 |
| --- | --- | --- | --- |
| Currency outside banks | 18,270 | 21,882 | 23,604 |
| Private sector deposits at central bank | 112 | 418 | 219 |
| Demand deposits at commercial banks | 13,005 | 12,753 | 14,719 |
| **Total money** | 31,387 | 35,053 | 38,542 |

Source: IMF, *International Financial Statistics*.

**COST OF LIVING**
(Consumer Price Index for Freetown; base: 1978 = 100)

| | 1990 | 1991 | 1992 |
| --- | --- | --- | --- |
| Food and drinks | 22,847.9 | 47,466.4 | 80,792.3 |
| Tobacco products and kola nuts | 49,483.6 | 131,347.6 | 164,407.7 |
| Housing | 11,727.0 | 22,237.3 | 41,895.2 |
| Clothing and footwear | 38,291.6 | 58,120.9 | 97,466.3 |
| **All items** (incl. others) | 23,215.9 | 47,055.8 | 77,877.3 |

**1993** (base: 1992 = 100): Food items 121.1; Beverages and tobacco 166.7; All items (incl. others) 127.9.

Source: Central Statistics Office, Tower Hill, Freetown.

**NATIONAL ACCOUNTS**
(Le million at current prices, year ending 30 June)

**National Income and Product**

| | 1991/92 | 1992/93 | 1993/94 |
| --- | --- | --- | --- |
| Compensation of employees | 50,894 | 71,373 | 89,173 |
| Operating surplus | 187,146 | 268,739 | 312,726 |
| **Domestic factor incomes** | 238,040 | 340,112 | 401,899 |
| Consumption of fixed capital | 14,507 | 19,248 | 24,641 |
| **Gross domestic product (GDP) at factor cost** | 252,547 | 359,360 | 426,540 |
| Indirect taxes, *less* subsidies | 24,987 | 36,713 | 48,305 |
| **GDP in purchasers' values** | 277,534 | 396,073 | 474,845 |
| Factor income received from abroad | 3,576 | n.a. | n.a. |
| *Less* Factor income paid abroad | 7,719 | n.a. | n.a. |
| **Gross national product (GNP)** | 273,391 | n.a. | n.a. |
| *Less* Consumption of fixed capital | 14,507 | 19,248 | 24,641 |
| **National income in market prices** | 258,884 | n.a. | n.a. |
| Other current transfers received from abroad | 8,430 | n.a. | n.a. |
| *Less* Other current transfers paid abroad | 422 | n.a. | n.a. |
| **National disposable income** | 266,892 | n.a. | n.a. |

Source: Central Statistics Office, Tower Hill, Freetown.

**Expenditure on the Gross Domestic Product**

| | 1991/92 | 1992/93* | 1993/94* |
| --- | --- | --- | --- |
| Government final consumption expenditure | 27,810 | 47,103 | 58,333 |
| Private final consumption expenditure | 205,031 | 311,223 | 401,766 |
| Increase in stocks | 26,886 | 28,866 | 446 |
| Gross fixed capital formation | 27,243 | 26,700 | 41,671 |
| **Total domestic expenditure** | 286,970 | 413,892 | 502,216 |
| Exports of goods and services | 77,527 | 93,558 | 84,188 |
| *Less* Imports of goods and services | 86,963 | 111,377 | 111,559 |
| **GDP in purchasers' values** | 277,534 | 396,073 | 474,845 |

* Provisional figures.

Source: Central Statistics Office, Tower Hill, Freetown.

**Gross Domestic Product by Economic Activity**

| | 1991/92 | 1992/93* | 1993/94* |
| --- | --- | --- | --- |
| Agriculture, hunting, forestry and fishing | 119,552 | 160,971 | 194,615 |
| Mining and quarrying | 29,156 | 32,805 | 33,489 |
| Manufacturing | 24,053 | 41,215 | 50,736 |
| Electricity, gas and water | 371 | 1,052 | 1,297 |
| Construction | 4,765 | 5,277 | 9,023 |
| Trade, restaurants and hotels | 45,100 | 67,466 | 75,406 |
| Transport, storage and communications | 19,898 | 31,801 | 40,258 |
| Finance, insurance, real estate and business services | 10,113 | 15,947 | 17,988 |
| Government services | 11,666 | 14,500 | 17,884 |
| Other community, social and personal services | 3,974 | 8,998 | 9,769 |
| **Sub-total** | 268,648 | 380,032 | 450,465 |
| Import duties | 11,649 | 18,993 | 27,410 |
| *Less* Imputed bank service charge | 2,764 | 2,951 | 3,390 |
| **GDP in purchasers' values** | 277,533 | 396,074 | 474,485 |

* Provisional figures.

Source: Central Statistics Office, Tower Hill, Freetown.

# SIERRA LEONE

## BALANCE OF PAYMENTS (US $ million)

|  | 1989 | 1990 | 1991 |
|---|---|---|---|
| Merchandise exports f.o.b. | 139.5 | 139.8 | 149.5 |
| Merchandise imports f.o.b. | −160.4 | −140.4 | −138.3 |
| **Trade balance** | −20.9 | −0.6 | 11.2 |
| Exports of services | 38.3 | 69.8 | 67.6 |
| Imports of services | −44.8 | −74.4 | −63.8 |
| Other income received | 0.2 | 0.7 | 0.9 |
| Other income paid | −39.8 | −71.8 | −14.9 |
| Private unrequited transfers (net) | 0.1 | 0.1 | 2.7 |
| Official unrequited transfers (net) | 7.2 | 6.8 | 7.1 |
| **Current balance** | −59.7 | −69.4 | 10.7 |
| Direct investment (net) | 22.4 | 32.4 | 7.5 |
| Other capital (net) | −40.3 | −33.2 | −9.8 |
| Net errors and omissions | 29.2 | 49.2 | 11.1 |
| **Overall balance** | −48.4 | −20.9 | 19.4 |

Source: IMF, *International Financial Statistics*.

# External Trade

## PRINCIPAL COMMODITIES (Le million)

| Imports | 1992 | 1993 | 1994 |
|---|---|---|---|
| Food and live animals | 29,747.9 | 31,437.8 | 30,559.6 |
| Beverages and tobacco | 734.9 | 2,246.4 | 2,262.0 |
| Crude materials (inedible) except fuels | 1,423.4 | 1,726.8 | 2,007.6 |
| Mineral fuels, lubricants, etc. | 11,875.2 | 12,450.0 | 16,316.8 |
| Animal and vegetable oils and fats | 1,801.6 | 2,837.0 | 1,813.2 |
| Chemicals | 7,122.6 | 7,165.8 | 6,440.5 |
| Basic manufactures | 9,199.2 | 8,508.8 | 9,606.0 |
| Machinery and transport equipment | 12,313.7 | 12,818.6 | 15,826.1 |
| Miscellaneous manufactured articles | 3,452.7 | 4,269.0 | 3,141.2 |
| **Total** | 77,671.2 | 83,460.3 | 87,972.7 |

| Exports | 1992 | 1993 | 1994 |
|---|---|---|---|
| Coffee | 1,351.0 | 1,301.3 | 1,549.1 |
| Cocoa beans | 1,053.1 | 2,115.9 | 1,704.2 |
| Palm kernels | 6.9 | — | — |
| Bauxite | 19,408.3 | 13,764.5 | 9,687.1 |
| Piassava | 50.1 | 49.9 | 51.1 |
| Diamonds | 15,360.0 | 11,089.3 | 15,075.1 |
| Rutile | 32,878.6 | 32,461.7 | 32,454.4 |
| Other items | 4,764.4 | 6,048.3 | 6,185.1 |
| Re-exports | 161.9 | 246.2 | 1,224.2 |
| **Total** | 75,034.3 | 67,077.3 | 67,930.3 |

## PRINCIPAL TRADING PARTNERS (Le '000)

| Imports | 1983 | 1984 | 1985 |
|---|---|---|---|
| China, People's Republic | 15,700 | 12,711 | 79,118 |
| France | 17,450 | 20,279 | 24,905 |
| Germany, Fed. Republic | 17,269 | 46,049 | 85,554 |
| Italy | 11,094 | 11,772 | 13,987 |
| Japan | 12,776 | 25,440 | 44,922 |
| Netherlands | 14,671 | 21,020 | 41,595 |
| United Kingdom | 33,246 | 47,815 | 110,959 |
| USA | 10,378 | 17,527 | 46,499 |
| **Total** (incl. others) | 286,923 | 418,286 | 781,604 |

(Le million)

| Exports | 1991 | 1992 | 1993 |
|---|---|---|---|
| Germany | 5,035.0 | 9,124.8 | 7,159.7 |
| Netherlands | 1,427.8 | 3,245.4 | 2,211.8 |
| Switzerland | 279.8 | 862.9 | 279.1 |
| United Kingdom | 5,607.1 | 6,620.3 | 13,215.0 |
| USA | 13,742.4 | 22,900.0 | 20,988.1 |
| **Total** (incl. others) | 44,008.7 | 74,872.4 | 65,019.1 |

# Transport

## ROAD TRAFFIC (motor vehicles in use at 31 December)

|  | 1991 | 1992 | 1993 |
|---|---|---|---|
| Passenger cars | 30,755 | 32,258 | 32,415 |
| Buses and coaches | 1,010 | 1,143 | 1,092 |
| Goods vehicles | 10,401 | 10,818 | 10,810 |
| Motorcycles | 10,134 | 10,491 | 10,198 |

Source: International Road Federation, *World Road Statistics*.

## INTERNATIONAL SEA-BORNE SHIPPING
(freight traffic, '000 metric tons)

|  | 1988 | 1989 | 1990 |
|---|---|---|---|
| Goods loaded | 1,200 | 1,280 | 1,802 |
| Goods unloaded | 510 | 527 | 533 |

Source: UN, *Monthly Bulletin of Statistics*.

## CIVIL AVIATION (estimated traffic)

|  | 1989 | 1990 | 1991 |
|---|---|---|---|
| Freight loaded (metric tons) | 655 | 670 | 685 |
| Freight unloaded (metric tons) | 1,380 | 1,415 | 1,460 |
| Passenger arrivals ('000) | 53 | 54 | 59 |
| Passenger departures ('000) | 52 | 50 | 60 |

Source: UN Economic Commission for Africa, *African Statistical Yearbook*.

# Tourism

|  | 1990 | 1991 | 1992 |
|---|---|---|---|
| Tourist arrivals ('000) | 98 | 98 | 91 |

Source: UN, *Statistical Yearbook*.

SIERRA LEONE
*Statistical Survey, Directory*

## Communications Media

|  | 1990 | 1991 | 1992 |
|---|---|---|---|
| Radio receivers ('000 in use) | 925 | 950 | 980 |
| Television receivers ('000 in use) | 42 | 43 | 45 |
| Daily newspapers | 1 | n.a. | 1 |
| Average circulation ('000 copies) | 10 | n.a. | 10 |

**1988** (provisional figures): Non-daily newspapers: 6 (average circulation 65,000 copies).

Source: UNESCO, *Statistical Yearbook*.

**Telephones** ('000 main lines in use): 15 in 1991 (Source: UN, *Statistical Yearbook*).

## Education

(1991/92)

| | Institutions | Teachers | Pupils Males | Pupils Females | Pupils Total |
|---|---|---|---|---|---|
| Primary | 1,792 | 10,051 | 184,880 | 130,266 | 315,146 |
| Secondary: | | | | | |
| General | 217 | 3,924 | 44,093 | 28,423 | 72,516 |
| Vocational | 24 | 496 | 2,056 | 2,223 | 4,279 |
| Teacher training* | 6 | 254 | n.a. | n.a. | 2,650 |
| Higher | 2* | 600† | n.a. | n.a. | 4,742† |

* 1984/85 figure(s).   † 1990 figure.

Source: mainly Department of Education, New England, Freetown.

# Directory

## The Constitution

Following a military coup on 29 April 1992, the Constitutions of 1978 and 1991 were suspended, and a governing council, known as the National Provisional Ruling Council (NPRC), was established. On 4 May a proclamation retroactively provided for the establishment of the NPRC (which was to comprise a maximum of 30 members, including a Chairman and a Vice-Chairman), the dissolution of the House of Representatives and the suspension of all political activity. In July the NPRC was designated the Supreme Council of State, and the Cabinet was reconstituted as the Council of Secretaries (headed by the Chief Secretary of State). The Council of Secretaries was to be responsible for government administration, subject to the authority of the NPRC. Three members of the NPRC were to act as Principal Liaison Officers, with responsibility for the supervision of government administration in a number of departments (which replaced the existing ministries).

In 1993 the Government announced the adoption of a transitional programme, which provided for the installation of a civilian government by January 1996, following multi-party presidential and legislative elections. In January 1994 a 19-member National Advisory Council, comprising representatives of various non-governmental organizations, promulgated a number of constitutional proposals, which were to be submitted for approval in a national referendum. The constitutional recommendations (which included a number of similar provisions to the 1991 Constitution) stipulated that: executive power was to be vested in the President, who was to be required to consult with the Cabinet (except in the event of a national emergency), and was to be restricted to a tenure of two four-year terms of office; only Sierra Leonean nationals of more than 40 years of age were to qualify to contest a presidential election; the successful presidential candidate was to secure a minimum of 50% of votes cast nationally, and at least 25% of the votes cast in each of the four provinces; the legislature was to comprise a House of Representatives, which was to be elected by universal adult suffrage for a term of five years, and a 30-member upper chamber, the Senate, which was to include a number of regional representatives and five presidential nominees; members of the House of Representatives were not to be permitted to hold ministerial portfolios concurrently. In October 1994 a draft Constitution was submitted for approval to the Government.

## The Government

### HEAD OF STATE

**Chairman of the Supreme Council of State:** Capt. VALENTINE E. M. STRASSER (took office 6 May 1992).

### SUPREME COUNCIL OF STATE
**National Provisional Ruling Council**
(June 1995)

Capt. VALENTINE E. M. STRASSER (Chairman)
Capt. JULIUS MAADA BIO (Deputy Chairman)
Capt. KOMBA S. MONDEH (Principal Liaison Officer)
Capt. CHARLES EMILE M'BAYO (Principal Liaison Officer)
Capt. KAREFA A. F. KARGBO (Principal Liaison Officer)
JOHN BENJAMIN (Secretary-General)
Brig. (retd) J. S. GOTTOR
Lt-Col DANIEL KOBINA ANDERSON
Lt-Col K. H. CONTEH
Lt-Col JOSEPH PHILIP GBONDO
Lt-Col AKIM A. GIBRIL
Lt-Col A. B. Y. KOROMA
Lt-Col S. F. Y. KOROMA
Lt-Col GABRIEL S. T. MANI
Lt-Commdr M. T. DIABBY
Maj. S. O. WILLIAMS
Lt-Col FALLAH SEWAH
Capt. IDRIS KAMARA
Capt. S. T. NYUMA
F. M. KAILIE
Sgt K. F. JALLOH
Cpl K. KARGBO
Lt-Col (retd) S. B. JUMU

### COUNCIL OF SECRETARIES
(June 1995)

**Chief Secretary of State and Secretary of State for Health and Social Services:** Lt-Col AKIM A. GIBRIL.

**Secretary of State for Marine Resources:** Dr ERNEST NDOMAHINA.

**Secretary of State for Youth, Sports and Social Mobilization:** SULAIMAN BANJA TEJAN-SIE.

**Secretary of State for Finance:** Dr JOHN KARIMU.

**Secretary of State for Foreign Affairs and International Co-operation:** Dr ABBAS BUNDU.

**Secretary of State for Development and Economic Planning:** VICTOR BRANDON.

**Secretary of State for Agriculture and Forestry:** LESLEY SCOTT.

**Secretary of State for Mineral Resources:** Lt-Col ROBERT YIRA KOROMA.

**Secretary of State for Trade, Industry and State Enterprises:** Dr KANDEH YUNKELLA.

**Secretary of State for Works:** Lt-Col JOSEPH PHILIP GBONDO.

**Secretary of State for Information, Broadcasting and Culture:** ARNOLD BISHOP-GOODING.

**Secretary of State for Labour:** ALEX BROWNE.

**Secretary of State for Energy and Power:** SYLVANUS E. A. TAYLOR-LEWIS.

**Secretary of State for Education:** CHRISTIANA THORPE.

**Secretary of State for Transport and Communications:** HINDOLO S. TRYE.

**Attorney-General and Secretary of State for Judicial Affairs:** CLAUDE CAMPBELL.

**Secretary of State for Lands, Housing and the Environment:** Dr MOHAMED SAMURA.

**Secretary of State for Internal Affairs and Rural Development:** SAM MALIGI.

# SIERRA LEONE

**Secretary of State for Tourism:** Maj. (retd) GABRIEL ABBAS TURAY.
**Secretary of State for the Eastern Province:** Maj. BASHIRU CONTEH.
**Secretary of State for the Northern Province:** Lt-Col A. B. Y. KOROMA.
**Secretary of State for the Southern Province:** Maj. SAMUEL WILLIAMS.

### DEPARTMENTS

**Office of the Chief Secretary of State:** Freetown.
**Department of Agriculture and Forestry:** Youyi Bldg, Freetown; telex 3418.
**Department of Development and Economic Planning:** Freetown.
**Department of Education:** New England, Freetown; tel. (22) 240846.
**Department of Energy and Power:** Electricity House, 4th Floor, Siaka Stevens St, Freetown; tel. (22) 222669.
**Department of Finance:** Secretariat Bldg, George St, Freetown; tel. (22) 226911; telex 3363.
**Department of Foreign Affairs and International Co-operation:** Gloucester St, Freetown; tel. (22) 224778; telex 3218.
**Department of Health and Social Services:** Youyi Bldg, 4th Floor, Brookfields, Freetown; tel. (22) 241500.
**Department of Information, Broadcasting and Culture:** Youyi Bldg, 8th Floor, Brookfields, Freetown; tel. (22) 240034; telex 3218.
**Department of Internal Affairs and Rural Development:** State Ave, Freetown; tel. (22) 223447.
**Department of Justice:** Guma Bldg, Lamina Sankoh St, Freetown; tel. (22) 226733.
**Department of Labour:** Freetown.
**Department of Lands, Housing and the Environment:** Freetown.
**Department of Marine Resources:** Youyi Bldg, Freetown.
**Department of Mineral Resources:** Youyi Bldg, 5th Floor, Brookfields, Freetown; tel. (22) 241500.
**Department of Tourism:** Freetown.
**Department of Trade, Industry and State Enterprises:** Ministerial Bldg, George St, Freetown; tel. (22) 225211; telex 3218.
**Department of Transport and Communications:** Ministerial Bldg, 5th Floor, George St, Freetown; tel. (22) 225211.
**Department of Works:** New England, Freetown; tel. (22) 240101.
**Department of Youth, Sports and Social Mobilization:** Freetown.

## Legislature

### HOUSE OF REPRESENTATIVES

The House of Representatives was dissolved following the military coup of 29 April 1992. Under the provisions of a transitional programme, which was initiated in 1993, elections to a new bicameral legislature were to take place by the end of 1995.

## Political Organizations

All political activity was suspended following the military coup of 29 April 1992. Under the provisions of a transitional programme, which was initiated in 1993, the registration of political parties was to take place in June 1995, prior to elections later that year. In April 1995 the military Government formally rescinded the ban on political activity.

Prior to the 1992 coup, the following were among the active political parties:

**All-People's Congress (APC):** 39 Siaka Stevens St, Freetown; f. 1960; sole authorized political party 1978–91; merged with the Democratic People's Party in March 1992; Leader Maj.-Gen. JOSEPH SAIDU MOMOH.
**National Labour Party (NLP):** f. 1991; Leader G. E. E. PALMER.
**National Unity Movement (NUM):** f. 1991; Leader DESMOND FASHOLE LUKE.
**Progressive People's Party (PPP):** based in London, England; f. 1991; Leader Col (retd) AMBROSE GENDA.
**Sierra Leone Democratic Party (SLDP):** obtained legal recognition in Dec. 1991; has operated from the United Kingdom, since the 1992 military coup; Leader EDISON GORVIE.
**United Front of Political Movements (UNIFOM):** f. Sept. 1991 as alliance of parties opposed to the fmr APC Govt; Chair. THAIMU BANGURA; Sec.-Gen. ALPHA LAVALIE.
**Civic Development Movement (CDEM):** Freetown; f. 1991.

*Directory*

**National Action Party (NAP):** Freetown; obtained official registration in Nov. 1991; Leader SHEKA KANU.
**National Democratic Alliance (NDA):** f. 1991; Leader CYRIL FORAY.
**National Democratic Party (NDP):** obtained official registration in Nov. 1991; Chair. Dr ALUSINE FOFANAH.
**People's Democratic Party (PDP):** obtained official registration in Sept. 1991; Leader THAIMU BANGURA.
**Sierra Leone People's Party (SLPP):** f. 1991; obtained official registration in Nov. 1991; Leader SALIA JUSU-SHERIFF.
**Unity Party (UP):** obtained official registration in 1992.

In 1995 the following rebel movements were active:

**National Front for the Restoration of Democracy (NFRD):** emerged 1994; based in Guinea.
**Revolutionary United Front (RUF):** engaged in armed conflict with Govt since 1991; forces numbered c. 1,000 in mid-1993; Leader FODAY SANKOH.
**Sierra Leonean Initiative for Peace:** f. 1994 to assist RUF in armed conflict with Govt; based in Liberia; Leader ABDULAI SOUARE.

## Diplomatic Representation

### EMBASSIES AND HIGH COMMISSIONS IN SIERRA LEONE

**China, People's Republic:** 29 Wilberforce Loop, Freetown; tel. (22) 231797; Ambassador: GAO JIANCHONG.
**Côte d'Ivoire:** 1 Wesley St, Freetown; tel. (22) 223983; Chargé d'affaires: EDO VAN AS.
**Egypt:** 174C Wilkinson Rd, POB 652, Freetown; tel. (22) 231499; telex 3300; Ambassador: MOHAMED ABDEL SALAM MOUSSA.
**France:** 13 Lamina Sankoh St, POB 510, Freetown; tel. (22) 222477; telex 3238; Ambassador: JEAN-CLAUDE FORTUIT.
**Gambia:** 6 Wilberforce St, Freetown; tel. (22) 225191; High Commissioner: (vacant).
**Germany:** Santanno House, 10 Howe St, POB 728, Freetown; tel. (22) 222511; telex 3248; fax (22) 226213; Chargé d'affaires a.i.: ASTRID ILPER.
**Guinea:** 4 Liverpool St, Freetown; tel. (22) 223080; Ambassador: IBRAHIM CHÉRIF HAIDARA.
**Holy See:** 23 Jomo Kenyatta Rd, PMB 526, Freetown; tel. (22) 242131; fax (22) 240509; Apostolic Delegate: Most Rev. LUIGI TRAVAGLINO, Titular Archbishop of Lettere.
**Italy:** 32A Wilkinson Rd, POB 749, Freetown; tel. (22) 230995; telex 3456; Ambassador: RANIERI FORNARI.
**Korea, Republic:** 22 Wilberforce St, POB 1383, Freetown; tel. (22) 224269; telex 3313; Ambassador: KIM CHANG-SOK.
**Lebanon:** 22 Wilberforce St, POB 727, Freetown; tel. (22) 223513; Ambassador: Dr FAWAZ FAWAD.
**Liberia:** 30 Brookfields Rd, POB 276, Freetown; tel. (22) 240322; telex 3229; Chargé d'affaires: SAMUEL B. PETERS.
**Nigeria:** 37 Siaka Stevens St, Freetown; tel. (22) 224202; telex 3258; fax (22) 224219; High Commissioner: MUHAMMED CHADI ABUBAKAR.
**United Kingdom:** Standard Chartered Bank Bldg, Lightfoot-Boston St, Freetown; tel. (22) 223961; fax (22) 1445251; High Commissioner: IAN MCCLUNEY.
**USA:** Walpole and Siaka Stevens Sts, Freetown; tel. (22) 226481; telex 3509; fax (22) 225471; Ambassador: LAURALEE PETERS.

## Judicial System

The legal structure comprises the Supreme, Appeal, High, Magistrate and Local Courts. The laws applicable in Sierra Leone are local statutes, statutes of general application in England on 1 January 1880, and Common and Equity Law.

**The Supreme Court:** The ultimate court of appeal in both civil and criminal cases. In addition to its appellate jurisdiction, the Court has supervisory jurisdiction over all other courts and any adjudicating authority in Sierra Leone, and also original jurisdiction, to the exclusion of all other courts, in all matters relating to the interpretation or enforcement of any provision of the Constitution.
   **Chief Justice:** S. BECCLES-DAVIES (acting).
   **Supreme Court Justices:** C. A. HARDING, AGNES AWUNOR-RENNER.
**The Court of Appeal:** The Court of Appeal has jurisdiction to hear and determine appeals from decisions of the High Court in both criminal and civil matters, and also from certain statutory tri-

SIERRA LEONE
*Directory*

bunals. Appeals against its decisions may be made to the Supreme Court.
**Justices of Appeal:** S. C. E. Warne, C. S. Davies, S. T. Navo, M. S. Turay, E. C. Thompson-Davis, M. O. Taju-Deen, M. O. Adophy, George Gelaga King, Dr A. B. Y. Timbo, Virginia A. Wright.
**High Court:** The High Court has unlimited original jurisdiction in all criminal and civil matters. It also has appellate jurisdiction against decisions of Magistrates' Courts.
**Judges:** Francis C. Gbow, Ebun Thomas, D. E. M. Williams, Laura Marcus-Jones, L. B. O. Nylander, A. M. B. Tarawallie, O. H. Alghalli, W. A. O. Johnson, N. D. Alhadi, R. J. Bankole Thompson, M. E. T. Thompson, C. J. W. Atere-Roberts (acting).
**Magistrates' Courts:** In criminal cases the jurisdiction of the Magistrates' Courts is limited to summary cases and to preliminary investigations to determine whether a person charged with an offence should be committed for trial.
**Local Courts** have jurisdiction, according to native law and custom, in matters which are outside the jurisdiction of other courts.

## Religion

A large proportion of the population holds animist beliefs, although there are significant numbers of Islamic and Christian adherents.

### ISLAM

In 1990 Islamic adherents represented an estimated 30% of the total population.
**Ahmadiyya Muslim Mission:** 15 Bath St, Brookfields, POB 353, Freetown; Emir and Chief Missionary Khalil A. Mobashir.
**Kankaylay (Sierra Leone Muslim Men and Women's Association):** 15 Blackhall Rd, Kissy, POB 1168, Freetown; tel. (22) 250931; f. 1972; 500,000 mems; Pres. Alhaji Ibrahim Bemba Turay; Lady Pres. Haja Isata Kebe; Vice-Pres. Haja Seray Sillah.
**Sierra Leone Muslim Congress:** POB 875, Freetown; Pres. Alhaji Muhammad Sanusi Mustapha.

### CHRISTIANITY

**Council of Churches in Sierra Leone:** 4a Kingharman Rd, Brookfields, POB 404, Freetown; tel. (22) 240568; telex 3210; f. 1924; 17 mem. churches; Pres. Rev. Henry A. E. Jenkins; Gen. Sec. Rev. Amadu F. Kamara.

#### The Anglican Communion

The Church of the Province of West Africa has two dioceses in Sierra Leone.
**Bishop of Bo:** Rt Rev. Samuel Sao Gbonda, MacRobert St, POB 21, Bo, Southern Province.
**Bishop of Freetown:** (vacant), Bishopscourt, Fourah Bay Rd, POB 128, Freetown.

#### Baptist Churches

**Sierra Leone Baptist Convention:** POB 64, Lunsar; Pres. Rev. Joseph S. Mans; Sec. Rev. N. T. Dixon.
The Nigerian Baptist Convention is also active.

#### Methodist Churches

**Methodist Church Sierra Leone:** Wesley House, George St, POB 64, Freetown; tel. (22) 222216; autonomous since 1967; Pres. of Conf. Rev. Gershon F. H. Anderson; Sec. Rev. Christian V. A. Peacock; 26,421 mems.
**United Methodist Church:** UMC House, 31 Wallace Johnson St, Freetown; Presiding Bishop T. S. Bangura; 36,857 mems.
Other active Methodist bodies include the African Methodist Episcopal Church, the Wesleyan Church of Sierra Leone, the Countess of Huntingdon's Connexion and the West African Methodist Church.

#### The Roman Catholic Church

Sierra Leone comprises one archdiocese and two dioceses. At 31 December 1993 there were an estimated 129,355 adherents in the country, representing about 2.8% of the total population.
**Inter-territorial Catholic Bishops' Conference of The Gambia, Liberia and Sierra Leone:** Santanno House, POB 893, Freetown; tel. (22) 228240; telex 3311; fax (22) 228252; f. 1971; Pres. Rt Rev. John O'Riordan, Bishop of Kenema (Sierra Leone).
**Archbishop of Freetown and Bo:** Most Rev. Joseph Henry Ganda, Santanno House, POB 893, Freetown; tel. (22) 224590.

#### Other Christian Churches

The following are represented: the Christ Apostolic Church, the Church of the Lord (Aladura), the Evangelical Church, the Missionary Church of Africa, the Sierra Leone Church and the United Brethren in Christ.

### AFRICAN RELIGIONS

Beliefs, rites and practices are very diverse, varying between ethnic groups and between families in the same group.

## The Press

### DAILY

**Daily Mail:** 29–31 Rawdon St, POB 53, Freetown; tel. (22) 223191; f. 1931; govt-owned; Editor Aiah Martin Mondeh; circ. 10,000.

### PERIODICALS

**African Crescent:** 15 Bath St, POB 353, Brookfields, Freetown; Editor Maulana-Khalil A. Mobashir.
**The Catalyst:** Christian Literature Crusade Bookshop, 35 Circular Rd, POB 1465, Freetown; tel. (22) 224382; Editor Dr Leopold Foullah.
**Concord Times:** 139 Pademba Rd, Freetown; 3 a week; Editor Kingsley Lington.
**Leonean Sun:** 49 Main Rd, Wellington, Freetown; tel. (22) 223363; f. 1974; monthly; Editor Rowland Martyn.
**Liberty Voice:** 139 Pademba Rd, Freetown; tel. (22) 242100; Editor A. Mahdieu Savage.
**New Citizen:** 5 Hanna Benka-Coker St, Freetown; tel. (22) 241795; Editor I. Ben Kargbo.
**The New Globe:** 49 Bathurst St, Freetown; tel. (22) 228245; weekly; Man. Editor Sam Tumoe; circ. 4,000.
**The New Shaft:** 60 Old Railway Line, Brookfields, Freetown; tel. (22) 241093; 2 a week; independent; Editor Franklin Bunting-Davies; circ. 10,000.
**Progress:** 1 Short St, Freetown; tel. (22) 223588; weekly; independent; Editor Fode Kandeh; circ. 7,000.
**Sierra Leone Chamber of Commerce Journal:** Sierra Leone Chamber of Commerce, Industry and Agriculture, Guma Bldg, 5th Floor, Lamina Sankoh St, POB 502, Freetown; tel. (22) 226305; telex 3712; fax (22) 228005; monthly.
**Unity Now:** 82 Pademba Rd, Freetown; tel. (22) 227466; Editor Frank Kposowa.
**The Vision:** 60 Old Railway Line, Brookfields; tel. (22) 241273; Editor Siaka Massaquoi.
**Weekend Spark:** 7 Lamina Sankoh St, Freetown; tel. (22) 223397; f. 1983; weekly; independent; Editor Rowland Martyn; circ. 20,000.

### NEWS AGENCY

**Sierra Leone News Agency (SLENA):** 15 Wallace Johnson St, PMB 445, Freetown; tel. (22) 224921; telex 3603; fax (22) 224439; f. 1980; Dir and Editor-in-Chief Rod Mac-Johnson.

## Publishers

**Njala University Publishing Centre:** Njala University College, PMB, Freetown; science and technology, university textbooks.
**Sierra Leone University Press:** Fourah Bay College, POB 87, Freetown; tel. (22) 22491; telex 3210; fax (22) 224439; f. 1965; biography, history, Africana, religion, social science, university textbooks; Chair. Prof. Ernest H. Wright.
**United Christian Council Literature Bureau:** Bunumbu Press, POB 28, Bo; tel. (32) 462; books in Mende, Temne, Susu; Man. Dir Robert Sam-Kpakra.

### Government Publishing House

**Government Printer:** New England, Freetown; tel. (22) 241146.

## Radio and Television

In 1992 there were an estimated 980,000 radio receivers and 45,000 television receivers in use.
**Sierra Leone Broadcasting Service:** New England, Freetown; tel. (22) 240403; telex 3334; f. 1934; state-controlled; programmes mainly in English and the four main Sierra Leonean vernaculars, Mende, Limba, Temne and Krio; weekly broadcast in French; television service established 1963; colour transmissions since 1978; Dir-Gen. Babatunde Roland-May.

SIERRA LEONE *Directory*

## Finance

(cap. = capital; m. = million; res = reserves;
dep. = deposits; brs = branches; amounts in leone)

### BANKING

#### Central Bank

**Bank of Sierra Leone:** Siaka Stevens St, POB 30, Freetown; tel. (22) 226501; telex 3232; fax (22) 224764; f. 1964; cap. and res 24,671.3m., dep. 80,361m. (Dec. 1994); Gov. STEVE SWARRAY (acting); Dep. Gov. YVONNE GIBRIL.

#### Other Banks

**Barclays Bank of Sierra Leone Ltd:** 25–27 Siaka Stevens St, POB 12, Freetown; tel. (22) 222501; telex 3220; fax (22) 222563; f. 1971; cap. and res 1,722.7m., dep. 12,676.6m. (Dec. 1994); Chair. AUGUSTUS D. A. M'CORMACK; Man. Dir E. LLOYD-DAVIES; 16 brs and 1 agency.

**International Bank for Trade and Industry (Sierra Leone) Ltd:** 22 Wilberforce St, PMB 679, Freetown; tel. (22) 223610; telex 3463; fax (22) 223657; f. 1982; operations suspended in April 1994; cap. 2m., res 127.1m., dep. 1,607.6m. (Dec. 1992); Chair. MOHAMED REMI-LEKUN TEJAN-COLE.

**Meridien BIAO Bank Sierra Leone Ltd:** Lightfoot-Boston St, PMB 1237, Freetown; tel. (22) 226515; telex 3233; fax (22) 226214; cap. 385m., res 16.1m., dep. 2,023.2m. (Dec. 1994); Chair. SIYANGA MALUMO; Man. Dir RAYMOND ABOU SAMRA.

**National Development Bank Ltd:** Leone House, 6th Floor, 21–23 Siaka Stevens St, PMB, Freetown; tel. (22) 226791; telex 3589; fax (22) 224468; f. 1968; provides medium- and long-term finance and technical assistance to development-orientated enterprises; cap. and res 1,568.2m., dep. 1,229.6m. (Dec. 1994); Man. Dir CHRISTIAN J. SMITH; 3 brs.

**Sierra Leone Commercial Bank Ltd:** 29–31 Siaka Stevens St, Freetown; tel. (22) 225264; telex 3275; fax (22) 225292; f. 1973; state-owned; cap. 45m., res 1,299.8m., dep. 6,753.2m. (Dec. 1994); Chair. I. I. MAY-PARKER; Man. Dir S. B. KANU; 7 brs.

**Standard Chartered Bank Sierra Leone Ltd:** 12 Lightfoot-Boston St, POB 1155, Freetown; tel. (22) 229294; telex 3523; fax (22) 225760; f. 1971; cap. 20.1m., res 1,105.6m., dep. 10,942.1m. (Dec. 1994); Chair. LLOYD A. DURING; Man. Dir JOHN JANES; 12 brs.

### INSURANCE

**Aureol Insurance Co Ltd:** Kissy House, 54 Siaka Stevens St, POB 647, Freetown; tel. (22) 223435; telex 3222; fax (22) 229336; f. 1987; Chair. LLOYD DURING; Man. Dir S. G. BENJAMIN.

**National Insurance Co Ltd:** 18–20 Walpole St, PMB 84, Freetown; tel. (22) 223892; telex 3344; fax (22) 226097; f. 1972; state-owned; Chair. J. T. SARJAH-WRIGHT; CEO A. N. YASKEY.

**New India Assurance Co Ltd:** 18 Wilberforce St, POB 340, Freetown; tel. (22) 226453; telex 3510; fax (22) 222494; Man. Dir V. KRISHNAN.

**Reliance Insurance Trust Corp. Ltd:** 24 Siaka Stevens St, Freetown; tel. (22) 225115; telex 3664; fax (22) 228051; fax (22) 228051; f. 1985; Chair. S. S. OMISSIONS; Man. Dir E. B. KOROMA.

**Sierra Leone Insurance Co Ltd:** 31 Lightfoot Boston St, POB 836, Freetown.

## Trade and Industry

### CHAMBER OF COMMERCE

**Sierra Leone Chamber of Commerce, Industry and Agriculture:** Guma Bldg, 5th Floor, Lamina Sankoh St, POB 502, Freetown; tel. (22) 226305; telex 3712; fax (22) 228005; f. 1961; 215 mems; Pres. Alhaji MOHAMED MUSA KING.

### GOVERNMENT ORGANIZATION

**Government Gold and Diamond Office (GGDO):** c/o Bank of Sierra Leone, Siaka Stevens St, Freetown; tel. (22) 222600; telex 3566; fax (22) 229064; f. 1985 to succeed Precious Minerals Marketing Co (PMMC) as govt regulatory agency for diamonds and gold; combats illicit trade; Chair. W. A. JONES.

### EMPLOYERS' ASSOCIATIONS

**Sierra Leone Employers' Federation:** POB 562, Freetown; Chair. DONALD C. SMYTHE-MACAULAY; Exec. Officer A. E. BENJAMIN.

**Sierra Leone Chamber of Mines:** POB 456, Freetown; tel. (22) 226082; f. 1965; comprises the principal mining concerns; Pres. D. J. S. FRASER; Exec. Officer N. H. T. BOSTON.

### TRADE UNIONS

**Artisans', Ministry of Works Employees' and General Workers' Union:** 4 Pultney St, Freetown; f. 1946; 14,500 mems; Pres. IBRAHIM LANGLEY; Gen. Sec. TEJAN A. KASSIM.

**Sierra Leone Labour Congress:** 35 Wallace Johnson St, POB 1333, Freetown; tel. (22) 226869; f. 1966; approx. 51,000 mems in 19 affiliated unions; Pres. H. M. BARRIE; Sec. Gen. KANDEH YILLA.

Principal affiliated unions:

**Clerical, Mercantile and General Workers' Union:** 35 Wallace Johnson St, Freetown; f. 1945; 3,600 mems; Pres. M. D. BENJAMIN; Gen. Sec. M. B. WILLIAMS.

**Sierra Leone Association of Journalists:** Freetown; Pres. SIAKA MASSAQUOI.

**Sierra Leone Dockworkers' Union:** 165 Fourah Bay Rd, Freetown; f. 1962; 2,650 mems; Pres. D. F. KANU; Gen. Sec. A. C. CONTEH.

**Sierra Leone Motor Drivers' Union:** 10 Charlotte St, Freetown; f. 1960; 1,900 mems; Pres. A. W. HASSAN; Gen. Sec. ALPHA KAMARA.

**Sierra Leone Teachers' Union:** 27 Goderich St, Freetown; f. 1951; 5,500 mems; Pres. M'BAN KABU; Sec.-Gen. A. O. TIMBO.

**Sierra Leone Transport, Agricultural and General Workers' Union:** 4 Pultney St, Freetown; f. 1946; 1,600 mems; Pres. S. O. SAWYERR-MANLEY; Gen. Sec. S. D. KARGBO.

**United Mineworkers' Union:** 35 Wallace Johnson St, Freetown; f. 1944; 6,500 mems; Pres. H. M. BARRIE; Gen. Sec. S. D. GBENDA.

Also affiliated to the Sierra Leone Labour Congress: **General Construction Workers' Union, Municipal and Local Government Employees' Union, Sierra Leone National Seamen's Union.**

### CO-OPERATIVES AND MARKETING BOARDS

In 1975 there were 1,024 primary co-operatives with a total membership of 46,762. There were 734 thrift and credit co-operative societies, 12 consumer co-operatives, five secondary societies, 270 marketing societies, eight producer co-operatives, and a central bank for all co-operatives. The Co-operative Department, which is based in Freetown with eight area offices throughout the provinces, is supervised by a Registrar of Co-operatives within the Department of Trade, Industry and State Enterprises.

## Transport

### RAILWAYS

**Marampa Mineral Railway:** Delco House, POB 735, Freetown; tel. (22) 222556; telex 3460; 84 km of track linking iron ore mines at Marampa with Pepel port; mining operations at Marampa have been suspended since 1985; Gen. Man. SYL KHANU.

### ROADS

In 1992 there were an estimated 11,674 km of classified roads, including 1,390 km of main roads and 1,630 km of secondary roads; about 1,284 km of the total network was paved. In 1993 the Government announced a seven-year road rehabilitation programme, which, at an estimated cost of US $100m., was to be financed by the World Bank.

**Sierra Leone Road Transport Corpn:** Blackhall Rd, POB 1008, Freetown; tel. (22) 250442; telex 3395; fax (22) 250000; f. 1965; state-owned; operates transport services throughout the country; Gen. Man. DANIEL R. W. FAUX.

### INLAND WATERWAYS

Recognized launch routes, including the coastal routes from Freetown northward to the Great and Little Scarcies rivers and southward to Bonthe, total almost 800 km. Although some of the upper reaches of the rivers are navigable only between July and September, a considerable volume of traffic uses the rivers.

### SHIPPING

**Sierra Leone National Shipping Co Ltd:** 45 Cline St, POB 935, Freetown; tel. (22) 250881; telex 3260; fax (22) 223222; f. 1972; state-owned; shipping, clearing and forwarding agency; representatives for foreign lines; Gen. Man. PAUL K. NIELSEN.

**Sierra Leone Ports Authority:** Queen Elizabeth II Quay, PMB 386, Cline Town, Freetown; tel. (22) 250111; telex 3262; fax (22) 250616; f. 1965; parastatal body, supervised by the Dept of Transport and Communications; operates the port of Freetown, which has full facilities for ocean-going vessels; Gen. Man. Capt. H. M. FRIEDRICHS.

**Sierra Leone Shipping Agencies Ltd:** Deep Water Quay, Cline-town, POB 74, Freetown; tel. (22) 250882; telex 3260; fax (22) 250400; f. 1949; Man. Dir W. SCHNEIDER.

SIERRA LEONE

**UMARCO (Freetown) Ltd:** POB 417, Freetown; telex 3216; shipping agents; Gen. Man. R. HUGHES.

### CIVIL AVIATION

There is an international airport at Lungi.

**Directorate of Civil Aviation:** Department of Transport and Communications, Ministerial Bldg, 5th Floor, George St, Freetown; tel. (22) 222106; Dir T. T. A. VANDY.

**Sierra Leone National Airlines:** 25 Pultney St, POB 285, Freetown; tel. (22) 222075; telex 3242; fax (22) 222026; f. 1982; state-owned; operates domestic and regional services, and scheduled flights to Paris; Chair. S. A. PALMER.

## Tourism

The main attractions for tourists are the beaches, the mountains and the game reserves. In 1992 an estimated 91,000 tourists visited Sierra Leone, while receipts from the tourism sector totalled US $17m.

**National Tourist Board:** International Conference Centre, Aberdeen Hill, POB 1435, Freetown; tel. (22) 272520; fax (22) 272197; f. 1990; Gen. Man. CECIL J. WILLIAMS.

# SINGAPORE

## Introductory Survey

### Location, Climate, Language, Religion, Flag, Capital

The Republic of Singapore lies in South-East Asia. The country comprises one main island and about 60 offshore islands, situated approximately 137 km (85 miles) north of the Equator, off the southernmost tip of the Malay Peninsula, to which it is linked by a causeway. The climate is equatorial, with a uniformly high daily and annual temperature varying between 24°C and 27°C (75°F–80°F). Relative humidity is high (often exceeding 90%), and the average annual rainfall is 236 cm (93 ins). There are no well-defined wet and dry seasons. There are four official languages—Malay (the national language), Chinese (Mandarin), Tamil and English. The language of administration is English. Chinese dialects were spoken, as a first language, by 37% of the population in 1990. The principal religions are Daoism, Buddhism, Islam, Christianity and Hinduism. The national flag (proportions 3 by 2) has two equal horizontal stripes, of red and white, with a white crescent moon and five white stars in the upper hoist. The capital is Singapore City.

### Recent History

In 1826 the East India Company formed the Straits Settlements by the union of Singapore and the dependencies of Penang and Malacca on the Malay Peninsula. They came under British rule in 1867 as a crown colony. Singapore was occupied by Japan for three years during the Second World War. At the end of the war, following Japan's defeat, Singapore was governed by a British military administration. When civil rule was restored in 1946, Singapore was detached from the other Straits Settlements and became a separate crown colony. A new Constitution, adopted in February 1955, introduced some measure of self-government, and in June 1959 the state achieved complete internal self-government, with Lee Kuan Yew as Prime Minister. The Federation of Malaysia came into being in September 1963, with Singapore as a constituent state. On 9 August 1965, following irreconcilable differences with the central Government in Malaysia, Singapore seceded from the federation and became an independent country. In September 1965 it joined the UN, and in October it became a member of the Commonwealth. In December Singapore was proclaimed a republic, with a President as constitutional Head of State. In May 1973 the last major ties with Malaysia, concerning currency and finance, were renounced. In September 1972 Lee Kuan Yew's ruling People's Action Party (PAP) won all 65 parliamentary seats in a general election that was also contested by five opposition parties.

After independence the Government supported a strong US military presence in South-East Asia. However, with the collapse of US influence in the area during 1974 and 1975, Singapore adopted a conciliatory attitude towards the People's Republic of China and its communist neighbours. The Government called for the removal of foreign bases from member states of the Association of South East Asian Nations (ASEAN—see p. 109), and advocated a policy of neutrality. From 1976 Singapore aimed to consolidate its trade links with China, although diplomatic relations were not established until 1982.

At general elections in December 1976 and December 1980, the PAP won all 69 seats in the enlarged Parliament. The PAP's monopoly ended in October 1981, however, when the Secretary-General of the opposition Workers' Party, J. B. Jeyaretnam, won a by-election. This posed no direct threat, but, in order to reassert its authority, the Government increased its control over trade unions and restructured the ownership of major newspapers.

At the general election in December 1984 the PAP was again returned to power with a large majority in Parliament (which was now enlarged to 79 seats), but the party lost two seats to opposition parties, and its share of the total votes was reduced to 62.9% from 75% in 1980. A constitutional amendment, approved in July 1984, provided for up to three 'non-constituency' parliamentary seats for the opposition (with restricted voting rights) if none were won in the election. One extra seat was subsequently offered to the losing opposition candidate with the highest percentage of votes. This seat was refused, however, in January 1985 by the Workers' Party. In March the state President, Devan Nair, resigned. A new President, Wee Kim Wee (hitherto the Chairman of the Singapore Broadcasting Corporation), was elected in August.

During 1986 the Government exhibited signs of increasing intolerance towards its critics. In August amendments to the Parliament (Privileges, Immunities and Powers) Act were hurriedly adopted, enabling Parliament to fine, expel or imprison members who were deemed to have abused their parliamentary privileges. In the same month Parliament also approved a Newspaper and Printing Presses (Amendment) Act, which empowered the Government to restrict the distribution of foreign publications that were deemed to be interfering in domestic political affairs; the circulation of several foreign periodicals was subsequently restricted, and in 1987 Lee Kuan Yew sued two foreign publications for libel in courts in Malaysia and Hong Kong.

In November 1986 Jeyaretnam (who was one of the two opposition members of Parliament) was sentenced to one month's imprisonment and fined S $5,000 (enough, according to the Constitution, to deprive him of his parliamentary seat and prevent him from standing for election for five years), when the Supreme Court upheld a conviction for perjury in connection with bankruptcy proceedings brought against the Workers' Party four years previously. In February 1987 Jeyaretnam was also fined by a parliamentary committee for abuse of privilege, having made allegations of government interference in the judiciary, and further fines were imposed on him for publishing 'distorted' accounts of an earlier hearing of the committee and (in May) for alleged contempt of Parliament and abuse of parliamentary privilege. In October Jeyaretnam's removal from the Law Society register was ordered by a three-judge court. An appeal to the Judicial Committee of the Privy Council in the United Kingdom (then the highest court of appeal for Singapore) resulted, in October 1988, in his reinstatement as a practising lawyer. During the course of the appeal, investigations into Jeyaretnam's previous convictions revealed that they had been 'fatally flawed'. However, since the criminal case had been considered in the District Court, where there was no right of appeal to the Privy Council, the original convictions prevented Jeyaretnam from re-entering Parliament without a presidential pardon. In May 1989 Wee Kim Wee refused to grant a pardon to Jeyaretnam.

In May and June 1987 the Government detained 22 persons (including 10 Roman Catholic church workers and four members of Jeyaretnam's Workers' Party) without trial, under the Internal Security Act, for alleged involvement in a 'Marxist conspiracy' to subvert state organizations. The arrests were denounced by Jeyaretnam, who claimed that the Government wished to intimidate Singaporeans so that they would not support opposition parties. In November the Government was also criticized by international human rights groups, including Amnesty International, for its refusal to present evidence of such a conspiracy in court; they requested an inquiry into the alleged torture of detainees, and urged Singapore to sign and observe the International Covenant on Civil and Political Rights. By December most of the alleged conspirators had been released, but eight of them were rearrested in April 1988, after complaining that they had been tortured while in detention. Four prisoners were released by June 1988, and in December a further four detainees were released in accordance with a ruling by the Court of Appeal, based on a fault in their detention orders. They were immediately rearrested. The trial had, however, established a precedent for the judicial review of cases brought under the Internal Security Act, including the acceptability to the courts of evidence used in warrants for the arrest of suspects. In January 1989 Parliament approved legislation ensuring that the judiciary could examine such detentions only on technical grounds, and abolishing the right of appeal to the Privy Council in cases brought under the Internal Security Act. In March three detainees were released.

The two remaining prisoners (of the original 22) remained in detention until June 1990.

A general election was held in September 1988. The electoral system was altered so that 39 of the existing 79 constituencies were replaced by 13 'group representation constituencies', which had to be contested by teams of three representatives for each party, at least one of whom was to be a member of an ethnic minority (i.e. non-Chinese). The declared aim was to ensure the presence of racial minorities in Parliament; in practice, however, opposition parties with few resources were handicapped by the difficulty of presenting three candidates. The PAP won 80 of the elective seats (which now totalled 81); one was gained by the leader of the Singapore Democratic Party (SDP), Chiam See Tong. Two 'non-constituency' seats were offered to Francis Seow (Workers' Party) and Lee Siew Choh (Socialist Front). In December, however, while Seow (who had already been detained in May under the Internal Security Act for organizing a meeting between a US diplomat and lawyers critical of the Government) was in the USA, undergoing medical treatment, he was convicted *in absentia* for tax evasion and fined S$19,000, which meant that he was legally prevented from taking his seat in Parliament. In January 1989 Lee began his eighth term as Prime Minister, and announced that he would retire from the premiership before the expiry of the term. This announcement was followed by a statement from Goh Chok Tong (the First Deputy Prime Minister and Lee's chosen successor) that Lee was adopting a secondary and more advisory role in the government of the country. In August Parliament unanimously re-elected Wee Kim Wee for a further four-year term as President.

In early 1990 Parliament approved legislation enabling the Government to nominate as many as six unelected MPs. This provoked limited opposition from PAP MPs. The politically neutral nominated MPs would be appointed for two years and would be able to vote on all legislative proposals except those concerning financial and constitutional affairs.

On 28 November 1990 Lee was duly replaced as Prime Minister by Goh Chok Tong. Lee remained in the Cabinet as Senior Minister to the Prime Minister's Office and retained the position of Secretary-General of the PAP. The other major changes to Lee's former Cabinet were the promotion of his son, Brig.-Gen. Lee Hsien Loong, to be a Deputy Prime Minister and the creation of a new Ministry for Information and the Arts, under Brig.-Gen. George Yeo, previously the Minister of State for Finance and Foreign Affairs.

In January 1991 the Constitution was amended to provide for a popularly-elected presidency with extensive powers of veto on proposed financial legislation, a role as final arbiter in cases of detention for reasons of national security, and influence in civil and military appointments. The changes to the functions of the President, formerly elected by Parliament to a largely ceremonial position, were initially proposed by Lee in 1984, and were criticized by members of opposition parties as being intended to accommodate Lee, following his resignation as Prime Minister. However, Lee stated, during the 1988 election campaign, that he would not be a candidate in the first presidential election under the new system. Parliament approved the legislation to amend the Constitution by 75 votes to one (the single dissenting vote was cast by the only opposition MP with full voting rights, Chiam See Tong). Under the amendment, Wee Kim Wee was to continue in office until October 1993. Legislation empowering him with the authority of an elected president took effect from 30 November 1991. Candidates for the presidency were limited to those who had held the post of a minister, chief justice or senior civil servant or were at the head of a large company. The candidates were to be scrutinized by a new presidential election committee, which was to comprise the head of the Society of Accountants, the Chairman of the Public Service Commission and a member of the Presidential Council of Human Rights. The latter two officials were appointed by the Government, prompting fears that the selected candidates would be those favoured by the PAP. The constitutional amendment also included a clause increasing the number of candidates required to contest a 'group representation constituency' in a general election to a minimum of three and a maximum of four, one of whom was to be a member of an ethnic minority.

In early 1991 the Government promoted the acceptance of five 'shared values', based on Confucian philosophy, as the basis of a national ideology, first discussed in January 1989. Critics alleged that the ideology would be used to reinforce support for the PAP and to obviate opposition challenges. Goh attempted, in principle, to introduce a more 'open' consultative form of government. He instituted an extensive programme of community visits to assess popular opinion, showing solicitude for the views of the minority Malay and Indian communities. Although film censorship was relaxed, restrictions on the foreign press remained in force and the Internal Security Act was not repealed. In June 1991 Goh implemented a minor cabinet reshuffle, relinquishing the defence portfolio to Dr Yeo Ning Hong, hitherto the Minster of Communications and Second Minister of Defence (Policy), and elevating younger members of the Cabinet to full ministerial status.

In early August 1991 Goh, seeking a popular mandate for his style of government, announced that there would be a general election at the end of the month. Under a plan conceived by Chiam, the opposition parties contested only 40 of the 81 seats, thus guaranteeing an absolute majority for the incumbent PAP. Chiam issued an appeal to the electorate to take the opportunity to elect a strong opposition. Goh indicated, during his campaign, that a failure to receive a popular endorsement would result in a return to a more authoritarian and paternalistic form of government. At the election, held on 31 August, the PAP's share of the vote declined from 63.2% in 1988 to 61.0%, and the party won 77 seats, compared with 80 in 1988. Chiam's SDP secured three seats, and the Workers' Party one seat. In early September there was a minor cabinet reshuffle, largely to replace a defeated minister. Jeyaretnam was unable to contest the election, as his disqualification remained in force until the beginning of November 1991. In response to Jeyaretnam's accusations that he had been deliberately excluded from the election and also because the election schedule had prevented the PAP from presenting enough new candidates, Goh had announced, prior to the polls, that he would organize by-elections within 12–18 months of the general election.

In October 1991 Seow, who had been in exile in the USA since 1988, was convicted *in absentia* of a further 60 offences involving tax evasion, rendering him ineligible to contest any potential by-election. Later that month Jeyaretnam paid S$392,838 in legal costs to Lee, thus avoiding bankruptcy, which would have prevented his candidacy. Lee had instituted a successful defamation suit against Jeyaretnam in 1990, over remarks made by Jeyaretnam at a 1988 election rally. In January 1992 another unsuccessful opposition candidate was arrested and charged with parking violations.

Following the 1991 general election, Lee, who had temporarily withdrawn from public attention after Goh's accession to the premiership, resumed a prominent role in domestic politics. He attributed the decline in PAP support to neglect of the Mandarin-educated ethnic Chinese majority, and advocated a greater emphasis on Chinese culture and language. In January 1992 a minor cabinet reorganization was necessitated by the resignation of the Minister of Education. In April Goh announced that the level of electoral support among inhabitants would be one of the criteria used to determine the order in which refurbishments would be undertaken in public housing estates. Since about 86% of Singaporeans live in public housing, this was widely interpreted as a warning against voting for the opposition in the forthcoming by-elections.

Prior to the convening of Parliament in mid-September 1992 the Government appointed the maximum of six nominated MPs. This was widely regarded as an attempt to discourage support for opposition candidates in the impending by-elections. In October the implementation of legislation prohibiting MPs from using the ground floors of public housing blocks as office space adversely affected all four opposition MPs, who were unable to afford commercial rents, owing to a shortage of party funds.

In November 1992 Goh announced to the Central Executive Committee of the PAP that the renewal of national leadership was the party's most urgent consideration. This statement was followed two days later by the public disclosure that both Deputy Prime Ministers, Lee Hsien Loong and Ong Teng Cheong, had been diagnosed as suffering from cancer. The revelation strengthened Goh's position as Prime Minister, since many had previously regarded his incumbency as an interim arrangement prior to Lee Hsien Loong's accession to the premiership. At the beginning of December Goh was unanimously elected to replace Lee Kuan Yew (who proposed his candidacy) as Secretary-General of the PAP.

In December 1992 Goh resigned his parliamentary seat (which formed part of a four-member 'group representation constituency') in order to contest a by-election. Jeyaretnam was unable to contest the by-election as only three candidates from the Workers' Party registered with the authorities. The results of the by-election were regarded as an endorsement of Goh's leadership, as the four PAP candidates received 72.9% of the votes cast, while the opposition SDP secured 24.5%. Goh subsequently appointed his political associate, Suppiah Dhanabalan, Minister of Trade and Industry, pending the complete recovery from illness of Lee Hsien Loong. Suppiah had resigned as Minister of National Development in August, owing to alleged differences of opinion with Lee Hsien Loong.

In March 1993 Chee Soon Juan, who contested the December by-election as a candidate for the SDP, was dismissed from his post as a lecturer at the National University of Singapore for 'dishonest conduct'. After an unsuccessful appeal against his dismissal Chee began a 'hunger strike' to protest against his treatment. The Government denied that the dismissal was politically motivated, and proceedings were initiated by university officials to sue Chee for defamation. In June, following a rejection by the SDP Central Committee of a motion of censure proposed by Chiam against Chee for bringing the party into disrepute, Chiam resigned as Secretary-General of the party. Chee replaced him as Acting Secretary-General, pending party elections in early 1995. In August 1993 the SDP expelled Chiam for alleged indiscipline; however, a High Court ruling in December declared the expulsion 'illegal and invalid'. (This enabled Chiam to retain his seat in Parliament, as under the Constitution a member of the legislature was obliged to relinquish his seat if he resigned or was expelled from the party he had been elected to represent.) The following month, under a judicial ruling, a 'breakaway' central executive committee, formed in 1993 by a faction of the SDP that remained loyal to Chiam, was declared void. Chee subsequently published a book entitled *Dare to Change*, which demanded greater democracy and was adopted as official party policy by the SDP in June 1994. The SDP policy also described the need to develop a united opposition in preparation for the next general election; however, Goh declared his intention to continue the present administration for a full term, making it unlikely that an election would be held before 1996. In January 1995 Chee was elected Secretary-General of the SDP and, a week later, Chiam (who had declined his nomination for the post) was asked to resign from the party for failing to state publicly his loyalty to Chee.

Meanwhile, in August 1993 Ong Teng Cheong was elected President with 58.7% of the votes cast. Contrary to expectation, however, the only other candidate, Chua Kim Yeow, a former government official, who adopted an apolitical position, secured a substantial proportion (41.3%) of the vote. The candidacies of both Jeyaretnam and Tan Soo Phuan, another member of the Workers' Party, were rejected by the Presidential Election Committee on the grounds that they were unsuitable 'in regard to integrity, good character and reputation'.

In October 1993 two journalists and three economists were brought to trial under the Official Secrets Act for prematurely disclosing an official economic growth estimate. The gravity with which the Government viewed the case was demonstrated by the appearance of the Attorney-General, Chan Sek Keong, for the prosecution. In March 1994 all five defendants were convicted of breaching the Official Secrets Act (although they did not receive custodial sentences), thus re-establishing the Government's strict control of official information.

In mid-December 1993 Goh announced a cabinet reorganization, most of which took effect in early January 1994. Owing to the complete remission of Lee Hsien Loong's illness, he was to supervise the trade and industry and defence portfolios, although each ministry was assigned a separate minister. Among other changes, Wong Kan Seng and Prof. Shanmugam Jayakumar exchanged the foreign and home affairs portfolios, although Jayakumar retained responsibility for law. When the term of office of the six nominated MPs expired in 1994, two of them were re-appointed following a general consensus that the contribution they had made warranted a retention of the system of nominees. A Maintenance of Parents Bill, introduced by a nominated MP, Dr Walter Woon, in July, which offered destitute parents the right to claim maintenance from their children and sought to alleviate the problem of the ageing population, had received widespread support. Senior Minister Lee suggested in May that, in order to avoid elderly persons' gaining undue influence over government policies, an extra vote might be given to Singaporeans (aged 35–60 years) who were married with children.

In May 1995 presidential authority was effectively limited when a three-member tribunal, headed by the Chief Justice, decided that the President could not block legislation restricting his power of veto to non-constitutional legislation.

The collapse of the British banking group, Barings PLC, in February 1995, following unchecked losses incurred by a British trader based in Singapore (on the Singapore International Monetary Exchange Ltd—SIMEX—and the Osaka Securities Exchange in Japan), prompted the Singaporean Ministry of Finance to launch a formal investigation, and SIMEX to review the regulation of the futures exchange. The Government was anxious that the affair should not harm the financial reputation of Singapore. The trader, Nick Leeson (who had fled from Singapore before the losses were exposed), was detained in early March in Germany, from where, in April, the Singaporean authorities applied for his extradition. Leeson was charged on 12 counts of forgery and fraud.

As a member of ASEAN, Singapore was active during the 1980s in encouraging a peaceful settlement in Cambodia, favouring the establishment of a neutral government in that country. Relations with Indonesia improved in the late 1980s: the process of establishing joint military training facilities with Indonesia, which had begun in 1986, was accomplished in February and March 1989 by the signing of two agreements. In September 1994 Singapore and Malaysia agreed to settle their long-standing dispute over the ownership of Pedra Branca Island (Batu Puteh) by referring the case to the International Court of Justice in The Hague, the Netherlands. During 1994 Indonesia and Singapore continued discussions through bilateral ministerial committees on issues including the mutual development of water resources and tourism.

In mid-March 1995 the execution of a Filipino woman, following her conviction by a Singapore court for a double murder committed in 1991, provoked a furious public response in the Philippines, where it was widely held that the Singapore authorities had acted unjustly by refusing appeals from international organizations—and the Philippine President, Fidel Ramos, himself—for a stay of execution pending the presentation of fresh evidence. The convicted woman's defence lawyers had claimed that the evidence cast doubt on her guilt. President Ramos postponed indefinitely a scheduled visit to the Philippines by Prime Minister Goh and recalled the Philippine Ambassador to Singapore. Singapore, in retaliation, recalled its Ambassador to the Philippines for consultations. President Ramos established a commission to review the case, which subsequently disputed the guilty verdict. In April Singapore agreed to allow a third party to re-evaluate the post-mortem examination of one of the victims, in an effort to reduce tension between the two countries.

In November 1990 representatives of the Governments of the USA and Singapore signed an agreement providing the US navy and air force with increased access to existing bases in Singapore following the planned US withdrawal from military installations in the Philippines. In January 1992 the two countries reached an agreement, in principle, on the relocation of a naval logistic command headquarters from Subic Bay, in the Philippines. However, relations with the USA were strained, in early 1994, by the sentencing of a US citizen to corporal punishment with a rattan cane, following his conviction in Singapore for vandalism. The US President, Bill Clinton, urged Singapore to reconsider the sentence, which he declared 'extreme'. Following an appeal for clemency to the Singaporean President, the sentence was reduced from six strokes to four and was carried out in May. Relations with the USA were further strained in January 1995, when a Singaporean court found five defendants guilty of contempt of court following the publication of an article in the US-owned *International Herald Tribune* in October 1994. The Government claimed that the article had insinuated that Singapore's judiciary was 'compliant' to official pressure to drive opposition politicians into bankruptcy.

Despite the establishment of important economic links during the 1980s, Singapore's relations with the People's Republic of China were adversely affected by the perceived threat of Chinese domination, owing to the preponderance of ethnic Chinese in Singapore (77% at mid-1994). Relations were also strained by Singapore's close military and economic ties with Taiwan. In October 1990, however, Singapore and the People's Republic of China established diplomatic relations at ambassadorial level. This development was prompted mainly by the resumption of diplomatic relations between the People's Republic of China and Indonesia, and followed a visit by the Chinese Premier, Li Peng, to Singapore in August. Singapore's relations with Taiwan were apparently unaffected by these events and Goh made his first official visit to that country in October 1993.

## Government

Legislative power is vested in the unicameral Parliament, with 81 members who are elected by universal adult suffrage for five years (subject to dissolution—within three months of which a general election must be held) in single-member and multi-member constituencies. The President is directly elected by universal adult suffrage for a six-year term as a constitutional Head of State, vested with certain powers of veto in financial matters, public appointments and detentions for reasons of national security. Effective executive authority rests with the Cabinet, led by the Prime Minister, which is appointed by the President and responsible to Parliament.

## Defence

In June 1994 the Singapore armed forces had an estimated total strength of 54,000 troops: 45,000 in the army, an estimated 3,000 in the navy and 6,000 in the air force. Military service is compulsory for two years. Paramilitary forces comprised 11,600 police and a civil defence force numbering an estimated 100,000. Singapore is a participant in the Five-Power Defence Arrangements (with Australia, Malaysia, New Zealand and the United Kingdom). Government expenditure on defence for the financial year 1994/95 was approximately S $3,000m.

## Economic Affairs

In 1993, according to estimates by the World Bank, Singapore's gross national product (GNP), measured at average 1991–93 prices, was US $55,372m., equivalent to US $19,310 per head. During 1985–93, it was estimated, GNP per head increased, in real terms, at an average annual rate of 6.1%. Over the same period the population increased by an annual average of 1.9%. Singapore's gross domestic product (GDP) increased, in real terms, by an annual average of 6.7% in 1980–92, and by 9.9% in 1993.

Agriculture (including hunting, forestry and fishing) contributed an estimated 0.2% of GDP in 1994, and engaged 0.3% of the employed labour force in 1992. Plants, vegetables and orchid flowers are the principal crops. During 1980–92 agricultural GDP declined at an average annual rate of 6.6%.

Industry (including mining, manufacturing, construction and power) contributed 34.3% of GDP, and (with agriculture) engaged 33.0% of the employed labour force, in 1994. During 1980–92 industrial GDP increased by an annual average of 6.0%.

Mining (chiefly the quarrying of granite) accounted for only about 0.03% of GDP in 1994 and 0.03% of employment in 1992.

Manufacturing contributed an estimated 25.6% of GDP, and engaged 25.6% of the employed labour force, in 1994. The principal branches of manufacturing (measured in terms of the value of output) are electrical machinery, particularly radios and televisions; petroleum-refining and related products; metal products; chemicals; transport equipment (especially shipbuilding); machinery; food products; and clothing. During 1980–92 manufacturing GDP increased by an annual average of 7.1%.

Singapore relies on imports of hydrocarbons to fuel its three thermal power stations. In 1994 imports of mineral fuels accounted for 8.8% of merchandise imports.

Finance and business services provided an estimated 28.1% of GDP, and engaged 12.0% of the employed labour force, in 1994. Singapore is an important foreign-exchange dealing centre in Asia and the Pacific. Banking is also a significant sector, with a total of 140 commercial banks in operation in April 1995. Tourism is an important source of foreign exchange. In 1993 tourist arrivals totalled 6.4m., and receipts from tourism reached S $9,350m.; tourist arrivals increased to 6.9m. in 1994. In 1994 transport and communications contributed an estimated 11.4% of GDP. Singapore is the world's busiest port in tonnage terms, and handled vessels with a total displacement of 624m. grt in 1993.

In 1993 Singapore recorded a visible trade deficit of US $8,065m., but there was a surplus of US $2,039m. on the current account of the balance of payments. In 1994 the principal source of imports (22.0%) was Japan; other major suppliers were Malaysia (16.4%) and the USA (15.3%). The principal market for exports (19.7%) was Malaysia; other major purchasers were the USA (18.8%), Hong Kong (8.7%), Japan (7.0%) and Thailand (5.6%). Principal imports in 1994 included electrical and non-electric machinery, crude petroleum, chemicals and food and live animals. Principal exports included electrical and non-electric machinery, petroleum products and chemicals. Singapore is an important entrepôt, and re-exports accounted for 37.3% of total exports in 1988.

For the financial year ending 31 March 1993 there was an estimated budgetary surplus of S $4,854m. (equivalent to 5.3% of GDP). The annual rate of inflation averaged 1.8% in 1985–93; consumer prices increased by an average of 3.6% in 1994. Only about 2.7% of the labour force were unemployed in June 1993. Owing to the labour shortage (mainly in the industrial and construction sectors), there were about 250,000 foreign workers in Singapore in 1991.

Singapore is a member of the Asian Development Bank (see p. 107), of the Association of South East Asian Nations (ASEAN—see p. 109), and of the Colombo Plan (see p. 238). As a member of ASEAN, Singapore signed an accord in January 1992, pledging to create a free trade zone by 2008, to be known as the ASEAN Free Trade Area (AFTA).

In the late 1980s and early 1990s many state-owned corporations were transferred to the private sector. Foreign and local companies were encouraged to invest overseas and, particularly, to transfer labour-intensive operations to neighbouring countries. In late 1992, following a deceleration of growth rates in 1991 and early 1992, economic expansion began to accelerate, owing to significant public expenditure on infrastructural improvements, ensuring rapid growth in the construction sector. The 1993/94 budget reduced corporate and personal taxation, in an attempt to encourage Singaporeans to invest overseas to take advantage of economic development in the region (particularly in the People's Republic of China and Viet Nam). The tax changes were also designed to maintain Singapore's competitiveness as an investment location. In 1994 the manufacturing sector, led by the electronics industry, achieved significant levels of growth, which were largely accounted for by a world-wide expansion in computer sales; however, growth in the financial services and business sector showed a decline compared with 1993. The overall economic performance remained buoyant in 1994 and was expected to continue so in 1995, owing to Singapore's central location in the region, the existence of a highly skilled work force and efficient infrastructure, which together encouraged international investment in the country. However, a continuing chronic labour shortage and associated wage rises were thought likely to affect Singapore's future competitiveness if they remained unchecked; at the end of 1994 domestic cost pressures had started to increase. The 1995/96 budget introduced further tax incentives for international investors and provided for greater tax deductions for Singaporean companies seeking to expand in the region, as part of the Government's declared policy of encouraging regional investment.

## Social Welfare

The Ministry of Community Development, aided by 159 voluntary bodies which are co-ordinated by the National Council of Social Service, provides a wide range of welfare services to individuals and families in need. Singapore has no state pensions or sickness benefit, but there is a central provident fund into which contributions must be paid by employers and employees. In 1993 Singapore had five government hospitals, six government-restructured hospitals and 10 private hospitals, with a total of 10,469 beds. In that year a total of 4,146 physicians were registered to practise in Singapore, and a further 11,649 nurses and midwives were recorded by the Singapore Nursing Board. Of total expenditure by the central Government in the financial year 1991/92, S $994m. (6.2%) was for health services, and a further S $344m. (2.2%) for social security and welfare.

## Education

Primary and secondary education is available in the four official languages of Malay, Chinese, Tamil and English. In 1978, as part of a policy of bilingualism, examinations in

# SINGAPORE

English and Mandarin Chinese became compulsory for pupils seeking to enter secondary education. In 1987 English became the medium of instruction in all schools. Primary education begins at six years of age and lasts for six years, comprising a cycle of four years followed by a cycle of two years. Secondary education lasts for seven years from the age of 12, comprising a cycle of four years and a cycle of three years. Outside the school system there are several higher education centres and vocational institutes, providing craft and industrial training, and technical institutes providing advanced craft training. Total enrolment in the seven universities and colleges was 76,985 at the end of June 1994. Adult education courses are conducted by a statutory board. Education is not compulsory, but in 1991 the number of children attending primary and secondary schools was equivalent to 86% of children in the relevant age-group. In that year secondary school enrolment was equivalent to 69% of children in the relevant age-group. At the 1990 census the average rate of adult illiteracy, among persons aged 15 years and over, was 10.9% (males 4.9%; females 17.0%). In 1993 the general rate of literacy among persons aged 10 years and over was estimated to be 91.6%. Expenditure on education by the central Government in the financial year 1991/92 was S$3,655m. (22.9% of total spending).

## Public Holidays

**1995:** 2 January (for New Year's Day), 31 January–1 February (Chinese New Year), 3 March* (Hari Raya Puasa, end of Ramadan), 14 April (Good Friday), 1 May (Labour Day), 10 May* (Hari Raya Haji, feast of the Sacrifice), 15 May (for Vesak Day), 9 August (National Day), 23 October (Deepavali), 25 December (Christmas Day).

**1996:** 1 January (New Year's Day), 19–20 February (Chinese New Year), 21 February* (Hari Raya Puasa, end of Ramadan), 5 April (Good Friday), 29 April* (Hari Raya Haji, feast of the Sacrifice), 1 May (Labour Day), 25 May (Vesak Day), 9 August (National Day), October/November (Deepavali), 25 December (Christmas Day).

* These holidays are dependent on the Islamic lunar calendar and may vary by one or two days from the dates given.

## Weights and Measures

The metric system is in force, but the following local units are also used:

Weight: 1 tahil = 1+ oz (37.8 grams).
 16 tahils = 1 kati = 1+ lb (604.8 grams).
 100 katis = 1 picul = 133+ lb (60.48 kg).
 40 piculs = 1 koyan = 5,333+ lb (2,419.2 kg).
Capacity: 1 chupak = 1 quart (1.1365 litres).
 1 gantang = 1 gallon (4.5461 litres).

# Statistical Survey

Source (unless otherwise stated): *Yearbook of Statistics*, Department of Statistics, 8 Shenton Way 10-01, Treasury Bldg, Singapore 0106; tel. 3239684; telex 63001; fax 3239689.

## Area and Population

### AREA, POPULATION AND DENSITY

| | |
|---|---:|
| Area (sq km) | 641.4* |
| Population (census results)† | |
| 24 June 1980 | 2,282,100 |
| 30 June 1990 | |
| Males | 1,370,059 |
| Females | 1,335,056 |
| Total | 2,705,115 |
| Population (official estimates at mid-year)† | |
| 1992 | 2,818,200 |
| 1993 | 2,873,800‡ |
| 1994 | 2,930,200‡ |
| Density (per sq km) at mid-1994 | 4,568.4 |

* 247.6 sq miles.
† Figures refer to the resident population of Singapore.
‡ Males 1,476,300; Females 1,453,900.

### ETHNIC GROUPS* (official estimates at mid-year 1994)

| | |
|---|---:|
| Chinese | 2,269,600 |
| Malays | 415,900 |
| Indians | 209,400 |
| Others | 35,300 |
| **Total** | 2,930,200 |

* Figures refer to the resident population of Singapore.

### BIRTHS AND DEATHS

| | Registered live births Number | Rate (per 1,000)† | Registered deaths* Number | Rate (per 1,000)† |
|---|---:|---:|---:|---:|
| 1987 | 43,616 | 16.6 | 13,173 | 4.7 |
| 1988 | 52,957 | 19.8 | 13,690 | 4.9 |
| 1989 | 47,669 | 17.5 | 14,069 | 4.9 |
| 1990 | 51,142 | 18.4 | 13,891 | 4.8 |
| 1991 | 49,114 | 17.3 | 13,876 | 4.7 |
| 1992 | 49,402 | 17.0 | 14,337 | 4.7 |
| 1993 | 50,225 | 17.0 | 14,461 | 4.6 |
| 1994 | 49,602 | 16.4‡ | 14,946 | 4.7‡ |

* Data are tabulated by year of registration, rather than by year of occurrence.
† Figures refer to the resident population of Singapore.
‡ Provisional.

**Expectation of life** (UN estimates, years at birth, 1992): Males 73.7; Females 78.3 (Source: UN, *Statistical Yearbook for Asia and the Pacific*).

# SINGAPORE

**EMPLOYMENT** (ISIC Major Divisions, '000 persons aged 15 years and over, at June of each year)

|  | 1992 | 1993 | 1994 |
|---|---|---|---|
| Agriculture, hunting, forestry and fishing | 5.0 | 4.2 | 5.2 |
| Mining and quarrying | 0.5 | | |
| Manufacturing | 434.1 | 429.5 | 422.5 |
| Electricity, gas and water | 8.0 | 7.5 | 8.5 |
| Construction | 103.2 | 102.1 | 108.8 |
| Trade, restaurants and hotels | 356.0 | 363.6 | 376.9 |
| Transport, storage and communications | 158.4 | 166.8 | 174.7 |
| Financing, insurance, real estate and business services | 171.4 | 173.4 | 198.6 |
| Community, social and personal services | 339.2 | 344.1 | 353.6 |
| Activities not adequately defined | 0.2 | 0.8 | 0.5 |
| **Total employed** | **1,576.2** | **1,592.0** | **1,649.3** |
| Males | 944.3 | 952.3 | 987.1 |
| Females | 631.8 | 639.7 | 662.2 |

## Agriculture

**PRINCIPAL CROPS** (metric tons, unless otherwise indicated)

|  | 1992 | 1993 | 1994 |
|---|---|---|---|
| Plants (million)* | — | 233 | 188 |
| Vegetables | 5,189 | 4,800 | 5,644 |
| Orchid flowers (million stalks) | 42.2 | 37.0 | 32.8 |

* Includes potted, non-potted, ornamental and aquatic plants, and tissue-cultured seedlings.

**LIVESTOCK PRODUCTS**

|  | 1992 | 1993 | 1994 |
|---|---|---|---|
| Poultry meat ('000 metric tons) | 5 | 4 | n.a. |
| Hen eggs (million) | 276 | 311 | 328 |
| Other poultry eggs (million) | 31 | 44 | 18 |

Source: Primary Production Department.

## Fishing

**FISH LANDED AND AUCTIONED*** (metric tons)

|  | 1992 | 1993 | 1994 |
|---|---|---|---|
| Total | 108,589 | 103,589 | 92,550 |

* Including fish landed in Singapore by non-Singapore vessels. The total catch (live weight) of Singapore vessels was 9,198 metric tons in 1992 and 9,279 metric tons in 1993.

## Industry

**PETROLEUM PRODUCTS** ('000 metric tons)

|  | 1990 | 1991 | 1992 |
|---|---|---|---|
| Liquefied petroleum gas* | 460 | 475 | 490 |
| Naphtha | 4,242 | 4,953 | 5,100 |
| Motor spirit (petrol) | 3,377 | 3,391 | 3,420 |
| Kerosene | 2,500 | 2,600 | 2,700 |
| Jet fuel | 6,370 | 6,425 | 6,460 |
| Distillate fuel oils | 14,564 | 15,715 | 16,000 |
| Residual fuel oil | 11,845 | 11,930 | 13,000 |
| Lubricating oils | 700 | 730 | 750 |
| Petroleum bitumen (asphalt) | 610 | 510 | 670 |

* Estimates.

Source: UN, *Industrial Commodity Statistics Yearbook*.

**SELECTED OTHER PRODUCTS**

|  | 1988 | 1989 | 1990 |
|---|---|---|---|
| Paints ('000 litres) | 48,103.6 | 52,746.9 | 58,245.9 |
| Broken granite ('000 metric tons) | 6,914.0 | 7,007.5 | 6,371.7 |
| Bricks ('000 units) | 103,136 | 116,906 | 128,386 |
| Soft drinks ('000 litres) | 269,689.4 | 252,977.6 | 243,175.1 |
| Plywood, plain and printed ('000 sq m) | 31,307.0 | 28,871.3 | 26,106.9 |
| Vegetable cooking oil (metric tons) | 75,022 | 103,003 | 102,854 |
| Animal fodder (metric tons) | 110,106 | 115,341 | 104,541 |
| Electricity (million kWh) | 13,017.5 | 14,039.0 | 15,617.6 |
| Gas (million kWh) | 681.1 | 722.4 | 807.1 |
| Cassette tape recorders ('000 sets) | 15,450 | 14,006 | 18,059 |

**1991:** Electricity (million kWh) 16,597; Gas (terajoules) 3,187.
**1992:** Electricity (million kWh) 17,543; Gas (terajoules) 3,396 (Source: UN, *Industrial Commodity Statistics Yearbook*).

## Finance

### CURRENCY AND EXCHANGE RATES

**Monetary Units**
100 cents = 1 Singapore dollar (S $).

**Sterling and US Dollar Equivalents** (31 December 1994)
£1 sterling = S $2.281;
US $1 = S $1.458;
S $100 = £43.84 = US $68.59.

**Average Exchange Rate** (Singapore dollars per US $)

| 1992 | 1.6290 |
|---|---|
| 1993 | 1.6158 |
| 1994 | 1.5274 |

**OFFICIAL FOREIGN ASSETS**
(S $ million, valuation at cost, 31 December)

|  | 1992 | 1993 | 1994 |
|---|---|---|---|
| Gold and foreign exchange | 65,239.0 | 77,290.7 | 84,559.4 |
| Reserve position in the IMF | 346.4 | 361.2 | 381.5 |
| SDRs | 203.0 | 214.9 | 224.6 |
| **Total** | **65,788.4** | **77,866.8** | **85,165.5** |

**GOVERNMENT BUDGET** (S $ million, year ending 31 March)

| Revenue | 1991/92* | 1992/93† | 1993/94‡ |
|---|---|---|---|
| Tax revenue | 12,466.1 | 13,731.0 | 14,467.2 |
| Fees and charges | 2,062.7 | 2,045.8 | 1,938.7 |
| Investment | 3,827.5 | 3,337.2 | 3,653.4 |
| Others | 1,168.6 | 1,003.0 | 829.3 |
| **Total** | **19,524.9** | **20,117.0** | **20,888.6** |

| Expenditure | 1991/92* | 1992/93† | 1993/94‡ |
|---|---|---|---|
| Recurrent expenditure | 10,893.7 | 11,064.5 | 11,662.2 |
| Expenditure on manpower | 2,081.2 | 2,093.8 | 2,452.4 |
| Other operating expenditure | 3,956.5 | 4,742.7 | 5,067.8 |
| Grants in aid | 1,853.3 | 1,734.8 | 1,875.7 |
| Pensions | 282.5 | 344.6 | 357.8 |
| Public debt-servicing | 2,720.2 | 2,148.6 | 1,908.5 |
| Development expenditure | 3,601.1 | 4,198.2 | 5,764.2 |
| Government development | 1,593.7 | 2,071.6 | 3,089.1 |
| Capital grants | 1,413.0 | 1,520.2 | 1,776.0 |
| Public housing | 594.4 | 606.4 | 899.1 |
| **Total** | **14,494.8** | **15,262.7** | **17,426.4** |

* Actual.  † Preliminary estimates.  ‡ Budget forecasts.

# SINGAPORE

*Statistical Survey*

## NATIONAL ACCOUNTS (S $ million at current prices)
### Composition of the Gross National Product

|  | 1992 | 1993 | 1994* |
|---|---|---|---|
| Gross domestic product (GDP) at factor cost | 74,360.7 | 84,953.9 | 96,242.2 |
| Indirect taxes, *less* subsidies | 6,275.9 | 7,394.4 | 9,071.0 |
| **GDP in purchasers' values** | 80,636.6 | 92,348.3 | 105,313.2 |
| Net factor income from abroad | 1,215.7 | 732.8 | −433.6 |
| **Gross national product (GNP)** | 81,852.3 | 93,081.1 | 104,879.6 |

* Preliminary.

### Expenditure on the Gross Domestic Product

|  | 1992 | 1993 | 1994* |
|---|---|---|---|
| Government final consumption expenditure | 7,511.9 | 8,468.1 | 8,942.3 |
| Private final consumption expenditure | 35,081.2 | 39,070.4 | 42,341.7 |
| Increase in stocks | 547.5 | 2,515.8 | −2,342.2 |
| Gross fixed capital formation | 28,797.0 | 32,925.4 | 36,267.1 |
| Statistical discrepancy | −989.3 | 714.1 | 229.0 |
| **Total domestic expenditure** | 70,948.3 | 83,693.8 | 85,437.9 |
| Trade in goods and services (net) | 9,688.3 | 8,654.5 | 19,875.3 |
| **GDP in purchasers' values** | 80,636.6 | 92,348.3 | 105,313.2 |

* Preliminary.

### Gross Domestic Product by Economic Activity

|  | 1992 | 1993 | 1994 |
|---|---|---|---|
| Agriculture and fishing | 170.8 | 166.7 | 179.8 |
| Quarrying | 38.7 | 38.3 | 34.5 |
| Manufacturing | 21,232.1 | 24,615.5 | 28,383.1 |
| Electricity, gas and water | 1,353.3 | 1,571.1 | 1,725.6 |
| Construction | 6,211.7 | 6,771.2 | 7,881.3 |
| Wholesale and retail trade | 14,690.2 | 16,054.1 | 17,918.9 |
| Transport and communications | 10,221.8 | 11,471.1 | 12,673.9 |
| Finance and business services | 22,379.1 | 26,778.8 | 31,103.2 |
| Other services | 8,898.0 | 9,783.2 | 10,942.9 |
| **Sub-total** | 85,195.7 | 97,250.0 | 110,843.2 |
| Import duties | 735.6 | 853.4 | 762.4 |
| *Less* Imputed bank service charge | 5,295.7 | 5,755.2 | 6,292.4 |
| **GDP in purchasers' values** | 80,635.6 | 92,348.2 | 105,313.2 |

## BALANCE OF PAYMENTS (US $ million)

|  | 1991 | 1992 | 1993 |
|---|---|---|---|
| Merchandise exports f.o.b. | 57,156 | 62,068 | 71,959 |
| Merchandise imports f.o.b. | −60,948 | −67,850 | −80,025 |
| **Trade balance** | −3,791 | −5,782 | −8,065 |
| Exports of services | 16,821 | 18,794 | 20,879 |
| Imports of services | −9,863 | −10,231 | −11,635 |
| Other income received | 7,464 | 8,407 | 9,091 |
| Other income paid | −6,140 | −6,844 | −7,534 |
| Private unrequited transfers (net) | −340 | −405 | −482 |
| Official unrequited transfers (net) | −159 | −190 | −215 |
| **Current balance** | 3,992 | 3,748 | 2,039 |
| Direct capital investment (net) | 4,444 | 5,982 | 6,062 |
| Portfolio investment (net) | −802 | −819 | −944 |
| Other capital (net) | −2,708 | 397 | 4,335 |
| Net errors and omissions | −728 | −3,208 | −3,913 |
| **Overall balance** | 4,198 | 6,100 | 7,578 |

Source: IMF, *International Financial Statistics*.

# External Trade

## PRINCIPAL COMMODITIES (distribution by SITC, S $ million)

| Imports c.i.f. | 1992 | 1993 | 1994 |
|---|---|---|---|
| Food and live animals | 4,837.1 | 5,033.3 | 5,217.9 |
| Cereals and cereal preparations | 471.4 | 513.2 | 518.8 |
| Beverages and tobacco | 1,651.5 | 2,074.0 | 2,141.3 |
| Crude materials (inedible) except fuels | 1,867.4 | 1,968.1 | 1,938.5 |
| Crude rubber, etc. | 595.6 | 507.7 | 532.8 |
| Wood, lumber and cork | 305.5 | 317.0 | 344.2 |
| Mineral fuels, lubricants, etc. | 14,987.2 | 14,911.8 | 13,787.8 |
| Petroleum and petroleum products | 14,970.5 | 14,902.6 | 13,778.4 |
| Animal and vegetable oils and fats | 877.5 | 833.7 | 640.9 |
| Chemicals | 8,854.7 | 9,614.9 | 10,113.6 |
| Basic manufactures | 15,045.8 | 16,013.4 | 16,523.4 |
| Textile yarn, fabrics, etc. | 3,255.0 | 3,162.5 | 3,072.2 |
| Iron and steel | 3,004.6 | 3,288.8 | 3,222.2 |
| Machinery and transport equipment | 56,330.5 | 71,915.9 | 88,306.3 |
| Non-electric machinery | 22,862.2 | 27,640.8 | 32,743.5 |
| Electrical machinery, apparatus, etc. | 26,199.9 | 35,916.4 | 47,902.3 |
| Miscellaneous manufactured articles | 11,718.4 | 13,414.9 | 15,427.7 |
| Other commodities and transactions | 1,359.4 | 1,822.7 | 2,298.4 |
| **Total** | 117,529.7 | 137,602.8 | 156,395.8 |

| Exports f.o.b. | 1992 | 1993 | 1994 |
|---|---|---|---|
| Food and live animals | 2,986.7 | 2,909.8 | 3,542.4 |
| Coffee, tea, cocoa and spices | 794.5 | 728.4 | 1,081.7 |
| Beverages and tobacco | 1,969.0 | 2,389.4 | 2,447.5 |
| Crude materials (inedible) except fuels | 2,278.3 | 2,132.4 | 2,193.2 |
| Crude rubber, etc. | 986.2 | 807.5 | 819.1 |
| Mineral fuels, lubricants, etc. | 13,509.8 | 14,611.7 | 14,074.8 |
| Petroleum and petroleum products | 11,096.9 | 11,879.9 | 11,411.6 |
| Animal and vegetable oils and fats | 746.7 | 610.1 | 574.1 |
| Chemicals | 6,731.8 | 7,662.8 | 8,418.0 |
| Basic manufactures | 7,114.5 | 7,756.1 | 8,855.8 |
| Wood and cork manufactures (excl. furniture) | 489.0 | 504.7 | 432.7 |
| Textile yarn, fabrics, etc. | 1,760.5 | 1,980.1 | 2,153.8 |
| Machinery and transport equipment | 56,939.3 | 69,640.6 | 94,198.7 |
| Non-electric machinery | 28,575.0 | 35,214.2 | 45,095.7 |
| Electrical machinery, apparatus, etc. | 25,553.3 | 31,284.3 | 45,949.3 |
| Transport equipment | 2,811.0 | 3,142.1 | 3,153.6 |
| Miscellaneous manufactured articles | 9,593.0 | 9,768.0 | 11,185.2 |
| Clothing (excl. footwear) | 2,947.8 | 2,500.3 | 2,322.3 |
| Other commodities and transactions | 1,481.9 | 1,992.7 | 1,837.6 |
| **Total** | 103,351.0 | 119,473.4 | 147,327.2 |

## PRINCIPAL TRADING PARTNERS* (S $ million)

| Imports c.i.f. | 1992 | 1993 | 1994 |
|---|---|---|---|
| Australia | 1,997.6 | 2,384.4 | 2,392.9 |
| China, People's Repub. | 3,667.6 | 3,877.1 | 4,412.0 |
| Germany | 3,839.3 | 4,203.0 | 5,269.6 |
| Hong Kong | 3,587.0 | 4,338.8 | 5,285.4 |
| Iran | 825.7 | 1,048.8 | 901.3 |
| Japan | 24,753.1 | 30,110.9 | 34,422.1 |
| Malaysia | 17,287.2 | 22,669.6 | 25,600.0 |
| Saudi Arabia | 6,018.3 | 5,359.1 | 5,607.0 |
| Thailand | 4,365.3 | 5,676.2 | 7,470.8 |
| United Kingdom | 3,280.7 | 3,592.9 | 4,325.7 |
| USA | 19,340.5 | 22,359.8 | 23,901.9 |

SINGAPORE

| Exports f.o.b. | 1992 | 1993 | 1994 |
|---|---|---|---|
| Australia | 2,456.8 | 2,701.9 | 3,490.3 |
| France | 1,582.8 | 1,758.8 | 1,998.6 |
| Germany | 4,388.6 | 4,746.7 | 5,229.8 |
| Hong Kong | 8,080.8 | 10,363.9 | 12,814.2 |
| Japan | 7,856.7 | 8,921.3 | 10,342.6 |
| Malaysia | 12,925.4 | 16,942.2 | 29,089.5 |
| Thailand | 6,441.8 | 6,804.9 | 8,189.3 |
| United Kingdom | 3,003.3 | 3,575.3 | 3,985.0 |
| USA | 21,778.9 | 24,291.8 | 27,637.0 |

* No figures are available for trade with Indonesia.

## Transport

**ROAD TRAFFIC** (registered vehicles)

|  | 1992 | 1993 | 1994 |
|---|---|---|---|
| Private cars* | 285,500 | 303,864 | 321,556 |
| Motor cycles and scooters | 116,532 | 119,939 | 126,156 |
| Motor buses | 9,658 | 9,716 | 10,198 |
| Goods vehicles (incl. private) | 119,335 | 122,739 | 123,844 |
| Others | 26,559 | 28,064 | 29,857 |
| **Total** | 557,584 | 584,322 | 611,611 |

* Including private and company cars.

**SHIPPING** (vessels of over 75 net registered tons)

|  | Ships Entered | Ships Cleared | Cargo Discharged ('000 freight tons) | Cargo Loaded ('000 freight tons) |
|---|---|---|---|---|
| 1992 | 81,334 | 81,245 | 136,468.2 | 101,977.7 |
| 1993 | 92,700 | 92,477 | 158,959.7 | 114,763.4 |
| 1994* | 101,000 | 101,000 | 164,400.0 | 125,600.0 |

* Figures are provisional.

Note: One freight ton equals 40 cubic feet (1.133 cubic metres) of cargo.

**Merchant shipping fleet** ('000 grt at 30 June): 8,488.2 in 1991; 9,905.1 in 1992; 11,034.8 in 1993. Source: Lloyd's Register of Shipping.

**CIVIL AVIATION**

|  | 1992 | 1993 | 1994 |
|---|---|---|---|
| Passengers |  |  |  |
| Arrived | 8,446,027 | 9,421,358 | 10,134,100 |
| Departed | 8,432,221 | 9,374,970 | 10,068,537 |
| In Transit | 1,221,907 | 1,190,886 | 1,442,040 |
| Mail (metric tons) |  |  |  |
| Landed | 5,948 | 7,927 | 8,538 |
| Dispatched | 6,073 | 6,759 | 8,401 |
| Freight (metric tons) |  |  |  |
| Landed | 386,793 | 444,019 | 529,334 |
| Dispatched | 332,212 | 394,397 | 480,430 |

## Tourism

|  | 1992 | 1993 | 1994 |
|---|---|---|---|
| Tourist arrivals* | 5,989,900 | 6,425,800 | 6,898,951 |

* Figures exclude arrivals of Malaysians by land.

**Tourist receipts** (S $ million): 8,554 in 1992; 9,350 in 1993.

Source: Singapore Tourist Promotion Board.

## Communications Media

(at 31 December)

|  | 1992 | 1993 | 1994 |
|---|---|---|---|
| Radio licences issued | 190,900 | 198,959 | 210,370 |
| Television licences issued | 614,309 | 639,139 | 645,529 |
| Rediffusion subscribers | 37,270 | 33,423 | 29,200 |

**Radio receivers*** (1992): 1,790,000 in use.

**Television receivers*** (1992): 1,050,000 in use.

**Daily newspapers** (1993): 8 (estimated combined circulation of 1,004,800 copies).

**Non-daily newspapers*** (1988, estimate): 7 (estimated combined circulation of 470,000 copies).

**Telephones:** (1993): 1,230,000.

* Source: UNESCO, *Statistical Yearbook*.

## Education

(June 1994)

|  | Institutions* | Students | Teachers |
|---|---|---|---|
| Primary | 194 | 251,097 | 10,553 |
| Secondary† | 184 | 197,981 | 9,675 |
| Technical and vocational institutes | 11 | 12,492 | 1,359 |
| Universities and colleges‡ | 7 | 76,985 | 6,235 |
| **Total** | 396 | 538,555 | 27,773 |

* A full school containing both primary and secondary classes is treated as one primary and one secondary school.
† Secondary institutions include secondary schools, junior colleges, pre-university centres and centralized institutes.
‡ Including part-time students and teachers.

# Directory

## The Constitution

A new Constitution came into force on 3 June 1959, with the establishment of the self-governing State of Singapore. This was subsequently amended as a consequence of Singapore's affiliation to Malaysia (September 1963 to August 1965) and as a result of its adoption of republican status on 22 December 1965. The Constitution was also amended in January 1991 to provide for the election of a President by universal adult suffrage, and to extend the responsibilities of the presidency, which had previously been a largely ceremonial office. The main provisions of the Constitution are summarized below:

### HEAD OF STATE

The Head of State is the President, elected by universal adult suffrage for a six-year term. He normally acts on the advice of the Cabinet, but is vested with certain functions and powers for the purpose of safeguarding the financial reserves of Singapore and the integrity of the Public Services.

### THE CABINET

The Cabinet, headed by the Prime Minister, is appointed by the President and is responsible to Parliament.

### THE LEGISLATURE

The Legislature consists of a Parliament of 81 members, presided over by a Speaker who may be elected from the members of Parliament themselves or appointed by Parliament although he may not be a member of Parliament. Members of Parliament are elected by universal adult suffrage for five years (subject to dissolution) in single-member and multi-member constituencies.*

A 21-member Presidential Council, chaired by the Chief Justice, examines material of racial or religious significance, including legislation, to see whether it differentiates between racial or religious communities or contains provisions inconsistent with the fundamental liberties of Singapore citizens.

### CITIZENSHIP

Under the Constitution, Singapore citizenship may be acquired either by birth, descent or registration. Persons born when Singapore was a constituent State of Malaysia could also acquire Singapore citizenship by enrolment or naturalization under the Constitution of Malaysia.

* A constitutional amendment was introduced in May 1988, whereby 39 constituencies were merged to form 13 'group representation constituencies' which would return 'teams' of three Members of Parliament. At least one member of each team was to be of minority (non-Chinese) racial origin. In January 1991 the Constitution was further amended, stipulating that the number of candidates contesting 'group representation constituencies' should be a minimum of three and a maximum of four.

## The Government

### HEAD OF STATE

**President:** ONG TENG CHEONG (took office 2 September 1993).

### THE CABINET
(June 1995)

**Prime Minister:** GOH CHOK TONG.
**Senior Minister in the Prime Minister's Office:** LEE KUAN YEW.
**Deputy Prime Minister:** Brig.-Gen. (retd) LEE HSIEN LOONG.
**Minister of Law and of Foreign Affairs:** Prof. SHANMUGAM JAYAKUMAR.
**Minister of Finance:** Dr RICHARD HU TSU TAU.
**Minister of Education:** LEE YOCK SUAN.
**Minister of Home Affairs:** WONG KAN SENG.
**Minister of Trade and Industry:** YEO CHEOW TONG.
**Minister of Information, of the Arts and of Health:** Brig.-Gen. GEORGE YONG BOON YEO.
**Minister of Labour and Minister of Defence:** Dr LEE BOON YANG.
**Minister of Communications and of the Environment:** MAH BOW TAN.
**Minister without Portfolio:** LIM BOON HENG.

**Acting Minister of National Development and Senior Minister of State for Foreign Affairs:** LIM HNG KIANG.
**Acting Minister of Community Development, Minister of State for the Environment and Minister in charge of Muslim Affairs:** ABDULLAH TARMUGI.

Note: In late June 1995 Dr TONY TAN KENG YAM was designated Deputy Prime Minister and Minister of Defence, with effect from August 1995.

### MINISTRIES

**Office of the Prime Minister:** Istana Annexe, Istana, Singapore 0923; tel. 2358577; fax 7324627.
**Ministry of Communications:** 460 Alexandra Rd, PSA Bldg 39-00, Singapore 0511; tel. 2707988; fax 3757734.
**Ministry of Community Development:** 512 Thomson Rd, MCD Bldg, Singapore 1129; tel. 2589595; fax 3548324.
**Ministry of Defence:** 2366 Gombak Drive, Singapore; tel. 7608188; telex 21373.
**Ministry of Education:** Kay Siang Rd, Singapore 1024; tel. 4739111; telex 34366.
**Ministry of the Environment:** 40 Scotts Rd, Environment Bldg, Singapore 0922; tel. 7327733; fax 7319456.
**Ministry of Finance:** 8 Shenton Way, Treasury Bldg, Singapore 0106; tel. 2259911; telex 34371; fax 3209435.
**Ministry of Foreign Affairs:** 250 North Bridge Rd, 07-00 Raffles City Tower, Singapore 0617; tel. 3361177; telex 21242; fax 3394330.
**Ministry of Health:** 16 College Rd, College of Medicine Bldg, Singapore 0316; tel. 2237777; telex 34360; fax 2241677.
**Ministry of Home Affairs:** Phoenix Park, Tanglin Rd, Singapore 1024; tel. 2359111; telex 34360.
**Ministry of Information and the Arts:** 460 Alexandra Rd, PSA Bldg, Singapore 0511; tel. 2707988; fax 2799765.
**Ministry of Labour:** 18 Havelock Rd, 07-01, Singapore 0105; tel. 5341511; fax 5344840.
**Ministry of Law:** 250 North Bridge Rd, Raffles City Tower 21-00, Singapore 0617; tel. 3361177; fax 3305891.
**Ministry of National Development:** 5 Maxwell Rd, 21/22-00, Tower Block, MND Complex, Singapore 0106; tel. 2221211; telex 34369; fax 3226254.
**Ministry of Trade and Industry:** 8 Shenton Way, Treasury Bldg 48-01, Singapore 0106; tel. 2259911; telex 24702; fax 3239260.

## President and Legislature

### PRESIDENT

**Election, 28 August 1993**

| Candidate | Percentage of Votes |
|---|---|
| ONG TENG CHEONG | 58.7 |
| CHUA KIM YEOW | 41.3 |

### PARLIAMENT

**Speaker:** TAN SOO KHOON.

**General Election, 31 August 1991**

|  | % of Votes | Seats |
|---|---|---|
| People's Action Party | 61.0 | 77* |
| Singapore Democratic Party | 12.0 | 3 |
| Workers' Party | 14.3 | 1 |
| National Solidarity Party | 7.3 | — |
| Singapore Justice Party | 1.9 | — |
| Pertubuhan Kebangsaan Melayu Singapura | 1.6 | — |
| Independents | 1.9 | — |
| **Total** | **100.0** | **81** |

* 41 seats were unopposed.

# Political Organizations

**Angkatan Islam** (Singapore Muslim Movement): Singapore; f. 1958; Pres. MOHAMED BIN OMAR; Sec.-Gen. IBRAHIM BIN ABDUL GHANI.

**Barisan Bersatu Singapura** (Singapore United Front): Singapore; f. 1973; Chair. TAN CHEE KIAN; Sec.-Gen. SEOW KHEE LENG.

**National Solidarity Party:** Singapore; f. 1986; Pres. KUM TENG HOCK; Sec.-Gen. RASIAH THIAGARAJAH.

**People's Action Party (PAP):** 510 Thomson Rd, SLF Bldg 07-02, Singapore 1129; tel. 2589898; fax 2599222; f. 1954; governing party since 1959; 12-member Cen. Exec. Cttee; Chair. (vacant); Sec.-Gen. GOH CHOK TONG.

**Pertubuhan Kebangsaan Melayu Singapura (PKMS)** (Singapore Malay National Organization): 218F Changi Rd, PKM Bldg, 4th Floor, Singapore 1441; tel. 3455275; fax 3458724; f. in 1950 as the United Malay National Organization (UMNO) of Malaysia; renamed as UMNO Singapore in 1954 and as PKMS in 1967; seeks to advance the implementation of the special rights of Malays in Singapore, as stated in the Constitution, to safeguard and promote the advancement of Islam and to encourage racial harmony and goodwill in Singapore; Pres. ATAN RAFIEE (acting); Sec.-Gen. MOHAMMED AZIZ IBRAHIM.

**Singapore Democratic Party:** 1 North Bridge Rd, 17-08 High Street Centre, Singapore 0617; tel. 3380378; fax 3383893; f. 1980; Chair. LING HOW DOONG; Sec.-Gen. CHEE SOON JUAN (acting).

**Singapore Justice Party:** Singapore; f. 1972; Pres. A. R. SUIB; Sec.-Gen. MUTHUSAMY RAMASAMY.

**United People's Front (UPF):** 715 Colombo Court, 7th Floor, Singapore 0617; f. 1975; a coalition of several small parties; Chair. ANG BEE LIAN; Gen. Sec. HARBANS SINGH.

**Workers' Party:** 411B Jalan Besar, Singapore 0820; tel. 2984765; f. 1957, merged with Barisan Sosialis (Socialist Front) in 1988; seeks to establish a democratic socialist govt with a constitution guaranteeing fundamental citizens' rights; Chair. Dr TAN BIN SENG; Sec.-Gen. J. B. JEYARETNAM.

Other parties are the Alliance Party Singapura, the Democratic Progressive Party, the Singapore National Front, the National Party of Singapore, the Partai Rakyat, the People's Front, the Parti Kesatuan Ra'ayat (United Democratic Party), the People's Republican Party, the Persatuan Melayu Singapura, the Singapore Chinese Party, the Singapore Indian Congress, the United National Front and the United People's Party.

# Diplomatic Representation

### EMBASSIES AND HIGH COMMISSIONS IN SINGAPORE

**Argentina:** 302 Orchard Rd, 03/04 Tong Bldg, 15th Floor, Singapore 0923; tel. 2354231; telex 23714; fax 2354382; Ambassador: JUAN AGUSTÍN CABALLERO.

**Australia:** 25 Napier Rd, Singapore 1025; tel. 7379311; telex 21238; fax 7337134; High Commissioner: TED DELOFSKI.

**Bangladesh:** 101 Thomson Rd, 06-07, United Sq., Singapore 1130; tel. 2550075; telex 23312; fax 2551824; High Commissioner: M. A. MALIK.

**Belgium:** 10 Anson Rd, 09-24 International Plaza, Singapore 0207; tel. 2207677; telex 23301; fax 2226976; Ambassador: Baron OLIVIER GILLES DE PÉLICHY.

**Brazil:** 302 Orchard Rd, 1503/4 Tong Bldg, Singapore 0923; tel. 7346777; telex 36204; Ambassador: A. B. PORTO DE OLIVEIRA.

**Brunei:** 325 Tanglin Rd, Singapore 1024; tel. 7339055; telex 24097; fax 7375275; High Commissioner: (vacant).

**Bulgaria:** 15 Scotts Rd, 09-08/09 Thong Teck Bldg, Singapore 0922; tel. 7371111; telex 50074; fax 2355768; Ambassador: OGNYAN MITEV.

**Canada:** 80 Anson Rd, 14-00 and 15-01 IBM Towers, Singapore 0207; tel. 225-6363; telex 21277; fax 2252450; High Commissioner: GAVIN STEWART.

**Chile:** 105 Cecil St, The Octagon 14-01/02, Singapore 0106; tel. 2238577; telex 34187; fax 2250677; Ambassador: CARLOS TUDELA.

**China, People's Republic:** 70-76 Dalvey Rd, Singapore 1025; tel. 7343360; telex 36878; fax 7338590; Ambassador: YANG WENCHANG.

**Denmark:** 101 Thomson Rd, 13-01/02 United Sq., Singapore 1130; tel. 2503383; telex 24576; fax 2533764; Ambassador: JENS PETER LARSEN.

**Egypt:** 75 Grange Rd, Singapore 1024; tel. 7371811; telex 23293; fax 7323422; Ambassador: MOHAMED AL-GHOBARY.

**Finland:** 101 Thomson Rd, 21-03 United Sq., Singapore 1130; tel. 2544042; telex 21489; fax 2534101; Ambassador: TIMO KOPONEN.

**France:** 5 Gallop Rd, Singapore 1025; tel. 4664866; telex 21351; fax 4690907; Ambassador: GÉRARD COSTE.

**Germany:** 545 Orchard Rd, 14-01 Far East Shopping Centre, Singapore 0923; tel. 7371355; telex 21312; fax 7372653; Ambassador: Dr KARL SPALCKE.

**Holy See:** 55 Waterloo St 6, Singapore 0718 (Apostolic Nunciature); tel. 3372466; fax 3372466; Apostolic Nuncio: Most Rev. LUIGI BRESSAN, Titular Archbishop of Severiana (resident in Bangkok, Thailand).

**India:** 31 Grange Rd, India House, Singapore 0923; tel. 7376777; telex 25526; fax 7326909; High Commissioner: B. M. C. NAYAR.

**Indonesia:** 7 Chatsworth Rd, Singapore 1024; tel. 7377422; telex 21464; Ambassador: TUK SETYOHADI.

**Israel:** 58 Dalvey Rd, Singapore 1025; tel. 2350966; telex 21975; fax 7337008; Ambassador: DANIEL MEGIDDO.

**Italy:** 101 Thomson Rd, 27-02 United Sq., Singapore 1130; tel. 2506022; telex 21177; fax 2533301; Ambassador: Dr RAFFAELE MINIERO.

**Japan:** 16 Nassim Rd, Singapore 1025; tel. 2358855; telex 21353; fax 7320781; Ambassador: TAKEHIRO TOGO.

**Korea, Democratic People's Republic:** 101 Thomson Rd, 10-01A-04 United Sq., Singapore 1130; tel. 2561188; fax 2543191; Ambassador: SOHN MYONG HYNN.

**Korea, Republic:** 101 Thomson Rd, United Sq., 10-02/04, Goldhill Sq, Singapore 1130; tel. 2561188; Ambassador: HAN CHANG-SIK.

**Malaysia:** 301 Jervois Rd, Singapore 1024; tel. 2350111; telex 21460; fax 7336135; High Commissioner: Dato' ZAINAL ABIDIN MOKHTAR.

**Myanmar:** 15 St Martin's Drive, Singapore 1025; tel. 7342637; telex 21467; fax 2355963; Ambassador: U NYUNT SWE.

**Netherlands:** 541 Orchard Rd, 13-01/04 Liat Towers, Singapore 0923; tel. 7371155; telex 33815; fax 7371940; Ambassador: J. G. WILBRENNINCK.

**New Zealand:** 391A Orchard Rd, 15-06/10 Ngee Ann City, Tower A, Singapore 0923; tel. 2359966; telex 21244; fax 7339924; High Commissioner: COLIN BELL.

**Norway:** 16 Raffles Quay, 44-01 Hong Leong Bldg, Singapore 0104; tel. 2207122; fax 2202191; Ambassador: ODD LAURITZ FOSSEIDBRÅTEN.

**Pakistan:** 20A Nassim Rd, Singapore 1025; tel. 7376988; telex 36777; fax 7374096; High Commissioner: SALIM NAWAZ KHAN GANDAPUR.

**Panama:** 16 Raffles Quay, 41-06 Hong Leong Bldg, Singapore 0104; tel. 2218677; fax 2240892; Ambassador: JORGE LUIS ALEMÁN.

**Philippines:** 20 Nassim Rd, Singapore 1025; tel. 7373977; fax 7339544; Ambassador: (vacant).

**Poland:** 100 Beach Rd, 33-11 Shaw Towers, Singapore 0718; tel. 2942513; telex 26355; fax 2950016; Chargé d'affaires a.i.: KRZYSZTOF KIJAK.

**Romania:** 48 Jalan Harom Setangkai, Singapore 1025; tel. 4683424; telex 22184; fax 4683425; Ambassador: ION DOROBANTU.

**Russia:** 51 Nassim Rd, Singapore 1025; tel. 2351834; telex 23404; fax 7334780; Ambassador: MIKHAIL M. BELY.

**Saudi Arabia:** 10 Nassim Rd, Singapore 1025; tel. 7345878; telex 25318; fax 7385291; Chargé d'affaires: MOHAMMAD A. AL-HAMDAN.

**Sri Lanka:** Newton Rd, 13-07 Goldhill Plaza, Singapore 1130; tel. 2544595; telex 26869; fax 2507201; High Commissioner: W. D. O. TILLEKERATNE.

**Sweden:** Devonshire Wing, 111 Somerset Rd, 05-08 PUB Bldg, Singapore 0923; tel. 7342771; telex 23450; fax 7322958; Ambassador: FINN BERGSTRAND.

**Switzerland:** 1 Swiss Club Link, Singapore 1128; tel. 4685788; telex 21501; fax 4668245; Ambassador: Dr JÜRG STREULI.

**Thailand:** 370 Orchard Rd, Singapore 0923; tel. 7373372; telex 35891; fax 7320778; Ambassador: VIKROM KOOMPIROCHANA.

**Turkey:** 20B Nassim Rd, Singapore 1025; tel. 7329211; fax 7381786; Ambassador: MEHMET GÜNEY.

**United Kingdom:** Tanglin Rd, Singapore 1024; tel. 4739333; fax 4752320; High Commissioner: GORDON DUGGAN.

**USA:** 30 Hill St, Singapore 0617; tel. 3380251; fax 3384550; Ambassador: TIMOTHY A. CHORBA.

**Viet Nam:** Singapore; Ambassador: NGUYEN MANH HUNG.

# Judicial System

The judicial power of Singapore is vested in the Supreme Court and in the Subordinate Courts. The Supreme Court consists of the High Court and the Court of Appeal. The Chief Justice is appointed by the President if the latter, acting at his discretion, concurs

SINGAPORE                                                                                                              *Directory*

with the advice of the Prime Minister. The other judges of the Supreme Court are appointed in the same way, in consultation with the Chief Justice. At 1 March 1995 there were 13 judges, including the Chief Justice, and four judicial commissioners, in the Supreme Court. Under a 1979 constitutional amendment, the position of judicial commissioner of the Supreme Court was created 'to facilitate the disposal of business in the Supreme Court'. A judicial commissioner has the powers and functions of a judge, and is appointed for such period as the President thinks fit.

The Subordinate Courts consist of District Courts, Magistrates' Courts, Juvenile Courts, Coroners' Courts and the Small Claims Tribunal. District Judges, Magistrates and Coroners are appointed by the President on the recommendation of the Chief Justice. At 1 March 1995 there were 34 District and Magistrates' Courts, one Juvenile Court and one Coroners' Court. A Referee, appointed by the President on the recommendation of the Chief Justice, presides over the Small Claims Tribunal.

District Courts and Magistrates' Courts have original criminal and civil jurisdiction. District Courts try offences for which the maximum penalty does not exceed 10 years of imprisonment and in civil cases where the amount claimed does not exceed S $100,000. Magistrates' Courts try offences for which the maximum term of imprisonment does not exceed three years. The jurisdiction of Magistrates' Courts in civil cases is limited to claims not exceeding S $30,000. The Coroners' Court conducts inquests. The Small Claims Tribunal has jurisdiction over claims relating to a dispute arising from any contract for the sale of goods or the provision of services involving an amount that does not exceed S $2,000. The Juvenile Court deals with offences committed by young persons aged under 16 years.

The High Court has unlimited original jurisdiction in criminal and civil cases. In its appellate jurisdiction it hears criminal and civil appeals from the District Courts and Magistrates' Courts. The amendment to the Supreme Court of Judicature Act, which took effect on 1 July 1993, removed the separate Court of Appeal and Court of Criminal Appeal and created a single permanent Court of Appeal for both civil and criminal appeals. The Court of Appeal hears appeals from any judgment or order of the High Court in any civil matter, either in original or appellate jurisdiction, and hears appeals against decisions made by the High Court in the exercise of its original criminal jurisdiction.

With the enactment of the Judicial Committee (Repeal) Act 1994 in April of that year, the right of appeal from the Court of Appeal to the Judicial Committee of the Privy Council was abolished. The Court of Appeal is now the final appellate court in the Singapore legal system. The Court of Appeal will continue to treat prior decisions of its own or of the Privy Council as normally binding, but may, when it appears right to do so, depart from such prior decisions. Bearing in mind the danger of retrospectively disturbing contractual, proprietary or other legal rights, this power will be exercised sparingly.

**Attorney-General:** CHAN SEK KEONG.

**Chief Justice:** YONG PUNG HOW.

**Judges of Appeal:** M. KARTHIGESU, L. P. THEAN.

**Judges of the High Court:** T. S. SINNATHURAY, LAI KEW CHAI, GOH JOON SENG, CHAO HICK TIN, S. RAJENDRAN, WARREN L. H. KHOO, G. P. SELVAM, M. P. H. RUBIN, KAN TING CHIU, LAI SIU CHIU.

**Judicial Commissioners:** K. S. RAJAH, AMARJEET SINGH, LIM TEONG QWEE, JUDITH PRAKASH.

# Religion

According to the 1990 census, 68% of ethnic Chinese, who constituted 77.6% of the population, professed either Buddhism or Daoism (including followers of Confucius, Mencius and Lao Zi) and 14% of Chinese adhered to Christianity. Malays, who made up 14.1% of the population, were 99.7% Muslim. Among Indians, who constituted 7.1% of the population, 53.2% were Hindus, 26.3% Muslims, 12.8% Christians and 6.9% Sikhs, Jains or adherents of other faiths. There are small communities of Zoroastrians and Jews. Freedom of worship is guaranteed by the Constitution.

## BAHÁ'Í FAITH

**National Spiritual Assembly:** Singapore; tel. 2814890; fax 2833931.

## BUDDHISM

**Buddhist Union:** 28 Jalan Senyum, Singapore 1441; tel. 4435959.

**Singapore Buddhist Federation:** 50 Lorong 34, Geylang, Singapore 1439; tel. 7444635; fax 7473618.

**Singapore Buddhist Sangha Organization:** 50 Lorong 34, Geylang, Singapore 1439; tel. 7444635; fax 7473618.

**Evangelical Fellowship of Singapore (EFOS):** Singapore; f. 1980.

## CHRISTIANITY

**National Council of Churches:** 1 Sophia Rd, 04-34 Peace Centre, Singapore 0922; tel. 3372150; fax 3360368; f. 1948; six mem. churches, six assoc. mems; Pres. Bishop HO CHEE SIN (Methodist Church in Singapore); Gen. Sec. Canon SAMUEL SIA.

**Singapore Council of Christian Churches (SCCC):** Singapore; f. 1956.

### The Anglican Communion

The Anglican diocese of Singapore (also including Indonesia, Laos, Thailand, Viet Nam and Cambodia) is extra-provincial and is directly subordinate to the Archbishop of Canterbury, the Primate of All England.

**Bishop of Singapore:** The Rt Rev. Dr MOSES LENG KONG TAY, Bishopsbourne, 4 Bishopsgate, Singapore 1024; tel. 4741661.

### Orthodox Churches

The Orthodox Syrian Church and the Mar Thoma Syrian Church are both active in Singapore.

### The Roman Catholic Church

Singapore comprises a single archdiocese, directly responsible to the Holy See. At 31 December 1993 there were an estimated 120,591 adherents in the country, representing 4.3% of the total population.

**Archbishop of Singapore:** Most Rev. GREGORY YONG SOOI NGEAN, Archbishop's House, 31 Victoria St, Singapore 0718; tel. and fax 3378818.

### Other Christian Churches

**Brethren Assemblies:** Bethesda Hall, 601 Ang Mo Kio Ave 4, Singapore 2056; tel. 4587474; fax 4566771; f. 1864; Hon. Sec. Dr PETER WEE HUAT LEONG; Bethesda (Katong) Church, 19 Pennefather Rd, Singapore 1542; Hon. Sec. T. C. KOH.

**Methodist Church in Singapore:** 10 Mount Sophia, Singapore 0922; tel. 3375155; fax 3389575; f. 1885; 26,114 mems (July 1994); Bishop HO CHEE SIN.

**Presbyterian Church:** Moderator Rev. DEREK J. KINGSTON; 3 Orchard Rd, cnr Penang Rd, Singapore 0923; tel. 3376681; fax 3391979; f. 1856; services in English, Chinese (Mandarin), Indonesian and German; 1,500 mems.

**Singapore Baptist Convention:** c/o Baptist Book Store, 01-25 Goldhill Plaza, Newton Rd, Singapore 1130; tel. 2538004; fax 2538214; Chair. Rev. M. S. SONG; Sec. RUSSELL MORRIS.

Other denominations active in Singapore include the Lutheran Church and the Evangelical Lutheran Church.

## HINDUISM

**Hindu Advisory Board:** c/o 397 Serangoon Rd, Singapore 0821; tel. 2963469; fax 2929766; f. 1917; Chair. P. SELVADURAI.

**Hindu Endowments Board:** 397 Serangoon Rd, Singapore 0821; f. 1967; tel. 2963469; fax 2929766.

## ISLAM

**Majlis Ugama Islam Singapura (MUIS)** (Islamic Religious Council): Islamic Centre of Singapore, 273 Braddell Road, Singapore 2057; tel. 2568188; fax 2537572; f. 1968; Pres. Haji ZAINUL ABIDIN RASHEED.

**Muslim Missionary Society Singapore (Jamiyah):** 31 Lorong 12, Geylang, Singapore 1439; tel. 7431211; telex 34725; fax 7450160; Pres. Haji ABU BAKAR MAIDIN; Sec.-Gen. JAAFAR MAJORI.

## SIKHISM

**Sikh Advisory Board:** c/o 2 Towner Rd, 03-01, Singapore 1232; tel. and fax 2996440. Chair. HARBANS SINGH.

# The Press

Compulsory government scrutiny of newspaper management has been in operation since 1974. All newspaper enterprises must be public companies. In August 1986 there were more than 3,700 foreign publications circulating in Singapore. The Newspaper and Printing Presses (Amendment) Act 1986 empowers the Government to restrict the circulation of foreign periodicals that are deemed to exert influence over readers on domestic political issues. An amendment to the Newspaper and Printing Presses Act was promulgated in October 1990. Under this amendment, all publications of which the 'contents and editorial policy were determined

# SINGAPORE

outside Singapore' and which dealt with politics and current events in South-East Asia would be required to obtain a ministerial licence, renewable annually. The permit would limit the number of copies sold and require a deposit in case of legal proceedings involving the publication. Permits could be refused or revoked without any reason being given. In November, however, a statement was issued exempting 14 of the 17 foreign publications affected by the amendment, which came into effect in December.

## DAILIES

### English Language

**Business Times:** Times House, 390 Kim Seng Rd, Singapore 0923; tel. 7370011; telex 21239; fax 7335271; f. 1976; Editor PATRICK DANIEL; circ. 36,000 (Singapore only).

**The New Paper:** Times House, 390 Kim Seng Rd, Singapore 0923; tel. 7370011; fax 7375375; f. 1988; Editor P. N. BALJI; circ. 90,315 (Singapore only).

**The Straits Times:** Times House, 390 Kim Seng Rd, Singapore 0923; tel. 7370011; telex 21239; fax 7320131; f. 1845; Editor-in-Chief CHEONG YIP SENG; circ. 392611 (Singapore only).

### Chinese Language

**Lianhe Wanbao:** Times House, 390 Kim Seng Rd, Singapore 0923; tel. 7370011; telex 21239; fax 7320131; f. 1983; evening; Editor LOY TECK JUAN; circ. 85,500.

**Lianhe Zaobao:** News Centre, 82 Genting Lane, Singapore 1334; tel. 7438800; fax 7427226; f. 1983; Editor LIM JIM KOON; circ. 206,795.

**Shin Min Daily News (S) Ltd:** Times House, 390 Kim Seng Rd, Singapore 0923; tel. 7370011; telex 21239; fax 7320131; f. 1967; Editor SENG HAN THONG; circ. 90,000.

### Malay Language

**Berita Harian:** Times House, 390 Kim Seng Rd, Singapore 0923; tel. 7370011; telex 21239; fax 2355402; f. 1957; morning; Editor ZAINUL ABIDIN RASHEED; circ. 60,000 (Singapore only).

### Tamil Language

**Tamil Murasu:** 161 Kampong Ampat, 05-03 Goldlion Bldg, Singapore 1336; tel. 2840076; fax 2842737; f. 1935; Editor V. T. ARASU; circ. 10,000 (daily), 13,500 (Sunday).

## WEEKLIES

### English Language

**Sunday Times:** Times House, 390 Kim Seng Rd, Singapore 0923; tel. 7370011; telex 21239; fax 7320131; f. 1845; Editor-in-Chief CHEONG YIP SENG; circ. 387,000 (Singapore only).

### Malay Language

**Berita Minggu:** Times House, 390 Kim Seng Rd, Singapore 0923; tel. 7370011; telex 21239; fax 7320131; f. 1957; Sunday; Editor ZAINUL ABIDIN RASHEED; circ. 73,231 (Singapore only).

## SELECTED PERIODICALS

### English Language

**Accent:** Block 305, 1 Ubi Ave, 02-169, Singapore 1440; tel. 7478088; telex 39283; fax 7472811; f. 1983; 2 a month; lifestyle; Senior Editor DORA TAY; circ. 65,000.

**Cherie Magazine:** 12 Everton Rd, Singapore 0208; tel. 2229733; fax 2843859; f. 1983; bimonthly; women's; Editor JOSEPHINE NG; circ. 20,000.

**8 Days:** SBC Enterprises Pte Ltd, 21-02/05 Goldhill Plaza, 51 Newton Rd, Singapore 1130; tel. 2556288; telex 39265; fax 2568921; f. 1990; weekly; CEO TAN JU KUANG; circ. 75,000.

**Fame Magazine:** Singapore; tel. 2966166; fax 2987551; f. 1990; monthly; entertainment; Editor MAUREEN KOH; circ. 30,000.

**Go:** Times Periodicals Pte Ltd, 422 Thomson Rd, Singapore 1129; tel. 2550011; fax 2568016; f. 1980; monthly; women's; Editor SANDRA CAMPBELL; circ. 27,000.

**Her World:** Times Periodicals Pte Ltd, 422 Thomson Rd, Singapore 1129; tel. 2550011; fax 2568016; f. 1956; monthly; women's; Editor TAN WANG JOO; circ. 57,000.

**Home and Decor:** Times Periodicals Pte Ltd, 422 Thomson Rd, Singapore 1129; tel. 2550011; fax 2568016; 6 a year; home-owners; Editor SOPHIE KHO; circ. 12,000.

**Lifestyle:** 1 New Industrial Rd, Times Centre, Singapore 1953; tel. 2848844; telex 25713; fax 2881186; f. 1987; bimonthly; English and Chinese; general interest; Editor DIANA TAN; circ. 250,000.

**Man—Life & Style:** 55 Cuppage Rd, 08-06 Cuppage Centre, Singapore 0922; tel. 7386166; fax 7386122; f. 1986; monthly; men's; Editor SU MANN ONG; circ. 20,000.

**Mondial Collections:** Singapore; telex 35983; f. 1990; bimonthly; arts; Chair. CHRIS CHENEY; circ. 100,000.

**NSman:** 5200 Jalan Bukit Merah, Singapore 0315; tel. 2786011; fax 2737441; f. 1973; bimonthly; men's; Editor SAMUEL EE; circ. 95,000.

**Republic of Singapore Government Gazette:** Singapore National Printers Ltd, 303 Upper Serangoon Rd, POB 485, Singapore 1334; tel. 2820611; telex 24462; fax 2854894; weekly; Friday.

**Reservist:** 5200 Jalan Bukit Merah, Singapore 0315; tel. 2786011; fax 273441; f. 1973; bimonthly; men's; Editor SAMUEL EE; circ. 130,000.

**Singapore Business:** Times Periodicals Pte Ltd, 390 Kim Seng Rd, Singapore 0923; tel. 7370011; telex 21239; fax 7335271; f. 1977; monthly; Editor PATRICK DANIEL; circ. 13,000.

**Singapore Medical Journal:** Singapore Medical Association, Level 2, Alumni Medical Centre, 2 College Rd, Singapore 0316; tel. 2231264; fax 2247827; 6 a year; Editor Prof. CHEE YAM CHENG.

**Times Guide to Computers:** 1 New Industrial Rd, Times Centre, Singapore 1953; tel. 2848844; fax 2850161; f. 1986; annually; computing and communications; Asst Vice-Pres. LESLIE LIM; circ. 30,000.

**Visage:** Ubi Ave 1, 02-169 Block 305, Singapore 1440; tel. 7478088; fax 7472811; f. 1984; monthly; Editor-in-Chief TENG JUAT LENG; circ. 63,000.

**WEEKENDeast:** 82 Genting Lane, News Centre, Singapore 1334; tel. 7401200; fax 7451022; f. 1986; Editor VICTOR SOH; circ. 75,000.

**Woman's Affair:** 140 Paya Lebar Rd, 04-10 A-Z Bldg, Singapore 1440; tel. 7478088; fax 7479119; f. 1988; 2 a month; Editor DORA TAY; circ. 38,000.

**Young Families:** Times Periodicals Pte Ltd, 422 Thomson Rd, Singapore 1129; tel. 2550011; fax 2568016; quarterly; family; also in Chinese; Editor ANGELINE THIEN; circ. 70,000.

### Chinese Language

**Characters:** 1 Kallang Sector, 04-04/04-05 Kolam Ayer Industrial Park, Singapore 1334; tel. 7458733; fax 7458213; f. 1987; monthly; television and entertainment; Editor SAM NG; circ. 45,000.

**The Citizen:** People's Association, Kallang, Singapore 1439; tel. 3405105; telex 38891; fax 4401553; monthly; English and Chinese; Man. Editor OOI HUI MEI.

**Movie & TV Weekly:** Henderson Rd 06-04, Block 203A, Henderson Industrial Park, Singapore 0315; tel. 2733000; fax 2749538; f. 1984; monthly; Editor CHAN ENG; circ. 95,000.

**Punters' Way:** 1 Kallang Sector, 04-04/04-05 Kolam Ayer Industrial Park, Singapore 1334; tel. 7458733; fax 7458213; f. 1977; biweekly; English and Chinese; sport; Editor T. S. PHAN; circ. 90,000.

**Racing Guide:** 1 New Industrial Rd, Times Centre, Singapore 1953; tel. 2848844; telex 25713; fax 2881186; f. 1987; 2 a week; English and Chinese; sport; Editorial Consultant BENNY ORTEGA; Chinese Editor KUEK CHIEW TEONG; circ. 20,000.

**Radio & TV Times (Chinese):** 51 Newton Rd, 22-06/08 Goldhill Plaza, Singapore 1130; tel. 2556288; telex 39265; fax 2540747; f. 1981; weekly; Editors TEO SONG LENG, WONG OI KUAN, ONG SOON NYUK; circ. 130,000.

**Singapore Literature:** Singapore Literature Society, 122B Sims Ave, Singapore 1438; quarterly; Pres. YAP KOON CHAN; Editor LUO-MING.

**Tune Monthly Magazine:** Henderson Rd 06-04, Block 203A, Henderson Industrial Park, Singapore 0315; tel. 2733000; fax 2749538; f. 1988; monthly; women's and fashion; Editor CHAN ENG; circ. 25,000.

**Young Generation:** EPB Publishers Pte Ltd, Block 162, Bukit Merah Central, 04-3545, Singapore 0315; tel. 2780881; telex 56289; fax 2766970; monthly; Editors WINSTON LAM, KOH SWEE YANG; circ. 80,000.

## NEWS AGENCIES

### Foreign Bureaux

**Agence France-Presse (AFP):** Maxwell Rd, POB 1847, Singapore 9036; tel. 2228581; telex 21255; fax 2247465; Bureau Chief MICHELE COOPER.

**Agenzia Nazionale Stampa Associata (ANSA)** (Italy): 18 Grove Drive, Singapore 1027; tel. 4690265; telex 38629; fax 4671912; Bureau Chief LICINIO GERMINI.

**Associated Press (AP)** (USA): 6 Battery Rd, 23-02 Standard Chartered Bank Bldg, Singapore 0104; tel. 2201849; telex 21232; Bureau Chief KENNETH L. WHITING.

**Central News Agency Inc. (CNA)** (Taiwan): 151 Cavenagh Rd, Ilex 08-151, Cavenagh Court, Singapore 0922; tel. and fax 7324193; Bureau Chief LEE PEI-HSIUNG.

# SINGAPORE

**Informatsionnoye Telegrafnoye Agentstvo Rossii—Telegrafnoye Agentstvo Suverennykh Stran (ITAR—TASS)** (Russia): 154-A Avenue Park, Sixth Ave, Singapore 1027; tel. 4684266; Correspondent STANISLAV V. BYCHKOV.

**Inter Press Service (IPS)** (Italy): Marine Parade Rd, 10-42 Lagoon View, Singapore 1544; tel. 4490432; Correspondent SURYA GANGADHARAN.

**Jiji Tsushin-sha (Jiji Press)** (Japan): 10 Anson Rd, 26-05 International Plaza, Singapore 0207; tel. 2244212; telex 28538; fax 2240711; Correspondent TAKASHI YAGI.

**Kyodo News Service** (Japan): 138 Cecil St, Cecil Court, Singapore; tel. 2233371; telex 36023; fax 2249208; Chief SHUICHI NAKAMURA.

**Reuters Singapore Pte Ltd:** 18 Science Park Drive, Singapore 0511; tel. 2253848; telex 21290; fax 2259317; Man. Dir ANIRUDDHA JOSHI.

**Rossiyskoye Informatsionnoye Agentstvo—Novosti (RIA—Novosti)** (Russia): 8 Namly Grove, Singapore 1026; tel. 4667998; telex 21703; fax 4690784; Correspondent MIKHAIL I. IDAMKIN.

**United Press International (UPI)** (USA): Singapore; tel. 3373715; fax 3389867; Man. C. J. HWU.

Bernama (Malaysia), United News (India) and Xinhua (People's Republic of China) are also represented.

## Publishers

### ENGLISH LANGUAGE

**Addison-Wesley (S) Pte Ltd:** 15 Beach Rd, 05-09/10 Beach Centre, Singapore 0718; tel. 3397503; telex 20904; fax 3399709; educational, computing and professional books; Man. Dir PAUL GOULDING.

**Butterworths Asia:** Singapore; tel. 2203684; fax 2255026; f. 1932; law texts and journals; Man. Dir STEPHEN STOUT.

**Caldecott Publishing Pte Ltd:** 298 Tiong Bahru Rd, 19-01/06 Tiong Bahru Plaza, Singapore 0316; tel. 2789822; fax 2724800.

**Chopmen Publishers:** 37 Jalan Pemimpin, 04–02 Union Industrial Bldg, Singapore 2059; tel. 3531101; fax 3542212; f. 1963; scholarly, academic, children's and general; Man. Dir N. T. S. CHOPRA.

**EPB Publishers Pte Ltd:** Block 162, 04-3545 Bukit Merah Central, Singapore 0315; tel. 2780881; telex 56289; fax 2782456; fmrly Educational Publications Bureau Pte Ltd; textbooks and supplementary materials, general, reference and magazines; English and Chinese; Gen. Man. AU PUI CHUAN.

**Federal Publications (S) Pte Ltd:** 1 New Industrial Rd, Singapore 1953; tel. 2848844; fax 2889254; f. 1957; educational, children's, general and reference books, academic; Gen. Man. Y. H. MEW.

**FEP International Pte Ltd:** 108 Pasir Panjang Rd, Singapore 0511; tel. 4743135; telex 25601; fax 4752389; f. 1960; textbooks, reference, children's and dictionaries; Gen. Man. RICHARD TOH.

**Flame of the Forest:** Block 1003, Yishun Industrial Park A, 02-432, Singapore; tel. 7532071; fax 7532407; Man. Dir ALEX CHACKO.

**Graham Brash (Pte) Ltd:** Singapore; tel. 2993441; telex 23718; fax 2991967; f. 1956; general, academic, educational; English, Chinese and Malay; Man. Dir K. C. CAMPBELL.

**HarperCollins, Asia Pte Ltd:** 970 Toa Payoh North, 04/24/26, Singapore 1231; tel. 2501985; fax 2501360; f. 1983; educational, children's, reference and general; Man. Dir FRANK FOLEY.

**Institute of Southeast Asian Studies:** Heng Mui Keng Terrace, Pasir Panjang Rd, Singapore 0511; tel. 7780955; telex 37068; fax 7781735; f. 1968; scholarly works on contemporary South-East Asia and the Pacific; Dir Prof. CHAN HENG CHEE.

**Intellectual Publishing Co:** 113 Eunos Ave 3, 04-08 Gordon Industrial Bldg, Singapore 1440; tel. 7466025; telex 55708; fax 7489108; f. 1971; Propr POH BE LECK.

**Landmark:** Singapore; Gen. Man. GOH ECK KHENG.

**Longman Singapore Publishers (Pte) Ltd:** 25 First Lok Yang Rd, Jurong Town, Singapore 2262; tel. 2682666; telex 24268; fax 2641740; textbooks, medicine, science, technology; Man. Dir WEE HIAN KING.

**McGraw-Hill Book Co:** 21 Neythal Rd, Jurong, Singapore 2262; tel. 2654633; telex 36791; fax 2652972; f. 1969; general educational; Man. Dir R. RADHAKRISHNAN.

**Oxford University Press Pte Ltd:** Singapore; tel. 2597122; fax 2598622; f. 1955; educational, academic and general; Man. Dir CLARENCE LIM.

**Reed International (Singapore) Pte Ltd:** 37 Jalan Pemimpin, 07–04, Block B, Union Industrial Bldg, Singapore 2057; tel. 2583255; telex 24299; fax 2588279; educational and consumer; Man. Dir CHARLES CHER.

**Simon & Schuster Asia Pte Ltd:** 24 Pasir Panjang Rd, 04-31 PSA Multi Storey Complex, Singapore 0511; tel. 2789611; telex 37270; fax 2734400; f. 1975; educational; Man. Dir GUNAWAN HADI.

**Singapore University Press Pte Ltd:** National University of Singapore, Yusof Ishak House, Kent Ridge, Singapore 0511; tel. 7761148; fax 7740652; f. 1971; scholarly; Editor and Man. PATRICIA TAY.

**Stamford College Publishers:** 246 MacPherson Rd, Betime Bldg, Singapore 1334; tel. 3393688; telex 25596; fax 3395825; f. 1970; general, educational and journals; Man. LAWRENCE THOMAS.

**Times Editions Pte Ltd:** Times Centre, 1 New Industrial Rd, Singapore 1953; tel. 2848844; fax 2854871; f. 1978; political, social and cultural books, general works on Asia; Vice-Pres. and Gen. Man. SHIRLEY HEW.

**World Scientific Publishing Co Pte Ltd:** Farrer Road, POB 128, Singapore 9128; tel. 3825663; telex 28561; fax 3825919; f. 1980; academic texts and science journals; Man. Dir DOREEN LIU.

### MALAY LANGUAGE

**Malaysia Press Sdn Bhd** (Pustaka Melayu): 745–747 North Bridge Rd, Singapore 0719; tel. 2933454; fax 2911858; f. 1962; textbooks and educational; Man. Dir ABU TALIB BIN ALLY.

**Pustaka Nasional Pte Ltd:** 2 Joo Chiat Rd, 05-1131 Joo Chiat Complex, Singapore 1542; tel. 7454321; fax 7452417; Malay and Islamic religious books; Man. Dir SYED AHMAD BIN MUHAMAD.

### CHINESE LANGUAGE

**Shanghai Book Co (Pte) Ltd:** 231 Bain St, 02-73 Bras Basah Complex, Singapore 0718; tel. 3360144; telex 29297; fax 3360490; f. 1925; educational and general; Man. Dir CHEN MONG HOCK.

**Shing Lee Publishers Pte Ltd:** 120 Hillview Ave, 05-06/07 Kewalram Hillview, Singapore 2366; tel. 7601388; telex 39255; fax 7625684; f. 1935; educational and general; Man. PEH CHIN HUA.

**Union Book Co (Pte) Ltd:** 231 Bain St 03-01, Bras Basah Complex, Singapore 0718; tel. 3380696; fax 3386306; general and reference; Gen. Man. CHOW LI-LIANG.

### TAMIL LANGUAGE

**EVS Enterprises:** 629 Upper Serangoon Rd, Singapore 1953; tel. 2830002; f. 1967; children's books, religion and general; Man. E. V. SINGHAN.

### Government Publishing House

**SNP Corporation Ltd:** 303 Upper Serangoon Rd, Singapore 1334; tel. 2820611; telex 24462; fax 2854894; f. 1973; printers and publishers; Chair. LUM CHOONG WAH.

### PUBLISHERS' ORGANIZATIONS

**National Book Development Council of Singapore (NBDCS):** Singapore; promotes reading and jointly organizes the annual Singapore Book Fair with the Singapore Book Publishers' Association.

**Singapore Book Publishers' Association:** c/o Chopmen Publrs, 865 Mountbatten Rd, 05-28 Katong Shopping Centre, Singapore 1543; tel. 3441495; fax 3440180; Pres. N. T. S. CHOPRA.

## Radio and Television

In 1994 210,370 radio licences and 645,529 television licences were issued.

**Singapore Broadcasting Authority:** 1 Maritime Square, 09-59 World Trade Centre, Singapore 0409; tel. 2708191; fax 2786009; f. 1994; regulates and promotes the broadcasting industry in Singapore; licenses broadcasting services, collects licence fees, oversees quality of programming through the issuing of guidelines on subject matter and censorship (including global computer information exchange), also acts as representative of Singapore on matters relating to international broadcasting; Chair. GOH KIM LEONG; CEO Col. HO MENG KIT.

**Singapore International Media (SIM):** Caldecott Hill, Andrew Rd, Singapore 1129; tel. 2560401; telex 39265; fax 2538808; f. 1994 following the privatization of the Singapore Broadcasting Corpn; holding co for four operating broadcasting cos: Television Corpn of Singapore; Television Twelve, Radio Corpn of Singapore and SIM Communications; Chair. Dr CHEONG CHOONG KONG; Gen. Man. MOSES LEE.

### RADIO

**Far East Broadcasting (FEBA Ltd):** POB 751, Robinson Rd, Singapore 9015; tel. 2225418; telex 25281; fax 2221805; f. 1960; Chair. GOH EWE KHENG; Exec. Dir Rev. Dr DAVID L. CHEN.

# SINGAPORE

**Radio Corpn of Singapore Pte Ltd (RCS):** Farrer Rd, Locked Bag Service 008, Singapore 9128; tel. 2518622; fax 2569533; f. 1936; operates 10 domestic services, in English (four), Chinese (Mandarin) (three), Malay (two) and Tamil; manages three International services for Radio Singapore International (RSI) in English and Malay; CEO ANTHONY CHIA.

**Radio Heart:** Singapore; f. 1991; first private radio station; 2 channels broadcasting a total of 280 hours.

**Rediffusion (Singapore) Pte Ltd:** 6 Harper Rd, 04-01/08 Leong Huat Bldg, Singapore 1336; tel. 3832633; fax 3832622; f. 1949; commercial wired broadcasting service; broadcasts two programmes in Mandarin (18 hours daily) and English (24 hours daily) to more than 90,000 listeners (1994); Man. Dir WONG BAN KUAN.

**SIM Communications:** Singapore; f. 1994.

### TELEVISION

**Asia Business News (ABN):** Singapore; f. 1994; satellite broadcaster of Asian business news; US controlled; Chief Exec. PAUL FRANCE.

**Singapore CableVision:** Singapore; f. 1993; subscription television service; three channels.

**Television Corpn of Singapore Private Ltd (TCS):** Caldecott Broadcast Centre, Andrew Rd, Singapore 1129; tel. 2560401; fax 2538808; f. 1963; three channels; colour transmissions since 1974; total weekly average of 254 hours; programmes in Chinese (Mandarin), Tamil and English; teletext service on two channels since 1983; Chair. KWA CHONG SENG; CEO LEE CHEOK YEW.

**Television Twelve:** 12 Prince Edward Rd, 05-00 Bestway Bldg, Singapore 0207; tel. 2258133; fax 2253238; f. 1994; one VHF channel (Channel 12), one UHF channel (to be launched in late 1995); total weekly average of 59 hours; programmes in English, Malay and other languages (a new channel will broadcast programmes in Tamil); Pres. and CEO SANDRA BUENAVENTURA.

# Finance

(cap. = capital; dep. = deposits; m. = million;
brs = branches; amounts in Singapore dollars)

### BANKING

The Singapore monetary system is regulated by the Monetary Authority of Singapore (MAS) and the Ministry of Finance. The MAS performs all the functions of a central bank, except the issuing of currency, a function which is carried out by the Board of Commissioners of Currency. In April 1995 there were 140 commercial banks (12 local, 138 foreign) and 57 representative offices in Singapore. Of the banks, 34 had full licences, 14 had restricted licences and 92 foreign banks had 'offshore' banking licences.

### Government Financial Institutions

**Board of Commissioners of Currency, Singapore:** 79 Robinson Rd, 01-01 CPF Bldg, Singapore 0106; tel. 2222211; telex 24722; fax 2257671; Chair. Dr RICHARD HU TSU TAU; Dep. Chair. NGIAM TONG DOW; Gen. Man. LAU KIM BOO.

**Monetary Authority of Singapore (MAS):** 10 Shenton Way, MAS Bldg, Singapore 0207; tel. 2255577; telex 28174; fax 2299491; Chair. Dr RICHARD HU TSU TAU; Man. Dir LEE EK TIENG.

### Domestic Full Commercial Banks

**Bank of Singapore Ltd:** 101 Cecil St, 01-02 Tong Eng Bldg, Singapore 0106; tel. 2239266; telex 26894; fax 2247731; f. 1955; subsidiary of Oversea-Chinese Banking Corpn Ltd; cap. 50m., dep. 1,556.8m. (Dec. 1993); Chair. TAN TOCK SAN; CEO SEAH BUCK TIANG; 5 brs.

**Chung Khiaw Bank Ltd:** 10 Anson Rd, 01-01 International Plaza, Singapore 0207; tel. 2228622; telex 22027; fax 5382528; f. 1950; subsidiary of United Overseas Bank Ltd; cap. 100m., dep. 4,798.4m. (Dec. 1993); Chair. WEE CHO YAW; Pres. ERNEST WONG YUEN WENG; 14 local brs, 2 overseas brs.

**DBS Bank (Development Bank of Singapore Ltd):** 6 Shenton Way, DBS Bldg, Tower One, Singapore 0106; tel. 2201111; telex 24455; fax 2211306; f. 1968; 44% govt-owned; cap. 905.8m., dep. 31.6m. (Dec. 1993); Pres. PATRICK YEOH KHWAI HOH; Chair. NGIAM TONG DOW; 46 local brs, 11 overseas brs.

**Far Eastern Bank Ltd:** 156 Cecil St, 01-00 FEB Bldg, Singapore 0106; tel. 2219055; telex 23029; fax 5382528; f. 1959; subsidiary of United Overseas Bank Ltd; cap. 24.4m., dep. 324.8m. (Dec. 1993); Chair. WEE CHO YAW; Pres. ERNEST WONG YUEN WENG; 4 brs.

**Four Seas Bank Ltd:** 110 Robinson Rd, Singapore 0106; tel. 2249898; telex 23670; fax 2244936; f. 1907; subsidiary of Oversea-Chinese Banking Corpn. Ltd; cap. 60m., dep. 1,189.6m. (Dec. 1993); Chair. TAN PUAY YONG; Dir and Gen. Man. EDDIE TANG; 3 brs.

**Industrial and Commercial Bank Ltd:** 2 Shenton Way, 01-01 ICB Bldg, Singapore 0106; tel. 2211711; telex 21112; fax 2259777; f. 1954; cap. 168.0m., dep. 667.9m. (Dec. 1993); Chair. WEE CHO YAW; Pres. ERNEST WONG YUEN WENG; 15 brs.

**International Bank of Singapore Ltd:** 60 Robinson Rd, Singapore 0106; tel. 2234488; telex 23579; fax 2240236; f. 1975; subsidiary of Overseas Union Bank Ltd; cap. 100m., dep. 853.8m. (Dec. 1993); Exec. Dir and CEO Dr TAN NG CHEE; Dir and Chief Operating Officer GRACY CHOO; 3 local brs, 4 overseas brs.

**Keppel Bank of Singapore Ltd:** 10 Hoe Chiang Rd, Keppel Towers, Singapore 0208; tel. 2228222; telex 21911; fax 2252256; f. 1959; fmrly Asia Commercial Bank Ltd; cap. 457.5m., dep. 4,597.1m. (Dec. 1993); Chair. SIM KEE BOON; Pres. BENEDICT KWEK; 16 brs.

**Lee Wah Bank Ltd:** 1 Coleman St, 01-14 The Adelphi, Singapore 0617; tel. 5339898; telex 21529; fax 5392528; f. 1920; subsidiary of United Overseas Bank Ltd; cap. 20m., dep. 2,336.4m. (Dec. 1993); Chair. WEE CHO YAW; Pres. ERNEST WONG YUEN WENG; 3 local brs, 9 overseas brs.

**Oversea-Chinese Banking Corpn Ltd:** 65 Chulia St, 08-00 OCBC Centre, Singapore 0104; tel. 5357222; telex 21209; fax 5337955; f. 1932; cap. 850.6m., dep. 23,431.4m. (Dec. 1993); Chair. and CEO Dr TONY TAN KENG YAM; 57 local brs, 14 overseas brs.

**Overseas Union Bank Ltd:** 1 Raffles Place, OUB Centre, Singapore 0104; tel. 5338686; telex 24475; fax 5332293; f. 1949; cap. 446.8m., dep. 11,447.2m. (Dec. 1993); Group Chair. and CEO Dr LIEN YING CHOW; Pres. and CEO PETER SEAH LIM HUAT; 36 local brs, 11 overseas brs.

**Tat Lee Bank Ltd:** 63 Market St, Tat Lee Bank Bldg, Singapore 0104; tel. 5339292; telex 26767; fax 5331043; f. 1974; cap. 344.5m., dep. 4,556.6m. (Dec. 1993); Chair. and CEO GOH TJOEI KOK; Pres. GOH ENG CHEW; 29 local brs, 1 overseas br.

**United Overseas Bank Ltd:** 80 Raffles Place, UOB Plaza, Singapore 0104; tel. 5339898; telex 21539; fax 5342334; f. 1935; cap. 663.10m., dep. 19,049.7m. (Dec. 1993); Chair. WEE CHO YAW; Pres. ERNEST WONG YUEN WENG; 47 local brs, 13 overseas brs.

### Savings Bank

**Post Office Savings Bank:** 73 Bras Basah Rd, POSB Centre, Singapore 0718; tel. 3393333; telex 25450; fax 3341282; govt statutory body; Chair. MOSES LIM KIM POO; Gen. Man. BERTIE CHENG; 135 brs and 10 automated brs.

### Foreign Banks

Full Commercial Banks

**ABN AMRO Bank NV** (Netherlands): 18 Church St, Singapore 0104; tel. 5355511; telex 24396; fax 5323108; Gen. Man. P. H. M. VAN AMERONGEN.

**Ban Hin Lee Bank Bhd** (Malaysia): 105 Cecil St, 01-00 The Octagon, Singapore 0106; tel. 2272133; telex 24191; fax 2272088; Dir YEAP LAM YANG; Sr Man. PHILIP HONG.

**Bangkok Bank Public Co Ltd** (Thailand): 180 Cecil St, Bangkok Bank Bldg, Singapore 0106; tel. 2219400; telex 21359; fax 2255852; Sr Vice-Pres. and Gen. Man. AMNUEY LILAONITKUL.

**Bank of America NT & SA** (USA): 78 Shenton Way, Singapore 0207; tel. 2236688; telex 24570; fax 3203068; merged with Security Pacific National Bank in 1992; Exec. Vice-Pres. and Regional Gen. Man. COLM MCCARTHY.

**Bank of China** (People's Republic of China): 4 Battery Rd, Bank of China Bldg, Singapore 0104; tel. 5352411; telex 23046; fax 5343401; Gen. Man. ZHOU ZHI-GONG.

**Bank of East Asia Ltd** (Hong Kong): 137 Market St, Bank of East Asia Bldg, Singapore 0104; tel. 2241334; telex 21049; fax 2251805; Gen. Man. PETER Y.K. TSANG.

**Bank of India** (India): 4 Shenton Way, 01-01/05 Shing Kwan House, Singapore 0106; tel. 2220011; telex 21482; fax 2254407; Chief Exec. N. S. NAYAK.

**Bank of Tokyo Ltd** (Japan): 16 Raffles Quay, 01-06 Hong Leong Bldg, Singapore 0104; tel. 2208111; telex 24363; fax 2244965; Gen. Man. TAKASHI ISHIDA; Dep. Gen. Mans MASAO TSUJI, IZUMI HAGIWARA.

**Banque Indosuez** (France): 6 Raffles Quay, 17-00 John Hancock Tower, Singapore 0104; tel. 5354988; telex 24435; fax 5322422; f. 1905; Gen. Man. JEAN-CLAUDE BERGADAA.

**Chase Manhattan Bank NA** (USA): 50 Raffles Place, Shell Tower, Singapore 0104; tel. 5304111; telex 21370; fax 2247950; Vice-Pres. and Country Man. GABRIEL TEO CHEN THYE.

**Citibank NA** (USA): 5 Shenton Way, 06-00 UIC Bldg, Singapore 0106; tel. 2242611; telex 24584; fax 2249844; Vice-Pres. and Country Corporate Officer DAVID P. CONNER.

**HL Bank** (Malaysia): 20 Collyer Quay, 01-02 and 02-02 Tung Centre, Singapore 0104; tel. 5352466; telex 24177; fax 5339340; fmrly MUI Bank Bhd; Gen. Man. NICHOLAS CHIA.

## SINGAPORE

**Hongkong and Shanghai Banking Corpn** (Hong Kong): 21 Collyer Quay, 01-00 HongkongBank Bldg, Singapore 0104; tel. 5305000; telex 21259; fax 2250663; CEO (Singapore) J. C. S. Rankin.

**Indian Bank** (India): 3 Raffles Place, Bharat Bldg, Singapore 0104; tel. 5343511; telex 26308; fax 5331651; Dep. Gen. Man. N. Sundaresan.

**Indian Overseas Bank** (India): 64 Cecil St, IOB Bldg, Singapore 0104; tel. 2251100; telex 23098; fax 2244490; Chief Exec. Balasubramanian Swaminathan.

**Kwangtung (Guangdong) Provincial Bank** (People's Republic of China): 60 Cecil St, 01-00 KPB Bldg, Singapore 0104; tel. 2239622; telex 26166; fax 2259970; Gen. Man. Qiu Weifa (acting).

**Malayan Banking Bhd (Maybank)** (Malaysia): 2 Battery Rd, 01-00 Maybank Chambers, Singapore 0104; tel. 5352266; telex 21036; fax 5327909; Sr Gen. Man. Spencer Lee.

**PT Bank Negara Indonesia (Persero)** (Indonesia): 158 Cecil St, 01 to 04-00 Dapenso Bldg, Singapore 0106; tel. 2257755; telex 21749; fax 2254757; Gen. Man. Muhammad Muchtar Panjaitan.

**Sakura Bank Ltd** (Japan): 16 Raffles Quay, 01-04 Hong Leong Bldg, Singapore 0104; tel. 2209761; telex 21319; fax 2250962; Gen. Man. Takehisa Hiraiwa.

**Standard Chartered Bank PLC**: (UK): 6 Battery Rd, Singapore 0104; tel. 2258888; telex 24290; fax 2259136; Exec. Dir (Asia-Pacific Region) David G. Moir; Chief Exec. (Singapore) Theresa Foo.

**UCO Bank** (India): 3 Raffles Place, Bharat Bldg, Singapore 0104; tel. 5325944; telex 21682; fax 5325044; Chief Exec. R. Gangadharan.

**United Malayan Banking Corpn Bhd** (Malaysia): 150 Cecil St, 01-00 Wing On Life Bldg, Singapore 0106; tel. 2253111; telex 20309; fax 2247871; Assistant Gen. Man. (Head of Singapore Operations) Tommy Lou Jenn Chee.

### Restricted Banks

**American Express Bank Ltd** (USA): 16 Collyer Quay, Hitachi Tower, Singapore 0104; tel. 5384833; telex 21172; fax 5343022; Exec. Dir and Country Man. Elie J. Baroudi.

**Banca Commerciale Italiana** (Italy): 36 Robinson Rd, 03-01 City House, Singapore 0106; tel. 2201333; telex 24545; fax 2252004; Sr Vice-Pres. Giacomo Ghillani.

**Banque Nationale de Paris** (France): 20 Collyer Quay, 01-01 Tung Centre, Singapore 0104; tel. 2240211; telex 24315; fax 2243459; CEO Alain Bailly; Dep. Gen. Man. Christian Giraudon.

**Bayerische Landesbank Girozentrale** (Germany): 300 Beach Rd, 37-01 The Concourse, Singapore 0719; tel. 2933822; telex 21445; fax 2932151; Gen. Man. and Chief Exec. Michael King.

**Chiao Tung Bank Co Ltd** (Taiwan): 4 Shenton Way, 08-01 Shing Kwan House, Singapore 0106; tel. 2239197; telex 22662; fax 2240561; Sr Vice-Pres. and Gen. Man. Maria Lu Dan-Hun.

**Crédit Suisse** (Switzerland): 80 Raffles Place, 49-01 UOB Plaza 1, Singapore 0104; tel. 5386322; telex 24650; fax 5312708; Br. Head Robert S. Lette.

**Deutsche Bank AG** (Germany): 6 Shenton Way, 15-08 DBS Bldg, Tower Two, Singapore 0104; tel. 2244677; telex 21189; fax 2259442; Gen. Mans Guido Mundt, Winston Tan Tien Hin.

**Dresdner Bank AG** (Germany): 20 Collyer Quay, 22-00 Tung Centre, Singapore 0104; tel. 2228080; telex 29366; fax 2244008; Gen. Mans Dr Manfred Barth, Raymond B. T. Koh, G. B. Low, Tan Eng Huat.

**First Commercial Bank** (Taiwan): 76 Shenton Way, 01-02 Ong Bldg, Singapore 0207; tel. 2215755; telex 24693; fax 2251905; Vice-Pres. and Gen. Man. Chiang Jin-Der.

**Habib Bank Ltd** (Pakistan): 141 Market St, International Factors Bldg, Singapore 0104; tel. 2230388; telex 21679; fax 2259562; Sr Vice-Pres. and Chief Man. Syed Pervaiz Mehdi.

**Korea Exchange Bank** (Republic of Korea): 2 Finlayson Green, 01-00 Asia Insurance Bldg, Singapore 0104; tel. 2241633; telex 21956; fax 2243701; Gen. Man. Cho Do Jae.

**Mitsubishi Bank Ltd** (Japan): 20 Collyer Quay, 12-01 Tung Centre, Singapore 0104; tel. 2205666; telex 21913; fax 2254739; Gen. Man. Hiizu Ichikawa.

**Moscow Narodny Bank Ltd** (UK): 50 Robinson Rd, MNB Bldg, Singapore 0106; tel. 2209422; telex 21726; fax 2250140; Gen. Man. I. G. Souvorov.

**Sumitomo Bank Ltd** (Japan): 6 Shenton Way, 27-08 DBS Bldg Tower Two, Singapore 0106; tel. 2201611; telex 21656; fax 2259647; Gen. Man. Hiroshi Tadano.

### 'Offshore' Banks

**ABSA Bank Ltd** (South Africa): 8 Robinson Rd, 03, Cosco Bldg, Singapore 0104; tel. 5366628; telex 24667; fax 5366612; Gen. Man. Tony G. Rogers.

**Allied Irish Banks PLC** (Ireland): 21 Collyer Quay, 11-01 HongkongBank Bldg, Singapore 0104; tel. 2258666; telex 25231; fax 2244928; Gen. Man. Seamus Doherty.

**Arab Bank PLC** (Jordan): 80 Raffles Place, 55-01 UOB Plaza 1, Singapore 0104; tel. 5330055; telex 22955; fax 5322150; Exec. Vice-Pres. and Area Head James J. Liu.

**Arab Banking Corpn (BSC)** (Bahrain): 20 Raffles Place, 11-03 Ocean Towers, Singapore 0104; tel. 5330315; telex 28989; fax 5335926; Gen. Man. Justin Goh Cheow Siah.

**Asahi Bank Ltd** (Japan): 50 Raffles Place, 25-01/06 Shell Tower, Singapore 0104; tel. 5354822; telex 22059; fax 5331462; Gen. Man. Masuhiro Omori.

**Australia and New Zealand Banking Group Ltd** (Australia): 10 Collyer Quay, 17-01/07 Ocean Bldg, Singapore 0104; tel. 5358355; telex 23336; fax 5396111; Gen. Man. Peter John Meers.

**Banca Nazionale del Lavoro SpA** (Italy): 111 Somerset Rd, 09-07 PUB Bldg, Singapore 0923; tel. 7363688; telex 28351; fax 7362074; Regional Gen. Man. Giovanni Bastreri.

**Banco do Brasil SA** (Brazil): 65 Chulia St, 38-01 OCBC Centre, Singapore 0104; tel. 5351177; telex 25668; fax 5354138; Gen. Man. Roberto da Silva Vargas.

**Banco Santander SA** (Spain): 20 Raffles Place, 27-01/08 Ocean Towers, Singapore 0104; tel. 5386878; telex 25024; fax 5386879; Gen. Man. Rafael Gómez Abolafio.

**Bank Brussels Lambert** (Belgium): 1 Raffles Place, 42-00 OUB Centre, Singapore 0104; tel. 5324088; telex 20294; fax 5305750; Gen. Man. Paul Houdijk.

**Bank Bumiputra Malaysia Bhd** (Malaysia): 150 Cecil St, 03-01/02, Wing On Life Bldg, Singapore 0106; tel. 2222133; telex 34837; fax 2222125; Gen. Man. Awaluddin bin Mohd Yassin.

**Bank of Hawaii** (USA): 4 Shenton Way, 19-01 Shing Kwan House, Singapore 0106; tel. 2210500; telex 21925; fax 2241144; Sr Vice-Pres. and Gen. Man/Reg. Man. Elson Ng Keng Kwang.

**Bank of Montreal** (Canada): 150 Beach Rd, 26-01 Gateway West, Singapore 0718; tel. 2963233; telex 20660; fax 2965044; Dir and Gen. Man. Marc Vandal.

**Bank of New York** (USA): 10 Collyer Quay, 14-02/03 Ocean Bldg, Singapore 0104; tel. 5359188; telex 23213; fax 5344208; Vice-Pres. and Gen. Man. George A. Fowler.

**Bank of New Zealand** 5 Temasek Blvd, 15-01 Suntec City Tower, Singapore 0103; tel. 3322990; telex 22149; fax 3322991; Gen. Man. W. A. Gloyne.

**Bank of Nova Scotia** (Canada): 10 Collyer Quay, 15-01/04 Ocean Bldg, Singapore 0104; tel. 5358688; telex 22177; fax 5322440; Man. Heng Yong Kung.

**Bank of Yokohama Ltd** (Japan): 50 Raffles Place, 30-04 Shell Tower, Singapore 0104; tel. 2217733; telex 20224; fax 2246410; Gen. Man. Yukihiko Ogawa.

**Bankers' Trust Co** (USA): 50 Raffles Place, 26-01/06 Shell Tower, Singapore 0104; tel. 2229191; telex 28626; fax 2250813; Gen. Man. Ho Tian Yee.

**Banque Française du Commerce Extérieur** (France): 50 Raffles Place, 35-01 Shell Tower, Singapore 0104; tel. 2241455; telex 28277; fax 2248651; Gen. Man. Jacques Michel.

**Banque Internationale à Luxembourg SA** (Luxembourg): 105 Cecil St, 10-01/04 The Octagon, Singapore 0106; tel. 2227622; telex 21396; fax 2243316; Jt Gen. Mans Malcolm Fleming, Han Eng Juan.

**Banque Paribas** (France): 80 Raffles Place, 43-01 UOB Plaza 1, Singapore 0104; tel. 4395000; telex 20414; fax 5384300; Area Man. Alain Kokocinski.

**Banque Worms** (France): 143 Cecil St, 23-00 GB Bldg, Singapore 0106; tel. 2259733; telex 22793; fax 2245636; Gen. Man. Dominique Beretti.

**Barclays Bank PLC** (UK): 50 Raffles Place, 23-01 Shell Tower, Singapore 0104; tel. 2248555; telex 26877; fax 2244717; Country Man. (Singapore) Kevin Wall.

**Berliner Handels- und Frankfurter Bank (BHF-Bank)** (Germany): 150 Beach Rd, 03-00 Gateway West, Singapore 0718; tel. 2912177; telex 28484; fax 2912755; Sr Vice-Pres and Gen. Man. Frank Behrends; Gen. Man. Klaus Gerhard Borig.

**Canadian Imperial Bank of Commerce** (Canada): 16 Collyer Quay, 04-02, Singapore 0104; tel. 5352323; telex 24005; fax 5357565; Exec. Vice-Pres. (Asia-Pacific) Y. J. Mirza.

**Chemical Bank** (USA): 150 Beach Rd, 23-00 Gateway West, Singapore 0718; tel. 2911298; telex 23022; fax 2901756; merged with Manufacturers' Hanover Trust Co in 1992; Man. Dir and Regional Man. Edward Anthony Whitaker, Jr.

**Cho Hung Bank** (Republic of Korea): 4 Shenton Way, 09-01/05 Shing Kwan House, Singapore 0106; tel. 2225955; telex 25049; fax 2219213; Gen. Man. Chung Ki Nam.

## SINGAPORE

**Christiania Bank og Kreditkasse** (Norway): 331 North Bridge Rd, 21-01 Odeon Towers, Singapore 0718; tel. 3382728; telex 42888; fax 3382729; Sr Vice-Pres. and Br. Man. CLAUS RHEIN-KNUDSEN.

**Commercial Bank of Korea Ltd** (Republic of Korea): 5 Shenton Way, 17-03 UIC Bldg, Singapore 0106; tel. 2235855; telex 20465; fax 2259530; Gen. Man. HAN KI CHUL.

**Commerzbank Aktiengesellschaft** (Germany): 8 Shenton Way, 32-01 Treasury Bldg, Singapore 0106; tel. 2234855; telex 27189; fax 2253943; Gen. Mans WILFRIED H. GRAF, GERHARD HELD.

**Commonwealth Bank of Australia** (Australia): 50 Raffles Place, 22-04 Shell Tower, Singapore 0104; tel. 2243877; telex 20920; fax 2245812; Gen. Man. JOHN PATRICK O'DONNELL.

**Compagnie Financière de CIC et de l'Union Européenne (Union Européenne de CIC)** (France): 36 Robinson Rd, 11-01 City House, Singapore 0106; tel. 2250333; telex 29070; fax 2244934; affiliated to Crédit Industriel et Commercial banking group; Gen. Man. JEAN-LUC ANGLADA.

**Co-operatieve Centrale Raiffeisen-Boerenleenbank BA (Rabobank Nederland)** (Netherlands): 50 Raffles Place, 32-01 Shell Tower, Singapore 0104; tel. 2259896; telex 42479; fax 2246692; Gen. Man. (Far East) JOHANNES M. HANNAART.

**Crédit Lyonnais** (France): 65 Chulia St, 37-01 OCBC Centre, Singapore 0104; tel. 5359477; telex 27225; fax 5322834; Gen. Man. ANDRÉ FROISSANT.

**Credito Italiano SpA** (Italy): 80 Raffles Place, 51-01 UOB Plaza 1, Singapore 0104; tel. 5324811; telex 23783; fax 5344300; Chief Man. DANTE PASQUALINI.

**Dai-Ichi Kangyo Bank Ltd** (Japan): 1 Raffles Place, 47-00 OUB Centre, Singapore 0104; tel. 5332626; telex 21622; fax 5332190; Gen. Man. TONAMI HIRAYAMA.

**Daiwa Bank Ltd** (Japan): 8 Shenton Way, 30-01 Treasury Bldg, Singapore 0106; tel. 2201791; telex 22123; fax 2246840; Gen. Man. TAKAYUKI SHIMADA.

**Den Danske Bank Aktieselskab** (Denmark): 50 Raffles Place, 24-01 Shell Tower, Singapore 0104; tel. 2241277; telex 28030; fax 2243320; Gen. Man. POUL KOSS.

**First National Bank of Boston** (USA): 150 Beach Rd, 07-00 Gateway West, Singapore 0718; tel. 2962366; telex 23689; fax 2960998; Vice-Pres. and Gen. Man. PETER J. ROBB.

**Fuji Bank Ltd** (Japan): 1 Raffles Place, 20-00 OUB Centre, Singapore 0104; tel. 5343500; telex 24610; fax 5327310; Gen. Man. TORU ISHIHARA.

**Hanil Bank** (Republic of Korea): 1 Raffles Place, 23-02 OUB Centre, Singapore 0104; tel. 5386696; telex 26857; fax 5380056; Gen. Man. CHUNG TAE WOONG.

**Hill Samuel Bank Ltd** (UK): 6 Shenton Way, 19-00 DBS Bldg, Tower Two, Singapore 0106; tel. 5341191; telex 28258; fax 5322493; Gen. Man. KEVIN WILKINSON.

**Hokkaido Takushoku Bank Ltd** (Japan): 65 Chulia St, 48-01/08 OCBC Centre, Singapore 0104; tel. 5332155; telex 24414; fax 5354047; Gen. Man. SEIZO HIRAKI.

**Industrial Bank of Japan Ltd** (Japan): 16 Collyer Quay, 14-00 Hitachi Tower, Singapore 0104; tel. 5387366; telex 21880; fax 5387779; Gen. Man. HAJIME YOSANO.

**Industrial Bank of Korea** (Republic of Korea): 16 Collyer Quay, 24-02 Hitachi Tower, Singapore 0104; tel. 5335155; telex 26643; fax 5335177; Gen. Man. CHANG CHUNG HOON.

**Industrial and Commercial Bank of China** (People's Republic of China): 6 Raffles Quay, 12-01 John Hancock Tower, Singapore 0104; tel. 5381066; telex 20130; fax 5381370; Gen. Man. ZHAO LIANG.

**Internationale Nederlanden Bank NV** (Netherlands): 50 Raffles Place, 34-01/06 Shell Tower, Singapore 0104; tel. 5334182; telex 21178; fax 5338329; Gen. Man. W. F. NAGEL.

**Istituto Bancario San Paolo di Torino SpA** (Italy): 20 Collyer Quay, 14-01/02 Tung Centre, Singapore 0104; tel. 2258477; telex 29317; fax 2250744; Gen. Man. ROBERTO ALESSANDRIA.

**Kansallis-Osake-Pankki** (Finland): 150 Beach Rd, 12-00 Gateway West, Singapore 0718; tel. 2917262; telex 28438; fax 2910948; Gen. Man. RAIMO VALO (acting).

**Korea First Bank** (Republic of Korea): 65 Chulia St, 38-05/07 OCBC Centre, Singapore 0104; tel. 5358477; telex 20853; fax 5352810; Gen. Man. CHA SANG MAN.

**Kredietbank NV** (Belgium): 1 Raffles Place, 40-00 OUB Centre, Singapore 0104; tel. 5337088; telex 23201; fax 5331968; Gen. Man. GUY LIBOT.

**Krung Thai Bank Public Co Ltd** (Thailand): 65 Chulia St, 32-05/08 OCBC Centre, Singapore 0104; tel. 5336691; fax 5330930; Gen. Man. DIREK MAITRIBORIRAK.

**Long-Term Credit Bank of Japan Ltd** (Japan): 80 Raffles Place, 27-01 UOB Plaza 1, Singapore 0104; tel. 5359633; telex 23813; fax 5326048; Gen. Man. KOZO TABAYASHI.

**MeesPierson NV** (Netherlands): Singapore 0104; tel. 5394788; telex 26293; fax 5382205; Gen. Man. HENRI CAREL VAN'T HOFF.

**Mitsubishi Trust and Banking Corpn** (Japan): 6 Battery Rd, 08-01 Singapore 0104; tel. 2259155; telex 20184; fax 2241857; Gen. Man. MICHIO HOSHINO.

**Mitsui Trust & Banking Co Ltd** (Japan): 6 Shenton Way, 35-01 and 36-01 DBS Bldg, Singapore 0106; tel. 2208553; telex 23796; fax 2241669; Gen. Man. KAZUO YASUDA.

**Monte dei Paschi di Siena (MPS-Bank)** (Italy): 10 Collyer Quay, 13-01/05 Ocean Bldg, Singapore 0104; tel. 5352533; telex 24617; fax 5327996; Gen. Man. GIANCARLO POMPEI.

**Morgan Grenfell & Co Ltd** (United Kingdom): 20 Raffles Place, 26-01 Ocean Towers, Singapore 0104; tel. 5332828; telex 28325; fax 5382673; Gen. Man. LEE CHEE SENG.

**Morgan Guaranty Trust Co of New York** (USA): 6 Shenton Way, 32-08 DBS Bldg Tower Two, Singapore 0106; tel. 2208144; telex 24460; fax 3269981; Man. Dir and Gen. Man. JAKOB STOTT.

**National Australia Bank Ltd** (Australia): 5 Tamasek Blvd, 15-01 Suntec City Tower, Singapore 0103; tel. 3380038; telex 21583; fax 3380039; Gen. Man. W. A. GLOYNE.

**National Bank of Canada** (Canada): 331 North Bridge Rd, 11-04/06 Odeon Towers, Singapore 0718; tel. 3393455; telex 42216; fax 3392866; Vice-Pres. and Gen. Man. ANTONIO MELOTTI.

**National Bank of Kuwait SAK** (Kuwait): 20 Collyer Quay, 20-00 Tung Centre, Singapore 0104; tel. 2225348; telex 20538; fax 2245438; Gen. Man. R. J. MCKEGNEY.

**National Westminster Bank PLC** (United Kingdom): 50 Raffles Place, 05-01 Shell Tower, Singapore 0104; tel. 5301000; telex 28491; fax 2259827; Gen. Man. (South and South-East Asia) PHILIP W. FORREST.

**NationsBank NA** (Carolinas) (USA): 5 Shenton Way, 11-01 UIC Bldg, Singapore 0106; tel. 2205755; telex 20681; fax 2257513; Sr Vice-Pres. and Regional Man. GREGORY J. BRUSBERG.

**Nippon Credit Bank Ltd** (Japan): 6 Battery Rd, 25-01, Singapore 0104; tel. 2229233; telex 33945; fax 2242139; Gen. Man. HITOSHI TAKAHASHI.

**Norddeutsche Landesbank Girozentrale** (Germany): 6 Shenton Way, 16-08 DBS Bldg Tower Two, Singapore 0106; tel. 3231223; fax 3230223; Gen. Man. and Chief Exec. JUERGEN LANGMAACK.

**Den Norske Bank AS** (Norway): 8 Shenton Way, 48-02 Treasury Bldg, Singapore 0106; tel. 2206144; telex 21737; fax 2249743; Gen. Man. JON A. JACOBSEN.

**Norinchukin Bank** (Japan): 80 Raffles Place, 53-01 UOB Plaza 1, Singapore 0104; tel. 5351011; telex 21461; fax 5352883; Gen. Man. HAJIME TANIMURA.

**Norwest Bank Minnesota NA** (USA): 100 Cecil St, 14-02 The Globe, Singapore 0106; tel. 2260809; telex 26908; fax 2260874; Br. Man. DAVID CHIN SIEW KEE.

**Philippine National Bank** (Philippines): 180 Cecil St, 10-01/02 Bangkok Bank Bldg, Singapore 0106; tel. 2228261; telex 21792; fax 2255704; Vice-Pres. and Gen. Man. MANUEL C. ARCEÑO, Jr.

**Postipankki Ltd** (Finland): 80 Raffles Place, 52-01 UOB Plaza 1, Singapore 0104; tel. 5389611; telex 23334; fax 5388586; Gen. Man. TAPIO OTAMAA.

**PT Bank Ekspor Impor Indonesia (Persero)** (Indonesia): 16 Collyer Quay, 28-00 Hitachi Tower, Singapore 0104; tel. 5320200; telex 23697; fax 5320206; Gen. Man. RAHADI SALMUN.

**Republic National Bank of New York** (USA): 143 Cecil St, 01-00 GB Bldg, Singapore 0106; tel. 2240077; telex 20237; fax 2255769; Gen. Man. JOHN C. HANSON.

**Royal Bank of Canada** (Canada): 140 Cecil St, 01-00 PIL Bldg, Singapore 0106; tel. 2247311; telex 20435; fax 2245635; Vice-Pres. (S-E Asia) and Gen. Man. GERALD J. LIPMAN.

**Royal Bank of Scotland PLC** (United Kingdom): 6 Battery Rd, 27-01, Singapore 0104; tel. 2251233; telex 25670; fax 2251254; Regional Man. G. A. LESLIE.

**Sanwa Bank Ltd** (Japan): 6 Raffles Quay, 24-01 John Hancock Tower, Singapore 0104; tel. 5384838; telex 28573; fax 5384636; Gen. Man. YOSHIHIKO TANAKA.

**Siam Commercial Bank Public Company Ltd** (Thailand): 16 Collyer Quay, 25-01 Hitachi Tower, Singapore 0104; tel. 5364338; telex 24419; fax 5384728; Vice-Pres. and Gen. Man. TAK BUNNAG.

**Skandinaviska Enskilda Banken** (Sweden): 50 Raffles Place, 36-01 Shell Tower, Singapore 0104; tel. 2235644; telex 25188; fax 2253047; CEO RALF ENCE.

**Société Générale** (France): 80 Robinson Rd, 25-00, Singapore 0106; tel. 2227122; telex 27213; fax 2252609; Gen. Man. CHARLES M. O. PIERRON.

**State Bank of India** (India): 6 Shenton Way, 22-00 DBS Bldg Tower Two, Singapore 0106; tel. 2222033; telex 23184; fax 2253348; Gen. Man. S. M. PRABAKARAN.

# SINGAPORE

**Sumitomo Trust & Banking Co Ltd** (Japan): 5 Shenton Way, 35-00 UIC Bldg, Singapore 0106; tel. 2249055; telex 20717; fax 2242873; Gen. Man. SENJI HORIUCHI.

**Svenska Handelsbanken** (Sweden): 65 Chulia St, 21-00 OCBC Centre, Singapore 0104; tel. 5323800; telex 29012; fax 5344909; Gen. Man. CARL-OTTO BECKVID.

**Swiss Bank Corpn** (Switzerland): 5 Temasek Blvd, 18-00 Suntec City Tower, Singapore 0103; tel. 4318000; telex 24140; fax 4318188; Exec. Dir and Head of Singapore Br. RUDOLF H. FLURY.

**Thai Farmers Bank Public Co Ltd** (Thailand): 6 Battery Road, 13-06, Singapore 0104; tel. 2238516; fax 2237095; Gen. Man. PATTANGAPONG TANSOMBOON.

**Tokai Bank Ltd** (Japan): 24 Raffles Place, 22-01/06 Clifford Centre, Singapore 0104; tel. 5358222; telex 21848; fax 5325453; Gen. Man. TATSURO SUZUKI.

**Toyo Trust and Banking Co Ltd** (Japan): 6 Battery Rd, 24-01, Singapore 0104; tel. 2250177; telex 20091; fax 2247367; Gen. Man. TOSHIHIKO NAKAHASHI.

**Unibank of Denmark A/S** (Denmark): 21 Collyer Quay, 18-00 HongkongBank Bldg, Singapore 0104; tel. 2250511; telex 29246; fax 2251205; Gen. Man. STEFFEN JOHANSEN.

**Union Bank of Finland Ltd** (Finland): 50 Raffles Place, 15-01 Shell Tower, Singapore 0104; tel. 2258211; telex 34253; fax 2255469; Gen. Man. MIKAEL WAHRN.

**Union Bank of Switzerland** (Switzerland): 80 Raffles Place, 36-00 UOB Plaza 1, Singapore 0104; tel. 5382888; telex 21549; fax 5316303; Exec. Vice-Pres. and CEO LIM HO KEE; Br. Man. JANICE ANG.

**Union de Banques Arabes et Françaises (UBAF)** (France): 11 Collyer Quay, 11-01/03 The Arcade, Singapore 0104; tel. 2246966; telex 28000; fax 2255071; Gen. Man. GUY THOMAS ALEJANDRO.

**Westdeutsche Landesbank Girozentrale** (Germany): 21 Collyer Quay, 10-00 HongkongBank Bldg, Singapore 0104; tel. 2279001; telex 26177; fax 2278253; Sr Vice-Pres. and Gen. Man. KLAUS R. GERRITZEN.

**Westpac Banking Corpn** (Australia): 65 Chulia St, 43-01 OCBC Centre, Singapore 0104; tel. 5338673; telex 21763; fax 5326781; Chief Man. GREGORY M. MIZON.

**Yasuda Trust and Banking Co Ltd** (Japan): 50 Raffles Place, 16-02 Shell Tower, Singapore 0104; tel. 2237266; telex 33285; fax 2241613; Gen. Man. SHOJI MASUBUCHI.

### Association

**Association of Banks in Singapore:** 10 Shenton Way, 12-08 MAS Bldg, Singapore 0207; tel. 2244300; telex 29291; fax 2241785; Dir ONG-ANG AI BOON.

### STOCK EXCHANGE

**Stock Exchange of Singapore (SES):** 20 Cecil St, 26-01/08 The Exchange, Singapore 0104; tel. 5353788; telex 21853; fax 5356994; f. 1930; 106 mems; Chair. CHUA KIM YEOW; Pres. LIM CHOO PENG.

### FINANCIAL FUTURES EXCHANGE

**Singapore International Monetary Exchange Ltd (SIMEX):** 1 Raffles Place, 07-00/08-00 OUB Centre, Singapore 0104; tel. 5357382; telex 38000; fax 5357282; energy and financial futures and options exchange; 82 corp. mems (April 1995); Chair. ELIZABETH SAM; Pres. ANG SWEE TIAN.

### INSURANCE

The insurance industry is supervised by the Monetary Authority of Singapore (see Banking). In April 1995 there were 142 insurance companies, comprising 58 direct insurers (eight life insurance, 44 general insurance, six composite insurers), 36 professional reinsurers (two life reinsurers, 28 general reinsurers, six composite reinsurers) and 48 captive insurers.

#### Domestic Companies
#### Life Insurance

**Asia Life Assurance Society Ltd:** 2 Finlayson Green, 05-05 Asia Insurance Bldg, Singapore 0104; tel. 2243181; telex 23971; fax 2239120; f. 1948; Chair. and Man. Dir TAN ENG HENG.

**John Hancock Life Assurance Co Ltd:** 6 Raffles Quay, 21-00 John Hancock Tower, Singapore 0104; tel. 5383333; fax 5383233; f. 1954; Pres. and CEO MALCOLM J. J. ARNEY.

**OUB Manulife Pte Ltd:** 10 Anson Rd, 06-18 International Plaza, Singapore 0207; tel. 2241222; telex 36373; fax 2248386; Pres. GARRY T. DICK.

**Prudential Assurance Co Singapore (Pte) Ltd:** 10 Collyer Quay, 09-01 Ocean Bldg, Singapore 0104; tel. 5395900; telex 26256; fax 5324043; CEO SUEE CHIEH TAN.

**UOB Life Assurance Ltd:** 156 Cecil St, 07-01/02 Far Eastern Bank Bldg, Singapore 0106; tel. 2278477; fax 2243012; Man. Dir RAYMOND KWOK CHONG SEE.

#### General Insurance

**AGF Insurance (Singapore) Pte Ltd:** 50 Raffles Place, 38-01 Shell Tower, Singapore 0104; tel. 5381188; telex 36028; fax 5388171; Man. Dir JEAN NOEL ROUSELLE.

**Allianz Insurance (Singapore) Pte Ltd:** 156 Cecil St, 09-01 Far Eastern Bank Bldg, Singapore 0105; tel. 2227733; telex 25094; fax 2242718; Gen. Man. Dr ULRICH FRIEDRICH DELIUS.

**Asia Insurance Co Ltd:** 2 Finlayson Green, 03-00 Asia Insurance Bldg, Singapore 0104; tel. 2243181; telex 23971; fax 2214355; f. 1923; cap. p.u. S $100m.; Chair. TAN ENG HENG; Man. Dir FONG AH SOO.

**Axa Sime Assurance Pte Ltd:** 47 Scotts Rd, 03-00 Goldbell Towers, Singapore 0922; tel. 7382818; telex 26362; fax 7382822; fmrly East West-USI Insurance Pte Ltd; Man. Dir ANTHONY TAN.

**Cosmic Insurance Corpn Ltd:** 410 North Bridge Rd, 04-01 Cosmic Insurance Bldg, Singapore 0718; tel. 3387633; telex 20307; fax 3397805; f. 1971; Gen. Man. TEO KWANG WHEE.

**ECICS-COFACE Guarantee Co (Singapore) Ltd:** 141 Market St, 10-00 International Factors Bldg, Singapore 0104; tel. 2270118; telex 21524; fax 2270170; Chair. H. R. HOCHSTADT; Dir KWAH THIAM HOCK.

**First Capital Insurance Ltd:** 80 Robinson Rd, 09-02/03, Singapore 0106; tel. 2222311; fax 2223547; Gen. Man. PETER LEE BONG SOO.

**India International Insurance Pte Ltd:** 64 Cecil St, 04-00/06-00 IOB Bldg, Singapore 0104; tel. 2238122; telex 34894; fax 2257743; f. 1987; all non-life insurance; Chair. S. V. MONY; CEO R. ATHAPPAN.

**Industrial and Commercial Insurance Ltd:** 156 Cecil St, 09-01 Far Eastern Bank Bldg, Singapore 0106; tel. 2227733; telex 20368; fax 2243568; Man. Dir HWANG SOO JIN.

**Kemper International Insurance Co (Pte) Ltd:** 143 Cecil St, 06-01 GB Bldg, Singapore 0106; tel. 2249477; telex 28327; fax 2250241; Dep. Man. (Southeast Asia) CHEW LOY HEOK.

**The Nanyang Insurance Co Ltd:** 302 Orchard Rd, 09-01 Tong Bldg, Singapore 0923; tel. 7388211; telex 22923; fax 7388133; Principal Officer SEOW NEE SHEK.

**Overseas Union Insurance Ltd:** 50 Collyer Quay, 02-02 Overseas Union House, Singapore 0104; tel. 2251133; telex 23737; fax 2246307; f. 1956; Gen. Man. PETER YAP KIM KEE.

**People's Insurance Co Ltd:** 10 Collyer Quay, 04-01 Ocean Bldg, Singapore 0104; tel. 5326022; telex 26714; fax 5333871; f. 1957; Man. Dir and CEO CHEW LOY KIAT.

**Provincial Insurance Asia Pte Ltd:** 79 Anson Rd, 12-00, Singapore 0207; tel. 2218611; telex 50501; fax 2263360; Principal Officer PETER KOH.

**Singapore Aviation and General Insurance Co (Pte) Ltd:** 25 Airline Rd, 06-A Airline House, Singapore 1781; tel. 5423333; telex 21241; fax 5450221; f. 1976; Man. ANNE ANG.

**Sun Alliance Insurance (Singapore) Ltd:** 20 Raffles Place, 16-01 Ocean Towers, Singapore 0104; tel. 5351522; fax 5350855; Man. Dir ROBIN HUKE.

**Taisho Marine and Fire Insurance (Asia) Ptd Lte:** 16 Raffles Quay, 24-01 Hong Leong Bldg, Singapore 0104; tel. 2209644; telex 21742; fax 2256371; Man. Dir KOJI YOSHIMURA.

**Tat Lee Insurance Ltd:** 63 Market St, 11-07/10 Tat Lee Bank Bldg, Singapore 0104; tel. 5333355; telex 55300; fax 5339390; Chair. GOH ENG CHEW; Prin. Officer FONG SIEW HONG.

**The Tokio Marine & Fire Insurance Co (Singapore) Pte Ltd:** 6 Shenton Way, 23-08 DBS Bldg Tower Two, Singapore 0106; tel. 2216111; telex 23975; fax 2240895; Man. Dir TOSHIO OKUBO.

**United Overseas Insurance Ltd:** 156 Cecil St, 09-01 Far Eastern Bank Bldg, Singapore 0106; tel. 2227733; telex 25094; fax 2242718; Man. Dir HWANG SOO JIN.

**Winterthur Insurance (Far East) Pte Ltd:** 143 Cecil St, 17-01 GB Bldg, Singapore 0106; tel. 2210759; telex 33652; fax 2251002; Man. Dir FRANÇOIS VUFFRAY.

**Yasuda Fire and Marine Insurance Co (Asia) Pte Ltd:** 50 Raffles Place, 03-03 Shell Tower, Singapore 0104; tel. 2235293; telex 26329; fax 2257947; Principal Officer YONG TIEN HUP (acting).

**Zürich Insurance (Singapore) Pte Ltd:** 30 Robinson Rd, 11-01 Robinson Towers, Singapore 0104; tel. 2285151; telex 22109; fax 2255749; Man. Dir ERIC PRYDE.

#### Composite Insurance

**Great Eastern Life Assurance Co Ltd:** 65 Chulia St, 18-01 OCBC Centre, Singapore 0104; tel. 5324331; telex 34421; fax 5322214; f. 1908; Man. Dir ALLEN J. PATHMARAJAH.

# SINGAPORE

**Insurance Corpn of Singapore Ltd:** 137 Cecil St, ICS Bldg, Singapore 0106; tel. 2218686; telex 28414; fax 2247719; f. 1969; Principal Officer LARRY CHAN.

**Keppel Insurance Pte Ltd:** 10 Hoe Chiang Rd, 13-00 Keppel Towers, Singapore 0208; tel. 2256111; telex 23207; fax 2212188; Gen. Man. ALBERT KOH.

**NTUC Income Insurance Co-operative Ltd:** 75 Bras Basah Rd, NTUC Income Centre, Singapore 0718; tel. 3363322; telex 26261; fax 3381500; Gen. Man. TAN KIN LIAN.

**Overseas Assurance Corpn Ltd:** 260 Tanjong Pagar Rd, 09-00 Singapore 0208; tel. 2251122; telex 21443; fax 2246215; f. 1920; Principal Officer LAW SONG KENG.

### Associations

**General Insurance Association of Singapore:** 1 Shenton Way, 13-07 Robina House, Singapore 0106; tel. 2218788; telex 20814; fax 2272051; Pres. DAVID CHAN MUN WAI.

**Life Insurance Association:** 1 Selegie Rd, 06-17A Paradiz Centre, Singapore 0718; tel. 3383340; fax 3360654; f. 1967; Pres. LAW SONG-KENG.

**Singapore Reinsurers' Association:** 1 Shenton Way, 14-01 Robina House, Singapore 0106; tel. 2206077; telex 23443; fax 2248910; Chair. H. J. WARNHOLTZ.

**Singapore Insurance Brokers' Association:** c/o 138 Cecil St, 15-00 Cecil Court, Singapore 0106; tel. 2227777; fax 2220022; Pres. ROBERT CHANG.

## Trade and Industry

### CHAMBERS OF COMMERCE

**Singapore Federation of Chambers of Commerce and Industry:** 47 Hill St, 03-01 Chinese Chamber of Commerce Bldg, Singapore 0617; tel. 3389761; fax 3395630; f. 1978; ROBERT CHUA; Hon. Sec.-Gen. CHIN TECK HUAT; mems comprise the following:

> **Singapore Chinese Chamber of Commerce and Industry:** 47 Hill St, Singapore 0617; tel. 3378381; fax 3390605.
> **Singapore Indian Chamber of Commerce and Industry:** 101 Cecil St, 23-01 Tong Eng Bldg, Singapore 0106; tel. 2222855; fax 2231707.
> **Singapore International Chamber of Commerce:** 6 Raffles Quay, 10-01 John Hancock Tower, Singapore 0104; tel. 2241255; fax 2242785.
> **Singapore Malay Chamber of Commerce:** 10 Anson Rd, 24-07 International Plaza, Singapore 0207; tel. 2211066; fax 2235811.

### DEVELOPMENT ORGANIZATIONS

**Asian Infrastructure Fund (AIF):** Singapore; f. 1994; promotes and directs investment into regional projects.

**Economic Development Board (EDB):** 250 North Bridge Rd, 24-00 Raffles City Tower, Singapore 0617; tel. 3395805; fax 3396077; f. 1961; statutory body for industrial planning, development and promotion of investments in manufacturing, services and local business; Chair. PHILIP YEO; Man. Dir SWEE SAY LIM.

**Government of Singapore Investment Corporation Pte Ltd (GSIC):** 250 North Bridge Rd, 33-00 Raffles City Tower, Singapore 0617; tel. 3363366; telex 20484; fax 3308722; f. 1981; Chair. LEE KUAN YEW; Man. Dir LEE EK TIENG.

**Housing and Development Board:** 3541 Bukit Merah Rd, HDB Centre, Singapore 0315; tel. 2739090; telex 22020; fax 2796097; f. 1960; public housing authority; Chair. HSUAN OWYANG.

**Jurong Town Corpn:** 301 Jurong Town Hall Rd, Jurong Town Hall, Singapore 2260; tel. 5600056; telex 35733; fax 5655301; f. 1968; statutory body responsible for developing and maintaining industrial estates; Chair. YEO SENG TECK; Gen. Man. FRANCIS MAK.

**National Science and Technology Board (NSTB):** Singapore; f. 1990; statutory board; responsible for the development of science and technology.

**Singapore Institute of Standards and Industrial Research:** 1 Science Park Drive, Singapore 0511; tel. 7787777; fax 7780086.

**Trade Development Board:** 1 Maritime Sq., Telok Blangah Rd, 10-40 World Trade Centre, Singapore 0409; tel. 2719388; telex 28617; fax 2740770; f. 1983 to develop and expand international trade; statutory body; Chair. ALAN YEO; CEO BARRY DESKER.

### INDUSTRIAL AND TRADE ASSOCIATIONS

**Association of Singapore Marine Industries (ASMI):** 1 Maritime Sq., 09-09/10 World Trade Centre, Singapore 0409; tel. 2707883; fax 2731867; f. 1968; 10 hon. mems, 76 assoc. mems, 54 ord. mems; Pres. TONG CHONG HEONG; Exec. Sec. Maj. (rtd) ONG CHEW LIANG.

**Malayan Pineapple Industry Board:** 10 Collyer Quay, 19-06 Ocean Bldg, Singapore 0104; tel. 5338827; f. 1957; controls pineapple cultivation, canning and marketing; Chair. AHMAD BIN OMAR.

**Singapore Commodity Exchange:** 111 North Bridge Rd, 23-04/05 Peninsula Plaza, Singapore 0617; tel. 3385600; fax 3389116; f. 1968 as Rubber Association of Singapore, adopted present name 1994; to regulate, promote, develop and supervise commodity futures trading in Singapore, including the establishment and dissemination of official prices for all grades and types of rubber; provides clearing facilities; endorses certificates of origin and licences for packers, shippers and mfrs; Chair. PATRICK HAYS; Gen. Man. CHONG KIM SENG.

**Singapore Manufacturers' Association:** 20 Orchard Rd, The SMA House, Singapore 0923; tel. 3388787; telex 24992; fax 3383358; f. 1932; Pres. ROBERT CHUA TECK CHEW; Exec. Dir CHIN TECK HUAT.

### STATE CORPORATION

**Singapore Telecom:** Singapore; 10% transferred to the private sector in 1993; Chair. KOH BOON HWEE; Pres. WONG HUNG KHIM.

### CO-OPERATIVES

At 31 December 1981 Singapore had 78 co-operative societies classified into 12 types, comprising 40 thrift and credit societies, eight consumer societies, 17 multi-purpose societies, three housing/land-purchase societies, one transport society, two producer societies, one insurance society, one medical society, two service societies, two school co-operative societies and one co-operative union. These societies, with paid-up share capital of S $53m. and statutory reserve funds of S $10.7m., had a combined membership of 273 institutional mems and 180,229 personal mems.

### EMPLOYERS' ORGANIZATION

**Singapore National Employers' Federation:** 19 Tanglin Rd, 10-01/04 Tanglin Shopping Centre, Singapore 1024; tel. 2358911; fax 2353904; f. 1948; Pres. STEPHEN LEE; Exec. Dir TAN PENG BOO.

### TRADE UNIONS

In 1993 there were 82 registered trade unions, of which 75 were affiliated to the Singapore National Trades Union Congress. Non-affiliated unions were mostly small, occupational or in-house unions.

In December 1993 the largest private-sector union, the United Workers of Electronics and Electrical Industries, had 36,829 members, while the largest public-sector union, the Amalgamated Union of Public Employees, had 20,253 members.

**National Trades Union Congress (NTUC):** Trade Union House, Shenton Way, Singapore 0106; tel. 2226555; telex 24543; f. 1961; 75 affiliated unions, 236,118 mems (Dec. 1993); Pres. OSCAR OLIVEIRO; Sec.-Gen. LIM BOON HENG.

## Transport

### RAILWAYS

In 1993 there was 26 km of 1-m gauge railway, linked with the Malaysian railway system and owned by the Malayan Railway Pentadbiran Keretapi Tanah Melayu—KTM. The main line crosses the Johore causeway (1.2 km) and terminates near Keppel Harbour. Branch lines link it with the industrial estate at Jurong.

Construction began in 1983 on the Mass Rapid Transit (MRT) system. The first section was completed in 1987, and the remaining sections by 1990. The network consists of three lines with 42 stations (26 elevated, 15 under ground and one at ground level). The system extends for 67 km (44.8 km elevated, 19.0 km under ground and 3.2 km at ground level). A further 16-km line was due to begin operating in 1996.

**Mass Rapid Transit Corpn:** 251 North Bridge Rd, Singapore 0617; tel. 3390955; telex 39954; fax 3398816; 66 trains; Chair. Brig.-Gen. WESLEY D'ARANJO; Exec. Dir LOW TIEN SIO.

### ROADS

In 1994 Singapore had a total of 2,989 km of roads, of which 111.6 km were motorway; in that year 2,905 km were paved roads. In 1990 the Government introduced a quota system to control the number of vehicles using the roads. In 1994 an electronic road-pricing system took effect, whereby each vehicle is charged according to road use in congested areas.

### SHIPPING

The Port of Singapore is the world's busiest in tonnage terms; Singapore handled 92,600 vessels with a total displacement of 624m. grt in 1993. It is used by about 600 shipping lines.

The Port of Singapore Authority operates six cargo terminals: Tanjong Pagar, Keppel, Pasir Panjang, Sembawang, Jurong and the newest container terminal, Brani.

# SINGAPORE

Tanjong Pagar Terminal (3.3 km) is the main gateway for containerized cargo and has the capacity to accommodate 58,500 20-foot equivalent units (TEUs). In 1990 it handled 5.02m. TEUs.

Keppel Terminal has four main berths, three feeder berths and, by 1994 (following redevelopment), five feeder container berths.

Pasir Panjang Terminal, Singapore's main gateway for conventional cargo, handled 7.1m. tons of cargo, with three deep-water berths and 10 coastal berths in 1990. Pasir Panjang Terminal has a total of seven deep-water berths, 14 coastal berths and 120,000 sq. m of covered storage space. A new container terminal at Pasir Panjang was to be built in four phases over 25 years, increasing the Port of Singapore Authority's handling capacity to 36m. TEUs. Construction began in 1993, and the first three berths were scheduled for operations in 1997.

Sembawang Terminal has four main berths and one cross berth. It handles low-value, high-volume homogeneous cargo such as timber and rubber. This terminal is also the main gateway for car carriers.

Jurong Terminal, which handles general and dry-bulk cargo, is situated in south-western Singapore, and serves the Jurong Industrial Estate.

Brani Terminal, built on an offshore island connected to the mainland by a 330m four-lane causeway, when completed in 1995, was to have five main berths and four feeder berths, with a capacity to handle 5.5m. TEUs annually.

At the end of December 1993 Singapore's merchant fleet totalled 2,394 vessels, with a combined displacement of 12,164,270 grt.

**Port of Singapore Authority:** 460 Alexandra Rd, PSA Bldg, Singapore 0511; tel. 2747111; telex 21507; fax 2744677; f. 1964; statutory board under the Ministry of Communications; responsible for the provision and maintenance of port facilities and services, the control of navigation in port waters and the promotion and development of the port; Chair. Dr YEO NING HONG; Exec. Dir DAVID LIM.

### Major Shipping Lines

**American President Lines Ltd:** 19 Keppel Rd, 02-01 Jit Poh Bldg, Singapore 0208; tel. 2259966; telex 21337; fax 2214922; container services to North and South Asia, the USA, the Middle East, India and Pakistan; Man. Dir JAMES RICHARDS.

**Austasia Line Pte Ltd:** Singapore; tel. 2201244; telex 21020; fax 2250464; Man. Dir W. H. ASKEW.

**Barwil Agencies Pte Ltd:** 200 Cantonment Rd, 07-02 Southpoint, Singapore 0208; tel. 2252577; telex 23057; fax 2252538; services to the USA, Canada and the Persian (Arabian) Gulf; Man. Dir Capt. KARE BJASTAD.

**Everett Steamship Corpn SA:** 24 Raffles Place, 17-03 Clifford Centre, Singapore 0104; tel. 5325481; telex 21306; fax 5325486; cargo services; shipping agents; Gen. Man. P. M. PANDOLFO.

**Guan Guan Shipping Pte Ltd:** 23 Telok Ayer St, Singapore 0104; tel. 5343988; telex 21395; fax 5343504; f. 1955; shipowners and agents; cargo services to East and West Malaysia, Indonesia, Pakistan, Sri Lanka, Bengal Bay ports, Persian (Arabian) Gulf ports, Hong Kong and China; Man. Dir R. THIO.

**Hin Leong Marine International (Pte) Ltd:** 1 Playfair Rd, Singapore 1336; tel. 2835694; telex 38835; Marine Supt V. LIM.

**Nedlloyd Lines Singapore Pte Ltd:** 138 Robinson Rd, 01-00 Hong Leong Centre, Singapore 0106; tel. 2218989; telex 21261; fax 2255267; f. 1963; Gen. Man. P. R. PUTMAN CRAMER.

**Neptune Orient Lines Ltd:** 456 Alexandra Rd, PDS 06-00 NOL Bldg, Singapore 0511; tel. 2789000; telex 51168; fax 2784900; f. 1968; liner containerized services on the Far East/Europe, Far East/North America, Straits/Australia, South Asia/Europe and South-East Asia, Far East/Mediterranean routes; tankers, bulk carriers and dry cargo vessels on charter; Chair. H. R. HOCHSTADT; Man. Dir LUA CHENG ENG.

**New Straits Shipping Co Pte Ltd:** 51 Anson Rd, 09-53 Anson Centre, Singapore 0207; tel. 2201007; telex 23150; fax 2240785.

**Pacific International Lines Pte Ltd:** 140 Cecil St, 03-00 PIL Bldg, Singapore 0106; tel. 2218133; telex 24190; fax 2258741; shipowners, agents and managers; liner services to the Far East, India, the Red Sea, the Persian (Arabian) Gulf, West and East Africa; container services to South-East Asia; world-wide chartering, freight forwarding; Exec. Chair. Y. C. CHANG; Man Dir S. S. TEO.

**Pacific Navigation Co Pte Ltd:** 3 Shenton Way, 21-08 Shenton House, Singapore 0106; tel. 2225688; telex 26003; fax 2259897; Man. Dir B. FORSELL.

**Petroships Private Ltd:** 460 Alexandra Rd 25-04, PSA Bldg, Singapore 0511; tel. 2731122; telex 24176; fax 2732200; Man. Dir YONG CHEE MIN.

**Syabas Tankers Pte Ltd:** 10 Anson Rd, 34-10 International Plaza, Singapore 0207; tel. 2259522; telex 26049.

### CIVIL AVIATION

Singapore's international airport at Changi was opened in 1981. In late 1990 a second passenger terminal came into operation, which more than doubled the airport's capacity, to 24m. passengers per year. There is a second airport at Seletar.

**Civil Aviation Authority of Singapore:** Singapore Changi Airport, POB 1, Singapore 9181; tel. 5421122; telex 21231; fax 5421231; responsible for airport maintenance and security, the development of air transport; Chair. SIM KEE BOON; Dir-Gen. WONG WOON LIONG.

**Region Air:** Singapore; f. 1994; operates regional flights to Vung Tao in Viet Nam twice a week; Owner ONGH BENG SENG.

**SilkAir:** 55 Airport Blvd, SATS Bldg, 03-0, Singapore 1781; tel. 5428111; telex 40135; fax 5426286; f. 1975; fmrly Tradewinds Private; wholly-owned subsidiary of Singapore Airlines Ltd; began scheduled services in 1989; Chair. SYN CHUNG WAH; Gen. Man. MICHAEL CHAN.

**Singapore Airlines Ltd (SIA):** Airline House, 25 Airline Rd, Singapore 1781; tel. 5423333; telex 21241; fax 5456375; f. 1972; passenger services to 70 cities in 40 countries; Chair. J. Y. PILLAY; Man. Dir and Chief Exec. CHEONG CHOONG KONG.

# Tourism

Singapore's tourist attractions include a blend of cultures and excellent shopping facilities. Tourist arrivals totalled 6,898,951 in 1994, an increase of 7.4% compared with 1993.

**Singapore Tourist Promotion Board:** 250 North Bridge Rd, Raffles City Tower 36-04, Singapore 0617; tel. 3396622; telex 33375; fax 3399423; f. 1964; Chair. EDMUND CHENG WAI WING; Chief Exec. TAN CHIN NAM.

# SLOVAKIA

## Introductory Survey

**Location, Climate, Language, Religion, Flag, Capital**

The Slovak Republic (formerly a constituent republic of the Czech and Slovak Federative Republic, or Czechoslovakia) is a land-locked state located in central Europe, bordered to the north by Poland, to the east by Ukraine, to the south by Hungary, to the west by Austria and to the north-west by the Czech Republic. The climate is typically continental, with cold, dry winters and hot, humid summers. Average temperatures in Bratislava range from −0.7°C (30.7°F) in January to 21.1°C (70.0°F) in July. Average annual rainfall in the capital is 649 mm (25.6 ins). The official language is Slovak, a member of the west Slavonic group (and closely related to Czech), although Hungarian, Czech and the languages of other ethnic minorities living in Slovakia are also spoken. The major religion is Christianity, the Roman Catholic Church being the largest denomination, followed by the Evangelical Church of the Augsburg Confession. The national flag (proportions 3 by 2) consists of three equal horizontal stripes, of white, blue and red; in the centre hoist there is a white-rimmed red shield containing a silver archiepiscopal (double-barred) cross surmounted on the central (and highest) of three blue hillocks. The capital is Bratislava.

**Recent History**

Slovaks and Czechs (who are closely related members of the western Slavic peoples) were first united, in the ninth century AD, in the Great Moravian Empire. Following the Empire's dissolution, in 907, however, they were divided. While the Slovaks came under Hungarian rule (which was to last, in different forms, until the early 20th century), the Czechs established a kingdom that remained an important political force until the incorporation of the Czech Lands into the Habsburg Empire in the 16th and 17th centuries.

A movement of nationalist revival evolved in Slovakia in the late 18th and 19th centuries, which was closely linked with a similar movement in the Czech Lands. During the First World War (1914–18) Slovaks joined with Czechs in campaigning for an independent state, which would be composed of the Czech Lands and Slovakia. At the end of the war the Republic of Czechoslovakia was established, on 28 October 1918, as one of the successor states to the Austro-Hungarian Empire. The country's boundaries were established by the Treaty of Trianon of 1920, under which a large Hungarian minority was incorporated into Slovakia. Despite the economic and social advances made by the new republic, there were demands by Slovaks for autonomy within a federal system (as envisaged by the Pittsburgh Agreement of May 1918, signed by leading Czech and Slovak emigrés in the USA). However, Czechoslovakia's first Constitution, promulgated in 1920, made no provision for a proper federal system, and Slovak proposals for self-government were rejected by the central authorities in Prague (the capital). A further cause of Slovak disaffection was the fact that the Czech Lands were the focus of the country's economic development, while Slovakia remained largely undeveloped. There was also an ideological divide between the two parts of the country: while the majority of Slovaks were strict Roman Catholics, the central Government in Prague was professedly anticlerical.

The centrist policies of the Czechs led to a more radical approach on the part of the Slovaks. In October 1938, following the Munich Agreement of 29 September (under which the predominantly German-populated areas of Czechoslovakia were ceded to Germany), Slovak nationalists declared Slovak autonomy. On 14 March 1939, one day before Nazi armed forces occupied the Czech Lands, Hitler agreed to the establishment of a separate Slovak state, under the pro-Nazi 'puppet' regime of Fr Jozef Tiso. The wartime Slovak state (March 1939–April 1945) was based on a combination of German and Italian fascist principles. Any opposition to the Tiso regime was ruthlessly suppressed, and the treatment of Jews, especially after the adoption of the Jewish Code in 1941, was particularly severe. In August 1944, however, an armed resistance (the Slovak National Uprising) against Tiso's regime was begun. It lasted two months before being suppressed by German troops.

Following the restoration of the Czechoslovak state in 1945, at the end of the Second World War, certain concessions were made to Slovak demands for autonomy, including the establishment of a regional legislature with restricted powers (the Slovak National Council) and an executive, both in Bratislava, the Slovak capital. However, this limited progress towards a federal system was largely negated by the seizure of power by the communists (led by Gustav Husák) in Slovakia in late 1947, and in the whole of the country in 1948. In May 1948 a new Constitution was approved, which declared Czechoslovakia to be a 'people's democracy'. The communists' consolidation of power was completed in the following month with the election to the post of President of Klement Gottwald, a Czech and the leader of the Communist Party of Czechoslovakia (CPCz). Gottwald had been Prime Minister in a coalition government since 1946, the year when the CPCz had become the largest party in the Czechoslovak legislature.

In the first years of communist rule in Czechoslovakia there was widespread repression, not only of political opponents of the CPCz, but also of members of the party itself (the notorious 'show trials' of the early 1950s, for example). Expressions of Slovak nationalism were also severely suppressed, and in 1954 Husák and other alleged nationalists were imprisoned on charges of Slovak separatism. The new Constitution of 1960 restricted Slovak autonomy: the executive in Bratislava was dissolved, while legislative authority was removed from the Slovak National Council.

It was not until the 1960s, when reformist policies began to be adopted within the CPCz, that the issue of Slovak autonomy re-emerged in public debate. In January 1968 Alexander Dubček (a Slovak and hitherto the leader of the Communist Party of Slovakia, CPS) was appointed First Secretary of the CPCz. The wide-ranging political and economic reforms introduced by Dubček and the new Government included plans for the creation of a federal system of two equal republics. This period of political tolerance and freedom of expression (which subsequently became known as the 'Prague Spring') was abruptly ended in August 1968 by the armed intervention of some 600,000 troops of the USSR and its Warsaw Pact allies (except Romania). Dubček was replaced by Husák as First (subsequently General) Secretary of the CPCz, and there was a severe purge of party members, in particular reformists and associates of Dubček. Nevertheless, the federal system was realized in January 1969: separate Czech and Slovak Socialist Republics were established, each with its own government and legislature (National Council). Supreme legislative and executive power, meanwhile, were vested, respectively, in the Federal Assembly and the Federal Government. However, the reimposition of centralized communist rule, under the leadership of Husák, left the new regional institutions largely powerless.

In 1975 Husák was appointed President of Czechoslovakia, while also remaining as General Secretary of the CPCz. He was replaced in the latter post in 1987 by Miloš Jakeš, a Czech member of the CPCz Presidium. Although the new administration under Jakeš publicly avowed its commitment to introduce political and economic reforms similar to those taking place in the USSR, political liberalization was not forthcoming. The Government continued its repressive treatment of both the Roman Catholic Church and the several dissident groups that had been established since the late 1970s (the most important being Charter 77). Nevertheless, the dissident movement broadened its influence during the 1980s, and was instrumental in organizing a series of anti-Government demonstrations, beginning in 1988, which were to culminate in the anti-communist revolution of late 1989. (For further details of the so-called 'velvet revolution' and subsequent events, see chapter on the Czech Republic.)

The elections to the Federal Assembly and to the Czech and Slovak National Councils, which took place on 8–9 June 1990, were the first to be held freely in Czechoslovakia since 1946.

Of the Slovak parties and movements, Public Against Violence (PAV), which, with its Czech counterpart, Civic Forum, had been the principal force in effecting the end of communist rule in late 1989, emerged with the largest representation at both federal and republican level. A coalition Slovak Government, dominated by PAV, was subsequently formed, with Vladimír Mečiar, a founding member of PAV, as Prime Minister.

The future of Czech-Slovak relations emerged in the latter half of 1990 as the dominant topic of political debate. While most Czech and Slovak citizens appeared to favour the preservation of a common state, there was increasing support in Slovakia for a more decentralized form of the existing federation. Among the Slovak political parties, the Christian Democratic Movement (CDM), which formed part of the Slovak coalition Government, advocated greater Slovak autonomy within a common state. More radical parties, however—most notably the Slovak National Party (SNP), which held seats in both the federal and republican legislatures—advocated the complete secession of Slovakia from the federation.

The debate over the future of the country (which since April 1990 had been officially known as the Czech and Slovak Federative Republic) led to increasing political turmoil in Slovakia during 1991. In March Mečiar was forced to resign as Slovak Prime Minister, accused of harming Czech-Slovak relations by his increasingly aggressive advocacy of full autonomy for Slovakia. Mečiar left PAV and formed a new party, the Movement for a Democratic Slovakia (MDS). He was replaced as Prime Minister by Ján Čarnogurský, the leader of the CDM. Discussions on the future constitutional structure of Czechoslovakia were held throughout the remainder of 1991, but achieved little progress. Proposals by the Czechoslovak President, Václav Havel, for a referendum to decide the country's future were repeatedly rejected by the Federal Assembly.

New elections to the federal and republican legislatures were held on 5–6 June 1992. The MDS, led by Mečiar, emerged clearly as the dominant Slovak party both in the Federal Assembly and the Slovak National Council. In the latter body the MDS won 74 of the total 150 seats, compared with only 18 by the CDM and 15 by the SNP. The Party of the Democratic Left (PDL—the successor to the CPS) won the second largest representation in the Council (29 seats). A coalition of Hungarian national parties obtained the remaining 14 seats. In late June Mečiar was reinstated as Prime Minister, at the head of a new, MDS-dominated Slovak Government.

Following the Slovak National Council's overwhelming approval of a declaration of Slovak sovereignty on 17 July 1992, the dismantling of the Czechoslovak federation appeared to be inevitable. In late July Mečiar and his Czech counterpart, Václav Klaus, reached agreement on the necessary measures to permit the separation of the two republics, and the modalities of the division were discussed in the following months. On 1 September the new Slovak Constitution was adopted with overwhelming support by the Slovak National Council. However, it subsequently appeared that some Slovak leaders still preferred the concept of a more decentralized federation rather than a complete division of the republics. It was mainly MDS deputies in the Federal Assembly who succeeded, on two occasions, in preventing the adoption of legislation to permit the constitutional dissolution of Czechoslovakia. In late November, however, the Federal Assembly finally approved the disputed legislation (albeit at the third attempt and by a margin of only three votes); accordingly, Czechoslovakia was to be divided on 1 January 1993.

During the remainder of 1992 there was an acceleration of the process of dividing federal assets and liabilities, as well as the armed forces, between the Czech and Slovak Republics. However, some federal property, it was agreed, would be shared by the two republics for the immediate future (the existing currency, the Czechoslovak koruna, was indeed retained until February 1993, when two separate currencies were introduced). In late December 1992 the two republics signed a treaty of good-neighbourliness, friendly relations and co-operation, and subsequently established formal diplomatic relations. With the dissolution of all federal structures at midnight on 31 December, the Czech Republic and the Slovak Republic came into existence. Recognition was quickly accorded to the new countries by all those states that had maintained relations with Czechoslovakia, as well as by various international bodies. Slovakia was thus automatically admitted, as was the Czech Republic, to the UN, the Conference on Security and Co-operation in Europe (subsequently renamed the OSCE, see p. 198), the IMF and the World Bank, among other organizations. The entirely peaceful nature of the dissolution of Czechoslovakia (notably at the time of the conflict in the former Yugoslavia) was believed to have contributed to the rapid international recognition of both republics.

Slovakia's existing MDS-dominated Government remained in place, and the National Council was retained as the republic's legislature (although its full official title was now the National Council of the Slovak Republic). In late January 1993 the National Council held two rounds of voting to elect Slovakia's President; however, none of the four candidates (representing the leading parties in the legislature, the MDS, the PDL, the CDM and the SNP) received the required three-fifths' majority. In a subsequent round of voting, in mid-February, the sole candidate, Michal Kováč, the Deputy Chairman of the MDS and the former Chairman of Czechoslovakia's Federal Assembly, was appointed President. (Prior to his death, in November 1992, it had been considered probable that Alexander Dubček would be elected Slovakia's first President.) The presidential election campaign was conducted against a background of growing internal divisions within the MDS, which culminated in March 1993 with the dismissal of Milan Kňažko from his post of Deputy Prime Minister and Minister of Foreign Affairs; he had been the most outspoken critic of Mečiar within the MDS. Kňažko subsequently formed a liberal party, the Alliance of Democrats of the Slovak Republic (ADSR), in opposition to Mečiar's Government. The resignation, also in March, of the Minister of the Economy, Ľudovít Černák (the leader of the SNP), meant that, with the exception of two independent ministers, the Government was now composed exclusively of members of the MDS.

The growing instability of Mečiar's Government was reflected in a series of further defections from the MDS, as a result of which the MDS (plus affiliates) lost its majority in the legislature. In order to regain this majority, the MDS held negotiations with the SNP in the latter half of 1993, with a view to forming a new coalition Government; this was finalized in early November, with the SNP holding several key portfolios. One of Mečiar's ministerial nominees was rejected by President Kováč, who had by this time become severely critical of the Prime Minister. Mečiar's outspoken views led the President to demand his resignation as Prime Minister in December, a demand that was ignored by Mečiar.

Mečiar's position was again undermined in early 1994 by a number of resignations and defections. In February six SNP deputies left the party to form what became the National Democratic Party—New Alternative (NDP—NA), led by Ľudovít Černák. In the same month the Minister of Foreign Affairs, Jozef Moravčík, and the Deputy Prime Minister, Roman Kováč, resigned from the Government, subsequently establishing another new opposition party, the Democratic Union of Slovakia (DUS). In early March the National Council approved a motion expressing 'no confidence' in Mečiar's Government by 78 votes to two (the MDS and SNP both abstained from voting). Following the resignation of Mečiar's administration, a new five-party coalition was hastily agreed, and sworn in by President Kováč in mid-March. The new Government, with Moravčík as Prime Minister, was composed of members of the CDM and the PDL, as well as the three new formations: the NDP—NA, the DUS and the ADSR (although the latter was subsequently absorbed into the DUS). With the support of Hungarian parties and independents, the Government held 83 of the 150 seats in the National Council. However, the Government was to act only in an interim capacity until the holding of early legislative elections in late September. The new administration, like its counterpart in the Czech Republic, adopted a policy of closer integration with western European states (whereas Mečiar's Government had been more orientated towards Russia, Ukraine and other eastern European countries). Moreover, Moravčík successfully improved relations with Hungary, giving assurances that the rights of Slovakia's Hungarian minority would be fully respected. The new Government also made considerable economic progress, reducing substantially the rate of inflation and reviving the state privatization programme (which had been largely curbed under Mečiar).

Despite the achievements of Moravčík's coalition Government, the MDS emerged as the leading party at elections to the National Council, held on 30 September and 1 October 1994 (with the participation of approximately 76% of the electorate). The renewed success of the MDS (which, in alliance with the smaller Farmers' Party of Slovakia, secured some 35% of the total votes cast, thus gaining 61 seats in the Council) was attributed to the highly populist character of Mečiar's election campaign. The Common Choice bloc (an alliance of left-wing parties, led by the PDL) secured the second largest share of the seats in the legislature (18, fewer than had been expected), followed by a coalition of Hungarian parties (17) and the CDM (also 17). The remaining seats were taken by the DUS (15), the Association of Workers of Slovakia (AWS—formed earlier in the year, following a split in the PDL—13 seats) and the SNP (nine seats).

Inter-party negotiations were held throughout October 1994 with the aim of establishing a new coalition, but they proved inconclusive. Thus, in late October, President Kováč requested Mečiar to form a new Government. However, Mečiar was initially able to win the support only of the SNP (whose nine seats in the Council, combined with the MDS's 61, would leave such a coalition short of a parliamentary majority). With no new Government installed, Moravčík's administration was forced to remain in office in a temporary capacity, despite its official resignation in early November. Finally, in mid-December a coalition of the MDS, the SNP and the AWS was announced, with Mečiar as Prime Minister (the third time he had held this office). The new Government immediately used its majority in the National Council to annul all decisions on privatization that had been made by the previous administration after 6 September. President Kováč opposed the legislation and returned it to the Council, which approved it again in January 1995. Opposition deputies then submitted the controversial legislation to the Constitutional Court, which, in May, declared the National Council's suspension of the privatization programme to have been illegal.

The growing personal enmity between Prime Minister Mečiar and President Kováč culminated in May 1995, when deputies of the MDS (and its allies) expressed 'no confidence' in the President, in a vote held in the National Council. The vote followed allegations that the Slovak Intelligence Service had provided Kováč with confidential information concerning the activities of political parties (in particular the MDS) and of state officials. However, the vote failed to gain the necessary three-fifths' majority, and Kováč remained in office. The CDM and the DUS organized mass rallies in Bratislava and Košice in support of Kováč, while opinion polls suggested that public support for the President remained high.

A priority of Slovak foreign policy is to preserve good relations with the Czech Republic and other neighbouring states. Slovakia is a member, together with the Czech Republic, Hungary and Poland, of the Visegrad Group, which promotes economic and other integration in the central European region. However, Slovakia's relations with Hungary have been strained by the issue of the large Hungarian minority (numbering almost 600,000) resident in Slovakia, who are campaigning for cultural and educational autonomy. The two countries are also involved in a dispute over the Gabčíkovo-Nagymaros hydroelectric project, a scheme initiated by the Governments of Czechoslovakia and Hungary in 1978, which involved the construction of two dams and the diversion of the River Danube. Despite Hungary's decision in 1989 to abandon the project (following pressure by environmentalist groups), the Czechoslovak Government announced that it would proceed unilaterally with its part of the construction (which was nearing completion in late 1992). In March 1993 Slovakia and Hungary agreed to forward the dispute to the International Court of Justice in The Hague, the Netherlands; no judgment was expected to be made for several years. Despite the Gabčíkovo-Nagymaros dispute, Slovak-Hungarian relations had improved considerably by March 1995, when an historic Treaty of Friendship and Co-operation was signed. The Treaty, notably, guaranteed the rights of ethnic minorities in each republic, while confirming the existing state border.

### Government

Supreme legislative power is vested in the National Council of the Slovak Republic, the 150 members of which are elected for a term of four years by universal adult suffrage. The President of the Republic (Head of State) is elected by the National Council for a five-year term. The President, who is also Commander-in-Chief of the Armed Forces, may serve no more than two consecutive terms. He/she appoints the Prime Minister and, on the latter's recommendation, the other members of the Government (the supreme body of executive power). For administrative purposes, Slovakia is divided into 38 districts (okresy).

### Defence

The division of the Czechoslovak armed forces was initiated in the latter half of 1992 and had almost been accomplished by 1 January 1993, when Czechoslovakia was dissolved and the Czech Republic and the Slovak Republic were established. In June 1994 the total strength of Slovakia's armed forces was 47,000: army 33,000 and an air force of 14,000. Paramilitary forces numbered 3,950: 600 border guards, 250 internal security forces and 3,100 civil defence troops. Military service is compulsory and lasts for 18 months. The 1994 Slovak budget allocated 10,400m. koruny to defence. In February 1994 Slovakia joined NATO's 'partnership for peace' programme (see p. 192), with the eventual aim of full membership of NATO.

### Economic Affairs

In 1993, according to estimates by the World Bank, Slovakia's gross national product (GNP), measured at average 1991–93 prices, was US $10,145m., equivalent to $1,900 per head. During 1985–93, it was estimated, GNP per head declined by an annual average of 2.6%. During the same period the population increased by an annual average of 0.4%. Slovakia's gross domestic product (GDP) declined, in real terms, by 14.5% in 1991, by 2.4% in 1992 and by 4.1% in 1993; however, in 1994 real GDP increased by 4.8%.

In 1993, according to preliminary figures, agriculture (including forestry and fishing) contributed 6.6% of GDP and provided 12.0% of employment. Subsistence agriculture traditionally dominated Slovakia's economy; however, during the communist period (1948–89) activity in the sector declined, as industry was promoted as the republic's principal economic sector. In the early 1990s approximately 2.5m. ha were used for agricultural purposes, of which 1.5m. ha were arable land. The principal crops are wheat and other grains, sugar beet, potatoes and other vegetables. Livestock breeding is also important. In 1992 agricultural production declined by 11.9%, compared with 1991; it fell by a further 15.9% in 1993.

Industry (including mining, manufacturing, construction and power) contributed 43.6% of GDP in 1993, according to provisional figures; in the same year 35.8% of the employed labour force were engaged in industry. In the early 1990s the structure of Slovak industrial activity included chemical, pharmaceutical, textile, clothing, glass, leather, footwear, construction and construction materials industries. During the communist period the arms industry was greatly expanded in Slovakia (in the 1980s about 10% of the total work-force were employed in arms-related industries). However, subsequent to the anti-communist revolution of 1989, activity in the arms industry was reduced, following government efforts to convert many factories to the production of non-military goods. In 1993 industrial production declined by 13.5%, compared with 1992; however, in 1994 production in the sector increased by 6.4%.

In 1993, according to preliminary figures, mining and quarrying provided 1.4% of employment. The principal minerals extracted include brown coal and lignite, copper, zinc, lead, iron ore and magnesite. There are also deposits of crude petroleum, natural gas and mercury, as well as materials used in construction (including limestone, gravel and brick loam). However, Slovakia remains heavily dependent on imported fuel and energy products (mineral fuels and lubricants accounted for more than 20% of the value of total merchandise imports in 1993). The large-scale nuclear power station at Jaslovské-Bohunice, in operation since the early 1980s, generated 53.6% of Slovakia's electricity in 1993. A new nuclear power station, at Mochovce, was not expected to be completed until 2000.

In 1993 Slovakia recorded a trade deficit of 33,821m. koruny. In the following year there was a surplus of US $129m. on the current account of the balance of payments. Slovakia's principal trading partner is the Czech Republic, which accounted for 42.4% of Slovakia's total exports and for 35.5% of its imports in 1993. Other important trading partners include Germany, Russia, Austria and Hungary. Slovakia's principal imports in 1993 were machinery and transport equipment (29.2% of the value of total imports), mineral fuels and lubricants (21.1%), and basic manufactures (15.0%). The principal exports in that year were basic manufactures (38.8% of the value of total exports), machinery and transport equipment (19.4%), and miscellaneous manufactured articles (13.4%).

In 1993 Slovakia recorded a budgetary deficit of 23,011m. koruny. Slovakia's total external debt at the end of 1993 was US $3,330m., of which $2,058m. was long-term public debt. In that year the cost of debt-servicing was equivalent to 8.2% of the value of exports of goods and services. In 1993 the average annual rate of inflation was 25.1%; the rate declined to 11.7% in 1994. In April 1995 355,600 people were registered as unemployed (some 14.0% of the labour force).

Slovakia is a member of the IMF and the World Bank, as well as of the European Bank for Reconstruction and Development, as a 'Country of Operations' (see p. 140). In October 1993 Slovakia signed an association agreement with the European Community (now European Union).

Following the division of Czechoslovakia in January 1993, the Slovak Government declared its aim to redress some of the adverse effects resulting from the programme of economic reforms implemented by the first post-communist Czechoslovak Government in the early 1990s. One particularly serious problem affecting Slovakia was the rapid increase in the level of unemployment, which had reached 14% by early 1994 (while the comparable rate in the Czech Republic was only 4%). This development was partly the result of the Czechoslovak Government's decision to reduce drastically the production of military equipment (which had been based largely in Slovakia, as had some 70% of Czechoslovakia's heavy industry), with the resultant loss of some 40,000 jobs in the republic in 1991–92. Following independence, however, it was declared that Slovakia would seek to revive the arms production industry as a valuable source of export revenue. There were also plans to establish customs-free zones to stimulate production and attract wider foreign investment. At mid-1992 there were some 2,100 joint-venture projects with foreign participation in operation in Slovakia (compared with almost 8,000 in the Czech Republic). The first signs of an economic recovery emerged in 1994, when overall GDP increased by almost 5%. The Slovak koruna was introduced as the national currency in February 1993, replacing the Czechoslovak koruna.

### Social Welfare

Following the dissolution of Czechoslovakia in January 1993, the Slovak Government announced modifications to the inherited Czechoslovak social welfare system. The health service was to remain largely under state control in Slovakia, although there were plans to privatize certain elements, particularly spas and pharmacies. A National Insurance Company came into being on 1 January 1993 and consisted of separate funds for general health insurance, sickness insurance and pensions insurance. Payments into the funds were to be made by employees, employers, the self-employed and the state. Further reforms to the social-welfare system were hampered by political uncertainties during 1993. In 1992 there were 6.5 physicians and 76.7 hospital beds per 1,000 inhabitants of Slovakia. The 1992 Slovak budget allocated 88,987m. koruny to social services (71.9% of total budgetary spending).

### Education

Education in Slovakia is provided free of charge at all levels. Children between the ages of three and six may attend kindergarten (materská škola). Compulsory education begins at six years of age, when children enter basic school (základná škola), which takes nine years to complete (although the ninth year is optional). Secondary education lasts for four years. There are three types of secondary school: the grammar school (gymnázium), which prepares students for higher education, and of which there were 175 in the 1993/94 academic year, secondary specialized school (stredná odborná škola, 339) and secondary vocational school (stredné odborné učilište, 344), with a total enrolment of 318,133 students. In the same year there were 14 institutions of higher education, with a total enrolment of 61,257 students. Children who, owing to handicaps, cannot attend regular schools may receive instruction at special schools. There are also private and church-affiliated schools (basic and secondary).

### Public Holidays

**1995:** 1 January (New Year's Day), 17 April (Easter Monday), 1 May (May Day), 8 May (Anniversary of Liberation), 5 July (Day of the Slav Apostles), 29 August (Anniversary of the Slovak National Uprising), 1 November (Reconciliation Day), 24–26 December (Christmas).

**1996:** 1 January (New Year's Day), 8 April (Easter Monday), 1 May (May Day), 8 May (Anniversary of Liberation), 5 July (Day of the Slav Apostles), 29 August (Anniversary of the Slovak National Uprising), 1 November (Reconciliation Day), 24–26 December (Christmas).

### Weights and Measures

The metric system is in force.

# Statistical Survey

Source: Statistical Office of the Slovak Republic, Miletičova 3, 824 67 Bratislava; tel. (7) 205-6341; fax (7) 566-1361.

## Area and Population

### AREA, POPULATION AND DENSITY

| | |
|---|---:|
| Area (sq km) | 49,036* |
| Population (census results) | |
| 3 March 1991 | |
| Males | 2,574,061 |
| Females | 2,700,274 |
| Total | 5,274,335 |
| Population (official estimates at 31 December) | |
| 1991 | 5,295,877 |
| 1992 | 5,314,155 |
| 1993 | 5,336,455 |
| Density (per sq km) at 31 December 1993 | 108.8 |

* 18,933 sq miles.

### POPULATION BY NATIONALITY
(at 31 December 1993)

| | Number | % |
|---|---:|---:|
| Slovak | 4,573,711 | 85.71 |
| Hungarian | 568,545 | 10.65 |
| Gypsy | 82,591 | 1.55 |
| Czech, Moravian, Silesian | 56,801 | 1.06 |
| Ruthenian and Ukrainian | 31,187 | 0.58 |
| German | 5,386 | 0.10 |
| Polish | 2,973 | 0.06 |
| Russian | 1,614 | 0.03 |
| Others (incl. undeclared) | 13,647 | 0.26 |
| **Total** | **5,336,455** | **100.00** |

# SLOVAKIA

## REGIONS

| | Area (sq km) | Population (31 Dec. 1993) | Density (per sq km) |
|---|---|---|---|
| Western Slovakia | 14,493 | 1,722,486 | 119 |
| Central Slovakia | 17,982 | 1,630,833 | 91 |
| Eastern Slovakia | 16,193 | 1,534,351 | 95 |
| Bratislava (city) | 368 | 448,785 | 1,220 |
| **Total*** | 49,036 | 5,336,455 | 109 |

* Until 1990 Slovakia comprised three large regions and the city of Bratislava, subdivided into 38 administrative districts (okresy). After 1990 only the okresy were retained for official administrative purposes. A new system of local administration was under discussion in 1993–1995.

## PRINCIPAL TOWNS
(estimated population at 31 December 1993)

| | | | | |
|---|---|---|---|---|
| Bratislava (capital) | 448,785 | Trnava | | 71,624 |
| Košice | 238,886 | Martin | | 60,155 |
| Prešov | 90,963 | Trenčín | | 57,748 |
| Nitra | 86,679 | Poprad | | 54,505 |
| Žilina | 85,686 | Prievidza | | 54,246 |
| Banská Bystrica | 84,575 | Zvolen | | 43,929 |

## BIRTHS, MARRIAGES AND DEATHS

| | Registered live births Number | Rate (per 1,000) | Registered marriages Number | Rate (per 1,000) | Registered deaths Number | Rate (per 1,000) |
|---|---|---|---|---|---|---|
| 1989 | 80,116 | 15.2 | 36,525 | 6.9 | 53,902 | 10.2 |
| 1990 | 79,989 | 15.1 | 40,435 | 7.6 | 54,619 | 10.3 |
| 1991 | 78,569 | 14.9 | 32,721 | 6.2 | 54,618 | 10.3 |
| 1992 | 74,640 | 14.1 | 33,880 | 6.4 | 53,423 | 10.1 |
| 1993 | 73,256 | 13.8 | 30,771 | 5.8 | 52,707 | 9.9 |

## EMPLOYMENT (at 31 December)*

| | 1991 | 1992 | 1993† |
|---|---|---|---|
| Agriculture, hunting, forestry and fishing | 271,789 | 256,489 | 259,000 |
| Mining and quarrying | 36,577 | 31,781 | 31,000 |
| Manufacturing | 625,118 | 578,519 | 550,000 |
| Electricity, gas and water | 45,183 | 47,147 | 61,000 |
| Construction | 241,198 | 197,764 | 133,000 |
| Trade, restaurants and hotels | 207,838 | 255,524 | 284,000 |
| Transport, storage and communications | 169,330 | 161,296 | 187,000 |
| Financing, insurance, real estate and business services | 124,382 | 169,762 | 188,000 |
| Public administration and defence, compulsory social security, education, health and social work | 344,631 | 414,862 | 422,000 |
| Other community, social and personal services | 85,538 | 61,418 | 51,000 |
| **Total** | 2,151,584 | 2,174,562 | 2,166,000 |

* Figures exclude women on maternity leave (annual averages): 143,991 in 1991; 122,990 in 1992; 108,143 in 1993.
† Preliminary figures.

# Agriculture

## PRINCIPAL CROPS ('000 metric tons)

| | 1991 | 1992 | 1993 |
|---|---|---|---|
| Wheat | 2,124 | 1,697 | 1,528 |
| Barley | 960 | 1,038 | 823 |
| Maize | 711 | 676 | 674 |
| Rye | 131 | 76 | 69 |
| Oats | 44 | 41 | 36 |
| Potatoes | 669 | 658 | 857 |
| Dry peas | 96 | 138 | 110 |
| Sunflower seed | 101 | 79 | 64 |
| Rapeseed | 97 | 48 | 58 |
| Cabbages (white) | 107 | 55 | 89 |
| Tomatoes | 96 | 76 | 82 |
| Peppers | 41 | 37 | 33 |
| Onions | 53 | 53 | 41 |
| Carrots | 62 | 53 | 75 |
| Grapes | 119 | 119 | 81 |
| Sugar beet | 1,501 | 1,326 | 1,107 |
| Apples | 96 | 59 | 107 |
| Tobacco (leaves) | 5 | 3 | 2 |
| Flax fibre | 2 | 3 | 3 |

## LIVESTOCK ('000 head at end of year)

| | 1991 | 1992 | 1993 |
|---|---|---|---|
| Cattle | 1,397 | 1,182 | 993 |
| Pigs | 2,428 | 2,269 | 2,179 |
| Sheep | 531 | 572 | 411 |
| Goats | 16 | 20 | 25 |
| Horses | 13 | 12 | 11 |

## LIVESTOCK PRODUCTS
('000 metric tons, unless otherwise indicated)

| | 1991 | 1992 | 1993 |
|---|---|---|---|
| Beef and veal* | 207.9 | 172.7 | 176.5 |
| Mutton, lamb and goats' meat* | 8.9 | 7.1 | 6.8 |
| Pig meat* | 328.4 | 313.2 | 294.2 |
| Poultry meat* | 98.7 | 88.4 | 70.0 |
| Cows' milk (million litres) | 1,526 | 1,331 | 1,214 |
| Butter† | 29.0 | 18.6 | 17.8 |
| Cheese† | 33.7 | 30.8 | 33.2 |
| Poultry eggs (million) | 1,825 | 1,721 | 1,527 |
| Wool | 1.3 | 1.2 | 1.2 |

* Slaughter weight. † Factory production only.

# Forestry

## ROUNDWOOD REMOVALS ('000 cubic metres)

| | 1991 | 1992 | 1993 |
|---|---|---|---|
| Production | 4,399 | 3,956 | 3,515 |
| Deliveries | 4,339 | 3,787 | 3,532 |
| Industrial | 3,834 | 3,419 | 3,195 |
| Fuel wood | 505 | 367 | 337 |

## SAWNWOOD PRODUCTION ('000 cubic metres)

| | 1991 | 1992 | 1993 |
|---|---|---|---|
| Coniferous (softwood) | 641 | 336 | 346 |
| Broadleaved (hardwood) | 343 | 349 | 205 |

# SLOVAKIA

## Mining

('000 metric tons, unless otherwise indicated)

|  | 1989 | 1990 | 1991 |
|---|---|---|---|
| Brown coal | 3,893 | 3,456 | 2,810 |
| Lignite | 1,376 | 1,310 | 1,338 |
| Iron ore (gross weight) | 1,674 | 1,728 | 1,627 |
| Crude petroleum | n.a. | 73 | 72 |
| Salt (refined) | n.a. | 50 | 54 |
| Magnesite (crude) | n.a. | 2,704 | 1,553 |
| Antimony concentrate (metric tons)* | n.a. | 2,256 | — |
| Copper concentrates (metric tons)* | 15,363 | 13,477 | 11,313 |
| Lead concentrates (metric tons)* | 3,124 | 3,853 | 4,634 |
| Mercury (metric tons) | 129 | 124 | 75 |
| Zinc concentrates (metric tons)* | 4,369 | 5,164 | 6,851 |

* Figures refer to the metal content of ores and concentrates.

**1992** ('000 metric tons): Iron ore 1,414; Crude petroleum 62.
**1993** ('000 metric tons): Iron ore 1,092; Crude petroleum 67.

## Industry

### SELECTED PRODUCTS

('000 metric tons, unless otherwise indicated)

|  | 1991 | 1992 | 1993 |
|---|---|---|---|
| Wheat flour | 388 | 409 | 419 |
| Refined sugar | 189.0 | 149.2 | 142.6 |
| Beer ('000 hectolitres) | 4,082 | 3,686 | 3,697 |
| Cigarettes (million) | 8,721 | n.a. | n.a. |
| Cotton yarn (metric tons) | 18,931 | 16,952 | 14,264 |
| Cotton fabrics ('000 metres) | 62,335 | 68,767 | n.a. |
| Linen fabrics ('000 metres) | 10,671 | 7,437 | 6,236 |
| Woollen fabrics ('000 metres) | 8,798 | 7,436 | 6,934 |
| Footwear ('000 pairs) | 27,466 | 22,875 | 18,322 |
| Paper and paperboard | 331.6 | 363.9 | 267.2 |
| Sulphuric acid (100%) | 93.7 | n.a. | n.a. |
| Nitrogenous fertilizers (a)* | 178.3 | 200.3 | 149.8 |
| Phosphate fertilizers (b)* | 122.0 | n.a. | n.a. |
| Potassic fertilizers (c)* | 11.5 | n.a. | n.a. |
| Chemical fibres | 86.6 | 78.6 | 66.4 |
| Plastic materials | 435.6 | 425.7 | 365.8 |
| Coke | 2,137 | 2,040 | 1,876 |
| Cement | 2,680 | 3,374 | 2,656 |
| Pig-iron | 3,163 | 2,952 | 3,205 |
| Crude steel | 4,107 | 3,798 | 3,922 |
| Copper (metric tons) | 25,496 | 11,486 | n.a. |
| Aluminium (metric tons) | 49,387 | 32,670 | 17,815 |
| Household refrigerators and freezers (number) | 514,965 | 551,695 | 482,102 |
| Washing machines (number) | 144,112 | 122,207 | n.a. |
| Radio receivers (number) | 65,110 | 7,600 | 1,683 |
| Television receivers (number)† | 214,795 | 216,491 | n.a. |
| Passenger cars and delivery vans (number) | 3,806 | n.a. | n.a. |
| Lorries (number) | 6,877 | n.a. | n.a. |
| Motorcycles (number) | 33,222 | n.a. | n.a. |
| Electric energy (million kWh) | 22,732 | 22,255 | 24,429 |

* Production in terms of (a) nitrogen; (b) phosphoric acid; or (c) potassium pentoxide.
† Colour television receivers only.

## Finance

### CURRENCY AND EXCHANGE RATES

**Monetary Units**
100 halierov (singular: halier) = 1 Slovenská koruna (Slovak crown or Sk; plural: koruny).

**Sterling and Dollar Equivalents** (31 December 1994)
£1 sterling = 48.93 koruny;
US $1 = 31.28 koruny;
1,000 koruny = £20.44 = $31.97.

**Average Exchange Rate** (Czechoslovak koruny per US $)
1990    17.95
1991    29.48
1992    28.26

Note: The foregoing information on average exchange rates refers to the Czechoslovak koruna, but the sterling and dollar equivalents apply to the Slovak koruna. In February 1993 Slovakia introduced its own currency, to replace (at par) the Czechoslovak koruna. The average exchange rates (koruny per US$) were: 30.770 in 1993; 32.045 in 1994.

### BUDGET (million koruny)

| Revenue | 1992 | 1993 |
|---|---|---|
| Tax revenue | 105,583 | 82,213 |
|   Income taxes | 45,152 | 25,133 |
|   Indirect taxes | 29,572 | 44,535 |
|   Other taxes | 30,858 | 349 |
|   Repayment of taxes payable by 1992 | — | 12,196 |
| Non-tax revenue | 10,293 | 23,002 |
| Insurance premiums | — | 40,674 |
| Customs duty | — | 4,453 |
| **Total** | **115,876** | **150,342** |

| Expenditure | 1992 | 1993 |
|---|---|---|
| Current expenditure | 110,519 | 148,472 |
|   Public consumption of the population | 82,231 | 97,927 |
|   Public consumption of the state | 17,639 | 28,694 |
|   Interest payments | 1,106 | 5,609 |
|   Grants | 9,543 | 16,242 |
|     To entrepreneurial sphere | 8,008 | 15,151 |
|     To local budgets | 1,535 | 1,091 |
| Capital expenditure | 13,098 | 12,851 |
| Debt service | — | 12,030 |
| **Total** | **123,617** | **173,353** |

**COST OF LIVING** (Consumer Price Index for employee households; base: January 1989 = 100)

|  | 1991 | 1992 | 1993 |
|---|---|---|---|
| Food | 172.7 | 186.0 | 226.7 |
| Beverages | 135.7 | 142.0 | 180.0 |
| Other goods | 191.1 | 209.9 | 255.3 |
| Services | 147.7 | 179.4 | 229.0 |
| **All items** | **172.4** | **190.8** | **234.8** |

**NATIONAL ACCOUNTS** (million koruny at current prices)*

**Expenditure on the Gross Domestic Product**

|  | 1992 | 1993 |
|---|---|---|
| Government final consumption expenditure | 73,600 | 85,500 |
| Private final consumption expenditure | 162,500 | 199,000 |
| Increase in stocks | −16,000 | −19,000 |
| Gross fixed capital formation | 97,600 | 93,500 |
| Statistical discrepancy | 3,900 | 1,600 |
| **Total domestic expenditure** | **321,600** | **360,600** |
| Exports of goods and services | 233,700 | 227,800 |
| *Less* Imports of goods and services | 247,500 | 248,200 |
| **GDP in purchasers' values** | **307,800** | **340,200** |

## SLOVAKIA

**Gross Domestic Product by Economic Activity**

|  | 1992 | 1993 |
|---|---|---|
| Agriculture and forestry | 18,955 | 22,357 |
| Industry† | 116,883 | 125,541 |
| Construction | 20,820 | 22,667 |
| Marketed services | 85,239 | 95,271 |
| Transport and communications | 27,803 | 37,966 |
| Non-market and housing services | 65,903 | 74,364 |
| VAT and net import taxes |  |  |
| **Total** | 307,800 | 340,200 |

* Preliminary figures.
† Principally mining, manufacturing, electricity and gas.

# External Trade

**COMMODITY GROUPS**
(distribution by SITC, million koruny)

| Imports c.i.f. | 1991* | 1992* | 1993 |
|---|---|---|---|
| Food and live animals | 5,023 | 5,065 | 14,767 |
| Crude materials (inedible) except fuels | 14,069 | 8,300 | 10,442 |
| Mineral fuels, lubricants, etc. | 39,080 | 30,562 | 42,603 |
| Chemicals and related products | 9,722 | 10,726 | 22,827 |
| Basic manufactures | 8,848 | 9,409 | 30,206 |
| Machinery and transport equipment | 26,449 | 36,013 | 58,828 |
| Miscellaneous manufactured articles | 6,668 | 9,098 | 18,106 |
| **Total** (incl. others) | 110,864 | 110,051 | 201,545 |

| Exports f.o.b. | 1991* | 1992* | 1993 |
|---|---|---|---|
| Food and live animals | 6,671 | 7,822 | 9,216 |
| Crude materials (inedible) except fuels | 4,352 | 5,739 | 8,251 |
| Mineral fuels, lubricants, etc. | 1,115 | 838 | 8,254 |
| Chemicals and related products | 11,790 | 11,736 | 20,155 |
| Basic manufactures | 35,065 | 43,978 | 64,999 |
| Machinery and transport equipment | 21,783 | 18,204 | 32,560 |
| Miscellaneous manufactured articles | 15,181 | 15,952 | 22,493 |
| **Total** (incl. others) | 96,800 | 104,915 | 167,724 |

*Excluding trade with the Czech Republic.

**PRINCIPAL TRADING PARTNERS** (million koruny)

| Imports c.i.f. | 1991* | 1992* | 1993 |
|---|---|---|---|
| Austria | 9,215 | 11,130 | 12,284 |
| Belgium | 1,061 | 1,070 | 1,662 |
| Brazil | 1,465 | 862 | 274 |
| Czech Republic | — | — | 71,477 |
| France | 2,104 | 2,552 | 3,054 |
| Germany | 15,553 | 22,850 | 22,955 |
| Hungary | 3,284 | 2,833 | 2,663 |
| Iran | 1,625 | 10 | 35 |
| Italy | 3,113 | 6,205 | 6,058 |
| Netherlands | 1,463 | 1,895 | 2,696 |
| Poland | 3,990 | 3,484 | 3,906 |
| USSR (former) | 47,489 | 38,187 | 46,493 |
| United Kingdom | 1,043 | 1,249 | 2,569 |
| USA | 1,250 | 1,820 | 3,566 |
| Yugoslavia (former) | 2,518 | 1,558 | 1,380 |
| **Total** (incl. others) | 110,864 | 110,051 | 201,545 |

| Exports f.o.b. | 1991* | 1992* | 1993 |
|---|---|---|---|
| Austria | 5,702 | 7,771 | 8,336 |
| Czech Republic | — | — | 71,124 |
| France | 2,364 | 3,978 | 2,667 |
| Germany | 19,154 | 25,618 | 25,490 |
| Hungary | 6,582 | 7,255 | 7,615 |
| Italy | 4,947 | 5,746 | 4,571 |
| Netherlands | 2,614 | 2,466 | 2,647 |
| Poland | 7,729 | 4,303 | 4,893 |
| Romania | 1,188 | 1,282 | 741 |
| Syria | 2,511 | 2,096 | 1,462 |
| USSR (former) | 24,139 | 17,584 | 13,959 |
| United Kingdom | 1,064 | 1,935 | 1,699 |
| Yugoslavia (former) | 3,910 | 3,706 | 2,783 |
| **Total** (incl. others) | 96,800 | 104,915 | 167,724 |

* Excluding trade with the Czech Republic.

# Transport

|  | 1991 | 1992 | 1993 |
|---|---|---|---|
| Railway transport |  |  |  |
| Freight ('000 tons) | 83,873 | 76,123 | 64,825 |
| Passengers (million) | 112 | 107 | 87 |
| Public road transport |  |  |  |
| Freight ('000 tons) | 72,309 | 79,852 | 37,826 |
| Passengers (million) | 939 | 855 | 826 |
| Waterway transport |  |  |  |
| Freight ('000 tons) | 1,946 | 1,648 | 1,399 |

**ROAD TRAFFIC** (motor vehicles in use)

|  | 1991 | 1992 | 1993 |
|---|---|---|---|
| Passenger cars | 906,129 | 953,239 | 994,933 |
| Buses and coaches | 13,770 | 13,338 | 12,655 |
| Goods vehicles | 150,456 | 152,555 | 147,673 |
| Motorcycles and scooters | 282,754 | 241,855 | 233,705 |

# Tourism

**FOREIGN TOURIST ARRIVALS***
(visitors at accommodation facilities)

| Country of origin | 1991 | 1992 | 1993 |
|---|---|---|---|
| Austria | 30,959 | 38,536 | 35,381 |
| France | 15,681 | 18,828 | 20,692 |
| Germany | 128,872 | 132,072 | 114,211 |
| Hungary | 72,674 | 54,696 | 39,896 |
| Italy | 36,627 | 38,034 | 30,227 |
| Netherlands | 16,908 | 27,367 | 26,295 |
| Poland | 92,311 | 95,270 | 80,585 |
| USSR (former) | 13,116 | 22,958 | n.a. |
| USA | 16,430 | 21,154 | 17,873 |
| Yugoslavia (former) | 64,602 | 28,926 | n.a. |
| **Total** (incl. others) | 576,299 | 566,494 | 652,815 |

* Excluding visitors from the Czech Republic.

## Communications Media

|  | 1990 | 1991 | 1992 |
|---|---|---|---|
| Telephones in use | 1,254,709 | 1,305,443 | 1,362,178 |
| Radio receivers (licensed) | 1,094,142 | 1,093,901 | 1,068,185 |
| Television receivers (licensed) | 1,309,045 | 1,309,083 | 1,279,101 |
| Book production: titles* | 2,734 | 3,305 | 2,842 |
| Newspapers and periodicals: titles | 689 | 571 | 707 |

* Including printed music, teaching materials, maps and atlases.

## Education

(1993/94)

|  | Institutions | Teachers* | Students |
|---|---|---|---|
| Kindergarten | 3,482 | 15,834 | 183,972 |
| Primary (basic) | 2,483 | 38,874 | 690,189 |
| Secondary |  |  |  |
| Grammar | 175 | 4,815 | 68,004 |
| Specialized | 339 | 8,494 | 111,664 |
| Vocational | 344 | 5,929 | 138,465 |
| Higher | 14 | 7,769 | 61,257 |

* Teachers in full-time employment.

# Directory

## The Constitution

On 1 September 1992 the Slovak National Council adopted the Constitution of the Slovak Republic (which entered into force on 1 January 1993), the main provisions of which are summarized below:

### FUNDAMENTAL PROVISIONS

The Slovak Republic is a democratic and sovereign state, ruled by law. It is bound neither to an ideology, nor to a religion. State power belongs to the people, who exercise it either through their representatives or directly. The state authorities shall act only on the basis of the Constitution and to the extent and in the manner stipulated by law.

The territory of the Slovak Republic is integral and indivisible. The conditions for naturalization or deprival of state citizenship of the Slovak Republic are regulated by law. No person may be deprived of citizenship against his will. The Slovak language is the state language in the republic. The use of languages other than the state language in administrative relations is regulated by law. The capital of the republic is Bratislava.

### BASIC RIGHTS AND FREEDOMS

The people are free and equal, and the rights and freedoms of every citizen are guaranteed, irrespective of sex, race, colour, language, faith, political or other conviction, national or social origin, nationality or ethnic origin. No person may be tortured, nor be subjected to cruel, inhuman or humiliating treatment or punishment. Capital punishment is not practised.

Every person has the right to own property. The place of abode is inviolable. The freedom of migration and the freedom of domicile are guaranteed.

The freedom of expression and the right to information are guaranteed. Censorship is prohibited. The right to assemble peacefully is guaranteed. Every person has the right to be a member of a union, community, society or any other association. Citizens have the right to found political parties and movements. Such parties and movements, as well as other associations, are separate from the state.

The citizens have the right to participate in the administration of public affairs, either directly or through the free election of their representatives. The right to vote is universal, direct and equal and is exercised by secret ballot.

The universal advancement of citizens who are members of national minorities and ethnic groups is guaranteed, above all the right to develop their own culture, to broadcast and receive information in their mother tongue, to join national associations and to found and maintain educational and cultural institutions. The languages of national minorities may also be used in administrative relations.

Every person has the right to the free choice of profession and vocational training as well as to do business and to perform other commercial activities. Employees are entitled to fair and satisfactory working conditions. Citizens may form free associations to protect their economic and social interests. Trade unions are independent of the state. The right to strike is guaranteed.

Every citizen is entitled to adequate old-age and disability benefits; widow's allowances; free health care; family suppport; and education.

### NATIONAL COUNCIL OF THE SLOVAK REPUBLIC

Supreme legislative power is vested in the National Council of the Slovak Republic, which has 150 deputies, elected for a four-year term. The deputies represent the citizens and are elected by them in general, equal and direct elections, by secret ballot.

The National Council has the power to: adopt the Constitution, constitutional and other laws and supervise their execution; elect and recall the President of the Slovak Republic by secret ballot; decide on proposals to call a referendum; prior to their ratification, give consent to international political, economic or other agreements; establish ministries and other bodies of state administration; supervise the activities of the Government and pass a vote of confidence or censure on the Government or its members; approve the state budget and supervise its execution; elect judges, including the Chairman and Vice-Chairmen of the Supreme Court and of the Constitutional Court; adopt a resolution to declare war if the Slovak Republic is attacked, or if such a declaration ensues from the obligations of international treaties.

### THE PRESIDENT OF THE REPUBLIC

The President is the Head of State of the Slovak Republic. He/she is elected by the National Council by secret ballot for a five-year term. The President is responsible to the National Council. He/she may not be elected for more than two consecutive terms.

The President represents the Slovak Republic internationally, negotiates and ratifies international agreements; receives and gives credentials to envoys; convenes constituent sessions of the National Council; may dissolve the National Council; signs laws; appoints and recalls the Prime Minister and other members of the Government and receives their resignation; grants amnesty, pardons and commutes sentences imposed by courts; may declare a state of emergency on the basis of constitutional law; may declare a referendum.

### THE GOVERNMENT

The Government of the Slovak Republic is the highest organ of executive power. It is composed of the Prime Minister and Ministers. The Prime Minister is appointed by the President of the Republic. On the Prime Minister's recommendation, the President appoints and recalls the members of the Government and puts them in charge of their ministries. For the execution of office, the Government is responsible to the National Council.

The Government has the power to prepare bills; issue decrees; adopt fundamental provisions for economic and social policy; authorize drafts for the state budget and closing account of the year; decide international agreements; decide principal questions of internal and international policy; submit bills to the National Council; request the legislature for a vote of confidence.

## The Government

### HEAD OF STATE

**President of the Republic:** MICHAL KOVÁČ (elected 15 February 1993).

SLOVAKIA                                                                                                                    *Directory*

## GOVERNMENT
(June 1995)

The Government is composed of members of the Movement for a Democratic Slovakia (MDS), the Slovak National Party (SNP) and the Association of Workers of Slovakia (AWS).

**Prime Minister:** VLADIMÍR MEČIAR (MDS).

**Deputy Prime Ministers:** KATARÍNA TÓTHOVÁ (MDS), JOZEF KALMAN (AWS).

**Deputy Prime Minister and Minister of Finance:** SERGEJ KOZLÍK (MDS).

**Minister of Foreign Affairs:** JURAJ SCHENK (MDS).

**Minister of Defence:** JÁN SITEK (SNP).

**Minister of the Economy:** JÁN DUCKÝ (MDS).

**Minister of Privatization:** PETER BISÁK (AWS).

**Minister of the Environment:** JOZEF ZLOCHA (MDS).

**Minister of the Interior:** L'UDOVÍT HUDEK (MDS).

**Minister of Labour, Social Affairs and the Family:** OL'GA KELTOŠOVÁ (MDS).

**Minister of Culture:** IVAN HUDEC (MDS).

**Minister of Justice:** JOZEF LIŠČÁK (AWS).

**Minister of Education:** EVA SLAVKOVSKÁ (SNP).

**Minister of Health:** L'UBOMÍR JAVORSKÝ (MDS).

**Minister of Agriculture:** PETER BACO (MDS).

**Minister of Transport, Posts and Telecommunications:** ALEXANDER REZES (MDS).

**Minister of Construction and Public Works:** JÁN MRÁZ (AWS).

### MINISTRIES

**Office of the Government of the Slovak Republic:** nám. Slobody 1, 842 18 Bratislava; tel (7) 415-111; fax (7) 492-795.

**Ministry of Agriculture:** Dobrovičova 12, 812 66 Bratislava; tel. (7) 368-561; fax (7) 456-579.

**Ministry of Construction and Public Works:** Špitálska 8, 816 44 Bratislava; tel. (7) 441-111; fax (7) 367-054.

**Ministry of Culture:** Dobrovičova 12, 813 31 Bratislava; tel. (7) 367-726; fax (7) 323-528.

**Ministry of Defence:** Kutuzovova 7, 832 28 Bratislava; tel. (7) 258-861; fax (7) 258-781.

**Ministry of the Economy:** Mierová 19, 827 15 Bratislava; tel. (7) 2998-111; fax (7) 230-122.

**Ministry of Education:** Hlboká 2, 812 20 Bratislava; tel. (7) 495-772; fax (7) 497-098.

**Ministry of the Environment:** Hlboká 2, 812 35 Bratislava; tel. (7) 492-532; fax (7) 497-267.

**Ministry of Finance:** Štefanovičova 5, 813 08 Bratislava; tel. (7) 498-431; fax (7) 498-065.

**Ministry of Foreign Affairs:** Stromová 1, 833 36 Bratislava; tel. (7) 3704-111; fax (7) 376-364.

**Ministry of Health:** Špitálska 6, 813 25 Bratislava; tel. (7) 361-482; fax (7) 361-508.

**Ministry of the Interior:** Pribinova 2, 812 72 Bratislava; tel. (7) 323-659; fax (7) 367-746.

**Ministry of Justice:** Župné nám. 13, 813 11 Bratislava; tel. (7) 353-204; fax (7) 330-732.

**Ministry of Labour, Social Affairs and the Family:** Špitálska 4–6, 816 43 Bratislava; tel. (7) 442-415; fax (7) 362-150.

**Ministry of Privatization:** Drieňová 24, 820 09 Bratislava; tel. (7) 234-332; fax (7) 294-548.

**Ministry of Transport, Posts and Telecommunications:** Miletičova 19, 820 06 Bratislava; tel. (7) 254-753; fax (7) 254-800.

## Legislature

### NATIONAL COUNCIL OF THE SLOVAK REPUBLIC

**Chairman:** IVAN GAŠPAROVIČ.

**Deputy Chairmen:** JÁN L'UPTÁK, AUGUSTÍN MARIÁN HÚSKA, MARIÁN ANDEL.

### General Election, 30 September and 1 October 1994

| Parties and Alliances | % of votes | Seats |
|---|---|---|
| Movement for a Democratic Slovakia/Farmers' Party of Slovakia | 34.96 | 61 |
| Common Choice bloc* | 10.41 | 18 |
| Hungarian Coalition† | 10.18 | 17 |
| Christian Democratic Movement | 10.08 | 17 |
| Democratic Union of Slovakia | 8.57 | 15 |
| Association of Workers of Slovakia | 7.34 | 13 |
| Slovak National Party | 5.40 | 9 |
| Others | 13.06 | — |
| **Total** | **100.00** | **150** |

* An alliance of the Party of the Democratic Left, the Social Democratic Party of Slovakia, the Green Party in Slovakia and the Farmers' Movement of Slovakia.
† A coalition of Coexistence (Együttélés), the Hungarian Christian Democratic Movement and the Hungarian People's Party.

## Political Organizations

**Association of Workers of Slovakia** (Združenie robotníkov Slovenska): Horná 83, 974 01 Banská Bystrica; tel. (88) 742-703; f. 1994; Chair. JÁN L'UPTÁK.

**Christian Democratic Movement** (Krest'ansko-demokratické hnutie): Žabotova 2, 811 04 Bratislava; tel. (7) 496-308; fax (7) 496-313; f. 1990; Chair. JÁN ČARNOGURSKÝ.

**Coexistence** (Spolužitie/Együttélés): Pražská 7, POB 44, 814 09 Bratislava; tel. and fax (7) 497-877; represents ethnic Hungarian interests; Leader MIKLÓS DURAY.

**Democratic Party** (Demokratická strana): Šancová 70, 813 47 Bratislava; tel. (7) 496-885; fax (7) 495-894; f. 1944; in 1994 absorbed the Civic Democratic Union, Civic Democratic Party of Slovakia, Democrats '92, Czech-Slovak Understanding and the Green League; conservative; Chair. PETER OSUSKÝ; 3,000 mems.

**Democratic Union of Slovakia** (Demokratická únia Slovenska): Medená 10, 811 04 Bratislava; tel. and fax (7) 361-637; f. 1994; formed by former members of the Movement for a Democratic Slovakia; in 1995 absorbed the National Democratic Party—New Alternative; Chair. JOZEF MORAVČÍK; First Dep. Chair. MILAN KŇAŽKO.

**Farmers' Movement of Slovakia** (Hnutie pol'nohospodárov Slovenska): Sama Chalúpku 18, 071 01 Bratislava; tel. (7) 215-291; Chair. JOZEF KLEIN.

**Farmers' Party of Slovakia** (Rol'nícka strana Slovenska): Trenčianska 55, 821 09 Bratislava; tel. (7) 215-800; Chair. PAVEL DELINGA.

**Green Party in Slovakia** (Strana zelených na Slovensku): Palisády 56, 811 06 Bratislava; tel. (7) 323-231; fax (7) 364-848; Chair. JOZEF POKORNÝ.

**Hungarian Christian Democratic Movement:** Žabotova 2, Bratislava; tel. (7) 495-164; fax (7) 495-264; Leader BÉLA BUGÁR.

**Hungarian People's Party:** Žabotova 2, 811 04 Bratislava; tel. (7) 497-684; fax (7) 495-791; Chair. LÁSZLÓ A. NAGY.

**Movement for a Democratic Slovakia** (Hnutie za demokratické Slovensko): Tomášikova 32A, 821 02 Bratislava; tel. (7) 230-144; fax (7) 293-855; f. 1991; Chair. VLADIMÍR MEČIAR.

**Party of the Democratic Left** (Strana demokratickej l'avice): Gunduličova 8, 811 05 Bratislava; tel. (7) 333-617; telex 92722; fax (7) 335-574; f. 1991 to replace the Communist Party of Slovakia; Chair. PETER WEISS.

**Slovak National Party** (Slovenská národná strana): Šafárikovo nám. 3, 811 02 Bratislava; tel. (7) 323-869; fax (7) 366-188; Chair. JÁN SLOTA.

**Social Democratic Party of Slovakia** (Sociálno-demokratická strana Slovenska): Žabotova 2, 811 04 Bratislava; tel. (7) 494-623; fax (7) 494-621; re-established 1990; Chair. JAROSLAV VOLF.

## Diplomatic Representation

### EMBASSIES IN SLOVAKIA

**Angola:** Jančova 8, 811 02 Bratislava; tel. (7) 413-549; fax (7) 314-546; Ambassador: EMANUEL QUARTA 'PUNZA'.

**Austria:** Venturska 10, 811 01 Bratislava; tel. (7) 334-885; fax (7) 335-086; Ambassador: MAXIMILIAN PAMMER.

**Belgium:** Fraňa král'a 5, 811 05 Bratislava; tel. (7) 491-338; fax (7) 494-296; Ambassador: DENIS BANNEEL.

**Bulgaria:** Kuzmányho 1, 811 06 Bratislava; tel. (7) 335-971; Ambassador: IVAN SLAVOV.

# SLOVAKIA

**China, People's Republic:** Údolná 7, 811 06 Bratislava; tel. (7) 314-577; fax (7) 316-551; Ambassador: TANG ZHANQING.

**Croatia:** Grösslingova 47, 811 09 Bratislava; tel. (7) 361-413; fax (7) 361-403; Ambassador: IVICA TOMIĆ.

**Cuba:** Matuškova 10, 831 01 Bratislava; tel. (7) 377-960; fax (7) 3789-067; Ambassador: (vacant).

**Czech Republic:** Panenská 33, 810 00 Bratislava; tel. (7) 334-361; fax (7) 333-410; Ambassador: FILIP ŠEDIVÝ.

**France:** Hlavné nám. 7, 811 01 Bratislava; tel. (7) 335-725; fax (7) 335-719; Ambassador: MICHEL PERRIN.

**Germany:** Palisády 47, 813 03 Bratislava; tel. (7) 315-300; fax (7) 315-363; Ambassador: HEIKE H. ZENKER.

**Holy See:** Uršulínska 3, 811 01 Bratislava (Apostolic Nunciature); tel. (7) 333-040; fax (7) 332-504; Apostolic Nuncio: Mgr LUIGI DOSSENA, Titular Archbishop of Carpi.

**Hungary:** Sedlárska 3, 814 25 Bratislava; tel. (7) 330-541; fax (7) 335-484; Ambassador: JENŐ BOROS.

**Italy:** Červeňova 19, 811 03 Bratislava; tel. (7) 313-195; fax (7) 313-202; Ambassador: ERMANNO SQUADRILLI.

**Malta:** Miletičova 5, 821 08 Bratislava; tel. (7) 207-2438; fax (7) 2072-449; Ambassador: HELMUT LIEDERMANN.

**Netherlands:** Fraňa Kral'a 5, 811 05 Bratislava; tel. (7) 491-577; fax (7) 491-075; Ambassador: HUGO GAJUS SCHELTEMA.

**Poland:** Hummelova 4, 814 91 Bratislava; tel. (7) 315-220; fax (7) 315-143; Ambassador: JERZY KOROLEC.

**Romania:** Fraňa Král'a 11, 811 05 Bratislava; tel. (7) 491-665; Ambassador: MIHAI DINUCU.

**Russia:** Godrova 4, 811 06 Bratislava; tel. (7) 313-468; fax (7) 334-910; Ambassador: SERGEY V. YASTRZHEMBSKY.

**South Africa:** Jančova 8, 811 02 Bratislava; tel. (7) 311-582; fax (7) 312-581; Ambassador: R. V. FRANKEN.

**Spain:** Grösslingova 35, 811 09 Bratislava; tel. (7) 362-294; fax (7) 362-320; Ambassador: (vacant).

**Turkey:** Grösslingova 35, 811 09 Bratislava; tel. (7) 361-050; fax (7) 361-937; Ambassador: AYDIN SAHINBAS.

**Ukraine:** Radvaňská 35, 811 01 Bratislava; tel. (7) 331-672; fax (7) 312-651; Ambassador: (vacant).

**United Kingdom:** Grösslingova 35, 811 09 Bratislava; tel. (7) 364-420; fax (7) 364-396; Ambassador: PETER GALE HARBORNE.

**USA:** Hviezdoslavovo nám. 4, 811 02 Bratislava; tel. (7) 330-861; fax (7) 335-439; Ambassador: THEODORE E. RUSSELL.

**Yugoslavia:** Palkovičova 16, 821 08 Bratislava; tel. (7) 499-422; fax (7) 499-477; Ambassador: (vacant).

# Judicial System

Justice in Slovakia is performed by the district courts (first level), county courts (second level) and the Supreme Court of the Slovak Republic. The Constitutional Court was restored in 1993.

**Chairman of the Supreme Court:** Prof. KAROL PLANK.

**Prosecutor-General:** MICHAL VALO.

**Chairman of the Constitutional Court:** MILAN ČIČ.

# Religion

The principal religion in Slovakia is Christianity, of which the largest denomination (representing some 68% of the total population) is the Roman Catholic Church. About 10% of the population profess no religious belief.

## CHRISTIANITY

### The Roman Catholic Church

Slovakia consists of one archdiocese and 6 dioceses, including one (directly responsible to the Holy See) for Catholics of the Slovak (Byzantine) rite, also known as 'Greek' Catholics or Uniates. At 31 December 1993 there were, in total, 3,619,004 adherents of the Roman Catholic Church in Slovakia.

**Bishops' Conference:** Konferencia biskupov Slovenska, Kapitulská 11, 814 99 Bratislava; tel. and fax (7) 335-234; f. 1993; Pres. Rt Rev. RUDOLF BALÁŽ, Bishop of Banská Bystrica.

*Latin Rite*

**Archbishop of Trnava:** Most Rev. JÁN SOKOL, Arcibiskupský úrad, nám. sv. Mikuláša 3, 917 66 Trnava; tel. (805) 262-35; fax (805) 262-37.

*Slovak Rite*

**Bishop of Prešov:** Rt Rev. JÁN HIRKA, Gréckokatolícky biskupský úrad, Hlavná ul. 1, 080 01 Prešov; tel. (91) 346-22; fax (91) 227-23; 208,238 adherents (Dec. 1993); 228 parishes.

### The Orthodox Church

**Orthodox Church of the Czech Lands and Slovakia:** V Jámě 6, POB 655, 111 21 Prague 1, Czech Republic; tel. (2) 260-017; divided into four eparchies in the former Czechoslovakia: Prague and Olomouc (Czech Republic), Prešov and Michalovce (Slovakia); Archbishop of Prague and Metropolitan of the Czech Lands and Slovakia DOROTHEOS; 53,613 mems (March 1991); 127 parishes; Theological Faculty in Charles University, Prague, Czech Republic.

**Archbishop of Prešov:** Rev. NIKOLAJ, Budovatelská 1, 080 01 Prešov.

**Bishop of Michalovce:** Rev. JOHN, Štefánikova, 071 44 Michalovce.

### Protestant Churches

**Baptist Union of Slovakia:** Súl'ovská 2, 821 05 Bratislava; tel. and fax (7) 221-145; f. 1994; 2,000 mems; Pres. Rev. JURAJ KOHÚT; Gen. Sec. Rev. JURAJ PRIBULA.

**Evangelical Church of the Augsburg Confession in Slovakia** (Lutheran Church): Palisády 46, 811 06 Bratislava; tel. (7) 332-842; fax (7) 330-500; presided over by the Bishop-General and Inspector-General; 327 parishes in 14 seniorates and two districts; 326,100 mems (Feb. 1995); Bishop-Gen. JÚLIUS FILO; Inspector-Gen. JÁN HOLČÍK.

**Reformed Christian Church of Slovakia:** Jókaiho 34, 945 01 Komárno; tel. (819) 2788; fax (819) 3716; 89,295 mems and 310 parishes (March 1991); Bishop Dr EUGEN MIKÓ; Gen. Sec. Mgr BARTOLOMEJ GÖÖZ.

### Other Christian Churches

**Apostolic Church:** Sreznevského 2, 831 03 Bratislava; tel. and fax (95) 644-1422; f. 1956; 2,000 mems; Pres. JOZEF BRENKUS.

## JUDAISM

**Union of the Jewish Religious Communities in the Slovak Republic** (Ústredný zväz židovských náboženských obcí ve Slovenskej republike): Kozia ul. 21/II, 814 47 Bratislava; tel. (7) 312-167; fax (7) 311-106; 3,300 mems; Exec. Chair. FERO ALEXANDER; Rabbis BARUCH MYERS (Bratislava), LAZAR KLEINMAN.

# The Press

In 1994 there were 787 newspapers and periodicals (80 of which were new titles) published in Slovakia: 20 daily newspapers, 465 nationwide periodicals and 302 regional periodicals.

The publications listed below are in Slovak, unless otherwise indicated.

## PRINCIPAL DAILIES

### Banská Bystrica

**Smer dnes** (Direct Today): Čs. armády 26, 974 01 Banská Bystrica; tel. (88) 254-78; telex 70261; fax (88) 255-06; f. 1948; independent; Editor-in-Chief IVAN BAČA; circ. 20,000.

**Večerník** (Evening Paper): nám. SNP 3, 974 00 Banská Bystrica; tel. (88) 539-01; fax (88) 526-03; Editor-in-Chief EVA BENČÍKOVÁ; circ. 5,000.

### Bratislava

**Hlas l'udu** (Voice of the People): Pribinova 21, 819 46 Bratislava; tel. (7) 334-560; fax (7) 334-521; f. 1949; morning; West Slovakia region; Editor-in-Chief GENAD PEŇKOVSKÝ; circ. 22,000.

**Hospodárske noviny** (Economic News): Pribinova 25, 810 11 Bratislava; tel. (7) 324-026; fax (7) 210-3608; morning; Editor-in-Chief PETER KASALOVSKÝ.

**Národná obroda** (National Renewal): Trnavská cesta 112, POB 63, 830 00 Bratislava; tel. (7) 5220-433; fax (7) 5220-594; f. 1990; independent; Editor-in-Chief JURAJ VEREŠ; circ. 45,000.

**Nový čas** (New Time): Gorkého 5, 812 78 Bratislava; tel. (7) 363-070; fax (7) 363-104; f. 1991; morning; Editor-in-Chief ZUZANA RAČKOVÁ; circ. 230,000.

**Práca** (Labour): Odborárske nám. 3, 814 99 Bratislava; tel. (7) 650-60; fax (7) 212-985; f. 1946; publ. by the Confederation of Trade Unions of the Slovak Republic; Editor-in-Chief EDUARD FAŠUNG; circ. 80,000.

**Pravda** (Truth): Pribinova 25, 810 11 Bratislava; tel. (7) 367-503; telex 92702; fax (7) 210-4759; f. 1920; independent; left-wing; Editor-in-Chief PETER SITÁNY; circ. 165,000.

**Rol'nícke noviny** (Agricultural News): Dobrovičova 12, 813 78 Bratislava; tel. (7) 368-449; telex 93211; fax (7) 321-282; f. 1946; Editor-in-Chief JURAJ ŠESTÁK; circ. 20,000.

# SLOVAKIA

**Slovenská republika** (Slovak Republic): Ružová dolina 6, 824 70 Bratislava; tel. (7) 201-1505; fax (7) 310-539; Editor-in-Chief Ján Smolec; circ 78,000.

**Sme** (We Are): Mytná 33, 810 05 Bratislava; tel. (7) 498-726; fax (7) 498-306; f. 1993; Editor-in-Chief Karol Ježík; circ. 50,000.

**Smena** (Shift): Dostojevského rad 1, 819 24 Bratislava; tel. (7) 326-250; fax (7) 362-655; f. 1947; youth daily; Editor-in-Chief L'ubomír Stanček; circ. 24,000.

**Šport** (Sport): Svätoplukova 2, 819 23 Bratislava; tel. (7) 600-53; telex 93334; fax (7) 211-380; Editor-in-Chief Zdeno Simonides; circ. 85,000.

**Új szó** (New Word): Pribinova 25, 819 15 Bratislava; tel. (7) 323-220; telex 92308; fax (7) 364-529; f. 1948; midday; Hungarian-language paper; Editor-in-Chief József Szilvássy; circ. 48,000.

**Večerník** (Evening Paper): Pribinova 25, 819 16 Bratislava; tel. (7) 325-085; fax (7) 210-4521; f. 1956; evening; Editor-in-Chief Martin Podstupka; circ. 30,000.

### Košice

**Košický večer** (Košice Evening): tr. SNP 24, 042 97 Košice; tel. (95) 429-820; fax (95) 421-214; f. 1990; Editor-in-Chief Mikuláš Jesenský; circ. 25,000.

**Lúč** (Ray): B. Němcovej 32, 042 62 Košice; tel. (95) 633-2117; fax (95) 359-090; f. 1992; East Slovakia region; Editor-in-Chief Edita Pačajová-Kardošová; circ. 15,000.

**Slovenský východ** (Slovak East): Letná 45, 042 66 Košice; tel. (95) 539-79; fax (95) 539-50; East Slovakia region; Editor-in-Chief Dušan Klinger; circ. 30,000.

### Prešov

**Prešovský večerník** (Prešov Evening Paper): Jarkova 4, 080 01 Prešov; tel. (91) 724-563; fax (91) 723-398; f. 1990; Editor-in-Chief Peter Ličák; circ. 13,000.

### PRINCIPAL PERIODICALS

**Deák-Avízo:** Teslova 26, 821 02 Bratislava; tel. (7) 627-10; fax (7) 672-39; weekly; advertising and information; Dir Ladislav Fogarassy; circ. 32,500.

**Dievča** (Girl): Mudroňova 12, 815 05 Bratislava; tel. (7) 311-920; monthly; publ. by the Slovak Union of Women; Editor-in-Chief Dana Viestová; circ. 18,000.

**Domino Efekt:** Hlavná 68, 040 01 Košice; tel. and fax (95) 622-7692; f. 1992; weekly; Editor-in-Chief Andrej Hrico; circ. 20,000.

**Elektrón + Zenit:** Pražská 11, 812 84 Bratislava; tel. (7) 417-225; fax (7) 493-385; monthly; science and technology for young people; Editor-in-Chief Ladislav Gyorffy; circ. 22,000.

**Eurotelevízia** (Eurotelevision): Pribinova 25, 819 14 Bratislava; tel. (7) 210-4194; telex 92661; fax (7) 210-4152; weekly; Editor-in-Chief Taňa Lucká; circ. 420,000.

**Eva:** Pribinova 25, 819 39 Bratislava; tel. (7) 210-3340; fax (7) 210-4128; monthly; magazine for women; Editor-in-Chief Dr Gita Pechová; circ. 180,000.

**Express:** Pribinova 25, 819 05 Bratislava; tel. (7) 210-4031; fax (7) 325-185 f. 1969; weekly digest of the foreign press; Editor-in-Chief Ján Machaj; circ. 67,000.

**Extra S:** Hálkova 11, 831 03 Bratislava; tel. (7) 369-715; fax (7) 325-154; social, economic and political weekly; Editor-in-Chief Imrich Demovič; circ. 20,000.

**International:** Štúrova 4, 815 80 Bratislava; tel. (7) 367-808; fax (7) 309-224; weekly; current affairs; Editor-in-Chief Tatiana Jaglová; circ. 60,000.

**Kamarát** (Friend): POB 73, 820 14 Bratislava; tel. and fax (7) 240-8777; f. 1950; fortnightly magazine for teenagers; Editor-in-Chief Vladimír Topercer; circ. 30,000.

**Katolícke noviny** (Catholic News): Kapitulská 20, 815 21 Bratislava; tel. (7) 333-790; fax (7) 333-178; f. 1849; weekly; Editor-in-Chief Juraj Chovan; circ. 116,000.

**Krásy Slovenska** (Beauty of Slovakia): Vajnorská 100A, 832 58 Bratislava; tel. (7) 258-454; illustrated monthly; Editor-in-Chief Elena Puková; circ. 10,000.

**Línia:** Pribišova 19A, 841 05 Bratislava; tel. (7) 714-411; fax (7) 714-420; quarterly; life-style; Editor-in-Chief Martin Brčak; circ. 45,000.

**Móda** (Fashion): Štefánikova 4, 812 64 Bratislava; tel. (7) 765-704; fax (7) 491-191; quarterly; Editor-in-Chief Dana Lapšanská; circ. 20,000.

**Nové slovo bez rešpektu** (New Word Without Respect): Pribinova 25, 819 07 Bratislava; tel. (7) 364-334; fax (7) 210-4798; f. 1944; weekly; politics, culture, economy; Editor-in-Chief Emil Polák; circ. 9,000.

**Ohník** (Little Flame): Pražská 11, 812 84 Bratislava; tel. (7) 417-233; monthly; youth; Editor-in-Chief Stanislav Bebjak; 35,000.

**Plus 7 dní:** Ružová dolina 27, 825 06 Bratislava; tel. (7) 656-83; fax (7) 201-6309; weekly social magazine; Editor-in-Chief Miloš Luknár; circ. 60,000.

**Poradca podnikateľa** (Entrepreneurs' Advice): Národná 13, POB 29, 010 01 Žilina; tel. (89) 621-101; fax (89) 222-56; monthly; Editor-in-Chief Mária Mestická; circ. 70,000.

**Rodina** (Family): Pribinova 25, POB 122, 810 11 Bratislava; tel. (7) 210-4027; monthly; family magazine; Editor-in-Chief M. Város; circ. 145,000.

**Romano ľil nevo:** Jarková 4, 080 01 Prešov; tel. (91) 733-439; f. 1991; in Romany; publ. by the Cultural Union of the Roma in Slovakia; Editor-in-Chief Palis R. Žiga; circ. 7,000.

**Slovenka** (Slovak Woman): Jaskový rad 5, 833 80 Bratislava; tel. (7) 373-169; fax (7) 376-118; f. 1949; weekly; illustrated magazine; Editor-in-Chief Drahoslava Výžinkárová; circ. 220,000.

**Slovenské národné noviny** (Slovak National News): Matica slovenská, Mudroňová 1, 036 52 Martin; tel. and fax (842) 345-35; f. 1845; weekly; organ of Matica slovenská cultural organization; Editor-in-Chief Miloš Majer; circ. 7,000.

**Slovenský profit:** Pribinova 25, 810 11 Bratislava; tel. (7) 210-3817; fax (7) 210-4581; economic weekly; Editor-in-Chief Jozef Gál; circ. 40,000.

**Stop:** Exnárova 57, 820 12 Bratislava; tel. and fax (7) 220-554; fortnightly; motoring; Editor-in-Chief L'uboš Kríž; circ. 47,000.

**Szabad újság** (Free Journal): Michalská 9, 814 99 Bratislava; tel. (7) 333-012; fax (7) 330-519; f. 1991; Hungarian-language economic weekly; Editor-in-Chief Géza Szabó; circ. 40,000.

**Trend:** Rezedova 5, 820 07 Bratislava; tel. (7) 5223-565; fax (7) 231-336; f. 1991; weekly; for entrepreneurs; publ. by Trendy Ltd; Editor-in-Chief Tatiana Repková; circ. 25,000.

**Vasárnap** (Sunday): Pribinova 25, 819 15 Bratislava; tel. (7) 323-220; fax (7) 364-529; f. 1948; weekly; independent Hungarian-language magazine; Editor-in-Chief József Szilvássy; circ. 97,000.

**Výber** (Digest): Kominárska 2, 832 03 Bratislava; tel. (7) 203-4486; fax (7) 203-4521; f. 1968; weekly; digest of home and foreign press; Editor-in-Chief Miroslava Avramovová; circ. 15,000.

**Život** (Life): Pribinova 25, 819 37 Bratislava; tel. (7) 210-4135; fax (7) 210-4145; f. 1951; illustrated family weekly; Editor-in-Chief Milan Város; circ. 255,000.

**Zmena** (Change): Záhradnícka 93, POB 7, 818 07 Bratislava; tel. and fax (7) 211-754; f. 1989; weekly; independent; Editor-in-Chief Maroš Puchovský; circ. 30,000.

### NEWS AGENCIES

**Tlačová agentúra Slovenskej republiky (TASR)** (News Agency of the Slovak Republic); Pribinova 23, 819 28 Bratislava; tel. (7) 362-578; fax (7) 363-405; f. 1992; has overseas bureaux in the USA, Russia, Poland, Hungary, Czech Republic, Belgium and Germany; Gen. Man. Dušan Kleiman.

#### Foreign Bureaux

**Česká tisková kancelář (ČTK)** (Czech Republic): Pribinova 25, 819 02 Bratislava; tel. (7) 210-4633; fax (7) 210-4605.

**Informatsionnoye Telegrafnoye Agentstvo Rossii—Telegrafnoye Agentstvo Suverennych Stran (ITAR—TASS)** (Russia): Jancova 8A, 811 01 Bratislava; tel. (7) 315-797; Correspondent Valery I. Rzhevsky.

The following news agencies are also represented in Slovakia: Reuters (UK), Deutsche Presse-Agentur (Germany), Austria Presse-Agentur (Austria), Agence France-Presse (France), Magyar Távirati Iroda (Hungary) and RIA—Novosti (Russia).

### PRESS ASSOCIATIONS

**Slovenský syndikát novinárov** (Slovak Syndicate of Journalists): Župné nám. 7, 815 68 Bratislava; tel. (7) 335-071; fax (7) 334-534; f. 1968; reorganized 1990; 2,070 mems; Chair. Július Gembický.

**Združenie slovenských novinárov** (Association of Slovak Journalists): Šafárikovo nám. 4, 811 02 Bratislava; tel. and fax (7) 363-184; f. 1992; 700 mems; Chair. Ján Smolec.

# Publishers

**Alfa:** Hurbanovo nám. 3, 815 89 Bratislava; tel. (7) 331-441; fax (7) 594-43; technical and economic literature, dictionaries; Dir Martin Parajka.

**Matica slovenská:** Novomeského 32, 036 52 Martin; tel. (842) 324-54; fax (842) 331-88; f. 1863; literary science, bibliography,

# SLOVAKIA

biography and librarianship; literary archives and museums; Man. Dr MIROSLAV BIELIK.

**Mladé letá** (Young Years): nám. SNP 12, 815 19 Bratislava; tel. (7) 364-475; telex 92721; fax (7) 364-563; f. 1950; literature for children and young people; Dir Ing. OLDRICH POLÁK.

**Obzor** (Horizon): Špitálska 35, 815 85 Bratislava; tel. (7) 361-015; fax (7) 361-237; f. 1953; educational encyclopaedias, popular scientific, fiction, textbooks, law; Editor-in-Chief MARGITA SVITKOVÁ.

**Osveta** (Education): Osloboditel'ov 21, 036 54 Martin; tel. (842) 341-21; fax (7) 350-36; f. 1953; medical, health, photographic, fiction; Gen. Dir Ing. MARTIN FARKAŠ.

**Práca** (Labour): Štefánikova 19, 812 71 Bratislava; tel. (7) 333-779; fax (7) 330-046; f. 1946; law, guides, cookery, fiction, etc.; Dir MIROSLAV BERNÁTH.

**Príroda a.s.** (Nature): Križkova 9, 811 04 Bratislava; tel. (7) 497-335; fax (7) 497-564; f. 1949; school textbooks, encyclopedias, etc.; Chair. Ing. EMILIA JANKOVITSOVÁ.

**Slovenské pedagogické nakladetel'stvo:** Sasinkova 5, 815 60 Bratislava; tel. (7) 566-1685; fax (7) 526-1894; f. 1920; pedagogical literature, educational, school texts, dictionaries; Dir RUDOLF STRECHAJ.

**Slovenský spisovatel a.s.** (Slovak Writer): Laurinská 2, 813 67 Bratislava; tel. (7) 333-903; fax (7) 335-411; fiction, poetry; Dir MARTIN CHOVANEC.

**Smena** (Change): Pražská 11, 812 84 Bratislava; tel. (7) 498-018; fax (7) 493-305; f. 1949; fiction, literature for young people, newspapers and magazines; Dir Ing. JAROSLAV ŠIŠOLÁK.

**Šport:** Vajnorská 100/A, 832 58 Bratislava; tel. (7) 691-95; telex 93330; sport, physical culture, guide books, periodicals; Dir Dr BOHUMIL GOLIAN.

**Tatran:** Michalská 9, 815 82 Bratislava; tel. (7) 335-849; fax (7) 335-777; f. 1949; fiction, art books, children's books, literary theory; Dir Ing. PETER TVRDOŇ.

**Veda** (Science): Bradáčova 7, 852 86 Bratislava; tel. (7) 832-254; fax (7) 832-254; f. 1953; publishing house of the Slovak Academy of Sciences; scientific and popular scientific books and periodicals; Man. EVA MAJESKÁ.

**Východoslovenské vydavatel'stvo** (East Slovakia Publishing House): Alejová 3, 040 11 Košice; tel. (95) 765-206; fax (95) 765-204; f. 1960; regional literature, children's literature, fiction, general; Dir Dr IMRICH GOFUS.

### PUBLISHERS' ASSOCIATION

**Združenie vydavatel'ov a kníhkupcov** (Publishers' and Booksellers' Asscn): Michalská 9, 815 82 Bratislava; tel. (7) 330-141; Sec. MARTIN UŠIAK.

### WRITERS' UNION

**Asociácia organizácií spisovatel'ov Slovenska** (Asscn of Writers' Organizations in Slovakia): Laurinská 2, 815 08 Bratislava; tel. (7) 335-368; f. 1949; reorganized 1990; 330 mems; Pres. JÁN BUZÁSSY; Sec. PETER ANDRUŠKA.

## Radio and Television

There were 1.1m. licences for radio receivers and 1.3m. licences for television receivers in 1992. Radio and television stations are licensed through the Slovak Council for Radio and Television.

### RADIO

**Slovenský rozhlas** (Slovak Radio): Mýtna 1, 811 06 Bratislava; tel. (7) 493-174; telex 93352; fax (7) 498-923; f. 1926; Dir-Gen. JÁN TUŽINSKÝ.

### TELEVISION

**Slovenská televízia** (Slovak Television): Mlynská dolina 28, 845 45 Bratislava; tel. (7) 725-948; telex 92277; fax (7) 725-227; f. 1956; public broadcasting co; Dir-Gen. JOZEF DARMO.

## Finance

(cap. = capital; res = reserves; dep. = deposits; m. = million; brs = branches; amounts in Slovak koruny)

### BANKING
#### Central Bank

**Národná banka Slovenska** (National Bank of Slovakia): Gorkého 14, 818 54 Bratislava; tel. (7) 319-1111; fax (7) 364-721; f. 1993; determines monetary policy, issues banknotes and coins, manages circulation of money, co-ordinates payment connections and accounting of banks, supervises activities of banks; Gov. VLADIMÍR MASÁR; Vice-Gov. Ing. MARIÁN JUŠKO.

#### Commercial Banks

**Devín banka, a.s.:** Františkánske nám. 8, 813 10 Bratislava; tel. (7) 333-479; fax (7) 332-311; f. 1992; cap. 499m.; Gen. Dir Ing. VLADISLAV BACHÁR; 2 brs.

**Investičná a rozvojová banka, a.s. Bratislava** (Investment and Development Bank, Inc.): Štúrova 5, 818 55 Bratislava; tel. (7) 389-1111; telex 92309; fax (7) 363-484; f. 1992; cap. 650.0m., res 1579.1m., dep. 37,716.7m. (Dec. 1993); Pres. JOZEF TKÁČ; 47 brs.

**Istrobanka, a.s.:** Laurinská 1, 810 00 Bratislava; tel. (7) 397-111; telex 92194; fax (7) 331-744; f. 1992; cap. 1,000m., dep. 3,507m. (Dec. 1994); Man. Dir Ing. IVAN ŠRAMKO; 11 brs.

**L'udová banka Bratislava, a.s** (People's Bank, Inc.): nám. SNP 15, 810 00 Bratislava; tel. (7) 367-049; fax (7) 363-794; f. 1992; cap. 426m., dep. 4,300m. (Dec. 1994); Chair. of Bd KARL MAYR-KERN; 5 brs.

**Poštová banka, a.s. Bratislava** (Postal Bank, Inc.): Gorkého 3, 814 99 Bratislava; tel. (7) 330-155; fax (7) 331-413; f. 1993; cap. 600m. (1994); Pres. Ing. MILAN LÔNČÍK.

**Priemyselná banka, a.s. Košice** (Industrial Bank, Inc.): Božený Němcovej 30, 040 61 Košice; tel. (95) 353-26; telex 77315; fax (95) 303-11; f. 1992; cap. and res 1,224.1m., dep. 4,225.0m. (Dec. 1994); Gen. Dir Doc. Ing. JAROSLAV MARIČÁK; 7 brs.

**Prvá komunálna banka, a.s.** (First Communal Bank, Inc.): Hodžova 9, 010 11 Žilina; tel. (89) 624-093; fax (89) 624-129; f. 1993; cap. 482.1m. (1994); Gen. Dir Ing. JOZEF MIHALIK.

**Slovenská kreditná banka, a.s.** (Slovak Credit Bank, Inc.): nám. SNP 13, 814 99 Bratislava; tel. (7) 455-111; fax (7) 321-021; f. 1993; cap. 520m. (1994); Gen. Dir ŠTEFAN VESELOVSKÝ.

**Slovenská pol'nohospodárska banka, a.s.** (Slovak Agricultural Bank, Inc.): Vajnorská 21, 812 65 Bratislava; tel. (7) 215-007; fax (7) 215-121; f. 1990; cap. 800m.; Gen. Dir Ing. L'UDOVÍT PÓSA; 15 brs.

**Slovenská záručná banka š.p.ú.** (Slovak Guarantee Bank): Kutlíkova 17, POB 223, 852 99 Bratislava; tel. (7) 836-732; fax (7) 836-909; f. 1991; cap. 376.2m.; Gen. Dir Ing. JOZEF DRŠKA; 2 brs.

**Tatra banka, a.s.:** Vajanského nábr. 5, 810 06 Bratislava; tel. (7) 452-111; telex 92644; fax (7) 334-656; f. 1990; cap. and res 850m., dep. 6,900m. (Dec. 1994); Gen. Dir Ing. MILAN VRŠKOVÝ; 10 brs.

**Všeobecná úverová banka, a.s.** (General Credit Bank, Inc.): nám. SNP 19, 818 56 Bratislava; tel. (7) 364-843; telex 93347; fax (7) 326-867; f. 1990; cap. 4,078m., res 7,380m., dep. 130,189m. (Dec. 1994); Chair. and Pres. Ing. JOZEF MUDRÍK; 40 brs.

#### Savings Bank

**Slovenská sporitel'ňa, a.s.** (Slovak Savings Bank): nám. SNP 18, 816 07 Bratislava; tel. (7) 367-300; fax (7) 367-087; f. 1953; cap. 2,134.0m., res 7,075.0m., dep. 121,761.0m. (Dec. 1994); Dir NORBERT TENCZER; 701 brs and agencies.

### COMMODITY AND STOCK EXCHANGES

**Bratislavská medzinárodná komoditná burza** (Bratislava International Commodity Exchange): Ružinovská 1, 821 02 Bratislava; tel. (7) 522-6311; fax (7) 522-6318; Gen. Sec. IGOR KREJČÍ.

**Burza cenných papierov v Bratislave a.s.** (Bratislava Stock Exchange): Hlavné nám. 8, POB 151, 814 99 Bratislava; tel. (7) 335-844; fax (7) 335-725; Man. MARIÁN SASIK.

### INSURANCE

**Slovenská poist'ovňa** (Slovak Insurance Co): Strakova 1, 815 74 Bratislava; tel. (7) 332-949; telex 93375; fax (7) 331-272; Gen. Man. MIKULÁŠ TRSTENSKÝ.

## Trade and Industry

### STATE PROPERTY AGENCY

**National Property Fund:** Bratislava; f. 1993; supervises the privatization process; Chair. ŠTEFAN GAVORNÍK.

### CHAMBER OF COMMERCE

**Slovenská obchodná a priemyselná komora** (Slovak Chamber of Commerce and Industry): Gorkého 9, 816 03 Bratislava; tel. (7) 362-787; fax (7) 362-222; Pres. Ing. PETER MIHÓK.

### INVESTMENT AGENCY

**Slovak National Agency for Foreign Investment and Development (SNAFID):** Manesovo nám. 2, 851 01 Bratislava; tel. (7) 847-219; fax (7) 849-806; Dir RADOVAN PEKNIK.

SLOVAKIA                                                                                                                                              *Directory*

### MAJOR STATE-OWNED ENTERPRISES

**Chemko:** 072 22 Strážske; tel. (946) 913-21; telex 77247; fax (946) 915-26; f. 1952; chemical products; Dir Ing. IVAN WILHALM; 3,065 employees.

**Chemosvit CHEM:** Štúrova 101, 059 21 Svit; tel. (92) 550-11; telex 78232; fax (92) 569-55; f. 1972; plastics, packaging materials, machinery, transport services; Dir Ing. MICHAL L'ACH; 3,600 employees.

**Duslo:** Kopanica 1778, 927 03 Šal'a; tel. (706) 2561-6; telex 93732; fax (706) 5643; f. 1972; ammonia, nitrogenous fertilizers, antioxidants, etc.; Exec. Dir JOZEF KOLLÁR; 5,080 employees.

**Makyta:** 1. mája 882/46, 020 25 Púchov; tel. (825) 2211; fax (825) 2975; f. 1972; Exec. Dir MARIÁN VIDOMAN; 4,578 employees.

**Mier:** Pílska 9, 955 13 Topol'čany; tel. (815) 218-65; fax (815) 216-58; f. 1988; manufacture of furniture, upholstery, etc.; Man. Ing. KAROL PITTNER; 2,873 employees.

**Nováské chemické závody** (Nováky Chemical Works): M. R. Štefánika 1, 972 71 Nováky; tel. (862) 9295; fax (862) 922-221; f. 1972; suspension and emulsion polyvinyl chloride and co-polymers; Man. Ing. FRANTIŠEK KOPAL; 3,342 employees.

**Oravské ferozliatinárske závody** (Orava Ferro-alloys Works): 027 53 Istebné nad Oravou; tel. (845) 891-301; telex 75311; fax (845) 891-320; f. 1952; production of ferro-alloys; Gen. Dir Ing. VLADIMÍR KLOCOK; 2,200 employees.

**Severoslovenské celulózky a papierne** (North Slovak Cellulose and Paper Works): Bystrická cesta 13, 034 01 Ružomberok; tel. (848) 322-223; fax (848) 327-701; f. 1988; production of cellulose, pulp, paper, cardboard, softwood timber, etc.; Man. Ing. IGOR VINCE; 3,660 employees.

**Slovenský hodvab:** Tovarenska 532/20, 905 35 Senica; tel. (802) 2751; telex 93611; fax (802) 5150; f. 1978; man-made fibres and synthetic polymer; Man. Ing. JOZEF FUTRIKANIČ; 2,285 employees.

**Trikota:** Zigmundikova 296/6, 922 03 Vrbove; tel. (838) 924-49; telex 93648; fax (838) 923-18; f. 1972; production of knitted garments and fabrics, rubber-elastic articles; Man. Ing. IVAN HAVRLENT; 2,206 employees.

**Trnavské automobilové závody** (Trnava Automobile Works): Strojárenská, 917 48 Trnava; tel. (805) 203-51; telex 93104; fax (805) 311-09; f. 1986; vehicles, special machines, spare parts, sheet metal products, etc.; Man. Ing. JOZEF PUSCHENREITER; 5,807 employees.

**Vagonka:** Kežmarská cesta, 058 80 Poprad; tel. (92) 461; telex 78222; fax (92) 220-18; f. 1983; structural steelwork, boilers, air conditioning and ventilating systems, trailers and semi-trailers for trucks, railway wagons and coaches; Man. Ing. FRANTIŠEK KRÁLIK; 3,287 employees.

**ZTS Dubnica:** Továrenská ul., 018 41 Dubnica nad Váhom; tel. (827) 210-17; fax (827) 226-91; f. 1937; military equipment, machines for rubber and glass industries, automatic forging machines, multi-purpose vehicles, special tools, pumping systems; Man. Ing. PETER KONČIER; 6,500 employees.

**ZTS TEES:** 036 01 Martin; tel. (842) 323-07; telex 75135; fax (842) 310-36; f. 1949; agricultural machinery; Exec. Dir. JÁN SEGL'A; 6,145 employees.

**ZVS Dubnica nad Váhom:** L'. Štúra, 018 41 Dubnica nad Váhom; tel. (827) 221-88; fax (827) 225-29; f. 1981; ammunition, industrial electronics, transformers, medical instruments; Gen. Dir Ing. ALEXANDER HRUBOŠ; 2,548 employees.

### TRADE UNIONS

**Confederation of Trade Unions of the Slovak Republic** (Konfederácia odborových zväzov Slovenskej republiky): Odborárské nám. 3, 815 70 Bratislava; tel. (7) 622-65; fax (7) 213-303; Pres. ALOJZ ENGLIŠ; affiliated unions include:

**Metalworkers' Federation:** Vajnorská 1, 815 70 Bratislava; tel. (7) 214-225; fax (7) 360-613; Pres. JOZEF KRUMPOLEC.

**Trade Union of Workers in Agriculture:** Vajnorská 1, 815 70 Bratislava; tel. (7) 213-942; fax (7) 211-673; Pres. EMIL KUČERA.

**Trade Union of Workers in the Chemical Industry:** Osadná 6, 831 03 Bratislava; tel. (7) 320-226; fax (7) 273-538; Pres. JURAJ BLAHÁK.

**Trade Union of Workers in Construction and Construction Materials:** Vajnorská 1, 815 70 Bratislava; tel. (7) 214-180; fax (7) 212-764; Pres. DUŠAN BARČÍK.

**Trade Union of Workers in Cultural and Social Organizations:** Vajnorská 1, 815 70 Bratislava; tel. and fax (7) 213-760; Pres. JARMILA JÁNOŠOVÁ.

**Trade Union of Workers in Energy:** Vajnorská 1, 815 70 Bratislava; tel. and fax (7) 211-622; Pres. JOZEF KOLLÁR.

**Trade Union of Workers in the Food-processing Industry:** Vajnorská 1, 815 70 Bratislava; tel. (7) 678-24; Pres. MILAN PIEŠŤANSKÝ.

**Trade Union of Workers in the Glass Industry:** Studentská, 911 01 Trenčín; tel. (831) 372-00; Pres. MILAN MLYNČÁR.

**Trade Union of Workers in the Health and Social Services:** Vajnorská 1, 815 70 Bratislava; tel. (7) 213-965; fax (7) 215-330; Pres. DANIEL REPÁŠ.

**Trade Union of Workers in Radio, Television and Newspapers:** Vajnorská 1, 815 70 Bratislava; tel. (7) 211-844; Pres. PETER JÁCHIN.

**Trade Union of Workers in the Textile, Clothing and Leather Industry:** Vajnorská 1, 815 70 Bratislava; tel. (7) 213-389; fax (7) 651-82; Pres. Ing. PAVOL JAKUBÍK.

**Trade Union of Workers in the Wood-working, Furniture and Paper Industries:** Vajnorská 1, 815 70 Bratislava; tel. (7) 213-660; fax (7) 213-163; Pres. BORISLAV MAJTÁN.

## Transport

### RAILWAYS

In 1994 the total length of railways in Slovakia was 3,662 km, of which 1,011 km were double-tracked, 1,408 km electrified, 50 km narrow-gauged and 102 km broad-gauged. A 43-km underground railway system in Bratislava was scheduled for completion in 1997.

**Železnice Slovenskej republiky** (Slovak State Railways): Klemensova 8, 813 61 Bratislava; tel. (7) 325-242; fax (7) 362-296; f. 1993; Dir Gen. Ing. MILAN CHÚPEK.

### ROADS

In 1993 there were 17,737 km of roads in Slovakia, including 198 km of motorways (with a further 646 km of motorways planned).

**Slovenská správa ciest** (Slovak Road Administration): Továrenská 7, 813 44 Bratislava; tel. (7) 325-583; fax (7) 361-783; Dir Ing. JÁN MIKOLAJ.

### INLAND WATERWAYS

The total length of navigable waterways in Slovakia (on the River Danube) is 172 km. The Danube provides a link with Germany, Austria, Hungary, Yugoslavia, Bulgaria, Romania and the Black Sea. The main river ports are Bratislava and Komárno.

**Štátna plavebná správa** (State Administration of Shipping): Prístavná 10, 816 14 Bratislava; tel. (7) 363-022; fax (7) 323-286; Dir Ing. KAROL ANDA.

**Slovenská plavba Dunajská** (Slovak Danube Shipping): Pribinova 24, 815 24 Bratislava; tel. (7) 367-504; fax (7) 363-002; Ing. STANISLAV HOLÁK.

### CIVIL AVIATION

There are five international airports in Slovakia: Bratislava (M. R. Štefánik Airport), Košice, Piešt'any, Poprad and Sliač. By 1995 no national carrier had yet been established, and ČSA (Czechoslovak Airlines) continued to serve as the national airline for both Slovakia and the Czech Republic.

**ČSA (Československé aerolinie, a.s.)** (Czechoslovak Airlines): Štúrova 13, 811 02 Bratislava; tel. (7) 361-073; fax (7) 361-070; f. 1923; services to most European capitals, the Near, Middle and Far East, North America and North Africa; Dir (Slovakia) M. GAJDOS.

**Slovenská správa letísk** (Slovak Airports Administration): M. R. Štefánik Airport, 823 11 Bratislava; tel. (7) 224-633; fax (7) 222-146; Man. Dir IGOR DULA.

**Tatra Air, a.s.:** M. R. Štefánik Airport, 823 11 Bratislava; tel. (7) 292-318; fax (7) 294-259; f. 1990; joint-stock airline co; Exec. Dir BOHUŠ HURAJ.

## Tourism

Slovakia's tourist attractions include ski resorts in the High and Low Tatras and other mountain ranges, more than 20 spa resorts (with thermal and mineral springs), numerous castles and mansions and historic towns, including Bratislava, Košice, Nitra, Bardejov, Kežmarok and Levoča. In 1993 652,815 foreign tourists visited Slovakia. In the following year revenue from tourism was US $568m.

**SATUR:** Bratislava; f. 1993 from the former Czechoslovak state travel agency Čedok; has 52 brs throughout Slovakia.

**Slovakoturist:** Volgogradská 1, Bratislava; tel. (7) 552-47.

**Tatratour:** Františkánske nám. 3, 811 01 Bratislava; tel. (7) 335-536; telex 92211; fax (7) 335-538.

# SLOVENIA

## Introductory Survey

### Location, Climate, Language, Religion, Flag, Capital

The Republic of Slovenia (formerly the Socialist Republic of Slovenia, a constituent republic of the Socialist Federal Republic of Yugoslavia) is situated in south-central Europe. It is bounded by Austria to the north, Hungary to the north-east, Croatia to the south and east and by Italy to the west, and it has a short (40-km—25-mile) western coastline on the Adriatic Sea. The climate is Alpine in the mountainous areas, Mediterranean along the coast and continental in the interior. Average temperatures range from between 0°C (32°F) and 22°C (71.6°F) inland, and between 2°C (35.6°F) and 24°C (75.2°F) on the coast. Average annual rainfall ranges from 800 mm (31.5 ins) in the east to 3,000 mm (118.1 ins) in the north-west. The official language is Slovene, and in ethnically-mixed regions also Hungarian and Italian. The majority religion in Slovenia is Roman Catholicism, although there are small communities of other Christian (in particular Eastern Orthodox) denominations and of Muslims and Jews. The national flag (proportions 3 by 2) consists of three horizontal stripes of white, blue and red, with a shield in the upper hoist depicting a white three-peaked mountain (the Triglav), below which are two horizontal wavy blue lines and above which are three six-pointed yellow stars. The capital is Ljubljana.

### Recent History

Following the collapse of the Austro-Hungarian empire, the Kingdom of Serbs, Croats and Slovenes was proclaimed on 4 December 1918. (The territory of Slovenia was formally ceded by Austria by the Treaty of Saint-Germain in 1919.) In 1929 the name of the country was changed to Yugoslavia. Yugoslavia collapsed under German attack in 1941, and during the Second World War Germany claimed and annexed lower Styria and Yugoslav Carinthia, while Italy annexed Istria and the territory around Ljubljana. (There was a continuing dispute with Italy over Istria; in 1954 Italy was awarded the city of Trieste, and Yugoslavia the remainder of the territory, giving Slovenia access to the sea.) Hungary occupied the plains along the Mura in north-eastern Slovenia.

The Slovene Liberation Front, formed in 1941, joined with the Communist-led all-Yugoslav Partisan Army of Josep Broz (Tito). This army was eventually recognized as an ally by the British and Americans. There was also a Slovene force which fought and fled with the Germans.

Following the post-war proclamation of the Federal People's Republic of Yugoslavia (from 1963 the Socialist Federal Republic of Yugoslavia—SFRY), Slovenia became the most prosperous of the Yugoslav republics, but was increasingly suspicious of Serb domination. On 27 September 1989 the Slovene Assembly voted in favour of radical amendments to the Constitution of Slovenia, confirming Slovenia's sovereignty and its right to secede from the SFRY. Political pluralism and the holding of free elections were envisaged, and the establishment of opposition parties (the local League of Communists of Slovenia—LCS—having hitherto been the only legal party) was formally authorized. Slovenia was warned that the amendments contravened the Federal Constitution, and the Serbian leader, Slobodan Milošević, attempted to arrange protests in Slovenia against the Slovene leadership; however, the demonstrations, planned for December, were banned in November. In response Milošević instructed all Serbian enterprises to sever links with Slovenia, which retaliated by closing its border with Serbia and by imposing reciprocal economic sanctions. Thousands of demonstrators in Montenegro and Serbia staged protests against the perceived threat to the unity of the SFRY, and relations between Slovenia and the other republics deteriorated sharply.

In January 1990 the Slovenian delegation withdrew from the 14th (Extraordinary) Congress of the League of Communists of Yugoslavia (LCY), after the overwhelming rejection of their proposals to reform the federal party and to give greater autonomy to the respective Leagues of Communists (LCs) of the republics. The Congress ended in disarray, and the LCY suffered a further reverse in February, when its Central Committee was unable to secure the quorum necessary to set a date for the reconvening of the Congress. A boycott by the entire Slovene contingent was supported by members of the LCs of Croatia and Macedonia. The LCS suspended its links with the LCY, withdrawing in February and changing its name to the Party of Democratic Reform (Stranka Democratskih Reformi—SDR). In that month Stefan Korosec of Slovenia was removed from the position of Secretary of the Presidium of the LCY Central Committee, in advance of the expiry of his mandate, and was replaced by a Serb. In March Slovenia was redesignated the Republic of Slovenia. Opposition parties were formed meanwhile, and six of the main parties formed a coalition called the Democratic Opposition of Slovenia (DEMOS) in December 1989. In the multi-party elections of April 1990, DEMOS won a majority in the republican parliament, and subsequently formed a Government under Lojze Peterle, the leader of the Slovenian Christian Democrats (Slovenski krščanski demokrati—SKD). However, the leader of the SDR, Milan Kučan (an outspoken opponent of Milošević), was elected President of the State Presidency (defeating Peterle in the second round of voting) and the SDR remained the largest single party in the legislature.

On 2 July 1990 the Slovenian legislature declared the sovereignty of the Republic and resolved that republican laws should take precedence over federal laws. This was confirmed by an amendment to the republican Constitution, approved by the republican parliament on 27 September. The republic also assumed control over the local territorial defence force, thereby bringing Slovenia into direct confrontation with the Serb-dominated federal army, which attempted to reassert its authority by confiscating the weapons and seizing the headquarters of the republican force. Slovenian and Croatian proposals to reform the Yugoslav Federation were rejected, and Serbia imposed economic sanctions on the secessionist states' goods. In a referendum held in Slovenia on 23 December 1990, none the less, some 89% of those who voted (about 94% of the electorate) endorsed Slovenian independence.

Relations between Slovenia and the SFRY deteriorated further when, in January 1991, the SFRY Presidency ordered the federal army to disarm all paramilitary groups; the Slovenian authorities refused to implement the order. Slovenia (along with Croatia—with which friendship and military co-operation treaties had been signed) none the less expressed a willingness to consider a looser 'federation of sovereign states', even after approving a programme for Slovenian dissociation from the SFRY in February. However, following the Serbian-led crisis in the Federal State Presidency in March (see the Recent History of Yugoslavia), the Slovenian Government became more resolved to withdraw from the federation. In May Slovenia declared its intention to secede before the end of June, and legislation was adopted that would enable eventual independence, including the establishment of a Slovenian territorial army. Tensions with the federal authorities were exacerbated when Slovenia attempted to take control of the collection of customs duties.

Slovenia unilaterally declared independence from the SFRY on 25 June 1991. In response, Serbian-dominated federal troops were mobilized on 27 June, and tanks were dispatched from Belgrade. Sporadic fighting ensued, and, despite attempts by the European Community (EC, now European Union—EU—see p. 143) to arrange a cease-fire, there was an aerial bombardment of Ljubljana on 2 July (the first of a European city since the Second World War). On the same day, however, the Slovenian Government agreed to the implementation of an EC-brokered cease-fire, and the federal army, which had not fared well in the fighting, began its withdrawal from Slovenia on 3 July. In all, 18 people had been killed in the conflict. On 8 October (following the expiry of a three-month moratorium on dissociation—agreed as part of the EC cease-fire accord) Slovenia proclaimed its full independence, introduced its own currency (the tolar), and recalled all its citizens serving in federal institutions. All federal army units had withdrawn from Slovenia by 26 October.

Slovenia was recognized by Germany in December 1991 and by the EC as a whole in January 1992. The USA recognized the country in April of that year, and withdrew sanctions against Slovenia (previously imposed on all of the former Yugoslavia) in August. Slovenia was admitted to the UN in May. The Peterle Government experienced increasing problems in functioning as the struggle for independence became less of a unifying factor. Later in October 1991 the Slovenian Democratic Union, one of the larger and most influential of the DEMOS parties, split into two factions, both of which remained in the coalition. A minority liberal wing rallied around the Minister of Foreign Affairs, Dr Dmitrij Rupel, who was elected leader of the new Democratic Party (Demokratska stranka—DS), while the majority of the party's parliamentary delegates supported a more right-wing programme and formed the National Democratic Party (Narodni Demokrati), led by the Minister of Justice and Administration, Dr Rajko Pirnat. DEMOS, undermined by such factionalism, was dissolved in December, although it was envisaged that the Peterle administration would remain in power until new elections (to take place under the terms of the new Constitution that was adopted in the same month) could be organized. However, the Government lost a parliamentary motion of 'no-confidence' in April 1992, and Peterle resigned. He was replaced by Dr Janez Drnovšek, leader of the Liberal Democratic Party (Liberalno demokratska stranka—LDS) and a former President of the SFRY Presidency.

Parliamentary and presidential elections took place on 6 December 1992. About 85% of the registered electorate participated in elections to the Državni Zbor (National Assembly), which were contested by 25 parties and coalitions. Although the LDS was the party returning the greatest number of deputies to the 90-member body (17 directly-elected, five elected on a proportional basis—see Government, below), it failed to secure a majority of seats in the legislature. Among the groupings that enjoyed considerable success were the SKD, with a total of 15 seats, the Associated List (Združena lista—ZL—a four-party electoral alliance), with 14 seats, and the extreme right-wing Slovenian National Party (Slovenska nacionalna stranka), which won 12 seats. In the presidential election Milan Kučan (standing as an independent candidate) was elected to what had, under the terms of the 1991 Constitution, become a largely ceremonial post, winning 63.9% of the votes cast. His nearest rival, Ivan Bizjak, of the SKD, took 21.1% of the votes. Participation by voters was about 76%. On the same day voting took place for the 22 directly-elected members of the advisory Državni Svet (National Council, as created under the 1991 Constitution); its remaining 18 members were chosen by an electoral college shortly afterwards.

In January 1993 Drnovšek formed a coalition Government, comprising members of the LDS, the SKD, the ZL (later renamed the Associated List of Social Democrats—Združena lista socialnih demokratov—ZLSD), the Greens of Slovenia (Zeleni Slovenije—ZS) and the Social Democratic Party of Slovenia (Socialdemokratska stranka Slovenije—SDSS). Peterle was appointed Minister of Foreign Affairs, and Bizjak Minister of Internal Affairs, in the new Government. However, the cohesion of the administration was notably undermined during 1993 by tensions between Kučan and the President of the SDSS, Janez Janša, Slovenia's Minister of Defence since March 1990. In June 1993 Janša was among six prominent politicians who sent an open letter to the President, accusing him of protecting former officials of the communist regime who were profiting from the lack of regulation of the transition period at a time of widespread unemployment and general economic decline.

In October 1993, following a series of strikes (in support of demands for salary increases) by police officers and employees of the Ministry of Internal Affairs, parliament approved emergency legislation denying police and other employees of security services the right to strike. The imposition by the Government of a 'freeze' on salaries, as part of efforts to control inflation, provoked considerable disquiet in early 1994.

Persistent rumours that Slovenia was involved in the sale of weaponry to Bosnian government forces (and also to Croatia), in contravention of the UN embargo on the transfer of armaments to countries of the former Yugoslavia, in force since late 1991, were apparently confirmed by the discovery at Maribor airport, in July 1993, of a large consignment of military equipment destined for Bosnia and Herzegovina.

Janša denied allegations that the weapons were being transferred to Bosnia and Herzegovina (in what had been purported to be a transhipment of humanitarian aid) with his knowledge, and countered that Kučan and other senior members of his administration had been aware of such transactions. In December the Maribor municipal court abandoned legal proceedings against six suspects in the affair, on the grounds of insufficient evidence, although it was stated that the prosecution of two other defendants would be pursued. In January 1994 the Maribor authorities, concluding that Janša had been complicit in the contravention of the UN embargo, referred the case to the Public Prosecutor in Ljubljana. In the subsequent trial, however, all the defendants in the case were acquitted.

Janša was dismissed from the Government in late March 1994, after a ministerial commission found that security forces under the command of the Ministry of Defence had abused their authority in ill-treating a former ministry employee who was said to have attempted military espionage. Janša's dismissal was followed, in early April, by the withdrawal of the SDSS from the Government, protesting at what it regarded to be a breach of the coalition agreement. However, the party maintained that it had for some time intended to leave the Government, owing to the persistence of corruption at high levels and also to the change in the coalition's structure arising from the merger, in mid-March, of the LDS with three other organizations to form a new party, Liberal Democracy of Slovenia (Liberalna demokracija Slovenije—LDS). The new LDS, with Drnovšek as its leader, also included the DS and ZS—Eco-Social Party (comprising the parliamentary members of the ZS), and numbered 30 deputies in the Državni Zbor. Drnovšek subsequently formed a new coalition Government with the SKD and the ZLSD.

In late May 1994 Bizjak resigned as Minister of Internal Affairs, in response to allegations that security forces controlled by his ministry had been involved in criminal activities in Austria; his successor, Andrej Šter, was also a member of the SKD. Revelations of irregularities in the allocation of government housing loans resulted in the resignation of the LDS Minister of Justice, Miha Kozinc, in the following month; there was further controversy in July, when it emerged that the newly-designated Minister of Justice, Meta Zupančič, had been accused of professional misconduct in her capacity as a lawyer. Also in June the labour, family and social affairs portfolio was allocated to Rina Klinar of the ZLSD. In mid-September the resignation of Herman Rigelnik, of the LDS, as President of the Državni Zbor (and as a member of parliament) prompted the resignation from the Government of Peterle, who protested that Rigelnik's immediate replacement by another LDS member, Jožef Školjč, was evidence of the excessive concentration of authority in the hands of the LDS. Although the SKD remained within the government coalition, Drnovšek refused to accede to the party's demand that Peterle's successor should also be a member of the SKD. It was not until late January 1995 that an agreement was reached whereby Zoran Thaler of the LDS was appointed Minister of Foreign Affairs, while Janko Deželak of the SKD assumed the post of Minister of Economic Relations and Development (a portfolio hitherto held by the LDS).

Areas of disputed border territory with Croatia, most notably the Istrian Bay of Piran, undermined otherwise harmonious relations between the two countries following independence. In May 1993 Croatia was reported to have ceased construction of border control facilities in Secovlje, in Slovenia's Piran region, following a protest by Slovenia. In July, however, tensions between the two countries prevented the signing of agreements on friendship and co-operation and on the regulation of bilateral payments (although protocols governing other issues, including trade and economic relations, were concluded). In November Slovenian proposals to decommission the country's nuclear power plant, at Krsko (constructed by the former federal authorities to supply energy to both Slovenia and Croatia), prompted protests by Croatia, which was reliant on the installation for one-quarter of its energy requirements. Shortly afterwards Slovenia warned that it would suspend power supplies to Croatia unless that country paid for supplies already received. In late January 1994, however, Drnovšek and his Croatian counterpart, Nikica Valentić, held discussions in Slovenia, during which broad agreement was reached on several issues of contention. None the less, little progress was achieved in subsequent bilateral efforts formally to delineate the joint border, and the resumed construction by Croatia of border facilities on Slovenian territory provoked renewed protests by the Slovenian Government. In October the Croatian Government submitted a formal protest to Slovenia, following the approval by the Državni Zbor of legislation providing for a reorganization of local government boundaries in Slovenia (prior to municipal elections in December), as part of which four villages in the disputed area were included within the Slovene municipality of Piran. A subsequent proposal by the Slovenian Government to revise the law to exclude the villages was rejected by parliament, although deputies agreed to delay implementation of the law (and thus the holding of elections) in three villages, pending a resolution of the border issue. In February 1995 a meeting of the Slovenian-Croatian joint border commission agreed that, since the process of delineating the border would be lengthy, this should be pursued separately from other bilateral concerns. Slovenia and Croatia agreed to divide ownership of the Krsko nuclear station equally between the two countries.

Slovenia and Croatia are united in their opposition to movements for Istrian autonomy and to any revision to their detriment of the 1975 Treaty of Osimo, which had defined the borders between the SFRY and Italy, and had provided for the payment by the SFRY of compensation for Italian property transferred to Yugoslav sovereignty after 1947. Although Slovenia asserted that its debt in this matter (in accordance with the Treaty of Osimo and the 1983 Treaty of Rome) had been discharged in full, in 1993 some 35,000 Italians were reported to be demanding compensation for, or the restitution of, property in Slovenia.

In July 1994 the Italian Government of Silvio Berlusconi stated that, until the Slovenian authorities agreed to compensate Italian nationals who had fled or been expelled after 1947 from territory now held by Slovenia and whose property had been confiscated under communist rule, Italy would block efforts by Slovenia to achieve further integration with Western Europe. Italy thus prevented scheduled negotiations on an association agreement between Slovenia and the EU. In August 1994 Slovenia accused Italy of violating bilateral accords by the enactment (in 1992) of legislation allowing residents of former Italian territories to acquire Italian nationality without renouncing that of their country of residence, and in September 1994 the Slovenian authorities stated that Italy had failed to respond to a request to nominate a bank account into which compensation payments could be made by Slovenia. Despite continued bilateral contacts, in late November Italy again prevented negotiations between Slovenia and the EU, and in February 1995 Thaler warned that Slovenia would be unwilling to make concessions to Italy so as to facilitate closer links with the EU. In early March, none the less, the new Italian Government of Lamberto Dini agreed to sanction EU-Slovenian negotiations, and the first round of discussions began in early April: Slovenia signed an association agreement with the EU in mid-June.

Following independence, Slovenia was keen to forge close relations with Western Europe, and developed important trading links with the countries of the EC and also with Austria. In May 1992 a co-operation agreement was signed with the European Free Trade Association (see p. 142); this was followed by a broader agreement on free trade in February 1995. In April 1993 Slovenia was the first former Yugoslav republic to sign a trade and economic co-operation accord with the EC, and negotiations for a full association agreement finally began in April 1995 (see above). Bilateral accords were also contracted with countries of the former eastern bloc, including Hungary, the Czech Republic, Poland and Estonia, in 1993–94. Slovenia joined the Council of Europe (see p. 134) in May 1993, and in December was granted observer status at the Western European Union (see p. 221) conference in Paris, France. In March 1994 it was confirmed that Slovenia was to join NATO's 'partnership for peace' programme (see p. 192), and was thus the first non-member of that organization's North Atlantic Co-operation Council to do so.

In mid-1993, according to the Slovenian authorities, some 60,000 refugees from the conflict in Bosnia and Herzegovina were sheltering in Slovenia. In August of that year the Drnovšek Government rejected proposals, made by the office of the UN High Commissioner for Refugees, for the permanent integration of refugees into Slovenian society. In August 1994 the Slovenian authorities reported that some 29,000 temporary refugees from Bosnia and Herzegovina were officially registered in Slovenia, although it was believed that there were large numbers of unregistered refugees in the country.

### Government

Under the terms of the 1991 Constitution, effective legislative power is vested in the Državni Zbor (National Assembly), to which 90 deputies are elected for a term of four years, by secret ballot, on the basis of universal adult suffrage. Of its members, 38 are directly elected, and 50 are selected on a proportional basis, by an electoral commission, from among those parties that have secured at least 3% of the total votes cast; two further members are non-elected representatives of the Hungarian and Italian minorities. The Državni Svet (National Council), which is elected for five years, comprises 22 directly-elected members, and 18 members chosen by an electoral college to represent various social, economic, trading, political and local interest groups; the Council's role is mainly advisory, but it is competent to veto decisions of the Državni Zbor. The Prime Minister must be able to command a majority in the Državni Zbor. Any government must be approved by the Državni Svet. The President of the Republic has largely ceremonial powers, and is directy elected for a maximum of two five-year terms.

For administrative purposes, Slovenia is divided into 148 municipalities, 11 of which are urban.

### Defence

Military service is compulsory and lasts for seven months. In June 1994 the active Slovenian armed forces numbered 8,100: army 8,000 (including 4,500 conscripts), air force 100. Reserve forces totalled 70,000. There was a paramilitary police force of 4,500 (with 5,000 reserves). A small coastal defence unit was inaugurated in early 1993, and had 35 active members (and 460 reservists) in mid-1994. The estimated defence budget for 1994 was SIT 23,509m. (2.9% of total forecast expenditure).

### Economic Affairs

In 1993, according to estimates by the World Bank, Slovenia's gross national product, measured at average 1991–93 prices, was US $12,566m., equivalent to $6,310 per head. During 1985–93 the population increased by an annual average of 0.6%. Slovenia's gross domestic product (GDP) was $12,672m. in 1993 (according to the Bank of Slovenia), equivalent to $6,366 per head. GDP declined, in real terms, by 5.4% in 1992, but increased by 1.3% in 1993 and by an estimated 5.0% in 1994.

Agriculture (including hunting, forestry and fishing) contributed an estimated 4.9% of GDP in 1994, and engaged some 10.7% of the employed labour force in May 1993. The principal crops are cereals (particularly maize and wheat), potatoes, sugar beet and fruits (especially grapes). Slovenia's forests, which cover about one-half of the country, are an important natural resource. Agricultural GDP declined by 5.9% in 1992, and by 3.6% in 1993.

Industry (including mining, manufacturing, construction and power) contributed 36.9% of GDP in 1994, and engaged 44.1% of the employed labour force in May 1993. Industrial GDP declined by 11.6% in 1992 and by 2.5% in 1993; however, production was estimated to have increased by 6.4% in 1994.

Mining and quarrying contributed 1.1% of GDP in 1994, and engaged 1.2% of the employed labour force in 1991. The principal activity is coal-mining; lead and zinc are also extracted, together with relatively small amounts of natural gas, petroleum and salt. Slovenia also has small deposits of uranium. The GDP of the mining sector increased by 3.1% in 1992, but declined by 8.8% in 1993.

Manufacturing contributed 29.3% of GDP in 1994, and engaged 35.7% of the employed labour force in 1991. The principal activities in 1993, in terms of contribution to industry (excluding power), included the manufacture of electrical equipment, food-processing, textiles, paper and paper products, chemicals and wood and wood products. Manufacturing GDP declined by 12.9% in 1992, and by 2.0% in 1993.

Energy is generated principally by hydroelectric installations. A nuclear power station was constructed in Slovenia by the former Yugoslav authorities to provide energy for both Slovenia and Croatia; agreement was reached in early 1995 regarding the division of its ownership equally between Slovenia and Croatia. Imports of fuel products comprised 7.1% of the value of merchandise imports in 1994.

The services sector contributed 56.9% of GDP in 1994, and engaged 42.9% of the employed labour force in 1991. Expenditure by tourists normally contributes about 5.5% of annual GDP. Tourist activity was adversely affected by the political instability of 1991, but from 1993 there was an appreciable recovery in tourist numbers. Financial services are well developed, contributing 3.9% of total GDP in 1994. Reforms in the banking and insurance sectors, in progress in the mid-1990s, were intended to ensure conformity with criteria for membership of the European Union (EU, see p. 143). The GDP of the services sector declined by 1.2% in 1992, but increased by 3.6% in 1993.

In 1994 Slovenia recorded a visible trade deficit of US $146.1m., while there was a surplus of $478.1m. on the current account of the balance of payments. Slovenia's principal trading partners in 1994 were Germany (which contributed 23.8% of imports and purchased 30.3% of exports), Italy, France, Austria and Croatia. In 1994 EU members supplied 57.1% of imports and purchased 59.3% of Slovenia's exports. The principal exports in 1994 were machinery and transport equipment, basic manufactures, miscellaneous manufactured articles and chemicals. The major imports in that year were machinery and transport equipment, basic manufactures, chemicals, miscellaneous manufactured articles, food and live animals, fuel products and other inedible raw materials.

In 1993 Slovenia recorded a budgetary surplus of SIT 6,393m. (equivalent to 0.1% of GDP in that year). Budget estimates for 1994 forecast a deficit of SIT 17,206m. (1.0% of GDP). Slovenia's external debt, according to national estimates, totalled US $2,258m. at the end of 1994, of which $1,331m. was long-term public debt. In that year the cost of debt-servicing was equivalent to 5.5% of the value of exports of goods and services. (These figures apply only to loans used directly by Slovenian beneficiaries; the division of the federal debt—approximately $2,600m.—was among the subjects of negotiations on the succession of the former Yugoslavia.) Annual inflation averaged 201.3% in 1992, although the rate declined to an average of 32.3% in 1993 and to 19.8% in 1994. Some 9.0% of the total labour force were unemployed in May 1994.

Slovenia has joined several international organizations, including the IMF, the World Bank and (as a 'Country of Operations') the European Bank for Reconstruction and Development (see p. 140). A free-trade agreement was reached with the European Free Trade Association (see p. 142) in February 1995, and Slovenia concluded an association agreement with the EU in June of that year. Slovenia became a contracting party to the General Agreement on Tariffs and Trade in September 1994, and expected to have fulfilled conditions for membership of the World Trade Organization by the end of 1994.

Despite accounting for only 8% of the population, Slovenia was the wealthiest republic of the former Yugoslavia. The economy was severely disrupted following Slovenia's dissociation from the Yugoslav Federation: the international economic blockade of Serbia and Montenegro, together with the conflicts in Croatia and in Bosnia and Herzegovina, resulted in the loss of one-third of Slovenia's traditional export markets, federal investment was lost, and the recession in all sectors in the immediate post-independence period was considerable. None the less, largely owing to its advantageous geographical location and well-developed infrastructure, Slovenia's prospects for growth are generally favourable. By the end of 1994 Slovenia had achieved considerable success in containing the rate of inflation, in accumulating foreign reserves and in slowing (or reversing) the rate of decline in all sectors, while strong trading links had been forged with Western Europe and with other countries of the former communist bloc. However, there was concern that the export-led growth of 1993–94 might again fuel inflation, and that rates of exchange, taxation and interest might deter much-needed investment. In addition, while there were more than 50,000 private companies in early 1995, the privatization of larger industrial units (which had proceeded more slowly than anticipated, but was scheduled for completion by the end of 1995) prompted fears of a further rise in unemployment.

### Social Welfare

There is an extensive social welfare system in Slovenia, which has the highest living standards among the former Yugoslav republics. In 1992 there were, for every 100,000 inhabitants, 69 general practitioners, 131 medical specialists and 53 dentists; there was a total of 11,839 hospital beds. State pensions and welfare benefits are paid.

### Education

Article 57 of the Slovenian Constitution guarantees free education for all. A one-year pre-primary programme ('small school') is obligatory, as is primary education between the ages of seven and 15. In ethnically-mixed regions, two methods of schooling have been developed: bilingual or with instruction in the minority languages. Secondary education offers vocational programmes (two or three years' duration) and technical or professional study (four or five years' duration). Slovenia's two universities are situated in Ljubljana (founded 1919) and Maribor (founded 1961), with 28,522 and 11,717 students, respectively, in 1993/94; there were a further 28 higher education institutions in that year.

### Public Holidays

**1995:** 1–2 January (New Year), 8 February (Prešeren Day, Day of Culture), 16–17 April (Easter), 27 April (Resistance Day), 1–2 May (Labour Days), 4 June (Whit Sunday), 25 June (National Statehood Day), 15 August (Assumption), 31 October (Reformation Day), 1 November (All Saints' Day), 25 December (Christmas Day), 26 December (Independence Day).

**1996:** 1–2 January (New Year), 8 February (Prešeren Day, Day of Culture), 7–8 April (Easter), 27 April (Resistance Day), 1–2 May (Labour Days), 26 May (Whit Sunday), 25 June (National Statehood Day), 15 August (Assumption), 31 October (Reformation Day), 1 November (All Saints' Day), 25 December (Christmas Day), 26 December (Independence Day).

### Weights and Measures

The metric system is in force.

…SLOVENIA

# Statistical Survey

Source (unless otherwise indicated): *Statistični letopis* (Statistical Yearbook), published by Statistical Office of the Republic of Slovenia, 61000 Ljubljana, Vožarski pot 12; tel. (61) 1255322; fax (61) 216932.

## Area and Population

### AREA, POPULATION AND DENSITY

| | |
|---|---|
| Area (sq km) | 20,253* |
| Population (census results) | |
| 31 March 1981 | 1,891,864 |
| 31 March 1991 | |
| Males | 952,611 |
| Females | 1,013,375 |
| Total | 1,965,986 |
| Population (official estimates at 31 December) | |
| 1991 | 1,998,912 |
| 1992 | 1,994,084 |
| 1993 | 1,989,408 |
| Density (per sq km) at 31 December 1993 | 98.2 |

* 7,820 sq miles.

**Population** (official estimate at mid-1994): 1,988,850.

### POPULATION BY ETHNIC GROUP (1991 census)

| Ethnic group | Number | % |
|---|---|---|
| Slovenes | 1,727,018 | 87.8 |
| Croats | 54,212 | 2.8 |
| Serbs | 47,911 | 2.4 |
| Slav Muslims | 26,842 | 1.4 |
| Yugoslavs | 12,307 | 0.6 |
| Hungarians | 8,503 | 0.4 |
| Macedonians | 4,432 | 0.2 |
| Montenegrins | 4,396 | 0.2 |
| Albanians | 3,629 | 0.2 |
| Italians | 3,064 | 0.2 |
| **Total** (incl. others) | 1,965,986 | 100.00 |

### PRINCIPAL TOWNS (estimated population at 31 December 1993)

| | | | |
|---|---|---|---|
| Ljubljana (capital) | 270,759 | Velenje | 27,142 |
| Maribor | 103,512 | Koper (Capodistria) | 24,746 |
| Celje | 39,942 | Novo mesto | 22,637 |
| Kranj | 36,808 | | |

### BIRTHS, MARRIAGES AND DEATHS

| | Registered live births | | Registered marriages | | Registered deaths | |
|---|---|---|---|---|---|---|
| | Number | Rate (per 1,000) | Number | Rate (per 1,000) | Number | Rate (per 1,000) |
| 1986 | 25,570 | 12.9 | 10,621 | 5.4 | 19,499 | 9.8 |
| 1987 | 25,592 | 12.9 | 10,307 | 5.2 | 19,837 | 10.0 |
| 1988 | 25,209 | 12.6 | 9,217 | 4.6 | 19,126 | 9.6 |
| 1989 | 23,447 | 11.7 | 9,776 | 4.9 | 18,669 | 9.3 |
| 1990 | 22,368 | 11.2 | 8,517 | 4.3 | 18,555 | 9.3 |
| 1991 | 21,583 | 10.8 | 8,173 | 4.1 | 19,324 | 9.7 |
| 1992 | 19,982 | 10.0 | 9,119 | 4.6 | 19,333 | 9.7 |
| 1993 | 19,793 | 9.9 | 9,022 | 4.5 | 20,012 | 10.0 |

**Expectation of life** (years at birth, 1992–93): males 69.4; females 77.3.

### ECONOMICALLY ACTIVE POPULATION
(persons aged 15 years and over, 1991 census)

| | Males | Females | Total |
|---|---|---|---|
| Agriculture, hunting, forestry and fishing | 62,310 | 58,750 | 121,060 |
| Mining and quarrying | 9,408 | 979 | 10,387 |
| Manufacturing | 175,831 | 137,693 | 313,524 |
| Electricity, gas and water | 8,727 | 2,489 | 11,216 |
| Construction | 34,548 | 7,075 | 41,623 |
| Trade, restaurants and hotels | 37,812 | 65,327 | 103,139 |
| Transport, storage and communications | 40,553 | 12,133 | 52,686 |
| Financing, insurance, real estate and business services | 22,773 | 21,704 | 44,477 |
| Community, social and personal services* | 69,181 | 107,327 | 176,508 |
| Activities not adequately defined | 2,543 | 1,626 | 4,169 |
| **Total employed** | 463,686 | 415,103 | 878,789 |
| Unemployed | 40,696 | 26,281 | 66,977 |
| **Total labour force** | 504,382 | 441,384 | 945,766 |

* Including members of the armed forces, totalling 2,430 (males 2,375; females 55).

Source: ILO, *Year Book of Labour Statistics*.

**May 1993** (sample survey, '000 persons aged 15 years and over): Agriculture, etc. 90; Industry 373 (incl. Construction 46); Services 381; Not stated 2; Total employed 845 (males 451, females 395); Unemployed 85 (males 49, females 36); Total labour force 931 (males 500, females 430).

## Agriculture

### PRINCIPAL CROPS ('000 metric tons)

| | 1991 | 1992 | 1993 |
|---|---|---|---|
| Wheat | 180.7 | 178.4 | 167.8 |
| Barley | 26.5 | 26.6 | 26.4 |
| Maize | 336.4 | 207.5 | 248.8 |
| Rye | 7.4 | 7.0 | 5.8 |
| Oats | 5.3 | 5.8 | 5.2 |
| Potatoes | 425.1 | 368.0 | 367.2 |
| Cabbages and kale | 50.0 | 38.7 | 42.8 |
| Tomatoes | 6.9 | 6.8 | 6.9 |
| Onions (dry) | 9.3 | 8.3 | 8.2 |
| Carrots | 5.7 | 4.7 | 5.1 |
| Grapes | 108.1 | 124.0 | 128.3 |
| Sugar beet | 165.6 | 96.6 | 132.6 |
| Apples | 72.9 | 85.2 | 91.3 |
| Pears | 13.8 | 16.5 | 13.5 |
| Peaches and nectarines | 7.2 | 8.5 | 10.2 |
| Plums | 4.8 | 9.1 | 5.5 |

### LIVESTOCK ('000 head at 1 January)

| | 1992 | 1993 | 1994 |
|---|---|---|---|
| Cattle | 484 | 504 | 238 |
| Pigs | 529 | 602 | 55 |
| Sheep | 28 | 21 | 12 |
| Horses | 11 | 9 | 9 |
| Poultry | 13,134 | 11,434 | 10,592 |

## SLOVENIA

### LIVESTOCK PRODUCTS
('000 metric tons)

|  | 1991 | 1992 | 1993 |
|---|---|---|---|
| Beef and veal | 50.8 | 38.1 | 38.4 |
| Pig meat | 41.0 | 41.0 | 47.1 |
| Poultry meat | 73.3 | 58.1 | 49.5 |
| Cows' milk | 643 | 352* | 280* |
| Cheese | 12.3 | 12.4 | 10.3* |
| Butter | 2.0 | 2.5 | 2.2* |
| Poultry eggs | 26.5 | 25.0† | 25.4† |

* FAO estimate.  † Unofficial figure.
Source: partly FAO, *Production Yearbook*.

## Forestry

### ROUNDWOOD REMOVALS ('000 cubic metres)

|  | 1991 | 1992 | 1993 |
|---|---|---|---|
| Sawlogs and veneer logs | 811.9 | 730.0 | 645.2 |
| Pitprops (mine timber) | 25.9 | 23.0 | 18.0 |
| Pulpwood | 172.9 | 194.3 | 154.8 |
| Other industrial wood | 239.4 | 203.3 | 140.2 |
| Fuel wood | 163.8 | 118.8 | 107.2 |
| **Total** | **1,413.9** | **1,269.4** | **1,065.4** |

### SAWNWOOD PRODUCTION ('000 cubic metres)

|  | 1991 | 1992 | 1993 |
|---|---|---|---|
| Coniferous (softwood) | 424 | 394 | 381 |
| Non-coniferous (hardwood) | 175 | 190 | 144 |
| **Total** | **599** | **584** | **525** |

## Fishing
(metric tons, live weight)

|  | 1991 | 1992 | 1993 |
|---|---|---|---|
| Freshwater fishes | 805 | 938 | 917 |
| Marine fishes | 4,865 | 3,593 | 1,951 |
| Crustaceans and molluscs | 147 | 175 | 101 |
| **Total catch** | **5,817** | **4,706** | **2,969** |

## Mining
('000 metric tons, unless otherwise indicated)

|  | 1991 | 1992 | 1993 |
|---|---|---|---|
| Brown coal | 1,252 | 1,323 | 1,200 |
| Lignite | 3,906 | 4,233 | 3,921 |
| Crude petroleum | 2.4 | 2.1 | 1.9 |
| Lead and zinc ore* | 162 | 152 | 62 |
| Salt (unrefined) | 8.0 | 710 | 12.3 |
| Natural gas (million cubic metres) | 19.3 | 16.5 | 13.4 |

* Figures refer to gross weight. In 1991 the estimated metal content (in '000 metric tons) was: Lead 2.8; Zinc 8.9 (Source: UN, *Industrial Statistics Yearbook*).

## Industry

### SELECTED PRODUCTS
('000 metric tons, unless otherwise indicated)

|  | 1991 | 1992 | 1993 |
|---|---|---|---|
| Wine ('000 hectolitres) | 515.6 | 553.8 | 635.4 |
| Beer ('000 hectolitres) | 2,286 | 1,813 | 1,979 |
| Cigarettes (million) | 4,535 | 5,278 | 4,851 |
| Wool yarn (metric tons) | 6,233 | 7,144 | 7,220 |
| Cotton yarn (metric tons) | 14,821 | 13,379 | 13,346 |
| Woven cotton fabrics (million sq metres)* | 102 | 79 | 80 |
| Woven woollen fabrics ('000 sq metres)* | 8,957 | 13,139 | 11,018 |
| Footwear (excl. rubber) ('000 pairs) | 9,124 | 9,492 | 8,840 |
| Veneer sheets (cubic metres) | 26,805 | 22,825 | 21,297 |
| Plywood (cubic metres) | 11,541 | 11,218 | 9,720 |
| Mechanical wood pulp (metric tons) | 61,089 | 30,893 | 27,699 |
| Chemical wood pulp (metric tons) | 85,292 | 71,898 | 41,352 |
| Paper | 290 | 263 | 244 |
| Hydrochloric acid (metric tons) | 17,667 | 17,636 | 16,838 |
| Sulphuric acid (metric tons) | 85,978 | 120,959 | 113,501 |
| Motor spirit (petrol) | 104 | n.a. | 78 |
| Distillate fuel oils | 241 | n.a. | 227 |
| Rubber tyres ('000)† | 4,362 | 5,076 | 5,610 |
| Clay building bricks (million) | 304 | 275 | 252 |
| Roofing tiles (million) | 26 | 35 | 34 |
| Cement | 974 | 801 | 707 |
| Crude steel | 287 | 297 | 355 |
| Aluminium (metric tons) | 90,164 | 84,809 | 82,682 |
| Refined lead (metric tons)‡ | 9,571 | 7,768 | 6,424 |
| Refrigerators for household use ('000) | 744 | 661 | 665 |
| Washing machines (household) ('000) | 317 | 200 | 199 |
| Television receivers ('000) | 103 | n.a. | 58 |
| Passenger motor cars (number)§ | 80,638 | 82,217 | 58,291 |
| Motorcycles (number) | 37,956 | 20,310 | 29,580 |
| Bicycles ('000) | 218 | 190 | 186 |
| Electric energy (million kWh) | 12,720 | 12,059 | 11,682 |

* Including fabrics of substitute materials.
† Tyres for road motor vehicles only.
‡ Primary metal only, excluding lead recovered from scrap.
§ Including vehicles assembled from imported parts.

## Finance

### CURRENCY AND EXCHANGE RATES

**Monetary Units**
 100 stotins = 1 tolar (SlT).

**Sterling and Dollar Equivalents** (31 December 1994)
 £1 sterling = 197.65 tolars;
 US $1 = 126.46 tolars (Bank of Slovenia rates);
 1,000 tolars = £5.060 = $7.908.

**Average Exchange Rate** (tolars per US $)
 1992   81.287
 1993  113.242
 1994  128.809

Note: The tolar was introduced in October 1991, replacing (initially at par) the Yugoslav dinar.

### BUDGET (million tolars)*

| Revenue | 1992 | 1993 | 1994† |
|---|---|---|---|
| Taxation | 440,998 | 630,069 | 739,888 |
|   Individual income taxes | 69,232 | 97,997 | 115,700 |
|   Domestic taxes on goods and services | 107,491 | 158,842 | 213,360 |
|   Import taxes | 32,460 | 51,463 | 65,300 |
|   Social security contributions | 225,461 | 314,575 | 329,878 |
| Other receipts | 26,786 | 45,590 | 44,588 |
| **Total** | **467,984** | **675,659** | **784,476** |

# SLOVENIA

*Statistical Survey*

| Expenditure | 1992 | 1993 | 1994† |
|---|---|---|---|
| Central Government | 211,342 | 299,235 | 370,003 |
| Wages, contributions and purchases of goods and services | 57,863 | 87,205 | 99,198 |
| Defence (incl. capital expenditure) | 18,299 | 20,463 | 23,509 |
| Social transfers (except to Pension fund) | 34,825 | 59,344 | 70,782 |
| Transfers to social services (excl. health) | 20,103 | 28,206 | 32,711 |
| Interest payments | 4,795 | 18,357 | 29,543 |
| Subsidies and other transfers to enterprises | 28,373 | 31,316 | 31,355 |
| Capital expenditure (excl. defence) | 24,813 | 29,503 | 50,461 |
| Local governments | 50,334 | 74,092 | 81,951 |
| Wages, contributions and purchases of goods and services | 10,763 | 15,203 | 17,700 |
| Transfers to social services | 21,009 | 29,346 | 35,058 |
| Subsidies and other transfers to enterprises | 15,763 | 24,663 | 23,333 |
| Pension Fund | 127,724 | 186,053 | 222,636 |
| Health care | 72,853 | 108,287 | 125,192 |
| **Total** (incl. others) | 465,683 | 669,266 | 801,682 |

* Figures represent a consolidation of the accounts of the central Government, local administrative authorities and extrabudgetary funds.
† Forecasts.

Source: Bank of Slovenia, *Monthly Bulletin*.

## BANK OF SLOVENIA RESERVES
(US $ million at 31 December)

|  | 1992 | 1993 | 1994 |
|---|---|---|---|
| IMF special drawing rights | — | — | 0.1 |
| Reserve position in IMF | — | 17.6 | 14.7 |
| Foreign exchange | 715.5 | 770.1 | 1,480.1 |
| **Total** (excl. gold) | 715.5 | 787.7 | 1,494.9 |

Source: Bank of Slovenia, *Monthly Bulletin*.

## MONEY SUPPLY (million tolars at 31 December)

|  | 1992 | 1993 | 1994 |
|---|---|---|---|
| Currency outside banks | 24,183 | 32,721 | 47,284 |

Source: Bank of Slovenia, *Monthly Bulletin*.

## COST OF LIVING
(Index of retail prices; base: previous year = 100)

|  | 1992 | 1993 | 1994 |
|---|---|---|---|
| All items | 301.3 | 132.3 | 119.8 |

Source: Bank of Slovenia, *Monthly Bulletin*.

## NATIONAL ACCOUNTS (million tolars at current prices)
### Composition of the Gross Domestic Product

|  | 1992 | 1993 | 1994* |
|---|---|---|---|
| Compensation of employees | 652,813 | 876,581 | 1,076,635 |
| Operating surplus | 33,753 | 123,863 | 137,435 |
| **Domestic factor incomes** | 686,566 | 1,000,444 | 1,214,070 |
| Consumption of fixed capital | 202,926 | 250,429 | 327,390 |
| **GDP at factor cost** | 889,492 | 1,250,873 | 1,541,460 |
| Indirect taxes | 141,815 | 217,359 | 303,260 |
| Less Subsidies | 26,047 | 33,259 | 36,620 |
| **GDP in purchasers' values** | 1,005,261 | 1,434,974 | 1,808,100 |

* Figures are provisional.

### Expenditure on the Gross Domestic Product

|  | 1992 | 1993 | 1994* |
|---|---|---|---|
| Government final consumption expenditure | 206,295 | 297,448 | 374,930 |
| Private final consumption expenditure | 531,892 | 791,843 | 976,010 |
| Increase in stocks | −2,754 | 14,950 | 17,940 |
| Gross fixed capital formation | 177,018 | 259,040 | 357,475 |
| Statistical discrepancy | 394 | 27,968 | 11,875 |
| **Total domestic expenditure** | 912,845 | 1,391,249 | 1,738,230 |
| Exports of goods and services | 639,932 | 842,625 | 1,044,130 |
| Less Imports of goods and services | 547,516 | 798,900 | 974,260 |
| **GDP in purchasers' values** | 1,005,261 | 1,434,974 | 1,808,100 |

* Figures are provisional.

### Gross Domestic Product by Economic Activity

|  | 1992 | 1993 | 1994* |
|---|---|---|---|
| Agriculture, hunting, forestry and fishing | 49,631 | 64,804 | 82,189 |
| Mining and quarrying | 17,156 | 14,692 | 18,604 |
| Manufacturing | 298,095 | 395,894 | 487,147 |
| Electricity, gas and water supply | 24,362 | 37,143 | 52,808 |
| Construction | 38,621 | 60,689 | 76,006 |
| Wholesale and retail trade | 105,172 | 148,838 | 187,338 |
| Hotels and restaurants | 24,260 | 36,614 | 52,988 |
| Transport, storage and communications | 65,818 | 105,454 | 136,373 |
| Finance and insurance services | 34,394 | 51,820 | 64,631 |
| Real estate and business services | 95,429 | 129,164 | 158,106 |
| Public administration and defence | 40,405 | 60,460 | 76,482 |
| Education | 43,612 | 66,429 | 83,700 |
| Health and social work | 47,376 | 75,708 | 95,393 |
| Other community, social and personal services | 48,888 | 76,999 | 92,399 |
| **Sub-total** | 933,218 | 1,324,706 | 1,664,163 |
| Import duties | 32,550 | 51,860 | 65,000 |
| Other indirect taxes† | 56,079 | 86,745 | 114,635 |
| Less Imputed bank service charge | 16,586 | 28,338 | 35,698 |
| **GDP in purchasers' values** | 1,005,261 | 1,434,974 | 1,808,100 |

* Figures are provisional.
† Including other adjustments.

Source: Bank of Slovenia, *Monthly Bulletin*.

### BALANCE OF PAYMENTS (US $ million)

|  | 1992 | 1993 | 1994 |
|---|---|---|---|
| Merchandise exports f.o.b. | 6,682.9 | 6,082.9 | 6,806.3 |
| Merchandise imports f.o.b. | −5,891.8 | −6,237.1 | −6,952.4 |
| **Trade balance** | 791.1 | −154.2 | −146.1 |
| Exports of services | 1,219.3 | 1,357.9 | 1,675.2 |
| Imports of services | −1,039.0 | −1,047.5 | −1,064.8 |
| Other income received | 69.8 | 117.2 | 127.4 |
| Other income paid | −161.1 | −164.3 | −164.3 |
| Unrequited transfers (net) | 46.0 | 40.8 | 50.7 |
| **Current balance** | 926.2 | 149.9 | 478.1 |
| Direct investment (net) | 112.9 | 111.9 | 88.1 |
| Portfolio investment (net) | −8.9 | 3.1 | −32.5 |
| Other capital (net) | −116.8 | −150.9 | 41.1 |
| Net errors and omissions | −280.8 | −3.0 | 67.6 |
| **Overall balance** | 632.6 | 111.1 | 642.4 |

Source: Bank of Slovenia, *Monthly Bulletin*.

SLOVENIA

# External Trade

**PRINCIPAL COMMODITIES**
(distribution by SITC, US $ million)

| Imports c.i.f. | 1992 | 1993 | 1994* |
|---|---|---|---|
| Food and live animals | 463.6 | 478.3 | 550 |
| Crude materials (inedible) except fuels | 418.7 | 344.9 | 469 |
| Mineral fuels, lubricants, etc. | 660.5 | 699.6 | 511 |
| Chemicals | 760.2 | 749.6 | 888 |
| Basic manufactures | 1,203.6 | 1,147.4 | 1,413 |
| Machinery and transport equipment | 1,620.9 | 1,969.2 | 2,301 |
| Miscellaneous manufactured articles | 645.8 | 782.9 | 796 |
| **Total** (incl. others) | 6,141.0 | 6,501.0 | 7,247 |

| Exports f.o.b. | 1992 | 1993 | 1994* |
|---|---|---|---|
| Food and live animals | 342.3 | 239.1 | 274 |
| Crude materials (inedible) except fuels | 137.0 | 107.7 | 131 |
| Mineral fuels, lubricants, etc. | 172.9 | 313.4 | 66 |
| Chemicals | 606.1 | 552.5 | 704 |
| Basic manufactures | 1,812.4 | 1,585.5 | 1,863 |
| Machinery and transport equipment | 1,962.3 | 1,664.3 | 2,063 |
| Miscellaneous manufactured articles | 1,552.2 | 1,557.3 | 1,635 |
| **Total** (incl. others) | 6,681.2 | 6,082.9 | 6,806 |

* Source: Bank of Slovenia, *Monthly Bulletin*.

**PRINCIPAL TRADING PARTNERS** (US $ million)

| Imports c.i.f. | 1992 | 1993 | 1994* |
|---|---|---|---|
| Austria | 499.7 | 553.2 | 753 |
| Belgium | 58.6 | 64.5 | 83 |
| Croatia | 851.6 | 595.4 | 492 |
| Czechoslovakia (former)† | 116.5 | 152.2 | 235 |
| France | 492.5 | 521.7 | 599 |
| Germany | 1,394..3 | 1,626.0 | 1,727 |
| Hungary | 152.2 | 165.0 | 192 |
| Iran | 19.7 | 87.1 | n.a. |
| Italy | 838.9 | 1,051.2 | 1,252 |
| Japan | 88.1 | 125.1 | 125 |
| Macedonia, former Yugoslav republic‡ | n.a. | 89.3 | 80 |
| Netherlands | 104.1 | 122.0 | 167 |
| Spain | 58.8 | 70.8 | 115 |
| Sweden | 63.5 | 65.4 | 83 |
| Switzerland | 99.6 | 126.5 | 153 |
| USSR (former)§ | 251.4 | 216.8 | 164 |
| United Kingdom | 73.8 | 103.0 | 129 |
| USA | 167.2 | 187.9 | 196 |
| Yugoslavia, Federal Republic‡ | 366.7 | 0.3 | 0 |
| **Total** (incl. others) | 6,141.0 | 6,501.0 | 7,247 |

| Exports f.o.b. | 1992 | 1993 | 1994* |
|---|---|---|---|
| Austria | 340.7 | 303.0 | 374 |
| Bosnia and Herzegovina‡ | n.a. | 20.1 | 68 |
| Croatia | 951.6 | 738.5 | 725 |
| Czechoslovakia (former)† | 91.9 | 86.1 | 113 |
| France | 616.0 | 527.7 | 586 |
| Germany | 1,805.4 | 1,797.6 | 2,065 |
| Hungary | 73.0 | 87.7 | 99 |
| Italy | 879.7 | 755.9 | 922 |
| Macedonia, former Yugoslav republic‡ | n.a. | 198.2 | 218 |
| Netherlands | 92.1 | 89.8 | 99 |
| Poland | 69.2 | 87.4 | 96 |
| USSR (former)§ | 225.6 | 297.5 | 316 |
| United Kingdom | 141.1 | 148.1 | 208 |
| USA | 195.1 | 216.0 | 248 |
| Yugoslavia, Federal Republic‡ | 556.1 | 7.6 | 15 |
| **Total** (incl. others) | 6,681.2 | 6,082.9 | 6,806 |

* Source: Bank of Slovenia, *Monthly Bulletin*.
† In 1993 trade with the Czech Republic (in $ million) was: Imports 121.4; Exports 55.9.
‡ Until June 1992 most of Slovenia's trade with Bosnia and Herzegovina and with the former Yugoslav republic of Macedonia (FYRM) was not recorded separately from trade with the Federal Republic of Yugoslavia (FRY, i.e. Serbia and Montenegro). For 1992 trade with countries of the former Yugoslavia (excluding Croatia) is shown jointly as trade with the FRY, but it includes recorded trade with Bosnia and Herzegovina (imports $20m., exports $23m.) and with the FYRM (imports $78m., exports $133m.).
§ In 1993 trade with Russia (in $ million) was: Imports 202.4; Exports 248.6.

# Transport

**RAILWAYS** (traffic)

| | 1991 | 1992 | 1993 |
|---|---|---|---|
| Passenger journeys ('000) | 13,837 | 12,286 | 12,636 |
| Passenger-kilometres (million) | 814 | 547 | 566 |
| Freight carried ('000 metric tons) | 17,233 | 13,045 | 11,900 |
| Freight ton-kilometres (million) | 3,246 | 2,573 | 2,262 |

**ROAD TRAFFIC**
(registered motor vehicles at 31 December)

| | 1991 | 1992 | 1993 |
|---|---|---|---|
| Motorcycles and mopeds | 14,344 | 13,568 | 9,967 |
| Passenger cars | 594,289 | 606,820 | 632,563 |
| Buses and coaches | 2,855 | 2,676 | 2,527 |
| Lorries and vans | 39,367 | 40,192 | 41,297 |
| Agricultural tractors | 96,280 | 97,314 | 98,125 |

**CIVIL AVIATION** (traffic)

| | 1991 | 1992 | 1993 |
|---|---|---|---|
| Kilometres flown ('000) | 8,035 | 5,808 | 7,593 |
| Passengers carried ('000) | 697 | 333 | 431 |
| Passenger-kilometres (million) | 576 | 417 | 475 |
| Freight carried (metric tons) | 1,670 | 1,885 | 4,119 |
| Freight ton-kilometres ('000) | 1,216 | 1,918 | 3,731 |

## Tourism

**FOREIGN TOURIST ARRIVALS** ('000)

| Country of origin | 1992 | 1993 | 1994* |
|---|---|---|---|
| Austria | 95.9 | 112.5 | 130.8 |
| Belgium | 4.0 | 7.4 | n.a. |
| Bosnia and Herzegovina | 55.0 | 22.9 | n.a. |
| Croatia | 91.7 | 71.1 | n.a. |
| Czech Republic | n.a. | 14.0 | 19.0 |
| Czechoslovakia | 9.6 | — | — |
| France | 8.0 | 10.2 | 13.6 |
| Germany | 62.6 | 94.3 | 131.4 |
| Hungary | 11.6 | 18.5 | 20.2 |
| Italy | 162.5 | 157.6 | 176.6 |
| Macedonia, former Yugoslav republic | 15.1 | 13.4 | n.a. |
| Netherlands | 8.4 | 12.5 | 19.2 |
| Russia | 5.9† | 8.3 | 12.4 |
| United Kingdom | 10.4 | 11.6 | 14.5 |
| USA | 7.4 | 10.1 | 13.8 |
| Yugoslavia, Federal Republic | 31.8 | 12.4 | n.a. |
| **Total** (incl. others) | 616.6 | 624.4 | 627.3 |

* Source: Centre for Tourism and Economic Promotion, Ljubljana.
† Including arrivals from other countries of the former USSR.

## Education

(1993/94, unless otherwise indicated)

| | Institutions | Students | Teachers |
|---|---|---|---|
| Pre-primary education | 773 | 67,178 | 6,343 |
| Primary education | 821 | 213,885 | 15,067 |
| Secondary education (first stage) | | | |
| Secondary education (second stage) | 145 | 99,974 | 7,361 |
| Special schools* | 78 | 4,611 | 993 |
| Higher education | 30 | 40,239 | 3,172 |

* Figures refer to 1992/93.

## Communications Media

| | 1991 | 1992 | 1993 |
|---|---|---|---|
| Telephone subscribers ('000) | 458.7 | 494.3 | 527.8 |
| Radio licences ('000) | 590.6 | 581.9 | 596.1 |
| Television licences ('000) | 444.1 | 441.2 | 454.4 |
| Books (titles published) | 2,459 | 2,136 | 2,440 |
| Daily newspapers | 5 | 6* | n.a. |
| Non-daily newspapers | 199 | 153 | n.a. |
| Other periodicals | 484 | 482 | n.a. |

* Combined average circulation 308,000 copies.

Source: partly UNESCO, *Statistical Yearbook*.

# Directory

## The Constitution

The Constitution of the Republic of Slovenia was enacted on 23 December 1991. Its provisions for the independence and sovereignty of Slovenia had been endorsed by a plebiscite held on 23 December 1990. The following is a summary of the Constitution's main articles:

### INTRODUCTION

Slovenia is a democratic republic, governed by the rule of law. Slovenia is a territorially indivisible state. Human rights and fundamental freedom—including the rights of the autochthonous Italian and Hungarian ethnic communities—are protected. Slovenia attends to the welfare of the autochthonous Slovenian minorities in neighbouring countries and of Slovenian emigrants and migrant workers abroad.

The separation of church and state is guaranteed. Religious groups enjoy equal rights under the law and are guaranteed freedom of activity.

The autonomy of local government in Slovenia is guaranteed. The capital of the republic is Ljubljana. The official language of Slovenia is Slovene. In those areas where Italian or Hungarian ethnic communities reside, the official language is also Italian or Hungarian.

### HUMAN RIGHTS AND FUNDAMENTAL FREEDOMS

All persons are guaranteed equal human rights and fundamental freedoms, irrespective of national origin, race, sex, language, religion, political or other beliefs, financial status, birth, education or social status, and all persons are equal before the law. Human life is inviolable, and there is no capital punishment. No person may be subjected to torture, inhuman or humiliating punishment or treatment. The right of each individual to personal liberty is guaranteed.

Respect for the humanity and dignity of the individual is guaranteed in all criminal or other proceedings. The use of violence of any sort on any person whose liberty has been restricted in any way is forbidden. Except for certain situations (as determined by statute), all court proceedings are conducted in public and all judgments are delivered in open court. Each person is guaranteed the right of appeal. Any person charged with a criminal offence is presumed innocent until proven guilty by due process of the law.

Each person has the right to freedom of movement, to choose his place of residence, to leave the country and to return at any time he wishes. The right to own and to inherit property is guaranteed. The dwellings of all persons are inviolable, and the protection of personal data relating to the individual is guaranteed. Freedom of expression of thought, freedom of speech and freedom to associate in public, together with freedom of the press and of other forms of public communication and expression, are guaranteed. The right to vote is universal and equal. Each citizen who has attained the age of 18 years is eligible both to vote and to stand for election.

The freedom of work is guaranteed. Each person may freely choose his employment. Forced labour is forbidden. All citizens who fulfil such conditions as are laid down by statute, have the right to social security. The State regulates compulsory health, pension, disability and other social insurance, and ensures the proper administration thereof. Education is free, and the State provides the opportunity for all citizens to obtain a proper education.

Each person is entitled freely to identify with his national grouping or ethnic community, to foster and give expression to his culture and to use his own language and script. All incitement to ethnic, racial, religious or other discrimination, as well as the inflaming of ethnic, racial, religious or other hatred or intolerance, is unconstitutional, as is incitement to violence or to war. The autochthonous Italian and Hungarian ethnic communities are guaranteed the right freely to use their national symbols and to establish organizations, to foster economic, cultural, scientific and research activities, as well as activities associated with the mass media and publishing. These two communities have the right to education and schooling in their own languages. They are also entitled to establish autonomous organizations in order to exercise their rights. The Italian and Hungarian communities are directly represented both at the local level and in the National Assembly. The status and special rights of Gypsy communities living in Slovenia are determined by statute.

## ECONOMIC AND SOCIAL RELATIONS

The State is responsible for the creation of opportunities for employment. Each person has the right to a healthy environment, and the State is responsible for such an environment. The protection of animals from cruelty is regulated by statute. State and local government bodies are responsible for the preservation of the natural and cultural heritage.

Free enterprise is guaranteed. The establishment of trade unions, and the operation and membership thereof, is free. Workers enjoy the right to strike. The State creates the conditions necessary to enable each citizen to obtain proper housing.

## ADMINISTRATION OF THE STATE

### The National Assembly (Državni Zbor)

The National Assembly consists of 90 deputies, representing the citizens of Slovenia. Deputies are directly elected by secret ballot, on the basis of universal adult suffrage, for a four-year term. The Italian and Hungarian ethnic communities are entitled to elect one deputy each to the National Assembly. The President of the National Assembly (Speaker) is elected by a majority vote of all elected deputies.

The National Assembly enacts laws; makes other decisions; authorizes adherence to international agreements; may call a referendum; may proclaim a state of war or a state of emergency, at the initiative of the Government; may establish parliamentary inquiries with respect to matters of public importance.

### The National Council (Državni Svet)

The National Council represents social, economic, trade and professional, and local interests. It is composed of 40 councillors: four representing employers; four representing employees; four representing farmers, small business persons and independent professional persons; six representing non-profit-making organizations; and 22 representing local interests. Councillors are elected for a five-year term.

The National Council may: propose the enactment of statutes by the National Assembly; demand that the National Assembly reconsider statutes prior to their proclamation; demand the holding of a referendum; and demand the establishment of a parliamentary inquiry. The National Assembly may require the National Council to provide its opinions on specific matters. A councillor of the National Council may not be simultaneously a deputy of the National Assembly.

### The President of the Republic

The President of the Republic of Slovenia is Head of State and Commander-in-Chief of the Defence Forces. The President is elected on the basis of universal, equal and direct suffrage by secret ballot. The President's term of office is five years (with a maximum of two consecutive terms). Only a citizen of Slovenia may be elected President of the Republic. Presidential elections are called by the President of the National Assembly. The office of President of the Republic is incompatible with other public offices or other employment. In the event that the President of the Republic is permanently incapacitated, dies, resigns or is otherwise permanently unable to perform his functions, the President of the National Assembly temporarily occupies the office of the President of the Republic until such time as a replacement is elected.

The President of the Republic is empowered to: call elections to the National Assembly; proclaim statutes; appoint state officers and functionaries; accredit, and revoke the accreditation of, Slovenian ambassadors to foreign states, and to accept the credentials of foreign diplomatic representatives; grant amnesties; and confer state honours, decorations and honorary titles.

If, in the course of carrying out his office, the President of the Republic acts in a manner contrary to the Constitution or commits a serious breach of the law, he may be brought before the Constitutional Court upon the request of the National Assembly. The President may be dismissed from office upon the vote of no less than two-thirds of all of the judges of the Constitutional Court.

### The Government

The Government is composed of the Prime Minister and ministers. The Government is independent, and individual ministers are independent within their own particular portfolios. Ministers are accountable to the National Assembly. After consultations with the leaders of the various political groups within the National Assembly, the President of the Republic proposes to the National Assembly a candidate for the office of Prime Minister. The Prime Minister is elected by the National Assembly by a majority vote. Ministers in the Government are appointed or dismissed by the National Assembly, upon the proposal of the Prime Minister. The Prime Minister is responsible for the political unity, direction and administrative programme of the Government and for the co-ordination of the work of the various ministers. The National Assembly may, upon the motion of no fewer than 10 deputies and by a majority vote, elect a new Prime Minister (such a vote is deemed a vote of 'no confidence' in the Government). Furthermore, the National Assembly may bring the Prime Minister or any minister before the Constitutional Court to answer charges relating to breaches of the Constitution.

### The Judiciary

Judges independently exercise their duties and functions in accordance with the Constitution and with the law. The Supreme Court is the highest court for civil and criminal cases in the republic. The National Assembly elects judges upon the recommendation of the Judicial Council, which is composed of 11 members. The office of a judge is incompatible with office in any other state body, local government body or organ of any political party.

### The Office of the Public Prosecutor

The Public Prosecutor is responsible for the preferment of criminal charges, for prosecuting criminal matters in court and for the performance of such other duties as are prescribed by statute.

## LOCAL SELF-GOVERNMENT

Slovenians exercise local government powers and functions through self-governing municipalities and other local government organizations. A municipality may comprise a single community or a number of communities, whose inhabitants are bound together by common needs and interests. The State supervises the proper and efficient performance of municipalities and wider self-governing local administrative bodies. Municipalities raise their own revenue. Municipalities are at liberty to join other municipalities in establishing wider self-governing local administrative bodies or regional local government bodies to exercise administrative powers and to deal with matters of wider common interest. Citizens may join together and form self-governing local bodies to further their common interests.

## PUBLIC FINANCE

The State and local government bodies fund the performance of their respective duties and functions from taxes and other mandatory charges levied by them and from such other income as they may derive from their assets. All revenues raised, and all monies expended, for public purposes by the State and by local government bodies must be accounted for in their respective budgets.

The Auditor General's office is the body with ultimate responsibility for auditing state finances, the state budget and monies expended for public purposes. The Auditor General's office is independent in the performance of its functions. Officers of the Auditor General's office are appointed by the National Assembly.

The Bank of Slovenia is the central bank. It is independent in its operations and accountable to the National Assembly. The Governor of the Bank of Slovenia is appointed by the National Assembly.

## THE CONSTITUTIONAL COURT

The Constitutional Court is composed of nine judges, elected by the National Assembly, upon the nomination of the President of the Republic, for a term (non-extendable) of nine years. The President of the Constitutional Court is elected by the judges from amongst their own number to hold office for a period of three years.

The Constitutional Court is empowered to decide upon matters relating to: the conformity of statutes with the Constitution and with international agreements; complaints of breaches of the Constitution involving individual acts infringing human rights and fundamental freedoms; juridical disputes between the state and local government bodies or among such local government bodies; juridical disputes between the National Assembly, the President of the Republic and the Government; and unconstitutional acts or activities of political parties.

# SLOVENIA

## The Government

### HEAD OF STATE

**President:** MILAN KUČAN (directly elected on 6 December 1992).

### GOVERNMENT
(June 1995)

A coalition of Liberal Democracy of Slovenia (LDS), the Associated List of Social Democrats (ZLSD), the Slovenian Christian Democrats (SKD) and independents (Ind.).

**Prime Minister:** Dr JANEZ DRNOVŠEK (LDS).
**Minister of Economic Affairs:** Dr MAKS TAJNIKAR (ZLSD).
**Minister of Economic Relations and Development:** JANKO DEŽELAK (SKD).
**Minister of Finance:** MITJA GASPARI (Ind.).
**Minister of Defence:** JELKO KACIN (LDS).
**Minister of Internal Affairs:** ANDREJ ŠTER (SKD).
**Minister of Justice:** META ZUPANČIČ (Ind.).
**Minister of Labour, Family and Social Affairs:** RINA KLINAR (ZLSD).
**Minister of the Environment and Regional Planning:** Dr PAVEL GANTAR (LDS).
**Minister of Foreign Affairs:** ZORAN THALER (LDS).
**Minister of Agriculture and Forestry:** Dr JOŽE OSTERC (SKD).
**Minister of Transport and Communications:** IGOR UMEK (SKD).
**Minister of Health:** Dr BOŽIDAR VOLJČ (LDS).
**Minister of Education and Sport:** Dr SLAVKO GABER (LDS).
**Minister of Culture:** SERGIJ PELHAN (ZLSD).
**Minister of Science and Technology:** Dr RADO BOHINC (ZLSD).
**Minister without Portfolio (responsible for legislation):** LOJZE JANKO (Ind.).
**Minister without Portfolio (responsible for local self-government):** BOŠTJAN KOVAČIČ (LDS).

### MINISTRIES

**Office of the President:** 61000 Ljubljana, Erjavčeva 17; tel. (61) 1259280; fax (61) 1251275.

**Office of the Prime Minister:** 61000 Ljubljana, Gregorčičeva st. 20; tel. (61) 224200; telex 06231284; fax (61) 224240.

**Ministry of Agriculture and Forestry:** 61000 Ljubljana, Parmova 33; tel. (61) 323643; fax (61) 313631.

**Ministry of Culture:** 61000 Ljubljana, Cankarjeva 5; tel. (61) 1259071; fax (61) 210814.

**Ministry of Defence:** 61000 Ljubljana, Kardeljeva ploščad 24–26; tel. (61) 1331111; fax (61) 1319145.

**Ministry of Economic Affairs:** 61000 Ljubljana, Kotnikova 5; tel. (61) 1713311; fax (61) 1331031.

**Ministry of Economic Relations and Development:** 61000 Ljubljana, Kotnikova 5; tel. (61) 1713311; fax (61) 1713544.

**Ministry of Education and Sport:** 61000 Ljubljana, Župančičeva 6; tel. (61) 1765443; fax (61) 214820.

**Ministry of the Environment and Regional Planning:** 61000 Ljubljana, Župančičeva 6; tel. (61) 1765211; fax (61) 224548.

**Ministry of Finance:** 61000 Ljubljana, Župančičeva 3; tel. (61) 1765211; fax (61) 214640.

**Ministry of Foreign Affairs:** 61000 Ljubljana, Gregorčičeva 25; tel. (61) 1250300; fax (61)1256275.

**Ministry of Health:** 61000 Ljubljana, Štefanova 5; tel. (61) 1251028; fax (62) 217752.

**Ministry of Internal Affairs:** 61000 Ljubljana, Štefanova 2; tel. (61) 1325125; fax (61) 214330.

**Ministry of Justice:** 61000 Ljubljana, Župančičeva 3; tel. (61) 1765279; fax (61) 210200.

**Ministry of Labour, Family and Social Affairs:** 61000 Ljubljana, Kotnikova 5; tel. (61) 1713311; fax (61) 1713456.

**Ministry of Science and Technology:** 61000 Ljubljana, Slovenska 50; tel. (61) 1311107; fax (61) 1324140.

**Ministry of Transport and Communications:** 61000 Ljubljana, Prešernova 23; tel. (61) 1256256; fax (61) 218707.

## President and Legislature

### PRESIDENT

**Election, 6 December 1992**

| Candidate | % of votes |
|---|---|
| MILAN KUČAN | 63.93 |
| IVAN BIZJAK | 21.14 |
| JELKO KACIN | 7.29 |
| STANISLAV BUSAR | 1.93 |
| DARJA LAVTIŽAR-BEBLER | 1.82 |
| ALENKA ŽAGAR-SLANA | 1.74 |
| LJUBO SIRC | 1.51 |
| FRANCE TOMŠIČ | 0.63 |
| **Total** | **100.00** |

### DRŽAVNI ZBOR
(National Assembly)

**President:** JOŽEF ŠKOLJČ; 61000 Ljubljana, Šubičeva st. 4; tel. (61) 1258022; fax (61) 1258160.

**General Election, 6 December 1992**

| Party | Directly elected | Indirectly elected | % of votes |
|---|---|---|---|
| Liberal Democratic Party (LDS)* | 17 | 5 | 23.5 |
| Slovenian Christian Democrats (SKD) | 8 | 7 | 14.5 |
| Associated List (ZL)† | 8 | 6 | 13.6 |
| Slovenian National Party (SNS) | 3 | 9 | 10.0 |
| Slovenian People's Party (SLS) | 2 | 8 | 8.7 |
| Democratic Party (DS)* | — | 6 | 5.0 |
| Greens of Slovenia (ZS)* | — | 5 | 3.7 |
| Social Democratic Party of Slovenia (SDSS) | — | 4 | 3.3 |
| Others | — | — | 17.9 |
| **Total** | **38** | **50** | **100.0** |

* In March 1994 the LDS, the DS, the ZS—Eco-Social Party (as the parliamentary grouping of the ZS had become) and the Socialist Party of Slovenia (not represented in the Državni Zbor) merged to form Liberal Democracy of Slovenia (LDS). The new party numbered 30 members of parliament.

† Later renamed the Associated List of Social Democrats (ZLSD).

Note: During 1993–94 there were numerous changes in party allegiances within the Državni Zbor. In mid-1994 the composition of the assembly was reported to be LDS 30; SKD 15; ZSLD 14; SLS 12; SDSS 6; SNS 4; Democratic Party of Slovenia (founded by DS members who opted not to join the LDS) 4; Independent Deputies Group (founded by former members of the SNS) 3.

### DRŽAVNI SVET
(National Council)

**President:** Dr IVAN KRISTAN; 61000 Ljubljana, Šubičeva st. 4; tel. (61) 1261222; fax (61) 212251.

## Political Organizations

**Associated List of Social Democrats** (Združena lista socialnih demokratov—ZLSD): 61000 Ljubljana, Levstikova 15; tel. (61) 215897; fax (61) 1261170; f. 1992 as the Associated List, an electoral alliance of the Democratic Party of Pensioners, Social Democratic Reform of Slovenia, the Social Democratic Union and the Workers' Party of Slovenia; in 1993 it became a single party and adopted its current name; Pres. JANEZ KOCIJANČIČ; 23,000 mems.

**Christian Social Union:** Ljubljana; f. 1995; Pres. FRANC MIKLAVIČ; Sec.-Gen. IVAN KEPIČ.

**Democratic Party of Slovenia:** 61000 Ljubljana, Tomšičeva 5; tel. (61) 1261073; fax (61) 1255077; f. 1994 by mems of Democratic Party who opted not to join the LDS (see below); Pres. TONE PERŠAK; 2,200 mems.

**Greens of Slovenia** (Zeleni Slovenije—ZS): 61000 Ljubljana; f. 1993, following split in fmr ZS (f. 1989); Leader VANE GOŠNIK.

**Independent Deputies Group:** 61000 Ljubljana; tel. (61) 150256; f. 1993 by five parliamentary mems of SNS (see below); Leader SAŠO LAP.

SLOVENIA

**Liberal Democracy of Slovenia** (Liberalna demokracija Slovenije—LDS): 61000 Ljubljana, trg Republike 3; tel. (61) 312659; fax (61) 1256150; f. 1994 by merger of Greens of Slovenia—Eco-Social Party, Democratic Party, Liberal Democratic Party and Socialist Party of Slovenia; Pres. Dr JANEZ DRNOVŠEK; 18,000 mems.

**National Democratic Party** (Narodni Demokratska stranka—NDS): 61000 Ljubljana; withdrew from SKD 1994; Pres. MARJAN VIDMAR.

**Party of Democratic Reform** (Stranka Demokratskih Reformi—SDR): 61000 Ljubljana, Šubičeva st. 4; former League of Communists of Slovenia, disaffiliated from the League of Communists of Yugoslavia and changed name in 1990; left-wing; Pres. CIRIL RIBIČIČ; Parl. Group Leader MIRAN POTIČ.

**Slovenian Christian Democrats** (Slovenski krščanski demokrati—SKD): 61000 Ljubljana, Beethovnova 4; tel. (61) 1262179; fax (61) 211738; f. 1989; centrist, conservative party; mem. of European Union of Christian Democrats and of European Democratic Union; Pres. LOJZE PETERLE; Sec. Gen. VIDA ČADONIČ-ŠPELIČ; Parl. Group Leader IGNAC POLAJNAR; 34,000 mems.

**Slovenian National Party** (Slovenska nacionalna stranka—SNS): 61000 Ljubljana, Tivolska 13; tel. (61) 224241; fax (61) 213294; f. 1991; right-wing nationalist party; Pres. ZMAGO JELINČIČ; Sec.-Gen. JURE JESENKO; 4,000 mems.

**Slovenian National Right** (Slovenska Nacionalna Desnica—SND): f. 1993 by a 'breakaway' faction of the SNS.

**Slovenian People's Party** (Slovenska ljudska stranka—SLS): 61000 Ljubljana, Zarnikova 3; tel. (61) 301891; fax (61) 301871; f. 1989 as the Slovenian Farmers' Association; conservative; Pres. MARJAN PODOBNIK; 40,000 mems.

**Social Democratic Party of Slovenia** (Socialdemokratska stranka Slovenije—SDSS): 61000 Ljubljana, Komenskega 11; tel. (61) 314086; fax (61) 301143; f. 1989; centre-left; Pres. JANEZ JANŠA; Sec.-Gen. BRANKO GRIMS; Parl. Group Leader IVO HVALICA; 10,000 mems.

**United List of Social Democrats of Slovenia:** 61000 Ljubljana; f. 1990; Pres. Dr RADO BOHINC.

## Diplomatic Representation

### EMBASSIES IN SLOVENIA

**Albania:** 61000 Ljubljana, Ob Ljubljanici 12; tel. (61) 1322324; fax (61) 1323129; Ambassador: NAPOLEON DHIMITER ROSHI.

**Austria:** 61000 Ljubljana, Štrekljeva 5; tel. (61) 213436; fax (61) 221717; Ambassador: Dr JUTTA STEFAN-BASTL.

**Bosnia and Herzegovina:** 61000 Ljubljana, Likozarjeva 6; tel. (61) 1322214; fax (61) 1322230; Ambassador: UGLJEŠA UZELAC.

**Bulgaria:** 61000 Ljubljana, Ziherlova 6; tel. and fax (61) 213643; Chargé d'affaires a.i.: GANCHO GANEV.

**China, People's Republic:** 61000 Ljubljana, Stara Slovenska 1; tel. (61) 1402383; fax (61) 1404007; Ambassador: LU PEIXIN.

**Croatia:** 61000 Ljubljana, Grubarjevo nabrežje 6; tel (61) 211635; fax (61) 1258106; Ambassador: MILJENKO ŽAGAR.

**Czech Republic:** 61000 Ljubljana, Kolarjeva 30; tel. (61) 1331354; fax (61) 1328035; Ambassador: PETR KYPR.

**France:** 61109 Ljubljana, Robbova 18/VI; tel. (61) 1734441; fax (61) 1734442; Ambassador: BERNARD PONCET.

**Germany:** 61000 Ljubljana, Prešernova 27, p.p. 85; tel. (61) 216166; fax (61) 1254210; Ambassador: Dr GÜNTHER SEIBERT.

**Holy See:** 61000 Ljubljana, Tabor 3; tel. (61) 1314133; fax (61) 1315130; Apostolic Nuncio: (vacant).

**Hungary:** 61000 Ljubljana, Dunajska 22, VI; tel. (61) 1315168; fax (61) 1317143; Ambassador: Dr ISTVÁN BALOGH.

**Italy:** 61000 Ljubljana, Snežniška 8; tel. (61) 1262194; fax (61) 1253302; Ambassador: LUIGI SOLARI.

**Macedonia, former Yugoslav republic:** 61000 Ljubljana, Dunajska 104; tel. (61) 1684454; fax (61) 1685181; Ambassador: DIMITAR MIRČEV.

**Romania:** 61000 Ljubljana, Nanoška 8; tel. and fax (61) 268702; Chargé d'affaires: MARIAN PAVELESCU.

**Russia:** 61000 Ljubljana, Rožna dolina, Cesta II, št 7; tel. (61) 261189; fax (61) 1254141; Chargé d'affaires: YURIY S. GIRENKO.

**Turkey:** 61000 Ljubljana, Livarska 4; tel. (61) 1322012; fax (61) 1323158; Ambassador: ILHAN YIGITBASIOGLU.

**United Kingdom:** 61000 Ljubljana, trg Republike 3, VI; tel. (61) 1257191; fax (61) 1250174; Ambassador: GORDON MACKENZIE JOHNSTON.

**USA:** 61000 Ljubljana, Pražakova 4; tel. (61) 301427; fax (61) 301401; Ambassador: ALLAN WENDT.

## Judicial System

The 1991 Constitution guarantees the independence of the judiciary.

The 44 district courts decide minor cases (criminal acts incurring a maximum sentence of three years' imprisonment, property disputes where the value of the disputed property is not more than SIT 2m., and certain other civil cases). The 11 regional courts act as courts of the first instance in all cases other than those for which the district courts have jurisdiction. Four regional courts act as courts of the second instance. In addition, labour courts have jurisdiction in labour disputes, and social courts adjudicate in disputes over pensions, welfare allocations and other social benefits. A higher labour and social court has jurisdiction in the second instance. The Supreme Court is the highest authority for civil and criminal law. There is also a Constitutional Court, composed of nine judges, each elected for a single term of nine years, which determines, *inter alia*, the conformity of national legislation and all other regulations with the Constitution.

**Constitutional Court of the Republic of Slovenia:** 61000 Ljubljana, Beethovnova 10; tel. (61) 210448; fax (61) 210451; Pres. Dr PETER JAMBREK.

**Supreme Court:** 61000 Ljubljana, Tavčarjeva 9; tel. (61) 1323133; fax (61) 303051; Pres. FRANCKA STRNOLE-HLASTEC.

**Office of the Public Prosecutor:** 61000 Ljubljana, Tavčarjeva 9; Public Prosecutor ANTON DROBNIČ.

**Office of the Public Attorney:** 61000 Ljubljana, Cankarjeva 5; Public Attorney JOŽE GREGORIČ.

## Religion

Most of the population are Christian, predominantly adherents of the creeds of the Roman Catholic Church. The Archbishop of Ljubljana is the most senior Roman Catholic prelate in Slovenia. There is also a Slovene Old Catholic Church, but there are few Protestant Christians, despite the importance of a Calvinist sect (Church of Carniola) to the development of Slovene literature in the 16th century. There are some members of the Eastern Orthodox Church, some who profess Islam and a small Jewish community.

### CHRISTIANITY

#### The Roman Catholic Church

The Roman Catholic Church in Slovenia comprises one archdiocese and two dioceses. At 31 December 1993 there were an estimated 1,666,915 adherents (equivalent to about 84% of the total population).

**Bishops' Conference:** Slovenska Škofovska Konferenca, 61000 Ljubljana, p.p. 121/III, Ciril Metodov trg 4; tel. (61) 1314166; fax (61) 314169; f. 1993; Pres. Most Rev. ALOJZIJ ŠUŠTAR, Archbishop of Ljubljana.

**Archbishop of Ljubljana:** Most Rev. ALOJZIJ ŠUŠTAR, 61001 Ljubljana, p.p. 121/III, Ciril Metodov trg 4; tel. (61) 310673; fax (61) 314169.

#### Old Catholic Church

**Slovene Old Catholic Church:** Ljubljana, trg Francoske revolucije 1/I; Maribor, Vita Kraigherja 2; f. 1948; Bishop Rev. JOSIP KVOČIĆ.

#### The Protestant Church

**Evangelical Lutheran Church of Slovenia:** Headquarters: 69000 Murska Sobota, Slovenska 15; tel. and fax (69) 22304; f. 1561; 18,900 mems; Chair. LUDVIK NOVAK.

## The Press

The publications listed below are in Slovene, unless otherwise indicated.

### PRINCIPAL DAILIES

**Delo:** 61000 Ljubljana, Dunajska 5; tel. (61) 1318255; telex 31255; fax (61) 1334032; f. 1959; morning; Editor TIT DOBERŠEK; circ. 90,000.

**Dnevnik:** 61000 Ljubljana, Kopitarjeva 2; tel. (61) 125261; telex 31177; fax (61) 312775; f. 1951; evening; independent; Editor-in-Chief ZLATKO ŠETINC; Exec.-Editor ROBERT MECILOŠEK; circ. 74,000.

**Primorski Dnevnik:** CP 559, Trieste, Italy; tel. (40) 7796600; fax (40) 772418; Man. Editor VOJIMIR TAVCAR.

**Republika:** 62000 Maribor, Svelozarevska 14; tel. (62) 26951; fax (62) 227645; f. 1992; Editor-in-Chief MARJAN SEDMAK; circ. 30,000.

# SLOVENIA

**Slovenec:** 61000 Ljubljana, Dunajska 9; tel. (61) 320841; fax (61) 320179; f. 1991; Editor-in-Chief JOZE MLAKAR; circ. 32,000.

**Slovenske novice:** 61000 Ljubljana, Dunajska 5; tel. (61) 115315; fax (61) 318193; f. 1991; Editor-in-Chief and Man. Editor MARJAN BAUER; circ. 46,000.

**Večer:** 62101 Maribor, E. Svetozarevska 14; tel. (62) 224221; telex 33183; fax (62) 227736; f. 1949; Man. Dir BOŽO ZORKO; Editor-in-Chief MILAN PREDAN; circ. 65,000.

## PERIODICALS

**Antena:** 61000 Ljubljana, Slovenska 15; tel. (61) 221991; fax (61) 221967; f 1965; weekly; youth magazine concerned with popular culture; Editor-in-Chief ALEKSANDER LUCU; circ. 25,000.

**Ars Vivendi:** 61000 Ljubljana, Poljanska 6; tel. and fax (61) 317058; f. 1987; quarterly; visual arts and design; publ. in Slovene and English; Editor-in-Chief SONJA TOMAŽIČ; circ. 10,000.

**Auto magazin:** 61000 Ljubljana, Dunajska 5; tel. (61) 319180; telex 31255; fax (61) 319873; f. 1967; fortnightly; cars, motor-cycles and sports; Editor MARTIN ČESENJ; circ. 26,000.

**Delavska enotnost:** 61000 Ljubljana, Dalmatinova 4; tel. (61) 1310033; fax (61) 1313942; f. 1942; weekly; trade union issues; Dir and Editor-in-Chief MARJAN HORVAT; circ. 16,000.

**Delo Plus:** 61000 Ljubljana, Dunajska 5; tel. (61) 118255; fax (61) 302339; weekly tabloid; Editor-in-Chief MARJAN RAZTRESEN.

**Dolenjski List:** 68000 Novo Mesto, Glavni trg 24; tel. (68) 23606; fax (68) 24200; f. 1950; weekly; general and local information; Editor-in-Chief DRAGO RUSTJA; circ. 24,000.

**Druzina:** 61000 Ljubljana, p.p. 95, Trubarjeva 82; tel. (61) 1316202; fax (61) 1316152; f. 1952; Christian; Editor-in-Chief JANEZ GRIL; circ. 70,000.

**Ekipa:** 61260 Ljubljana, Vevska 52; tel. (61) 482469; fax (61) 483710; weekly; Editor-in-Chief SLAVKO SAKELSEK.

**Finance:** 61000 Ljubljana, Dunajska 5; tel. (61) 319380; fax (61) 1312223; f. 1992; 2 a week; Editor-in-Chief DUŠAN SNOJ; circ. 8,500.

**Gea:** 61000 Ljubljana, Nazoreva 1; tel. (61) 210339; fax (61) 1259259; f. 1943; monthly; popular science; Editor BORIS BOGATAJ; circ. 6,500.

**Glasbena Mladina:** 61000 Ljubljana, Kersnikova 4; tel. (61) 322570; monthly; music; Editor-in-Chief KAJA SIVIČ.

**Gorenjski glas:** 64000 Kranj, Zoisova 1; tel. (64) 223111; fax (64) 222917; f. 1947; 2 a week; general and regional information; Editor-in-Chief MARKO VALJAVEC; circ. 25,000.

**Gospodarski vestnik:** 61000 Ljubljana, Dunajska 5; tel. (61) 135315; fax (61) 1322115; f. 1952; weekly; business; Editor-in-Chief DUŠAN SNOJ; circ. 9,500.

**Jana:** 61000 Ljubljana, Dunajska 5; tel. (61) 1318255; fax (61) 319873; f. 1972; weekly; women's interest; Editor-in-Chief BERNARDA JEKLIN; circ. 62,000.

**Kaj:** 62000 Maribor, Svetozarevska 14; tel. (62) 26951; fax (62) 227736; f. 1984; weekly; popular; Editor-in-Chief MILAN PREDAN; circ. 16,500.

**Kmečki glas:** 61000 Ljubljana, p.p. 47, Železna 14; tel. (61) 1735350; fax (61) 1735376; Dir BORIS DOLNIČAR; circ. 38,500.

**Lipov List:** 61000 Ljubljana, Miklosičeva 38/6; tel. (61) 312087; fax (61) 557650; tabloid; Editor-in-Chief BORIS BALZELJ.

**Manager:** 61000 Ljubljana, Dunajska 5; tel. (61) 319380; fax (61) 1322115; f. 1990; monthly; business management; Editor-in-Chief DUŠAN SNOJ; circ. 5,000.

**Mladina:** 61000 Ljubljana, Resljeva 16; tel. (61) 1328175; fax (61) 1331239; f. 1942; weekly; news magazine; Editor-in-Chief ROBERT BOTTERI; circ. 30,000.

**Moj Mikro:** 61000 Ljubljana, Dunajska 5; tel. (61) 319798; fax (61) 319873; monthly; personal computers; Editor-in-Chief ALJOSA VRECAR.

**Naš Caš** (Our Time): 63320 Velenje, Foltova 10; tel. (63) 855450; fax (63) 851990; f. 1956; weekly; general and regional information; Editor-in-Chief STANE VOVK; circ. 6,250.

**Nedeljski Dnevnik:** 61000 Ljubljana, Kopitarieva 2; tel. (61) 1325261; telex 31177; fax (61) 1321020; f. 1961; weekly; popular; Editor-in-Chief VASO GASAR; circ. 171,000.

**Nova Doba** (New Era): 63000 Celje, Askerceva 15; tel. (63) 441215; fax (63) 25849; weekly; tabloid; Editor-in-Chief JANEZ SEVER.

**Nova Revija:** 61000 Ljublijana, Cankarjeva 10B; tel. (61) 219125; fax (61) 223087; monthly; literary; Editor-in-Chief NIKO GRAFEN-AUER.

**Novi Tednik** (New Weekly): 63000 Celje, p.p. 161, V. Kongresa trg 3A; tel. (63) 29431; fax (63) 441032; f. 1945; weekly; general and local information; Editor-in-Chief BRANE STAMEJČIČ; circ. 16,980.

**Obrtnik:** 61000 Ljubljana, Celovška 71; tel. (61) 1593241; fax (61) 559270; f. 1971; monthly; small businesses; Editor-in-Chief MIRAN JAREC; circ. 58,000.

**Pavliha:** 61000 Ljubljana, Slovenska 15; tel. (61) 221661; monthly; satire; Editor-in-Chief JOZE PETELIN.

**PIL:** 61000 Ljubljana, Nazorjeva 1; tel. (61) 210261; fax (61) 210313; Editor-in-Chief SUZANA SOSTER.

**Primorske Novice:** 66000 Koper, Ulica OF 12; tel. (66) 23561; fax (66) 25200; f. 1947; bi-weekly; general and regional information; Editor-in-Chief SLOBODAN VALENTINČIČ; circ. 28,000.

**Radio Tednik:** Plus 62250, Raiceva 6; tel. (62) 771261; fax (62) 771223; weekly; Editor-in-Chief FRANC LACEN.

**Razgledi:** 61001 Ljubljana, Dunajska 5, POB 188; tel. (61) 1318255; telex 31255; fax (61) 1334032; f. 1952; fortnightly; political and cultural; Editor MARKO CRNKOVIĆ; circ. 5,000.

**7D:** 62000 Maribor, Svetozarevska 14; tel. (62) 211264; fax (62) 227736; f. 1972; weekly; general, travel; Editor-in-Chief MILAN PREDAN; circ. 26,600.

**Slovenia Weekly:** 61000 Ljubljana, Metodov trg 19; tel. (61) 1334292; fax (61) 1332301; f. 1994; weekly; information about Slovenia; Editor UROS MAHKOVEC.

**Slovenian Business Report:** 61000 Ljubljana, Dunajska 5; tel. (61) 312363; fax (61) 1332301; monthly; in English; Editor-in-Chief TOMAŽ GERDINA.

**Slovenija:** 61000 Ljubljana, Cankarjeva 1; tel. (61) 210716; fax (61) 210732; f. 1987; quarterly; news about Slovenia in English; Man. Ed. JOZE PRESEREN.

**Slovenske brazde:** 61000 Ljubljana, Zarnikova 3; tel. (61) 301891; fax (61) 301871; f. 1990; weekly; Man. Ed. NACE POTOCNIK.

**Stop:** 61000 Ljubljana, Dunajska 5; tel. (61) 1318255; fax (61) 319190; f. 1967; weekly; leisure, film, theatre, pop music, radio and television programmes; Editor IGOR SAVIČ; circ. 50,000.

**Tednik Ptuj:** 62250 Ptuj, Rječeva 6; tel. (62) 771261; fax (62) 771223; f. 1948; weekly; politics, local information; Editor-in-Chief FRANC LAČEN; circ. 15,000.

**Treti Dan** (Third Day): 61000 Ljubljana, Jucicev trg 2; tel. (61) 211136; fax (61) 223836; weekly; Editor-in-Chief JOZE KURILCIC.

**Tribuna:** 61000 Ljubljana, Kersnikova 4; tel. (61) 319496; fax (61) 319448; student newspaper; Editor-in-Chief BOJAN KORENINI.

**Vestnik Murska Sobota:** 69000 Murska Sobota, Arhitekta Novaka 13; tel. (69) 31960; fax (69) 32175; weekly; popular; Editor-in-Chief JANKO VOTEK; circ. 25,500.

**Zdravje** (Health): 61000 Ljubljana, Dunajska 5; tel. (61) 319360; monthly; Editor-in-Chief JOZE VETROVEC.

## PRESS AGENCY

**Slovenska Tiskovna Agencija (STA):** 61101 Ljubljana, Cankarjeva 5, p.p. 145; tel. (61) 1262222; fax (61) 301321; f. 1991; Dir DUŠICA JURMAN; Dir-Gen. and Editor-in-Chief TADEJ LABERNIK.

# Publishers

**Cankarjeva založba:** 61000 Ljubljana, Kopitarjeva 2; tel. (61) 323841; telex 31821; fax (61) 318782; f. 1945; philosophy, science and popular science; dictionaries and reference books; Slovenian and translated literature; import and export; international co-productions; Dir-Gen. JANEZ STANIČ.

**DZS d.d.:** 61000 Ljubljana, Mestni trg 26; tel. (61) 211711; fax (61) 215675; f. 1945; Slovenian textbooks, manuals, Slovenian authors, world classics, natural sciences, art books, dictionaries; import and export; Mans ANDREJ POGLAJEN, IRENA JUNKAR.

**Mladinska knjiga:** 61000 Ljubljana, Slovenska 29; tel. (61) 161300; telex 31345; fax (61) 215320; f. 1945; books for youth and children, including general, fiction, science, travel and school books; international co-operation; Dir MILAN MATOS.

**Slovenska Matica:** 61000 Ljubljana, Kongresni trg 8; tel. (61) 214200; f. 1864; poetry, science, philosophy; Pres. Prof. Dr JOŽA MAHNIČ.

**Založba Obzorja:** 62000 Maribor, Partizanska 3–5; tel. (62) 28971; telex 33255; fax (62) 26696; f. 1950; popular science, general literature, periodicals, etc.; Man. Dir FRANC FILIPIĆ.

**Zdo Založba Lipa Koper:** 66000 Koper, Muzejski trg 7; tel. (66) 23291; fax (66) 23293; fiction; Dir Prof. JOŽE A. HOČEVAR.

SLOVENIA
*Directory*

## Radio and Television

Radiotelevizija Slovenija is the state broadcasting authority. There are, in addition, more than 20 regional and local radio stations, two regional television stations (operating as part of Televizija Slovenia) and one private television station broadcasting nationally; more than 20 local cable television stations also operate.

**Radiotelevizija Slovenija** (Slovenian Radio and Television): 61000 Ljubljana, Kolodvorska 2–4; tel. (61) 1311333; telex 32283; fax (61) 1319171; f. 1928 (radio), 1958 (television); 3 radio programmes and 2 television programmes nationally; broadcasts in Slovene, Hungarian and Italian; foreign broadcasts in English, German and French; Dir-Gen. ZARKO PETAN; Dir (radio) ANDREJ ROT; Dir (television) JANEZ LOMBERGAR (acting).

**Kanal A:** 61101 Ljubljana, Tivolska 50, p.p. 41; tel. (61) 1334133; fax (61) 1334222; f. 1990; private television company; Editor-in-Chief NATALIJA GORŠČAK.

## Finance

### BANKS

(cap. = capital; res = reserves; dep. = deposits; m. = million; amounts in Slovene tolars unless otherwise stated; brs = branches)

The Slovenian banking sector is currently undergoing a rationalization process, involving a conversion to Western-style commercial banking (new regulations having come into effect in January 1995) and the merging of smaller banks.

#### National Bank

**Banka Slovenije** (Bank of Slovenia): 61001 Ljubljana, Slovenska 35, p.p. 440; tel. (61) 1257333; telex 31214; fax (61) 215516; formerly National Bank of Slovenia, as part of the Yugoslav banking system; assumed central bank functions in 1991; bank of issue since Oct. 1991; cap. and res 21,494m., dep. 165,198m., total assets 238,392m. (Dec. 1994); Gov. Dr FRANCE ARHAR; Dep. Gov. BOGOMIR KOS.

#### Selected Banks

**Abanka d.d. Ljubljana** (Abanka Joint-Stock Company): 61001 Ljubljana, Slovenska 58, POB 368; tel. (61) 1718100; telex 31228; fax (61) 1325165; f. 1955 as Ljubljana Branch of Yugoslav Bankfor Foreign Trade, adopted current name 1989; total assets US $427m. (Sept. 1994); Pres. and Chief Exec. MIROSLAV KERT; 35 brs.

**Bank Austria d.d.:** 61000 Ljubljana, Wolfova 1; tel. (61) 1262225; telex 39153; fax (61) 211217; Dir PETER SETZER.

**Banka Celje d.d.:** 63000 Celje, Vodnikova 2; tel. (63) 431000; telex 36537; fax (63) 25118; Dir. NIKO KAČ.

**Banka Creditanstalt d.d.:** 61000 Ljubljana, Kotnikova 5; tel. (61) 1321714; fax (61) 1325206; f. 1990; Gen. Man. MARJAN KANDUS; 4 brs.

**Dolenjska Banka d.d.:** 68000 Novo Mesto, Seidlova 3; tel. (68) 321130; telex 35736; fax (68) 321019; Man. Dir FRANCI BORSAN.

**Komercialna Banka Nova Gorica d.d.:** 65000 Nova Gorica, Kidričeva 11; tel. (65) 27811; telex 38347; fax (65) 27481; f. 1978; name changed 1994; Man. Dir DUŠAN ŠINIGOJ; 25 brs.

**Kreditna Banka Maribor d.d.:** 62001 Maribor, Vita Kraigherja 4; tel. (62) 223311; telex 33167; fax (62) 224333; f. 1955, name changed 1993; Pres. and Chief Exec. ANDREJ HAZABENT; 3 brs.

**Ljubljanska Banka Dolenjska Banka d.d.:** 68000 Novo Mesto, Kettejev Drevored 1; tel. (68) 22213; telex 35736; fax (68) 28213; f. 1978; Dir FRANCI BORSAN; 20 brs.

**Ljubljanska Banka Domžale Banka d.d.:** 61230 Domžale, Ljubljanska 62; tel. (61) 715422; fax (61) 722422; f. 1978; Dir VILJEM DRŽANIČ.

**Ljubljanska Banka Gorenjska Banka d.d.:** 64000 Kranj, Bleiweisova 1; tel. (61) 217271; telex 37108; fax (64) 218167; f. 1978; Dir ZLATKO KAVČIČ; 27 brs.

**Ljubljanska Banka Koroška Banka d.d.:** 62380 Slovenj Gradec, Glavni trg 30; tel. (602) 42371; fax (602) 42382; f. 1978; Dir PETER OROŽEN.

**Ljubljanska Banka Pomurska Banka d.d.:** 69000 Murska Sobota, trg Zmage 7; tel. (69) 32710; fax (69) 31296; f. 1978; Dir VICTOR ŠBÜL.

**Ljubljanska Banka Posarska Banka d.d.:** 68270 Krško, trg Matije Gubca 1; tel. (608) 21330; fax (608) 22535; f. 1978; Dir DEJAN AVSEC.

**Ljubljanska Banka Splošna Banka d.d. Velenje:** 63320 Velenje, Rudarska 3; tel. (63) 854251; fax (63) 854282; f. 1978; Dir RAFKO BERLOČNIK.

**Nova Ljubljanska Banka d.d.:** 61001 Ljubljana, trg Republike 2; tel. (61) 1250155; telex 31256; fax (61) 222422; f. 1994; commercial, investment and savings bank; cap. US $2,862m. (July 1994); dep. US $1,448m. (July 1994); Pres. and CEO MARKO VOLJČ; 70 brs.

**SKB Banka d.d.:** 61000 Ljubljana, Ajdovščina 4; tel. (61) 312396; telex 39144; fax (61) 302808; f. 1965; cap. US $96.3m., dep. $330.3m. (Dec. 1992); Pres. IVAN NERAD; more than 40 brs.

**Splošna Banka Koper d.d.:** 66000 Koper, Pristaniška 14; tel. (66) 451100; telex 34187; fax (66) 37842; f. 1978; Dir. VOJKO ČOK; 23 brs.

**UBK Univerzalna Banka:** 61111 Ljubljana, Tržaška 116; tel. (61) 1231131; fax (61) 273082.

### STOCK EXCHANGE

**Ljubljana Stock Exchange d.d.:** 61000 Ljubljana, Slovenska 56; tel. (61) 1710211; fax (61) 1710213; f. 1989, operative 1990; Pres. and Chief Exec. DRAŠKO VESELINOVIĆ.

## Trade and Industry

### STATE PROPERTY AGENCIES

**Agency for Restructuring and Privatization:** 61000 Ljubljana, Kotnikova 28; tel. (61) 1312122; fax (61) 1316011; Dir MIRA PUC.

**Development Fund of the Republic of Slovenia:** 61000 Ljubljana, Kotnikova 28; tel. (61) 1312122; fax (61) 1312061; Dir UROŠ KORŽE.

### CHAMBERS OF COMMERCE

**Chamber of Economy of Slovenia:** 61000 Ljubljana, Slovenska 41; tel. (61) 1250122; fax (61) 218242; Pres. DAGMAR ŠUSTER.

> **Slovene Businessmen's Association:** 61000 Ljubljana, Slovenska 41; tel. (61) 1250122; fax (61) 218242; f. 1994 as autonomous part of Chamber of Economy of Slovenia; Pres. FRANC ZAVODNIK; 1,300 mems.

**Chamber of Small Businesses of Slovenia:** 61000 Ljubljana, Celovška 71; tel. (61) 1593241; fax (61) 559270; Pres. MIHA GRAH; 50,000 mems.

### TRADE UNIONS

**The Association of Independent Trade Unions of Slovenia:** 61000 Ljubljana, Dalmatinova 4; tel. (61) 317983; fax (61) 316895; Pres. DUŠAN SEMOLIČ.

**Independence—Confederation of New Trade Unions of Slovenia:** 61000 Ljubljana, Linhartova 13; tel. (61) 1329141; fax (61) 302868; Pres. FRANCE TOMŠIČ.

## Transport

### RAILWAYS

The rail link between western Europe and Greece, Turkey and the Near and Middle East runs through Slovenia. In 1993 there were 1,201 km of railway lines in Slovenia, of which 499 km were electrified. The renovation and modernization of some 200 km of track during 1994–96 was to be undertaken with financial assistance from the European Union and the European Bank for Reconstruction and Development.

**Slovenske Železnice** (SŽ—Slovenian Railways): 61000 Ljubljana, Kolodvorska 11; tel. (61) 325989; fax (61) 317262.

### ROADS

In 1994 the country had 14,794 km of roads, of which some 90% were tarmac-covered. A 56-km motorway links Ljubljana, Postojna and Razdrto with the coastal region in the south-west, and a 25-km motorway connects the capital with Kranj and the Gorenjska region in the north-east. Construction of a further 128 km of main roads, including 88 km of motorway, was scheduled to begin in late 1994.

### SHIPPING

Slovenia's principal international trading port, at Koper, handles some 6m. tons of freight annually, and has terminals for general, bulk and liquid cargo, containers and 'roll on, roll off' traffic, as well as warehousing facilities. The port is a duty-free zone. There are also major ports at Portorož and Izola.

**Port of Koper:** 66000 Koper, Vojkovo nabrežje 38; tel. (66) 456100; telex 34110; fax (66) 34418.

## Principal Shipping Company

**Splošna Plovba Piran:** 66320 Portorož, Obala 55; tel. (66) 73881; telex 34122; fax (66) 34078; transport of all types of cargo; regular liner service.

### CIVIL AVIATION

There are three international airports in Slovenia, at Brnik (Ljubljana), Maribor and Portorož.

**Adria Airways:** 61000 Ljubljana, Kuzmičeva 7; tel. (61) 1334336; telex 31268; fax (61) 323356; f. 1961; operates international scheduled services to destinations in Europe and the Near and Middle East; Pres. PETER GRASEK.

**Solinair** commenced a daily service to Vienna (Austria) in April 1992.

# Tourism

Slovenia offers a variety of attractions for the tourist, including Mediterranean beaches to the west, the Alps to the north and the 'karst' limestone regions, with more than 6,000 caves. The number of foreign tourist arrivals (including visitors from other parts of former Yugoslavia) was 627,283 in 1994, compared with 1,885,500 in 1990. According to the Bank of Slovenia, income from tourism was more than US $900m. in 1994.

**Centre of Tourism and Economic Promotion (Chamber of Economy of Slovenia):** 61000 Ljubljana, Igriška 5; tel. (61) 156172; fax (61) 157323; Dir RUDI TAVČAR.

**Tourist Association of Slovenia:** 61000 Ljubljana, Milošičeva 38; tel. (61) 1320141; fax (61) 1332338; Pres. Dr MARJAN ROŽIČ.

# SOLOMON ISLANDS

## Introductory Survey

**Location, Climate, Language, Religion, Flag, Capital**

Solomon Islands is a scattered Melanesian archipelago in the south-western Pacific Ocean, east of Papua New Guinea. The country includes most of the Solomon Islands (those to the north-west being part of Papua New Guinea), Ontong Java Islands (Lord Howe Atoll), Rennell Island and the Santa Cruz Islands, about 500 km (300 miles) to the east. The climate is equatorial, with small seasonal variations, governed by the trade winds. In Honiara the average temperature is about 27°C (81°F) and the average annual rainfall about 2,160 mm (85 ins). The official language is standard English, although pidgin English is more widely used and understood. More than 80 different local languages exist, and no vernacular is common to the whole country. More than 95% of the inhabitants profess Christianity, and most of the remainder follow traditional beliefs. The national flag (proportions 2 by 1) comprises two triangles, one of blue (with its base at the hoist and its apex in the upper fly) and one of dark green (with its base in the fly and its apex in the lower hoist), separated by a narrow yellow diagonal stripe (from lower hoist to upper fly), with five white five-pointed stars (arranged to form a diagonal cross) in the upper hoist. The capital is Honiara, on the island of Guadalcanal.

**Recent History**

The northern Solomon Islands became a German protectorate in 1885 and the southern Solomons a British protectorate in 1893. Rennell Island and the Santa Cruz Islands were added to the British protectorate in 1898 and 1899. Germany ceded most of the northern Solomons and Ontong Java Islands to the United Kingdom between 1898 and 1900. The whole territory, known as the British Solomon Islands Protectorate, was placed under the jurisdiction of the Western Pacific High Commission (WPHC), with its headquarters in Fiji.

The Solomon Islands were invaded by Japan in 1942, but, after a fierce battle on Guadalcanal, most of the islands were recaptured by US forces in 1943. After the Second World War the protectorate's capital was moved from Tulagi Island to Honiara. In January 1953 the headquarters of the WPHC also moved to Honiara. Meanwhile, elected local councils were established on most of the islands, and by 1966 almost the whole territory was covered by such councils.

Under a new Constitution, introduced in October 1960, a Legislative Council and an Executive Council were established for the protectorate's central administration. Initially, all members of both bodies were appointed, but from 1964 the Legislative Council included elected members, and the elective element was gradually increased. Another Constitution, introduced in March 1970, established a single Governing Council of 17 elected members, three *ex-officio* members and (until the end of 1971) up to six public service members. A new Governing Council of 24 directly elected members was formed in 1973, when a ministerial system was introduced.

A further new Constitution, adopted in April 1974, instituted a single Legislative Assembly, containing 24 members who chose a Chief Minister with the right to appoint his own Council of Ministers. A new office of Governor of the Protectorate was also created, to assume almost all of the functions previously exercised in the territory by the High Commissioner for the Western Pacific. Solomon Mamaloni, leader of the newly founded People's Progressive Party (PPP), was appointed the first Chief Minister in August 1974. The territory was officially renamed the Solomon Islands in June 1975, although it retained protectorate status.

In January 1976 the Solomon Islands received internal self-government, with the Chief Minister presiding over the Council of Ministers in place of the Governor. In June elections were held for an enlarged Legislative Assembly, and in July the Assembly elected one of its new members, Peter Kenilorea, to the position of Chief Minister. Solomon Islands (as it was restyled) became an independent state, within the Commonwealth, on 7 July 1978. The Legislative Assembly became the National Parliament and designated Kenilorea the first Prime Minister.

The main political issue confronting the new nation was the proposed decentralization of authority to the regions, support for which was particularly strong in the Western District, the most commercially developed part of the country. In 1979 the PPP merged with the Rural Alliance Party to form the People's Alliance Party (PAP), with Solomon Mamaloni as its leader.

The first general election since independence took place in August 1980. Independent candidates won more seats than any of the three parties. Parliament again elected Kenilorea Prime Minister by an overwhelming majority. In August 1981, however, Parliament approved a motion expressing 'no confidence' in Kenilorea, and chose Mamaloni to succeed him as Prime Minister. In February 1984 notice was given to foreign governments that no warship or military aircraft would be allowed to enter Solomon Islands' airspace or territorial waters unless there had first been a written assurance that it was neither nuclear-powered nor carrying nuclear weapons.

After a scheduled general election to the National Parliament in October 1984, a majority among the minor parties and independent members was decisive in electing Sir Peter Kenilorea (as he had become) to the post of Prime Minister. The new Government consisted of a coalition of nine members of Kenilorea's Solomon Islands United Party (SIUPA), three members of the newly formed Solomone Ano Sagufenua (SAS) party and three independents. The five provincial ministries, established by Mamaloni, were abolished, in accordance with Kenilorea's declared policy of restoring to central government control some of the powers held by the provincial governments.

In October 1985 a new political party, the Nationalist Front for Progress (NFP), was formed, under the leadership of Andrew Nori. He declared that the party aimed to provide an open forum for those wishing to seek solutions to land disputes. The SAS subsequently withdrew its support from the coalition, and Kenilorea formed a new Cabinet, comprising nine members of the SIUPA, three of the NFP and three independents. Kenilorea resigned following the proposal of a third motion expressing 'no confidence' (the previous two having been defeated), and in December he was replaced as Prime Minister by Ezekiel Alebua, the former Deputy Prime Minister. Under Alebua's leadership, Kenilorea became Deputy Prime Minister, and most members of the previous administration retained their posts.

A report by a specially commissioned constitutional review committee, chaired by Mamaloni, was published in March 1988, and proposed that Solomon Islands become a federal republic, while remaining within the Commonwealth. It also recommended that the President of the Republic be a native of the territory. In January 1989 the PAP announced that Solomon Islands would be declared a republic if the party won the next general election, scheduled to take place on 22 February. At the election, several PAP-sponsored candidates successfully sought election as independents. The PAP obtained 11 of the 38 seats, while Alebua's party, the United Party, failed to offer candidates in the majority of constituencies and won only four seats. In March Mamaloni defeated Bartholomew Ulufa'alu, the leader of the Solomon Islands Liberal Party, in a parliamentary ballot and was elected Prime Minister. His Cabinet included the former Governor-General of Solomon Islands, Sir Baddeley Devesi (who had been replaced by Sir George Lepping in July 1988), and was described as the first since independence solely to comprise the members of a single party (following the dissolution of the SAS, whose leader, Allan Qurusu, became an independent member of the Cabinet).

In May 1989 Nori, leader of the NFP and of the parliamentary opposition, challenged the legality of Lepping's appointment, and consequently that of the Government, on the grounds that the Governor-General had not formally resigned his public service commission. The Chief Justice declared Lepping's appointment void (he was appointed again in June), but ruled that his exercise of the office of Governor-General remained valid. Dissatisfaction with Mamaloni's leadership was expressed throughout 1990, and in October he resigned as leader of the PAP, one week before Parliament was due to vote on another motion of 'no confidence' in his premiership. Mamaloni declared that he would remain as an independent Prime Minister, and dismissed five members of the Cabinet, replacing them with four members of the opposition and a PAP back-bencher. Kenilorea became Minister for Foreign Affairs and Trade Relations. Persistent demands for Mamaloni's resignation by more than one-half of the members of Parliament were defied by the Prime Minister. The PAP subsequently asked the remaining 10 ministers to resign their posts in the interests of party unity, but they refused, and in February 1991 were expelled from the party. By establishing a coalition Government and dividing the opposition and the ruling party, Mamaloni's action was widely interpreted as a return to the political traditions of Solomon Islands, based on personalities rather than on organized parties.

The country's economic situation deteriorated throughout 1991, and in November prompted the Solomon Islands Council of Trade Unions to issue an ultimatum demanding Mamaloni's resignation, in order to avert mass industrial action. The opposition (under the new leadership of Joses Tuhanuku) similarly attacked the Government, accusing it of failing to acknowledge the extent of the country's financial difficulties.

At legislative elections on 26 May 1993 the Group for National Unity and Reconciliation, led by Mamaloni, won 21 of the 47 seats in the recently-enlarged National Parliament. Although Mamaloni's party secured the largest number of seats, it failed to achieve the majority necessary to form a government, and on 31 May the main opposition parties and independents agreed to form the National Coalition Partners. At parliamentary elections to the premiership on 18 June an independent member, Francis Billy Hilly (supported by the newly-formed alliance), defeated Mamaloni by a single vote. Among the new Government's stated aims were the immediate investigation of allegations of widespread corruption in the business and public sectors, reductions in government borrowing and public-sector expenditure, a review of foreign policy and the decentralization of certain public services to the provinces. A subsequent challenge by Mamaloni to the validity of Hilly's election was rejected by the High Court in September. However, the Government was seriously destabilized when, following the dismissal of a cabinet minister and the resignation of two others in November, the opposition demanded the resignation of the Prime Minister, claiming that his Government no longer held a majority in the National Parliament. The appointment of three new cabinet members and a reorganization of portfolios in February 1994 appeared to resolve the crisis, although concern remained at the apparent lack of cohesion within the governing alliance.

An attempt in mid-1994 by the head of a Malaysian logging company to bribe the Minister for Commerce, Employment and Trade, in order to secure favourable treatment for his business in Solomon Islands (amid evidence of several similar attempts), highlighted the vulnerability of the country's forestry industry to unscrupulous foreign operators. In recognition of this situation, during a reorganization of cabinet portfolios in July, Hilly transferred the Minister for Commerce to the Ministry of Forests, Environment and Conservation. In September Nori resigned as Minister of Finance, following allegations concerning his personal finances.

In October 1994 a constitutional crisis resulted in several weeks of political confusion, following attempts by the Governor-General, Moses (later Sir Moses) Pitakaka, to dismiss Hilly on the grounds that he no longer held a parliamentary majority. Hilly remained in office, however, with the support of a High Court ruling, and confusion intensified when Pitakaka appointed the opposition leader, Mamaloni, to the position of Prime Minister. Hilly finally resigned on 31 October, and the post was declared vacant. In a parliamentary election to the premiership on 8 November, Mamaloni defeated the former Governor-General, Devesi, by 29 votes to 18. Among the new Government's stated objectives were several major political changes, including proposals to increase the size of the National Parliament and to extend its term to five years, to limit the number of political groups in the country and to allow the party with the largest number of seats in the legislature to form a government, regardless of whether it held a majority. Mamaloni also expressed his intention to conduct a thorough review of the country's current logging policy. Consequently, during late 1994 it was announced that many of the regulations introduced by the previous Government, in an attempt to conserve the islands' forestry resources, were to be repealed or relaxed (see Economic Affairs).

In April 1995 security forces were dispatched to Pavuvu Island (some 50 km north-west of Honiara), following angry protests by islanders who were resisting a compulsory resettlement programme, which the Government had agreed to implement in return for the sale of logging rights (for some 1m. cu m of timber on the island) to a Malaysian company. Some 56 islanders were detained by the security forces after widespread threats by the island's several thousand inhabitants to destroy any logging equipment brought onto Pavuvu.

The Government aroused further controversy in April 1995, when it decided to allow a British ship transporting nuclear material from France to Japan to pass through its waters. The decision attracted criticism from environmentalists and other island nations in the region, many of which had refused the ship permission to cross their maritime borders.

In October 1986 Solomon Islands was one of a group of South Pacific island states to conclude a five-year fishing agreement with the USA, whereby the US tuna fleet was granted a licence to operate vessels within Solomon Islands' exclusive fishing zone. In 1988 Parliament adopted legislation allowing US vessels to fish in only 10% of the zone. Attempts by the South Pacific Forum in 1988 and 1989 to ban drift-net fishing in the region were supported by Solomon Islands, and in December 1991 Japan agreed to cease its drift-net operations by the end of 1992.

In March 1987 talks were held between representatives of the Papua New Guinea and Solomon Islands Governments, following reports of violence on the Shortland Islands and Choiseul Island (in Solomon Islands), whose inhabitants complained that their waters had been 'invaded' by fishermen from Papua New Guinea's North Solomons province. The negotiations resulted in a decision to sign, in June 1987, an agreement on a maritime boundary between the two countries. In 1990, however, relations between Solomon Islands and Papua New Guinea deteriorated, following allegations by the Solomon Islands' Government that patrol boats from Papua New Guinea were interfering with the traditional crossing between Bougainville Island (Papua New Guinea) and the Shortland Islands, while the Papua New Guinea Government accused Solomon Islands of harbouring members of a rebel group, the Bougainville Revolutionary Army (BRA), and of providing them with supplies. In May 1990 Solomon Islands and Papua New Guinea signed an agreement on joint border surveillance and agreed to host peace negotiations between the BRA and the Papua New Guinea Government, at the latter's request. Following the reopening in 1991 of Papua New Guinea's High Commission in Honiara, the two countries held further discussions, and the Solomon Islands Government reiterated its view that the Bougainville crisis was an internal matter for Papua New Guinea, despite widespread support from the parliamentary opposition for the independence movement on the island. In March 1992, however, relations worsened considerably when Papua New Guinea forces carried out two unauthorized incursions into the Shortland Islands, in which a fuel depot was destroyed. A formal apology from the Papua New Guinea Government, together with a personal apology from the Prime Minister, Rabbie Namaliu, for the incidents, were not accepted. In September a similar raid resulted in the deaths of two Solomon Islanders. Alleging Australian involvement in the incursions, Mamaloni suspended surveillance flights by the Australian air force over its territory, and relations between the two countries deteriorated significantly. Despite the initiation of discussions between Solomon Islands and Papua New Guinea in January 1993, further incursions were reported in April. Mamaloni continued to deny that his country was supplying arms to the Bougainville rebels, and appealed for international assistance in policing the border. Following the election of a new Government in May in Solomon Islands, however, relations appeared to improve, and in August negotiations between the two countries resulted in an agreement to close the BRA office in Honiara. Further discussions in November resulted in the conclusion of a draft treaty on bilateral relations and the border issue.

In March 1988 Solomon Islands signed an agreement with Vanuatu and Papua New Guinea to form the 'Melanesian Spearhead Group' (MSG). The new group regarded as its principal aims the preservation of Melanesian cultural traditions and the attainment of independence by the French Overseas Territory of New Caledonia. In July 1989 Solomon Mamaloni spoke in favour of a closer political union between the three countries and the establishment of a Melanesian federation. In March 1990 the MSG admitted the FLNKS (the main Kanak, or Melanesian, political group in New Caledonia). In mid-1994 the group concluded an agreement regarded as the first step towards the establishment of a free-trade area by the three countries.

In April 1989 Solomon Islands ratified the South Pacific Nuclear-Free Zone Treaty.

## Government

Under the 1978 Constitution, executive authority is vested in the British monarch, as Head of State, and is exercisable by the monarch's representative, the Governor-General, who is appointed on the advice of Parliament and acts on the advice of the Cabinet. Legislative power is vested in the unicameral National Parliament, with 47 members elected by universal adult suffrage for four years (subject to dissolution) in single-member constituencies. The Cabinet is composed of the Prime Minister, elected by Parliament, and other ministers appointed by the Governor-General on the Prime Minister's recommendation. The Cabinet is responsible to Parliament. The country comprises four Districts, within which there are nine local government councils, elected by universal adult suffrage. The Constitution provides for further devolution of power to provincial authorities.

## Defence

There is a unit within the Police Force, the Police Field Force, which receives technical training and logistical support from Australia and New Zealand. The Force has seven patrol boats and undertakes surveillance activities in Solomon Islands' maritime economic zone. In late 1994 it was announced that a national reconnaissance and surveillance force was to be created by 1998.

## Economic Affairs

In 1993, according to estimates by the World Bank, Solomon Islands' gross national product (GNP), measured at average 1991–93 prices, was US $261m., equivalent to US $750 per head. During 1985–93, it was estimated, GNP per head increased, in real terms, at an average annual rate of 2.5%. Over the same period the population increased by an annual average of 2.9%. Solomon Islands' gross domestic product (GDP) increased, in real terms, by an annual average of 3.7% in 1982–91.

Agriculture (including hunting, forestry and fishing) contributed 48.4% of GDP (measured at constant 1984 prices) in 1991, and employed 23.7% of wage-earners in 1992. It was estimated that primary production contributed about 70% of GDP in the late 1980s. Around 90% of the working population are involved in subsistence agriculture. The principal cash crops are coconuts, cocoa, rice and oil palm. Spices are cultivated for export on a small scale, while in the early 1990s the production of honey was becoming increasingly important. The main subsistence crops are sweet potatoes, taro, yams, garden vegetables and fruit. Pigs and cattle are also reared. Seaweed farming has been introduced, and sea shells are exported. Fish accounted for 29.5% of export earnings in 1992, while timber provided 37.1%, copra 6.6% and palm oil a further 10.7%. The forestry sector is an extremely important source of revenue, contributing some 40% to the islands' economy. A dramatic increase in the production of timber in the early 1990s prompted several international organizations, including the World Bank, to express alarm at the current rate of logging in the country, which, if continued, would result in the depletion of existing stocks within eight years. In March 1994 the Government announced plans to reduce logging quotas to a sustainable level of some 0.3m.–0.4m. cu m per year (from the previous level of 1m. cu m), to increase the proportion of timber processed in the islands to some 20% of total production, and to ban the export of round logs from 1997. The election of a new Prime Minister in November 1994, however, resulted in the reversal of many of these measures and the introduction of policies which aimed to increase logging activity (including a 50% reduction in export duties for round logs and a postponement of the ban due to take effect in 1997). Agricultural GDP increased by an annual average of 2.5% in 1982–91.

Industry (including mining, manufacturing, construction and power) contributed 8.6% of GDP in 1991 (at 1984 prices), and employed 13.2% of wage-earners in 1992. Industrial GDP increased by an annual average of 3.7% in 1982–91.

Mining employed 0.5% of the working population in 1988. Gold is the sole mineral export, and earned SI $1.6m. for 53kg in 1990. An important mining project on Guadalcanal was to begin operations in mid-1997, with a projected yield of 100,000 oz per year for eight years. Other (undeveloped) mineral resources include deposits of copper, lead, zinc, silver, cobalt, asbestos, phosphates, nickel and high-grade bauxite. Nickel deposits of some 25m. metric tons of ore on Isabel and San Jorge islands were expected to be mined in the mid-1990s at a rate of 924,000 metric tons per year.

Manufacturing (including mining and quarrying) contributed 3.7% of GDP (at 1984 prices), and employed 7.6% of wage-earners in 1992. The most important branches are food-processing, coconut-based products, saw-milling, logging and handicrafts. In the late 1980s new industrial sites were developed on Guadalcanal. Manufacturing GDP increased by an annual average of 3.5% in 1982–91.

Energy is derived principally from hydroelectric power. Mineral fuels accounted for 7.6% of the total value of imports in 1990. In 1992 exploratory projects revealed several potential petroleum-producing areas in the islands.

Tourism was to be encouraged by a 10-year development plan, announced in 1989. In 1992 some 17,191 people visited Solomon Islands, of whom less than half were tourists. Earnings from the sector were estimated at some SI $6.4m. in 1993.

In 1992 Solomon Islands recorded a visible trade surplus of US $14.3m., but there was a deficit of US $1.9m. on the current account of the balance of payments. In 1991 the principal source of imports (32.4%) was Australia, while the principal market for exports (45.8%) was Japan. Other major trading partners are the United Kingdom, the Republic of Korea, Thailand, New Zealand and Singapore. The principal exports in 1992 were fish and other marine products, timber, copra, palm oil and cocoa. The principal imports were machinery and transport equipment, basic manufactures, foodstuffs and mineral fuels.

Budgetary estimates for 1992 envisaged recurrent expenditure of SI $161.6m., and total revenue of SI $228.4m. Overseas aid totalled US $35.6m. in 1991. Solomon Islands' total external debt totalled US $101.1m. in 1993, of which US $95.0m. was long-term public debt. In 1992 (when the external debt totalled US $95.1m.) the cost of debt-servicing was equivalent to 5.7% of the value of exports of goods and services. The average annual rate of inflation in 1985–93 was 12.4%; consumer prices increased by an average of 17.2% in 1993.

Solomon Islands is a member of the South Pacific Commission (see p. 215), the South Pacific Forum (see p. 217) and the UN Economic and Social Commission for Asia and the Pacific (ESCAP—see p. 27).

During the 1980s and early 1990s Solomon Islands' economic development was adversely affected by inadequate transport facilities and inclement weather (particularly cyclones), and also by fluctuations in prices on the international market for its major agricultural exports. Successive budget deficits and a substantial current account deficit were financed by heavy borrowing and foreign aid. A five-year plan (1989/90–1993/94) aimed to develop the coconut, cocoa and timber industries, while a project to establish 21 rural training centres was undertaken with aid from the European Community (now European Union) in 1993. In late 1994 the Government, under its newly-elected Premier, announced policies that aimed to achieve self-sufficiency for Solomon Islands through import substitution, increased trade with Asia, privatization (particularly in the tourism and forestry sectors) and greater emphasis on investment in production rather than in social services.

## Social Welfare

The Ministry of Health and Medical Services is responsible for government health projects. In 1985 the country had eight hospital establishments, with a total of 729 beds, and in 1989 there was one physician for every 5,190 inhabitants in the islands. Of total budgetary expenditure by the central Government in 1988, about SI $8.6m. (6.2%) was for health, and a further SI $1.1m. (0.8%) for social security and welfare. A National Provident Fund was established in 1976 to provide social security benefits to all persons in paid employment.

## SOLOMON ISLANDS

### Education

Education is not compulsory in Solomon Islands. Primary education generally begins at six years of age and lasts for six years. Secondary education, normally beginning at the age of 12, lasts for up to six years. In 1992 an estimated 90% of children (99% of boys; 81% of girls) in the relevant age-group were enrolled in primary education, while 16% of children (19% of boys; 12% of girls) in the relevant age-group attended secondary schools. In 1992 there were 522 primary schools, with a total of 53,320 pupils, and in 1988 there were 20 secondary schools, with a total of 6,666 pupils in 1992. In 1987 eight of the country's secondary schools were national secondary schools, which are run either by the Government or by one of the churches, and the remaining 12 were provincial secondary schools, which are run by provincial assemblies and provide courses of a practical nature, mainly in agriculture and development studies. There are two teacher-training schools and a technical institute. Scholarships are available for higher education at various universities overseas, which in 1987 were attended by 413 students from Solomon Islands. In 1977 the Solomon Islands Centre of the University of the Pacific opened in Honiara. Government expenditure on education was SI $24m. (7.9% of total spending) in 1991.

### Public Holidays

**1995:** 1 January (New Year's Day), 14–17 April (Easter), 5 June (Whit Monday), 17 June (Queen's Official Birthday), 7 July (Independence Day), 25 December (Christmas Day), 26 December (Boxing Day).

**1996:** 1 January (New Year's Day), 5–8 April (Easter), 27 May (Whit Monday), 15 June (Queen's Official Birthday), 7 July (Independence Day), 25 December (Christmas Day), 26 December (Boxing Day).

# Statistical Survey

Source (unless otherwise stated): Statistics Office, POB G6, Honiara; tel. 23700; telex 66337; fax 20392

### AREA AND POPULATION

**Area:** 27,556 sq km (10,639 sq miles).

**Population:** 196,823 (males 102,808; females 94,015) at census of 7 February 1976; 285,176 (males 147,972; females 137,204) at census of 23–24 November 1986; 355,000 (official estimate) at mid-1993.

**Density** (mid-1993): 12.9 per sq km.

**Ethnic Groups** (census of November 1986): Melanesians 268,536; Polynesians 10,661; Micronesians 3,929; Europeans 1,107; Chinese 379; Others 564.

**Principal Town:** Honiara (capital), population 35,288 (official estimate) at mid-1990.

**Births and Deaths** (1991): Birth rate 41.5 per 1,000; Death rate 7.3 per 1,000. Source: UN, *Statistical Yearbook for Asia and the Pacific*.

**Expectation of Life** (UN estimates, years at birth, 1985–90): 69.0 (males 67.2; females 71.2). Source: UN, *World Population Prospects: The 1992 Revision*.

**Employment** (employees only, June 1992): Agriculture, hunting, forestry and fishing 6,355; Manufacturing (incl. mining and quarrying) 2,040; Electricity and water 386; Construction 1,109; Trade, restaurants and hotels 3,201; Transport, storage and communications 1,418; Finance, insurance, real estate and business services 1,195; Community, social and personal services 11,138; Total 26,842. Source: UN, *Statistical Yearbook for Asia and the Pacific*. In 1988 some 81% of the employed labour force were males.

### AGRICULTURE, ETC.

**Principal Crops** (FAO estimates, metric tons, 1993): Coconuts 170,000; Copra 30,000*; Palm oil 30,000*; Palm kernel 6,000*; Rice 2,355† (1986); Cocoa beans 3,000*; Sweet potatoes 52,000; Other roots and tubers 47,000; Vegetables and melons 6,000; Fruit 14,000. Source: FAO, *Production Yearbook*.
* Unofficial estimate.  † Official estimate.

**Livestock** (FAO estimates, '000 head, year ending September 1993): Cattle 12; Pigs 54. Source: FAO, *Production Yearbook*.

**Livestock Products** (FAO estimates, '000 metric tons, 1993): Beef and veal 1 (1992); Pigmeat 2. Source: FAO, *Production Yearbook*.

**Forestry** (roundwood removals, '000 cu m): Industrial wood 330 in 1990; 330 per year (FAO estimate) in 1991 and 1992; Fuel wood 138 per year (FAO estimate) in 1990, 1991 and 1992. Source: FAO, *Yearbook of Forest Products*.

**Fishing** (metric tons, live weight): Total catch 54,766 in 1990; 69,292 in 1991; 60,000 (FAO estimate) in 1992. Source: FAO, *Yearbook of Fishery Statistics*.

### MINING

**Gold** (1991): 30 kg. Source: UN, *Industrial Statistics Yearbook*.

### INDUSTRY

**Production** (metric tons, 1993, unless otherwise stated): Copra 29,057; Coconut oil 4,286; Palm oil 30,986; Cocoa 3,297; Frozen fish* 17,100 (1990); Electric energy* 30 million kWh (1991).
* Source: UN, *Industrial Statistics Yearbook*.

### FINANCE

**Currency and Exchange Rates:** 100 cents = 1 Solomon Islands dollar (SI $). *Sterling and US Dollar Equivalents* (30 September 1994): £1 sterling = SI $5.229; US $1 = SI $3.316; SI $100 = £19.125 = US $30.160. *Average Exchange Rate* (SI $ per US $): 2.7148 in 1991; 2.9281 in 1992; 3.1877 in 1993.

**Budget** (estimates, SI $ million 1992): Expenditure 255.9 (Recurrent 161.6, Development 94.3); Revenue 228.4.

**Development Expenditure** (estimates, SI $ '000, 1990): Human resources and community development 28,125; Natural resources 30,442; Commerce, industry and finance 13,375; Physical infrastructure 18,981; Government and security 6,691; Total 97,614.

**Overseas Aid** (external grants, SI $ '000, 1989): Australia 26,138; EC 8,259; Japan 21,192; United Kingdom 11,252; World Health Organization 4,464; Total (incl. others) 78,871.

**International Reserves** (US $ million at 31 December 1993): IMF special drawing rights 0.04; Reserve position in IMF 0.74; Foreign exchange 19.29; Total 20.07. Source: IMF, *International Financial Statistics*.

**Money Supply** (SI $ million at 31 December 1993): Currency outside banks 42.11; Demand deposits at deposit money banks 81.82; Total money 123.93. Source: IMF, *International Financial Statistics*.

**Cost of Living** (Consumer Price Index for Honiara; base: 1990 = 100): 115.1 in 1991; 118.3 in 1992; 138.7 in 1993. Source: IMF, *International Financial Statistics*.

**Gross Domestic Product by Economic Activity** (official estimates, SI $ million at constant 1984 market prices, 1991): Agriculture 117.6; Mining and exploration −0.7; Manufacturing 9.0; Electricity, gas and water 2.2; Construction 10.5; Trade 23.3; Transport and communications 17.5; Finance 8.0; Other services 55.8; GDP 243.1. Source: Asian Development Bank, *Key Indicators of Developing Asian and Pacific Countries*.

**Balance of Payments** (US $ million, 1992): Merchandise exports f.o.b. 101.74; Merchandise imports f.o.b. −87.43; *Trade balance* 14.31; Exports of services 36.03; Imports of services −78.04; Other income received 0.99; Other income paid −10.89; Private unrequited transfers (net) 1.78; Official unrequited transfers (net) 33.95; *Current balance* −1.88; Direct investment (net) 14.17; Other capital (net) 8.26; Net errors and omissions −6.16; *Overall balance* 14.40. Source: IMF, *International Financial Statistics*.

### EXTERNAL TRADE

**Principal Commodities** (SI $ '000, 1990): *Imports c.i.f.:* Food and live animals 14,202; Beverages and tobacco 23,806; Crude materials (inedible) except fuels 35,112; Mineral fuels, lubricants, etc. 18,144; Animal and vegetable oils and fats 12,425; Chemicals 6,973; Basic manufactures 21,910; Machinery and transport equipment 37,834; Miscellaneous manufactured articles 59,435; Other commodities and transactions 9,124; Total 238,965. *1991* (provisional, SI $'000): Total imports c.i.f.: 299,593. *Exports f.o.b.:* Fish 53,184; Copra 10,936; Timber 60,814); Sea shells 6,457; Cocoa 11,053; Rice 12,865; Palm oil and kernels 19,321; Total (incl. others) 178,109. *1991* (provisional, SI $'000): Total exports f.o.b.:

SOLOMON ISLANDS

226,472 (Fish 106,417); Timber 53,557. *1992* (provisional, SI $ '000): Total exports f.o.b.: 297,866 (Fish 87,950; Timber 110,452).

**Principal Trading Partners** (provisional, US $ million, 1991): *Imports:* Australia 34.9; Japan 23.1; New Zealand 7.8; Singapore 16.2; USA 4.5; Total (incl. others) 107.6. *Exports:* Australia 1.2; Japan 36.8; Republic of Korea 7.4; Thailand 2.4; Total (incl. others) 80.2.

Source: UN, *Statistical Yearbook for Asia and the Pacific*.

### TRANSPORT

**Road Traffic** (motor vehicles in use at 30 June 1986): Passenger cars 1,350; Commercial vehicles 2,026.

**Shipping** (international traffic, '000 metric tons, 1990): Goods loaded 278; Goods unloaded 349. Source: UN, *Monthly Bulletin of Statistics*.

**Civil Aviation** (traffic on scheduled services, 1990): Passengers carried 69,000; Passenger-km 13 million. Source: UN, *Statistical Yearbook*.

### TOURISM

**Total Visitor Arrivals:** 11,811 in 1990; 13,013 in 1991; 17,191 (Air 12,305, Sea 4,886) in 1992.

### COMMUNICATIONS MEDIA

**Non-Daily Newspapers** (1988): 4; estimated circulation 12,000*.
**Radio Receivers** (1992): 41,000 in use*.
**Television Receivers** (1992): 2,000 in use*.
**Telephones** (1991): 5,000 main lines in use†.

\* Source: UNESCO, *Statistical Yearbook*.
† Source: UN, *Statistical Yearbook*.

### EDUCATION

**Pre-Primary** (1992): 12,705 pupils.
**Primary** (1992): 522 schools; 2,490 teachers; 53,320 pupils.
**Secondary** (1992): 20 schools (1988); 364 teachers (1991); 6,666 pupils.
**Overseas centres** (1988): 405 students.

Source: mainly, UNESCO, *Statistical Yearbook*.

# Directory

## The Constitution

A new Constitution came into effect at independence on 7 July 1978.

The main provisions are that Solomon Islands is a constitutional monarchy with the British sovereign (represented locally by a Governor-General, who must be a Solomon Islands citizen) as Head of State, while legislative power is vested in the unicameral National Parliament composed of 47 members, elected by universal adult suffrage for four years (subject to dissolution), and executive authority is exercised by the Cabinet, led by the Prime Minister. The Governor-General is appointed for up to five years, on the advice of Parliament, and acts in almost all matters on the advice of the Cabinet. The Prime Minister is elected by and from members of Parliament. Other ministers are appointed by the Governor-General, on the Prime Minister's recommendation, from members of Parliament. The Cabinet is responsible to Parliament. Emphasis is laid on the devolution of power, and traditional chiefs and leaders have a special role within these arrangements. Local government is conducted by the Honiara Town Council (for the capital) and eight provincial assemblies for Western, Makira, Isabel (Ysabel), Malaita, Guadalcanal, Central, Rennell and Belona and Temotu Provinces.

The Constitution contains comprehensive guarantees of fundamental human rights and freedoms, and provides for the introduction of a 'leadership code' and the appointment of an Ombudsman and a Public Solicitor. It also provides for 'the establishment of the underlying law, based on the customary law and concepts of the Solomon Islands people'. Solomon Islands citizenship was automatically conferred on the indigenous people of the islands and on other residents with close ties with the islands upon independence. The acquisition of land is reserved for indigenous inhabitants or their descendants.

## The Government

**Head of State:** HM Queen Elizabeth II.
**Governor-General:** Sir Moses Pitakaka (sworn in 7 July 1994).

### THE CABINET
(June 1995)

**Prime Minister:** Solomon Mamaloni.
**Deputy Prime Minister and Minister for Home Affairs:** Dennis Lulei.
**Minister for Foreign Affairs:** Danny Philip.
**Minister for Finance:** Christopher C. Abe.
**Minister for Commerce, Employment and Trade:** George Luialamo.
**Minister for Agriculture and Fisheries:** Edmond Andresen.
**Minister for Energy, Minerals and Mines:** Eric Seri.
**Minister for Education and Training:** Alfred Maetia.
**Minister for Provincial Government and Rural Development:** Allan Qurusu.
**Minister for Forestry, Environment and Conservation:** Allan Kemakeza.
**Minister for Sports, Youth, Women's Affairs and Recreation:** Brown Beu.
**Minister for Transport, Works and Utilities:** John Fisango.
**Minister for Health and Medical Services:** Gordon Mara.
**Minister for Development Planning:** David Sitai.
**Minister for Culture and Tourism:** William Haomae.
**Minister for Lands and Housing:** Francis Orodani.
**Minister for Posts and Communications:** John Musoata.
**Minister for Justice:** Oliver Zapo.
**Minister for Police and National Security:** Victor Ngele.

### MINISTRIES

**Office of the Prime Minister:** POB G1, Honiara; tel. 21863; telex 66311.
**Ministry of Agriculture and Fisheries:** POB G13, Honiara; tel. 21326; fax 21955.
**Ministry of Commerce, Employment and Trade:** POB G26, Honiara; tel. 21140; telex 66311.
**Ministry of Culture and Tourism:** POB G20, Honiara; tel. 21640; fax 21689.
**Ministry of Development Planning:** Honiara.
**Ministry of Education and Training:** POB 584, Honiara; tel. 23900.
**Ministry of Energy, Minerals and Mines:** Honiara.
**Ministry of Finance:** POB 26, Honiara; tel. 23700; telex 66337; fax 20392.
**Ministry of Foreign Affairs:** POB G10, Honiara; tel. 22223; telex 66311.
**Ministry of Forestry, Environment and Conservation:** POB G24, Honiara; tel. 22944; telex 66306.
**Ministry of Health and Medical Services:** POB 349, Honiara; tel. 23600.
**Ministry of Home Affairs:** POB G11, Honiara; tel. 22262.
**Ministry of Justice:** POB 404, Honiara; tel. 22915; fax 25610.
**Ministry of Lands and Housing:** Honiara.
**Ministry of Police and National Security:** Honiara.
**Ministry of Posts and Communications:** POB G25, Honiara; tel. 21821; telex 66310; fax 21472.
**Ministry of Provincial Government and Rural Development:** POB G35, Honiara.
**Ministry of Sports, Youth, Women's Affairs and Recreation:** POB G39, Honiara; tel. 25490; fax 25684.

SOLOMON ISLANDS                                                                                          *Directory*

**Ministry of Transport, Works and Utilities:** POB G8, Honiara; tel. 21141; telex 66352.

## Legislature
### NATIONAL PARLIAMENT
**Speaker:** Paul Tovua.

**General Election, 26 May 1993**

| Party | Seats |
| --- | --- |
| Group for National Unity and Reconciliation | 21 |
| People's Alliance Party | 7 |
| Independents | 6 |
| National Action Party of Solomon Islands | 5 |
| Solomon Islands Labour Party | 4 |
| United Party | 4 |
| **Total** | **47** |

## Political Organizations

Parties in the National Parliament can have a fluctuating membership and an influence disproportionate to their representation. There is a significant number of independents who are loosely associated in the amorphous, but often decisive, 'Independent Group'. The following parties represent the main groupings:

**Group for National Unity and Reconciliation:** Honiara; f. 1993 to contest the general election; Leader Solomon Mamaloni.

**National Action Party of Solomon Islands (NAPSI):** Honiara; f. 1993; Leader Francis Saemala.

**Nationalist Front for Progress (NFP):** POB 821, Honiara; tel. 22472; f. 1985; seeks to promote rural progress and the settlement of land disputes; Leader Andrew Nori.

**People's Alliance Party (PAP):** POB 722, Honiara; f. 1979 by a merger of the People's Progressive Party (f. 1973) and the Rural Alliance Party (f. 1977); advocates the establishment of a federal republic; Leader Sir David Kausimae; Sec. Edward Kingmele.

**Solomon Islands Labour Party:** Honiara; f. 1988; Leader Joses Tuhanuku.

**Solomon Islands Liberal Party (SILP):** Honiara; f. 1976 as the National Democratic Party (NADEPA); present name adopted in 1986; Leader Bartholomew Ulufa'alu.

**United Party (UP):** Honiara; f. 1979; favours strong central govt; Leader Ezekiel Alebua.

## Diplomatic Representation
### EMBASSIES AND HIGH COMMISSIONS IN SOLOMON ISLANDS

**Australia:** Mud Alley, POB 589, Honiara; tel. 21561; fax 23691; High Commissioner: Rob Flynn.

**China (Taiwan):** Lengakiki Ridge, POB 586, Honiara; tel. 22590; telex 66395; fax 21378; Ambassador: William Hsing-chung Chao.

**Japan:** National Provident Fund Bldg, Mendana Ave, POB 560, Honiara; tel. 22953; telex 66385; fax 21006; Chargé d'affaires: Noburo Kawagishi.

**New Zealand:** Mendana Ave, POB 697, Honiara; tel. 21502; fax 22377; High Commissioner: J. R. T. Barrett.

**Papua New Guinea:** POB 1109, Honiara; tel. 21737; fax 20687; High Commissioner: Joseph Assaigo.

**United Kingdom:** Telekom House, Mendana Ave, POB 676, Honiara; tel. 21705; fax 21549; High Commissioner: Raymond Francis Jones.

## Judicial System

The High Court is a Superior Court of Record with unlimited original jurisdiction and powers (except over customary land) as prescribed by the Solomon Islands Constitution or by any law for the time being in force in Solomon Islands. The Judges of the High Court are the Chief Justice, resident in Solomon Islands and employed by its government and the Puisne Judge. Appeals from this Court go to the Court of Appeal, the members of which are senior judges from Australia, New Zealand and Papua New Guinea. The Chief Justice and judges of the High Court are *ex officio* members of the Court of Appeal.

In addition there are Magistrates' Courts staffed by qualified and lay magistrates exercising limited jurisdiction in both civil and criminal matters. There are also Local Courts staffed by elders of the local communities which have jurisdiction in the areas of established native custom, petty crime and local government by-laws. In 1975 Customary Land Appeal Courts were established to hear land appeal cases from Local Courts, which have exclusive original jurisdiction over customary land cases.

**The High Court:** POB G21, Honiara; tel. 21632; fax 22702.
**President of the Court of Appeal:** Peter David Connolly.
**Chief Justice of the High Court:** John Baptist Muria.
**Puisne Judge:** Albert Rocky Palmer.
**Registrar and Commissioner of the High Court:** Sam Awich.
**Chief Magistrate:** Denzil Seneviratne.
**Attorney-General:** R. Teutao.
**Director of Public Prosecutions:** Francis Mwanesalua.
**Solicitor-General:** Primo Afeau.
**Public Solicitor:** J. Remobatu (acting).
**Chair of Law Reform Commission:** Frank Kabui.

## Religion

More than 95% of the population profess Christianity, and the remainder follow traditional beliefs. According to the census of 1976, about 34% of the population adhered to the Church of Melanesia (Anglican), 19% were Roman Catholics, 17% belonged to the South Seas Evangelical Church, 11% to the United Church (Methodist) and 10% were Seventh-day Adventists. Most denominations are affiliated to the Solomon Islands Christian Association. In many areas Christianity is practised alongside traditional beliefs, especially ancestor worship.

### CHRISTIANITY

**Solomon Islands Christian Association:** POB 1335, Honiara; tel. 23350; fax 26150; f. 1967; three full mems, two assoc. mems and eight mem. orgs; Chair. Most Rev. Adrian Smith; Exec. Sec. Wainga T. Tion.

#### The Anglican Communion

Anglicans in Solomon Islands are adherents of the Church of the Province of Melanesia, comprising six dioceses: five in Solomon Islands (Central Melanesia, Malaita, Temotu, Isabel and Hanuato'o, which was established in June 1991) and the diocese of Vanuatu (which also includes New Caledonia). A new diocese, covering the Banks and Torres Islands in northern Vanuatu, was to be established in 1995. The Archbishop is also Bishop of Central Melanesia and is based in Honiara. The Church had an estimated 180,000 members in 1988.

**Archbishop of the Province of Melanesia:** Most Rev. Ellison Pogo, Archbishop's House, POB 19, Honiara; tel. 21892; telex 66455; fax 21098.

**Provincial Secretary:** Nicholas Ma'aramo, Provincial Headquarters, POB 19, Honiara; tel. 21892; fax 21098.

#### The Roman Catholic Church

For ecclesiastical purposes, Solomon Islands comprises one archdiocese and two dioceses. At 31 December 1993 there were an estimated 67,633 adherents in the country. The Bishops participate in the Bishops' Conference of Papua New Guinea and Solomon Islands (based in Papua New Guinea).

**Archbishop of Honiara:** Most Rev. Adrian Thomas Smith, Holy Cross, POB 237, Honiara; tel. 22387; fax 22869.

#### Other Christian Churches

**Assembly of God:** Honiara; f. 1971; Gen. Supt Rev. Jeriel Ofea Ausuta.

**Christian Fellowship Church:** Church, Paradise, Munda, Western Province; f. 1960; over 5,000 mems in 24 villages; runs five primary schools; Leader: Holy Mama (Job Duddley).

**Seventh-day Adventist Church:** POB 63, Honiara; tel. 30271; telex 66378; fax 30653; Pres. of Western Pacific Region Pastor J. R. Lee; Sec. Wilfred Billy.

**South Sea Evangelical Church:** POB 16, Honiara; tel. 22388; fax 20302; Pres. Bobbi Kusilifu; Gen. Sec. Charles J. Razcasi.

**United Church of Papua New Guinea and Solomon Islands:** POB 18, Honiara; tel. 22488; fax 20453; f. 1968; a Methodist church; Bishop of Solomon Islands Region: Rev. Lesly Boseto.

### BAHÁ'Í FAITH

**National Spiritual Assembly:** POB 245, Honiara; tel. 22475; fax 25368.

SOLOMON ISLANDS
*Directory*

### ISLAM

**Solomon Islands Muslim League:** Honiara; Gen. Sec. Dr MUSTAPHA RAMO; 66 mems. In early 1995 the organization was still awaiting official registration as a religious group in Solomon Islands.

## The Press

**Agrikalsa Nius** (Agriculture News): POB G13, Honiara; tel. 21211; fax 21955; f. 1986; monthly; Editor ALFRED MAESULIA; circ. 1,000.

**Citizens' Press:** Honiara; monthly.

**Link:** Solomon Islands Development Trust, POB 147, Honiara; tel. 21130; fax 21131; every 2 months.

**The Nius:** POB 718, Honiara; tel. 21300; monthly; Dept of Information publication; Editor BRIAN BETI (acting); circ. 4,000.

**Solomon Star:** POB 255, Honiara; tel. 22913; fax 21572; f. 1982; weekly; English; Editor JOHN W. LAMANI; circ. 4,000.

**Solomon Times:** POB 212, Honiara; weekly; Chief Editor and Man. Dir EDWARD KINGMELE.

**Solomons Voice:** POB 1235, Honiara; tel. 22275; fax 20090; f. 1992; weekly; circ. 10,000.

## Radio and Television

In 1992 there were an estimated 41,000 radio receivers and 2,000 television receivers in use. A broadcast television service was to be established in late 1995 or early 1996.

**Solomon Islands Broadcasting Corporation:** POB 654, Honiara; tel. 20051; fax 23159; f. 1976; daily transmissions are mainly in Pidgin with some English news bulletins and programmes; broadcasts total 116 hours per week; Programme Dir DAVID PALAPU; Gen. Man. JAMES T. KILUA.

## Finance

The financial system is regulated and monitored by the Central Bank of Solomon Islands. There are three commercial banks and a development bank. Financial statutory corporations include the Home Finance Corpn (which took over from the Housing Authority in 1990) and the Investment Corporation of Solomon Islands (the state holding company). In 1989 there were 80 credit unions, with a total of 9,300 members (with total assets of SI $2.1m.).

### BANKING

(cap. = capital; res = reserves; dep. = deposits; brs = branches; amounts in Solomon Islands dollars)

#### Central Bank

**Central Bank of Solomon Islands:** POB 634, Honiara; tel. 21791; telex 66320; fax 23513; f. 1983; sole bank of issue; cap. 2.6m., res 44.4m., dep. 9.0m. (Dec. 1992); Gov. R. HOUENIPWELA; Deputy Gov. J. KAITU.

#### Development Bank

**Development Bank of Solomon Islands:** POB 911, Honiara; tel. 21595; fax 23715; f. 1978; auth. cap. 10m., cap. p.u. 8m. (Dec. 1988); Chair. BEN FOUKONA; Man. Dir VINCENT YEE; 6 brs.

#### Commercial Banks

**Australia and New Zealand Banking Group Ltd** (Australia): Mendana Ave, POB 10, Honiara; tel. 21835; telex 66321; fax 22957; Man. R. GOUDSWAARD.

**National Bank of Solomon Islands Ltd:** Mendana Ave, POB 37, Honiara; tel. 21874; telex 66319; fax 23478; f. 1981; 51% govt-owned, 49% owned by the Commonwealth Bank of Australia (to be acquired by the Bank of Hawaii in late 1995); cap. 2.0m., res 12.8m., dep. 107.6m. (June 1993); Chair. RAYMOND G. WILKIE; Gen. Man. MICK KRANAS; 10 brs and 48 agencies.

**Westpac Banking Corporation** (Australia): NPF Bldg, 21 Mendana Ave, POB 466, Honiara; tel. 21222; telex 66433; fax 23419; Man. ALAN TAYLOR.

### INSURANCE

About 10 major British insurance companies maintain agencies in Solomon Islands.

## Trade and Industry

### CHAMBER OF COMMERCE

**Solomon Islands Chamber of Commerce:** POB 64, Honiara; tel. 22960; telex 66448; Chair. BARTHOLOMEW ULUFA'ALU.

### EMPLOYERS' ORGANIZATIONS

**Chinese Association:** China Town, Honiara; asscn of businessmen from the ethnic Chinese community.

**Federation of Employers:** POB 650, Honiara; tel. 25251.

**Solomon Islands Farmers' Association:** Honiara; founded a credit union in 1990; Pres. BARTHOLOMEW ULUFA'ALU.

### INDUSTRIAL AND DEVELOPMENT ORGANIZATIONS

**Association of Mining and Exploration Companies:** c/o POB G24, Honiara; f. 1988; Pres. NELSON GREG YOUNG.

**Commodities Export Marketing Authority:** POB 54, Honiara; telex 66316; sole exporter of copra; agencies at Honiara and Yandina; Gen. Man. SOLOMON ILALA.

**Livestock Development Authority (LDA):** POB 525, Honiara; tel. 21650; fax 22214; f. 1977; Gen. Man. RICHARD NAMO.

**Solomon Islands Development Trust (SIDT):** POB 147, Honiara; tel. 21130; fax 21131; development org.

### CO-OPERATIVE SOCIETIES

In 1986 there were 156 primary co-operative societies, working mostly outside the capital. There are two associations running and aiding co-operative societies in Solomon Islands:

**Central Co-operative Association (CCA):** Honiara.

**Western General Co-operative Association (WGCA):** Gizo, Western Province.

### TRADE UNIONS

There are 14 registered trade unions in Solomon Islands.

**Solomon Islands Council of Trade Unions (SICTU):** National Centre for Trade Unions, Honiara; f. 1986; the principal affiliated unions are:

**Solomon Islands Medical Association:** Honiara.

**Solomon Islands National Teachers' Association (SINTA):** POB 967, Honiara; f. 1985; Pres. G. INIOMEA; Gen. Sec. A. J. AIHUNU.

**Solomon Islands National Union of Workers (SINUW):** Honiara, POB 271; Pres. DAVID TUHANUKU.

**Solomon Islands Post and Telecommunications Union:** Honiara.

**Solomon Islands Public Employees' Union (SIPEU):** POB 360, Honiara; tel. 21967; fax 23110; Pres. JOHNSON ACROM; Gen. Sec. CLEMENT WAIWARI.

**Solomon Islands Seamen's Association:** Honiara.

## Transport

### ROADS

There are about 1,300 km of roads maintained by the central and provincial governments; in 1976 main roads covered 455 km. In addition, there are 800 km of privately maintained roads mainly for plantation use. Road construction and maintenance is difficult because of the nature of the country, and what roads there are serve as feeder roads to the main town of an island.

Honiara has a main road running about 65 km each side of it along the north coast of Guadalcanal, and Malaita has a road 157 km long running north of Auki and around the northern end of the island to the Lau Lagoon, where canoe transport takes over; and one running south for 35 km to Masa. On Makira a road links Kira Kira and Kakoranga, a distance of 35 km. Before it abandoned mining investigations in 1977, the Mitsui Mining and Smelting Co built 40 km of road on Rennell Island.

### SHIPPING

Regular shipping services (mainly cargo) exist between Solomon Islands and Australia, New Zealand, Papua New Guinea, Hong Kong, Japan, Singapore and European ports. In 1994 internal shipping was provided by 93 passenger/cargo ships, 13 passenger-only ships, 61 fishing vessels and 17 tugs. The four main ports are at Honiara, Yandina, Noro and Gizo. The international seaports of Honiara and Noro are controlled by the Solomon Islands Ports Authority.

**Solomon Islands Ports Authority:** POB 307, Honiara; tel. 22646; fax 23994; f. 1956; Chair. DAVID VOUZA; Gen. Man. N. B. KABUI.

**Tradco Shipping Ltd:** POB 114, Honiara; tel. 22588; telex 66313; fax 23887; f. 1984; shipping agents, agents for Lloyd's.

Shipping companies operating freight services to Solomon Islands include Sofrana-Unilines, Kyowa Shipping Co Ltd, New Guinea Pacific Line, Chief Container Service, Thongsoon Lines Pte Ltd and Bank Line. CTC Cruises, Royal Viking Line and P & O-Sitmar

# SOLOMON ISLANDS

Cruises are among the companies that operate passenger services to the islands.

### CIVIL AVIATION

Two airports are open to international traffic and a further 25 serve internal flights. Air Niugini (Papua New Guinea), Air Nauru, and Qantas (Australia) fly to the principal airport of Henderson, 13 km from Honiara. Work to extend the runway at Henderson began in early 1995.

**Director of Civil Aviation:** MICHAEL ANITA.

**Solomon Airlines Limited:** POB 23, Honiara; tel. 20031; telex 16312; fax 23992; f. 1968; govt-owned; international and domestic operator; scheduled services between Honiara and Port Moresby (Papua New Guinea), Nadi (Fiji), Auckland (New Zealand), Brisbane (Australia) and Port Vila (Vanuatu); Gen. Man. JIM BRADFIELD.

## Tourism

Tourism is hindered by the relative inaccessibility of the islands and the inadequacy of tourist facilities. In 1992 visitor arrivals totalled 17,191, less than half of whom were tourists. Most visitors come from Australia, New Zealand and Papua New Guinea. The industry earned an estimated SI $6.4m. in 1993.

**Solomon Islands Tourist Authority:** POB 321, Honiara; tel. 22442; fax 23986; f. 1980; Chair. NELSON BOSO; Gen. Man. WILSON C. MAELAUA.

# SOMALIA

## Introductory Survey

**Location, Climate, Language, Religion, Flag, Capital**

The Somali Democratic Republic lies on the east coast of Africa, with Ethiopia to the north-west and Kenya to the west. There is a short frontier with Djibouti to the north-west. Somalia has a long coastline on the Indian Ocean and the Gulf of Aden, forming the 'Horn of Africa'. The climate is generally hot and dry, with an average annual temperature of 27°C (80°F). It is hotter in the interior and on the Gulf of Aden, but cooler on the Indian Ocean coast. Average annual rainfall is less than 430 mm (17 in). The national language is Somali but Arabic is also in official use. English and Italian are also widely spoken. The state religion is Islam, and the majority of Somalis are Sunni Muslims. There is a small Christian community, mostly Roman Catholics. The national flag (proportions 3 by 2) is pale blue, with a large five-pointed white star in the centre. The capital is Mogadishu.

**Recent History**

Somalia was formed by a merger of two former colonial territories: British Somaliland, in the north, and its larger and more populous neighbour, Italian Somaliland. The United Kingdom established a protectorate in British Somaliland in 1886, following the withdrawal of Egyptian garrisons from the area. Italian Somaliland originated in 1889, when Italy concluded agreements with two local rulers, who placed their territories under Italian protection. Italy's occupation of the region was subsequently extended along the coast and inland, and Italian control was completed in 1927.

Italian forces in Somaliland and Eritrea invaded and occupied neighbouring Abyssinia (Ethiopia) in 1935–36. During the Second World War British Somaliland was temporarily conquered by Italian troops, but in 1941 it was recaptured by a British counter-offensive, which also forced the Italians to withdraw from Eritrea, Italian Somaliland and Ethiopia. A British military administration was then established in British and Italian Somaliland.

Under the provisions of the post-war peace treaty of February 1947, Italy renounced all rights to Italian Somaliland. In December 1950, however, the pre-war colony became the UN Trust Territory of Somalia, with Italy returning as the administering power for a transitional period, fixed at 10 years, prior to independence. During the 1950s the Italian administration expanded education and other social services. Under Italian supervision, the territory's first general election on the basis of universal adult suffrage was held in March 1959, when 83 of the 90 seats in the Legislative Assembly were won by the Somali Youth League (SYL), a pro-Western party, founded in 1943 and led by the Prime Minister, Seyyid Abdullah Issa. The SYL favoured the creation of a single state embracing all Somali-inhabited areas, including those in French Somaliland (now Djibouti), Ethiopia and Kenya.

Meanwhile, British Somaliland reverted to civilian rule in 1948. The British colonial authorities prepared the territory for self-government, and the first general election took place in March 1959. Fresh elections, for a new legislative council, were held in February 1960, with all parties in favour of early independence and the unification of all Somali territories. Representatives of British Somaliland and the Trust Territory of Somalia met in April and agreed on a merger of the two territories in an independent republic. British Somaliland was granted independence on 26 June 1960, and the merger scheme received unanimous approval by the legislature on the following day.

Accordingly, the union of former British and Italian Somaliland took effect on 1 July 1960, when the independent Somali Republic was proclaimed. On the same day representatives of the two component territories elected Dr Aden Abdullah Osman, hitherto President of the Somalia Legislative Assembly (the legislature of the southern territory), to be the first President of the new Republic. The legislatures of the two Somali regions merged to form a single chamber, the National Assembly. The two dominant parties in former British Somaliland joined with the SYL to form a tripartite coalition government. Dr Abdirashid Ali Shermarke of the SYL became Prime Minister, following Issa's resignation.

As the dominant party during the 1960s, the SYL pursued Somali territorial claims to parts of Ethiopia and Kenya. Somalia became increasingly dependent on aid from the USSR and other communist states. A frontier dispute between the United Kingdom and Somalia regarding Kenya's Northern Frontier District resulted in the severing of diplomatic relations by Somalia in 1963. A further dispute over frontiers with Ethiopia led to fighting in 1964. Following a general election in March 1964, Dr Shermarke resigned as Prime Minister in June. He was replaced by Abdirazak Haji Hussein, formerly the Minister of Works, who formed a cabinet exclusively from members of the SYL. In June 1967, however, Dr Shermarke was elected by the National Assembly to replace President Osman. He appointed a new Cabinet, led by Mohamed Haji Ibrahim Egal, the former Prime Minister of British Somaliland. Diplomatic relations with Kenya and the United Kingdom were resumed in 1968, although relations with Ethiopia deteriorated as a result of Somalia's claim to the Ogaden district and its support for the Western Somali Liberation Front (WSLF).

On 15 October 1969 President Shermarke was assassinated by a police-officer. Six days later the army seized control in a coup on the eve of a planned presidential election. Power was assumed by the armed forces Commander-in-Chief, Maj.-Gen. Mohamed Siad Barre. The 1960 Constitution was suspended, political parties were abolished and the National Assembly dissolved. A new Government was formed by the Supreme Revolutionary Council (SRC), chaired by Siad Barre, which proclaimed the Somali Democratic Republic. In October 1970 Siad Barre declared Somalia a socialist state, and began a revolutionary programme of national unification and social and economic reform. In July 1976 the SRC dissolved itself, and power was transferred to the newly-formed Somali Revolutionary Socialist Party (SRSP). All members of the SRC became members of the ruling party's Central Committee, and Siad Barre became the Secretary-General of the SRSP.

A new Constitution came into force in September 1979. Elections were held in December for a new legislature, the People's Assembly, which, at its first session in January 1980, elected Siad Barre as President of the Republic. A government reshuffle in March 1982 was notable for the increasing influence of Siad Barre's Marehan clan at the expense of the northern Mijertyn and Isaaq clans, from which the main insurgent opposition groups drew their support. Arrests of prominent politicians in June further reduced the influence of the northern clans. During 1983 Siad Barre encountered opposition in the northern region, where a mutiny occurred in February and riots took place later in the year. Constitutional amendments, approved by the Assembly in November 1984, effectively transferred all powers of government to the President.

Despite continuing internal unrest, at elections to the National Assembly, in December 1984, a single list of SRSP candidates was reportedly endorsed by 99.9% of voters. In February 1985 Siad Barre announced government changes, and declared that the priority of the new Council of Ministers would be defence and the economy; in August a new Ministry of the Treasury was created, in accordance with the policy of economic reforms.

A presidential election, in which Siad Barre was the sole candidate, took place in December 1986, confirming his presidency for a further seven-year term by 99.93% of a reported 4.9m. votes cast. Despite a government reshuffle in February 1987, in which Lt-Gen. Mohamed Ali Samater (hitherto First Vice-President and Minister of Defence) was appointed to the newly-created post of Prime Minister, the President continued to dominate Somalia's political life. During 1987 attacks on military targets by insurgents increased and there were indications that a struggle for the presidential succession was in progress. In June it was reported that a coup plot, in which Samater was rumoured to have been involved, had been foiled.

None the less, Samater remained as Prime Minister following government changes in December, in which the President's half-brother, Dr Abd ar-Rhaman Jama Barre, previously Minister of Foreign Affairs, was appointed Minister of Finance.

In October 1981 the Somali Salvation Front, some of whose members had staged an unsuccessful military coup in 1978, joined with two other opposition groups to form the Democratic Front for the Salvation of Somalia (DFSS, later renamed the Somali Salvation Democratic Front—SSDF). Together with another group founded in 1981, the Somali National Movement (SNM), and with substantial Ethiopian military support, DFSS guerrillas invaded the central border area of Somalia in July 1982. The invasion was contained by the Somali national forces but, despite military aid from the USA and from Italy, it was not possible to expel the rebel troops from the country. Following a meeting between Siad Barre and Lt-Col Mengistu, the Ethiopian leader, in January 1986, Ethiopian military support for the insurgent groups was reduced, particularly in respect of the DFSS. In May 1988 the SNM claimed to have captured the north-western town of Hargeysa, together with the town of Burao and the Red Sea port of Berbera. The Government denied this claim, but by July it was clear that some areas, at least, of these towns had been captured. Heavy fighting in the north during mid-1988 reportedly led to the recapture by government forces of Burao and Hargeysa. After the evacuation of all foreigners in the Hargeysa area in June 1988, it became impossible to corroborate the rival claims of the Government and the SNM regarding the hostilities. In January 1989 the SNM declared that it remained in control of 95% of the region. In a renewed offensive in February the SNM was reported to have captured the town of Odweina, killing about 500 government troops, and to have perpetrated a further attack to the east of Burao. In March Siad Barre announced the creation of a national committee to administer the north-western and Togdhere regions of the country.

In February 1989 the appointment of Hussein Abd ar-Rahman Mattan as Minister of Defence (the first civilian to occupy this post for 20 years) was regarded as further evidence of the Government's desire to seek a political, rather than a military, solution to the war in the north. Proposals for a multi-party political system were discussed at the third congress of the SRSP in July, but it was decided that Somalia was not ready for such a change. Elections to the People's Assembly, scheduled for December, were also postponed for a year.

Disturbances erupted in Mogadishu in mid-July 1989. They were reportedly precipitated by the arrest, earlier in the month, of several leading Muslim clergymen, and allegedly involved members of the United Somali Congress (USC) and the National United Front of Somalia (NUFS). The suppression of the demonstrations by the army and the police reportedly left more than 400 people dead and 1,000 wounded. A US-based human rights organization, Africa Watch, claimed that 46 of those killed had been summarily executed after the disturbances. Two government ministers were dismissed later in the month, accused of threatening state security.

In August 1989, amid reports that Somalia's ruling Marehan clan had lost the crucial support of the Ogadeni clan, the President offered to relinquish power, and announced that the next elections would take place in the context of a multi-party system. At the same time there were reports of fighting between government troops and members of the Ogadeni clan in southern Somalia, and Western sources claimed that the only areas of the country that remained under government control were Mogadishu, parts of Hargeysa and Berbera. In September it was reported that Ogadeni deserters from the army had formed two new opposition groupings: the Somali Patriotic Movement (SPM) in the south, and the Somali National Army (SNA) in central Somalia.

Meanwhile, the USC gained support in the south, where its forces were fighting alongside those of the SPM. In the north the emergence of a new opposition movement, the Somali Democratic Alliance (SDA), led by Mohamed Farah Abdullah, increased the challenge to Siad Barre's authority. The President responded to these pressures by dismissing the Government in January 1990 and offering posts in a successor administration to prominent opposition leaders. All refused to join the new Government, which, although still under the leadership of Siad Barre's close associate, Lt-Gen. Samater, was reduced in number (to 20 members) and consisted mainly of young bureaucrats.

In late March 1990 the Government renewed its military offensive in the north against the SNM. As the conflict escalated, more than 100 alleged dissidents, mainly of northern origin, were arrested in Mogadishu. In May a partial curfew was imposed in Mogadishu, which was experiencing rising levels of violent disturbances. Disorder was also reported in central Somalia, where fierce fighting broke out between the Mijertyn and Dashiishe tribes.

In early July 1990 the Council of Ministers endorsed the proposals of August 1989 for the democratization of Somalia's political system. It was decided that, following a review by the People's Assembly, a new constitution be submitted to a national referendum in late October, and that multi-party legislative and local government elections would be held in February 1991. In mid-August 1990 the USC, the SNM and the SPM announced that they had agreed to co-ordinate their separate military campaigns to overthrow Siad Barre. In early September the President dismissed the Samater Government, citing its failure to end the country's political and economic crises, and appointed in its place an administration led by Mohamed Hawadle Madar, a member of the Isaaq clan. The appointment of a new Government, accompanied by the release of some political prisoners, was regarded as a conciliatory gesture towards the rebel movements. In mid-October the Government announced the immediate introduction of the new Constitution and a new electoral code. Siad Barre relinquished the post of Secretary-General of the SRSP, in accordance with the provisions of the new Constitution, which stipulated that the President should hold no responsibilities other than those of the presidency.

Despite the apparent readiness of the new Government to hasten the process of political reform, the principal insurgent groups showed no signs of relaxing their military campaigns. In early November 1990 the SNM rejected the Government's invitation to all opposition groups to participate in a conference of national reconciliation, to be held in Cairo, Egypt. In mid-November the USC was reported to have occupied briefly the town of Johar, 100 km north of Mogadishu, and in late November forces of the SPM seized control of Kismayu, in southern Somalia. On 25 December, in accordance with the new Constitution, legislation was introduced to permit the establishment of political parties opposed to the Government.

On 1 January 1991 the USC announced that its military campaign had culminated in the capture of most areas of Mogadishu and that it had besieged the home of President Siad Barre. It rejected offers by Egypt and Italy to mediate in the conflict. On 27 January Siad Barre was reported to have fled the capital with those forces which remained loyal to him, and the USC took power. It immediately invited all former opposition groups to participate in a national conference to discuss the democratization of Somalia. On 29 January the USC appointed Ali Mahdi Mohamed (who had been a government minister in the 1960s) as President, in a temporary capacity, and he, in turn, invited Umar Arteh Ghalib (a former foreign affairs minister) to form a government which would prepare the country for democracy. The new, provisional Government was approved by the President on 2 February. However, the SNM and the SPM both opposed the appointment of Ali Mahdi as interim President, and demanded his resignation. At the beginning of February the USC emphasized that it did not intend to form a permanent government independently of the other insurgent movements that had collaborated in the overthrow of Siad Barre.

By mid-March 1991, however, Somalia was reported to be close to anarchy. A consolidation of the divisions between the various Somali clans appeared to be taking place, while former President Siad Barre was reported to have relocated to his native region of Gedo, near the border with Kenya, accompanied by loyal armed forces. The SNM and other opposition movements rejected the USC's invitation to take part in a national conference, and the SNM was reported to have formed an 11-member administration and a legislature to govern the former territory of British Somaliland. In mid-April the forces of the USC were reported to have defeated troops loyal to the former President after the latter had launched an offensive to recapture Mogadishu. In the same month it was reported that other forces loyal to Siad Barre had joined the southern clans in opposition to the USC, and that they were receiving support from the Kenyan Government. In early May it was announced that the USC and the SNM had accepted proposals by Egypt and Italy (both of which had attempted to mediate between the rival Somali factions) to attend a peace conference in Cairo in July. However, hopes of a reconciliation were frustrated on 16 May, when the SNM announced its official support for the secession of the former territory of British Somaliland, which the leaders of the northern-based clans were demanding. In late May the SNM Central Committee elected its Chairman, Abd ar-Rahman Ahmed Ali 'Tur', to be President of the newly-proclaimed 'Republic of Somaliland'. In early June the Committee approved a government comprising 17 ministers to administer the territory for a period of two years, after which free elections were to be held.

The SNM declined an invitation issued by the USC to participate in a conference of national reconciliation in June 1991, stating that the conference did not concern 'Somaliland'. The conference, convened in Djibouti, under the auspices of the Government of that country, was attended by representatives of the USC, the SDM, the SPM and the DFSS, and was chaired by former President Osman. The conference mandated delegates from the four organizations to travel to 'Somaliland' to persuade the SNM to abandon its declaration of independence. The SNM insisted, however, that 'Somaliland's' secession from Somalia was irreversible.

At a second reconciliation conference, held in Djibouti in mid-July 1991, the four groups which had met in June were joined by the United Somali Front (USF) and the Somali Democratic Alliance (SDA). The leaders of the six groups signed a manifesto which, *inter alia*, committed them to defeat the forces of Siad Barre (which had regrouped as the Somali National Front—SNF), to readopt the 1960 Constitution which Barre had suspended in 1969, and to implement a general cease-fire. The manifesto also confirmed Ali Mahdi in his position as Somalia's President, for a period of two years pending free elections. The participants in the conference agreed that a transitional government was to be formed under Ali Mahdi's presidency, in which each of the groups would be represented, with an equitable distribution of major posts and portfolios. Ali Mahdi was sworn in as President on 18 August 1991. In early September the President reappointed Umar Arteh Ghalib as Prime Minister, and in early October the latter announced the composition of the new Government. The new Council of Ministers was unusually large, comprising 72 ministers and deputy ministers, in order to ensure equal representation for the six participating groups.

In June 1991 a major rift within the USC was reported, with supporters of President Ali Mahdi fighting those of the USC's military commander, Gen. Mohamed Farah Aidid, on the streets of Mogadishu. Gen. Aidid apparently objected to Ali Mahdi's assumption of the presidency, since he had headed the military campaign to bring about the overthrow of Siad Barre. Moreover, the rival factions represented two 'sub-clans' of the Hawiye tribal grouping: although there was no tradition of enmity between the two sub-clans, rivalry was now fostered by the leaders, and clan loyalty quickly became entrenched. In July Gen. Aidid was elected Chairman of the USC by its Central Committee. The internal conflict appeared to have abated following Ali Mahdi's inauguration as President in August: Gen. Aidid pledged to support the new President, and the two signed a co-operation agreement. In early September, however, at least 300 people were killed, and more than 1,000 injured, in three days of armed confrontation in Mogadishu between supporters of the rival factions. A reconciliation committee of elders and members of neutral clans was subsequently established to resolve the conflict, and a cease-fire was agreed by both sides as a result of the new committee's arbitration. None the less, bitter divisions remained, and Gen. Aidid rejected the legitimacy of the Government appointed in early October. (Posts were reserved for supporters of Gen. Aidid's faction in the Council of Ministers, but Aidid denounced the new administration.) On 17 November his faction launched a full-scale attack on the President's positions in the capital (which largely represented the extent of Ali Mahdi's control of the country), and captured most of the city, forcing Ali Mahdi to flee. Gen. Aidid claimed to have overthrown the President, but by the end of November Ali Mahdi appeared to have regained control of much of the north of Mogadishu. At 30 November it was estimated that 1,000 people had been killed, and 6,000 injured. The fighting intensified in early December, and in mid-December Ali Mahdi appealed to the UN to send a peace-keeping force to intervene in the conflict. The UN announced that a special envoy was to visit Mogadishu in early January 1992. However, the envoy's attempts to negotiate a cease-fire were thwarted by Gen. Aidid's refusal to agree to UN involvement in Somalia's internal affairs, and the mission was followed by an escalation in violence. In mid-January Gen. Aidid's determination to seize political power was exemplified by his appointment of his own, 21-member administration. By the end of March 1992 it was estimated that 14,000 people had been killed and 27,000 wounded in the hostilities in Mogadishu, most of them civilians.

Throughout 1991 Somalia outside of Mogadishu (excluding 'Somaliland') was riven by battles for territory between armed groups, mostly divided along clan lines. By contrast, 'Somaliland' enjoyed several months of relative peace and stability following its declaration of independence, and work began, with the assistance of non-governmental aid organizations, on the task of rebuilding the territory's infrastructure. 'Somaliland', however, was not recognized as an independent state by the international community, and consequently did not receive the substantial financial aid that its economy required. Sub-clan rivalries within the Isaaq clan, to which the majority of the population in 'Somaliland' belong, emerged in December, when an armed group opposing the SNM took control of the port of Berbera. Forces of the SNM recaptured the port, but in January fighting between rival factions within the army was reported in Burao.

In March 1992 serious fighting erupted again in Berbera. President Abd ar-Rahman Ahmed Ali 'Tur' dispatched forces of his own sub-clan, the Habr Younis, to wrest control of the port from the Issa Musa sub-clan. Six months of hostilities ensued in Berbera and the town of Burao. In October peace talks were initiated by elders of the sub-clans concerned, which resulted in a cessation of the conflict. The SNM Government was also threatened by non-Isaaq ethnic groups within the borders of 'Somaliland' who opposed the secession of the territory. Islamic fundamentalist groups, which were funded by Sudan and Iran, also presented a threat to security.

In late January 1992 the UN had imposed an embargo on the sale of armaments to Somalia. In mid-February, at a conference at the UN headquarters in New York, the UN, the Organization of African Unity (OAU), the League of Arab States (the Arab League) and the Organization of the Islamic Conference (OIC) issued a joint appeal for a cease-fire, stating that it was a prerequisite for the granting of humanitarian aid to Somalia. Representatives from the rival factions involved in the battle for Mogadishu subsequently joined the conference, and agreed to the terms of a cease-fire accord devised by the international organizations. In early March, in discussions with a joint mission of the UN, the OAU, the OIC and the Arab League in Mogadishu, Gen. Aidid agreed to some form of monitoring of the cease-fire by a foreign observer mission. Both Gen. Aidid and Ali Mahdi signed the cease-fire accord on 3 March, and a fragile cease-fire in Mogadishu ensued. The terms of the accord provided for a visit, in late March, by a UN technical team, whose task was to survey the situation in Mogadishu, in advance of an unarmed observer mission which was to be dispatched to monitor violations of the accord. In late April the UN Security Council approved the establishment of a 'UN Operation in Somalia' (UNOSOM, see p. 51), to comprise a 50-strong observer mission to monitor the cease-fire. The Security Council also agreed in principle to the dispatch of a peace-keeping force to protect UN personnel and supplies at Mogadishu's port, and to escort food supplies to distribution points. The Security Council, however, needed to obtain consent for the peace-keeping force from both parties involved in the conflict, and Gen. Aidid was opposed to the deployment of foreign military personnel in Somalia. At the end of April the UN Secretary-General appointed a special representative to Somalia, whose task would be to oversee UN activities there. The representative left for Somalia at the beginning of May.

In the second half of April 1992 the SNF advanced on Mogadishu, with Siad Barre apparently intending to recapture the capital. Forces of the SNF came to within 40 km of the capital, but Gen. Aidid's forces decisively repelled them and pursued them to the south of the country. At the end of April the USC captured the town of Garba Harre, in the south-west, which had served as Siad Barre's base since his overthrow. Siad Barre fled, with about 200 supporters, over the border into Kenya. Kenya was not prepared to grant the former dictator political asylum, and in mid-May Siad Barre left for

Nigeria, the Government of which had temporarily offered him refugee status. In mid-May Gen. Aidid's forces and those of the SPM, the SDM and the Southern Somali National Movement (SSNM), with which he had formed a military alliance known as the Somali Liberation Army (SLA), captured Kismayu, which had been held by the SNF, a rival faction of the SPM and the SSDF. By June the SLA was in control of the majority of central and southern Somalia, making Gen. Aidid the most powerful of the country's warlords. In late June the UN secured agreement from the principal factions in Mogadishu for the deployment of the 50-strong observer mission envisaged in the March cease-fire accord.

In mid-August 1992, after much prevarication, Gen. Aidid finally agreed to the deployment of 500 troops charged with escorting food aid from Mogadishu's port and airport to distribution points. By late September the armed UN group had arrived but were yet to be deployed. In late August the UN Security Council approved the UN Secretary-General's recommendation to send four additional armed units (with a total of about 3,000 men) to Somalia, in order to protect humanitarian convoys and distribution centres in many parts of the country. This proposed strengthening of UNOSOM was intended to facilitate the safe delivery of food aid to alleviate the dire famine affecting the majority of the country: thousands of people were dying every day from starvation, while 1.5m. of the population were estimated to be close to death and 4.5m. in need of urgent assistance. Relief efforts by international aid agencies and the UN itself were being gravely impeded by systematic looting of supplies by armed groups, and by insecurity in different areas, posing a threat to relief workers.

Also in August 1992 the coalition of Gen. Aidid's faction of the USC with the SPM, the SDM and the SSNM was consolidated with the formation of the Somali National Alliance (SNA), of which Gen. Aidid was the leader. Meanwhile, Ali Mahdi strengthened ties with other armed groups hostile to Gen. Aidid, notably the SSDF and a faction of the SPM, and forged links with the SNA's main opponent in the south, Gen. Mohamed Siad Hersi 'Morgan' (who had led the SNF since the departure of his father-in-law, Siad Barre). In mid-October, after several months of relative calm in southern Somalia, Gen. Morgan's forces ousted those of the SNA from Bardera, which had served as Gen. Aidid's headquarters in that part of the country. The town was recaptured by the SNA, however, at the end of the month. Kismayu subsequently became the focus for hostilities between the SNF and the SNA (the SNA faction of the SPM holding control of the town).

In September 1992 'Somaliland' stated its categorical opposition to the deployment of UN troops within its borders. By early November UNOSOM's 500 armed troops had still not been deployed: Gen. Aidid placed conditions on their deployment in Mogadishu's port that were unacceptable to the UN. In mid-November UNOSOM secured Mogadishu's airport with the agreement of the clan controlling it. In late November a ship carrying grain for the World Food Programme's relief efforts was prevented from docking and was attacked by shells. By late November the 3,000 additional UN troops had not been dispatched, since Gen. Aidid objected to the presence of more foreign soldiers in Somalia. In response to a letter sent to the UN Security Council towards the end of the month regarding the intolerable situation in Somalia, the USA offered to lead a military operation in the country, with a US contingent of up to 30,000 men. In early December the Security Council sanctioned the proposed US operation, authorizing UN member states to use 'all necessary means to establish as soon as possible a secure environment for humanitarian relief operations in Somalia'. A few days later an advance contingent of 1,800 US marines landed on the beaches of Mogadishu and swiftly took control of the port and airport. Gen. Aidid and Ali Mahdi had instructed their supporters that the US forces were amicable, and consequently they encountered little resistance. The arrival of the foreign force, however, provoked fierce fighting in Kismayu, Baidoa and the north-east, with rival factions attempting to gain territory before the expected imposition of a cease-fire. The US members of the United Task Force (UNITAF) were subsequently reinforced by troops from 21 countries, with France, Belgium, Saudi Arabia, Zambia, Canada, Morocco and Australia providing substantial contingents. By the end of December UNITAF comprised 23,000 military personnel (rising to 33,000 in mid-January 1993), of whom about three-quarters were from the USA. In the second half of December UNITAF secured eight major relief centres in central and southern Somalia, including Baidoa, Bardera and Kismayu. No concerted resistance was mounted by the armed groups controlling the towns.

Shortly after the arrival of UNITAF, Gen. Aidid and Ali Mahdi signed a peace agreement at talks chaired by the US Special Envoy to Somalia. This agreement provided for an end to hostilities between the two factions of the USC. In late December 1992 the respective factions began to move vehicles mounted with heavy weaponry out of the capital. Gen. Aidid and Ali Mahdi subsequently met again and agreed to implement fully their initial peace accord, which had been flouted by both sides. A peace demonstration led by the two leaders, in which about 10,000 people participated, followed this new agreement. At the end of December, however, heavy fighting was reported between the SNA and fighters of the Murusade clan in north-west Mogadishu.

In early January 1993 peace negotiations were held in Addis Ababa, Ethiopia, under the auspices of the UN, and were attended by 14 of Somalia's political organizations. The talks resulted in agreements on an immediate cease-fire, disarmament under UN supervision and the holding of a conference of national reconciliation in March. A committee composed of members of the most important political groups was established, which was to prepare an agenda for the conference. Gen. Aidid had obstructed an agreement at first, but reports that UNITAF had destroyed a significant cache of weapons belonging to the General (killing about 30 of his supporters in the process) appeared to precipitate his consent to the proposals. The destruction of the weapons store was part of an unofficial campaign of disarmament launched by UNITAF: in early and mid-January US forces seized large quantities of weapons from arms markets and caches in Mogadishu, and Belgian troops seized weapons from residences in Kismayu.

Despite the cease-fire agreement, hostilities were resumed in various parts of the country almost immediately. A fresh outbreak of fighting was reported between the SNA and SSDF in the north-east, and the SNF continued its campaign to wrest control of the south from the SNA. In early February 1993 UNITAF repulsed attacks on Kismayu, launched by Gen. Morgan, but later in the month the SNF made gains in the city, prompting violent anti-UNITAF demonstrations by SNA supporters in Mogadishu, who accused UNITAF of assisting Gen. Morgan. Fighting between UNITAF troops and armed Somali youths continued in the capital for several days: at least seven Somalis were shot dead by the international force. In the battle for Kismayu more than 100 people were killed in the last week of February. Gen. Morgan finally yielded to demands by UNITAF to withdraw from the city at the end of the month, and in early March both the SNF and SNA surrendered heavy weapons to UNITAF.

In early March 1993 the preparatory committee for the national reconciliation conference reached agreement on an agenda, and the conference duly opened on 15 March in Addis Ababa, Ethiopia, at the headquarters of the UN Economic Commission for Africa. Conference proceedings were adjourned almost immediately when Gen. Aidid withdrew in protest at a renewed SNF attack on Kismayu. UNITAF forces were prevented from apprehending the SNF fighters by a tactically-placed shield of women and children; a 500-strong detachment of US marines was dispatched from Mogadishu to restore order in the south. When discussions at the conference resumed, the major point of disagreement was Gen. Aidid's desire for the remit of the conference to be limited to the establishment of regional administrations, while the organizations opposed to the SNA were intent on the formation of a central national government. After 13 days of negotiations, a compromise solution, proposed by the Ethiopian President, Meles Zenawi, secured general agreement. Under the terms of the accord, a Transitional National Council was to be established, which would administer the country for about two years until the holding of national elections. The council was to be composed of 74 members: one from each of the 15 organizations represented at the conference, three from each of the 18 proposed administrative regions (with each region appointing at least one woman) and five from Mogadishu. (A draft national transitional charter, enshrining the recommendations of the accord, was presented in November.)

Agreement on the future government of Somalia was reached hours after the UN Security Council approved the establishment of UNOSOM II, which was to take over responsibility for maintaining security from UNITAF by 1 May 1993. UNOSOM II was to be the UN's largest ever peace-keeping operation, comprising 28,000 military personnel and 2,800 civilian staff, and was to be the first UN peace-keeping operation where peace-enforcement without consent from parties within the country was authorized. UNOSOM II was, in addition, to be responsible for overseeing the rehabilitation of the country and the repatriation of Somali refugees. In January US forces had begun to be redeployed, and were replaced by military personnel from other countries. The USA was expected, however, to maintain a contingent of 5,000 in UNOSOM II. Hostilities in and around Kismayu continued subsequent to the successful national reconciliation conference, although none of the parties involved threatened to withdraw from the agreement reached. By early April Gen. Morgan appeared to be in control of the city, with the SNA accusing UNITAF of supporting the SNF by doing nothing to oppose its advances (a claim that was not wholly refuted by the Belgian forces responsible for Kismayu). On 4 May the USA handed over responsibility for international efforts in Somalia to UNOSOM II. A few days later Belgian troops (now under UN command) were involved in an armed confrontation with SPM forces who were attempting to enter Kismayu. In early June 24 Pakistani members of UNOSOM II were killed, and more than 50 injured, when the UN soldiers, who were attempting to inspect a weapons cache belonging to the SNA, were attacked by armed supporters of Gen. Aidid; 23 of the Somali fighters were killed in the confrontation. On the following day the Security Council adopted Resolution 837, which condemned the attack on UN forces and sought to bring to justice those responsible. UNOSOM forces, bolstered by US units redeployed from the Persian (Arabian) Gulf, embarked on a series of armed initiatives, including air strikes, against suspected strategic positions of the SNA. An exchange of gunfire between Pakistani troops and Somali militiamen, during a demonstration organized in protest at the intensification of the UN's campaign of enforced disarmament, resulted in the deaths of more than 20 Somali civilians. Despite the increased scale of UNOSOM operations, Aidid avoided injury or capture during June, prompting the Security Council to issue a formal warrant for his arrest. The violent deaths of three Italian UNOSOM troops in early July provoked Italian media claims that the military emphasis of the mission, promoted by the USA in pursuit of Gen. Aidid, was threatening the security of UN personnel and jeopardizing diplomatic initiatives undertaken by the Italian Government. The Italian Minister of Foreign Affairs urged UNOSOM to redirect its efforts towards securing a political solution to the conflict. The situation was exacerbated by a US helicopter attack on a suspected pro-Aidid command centre, which resulted in the deaths of 50–100 Somalis, and the murder, in retaliation, of four foreign journalists by enraged Somali crowds.

The allegedly belligerent methods employed by the UN in Somalia were subject to renewed scrutiny following sustained hostilities between UNOSOM forces and Somali militia during August 1993 (resulting in fatalities on both sides), culminating in a major embarrassment for the USA when, owing to inaccurate intelligence reports, the first operation involving US Ranger élite forces (a 400-strong contingent was dispatched to Somalia in late August) resulted in the forced occupation of the offices of a French humanitarian aid organization and the building being used by the UN Development Programme (eight of whose employees were temporarily taken captive by the US force). Further misgivings were expressed in early September, following the deaths of an estimated 200 Somalis (including women and children), after the armed intervention of a US helicopter in support of UN forces under fire in the midst of a crowd of civilians, in the capital. The UN Secretary-General attributed the tragedy to the Somali militia's practice of sheltering behind civilians while firing. By the end of September the number of UN troop casualties recorded since May had risen to more than 50 (including seven Nigerian troops, ambushed by Somali gunmen early in the month), reinforcing the urgency of UN Security Council Resolution 865, adopted on 22 September, that the Somali police and judicial systems should be promptly rehabilitated, and that UNOSOM II's mission should be ended by March 1995, with the installation of an elected Somali government. US forces enjoyed a minor success during September, when Osman Hassan Ali 'Ato', a financier to Aidid, was apprehended, together with three other suspected members of the SNA, under Resolution 837.

Uncompromising media coverage of the aftermath of the deaths of three US troops in late September 1993, and a violent exchange in the capital in early October (which resulted in the deaths of some 300 Somalis, 18 US troops and the capture, by local militiamen, of a US helicopter pilot and a Nigerian soldier), prompted widespread public outrage in the USA, and encouraged US congressional demands for a reassessment of the US role in Somalia. The US President, Bill Clinton, subsequently indicated a shift in US policy toward fostering multilateral political contacts in Somalia, and announced that all US troops were to be withdrawn by the end of March 1994, regardless of the outcome of attempts to negotiate a political settlement to the conflict by that date. (In the mean time the US military presence was to be significantly increased in order to ensure the security of its UN personnel and swiftly to achieve outstanding humanitarian objectives.) President Clinton's decision, announced during October, to withdraw the Ranger forces (which had actively sought to apprehend Aidid), prompted speculation (dismissed by Clinton) that the release of the US pilot and the Nigerian solider, secured in mid-October following four days of discussions between representatives of the US Government and Gen. Aidid, had been achieved as part of an undisclosed agreement negotiated between the two sides. Despite Aidid's declaration of a unilateral cease-fire prior to the talks, and subsequent indications of his willingness to enter into negotiations with the USA (in preference to the UN), fighting between pro-Aidid and pro-Mahdi factions escalated towards the end of October. In mid-November, responding to US pressure to sponsor Aidid's participation in the pursuit of a politically-negotiated peace, the UN Security Council adopted Resolution 885, which provided for the establishment of a commission of inquiry to investigate attacks on UNOSOM personnel, but suspended actions to apprehend further suspects (including Aidid). In late November the SNA refused to attend a UN-sponsored peace conference in Addis Ababa, in protest at the continued detention of SNA members under Resolution 837. In early December, however, Aidid and Ali Mahdi (who in November was reported to have assumed the leadership of the Somali Salvation Alliance—SSA, a new alliance of 12 factions opposed to Aidid) attended renewed negotiations in Addis Ababa, again sponsored by the UN (with the mediation of the Ethiopian Government), but discussions disintegrated with little progress.

Despite encouraging reports of renewed contacts between Aidid and representatives of the SSA, mediated by the Kenyan President, Daniel arap Moi, in Nakuru (Kenya) in early January 1994, and of attempts by more than 200 senior members of five Hawiye clans (including the pro-Aidid Habr Gidir and the pro-Mahdi Abgal clans) to negotiate a peace agreement in Mogadishu in mid-January, Aidid's unilateral declaration of intent to establish an interim government in the capital by the end of March, delivered in Uganda in late January, frustrated hopes of an imminent settlement. A succession of violent incidents involving UN forces and Somali civilians and militia resulted in a number of Somali deaths during January, perpetuating anti-UN sentiment. Relations were little improved by the UN's release of eight SNA supporters, apprehended in connection with alleged attacks on UNOSOM personnel, who subsequently complained of ill-treatment by UN troops during their period of detention.

In February 1994, in the context of the imminent withdrawal of UNOSOM contingents from the US and other Western nations (the US decision to recall all troops by the end of March had inspired similar commitments from Germany, Belgium, France, Sweden and Italy), the UN Security Council approved Resolution 897, reducing the troop strength of the mission to a maximum of 22,000, with a renewed mandate which prioritized the establishment of transitional institutions of government as detailed in the March 1993 Addis Ababa agreement, the rehabilitation of the apparatus of national law and order, and the protection of centres of communications, in order to facilitate reconstruction and humanitarian initiatives.

In late March 1994, following almost two weeks of negotiations, initiated by the UN, an agreement on the restoration of peace was signed by Gen. Aidid and Ali Mahdi (on behalf of the SSA) in Nairobi, Kenya. The agreement committed both sides to a cease-fire, disarmament and the organization of a conference of national reconciliation on 15 May to elect a President, Vice-Presidents and a Prime Minister. (A similar

# SOMALIA

agreement, concluded in Nairobi days later between community leaders from the lower Juba region, sought to restore order to the port of Kismayu, where fighting between factions had intensified in mid-February.) Electoral procedures and a future legislative structure were to be decided at a meeting of all signatories to the 1993 Addis Ababa agreement and the SNM, to be convened in April. By mid-1994, however, no such meeting had taken place, with accusations of failure to adhere to the terms of the Nairobi agreement proceeding from both Aidid and the SSA. Prospects for the successful organization of the meeting were further complicated by serious divisions within the SNM, arising from a declaration made by Abd ar-Rahman Ahmed Ali 'Tur', the former head of the self-proclaimed 'Republic of Somaliland', that the region should seek reintegration within a reconciled national territory of Somalia (an opinion which was strenuously opposed by President Egal—see below). In mid-April, after two weeks of fighting, Gen. Aidid's SNA wrested control of the southern coastal town of Merca (previously held by the SSNM—former allies of the SNA who had realigned behind the SSA in late 1993).

In June 1994 the UN Security Council agreed to renew UNOSOM's mandate by only four rather than the customary six months, and in late August it was agreed to reduce the strength of the mission (currently at 18,760) by 1,500. Pressure for UNOSOM to withdraw completely from Somalia was increased by further attacks on UN personnel: a Zimbabwean soldier was killed in late July, and seven Indian peacekeepers and three Indian doctors working for the UN were killed in late August. In late September a UN delegation visited Somalia with the intention of assessing the realistic possibilities for political reconciliation, in the absence of which UNOSOM would be withdrawn. The delegation attempted to organize a national reconciliation conference but Gen. Aidid and Ali Mahdi refused to agree on its terms and opened separate conferences, attended by their respective supporting factions. In the absence of any progress towards a political settlement of Somalia's divisions and in the context of increasing threats to the safety of UN personnel, the Security Council extended UNOSOM's mandate in early November to a final date of 31 March 1995, by which time the whole operation was to have been withdrawn.

In late June 1994 heavy fighting broke out in Mogadishu between Gen. Aidid's and Ali Mahdi's factions, resulting in the deaths of over 30 people. In July Gen. Aidid's fighters took the central town of Belet Huen from the Hawadle. In September several clashes between UN troops and Somali militias were reported, in which an unknown number of Somalis were killed. In late October fierce fighting erupted in the Bermuda area of Mogadishu, this time between Ali Mahdi's Abgal clan and the Murusade clan, although the two groups had previously been in alliance (there were rumours that Gen. Aidid had engineered the estrangement). Hostilities continued into early November, with over 40 people killed and many more wounded; fighting broke out again between the same clans in early December and continued sporadically into January 1995, resulting in as many as 200 fatalities. In early January a peace agreement was brokered by elders from the Abgal and Murusade communities. As the deadline for UNOSOM's departure approached, the competition for control of installations currently in UN hands, in particular the port and airport, became the focus of factional hostility.

In late November 1994 UN forces began to withdraw from positions outside Mogadishu in the first stages of UNOSOM's departure. In December Harti and Marehan clansmen fought for control of the port of Kismayu in the wake of the UN's withdrawal from that town. The operation to ensure the safe evacuation of the UN troops and civilian personnel, as well as most of the equipment brought in under UNOSOM, was organized and led by the USA, and was given the name 'Operation United Shield'. The USA stationed several thousand marines in warships off the Somali coast as early as December 1994, and in early 1995 they were joined by a multinational force of naval and airforce units comprising some 10,000 armed personnel. The strength of this force was intended to provide sufficient protection to the departing UN personnel to avoid any further killings (by early 1995 some 136 members of UNOSOM had been killed since the beginning of the operation). Contingents of UN soldiers began to be airlifted out of the country.

*Introductory Survey*

In early February 1995 UN troops left their compound in Mogadishu, which had served as UNOSOM's headquarters, and withdrew to positions in the port and airport. The compound buildings were immediately plundered for remaining equipment and materials by Somali looters. In mid-February thousands of SNA supporters demonstrated against the return of US forces, although Gen. Aidid gave assurances that they would not be attacked. Gen. Aidid and Ali Mahdi reached agreement on joint management of the port and airport: they each appointed six representatives to a committee that was to be responsible for administering the facilities once the UN had left. They subsequently agreed on a cessation of hostilities, including the removal of weapons from the streets of the capital during the UN withdrawal. This was not adhered to, however, with fighting reported around both the port and airport areas in late February. The combatants in the airport area appeared to be rival factions of the Habr Gidir sub-clan, with some supporting Gen. Aidid and others his former aide, Osman Hassan Ali 'Ato'. At the end of February 1,800 US and 400 Italian marines landed on Mogadishu's beaches, and command of the remaining 2,400 UN troops and of the whole operation was passed from the UN to the US commander. The marines secured the port and airport, and evacuated the last UN soldiers in an operation the execution of which was designed to minimize casualties, although several Somalis were killed and more injured as they threatened US positions. The departure of the last UN personnel on 2 March was closely followed by that of the US and Italian marines themselves. UNOSOM was thus terminated almost one month earlier than had originally been planned. Somali looters overran the airport, but armoured cars from Gen. Aidid's faction, reportedly accompanied by UN-trained police-officers, took control of the area. Ali Mahdi's Abgal clansmen, however, gained control of the eastern section of the airport and skirmishes were reported between the two sides. Nevertheless, Gen. Aidid and Ali Mahdi agreed on the reopening of the port and set out detailed terms for the 'technical peace committee' that was to administer the port and airport. In March fighting was reported in the Bay area of southern Somalia following the introduction of Islamic law, *Shari'a*, there. In mid-April Ali Mahdi accused the SNA of trying to buy arms in Ethiopia. In early May the heaviest fighting since the UN withdrawal was reported in the Bermuda area of Mogadishu.

Significant divisions within the SNA became more apparent in June 1995, following an attempt, made by a group of disaffected party members, to replace Aidid with Osman Hassan Ali 'Ato' as Chairman of the party. SNA members loyal to Aidid, however, immediately broadcast a rejection of the legitimacy of the actions of the Ali 'Ato' faction and announced the expulsion of the faction from the SNA. On 15 June a conference of reconciliation, convened in southern Mogadishu by representatives of 15 pro-Aidid factions, elected Aidid President of the Republic of Somalia for a three-year term. Five Vice-Presidents, representing the interests of distinct clans, were also elected, and the composition of a comprehensive cabinet was subsequently announced. However, Aidid's presidency and mandate to govern were immediately rejected in a joint statement issued by Ali Mahdi and Osman Hassan Ali 'Ato'.

Meanwhile, in May 1993, Mohamed Ibrahim Egal, who had been Somalia's Prime Minister in 1967–69, was elected as the new President of 'Somaliland'. In June Egal announced the composition of a 14-member council of ministers for 'Somaliland'. By late September a two-year transitional programme for reconstruction had been approved by a 47-member bicameral parliament (composed of a council of elders and a council of representatives). The administration's hopes that the prevailing atmosphere of peace in the north-western region would inspire the international community's prompt recognition of 'Somaliland' were largely frustrated, in October, by the OAU Secretary-General's rejection of the territory's independent status. Relations between the Egal adminstration and UNOSOM officials improved in late 1993, following the assurances of the UN Secretary-General that the mission would not interfere in the region's affairs but would provide funding for reconstruction and the rehabilitation of the police force. In late February 1994 Egal announced that a referendum would be organized in the north-western region in May, in order to ascertain the level of popular support for an independent 'Somaliland'. By early 1995, however, no such referendum had taken place. In August 1994 Egal expelled UN representatives from 'Somaliland', accusing them of interfering in the country's internal affairs. This was apparently precipitated by talks held between the new UN Special Representative to Somalia, James Victor Gbeho (appointed in July), and Ahmed Ali 'Tur', who was courted by both the UN and Gen. Aidid following his disavowal of secession for 'Somaliland'. In October the rift between Egal and Ahmed Ali 'Tur' culminated in violent confrontations in Hargeysa between military units remaining loyal to Egal and those defecting to support Ahmed Ali 'Tur'. Fighting continued during November, with conflicting reports as to which side was in control of the city and its airport. There were reports of many fatal casualties, including a defence minister of Egal's administration. In mid-December it was estimated that three-quarters of the population of Hargeysa had fled, many thousands of them seeking refuge in Ethiopia (see below). The rebel militias continued launching attacks on government positions in Hargeysa during the early part of 1995, although their success was difficult to ascertain. Fighting spread to other parts of 'Somaliland' and in April 1995 government forces were in armed conflict with fighters from the Garhadji clan who had recently formed an alliance with Issa militiamen belonging to the anti-secessionist USF. Despite Egal's obviously weakened position he persevered with the introduction of a new currency for the territory, the 'Somaliland Shilling', which was to be completed by the end of January 1995.

The departure of Western UN contingents by mid-1994 prompted international reappraisal and renewed criticism of UN operations in Somalia, despite the organization's promotion of its success in containing the humanitarian crisis and rehabilitating local administration, the judiciary and the police force. In mid-March a Canadian serviceman was sentenced to five years' imprisonment by a Canadian court martial for his involvement in the murder of a Somali civilian in March 1993, while serving with UNOSOM. Five other members of the élite Canadian Airborne Regiment were awaiting trial on the same charge. In late March 1994 it was reported that the unpublished report of an internal commission of inquiry, appointed by the UN in November 1993, was highly critical of several aspects of UN operations in Somalia, recommending that financial compensation should be considered for innocent Somali victims of UN peace-enforcement actions, and questioning the appropriateness, within the UN mandate, of some actions undertaken by US forces. The UN suffered a further embarrassment in April 1994, when US $2.6m. of UN personnel salaries was stolen from the organization's compound in Mogadishu. In January 1995 a Belgian paratrooper was sentenced by a Belgian military tribunal to five years' imprisonment for his involvement in a shooting incident in which two Somalis were killed in a dispute relating to illegal arms sales.

In 1992 severe drought, combined with the disruption to agriculture and relief efforts caused by conflict in many parts of the country, resulted in deaths from starvation and famine-related diseases at atrociously high levels: 500,000 people were estimated to have died during the year. UNITAF's operations greatly increased the amount of food reaching people in need, and by late February 1993 deaths from starvation had been virtually eliminated. The lives of relief workers were, however, at greater risk: three foreign and a large number of Somali aid workers were killed in the first three months of 1993. At a conference on humanitarian assistance to Somalia which immediately preceded the national reconciliation conference in March, US $142m. was pledged by international donors to Somalia for 1993, although it was to be conditional on security being maintained in the country. As a result of good rains in 1993–94 harvests were much better than in previous years and the country was expected to become self-sufficient in food once again. The UN World Food Programme had by the end of 1994 assisted thousands of displaced people returning to their villages in the cultivation of crops. There remained, however, much to do in the rehabilitation of infrastructure and health care in many parts of Somalia. In the course of 1994 the incidence of attacks on foreign aid workers increased and, in anticipation of the departure of UNOSOM, which had provided a measure of protection, aid organizations withdrew many of their personnel from Somalia, thus impeding many relief and rehabilitation projects. In late December the UN made an appeal for $70.3m. in assistance for Somalia until July 1995.

The escalation of hostilities between the Siad Barre Government and the rebel forces increased the flow of refugees from Somalia to Ethiopia and Kenya. During 1988–91 an estimated 600,000 Somalis fled from the civil war into Ethiopia, with more than 150,000 arriving in the first half of 1991. Following the SNM's assumption of control in northern Somalia in January of that year, thousands of refugees returned from Ethiopia. Many more returned to their home territory in 'Somaliland' in late 1991 and early 1992, as a result of the ethnic conflict in south-western Ethiopia, although adequate facilities did not exist to ensure their rehabilitation. The intensification of hostilities in the south of Somalia from April 1992 precipitated a huge movement of refugees into Kenya: by the end of 1992 there were approximately 400,000 Somali refugees in that country. In December 1992 it was estimated that there were more than 300,000 Somali refugees in Ethiopia, up to 100,000 in Yemen, and hundreds of thousands in the Persian (Arabian) Gulf region, in Europe and North America. In early 1993 the International Committee of the Red Cross estimated that three-quarters of Somalia's population had been internally displaced by the civil conflict, although by late 1994 many thousands had returned to their villages, with peace prevailing in many areas. During 1994 the office of the UN High Commissioner for Refugees estimated that 60,000 Somalis returned from Kenya, with a further 9,000 returnees arriving in the first two months of 1995. However, in November 1994 thousands of civilians fled fighting in Hargeysa, the capital of 'Somaliland', crossing the border into Ethiopia: over 30,000 had arrived by the end of the month, according to Ethiopian figures.

In April 1988 a decade of hostile relations between Somalia and Ethiopia, following the war in 1977–78 over the Ogaden area of Ethiopia (which is inhabited by ethnic Somalis), ended with a peace accord. It was agreed to re-establish diplomatic relations, to withdraw troops from border areas and to exchange prisoners of war. Following the overthrow of the Mengistu regime in May 1991, the new Government in Ethiopia declared itself neutral with regard to the factions fighting for control of Somalia. In early 1992 a delegation from Eritrea, which had declared its independence from Ethiopia in 1991, undertook extensive discussions with clan leaders from both sides of the conflict in Mogadishu, in an attempt to ease the crisis. Ethiopia hosted a peace conference for the warring Somali factions in early 1993 (see above).

In April 1991 the USC accused Kenya of assisting Siad Barre and of harbouring his supporters. Kenya's President Moi subsequently stated that his Government supported none of the rival factions, and in late 1991 Kenya sent a delegation to mediate between the parties involved in the hostilities in Mogadishu. During 1992 Gen. Aidid repeatedly accused the Kenyan Government of assisting Gen. Morgan and the SNF, a claim that Kenya consistently refuted.

The sporadic fighting in the Ogaden, which had continued since 1978, and prolonged periods of drought caused an influx of large numbers of Ethiopian refugees during the 1980s; by 1988 there were an estimated 840,000 refugees in camps in Somalia. By January 1992, however, few refugees remained in Somalia, with more than 350,000 having returned to Ethiopia in the first half of 1991 as a result of the continued armed conflict and drought in Somalia.

Soviet support for Somalia, which had been considerable since the 1969 revolution, ceased in 1977 as a result of the Ogaden War, with the USSR choosing to take Ethiopia's side in the conflict. In April 1987 a US military delegation visiting Somalia agreed to increase US military aid, and in August US troops participated in joint military exercises with Somali forces in Somalia. However, in February 1990 the USA suspended virtually all aid to Somalia, in protest at the 'long pattern of human rights abuses' of the Siad Barre regime. The USA provided about two-thirds of the financing of UNOSOM from late 1992 to early 1995, with the total amount spent on the operation estimated at US $2,500m.

## Government

Despite agreement at a conference of national reconciliation in July 1991 on the formation of a transitional government, by late 1991 Somalia was in a state of near anarchy, with no recognizable government. In March 1993, at a new national reconciliation conference, it was agreed to establish a 74-member Transitional National Council, which was to govern the country for about two years, pending the organization of free elections (see Recent History). The UN Operation in Somalia, UNOSOM II, was, however, to have substantial responsibility for the administration of the country during this period, and no transitional institutions of national government had been installed by mid-1995.

### Defence

Of total armed forces of 64,500 in June 1990, the army numbered 60,000, the navy 2,000 and the air force 2,500. In addition, there were 29,500 members of paramilitary forces, including 20,000 members of the People's Militia. Following the overthrow of the Siad Barre regime in January 1991, there were no national armed forces. Somalia was divided into areas controlled by different armed groups, which were based on clan, or sub-clan, membership. In March 1994 the UN announced that 8,000 former Somali police-officers had been rehabilitated throughout the country, receiving vehicles and uniforms from the UN. Following the UN withdrawal from Somalia in early 1995, these police-officers ceased receiving payment and their future and their hitherto neutral stance appeared vulnerable.

### Economic Affairs

In 1990, according to estimates by the World Bank, Somalia's gross national product (GNP), measured at average 1988–90 prices, was US $946m., equivalent to $150 per head. During 1980–90, it was estimated, GNP increased, in real terms, at an average annual rate of 1.1%, although GNP per head declined by 2.3% per year in the period 1985–93. Over the period 1985–93 the population increased by an annual average of 3.1%. Somalia's gross domestic product (GDP) increased, in real terms, by an annual average of 2.4% in 1980–92.

Agriculture (including forestry and fishing) contributed 66% of GDP in 1990. Some 68% of the working population were employed in agriculture in 1993. Agriculture is based on the breeding of livestock, which accounted for 49% of GDP in 1989 and 38.4% of the total value of exports in 1988. It was forecast that 27,000 metric tons of bananas would be exported from Somalia in 1995. Bananas are the principal cash crop, accounting for 40.3% of export earnings in 1988. During 1980–90 the GDP of the agricultural sector increased by an annual average of 3.3%; in 1991, however, agricultural production declined by 8.8%.

Industry (including mining, manufacturing, construction and power) contributed 8.6% of GDP in 1988, and employed an estimated 10.5% of the working population in 1991. Industrial GDP increased by an average of 1.0% annually in 1980–90.

Mining contributed 0.3% of GDP in 1988. Somalia's mineral resources include salt, tin, zinc, copper, gypsum, manganese, uranium and iron ore. Deposits of petroleum and natural gas have been discovered but remain unexploited: US petroleum companies were granted exploration rights covering two-thirds of the country by Siad Barre, and were expected to start investigations once there was a durable peace.

Manufacturing contributed almost 5% of GDP in 1988. The most important sectors are food-processing, especially sugar-refining, the processing of hides and skins, and the refining of petroleum. Manufacturing GDP decreased by an average of 1.7% annually in 1980–90.

Energy is derived principally from oil-fired generators. Imports of fuel products comprised 14% of the value of merchandise imports in 1990.

In 1989 Somalia recorded a visible trade deficit of US $278.6m., and there was a deficit of $156.7m. on the current account of the balance of payments. In 1982 the principal source of imports (34.4%) was Italy, while Saudi Arabia was the principal market for exports (86.5%). Other major trading partners in that year were the United Kingdom, the Federal Republic of Germany, Kenya and Ethiopia. The principal exports in 1988 were livestock and bananas. The principal imports were petroleum, fertilizers, foodstuffs and machinery.

In 1988 Somalia recorded a budget deficit of 10,009.4m. Somali shillings. A provisional budget for 1991 was projected to balance at 268,283.2m. Somali shillings. Somalia's total external debt was US $2,501m. at the end of 1993, of which $1,897m. was long-term public debt. In 1990 the cost of debt-servicing was equivalent to 11.7% of the value of exports of goods and services. In 1991 the annual rate of inflation was estimated at more than 100%; it was estimated to have averaged 45.7% annually during 1980–88.

Somalia is a member of the African Development Bank (see p. 102) and the Islamic Development Bank (see p. 180).

Somalia's long history of civil unrest (exacerbated by the overthrow of President Siad Barre in January 1991), together with unreliable climatic conditions, have undermined the traditional agricultural base of the economy. Agricultural production in 1991–92 was estimated at just 5%–10% that of 1987–88, although in 1993–94 good rainfall resulted in much improved harvests (small-scale exports of fruit and livestock resumed). In the absence of government and a conventional economic system, economic activity is largely controlled by clan-based militias. These have exploited the presence of foreign relief organizations (looting supplies and exacting protection money from them), and in particular the massive presence of the UN in 1993–95 (see Recent History). During this period the UN became the largest employer in the country and introduced a large amount of foreign currency. With the withdrawal of the UN operation in early 1995, hundreds of Somalis lost their employment and the country's largest source of income was removed. As a result of the sustained civil conflict, considerable damage has been inflicted on the infrastructure of many urban areas, notably the capital. Large-scale reconstruction and the exploitation of Somalia's underdeveloped resources (including large areas of uncultivated arable land between the Juba and Shebelle rivers, and rich fishing grounds along the country's coastline) were expected to be hampered by unwieldy foreign debt, in the seemingly unlikely event of the prompt negotiation of a durable peace accord. The relative stability of the self-proclaimed 'Republic of Somaliland', following its secession in 1991, contributed to an improvement in the economy of that territory, with an estimated increase in GNP per head of 20% in 1991–94. The Egal administration announced the introduction of tax, banking and customs systems in late 1993, and a new currency was introduced in late 1994. However, during 1994 the 'Somaliland' government was placed increasingly under threat by rebels from the armed forces, which, together with the refusal of the international community to recognize the territory's independence, jeopardized the future prosperity of 'Somaliland'.

### Social Welfare

There is no state system of social insurance, but in the late 1980s there were plans for improving social welfare facilities. Medical treatment at government-administered hospitals and dispensaries is provided free of charge. In 1988 Somalia had 8,200 hospital beds, and there were 1,250 physicians working in the country. In the same year 255.2m. Somali shillings (equivalent to 1.0% of total government spending) were allocated to the health sector. In 1992 only 10–15 of Somalia's 70 hospitals were functioning, as a result of the civil unrest.

### Education

All private schools were nationalized in 1972, and education is now provided free of charge. Despite the introduction of the Somali script in 1972, the level of literacy remains low. According to estimates by UNESCO, the average rate of adult illiteracy declined from 83.1% in 1985 to 75.9% (males 63.9%; females 86.0%) in 1990. Primary education, lasting for eight years, is officially compulsory for children aged six to 14 years. However, the total enrolment at primary schools of children in this age-group declined from 14% (boys 18%; girls 10%) in 1980 to only 8% (boys 11%; girls 6%) in 1985. Secondary education, beginning at the age of 14, lasts for four years but is not compulsory. In 1985 the enrolment at secondary schools included 4% of children (boys 5%; girls 3%) in the relevant age-group. In 1985 enrolment at primary and secondary schools was equivalent to 10% of the school-age population (boys 13%; girls 7%). Current expenditure on education in the Government's 1988 budget was 478.1m. Somali shillings (equivalent to 1.9% of total current spending). Following the overthrow of Siad Barre's Government in January 1991 and the descent of the country into anarchy, Somalia's education system collapsed. In January 1993 a primary school was opened in the building of Somalia's sole university, the Somali National University in Mogadishu (which had been closed in early 1991). The only other schools operating in the country were a number run by fundamentalist Islamic groups and some that had been reopened in 'Somaliland' in mid-1991.

### Public Holidays

**1995:** 1 January (New Year's Day), 3 March* (Id al-Fitr, end of Ramadan), 1 May (Labour Day), 10 May* (Id al-Adha, Feast of the Sacrifice), 9 June* (Ashoura), 26 June (Independence Day), 1 July (Foundation of the Republic), 9 August* (Mouloud, Birth of the Prophet).

## SOMALIA

**1996:** 1 January (New Year's Day), 21 February* (Id al-Fitr, end of Ramadan), 29 April* (Id al-Adha, Feast of the Sacrifice), 1 May (Labour Day), 28 May* (Ashoura), 26 June (Independence Day), 1 July (Foundation of the Republic), 28 July* (Mouloud, Birth of the Prophet).

* These holidays are dependent on the Islamic lunar calendar and may vary by one or two days from the dates given.

### Weights and Measures
The metric and imperial systems are both used.

# Statistical Survey

Sources (unless otherwise stated): Economic Research and Statistics Department, Central Bank of Somalia, Mogadishu, and Central Statistical Department, State Planning Commission, POB 1742, Mogadishu; tel. (1) 80385; telex 715.

## Area and Population

### AREA, POPULATION AND DENSITY

| | |
|---|---:|
| Area (sq km) | 637,657* |
| Population (census results)† | |
| 7 February 1975 | 3,253,024 |
| 1986–87 (provisional) | |
| Males | 3,741,664 |
| Females | 3,372,767 |
| Total | 7,114,431 |
| Density (per sq km) at 1986–87 census | 11.2 |

* 246,201 sq miles.
† Excluding adjustment for underenumeration.

### PRINCIPAL TOWNS (estimated population in 1981)

| | |
|---|---:|
| Mogadishu (capital) | 500,000 |
| Hargeysa | 70,000 |
| Kismayu | 70,000 |
| Berbera | 65,000 |
| Merca | 60,000 |

### BIRTHS AND DEATHS (UN estimates, annual averages)

| | 1975–80 | 1980–85 | 1985–90 |
|---|---:|---:|---:|
| Birth rate (per 1,000) | 50.4 | 50.4 | 50.4 |
| Death rate (per 1,000) | 22.7 | 21.8 | 20.1 |

**Expectation of life** (UN estimates, years at birth, 1985–90): 45.0 (males 43.4; females 46.6).

Source: UN, *World Population Prospects: The 1992 Revision*.

### ECONOMICALLY ACTIVE POPULATION
(estimates, '000 persons, 1991)

| | Males | Females | Total |
|---|---:|---:|---:|
| Agriculture, etc. | 1,157 | 1,118 | 2,275 |
| Industry | 290 | 46 | 336 |
| Services | 466 | 138 | 604 |
| **Total labour force** | 1,913 | 1,302 | 3,215 |

Source: UN Economic Commission for Africa, *African Statistical Yearbook*.

**Mid-1993** (estimates in '000): Agriculture, etc. 2,539; Total 3,714 (Source: FAO, *Production Yearbook*).

## Agriculture

### PRINCIPAL CROPS ('000 metric tons)

| | 1991 | 1992 | 1993 |
|---|---:|---:|---:|
| Maize | 100* | 101* | 120† |
| Sorghum | 145* | 92* | 150† |
| Rice (paddy)† | 10 | 8 | 15 |
| Cassava (Manioc)† | 45 | 40 | 45 |
| Pulses† | 13 | 10 | 13 |
| Groundnuts† | 2 | 1 | 2 |
| Sesame seed† | 35 | 18 | 30 |
| Sugar cane† | 290 | 280 | 200 |
| Grapefruit† | 15 | 7 | 15 |
| Bananas† | 90 | 80 | 90 |
| Vegetables† | 47 | 26 | 47 |

* Unofficial figure. † FAO estimate(s).

Source: FAO, *Production Yearbook*.

### LIVESTOCK (FAO estimates, '000 head, year ending September)

| | 1991 | 1992 | 1993 |
|---|---:|---:|---:|
| Cattle | 2,000 | 1,000 | 1,500 |
| Sheep | 9,500 | 6,000 | 6,500 |
| Goats | 15,000 | 12,000 | 12,500 |
| Pigs | 7 | 2 | 6 |
| Asses | 25 | 20 | 23 |
| Mules | 23 | 18 | 20 |
| Camels | 6,500 | 6,000 | 6,100 |

Poultry (FAO estimates, million): 2 in 1991; 1 in 1992; 3 in 1993.

Source: FAO, *Production Yearbook*.

### LIVESTOCK PRODUCTS (FAO estimates, '000 metric tons)

| | 1991 | 1992 | 1993 |
|---|---:|---:|---:|
| Cows' milk | 225 | 120 | 180 |
| Goats' milk | 462 | 370 | 385 |
| Sheep's milk | 277 | 175 | 190 |
| Beef and veal | 24 | 13 | 20 |
| Mutton and lamb | 25 | 18 | 19 |
| Goat meat | 46 | 39 | 39 |
| Poultry eggs | 1.8 | 0.8 | 2.0 |
| Cattle hides | 4.4 | 2.4 | 3.6 |
| Sheepskins | 4.7 | 3.5 | 3.6 |
| Goatskins | 7.1 | 6.0 | 6.0 |

Source: FAO, *Production Yearbook*.

SOMALIA                                                                                                                                    Statistical Survey

## Forestry

**ROUNDWOOD REMOVALS** (FAO estimates, '000 cubic metres)

|  | 1990 | 1991 | 1992 |
|---|---|---|---|
| Sawlogs, veneer logs and logs for sleepers* | 28 | 28 | 28 |
| Other industrial wood | 73 | 75 | 78 |
| Fuel wood | 8,153 | 8,378 | 8,649 |
| **Total** | 8,254 | 8,481 | 8,755 |

* Assumed to be unchanged since 1975.

Source: FAO, *Yearbook of Forest Products*.

## Fishing

('000 metric tons, live weight)

|  | 1990 | 1991 | 1992* |
|---|---|---|---|
| Freshwater fishes | 0.4* | 0.3 | 0.3 |
| Marine fishes | 16.2* | 15.0 | 14.3 |
| Spiny lobsters | 0.5 | 0.5 | 0.4 |
| Marine molluscs | 0.4 | 0.3 | 0.3 |
| **Total catch** | 17.5* | 16.1 | 15.3 |

* FAO estimate(s).

Source: FAO, *Yearbook of Fishery Statistics*.

## Mining

|  | 1989 | 1990 | 1991 |
|---|---|---|---|
| Salt ('000 metric tons)* | 30 | 30 | 30 |

* Data from the US Bureau of Mines.

Source: UN, *Industrial Statistics Yearbook*.

## Industry

**SELECTED PRODUCTS**
('000 metric tons, unless otherwise indicated)

|  | 1986 | 1987 | 1988 |
|---|---|---|---|
| Sugar* | 30.0 | 43.3 | 41.2 |
| Canned meat (million tins) | 1.0 | — | — |
| Canned fish | 0.1 | — | — |
| Pasta and flour | 15.6 | 4.3 | — |
| Textiles (million yards) | 5.5 | 3.0 | 6.3 |
| Boxes and bags | 15.0 | 12.0 | 5.0 |
| Cigarettes and matches | 0.3 | 0.2 | 0.1 |
| Petroleum products | 128 | 44 | 30 |
| Electric energy (million kWh)† | 253 | 255 | 257 |

Sugar ('000 metric tons)*: 50 in 1989; 25 in 1990; 30 in 1991.

Electric energy (million kWh)†: 258 in 1989; 230 in 1990; 210 in 1991.

* Source: FAO.
† Source: UN, *Industrial Statistics Yearbook*.

## Finance

**CURRENCY AND EXCHANGE RATES**

**Monetary Units**
100 cents = 1 Somali shilling (So. sh.).

**Sterling and Dollar Equivalents** (31 October 1994)
£1 sterling = 7,990 Somali shillings;
US $1 = 4,900 Somali shillings;
10,000 Somali shillings = £1.252 = $2.041.

**Average Exchange Rate** (Somali shillings per US $)
1987   105.18
1988   170.45
1989   490.68

**CURRENT BUDGET** (million Somali shillings)

| Revenue | 1986 | 1987 | 1988 |
|---|---|---|---|
| Total tax revenue | 8,516.4 | 8,622.4 | 12,528.1 |
| Taxes on income and profits | 1,014.8 | 889.7 | 1,431.0 |
| Income tax | 380.5 | 538.8 | 914.8 |
| Profit tax | 634.3 | 350.9 | 516.2 |
| Taxes on production, consumption and domestic transactions | 1,410.4 | 1,274.2 | 2,336.4 |
| Taxes on international transactions | 6,091.2 | 6,458.5 | 8,760.6 |
| Import duties | 4,633.2 | 4,835.2 | 6,712.1 |
| Total non-tax revenue | 6,375.2 | 8,220.4 | 7,623.4 |
| Fees and service charges | 274.1 | 576.1 | 828.8 |
| Income from government property | 633.4 | 656.4 | 2,418.9 |
| Other revenue | 5,467.2 | 6,987.9 | 4,375.7 |
| **Total** | 14,891.6 | 16,842.8 | 20,151.5 |

| Expenditure | 1986 | 1987 | 1988 |
|---|---|---|---|
| Total general services | 11,997.7 | 19,636.7 | 24,213.6 |
| Defence | 2,615.9 | 3,145.0 | 8,093.9 |
| Interior and police | 605.0 | 560.7 | 715.4 |
| Finance and central services | 7,588.3 | 14,017.8 | 12,515.6 |
| Foreign affairs | 633.0 | 1,413.9 | 2,153.1 |
| Justice and religious affairs | 248.5 | 290.2 | 447.0 |
| Presidency and general administration | 93.0 | 148.0 | 217.4 |
| Planning | 189.0 | 24.9 | 24.3 |
| National Assembly | 25.0 | 36.2 | 46.9 |
| Total economic services | 1,927.6 | 554.1 | 600.3 |
| Transportation | 122.2 | 95.2 | 94.5 |
| Posts and telecommunications | 94.3 | 76.7 | 75.6 |
| Public works | 153.9 | 57.5 | 69.8 |
| Agriculture | 547.2 | 59.4 | 55.3 |
| Livestock and forestry | 459.0 | 89.5 | 109.9 |
| Mineral and water resources | 318.8 | 85.2 | 93.1 |
| Industry and commerce | 131.0 | 45.1 | 43.9 |
| Fisheries | 101.2 | 45.5 | 58.2 |
| Total social services | 1,050.5 | 900.1 | 930.8 |
| Education | 501.6 | 403.0 | 478.1 |
| Health | 213.8 | 203.5 | 255.2 |
| Information | 111.5 | 135.0 | 145.8 |
| Labour, sports and tourism | 139.6 | 49.3 | 51.7 |
| Other | 84.0 | 109.3 | — |
| **Total** | 14,975.8 | 21,091.0 | 25,744.7 |

**1989** (estimates): Budget to balance at 32,429m. Somali shillings.
**1990** (estimates): Budget to balance at 86,012.0m. Somali shillings.
**1991** (estimates): Budget to balance at 268,283.2m. Somali shillings.

**CENTRAL BANK RESERVES** (US $ million at 31 December)

|  | 1987 | 1988 | 1989 |
|---|---|---|---|
| Gold* | 8.3 | 7.0 | 6.9 |
| Foreign exchange | 7.3 | 15.3 | 15.4 |
| **Total** | 15.6 | 22.3 | 22.3 |

* Valued at market-related prices.

Source: IMF, *International Financial Statistics*.

# SOMALIA

## Statistical Survey

### MONEY SUPPLY (million Somali shillings at 31 December)

|  | 1987 | 1988 | 1989 |
|---|---|---|---|
| Currency outside banks | 12,327 | 21,033 | 70,789 |
| Private-sector deposits at central bank | 1,771 | 1,555 | 5,067 |
| Demand deposits at commercial banks | 15,948 | 22,848 | 63,971 |
| **Total money** | 30,046 | 45,436 | 139,827 |

Source: IMF, *International Financial Statistics*.

### COST OF LIVING
(Consumer Price Index for Mogadishu; base: 1985 = 100)

|  | 1986 | 1987 | 1988 |
|---|---|---|---|
| Food | 123.6 | 161.4 | 319.8 |
| Beverages and tobacco | 117.5 | 155.5 | 249.3 |
| Clothes | 119.2 | 153.4 | 271.3 |
| Rent | 131.5 | 169.5 | 250.6 |
| Water, fuel and power | 156.0 | 203.2 | 222.8 |
| Transport and petrol | 130.2 | 155.4 | 260.1 |
| Miscellaneous items | 121.5 | 140.9 | 253.0 |
| **All items** | 125.8 | 161.2 | 292.9 |

### NATIONAL ACCOUNTS

**Expenditure on the Gross Domestic Product***
(estimates, million Somali shillings at current prices)

|  | 1988 | 1989 | 1990 |
|---|---|---|---|
| Government final consumption expenditure | 33,220 | 58,530 | 104,760 |
| Private final consumption expenditure | 240,950 | 481,680 | 894,790 |
| Increase in stocks | 14,770 | n.a. | n.a. |
| Gross fixed capital formation | 44,780 | 134,150 | 240,030 |
| **Total domestic expenditure** | 333,720 | 674,360 | 1,239,580 |
| Exports of goods and services | 7,630 | 8,890 | 8,660 |
| *Less* Imports of goods and services | 49,430 | 57,660 | 58,460 |
| **GDP in purchasers' values** | 291,920 | 625,580 | 1,189,780 |

* Figures are rounded to the nearest 10m. Somali shillings.

Source: UN Economic Commission for Africa, *African Statistical Yearbook*.

**Gross Domestic Product by Economic Activity**
(million Somali shillings at constant 1985 prices)

|  | 1986 | 1987 | 1988 |
|---|---|---|---|
| Agriculture, hunting, forestry and fishing | 54,868 | 59,378 | 61,613 |
| Mining and quarrying | 291 | 291 | 291 |
| Manufacturing | 4,596 | 4,821 | 4,580 |
| Electricity, gas and water | 77 | 62 | 57 |
| Construction | 3,289 | 3,486 | 2,963 |
| Trade, restaurants and hotels | 8,587 | 9,929 | 8,599 |
| Transport, storage and communications | 6,020 | 6,153 | 5,873 |
| Finance, insurance, real estate and business services | 3,743 | 4,095 | 3,890 |
| Government services | 1,631 | 1,530 | 1,404 |
| Other community, social and personal services | 2,698 | 2,779 | 2,863 |
| **Sub-total** | 85,800 | 92,524 | 92,133 |
| *Less* Imputed bank service charges | 737 | 748 | 748 |
| **GDP at factor cost** | 85,064 | 91,776 | 91,385 |
| Indirect taxes, *less* subsidies | 5,301 | 4,250 | 3,262 |
| **GDP in purchasers' values** | 90,365 | 96,026 | 94,647 |

**GDP at factor cost** (estimates, million Somali shillings at current prices): 249,380 in 1988; 500,130 in 1989; 923,970 in 1990 (Source: UN Economic Commission for Africa, *African Statistical Yearbook*).

### BALANCE OF PAYMENTS (US $ million)

|  | 1987 | 1988 | 1989 |
|---|---|---|---|
| Merchandise exports f.o.b. | 94.0 | 58.4 | 67.7 |
| Merchandise imports f.o.b. | −358.5 | −216.0 | −346.3 |
| **Trade balance** | −264.5 | −157.6 | −278.6 |
| Imports of services (net) | −127.7 | −104.0 | −122.0 |
| Other income paid (net) | −52.0 | −60.6 | −84.4 |
| Private unrequited transfers (net) | −13.1 | 6.4 | −2.9 |
| Official unrequited transfers (net) | 343.3 | 217.3 | 331.2 |
| **Current balance** | −114.0 | −98.5 | −156.7 |
| Capital (net) | −25.1 | −102.8 | −31.9 |
| Net errors and omissions | 40.7 | 21.1 | −0.8 |
| **Overall balance** | −98.4 | −180.2 | −189.4 |

Source: IMF, *International Financial Statistics*.

## External Trade

### PRINCIPAL COMMODITIES (million Somali shillings)

| Imports* | 1986 | 1987 | 1988 |
|---|---|---|---|
| Foodstuffs | 1,783.3 | 3,703.6 | 1,216.1 |
| Beverages and tobacco | 298.1 | 183.6 | 6.2 |
| Textiles, household goods | 156.0 | 304.1 | 115.5 |
| Medicinal and chemical products | 89.2 | 133.9 | 97.9 |
| Manufacturing raw materials | 230.0 | 626.9 | 661.4 |
| Fertilizers | 1.8 | 238.0 | 2,411.4 |
| Petroleum | 2,051.0 | 3,604.2 | 3,815.9 |
| Construction materials | 981.4 | 2,001.9 | 307.8 |
| Machinery and parts | 1,098.3 | 1,203.6 | 957.1 |
| Transport equipment | 1,133.8 | 1,027.6 | 195.2 |
| Agricultural machinery | 4.2 | 62.7 | 113.4 |
| **Total** (incl. others) | 8,443.4 | 13,913.7 | 11,545.5 |

* Figures cover only imports made against payments of foreign currencies. The total value of imports in 1986 was 20,474 million Somali shillings.

| Exports | 1986 | 1987 | 1988 |
|---|---|---|---|
| Livestock | 4,420.3 | 7,300.0 | 3,806.5 |
| Bananas | 1,207.2 | 2,468.8 | 3,992.3 |
| Fish | 45.2 | 70.4 | 291.8 |
| Hides and skins | 294.0 | 705.2 | 492.0 |
| Myrrh | 43.6 | 229.9 | 252.8 |
| **Total** (incl. others) | 6,372.5 | 10,899.9 | 9,914.1 |

**1991** (estimates, US $ million): Imports 160; Exports 80.

### PRINCIPAL TRADING PARTNERS ('000 Somali shillings)

| Imports | 1980 | 1981 | 1982 |
|---|---|---|---|
| China, People's Republic | 46,959 | 40,962 | 89,772 |
| Ethiopia | 43,743 | 146,853 | 155,775 |
| Germany, Fed. Republic | 104,117 | 430,548 | 214,873 |
| Hong Kong | 5,351 | 13,862 | 3,972 |
| India | 41,467 | 19,638 | 4,801 |
| Iraq | 2,812 | 67,746 | 402 |
| Italy | 756,800 | 662,839 | 1,221,146 |
| Japan | 28,900 | 54,789 | 48,371 |
| Kenya | 86,515 | 105,627 | 198,064 |
| Saudi Arabia | 120,208 | 160,583 | 82,879 |
| Singapore | 18,569 | 15,592 | 73,652 |
| Thailand | 19,296 | 40,527 | 106,474 |
| United Kingdom | 172,613 | 935,900 | 238,371 |
| USA | 201,662 | 141,823 | 154,082 |
| **Total** (incl. others) | 2,190,627 | 3,221,715 | 3,548,805 |

# SOMALIA

| Exports | 1980 | 1981 | 1982 |
|---|---|---|---|
| Djibouti | 6,640 | 3,209 | 2,458 |
| Germany, Fed. Republic | 11,376 | 1,956 | 20,086 |
| Italy | 107,661 | 58,975 | 77,870 |
| Kenya | 2,425 | 6,929 | 4,211 |
| Saudi Arabia | 583,768 | 803,631 | 1,852,936 |
| United Kingdom | 1,233 | — | 3,169 |
| USA | 1,301 | — | 6,970 |
| Yemen, People's Dem. Republic | 3,182 | — | — |
| **Total** (incl. others) | 844,012 | 960,050 | 2,142,585 |

Source: the former Ministry of Planning, Mogadishu.

**1986:** *Imports* (estimates, million Somali shillings) USA 1,816; Japan 836; China, People's Republic 553; United Kingdom 773; France 341; Germany, Fed. Republic 1,481; Total (incl. others) 8,443; *Exports* (estimates, million Somali shillings) USA 5; China People's Republic 4; United Kingdom 31; France 27; Germany, Fed. Republic 11; Total (incl. others) 6,373. (Source: UN Economic Commission for Africa, *African Statistical Yearbook*.)

## Transport

**ROAD TRAFFIC** (estimates, '000 motor vehicles in use)

|  | 1989 | 1990 | 1991 |
|---|---|---|---|
| Passenger cars | 2 | 1 | 1 |
| Commercial vehicles | 8 | 8 | 1 |

Source: UN Economic Commission for Africa, *African Statistical Yearbook*.

**SHIPPING**
**Merchant Fleet** (at 30 June)

|  | 1979 | 1980 | 1981 |
|---|---|---|---|
| Displacement ('000 gross registered tons) | 55 | 46 | 35 |

**1983:** 18,775 grt.

**International Sea-borne Freight Traffic** ('000 metric tons)

|  | 1989 | 1990 | 1991 |
|---|---|---|---|
| Goods loaded | 325 | 324 | n.a. |
| Goods unloaded | 1,252* | 1,118 | 1,007* |

* Estimate.

Source: UN Economic Commission for Africa, *African Statistical Yearbook*.

**CIVIL AVIATION** (traffic on scheduled services)

|  | 1989 | 1990 | 1991 |
|---|---|---|---|
| Kilometres flown (million) | 3 | 3 | 1 |
| Passengers carried ('000) | 89 | 88 | 46 |
| Passenger-km (million) | 248 | 255 | 131 |
| Freight ton-km (million) | 8 | 9 | 5 |

Source: UN, *Statistical Yearbook*.

## Communications Media

|  | 1990 | 1991 | 1992 |
|---|---|---|---|
| Radio receivers ('000 in use) | 320 | 330 | 350 |
| Television receivers ('000 in use) | 105 | 108 | 113 |
| Telephones ('000 in use)* | 9 | 9 | n.a. |
| Daily newspapers | 1 | n.a. | 1 |

* UN estimates.

Sources: UNESCO, *Statistical Yearbook*; UN Economic Commission for Africa, *African Statistical Yearbook*.

## Education
(1985)

|  | Institutions | Teachers | Pupils |
|---|---|---|---|
| Pre-primary | 16 | 133 | 1,558 |
| Primary | 1,224 | 10,338 | 196,496 |
| Secondary: |  |  |  |
| General | n.a. | 2,149 | 39,753 |
| Teacher training | n.a. | 30* | 613* |
| Vocational | n.a. | 637 | 5,933 |
| Higher | n.a. | 817† | 15,672† |

* Figures refer to 1984.   † Figures refer to 1986.

Source: UNESCO, *Statistical Yearbook*.

**1990** (UN estimates): 377,000 primary-level pupils; 44,000 secondary-level pupils; 10,400 higher-level pupils.

**1991:** University teachers 549; University students 4,640.

# Directory

## The Constitution

The Constitution promulgated in 1979 and amended in 1990 was revoked following the overthrow of President Siad Barre in January 1991. Proposals to reinstate the independence Constitution of 1960 were subsequently abandoned. A preparatory commission for a Transitional National Council, formed in March 1993, presented a draft transitional national charter in November 1993, providing the constitutional framework for the country during a two-year transitional period.

## The Government
(June 1995)

On 27 March 1993 a conference of the main political factions agreed to form a 74-member Transitional National Council (TNC) as the country's supreme authority, with a mandate to hold elections within two years. The TNC was to comprise three representatives from each of the country's 18 administrative regions, five representatives from Mogadishu and one representative from each of the 15 political factions that signed the agreement. The UN Operation in Somalia, UNOSOM, was, however, to have substantial responsibility for the administration of the country during this period. The TNC failed to become operational and UNOSOM withdrew from Somalia in early 1995, with no progress having been made towards establishing a national government for the country.

### MINISTRIES

**Office of the President:** People's Palace, Mogadishu; tel. (1) 723.
**Ministry of Agriculture:** Mogadishu; tel. (1) 80716.
**Ministry of Civil Aviation and Transport:** Mogadishu; tel. (1) 23025.
**Ministry of Commerce:** Mogadishu; tel. (1) 33089.
**Ministry of Defence:** Mogadishu; tel. (1) 710; telex 726.
**Ministry of Finance and Economy:** Mogadishu; tel. (1) 33090.
**Ministry of Foreign Affairs:** Mogadishu; tel. (1) 721; telex 639.
**Ministry of Health:** Mogadishu; tel. (1) 31055; telex 776.

# SOMALIA

**Ministry of Higher Education and Culture:** POB 1182, Mogadishu; tel. (1) 35042.
**Ministry of Industry:** Mogadishu; telex 747.
**Ministry of Information and National Guidance:** POB 1748, Mogadishu; tel. (1) 20947; telex 621.
**Ministry of the Interior:** Mogadishu.
**Ministry of Justice and Islamic Affairs:** Mogadishu; tel. (1) 36062.
**Ministry of Labour, Youth and Sports:** Mogadishu; tel. (1) 33086.
**Ministry of National Planning:** POB 1742, Mogadishu; tel. (1) 80384; telex 715.
**Ministry of Public Works:** Mogadishu; tel. (1) 21051; telex 700.
**Ministry of Telecommunications:** Mogadishu; tel. (1) 29005; telex 615.

## Political Organizations

**Islamic Union Party (Ittihad):** operates in northern Somalia; aims to unite ethnic Somalis from Somalia, Ethiopia, Kenya and Djibouti in an Islamic state.
**Somali Democratic Alliance (SDA):** f. 1989; represents Gadabursi ethnic grouping in north-west; opposes Isaaq-dominated SNM and its declaration of an independent 'Republic of Somaliland'; Leader MOHAMED FARAH ABDULLAH.
**Somali Democratic Movement (SDM):** represents Rahenweyne clan; organization split in early 1992, with this faction in alliance with Ali Mahdi Mohamed's USC; Leader ABDULKADIR MOHAMED ADAN.
**Somali Eastern and Central Front (SECF):** f. 1991; opposes SNM's declaration of the independent 'Republic of Somaliland'; Chair. HIRSI ISMAIL MOHAMED.
**Somali National Alliance (SNA):** f. 1992 as alliance between the Southern Somali National Movement (which withdrew in 1993) and the factions of the United Somali Congress, Somali Democratic Movement and Somali Patriotic Movement given below; Chair. Gen. MOHAMED FARAH AIDID.
  **Somali Democratic Movement (SDM):** represents Rahenweyne clan; Chair. YUSUF ALI YUSUF.
  **Somali Patriotic Movement (SPM):** f. 1989; represents Ogadenis (of the southern Darod clan); Chair. GEDI UGAS MADHAR.
  **United Somali Congress (USC):** f. 1989; overthrew Siad Barre in 1991; party split in mid-1991, with this faction dominated by the Habr Gidir sub-clan of the Hawiye clan, Somalia's largest ethnic group; Chair. Gen. MOHAMED FARAH AIDID; Sec.-Gen. ABD AL-KARIM AHMED ALI.
**Somali National Front (SNF):** f. 1991; guerrilla force active in southern Somalia, promoting Darod clan interests and seeking restoration of SRSP Govt; Leader Gen. MOHAMED SIAD HERSI 'MORGAN'.
**Somali National Movement (SNM):** Hargeysa; f. 1981 in London; conducted guerrilla operations in north and north-west Somalia, with early support from Ethiopia, until 1991; support drawn mainly from nomadic Isaaq clan; in May 1991 declared independent 'Republic of Somaliland' with the capital at Hargeysa; mems hold a majority of ministerial portfolios in 'Govt of Somaliland'; in 1994 Mohamed Ibrahim Egal, the elected President of 'Somaliland', disputed that the SNM was still led by Ahmed Ali 'Tur' (see Recent History); Chair. ABD AR-RAHMAN AHMED ALI 'TUR'; Vice-Chair. HASAN ISA JAMA.
**Somali Patriotic Movement (SPM):** f. 1989 in southern Somalia; represents Ogadenis (of the Darod clan) in southern Somalia; this faction of the SPM has allied with the SNF in opposing the SNA; Chair. Gen. ADEN ABDULLAHI NOOR ('GABIO').
**Somali Revolutionary Socialist Party (SRSP):** f. 1976 as the sole party; overthrown in Jan. 1991; conducts guerrilla operations in Gedo region, near border with Kenya; Sec.-Gen. (vacant); Asst Sec.-Gen. AHMED SULEIMAN ABDULLAH.
**Somali Salvation Democratic Front (SSDF):** f. 1981, as the Democratic Front for the Salvation of Somalia (DFSS), as a coalition of the Somali Salvation Front, the Somali Workers' Party and the Democratic Front for the Liberation of Somalia; operates in central Somalia, although a smaller group has opposed the SNA around Kismayu in alliance with the SNF; Chair. Col ABDULLAHI YUSSUF AHMED.
**Southern Somali National Movement (SSNM):** based on coast in southern Somalia; Chair. ABDI WARSEMEH ISAR.
**United Somali Congress (USC):** f. 1989 in central Somalia; overthrew Siad Barre in Jan. 1991; party split in mid-1991 with this faction dominated by the Abgal sub-clan of the Hawiye clan, Somalia's largest ethnic group; Leader ALI MAHDI MOHAMED; Sec.-Gen. MUSA NUR AMIN.

**United Somali Front (USF):** f. 1989; represents Issas in the north-west of the country; Chair. ABD AR-RAHMAN DUALEH ALI; Sec.-Gen. MOHAMED OSMAN ALI.
**United Somali Party:** opposes SNM's declaration of the independent 'Republic of Somaliland'; Leader MOHAMED ABDI HASHI.

In November 1993 interim President Ali Mahdi Mohamed was reported to have assumed the leadership of the **Somali Salvation Alliance (SSA)**, a new alliance of 12 factions opposed to Gen. Aidid, including the Somali African Muki Organization (SAMO), the Somali National Union (SNU), the USF, the SDA, the SDM, the SPM, the USC (pro-Mahdi faction), the SSDF, the Somali National Democratic Union (SNDU), the SNF and the SSNM. In May 1994 the SNU announced its intention to leave the alliance and join the SNA. The majority of Somalia's political organizations have split into two factions, with one aligned to the SNA and the other to the SSA.

## Diplomatic Representation

### EMBASSIES IN SOMALIA

Note: Following the overthrow of Siad Barre in January 1991, all foreign embassies in Somalia were closed and all diplomatic personnel left the country. Some embassies were reopened, including those of France, Sudan and the USA, following the arrival of the US-led United Task Force (UNITAF) in December 1992; however, nearly all foreign diplomats left Somalia in anticipation of the withdrawal of the UN peace-keeping force, UNOSOM, in early 1995 (see Recent History).

**Algeria:** POB 2850, Mogadishu; tel. (1) 81696; Ambassador: HAMID BENCH ERCHALI.
**Bulgaria:** Hodan District, Km 5, off Via Afgoi, POB 1736, Mogadishu; tel. (1) 81820; Chargé d'affaires a.i.: PEYO BOZOV.
**China, People's Republic:** POB 548, Mogadishu; tel. (1) 20805; Ambassador: XU YINGJIE.
**Cuba:** Mogadishu.
**Djibouti:** Mogadishu; telex 771; Ambassador: ABDI ISMAEL WABERI.
**Egypt:** Via Maka al-Mukarama Km 4, POB 76, Mogadishu; tel. (1) 80781; Chargé d'affaires: MUBAD AL-HADI.
**Ethiopia:** POB 368, Mogadishu; telex 3089; Chargé d'affaires a.i.: YAMANI ABDI.
**France:** Corso Primo Luglio, POB 13, Mogadishu; tel. (1) 21715; telex 625; Ambassador: (vacant).
**Germany:** Via Mahamoud Harbi, POB 17, Mogadishu; tel. (1) 20547; telex 3613; Ambassador: M. A. PETERS.
**India:** Via Jigjiga, Shingani, POB 955, Mogadishu; tel. (1) 21262; telex 716; Ambassador: KRISHAN MOHAN LAL.
**Iran:** Via Maka al-Mukarama, POB 1166, Mogadishu; tel. (1) 80881; telex 616; Chargé d'affaires: ALI AMOUEI.
**Iraq:** Via Maka al-Mukarama, POB 641, Mogadishu; tel. (1) 80821; telex 638; Ambassador: HIKMAT A. SATTAR HUSSAIN.
**Italy:** Via Alto Giuba, POB 6, Mogadishu; tel. (1) 20544; telex 777; Ambassador: MARIO SCIALOJA.
**Kenya:** Via Mecca, POB 618, Mogadishu; tel. (1) 80857; telex 610; Ambassador: JOHN OLE SIPARO.
**Korea, Democratic People's Republic:** Via Km 5, Mogadishu; Ambassador: KIM RYONG SU.
**Kuwait:** First Medina Rd, Km 5, POB 1348, Mogadishu; telex 608; Chargé d'affaires: MATTAR THAJIL AL-SALMAN.
**Libya:** Via Medina, POB 125, Mogadishu.
**Nigeria:** Via Km 5, Mogadishu; tel. (1) 81362; telex 637; Ambassador: DAHIRU MOHAMED ABU BAKAR.
**Oman:** Via Afgoi, POB 2992, Mogadishu; tel. (1) 81658; telex 796; Ambassador: AHMED EBRAHIM QASIM.
**Pakistan:** Via Afgoi, Km 5, POB 339, Mogadishu; tel. (1) 80856; Chargé d'affaires: TAHIR IQBAL BUTT.
**Qatar:** Via Km 4, POB 1744, Mogadishu; tel. (1) 80746; telex 629; Ambassador: ABDUL YUSUF AL-JAIDA.
**Romania:** Via Lido, POB 651, Mogadishu; Ambassador: GHEORGHE MANCIU.
**Saudi Arabia:** Via Benadir, POB 603, Mogadishu; tel. (1) 22087; telex 618; Ambassador: ABDULLAH AL-MUHAYYIM.
**Sudan:** Via Mecca, POB 552, Mogadishu; Ambassador: MUSTAFA ABD AL-BADR MOHAMED HASAN.
**Syria:** Via Medina, POB 986, Mogadishu; telex 636; Chargé d'affaires: SHAYESH TERKAWI.
**Turkey:** Via Km 6, POB 2833, Mogadishu; tel. (1) 81975; telex 784; Ambassador: HIKMET SENGENC.

**United Arab Emirates:** Via Afgoi, Km 5, Mogadishu; tel. (1) 23178; telex 614; Ambassador: ABDULHADI A. AL-KHAJAH.
**United Kingdom:** Hassan Geedi Abtow 7/8, POB 1036, Mogadishu; tel. (1) 20288; telex 3617; Ambassador: (vacant).
**USA:** Via Afgoi, Km 5, POB 574, Mogadishu; tel. (1) 39971; telex 789; Special Envoy: DANIEL H. SIMPSON.
**Yemen:** Via Km 5, POB 493, Mogadishu; Ambassador: AWADH ABDALLA MASHBAH.
**Yugoslavia:** Via Mecca, POB 952, Mogadishu; tel. (1) 81729; telex 3778; Ambassador: DRAGOLJUB KONTIĆ.
**Zimbabwe:** Mogadishu.

## Judicial System

Constitutional arrangements in operation until 1991 provided for the Judiciary to be independent of the executive and legislative powers. Laws and acts having the force of law were required to conform to the provisions of the Constitution and to the general principles of Islam.

**The Supreme Court:** Mogadishu; the court of final instance in civil, criminal, administrative and auditing matters; Chair. Sheikh AHMAD HASAN.

**Military Supreme Court:** f. 1970, with jurisdiction over members of the armed forces.

**National Security Court:** heard cases of treason.

**Courts of Appeal:** sat at Mogadishu and Hargeysa, with two Divisions: General and Assize.

**Regional Courts:** There were eight Regional Courts, with two Divisions: General and Assize.

**District Courts:** There were 84 District Courts, with Civil and Criminal Divisions. The Civil Division had jurisdiction over all controversies where the cause of action had arisen under Shari'a (Islamic) Law or Customary Law and any other Civil controversies where the matter in dispute did not involve more than 3,000 shillings. The Criminal Division had jurisdiction with respect to offences punishable with imprisonment not exceeding three years, or fine not exceeding 3,000 shillings, or both.

**Qadis:** Districts Courts of civil jurisdiction under Islamic Law.

In September 1993, in accordance with Resolution 865 of the UN Security Council, a judiciary re-establishment council, composed of Somalis, was created in Mogadishu to rehabilitate the judicial and penal systems.

**Judiciary Re-establishment Council (JRC):** Mogadishu; Chair. Dr ABD AL-RAHMAD Haji GA'AL.

## Religion

### ISLAM

Islam is the state religion. Most Somalis are Sunni Muslims.
**Imam:** Gen. MOHAMED ABSHIR.

### CHRISTIANITY

#### The Roman Catholic Church

Somalia comprises a single diocese, directly responsible to the Holy See. At 31 December 1993 there were an estimated 200 adherents.

**Bishop of Mogadishu:** (vacant); POB 273, Ahmed bin Idris, Mogadishu; tel. (1) 20184.

#### The Anglican Communion

Within the Episcopal Church in Jerusalem and the Middle East, the Bishop in Egypt has jurisdiction over seven African countries, including Somalia.

## The Press

Prior to the overthrow of the Siad Barre regime in 1991, all newspapers were published by the Ministry of Information and National Guidance.

**The Country:** POB 1178, Mogadishu; tel. (1) 21206; telex 621; f. 1991; daily.

**Dalka:** POB 388, Mogadishu; f. 1967; current affairs; weekly.

**Heegan** (Vigilance): POB 1178, Mogadishu; tel. (1) 21206; telex 621; f. 1978; weekly; English; Editor MOHAMOUD M. AFRAH.

**Horseed:** POB 1178, Mogadishu; tel. (1) 21206; telex 621; weekly; in Italian and Arabic.

**New Era:** POB 1178, Mogadishu; tel. (1) 21206; telex 621; quarterly; in English, Somali and Arabic.

**Somalia in Figures:** Ministry of National Planning, POB 1742, Mogadishu; tel. (1) 80384; telex 715; govt publication; statistical information; 3 a year; in English.

**Xiddigta Oktobar** (October Star): POB 1178, Mogadishu; tel. (1) 21206; telex 621; in Somali; daily.

### NEWS AGENCIES

**Horn of Africa News Agency:** Mogadishu; f. 1990.

**Somali National News Agency (SONNA):** POB 1748, Mogadishu; tel. (1) 24058; telex 621; Dir MUHAMMAD HASAN KAHIN.

#### Foreign Bureaux

**Agence France-Presse (AFP)** (France): POB 1178, Mogadishu; telex 615; Rep. MOHAMED ROBLE NOOR.

**Agenzia Nazionale Stampa Associata (ANSA)** (Italy): POB 1399, Mogadishu; tel. (1) 20626; telex 3761; Rep. ABDULKADIR MOHAMOUD WALAYO.

## Publishers

**Government Printer:** POB 1743, Mogadishu.

**Somalia d'Oggi:** Piazzale della Garesa, POB 315, Mogadishu; law, economics and reference.

## Radio and Television

In 1992, according to UNESCO, there were an estimated 350,000 radio receivers and 113,000 television receivers in use. Some radio receivers are used for public address purposes in small towns and villages. A television service, financed by Kuwait and the United Arab Emirates, was inaugurated in 1983. Programmes in Somali and Arabic are broadcast for two hours daily, extended to three hours on Fridays and public holidays. Reception is limited to a 30-km radius of Mogadishu.

**Radio Awdal:** Boorama, 'Somaliland'; operated by the Gadabursi clan.

**Radio Hargeysa, the Voice of the 'Republic of Somaliland':** POB 14, Hargeysa; tel. 155; serves the northern region ('Somaliland'); broadcasts in Somali, and relays Somali and Amharic transmission from Radio Mogadishu; Dir of Radio IDRIS EGAL NUR.

**Radio Mogadishu, Voice of the Somali People** (Radio Mogadishu, codka ummad weeynta Soomaaliyeed): southern Mogadishu; f. mid-1993 by supporters of Gen. Aidid after the facilities of the former state-controlled radio station, Radio Mogadishu (of which Gen. Aidid's faction took control in 1991), were destroyed by UNOSOM; Chair. FARAH HASAN AYOBOQORE.

**Radio Mogadishu, Voice of the Somali Republic:** northern Mogadishu; f. 1992 by supporters of Ali Mahdi Mohamed.

**Voice of Peace:** POB 1631, Addis Ababa, Ethiopia; f. 1993; aims to promote peace and reconstruction in Somalia; receives support from UNICEF and the OAU.

## Finance

(cap. = capital; res = reserves; m. = million; brs = branches; amounts in Somali shillings)

### BANKING

All banks were nationalized in May 1970.

#### Central Bank

**Central Bank of Somalia (Bankiga Dhexe ee Soomaaliya):** Corso Somalia 55, POB 11, Mogadishu; telex 604; f. 1960; bank of issue; cap. and res 132.5m. (Sept. 1985); Gov. ALI ABDI AMALOW; Gen. Mans MOHAMED MOHAMED NUR, BASHIR ISSE ALI; brs in Hargeysa and Kismayu.

#### Commercial Bank

**Commercial Bank of Somalia:** Place Lagarde, POB 2004, Mogadishu; tel. (1) 351282; telex 5879; f. 1990 to succeed the Commercial and Savings Bank of Somalia; cap. 1,000m. (May 1990); 33 brs.

#### Development Bank

**Somali Development Bank:** Via Primo Luglio, POB 1079, Mogadishu; tel. (1) 21800; telex 635; f. 1968; cap. and res 2,612.7m. (Dec. 1988); Pres. MAHMUD MOHAMED NUR; 4 brs.

## INSURANCE

**Cassa per le Assicurazioni Sociali della Somalia:** POB 123, Mogadishu; f. 1950; workers' compensation; Dir-Gen. Hassan Mohamed Jama; nine brs.

**State Insurance Company of Somalia:** POB 992, Mogadishu; telex 710; f. 1974; Gen. Man. Abdullahi Ga'al; brs throughout Somalia.

# Trade and Industry

## CHAMBER OF COMMERCE

**Chamber of Commerce, Industry and Agriculture:** Via Asha, POB 27, Mogadishu; Chair. Mohamed Haji Ibrahim Egal.

## TRADE ORGANIZATION

**National Agency of Foreign Trade:** POB 602, Mogadishu; major foreign trade agency; state-owned; brs in Berbera and over 150 centres throughout Somalia; Dir-Gen. Jama aw Muse.

## DEVELOPMENT ORGANIZATIONS

**Agricultural Development Corporation:** POB 930, Mogadishu; telex 713; f. 1971 by merger of fmr agricultural and machinery agencies and grain marketing board; supplies farmers with equipment and materials at reasonable prices; buys Somali growers' cereal and oil seed crops; Dir-Gen. Mohamed Farah Anshur.

**Livestock Development Agency:** POB 1759, Mogadishu; Dir-Gen. Hassan Weli Scek Hussen; brs throughout Somalia.

**Somali Co-operative Movement:** Mogadishu; Chair. Hassan Hawadle Madar.

**Somali Oil Refinery:** POB 1241, Mogadishu; Chair. Nur Ahmed Darawish.

**Water Development Agency:** POB 525, Mogadishu; Dir-Gen. Khalif Haji Farah.

## TRADE UNION

**General Federation of Somali Trade Unions:** POB 1179, Mogadishu; Chair. Muhammad Farah Isa Gashan.

# Transport

## RAILWAYS

There are no railways in Somalia.

## ROADS

In 1991 there were an estimated 21,700 km of roads, of which 5,200 km were main roads, and 4,500 were secondary roads. In the same year, an estimated 6,000 km of road were paved. A 122-km road between Berbera and Burao, financed by the United Arab Emirates, was inaugurated in 1981, and work on a 257-km road between Goluen and Gelib, completing a link between Mogadishu and Kismayu, was begun in 1977, with financial aid from the EC and the Arab Fund for Economic and Social Development. In September 1988 work began on a 120-km US-funded road between Mogadishu and Cadale. In July 1989 the European Development Fund granted US $54m. for the construction of a 230-km road between Gelib and Bardera, to provide access to the Juba valley.

## SHIPPING

Merca, Berbera, Mogadishu and Kismayu are the chief ports. Facilities at Kismayu were undergoing rehabilitation in 1986. These improvements were to enable the port to handle livestock, other agricultural commodities, liquids and general cargo. In late 1986 arrangements were finalized for a US $24m. programme, financed by the World Bank, for further improvements at Kismayu and for modernization products at Berbera and Mogadishu.

In the context of continuing civil unrest, the dispatch of a UN-sponsored port management team for Mogadishu, for an initial period of six months, was announced in May 1993. Following the departure of the UN in early 1995, the two main factions in Mogadishu established a joint committee to administer the port as well as the airport.

Linea Messina, Medite Line and Lloyd Triestino provide regular services. Other lines call irregularly.

**Somali Ports Authority:** POB 935, Mogadishu; tel. (1) 30081; telex 708; Port Dir Ugas Khalif.

**Juba Enterprises Beder & Sons Ltd:** POB 549, Mogadishu; privately-owned.

**National Shipping Line:** POB 588, Mogadishu; tel. (1) 23021; telex 611; state-owned; Gen. Man. Dr Abdullahi Mohamed Salad.

**Shosman Commercial Co Ltd:** North-Eastern Pasaso; privately-owned.

**Somali Shipping Corporation:** POB 2775, Mogadishu; state-owned.

## CIVIL AVIATION

Mogadishu has an international airport. There are airports at Hargeysa and Baidoa and six other airfields. It was reported that a daily service had been inaugurated in April 1994 between Hargeysa (in the self-declared 'Republic of Somaliland') and Nairobi, Kenya.

**Somali Airlines:** Via Medina, POB 726, Mogadishu; tel. (1) 81533; telex 3619; f. 1964; state-owned; operates internal passenger and cargo services and international services to destinations in Africa, Europe and the Middle East; Pres. Mohamoud Mohamed Gulaid.

In addition, two airlines, Bulisafia and African Air, operate services from Mogadishu international airport.

# SOUTH AFRICA

## Introductory Survey

### Location, Climate, Language, Religion, Flag, Capital

The Republic of South Africa occupies the southern extremity of the African mainland. It is bordered by Namibia to the north-west, by Botswana and Zimbabwe to the north, by Mozambique to the north-east, and by Swaziland to the east. Lesotho is completely surrounded by South African territory. The climate is generally sub-tropical, but with considerable regional variations. Temperatures in Cape Town, on the south-west coast, vary from 7°C (45°F) to 26°C (79°F), with an annual average of about 17°C (63°F). Annual rainfall averages 510 mm (20 ins) at Cape Town, and 1,101 mm (43 ins) at Durban, on the east coast. The official languages are Afrikaans, English, isiNdebele, Sesotho sa Leboa, Sesotho, siSwati, Xitsonga, Setswana, Tshivenda, isiXhosa and isiZulu. About 70% of the population are black, 18% are white, 9% are Coloured (of mixed race), and 3% are Asian (mainly of Indian origin). Most of the inhabitants profess Christianity. There are also small minorities of Hindus (nearly all Asians) and Muslims (mainly Coloureds and Asians). The national flag (proportions 3 by 2) has a green 'Y' shape extending from the upper and lower hoist corners to the centre of the fly end, bordered in white on its outer edges, and in light orange on its inner edges near the hoist; the areas above and below the horizontal band of the 'Y' are red and blue respectively, with a black triangle at the hoist. The administrative capital is Pretoria, the legislative capital is Cape Town, and the judicial capital is Bloemfontein.

### Recent History

On 31 May 1910 four British dependencies were merged to form the Union of South Africa, a dominion under the British Crown. Under the Statute of Westminster, which was approved by the British Parliament in December 1931 and accepted by South Africa in June 1934, the Union was recognized as an independent country. From the establishment of South Africa until 1984, national administration was the exclusive preserve of the white population.

The National Party (NP), which acceded to power in 1948, introduced the doctrine of apartheid (in theory the separate but equal development of all racial groups, in practice leading to white, particularly Afrikaner, supremacy). The principal opposition to government policy during the 1950s took the form of a campaign of civil disobedience, led by the multiracial African National Congress of South Africa (ANC). In 1955 the ANC and other organizations formed the Freedom Congress, which drafted the 'Freedom Charter', demanding equal political rights for all racial groups. In 1959 some members of the ANC formed the exclusively black Pan-Africanist Congress (PAC). In 1960 the ANC and the PAC conducted a campaign against the notorious 'pass laws' (which required blacks to be in possession of special documentation in designated white urban areas); at one demonstration, which took place, at Sharpeville in March, 67 blacks were killed by security forces. This incident prompted international outrage, and further demonstrations within South Africa, as a result of which the ANC and the PAC were declared illegal. Both movements subsequently formed military wings, based outside South Africa, to conduct campaigns of sabotage. An influential leader of the ANC, Nelson Mandela, was detained in 1962 and sentenced to life imprisonment on a charge of sabotage in 1964, but remained a focus for opposition to apartheid.

On 31 May 1961, following a referendum among white voters in October 1960, South Africa became a republic, and left the Commonwealth. Dr Hendrik Verwoerd was Prime Minister from 1958 until his assassination in September 1966. His basic policies were continued by his successor, B. J. Vorster, formerly Minister of Justice.

As an integral part of the policy of apartheid, the territorial segregation of African ethnic groups was enforced, on the grounds that the Native Reserves (comprising only 13% of national territory) constituted the historic 'homelands' (Bantustans) of different African nations. Legislation introduced in 1959 established eight 'national' units in respect of the black population, and provided for the appointment of Commissioners-General, to serve as links between the 'national' units and the central Government. In 1963 Transkei was accorded 'self-governing' status, with an Executive Council, headed by a Chief Minister, to be elected by a Legislative Assembly. Bophuthatswana (June 1972), Ciskei (August 1972), Lebowa (October 1972), Gazankulu (February 1973), KwaZulu (April 1973), Qwaqwa (November 1974), and KwaNdebele (October 1977) were subsequently granted 'self-government'. KaNgwane was granted a certain measure of 'self-government' in 1981, but did not receive formal 'self-governing' status until August 1984 (after plans by the South African Government to transfer KaNgwane and the Ingwavuma area of KwaZulu to the Kingdom of Swaziland were disallowed by the Supreme Court in 1982). Transkei was declared 'independent' in October 1976, Bophuthatswana in December 1977, Venda in September 1979 and Ciskei in December 1981. (Plans by the South African authorities to grant 'independence' to the six 'self-governing homelands' were finally abandoned in 1990, following the adoption of a programme of political reforms—see below). The population of the 'independent homelands' was not entitled to South African citizenship. The 'independent homelands' were not recognized by any government other than that of South Africa.

The numerous discriminatory laws regulating the lives of the country's black, 'Coloured' (a term used to denote people of mixed race) and 'Indian' (Asian) populations, combined with stringent security legislation, led to the detention without trial of many of the Government's opponents, the banning of black political organizations outside the 'homelands', and the forced removal of hundreds of thousands of blacks in accordance with the provisions of the Group Areas Act of 1966 (which imposed residential segregation of the races) and the 'homelands' policy. In June 1976 violent riots occurred in Soweto (South-Western Townships), near Johannesburg, and rapidly spread to other black urban areas. Vorster used the executive's virtually limitless powers, conferred by the newly-adopted Internal Security Act, to suppress riots and strikes. Several hundred people died in confrontations with the security forces, and many more were detained without trial. Allegations of human rights violations by security forces culminated in international indignation at the death in detention of a black community leader, Steve Biko, in September 1977. In 1978 black, Coloured and Indian activists founded the Azanian People's Organization (AZAPO).

The parliamentary majority of the NP was considerably strengthened at the November 1977 general election. In September 1978 Vorster resigned as Prime Minister, and was succeeded by P. W. Botha, hitherto the Minister of Defence. In 1979, following the disclosure of corruption and misappropriation of public funds, Vorster resigned from the largely honorary post of State President. At the general election of April 1981 the NP lost several seats in the House of Assembly to the opposition Progressive Federal Party (PFP). In February of that year a new, 60-member advisory body, the President's Council, comprising representatives of the white, Coloured and Indian population, was formed to consider constitutional reform. Its recommendations to include Coloureds and Indians (but not blacks) in a three-chamber Parliament, with a multiracial government (led by an executive President), exacerbated inter-party differences: the 'verligte' (liberal) wing of the NP, led by Botha, advocated the establishment of a confederation of South Africa and the 'homelands', with separate citizenships but a common South African nationality, and was strongly opposed by the 'verkrampte' (uncompromising) wing of the party. In March 1982 16 extreme right-wing parliamentary deputies who had opposed the constitutional recommendations were expelled from the NP; they subsequently formed a new political association, the Conservative Party of South Africa (CP), in conjunction with other right-wing elements.

Throughout 1983 and 1984, despite opposition from both the CP and the liberal PFP, Botha pursued his policy of constitutional reform. The majority vote of the Coloured Labour Party (LP) in 1983 to participate in the reform programme caused divisions within the party. The constitutional body representing the Indian population, the South African Indian Council (SAIC), provisionally agreed to the proposals, subject to approval by an Indian community referendum. This decision was, however, opposed by the Transvaal Anti-SAIC Committee, an organization that had been formed in 1981 in protest at participation in elections to the SAIC. In August 1983 the Committee established the United Democratic Front (UDF), to organize resistance on a national scale to Indian and Coloured participation in the constitutional reforms. The UDF rapidly became the principal legal opposition movement.

The constitutional reforms were approved by the House of Assembly in September 1983, and by about 66% of voters in an all-white referendum in November. In the same month, the PFP decided to take part in the reformed system. However, six 'homeland' leaders, including Chief Mangosuthu Gatsha Buthelezi, the Chief Minister of KwaZulu (who had consistently opposed the 'homelands' policy), rejected the constitutional reforms on the grounds that blacks remained excluded from participation in the central Government. Despite a previous pledge by the Prime Minister to assess Coloured and Indian opinion on the reforms, elections to the Coloured and Indian chambers of the new Parliament, known as the House of Representatives and the House of Delegates respectively, took place in August 1984, without prior referendums. As a result, the boycott that had been organized by the UDF was widely-observed: about 18% of the eligible Coloured population voted in the elections to the House of Representatives, with the LP winning 76 of the 80 directly-elected seats, while only 16.6% of the total Indian population eligible to vote participated in the elections to the House of Delegates, with the National People's Party (NPP) winning 18 and the Solidarity Party 17 of the 40 directly-elected seats. (The House of Assembly, as elected in 1981, remained in office.)

Despite the opposition of large sectors of the black, Coloured and Indian populations, the new Constitution came into effect in September 1984. Under the terms of the Constitution, legislative power was vested in the State President and the multiracial, tricameral Parliament, comprising the 178-member House of Assembly (for the representation of whites), the 85-member House of Representatives (for the representation of Coloureds) and the 45-member House of Delegates (for the representation of Indians). Each House was to be solely responsible for the legislation affecting matters considered by the State President to be the 'own' affairs of its particular population group (subject to the final approval of the President). Legislation for general affairs (concerning all population groups) was to be approved by all three Houses and the State President; disagreement between the Houses on general affairs was to be referred to the President's Council. The Constitution provided for the establishment of three Ministers' Councils, one for each population group (comprising certain designated Ministers, who were members of the population group in question). The State President was to exercise executive power in consultation with the Ministers' Council concerned in the case of 'own' affairs, or with the Cabinet (which was to be appointed by him) in the case of general affairs. Following the adoption of the Constitution in September, the post of Prime Minister was abolished, and P. W. Botha was unanimously elected to the new office of State President (which combined the powers of Head of State and Prime Minister) by an electoral college, comprising 50 members of the House of Assembly, 25 of the House of Representatives, and 13 of the House of Delegates. The President's Council, the new Cabinet (formerly Executive Council) and the three Ministers' Councils were subsequently established. The Cabinet comprised only two non-white members, the Chairmen of the Indian and Coloured Ministers' Councils, neither of whom was given a portfolio.

During 1985–86 a number of the laws on which apartheid was based were modified or repealed under President Botha's continuing programme of reform, prompting strong right-wing opposition. The Immorality Act (1927) and the Prohibition of Mixed Marriages Act (1949), which banned sexual relations and marriage between members of different races, were repealed in April 1985, and in the following month it was announced that the Prohibition of Political Interference Act (1967), prohibiting members of different racial groups from belonging to the same political party, was to be abrogated. In April 1986 the Government promulgated legislation that provided for the removal of a number of restrictions on the movement, residence and employment of blacks in white urban areas. (However, citizens of the 'independent homelands' were not entitled to benefit from the new legislation.) On 1 July the 'pass laws' were officially repealed, with the introduction of uniform identity documents for all South African citizens. On the same day reforms concerning the structure of local and provincial government were implemented, and legislation granting blacks limited rights to own property in black urban areas entered into force. In the same month it was announced that citizens of the four 'independent homelands' who were residing and working permanantly in South Africa were to regain South African citizenship; in effect, however, only a small proportion of the population of the 'homelands' was eligible. Following discussions, initiated by Buthelezi in April 1986, regarding the establishment of a joint authority for his 'homeland', KwaZulu, and the province of Natal, the Government agreed to the formation of an administrative body, the Joint Executive Authority (which was installed in November 1987).

The introduction of the new Constitution in September 1984 prompted severe rioting in the black townships, which was violently repressed by the security forces. There were also recurrent boycotts of classes by black students, in protest against the inferior quality of black education. Violence took place within the black community, directed at those who were regarded as collaborators with the Government, in particular black local government councillors and members of the security forces; factional clashes also occurred, notably between supporters of the ANC and of the Inkatha Movement, a Zulu organization led by Buthelezi. In July 1985 the Government declared a state of emergency in 36 districts, which increased the already considerable powers of the security forces; by the end of the state of emergency in March 1986, it was estimated that 757 people had been killed, and almost 8,000 arrested.

On 12 June 1986 President Botha declared a nationwide state of emergency, on the grounds that national security was endangered by subversive elements. It was speculated that the imposition of the state of emergency was connected to a delay in the adoption of legislation extending the powers of the Minister of Law and Order and of the security forces, owing to opposition from the Indian and Coloured legislative chambers. Press censorship subsequently became progressively stricter, and the powers of the security forces were extended, in spite of judicial rulings that several regulations providing for summary arrest and detention under the state of emergency were ambiguous or unlawful. In October the UDF was declared an 'affected organization' (thereby prohibited from receiving financial assistance from abroad). Opposition to the Government emerged from trade unions: the Congress of South African Trade Unions (COSATU), an influential federation of trade unions which was formed in December 1985, demanded the abolition of press restrictions, the release of Mandela and the withdrawal of foreign investment.

In early 1987 a number of 'verligte' members defected from the NP, owing to its increasingly conservative attitude to reform. At a general election to the House of Assembly in May, the NP was returned to power, obtaining 52.7% of votes cast and winning 123 of the 166 directly elective seats. The CP, which secured 26.8% of the vote, increased its representation from 17 to 22 elective seats, thereby replacing the PFP as the official opposition. Following the election, the Government demonstrated an increasingly repressive attitude to the unrest accompanying pressure for fundamental reform. The state of emergency was renewed in June 1987, and further stringent press restrictions were imposed. In August the Rev. Allan Hendrickse (the leader of the LP) announced his resignation as the sole Coloured minister in the Cabinet, owing to his disagreement with certain of the Cabinet's decisions. In October three members of the PFP resigned to form, in conjunction with prominent independents, the National Democratic Movement (NDM), a broad parliamentary and extra-parliamentary party opposed to apartheid.

During 1987 the involvement of trade unionists in allegedly subversive activities resulted in many arrests. In February 1988 the Government restricted the activities of COSATU to purely trade union affairs, and prohibited 17 opposition organizations, including the UDF and AZAPO (thereby effectively banning almost all peaceful extra-parliamentary opposition to apartheid). In March Dr Denis Worrall, a 'verligte' defector from the NP who had been excluded from the NDM, announced the formation of the Independent Party.

In April 1988 President Botha announced several planned reforms, including a proposal that black voters should be allowed to participate in the election of the President and should be offered representation on the advisory President's Council. There was, however, no suggestion that black voters should participate in the election of the legislature. In June Parliament approved legislation that provided for the establishment of a multiracial consultative body, which was to include black members. In March 1989 the Group Areas Act was amended to permit some racially-mixed residential areas.

In spite of the Government's continuing programme of reforms, the suppression of dissidents increased. The state of emergency was renewed for a further 12 months in June 1988, and even more rigorous restrictions were placed upon the media. Strict limitations on strike action came into effect from September, despite protests both from trade unions and employers, and in March 1989 Parliament approved legislation requiring political organizations to disclose the source, amount and purpose of any foreign funding. During 1988 more than 30 organizations (of which all but one were opposed to apartheid) were banned under the emergency regulations. It was estimated that more than 50,000 people were detained under the emergency regulations between 1985 and 1988.

During early 1989 a crisis emerged within the NP: in mid-January President Botha withdrew from his official duties, owing to ill health, and in early February he resigned as leader of the party, and was succeeded by F. W. de Klerk, hitherto Minister of National Education. Despite almost unanimous demands from the party that he should share power with de Klerk before retiring at the next general election, Botha refused to allow his power as State President to be eroded, and in mid-March he resumed his official duties. In April the PFP, the Independent Party and the NDM merged to form, in conjunction with a group of liberal Afrikaner intellectuals, the Democratic Party (DP), which was headed jointly by the leaders of the three parties: respectively Dr Zacharias de Beer, Dr Worrall and Wynand Malan.

The state of emergency was extended for a further 12 months in June 1989. In early August President Kenneth Kaunda of Zambia announced that he was to receive de Klerk later in that month. President Botha claimed that members of his Cabinet had omitted to inform him of this prospective visit, of which he disapproved, owing to President Kaunda's support for the ANC. Following a confrontation with the Cabinet, which defied his authority and supported de Klerk, Botha resigned as State President in mid-August. Shortly afterwards de Klerk was appointed acting President.

Elections to the three Houses of Parliament took place concurrently in early September 1989. At the general election to the House of Assembly the NP received 48.6% of votes cast and won 93 of the 166 elective seats, while the CP secured 31.3% of the vote and 39 seats, and the DP, with 20% of the vote, obtained 33 seats. Less than 12% of the Coloured electorate voted in the general election to the House of Representatives, at which the LP won 69 of the 80 directly elective seats. Some 20% of the Indian electorate voted in the general election to the House of Delegates: the Solidarity Party secured 16 of the 40 directly elective seats, while the NPP won nine. In mid-September, following his inauguration as State President, de Klerk stated that the implementation of constitutional reforms was his highest priority. In the following month eight long-term political prisoners were released by the new Government; these included Walter Sisulu, a secretary-general of the ANC who had been detained since 1964.

On 2 February 1990 de Klerk announced several radical reforms, including the legalization of the ANC, the PAC, the South African Communist Party (SACP), the UDF and more than 30 other banned political organizations. Mandela and a further 120 political prisoners were to be released unconditionally. In addition, most emergency regulations restricting the media were to be removed, as were repressive measures imposed upon former political detainees. Further measures included the repeal of the Separate Amenities Act of 1953 (which imposed social segregation with regard to public amenities and the limitation of detention without trial to a maximum of six months. President de Klerk confirmed that the Government intended to initiate negotiations with the black opposition, with the aim of drafting a new democratic constitution.

Leaders of the extreme right-wing parties reacted to de Klerk's reforms with threats of violence.

Mandela's release from prison, on 11 February 1990, received much international attention. In March he was elected Deputy President of the ANC. In spite of appeals by Mandela for reconciliation between rival factions within the black community, the continuing violence in Natal between supporters of the Inkatha Movement and mainly Xhosa-speaking supporters of the ANC intensified in March and April, and unrest erupted in several black townships. The first formal discussions between the ANC and the de Klerk Government took place in early May. Shortly afterwards Botha resigned from the NP in protest against its programme of political reforms. In mid-May legislation was introduced that granted temporary immunity from prosecution to political exiles, including leaders of the ANC, who had committed crimes. (The legislation was renewed in subsequent years.) In June President de Klerk repealed the state of emergency in all provinces except Natal. In mid-July Buthelezi reconstituted the Inkatha Movement as the Inkatha Freedom Party (IFP—also popularly known as Inkatha), in order to participate in future constitutional negotiations. At a second series of discussions in early August, the ANC and the Government reached an agreement whereby, in preparation for constitutional negotiations, the ANC was to suspend its guerrilla activities, and the Government was to release more than 3,000 political prisoners and to facilitate the return to South Africa of an estimated 40,000 exiles. However, the ANC subsequently continued to train recruits for its military wing (known as Umkhonto we Sizwe—MK) and to stockpile ammunition, thereby contravening the terms of its cease-fire and causing the Government to delay the release of political prisoners and the repatriation of exiles.

During August 1990 factional fighting between supporters of the IFP and of the ANC, which was no longer confined to Natal, escalated in the black townships surrounding Johannesburg; more than 500 people were reported to have been killed by the end of that month. Intense fighting continued during September, when temporary curfews were imposed in several districts. Nevertheless, in the following month the state of emergency was revoked in Natal. In mid-October the Separate Amenities Act was repealed, prompting right-wing protests, particularly from the Afrikaanse Weerstandsbeweging (AWB), a paramilitary organization which had been formed in 1973 under the leadership of Eugene Terre'Blanche. During October the NP opened its membership to all races. Large-scale fighting erupted again in black townships during December, causing the Government to impose temporary curfews on some districts in the Witwatersrand area. In mid-December Oliver Tambo, the President of the ANC, returned after more than 30 years in exile.

In early January 1991 the ANC proposed that a multi-party conference should be convened to formulate the procedures under which constitutional negotiations should take place. At the end of the month Mandela and Buthelezi held a widely-publicized meeting, at which both leaders appealed to their respective followers to end hostilities. In early February President de Klerk announced that he was to introduce draft legislation to repeal the principal remaining apartheid laws: the Land Acts of 1913 and 1936 (which stipulated that the black population was entitled to own only 13.6% of the land), the Group Areas Act, the Black Communities Act of 1984 (which enforced the separate status of black townships) and the Population Registration Act of 1950 (which decreed that all South Africans should be registered at birth according to race) were subsequently abolished. In the same month the Government agreed to assume joint administrative powers in Ciskei, following increasing pressure within the 'independent homeland' for its reincorporation into South Africa and for the resignation of its military ruler. In mid-February the Government and the ANC reached agreement on a wide range of issues, including the release of political prisoners, the return of exiles and the curtailment of activities by the MK. (Nevertheless, the MK continued to operate during 1991, and in December of that year an estimated 350 political prisoners remained in detention.) In early April an increase in township violence caused the ANC to issue an ultimatum, in which it threatened to withdraw from negotiations unless the Government made several undertakings, including the removal from office of the Minister of Defence and the Minister of Law and Order, the dismissal of members of the security forces who had been implicated in the murders of opposition activists and the banning of the possession of weapons at public gatherings. Apart from implementing a ban on traditional weapons in areas of unrest, the Government rejected these demands, and the ANC suspended negotiations. In May Winnie Mandela, the (later estranged) wife of the ANC leader, was found guilty of charges of assault and kidnapping, and was sentenced to six years' imprisonment, causing considerable embarrassment for the ANC. (She remained at liberty, pending an appeal against the verdict, and in June 1993 the conviction for assault was overturned and her sentence was commuted to a fine and a suspended term of imprisonment.) In early July 1991, at a national congress of the ANC, Nelson Mandela was elected as its President and Cyril Ramaphosa, hitherto leader of the National Union of Mineworkers, was elected Secretary-General of the organization. The congress gave its executive a strong mandate to continue negotiations with the Government.

In mid-July 1991 the Government admitted that it had made secret payments to the IFP in 1989 and 1990; however, President de Klerk and Buthelezi maintained that they had not known about the covert transfer of funds. The admission came at a time of intense speculation that Inkatha was supported by the security forces. Shortly afterwards, in response to renewed pressure from the ANC, compounded by international outrage at the affair, President de Klerk announced the demotion of the Minister of Defence and the Minister of Law and Order to minor cabinet posts. In mid-August 1991 the Government declared an amnesty for all political exiles; their repatriation was to take place under the auspices of the UN. During that month the UDF was dissolved. In mid-September the Government, the ANC, the IFP and the leaders of 23 other political organizations signed a national peace accord that detailed a code of conduct for the security forces and for political groupings, in an attempt to end township violence; however, an escalation in unrest during September and October appeared to undermine the accord. In October a judicial commission of inquiry, headed by Justice Richard Goldstone, was established to assess the causes of civil violence.

At the end of November 1991 the Government and several political groupings met to prepare for multi-party constitutional negotiations. A multi-party conference on South Africa's future, known as the Convention for a Democratic South Africa (CODESA), was convened in late December, and was to be followed by the election of a multiracial interim government. CODESA was attended by the Government and 18 political organizations, including the ANC, NP, DP, LP, NPP, New Solidarity (formerly the Solidarity Party) and representatives of the 'independent' and 'self-governing' 'homelands' (including the IFP, which represented KwaZulu); the conference was boycotted by the PAC, AZAPO and the CP. CODESA was empowered to draft legislation, although such draft legislation could only be enacted by Parliament. The negotiating body's stated aim to create an undivided South Africa was rejected by the IFP, which favoured the concept of a South African federation of independent states, and by the Bophuthatswana administration, which demanded total independence from South Africa. CODESA was reconvened in January 1992.

In late February 1992, after the CP defeated the NP at an important by-election, President de Klerk announced a forthcoming referendum of the white population, in order to determine the level of support for the negotiation of a democratic constitution: the referendum, which was held in mid-March, resulted in an overwhelming white mandate for the continuation of the process of reform.

In May 1992 constitutional negotiations were suspended, owing to the Government's insistence on a veto on CODESA's decisions. The ANC subsequently announced a forthcoming protest campaign of mass action by its supporters. In mid-June several residents of Boipatong, a black township, were massacred, apparently by Inkatha supporters and allegedly with the complicity of the security forces. Following a visit to the township by President de Klerk, 30 demonstrators were killed as the security forces suppressed an anti-Government protest. In response the ANC announced its withdrawal from all bilateral contact with the Government, pending the Government's agreement to a number of demands, including the immediate release of all remaining political prisoners and effective action to curtail township violence. In mid-July President de Klerk announced the imminent dissolution of several units of the armed forces and security forces. Later in that month the UN Security Council, acting upon a request by Mandela, sent a special representative to South Africa, who effected a tentative *rapprochement* between the Government and the ANC. The UN Security Council subsequently authorized the deployment of 30 UN observers in South Africa to monitor political violence (the phased arrival of these commenced in September).

During the first week in August 1992 the ANC, SACP and COSATU orchestrated an unprecedented level of mass action against the Government, including political rallies and a two-day general strike. In late August it was reported that the country's Head of Military Intelligence had organized special units to assassinate opponents. Later in that month the Government announced a major restructuring of the security forces and, in response to a recommendation by the UN, the forthcoming establishment of an independent inquiry into complicity by the security forces on serious crimes. During August several parliamentary deputies belonging to the CP defected to form a new extreme right-wing party, the Afrikaner Volksunie (AVU).

In mid-1992 the ANC (which from 1990 had campaigned in support of the abolition of the 'homeland' system) announced that it was to organize a series of demonstrations in protest against 'homeland' leaders who wished their territories (Bophuthatswana, Ciskei, KwaZulu and Qwaqwa) to retain a strong measure of autonomy in the future South Africa. In September, however, Ciskei security forces killed 28 ANC demonstrators, and injured about 200, prompting international outrage. The ANC accused the South African security forces (some of whose members had been seconded to Ciskei) of complicity in the incident. President de Klerk promised an inquiry into the affair, and, in mid-September, announced that measures to reduce the 'independence' of the 'homelands' would be implemented. In late 1992 the leaders of Bophuthatswana, Ciskei and KwaZulu, in conjunction with the IFP, the AVU and the CP, formed a pressure group (the Concerned South Africans Group—COSAG) to campaign for a maximum degree of regional autonomy within the new South Africa.

In late September 1992, following intense negotiations between representatives of the ANC and the Government, a peace summit was attended by the leaders of the two sides, at which the Government accepted the ANC's preconditions for the resumption of constitutional negotiations: the release of several hundred political prisoners and the implementation of measures to reduce the level of violence in the black townships. A 'record of understanding' was signed, which stated that the new Constitution would be drafted by an elected constitutional assembly and that there would be a non-racial elected interim government. The IFP immediately announced its disapproval of perceived connivance between the ANC and the Government, and in December Buthelezi published a draft constitution for a planned state comprising the KwaZulu 'homeland' and the province of Natal, which was to retain a strong measure of autonomy within a future South African federation. In mid-October the Constitution was amended to permit blacks to serve in the Cabinet. Later in that month legislation was approved which granted immunity from prosecution to perpetrators of politically-motivated offences committed prior to 8 October 1990. A minor reshuffle of cabinet portfolios was implemented at the beginning of December 1992. Shortly afterwards talks were held between representatives of the ANC and the Government. In late December President de Klerk restructured the leadership of the armed forces.

Bilateral discussions between the ANC and the Government continued in January 1993. The two sides appeared to disagree over the timetable for the transition to democracy and the distribution of power within the future interim government (with de Klerk insisting on a degree of predetermined power-sharing). At the end of January President de Klerk announced that legislation to dissolve the President's Council would be submitted to Parliament, and that certain racially-based government departments (including those responsible for education) were to be abolished. Further bilateral talks between the ANC and the Government took place in mid-February, at which both sides agreed to the immediate resumption of multi-party discussions. These negotiations were expected to continue until the end of June, following which (subject to approval at the multi-party negotiations) a multi-party Transitional Executive Council (with control over certain key ministries), an independent elections commission and an independent media commission were to be established to prepare for free and fair elections. Between the end of 1993 and April 1994 a constituent assembly (and an interim government) were to be elected by proportional representation; the constituent assembly, whose proposals would require ratification by a two-thirds majority of its members, was to draft and adopt a new constitution. Political parties with seats in the constituent assembly would be represented proportionately in the Cabinet which, with the President, would compose the interim government. Within five years further elections would be held and a majority government would be inaugurated. Differences remained between the Government and the ANC over the system of government of the future state (with the Government demanding substantial regional devolution of power and the ANC preferring a centrally-governed unitary state) and over the Government's refusal to allow control of the security forces to be assumed by the Transitional Executive Council.

During February 1993, and at the beginning of March, the Government held talks with both the PAC and the IFP. In early March the Government and 25 delegations from national political parties (including the formerly uncooperative PAC, IFP and CP) and the 'homeland' Governments met to plan the resumption of multi-party negotiations; it was decided that these were to commence in April and that CODESA was to be reconstituted as a new negotiating forum (in which the PAC, the IFP and the CP were to be granted equal status with the other representatives). At the beginning of April one Indian and two Coloured parliamentary deputies received ministerial portfolios in an extensive reorganization of the Cabinet.

In early April 1993, soon after the recommencement of constitutional negotiations, Chris Hani, the General Secretary of the SACP and the former leader of the MK, was assassinated by a white right-wing extremist; several members of the CP were implicated in the affair, and three of them were subsequently charged in connection with the murder, which appeared to be part of a right-wing plot to disrupt the constitutional negotiations. (In October two of the alleged conspirators received the death sentence, while the remaining defendant was acquitted.) The assassination precipitated widespread violent unrest, which was suppressed by the security forces. The ANC, SACP and COSATU organized a national strike on the day of Hani's funeral, and announced that a period of mass action would ensue in support of demands for the swift agreement of a date for multi-party elections and the immediate introduction of multi-party control of the army and security forces. In late April Oliver Tambo, the former ANC President, died. It was reported during April that several retired senior officers in the army and security forces had formed a secret committee to mobilize white right-wing resistance to political reform, with the possible aim of establishing a separate Afrikaner state. In early May the committee established an informal alliance of 21 right-wing organizations (which included the AVU, the CP and the AWB), known as the Afrikaner Volksfront (AVF), to co-ordinate opposition to the negotiating process. In the same month reports emerged that right-wing extremists had planned to assassinate the Chairman of the SACP, Joe Slovo, prompting increased speculation regarding the existence of a conspiracy to disrupt the negotiations.

In May 1993 23 of the 26 delegations participating in the negotiating forum signed a 'declaration of intent', affirming their commitment to the constitutional process and agreeing that a date for the multi-party elections (which would take place no later than April 1994) would be decided within a period of four weeks. (Decisions were reached by the forum when, in the opinion of the Chairman, sufficient participants had reached a consensus.) After bilateral negotiations with the AVU, the ANC recognized, in principle, demands for a devolution of power to regional government. Following the arrest of a number of members of the PAC and its military wing, the Azanian People's Liberation Army (APLA), later in May, the party temporarily withdrew from the negotiating forum. In the same month the Ciskei authorities announced an unconditional amnesty for all those implicated in the massacre of ANC demonstrators in September 1992. In early June 1993, in accordance with the 'declaration of intent', the negotiating forum provisionally scheduled the elections for 27 April 1994, despite opposition from a number of the delegations belonging to COSAG. Confirmation of that date was subsequently postponed, after the IFP and the other constituent members of COSAG temporarily withdrew from negotiations, in protest at the forum's rejection of their motion in favour of the establishment of a federal state. In mid-June legislation providing for the abolition of the President's Council was approved by Parliament. Later that month the 26 delegations pledged to cease violence in the pursuance of political aims; however, the PAC subsequently indicated that it was not prepared to suspend the activities of the APLA (which had been implicated in a number of attacks against whites earlier that year). Shortly before the date of the elections was due to be confirmed, armed right-wing extremists, many of whom were members of the AWB, staged a violent protest in support of demands for the establishment of a separate Afrikaner state, occupying the negotiating centre and assaulting black delegates and journalists. The ANC subsequently criticized the failure of the security forces to prevent the attack, and demanded the arrest of right-wing leaders; some 25 members of the AWB were later detained. At the end of June the negotiating forum reached an agreement in an effort to reconcile the demands of the Government and the ANC (that the country's Constitution be drafted by an elected constituent assembly) with those of COSAG (that it be drafted by the forum itself): the Constitution was to be prepared by a constituent assembly, with adherence to entrenched principles, which were to be determined by the forum.

In early July 1993 the negotiating forum confirmed that the elections would take place on 27 April, despite continuing opposition from COSAG. The IFP, CP and KwaZulu delegations subsequently withdrew from the negotiations, while the remaining representatives in the forum continued discussions on the precepts of a multiracial interim constitution, which was to remain in force pending the preparation and adoption of the country's future constitution. The confirmation of the election date prompted increased factional violence (which was concentrated in the townships of the East Rand region, near Johannesburg, and in Natal) between supporters of the IFP and those of the ANC. In late July 12 people, mainly whites, were killed in an attack at a church in Kenilworth, near Cape Town; the APLA denied responsibility for the massacre, which increased speculation regarding the existence of a 'third force', an unidentified group that appeared to be inciting factional violence in order to undermine the negotiating process. At the end of July a draft interim Constitution, which had been prepared by legal advisors on the basis of instructions from the negotiating forum, was promulgated. The interim Constitution entrenched equal rights for citizens regardless of race, and vested executive power in a President and a Cabinet, which was to comprise representatives of the political parties that held a stipulated number of seats in the legislature. Legislative authority was vested in a bicameral Parliament, comprising a 400-member National Assembly (which was to be elected by proportional representation) and a Senate (with 10 members elected by each regional legislature). The National Assembly and Senate were together to form a 'constitution-making body' (later designated as the Constitutional Assembly), which was to draft a new constitution, with adherence to the principles stipulated by the negotiating forum. Failure to adopt the draft by a majority of two-thirds within a period of two years would require the new document to be submitted for approval at a national referendum. Although the interim Constitution included provisions for the establishment of regional legislatures (while retaining the concept of a unitary state), it was rejected by COSAG, and the IFP, KwaZulu and CP delegations continued to boycott negotiations. In early August, as a concession to COSAG, a number of amendments to the interim Constitution were introduced, whereby regional legislatures were to be granted primary responsibility for several areas of government, and joint powers with central government in the principal administrative areas. However, the revised draft failed to secure the support of the dissenting delegations.

In August 1993, in response to demands by the ANC, it was announced that a National Peace-keeping Force (NPKF), comprising members of the existing security forces, including those of the 'homelands', and elements of the military wings of negotiating parties, was to be established, in an attempt to quell escalating political violence in the townships. Later in August an independent commission of inquiry, which had been established in January at the request of Mandela, concluded that members of the ANC had been responsible for human rights violations of political prisoners during the campaign against apartheid. In early September the negotiating forum approved legislation providing for the establishment of a multiracial Transitional Executive Council (TEC), which was to rule in conjunction with the existing Government pending the elections, thereby allowing blacks to participate in central government for the first time. The TEC, which was to include seven sub-councils responsible for several areas of adminstration, was to comprise representatives of the groups involved in the negotiating process; however, six of those entitled to membership (the IFP, the CP, the governments of Bophuthatswana, Ciskei and KwaZulu, and the PAC) refused to participate. Later in September Parliament adopted legislation providing for the installation of the TEC, and the establishment of an Independent Electoral Commission (IEC), and an independent media commission and broadcasting authority (which were to ensure impartial news coverage prior to the elections). Mandela subsequently urged foreign Governments to withdraw the remaining economic sanctions against South Africa, but stipulated that the embargo on armaments continue until the formation of an interim government of national unity after the elections. Also in September the Government assumed control of financial administraton in the 'self-governing homeland' of Lebowa, following a strike by civil servants in protest at the local authorities' failure to pay public sector salaries.

In early October 1993 the constituent members of COSAG, together with the AVF, formed the Freedom Alliance (FA), with the stated objective of negotiating concessions regarding regional autonomy. The Bophuthatswana and Ciskei delegations subsequently withdrew from the negotiating forum, while the FA demanded the dissolution of the forum in favour of a convention of South African leaders (apparently with the aim of upgrading its position in the negotiating process to a par with that of the Government and the ANC). Following unsuccessful efforts to persuade the FA to join the negotiating process, President de Klerk indicated that failure to reach an agreement on the interim Constitution might necessitate a referendum to determine national commitment to democracy. The ANC, however, declared that a referendum should only be conducted as a means of endorsing a negotiated settlement, and insisted on adherence to the scheduled transition to democratic rule. Also in October members of the armed forces killed five blacks, including two children, in an attack against an alleged base of the APLA in Transkei; the ANC condemned the incident, while tension between the South African Government and the Transkei authorities temporarily disrupted the negotiating process. In November the negotiating forum repealed legislation providing for detention without trial. Later that month agreement was reached regarding the establishment of a new security force, which was to be under the control of both central and provincial government, and a reconstituted national defence force, which was to comprise members of the existing armed forces of South Africa and the 'independent homelands', and the military wings of political organizations.

On 18 November 1993, following intensive discussions, 19 of the 21 delegations remaining in the negotiating forum approved the interim Constitution, which incorporated several amendments to the draft promulgated in July. A number of significant compromises between the Government and the ANC had been achieved: the Government abandoned its demand that cabinet decisions require a two-thirds majority (thereby accepting that power-sharing would not be constitutionally entrenched), while the ANC agreed to a fixed five-year period for transition to civilian rule. The President was to be elected by the National Assembly, and was to exercise executive power in consultation with at least two Deputy Presidents, who were to be nominated by parties with a minimum of 80 seats in the National Assembly (equivalent to 20% of the national vote). A Constitutional Court (which was to ensure adherence to the principles stipulated by the negotiating forum) was to be appointed by the President from a list of candidates nominated by an independent judicial commission. In accordance with demands by the ANC, a 'single-ballot system' was adopted, whereby the electorate would vote for the same party at regional and national elections. As a concession to the FA, the interim Constitution included a provision that entitled the legislatures of the nine redesignated provinces to draft their own constitutions, subject to the principles governing the national Constitution, in addition to the amendments defining the powers of regional government that had been approved in August. (However, the central Government retained substantial powers to intervene in a number of significant areas of regional administration.) Despite the efforts of the Government and the ANC to secure its support, the FA, together with the PAC, rejected the interim Constitution. (It was widely feared that failure to include the major political factions, particularly the IFP, in the negotiating process would result in a deterioration in internal stability, and ultimately in civil conflict.)

In early December 1993 the 21 delegations participating in the negotiating forum agreed unanimously to the reincorporation of the four 'independent homelands' into South Africa on 27 April 1994, when the interim Constitution was to enter into force. On 1 January South African citizenship was to be restored to the population of the 'homelands', who would be entitled to vote in the elections. However, the governments of Bophuthatswana and Ciskei refused to recognize the decision. On 7 December 1993 the TEC commenced sessions, but was, as expected, boycotted by a number of delegations. Members of the AWB temporarily occupied an Afrikaner fort near Pretoria in protest at the inauguration of the TEC. In mid-December the IEC and the seven TEC sub-councils were established. In the same month the Government and the ANC continued negotiations with the FA, in a further effort to persuade it to accept the interim Constitution and to participate in the TEC; however, bilateral discussions between the ANC and the AVF ended in failure, after the ANC insisted on an immediate commitment from the FA to join the transitional process as a precondition to further amendments to the interim Constitution. On 22 December Parliament ratified the interim Constitution, thereby effecting its own dissolution as an organ of the apartheid regime.

In December 1993 the judicial commission of inquiry into political violence that had been established in October 1991 concluded that several members of the KwaZulu security forces, who had been trained by the South African armed forces, had killed ANC members in Natal (apparently with the aim of inciting unrest). In early January 1994 the APLA was implicated in further indiscriminate killings of civilians; the PAC, however, denied responsibility for the violence, and in mid-January, following the withdrawal of support from the Govenments of Tanzania and Zimbabwe, announced that it had suspended the activities of the APLA and indicated that it intended to contest the elections. (The cessation of violence was subsequently opposed by some elements within the organization.) Meanwhile, the Government and the ANC resumed negotiations with the FA, which continued to insist on greater regional autonomy, with an additional demand for the use of separate ballot papers for national and regional representatives. In early January, however, the unity of the groups opposed to the transitional process was undermined by the decision of the Ciskei government to join the TEC, and its subsequent withdrawal from the FA. Later that month the IFP and the AVF demonstrated their continuing opposition to participation in the elections at separate conventions; the AVF effectively declared independence from South Africa, with the establishment of a representative council as a parallel administration to the TEC. Also in January President de Klerk, Mandela and a number of delegates representing black and white communities signed an agreement on local government reform, which also provided for the amalgamation of black and white municipal councils prior to local government elections (which were to take place within a period of two years). Mandela subsequently urged township residents to end the boycott of rent and rates (which had been initiated in 1986 as part of the campaign against apartheid), in exchange for a government pledge to improve the quality of services in the townships. At the end of January 1994, following an attack against ANC leaders in an East Rand township, in which a journalist was killed, it was announced that the NPKF was to be deployed in areas of unrest in March.

In February 1994, in accordance with a decision by the TEC, President de Klerk announced that voting would take place between 26 and 28 April. The elections were to be monitored by international representatives, including some 2,800 UN observers. Nineteen political parties had registered to contest the elections by the stipulated date on 12 February (which was subsequently extended to March). The ANC's list of candidates incorporated members of the SACP, COSATU, the 'homeland' governments and parties representing the Indian and Coloured communities; the inclusion of Winnie Mandela (who had been elected President of the ANC's Women's League in December 1993) attracted widespread criticism. The IFP confirmed that it intended to boycott the elections, after the Zulu tribal monarch, King Goodwill Zwelithini (who was Buthelezi's nephew), rejected the interim Constitution and declared sovereignty over the territory traditionally owned by the Zulus, prompting increased fears of civil conflict. (It was reported, however, that there was considerable support within the IFP for participation in the elections.) In mid-February, after continuing trilateral negotiations between the Government, the ANC and the FA proved unsuccessful, Nelson Mandela announced a number of proposed amendments to the interim Constitution, in an effort to comply with the demands of the IFP and the AVF. The new constitutional amendments recognized the right to regional self-determination, including the concept of a separate Afrikaner state; introduced a 'double-ballot system', whereby the electorate was to vote separately for national and provincial candidates; allowed each province to determine its legislative and executive structure and to manage its own finances; guaranteed the powers of provincial government; and redesignated Natal as KwaZulu/Natal. The FA, however, rejected the concessions, on the grounds that the powers of regional government remained inadequate, and refused to attend discussions on the proposed amendments, which were, nevertheless, adopted by the negotiating forum. (The dissolved Parliament was reconvened to ratify the constitutional amendments.) Also in February, despite objections from the IFP, the Internal Stability Units (a specialized division of the security forces) were withdrawn from the East Rand and replaced by members of the armed forces, under a joint initiative by the Government and the ANC to restore peace in the region. During that month a series of bomb attacks, which were attributed to right-wing extremists, took place in Orange Free State and Transvaal. In early March, after the ANC and IFP agreed to accept international mediation regarding the issue of regional autonomy, Buthelezi announced that he was to register the IFP provisionally to contest the elections. The leader of the AVU, Gen. (retd) Constand Viljoen (who had increasingly dissociated himself from extreme right-wing elements in the AVF) also provisionally registered a new party, the Freedom Front (FF). Despite the insistence of the AVF that its constituent groups were to boycott the elections, the FF subsequently submitted a list of candidates, which included several prominent members of the CP (thereby consolidating the division within the right wing). The IFP, however, failed to present a list of candidates by the stipulated date, while Zwelithini continued to urge his followers to boycott the elections.

In early March 1994 the President of Bophuthatswana, Lucas Mangope (who was a member of the FA), announced that the population of the 'homeland' would not participate in the elections. A series of strikes and demonstrations by civil servants (who were concerned about their future status following the reincorporation of the 'homelands' into South Africa) subsequently escalated into widespread protests against the Mangope regime. Mangope fled from the capital, Mmabatho, after disaffected members of the security forces demanded that he allow participation in the elections and refused to take action against the demonstrators. At the apparent instigation of the AVF, some 5,000 armed right-wing extremists, principally members of the AWB, entered Bophuthatswana and occupied Mmabatho, with the aim of reinstating Mangope. Shortly afterwards the Government dispatched some 2,000 members of the armed forces to Bophuthatswana, which, together with disaffected local troops, regained control of the 'homeland'; it was reported that more than 60 people had been killed in the fighting. The Government and the TEC formally deposed Mangope (whose removal signified the effective dissolution of the FA), and announced that voting was to take place in the 'homeland'. Later in March members of the armed forces were deployed in Ciskei to maintain civil order, following the resignation of the 'homeland's' military ruler in response to a strike by reformist members of the security forces. (The TEC and the Government assumed joint responsibility for administration in Bophuthatswana and Ciskei pending the elections.) In the same month President de Klerk announced the conclusions of a report by the judicial commission of inquiry into political violence, which implicated three senior officials in the security forces and prominent members of the IFP in a conspiracy to organize political assassinations, with the aim of undermining national stability prior to the elections (apparently confirming suspicions regarding the existence of the 'third force'). The report was strongly condemned by the security forces and the IFP, which denied the accusations. President de Klerk subsequently stated that the allegations would be investigated by an international task force; his decision to suspend a number of members of the security forces, including the three officials (who had apparently supplied armaments to the IFP) prompted criticism from security force leaders.

Following renewed clashes between members of the IFP and the ANC in KwaZulu/Natal in March 1994, the ANC urged the Government to dispatch troops to the region, despite Buthelezi's provisional agreement to allow the IEC to organize elections in the province. In late March an estimated 53 people were killed after a demonstration by Zulus in support of the demands of Zwelithini culminated in violent clashes with security forces at ANC headquarters in Johannesburg. At the end of that month President de Klerk, with the approval of the ANC, imposed a state of emergency in KwaZulu/Natal; some 3,000 troops were subsequently deployed in the province to maintain civil order during the election period. (However, political violence continued in KwaZulu/Natal, and a demonstration by Zulus who were armed with traditional weapons took place in April, despite the state of emergency.) In early April some 1,800 troops belonging to the NPKF, which included a substantial number of the MK, replaced members of the armed forces deployed in the East Rand (but were withdrawn later that month, after proving to be ineffective). Meanwhile, a proposal by the ANC that the position of the Zulu monarch be entrenched in the interim Constitution was rejected by the IFP, on the grounds that the offer only allowed Zwelithini ceremonial functions, and made no provision for the autonomy of the Zulu nation. Subsequent negotiations between the Government, the ANC and the IFP, with the assistance of international mediators, were impeded by procedural issues, owing to the refusal of the Government and the ANC to discuss Buthelezi's demand that the elections be rescheduled. In mid-April a planned demonstration by the IFP in Johannesburg in protest at the killing of Zulus in late March was prohibited by the authorities, amid increasing fears of civil conflict. Later in April, however, following mediation by a Kenyan academic, who was acquainted with Buthelezi, an agreement was reached whereby the IFP was to participate in the elections, in exchange for guarantees that the institutions of the Zulu monarch and kingdom were to be recognized in the interim Constitution. Under the terms of a proposed draft constitution for KwaZulu/Natal, the Zulu monarch was to be granted additional territorial powers and sovereignty with regard to traditional law and custom; outstanding issues were to be negotiated after the elections. Parliament was consequently reconvened to adopt the appropriate amendments to the interim Constitution. (The stipulated date for registration of parties had effectively been extended indefinitely to allow the IFP to participate in the elections.) The IFP's decision prompted general relief; however, the AVF announced that it would continue to boycott the elections. A series of bomb attacks during April was widely perceived as a campaign by right-wing extremists to disrupt the elections. At the end of April about 32 members of the AWB, including prominent party officials, were arrested in connection with the bombing offensive, in which a total of 21 people were killed. Terre'Blanche subsequently threatened that the campaign would continue unless the Government acceded to demands for Afrikaner self-determination. Under the terms of an accord between the Government, the ANC and the FF earlier in April, the level of support for the FF in the elections was to be used to determine whether a separate Afrikaner state might be established in any region with the approval of the majority of the resident population. Prior to the elections, the Government also reached an agreement with the PAC, which provided for the inclusion of members of the APLA in the new national defence force, in exchange for a guaranteed cessation of hostilities.

On 27 April 1994 the interim Constitution came into force, with voting commencing on the previous day, as scheduled. However, a number of logistical difficulties (which were compounded by the IFP's late decision to contest the elections) and a shortage of voting materials were reported, and widespread delays occurred. On 28 April, in accordance with a decision by the IEC, voting was extended by one day in KwaZulu/Natal and other regions affected by administrative confusion. A number of reports of electoral malpractice (which had apparently been facilitated by the organizational difficulties) emerged; in particular, the ANC accused the IFP of assuming control of polling stations in KwaZulu/Natal. Nevertheless, the IEC declared that the elections had been free and fair. The promulgation of the official election results was subsequently delayed, owing, in part, to the necessity of adjudication regarding disputed ballots in KwaZulu/Natal, which involved negotiations between the IFP and the ANC; it was finally agreed that the IFP would be allocated 50.3% of the vote in the province, thereby allowing it a majority of one seat in the regional legislature. On 2 May, after partial results indicated a substantial majority in favour of the ANC, de Klerk conceded defeat, prompting widespread jubilation. Shortly afterwards it was announced that the ANC had secured 62.65% of votes cast, while the NP had won 20.39%, the IFP 10.54% and the FF 2.17% of the votes. Consequently, the ANC narrowly failed to obtain a parliamentary majority of two-thirds, which, under the terms of the interim Constitution, would allow its members to draft and adopt the new constitution without consulting other parties. The NP, which secured a majority in the province of Northern Cape, received the stipulated percentage of the national vote entitling it to nominate a Deputy President. Mandela subsequently appointed a senior official of the ANC, Thabo Mbeki, as First Deputy President, while de Klerk, as expected, was nominated as Second Deputy President.

Mandela was officially elected as President by the National Assembly on 9 May 1994, and was inaugurated on the following day at a ceremony which was attended by a large number of international Heads of State. A Cabinet of National Unity, comprising 18 representatives of the ANC, six of the NP and three of the IFP, was subsequently formed. Joe Slovo was appointed Minister of Housing and Welfare, while a former Commander of the MK, Joe Modise, became Minister of Defence; the NP retained a number of portfolios, including that of finance. Despite speculation that he would refuse a cabinet post, Buthelezi accepted the portfolio of home affairs. The appointment of Winnie Mandela as a deputy minister was widely interpreted as an attempt to prevent her from criticizing the new administration. Later in May the provincial legislatures elected a 90-member Senate, comprising 60 representatives of the ANC, 17 of the NP, five of the IFP and FF respectively, and three of the DP. The ANC consequently held a slightly higher majority in the Constitutional Assembly than in the National Assembly, but failed, nevertheless, to obtain a majority of two-thirds. The Secretary-General of the ANC, Cyril Ramaphosa, was subsequently elected Chairman of the Constitutional Assembly.

Following the inauguration of the new Cabinet, the Government adopted a Reconstruction and Development Programme (RDP), which comprised extensive measures for social and economic development, including the reformation of the education and health services. The Government also announced plans to establish a 'Truth and Reconciliation Commission', comprising eminent citizens, which would investigate violations of human rights perpetrated under the apartheid regime; the Commission was to be empowered to grant indemnity to individuals who confessed to politically-motivated crimes committed before 5 December 1993 (when the TEC was effectively installed). Although the FF had failed to obtain the level of support in the elections stipulated as a precondition to the consideration of its demands, the Government subsequently agreed to the establishment of a 'volkstaat council', in which Viljoen and other right-wing Afrikaners were to debate the issue of self-determination. Meanwhile, it was disclosed that de Klerk had authorized the transfer of state-owned land (comprising one-third of the territory of KwaZulu/Natal) to Zwelithini shortly before the elections. The ANC denied knowledge of the agreement, which, it was speculated, had been designed to prevent attempts to include the territory in the ANC's land reform programme (whereby communities or individuals were entitled to claim restitution for land dispossessed under regional legislation from 1913). In addition to contention over this issue, the allocation of portfolios in the government of KwaZulu/Natal prompted acrimony between the ANC and IFP, while considerable support emerged within the ANC for legal action regarding a number of election results in the province, following increasing indications that extensive malpractice had taken place.

In early June 1994 the NPKF was dissolved; the new South African National Defence Force (SANDF) was to be constituted over a period of three years (to allow the integration of former members of the MK and APLA). ANC officials proposed that the 'self-defence units' (ANC paramilitary groups which patrolled townships and frequently clashed with rival IFP factions) be disbanded and incorporated into regional security forces. In the same month ANC officials agreed to abandon plans to take legal action over the alleged electoral irregularities in KwaZulu/Natal, following an appeal by Mandela in the interests of national reconciliation; the decision was reportedly influenced by IFP concessions regarding the allocation of portfolios in the provincial Government. In mid-June a cabinet committee, headed by the Minister of Land Affairs, decided that Zwelithini was to remain the statutory trustee of the territory in KwaZulu/Natal that had been transferred to his control prior to the elections. At the end of June nine former MK officials were allocated prominent positions within the SANDF. (The commander of the former defence forces, Gen. George Meiring, had been reappointed Chief of the SANDF in May.) In July Derek Keys resigned the finance portfolio, citing personal reasons (although he agreed to remain in office until October). The Government subsequently reaffirmed its commitment to its stated policy of fiscal restraint, following general concern that Keys's resignation reflected disagreement within the Cabinet over the economy. Christo Liebenberg, a prominent former banker with no official political affiliations, was appointed to succeed Keys. In mid-July, following hostilities in the East Rand in which a number of people were killed, ANC and IFP factions met for discussions and agreed, in principle, that the ANC 'self-defence units' be disbanded. In August de Klerk accused the ANC of misusing its parliamentary majority, after ANC deputies were elected to chair 24 standing committees in the National Assembly, while the NP secured the chairmanship of only four committees. The dispute prompted increased demands from NP parliamentary deputies that the party withdraw from the coalition administration and function as official opposition to the Government. At a national conference of COSATU in early September, Mandela appealed to unions to refrain from strike action in the interests of national reconciliation, following widespread industrial unrest.

In early September 1994 the Government officially ended the state of emergency in KwaZulu/Natal, which had been imposed in March in response to increasing factional violence during the electoral campaign. Later that month, however, divisions between Buthelezi and Zwelithini prompted renewed fears of conflict in the province: Buthelezi protested at Zwelithini's failure to consult him prior to inviting Mandela to attend annual celebrations commemorating the 19th century Zulu king, Shaka. The dispute followed reports that Buthelezi's former dominance of Zwelithini had been undermined by the transfer of control over royal finances and personal security forces from provincial to central government after the elections, and that the King planned to replace him as senior adviser (self-styled traditional 'Prime Minister') with a senior ANC official, Prince Mcwayizeni Zulu. Zwelithini issued a statement severing contact with Buthelezi and cancelling the Shaka Day festival, after IFP supporters rioted outside the royal residence during a meeting between the King, Buthelezi and Mandela. SANDF troops were subsequently dispatched to protect Zwelithini, amid fears of violent repercussions. In defiance of Zwelithini's order, Buthelezi conducted the Shaka Day celebrations, which were principally attended by IFP supporters; despite widespread concern, the festivities took place peacefully. Shortly afterwards Buthelezi, together with a group of personal bodyguards, interrupted a television broadcast and apparently assaulted one of Zwelithini's advisers, after he declared during an interview that Buthelezi was unjustified in designating himself as Prime Minister to the King. The incident prompted widespread demands that Buthelezi resign from the Cabinet; both the SACP and the NP condemned his actions, although the CP claimed that the disturbance had been fabricated by the Government in an attempt to discredit him. Following a motion of censure by the Cabinet, Buthelezi issued a public apology; however, Mandela rejected his offer to resign from office.

In early October 1994 Modise announced that some 7,500 former members of the MK and APLA had absconded from the SANDF and had refused to resume duties unless the Government addressed grievances regarding the protracted process of their integration into the SANDF and at alleged discrimination against them. (In September several hundred former members of the MK had marched to Mandela's presidential office in Pretoria to present a number of demands for improvements in salaries and living conditions in the SANDF.) Later in October Mandela met representatives of the disaffected members of the SANDF, and apparently indicated that their complaints would be investigated. He subsequently announced, however, that any members of the SANDF who failed to report for duty within seven days would be regarded as deserters and consequently dismissed. In mid-October the ANC temporarily suspended participation in the provincial Cabinet of Western Cape, in protest at the failure of the NP Premier, Hermanus Kriel, to consult ANC ministers regarding the restructuring of the local civil service and other issues. In the same month the Minister of Justice, Abdullah Mohammed Omar, submitted draft legislation providing for the establishment of the Truth and Reconciliation Commission; Omar had resisted demands by right-wing organizations, particularly the CP, that the final date for amnesty be extended to 27 April 1994, thereby qualifying a number of right-wing activists (including the AWB members implicated in the pre-election bombing campaign) for indemnity from prosecution. At the end of October it was announced that the salaries of the President and the Deputy Presidents be reduced by 20%, and those of other cabinet members by 10%, as part of austerity measures which were designed to create funds for the RDP. (The high salaries allocated to members of the Government, in conjunction with the continuing privations of much of the black population, had attracted widespread criticism.) Meanwhile, Buthelezi warned that the IFP would refuse to participate in forthcoming local government elections unless the status of the Zulu kingdom were determined by constitutional negotiations with foreign mediation, and urged traditional leaders to boycott the transitional organs of local government. In late October the IFP majority in the provincial legislature of KwaZulu/Natal adopted legislation that provided for the establishment of an advisory council of Zulu chiefs, the House of Traditional Leaders, in which Zwelithini would be equal in status to other chiefs (including Buthelezi). Zwelithini subsequently protested that he had not been consulted regarding the legislation, which he described as an attempt by the IFP to seize power, and demanded that it be rescinded immediately. The IFP, however, maintained that the House of Traditional Leaders would be installed, despite the opposition of both Zwelithini and the ANC (which indicated that it would institute a legal challenge against the validity of the legislation). In early November the Government announced the dismissal of more than 2,000 members of the SANDF, who had failed to return to base by the stipulated date.

In November 1994 the Government adopted legislation that formally restored the rights of land ownership to members of the black population who had been dispossessed following the introduction of discriminatory legislation beginning in 1913; the Restitution of Land Rights Act provided for the establishment of a special commission and court, which were, respectively, to investigate and arbitrate claims. The introduction of the Act was opposed by IFP and FF deputies in the National Assembly, while the South African Agricultural Union (which represented white farmers) also rejected the legislation, despite a number of amendments made to the original draft as a result of consultations with the Union. In early December the Government announced plans to restrict illegal immigration from neighbouring countries, which was cited as a contributory factor to the increase in crime. In the same month a number of people were injured in fighting in central Johannesburg between security forces and several hundred black squatters, who had defied a court order evicting them from properties; the Johannesburg Tenants Association attributed the violence to the failure of the Government to address the needs of the homeless. (The Government had previously indicated that township residents who continued the boycott of rent and rates initiated in protest at local authorities during the apartheid era would be evicted.) At a national conference of the ANC, which took place at Bloemfontein in late December, Mandela and Ramaphosa were returned unopposed as party President and Secretary-General, respectively; Jacob Zuma, the leader of the ANC in KwaZulu/Natal, was elected Chairman, replacing Mbeki, who became Vice-President. Elections to the National Executive Committee indicated an increase in support for members who had maintained an uncompromising attitude to party issues (notably Winnie Mandela, who received the fifth highest number of votes). Delegates endorsed controversial proposals for the privatization of state-owned enterprises, but, following opposition from COSATU, agreed that proceeds from the sale of public assets would be used solely to reimburse national debt (rather than to finance the RDP, as originally envisaged by the Government). Also in December the Government of Pretoria-Witwatersrand-Vereeniging voted in favour of renaming the province Gauteng.

In early January 1995 the existing National Intelligence Service (NIS) was officially dissolved and replaced with two new bodies, incorporating elements of the ANC's security department and agencies of the former 'homelands': the South African Secret Service, under the command of the former head of the NIS, was to control international intelligence, while the National Intelligence Agency, headed by a former ANC security official, was to be responsible for internal intelligence. Later in January Sankie Mthembi-Nkondo (hitherto a deputy minister) became Minister of Housing, following the death of Slovo. In the same month, amid reports of increasing political violence between ANC and IFP supporters in KwaZulu/Natal, Buthelezi was elected Chairman of the House of Traditional Leaders. A national association of traditional leaders subsequently protested that it was unsuitable for Buthelezi to hold such a position in conjunction with his ministerial office and leadership of the IFP. Meanwhile, controversy emerged over the disclosure that de Klerk had secretly granted political indemnity to some 3,500 members of the security force and two former cabinet ministers shortly before the elections in April 1994. Omar (a member of the ANC) declared that the decrees providing for indemnity were invalid; de Klerk maintained that the amnesties had been granted legally, while the NP Minister of Mineral and Energy Affairs, Roelof Botha, claimed that they had not been formally enacted, apparently reflecting inter-party division. After an acrimonious meeting, at which Mandela reportedly questioned de Klerk's commitment to the aims of the Government, the Cabinet agreed by consensus that the amnesties were invalid. De Klerk subsequently declared that he had been insulted, and threatened to withdraw the NP from the Government. Following a meeting between Mandela and de Klerk, however, the two leaders agreed to resolve their differences and reaffirmed their mutual commitment to the coalition administration. At the end of January 1995 security forces threatened to present evidence implicating leading politicians in crimes perpetrated under the aegis of the apartheid administration unless the Government accede to a number of demands with respect to the Truth and Reconciliation Commission, principally that the identities of individuals who had committed political crimes remain secret, and that politicians acknowledge principal responsibility for such crimes. The human rights organization, Amnesty International, had previously expressed concern at delays in the establishment of the Commission, and claimed that individuals who had been involved in the violation of human rights continued to be employed in the security forces.

In accordance with the interim Constitution, an 11-member Constitutional Court was installed in February 1995; the Court was to ensure that the executive, legislative and judicial organs of government adhered to the principles entrenched in the interim Constitution, and was to endorse a final constitutional text with respect to these principles. In the same month Mandela confirmed that he would not contest the elections in 1999. Meanwhile, Dr Allan Boesak, a prominent former anti-apartheid activist, was obliged to resign as the South African permanent representative at the UN, after it was alleged that he had misappropriated donations to the Foundation for Peace and Justice, a charity which he administered. The activities of Winnie Mandela also attracted increasingly adverse publicity: following rumours in December that she had been involved in a clandestine business transaction with the Angolan Head of State, she was accused by senior members of the ANC Women's League of misappropriating funds that the Pakistani Prime Minister, Benazir Bhutto, had donated to the League in 1994. Later in February Winnie Mandela defied a presidential order that she cancel an official visit abroad to attend reconciliation discussions with a group of ANC members who had resigned from the Executive Committee of the Women's League in protest at her alleged authoritarianism.

After publicly denouncing the Government for concentrating on the appeasement of the white population while failing to address the continuing hardship of the black majority, she was threatened with dismissal from the Cabinet and forced to apologize. During her absence security forces raided her premises in search of evidence to support additional allegations that she had received payments from a construction company in return for using her influence to obtain housing contracts in black townships. In mid-February the ANC instituted a strict code of conduct for its members and established a disciplinary committee to investigate the allegations of corruption involving party officials.

In late February 1995 Buthelezi claimed that the ANC and NP had reneged on a pledge (which had been made shortly before the elections in April 1994) to invite international mediators to arbitrate on IFP demands for the devolution of power to KwaZulu/Natal, and announced that IFP deputies were consequently to suspend participation in Parliament and the Constitutional Assembly. (However, IFP ministers, including Buthelezi, remained in the Cabinet.) At the end of February 1995 Mandela ordered that additional security forces be deployed in parts of KwaZulu/Natal and other regions, in response to concern at increasing violence. At a special party congress, which took place in early March, the IFP agreed to resume participation in Parliament and in the Constitutional Assembly, but issued a resolution to the effect that IFP deputies would continue the boycott of the Constitutional Assembly if Mandela failed to invite international mediators for negotiations on the issue of regional autonomy. Later that month Buthelezi denied allegations by Zwelithini regarding the existence of a conspiracy to remove him from power, and demanded that the King convene a gathering of Zulus within two months to determine the future of KwaZulu/Natal. Zwelithini, however, rejected the ultimatum and initiated a legal appeal that the installation of the House of Traditional Leaders be declared unconstitutional. In mid-March Mandela announced that local government elections would take place on 1 November. Buthelezi had previously indicated that he would support voter registration, but that the IFP's participation in the elections remained conditional on the Government's acceptance of demands for regional autonomy. Although the CP had announced that it intended to participate in the elections, it was reported that extreme right-wing groups, including the AWB, planned to conduct separate 'elections' (which would take place concurrently with the official elections). The registration of voters was scheduled to end in April; however, the date was subsequently extended until early June, owing to the low level of registration, particularly among the black population. At the end of March members of the IFP staged demonstrations in several towns (which, despite widespread concern, took place peacefully), in commemoration of the deaths of Zulu protesters outside the ANC headquarters in Johannesburg in March 1994. The IFP claimed that the ANC was responsible for the incident and demanded that security forces institute investigations. Meanwhile, Winnie Mandela's position in the Cabinet appeared to be increasingly untenable, as a result of her continued autocratic behaviour. She refused to meet Mbeki (who had been assigned by Mandela to examine the allegations against her), pending the outcome of her legal appeal against the search of her property by security forces. (A judicial ruling that the warrant authorizing the search was invalid subsequently prompted her to institute legal proceedings against security officials.) In late March Mandela finally removed her from the Cabinet, after she publicly criticized government expenditure on the visit to South Africa of the British monarch, Queen Elizabeth II. The presidential decision to dismiss Winnie Mandela received widespread support, both from within the ANC and from other political parties.

At a party conference on constitutional policy, which took place in early April 1995, the ANC rejected NP proposals that the principle of power-sharing be entrenched in the final constitution, thereby extending the tenure of the coalition Government. (Controversy over this issue had reportedly resulted in divisions within the Constitutional Assembly.) The conference also failed to accept IFP demands for international mediation on regional autonomy, and adopted constitutional proposals that provided for a Senate comprising members of provincial legislatures, which would be empowered to veto provincial legislation. Buthelezi implemented his threat to suspend IFP participation in the Constitutional Assembly, and indicated that the IFP would not accept a constitution that had been drafted by the remaining parties in the Assembly (while rejecting the ANC's constitutional recommendations). De Klerk subsequently intervened in the dispute between the ANC and the IFP, reportedly proposing that he, Mbeki and Buthelezi meet to discuss the issue of international mediation on provincial autonomy. Mbeki, however, maintained that the ANC would not consider international mediation and that constitutional discussions should be conducted in the forum of the Constitutional Assembly. In the same month the Cabinet adopted draft legislation providing for the establishment of the Truth and Reconciliation Commission: the final date for political indemnity of 5 December was retained, despite the protests of right-wing organizations, while provisions empowering the Commission to conduct amnesty hearings in camera had been removed. (Civil rights activists had expressed concern that the Truth and Reconciliation Commission would offer immunity against legal action to perpetrators of human rights violations, and had particularly objected to the provisions for secret hearings.)

Also in April 1995 Winnie Mandela instituted legal action against the President, on the grounds that he had failed to provide an explanation for her dismissal, and to consult with leaders of the other political parties in the coalition Government, as stipulated in the interim Constitution. (Buthelezi had supplied her with a written statement confirming that Mandela had not consulted him.) Mandela acknowledged that her dismissal was technically invalid (thereby obviating embarassing legal proceedings) and temporarily reinstated her, pending discussions with other political leaders. Shortly afterwards he confirmed her removal from the Cabinet, after consulting with de Klerk and Buthelezi. It was reported, however, that Winnie Mandela planned to initiate further legal action, on the grounds that the President had again failed to cite reasons for her dismissal. Later in April Mbeki announced that a government inquiry had exonerated Boesak of misappropriating aid funds (although he was reprimanded for mismanaging the charity), while Mandela reportedly promised to allocate him an important position in the diplomatic service. In response to criticism that it had pre-empted continuing investigations by the security forces, however, the Government conceded that the results of its inquiry were inconclusive.

In early May 1995, following reports that factional hostilities in KwaZulu/Natal had increased, Mandela accused Buthelezi of inciting political violence and threatened to suspend government funds to the province, subsequently adding that he would amend the interim Constitution in order to acquire the requisite powers. His statement was widely criticized, and it was announced shortly afterwards that Mandela and Buthelezi had agreed to resolve their differences and to negotiate regarding the issue of international mediation. Later in May Mandela consented to foreign mediation on constitutional discussions, but maintained that the terms of reference for such arbitration should be identified beforehand (Buthelezi had previously stated that this was unnecessary). In the same month the National Assembly approved the draft legislation providing for the establishment of the Truth and Reconciliation Commission; only the FF deputies opposed the enactment of the legislation. At the end of May the IFP and ANC agreed formally to exchange constitutional proposals in order to establish a basis for negotations. Meanwhile, COSATU announced a campaign of demonstrations, culminating in a one-day strike, in support of demands for amendments to draft legislation on labour relations which was to be submitted to Parliament later in the year; the unions' demands included the right to institute strike action and the official introduction of centralized wage-bargaining. In early June the Constitutional Court abolished the death penalty, deeming that it contravened the provisions in the interim Constitution that protected fundamental human rights.

South Africa became increasingly isolated politically in southern Africa after Zimbabwe (formerly Rhodesia) underwent the transition to independence in April 1980. Zimbabwe severed diplomatic relations with South Africa in September 1980, although economic links were retained. Malawi was the only African state to maintain official diplomatic relations with South Africa during the 1980s. Among regional difficulties concerning South Africa during the 1980s was the conflict in Namibia, involving frequent clashes between guerrillas of the South West Africa People's Organisation of Namibia (SWAPO) and South African troops (see chapter on Namibia). The South African army also made long-distance raids across Namibia's border with Angola. Both the UN and the Organization of African Unity (OAU—see p. 200) recognized SWAPO as the 'authentic representative of the Namibian people', and the International Court of Justice and the UN declared South Africa's presence in Namibia to be illegal. After prolonged attempts to achieve a negotiated settlement for Namibia progress was halted by South African and US insistence that Cuban troops be withdrawn from Angola. Following the collapse of the semi-autonomous internal administration, South Africa resumed direct rule of Namibia in January 1983. In February 1984 South Africa and Angola agreed on a cease-fire along the Angola–Namibia border, and established a joint commission to monitor the withdrawal of South African troops from Angola. In June 1985 a 'transitional government' was established in Namibia, but this regime failed to secure international recognition. In October 1987 South Africa admitted that it continued to maintain a 'limited presence' of troops inside Angola. In the following month, the UN demanded the withdrawal of South African troops from Angola. Having eventually agreed to comply with this demand, South African troops nevertheless continued to be active in Angola during the first half of 1988. In May negotiations began between Angola, Cuba and South Africa, with the USA acting as mediator. On 22 December 1988 Angola, Cuba and South Africa signed a formal treaty designating 1 April 1989 as the commencement date for the process leading to Namibian independence, as well as a treaty requiring all 50,000 Cuban troops to be withdrawn from Angola by July 1991. Elections were held in Namibia in November 1989, and independence for the former South African territory was achieved on 21 March 1990, under a SWAPO-controlled Government. The strategic port of Walvis Bay and 12 offshore islands, to which Namibia laid claim, remained under South African jurisdiction. However, in September 1991 the two countries agreed to administer Walvis Bay and the 12 islands jointly, pending a final settlement on the sovereignty of the disputed territories. In August 1993 South Africa relinquished sovereignty over Walvis Bay and the 12 islands, which were officially transferred to Namibia in March 1994.

In March 1984 South Africa signed a mutual non-aggression pact with Mozambique, known as the Nkomati accord, in which each Government undertook to prevent opposition forces in its territory from launching attacks against the other, and a joint security commission was established. The pact implied that South Africa would withdraw its covert support for the Resistência Nacional Moçambicana (Renamo), while Mozambique would prevent the ANC from using its territory as a base for attacks on South Africa. However, Renamo guerrillas remained active in Mozambique. In September 1985 the South African Government conceded that there had been 'technical' violations of the accord. The joint security commission ceased to meet in 1985. Relations between South Africa and Mozambique were severely strained in October 1986, when President Machel of Mozambique was killed in an air crash within South African territory. Although the South African authorities concluded that pilot error, and not sabotage, had caused the crash, the Mozambican Government declared that investigations were to continue into the possibility of South African involvement. In July the massacre of 424 people in Mozambique, allegedly by Renamo, provoked renewed accusations by the Mozambique Government of South African support for the rebels. South Africa denied any involvement in the massacre. In May 1988 Mozambican and South African officials agreed to reactivate the Nkomati accord and to re-establish the joint security commission, and in September President Botha visited President Joaquim Chissano of Mozambique, his first state visit to a black African nation. Following his election as President, Mandela made an official visit to Mozambique in July 1994. In August of that year South Africa, Mozambique and Swaziland signed a security co-operation accord, in an effort to combat the continuing illicit transport of armaments.

In 1984 Swaziland revealed that it had signed a security pact with South Africa in February 1982. In December 1986, however, bilateral relations were threatened by the abduction by South African forces of six suspected ANC agents from Swazi territory. Relations deteriorated further in April 1987, when several suspected ANC members were assassinated in Swaziland, reportedly by South African police units. Following criticism by the Lesotho authorities of alleged South African involvement in a raid in December 1985 on the capital, Maseru, South Africa imposed harsh restrictions at its border with Lesotho (which is completely surrounded by South African territory). These restrictions were relaxed following the Lesotho coup in January 1986 and negotiations with the new Lesotho Government (see chapter on Lesotho). In December 1987 South Africa imposed security checks at its border with Botswana, following alleged mass infiltration by the ANC into South Africa from Botswana. South Africa appeared to widen its campaign against the ANC in March 1988, when several attacks were launched on ANC targets in European capitals. During 1990–92, following the implementation of a far-reaching programme of political reforms in February 1990 (see above), President de Klerk engaged in unprecedented diplomatic activity, visiting several European and African states, and the USA. During 1991 and 1992 South Africa established diplomatic relations with several states, including Angola, Côte d'Ivoire, Japan and Russia. Following the installation of an interim Government of National Unity in May 1994, about 50 countries had established diplomatic relations with South Africa by March of the following year.

In 1979 the Southern African Development Co-ordination Conference (SADCC) was established by southern African countries, to work towards a reduction of their economic dependence on South Africa. The SADCC reformed in August 1992 as the Southern African Development Community (SADC—see p. 219), which aimed to achieve closer economic integration between its member states. During the 1980s, despite appeals by anti-apartheid groups within and outside the country for the imposition of economic sanctions, South Africa retained vital trading links with many Western countries, and its economy was supported by considerable foreign investment. Nevertheless, following the violent events of 1984–85, the UN Security Council imposed a number of economic sanctions and restrictions on sport and cultural relations. The US Government (which had hitherto maintained a policy of 'constructive engagement' with South Africa) imposed a series of limited economic sanctions, as did members of the European Community (EC—now European Union—see p. 143) and Scandinavian countries. In August 1986 the Heads of Government of seven Commonwealth countries agreed (with the exception of the United Kingdom) to adopt wide-ranging sanctions. In the following month, the US Congress overruled President Reagan's veto of a series of strong economic measures against South Africa. Although Japan had imposed limited sanctions in 1985 and 1986, it became South Africa's leading trading partner in 1987. In March 1988, however, major Japanese companies began to cease direct exports to South Africa.

Following the implementation of political reforms in South Africa from February 1990, international sanctions were reviewed. In December the EC removed sanctions on new investment in South Africa. During 1991 South Africa was readmitted to international sporting competition, after many years of exclusion. In July the USA officially withdrew sanctions (which were, however, retained by a number of US states and cities). In September of that year South Africa was granted its first international loan issue since 1985. In October 1991 Commonwealth Heads of Government endorsed the withdrawal of cultural sanctions against South Africa; however, sanctions on finance, arms and trade and investment remained. Japan ended all its sanctions during that month. In 1992 the EC withdrew a number of sanctions against South Africa. In September 1993, following the adoption of legislation providing for the installation of a multiracial transitional administration (see above), the international community ended the remaining economic sanctions against South Africa. The UN Security Council ended its mandatory embargo on armaments, following the establishment of an interim Government of National Unity in May 1994. South Africa became a member of the Commonwealth on 1 June, and joined the OAU later that month. In August South Africa was also admitted to the SADC.

### Government

Under the terms of the interim Constitution, which came into effect on 27 April 1994, legislative power is vested in a bicameral Parliament, comprising a National Assembly and a Senate. The 400-member National Assembly is elected by universal adult suffrage under a system of proportional representation. The 90-member Senate comprises 10 representatives elected by each of the provincial legislatures (see below). The President, who is elected by the National Assembly from among its members, exercises executive power in consultation with at least two Deputy Presidents. Any party that holds a minimum of 80 seats in the National Assembly (equivalent to 20% of the national vote) is entitled to nominate a Deputy President. The Constitution provides for an interim Government of National Unity, with a Cabinet in which each party with a minimum of 20 seats in the National Assembly (equivalent to 5% of the national vote) is entitled to a proportionate number of ministerial portfolios. The President allocates cabinet portfolios in consultation with party leaders. The National Assembly and Senate together form a Constitutional Assembly, which is to draft and adopt a new constitution within a period of two years of its first session. A Constitutional Court ensures that the executive, legislative and judicial organs of government adhere to a number of principles entrenched in the interim Constitution (which include provisions for multi-party democracy, the delineated powers of provincial government, fundamental human rights and the independence of the judiciary), and is to endorse a final constitutional text with respect to these principles.

Each of the nine provinces has a legislature, which is elected under a system of proportional representation. Each legislature is entitled to draft a constitution for the province, subject to the principles governing the national Constitution, and to elect a Premier, who heads a Cabinet. Parties that hold a minimum of 10% of seats in the provincial legislature are entitled to a proportionate number of portfolios in the provincial Cabinet.

**Defence**

In June 1994 the armed forces totalled 78,500: army an estimated 58,000, navy 4,500, air force 10,000 and a medical corps numbering 6,000. In the same year there were some 35,400 conscripts; conscription ended when the interim Constitution entered into force in April 1994. Following the installation of a new Government in May 1994, it was announced that a new South African National Defence Force (SANDF) was to be established over a period of three years. The SANDF, which was expected to number 67,000–70,000, was to comprise members of the South African armed forces, including an estimated 30,000 personnel from the former military wing of the ANC, the Pan-Africanist Congress and the former 'homelands'). A new national security force was also to be established. The defence budget for 1993/94 was R 14,200m.

**Economic Affairs**

In 1993, according to estimates by the World Bank, South Africa's gross national product (GNP), measured at average 1991–93 prices, was US $118,057m., equivalent to $2,900 per head. During 1985–93, it was estimated, GNP per head declined, in real terms, by an annual average of 1.5%, while the population increased by an annual average of 2.4%. South Africa's gross domestic product (GDP) increased, in real terms, by an annual average of 1.1% in 1980–93; real GDP increased by 1.1% in 1993, and by 2.3% in 1994.

In the following paragraphs the percentages given for sectoral contributions to GDP refer to the combined GDP of South Africa and the former 'independent homelands', while percentages of the working population exclude the 'independent homelands'.

Agriculture (including forestry and fishing) contributed 4.5% of GDP in 1994. About 12.9% of the employed labour force were engaged in the sector in 1991. Maize (also the principal subsistence crop), fruit and sugar are exported, and livestock-rearing is also important: wool is another significant export. During 1980–92 agricultural GDP increased by an annual average of 1.7%; output declined by 18.4% in 1992, but increased by 16.7% in 1993 and by 7.7% in 1994.

Industry (including mining, manufacturing, construction and power) contributed 38.0% of GDP in 1994, and engaged 30.4% of the employed labour force in 1991. During 1980–92 industrial GDP declined by an annual average of 0.1%.

Mining contributed 8.4% of GDP in 1994, and engaged 8.8% of the employed labour force in 1991. South Africa is the world's leading producer of gold, which is the major mineral export, accounting for 25% of total export earnings in 1990. Coal, platinum, iron ore, diamonds, chromium, manganese, vanadium, vermiculite, antimony, limestone, asbestos, fluorspar, uranium, copper, lead and zinc are also important mineral exports. There are reserves of petroleum, natural gas, sillimanite, titanium and zirconium.

Manufacturing contributed 22.6% of GDP in 1994, and engaged about 14.9% of the employed labour force in 1991. In 1991 the principal sectors (measured by value of output) were chemicals, petroleum and coal products, food products, transport equipment, iron and steel, metal products, machinery, paper and textiles. Manufacturing GDP declined at an average rate of 0.2% per year during 1980–92.

Energy is derived principally from coal-based electricity; this is supplemented by nuclear power and by hydroelectric power. The construction of a plant to convert natural gas into liquid fuel was completed in 1992.

In 1993 the Southern African Customs Union (SACU, see below) recorded a visible trade surplus of US $5,781m., and a surplus of $1,805m. on the current account of the balance of payments. In 1994 the principal source of SACU's imports (an estimated 17.2%) was Germany; other major suppliers of imports were the United Kingdom, the USA and Japan. The principal market for exports in 1993 was Switzerland (10.0%); other important purchasers in that year were the USA, the United Kingdom and Japan. The principal exports in 1994 were metals and metal products, precious and semi-precious stones, mineral products and chemicals. The principal imports were machinery and electrical equipment, transport equipment and chemical products.

In the financial year ending 31 March 1994 South Africa recorded a budgetary deficit of R 36,832m. For 1994/95 there was an estimated budgetary deficit of R 36,500m. At the end of 1994 the Government's total debt was R 237,706m., of which R 8,058m. was foreign debt. The annual rate of inflation averaged 14.4% in 1985–93; consumer prices increased by 9.7% in 1993 and by 9.0% in 1994. According to official figures, the rate of unemployment in early 1995 was 29.0% of the labour force.

South Africa is a member of SACU, with Botswana, Lesotho, Namibia and Swaziland, the Southern African Development Community (SADC, see p. 219), and the Organization of African Unity (OAU, see p. 200).

Despite South Africa's mineral wealth and highly-developed manufacturing sector, economic progress was hindered during the 1980s following the imposition of economic sanctions by the international community in protest at apartheid. Disinvestment by foreign companies resulted in a major outflow of capital. By early 1992 a number of economic sanctions against South Africa had been withdrawn, in response to the Government's programme of political reforms (see Recent History). In late 1993 the remaining economic sanctions were ended, relations with international financial institutions were normalized, and an agreement with foreign creditor banks regarding the country's outstanding debt was reached. These developments, together with an increase in agricultural production (which had been adversely affected by drought), contributed to an improvement in the economy. Following democratic elections in April 1994, foreign Governments pledged financial assistance and granted significant trade concessions to South Africa. The new Government initiated a Reconstruction and Development Programme (RDP), which comprised extensive measures for social and economic development, including plans to reduce unemployment and to diversify the economy into value-added manufacturing. The implementation of the RDP was impeded by the necessity for fiscal restraint (as prescribed by the Bretton Woods institutions). The programme was to be financed by reductions in government expenditure, including an extensive restructuring of the civil service. However, plans to privatize state-owned enterprises proved controversial, and it was agreed that the proceeds would be used only to reduce the national debt. It was feared, moreover, that an increase in industrial unrest in late 1994 (in support of demands for increases in salary), in conjunction with the continuing high rate of crime and political violence, would act as a disincentive to potential foreign investors. In March 1995 the Government abolished the financial rand (which had been introduced in response to economic sanctions during the apartheid administration) and established a unitary currency system. The adoption of a proposed trade agreement between South Africa and the European Union (EU, see p. 143) was delayed by dissent between the member states of the EU.

# SOUTH AFRICA

## Social Welfare

Social welfare services protect the old, the blind, the war disabled, the unemployed and those injured at work. Medical services, which are administered at provincial level, ceased to be provided on a racial basis in May 1990. Nevertheless, there remains considerable disparity in the provision of health care to whites and non-whites. The majority of white South Africans contribute to private medical aid schemes, while most of the black population are dependent on medical services provided by the State. In 1990 there were 20,771 medical practitioners and 724 general and specialized hospitals. Health care was allocated R 13,969m. (10.6% of total projected expenditure) in the budget proposals for 1993/94. In 1994 the new Government initiated a new national health plan under the Reconstruction and Development Programme, which included the introduction of free health care for children under six years of age and pregnant women, provision of free food for primary school children in poor communities, and the establishment of additional community health centres.

## Education

School attendance is compulsory for children of all population groups between the ages of seven and 16 years, although in 1992 an estimated 1.7m. school-age children were not attending schools. During the 1980s universities, which were formerly racially segregated, began to admit students of all races. In 1991 there were 21 universities and 15 'technikons' (tertiary education institutions offering technological and commercial vocational training). From January 1991 state schools were permitted to admit pupils from all races. By early 1995 the estimated rate of adult illiteracy had declined to 30%. In 1992 the total enrolment at primary and secondary schools was equivalent to 94% of the school-age population (91% of boys; 96% of girls). A report on education in South Africa, compiled in 1984, estimated that 50% of the adult population were illiterate. The illiteracy rate was 7% among whites, 29% among Asians, 38% among Coloureds, and nearly 68% among blacks. Free education in all state schools was introduced from January 1995. Education was allocated 21.0% of total projected expenditure by the central Government in the budget for 1992/93.

## Public Holidays

**1995:** 1 January (New Year's Day), 21 March (Human Rights Day), 14–17 April (Easter), 27 April (Freedom Day), 1 May (Workers' Day), 16 June (Youth Day), 9 August (National Women's Day), 24 September (Heritage Day), 16 December (Day of Reconciliation), 25–27 December (Christmas).

**1996:** 1 January (New Year's Day), 21 March (Human Rights Day), 5–8 April (Easter), 27 April (Freedom Day), 1 May (Workers' Day), 16 June (Youth Day), 9 August (National Women's Day), 24 September (Heritage Day), 16 December (Day of Reconciliation), 25–27 December (Christmas).

## Weights and Measures

The metric system is in use.

# Statistical Survey

Source (unless otherwise indicated): Central Statistical Service, Steyn's Arcade, 274 Schoeman St, Private Bag X44, Pretoria 0001; tel. (12) 3108911; telex 320450; fax (12) 3108500.

## Area and Population

### AREA, POPULATION AND DENSITY*

| | |
|---|---:|
| Area (sq km) | 1,221,037† |
| Population (census results)‡ | |
| 5 March 1985 | 23,385,645 |
| 7 March 1991 | |
| Males | 12,834,016 |
| Females | 13,454,374 |
| Total | 26,288,390 |
| Population (official estimate at mid-year) | |
| 1994 | 40,436,000 |
| Density (per sq km) at mid-1994 | 33.1 |

* Excluding data for Walvis Bay (area 1,124 sq km or 434 sq miles, population 23,641 in 1970), sovereignty over which was transferred from South Africa to Namibia on 1 March 1994.

† 471,445 sq miles.

‡ Excluding the former 'homelands' of Transkei, Bophuthatswana, Venda and Ciskei (the TBVC states). The TBVC states had a combined area of about 95,500 sq km and an estimated population of 7,169,000 at mid-1994. Census results also exclude any adjustment for underenumeration. At the 1985 census the extent of underenumeration was estimated to have been: Africans 20.4%; Asians 6.5%; Coloureds 3.5%; Europeans 5.5%. At the 1991 census underenumeration was estimated at 15.1%. The adjusted total for 1991 is 30,986,920 (males 15,479,528; females 15,507,392).

### ETHNIC GROUPS (estimates, 27 April 1994)*

| | |
|---|---:|
| Africans (Blacks) | 30,645,157 |
| Europeans (Whites) | 5,171,419 |
| Coloureds | 3,435,114 |
| Asians | 1,032,943 |
| **Total** | **40,284,634** |

* Figures have been estimated independently, so the total is not the sum of the components.

### POPULATION BY PROVINCE (estimates, 27 April 1994)

| | |
|---|---:|
| Western Cape | 3,633,077 |
| Eastern Cape | 6,436,790 |
| Northern Cape | 737,306 |
| KwaZulu/Natal | 8,505,338 |
| Orange Free State | 2,726,840 |
| North-West | 3,252,991 |
| Northern Transvaal | 5,201,630 |
| Eastern Transvaal | 2,921,559 |
| Gauteng* | 6,869,103 |
| **Total** | **40,284,634** |

* Formerly called Pretoria-Witwatersrand-Vereeniging.

### PRINCIPAL TOWNS (population at 1991 census)

| | City Proper | Metropolitan Area |
|---|---:|---:|
| Cape Town* | 854,616 | 2,350,157 |
| Durban | 715,669 | 1,137,378 |
| Johannesburg | 712,507 | 1,916,061 |
| Pretoria* | 525,583 | 1,080,187 |
| Port Elizabeth | 303,353 | 853,205 |
| Umlazi | 299,275 | n.a. |
| Roodepoort | 162,632 | 870,066 |
| Pietermaritzburg | 156,473 | 228,549 |
| Germiston | 134,005 | n.a. |
| Bloemfontein* | 126,867 | 300,150 |
| Boksburg | 119,890 | n.a. |
| Benoni | 113,501 | n.a. |
| East London | 102,325 | 270,127 |
| Kimberley | 80,082 | 167,060 |
| Springs | 72,647 | 700,906 |
| Vereeniging | 71,255 | 773,594 |

* Pretoria is the administrative capital, Cape Town the legislative capital and Bloemfontein the judicial capital.

# SOUTH AFRICA

## Statistical Survey

### BIRTHS AND DEATHS (official estimates, annual averages)

|  | 1975–80 | 1980–85 | 1985–90 |
|---|---|---|---|
| Birth rate (per 1,000) | 34.3 | 33.1 | 32.1 |
| Death rate (per 1,000) | 12.1 | 11.0 | 9.9 |

**1992/93** (sample survey, year to October): Birth rate 27.1 per 1,000; Death rate 9.0 per 1,000.

**Expectation of life** (UN estimates, years at birth, 1985–90): 60.4 (males 57.5; females 63.5) (Source: UN, *World Population Prospects: The 1992 Revision*).

### IMMIGRATION AND EMIGRATION

|  | 1991 | 1992 | 1993 |
|---|---|---|---|
| **Immigrants** |  |  |  |
| Africa | 2,065 | 1,266 | 1,701 |
| Europe | 5,767 | 3,869 | 4,541 |
| Asia | 3,650 | 3,005 | 3,165 |
| Americas | 702 | 423 | 321 |
| Oceania | 195 | 118 | 93 |
| **Total** (incl. unspecified) | 12,379 | 8,686 | 9,824 |
| **Emigrants** |  |  |  |
| Africa | 212 | 139 | 227 |
| Europe | 2,408 | 2,633 | 1,000 |
| Asia | 62 | 89 | 120 |
| Americas | 593 | 606 | 292 |
| Oceania | 978 | 821 | 373 |
| **Total** (incl. unspecified) | 4,256 | 4,289 | 2,013 |

### ECONOMICALLY ACTIVE POPULATION
(persons aged 16 years and over, 1991 census)*

|  | Males | Females | Total |
|---|---|---|---|
| Agriculture, hunting, forestry and fishing | 892,646 | 331,789 | 1,224,435 |
| Mining and quarrying | 813,988 | 26,759 | 840,747 |
| Manufacturing | 1,008,273 | 408,854 | 1,417,127 |
| Electricity, gas and water | 92,189 | 10,740 | 102,928 |
| Construction | 492,992 | 33,381 | 526,373 |
| Trade, restaurants and hotels | 805,613 | 552,680 | 1,358,292 |
| Transport, storage and communications | 427,931 | 69,191 | 497,122 |
| Financing, insurance, real estate and business services | 262,564 | 241,406 | 503,970 |
| Community, social and personal services | 993,602 | 1,646,920 | 2,640,521 |
| Activities not adequately defined | 265,842 | 128,361 | 394,203 |
| **Total employed** | 6,055,640 | 3,450,081 | 9,505,718 |
| Unemployed | 987,415 | 1,131,234 | 2,118,649 |
| **Total labour force** | 7,043,053 | 4,581,314 | 11,624,368 |

* Excluding Transkei, Bophuthatswana, Venda and Ciskei. The data include an adjustment for underenumeration. Figures have been assessed independently, so that totals are not always the sum of the component parts.

Source: ILO, *Year Book of Labour Statistics*.

**October 1993** (household survey, persons aged 15 years and over, excluding Transkei, Bophuthatwana, Venda and Ciskei): Total labour force 12,353,324 (males 6,989,157; females 5,364,167), of whom 8,767,587 (males 5,305,942; females 3,461,645) were employed and 3,585,737 (males 1,683,215; females 1,902,522) were unemployed.

## Agriculture

### PRINCIPAL CROPS ('000 metric tons)

|  | 1991 | 1992 | 1993 |
|---|---|---|---|
| Maize | 8,179 | 3,061 | 9,425* |
| Sorghum | 260 | 101 | 380* |
| Wheat | 2,147 | 1,318 | 1,958† |
| Barley | 173 | 100* | 190† |
| Oats | 29 | 20 | 35† |
| Dry beans | 120 | 34 | 52* |
| Cottonseed | 86 | 36 | 28* |
| Cotton (lint) | 49 | 20 | 16* |
| Sugar cane | 20,078 | 14,788 | 11,240* |
| Tobacco (leaves) | 30 | 36 | 35* |
| Potatoes | 1,311 | 1,190 | 1,200† |
| Sweet potatoes | 56 | 56 | 50† |
| Soybeans | 126 | 68 | 63* |
| Groundnuts (in shell) | 110 | 114* | 174* |
| Sunflower seed | 597 | 176 | 329† |
| Cabbages | 221 | 228 | 230† |
| Tomatoes | 452 | 457 | 460† |
| Pumpkins, squash and gourds | 171 | 170 | 170† |
| Onions (dry) | 243 | 220 | 230† |
| Carrots | 89 | 99 | 100† |
| Watermelons | 45 | 51 | 50† |
| Apples | 515 | 483 | 597* |
| Grapefruit and pomelo | 132 | 113* | 115* |
| Grapes | 1,570 | 1,673 | 1,490† |
| Lemons and limes | 62 | 70 | 54* |
| Oranges | 628 | 690 | 677* |
| Peaches and nectarines* | 157 | 168 | 158* |
| Pears | 201 | 195 | 260* |
| Bananas | 239 | 179 | 180† |
| Mangoes | 32 | 32 | 32† |
| Avocados | 49 | 46 | 47† |
| Apricots | 48 | 49 | 50* |
| Pineapples | 163 | 176 | 165* |

* Unofficial figure.   † FAO estimate.

Source: FAO, *Production Yearbook*.

### LIVESTOCK ('000 head, year ending September)

|  | 1991 | 1992 | 1993 |
|---|---|---|---|
| Cattle* | 13,512 | 13,311 | 13,239 |
| Pigs† | 1,490 | 1,490 | 1,499 |
| Sheep* | 32,580 | 32,110 | 30,000 |
| Goats† | 5,900 | 5,900 | 5,915 |
| Horses† | 230 | 230 | 230 |
| Asses† | 210 | 210 | 210 |
| Mules† | 14 | 14 | 14 |

* Unofficial figures.   † FAO estimates.

Chickens (FAO estimates, million): 40 in 1991; 40 in 1992; 41 in 1993.

Source: FAO, *Production Yearbook*.

### LIVESTOCK PRODUCTS ('000 metric tons)

|  | 1991 | 1992 | 1993 |
|---|---|---|---|
| Beef and veal* | 700 | 745 | 729 |
| Mutton and lamb† | 133 | 130 | 132 |
| Goat meat† | 35 | 35 | 35 |
| Pig meat | 123 | 129 | 130 |
| Poultry meat† | 394 | 374 | 384 |
| Edible offals† | 184 | 191 | 186 |
| Cows' milk | 2,300* | 2,390* | 2,400† |
| Butter | 21.4 | 15.3 | 16.0† |
| Cheese | 42.3 | 39.1 | 38.0† |
| Condensed and evaporated milk | 18.7 | 17.9 | 18.0† |
| Dried milk | 12.4 | 10.5 | 10.5† |
| Hen eggs | 218.1 | 225.2 | 223.0* |
| Wool: |  |  |  |
| greasy | 102.6 | 97.0 | 90.0† |
| clean | 51.0 | 48.5* | 45.0 |
| Cattle hides (fresh)† | 93.8 | 97.5 | 94.8 |
| Sheepskins (fresh)† | 31.0 | 31.0 | 31.0 |

* Unofficial figure(s).   † FAO estimate(s).

Sources: FAO, *Production Yearbook* and *Quarterly Bulletin of Statistics*.

SOUTH AFRICA

## Forestry
(including Namibia)

**ROUNDWOOD REMOVALS** ('000 cubic metres, excluding bark)

|  | 1989 | 1990 | 1991 |
|---|---|---|---|
| Sawlogs, veneer logs and logs for sleepers | 4,468* | 5,193† | 4,786† |
| Pulpwood* | 4,841 | 4,841 | 4,841 |
| Other industrial wood* | 2,974 | 2,974 | 2,974 |
| Fuel wood* | 7,078 | 7,078 | 7,078 |
| **Total** | 19,361* | 20,086 | 19,679 |

**1992:** Output as in 1991 (FAO estimates).
* FAO estimate(s).  † Unofficial figure.
Source: FAO, *Yearbook of Forest Products*.

**SAWNWOOD PRODUCTION**
('000 cubic metres, incl. railway sleepers)

|  | 1989* | 1990† | 1991† |
|---|---|---|---|
| Coniferous (softwood) | 1,623 | 1,734 | 1,619 |
| Broadleaved (hardwood) | 251 | 202 | 173 |
| **Total** | 1,873 | 1,936 | 1,792 |

* FAO estimates.  † Unofficial figures.
**1992:** Production as in 1991 (FAO estimates).
Source: FAO, *Yearbook of Forest Products*.

## Fishing
('000 metric tons, live weight)

|  | 1990 | 1991 | 1992 |
|---|---|---|---|
| Freshwater and diadromous fishes | 2.7 | 3.3 | 2.4 |
| Cape hakes (Stokvisse) | 135.2 | 136.5 | 135.8 |
| Cape horse mackerel (Maasbanker) | 51.1 | 35.6 | 33.6 |
| Southern African pilchard | 56.9 | 52.0 | 53.4 |
| Whitehead's round herring | 44.7 | 33.5 | 47.3 |
| Southern African anchovy | 150.1 | 150.6 | 347.3 |
| Snoek (Barracouta) | 20.8 | 21.9 | 18.4 |
| Silver scabbardfish | 14.6 | 12.1 | 14.2 |
| Chub mackerel | 14.3 | 13.5 | 4.3 |
| Other marine fishes (incl. unspecified) | 33.0 | 27.4 | 28.9 |
| **Total fish** | 523.4 | 486.4 | 685.7 |
| Crustaceans | 6.0 | 3.5 | 3.6 |
| Chokker squid | 5.0 | 7.0 | 2.8 |
| Other molluscs | 3.2 | 4.0 | 3.2 |
| **Total catch*** | 537.6 | 501.0 | 695.3 |

* Excluding aquatic plants (FAO estimates, '000 metric tons): 11.0 in 1990; 11.0 in 1991; 11.5 in 1992.
Source: FAO, *Yearbook of Fishery Statistics*.

## Mining
('000 metric tons, unless otherwise indicated)

|  | 1989 | 1990 | 1991 |
|---|---|---|---|
| Hard coal | 173,913 | 174,784 | 175,251 |
| Iron ore[1] | 18,754 | 18,962 | 18,119 |
| Copper ore[1] | 181.7 | 178.7 | 192.9 |
| Nickel ore*[2,3] | 35.5 | 36.3 | 30.0 |
| Lead concentrates[1] | 78.2 | 70.2 | 76.3 |
| Zinc ore[1] | 77.3 | 74.8 | 66.6 |
| Tin concentrates (metric tons)[1] | 1,306 | 1,140 | 1,042 |
| Manganese ore*[1] | 2,017.1 | 1,836.1 | 1,368.0 |
| Chromium ore*[1] | 1,558 | 1,416 | n.a. |
| Rutile—Titanium dioxide (metric tons) | 64,367 | 64,056 | 75,000 |
| Vanadium ore (metric tons)*[1,3] | 18,567 | 17,106 | 13,435 |
| Zirconium concentrates (metric tons)*[3] | 150,000 | 151,136 | 230,000 |
| Antimony concentrates (metric tons)[1] | 5,201 | 4,815 | 4,500 |
| Silver ore (metric tons)[1] | 180 | 161 | 171 |
| Uranium ore (metric tons)[1] | 2,943 | 2,487 | 1,654 |
| Gold (metric tons)[1] | 605.5 | 603.0 | 601.0 |
| Kaolin | 140 | 132 | 134 |
| Magnesite—crude | 75.7 | 114.2 | n.a. |
| Natural phosphates[3] | 2,963 | 3,165 | n.a. |
| Fluorspar—Fluorite[4] | 368.3 | 311.0 | 270.3 |
| Salt—unrefined | 692 | 728 | 665 |
| Diamonds: industrial ('000 metric carats)[3] | 5,106 | 4,882 | 4,612 |
| gem ('000 metric carats)[3] | 4,010* | 3,826 | 3,800 |
| Gypsum—crude | 407 | 384 | 420 |
| Asbestos | 157 | 146 | 149 |
| Mica (metric tons) | 1,708 | 1,765 | n.a. |

* Provisional or estimated figure.
[1] Figures relate to the metal content of ores or concentrates.
[2] Nickel content of matte and refined nickel.
[3] Data from the US Bureau of Mines.
[4] Acid, metallurgical and ceramic grade.
Source: UN, *Industrial Statistics Yearbook*.

**1992** ('000 metric tons, unless otherwise indicated): Hard coal 174,000 (estimate); Iron ore 28,224 (gross weight); Copper ore 167; Lead concentrates 75.4 (provisional); Tin concentrates (metric tons) 600.

**1993** (provisional): Iron ore 29,388 (gross weight); Copper ore 166; Lead concentrates ('000 metric tons) 98.4; Tin concentrates (metric tons) 490.

Note: The metal content of iron ore is 60%–65%.

Sources (for 1992 and 1993): UN, *Monthly Bulletin of Statistics*; UN Conference on Trade and Development, *International Tin Statistics*.

## Industry

**SELECTED PRODUCTS**
('000 metric tons, unless otherwise indicated)

|  | 1991 | 1992 | 1993 |
|---|---|---|---|
| Wheat flour | 1,734 | 1,833 | 1,867 |
| Sugar—refined | 1,359 | 1,316 | 1,098 |
| Wine ('000 hectolitres) | 3,899 | 3,779 | 3,647 |
| Beer ('000 hectolitres) | 17,710 | 18,290 | n.a. |
| Cigarettes (million) | 40,163 | 35,563 | 34,499 |
| Pipe tobacco (metric tons) | 5,832 | 7,451 | 7,759 |
| Cotton yarn—incl. mixed | 69.9 | 64.1 | 63.4 |
| Woven cotton fabrics (million sq metres) | 169.8 | 129.6 | 150.3 |
| Footwear (million pairs) | 52.1 | 44.5 | 45.9 |
| Mechanical wood pulp*† | 370 | 370 | n.a. |
| Chemical wood pulp*† | 1,490 | 1,490 | n.a. |
| Newsprint paper | 252 | 255 | 316 |
| Other printing and writing paper | 886 | 940 | 968 |
| Other paper and paperboard*† | 1,160 | 1,160 | n.a. |
| Synthetic rubber | 89.6 | 34.6 | n.a. |
| Rubber tyres ('000) | 7,418 | 7,333 | 7,780 |
| Nitrogenous fertilizers | 1,088 | 1,010 | 1,109 |
| Phosphate fertilizers | 200 | 165 | 182 |

## SOUTH AFRICA

| — continued | 1991 | 1992 | 1993 |
|---|---|---|---|
| Motor spirit—petrol (million litres)‡ | 8,530 | 8,761 | n.a. |
| Kerosene (million litres)‡ | 617 | 629 | n.a. |
| Jet fuel (million litres)‡ | 861 | 1,000 | n.a. |
| Distillate fuel oils (million litres)‡ | 5,388 | 5,310 | n.a. |
| Residual fuel oils (million litres)‡ | 1,891 | 2,401 | n.a. |
| Lubricating oils (million litres)‡ | 335 | 329 | n.a. |
| Petroleum bitumen—asphalt | 261 | 276 | n.a. |
| Coke-oven coke* | 1,835 | n.a. | n.a. |
| Cement | 6,147 | 5,850 | 5,818 |
| Pig-iron | 7,117 | n.a. | n.a. |
| Crude steel | 9,360 | 9,061 | n.a. |
| Refined copper—unwrought | 136 | 120 | 126 |
| Radio receivers and record players ('000) | 775 | n.a. | n.a. |
| Television receivers ('000) | 486 | 376 | 321 |
| Passenger motor cars—assembled ('000) | 238.3 | 206.6 | 228 |
| Lorries—assembled ('000) | 97.2 | 93.6 | 97 |
| Electric energy (million kWh) | 148,919 | 149,427 | 155,812 |

* Estimates.
† Including data for Namibia.
‡ Excluding data for Transkei, Bophuthatswana, Venda and Ciskei.

Sources: National Productivity Institute, Pretoria; UN, *Industrial Statistics Yearbook*; FAO, *Yearbook of Forest Products*.

## Finance

### CURRENCY AND EXCHANGE RATES

**Monetary Units**
100 cents = 1 rand (R).

**Sterling and Dollar Equivalents** (31 December 1994)
£1 sterling = 5.545 rand;
US $1 = 3.544 rand;
100 rand = £18.03 = $28.21.

**Average Exchange Rate** (US $ per rand)
1992   0.35092
1993   0.30641
1994   0.28177

**BUDGET** (million rand, year ending 31 March)*

| Revenue | 1991/92 | 1992/93 | 1993/94 |
|---|---|---|---|
| Income tax | 42,451 | 45,270 | 48,170 |
| Value-added tax | 18,528 | 17,165 | 24,979 |
| Other taxes | 4,013 | 4,951 | 5,782 |
| Customs duty | 2,736 | 2,961 | 3,413 |
| Surcharge on imports | 1,455 | 1,521 | 1,756 |
| Fuel levy | 5,421 | 7,083 | 7,888 |
| Excise duty | 3,797 | 4,436 | 4,967 |
| Other revenue | 158 | 162 | 77 |
| **Sub-total** | 78,559 | 83,549 | 97,032 |
| *Less* Transfers to neighbouring countries | 2,675 | 2,809 | 3,089 |
| **Total** | 75,884 | 80,740 | 93,943 |

| Expenditure | 1991/92 | 1992/93 | 1993/94 |
|---|---|---|---|
| Defence | 10,488 | 10,803 | 10,683 |
| Other general services | 8,625 | 9,052 | 9,805 |
| Education | 19,929 | 24,393 | 27,761 |
| Health | 10,630 | 12,709 | 13,969 |
| Other social services | 11,282 | 14,656 | 16,254 |
| Interest on public debt | 14,460 | 17,530 | 22,150 |
| Other expenditure | 21,389 | 28,954 | 30,788 |
| **Total** | 96,803 | 118,097 | 131,410 |

* Figures represent revenue and expenditure on State Revenue Fund. Accounts of Transnet and Telcom are not included.
† Revenue from provincial administrations, Bophuthatswana, Ciskei, Transkei, Venda and the other former 'homelands'.

**INTERNATIONAL RESERVES** (US $ million at 31 December)

|  | 1990 | 1991 | 1992 |
|---|---|---|---|
| Gold* | 1,415 | 2,074 | 1,992 |
| IMF special drawing rights | 2 | 2 | — |
| Foreign exchange | 1,006 | 897 | 991 |
| **Total** | 2,423 | 2,973 | 2,984 |

* National valuation, based on market prices.
Source: IMF, *International Financial Statistics*.

**MONEY SUPPLY** (million rand at 31 December)

|  | 1988 | 1989 | 1990 |
|---|---|---|---|
| Currency outside banks | 6,128 | 7,314 | 8,251 |
| Demand deposits at deposit money banks | 33,375 | 35,559 | 41,031 |
| **Total** (incl. others) | 39,934 | 43,343 | 49,858 |

Source: IMF, *International Financial Statistics*.

**COST OF LIVING** (Consumer Price Index; base: 1990 = 100)

|  | 1992 | 1993 | 1994 |
|---|---|---|---|
| Food | 149.3 | 160.0 | 181.7 |
| Fuel and light | 126.5 | 146.5 | 160.5 |
| Clothing | 122.2 | 130.9 | 135.8 |
| **All items** (incl. others) | 131.3 | 144.1 | 157.0 |

**NATIONAL ACCOUNTS** (million rand at current prices)

Note: Data cover the whole of South Africa (including African 'homelands' that had been declared 'independent').

**National Income and Product**

|  | 1992 | 1993 | 1994 |
|---|---|---|---|
| Compensation of employees | 190,003 | 210,024 | 231,467 |
| Operating surplus | 68,810 | 80,772 | 91,557 |
| **Domestic factor incomes** | 258,813 | 290,796 | 323,024 |
| Consumption of fixed capital | 50,272 | 54,121 | 59,537 |
| **Gross domestic product (GDP) at factor cost** | 309,085 | 344,917 | 382,561 |
| Indirect taxes | 38,803 | 46,015 | 57,736 |
| *Less* Subsidies | 6,925 | 7,861 | 7,544 |
| **GDP in purchasers' values** | 340,963 | 383,071 | 432,753 |
| Factor income received from abroad | 2,606 } | −9,458 | −10,561 |
| *Less* Factor income paid abroad | 11,751 } |  |  |
| **Gross national product** | 331,818 | 373,613 | 422,192 |
| *Less* Consumption of fixed capital | 50,272 | 54,121 | 59,537 |
| **National income in market prices** | 281,546 | 319,492 | 362,655 |
| Other current transfers from abroad (net) | 300 | 429 | 205 |
| **National disposable income** | 281,846 | 319,921 | 362,860 |

**Expenditure on the Gross Domestic Product**

|  | 1992 | 1993 | 1994 |
|---|---|---|---|
| Government final consumption expenditure | 70,196 | 79,047 | 91,349 |
| Private final consumption expenditure | 207,769 | 230,630 | 256,320 |
| Increase in stocks | −2,608 | 2,407 | 10,209 |
| Gross fixed capital formation | 56,711 | 58,837 | 68,101 |
| Statistical discrepancy | −3,890 | −2,708 | −1,493 |
| **Total domestic expenditure** | 328,178 | 368,213 | 424,486 |
| Exports of goods and services | 78,070 | 91,013 | 102,682 |
| *Less* Imports of goods and services | 65,285 | 76,155 | 94,415 |
| **GDP in purchasers' values** | 340,963 | 383,071 | 432,753 |
| **GDP at constant 1990 prices** | 267,257 | 270,181 | 276,464 |

# SOUTH AFRICA

*Statistical Survey*

**Gross Domestic Product by Economic Activity** (at factor cost)

|  | 1992 | 1993 | 1994 |
|---|---|---|---|
| Agriculture, forestry and fishing | 12,865 | 15,054 | 17,930 |
| Mining and quarrying | 26,502 | 30,505 | 33,168 |
| Manufacturing | 74,295 | 81,167 | 89,766 |
| Electricity, gas and water | 12,764 | 13,969 | 15,751 |
| Construction (contractors) | 10,305 | 11,249 | 12,265 |
| Wholesale and retail trade, catering and accommodation | 49,137 | 55,699 | 61,648 |
| Transport, storage and communication | 25,232 | 26,780 | 28,976 |
| Finance, insurance, real estate and business services | 48,864 | 56,595 | 63,411 |
| Government services | 47,445 | 52,543 | 58,678 |
| Other community, social and personal services | 5,917 | 6,857 | 7,573 |
| Other producers (non-profit institutions and domestic servants) | 6,605 | 7,243 | 7,954 |
| **Sub-total** | 319,931 | 357,661 | 397,120 |
| *Less* Imputed bank service charges | 10,846 | 12,744 | 14,559 |
| **Total** | 309,085 | 344,917 | 382,561 |

## BALANCE OF PAYMENTS (US $ million)*

|  | 1991 | 1992 | 1993 |
|---|---|---|---|
| Merchandise exports f.o.b. | 23,289 | 23,645 | 24,068 |
| Merchandise imports f.o.b. | −17,156 | −18,216 | −18,287 |
| **Trade balance** | 6,134 | 5,429 | 5,781 |
| Exports of services | 2,714 | 2,999 | 3,110 |
| Imports of services | −4,083 | −4,686 | −4,969 |
| Other income received | 1,773 | 1,670 | 1,333 |
| Other income paid | −4,350 | −4,131 | −3,580 |
| Private unrequited transfers (net) | −28 | 32 | 68 |
| Official unrequited transfers (net) | 100 | 74 | 62 |
| **Current balance** | 2,258 | 1,388 | 1,805 |
| Direct investment (net) | −8 | −5 | −8 |
| Portfolio investment (net) | 78 | 1,496 | 225 |
| Other capital (net) | 406 | −1,305 | −1,881 |
| Net errors and omissions | −1,228 | −1,443 | −2,936 |
| **Overall balance** | 1,506 | 131 | −2,795 |

* Including Botswana, Lesotho, Namibia and Swaziland.

Source: IMF, *International Financial Statistics*.

# External Trade

Figures refer to the Southern African Customs Union, comprising South Africa, Namibia, Botswana, Lesotho and Swaziland. Trade between the component territories is excluded.

## PRINCIPAL COMMODITIES (million rand)

| Imports f.o.b. | 1992 | 1993 | 1994* |
|---|---|---|---|
| Chemical products, etc. | 5,789.1 | 6,598.8 | 8,291.7 |
| Plastics and plastic articles, rubber and rubber articles | 2,249.7 | 2,638.9 | 3,255.9 |
| Paper, paperboard, etc. | 1,463.1 | 1,740.1 | 2,182.6 |
| Textiles and textile articles | 2,437.2 | 2,654.0 | 3,295.0 |
| Base metals and articles of base metal | 2,502.2 | 2,605.7 | 3,399.5 |
| Machinery and mechanical appliances, electrical equipment, parts thereof | 14,944.0 | 17,130.9 | 24,804.5 |
| Transport equipment | 6,619.0 | 8,915.9 | 11,283.6 |
| Optical and photographic instruments, surgical instruments, etc. | 2,241.6 | 2,716.1 | 3,299.7 |
| **Total** (incl. others) | 52,514.1 | 59,017.7 | 75,601.6 |

| Exports f.o.b. | 1992 | 1993 | 1994* |
|---|---|---|---|
| Vegetable products | 2,290.7 | 2,436.5 | 4,197.3 |
| Prepared foodstuffs; beverages, spirits and vinegar; tobacco | 1,856.8 | 1,812.5 | 2,826.0 |
| Mineral products | 7,083.3 | 8,443.7 | 7,712.4 |
| Chemical products, etc. | 3,220.8 | 3,377.9 | 4,756.8 |
| Textiles and textile articles | 1,809.0 | 1,812.1 | 1,923.4 |
| Pearls, precious and semi-precious stones, precious metals, etc. | 7,160.4 | 10,137.7 | 10,213.3 |
| Base metals and articles of base metal | 9,484.8 | 9,905.2 | 11,853.0 |
| **Total** (incl. others)† | 68,996.8 | 79,214.2 | 90,328.2 |

* Preliminary figures.

† Figures include exports of gold. The net value of gold output (in million rand) was: 18,195 in 1992; 22,229 in 1993; 22,661 in 1994.

Source: South African Reserve Bank, Pretoria.

## SELECTED TRADING PARTNERS (million rand)

| Imports | 1992 | 1993 | 1994* |
|---|---|---|---|
| Australia | 629 | 693 | 1,074 |
| Belgium | 1,138 | 1,273 | 1,739 |
| China, People's Republic | 652 | 1,003 | 1,284 |
| France | 2,052 | 2,094 | 2,717 |
| Germany | 8,588 | 9,281 | 12,986 |
| Hong Kong | 885 | 1,110 | 1,464 |
| Italy | 1,843 | 2,085 | 2,985 |
| Japan | 5,563 | 7,445 | 7,893 |
| Netherlands | 1,248 | 1,386 | 1,892 |
| Singapore | 645 | 788 | 994 |
| Switzerland | 1,223 | 1,310 | 1,935 |
| Taiwan | 1,767 | 2,039 | 2,604 |
| United Kingdom | 5,381 | 6,549 | 8,961 |
| USA | 7,142 | 7,766 | 8,584 |
| **Total** (incl. others) | 52,514 | 59,018 | 75,602 |

* Preliminary figures.

Source: South African Reserve Bank, Pretoria.

| Exports | 1991 | 1992 | 1993 |
|---|---|---|---|
| Belgium | 1,644 | 1.998 | 2,314 |
| France | 950 | n.a. | n.a. |
| Germany | 3,392 | 3,008 | 3,084 |
| Hong Kong | 1,354 | 1,471 | 1,750 |
| Israel | n.a. | 973 | 1,680 |
| Italy | 1,598 | 1,656 | 1,465 |
| Japan | 4,074 | 3,761 | 4,363 |
| Korea, Republic | n.a. | 993 | 1,275 |
| Netherlands | 2,373 | 1,928 | 2,151 |
| Switzerland | 5,719 | 5,382 | 7,896 |
| Taiwan | n.a. | 2,149 | 2,166 |
| United Kingdom | 5,039 | 4,525 | 4,740 |
| USA | 3,967 | 4,858 | 5,454 |
| Zambia | n.a. | 1,112 | 1,307 |
| Zimbabwe | n.a. | 1,553 | 1,748 |
| **Total** (incl. others) | 64,355 | 68,999 | 79,214 |

Source: National Productivity Institute, Pretoria.

# Transport

**RAILWAYS** (traffic, year ending 31 March)

|  | 1989 | 1990 | 1991 |
|---|---|---|---|
| Freight carried ('000 metric tons) | 174,160 | 183,420 | 171,300 |
| Passenger journeys ('000) | 579,524 | 552,264 | 527,737 |

Source: Department of Transport, Pretoria.

# SOUTH AFRICA

**ROAD TRAFFIC** (motor vehicles in use at 30 June)

|  | 1990 | 1991 | 1992 |
|---|---|---|---|
| Passenger cars | 3,408,605 | 3,489,947 | 3,522,129 |
| Buses and coaches | 28,107 | 28,545 | 28,354 |
| Vans | 196,243 | 208,256 | 217,037 |
| Goods vehicles | 1,273,257 | 1,303,995 | 1,338,737 |
| Motor cycles | 298,941 | 294,006 | 285,034 |

**SHIPPING** (year ending 31 March)

**Cargo Handled** ('000 metric tons)

|  | 1993/94 |
|---|---|
| Landed | 16,449 |
| Shipped | 104,889 |

Source: Department of Transport, Pretoria.

**Vessels Handled**

|  | 1993/94 |
|---|---|
| Number | 12,526 |
| Displacement ('000 gross tons) | 431,353 |

Source: Department of Transport, Pretoria.

**CIVIL AVIATION** (traffic on scheduled services)

|  | 1991 | 1992 | 1993 |
|---|---|---|---|
| Kilometres flown (million) | 39.9 | 83.8 | 128.3 |
| Passengers carried ('000) | 11,736.8 | 16,433.5 | 18,763.0 |
| Freight ton-km (million) | 228.5 | 278.5 | 344.3 |

Source: Department of Transport, Pretoria.

## Tourism

**FOREIGN TOURIST ARRIVALS** (number of visitors by region of origin)

|  | 1991 | 1992 | 1993 |
|---|---|---|---|
| Africa | 1,193,743 | 2,327,959 | 2,698,089 |
| Europe | 367,641 | 395,319 | 429,867 |
| Asia | 59,312 | 67,508 | 87,480 |
| America | 67,104 | 75,013 | 91,699 |
| Oceania | 19,986 | 24,821 | 30,115 |
| **Total** (incl. unspecified) | 1,709,554 | 2,892,822 | 3,369,762 |

## Communications Media

|  | 1990 | 1991 | 1992 |
|---|---|---|---|
| Radio receivers ('000 in use) | 11,500 | 11,800 | 12,100 |
| Television licences ('000) | 2,422 | 2,460 | 2,573 |
| Telephones ('000 in use) | 5,017 | 5,128 | 5,208 |
| Daily newspapers |  |  |  |
|   Number | 19 | 19 | 19 |
|   Average circulation ('000)* | 2,658 | 2,596 | 2,621 |

* Estimates.

Sources: Central Statistical Service, Pretoria; UNESCO, *Statistical Yearbook*.

## Education

Primary and Secondary Levels (1993, preliminary figures)

|  | Africans | Whites | Coloureds | Asians |
|---|---|---|---|---|
| Teachers Primary, Secondary and Special | 196,169 | 75,919 | 50,520 | 14,703 |
| Pupils Primary, Secondary and Special | 6,486,588 | 1,041,707 | 897,002 | 256,579 |

Tertiary Level (1993, preliminary figures)

|  | Africans | Whites | Coloureds | Asians |
|---|---|---|---|---|
| University |  |  |  |  |
|   Students | 135,482 | 153,513 | 17,406 | 23,491 |
|   Teachers | 9,521 | 17,388 | 3,734 | 1,404 |
| Teacher Training |  |  |  |  |
|   Students | 43,368 | 8,481 | 6,449 | 1,640 |
|   Teachers | 4,777 | 2,867 | 940 | 286 |
| Technical |  |  |  |  |
|   Students | 28,060 | 53,575 | 6,021 | 5,388 |
|   Teachers | 2,042 | 3,407 | 529 | 184 |
| Technikons |  |  |  |  |
|   Students | 42,674 | 74,887 | 11,820 | 7,787 |
|   Teachers | 1,730 | 4,580 | 586 | 445 |

Source: Department of National Education, Pretoria.

# Directory

## The Constitution

Following multi-party negotiations (see Recent History), the interim Constitution of the Republic of South Africa was ratified on 22 December 1993, and officially came into effect on 27 April 1994; it was to remain in force pending the adoption of a new constitution (see below), prior to elections for a new legislature, and the installation of a majority government, in 1999. The main provisions of the interim Constitution are summarized below:

### FUNDAMENTAL RIGHTS

Fundamental human rights are protected under a bill of rights. Communities or individuals are entitled to claim restitution for land dispossessed under legislation from 1913. A state of emergency may be declared only if it is considered necessary for the restoration of civil order, and is limited to 21 days, renewable with the support of two-thirds of deputies in the National Assembly. Under a state of emergency, indefinite detention without trial is permitted, subject to judicial review after 10 days.

### PARLIAMENT

Legislative power is vested in a bicameral Parliament, comprising a National Assembly and a Senate. The 400-member National Assembly is elected by proportional representation, with 200 members elected from national party lists and 200 from regional party lists. National and provincial legislatures are elected separately, under a 'double-ballot' electoral system. Each provincial legislature elects 10 representatives to the 90-member Senate, which is headed by a President. Parliamentary decisions are generally reached by a simple majority, although constitutional amendments require a majority of two-thirds.

### ADOPTION OF THE NEW CONSTITUTION

The National Assembly and the Senate together form a Constitutional Assembly, which is to draft and adopt a new constitution

# SOUTH AFRICA

with adherence to 33 entrenched Constitutional Principles (guaranteeing multi-party democracy, the delineated powers of provincial government, fundamental human rights and the independence of the judiciary). The Constitutional Assembly is advised by a five-member independent panel of constitutional experts, which it appoints. A new constitutional text is to be submitted for endorsement by a Constitutional Court, which certifies that its provisions comply with the Constitutional Principles. In the event that the Constitutional Assembly fails to adopt a new constitution by a majority of two-thirds within a period of two years of its first session, the proposed text is to be submitted for approval by 60% of the electorate at a national referendum. If the proposed constitution is not approved by referendum, the President is to dissolve Parliament by proclamation, whereupon elections are to take place. The new Constitutional Assembly is subsequently to approve the text by a majority of 60% within a period of one year of its first session.

## THE NATIONAL EXECUTIVE

The Head of State is the President, who is elected by the National Assembly from among its members, and exercises executive power in consultation with at least two Deputy Presidents. Any party that holds a minimum of 80 seats in the National Assembly (equivalent to 20% of the national vote) is entitled to nominate a Deputy President. If no party secures 80 seats, the First Deputy President is elected by the party that holds the highest number of seats, and the Second Deputy President by the party that holds the second highest number of seats, in the National Assembly. In the event of the absence from office of the President, the Deputy Presidents assume his functions on a rotational basis. The President may be removed by a motion of no-confidence or by impeachment. The Cabinet constitutes an interim Government of National Unity, and comprises a maximum of 27 ministers. Each party with a minimum of 20 seats in the National Assembly (equivalent to 5% of the national vote) is entitled to a proportional number of ministerial portfolios. The President allocates cabinet portfolios in consultation with party leaders, who are entitled to request the replacement of ministers. Cabinet decisions are reached by consensus.

## JUDICIAL AUTHORITY

There is a Supreme Court, headed by a Chief Justice, which is independent from the executive. An 11-member Constitutional Court, headed by a President, ensures that the executive, legislative and judicial organs of government adhere to the Constitutional Principles, and is empowered to reverse legislation adopted by Parliament. Members of the Constitutional Court are appointed by the President, in consultation with the Cabinet, and hold office for a non-renewable period of seven years. An independent Judicial Service Commission, which includes the Chief Justice and the President of the Constitutional Court, makes recommendations regarding the appointment of judges, and advises central and provincial government on all matters relating to the judiciary.

## PROVINCIAL GOVERNMENT

There are nine provinces: Eastern Cape, Eastern Transvaal, Kwa-Zulu/Natal, Northern Cape, Northern Transvaal, North-West, Orange Free State, Gauteng and Western Cape. Each province is entitled to determine its legislative and executive structure. The interim Constitution guarantees the powers of provincial government and recognizes the right to regional autonomy. Each province has a legislature, comprising between 30 and 100 members (depending on the size of the local electorate), who are elected by proportional representation. Each legislature is entitled to draft a constitution for the province, subject to the principles governing the national constitution, and elects a Premier, who heads a Cabinet. Parties that hold a minimum of 10% of seats in the legislature are entitled to a proportional number of portfolios in the Cabinet. Provincial legislatures are allowed primary responsibility for a number of areas of government, and joint powers with central government in the principal administrative areas.

## LOCAL GOVERNMENT

Local negotiating forums are to supervise the organization of elections to multiracial municipal councils. White and black voters are to elect 30% of members respectively, while the remainder of seats in the new councils are to be elected on a non-racial basis. Municipal budgets are approved by a majority of two-thirds of members of the council.

# The Government

## HEAD OF STATE

**President:** NELSON ROLIHLAHLA MANDELA (took office 10 May 1994).
**First Deputy President:** THABO MBEKI.
**Second Deputy President:** FREDERIK WILLEM DE KLERK.

## CABINET
(June 1995)

An interim Government of National Unity, comprising representatives of the African National Congress of South Africa (ANC), the National Party (NP), and the Inkatha Freedom Party (IFP).

**Minister of Foreign Affairs:** ALFRED B. NZO (ANC).
**Minister of Public Enterprises:** Princess STELLA SIGCAU (ANC).
**Minister of Justice:** ABDULLAH MOHAMMED OMAR (ANC).
**Minister of Defence:** JOE MODISE (ANC).
**Minister of Posts, Telecommunications and Broadcasting:** PALLO JORDAN (ANC).
**Minister of Correctional Services:** Dr SIPHO E. MZIMELA (IFP).
**Minister of Education:** Prof. SIBUSISO M. E. BENGU (ANC).
**Minister of Mineral and Energy Affairs:** ROELOF FREDERIK BOTHA (NP).
**Minister of Agriculture:** Dr ANDRÉ ISAK VAN NIEKERK (NP)
**Minister of Health:** Dr NKOSAZANA C. DHLAMINI ZUMA (ANC).
**Minister of Safety and Security:** SYDNEY MUFAMADI (ANC).
**Minister of Transport:** S. R. MAHARAJ (ANC).
**Minister of Provincial Affairs and of Constitutional Development:** ROELOF PETRUS MEYER (NP).
**Minister of Labour:** TITO T. MBOWENI (ANC).
**Minister of Arts, Culture, Science and Technology:** Dr BEN S. NGUBANE (IFP).
**Minister of Finance:** CHRISTO F. LIEBENBERG (Independent).
**Minister of Welfare and Population Development:** ABRAHAM WILLIAMS (NP).
**Minister of Sport and Recreation:** STEVE TSHWETE (ANC).
**Minister of Housing:** SANKIE MTHEMBI-NKONDO (ANC).
**Minister of Trade and Industry:** TREVOR A. MANUEL (ANC).
**Minister of Environment Affairs and Tourism:** Dr DAWIE J. DE VILLIERS (NP).
**Minister of Land Affairs:** DEREK M. HANEKOM (ANC).
**Minister of Home Affairs:** Chief MANGOSUTHU GATSHA BUTHELEZI (IFP).
**Minister of Public Service and Administration:** Dr ZOLA S. T. SKWEYIYA (ANC).
**Minister of Public Works:** JEFF T. RADEBE (ANC).
**Minister of Water Affairs and Forestry:** Prof. KADER ASMAL (ANC).
**Minister of General Affairs:** CHRIS L. FISMER (ANC).
**Minister in the Office of the President:** JAY NAIDOO (ANC).

## MINISTRIES

**Office of the President:** Union Bldgs, West Wing, Government Ave, Pretoria 0002; Private Bag X1000, Pretoria 0001; tel. (12) 3284708; fax (12) 3238246.

**Ministry of Agriculture:** Agriculture Bldg, DA 113, cnr Hamilton St and Soutpansberg Rd, Pretoria 0002; Private Bag X116, Pretoria 0001; tel. (12) 3197235; fax (12) 217219.

**Ministry of Arts, Culture, Science and Technology:** Private Bag X727, Pretoria 0001; tel. (12) 3244096; fax (12) 3242687.

**Ministry of Correctional Services:** Poyntons Bldg, West Block, cnr Church and Schubart Sts, Pretoria 0002; Private Bag X853 Pretoria 0001; tel. (12) 3238198; fax (12) 3234111.

**Ministry of Defence:** Armscor Building, Block 1, Nossob St, Erasmusrand 0181; Private Bag X247, Pretoria 0001; tel. (12) 4281912; fax (12) 3470118.

**Ministry of Education:** Private Bag X603, Pretoria 0001; tel. (12) 3260126; fax (12) 3242687.

**Ministry of Environmental Affairs and Tourism:** Private Bag X883, Pretoria 0001; tel. (12) 219587; fax (12) 3235989.

**Ministry of Finance:** 240 Vermeulen St, Pretoria 0002; Private Bag X115, Pretoria 0001; tel. (12) 3238911; fax (12) 3233262.

**Ministry of Foreign Affairs:** Union Bldgs, East Wing, Government Ave, Pretoria 0002; Private Bag X152, Pretoria 0001; tel. (12) 3510005; telex 321348; fax (12) 3510253.

**Ministry of General Affairs:** Union Bldgs, East Wing, Rm 949, Pretoria 0002; Private Bag X999, Pretoria 0001; tel. (12) 3192023; fax (12) 3192001.

**Ministry of Health:** 2027 Civitas Bldg, cnr Andries and Struben Sts, Pretoria 0002; Private Bag X399, Pretoria 0001; tel. (12) 3284773; fax (12) 3255526.

**Ministry of Home Affairs:** 1005 Civitas Bldg, cnr Andries and Struben Sts, Pretoria 0002; Private Bag X741, Pretoria 0001; tel. (12) 3268081; fax (12) 216491.

**Ministry of Housing:** 240 Walker St, Sunnyside, Pretoria 0002; Private Bag X645, Pretoria 0001; tel. (12) 441879; fax (12) 3418513.

**Ministry of Justice:** Presidia Bldg, 8th Floor, cnr Pretorius and Paul Kruger Sts, Pretoria 0002; Private Bag X276, Pretoria 0001; tel. (12) 3238581; fax (12) 211708.

**Ministry of Labour:** Private Bag X9090, Pretoria 0001; tel. (12) 3226523.

**Ministry of Land Affairs:** 184 Jacob Mare St, cnr Jacob Mare and Paul Kruger Sts, Pretoria 0002; Private Bag X844, Pretoria 0001; tel. (12) 3235212; fax (12) 211244.

**Ministry of Mineral and Energy Affairs:** NG Sinodale Centre, cnr Andries and Visagie Sts, Pretoria 0002; Private Bag X646, Pretoria 0001; tel. (12) 3228695; fax (12) 3228699.

**Ministry of Posts, Telecommunications and Broadcasting:** cnr Bosman and Vermeulen Sts, Telkom Towers South, 25th Floor, Pretoria 0001; tel. (12) 3261110; fax (12) 3232275.

**Ministry of Provincial Affairs and of Constitutional Development:** 260 Walker Street, Sunnyside, Pretoria 0002; Private Bag X802, Pretoria 0001; tel. (12) 3411380; fax (12) 3411389.

**Ministry of Public Enterprises:** Cafe Rich Bldg, Parliament St, Pretoria 0002; Private Bag X482, Pretoria 0001; tel. (12) 3241883; fax (12) 3241889.

**Ministry for the Public Service and Administration:** Private Bag X884, Pretoria 0001; tel. (12) 3230331; fax (12) 3286529.

**Ministry of Public Works:** Central Government Bldg, cnr Bosman and Vermeulen Sts, Pretoria 0002; Private Bag X90, Pretoria 0001; tel. (12) 3241510; fax (12) 3256398.

**Ministry of Safety and Security:** Wachthuis, 7th Floor, 231 Pretorius St, Pretoria 0002; Private Bag X463, Pretoria 0001; tel. (12) 3238880; fax (12) 3205065.

**Ministry of Sport and Recreation:** Frans du Toit Bldg, cnr Schoeman and Paul Kruger Sts, Pretoria 0002; Private Bag X869, Pretoria 0001; tel. (12) 211781; fax (12) 218493.

**Ministry of Trade and Industry:** House of Trade and Industry, 11th Floor, Prinsloo St, Pretoria 0002; Private Bag X274, Pretoria 0001; tel. (12) 3227677; fax (12) 3227851.

**Ministry of Transport:** Forum Bldg, cnr Struben and Bosman Sts, Pretoria 0002; Private Bag X193, Pretoria 0001; tel. (12) 3283084.

**Ministry of Water Affairs and Forestry:** Residensie Bldg, 185 Schoeman St, Pretoria 0002; Private Bag X313, Pretoria 0001; tel. (12) 2992525; fax (12) 3284254.

**Ministry of Welfare and Population Development:** Hallmark Bldg, Vermeulen St, Pretoria 0002; Private Bag X885, Pretoria 0001; tel. (12) 3284600; fax (12) 3257071.

## Legislature

### PARLIAMENT

#### Senate

**President:** Hendrik Jacobus (Kobie) Coetsee.

The 90-member Senate has 10 representatives elected by each provincial legislature. Following legislative elections in April 1994, the Senate comprised 60 representatives of the African National Congress of South Africa, 17 of the National Party, five each of the Inkatha Freedom Party and the Freedom Front, and three of the Democratic Party.

#### National Assembly

**Speaker:** Dr Frene Noshir Ginwala.

**General Election, 26–29 April 1994**

| Party | Votes | % of votes | Seats |
|---|---|---|---|
| African National Congress of South Africa | 12,237,655 | 62.65 | 252 |
| National Party | 3,983,690 | 20.39 | 82 |
| Inkatha Freedom Party | 2,058,294 | 10.54 | 43 |
| Freedom Front | 424,555 | 2.17 | 9 |
| Democratic Party | 338,426 | 1.73 | 7 |
| Pan-Africanist Congress | 243,478 | 1.25 | 5 |
| African Christian Democratic Party | 88,104 | 0.45 | 2 |
| Africa Muslim Party | 27,690 | 0.14 | — |
| African Moderates Congress Party | 27,690 | 0.14 | — |
| Dikwankwetla Party | 19,451 | 0.10 | — |
| Federal Party | 17,663 | 0.09 | — |
| Minority Front | 13,433 | 0.07 | — |
| SOCCER Party | 10,575 | 0.05 | — |
| African Democratic Movement | 9,886 | 0.05 | — |
| Women's Rights Peace Party | 6,434 | 0.03 | — |
| Ximako Progressive Party | 6,320 | 0.03 | — |
| Keep It Straight and Simple Party | 5,916 | 0.03 | — |
| Workers' List Party | 4,169 | 0.02 | — |
| Luso South African Party | 3,293 | 0.02 | — |
| **Total*** | **19,533,498** | **100.00** | **400** |

* Excluding spoilt ballot papers, which numbered 193,081.

## Provincial Governments

### EASTERN CAPE
**Premier:** Raymond Mhlaba (ANC).
**Speaker of the Legislature:** Gugile Nkwinti (ANC).

### EASTERN TRANSVAAL
**Premier:** Matthew Phosa (ANC).
**Speaker of the Legislature:** Mbalekelwa Ginindza (ANC).

### NORTHERN CAPE
**Premier:** M. A. Dipico (ANC).
**Speaker of the Legislature:** Ethne Papenfus (DP).

### NORTHERN TRANSVAAL
**Premier:** Ngoako Ramathlodi (ANC).
**Speaker of the Legislature:** T. G. Mashamba (ANC).

### NORTH WEST
**Premier:** Popo Molefe (ANC).
**Speaker of the Legislature:** Jerry Thibedi (ANC).

### ORANGE FREE STATE
**Premier:** Patrick Lekota (ANC).
**Speaker of the Legislature:** Rev. Motlalepule Chabuka (ANC).

### GAUTENG
**Premier:** Gabriel Sexwale (ANC).
**Speaker of the Legislature:** Trevor Fowler (ANC).

### WESTERN CAPE
**Premier:** Hermanus Kriel (NP).
**Speaker of the Legislature:** Willem Doman (NP).

### KWAZULU/NATAL
**Premier:** Dr Frank Mdlalose (IFP).
**Speaker of the Legislature:** Gideon H. S. Mdlalose (IFP).

## Political Organizations

**African Christian Democratic Party (ACDP):** f. 1993; Leader Dr Johann van der Westhuizen.

**African National Congress of South Africa (ANC):** 51 Plein St, Johannesburg 2001, POB 61884, Marshalltown 2107; tel. (11) 3307000; fax (11) 290097; f. 1912; Nat. Exec. Cttee of 60 mems; became the principal party in new Govt, following democratic elections in 1994; Pres. Nelson Mandela; Chair. Jacob Zuma; Sec.-Gen. Cyril Ramaphosa.

# SOUTH AFRICA

**Afrikaner Volksfront:** Pretoria; f. 1994; loose alliance of 30 organizations seeking Afrikaner self-determination; Chair. Dr FERDINAND HARTZENBERG; Vice-Chair. Dr WILLIE SNYMAN.

**Afrikaner Weerstandsbeweging (AWB)** (Afrikaner Resistance Movement): POB 274, Ventersdorp 2710; tel. (11) 2005; fax (11) 2032; f. 1973; extreme right-wing paramilitary group; Leader EUGENE TERRE'BLANCHE; Sec.-Gen. PIET 'SKIET' RUDOLPH.

**Azanian People's Organization (AZAPO):** POB 4230, Johannesburg 2000; tel. (11) 299055; f. 1978 to seek the establishment of a unitary, democratic, socialist republic; excludes white mems; banned 1988–90; 84 brs; Pres. MOSIBUDI MANGENA; Sec.-Gen. JAIRUS KGOKONG.

**Blanke Bevrydingsbeweging (BBB)** (White Protection Movement): f. 1987; extreme right-wing activist group; banned 1988–90; Leader Prof. JOHAN SCHABORT.

**Boerestaat Party** (Boer State Party): f. 1988; seeks the establishment of an Afrikaner state; mil. wing (f. 1990) known as Boere Weerstandsbeweging (BWB); Leader ROBERT VAN TONDER.

**Boere Vryheidsbeweging** (Boer Freedom Movement): f. 1989 by fmr mems of the Afrikaanse Weerstandsbeweging.

**Cape Democrats:** f. 1988; white support; liberal.

**Conservative Party of South Africa (CP):** POB 1842, Pretoria 0001; tel. (12) 3423408; fax (12) 3423912; f. 1982 by extreme right-wing MPs expelled from National Party; includes mems of fmr National Conservative Party; seeks the establishment of a separate Afrikaner state; Leader Dr FERDINAND HARTZENBERG.

**Democratic Party (DP):** Ruskin House, 5th Floor, 2 Roeland St, Cape Town 8001; POB 1475, Cape Town 8000; tel. (21) 451431; fax (21) 4615276; f. 1989 by merger of Independent Party, National Democratic Movement and Progressive Federal Party; membership open to all racial groups; supported the establishment of a democratic, non-racial society by peaceful means; Leader TONY LEON; Sec.-Gen. D. VENTER.

**Democratic Reform Party (DRP):** f. 1988; Coloured support; Leader CARTER EBRAHIM.

**Democratic Workers' Party (DWP):** Cape Town; f. 1984 by breakaway faction of the People's Congress Party; mainly Coloured support, but open to all races; Leader DENNIS DE LA CRUZ.

**Federal Independent Democratic Alliance (FIDA):** POB 10528, Johannesburg 2000; tel. (11) 4034268; fax (11) 4031557; f. 1987; black support; centrist; Leader JOHN GOGOTYA.

**Freedom Front:** f. 1994 by mems of the right-wing, to contest democratic elections; included some mems of the Conservative Party of South Africa; Leader Gen. (retd) CONSTAND VILJOEN.

**Freedom Party:** Coloured support; Leader ARTHUR BOOYSEN.

**Herstigte Nasionale Party (HNP)** (Reconstituted National Party): POB 1888, Pretoria 0001; tel. (12) 3423410; fax (12) 3423417; f. 1969 by extreme right-wing MPs expelled from National Party; advocates 'Christian Nationalism'; Leader JAAP MARAIS; Chair. WILLEM MARAIS; Gen. Sec. L. J. VAN DER SCHYFF.

**Inkatha Freedom Party (IFP):** POB 4432, Durban 4000; tel. (31) 3074962; fax (31) 3074964; f. as Inkatha Movement, a liberation movement with mainly Zulu support; relaunched in 1990 as a multiracial political party; represented in new Govt, following democratic elections in 1994; Leader Chief MANGOSUTHU GATSHA BUTHELEZI; Sec.-Gen. Dr ZIBA JIYANE.

**National Party (NP):** Private Bag X402, Pretoria 0001; tel. (12) 3483100; fax (12) 3485645; f. 1912; ruling party 1948–94; opened membership to all racial groups in 1990; represented in new Govt, following democratic elections in 1994; Leader FREDERIK WILLEM DE KLERK.

**National People's Party:** Private Bag X54330, Durban 4000; Indian support; Leader AMICHAND RAJBANSI.

**New Freedom Party of Southern Africa:** 15 Eendrag St, Bellville 7530; Coloured support.

**New Solidarity:** POB 48687, Qualbert 4078; tel. (11) 3055692; fax 3011077; f. 1989; Indian support; Leader Dr J. N. REDDY.

**Die Orangjewerkers:** seeks to establish several small, self-governing white states; Leader HENDRIK FRENSCH VERWOERD.

**Pan-Africanist Congress (PAC):** POB 25245, Ferreirastown 2048; tel. (11) 8360407; fax (11) 8383705; f. 1959 by breakaway faction of the ANC; banned 1960–90; advocated the establishment a democratic society through black and not multiracial orgs; Pres. CLARENCE MAKWETU; Sec.-Gen. MAXWELL NEMADZIVHANANI.

**Progressive Independent Party (PIP):** Indian support; Leader FAIZ KHAN.

**South African Communist Party (SACP):** c/o POB 1027, Johannesburg 2000; tel. (11) 8366867; fax (11) 8368366; f. 1921 as Communist Party of South Africa; refounded, under present name, 1953; banned 1950–90; supports new Govt, following democratic elections in 1994; Chair. RAYMOND MHLABA (acting); Gen. Sec. CHARLES NQAKULA.

**Transvaal Indian Congress:** f. 1902, reactivated 1983; Pres. Dr ESSOP JASSAT.

**United Christian Conciliation Party:** Johannesburg; f. 1986; multiracial; Pres Bishop ISAAC MOKOENA, TAMASANQA LINDA.

**United Democratic Reform Party:** POB 14048, Reigerpark 1466; f. 1987 by merger of People's Congress Party, Progressive Reform Party and Democratic Party; Coloured and Indian support; Leader JAKOBUS (JAC) ALBERT RABIE; Nat. Chair. NASH PARMANAND.

**Workers' Organization for Socialist Action (WOSA):** Cape Town; f. 1990; Chair. Dr NEVILLE ALEXANDER; Gen. Sec. C. BRECHER.

Other political parties that contested the 1994 elections included the Africa Muslim Party; the African Moderates Congress Party; the Dikwankwetia Party; the Federal Party; the Minority Front; the SOCCER Party; the African Democratic Movement; the Women's Rights Peace Party; the Ximako Progressive Party; the Keep it Straight and Simple (KISS) Party; the Workers' List Party; and the Luso South African Party.

## Diplomatic Representation

### EMBASSIES AND HIGH COMMISSIONS IN SOUTH AFRICA

**Algeria:** 730 Arcadia St, Hatfield, Pretoria; tel. (12) 3425074; fax (12) 3425078.

**Angola:** Pretoria; (12) 466104; Ambassador: MANUEL AGUFTO.

**Argentina:** 200 Standard Plaza, 440 Hilda St, Hatfield, Pretoria 0083; tel. (12) 433527; fax (12) 433521; Ambassador: H. PORTA.

**Australia:** 292 Orient St, Arcadia, St, Pretoria 0083; Private Bag X150, Pretoria 0001; tel. (12) 3423740; fax (12) 3424222; High Commissioner: R. A. BURNS.

**Austria:** Apollo Centre, 10th Floor, 405 Church St, Pretoria 0002; POB 851, Pretoria 0001; tel. (12) 462483; telex 320541; fax (12) 461151; Ambassador: Dr ARNOLD MOEBIUS.

**Belgium:** 275 Pomona St, Muckleneuk, Pretoria 0002; tel. (12) 443201; telex 320508; fax (12) 443216; Ambassador: R. VAN OVERBERGHE.

**Botswana:** Pretoria; tel. (12) 3424760; High Commissioner: O. J. TEBAPE.

**Brazil:** 353 Festival St, Arcadia 0083, POB 3269, Pretoria 0001; tel. (12) 435559; telex 321364; fax (12) 3421419; Chargé d'affaires: RICARDO DRUMMOND DE MELLO.

**Bulgaria:** Pretoria; tel. (12) 3423720.

**Canada:** 1103 Arcadia St, cnr Hilda St, Hatfield 0083; POB 26006, Pretoria 0007; tel. (12) 3426923; telex 32212; fax (12) 3423837; High Commissioner: MARC A. BRAULT.

**Chile:** Campus Centre 1102, 5th Floor, Burnett St, Hatfield 0083; POB 2073, Pretoria 0001; tel. (12) 3421511; telex 322567; fax (12) 3421658; Ambassador: C. BUSTOS.

**China (Taiwan):** 1147 Schoeman St, Pretoria 0083, POB 649, Pretoria 0001; tel. (12) 436071; fax (12) 435816; Ambassador: I-CHENG LOH.

**Congo:** Pretoria; tel. (12) 3425507; fax (12) 3425510.

**Cuba:** Pretoria; tel. (12) 3462215; fax (12) 3462216.

**Czech Republic:** 936 Pretorius St, Arcadia, POB 3326, Pretoria 0083; tel. (12) 3423477; fax (12) 432033; Chargé d'affaires a.i.: JINDŘICH BABICKÝ.

**Denmark:** POB 2942, Pretoria 0001; tel. (12) 3220595; telex 323133; fax (12) 3220596; Ambassador: PETER BRÜCKNER.

**Egypt:** Pretoria; tel. (12) 3431590.

**Ethiopia:** Lymnwood, Pretoria; tel. (12) 3489242; fax (12) 476773; Ambassador: MOHAMMED ALI.

**Finland:** 628 Leyds St, Muckleneuk, Pretoria; POB 443, Pretoria 0001; tel. (12) 3430275; telex 350063; fax (12) 3433095; Ambassador: BJÖRN EKBLOM.

**France:** 807 George Ave, Arcadia, Pretoria 0083; POB 4619, Pretoria 0001; tel. (12) 435564; telex 321319; fax (12) 433481; Ambassador: JOËLLE M. P. BOURGOIS.

**Gabon:** Pretoria; tel. (12) 3424376.

**Germany:** POB 2023, Pretoria 0001; tel. (12) 3443854; telex 321386; fax (12) 3439401; Ambassador: (vacant).

**Greece:** 995 Pretorius St, Arcadia, Pretoria 0083; tel. (12) 437351; telex 320520; fax (12) 434313; Ambassador: P. A. TSAMOULIS.

**Holy See:** 800 Pretorius St, Arcadia, Pretoria 0083; tel. (12) 3443815; fax (12) 3443595; Apostolic Nuncio: Most Rev. AMBROSE B. DE PAOLI, Titular Archbishop of Lares.

# SOUTH AFRICA

**Hungary:** 959 Arcadia St, Arcadia, Pretoria 0083; POB 27077, Sunnyside 0132; tel. (12) 433030; fax (12) 433029; Ambassador: Dr ANDRÁS GERGELY.

**India:** Pretoria; tel. (12) 3425392; Chargé d'affaires: TALMIZ AHMED.

**Indonesia:** Pretoria; tel. (12) 3423356; fax (12) 3423369.

**Ireland:** Tulbach Park, 1234 Church St, Pretoria; tel. (12) 3425062; fax (12) 3424752; Ambassador: EAMON TUATHAIL.

**Israel:** Dashing Centre, 3rd Floor, 339 Hilda St, Hatfield, Pretoria 0083; POB 3726, Pretoria 0001; tel. (12) 4212222; fax (12) 3421442; Ambassador: ALON LIEL.

**Italy:** 796 George Ave, Arcadia, Pretoria 0083; tel. (12) 435541; telex 321397; fax (12) 435547; Ambassador: BRUNO CABRAS.

**Japan:** Sanlam Bldg, 353 Festival St, Hatfield, Pretoria 0083; POB 11434, Brooklyn 0011; tel. (12) 3422100; telex 322134; fax (12) 433922; Ambassador: K. SEZAKI.

**Kenya:** Pretoria; tel. (12) 3425066; fax (12) 3425069.

**Korea, Republic:** Pretoria; tel. (12) 462508.

**Lesotho:** Pretoria; tel. (12) 3226090.

**Malawi:** Delta Bldg, 1st Floor, 471 Monica Rd, Pretoria 0081; POB 11172, Brooklyn 0011; tel. (12) 477827; telex 322017; fax (12) 3484649; High Commissioner: N. T. MIZERE.

**Mauritius:** 1163 Pretorius St, Hatfield, Pretoria 0083; tel. (12) 3421283; fax (12) 3421286; High Commissioner: J. M. MAUNICK.

**Mexico:** Southern Life Plaza, First Floor, Hatfield, Pretoria 0083; tel. (12) 3425190; Ambassador: CASSO LUISELLI FERNÁNDEZ.

**Morocco:** Pretoria; tel. (12) 3430230.

**Mozambique:** 199 Beckett St, Arcadia, Pretoria 0083; tel. (12) 3437840; Ambassador: MUSSAGI JAICHANDI

**Namibia:** Tulbach Park, 1234 Church St, Colbyn, Pretoria; tel. (12) 3423520; High Commissioner: J. HOEBEB.

**Netherlands:** 825 Arcadia St, Pretoria; POB 117, Pretoria 0001; tel. (12) 3443910; telex 321332; fax (12) 3439950; Ambassador: E. RÖELL.

**Nigeria:** Pretoria; tel. (12) 3432021; fax (12) 3431668.

**Norway:** POB 9843, Pretoria 0001; tel. (12) 3234790; telex 320039; fax (12) 3234789; Ambassador: J. K. OTTERBECH.

**Pakistan:** Pretoria; tel. (12) 3464605.

**Paraguay:** POB 95774, Waterkloof, Pretoria 0145; tel. (12) 3471047; fax (12) 3470403; Ambassador: RAÚL DOS SANTOS.

**Peru:** Infotech Bldg, Suite 202, 1090 Arcadia St, Hatfield, Pretoria 0083; tel. (12) 3424944; fax (12) 3424944; Ambassador: JORGE BALEDEZ.

**Poland:** 14 Amos St, Colbyn, Pretoria 0083; tel. (12) 432631; Ambassador: S. CIENIUCH.

**Portugal:** 599 Leyds St, Muckleneuk, Pretoria 0002; tel. (12) 3412340; telex 321365; fax (12) 3413975; Ambassador: Dr J. M. L. RITTO.

**Romania:** 117 Charles St, Brooklyn 0181; POB 11295, Pretoria 0011; tel. (12) 466941; fax (12) 466947; Ambassador: (vacant).

**Russia:** First National Bank Plaza, 3rd Floor, Pretoria 0001; Ambassador: (vacant).

**Rwanda:** Pretoria; tel. (12) 3421740.

**Senegal:** Pretoria; tel. (12) 3426230; Ambassador: SALOUM KANDÉ.

**Slovakia:** 930 Arcadia St, Pretoria 0083; tel. (12) 3422051; fax (12) 3423688; Ambassador: LADISLAV VLAŠIČ.

**Spain:** 169 Pine St, Arcadia, Pretoria 0083; tel. (12) 3443875; telex 320705; fax (12) 3434891; Ambassador: MARIANO UCELAY.

**Sudan:** Pretoria; tel. (12) 3424538; Ambassador: NAFRELDIN MUHAMMED.

**Sweden:** Old Mutual Centre, 167 Andries St, POB 1664, Pretoria 0001; tel. (12) 211050; telex 321193; fax (12) 3232776; Ambassador: B. HEINEBÄCK.

**Switzerland:** 818 George Avenue, Pretoria 0002; POB 2289, Pretoria 0001; tel. (12) 436707; telex 322106; fax (12) 436771; Ambassador: R. WERMUTH.

**Tanzania:** Pretoria; tel. (12) 3424393; High Commissioner: AMI MPUNGWE.

**Tunisia:** Pretoria; tel. (12) 3426282; Ambassador: HATEM ATALLAH.

**Turkey:** 1067 Church St, Hatfield, Pretoria 0083; tel. (12) 3426053.

**United Kingdom:** 255 Hill St, Pretoria 0002; tel. (12) 433121; fax (12) 433207; High Commissioner: Sir ANTHONY REEVE.

**USA:** Thibault House, 7th Floor, 877 Pretorius St, Pretoria; tel. (12) 3421048; telex 322143; fax (12) 3422244; Ambassador: PRINCETON N. LYMAN.

**Uruguay:** 301 M.I.B. House, 119 Burnett St, Hatfield Square, Hatfield 0083; POB 3247, Pretoria 0001; tel. (12) 432829; fax (12) 432833; Ambassador: Dr FÉLIX PITTIER.

**Zambia:** Pretoria; tel. (12) 3421541; High Commissioner: J. M. KABINGA.

**Zimbabwe:** Pretoria; tel. (12) 3425125; High Commissioner: Dr ANDREW HAMA MTETWA.

## Judicial System

The common law of the Republic of South Africa is the Roman-Dutch law, the uncodified law of Holland as it was at the time of the secession of the Cape of Good Hope in 1806. The law of England is not recognized as authoritative, though the principles of English law have been introduced in relation to civil and criminal procedure, evidence and mercantile matters.

The Supreme Court consists of an Appellate Division, and a number of Provincial and Local Divisions. The provinces are further divided into districts and regions with Magistrates' Courts, whose criminal and civil jurisdiction is clearly defined. From these courts appeals may be taken to the Provincial and Local Divisions of the Supreme Court, and thence to the Appellate Division. In accordance with the provisions of the interim Constitution, an 11-member Constitutional Court ensures that the executive, legislative and judicial organs of government adhere to 33 principles entrenched in the Constitution, and is empowered to reverse legislation adopted by Parliament. A Judicial Service Commission makes recommendations regarding the appointment of judges and advises central and provincial government on all matters relating to the judiciary.

### THE SUPREME COURT
#### Appellate Division
**Chief Justice:** MICHAEL CORBETT.

### THE CONSTITUTIONAL COURT
**President:** ARTHUR CHASKALSON.

## Religion

The majority of the population professes the Christian faith.

### CHRISTIANITY

**The South African Council of Churches:** Khotso House, 62 Marshall St, POB 4921, Johannesburg 2000; tel. (11) 4921380; fax (11) 4921448; f. 1936; 26 mem. churches; Pres. Dr K. MGOJO; Gen. Sec. HLOPHE BAM.

#### The Anglican Communion

Most Anglicans in South Africa are adherents of the Church of the Province of Southern Africa, comprising 23 dioceses (including Lesotho, Namibia, St Helena, Swaziland and two dioceses in Mozambique). The Church had more than 2m. members in 1988.

**Archbishop of Cape Town and Metropolitan of the Province of Southern Africa:** Most Rev. DESMOND M. TUTU, Bishopscourt, Claremont 7700; tel. (21) 7612531; fax (21) 7614193.

#### The Dutch Reformed Church (Nederduitse Gereformeerde Kerk—NGK)

In 1991 there were 946,971 white, 228,099 Coloured and 294,830 African members of the Dutch Reformed Church in South Africa. Separate worship for whites and non-whites was instituted in 1863; in 1986 all congregations were desegregated.

**General Synod:** POB 4445, Pretoria 0001; tel. (12) 3227658; fax (12) 3223803; Moderator Prof. PIETER POTGIETER; Scribe Dr F. M. GAUM; CEO Prof. P. G. MEIRING.

#### The Evangelical Lutheran Churches

In 1980 there were 39,620 white, 95,640 Coloured and 698,400 African members of the Evangelical Lutheran Church in South Africa.

**Evangelical Lutheran Church in Southern Africa (ELCSA):** POB 7095, 1622 Bonaero Park; tel. (11) 9731851; telex 451751; fax (11) 3951862; f. 1975 by merger of four non-white churches; now the major Lutheran body in southern Africa; 703,349 mems; Gen. Sec. Rev. T. MBULI.

**Evangelical Lutheran Church in Southern Africa (Cape):** 240 Long St, Cape Town 8001; tel. (21) 244932; fax (21) 249618; 6,500 mems; Pres. Rev. NILS LOHWER.

**Evangelical Lutheran Church in Southern Africa (Natal–Transvaal):** POB 7095, Bonaero Park 1622; tel. (21) 9731851; fax (21) 3951862; Pres. Bishop D. R. LILJE.

**Lutheran Communion in Southern Africa:** POB 7170, Bonaero Park 1622; tel. 9731873; fax 3951615; f. 1991; Pres. Rev. M. WESSELS; Exec. Dir F. F. GRAZ.

# SOUTH AFRICA

### The Roman Catholic Church

South Africa comprises four archdioceses, 21 dioceses and one Apostolic Prefecture. At 31 December 1993 there were an estimated 2,931,776 adherents in the country, representing about 7.9% of the total population.

**Southern African Catholic Bishops' Conference (SACBC):** Khanya House, 140 Visagie St, Pretoria 0002; POB 941, Pretoria 0001; tel. (12) 3236458; fax (12) 3266218; f. 1951; 34 mems representing South Africa, Botswana, Namibia and Swaziland; Pres. Rt Rev. LOUIS NDLOVU, Bishop of Manzini; Sec.-Gen. Br JUDE PIETERSE.

**Archbishop of Bloemfontein:** Most Rev. PETER BUTELEZI, Archbishop's House, 7A Whites Rd, Bloemfontein 9300; POB 362, Bloemfontein 9300; tel. and fax (51) 481658.

**Archbishop of Cape Town:** Most Rev. LAWRENCE HENRY; Cathedral Place, 12 Bouquet St, Cape Town 8001; POB 2910, Cape Town 8001; tel. (21) 4622417; fax (21) 4619330.

**Archbishop of Durban:** Most Rev. WILFRID NAPIER, Archbishop's House, 154 Gordon Rd, Durban 4001; POB 47489, Greyville 4023; tel. (31) 3031417; fax (31) 231848.

**Archbishop of Pretoria:** Most Rev. GEORGE DANIEL, Archbishop's House, 125 Main St, Waterkloof 0181; POB 17245, Groenkloof, Pretoria 0027; tel. (12) 462048; fax (12) 462452.

### Other Christian Churches

In addition to the following Churches, there are a large number of Pentecostalist groups, and more than 3,000 African independent Churches.

**African Gospel Church:** POB 32312, 4060 Mobeni; tel. (31) 9074377; Moderator Rev. F. D. MKHIZE; Gen. Sec. O. MTOLO; 100,000 mems.

**Afrikaanse Protestaante Kerk** (Afrikaans Protestant Church): POB 11488, Pretoria 0001; tel. (12) 3443960; fax (12) 3445480; f. 1987 by fmr mems of the Dutch Reformed Church (Nederduitse Gereformeerde Kerk) in protest at the proposed racial integration of church congregations; Leader Prof. WILLIE LUBBE; c. 43,000 mems.

**Apostolic Faith Mission of South Africa:** POB 890197, Lyndhurst 2106; tel. (11) 7868550; fax (11) 8871182; f. 1908; Gen. Sec. Dr J. L. LANGERMAN; 136,000 mems.

**Assemblies of God:** POB 1402, Alberton 1450; tel. (11) 8696095; f. 1915; Chair. Rev. J. S. W. BOND; Gen. Sec. Rev. M. NKOMONDE; 250,000 mems.

**Baptist Union of Southern Africa:** POB 1085, Roodepoort 1725; tel. (11) 7603038; f. 1877; Pres. Rev. A. SCHEEPERS; Gen. Sec. Rev. T. G. RAE; 61,000 mems.

**Black Dutch Reformed Church:** POB 137, Bergvlei 2012; Leader Rev. SAM BUTI; c. 1m. mems.

**Church of England in South Africa:** POB 185, Gillitts 3603; tel. (31) 752876; fax (31) 7655150; 207 churches; Bishops: Rt Rev. J. BELL, Rt Rev. J. NGUBANE, Rt Rev. F. RETIEF, Rt Rev. M. MORRISON.

**Evangelical Presbyterian Church in South Africa:** POB 31961, Braamfontein 2017; tel. (11) 3391044; Gen. Sec. Rev. S. NGOBE; Gen. Sec. Rev. J. S. NGOBE; Treas. Rev. H. D. MASANGU; 60,000 mems.

**The Methodist Church of Southern Africa:** Methodist Connexional Office, POB 50216, Musgrave 4062; tel. (31) 224214; fax (31) 217674; f. 1883; Pres. Bishop M. STANLEY MOGOBA; Sec. Rev. VIVIAN W. HARRIS; 758,178 mems.

**Moravian Church in Southern Africa:** POB 24111, Lansdowne 7780; tel. (21) 6962926; fax (21) 6963887; f. 1737; Head Rev. MARTIN WESSELS; 102,132 mems.

**Nederduitsch Hervormde Kerk van Afrika:** POB 2368, Pretoria 0001; tel. (12) 3228885; fax (12) 3227909; Chair. Dr D. J. C. VAN WYK; Gen. Sec. Dr S. P. PRETORIUS; 193,561 mems.

**Nederduitse Gereformeerde Kerk in Afrika:** Portland Place, 37 Jorissen St, 2017 Johannesburg; tel. (11) 4031027; 6 synods (incl. 1 in Swaziland); Moderator Rev. S. P. E. BUTI; Gen. Sec. W. RAATH; 350,870 mems.

**Presbyterian Church of Africa:** POB 54840, Umlazi 4031; tel. (31) 9072366; f. 1898; 8 presbyteries (incl. 1 in Malawi and 1 in Zimbabwe); Chief Clerk Rev. S. A. KHUMALO; 1,231,000 mems.

**Presbyterian Church of Southern Africa:** POB 475, Witwatersrand 2050; tel. (11) 3391017; fax (11) 4031921; f. 1897; Moderator Rt Rev. R. J. BOTSIN; Gen. Sec. and Clerk of the Assembly Rev. A. RODGER; 90,000 mems.

**Reformed Church in South Africa** (Die Gereformeerde Kerke): POB 20004, Noordbrug 2522, Potchefstroom; tel. (148) 2973986; fax (148) 2931042; f. 1859; Prin. Officer L. J. SWART; 158,973 mems.

**Seventh-day Adventist Church:** POB 468, Bloemfontein 9300; tel. (51) 478271; fax (41) 488059; Pres. Pastor D. W. B. CHALALE; Sec. Pastor B. H. PARKERSON; 145,287 mems.

**United Congregational Church of Southern Africa:** POB 61305, Marshalltown 2107; tel. (11) 8366537; fax (11) 8369249; f. 1799; Gen. Sec. Rev. S. M. ARENDS; 234,451 mems.

**Zion Christian Church:** Zion City, Moria; f. 1910; South Africa's largest black religious group, with c. 4m. mems; Leader Bishop BARNABAS LEKGANYANE.

## BAHÁ'Í FAITH

**National Spiritual Assembly:** 10 Acorn Lane, Houghton Estate, Houghton 2198; POB 2142, Houghton 2041; tel. (11) 4872077; fax (11) 4871809; f. 1956; 8,000 mems resident in 180 localities; Sec. SHOHREH RAWHANI.

## JUDAISM

There are about 100,000 Jews in South Africa.

**South African Jewish Board of Deputies:** POB 87557, Houghton 2041; tel. (11) 4861434; fax (11) 6464946; f. 1912; the representative institution of South African Jewry; Pres. G. LEISSNER; Chair. M. SMITH; Nat. Dir S. KOPELOWITZ.

# The Press

In December 1993 legislation was adopted that provided for the establishment of an Independent Media Commission, which was to ensure the impartiality of the press.

**Bureau of Information:** Midtown Bldg, cnr Vermeulen and Pretorius Sts, Pretoria; Private Bag X745, Pretoria 0001; tel. (12) 3142911; fax (12) 3233831; govt agency.

**Directorate of Publications:** Pleinpark Bldg, 13th Floor, Plein St, Cape Town; Private Bag X9069, Cape Town 8000; tel. (21) 456518; fax (21) 456511; f. 1974; Govt agency responsible under Publications Act 1974 for censorship of films and video cassettes and the examination of publs submitted to it for adjudication; Dir Prof. Dr A. COETZEE.

**South African Media Council:** Nedbank Gardens, 8th Floor, 33 Bath Ave, Rosebank 2196; POB 31559, Braamfontein; tel. (11) 4032878; fax (11) 4032879; f. 1983 by the Newspaper Press Union and the Conf. of Editors to promote press freedom; 14 media and 14 public representatives; Chair. Prof. KOBUS VAN ROOYEN.

### DAILIES

#### Western Cape

**The Argus:** 122 St George's St, POB 56, Cape Town 8000; tel. (21) 48184911; telex 527383; fax (21) 4884075; f. 1857; evening and Sat.; English; independent; Editor-in-Chief ANDREW DRYSDALE; circ. 106,574 (eves); 120,719 (Sat.).

**Die Burger:** 40 Heerengracht, POB 692, Cape Town 8000; tel. (21) 4062222; telex 527751; fax (21) 4062913; f. 1915; morning; Afrikaans; Editor E. DOMMISSE; circ. 89,600 (Mon.–Fri.), 95,800 (Sat.).

#### Eastern Cape

**Die Burger (Oos-Kaap):** 52 Cawood St, POB 525, Port Elizabeth 6000; tel. (41) 542431; fax (41) 545166; f. 1937; morning; Afrikaans; Editor J. CROWTHER; circ. 11,400.

**Cape Times:** Newspaper House, 122 St George's St, POB 56, Cape Town 8000; tel. (21) 4884911; fax (21) 4884717; f. 1876; morning; English; Editor KOOS VIVIERS; circ. 61,000.

**Daily Dispatch:** 33 Caxton St, POB 131, East London 5200; tel. (431) 430010; telex 250678; fax (431) 435159; f. 1872; morning; English; Editor Prof. G. STEWART; circ. 35,940.

**Eastern Province Herald:** Newspaper House, 19 Baakens St, POB 1117, Port Elizabeth 6000; tel. (41) 5047911; telex 243351; fax (41) 554966; f. 1845; morning; English; Editor DEREK SMITH; circ. 30,000 (Mon.–Fri.), 25,000 (Sat.).

**Evening Post:** Newspaper House, 19 Baakens St, POB 1121, Port Elizabeth 6000; tel. (41) 5047911; telex 243351; fax (41) 554966; f. 1950; evening; English; Editor CLIFF FOSTER; circ. 19,400.

#### Northern Cape

**Diamond Fields Advertiser:** POB 610, Kimberley 8300; tel. (531) 26261; telex 280229; fax (531) 25881; morning; English; Editor Prof. J. G. WILLIAMS; circ. 8,000.

#### KwaZulu/Natal

**The Daily News:** 18 Osborne St, Greyville 4001, POB 47549, Greyville 4023; tel. (31) 3082100; fax (31) 3082111; f. 1878; Mon.–Fri., evening; English; Editor P. DAVIS; circ. 85,000.

**Natal Mercury:** 18 Osborne St, Greyville, POB 950, Durban 4001; tel. (31) 3082300; telex 622301; fax (31) 3082333; f. 1852; morning; English; Editor J. PATTEN; circ. 61,000.

# SOUTH AFRICA

**Natal Witness:** 244 Longmarket St, POB 362, Pietermaritzburg 3200; tel. (331) 942011; telex 643385; fax (331) 940468; f. 1846; morning; English; Editor D. J. WILLERS; circ. 28,000.

### Orange Free State

**Die Volksblad:** 79 Voortrekker St, POB 267, Bloemfontein 9300; tel. (51) 473351; telex 267612; fax (51) 306949; f. 1904; morning; Afrikaans; Editor PAUL MARAIS; circ. 28,000 (Mon.–Fri.), 23,000 (Sat.).

### North-West

**Rustenburg Herald:** 28 Steen St, POB 2043, Rustenburg 0300; tel. (1421) 28329; fax (1421) 28350; f. 1924; English and Afrikaans; Editor C. THERON; circ. 11,000.

### Gauteng

**Beeld:** 32 Miller St, POB 5425, Johannesburg 2000; tel. (11) 4021460; fax (11) 4021871; f. 1974; morning; Afrikaans; Editor SARIE DE SWART; circ. 100,000 (Mon.–Fri.), 81,000 (Sat.).

**Business Day:** 11 Diagonal St, POB 1138, Johannesburg 2000; tel. (11) 4972711; telex 488921; fax (11) 8360805; f. 1985; morning; English; financial; Editor JIM JONES; circ. 32,890.

**The Citizen:** POB 7712, Johannesburg 2000; tel. (11) 4022900; telex 424053; fax (11) 4026862; f. 1976; morning; English; Editor M. A. JOHNSON; circ. 14,000 (Mon.–Fri.), 108,000 (Sat.).

**The Pretoria News:** 216 Vermeulen St, Pretoria 0002; tel. (12) 3255382; telex 322174; fax (12) 3257300; f. 1898; evening; English; Editor D. DU PLESSIS; circ. 25,822 (Mon.–Fri.), 15,442 (Sat.).

**Sowetan:** 61 Commando Rd, Industria West, POB 6663, Johannesburg 2000; tel. (11) 4740128; telex 5425992; fax (11) 4748834; f. 1981; Mon.–Fri.; English; Editor Z. AGGREY KLAASTE; circ. 225,000.

**The Star:** 47 Sauer St, POB 1014, Johannesburg 2000; tel. (11) 6339111; telex 487083; fax (11) 8368398; f. 1887; English; Editor PETER J. SULLIVAN; circ. 209,000 (Mon.–Fri.), 156,000 (Sat.).

**Transvaaler:** 28 Height St, Doornfontein, POB 845, Johannesburg 2000; tel. (11) 7769111; fax (11) 4020037; afternoon; Afrikaans; Editor G. JOHNSON; circ. 40,000.

## WEEKLIES AND FORTNIGHTLIES

### Western Cape

**Eikestadnuus:** 44 Alexander St, POB 28, Stellenbosch 7600; tel. (2231) 72840; fax (2231) 99538; weekly; English and Afrikaans; Editor R. GERBER; circ. 7,000.

**Fair Lady:** 40 Heerengracht, POB 1802, Cape Town 8000; tel. (21) 4062044; telex 527751; fax (21) 4062930; fortnightly; English; Editor LIZ BUTLER; circ. 150,284.

**Huisgenoot:** 40 Heerengracht, POB 1802, Cape Town 8000; tel. (21) 4062575; telex 527751; fax (21) 4062937; f. 1916; weekly; Afrikaans; Editor NIEL HAMMANN; circ. 517,000.

**Sarie:** POB 1802, Cape Town 8000; tel. (21) 4062203; telex 527751; fax (21) 4062913; fortnightly; Afrikaans; women's interest; Editor A. ROSSOUW; circ. 227,000.

**South:** 6 Russel St, Castle Mews, Woodstock 7925; POB 13094, Sir Lowry Rd 7900; tel. (21) 4622012; fax (21) 4615407; weekly; black interest; Editor Dr GUY BERGER; circ. 25,000.

**The Southern Cross:** POB 2372, Cape Town 8001; tel. (21) 455007; fax (21) 453850; f. 1920; weekly; English; Roman Catholic; Editor M. SHACKLETON; circ. 10,000.

**Tyger-Burger:** 40 Heerengracht, POB 2271, Cape Town 8000; tel. (21) 4062121; telex 527751; fax (21) 4062913; weekly; Afrikaans and English; Editor BAREND VENTER.

**Die Voorligter:** POB 1444, Cape Town 8000; f. 1937; journal of the Dutch Reformed Church of South Africa; Editor Dr F. M. GAUM; circ. 133,000.

**Weekend Argus:** 122 St George's Mall, POB 56, Cape Town 8000; tel. (21) 4884911; telex 527383; fax (21) 4884075; f. 1857; weekly; English; Editor JONATHAN HOBDAY; circ. 125,000.

**You Magazine:** 40 Heerengracht, POB 7167, Cape Town 8000; tel. (21) 4062115; telex 527751; fax (21) 4062915; f. 1987; weekly; English; Editor-in-Chief NIGEL HAMMAN; circ. 232,000.

### Eastern Cape

**Imvo Zabantsundu** (Black Opinion): 35 Edes St, POB 190, King William's Town 5600; tel. (433) 23550; fax (433) 33865; f. 1884; weekly; English and Xhosa; Editor D. J. DE VILLIERS; circ. 31,000.

**Weekend Post:** POB 1141, Port Elizabeth 6000; tel. (41) 5047911; telex 243047; fax (41) 554966; English; Editor N. M. WOUDBERG; circ. 38,000.

### Northern Cape

**Die Gemsbok:** POB 60, Upington 8800; tel. 27017; fax 24055; English and Afrikaans; Editor D. JONES; circ. 8,000.

### KwaZulu/Natal

**Farmers' Weekly:** POB 32083, Mobeni 4060; tel. (31) 422041; telex 624422; fax (31) 426068; f. 1911; weekly; agriculture and horticulture; Editor M. FISHER; circ. 17,000.

**Ilanga:** 128 Umgeri Rd, POB 2159, Durban 4000; tel. (31) 3094350; fax (31) 3091938; f. 1903; 2 a week; Zulu; Editor P. G. MTHEMBU; circ. 126,000.

**Keur:** POB 32083, Mobeni 4060; tel. (31) 422041; telex 5624422; fax (31) 426068; f. 1967; Afrikaans; Editor CARL STEYN; circ. 91,000.

**Ladysmith Gazette:** POB 10019, Ladysmith 3370; tel. (361) 26801; fax (361) 22283; f. 1902; weekly; English, Afrikaans and Zulu; Editor BEVIS FAIRBROTHER; circ. 7,000.

**Natal On Saturday:** 18 Osborne St, Greyville 4001, POB 47549, Greyville 4023; tel. (31) 3082500; fax (31) 3082355; f. 1878; English; Editor G. PARKER; circ. 84,000.

**Personality:** POB 32083, Mobeni 4060; tel. (31) 422041; telex 624422; fax (31) 426068; weekly; Editor WENDY CHRISTOPHER; circ. 107,000.

**Post:** 18 Osborne St, Greyville 4001, POB 47549, Greyville 4023; tel. (31) 3082400; fax (31) 3082427; f. 1935; weekly; English; general; Editor BRIGLALL RAMGUTHEE; circ. 54,000.

**Rooi Rose:** POB 32083, Mobeni 4060; tel. (31) 422041; telex 624422; fax (31) 426068; Afrikaans; fortnightly; women's interest; Editor J. KRUGER; circ. 165,000.

**Scope:** POB 32083, Mobeni 4060; tel. (31) 422041; telex 5624422; fax (31) 426068; f. 1966; fortnightly; general interest for men; Editor D. MULLANY; circ. 169,700.

**Sunday Tribune:** 18 Osborne St, POB 47549, Greyville 4023; tel. (31) 3082100; telex 622301; fax (31) 3082715; f. 1937; English; weekly; Editor DAVID WIGHTMAN; circ. 125,710.

**Umafrika:** POB 11002, Mariannhill 3601; tel. (31) 7002720; fax (31) 7003707; f. 1911; weekly; Zulu and English; Editor CYRIL MADLALA; circ. 60,000.

### Orange Free State

**Vista:** POB 1027, Welkom 9460; tel. (57) 3571304; fax (57) 3532427; f. 1971; 2 a week; English and Afrikaans; Editor P. GOUWS; circ. 26,000 (Tues.), 26,000 (Fri.).

### Gauteng

**African Jewish Newspaper:** POB 6169, Johannesburg 2000; tel. (11) 6468292; f. 1931; weekly; Yiddish; Editor LEVI SHALIT.

**Die Afrikaner:** POB 1888, Pretoria 0001; tel. (12) 3423410; fax (12) 3423417; f. 1970; Wednesday; organ of Herstigte Nasionale Party; Editors A. J. H. FERGUSON, H. VAN DE GRAAF; circ. 10,000.

**Benoni City Times en Oosrandse Nuus:** 28 Woburn Ave, POB 494, Benoni 1500; tel. (11) 8451680; telex 748942; fax (11) 4224796; English and Afrikaans; Editor H. LEE; circ. 27,000.

**City Press:** POB 3413, Johannesburg 2000; tel. (11) 4021632; fax (11) 4026662; f. 1983; weekly; English; Editor KHULU SIBIYA; circ. 160,000.

**Finance Week:** Private Bag 78816, Sandton 2146; tel. (11) 4440555; fax (11) 4440424; f. 1979; Editor A. J. GREENBLO; circ. 16,000.

**Financial Mail:** 11 Diagonal St, POB 9959, Johannesburg 2000; tel. (11) 4972711; telex 488921; fax (11) 8341686; weekly; English; Editor N. BRUCE; circ. 34,000.

**The Herald Times:** POB 31015, Braamfontein 2017; tel. (11) 8876500; telex 431078; weekly; Jewish interest; Man. Dir R. SHAPIRO; circ. 5,000.

**Mining Week:** Johannesburg; tel. (11) 7892144; telex 422125; f. 1979; fortnightly; Editor VAL PIENAAR; circ. 10,000.

**The New Nation:** POB 10674, Johannesburg 2000; tel. (11) 3332721; telex 482226; fax (11) 3332733; f. 1986; weekly; English; Editor ZWELAKHE SISULU; circ. 64,000.

**Die Noord-Transvaler:** POB 220, Ladanna, Pietersburg 0704; tel. (152) 931831; fax (152) 932586; weekly; Afrikaans; Editor A. BUYS; circ. 12,000.

**Northern Review:** 16 Grobler St, POB 45, Pietersburg 0700; tel. (152) 2959167; fax (152) 2915148; weekly; English and Afrikaans; Editor R. S. DE JAGER; circ. 8,000.

**Potchefstroom and Ventersdorp Herald:** POB 515, Potchefstroom 2520; tel. (148) 930750; fax (148) 930750; f. 1908; 2 a week; English and Afrikaans; Editor H. STANDER; Man. G. WESSELS; circ. 4,000 (Tues.), 5,000 (Fri.).

**Rapport:** POB 8422, Johannesburg 2000; tel. (11) 4022620; telex 422027; fax (11) 4026163; f. 1970; weekly; Afrikaans; Editor IZAK DE VILLIERS; circ. 353,020.

**South African Industrial Week:** Johannesburg; Man. Editor W. MASTINGLE; circ. 19,000.

SOUTH AFRICA	*Directory*

**Springs and Brakpan Advertiser:** POB 138, Springs 1560; tel. (11) 8121600; fax (11) 8121908; English and Afrikaans; Editor L. NEILL; circ. 11,000.

**Sunday Times:** POB 1090, Johannesburg 2000; tel. (11) 4972711; telex 488921; fax (11) 4972664; English; Editor K. F. OWEN; circ. 564,000.

**Vaalweekblad:** 27 Ekspa Bldg, D.F. Malan St, POB 351, Vanderbijlpark 1900; tel. (16) 817010; fax (16) 810604; weekly; Afrikaans and English; Editor J. J. DOMINICUS; circ. 12,000.

**Vrye Weekblad:** 153 Bree St, Newtown, Johannesburg 2001; tel. (11) 8362151; fax (11) 8385901; f. 1988; weekly; Afrikaans; anti-apartheid; Editor MAX DU PREEZ; circ. 13,000.

**Weekly Mail and Guardian:** 139 Smit St, Braamfontein, Johannesburg; POB 32362, Braamfontein 2017; tel. (11) 4037111; fax (11) 4031025; f. 1985; English; Editor ANTON HARBER; circ. 30,000.

## MONTHLIES
### Western Cape

**Boxing World:** Unit 17, Park St, POB 164, Steenberg 7945; tel. 7015070; fax 7015863; Editor BERT BLEWETT; circ. 10,000.

**Car:** POB 180, Howard Place 7450; tel. (21) 5311391; (21) fax 5313333; Editor J. WRIGHT; circ. 129,573.

**Drum:** POB 784696, Sandton 2146; tel. (11) 7837227; fax (11) 7838822; f. 1951; English; Editor BARNEY COHEN; circ. 135,850 in southern Africa.

**Femina:** 2 the Avalon, POB 3647, Cape Town 8000; tel. (21) 4623070; telex 522991; fax (21) 4612500; Editor JANE RAPHAELY; circ. 109,321.

**Finansies & Tegniek:** POB 53171, Troyville 2139; tel. (11) 4026372; fax (11) 4041701; Afrikaans; Editor G. L. MARAIS; circ. 22,733.

**Learning Roots:** POB 1161, Cape Town 8000; tel. (21) 6968414; fax (21) 6968346; f. 1980; newsletter for black schools in the Western Cape; circ. 50,000.

**Nursing RSA Verpleging:** Private Bag XI, Pinelands 7430; tel. (21) 5312691; fax (21) 5314126; f. 1986; professional nursing journal; Editor LILLIAN MEDLIN; circ. 10,000.

**Reader's Digest** (South African Edition): POB 2677, Cape Town 8000; tel. (21) 254460; telex 520333; fax (21) 4191090; English; Editor-in-Chief W. PANKHURST; circ. 371,000.

**South African Medical Journal:** Private Bag XI, Pinelands 7430; tel. (21) 5313081; fax (21) 5314126; f. 1926; publ. by the Medical Asscn of South Africa; Editor Dr DANIEL J. NCAYIYANA; circ. 20,000.

**Die Unie:** POB 196, Cape Town 8000; tel. (21) 4616340; fax (21) 4619238; f. 1905; educational; publ. by the South African Teachers' Union; Editor M. J. L. OLIVIER; circ. 7,500.

**Woman's Value:** POB 1802, Cape Town 8000; tel. (21) 4062205; telex 527751; fax (21) 4062929; English; Editor RIETA BURGERS; circ. 146,000.

**Wynboer:** K. W. V. Van ZA Bpkt, POB 528, Suider-Paarl 7624; tel. (2211) 73267; telex 527107; fax (2211) 631562; f. 1931; viticulture and the wine and spirit industry; Editor HENRY HOPKINS; circ. 10,000.

### KwaZulu/Natal

**Bona:** POB 32083, Mobeni 4060; tel. (31) 422041; telex 624422; fax (31) 426068; f. 1956; English, Sotho, Xhosa and Zulu; Editor R. BAKER; circ. 263,000.

**Home Front:** POB 2549, Durban 4000; tel. (31) 3071574; fax (31) 3054148; f. 1928; ex-servicemen's magazine; Editor REG SWEET; circ. 14,000.

**Living and Loving:** POB 32083, Mobeni 4060; tel. (31) 422041; telex 624422; fax (31) 426068; English; Editor ANGELA STILL; circ. 113,000.

**South African Garden and Home:** POB 32083, Mobeni 4060; tel. (31) 422041; telex 624422; fax (31) 426068; f. 1947; Editor MARGARET WASSERFALL; circ. 146,070.

**Tempo:** POB 16, Pinetown 3600; tel. (31) 7013225; fax (31) 7012166; f. 1984; weekly; Afrikaans; Editor Dr HILDA GROBLER; circ. 7,000.

**World Airnews:** POB 35082, Northway, Durban 4065; tel. (31) 841319; fax (31) 837115; f. 1973; aviation news; Editor T. CHALMERS; circ. 13,000.

**Your Family:** POB 32083, Mobeni 4060; tel. (31) 422041; telex 624422; fax (31) 426068; f. 1973; English; cooking, crafts, DIY; Editor ANGELA WALLER-PATON; circ. 216,000.

### Orange Free State

**Wamba:** POB 1097, Bloemfontein; educational; publ. in seven vernacular languages; Editor C. P. SENYATSI.

### Gauteng

**Centre News:** Johannesburg; tel. (11) 5591781; English; publ. by R.J.J. Publications; circ. 30,000.

**The Mail of Rosebank News:** Johannesburg; tel. (11) 3391781; English; publ. by R.J.J. Publications; circ. 40,000.

**Nursing News:** POB 1280, Pretoria 0001; tel. (12) 3432315; fax (12) 3440750; f. 1978; newspaper of the South African Nursing Asscn; English and Afrikaans; circ. 110,000.

**Pace:** POB 48985, Roosevelt Park 2129; tel. (11) 8890600; fax (11) 8805942; Man. Editor FORCE KOSHANI; circ. 131,000.

**Postal and Telkom Herald:** POB 9186, Johannesburg 2000; tel. (11) 7255422; fax (11) 7256540; f. 1903; English and Afrikaans; Staff Asscn (Workers' Union); Editor F. A. GERBER; circ. 13,000.

**Technobrief:** POB 395, Pretoria 0001; tel (12) 8414304; fax (12) 8413789; f. 1991; publ. by the Council for Scientific and Industrial Research (CSIR); Editor HOEPEL SCHEEPERS; circ. 12,000.

**Telescope:** POB 925, Pretoria 0001; tel. (12) 3112495; fax (12) 3114031; f. 1970; English, Afrikaans and ethnic languages; telecom staff newspaper; Editor WERNA HOUGH; circ. 50,000.

## QUARTERLIES
### Western Cape

**New Era:** Cape Town.

**South African Law Journal:** POB 30, Cape Town 8000; tel. (2721) 7975101; fax (2721) 7627424; f. 1884; Editor ELLISON KAHN; circ. 2,500.

### Gauteng

**The Motorist/Die Motoris:** POB 31015, Braamfontein 2017; tel. (11) 8876500; fax (11) 8876551; f. 1966; journal of the Automobile Asscn of SA; Editor MICHAEL WANG; circ. 184,000.

**South African Journal of Economics:** 4-44 EBW Bldg, University of Pretoria, Pretoria 0002; tel. (12) 4203525; fax (12) 437589; English and Afrikaans; Man. Editor Prof. D. J. J. BOTHA.

**Viva SA:** POB 1758, Pretoria 0001; tel. (12) 3226404; fax (12) 3207803; f. 1952; publ. by the Foundation for Education, Science and Tech.; Editor JOHAN VAN ROOYEN; circ. 5,000.

## NEWS AGENCIES

**South African Press Association:** Kine Centre, 1st Floor, Commissioner St, POB 7766, Johannesburg 2000; tel. (11) 3310661; telex 488061; fax (11) 3317473; f. 1938; 40 mems; Chair. J. S. CRAIB; Man. W. J. H. VAN GILS; Editor MARK A. VAN DER VELDEN.

### Foreign Bureaux

**Agence France-Presse (AFP):** Nixdorf Centre, 6th Floor, 37 Stanley Ave, Milpark; POB 3462, Johannesburg 2000; tel. (11) 4822170; telex 422660; fax (11) 7268756; Bureau Chief MARC HUTTEN.

**Agencia EFE** (Spain): Johannesburg; Chief JOSÉ BUJANDA PAN.

**Agenzia Nazionale Stampa Associata (ANSA)** (Italy): POB 32312, Camps Bay, Cape Town 8040; tel. (21) 7903991; telex 522211; fax (21) 7904444; Correspondent LICINIO GERMINI.

**Associated Press (AP)** (USA): 15 Napier St, Richmond, Johannesburg 2092; tel. (11) 7267022; fax (11) 7267834; Bureau Chief JOHN DANISZEWSKI.

**Central News Agency** (Taiwan): Kine Centre, 1st Floor, 141 Commissioner St, Johannesburg 2001; tel. (11) 3316654; fax (11) 3319463; Chief CHANG JER SHONG.

**Deutsche Presse-Agentur (dpa)** (Germany): 96 Jorrisen St, POB 32521, Braamfontein 2017; tel. (11) 3391148; telex 426038; Chief GEORGE SPIEKER.

**Informatsionnoye Telegrafnoye Agentstvo Rossii—Telegrafnoye Agentstvo Suverennykh Stran (ITAR—TASS)** (Russia): 1261 Park St, Atfield, Pretoria; tel. (12) 436677; telex 320142; fax (12) 3425017; Bureau Chief YURI K. PICHUGIN.

**Inter-Press Service (IPS)** (Italy): POB 260425, Excom 2023, Johannesburg; Correspondent NEIL LEWIS.

**Kyodo News Service** (Japan): Royal St Mary's Bldg, 4th Floor, 85 Eloff St, POB 7772, Johannesburg 2000; tel. (11) 3334207; telex 483731; fax (11) 3378918; Rep. NORIO YATAKA.

**Reuters Ltd** (UK): Surrey House, 7th and 8th Floors, 35 Rissik St, Johannesburg; Man. CHRIS INWOOD.

**United Press International (UPI)** (USA): Nedbank Centre, 2nd Floor, POB 32661, Braamfontein 2017; tel. (11) 4033910; telex 423428; fax (11) 4033914; Bureau Chief PATRICK COLLINS.

## PRESS ASSOCIATION

**Newspaper Press Union of South Africa:** Nedbank Gardens, 8th Floor, 33 Bath Ave, Rosebank 2196; tel. (21) 3396344; fax (21) 3393393; f. 1882; 220 mems; Pres. R. H. PAULSON; Gen. Man. P. S. C. POTÉ.

SOUTH AFRICA

# Publishers

**Acorn Books:** POB 4845, Randburg 2125; tel. (11) 8805768; fax (11) 8805768; f. 1985; general, natural history.

**Albertyn Publishers (Pty) Ltd:** Andmar Bldg, Van Ryneveld St, Stellenbosch 7600; tel. (21) 8871202; fax (21) 8871292; f. 1971; encyclopaedias; Editorial Man. S. Carstens.

**Amagi Publications:** Bisho.

**BLAC Publishing House:** POB 17, Athlone, Cape Town; f. 1974; general fiction, poetry; Man. Dir James Matthews.

**Jonathan Ball Publishers:** POB 33977, Jeppestown 2043; tel. (11) 6222900; fax (11) 6223553; history, politics, business, leisure.

**Bible Society of South Africa:** POB 6215, Roggebaai 8012; tel. (21) 212040; telex 527964; fax (21) 4194846; f. 1820; Gen. Sec. Dr D. Tolmie.

**Bok Books:** POB 20194, Durban North 4016; tel. (31) 5792177; (31) fax 5792407.

**Book Promotions (Pty) Ltd:** POB 23320, Claremont 7735; tel. (21) 720332; fax (21) 720383; Man. Dir. R. Mansell.

**Book Studio (Pty) Ltd:** POB 121, Hout Bay 7872.

**Books of Africa (Pty) Ltd:** POB 10, Muizenberg 7950; tel. (21) 888316; f. 1947; biography, history, Africana, art; Man. Dir T. V. Bulpin.

**Brenthurst Press (Pty) Ltd:** POB 87184, Houghton 2041; tel. (11) 6466024; fax (11) 4861651; f. 1974; Southern African history; Man. Editor Mrs C. Kemp.

**Butterworth Publishers (Pty) Ltd:** POB 792, Durban 4000; tel. (31) 294247; telex 620730; fax (31) 283255; Man. Dir William J. Last.

**Clever Books:** POB 20113, Alkantrant 0005.

**College of Careers/Faircare Books:** POB 2081, Cape Town 8000; tel. (21) 452041; f. 1946; general, educational; Man. Dir Richard S. Pooler.

**Cornea Publications:** Welgemoed.

**CUM Books:** POB 1599, Vereeniging 1930; tel. (16) 214781; fax (16) 211748.

**Da Gama Publishers (Pty) Ltd:** M.W.U. Bldg, 6th Floor, 19 Melle St, Braamfontein 2017; tel. (11) 4033763; fax (11) 4031263; travel; Publr Dermot Swaine.

**Digma Publications:** POB 95466, Waterkloof 0145; tel. (11) 3463840; fax (11) 3463845.

**A. Donker (Pty) Ltd:** POB 33977, Jeppestown 2043; tel. (11) 6222900; fax (11) 6223553.

**Dreyer Printers and Publishers:** POB 286, Bloemfontein 9300; tel. (51) 479001; fax (51) 471281.

**Educational Workshop:** POB 26347, Hout Bay 7872; pre-school educational.

**Educum Publishers:** POB 3068, Halfway House 1685.

**Eksamenhulp:** POB 55555, Arcadia 0007.

**Fisichem Publishers:** POB 6052, Stellenbosch 7600.

**Flesch, W. J., & Partners:** 4 Gordon St, Gardens, POB 3473, Cape Town 8000; tel. (21) 4617472; fax (21) 4613758; f. 1954; Prin. Officer S. Flesch.

**Fortress Publishers:** POB 679, Germiston 1400; tel. (11) 8276205; fax (11) 8738370; f. 1973; military history, biographies, financial; Man. Dir I. Uys.

**T. W. Griggs & Co:** 341 West St, Durban 4001; tel. (31) 3048571; Africana.

**F.J.N. Harman Publishers:** Menlo Park; tel. (12) 469575; f. 1981; educational; Man. Dir F. J. N. Harman.

**Harper Collins Publishers (SA) (Pty) Ltd:** POB 33977, Jeppestown 2043; tel. (11) 6222900; fax (11) 6223553; f. 1970; book distributors; Man. Dir M. J. Edwards.

**HAUM:** Prima Park 4 and 6, cnr Klosser and King Edward Rds, Porow 7500; tel. (21) 926123; f. 1894; Man. C. J. Hage. Subsidiaries include:

**De Jager-HAUM Publishers:** POB 629, Pretoria 0001; tel. (12) 3228474; fax (12) 3222424; f. 1974; general, medical and university textbooks, school textbooks and books in African languages; Man. Dir C. Richter.

**Juventus Publishers:** POB 629, Pretoria 0001; tel. (12) 3220806; fax (12) 3222424; f. 1980; juvenile, educational; Man. Marietjie Coetzee.

**University Publishers & Booksellers (Pty) Ltd:** POB 29, Stellenbosch 7599; tel. (21) 8870337; fax (21) 8832975; f. 1947; educational; Man. Dir B. B. Liebenberg.

**Heinemann Publishers SA (Pty) Ltd:** POB 371, Isando 1600; educational; tel. (11) 9741190; fax (11) 9744311; Man. Dir K. Kroeger.

**Home Economics Publishers:** POB 7091, Stellenbosch 7600; 74630.

**Human and Rousseau (Pty) Ltd:** POB 5050, Cape Town 8000; tel. (21) 251280; fax (21) 4192619; f. 1959; English, Afrikaans, Xhosa and Zulu; general adult and children's trade books; Gen. Man. C. T. Breytenbach.

**Incipit Publishers:** POB 28754, Sunnyside, Pretoria 0132; tel. and fax (12) 463802; f. 1987; music; Man. Marianne Feenstra.

**Inter-Kampus Publications:** Baillie Park; study aids.

**Juta and Co Ltd:** POB 14373, Kenwyn 7790; tel. (11) 7975101; fax (11) 7615010; f. 1853; legal, technical, academic, educational; Man. Dir J. E. Duncan.

**Klipbok Publishers:** POB 170, Durbanville 7550.

**Knowledge Unlimited (Pty) Ltd:** POB 781337; Sandton 2146; tel. (11) 6521800; fax (11) 3142984; children's fiction, educational; Man. Dir Mike Jacklin.

**Konsensus Publishers:** Orion St 213, Waterkloof 0180.

**Lemur Books (Pty) Ltd:** POB 1645, Alberton 1450; tel. (11) 9072029; fax (11) 8690890; military, political, history, hunting, general; Man. Dir F. Lategan.

**Lexicon Publishers (Pty) Ltd:** POB 371, Isando 1600, tel. (11) 9741181; fax (11) 9744311; education and general; Man. Dir J. Savage.

**Lovedale Press:** Private Bag X1346, Alice; tel. (0404) 31135; fax (0404) 31871; f. 1841; Gen. Man. Rev. B. B. Finca.

**Lux Verbi:** POB 1822, Cape Town 8000; tel. (21) 253505; telex 526922; fax (21) 4191865; Exec. Chair. W. J. van Zijl.

**Macdonald Purnell (Pty) Ltd:** POB 51401, Randburg 2125; tel. (11) 7875830; telex 424985; South African flora, fauna, geography and history; Man. Dir E. Anderson.

**Marler Publications (Pty) Ltd:** POB 27815, Sunnyside, Pretoria 0132; tel. (12) 573770; f. 1987; educational; Man. Dir C. J. Muller.

**Maskew Miller Longman (Pty) Ltd:** Howard Drive, Pinelands 7405, POB 396, Cape Town 8000; tel. (21) 5317750; telex 5726053; fax (21) 5314049; f. 1983; educational and general; Chief Exec. M. A. Peacock.

**Methodist Publishing House:** POB 708, Cape Town 8000; tel. (21) 4618214; fax (21) 4618249; religious and theology; Gen. Man. D. R. Leverton.

**Nasionale Boekhandel:** POB 122, Parow 7500; tel. (21) 5911131; telex 526951; fiction, general, educational, academic; English, Afrikaans and several African languages; Man. Dir P. J. Botma.

**Nasou:** POB 5197, Cape Town 8000; tel. (21) 4063313; fax (21) 4062922; educational; Gen. Man. L. I. Naudé.

**N.G. Kerkboekhandel (Pty) Ltd:** POB 3068, Halfway House 1685; tel. (21) 3153647; fax (21) 3152757; f. 1947; Sen. Publr Neels du Plooy.

**Oudiovista Productions (Pty) Ltd:** Parow; tel. (21) 5911131; telex 527751; Man. Dir P. J. Botma.

**Owen Burgess Publications (Pty) Ltd:** Hillcrest.

**Oxford University Press:** Harrington House, 37 Barrack St, POB 1141, Cape Town 8000; tel. (21) 457266; fax (21) 457265; f. 1914; Man. Dir Kate McCallum.

**Perskor Publishers:** POB 3068, Halfway House 1685 tel. (11) 3153647; fax (11) 3152757; f. 1940; general and educational; Sr Gen. Man. W. F. Struik.

**David Philip Publishers (Pty) Ltd:** POB 23408, Claremont 7735; tel. (21) 644136; fax (21) 643358; f. 1971; general, academic, literature, reference, fiction, juvenile; Dirs D. H. Philip, M. Philip, R. Martin, B. Impey.

**Pretoria Boekhandel:** POB 23334, Innesdale, Pretoria 0031; tel. (12) 761531; f. 1971; Prin. Officer L. S. van der Walt.

**Random House SA (Pty) Ltd:** POB 337, Bergvlei, Sandton 2012; tel. (11) 7862983; telex 423981; fax (11) 8875077; f. 1966 as Century Hutchinson (SA); Man. Dir S. Johnson.

**Ravan Press (Pty) Ltd:** POB 145, Randburg 2125; tel. (11) 7897636; fax (11) 7897653; f. 1972; political, sociological, fiction, business studies, gender, history, autobiography, biography, educational and children's; Man. Dir Glenn Moss.

**Saayman and Weber (Pty) Ltd:** POB 673, Cape Town 8000; f. 1980.

**Sasavona Publishers and Booksellers:** Private Bag X8, Braamfontein 2017; tel. (11) 4032502; Northern Sotho, Tshwa, Tsonga, Tswana, Venda and Zulu; Man. A. E. Kaltenrieder.

**Shuter and Shooter (Pty) Ltd:** 199 Pietermaritz St, Pietermaritzburg 3201; POB 109, Pietermaritzburg 3200; tel. (331) 946830; fax (331) 427419; f. 1921; educational, general and African languages; Man. Dir D. F. Ryder.

# SOUTH AFRICA

**The Struik Publishing Group (Pty) Ltd:** POB 1144, Cape Town 8000; tel. (21) 4624360; fax (21) 4619378; Dirs G. Struik, A. D. L. Cruzen, M. C. H. James, C. M. Hanley, N. D. Pryke, J. D. Wilkins, J. L. Schoeman, A. S. Verschoyle.

**Study Aids Ltd:** 13 Darrock Ave, Albemarle Park, Germiston 1401; study aids.

**Hans Strydom Publishers:** Private Bag 10, Mellville 2109.

**Sunray Publishers:** 96 Queen St, Durban 4001; tel. (31) 3052543.

**Tafelberg Publishers Ltd:** 28 Wale St, POB 879, Cape Town 8000; tel. (21) 241320; fax (21) 242510; f. 1950; children's, young persons', fiction and non-fiction, arts and crafts; Gen. Man. J. J. Labuschagne.

**Thomson Publications:** Johannesburg 2123; tel. (11) 7892144; telex 422125; fax (11) 7893196; f. 1948; trade and technical; Man. Dir Joe M. Brady.

**UCCSA Publications Dept:** POB 31083, Braamfontein 2017; tel. (11) 8360065; f. 1946; Gen. Man. W. Westenborg.

**University of Natal Press:** Private Bag X01, Scottsville 3209; tel. (331) 2605225; fax (331) 2605599; Publisher M. P. Moberly.

**University of South Africa:** POB 392, Pretoria 0001; tel. (12) 4293111; telex 350068; fax (12) 4293221; Registrar M. H. Stockhoff.

**University Publishers and Booksellers (Pty) Ltd:** POB 29, Stellenbosch 7599; tel. (21) 8870337; fax (21) 8832975; educational; Man. Dir B. B. Liebenberg.

**Van der Walt and Son, J. P. (Pty) Ltd:** POB 123, Pretoria 0001; tel. (12) 3252100; fax (12) 3255498; f. 1947; general; Man. Dir C. J. Steenkamp.

**Chris van Rensburg Publications (Pty) Ltd:** POB 29159, Mellville 2109; tel. (31) 7264350; yearbooks, general; Man. Dir. C. C. van Rensburg.

**Van Schaik, J. L. Publishers:** 1064 Arcadia St, Hatfield 0083; tel. (11) 3422765; fax (11) 433563; f. 1914; reference, general, educational; English, Afrikaans and vernaculars; Gen. Man. G. Louw.

**Via Afrika Ltd:** POB 151, Pretoria 0001; tel. (12) 3421964; fax (12) 3421964; f. 1970; educational, technical and general; Gen. Man. D. Schroeder.

**Waterkant Publishers:** POB 4539, Cape Town 8000; tel. (21) 215540; fax (21) 4191865; f. 1980; Exec. Chair. W. J. van Zijl.

**Witwatersrand University Press:** Private Bag 3, Witwatersrand 2050; tel. (11) 4845910; fax (11) 4845971; f. 1923; academic; Head Eve Horwitz.

### PUBLISHERS' ASSOCIATION

**Publishers' Association of South Africa:** Private Bag 91932, Auckland Park 2092; tel. (11) 7267470; fax (11) 4823409; f. 1992; represents publrs in dealing with govt depts, local authorities and other institutions; Chair. M. A. Peacock; Sec. K. McCallum.

## Radio and Television

In 1992 there were some 2.6m. television licenses issued and (according to UNESCO) 12.1m. radio receivers in use.

In December 1993 legislation providing for the establishment of an Independent Broadcasting Authority was adopted, effectively ending state control of radio and television. All stations were required to reapply for licences.

**South African Broadcasting Corporation (SABC):** Private Bag X1, Auckland Park 2006; tel. (11) 7149111; telex 424116; fax (11) 7143106; f. 1936; statutory body; revenue from licences and advertising; operates 22 internal radio services broadcasting in 11 languages, one external radio service broadcasting in seven languages, and three TV channels broadcasting in seven languages; Chair. of Bd Dr Ivy Matsepe-Casaburri; CEO Zwelakhe Sisulu.

### RADIO

**SABC-Radio:** Private Bag X1, Auckland Park 2006; tel. (11) 7149111; telex 424116; fax (11) 7143106.

*Domestic Services*

Radio South Africa; Afrikaans Stereo; Radio 5; Radio 2000; Highveld Stereo; Good Hope Stereo; Radio Kontrei; RPN Stereo; Jacaranda Stereo; Radio Algoa (regional services); Radio Lotus (Indian service in English); Radio Metro (African service in English); Radio Lebowa; Radio Ndebele; Radio Sesotho; Setswana Stereo; Radio Swazi; Radio Tsonga; Radio Xhosa; Radio Zulu.

*External Service*

**Channel Africa Radio:** POB 91313, Auckland Park 2006; tel. (11) 7142551; fax (11) 7142546; f. 1966; SABC's external service; broadcasts 217 hours per week in Chichewa, English, French, Lozi, Portuguese, Swahili and Tsonga to Africa; Exec. Editor Lionel Williams.

### TELEVISION

**SABC-Television:** Private Bag X41, Auckland Park 2006; tel. (11) 7149111; telex 424116; fax (11) 7145055; transmissions began in 1976; operates television services in seven languages over three channels; English and Afrikaans programmes on Channel one (TV1); Channel two (CCV-TV) broadcasts in English, Northern and Southern Sotho, Tswana, Xhosa and Zulu; Channel three (NNTV) broadcasts documentaries, educational programmes and sport.

## Finance

(cap. = capital; res = reserves; dep. = deposits; m. = million; brs = branches; amounts in rand)

### BANKING

#### Central Bank

**South African Reserve Bank:** 370 Church St, POB 427, Pretoria 0001; tel. (12) 3133911; telex 322411; fax (12) 3133197; f. 1921; cap. and res 132m., dep. 3,702m. (March 1994); Gov. Dr Christian Stals; Sr Dep. Gov. Dr B. P. Groenewald; 8 brs.

#### Commercial Banks

**ABSA Bank Ltd:** Sanlam Centre, 31st Floor, 208 Jeppe St, Johannesburg 2001; tel. (11) 3303349; telex 489399; fax (11) 3333941; f. 1990; cap. and res 4,119.2m., dep. 73,456.7m. (March 1994); Chair. David C. Brink.

**African Bank Ltd:** 56 Marshall St, POB 61352, Johannesburg 2107; tel. (11) 8362331; telex 483089; fax (11) 8382845; f. 1975 to operate in the fmr 'homelands'; cap. and res 14,360.7m., dep. 416,238.1m. (March 1993); Chair. Dr S. M. Motsuenyane; 1 br.

**Bank of Lisbon International Ltd:** Bank of Lisbon Bldg, 1st Floor, 37 Sauer St, Johannesburg 2001; POB 11343, Johannesburg 2000; tel. (11) 8322477; telex 485076; fax (11) 8384816; f. 1965; cap. and res 26.9m., dep. 610.6m. (Sept. 1991); Chair. C. S. Margo; Man. Dir Dr Durval Marques; 28 brs.

**Boland Bank Ltd:** 333 Main St, POB 4, Paarl 7622; tel. (2211) 72911; telex 522136; fax (2211) 72811; f. 1900; cap. and res 263.5m., dep. 3,573.7m. (March 1994); Chair. C. H. Wreie; CEO M. S. du P. Le Roux; 98 brs.

**First National Bank of Southern Africa Ltd:** 1 First Place, Bankcity, Johannesburg 2001; POB 1153, Johannesburg 2000; tel. (11) 3712111; telex 486939; fax (11) 3712402; f. 1971 as Barclays National Bank; cap. and res 3,129.9m., dep. 50,123.6m. (Sept. 1993); Chair. B. E. Hersov; Man. Dir B. J. Swart; 1,360 brs.

**French Bank of Southern Africa Ltd:** 4 Ferreira St, Marshalltown, Johannesburg 2001; POB 61523, Marshalltown 2107; tel. (11) 8322433; telex 482896; fax (11) 8360625; f. 1949; subsidiary of Banque Indosuez (France); cap. and res 97.6m., dep. 1,968.8m. (Dec. 1993); Chair. P. Brault; Man. Dir B. Destoppeleire; 3 brs.

**Nedcor Bank:** 100 Main St, Johannesburg 2001, POB 1144, Johannesburg 2000; tel. (11) 6307111; telex 482765; fax (11) 6302465; f. 1888; cap. and res 2,340m., dep. 43,289m. (Sept. 1994); Chair. Dr J. B. Maree; CEO R. C. M. Laubscher; 317 brs.

**The New Republic Bank Ltd:** NRB House, 110 Field St, Durban 4001; tel. (31) 3047544; telex 625354; fax (31) 3053547; f. 1971; cap. 89m., dep. 901m. (1993); Man. Dir M. Mia; 13 brs.

**The South African Bank of Athens Ltd:** Bank of Athens Bldg, 116 Marshall St, POB 7781, Johannesburg 2001; tel. (11) 8321211; telex 486976; fax (11) 8381001; f. 1947; subsidiary of National Bank of Greece; cap. and res 23.3m., dep. 365m. (Dec. 1993); Chair. G. Mirkos; Man. Dir A. Stringos; 13 brs.

**The Standard Bank of South Africa Ltd:** Standard Bank Centre, 5 Simmonds St, Johannesburg 2001, POB 7725, Johannesburg 2000; tel. (11) 6369111; telex 484191; fax (11) 6364207; f. 1862; cap. and res 2,739.9m., dep. 48,221.3m. (Dec. 1992); Chair. Dr Conrad B. Strauss; Man. Dir M. H. Vosloo; 854 brs.

#### Merchant Banks

**ABSA Merchant Bank Ltd:** Carlton Centre, 40th Floor, Commissioner St, Johannesburg 2001; tel. (11) 3315741; telex 486965; fax (11) 3311040; f. 1977 as Volkskas Merchant Bank Ltd, name changed 1991; cap. and res 96.9m., dep. 699m. (March 1991); Man. Dir J. J. Brown; 1 br.

**Central Merchant Bank Ltd** (Sentrale Aksepbank Bpk): Sanlamsentrum, Jeppe St, POB 2683, Johannesburg 2001; tel. (11) 2289111; telex 487310; f. 1969; cap. and res 59m., dep. 348.1m.

SOUTH AFRICA                                                                                                                                                    *Directory*

(June 1986); Chair. Dr F. J. DU PLESSIS; Man. Dir D. H. ANDERSON; 4 brs.

**Corporate Merchant Bank Ltd:** Johannesburg; tel. (11) 3320111; telex 485143; fax (11) 237802; f. 1969; cap. and res 31.5m., dep. 393.4m. (March 1989); Exec. Chair. L. P. KORSTEN.

**FirstCorp Merchant Bank Ltd:** 4 First Place, Johannesburg 2001; POB 9773, Johannesburg 2000; tel. (11) 3718336; telex 487092; fax (11) 3718686; f. 1987; cap. and res 131.5m., dep. 2,300.2m. (Sept. 1992); Chair. B. J. SWART; CEO D. M. LAWRENCE.

**Mercabank Ltd:** Sanlam Center, Jeppe St, POB 1281, Johannesburg 2001; tel. (11) 3373353; telex 483007; f. 1970; cap. and res 40m., dep. 159.1m. (June 1986); Chair. C. G. ERASMUS; Man. Dir R. E. SHERRELL.

**Rand Merchant Bank Ltd:** 25 Fredman Drive, Sandton 2199, POB 786273, Sandton 2146; tel. (11) 8833622; telex 427602; fax (11) 7838651; cap. and res 303.8m., dep. 2,677.6m. (June 1993); Chair. GERRIT FERREIRA; Man. Dir P. K. HARRIS; 2 brs.

**Standard Merchant Bank Ltd:** 78 Fox St, 16th Floor, Johannesburg 2001, POB 61344, Marshalltown 2107; tel. (11) 6369115; telex 487629; fax (11) 6362371; f. 1964; cap. and res 234.9m., dep. 3,555.5m. (Dec. 1993); Chair. D. R. GEERINGH; Man. Dir J. H. MAREE.

### Savings Banks

**British Kaffrarian Savings Bank Society:** POB 1432, King William's Town 5600; tel. (433) 21478; telex 5250117; f. 1860; dep. 28.8m.; CEO D. E. DAUBERMANN.

**Pretoria Bank Ltd:** Woltemade Bldg, 118 Paul Kruger St, POB 310, Pretoria; cap. 601,250; dep. 7.6m.; Chair. M. D. MARAIS; Gen. Man. I. W. FERREIRA.

**Staalwerkerssparbank:** 417 Church St, POB 1747, Pretoria; cap. 240,630; dep. 2.5m.; Chair. and Man. Dir L. J. VAN DEN BERG.

### Investment Bank

**Investec Bank Ltd:** 55 Fox St, POB 11177, Johannesburg 2000; tel. (11) 4982000; telex 488381; fax (11) 4982100; cap. and res 971.4m., dep. 4,172m. (March 1994); Chair. B. KARDOL; Man. Dir S. KOSEFF; 4 brs.

### Development Bank

**Development Bank of Southern Africa:** POB 1234, Halfway House 1685; tel. (11) 3133911; telex 425546; fax (11) 3133086; f. 1983; CEO A. B. LA GRANGE.

### Discount Houses

**Discount House Merchant Bank Ltd:** 66 Marshall St, Johannesburg 2001; POB 61574, Marshalltown 2107; tel. (11) 8367451; fax (11) 8369636; f. 1957; cap. 18.8m.; Exec. Chair. C. J. H. DUNN; Man. Dir M. R. THOMPSON.

**Interbank Ltd:** 108 Fox St, POB 6035, Johannesburg; tel. (11) 8344831; fax (11) 8345357; f. 1971; cap. 15.5m., dep. 564m. (1990); Chair. A. KELLY; Man. Dir M. SWART.

**The National Discount House of South Africa Ltd:** Loveday House, 1st Floor, 15 Loveday St, Johannesburg; tel. (11) 8323151; telex 485081; f. 1961; auth. cap. 10m., dep. 357.1m. (1987); Chair. M. MACDONALD; Man. Dir G. G. LUND.

### Bankers' Association

**Institute of Bankers in South Africa:** POB 61420, Marshalltown 2107; tel. (11) 8321371; fax (11) 8346592; f. 1904; 15,000 mems; CEO JALDA HODGES.

## STOCK EXCHANGE

**Johannesburg Stock Exchange:** POB 1174, Johannesburg 2000; tel. (11) 8336580; telex 487663; f. 1887; Exec. Pres. R. A. NORTON.

## INSURANCE

**ACA Insurers Ltd:** 35 Symons Rd, Auckland Park; tel. (11) 7268900; telex 4896262; f. 1948; Man. Dir L. G. Y. NEMORIN.

**Aegis Insurance Co Ltd:** Aegis Insurance House, 91 Commissioner St, Johannesburg; tel. (11) 8367621; telex 487512; fax (11) 8384559; Man. Dir B. H. SEACH.

**African Mutual Trust & Assurance Co Ltd:** 34 Church St, POB 27, Malmesbury; f. 1900; Chief Gen. Man. R. A. L. CUTHBERT.

**Allianz Insurance Ltd:** Allianz House, 13 Fraser St, Johannesburg 2001; POB 62228, Marshalltown 2107; tel. (11) 4970400; telex 487103; fax (11) 8383827; Man. Dir Dr A. GOSSNER.

**Anglo American Life Assurance Co Ltd:** Life Centre, 45 Commissioner St, POB 6946, Johannesburg 2000; telex 487780; Exec. Chair. Dr Z. J. DE BEER; Man. Dir Dr M. BERNSTEIN.

**Commercial Union of South Africa Ltd:** Commercial Union House, 26 Loveday St, POB 3555, Johannesburg 2000; tel. (11) 4911911; fax (11) 8382600; f. 1964; Chair. A. M. D. GNODDE; Man. Dir J. A. KINVIG.

**Credit Guarantee Insurance Corpn of Africa Ltd:** 31 Dover St, POB 125, Randburg 2125; tel. (11) 8897000; telex 420508; fax (11) 8861027; f. 1956; Man. Dir C. T. L. LEISEWITZ.

**Fedlife Assurance Ltd:** Fedlife House, 1 de Villiers St, POB 666, Johannesburg 2000; tel. (11) 3326000; fax (11) 4921102; f. 1944; Chair. J. A. BARROW; Man. Dir A. I. BASSERABIE.

**General Accident Insurance Co of South Africa Ltd:** POB 32424, Braamfontein 2017; tel. (11) 4086000; telex 9450092; fax (11) 3397732; Man. Dir I. L. MAXWELL.

**I. G. I. Insurance Co Ltd:** 162 Anderson St, POB 8199, Johannesburg 2000; tel. (11) 3351911; telex 485393; fax (11) 290491; f. 1954; Chair. I. M. A. LEWIS; Man. Dir P. S. DENNISS.

**Liberty Life Association of Africa Ltd:** Liberty Life Centre, 1 Ameshoff St, Johannesburg 2001; POB 10499, Johannesburg 2000; tel. (11) 4082100; telex 422530; fax (11) 4033171; f. 1958; Chair. DONALD GORDON; Man. Dir A. ROMANIS.

**Metropolitan Life Ltd:** 7 Coen Steytler Avenue, Foreshore, POB 93, Cape Town 8001; POB 93, Cape Town 8000; tel. (21) 241134; telex 550120; fax (21) 253315; Chair. Dr NTHATO MOTLANA; Man. Dir M. L. SMITH.

**Momentum Life Assurers Ltd:** Momentum Park, 267B West Ave, Verwoerdburgstad 0157, POB 7400 Hennopsmeer 0046; tel. (11) 6718911; fax (11) 6636336; f. 1967; Man. Dir J. D. KRIGE.

**Mutual & Federal Insurance Co Ltd:** Mutual Federal Centre, 28th Floor, 69 President St, Johannesburg 2001; tel. (11) 3749111; telex 487641; f. 1970; Chair. G. A. MACMILLAN; Man. Dir K. T. M. SAGGERS.

**Old Mutual** (South African Mutual Life Assurance Society): Mutualpark, Jan Smuts Drive, POB 66, Cape Town 8001; tel. (21) 5099111; telex 527201; fax (21) 5094444; f. 1845; Chair. and Man. Dir M. J. LEVETT.

**President Insurance Co Ltd:** Rentmeester Park, 74 Watermeyer St, Val de Grace 0184; tel. (12) 868100; telex 323281; Man. Dir J. K. WASSERFALL.

**Protea Assurance Co Ltd:** Protea Assurance Bldg, Greenmarket Sq., POB 646, Cape Town 8000; tel. (21) 4887911; telex 9550038; fax (21) 4887110; Man. Dir A. L. TAINTON.

**The Rand Mutual Assurance Co Ltd:** POB 61413, Marshalltown 2107; tel. (11) 8388211; telex 487057; fax (11) 4921253; f. 1894; Chair. P.J. EUSTACE; Gen. Man. A. B. MAY.

**Santam Ltd:** Santam Bldg, Burg St, Cape Town 8001, POB 653, Cape Town 8000; tel. (21) 242254; telex 527822; fax (21) 244572; f. 1918; Chair. Dr C. H. J. VAN ASWEGEN; Man. Dir J. J. GELDENHUYS.

**South African Eagle Insurance Co Ltd:** Eagle House, 70 Fox St, Johannesburg 2001; POB 61489, Marshalltown 2107; tel. (11) 3709111; telex 485370; fax (11) 8365541; CEO P. T. MARTIN.

**South African National Life Assurance Co (SANLAM):** Strand Rd, Bellville, POB 1, Sanlamhof 7532; tel. (11) 9479111; telex 520191; fax (11) 9478066; f. 1918; Chair. M. H. DALING; Man. Dir DESMOND SMITH.

**South African Trade Union Assurance Society Ltd:** Traduna Centre, 118 Jorissen St, Braamfontein, Johannesburg 2001; f. 1941; Chair. E. VAN TONDER; Gen. Man. A. SUMNER.

**The Southern Life Association Ltd:** Great Westerford, Main Rd, Rondebosch, Cape Town 7700; tel. (21) 6580911; telex 527621; fax (21) 6891323; f. 1891; Chair. T. N. CHAPMAN.

**Standard General Insurance Co Ltd:** Standard General House, 12 Harrison St, POB 4352, Johannesburg 2000; tel. (11) 8362723; telex 487320; fax (11) 8344935; f. 1943; Man. Dir Dr R. GRANDI.

**Swiss South African Reinsurance Co Ltd:** Swiss Park, 10 Queens Rd, Parktown, POB 7049, Johannesburg 2000; tel. (11) 4895600; telex 427556; fax (11) 6432929; f. 1950; Chair. and Man. Dir L. KEEL.

**UBS Insurance Co Ltd:** United Bldgs, 6th Floor, cnr Fox and Eloff Sts, Johannesburg; Chair. P. W. SCEALES; Gen. Man. J. L. S. HEFER.

**Westchester Insurance Co (Pty) Ltd:** Mobil Court, POB 747, Cape Town 8000; tel. (21) 4034000.

### Association

**The South African Insurance Asscn:** POB 2163, Johannesburg 2000; tel. (11) 8384881; fax (11) 8386140; f. 1973; asscn of short-term insurers; CEO B. SCOTT.

# Trade and Industry

## CHAMBER OF COMMERCE

**South African Chamber of Business (SACOB):** POB 91267, Auckland Park 2006; tel. (11) 4822524; fax (11) 450093; f. 1990

SOUTH AFRICA

by merger of Asscn of Chambers of Commerce and Industry and South African Federated Chamber of Industries; 102 chambers of commerce and industry are mems; Pres. LES WEIL; Dir-Gen. R. W. K. PARSONS.

## DEVELOPMENT ORGANIZATIONS

**Industrial Development Corporation of South Africa Ltd:** POB 784055, Sandton 2146; tel. (11) 8831600; telex 427174; fax (11) 8831655; f. 1940; Chair. C. H. WIESE; Man. Dir W. C. VAN DER MERWE.

**The Independent Development Trust:** 129 Bree St, Cape Town 8001, POB 16114, Vlaeberg 8018; tel. (21) 238030; fax (21) 234512; f. 1990; finances, health and rural devt, housing and urban devt, micro-enterprise, education, school and clinic-building projects; Chair. Dr MAMPHELA RAMPHELE.

**National Productivity Institute:** POB 3971, Pretoria 0001; tel. (12) 3411470; telex 320485; fax (12) 441866; f. 1968; Exec. Dir Dr J. H. VISSER.

## CHAMBERS OF INDUSTRIES

**Cape Chamber of Commerce and Industry:** Cape Chamber House, 19 Louis Gradner St, Foreshore, Cape Town 8001; tel. (21) 4184300; fax (21) 4181800; f. 1994; Exec. Dir ALAN LIGHTON; 3,800 mems.

**Durban Regional Chamber of Business:** POB 1506, Durban 4000; tel. (31) 3013692; fax (31) 3045255; Dir G. W. TYLER; 8,500 mems.

**Johannesburg Chamber of Commerce and Industry:** JCC House, Empire Road, Milpark, Johannesburg 2001; tel. (11) 7265300; telex 425594; fax (11) 7268421; CEO M. DE JAGER; 5,000 mems.

**Midland Chamber of Industries:** MCI Bldg, 22 Grahamstown Rd, Port Elizabeth 6001; tel. (41) 544430; telex 242815; fax (41) 571851; f. 1917; Dir W. B. WASMÜTH; 502 mems.

**Northern Transvaal Chamber of Industries:** Showground Office, Soutter St, Pretoria 0001; tel. (12) 3271487; telex 320245; fax (12) 3271501; f. 1929; Exec. Dir J. G. TOERIEN; 350 mems (secondary industries).

**Orange Free State Chamber of Business:** Kellner Heights, 37 Kellner St, POB 87, Bloemfontein 9300; tel. (51) 473368; fax (51) 475064; Dir J. J. VAN RENSBURG.

**Pietermaritzburg Chamber of Industries:** POB 637, Pietermaritzburg 3200; tel. (331) 452747; fax (331) 944151; f. 1910; Dir R. J. ALLEN; 300 mems.

**Wesvaal Chamber of Business:** POB 7, Klerksdorp 2570; tel. (18) 4627401; fax (18) 4627402; Pres. J. LENNOX.

## INDUSTRIAL ORGANIZATIONS

**Armaments Corporation of SA Ltd (ARMSCOR):** Private Bag X337, Pretoria 0001; tel. (12) 4281911; telex 320217; fax (12) 4285635; Exec. Chair. J. G. J. VAN VUUREN.

**Building Industries Federation (South Africa):** POB 1619, Halfway House 1685; tel. (11) 3151010; fax (11) 3151644; f. 1904; 5,300 mems.

**Chamber of Mines of South Africa:** 5 Hollard St, POB 61809, Marshalltown 2107; tel. (11) 4987100; fax (11) 8341884; f. 1889; Pres. A. H. MUNRO.

**Clothing Federation of South Africa:** 42 Van der Linde St, Bedfordview 2008, POB 75755, Gardenview 2047; tel. (11) 6228125; fax (11) 6228316; f. 1945; Dir H. W. VAN ZYL.

**ESKOM:** POB 1091, Johannesburg 2000; tel. (11) 8008111; telex 424481; f. 1923; electricity supply; Chair. Dr JOHN B. MAREE.

**FOSKOR Ltd:** POB 1, Phalaborwa 1390; tel. (1524) 892911; telex 361012; fax (1524) 5531; Man. Dir D. R. V ORSTER.

**Grain Milling Federation:** Johannesburg; f. 1944; Sec. J. BARENDSE.

**Industrial Rubber Manufacturers' Asscn of South Africa:** POB 91267, Auckland Park 2006; tel. (11) 4822524; fax (11) 7261344; f. 1978; Chair. Dr D. DUNCAN.

**Master Diamond Cutters' Asscn of South Africa:** S.A. Diamond Centre, Suite 511, 5th Floor, 240 Commissioner St, Johannesburg 2001; tel. (11) 3348890; fax (11) 3341748; f. 1928; 76 mems.

**Motor Industries' Federation:** POB 2940, Randburg 2125; tel. (11) 7892542; fax (11) 7894525; f. 1910; Dir W. FOURIE; 7,800 mems.

**National Asscn of Automobile Manufacturers of South Africa:** Nedbank Plaza, 1st Floor, cnr Church and Beatrix Sts, Pretoria 0002; POB 40611, Arcadia 0007; tel. (12) 3232003; fax (12) 3263232; f. 1935; Dir N. M. W. VERMEULEN.

**National Chamber of Milling, Inc:** Braamfontein; tel. (11) 4033739; f. 1936; Dir Dr J. B. DE SWARDT.

**National Textile Manufacturers' Asscn:** POB 1506, Durban 4000; tel. (31) 3013692; fax (31) 3045255; f. 1947; Sec. PETER McGREGOR; 9 mems.

*Directory*

**Plastics Federation of South Africa:** 18 Plantation Rd, Unit 2, Eastleigh, POB 1128, Edenvale 1610; tel. (11) 6097956; fax (11) 4522643; f. 1979; Exec. Dir W. NAUDÉ; 3 mems.

**Printing Industries Federation of South Africa:** Printech Ave, Laser Park, POB 1084, Honeydew 2040; tel. (11) 7943810; fax (11) 7943964; f. 1916; Chief Exec. C. W. J. SYKES.

**SOEKOR (Pty) Ltd:** POB 307, Parow 7500; tel. (21) 9383911; fax (21) 9383144; f. 1965 as Southern Oil Exploration Corpn; responsible for all offshore oil and gas prospecting in South Africa; CEO M. J. HEÜSER.

**South African Brewing Industry Employers' Asscn:** Private Bag 34, Auckland Park 2006; tel. (11) 7265300; telex 425594; f. 1927; Sec. L. I. GOLDSTONE; 2 mems.

**South African Cement Producers' Asscn:** Private Bag X11, Halfway House 1685; tel. (11) 3150300; fax (11) 3150054.

**South African Dairy Foundation:** POB 72300, Lynnwood Ridge 0040; tel. (2712) 3485345; telex 322022; fax (2712) 3486284; f. 1980; Sec. F. J. NELL; 59 mems.

**South African Federation of Civil Engineering Contractors:** POB 644, Bedfordview 2008; tel. (11) 4551700; fax (11) 4551153; f. 1939; Exec. Dir Dr W. G. VANCE; 230 mems.

**South African Fruit and Vegetable Canners' Asscn (Pty) Ltd:** Canning Fruit Board Bldg, 258 Main St, POB 6172, Paarl 7622; tel. (2211) 611308; fax (2211) 25930; f. 1953; Sec. T. R. M. MALONE; 12 mems.

**South African Inshore Fishing Industry Asscn (Pty) Ltd:** POB 2066, Cape Town 8000; tel. (21) 251500; telex 527259; f. 1953; Chair. W. A. LEWIS; Man. S. J. MALHERBE; 4 mems.

**South African Lumber Millers' Asscn:** Private Bag 686, Isando 1600; tel. (11) 9741061; fax (11) 9749779; f. 1941; Exec. Dir J. H. MORTIMER; 88 mems.

**South African Oil Expressers' Asscn:** Cereal Centre, 6th Floor, 11 Leyds St, Braamfontein 2017; tel. (11) 7251280; telex 422526; f. 1937; Sec. Dr R. DU TOIT; 14 mems.

**South African Paint Manufacturers' Asscn:** 39 Field St, Durban 4001, POB 1506, Durban 4000; tel. (31) 3013692; fax (31) 3045255.

**South African Petroleum Industry Association (SAPIA):** Cape Town; Dir. COLIN MCCLELLAN.

**South African Sugar Asscn:** Norwich Life House, 6 Durban Club Place, Durban 4001; POB 507, Durban 4000; tel. (31) 3056161; telex 622215; fax (31) 3044939; Exec. Dir MICHAEL J. A. MATHEWS.

**South African Wool Board:** POB 2191, Port Elizabeth 6056; tel. (41) 544301; telex 242329; fax (41) 546760; f. 1946; 12 mems: nine appointed by wool-growers and three by the Minister of Agriculture; Chair. H. F. PRINSLOO; CEO Dr J. W. GIESELBACH.

**South African Wool Textile Council:** POB 2201, North End, Port Elizabeth 6056; tel. (41) 545252; fax (41) 545629; f. 1953; Sec. C. THOMAS.

**Steel and Engineering Industries Federation of South Africa (SEIFSA):** POB 1338, Johannesburg 2000; tel. (11) 8336033; fax (11) 8381522; f. 1943; Exec. Dir. B. ANGUS; 3,000 mems; includes the following asscns:

**Electrical Engineering and Allied Industries Asscn:** POB 1338, Johannesburg 2000; tel. (11) 8336033; fax (11) 8381522; f. 1936; 315 mems.

**Iron and Steel Producers' Asscn of South Africa:** POB 1338, Johannesburg 2000; tel. (11) 8336033; fax (11) 8381522; 11 mems.

**Light Engineering Industries Asscn of South Africa:** POB 1338, Johannesburg 2000; tel. (11) 8336033; fax (11) 8381522; f. 1936; 342 mems.

**Non-ferrous Metal Industries Asscn of South Africa:** Metal Industries House, 42 Anderson St, POB 1338, Johannesburg 2000; tel. (11) 8336033; fax (11) 8381522; f. 1943; 26 mems.

**Radio and Television Manufacturers' Asscn of South Africa:** POB 1338, Johannesburg 2000; tel. (11) 8336033; fax (11) 8381522; 14 mems.

**Radio, Appliance and Television Asscn of South Africa:** Metal Industries House, 42 Anderson St, POB 1338, Johannesburg 2000; tel. (11) 8336033; fax (11) 8381522; f. 1942; 48 mems.

**Sheet Metal Industries Asscn of South Africa:** POB 1338, Johannesburg 2000; tel. (11) 8336033; fax (11) 8381522; f. 1948; 165 mems.

**South African Asscn of Shipbuilders and Repairers:** POB 1338, Johannesburg 2000; tel. (11) 8336033; fax (11) 8381522; 11 mems.

**South African Engineers' and Founders' Asscn:** POB 1338, Johannesburg 2000; tel. (11) 8336033; fax (11) 8381522; f. 1945; 768 mems.

SOUTH AFRICA
*Directory*

**Sugar Manufacturing and Refining Employers' Asscn:** 11th Floor, 6 Durban Club Place, POB 2278, Durban 4001; tel. (31) 3043551; fax (31) 3074241; f. 1947; Chair. L. B. DE WET.

**Tobacco Employers' Organisation:** PB 34, Auckland Park 2006; tel. (11) 7265300; telex 425594; f. 1941; Sec. L. I. GOLDSTONE; 3 mems.

### TRADE ORGANIZATION

**South African Foreign Trade Organization (SAFTO):** POB 782706, Sandton 2146; tel. (11) 8833737; telex 424111; fax (11) 8836569; f. 1963; Chair. R. A. NORTON; CEO J. L. VAN ZYL; 1,500 mems.

### TRADE UNIONS

In 1989 the number of registered unions totalled 212, with a membership of 2,130,117, representing about 17% of the economically active population. In addition there were an estimated 85 unregistered unions in 1989, with a membership of about 550,000.

#### Trade Union Federations

**Congress of South African Trade Unions (COSATU):** POB 1019, Johannesburg 2000; tel. (11) 3394911; fax (11) 3394060; f. 1985; multiracial fed. of 16 trade unions representing c. 1.4m. mems; Gen. Sec. SAM SHILOWA.

Principal affiliates include:

**Chemical Workers' Industrial Union:** POB 18349, Dalbridge 4014; tel. (11) 259510; fax (11) 256680; Pres. D. GUMEDE; Gen. Sec. R. CROMPTON.

**Construction and Allied Workers' Union:** POB 1962, Johannesburg 2000; tel. (11) 230544; Pres. D. NGCOBO; Gen. Sec. L. MADUMA.

**Food and Allied Workers' Union:** POB 234, Salt River 7925; tel. (21) 6379040; fax (21) 6383761; Pres. ERNEST THERON; Gen. Sec. M. GXANYANA.

**Health and Allied Workers' Union:** POB 47011, Greyville 4023; tel. (11) 3063993; Gen. Sec. S. NGCOBO.

**National Education, Health and Allied Workers' Union:** POB 7549, Johannesburg 2000; tel. (11) 299665; Pres. R. MKHIZE; Gen. Sec. S. NJIKELANA.

**National Union of Metalworkers of South Africa (NUMSA):** POB 260483, Excom 2023; tel. (11) 8322031; fax (11) 8384092; Pres. M. TOM; Gen. Sec. ENOCH GODONGWANA; 240,000 mems (1994).

**National Union of Mineworkers:** POB 2424, Johannesburg 2000; tel. (11) 8337012; Pres. JAMES MOTLATSI; Gen. Sec. MARCEL GOLDING; 350,000 mems.

**Paper, Printing, Wood and Allied Workers' Union:** POB 3528, Johannesburg 2000; tel. (11) 8344661; Pres. M. NDOU; Gen. Sec. S. KUBHEKA.

**Post and Telecommunications Workers' Association:** POB 260100, Excom 2023; tel. (11) 234351; Pres. K. MOSUNKULU; Gen. Sec. V. A. KHUMALO.

**South African Clothing and Textile Workers' Union:** POB 18359, Dolbridge 4014; tel. (11) 3011391; fax (11) 3017050; Pres. A. NTULI; Gen. Sec. J. COPALYN; 185,000 mems.

**South African Railways and Harbours Workers' Union:** POB 8059, Johannesburg 2000; tel. (11) 8343251; fax (11) 8344664; Pres. J. LANGA; Gen. Sec. M. SEBEKOANE.

**Transport and General Workers' Union:** POB 9451, Johannesburg 2000; tel. (11) 3319321; fax (11) 3315418; Pres. A. NDLOVU; Gen. Sec. R. HOWARD.

**National Council of Trade Unions (NACTU):** POB 10928, Johannesburg 2000; tel. (11) 3368031; fax (11) 3337625; f. 1986; black fed. of 22 trade unions representing c. 450,000 mems (1987); Pres. JAMES MDLALOSE; Gen. Sec. CUNNINGHAM MCGUKAMU.

Principal affiliates include:

**Building, Construction and Allied Workers' Union:** POB 96, Johannesburg 2000; tel. (11) 236311; Pres. J. SEISA; Gen. Sec. V. THUSI.

**Food Beverage Workers' Union of South Africa:** POB 4871, Johannesburg 2000; tel. (11) 299527; Pres. M. L. KWELEMTINI; Gen. Sec. L. SIKHAKHANE.

**Hotel, Liquor and Catering Trade Employees' Union:** POB 1409, Johannesburg 2000; tel. (11) 234039; Pres. E. NKOSI (acting); Gen. Sec. K. KEELE (acting).

**Metal and Electrical Workers' Union of South Africa:** POB 3669, Johannesburg 2000; tel. (11) 8369051; fax (11) 8369002; f. 1989; Pres. RAYMOND KHOZA; Gen. Sec. TOMMY OLIPHANT; 30,000 mems (1991).

**National Union of Farm Workers:** POB 10928, Johannesburg 2000; tel. (11) 233054; fax (11) 237625; Pres. E. MUSEKWA; Gen. Sec. T. MOLETSANE.

**National Union of Public Service Workers:** POB 10928, Johannesburg 2000; tel. (11) 232812; Pres. K. NTHUTE; Gen. Sec. S. RADEBE.

**South African Chemical Workers' Union:** POB 236, Johannesburg 2000; tel. (11) 288907; Pres. W. THUTHANI; Gen. Sec. O. H. NDABA.

**Steel, Engineering and Allied Workers' Union of South Africa:** POB 4283, Johannesburg 2001; tel. (11) 294867; fax (11) 294869; Pres. G. MABIDIKAMA; Gen. Sec. N. RAMAEMA.

**Transport and Allied Workers' Union of South Africa:** POB 4469, Johannesburg 2000; Pres. A. MAHLATJIE; Gen. Sec. M. RAMELA.

**SAAWU Federation of Unions:** POB 10419, Marine Parade 4050; tel. (11) 3019127; 19 mems; Pres. M. MABOSO; Gen. Sec. S. K. B. KIKINE.

**South African Confederation of Labour:** POB 19299, Pretoria West 0117; tel. (12) 793271; 7 mems; Pres. I. J. ELS; Sec. L. N. CELLIERS.

#### Unaffiliated Trade Union

**United Workers' Union of South Africa:** f. 1986; controlled by the Inkatha Freedom Party.

## Transport

Most of South Africa's railway network and the harbours and airways are administered by the state-owned Transnet Ltd. There are no navigable rivers. Private bus services are regulated to complement the railways.

**Transnet Ltd:** POB 72501, Parkview 2122; tel. (11) 4887000; fax (11) 4887010; Man. Dir Dr ANTON T. MOOLMAN.

### RAILWAYS

With the exception of commuter services, the South African railways system is operated by Spoornet Ltd (the rail division of Transnet). The network comprised 21,303 route-km in 1993. Transnet Ltd also operates an extensive network of road transport services, which serves primarily to develop rural areas, but also acts as feeder to the railways. The electrified lines totalled 18,455 track-km in 1989. Rail services between South Africa and Mozambique were resumed in April 1994.

**Spoornet Ltd:** Paul Kruger Bdg, 30 Wolmarans St, Johannesburg 2001; tel. (11) 7738785; telex 424087; fax (11) 7742665; CEO A. S. LE ROUX.

### ROADS

In 1991 the total road network was 182,329 km, excluding roads in the former 'independent homelands'. This total comprised 2,040 km of motorways, 53,395 km of main roads and 126,894 km of secondary roads. Some 30.4% of the network was paved.

**South African Roads Board:** Dept of Transport, Private Bag X193, Pretoria 0001; responsible for location, planning, design, construction and maintenance of national roads.

### SHIPPING

The principal harbours are at Cape Town, Port Elizabeth, East London and Durban. The deep-water port at Richards Bay has been extended and its facilities upgraded. Saldanha Bay is a major bulk-handling port.

More than 30 shipping lines serve South African ports. At mid-1992 South Africa's merchant fleet had a total displacement of 336,000 grt.

**Chief Directorate of Shipping:** Dept of Transport, Private Bag X193, Pretoria 0001; tel. (12) 2909111; telex 321195; fax (12) 2902040; advises the Govt on matters connected with sea transport to, from or between South Africa's ports, incl. safety at sea, and prevention of pollution by oil.

### CIVIL AVIATION

Civil aviation is controlled by the Minister of Transport. The Air Services Licensing Council and the International Air Services Council are responsible for licensing and control of domestic and international air services. Executive and administrative work of the Air Council is carried out by the Department of Transport.

**South African Airways (SAA):** Airways Towers, POB 7778, Johannesburg 2000; tel. (11) 7739433; telex 425020; fax (11) 7739858; f. 1934; state-owned; internal passenger services linking all the principal towns; international services to Africa, Europe, N and S America and Asia; Chief Exec. MIKE MYBURGH.

**COMAIR (Commercial Airways (Pty) Ltd):** POB 7015, Bonaero Park 1622; tel. (11) 9210111; telex 746738; fax (11) 9733913;

# SOUTH AFRICA

f. 1946; scheduled domestic, regional and international services; Chair. D. NOVICK; Man. Dir P. VAN HOVEN.

**Airlink Airline:** POB 7529, Bonaero Park 1622; tel. (11) 9732941; fax (11) 9732501; f. 1992; internal scheduled and chartered flights; Man. Dirs RODGER FOSTER and BARRIE WEBB.

**Protea Airways (Pty) Ltd:** Bonaero Drive, Bonaero Park 1620, POB 7049, Bonaero Park 1622; tel. (11) 3951806; fax (11) 3951337; charter services; Chair. and Man. Dir J. T. MORRISON.

**Safair Freighters (Pty) Ltd:** POB 938, Kempton Park 1620; tel. 9731921; telex 742242; fax 9734620; f. 1969; subsidiary of South African Marine Corpn; scheduled internal cargo services and charter international cargo flights; Chair. A. Z. FARR; Man. Dir Dr P. J. VAN ASWEGEN.

**Air Cape (Pty) Ltd:** POB D.F. Malan Airport, Cape Town 7525; tel. (21) 9340344; telex 520246; fax (21) 9348379; scheduled internal passenger services and charters, engineering services and aerial surveys; Chair. Dr P. VAN ASWEGEN; Gen. Man. G. A. NORTJE.

**Flitestar Ltd:** POB 839, Cape Town 8000; tel. (21) 9340344; telex 520246; fax (21) 9340344; scheduled passenger services; fmrly Trek Airways; Chair. G. A. MACMILLAN; Man. Dir J. V. BLAKE.

# Tourism

Tourism is an important part of South Africa's economy. The chief attractions for visitors are the climate, scenery and wildlife reserves. Tourist receipts provided an estimated US $934m. in foreign exchange in 1990. In 1993 3,369,762 tourists visited South Africa.

**South African Tourism Board:** 442 Rigel Ave South, Erasmusrand 0181, Private Bag X164, Pretoria 0001; tel. (12) 3470600; fax (12) 454889; f. 1947; 13 overseas brs; Exec. Dir MARUSO MSIMANG.

# SPAIN

## Introductory Survey

**Location, Climate, Language, Religion, Flag, Capital**

The Kingdom of Spain, in south-western Europe, forms more than four-fifths of the Iberian peninsula. The country also includes the Balearic Islands in the Mediterranean Sea, the Canary Islands in the Atlantic Ocean and a few small enclaves in Morocco. Mainland Spain is bounded to the north by France and to the west by Portugal. To the east is the Mediterranean Sea, and Morocco lies 30 km to the south. The climate is less temperate than in most of western Europe, with hot summers and, in the hilly interior, cold winters. The principal language is Castilian Spanish. Catalan is widely spoken in the north-east, Basque in the north and Galician in the north-west. The overwhelming majority of the population are Roman Catholics, but the 1978 Constitution laid down that Spain had no official state religion. The national flag (proportions 3 by 2) carries three horizontal stripes, of red, yellow (half the depth) and red. The state flag carries, in addition, the national coat of arms. The capital is Madrid.

**Recent History**

After winning the civil war of 1936–39, the Nationalist forces, led by Gen. Francisco Franco y Bahamonde, established an authoritarian rule which provided peace and stability, while restricting individual liberties and severely repressing challenges to its power. In 1942 Gen. Franco revived the traditional legislative assembly, the Cortes ('Courts'), with limited powers. After keeping Spain neutral in the Second World War, Gen. Franco announced in 1947 that the monarchy (abolished in 1931) would be restored after his death or retirement. In 1967, in the first elections since the civil war, a portion of the Cortes was directly elected under a limited franchise. In July 1969 Gen. Franco nominated Prince Juan Carlos de Borbón (grandson of the last reigning monarch, King Alfonso XIII) as his successor, and in June 1973 relinquished the post of President of the Council of Ministers to Admiral Luis Carrero Blanco, who was killed in December. Responsibility for the assassination was claimed by Euskadi ta Askatasuna (ETA), the Basque separatist organization. Carlos Arias Navarro became Prime Minister in January 1974.

Gen. Franco died in November 1975. He was succeeded as Head of State by King Juan Carlos, and in December a more liberal Council of Ministers was formed. In 1976 restrictions on political activity were lifted, but the slow progress of the reforms resulted in widespread demonstrations. In July Arias Navarro resigned at the King's request, and was replaced by Adolfo Suárez González. The introduction of democratic government then proceeded rapidly. Political reforms included the establishment of an elected bicameral legislature. Most of the numerous *de facto* political parties were able to take part in the general elections for the Cortes, held in June 1977. An overall majority was won by the Unión de Centro Democrático (UCD), a coalition party headed by the Prime Minister. In December 1978 a new Constitution was endorsed by referendum and ratified by the King. It confirmed Spain as a parliamentary monarchy, with freedom for political parties, and guaranteed the right of Spain's 'nationalities and regions' to autonomy.

General elections were held in March 1979, resulting in little change in the distribution of seats in the Cortes, although there was stronger support for the regionalist parties. The new Government was again headed by Adolfo Suárez. Basque and Catalan autonomous parliaments were established in March 1980 and, in both elections, the UCD was heavily defeated by the moderate regionalist parties. Confidence in Suárez diminished and in January 1981, as a result of growing opposition from right-wing factions within the UCD, he unexpectedly resigned. Leopoldo Calvo Sotelo, hitherto the Deputy Prime Minister, succeeded him.

In February 1981 a group of armed Civil Guards, led by Lt-Col Antonio Tejero, stormed into the Cortes, taking hostage 350 Deputies. The military commander of Valencia, Lt-Gen. Jaime Milans del Bosch, declared a state of emergency in that region and sent tanks on to the streets of the city of Valencia. King Juan Carlos acted swiftly to secure the loyalty of other military commanders, and by the following morning had been able to persuade Lt-Gen. Milans del Bosch himself to stand down. Lt-Col Tejero surrendered, and the Deputies were released unharmed. More than 30 military officers were subsequently brought to trial, and both Lt-Col Tejero and Lt-Gen. Milans received heavy prison sentences. In mid-1990, however, Lt-Gen. Milans was released. In September 1993 the Government refused to grant a pardon to Lt-Col Tejero.

Immediately after the attempted coup, Calvo Sotelo formed a new Council of Ministers, resisting pressure to establish a coalition government. The Prime Minister addressed various contentious issues during his term of office, including his decision to take Spain into NATO. At the election for the first Galician Parliament, held in October 1981, the Alianza Popular (CAP) won two seats more than the UCD.

The ministerial reshuffle of December 1981 reflected the growing tensions within the ruling party, and failed to stem desertions from the UCD. The overwhelming Socialist victory at the election for the Parliament of Andalucía in May 1982 was a grave set-back for the central Government. Defections from the UCD continued, the most damaging being the departure of Adolfo Suárez, who, following the replacement of Calvo Sotelo as party leader by Landelino Lavilla Alsina, left in July to found a rival party, the Centro Democrático y Social (CDS). By August the UCD no longer commanded a workable majority, and early general elections were called. In October, however, shortly before the elections, a right-wing plot to stage a pre-emptive military coup was uncovered. Four colonels were arrested (three of whom were subsequently sentenced to prison terms), and Lt-Gen. Milans del Bosch was also implicated. The elections resulted in a decisive victory for the Partido Socialista Obrero Español (PSOE—Socialist Workers' Party), led by Felipe González Márquez, who formed a new Council of Ministers in December 1982.

One of the most serious problems facing the new Government was the continuing tension in the Basque region (see below). The Government's proposals for the rationalization of Spain's industry and bureaucracy, instigated in 1983, met with strong opposition from the trade unions. In July 1985 Felipe González carried out his first major government reorganization. Following the massive public demonstration against a new education law (imposing stricter controls over privately-run schools in receipt of state subsidies) in November 1984, there were further protests against the Government's restructuring policies and against the lack of new jobs in 1985. In June hundreds of thousands of workers, motivated by the Unión General de Trabajadores (UGT—the socialist trade union) and supported by the Confederación Sindical de Comisiones Obreras (CCOO—the left-wing trade union), took to the streets to protest against proposed reforms in the social security system and consequent reductions in pension rights. There was also a good response to the CCOO's 24-hour general strike call. In November there were large-scale demonstrations against Spain's continued membership of NATO. In March 1986, the long-awaited referendum on the question of Spain's membership of NATO was held. Contrary to expectations, the Spanish people voted to remain within the alliance, following the Prime Minister's reversal on the issue and an extensive pro-NATO campaign by the Government.

In April 1986 the Cortes were dismissed in preparation for an early general election in June. The PSOE was returned to power, winning 184 of the 350 seats in the Congress of Deputies (18 fewer than at the 1982 election), while the conservative Coalición Popular (CP), which incorporated the AP, the Partido Demócrata Popular (subsequently Democracia Cristiana) and the Partido Liberal, won 105 seats. The new Council of Ministers, appointed in late July and again led by Felipe González, contained four new members.

Following its defeat in the general election of mid-1986, the CP fell into disarray and in December Manuel Fraga, leader of the AP, the principal component of the conservative grouping, resigned. In March 1987 a motion of censure against the

Government, presented by the AP under its new leader, Antonio Hernández Mancha, was defeated. Industrial unrest continued, however; frequent strikes against the Government's economic policies, notably its commitment to pay restraint, took place, the public transport sector being particularly badly affected. At Reinosa (Cantabria) steelworkers protesting against the Government's rationalization programme were repeatedly involved in violent clashes with the police.

In June 1987 the results of the elections for the European Parliament, for 13 of the 17 regional parliaments and for the municipal governments confirmed the continuing decline in support for the PSOE. The AP also sustained losses, while the centre-left CDS was able to strengthen its position. The growing rift between the Prime Minister and the UGT, the socialist trade union, became increasingly evident during 1987, and in October Nicolás Redondo, the UGT leader, and a union colleague resigned from their seats as PSOE deputies in the Cortes, in protest against the Government's economic policies. The UGT and the left-wing CCOO then combined forces to organize a new campaign of protests against the Government, which continued throughout 1988. Intermittent strike action by teachers, in support of their demands for higher salaries, lasted for several months. Protests by civil servants, miners, farmers and workers in the transport, health and industrial sectors also took place. In northern Spain in May redundant shipyard workers became involved in violent confrontations with the security forces. In July 1988 Felipe González announced an extensive reshuffle of the Council of Ministers. In December the country was paralysed by a one-day general strike (the first since 1934), which was supported by almost 8m. workers. Massive protest marches against the Government's economic policies took place throughout Spain. In April 1989 Madrid was brought to a halt by strikers demanding pay increases of up to 8%, action by transport workers again being particularly effective. Similar strikes elsewhere in Spain followed.

In January 1989 Manuel Fraga returned to the leadership of the AP, which was relaunched as the Partido Popular (PP) and was subsequently joined by Democracia Cristiana and the Partido Liberal. At elections to the European Parliament in June 1989, the PSOE maintained its support, losing only one seat, whereas the PP lost two seats. In September the dissolution of the Cortes was announced, in preparation for the holding of a general election eight months earlier than necessary. The unity of the PSOE was undermined by the establishment of a dissident faction and by the defection to the Izquierda Unida (IU, an alliance comprising the Partido Comunista de España (PCE) and other left-wing parties) of 100 PSOE members. Nevertheless, at the election, held on 29 October 1989, the PSOE was returned to power on a provisional basis, pending investigations into allegations of polling irregularities. After several months of controversy, the PSOE's final representation in the Congress of Deputies was reduced to 175 of the 350 seats, the PP holding 107 seats. The PSOE, however, was able to retain a majority by subsequently entering into a tactical alliance with the CDS, the Catalan Convergència i Unió (CiU) and the Partido Nacionalista Vasco (PNV—Basque Nationalist Party).

In early 1990 the Government faced a crisis following the revelation of a scandal involving Juan Guerra, the brother of the Deputy Prime Minister. It was alleged in a Madrid newspaper that Juan Guerra had made improper use of his political connections to further his business interests and, as a result, had amassed a considerable personal fortune. Alfonso Guerra denied any knowledge of his brother's business activities. Nevertheless, the opposition parties demanded that the Deputy Prime Minister resign. In March 1995, having appeared in court for the fifth time, Juan Guerra received an 18-month prison sentence for misuse of a government office building.

In April 1990 a new corruption scandal, this time involving the financing of the opposition PP, was revealed. Rosendo Naseiro, the party treasurer, was arrested in connection with allegations of bribery. A number of other party officials and businessmen were also detained. It was alleged that the PP had received funds from companies that were seeking planning permission or hoping to win municipal contracts. The allegations were substantiated by the publication of transcripts of recorded telephone conversations between PP officials. Furthermore, it was suggested that both José María Aznar, the new leader of the PP, and Manuel Fraga, his predecessor, had been aware of these illegal activities. The integrity of the PP, and indeed of other political parties, was therefore questioned. Many observers believed that parties were deriving a substantial portion of their income in this way. In December 1994, during the course of a congressional inquiry into the financing of political parties, Naseiro strenuously denied the allegations against him. Discrepancies in the PP's accounts, however, appeared to confirm suggestions that Fraga had received 363m. pesetas from Naseiro (to finance the former's Galician presidential campaign) of which only 199m. had been declared.

In January 1991, prior to the conclusion of a judicial inquiry into the affairs of his brother, Alfonso Guerra resigned as Deputy Prime Minister. He was replaced by Narcís Serra, hitherto Minister of Defence. An extensive government reorganization followed in March. Local elections were held in May, to coincide with elections to the regional parliaments. Although remaining the most widely-supported party, the PSOE lost control of several major cities. The CDS suffered heavy losses, as a result of which Adolfo Suárez, the party leader and former Prime Minister, resigned.

In June 1991 Carlos Navarro, a senior PSOE treasurer, was obliged to resign, following the exposure of a scandal concerning alleged illicit donations to the ruling party. In January 1992, as labour unrest and protests against the Government's programme of industrial restructuring and attendant job losses continued, a fresh scandal arose, leading to the resignation of the Minister of Health and Consumer Affairs, Julián García Valverde. It was alleged that in 1990, while head of RENFE (the state railways organization), García Valverde had been responsible for fraudulent land purchases. Public concern at apparent widespread corruption increased further in February, when a new financial scandal was revealed, this time involving the Governor of the Central Bank, Mariano Rubio, who was accused of irregularities relating to his personal investments.

In May 1992 a half-day general strike in protest at proposed reductions in both rates of and rights to unemployment benefit attracted less support than anticipated. In November, however, more than 1m. public-sector workers took part in a strike against the 'freezing' of wages (educational establishments and postal services being the worst affected areas). In March 1993 a 'green march' by disgruntled farmers culminated in a demonstration by as many as 100,000 in Madrid and nationwide protests against the Government's agricultural policies.

In early 1993 the PSOE's reputation was further damaged by new revelations concerning the party's financing. Having refused to permit inspection of its accounts, in late 1992 the PSOE headquarters had been forcibly searched on the orders of the judge investigating the allegations. The 'Filesa case', as the principal scandal became known, was named after a bogus Barcelona holding company which, it was claimed, had been administered by senior PSOE officials, including Carlos Navarro. It was alleged that during 1989–91 illicit contributions, totalling an estimated 1,000m. pesetas, had been made to Filesa by both private companies and public corporations, in return for fictitious consultancy work. In May 1995 the Supreme Court concluded its inquiry into the affair. PSOE officials, business executives and bankers were among the 39 who were to be brought to trial on various charges.

In April 1993, therefore, with the repercussions of the Filesa scandal continuing and the Spanish economy in recession, the Prime Minister called an early general election. In May the ruling party's difficulties were compounded by fresh allegations of misconduct, this time concerning the funding in 1986 of the campaign for the referendum to remain in NATO and for the legislative elections of that year. At the general election of 6 June 1993 the PSOE failed to obtain an absolute majority in the Congress of Deputies, where its strength declined to 159 of the 350 seats. The PP increased its representation to 141 seats, while the IU won 18 seats, the CiU 17 and the PNV five. The CDS lost all its seats. The PSOE's negotiations with the CiU (which insisted upon greater control over taxes in return for support) and with the PNV failed to result in the conclusion of a formal coalition agreement. In July, therefore, Felipe González commenced his fourth term as Prime Minister, at the head of a minority administration. Although most senior ministers of the outgoing Government retained their portfolios, the incoming Council of Ministers incorporated several new members and included a number of independents.

The Prime Minister appealed for support for drastic measures to address Spain's serious economic crisis. In November 1993, however, thousands of demonstrators took to the streets to protest against the Government's economic policies. At the end of the month the Government failed in its protracted attempts to negotiate with the trade unions and employers' organizations a three-year 'social pact', relating to wage restraint and reforms of the labour market to permit greater flexibility. A 24-hour general strike, called in January 1994 to protest in particular against the Government's labour policy, attracted varying degrees of support. The controversial labour legislation, as amended to comply with CiU requests, was finally approved by the Congress of Deputies in late March. Earlier in the month an acrimonious dispute had arisen in the chamber, when the PP accused the ruling party of procedural misconduct during a vote on the issue of labour reform. At the PSOE Congress convened in the same month, the differences between Felipe González and Alfonso Guerra, who opposed the party's deviation from orthodox socialism, were acknowledged.

In November 1993, meanwhile, the Government suffered a further set-back upon the resignation of José Luis Corcuera as Minister of the Interior, owing to controversy resulting from his inclusion in a new security law of an article aimed at combating the increasing problem of drug abuse. The Constitutional Court subsequently ruled against the article, which had permitted the police forcibly to search homes without a warrant. Moreover, in the same month the Government was embarrassed by the discovery of an illegal telephone 'tapping' network, centred on a respected Barcelona newspaper. The existence of a complex espionage and extortion operation was subsequently revealed, in which former agents of the country's military intelligence service, CESID, were implicated. The opposition PP accused the Deputy Prime Minister, Narcís Serra, of ultimate responsibility for the affair.

In April 1994 the Government was discredited to an even greater extent, when details of further corruption scandals were disclosed. Fresh accusations of tax evasion and 'insider' stock trading were made against Mariano Rubio, the former Governor of the Central Bank. In May he was arrested and imprisoned, along with Manuel de la Concha, a former chairman of the Madrid stock exchange. The most serious political crisis to confront the ruling party to date, however, involved another government appointee, Luis Roldán, the former head of the paramilitary Civil Guard, who in April absconded while being investigated on charges of tax fraud and embezzlement of government funds. It was alleged that Roldán's substantial personal wealth was derived from the misappropriation of the Ministry of the Interior's covert-operations reserves (notably for the financing of GAL—see below). Antoni Asunción, appointed Minister of the Interior only in November 1993, was obliged to resign. In May 1994 the Minister of Agriculture resigned, following an admission of his failure, 10 years previously, to fulfil tax obligations on personal investments also handled by Manuel de la Concha. Furthermore, a number of former government ministers, including Carlos Solchaga, Minister of Finance during Mariano Rubio's tenure of office and a close associate of Felipe González, announced their intention to relinquish their seats in the Cortes. At elections to the European Parliament in June 1994, the PP won 28 of the country's 64 seats, while the PSOE's strength was reduced to 22 seats. At the concurrent election to the regional Parliament of Andalucía, a traditional socialist stronghold, the PSOE also suffered a set-back, losing its majority.

Following the failure in December 1993 of the Banco Español de Crédito (Banesto) and the revelation of its huge debts and of irregularities, in June 1994 Mario Conde, the bank's flamboyant former head, was accused of having conducted fraudulent operations. He was formally charged in November 1994, along with several other former executives of the bank. In December Conde and a close associate were imprisoned, but were released on bail in the following month. The inquiry into Banesto's operations continued in early 1995. Confidence in the country's financial system was further undermined by the arrest in October 1994 of Javier de la Rosa, the prominent Barcelona financier, pending the investigation of charges of fraud. He was released on bail in February 1995.

In November 1994 the Prime Minister was accused of personal involvement in yet another corruption scandal. It was alleged that his brother-in-law, Francisco Palomino, had sold a loss-making family business to a company that subsequently engaged him as a non-executive director, and which was then awarded a contract for the installation of electronic systems in the Prime Minister's nuclear-proof bunker. The PP's demand for a parliamentary commission of inquiry into the affair was rejected.

In February 1995 Luis Roldán was captured in Laos and promptly extradited via Thailand. The case against him, however, was jeopardized by the Laotian authorities' disclosure that Roldán's extradition documents had been forged. The Spanish Government was further embarrassed when, at a court hearing in March, Roldán accused the Deputy Prime Minister, among others, of corruption.

Meanwhile, in mid-1988 the Government had been embarrassed by suggestions that it had been involved in the establishment of the counter-terrorist grouping, Grupos Antiterroristas de Liberación (GAL), which had been formed in 1983 with the aim of combating ETA. It was alleged that members of the Basque police force had given support to these death squads, which were suspected of responsibility for the murders of numerous ETA members exiled in France. The Ministry of the Interior in Madrid was also implicated in the scandal. In July 1988 a senior police officer in Bilbao, José Amedo, and an accomplice, Michel Domínguez, were formally charged with organizing the groups of mercenaries. Their trial concluded in mid-1991, both defendants receiving long prison sentences. In July 1994, however, both Amedo and Domínguez were granted day release. In December, following further questioning of the pair and the reopening of the case, Julián Sancristóbal, a former director-general of state security in the Ministry of the Interior, was arrested on suspicion of financing and assisting GAL. The Prime Minister denied that the Government had been connected in any way with the so-called 'dirty war' against ETA, and dismissed opposition demands for the holding of an early general election. At the end of the month the Minister of Justice and the Interior was obliged to appear before a congressional commission of inquiry.

In January 1995 the investigating judge, Baltasar Garzón, ordered the arrest of the former personal assistant of Rafael Vera, ex-Secretary of State for Security, on suspicion of embezzlement. Vera himself was detained in the following month, accused of involvement in a kidnapping in 1983 and of misappropriation of public funds. Nevertheless, in January 1995, as the Prime Minister came under increasing pressure over the GAL affair, the leader of the CiU confirmed his party's support for the Government until the expiry of its mandate in 1997. The crisis deepened in March, however, following the identification by forensic scientists of the remains of José Antonio Lasa and José Ignacio Zabala, two ETA members apparently tortured before being murdered by GAL in 1983. An inquiry into their fate had been closed in 1988, ostensibly owing to lack of evidence. A new inquiry into their deaths was instigated. In April 1995, concluding that GAL had been established and financed by the Ministry of the Interior, Judge Baltasar Garzón indicted a total of 14 former officials, including Vera and Sancristóbal.

In late June 1995 Felipe González accepted the resignations of the Deputy Prime Minister and of the Minister of Defence, following the exposure of a scandal relating to the illegal recording by CESID of the private telephone conversations of numerous prominent figures. Public outrage was compounded by the revelation that the victims included King Juan Carlos. In the ensuing minor government reorganization, Narcís Serra was not replaced. Despite the gravity of the latest scandals and the PSOE's heavy losses at the municipal and regional elections of May (in which month the country's doctors embarked upon a strike in support of pay increases), the Prime Minister continued to reject demands for his resignation.

Autonomous parliaments had been established in the Basque Country and in Cataluña in 1980, elections being held in March. The parliaments of Galicia and Andalucía were established in October 1981 and May 1982 respectively, the remaining 13 being elected in May 1983. Elections to the Catalan Parliament took place in March 1992. The CiU, led by Jordi Pujol i Soley, was returned to office, as was the PP Government of Manuel Fraga at the Galician elections in October 1993. Following elections to the Basque Parliament in October 1994, José Antonio Ardanza of the moderate PNV continued as President of the regional Government, this time heading a tripartite coalition. In the same month the Cantabrian President, Juan Hormaechea, received a six-year prison sentence upon conviction on charges of corruption, and subsequently resigned. At elections for 13 of the 17 regional parliaments in May 1995, the PSOE suffered serious reverses. (See Legislative Assemblies of the Autonomous Regions, pp. 2805–2806, for current details of all Parliaments.)

In the Basque region, meanwhile, terrorist activity by the separatist organization, ETA, continued. Between 1978 and 1992 a total of 711 murders was attributed to the group. The indiscriminate bombing of a crowded Bilbao bank in February 1983 provoked public outrage. Following a bomb attack in Madrid in July 1986 on a bus transporting members of the paramilitary Civil Guard, as a result of which 13 guardsmen died, it was disclosed that the Basque regional Government had held secret discussions with ETA. The central Government maintained its offer of social reintegration, instigated in mid-1984, to former ETA members. The explosion in June 1987 of a bomb beneath a crowded Barcelona supermarket, which killed 21 shoppers and injured 45, was the most devastating ETA attack ever. For the first time, Herri Batasuna (HB), the political wing of ETA, condemned a terrorist attack. In August the central Government publicly acknowledged the existence of secret contacts with ETA leaders. In September, however, ETA rejected the Government's renewed offer of dialogue. Co-operation with the authorities of France and Algeria (where numerous ETA members were discovered to be living) was strengthened, and in October the French police arrested 67 Basque suspects. In December, however, five children were among the 12 killed in a bomb attack on the married quarters of a civil guard barracks in Zaragoza, which provoked a further public outcry. In January 1988, after protracted negotiations, six Basque parties (excluding HB) signed a pact rejecting terrorism as a means of determining the region's future.

In January 1989 a unilateral truce was declared by ETA, in an effort to reopen negotiations with the Government, broken off in early 1988. Secret discussions between representatives of the Government and of ETA commenced in Algeria. In April 1989, however, the peace talks broke down, and the Basque separatist organization resumed its campaign of violence, civilians, as well as members of the security forces, again being among the victims. In February 1990 a resolution declaring the right of the Basque people to self-determination was approved by the Basque Parliament.

In November 1989, during an attack on a group of Basque politicians in a Madrid restaurant, one HB deputy-elect, Josu Muguruza, was murdered and another seriously wounded. Responsibility for the shooting was claimed by GAL. In July 1990 seven suspects, including a policeman, were arrested in connection with the murder. In March 1993 one of the defendants received a prison sentence of 100 years.

The authorities continued to make arrests and to convict members of ETA. In April 1990 the detention near Sevilla of a French Basque, who was driving a car laden with explosives, enabled the security forces in south-western France to arrest a total of 17 ETA suspects. The separatist movement suffered a further set-back in September, when José Javier Zabaleta Elósegui ('Waldo'), alleged to be ETA's second-in-command, was arrested in France. The French authorities made further arrests, and in November more than 30 suspected members of ETA were detained in Spain.

Nevertheless, ETA's campaign of violence continued. In late 1990 a series of car bombings claimed several lives. In December, following the killing of six policemen in Sabadell in such an attack, the Prime Minister reaffirmed that the Government would not negotiate with the terrorist organization. In March 1991 Jesús Arkautz Arana ('Josu Mondragón'), another key ETA leader, was apprehended by the French security forces in Biarritz. ETA attacks continued throughout 1991, one of the most serious incidents occurring in May, when a car bomb planted at a civil guard barracks in Vic, near Barcelona, killed nine persons, including four children. On the following day two terrorist suspects, one of whom was believed to be the head of ETA's Barcelona unit, were shot dead during a raid by the civil guard. In December, following an apparent rift within ETA over the organization's future policy, the central Government denied that it was planning to resume direct negotiations with the terrorists. Attacks in early 1992 included the killing of four soldiers and one civilian in February, when a car bomb exploded next to a military vehicle in Madrid. The capture near Biarritz in March of Francisco Múgica Garmendia ('Pakito'), ETA's military leader, along with other senior commanders, represented a particular achievement in the Government's increasingly successful anti-terrorist campaign. Between mid-1992 and early 1993 more than 500 ETA suspects were arrested. In July 1992 ETA's offer of a truce (to coincide with the forthcoming Olympic Games in Barcelona), in return for the reopening of dialogue, was rebuffed by the Government, which continued to insist upon the group's permanent renunciation of violence. Hopes that ETA's campaign might be ended were raised in February 1993, upon the discovery of a major arsenal in France and the capture of Rafael Caride, thought to be ETA's operational head. In June, however, following the conclusion of the trial in Paris of six ETA members (including 'Pakito', who received a 10-year prison sentence), two car bombs exploded in Madrid, one of which killed five senior military officers and two others.

The Basque people's growing revulsion at ETA's actions, demonstrated by HB's loss of two of its four seats in the Congress of Deputies at the recent general election, was intensified by the abduction in July 1993 of industrialist Julio Iglesias Zamora, leading to a resurgence of the peace movement within the region. In August there were violent clashes in San Sebastián and Bilbao between peace demonstrators and supporters of ETA. In the same month the Basque and French authorities arrested eight ETA suspects believed to be part of an extortion network responsible for the attempted blackmailing of numerous Basque enterprises. It was reported that a new ETA leadership had been established in Paris. In September there was renewed unrest in the Basque region, following the deaths in custody of two ETA suspects and the disclosure of medical evidence suggesting violent treatment of a third detainee. Arrests in both Spain and France continued, and in mid-October the French police apprehended 15 suspected ETA members in one operation alone. Detentions in Spain of terrorist suspects totalled 127 in 1993. In late October Iglesias Zamora was released, reportedly upon the payment of a large ransom by his family. In the same month an air force general was murdered by ETA gunmen in Madrid, and in November a senior member of the Ertzaintza (Basque police force) was shot and later died.

In January 1994, in response to an offer to HB by Basque socialist leaders of negotiations in return for an ETA truce, the Minister of the Interior reiterated the central Government's commitment to its anti-terrorist policy and declined the Basque invitation. In March a total of 10 ETA units were believed to be operational in Spain. In the same month Henri Parot, a French member of ETA, was sentenced to a total of 1,802 years' imprisonment for the bomb attack on the Zaragoza barracks in 1987. Attacks by ETA continued in 1994. In February an army colonel was shot dead in Barcelona, as was a general in Madrid in June. In March, however, an ETA member was killed by his own bomb in Vitoria. Further car bombs claimed the lives of a Basque civil guard in Bilbao in April and of an army lieutenant in Madrid in May, in which month three people were also seriously injured in bomb attacks on Basque beaches. In May 1994 the newly-appointed Minister of Justice and the Interior declared that there would be no dialogue of any kind between the Government and ETA. In June 13 alleged ETA activists were detained in Guipúzcoa, and a large cache of weapons and explosives was subsequently discovered. In early July Pedro Picabea Ugalde ('Kepa'), believed to be responsible for 24 murders and for the abduction of Iglesias Zamora, was arrested by the French authorities. In the same month a car bomb in Madrid killed a senior army general and two others.

In late August 1994 the arrest in France of Idoia López Riaño ('Margarita' or 'La Tigresa'), accused of a total of 22 murders, coincided with the Spanish Government's success in achieving the extradition from Uruguay of three ETA members. (France approved the extradition of López Riaño in May 1995.) At the end of August the ETA leadership ordered its imprisoned members to embark upon a hunger strike, in an attempt to reassert its authority and to obstruct the process of 'reinsertion' into society. About 100 of the 600 ETA prisoners had expressed an interest in the Government's offer of reintegration, in return for the renunciation of violence. In September the all-party anti-terrorist pact was jeopardized by the PP's opposition to the Government's new partial-parole initiative for selected ETA prisoners. In the same month the discovery by the French police of an explosives factory near Bayonne led to six arrests. The brother of the imprisoned 'Pakito' was among those apprehended.

The results of the election to the Basque Parliament in October 1994 demonstrated the continuing decline in support for HB. ETA suffered a major reverse in mid-November, when several activists were arrested, including Félix Alberto López de la Calle ('Mobutu'), the terrorist group's alleged second-in-command, who was detained in the French city of Toulon, and José Luis Martín Carmona ('Koldo'), believed to be the head of the notorious 'Vizcaya cell', who was captured near Bilbao following a gun battle in which another ETA member was shot dead.

In January 1995, as attacks on police officers continued, Gregorio Ordóñez, a member of the Basque Parliament and the PP candidate for the mayoralty of San Sebastián at the forthcoming municipal elections, was shot dead, the first politician since 1992 to be murdered by ETA. Thousands of Basque citizens took to the streets of San Sebastián and Bilbao to protest against the assassination. In the following month ETA's attempts to reconstruct its Barcelona unit were thwarted by the arrest of several activists. In April in Madrid José María Aznar, leader of the opposition PP, narrowly survived a car-bomb attempt on his life, which injured 19 others. ETA warned that its campaign of violence would continue if the Basque country were not granted self-determination. In May a Basque businessman, José María Aldaya, was abducted by ETA. The French authorities assisted in an extensive operation to locate the kidnapped man. A demonstration in San Sebastián to demand his release attracted 70,000.

Catalan and Galician nationalist groups, meanwhile, had continued their terrorist activities, the Catalan organization, Terra Lliure, claiming its first victim in September 1987 and the Galician Exército Guerrilheiro do Pobo Galego Ceibe (EGPGC) carrying out its first murder, of a civil guard, in February 1989. In mid-1989 the Catalan Government was reported to be negotiating with Terra Lliure. In July 1991 the dissolution of Terra Lliure was announced, following the group's renunciation of the use of violence. In mid-1992, however, a dissident faction planted several bombs. The trial of 25 alleged members of Terra Lliure commenced in April 1995. In October 1990 a series of bombings occurred in Galicia. Three persons (including two suspected terrorists) were killed and 49 injured when a bomb exploded at a discothèque in Santiago de Compostela. The EGPGC's campaign continued intermittently. In September 1991 the alleged leader of the group was apprehended by the authorities and, upon the arrest in November of eight suspected EGPGC members, it was believed that the organization had been annihilated. In June 1994 six EGPGC activists received prison sentences, while two others were acquitted.

In January 1985 the police arrested 17 members of Grupos de Resistencia Antifascista Primero de Octubre—GRAPO, an extreme left-wing organization. Detainees included the alleged leader of GRAPO, Mercedes Padrós Corominas. After a period of inactivity, GRAPO resumed its guerrilla campaign in 1988. In December 1989 GRAPO announced an intensification of its activities, shooting dead two civil guards shortly afterwards. In January 1990, as a hunger strike by more than 50 GRAPO prisoners progressed, the Minister of Justice confirmed that the Government would not negotiate with the terrorist organization. In late March a doctor who had attended the hunger strikers was murdered. In September GRAPO claimed responsibility for various bomb attacks, targets including the stock exchange and the Ministry of Finance in Madrid and the PSC-PSOE headquarters in Barcelona. Two further bombs at government offices in Barcelona in November again caused extensive damage. GRAPO remained active in 1992, the bombing of a gas pipeline in Zaragoza in February being attributed to the grouping. Between its foundation in 1975 and 1992, GRAPO was believed to be responsible for a total of 70 murders. In December 1992 Laureano Ortega and two other leaders of the grouping were captured in Santander. In March 1993, however, three bombs planted by GRAPO exploded at offices in Madrid. In the following month, in Zaragoza, three GRAPO members were killed when the bomb that they were transporting exploded. Bomb attacks similar to those in March were carried out in May and in January 1994. At the end of the latter month four GRAPO suspects were arrested. Several members of GRAPO, including Laureano Ortega, received long prison sentences upon the conclusion of their trial in June 1995.

In foreign relations, in December 1988 Spain and the USA renewed their bilateral defence agreement, permitting the USA's use of bases in Spain, for a further eight years. Spain was admitted to Western European Union (see p. 221) in November 1988. Spanish ratification of the Maastricht Treaty on European Union (EU, see p. 149) was completed in November 1992. The dispute between Spain and the United Kingdom over the sovereignty of the neighbouring British dependent territory of Gibraltar remained unresolved. In May 1991 Felipe González was reported to have put forward proposals for nominal joint Spanish-British sovereignty of the territory, whereby Gibraltar would be granted effective autonomy. Negotiations were resumed in March 1993. Relations between Spain and the United Kingdom, already strained in early 1995 by British support for Canada in that country's dispute with the EU over North Atlantic fishing rights, deteriorated further in May upon Spain's announcement that, in protest at the apparent inadequacy of British efforts, it was to implement stricter border controls to combat the problem of drug and tobacco smuggling from Gibraltar. In November 1992 Spain dispatched a substantial contingent of troops to Bosnia, the first Spanish soldiers to serve in a UN peace-keeping operation. By May 1995, however, a total of 14 Spanish lives had been lost in the former Yugoslav republic. More than 1,400 Spanish troops remained in Bosnia in mid-1995.

### Government

Under the Constitution approved in 1978, Spain is an hereditary monarchy, with the King as Head of State. He appoints the President of the Government (Prime Minister) and, on the latter's recommendation, other members of the Council of Ministers. Legislation is initiated for discussion in the Cortes (national assembly) in Madrid, in the Parliaments of the Autonomous Communities, or by popular petition. The King's actions in state affairs must receive the prior approval of the Cortes, to which the Government is responsible. The Council of State is the supreme consultative organ and comprises 23 members.

Legislative power is vested in the Cortes Generales, comprising two Houses, elected by direct universal adult suffrage for four years (subject to dissolution). The Congress of Deputies has 350 members, elected by proportional representation, and the Senate has 208 directly-elected members, plus 47 regional representatives. A party can gain representation only if it obtains at least 3% of the votes.

Spain comprises 50 provinces, each with its own Council (Diputación Provincial) and Civil Governor.

The process of regional self-government was initiated in 1967. In October 1979 the statutes of the first of 17 Autonomous Communities were approved by referendum. The first Parliaments (Basque and Catalan) were elected in March 1980. The Galician Parliament was elected in October 1981, and that of Andalucía in May 1982. The remaining 13 were elected in May 1983, thus completing the process of devolution (see pp. 2805–2806). The regions possess varying degrees of autonomy. Each Parliament is elected for four years.

### Defence

Military service is compulsory in Spain and lasts for nine months. Exemption may be granted on family, medical and other grounds, and legislation relating to conscientious objection was approved in 1984. In June 1994 the total strength of the armed forces was 206,500 (including 133,200 conscripts), comprising: army 145,000, navy 33,100 (including 7,150 marines), and air force 28,400. The paramilitary Guardia Civil numbered 72,000. Spain became a member of NATO in May 1982 and of Western European Union in November 1988. In June 1994 the number of Spanish troops deployed in Bosnia, as part of UNPROFOR, totalled 1,415. The US military presence in Spain comprised a naval force of 4,100 and an air force of 400 in mid-1994. The 1995 defence budget was 866,100m. pesetas. Legislation to permit the entry of women to all sections of the armed forces took effect in early 1989.

### Economic Affairs

In 1993, according to estimates by the World Bank, Spain's gross national product (GNP), measured at average 1991–93 prices, was US $533,986m., equivalent to US $13,650 per head. During 1985–93, it was estimated, GNP per head increased, in real terms, at an average annual rate of 3.1%. Over the same period, the population increased by an annual average rate of 0.2%. Spain's gross domestic product (GDP) increased, in real terms, by an average annual rate of 3.2% in 1980–92.

According to official estimates, GDP declined by 1.1% in 1993, compared with the previous year, but grew by 2.0% in 1994.

Agriculture (including forestry and fishing) contributed an estimated 3.7% of GDP in 1993. In that year 10.1% of the labour force were employed in agriculture. The principal crops are barley, wheat, sugar beet, vegetables, citrus fruits, grapes and olives; wine and olive oil are important products. During 1985–93 agricultural production increased by an average annual rate of 1.0%. Production was affected by drought in 1993–95. The 1995 cereal harvest was expected to be the lowest for 25 years. The fishing industry is significant. The Spanish fishing fleet is one of the largest in the world, and has been involved in various international disputes.

Industry (including mining, manufacturing, utilities and construction) contributed an estimated 32.8% of GDP in 1993. In that year 30.7% of the labour force were employed in the sector. During 1980–86 industrial GDP increased by an average annual rate of 0.4%. Having risen by 5.2%, compared with the previous year, in 1989, production declined in 1990. Industrial output decreased by 1.1% in 1991, by 1.7% in 1992 and by 4.6% in 1993. In 1994, however, production rose by 7.1%.

The mining and quarrying industry provided 0.6% of GDP in 1990 and employed less than 0.5% of the labour force in 1993. Hard coal and brown coal are the principal minerals extracted. There are small reserves of crude petroleum. Some natural gas requirements are obtained from the Bay of Biscay, the remainder being imported by pipeline from Algeria.

Manufacturing contributed 17.4% of GDP in 1992. In 1993 the sector employed 20.3% of the labour force. Spain is one of the world's largest exporters of passenger cars. In 1994 production reached a record 1.8m. cars, of which 74% were exported. Other important industries are shipbuilding, chemicals, steel, textiles and footwear; some of these sectors underwent a process of rationalization in the 1980s. Investment is being made in new manufacturing industries, such as information technology and telecommunications equipment.

Energy is derived principally from petroleum, most of which is imported. In 1992 imports of mineral fuels and petroleum products accounted for 10.0% of total import costs. Nuclear energy supplied 36.0% of total electricity production in 1993.

The tourism industry makes an important contribution to the Spanish economy, receipts in 1994, when the number of tourist arrivals totalled 61.4m., reaching a record 2,867,800m. pesetas. Remittances from emigrants are also significant.

In 1993 Spain recorded a visible trade deficit of US $16,065m., and there was a deficit of US $6,258m. on the current account of the balance of payments. In terms of local currency, both deficits increased in 1994. In 1992 the principal sources of imports were Germany (16.4%) and France (16.0%), while the latter was the main export market, purchasing 20.2%, followed by Germany (15.7%). Italy, the United Kingdom and other EU countries, and the USA, are also important trading partners. The principal imports in 1992 were mineral fuels and petroleum products, machinery, electrical equipment, vehicles and chemical products. The main exports were motor cars, machinery, vegetable products and metals and their manufactures.

The austere 1995 draft budget envisaged a deficit of 3,168,900m. pesetas, equivalent to 4.6% of projected GDP. At June 1992 external debt totalled almost US $73,900m. In 1985–93 the annual rate of inflation averaged 6.1%; annual inflation declined from an average rate of 4.9% in 1993 to 4.3% in 1994. In the first quarter of 1995 the number of registered unemployed declined steadily, reaching 2.5m. in April, equivalent to 16.2% of the economically active population.

Spain became a member of the EU (see p. 143) in January 1986, and joined the exchange rate mechanism of the EMS (see p. 161) in June 1989. For 1994–99 the European Regional Development Fund committed ECU 15,944.2m. towards projects in Spain. Spain is also a member of the OECD (see p. 194).

Following a period of strong expansion, in 1993 Spain experienced its worst recession for 30 years. The economy recovered in 1994, however, and a growth rate of 3% was envisaged in 1995. Despite fears that the failure of a major bank in December 1993 and the political instability arising from a series of corruption scandals (see Recent History) would lead to a sharp decline, in 1994 direct foreign investment in Spain reached a record 2,347,806m. pesetas, an increase of 26.5% compared with the previous year, and continued to rise in 1995. Owing to the international currency crisis, the peseta was devalued by 7% in March 1995, the fourth realignment since September 1992. Interest rates were raised in attempts to support the currency and to curb inflationary pressure. In 1994 the Government was obliged to modify its 1992–96 convergence plan (to prepare Spain for European economic and monetary union, as agreed at the EU summit meeting in Maastricht in December 1991), which had involved drastic cuts in planned public spending, including decreases in subsidies to employers and reductions in rights to unemployment benefits. In February 1993 the Government had announced an emergency economic programme. Measures included the extension of temporary employment contracts and assistance to small and medium-sized companies. Nevertheless, in 1995 the level of unemployment (by far the highest rate in the EU), although declining, remained a serious economic and social problem. In southern Spain the worst drought of the century continued to cause concern in mid-1995.

### Social Welfare

National Insurance is compulsory for all employed or self-employed Spaniards. The National Insurance Scheme covers temporary incapacity to work, accident insurance, assistance to dependants, permanent incapacity, widows' pensions, old-age pensions and unemployment. Contributions are paid by the employer, the employee and the State. In 1989 maternity leave was extended to 16 weeks. In December 1992 Spain had 796 hospitals (of which 460 were private), with a total of 172,675 beds. There were 156,100 physicians and 11,808 stomatologists working in the country. The 1995 draft budget allocated 2,537,700m. pesetas (14.6% of total expenditure) to health and consumer affairs.

### Education

In 1992/93 more than 1.0m. children were attending pre-school institutions, while more than 2.5m. were enrolled at primary schools. Under reforms implemented in 1991, basic education is compulsory, and available free of charge, from the ages of six to 16 years. It comprises primary education, which begins at six years of age and lasts for six years, and secondary education, composed of two two-year cycles, followed between the ages of 12 and 16. Thereafter, students may take either a vocational training course, lasting one or two years, or the two-year Bachillerato course, in preparation for university entrance. Private schools, many of which are administered by the Roman Catholic Church, are responsible for the education of more than 30% of Spanish children. In autonomous communities the teaching of languages other than Spanish (such as Catalan) is regulated by decree.

Almost 1.2m. students were attending university in 1992/93. There are about 20 state universities, one open university (UNED, established in 1972), four polytechnics (in Madrid, Barcelona, Valencia and Las Palmas), two independent universities (in Bilbao and Pamplona), autonomous universities in Madrid and Barcelona, and eight technical universities. There are three cycles within university education. The first cycle lasts for three years and leads to the degree of Diplomatura. The second cycle lasts for two or three years and leads to the degree of Licenciatura. The degree of Doctor is awarded upon completion of the two-year third cycle and the writing of a thesis. Higher Technical studies in engineering and architecture are followed at Escuelas Técnicas de Grado Medio and Escuelas Técnicas de Grado Superior. The 1995 draft budget allocated 1,152,500m. pesetas (6.6% of total expenditure) to education and science.

### Public Holidays

**1995:** 1 January (New Year's Day), 6 January (Epiphany), 13 April (Maundy Thursday, except Barcelona), 14 April (Good Friday), 17 April (Easter Monday, Barcelona and Palma de Mallorca only), 1 May (St Joseph the Workman), 15 May (St Isidro, Madrid only), 15 June (Corpus Christi), 24 June (King Juan Carlos' Saint's Day), 25 July (St James of Compostela), 15 August (Assumption), 12 October (National Day, anniversary of the discovery of America), 1 November (All Saints' Day), 1 December (Constitution Day), 8 December (Immaculate Conception, except Barcelona), 25 December (Christmas Day), 26 December (Boxing Day, Barcelona and Palma de Mallorca only).

**1996:** 1 January (New Year's Day), 6 January (Epiphany), 4 April (Maundy Thursday, except Barcelona), 5 April (Good

# SPAIN

Friday), 8 April (Easter Monday, Barcelona and Palma de Mallorca only), 1 May (St Joseph the Workman), 15 May (St Isidro, Madrid only), 6 June (Corpus Christi), 24 June (King Juan Carlos' Saint's Day), 25 July (St James of Compostela), 15 August (Assumption), 12 October (National Day, anniversary of the discovery of America), 1 November (All Saints' Day), 2 December (Constitution Day), 8 December (Immaculate Conception, except Barcelona), 25 December (Christmas Day), 26 December (Boxing Day, Barcelona and Palma de Mallorca only).

In addition, various regional holidays are observed.

**Weights and Measures**

The metric system is in force.

# Statistical Survey

Source (unless otherwise stated): Instituto Nacional de Estadística, Paseo de la Castellana 183, 28046 Madrid; tel. (1) 5839100; telex 22224; fax (1) 5839486.

## Area and Population

### AREA, POPULATION AND DENSITY

| | |
|---|---:|
| Area (sq km) | |
| Land | 499,542 |
| Inland water | 5,240 |
| Total | 504,782* |
| Population (census results) | |
| 1 March 1981 | 37,682,355 |
| 1 March 1991 | |
| Males | 19,036,446 |
| Females | 19,835,822 |
| Total | 38,872,268 |
| Population (official estimates at mid-year) | |
| 1992 | 39,005,690 |
| 1993 | 39,082,551 |
| 1994 | 39,143,394 |
| Density (per sq km) at mid-1994 | 77.5 |

* 194,897 sq miles.

**PROVINCES** (population at 1 March 1991)

| | Area (sq km) | Population | Density (per sq km) |
|---|---:|---:|---:|
| Alava | 3,047 | 272,447 | 89.41 |
| Albacete | 14,862 | 342,677 | 23.06 |
| Alicante | 5,863 | 1,292,563 | 220.46 |
| Almería | 8,774 | 455,496 | 51.91 |
| Avila | 8,048 | 174,378 | 21.66 |
| Badajoz | 21,657 | 650,388 | 30.03 |
| Baleares (Balearic Is) | 5,014 | 709,138 | 141.43 |
| Barcelona | 7,733 | 4,654,407 | 601.89 |
| Burgos | 14,309 | 352,772 | 24.65 |
| Cáceres | 19,945 | 411,464 | 20.63 |
| Cádiz | 7,385 | 1,078,404 | 146.03 |
| Cantabria (Santander) | 5,289 | 527,326 | 99.70 |
| Castellón | 6,679 | 446,744 | 66.89 |
| Ciudad Real | 19,749 | 475,435 | 24.07 |
| Córdoba | 13,718 | 754,452 | 54.99 |
| La Coruña | 7,876 | 1,096,966 | 139.28 |
| Cuenca | 17,061 | 205,198 | 12.03 |
| Gerona (Girona) | 5,886 | 509,628 | 86.58 |
| Granada | 12,531 | 790,515 | 63.08 |
| Guadalajara | 12,190 | 145,593 | 11.94 |
| Guipúzcoa | 1,997 | 676,488 | 338.75 |
| Huelva | 10,085 | 443,476 | 43.97 |
| Huesca | 15,613 | 207,810 | 13.31 |
| Jaén | 13,498 | 637,633 | 47.24 |
| León | 15,468 | 525,896 | 33.99 |
| Lleida (Lérida) | 12,028 | 353,455 | 29.37 |
| Lugo | 9,803 | 384,365 | 39.21 |
| Madrid | 7,995 | 4,947,555 | 618.83 |
| Málaga | 7,276 | 1,160,843 | 159.54 |
| Murcia | 11,317 | 1,045,601 | 92.39 |
| Navarra | 10,421 | 519,277 | 49.83 |
| Orense | 7,278 | 353,491 | 48.57 |
| Oviedo (Principado de Asturias) | 10,565 | 1,093,937 | 103.54 |
| Palencia | 8,035 | 185,479 | 23.08 |
| Las Palmas | 4,072 | 767,969 | 188.59 |
| Pontevedra | 4,477 | 896,847 | 200.32 |
| La Rioja | 5,034 | 263,434 | 52.33 |
| Salamanca | 12,336 | 357,801 | 29.00 |
| Santa Cruz de Tenerife | 3,170 | 725,815 | 228.96 |
| Segovia | 6,949 | 147,188 | 21.18 |
| Sevilla | 14,001 | 1,619,703 | 115.68 |
| Soria | 10,287 | 94,537 | 9.19 |
| Tarragona | 6,283 | 542,004 | 86.27 |
| Teruel | 14,785 | 143,680 | 9.72 |
| Toledo | 15,368 | 489,543 | 31.85 |
| Valencia | 10,763 | 2,117,927 | 196.78 |
| Valladolid | 8,202 | 494,207 | 60.25 |
| Vizcaya | 2,217 | 1,155,106 | 521.02 |
| Zamora | 10,559 | 213,668 | 20.24 |
| Zaragoza | 17,252 | 837,327 | 48.54 |
| **Total** | 504,750 | 38,872,268* | 77.01 |

* Includes Spanish North Africa, an integral part of Spain. Ceuta had a population of 67,615 in 1991, while Melilla's population was 56,600.

# SPAIN

## PRINCIPAL TOWNS* (population at 1 March 1991)

| | | | |
|---|---|---|---|
| Madrid (capital) | 3,010,492 | Pamplona | 180,372 |
| Barcelona | 1,643,542 | Leganés | 171,589 |
| Valencia | 752,909 | Donostia-San Sebastián | 171,439 |
| Sevilla (Seville) | 683,028 | Cartagena | 168,023 |
| Zaragoza (Saragossa) | 594,394 | Salamanca | 162,888 |
| Málaga | 522,108 | Burgos | 160,278 |
| Bilbao | 369,839 | Alcalá de Henares | 159,355 |
| Las Palmas de Gran Canaria | 354,877 | Terrassa | 158,063 |
| Valladolid | 330,700 | Almería | 155,120 |
| Murcia | 328,100 | Cádiz | 154,347 |
| Córdoba | 302,154 | Fuenlabrada | 144,723 |
| Palma de Mallorca | 296,754 | León | 144,021 |
| Vigo | 276,109 | Huelva | 142,547 |
| L'Hospitalet de Llobregat | 272,578 | Alcorcón | 139,662 |
| Alicante | 265,473 | Getafe | 139,190 |
| Gijón | 259,067 | Castellón de la Plana | 134,213 |
| Granada | 255,212 | Santa Coloma de Gramanet | 133,138 |
| La Coruña (Corunna) | 246,953 | Albacete | 130,023 |
| Badalona | 218,725 | Logroño | 122,254 |
| Vitoria-Gasteiz | 206,116 | Badajoz | 122,225 |
| Santa Cruz de Tenerife | 200,172 | Lleida (Lérida) | 112,093 |
| Oviedo | 196,051 | La Laguna | 110,895 |
| Móstoles | 192,018 | Tarragona | 110,153 |
| Santander | 191,079 | Barakaldo | 105,088 |
| Sabadell | 189,404 | Jaén | 103,260 |
| Elche | 188,062 | Ourense | 102,758 |
| Jerez de la Frontera | 183,316 | Mataró | 101,510 |
| | | Algeciras | 101,256 |

* Population figures refer to *municipios*, each of which may contain some rural area as well as the urban centre.

## BIRTHS, MARRIAGES AND DEATHS

| | Registered live births | | Registered marriages | | Registered deaths | |
|---|---|---|---|---|---|---|
| | Number | Rate (per 1,000) | Number | Rate (per 1,000) | Number | Rate (per 1,000) |
| 1986 | 438,750 | 11.4 | 207,929 | 5.4 | 310,413 | 8.0 |
| 1987 | 426,782 | 11.0 | 215,771 | 5.6 | 310,073 | 8.0 |
| 1988 | 418,919 | 10.8 | 219,027 | 5.6 | 319,437 | 8.2 |
| 1989 | 408,434 | 10.5 | 221,470 | 5.7 | 324,796 | 8.4 |
| 1990 | 401,425 | 10.3 | 220,533 | 5.7 | 333,142 | 8.6 |
| 1991 | 395,989 | 10.2 | 218,121 | 5.6 | 337,691 | 8.7 |
| 1992 | 396,747 | 10.2 | 217,512 | 5.6 | 331,515 | 8.5 |
| 1993* | 380,564 | 9.7 | 196,304 | 5.0 | 338,666 | 8.7 |

* Provisional.

**Expectation of life** (UN estimates, years at birth 1985–90): 77.0 (males 73.8, females 80.0) (Source: UN, *World Population Prospects: The 1992 Revision*).

## EMPLOYMENT (average of quarterly sample surveys, '000 persons aged 16 years and over, excl. Ceuta and Melilla)*

| | 1991 | 1992 | 1993 |
|---|---|---|---|
| Agriculture, hunting, forestry and fishing | 1,345.1 | 1,252.7 | 1,197.8 |
| Mining and quarrying | 75.3 | 67.2 | 58.2 |
| Manufacturing | 2,728.4 | 2,660.1 | 2,401.7 |
| Electricity, gas and water | 86.5 | 76.9 | 79.9 |
| Construction | 1,273.5 | 1,196.3 | 1,088.5 |
| Trade, restaurants and hotels (incl. repair services) | 2,591.4 | 2,537.1 | 2,692.0 |
| Transport, storage and communications | 727.1 | 728.0 | 694.9 |
| Financing, insurance, real estate and business services | 733.8 | 741.4 | 926.6 |
| Community, social and personal services (excl. repair services) | 3,048.5 | 3,106.5 | 2,697.9 |
| **Total** | 12,609.4 | 12,366.2 | 11,837.5 |
| Males | 8,530.8 | 8,277.8 | 7,850.3 |
| Females | 4,078.6 | 4,088.4 | 3,987.3 |

* Including regular members of the armed forces (totalling 80,900 in 1991, 87,100 in 1992 and 93,200 in 1993), but excluding persons on compulsory military service.

Source: ILO, *Year Book of Labour Statistics*.

# Agriculture

## PRINCIPAL CROPS ('000 metric tons)

| | 1991 | 1992 | 1993 |
|---|---|---|---|
| Wheat | 5,468 | 4,357 | 5,002 |
| Rice (paddy) | 582 | 564 | 316 |
| Barley | 9,262 | 6,105 | 9,520 |
| Maize | 3,233 | 2,758 | 1,699 |
| Rye | 237 | 222 | 304 |
| Oats | 404 | 313 | 405 |
| Potatoes | 5,182 | 5,181 | 3,977 |
| Olive oil | 647 | 678 | 636 |
| Cabbages | 411 | 402 | 356 |
| Tomatoes | 2,665 | 2,647 | 2,699 |
| Onions | 1,019 | 1,020 | 897 |
| Grapes | 5,197 | 5,715 | 4,453 |
| Sugar cane | 165 | 167 | 170* |
| Sugar beet | 6,679 | 7,234 | 8,650 |
| Oranges | 2,651 | 2,926 | 2,426 |
| Mandarins | 1,340 | 1,521 | 1,536 |
| Lemons | 555 | 743 | 597 |
| Bananas | 373 | 368 | 358 |
| Almonds | 258 | 282 | 251 |

* FAO estimate.

Source: FAO, *Production Yearbook*.

## LIVESTOCK ('000 head at September each year)

| | 1991 | 1992 | 1993 |
|---|---|---|---|
| Horses* | 273 | 263 | 263 |
| Mules* | 70 | 60 | 60 |
| Asses* | 90 | 90 | 90 |
| Cattle | 5,063 | 4,976 | 4,800 |
| Pigs | 17,247 | 18,260 | 18,000† |
| Sheep | 24,625 | 24,615 | 24,800† |
| Goats | 2,972 | 2,837 | 2,800* |

* FAO estimate(s).   † Unofficial figure.

Source: FAO, *Production Yearbook*.

SPAIN

**LIVESTOCK PRODUCTS** ('000 metric tons)

|  | 1991 | 1992 | 1993 |
|---|---|---|---|
| Beef and veal | 509 | 539 | 530* |
| Mutton and lamb | 228 | 232 | 233* |
| Goat meat | 16 | 17 | 17† |
| Pig meat | 1,877 | 1,918 | 1,950* |
| Horse meat | 6 | 6 | 7† |
| Poultry meat | 840* | 868* | 863 |
| Cows' milk | 5,699 | 5,730 | 5,800* |
| Sheep's milk | 270 | 275 | 275† |
| Goats' milk | 410 | 430 | 430† |
| Butter | 37.5 | 29.0 | 27.0* |
| Cheese | 145.0 | 147.0† | 147.0† |
| Hen eggs | 640.6 | 625.2* | 603.2* |
| Other poultry eggs† | 1.3 | 1.3 | 1.3 |
| Honey | 25.3 | 25.0† | 25.0† |
| Wool (greasy) | 32.2* | 30.5† | 31.0† |
| Cattle hides | 44.1 | 46.0† | 45.0† |
| Sheepskins | 23.7 | 25.0† | 25.0† |

* Unofficial figure(s).   † FAO estimate(s).

Source: FAO, *Production Yearbook*.

## Forestry

**ROUNDWOOD REMOVALS** ('000 cubic metres, excl. bark)

|  | 1990 | 1991 | 1992 |
|---|---|---|---|
| Sawlogs, veneer logs and logs for sleepers | 5,776 | 6,004 | 4,745 |
| Pulpwood | 9,300 | 9,300* | 9,467 |
| Other industrial wood | 900 | 900 | 900* |
| Fuel wood | 2,190 | 1,990 | 1,990* |
| **Total** | **18,166** | **18,194** | **17,102** |

* FAO estimate.

Source: FAO, *Yearbook of Forest Products*.

**SAWNWOOD PRODUCTION**
('000 cubic metres, incl. railway sleepers)

|  | 1990 | 1991 | 1992 |
|---|---|---|---|
| Coniferous (softwood) | 2,697 | 2,559 | 1,686 |
| Broadleaved (hardwood) | 570 | 877 | 782 |
| **Total** | **3,267** | **3,436** | **2,468** |

Source: FAO, *Yearbook of Forest Products*.

## Fishing

('000 metric tons, live weight)

|  | 1990 | 1991 | 1992 |
|---|---|---|---|
| Greenland halibut | 1.8 | 6.7 | 34.5 |
| Atlantic cod* | 28.3 | 26.4 | 20.0 |
| Blue whiting (Poutassou)* | 43.4 | 38.8 | 42.0 |
| European hake* | 43.4 | 41.4 | 48.0 |
| Argentine hake | 10.6 | 6.0 | 3.1 |
| Cape hakes | 60.0 | 13.3 | 20.5 |
| Atlantic horse mackerel* | 44.9 | 46.0 | 44.0 |
| European pilchard (sardine)* | 239.9 | 224.3 | 228.0 |
| European anchovy* | 38.6 | 34.3 | 36.2 |
| Skipjack tuna | 105.9 | 111.8 | 112.9 |
| Albacore | 26.0 | 19.2 | 22.0 |
| Yellowfin tuna | 114.0 | 104.9 | 93.8 |
| Atlantic mackerel* | 30.6 | 28.1 | 25.0 |
| Blue mussel | 173.3 | 195.2 | 138.9 |
| Squids* | 64.0 | 53.8 | 79.0 |
| Octopuses* | 38.7 | 54.6 | 57.7 |
| **Total catch** (incl. others)* | **1,400.0** | **1,320.0** | **1,330.0** |

* FAO estimates.

Source: FAO, *Yearbook of Fishery Statistics*.

## Mining

('000 metric tons, unless otherwise indicated)

|  | 1989 | 1990 | 1991 |
|---|---|---|---|
| Hard coal | 14,525 | 14,743 | 13,916 |
| Brown coal (including lignite) | 21,926 | 21,070 | 19,646 |
| Crude petroleum | 1,038 | 795 | 1,067 |
| Natural gas (petajoules) | 61 | 59 | 55 |
| Iron ore* | 2,128 | 1,439 | 1,604 |
| Copper* | 28.5 | 14.2 | 7.7 |
| Iron pyrites | 1,930 | 1,638 | n.a. |
| Lead* | 62.8 | 58.5 | 45.7 |
| Zinc* | 269.7 | 260.9 | 261.2 |
| Potash salts (crude) | 842 | 781 | 585 |
| Fluorspar* | 172.3 | 153.7 | 90.0 |
| Salt (unrefined) | 3,223 | 3,377 | 3,175 |
| Gypsum (crude) | 7,033 | 7,673 | 3,501 |

* Figures refer to the metal content of ores.

Source: UN, *Industrial Statistics Yearbook*.

## Industry

**SELECTED PRODUCTS**
('000 metric tons, unless otherwise indicated)

|  | 1989 | 1990 | 1991 |
|---|---|---|---|
| Wine ('000 hectolitres) | 28,000* | 22,940* | 31,070 |
| Aluminium (primary) | 352.4 | 355.3 | 355.2 |
| Copper (primary) | 133.7 | 140.6 | 157.9 |
| Lead (primary) | 68.3 | 70.0 | n.a. |
| Pig iron | 5,464 | 5,733 | 5,600 |
| Steel ingots | 12,397* | 12,658* | 12,700 |
| Zinc (primary) | 237.5* | 239.7* | n.a. |
| Cement (Portland) | 27,375 | 28,092 | 27,576 |
| Sulphuric acid | 3,325 | 2,848 | n.a. |
| Nitric acid | 1,249 | 1,203 | n.a. |
| Soda ash | 817 | 816 | 500 |
| Caustic soda | 590 | 569 | n.a. |
| Motorcycles ('000) | 351 | 364 | n.a. |
| Passenger cars ('000) | 1,651 | 1,696 | 1,830 |
| Merchant ships launched ('000 gross tons) | 117 | 111 | 69 |
| Electricity (million kWh) | 147,842 | 151,759 | 155,704 |

* Provisional.

Source: UN, *Industrial Statistics Yearbook*.

## Finance

**CURRENCY AND EXCHANGE RATES**

**Monetary Units**
 100 céntimos = 1 Spanish peseta.

**Sterling and Dollar Equivalents** (31 December 1994)
 £1 sterling = 205.9 pesetas;
 US $1 = 131.6 pesetas;
 1,000 Spanish pesetas = £4.856 = $7.597.

**Average Exchange Rate** (pesetas per US $)
 1992   102.38
 1993   127.26
 1994   133.96

# SPAIN

*Statistical Survey*

## BUDGET ('000 million pesetas, provisional)

| Revenue | 1993 | 1994 | 1995 |
| --- | --- | --- | --- |
| Direct taxation | 6,068.1 | 6,057.9 | 6,683.7 |
| Personal income tax | 4,818.0 | 4,860.0 | 5,399.0 |
| Corporate tax | 1,149.0 | 1,090.0 | 1,169.7 |
| Indirect taxation | 4,420.0 | 5,108.5 | 5,563.7 |
| Value-added tax | 2,682.0 | 3,190.0 | 3,533.8 |
| Special taxes and petroleum revenue | 1,578.1 | 1,768.9 | 1,872.6 |
| Rates and other taxes | 274.5 | 316.6 | 341.2 |
| Current transfers | 437.7 | 555.4 | 521.3 |
| Estate taxes | 1,269.0 | 869.2 | 759.3 |
| Transfer of real investments | 4.3 | 11.4 | 7.9 |
| Capital transfers | 255.4 | 282.9 | 272.4 |
| **Total** (incl. others) | 12,729.0* | 13,201.9 | 14,149.5 |

* Revised total is 12,684,700 million pesetas.

| Expenditure | 1993 | 1994 | 1995 |
| --- | --- | --- | --- |
| Pensions | 760.9 | 809.3 | 838.5 |
| Interior | 494.5 | 754.0 | 794.6 |
| Justice | 222.7 | | |
| Defence | 757.2 | 805.0 | 866.1 |
| Public works, transport and environment | 1,085.3 | 1,261.9 | 1,306.6 |
| Education and science | 1,058.7 | 1,075.5 | 1,152.5 |
| Agriculture, fisheries and food | 174.9 | 159.9 | 199.4 |
| Industry and energy | 179.4 | 187.0 | 190.5 |
| Health and consumer affairs | 1,873.9 | 2,034.4 | 2,537.7 |
| Labour and social security | 1,356.8 | 1,636.5 | 1,528.7 |
| Economy and finance | 198.4 | 198.8 | 205.2 |
| Territorial bodies | 2,809.0 | 3,066.7 | 3,163.8 |
| EC/EU contributions | 798.5 | 937.9 | 857.0 |
| Public debt | 2,340.7 | 2,860.6 | 2,920.7 |
| **Total** (incl. others) | 14,752.6† | 16,513.9 | 17,318.4 |

† Revised total is 16,458,600 million pesetas.

## INTERNATIONAL RESERVES (US $ million at 31 December)

| | 1992 | 1993 | 1994 |
| --- | --- | --- | --- |
| Gold* | 4,217 | 4,217 | 4,217 |
| IMF special drawing rights | 184 | 216 | 255 |
| Reserve position in IMF | 1,144 | 1,031 | 1,109 |
| Foreign exchange | 44,176 | 39,798 | 40,205 |
| **Total** | 49,721 | 45,262 | 45,786 |

* Valued at market-related prices.

Source: IMF, *International Financial Statistics*.

## MONEY SUPPLY ('000 million pesetas at 31 December)

| | 1992 | 1993 | 1994 |
| --- | --- | --- | --- |
| Currency outside banks | 6,025 | 6,509 | 7,165 |
| Demand deposits at deposit money banks | 10,944 | 10,878 | 11,411 |

Source: IMF, *International Financial Statistics*.

## COST OF LIVING (Consumer Price Index. Base: 1980 = 100)

| | 1991 | 1992 | 1993 |
| --- | --- | --- | --- |
| Food | 255.1 | 264.5 | 267.4 |
| Fuel and light | 210.1 | 224.2 | 241.3 |
| Clothing | 266.8 | 280.6 | 282.8 |
| Rent | 153.5* | 160.1* | 285.4 |
| **All items** (incl. others) | 257.6 | 272.8 | 285.3 |

* Base: 1983 = 100.

Source: ILO, *Year Book of Labour Statistics*.

## NATIONAL ACCOUNTS (million pesetas at current prices)

### National Income and Product (estimates)

| | 1991 | 1992 | 1993 |
| --- | --- | --- | --- |
| Compensation of employees | 25,660,994 | 27,488,618 | 28,174,651 |
| Operating surplus | 18,777,380 | 19,969,319 | 21,276,530 |
| **Domestic factor incomes** | 44,438,374 | 47,457,937 | 49,451,181 |
| Consumption of fixed capital | 6,025,953 | 6,440,502 | 6,949,800 |
| **Gross domestic product at factor cost** | 50,464,327 | 53,898,439 | 56,400,981 |
| Indirect taxes | 5,888,830 | 6,603,615 | 6,422,864 |
| *Less* Subsidies | 1,452,361 | 1,499,946 | 1,919,558 |
| **GDP in purchasers' values** | 54,900,796 | 59,002,108 | 60,904,287 |
| Factor income received from abroad | 1,172,247 | 1,485,564 | 1,603,729 |
| *Less* Factor income paid abroad | 1,726,304 | 2,193,923 | 2,253,456 |
| **Gross national product** | 54,346,739 | 58,293,749 | 60,254,560 |
| *Less* Consumption of fixed capital | 6,025,953 | 6,440,502 | 6,949,800 |
| **National income in market prices** | 48,320,786 | 51,853,247 | 53,304,760 |
| Other current transfers received from abroad | 1,060,544 | 1,170,259 | 1,249,768 |
| *Less* Other current transfers paid abroad | 748,923 | 952,824 | 962,547 |
| **National disposable income** | 48,632,407 | 52,070,682 | 53,591,981 |

### Expenditure on the Gross Domestic Product (estimates)

| | 1991 | 1992 | 1993 |
| --- | --- | --- | --- |
| Government final consumption expenditure | 8,881,875 | 10,027,272 | 10,669,059 |
| Private final consumption expenditure | 34,244,386 | 37,219,873 | 38,510,798 |
| Increase in stocks | 461,070 | 529,274 | 83,161 |
| Gross fixed capital formation | 13,041,336 | 12,868,614 | 12,040,116 |
| **Total domestic expenditure** | 56,628,667 | 60,645,033 | 61,303,134 |
| Exports of goods and services | 9,409,431 | 10,409,836 | 11,784,205 |
| *Less* Imports of goods and services | 11,137,302 | 12,052,761 | 12,183,052 |
| **GDP in purchasers' values** | 54,900,796 | 59,002,108 | 60,904,287 |

### Gross Domestic Product by Economic Activity (estimates)

| | 1991 | 1992 | 1993 |
| --- | --- | --- | --- |
| Agriculture, hunting, forestry and fishing | 2,237,546 | 2,021,623 | 2,109,564 |
| Mining and quarrying | | | |
| Manufacturing | 13,752,386 | 13,837,513 | 13,863,084 |
| Electricity, gas and water | | | |
| Construction | 5,113,875 | 5,091,487 | 4,981,437 |
| Services | 30,389,785 | 34,180,511 | 36,478,763 |
| **Sub-total** | 51,493,592 | 55,131,134 | 57,432,848 |
| Import duties | 350,385 | 283,891 | 159,071 |
| Value-added tax on products | 3,056,819 | 3,587,083 | 3,312,368 |
| **GDP in purchasers' values** | 54,900,796 | 59,002,108 | 60,904,287 |

# SPAIN

## BALANCE OF PAYMENTS (US $ million)

|  | 1991 | 1992 | 1993 |
|---|---|---|---|
| Merchandise exports f.o.b. | 58,901 | 63,921 | 58,713 |
| Merchandise imports f.o.b. | −89,654 | −94,954 | −74,778 |
| **Trade balance** | **−30,753** | **−31,034** | **−16,065** |
| Exports of services | 30,833 | 36,265 | 31,632 |
| Imports of services | −17,366 | −22,093 | −19,375 |
| Other income received | 7,342 | 9,445 | 7,380 |
| Other income paid | −12,835 | −16,874 | −14,340 |
| Private unrequited transfers (net) | 2,201 | 2,613 | 1,657 |
| Official unrequited transfers (net) | 3,859 | 3,197 | 2,854 |
| **Current balance** | **−16,718** | **−18,481** | **−6,258** |
| Direct investment (net) | 6,919 | 6,758 | 4,733 |
| Portfolio investment (net) | 18,725 | −790 | 25,699 |
| Other capital (net) | 6,332 | 448 | −27,920 |
| Net errors and omissions | −1,117 | −5,407 | −1,005 |
| **Overall balance** | **14,141** | **−17,472** | **−4,750** |

Source: IMF, *International Financial Statistics*.

## External Trade

### PRINCIPAL COMMODITIES (million pesetas)

| Imports c.i.f. | 1990 | 1991 | 1992 |
|---|---|---|---|
| **Live animals and animal products** | 373,979.8 | 411,313.4 | 462,720.8 |
| Fish, crustaceans and molluscs | 233,300.6 | 239,431.4 | 269,193.7 |
| **Vegetable products** | 291,108.6 | 330,557.6 | 341,223.9 |
| **Products of the food industries, drinks and tobacco** | 313,435.0 | 376,394.0 | 431,817.3 |
| **Mineral products** | 1,191,395.8 | 1,184,825.7 | 1,148,003.5 |
| Mineral fuels and petroleum products | 1,061,373.2 | 1,054,680.5 | 1,022,639.9 |
| **Products of the chemical industries and related industries** | 704,163.7 | 775,859.3 | 860,016.9 |
| Organic chemical products | 279,561.2 | 294,188.7 | 307,747.8 |
| **Artificial plastic materials, rubber and their manufactures** | 352,149.9 | 375,197.3 | 411,820.8 |
| Artificial plastic materials and their manufactures | 239,781.3 | 263,554.6 | 282,719.1 |
| **Materials used in the manufacture of paper, paper, etc.** | 269,278.8 | 288,877.8 | 302,530.4 |
| Paper, cardboard and their manufactures | 189,802.8 | 211,127.8 | 223,230.8 |
| **Textiles and their manufactures** | 400,617.9 | 513,548.9 | 601,167.1 |
| **Base metals and their manufactures** | 642,217.8 | 660,744.2 | 668,303.6 |
| Cast iron, iron and steel | 290,383.7 | 269,800.0 | 265,560.0 |
| **Machines and apparatus, electrical equipment** | 2,210,909.2 | 2,347,015.2 | 2,346,847.5 |
| Nuclear reactors, boilers, mechanical machines, apparatus and appliances | 1,450,843.6 | 1,496,113.0 | 1,473,288.4 |
| Electrical machines and apparatus | 760,065.6 | 850,902.2 | 873,559.1 |
| **Transport equipment** | 1,204,728.3 | 1,310,860.8 | 1,500,990.3 |
| Motor cars, tractors, mopeds, etc. | 964,021.2 | 1,021,116.7 | 1,289,394.1 |
| **Optical, photographic and cinematographic, precision instruments and apparatus** | 327,685.9 | 354,267.5 | 360,864.4 |
| Optical, photographic and cinematographic apparatus | 277,074.2 | 294,709.2 | 300,944.5 |
| **Total** (incl. others) | 8,898,365.6 | 9,636,773.4 | 10,204,760.0 |

| Exports f.o.b. | 1990 | 1991 | 1992 |
|---|---|---|---|
| **Vegetable products** | 427,096.3 | 487,038.8 | 542,964.3 |
| Vegetables, plants, edible roots and tubers | 117,953.3 | 138,678.9 | 162,036.0 |
| Edible fruits, citrus and melon peel | 227,003.8 | 264,474.7 | 294,123.2 |
| **Products of the food industries, drinks and tobacco** | 242,392.3 | 270,102.8 | 299,130.7 |
| **Mineral products** | 317,247.4 | 246,042.1 | 253,617.5 |
| Mineral fuels and petroleum products | 265,161.0 | 196,421.7 | 204,608.3 |
| **Products of the chemical industries and related industries** | 338,719.8 | 360,716.7 | 395,608.7 |
| Organic chemical products | 131,318.4 | 138,244.2 | 142,609.2 |
| **Artificial plastic materials, rubber and their manufactures** | 255,372.8 | 259,707.5 | 276,720.3 |
| Artificial plastic materials and their manufactures | 142,248.1 | 147,102.4 | 153,685.2 |
| **Materials used in the manufacture of paper, paper, etc.** | 161,356.2 | 164,980.5 | 188,627.4 |
| **Textiles and their manufactures** | 228,420.7 | 227,265.0 | 252,484.0 |
| **Footwear, hats, umbrellas, sunshades, etc.** | 155,382.8 | 141,418.2 | 136,374.7 |
| Shoes, boots, etc. | 152,966.5 | 139,813.7 | 134,778.9 |
| **Manufactures of stone, cement, etc.; ceramics; glass and its manufactures** | 171,232.0 | 184,305.9 | 207,728.2 |
| Manufactures of cast iron, iron and steel | 137,971.2 | 134,696.6 | 146,055.9 |
| **Base metals and their manufactures** | 537,119.9 | 567,256.3 | 577,380.5 |
| Cast iron, iron and steel | 234,621.2 | 249,447.5 | 231,791.1 |
| **Machines and apparatus, electrical equipment** | 869,677.6 | 979,986.9 | 1,077,728.7 |
| Nuclear reactors, boilers, mechanical machines, apparatus and appliances | 590,565.4 | 653,055.8 | 679,240.6 |
| Electrical machines and apparatus | 279,112.2 | 326,931.1 | 398,488.1 |
| **Transport equipment** | 1,301,939.1 | 1,545,334.5 | 1,786,623.2 |
| Motor cars, tractors, mopeds, etc. | 1,106,105.5 | 1,354,111.2 | 1,539,888.8 |
| **Total** (incl. others) | 5,630,558.6 | 6,064,708.6 | 6,657,585.0 |

### PRINCIPAL TRADING PARTNERS* (million pesetas)

| Imports c.i.f. | 1990 | 1991 | 1992 |
|---|---|---|---|
| Algeria | 88,464.6 | 106,123.9 | 103,652.9 |
| Belgium-Luxembourg-Netherlands | 603,548.3 | 625,759.6 | 680,147.7 |
| China, People's Republic | 75,332.4 | 119,045.7 | n.a. |
| France | 1,309,425.3 | 1,464,042.9 | 1,631,212.0 |
| Germany | 1,463,963.7 | 1,559,078.1 | 1,676,588.9 |
| Italy | 906,241.5 | 964,775.0 | 1,003,363.8 |
| Japan | 397,851.9 | 454,254.9 | 477,066.0 |
| Libya | 119,961.6 | 127,880.6 | 126,080.6 |
| Mexico | 145,863.0 | 137,896.1 | 135,930.5 |
| Nigeria | 162,030.0 | 184,635.6 | 133,973.7 |
| Portugal | 223,804.8 | 264,014.2 | 276,667.0 |
| Saudi Arabia | 62,127.0 | 108,441.9 | 108,817.5 |
| Sweden | 161,630.3 | 151,592.9 | 135,728.8 |
| Switzerland | 130,158.7 | 143,764.4 | 157,699.5 |
| Taiwan | 82,109.5 | 109,290.2 | n.a. |
| United Kingdom | 602,017.0 | 727,869.5 | 744,986.0 |
| USA | 748,067.1 | 769,855.4 | 749,750.3 |
| **Total** (incl. others) | 8,898,365.6 | 9,636,773.4 | 10,204,760.0 |

SPAIN

| Exports f.o.b. | 1991 | 1992 | 1993 |
|---|---|---|---|
| Algeria | 57,480.8 | 66,503.7 | 76,842.0 |
| Belgium-Luxembourg-Netherlands | 438,769.6 | 460,531.6 | 504,816.7 |
| France | 1,161,637.7 | 1,243,036.5 | 1,346,770.9 |
| Germany | 758,334.9 | 992,275.7 | 1,043,152.7 |
| Italy | 600,176.9 | 705,402.0 | 716,439.6 |
| Japan | 64,491.4 | 60,984.4 | 61,944.9 |
| Mexico | 59,542.5 | 62,939.9 | 99,171.1 |
| Morocco | 68,303.0 | 62,015.7 | 72,823.9 |
| Portugal | 345,394.5 | 408,730.7 | 500,551.1 |
| Sweden | 54,571.1 | 63,457.2 | 65,947.2 |
| Switzerland | 91,985.8 | 90,376.8 | 89,772.7 |
| United Kingdom | 509,678.3 | 474,480.8 | 502,936.5 |
| USA | 329,500.0 | 297,334.2 | 316,754.3 |
| **Total** (incl. others) | 5,630,558.6 | 6,064,708.6 | 6,657,585.0 |

\* Imports by country of production; exports by country of last consignment. For exports the distribution by country excludes stores and bunkers for ships and aircraft.

## Transport

**RAILWAYS** (RENFE only)

|  | 1990 | 1991 | 1992 |
|---|---|---|---|
| Number of passengers ('000) | 386,000 | 435,000 | 475,400 |
| Passenger-kilometres (million) | 16,733 | 16,353 | 17,645 |
| Freight ('000 tons) | 37,300 | 35,500 | 30,370 |
| Freight ton-kilometres (million) | 11,613 | 10,808 | 9,582 |

Source: Ministry of Public Works, Transport and Environment.

**ROAD TRAFFIC** (motor vehicles in use at 31 December)

|  | 1990 | 1991 | 1992 |
|---|---|---|---|
| Passenger cars | 12,010,717 | 12,537,099 | 13,102,285 |
| Buses | 45,963 | 46,604 | 47,180 |
| Lorries | 2,339,250 | 2,495,226 | 2,649,596 |
| Motor cycles | 3,073,553 | 3,575,000 | 3,251,879 |

Source: International Road Federation, *World Road Statistics*.

**SHIPPING** (freight traffic)

|  | 1988 | 1989 | 1990 |
|---|---|---|---|
| Vessels entered ('000 gross tons): |  |  |  |
| Coastwise | 153,323 | 156,115 | 157,978 |
| International | 283,004 | 302,546 | 323,124 |
| Goods loaded ('000 metric tons): |  |  |  |
| Coastwise | 36,098 | 38,378 | 34,400 |
| International | 45,349 | 43,301 | 43,208 |
| Goods unloaded ('000 metric tons): |  |  |  |
| Coastwise | 36,349 | 37,597 | 35,223 |
| International | 108,637 | 119,595 | 125,881 |

**1991**: Total goods loaded and unloaded ('000 metric tons) 247,951.
**1992** (provisional): Total goods loaded and unloaded ('000 metric tons) 245,025.

Merchant shipping fleet ('000 grt at 30 June): 3,807.1 in 1990; 3,617.2 in 1991; 3,224.6 in 1992. Source: Lloyd's Register of Shipping.

**CIVIL AVIATION** (traffic)

|  | 1988 | 1989 | 1990 |
|---|---|---|---|
| Passengers ('000): |  |  |  |
| Scheduled | 37,163 | 40,215 | 43,474 |
| Non-scheduled | 31,125 | 30,657 | 29,669 |
| Number of flights: |  |  |  |
| Scheduled | 414,226 | 455,213 | 500,004 |
| Non-scheduled | 244,152 | 259,836 | 251,958 |
| Freight carried (metric tons): |  |  |  |
| Scheduled | 339,983 | 369,241 | 387,697 |
| Non-scheduled | 33,442 | 39,352 | 43,499 |

## Tourism

**FOREIGN TOURIST ARRIVALS**
(by country of origin, incl. Spaniards resident abroad)

|  | 1992 | 1993 | 1994 |
|---|---|---|---|
| Belgium | 1,361,774 | 1,470,061 | 2,076,267 |
| France | 11,792,108 | 12,085,945 | 13,696,012 |
| Germany | 7,762,127 | 8,712,051 | 9,678,673 |
| Italy | 1,852,567 | 2,018,529 | 2,818,988 |
| Morocco | 2,034,737 | 2,127,530 | n.a. |
| Netherlands | 2,117,030 | 2,060,886 | 2,271,429 |
| Portugal | 11,567,533 | 11,358,644 | 10,249,070 |
| Switzerland | 1,109,871 | 1,169,603 | 1,990,268 |
| United Kingdom | 6,515,540 | 7,484,680 | 9,170,041 |
| USA | 825,387 | 783,592 | 997,146 |
| **Total** (incl. others) | 55,330,716 | 57,258,615 | 61,428,034 |

Source: Ministry of Trade and Tourism, Madrid.

## Communications Media

|  | 1990 | 1991 | 1992 |
|---|---|---|---|
| Telephones ('000 in use) | 12,603 | n.a. | n.a. |
| Radio receivers ('000 in use) | 12,000 | 12,100 | 12,200 |
| Television receivers ('000 in use) | 15,500 | 15,600 | 15,700 |
| Book production |  |  |  |
| Titles | 36,239 | 39,082 | 41,816 |
| Copies ('000) | 184,949 | 198,093 | 194,785 |

**Daily newspapers** (1992): 148 (with an estimated combined average circulation of 4,100,000 copies per issue).
**Non-daily newspapers** (1988): 85.
**Other periodicals** (1986): 1,998.

Source: mainly UNESCO, *Statistical Yearbook*.

## Education

(1992/93)

|  | Teachers | Pupils/Students |
|---|---|---|
| Pre-primary | 49,125 | 1,052,488 |
| Primary | 121,893* | 2,554,083 |
| Secondary |  |  |
| General | } 293,106* | { 3,590,525 |
| Vocational |  | { 1,164,805 |
| Higher† |  |  |
| Universities, etc. | 70,443 | 1,183,331 |
| Distance-learning | 854 | 91,113 |
| Other | 2,115 | 47,880 |

\* Estimate. † Provisional.

Sources: Ministry of Education and Science, Madrid, and Instituto Nacional de Estadística.

# Directory

## The Constitution

The Constitution of the Kingdom of Spain was approved by popular referendum on 6 December 1978, and promulgated on 29 December 1978.

According to the final provisions, all the fundamental laws of the Franco regime are repealed, together with all measures incompatible with the Constitution.

The following is a summary of the main provisions:

### PRELIMINARY PROVISIONS

Spain is established as a social and democratic State whose supreme values are freedom, justice, equality and political pluralism. National sovereignty and power reside with the Spanish people, the political form of the State being a parliamentary Monarchy.

The Constitution is based on the indissoluble unity of the Spanish nation, and recognizes and guarantees the right to autonomy of the nationalities and regions.

### FUNDAMENTAL RIGHTS, DUTIES AND FREEDOMS

Standards concerning fundamental rights and freedoms recognized in the Constitution are to be interpreted in accordance with the Universal Declaration of Human Rights and other international treaties and agreements of a similar nature ratified by Spain.

All Spaniards are equal under the law and no Spaniard by birth may be deprived of his nationality. The age of majority is 18, suffrage is free and universal and every person has a right to public service.

The main freedoms listed are described below, bearing in mind that the Constitution contains the proviso that no person, group or action pose a threat to public order and safety. Free entry to and exit from Spain, freedom of thought, belief and expression are guaranteed, as is the right of access to state and public communications media by significant social and political groups and to administrative archives and registers by individuals, except in matters concerning that state security and defence, and the private life and home of the individual, which are inviolable.

The Constitution states that there is no state religion but that it will maintain co-operation with the Roman Catholic Church and other religious groups.

Freedom of association is guaranteed, except for criminal, paramilitary and secret associations, all associations being bound to inscribe themselves in a public register; the right to form trade unions and to strike is also guaranteed, military personnel being subject to special laws in these cases.

Every person has a right to work for a just remuneration, including paid holiday, under conditions of safety, hygiene and a healthy environment. The State is to be run on the principles of a market economy. Taxation is determined according to means and consumer protection is encouraged by the State. Social security payments are provided for and it is stipulated that special care be taken of the handicapped and the elderly.

In criminal matters, the death penalty is abolished except under military criminal law in time of war. Extradition functions on the principle of reciprocity but the terms do not apply to political crimes; acts of terrorism however, not being considered as such. All persons are presumed innocent before trial, and a habeas corpus clause provides for a detainee to be freed within 72 hours of arrest or brought before a court.

### THE CROWN

The King is the Head of State, the symbol of its unity and permanence, and the highest representative of the Spanish State in international relations. The person of the King is inviolable. His decisions and acts must be approved by the Government, without which they are deemed invalid, and responsibility for the King's actions is borne by those who approve them. The Crown is hereditary descending to the sons of the Sovereign in order of seniority or, if there are no sons, to the daughters. Persons marrying against the wishes of the King or Cortes (national assembly) are excluded from the succession. The Constitution lays down the procedure for establishing the Regency.

The King's duties are as follows:

To approve and promulgate laws;

To convene and dissolve the Cortes Generales and to call elections and referendums (according to the Constitution);

To propose a candidate for the presidency of the Cortes and dismiss him;

To appoint the members of the Cortes on the proposal of the President;

To issue decrees approved by the Council of Ministers, and to confer civil and military posts and grant honours and distinctions in accordance with the laws;

To be informed of the affairs of State, and to preside over the Council of Ministers when he deems it necessary on the request of the President of the Government;

To command the Armed Forces;

To grant mercy according to the law (which may not authorize general pardons);

To accredit ambassadors and other diplomatic representatives;

To express the State's assent to bind itself to international treaties;

To declare war and peace on the prior authorization of the Cortes.

### THE CORTES GENERALES
(National Assembly)

The Cortes represent the Spanish people and comprise the Congress of Deputies (Lower House) and the Senate (Upper House).

The Congress has a minimum of 300 deputies and a maximum of 400, elected by universal, free, equal, direct and secret suffrage. Each province forms one constituency, the number of deputies in each one being determined according to population and elected by proportional representation for four years, Ceuta and Melilla having one deputy each. Elections must be held between 30 and 60 days after the end of each parliamentary mandate, and Congress convened within 25 days of the elections.

The Senate is based on territorial representation. Each province elects four senators for four years. Each island or group of islands forms one constituency. Gran Canaria, Mallorca and Tenerife return three senators each, the others one each. The Autonomous Communities return, in addition, one senator, plus one more for each million inhabitants, appointed by the legislative assembly of the community.

Each House lays down its own rules of procedure and elects its own president and governing body. Each year there are two ordinary sessions of the Cortes, of four and five months each, and a standing committee of 21 members in each House looks after affairs while the Cortes is in recess or during electoral periods. Plenary sessions are normally public. Measures are adopted by a majority in both Houses providing that a majority of the members is present. If agreement is not reached between the Congress and the Senate, a joint committee must attempt to solve the differences by drawing up a text to be voted on again by both Houses. In the case of further non-agreement, the issue is decided by an absolute majority vote in Congress. Members may not vote by proxy.

### LEGISLATION

Laws may not be retroactive.

Organic laws concern the development of fundamental rights and public freedoms, the approval of statutes of autonomy, the general electoral system, and other matters specified in the Constitution. Any approval, modification or repeal of these laws requires an absolute majority in Congress. The Cortes may delegate the power to issue measures called Legislative Decrees with the status of law to a governmental legislative body. In urgent cases the Government may issue provisional measures in the form of Decree-Laws not affecting the fundamental laws and rights of the nation, which must be voted upon by the Cortes within 30 days.

All laws must be sanctioned by the King within 15 days of their approval by the Cortes.

Provision is made for the popular presentation of bills if they are supported by 500,000 reputable signatures. Petitions to the Cortes by public demonstration are prohibited.

### THE GOVERNMENT

The Government is the executive power and is composed of a President proposed by the King on the Cortes' approval and voted into office by Congress by absolute majority. If no President is elected within two months, the King will dissolve the Cortes and convene new elections with the President of Congress's approval. The President of the Government designates the Ministers.

SPAIN

The Council of State is the supreme consultative organ of the Government. (An Organic law will regulate its composition.)
Further articles provide for the procedure for declaring a state of alarm, emergency or siege.

### THE JUDICIARY

Justice derives from the people and is administered in the name of the King by judges and magistrates subject only to the law. The principle of jurisdictional unity is the basis of the organization and functioning of the Courts, which are established in an Organic Law of judicial power. Emergency courts are prohibited.

The Judiciary is governed by the General Council of Judicial Power, presided over by the President of the Supreme Court and made up of 20 members appointed by the King for five years, of whom 12 are judges or magistrates, four are nominated by Congress and four by the Senate, these eight being elected by a three-fifths majority from lawyers and jurists of more than 15 years' professional service.

The Attorney-General is appointed by the King on the Government's approval. Citizens may act on juries.

### TERRITORIAL ORGANIZATION

The State is organized into municipalities, provinces and Autonomous Communities, all of which have local autonomy. The Constitution states that the differences between the Statutes of the Autonomous Communities shall not imply economic or social privileges.

### THE AUTONOMOUS COMMUNITIES

The peripheral provinces, with their own historical, cultural and economic characteristics, are entitled to accede to self-government, but the Constitution states that in no case will the federation of the Autonomous Communities be permitted.

Article 148 lists the matters in which the Communities may assume competence, among which are: land use and building, public works and transport, ports, agriculture, environment, minerals, economic development, culture, tourism, social aid, health and local policing, all within the framework of national laws and policy and as long as nothing outside the regional boundaries is involved. Areas solely under state control are listed in article 149. In the specific case of financial autonomy, revenue proceeds from the State and from each Autonomous Community's own taxes, and a State Compensation Fund acts to correct any imbalances between the Communities. State competence will always prevail over regional competence should conflict arise over matters not under the exclusive control of the Autonomous Communities.

Although the State will delegate state power wherever possible, legislative measures must always be guided by state law. The State, in the general public interest, may pass laws by absolute majority to establish the principles for the harmonization of measures taken by the Autonomous Communities, even concerning matters directly under their authority.

The institutional organization of the Communities is based on a Legislative Assembly elected by universal suffrage and proportional representation, a Governing Council with executive and administrative functions, and a President elected by the Assembly from its members and appointed by the King to be the supreme representative of the Community to the State, and the ordinary representative of the State in the Community, and finally a High Court of Justice, inferior only to the Supreme Court.

### THE CONSTITUTIONAL COURT

This court monitors observance of the Constitution and comprises 12 members appointed by the King, of whom four are elected by Congress and four by the Senate by three-fifths majority, two on the proposal of the Government and two on the proposal of the General Council of Judicial Power. The members must satisfy the conditions for membership of the aforesaid Council. They are appointed for nine years, with three members resigning every three years.

Three further articles establish the procedure for constitutional reform.

# The Government

### HEAD OF STATE

**King of Spain, Head of State, Commander-in-Chief of the Armed Forces and Head of the Supreme Council of Defence:** HRH King JUAN CARLOS (succeeded to the Throne, 22 November 1975).

### COUNCIL OF MINISTERS
(July 1995)

**Prime Minister and President of the Council:** FELIPE GONZÁLEZ MÁRQUEZ.

**Minister of Foreign Affairs:** JAVIER SOLANA MADARIAGA.

**Minister of Justice and the Interior:** JUAN ALBERTO BELLOCH JULBE.

**Minister of Defence:** GUSTAVO SUÁREZ PERTIERRA.

**Minister of Economy and Finance:** PEDRO SOLBES MIRA.

**Minister of Public Works, Transport and Environment:** JOSÉ BORRELL FONTELLES.

**Minister of Education and Science:** JERÓNIMO SAAVEDRA ACEVEDO.

**Minister of Labour and Social Security:** JOSÉ ANTONIO GRIÑÁN MARTÍNEZ.

**Minister of Industry and Energy:** JUAN MANUEL EGUIAGARAY UCELAY.

**Minister of Trade and Tourism:** JAVIER GÓMEZ-NAVARRO NAVARRETE.

**Minister of Agriculture, Fisheries and Food:** LUIS ATIENZA SERNA.

**Minister of the Presidency:** ALFREDO PÉREZ RUBALCABA.

**Minister of Public Administration:** JOAN LERMA BLASCO.

**Minister of Culture:** CARMEN ALBORCH BATALLER.

**Minister of Health and Consumer Affairs:** MARÍA ANGELES AMADOR MILLÁN.

**Minister of Social Affairs:** CRISTINA ALBERDI ALONSO.

### MINISTRIES

**Prime Minister's Chancellery:** Complejo de la Moncloa, Edif. INIA, 28071 Madrid; tel. (1) 3353535; fax (1) 3353383.

**Ministry of Agriculture, Fisheries and Food:** Paseo Infanta Isabel 1, 28014 Madrid; tel. (1) 3475000; telex 47062; fax (1) 3475618.

**Ministry of Culture:** Plaza del Rey, 28071 Madrid; tel. (1) 5320093; telex 27286; fax (1) 5319212.

**Ministry of Defence:** Paseo de la Castellana 109, Madrid 28046; tel. (1) 5555000; telex 41523; fax (1) 5563958.

**Ministry of Economy and Finance:** Paseo de la Castellana 162, 28071 Madrid; tel. (1) 5837411; telex 48387; fax (1) 3495240.

**Ministry of Education and Science:** Alcalá 34, 28071 Madrid; tel. (1) 5311202; telex 23102; fax (1) 5229256.

**Ministry of Foreign Affairs:** Plaza de la Provincia 1, 28071 Madrid; tel. (1) 3664800; telex 22645; fax (1) 3667098.

**Ministry of Health and Consumer Affairs:** Paseo del Prado 18–20, 28071 Madrid; tel. (1) 5961000; telex 22608; fax (1) 5961547.

**Ministry of Industry and Energy:** Paseo de la Castellana 160, 28071 Madrid; tel. (1) 3494000; telex 42112; fax (1) 4582019.

**Ministry of the Interior:** Amador de los Rios 5, 28071 Madrid; tel. (1) 5371000; telex 46092; fax (1) 5371177.

**Ministry of Justice:** San Bernando 47, Madrid 8; tel. (1) 3902000; fax (1) 5221538.

**Ministry of Labour and Social Security:** Nuevos Ministerios, Agustín de Bethancourt 4, 28003 Madrid; tel. (1) 5536000; telex 45843; fax (1) 5534033.

**Ministry of Public Administration:** Paseo de la Castellana 3, 28046 Madrid; tel. (1) 5861000; telex 45567; fax (1) 3192448.

**Ministry of Public Works, Transport and Environment:** Nuevos Ministerios, 28071 Madrid; tel. (1) 5977000; telex 46388; fax (1) 5978542.

**Ministry of Social Affairs:** Calle de José Abascal 39, 28071 Madrid; tel. (1) 3477000; fax (1) 4423454.

**Ministry of Trade and Tourism:** Paseo de la Castellana 162, 28071 Madrid; tel. (1) 3493500; fax (1) 4578066.

### COUNCIL OF STATE

The Council of State has 29 Members.

**President:** FERNANDO LEDESMA.

SPAIN                                                                                                              Directory

# Legislature

### LAS CORTES GENERALES

**Congreso de los Diputados**
(Congress of Deputies)

**President:** FELIX PONS IRAZAZÁBAL.

**General Election, 6 June 1993**

|  | Seats |
|---|---|
| Partido Socialista Obrero Español (PSOE) | 159 |
| Partido Popular (PP) | 141 |
| Izquierda Unida (IU) | 18 |
| Convergència i Unió (CiU) | 17 |
| Partido Nacionalista Vasco (PNV) | 5 |
| Coalición Canaria (CC) | 4 |
| Herri Batasuna (HB) | 2 |
| Esquerra Republicana de Catalunya (ERC) | 1 |
| Partido Aragonés (PAR) | 1 |
| Eusko Alkartasuna (EA) | 1 |
| Unión Valenciana (UV) | 1 |
| **Total** | **350** |

**Senado**
(Senate)

The Senate comprises 255 directly-elected members, the remaining 47 regional representatives being chosen by the assemblies of the autonomous regions.

**President:** JUAN JOSÉ LABORDA MARTÍN.

**General Election, 6 June 1993**

|  | Seats Directly elected | Regional representatives |
|---|---|---|
| Partido Socialista Obrero Español (PSOE) | 116 | 20 |
| Partido Popular (PP) | 106 | 13 |
| Convergència i Unió (CiU) | 15 | 5 |
| Coalición Canaria (CC) | 6 | 1 |
| Partido Nacionalista Vasco (PNV) | 5 | 2 |
| Izquierda Unida (IU) | 2 | 2 |
| Partido Aragonés (PAR) | 1 | 1 |
| Eusko Alkartasuna (EA) | 1 | 1 |
| Unión Valenciana (UV) | 1 | 1 |
| Partido Riojano | 1 | 1 |
| Herri Batasuna (HB) | 1 | — |
| **Total** | **255** | **47** |

# Legislative Assemblies of the Autonomous Regions

For full names of political parties, see pp. 2807–2808.

### ANDALUCÍA

**President of the Government:** MANUEL CHAVES GONZÁLEZ (PSOE).
**President of the Parliament:** DIEGO VALDERAS (IU).

**Election, 12 June 1994**

|  | Seats |
|---|---|
| PSOE | 45 |
| PP | 41 |
| IU-CA*-Los Verdes | 20 |
| PA | 3 |
| **Total** | **109** |

* Convocatoria por Andalucía.

### ARAGÓN

**President of the Government:** SANTIAGO LANZUELA (PP).
**President of the Parliament:** (to be appointed – PAR).

**Election, 28 May 1995**

|  | Seats |
|---|---|
| PP | 27 |
| PSOE | 19 |
| PAR | 14 |
| IU | 5 |
| ChA | 2 |
| **Total** | **67** |

### ASTURIAS

**President of the Government:** SERGIO MARQUÉS (PP).
**President of the Parliament:** OVIDIO SÁNCHEZ (PP).

**Election, 28 May 1995**

|  | Seats |
|---|---|
| PP | 21 |
| PSOE | 17 |
| IU | 6 |
| PAS*-UNA | 1 |
| **Total** | **45** |

* Partiu Asturianista.

### BALEARES (BALEARIC ISLANDS)

**President of the Government:** GABRIEL CAÑELLAS FONS (PP).
**President of the Parliament:** CRISTÓBAL SOLER.

**Election, 28 May 1995**

|  | Seats |
|---|---|
| PP | 30 |
| PSOE | 16 |
| PSM-NM* | 6 |
| IU | 3 |
| UM | 2 |
| Others | 2 |
| **Total** | **59** |

* Partit Socialista de Mallorca-Nacionalistes de Mallorca.

### BASQUE COUNTRY (EUSKADI)

**President (Lehendakari) of the Government:** JOSÉ ANTONIO ARDANZA (PNV).
**President of the Parliament:** JOSEBA LEIZAOLA (PNV).

**Election, 23 October 1994**

|  | Seats |
|---|---|
| EAJ*-PNV | 22 |
| PSE-EE | 12 |
| HB | 11 |
| PP | 11 |
| EA | 8 |
| IU-EB† | 6 |
| UA | 5 |
| **Total** | **75** |

* Eusko Alderdi Jeltzalea.
† Ezker Batua.

### CANARIAS (CANARY ISLANDS)

**President of the Government:** MANUEL HERMOSO ROJAS (AIC).
**President of the Parliament:** JOSÉ MIGUEL BRAVO DE LAGUNA (PP).

**Election, 28 May 1995**

|  | Seats |
|---|---|
| CC | 21 |
| PP | 18 |
| PSOE | 16 |
| PCN | 4 |
| AHI | 1 |
| **Total** | **60** |

## CANTABRIA

**President of the Government:** José Joaquín Martínez Sieso (PP—designate).
**President of the Parliament:** Adolfo Pajares Compostizo (PP).

**Election, 28 May 1995**

|  | Seats |
|---|---|
| PP | 13 |
| PSOE | 10 |
| UPCA | 7 |
| PRC | 6 |
| IU | 3 |
| Total | 39 |

## CASTILLA Y LEÓN

**President of the Government:** Juan José Lucas Jiménez (PP).
**President of the Parliament:** Manuel Estella Hoyos (PP).

**Election, 28 May 1995**

|  | Seats |
|---|---|
| PP | 50 |
| PSOE | 27 |
| IU | 5 |
| UPL | 2 |
| Total | 84 |

## CASTILLA-LA MANCHA

**President of the Government:** José Bono Martínez (PSOE).
**President of the Parliament:** (to be appointed).

**Election, 28 May 1995**

|  | Seats |
|---|---|
| PSOE | 24 |
| PP | 22 |
| IU | 1 |
| Total | 47 |

## CATALUÑA (CATALUNYA)

**President of the Government:** Jordi Pujol i Soley (CiU).
**President of the Parliament:** Joaquim Xicoy (CiU).

**Election, 15 March 1992**

|  | Seats |
|---|---|
| CiU | 71 |
| PSC | 39 |
| ERC | 11 |
| IC | 7 |
| PP | 7 |
| Total | 135 |

## EXTREMADURA

**President of the Government:** Juan Carlos Rodríguez Ibarra (PSOE).
**President of the Parliament:** Teresa Rejas (IU).

**Election, 28 May 1995**

|  | Seats |
|---|---|
| PSOE | 31 |
| PP | 27 |
| IU | 6 |
| Ex-U. | 1 |
| Total | 65 |

## GALICIA (GALIZA)

**President of the Government (Xunta):** Manuel Fraga Iribarne (PP).
**President of the Parliament:** Victorino Núñez Rodríguez (PP).

**Election, 17 October 1993**

|  | Seats |
|---|---|
| PP | 43 |
| PS de G-PSOE | 19 |
| BNG | 13 |
| Total | 75 |

## MADRID

**President of the Government:** Alberto Ruiz Gallardón (PP).
**President of the Parliament:** (to be appointed).

**Election, 28 May 1995**

|  | Seats |
|---|---|
| PP | 54 |
| PSOE | 32 |
| IU | 17 |
| Total | 101 |

## MURCIA

**President of the Government:** Ramón Luis Valcárcel (PP).
**President of the Parliament:** (to be appointed).

**Election, 28 May 1995**

|  | Seats |
|---|---|
| PP | 26 |
| PSOE | 15 |
| IU | 4 |
| Total | 45 |

## NAVARRA

**President of the Government:** Javier Otano (PSN-PSOE).
**President of the Parliament:** Dolores Eguren (PSN-PSOE).

**Election, 28 May 1995**

|  | Seats |
|---|---|
| PP-UPN | 17 |
| PSN-PSOE | 11 |
| CDN | 10 |
| HB | 5 |
| IU | 5 |
| EA | 2 |
| Total | 50 |

## LA RIOJA

**President of the Government:** Pedro María Sanz (PP).
**President of the Parliament:** (to be appointed).

**Election, 28 May 1995**

|  | Seats |
|---|---|
| PP | 17 |
| PSOE | 12 |
| IU | 2 |
| PR | 2 |
| Total | 33 |

SPAIN                                                                                                          *Directory*

### VALENCIA
**President of the Government:** EDUARDO ZAPLANA (PP).
**President of the Parliament:** VICENTE GONZÁLEZ LIZONDO (UV).

**Election, 28 May 1995**

|          | Seats |
|----------|------:|
| PP       | 42    |
| PSPV-PSOE| 32    |
| EU-EV*   | 10    |
| UV       | 5     |
| **Total**| **89**|

* Els Verds (Greens).

## Political Organizations

In mid-1994 more than 1,000 political parties were officially registered.

### PRINCIPAL NATIONAL PARTIES

**Frente Nacional:** Núñez de Balboa 31, 28001 Madrid; f. 1986; extreme right-wing; Pres. BLAS PIÑAR LÓPEZ; agreed to merge with Juntas Españolas de Integración (f. 1984 by fmr ministers of Franco Govt), Feb. 1993.

**Izquierda Unida (IU):** see note below.

**Partido de Acción Socialista (PASOC):** Plaza de Canalejas 6, 3°, 28014 Madrid; tel. (1) 5328994; fax (1) 5226951; f. 1879; took present name 1982; formerly Partido Socialista Obrero Español—Histórico (PSOE(h), Partido Socialista); Pres. PABLO CASTELLANO; Sec.-Gen. ALONSO PUERTA.

**Partido Comunista de España (PCE):** Marqués de Monteagudo 8, 28028 Madrid; tel. (1) 3569807; f. 1922; Euro-communist; 62,342 mems (Dec. 1987); absorbed Partido Comunista Obrero Español (PCOE) in 1986, and most of Partido Comunista de los Pueblos de España (PCPE) in Jan. 1989; Sec.-Gen. JULIO ANGUITA.

**Partido Feminista de España:** Magdalena 29, 1A, 28012 Madrid; tel. (1) 3694488; fax (1) 3694488; f. 1979; feminist party; Leader LIDIA FALCÓN O'NEILL.

**Partido Popular (PP):** Génova 13, 28004 Madrid; tel. (1) 3192027; telex 47444; fax (1) 3084618; f. 1976; fmrly Alianza Popular, name changed Jan. 1989; absorbed Democracia Cristiana (fmrly Partido Demócrata Popular) and Partido Liberal in early 1989; centre-right, Christian Democrat; 334,710 mems; Pres. JOSÉ MARÍA AZNAR; Sec.-Gen. FRANCISCO ALVAREZ CASCOS.

**Partido Socialista Obrero Español (PSOE):** Ferraz 68 y 70, 28008 Madrid; tel. (1) 5820444; telex 47554; fax (1) 5820422; f. 1879; socialist workers' party; affiliated to the Socialist International; merged with the Partido Socialista Popular in 1978; joined by Partido de los Trabajadores de España-Unidad Comunista (PTE-UC) in 1991; 351,770 mems (1994); Pres. RAMÓN RUBIAL; Sec.-Gen. FELIPE GONZÁLEZ MÁRQUEZ.

**Unión Centrista (UC):** Madrid; f. 1995 by fmr mems of Centro Democrático y Social (CDS), Greens and others; Co-ordinator FERNANDO GARCÍA FRUCTUOSO.

**Los Verdes:** Apdo 565, 38400 Puerto de la Cruz, Tenerife; f. 1984; green party; opposes nuclear energy, bull-fighting and development of tourism in the Canary Islands; proposes progressive abolition of armed forces; 19 ecological groups merged in Jan. 1993.

Note: Since 1989 the left-wing parties, including the PCE, PASOC, Izquierda Republicana and independents, have united to contest elections as the **Izquierda Unida (IU)**, which had 57,303 members in 1993.

### REGIONAL PARTIES

There are branches of the main national parties in most Spanish regions, and numerous regional parties including the following:

**Agrupación Herreña Independiente (AHI):** El Hierro; Canary Islands group.

**Agrupaciones Independientes de Canarias (AIC):** Galcerán 7-9, 38004 Santa Cruz de Tenerife; federation of Canary Island groupings (incl. Agrupación Tinerfeña de Independientes—ATI; Pres. MANUEL HERMOSO ROJAS; Sec.-Gen. PAULINO RIVERO); supported by Centro Canario Independiente (CCI; Leader LORENZO OLARTE); Pres. RAFAEL PEDRERO: Sec.-Gen. VICTORIANO RÍOS.

**Asamblea Majorera (AM):** La Venta 4 y 6, Apdo 195, 35600 Puerto del Rosario, Fuerteventura; tel. (28) 850798; fax (28) 531591; f. 1977; progressive, left-wing Canary Islands nationalist party; Sec.-Gen. JOSÉ MIGUEL BARRAGÁN CABRERA.

**Bloque Nacionalista Galego (BNG)** (Galician Nationalist Block): left-wing radical party; joined by Partido Nacionalista Galego (PNG) in Nov. 1991; Leader XOSÉ MANUEL BEIRAS.

**Chunta Aragonesista (ChA):** c/o Parliament of Aragón, Zaragoza; regional party of Aragón.

**Coalición Canaria (CC):** Canary Islands coalition of six parties, incl. AIC and most of Iniciativa Canaria (ICAN).

**Congreso Nacional de Canarias (CNC):** Avda 3 de mayo 81, 1° y 2°, Santa Cruz de Tenerife; tel. (22) 283353; fax (22) 283353; f. 1986; opposes membership of the EU and advocates membership of the OAU; seeks independence for the Canary Islands; Leader ANTONIO CUBILLO FERREIRA.

**Convergencia de Demócratas Navarros (CDN):** c/o Parliament of Navarra, Pamplona; f. 1995 following split in UPN; Leader JUAN CRUZ ALLI.

**Convergència i Unió (CiU):** València 231, 08007 Barcelona; tel. (3) 4870111; telex 97363; f. 1979 as an electoral coalition; Leader JORDI PUJOL I SOLEY; an alliance of the following two parties:

    **Convergència Democràtica de Catalunya (CDC):** València 231, 08007 Barcelona; Apdo 36245, 08080 Barcelona; tel. (3) 4870111; telex 97363; fax (3) 2158428; f. 1974; Catalan nationalist; centre; 33,724 mems (1992); Pres. JORDI PUJOL I SOLEY; Sec.-Gen. MIQUEL ROCA I JUNYENT.

    **Unió Democràtica de Catalunya:** València 246, 08007 Barcelona; tel. (3) 4873711; fax (3) 4875784; f. 1931; 29,169 mems (1993); Pres. of National Council JOAN RIGOL I ROIG; Pres. of Exec. Cttee JOSEP ANTONI DURAN I LLEIDA.

**Esquerra Republicana de Catalunya (ERC)** (Republican Left of Catalonia): Carrer Villarroel 45, ent., 08011 Barcelona; tel. (3) 4536005; fax (3) 3237122; f. 1931; advocates complete independence for Catalonia; Pres. HERIBERT BARRERA; Sec.-Gen. ANGEL COLOM.

**Esquerra Unida (EU):** c/o Parliament of Valencia, Valencia; left-wing.

**Euskal Ezkerra (EuE):** f. following split in Euskadiko Ezkerra (EE); left-wing Basque party; Sec.-Gen. XABIER GURRUTXAGA.

**Eusko Alkartasuna (EA)** (Basque Solidarity): San Prudencio 3, bajo, 01005 Vitoria; tel. (45) 232762; fax (45) 232953; f. 1986 (as Eusko Abertzaleak—Basque Nationalists) by breakaway group of progressive PNV mems; 15,000 mems; Pres. CARLOS GARAIKOETXEA; Sec.-Gen. INAXIO OLIVERI VITORIA-GASTEIZ.

**Extremadura Unida (Ex-U):** c/o Parliament of Extremadura, Cáceres.

**Federación Socialista Madrileña (FSM):** Santa Engracia 165, Madrid; Pres. JOSÉ ACOSTA; Sec.-Gen. JAIME LISSAVETZKY.

**Herri Batasuna (HB)** (People's Unity): Astarloa 8, 3°, 48001 Bilbao; tel. (4) 4240799; fax (4) 4235932; f. 1978; achieved legal recognition in 1986; Basque nationalist.

**Iniciativa Canaria (ICAN):** El Hierro; Canary Islands grouping of Communists and left-wing nationalists.

**Iniciativa per Catalunya (IC):** Ciutat 7, 08002 Barcelona; tel. 3027493; fax 4124252; f. 1987; left-wing alliance comprising the Parti Socialista Unificat de Catalunya (PSUC, see below), Entesa des Nacionalistes d'Esquerra (ENE) and individual citizens; Pres. RAFAEL RIBÓ MASSÓ.

    **Partit Socialista Unificat de Catalunya (PSUC):** Ciutat 7, 08002 Barcelona; tel. 3010612; telex 51793; fax 4120738; f. 1936; Communist; Sec.-Gen. RAFAEL RIBÓ MASSÓ.

**Partido Andaluz de Progreso (PAP):** Sevilla; f. 1993; nationalist; Sec.-Gen. PEDRO PACHECO.

**Partido Aragonés (PAR):** c/o Parliament of Aragón, Zaragoza; tel. (76) 214127; telex 58579; fax (76) 237403; f. 1977; fmrly Partido Aragonés Regionalista; Pres. JOSÉ MARÍA MUR BERNAD; Sec.-Gen. EMILIO EIROA GARCÍA.

**Partido Nacionalista Vasco (PNV):** c/o Parliament of Euskadi, Bilbao; tel. (4) 4244100; telex 32609; conservative Basque nationalist; seeks to achieve autonomous region through peaceful means; 31,000 mems (1993); Pres. XABIER ARZALLUS; Sec. JOSU BERGARA ETXEBARRIA.

**Partido Regionalista de Cantabria (PRC):** Madrid; centre-right party of Cantabria Region; Sec.-Gen. MIGUEL ANGEL REVILLA.

**Partido Riojano (PR):** Portales 17, 1°, 26001 Logroño; tel. (41) 238199; fax (41) 254396; Pres. LEOPOLDO VIROSTA GAROZ; Sec.-Gen. MIGUEL GONZÁLEZ DE LEGARRA.

**Partido Socialista de Euskadi-Euskadiko Ezkerra (PSE-EE)** (Basque Socialist Party-Basque Left): Plaza de San José 3, Bilbao 9; tel. (4) 4241606; f. 1993 by merger of PSE-PSOE and EE; Pres. JOSÉ MARÍA (TXIKI) BENEGAS; Sec.-Gen. RAMÓN JAÚREGUI.

**Partido Socialista de Navarra (PSN):** c/o Parliament of Navarra, Pamplona; Pres. JAVIER OTANO.

**Partido dos Socialistas de Galicia (PS de G-PSOE)** (Galician Socialist Party): Pino 1-9, 15704 Santiago de Compostela; tel. (81) 589622; Sec.-Gen. FRANCISCO VÁZQUEZ.

**Partido Socialista Obrero Español de Andalucía** (Spanish Socialist Workers' Party of Andalucía): San Vicente 37-41, 41002

Sevilla; tel. (5) 4386761; fax (5) 4388564; Sec.-Gen. CARLOS SANJUAN DE LA ROCHA.

**Partido Socialista del País Valenciano (PSPV-PSOE)** (Valencian Socialist Party): Almirante 3, 46003 Valencia; Pres. ANTONIO GARCÍA MIRALLES; Sec.-Gen. JOAN LERMA BLASCO.

**Partit dels Socialistes de Catalunya (PSC-PSOE):** Calle Nicaragua 75, 08029 Barcelona; tel. (3) 3210100; telex 50463; fax (3) 4397811; f. 1978 by merger of various Catalan parties of socialist ideology; Pres. JOAN REVENTÓS I CARNER; First Sec. JOSEP MARÍA (RAIMON) OBIOLS I GERMÀ.

**Plataforma Canaria Nacionalista (PCN):** Canary Islands nationalist group.

**Poder Andalucista (PA):** c/o Parliament of Andalucía, Sevilla; tel. (5) 4226855; fax (5) 4210446; f. 1977; fmrly Partido Andalucista; Sec.-Gen. MIGUEL ANGEL ARREDONDA CRECENTE.

**Unidad Alavesa (UA):** f. 1989; splinter group of PP; supports rights of province of Alava, within Basque Country; Pres. JOSÉ LUIS AÑÚA AJURIA; Sec.-Gen. PABLO MOSQUERA.

**Unió Mallorquina (UM):** Avda de Juan March Ordinas 8, entresuelo 2°, 07004 Palma de Mallorca; centre-right party; supports PRD; Pres. JERÓNIMO ALBERTÍ; Sec.-Gen. PEDRO JUAN MOREY BALLESTER.

**Unión Demócrata Foral (UDF):** centre party of Navarra region; allied to UPN.

**Unión para el Progreso de Cantabria (UPCA):** c/o Parliament of Cantabria, Santander; f. 1990, following split in regional PP, revived 1993; Leader JUAN HORMAECHEA CAZÓN.

**Unión del Pueblo Leonés (UPL):** c/o Parliament of Castilla y León, Valladolid; León separatist party.

**Unión del Pueblo Navarro (UPN):** Plaza Príncipe de Viana 1, 4° Dcha, 31002 Pamplona; tel. (48) 210810; fax (48) 210870; f. 1979; social Christian; Pres. JESÚS AIZPUN; Sec. RAFAEL GURREA.

**Unión Valenciana (UV):** Avda de César Giorgeta 16, 2A, 46007 Valencia; Pres. VICENTE GONZÁLEZ LIZONDO; Sec.-Gen. MANUEL CAMPILLOS MARTÍNEZ.

**Unitat del Poble Valencià (UPV):** Almirante 3, 46003 Valencia; tel. (6) 3915005; fax (6) 3915256; f. 1982; left-wing nationalist party; Leader PERE MAYOR PENADÉS.

### OTHER ORGANIZATIONS

Illegal terrorist organizations include the extreme left-wing Grupos de Resistencia Antifascista Primero de Octubre (GRAPO, First of October Anti-Fascist Resistance Groups, f. 1975); the Basque separatist Euskadi ta Askatasuna (ETA, Basque Homeland and Liberty, f. 1959), divided into ETA Político-militar and the more extremist ETA-Militar, and the Comandos Autónomos Anticapitalistas (CAA), a splinter group of ETA-M. The Grupos Antiterroristas de Liberación (GAL) were formed in 1983 to oppose ETA, and were subsequently revealed to have received government funding (see Recent History). The Grupo de Liberación Vasca appeared in 1984. Catalan nationalist movements include the right-wing anti-separatist Milicia Catalana (f. 1986 to oppose Terra Lliure), Moviment de Defensa de la Terra (MDT) and Ejército Rojo Catalán de Liberación (ERCA); Terra Lliure (Free Land, f. 1975), which had links with ETA, was dissolved in July 1991, but a dissident faction subsequently became active. A Galician nationalist movement, Exército Guerrilheiro do Pobo Galego Ceibe (EGPGC), was active between 1987 and 1991.

## Diplomatic Representation

### EMBASSIES IN SPAIN

**Algeria:** General Oráa 12, Apdo 6025, 28006 Madrid; tel. (1) 5629705; telex 41497; fax (1) 5629877; Ambassador: ABDELAZIZ RAHABI.

**Andorra:** Madrid; Ambassador: PERE ALTIMIR PINTAT.

**Angola:** D. Ramón de la Cruz 1, 3°, 28001 Madrid; tel. (1) 4356166; telex 47171; fax (1) 5779010; Ambassador: ASSUNÇÃO AFONSO DE SOUSA DOS ANJOS.

**Argentina:** Paseo de la Castellana 53, 28046 Madrid; tel. (1) 4424500; telex 27415; fax (1) 4423559; Ambassador: GUILLERMO JACOVELLA.

**Australia:** Paseo de la Castellana 143, 2°, Edif. Cuzco 1, 28046 Madrid; tel. (1) 5790428; fax (1) 5700204; Ambassador: WARWICK R. PEARSON.

**Austria:** Paseo de la Castellana 91, 9°, 28046 Madrid; tel. (1) 5565315; telex 22694; fax (1) 5973579; Ambassador: RICHARD WOTAVA.

**Belgium:** Paseo de la Castellana 18, 6°, 28046 Madrid; tel. (1) 5776300; telex 23715; fax (1) 4318166; Ambassador: THIERRY MUÛLS.

**Bolivia:** Velázquez 20, 7°, 28001 Madrid; tel. (1) 5780835; fax (1) 5773946; Ambassador: RAÚL LEMA PATIÑO.

**Brazil:** Fernando el Santo 6, 28010 Madrid; tel. (1) 3080459; telex 23291; fax (1) 3080465; Ambassador: LUIZ FELIPE DE SEIXAS-CORREA.

**Bulgaria:** Santa María Magdalena 15, 28016 Madrid; tel. (1) 3456651; telex 22407; fax (1) 3591201; Ambassador: MIKHAIL PETKOV.

**Cameroon:** Rosario Pino 3, 28020 Madrid; tel. (1) 5711160; telex 27772; fax (1) 5712504; Ambassador: PHILIPPE MATANGA.

**Canada:** Núñez de Balboa 35, Edif. Goya, 28001 Madrid; tel. (1) 4314300; telex 27347; fax (1) 4312367; Ambassador: DAVID WRIGHT.

**Chile:** Lagasca 88, 6°, 28001 Madrid; tel. (1) 4319160; telex 43816; fax (1) 5775560; Ambassador: ALVARO BRIONES.

**China, People's Republic:** Arturo Soria 113, 28027 Madrid; tel. (1) 5194242; telex 22808; fax (1) 5194675; Ambassador: YUAN TAO.

**Colombia:** General Martínez Campos 48, 28010 Madrid; tel. (1) 3103800; telex 23959; fax (1) 3102869; Ambassador: HUMBERTO DE LA CALLE.

**Costa Rica:** Paseo de la Castellana 166, 5°, 28046 Madrid; tel. (1) 3459622; telex 49299; fax (1) 3459622; Ambassador: ANTONIO LÓPEZ ESCARRÉ.

**Côte d'Ivoire:** Serrano 154, 28006 Madrid; tel. (1) 5626916; telex 45971; Ambassador: JEAN-VINCENT ZINSOU.

**Croatia:** Velázquez 44, 2°, 28001 Madrid; tel. (1) 5776881; fax (1) 5776905; Ambassador: SERGEJ MORSAN.

**Cuba:** Paseo de la Habana 194, 28036 Madrid; tel. (1) 3592500; telex 23858; fax (1) 3596145; Ambassador: ROSARIO NAVAS MORATA.

**Cyprus:** Serrano 43–45, Oficina 19, 6°, 28001 Madrid; tel. (1) 4359630; fax (1) 5755473; Ambassador: ELIAS ELIADES.

**Czech Republic:** Caídos de la División Azul 22-A, 28016 Madrid; tel. (1) 3503604; telex 22466; fax (1) 3591146; Ambassador: PAVLINA REZNIČKOVA.

**Denmark:** Claudio Coello 91, 4°, 28006 Madrid; tel. (1) 4318445; telex 27265; fax (1) 4319168; Ambassador: JOHN H. BERNHARD.

**Dominican Republic:** Paseo de la Castellana 30, 28046 Madrid; tel. (1) 4315395; Ambassador: Dr RAFAEL GAUTREAU.

**Ecuador:** Príncipe de Vergara 73, 7°, 28006 Madrid; tel. (1) 5627215; telex 42038; fax (1) 5613067; Ambassador: FEDERICO ARTETA RIVERA.

**Egypt:** Velázquez 69, 28006 Madrid; tel. (1) 5776308; telex 42389; fax (1) 5781732; Ambassador: MOHAMED ALAA EL-DIN BARAKAT.

**El Salvador:** Serrano 114, 28006 Madrid; tel. (1) 5628002; telex 23137; fax (1) 5630584; Ambassador: GUILLERMO PAZ LARÍN.

**Equatorial Guinea:** Claudio Coello 91, 5°, 28006 Madrid; tel. (1) 5782418; telex 46800; Ambassador: BRUNO ESONO ONDO.

**Finland:** Paseo de la Castellana 15, 4°, 28046 Madrid; tel. (1) 3196172; telex 22007; fax (1) 3083901; Ambassador: EEVA-KRISTIINA FORSMAN.

**France:** Salustiano Olózaga 9, 28001 Madrid; tel. (1) 4355560; telex 27798; fax (1) 4356655; Ambassador: ANDRÉ GADAUD.

**Gabon:** Angel de Diego Roldán 14–16, 28016 Madrid; tel. (1) 4138211; telex 27437; fax (1) 4131153; Ambassador: JULES MARIUS OGOUEBANDJA.

**Germany:** Fortuny 8, 28010 Madrid; tel. (1) 3199100; telex 27768; fax (1) 3102104; Ambassador: Dr HENNING WEGENER.

**Greece:** Avda del Dr Arce 24, 28002 Madrid; tel. (1) 5644653; telex 44135; fax (1) 5644669; Ambassador: CHARALAMBOS KÓRAKAS.

**Guatemala:** Rafael Salgado 3, 4° Izqda, 28036 Madrid; tel. (1) 3440347; telex 48618; fax (1) 4587894; Ambassador: JUAN JOSÉ SERRA CASTILLO.

**Haiti:** Marqués del Duero 3, 1° Izqda, 28001 Madrid; tel. (1) 5752624; fax (1) 4314600; Ambassador: (vacant).

**Holy See:** Avda de Pío XII 46, 28016 Madrid (Apostolic Nunciature); tel. (1) 7668311; telex 47768; fax (1) 7667085; Apostolic Nuncio: (vacant).

**Honduras:** Rosario Pino 6, 4°, 28023 Madrid; tel. (1) 5714133; fax (1) 5721319; Ambassador: Dr EDGARDO PAZ BARNICA.

**Hungary:** Angel de Diego Roldán 21, 28016 Madrid; tel. (1) 4137011; fax (1) 4134138; Ambassador: Dr PÁL SCHMITT.

**India:** Avda Pío XII 30–32, 28016 Madrid; tel. (1) 3450406; telex 22605; fax (1) 3451112; Ambassador: G. D. ATUK.

**Indonesia:** Agastia 65, 28043 Madrid; tel. (1) 4130394; telex 43822; fax (1) 5194950; Ambassador: (vacant).

**Iran:** Jerez 5, Villa El Altozano (Chamartín), 28016 Madrid; tel. (1) 3450112; telex 22322; fax (1) 3451190; Ambassador: BAHRAM GHASSEMI.

**Iraq:** Ronda de Sobradiel 67 (Parque Conde de Orgaz), 28043 Madrid; tel. (1) 7593575; telex 23806; fax (1) 7593180; Ambassador: (vacant).

**Ireland:** Claudio Coello 73, 1°, 28001 Madrid; tel. (1) 5763500; fax (1) 4351677; Ambassador: RICHARD RYAN.

**Israel:** Velázquez 150, 7°, 28002 Madrid; tel. (1) 4111357; telex 46996; fax (1) 5645974; Ambassador: YAACOV COHEN.

**Italy:** Lagasca 98, 28006 Madrid; tel. (1) 5776529; telex 22414; fax (1) 5757776; Ambassador: ANTONIO CIARRAPICO.

**Japan:** Joaquín Costa 29, 28002 Madrid; tel. (1) 5625546; telex 27652; fax (1) 2627868; Ambassador: TATSUO YAMAGUCHI.

**Jordan:** General Martínez Campos 41, 5°, 28010 Madrid; tel. (1) 4191100; telex 23755; fax (1) 3082536; Ambassador: (vacant).

**Korea, Republic:** Miguel Angel 23, 4°, 28010 Madrid; tel. (1) 3100053; fax (1) 3196297; Ambassador: KWANG JE CHO.

**Kuwait:** Paseo de la Castellana 141, 28046 Madrid; tel. (1) 5720162; telex 23753; fax (1) 2796350; Ambassador: ABDEL RAZZAK ABDEL KADER AL-KANDARI.

**Latvia:** Pedro de Valdivia 9, 28006 Madrid; tel. (1) 5631745; Ambassador: AINA NAGOBADS-ABOLS.

**Lebanon:** Paseo de la Castellana 178, 3° Izqda, 28046 Madrid; tel. (1) 3451368; telex 45964; fax (1) 3455631; Ambassador: ROBERT ARAB.

**Libya:** Pisuerga 12, 28002 Madrid; tel. (1) 5635753; telex 27814; fax (1) 5641904; Head of People's Bureau: NURI MOHAMED ABDALLA BET EL-MAL.

**Lithuania:** Fortuny 19, 1a Izqda, 28010 Madrid; tel. (1) 3102075; fax (1) 3104018; Ambassador: GIEDRUS CEKUDIS.

**Luxembourg:** Claudio Coello 78, 1°, 28001 Madrid; tel. (1) 4359164; telex 49229; fax (1) 5774826; Ambassador: JEAN FALTZ.

**Malaysia:** Paseo de la Castellana 91, 5°, 28046 Madrid; tel. (1) 5550684; telex 42108; fax (1) 5555208; Ambassador: MOHD AZHARI BIN ABDUL KARIM.

**Malta:** Fortuny 3, 3° Dcha, 28010 Madrid; tel. (1) 3198717; fax (1) 3198277; Ambassador: EVARIST V. SALIBA.

**Mauritania:** Velázquez 90, 3°, 28006 Madrid; tel. (1) 5757006; telex 23135; fax (1) 4359531; Ambassador: CHEIKH OULD BAHA.

**Mexico:** Carrera de San Jerónimo 46, 28014 Madrid; tel. (1) 3692814; fax (1) 4202292; Ambassador: RODOLFO ECHEVERRÍA RUIZ.

**Monaco:** Villanueva 12, 28001 Madrid; tel. (1) 5782048; fax (1) 4357132; Ambassador: JEAN AUSSEIL.

**Morocco:** Serrano 179, 28002 Madrid; tel. (1) 5631090; telex 27799; fax (1) 5617887; Ambassador: ALI BENBOUCHTA.

**Netherlands:** Paseo de la Castellana 178–180, 28046 Madrid; tel. (1) 3590914; telex 27316; fax (1) 3592150; Ambassador: Baron W. O. BENTINCK VAN SCHOONHETEN.

**New Zealand:** Plaza de la Lealtad 2, 3°, 28014 Madrid; tel. (1) 5230226; fax (1) 5230171; Ambassador: PAUL TIPPING.

**Nicaragua:** Paseo de la Castellana 127, 1°B, 28046 Madrid; tel. (1) 5555510; telex 45382; fax (1) 4555737; Ambassador: FILADELFO CHAMORRO CORONEL.

**Nigeria:** Segre 23, Apdo 14.287, 28002 Madrid; tel. (1) 5630911; telex 44395; fax (1) 5636320; Ambassador: YARO YUSUFU MAMMAN.

**Norway:** Paseo de la Castellana 31, Edif. 'La Pirámide', 28046 Madrid; tel. (1) 3103116; telex 23331; fax (1) 3190969; Ambassador: HELGE VINDENES.

**Pakistan:** Avda do Pio XII, 28016 Madrid; tel. (1) 3458986; telex 41215; fax (1) 3458158; Ambassador: TAUQIR HUSSAIN.

**Panama:** Claudio Coello 86, 28003 Madrid; tel. (1) 5765001; fax (1) 5767161; Ambassador: Dr ARÍSTIDES ROYO SÁNCHEZ.

**Paraguay:** Castelló 30, 1° Izqda, 28001 Madrid; tel. (1) 5763186; fax (1) 4358858; Ambassador: ANGEL JUAN SOUTO HERNÁNDEZ.

**Peru:** Príncipe de Vergara 36, 5D, 28001 Madrid; tel. (1) 4314242; fax (1) 5776861; Ambassador: ROBERTO VILLARÁN KOECHLIN.

**Philippines:** Claudio Coello 92, 28006 Madrid; tel. (1) 5765403; fax (1) 5758360; Ambassador: ISABEL CARO WILSON.

**Poland:** Guisando 23 bis, 28035 Madrid; tel. (1) 3736605; fax (1) 3736624; Ambassador: WŁADYSŁAW KLACZYŃSKI.

**Portugal:** Pinar 1, 28006 Madrid; tel. (1) 5617800; telex 22205; fax (1) 4110172; Ambassador: LEONARDO MATHIAS.

**Qatar:** Paseo de la Castellana 15, 28046 Madrid; tel. (1) 3198400; telex 48537; fax (1) 3196619; Chargé d'affaires a.i.: Sheikh FAHAD AWEADA MOHD AL-THANI.

**Romania:** Avda Alfonso XIII 157, 28016 Madrid; tel. (1) 3504436; telex 22433; fax (1) 3452917; Ambassador: DARIE AUREL NOVACEANU.

**Russia:** Velázquez 155, 28002 Madrid; tel. (1) 5622264; telex 45632; fax (1) 5629712; Ambassador: VIKTOR G. KOMPLETOV.

**Saudi Arabia:** Paseo de la Habana 163, 28036 Madrid; tel. (1) 3451250; telex 22710; fax (1) 3507876; Ambassador: MOHAMED N. IBRAHIM.

**Slovakia:** Pinar 20, 28006 Madrid; tel. (1) 5641241; telex 22466; fax (1) 5636467; Ambassador: MILAN TRAVNÍČEK.

**Slovenia:** Salustiano Olózaga 5, 4° Izqda, 28001 Madrid; tel. (1) 5756556; fax (1) 5750091.

**South Africa:** Claudio Coello 91, 28006 Madrid; tel. (1) 4356688; telex 44049; fax (1) 5777414; Ambassador: AWIE MARAIS.

**Sweden:** Caracas 25, Apdo 14159, 28080 Madrid; tel. (1) 3081535; telex 27405; fax (1) 3081903; Ambassador: TOMAS BERTELMAN.

**Switzerland:** Núñez de Balboa 35, 7°, 28001 Madrid; tel. (1) 4313400; telex 23079; fax (1) 5776898; Ambassador: RUDOLF SCHALLER.

**Syria:** Plaza de Platería Martínez 1, 28014 Madrid; tel. (1) 4203946; telex 43529; fax (1) 4202681; Ambassador: MOHAMMAD ZUHAIR AL-AQAD.

**Thailand:** Segre 29, 28002 Madrid; tel. (1) 5632903; telex 49044; fax (1) 5640033; Ambassador: CHITRIK SRESHTHAPUTRA.

**Tunisia:** Plaza de Alonso Martínez 3, 28004 Madrid; tel. (1) 4473508; telex 27672; fax (1) 5938416; Ambassador: ABDELHAMID FEHRI.

**Turkey:** Rafael Calvo 18, 28010 Madrid; tel. (1) 3198111; telex 44345; fax (1) 3086602; Ambassador: NABI ŞENSOY.

**United Arab Emirates:** Capitán Haya 40, 28020 Madrid; tel. (1) 5701003; telex 42765; fax (1) 5715176; Ambassador: Sheikh ABDULLA BEN ZAYED BEN SAQR AL-NAHAYYAN.

**United Kingdom:** Fernando el Santo 16, 28010 Madrid; tel. (1) 3190200; telex 27656; fax (1) 3190423; Ambassador: A. D. BRIGHTY.

**USA:** Serrano 75, 28006 Madrid; tel. (1) 5774000; telex 27763; fax (1) 5641652; Ambassador: RICHARD GARDNER.

**Uruguay:** Paseo del Pintor Rosales 32, 1° D, 28008 Madrid; tel. (1) 5428038; telex 22441; fax (1) 5428177; Ambassador: JULIO AZNAREZ BECHTOLD.

**Venezuela:** Avda Capitán Haya 1, Edif. Eurocentro, Planta 13, 28020 Madrid; tel. (1) 5558452; telex 23699; fax (1) 5971583; Ambassador: FRANCISCO PAPARONI M.

**Yugoslavia:** Velázquez 162, 28002 Madrid; tel. (1) 5635045; telex 44280; fax (1) 5630440; Ambassador: (vacant).

**Zaire:** Avda del Dr Arce 7, 28002 Madrid; tel. (1) 2624710; telex 27816; Ambassador: KUNTALA KINA.

# Judicial System

**Consejo General del Poder Judicial—CGPJ** (General Council of Judicial Power): Marqués de la Ensenada 8, 28004 Madrid; tel. (1) 3199700; the highest governing body of the judiciary; comprises the President of the Supreme Court, 20 members elected (since 1985) by the Cortes and appointed by the King for a five-year term (10 by the Congress of Deputies and 10 by the Senate); supervises the judicial system; independent of the Ministry of Justice; Pres. PASCUAL SALA SÁNCHEZ.

**General Prosecutor:** CARLOS GRANADOS PÉREZ.

### SUPREME COURT

**Tribunal Supremo:** Palacio de Justicia, Plaza de la Villa de París s/n, 28004 Madrid; tel. (1) 3971000; is composed of five courts, each with its president and its respective judges.

**President:** PASCUAL SALA SÁNCHEZ.

**First Court:** civil; President and 10 judges; Pres. PEDRO GONZÁLEZ POVEDA.

**Second Court:** criminal; 14 judges; Pres. (vacant).

**Third Court:** litigious-administrative; 33 judges; Pres. ANGEL RODRÍGUEZ GARCÍA.

**Fourth Court:** company; 13 judges; Pres. MIGUEL ANGEL CAMPOS ALONSO.

**Fifth Court:** military; 8 judges; Pres. JOSÉ JIMÉNEZ VILLAREJO.

### HIGH COURTS

**Audiencia Nacional** (National Court): García Gutiérrez 1, Madrid 4; tel. (1) 4101941; established in 1977; consists of five divisions, each with its president and respective judges and a central criminal court; attached to Second Court; deals primarily with crimes associated with a modern industrial society, such as forgery and drugs-trafficking; also comprises company and litigation courts; Pres. CLEMENTE AUGER.

**Audiencias Superiores de Justicia de las Comunidades Autónomas** (Autonomous Communities' Superior Courts of Justice): consist of civil and criminal division, administrative division and labour division.

**Audiencias Provinciales** (Provincial Courts): hear oral public proceedings, in single instance, for prosecutions of offences pun-

SPAIN — Directory

ishable by major prison terms, and appeals against decisions, sentences and judgments of lower courts.

### OTHER COURTS

Lower courts are the Criminal, Administrative, Labour, Juvenile and Prison Supervisory Courts of First Instance and Trial Courts. In municipalities where there are no Courts of First Instance and Trial, there is a Magistrates' Court.

## Religion

### CHRISTIANITY

Most of Spain's inhabitants profess adherence to Roman Catholicism, and the country contains some 61,000 churches, with about 500 persons in each parish. In 1976 there were 34,415,600 Roman Catholics in Spain. Opus Dei (see International Organizations, p. 263) plays an important role in Spanish society. There are some 30,000 Protestants in Spain.

#### The Roman Catholic Church

For ecclesiastical purposes, Spain (including Spanish North Africa) comprises 14 archdioceses and 53 dioceses. The archdiocese of Barcelona is directly responsible to the Holy See, while the remaining 13 are metropolitan sees. Each diocese is suffragan to a metropolitan see.

**Bishops' Conference:** Conferencia Episcopal Española, Calle Añastro 1, 28033 Madrid; tel. (1) 3439600; telex 42922; fax (1) 3439616; f. 1977; Pres. ELÍAS YANES ALVAREZ, Archbishop of Zaragoza.

**Archbishop of Toledo and Primate of Spain:** FRANCISCO ALVAREZ MARTÍNEZ, Arco de Palacio 1, 45002 Toledo; tel. (25) 224100; fax (25) 222639.

**Archbishop of Barcelona:** Cardinal RICARD MARIA CARLES.

**Archbishop of Burgos:** SANTIAGO MARTÍNEZ ACEBES.

**Archbishop of Granada:** JOSÉ MÉNDEZ ASENSIO.

**Archbishop of Madrid:** ANTONIO MARÍA ROUCO VARELA.

**Archbishop of Mérida-Badajoz:** ANTONIO MONTERO MORENO.

**Archbishop of Oviedo:** GABINO DÍAZ MERCHÁN.

**Archbishop of Pamplona:** FERNANDO SEBASTIÁN AGUILAR.

**Archbishop of Santiago de Compostela:** (vacant).

**Archbishop of Sevilla:** CARLOS AMIGO VALLEJO.

**Archbishop of Tarragona:** RAMÓN TORRELLA CASCANTE.

**Archbishop of Valencia:** AUGUSTÍN GARCÍA-GASCO VICENTE.

**Archbishop of Valladolid:** JOSÉ DELICADO BAEZA.

**Archbishop of Zaragoza:** ELÍAS YANES ALVAREZ.

#### The Anglican Communion

Anglicans in Spain are adherents of the Spanish Reformed Episcopal Church (Iglesia Española Reformada Episcopal), founded in 1880. The Church had 17 congregations, with a total of about 2,510 members, in 1994.

**Bishop:** Rt Rev. ARTURO SÁNCHEZ, Calle Beneficienca 18, 28004 Madrid; tel. (1) 4452560; fax (1) 5944572; f. 1880.

#### Other Christian Churches

**Baptist Evangelical Union of Spain:** Cerinola 3–6°, IA, Barcelona 22; tel. (3) 2110489; Sec. Rev. ADOLFO MONSO CABRE; Pres. PEDRO BONET.

**Iglesia Evangélica Española** (Spanish Evangelical Church): Noviciado 5, 08015 Madrid; tel. (1) 5313947; fax (1) 5234137; f. 1869 by merger of Presbyterians, Methodists, Congregationalists and Lutherans; 3,000 mems (1994); Pres. ENRIQUE CAPÓ; Sec. ALFREDO ABAD.

**Iglesia Ortodoxa Griega** (Greek Orthodox Church): Nicaragua 12, 28016 Madrid; tel. (1) 3454085; fax (1) 3509374.

### ISLAM

In the early 1990s there were an estimated 300,000 Muslims in Spain.

**Centro Islamico:** Alfonso Cano 3, 28010 Madrid; tel. (1) 4480554.

### JUDAISM

There are an estimated 15,000 Jews in Spain.

**Comunidad Israelita** (Jewish Community): Balmes 3, 28010 Madrid; tel. (1) 4459835; fax (1) 5941517.

### OTHER RELIGIOUS GROUPS

There are minorities of Muslims (300,000 adherents), Jews (15,000 adherents), Bahá'ís (2,000 adherents) and Buddhists.

## The Press

Freedom of thought, belief and expression are guaranteed in the 1978 Constitution, as is the right to receive and disseminate true information, provided that, in the exercise of these rights, the laws regulating professional secrecy are observed and that personal privacy and honour are respected. The Constitution also states that these rights may not be restricted by pre-censorship.

There are no truly national newspapers, although some, such as *ABC*, *Ya* and *El País* may readily be obtained outside the region in which they are published. Since 1982 *El País* has been printed simultaneously in Madrid and Barcelona. In 1986 regional editions were established in Andalucía and Valencia, and in 1993 in the Canary Islands and Vigo. Since 1978 there has been a marked decline in the local press and an increase in the importance of the regional press. In 1990 there were about 120 newspapers in Spain, with a total daily circulation of 3.3m.

### PRINCIPAL NEWSPAPERS
(arranged alphabetically by province)

#### Albacete

**La Tribuna de Albacete:** Salamanca 17, Apdo 369, Albacete; tel. (67) 210121; telex 29696; fax (67) 211275; daily; Dir CARLOS ZULOAGA LÓPEZ.

#### Alicante

**Ciudad de Alcoy:** San Juan de la Ribera 30, 03800 Alcoy; tel. (6) 5544577; fax (6) 5542106; daily; Dir JOSÉ VICENTE BOTELLA.

**Información:** Avda Dr Rico 17, Apdo 214, 03005 Alicante; tel. (6) 5123199; telex 66733; fax (6) 5227527; f. 1941; morning; Dir VICENTE MARTÍNEZ CARRILLO; circ. 21,269.

**El Periódico de Elche:** Polígono Industrial Altabix, Calle Elda s/n, 03203 Elche; tel. (6) 5456586; fax (6) 5456519; Dir VICENTE MARCO VALLADOLID.

#### Almería

**La Crónica del Sur:** Andalucía 8, Ciudad Jardín, 04007 Almería; tel. (51) 258511; telex 75366; fax (51) 243863; f. 1982; daily; ultra-right wing; Dir JOAQUÍN ABAD; Editor-in-Chief JOSÉ MANUEL BRETONES; circ. 1,372.

**La Voz de Almería:** Avda de Monserrat 50, 04006 Almería; tel. (51) 250888; telex 75348; fax (51) 256458; morning; Dir PEDRO MANUEL DE LA CRUZ ALONSO; circ. 6,633.

#### Asturias—see Oviedo

#### Avila

**El Diario de Avila:** Carretera de Valladolid s/n, 05004 Avila; tel. (20) 252052; fax (20) 251406; f. 1888; morning; Dir JOSÉ MANUEL SERRANO ALVAREZ; circ. 8,000.

#### Badajoz

**Hoy:** Carretera Madrid–Lisboa s/n, 06008 Badajoz; tel. (24) 252511; telex 28643; fax (24) 243004; f. 1933; morning; Catholic; Badajoz and Cáceres editions; Dir TERESIANO RODRÍGUEZ NÚÑEZ; circ. 21,815.

#### Barcelona

**Avui:** Consell de Cent 425, 08009 Barcelona; tel. (3) 2656000; telex 54063; fax (3) 2658251; f. 1976; morning; in Catalan; Man. XAVIER LLOBET COLOM; Dir VICENC VILLATORO LAMOLLA; circ. 50,000.

**Diari de Sabadell:** Sant Quirze 37–41, 1°, 08201 Sabadell; tel. (3) 7261100; fax (3) 7255543; f. 1977; 5 a week; Dir RAMÓN RODRÍGUEZ ZORRILLA; circ. 9,100.

**Diario Regió 7:** Sant Antoni M. Claret 32, 08240 Manresa; tel. (3) 8772233; fax (3) 8740352; f. 1978; 5 a week; Dir GONÇAL MAZCUÑAN I BOIX; circ. 8,400 (Sat. 12,000).

**Diario de Terrassa:** Galileo 347, 08224 Terrassa; tel. (3) 7886166; fax (3) 7887458; daily; Dir ANA MUÑOZ NÚÑEZ; circ. 5,590.

**Foto-Sport:** Valencia 49–51, 08015 Barcelona; tel. (3) 2269494; fax (3) 2268421; daily; Dirs JOSÉ SANCLEMENTE, DALMAU CODINA.

**El Mundo Deportivo:** Tallers 62–64, 4°, 08001 Barcelona; tel. (3) 3012828; fax (3) 3019480; f. 1906; morning; sport; Dir SANTI NOLLA ZAYAS; circ. 120,000.

**Nou Diari de Barcelona:** Tamarit 155, 08015 Barcelona; tel. (3) 3294446; telex 98766; fax (3) 3290227; f. 1792; morning; in Catalan.

**El País:** Zona Franca, Sector B, Calle D, 08004 Barcelona; tel. (3) 4010500; telex 97940; fax (3) 3353925; daily; f. 1982; Assistant Editor-in-Chief LLUÍS BASSETS; circ. 80,000 (Sun. 143,000).

**El Periódico:** Consell de Cent 425–427, 08009 Barcelona; tel. (3) 2655353; telex 51950; fax (3) 4846512; daily; f. 1978; Dir ANTONIO FRANCO ESTADELLA; circ. 190,000 (Sun. 380,000).

SPAIN

**La Vanguardia:** Pelayo 28, 08001 Barcelona; tel. (3) 3015454; telex 54530; fax (3) 3185587; f. 1881; morning; Dir JUAN TAPIA; Editor JAVIER DE GODÓ Y MUNTAÑOLA; circ. 208,029; (Sun. 316,425).

### Burgos

**Diario de Burgos:** San Pedro de Cardeña 34, Apdo 46, 09002 Burgos; tel. (47) 268375; telex 39703; fax (47) 268003; f. 1891; morning; Catholic; independent; Dir VICENTE RUIZ DE MENCIA; circ. 15,028 (Sun. 21,600).

### Cáceres

**Extremadura:** Camino Llano 9, Apdo 26, 10002 Cáceres; tel. (27) 210661; fax (27) 210372; f. 1923; morning; Dir JOSÉ HIGUERO MANZANO; circ. 10,680.

### Cádiz

**Area:** Gibraltar 13–15, Apdo 15, 11300 La Línea de la Concepción; tel. (56) 761478; telex 78038; fax (56) 763050; morning; Dir ANTONIO GÓMEZ RUBIO; circ. 2,601.

**Diario de Cádiz:** Ceballos 1, Apdo 57, 11003 Cádiz; tel. (56) 226605; telex 76099; fax (56) 211601; f. 1867; morning; independent; Dir JOSÉ JOLY PALOMINO; circ. 29,289.

**Diario de Jerez:** Patricio Garvey s/nº, Apdo 316, Jerez de la Frontera; tel. (56) 321411; fax (56) 320011; f. 1984; Dir MANUEL DE LA PEÑA MUÑOZ.

**Europa Sur:** José Antonio 9–3°, Edificio los Gálvez, Apdo 453, Algeciras; tel. (56) 666811; fax (56) 631167; f. 1989; daily; Dir JUAN CARLOS JIMÉNEZ LAZ; circ. 15,000.

**El Periódico del Guadalete:** Córdoba 16, 11405 Jerez de la Frontera; tel. (56) 302511; fax (56) 307912; Dir ALEJANDRO RAMÍREZ FERNÁNDEZ; Cádiz edn: *Cádiz Información*, Ancha 5, 11001 Cádiz; tel. (56) 220910; fax (56) 221291.

### Cantabria (Santander)

**Alerta:** Marcelino Sanz de Sautuola 12, 39003 Santander; tel. (42) 213500; fax (42) 362100; f. 1937; morning; Dir JUAN LUIS FERNÁNDEZ; circ. 30,619.

**El Diario Montañés:** Canda Landaburu s/n, La Albericia, 39012 Santander; tel. (42) 346622; fax (42) 341007; f. 1902; morning; independent; Dir MANUEL ANGEL CASTAÑEDA; circ. 35,000 (Sun. 50,000).

### Castellón

**Castellón Diario Independiente:** Carretera de Valencia–Barcelona, km 68,700, Apdo 505, 12080 Castellón de la Plana; tel. (64) 209599; telex 65819; fax (64) 243650; daily; Dir FRANCISCO PLANELLES SEGARRA.

**Mediterráneo:** Carretera de Almassora s/n, 12005 Castellón de la Plana; tel. (64) 207211; telex 65454; fax (64) 218424; f. 1938; morning; Dir JAVIER ANDRÉS BELTRÁN; circ. 6,367.

### Ciudad Real

**Lanza:** Ronda del Carmen s/n (antiguo Hospital provincial), 13004 Ciudad Real; tel. (26) 220339; telex 26059; fax (26) 222977; morning; Dir JOSÉ ANTONIO CASADO; circ. 5,000.

**La Tribuna de Ciudad Real:** Plaza del Pilar 7, 13001 Ciudad Real; tel. (26) 215301; fax (26) 215306.

### Córdoba

**Córdoba:** Ing. Juan de la Cierva 18 (Polígono Industrial de la Torrecilla), Apdo 2, 14013 Córdoba; tel. (57) 291711; telex 76548; fax (57) 204648; f. 1941; morning; Dir ANTONIO RAMOS ESPEJO; Editor-in-Chief ANTONIO GALÁN ORTIZ; circ. 8,524.

**Córdoba 92:** Virgen del Valle 4, 14012 Córdoba; daily; Dir MARÍA DEL AMOR MARTÍN FERNÁNDEZ.

### La Coruña

**El Correo Gallego:** Preguntoiro 29, Santiago de Compostela; tel. (81) 582600; telex 82372; fax (81) 562396; morning; Dir JOSÉ MANUEL REY NOVOA; circ. 6,595.

**O Correo Galego:** f. 1994; Galician edn of above; circ. 10,000.

**El Ideal Gallego:** Polígono de Pocomaco Parcela C-12, Mesoiro, 15190 La Coruña; tel. (81) 299000; telex 82123; fax (81) 299327; f. 1917; morning; Dir ALBINO MALLO ALVAREZ; circ. 20,000.

**La Voz de Galicia:** Concepción Arenal 11–13, 15006 La Coruña; tel. (81) 180180; telex 82121; fax (81) 295918; f. 1882; morning; commercial; Dir JUAN RAMÓN DÍAZ GARCÍA; circ. 82,275 (Sun. 126,789).

### Cuenca

**El Día de Cuenca:** Polígono 'El Cantorral' 13, 16004 Cuenca; tel. (66) 212291; telex 48509; fax (66) 213200; f. 1984; Dir SANTIAGO MATEO SAHUQUILLO; circ. 5,500.

### Gerona

**Diari de Girona:** Carretera de Barcelona 29, 17001 Gerona; tel. (72) 476277; fax (72) 476240; f. 1891; morning; Dir JORDI BOSCH I MOLINET; circ. 8,500; filed for bankruptcy June 1995.

**El Punt:** Figuerola 28, 17001 Gerona; tel. (72) 221010; fax (72) 218630; f. 1979; Dir EMILI GISPERT I NEGRELL; circ. 15,000.

### Granada

**Ideal:** Cádiz s/n, Polígono de Asegra, 18210 Peligros; tel. (58) 405161; fax (58) 405072; f. 1932; morning; Dir MELCHOR SÁIZ-PARDO RUBIO; circ. 40,000; edns also in Jaén and Almería.

### Guipúzcoa

**El Diario Vasco:** Barrio de Ibaeta s/n, Apdo 201, 20009 San Sebastián; tel. (43) 212233; telex 38113; fax (43) 211867; f. 1934; morning; Liberal; Dir MIGUEL LARREA (acting); circ. 80,714 (weekdays), 67,332 (Mondays).

**Egin:** Polígono Eciago 10B, Apdo 1397, 20120 Hernani; tel. (43) 554712; telex 36629; fax (43) 551207; morning; Dir JABIER SALUTREGI; circ. 42,814.

**Euskaldunon Egunkaria:** Industrialdea 01-02, Pabilioiak, 20160 Lasarte-Oria; tel. (43) 371545; fax (43) 365493; f. 1990; daily; entirely in Basque; Dir MARTÍN UGALDE; circ. 15,000.

### Huelva

**Huelva Información:** Plaza San Pedro 7, Apdo 176, 21001 Huelva; tel. (55) 257989; telex 75619; fax (55) 259467; Dir-Gen. RAMÓN FERNÁNDEZ BEVIÁ; circ. 7,653.

### Huesca

**Diario del Altoaragón:** La Palma 9, 22001 Huesca; tel. (74) 223993; fax (74) 245444; fmrly *Nueva España*; morning; Dir ANTONIO ANGULO ARAGUÁS.

### Jaén

**Jaén:** Calle Torredonjimeno 1, Polígono los Olivares, 23009 Jaén; tel. (53) 221881; fax (53) 221877; f. 1941; morning; Dir JOSÉ LUIS MORENO CODINA; circ. 5,500.

### León

**La Crónica de León:** Paseo de la Facultad 53 bajo, 24004 León; tel. (87) 212512; telex 89649; fax (87) 213152; f. 1986; daily; Dir OSCAR CAMPILLO.

**Diario de León:** Lucas de Tuy 7, 24002 León; tel. (87) 227400; telex 89834; fax (87) 232614; morning; Dir FRANCISCO J. MARTÍNEZ CARRIÓN; circ. 5,743.

**El Faro Astorgano:** Prensa Astorgana 2, Apdo 13, 24700 Astorga; tel. (87) 617012; fax (87) 617025; f. 1980; 5 a week; Dir PAULINO SUTIL JUAN; Editor ISIDRO MARTÍNEZ RODRÍGUEZ; circ. 2,250.

### Lérida

**Diari de Lleida:** Academia 17, 25002 Lérida; tel. (73) 270100; fax (73) 275424; f. 1885; morning; Dir JOSEP RAMÓN CORREAL MÒDOL; Editor GINA DOMINGO MASANÉS; circ 14,000.

**La Mañana:** Polígono Industrial Segre 118, Apdo 11, 25080 Lérida; tel. (73) 204600; f. 1938; morning; Dir JOSEP RAMÓN CORREAL MÒDOL; Editor AURELIO BAUTISTA CID; circ. 7,510.

**Segre:** Río 6, Apdo 543, 25007 Lérida; tel. (73) 248000; fax (73) 246031; f. 1982; morning; Dir JUAN CAL SÁNCHEZ; circ. 13,000.

### Lugo

**El Progreso de Lugo:** Progreso 12, Apdo 5, 27001 Lugo; tel. (82) 298100; telex 86509; fax (82) 298101; f. 1908; morning; independent; Dir JOSÉ DE CORA PARADELA; circ. 12,354.

### Madrid

**ABC:** Juan Ignacio Luca de Tena 7, 28027 Madrid; tel. (1) 3399000; fax (1) 3203680; f. 1905; morning; Monarchist, independent; Dir LUIS MARÍA ANSÓN; circ. 334,696 (Sun. 765,668).

**As:** Cuesta de San Vicente 26, 28008 Madrid; tel. (1) 2472300; telex 22411; fax (1) 2486121; f. 1967; morning, sporting paper; Dir JULIÁN GARCÍA CANDAU; Editors GERARDO GARCÍA SIMÓN, CARLOS JIMÉNEZ; circ. 143,341.

**Cinco Días:** Gran Vía 32, 2a planta, 28013 Madrid; tel. (1) 5210164; telex 47466; fax (1) 5231128; morning, incl. Sat. and Sun.; economic; Dir JESÚS MOTA HERVÍAS; circ. 30,000.

**Diario 16:** Basauri 17, Edif. Valrrealty, La Florida, 28023 Madrid; tel. (1) 5589800; telex 45934; fax (1) 5589896; f. 1976; morning; Dir JOSÉ LUIS GUTIÉRREZ; circ. 178,957 (Sun. 209,491).

**Expansión de la Actualidad Económica Diaria:** Recoletos 1, 5°, 28001 Madrid; tel. (1) 3373220; telex 41889; fax (1) 5756502; daily; Dir JESÚS MARTÍNEZ VÁZQUEZ.

SPAIN                                                                                                                           *Directory*

**Gaceta de los Negocios:** O'Donnell 12, 28009 Madrid; tel. (1) 5863300; telex 41462; fax (1) 5776233; f. 1989; daily; business and finance; Dir Carlos E. Rodríguez; circ. 80,000.

**Iberian Daily Sun:** Zurbano 74, 28010 Madrid; tel. (1) 4427700; fax (1) 4427854; morning; English language; Dir Pedro Serra Bauza; circ. 5,523.

**Marca:** Recoletos 14, 1°, 28001 Madrid; tel. (1) 3373220; telex 22843; fax (1) 3373260; f. 1938 as weekly in San Sebastián, 1942 as daily in Madrid; morning; sports; Dir Luis Infante; circ. 310,000.

**El Mundo (del Siglo Veintiuno):** Sánchez Pacheco 61, 28002 Madrid; tel. (1) 5864800; telex 49353; fax (1) 5195192; f. 1989; daily; Dir Pedro J. Ramírez; circ. 230,000 (Sun. 215,000).

**El País:** Miguel Yuste 40, 28037 Madrid; tel. (1) 3378200; telex 42187; fax (1) 3048766; f. 1976; morning; Dir Jesús Ceberio; circ. 408,550 (Sun. 1,121,590); also publishes weekly international edn; f. 1983, circ. 25,000.

**La Región Internacional:** Menéndez Pelayo 3, 1°, 28009 Madrid; tel. (1) 5775685; fax (1) 2752053; f. 1967; 4 a week; distributed world-wide to Spanish residents abroad; Man. Dir Marcelo R. Carbone; circ. 66,000.

**Ya:** Mateo Inurria 15, 28036 Madrid; tel. (1) 2592800; telex 27740; fax (1) 2590063; f. 1935; morning; independent; Catholic, right-wing; Pres. Javier Baviano; Dir Rafael González; circ. 46,500.

### Málaga

**El Diario de la Costa del Sol:** Málaga; tel. (52) 347750; fax (52) 347758; Dirs Agustín Lomeña Cantos, Manolo Jota.

**El Sol del Mediterráneo:** Marbella; tel. (52) 828602; fax (52) 827760; morning; independent; Dir Rafael de Loma.

**Sur:** Avda Dr Marañón 48, 29009 Málaga; tel. (52) 393900; telex 79013; fax (52) 279504; f. 1937; morning; Dir Joaquín Marín Alarcón; circ. 60,000; also publishes free English weekly, circ. 50,000.

**La Tribuna de Marbella:** Marbella; tel. (52) 826894; fax (52) 826782; f. 1985; Dir José Luis Yagüe Ormad.

### Murcia

**La Opinión de Murcia:** Plaza Condestable 3, 30009 Murcia; tel. (68) 281888; fax (68) 281417; f. 1988; Dir Paloma Reverte de Luis; circ. 180,000.

**La Verdad:** Ronda de Levante 15, 30008 Murcia; tel. (68) 234000; fax (68) 231913; f. 1903; morning; independent; Dir Antonio González Conejero; circ. 39,000.

### Navarra

**Diario de Navarra:** Zapatería 49, Apdo 5, 31001 Pamplona; tel. (48) 236050; telex 37716; fax (48) 244156; f. 1903; morning; independent; Dir José Javier Uranga Santesteban; circ. 39,491.

**Diario de Noticias:** Pamplona; f. 1994; daily; Dir Fernando Múgica; circ. 13,757.

### Orense

**La Región de Orense:** Polígono de San Ciprián de Viñas, Orense; tel. (88) 222211; telex 46174; fax (88) 242010; f. 1910; morning; Dir Alfonso Sánchez Izquierdo; circ. 12,100.

**La Región de Orense, Edición Internacional:** Cardenal Quiroga 11–15, Orense; tel. 222211; 104 a year; Dir Francisco Campos; circ. 44,259.

### Oviedo (Asturias)

**El Comercio:** Calle Ferrocarril 1, 33207 Gijón; tel. (8) 5351946; telex 87513; fax (8) 5342226; f. 1878; morning; Editor Francisco Carantoña Dubert; circ. 32,714.

**La Nueva España:** Calvo Sotelo 7, Edificio Sedes, 33007 Oviedo; tel. (8) 530550; telex 84122; fax (8) 5232899; f. 1937; morning; Dir Melchor Fernández; circ. weekdays 44,000, Sunday 115,000.

**La Voz de Asturias:** Polígono Puente Nora s/n, 33420 Lugones; tel. (8) 5101500; telex 84004; fax (8) 5101505; f. 1923; morning; independent; Dir Faustino F. Álvarez; circ. 23,500.

**La Voz de Avilés:** Avda Gijón 70, Avilés; tel. (85) 540126; fax (85) 544340; morning; Man. María Jesús Wes López; Dir Juan Manuel Wes López; circ. 3,541.

### Palencia

**El Diario Palentino–El Día de Palencia:** Mayor Principal 67, Apdo 17, 34001 Palencia; tel. (88) 744822; f. 1882; morning; independent; Dir José María Ruiz de Gopegui y Santoyo; circ. 10,000.

### Pontevedra

**Atlántico Diario:** Avda de las Camelias 104, 36211 Vigo; tel. (86) 203132; telex 46174; fax (86) 230787; f. 1987; daily; Dir Manuel Orío Avila; circ. 9,000.

**Diario 16 de Galicia:** La Gandariña 124, 36214 Vigo; tel. (86) 372111; f. 1988; daily; Dir Segundo Mariño Vázquez; circ. 50,000.

**Diario de Pontevedra:** Secundino Esperón 5 bajo, 36002 Pontevedra; tel. (86) 856554; fax (86) 863275; morning; Dir Pedro Antonio Rivas Fontenla; circ. 3,903.

**Faro de Vigo:** Colón 30, Apdo 91, 36201 Vigo; tel. (86) 453000; telex 83011; fax (86) 452005; f. 1853; morning; Dir Ceferino de Blas; circ. 38,309.

### La Rioja (Logroño)

**La Rioja:** Vara del Rey 74, Apdo 28, 26002 Logroño; tel. (41) 237133; telex 37057; fax (41) 248934; f. 1889; morning; Dir Francisco Martín Losa; Editor Domingo Martínez Benavente; circ. 15,000.

### Salamanca

**El Adelanto:** Gran Vía 56, 37001 Salamanca; tel. (23) 216595; telex 26816; fax (23) 219435; f. 1883; morning; independent; Dir Carlos del Pueyo; Editor and Man. Mariano Núñez-Varadé Ramo; circ. 9,200.

**La Gaceta Regional:** Peña Primera 18–24, 37002 Salamanca; tel. (23) 218607; fax (23) 213929; morning; Dir Iñigo Domingués de Calatayud; circ. 7,069.

### Santander—see Cantabria

### Segovia

**El Adelantado de Segovia:** San Agustín 7, 40001 Segovia; tel. (11) 437261; fax (11) 442432; f. 1901; evening; Dir Fernando Ganuza Laita; circ. 5,000.

### Sevilla

**ABC:** Cardenal Illandain 9, 41013 Sevilla; tel. (5) 4616200; telex 72300; f. 1929; morning; monarchist; independent; Dir Francisco Jiménez Alemán; circ. 56,692 (see also under Madrid).

**El Correo de Andalucía:** Avda de la Prensa 1, 41007 Sevilla; tel. (5) 4517911; telex 72148; fax (5) 4517635; f. 1899; morning; independent; Dir Manuel Gómez Cardeña; circ. 25,600.

**Diario 16—Andalucía:** Polígono Calonge, Calle B, 13, 41007 Sevilla; tel. (5) 4431561; telex 72719; fax (5) 4361058; morning.

**El País:** Paseo de las Delicias 1, 41001 Sevilla; tel. (5) 4223378; telex 73061; f. 1986; regional edition of the Madrid daily; circ. 74,000.

### Soria

**Diario de Soria:** Alberca 4, 42003 Soria; tel. (75) 212063; fax (75) 221504; daily; Dir José Manuel Serrano Alvarez.

### Tarragona

**Diario de Tarragona:** Doménech Guansé 2, 43005 Tarragona; tel. (77) 211816; telex 56743; fax (77) 223013; f. 1808; morning; Dir Antonio Coll i Gilabert; Editor Luis Antonio Sánchez-Friera; circ. 12,500.

### Teruel

**Diario de Teruel:** Amantes 22, 44001 Teruel; tel. (74) 601662; fax (74) 600682; evening; Dir José Hernández; circ. 2,853.

### Toledo

**El Día de Toledo:** Plaza Zocodover 7, 3° Izqda, 45001 Toledo; tel. (25) 221171; telex 48509; fax (25) 214065; f. 1987; daily; Dir Santiago Mateo Sahuquillo; circ. 3,500.

**La Voz del Tajo:** Banderas de Castilla 2, 45600 Talavera de la Reina; tel. (25) 812400; fax (25) 812454; f. 1951; daily; Editors-in-Chief Elena Bressel, Joaquín del Rio; circ. 10,000.

### Valencia

**Levante:** Traginers 7, 46014 Valencia; tel. (6) 3790800; telex 63596; fax (6) 3502542; f. 1939; morning; Dir Ferran Belda; circ. 31,316, Sunday 87,341.

**El País:** Embajador Vich 3, 3°, 46002 Valencia; tel. (6) 3521171; telex 63131; f. 1986; regional edition of the Madrid daily.

**Las Provincias:** Calle Gremis 4, 46014 Valencia; tel. (6) 3502211; telex 62770; fax (6) 3598288; f. 1866; morning; Rightist, independent; Dir María Consuelo Reyna Domenench; circ. 56,751, (Sun. 82,421).

### Valladolid

**El Norte de Castilla:** Vázquez de Menchaca 10 (Polígono de Argales), 47008 Valladolid; tel. (83) 412100; fax (83) 412111; f. 1854; morning; agricultural and economic interests; Dir Carlos Roldán; circ. 27,107 (Sun. 38,210).

### Vizcaya

**El Correo:** Pintor Losada 7, Apdo 205, 48004 Bilbao; tel. (4) 4120100; telex 32082; fax (4) 4125377; *El Correo Español* f. 1937,

*El Pueblo Vasco* f. 1910, amalgamated 1938; morning; independent; Dir José Antonio Zarzalejos Nieto; circ. 133,000.

**Deia:** Elcano 25, 3°, 48004 Bilbao; tel. (4) 4120211; telex 31376; morning; Basque; Dir Anton Eguia Cuadra; circ. 50,690.

### Zamora

**El Correo de Zamora:** Rua de los Francos 20, 49001 Zamora; tel. (88) 515611; fax (88) 515744; f. 1896; morning; Dir Miguel Angel Pérez Gallego (acting); Editor Vicente Díez García; circ. 10,500.

**La Opinión de Zamora:** Plaza del Mercado 15, 49003 Zamora; tel. (88) 534759; fax (88) 532514.

### Zaragoza

**El Día:** Zaragoza; tel. (76) 328111; telex 58676; fax (76) 319006; daily; independent; Dir Plácido Díez Bella.

**Diario 16 de Aragón:** Avda Cataluña 17, 50014 Zaragoza; tel. (76) 396767; fax (76) 294069; Dir Miguel Angel Liso Tejada; regional edition of the Madrid daily.

**Heraldo de Aragón:** Independencia 29, Apdo 175, 50001 Zaragoza; tel. (76) 221858; telex 58046; fax (76) 393959; f. 1895; morning; independent; Dir Antonio Bruned Mompeón; circ. 49,274.

**El Periódico de Aragón:** Paseo Pamplona 12–14, 50004 Zaragoza; tel. (76) 700400; fax (76) 700462; f. 1990; Dir Miguel Angel Liso Tejada.

**Siete de Aragón:** Huesca; f. 1993; weekly; Dir Lorenzo Lascorz; circ. 13,000.

### Balearic Islands

**Baleares:** Paseo Mallorca 9a, 07011 Palma de Mallorca; tel. (71) 457000; fax (71) 455740; f. 1939; morning; Dir Marisa Gallardo Garrido; circ. 11,777.

**El Día del Mundo de Baleares:** Gremios Herreros 42, Polígono de Son Castelló, 07009 Palma de Mallorca; tel. (71) 767600; fax (71) 767656; f. 1981; daily; Dir Gabriel Ramis; circ. 17,065.

**Diario de Ibiza:** Pasaje Vía Púnica 2, 07800 Ibiza; tel. (71) 301604; telex 69952; fax (71) 302458; morning; Dir Francisco Verdera Ribas; Publr Juan y Francisco Verdera Ribas; circ. 4,675.

**Diario Mallorca:** Conflent 1, 07012 Palma de Mallorca; tel. (71) 716343; telex 68804; fax (71) 719838; f. 1953; morning; Dir Juan Antonio Fuster Rosselló; circ. 23,517, Sunday 27,359.

**Diario Menorca:** Avda Central 5, Polígono Industrial Mahón, Mahón, Menorca; tel. (71) 351600; fax (71) 351983; f. 1941; morning; Dir Joan Bosco Marqués Bosch; circ. 5,550.

**Majorca Daily Bulletin:** Paseo Mallorca 9a, Palau de la Premsa, Apdo 304, 07011 Palma de Mallorca; tel. (71) 788400; fax (71) 719706; f. 1962; morning; English language; Propr and Dir Pedro A. Serra Bauzá; circ. 5,300.

**La Prensa de Ibiza:** Carretera de Sant Antoni, km 3700, Apdo 561, 07800 Ibiza; tel. (71) 191019; fax (71) 316970; f. 1988; daily; Dir Joan Serra Tur; circ. 4,000.

**Soller:** San Felio 17, Palma de Mallorca; tel. (71) 788400; fax (71) 719706; f. 1885; weekly; Dir José Bauzá Piza.

**Última Hora Matutino:** Edif. Palacio de la Prensa, Paseo de Mallorca 9a, 07011 Palma de Mallorca; tel. (71) 456000; telex 69140; fax (71) 454190; f. 1893; morning; Dir Pedro Comas Barceló; circ. 29,648.

### Canary Islands (Las Palmas)

**Canarias 7:** Apdo 2441, 35080 Las Palmas; tel. (28) 466000; telex 95327; fax (28) 468435; daily; Dir José Luis Torró Micó; circ. 25,529.

**Diario de Las Palmas:** Urb. El Cebadal, Vial XII-Parcela 19, 35008 Las Palmas; tel. (28) 263850; telex 96049; fax (28) 268821; f. 1895; evening; independent; Dir Santiago Betancourt Brito; Gen. Man. Juan Ignacio Jiménez Mesa; circ. 11,807.

**La Provincia:** Urb. El Cebadal, Vial XII-Parcela 19, 35008 Las Palmas; tel. (28) 274050; telex 96049; fax (28) 268821; f. 1911; morning; independent; Dir Diego Talavera; Gen. Man. Juan Ignacio Jiménez Mesa; circ. 28,674.

### Canary Islands (Santa Cruz de Tenerife)

**El Día:** Avda de Buenos Aires 71, Apdo 97, 38005 Santa Cruz; tel. (22) 211000; telex 92184; fax (22) 214247; f. 1910; morning; Gen. Man. and Dir José E. Rodríguez Ramírez; circ. 28,000 and Sunday 43,800.

**Diario de Avisos:** Salamanca 5, 38006 Santa Cruz; tel. (22) 272350; telex 92326; fax (22) 241039; f. 1890, re-f. 1976; morning; Dir Leopoldo Fernández Cabeza de Vaca; circ. 9,919.

**La Gaceta de Canarias:** Polígono Industrial Los Majuelos, Fernando Díaz Cutillas s/n, La Laguna; tel. (22) 655216; fax (22) 654460; f. 1989; Dir Jorge Bethencourt.

**Jornada Deportiva:** Avda Buenos Aires 71, Apdo 714, 38005 Santa Cruz; tel. 211000; telex 92184; fax (22) 213834; f. 1953; morning; general information; Gen. Man. José E. Rodríguez; circ. 10,000 (Tue.–Sat.), 26,000 (Mon.).

### PERIODICALS OF GENERAL INTEREST

**Aceprensa:** Núñez de Balboa 125, 28006 Madrid; tel. (1) 5628712; fax (1) 5631243; f. 1973; weekly; news and features; Dir Ignacio Aréchaga.

**El Alcalde:** San Agustín 15, 28014 Madrid; tel. (1) 4292403; f. 1967; monthly; Dir (vacant).

**El Alcázar:** San Romualdo 26, 28037 Madrid; tel. (1) 2545082; f. 1936 during the siege of the Alcázar; weekly; right-wing; Dir Félix Martialay; circ. 95,012.

**Algo 2000:** Aribau 28, 08011 Barcelona; tel. (3) 3237063; telex 50482; monthly; science and technology; Dir Oriol Pugés Gibert; circ. 65,000.

**Alianza:** Génova 13, 28004 Madrid; tel. (1) 3103265; fax (1) 3085587; monthly; publ. by Partido Popular; Dir Miguel Angel Rodríguez.

**Argia:** Industrialdea 1 eta 2 pabeloiak, 20160 Lasarte-Oria; tel. (43) 371545; fax (43) 361048; f. 1919; weekly; Dir Garbiñe Ubeda; circ. 10,000.

**Avant:** Portal de l'Angel 42, 2°, 08002 Barcelona; tel. (3) 3184550; weekly; Dir Juan Tafalla Monferrer.

**Banca Española:** Avda de Alfonso XIII 15, Bajo B, 28002 Madrid; tel. (1) 5191799; fax (1) 5191795; monthly; Dir César de la Mota.

**Bierzo 7:** Avda del Ferrocarril 18, 24400 Ponferrada; tel. (87) 404855; f. 1984; weekly; general; Dir Daniel Fernández Cuadrillero; Editor-in-Chief María Angeles Calvo Diez; circ. 3,000.

**Cambio 16:** Hermanos García Noblejas 41, 28037 Madrid; tel. (1) 4072700; telex 43974; fax (1) 4075850; f. 1972, weekly (Wed.); general; Dir Román Orozco.

**Canfali:** Vía Emilio Ortuño 8, Benidorm; tel. (65) 5851823; f. 1971; various editions, 3 a week or weekly; Dir Manuel Esquembre Bañuls; circ. 25,000.

**Carta de España:** Marqués de Urquijo 47, 28008 Madrid; tel. (1) 5475200; f. 1960; monthly; general; Dir Raimundo Aragón Bombín; circ. 20,000.

**El Caso Criminal:** Andalucía 6, 04007 Almería; tel. (51) 258511; fax (51) 243863; weekly; Dir Carlos Iglesias.

**El Ciervo:** Calvet 56, 08021 Barcelona; tel. (3) 2005145; fax (3) 2011015; f. 1951; monthly; Dir Lorenzo Gomis Sanahuja; circ. 5,000.

**Ciudad Nueva Internacional:** Andrés Tamayo 4, 28028 Madrid; tel. (1) 7259530; fax (1) 3611412; f. 1958; monthly; Dir José Luis Romero; circ. 9,000.

**Ciudadano:** Príncipe de Vergara 17, 3°, 28001 Madrid; tel. (1) 5782807; fax (1) 5782132; monthly; consumer news; Dir Carmen Martín Carrobles; circ. 70,000.

**Crónica, Mensual d'Actualitat:** Caspe 116, 08013 Barcelona; tel. (3) 2320311; monthly; Dir Antonio Batista Viladrich.

**El Decano de Guadalajara:** Constitución 2, Torre 1, 1°, Apdo 73, 19003 Guadalajara; tel. (49) 211567; fax (49) 228911; f. 1894; weekly; provincial news; Dir Salvador Toquero Cortés; circ. 10,000.

**Diez Minutos:** Santa Engracia 23, 28010 Madrid; tel. (1) 5938462; fax (1) 5930068; f. 1951; weekly; Dir Basilio Rogado; circ. 377,105.

**El Empresario:** Diego de León 50, 28006 Madrid; tel. (1) 4116161; fax (1) 5645269; monthly; Dir Carlota Domínguez; circ. 15,000.

**Época:** Alberto Alcocer 32, 28036 Madrid; tel. (1) 4582152; telex 41025; fax (1) 4576962; weekly; Dir Jaime Campmany.

**La Esfera:** Madrid; f. 1991; monthly; travel, culture and leisure; Dir Pedro Montoliú; circ. 185,000.

**Fantastic Magazine:** Consejo de Ciento 83, 6°, 08015 Barcelona; tel. (3) 4262394; fax (3) 4261450; monthly; cinema and video; Dir Elisenda Nadal Gañan; circ. 60,000.

**El Faro de la Costa:** Garcés Herrera 4, 18600 Motril; tel. (58) 820619; f. 1930; weekly; Dir Francisco-Fermín Jiménez García.

**Geo:** Marqués de Villamagna 4, 28001 Madrid; tel. (1) 4358100; telex 43419; fax (1) 5767881; f. 1987; monthly; Dir Javier Rubio Navarro; circ. 60,000.

**Guía Cocina:** Rocafort 104, 08015 Barcelona; tel. (3) 2233191; weekly; Dir Alicia Villoldo de Botana.

**Guía del Ocio de Barcelona:** Balmes 114, 2°, 08008 Barcelona; tel. (3) 2155088; fax (3) 4871434; f. 1977; weekly; Dir Pau Bolaños; circ. 50,000.

**¡Hola!:** Miguel Angel 1, 28010 Madrid; tel. (1) 4101311; f. 1944; weekly; general illustrated; Dir Eduardo Sánchez Junco; circ. 582,778.

**Insula:** Carretera de Irún, Km 12,200 (Variante de Fuencarral), 28049 Madrid; tel. (1) 3589689; fax (1) 3589505; f. 1946; monthly;

SPAIN *Directory*

literature and social sciences; Dir Víctor García de la Concha; Editor Carlos Alvarez-Ude; circ. 6,000.

**Interviú:** O'Donnell 12, 5a Planta, 28009 Madrid; tel. (1) 5863300; fax (1) 5863555; f. 1976; weekly; Pres. Antonio Asensio; Dir José Cavero; circ. 494,347.

**El Jueves:** Calle Atenas 11, bajos, 08006 Barcelona; tel. (3) 4174045; fax (3) 4189130; f. 1977; weekly; satirical; Dir José Antonio Fernández; circ. 170,000.

**Luna de Madrid:** Pintor Moreno Carbonero 18, 28028 Madrid; tel. (1) 2550505; f. 1983; monthly; for young people; Dir Jorge Gines; circ. 150,000.

**Mallorca Magazin:** San Felio 17, 07012 Palma de Mallorca; tel. (71) 216110; weekly; Dir Pedro A. Serra Bauzá.

**Más:** Juan de Austria 6, 28010 Madrid; tel. (1) 4457454; f. 1957; monthly; work-related activities; Dir Rogelio Rodríguez Blanco; circ. 57,402.

**Mucho Más:** Pedro Teixeira 8, 28020 Madrid; tel. (1) 5560048; telex 46148; fax (1) 5567044; weekly; TV; Dir Alicia Otero.

**Muy Interesante:** Marqués de Villamagna 4, 28001 Madrid; tel. (1) 4316631; telex 43419; fax (1) 5759128; f. 1981; monthly; Dir José Pardina; circ. 290,000.

**Natura:** Marqués de Villamagna 4, 28001 Madrid; tel. (1) 4358100; telex 43419; fax (1) 5767881; f. 1983; monthly; wildlife, archaeology, research; Dir Alberto Huerta; circ. 69,913.

**El Nuevo Lunes de la Economía y la Sociedad:** Plaza de España 18, 7°, Of. 3, 28008 Madrid; tel. (1) 5410134; fax (1) 2480406; weekly; Dir Rosa del Río.

**Nuevo Rumbo:** Desengaño 11, 1°, 28004 Madrid; tel. (1) 5210684; fax (1) 5329187; fortnightly; Dir José A. García Rubio.

**Nuevo Vale:** Gran Vía de Carlos III 124, 08034 Barcelona; tel. (3) 2800088; weekly; Dir Carmen del Vado; circ. 250,000.

**Pronto:** Avda Gran Vía Carlos III 124, 5°, 08034 Barcelona; tel. (3) 2800088; fax (3) 2805555; telex 97834; f. 1972; weekly; general information; Dir Antonio G. Abad; circ. 925,108.

**Semana:** Cuesta de San Vicente 26, 28008 Madrid; tel. (1) 2472300; telex 22134; fax (1) 2486121; f. 1942; weekly; general, illustrated; Dir Luis González de Linares Lamazou; circ. 340,590.

**Serra d'Or:** Ausiàs March 92–98, 08013 Barcelona; tel. (3) 2450303; fax (3) 4473594; f. 1959; monthly; culture; Dir Maur Boix i Selva; circ. 15,000.

**Supertele:** Santa Engracia 23, 28010 Madrid; tel. (1) 5938462; telex 49437; fax (1) 5930735; weekly; TV magazine.

**El Socialista:** Ferraz 70, 28008 Madrid; tel. (1) 4701112; telex 475553; fortnightly; Dir Pedro Bofill; circ. 185,000.

**Super Pop:** Gran Vía Carlos III 124, 5°, 08034 Barcelona; tel. (3) 2800088; fax (3) 2805555; f. 1976; fortnightly; teenage magazine; Dir Carmen Grasa; circ. 250,000.

**Tele Indiscreta:** Gran Vía de Carlos III 124, 5°, 08034 Barcelona; tel. (3) 2800088; fax (3) 2804855; weekly; popular illustrated; TV programmes; Dir Jordi Cebrián; circ. 700,000.

**Telenovela:** Santa Engracia 23, 28010 Madrid; tel. (1) 5938462; fax (1) 5938956; f. 1993; TV series; circ. 200,000.

**El Temps:** Avinguda del Baró de Càrcer 40-13, 46001 Valencia; tel. (6) 3524869; fax (6) 3520983; f. 1984; weekly; general information; Dir Assumpció Maresma; circ. 15,000.

**Tiempo:** O' Donnell 12, 3a, 28009 Madrid; tel. (1) 5781572; telex 49441; fax (1) 5776183; weekly; Dir José Oneto; circ. 156,310.

**Tiempo de Hoy:** O' Donnell 12, 3a Planta, 28009 Madrid; tel. (1) 5220072; telex 49441; fax 4015020; weekly; Dir José Oneto Revuelta.

**Tiempo de Viajar:** O'Donnell 12, 28009 Madrid; tel. (1) 5781572; telex 49441; fax (1) 5775400; monthly; travel; Dir Emilio Rey.

**TP Teleprograma:** Avda Cardenal Herrera Oria 3, 28034 Madrid; tel. (1) 3581122; fax (1) 3581348; f. 1966; weekly; TV, cinema and video; Dir Cristina Acebal; circ. 1,000,000.

**Tribuna de Actualidad:** Eladio López Vilches 18, 1°, 28033 Madrid; tel. (1) 3832218; f. 1988; weekly; Dir Fernando García Romanillos; circ. 200,000.

**Vida Nueva:** Enrique Jardiel Poncela 4, 28016 Madrid; tel. (1) 3453539; fax (1) 3450282; f. 1958; weekly; Dir Rosario Marín; Propr Promoción Popular Cristiana; circ. 20,000.

**La Voz del Valle:** Apdo 87, Puerto de la Cruz (Tenerife); tel. (22) 341684; monthly; Dir Millán Cazorla; circ. 5,000.

### SPECIALIZED PUBLICATIONS
#### Economics

**Actualidad Económica:** Recoletos 1, 7°, 28001 Madrid; tel. (1) 3373220; telex 49455; fax (1) 5768150; f. 1958; Mon.; Dir Ignacio de la Rica; circ. 39,497.

**Dinero:** O' Donnell 12, 28009 Madrid; tel. (1) 4096345; telex 41462; weekly; Dir Rafael Navas Castellón.

**El Economista:** Conde de Aranda 8, 28001 Madrid; tel. (1) 5771709; fax (1) 5782345; f. 1886; weekly; Dir Valentín González Alvarez.

**El Financiero:** Maldonado 55, 1°, 28006 Madrid; tel. (1) 4110653; fax (1) 4110752; monthly; Dir Francisco Bermejo.

**Información Comercial Española:** Paseo de la Castellana 162, 16°, 28046 Madrid; tel. (1) 3493965; fax (1) 3493634; monthly; Dir Ministerio de Comercio y Turismo.

**Mercado:** Valentín San Narciso 14, 28018 Madrid; tel. (1) 3035484; fax (1) 3034598; Dir Rodolfo Serrano Recio; weekly; circ. 30,000.

**El Mundo Financiero:** Hermosilla 93, 1°, Apdo 6.119, 28001 Madrid; tel. (1) 5773376; fax (1) 5778981; f. 1946; monthly; Dir José Luis Barceló; circ. 15,000.

**El Nuevo Lunes:** Plaza de España 18, Torre de Madrid 32°, Of. 4, 28008 Madrid; tel. (1) 2473101; f. 1981; weekly; circ. 27,000.

#### Law, Politics, Sociology, Religion

**Ecclesia:** Alfonso XI 4, 28014 Madrid; tel. (1) 5315400; fax (1) 5225561; weekly; f. 1941; Dir José Antonio Carro Celada; Propr Conferencia Episcopal Española; circ. 24,000.

**Iniciativa i Treball:** Ciutat 7, 08002 Barcelona; tel. (3) 3010554; telex 51793; f. 1936; fortnightly; organ of PSUC; Dir Jordi Guillot Niravet; circ. 6,000.

**La Ley:** Monterrey 1 (Ctra La Coruña km. 17,200), 28230 Las Rozas; tel. 6345362; Dir José Manuel Otero Lastres.

**Mundo Cristiano:** Paseo Castellana 210-2°B, 28046 Madrid; tel. (1) 3508311; fax (1) 3590230; f. 1963; monthly; Dir Jesús Urteaga Loidi; circ. 46,852.

**Revista de Administración Pública:** Plaza de la Marina Española 9, 28013 Madrid; tel. (1) 5325069; f. 1950; 3 a year; Dir Eduardo García de Enterría; publ. by the Centro de Estudios Constitucionales; circ. 2,300.

**Revista de Derecho Privado:** Valverde 32, 1°, 28004 Madrid; tel. (1) 5210246; monthly; Dir Manuel Albadalejo.

**Revista de Derecho Público:** Valverde 32, 1°, 28004 Madrid; tel. (1) 5210246; quarterly; Dir Luis Sánchez Agesta.

**Revista de Estudios Políticos:** Plaza de la Marina Española 9, Madrid 28013; tel. (1) 5325069; f. 1941; quarterly; Dir Pedro de Vega; publ. by Centro de Estudios Constitucionales; circ. 1,000.

#### Science and Medicine

**Arbor:** Serrano 117, 28006 Madrid; tel. (1) 2619800; f. 1944; monthly; science, thought and culture; Dir Miguel Angel Quintanilla; publ. by Consejo Superior de Investigaciones Científicas (CSIC).

**Conocer la Vida y el Universo:** O'Donnell 12, 28009 Madrid; tel. (1) 5781572; monthly; Dir Felipe Teruel.

**Investigación y Ciencia:** Muntaner 339, Pral 1a, 08021 Barcelona; tel. (3) 4143344; fax (3) 4145413; f. 1976; monthly; Dir Francisco Gracia Guillén; circ. 38,000.

**Jano:** Travesera de Gracia 17–21, 08021 Barcelona; tel. (3) 2000711; telex 51964; fax (3) 2091136; f. 1971; weekly; medical and paramedical; Dir Celia Ribera; circ. 40,000.

**Medicina Clínica:** Travesera de Gracia 17, 08021 Barcelona; tel. (3) 2000711; telex 51964; fax (3) 2091136; f. 1943; weekly; medicine; Dir C. Rozman; circ. 8,000.

**El Médico, Profesión y Humanidades:** Saned, Apolonio Morales 6–8, 28036 Madrid; tel. (1) 3594092; telex 47331; fax (1) 3453169; weekly; Dir Jenaro Báscuas; circ. 40,000.

**Noticias Médicas:** Gabriela Mistral 2, 28035 Madrid; tel. (1) 3860033; fax (1) 3739907; weekly; Dir Adolfo Berzosa Blanco; circ. 35,000.

**Tiempos Médicos:** Editores Médicos, SA, Gabriela Mistral 2, 28035 Madrid; tel. (1) 3860033; fax (1) 3739907; monthly; Dir Dr A. Chicharro; circ. 20,000.

**Tribuna Médica:** Londres 17, 28028 Madrid; tel. (1) 2557263; telex 47124; Dir Jesús Ibáñez Montoya; circ. 59,107.

#### Sport

**Caza y Pesca:** José Abascal 24, 28003 Madrid; tel. (1) 4473484; fax (1) 4474163; f. 1943; monthly; hunting, fishing, shooting; Publr Joaquín España Payá; Editor Joaquín España Aguado; circ. 37,000.

**Don Balón:** Avda Diagonal 435, 1°, 2a, 08036 Barcelona; tel. (3) 2092000; fax (3) 2092611; f. 1975; weekly; Dir Juan Pedro Martínez.

**Trofeo:** Telémaco 37, 28027 Madrid; tel. (1) 3200818; telex 27524; fax (1) 3203557; f. 1970; monthly; hunting, fishing, nature conservation; Dir J. Delibes; circ. 35,000.

SPAIN

### Women's Magazines

**Clara:** Muntaner 40–42, 08011 Barcelona; tel. (3) 4541004; fax (3) 4545949; f. 1992; monthly; Dir Assumpta Soria Badia; circ. 309,347.

**Cómplice:** Pedro Teixeira 8, 28020 Madrid; tel. (1) 5560048; telex 46148; fax (1) 4358701; f. 1985; monthly; Dir Martha Cardozo; circ. 80,991.

**Cosmopolitan:** Marqués de Villamagna 4, 28001 Madrid; tel. (1) 4358100; fax (1) 4358701; circ. 190,562.

**Dunia:** Marqués de Villamagna 4, 28001 Madrid; tel. (1) 4358100; telex 43419; fax (1) 5767881; f. 1976; fortnightly; Dir Teodoro Izquierdo; circ. 151,000.

**Elle:** Luchana 23, 5°, 28010 Madrid; tel. (1) 5931119; fax (1) 5934724; f. 1986; monthly; Dir Susana Martínez Vidal; circ. 180,000.

**Entorno de Mujer:** Madrid; f. 1991; monthly; Dir María Luisa Malibrán; Editor-in-Chief Zulema González; circ. 200,000.

**Greca:** Pedro Teixeira 8, 28020 Madrid; tel. (1) 5560048; telex 46148; fax 5563798; f. 1977; monthly; Dir Angeles Aledo; circ. 124,570.

**Labores del Hogar:** Muntaner 40–42, 08011 Barcelona; tel. (3) 4541004; fax (3) 4540551; f. 1925; monthly; home textile crafts; Dir Eulalia Ubach; circ. 156,765.

**Lecturas:** Muntaner 40-42, 08011 Barcelona; tel. (3) 4541004; telex 50482; fax (3) 4541322; f. 1921; Fri.; Dir Julio Bou Gibert; Man. Xavier Elies; circ. 341,841.

**Marie Claire 16:** Marqués de Villamagna 4, 28001 Madrid; tel. (1) 4316631; fax (1) 5751392; f. 1987; monthly; Dir Ana Rosa Semprún; circ. 98,242.

**Mía:** Marqués de Villamagna 4, 28001 Madrid; tel. (1) 4316631; fax (1) 5767881; f. 1986; weekly; Dir Ketty Rico; circ. 276,988.

**El Mueble Actual:** Rocafort 142, 8°, 08015 Barcelona; tel. (3) 2246503; monthly; Dir Isabel Castellet; circ. 38,823.

**Nuevo Estilo:** Axel Springer Revistas, Pedro Teixeira 8, 28020 Madrid; tel. (1) 5560048; fax (1) 5565526; f. 1977; monthly; decoration; circ. 144,000.

**Telva:** Paseo Recoletos 16, 28001 Madrid; tel. (1) 3370599; telex 49455; fax (1) 3373143; f. 1963; monthly; Dir Covadonga O'Shea; circ. 140,000.

**Vogue España:** Serrano 3, 4°, 28001 Madrid; tel. (1) 5783390; telex 27505; fax (1) 5777783; f. 1988; monthly; Dir Mara Malibrán; circ. 51,790.

**Woman:** O'Donnell 12, 28009 Madrid; tel. (1) 5777699; fax (1) 5766166; f. 1992; monthly; Dir Joanna Bonet; circ. 160,000.

### Miscellaneous

**A Hombros de Trabajadores:** Juan de Austria 9, 28010 Madrid; tel. (1) 4464290; monthly; trade unionism; Dir Juan González Castejón.

**Automóvil:** Ancora 40, 28045 Madrid; tel. (1) 3470100; telex 42022; fax (1) 3470143; monthly; motoring; Dir Carlos Hernández; circ. 75,000.

**Autopista:** Ancora 40, 28045 Madrid; tel. (1) 3470100; telex 42022; fax (1) 3470135; weekly; motoring; Dir Enrique Hernández; circ. 90,000.

**Avión Revue:** Ancora 40, 28045 Madrid; tel. (1) 3470100; fax (1) 3470143; f. 1982; monthly; aeroplanes; Dir José María Parés; circ. 30,000.

**Boletín Oficial del Estado:** Trafalgar 29, 28071 Madrid; tel. (1) 5382100; fax (1) 5382347; f. 1936; successor of *Gaceta de Madrid*, f. 1661; daily except Sundays; laws, decrees, orders, etc.; Dir (vacant).

**Coche Actual:** Ancora 40, 28045 Madrid; tel. (1) 3470100; telex 42022; fax (1) 3470119; fortnightly; cars; Dir José Luis Sarralole; circ. 110,000.

**Computerworld:** Rafael Calvo 18, 4° B, 28010 Madrid; tel. (1) 3194014; fax (1) 3196104; f. 1981; weekly; circ. 15,000.

**Fotogramas:** Consejo de Ciento 83, 6°, 08015 Barcelona; tel. (3) 4262394; fax (3) 4261450; f. 1946; monthly; cinema and video; Dir Elisenda Nadal Gañán; circ. 200,000.

**Historia y Vida:** Tallers 62 y 64, 08001 Barcelona; tel. (3) 3010404; monthly; history; Dir Josep Tomas Cabot; circ. 25,000.

**Historia 16:** Rufino González 34 bis, 28037 Madrid; tel. (1) 3271171; fax (1) 3271220; f. 1976; monthly; history; Dir José David Solar; circ. 25,000.

**El Magisterio Español:** López de Hoyos 5, 2° Izqda, 28006 Madrid; tel. (1) 5624105; fax (1) 5611200; f. 1866; Wed.; education; Dir Mercedes Eguíbar Galarza; circ. 23,691.

**Motociclismo:** Ancora 40, 28045 Madrid; tel. (1) 3470100; telex 42022; fax (1) 3470119; f. 1951; weekly; motor cycling; Dir Javier Herrero; Editor Juan Hernández; circ. 110,000.

**PC World/España:** Rafael Calvo 18-4°B, 28010 Madrid; tel. (1) 3194014; fax (1) 3196104; f. 1988; monthly; for users of personal computers.

**El Público:** Capitán Haya 44, 28020 Madrid; tel. (1) 5723311; fax (1) 5705199; f. 1983; every 2 months; theatre; circ. 5,000.

**Ser Padres Hoy:** Marqués de Villamagna 4, 28001 Madrid; tel. (1) 4358100; telex 43419; fax (1) 2767881; f. 1974; monthly; for parents; circ. 105,000.

**Tu Bebé:** Muntaner 40–42, 08011 Barcelona; tel. (3) 4541004; fax (3) 4541322; f. 1993; monthly; for parents; Dir Pedro Riaño; circ. 60,000.

## NEWS AGENCIES

**Agencia EFE, SA:** Espronceda 32, 28003 Madrid; tel. (1) 3467100; f. 1939; national and international news; 82 offices and correspondents abroad; sports, features and photographic branches; Pres. and Dir-Gen. Alfonso S. Palamares.

**Colpisa:** Padre Damián 43, 28036 Madrid; tel. (1) 3450496; telex 22972; fax (1) 3505975; f. 1972; Pres. Santiago Rey Fernández-Latorre; Dir Rogelio Rodríguez.

**Europa Press:** Paseo de la Castellana 210, 3a, 28046 Madrid; tel. (1) 4042300; Dir Jesús González Mateos.

**Iberia Press:** Rafael Calvo 15, 6°, 28010 Madrid; tel. (1) 3086758; telex 45029; fax (1) 3085943; f. 1977; Dir José Ramón Alonso.

**Logos Agencia de Información:** Mateo Inurria 15, 28036 Madrid; tel. (1) 2592800; telex 27740; f. 1929; domestic news; Pres. Juan José Brassac; Co-ordinator Rafael González Rodríguez.

### Foreign Bureaux

**Agence France-Presse:** Paseo de Recoletos 18, Madrid 1; tel. (1) 4358740; fax (1) 5755380; Man. Jean-Jacques Cazaux.

**Agenzia Nazionale Stampa Associata (ANSA)** (Italy): Calle Marqués de Cuba 12, 28014 Madrid; tel. (1) 4295965; telex 22676; fax (1) 4203316; Bureau Chief Riccardo Ehrman.

**Associated Press (AP)** (USA): POB 844, 28014 Madrid; tel. (1) 4295612; telex 27771; fax (1) 4423612; Bureau Chief Susan Linnee.

**Central News Agency** (Taiwan): Paseo de la Castellana 222, 28046 Madrid; tel. (1) 3154040; Correspondent Eduardo Sou-Er Mo Chang.

**Deutsche Presse-Agentur (dpa)** (Germany): Espronceda 32, 5°, 28003 Madrid; tel. (1) 4416484; telex 22480; fax (1) 4427706; Man. Rolf Hilpert.

**Informatsionnoye Telegrafnoye Agentstvo Rossii—Telegrafnoye Agentstvo Suverennykh Stran (ITAR—TASS)** (Russia): General Díaz Porlier 18, 5°, 28001 Madrid; tel. (1) 4314864; Correspondent Vladimir V. Shekhovtsov.

**Reuters** (UK): Paseo de la Castellana 36–38, 28046 Madrid; tel. (1) 5852100; telex 42967; fax (1) 4359666; Chief Correspondent Christian Levesque.

**United Press International (UPI)** (USA): Argensola 2, 28004 Madrid; tel. (1) 3086473; fax (1) 3086450; Correspondent Giles Tremlett.

**Wikalat al-Maghreb al Arabi** (Morocco): Espronceda 32, Madrid 3; tel. 4414599.

**Xinhua (New China) News Agency** (People's Republic of China): Arturo Soria 154, Bloque 3°, 1° F, 28043 Madrid; tel. (1) 4131620; telex 43319; fax (1) 4168543; Correspondent Hu Tairan.

## PRESS ASSOCIATIONS

### National Organizations

Madrid

**Asociación de Editores de Diarios Españoles (AEDE):** Espronceda 32, 6a, 28003 Madrid; tel. (1) 4421992; fax (1) 4414774; f. 1978; asscn of 83 private firms publishing 88 daily newspapers; Pres. Vicente Montiel; Sec.-Gen. Pedro Crespo de Lara.

**Federación de Asociaciones de la Prensa de España (FAPE):** Plaza del Callao 4, 7°C, 28013 Madrid; tel. (1) 5221950; fax (1) 5211573; f. 1922; Pres. Jesús de la Serna; Sec.-Gen. José M. Torre Cervignon; mems: 5,716 journalists in 50 associations.

**Unión de Periodistas:** Silva 22, 28004 Madrid; tel. (1) 5224810; fax (1) 5225179; f. 1978; journalists' asscn; Pres. Celso Collazo; Sec.-Gen. Eloy S. Castañares; 4,000 mems.

**Asociación de la Prensa de Madrid** (Madrid Press Asscn): Juan Bravo 6, 28006 Madrid; tel. (1) 5850010; fax (1) 5850070; f. 1895; Pres. Jesús de la Serna; Sec.-Gen. José María Lorente Toribio; 3,130 mems.

**Asociación de Corresponsales de Prensa Extranjera en España (ACPE):** Monte Esquinza 41, 28010 Madrid; f. 1923; foreign correspondents' asscn; Pres. Harry Debelius; 150 mems.

SPAIN

### Provincial Organizations

#### Barcelona
**Centre Internacional de Premsa de Barcelona:** Rambla de Catalunya 10, 1er, 08007 Barcelona; tel. (3) 4121111; fax (3) 3178386; f. 1988; Pres. CARLES SENTÍS I ANFRUNS; Man. ANGEL JIMÉNEZ LESEDUARTE.

#### Bilbao
**Asociación de la Prensa de Bilbao:** Bilbao; tel. 4241000; f. 1912; Pres. FERNANDO BARRENA BALLARIN; Man. JUAN RIBECHINI SALAVERRI; 120 mems.

#### Sevilla
**Asociación de la Prensa de Sevilla:** San Francisco 9, Sevilla 4; tel. 4225299; f. 1918; Pres. SANTIAGO SÁNCHEZ TRAVER; Sec. ANTONIO SILVA DE PABLOS.

#### Valencia
**Asociación de la Prensa Valenciana:** Calle del Marqués de Dos Aguas 5, 46002 Valencia; tel. 3513750; f. 1906; Pres. RICARDO TRIVIÑO LÓPEZ; Sec. JOSÉ MANUEL DASÍ MONZO.

There are also Press Associations in every provincial capital.

## Publishers

A total of 51,048 titles were published in 1994.

### Madrid

**Aguilar, SA de Ediciones:** Juan Bravo 38, 28006 Madrid; tel. (1) 2763800; telex 42710; fax (1) 4316481; f. 1923; world classics, literature, reference books, law, history, geography, cartography, political and social economics, science, medicine, psychology, technical, art, children's books, education, etc.; Pres. JESÚS DE POLANCO; Dir-Gen. IGNACIO CARDENEL.

**Alianza Editorial, SA:** Juan Ignacio Luca de Tena 15, 28027 Madrid; tel. (1) 3938888; fax (1) 7414343; f. 1959; advanced textbooks, fiction, general non-fiction, reference, paperbacks; Pres. ISABEL ANDRÉS; Gen. Man. RAFAEL MARTÍNEZ ALES.

**Altea, Taurus, Alfaguara, SA:** Juan Bravo 38, 28006 Madrid; tel. (3) 3224626; fax (3) 3224772; f. 1961; children's books, non-fiction and general fiction; Pres. JESÚS DE POLANCO; Gen. Dir EMILIANO MARTÍNEZ.

**Consejo Superior de Investigaciones Científicas:** Vitruvio 8, 28006 Madrid; tel. (1) 5629633; telex 42182; fax (1) 5629634; f. 1939; science, reference, religion, law, textbooks, etc.

**Ediciones Cátedra, SA:** Juan Ignacio Luca de Tena 15, 28027 Madrid; tel. (1) 3938787; telex 41071; fax (1) 7426631; f. 1973; literature, literary criticism, history, humanities, linguistics, arts, cinema, music, feminism; Pres. MARÍA ISABEL DE ANDRÉS BRAVO; Man. Dir GUSTAVO DOMÍNGUEZ.

**Ediciones de Cultura Hispánica:** Avda de los Reyes Católicos, Ciudad Universitaria, 28040 Madrid; tel. (1) 5838100; fax (1) 5838311; f. 1943; arts, law, history, economics for circulation in Latin America; Literary and Artistic Dir ANTONIO PAPELL.

**Ediciones Morata, SL:** Mejía Lequerica 12, 28004 Madrid; tel. (1) 4480926; telex 47891; fax (1) 4480925; f. 1920; medicine, chemistry, psychology, psychiatry, pedagogics; Dir FLORA MORATA; Editor FLORENTINA GÓMEZ MORATA.

**Ediciones OFFO, SA:** Los Mesejo 23, 28007 Madrid; tel. (1) 4330249; fax (1) 5010699; f. 1956; arts; Dir JOAQUÍN ZUAZO MARTÍNEZ.

**Ediciones Pirámide, SA:** Juan Ignacio Luca de Tena 15, 28027 Madrid; tel. (1) 3938989; telex 41071; fax (1) 7426631; f. 1973; scientific and technical books; Pres. MARÍA ISABEL ANDRÉS; Man. Dir GUILLERMO DE TOCA.

**Fundación Santa María—Ediciones SM:** Joaquín Turina 39, 28044 Madrid; tel. (1) 5085145; fax (1) 5089927; f. 1939; textbooks, children's literature; Man. Dir JORGE DELKÁDER TEIG.

**Editorial Biblioteca Nueva:** Almagro 38, 28010 Madrid; tel. (1) 3100436; f. 1945; literature, essays, poetry, psychology; Dir JOSÉ RUIZ-CASTILLO BASALA.

**Editorial Bruño (La Instrucción Popular, SA):** Maestro Alonso 21, 28028 Madrid; tel. (1) 3610448; fax (1) 3613133; f. 1897; education, children's books; Dir FRANCISCO FERNÁNDEZ CILLERUELO.

**Editorial Castalia:** Zurbano 39, 28010 Madrid; tel. (1) 3198940; fax (1) 3102442; f. 1946; classics, literature; Pres. AMPARO SOLER GIMENO; Dir FEDERICO IBÁÑEZ SOLER.

**Editorial Católica, SA:** Valportillo Primera 11, Polígono Industrial 28100 Alcobendas; tel. (1) 6234100; fax (1) 6234171; f. 1912; religious and philosophical; Dir-Gen. FRANCISCO VALTUEÑA.

**Editorial Dossat, SA:** Plaza de Santa Ana 9, 28012 Madrid; tel. (1) 433400; telex 42572; fax (1) 4293721; f. 1943; technology, science; Dir EUGENIANO BARRERA SAN MARTÍN.

**Editorial Edaf, SA:** Jorge Juan 30, 1°, 28001 Madrid; tel. (1) 4358260; fax (1) 4315281; f. 1967; literature, dictionaries, occult, natural health, paperbacks; Mans GERARDO FOSSATI, LUCIANO FOSSATI.

**Editorial Gredos, SA:** Sánchez Pacheco 81, 28002 Madrid; tel. (1) 4157408; telex 43229; fax (1) 5192033; f. 1944; reference, humanities, art, literature; Dir JOSÉ OLIVEIRA BUGALLO.

**Editorial Magisterio Español, SA:** Tutor 27, 28008 Madrid; tel. (1) 5429597; fax (1) 5427145; f. 1866; educational; Vice-Pres. ALFONSO VERICAT NÚÑEZ.

**Editorial Música Moderna, SA:** Apdo 2401, 28080 Madrid; tel. (1) 4169181; fax (1) 4153778; f. 1935; music; Man. FRANCISCO CARMONA GONZÁLEZ.

**Editorial Paraninfo, SA:** Magallanes 25, 28015 Madrid; tel. (1) 4463350; fax (1) 4456218; f. 1946; technical, reference and educational; Man. MIGUEL MANGADA FERBER.

**Editorial Prensa Española, SA:** Padilla 6, 28006 Madrid; tel. (1) 3200818; fax (1) 3203555; f. 1977; facsimiles, journalism, music; Man. Dir JOSÉ LUIS HERRERA.

**Editorial Reus, SA:** Calle de Preciados 23, 28013 Madrid; tel. (1) 5213619; fax (1) 5312408; f. 1852; law, literature; Dir ANGEL RODRÍGUEZ SAIZ.

**Editorial Rudolf Steiner:** Guipúzcoa 11, 1°, 28020 Madrid; tel. (1) 5531481; fax (1) 5348163; f. 1978; arts, sciences etc.; Man. ISABEL NOVILLO GILA AMBRUSTER.

**Editorial Tecnos, SA:** Juan Ignacio Luca de Tena 15, 28027 Madrid; tel. (1) 3938686; telex 41071; fax (1) 7426631; f. 1947; science, law, social and political science, philosophy, engineering and economics; Pres. GERMÁN SÁNCHEZ RUIPÉREZ; Man. FRANCISCO J. BOBILLO DE LA PEÑA.

**Espasa-Calpe, SA:** Carretera de Irún, km. 12,200, Apdo 547, 28049 Madrid; tel. (1) 3589689; telex 48850; fax (1) 3589505; f. 1925; encyclopaedias, history, dictionaries, literature, biographies, paperbacks, etc.; Pres. MANUEL RAMÍREZ ORTIZ; Dir-Gen. JORGE HERNÁNDEZ ALIQUES.

**Fondo de Cultura Económica, SA:** Vía de los Poblados 10, Edificio Indubuilding Goico 4–15, 28033 Madrid; tel. (1) 7632800; fax (1) 7635133; f. 1974; pocket collections, sciences, literature; Dir MARGARITA DE LA VILLA.

**Grupo Anaya, SA:** Juan Ignacio Luca de Tena 15, 28027 Madrid; tel. (1) 3938800; telex 41071; fax (1) 7426631; f. 1959; reference, sciences, arts, literature, education; Pres. ISABEL ANDRÉS BRAVO.

**Ibérico Europea de Ediciones, SA:** Serrano 44, 28001 Madrid; tel. (1) 2253527; f. 1966; sciences, literature, sports; Dir JOSÉ CARLOS CAMÍNS MOCHALES.

**Librería y Casa Editorial Hernando, SA:** José Garrido 8, 28019 Madrid; tel. (1) 4717762; textbooks, literature, science; Man. Dir PABLO MUÑOZ MATEA.

**Narcea, SA de Ediciones:** Dr Federico Rubio y Galí 9, 28039 Madrid; tel. (1) 5546484; fax (1) 5546487; f. 1968; humanities, pedagogy, psychology, spiritualism and textbooks; Man. Dir ANA MARÍA DE MIGUEL CARRO.

**Siglo XXI de España, Editores, SA:** Plaza 5, 28043 Madrid; tel. (1) 7594809; fax (1) 7594557; f. 1967; pocket collections, reference, social sciences; Pres. PABLO GARCÍA-ARENAL.

**Susaeta Ediciones, SA:** Campezo s/n, 28022 Madrid; tel. (1) 7472111; fax (1) 7479295; f. 1963; children's books; Dir JOSÉ IGNACIO SUSAETA ERBURU.

### Barcelona

**Barcino Editorial:** Montseny 9, 08012 Barcelona; tel. (3) 2186888; fax (3) 2186888; f. 1924; general; Dir JOSEP TREMOLEDA I ROCA.

**Biblograf, SA:** Calabria 108, 08015 Barcelona; tel. (3) 4240000; fax (3) 4236898; f. 1953; encyclopaedias, dictionaries, atlases, linguistics; Man. MARÍA ISABEL ANDRÉS BRAVO.

**Bosch, Casa Editorial, SA:** Comte d'Urgell 51 bis, Apdo 928, 08011 Barcelona; tel. (3) 4548437; fax (3) 3236736; f. 1934; law, social science, classics; Gen. Man. J. M. IAÑEZ.

**Luis de Caralt/Editor, SA:** Santa Amelia 22, Bajos, 08034 Barcelona; tel. (3) 2801399; fax (3) 2801993; f. 1942; literature, novels, biographies, history, art, books, non-fiction, pocket books; Man. EMILIO ARDEVOL.

**Carroggio, SA de Ediciones:** Numancia 72–74, 08029 Barcelona; tel. (3) 3223751; fax (3) 4192852; f. 1911; sciences, literature; Man. Dirs FERNANDO CARROGGIO.

**Círculo de Lectores, SA:** Valencia 344–346, 08009 Barcelona; tel. (3) 4587600; telex 52532; fax (3) 4585928; f. 1962; arts, literature, leisure; Man. Dir Dr HANS MEINKE.

**EDEBE:** Paseo San Juan Bosco 62, 08017 Barcelona; tel. (3) 2037408; fax (3) 2054670; f. 1968; children's and educational publications; Man. JOSÉ ALDUNATE JURÍO.

SPAIN

**EDHASA (Editora y Distribuidora Hispano-Americana, SA):** Avda Diagonal 519–521, 2°, 08029 Barcelona; tel. (3) 4395105; fax (3) 4194584; f. 1946; contemporary fiction, non-fiction, pocket books, travel, historical fiction; Editorial Dir and Man. JORDI NADAL.

**Ediciones Ceac, SA:** Perú 164, 08020 Barcelona; tel. (3) 3073004; telex 50564; fax (3) 3084392; f. 1957; textbooks, education, leisure; Dir GUILLERMO MENAL.

**Ediciones Destino, SA:** Consell de Cent 425, 08009 Barcelona; tel. (3) 2652305; fax (3) 2657537; f. 1942; general fiction, history, art, children's books; Dir ANDREU TEIXIDOR DE VENTÓS.

**Ediciones Editorial Vicens-Vives, SA:** Avda Sarriá 130–136, 08017 Barcelona; tel. (3) 2034400; fax (3) 2047062; f. 1961; school and university, educational; Dirs ROSARIO RAHOLA DE ESPONA, PERE-JOAN VICENS RAHOLA.

**Ediciones Océano-Exito, SA:** Milanesat 21–23, 08017 Barcelona; tel. (3) 2802020; fax (3) 2045958; f. 1950; general; Chair. JOSÉ LLUIS MONREAL; Gen. Man. JOSÉ MARÍA MARTÍ COSTA.

**Ediciones Martínez Roca, SA:** Enric Granados 84, bajos, 08008 Barcelona; tel. (3) 4153911; fax (3) 4153830; f. 1965; fiction, chess, occultism, history, sport, psychology, psychiatry, practical; Man. Dir FERNANDO CALVO.

**Ediciones Musicales Clipper's:** Calle Valencia 335, Pral. 2A, 08009 Barcelona; tel. (3) 2073913; telex 51539; fax (3) 4594738; f. 1939; Dir JULIO GUIU ARBELOA.

**Ediciones Nauta, SA:** Loreto 16, 08029 Barcelona; tel. (3) 4392204; telex 54495; fax (3) 4107314; f. 1962; luxury reference and belles lettres, atlases, business-management; Man. Dir J. L. RUIZ DE VILLA.

**Ediciones Omega, SA:** Platón 26, 08006 Barcelona; tel. (3) 2010599; fax (3) 2097362; f. 1948; biology, field guides, geography, geology, agriculture, photography; Chair. ANTONIO PARICIO; Mans ANTONIO and GABRIEL PARICIO.

**Ediciones Polígrafa, SA:** Balmes 54, 08007 Barcelona; tel. (3) 4882381; fax (3) 4877392; f. 1966; arts, leisure; Man. Dir MANUEL DE MUGA TOSET.

**Edicions 62, SA:** Provença 278, 08008 Barcelona; tel. (3) 4870062; fax (3) 2155468; f. 1963; Man. JUAN CAPDEVILA; Literary Dir JOSEP M. CASTELLET.

**Editores Técnicos Asociados, SA (Etasa):** Maignón 26, 08024 Barcelona; tel. (3) 2844178; fax (3) 2108082; f. 1963; Pres. CARLOS PALOMAR; Dir SERGE EYROLLES.

**Editorial Acervo, SL:** Julio Verne 5–7, 08006 Barcelona; tel. (3) 2122664; fax (3) 2122706; f. 1954; law, literature, history, science fiction; Man. Dir ANA PERALES HERRERO.

**Editorial Aedos, SA:** Consejo de Ciento 391, 08009 Barcelona; tel. (3) 4883009; telex 98772; fax (3) 4877659; f. 1939; agriculture and stockbreeding, veterinary surgery, biography, art and tourism; specialists in Catalan works; Dir CRISTINA CONCELLÓN RODRÍGUEZ.

**Editorial Argos-Vergara, SA:** Rambla Montserrat 19, Bajos, 08290 Cerdanyola; tel. and fax (3) 5808124; f. 1941; general; Pres. ALFREDO PLANA.

**Editorial Ariel, SA:** Calle Córcega 270, 08008 Barcelona; tel. (3) 2186400; telex 98255; fax (3) 2184773; f. 1941; social and political science, economics, history, sciences and law; Gen. Dir YMELDA NAVAJO; Editorial Dir MARCELO COVIÁN FASCE.

**Editorial Casanovas, SA:** Montserrat de Casanovas 49, 08032 Barcelona; tel. (3) 4290335; f. 1989.

**Editorial Claret, SA:** Roger de Llúria 5, 08010 Barcelona; tel. (3) 3010887; fax (3) 3174830; f. 1926; Dirs Claretian Fathers; religion, children's books, Catalan grammar and general books, slides, cassettes and videos, *Audio-visuals Claret*.

**Editorial Gustavo Gili, SA:** Rosellón 87–89, 08029 Barcelona; tel. (3) 3228161; fax (3) 3229205; f. 1902; technology, art, architecture, design, communication; Man. Dir GUSTAVO GILI T.

**Editorial Hispano-Europea, SA:** Bori y Fontestá 6, 08021 Barcelona; tel. (3) 2018500; telex 98772; fax (3) 4142635; f. 1954; technical, scientific, sport, pet books and reference; Propr and Man. Dir JORGE J. PRAT ROSAL.

**Editorial Juventud, SA:** Provenza 101, 08029 Barcelona; tel. (3) 4392000; fax (3) 4398383; f. 1923; general fiction, biography, history, art, music, textbooks, reference, dictionaries, travel books, children's books, paper-backs; Dir LUIS ZENDRERA.

**Editorial Labor, SA:** Rambla Montserrat 19, Bajos, 08290 Cerdanyola; tel. and fax (3) 5808124; f. 1915; medicine, technical, engineering, law, art, music, dictionaries, general; Pres. ALFREDO PLANA.

**Editorial Molino:** Calabria 166, 08015; Barcelona; tel. (3) 2260625; telex 98772; fax (3) 2266998; f. 1933; crime, cookery, children's books, reference books; Dirs PABLO DEL MOLINO STERNA, LUIS ANTONIO DEL MOLINO JOVER.

**Editorial Noguer, SA:** Santa Amelia 22, Bajos, 08034 Barcelona; tel. (3) 2801399; fax (3) 2801993; f. 1949; literature, non-fiction, art, children's and juveniles' books; mysteries, short stories, paperbacks, encyclopaedias, travel books, reports, historical and biographical; Pres. EMILIO ARDÉVOL.

**Editorial Planeta, SA:** Córcega 273–277, 08008 Barcelona; tel. (3) 4154100; telex 52632; fax (3) 2177140; f. 1948; popular, literature, children's; Pres. JOSÉ MANUEL LARA HERNÁNDEZ; Dir-Gen. FERNANDO LARA BOSCH.

**Editorial Reverté, SA:** Loreto 13–15, Local B, 08029 Barcelona; tel. (3) 4193336; fax (3) 4195189; f. 1947; engineering, general science, university and scientific books; Dir FELIPE REVERTÉ PLANELLS.

**Editorial Selecta Catalònia:** Ronda de Sant Pere 3, 08010 Barcelona; tel. (3) 3172331; fax (3) 3024793; f. 1946; books in Catalan; Man. SEBASTIÀ BORRÀS I TEY.

**Editorial Ramón Sopena, SA:** Provenza 93–97, 08029 Barcelona; tel. (3) 2303809; telex 52195; fax (3) 2303809; f. 1896; encyclopaedias, dictionaries, art, science, history, geography, juvenile literature, children's books; Man. RAMÓN SOPENA.

**Editorial Teide, SA:** Viladomat 291, 08029 Barcelona; tel. (3) 4104507; fax (3) 3224192; f. 1942; educational, scientific, technical and art; Man. Dir FEDERICO RAHOLA.

**Empresa Editorial Herder, SA:** Provenza 388, 08025 Barcelona; tel. (3) 4577700; fax (3) 2073448; f. 1943; philosophy, pedagogy, sociology; philology, psychology, theology, history, languages, dictionaries; Dir JAN-CORNELIUS SCHULZ.

**Grijalbo Mondadori, SA:** Aragó 385, 08013 Barcelona; tel. (3) 4587000; telex 53940; fax (3) 4580495; f. 1939; fiction, non-fiction, economics, reference books, dictionaries, guides; Pres. MAURIZIO COSTA; Gen. Man. GONZALO PONTÓN.

**Instituto Gallach de Librería y Ediciones, SL:** Milanesat 21–23, 08017 Barcelona; tel. (3) 2802020; fax (3) 2045958; f. 1924; illustrated and reference books, encyclopaedias; Chair. JOSÉ LLUIS MONREAL; Gen. Man. JOSÉ MARÍA MARTI COSTA.

**LEDA—Las Ediciones de Arte:** Riera San Miguel 37, 08006 Barcelona; tel. (3) 2379389; fax (3) 2155273; f. 1940; artistic books; Propr and Man. Dir DANIEL BASILIO BONET.

**Marcombo, SA de Boixareu Editores:** Gran Vía de les Corts Catalanes 594, 08007 Barcelona; tel. (3) 3180079; fax (3) 3189339; f. 1945; reference, sciences, textbooks; Pres. JOSEP M. BOIXAREU GINESTA; Man. Dir JOSEP M. BOIXAREU VILAPLANA.

**Masson, SA:** Avda Príncipe de Asturias 20, 08012 Barcelona; tel. (3) 4154544; fax (3) 4161219; medical and scientific books; Dir PEDRO DE LA ROSA.

**Montagud Editores:** Ausiàs Marc 25, 1°, 08010 Barcelona; tel. (3) 3182082; fax (3) 3025083; f. 1906; business; Chair. FRANCISCO ANTOJA GIRALT.

**Oikos-Tau, SA—Ediciones:** Montserrat 12–14, Vilassar de Mar, 08340 Barcelona; Apdo 5347, 08080 Barcelona; tel. (3) 7590791; fax (3) 7595851; f. 1963; economics, science, geography, history, marketing, management, agriculture, sociology, urban planning and education; Man. JORDI GARCIA-BOSCH.

**Plaza y Janés, Editores, SA:** Enrique Granados 86–88, 08008 Barcelona; tel. (3) 4151100; fax (3) 4156976; f. 1959; fiction and non-fiction, science, travel, reference; Dir-Gen. MANFRED GREBE.

**Salvat Editores, SA:** Mallorca 45, 08029 Barcelona; tel. (3) 4301441; fax (3) 4303398; f. 1923; art, history, dictionaries, encyclopaedias, English courses, music; Pres. JEAN-LOUIS LISIMACHIO.

**Toray, SA Ediciones:** Rambla Montserrat 19, Bajos, 08290 Cerdanyola; tel. and fax (3) 5808124; f. 1953; children's books; Pres. ALFREDO PLANA.

### Other Towns

**Dilagro SA—Librería Editorial:** Comercio 48, 25007 Lérida; tel. 233480; fax 236413; f. 1967; sciences, literature, textbooks, specialists in textbooks on agriculture; Man. JORGE MARIMÓN SARRÁ.

**Ediciones Deusto, SA:** Alameda Recalde 27, 7a, 48009 Bilbao; tel. (4) 4251500; fax (4) 4251515; f. 1960; diaries, newsletters, management and law books; Man. Dir JUAN RAMÓN GRIJELMO.

**Ediciones Mensajero, SA:** Apdo 73, 48080 Bilbao; tel. (4) 4470583; fax (4) 4472630; f. 1915; arts, biography, theology, psychology, pedagogy, social science and paperbacks; Dir ANGEL ANTONIO PÉREZ GÓMEZ.

**Ediciones Universidad de Navarra, SA (EUNSA):** Plaza de los Sauces, 1 y 2, Barañain/Pamplona; tel. 256850; fax (48) 256854; f. 1967; architecture, natural sciences, law, history, social sciences, theology, philosophy, medical, engineering, journalism, education, economics and business administration, biology, literature, library science, paperbacks, etc; Chair. DÁMASO RICO; Vice-Pres. JOSÉ A. MUSTIENES.

**Editorial Aranzadi SA:** Avda Carlos III 34, 31004 Pamplona; tel. (48) 249950; fax (48) 330919; f. 1930; law.

# SPAIN

**Editorial Everest, SA:** Carretera León-Coruña, Km 5, Apdo 339, 24080 León; tel. (87) 802020; telex 89916; fax (87) 801251; f. 1966; general; Dir José Antonio López Martínez.

**Editorial Galaxia:** Reconquista 1, 36201 Vigo; tel. (86) 432100; fax (86) 223205; f. 1950; literary works, reviews, popular, children's, Galician literature; Dir Carlos Casares Mouriño.

**Editorial Marfil, SA:** San Eloy 17, 03800 Alcoy; tel. (6) 5523311; fax (6) 5523496; f. 1947; textbooks, psychology, pedagogy, university texts, literature; Man. Verónica Cantó Doménech.

**International Book Creation, SA:** Juan de Ajuriaguerra 10, 48009 Bilbao; tel. (4) 4438195; f. 1964; art, history, geography, classical literature, biographies; Dir Juan Carlos Grijelmo Mintegui.

**Publicaciones Fher, SA:** Camilo Villabaso 9, 48002 Bilbao; tel. (4) 4218000; telex 32195; fax (4) 4432649; f. 1983; children's, leisure; Dir Ignacio Aguirre Aguirre.

## PUBLISHERS' ASSOCIATIONS

**Federación de Gremios de Editores de España** (Federation of Publishers' Associations of Spain): Juan Ramón Jiménez 45, 9° Izqda, 28036 Madrid; tel. (1) 3509105; fax (1) 3454351; Pres. Pere Vicens; Sec.-Gen. Ana Moltó.

**Associació d'Editors en Llengua Catalana** (Association of Publishers in Catalan Language): València 279, 1a, 08009 Barcelona; tel. (3) 2155091; fax (3) 2155273; Pres. Ramon Bastardes i Porcel.

**Gremi d'Editors de Catalunya:** València 279, 1a, 08009 Barcelona; tel. (3) 2155091; fax (3) 2155273; Pres. Jordi Ubeda Bauló.

**Gremio de Editores de Euzkadi:** Bilbao; tel. (4) 4242449; fax (4) 4242469; Pres. Javier Gogeascoechea Arrien.

**Gremio de Editores de Madrid:** Santiago Rusiñol 8, 28040 Madrid; tel. (1) 5544745; telex 47891; fax (1) 5532553; f. 1977; Pres. Juan de Isasa González-Ubieta; Sec.-Gen. Amalia Martín Pereda.

# Radio and Television

There were an estimated 12.2m. radio receivers and 15.7m. television receivers in use in Spain in 1992.

**RTVE—Radiotelevisión Española:** Casa de la Radio, Prado del Rey, 28023 Madrid; tel. (1) 5817000; telex 27366; fax (1) 3462064; state organization; controls and co-ordinates radio and television; Dir-Gen. Jordi García Candau.

**Compañía de Radio Televisión de Galicia (CRTVG):** Apdo 707, San Marcos, 15780 Santiago de Compostela; tel. (81) 564400; telex 86297; f. 1985; Galician language station; public company; Dir-Gen. Ramón Villot.

**Corporació Catalana de Ràdio i Televisió (CCRTV):** Avda Diagonal 477, 7°, 08036 Barcelona; tel. (3) 4109696; telex 97012; fax (3) 4194051; f. 1983; Catalan language station; public-company; two television channels and four radio stations; Dir-Gen. Jordi Vilajoana.

**EITB—Euskal Irrati Telebista (Radiotelevisión Vasca):** 48200 Iurreta s/n, Vizcaya; tel. (4) 6203000; telex 34440; fax (4) 6816416; f. 1982; Basque language station; public company; two television channels and five radio stations; Dir-Gen. Iñaki Zarraoa.

**Ràdio Televisió Valenciana (RTVV):** Avda de Blasco Ibáñez 34, 46022 Valencia; tel. (6) 3710055; f. 1984; public company; Dir-Gen. Amadeu Fabregat.

**Radio Televisión de Andalucía (RTVA):** Carretera San Juan de Aznalfarache a Tomares, Km 1350, 41920 San Juan de Aznalfarache, Sevilla; tel. (5) 4763111; fax (5) 4769755; public company; Dir-Gen. Joaquín Marín.

**Radio Televisión Madrid (RTVM):** Madrid; public company; Pres. José Antonio Moral Santín; Dir-Gen. Marcos Sanz.

**Radiotelevisión Murciana (RTVMU):** Murcia; Dir-Gen. Eduardo Alonso.

### Federation

**Federación de Organismos de Radio y Televisión Autonómicos (FORTA):** Madrid; f. 1989; groups autonomous orgs; Pres. Ramón Villot; Sec.-Gen. Joaquín Amat.

### RADIO

**Radio Nacional de España (RNE):** Casa de la Radio, Prado del Rey, 28223 Madrid; tel. (1) 3461000; telex 45891; fax (1) 5183240; 17 regional stations; Dir Diego Carcedo; Dir of Programmes and Broadcasts Salvador Barber.

**Radio Exterior España (REE):** Apdo 156.202, 28080 Madrid; tel. (1) 3461081; telex 42412; fax (1) 3461815; foreign service of RNE; broadcasts in 10 languages; includes a world service in Spanish; Dir Fermín Bocos.

### Regional Public Stations

**Catalunya Ràdio:** Avda Diagonal 614–616, 08021 Barcelona; tel. (3) 2019911; telex 97325; fax (3) 2006224; f. 1983; run by Catalan autonomous govt; four channels: Catalunya Ràdio, Ràdio Associació de Catalunya, Catalunya Música, Catalunya Informació; Dir Lluís Oliva.

**Euskadi Irratia:** Larramendi 1, 20006 San Sebastián; tel. (43) 423630; fax (43) 423895; run by Basque autonomous govt; broadcasts on FM and MW; also stations in Bilbao and Vitoria; Dir Julián Beloki.

**Radio Galega:** Sau Marcos, 15820 Santiago de Compostela; tel. (81) 540940; fax (81) 540919; f. 1985; run by Galician autonomous govt; Dir Xosé-Luís Blanco.

### Other Stations

There are more than 300 other radio stations.

**Antena 3 de Radio:** Oquendo 23, 28006 Madrid; tel. (1) 5870100; telex 49369; fax (1) 5622787; f. 1982; 90 regional stations; Dir Eduardo Alcalde Clemente.

**Cadena Dial:** Plaza de Callao 4, 28013 Madrid; several regional stations; owned by PRISA; Dir Francisco Herrera.

**Compañía de Radiodifusión Intercontinental (INTER):** Modesto Lafuente 42, Madrid 3; tel. (1) 2544603; stations in Madrid, Córdoba, Linares and Onteniente; Dir-Gen. Fernando Serrano-Suñer Polo.

**Onda Cero Radio:** Paseo Pintor Rosales 76, 28008 Madrid; tel. (1) 5386300; telex 41044; fax (1) 5386360; owned by ONCE; Dir-Gen. Santiago Galván.

**Onda Cero Radio Barcelona/Onda Rambla:** Ramblas 126, 08002 Barcelona; tel. (3) 3180870; fax (3) 3016843; Dir Francisco Olona.

**Ondas Galicia, SA:** Ramón Cabanillas 14, 15701 Santiago de Compostela; private station; Gen. Man. Eduardo de la Peña Vila.

**Radio 80:** Oquendo 23, 28006 Madrid; tel. (1) 2624533; telex 49387; fax (1) 5644341; f. 1982; 18 regional stations; Dir Manuel Martín Ferrand.

**Radio Autonomía Madrid, SA/Onda Madrid:** García de Paredes 65, 28010 Madrid; tel. (1) 5924100; fax (1) 5924674; f. 1985; broadcasts on 101.3 and 106.0 MHz; Dir Luis Rodríguez Olivares.

**Radio España de Madrid (Cultural Radio Española):** Manuel Silvela 9, 28010 Madrid; tel. (1) 4475300; telex 49294; fax (1) 4468988; f. 1924; part of Cadena Ibérica; Exec. Pres. Eugenio Fontán Pérez.

**Radio Minuto Madrid:** Gran Vía 32, 8a planta, 28013 Madrid; tel. (1) 3470800; fax (1) 3470779; f. 1983; Dir-Gen. Javier Suárez.

**Radio Miramar:** Barcelona; tel. (3) 3025566; fax (3) 3188583; Dir Francisco J. Olona Cabasses.

**Radio Noroeste:** Príncipe 22, Vigo; tel. 226965; fax 226969; private station; Man. Jesús Lorenzo Loureiro.

**Ràdio Olot:** Plaça del Mig s/n, Apdo 177, 17800 Olot (Girona); tel. 261750; fax 261357; f. 1951; Pres. Pere Macias Arau; Dir Joan Brilli i Mora.

**Radio Popular, SA—COPE:** Alfonso XI 4, 28014 Madrid; tel. (1) 3090034; telex 41948; fax (1) 5322008; f. 1959; 45 medium-wave and 121 FM stations; Dir-Gen. Silvio González Moreno.

**Radio Sabadell/882 COM—Catalunya Ona Mitjana:** Convent 22, 08202 Sabadell; tel. (3) 7272020; fax (3) 7271195; f. 1932; Dir Josep Anton Pages.

**Radio Tiempo (Sistemas Radiofónicos):** Teodoro Roviralta 31, 08022 Barcelona; tel. (3) 4170505; fax (3) 2120569; Dir-Gen. José María Rovira Milá.

**Ràdio Vic:** Osonenca de Ràdio i TV, St Antoni 2, Apartat Correus 30, 08500 Vic (Barcelona); tel. 8863731; fax 8863430; Dir Joan Orriols i Puig.

**Sociedad Española de Radiodifusión (SER):** Gran Vía 32, 28013 Madrid; tel. (1) 3470700; telex 27638; fax (1) 3470709; f. 1924; 235 regional stations; Dir-Gen. Augusto Delkáder; Man. Dir Daniel Gavela.

### Radio Association

**Asociación Española de la Radiodifusión Comercial (AERC):** Madrid; groups nearly all commercial radio stations; Pres. Alfonso Cavallé.

### TELEVISION

Legislation relating to the ending of TVE's monopoly and the regulation of private TV stations was approved in April 1988. Three new national channels were awarded licences in 1989.

**Televisión Española (TVE):** Prado del Rey, Apdo 26002, 28023 Madrid; tel. (1) 7110400; telex 27694; broadcasts on TVE-1 and La 2; 15 regional centres; broadcasts to Europe and the Americas on Canal Internacional; Dir Ramón Colom Esmatges.

SPAIN                                                                                                          *Directory*

### Public Regional Stations
The following autonomous stations have been established:

**Canal 9—Televisió Valenciana (TVV):** Poligon Ademuz, 46100 Burjassot (Valencia); tel. (6) 3641100; fax (6) 3634355; commenced regular transmissions Oct. 1989; Dir-Gen. AMADEU FABREGAT.

**Canal Sur Televisión, SA:** Sevilla; tel. (5) 5607600; fax (5) 5607778; commenced transmissions in 1989; regional station for Andalucía; controlled by RTVA; Dir FERNANDO IBÁÑEZ CONTRERAS.

**Euskal Telebista—ETB (TV Vasca):** 48278 Iurreta, Vizcaya; tel. (4) 6203000; telex 34441; fax (4) 6816526; f. 1983; broadcasts in Basque Country in Basque language on ETB-1 and in Spanish on ETB-2; mem. of EITB; Dir LUIS ALBERTO ARANBERRI.

**Tele 3:** Platena 44, 2°C, 30001 Murcia; tel. (68) 212224; fax (68) 214673; commenced test transmissions in early 1990; Dir-Gen. JESÚS MARTÍN-GIL GARCÍA.

**Televisió de Catalunya:** Apartat de Correus 30300, 08080 Barcelona; tel. (3) 4999333; telex 53280; fax (3) 4730671; f. 1983; broadcasts on TV-3 and Canal 33 in Catalan over north-eastern Spain; controlled by CCRTV; Dir JAUME FERRÚS.

**Televisión de Galicia (TVG):** Apdo 707, San Marcos, 15780 Santiago de Compostela; tel. (81) 540640; telex 86243; fax (81) 540719; f. 1985; broadcasts in Galician; controlled by CRTVG; Dir ARTURO MANEIRO VILA.

**Televisión Madrid (Telemadrid):** Zurbano 56, 28010 Madrid; tel. (1) 4107104; fax (1) 4106197; commenced transmissions in 1989; controlled by RTVM; Dir JOSÉ RAMÓN PÉREZ ORNIA.

Regional stations are also coming into operation in Aragón, Asturias, the Canary Islands, Cantabria, Castilla y León and Navarra.

### Private Stations

**Antena 3 de Televisión, SA:** Carretera Madrid–Irun, km 19.3, 28700 San Sebastián de los Reyes, Madrid; tel. (1) 6230500; fax (1) 6527144; f. 1989; transmissions include satellite news service; Pres. ANTONIO ASENSIO.

**Canal +:** Gran Vía 32, 1°, 28013 Madrid; tel. (1) 3965500; commenced transmissions in 1990; Pres. JESÚS POLANCO; Dir-Gen. CARLOS ABAD.

**Tele 5:** Plaza Pablo Ruiz Picasso s/n, Edif. Torre Picasso, 36°, 28020 Madrid; tel. (1) 3966100; fax (1) 5550044; commenced transmissions in 1990; Pres. MIGUEL DURÁN; Dir-Gen. MAURIZIO CARLOTTI.

### Network Operator

**Red Técnica Española de Televisión (Retevisión):** Paseo de la Castellana 83–85, 28046 Madrid; tel. (1) 5560214; telex 22989; fax (1) 5565241; f. 1989; state-owned company (to be transferred to private ownership) responsible for relaying of programmes throughout Spain from public and private radio and TV cos; Pres. MIGUEL ANGEL FEITO; Dir JOSÉ AZNAR.

### Cable and Satellite Television

In November 1992 it was announced that three of the seven channels available on Hispasat were to be awarded to Televisión Española. Teledeporte and Canal Clásico, along with the three private stations listed above (responsible for TeleNoticias, Cinemanía 2 and Telesatcinco) commenced regular satellite transmissions in September 1994. Various other cable and satellite channels, including Cineclassics, Cinemanía, Documanía, Minimax, TVE Inter, Super Channel, Galavisión, TV-5, CNN, RAI Uno, RAI Due, Eurosport and Screensport, can be received in Spain.

# Finance

(Amounts in pesetas unless stated otherwise; cap. = capital, p.u. = paid up, res = reserves, dep. = deposits, br. = branch, m. = million)

### BANKING

In 1991 there were about 100 private and commercial banks operating in Spain. A process of consolidation continues to take place in the banking system. In March 1988 the Banco de España announced that the Government was to resume authorizing the establishment of new banks with national capital (for the first time since 1978). The minimum capital requirement for the establishment of new banks was raised from 1,500m. to 3,000m. pesetas in 1995. In 1987 there were 77 savings banks (cajas de ahorro), which had 12,000 branches and took 43% of all Spanish deposits. By far the largest savings bank was La Caixa (Caja de Pensiones), based in Barcelona. In late 1989 La Caixa and La Caixa de Barcelona agreed to merge, establishing La Caja de Ahorros y Pensiones de Barcelona. Combined deposits totalled 3,800,000m. pesetas, thus far exceeding those of the largest commercial bank. In addition, there were 62 rural savings banks in 1987.

### Central Bank

**Banco de España:** Alcalá 50, 28014 Madrid; tel. (1) 4469055; telex 27783; fax (1) 5216356; f. 1829; granted exclusive right of issue in 1874; nationalized 1962; granted a degree of autonomy in 1994; responsible for formulation of monetary policy; Gov. LUIS ANGEL ROJO; 52 brs.

### Principal Commercial and Development Banks

**Argentaria—Corporación Bancaria de España (BCE):** Paseo de Recoletos 10, 28001 Madrid; tel. (1) 5377000; fax (1) 4291902; f. 1991; state holding co; groups the following public enterprises and also the Caja Postal and Banco Hipotecario, Banco Directo and Banco de Negocios Argentaria; partial transfer to private ownership in 1993 reached 48.3%; Pres. FRANCISCO LUZÓN.

**Banco de Crédito Agrícola (BCA):** Alcalá 44, Pl. 5, 28014 Madrid; tel. (1) 3470347; telex 47405; fax (1) 5216584; f. 1962; cap. 13,127m., res 14,159m., dep. 559,611m. (Dec. 1990); Pres. LUIS TARRAFETA PUYAL.

**Banco de Crédito Local (BCL):** Carrera de San Jerónimo 40, 28014 Madrid; tel. (1) 5376500; fax (1) 5376526; Pres. FRANCISCO LUZÓN; Man. Dir LUIS ESCAURIAZA IBÁÑEZ.

**Banco Exterior de España:** Carrera de San Jerónimo 36, 28014 Madrid; tel. (1) 5377000; telex 48739; fax (1) 4298342; f. 1929; commercial bank; cap. 52,683m., res 238,849m., dep. 4,769,012m. (Dec. 1993); Chair. FRANCISCO LUZÓN; 466 brs.

**Banc Catalá de Credit:** Pasaje Mercader 7 y 9, 08008 Barcelona; tel. (3) 4871212; fax (3) 2159731; f. 1964; cap. 10,500m., res 2,603m., dep. 108,157m. (Dec. 1992); Pres. ABEL MATUTES; 102 brs.

**Banca Catalana:** Diagonal 662–664, 08034 Barcelona; tel. (3) 4044000; telex 53185; fax (3) 4044344; f. 1961; cap. 38,506m., res 27,721m., total assets 880,459m. (Dec. 1993); Pres. ALFREDO SÁENZ ABAD; 396 brs.

**Banca March, SA:** Avda Alejandro Rosselló 8, 07002 Palma de Mallorca; tel. (71) 779100; telex 68611; fax (71) 469929; f. 1926; cap. 4,800m., res 33,004m., dep. 161,195m. (Dec. 1993); Pres. JOSÉ CARLOS MARCH DELGADO; Vice-Pres. SIMÓN J. GALMÉS CERDÓ; 136 brs.

**Banco de Andalucía:** Fernández y González 4–6, 41001 Sevilla; tel. (5) 4594700; telex 72246; fax (5) 4214513; f. 1844; cap. 2,716m., res 37,240m., dep. 279,761m. (Dec. 1993); Pres. FERNANDO DE SOLÍS Y ATIENZA; Dir-Gen. JOSÉ M. YÉLAMOS NAVARRO; 240 brs.

**Banco Arabe Español:** Paseo de la Castellana 257, 28046 Madrid; tel. (1) 3149595; fax (1) 3149768; f. 1975; shareholders from Spain, Libya and Kuwait; cap. 12,000m., res 6,594m., dep. 106,272m. (Dec. 1993); Pres. ABDULLA A. SAUDI; Gen. Man. LUIS VAÑÓ; 3 brs.

**Banco Atlántico:** Diagonal 407 bis, 08008 Barcelona; tel. (3) 4161840; telex 52267; fax (3) 2188317; f. 1901; cap. 20,893m., res 27,151m., dep. 895,838m. (Dec. 1993); Pres. ABDULLA AMMAR SAUDI; Man. Dir ANTONIO SÁNCHEZ PEDREÑO; 234 brs.

**Banco Banif de Gestión Privada:** Juan Bravo 2, 28006 Madrid; tel. (1) 3484848; telex 27368; fax (1) 3484892; f. 1949; fmrly Banco del Norte; cap. 3,500m., res 3,257m. (Dec. 1994); Pres. JOSÉ MANUEL ABURURÚA ASPIUNZA; 6 brs.

**Banco Bilbao Vizcaya (BBV):** Plaza de San Nicolás, 48005 Bilbao; tel. (4) 4202000; telex 32055; fax (4) 4202030; f. 1988 through merger; cap. 138,600m., res 464,582m., dep. 10,261,990m. (Dec. 1993); Pres. EMILIO YBARRA CHURRUCA; CEO PEDRO LUIS URIARTE; 2,762 brs.

**Banco de Castilla:** Plaza de los Bandos 10, 37002 Salamanca; tel. (23) 290000; telex 26860; fax (23) 211902; f. 1915; cap. 4,339m., res 19,747m., dep. 228,871m. (Dec. 1993); Dir-Gen. SANTIAGO BERROCAL; 151 brs.

**Banco Central Hispano (BCH):** Alcalá 49, 28014 Madrid; tel. (1) 5328810; telex 43402; fax (1) 5316461; f. 1991 through merger; cap. 86,038m., res 547,563m., dep. 11,788,379m. (Dec. 1993); Pres. JOSÉ MARÍA AMUSÁTEGUI; CEO ANGEL CORCÓSTEGUI; 4,297 brs.

**Banco del Comercio:** Paseo de la Castellana 108, Apdo 1023, 28046 Madrid; tel. (1) 3743500; telex 27481; fax (1) 5619842; f. 1964; fmrly Banco de Financiación Industrial (Indubán); finances and undertakes industrial promotions; cap. 4,844m., res 41,185m., dep. 746,431m. (Dec. 1993); Pres. JAVIER GÚRPIDE HUARTE; 222 brs.

**Banco del Desarrollo Económico Español (Bandesco), SA:** Paseo de la Castellana 33, 10A planta, 28046 Madrid; tel. (1) 3100662; telex 41581; fax (1) 4100666; f. 1963; cap. 2,092m., res 10,651m., dep. 36,674m. (Dec. 1993); Pres. RAFAEL PÉREZ ESCOLAR; 9 brs.

**Banco Español de Crédito (Banesto):** Paseo de la Castellana 7, 28046 Madrid; tel. (1) 3381000; telex 27755; fax (1) 5318340; f. 1902; following the bank's failure in Dec. 1993, administration was assumed by Banco de España; subsequently purchased by Banco Santander; Pres. ALFREDO SÁENZ.

**Banco de Fomento:** Paseo de la Castellana 92, 28046 Madrid; tel. (1) 5620900; telex 44288; fax (1) 4114110; f. 1963; cap. 6,623m., res 15,262m. (Dec. 1990); Pres. ALFONSO ESCÁMEZ LÓPEZ; Dir-Gen. JUAN SÁNCHEZ-CORTÉS Y ALGUACIL-CARRASCO; 161 brs. (Merger with Hispamer, to form Hispamer Banco Financiero, approved June 1995.)

**Banco de Galicia:** Policarpo Sanz 23, 36201 Vigo (Pontevedra); tel. (86) 822106; telex 83407; fax (86) 822101; f. 1918; cap. 1,521m., res 7,441m. (Dec. 1989); Dir-Gen. MANUEL HIERRO SOSA; 123 brs.

**Banco Gallego:** Plaza de Cervantes 15, 15704 Santiago de Compostela; tel. (81) 581000; telex 86014; fax (81) 221337; f. 1847; fmrly Banco de Crédito e Inversiones, name changed 1988; cap. 3,503m., res 1,361m., dep. 136,808m. (Dec. 1992); Pres. JUAN MANUEL URGOITI LÓPEZ OCAÑA; 151 brs.

**Banco General, SA:** Plaza Sagrados Corazones 1, 28036 Madrid; tel. (1) 5631442; telex 47149; fax (1) 5631262; f. 1935; cap. 1,000m., dep. 4,347m.; Pres. ANTONIO SÁEZ DE MONTAGUT Y ARITIO; Dir-Gen. FRANCISCO MONTESINOS ZÚÑIGA; 4 brs.

**Banco de Granada, SA:** Gran Vía de Colón 16, 18010 Granada; tel. (58) 225561; telex 78425; fax (58) 226203; f. 1964; cap. 4,515m., res 35m. (Dec. 1989); taken over by the Corporación Bancaria in January 1979; Pres. TOMÁS PAREJO CAMACHO; 152 brs.

**Banco Guipuzcoano:** Avda de la Libertad 21, 20004 San Sebastián; tel. (43) 418100; telex 36369; fax (43) 426828; f. 1899; cap. 3,500m., res 21,974m., dep. 336,339m. (Dec. 1994); Pres. JOSÉ MARÍA AGUIRRE GONZÁLEZ; Gen. Man. JUAN LUIS ARRIETA; 188 brs.

**Banco Herrero:** Fruela 11, 33007 Oviedo; tel. (85) 215291; telex 84340; fax (85) 221296; f. 1912; cap. 3,847m., res 18,781m., dep. 317,987m. (Dec. 1993); Pres. IGNACIO HERRERO GARRALDA; Vice-Pres. IGNACIO HERRERO ALVAREZ; 162 brs.

**Banco Industrial de Bilbao:** Cardenal Gardoquí 1, 48008 Bilbao; tel. (4) 4158211; telex 32087; fax (4) 4158399; finances medium-term investments and industrial participants; cap. 3,098m., res 18,922m. (Dec. 1989), dep. 97,098m. (Dec. 1988); Pres. JOSÉ MARÍA CONCEJO ALVAREZ; 3 brs.

**Banco Industrial de Cataluña:** Diagonal 662–664, 08034 Barcelona; tel. (3) 4044000; telex 53905; fax (3) 4044344; f. 1965; cap. 4,500m., res 384m., dep. 50,539m. (Nov. 1988); Pres. ALFREDO SÁENZ ABAD.

**Banco Pastor:** Edificio Pastor, Cantón Pequeño 1, 15003 La Coruña; tel. (81) 224100; telex 82178; fax (81) 222661; f. 1776; cap. 9,086m., res 38,187m., dep. 872,397m. (Dec. 1992); Pres. CARMELA ARIAS Y DÍAZ DE RÁBAGO; 400 brs.

**Banco de la Pequeña y Mediana Empresa (BPME):** Travesera de Gracia 11, 08021 Barcelona; tel. (3) 2020000; telex 97691; fax (3) 2099765; f. 1978; finances small and medium businesses; cap. 4,800m., res 2,484m., dep. 145,274m. (Dec. 1993); Pres. and CEO Prof. Dr JOSÉ JANÉ; 21 brs.

**Banco Popular Español:** Velázquez 34 (esquina a Goya), 28001 Madrid; tel. (1) 5207000; telex 44351; fax (1) 5779208; f. 1926; cap. 14,450m., res 196,587m., dep. 2,545,059m. (Dec. 1993); merging with Banco Popular Industrial (Eurobanco); Co-Pres LUIS VALLS TABERNER, JAVIER VALLS TABERNER; 1,607 brs.

**Banco de Sabadell:** Plaza de Catalunya 1, 08201 Sabadell; tel. (3) 7289289; telex 94400; fax (3) 7259733; f. 1881; cap. 10,062m., res 65,697m., dep. 1,133,990m. (Dec. 1993); Chair. JUAN COROMINAS; 365 brs.

**Banco Santander:** Paseo de Pereda 9–12, Apdo 45, 39004 Santander; tel. (42) 206100; telex 35833; fax (42) 226405; f. 1857; cap. 84,230m., res 257,744m., dep. 9,263,434m. (Dec. 1993); Pres. EMILIO BOTÍN-SANZ DE SAUTUOLA Y GARCÍA DE LOS RÍOS; Dir-Gen. ANA PATRICIA BOTÍN; 1,391 brs.

**Banco Santander de Negocios:** Plaza Marqués de Salamanca 3 y 4, 28006 Madrid; tel. (1) 4357766; telex 49865; fax (1) 2752362; f. 1877; fmrly Banco Comercial de Cataluña; cap. 4,500m., res 4,653m. (Dec. 1989); Pres. EMILIO BOTÍN-SANZ DE SAUTUOLA Y GARCÍA DE LOS RÍOS; Dir-Gen. ANA PATRICIA BOTÍN; 6 brs.

**Banco Saudi Español (Saudesbank):** Paseo de la Castellana 40, 28046 Madrid; tel. (1) 4355540; telex 46753; fax (1) 2754387; f. 1979; cap. 3,500m., res 1,551m., dep 27,878m. (Dec. 1991); Pres. AHMED ABDULLATIF; 4 brs.

**Banco Urquijo:** Príncipe de Vergara 131, 28002 Madrid; tel. (1) 3964300; telex 27854; fax (1) 3964323; f. 1870; cap. 15,398m., res 42,272m., dep 590,377m. (Dec. 1992); Pres. CARLOS MARCH; Man. Dir ISIDRO FERNÁNDEZ BARREIRO; 171 brs.

**Banco de Valencia:** Calle del Pintor Sorolla 2–4, 46002 Valencia; tel. (6) 3521862; telex 64072; fax (6) 3621852; f. 1900; cap. 11,045m., dep. 259,002m. (1994); Pres. JOSÉ MARÍA SIMÓ NOGUÉS; CEO and Gen. Man. DOMINGO PARRA SORIA; 238 brs.

**Banco Zaragozano:** Coso 47–49, 50003 Zaragoza; tel. (76) 399399; telex 58810; fax (76) 296941; f. 1910; cap. 10,875m., res 29,633m., dep. 555,441m. (Dec. 1993); Pres. JOSÉ RAMÓN ALVAREZ RENDUELES; 353 brs.

**Bancoval:** Alfonso XI 6, 28014 Madrid; tel. (1) 5892552; telex 47673; fax (1) 5892028; f. 1989; cap. 1,500m., res 2,886m., dep. 31,888m. (Dec. 1992); Chair. VICENTE SANTANA APARICIO; CEO JOSÉ LUIS VELASCO; 1 br.

**Bankinter, SA:** Paseo de la Castellana 29, 28046 Madrid; tel. (1) 3199500; telex 27285; fax (1) 3193387; f. 1965; finances industrial and business dealings with medium-and long-term loans and investments; cap. 24,360m., res 75,059m., dep. 1,388,922m. (Dec. 1993); Pres. JAIME BOTÍN-SANZ DE SAUTUOLA Y GARCÍA DE LOS RÍOS; Dir-Gen. JUAN ARENA DE LA MORA; 236 brs.

**Bankoa:** Avda de la Libertad 5, 20004 San Sebastián; tel. (43) 410100; telex 36621; fax (43) 429414; f. 1975 as Banco Industrial de Guipuzcoa; cap. 2,912m., res 4,135m., dep. 46,748m. (Dec. 1993); Pres. JOSÉ ORTIGÜELA ALONSO; 21 brs.

**Instituto de Crédito Oficial (ICO):** Paseo del Prado 4, Madrid 14; tel. (1) 5219380; telex 42093; fax (1) 5311915; state credit bank; Pres. MIGUEL MUÑIZ; Dir-Gen. NIEVES RODRÍGUEZ.

### Foreign Banks

In 1992 there were 47 foreign banks operating in Spain.

### Banking Associations

**Consejo Superior Bancario** (Central Committee of Spanish Banking): José Abascal 57, 28003 Madrid; tel. (1) 4410611; telex 22937; fax (1) 4412720; f. 1946; supervisory body; Pres. PEDRO PÉREZ FERNÁNDEZ.

**Asociación Española de Banca Privada (AEB)** (Spanish Banking Association): Velázquez 64–66, 28001 Madrid; tel. (1) 5777015; fax (1) 5777022; Pres. JOSÉ LUIS LEAL MALDONADO; Sec. MANUEL TORRES ROJAS.

**Confederación Española de Cajas de Ahorros (CECA)** (Spanish Confederation of Savings Banks): Alcalá 27, 28014 Madrid; tel. (1) 5965000; telex 23413; fax (1) 5965742; f. 1928; Pres. BRAULIO MEDEL CÁMARA; Dir-Gen. JUAN RAMÓN QUINTÁS; SEOANE.

**Fondo de Garantía de Depósitos (FGD):** José Ortega y Gasset 22, Madrid; tel. (1) 4312902; f. 1977; deposit guarantee fund; financing by Banco de España to cease in 1997; Pres. JUAN ANTONIO RUIZ DE ALDA.

## STOCK EXCHANGES

The stock market was deregulated in 1989.

**Bolsa de Bilbao:** Calle José M. Olabarri 1, 48001 Bilbao; tel. (4) 4237400; telex 32709; fax (4) 4240719; f. 1890; Dir LUIS I. FERNÁNDEZ DE TROCÓNIZ URIARTE; Sec. RAMÓN BERGARECHE GARAY.

**Bolsa de Madrid:** Plaza de la Lealtad 1, 28014 Madrid; tel. (1) 5892600; fax (1) 5891417; f. 1831; 44 mems; Chair. MANUEL PIZARRO; Exec. Vice-Pres. ANTONIO ZOIDO.

**Bolsa de Barcelona:** Paseo de Gracia 19, 08007 Barcelona; tel. (3) 4013555; fax (3) 4013625; f. 1915; Pres. JOAN HORTALA I ARAU.

**Bolsa de Valencia:** San Vicente 23, 46002 Valencia; tel. (6) 3870100; telex 62880; fax (6) 3870133; f. 1980; Pres. JOAQUÍN MALDONADO CHIARRI; Gen. Man. FRANCISCO ALVAREZ MOLINA.

### Regulatory Authority

**Comisión Nacional del Mercado de Valores (CNMV):** Paseo de la Castellana 19, 28046 Madrid; tel. (1) 5851500; fax (1) 3193373; f. 1988; national securities and exchange commission; Pres. LUIS CARLOS CROISSIER.

## INSURANCE

In 1993 total premiums reached 2,260,000m. pesetas.

**Aegon Unión Aseguradora, SA:** Príncipe de Vergara 156, 28002 Madrid; tel. (1) 5636222; telex 45534; fax (1) 5639715; f. 1902; merged with Unión Levantina in 1986 and Unión Previsora in 1987; life, health and personal insurance and reinsurance; total premiums 32,133m. (1992); Chair. JESÚS QUINTANAL SAN EMETERIO.

**AGF Unión Fénix:** Paseo Castellana 33, 28046 Madrid; tel. (1) 5960000; telex 27759; fax (1) 5960600; f. 1994; total premiums 88,797m. (1994); Pres. PIERRE PIERART.

**Asistencia Sanitaria Interprovincial de Seguros, SA (ASISA):** Caracas 12, 28010 Madrid; tel. (1) 3190191; telex 44454; fax (1) 4103836; total premiums 49,340m. (1992); Pres. FRANCISCO CARREÑO CASTILLA.

**Aurora-Polar, SA de Seguros y Reaseguros:** Plaza de Federico Moyúa 4, 48009 Bilbao; tel. (4) 4206200; telex 34282; fax (4) 4206239; f. 1900; total premiums 38,638m. (1992); Pres. EDUARDO AGUIRRE ALONSO-ALLENDE.

SPAIN                                                                                                                    Directory

**Banco Vitalicio de España, Compañía Anónima de Seguros:** Paseo de Gracia 11, 08007 Barcelona; tel. (3) 4840100; telex 54447; fax (3) 4840226; f. 1880; total premiums 115,415m. (1992); Pres. Alfonso Escámez López; Man. Dir José Luis Pérez Torres.

**Bilbao, Cía Anónima de Seguros y Reaseguros:** Paseo del Puerto 20, 48990 Neguri-Getxo (Vizcaya); tel. (4) 4898100; telex 32224; fax (4) 4602061; f. 1918; cap. p.u. 4,659m. (1990); total premiums 20,006m. (1991); gen. insurance, represented throughout Spain; Pres. Patrick de la Sota MacMahon; Man. Dir José María Alvear; 8 brs.

**Caja de Seguros Reunidos, SA (Caser):** Plaza de la Lealtad 4, 28014 Madrid; tel. (1) 5323843; telex 45466; fax (1) 5327245; f. 1942; total premiums 13,959.0m. (Dec. 1990); represented throughout Spain; Pres. José Joaquín Sancho Dronda.

**Catalana Occidente, SA de Seguros y Reaseguros:** Avda Alcalde Barnils s/n, Zona San Juan, 08190 Sant Cugat del Vallés (Barcelona); tel. (3) 5820500; fax (3) 5820641; insurance and reinsurance; total premiums 57,214.6m. (Dec. 1993); Pres. Jesús Serra Santamans.

**Compañía Española de Seguros y Reaseguros de Crédito y Caución, SA:** Raimundo Fernández Villaverde 61, 28003 Madrid; tel. (1) 5536800; telex 43163; fax (1) 3353372; total premiums 20,342.3m. (Dec. 1990); Pres. Jesús Serra Santamans.

**La Estrella, SA:** Gran Vía 7, 28013 Madrid; tel. (1) 3301400; telex 45197; fax (1) 5225654; f. 1901; all classes of insurance and reinsurance; total premiums 56,500m. (1994); Pres. Miguel Geijo; Man. Dir Jaime Varela; 124 brs.

**Euroseguros, SA:** Cedaceros 9, 28014 Madrid; tel. (1) 4294737; total premiums 97,994m. (1992); Pres. Javier Pérez de Laborda.

**Mapfre (Mutualidad de Seguros):** Carretera de Pozuelo a Majadahonda, Km. 3800, 28820 Majadahonda (Madrid); tel. (1) 6262100; telex 23898; fax (1) 6262308; car insurance; total premiums 98,093m. (1992); Pres. José A. Rebuelta García.

**Mapfre Seguros Generales, SA:** Ctra Pozuelo a Majadahonda Km 3,800, 28220 Majadahonda; tel. (1) 5811396; fax (1) 5811220; total premiums 33,436m. (1992); Pres. Rafael Galarraga Solores.

**Mapfre Vida, SA:** Avda General Perón 40, 28020 Madrid; tel. (1) 5811400; telex 46468; life and health insurance; total premiums 55,976m. (1993); Pres. Juan Fernández Layos.

**Mare Nostrum, SA de Seguros y Reaseguros:** Vía Roma 3, 07012 Palma de Mallorca; tel. (71) 203113; telex 68747; fax (71) 722246; f. 1942; total premiums 14,670.5m. (Dec. 1990); Pres. Pierre Barberis; Dir-Gen. Pedro Bauer Calín.

**Multinacional Aseguradora, SA:** Doctor Ferrán 3 y 5, 08034 Barcelona; tel. (3) 2040012; fax (3) 2056056; total premiums 24,356.9m. (Dec. 1990).

**Musini:** Padilla 46, 28006 Madrid; tel. (1) 5750138; telex 48799; fax (1) 5769047; f. 1968; total premiums 47,094m. (1992); CEO Alvaro Muñoz López.

**Mutua General de Seguros:** Diagonal 543, 08029 Barcelona; tel. (3) 3222112; fax (3) 3220871; f. 1907; total premiums 23,015m. (Dec. 1994); Chair. V. Gaminde Cortejarena; Gen. Man. J. M. Sampietro Villacampa; brs throughout Spain.

**Mutua Madrileña Automovilista:** Almagro 9, 28010 Madrid; tel. (1) 4107766; f. 1930; total premiums 60,355m. (1992); Pres. Gabriel Gancedo.

**Ocaso, SA, Compañía de Seguros y Reaseguros:** Calle Princesa 23, 28008 Madrid; tel. (1) 5380100; telex 44181; fax (1) 5418509; f. 1920; total premiums 40,889m. (1994); 269 brs in Spain, 1 in London, 1 in Puerto Rico; Chair. HE the Marchioness of Taurisano Doña Isabel Castelo d'Ortega; Gen. Man. Rafael Estévez Bartolomé.

**Plus Ultra:** Plaza de las Cortes 8, 28014 Madrid; tel. (1) 5899292; telex 22079; fax (1) 4298921; total premiums 34,176m. (1992); Pres. Gerardo Aróstegui Gómez.

**Sanitas, SA de Seguros:** Serrano 88, 28006 Madrid; tel. (1) 5852400; fax (1) 5751264; health insurance; total premiums 36,857m. (Dec. 1994); Pres. Juan José López-Ibor.

**Santa Lucía, SA:** Plaza de España 15, 28008 Madrid; tel. (1) 5419387; fax (1) 5410133; f. 1922; total premiums 61,292m. (1994); Pres. Carlos J. Alvarez Navarro.

**Schweiz Seguros:** Vía Augusta 153–157, 08021 Barcelona; tel. (3) 2020404; telex 59049; fax (3) 4146295; total premiums 23,727.6m. (Dec. 1990); Pres. Paul E. Christen.

**UAP Ibérica:** Paseo de la Castellana 79, 28046 Madrid; tel. (1) 5557000; telex 41697; fax (1) 5971418; total premiums 19,979.1m. (Dec. 1990); Pres. Christian Huot.

**Vidacaixa, SA:** Avda Diagonal 477, 2°, 08036 Barcelona; tel. (3) 2278700; fax (3) 4108061; total premiums 65,972m. (Dec. 1993); Pres. Isidro Fainé Casas.

**Zurich:** Vía Augusta 192–200, 08021 Barcelona; tel. (3) 2099111; fax (3) 2014849; total premiums 18,592.5m. (Dec. 1990).

### Insurance Associations

**Dirección General de Seguros:** Paseo de la Castellana 44, 28046 Madrid; tel. (1) 3397110; fax (1) 3397113; supervisory body; Dir-Gen. Antonio Fernández Toraño.

**Comisión Liquidadora de Entidades Aseguradoras (CLEA):** Príncipe de Vergara 43, Madrid; tel. (1) 4312063; fax (1) 5772774; f. 1984; empowered to liquidate companies dissolved by the Public Administration; Pres. Francisco García Esteban.

**Unión Española de Entidades Aseguradoras y Reaseguradoras (UNESPA):** Núñez de Balboa 101, 28006 Madrid; tel. (1) 5624730; fax (1) 4117003; professional association; Pres. Alvaro Muñoz; Sec. Jesús Sáinz de los Terreros.

## Trade and Industry

### CHAMBERS OF COMMERCE

**Cámara de Comercio Internacional** (International Chamber of Commerce): Claudio Coello 19, 1°, 28001 Madrid; tel. (1) 2753400; telex 23227; Pres. Josep María Figueras Bassols; Sec.-Gen. Luis Solá i Viliardell.

**Consejo Superior de Cámaras Oficiales de Comercio, Industria y Navegación de España** (Supreme Council of Official Chambers of Commerce, Industry, and Navigation of Spain): Calle Claudio Coello 19, 1°, 28001 Madrid; tel. (1) 5753400; telex 23227; fax (1) 4352392; f. 1922; Pres. Guillermo de la Dehesa; Dir-Gen. Fernando Gómez Aviles-Casco; Sec.-Gen. Fernando Ferrero García; comprises 85 Chambers throughout Spain, incl. the following:

**Cámara de Comercio, Industria y Navegación de Bilbao:** Alameda Recalde 50, 48008 Bilbao; tel. (4) 4104664; telex 32783; fax (4) 4436171.

**Cámara Oficial de Comercio e Industria de Madrid:** Calle Huertas 13, 28012 Madrid; tel. (1) 5383500; telex 27307; fax (1) 5383677; f. 1887; Pres. Adrián Piera Jiménez; Sec. José Díez Clavero; 258,000 mems.

**Cámara Oficial de Comercio, Industria y Navegación de Sevilla:** Plaza de la Contratación 8, 41004 Sevilla; tel. (54) 211204; telex 72407; fax (54) 225619.

**Cámara Oficial de Comercio, Industria y Navegación de Valencia:** Poeta Querol 15, 46002 Valencia; tel. (6) 3511301; telex 62243; fax (6) 3516349; f. 1886; Pres. Enrique Silla Criado; Sec.-Gen. José María Gil Suay.

**Cambra Oficial de Comerç, Indústria i Navegació de Barcelona:** Avda Diagonal 452–454, 08006 Barcelona; tel. (3) 4169300; telex 54713; fax (3) 4169301; f. 1886; Pres. Antoni Negre; Dir Jordi Oliveras.

### EXPORT PROMOTION

**Consejo Asesor de Exportación (CAE):** Secretaría de Estado de Comercio, Dirección General de Comercio Exterior, Paseo de la Castellana 162, 28046 Madrid; tel. (1) 5836011; fax (1) 5631823; f. 1986; 16 mems; Pres. Secretary of State for Trade.

**Instituto Español de Comercio Exterior (ICEX):** Paseo de la Castellana 14, 28046 Madrid; tel. (1) 3496100; telex 44838; fax (1) 4316128; f. 1982; fmrly INFE; state institute for export promotion.

### TRADE ASSOCIATIONS

**Agrupación de Exportadores del Centro de España (AGRECE):** Plaza de la Independencia 1, 28001 Madrid; tel. (1) 5383500; telex 27307; fax (1) 5383718; exporters.

**Agrupación de Importadores y Exportadores de Productos Agrícolas:** Londres 96, 08036 Barcelona; tel. (3) 2093478; agricultural products.

**Asociación de Comercio de Cereales y Oleaginosas de España (ACCOE):** Doctor Fleming 56, 3°, 28036 Madrid; tel. (1) 3504305; fax (1) 3455009; cereal traders; Pres. Pelayo Moreno Sánchez; Sec. Ricardo García San José.

**Asociación de Criadores Exportadores de Sherry (ACES):** Eguiluz 2, 1°, 11402 Jerez de la Frontera; tel. (56) 341046; fax (56) 346081; sherry exporters; Pres. José Luis García Ruiz.

**Asociación Española de Comercio Exterior (AECE):** Madrid; tel. (1) 2624147; telex 44575; fax (1) 2624148; f. 1983; traders' organization; Pres. Andrés Manzano García; Sec. Miguel Angel Jorquera Fernández.

**Asociación Española de Comercio Exterior de Cereales y Productos Análogos (AECEC):** Pedro Muguruza 3, 28036 Madrid; tel. (1) 2503160; telex 44763; fax (1) 4570527; cereal exporters; Pres. Antonio Gómez Vega; Sec. Guillermo Lorenzo.

**Asociación Española de Exportadores de Electrónica e Informática (SECARTYS):** Gran Vía de las Cortes Catalanas 456-Pral, 08015 Barcelona; tel. (3) 4236485; telex 81166; fax (3) 4254377; electronics exporters; Pres. José Beltrán; Sec. Ignacio Tormo.

SPAIN                                                                                                                                                                                                                                                           *Directory*

**Asociación Española de la Industria y Comercio Exportador de Aceite de Oliva (ASOLIVA):** José Abascal 40, 2°, 28003 Madrid; tel. (1) 4468812; telex 22232; fax (1) 5931918; olive oil exporters; Pres. Francisco Sensat Alemany.

**Asociación de Exportadores de Pescado y Cefalópodos Congelados (AEPYCC):** Diego de León 44, 28006 Madrid; tel. (1) 4112407; telex 44220; fax (1) 5618178; fish exporters; Pres. Manuel Freire Veiga; Sec. Ignacio Montenegro González.

**Comité de Gestión de la Exportación de Frutos Cítricos:** Monjas de Santa Catalina 8, 4°, 46002 Valencia; tel. (6) 3521102; telex 64340; fax (6) 3510718; citrus fruit exporters; Pres. Julio de Miguel Martínez de Bujanda; Sec. Ricardo Llerena.

**Confederación Española de Comercio de Pequeña y Mediana Empresa (PYME):** Diego de León 50, 28006 Madrid; tel. (1) 4116161; telex 45754; fax (1) 5645269; traders of small and medium businesses; Pres. Felipe Luis Maestro; Sec.-Gen. Javier Millán-Astray.

**Federación Española de Asociaciones de Productores Exportadores de Frutas y Hortalizas (FEPEX):** Miguel Angel 13, 4a Pl., 28010 Madrid; tel. (1) 3191050; telex 43165; fax (1) 3103812; fruit and vegetable producers and exporters; Pres. Andrés Cuartero Ruiz; Sec. José Naranjo.

**Federación Española de Exportadores de Frutos Cítricos (FECIT):** Hernán Cortes 4, 46004 Valencia; tel. (6) 3521284; telex 62297; fax (6) 3513187; citrus fruit exporters; Pres. Antonio Pelufo; Sec. Luis Ribera Peris.

**HISPACEMENT, SA (Asociación de Exportadores de Cemento):** Josep Tarradellas 123, 4a, 08029 Barcelona; tel. (3) 3223204; telex 52269; fax (3) 3216802; f. 1977; cement and clinker exporters.

**Servicio Comercial de la Industria Textil Lanera (SCITL):** Rosellón 216, 08008 Barcelona; tel. (3) 2150170; telex 52897; fax (3) 2158463; wool industry; Pres. Pedro Guitart; Sec. Antonio Aizpún.

### EMPLOYERS' ORGANIZATIONS

**Confederación Española de Organizaciones Empresariales (CEOE)** (Spanish Confederation of Employers' Organizations): Diego de León 50, 28006 Madrid; tel. (1) 5639641; telex 43532; fax (1) 5628023; f. 1977; covers industry, agriculture, commerce and service sectors; comprises 165 orgs; Pres. José María Cuevas; Sec.-Gen. Juan Jiménez Aguilar.

**Círculo de Empresarios:** Serrano 1, 4a Planta, 28001 Madrid; tel. (1) 5781472; telex 42427; fax (1) 5774871; f. 1977; comprises CEOs of more than 150 major companies; Pres. Carlos Espinosa de los Monteros; Sec.-Gen. Vicente Boceta Alvarez.

**Club de Empresarios:** Paseo de la Castellana 123-9°A, 28046 Madrid; tel. (1) 4567011; comprises 95 presidents of public enterprises; Pres. Antonio López.

**Confederación de Empresarios de Andalucía (CEA):** Avda San Francisco Javier, 9 Edif. Sevilla 2, 9a–26, 41018 Sevilla; tel. (54) 650555; telex 72828; fax (54) 641242; f. 1979; Pres. Manuel Otero Luna; Sec.-Gen. Santiago Herrero León; Dir-Gen. Antonio Carrillo Alcalá.

**Confederación Empresarial de Barcelona (CEB):** Vía Layetana 32–34, 08003 Barcelona; tel. (3) 4841200; telex 97826; fax (3) 4841230.

**Confederación Empresarial de Madrid:** Diego de León 50, 1°, 28006 Madrid; tel. (1) 4115317; fax (1) 5627537; small, medium and large businesses; Pres. Fernando Fernández Tapias; Sec. Agustín Mascareñas.

**Confederación Empresarial Valenciana (CEV):** Músico Peydró 36, 46001 Valencia; tel. (6) 3521534; telex 62203; fax (6) 3525703; f. 1977; Pres. José María Jiménez de Laiglesia; Sec.-Gen. Luis Espinosa Fernández.

**Confederación Empresarial Vasca (CONFEBASK):** Henao 5, 3°, 48009 Bilbao; tel. (4) 4238800; fax (4) 4232311; f. 1983; Pres. Baltasar Errazti Navarro; Sec.-Gen. Javier Hernández Bilbao.

**Confederación Española de la Pequeña y Mediana Empresa (CEPYME):** Diego de León 50, 3a, 28006 Madrid; tel. (1) 4116161; telex 45754; fax (1) 5645269; small and medium businesses; Pres. Manuel Otero Luna; Sec.-Gen. Elías Aparicio Bravo.

**Fomento del Trabajo Nacional:** Vía Layetana 32, 08003 Barcelona; tel. (3) 4841200; fax (3) 4841230; f. 1771; development of national labour; Pres. Juan Rosell Lastortras; Sec.-Gen. Juan Pujol Segarra.

**Tribunal de Defensa de la Competencia:** Avda Pío XII 17–19, Madrid 16; tel. (1) 3505400; fax (1) 3505406; f. 1963; Pres. Miguel Angel Fernández Ordóñez; Sec. Antonio Fernández Fábrega.

### STATE HOLDING COMPANIES

**Instituto Nacional de Hidrocarburos (INH):** Paseo de la Castellana 89, 28046 Madrid; tel. (1) 4565300; telex 48162; groups oil, gas and petrochemical companies; Chair. Oscar Fanjul.

**Instituto Nacional de Industria (INI)** (National Industrial Institute): Plaza del Marqués de Salamanca 8, 28071 Madrid; tel. (1) 5757650; telex 22213; fax (1) 5755641; f. 1941; public corporation; has direct or indirect control of over 200 companies in following industrial sectors: electric power, steelmaking, mining, defence, shipbuilding, capital equipment, aluminium, electronics, automotive industry, fertilizers, air transport, sea transport, engineering and construction, paper, handicrafts, foreign trade, financial services and industrial promotion; investment policy includes the modernization of industry, supply of energy, research and exchange of technology, promotion of exports and the expansion of regional industrialization; Chair. Javier Salas Collantes; Dir-Gen. Raúl Herranz de Miguel; Sec.-Gen. José María Zarate.

**Teneo:** f. 1992 through grouping of 29 cos; further 18 cos to be incorporated.

### INDUSTRIAL ASSOCIATIONS

There are numerous industrial associations throughout Spain, including the following:

**Agrupación de Fabricantes de Cemento de España (OFICEMEN):** José Abascal 53, 28003 Madrid; tel. (1) 4411688; fax (1) 4423817; cement manufacturers; Pres. Jorge Villavecchia; Dir-Gen. Rafael Fernández.

**Asociación Agraria de Jovenes Agricultores (ASAJA):** Madrid; tel. (1) 4685950; telex 22381; fax (1) 4683434; farmers; Pres. Ignacio Barco Fernández; Dir-Gen. Pedro Menchero; Sec.-Gen. (vacant); 200,000 mems.

**Asociación Española de Extractores de Aceite de Orujo de Aceitunas (ANEO):** Paseo Reina Cristina 6, 28014 Madrid; tel. (1) 4376585; fax (1) 5515013; olive oil extractors; Pres. Alvaro Espuny Rodríguez; Sec. Juan José Vázquez Cansino.

**Asociación Española de Fabricantes de Automóviles y Camiones (ANFAC):** Fray Bernardino Sahagún 24, 28036 Madrid; tel. (1) 3596716; fax (1) 3594488; car and lorry manufacturers; Pres. Carlos Espinosa de los Monteros; Sec. Enrique Fernández Laguilhoat.

**Asociación Española de Fabricantes de Equipos y Componentes para Automoción (SERNAUTO):** Castelló 120, 28006 Madrid; tel. (1) 5621041; telex 23295; fax (1) 5618437; association of manufacturers of parts and equipment for automobile industry; Pres. Antonio Escudero; Sec. Miguel Angel Obregón.

**Asociación Española de Productoras de Fibras Químicas (PROFIBRA):** Alta de San Pedro 1, 08003 Barcelona; tel. (3) 2682644; fax (3) 2682630; chemical fibre producers; Pres. Rafael Español Navarro; Sec.-Gen. Guillermo Graell Deniel.

**Asociación Nacional Española de Fabricantes de Hormigón Preparado (ANEFHOP):** Bretón de los Herreros 43-bajo, 28003 Madrid; tel. (1) 4416834; fax (1) 4418341; concrete manufacturers; Pres. Félix Rodríguez Massa; Dir-Gen. Francisco Javier Martínez de Eulate.

**Asociación Industrial Textil de Proceso Algodonero (AITPA):** Gran Vía de les Corts Catalanes 670, 08010 Barcelona; tel. (3) 3189200; fax (3) 3026235; cotton textile industry; Pres. Juan María Pares; Sec. Salvador Maluquer.

**Asociación Nacional de Fabricantes de Pastas Papeleras, Papel y Cartón (ASPAPEL):** Alcalá 85, 4°, 28009 Madrid; tel. (1) 5763002; fax (1) 5774710; paper and cardboard manufacturers; Pres. José Luis Asenjo Martínez; Dir-Gen. Jesús Garrido Arilla; Sec.-Gen. Armando García-Mendoza Raso.

**Confederación Española de Asociaciones de Electrónica e Informática (CEDEI):** Príncipe de Vergara 74, 28006 Madrid; tel. (1) 4111661; telex 43908; f. 1984; electronic and information industries; Pres. J. M. Navarrete.

**Confederación Española de Asociaciones Pesqueras (CEAPE):** Lagasca 40, 1° Izqda, 28001 Madrid; tel. (1) 5777883; fishing associations; Pres. Julio Vieira; Sec. Antonio García Espinosa.

**Confederación Española de Organizaciones Empresariales del Metal (CONFEMETAL):** Príncipe de Vergara 74, 5°, 28006 Madrid; tel. (1) 5625590; fax (1) 5628477; metal organizations; Pres. Carlos Pérez de Bricio Olariaga; Sec.-Gen. Andrés Sánchez de Apellaniz.

**Confederación Nacional de la Construcción (CNC):** Diego de León 50, 2°, 28006 Madrid; tel. (1) 2619715; fax (1) 2615269; construction industry; Pres. José Luis Alonso; Sec. José Luis Pastor Rodríguez-Ponga.

**Confederación Nacional de Empresarios de la Minería y de la Metalurgia (CONFEDEM):** Núñez de Balboa 37, 28001 Madrid; tel. (1) 4319402; mining and metallurgy; Pres. Ubaldo Usunáriz Balanzategui; Sec. Andrés Villalobos Beltrán.

**Consejo Intertextil Español (CIE):** Alta de San Pedro 1, Pral bis, 08003 Barcelona; tel. (3) 2682644; fax (3) 2682630; textile industry; Pres. Jaume Valls Roig; Sec. Guillermo Graell.

SPAIN
*Directory*

**CONSTRUNAVES—CNE, SA:** Orense 11, 1°, 28020 Madrid; tel. (1) 5560458; fax (1) 5555216; f. 1959; private shipbuilders' asscn; Man. Dir ENRIQUE SILVELA.

**Federación Empresarial de la Industria Química Española (FEIQUE):** Hermosilla 31, 1°, 28001 Madrid; tel. (1) 4317964; fax (1) 5763381; chemical industry; Dir-Gen. JOSÉ CAPMANY.

**Federación Española de Industrias de la Alimentación y Bebidas (FIAB):** Diego de León 44, 1° Izqda, 28006 Madrid; tel. (1) 4117211; telex 41659; fax (1) 4117344; f. 1977; food and drink industries; Pres. ARTURO GIL PÉREZ ANDUJAR; Sec. JORGE JORDANA BUTTICAZ DE POZAS.

**Federación de Industriales del Calzado Español (FICE):** Núñez de Balboa 116, 3°, Ofs 5 y 6, 28006 Madrid; tel. (1) 5627001; fax (1) 5620094; footwear; Pres. RAFAEL CALVO RODRÍGUEZ.

**Federación Nacional de la Industria Textil Lanera Española:** San Quirico 30, 08201 Sabadell; tel. (3) 7259311; fax (3) 7261526; wool industry; Pres. FRANCISCO LLONCH SOLER; Sec. BENET ARMENGOL OBRADORS.

**Unión de Empresas Siderúrgicas (UNESID):** Castelló 128, 3°, Apdo 13098, 28006 Madrid; tel. (1) 5624010; telex 22228; fax (1) 5626584; iron and steel makers; Pres. JUAN LUIS BURGOS MARÍN; Sec. RAFAEL CERECEDA.

### DEVELOPMENT ORGANIZATIONS

**Instituto Madrileño de Desarrollo (IMADE):** García de Paredes 92, 28010 Madrid; tel. (1) 4102063; telex 44594; fax (1) 3194290; f. 1984; public development institution for Madrid region; Dir-Gen. JOSÉ CARLOS LÓPEZ.

**Instituto Andaluz de la Reforma Agraria (IARA):** Avda San Fco Javier s/n, Edif. Sevilla 1, 1°, 41005 Sevilla; tel. (5) 463900; empowered to expropriate land under the agricultural reform programme; Pres. FRANCISCO VÁZQUEZ.

**Instituto de Fomento de Andalucía (IFA):** Avda San Francisco Javier 15, Edif. Capitolio, Planta 3a, 41005 Sevilla; tel. (5) 4661711; telex 72576; fax (5) 4660360; f. 1987; incorporates Instituto para la Promoción Industrial en Andalucía (IPIA); Pres. JOSÉ MANUEL ROMERO ALVAREZ; brs in Andalucía, Madrid, Brussels and Tokyo.

**Sociedad para el Desarrollo Industrial de Andalucía (SODIAN):** República Argentina 29 accessorio, Sevilla 11; tel. (5) 4278705.

**Sociedad para el Desarrollo Industrial de Canarias (SODICAN):** Villalva Hervás 4, 6°, 38002 Santa Cruz de Tenerife; tel. (22) 245677; telex 92054; fax (22) 245683; Pres. DANIEL VIERA LEÓN.

**Sociedad para el Desarrollo Industrial de Extremadura (SODIEX):** Doctor Marañon 2, Cáceres; tel. (27) 227700; telex 28950; fax (27) 243304; f. 1977.

**Sociedad para el Desarrollo Industrial de Galicia, SA (SODIGA):** Orense 6, La Rosaleda, 15701 Santiago de Compostela; tel. (81) 566100; telex 88454; fax (81) 566183.

### TRADE UNIONS

The following represent some of the more important trade unions:

**Confederación General del Trabajo (CGT)** (National Confederation of Labour): Magdalena 29, 2°, Tirso de Molina 5, 28012 Madrid; f. 1979 following split in CNT; reformist section; name changed 1989; anarchist; Sec.-Gen. EMILIO LINDOSA; 50,000 mems.

**Confederación Nacional del Trabajo (CNT):** San Martín 5, 46003 Valencia; tel. (6) 3518936; fax (6) 3942372; f. 1910; anarchist; Sec.-Gen. VICENTE VILLANOVA GARDÓ.

**Confederación Sindical de Comisiones Obreras (CCOO)** (Workers' Commissions): Fernández de la Hoz 12, 28010 Madrid; tel. (1) 3191750; telex 45226; fax (1) 3104804; f. 1956; independent left-wing; Pres. MARCELINO CAMACHO ABAD; Sec.-Gen. ANTONIO GUTIÉRREZ VEGARA; 930,000 mems (1992).

**Eusko Langilleen Alkartasuna/Solidaridad de Trabajadores Vascos (ELA/STV)** (Basque Workers' Solidarity): Barrainkua 15, 48009 Bilbao; tel. (4) 4243300; fax (4) 4243654; f. 1911; independent; Pres. JOSÉ MIGUEL LEUNDA ETXEBERRIA; Sec.-Gen. JOSÉ ELORRIETA AURREKOETXEA; 110,000 mems.

**Unión General de Trabajadores (UGT)** (General Union of Workers): Hortaleza 88, 28004 Madrid; tel. (1) 5897601; telex 45594; fax (1) 5897603; f. 1888; 15 affiliated federations; Sec.-Gen. CÁNDIDO MÉNDEZ; 720,691 mems (1992).

**Unión Sindical Obrera (USO)** (Workers' Trade Union): Príncipe de Vergara 13, 7°, 28001 Madrid; tel. (1) 5774113; fax (1) 5772959; f. 1960; independent; Sec.-Gen. MANUEL ZAGUIRRE CANO; 60,000 mems.

# Transport

### RAILWAYS

**Red Nacional de los Ferrocarriles Españoles (RENFE)** (National System of Spanish Railways): Avda Pío XII s/n, 28036 Madrid; tel. (1) 3232121; fax (1) 3150384; 12,570 km of wide-gauge track, of which 6,426 km were electrified (1992); in 1987 a 13-year modernization plan, envisaging a total investment of 2,090m. pesetas, was begun; the Madrid–Córdoba–Sevilla high-speed line opened in 1992, forming the first stage of a high-speed network that was to extend northwards via Barcelona to Irún on the border with France (and eventually to Paris) and southwards to Cádiz, Málaga and Huelva; Pres. MERCÈ SALA.

**Eusko Trenbideak—Ferrocarriles Vascos (ET/FV), SA:** Atxuri 6, 48006 Bilbao; tel. (4) 4339500; fax (4) 4336009; controlled by the Basque Government; 202 km of 1,000 mm gauge; passengers carried 43.6m. (1994); Man. Dir CARLOS GARCÍA CAÑIBANO.

**Ferrocarriles de Vía Estrecha (FEVE)** (Narrow Gauge Railways): General Rodrigo 6, Parque de las Naciones, 28003 Madrid; tel. (1) 5337000; telex 48690; fax (1) 5546319; f. 1965 by integration of private companies; operates mainly in suburban areas of northern cities; 1,202 km (1992) of narrow-gauge track (of which 124 km were electrified); passengers carried (1992): 11.7m.; goods loaded (1992): 4.1m. metric tons net; Pres. JOSÉ MARÍA GURRUCHAGA.

**Ferrocarrils de la Generalitat de Catalunya:** Avda Pau Casals 24, 8°, 08021 Barcelona; tel. (3) 2011114; fax (3) 2014683; 184 km, of which 107 km are electrified; Pres. ENRIC ROIG; Dir MIQUEL LLEVAT.

**Ferrocarrils de la Generalitat de Valencia:** Cronista Rivelles 1, 46009 Valencia; tel. (6) 3473750; telex 64936; fax (6) 3476789; f. 1986; 93-km line from Alicante to Denia; Pres. EUGENIO BURRIEL DE ORUETA.

A further 217 km are under private control.

There are underground railway systems in Madrid and Barcelona. The first section of the Valencia underground railway opened in October 1988, and systems are planned for Bilbao (first section due to open in late 1995) and Sevilla.

### ROADS

Total road network at December 1992 was 337,139 km, including 2,850 km of motorway and 21,512 km of main roads.

**Empresa Nacional de Transportes de Viajeros por Carretera (ENATCAR):** Alcalá 478, 28027 Madrid; tel. (1) 7542054; fax (1) 3271445; f. 1985; road transport organization; Pres. JOSÉ JULIÁN ELGORRIAGA GOYENECHE.

### SHIPPING

Spain has many ports. Among the most important are Barcelona, Bilbao, Santa Cruz de Tenerife, Gijón, Las Palmas, Sevilla and Valencia. The 2,190 ships of the merchant fleet totalled 3,224,604 grt in 1992.

**Asociación de Navieros Españoles (ANAVE):** Santa María Magdalena 30 C, 28016 Madrid; tel. (1) 3459001; telex 43137; fax (1) 3459209; shipowners' asscn; Pres. CARLOS BARREDA ALDÁMIZ-ECHEVARRÍA; Dir FERNANDO CASAS BLANCO.

**Empresa Nacional Elcano de la Marina Mercante:** General Martínez Campos 46, 28010 Madrid; tel. (1) 4195222; telex 27708; fax (1) 4107105; controlled by INI (state holding company); Pres. RAMÓN GARCÍA LÓPEZ DORIGA.

#### Principal Shipping Companies

**Compañía Española de Petróleos, SA (CEPSA):** Avda de América 32, 28028 Madrid; tel. (1) 3376000; telex 22938; fax (1) 7254116; f. 1929; Chair. LUIS MAGAÑA; petroleum and natural gas exploration; refining of petroleum and petro-chemicals; marketing.

**Compañía Logística de Hidrocarburos (CLH), SA:** Capitán Haya 41, Apdo 318, 28020 Madrid; tel. (1) 5825100; telex 23387; fax (1) 5562023; f. 1927; fmrly CAMPSA; petroleum distribution; Pres. JUAN SANCHO ROF.

**Compañía Remolcadores Ibaizabal, SA:** Muelle de Tomás Olabarri 4, 5°, 48930 Las Arenas-Getxo; tel. (4) 4645133; fax (4) 4645565; f. 1906; ocean-going, coastal, harbour, salvage, fire-fighting; Pres. EDUARDO AZNAR SAINZ; Dir JOSÉ MARÍA ANSOTEGUI.

**Compañía Trasatlántica Española, SA:** General Martínez Campos 46, 28010 Madrid; tel. (1) 3355100; telex 27667; fax (1) 3351800; f. 1850; cargo services; operates six lines; USA, Venezuela, Colombia, Mexico, Central America, Puerto Rico, Caribbean islands, Spain, Italy, Portugal, France; Pres. RAMÓN E. GARCÍA LÓPEZ-DORIGA.

**Compañía Trasmediterránea, SA:** Obenque 4, Edif. Transmediterránea, 28042 Madrid; tel. (1) 229100; telex 27666; fax (1)

229110; f. 1917; Spanish ports, Balearic and Canary Is and Spanish North African ports; Pres. TARRAFETA PUYAL.

**Ership:** Don Ramón de la Cruz 13, 28001 Madrid; tel. (1) 4355620; fmrly TAC; Pres. GUILLERMO ZATARAÍN GUTIÉRREZ DE LA CONCHA.

**Ibarra y Cía, SA:** Menéndez Pelayo 4, Apdo 15, 41004 Sevilla; tel. (5) 4421658; telex 72153; fax (5) 4410112; f. 1881; cargo vessels to South America from Italy, France, Spain and Portugal; Pres. LUIS DE YBARRA YBARRA.

**Marítima del Norte, SA:** Miño 4, 28002 Madrid; tel. (1) 5634644; telex 27718; fax (1) 5618962; f. 1958; refrigerated cargo vessels, liquefied gas tankers, off-shore supply vessels; Pres. JESÚS A. DE SENDAGORTA.

**Naviera García Minaur, SA:** Barroeta Aldamar 2–4°, 48001 Bilbao; tel. (4) 4236100; telex 32152; fax (4) 4241275; operates on seven lines between Northern Europe, the UK, South and Central America, the Mediterranean and West Africa; Pres. ALEJANDRO BARRAZA.

**Naviera Pinillos, SA:** Capitán Haya 21, 28020 Madrid; tel. (1) 5556711; telex 27665; fax (1) 5569777; f. 1940; services between Canary Is and other Spanish ports; Pres. ALBERTO HERRERA HERNÁNDEZ; Dir FERNANDO SALVADOR.

**Naviera Química, SA:** Las Mercedes 31, 3° Izqda, 48930 Arenas-Getxo; tel. (4) 4641099; telex 31056; fax (4) 4649481; f. 1967; transport of liquid chemicals, foodstuffs and oils in bulk; Man. Dir JUAN MARÍN SÁNCHEZ.

**Repsol Naviera Vizcaina, SA:** Juan de Aguriaguerra 35, 2°, 48009 Bilbao; tel. (4) 4251100; telex 32754; fax (4) 4251143; f. 1956; world-wide, but particularly Mediterranean, Near East and Persian Gulf to Spain and transatlantic trade; Chair. JUAN SANCHO ROF; Man. Dir JAVIER GONZÁLEZ JULIÁ.

### CIVIL AVIATION

More than 20 airports are equipped to receive international flights.

**IBERIA, Líneas Aéreas de España, SA** (Airlines of Spain): Velázquez 130, 28006 Madrid; tel. (1) 5878787; telex 27775; fax (1) 5857682; f. 1927; domestic and international passenger and freight services to Africa, Europe, North, Central and South America, the Middle East and Japan; Pres. JUAN SÁEZ.

**Air Europa/Air España:** Gran Vía Asima 23, Polígono Son Castello, 07009 Palma de Mallorca; tel. (71) 757737; telex 69158; fax (1) 758652; f. 1986; charter and scheduled services to Canary and Balearic Islands, North Africa, Western and Northern Europe; also Thailand, Egypt, Mexico, USA and Dominican Republic; Pres. JUAN JOSÉ HIDALGO ACERA.

**Aviación y Comercio, SA (AVIACO):** Maudes 51, 28003 Madrid; tel. (1) 5543600; telex 27641; fax (1) 5334613; f. 1948; subsidiary of IBERIA; scheduled domestic flights and services to London and Paris; Pres. JUAN SÁEZ; Dir-Gen. CARLOS RODRÍGUEZ FERNÁNDEZ.

**Bínter Canarias, SA:** Avda Alcalde Ramirez Bethencourt 8, POB 1277, 35080 Las Palmas; tel. (28) 380366; telex 95026; fax (28) 361347; f. 1988; subsidiary of IBERIA; scheduled services within Canary Islands and to Madeira; Pres. JAVIER ALVAREZ.

**Bínter Mediterránea:** Bloco Técnico Aeropuerto, 46940 Manises; tel. (22) 264346; fax (22) 264822; f. 1989; subsidiary of IBERIA; services to Balearic Islands, France, Italy, Middle East and North Africa; Pres. JAVIER ALVAREZ.

**LTE International Airways, SA:** Carrer del Ter 27, 07009 Palma de Mallorca; tel. (71) 419400; telex 68660; fax (71) 248886; f. 1987; charter flights between Spanish islands and Europe; Pres. HANS-JOACHIM DRIESSEN; Man. Dir MATEO JULIA.

**Oasis International Airlines:** Gobelas 17, La Florida, 28023 Madrid; tel. (1) 3728851; telex 27052; fax (1) 3728010; f. 1986; fmrly Andalus Air; charter services to Europe, Canary Islands and Caribbean; Pres. ANTONIO MATA.

**Spanair:** Aeropuerto de Palma, Apdo 50.086, Palma de Mallorca; tel. (71) 492012; telex 69994; fax (71) 492553; f. 1988; passenger scheduled services to Canary and Balearic Islands, charter services within Europe and to USA, Mexico and Dominican Republic; Pres. GONZALO PASCUAL; Man. Dir CARLOS BRAVO.

**Viva Air:** Camino de la Escollera 4, 07012 Palma de Mallorca; tel. (71) 219100; telex 69996; fax (71) 219133; f. 1988; 98% owned by Iberia; scheduled passenger services within Europe and to Africa and the Middle East; Dir-Gen. JOSÉ MARÍA DE CALIS BORES.

## Tourism

Spain's tourist attractions include its climate, beaches and historic cities. Since 1985 the Government has aimed at attracting more visitors to the interior and to the north-west of Spain. Hotel bedrooms totalled 1,132,350 in December 1994. Tourism makes an important contribution to the country's economy. In 1994 Spain received more than 61.4m. foreign visitors (compared with 14.3m. in 1965), and receipts from tourism totalled an estimated 2,867,800m. pesetas.

**Secretaría General de Turismo:** María de Molina 50, 28006 Madrid; tel. (1) 4114014; telex 23100; fax (1) 4114232; Sec.-Gen. MIGUEL GÓNGORA BENÍTEZ DE LUGO.

**Turespaña:** Castelló 117, 28006 Madrid; tel. (1) 4114229; telex 23100; fax (1) 5638638; fmrly Inprotur; autonomous organization; Dir-Gen. PALOMA NOTARIO BODELÓN.

# SPANISH EXTERNAL TERRITORIES

## SPANISH NORTH AFRICA

### Introductory Survey

**Location, Climate, Language, Religion**

Spanish North Africa comprises mainly two enclaves within Moroccan territory: Ceuta, on the north African coast opposite Gibraltar, the Strait here being about 25 km wide; and Melilla, situated on a small peninsula jutting into the Mediterranean Sea. Attached to Melilla, for administrative purposes, are Peñón de Vélez de la Gomera, a small fort on the Mediterranean coast, and two groups of islands, Peñón de Alhucemas and the Chafarinas. The average temperature is 17°C. Spanish and Arabic are spoken. Most Europeans are Roman Catholic, most North Africans being Muslim. There is a small Jewish community.

**Recent History**

The population of the enclaves is mostly Spanish. The proportion of Arab residents, however, particularly in Melilla, has greatly increased, owing to the large numbers of illegal immigrants from Morocco. Those born in the territories are Spanish citizens and subjects. An ancient port and walled city, Ceuta was retained by Spain upon Moroccan independence from France in 1956. Having developed as a military and administrative centre for the former Spanish Protectorate in Morocco, Ceuta now functions as a bunkering and fishing port. In 1974 the town became the seat of the Capitanía General de Africa. Two-thirds of Ceuta's land area are used exclusively for military purposes.

Melilla was the first Spanish town to rise against the Government of the Popular Front in July 1936, at the beginning of the Spanish Civil War. Like Ceuta, Melilla was retained by Spain when Morocco became independent in 1956. In addition to its function as a port, Melilla now serves as a military base, more than one-half of the enclave's land area being used solely for military purposes.

In October 1978 King Hassan of Morocco attempted to link the question of the sovereignty of Melilla to that of the return of the British dependent territory of Gibraltar to Spain. In November King Hassan stated his country's claim to Ceuta and Melilla. In October 1981 Spain declared before the UN that Ceuta and Melilla were integral parts of Spanish territory. In April 1982 the Istiqlal, a Moroccan political party, demanded action to recover the territories from Spain, and in March 1983 the Moroccan Government blocked the passage of goods across the frontiers of Ceuta and Melilla. In August the movement of Moroccan workers to Ceuta, Melilla and also Gibraltar was restricted. Following the opening of the Spanish frontier with Gibraltar, in early 1985, Morocco reiterated its claim to Ceuta and Melilla. King Hassan indicated, however, that he desired a political solution to the problem. Spain rejects any comparison between the two enclaves and Gibraltar.

From 1984 there was increasing unease over Spanish North Africa's future. The riots in Morocco in January 1984 and the signing of the treaty of union between Libya and Morocco in August gave rise to disquiet. In July 1985 the joint Libyan-Moroccan assembly passed a resolution calling for the 'liberation' of Ceuta and Melilla. In July 1985 the leaders of the nationalist parties of both Ceuta and Melilla visited Gibraltar for talks with the Chief Minister, in an effort to secure support for their cause. Details of the enclaves' new draft statutes, envisaging the establishment of two local assemblies, with jurisdiction over such matters as public works, agriculture, tourism, culture and internal trade, were announced in August and approved by the central Government in December 1985. Unlike Spain's other regional assemblies, however, those of Ceuta and Melilla were not to be vested with legislative powers, and this denial of full autonomy was much criticized in the two enclaves. In March 1986 up to 20,000 people took to the streets of Ceuta in a demonstration to demand autonomy.

Meanwhile, the introduction by Madrid of a new aliens law in July 1985 required all foreigners resident in Spain to register with the authorities or risk expulsion. In Ceuta most Muslims possessed the necessary documentation. However, in Melilla (where the Muslim community was estimated to number 27,000, of whom only 7,000 held Spanish nationality) thousands of Muslims staged a protest against the new legislation in November 1985, as a result of which the central Government gave an assurance that it would assist the full integration into Spanish society of Muslims in Ceuta and Melilla, and promised to improve conditions in the territories. In December an inter-ministerial commission, headed by the Minister of the Interior, was created to formulate plans for investment in the enclaves' transport, health services and other public facilities.

Tension in Melilla was renewed in December 1985, when 40,000 members of the Spanish community attended a demonstration in support of the new aliens law. In January 1986 the brutality with which the police broke up a peaceful rally by Muslim women provoked outrage in all quarters. In addition to the hunger strike already being undertaken by a number of Muslims, a two-day general strike was called. In February 1986, however, the Ministry of the Interior in Madrid and the leaders of the Muslim communities of Ceuta and Melilla reached agreement on the application of the aliens law. A joint commission to study the Muslims' grievances was to be established, and a census to determine those eligible for Spanish citizenship was to be carried out. The agreement was denounced as unconstitutional by the Spanish populations of the enclaves. In March the central Government announced that it was to grant 8,500m. pesetas to Melilla and 6,500m. to Ceuta for the purposes of infrastructural development. The Minister of the Interior visited the territories in April and reiterated that the implementation of the aliens law (the deadline for registration having been extended to 31 March 1986, following three postponements) would not entail mass expulsions of Muslim immigrants.

After negotiations with representatives of the Muslim community, in May the Government agreed to grant Spanish nationality to more than 2,400 Muslims resident in the enclaves. By mid-1986, however, the number of Muslims applying for Spanish nationality in Melilla alone had reached several thousand. As a result of the delays in the processing of the applications by the authorities, Aomar Muhammadi Dudú, the leader of the newly founded Muslim party, Partido de los Demócratas de Melilla (PDM), accused the Government of failing to fulfil its pledge to the Muslim residents.

At the general elections of June 1986 the ruling Partido Socialista Obrero Español (PSOE) was successful in Ceuta, but was defeated by the centre-right Coalición Popular (CP) in Melilla, the latter result indicating the strong opposition of local Spaniards to the Government's plan to integrate the Muslim population. Tight security surrounded the elections in Melilla, where 'parallel elections', resulting in a vote of confidence in the PDM leader, were held by the Muslim community. The elections were accompanied by several days of unrest, involving right-wing Christians and local Muslims, and there were further violent clashes between the police and Christian demonstrators demanding the resignation of the Government Delegate in Melilla, Andrés Moreno.

In August 1986 work began on the census of Muslim residents in Ceuta and Melilla. In the same month Juan Díez de la Cortina, Secretary-General of the extreme right-wing Partido Nacionalista (Español) de Melilla, was arrested on suspicion of planning a terrorist attack against the Government Delegate in Melilla. Following talks in Madrid between representatives of the main political parties in Melilla and the Ministry of the Interior, concessions to the enclave included the replacement of Andrés Moreno as Government Delegate by Manuel Céspedes. The Madrid negotiations were denounced by Aomar Muhammadi Dudú, the Muslim leader of Melilla, who nevertheless in September agreed to accept a senior post in the Ministry of the Interior in Madrid, with responsibility for relations with the Muslim communities of Spain.

In October 1986 it was reported that Dudú had travelled to Rabat for secret discussions with the Moroccan Minister of the Interior. In November Muslim leaders in Melilla announced that they wished to establish their own administration in the enclave, in view of the Madrid Government's failure to fulfil its promise of Spanish citizenship for Muslim residents. The Spanish Minister of the Interior, however, reiterated an assurance of the Government's intention to carry out the process of integration of the Muslim community. Later in the month, Muslim traders staged a four-day closure of their businesses to draw attention to their plight, and thousands of Muslims took part in a peaceful demonstration, reaffirming support for Dudú, who had resigned from his Madrid post after only two months in office. (Dudú subsequently went into exile in Morocco and lost the support of Melilla's Muslim community.) A similar protest, to have taken place in Ceuta in December, was banned by the Spanish authorities.

In January 1987 the Spanish Minister of the Interior paid an official visit to Morocco. King Hassan proposed the establishment of a joint commission to seek a solution to the problem of the Spanish enclaves, but the proposal was rejected by Spain. There was a serious escalation of tension in Melilla in early February, when a member of the Muslim community died from gunshot wounds, following renewed racial clashes. Police reinforcements were flown in from Spain to deal with the crisis. Numerous demonstrators were detained. Several prominent Muslims were charged with sedition and transferred to a prison in Almería, on the Spanish mainland, but were released shortly afterwards. The indictment of a total of 27 Muslims was completed in mid-1988. In March 1987 King Hassan of Morocco reaffirmed his support for the Muslims of the Spanish enclaves, and later warned that a serious crisis in relations between Rabat and Madrid would arise if Spain were to grant autonomy to the territories. King Hassan renewed his proposal for dialogue, ruling out the possibility of a 'green march' similar to the campaign organized in 1975, when 300,000 unarmed Moroccan volunteers had attempted to occupy the Spanish Sahara, which Spain had subsequently agreed to relinquish.

In April 1987 Spanish and Moroccan troops participated in joint manoeuvres on Moroccan territory adjacent to Melilla, as part of a programme of military co-operation. In early May thousands of Melilla residents attended a demonstration in favour of autonomy for the enclave. During a visit to Melilla a senior official of the ruling PSOE emphasized the need for the integration of Christians and Muslims, while asserting that Spanish sovereignty would continue and would form the basis of the territory's future autonomy statute. In July, following a visit to Rabat by the Spanish Minister of Foreign Affairs, King Hassan declared that agreement had been reached on the holding of talks on the question of Ceuta and Melilla. The Spanish Government, however, denied the existence of such an agreement, maintaining that the issue was not negotiable.

At the end of July 1987 Spain was obliged to order its fishing fleet to withdraw from Moroccan waters, upon the expiry of an agreement signed with Morocco in 1983 (prior to Spain's accession to the EC, now European Union—EU), allowing Spain access to the rich fishing grounds off the Moroccan coast in exchange for financial aid of US $550m. Having previously appeared unwilling to extend the treaty, in an attempt to link the issue of fishing rights to that of Spanish North Africa, Morocco unexpectedly agreed to a provisional renewal of the accord, whereby Spanish vessels would be permitted to continue operating in Moroccan waters until December 1987, pending the negotiation of a new agreement between Morocco and the EC. At the end of 1987, when the temporary accord expired, Spanish fishing vessels were once again expelled from Moroccan waters and were unable to resume operations until March 1988, upon the entry into force of a new four-year agreement between the EC and Morocco. (This agreement was renewed for a further four years in May 1992. In September 1994, however, Morocco demanded that the accord be renegotiated and that fishing quotas be drastically reduced—see below.)

In Ceuta, meanwhile, there was renewed unrest in August 1987, following the indiscriminate shooting dead of a Muslim by a member of the security forces. On a visit to that territory in September, the Spanish Minister of Justice emphasized the difficulty of elevating the status of the enclaves to that of an autonomous region. In February 1988 it was announced that, in accordance with EC regulations, Moroccan citizens would in due course require visas to enter Spain. Entry to Spanish North Africa, however, was to be exempt from the new ruling.

In March 1988 a group of seven Muslims began an indefinite occupation of the Melilla office responsible for the processing of applications for Spanish nationality, to protest against its alleged inefficiency. Of the 8,000 applications presented, it was claimed, fewer than one-half had been granted. After several months of negotiations, in March the central Government and main opposition parties in Madrid reached a broad consensus on the draft autonomy statutes for the Spanish External Territories.

Spain's relations with Morocco improved in June 1988, when the two countries signed an agreement on bilateral economic co-operation, whereby Spain was to grant credits totalling 125,000m. pesetas to Morocco. In the same month the Melilla representative to the Madrid Senate requested that the Government clarify all aspects of Spanish North Africa's security position, in view of the territories' exclusion from the NATO 'umbrella'.

In July 1988 a senior member of the ruling PSOE acknowledged that the party's Programme 2000 contained contradictory proposals regarding Ceuta and Melilla. Although it was envisaged that Spain would retain the territories, the possibility of a negotiated settlement with Morocco was not discounted. In late July, seven years after the enclaves' first official request for autonomy, the central Government announced that the implementation of the territories' autonomy statutes was to be accelerated. Revised draft statutes were submitted by the PSOE to the main opposition parties for consideration. The statutes declared Ceuta and Melilla to be integral parts of Spain and, for the first time, the Spanish Government undertook to guarantee financial support for the territories. A further innovation contained in the revised draft provided for the establishment of mixed commissions to oversee the movement of goods and services through the territories. As previously indicated by the Spanish Government, the two Spanish North African assemblies were to be granted 'normative' rather than legislative powers. Each new assembly would elect from among its members a city president.

It was subsequently revealed that the revised statutes encompassed only the enclaves of Ceuta and Melilla, thus excluding the associated Spanish North African islands (the Chafarinas Islands, the Peñón de Alhucemas, the Peñón de Vélez de la Gomera and the island of Perejil, Spanish sovereignty over the latter being uncertain), and that they had been erroneously incorporated in the preliminary statutes, approved by the Government in December 1985. Although remaining the responsibility of the Spanish Ministry of Defence, these islands were not, therefore, to become part of any Spanish autonomous region.

In August 1988 a Moroccan Minister of State asserted that Spain should negotiate a peaceful, political solution to the question of Ceuta and Melilla. In October the Moroccan Minister of Foreign Affairs formally presented his country's claim to Ceuta and Melilla to the UN General Assembly. An official visit by King Hassan to Spain, scheduled for November, was indefinitely postponed without explanation, and in Melilla a Muslim group acknowledged that it had been in receipt of financial assistance from the Moroccan Government. By December 1988 a total of 5,257 Muslims in Melilla had been granted Spanish citizenship since 1986, and a further 1,126 applications were pending. (By 1990 nearly all residents were in possession of an identity card.) On a visit to Ceuta in December 1988 a Spanish government official stated that the enclaves would be granted autonomy during the present Government's term of office.

In January 1989, however, King Hassan reiterated Morocco's claim to Ceuta and Melilla. A planned visit to Rabat by the Spanish Minister of Foreign Affairs was postponed, but in March the Spanish Minister of Defence, travelled to Morocco for consultations with King Hassan on security matters. In April the Spanish Government and the Partido Popular (PP), the main opposition party, reached agreement on the revised statutes for Ceuta and Melilla. In May the Spanish Prime Minister and King Hassan met in Casablanca for discussions on the situation in the Middle East. In September King Hassan paid an official visit to Spain. The question of Spanish North Africa was not discussed, although the King of Morocco reiterated his country's claim to the territories, while discounting the use of force as a means of settling the dispute. Spain and Morocco agreed to hold annual summit meetings, in order to improve relations.

At the general election held in October 1989 the ruling PSOE retained its Ceuta seats, despite allegations by the opposition PP that many names on the electoral register were duplicated. In Melilla, however, the election results were declared invalid, following the discovery of serious irregularities. Melilla's one seat in the Congress of Deputies and one of its two seats in the Senate in Madrid had originally been allocated to the PSOE, the PP winning the second seat in the Senate. At the repeated ballot held in March 1990, however, at which 52% of the electorate voted, both Senate seats and the one Congress seat were won by the PP, the latter result stripping the PSOE of its overall majority in the Madrid lower chamber. The Government Delegate in Melilla claimed that voting irregularities had again occurred.

In January 1990, meanwhile, the Partido Comunista de España (PCE) and its Moroccan counterpart, the Parti du Progrès et du Socialisme (PPS), had issued a joint communiqué urging the Governments of Spain and Morocco to open dialogue and work towards a satisfactory solution to the question of Ceuta and Melilla. Relations between Spain and Morocco were strained in March, when Spanish fishermen blockaded Algeciras and other ports (thereby disrupting communications with Ceuta) in protest at the Moroccan authorities' imposition of greatly-increased penalties on Spanish fishing vessels found to be operating without a licence in Moroccan waters. Following negotiations between the EC and Morocco, Spain agreed to grant financial compensation to Morocco.

In a newspaper article in March 1990 a Moroccan government minister repeated his country's claim to Spanish North Africa, maintaining that, with the accession of Namibia to independence, Ceuta and Melilla were the last vestiges of colonialism in Africa. In April the Spanish Government decided to open negotiations with the political groupings of Ceuta and Melilla, the autonomy statutes being presented for discussion in the territories. It was confirmed that the enclaves were to remain an integral part of Spain, and that they were to be granted self-government at municipal, rather than regional, level. The Spanish Government's decision provoked a strong reaction from Moroccan political parties, which were united in their denunciation of the perceived attempt to legalize Spanish possession of the territories. In June a two-hour strike in Ceuta, in support of demands for full autonomy for the enclave, was widely observed.

In July 1990 Istiqlal, the Moroccan opposition party, announced that it was initiating a new campaign to press for the 'liberation' of Ceuta and Melilla. In the following month Istiqlal organized a protest march through the streets of Martil, a Moroccan town 40 km from Ceuta. The Muslim community of Ceuta, however, expressed its concern at these developments.

In mid-August 1990 Spain granted its Government Delegate in Melilla direct powers to expel illegal residents from the territory. In the same month King Hassan and the Spanish Prime Minister met near Rabat for talks. Their discussions focused on the crisis caused by Iraq's recent invasion of Kuwait, and on their bilateral relations, particularly increased co-operation and security. In December 1990 a Spanish delegation, led by the Prime Minister, travelled to Morocco, where the first of the planned regular summit meetings between the Spanish and Moroccan premiers took place. Among the topics discussed was the forthcoming implementation (in May 1991) of new visa requirements for North Africans entering Spain, which had caused dismay in the Muslim community. Special arrangements were to apply to Moroccan citizens who worked in, or travelled regularly to, Ceuta and Melilla. At the meeting a Spanish credit to Morocco of 25,000m. pesetas (in addition to that agreed in 1988) was also arranged.

The outbreak of the Gulf war in early 1991 gave rise to renewed disquiet in Spanish North Africa. In February 800 Muslims marched through the streets of Melilla to protest against the war, in which the US military bases in Spain were to play a crucial role. In the same month, as anti-Western sentiment in North Africa increased, the Spanish Minister of Foreign Affairs embarked on a tour of five Maghreb countries. Discussions with his Moroccan counterpart took place in Rabat.

Elections for the 25-member municipal councils of Ceuta and Melilla were held in May 1991, and in each territory the PSOE Mayor was replaced. In Ceuta Francisco Fraiz Armada of the Progreso y Futuro de Ceuta (PFC), became Mayor. In Melilla, where the PP had secured 12 of the 25 seats, Ignacio Velázquez Rivera of the right-wing Partido Nacionalista de Melilla (PNM) was elected Mayor of the enclave.

In July 1991, in Rabat, the Spanish and Moroccan heads of government signed a treaty of friendship. In addition to the promotion of co-operation in the fields of economy, finance, fisheries, culture and the judiciary, agreement was also reached on Spanish military aid to Morocco. Shortly afterwards the Moroccan Minister of the Interior, Driss Basri, and a cabinet colleague unexpectedly accepted an invitation from the Spanish Minister of the Interior to visit Ceuta, their brief trip being the first ever visit by members of the Government of King Hassan.

The draft autonomy statutes of Ceuta and Melilla were submitted to the Congress of Deputies in Madrid for discussion in October 1991. During the debate the PP accused the PSOE of supporting Moroccan interests. In November thousands of demonstrators, many of whom had travelled from the enclaves, attended a protest march in Madrid (organized by the Governments of Ceuta and Melilla), in support of demands for full autonomy for the territories. In early 1992, however, the central Government confirmed that the assemblies of Ceuta and Melilla were not to be granted full legislative powers. In May a general strike in Ceuta, to protest against this denial of full autonomy, was widely supported.

In mid-1992 relations between Spain and Morocco were dominated by the issue of illegal immigration. In addition to the problem of the large numbers of Moroccans trying to enter Spain (many drownings in the Strait of Gibraltar being reported), there had been a sharp increase in the numbers of those from other (mainly West African) countries attempting to gain entry to Europe via Morocco and the two Spanish enclaves. In July the Spanish Minister of Foreign Affairs flew to Rabat for discussions on the problem.

In March 1993 it was revealed that Spain would require the permission of NATO before employing its most modern military equipment in the defence of the enclaves. In the same month, in an attempt to bring about the transfer of powers to the territories, the PP submitted its own draft statute for Melilla to the central Government, which immediately condemned the document as unconstitutional. All political parties in Melilla, except the PSOE, demanded that a local referendum be held on the issue of autonomy.

At the general election of June 1993 the PSOE of Ceuta lost its one seat in Congress and its two seats in the Senate to the PP. In Melilla the PSOE candidate defeated the incumbent PP Congress member; the PP also lost one of its two seats in the Senate. In September the Spanish Minister of Public Administration affirmed his commitment to the conclusion, within the next few months, of an agreement on the territories' statutes.

In February 1994 the Mayor of Ceuta, Francisco Fraiz Armada, was obliged to resign, following the Supreme Court's ratification of a lower court ruling that barred him from holding public office for six years. His disqualification resulted from his involvement in irregularities in the housing sector in 1984, when unauthorized evictions had been carried out. He was replaced by Basilio Fernández López, also of the PFC.

In March 1994 King Hassan declared his opposition to the forthcoming adoption of the autonomy statutes, repeating Morocco's claim to the territories. By May, however, the final statutes had still not been presented to the Cortes in Madrid. Representatives of Ceuta were particularly critical of the dilatory conduct of the Minister of Public Administration, and urged the central Government and the opposition PP to bring the matter to a speedy conclusion. In the same month King Juan Carlos of Spain received a delegation from Melilla, led by the Mayor, Ignacio Velázquez Rivera, who emphasized the necessity for a swift adoption of the enclave's autonomy statute and conveyed his citizens' concern at the Moroccan monarch's recent statement.

In September 1994 the final statutes of autonomy were approved by the Spanish Government, in preparation for their presentation to the Cortes. The statutes provided for 25-member local assemblies with powers similar to those of the municipal councils of mainland Spain. Morocco, however, announced that it was initiating a new diplomatic campaign to reassert its claim over the territories. Spain rejected as 'inappropriate' the Moroccan Prime Minister's efforts, in a speech to the UN General Assembly, to draw a comparison between the position of the enclaves and the forthcoming return to Chinese sovereignty of the British dependent territory of Hong Kong and of the Portuguese territory of Macau.

The proposals for limited self-government were generally acceptable in Melilla but not in Ceuta, where, in October 1994, a general strike received widespread support. An estimated 20,000 residents of Ceuta participated in a demonstration to demand equality with other Spanish regions and full autonomy for the enclave. Earlier in the month, following expressions of concern regarding the territories' protection in the event of Moroccan aggression, the Minister of Defence confirmed that Spain would continue to maintain an appropriate military presence in Ceuta and Melilla. In December more than 2,000 citizens of Ceuta attended a demonstration in Madrid in support of their demands for full autonomy.

Following their approval by the Congress of Deputies in December 1994, the autonomy statutes were ratified by the Senate in February 1995. This approval of the statutes by the Spanish Cortes was denounced by the Moroccan Government, which, upon taking office in March, declared that the recovery of Ceuta and Melilla was to be one of its major objectives. In April responsibility for two explosions in Ceuta was claimed by the Organización 21 de Agosto para la Liberación de los Territorios Marroquíes Usurpados, a group that had apparently remained inactive since 1975, and which the Spanish Government suspected was now receiving covert assistance from the Moroccan authorities.

At the end of April 1995 hundreds of Spanish fishing vessels, including some from Ceuta, were obliged once again to withdraw from Moroccan waters, following the EU's failure to renegotiate the agreement with Morocco. In May, as anti-Moroccan sentiment grew, there were violent scenes when Spanish fishermen and farmers attempted to obstruct the entry of Moroccan produce into the ports of southern Spain.

Elections for the new local assemblies were held in May 1995, to coincide with the municipal polls. At the latter, in Ceuta the PP won nine of the 25 seats, the PFC six, the nationalist Ceuta Unida four and the PSOE three. Basilio Fernández López of the PFC was re-elected Mayor, heading a coalition with Ceuta Unida and the PSOE. Mustafa Mizzian Ammar, leader of the Partido Democrático y Social de Ceuta (PDSC) became the first Muslim candidate ever to be elected in the territory. Fewer than 57% of those eligible voted in Ceuta. In Melilla, where the level of participation was less than 62%, the PP won 14 of the 25 seats, the PSOE five seats, Coalición por Melilla, a new Muslim grouping, four seats and the right-wing Unión del Pueblo Melillense (UPM) two seats. Ignacio Velázquez Rivera (PP/PNM) returned to the position of Mayor.

## Government

Following the adoption of statutes of autonomy and the establishment of local assemblies in 1995, Spanish North Africa remains an integral part of Spain, but has greater jurisdiction over matters such as public works, internal trade and tourism. Each enclave has its own President. Ceuta, Melilla and the island dependencies are known as plazas de soberanía, fortified enclaves over which Spain has full sovereign rights. In both Ceuta and Melilla civil authority is vested in an official (Delegado del Gobierno) directly responsible to the Ministry of the Interior in Madrid. This official is usually assisted by a government sub-delegate. There is also one delegate from each of the Ministries in Madrid.

### Defence

Military authority is vested in a commandant-general. The enclaves are attached to the military region of Sevilla. Spain had 10,000 troops deployed in Spanish North Africa in June 1994 (compared with 21,000 in mid-1987).

### Economic Affairs

In 1991 Ceuta's GDP was 33.6% below the average for the whole of Spain, while that of Melilla was 30.5% below. The GDP of the two territories in 1992 totalled 133,767m. pesetas, equivalent to 1,072,607 pesetas per head. Agricultural activity in the territories is negligible, and industry is on a limited scale. There is a local brewery in Ceuta. In 1989 the economically active population of the two enclaves totalled 49,400, of whom 15,200 were unemployed, 1,800 were employed in the construction sector, 1,400 in industry and 100 in agriculture; 30,800 were employed in the services sector. In late 1993 it was estimated that the territories' rate of unemployment was 26.7% of the labour force. A total of 8,338 persons were registered as unemployed in April 1995. Most of the population's food is imported, with the exception of fish which is obtained locally. Sardines and anchovies are the most important items. A large proportion of the tinned fish is sold outside Spain. More important to the economies of the cities is the port activity; most of their exports take the form of fuel supplied—at very competitive rates—to ships. Most of the fuel comes from the Spanish refinery in Tenerife. Ceuta's port is the busier, receiving a total of 8,203 ships in 1993. Apart from the ferries from Málaga and Almería in mainland Spain, Melilla's port is not so frequented, and its exports are correspondingly low. Ceuta's main exports are frozen and preserved fish, foodstuffs and beer. Most trade is conducted with other parts of Spain. Tourism makes a significant contribution to the territories' economies. The average annual rates of inflation in 1994 were 3.9% in Ceuta and 3.7% in Melilla.

Upon the accession in January 1986 of Spain to the EC (EU since November 1993), Ceuta and Melilla were considered as Spanish cities and European territory, and joined the organization as part of Spain. They retained their status as free ports. The statutes of autonomy, adopted in early 1995, envisaged the continuation of the territories' fiscal benefits.

In 1989 a campaign to attract more investment to Ceuta began, tax concessions and other incentives being offered. In the three years to 1990 the Spanish Government's investment in Melilla totalled 32,000m. pesetas. Ceuta received 9,000m. pesetas for the purposes of public works. In early 1993 investment of a further 18,000m. pesetas for housing and transport projects in Melilla was announced. In June 1994 the EU announced substantial regional aid: between 1995 and 1999 Ceuta and Melilla were to receive totals of ECU 28m. and ECU 45m., of which ECU 20m. and ECU 18m., respectively, were to be in the form of direct aid.

In Ceuta the apparent lack of banking controls and alleged corruption at senior levels drew criticism in April 1993, when evidence of the territory's use as a 'money-laundering' centre for the proceeds of drugs-trafficking was revealed. A sum of more than 25,000m. pesetas was believed to be involved. Furthermore, in December fraudulent operations, allegedly involving almost 100m. pesetas and in which two civil servants were implicated, were uncovered at the city hall of Ceuta.

### Social Welfare

In 1991 there were two general hospitals in Ceuta, with a total of 447 beds. Melilla had three general hospitals, the number of beds totalling 245. A total of 458 medical personnel were working in Ceuta, and 490 in Melilla in 1986. In the three years to 1990 the Spanish Government's expenditure on the health service of Ceuta totalled 347m. pesetas.

### Education

The education system is similar to that of mainland Spain. In addition to the conventional Spanish facilities, the Moroccan Government finances a school for 600 Muslim children in Melilla, the languages of instruction being Arabic and Spanish. The curriculum includes Koranic studies. In 1982 only 12% of Muslim children were attending school, but by 1990 the authorities had succeeded in achieving an attendance level of virtually 100%. The open university (UNED) maintains a branch in Melilla.

## Statistical Survey

### Ceuta

**Area:** 19.7 sq km.
**Population** (1 January 1994): 71,926 (35,705 males, 36,221 females).
**Density** (1 January 1994): 3,651 per sq km.
**Births, Marriages and Deaths** (1994): Live births 962; Marriages 440; Deaths 422.
**Finance:** Spanish currency: 100 céntimos = 1 peseta. *Sterling and Dollar Equivalents* (31 December 1994): £1 sterling = 205.9 pesetas; US $1 = 131.6 pesetas; 1,000 pesetas = £4.856 = $7.597. *Average exchange rate* (pesetas per US $): 102.38 in 1992; 127.26 in 1993; 133.96 in 1994.
**External Trade:** Ceuta is a duty-free port. Trade is chiefly with mainland Spain, the Balearic and Canary Islands and Melilla. Ceuta supplies fuel and water to ships entering the port. Other exports include frozen and preserved fish, beer and foodstuffs.
**Transport:** *Road Traffic:* vehicles registered (1994): 2,156; vehicles entered (1993): 205,886; vehicles departed (1993): 150,499. *Shipping* (1993): Ships entered 8,203. Goods unloaded 2,758,797 metric tons (of which fuel 685,117 metric tons, water 1,461,782 metric tons); Passenger departures 1,062,005; arrivals 1,215,010.
**Education** (1994/95): Pre-school 2,388 pupils, General basic 9,351 pupils, 24 schools; Secondary 3,438 pupils, 5 schools; Vocational (1987/88) 873 students, 3 centres.

### Melilla

**Area:** 12.5 sq km.
**Population:** (March 1982) 54,741 (incl. Peñón de Alhucemas 61, Chafarinas 191, Peñón de Vélez de la Gomera 60); (1 January 1990): 62,569; (1 March 1991): 63,670 (*de facto*) or 56,600 (*de jure*).
**Density** (1991): 5,087 per sq km.
**Births, Marriages and Deaths** (1988, provisional): Live births 997; Marriages 332; Deaths 396.
**Finance:** Spanish currency (see Ceuta). 1985 budget: 2,700m. pesetas.
**External Trade:** Melilla is a duty-free port. Most imports are from Spain but over 90% of exports go to non-Spanish territories. The chief export is fish.
**Transport:** *Road Traffic* (vehicles registered, 1987, provisional): 1,498. *Shipping* (1989): Ships entered 819; (1992, provisional): Goods loaded and unloaded 639,000 metric tons; Passenger departures and arrivals 476,000. *Civil Aviation* (1989): Goods loaded and unloaded 560 metric tons; Passenger departures and arrivals 168,000.
**Education** (1987/88): Pre-school 1,961 pupils, 61 centres; General basic 8,256 pupils, 245 schools; Secondary 1,863 pupils, 4 schools; Vocational 927 students, 1 centre.

## Directory

### Ceuta

#### GOVERNMENT
(June 1995)

**Delegación del Gobierno:** Beatriz de Silva 4, 11701 Ceuta; tel. (56) 51-25-23; fax (56) 51-36-71; Government Delegate in Ceuta María del Carmen Cedeira Morterero.

Mayor of Ceuta: Basilio Fernández López (PFC). Deputy elected to the Congress in Madrid: Francisco Antonio González Pérez (PP). Representatives to the Senate in Madrid: José Luis Morales Montero (PP), Francisco Olivencia Ruiz (PP). Commandant-General: Félix Miranda Robredo.

#### COUNCIL
**Election, 28 May 1995**

|  | Seats |
|---|---|
| Partido Popular (PP) | 9 |
| Progreso y Futuro de Ceuta (PFC) | 6 |
| Ceuta Unida (CEU) | 4 |
| Partido Socialista Obrero Español (PSOE) | 3 |
| Partido Socialista del Pueblo de Ceuta (PSPC) | 2 |
| Other | 1 |
| **Total** | **25** |

#### POLITICAL ORGANIZATIONS

**Ceuta Unida (CEU):** Ceuta; nationalist party; Sec.-Gen. José Antonio Querol.

# SPANISH EXTERNAL TERRITORIES

**Iniciativa por Ceuta (INCE):** Plaza de Africa 10, 1°, 11701 Ceuta; fax (56) 51-68-90; f. 1993; Muslim party; 380 mems; Pres. AHMED SUBAIRE; Sec. ABDELKADER MAIMON.

**Izquierda Unida:** Ceuta; left-wing electoral alliance; Leader ROSA RODRÍGUEZ.

**Partido Democrático y Social de Ceuta (PDSC):** Ceuta; Leader MUSTAFA MIZZIAN AMMAR.

**Partido Humanista:** B. Príncipe Alfonso, Ceuta; Leader MOHAMED ALI.

**Partido Nacionalista Ceutí (PNC):** Ceuta; nationalist party; Leader FRANCISCO ALCÁNTARA TRUJILLO.

**Partido Popular (PP):** Ceuta; fmrly Alianza Popular; centre-right; Leader JESÚS FORTES.

**Partido Socialista Obrero Español (PSOE):** Ceuta; socialist workers' party; Leader ANTONIO TROYANO PÉREZ.

**Partido Socialista del Pueblo de Ceuta (PSPC):** Carretera del Embalse 10, 11704 Ceuta; dissident group of PSOE; Leader JUAN LUIS ARÓSTEGUI.

**Partido Socialista de los Trabajadores (PST):** B. Príncipe Alfonso, Ceuta; Leader Sr ABBAS.

**Progreso y Futuro de Ceuta (PFC):** Marina de Ceuta, Ceuta; Leader FRANCISCO FRAIZ ARMADA.

There are branches of the major Spanish parties in Ceuta, and also various civic associations. The **Asociación Ceuta y Melilla (Acyme)** is based in Granada (Pres. FRANCISCO GODINO), and is opposed to the limited autonomy of the enclaves. The **Organización 21 de Agosto para la Liberación de los Territorios Marroquíes Usurpados** resumed its activities in 1995.

### RELIGION

The majority of the European inhabitants are Christians, almost all being adherents of the Roman Catholic Church. Most Africans are Muslims, totalling about 13,000 in 1991. The Jewish community numbers several hundred.

#### Christianity
#### The Roman Catholic Church

**Bishop of Cádiz and Ceuta:** ANTONIO CEBALLOS ATIENZA (resident in Cádiz); Vicars-General: FÉLIX GONZÁLEZ MORAL, ENRIQUE ARROYO CAMACHO, Plaza de Nuestra Señora de Africa, 11701 Ceuta; tel. (56) 51-32-08.

### THE PRESS

**Ceuta Información:** Edif. San Luis, Local 4, Ceuta; tel. (56) 51-42-83; fax (56) 51-47-49; daily; Dir MANUEL GONZÁLEZ BOLORINO (acting).

**El Faro de Ceuta:** Sargento Mena 8, Ceuta; tel. (56) 51-10-24; fax (56) 51-47-69; f. 1934; morning; Dir LUIS MANUEL AZNAR; circ. 5,000.

**El Pueblo de Ceuta:** Paseo de las Palmeras 22, Entreplanta 1, Ceuta; tel. (56) 51-76-50; fax (56) 51-45-82; daily; Dir JOSÉ LÓPEZ FRANCO.

### RADIO

**Onda Cero Radio:** Alfau 4, 3° Izq., Ceuta; tel. (56) 51-78-87; Dir NANI MELUL.

**Radio Ceuta:** Real 90, Ceuta; tel. (56) 51-18-10; f. 1934; commercial; owned by Sociedad Española de Radiodifusión (SER); Dir BEATRIZ PALOMO.

**Radio Nacional de España:** Real 90, Ceuta; tel. (56) 51-90-35; Dir DOLORES BEX.

**Radio Popular de Ceuta/COPE:** Sargento Mena 8, Ceuta; tel. (56) 51-32-83; Dir HIGINIO MOLINA.

### TELEVISION

**Canal Ceuta:** Sargento Mena 8; tel. (56) 51-20-57; Dir RAFAEL MONTERO PALACIOS.

**Tele Ceuta:** Marina Española 8 bis, Ceuta; tel. (56) 51-44-17; Dir MANUEL GONZÁLEZ BOLORINO.

### FINANCE

At the end of 1989 total deposits in the private banking sector stood at 42,500m. pesetas, deposits at savings banks totalling 18,600m. The main Spanish banks have branches in Ceuta.

**Banco Bilbao Vizcaya (BBV):** Serrano Orive 3, Ceuta; tel. (56) 51-84-44; 2 brs.

**Banco Central Hispano (BCH):** Paseo del Revellín 23, Ceuta; tel. (56) 51-11-39.

**Banco de España:** Plaza de España, Ceuta; tel. (56) 51-32-53.

**Banco Español de Crédito (Banesto):** Camoens 6, Ceuta; tel. (56) 51-30-09.

**Banco Exterior de España:** Paseo del Revellín 5, Ceuta; tel. (56) 51-21-56.

**Banco Meridional:** Jáudenes 30, Ceuta; tel. (56) 51-57-86.

**Banco Popular Español:** Paseo del Revellín 1, Ceuta; tel. (56) 51-53-40.

**Banco Santander:** Marina Española 10, Ceuta; tel. (56) 51-66-85; 2 brs.

**Banco Urquijo:** Antioco, Ceuta; tel. (56) 51-25-52.

### TRADE AND INDUSTRY

**Cámara Oficial de Comercio, Industria y Navegación:** Muelle Cañonero Dato s/n, 11701 Ceuta; tel. (56) 50-95-90; fax (56) 50-95-89; Pres. JOSÉ MARÍA CAMPOS MARTÍNEZ; Sec.-Gen. FRANCISCO OLIVENCIA RUIZ.

**Confederación de Empresarios de Ceuta:** Teniente Arrabal 2, 11701 Ceuta; tel. (56) 51-69-12; employers' confederation; Pres. JOSÉ MARÍA CAMPOS MARTÍNEZ; Sec.-Gen. EVARISTO RIVERA GÓMEZ.

### TRANSPORT

Much of the traffic between Spain and Morocco passes through Ceuta; there are ferry services to Algeciras, Spain. Plans for an airport are under consideration.

### TOURISM

Visitors are attracted by the historical monuments and museums, and by the availability of duty-free goods. In 1992 Ceuta had four hotels and 27 hostels and guest houses. Plans to build additional accommodation were under way.

**Oficina de Información de Turismo:** Muelle Cañonero Dato 1, Ceuta; tel. (56) 50-92-75.

# Melilla

### GOVERNMENT
(June 1995)

**Delegación del Gobierno:** Plaza de España s/n, 29871 Melilla; tel. (52) 67-58-40; fax (52) 67-26-57; Government Delegate in Melilla: MANUEL CÉSPEDES CÉSPEDES.

Mayor of Melilla: IGNACIO VELÁZQUEZ RIVERA (PP/PNM). Deputy elected to the Congress in Madrid: JULIO BASSETS RUTLLANT (PSOE). Representatives to the Senate in Madrid: GONZALO HERNÁNDEZ MARTÍNEZ (PSOE), CARLOS A. BENET CAÑETE (PP). Commandant-General: VICENTE CERVERA GARCÍA.

### COUNCIL

**Election, 28 May 1995**

| | Seats |
|---|---|
| Partido Popular (PP) | 14 |
| Partido Socialista Obrero Español (PSOE) | 5 |
| Coalición por Melilla | 4 |
| Unión del Pueblo Melillense (UPM) | 2 |
| Total | 25 |

### POLITICAL ORGANIZATIONS

**Coalición por Melilla:** Melilla; Berber party.

**Lucha por la Libertad de Melilla:** Melilla; extreme right-wing; opposed to granting of Spanish citizenship to Muslims.

**Movimiento para la Liberación de Melilla:** Melilla; f. 1986; clandestine group; advocates use of violence.

**Partido de Acción Social de Melilla:** Melilla; favours full autonomy.

**Partido de los Demócratas de Melilla (PDM):** Melilla; f. 1985; Muslim party; Leader ABDELKÁDER MOHAMED ALÍ.

**Partido Independiente Hispano Bereber:** Melilla; Pres. LAARBI BUMEDIEN.

**Partido Nacionalista de Melilla-Asociación Pro Melilla (PNM-Aprome):** Miguel Zazo 30, 29804 Melilla; extreme-right-wing nationalist party; allied to PP; Pres. AMALIO JIMÉNEZ; Sec.-Gen. ANTONIO CIENDONES GARCÍA.

**Partido Popular (PP):** Gral Marina 11, 1° Dcha, POB 384, 29804 Melilla; tel. (52) 68-10-95; fax (52) 68-44-77; centre-right; absorbed Melilla branch of Democracia Cristiana (DC) in July 1988; Pres. JORGE HERNÁNDEZ MOLLAR.

**Partido Progresista Liberal de Melilla (PPLM):** Melilla; Leader FRANCISCO CINTAS GARCÍA.

**Partido Socialista de Melilla-Partido Socialista Obrero Español (PSME-PSOE):** Cándido Lobera 7-1°, Melilla; tel. (52) 68-18-20; socialist workers' party; favours self-government but not full autonomy; Pres. José Torres Vega; Sec.-Gen. Julio Bassets Rutllant.

**Unión de Melillenses Independientes (UMI):** Melilla; advocates independence; Spokesman José Imbroda Domínguez.

**Unión del Pueblo Melillense (UPM):** Ejército Español 7, 1° al derecha, Apdo 775, 29801 Melilla; tel. (52) 681987; fax (52) 673545; f. 1985; right-wing; Pres. Juan José Imbroda Ortiz; Gen. Sec. Daniel Conesa Mínguez.

There are branches of the major Spanish parties in Melilla, and also various civic associations.

### RELIGION

As in Ceuta, most Europeans are Roman Catholics. The registered Muslim community numbered 20,800 in 1990. The Jewish community numbered 1,300.

### THE PRESS

**Diario Sur:** Edif. Monumental 3a, Oficina 17, Melilla; tel. (52) 68-18-54; fax (52) 68-39-08; Perm. Rep. Avelino Gutiérrez Pérez.

**Guía del Ocio:** Melilla; tel. (52) 68-37-34; leisure guide; Dir José Luis Céspedes Mercado.

**Melilla Costa del Sol:** Melilla; tel. (52) 68-68-48; f. 1985; Rep. Laureano Folgar Villasenín; circ. 2,500.

**Melilla Hoy:** Teniente Aguilar de Mera 1, Edif. Monumental 1a, 29801 Melilla; tel. (52) 68-40-24; fax (52) 68-48-44; f. 1985; Dir Irene Flores Saez; Editor-in-Chief Enrique Bohórquez López Doriga.

### RADIO

**Antena 3:** Edif. Melilla, Urbanización Rusadir, Melilla; tel. (52) 68-88-40; Dir Toñi Ramos Peláez.

**Cadena Rato:** Melilla; tel. (52) 68-58-71; Dir Angel Valencia.

**Radio Melilla Ser:** Falda de Carmellos s/n, Melilla; tel. (52) 68-17-08; commercial; owned by Sociedad Española de Radiodifusión (SER); Administrator Francisco Ruiz Ripoll.

**Radio Nacional de España (RNE):** Mantelete 1, Apdo 222, Melilla; tel. (52) 68-19-07; fax (52) 68-31-08; state-controlled; Rep. Pedro A. Medina Barrenechea.

### TELEVISION

A fibre optic cable linking Melilla with Almería was laid in 1990. From March 1991 Melilla residents were able to receive three private TV channels from mainland Spain: Antena 3, Canal+ and Tele 5.

### FINANCE

At the end of 1989 total deposits in the private banking sector stood at 29,300m. pesetas, deposits at savings banks totalling 16,400m. The following banks have branches in Melilla: Banco Bilbao Vizcaya (2 brs), Banco Central Hispano, Banco Español de Crédito (Banesto), Banco Meridional, Banco Popular Español and Banco de Santander (2 brs).

### TRADE AND INDUSTRY

**Cámara Oficial de Comercio, Industria y Navegación:** Cervantes 7, 29801 Melilla; tel. (52) 68-48-40; fax (52) 68-31-19; f. 1906; Pres. Francisco Marqués Vivancos; Sec.-Gen. María Jesús Fernández de Castro y Pedrajas.

**Confederación de Empresarios de Melilla:** Paseo Marítimo Mir Berlanga 26—Entreplanta, Apdo de Correos 445, 29806 Melilla; tel. (52) 67-82-95; telex 79407; fax (52) 67-61-75; f. 1979; employers' confederation; Pres. Margarita López Almendáriz; Sec.-Gen. Jerónimo Pérez Hernández.

### TRANSPORT

There is a daily ferry service to Málaga and a service to Almería. Melilla airport, situated 4 km from the town, is served by daily flights to Málaga and Almería, operated by Iberia. There are also services to Madrid and Granada. Plans to extend the runway were approved in early 1993.

### TOURISM

There is much of historic interest to the visitor. Melilla had 19 hotels in the late 1980s. Further hotels, including a luxury development, were under construction in 1990.

## The Peñón de Vélez de la Gomera, Peñón de Alhucemas and Chafarinas Islands

These rocky islets, situated respectively just west and east of al-Hocima (Alhucemas) and east of Melilla off the north coast of Morocco, are administered with Melilla. The three Chafarinas Islands lie about 3.5 km off Ras el-Ma (Cabo de Agua). The Peñón de Alhucemas is situated about 300 m from the coast. The Peñón de Vélez de la Gomera is situated about 80 km further west, lying 85 m from the Moroccan shore, to which it is joined by a narrow strip of sand. Small military bases are maintained on the Peñón de Vélez, Peñón de Alhucemas and on the Isla del Congreso, the most westerly of the Chafarinas Islands. A supply ship calls at the various islands every two weeks. Prospective visitors must obtain the necessary military permit in Ceuta or Melilla.

# SRI LANKA

## Introductory Survey

**Location, Climate, Language, Religion, Flag, Capital**

The Democratic Socialist Republic of Sri Lanka lies in southern Asia. It comprises one large island and several much smaller ones, situated in the Indian Ocean, about 80 km (50 miles) east of the southern tip of India. The climate is tropical, with an average annual temperature of about 27°C (81°F) in Colombo. There is very little seasonal variation in temperature: the monthly average in Colombo ranges from 25°C (77°F) to 28°C (82°F). The south-western part of the island receives rain from both the south-west and the north-east monsoons: average annual rainfall in Colombo is 2,365 mm (93 ins). Sinhala, Tamil and English are all recognized national languages. One of the official languages, Sinhala, is spoken by more than 70% of the population. Tamil was made the country's second official language in December 1988. Nearly 70% of the population are Buddhist, about 15% are Tamil-speaking Hindus and there are sizeable Christian (mostly Roman Catholic) and Muslim minorities. The national flag (proportions 2 by 1) consists mainly of a dark crimson rectangular panel, with a yellow border, in the fly. In the centre of the panel is a gold lion, carrying a sword, while in each corner (also in gold) there is a leaf of the bo (bodhi) tree, which is sacred to Buddhists. At the hoist are two vertical stripes, also edged in yellow, to represent Sri Lanka's minorities: one of green (for Muslims) and one of orange (for Tamils). The capital is Colombo. The seat of government returned to the ancient capital of Sri Jayawardenepura Kotte in 1982, in preparation for the transfer of the capital.

**Recent History**

Sri Lanka, known as Ceylon until 1972, gained its independence from the United Kingdom in February 1948. From then until 1956, for a brief period in 1960 and from 1965 to 1970 the country was ruled, latterly in coalition, by the United National Party (UNP), which was concerned to protect the rights of the Tamils, Hindu members of an ethnic minority (closely linked with the inhabitants of the southern Indian state of Tamil Nadu), who are concentrated in the north (and, to a lesser extent, in the east) of the main island. The socialist Sri Lanka Freedom Party (SLFP), formed in 1951 by Solomon Bandaranaike, emphasized the national heritage, winning the support of groups that advocated the recognition of Sinhala as the official language and the establishment of Buddhism as the predominant religion. The SLFP won the 1956 elections decisively and remained in power, except for a three-month interruption in 1960, until 1965, having formed a coalition Government with the Lanka Sama Samaj Party (LSSP), a Trotskyist group, in 1964. Following the assassination of Solomon Bandaranaike in 1959, his widow, Sirimavo Bandaranaike, assumed the leadership of the SLFP. At the 1970 elections the SLFP became the leading partner of a United Front coalition Government with the LSSP and the Communist Party (Moscow Wing).

In 1971 the United Front Government suppressed an uprising led by the left-wing Janatha Vimukthi Peramuna (JVP—People's Liberation Front). A state of emergency was declared, and the party was banned. In 1976 the main Tamil party, the Federal Party, and other Tamil groups formed the Tamil United Liberation Front (TULF), calling for a separate Tamil state (Eelam) in the northern and eastern parts of the country.

In December 1976 the communists supported strikes of transport unions, which were initiated by the UNP and the LSSP (which had been expelled from the coalition in 1975). The strikes ended in January 1977, and in February Sirimavo Bandaranaike prorogued the National State Assembly until 19 May. Several members of the SLFP resigned, and seven members of the Communist Party left the coalition Government, forming an independent group within the opposition. The state of emergency was lifted in February 1977, and a general election was held in July, accompanied by widespread violence. The UNP won the election, with an overwhelming majority, and Junius Richard Jayewardene became Prime Minister. In August riots broke out between the Sinhalese majority and the Tamil minority. The TULF, which had become the main opposition party, increased its demands for an independent Tamil state. In October a constitutional amendment was passed to establish a presidential system of government, and in February 1978 Jayewardene became the country's first executive President.

Continued violence and pressure from the Tamils during 1978 led the Government to make some concessions, such as the recognition of the Tamil language, in the new Constitution of the Democratic Socialist Republic of Sri Lanka, which came into force in September 1978. In view of this, the Ceylon Workers' Congress joined the Government, but the TULF remained undecided, mainly for fear of reprisals by Tamil extremists. Continuing violence prompted the declaration of a state of emergency in July 1979 in the northern district of Jaffna, where the Tamils are in a majority. At the same time, stringent anti-terrorist legislation was passed in Parliament (as the National State Assembly had been renamed in 1978), and a presidential commission was established to study the Tamil problem.

In June 1980 a general strike, called by left-wing trade unions seeking higher wages, led to the declaration of a state of emergency between July and August, and more than 40,000 government workers lost their jobs. In August the TULF agreed to the establishment of District Development Councils, providing for a wide measure of regional autonomy. Elections to these, held in June 1981, were boycotted by the SLFP, the LSSP and the Communist Party, and the UNP won control of 18 of the 24 Councils. Subsequent communal disturbances between Sinhalese and Tamils led to the imposition of a state of emergency in the north for five days in June, and throughout the country from August 1981 to January 1982. Tamil MPs proposed a motion of no confidence in the Government and subsequently boycotted Parliament until November 1981, when a peace initiative to ease racial tension was proposed by the Government.

In October 1980 the former Prime Minister, Sirimavo Bandaranaike, was found guilty of having abused power by a special presidential commission, which deprived her of all civic rights and effectively prevented her from standing in the next elections.

In August 1982 Parliament approved an amendment to the 1978 Constitution which enabled President Jayewardene to call a presidential election before his term of office expired, i.e. after four years instead of six. Sri Lanka's first presidential election was held in October, and Jayewardene was returned to office with 53% of the votes cast. The SLFP candidate, Hector Kobbekaduwa, polled 39%, despite his party's disarray and Sirimavo Bandaranaike's loss of civic rights; she was unable to campaign, but her cause was helped when one of her trial judges was found guilty of corruption.

Following this success, the President announced, with the approval of Parliament and the Supreme Court, that, instead of a general election, a referendum would be held to decide whether to prolong the life of Parliament for a further six years after the session ended in July 1983. A state of emergency was in force between October 1982 and January 1983, and all opposition newspapers were closed by the Government. Sirimavo Bandaranaike was allowed to campaign in the referendum, which took place in December 1982 and resulted in approval of the proposal to prolong Parliament until 1989. On a 71% turnout, 55% (3.1m.) voted in favour, with the dissenting minority of 2.6m. being concentrated mainly in and around Jaffna.

In May 1983 by-elections were held for seats where the UNP had fared badly in both the presidential election and the referendum, and the UNP won 14 of the 18 seats. This was accompanied by success for the UNP in the local government elections, held concurrently, although the TULF was successful in Tamil-speaking areas. The UNP had now defeated its opponents in four polls at national level between October 1982 and June 1983.

A state of emergency was declared in May 1983 to combat mounting terrorism, and in June Tamil terrorist activity led to army reprisals and the worst outbreak of violence for many years, with more than 400 deaths and particularly severe rioting in Jaffna and Colombo. A curfew and press censorship were imposed, and three left-wing parties (including the JVP) were banned. In July the 16 TULF MPs resigned in protest at the extension of Parliament, as approved by the referendum. In August Parliament passed a 'no-separation' amendment to the Constitution, depriving those espousing Tamil separatism of their civic rights. In October the 16 TULF MPs were found to have forfeited their seats because of their boycott. After much discussion and with the informal mediation of India, an All-Party Conference (APC) began in January 1984. The APC comprised representatives of the Buddhist, Christian and Muslim faiths as well as political leaders from the Sinhalese and Tamil communities. The Government proposed to establish provincial councils, with some regional autonomy, throughout the country. The TULF, however, demanded regional devolution which would enable the northern province, with its Tamil majority, to amalgamate with the eastern province where the Tamils were in a minority and thus create a Tamil state within the framework of a united Sri Lanka. The Sinhalese and the Muslims were implacably opposed to this proposal. The APC was finally abandoned in December 1984, without agreement on the crucial question of the extent of regional autonomy.

Further violent outbursts in the northern part of the island in November and December 1984 led to the proclamation of another state of emergency. There were widespread accusations of gross military indiscipline, and there was condemnation of government-sponsored settlement of Sinhalese in Tamil areas in the eastern province. A restricted zone was established between Mannar and Mullaitivu, to prevent contact with the Indian state of Tamil Nadu, where many of the Tamil militants were based.

In February 1986 there was a resurgence of violence in the northern and eastern provinces. In May a series of explosions in Colombo was widely believed to have been carried out by Tamil terrorists. In the same month, the Government intensified its campaign against the insurgents by increasing defence expenditure and by launching an offensive against the militant Tamils in the Jaffna peninsula. This offensive made little headway, but the government cause was helped by internecine fighting which broke out between two of the principal Tamil militant groups, the Tamil Eelam Liberation Organization (TELO) and the Liberation Tigers of Tamil Eelam (LTTE—also known as the Tamil Tigers), which, over the year, emerged as the dominant Tamil separatist group. In the same month Tamil terrorists renewed their attacks on Sinhalese villagers who had been settled by the Government in Tamil-dominated areas in the eastern province. In June the Government presented new devolution proposals to a newly-convened APC, in which the TULF was not invited to participate, while the SLFP boycotted the talks. The proposals again envisaged the formation of provincial councils, but did not satisfy the Tamils' demand for amalgamation of the northern and eastern provinces. The proposals were also rejected by the SLFP, on the grounds that they conceded too much to the Tamils.

In January 1987, in response to an announcement by the LTTE that they intended to seize control of the civil administration of Jaffna, the Government suspended, indefinitely, the distribution of all petroleum products to the peninsula. In the same month all the powers previously vested in the Prime Minister, Ranasinghe Premadasa, as Minister of Emergency Civil Administration were transferred to a new Ministry of National Security, directly supervised by the President. In February the Government launched an offensive against the terrorists in the Batticaloa district. The situation worsened in April, when the LTTE, having rejected an offer of a cease-fire by the Sri Lankan Government, carried out a series of outrages against the civilian population, including a bomb explosion in Colombo's main bus station, which killed more than 100 people. In response, the Government attempted to regain control of the Jaffna peninsula, the stronghold of the LTTE. During the resultant struggle between the LTTE and government forces, India demonstrated its support for the Tamils by violating Sri Lankan airspace to drop food and medical supplies in Jaffna. On 29 July, however, an important breakthrough was made when President Jayewardene and the Indian Prime Minister, Rajiv Gandhi, signed an accord regarding a settlement of the country's ethnic crisis. The main points of this accord were: the provision of an Indian Peace-Keeping Force (IPKF) to oversee its proper implementation; a complete cessation of hostilities, and the surrender of all weapons held by the Tamil militants; the amalgamation of the northern and eastern provinces into one administrative unit, with an elected provincial council (together with the creation of provincial councils in the seven other provinces); the holding of a referendum in the eastern province at a date to be decided by the Sri Lankan President, to determine whether the mixed population of Tamils, Sinhalese and Muslims supported an official merger with the northern province into a single Tamil-dominated north-east province; a general amnesty for all Tamil militants; the repatriation of some 130,000 Tamil refugees from India to Sri Lanka (by early 1991 the number of Tamil refugees in India had risen to an estimated 210,000, and in early 1992 the Indian Government began to repatriate them, allegedly on a voluntary basis); the prevention of the use of Indian territory by Tamil militants for military or propaganda purposes; the prevention of the military use of Sri Lankan ports by any country in a manner prejudicial to Indian interests; and the provision that Tamil and English should have equal status with Sinhala as official languages. The accord encountered widespread disapproval among the Sinhalese population and from the SLFP, who felt that it granted too much power to the Tamil minority.

In July and August 1987 more than 7,000 Indian troops were dispatched to Sri Lanka. After a promising start in August, the surrender of arms by the Tamil militant groups became more sporadic in September, and the implementation of the peace accord was impeded by further bitter internecine fighting among the Tamil militias (involving the LTTE in particular), which necessitated direct intervention by the IPKF. Under arrangements reported to have been negotiated in September with the Indian authorities, the LTTE was to be allocated a majority of seats on an interim council, which was to administer the northern and eastern provinces, pending the holding of elections. Despite this concession, the surrender of arms by the LTTE had virtually ceased by early October; the group had resumed its terrorist attacks on Sinhalese citizens, and had declared itself to be firmly opposed to the peace accord. In response to this resurgence in violence, the IPKF launched an offensive against the LTTE stronghold in the Jaffna peninsula in October. The Indian troops encountered fierce and prolonged resistance from the Tamil militants, which necessitated the deployment of thousands of reinforcements. By the end of the month, however, the IPKF had gained control of Jaffna city, while most of the LTTE militants had escaped to establish a new base for guerrilla operations, in the Batticaloa district of the eastern province. Both sides had suffered heavy casualties.

Because of the continuing violence, the Sri Lankan Government abandoned its plan to create an interim administrative council for the northern and eastern provinces. However, in November 1987, despite strong opposition from the SLFP and the resignation of the Minister of Agricultural Development and Research, Food and Co-operatives (who opposed the proposed merger of the northern and eastern provinces), Parliament adopted the legislation establishing provincial councils.

Another major threat to the successful implementation of the peace accord was the re-emergence in 1987 of the outlawed Sinhalese group, the JVP, which was based mainly in the south of the island. This group claimed that the accord conceded too much power to the Tamils. As part of its anti-accord campaign, the JVP was widely believed to have been responsible for an assassination attempt on President Jayewardene in August, in which one MP was killed and several cabinet ministers were seriously wounded, and to have murdered more than 200 UNP supporters by February 1988, including the Chairman of the UNP, Harsha Abeywardene, and the leader of the left-wing Sri Lanka Mahajana (People's) Party (SLMP), Vijaya Kumaratunga, who supported the accord. In May 1988 the Government revoked the five-year ban on the JVP in return for an agreement by the party to end its campaign of violence, but JVP leaders disowned the agreement as a hoax. The JVP was believed to be responsible for the murder of the UNP General Secretary, later in the same month.

In February 1988 a new opposition force emerged when an alliance, named the United Socialist Alliance (USA), was formed between the SLMP, the LSSP, the Communist Party of Sri Lanka, the Nava Sama Samaja Party, and (most notably) the Eelam People's Revolutionary Liberation Front (EPRLF).

Although the USA group, led by Chandrika Kumaratunga (the widow of the SLMP leader), comprised opposition parties, it expressed support for the peace accord.

Elections to seven of the provincial councils were held in April and June 1988 (in defiance of the JVP's threats and violence); elections in the northern and eastern provinces were postponed indefinitely. The UNP won a majority and effective control in all seven (with 57% of the elective seats), while the USA emerged as the main opposition group (with 41% of the seats). The SLFP boycotted the elections, in protest at the presence of the IPKF (which now numbered about 50,000). In September President Jayewardene officially authorized the merger of the northern and eastern provinces into a single north-eastern province, prior to provincial council elections there. The JVP reacted violently, and was widely believed to have been responsible for the murder of the Minister of Rehabilitation and Reconstruction, Lionel Jayatilleke, at the end of the month. In protest against the proposed elections in the new north-eastern province and the presidential election (due to be held in December), the JVP organized a series of disruptive strikes and violent demonstrations in the central, western and southern provinces in October. In an effort to curb the increasing violence, the Government applied extensive emergency regulations, imposed curfews in areas of unrest, and deployed armed riot police. Despite boycotts and threats by both the JVP and the LTTE, elections to the new north-eastern provincial council took place in November. The moderate and pro-accord Tamil groups, the EPRLF and the Eelam National Democratic Liberation Front (ENDLF), together with the Sri Lanka Muslim Congress (SLMC), were successful in the elections, while the UNP won only one seat. In early December Parliament unanimously approved a Constitution Amendment Bill to make Tamil one of the country's two official languages (with Sinhala), thus fulfilling one of the major commitments envisaged in the peace accord. On 19 December the presidential election took place, in circumstances of unprecedented disruption, and was boycotted by the LTTE and the JVP. None the less, about 55% of the total electorate was estimated to have voted. The Prime Minister, Ranasinghe Premadasa (the UNP's candidate), won by a narrow margin, with 50.4% of the total votes, while Sirimavo Bandaranaike, the President of the SLFP (whose civil rights had been restored in January 1986), received 44.9%. On the following day, as promised earlier in the month by the Government, Parliament was dissolved in preparation for the general election, which was to be held in February 1989 (six months in advance of the date when it was due).

In early January 1989 Premadasa was sworn in as Sri Lanka's new President, and an interim Cabinet was appointed. In the same month, the Government decided to repeal the state of emergency, which had been in force since May 1983, and to abolish the Ministry of National Security. At the same time, however, special security measures were invoked in an attempt to arrest the escalating violence. Shortly after his inauguration, Premadasa offered to confer with the extremists and invited all groups to take part in the electoral process. The JVP and the LTTE, however, intensified their campaigns of violence in protest at the forthcoming general election. In early February 1989 the moderate, pro-accord Tamil groups, the EPRLF, the ENDLF and the TELO, formed a loose alliance, under the leadership of the TULF, to contest the general election. In the election, which was held on 15 February and which was, again, marred by widespread violence, the UNP won 125 seats of the total of 225 that were contested. The new system of proportional representation, which was introduced at this election, was especially advantageous to the SLFP, which became the major opposition force in Parliament, with 67 seats. The comparatively low electoral participation of 64% confirmed, again, that intimidatory tactics, employed by the LTTE and the JVP, had had an effect on the voters. A few days later, President Premadasa appointed a new Cabinet, and in March he appointed the Minister of Finance, Dingiri Banda Wijetunga, as the country's new Prime Minister. Although both the LTTE and the JVP rejected a conciliatory offer made by the President in April, in a surprising development, representatives of the LTTE began discussions with government officials in Colombo in the following month.

Between January and April 1989, five battalions of the IPKF left Sri Lanka, and in May the Sri Lankan Government announced that it wanted all Indian troops to have left Sri Lanka by the end of July. India responded cautiously to Premadasa's demand, which had been made without warning or consultation, saying only that it would withdraw its troops at an 'early date'. Rajiv Gandhi stressed that the timetable for a complete withdrawal would have to be decided mutually, and that, before the Indian forces left, he wanted to ensure the security of the Tamils and the devolution of real power to the elected local government in the north-eastern province. In protest against the continued presence of the IPKF in Sri Lanka, the JVP organized demonstrations and strikes. As a result of the escalation in unrest and violence, the Government reimposed a state of emergency on 20 June. In the same month, shortly after the murders of several prominent Tamil leaders, including the Secretary-General of the TULF, Appapillai Amirthalingam, and the leader of the People's Liberation Organization of Tamil Eelam (PLOTE), Kadirkamam Uma Maheswaran, the peace negotiations between the Sri Lankan Government and the LTTE were temporarily discontinued. It was widely believed that the Government had demanded, and had not been given, a categorical denial that the LTTE were involved in the murders. In mid-September the Governments of Sri Lanka and India signed an agreement in Colombo, under which India promised to make 'all efforts' to withdraw its remaining 45,000 troops from Sri Lanka by the end of the year, and the IPKF was to declare an immediate unilateral cease-fire. In turn, the Sri Lankan Government pledged immediately to establish a peace committee for the north-eastern province in an attempt to reconcile the various Tamil groups and to incorporate members of the LTTE into the peaceful administration of the province.

The JVP suffered a very serious set-back when its leader, Rohana Wijeweera, and his principal deputy, Upatissa Gamanayake, were shot dead by the security forces in November 1989. In the following month the leader of the military wing of the JVP, Saman Piyasiri Fernando, was killed in an exchange of gunfire in Colombo. Between September 1989 and the end of January 1990 the Sri Lankan security forces effectively destroyed the JVP as a political force, thus substantially transforming the country's political scene. All but one member of the JVP's political bureau and most leaders at district level had been killed. It was estimated, however, that the number of civilians killed in the lengthy struggle between the JVP and the Government might have been as high as 25,000–50,000.

As the Indian troops increased the speed of their withdrawal from Sri Lanka in the latter half of 1989, the LTTE initiated a campaign of violence against its arch-rivals, the more moderate Indian-supported EPRLF, who were mustering a so-called Tamil National Army (TNA), with Indian help, in the north-eastern province, to resist the LTTE. The LTTE accused the EPRLF and its allies of forcibly conscripting thousands of Tamil youths into the TNA. Following months of peace talks with the Government, however, the political wing of the LTTE was recognized as a political party by the commissioner of elections in December. The LTTE leaders then proclaimed that the newly-recognized party would take part in the democratic process (it demanded immediate fresh elections in the north-eastern province) under the new name of the People's Front of the Liberation Tigers (PFLT). By the end of 1989 the inexperienced and undisciplined TNA had been virtually destroyed by the LTTE, who now appeared to have the tacit support of the central Government and had taken control of much of the territory in the north-eastern province.

Following further talks between the Governments of Sri Lanka and India, the completion date for the withdrawal of the IPKF was postponed until the end of March 1990. In early March the EPRLF-dominated north-eastern provincial council, under the leadership of Annamalai Varadharajah Perumal, renamed itself the 'National Assembly of the Free and Sovereign Democratic Republic of Eelam' and gave the central Government a one-year ultimatum to fulfil a 19-point charter of demands. Two weeks later, however, Perumal was reported to have fled to Madras in southern India. The last remaining IPKF troops left Sri Lanka on 24 March, a week ahead of schedule. In the next month the Government eased emergency regulations (including the ban on political rallies) in an effort to restore a degree of normality to the country after years of violence. At the same time, Sri Lanka's security forces, encouraged by the relative lull in violence, halted all military operations against the now much-weakened JVP and the Tamil militant groups. A fragile peace was maintained until June, when the LTTE abandoned its negotiations with the Government and renewed hostilities with surprise attacks on military and police installations in the north and north-east. Consequently, the Sri Lankan security forces were compelled to launch a counter-offensive. In mid-June the Government dissolved the north-eastern provincial council (despite protests by the EPRLF), and the holding of fresh elections in the province was postponed indefinitely pending the LTTE's agreement to participate in them (as earlier promised). In August the LTTE intensified its campaign of violence against the Muslim population in the eastern province, which retaliated with counter-attacks. At the end of August the Government launched a major offensive against the Tamil strongholds in the Jaffna peninsula. In January 1991 the LTTE suffered an apparent set-back when the Indian central Government dismissed the state government in Tamil Nadu, on account of the latter's alleged support for the Tamil militants in Sri Lanka. In early March it was widely suspected that the LTTE were responsible for the assassination of a senior cabinet member, the Minister of Plantation Industries and Minister of State for Defence, Ranjan Wijeratne (who had been in charge of both the government forces' successful offensive against the JVP, several years earlier, and the ongoing offensive against the LTTE), and for the bomb attack on an armed-forces building in Colombo in late June. More significantly, for its regional implications, the LTTE were believed to have been responsible for the assassination of the former Indian Prime Minister, Rajiv Gandhi, near Madras, the state capital of Tamil Nadu, in May. In January 1992 the leader of the LTTE, Velupillai Prabhakaran, and his intelligence chief were charged *in absentia* in a court in Madras in connection with the assassination of Rajiv Gandhi. Shortly afterwards the Indian Government proscribed the LTTE in India and banned its activities on Indian territory. By mid-1992 the fighting between the Sri Lankan army and the LTTE showed no sign of abating, despite several offers of a resumption of talks made by the Government to the Tamil militants.

In May 1991 President Premadasa consolidated his political position when the UNP won a decisive victory in the local government elections. In late August, however, the opposition, with the support of a number of UNP parliamentary members, began proceedings for the impeachment of the President. The impeachment motion listed 24 instances of alleged abuse of power, including illegal land deals, improperly aiding Tamil rebels, and failure to consult the Cabinet (thus violating the Constitution). The motion constituted a serious challenge to the authority of Premadasa and to the stability of his Government, but was rejected in October by the Speaker of Parliament on the grounds that some of the signatures on the resolution were invalid. Eight erstwhile UNP parliamentary members, including two former cabinet members, Lalith Athulathmudali and Gamini Dissanayake, who were expelled from the party (thus losing their parliamentary seats as well) by Premadasa for supporting the impeachment motion, formed a new party in December, called the Democratic United National Front (DUNF), to which they hoped to attract dissident members of the UNP.

The security forces suffered a serious set-back in August 1992, when 10 senior officers, including the northern military commander, Brig.-Gen. Denzil Kobbekaduwa, and the Jaffna peninsula commander, Brig. Wijaya Wimalaratne, were killed in a mine explosion near Jaffna. Tension between the Muslim and Tamil populations in the north-eastern district of Polonnaruwa drastically increased following the massacre of more than 170 Muslim villagers by suspected LTTE guerrillas in October. In the next month the LTTE were also widely believed to have been responsible for the murder of the naval commander, Vice-Admiral Clancy Fernando, in Colombo. The LTTE themselves also lost one of their most senior leaders when Commander Sathasivam Krishnakumar, Velupillai Prabhakaran's chief deputy, was killed at sea in January 1993.

In late April 1993 the opposition DUNF accused Premadasa's Government of having been responsible for the assassination of the party's leader, Lalith Athulathmudali. In response, Premadasa alleged that the perpetrators of the murder had been LTTE terrorists. The LTTE, however, denied any responsibility for the killing. The country was thrown into greater political turmoil on 1 May, when President Premadasa was assassinated in a bomb explosion in Colombo. The LTTE were officially blamed for the murder, although, again, they strenuously denied any involvement. A few days later Parliament unanimously elected the incumbent Prime Minister, Dingiri Banda Wijetunga, to serve the remaining presidential term (expiring in December 1994), and the erstwhile Minister of Industries, Science and Technology, Ranil Wickremasinghe, was appointed to replace him in the premiership. In provincial elections held in mid-May the UNP won control of four of the seven councils; no polling was carried out in the area covered by the now defunct north-eastern province. Although the ruling party received 47% of the votes, it was the first time since 1977 that its percentage of total votes had fallen below 50%, indication of an erosion of its support base that became more pronounced in the early part of 1994.

The Sri Lankan forces achieved considerable success in their fight against ethnic violence in the eastern province in 1993, but were forced to abandon a massive military offensive in the Jaffna peninsula in October owing to the ferocity of the LTTE resistance. In the following month both sides suffered heavy casualties in the course of the battle over the military base at Pooneryn on the Jaffna lagoon. As a result of this military débâcle, in which, according to official figures, more than 600 army and naval personnel were either killed or captured, the Government established a new combined security forces command for the Jaffna and Kilinochchi districts to counter the LTTE threat.

Despite the continuing violence, provincial elections were held in the eastern province and in the northern town of Vavuniya in early March 1994; the UNP secured the greatest number of seats, while independent Tamil groups also performed well. The LTTE and the TULF boycotted the poll. The ruling party suffered its first major electoral reverse for 17 years at the end of the month, however, when an opposition grouping known as the People's Alliance (of which the main constituent was the SLFP and which was headed by the former leader of the USA group, Chandrika Kumaratunga) won a clear majority in elections to the southern provincial council. In an attempt to regain lost support, the UNP proceeded to reintroduce various populist welfare policies, such as had been adopted by the former President, Ranasinghe Premadasa. In early May Wijetunga's Government defeated a parliamentary motion of no confidence by 111 votes to 71. On 24 June, in an apparent attempt to catch the opposition by surprise, the President dissolved Parliament and announced that early legislative elections were to be held on 16 August, ahead of the presidential election. Wijetunga's ploy failed, however: the People's Alliance obtained 48.9% of the votes, thus securing a narrow victory over the UNP, which received 44% of the poll. Under the prevailing system of proportional representation, this translated to 105 seats for the People's Alliance and 94 for the UNP in the 225-seat Parliament. The 17-year rule of the UNP had thus come to an end. On 18 August President Wijetunga gave up hope of forming a UNP minority Government and appointed Kumaratunga as Prime Minister, the People's Alliance having secured the support of the Sri Lanka Muslim Congress, the TULF, the Democratic People's Liberation Front and a small, regional independent group. A new Cabinet was appointed on the following day, all members of which belonged to the SLFP, with the exception of four ministers and the President. In line with her electoral pledge to abolish the executive presidency and to establish a parliamentary system in its place, the Prime Minister removed the finance portfolio from the President and assumed responsibility for it herself. Although Wijetunga retained the title of Minister of Defence, actual control of the ministry was expected to be exercised by the Deputy Minister of Defence. The Prime Minister's mother, Sirimavo Bandaranaike, was appointed as Minister without Portfolio. With regard to the Tamil question, overtures were made between the new Government and the LTTE concerning unconditional peace talks (commenced in mid-October) and at the end of August, as a gesture of goodwill, the Government partially lifted the economic blockade on LTTE-occupied territory. In addition, the Prime Minister created a new Ministry of Ethnic Affairs and National Integration and assumed the portfolio herself, thus revealing her determination to seek an early solution to the civil strife.

In early September 1994 Chandrika Kumaratunga was unanimously elected by the SLFP as its candidate for the forthcoming presidential poll, while Gamini Dissanayake, the leader of the opposition (who had left the DUNF and returned to the UNF in 1993), was chosen as the UNP's candidate. The election campaign was thrown into turmoil, however, on 24 October, when Dissanayake was assassinated by a suspected LTTE suicide bomber in a suburb of Colombo; more than 50 other people, including the General Secretary of the UNP, were killed in the blast. The Government declared a state of emergency and suspended the ongoing peace talks with the LTTE. Dissanayake had been an outspoken critic of these talks and had been the architect of the 1987 Indo-Sri Lankan accord. His widow, Srima Dissanayake, was chosen by the UNP to replace him as the party's presidential candidate. The state of emergency was revoked on 7 November (with the exception of the troubled areas in the north and east) to facilitate the fair and proper conduct of the presidential election, which was held on 9 November. Kumaratunga won the election, with 62.3% of the votes, while Srima Dissanayake obtained 35.9%. The Government viewed the victory as a clear mandate for the peace process initiated earlier that year. Sirimavo Bandaranaike was subsequently appointed Prime Minister, for the third time. The new President pledged to abolish the executive presidency before mid-July 1995, on the grounds that she believed that the post vested too much power in one individual.

The Government and the LTTE resumed peace talks in early January 1995, which resulted in the drawing up of a preliminary agreement on the cessation of hostilities as a prelude to political negotiations. This important development constituted the first formal truce since fighting was renewed in the north-east in June 1990. As an inducement to ending the violence, the Government offered to implement a US $816m. rehabilitation and development programme in the war-torn northern region. A further incentive was the Government's decision to employ foreign observers to monitor the cease-fire. Towards the end of the month, the LTTE modified its central demand and indicated that it would be willing to accept some form of devolution under a federal system, rather than full independence. In April, however, following several rounds of deadlocked negotiations, with both sides accusing each other of making unreasonable demands and proposals, the LTTE unilaterally ended the truce, withdrew from the peace talks and resumed hostilities against the government forces. (As feared, the LTTE had apparently used the 14-week truce period to fortify and consolidate its strategic positions, notably in the eastern province.) In response, the Government cancelled all the concessions made to the guerrillas during the peace negotiations and put the security forces on alert. As conditions for reinstigating peace talks, the LTTE demanded the dismantling of the army camp at Pooneryn in the south-west of the Jaffna peninsula, the complete removal of the economic embargo, the free movement of Tamil militia in the east and the relaxation of fishing restrictions around the northern coastline. A disturbing escalation in the violence was demonstrated at the end of the month by the LTTE's deployment, for the first time, of surface-to-air missiles. The Government's exasperation with the LTTE was highlighted during an interview for an Indian periodical, when President Kumaratunga categorically blamed Velupillai Prabhakaran, the leader of the guerrilla group, for the assassination of Rajiv Gandhi.

Negotiations have been held with India since 1964 on the repatriation of stateless Tamils of Indian origin residing in the central tea-plantation region, who had been brought to the island as labourers during British colonial rule (they are distinct from the Sri Lankan Tamils residing in the north and north-east). In 1985 India granted citizenship to 600,000 people, while Sri Lanka agreed to accept the remaining 469,000 as citizens. In April 1989 the Sri Lankan Government granted voting rights to 320,000 of these Tamils.

In foreign policy, Sri Lanka has adopted a non-aligned role. Sri Lanka is a founder member of the South Asian Association for Regional Co-operation (SAARC, see p. 241), formally established in 1985.

### Government

A presidential form of government was adopted in October 1977 and confirmed in the Constitution of September 1978. The Constitution provides for a unicameral Parliament as the supreme legislative body, its members being elected by a system of modified proportional representation. Executive powers are vested in the President, who is Head of State. He/she is directly elected for a term of six years, but he/she is not accountable to Parliament. He/she has the power to appoint or dismiss the Prime Minister and members of the Cabinet, and may assume any portfolio. He/she is empowered to dismiss Parliament. In 1982 the Constitution was amended, allowing the President to call a presidential election before his/her first term of office was completed. In 1983 the Constitution was further amended to include a 'no-separation' clause, making any division of Sri Lanka illegal, and any advocates of separatism liable to lose their civic rights.

Sri Lanka comprises nine provinces and 24 administrative districts, each with an appointed Governor and elected Development Council. In November 1987 a constitutional amendment was adopted, providing for the creation of eight provincial councils (the northern and eastern provinces were to be merged as one administrative unit). A network of 68 Pradeshiya Sabhas (district councils) was inaugurated throughout the country in January 1988.

### Defence

In June 1994 the armed forces totalled about 126,000 (including recalled reservists): army 105,000, navy 10,300, air force 10,700. There are also paramilitary forces of around 70,200 (including 15,200 Home Guard and a 3,000-strong anti-guerrilla unit). The defence budget for 1994 totalled Rs 24,100m. Military service is voluntary.

### Economic Affairs

In 1993, according to estimates by the World Bank, Sri Lanka's gross national product (GNP), measured at average 1991–93 prices, was US $10,658m., equivalent to $600 per head. During 1985–93, it was estimated, GNP per head increased, in real terms, at an average annual rate of 2.6%. Over the same period, the population increased by an annual average of 1.3%. Sri Lanka's gross domestic product (GDP) increased, in real terms, by an annual average of 4.0% in 1980–92. Real GDP grew by 6.9% in 1993 (the highest rate for 16 years and the highest rate in South Asia) and by 5.5% in 1994.

Agriculture (including hunting, forestry and fishing) contributed an estimated 21.7% of GDP in 1993. About 38.5% of the total working population were employed in the sector in that year. The principal cash crops are tea (which accounted for 14.2% of total export earnings in 1993), rubber and coconuts. In 1990 Sri Lanka overtook India as the world's largest tea exporter. Rice production is also important. Cattle, buffaloes, pigs and poultry are the principal livestock. During 1980–92 agricultural GDP increased by an annual average of 2.1%; agricultural output grew by 4.9% in 1993.

Industry (including mining and quarrying, manufacturing, construction and power) contributed an estimated 28.1% of GDP in 1993 and employed 20.9% of the working population. During 1980–92 industrial GDP increased by an annual average of 4.8%; industrial production grew by 15% in 1993.

Mining and quarrying contributed an estimated 1.1% of GDP in 1993, and employed 2.2% of the working population. Gemstones are the major mineral export (accounting for about 7.4% of total export earnings in 1993). Another commercially important mineral in Sri Lanka is graphite, and there are also deposits of iron ore, monazite, uranium, ilmenite sands, limestone and clay.

Manufacturing contributed an estimated 17.9% of GDP in 1993 and employed about 13.2% of the working population. Based on the value of output, the principal branches of manufacturing in 1990 were food products (providing 19.5% of the total), clothing (15.4%), petroleum and textiles. The garment industry is Sri Lanka's largest earner of foreign exchange, with sales of clothing providing about 45% of total export earnings in 1993. During 1980–92 manufacturing GDP increased by an annual average of 6.5%; manufacturing output rose by 10.5% in 1993 (most of the growth being in the private sector).

Energy is derived principally from hydroelectric power; of Sri Lanka's installed capacity of 1,410 MW in 1993, 1,137 MW was hydropower. Imports of petroleum and petroleum products comprised 7.7% of the value of total imports in 1993.

In 1993 Sri Lanka recorded a visible trade deficit of US $742.1m., and there was a deficit of $380.6m. on the current account of the balance of payments. Remittances from Sri Lankans working abroad increased from SDR 388m. in 1992 to SDR 454m. in 1993. In 1993 the principal source of imports (12.1%) was Japan, while the USA was the principal market for exports (35.3%). Other major trading partners were Germany, the United Kingdom and India. The principal exports in 1992 were clothing, tea and gemstones. The principal imports were machinery and transport equipment, textile yarn and fabrics, and food and live animals.

In 1994 there was an estimated budgetary deficit of Rs 83,500m. According to official figures, the budget deficit was equivalent to almost 10% of GDP in 1994. Sri Lanka's total external debt was US $6,783m. at the end of 1993, of which $5,936m. was long-term public debt. In that year the cost of debt-servicing was equivalent to 9.9% of earnings from the exports of goods and services. In April 1995 a consortium of aid donors, led by the World Bank, pledged total aid of $850m. for that year. During 1985–93 the average annual rate of inflation was 12.2%. The rate decreased to 11.7% in 1993 and 8.4% in 1994; by March 1995 the rate had declined further, to 5.5%. An estimated 13.8% of the labour force were unemployed in late 1993.

Sri Lanka is a member of the Asian Development Bank (ADB, see p. 107) and a founder member of the South Asian Association for Regional Co-operation (SAARC, see p. 241), which seeks to improve regional co-operation, particularly in economic development.

Unemployment, a persistent fiscal deficit and inflation, together with the economic dislocation resulting from the ethnic conflict, are among the country's main economic problems. Another major problem, since the late 1950s, has been a regular deficit on the current account of the balance of payments. In 1992, however, the Sri Lankan economy showed some signs of recovery, despite the continuing ethnic violence: both the trade deficit and the deficit on the current account of the balance of payments narrowed, partly owing to a rise in export earnings (particularly from exports of tea, garments and gems), an increase in remittances from expatriate workers, and a substantial recovery in the tourism sector. In the early 1990s, in an attempt to attract greater foreign investment and to promote economic growth, the Government introduced a series of wide-ranging economic reforms, including the transfer to private ownership of state-owned plantations and other enterprises, and the liberalization of exchange controls. By the end of 1993 15 state-owned industrial enterprises and two state-owned graphite mines had been fully transferred to private ownership, and in that year the actual inflow of foreign direct investment amounted to US $130m. Foreign investment also increased substantially in 1994. The left-wing People's Alliance Government, which came to power in August 1994, promised to continue the market-orientated policies of the previous administration with minimal change. In January 1995 President Kumaratunga announced a major privatization programme, which would encompass the country's aviation, transport, insurance and power-generation sectors.

## Social Welfare

There is an island network of hospitals, clinics and dispensaries, where treatment is provided free of charge. In 1982 Sri Lanka had 493 hospital establishments, with a total of 43,389 beds. There were 1,914 registered physicians (1.2 per 10,000 population), 301 dentists, 8,091 nursing personnel and 3,255 midwifery personnel in 1985. Unemployment benefits were introduced in 1977. Of total estimated budgetary expenditure by the central Government in 1993, Rs 7,064m. (5.3%) was for health services, and a further Rs 21,231m. (15.8%) for social security and welfare.

## Education

Education is officially compulsory for 10 years between five and 15 years of age, and it is available free of charge from lower kindergarten to university age. There are three types of school: state-controlled schools (mostly co-educational), denominational schools and Pirivenas (for Buddhist clergy and lay students). Primary education begins at the age of five and lasts for five years. Secondary education, beginning at 10 years of age, lasts for up to eight years, comprising a first cycle of six years and a second of two years. In 1992 the total enrolment at primary and secondary schools was equivalent to 87% of the school-age population (boys 86%; girls 89%). Primary enrolment in that year was equivalent to 107% of children in the relevant age-group (boys 110%; girls 106%); the comparable ratio for secondary enrolment was 73% (boys 70%; girls 77%). There are 26 teacher-training colleges, nine universities, 13 polytechnic institutes, eight junior technical colleges and an open university. Since 1977 there has been increased emphasis on informal education programmes for school leavers and special education programmes. Estimated budgetary expenditure on education by the central Government in 1993 was Rs 14,056m. (10.5% of total spending). Adult illiteracy declined from 24.5% in 1963 to 14.0% (males 9.2%; females 18.8%) in 1981. According to estimates by UNESCO, the rate in 1990 was 11.6% (males 6.6%; females 16.5%).

## Public Holidays

**1995:** 1 January (New Year's Day), 4 February (Independence Commemoration Day), 3 March (Id al-Fitr, Ramazan Festival Day), 14 April (Good Friday), 17 April (Easter Monday), 1 May (May Day), 10 May (Id al-Adha, Hadji Festival Day), 22 May (National Heroes' Day), 30 June (Special Bank Holiday), 9 August (Milad un-Nabi, Birth of the Prophet), 25 December (Christmas Day), 26 December (Boxing Day), 31 December (Special Bank Holiday).

**1996:** 1 January (New Year's Day), 4 February (Independence Commemoration Day), 21 February (Id al-Fitr, Ramazan Festival Day), 5 April (Good Friday), 8 April (Easter Monday), 29 April (Id al-Adha, Hadji Festival Day), 1 May (May Day), 22 May (National Heroes' Day), 30 June (Special Bank Holiday), 28 July (Milad un-Nabi, Birth of the Prophet), 25 December (Christmas Day), 26 December (Boxing Day), 31 December (Special Bank Holiday).

Note: A number of Hindu, Muslim and Buddhist holidays depend on lunar sightings. There is a holiday every lunar month on the day of the full moon.

## Weights and Measures

Legislation in November 1974 provided for the introduction of the metric system but imperial units are still used for some purposes.

# Statistical Survey

Source (unless otherwise stated): Department of Census and Statistics, 6 Albert Crescent, POB 563, Colombo 7; tel. (1) 665291.

## Area and Population

### AREA, POPULATION AND DENSITY

| | |
|---|---:|
| Area (sq km) | 64,454* |
| Population (census results) | |
| 9 October 1971 | 12,689,897 |
| 17 March 1981 | |
| Males | 7,568,253 |
| Females | 7,278,497 |
| Total | 14,846,750 |
| Population (official estimates at mid-year) | |
| 1991 | 17,247,000 |
| 1992 | 17,405,000 |
| 1993 | 17,619,000 |
| Density (per sq km) at mid-1993 | 273.4 |

* 24,886 sq miles. This figure refers to land area only, excluding inland water.

### ETHNIC GROUPS (census results)

| | 1971* | 1981 |
|---|---:|---:|
| Sinhalese | 9,131,000 | 10,979,561 |
| Sri Lankan Tamil | 1,424,000 | 1,886,872 |
| Indian Tamil | 1,175,000 | 818,656 |
| Sri Lankan Moors | 828,000 | 1,046,926 |
| Others | 132,000 | 114,735 |
| **Total** | 12,690,000 | 14,846,750 |

* Provisional.

### DISTRICTS (provisional, mid-1993)

| | Area (sq km, excl. inland water) | Population (official estimates, '000) | Density (persons per sq km) |
|---|---:|---:|---:|
| Colombo | 657 | 2,026 | 3,084 |
| Gampaha | 1,387 | 1,555 | 1,121 |
| Kurungela | 4,813 | 1,462 | 304 |
| Kandy | 1,916 | 1,269 | 662 |
| Galle | 1,636 | 971 | 594 |
| Kalutara | 1,589 | 961 | 605 |
| Ratnapura | 3,275 | 960 | 293 |
| Jaffna | 983 | 879 | 894 |
| Matara | 1,283 | 797 | 621 |
| Kegalle | 1,693 | 758 | 448 |
| Anuradhapura | 7,034 | 741 | 105 |
| Badulla | 2,857 | 724 | 253 |
| Puttalam Chilaar | 3,013 | 617 | 205 |
| Nuwara-Eliya | 1,741 | 535 | 307 |
| Hambantota | 2,579 | 531 | 206 |
| Amparai | 4,350 | 501 | 115 |
| Batticaloa | 2,686 | 433 | 161 |
| Matale | 1,993 | 429 | 215 |
| Moneragala | 5,560 | 361 | 65 |
| Polonnaruwa | 3,248 | 329 | 101 |
| Trincomalee | 2,631 | 323 | 123 |
| Mannar | 1,985 | 137 | 69 |
| Vavuniya | 1,967 | 117 | 59 |
| Kilinochchi | 1,235 | 107 | 87 |
| Mullativu | 2,517 | 96 | 38 |
| **Total** | 64,628 | 17,619 | 273 |

Source: Registrar General's Office.

### PRINCIPAL TOWNS
(provisional, estimated population at mid-1990)

| | | | |
|---|---:|---|---:|
| Colombo (capital) | 615,000 | Jaffna | 129,000 |
| Dehiwala-Mount Lavinia | 196,000 | Kotte | 109,000 |
| | | Kandy | 104,000 |
| Moratuwa | 170,000 | Galle | 84,000 |

Source: Registrar General's Office.

### BIRTHS, MARRIAGES AND DEATHS

| | Registered live births | | Registered marriages | | Registered deaths | |
|---|---:|---:|---:|---:|---:|---:|
| | Number | Rate (per 1,000) | Number | Rate (per 1,000) | Number | Rate (per 1,000) |
| 1986 | 361,735 | 22.4 | 128,294 | 8.0 | 96,145 | 6.0 |
| 1987 | 357,723 | 21.8 | 125,996 | 7.7 | 97,756 | 6.0 |
| 1988 | 344,179 | 20.7 | 132,520 | 8.0 | 95,934 | 5.8 |
| 1989* | 357,964 | 21.3 | 141,533 | 8.4 | 104,590 | 6.2 |
| 1990* | 341,223 | 20.1 | 151,935 | 8.9 | 97,713 | 5.7 |
| 1991* | 363,068 | 21.0 | 154,856 | 9.0 | 96,940 | 5.6 |
| 1992* | 350,431 | 20.1 | n.a. | n.a. | 98,017 | 5.6 |

* Provisional.

**Expectation of life** (years at birth, 1981): Males 67.8; females 71.7.
Source: UN, *Demographic Yearbook*.

### ECONOMICALLY ACTIVE POPULATION*
(sample survey, October–December 1993)

| | Males | Females | Total |
|---|---:|---:|---:|
| Agriculture, hunting, forestry and fishing | 1,377,645 | 633,588 | 2,011,197 |
| Mining and quarrying | 93,117 | 20,457 | 113,572 |
| Manufacturing | 313,772 | 376,439 | 690,193 |
| Electricity, gas and water | 24,290 | 5,377 | 29,666 |
| Construction | 237,932 | 20,705 | 258,630 |
| Trade, restaurants and hotels | 476,683 | 97,339 | 573,997 |
| Transport, storage and communications | 204,348 | 11,672 | 216,012 |
| Financing, insurance, real estate and business services | 56,293 | 17,752 | 74,041 |
| Community, social and personal services | 659,557 | 433,990 | 1,093,505 |
| Activities not adequately defined | 158,985 | 6,724 | 165,704 |
| **Total employed** | 3,602,622 | 1,624,044 | 5,226,547 |
| Unemployed | 408,908 | 430,585 | 839,494 |
| **Total labour force** | 4,011,530 | 2,054,629 | 6,066,041 |

* Figures have been estimated independently, so totals may not be the sum of the component parts.

Source: Sri Lanka Labour Force Survey—4th Quarter 1993.

SRI LANKA
*Statistical Survey*

## Agriculture

**PRINCIPAL CROPS** ('000 metric tons)

|  | 1991 | 1992 | 1993 |
|---|---|---|---|
| Rice (paddy) | 2,389 | 2,340 | 2,450* |
| Maize | 34 | 29 | 30* |
| Millet | 7 | 5 | 7* |
| Potatoes | 67 | 79 | 80* |
| Sweet potatoes | 74 | 60 | 65* |
| Cassava (Manioc) | 367 | 302 | 310* |
| Dry beans* | 28 | 19 | 21 |
| Groundnuts (in shell) | 4 | 3 | 3* |
| Sesame seed* | 5 | 4 | 4 |
| Coconuts | 1,660 | 1,809 | 1,597† |
| Copra | 60 | 70 | 60† |
| Green peppers | 100 | 74 | 75* |
| Onions (dry) | 42 | 54 | 54* |
| Sugar cane | 851 | 731 | 780* |
| Coffee (green) | 8 | 9 | 8* |
| Cocoa beans | 5 | 6 | 5* |
| Tea (made)† | 250 | 179 | 232 |
| Tobacco (leaves) | 9 | 9 | 9* |
| Natural rubber | 104 | 105 | 110* |

* FAO estimate(s). † Unofficial figure(s).
Source: FAO, *Production Yearbook*.

**LIVESTOCK** ('000 head, year ending 30 September)

|  | 1991 | 1992 | 1993 |
|---|---|---|---|
| Buffaloes | 824 | 896 | 870 |
| Cattle | 1,477 | 1,568 | 1,600 |
| Sheep | 20 | 17 | 19 |
| Goats | 460 | 502 | 500 |
| Pigs | 84 | 91 | 90 |

Chickens (million): 8† in 1991; 9† in 1992; 9* in 1993.
* FAO estimate(s). † Unofficial figure.
Source: FAO, *Production Yearbook*.

**LIVESTOCK PRODUCTS** ('000 metric tons)

|  | 1991 | 1992 | 1993 |
|---|---|---|---|
| Beef and veal | 23 | 24* | 24 |
| Goat meat | 2 | 2* | 2 |
| Pig meat | 2 | 2* | 2 |
| Poultry meat | 15 | 14* | 14 |
| Cows' milk | 189 | 194 | 190 |
| Buffaloes' milk | 64 | 83 | 80 |
| Goats' milk | 5* | 6* | 6 |
| Hen eggs | 44.5† | 45.7† | 45.4 |
| Cattle and buffalo hides | 3.8* | 7.5* | 7.7 |

* FAO estimate. † Unofficial figure.
Source: FAO, *Production Yearbook*.

## Forestry

**ROUNDWOOD REMOVALS**
('000 cu m, excluding bark)

|  | 1990 | 1991 | 1992 |
|---|---|---|---|
| Sawlogs, veneer logs and logs for sleepers | 55 | 28 | 42 |
| Pulpwood | 75 | 75* | 75* |
| Other industrial wood* | 533 | 540 | 547 |
| Fuel wood | 8,349 | 8,456 | 8,566 |
| **Total** | 9,012 | 9,099 | 9,230 |

* FAO estimate(s).
Source: FAO, *Yearbook of Forest Products*.

**SAWNWOOD PRODUCTION** ('000 cu m, incl. railway sleepers)

|  | 1990 | 1991 | 1992 |
|---|---|---|---|
| **Total** | 10 | 5 | 5 |

Source: FAO, *Yearbook of Forest Products*.

## Fishing*

('000 metric tons)

|  | 1990 | 1991 | 1992 |
|---|---|---|---|
| Inland waters: |  |  |  |
| Freshwater fishes | 31.3 | 23.8 | 21.0 |
| Indian Ocean: |  |  |  |
| Marine fishes | 128.7 | 168.0 | 177.1 |
| Other marine animals | 5.4 | 6.2 | 8.0 |
| **Total catch** | 165.4 | 198.1 | 206.2 |

* Excluding (a) quantities landed by Sri Lanka craft in foreign ports, and (b) quantities landed by foreign craft in Sri Lanka ports.
Source: FAO, *Yearbook of Fishery Statistics*.

## Mining

(metric tons, unless otherwise indicated)

|  | 1988 | 1989 | 1990* |
|---|---|---|---|
| Ilmenite concentrates ('000 metric tons) | 78.0 | 101.4 | 69.5 |
| Rutile concentrates | 5,255 | 5,589 | 5,460 |
| Zirconium concentrates | 20,900 | 21,983 | 19,727 |
| Natural graphite—exports | 6,356 | 3,992 | 5,469 |
| Salt—unrefined ('000 metric tons) | 107 | 148 | 53 |

* Provisional.
Sources: State Mining and Mineral Development Corporation and National Salt Corporation.

## Industry

**SELECTED PRODUCTS**

|  | 1988 | 1989 | 1990 |
|---|---|---|---|
| Beer ('000 hectolitres) | 92 | 60 | n.a. |
| Cigarettes (million) | 4,328 | 5,136 | 5,620 |
| Cotton yarn ('000 metric tons) | 6.8 | 6.7 | 3.9 |
| Cement ('000 metric tons) | 633 | 596 | 566 |
| Raw sugar ('000 metric tons) | 24 | 26 | 24 |

## Finance

**CURRENCY AND EXCHANGE RATES**
**Monetary Units**
100 cents = 1 Sri Lanka rupee.

**Sterling and Dollar Equivalents** (31 December 1994)
£1 sterling = 78.19 rupees;
US $1 = 49.98 rupees;
1,000 Sri Lanka rupees = £12.79 = $20.01.

**Average Exchange Rate** (rupees per US $)
1992  43.830
1993  48.322
1994  49.415

# SRI LANKA

## BUDGET (million rupees)

| Revenue* | 1991 | 1992 | 1993‡ |
|---|---|---|---|
| Taxation | 68,157 | 76,352 | 87,274 |
| Taxes on income, profits, etc. | 9,722 | 10,966 | 13,658 |
| Taxes on property | 3,541 | 3,597 | 3,454 |
| Sales taxes | 21,430 | 24,095 | 29,382 |
| Excises | 10,597 | 10,232 | 12,410 |
| Other domestic taxes on goods and services | 3,113 | — | — |
| Import duties | 18,617 | 20,819 | 20,615 |
| Export duties | 1,137 | 821 | 57 |
| Other current revenue | 7,989 | 9,417 | 11,149 |
| Entrepreneurial and property income | 5,964 | 6,262 | 6,927 |
| Administrative fees, charges, etc. | 1,634 | 2,162 | 2,843 |
| Capital revenue | 33 | 11 | 72 |
| **Total** | 76,179 | 85,780 | 98,495 |

| Expenditure† | 1991 | 1992 | 1993‡ |
|---|---|---|---|
| General public services | 7,292 | 8,335 | 10,868 |
| Defence | 10,317 | 12,876 | 15,413 |
| Public order and safety | 4,624 | 5,192 | 5,368 |
| Education | 9,129 | 12,541 | 14,056 |
| Health | 5,229 | 6,541 | 7,064 |
| Social security and welfare | 19,221 | 12,569 | 21,231 |
| Housing and community amenities | 919 | 1,186 | 1,078 |
| Fuel and energy | 6,840 | 5,560 | 4,361 |
| Agriculture, forestry, fishing and hunting | 7,262 | 7,531 | 6,807 |
| Mining, manufacturing and construction | 402 | 533 | 1,860 |
| Transport and communications | 12,229 | 5,571 | 10,432 |
| Other economic affairs and services | 3,214 | 4,983 | 3,003 |
| Other purposes | 29,675 | 29,724 | 33,001 |
| Interest payments | 22,073 | 25,940 | 28,926 |
| **Total** | 109,061 | 114,588 | 134,229 |
| Current | 83,756 | 89,639 | 100,451 |
| Capital | 25,305 | 24,949 | 33,778 |

\* Excluding grants (all capital) received from abroad.
† Excluding lending minus repayments.
‡ Provisional.

## INTERNATIONAL RESERVES (US $ million at 31 December)

| | 1992 | 1993 | 1994 |
|---|---|---|---|
| Gold* | 37 | n.a. | n.a. |
| Reserve position in IMF | 28 | 28 | 30 |
| Foreign exchange | 899 | 1,601 | 2,016 |
| **Total** | 964 | n.a. | n.a. |

\* National valuation, based on cost of acquisition.
Source: IMF, *International Financial Statistics*.

## MONEY SUPPLY (million rupees at 31 December)

| | 1992 | 1993 | 1994 |
|---|---|---|---|
| Currency outside banks | 27,280 | 32,133 | 38,906 |
| Demand deposits at commercial banks | 22,741 | 27,169 | 31,415 |

Source: IMF, *International Financial Statistics*.

## COST OF LIVING
(Consumer Price Index, Colombo; base: 1970 = 100)

| | 1991 | 1992 | 1993 |
|---|---|---|---|
| Food | 893.3 | 1,000.0 | 1,112.3 |
| Fuel and light | 1,654.8 | 1,715.1 | 2,005.9 |
| Clothing | 494.1 | 527.0 | 570.1 |
| Miscellaneous | 748.0 | 860.1 | 912.8 |
| **All items** | 818.7 | 912.0 | 1,019.1 |

## NATIONAL ACCOUNTS (million rupees at current prices)
### Gross Domestic Product by Economic Activity

| | 1991 | 1992 | 1993* |
|---|---|---|---|
| Agriculture, hunting, forestry and fishing | 81,926.4 | 88,839.7 | 103,440.5 |
| Mining and quarrying | 4,047.9 | 4,418.3 | 5,432.8 |
| Manufacturing | 62,797.9 | 72,292.9 | 85,313.9 |
| Construction | 24,857.6 | 27,563.8 | 32,794.5 |
| Electricity, gas, water and sanitary services | 6,499.6 | 7,416.8 | 10,362.1 |
| Transport, storage and communications | 35,268.9 | 40,463.0 | 47,339.0 |
| Wholesale and retail trade | 75,247.6 | 91,086.4 | 107,154.5 |
| Banking, insurance and real estate | 17,103.2 | 21,876.7 | 28,671.5 |
| Ownership of dwellings | 3,398.1 | 3,729.1 | 3,782.3 |
| Public administration and defence | 28,852.3 | 29,856.3 | 37,429.4 |
| Other services | 10,560.5 | 12,718.2 | 14,389.4 |
| **Sub-total** | 350,560.1 | 400,261.2 | 476,109.9 |
| Import duties | 19,160.0 | 24,494.2 | 23,527.1 |
| **Total** | 369,720.1 | 424,755.4 | 499,637.0 |

\* Provisional.

## BALANCE OF PAYMENTS (US $ million)

| | 1991 | 1992 | 1993 |
|---|---|---|---|
| Merchandise exports f.o.b. | 2,003.3 | 2,301.4 | 2,785.7 |
| Merchandise imports f.o.b. | −2,808.0 | −3,016.5 | −3,527.8 |
| **Trade balance** | −804.7 | −715.1 | −742.1 |
| Exports of services | 546.6 | 621.4 | 634.4 |
| Imports of services | −762.5 | −823.2 | −873.9 |
| Other income received | 54.5 | 68.1 | 110.7 |
| Other income paid | −232.5 | −246.2 | −229.7 |
| Private unrequited transfers (net) | 401.3 | 461.7 | 559.8 |
| Official unrequited transfers (net) | 202.4 | 182.6 | 160.2 |
| **Current balance** | −594.8 | −450.7 | −380.6 |
| Direct investment (net) | 43.8 | 121.0 | 187.6 |
| Portfolio investment (net) | 32.1 | 25.7 | 67.2 |
| Other capital (net) | 613.2 | 354.6 | 669.6 |
| Net errors and omissions | 225.6 | 173.3 | 131.1 |
| **Overall balance** | 319.9 | 223.9 | 674.9 |

Source: IMF, *International Financial Statistics*.

# SRI LANKA

## External Trade

Note: Data exclude military goods. Exports include stores and bunkers for foreign ships and aircraft.

### PRINCIPAL COMMODITIES
(distribution by SITC, US $ million)

| Imports c.i.f. | 1990 | 1991 | 1992 |
|---|---|---|---|
| **Food and live animals** | 477.2 | 612.4 | 504.6 |
| Dairy products and birds' eggs | 57.9 | 83.4 | 66.9 |
| Milk and cream | 55.3 | 79.3 | 64.0 |
| Cereals and cereal preparations | 168.1 | 151.1 | 147.4 |
| Wheat (unmilled) | 87.9 | 81.1 | 66.1 |
| Vegetables and fruit | 37.5 | 81.2 | 59.9 |
| Sugar, sugar preparations and honey | 131.8 | 163.0 | 118.4 |
| Raw beet and cane sugar | 109.6 | 157.2 | 111.3 |
| **Crude materials (inedible) except fuels** | 64.8 | 98.8 | 85.7 |
| **Mineral fuels, lubricants, etc.** | 333.2 | 434.9 | 309.3 |
| Petroleum, petroleum products, etc. | 328.5 | 428.2 | 298.8 |
| **Chemicals and related products** | 308.5 | 355.9 | 309.8 |
| Organic chemicals | 69.7 | 47.7 | 34.8 |
| Fertilizers (manufactured) | 64.7 | 76.0 | 49.2 |
| Plastic materials, etc. | 54.1 | 77.8 | 63.4 |
| **Basic manufactures** | 812.3 | 1,320.8 | 1,247.4 |
| Paper, paperboard and manufactures | 75.5 | 103.6 | 87.1 |
| Textile yarn, fabrics, etc. | 411.8 | 772.6 | 749.1 |
| Textile yarn | 40.7 | 89.8 | 80.1 |
| Cotton fabrics (woven) | 103.1 | 181.9 | 207.1 |
| Bleached and mercerized fabrics | 79.3 | 139.4 | 163.8 |
| Woven man-made fibre fabrics | 150.5 | 261.5 | 240.6 |
| Knitted, etc., fabrics | 71.4 | 141.6 | 130.5 |
| Non-metallic mineral manufactures | 132.4 | 164.9 | 166.9 |
| Pearls, precious and semi-precious stones | 74.3 | 81.9 | 78.9 |
| Diamonds, non-industrial, unset | 73.5 | 75.6 | 76.4 |
| Iron and steel | 80.1 | 114.8 | 103.2 |
| **Machinery and transport equipment** | 504.9 | 745.2 | 737.2 |
| Machinery specialized for particular industries (excl. metalworking) | 68.2 | 126.2 | 149.5 |
| Machinery for textiles and leather | 24.4 | 57.4 | 77.3 |
| General industrial machinery and equipment | 63.8 | 88.0 | 99.3 |
| Electrical machinery, apparatus and appliances | 116.2 | 136.3 | 155.2 |
| Road vehicles and parts* | 162.7 | 251.1 | 208.9 |
| Lorries and trucks | 41.6 | 76.5 | 75.4 |
| **Miscellaneous manufactured articles** | 103.6 | 238.4 | 214.2 |
| **Total** (incl. others) | 2,632.8 | 3,866.1 | 3,472.7 |

* Excluding tyres, engines and electrical parts.

Source: UN, *International Trade Statistics Yearbook*.

**1993** (million rupees): Sugar 5,621, Petroleum and petroleum products 13,978, Machinery and transport equipment 26,964; **Total** (incl. others) 181,381. Source: Customs, Sri Lanka.

| Exports f.o.b. | 1990 | 1991 | 1992 |
|---|---|---|---|
| **Food and live animals** | 626.6 | 754.3 | 507.5 |
| Vegetables and fruit | 61.3 | 88.6 | 82.8 |
| Edible nuts (fresh and dried) | 47.7 | 68.1 | 66.2 |
| Coconuts (fresh and dried) | 38.7 | 53.8 | 59.9 |
| Coffee, tea, cocoa and spices | 533.8 | 628.0 | 384.6 |
| Tea | 493.0 | 570.3 | 341.6 |
| Spices | 39.5 | 55.2 | 41.5 |
| **Crude materials (inedible) except fuels** | 147.3 | 147.7 | 128.5 |
| Rubber, crude | 76.9 | 82.6 | 69.8 |
| **Basic manufactures** | 255.5 | 358.9 | 351.0 |
| Textile yarn, fabrics, etc. | 24.9 | 54.1 | 82.3 |
| Non-metallic mineral manufactures | 177.3 | 199.7 | 191.8 |
| Pearls, precious and semi-precious stones | 162.4 | 170.3 | 161.1 |
| Diamonds, non-industrial, unset | 89.2 | 93.1 | 103.3 |
| **Machinery and transport equipment** | 54.3 | 77.9 | 45.5 |
| **Miscellaneous manufactured articles** | 687.9 | 1,154.0 | 1,321.9 |
| Clothing and accessories (excl. footwear) | 642.8 | 1,074.2 | 1,200.7 |
| **Total** (incl. others) | 1,912.2 | 2,652.7 | 2,490.0 |

Source: UN, *International Trade Statistics Yearbook*.

**1993** (million rupees): Tea 19,597, Rubber 3,086, Precious and semi-precious stones 10,269; **Total** (incl. others) 137,994. Source: Customs, Sri Lanka.

### PRINCIPAL TRADING PARTNERS ('000 rupees)

| Imports | 1991 | 1992 | 1993 |
|---|---|---|---|
| Australia | 1,513,107 | 2,230,348 | 2,888,899 |
| Belgium | 2,231,652 | 3,407,465 | 3,044,239 |
| China, People's Republic | 4,922,013 | 5,302,269 | 7,244,682 |
| France | 1,441,070 | 1,896,424 | 2,441,909 |
| Germany | 4,214,540 | 5,579,507 | 6,685,645 |
| India | 9,105,319 | 13,230,208 | 16,569,391 |
| Iran | 5,987,869 | 5,128,912 | 4,642,038 |
| Italy | 797,332 | 1,142,369 | 2,107,890 |
| Japan | 14,827,602 | 18,214,484 | 21,869,621 |
| Korea, Republic | 9,061,733 | 9,181,998 | 12,641,484 |
| Netherlands | 1,988,526 | 1,868,622 | n.a. |
| Pakistan | 3,050,563 | 2,891,659 | 2,670,441 |
| Singapore | 5,584,354 | 10,415,967 | 10,049,359 |
| United Kingdom | 6,880,462 | 7,574,747 | 8,930,085 |
| USA | 7,221,016 | 6,984,749 | 6,343,401 |
| **Total** (incl. others) | 127,830,821 | 149,780,179 | 181,381,167 |

Source: Customs, Sri Lanka.

| Exports* | 1991 | 1992 | 1993 |
|---|---|---|---|
| Australia | 1,011,239 | 1,054,342 | 136,052 |
| Canada | 1,324,082 | 1,699,931 | 1,752,848 |
| France | 2,628,467 | 3,949,077 | 4,161,803 |
| Germany | 6,156,786 | 9,282,303 | 10,992,079 |
| Iran | 3,227,470 | 2,116,432 | 979,524 |
| Italy | 1,537,728 | 2,074,377 | 2,054,031 |
| Japan | 4,203,700 | 5,610,967 | 7,149,653 |
| Netherlands | 2,442,717 | 4,282,604 | 5,200,349 |
| Pakistan | 1,322,961 | 1,251,625 | 1,713,329 |
| Saudi Arabia | 1,587,602 | 1,602,832 | 1,422,090 |
| Singapore | 2,791,499 | 1,457,424 | 2,352,912 |
| United Kingdom | 5,221,523 | 7,460,299 | 9,835,661 |
| USA | 23,127,675 | 36,711,670 | 48,652,648 |
| **Total** (incl. others) | 82,224,847 | 107,508,533 | 137,993,665 |

* Incl. re-exports.

Source: Customs, Sri Lanka.

SRI LANKA                                                                                             *Statistical Survey*

## Transport

**RAILWAYS** (traffic)

|  | 1991 | 1992 | 1993* |
|---|---|---|---|
| Passenger-km (million) | 2,690 | 2,613 | 2,852 |
| Freight ton-km (million) | 169 | 177 | 168 |

* Provisional.
Source: Sri Lanka Railways.

**ROAD TRAFFIC** (motor vehicles in use at 31 December)

|  | 1991 | 1992 | 1993 |
|---|---|---|---|
| Cars and cabs | 180,135 | 189,477 | 197,300 |
| Motor cycles | 450,372 | 516,205 | 570,136 |
| Buses | 43,259 | 46,162 | 47,692 |
| Lorries and vans* | 137,539 | 152,648 | 166,491 |
| Agricultural tractors and engines | 93,068 | 98,555 | 105,202 |
| **Total** | 904,373 | 1,003,047 | 1,086,821 |

* Including ambulances, hearses and dual-purpose vehicles.
Source: Department of Motor Traffic.

**SHIPPING**
Merchant Fleet ('000 gross registered tons at 30 June)

|  | 1990 | 1991 | 1992 |
|---|---|---|---|
| Total | 350 | 333 | 285 |

Source: UN, *Statistical Yearbook*.

**International Sea-borne Shipping***
(freight traffic, '000 metric tons)

|  | 1991 | 1992 | 1993 |
|---|---|---|---|
| Goods loaded | 4,721 | 4,271 | 5,443 |
| Goods unloaded | 8,970 | 9,260 | 11,055 |

* Ports of Colombo, Galle and Trincomalee.
Source: Sri Lanka Ports Authority.

**CIVIL AVIATION** (traffic on scheduled services)

|  | 1991 | 1992 | 1993 |
|---|---|---|---|
| Kilometres flown ('000) | 19,780 | 24,222 | 21,862 |
| Passengers carried | 832,740 | 1,045,589 | 993,847 |
| Passenger-km ('000) | 3,449,156 | 4,104,396 | 3,624,030 |

* Provisional.

## Tourism

**FOREIGN VISITORS BY ORIGIN**
(excluding cruise passengers and excursionists)

|  | 1990 | 1991 | 1992 |
|---|---|---|---|
| Western Europe | 190,612 | 195,041 | 252,852 |
| Asia | 79,776 | 92,543 | 107,103 |
| North America | 8,474 | 11,519 | 12,954 |
| Eastern Europe | 7,520 | 337 | 3,633 |
| Australasia | 7,854 | 12,247 | 12,759 |
| Others | 3,652 | 6,016 | 4,368 |
| **Total** | 297,888 | 317,703 | 393,669 |

Source: Department of Census and Statistics.
**Receipts from Tourism** (US $ million): 132.4 in 1990; 156.5 in 1991; 198.5 in 1992.
Source: Ceylon Tourist Board.
**Tourist Arrivals:** 392,215 in 1993; 407,511 in 1994 (incl. 253,899 from Western Europe).

## Communications Media

|  | 1990 | 1991 | 1992 |
|---|---|---|---|
| Telephones ('000 main lines in use) | 121 | 126 | n.a. |
| Radio receivers ('000) | 3,400 | 3,460 | 3,525 |
| Television receivers ('000) | 600 | n.a. | 865 |
| Books published (number of titles) | 2,455 | 2,535 | 4,225 |
| Daily newspapers (number) | 18 | n.a. | 10 |
| Daily newspapers (total circulation, '000) | 550* | n.a. | 480* |

* Estimate.
Sources: UN, *Statistical Yearbook*, and UNESCO, *Statistical Yearbook*.

## Education

|  | 1990 | 1991 | 1992 |
|---|---|---|---|
| Schools | 10,382 | 10,520 | 10,586 |
|   Primary | 4,402 | 4,398 | 4,337 |
|   Junior secondary | 3,586 | 3,593 | 3,596 |
|   Senior secondary | 1,937 | 2,070 | 2,175 |
|   Pirivenas* | 457 | 459 | 478 |
| Pupils | 4,232,356 | 4,258,697 | 4,289,334 |
| Teachers | 184,822 | 177,231 | 182,756 |

* For Buddhist clergy and lay students.
Source: Ministry of Education.

# Directory

## The Constitution

The Constitution of the Democratic Socialist Republic of Sri Lanka was approved by the National State Assembly (renamed Parliament) on 17 August 1978, and promulgated on 7 September 1978. The following is a summary of its main provisions.

### FUNDAMENTAL RIGHTS

The Constitution guarantees the fundamental rights and freedoms of all citizens, including freedom of thought, conscience and worship and equal entitlement before the law.

### THE PRESIDENT

The President is Head of State, and exercises all executive powers including defence of the Republic. The President is directly elected by the people for a term of six years, and is eligible for re-election. The President's powers include the right to:
 (i) choose to hold any portfolio in the Cabinet;
 (ii) appoint or dismiss the Prime Minister or any other minister;
 (iii) preside at ceremonial sittings of Parliament;
 (iv) dismiss Parliament at will; and
 (v) submit to a national referendum any Bill or matter of national importance which has been rejected by Parliament.

### LEGISLATURE

The Parliament is the legislative power of the people. It consists of such number of representatives of the people as a Delimitation Commission shall determine. The members of Parliament are directly elected by a system of modified proportional representation. By-elections are abolished, successors to members of Parliament being appointed by the head of the party which nominated the outgoing member at the previous election. Parliament exercises the judicial power of the people through courts, tribunals and institutions created and established or recognized by the Constitution or established by law. Parliament has control over public finance.

### OTHER PROVISIONS

**Religion**
Buddhism has the foremost place among religions and it is the duty of the State to protect and foster Buddhism, while assuring every citizen the freedom to adopt the religion of their choice.

**Language**
The Constitution recognizes two official languages, Sinhala and Tamil. Either of the national languages may be used by all citizens in transactions with government institutions.

**Amendments**
Amendments to the Constitution require endorsement by a two-thirds majority in Parliament. In February 1979 the Constitution was amended by allowing members of Parliament who resigned or were expelled from their party to retain their seats, in certain circumstances. In January 1981 Parliament amended the Constitution to increase its membership from 168 to 169. An amendment enabling the President to seek re-election after four years was approved in August 1982. In February 1983 an amendment providing for by-elections to fill vacant seats in Parliament was approved. An amendment banning parties that advocate separatism was approved by Parliament in August 1983. In November 1987 Parliament adopted an amendment providing for the creation of eight provincial councils (the northern and eastern provinces were to be merged as one administrative unit). In December 1988 Parliament adopted an amendment allowing Tamil the same status as Sinhala, as one of the country's two official languages.

## The Government

### HEAD OF STATE

**President:** CHANDRIKA BANDARANAIKE KUMARATUNGA (sworn in 12 November 1994).

### CABINET
(June 1995)

All members of the Cabinet belong to the Sri Lanka Freedom Party apart from the five indicated.

**President, Minister of Finance, of Defence, of Buddha Sasana, of Planning and of Ethnic Affairs and National Integration:** CHANDRIKA BANDARANAIKE KUMARATUNGA.
**Prime Minister:** SIRIMAVO R. D. BANDARANAIKE.
**Minister of Public Administration, of Local Government and of Plantation Industries:** RATNASIRI WICKRAMANAYAKE.
**Minister of Irrigation, and of Power and Energy and Deputy Minister of Defence:** Col ANURUDDHA RATWATTE.
**Minister of Home Affairs and Provincial Councils and of Co-operatives:** AMARASIRI DODANGODA.
**Minister of Foreign Affairs:** LAKSHMAN KADIRAGAMAR.
**Minister of Cultural and Religious Affairs:** LAKSHMAN JAYAKODY.
**Minister of Science, Technology and Human Resources Development:** BERNARD SOYSA (Lanka Sama Samaja Party).
**Minister of Agriculture, Lands and Forests:** D. M. JAYARATNA.
**Minister of Labour and Vocational Training:** MAHINDA RAJAPAKSE.
**Minister of Shipping and Ports and of Rehabilitation and Reconstruction:** MOHAMED H. M. ASHROFF (Sri Lanka Muslim Congress).
**Minister of Information and of Tourism and Aviation:** DHARMASIRI SENANAYAKE.
**Minister of Trade, Commerce and Food:** KINGSLEY WICKRAMARATNA.
**Minister of Industrial Development:** C. V. GUNARATNA.
**Minister of Rural Industries:** W. E. K. R. SAVUMYAMOORTHY THONDAMAN (Ceylon Workers' Congress).
**Minister of Education and Higher Education:** RICHARD PATHIRANA.
**Minister of Housing, Construction and Public Utilities:** NIMAL SIRIPALA DE SILVA.
**Minister of Posts and Telecommunications:** MANGALA SAMARAWEERA.
**Minister of Youth Affairs and Sports and of Rural Development:** D. M. S. B. DISSANAYAKE.
**Minister of Transport and Highways, of the Environment and of Women's Affairs:** SRIMANI ATHULATHMUDALI (Democratic United National Front).
**Minister of External Trade, and of Justice and Constitutional Affairs and Deputy Minister of Finance:** Prof. G. L. PEIRIS.
**Minister of Health and of Social Services:** A. H.M. FOWZIE.
**Minister of Fisheries and Aquatic Resources:** INDIKA GUNAWARDENA (Communist Party of Sri Lanka).

### MINISTRIES

**President's Secretariat:** Republic Sq., Colombo 1; tel. (1) 24801.
**Prime Minister's Office:** 150 R. A. de Mel Mawatha, Colombo 3; tel. (1) 433215; fax (1) 437017.
**Ministry of Agriculture, Lands and Forests:** 73/1 Galle Rd, Colombo 3; tel. (1) 26346; telex 21434.
**Ministry of Buddha Sasana:** Colombo.
**Ministry of Co-operatives:** 330 Union Place, Colombo 2.
**Ministry of Cultural and Religious Affairs:** 9th Floor, 'Rakshana Mandiraya', 21 Vauxhall St, Colombo 2; tel. (1) 437383.
**Ministry of Defence:** 15/5 Baladaksha Mawatha, POB 572, Colombo 3; tel. (1) 430860; telex 21139; fax (1) 541529.
**Ministry of Education and Higher Education:** 'Isurupaya', Pelawatta, Battaramulla; tel. 865141; fax 869326.
**Ministry of Ethnic Affairs and National Integration:** Colombo.
**Ministry of Finance:** Galle Face Secretariat, Colombo 1; tel. (1) 33937; telex 21409; fax (1) 449823.
**Ministry of Fisheries and Aquatic Resources:** New Secretariat, Colombo 10; tel. (1) 4461843; telex 21419; fax (1) 541184.
**Ministry of Foreign Affairs:** Republic Bldg, Colombo 1; tel. (1) 325371; telex 21139.
**Ministry of Handlooms and Textile Industries:** No. 375, 'Vilasitha Niwasa', Havelock Rd, Colombo 6; tel. (1) 508032; fax (1) 503211.
**Ministry of Health and Women's Affairs:** 5th Floor, Inland Revenue Bldg, Sir Chittampalam A. Gardiner Mawatha, POB 513, Colombo 2; tel. (1) 433711.
**Ministry of Housing, Construction and Public Utilities:** Colombo.
**Ministry of Industrial Development:** Colombo.

# SRI LANKA

**Ministry of Information:** 34 Malay St, Colombo 2; tel. (1) 545777.

**Ministry of Irrigation:** 500 T. B. Jayah Mawatha, Colombo 10; tel. (1) 36271.

**Ministry of Justice and Constitutional Affairs:** Hulftsdorp, Colombo 12; tel. (1) 323979.

**Ministry of Labour and Vocational Training:** 2nd Floor, Labour Secretariat, Narahenpita, Colombo 5; tel. (1) 81991; telex 22234.

**Ministry of Local Government:** 'Sethsiripaya', Sri Jayewardenepura Kotte, Battaramulla.

**Ministry of Media, Tourism and Aviation:** 45 St Michael's Rd, Colombo 3; tel. (1) 540221.

**Ministry of National Reconciliation:** Colombo.

**Ministry of Planning:** 'Sethsiripaya', 3rd Floor, Sri Jayewardenepura Kotte, POB 6, Battaramulla; tel. 562721.

**Ministry of Posts and Telecommunications:** Old CTO Bldg, Lotus Rd, Colombo 1; tel. (1) 22591; telex 21490.

**Ministry of Power and Energy:** 50 Sir Chittampalam A. Gardiner Mawatha, Colombo 2; tel. (1) 422051.

**Ministry of Privatization of Public Enterprises:** Colombo.

**Ministry of Public Administration, Home Affairs, Plantation Industries and Parliamentary Affairs:** Independence Sq., Colombo 7; tel. (1) 696211; telex 23238; fax (1) 695279.

**Ministry of Regional Development:** 244 Galle Rd, Colombo 4; tel. (1) 580146.

**Ministry of Rehabilitation and Reconstruction:** Colombo.

**Ministry of Rural Development:** Independence Sq., Colombo 7; tel. (1) 596007.

**Ministry of Science, Technology and Human Resources Development:** 73/1 Galle Rd, Colombo 3; tel. (1) 327553; telex 21248; fax (1) 449402.

**Ministry of Shipping and Ports:** Colombo.

**Ministry of Social Services:** Colombo; tel. (1) 94438.

**Ministry of State Plantations:** 18 Gregory's Rd, Colombo 7; tel. (1) 31747.

**Ministry of Trade, Commerce and Food:** 21 Rakshana Mandlraya, Vauxhall St, Colombo 2; tel. (1) 35601; telex 21245.

**Ministry of Transport and Highways:** 1 D. R. Wijewardene Mawatha, POB 588, Colombo 10; tel. (1) 687105; fax (1) 694547.

**Ministry of Youth Affairs and Sports:** 4th Floor, 111/1 Inland Revenue Bldg, Sir Chittampalam A. Gardiner Mawatha, POB 510, Colombo 2; tel. (1) 422263; fax (1) 546602.

## President and Legislature

### PRESIDENT

**Presidential Election, 9 November 1994**

| Candidate | Votes | Percentage of votes |
|---|---|---|
| CHANDRIKA BANDARANAIKE KUMARATUNGA (PA) | 4,709,205 | 62.28 |
| SRIMA DISSANAYAKE (UNP) | 2,715,283 | 35.91 |
| HUDSON SAMARASINGHE (Independent) | 58,886 | 0.78 |
| Dr HARISCHANDRA WIJETUNGA (Sinhalaye Mahasammatha Bhoomiputra Party) | 32,651 | 0.43 |
| A. J. RANASINGHE (Independent) | 22,752 | 0.30 |
| NIHAL GALAPPATHY (Sri Lanka Progressive Front) | 22,749 | 0.30 |
| Total | 7,561,526 | 100.00 |

### PARLIAMENT

**Speaker:** K. B. RATNAYAKE.

**General Election, 16 August 1994**

| Party | Seats |
|---|---|
| People's Alliance | 105 |
| United National Party (UNP) | 94 |
| Independent Group (Jaffna) (Eelam People's Democratic Party—EPDP) | 9 |
| Sri Lanka Muslim Congress (SLMC) | 7 |
| Tamil United Liberation Front (TULF) | 5 |
| Democratic People's Liberation Front (DPLF) | 3 |
| Sri Lanka Progressive Front | 1 |
| Independent Group (Nuwara Eliya) | 1 |
| Total | 225 |

Note: Direct elections were held in 22 districts for 196 of the 225 seats on the basis of a proportional representation system involving preferential voting; the remaining 29 were chosen from party lists according to each party's national share of the vote.

## Political Organizations

**All Ceylon Tamil Congress:** Congress House, 120 Main St, Jaffna; tel. (21) 22551; f. 1944; aims to secure Tamil self-determination; Gen. Sec. KUMAR PONNAMBALAM.

**Ceylon Workers' Congress (CWC):** 19 St Michael's Rd, POB 12, Colombo 3; tel. (1) 436332; telex 22894; fax (1) 436341; f. 1939; represents the interests of workers (mainly of Indian Tamil origin) on tea plantations; Pres. W. E. K. R. SAVUMYAMOORTHY THONDAMAN; Gen. Sec. MUTHU SANGARALINGAM SELLASWAMMY.

**Communist Party of Sri Lanka (CPSL):** 91 Dr N. M. Perera Mawatha, Colombo 8; tel. (1) 694945; fax (1) 691610; f. 1943; advocates establishment of socialist society; seeks broadening of democratic rights and processes, political solution to ethnic problem, defence of and presses for social justice; Chair. PIETER KEUNEMAN; Gen. Sec. RAJA COLLURE.

**Democratic People's Liberation Front (DPLF):** has operated as a national political party since Sept. 1988; political wing of the People's Liberation Organization of Tamil Eelam (PLOTE); Leader DHARMALINGAM SITHADTHAN.

**Democratic United National Front (DUNF):** f. 1991 by a dissident group of UNP politicians; 500,000 mems; Gen. Sec. G. M. PREMACHANDRA.

**Democratic Workers' Congress (DWC)** (Political Wing): 82-1/2 Sri Vijiragnana Mawatha, Dematagoda Rd, POB 1009, Colombo 9; tel. (1) 691279; fax (1) 435961; f. 1939 as trade union, f. 1978 as political party; aims to eliminate social and economic exploitation and inequality; 201,700 mems (1994); Pres. V. P. GANESAN; Political Gen. Sec. MANO GANESHAN.

**Desha Vimukthi Janatha Party** (National Liberation People's Party): has operated as a national political party since Sept. 1988.

**Deshapriya Janatha Viyaparaya (DJV)** (Patriotic People's Movement): militant, Sinhalese group; associated with the JVP.

**Eelam National Democratic Liberation Front (ENDLF):** Tamil; supports 1987 Indo-Sri Lankan peace accord; has operated as a national political party since Sept. 1988; Gen. Sec. G. GNANASEKARAN; Dep. Gen. Sec. P. MANOHARAN.

**Eelam People's Democratic Party (EPDP):** Tamil; Sec.-Gen. DOUGLAS DEVANANDA; Political Sec. N. RAMAIAH.

**Eelam People's Revolutionary Liberation Front (EPRLF):** Tamil rights group; c. 1,000 mems; Leader ANNAMALAI VARADHARAJAH PERUMAL; Gen. Sec. SURESH K. PREMACHANDRAN.

**Eelavar Democratic Front:** fmrly known as Eelam Revolutionary Organization of Students (EROS); Tamil separatist group; Leader VELUPILLAI BALAKUMAR.

**Eksath Lanka Jathika Peramuna:** f. by fmr mems of the UNP.

**Janatha Vimukthi Peramuna (JVP)** (People's Liberation Front): Colombo; f. 1964, banned following a coup attempt in 1971, regained legal status in 1977, banned again in Aug. 1983, but regained legal status in May 1988; Marxist; Sinhalese support; c. 2,000 mems; effectively eradicated as a result of military action in late 1989 and early 1990.

**Lanka Sama Samaja Party (LSSP)** (Lanka Equal Society Party): 457 Union Place, Colombo 2; tel. (1) 696903; f. 1935; Trotskyist; Leader BERNARD SOYSA; Gen. Sec. BATTY WEERAKOON.

**Liberal Party:** Leader Dr CHANAKA AMARATUNGA.

**Mahajana Eksath Peramuna (MEP)** (People's United Front): 75 Gothami Rd, Borella, Colombo 8; tel. (1) 595450; f. 1956; Sinhalese

# SRI LANKA

and Buddhist support; left-wing; advocates economic self-reliance; Pres. DINESH C. R. GUNAWARDENA.

**Muslim United Liberation Front:** has operated as a national political party since Sept. 1988.

**Nava Sama Samaja Party (NSSP)** (New Equal Society Party): 17 Barrak Lane, Colombo 2; tel. (1) 24053; f. 1977; Trotskyist; Gen. Sec. Dr VICKRAMABAHU BANDARA KARUNARATHNE; Popular leaders VASUDEVA NANAYAKKARA, Dr SUNIL RATHNAPRIYA, P. D. SARANAPALA (Sinhalese), V. THIRNNAKARASU (Tamil).

**People's Alliance (PA):** f. 1993 as a left-wing alliance, incl. communists and Trotskyists; Leader CHANDRIKA BANDARANAIKE KUMARATUNGA; Gen. Sec. Prof. G. L. PEIRIS.

**Sri Lanka Freedom Party (SLFP):** 301 T. B. Jayah Mawatha, Colombo 10; tel. (1) 696289; f. 1951; democratic socialist; advocates a non-aligned foreign policy, industrial development in both the state sector and the private sector, rapid modernization in education and in the economy, and safeguards for minorities; Pres. SIRIMAVO R. D. BANDARANAIKE; Dep. Pres. CHANDRIKA BANDARANAIKE KUMARATUNGA; Gen. Sec. DHARMASIRI SENANAYAKE.

**Sri Lanka Mahajana (People's) Party (SLMP):** 82 Sri Vajiragnana Mawatha, Colombo 9; tel. (1) 696038; f. 1984 by fmr mems of the SLFP; social democrats; Leader SARATH KONGAHAGE. Gen. Sec. PREMASIRI PERERA.

**People's Front of the Liberation Tigers (PFLT):** f. 1989; political wing of the LTTE (see below); Leader GOPALSWAMY MAHENDRARAJAH ('MAHATHYA'); Gen. Sec. YOGARATNAM YOGI.

**Singhalaye Nithahas Peramuna** (Sinhalese Freedom Front): Sri Panchananda Charity Bldg, Kelani Railway Station Rd, Colombo; f. 1994; nationalist, Buddhist; Pres. ARYA SENA TERA; Sec. Prof. NALIN DE SILVA.

**Sri Lanka Muslim Congress (SLMC):** f. 1980; has operated as a national political party since 1986; Pres. MOHAMED H. M. ASHROFF.

**Sri Lanka Progressive Front:** c/o Parliament, Colombo.

**Tamil Eelam Liberation Organization (TELO):** supports 1987 Indo-Sri Lankan peace accord; has operated as a national political party since Sept. 1988; Leader Sri SABARATNAM.

**Tamil United Liberation Front (TULF):** 238 Main St, Jaffna; tel. (21) 352; f. 1949; aims to establish a separate autonomous Tamil region, known as 'Eelam', with the right of self-determination; Pres. MURUGESU SIVASITHAMPARAM; Vice-Pres. R. SAMBANTHAN; Sec.-Gen. NEELAN TIRUCHELVAM.

**United National Party (UNP):** 400 Kotte Rd, Pitakotte; tel. (1) 865375; f. 1947; democratic socialist; aims at a non-aligned foreign policy, supports Sinhala as the official language and state aid to denominational schools; Leader RANIL WICKREMASINGHE; Chair. A. C. S. HAMEED; Gen. Sec. GAMINI ATUKORALE.

**Up-Country People's Front:** represents interests of workers (mainly of Indian Tamil origin) on tea plantations.

Tamil separatist groups also include the Liberation Tigers of Tamil Eelam (LTTE; Leader VELUPILLAI PRABHAKARAN; Political Spokesman ANTON BALASINGHAM), the Tamil Eelam Liberation Front (TELF; Gen. Sec. M. K. EELAVENTHAN), the People's Liberation Organization of Tamil Eelam (PLOTE; Leader DHARMALINGAM SITHADTHAN; Vice-Pres. KARUVAI A. SRIKANTHASAMI), the People's Revolutionary Action Group, the Ellalan Force and the Tamil People's Protection Party.

## Diplomatic Representation

### EMBASSIES AND HIGH COMMISSIONS IN SRI LANKA

**Australia:** 3 Cambridge Place, POB 742, Colombo 7; tel. (1) 698767; telex 21157; fax (1) 686939; High Commissioner: BILL TWEDDELL.

**Bangladesh:** 286 Bauddhaloka Mawatha, Colombo 7; tel. (1) 502397; telex 21454; fax (1) 508123; High Commissioner: SHAMSHER M. CHOWDHURY.

**Canada:** 6 Gregory's Rd, Cinnamon Gdns, POB 1006, Colombo 7; tel. (1) 695841; telex 21106; fax (1) 687049; High Commissioner: BENNO T. PFLANZ.

**China, People's Republic:** 191 Dharmapala Mawatha, Colombo 7; tel. (1) 596459; Ambassador: ZHANG CHENGLI.

**Cuba:** 30/58 Longdon Place, Colombo 7; tel. (1) 589778; telex 21240; Ambassador: ROLANDO LÓPEZ DEL AMO.

**Czech Republic:** 47–47A Horton Place, Colombo 7; tel. (1) 694766; telex 21206.

**Egypt:** 39 Dickman's Rd, Colombo 5; tel. (1) 508752; telex 21127; fax (1) 585292; Ambassador: HANY ABDEL HAMID AL-ABBADY.

**Finland:** 81 Barnes Place, Colombo 7; tel. (1) 698819; telex 22651; fax (1) 698820; Ambassador: SATU MARJATTA RASI (resident in New Delhi, India).

**France:** 89 Rosmead Place, Colombo 7; tel. (1) 699750; telex 21191; fax (1) 699039; Ambassador: JEAN-FRANÇOIS BOUFFANDEAU.

**Germany:** 40 Alfred House Ave, POB 658, Colombo 3; tel. (1) 580431; telex 21119; fax (1) 580440; Ambassador: Dr MICHAEL SCHMIDT.

**Holy See:** 220 Bauddhaloka Mawatha, Colombo 7 (Apostolic Nunciature); tel. (1) 582554; fax (1) 580906; Apostolic Nuncio: Most Rev. Dr OSVALDO PADILLA, Titular Archbishop of Pia.

**India:** 36–38 Galle Rd, Colombo 3; tel. (1) 421605; telex 21132; High Commissioner: NARESHWAR DAYAL.

**Indonesia:** 1 Police Park Terrace, Colombo 5; tel. (1) 580113; telex 21223; Ambassador: JUNIZAR JACUB.

**Iraq:** 19 Barnes Place, POB 79, Colombo 7; tel. (1) 698733; telex 21166; Ambassador: AMER NAJI.

**Italy:** 55 Jawatte Rd, Colombo 5; tel. (1) 588388; telex 21449; fax (1) 588622; Ambassador: LUIGI COSTA SANSEVERINO.

**Japan:** 20 Gregory's Rd, POB 822, Colombo 7; tel. (1) 693831; telex 21148; fax (1) 698629; Ambassador: MASAAKI KUNIYASU.

**Korea, Republic:** 98 Dharmapala Mawatha, Colombo 7; tel. (1) 699036; telex 21212; Ambassador: HONG JUNG PYO.

**Libya:** 120 Horton Place, Colombo 7; tel. (1) 695671; telex 21246; fax (1) 695671; Secretary of the People's Bureau: SALEM A. QUATEEN.

**Malaysia:** 47/1 Jawatta Rd, Colombo 7; tel. (1) 508973; telex 21181; fax (1) 508972; High Commissioner: ABDUL KADIR MOHD DEEN.

**Maldives:** 25 Melbourne Ave, Colombo 4; tel. (1) 586762; telex 22469; fax (1) 581200; High Commissioner: ABDUL AZEEZ YOOSUF.

**Myanmar:** 17 Skelton Gdns, Colombo 5; tel. (1) 587608; telex 22844; fax (1) 580460; Ambassador: U SHWE ZIN.

**Netherlands:** 25 Torrington Ave, Colombo 7; tel. (1) 589626; telex 21308; fax (1) 502855; Ambassador: B. R. KÖRNER.

**Norway:** 34 Ward Place, Colombo 7; tel. (1) 692263; telex 21340; fax (1) 695009; Ambassador: JON ATLE GAARDER (resident in New Delhi, India).

**Pakistan:** 211 De Saram Place, Colombo 10; tel. (1) 697939; High Commissioner: TARIQ ALTAF.

**Russia:** 62 Sir Ernest de Silva Mawatha, Colombo 7; tel. (1) 573555; telex 22751; Ambassador: OLEG V. KABANOV.

**Sweden:** 47/1 Horton Place, POB 1072, Colombo 7; tel. (1) 688452; telex 21253; fax (1) 688455; Chargé d'affaires a.i.: THORVALD ÅKESSON.

**Switzerland:** 63 Gregory's Rd, POB 342, Colombo 7; tel. (1) 695117; telex 21666; fax (1) 695176; Ambassador: MARIA LUISA CARONI.

**Thailand:** 43 Dr C. W. W. Kannangara Mawatha, Colombo 7; tel. (1) 597406; telex 22165; Ambassador: KHAJORU SOBHOA.

**United Kingdom:** 190 Galle Rd, Kollupitiya, POB 1433, Colombo 3; tel. (1) 437336; telex 21101; fax (1) 430308; High Commissioner: EDWARD J. FIELD.

**USA:** 210 Galle Rd, POB 106, Colombo 3; tel. (1) 448007; telex 21305; fax (1) 437345; Ambassador: TERESITA CURRIE SCHAFFER.

## Judicial System

The judicial system consists of the Supreme Court, the Court of Appeal, the High Court, District Courts, Magistrates' Courts and Primary Courts. The last four are Courts of the First Instance and appeals lie from them to the Court of Appeal and from there, on questions of law or by special leave, to the Supreme Court. The High Court deals with all criminal cases and the District Courts with civil cases. There are Labour Tribunals to decide labour disputes.

The Judicial Service Commission comprises the Chief Justice and two judges of the Supreme Court, nominated by the President. All judges of the Courts of First Instance (except High Court Judges) and the staff of all courts are appointed and controlled by the Judicial Service Commission. The Supreme Court consists of the Chief Justice and not fewer than six and not more than 10 other judges. The Court of Appeal consists of the President and not fewer than six and not more than 11 other judges.

**Chief Justice of the Supreme Court:** G. P. S. DE SILVA.

**Attorney-General:** TILAK MARAPANA.

## Religion

According to the census of March 1981, the distribution of the population by religion was: Buddhist 69.81%, Hindu 15.17%, Christian 7.62%, Muslim 7.36%, Others 0.04%.

SRI LANKA  *Directory*

## BUDDHISM

Theravada Buddhism is the predominant sect. There are an estimated 53,000 Buddhist Bhikkhus (monks), living in about 6,000 temples.

**All Ceylon Buddhist Congress:** 380 Bauddhaloka Mawatha, Colombo 7; tel. (1) 691695; f. 1919; Pres. Dudley Gunasekera; Jt Secs Ratna Goonetilleke, Nanda P. Kalutantri.

**Sri Lanka Regional Centre of the World Fellowship of Buddhists:** 380 Bauddhaloka Mawatha, Colombo 7; tel. (1) 691695; telex 21819; Pres. Desabandu Albert Edirisinghe; Hon. Sec. Nemsiri Mutukumara.

## HINDUISM

The majority of the Tamil population are Hindus. In March 1981 the Hindu population was 2,252,000.

## CHRISTIANITY

**National Christian Council of Sri Lanka:** 368/6 Bauddhaloka Mawatha, Colombo 7; tel. (1) 696701; fax (1) 697879; f. 1945; 13 mem. bodies; Gen. Sec. Shirley J. S. Peiris.

### The Anglican Communion

The Church of Ceylon (Sri Lanka) comprises two Anglican dioceses. In 1985 there were about 78,000 adherents.

**Bishop of Colombo:** Rt Rev. Kenneth Michael James Fernando, Bishop's House, 358/1 Bauddhaloka Mawatha, Colombo 7; tel. (1) 696208; fax (1) 693997; f. 1845.

**Bishop of Kurunagala:** Rt Rev. Andrew Oliver Kumarage, Bishop's House, Kandy Rd, Kurunagala; tel. (37) 22191; f. 1950.

### The Roman Catholic Church

For ecclesiastical purposes, Sri Lanka comprises one archdiocese and nine dioceses. At 31 December 1993 there were an estimated 1,191,256 adherents in the country.

**Catholic Bishops' Conference in Sri Lanka:** Lankarama, 19 Balcombe Place, Cotta Rd, Borella, Colombo 8; tel. (1) 697110; fax (1) 699619; f. 1975; Pres. Rt Rev. Dr Vianney Fernando, Bishop of Kandy; Sec.-Gen. Rt Rev. Dr Malcolm Ranjith, Auxiliary Bishop of Colombo.

**Archbishop of Colombo:** Most Rev. Dr Nicholas Marcus Fernando, Archbishop's House, 976 Gnanartha Pradeepaya Mawatha, Colombo 8; tel. (1) 695471; fax (1) 692009.

### The Church of South India

The Church comprises 21 dioceses, including one, Jaffna, in Sri Lanka. The diocese of Jaffna, with an estimated 11,200 adherents, was formerly part of the South India United Church (a union of churches of the Congregational and Presbyterian/Reformed traditions), which merged with the Methodist Church in South India and the four southern dioceses of the (Anglican) Church of India to form the Church of South India in 1947.

**Bishop in Jaffna:** Rt Rev. Dr S. Jebanesan, Bishop's House, Vaddukoddai; tel. (21) 226; fax (1) 582015.

### Other Christian Churches

**Dutch Reformed Church:** General Consistory Office, 363 Galle Rd, Colombo 6; tel. (1) 585861; fax (1) 582469; f. 1642; Pres. of Gen. Consistory Rev. Charles N. Jansz; Admin. Sec. Mabelle Ariyaratnam.

**Methodist Church:** Methodist Headquarters, 252 Galle Rd, Colombo 3; tel. (1) 575707; 28,000 mems (1985); Pres. of Conference Rev. Dr Kingsley T. Muttiah; Sec. of Conference Rev. Duleep R. Fernando.

Other denominations active in the country include the Sri Lanka Baptist Sangamaya.

## BAHÁ'Í FAITH

**Spiritual Assembly:** Bahá'í National Centre, 65 Havelock Rd, Colombo 5; tel. and fax (1) 587360; telex 21537.

# The Press

## NEWSPAPERS

Newspapers are published in Sinhala, Tamil and English. There are four main newspaper publishing groups:

**Associated Newspapers of Ceylon Ltd:** Lake House, D. R. Wijewardene Mawatha, POB 248, Colombo 10; tel. (1) 434544; telex 22262; fax (1) 449069; f. 1926; nationalized 1973; publr of *Daily News, Observer, Thinakaran, Janatha* and *Dinamina* (dailies), three Sunday papers: *Sunday Observer, Silumina* and *Thinakaran Vaara Manjari*, and 11 periodicals; Chair. (vacant); Sec. B. A. Jinadasa.

**Express Newspapers (Ceylon) Ltd:** 185 Grandpass Rd, POB 160, Colombo 14; tel. (1) 20881; publr of *Mithran, Virakesari* (dailies) and *Mithran Varamalar, Virakesari Vaaraveliyeedu* (Sunday); Editor A. Sivanesaselvan; Man. Dir M. G. Wenceslaus.

**Independent Newspapers Ltd:** 5 Gunasena Mawatha, POB 47, Colombo 12; tel. (1) 23883; telex 21306; fax (1) 545263; f. 1961; under private ownership; publr of *Dawasa* and *Sun* (dailies), *Riviresa, Weekend* and *Iranama* (weeklies) and *Sri* (monthly); Chair. Percy Gunasena.

**Upali Newspapers Ltd:** 223 Bloemendhal Rd, POB 133, Colombo 13; tel. and fax (1) 448103; telex 22814; f. 1981; publr of *The Island, Divaina* (dailies), two Sunday papers, *Sunday Island* and *Divaina*, and four weeklies, *Vidusara, Navaliya, Bindu* and *The Island International* (for sale abroad only); English and Sinhala; Editor-in-Chief Edmund Ranasinghe; Man. Dir J. H. Lanerolle.

### Dailies

**Daily News:** Lake House, D. R. Wijewardene Mawatha, POB 248, Colombo 10; tel. (1) 445433; telex 22262; fax (1) 449069; f. 1918; morning; English; Editor Manik de Silva; circ. 65,000.

**Dawasa:** 5 Gunasena Mawatha, POB 226, Colombo 12; tel. (1) 23864; f. 1961; morning; Sinhala; Editor Rohana Gamage; circ. 108,000.

**Dinamina:** Lake House, D. R. Wijewardene Mawatha, POB 248, Colombo 10; tel. (1) 21181; f. 1909; morning; Sinhala; Editor G. S. Perera; circ. 140,000.

**Dinakara:** 95 Maligakanda Rd, Colombo 10; tel. (1) 595754; f. 1978; morning; Sinhala; publ. by Rekana Publrs; Editor Mulen Perera; circ. 12,000.

**Divaina:** 223 Bloemendhal Rd, POB 133, Colombo 13; tel. (1) 24001; telex 21198; fax (1) 448103; f. 1982; morning and Sunday; publ. by Upali Newspapers Ltd; Chief Editor Upali Tennakoon.

**Eelanadu:** 165 Sivan Kovil West Rd, POB 49, Jaffna; tel. (21) 22389; f. 1959; morning; Tamil; Chair. S. Raveenthiranathan; Editor M. Sivanantham; circ. 15,000.

**The Island:** 223 Bloemendhal Rd, POB 133, Colombo 13; tel. (1) 324001; telex 21198; f. 1981; English; Editor Gamini Weerakoon; circ. 80,000.

**Janatha:** Janata Lake House, D. R. Wijewardene Mawatha, Colombo 10; tel. (1) 421181; f. 1953; evening; Sinhala; Editor M. Newton Pinto; circ. 15,000.

**Mithran:** 185 Grandpass Rd, Colombo 14; tel. (1) 20881; fax (1) 448205; f. 1966; morning; Tamil; Editor A. Sivanesaselvan; circ. 20,000.

**Observer:** Associated Newspapers of Ceylon Ltd, Lake House, D. R. Wijewardene Mawatha, POB 248, Colombo 10; tel. (1) 434544; telex 22262; fax (1) 449069; f. 1834; evening (weekdays) and Sunday morning; Editor Ajith Samaranayake; circ. 10,000 (evening), 95,000 (Sunday).

**Sun:** 5 Gunasena Mawatha, POB 226, Colombo 12; tel. (1) 23864; telex 21306; f. 1964; morning; English; Editor Rex de Silva; circ. 59,400.

**Thinakaran:** Lake House, D. R. Wijewardene Mawatha, POB 248, Colombo 10; tel. (1) 21181; f. 1932; morning; Tamil; Editor R. Sivagurunathan; circ. daily 14,000.

**Virakesari:** 185 Grandpass Rd, POB 160, Colombo 14; tel. (1) 20881; fax (1) 448205; f. 1931; morning; Tamil; Editor A. Sivanesaselvan; circ. 48,000.

### Sunday Newspapers

**Janasathiya:** 47 Jayantha Weerasekara Mawatha, Colombo 10; f. 1965; Sinhala; publ. by Suriya Publishers Ltd; Editor Sarath Nawana; circ. 50,000.

**Mithran Varamalar:** 185 Grandpass Rd, Colombo 14; tel. (1) 20881; fax (1) 448205; f. 1969; Tamil; Editor A. Sivanesaselvan; circ. 25,000.

**Riviresa:** 5 Gunasena Mawatha, Colombo 12; tel. (1) 23864; f. 1961; Sinhala Weekly; Editor Rohana Gamage; circ. 317,000.

**Silumina:** Lake House, D. R. Wijewardene Mawatha, POB 248, Colombo 10; tel. (1) 21181; f. 1930; Sinhala; Editor W. B. Mettananda; circ. 254,000.

**Sunday Island:** 223 Bloemendhal Rd, POB 133, Colombo 13; tel. (1) 24001; telex 21198; fax (1) 448103; f. 1981; English; Editor Ajith Samaranayake; circ. 200,000.

**Sunday Observer:** POB 248, Colombo; tel. (1) 421181; telex 22262; fax (1) 449069; f. 1923; English; Editor H. L. D. Mahindapala.

**Thinakaran Vaara Manjari:** Lake House, D. R. Wijewardene Mawatha, POB 248, Colombo 10; tel. (1) 21181; f. 1948; Tamil; Editor R. Sivagurunathan; circ. 21,000.

# SRI LANKA

**Virakesari Vaaraveliyeedu:** 185 Grandpass Rd, Colombo 14; tel. (1) 20881; fax (1) 448205; f. 1931; Tamil; Editor A. SIVANESASELVAN; circ. 48,000.

**Weekend:** 5 Gunasena Mawatha, POB 226, Colombo 12; tel. (1) 23864; telex 21306; f. 1965; English; Editor MANU GUNASENA; circ. 79,600.

## PERIODICALS
(weekly unless otherwise stated)

**Aththa:** 91 Dr N. M. Perera Mawatha, Colombo 8; tel. (1) 595328; f. 1965; Sinhala; publ. by the Communist Party of Sri Lanka; Editor B. A. SIRIWARDENE; circ. 28,000.

**Business Lanka:** Trade Information Service, 115 Sir Chittampalam A. Gardiner Mawatha, POB 1872, Colombo 2; tel. (1) 438523; telex 21457; fax (1) 438404; f. 1981; quarterly; information for visiting businessmen etc.; Editor Dep. Dir of Trade Information Service.

**Ceylon Commerce:** The National Chamber of Commerce of Sri Lanka, 450 D. R. Wijewardene Mawatha, POB 1375, Colombo 10; tel. (1) 447412; fax (1) 445409; monthly.

**Ceylon Medical Journal:** 6 Wijerama Mawatha, Colombo 7; tel. (1) 693324; fax (1) 698802; f. 1887; quarterly; Editors Prof. COLVIN GOONARATNA, Dr C. G. URAGODA.

**The Economic Times:** 146/54 Aramaya Rd, Colombo 9; tel. (1) 686337; f. 1970; Chief Editor Al-Haj A. C. A. GAFFOOR; Man. Editor THIMSY FAHIM.

**The Financial Times:** 323 Union Place, POB 330, Colombo 2; tel. (1) 26181; quarterly; commercial and economic affairs; Man. Editor CYRIL GARDINER.

**Gnanartha Pradeepaya:** Colombo Catholic Press, 2 Gnanartha Pradeepaya Mawatha, Borella, Colombo 8; tel. (1) 695984; f. 1866; Sinhala; Roman Catholic; Chief Editor Rev. Fr W. DON BENEDICT JOSEPH; circ. 26,000.

**Honey:** 5 Gunasena Mawatha, Colombo 12; tel. (1) 23882; f. 1976; illustrated family magazine; English; publ. by Independent Newspapers Ltd; publication temporarily suspended.

**Iranama:** 5 Gunasena Mawatha, Colombo 12; tel. (1) 23864; f. 1964.

**Janakavi:** 47 Jayantha Weerasekera Mawatha, Colombo 10; fortnightly; Sinhala; Assoc. Editor KARUNARATNE AMERASINGHE.

**Lanka Guardian:** 246 Union Place, Colombo 2; fortnightly; Editor MERVYN DE SILVA.

**Manasa:** 150 Dutugemunu St, Dehiwala; tel. (1) 553994; f. 1978; Sinhala; monthly; science of the mind; Editor SUMANADASA SAMARASINGHE; circ. 6,000.

**Mihira:** Lake House, D. R. Wijewardene Mawatha, Colombo 10; tel. (1) 21181; telex 22262; f. 1964; Sinhala children's magazine; Editor M. NEWTON PINTO; circ. 145,000.

**Morning Star:** 17 Frances Rd, Colombo 6; tel. and fax (1) 582015; f. 1841; English and Tamil; publ. by the Church of South India.

**Navalokaya:** Gampaha, WP; f. 1941; monthly; Sinhala; publ. by Communist Party of Sri Lanka; articles on literature, art, politics, education, science, etc.

**Nava Yugaya:** Lake House, D. R. Wijewardene Mawatha 1, Colombo 10; tel. (1) 21181; f. 1956; literary fortnightly; Sinhala; Editor S. N. SENANAYAKE; circ. 57,000.

**Pathukavalan:** POB 2, Jaffna; tel. (21) 22300; f. 1876; Tamil; publ. by St Joseph's Catholic Press; Editor Rev. Fr G. A. FRANCIS JOSEPH; circ. 7,000.

**Puthiya Ulaham:** 115, 4th Cross St, Jaffna; tel. (21) 22627; f. 1976; Tamil; six a year; publ. by Centre for Better Society; Editor Rev. Dr S. J. EMMANUEL; circ. 1,500.

**Samajawadhaya:** 91 Dr N. M. Perera Mawatha, Colombo 8; tel. (1) 595328; monthly; theoretical; publ. by the Communist Party of Sri Lanka.

**Sarasaviya:** Lake House, D. R. Wijewardene Mawatha, POB 1168, Colombo 10; tel. (1) 21181; f. 1963; Sinhala; films; Editor GRANVILLE SILVA; circ. 56,000.

**Sinhala Bauddhaya:** Maha Bodhi Mandira, 130 Rev. Hikkaduwe Sri Sumangala Nahimi Mawatha, Colombo 10; tel. (1) 698079; f. 1906; publ. by The Maha Bodi Society of Ceylon; Editor-in-Chief KIRTHI KALAHE; circ. 25,000.

**Sri:** 5 Gunasena Mawatha, Colombo 12; tel. (1) 23864; f. 1963; monthly; women's magazine.

**Sri Lanka Government Gazette:** Government Press, POB 507, Colombo; tel. (1) 93611; f. 1802; official govt bulletin; circ. 54,000.

**Sri Lanka News:** Lake House, D. R. Wijewardene Mawatha, POB 248, Colombo 10; tel. (1) 21181; telex 22262; fax (1) 549069; f. 1938; digest of news and features; Editor NORTON WEERASINGHE.

**Sri Lanka Today:** Government Dept of Information, 7 Sir Baron Jayatilaka Mawatha, Colombo 1; tel. (1) 28376; English; quarterly; Editor MANEL ABHAYARATNE.

**Subasetha:** Lake House, D. R. Wijewardene Mawatha, POB 248, Colombo 10; tel. (1) 21181; f. 1967; Sinhala; astrology, the occult and indigenous medicine; Editor Capt. K. CHANDRA SRI KULARATNE; circ. 80,000.

**Tharunee:** Lake House, D. R. Wijewardene Mawatha, POB 248, Colombo 10; tel. (1) 21181; telex 22262; f. 1969; Sinhala; women's journal; Editor SUMANA SAPRAMADU; circ. 95,000.

**Tribune:** Colombo; tel. (1) 33172; f. 1954; English; news review; Editor S. P. AMARASINGAM.

**Vanitha Vitti:** Wijeya Newspapaers Pvt Ltd, 8 Humipitiya Cross Rd, Colombo 2; tel. (1) 433272; f. 1957; monthly; women's magazine; Editor ANULA DE SILVA; circ. 50,000.

## NEWS AGENCIES

**Cesmos Economic News Agency:** Colpetty, Colombo.

**Lankapuvath** (National News Agency of Sri Lanka): Transworks House, Lower Chatham St, Colombo 1; tel. (1) 433173; telex 22582; fax (1) 433173; f. 1978; Chair. Prof. TISSA KARIYAWASAM; Chief Editor GEOFF WIJESINGHE.

**Press Trust of Ceylon:** Negris Bldg, POB 131, Colombo 1; tel. (1) 31174; Chair. R. BODINAGODA; Sec. and Gen. Man. A. W. AMUNUGAMA.

**Sandesa News Agency:** 23 Canal Row, Colombo 1; tel. (1) 421507; f. 1968; Dir GAMINI NAVARATNE.

### Foreign Bureaux

**Agence France-Presse (AFP):** Hotel Taprobane, Room 20, York St, Colombo 1; tel. (1) 546733; telex 21557; fax (1) 437372; Correspondent ANOSH AHAMOD.

**Deutsche Presse-Agentur (dpa)** (Germany): Independent Newspapers Ltd, 5 Gunasena Mawatha, Colombo 12; tel. (1) 545327; telex 21306; Correspondent REX DE SILVA.

**Iraqi News Agency:** Dinakara, 301 Darley Rd, Colombo 10; tel. (1) 595323; Correspondent SARATH COORAY.

**Novinska Agencija Tanjug** (Yugoslavia): 53/25A Torrington Ave, Colombo 7; tel. (1) 92924; Correspondent LADISLAV BRUNER.

**Press Trust of India (PTI):** 20–22 Regent Flats, Colombo 2; Correspondent K. DHARMARAJAN.

**Reuters** (UK): Stuart House, 45 Janadhipathi Mawatha, POB 131, Colombo 1; tel. (1) 31163; telex 21829; Correspondent DALTON DE SILVA.

**United Press International (UPI)** (USA): 65 Jambugasmulla Rd, Nugegoda; tel. (1) 853923; telex 22812; fax (1) 856496; Correspondent IQBAL ATHAS.

**Xinhua (New China) News Agency** (People's Republic of China): 21 Anderson Rd, Colombo 5; tel. (1) 589092; telex 21537; Chief Correspondent ZHAO XINKAO.

Prensa Latina (Cuba) is also represented.

## PRESS ASSOCIATIONS

**Press Association of Ceylon:** Negris Bldg, POB 131, Colombo 1; tel. (1) 31174; Pres. K. SIVAPIRAGASAM; Gen. Sec. U. L. D. CHANDRATILLAKE.

**Sri Lanka Foreign Correspondents' Association:** 20 1/1 Regent Flats, Sir Chittampalan Gardiner Mawatha, Colombo; tel. (1) 31224.

# Publishers

**Arts Council of Sri Lanka:** Department of Cultural Affairs, 255 Bauddhaloka Mawatha, Colombo 7; tel. (1) 581909; f. 1952; literature, painting, sculpture, performing arts, photography and puppetry; Pres. Prof. V. VITHARANA; Sec. D. M. GUNARATNA.

**W. E. Bastian and Co (Pvt) Ltd:** 23 Canal Row, Fort, Colombo 1; tel. (1) 432752; f. 1904; art, literature, technical; Dirs H. A. MUNIDEVA, K. HEWAGE, N. MUNIDEVA, G. C. BASTIAN.

**Colombo Catholic Press:** 2 Gnanartha Pradeepaya Mawatha, Borella, Colombo 8; tel. (1) 695984; f. 1865; religious; publrs of *The Messenger, Gnanartha Pradeepaya, The Weekly;* Exec. Dir and Editor Rev. Fr BERTRAM DABRERA.

**M. D. Gunasena and Co Ltd:** 217 Olcott Mawatha, POB 246, Colombo 11; tel. (4) 323981; fax (1) 323336; f. 1913; educational and general; Chair M. D. PERCY GUNASENA; Man. Dir M. D. ANANDA GUNASENA.

**Hansa Publishers Ltd:** Colombo; tel. (1) 24536; general.

**Lake House Printers and Publishers Ltd:** 41 W. A. D. Ramanayake Mawatha, POB 1458, Colombo 2; tel. (1) 433271; telex

# SRI LANKA

21266; fax (1) 449504; f. 1965; Chair. R. S. Wijewardene; Sec. S. W. K. H. Samaranayake.

**Saman Publishers Ltd:** 49/16 Iceland Bldg, Colombo 3; tel. (1) 23058; telex 21540; fax (1) 447972.

**Sarexpo International Ltd:** Caves Bookshop, 81 Sir Baron Jayatilleke Mawatha, POB 25, Colombo 1; tel. (1) 422676; telex 21241; fax (1) 447854; f. 1876; history, arts, law, medicine, technical, educational; Man. Dir C. J. S. Fernando.

**K. V. G. de Silva and Sons (Colombo) Ltd:** 415 Galle Rd, Colombo 4; tel. (1) 584146; telex 22658; fax (1) 588875; f. 1898; art, philosophy, scientific, technical, academic, 'Ceyloniana', fiction; Chair. K. V. J. de Silva.

**The Union Press (Pvt) Ltd:** 169/1 Union Place, POB 362, Colombo 2; tel. (1) 435912; f. 1942; Man. Dir Nirmalan Dhas.

### PUBLISHERS' ASSOCIATION

**Sri Lanka Publishers' Association:** 61 Sangaraja Mawatha, Colombo 10; tel. (1) 21181; Sec.-Gen. Eamon Kariyakarawana.

## Radio and Television

In 1992 there were 3.5m. radio receivers and 865,000 television receivers in use.

### RADIO

**Sri Lanka Broadcasting Corpn:** Independence Sq., POB 574, Colombo 7; tel. (1) 697491; telex 21408; fax (1) 695488; f. 1967; under Ministry of Media, Tourism and Aviation; controls all broadcasting in Sri Lanka; regional stations at Anuradhapura, Kandy and Matara; transmitting stations at Ambewela, Amparai, Anuradhapura, Diyagama, Ekala, Galle, Kanthalai, Mahiyangana, Maho, Matara, Puttalam, Ratnapura, Seeduwa, Senkadagala, Weeraketiya; home service in Sinhala, Tamil and English; foreign service also in Tamil, English, Sinhala, Hindi, Kannada, Malayalam, Nepali and Telugu; 893 broadcasting hours per week: 686 on domestic services, 182 on external services and 126 on education; Chair. W. P. S. Jayawardena; Dir-Gen. Janadasa Peiris.

**Trans World Radio:** POB 364, Colombo; tel. (1) 685235; fax (1) 685245; f. 1978; religious station; broadcasts 3 hours every morning and 3 hours each evening to Indian subcontinent; Dir J. Mark Blosser.

### TELEVISION

Experimental television, broadcasting within a 50-km radius of Colombo, was begun in April 1979 by the Independent Television Network and was taken over by the Government in June 1979. A national television network, the Sri Lanka Rupavahini Corporation (SLRC), was established in February 1982.

**Independent Television Network (ITN):** POB 574, Colombo 7; tel. (1) 564591; telex 22445; station at Wickramsinghapura; broadcasts 6 hrs daily.

**Sri Lanka Rupavahini Corpn (SLRC):** Independence Sq., POB 2204, Colombo 7; tel. (1) 501050; telex 22148; fax (1) 580929; f. 1982; stations at Kandy, Sooriyakanda, Namunukula, Piduruthalagala and Madukanda; broadcasts 9 hrs daily (12 hrs on Sat. and 18 hrs on Sun.); Chair. Mr Vasantaraja; Dir-Gen. Sunil Sarath Perera.

## Finance

(cap. = capital; res = reserves; dep. = deposits; m. = million; brs = branches; amounts in Sri Lanka rupees)

### BANKING

#### Central Bank

**Central Bank of Sri Lanka:** 34–36 Janadhipathi Mawatha, POB 590, Colombo 1; tel. (1) 421191; telex 21176; fax (1) 440353; f. 1950; cap. 15m., res 985m., dep. 61,022.7m. (Dec. 1994); Gov. and Chair. of the Monetary Board H. B. Disanayaka; Sec. C. E. Jayasuriya; 3 regional offices.

#### Commercial Banks

**Bank of Ceylon:** 4 Bank of Ceylon Mawatha, Colombo 1; tel. (1) 446811; telex 21126; fax (1) 447171; f. 1939; state-owned; cap. 530m., res 3,435.3m., dep. 62,653.1m. (Dec. 1992); Chair. Jehan K. Cassim; Gen. Man. Rohini L. Nanayakkara; 330 brs in Sri Lanka, one br. in the UK and one br. in Maldives.

**Commercial Bank of Ceylon Ltd:** Commercial House, 21 Bristol St, POB 856, Colombo 1; tel. (1) 430420; telex 21274; fax (1) 449889; f. 1969; 40% owned by Standard Chartered UK Holdings Ltd, 33% by Govt and 27% by public; cap. 125m., res 1,418.8m.,

*Directory*

dep. 13,855.3m. (Dec. 1993); Chair. S. K. Wickremesinghe; Man. Dir M. R. V. de Almeida; 33 brs.

**Hatton National Bank Ltd:** 10 R. A. de Mel Mawatha, POB 837, Colombo 3; tel. (1) 421885; telex 22152; fax (1) 546312; f. 1970; 26.4% owned by Browns Group, 44.8% by public and 28.8% by others; cap. 120m., res 976m., dep. 17,817.7m. (Dec. 1993); Chair. J. Chrisantha R. Cooray; Gen. Man. and CEO Rienzie T. Wijetilleke; 49 brs.

**People's Bank:** 75 Sir Chittampalam A. Gardiner Mawatha, POB 728, Colombo 2; tel. (1) 27841; telex 22206; fax (1) 546407; f. 1961; 92% owned by Govt, 8% by co-operatives; cap. 50m., res 1,542.1m., dep. 51,423.8m. (Dec. 1992); Chair. L. H. S. Peiris; Gen. Man. Nihal Jayawardena; 331 brs.

**Sampath Bank Ltd:** 55 D.R. Wijewardene Mawatha, POB 997, Colombo 10; tel. (1) 541332; telex 22760; fax (1) 434217; f. 1987; cap. 354.3m., res 348m., dep. 6,928m. (Dec. 1994); Chair. Dunstan D. de Alwis; Man. Dir Edgar Gunatunge; 20 brs and 2 personal banking units.

**Seylan Bank Ltd:** 33 Sir Baron Jayatilleke Mawatha, POB 400, Colombo 1; tel. (1) 437901; telex 23005; fax (1) 433072; f. 1988; cap. 300m., res 547m., dep. 16,186m. (Dec. 1993); Chair. J. L. B. Kotelawala; Gen. Man./CEO C. R. S. Perera; 80 brs.

#### Development Banks

**Agricultural and Industrial Credit Corpn of Ceylon:** POB 20, Colombo 3; tel. (1) 23783; f. 1943; loan cap. 30m.; Chair. V. P. Vittachi; Gen. Man. H. S. F. Goonewardena.

**Development Finance Corpn of Ceylon:** 73/5 Galle Rd, POB 1397, Colombo 3; tel. (1) 440366; telex 21681; fax (1) 440376; f. 1955; provides long- and medium-term credit, investment banking and consultancy services; Chair. C. A. Coorey; Gen. Man. and CEO M. R. Prelis; 2 brs.

**National Development Bank of Sri Lanka:** 40 Navam Mawatha, Colombo 2; tel. (1) 547474; telex 21399; fax (1) 540262; f. 1979; 15% state-owned; provides long-term finance for projects, equity financing and merchant banking services; Chair. Dr Nimal E. H. Sandaratne; Gen. Man. and Chief Exec./Dir R. M. S. Fernando.

**State Mortgage and Investment Bank:** 269 Galle Road, POB 156, Colombo 3; tel. (1) 573561; fax (1) 573567; f. 1979; Chair. R. N. B. Talwatte; Gen. Man. D. B. Rajapakse.

#### Merchant Bank

**Merchant Bank of Sri Lanka Ltd:** 189 Galle Rd, Colombo 3; tel. (1) 423800; telex 23245; fax (1) 423799; f. 1982; public ltd liability co; cap. p.u. 100m.; Chair. Jehan K. Cassim.

#### Foreign Banks

**ABN AMRO Bank NV** (Netherlands): 41 Janadhipathi Mawatha, POB 317, Colombo 1; tel. (1) 423361; telex 21590; fax (1) 447843; Gen. Man. P. R. Balaratnarajah.

**American Express Bank Ltd** (USA): 45 Janadhipathi Mawatha, Colombo 1; tel. (1) 431288; telex 21469; fax (1) 448295.

**ANZ Grindlays Bank PLC** (UK): 37 York St, POB 112, Colombo 1; tel. (1) 446150; telex 21130; fax (1) 446158; f. 1881; Chair. of Advisory Board G. C. B. Wijeyesinghe; Gen. Man. John Clark.

**Bank of Oman Ltd:** 67 Sir Chittampalam A. Gardiner Mawatha, Colombo 2; tel. (1) 447216; telex 21466; fax (1) 447220; Man. H. Sharieff.

**Bankers Trust Co** (USA): 41 Janadhipathi Mawatha, Colombo 1; tel. (1) 549299; telex 22001.

**Banque Indosuez** (France): 1st Floor, Ceylinco House, 69 Janadhipathi Mawatha, POB 303, Colombo 1; tel. (1) 436181; telex 21402; fax (1) 541537; f. 1979; Gen. Man. Francis Dubus.

**Citibank NA** (USA): 67 Dharmapala Mawatha, POB 888, Colombo 7; tel. (1) 447316; telex 21445; fax (1) 445487; Vice-Pres. Nihal Welikala.

**Deutsche Bank AG** (Germany): 86 Galle Rd, POB 314, Colombo 3; tel. (1) 447062; telex 21506; fax (1) 447067; Gen. Man. Stefan Mahrdt.

**Emirates Bank International Ltd** (United Arab Emirates): 64 Lotus Rd, POB 358, Colombo 1; tel. (1) 23467; telex 21769; Gen. Man. N. C. Vitarana.

**Habib Bank Ltd** (Pakistan): 140–142 Second Cross St, POB 1088, Colombo 11; tel. (1) 326565; telex 21258; fax (1) 447827; f. 1951; Sen. Vice-Pres. and Gen. Man. Muhammad Khalid.

**Hongkong and Shanghai Banking Corpn Ltd** (Hong Kong): 24 Sir Baron Jayatilleke Mawatha, POB 73, Colombo 1; tel. (1) 325435; telex 21152; fax (1) 448388; Man. Richard J. D. Law.

**Indian Bank** (India): 22 & 24 Mudalige Mawatha, POB 624, Colombo 1; tel. (1) 323402; telex 21348; fax (1) 447562; Chief Exec. S. Ramachandran.

# SRI LANKA

*Directory*

**Indian Overseas Bank** (India): Stuart House, 45 Janadhipathi Mawatha, POB 671, Colombo 1; tel. (1) 24422; telex 21515; Chief Man. R. SRINIVASAN; 1 br.

**Overseas Trust Bank Ltd** (Hong Kong): YMCA Bldg, 39 Bristol St, POB 835, Colombo 1; tel. (1) 547655; telex 21489.

**Public Bank Berhad** (Malaysia): Ground and First Floor, Jewelarts Bldg, 324 Galle Rd, Colombo 3; tel. (1) 576289; telex 23171; fax (1) 573958.

**Standard Chartered Bank PLC** (UK): 17 Janadhipathi Mawatha, POB 27, Colombo 1; tel. (1) 26671; telex 21117; fax (1) 432522; f. 1853; Man. J. M. MORRISON.

**State Bank of India:** 16 Sir Baron Jayatilleke Mawatha, POB 93, Colombo 1; tel. (1) 26133; telex 21286; fax (1) 547166; f. 1955; Chief Man. B. P. AGRAWAL.

## STOCK EXCHANGE

**Colombo Stock Exchange:** Mackinnons Bldg, 2nd Floor, York St, Colombo 1; tel. (1) 446581; telex 21124; fax (1) 445279; f. 1985; share market; 216 mems; Chair. AJIT M. DE S. JAYARATNE; Dir-Gen. DYLAN MOLDRICH.

## INSURANCE

**Ceylinco Insurance Co Ltd:** 2nd Floor, Ceylinco House, 69 Janadhipathi Mawatha, POB 439, Colombo 1; tel. (1) 325621; telex 21265; fax (1) 448463; Chair. and Man. Dir J. L. B. KOTELAWALA.

**National Insurance Corpn:** 47 Muttiah Rd, Colombo 2; tel. (1) 545738; general; Chair. T. M. S. NANAYAKKARA; Sec. A. C. J. DE ALWIS.

**Sri Lanka Insurance Corporation Ltd:** 'Rakshana Mandiraya', 21 Vauxhall St, POB 1337, Colombo 2; tel. (1) 325311; telex 21227; fax (1) 447742; f. 1961; all classes of insurance; Chair. S. G. UDALAMATTA.

# Trade and Industry

## CHAMBERS OF COMMERCE

**Federation of Chambers of Commerce and Industry of Sri Lanka:** 29 Gregory's Rd, Colombo 7; tel. (1) 698225; fax (1) 699530; f. 1973; Pres. PATRICK AMARASINGHE.

**All Ceylon Trade Chamber:** 212/45, 1/3 Bodhiraja Mawatha, Colombo 11; tel. (1) 432428; Pres. MUDLIYAR N. W. J. MUDALIGE; Gen. Sec. Y. P. MUTHUKUMARANA.

**Ceylon Chamber of Commerce:** 50 Navam Mawatha, POB 274, Colombo 2; tel. (1) 421745; telex 21494; fax (1) 449352; f. 1839; 493 mems; Chair. A. C. GUNASINGHE; Sec.-Gen. C. G. JAYASURIYA.

**Ceylon National Chamber of Industries:** Galle Face Court 2, Room 20, 1st Floor, POB 1775, Colombo 3; tel. (1) 423734; telex 21245; fax (1) 423734; f. 1960; 300 mems; Chair. LAL DE MEL; Chief Exec. JOE SOTHINATHAN.

**Mercantile Chamber of Commerce of Ceylon:** 99-2/62 Gaffoor Bldg, 2nd Floor, Main St, Colombo 1; tel. (1) 25451; f. 1930; 200 mems; Pres. A. H. RAJKOTWALA.

**The National Chamber of Commerce of Sri Lanka:** 450 D. R. Wijewardene Mawatha, POB 1375, Colombo 10; tel. (1) 447412; fax (1) 445409; f. 1948: Pres. Maj. D. L. WIJESINHA; Sec.-Gen. J. C. SAVANADASA.

**Sri Lanka National Council of the International Chamber of Commerce:** 51, CNAPT Centre, Sir Marcus Fernando Mawatha, POB 1733, Colombo 7; tel. (1) 691290; telex 21673; f. 1955; Chair. C. P. DE SILVA; Hon. Sec. H. E. P. COORAY.

## TRADE AND INDUSTRIAL ORGANIZATIONS

**Industrial Development Board of Ceylon (IDB):** 615 Galle Rd, Katubedda, Moratuwa; tel. 605326; telex 22625; fax 607002; f. 1969; under Ministry of Industrial Development; promotes industrial development through provincial network; Chair. W. A. J. ANTON FERNANDO; Gen. Man. A. G. DE Z. JAYATILLAKA.

**Centre for Entrepreneurship Development and Consultancy Services:** 615 Galle Rd, Katubedda, Moratuwa; tel. 607001; f. 1989; Dir K. D. JINADASA.

**Centre for Industrial Technology Information Services:** 615 Galle Rd, Katubedda, Moratuwa; tel. 605111; f. 1989; Dir Ms S. M. TENNEKOON (acting).

**Sri Lanka Export Development Board:** 115 Sir Chittampalam A. Gardiner Mawatha, Colombo 2; tel. (1) 438512; telex 21457; fax (1) 438404; Chair. K. GUNARATNAM.

**Board of Investment of Sri Lanka (BOI):** 14 Sir Baron Jayatilleke Mawatha, POB 1768, Colombo 1; tel. (1) 434403; telex 21332; fax (1) 447995; f. 1978, as the Greater Colombo Economic Commission, to promote investment and to administer the Export Processing Zones at Katunayake, Biyagama, Mihintale, Kandy and Koggala; Dir-Gen. A. DE VAS GUNAWARDENA.

**Ceylon Coir Fibre Exporters' Association:** c/o Jafferjee Bros, 150 St Joseph's St, POB 1180, Colombo 14; tel. (1) 432051; telex 21299; fax (1) 446085; Chair. G. H. I. JAFFERJEE.

**Ceylon Hardware Merchants' Association:** 20B Central Rd, Colombo 12; tel. and fax (1) 435920; telex 21261; Pres. S. THILLAINATHAN.

**Ceylon Planters' Society:** 40/1 Sri Dharmadara Mawatha, Ratmalana; tel. and fax (1) 715656; f. 1936; 1,778 mems (plantation mans); 24 brs and eight regional organizations; Pres. A. R. TAMBINAYAGAM; Sec. D. S. P. HETTIARACHCHI.

**Coconut Development Authority:** 11 Duke St, POB 386, Colombo 1; tel. (1) 421025; telex 21217; fax (1) 447602; f. 1972; state body; Chair. J. EDIRISINGHE.

**Coconut Products Traders' Association:** c/o Ceylon Chamber of Commerce, 50 Navam Mawatha, POB 274, Colombo 2; tel. (1) 421745; telex 21494; fax (1) 449352; f. 1925; Chair. I. PAULRAJ; Sec. C. G. JAYASURIYA.

**Colombo Rubber Traders' Association:** c/o Ceylon Chamber of Commerce, 50 Navam Mawatha, POB 274, Colombo 2; tel. (1) 421745; telex 21494; fax (1) 449352; f. 1918; Chair. M. S. RAHIM; Sec. C. G. JAYASURIYA.

**Colombo Tea Traders' Association:** c/o Ceylon Chamber of Commerce, 50 Navam Mawatha, POB 274, Colombo 2; tel. (1) 421745; telex 21494; fax (1) 449352; f. 1894; 179 mems; Chair. R. L. JURIANSZ; Sec. C. G. JAYASURIYA.

**Consolidated Exports and Trading Co Ltd:** 68/70 York St, POB 263, Colombo 1; tel. (1) 25167; telex 21164; fax (1) 449531; f. 1971; largest govt export organization; exports products manufactured, grown and mined in Sri Lanka; also handles imports; Chair. M. M. MOHINUDEEN.

**The Finance Houses' Association of Sri Lanka:** 84 Ward Place, Colombo 7; tel. (1) 699295; fax (1) 697205; f. 1958; represents the finance cos registered and licensed by the Central Bank of Sri Lanka; Chair. T. H. NOORAMITH; Sec. M. M. N. DE SILVA.

**Free Trade Zone Manufacturers' Association:** Plaza Complex, Unit 6 (Upper Floor), IPZ, Katunayake; tel. (30) 452813; Administrative Sec. TUWAN SAMAHOON.

**Janatha Estates Development Board:** 55/57 Vauxhall Rd, Colombo 2; tel. (1) 24083; telex 21276; f. 1975; manages 300 tea, rubber, coconut and spice plantations; 205,000 employees; 6 regional bds.

**Sea Food Exporters' Association:** c/o Andriesz & Co Ltd, 39 Nuge Rd, Peliyagoda; tel. 530021; telex 22247.

**Sri Lanka Apparel Exporters' Association:** Colombo; tel. (1) 575836; f. 1982; Chair. AJITA DE COSTA; Exec. Sec. S. KANNANGARA.

**Sri Lanka Association of Manufacturers and Exporters of Rubber Products:** c/o D. Samson Industries Ltd, 110 Kumaran Ratnam Rd, Colombo 2; tel. (1) 320978; telex 21871; fax (1) 440890; Chair. D. K. RAJAPAKSA; Vice-Chair. N. PALIHAKKARA.

**Sri Lanka Association of Printers:** 593 Kularatne Mawatha, Colombo 10; tel. (1) 687557; Pres. D. D. H. S. WICKREMARATNE.

**Sri Lanka Fruit and Vegetables Producers, Processors and Exporters' Association:** c/o Sri Lanka Export Development Board, 115 Sir Chittampalam A. Gardiner Mawatha, Colombo 2; tel. (1) 438513; telex 21547; fax (1) 438404; Sec. Y. ILANGAKOON.

**Sri Lanka Importers, Exporters and Manufacturers' Association:** Monte Christo Bldg, 816-1/1, Berving Terrace, Punchi Borella, Colombo 10; tel. (1) 691888; telex 21494; fax (1) 696321; f. 1955; Pres. WILLIAM J. T. PERERA.

**Sri Lanka Jewellery Manufacturing Exporters' Association:** World Trade Centre, Lower Chatham St, Colombo 1; tel. (1) 445141; fax (1) 445105; Pres. IFTHIKHAR AZIZ; Sec. CHANAKA ELLAWELA.

**Sri Lanka Pesticides Association:** POB 919, Colombo; tel. (1) 598292; Sec. L. C. DE SILVA.

**Sri Lanka Pharmaceutical Traders' Association:** 503 Union Place, POB 240, Colombo 2; tel. (1) 691083; Pres. J. ABEYWICKREMA; Hon. Sec. S. NADARAJAH.

**Sri Lanka Tea Board:** 574 Galle Rd, POB 1750, Colombo 3; tel. (1) 582236; telex 21304; fax (1) 585701; f. 1976 for development of tea industry through research and promotion in Sri Lanka and in world markets; Chair. RONNIE WEERAKOON; Dir-Gen. (vacant).

**Sri Lanka Wooden Furniture and Wood Products Manufacturers' and Exporters' Association:** c/o E. H. Cooray & Sons Ltd, 411 Galle Rd, Colombo 3; tel. (1) 509227; fax (1) 575198; Pres. PATRICK AMARASINGHE; Sec. PINSIRI FERNANDO.

**Sugar Importers' Association of Sri Lanka:** c/o C. W. Mackie & Co Ltd, 36 D. R. Wijewardena Mawatha, POB 89, Colombo 10; tel.

# SRI LANKA

(1) 423554; fax (1) 438069; Pres. M. THAVAYOGARAJAH; Sec. C. KAPUWATTA.

**Tea Promotion Bureau:** Sri Lanka Tea Board, 574/1 Galle Rd, Colombo 3; tel. (1) 582121; fax (1) 587341; Dir D. S. CHANDRASEKERA.

**Tea Research Institute of Sri Lanka:** St Coombs, Talawakele; tel. (52) 8386; fax (52) 8311; f. 1925 to conduct research into all aspects of tea production and manufacture, and to provide and publish information derived from this research; 5 brs; Dir (vacant).

**Trade Information Service:** Sri Lanka Export Development Board, 115 Sir Chittampalam A. Gardiner Mawatha, POB 1872, Colombo 2; tel. (1) 438523; telex 21457; fax (1) 438404; f. 1981 to collect and disseminate commercial information and to provide advisory services to trade circles; Dir Mrs G. I. UNAMBOOWE.

## THE CO-OPERATIVE MOVEMENT

The most important organizations in the consumer field are the Wholesale Stores Unions, which handle all foodstuffs and miscellaneous goods supplied by the Co-operative Wholesale Establishment, as well as running a large number of retail stores. The Co-operative Wholesale Establishment is at the head of the consumer co-operative movement. It was founded in 1943 and is administered by an autonomous Board of Directors.

## EMPLOYERS' ORGANIZATION

**Employers' Federation of Ceylon:** 30 Sulaiman Ave, POB 858, Colombo 5; tel. (1) 502204; fax (1) 508385; f. 1928; mem. International Organization of Employers; 365 mems; Chair. S. T. NAGENDRA; Sec.-Gen. E. F. G. AMERASINGHE.

## STATE INDUSTRIAL ORGANIZATIONS

### State Corporations

**BCC Lanka Ltd:** Hultsdorp Mills, POB 281, Colombo 12; tel. (1) 422111; telex 21123; fax (1) 447139; mfrs and shippers of coconut oil, household and toilet soaps, detergents, animal feed, etc.

**Ceylon Agro-Industries Ltd:** 346 Negombo Rd, Seeduwa; tel. (45) 3529; telex 21256; fax (45) 3537; f. 1992; mfrs and exporters of instant noodles and pulses; poultry processing; Gen. Man. Dr LIM BENG JOO.

**Ceylon Ceramics Corpn:** Thumbowila, Piliyandala; tel. 588533; eight factories; produces roofing tiles, terracotta tiles and bricks; Chair. TISSA JAYAWERA.

**Ceylon Fisheries Corpn:** Rock House Lane, Mutwal, Colombo 15; tel. (1) 523227; fax (1) 523385; f. 1964; main harbours at Mutwal and Galle; exports fish and fish products; Chair. Dr S. K. ONIL PERERA.

**Ceylon Galvanising Industries Ltd:** Lady Catherine Estate Drive, POB 35, Ratmalana; tel. (63) 6711; fax (63) 435649; f. 1967; cap. p.u. Rs 4.5m.; sales (1991) Rs 142m.; mfrs of galvanized steel sheets; Man. Dir V. BALASUBRAMANIAM; 50 employees.

**Ceylon Hotels Corpn:** 63 Janadhipathi Mawatha, POB 259, Colombo 1; tel. (1) 323715; fax (1) 422732; Chair. A. K. MALLIMARATCHI.

**Ceylon Leather Products Ltd:** 141 Church Rd, POB 1488, Colombo 15; tel. (1) 522776; telex 22210; fax (1) 521360; mfrs and exporters of leather, including footwear, sports and leather goods; Chair. NIMAL SAMARAKKODY.

**Ceylon Petroleum Corpn:** 113 Galle Rd, Colombo 3; tel. (1) 25231; telex 21167; terminal at Kolonnawa, Colombo; refinery at Sapugaskanda; subsidiary: Lanka Lubricants Ltd; Chair. DAHAM WIMALASENA.

**Ceylon Plywoods Corpn:** 420 Bauddhaloka Mawatha, Colombo 7; tel. (1) 595846; factory at Gintota, woodwork complex at Kosgama, timber extraction project at Kanneliya; Chair. N. G. PUVIMANASINGHE.

**Ceylon Silks Ltd:** 50/22 Mayura Place, POB 132, Colombo 6; tel. (1) 585298; f. 1962; cap. Rs12m.; mfrs of rayon and synthetic textiles; Gen. Man. P. M. D. GUNASEKERA; 800 employees.

**Ceylon State Hardware Corpn:** Kandy Rd, Yakkala; tel. 332154; telex 21248; hardware factory at Yakkala, cast iron foundry at Enderamulle; Chair. H. C. O. EBERT.

**Ceylon Steel Corpn:** Office and Works, Oruwela, Athurugiriya; tel. (1) 561212; telex 21416; fax (1) 561440; f. 1961; steel rolling; mfrs of wire products, steel castings, machine tools; welding electrodes; soldering lead; metallographic work and testing, etc.; Chair. C. M. PEREIRA.

**Lanka Mineral Sands Ltd:** 167 Sri Wipulasena Mawatha, POB 1212, Colombo 10; tel. (1) 694631; telex 21174; fax (1) 699132; ilmenite, rutile, zircon and monazite plants at Pulmoddai; Chair. W. B. A. JAYASEKERA.

**National Gem and Jewellery Authority:** 25 Galle Face Terrace, Colombo 3; tel. (1) 325364; fax (1) 576171; f. 1971 as State Gem Corpn; Chair. T. K. DASSANAYAKE; Gen. Man. S. WIJEGUNAWARDANE.

**Sri Lanka Gem and Jewellery Exchange:** 310 Galle Rd, Colombo 3; tel. (1) 574274; fax (1) 576171; f. 1990; import and export facilities, testing and certification, assaying and hallmarking, trading booths; Chief Exec. T. PIYADASA.

**National Paper Co Ltd:** 356 Union Place, Colombo 2; tel. (1) 446381; telex 21248; fax (1) 446381; paper boards, printing, pulp; Chair. A. B. PADMAPERUMA; Gen. Man. M. A. JUSTIN; factories at Valaichchenai and Embilipitiya.

**National Small Industries' Corpn:** Colombo; tel. (1) 22781.

**National Textile Corpn:** 16 Gregory's Rd, Colombo 7; tel. (1) 595891; factories at Veyangoda, Thulhiriya, Mattegama and Pugoda.

**Paranthan Chemicals Corpn:** 292 Galle Rd, POB 1489, Colombo 3; tel. (1) 575321; factory at Paranthan.

**Sri Lanka Cement Corpn:** 130 W. A. D. Ramanayaka Mawatha, POB 1382, Colombo 2; tel. (1) 540201; telex 21498; cement works at Puttalam, Kankesan and Ruhunu; combined capacity of cement works meets about 60% of the country's requirements and provides for export.

**Sri Lanka Fertilizer Corpn:** 294 Galle Rd, POB 841, Colombo 3; tel. (1) 575639; telex 21108; fax (1) 575624.

**Sri Lanka National Salt Corpn:** 110 Sir James Peries Mawatha, Colombo 2; tel. (1) 28128; salt urns at Hambantota, Palatupana, Palavi, Puttalam, Manmar, Elephant Pass, Kurinchativu, Nilaveli and Bundala.

**Sri Lanka State Flour Milling Corpn:** 7 Station Rd, Colombo 3; tel. (1) 21300; mill at Mutwal, Colombo 15.

**Sri Lanka Sugar Corpn:** 651 Alvitigala Mawatha, Colombo 5; tel. (1) 582231; factories at Kantalai and Hingurana.

**State Engineering Corpn:** 130 W. A. D. Ramanayake Mawatha, POB 194, Colombo 2; tel. (1) 21261.

**State Fertilizer Manufacturing Corpn:** POB 1344, Colombo; tel. (1) 521820; Sapugaskanda, Kelaniya; f. 1966; Chair. A. N. SENANAYAKA; Works Dir PREMARATNE GUNASEKARA.

**State Timber Corpn:** 82 Rajamalwatte Rd, Battaramulla; tel. 566602; telex 21675; f. 1968; extraction of timber, saw milling, running of timber sales depots, research into increased timber exploitation, timber seasoning, preservation, import of timber and special projects connected with timber industry.

### State-owned Companies

**Ceylon Cold Stores Ltd:** POB 220, Colombo; tel. (1) 328221; telex 21180; fax (1) 447422; mfrs, wholesalers, retailers of food and beverages; exports sea foods, spices, essential oils, fruit juices and processed meats; brs at Kandy and Trincomalee.

**United Motors Lanka Ltd:** 100 Hyde Park Corner, POB 697, Colombo 2; tel. (1) 448112; telex 21600; fax (1) 448113; nationalized 1972 and incorporated 1989; sales Rs 635.3m. (1992/93); imports, assembles and markets motor vehicles; imports motor spare parts, construction equipment, agricultural machinery, reconditioned vehicles and machinery, tyres and batteries; Chair. MAHENDRA AMARASURIYA; CEO GERALD A. HIDELARATCHI; 420 employees.

**Wellawatte Spinning and Weaving Mills:** 324 Havelock Rd, Colombo 6; tel. (1) 582381; nationalized 1976; textiles.

## TRADE UNIONS

**All Ceylon Federation of Free Trade Unions (ACFFTU):** 94 1/6 York Bldg, York St, Colombo 1; tel. and fax (1) 431847; seven affiliated unions; 80,000 mems; Pres. Mrs M. C. RAJAHMONEY; Sec.-Gen. ANTONY LODWICK.

**Ceylon Federation of Labour (CFL):** 457 Union Place, Colombo 2; tel. (1) 94273; f. 1957; 16 affiliated unions; 155,969 mems; Pres. Dr COLVIN R. DE SILVA; Gen. Sec. R. WEERAKOON.

**Ceylon Trade Union Federation (CTUF):** Colombo; tel. (1) 20365; f. 1941; 24 affiliated unions; 35,271 mems; Sec.-Gen. L. W. PANDITHA.

**Ceylon Workers' Congress (CWC):** 19 St Michael's Rd, POB 1294, Colombo 3; tel. (1) 436332; telex 22894; fax (1) 436341; f. 1939; represents mainly plantation workers of Indian Tamil origin; 400,000 mems; Pres. W. E. K. R. SAVUMYAMOORTHY THONDAMAN; Gen. Sec. MUTHU SANGARALINGAM SELLASWAMMY.

**Democratic Workers' Congress (DWC):** 82-1/2 Sri Vijiragnana Mawatha, Dematagoda Rd, POB 1009, Colombo 9; tel. (1) 691279; fax (1) 435961; f. 1939; 201,700 mems (1994); Pres. V. P. GANESAN; Gen. Sec. K. P. GOVINDARAJ.

**Government Workers' Trade Union Federation (GWTUF):** 457 Union Place, Colombo 2; tel. (1) 95066; 52 affiliated unions; 100,000 mems; Leader P. D. SARANAPALA.

# SRI LANKA

**Jathika Sevaka Sangamaya (JSS)** (National Employees' Union): 416 Kotte Rd, Pitakotte, Colombo; tel. (1) 565432; f. 1959; 357,000 mems; represents over 70% of unionized manual and clerical workers of Sri Lanka; Pres. W. A. NEVILLE PERERA; Sec. SIRINAL DE MEL.

**Lanka Jathika Estate Workers' Union (LJEWU):** 60 Bandaranayakepura, Sri Jayawardenepura Mawatha, Welikada, POB 1918, Rajagiriya; tel. (1) 865138; f. 1958; 350,000 mems; Pres. RANIL WICKREMASINGHE; Gen. Sec. RAJAH SENEVIRATNE.

**Public Service Workers' Trade Union Federation (PSWTUF):** POB 500, Colombo; tel. (1) 31125; 100 affiliated unions; 100,000 mems.

**Sri Lanka Nidahas Sewaka Sangamaya** (Sri Lanka Independent Employees' Union): 301 T. B. Jayah Mawatha, POB 1241, Colombo 10; tel. (1) 94074; f. 1960; 35 affiliated unions; 62,338 mems; affiliated to Sri Lanka Freedom Party; Pres. SIRIMAVO R. D. BANDARANAIKE; Gen. Sec. LESLIE DEVENDRA.

**Union of Post and Telecommunication Officers:** 11/4 Lotus Rd, POB 15, Colombo 1; tel. (1) 324100; fax (1) 341626; f. 1945; Pres. S. T. B. WICKRAMASINGHE; Sec. N. P. HETTIARACHCHI.

## Transport

### RAILWAYS

**Sri Lanka Railways:** POB 355, Colombo 10; tel. (1) 421281; telex 21674; fax (1) 546490; operates 1,979 track-km, of which 35 km is narrow gauge and 1,944 km broad gauge (incl. 100 km of double track); there are 9 railway lines across the country and 169 stations, with 123 sub-stations (1994); Gen. Man. P. W. A. K. SILVA.

### ROADS

In 1981 there were 152,423 km of roads in Sri Lanka, of which 27,171 km were main roads. The road network accounts for about 90% of inland passenger and freight traffic. In 1979 road passenger transport was opened to the private sector, which operates about 1,500 vehicles.

**Office of the Minister of Transport and Highways:** 1 D. R. Wijewardene Mawatha, POB 588, Colombo 10; tel. (1) 687105; fax (1) 694547; maintains 11,076 km of national highways and 3,571 bridges through the Road Development Authority.

**Department of Motor Traffic:** POB 533, Colombo 5; tel. (1) 94331.

**Sri Lanka Central Transport Board:** 200 Kirula Rd, POB 1435, Colombo 5; tel. (1) 581121; f. 1958; nationalized organization responsible for road passenger transport services consisting of a central transport board and 10 regional transport boards; fleet of 7,000 buses operating from 102 depots (1990); Chair. R. V. RUPESINGHE; Sec. H. W. GOONESEKERE.

### SHIPPING

Colombo is one of the most important ports in Asia and is situated at the junction of the main trade routes. The other main ports of Sri Lanka are Trincomalee, Galle and Jaffna. Trincomalee is the main port for handling tea exports.

**Ceylon Association of Steamer Agents (CASA):** 2nd Floor, Associated Motorways Bldg, 185 Union Place, Colombo 2; tel. (1) 440233; fax (1) 341461; f. 1966; primarily a consultative organization; represents mems in dealings with govt authorities; 81 mems; Chair. A. N. MARALANDE; Sec. W. KARUNATILLEKE.

**Sri Lanka Ports Authority:** 19 Church St, POB 595, Colombo 1; tel. (1) 325559; telex 21805; fax (1) 440651; f. 1976; responsible for all cargo handling operations and harbour maintenance in the ports of Colombo, Galle, Kankasanthurai and Trincomalee; Chair. A. P. HAPUDENIYA; Jt Man. Dirs H. A. WIJEGUNAWARDHANA, S. K. W. DIAS.

### Shipping Companies

**Ceylon Ocean Lines Ltd:** 74/5 Grandpass Rd, POB 1276, Colombo 14; tel. (1) 434928; telex 21156; fax (1) 446234; f. 1956; agents for shipping lines from Poland, the republics of the fmr USSR, Romania, Bulgaria and the People's Republic of China; also charters and container services; Chair. U. JAYASINGHE; Man. Dir S. SELVARATNAM.

**Ceylon Shipping Corpn Ltd:** 6 Sir Baron Jayatilleke Mawatha, POB 1718, Colombo 1; tel. (1) 328772; telex 21205; fax (1) 449486; f. 1971 as a govt corpn; became govt-owned limited liability co in 1992; operates fully-containerized service to Europe, the Far East, the Mediterranean and Canada (East Coast); Chair. R. J. WICKRAMASINGHE; Gen. Man. D. L. W. TALAGALA.

**Ceylon Shipping Lines Ltd:** 55 1/1 Iceland Bldg, Galle Rd, POB 891, Colombo 3; tel. (1) 327052; telex 21113; fax (1) 448651; travel agents, off dock terminal operators; Chair. E. A. WIRASINHA; Man. Dir T. D. V. GUNARATNE.

**Ceyoceanic Ltd:** 80 Reclamation Rd, POB 795, Colombo 11; tel. (1) 36071; telex 21834; Dir M. T. G. ANAAM.

**Colombo Dockyard Ltd:** Port of Colombo, POB 906, Colombo 15; tel. (1) 522461; telex 22794; fax (1) 446441; f. 1974; 51% owned by Onomichi Dockyard Co Ltd, Japan, and 49% by Sri Lankan public and government institutions; four dry-docks, seven repair berths (1,200 m), repair of ships up to 125,000 dwt, and builders of steel/aluminium vessels of up to 3,000 dwt; Chair. I. IDE; Man. Dir Dr SARATH OBEYSEKERA.

**Mercantile Shipping Co Ltd:** 108 Aluthmawatha Rd, Colombo 15; tel. 331792; telex 22085; fax (1) 331799.

**Sri Lanka Shipping Co Ltd:** 46/5 Navam Mawatha, POB 1125, Colombo 2; tel. (1) 336853; telex 21343; fax (1) 437420; f. 1956.

### INLAND WATERWAYS

There are more than 160 km of canals open for traffic.

### CIVIL AVIATION

Civil aviation is controlled by the Government's Department of Civil Aviation. There are airports at Batticaloa, Colombo (Katunayake for external flights and Ratmalana for internal), Gal Oya, Palali, Jaffna and Trincomalee.

**Air Lanka:** 37 York St, Colombo 1; tel. (1) 735555; telex 21401; fax (1) 735122; f. 1979; 100% state-owned; partial transfer to private ownership pending in 1995; domestic flights and international services to Europe, the Middle East, Far East and Asia; Chair. and Man. Dir Gen. D. SEPALA ATTYGALLE; Exec. Dirs D. S. J. PELPOLA, Air Vice-Marshal WALTER FERNANDO.

## Tourism

As a stopping place for luxury cruises and by virtue of the spectacle of its Buddhist festivals, ancient monuments and natural scenery, Sri Lanka is one of Asia's most important tourist centres. Good motor roads connect Colombo to the main places of interest.

Despite the continuing intercommunal violence, which began in 1983, the tourism sector performed well in 1992, with tourist arrivals increasing to 393,669 and receipts from tourism amounting to US $198.5m. In 1994 the total number of tourist arrivals rose to 407,511.

**Ceylon Tourist Board:** 78 Steuart Place, POB 1504, Colombo 3; tel. (1) 437059; telex 21867; fax (1) 437953; f. 1966; Chair. H. M. S. SAMARANAYAKE; Dir-Gen. (vacant).

# SUDAN

## Introductory Survey

### Location, Climate, Language, Religion, Flag, Capital

The Republic of Sudan lies in north-eastern Africa. It is bordered by Egypt to the north, by the Red Sea, Eritrea and Ethiopia to the east, by the Central African Republic, Chad and Libya to the west, and by Kenya, Uganda and Zaire to the south. The climate shows a marked transition from the desert of the north to the rainy equatorial south. Temperatures vary with altitude and latitude. The annual average for the whole country is about 21°C (70°F). Arabic is the official language, although other languages are spoken and English is widely understood. Most northern Sudanese are Muslims, while in the south most of the inhabitants are animists or Christians. The national flag (proportions 2 by 1) has three equal horizontal stripes, of red, white and black, with a green triangle at the hoist. The capital is Khartoum.

### Recent History

The Sudan (as the country was known before 1975) was ruled as an Anglo-Egyptian condominium from 1899 until achieving independence as a parliamentary republic on 1 January 1956. After a military coup in November 1958, the army took control of the state. A Supreme Council of the Armed Forces was set up and ruled until October 1964, when it was overthrown in a civilian revolution. The governments that followed failed to improve the economic situation or to deal with the problem of the insurgent southern provinces, and in May 1969 power was seized by a group of officers, led by Col Gaafar Mohammed Nimeri, who assumed the rank of major-general. All existing political institutions and organizations were abolished, and the 'Democratic Republic of the Sudan' was proclaimed, with supreme authority in the hands of the Revolutionary Command Council (RCC). In October 1971 a referendum confirmed Gen. Nimeri's nomination as President. A new Government was formed, the RCC was dissolved, and the Sudanese Socialist Union (SSU) was recognized as the only political party.

An early problem facing the Nimeri Government concerned the disputed status of the three southern provinces (Bahr al-Ghazal, Equatoria and Upper Nile), whose inhabitants are racially and culturally distinct from most of the country's population. Rebellion against rule from the north had first broken out in 1955, and fighting continued until March 1972, when an agreement to give the three provinces a degree of autonomy was concluded in Addis Ababa, Ethiopia, between members of the Sudan Government and representatives of the South Sudan Liberation Movement. A High Executive Council (HEC) for the Southern Region was established in April 1972, and Sudan's permanent constitution was endorsed in April 1973. Elections to the Regional People's Assembly for southern Sudan took place in November 1973, followed by elections to the National People's Assembly in April 1974.

The establishment of a National Assembly and a political party broadened the Government's base of power, though the army continued to play an important role in the country's affairs. During 1977 a policy of reconciliation was initiated, which brought several of Nimeri's former opponents into the administration. Regional and national elections were held in February 1978, with the provision that opposition candidates must be approved by the SSU. About one-half of the 274 elective seats in the National Assembly were won by SSU candidates. In May 1979, on the 10th anniversary of his accession to power, President Nimeri assumed the rank of field marshal. Elections were held in May 1980 for the National and Regional Assemblies, and in October legislative proposals to legalize a regional system of government were approved. The National People's Assembly was again dissolved in October 1981. When new elections were held in December, its membership had been reduced from 366 to 151, as many powers had been devolved to the regions. At the same time, the southern HEC was dissolved. The entire Sudanese Government was dismissed in November, although many individuals were later reinstated. In April 1982 a new Southern Region People's Assembly was elected.

In April 1983 President Nimeri was re-elected for a third six-year term. During 1983 Sudan's north–south conflict worsened significantly, and in June Nimeri finally decided to redivide the south into three smaller regions, each with its own assembly, in an effort to quell the unrest. In September Nimeri suddenly announced the imposition of strict Islamic law (the *Shari'a*), provoking anger in the largely non-Muslim south, where redivision was seen as a clear betrayal of the 1972 Addis Ababa Agreement. In the north discontent was reflected in strikes by workers in the public sector. In April 1984 President Nimeri finally proclaimed a state of emergency. Special emergency courts were established, and the army and police were given powers to search mail, to impose curfews and to detain suspects without trial. The stringent application of *Shari'a* law (seen by many as an excuse to suppress political dissent) aggravated tensions within the country and strained relations between Sudan and its allies, Egypt and the USA. In January 1985 the execution for 'heresy' of 76-year-old Mahmoud Mohamed Taha, the moderate leader of the outlawed Republican Brothers movement, provoked international protest.

In May 1984 Nimeri replaced his Council of Ministers with a 64-member Presidential Council, in accordance with the 'Shoura' (consultation) principle of *Shari'a* law. In July, however, the National People's Assembly rejected his proposed constitutional amendments to make Sudan a formal Islamic state. In October Nimeri adopted a more conciliatory approach: the state of emergency was ended, the special courts were suspended, and the President offered to revoke the redivision of the south if a majority of southerners desired it. The situation in the south continued to deteriorate, with the emergence of the Sudan People's Liberation Movement (SPLM), whose armed forces, the Sudan People's Liberation Army (SPLA), rapidly gained military control over large areas of the provinces of Bahr al-Ghazal and Upper Nile.

Meanwhile, in Khartoum, public discontent, provoked largely by rises in the price of food, culminated in March 1985 in a general strike, and on 6 April, while Nimeri was visiting the USA, he was deposed in a bloodless military coup. The country's new leader, Gen. Abdel-Rahman Swar al-Dahab (who had recently been made Minister of Defence and Commander-in-Chief of the army by Nimeri), appointed a Transitional Military Council (TMC) to govern the country, but he pledged a return to civilian rule after a one-year transitional period. An interim Cabinet was announced, whose members were mainly civilians, including three non-Muslim southerners. The Prime Minister, Dr Gizuli Dafallah, had been a prominent organizer of the general strike which preceded the coup. The SSU and the National People's Assembly were dissolved, and hundreds of Nimeri's officials were arrested. Nimeri himself went into exile in Cairo. A transitional Constitution was introduced in October 1985. Under its provisions, numerous new political groupings began to emerge, in preparation for a general election. In December 1985 the name of the country was officially changed to 'the Republic of Sudan'.

In the general election which took place in April 1986 no single party won an outright majority of seats in the new National Assembly, but the Umma Party (UP), led by Sadiq al-Mahdi (who had been Prime Minister in 1966–67), won the largest number of seats (99 out of 264 contested places), followed by the Democratic Unionist Party (DUP) of Osman al-Mirghani (63 seats). After lengthy negotiations, a coalition government was formed between the UP and DUP, with, in addition, four portfolios in the Council of Ministers allocated to southern parties. Sadiq al-Mahdi became Prime Minister and Minister of Defence, and a six-member Supreme Council was appointed to exercise collectively the functions of Head of State. With these appointments, the TMC was dissolved, signifying a return to civilian rule.

In response to the April 1985 coup, the SPLM initially declared a cease-fire, but presented the new regime with a series of demands concerning the southern region. Swar al-Dahab offered various concessions to the south, including the cancellation of the redivision and the reinstatement of the southern HEC. Despite this, the SPLM refused to negotiate with the TMC, and fighting resumed. The civil war in the south continued throughout 1985, with many southern towns held under siege. Following the 1986 election, in an effort to make the new Government acceptable to southerners, Col John Garang, the SPLM leader, was offered a place in the Council of Ministers. Although the SPLM announced that it would not recognize, or take part in, the new Government, negotiations took place during 1986 between the SPLM and the National Alliance for Salvation (NAS), a semi-official group of trade unionists and politicians who supported the Government, in an attempt to find a peaceful solution, and in July Sadiq al-Mahdi and Garang met in Addis Ababa. All contacts were discontinued, however, after the SPLM shot down a Sudan Airways aircraft in August, killing 60 civilians on board. In the same month, the SPLM launched a new offensive, with the aim of recapturing the four strategic southern towns of Juba, Wau, Malakal and Bentiu. The Government was also confronted by opposition in the north: in September 1985 a mutiny in several army units in Khartoum North and Omdurman was officially denounced as an attempted coup, and in November 1986 five senior military commanders were dismissed, following rumours of unrest in the army.

In May 1987, following increasing instability in the south, a temporary Council for the Southern Sudan (CSS) was established. This was intended to be a transitional body, pending the convening of a constitutional conference to decide the final system of government, but its influence on the army and the SPLM, the two contending *de facto* ruling powers which by now existed in the south, was negligible. On 14 May al-Mahdi unexpectedly asked the Supreme Council to dissolve his coalition Government, indicating that his decision had been prompted partly by internal dissension within the Council of Ministers. Disagreements within the DUP, between liberals and religious traditionalists, had led al-Mahdi, during April, to begin secret negotiations with the opposition National Islamic Front (NIF), with a view to forming a new coalition. In the event, neither the NIF nor the UP was willing to participate in the administration together, and al-Mahdi's reconstructed Council of Ministers, announced in June, differed little from its predecessor. Al-Mahdi announced that the coalition parties had agreed on mutually acceptable guidelines for the conduct of government policy; it was stated that laws based on a 'Sudanese legal heritage' would replace those unacceptable to non-Muslims, who would be exempted from Islamic taxation and special penalties. However, the SPLM rejected such a compromise and continued to demand a total abrogation of Islamic law as a precondition for peace negotiations, while the fundamentalist NIF restated its demand that the Islamic code be imposed on the country as a whole. On 25 July the Government imposed a 12-month state of emergency, aimed at bringing under control the country's worsening economic situation. In August the DUP temporarily withdrew from the coalition Government, after the party's proposed candidate for a vacancy on the Supreme Council had been rejected by the UP. In October, however, the two parties agreed to form a joint administration once again, the NIF having elected to remain in opposition.

In September 1987 representatives of southern Sudanese political parties and the SPLM met in Nairobi, Kenya; they issued a joint appeal for all Sudanese political forces to join the peace efforts, and requested that the Government should convene a national constitutional conference. However, the conflict in the south continued unabated. In November SPLM forces, allegedly with Ethiopian assistance, captured the town of Kurmuk (near the border with Ethiopia and lying within Sudan's northern provinces). While the capture of this town was of little strategic significance, it was nevertheless considered to be a psychological blow to the Government, since the SPLM had previously confined its operations to the south of the country. Kurmuk was recaptured by government forces in December, and in the same month the Government held secret negotiations for peace in London, the United Kingdom, with representatives of the SPLM. Although no agreement was reached, the SPLM was reported to have abandoned its demand for the abrogation of Islamic law as a precondition for talks. In April 1988 al-Mahdi announced that he had again asked the Supreme Council to dissolve his coalition Government, following a vote by the National Assembly in favour of the formation of a new 'government of national unity'. Al-Mahdi's formation of such a Government, comprising members of the UP, the DUP, the NIF and some southern Sudanese political parties, was completed in May. Few observers expected it to achieve its declared aim of resolving the problem of the war in the south, especially since the fundamentalist NIF had joined the coalition on condition that a replacement *Shari'a* code be introduced within 60 days of its formation. In November representatives of the SPLM met senior members of the DUP and reached agreement on proposals to end the civil war. A statement issued by the two sides stipulated that, in the period preceding the convening of a national constitutional conference, the Islamic legal code should be suspended, that military agreements between Sudan and other countries should be abandoned, and that the state of emergency be lifted and a cease-fire implemented in the south. In December, however, a state of emergency was again declared amidst reports that a military coup had been attempted. The DUP withdrew from the coalition government and its six cabinet ministers announced their resignation. The political crisis was caused by al-Mahdi's requesting the National Assembly to convene a national constitutional conference, whilst refusing to incorporate the agreement between the SPLM and the DUP (see above) into his proposal. In the same month the Government was forced to revoke substantial increases in the prices of basic commodities, following a national strike and demonstrations in Khartoum in protest at the measure.

In February 1989, in a major cabinet reshuffle, Dr Hassan at-Turabi, the leader of the NIF, was appointed Deputy Prime Minister, strengthening the position of the NIF in the Government. In late February al-Mahdi threatened to resign as Prime Minister unless senior army officers allowed him to form a new government and to work for peace in the south. (Senior army officers had issued an ultimatum demanding the introduction of political reforms and the formation of a government of national unity.) However, the army refused to guarantee that it would not intervene in Sudanese politics in the event of Sudan's continued perceived drift towards Libya and a lack of progress in negotiations to end the war in the south. In March al-Mahdi agreed to form a new, broad-based government which would begin negotiations with the SPLM. Thirty political parties and 17 trade unions had previously signed an agreement endorsing the peace agreement concluded by the DUP and the SPLM in November 1988 (see above). However, the NIF refused to endorse the agreement, which envisaged the suspension of Islamic laws as a prelude to the negotiation of a peace settlement to the civil war, and it was excluded from the new government formed on 23 March 1989. Peace negotiations between a government delegation and the SPLM commenced in Ethiopia in April, and at the beginning of May the SPLM leader, Col Garang, proclaimed a one-month cease-fire (subsequently extended to 30 June), renewing hopes for peace and aiding the work of famine relief. The negotiations culminated in an agreement to suspend Islamic laws pending the proposed convening, in September, of a constitutional conference at which the support of all political parties for a new, secular constitution would be sought. A further sign of conciliation was the announcement, in June, of the Government's decision to abrogate defence agreements with Egypt and Libya.

On 18 June 1989 it was reported that an attempt by the armed forces to restore the former President, Gen. Nimeri, to power had been thwarted, but on 30 June a bloodless coup, led by Brig. (later Lt-Gen.) Omar Hassan Ahmad al-Bashir, removed al-Mahdi's Government. Al-Bashir formed a 15-member Revolutionary Command Council for National Salvation (RCC), which declared its primary aim to be the resolution of the southern conflict. Al-Bashir, who became head of state, chairman of the RCC, Prime Minister and Minister of Defence, and commander-in-chief of the armed forces, rapidly dismantled the civilian ruling apparatus. The Constitution, the National Assembly and all political parties and trade unions were abolished, a state of emergency was declared, and civilian newspapers were closed. About 30 members of the former Government were detained, including al-Mahdi, although three of the ex-ministers were included in the new 21-member Cabinet which was announced in early July. Its composition included 16 civilians, of whom four were southerners, as well as several members who were understood to be sympathetic towards Islamic fundamentalism. Al-Bashir assigned a high priority to the suppression of financial corruption, and announced that special courts would be established to consider allegations of profiteering and hoarding.

The SPLM's response to the coup was cautious. In early July 1989 Lt-Gen. al-Bashir declared a one-month unilateral cease-fire and offered an amnesty to those opposing the Khartoum Government 'for political reasons'. In an effort to restart negotiations, al-Bashir requested Ethiopia, Egypt and Kenya to act as mediators. At the same time, however, the Government's announcement of proposals for a national referendum on *Shari'a* law alienated the SPLM, which demanded its suspension as a precondition for talks. A plan by the RCC to introduce military conscription appeared to foreshadow a possible escalation in the southern conflict.

Peace negotiations were renewed in Ethiopia in August 1989. By this time the SPLM's terms for a negotiated settlement to the conflict included the immediate resignation of the RCC prior to the establishment of an interim government, in which the SPLM, the banned political parties and other groupings would be represented. The new regime's proximity to the fundamentalist NIF had become apparent. The negotiations collapsed immediately over the issue of Islamic law. Col Garang was invited to attend a government-sponsored peace conference in Khartoum in September, but declined to do so while the curfew and the state of emergency remained in force. Delegates who did attend the conference were believed to be sympathetic to the fundamentalist NIF, and were thought to favour the secession of southern Sudan if it proved impossible to achieve a negotiated settlement to the conflict.

Hostilities, which had been in abeyance since the beginning of May 1989, resumed at the end of October, when the SPLM attacked and captured the town of Kurmuk. Further peace negotiations, mediated by the former US President, Jimmy Carter, began in Kenya at the beginning of December, but quickly collapsed over the issue of *Shari'a* law. By the end of January 1990 the SPLM was preparing a full-scale military assault on the garrison town of Juba. In March President Mobutu Sese Seko of Zaire conferred, separately, with both Lt-Gen. al-Bashir and Col Garang, in an attempt to restart the peace negotiations. Garang pronounced himself in favour of a cease-fire, as proposed by President Mobutu, but at the end of the month intense fighting was reported to have erupted around the government-held garrisons of Yei and Rumbrek, in south-western Sudan.

In late March 1990 57 people, including both army officers and civilians, were reported to have been arrested after allegedly having attempted to seize control of the Government. A reshuffle of the Cabinet in April was believed to have strengthened the influence of Islamic fundamentalists in Sudanese politics, as two of the new appointees were known to have close links with the NIF. It was claimed that a further military coup was attempted on 23 April, and this resulted in the execution, on the following day, of 28 army officers.

In May 1990 a senior official of the US Department of State met Col Garang, in an attempt to revive the peace negotiations, while US diplomats in Khartoum reportedly held talks with representatives of the Government, to the same end. However, reports in June cited the regular visits of Sudanese leaders to Iran, and the allocation of civil service posts to Islamic fundamentalists, as evidence of the military regime's increasingly fundamentalist character. These reports reduced still further the likelihood of any progress towards an early settlement of the southern conflict. Further attempted coups were reported to have taken place in September and November. Like those alleged to have been staged earlier in the year, their origins remained obscure.

In late January 1991 the Cabinet was reshuffled; three new ministries were created and several existing ministries were renamed. In early February the RCC enacted a decree which instituted a new, federal system of government. Sudan was divided into nine states—Khartoum, Central, Kordofan, Darfur, Northern, Eastern, Bahr al-Ghazal, Upper Nile and Equatoria—which were sub-divided into 66 provinces and 281 local government areas. The decree provided for each of the nine new states to have its own governor, deputy governor and cabinet of ministers, and to assume responsibility for local administration and the collection of some taxes. The central Government retained control over foreign policy, military affairs, the economy and the other principal areas of administration. The introduction of a new administrative structure was intended as a step towards ending the civil war in the south, but the SPLM immediately condemned the degree of power retained by the central Government. At the beginning of February it had been announced that a new penal code, based on *Shari'a* law, would take effect in March, but that it would not apply in the three southern states of Equatoria, Upper Nile and Bahr al-Ghazal, pending the establishment there of elected assemblies to resolve the issue. The SPLM nevertheless regarded the application of Islamic law in the northern states as unacceptable, citing the large numbers of non-Muslims resident there, and expressed their suspicion that the Government would seek to apply *Shari'a* law throughout the whole country.

A national conference to decide the country's political future was held during 29 April–2 May 1991. Some 1,600 delegates were reported to have been selected by the Government to attend the conference, at the opening of which it was announced that all political prisoners, including the former Prime Minister, Sadiq al-Mahdi, were to be released. Following the conference, al-Bashir announced that a political system based on Libyan-style 'people's congresses' was to be introduced into Sudan.

On 16 May 1991 Col Garang invited the Government to participate in peace negotiations. The Government declined to do so, however, claiming that the administrative reforms which it had introduced in February already represented a considerable degree of compromise. The overthrow, on 21 May, of the Ethiopian Government, led by Mengistu Haile Mariam, had implications for the SPLA forces, who had, in the past, enjoyed Ethiopian support. Armed clashes within Ethiopia between SPLA forces and those of the new Ethiopian Government were reported in late May. On 29 May the Sudanese Government declared its recognition of, and support for, the new Ethiopian regime. In June the Ethiopian Government was reported to have presented SPLA fighters in western Ethiopia with a deadline by which they had either to leave the country, to disarm or to accept refugee status. In October Sudan and Ethiopia signed a treaty of friendship and co-operation.

In mid-June 1991 the Government stated that it was prepared to consider proposals, made by a senior official of the US Department of State, which provided for the partial withdrawal of government forces from southern Sudan, for the withdrawal of the SPLA forces from government-held areas and for the declaration of Juba, the southern capital, as an 'open' city. On 14 June the SPLA declared its support for the Government's proposal that the President of Nigeria, Ibrahim Babangida, should act as a mediator in the southern conflict. However, this diplomatic progress was negated by a new government offensive against the SPLA.

In late August 1991 it was reported that Col Garang had been deposed as leader of the SPLA. However, it subsequently transpired that three of the SPLA's 13 commanders had defected from the organization in order to campaign for an independent southern Sudan. In early October it was reported that talks, mediated by the President of Nigeria, between representatives of the Government and the SPLA would shortly commence. At the end of the month, however, the talks were postponed as a result of the recent split within the leadership of the SPLA, the two rival factions of which were reported to be involved in fierce fighting in November. In December the Government declined to attend a peace conference organized by the former US President, Jimmy Carter, on the grounds that to do so would undermine its legitimacy. The conference had been scheduled to commence in Atlanta, USA, in early January 1992.

On 24 February 1992 a 300-member, transitional National Assembly was created. Members of the assembly, all of whom were appointed by al-Bashir, included the entire RCC, all government ministers and the governors of Sudan's nine states. The assembly was accorded legislative authority, with the power to examine all decrees issued by the RCC, and responsibility for preparing the country for parliamentary elections.

In early March 1992 government forces commenced an offensive against the SPLA in southern Sudan, and by May they were reported to have recaptured a number of towns. This success had apparently been facilitated by the continued division of the SPLA into two, rival factions. In late May a new round of peace negotiations commenced in Abuja, Nigeria, between a government delegation and two from the SPLA: one representing the faction led by Garang, and one from the dissident group based at Nasir. At the conclusion of the talks in June all parties agreed to continue negotiations at a future date. The final communiqué referred to Sudan as a 'multi-ethnic, multi-lingual, multi-cultural and multi-religious country'. However, the government refused to agree to hold a referendum on self-determination for the South.

In early July 1992 government forces were reported to have captured the town of Torit, near the Ugandan border, which had been the headquarters of Garang's faction of the SPLA. At the start of the rainy season, however, the SPLA launched a new offensive and there were signs that its two rival factions had achieved a degree of reconciliation since the Abuja peace negotiations, enabling them to offer a united response to the government advance. The shelling of Juba led to the suspension of relief flights to the city, and by mid-August its population was reported to be close to starvation. Meanwhile, the SPLA claimed that the government forces occupying the town had massacred 900 civilians there. Relief flights to the city resumed in November.

In early 1993 the NIF was reported to be opposed to the continued military character of the Government, and to favour the dissolution of the RCC. Regional councils were in the process of being elected, and the Government had reportedly undertaken, in 1992, to dissolve the RCC once the regional councils were in place. In mid-January al-Bashir effected an extensive reshuffle of the Cabinet, but stated that there would be no change in government policy and that the RCC would not be dissolved. Rather, in 1994 the gradual transfer of power to the regional councils would begin. Further talks between the Government and the SPLA ended inconclusively in January. By this time the SPLA was reported to have split into three rival factions.

In late February 1993 the Government revealed plans to hold both general and presidential elections in early 1994. However, it was emphasized at the same time that there would be no return to political pluralism. Immediately prior to the announcement of the elections, talks between the Government and Garang's faction of the SPLA had collapsed. In mid-March, in preparation for a new round of peace negotiations with the Government, Garang's faction of the SPLA announced a unilateral cease-fire.

Peace talks between the Government and the faction of the SPLA led by John Garang resumed in Abuja, Nigeria, in April 1993. After preliminary discussions on 8 April, at which it was agreed to continue to observe a cease-fire, the two sides met again for substantive talks on 26 April. Meanwhile, in Nairobi, talks were also taking place between a government delegation and SPLA-United, an alliance formed in early April between the Nasir faction, the 'Forces of Unity' and a faction led by Carabino Kuany Bol (see Directory, p. 2862). The Abuja talks adjourned on 18 May, having made little progress on the main issues dividing the parties. Although the Government claimed that the talks would resume in June, the SPLA side regarded them as having failed and pronounced the cease-fire at an end. The Nairobi talks resumed during 7–26 May, and ended with agreement on the concept of a unified federal state and on the rights of state governments to introduce laws supplementary to federal legislation—allowing the implementation of *Shari'a* law in the north, but not in the south. No agreement was reached, however, on the length of the transition period before the holding of a referendum on future divisions of power.

The collapse of the Abuja negotiations was quickly followed by allegations of cease-fire violations from both the Government and rebel factions, and in July 1993 the faction of the SPLA led by Garang announced that it had launched a major offensive after attacks by government troops, aided by rival SPLA factions. According to government sources, the renewed fighting caused the influx of some 100,000 starving people into the area around the southern provincial capital of Malakal. In August government forces attacked SPLA-held towns near the Ugandan border, in an attempt to sever supply routes to rebel forces in southern and western Sudan. They were reported to have gained control of the town of Morobo and to have blocked the road route for relief supplies to Bahr al-Ghazal and Western Equatoria. Also in August, the Nuba people were reported to be threatened by government forces in central Sudan. Independent observers urged the UN to establish 'safe havens' for refugees and to extend its Operation Lifeline Sudan to the Nuba Mountains. In early September the SPLA was reported to have checked the government forces' advance in southern Sudan. A reshuffle of the Cabinet in July 1993 was regarded as having further strengthened the position of the NIF within the Government, and as another step towards the establishment of a civilian administration.

On 19 October 1993 al-Bashir announced political reforms in preparation for presidential and legislative elections in 1994 and 1995 respectively. The RCC had been dissolved three days previously—after it had appointed al-Bashir as President and as head of a new civilian Government. Cabinet ministers were requested to remain in office until elections took place. On 20 October al-Bashir appointed a new Minister of Defence—a portfolio that he had formerly held himself—and a new Vice-President. Western observers regarded the dissolution of the RCC as reinforcing the position of the NIF within the Government during the transition to civilian rule. At the end of October the Cabinet was reshuffled.

In January 1994 the two principal rival factions of the SPLA were reported to have agreed on a cease-fire. In late January government forces were reported to have launched ground and air offensives against rebel forces in southern Sudan, forcing thousands of civilians to flee across the Ugandan border. The intensity of the offensives led to speculation that the Government was attempting finally to end the civil war. In mid-February the SPLA claimed that it had repulsed a government advance in Southern Equatoria.

In early February 1994, by constitutional decree, Sudan was redivided into 26 states instead of the nine that had formed the basis of administration since 1991. The executive and legislative powers of each state government were to be expanded, and southern states were expected to be exempted from *Shari'a* law.

In late March 1994 delegations representing the Government and two factions of the SPLA travelled to Nairobi, Kenya, in order to participate in peace talks held under the auspices of the Intergovernmental Authority on Drought and Development (IGADD, see p. 239), which in September 1993 had formed a committee on the Sudanese conflict comprising the Heads of State of Kenya, Ethiopia, Uganda and Eritrea. All parties to the talks agreed to allow the free passage of relief supplies to southern Sudan, and it was reported that an agenda forming the basis of future negotiations had been agreed.

On 10 April 1994 the Government adopted legislation providing for the appointment, by the President, of an independent commission to supervise legislative elections scheduled to take place in the second half of 1994, and for a constitutional referendum. In order to combat corruption, election campaigns would be financed exclusively by the State.

On 16 May 1994 the Government held a conference in Juba province, at the conclusion of which a declaration was issued that urged national unity and appealed to all rebel forces to embrace conventional politics. On 18 May a second round of IGADD-sponsored peace talks between representatives of the Government and two factions of the SPLA commenced in Nairobi, but this was adjourned until mid-July two days later, in order to allow the participants time to study a draft declaration of principles on which future negotiations might be based. On 20 June the President of the proscribed UP and former Prime Minister, Sadiq al-Mahdi, was arrested for allegedly having plotted to overthrow the Government. However, no charges were subsequently brought against him and he was released on 3 July.

On 13 July 1994 a restructuring of the Cabinet was announced in which Lt-Col Altayed Ibrahim Muhammad Khair was appointed Minister of the Interior. The changes to the Government were regarded as having strengthened the position of those within it who opposed any compromise with the SPLA. A third round of IGADD-sponsored peace negotiations was held in Nairobi on 18–28 July. On 23 July the Government announced a unilateral cease-fire, to which the faction of the SPLA led by John Garang reportedly responded on 28 July with a ceasefire of its own. The negotiations were adjourned until early September. During the interim delegations were to study proposed solutions to the southern conflict which might take effect after a transitional period. However, when the negotiations resumed divergent positions on the issues of the governance of the south and the role of religion in government quickly led to deadlock. Later in September, however, the IGADD committee on the Sudanese conflict held a further meeting in Nairobi and resolved to continue its Sudanese peace initiative. In late September President al-Bashir announced the creation of an 89-member peace council. In mid-November it was formally inaugurated, as the Supreme Council for Peace, and enlarged to 96 members at the end of that month. The severing, in December, of diplomatic relations between Sudan and Eritrea led Sudan to inform the IGADD in early 1995 that it no longer considered Eritrea to be a suitable intermediary in the Sudanese conflict. In early February the Cabinet was reshuffled. Once again the pattern of changes suggested a reinforcement of the Islamic character of the Government.

In addition to the consequences of internal rebellion and economic crisis, Sudan has experienced drought and famine, and the problem has been compounded by a very large number of refugees in the southern provinces, mainly from Ethiopia and Chad. In March 1990 a report by the human rights organization, Africa Watch, claimed that as many as 500,000 Sudanese civilians had been killed by war and 'man-made' famine since 1986. International relief operations to provide food aid, in years of drought and failed harvests, have done little to solve the problems of underinvestment in, and mismanagement of, Sudanese agriculture, and the economic impoverishment which has resulted from drought and famine.

In December 1992 the UN Security Council adopted a resolution that condemned the abuse of human rights in southern Sudan. The Government, however, denied that any abuse had taken place and announced that it would investigate such allegations independently. In February 1993 the human rights organization, Amnesty International, also alleged the widespread abuse of human rights by government forces in southern Sudan. In the same month the USA was reported to be considering whether to establish 'safety zones' in southern Sudan in order to combat famine and disease there, an idea for which Garang's faction of the SPLA expressed its support. In late February US relief organizations were reported to have urged the new US Administration of President Clinton to play a leading role in providing aid to Sudan. In February 1994 the UN launched an appeal for US $279m. to provide food and emergency aid in order to compensate for the failure of harvests in northern Sudan. The UN World Food Programme estimated that some 3.7m. Sudanese would require food aid in 1994. In late December Sudan appealed to the international community for more aid for refugees, whose number was now estimated at more than 1m. The office of the UN High Commissioner for Refugees was reported to have halved to $6m. the amount of aid it had pledged for refugees in Sudan in 1995. In January 1995 the UN launched an international appeal to raise $101m. to provide food aid for an estimated 1.2m. needy Sudanese in 1995.

Following an unsuccessful coup attempt in July 1976, Sudan severed diplomatic relations with Libya and established a mutual defence pact with Egypt. Diplomatic links between Sudan and Libya were restored in February 1978, but relations became strained in 1981, during Libya's occupation of Chad, and President Nimeri frequently accused Libya of supporting plots against him. After the 1985 coup, Libya was the first country to recognize the new regime, and relations between the two countries improved significantly; a military co-operation agreement was signed in July. Although Libya's military involvement in Chad declined, some Libyan forces remained in north-western Sudan, despite repeated Sudanese demands for their withdrawal. The regime that took power in Sudan in 1985 adopted a foreign policy of non-alignment, in contrast to Nimeri's strongly pro-Western attitude, and sought improved relations with Ethiopia and the USSR, to the concern of Sudan's former allies, Egypt and the USA. Relations with Ethiopia fluctuated after November 1987, however, while the USSR eschewed any involvement in Sudanese affairs.

President Nimeri was one of very few Arab leaders to support President Sadat of Egypt's initiative for peace with Israel in 1978. Sudan's close relations with Egypt were consolidated in October 1982, when a 'charter of integration' was signed. The first session of the joint 'Nile Valley Parliament', created by the charter, was convened in May 1983 with 60 Sudanese and 60 Egyptian members. After the coup of April 1985, the leaders of the two countries exchanged official visits, and reaffirmed links between Khartoum and Cairo, despite the change of government in Sudan. After the 1986 election Sadiq al-Mahdi sought to introduce a more independent policy for Sudan. In February 1987, however, al-Mahdi paid an official visit to Cairo, when a new agreement on economic and cultural co-operation was signed. Relations with Egypt deteriorated in January 1991, as a result of the Sudanese Government's support for Iraq in its conflict with the multinational force that brought about the withdrawal of Iraqi occupying troops from Kuwait. Egypt has also expressed concern at the perceived growth of Islamic 'fundamentalism', and has accused Sudan of attempting to support Islamic revolution and to destabilize the region. Sudan and Egypt are also involved in a dispute over the Halaib border area, and in February 1992 relations deteriorated sharply following the announcement that Sudan had awarded a Canadian company a concession to explore for oil there. In April two Sudanese policemen were killed in a clash between border guards in the Halaib area and relations deteriorated further as Egypt repeatedly accused Sudan of supporting illegal Islamic fundamentalist groups in Egypt—matched by Sudanese allegations that Egypt was supporting the SPLA. In August the Sudanese Government announced that it wished to seek international arbitration on the Halaib issue, claiming that Egypt had been settling families in the area in an effort to bring it under Egyptian control. A series of bilateral meetings held during the second half of 1992 failed to resolve the issue, and in January 1993 Sudan complained to the UN Security Council that Egyptian troops had infringed Sudan's territorial integrity. In March Egypt announced the construction of a new road link to Halaib. Sudan retaliated by appropriating the Khartoum campus of Cairo University (see Education, below). In June Sudan announced that it was closing two Egyptian consulates in Sudan and two of its own consulates in Egypt. A meeting between al-Bashir and the Egyptian President, Hosni Mubarak, during a summit meeting of the OAU at the end of June appeared, however, to ease tensions between the two countries, and was followed by a meeting of their respective Ministers of Foreign Affairs at the end of July. In May 1994 Sudan accused Egypt of establishing military posts on Sudanese territory, and at the end of the month the Sudanese Ministry of Foreign Affairs announced that Sudan wished to refer its dispute with Egypt to the International Court of Justice (ICJ) in The Hague, the Netherlands, for arbitration. In early September the Sudanese Ministry of Foreign Affairs alleged that Egyptian armed forces had carried out attacks in the Halaib area, and that they had kidnapped a Sudanese officer. In late September Sudan expelled an Egyptian diplomat for actions incompatible with his status. Egypt responded by expelling two Sudanese diplomats, accusing them of security offences.

In March 1990, after Lt-Gen. al-Bashir had visited Col Qaddafi, the Libyan leader, in Tripoli, Sudan and Libya signed a 'declaration of integration' that envisaged the complete union of the two countries within four years. An agreement on integration was signed in September. In January 1995 Sudan, Libya and Chad were reported to be discussing integration after eventual legislative elections in Chad.

There was evidence of increasing economic and military links between Sudan and Iran in 1991. Some 2,000 Iranian Revolutionary Guards were allegedly dispatched to Sudan to assist with the training of the Sudanese army, and in December President Rafsanjani of Iran made an official visit to Sudan, during which a trade agreement between the two countries was concluded. In November 1993 Iran was reported to have financed Sudan's purchase of some 20 Chinese ground-attack aircraft. The USA has frequently expressed concern about Sudan's links with Iran. Allegations of Sudanese involvement in terrorism resulted in the detention in the USA, in June 1993, of five Sudanese residents suspected of involvement in a plot to blow up buildings and road tunnels in New York, and to assassinate President Mubarak of Egypt on a visit to the USA. The Sudanese Government denied any connection with such a plot, but in August the USA added Sudan to its list of countries accused of sponsoring terrorism.

Sudan's relations with the United Kingdom deteriorated in December 1993, when the Archbishop of Canterbury, Dr George Carey, cancelled a planned visit to Khartoum but made another, behind SPLA lines, in the south. This resulted in the mutual expulsion of ambassadors by Sudan and the United Kingdom. The release by the Sudanese to the French authorities, in August 1994, of the Venezuelan-born terrorist, Illich Ramirez Sanchez ('Carlos'), was regarded by many observers as an attempt by the Government to improve its international standing.

### Government

Under the terms of the 1985 interim Constitution, legislative power was vested in the 301-seat National Assembly. There was a Supreme Council, comprising a President and five other members, which collectively exercised the functions of Head of State. Executive power was exercised by the Council of Ministers (headed by the Prime Minister), which was responsible to the National Assembly.

In February 1992 a 300-member transitional National Assembly was appointed by Lt-Gen. al-Bashir. The Assembly was vested with legislative authority and was charged with preparing the country for parliamentary elections.

In October 1993 the Revolutionary Command Council for National Salvation, which had assumed power after the military coup of 30 June 1989, was dissolved after appointing Lt-Gen. al-Bashir as President and head of a new civilian Government. In February 1994 Sudan was redivided into 26 states rather than the nine that had formed the basis of administration since 1991. A governor assumed responsibility for each state, assisted by five—in the case of the southern states six—state ministers.

### Defence

In June 1994 the armed forces totalled 118,500: army 115,000, navy an estimated 500, air force 3,000. Paramilitaries formed a Popular Defence Force with an active strength of 15,000 and 60,000 reserves. Defence expenditure for 1994 was budgeted at £S15,220m. (including internal security). Sudan has a defence agreement with Egypt and has received military aid from the USA. A military co-operation agreement was signed with the People's Republic of China in January 1982, and another with Libya in July 1985. Military service is compulsory for males aged 18–30 years and lasts for up to 36 months.

### Economic Affairs

In 1990, according to estimates by the World Bank, Sudan's gross national product (GNP), measured at average 1988–90 prices, was US $10,107m., equivalent to $400 per head. During 1980–90, it was estimated, GNP increased, in real terms, at an average annual rate of 0.3%, but real GNP per head declined by 2.4% per year. During 1985–93 the population increased by an annual average of 2.8%. According to World Bank estimates, Sudan's gross domestic product (GDP), expressed in constant 1986/87 prices, increased by an annual average of 1.5% in 1979/80–1988/90, fell by 1.5% in 1989/90 and rose by 0.7% in 1990/91.

Agriculture (including forestry and fishing) contributed 34% of GDP in 1992. About 56.6% of the labour force were employed in the sector in 1993. The principal cash crop is cotton, which accounted for about 50% of export earnings in 1991. The principal subsistence crops are sorghum and wheat. According to FAO estimates, during 1985–94 agricultural production increased by an annual average of 0.5%.

Industry (including mining, manufacturing, construction and power) contributed 17% of GDP in 1992, and employed 7.9% of the labour force in 1983. During 1980–90 industrial production increased by an annual average of 2.9%.

The contribution of mining to GDP is insignificant. Sudan has reserves of petroleum, marble, mica, chromite, gypsum and gold.

Manufacturing contributed 9% of GDP in 1992. The most important sector is food-processing, especially sugar-refining, while the textile industry, cement production and petroleum-refining are also significant. Some 4.6% of the labour force were employed in manufacturing in 1983.

Energy is derived principally from hydroelectric power and thermal power. Imports of mineral fuels comprised about 23% of the total value of imports in 1991.

In 1992 Sudan recorded a visible trade deficit of US $596.8m., and there was a deficit of $506.2m. on the current account of the balance of payments. In 1987 the principal source of imports (10.5%) was the United Kingdom, which also provided the principal market for Sudanese exports (8.2%). Other major trading partners in that year were the USA, Japan and the Federal Republic of Germany. The principal exports in 1987 were cotton, sesame seed, millet and sorghum, and gum arabic, and the principal imports were petroleum and petroleum products, wheat and meslin and machinery.

It was estimated that Sudan's budget deficit would reach £S13,200m. in the 1989/90 financial year. At the end of 1993 Sudan's total external debt was US $16,560m., of which $8,994m. was long-term public debt. During 1988–93 the average annual rate of inflation was 93.3%; consumer prices increased by an average of 101.4% in 1993. In early 1995 the rate was reported to be 65%.

Sudan is a member of the African Development Bank (see p. 102), the Arab Bank for Economic Development in Africa (see p. 183), the Arab Fund for Economic and Social Development (see p. 237), the Arab Monetary Fund (see p. 237), the Council of Arab Economic Unity (see p. 133) and the Islamic Development Bank (see p. 180).

Sudan's economic problems are largely due to mismanagement in the 1970s, when the development of the country's agricultural potential was neglected, and the Government began to borrow heavily, resulting in the country's present unmanageably large foreign debt. Sudan's foreign debt is the biggest obstacle to its economic recovery. In September 1990 the IMF adopted a Declaration of Non-co-operation regarding Sudan, noting that the country had remained in arrears in its obligations to the Fund since July 1984. In February 1994 Sudan's arrears in payments to the IMF were estimated to be the largest ever recorded, at US $1,700m. In February 1992 the Government introduced a comprehensive economic reform programme, but the reforms failed to satisfy the IMF, and in April 1993 the World Bank ceased funding Sudanese projects after the country had failed to pay arrears owed to the Bank. In February 1994 the Executive Board of the IMF voted to commence proceedings to withdraw Sudan's membership of the Fund. However, withdrawal proceedings were suspended in early 1995, after the Government had committed itself to structural adjustments and to repaying its arrears to the IMF. The other major obstacle to recovery is the conflict in southern Sudan, which is estimated to cost the country $1m.–$2m. each day.

### Social Welfare

The Ministry of Health organizes the public health services. In 1981 there were 158 hospitals with 17,205 beds, 220 health centres, 887 dispensaries, 1,619 dressing stations and 1,095 primary health care units. In 1984 there were 2,095 physicians working in Sudan, while nursing and midwifery personnel totalled 12,986. In 1986 medical personnel included 2,405 physicians, and the total number of beds in medical establishments was 18,571.

### Education

The Government provides free primary education from the ages of seven to 12 years. Secondary education begins at 13 years of age and lasts for up to six years, divided into two cycles of three years each. The average rate of adult illiteracy was estimated by UNESCO at 72.9% (males 57.3%; females 88.3%) in 1990, compared with 85.3% in 1966. In 1991 the total enrolment at primary and secondary schools was equivalent to 38% of children in the appropriate age-groups (42% of boys; 33% of girls). About 15% of current government expenditure in 1985 was for primary and secondary education. Pupils from secondary schools are accepted at the University of Khartoum, subject to their reaching the necessary standards. The Khartoum branch of Cairo University was appropriated and renamed Nilayn University by the Sudanese Government in April 1993. There are three universities at Omdurman: Omdurman Islamic University; Omdurman Ahlia University; and Ahfad University for Women. New universities were opened at Juba and Wadi Medani (University of Gezira) in 1977. There is also a University of Science and Technology in Khartoum.

### Public Holidays

**1995:** 1 January (Independence Day), 3 March (Unity Day and Id al-Fitr*, end of Ramadan), 6 April (Uprising Day, anniversary of 1985 coup), 24 April (Sham an-Nassim, Coptic Easter Monday), 10 May* (Id al-Adha, Feast of the Sacrifice), 31 May* (Islamic New Year), 1 July (Decentralization Day), 9 August* (Mouloud, Birth of the Prophet), 25 December (Christmas).

**1996:** 1 January (Independence Day), 21 February* (Id al-Fitr, end of Ramadan), 3 March (Unity Day), 6 April (Uprising Day, anniversary of 1985 coup), 15 April (Sham an-Nassim, Coptic Easter Monday), 29 April* (Id al-Adha, Feast of the Sacrifice), 19 May* (Islamic New Year), 1 July (Decentralization Day), 28 July* (Mouloud, Birth of the Prophet), 25 December (Christmas).

* The dates of Islamic holidays are determined by sightings of the moon, and may be slightly different from those given above.

### Weights and Measures

The metric system is gradually replacing traditional weights and measures.

SUDAN

# Statistical Survey

Source (unless otherwise stated): Department of Statistics, Ministry of Finance and Economic Planning, POB 700, Khartoum; tel. 77003.

## Area and Population

### AREA, POPULATION AND DENSITY

| | |
|---|---|
| Area (sq km) | 2,505,813* |
| Population (census results) | |
| 1 February 1983 | 20,594,197 |
| 15 June 1993 | 24,940,683† |
| Density (per sq km) at June 1993 | 10.0 |

* 967,500 sq miles.  † Provisional result.

### PROVINCES* (1983 census, provisional)

| | Area (sq miles) | Population | Density (per sq mile) |
|---|---|---|---|
| Northern | 134,736 | 433,391 | 3.2 |
| Nile | 49,205 | 649,633 | 13.2 |
| Kassala | 44,109 | 1,512,335 | 34.3 |
| Red Sea | 84,977 | 695,874 | 8.2 |
| Blue Nile | 24,009 | 1,056,313 | 44.0 |
| Gezira | 13,546 | 2,023,094 | 149.3 |
| White Nile | 16,161 | 933,136 | 57.7 |
| Northern Kordofan | 85,744 | 1,805,769 | 21.1 |
| Southern Kordofan | 61,188 | 1,287,525 | 21.0 |
| Northern Darfur | 133,754 | 1,327,947 | 9.9 |
| Southern Darfur | 62,801 | 1,765,752 | 28.1 |
| Khartoum | 10,883 | 1,802,299 | 165.6 |
| Eastern Equatoria | 46,073 | 1,047,125 | 22.7 |
| Western Equatoria | 30,422 | 359,056 | 11.8 |
| Bahr al-Ghazal | 52,000 | 1,492,597 | 28.7 |
| Al-Bohayrat | 25,625 | 772,913 | 30.2 |
| Sobat | 45,266 | 802,354 | 17.7 |
| Jonglei | 47,003 | 797,251 | 17.0 |
| **Total** | **967,500** | **20,564,364** | **21.3** |

* In 1991 a federal system of government was inaugurated, whereby Sudan was divided into nine states, which were sub-divided into 66 provinces and 281 local government areas. A constitutional decree, issued in February 1994, redivided the country into 26 states.

### PRINCIPAL TOWNS (population at 1983 census)

| | | | |
|---|---|---|---|
| Omdurman | 526,192 | Wadi Medani | 145,015 |
| Khartoum (capital) | 473,597 | Al-Obeid | 137,582 |
| Khartoum North | 340,857 | Atbara | 73,009* |
| Port Sudan | 206,038 | | |

* Provisional.

### BIRTHS AND DEATHS (UN estimates, annual averages)

| | 1975–80 | 1980–85 | 1985–90 |
|---|---|---|---|
| Birth rate (per 1,000) | 47.1 | 45.9 | 44.6 |
| Death rate (per 1,000) | 19.4 | 17.3 | 15.8 |

**Expectation of life** (UN estimates, years at birth, 1985–90): 49.8 (males 48.6; females 51.0).

Source: UN, *World Population Prospects: The 1992 Revision*.

### ECONOMICALLY ACTIVE POPULATION* (1983 census, provisional)

| | Males | Females | Total |
|---|---|---|---|
| Agriculture, hunting, forestry and fishing | 2,638,294 | 1,390,411 | 4,028,705 |
| Mining and quarrying | 5,861 | 673 | 6,534 |
| Manufacturing | 205,247 | 61,446 | 266,693 |
| Electricity, gas and water | 42,110 | 1,618 | 43,728 |
| Construction | 130,977 | 8,305 | 139,282 |
| Trade, restaurants and hotels | 268,382 | 25,720 | 294,102 |
| Transport, storage and communications | 209,776 | 5,698 | 215,474 |
| Financing, insurance, real estate and business services | 17,414 | 3,160 | 20,574 |
| Community, social and personal services | 451,193 | 99,216 | 550,409 |
| Activities not adequately described | 142,691 | 42,030 | 184,721 |
| Unemployed persons not previously employed | 387,615 | 205,144 | 592,759 |
| **Total** | **4,499,560** | **1,843,421** | **6,342,981** |

* Excluding nomads, homeless and institutional households.

**Mid-1993** (estimates in '000): Agriculture, etc. 5,066; Total 8,943 (Source: FAO, *Production Yearbook*).

## Agriculture

### PRINCIPAL CROPS ('000 metric tons)

| | 1991 | 1992 | 1993 |
|---|---|---|---|
| Wheat† | 680 | 895 | 453 |
| Maize | 61† | 51† | 90* |
| Millet | 308 | 449† | 221† |
| Sorghum (Durra)† | 3,540 | 4,042 | 2,386 |
| Rice (paddy) | 1 | 1* | 1* |
| Sugar cane* | 4,500 | 4,600* | 4,650* |
| Potatoes* | 16 | 17 | 14 |
| Sweet potatoes* | 7 | 7 | 7 |
| Cassava (Manioc) | 8* | 9* | 8 |
| Yams* | 128 | 129 | 125 |
| Onions* | 40 | 40 | 40 |
| Dry beans | 3 | 3 | 5 |
| Dry broad beans | 45* | 35† | 45* |
| Chick-peas | 2 | 2* | 2* |
| Other pulses* | 60 | 62 | 63 |
| Oranges* | 15 | 15 | 15 |
| Tangerines, mandarins, clementines and satsumas* | 1 | 1 | 1 |
| Lemons and limes* | 55 | 55 | 55 |
| Grapefruit* | 63 | 63 | 62 |
| Mangoes* | 130 | 135 | 135 |
| Dates* | 140 | 142 | 140 |
| Bananas* | 63 | 64 | 63 |
| Groundnuts (in shell) | 179† | 315 | 390* |
| Seed cotton | 273 | 261† | 185* |
| Cottonseed* | 177 | 170 | 120 |
| Cotton lint† | 92 | 87 | 61 |
| Sesame seed | 117† | 125* | 120* |
| Castor beans | 7 | 6† | 6* |
| Tomatoes* | 165 | 170 | 160 |
| Pumpkins, etc.* | 55 | 55 | 55 |
| Aubergines* | 75 | 75 | 70 |
| Melons* | 21 | 21 | 20 |
| Water melons* | 123 | 123 | 120 |

* FAO estimate(s).  † Unofficial figure(s).

Source: FAO, *Production Yearbook*.

## SUDAN

### LIVESTOCK ('000 head, year ending September)

|  | 1991 | 1992 | 1993* |
|---|---|---|---|
| Cattle | 21,028 | 21,600† | 21,600 |
| Sheep | 20,700 | 22,600† | 22,500 |
| Goats | 15,277 | 15,700* | 16,200 |
| Horses* | 22 | 23 | 23 |
| Asses* | 680 | 681 | 670 |
| Camels | 2,757 | 2,800 | 2,850 |

**Poultry** (million): 33 in 1991; 35† in 1992; 35* in 1993.
* FAO estimate(s).   † Unofficial figure.
Source: FAO, *Production Yearbook*.

### LIVESTOCK PRODUCTS ('000 metric tons)

|  | 1991 | 1992 | 1993 |
|---|---|---|---|
| Beef and veal | 231 | 250* | 258 |
| Mutton and lamb | 72 | 74 | 75 |
| Goat meat | 35 | 35* | 36 |
| Poultry meat* | 22 | 23 | 24 |
| Other meat | 68 | 67* | 65 |
| Cows' milk | 2,299 | 2,393* | 2,500 |
| Sheep's milk* | 480 | 494 | 505 |
| Goats' milk | 528 | 563* | 565 |
| Butter and ghee* | 13.5 | 13.6 | 13.5 |
| Cheese* | 68.5 | 69.6 | 70.7 |
| Poultry eggs | 34.3 | 35.2 | 34.0 |
| Wool: |  |  |  |
| greasy* | 19.0 | 19.5 | 20.0 |
| clean* | 8.6 | 8.8 | 9.0 |
| Cattle hides* | 35.5 | 38.3 | 39.5 |
| Sheepskins* | 10.8 | 11.0 | 11.3 |
| Goatskins* | 6.5 | 6.7 | 6.9 |

* FAO estimate(s).   † Unofficial figure.
Source: FAO, *Production Yearbook*.

## Forestry

### ROUNDWOOD REMOVALS ('000 cubic metres)

|  | 1990 | 1991* | 1992* |
|---|---|---|---|
| Sawlogs, veneer logs and logs for sleepers | 5 | 5 | 5 |
| Other industrial wood* | 2,104 | 2,164 | 2,225 |
| Fuel wood* | 20,682 | 21,270 | 21,874 |
| Total | 22,791 | 23,439 | 24,104 |

* FAO estimates.
Source: FAO, *Yearbook of Forest Products*.

### GUM ARABIC PRODUCTION (metric tons, year ending 30 June)

|  | 1984/85 | 1985/86 | 1986/87 |
|---|---|---|---|
| Gum kashab | 11,313 | 18,047 | 37,500 |
| Gum talh | 2,775 | 2,375 | 2,500 |
| Total | 14,066 | 20,422 | 40,000 |

Source: Bank of Sudan.
**1990:** Total production (metric tons): 40,000.

## Fishing

(metric tons, live weight)

|  | 1990 | 1991 | 1992* |
|---|---|---|---|
| Inland waters | 30,234 | 31,803 | 30,200 |
| Indian Ocean | 1,500 | 1,500 | 1,500 |
| Total catch | 31,734 | 33,303 | 31,700 |

* FAO estimates.
Source: FAO, *Yearbook of Fishery Statistics*.

## Mining

(estimated production)

|  | 1989 | 1990 | 1991 |
|---|---|---|---|
| Salt (unrefined) ('000 metric tons) | 91 | 68 | 77 |
| Chromium ore ('000 metric tons)* | 9 | 5 | n.a. |
| Gold ore (kilograms)* | 500 | 100 | 50 |

* Figures refer to the metal content of ores.
Source: UN, *Industrial Statistics Yearbook*.

## Industry

### PETROLEUM PRODUCTS (estimates, '000 metric tons)

|  | 1989 | 1990 | 1991 |
|---|---|---|---|
| Motor spirit (petrol) | 112 | 95 | 98 |
| Aviation gasoline | 4 | 3 | 5 |
| Naphtha | 20 | 20 | 22 |
| Jet fuels | 77 | 75 | 82 |
| Kerosene | 18 | 15 | 21 |
| Distillate fuel oils | 315 | 331 | 329 |
| Residual fuel oils | 310 | 304 | 314 |
| Liquefied petroleum gas | 5 | 7 | 6 |

Source: UN, *Industrial Statistics Yearbook*.

### SELECTED OTHER PRODUCTS (year ending 30 June)

|  | 1983/84 | 1984/85 | 1985/86 |
|---|---|---|---|
| Cement ('000 metric tons) | 198 | 146 | 151 |
| Wheat flour ('000 metric tons) | 266 | 280 | n.a. |
| Raw sugar ('000 metric tons) | 419 | 497 | 452 |
| Cigarettes (million) | 1,600 | 2,400 | 2,900 |

Source: Bank of Sudan.

## Finance

### CURRENCY AND EXCHANGE RATES

**Monetary Units**
1,000 millièmes = 100 piastres = 1 Sudanese pound (£S).

**Sterling and Dollar Equivalents** (31 December 1994)
£1 sterling = £S625.8;
US $1 = £S400.0;
£S1,000 = £1.598 sterling = $2.500.

**Average Exchange Rate**
Between October 1987 and October 1991 the official rate of exchange was fixed at US $1 = £S4.50. In October 1991 a new rate of US $1 = £S14.99 was introduced. The average exchange rate for 1991 was $1 = £S5.43. In February 1992 the currency was devalued by 83.4%, with the exchange rate fixed at $1 = £S90.09. This rate was subsequently adjusted. The average rate per US $ was about £S69 in 1992, £S154 in 1993 and £S278 in 1994.

### CENTRAL GOVERNMENT BUDGET
(estimates, £S million, year ending 30 June)

| Revenue | 1983/84 | 1984/85 | 1985/86 |
|---|---|---|---|
| Direct taxes | 404.5 | 300.5 | 351.6 |
| Indirect taxes | 839.9 | 984.6 | 1,222.6 |
| Others | 224.6 | 200.4 | 216.2 |
| Total | 1,469.0 | 1,485.5 | 1,790.4 |

# SUDAN

## Statistical Survey

| Expenditure | 1983/84 | 1984/85 | 1985/86 |
|---|---|---|---|
| **Ordinary budget:** | | | |
| Economic services | 74.3 | 196.0 | 208.0 |
| Social Services | 69.9 | 160.8 | 182.0 |
| Loan repayments | 212.0 | 118.0 | 465.4 |
| Defence and security | 260.6 | 462.0 | 473.1 |
| Regional Governments | 270.3 | 360.5 | 557.0 |
| Others | 755.6 | 1,214.9 | 1,492.8 |
| **Development budget:** | | | |
| Agricultural sector | 135.4 | 139.1 | 96.3 |
| Industrial sector | 119.2 | 110.1 | 74.6 |
| Transport and communications | 67.6 | 52.1 | 57.9 |
| Services sector | 59.4 | 54.3 | 32.5 |
| Others | 101.4 | 97.4 | 107.8 |
| **Total** | 2,130.7 | 2,965.2 | 3,747.0 |

**1986/87** (estimates, £S million, year ending 30 June): revenue 2,682.8 (tax revenue 1,670.0, non-tax revenue 1,012.8); expenditure 5,542.0 (current expenditure 3,616.2, development 1,380.8, debt servicing 520.0, equity 25.0).
**1987/88** (estimates, £S million, year ending 30 June): revenue 3,905.5 (tax revenue 2,379.2, non-tax revenue 1,348.0); expenditure 6,790.0 (current expenditure 5,232.2, development 1,533.4).
**1988/89** (estimates, £S million, year ending 30 June): revenue 5,885; expenditure 9,767 (development 2,518).
**1989/90** (estimates, £S million, year ending 30 June): revenue 8,600; expenditure 21,600 (development 4,000).
**1990/91** (estimates, £S million, year ending 30 June): revenue 14,457; expenditure 16,163 (development 5,200); expenditure subsequently revised to 13,900.
**1991/92** (estimates, £S million, year ending 30 June): revenue 32,600; expenditure 42,500.
**1992/93** (estimates, £S million, year ending 30 June): revenue 73,700; expenditure 156,000.

## INTERNATIONAL RESERVES (US $ million at 31 December)

| | 1991 | 1992 | 1993 |
|---|---|---|---|
| Foreign exchange | 7.6 | 24.2 | 37.7 |
| **Total** | 7.6 | 24.2 | 37.7 |

Source: IMF, *International Financial Statistics*.

## MONEY SUPPLY (£S'000 million at 31 December)

| | 1991 | 1992 | 1993 |
|---|---|---|---|
| Currency outside banks | 21.66 | 43.52 | 94.54 |
| Demand deposits at deposit money banks | 18.71 | 45.67 | 62.50 |
| **Total money** (incl. others) | 44.31 | 89.19 | 157.04 |

Source: IMF, *International Financial Statistics*.

## COST OF LIVING
(Consumer Price Index for low-income households; base: 1980 = 100)

| | 1987 | 1988 | 1989 |
|---|---|---|---|
| Food | 679.3 | 1,107.2 | 1,602.2 |
| Fuel and light | 548.4 | 567.9 | 1,472.0 |
| Clothing | 777.3 | 868.3 | 2,248.0 |
| Rent | 547.8 | 562.0 | 1,217.0 |
| **All items** (incl. others) | 649.9 | 965.2 | 1,603.7 |

**1990** (base: January 1988 = 100): Food 392.1; Fuel and light 357.4; Clothing 402.5; Rent 200.4; All items (incl. others) 385.0.
**1991** (base: January 1988 = 100): Food 804.3; Fuel and light 789.5; Clothing 834.3; Rent 529.8; All items (incl. others) 790.1.

Source: ILO, *Year Book of Labour Statistics*.

## NATIONAL ACCOUNTS
(£S million in current prices, year ending 30 June)

| | 1988/89 | 1989/90 | 1990/91 |
|---|---|---|---|
| Gross domestic product | 82,562 | 110,111 | 192,660 |

Source: IMF, *International Financial Statistics*.

## Expenditure on the Gross Domestic Product
(estimates, £S million in current prices)

| | 1989 | 1990 | 1991 |
|---|---|---|---|
| Government final consumption expenditure | 13,194 | 19,226 | 29,407 |
| Private final consumption expenditure | 55,905 | 81,483 | 122,621 |
| Gross fixed capital formation | 12,371 | 18,005 | 27,851 |
| **Total domestic expenditure** | 81,470 | 118,714 | 179,879 |
| Exports of goods and services | 6,108 | 4,524 | 4,321 |
| *Less* Imports of goods and services | 14,015 | 12,493 | 11,737 |
| **GDP in purchasers' values** | 73,563 | 110,745 | 172,463 |
| **GDP at constant 1980 prices** | 4,758 | 4,496 | 4,496 |

Source: UN Economic Commission for Africa, *African Statistical Yearbook*.

## Gross Domestic Product by Economic Activity
(estimates, £S million)

| | 1989 | 1990 | 1991 |
|---|---|---|---|
| Agriculture, forestry and fishing | 17,746 | 28,427 | 50,017 |
| Mining and quarrying | 49 | 77 | 93 |
| Manufacturing | 4,864 | 7,148 | 10,167 |
| Electricity, gas and water | 1,558 | 2,183 | 3,095 |
| Construction | 2,415 | 3,598 | 5,132 |
| Trade, restaurants and hotels | 11,302 | 15,857 | 21,739 |
| Transport, storage and communications | 6,161 | 9,100 | 12,720 |
| Finance, insurance, real estate and business services | 2,603 | 3,636 | 4,863 |
| Public administration and defence | 6,280 | 9,428 | 13,277 |
| Other community, social and personal services | 1,482 | 2,241 | 3,197 |
| **GDP at factor cost** | 54,460 | 81,695 | 124,300 |
| Indirect taxes, *less* subsidies | 19,103 | 29,050 | 48,163 |
| **GDP in purchasers' values** | 73,563 | 110,745 | 172,463 |

Source: UN Economic Commission for Africa, *African Statistical Yearbook*.

## BALANCE OF PAYMENTS (US $ million)

| | 1990 | 1991 | 1992 |
|---|---|---|---|
| Merchandise exports f.o.b. | 326.5 | 302.5 | 213.4 |
| Merchandise imports f.o.b. | −648.8 | −1,138.2 | −810.2 |
| **Trade balance** | −322.3 | −835.7 | −596.8 |
| Exports of services | 172.5 | 77.0 | 155.5 |
| Imports of services | −228.0 | −197.3 | −204.1 |
| Other income received | 12.4 | 2.7 | — |
| Other income paid | −145.0 | −132.2 | −93.5 |
| Private unrequited transfers (net) | 59.8 | 45.2 | 123.7 |
| Official unrequited transfers (net) | 81.4 | 82.5 | 109.0 |
| **Current balance** | −369.2 | −957.8 | −506.2 |
| Capital (net) | 112.3 | 587.0 | 316.4 |
| Net errors and omissions | 10.9 | 97.9 | 31.0 |
| **Overall balance** | −246.0 | −272.9 | −158.8 |

Source: IMF, *International Financial Statistics*.

# External Trade

**PRINCIPAL COMMODITIES** (£S million)

| Imports c.i.f. | 1985 | 1986 | 1987 |
|---|---|---|---|
| Wheat and meslin (unmilled) | 78.6 | 57.0 | 199.5 |
| Tea | 94.7 | 71.9 | 39.8 |
| Petroleum products | 298.7 | 257.7 | 483.4 |
| Insecticides | 59.5 | 90.1 | 83.2 |
| Paper, paperboard and paper products | 48.2 | 36.4 | 30.8 |
| Cotton fabrics | 3.9 | 15.0 | 38.7 |
| Telecommunication apparatus | 0.6 | 2.1 | 88.8 |
| Electric power machinery | 61.6 | 64.0 | 76.6 |
| Passenger motor cars | 53.5 | 114.6 | 101.6 |
| Lorries and trucks | 76.1 | 136.8 | 125.2 |
| Buses | 30.4 | 51.9 | 34.1 |
| Parts for road motor vehicles | 46.9 | 79.8 | 75.7 |
| **Total** (incl. others) | 2,128.8 | 2,402.2 | 2,612.9 |

| Exports f.o.b.* | 1985 | 1986 | 1987 |
|---|---|---|---|
| Sheep, lambs and goats | 145.6 | 66.9 | 38.9 |
| Millet and sorghum | n.a. | 13.9 | 248.8 |
| Cattle hides | 38.8 | 33.7 | 39.0 |
| Sesame seed | 97.8 | 58.9 | 134.8 |
| Cotton | 374.3 | 366.7 | 455.2 |
| Gum arabic | 66.0 | 141.7 | 267.1 |
| **Total** (incl. others) | 844.7 | 833.2 | 1,497.1 |

* Excluding exports of camels by land routes.

**1988** (£S million): Imports c.i.f. 4,772.1; Exports f.o.b. 2,290.9.

**PRINCIPAL TRADING PARTNERS** (£S million)

| Imports c.i.f. | 1985 | 1986 | 1987 |
|---|---|---|---|
| Africa | 149.4 | 186.5 | 215.0 |
| EC | 855.5 | 970.9 | 918.9 |
| France | 107.1 | 86.9 | 90.5 |
| Germany, Federal Republic | 184.2 | 204.8 | 190.0 |
| United Kingdom | 240.9 | 282.5 | 273.2 |
| Eastern Europe | 37.1 | 57.7 | 48.9 |
| USSR | 0.5 | 2.4 | 2.0 |
| USA | 161.4 | 185.6 | 271.7 |
| Japan | 188.5 | 120.7 | 193.7 |
| China, People's Republic | 67.2 | 68.2 | 27.1 |
| **Total** (incl. others) | 2,128.8 | 2,402.2 | 2,612.9 |

| Exports f.o.b. | 1985 | 1986 | 1987 |
|---|---|---|---|
| Africa | 5.6 | 13.9 | 9.1 |
| EC | 181.5 | 233.9 | 735.0 |
| France | 20.8 | 47.8 | 59.8 |
| Germany, Federal Republic | 47.9 | 47.1 | 109.3 |
| United Kingdom | 22.6 | 33.8 | 122.5 |
| Eastern Europe | 97.7 | 96.3 | 28.4 |
| USSR | 10.8 | 21.8 | 3.6 |
| USA | 27.9 | 45.0 | 70.3 |
| Japan | 68.5 | 55.4 | 94.5 |
| China, People's Republic | 0.8 | 0.5 | 0.1 |
| **Total** (incl. others) | 844.7 | 833.2 | 1,497.1 |

Source (for all external trade tables): UN Economic Commission for Africa, *African Statistical Yearbook*.

**1989**: Exports f.o.b. £S3,023.2 million (Source: IMF, *International Financial Statistics*).

# Transport

**RAILWAY TRAFFIC** (year ending 30 June)

| | 1980/81 | 1981/82 | 1982/83 |
|---|---|---|---|
| Freight ton-km (million) | 1,594 | 1,600 | 3,190 |
| Passenger-km (million) | 1,170 | 1,149 | 1,031 |

**1988**: Freight ton-km (million): 752; Passenger-km (million): 759.

**ROAD TRAFFIC** (registered motor vehicles)

| | 1979 | 1980 | 1981 |
|---|---|---|---|
| Passenger cars | 70,171 | 84,958 | 1,004,688 |
| Buses | 6,295 | 2,956 | 3,590 |
| Lorries and vans | 50,108 | 40,107 | 40,839 |
| Motor cycles | 3,306 | 4,131 | 5,542 |
| **Total** (incl. others) | 137,029 | 138,695 | 181,821 |

Source: Ministry of National Planning, Khartoum, *Transport Statistical Bulletin*.

**INTERNATIONAL SEA-BORNE SHIPPING** (estimated freight traffic, '000 metric tons)

| | 1988 | 1989 | 1990 |
|---|---|---|---|
| Goods loaded | 1,390 | 1,310 | 1,195 |
| Goods unloaded | 3,480 | 3,681 | 3,467 |

Source: UN, *Monthly Bulletin of Statistics*.

**CIVIL AVIATION** (traffic on scheduled services)

| | 1990 | 1991 | 1992 |
|---|---|---|---|
| Kilometres flown (million) | 10 | 6 | 12 |
| Passengers carried ('000) | 454 | 363 | 480 |
| Passenger-km (million) | 589 | 426 | 511 |
| Total ton-km (million) | 67 | 50 | 85 |

Source: UN, *Statistical Yearbook*.

# Tourism

| | 1989 | 1990 | 1991 |
|---|---|---|---|
| Tourist arrivals ('000) | 23 | 25* | 20* |

* Estimate.

Source: UN Economic Commission for Africa, *African Statistical Yearbook*.

SUDAN                                                                                               Statistical Survey, Directory

## Communications Media

|  | 1981 | 1982 | 1983 |
|---|---|---|---|
| Radio receivers ('000 in use) | n.a. | n.a. | 5,000 |
| Television receivers ('000 in use) | n.a. | n.a. | 1,000 |
| Telephones ('000 in use) | 68 | n.a. | n.a. |
| Daily newspapers: |  |  |  |
| Number | n.a. | 6 | n.a. |
| Average circulation ('000 copies) | n.a. | 105 | n.a. |
| Non-daily newspapers: |  |  |  |
| Number | n.a. | 9 | n.a. |
| Average circulation ('000 copies) | n.a. | 121 | n.a. |
| Other periodicals: |  |  |  |
| Number | n.a. | 25 | n.a. |
| Average circulation ('000 copies) | n.a. | 200 | n.a. |

**1987** ('000 in use): Telephones 74.
**1988** ('000 in use): Radio receivers 5,550; Television receivers 1,250.
**1989** ('000 in use): Radio receivers 5,755; Television receivers 1,500.
**1990** ('000 in use): Radio receivers 6,295; Television receivers 1,800.
**1991** ('000 in use): Radio receivers 6,480; Television receivers 2,000.
**1992** ('000 in use): Radio receivers 6,670; Television receivers 2,060.

Source: mainly UNESCO, *Statistical Yearbook*.

## Education

(1991)

|  | Institutions | Teachers | Pupils/Students |
|---|---|---|---|
| Pre-primary | 6,525 | 8,478 | 350,306 |
| Primary | 8,016 | 64,227 | 2,168,180 |
| Secondary: |  |  |  |
| General | n.a. | 29,208 | 683,982 |
| Teacher training | n.a. | 640 | 5,328 |
| Vocational | n.a. | 794 | 28,988 |
| Universities etc.* | n.a. | 2,522 | 60,134 |

* Figures refer to 1989.

Source: UNESCO, *Statistical Yearbook*.

# Directory

## The Constitution

Following the coup of 6 April 1985, the Constitution of April 1973 was suspended, pending the drafting and promulgation of a new Constitution. A transitional Constitution, approved in October 1985, was suspended following the military coup of 30 June 1989.

## The Government

### HEAD OF STATE

**President:** Lt-Gen. OMAR HASSAN AHMAD AL-BASHIR (took power as Chairman of the Revolutionary Command Council for National Salvation (RCC) on 30 June 1989; appointed President by the RCC on 16 October 1993).

**First Vice-President:** Maj.-Gen. ZUBAIR MUHAMMAD SALIH.

**Second Vice-President:** GEORGE KONGOR AROP.

### CABINET
(June 1995)

**Prime Minister:** Lt-Gen. OMAR HASSAN AHMAD AL-BASHIR.
**Minister of Defence:** Lt-Gen. HASSAN ABD AR-RAHMAN ALI.
**Minister of the Interior:** Lt-Col ALTAYEB IBRAHIM MUHAMMAD KHAIR.
**Minister of Cabinet Affairs:** AWAD AHMAD AL-JAZ.
**Minister of Foreign Affairs:** ALI UTHMAN MUHAMMAD TAHA.
**Minister of Finance:** ABD AR-RAHIM HAMDI.
**Minister of Irrigation and Water Resources:** Dr YAQUB ABU SHURA MUSA.
**Minister of Transport:** AL-FATIH MUHAMMAD.
**Minister of General Education:** KABOSHO KUKU.
**Minister of Higher Education and Scientific Research:** Prof. IBRAHIM AHMAD OMAR.
**Minister of Housing and Social Affairs:** Dr HUSSEIN ABU SALEH.
**Minister of Energy and Mining:** Naval Staff Col SALIH AD-DIN MUHAMMAD AHMAD KARRAR.
**Minister of Surveys and Aviation:** Maj-Gen. AT-TIGANIA ADAM TAHIR.
**Minister of Economic Planning and Investment:** IBRAHIM OBAIDULLAH.
**Minister of Health:** GULWAK DENG.
**Minister of Industry:** BADR ED-DIN SULEIMAN
**Minister of Commerce:** Dr TAJ AS-SIR MUSTAFA ABD AS-SALAM.
**Minister of Justice:** ABDEL AZIZ SHIDDU.
**Minister of Culture and Information:** SULEIMAN MUHAMMAD SULEIMAN.
**Minister of Tourism and the Environment:** MUHAMMAD TAHIR EILLA
**Minister of Labour and Administrative Reform:** Brig.-Gen. DOMINIC KASSIANO BAKHIT.
**Minister of Agriculture and Natural Resources:** Dr AHMAD ALI GENIEF.
**Minister of Roads and Communications:** UTHMAN ABD AL-QADIR AL-LATIF.
**Minister of Social Planning:** MUHAMMAD OSMAN KHALIFA.
**Minister of State in the Offices of the Federal Administration:** ABDUL RAHMAN NOUR ED-DIN MUSTAFA.
**Minister of Local Government:** Lt-Gen. GALWAK.
**Minister of Peace and Rehabilitation:** ABDULLAH DENG NHIAL.
**Minister of State for Presidential Affairs:** MAHDI IBRAHIM MUHAMMAD.
**Minister of State for Defence:** OSMAN MUHAMMAD AL-HASSAN.
**Minister of State for Electricity:** (vacant).
**Minister of State for Energy:** HASSAN DAHAWI.
**Minister of State for Finance:** ABD AL-WAHAB AHMAD HAMZA.
**Minister of State for Social Planning:** IBRAHIM ABU AWE.
**Minister of State for Agriculture:** ABDUL-GADIR AHMED WAMBI.
**Minister of State for Labour and Administrative Reform:** MAJDHUB AL-KHALIFAH AHMAD.
**Minister of State for Trade and Industry:** NASR AD-DIN MUHAMMAD UMAR.
**Minister of State for Foreign Affairs:** GHAZI SALAH ED-DIN.
**Minister of State for Information:** MUSA MUHAMMAD MUSA.
**Minister of State for the Interior:** IHSAN ABDALLAH EL-GHASHANI.

### MINISTRIES

**Ministry of Agriculture and Natural Resources:** Khartoum; tel. (11) 72300.
**Ministry of Culture and Information:** Khartoum; tel. (11) 79850; telex 22275.
**Ministry of Defence:** Khartoum; tel. (11) 74910; telex 22411.
**Ministry of Education:** Khartoum; tel. (11) 78900.
**Ministry of Energy and Mining:** POB 2087, Khartoum; tel. (11) 75595; telex 22256.

# SUDAN

**Ministry of Finance and Economic Planning:** POB 700, Khartoum; tel. (11) 77003; telex 22324.
**Ministry of Foreign Affairs:** Khartoum; tel. (11) 73101.
**Ministry of Health:** Khartoum; tel. (11) 73000.
**Ministry of the Interior:** Khartoum; tel. (11) 79990; telex 22604.
**Ministry of Irrigation and Water Resources:** Khartoum; tel. (11) 77533.
**Ministry of Transport and Communications:** POB 300, Khartoum; tel. (11) 79700.

## Legislature

The National Assembly was dissolved following the coup of 30 June 1989. In February 1992 Lt-Gen. al-Bashir appointed a 300-member, transitional National Assembly (Speaker MUHAMMAD AL-AMIN KHALIFA). The transitional Assembly was granted legislative authority, and it was instructed to make preparations for parliamentary elections. The election of provincial representatives to the transitional National Assembly reportedly took place in March 1995.

**President:** MUHAMMAD AL-AMIN KHALIFAH YUNIS.

## Political Organizations

All political organizations were banned following the military coup of 30 June 1989. The more influential parties prior to the coup included.

**Baath Party:** Khartoum.
**Democratic Unionist Party (DUP):** Khartoum; Leader OSMAN AL-MIRGHANI.
**Muslim Brotherhood:** Khartoum; Islamic fundamentalist movement; Leader Dr HABIR NUR AD-DIN.
**National Alliance for Salvation (NAS):** Khartoum; f. 1985; grouping of professional asscns, trade unions and political parties.
**National Congress Party:** Khartoum; f. 1985; aims include national unity, decentralization, non-alignment; Leader Dr RIYAD BAYYUMI.
**National Islamic Front (NIF):** Khartoum; Sec.-Gen. Dr HASSAN AT-TURABI.
**Nationalist Unionist Party:** Khartoum; Leader UTHMAN AL-MIRGHANI.
**Progressive People's Party (PPP):** Khartoum.
**Southern Sudanese Political Association (SSPA):** Juba; largest Southern party; advocates unity of the Southern Region.
**Sudan African National Union (SANU):** Malakal; Southern party; supports continuation of regional rule.
**Sudanese African Congress (SAC):** Juba.
**Sudanese African People's Congress (SAPCO):** Juba.
**Sudanese Communist Party:** Khartoum; Sec.-Gen. IBRAHIM NUGUD.
**Sudanese National Party (SNP):** Khartoum; Leader PHILIP ABBAS GHABOUSH.
**Sudanese People's Federal Party (SPFP):** Khartoum.
**Umma Party (UP):** Khartoum; Mahdist party based on the Koran and Islamic traditions; Pres. SADIQ AL-MAHDI.

Opposition movements include the **Sudan People's Liberation Movement (SPLM)** (Leader Col JOHN GARANG), its military wing, the **Sudan People's Liberation Army (SPLA)**, and the **Liberation Front for Southern Sudan (LFSS)**. A rival faction to the original SPLM, the South Sudan Independence Movement (SSIM, led by RIEK MACHAR), was formed in mid-1991; and another, the Forces of Unity faction (led by WILLIAM NYUON), in 1992. SPLA–United, an alliance between the faction led by Riek Machar, the Forces of Unity and a further faction (led by CARABINO KUANY BOL), emerged in April 1993. Many of the movements opposed to the Government are grouped together in the **Sudanese National Democratic Forum.** The **Sudan Federal Democratic Alliance** (SFDA) (Chair. AHMED DREIGE) was formed in London in February 1994. It advocates a new federal structure for Sudan, based on decentralization.

## Diplomatic Representation

### EMBASSIES IN SUDAN

**Algeria:** POB 80, St 31, New Extension, Khartoum; tel. (11) 41954; Ambassador: SALIH BEN KOBBI.
**Bulgaria:** POB 1690, St 31, Middle Road, New Extension, Khartoum; tel. (11) 43414; Ambassador: T. F. MITEV.
**Chad:** POB 1514, 21, St 17, New Extension, Khartoum; tel. (11) 42545; Ambassador: MBAILAOU BERAL MOISE.
**China, People's Republic:** POB 1425, 93, St 22, Khartoum; tel. (11) 222036; Ambassador: HUI ZHEN.
**Czech Republic:** POB 1047, 39, St 39, Khartoum; tel. (11) 43448.
**Egypt:** POB 1126, Al-Gamma St, Khartoum; tel. (11) 72836; telex 22545; Ambassador: HASSAN ABD AL-HAK GAD AL-HAK.
**Ethiopia:** POB 844, 6, 11A St 3, New Extension, Khartoum; Chargé d'affaires: Dr AWOKE AGONGFER.
**France:** POB 377, Plot No. 163, Block 8, Burri, Khartoum; tel. (11) 225608; telex 22220; Ambassador: MARCEL LAUGEL.
**Germany:** POB 970, Baladia St, Block No. 8DE, Plot No. 2, Khartoum; tel. (11) 77990; telex 22211; Ambassador: PETER MENDE.
**Greece:** POB 1182, Sharia al-Gamhouria, Block 5, No. 30, Khartoum; tel. (11) 73155; Ambassador: VASSILIS COUZOPOULOS.
**Holy See:** POB 623, Kafouri Belgravia, Khartoum (Apostolic Nunciature); tel. (11) 74692; telex 26032; Apostolic Pro-Nuncio: Most Rev. ERWIN JOSEF ENDER, Titular Archbishop of Germania in Numidia.
**India:** POB 707, 61 Africa Rd, Khartoum; tel. (11) 40560; telex 22228; Ambassador: VIRENDRA P. SINGH.
**Iran:** House No. 8, Square 2, Mogran, Khartoum; tel. (11) 48843; Chargé d'affaires: NIMATALLAH GADIR.
**Iraq:** Khartoum; tel. (11) 45428; telex 24035; Ambassador: TARIQ MOHAMMED YAHYA.
**Italy:** POB 793, St 39, Khartoum; tel. (11) 45326; telex 24034; Ambassador: ROSARIO GUIDO NICOSIA.
**Japan:** POB 1649, 24, Block AE, St 3, New Extension, Khartoum; tel. (11) 44554; telex 24019; Ambassador: YOSHINORI IMAGAWA.
**Jordan:** 25, St 7, New Extension, Khartoum; tel. (11) 43264; telex 24047; Ambassador: MOHAMMED JUMA ASANA.
**Kenya:** POB 8242, Khartoum; tel. (11) 40386; telex 24190; Ambassador: GIDEON NYAMWEYA NYAANGA.
**Korea, Democratic People's Republic:** POB 322, House No. 59, 1 St 31, New Extension, Khartoum; tel. (11) 75645; Ambassador: JOM YONG HWANG.
**Korea, Republic:** POB 2414, House 2, St 1, New Extension, Khartoum; tel. (11) 451136; telex 24029; fax (11) 452822; Ambassador: SAE DON CHANG.
**Kuwait:** POB 1457, Africa Ave, near the Tennis Club, Khartoum; tel. (11) 81525; telex 24043; Ambassador: (vacant).
**Libya:** POB 2091, 50 Africa Rd, Khartoum; Secretary of People's Bureau: GUMMA AL-FAZANI.
**Morocco:** POB 2042, 32, St 19, New Extension, Khartoum; tel. (11) 43223; Ambassador: MOHAMMED KAMLICHI.
**Netherlands:** POB 391, St 47, House No. 47, Khartoum; tel. (11) 47271; telex 24013; Chargé d'affaires: J. BOJ.
**Nigeria:** POB 1538, St 17, Sharia al-Mek Nimr, Khartoum; tel. (11) 79120; telex 22222; Ambassador: IBRAHIM KARLI.
**Oman:** POB 2839, St 1, New Extension, Khartoum; tel. (11) 45791; Ambassador: MOSLIM EBIN ZAIDAN AL-BARAMI.
**Pakistan:** POB 1178, House No. 6, Block 12AE, St 3, New Extension, Khartoum; tel. (11) 42518; telex 24219; Ambassador: KHALID NIZAMI.
**Poland:** POB 902, 73 Africa Rd, Khartoum; tel. (11) 44248; Chargé d'affaires a.i.: WALDEMAR POPIOLEK.
**Qatar:** POB 223, St 15, New Extension, Khartoum; tel. (11) 42208; telex 22223; Chargé d'affaires a.i.: HASSAN AHMED ABDULLAH ABU HINDI.
**Romania:** POB 1494, Kassala Rd, Plot No. 172–173, Kafouri Area, Khartoum North; tel. (11) 613445; telex 24188; Chargé d'affaires a.i.: GHEORGHE GUSTEA.
**Russia:** POB 1161, B1, A10 St, New Extension, Khartoum; Ambassador: VALERI YAKOVLEVICH SUKHIN.
**Saudi Arabia:** St 11, New Extension, Khartoum; tel. (11) 41938; Ambassador: SAYED MOHAMMED SIBRI SULIMAN.
**Somalia:** POB 1857, St 23–25, New Extension, Khartoum; tel. (11) 44800; Ambassador: MUHAMMAD Sheikh AHMED.
**Spain:** POB 2621, St 3, New Extension, Khartoum; tel. (11) 45072; telex 22476; Ambassador: TOMÁS SOLÍS GRAGERA.
**Switzerland:** POB 1707, Amarat, Street 15, Khartoum; tel. (11) 451010; Chargé d'affaires: GIAMBATTISTA MONDADA.
**Syria:** POB 1139, St 3, New Extension, Khartoum; tel. (11) 44663; Ambassador: MOHAMMED AL-MAHAMEED.
**Turkey:** POB 771, 31, St 29, New Extension, Khartoum; tel. (11) 451197; fax 451197; Ambassador: ERDINÇ ERDÜN.
**Uganda:** House No. 6, Square 42, Khartoum East; tel. (11) 78409; telex 22811; Ambassador: E. OBITRE-GAMA.

**United Arab Emirates:** POB 1225, St 3, New Extension, Khartoum; tel. (11) 44476; telex 24024; Ambassador: MOHAMMED SULTAN AS-SUAIDI.
**United Kingdom:** POB 801, St 10, off Baladia St, Khartoum; tel. (11) 451029; telex 22189; Ambassador: ALAN F. GOULTY.
**USA:** POB 699, Sharia Ali Abdul Latif, Khartoum; tel. (11) 74700; telex 22619; Ambassador: DON PETTERSON.
**Yemen:** POB 1010, St 11, New Extension, Khartoum; tel. (11) 43918; Ambassador: ABD AS-SALAM HUSSEIN.
**Yugoslavia:** POB 1180, St 31, 49A, Khartoum 1; tel. (11) 41252; Ambassador: VLADIMIR PETKOVSKI.
**Zaire:** POB 4195, St 13, New Extension, Block 12CE, 23, Khartoum; tel. (11) 42424; telex 24192; Ambassador: MGBAMA MPWA.

## Judicial System

Until September 1983 the judicial system was divided into two sections, civil and Islamic, the latter dealing only with personal and family matters. In September 1983 President Nimeri revoked all existing laws in favour of a new system of Islamic (*Shari'a*) law. Under the provisions of the new penal code, alcohol and gambling were prohibited, while imprisonment was largely replaced by the death sentence or dismemberment. Crimes of murder and related offences were judged in accordance with the Koran. Following the coup in April 1985, the *Shari'a* courts were abolished, and it was announced that the previous system of criminal courts was to be revived. In June 1986 the Prime Minister, Sadiq al-Mahdi, reaffirmed that the *Shari'a* law was to be abolished. It was announced in June 1987 that a new legal code, based on a 'Sudanese legal heritage', was to be introduced. In July 1989 the military Government established special courts to investigate violations of emergency laws concerning corruption. It was announced in June 1991 that these courts were to be incorporated in the general court administration. Islamic law was reintroduced in March 1991, but was not applied in the southern states of Equatoria, Bahr al-Ghazal and Upper Nile.

**Chief Justice:** JALLAL ALI LUTFI.

## Religion

The majority of the northern Sudanese population are Muslims, while in the south the population are mostly either animists or Christians.

### ISLAM

Islam is the state religion. Sudanese Islam has a strong Sufi element, and is estimated to have more than 15m. adherents.

### CHRISTIANITY

**Sudan Council of Churches:** Inter-Church House, St 35, New Extension, POB 469, Khartoum; tel. (11) 42859; telex 24099; f. 1967; 12 mem. churches; Chair. Most Rev. PAOLINO LUKUDU LORO (Roman Catholic Archbishop of Juba); Gen. Sec. Rev. CLEMENT H. JANDA.

#### Roman Catholic Church

*Latin Rite*

Sudan comprises two archdioceses and seven dioceses. At the end of 1993 there were about 2.3m. adherents in the country, representing about 7% of the total population.

**Sudan Catholic Bishops' Conference:** General Secretariat, POB 6011, Khartoum; tel. (11) 225075; telex 24261; f. 1971; Pres. Most Rev. GABRIEL ZUBEIR WAKO, Archbishop of Khartoum.
**Archbishop of Juba:** Most Rev. PAOLINO LUKUDU LORO, Catholic Church, POB 32, Juba, Equatoria State; tel. 2930; fax 24261.
**Archbishop of Khartoum:** Most Rev. GABRIEL ZUBEIR WAKO, Catholic Church, POB 49, Khartoum; tel. (11) 82176.

*Maronite Rite*

**Maronite Church in Sudan:** POB 244, Khartoum; Rev. Fr YOUSEPH NEAMA.

*Melkite Rite*

**Patriarchal Vicariate of Egypt and Sudan:** Patriarcat Grec-Melkite Catholique, 16 rue Daher, Cairo, Egypt; tel. (2) 905790 (Vicar Patriarchal: Most Rev. PAUL ANTAKI, Titular Archbishop of Nubia); Vicar in Sudan: Fr GEORGE BANNA, POB 766, Khartoum; tel. (11) 76466.

#### Orthodox Churches

**Coptic Orthodox Church:** Bishop of Nubia, Atbara and Omdurman: Rt Rev. BAKHOMIOS; Bishop of Khartoum, Southern Sudan and Uganda: Rt Rev. ANBA YOUANNIS.

**Greek Orthodox Church:** POB 47, Khartoum; tel. (11) 72973; Metropolitan of Nubia: Archbishop DIONYSSIOS HADZIVASSILIOU.
The Ethiopian Orthodox Church is also active.

#### The Anglican Communion

Anglicans are adherents of the (Episcopal) Church of the Province of the Sudan. The Province, with four dioceses and about 1m. adherents, was inaugurated in October 1976.

**Archbishop in Sudan:** Most Rev. BENJAMINA W. YUGUSUK (Bishop of Juba), c/o PO Box 47429, Nairobi, Kenya.

#### Other Christian Churches

**Evangelical Church:** POB 57, Khartoum; c. 1,500 mems; administers schools, literature centre and training centre; Chair Rev. RADI ELIAS.
**Presbyterian Church:** POB 40, Malakal; autonomous since 1956; 67,000 mems (1985); Gen. Sec. Rev. THOMAS MALUIT.
**Sudan Interior Mission (SIM):** Dir R. WELLING, POB 220, Khartoum; tel. (11) 452790; fax 447213; f. 1937.
The Africa Inland Church and the Sudanese Church of Christ are also active.

## The Press

### DAILIES

Press censorship was imposed following the coup of 30 June 1989. The only publications permitted were the armed forces' weekly newspaper, *Al-Guwwat al-Musallaha*, and the government-controlled dailies, *Al-Engaz al-Watan* and *As-Sudan al-Hadeeth*. The principal publications in circulation prior to the coup included:

**Al-Ayyam** (The Days): POB 2158, Khartoum; tel. (11) 74321; f. 1953; Arabic; Chair. and Editor-in-Chief HASSAN SATTI; circ. 60,000 (publication suspended since August 1986).
**Al-Engaz al-Watan:** Khartoum; state-controlled.
**Al-Khartoum:** Khartoum; Arabic.
**Al-Midan** (The Field): Khartoum; Arabic; supports Sudanese Communist Party.
**Ar-Rayah** (The Banner); Khartoum; Arabic.
**As Sudan al-Hadeeth:** Khartoum; state-controlled.
**Sudan Times:** Khartoum; English; Editor BONA MALWAL.
**As-Sudani** (The Sudanese): Khartoum.
**Ath-Thawra** (The Revolution): Khartoum; Arabic.
**Al-Usbu** (The Week): Khartoum; Arabic.

### PERIODICALS

**Al-Guwwat al-Musallaha** (The Armed Forces): Khartoum; f.1969; publs a weekly newspaper and monthly magazine for the armed forces; Editor-in-Chief Maj. MAHMOUD GALANDER; circ. 7,500.
**New Horizon:** POB 2651, Khartoum; tel. (11) 77913; telex 22418; f. 1976; publ. by the Sudan House for Printing and Publishing; weekly; English; political and economic affairs, development, home and international news; Editor-in-Chief MATTHEW OBUR AYANG; circ. 7,000.
**Sudanow:** POB 2651, Khartoum; tel. (11) 77913; telex 22956; f. 1976; publ. by the Sudan House for Printing and Publishing; monthly; English; political and economic affairs, arts, social affairs and diversions; Editor-in-Chief AHMED KAMAL ED-DIN; circ. 10,000.

### NEWS AGENCIES

**Sudan News Agency (SUNA):** Sharia al-Gamhouria, POB 1506, Khartoum; tel. (11) 75770; telex 22418; Dir-Gen. TAYYIB HAI ATIYAH.
**Sudanese Press Agency:** Khartoum; f. 1985; owned by journalists.

#### Foreign Bureaux

**Agence France-Presse (AFP):** POB 1911, Khartoum; telex 22418; Rep. MUHAMMAD ALI SAID.
**Middle East News Agency (MENA) (Egypt):** POB 740, Dalala Bldg, Khartoum.
**Xinhua (New China) News Agency** (People's Republic of China): POB 2229, No. 100, 12 The Sq., Riad Town, Khartoum; tel. (11) 224174; telex 24205; Correspondent SUN XIAOKE.
The Iraqi News Agency and the Syrian News Agency also have bureaux in Khartoum.

## Publishers

**Ahmad Abd ar-Rahman at-Tikeine:** POB 299, Port Sudan.
**Al-Ayyam Press Co Ltd:** POB 363, Aboulela Bldg, United Nations Sq., Khartoum; f. 1953; general fiction and non-fiction, arts,

# SUDAN

poetry, reference, newspapers, magazines; Man. Dir BESHIR MUHAMMAD SAID.

**As-Sahafa Publishing and Printing House:** POB 1228, Khartoum; f. 1961; newspapers, pamphlets, fiction and govt publs.

**As-Salam Co Ltd:** POB 944, Khartoum.

**Claudios S. Fellas:** POB 641, Khartoum.

**Khartoum University Press:** POB 321, Khartoum; tel. (11) 76653; telex 22738; f. 1964; academic, general and educational in Arabic and English; Man. Dir KHALID AL-MUBARAK.

### Government Publishing House

**El-Asma Printing Press:** POB 38, Khartoum.

## Radio and Television

In 1992, according to UNESCO, there were an estimated 6.7m. radio receivers and 2.1m. television receivers in use.

### RADIO

**Sudan National Broadcasting Corpn:** POB 1094, Omdurman; tel. (11) 52100; state-controlled service broadcasting daily in Arabic, English, French and Swahili; Dir-Gen. SALAH AD-DIN AL-FADHIL USUD

### TELEVISION

An earth satellite station operated on 36 channels at Umm Haraz has much improved Sudan's telecommunication links. A nation-wide satellite network is being established with 14 earth stations in the provinces. A microwave network of television transmission covered 90% of inhabited areas in 1983. There are regional stations at Gezira (Central Region) and Atbara (Northern Region).

**Sudan Television:** POB 1094, Omdurman; tel. 550022; telex 28002; f. 1962; state-controlled; 60 hours of programmes per week; Head of Directorate HADID AS-SIRA.

## Finance

(cap. = capital; res = reserves; dep. = deposits;
m. = million; brs = branches; amounts in Sudanese pounds unless otherwise stated)

### BANKING

All domestic banks are controlled by the Bank of Sudan. Foreign banks were permitted to resume operations in 1976. In December 1985 the government banned the establishment of any further banks. It was announced in December 1990 that Sudan's banking system was to be reorganized to accord with Islamic principles.

### Central Bank

**Bank of Sudan:** POB 313, Gamaa Ave, Khartoum; tel. (11) 78064; telex 22352; f. 1960; bank of issue; cap. and res 70.1m. (Dec. 1989); Gov. SABIR MUHAMMAD HASSAN; 9 brs.

### Commercial Banks

**Al-Baraka Bank:** POB 3583, Al-Baraka Tower, Sharia al Kasr, Khartoum; tel. (11) 80688; telex 22555; fax (11) 78948; f. 1984; investment and export promotion; cap. 55.3m., total assets 1,446m. (Dec. 1991); Pres. Sheikh SALIH ABDALLA KAMIL; 15 brs.

**Bank of Khartoum:** POB 1008, 8 Gamhouria Ave, Khartoum; tel. (11) 72880; telex 22181; fax (11) 81072; f. 1913; cap. 20m., res 236.4m., total assets 5,324.1m. (1990); Chair. of Bd and Gen. Man. Dr SABIR MUHAMMAD EL-HASSAN; 47 brs.

**Islamic Bank for Western Sudan:** POB 3575, United Nations Sq., Khartoum; tel. (11) 79918; telex 23046; f. 1984; cap. 393m., total assets 8,908m. (Dec. 1994); Chair. IBRAHIM MOUNIEM MANSOUR; Gen. Man. ESH-SHARIEF EL-KHATIM; 28 brs.

**National Bank of Sudan:** POB 1183, Kronfli Bldg, Al-Qasr Ave, Khartoum; tel. (11) 78153; telex 22058; fax (11) 79497; f. 1982; cap. 39.2m. (Dec. 1991); Chair. Dr BASHIR EL-BAKRI; Gen. Man. SAYED ISAM ALUZRI; 4 brs.

**National Export/Import Bank:** POB 2732, En-Niel Ave, Khartoum; tel. (11) 81961; telex 22928; f. 1983; cap. 50m. (Dec. 1990); Pres. and Gen. Man. ABD AR-RAHMAN AHMAD OSMAN; 8 brs.

**People's Co-operative Bank:** POB 922, Khartoum; tel. (11) 73555; telex 22247; Chair. KARAMALLAH AL-AWAD.

**Sudan Commercial Bank:** POB 1116, Al-Qasr Ave, Khartoum; tel. (11) 79836; telex 22434; fax (11) 74194; f. 1960; cap. 10m., total assets 5,025.1m. (Dec. 1992); Chair. EL-TAYB ELOBEID BADR; 18 brs.

**Sudanese French Bank:** POB 2775, Zubair Basha St, Khartoum; tel. (11) 76542; telex 22204; fax (11) 71740; f. 1978 as Sudanese Investment Bank; cap. 5m. (Dec. 1993); Chair. GHAZI SULIMAN; 11 brs.

**Tadamun Islamic Bank of Sudan:** POB 3154, Baladin Ave, Khartoum; tel. (11) 71845; telex 22158; (11) fax 73840; f. 1983; cap. 49.7m., dep. 6,961.6m., total assets 7,531.3m. (Aug. 1993); Chair. ALIGANI HASSAN HILAL; 15 brs.

**Unity Bank:** Barlaman Ave, POB 408, Khartoum; tel. (11) 74200; telex 22231; f. 1970; cap. 10m., total assets 2,408m. (Dec. 1990); Chair. and Gen. Man. FAWZI IBRAHIM WASFI; 27 brs.

### Foreign Banks

**Blue Nile Bank Ltd:** POB 984, Zubeir Pasha Ave, Khartoum; tel. (11) 78925; telex 22905; f. 1983; cap. 31.9m., total assets 197.2m. (Dec. 1991); jtly controlled by the Govts of Sudan and the Repub. of Korea; Chair. CHAN SUP LEE.

**Citibank NA** (USA): POB 8027, SDC Bldg, St 19, New Extension, Khartoum; tel. (11) 47615; telex 22454; f. 1978; cap. and res 48m., total assets 400m. (Dec. 1989); Gen. Man. ADNAN MOHAMED.

**Faisal Islamic Bank (Sudan)** (Saudi Arabia): POB 10143, Ali Abdel Latif Ave, Khartoum; tel. (11) 81848; telex 22519; fax (11) 80193; f. 1977; cap. 117.7m., total assets 16,490m. (Dec. 1993); Chair. Prince MUHAMMAD AL-FAISAL AS-SAUD.

**Habib Bank** (Pakistan): POB 8246, Baladiya Ave, Khartoum; tel. (11) 81497; telex 22490; f. 1982; cap. and res 13.8m., total assets 27.3m. (Dec. 1987); Gen. Man. BAZ MUHAMMAD KHAN.

**Mashreq Bank PSC:** POB 371, Baladia St, Khartoum; tel. (11) 72969; telex 22124; fax (11) 72743; Regional Chief Man. Sayed ARIF HUSAIN.

**Middle East Bank Ltd** (United Arab Emirates): POB 1950, Kronfli Bldg, Al-Qasr Ave, Khartoum; tel. (11) 73794; telex 22516; fax (11) 73696; f. 1982; cap. and res 9.9m., total assets 8.9m. (Dec. 1987); Chief Man. FAISAL HASSOUN.

**National Bank of Abu Dhabi** (United Arab Emirates): POB 2465, Atbara St, Khartoum; tel. (11) 74870; telex 22249; f. 1976; cap. and res 16.9m., total assets 12.5m. (Dec. 1987); Man. GAAFAR OSMAN.

### Development Banks

**Agricultural Bank of Sudan:** POB 1363, Khartoum; tel. (11) 77432; telex 22610; fax (11) 78296; f. 1957; cap. p.u. 200m.; provides finance for approved agricultural projects; Dir-Gen. BADR AD-DIN TAHA; 40 brs.

**Arab-African International Bank:** POB 2721, Khartoum; tel. 75573; telex 22624; Rep. SHEIKH HASSAN BELAIL.

**Islamic Co-operative Development Bank (ICDB):** POB 62, Khartoum; tel. (11) 80223; telex 22906; fax (11) 77715; f. 1983; cap. 16.4m. (Dec. 1990); 6 brs.

**National Development Bank:** POB 655, Khartoum; tel. (11) 79496; telex 22835; f. 1982; finances or co-finances economic and social development projects; cap. 5m. (Dec. 1992); Chair. MUHAMMAD DAOUD ALKHALIFA.

**Nilein Industrial Development Bank:** POB 1722, United Nations Sq., Khartoum; tel. (11) 80929; telex 22456; fax (11) 80776; f. 1993 by merger of An-Nilein Bank and the Industrial Bank of Sudan; provides tech. and financial assistance for private-sector industrial projects and acquires shares in industrial enterprises; Chair. ELSAED OSMAN MAHGOUB.

**Sudanese Estates Bank:** POB 309, Al-Baladiya Ave, Khartoum; tel. (11) 77917; telex 22439; fax (11) 79465; f. 1967; mortgage bank financing private-sector urban housing development; cap. 59m. (Dec. 1992); Chair. Eng. MUHAMMAD ALI EL-AMIN; 6 brs.

**Sudanese Savings Bank:** POB 159, Wad Medani; tel. 3013; telex 50005; f. 1974; cap. 10m., total assets 1,613.4m. (Dec. 1991); Chair. MANSOUR AHMAD ESH-SHEIKH; 22 brs.

### STOCK EXCHANGE

**Sudanese Stock Exchange:** Khartoum; f. 1995; 24 mems.

### INSURANCE COMPANIES

**African Insurance Co (Sudan) Ltd:** POB 149, Al-Baladiya Ave, Muhammad Hussein Bldg, Khartoum; f. 1977; fire, accident, marine and motor; Gen. Man. AN-NOMAN AS-SANUSI.

**Blue Nile Insurance Co (Sudan) Ltd:** POB 2215, Khartoum; telex 22389; Gen. Man. MUHAMMAD AL-AMIN MIRGHANI.

**General Insurance Co (Sudan) Ltd:** POB 1555, El-Mek Nimr St, Khartoum; tel. (11) 80616; telex 22303; f. 1961; Gen. Man. ABD AL-FATTAH MUHAMMAD SIYAM.

**Islamic Insurance Co Ltd:** POB 2776, Al-Faiha Commercial Bldg, Khartoum; tel. (11) 72656; telex 22167; f. 1979; all classes.

**Khartoum Insurance Co Ltd:** POB 737, Khartoum; tel. (11) 78647; telex 22241; f. 1953; Chair. MUDAWI M. AHMAD; Gen. Man. ABD AL-MENIM AL-HADARI.

**Middle East Insurance Co Ltd:** POB 3070, Khartoum; tel. (11) 72202; telex 22191; f. 1981; fire, marine, motor, general liability; Chair. AHMAD I. MALIK; Gen. Man. ALI AL-FADL.

**Sudanese Insurance and Reinsurance Co Ltd:** POB 2332, Sharia al-Gamhouria, Nasr Sq., Khartoum; tel. (11) 70812; telex 22292; f. 1967; Gen. Man. IZZ AD-DIN AS-SAID MUHAMMAD.

**United Insurance Co (Sudan) Ltd:** POB 318, Makkawi Bldg, Sharia al-Gamhouria, Khartoum; tel. (11) 76630; telex 22390; fax (11) 70783; f. 1968; Dir-Gen. MUHAMMAD ABDEEN BABIKER.

# Trade and Industry

## STATE CORPORATIONS

**Agricultural Research Corporation:** POB 126, Wadi Medani; tel. (51) 2226; telex 50009; fax (51) 3213; f. 1967; Gen. Man. Dr OSMAN AGEEB.

**Alaktan Trading Co:** POB 2067, Khartoum; tel. (11) 81588; telex 22272; Gen. Man. ABD AR-RAHMAN ABD AL-MONEIM.

**Animal Production Public Corporation:** POB 624, Khartoum; tel. (11) 40611; telex 24048; Gen. Man. Dr FOUAD RAMADAN HAMID.

**General Petroleum Corporation:** POB 2986, Khartoum; tel. (11) 71554; telex 22638; f. 1976; Chair. Dr OSMAN ABDULWAHAB; Dir-Gen. Dr ABD ER-RAHMAN OSMAN ABD ER-RAHMAN.

**Gum Arabic Co:** POB 857, Khartoum; tel. (11) 77288; telex 22314; f. 1969; Gen. Man. OMER EL-MUBARAK ABU ZEID.

**Industrial Production Corporation:** POB 1034, Khartoum; tel. (11) 71278; telex 22236; Dir-Gen. OSMAN TAMMAM; Dep. Chair. ABD AL-LATIF WIDATALLA; incorporates:

  **Cement and Building Materials Sector Co-ordination Office:** POB 2241, Khartoum; tel. (11) 74269; telex 22079; Dir T. M. KHOGALI.

  **Food Industries Corporation:** POB 2341, Khartoum; tel. (11) 75463; Dir MUHAMMAD AL-GHALI SULIMAN.

  **Leather Trading and Manufacturing Co Ltd:** POB 1639, Khartoum; tel. (11) 78187; telex 22298; f. 1986; Man. Dir IBRAHIM SALIH ALI.

  **Oil Corporation:** POB 64, Khartoum North; tel. (11) 32044; telex 22198; Gen. Man. BUKHARI MAHMOUD BUKHARI.

  **Spinning and Weaving General Co Ltd:** POB 765, Khartoum; tel. (11) 74306; telex 22122; f. 1975; Dir MUHAMMAD SALIH MUHAMMAD ABDALLAH.

  **Sudan Tea Co:** POB 1219, Khartoum; tel. (11) 81261; telex 22320.

  **Sudanese Mining Corporation:** POB 1034, Khartoum; tel. (11) 70840; telex 22298; Dir IBRAHIM MUDAWI BABIKER.

  **Sugar and Distilling Industry Corporation:** POB 511, Khartoum; tel. (11) 78417; telex 22665; Man. MIRGHANI AHMAD BABIKER.

**Mechanized Farming Corporation:** POB 2482, Khartoum; Man. Dir AWAD AL-KARIM AL-YASS.

**National Cotton and Trade Co Ltd:** POB 1552, Khartoum; telex 22267; Gen. Man. ZUBAIR MUHAMMAD AL-BASHIR.

**Port Sudan Cotton Trade Co Ltd:** POB 261, Port Sudan; telex 22270; POB 590, Khartoum; Gen. Man. SAID MUHAMMAD ADAM.

**Public Agricultural Production Corporation:** POB 538, Khartoum; Chair. and Man. Dir ABDALLAH BAYOUMO; Sec. SAAD AD-DIN MUHAMMAD ALI.

**Public Corporation for Building and Construction:** POB 2110, Khartoum; tel. (11) 74544; Dir NAIM AD-DIN.

**Public Corporation for Irrigation and Excavations:** POB 619, Khartoum; tel. (11) 80167; Gen. Sec. OSMAN AN-NUR.

**Public Corporation for Oil Products and Pipelines:** POB 1704, Khartoum; tel. (11) 78290; Gen. Man. ABD AR-RAHMAN SULIMAN.

**Public Electricity and Water Corporation:** POB 1380, Khartoum; Gen. Man. MUHAMMAD AL-MAHDI MIRGHANI.

**Rahad Corporation:** POB 2523, Khartoum; tel. (11) 75175; financed by the World Bank, Kuwait and the USA; by 1983 300,000 ha had been irrigated and 70,000 people settled in 15,000 tenancies; Man. Dir HASSAN SAAD ABDALLA.

**The State Trading Corporation:** POB 211, Khartoum; tel. (11) 78555; telex 22355; Chair. E. R. M. TOM.

  **Automobile Corporation:** POB 221, Khartoum; tel. (11) 78555; telex 22230; importer of vehicles and spare parts; Gen. Man. DAFALLA AHMAD SIDDIQ.

  **Engineering Equipment Corporation:** POB 97, Khartoum; tel. (11) 73731; telex 22274; importers and distributors of agricultural, engineering and electronic equipment; Gen. Man. IZZ AD-DIN HAMID.

  **Gezira Trade and Services Co:** POB 215, Khartoum; tel. (11) 72687; telex 22302; fax (11) 79060; f. 1980; largest importer of general merchandise and services in storage, shipping and insurance; exporter of oilseeds and cereals.

  **Khartoum Commercial and Shipping Co:** POB 221, Khartoum; tel. (11) 78555; telex 22311; import, export and shipping services, insurance and manufacturing; Gen. Man. IDRIS M. SALIH.

  **Silos and Storage Corporation:** POB 1183, Khartoum; stores and handles agricultural products; Gen. Man. AHMAD AT-TAIEB HARHOOF.

**Sudan Cotton Co Ltd:** POB 1672, Khartoum; tel. (11) 71567; telex 22245; fax (11) 70703; f. 1970; exports raw cotton; Chair AHMED EN-NOUR ALI; Man. Dir ABD AR-RAHMAN ABD AL-MONEIM.

**Sudan Gezira Board:** POB 884, HQ Barakat Wadi Medani, Gezira Province; tel. 2412; telex 50001; Sales Office, POB 884, Khartoum; tel. 40145; responsible for Sudan's main cotton-producing area; the Gezira scheme is a partnership between the govt, the tenants and the board. The govt provides the land and is responsible for irrigation. Tenants pay a land and water charge and receive the work proceeds. The role of the board is to provide agricultural services at cost, technical supervision and execution of govt agricultural policies relating to the scheme. Tenants pay a percentage of their proceeds to the Social Development Fund. The total potential cultivable area of the Gezira scheme is c. 850,000 ha and the total area under systematic irrigation is c. 730,000 ha. In addition to cotton, groundnuts, sorghum, wheat, rice, pulses and vegetables are grown for the benefit of tenant farmers; Man. Dir IZZ ED-DIN OMAR EL-MAKKI.

**Sudan Oilseeds Co Ltd:** POB 167, Parliament Ave, Khartoum; tel. (11) 80120; telex 22312; f. 1974; 58% state-owned; exporter of oilseeds (groundnuts, sesame seeds and castor beans); importer of foodstuffs and other goods; Chair. SADIQ KARAR AT-TAYEB; Gen. Man. KAMAL ABD AL-HALIM.

## CHAMBER OF COMMERCE

**Sudan Chamber of Commerce:** POB 81, Khartoum; tel. (11) 72346; f. 1908; Pres. SAAD ABOU AL-ELA; Sec.-Gen. HAROUN AL-AWAD.

## INDUSTRIAL ASSOCIATION

**Sudanese Industries Association:** POB 2565, Africa St, Khartoum; tel. (11) 73151; f. 1974; Chair. FATH AR-RAHMAN AL-BASHIR; Exec. Dir A. IZZ AL-ARAB YOUSUF.

## DEVELOPMENT CORPORATIONS

**Sudan Development Corporation (SDC):** POB 710, 21 al-Amarat, Khartoum; tel. (11) 42425; telex 24078; fax (11) 40473; f. 1974 to promote and co-finance development projects with special emphasis on projects in the agricultural, agri-business, and industrial sectors; cap. p.u. US $200m. (Dec. 1990); Chair. and Man. Dir Sayed ABDALLAH AHMED AR-RAMADI; affiliates:

  **Sudan Rural Development Co Ltd (SRDC):** POB 2190, Khartoum; tel. (11) 73855; telex 22813; f. 1980; SRDC has 27% shareholding; cap. p.u. US $2m.; Gen. Man. OMRAN MUHAMMAD ALI.

  **Sudan Rural Development Finance Co (SRDFC):** POB 2190, Khartoum; tel. (11) 73855; telex 22813; fax (11) 73235; f. 1980; Gen. Man. Dr HASHIM M. HASHIM EL-HADIA.

## TRADE UNIONS

All trade union activity was banned following the coup of 30 June 1989. The following organizations were active prior to that date. Many of their officers are reported to have been imprisoned.

### Federations

**Sudan Workers Trade Unions Federation (SWTUF):** POB 2258, Khartoum; tel. (11) 77463; includes 42 trade unions representing c. 1.75m. public-service and private-sector workers; affiliated to the Int. Confed. of Arab Trade Unions and the Org. of African Trade Union Unity; Pres. MUHAMMAD OSMAN GAMA; Gen. Sec. YOUSUF ABU SHAMA HAMED.

### Principal Affiliates

**Agricultural Sector Workers' Trade Union:** Workers' Club, Khartoum North; Pres. AWAD WIDATALLA; Sec. MUHAMMAD OSMAN SALIM; 30,000 mems.

**Gezira Scheme Workers' Trade Union:** Barakat; Pres. IBRAHIM MUHAMMAD AHMAD ASH-SHEIKH; Sec. AS-SIR ABDOON; 11,500 mems.

**Health Workers' Trade Union:** Khartoum Civil Hospital, Khartoum; Pres. Dr HARITH HAMED; Sec. GAAFAR MUHAMMAD SID AHMAD; 25,000 mems.

**Local Government Workers' Trade Union:** Workers' Union, Khartoum; Pres. ISMAIL MUHAMMAD FADL; Sec. SALEM BEDRI HUMAM; 25,000 mems.

**Post, Telegraph and Telephone Workers' Trade Union:** Workers' Club, Khartoum; Pres. Mansoul al-Manna; Sec. Yassin Abd al-Galil; 8,463 mems.

**Public Service Workers' Trade Union:** Al-Baladiya Ave, Khartoum; Pres. Mohi ad-Din Bakheit; Sec. Ali Idris al-Hussein; 19,800 mems.

**Railway Workers' Trade Union:** Railway Workers' Club, Atbara; Pres. Muhammad al-Hassan Abdallah; Sec. Osman Ali Fadl; 32,000 mems.

**Sudan Irrigation Workers' Trade Union:** Ministry of Education, Wadi Medani; Pres. Muhammad Habib; Sec. Muhammad Ahmad; 19,150 mems.

**Taxi Workers' Trade Union:** Workers' Union, Khartoum; Pres. Ar-Rayan Yousif; Sec. At-Tayeb Khalafalla; 15,000 mems.

**Sudanese Federation of Employees and Professionals Trade Unions:** POB 2398, Khartoum; tel. (11) 73818; f. 1975; includes 54 trade unions representing 250,000 mems; Pres. Ibrahim Awadallah; Sec.-Gen. Kamal ad-Din Muhammad Abdallah.

### Principal Affiliates

**Bank Officials' Union:** POB 313, Bank of Sudan, Gamaa Ave, Khartoum; Pres. Muhammad Sallam; Sec. Abdallah Mahmoud Abdallah.

**Gezira Board Officials' Union:** Barakat; Pres. Galal Hamid; Sec. Osman Abd ar-Rahim Kheirawy.

**Local Government Officials' Union:** Dept of Local Government, Khartoum; Pres. Salah Ibrahim Khalil; Sec. Muhammad Awad Gabir.

**Post, Telegraph and Telephone Officials:** PO, Khartoum; Pres. Abd ar-Rahman al-Khider Ali; Sec. Awad al-Karim Osman.

**Railway Officials' Union:** POB 65, Sudan Railways Corporation, Atbara; Pres. Hassan Haq Musa; Sec. Gen. Abbas Bashir ar-Raieh.

**Teachers' Union:** Teachers' House, Khartoum; Pres. Abdallah Ali Abdallah; Sec. Hassan Ibrahim Marzoug.

## CO-OPERATIVE SOCIETIES

There are about 600 co-operative societies, of which 570 are officially registered.

**Central Co-operative Union:** POB 2492, Khartoum; tel. (11) 80624; largest co-operative union operating in 15 provinces.

## TRADE FAIR

**Sudan Exhibitions and Fairs Corporation (Sudanexpo):** POB 2366, Khartoum; tel. (11) 77702; telex 22407; f. 1976; Dir-Gen. Malik Amin Nabri.

# Transport

## RAILWAYS

The total length of railway in operation in 1991 was 4,725 route-km. The main line runs from Wadi Halfa, on the Egyptian border, to al-Obeid, via Khartoum. Lines from Atbara and Sinnar connect with Port Sudan. There are lines from Sinnar to Damazine on the Blue Nile (227 km) and from Aradeiba to Nyala in the southwestern province of Darfur (689 km), with a 445-km branch line from Babanousa to Wau in Bahr al-Ghazal province.

**Sudan Railways Corporation:** POB 43, Atbara; tel. 2000; telex 40002; f. 1875; Chair. and Gen. Man. Dr el-Fatih Mohammad Ali.

## ROADS

Roads in northern Sudan, other than town roads, are only cleared tracks and often impassable immediately after rain. Motor traffic on roads in the former Upper Nile province is limited to the drier months of January–May. There are several good gravelled roads in Equatoria and Bahr al-Ghazal provinces which are passable all the year, but in these districts some of the minor roads become impassable after rain. Rehabilitation of communications in southern Sudan is hampered by the continuing hostilities in the area.

The Wadi Medani to Gedaref highway, financed by a loan from the People's Republic of China, was completed in March 1977. Over 48,000 km of tracks are classed as 'motorable'; there were 3,160 km of main roads and 739 km of secondary roads in 1985. A 1,190-km tarmac road linking the capital with Port Sudan was completed during 1980. In July 1991 construction began on a 270-km road linking Jaili with Atbara, as part of a scheme to provide an alternative route from Khartoum to the coast.

**National Transport Corporation:** POB 723, Khartoum; Gen. Man. Mohi ad-Din Hassan Muhammad Nur.

**Public Corporation for Roads and Bridges:** POB 756, Khartoum; tel. (11) 70794; f. 1976; Chair. Abd ar-Rahman Haboud; Dir-Gen. Abdou Muhammad Abdou.

## INLAND WATERWAYS

The total length of navigable waterways served by passenger and freight services is 4,068 km, of which approximately 1,723 km is open all year. From the Egyptian border to Wadi Halfa and Khartoum navigation is limited by cataracts to short stretches but the White Nile from Khartoum to Juba is almost always navigable.

**River Transport Corporation (RTC):** POB 284, Khartoum North; operates 2,500 route-km of steamers on the Nile; Chair. Ali Amir Taha.

**River Navigation Corporation:** Khartoum; f. 1970; jtly owned by Govts of Egypt and Sudan; operates services between Aswan and Wadi Halfa.

## SHIPPING

Port Sudan, on the Red Sea, 784 km from Khartoum, and Suakin, are the only commercial seaports.

**Axis Trading Co Ltd:** POB 1574, Khartoum; tel. (11) 75875; telex 22294; Chair. H. A. M. Suliman.

**Red Sea Shipping Corporation:** POB 116, Khartoum; tel. (11) 77688; telex 22306; Gen. Man. Osman Amin.

**Sea Ports Corporation:** Port Sudan; tel. 2910; telex 70012; f. 1906; Gen. Man. Muhammad Tahir Aila.

**Sudan Shipping Line Ltd:** POB 426, Port Sudan; tel. 2655; telex 22518; and POB 1731, Khartoum; tel. (11) 80017; telex 22301; f. 1960; 10 vessels totalling 54,277 dwt operating between the Red Sea and western Mediterranean, northern Europe and United Kingdom; Chair. Ismail Bakheit; Gen. Man. Salah ad-Din Omer al-Aziz.

**United African Shipping Co:** POB 339, Khartoum; tel. (11) 80967; Gen. Man. Muhammad Taha al-Gindi.

## CIVIL AVIATION

**Civil Aviation Authority:** Khartoum; tel. (11) 72264; telex 22650; Dir-Gen. Brig. Mahgoub Muhammad Mahdi.

**Sudan Airways Co. Ltd:** POB 253, SDC Bldg Complex, Amarat St 19, Khartoum; tel. (11) 47953; telex 24212; fax (11) 47987; f. 1947; internal flights and international services to Africa, the Middle East and Europe; Chair. Col Salih ad-Din Muhammad Ahmad Karrar.

# Tourism

**Public Corporation of Tourism and Hotels:** POB 7104, Khartoum; tel. (11) 81764; telex 22436; f. 1977; Dir-Gen. Maj.-Gen. El-Khatim Muhammad Fadl.

# SURINAME

## Introductory Survey

**Location, Climate, Language, Religion, Flag, Capital**

The Republic of Suriname lies on the north-east coast of South America. It is bordered by Guyana to the west, by French Guiana to the east, and by Brazil to the south. The climate is sub-tropical, with fairly heavy rainfall and average temperatures of between 21°C (70°F) and 30°C (86°F). Average annual rainfall varies from 3,720 mm (146 ins) in the north to 804 mm (32 ins) in the south. The official language is Dutch (spoken by 37% of the population in 1964). The other main languages are Hindustani (32%) and Javanese (15%). The majority of the people can speak the native language Sranang Tongo, a Creole language known as Negro English or taki-taki, while Chinese, English, French and Spanish are also used. The principal religions are Christianity (professed by 45% of the population in 1964), Hinduism (28%) and Islam (20%). The national flag (proportions 3 by 2) has five horizontal stripes: a broad central band of red (with a five-pointed yellow star in the centre), edged with white, between bands of green. The capital is Paramaribo.

**Recent History**

Settlers from England landed in Suriname in the 1630s, and the territory was alternately a British and a Dutch colony until it was eventually awarded to the Netherlands by the Treaty of Vienna in 1815. The colony's economy depended on large sugar plantations, for which labour was provided by slaves of African origin. Following the abolition of slavery in 1863, immigration of labourers from India and the then Dutch East Indies was encouraged, and many of them settled permanently in Suriname. This history explains the country's current ethnic diversity: there are small communities of the original Amerindian population (mainly in the interior) and of ethnic Chinese descent and Europeans; a Creole population, largely of African descent, constitutes about one-third of the population, as do the Asian-descended 'East' Indians (known locally as Hindustanis); the Indonesian-descended 'Javanese' form about 15% of the population, and another Creole group, the 'boschnegers' or Bush Negroes, forms a further 10% (the Bush Negroes are the Dutch-speaking descendants of escaped slaves, long-established in the rain-forest as a tribalized society of four clans). Under a Charter signed in December 1954, Suriname (also known as Dutch Guiana) became an equal partner in the Kingdom of the Netherlands, with the Netherlands Antilles and the Netherlands itself, and gained full autonomy in domestic affairs.

The Hindustani-dominated Government, in power since 1969 and led by Dr Jules Sedney, resigned in February 1973. General elections in November 1973 were won by an alliance of parties, the Nationale Partij Kambinatie (NPK), which favoured complete independence from the Netherlands, and in December Henck Arron, leader of the Nationale Partij Suriname (NPS—a predominantly Creole party), became Prime Minister. In May 1975 it was agreed that Suriname would become independent on 25 November, and that the Dutch Government would provide, over a period of 15 years, 3,500m. guilders in aid. Dr Johan Ferrier, hitherto the Governor of Suriname, became the new republic's first President. After independence, some 40,000 Surinamese emigrated to the Netherlands, leaving Suriname with a severely underskilled work-force. Border disputes with French Guiana and Guyana also ensued. The general election of October 1977 resulted in a clear majority for the ruling NPK, and Henck Arron continued as Prime Minister.

The Government of Henck Arron was overthrown in February 1980 by a group of soldiers, who formed an eight-man military council, the Nationale Militaire Raad (NMR). President Ferrier refused to agree to the retention of supreme power by this council, and in March he appointed a civilian administration led by Dr Henk Chin-A-Sen, a former leader of the Partij Nationalistische Republiek. In August the Army Chief of Staff, NMR member Sgt-Maj. (later Lt-Col) Désiré (Desi) Bouterse (subsequently Commander-in-Chief of the armed forces), staged a coup. President Ferrier was replaced by Chin-A-Sen. The legislature was dissolved, and a state of emergency declared. An unsuccessful Hindustani-inspired coup against Lt-Col Bouterse, led by Sgt-Maj. Wilfred Hawker, was staged in March 1981. In September the President announced details of a draft Constitution, which sought to limit the army to a supervisory role in government. This move, however, was countered by the army with the formation of the Revolutionary People's Front, a comprehensive political alliance headed by Bouterse and two other members of the NMR, Maj. Roy Horb and Lt (later Commdr) Iwan Graanoogst, together with three leaders of workers' and students' organizations. In February 1982 the NMR, led by Bouterse, seized power from Chin-A-Sen and his civilian Government. (Chin-A-Sen later emigrated to the Netherlands, where, in January 1983, he formed the Movement for the Liberation of Suriname, which aimed to remove Bouterse from power by peaceful means.) The Vice-President of the Supreme Court, L. Fred Ramdat Misier, was appointed interim President. In March 1982 a further coup attempt by Hawker failed, and he was executed.

A state of siege was declared, and martial law was imposed. In order to prevent the Netherlands from suspending its aid, a 12-member Cabinet of Ministers with a civilian majority was appointed at the end of March 1982, and a moderate economist, Henry Neyhorst, became Prime Minister, although Bouterse remained effectively in control. Failure to effect promised social and economic changes lost Bouterse the support of left-wing groups and the trade unions, which supported the business community in demanding a return to constitutional rule. The military regime responded by tightening censorship and by attempting to suppress the opposition. In October the arrest of Cyriel Daal, the leader of Suriname's principal trade union (De Moederbond), prompted strikes and demonstrations. Threatened with a general strike in November, Bouterse agreed to arrange for the election of a constituent assembly to draft a new constitution by March 1983, to be followed by the establishment of an elected government, but he subsequently reneged on his commitment. In December 1982 members of the armed forces burned down several buildings used by the opposition. During the ensuing disturbances, 15 leading citizens, including Cyriel Daal, were murdered. The Government resigned, the Netherlands and the USA halted all aid, and the country was placed under rule by decree. A temporary, largely military, Government was appointed. An attempted coup in January 1983, the sixth since February 1980, resulted in the dismissal of two-thirds of the officers of the armed forces and the death of Maj. Roy Horb. In February Dr Errol Alibux, a former Minister of Social Affairs, was appointed Prime Minister. He formed a new Cabinet of Ministers, composed of members of two left-wing parties, the Progressieve Arbeiders en Landbouwers Unie (PALU) and the Revolutionaire Volkspartij. The new Government immediately lifted the restrictions imposed in December 1982.

In January 1984, after a series of widely-observed strikes and an increasing demand for the restoration of civilian rule and the holding of free elections, Bouterse dismissed the Cabinet of Ministers. He reached an agreement with the strikers after withdrawing planned tax increases. An interim Government, with Wim Udenhout, a former adviser to Bouterse, as Prime Minister, was created in February to prepare plans for a gradual restoration of constitutional rule; it included nominees of the trade unions and of the business sector. Bouterse hoped to consolidate his position by securing a political base through Standvaste (the 25 February Movement), which he had founded in November 1983. In December 1984 plans for a nominated National Assembly (comprising representatives of Standvaste, the trade unions and the business sector) were announced. The Netherlands Government, however, refused to consider the changes as a significant move towards democratic rule, and regarded them as insufficient to merit the resumption of Dutch aid. In spite of this rejection, the new National Assembly was inaugurated in January 1985. A new Cabinet of Ministers, based on the previous administration, was formed by Udenhout.

The tripartite system of government broke down in April 1985, after the withdrawal from the Cabinet of Ministers of three of the four trade union nominees. The reconstituted Cabinet of Ministers, formed in June, contained new members with links to traditional political parties. In November the ban on political parties was lifted, and a new constitution was promised as a prelude to an eventual return to civilian rule. In the same month the former Prime Minister, Henck Arron of the NPS, together with Jaggernath Lachmon of the Hindustani-based Vooruitstrevende Hervormings Partij (VHP) and Willy Soemita of the Kaum-Tani Persuatan Indonesia (KTPI), accepted an invitation to join the NMR, renamed the Supreme Council (Topberaad). By July 1986 only two military officers remained on the Topberaad.

In July 1986 Bouterse appointed a new Cabinet of Ministers, which included representatives from industry, business, political parties, trade unions and Standvaste. Pretaap Radhakishun, a business executive and member of the VHP, was appointed Prime Minister. The Cabinet drafted a new Constitution, which was approved by the National Assembly on 31 March 1987. A national referendum was held in September 1987, when the draft, despite the voicing of some anxieties about certain ambiguities in the distribution of power, was approved by 93% of the voters.

A series of attacks on military posts on the eastern border of the country was begun in July 1986 by a group of anti-Government guerrillas, believed to number between 100 and 300, who were demanding the restoration of democracy. The group, which was led by Ronnie Brunswijk (a former presidential bodyguard), consisted mainly of Bush Negroes, who claimed that government resettlement policies threatened the autonomy of their tribal society, which had been guaranteed by treaties with the former Dutch authorities, signed in 1760. It was reported that financial support for the guerrillas (known as the Jungle Commando, or Surinamese Liberation Army—SLA) was being provided by Surinamese exiles in the Netherlands, in particular by members of the Movement for the Liberation of Suriname.

Guerrilla attacks against military posts and state-owned industries escalated during August and September 1986, and erupted into fierce fighting with government troops. By November most of the eastern district of Marowijne was under guerrilla control, and the rebels had also occupied the area near Zanderij (later renamed Johan Adolf Pengel) International Airport, 50 km south of Paramaribo. Rebel attacks on the mining town of Moengo forced the closure of the country's principal bauxite mines. The town was recaptured by the armed forces in December, but the mines remained closed. At the beginning of December a state of emergency was declared in eastern and southern Suriname, and a curfew was imposed. Reports that civilians had been massacred by government troops in the search for guerrillas led to protests by the Netherlands and US Governments. (A report published in February 1988 by the UN Commission on Human Rights claimed that the armed forces were responsible for the deaths of between 150 and 200 civilians between June 1986 and August 1987.) Relations with the Netherlands deteriorated further in January 1987, when the Dutch Ambassador to Suriname was accused of complicity in guerrilla activity, and his recall was requested. By December 1986 an estimated 4,500 Surinamese refugees had crossed into French Guiana to escape the fighting.

In February 1987 the sabotage of electricity pylons by the guerrillas, and damage to equipment by workers, forced the indefinite closure of the main bauxite smelting and refining plants. In that month five members of the Cabinet of Ministers, including Radhakishun, resigned. Jules Wijdenbosch, hitherto the Minister of Internal Affairs and a member of Standvaste, was appointed Prime Minister. The entire Cabinet resigned at the end of March 1987, and a new Cabinet, led by Wijdenbosch, was appointed by Bouterse on 7 April.

It was announced in March 1987 that a general election for a new National Assembly was to be held in November. During the period preceding the election several political parties resumed their activities. Standvaste was reconstituted, under Wijdenbosch, as the National Democratic Party (NDP), which was officially inaugurated in July 1987. In August the three major opposition parties, the NPS, the VHP and the KTPI (whose name was changed to the Kerukanan Tulodo Pranatan Ingil in October 1987), held a rally, attended by more than 60,000 people, to launch an electoral alliance, the Front voor Demokratie en Ontwikkeling (FDO—Front for Democracy and Development). The leaders of the parties strongly criticized the Government's economic policies. The rally was rapidly followed by a mass meeting held by the armed forces, and by the announcement that Bouterse and Granoogst were to withdraw from the Topberaad, having been 'insulted' by the FDO. Shortly afterwards, however, Bouterse and the leaders of the FDO signed the 'Leonsberg Accord', in which the alliance declared that it would strive for the best possible relationship with the armed forces, while Bouterse stated that the army would respect the outcome of the election. Brunswijk's SLA observed a cease-fire for the election.

The general election to the 51-seat National Assembly was held on 25 November 1987. The FDO won a decisive victory, obtaining 40 of the 41 seats that it contested; the PALU and the Progressieve Bosneger Partij each won four seats, while the NDP won three. In January 1988 the National Assembly unanimously elected Ramsewak Shankar (a former Minister of Agriculture) as President of the Republic, and Henck Arron was elected Vice-President and thus (in accordance with the Constitution) Prime Minister, leading the 14-member Cabinet of Ministers, which comprised members of the alliance. In December 1987 Bouterse was appointed leader of a five-member Military Council, established under the new Constitution to 'guarantee a peaceful transition' to democracy. Full diplomatic relations with the Netherlands were restored during 1988, and in July the Dutch Government agreed to resume aid to Suriname. However, relations remained tense, owing mainly to the Dutch administration's suspicions concerning the Surinamese army.

In June 1988 negotiations finally began between the Government and representatives of the SLA, with the Committee of Christian Churches, led by the Roman Catholic Bishop of Paramaribo, acting as mediator. Prospects for a settlement appeared to be favourable after President Shankar announced, in January 1989, that a legal commission had been established to study the possibility of a general amnesty for personnel from both sides involved in the conflict. (This move was considered a likely explanation for Bouterse's acceptance of direct negotiations with Brunswijk.) The SLA claimed that the amnesty would prevent investigation of alleged abuses of human rights by the army, and appeared to remain suspicious of any agreement.

After preliminary discussions in June 1989, and further negotiations in July, representatives of the Government and the SLA, meeting in French Guiana, signed an agreement at Kourou. The National Assembly ratified the Kourou Accord in August. Its main provisions were: a general amnesty for those involved in the recent conflicts; the ending of the state of emergency imposed in December 1986; the incorporation of many members of the SLA into a special police unit for the interior of the country; and significant investment in the interior. The armed forces declared their opposition to the Accord and withdrew all co-operation with the Government, but took no direct action against continuing negotiations.

There was renewed pressure on the Accord at the end of August 1989 (timed to coincide with the ending of the state of emergency) and in September and October, with the outbreak of more guerrilla activity. On this occasion the violence was primarily in the west of the country and threatened seriously to disrupt agricultural production. Those responsible, a group of Amerindians who had adopted the name of Tucayana Amazonica, criticized some of the provisions of the Kourou Accord, principally the involvement of the SLA in the proposed police force for the interior; they also requested the restoration of the Bureau for Amerindian Affairs. Several of their demands were similar to those of the army command, and there were allega-tions that Tucayana were being armed and encouraged by the military, exploiting the traditional antipathy between the Amerindians and many of the Bush Negroes. In October, however, the Tucayana spokesmen were augmented by elected representatives of the Amerindian communities, the Commission of Eight, and the two groups met representatives of the National Assembly, who stated that the Government was prepared to supplement, but not rescind, the Kourou Accord.

Also in October 1989 Tucayana received the support of another new insurgent group, the Mandela Bush Negro Liberation Movement (BBM), which declared itself to be dissatisfied with the Kourou Accord. The BBM was formed by members of the most westerly (and, hitherto, least involved in the civil war) of the Bush Negro clans, the Mauauriërs. In the same month, however, Brunswijk's SLA secured the support of another new insurgent group, the Union for Liberation and Democracy (UBD), which occupied the mining town of Moengo. Apparently composed of radical former members of the SLA, the UBD declared its support for the Kourou Accord.

In November and December 1989 Bouterse held direct negotiations with Brunswijk, and also met representatives of Tucayana and, to the annoyance of the SLA leadership, two of the SLA's own more recalcitrant field commanders. Brunswijk was reported to be experiencing difficulties with formerly loyal mercenaries and in his relations with the UBD in Moengo. That he retained considerable popular support was demonstrated, however, at the SLA's first mass meeting in Moengo, in January 1990.

In February 1990 both Brunswijk and the Tucayana leadership enforced their authority over dissatisfied elements in their groups. Some of the dissident Tucayana, however, alleged that they were part of a force trained by the Surinamese military to defend marijuana (hemp) plantations in the west (the army leadership denied any involvement in drugs-trafficking). The military authorities were criticized by the US Ambassador for their involvement in politics, and were further embarrassed by a demand for the investigation into the murders, in 1982, of 15 prominent citizens. At the end of February Bouterse relinquished his mandate to negotiate with the rebel groups, and the responsibility was assumed by a commission headed by President Shankar, which met Brunswijk and Tucayana in March. Later in that month, however, negotiations were imperilled by the arrest of Brunswijk and his aides, by military personnel, when they were in Paramaribo for meetings with the Government. The Government ordered their release and then introduced legislation to remove the power of arrest from the military police. The SLA announced that, henceforth, it would prefer negotiations to take place outside Suriname.

In June 1990 Brunswijk was placed under arrest in Cayenne, French Guiana, reportedly in possession of a false passport and undeclared currency. There he announced his intention to abandon the military struggle in Suriname and to seek residence in the Netherlands. In early July, however, Brunswijk returned to Suriname. In June the armed forces recaptured the rebel stronghold of Moengo. In September another rebel base, at Langetabbetje, was recovered by the armed forces.

On 22 December 1990 Bouterse resigned as Commander-in-Chief of the armed forces, after President Shankar failed to issue an official protest at the Netherlands' treatment of Bouterse, who was denied access to the country while in transit at Amsterdam's airport. Suspicions that Bouterse's resignation might portend a military coup were realized on 24 December, when the acting Commander-in-Chief of the armed forces, Graanoogst, seized power from the Government. The coup, which took place without bloodshed, was immediately condemned by the Netherlands Government, which suspended development aid to Suriname. Johan Kraag (honorary chairman of the NPS and a former Minister of Labour) was appointed provisional President on 29 December, and promptly invited Bouterse to resume command of the armed forces, thus substantiating speculation that Kraag was merely acting on behalf of Bouterse. A transitional Government (led by Jules Wijdenbosch, who had been Prime Minister in 1987) was sworn in on 7 January 1991, and it was announced that a general election would take place within 100 days. The period was later extended to 150 days. In March Brunswijk and Bouterse met in the rebel stronghold of Drietabbetje to sign a peace accord, in an attempt to put an end to four years of hostilities. In late April four rebel groups, the SLA, Tucayana, the BBM and Angula, signed a further agreement with the Government, promising to respect the law and not to obstruct the conduct of free elections. The elections, which were monitored by a delegation from the Organization of American States (OAS, see p. 204), were held on 25 May 1991. The Nieuw Front (NF), an electoral alliance comprising the members of the former FDO and the Surinaamse Partij van de Arvid secured 30 seats in the National Assembly, tbwhile the NDP won 12. The remaining nine seats were gained by a new coalition, Democratisch Alternatief 1991 (DA '91), mainly comprising former members of the FDO critical of the Government's failure to curb the political influence of the military. Despite the fact that it had not secured the two-thirds'

majority in the Assembly necessary to elect automatically its presidential candidate, Runaldo R. Venetiaan, the NF refused to consider the possibility of any agreement involving the formation of a coalition government or the cession of ministerial posts or policy commitments to either the NDP or DA '91. When a series of meetings of the National Assembly in July failed to result in any one presidential candidate securing a majority, the Chairman of the Assembly, Jaggernath Lachman, in accordance with provisions incorporated in the Constitution, convened the Vereinigde Volksvergadering (United People's Assembly), a body comprising the members of the National Assembly and representatives of the municipal and district councils, in order to elect a President. On 7 September Venetiaan was elected with an overwhelming 78.9% of the votes. Jules Wijdenbosch, the NDP candidate, won 14.7% of the votes and Hans Prade, the candidate for DA '91, secured the remaining 6.4%. The new Cabinet was appointed on 17 September.

In July 1991, following renewed allegations by international media implicating senior military personnel in the illegal trafficking of cocaine in Suriname, the Minister of Defence, Lt-Col Rupert Christopher, tendered his resignation and requested that he be suspended from the armed forces. However, at the request of President Kraag, he later withdrew his resignation. Reports accusing senior military officials, including Bouterse, of supervising shipments of cocaine *en route* from Colombia to Europe were refuted by the military. Following his election in September, President Venetiaan announced that the Government would seek technical and military assistance abroad should the problem of illegal drugs-trafficking in Suriname prove beyond his control. In October Venetiaan announced the reduction of the armed forces by two-thirds and a reduction in the defence budget of 50%. These measures were introduced as part of a government programme of 'socialization' of the armed forces. In addition, amendments to the Constitution, which were approved in March 1992, included measures to curb the political influence of the military, removing all its constitutional duties except those of national defence and the combating of organized subversion, and banning serving members of the security forces from holding representative public office. In early April the Military Council, established under the 1987 Constitution, was abolished.

In early 1991 senior officials from the Netherlands began conducting informal discussions with political parties in Suriname sympathetic to the possibility of creating a commonwealth association between the two nations. According to the proposals, which aimed to put an end to the military dominance of Bouterse, the Netherlands would assume responsibility for the national security and foreign affairs of Suriname; there would also be some form of monetary union. Following his election in September 1991, President Venetiaan cited an improvement in relations with other countries, and in particular with the Netherlands, the USA and Venezuela, as a priority of the new Government. He considered an amelioration of the tensions in foreign relations to be essential to the prevention of a recurrence of military intervention in the political affairs of Suriname.

Following peace negotiations in early 1992 between the Government, the SLA and Tucayana, hostilities were suspended in May. In early August a peace agreement was signed by the Government and the two rebel groups; the BBM also committed itself to the agreement. Under the terms of the agreement, the amnesty law envisaged under the Kourou Accord of 1989, covering all civil conflicts since 1985 and amended to include insurgent groups formed since the ratification of the Kourou Accord, was to be implemented. All weapons were to be surrendered to the Government, under the supervision of the OAS. Following disarmament, members of all the groups would be eligible for recruitment into a special police force for the interior of the country. In addition, the Government gave assurances that the interior would receive priority in its programmes for economic development and social welfare.

In November 1992 Bouterse resigned as Commander-in-Chief of the armed forces, prompting an anxious reaction by the public, who recalled that an identical move by Bouterse had preceded the coup of December 1990. Bouterse's resignation came as the result of a dispute with the Government over its decision to allow the staging of a march to commemorate the 10th anniversary of the massacre of 15 civilian opponents of Bouterse's military regime.

In April 1993 Venetiaan's appointment of Col (retd) Arthy Gorré as Commander-in-Chief of the armed forces resulted in a confrontation between the Government and senior military officers. (Gorré had supported the 1980 coup staged by Bouterse but had resigned from the armed forces in 1987, following a disagreement with the latter. Graanoogst, who had occupied the position of Commander-in-Chief on an interim basis since Bouterse's resignation in November 1992, refused to concede the post to Gorré. Graanoogst was supported in his decision by his fellow members of the military high command and by Bouterse, who, despite his resignation, remained effectively in control of the armed forces. Venetiaan subsequently deferred Gorré's appointment until mid-May, when it was endorsed by a majority in the National Assembly, despite veiled threats of a military coup and an attack on the national television station, which had allegedly been instigated by Bouterse in an attempt to intimidate the legislature. All four members of the military high command subsequently acceded to a request by the National Assembly for their resignations. Three of them, including Graanoogst, later accepted posts as advisers to the Government, thus assuaging fears of an escalation of the conflict. Indications that the Netherlands might intervene to assist the Government were also considered influential in averting further military defiance of civilian rule.

In September 1993 Venetiaan conducted a reorganization of cabinet portfolios. In the following month a demonstration, organized by opposition parties and led by Bouterse, took place in the capital in protest at austerity measures introduced by the Government under its structural adjustment programme. Earlier in the month the DA '91 organized a one-day general strike, although, reportedly, it failed to elicit widespread support.

In April 1994 a previously unknown insurgent group, the Suriname Liberation Front, seized a hydroelectric plant at Afobaka, 100 km south of Paramaribo, taking 30 hostages. The rebels' demands included the resignation of the Government, a decentralization of power, and the introduction of measures to improve the situation of the country's poor. A Surinamese commando unit succeeded in releasing the hostages, killing some eight guerrillas; the remaining insurgents were reported to have escaped.

In November 1994 there were violent confrontations in Paramaribo between the security forces and some 4,000 demonstrators who were protesting at increased food prices. The increases had been implemented by the Government in an attempt to regain control over a widening budget deficit and rapidly rising inflation.

Suriname has a territorial dispute with Guyana over an estimated 15,000 sq km (6,000 sq miles) of land in the Corentyne region, and another with French Guiana over land to the east of the Litani river. In 1988 France warned Suriname not to allow its forces to enter French Guiana in the course of its struggle against rebel forces. In April 1990, with the mediation of the UN High Commissioner for Refugees, France and Suriname agreed terms providing for the repatriation of an estimated 10,000 Surinamese refugees from French Guiana. In October French Guiana was reported to have begun forcible repatriation of Surinamese refugees. In April 1992, under a plan agreed between France, Suriname and the UN, which had been prompted by the ongoing peace negotiations in Suriname (see above), some 6,000 Surinamese refugees were offered voluntary repatriation. The deadline for the French-funded resettlement scheme, originally scheduled for 30 September, was later extended by the French Government to 31 December. In late July the Suriname Government delivered an official protest to the French authorities concerning the alleged compulsory repatriation of refugees.

### Government

Under the provisions of the 1987 Constitution, legislative power is held by the National Assembly, with 51 members, elected by universal adult suffrage for a five-year term. The Assembly elects the President and the Vice-President of the Republic. Executive power is vested in the President, who appoints the Cabinet of Ministers, led by the Vice-President, who is also the Prime Minister. The Cabinet is responsible to the National Assembly. A Council of State, comprising civilians and members of the armed forces, advises the President and the Cabinet of Ministers on policy, and has power of veto over legislation approved by the Assembly. Suriname comprises nine administrative districts.

### Defence

Suriname's armed forces numbered 1,790 men and women in June 1994. There is an army of 1,400, a navy of 240, and an air force of about 150. The defence budget for 1993 was Sf 110.7m.

In March 1992 constitutional amendments providing for the abolition of conscription and the disbanding of the paramilitary National Militia (numbering some 900) were deferred to a second stage of revision by the National Assembly.

### Economic Affairs

In 1993, according to estimates by the World Bank, Suriname's gross national product (GNP), measured at average 1991–93 prices, was US $488m., equivalent to $1,210 per head. During 1985–93, it was estimated, GNP per head increased, in real terms, at an average annual rate of 2.2%. Over the same period there was no discernible increase in the population. Suriname's gross domestic product (GDP) increased, in real terms, by an annual average of 1.1% in 1985–90, and by 2.8% in 1991. However, GDP was estimated to have declined by 3% in 1994.

Agriculture (including hunting, forestry and fishing) contributed 13.8% of GDP in 1992. This sector employed 15.3% of the working population in 1993. The principal crop is rice, which supplies domestic demand and provided 6.1% of export earnings in 1991. The other major agricultural export (since 1986, when guerrilla activity disrupted the oil palm industry) is bananas, which earned 2.5% of total export earnings in 1991. Sugar cane, citrus fruits, plantains and bacoven are cultivated for export, while Suriname also produces coconuts, maize and vegetables. Livestock is being developed, as are the extensive timber reserves (94.9% of Suriname's total land area was wooded in 1992). Commercial fishing is important, particularly of shrimps (which provided 9.0% of total export revenue in 1991). During 1980–85 agricultural production increased by an average of 6.1% per year; in 1985–90, however, following the outbreak of guerrilla activity, it declined by 6.3% per year. Production increased by an estimated 5.2% annually in 1990–94.

Industry (including mining, manufacturing, public utilities and construction) contributed 22.4% of GDP in 1992, and employed nearly 20% of the working population in 1984. The principal activity is the bauxite industry, which dominates both the mining and manufacturing sectors, but which was severely affected following the outbreak of guerrilla activity in 1986.

Mining and quarrying contributed 2.1% of GDP in 1992, and employed 4.6% of the working population in 1984. The principal product is bauxite (used in the manufacture of aluminium), of which Suriname is one of the world's leading producers. Suriname also has extensive deposits of iron ore and reserves of manganese, copper, nickel, platinum, gold and kaolin. In 1981 petroleum-bearing sand was discovered in the Saramacca district, and offshore reserves have also been found.

Manufacturing contributed 10.3% of GDP in 1992, and employed 11.0% of the working population in 1984. Bauxite refining and smelting is the principal industry (alumina and aluminium accounted for 79.5% of export revenue in 1991), but there are also important food-processing industries and manufacturers of cigarettes, beverages and chemical products.

Energy is currently derived principally from hydrocarbon fuels, mainly imported; in 1991 refined petroleum products accounted for 15.5% of total import costs. The country has considerable potential for the development of hydroelectric power; there is a hydroelectric station for the aluminium industry, and in January 1989 the Government announced that work would resume on a 500-MW plant in west Suriname (delayed since 1980).

In 1992 Suriname recorded a visible trade surplus of US $68.4m., and there was a surplus of $11.0m. on the current account of the balance of payments. In 1991 the principal source of imports was the USA (38.4% of total imports); other significant suppliers were the Netherlands (22.2%) and Trinidad and Tobago (11.2%). The principal markets for exports in 1991 were Norway (taking 33.8% of the total), the Netherlands (26.0%) and the USA (12.8%). The principal imports in 1991 were raw materials and semi-manufactured goods, investment goods and fuels and lubricants. The principal exports in that year were bauxite and its derivatives, and shrimps, rice and bananas.

In 1992 there was a budgetary deficit of Sf 384.8m. At the end of 1990 the total external public debt stood at an estimated US $123m. The annual rate of inflation averaged 34.3% in 1985–93. Consumer prices increased by an average of 143.5% in 1993. At the end of 1987 some 33% of the labour force were unemployed, despite the exodus of a large number of refugees who fled the civil war into French Guiana and the continued expulsion of illegal Guyanese immigrants.

In February 1995 Suriname was granted full membership of the Caribbean Community and Common Market (CARICOM, see p. 114).

Economic activity is relatively diversified in range, but the dominant sector is the bauxite industry. The outbreak of guerrilla activity in 1986, however, severely disrupted the mining, manufacturing and agricultural sectors and served to discourage foreign investment. Foreign exchange earnings declined in the late 1980s as a result of falling prices on the international market for alumina and aluminium, Suriname's principal exports. In December 1990, following the military coup, the Netherlands, Suriname's principal source of aid, suspended all development aid; aid was resumed in November 1991, however, following free elections in Suriname. In January 1993 the Government introduced a structural adjustment programme (SAP); measures included a devaluation of the currency, the transfer to private ownership of state enterprises, reductions in government spending and in the number of public employees, and the removal of subsidies on basic goods. However, balance-of-payments support provided by the Netherlands, which was contingent upon implementation of the SAP, was withdrawn in August 1993. In June 1993 the Government introduced a free-market rate for the Suriname guilder. In July 1994 the Government abolished the official exchange rate and introduced a new unified exchange rate system, removing all remaining exchange controls. In that year Suriname's economy experienced hyperinflation (inflation for the year was reported to be 369%), rapid currency depreciation and an increasing budgetary deficit. In early 1995 the Government agreed to monitoring of the economy, on a non-binding basis, by the IMF in the hope that this might facilitate the release of suspended balance-of-payments support by the Netherlands. In March the Government introduced gold-linked debt security certificates in an effort to reduce excess liquidity and curb inflation.

### Social Welfare

There is a modern medical service, financed by Dutch and European Union funds, but social welfare has remained largely dependent on private initiative within the various religious communities. In 1985 Suriname had a total of 1,964 hospital beds, and there were 219 physicians working in the country. Of total expenditure by the central Government in 1986, Sf 34.4m. (4.0%) was for health, and a further Sf 57.7m. (6.7%) for social security and welfare.

### Education

Primary education is compulsory for children between six and 12 years of age, and is followed by a further seven years of secondary education, comprising a first cycle of four years and a second cycle of three years. All education in government and denominational schools is provided free of charge. In 1988 the total enrolment at primary and secondary schools was equivalent to 87% of the school-age population (86% of males; 88% of females). In that year, primary enrolment included 100% of children in the relevant age-group. The comparable ratio for secondary enrolment was 45% (males 43%; females 47%). The traditional educational system, inherited from the Dutch, was amended after the 1980 revolution to place greater emphasis on serving the needs of Suriname's population. This included a literacy campaign and programmes of adult education. In 1990, according to an official estimate, the rate of adult illiteracy was only 5.1% (males 4.9%; females 5.3%). Higher education is provided by technical and vocational schools and by the University of Suriname at Paramaribo, which has faculties of law, economics, medicine, social sciences and technology. Expenditure on education by all levels of government in 1990 was Sf 250m. (8.3% of GNP).

### Public Holidays

**1995:** 1 January (New Year's Day), March* (Phagwa), 3 March (Id al-Fitr, end of Ramadan), 14–17 April (Easter), 1 May (Labour Day), 1 July (National Union Day), 25 November (Independence Day), 25–26 December (Christmas).

**1996:** 1 January (New Year's Day), 21 February (Id al-Fitr, end of Ramadan), March* (Phagwa), 5–8 April (Easter), 1 May (Labour Day), 1 July (National Union Day), 25 November (Independence Day), 25–26 December (Christmas).

* Exact date dependent upon sightings of the moon.

### Weights and Measures

The metric system is in force.

# Statistical Survey

Source (unless otherwise stated): Algemeen Bureau voor de Statistiek, Kromme Elleboogstraat 10, POB 244, Paramaribo; tel. 473927.

## AREA, POPULATION AND DENSITY

**Area:** 163,265 sq km (63,037 sq miles).

**Population:** 379,607 at census of 31 December 1971; 355,240 (males 175,814; females 179,426) at census of 1 July 1980; 404,310 (official estimate, provisional) at 31 December 1991.

**Density** (31 December 1991): 2.5 per sq km.

**Ethnic Groups** (1980 census, percentage): Creole 34.70; Hindustani 33.49; Javanese 16.33; Bush Negro 9.55; Amerindian 3.10; Chinese 1.55; European 0.44; Others 0.84.

**Administrative Districts** (population at 1980 census, according to new boundaries of 1985): Paramaribo 169,798; Nickerie 32,690; Coronie 2,777; Saramacca 10,808; Wanica 60,725; Commewijne 20,063; Marowijne 16,125; Brokopondo 6,621; Para 12,827; Sipaliwini 23,226.

**Births and Deaths** (1991): Registered live births 9,104 (birth rate 22.5 per 1,000); Registered deaths 2,573 (death rate 6.4 per 1,000).

**Expectation of Life** (UN estimates, years at birth, 1985–90): 68.8 (males 66.4, females 71.3). Source: UN, *World Population Prospects: The 1992 Revision*.

**Economically Active Population** (1984): Agriculture, hunting, forestry, wood processing and fishing 16,700; Mining and quarrying 4,600; Manufacturing 10,960; Electricity, gas and water 1,420; Construction 2,800; Trade, restaurants and hotels 12,840; Transport, storage and communications 3,830; Financial institutions and commercial services 2,100; Government 40,190; Other services 3,800; Total employed 99,240.

## AGRICULTURE, ETC.

**Principal Crops** (FAO estimates, '000 metric tons, 1993): Rice (paddy) 260; Sugar cane 45; Citrus fruit 18; Bananas and plantains 63; Coconuts 10; Roots and tubers 4; Vegetables 30. Source: FAO, *Production Yearbook*.

**Livestock** (FAO estimates, '000 head, 1993): Cattle 97; Goats 9; Sheep 9; Pigs 36; Chickens 6,000. Source: FAO, *Production Yearbook*.

**Forestry** ('000 cu metres, 1992): Roundwood removals: Sawlogs, veneer logs and logs for sleepers 109; Other industrial wood (FAO estimate) 26; Fuel wood 19; Total 154. Sawnwood production: Total (incl. railway sleepers) 43. Source: FAO, *Yearbook of Forest Products*.

**Fishing** (FAO estimates, metric tons, 1992): Freshwater fishes 564; Marine fishes 10,108; Penaeus shrimps 261; Total catch 10,933. Source: FAO, *Fishery Statistics Yearbook*.

## MINING

**Production:** ('000 metric tons, 1991): Crude petroleum 234 (estimate); Bauxite 3,136. Source: UN, *Industrial Statistics Yearbook*.

Bauxite (estimates, '000 metric tons): 3,160 in 1992; 3,200 in 1993. Source: UN, *Monthly Bulletin of Statistics*.

## INDUSTRY

**Production** ('000 litres, 1992): Soft drinks 10,168; Beer 6,669 (estimate); Alcohol 69 (1991). ('000 metric tons, 1992): Alumina 1,573; Aluminium 32.4. (metric tons, 1992): Raw sugar 42 (1989); Shrimps 2,878 (estimate); Cement 14,339; Palm oil 1,988. Other products (1992): Cigarettes 419 million; Shoes (pairs) 111,624; Plywood (cubic metres) 7,627; Particle board (cubic metres) 106 (1991); Electricity (million kWh) 1,599.

## FINANCE

**Currency and Exchange Rates:** 100 cents = 1 Suriname gulden (guilder) or florin (Sf). *Sterling and Dollar Equivalents* (31 December 1994): £1 sterling = 640.7 guilders; US $1 = 409.5 guilders; 1,000 Suriname guilders = £1.561 = $2.442. *Exchange Rate:* The official rate was fixed at US $1 = 1.78876 guilders (central rate) or $1 = 1.785 guilders (market rate) in December 1971. A new free market rate was introduced in June 1993, and a unified, market-determined rate took effect in July 1994.

**Budget** (Sf million, 1992): *Revenue:* Direct taxation 467.0; Indirect taxation 383.2; Other revenue (incl. bauxite levy) 240.7; Grants 277.1; Aid 62.7; Total 1,430.7. *Expenditure:* Compensation of employees 886.9; Interest payments 188.1; Transfers 254.6; Lending 8.4; Material costs, etc. 406.5; Development expenditure 71.0; Total 1,815.5.

**International Reserves** (US $ million at 31 December 1992): Gold 16.21; Total 16.21. Source: IMF, *International Financial Statistics*.

**Money Supply** (Sf million at 31 December 1992): Currency outside banks 1,347.2; Demand deposits at deposit money banks 1,818.4; Total money (incl. others) 3,221.1. Source: IMF, *International Financial Statistics*.

**Cost of Living** (Consumer Price Index in Paramaribo; base: April 1968 to March 1969 = 100): 1,024.0 in 1991; 1,471.1 in 1992; 3,582.4 in 1993.

**Expenditure on the Gross Domestic Product** (Sf million at current prices, 1991): Government final consumption expenditure 1,069.4; Private final consumption expenditure 1,713.3; Increase in stocks 69.6; Gross fixed capital formation 626.0; *Total domestic expenditure* 3,478.3; Exports of goods and services 657.3; *Less* Imports of goods and services 793.9; GDP in purchasers' values 3,341.7. Source: UN, *National Accounts Statistics*.

**Gross Domestic Product by Kind of Economic Activity** (Sf million at current factor cost, 1992): Agriculture, forestry and fishing 684.0; Mining and quarrying 103.5; Manufacturing 508.8; Electricity, gas and water 151.0; Construction 349.0; Trade, restaurants and hotels 1,089.4; Transport, storage and communications 262.9; Finance, insurance, real estate and business services 932.4; Government services 843.3; Community, social, personal and other services 36.2; Sub-total 4,960.4; *Less* Imputed bank service charge 316.9; GDP at factor cost 4,643.5; Indirect taxes, *less* subsidies 366.8; GDP in purchasers' values 5,010.3.

**Balance of Payments** (US $ million, 1992): Merchandise exports f.o.b. 341.0; Merchandise imports f.o.b. −272.5; *Trade balance* 68.4; Exports of services 22.6; Imports of services −98.7; Other income received 0.7; Other income paid −8.2; Private unrequited transfers (net) −7.3; Official unrequited transfers (net) 33.4; *Current balance* 11.0; Direct investment (net) −30.4; Portfolio investment (net) 1.5; Other capital (net) −19.6; Net errors and omissions 25.4; *Overall balance* −12.0. Source: IMF, *International Financial Statistics*.

## EXTERNAL TRADE

**Principal Commodities** (Sf million, 1991): *Imports c.i.f.:* Raw materials and semi-manufactured goods 319.6; Investment goods 178.2; Fuels and lubricants 141.3; Foodstuffs 68.6; Cars and motorcycles 44.7; Total (incl. others) 909.4. *Exports f.o.b.* (incl. re-exports): Alumina 452.4; Aluminium 57.3; Rice 39.2; Shrimps 57.4; Bananas 16.3; Total (incl. others) 641.3.

**Principal Trading Partners** (Sf million, 1991): *Imports c.i.f.:* Brazil 27.5; Japan 33.9; Netherlands 201.4; Netherlands Antilles 31.7; Trinidad and Tobago 101.9; United Kingdom 14.8; USA 348.7; Total (incl. others) 909.0. *Exports f.o.b.:* Brazil 52.5; Japan 49.9; Netherlands 168.7; Norway 219.1; United Kingdom 11.4; USA 82.7; Total (incl. others) 648.1.

## TRANSPORT

**Road Traffic** (motor vehicles in use at 31 December 1993): Passenger cars 42,509; Goods vehicles 13,881; Buses 1,861. Source: IRF, *World Road Statistics*.

**International Sea-borne Shipping:** (estimated freight traffic, '000 metric tons, 1990): Goods loaded 5,776; Goods unloaded 1,286. Source: UN, *Monthly Bulletin of Statistics*.

**Civil Aviation** (traffic on scheduled services, 1990): Passengers carried ('000) 133; Passenger-km (million) 404; Total ton-km (million) 54. Source: UN, *Statistical Yearbook*.

## TOURISM

**Tourist Arrivals:** 28,000 in 1990; 30,000 in 1991; 30,000 in 1992. Source: UN, *Statistical Yearbook*.

**Tourist Receipts** (US $ million): 11 in 1990; 11 in 1991; 11 in 1992. Source: UN, *Statistical Yearbook*.

## COMMUNICATIONS MEDIA

**Radio Receivers** (1993): 290,256 in use.

**Television Receivers** (1993): 59,598 in use.

**Telephones** (1992): 43,522 in use.

**Daily Newspapers** (1992): 3 (estimated average circ. 43,000). Source: UNESCO, *Statistical Yearbook*.

**Non-daily Newspapers** (1988, estimates): 2 (average circ. 10,000). Source: UNESCO, *Statistical Yearbook*.

## EDUCATION

**Pre-primary** (1991/92): 223 schools; 15,895 pupils.

**Primary** (1991/92): 223 schools; 2,918 teachers; 63,083 pupils.

**Secondary** (1991/92): 89 schools; 1,684 teachers; 26,708 pupils.

**Vocational Training:** 1 school (1984/85); 1,374 staff (1987); 9,292* pupils (1988).

**Teacher Training:** 1 school (1991/92); 332* staff (1987); 1,143 pupils (1991/92).

**University:** 1 institution (1989/90); 254* teachers (1990); 2,373* students (1990).

**Other Higher** (1990): 241* teachers; 1,949* students.

* Source: UNESCO, *Statistical Yearbook*.

# Directory

## The Constitution

The 1987 Constitution was approved by the National Assembly on 31 March and by 93% of voters in a national referendum in September.

### THE LEGISLATURE

Legislative power is exercised jointly by the National Assembly and the Government. The National Assembly comprises 51 members, elected for a five-year term by universal adult suffrage. The Assembly elects a President and a Vice-President and has the right of amendment in any proposal of law by the Government. The approval of a majority of at least two-thirds of the number of members of the National Assembly is required for the amendment of the Constitution, the election of the President, the decision to organize a plebiscite and a People's Congress and for the amendment of electoral law. If it is unable to obtain a two-thirds majority, the Assembly may convene a People's Congress and supplement its numbers with members of local councils.

### THE EXECUTIVE

Executive authority is vested in the President, who is elected for a term of five years as Head of State, Head of Government, Head of the Armed Forces, Chairman of the Council of State, the Cabinet of Ministers and the Security Council.

The Government comprises the President, the Vice-President and the Cabinet of Ministers. The Cabinet of Ministers is appointed by the President from among the members of the National Assembly. The Vice-President is the Prime Minister and leader of the Cabinet, and is responsible to the President.

In the event of war, a state of siege, or exceptional circumstances to be determined by law, a Security Council assumes all government functions.

## THE COUNCIL OF STATE

The Council of State comprises the President (its Chairman) and 14 additional members, composed of two representatives of the combined trade unions, one representative of the associations of employers, one representative of the National Army and 10 representatives of the political parties in the National Assembly. Its duties are to advise the President and the legislature and to supervise the correct execution by the Government of the decisions of the National Assembly. The Council may present proposals of law or of general administrative measures to the Government. The Council has the authority to suspend any legislation approved by the National Assembly which, in the opinion of the Council, is in violation of the Constitution. In this event, the President must decide within one month whether or not to ratify the Council's decision.

## The Government

**President:** RUNALDO R. VENETIAAN (assumed office on 7 September 1991).

**Council of State:** Chair. President of the Republic; 14 mems (10 to represent the political parties in the National Assembly, one for the armed forces, two for the trade unions and one for employers).

### CABINET OF MINISTERS
(June 1995)

**Vice-President and Prime Minister:** JULES R. AJODHIA (VHP).
**Minister of Finance:** HUMPHREY STANLEY HILDENBURG (NPS).
**Minister of Planning and International Co-operation:** RONALD ASSEN (NPS).
**Minister of Education and Community Development:** GERARD OTMAR HIWAT (NPS).
**Minister for Natural Resources and Energy:** RUDY DEMON (NPS).
**Minister of Regional Affairs:** ROMEO VAN RUSSEL (NPS).
**Minister of Foreign Affairs:** SUBHAS CHANDRA MUNGRA (VHP).
**Minister of Justice and the Police:** SOESHIEL K. GIRJASING (VHP).
**Minister of Public Health:** MOHAMED R. KHUDABUX (VHP).
**Minister of Public Works:** RADJKOEMAR RANDJIETSING (VHP).
**Minister of Trade and Industry:** RICHARD B. KALLOE (VHP).
**Minister of Social Affairs and Housing:** WILLY SOEMITA (KTPI).
**Minister of Internal Affairs:** SABAN SABIRAN (KTPI).
**Minister of Agriculture, Animal Husbandry and Fisheries:** JOHAN SISAL (KTPI).
**Minister of Defence:** SIEGFRIED F. GILDS (SPA).
**Minister of Labour:** JACK KROSS (SPA).
**Minister of Transport, Communications and Tourism:** JOHN A. DEFARES (SPA).

### MINISTRIES

**Ministry of Agriculture, Animal Husbandry and Fisheries:** Cultuurtuinlaan 10, POB 1807, Paramaribo; tel. 474177; telex 118; fax 470301.
**Ministry of Defence:** Kwattaweg 29, Paramaribo; tel. 474244; fax 420055.
**Ministry of Trade and Industry:** Nieuwe Haven, Paramaribo; tel. 479886; fax 477602.
**Ministry of Education and Community Development:** Dr Samuel Kafilludistraat 117-123, Paramaribo; tel. 498850; fax 495083.
**Ministry of Finance:** Onafhankelijkheidsplein 3, Paramaribo; tel. 472619; fax 476314.
**Ministry of Foreign Affairs:** Gravenstraat 8, Paramaribo; tel. 471209; telex 132; fax 410851.
**Ministry of Internal Affairs:** Onafhankelijkheidsplein 2, Paramaribo; tel. 476461; fax 421170.
**Ministry of Justice and the Police:** Gravenstraat 1, Paramaribo; tel. 473033; fax 412109.
**Ministry of Labour:** Wagenwegstraat 22, POB 911, Paramaribo; tel. 477045; fax 410465.
**Ministry of Natural Resources and Energy:** Dr J. C. de Mirandastraat 13-15, Paramaribo; tel. 473420; fax 472911.
**Ministry of Planning and International Co-operation:** Dr S. Redmondstraat 118, Paramaribo; tel. 473628; fax 421056.
**Ministry of Public Health:** Gravenstraat 64 boven, POB 201, Paramaribo; tel. 474841; fax 410702.
**Ministry of Public Works:** Verlengde Coppenamestraat 167, Paramaribo; tel. 462500; fax 464901.
**Ministry of Regional Affairs:** Van Rooseveltkade 2, Paramaribo; tel. 471574.
**Ministry of Social Affairs and Housing:** Waterkant 30-32, Paramaribo; tel. 472610; fax 470516.
**Ministry of Transport, Communications and Tourism:** Prins Hendrikstraat 26-28, Paramaribo; tel. 420422; fax 420425.

## President and Legislature

### PRESIDENT

**Election, 7 September 1991\***

| Candidate | Number of votes | % of votes |
|---|---:|---:|
| RUNALDO R. VENETIAAN (NF) | 645 | 78.9 |
| JULES WIJDENBOSCH (NDP) | 120 | 14.7 |
| HANS PRADE (DA '91) | 52 | 6.4 |
| **Total** | **817** | **100.0** |

\* Figures refer to the election by the Vereinigde Volksvergadering (United People's Assembly). Under the provisions of the Constitution, this body, comprising the members of the National Assembly and representatives of the municipal and district councils, is convened by the Chairman of the National Assembly to elect a President when the National Assembly has failed to do so.

### NATIONAL ASSEMBLY

**Chairman:** JAGGERNATH LACHMON (VHP).

**Election, 25 May 1991**

| Party | Seats |
|---|---:|
| Nieuw Front\* | 30 |
| National Democratic Party | 12 |
| Democratisch Alternatief 1991† | 9 |
| **Total** | **51** |

\* Electoral alliance (see below) whose member parties obtained seats as follows: NPS 12, VHP 9, KTPI 7, SPA 2.
† Electoral alliance (see below) whose member parties obtained seats as follows: HPP 3, BEP 3, Pendawa Lima 2, AF 1.

## Political Organizations

**Democratic Party (DP):** Paramaribo; f. 1992; Chair. ERNIE BRUNINGS; Leader FRANK PLAYFAIR.

**Democratisch Alternatief 1991 (DA '91)** (Democratic Alternative 1991): POB 1774, Paramaribo; tel. 470276; f. 1991 as an electoral alliance comprising the AF, BEP and HPP; tel. 410350; fax 498363; social-democratic.

    **Alternatief Forum (AF)** (Alternative Forum): Paramaribo.

    **Bosneger Eenheids Partij (BEP)** (Bush Negro Unity Party): Paramaribo.

    **Hernieuwde Progressieve Partij (HPP)** (Renewed Progressive Party): Paramaribo.

**National Democratic Party (NDP):** Paramaribo; f. 1987 by Standvaste (the 25 February Movement); army-supported; Chair. Lt-Col DÉSIRÉ (DESI) BOUTERSE.

**Nieuw Front (NF)** (New Front): Paramaribo; f. 1987 as Front voor Demokratie en Ontwikkeling (FDO) (Front for Democracy and Development), an electoral alliance comprising the KTPI, the NPS and the VHP.

    **Kerukanan Tulodo Pranatan Ingil (KTPI)** (Party for National Unity and Solidarity): Weidestraat, Paramaribo; f. 1947 as the Kaum-Tani Persuatan Indonesia; largely Indonesian; Leader WILLY SOEMITA.

    **Nationale Partij Suriname (NPS)** (Suriname National Party): Wanicastraat 77, Paramaribo; f. 1946; predominantly Creole; Sec. OTMAR ROEL RODGERS.

    **Surinaamse Partij van de Arvid (SPA)** (Suriname Labour Party): Paramaribo; f. 1987; affiliated with C-47 trade union; social democratic party; joined FDO in early 1991; Leader FRED DERBY.

    **Vooruitstrevende Hervormings Partij (VHP)** (Progressive Reform Party): Lim A Postraat, Paramaribo; f. 1949; leading left-wing party; predominantly Indian; Leader JAGGERNATH LACHMON.

**Partij Nationalistische Republiek (PNR):** f. 1963; resumed political activities 1987.

**Pendawa Lima:** Paramaribo; f. 1975; predominantly Indonesian.

# SURINAME

**Progressieve Arbeiders en Landbouwers Unie (PALU)** (Progressive Workers' and Farm Labourers' Union): Paramaribo; socialist party; Chair. Ir IWAN KROLIS.

**Progressieve Bosneger Partij (PBP):** f. 1968; resumed political activities 1987; represents members of the Bush Negro ethnic group; associated with the Pendawa Lima (see above).

**Progressieve Nationale Partij (PNP):** Paramaribo; resumed political activities 1987.

**Progressieve Surinaamse Volkspartij (PSV):** Paramaribo; f. 1946; resumed political activities 1987; Christian democratic party.

Insurgent groups are as follows:

**Angula:** f. 1990; composed mainly of Saramaccaner Bush Negro clan; Leader CARLOS MAASSI.

**Mandela Bush Negro Liberation Movement (BBM):** Upper Saramacca region; f. 1989 by mems of the Mataurïer Bush Negro clan; Leader 'BIKO' (LEENDERT ADAMS).

**Suriname Liberation Front:** Leader CORNELIS MAISI.

**Surinamese Liberation Army (SLA—Jungle Commando):** Langetabbetje (Suriname), via St Laurent du Maroni, French Guiana; f. 1986; Bush Negro guerrilla group; Leader RONNIE BRUNSWIJK.

**Tucayana Amazonica:** Bigi Poika; f. 1989 by Amerindian insurgents objecting to Kourou Accord between Govt and Bush Negroes of the SLA; Leader THOMAS SABAJO ('Commander THOMAS'); Chair. of Tucayana Advisory Group (Commission of Eight) ALEX JUBITANA.

**Union for Liberation and Democracy (UBD):** Moengo; f. 1989 by radical elements of SLA; Bush Negro; Leader KOFI AJONGPONG.

## Diplomatic Representation

### EMBASSIES IN SURINAME

**Belgium:** Kwasistraat 10, Paramaribo; tel. 499994; Chargé d'affaires: Dr W. DE SMET.

**Brazil:** Maratakkastraat 2, Paramaribo; tel. 400200; telex 185; fax 400205; Ambassador: SERGIO DA VEIGA WATSON.

**China, People's Republic:** Dr Axwijkstraat 45, POB 3042, Paramaribo; tel. 451540; telex 197; Ambassador: TANG BAISHENG.

**France:** Gravenstraat 5–7 boven, POB 2648, Paramaribo; tel. 476455; telex 181; Ambassador: JACQUES NIZART.

**Guyana:** Gravenstraat 82, Paramaribo; tel. 472509; telex 236; Chargé d'affaires a.i.: DONALD ABRAMS.

**India:** Rode Kruislaan 10, Paramaribo; tel. 498018; Ambassador: INDERVIR CHOPRA.

**Indonesia:** Van Brussellaan 3, POB 157, Paramaribo; tel. 497070; telex 120; Ambassador: SOEKADARI HONGGOWONGSO.

**Japan:** Gravenstraat 23–25, POB 2921, Paramaribo; tel. 474860; telex 370; fax 412208; Ambassador: TATSUO ISHIZAKI.

**Libya** (People's Bureau): Dario Saveedralaan 4, Paramaribo; tel. 490717; Chargé d'affaires: A. TAHER AFTEES.

**Netherlands:** Dr J. C. de Mirandastraat 10 boven, Paramaribo; tel. 477211; telex 125; fax 477792; Ambassador: PETER KOCH.

**Russia:** Anton Dragtenweg 7, POB 8127, Paramaribo; tel. 472387; telex 354; Chargé d'affaires a.i.: V. SHCHERBAKOV.

**USA:** Dr Sophie Redmondstraat 129, POB 1821, Paramaribo; tel. 472900; telex 373; fax 410025; Ambassador: JOHN LEONARD.

**Venezuela:** Gravenstraat 23–25, POB 3001, Paramaribo; tel. 475401; telex 146; fax 475602; Chargé d'affaires: HÉCTOR C. AZÓCAR.

## Judicial System

The administration of justice is entrusted to a Court of Justice, the six members of which are nominated for life, and three Cantonal Courts.

**President of the Court of Justice:** R. E. TH. OOSTERLING.
**Attorney-General:** C. G. DE RANDAMIE.

## Religion

Many religions are represented in Suriname. Christianity, Hinduism and Islam predominate.

### CHRISTIANITY

**Committee of Christian Churches:** Paramaribo; Chair. Rev. JOHN KENT (Praeses of the Moravian Church).

#### The Roman Catholic Church

For ecclesiastical purposes, Suriname comprises the single diocese of Paramaribo, suffragan to the archdiocese of Port of Spain (Trinidad and Tobago). The Bishop participates in the Antilles Episcopal Conference (currently based in Port of Spain, Trinidad and Tobago). At 31 December 1993 there were an estimated 92,000 adherents in the diocese, representing 22.7% of the population.

**Bishop of Paramaribo:** Rt Rev. ALOYSIUS FERDINANDUS ZICHEM, Bisschopshuis, Gravenstraat 12, POB 1230, Paramaribo; tel. 473306; fax 471602.

#### The Anglican Communion

Within the Church in the Province of the West Indies, Suriname forms part of the diocese of Guyana. The Episcopal Church is also represented.

**Anglican Church:** St Bridget's, Hoogestraat 44, Paramaribo.

#### Protestant Churches

**Evangelisch-Lutherse Kerk in Suriname:** Waterkant 102, POB 585, Paramaribo; Pres. ILSE LABADIE; 4,300 mems.

**Moravian Church in Suriname:** Maagdenstraat 50, POB 1811, Paramaribo; tel. 473073; f. 1735; Praeses JOHN KENT; Gen. Sec. B. J. PARABIRSING; 57,400 mems (1985).

Also represented are the Christian Reformed Church, the Dutch Reformed Church, the Evangelical Methodist Church, Pentecostal Missions, the Seventh-day Adventists and the Wesleyan Methodist Congregation.

### HINDUISM

**Sanatan Dharm:** Koningstraat 31–33, POB 760, Paramaribo; tel. 477790; f. 1930; Pres. Dr R. M. NANNAN-PANDAY; Sec. R. KAMTASING; over 150,000 mems.

### ISLAM

**Surinaamse Moeslim Associatie:** Kankantriestraat 55–57, Paramaribo; Chair. A. ABDOELBASHIRE.

**Surinaamse Islamitische Organisatie (SIO):** Watermolenstraat 10, POB 278, Paramaribo; tel. 475220; f. 1978; Pres. Dr I. JAMALUDIN; Sec. C. HASRAT; 6 brs.

**Stichting Islamitische Gemeenten Suriname:** Verlengde Mahonielaan 39, Paramaribo; Chair. Dr T. SOWIRONO.

**Federatie Islamitische Gemeenten in Suriname:** Paramaribo; Chair. K. KAAIMAN.

### JUDAISM

The Dutch Jewish Congregation and the Dutch Portuguese-Jewish Congregation are represented in Suriname.

**Jewish Community:** The Synagogue, Heerenstraat, Paramaribo; f. 1854.

### OTHER RELIGIONS

**Arya Dewaker:** Dr S. Kafilludistraat 1, Paramaribo; tel. 400706; members preach the Vedic Dharma; disciples of Maha Rishi Swami Dayanand Sarswati, the founder of the Arya Samaj in India; f. 1929; Chair. Dr R. BANSRADJ; Sec.-Gen. S. HANOEMAN.

The Bahá'í faith is also represented.

## The Press

### DAILIES

**De Ware Tijd:** Malebatrumstraat 11, POB 1200, Paramaribo; tel. 472823; f. 1957; morning; Dutch; independent/liberal; Editor L. E. MORPURGO.

**De West:** Dr J. C. de Mirandastraat 2–6, POB 176, Paramaribo; tel. 473338; fax 470322; f. 1909; midday; Dutch; liberal; Editors G. D. C. FINDLAY, G. R. H. FERRIER; circ. 15,000–18,000.

### PERIODICALS

**Adverten tieblad van de Republiek Suriname:** Gravenstraat 120, POB 56, Paramaribo; tel. 473501; fax 454782; f. 1871; 2 a week; Dutch; government and official information bulletin; Editor E. D. FINDLAY; circ. 1,000.

**CLO Bulletin:** Gemenelandsweg 95, Paramaribo; f. 1973; irregular; Dutch; labour information published by civil servants' union.

**Kerkbode:** Paramaribo; weekly; religious.

**Omhoog:** Gravenstraat 21, POB 1802, Paramaribo; tel. 472521; fax 473904; weekly; Dutch; Catholic bulletin; Editor S. MULDER.

**Protestantenblad:** POB 2542, Paramaribo; tel. 472344; f. 1895; monthly; religious.

### NEWS AGENCIES

**Surinaams Nieuws Agentschap (SNA)** (Suriname News Agency): Gravenstraat 39C, Paramaribo; telex 258; two daily bulletins in Dutch, one in English; Dir E. G. J. DE MEES.

SURINAME                                                                                                          *Directory*

**Foreign Bureau**

**Inter Press Service (IPS)** (Italy): Malebatrumstraat 1–5, POB 5065, Paramaribo; tel. 471818; telex 62200; Correspondent Eric Karwofodi.

## Publishers

**Anton de Kom Universiteit van Suriname:** Universiteitscomplex, Leysweg 1, POB 9212, Paramaribo; tel. 465558; fax 462291.

**Educatieve Uitgeverij Sorava NV:** Latourweg 10, POB 8382, Paramaribo; tel. and fax 480808.

**Publishing Services Suriname:** Van Idsingastraat 133, Paramaribo; tel. 472746; fmrly I. Krishnadath.

**Ministerie van Onderwijs en Volksontwikkeling** (Ministry of Education and Community Development): Dr Samuel Kafilludistraat 117-123, Paramaribo; tel. 498850; fax 495083.

**Pkin Fowru Productions:** Jupiterstraat 30, Paramaribo; tel. 455792.

**Stichting Al Qalam:** Lawtonlaan 6, Paramaribo.

**Stichting Volksboekwinkel:** Keizerstraat 197, POB 3040, Paramaribo; tel. 472469.

**Stichting Volkslectuur:** Dr S. Redmondstraat 231, Paramaribo; tel. 497935.

**Stichting Wetenschappelijke Informatie:** Prins Hendrikstraat 38, Paramaribo; tel. 475232.

**VACO, NV:** Domineestraat 26, POB 1841, Paramaribo; tel. 472545; fax 410563; Dir Eduard Hogenboom.

### PUBLISHERS' ASSOCIATION

**Publishers' Association Suriname:** Domineestraat 32, POB 1841, Paramaribo; tel. 472545; fax 410563.

## Radio and Television

In 1993 there were an estimated 290,256 radio receivers and 59,598 television receivers in use.

**Telecommunication Corporation Suriname (Telesur):** Heiligenweg 1, POB 1839, Paramaribo; tel. 473944; telex 131; fax 477800; supervisory body; Dir Ir L. C. Johanns (acting).

### RADIO

**Ampi's Broadcasting Corporation (ABC):** Maystraat 57, Paramaribo; tel. 465092; f. 1975; re-opened in 1993; commercial; Dutch and some local languages; Dir J. Kamperveen.

**Kara's Broadcasting Co (KBC):** Verlengde Keizerstraat 5–7, POB 3025, Paramaribo; tel. 475032; fax 474946; f. 1985; commercial; Dutch and some local languages; Dir Orlando Karamat Ali.

**Radio Apintie:** Verlengde Gemenelandsweg 37, POB 595, Paramaribo; tel. 400500; fax 400684; f. 1958; commercial; Dutch and some local languages; Gen. Man. Ch. Vervuurt.

**Radio Boskopou:** Roseveltkade 1, Paramaribo; tel. 410300; govt-owned; Sranang Tongo and Dutch; Head Mr van Varseveld.

**Radio Nickerie (RANI):** Waterloostraat 3, Nieuw Nickerie; tel. 231462; commercial; Hindi and Dutch; Dir. Djoties Lalta.

**Radio Paramaribo:** Verlengde Coppenamestraat 34, POB 975, Paramaribo; tel. 499995; fax 493121; f. 1957; commercial; Dutch and some local languages; Dir R. Pierkhan.

**Radio Radhika:** Indira Gandhiweg 165, Paramaribo; tel. 482910; re-opened in 1989; Dutch, Hindi; Dir Roshni Radhakisun.

**Radio Sangeet Mala:** Indira Gandhiweg 40, Paramaribo; tel. 482390; Dutch, Hindi; Dir Radjen Soekhradj.

**Stichting Radio Omroep Suriname (SRS):** Jacques van Eerstraat 20, POB 271, Paramaribo; tel. 498115; fax 498116; f. 1965; commercial; govt-owned; Dutch and some local languages; Dir L. Darthuizen.

### TELEVISION

**Algemene Televisie Verzorging (ATV):** Adrianusstraat 1, POB 2995, Paramaribo; tel. 470425; telex 488; fax 479260; f. 1985; govt-owned; commercial; Dutch, English, Portuguese, Spanish and some local languages; Man. Roy M. Doorson.

**Surinaamse Televisie Stichting (STVS):** Cultuurtuinlaan 34, POB 535, Paramaribo; tel. 473100; telex 271; fax 477216; f. 1965; govt-owned; commercial; local languages; Dutch and English; Dir Frits J. Pengel.

## Finance

(cap. = capital; res = reserves; dep. = deposits; m. = million; amounts in Suriname guilders unless otherwise stated)

### BANKING

#### Central Bank

**Centrale Bank van Suriname:** 16–24 Waterkant, POB 1801, Paramaribo; tel. 473741; telex 152; fax 476444; f. 1957; cap. and res 34.5m. (Dec. 1987); Chair. H. H. Pinas; Man. Dir O. H. Ezechiëls.

#### Commercial Banks

**Algemene Bank Nederland NV:** Kerkplein 1, POB 1836, Paramaribo; tel. 471555; telex 122; fax 411325; f. 1970; Man. Dirs F. P. Vos, L. J. M. van de Lande; br. at Nieuw Nickerie; 8 brs.

**Handels-Krediet-en Industriebank (Hakrinbank NV):** Dr Sophie Redmondstraat 11–13, POB 1813, Paramaribo; tel. 477722; telex 136; fax 472066; f. 1936; cap. 18.9m., res 197.5m., dep. 1,309.6m. (Dec. 1994); Pres. Drs J. J. F. Tjang-A-Sjin; Man. Dir Drs T. L. M. van Philips; 8 brs.

**Landbouwbank NV:** Lim A Postraat 32, POB 929, Paramaribo; tel. 475945; telex 240; fax 411965; f. 1972; agricultural bank; cap. 5m., res 4.6m., dep. 76.0m. (Dec. 1987); Chair. R. Schillevoort; Dir J. G. Bundel.

**De Surinaamsche Bank NV:** Gravenstraat 26–30, POB 1806, Paramaribo; tel. 471100; telex 134; fax 477835; f. 1865; cap. 16.3m., res 81.9m., dep. 3,387.5m. (Dec. 1993); Chair. A. R. Frijmersum; Man. Dir Drs E. J. Müller; 11 brs.

**Surinaamse Hypotheekbank NV:** Lim A Postraat 9, Paramaribo; f. 1951; cap. and res 0.3m. (Dec. 1986); Dir M. A. A. Oemar.

**Surinaamse Postspaarbank:** Knuffelsgracht 10–14, POB 1879, Paramaribo; tel. 472904; telex 280; fax 411965; f. 1904; savings and commercial bank; cap. and res 50.3m., dep. 269.7m. (Dec. 1992); Man. Rudi R. Lo Fo Wong (acting); 2 brs.

**Surinaamse Volkscredietbank:** Waterkant 104, POB 1804, Paramaribo; tel. 472616; telex 425; fax 473257; f. 1949; cap. and res 5.4m. (Dec. 1983); Man. Dir Lino J. Stomp; 3 brs.

#### Development Bank

**Nationale Ontwikkelingsbank van Suriname NV:** Coppenamestraat 160–162, POB 677, Paramaribo; tel. 465000; telex 359; fax 497192; f. 1963; govt-supported development bank; cap. and res 34m. (Dec. 1992); Man. Dir J. Tsai Meu Chong.

### INSURANCE

**AEGON Levensverzekering NV:** Lim A Postraat 28–30, POB 410, Paramaribo; tel. 472879; f. 1973; Dir. A. R. Frijmersum.

**American Life Insurance Company (ALICO):** Van het Hogerhuysstraat 55, POB 3026, Paramaribo; tel. 472525; fax 477219; Gen. Man. J. A. Harten.

**Assuria NV:** Grote Combéweg 37, POB 1501, Paramaribo; tel. 477955; fax 472390; f. 1961; life and indemnity insurance; Man. Dir Dr S. Smit.

**Assuria Schadeverzekering NV:** Gravenstraat 5–7, POB 1030, Paramaribo; tel. 473400; telex 243; fax 476669; Dir. M. R. Cabenda.

**British American Insurance Company:** Klipstenenstraat 29, POB 370, Paramaribo; tel. 476523; Man. H. W. Soesman.

**The Manufacturers' Life Insurance Company:** c/o Assuria NV, Grote Combeweg 37, Paramaribo; tel. 473400; telex 184; fax 472390; Man. S. Smit.

**Nationale Nederlanden Levensverzekering Maatschappij NV:** Noorderkerkstraat 5–7, POB 1845, Paramaribo; tel. 471541; telex 284; f. 1955; subsidiary: Fatum Schadeverzekering NV; Man. Dir S. I. Sjiem Fat.

**Self Reliance:** Herenstraat 22, Paramaribo; tel. 472582; life insurance; Dir N. J. Veira.

**Suram NV (Suriname American International Insurance Company):** Lim A Postraat 7, Paramaribo; tel. 473908; Man. P. J. Kappel.

## Trade and Industry

### CHAMBERS OF COMMERCE

**Kamer van Koophandel en Fabrieken** (Chamber of Commerce and Industry): Dr J. C. de Mirandastraat 10, POB 149, Paramaribo; tel. 474779; fax 474779; f. 1910; Chair. R. J. M. Smits; Sec. E. Graanoogst; 13,002 mems.

**Surinaams–Nederlandse Kamer voor Handel en Industrie** (Suriname–Netherlands Chamber of Commerce and Industry):

# SURINAME

Hotel Krasnapolsky, Domineestraat 39, POB 1861, Paramaribo; tel. 471133, ext. 438; fax 422829.

## DEVELOPMENT ORGANIZATIONS

**Centre for Industrial Development and Export Promotion:** Rust en Vredestraat 79–81, POB 1275, Paramaribo; tel. 474830; telex 285; fax 476311; f. 1981; Man. R. A. LETER.

**Stichting Planbureau Suriname** (National Planning Bureau of Suriname): Dr Sophie Redmondstraat 118, POB 172, Paramaribo; tel. 476241; telex 170; fax 475001; responsible for financial administration of development programmes and projects; long- and short-term planning; Gen. Sec. A. J. S. HOK A HIN.

## EMPLOYERS' ASSOCIATION

**Vereniging Surinaams Bedrijfsleven (VSB)** (Suriname Trade and Industry Association): Prins Hendrikstraat 18, POB 111, Paramaribo; tel. 475286; fax 472287; f. 1950; Chair. M. A. MEYER; Exec. Sec. G. R. BIJNOE; 290 mems.

## MANUFACTURERS' ASSOCIATION

**Associatie van Surinaamse Fabrikanten (ASFA)** (Suriname Manufacturers' Asscn): Domineestraat 33 boven, POB 3046, Paramaribo; tel. 476585; fax 421160; Chair. C. GLANS; Sec. M. R. EMANUELS; 317 mems.

## TRADE UNIONS

**Council of the Surinamese Federation of Trade Unions (RVS):** f. 1987; comprises:

**Algemeen Verbond van Vakverenigingen in Suriname 'De Moederbond' (AVVS)** (General Confederation of Trade Unions): Verlengde Coppenamestraat 134, POB 230, Paramaribo; rightwing; Pres. I. GREP; 15,000 mems.

**Centrale 47 (C-47):** Wanicastraat 230, Paramaribo; includes bauxite workers; Chair. FRED DERBY; 7,654 mems.

**Centrale Landsdienaren Organisatie (CLO)** (Central Organization for Civil Service Employees): Gemenelandsweg 93, Paramaribo; Pres. HENDRIK SYLVESTER; 13,000 mems.

**Progressieve Werknemers Organisatie (PWO)** (Progressive Workers' Organization): Limesgracht 80, Paramaribo; f. 1948; covers the commercial, hotel and banking sectors; Chair. RAMON W. CRUDEN; Sec. M. E. MENT; 4,000 mems.

# Transport

## RAILWAYS

There are no public railways operating in Suriname.

**Paramaribo Government Railway:** Onverwacht, Paramaribo; single-track narrow-gauge railway from Onverwacht, via Zanderij, to Brownsweg (87 km—54 miles); not operational; Dir M. NAHAR.

**Suriname Bauxite Railway:** POB 1893, Paramaribo; 70 km (44 miles), standard gauge, from the Backhuis Mountains to Apoera on the Corantijn river; owing to the abandonment of plans to mine bauxite in the Backhuis mountains, the railway transports timber and crushed stone; Pres. EMRO HOLDER.

## ROADS

In 1990 Suriname had 9,153 km (5,688 miles) of roads, of which 1,570 km (976 miles) were main roads. The principal east–west road, 390 km (242 miles) in length, links Albina, on the eastern border, with Nieuw Nickerie, in the west. An east–west road, further to the south, was completed in 1978.

## SHIPPING

Suriname is served by many shipping companies and has about 1,500 km (930 miles) of navigable rivers and canals. A number of shipping companies conduct regular international services (principally for freight) to and from Paramaribo including EWL, Fyffesgroup, the Alcoa Steamship Co, Baank Shipping, Continental Shipping, Bromet Shipping and Ten Shipping (in addition to those listed below). There are also two ferry services linking Suriname with Guyana, across the Corentijn River, and with French Guiana, across the Marowijne River.

**Dienst voor de Scheepvaart:** Cornelis Jongbawstraat 2, POB 888, Paramaribo; tel. 474575; telex 163; fax 472940; government authority supervising and controlling shipping in Surinamese waters; Dir of Maritime Affairs E. FITZ JIM.

**Scheepvaart Maatschappij Suriname NV (SMS)** (Suriname Shipping Line Ltd): Waterkant 44, POB 1824, Paramaribo; tel. 472447; telex 164; fax 474814; f. 1936; services to the Netherlands, Belgium, Germany, Brazil, Colombia, Guyana, Mexico, Venezuela, US Gulf and Caribbean ports; regular cargo and passenger services in the interior; Man. Dir. R. E. HASSELBAINK.

**NV VSH Scheepvaartmij United Suriname Shipping Company:** Van het Hogerhuysstraat 9–11, POB 1860, Paramaribo; tel. 472558; telex 144; fax 475515; shipping agents and freight carriers; Man. PATRICK HEALY.

**Staatsolie Maatschappij Suriname NV:** Industrieterrein 21, POB 4069, Paramaribo; tel. 499649; telex 217; fax 491105; Man. Dir Dr S. E. JHARAP.

**Suriname Coast Traders NV:** Flocislaan 4, Industrieterrein Flora, POB 9216, Paramaribo; tel. 463020; telex 298; fax 463831.

## CIVIL AVIATION

The main airport is Johan Adolf Pengel International Airport (formerly Zanderij International Airport), 45 km from Paramaribo. Domestic flights operate from Zorg-en-Hoop Airport, located in a suburb of Paramaribo. There are 35 airstrips throughout the country.

**Surinaamse Luchtvaart Maatschappij NV (SLM)** (Suriname Airways): Coppenamelaan 136, POB 2029, Paramaribo; tel. 465700; telex 292; fax 491213; f. 1962; services to Amsterdam (the Netherlands) and to destinations in North America, South America and the Caribbean; Pres. R. CALOR.

**Gonini Air Service Ltd:** Doekhiweg 1, Zorg-en-Hoop Airport, POB 1614, Paramaribo; tel. 499098; fax 498363; f. 1976; privately-owned; licensed for scheduled and unscheduled national and international services (charters, lease, etc.); Man. Dir GERARD BRUNINGS.

**Gum Air NV:** Rijweg naar Kwatta 254, Paramaribo; tel. 497670; privately-owned; unscheduled domestic flights; Man. Mr GUMMELS.

# Tourism

Efforts were being made to promote the previously undeveloped tourism sector in the 1990s. Attractions include the varied cultural activities, a number of historical sites and an unspoiled interior with many varieties of plants, birds and animals. There are 13 nature reserves and one nature park. In 1992 tourist arrivals were estimated to total 30,000.

**Suriname Tourism Department:** Cornelis Jongbawstraat 2, Paramaribo; tel. 410357; f. 1981; Co-ordinator ARMAND LI-A-YOUNG (acting).

# SWAZILAND

## Introductory Survey

**Location, Climate, Language, Religion, Flag, Capital**

The Kingdom of Swaziland is a land-locked country in southern Africa, bordered by South Africa to the north, west, south and south-east, and by Mozambique to the east. The average annual temperature is about 16°C (61°F) on the Highveld, and about 22°C (72°F) in the sub-humid Lowveld, while annual rainfall ranges from 1,000 mm (40 ins) to 2,280 mm (90 ins) on the Highveld, and from 500 mm (20 ins) to 890 mm (35 ins) in the Lowveld. English and siSwati are the official languages. About 60% of the population profess Christianity, while most of the remainder adhere to traditional beliefs. The national flag (proportions 3 by 2) is blue, with a yellow-edged horizontal crimson stripe (one-half of the depth) in the centre. On this stripe is a black and white Swazi shield, superimposed on two spears and a staff, all lying horizontally. The capital is Mbabane.

**Recent History**

Swaziland, which was previously under the joint rule of the United Kingdom and the South African (Transvaal) Republic, became a British protectorate in 1903, and one of the High Commission Territories in 1907, the others being the colony of Basutoland (now the Kingdom of Lesotho) and the protectorate of Bechuanaland (now the Republic of Botswana). The British Act of Parliament that established the Union of South Africa in 1910 also provided for the inclusion in South Africa of the three High Commission Territories, subject to consultation with the local inhabitants.

Swaziland's first Constitution, which was introduced by the British Government, entered into force in January 1964. The Paramount Chief (Ngwenyama—the Lion), King Sobhuza II, subsequently established a traditionalist political party, the Imbokodvo National Movement (INM). In elections, which took place in June of that year, the INM secured all of the seats in the new Legislative Council. In 1965, in response to continued pressure from the INM, the British Government agreed to a revision of the Constitution, and established a committee to draft proposed constitutional amendments. A new Constitution, which was promulgated in 1966 and came into effect in April 1967, provided for the introduction of internal self-government, pending the attainment of full independence by the end of 1969. Executive power was vested in King Sobhuza as the hereditary monarch and constitutional Head of State. The Legislative Council was dissolved in March 1967; in elections to the new bicameral Parliament, which took place in April, the INM secured all 24 elective seats in the House of Assembly. (However, the Ngwane National Liberatory Congress—NNLC—received 20% of the votes cast.) In May King Sobhuza announced the formation of Swaziland's first Cabinet, and appointed the leader of the INM, Prince Makhosini Dlamini, as Prime Minister. On 6 September 1968 Swaziland was granted full independence within the Commonwealth, and a new Constitution (which was based on the existing Constitution) was adopted.

In legislative elections, which took place in May 1972, the INM secured 21 seats in the House of Assembly, while the NNLC won the remaining three elective seats. A constitutional crisis was subsequently precipitated, after the INM attempted to deport one of the NNLC Assembly members, on the grounds that he was not a Swazi citizen. The deportation order was overruled by the High Court, whereupon the Immigration Act was amended to remove the High Court's jurisdiction over it. This measure was, in turn, declared by the High Court to be unconstitutional. In April 1973, in accordance with a parliamentary resolution, King Sobhuza repealed the Constitution, imposed a state of emergency under which all political activity was suspended, introduced legislation providing for detention without trial for a period of 60 days, and announced the formation of a national army. A new Constitution, which was promulgated on 13 October 1978, confirmed the King's control of executive and legislative decisions, and provided for a bicameral parliament (Libandla), comprising a House of Assembly and a Senate. The functions of the Libandla were confined to debating government proposals and advising the King. The existing 40 traditional local councils, known as Tinkhundla (singular: Inkhundla), were each to nominate two members to an 80-member electoral college, which was, in turn, to elect 40 deputies to the House of Assembly. Members of the House of Assembly were to select 10 members of the Senate, while the King was to nominate a further 10 members to each chamber. The King was to appoint the Cabinet, which was to be headed by the Prime Minister. Under the terms of the new Constitution, all political parties (including the INM) were prohibited. Legislative elections took place later that year, and the Libandla was inaugurated in January 1979. The Prime Minister, Maj.-Gen. Maphevu Dlamini (who had replaced Prince Makhosini in March 1976), died in October 1979, and was succeeded by Prince Mabandla N. F. Dlamini. In June 1982 the Swaziland National Council, an advisory body on matters of Swazi tradition, comprising members of the royal family, was redesignated as the Supreme Council of State (Liqoqo).

King Sobhuza died in August 1982. In accordance with Swazi tradition, the powers of Head of State devolved upon the Queen Mother (Indlovukazi—Great She Elephant) Dzeliwe, who was authorized to act as Regent until King Sobhuza's designated successor, Prince Makhosetive (born in April 1968), attained the age of 21. Shortly afterwards, Queen Regent Dzeliwe appointed the Liqoqo, which was to advise her in all affairs of State. Competition to secure supreme executive power subsequently emerged between Prince Mabandla and several prominent members of the Liqoqo, who were led by Prince Mfanasibili Dlamini. In March 1983 Prince Mabandla was replaced as Prime Minister by a traditionalist, Prince Bhekimpi Dlamini. In August, under the powers of the 'Authorized Person' (an important hereditary post, held by Prince Sozisa Dlamini, the Chairman of the Liqoqo), Queen Regent Dzeliwe was deposed, apparently as a result of her reluctance to dismiss Prince Mabandla. Following an attempt by Queen Regent Dzeliwe to appeal against her deposition, Prince Mfanasibili and his followers obtained an official declaration, which stated that the High Court had no jurisdiction in matters concerning Swazi custom and tradition. Widespread opposition to the deposition of Queen Regent Dzeliwe was suppressed, and in September Queen Ntombi, the mother of Prince Makhosetive, was officially invested as Regent. In November elections to the Libandla took place. In the same month a new Cabinet was appointed, in which only Prince Bhekimpi, and the Minister of Foreign Affairs, Richard Dlamini, were retained.

In June 1984 Richard Dlamini and the Minister of Finance, Dr Sishayi Nxumalo, were dismissed, as a result of pressure from Prince Mfanasibili and another leading member of the Liqoqo, Dr George Msibi. Their removal from office followed the conduction of an investigation by Dr Nxumalo into allegations that several prominent Swazi politicians, including Prince Mfanasibili, had been involved in the misappropriation of funds owed to the Southern African Customs Union. Following pressure from the South African Government, plans to continue the investigation of the alleged misappropriation of customs revenue were announced; in September, however, the Government issued a decree granting immunity to members of the Liqoqo on matters arising from their official activities. In the same month it was announced that Prince Sozisa, who had allegedly staged an attempted coup in June, had been dismissed as Chairman of the Liqoqo. In November Dr Nxumalo was arrested, and, together with four senior members of the army and security forces, was subsequently convicted on charges of conspiring to overthrow the Government.

In October 1985, following protests by prominent members of the royal family at the Liqoqo's monopoly of power, Queen Regent Ntombi dismissed Prince Mfanasibili and Dr Msibi. It was subsequently announced that the Liqoqo was to be reconstituted in its former capacity as an advisory body on matters pertaining to traditional law and custom. In December Dr Nxumalo and the other four prisoners were pardoned by Queen Regent Ntombi and released. In January 1986 it was announced that Prince Makhosetive was to be crowned in April, almost three years earlier than expected, in order to end the competition for power among vying royal factions. In February Prince Mfanasibili and his associate, Majiji Simelane, were arrested on charges of attempting to subvert justice.

Prince Makhosetive was crowned on 25 April 1986, and assumed the title of King Mswati III. In May King Mswati dissolved the Liqoqo, thereby consolidating his power. In the same month Prince Mfanasibili and Simelane were convicted on charges of fabricating evidence to ensure the continued detention of Dr Nxumalo and the four other prisoners, and received custodial sentences. In July King Mswati reorganized the Cabinet, and, in October, he appointed a former senior member of the security forces, Sotsha Dlamini, as Prime Minister, replacing Prince Bhekimpi. In May 1987 12 prominent officials, including Prince Bhekimpi and Prince Mfanasibili, were charged with sedition and treason, in connection with the removal from power of Queen Regent Dzeliwe in 1983. The Minister of Natural Resources, Land Utilization and Energy, Mhambi Mnisi, was dismissed in June; he and Dr Msibi subsequently fled to South Africa. In November King Mswati established a special tribunal to preside over all cases involving alleged offences against the King or the Queen Regent; defendants appearing before the tribunal were not to be granted the right to legal representation or appeal. In March 1988 10 of those accused of involvement in the deposition of Queen Regent Dzeliwe were convicted of treason by the special tribunal, and received custodial sentences, while the remaining two defendants were acquitted. In July, however, it was reported that all those convicted in March had been released. (Prince Mfanasibili was returned to prison to serve the remainder of the sentence that he had received in May 1986.)

In November 1987 elections to the Libandla took place, one year earlier than scheduled. Later that month King Mswati reappointed Sotsha Dlamini as Prime Minister, and formed a new Cabinet, in which only three members of the previous Government were retained. In 1988 widespread dissatisfaction with the electoral system, which was based on the Tinkhundla, emerged. In October a majority of members of the Libandla supported a motion in favour of a comprehensive review of the legislative structure. Sotsha Dlamini, however, rejected the motion, on the grounds that it would be contrary to Swazi tradition to challenge an established institution. In March 1989 it was reported that a conspiracy to release Prince Mfanasibili from prison and to overthrow the Government had been suppressed. Nine prominent Swazis were detained (of whom six were subsequently released). In April King Mswati announced his continuing support for the existing electoral system. In July he dismissed Sotsha Dlamini for alleged disobedience, replacing him with Obed Dlamini, a former leader of the Swaziland Federation of Trade Unions (SFTU). This appointment was widely regarded as a measure to appease increasing discontent within some sectors of the labour force; nevertheless, unrest continued throughout 1989. In August it was announced that Prince Mfanasibili had been charged with treason in connection with the alleged coup attempt in March. (He was later acquitted, but remained in detention.)

In early 1990 an opposition movement, known as the People's United Democratic Movement (PUDEMO), which had been established in 1983, distributed pamphlets that questioned the legitimacy of the monarchy in its existing form and demanded constitutional reform. Security forces subsequently arrested a number of suspected members of PUDEMO, who were variously charged with treason, sedition or conspiring to form a political party. In August, in response to increasing dissatisfaction, King Mswati announced that public forums were to be convened to discuss electoral reform. By the end of October all the defendants belonging to PUDEMO had been acquitted of the principal charges, although six were convicted of illegally attending a political gathering. In November a student boycott, in protest at the conviction of two students belonging to PUDEMO, was violently suppressed by the security forces; some 86 students were reported to have been injured. In the same month King Mswati replaced the reformist Minister of Justice, Reginald Dhladhla, with a former Deputy Prime Minister, Zonke Khumalo. It was widely believed that the dismissal of Dhladhla had been undertaken on the advice of the Swaziland National Council, a body that had been reconstituted from the former Liqoqo, resulting in public concern that it continued to exert undue influence on government policies. Later in November five members of PUDEMO (who had previously been acquitted of all charges) were arrested under legislation that permitted the detention of alleged suspects without trial. In March 1991 the prisoners, who had staged a series of hunger strikes, were released, as a result of international pressure, particularly from the Governments of the United Kingdom and the USA; Prince Mfanasibili was also released. In an attempt to advance its objectives through legal bodies, PUDEMO subsequently established a number of affiliated organizations, including the Human Rights Association of Swaziland (HUMARAS) and the Swaziland Youth Congress (SWAYOCO), which, however, failed to receive recognition from the Government. In early October the Court of Appeal annulled the sentences of two prisoners, who, in October 1990, had been convicted on charges of illegally attending a political gathering.

In September and October 1991 a committee, known as Vusela (Greetings), which had been established by King Mswati to review the electoral system, conducted a series of public forums throughout the country to elicit popular opinion on political reforms. Widespread demands for the abolition of the existing electoral system were reported, while substantial criticism of the composition of the Vusela committee also emerged. In subsequent months a number of peaceful demonstrations, staged by members of SWAYOCO in support of the establishment of a democratic system of government, were suppressed by security forces. In October King Mswati announced an extensive reorganization of the Cabinet, including the appointment of 10 new ministers and the creation of five new or reconstituted ministries. In February 1992 PUDEMO declared itself a legal opposition party, in contravention of the prohibition on political associations, rejected King Mswati's efforts to institute political reform, and demanded that a constitutional referendum be conducted. A further two opposition movements, the Swaziland United Front (SUF) and the Swaziland National Front (SWANAFRO), subsequently re-emerged. In February King Mswati appointed a second committee (Vusela 2), which was to draft a report on the conclusions of the first committee and to present recommendations for consideration by the King. A member of PUDEMO and a number of HUMARAS were represented in the Vusela 2 committee, but resigned later that year, on the grounds that the committee remained in favour of the existing electoral system.

In October 1992 King Mswati approved a number of proposals, which had been submitted by the Vusela 2 committee. Under new amendments to the electoral system, the House of Assembly (which was redesignated as the National Assembly) was to be expanded to 65 deputies (of whom 55 were to be directly elected by secret ballot from candidates nominated by the Tinkhundla, and 10 appointed by the King), and the Senate to 30 members (of whom 10 were to be selected by the National Assembly and 20 appointed by the King); in addition, the legislation providing for detention without trial was to be abrogated, and a new constitution, which incorporated the amendments, enshrined an hereditary monarchy and confirmed the fundamental rights of the individual and the independence of the judicial system, was to be drafted. However, opposition groups protested at the committee's failure to recommend the immediate restoration of a multi-party political system; the issue was to be postponed until the forthcoming elections in order to determine the extent of public support. PUDEMO announced its opposition to the electoral reforms, and demanded that the Government organize a national convention to determine the country's constitutional future. King Mswati subsequently dissolved the Libandla, one month prior to the expiry of its term of office, and announced that he was to rule by decree, with the assistance of the Cabinet (which was redesignated as the Council of Ministers), pending the adoption of the new Constitution and the holding of parliamentary elections. A third committee (Vusela 3) was established to instruct the population about the forthcoming amendments to the electoral system. Later in October King Mswati announced that elections to the National Assembly were to take place in the first half of 1993. At a series of public meetings, which were convened by the Vusela 3 committee from December 1992, doubts regarding the viability of the reformed electoral system were expressed; in early 1993, in response to public concern, it was announced that legislation preventing the heads of the Tinkhundla from exerting undue influence in the nomination of candidates had been introduced.

In December 1992 an informal alliance of organizations that advocated democratic reform (principally comprising HUMARAS, PUDEMO and SWAYOCO), known as the Confederation for Full Democracy in Swaziland, was established. In the same month PUDEMO rejected a proposal by SWAYOCO that a 'Vusela Resistance Movement' be established, to impede the implementation of economic reforms by disrupting essential services. In early 1993, in response to attempts by the opposition to organize a campaign against the elections, additional security measures were imposed in order to prevent political meetings from taking place. In March more than 50 opposition supporters, including leaders of PUDEMO and SWAYOCO, were arrested and charged in connection with the organization of illegal political gatherings. Although those arrested were subsequently released on bail, legal restrictions prevented them from participating in opposition activity, thereby effectively undermining efforts to co-ordinate a campaign in protest at the elections. Despite the opposition's failure to organize an official electoral boycott, however, the subsequent low level of voter registration appeared to reflect widespread objections to the reforms. Only a small proportion of the electorate had registered by the stipulated date in June (which was consequently extended to the end of that month).

The first round of elections to the expanded National Assembly, which was contested by 2,094 candidates nominated by the Tinkhundla, finally took place on 25 September 1993. At the end of September King Mswati repealed the legislation providing for detention without trial for a period of 60 days. The second round of parliamentary elections, which took place on 11 October, was contested by the three candidates in each Inkhundla who had obtained the highest number of votes in the first poll; the majority of members of the former Cabinet (which had been dissolved in late September), including Obed Dlamini, failed to secure seats in the National Assembly. (King Mswati subseqently appointed an acting Prime Minister, with responsibility for all ministerial portfolios, pending the formation of a new cabinet.) Shortly afterwards, Prince Mfanasibili questioned the loyalty to King Mswati of the elected parliamentary deputies, and claimed that certain elements planned to transfer executive power to the Prime Minister and redesignate the Head of State as a constitutional monarch. Later in October King Mswati nominated a further 10 deputies to the National Assembly, which elected 10 of its members to the Senate; King Mswati subsequently appointed the remaining 20 Senators, who included Obed Dlamini and Prince Bhekimpi. In early November the former Minister of Works and Construction, Prince Jameson Mbilini Dlamini, who was considered to be a traditionalist, was appointed Prime Minister, and a new Cabinet (which included Dr Nxumalo, in the office of Deputy Prime Minister) was formed.

In February 1994, following a report by the US Department of State concerning human rights in Swaziland, which stated that the parliamentary elections had been 'undemocratic', the Government claimed that the majority of the Swazi people were opposed to the establishment of a multi-party political system. It was announced, however, that King Mswati was to appoint a 15-member commission, comprising representatives of state organs and non-governmental organizations, to draft a new constitution, and a national policy council, which was to prepare a manifesto of the Swazi people. In March elections to the Tinkhundla, which were scheduled to take place later that month in accordance with the reforms, were postponed, owing to lack of preparation. (The heads of the Tinkhundla had previously been appointed by the King.)

In September 1994 the Confederation for Full Democracy in Swaziland claimed that the parliamentary elections in 1993 were effectively invalid, owing to the low level of voter participation, and warned that failure on the part of the Government to organize democratic elections would result in civil conflict. In October elections to the Tinkhundla took place; it was reported, however, that a high proportion of the electorate had abstained from voting. In January 1995 a number of incendiary attacks, which were widely attributed to pro-democracy activists, were staged against property of government officials, culminating in an incident in early February, in which the parliament building was severely damaged by fire. SWAYOCO (which had previously threatened violence if the Government failed to rescind the ban on political parties) denied initial reports that it was responsible for the attacks. In March the Cabinet was reorganized, after King Mswati dismissed two ministers who were allegedly in possession of vehicles that had been stolen from the former Bophuthatswana 'homeland' government. Later that month the SFTU initiated a two-day general strike (which was widely observed) in support of a number of demands, including the introduction of legislation providing for the reinstatement of employees who had been dismissed. The unions subsequently agreed to suspend further strike action, after the Government established a five-member independent committee to consider the SFTU's demands.

Swaziland pursued a policy of dialogue and co-operation with white-ruled South Africa, while attaching considerable importance to maintaining good relations with other black African states. In early 1982 Swaziland and South Africa began discussions concerning the possibility of transferring to Swaziland the South African-controlled KaNgwane 'homeland' and the district of Ngwavuma in the KwaZulu 'homeland', with a population of 750,000 Swazis. The plan was finally abandoned in August 1984, when South Africa granted KaNgwane 'self-government' status, despite Swaziland's objections.

In the late 1970s members of the African National Congress of South Africa (ANC), a nationalist organization then banned in South Africa, increasingly used Swaziland as a base from which to conduct guerrilla attacks over the border into South Africa. In February 1982 Swaziland and South Africa signed a secret non-aggression pact. As a result, several members of the ANC were arrested and expelled from Swaziland. Following the signing, in March 1984, of the Nkomati accord between South Africa and Mozambique (which banned both countries from harbouring dissidents), many ANC members fled from Mozambique to neighbouring Swaziland. Clashes between ANC guerrillas and the Swazi security forces escalated. By July 1984, more than 80 ANC members were reported to have been expelled, and in August Swaziland and Mozambique signed a security pact designed to prevent further hostilities. Tension between the Swaziland Government and the ANC intensified following the murder, in December 1984, of the deputy chief of the Swazi security police. Although the ANC denied any involvement in the killing, the Government initiated a campaign to arrest all ANC fugitives remaining in the country. In August 1986 leading Swazi politicians expressed opposition to the imposition of economic sanctions against South Africa, owing to Swaziland's economic dependence on that country. South African security forces abducted six alleged ANC supporters from Swaziland in December. The detention and deportation of ANC members by the Swazi Government continued between 1986 and 1988. Over the same period, several suspected ANC members were killed in Swaziland by gunmen who were widely assumed to be South African. Following the legalization of the ANC in 1990 (see chapter on South Africa), the Swazi Prime Minister, Obed Dlamini, pledged to conduct an inquiry (which, however, he failed to initiate) into previous government operations against ANC members.

In the 1980s social tension was caused by the presence in Swaziland of large numbers of refugees, who had fled from Mozambique in an attempt to escape the civil conflict in that country (see chapter on Mozambique). In June 1990 the Governments of Swaziland and Mozambique signed an extradition agreement providing for the repatriation of alleged criminals and illegal immigrants, which was designed to reduce the incidence of smuggling between the two countries. In 1992, however, tension at the border with Mozambique increased, following reports of raids against Swazi farms by members of the Mozambican armed forces. Following the ratification of a Mozambican peace accord in October 1992, an agreement, which was signed by the Governments of Swaziland and Mozambique and the UN High Commissioner for Refugees in August 1993, provided for the repatriation of some 24,000 Mozambican nationals resident in Swaziland; in October 500 Mozambican refugees returned from Swaziland under the programme. In December the number of Swazi troops deployed at the border with Mozambique was increased, following clashes between Swazi and Mozambican forces in the region. Mozambique subsequently protested at alleged border incursions by members of the Swazi armed forces. In early 1995 a joint security commission of Swazi and Mozambican officials met for discussions, following a further border incursion by Swazi forces, who had allegedly abducted two Mozambican citizens.

### Government

The Constitution of 13 October 1978 vests supreme executive and legislative power in the hereditary King, who is the Head of State, and provides for a bicameral legislature (Libandla), comprising a House of Assembly and a Senate. The functions of the Libandla are confined to debating government proposals and advising the King. Executive power is exercised through the Cabinet (later redesignated as the Council of Ministers), which is appointed by the King. The Swaziland National Council, which comprises members of the royal family and is headed by the King and the constitutional dual monarch, the Queen Mother, provides advice on matters regulated by traditional law and custom.

Following a number of amendments to the electoral system, which were approved by the King in October 1992, the House of Assembly (which was redesignated as the National Assembly) was expanded to 65 deputies (of whom 55 are directly elected from candidates nominated by traditional local councils, known as Tinkhundla, and 10 appointed by the King), and the Senate to 30 members (of whom 20 are appointed by the King and 10 elected by the National Assembly). Elections to the National Assembly are conducted by secret ballot, in two rounds of voting; the second round of the elections is contested by the three candidates from each of the Tinkhundla who secure the highest number of votes in the first poll. In early 1994 it was announced that the King was to appoint a 15-member commission, comprising representatives of state organs and non-governmental organizations, which was to draft a new constitution incorporating the amendments.

Swaziland is divided into 273 regional tribal areas, comprising 55 Tinkhundla, which are elected.

### Defence

The Umbutfo Swaziland Defence Force, created in 1973, totalled 2,657 regular troops in November 1983. Swaziland also has a paramilitary police force. Military service is compulsory and lasts for two years. Of total budgetary expenditure by the central Government in the financial year 1993/94, E 69.8m. (6.6%) was for defence.

### Economic Affairs

In 1993, according to estimates by the World Bank, Swaziland's gross national product (GNP), measured at average 1991–93 prices, was US $933m., equivalent to $1,050 per head. In 1985–93, it was estimated, GNP per head increased, in real terms, at an average annual rate of 3.8%, while the population increased by an annual average of 3.8% over the same period. During 1987–92, it was estimated, Swaziland's gross domestic product (GDP) increased, in real terms, by an annual average of 3.5%.

Agriculture (including forestry) contributed an estimated 11.8% of GDP in 1993. About 63.8% of the labour force were employed in the agricultural sector in that year. The principal cash crops are sugar cane (sugar accounted for 24.6% of export earnings in 1992), cotton, citrus fruits, pineapples and maize. Tobacco and rice are also cultivated. Livestock-rearing is traditionally important. Commercial forestry (which employs a significant proportion of the population) provides wood for the manufacture of pulp. During 1985–93, it was estimated, agricultural GDP declined by an annual average of 2.1%.

Industry (including mining, manufacturing and construction) contributed an estimated 40.4% of GDP in 1993. During 1985–93, it was estimated, industrial GDP increased by an annual average of 12.2%.

Mining contributed an estimated 1.8% of GDP in 1993. Swaziland has extensive reserves of coal, which is exported with diamonds and gold. Asbestos is also an important mineral export. In addition, Swaziland has reserves of tin, kaolin, talc, iron ore, pyrophyllite and silica. During 1987–92, it was estimated, mining GDP increased by an annual average of 3.8%.

Manufacturing contributed an estimated 34.1% of GDP in 1993, and is mainly based on the processing of agricultural, livestock and forestry products. In 1985 the principal branches of manufacturing (measured by value of output) were food products (53% of the total), paper, textiles, wood products, beverages and metal products. During 1985–93, it was estimated, manufacturing GDP increased by an annual average of 15.6%.

Swaziland imports most of its energy requirements from South Africa. However, the Swazi Government aims to increase domestic energy output by constructing a hydroelectric dam. Mineral fuels accounted for 10.2% of imports in 1993.

In 1993 Swaziland recorded a visible trade deficit of US $124.5m., while there was a deficit of $37.2m. on the current account of the balance of payments. In 1992/93 the principal source of imports was South Africa (93.9%); other suppliers were the United Kingdom, the Netherlands and Switzerland. In 1991 South Africa was the principal market for exports (taking 47.0% of the total); the United Kingdom was also a significant purchaser. The principal exports in 1992 were foodstuffs (particularly sugar, and canned and fresh fruits), wood and wood products, and mineral products. The principal imports in 1993 were machinery and transport equipment, food and live animals, miscellaneous manufactured articles, and mineral fuels and lubricants.

In the financial year ending 31 March 1994 there was an estimated budgetary deficit of E 119.9m. Swaziland's external debt totalled US $225.6m. at the end of 1993, of which $217.8m. was long-term public debt. In that year the cost of debt-servicing was equivalent to 3.8% of the value of exports of goods and services. In 1985–93 the average annual rate of inflation was 11.8%; consumer prices increased by 14.3% in 1994. It was estimated that 30% of the labour force were unemployed in 1994.

Swaziland is a member both of the Southern African Development Community (see p. 219), and of the Southern African Customs Union, which also includes Botswana, Lesotho, Namibia and South Africa. In November 1993 Swaziland was among the members of the Preferential Trade Area for Eastern and Southern African States (see p. 240) to sign a treaty providing for the establishment of a Common Market for Eastern and Southern Africa.

During the 1980s Swaziland's economic development was undermined by a decline in international prices for sugar and asbestos, in conjunction with the adverse effects of unfavourable weather conditions on the agricultural sector. In addition, the Swazi economy was vulnerable to fluctuations in the economy of neighbouring South Africa: although Swaziland may determine the exchange rate of its currency, the lilangeni, this has remained at par with the South African rand. From the mid-1980s, following successive years of balance-of-payments deficits and a high level of unemployment, the Government achieved significant economic growth through the implementation of measures that were designed to promote foreign investment in the agricultural, mining and manufacturing sectors and improve the country's infrastructure. A policy of restraining budgetary expenditure and of imposing financial controls on public enterprises was also adopted. In the early 1990s the agricultural sector was adversely affected by a prolonged drought in the region; however, significant growth in value-added production in the industrial sector was recorded. In March 1995 a substantial decline in the projected budgetary deficit for the 1995/96 financial year was expected to result from an increase in revenue from the Southern African Customs Union (which accounted for about 46% of total revenue in 1994). However, negotiations between the member states of the Union were likely to conclude in a new arrangement for the distribution of revenue, which would be less advantageous to the Swazi Government.

### Social Welfare

In 1986 Swaziland had 10 hospitals and an additional 14 health centres. In 1985 there were 36 physicians and 1,054 nurses working in the country. Of total budgetary expenditure by the central Government in the financial year 1993/94, E 85.4m. (8.0%) was for health, and a further E 6.23m. (0.6%) for social security and welfare.

### Education

Education is not compulsory in Swaziland. Primary education begins at six years of age and lasts for seven years. Secondary education begins at 13 years of age and lasts for up to five years, comprising a first cycle of three years and a second of two years. In 1992 91% of children in the relevant age group were enrolled at primary schools (boys 89%; girls 93%), while secondary enrolment was equivalent to 50% of children in the appropriate age group (boys 51%; girls 48%). Swaziland has a university, with campuses at Luyengo and Kwaluseni, and

# SWAZILAND

a number of other institutions of higher education. In 1986 the rate of adult illiteracy averaged 32.7% (males 30.3%; females 34.8%). Of total expenditure by the central Government in the financial year 1993/94, E 241.2m. (22.7%) was for education.

## Public Holidays

**1995:** 1 January (New Year's Day), 13 March (Commonwealth Day), 14–17 April (Easter), 19 April (Birthday of King Mswati), 25 April (National Flag Day), 25 May (Ascension Day), 22 July (Birthday of the late King Sobhuza), 24 August (Umhlanga—Reed Dance—Day), 6 September (Somhlolo—Independence—Day), 24 October (United Nations Day), 25–26 December (Christmas and Boxing Day).

**1996:** 1 January (New Year's Day), 11 March (Commonwealth Day), 5–8 April (Easter), 19 April (Birthday of King Mswati), 25 April (National Flag Day), 16 May (Ascension Day), 22 July (Birthday of the late King Sobhuza), 24 August (Umhlanga—Reed Dance—Day), 6 September (Somhlolo—Independence—Day), 24 October (United Nations Day), 25–26 December (Christmas and Boxing Day).

The Incwala Ceremony is held in December or January, but the exact date is variable each year.

# Statistical Survey

Source (unless otherwise stated): Central Statistical Office, POB 456, Mbabane.

## AREA AND POPULATION

**Area:** 17,363 sq km (6,704 sq miles).

**Population** (excluding absentee workers): 494,534 (males 231,861, females 262,673) at census of 25 August 1976; 681,059 (males 321,579, females 359,480) at census of 25 August 1986; 823,000 (official estimate) at mid-1992.

**Density** (mid-1992): 47.4 per sq km.

**Ethnic Groups** (census of August 1986): Swazi 661,646; Other Africans 14,468; European 1,825; Asiatic 228; Other non-Africans 412; Mixed 2,403; Unknown 77; Total 681,059.

**Principal Towns** (population at census of August 1986): Mbabane (capital) 38,290; Manzini 18,084.

**Births and Deaths** (UN estimates, 1985–90): Average annual birth rate 38.0 per 1,000; average annual death rate 11.8 per 1,000. Source: UN, *World Population Prospects: The 1992 Revision*.

**Expectation of Life** (UN estimates, years at birth, 1985–90): 55.5 (males 53.7; females 57.3). Source: UN, *World Population Prospects: The 1992 Revision*.

**Economically Active Population** (census of August 1986): 160,355 (males 105,191, females 55,164). Source: ILO, *Year Book of Labour Statistics*.

## AGRICULTURE

**Principal Crops** ('000 metric tons, 1992): Rice (paddy) 3*; Maize 84†; Potatoes 6*; Sweet potatoes 4*; Pulses 4*; Cottonseed 33*; Cotton (lint) 16; Oranges 35*; Grapefruit 52*; Pineapples 55*; Sugar cane 3,500*.

\* FAO estimate.
† Unofficial figure.

**Livestock** (FAO estimates, '000 head, year ending September 1993): Horses 1; Asses 12; Cattle 753; Pigs 31; Sheep 23; Goats 406.

**Livestock Products** (FAO estimates, '000 metric tons, 1992): Beef and veal 12; Goat meat 3; Cows' milk 42; Cattle hides 1.6.

Source: FAO, *Production Yearbook*.

## FORESTRY

**Roundwood Removals** ('000 cubic metres, 1981): Sawlogs, veneer logs and logs for sleepers 319; Pitprops (Mine timber) 65; Pulpwood 1,268; Other industrial wood 11 (FAO estimate); Fuel wood 560 (FAO estimate); Total 2,223.

**1982 – 91:** Annual output as in 1981 (FAO estimates).

**Sawnwood Production** ('000 cubic metres, 1982): 103.

**1983 – 91:** Annual output as in 1982.

Source: FAO, *Yearbook of Forest Products*.

## MINING

**Production** (estimates, 1994): Coal 28,100 metric tons; Asbestos 227,700 metric tons; Quarrystone 211,500 cubic metres; Diamonds 52,800 carats.

## INDUSTRY

**1994:** Electric energy 568m. kWh; Wood pulp 170,800 metric tons; Raw sugar 457,300 metric tons.

## FINANCE

**Currency and Exchange Rates:** 100 cents = 1 lilangeni (plural: emalangeni). *Sterling and Dollar Equivalents* (31 December 1994): £1 sterling = 5.545 emalangeni; US $1 = 3.544 emalangeni; 100 emalangeni = £18.03 = $28.21. *Average Exchange Rate* (US $ per lilangeni): 0.35092 in 1992; 0.30641 in 1993; 0.28177 in 1994. Note: The lilangeni is at par with the South African rand.

**Budget** (million emalangeni, year ending 31 March 1994): *Revenue:* Taxes on income, etc. 315.8; Sales taxes 122.9; Import duties 454.5; Total (incl. others) 981.7. *Expenditure:* General public services 244.62; Defence 69.78; Public order and safety 98.33; Education 241.17; Health 85.35; Social security and welfare 6.23; Housing and community amenities 37.64; Recreational, cultural and religious affairs 6.23; Economic services 256.92 (Agriculture, forestry and fishing 50.43); Other purposes 18.47; Total 1,064.74 (Current 821.43, Capital 243.31).

**1995** (estimates, million emalangeni, year ending 31 March): Total revenue (incl. grants received) 1,202.8; Total expenditure (incl. net lending 1,484.5. Source: Ministry of Finance.

**International Reserves** (US $ million at 31 December 1994): IMF special drawing rights 8.60; Reserve position in IMF 4.38; Foreign exchange 283.99; Total 296.97. Source: IMF, *International Financial Statistics*.

**Money Supply** (million emalangeni at 31 December 1994): Currency outside banks 69.59; Demand deposits at commercial banks 241.75; Total money (incl. others) 311.59. Source: IMF, *International Financial Statistics*.

**Cost of Living** (Retail Price Index, excluding rent, for low-income wage-earners' families in Mbabane and Manzini; base: 1990 = 100): 101.6 in 1991; 121.6 in 1992; 137.2 in 1993. Source: UN, *Monthly Bulletin of Statistics*.

**Gross Domestic Product by Kind of Economic Activity** (million emalangeni in current purchasers' values, 1993): Agriculture and forestry 306.6; Mining and quarrying 47.6; Manufacturing 888.7; Electricity, gas and water 36.6; Construction 82.2; Trade, restaurants and hotels 209.3; Transport and communications 151.4; Finance, insurance, real estate etc, 170.4; Government services 566.4; Other community, social and personal services 90.4; Other services 59.2; *Sub-total* 2,608.9; *Less* Imputed bank service charge 106.1; *GDP at factor cost* 2,502.7; Indirect taxes, *less* subsidies 558.5; *GDP in purchasers' values* 3,061.2.

**Balance of Payments** (US $ million, 1993): Merchandise exports f.o.b. 649.8; Merchandise imports f.o.b. –774.4; *Trade balance* –124.5; Exports of services 99.3; Imports of services –113.8; Other income received 125.7; Other income paid –138.6; Private unrequited transfers (net) 0.4; Government unrequited transfers (net) 114.4; *Current balance* –37.2; Direct investment (net) 29.0; Portfolio investment (net) –1.1; Other capital (net) –64.8; Net errors and omissions 26.3; *Overall balance* –47.6. Source: IMF, *International Financial Statistics*.

## EXTERNAL TRADE

**Principal Commodities:** *Imports* ('000 emalangeni, 1993): Food and live animals 441,018; Beverages and tobacco 62,668; Crude materials 130,092; Mineral fuels, lubricants 302,092; Animal and vegetable oils and fats 15,988; Chemical products 282,466; Machinery and transport equipment 783,080; Miscellaneous manufactured articles 315,984; Total (incl. others) 2,971,429. *Exports* (million emalangeni, 1992): Foodstuffs 510.4 (Sugar 424.0, Canned and fresh fruit 86.4); Wood and wood products 70.1; Mineral products 66.6; Total (incl. others) 1,724.1. Figures refer to domestic exports, excluding re-exports. Source: Central Bank of Swaziland.

**Principal Trading Partners** ('000 emalangeni): *Imports* (year ending 31 March 1993): France 1,552.2; Netherlands 10,726.9; South Africa 2,428,294.0; Switzerland 7,499.6; United Kingdom 75,117.8; Total (incl. others) 2,587,338.5. *Exports* (excl. re-exports, 1991): South Africa 804,103.7; United Kingdom 56,561.3; Total (incl. others) 1,711,539.0.

## TRANSPORT

**Railways** (traffic estimates, million, 1991): Passenger-km 1,210 (1988); Freight net ton-km 2,910. Source: UN Economic Commission for Africa, *African Statistical Yearbook*.

Total freight ('000 tons, 1993): 4,203.

**Road Traffic** (motor vehicles in use, 1990): Passenger cars 26,415; Buses and coaches 2,544; Goods vehicles 21,752; Tractors (excl. agricultural) 6,811; Motor cycles and scooters 2,628 (1991). Source: International Road Federation, *World Road Statistics*.

**Civil Aviation** (traffic on scheduled services, 1992): Passengers carried 56,000; Passenger-km 41 million. Source: UN, *Statistical Yearbook*.

## TOURISM

**Tourist Arrivals by Nationality** (1992): South Africa 137,000; United Kingdom 31,181; Total (incl. others) 268,071. Figures cover only tourists staying in hotels. Including other visitors, the total number of arrivals was 1,568,198.

**Total Receipts** (million emalangeni): 76.4 in 1991; 85.7 in 1992; 93.9 in 1993.

## COMMUNICATIONS MEDIA

**Radio Receivers** (1992): 129,000 in use.
**Television Receivers** (1992): 16,000 in use.
Source: UNESCO, *Statistical Yearbook*.
**Daily Newspapers** (1995): 2.
**Telephones** (1992): 25,888 in use.

## EDUCATION

**Primary** (1994): Institutions 535; Teachers 5,887; Students 192,599.

**General Secondary** (1994): Institutions 165; Teachers 2,872; Students 52,571.

**Teacher Training** (1993/94): Institutions 3; Teachers 88; Students 924.

**Technical and Vocational Training** (1993/94): Institutions 2; Teachers 140; Students 2,034.

**University Education** (1993/94): Institution 1; Teachers 190; Students 1,730.

# Directory

## The Constitution

The Constitution of 13 October 1978 vests supreme executive and legislative power in the hereditary King (Ngwenyama—the Lion). Succession is governed by traditional law and custom. In the event of the death of the King, the powers of Head of State are transferred to the constitutional dual monarch, the Queen Mother (Indlovukazi—Great She Elephant), who is authorized to act as Regent until the designated successor attains the age of 21. The Constitution provides for a bicameral legislature (Libandla), comprising a House of Assembly and a Senate. The functions of the Libandla are confined to debating government proposals and advising the King. Executive power is exercised through the Cabinet (later redesignated as the Council of Ministers), which is appointed by the King. The Swaziland National Council, which comprises members of the royal family, and is headed by the King and Queen Mother, advises on matters regulated by traditional law and custom. The Constitution affirms the fundamental rights of the individual.

Following a number of amendments to the electoral system, which were approved by the King in October 1992, the House of Assembly (which was redesignated as the National Assembly) was expanded to 65 deputies (of whom 55 are directly elected from candidates nominated by traditional local councils, known as Tinkhundla, and 10 appointed by the King), and the Senate to 30 members (of whom 20 are appointed by the King and 10 elected by the National Assembly). Elections to the National Assembly are conducted by secret ballot, in two rounds of voting; the second round of the elections is contested by the three candidates from each of the Tinkhundla who secure the highest number of votes in the first poll. In early 1994 it was announced that the King was to appoint a 15-member commission, comprising representatives of state organs and non-governmental organizations, which was to draft a new constitution incorporating the amendments.

## The Government

### HEAD OF STATE

HM King MSWATI III (succeeded to the throne 25 April 1986).

### COUNCIL OF MINISTERS
(June 1995)

**Prime Minister:** Prince JAMESON MBILINI DLAMINI.
**Deputy Prime Minister:** Dr SISHAYI NXUMALO.
**Minister of Justice:** Chief MAWENI SIMELANE.
**Minister of Foreign Affairs:** SOLOMON DLAMINI.
**Minister of Finance:** Dr DERRICK VON WISSEL.
**Minister of the Interior:** Prince SOBANDLA DLAMINI.
**Minister of Education:** ARTHUR KHOZA.
**Minister of Agriculture and Co-operatives:** Chief DAMBUZA LUKHELE.
**Minister of Labour and Public Service:** ALBERT SHABANGU.
**Minister of Economic Planning and Development:** THEMBA MASUKU.
**Minister of Commerce and Industry:** MAJAHENKABA DLAMINI.
**Minister of Health:** MUNTU MSWANE.
**Minister of Broadcasting, Information and Tourism:** Prince KHUZULWANDLE DLAMINI.
**Minister of Works and Construction:** Prince MAHLALENGANGENI DLAMINI.
**Minister of Natural Resources and Land Utilization and Energy:** ABSALOM DLAMINI.
**Minister of Transport and Communications:** EPHRAEM MAGAGULA.
**Minister of Housing and Urban Development:** JOHN CARMICHAEL.

### MINISTRIES

**Office of the Prime Minister:** POB 395, Mbabane; tel. 42251.
**Ministry of Agriculture and Co-operatives:** POB 162, Mbabane; tel. 42731; telex 2343; fax 44700.
**Ministry of Broadcasting, Information and Tourism:** POB 338, Mbabane; tel. 42761; fax 42774.
**Ministry of Commerce and Industry:** POB 451, Mbabane; tel. 43201; telex 2232; fax 43833.
**Ministry of Economic Planning and Development:** POB 602, Mbabane; tel. 43765; fax 42157.
**Ministry of Education:** POB 39, Mbabane; tel. 42491; telex 2293; fax 43880.
**Ministry of Finance:** POB 443, Mbabane; tel. 42141; telex 2109; fax 43187.
**Ministry of Foreign Affairs:** POB 518, Mbabane; tel. 42661; telex 2036; fax 42669.
**Ministry of Health:** POB 5, Mbabane; tel. 42431; fax 42092.
**Ministry of Housing and Urban Development:** POB 1832, Mbabane; tel. 46510; fax 45224.
**Ministry of the Interior:** POB 432, Mbabane; tel. 42941; telex 2328; fax 44303.
**Ministry of Justice:** POB 924, Mbabane; tel. 43531; fax 43533.
**Ministry of Labour and Public Service:** POB 170, Mbabane; tel. 43521; fax 45379.
**Ministry of Natural Resources, Land Utilization and Energy:** POB 57, Mbabane; tel. 46244; telex 2301; fax 42436.
**Ministry of Transport and Communications:** POB 58, Mbabane; tel. 42321; fax 42364.

SWAZILAND

**Ministry of Works and Construction:** POB 58, Mbabane; tel. 42321; telex 2104; fax 42364.

## Legislature

### LIBANDLA
### The Senate

**President:** LAWREN MNINA.

There are 30 senators, of whom 20 are appointed by the King and 10 elected by the National Assembly.

### National Assembly

**Speaker:** MUSA SIBANDZE.

There are 65 deputies, of whom 55 are directly elected from candidates nominated by the Tinkhundla and 10 appointed by the King. Elections to the National Assembly took place, in two rounds of voting, on 25 September and 11 October 1993.

## Political Organizations

Party political activity was banned by royal proclamation in April 1973, and formally prohibited under the 1978 Constitution. Since 1991, following indications that the Constitution was to be revised, a number of political associations have re-emerged.

**Imbokodvo National Movement (INM):** f. 1964 by King Sobhuza II; traditionalist movement, but also advocates policies of development and the elimination of illiteracy; Leader (vacant).

**Ngwane National Liberatory Congress (NNLC):** Ilanga Centre, Martin St, POB 766, Manzini; tel. 53935; f. 1962, by a breakaway faction of the SPP; advocates democratic freedoms and universal suffrage, and seeks abolition of the Tinkhundla electoral system; Pres. Dr AMBROSE ZWANE; Sec.-Gen. DUMISA DLAMINI.

**Confederation for Full Democracy in Swaziland:** f. 1992; alliance of organizations advocating democratic reform.

    **People's United Democratic Movement (PUDEMO):** f. 1983; seeks constitutional reform to limit the powers of the monarchy; established affiliated organizations in 1991, incl. the Human Rights Association of Swaziland and the Swaziland Youth Congress; Pres. KISLON SHONGWE; Sec.-Gen. DOMINIC MNGOMEZULU.

**Swaziland National Front (SWANAFRO):** Mbabane; Pres. ELMOND SHONGWE; Sec.-Gen. GLENROSE DLAMINI.

**Swaziland Progressive Party (SPP):** POB 6, Mbabane; tel. 22648; f. 1929 as Swazi Progressive Association; Pres. J. J. NQUKU.

**Swaziland United Front (SUF):** POB 14, Kwaluseni; f. 1962, by a breakaway faction of the SPP; Leader MATSAPA SHONGWE.

## Diplomatic Representation

### EMBASSIES AND HIGH COMMISSIONS IN SWAZILAND

**China (Taiwan):** Embassy House, Warner St, POB 56, Mbabane; tel. 42379; telex 2167; fax 46688; Ambassador: ENTI LIU.

**Israel:** Mbabane House, Warner St, POB 146, Mbabane; tel. 42626; telex 2098; fax 45857; Ambassador: (vacant).

**Mozambique:** Princess Drive, POB 1212, Mbabane; tel. 43700; telex 2248; fax 43692; Ambassador: ANTONIO C. F. SUMBANA.

**United Kingdom:** Allister Miller St, Mbabane; tel. 42581; fax 42585; High Commissioner: RICHARD GOZNEY.

**South Africa:** Standard Bank Bldg, Allister Miner St; tel. 45209; fax 44335.

**USA:** Central Bank Bldg, Warner St, POB 199, Mbabane; tel. 46441; telex 2285; fax 46446; Ambassador: JOHN SPROTT.

## Judicial System

The judiciary is headed by the Chief Justice. There is a High Court (which is a Superior Court of Record) with six subordinate courts in all the administrative districts, and there is a Court of Appeal which sits at Mbabane.

There are 17 Swazi Courts, including two Courts of Appeal and a Higher Court of Appeal, which have limited jurisdiction in civil and criminal cases. Their jurisdiction excludes non-Swazi nationals.

**Chief Justice:** DAVID HULL.

*Directory*

## Religion

About 60% of the adult Swazi population profess Christianity. Most of the remainder hold traditional beliefs.

### CHRISTIANITY

**Conference of Churches:** POB 384, Mbabane; tel. 53071; f. 1929; mems: 14 church denominations and one Christian org.; Head Rev. ISAAC HLETA.

**Council of Swaziland Churches:** POB 1095, Manzini; tel. 53628; f. 1976; eight mem. churches; Chair. Rt Rev. LOUIS NDLOVU (Roman Catholic Bishop of Manzini); Gen. Sec. EUNICE SOWAZI.

### The Anglican Communion

Swaziland comprises a single diocese within the Church of the Province of Southern Africa. The Metropolitan of the Province is the Archbishop of Cape Town, South Africa.

**Bishop of Swaziland:** Rt Rev. LAWRENCE BEKISISA ZULU, POB 118, Mbabane; tel. 43624; fax 46759.

### The Roman Catholic Church

For ecclesiastical purposes, Swaziland comprises the single diocese of Manzini, suffragan to the archdiocese of Pretoria, South Africa. At 31 December 1993 there were an estimated 46,000 adherents in Swaziland, equivalent to about 5.8% of the total population. The Bishop participates in the Southern African Catholic Bishops' Conference (based in Pretoria, South Africa).

**Bishop of Manzini:** Rt Rev. LOUIS NCAMISO NDLOVU, Bishop's House, Sandlane St, POB 19, Manzini; tel. 52348; fax 54876.

### Other Christian Churches

**Lutheran Development Service:** POB 388, Mbabane; tel. 42562; fax 43870.

**Mennonite Central Committee:** POB 329, Mbabane; tel. 42805; fax 44732; Co-ordinators JON RUDY, CAROLYN RUDY.

**The Methodist Church in Southern Africa:** POB 218, Mbabane; tel. 42658.

**United Christian Church of Africa:** POB 6, Mbabane; tel. 22648; f. 1944; Pres. Rt Rev. JEREMIAH NDINISA; Founder and Gen. Sec. Dr J. J. NQUKU.

The National Baptist Church, the Christian Apostolic Holy Spirit Church in Zion and the Religious Society of Friends (Quakers) are also active.

### BAHÁ'Í FAITH

**National Spiritual Assembly:** POB 298, Mbabane; tel. 43457; mems resident in 153 localities.

## The Press

**The Swazi News:** Allister Miller St, POB 156, Mbabane; tel. 42220; telex 2097; fax 42438; f. 1983; weekly (Sat.); English; owned by *The Times of Swaziland*; Editor JABU E. MATSEBULA; circ. 7,000.

**Swaziland Observer:** Swazi Plaza, POB A385, Mbabane; tel. 23383; telex 2322; f. 1981; daily (Mon. – Sat.); English; Man. Editor MASI MUBISI; circ. 11,000.

**Swaziview:** POB 1532, Mbabane; tel. 42716; monthly magazine; general interest; circ. 3,500.

**The Times of Swaziland:** Allister Miller St, POB 156, Mbabane; tel. 42220; telex 2097; fax 42438; f. 1897; English; daily (Mon. – Fri.); monthly; Editor MUSHUMI NOLA; circ. 25,000.

**Tindzaba News:** monthly magazine; English, siSwati; publ. by Swaziland Broadcasting and Information Service.

**Umbiki:** Allister Miller St, POB 464, Mbabane; tel. 42761; telex 2035; monthly; siSwati; publ. by Swaziland Broadcasting and Information Service.

## Publishers

**Apollo Services (Pty) Ltd:** POB 35, Mbabane; tel. 42711.

**GBS Printing and Publishing (Pty) Ltd:** POB 1384, Mbabane; tel. 52779.

**Longman Swaziland (Pty) Ltd:** POB 2207, Manzini; tel. 53891.

**Macmillan Boleswa Publishers (Pty) Ltd:** POB 1235, Manzini; tel. 84533; telex 2221; fax 85247; Man. Dir L. A. BALARIN.

**Swaziland Printing & Publishing Co Ltd:** POB 28, Mbabane; tel. 42716.

**Whydah Media Publishers Ltd:** POB 1532, Mbabane; tel. 42716; f. 1978.

SWAZILAND

## Radio and Television

In 1992 there were an estimated 129,000 radio receivers and 16,000 television receivers in use.

### RADIO

**Swaziland Broadcasting and Information Service:** POB 338, Mbabane; tel. 42761; telex 2035; f. 1966; broadcasts in English and siSwati; Dir N. Z. MALINGA.

**Swaziland Commercial Radio (Pty) Ltd:** POB 1586, Alberton 1450, South Africa; tel. (11) 8848400; fax (11) 8831982; privately-owned commercial service; broadcasts to southern Africa in English and Portuguese; music and religious programmes; Man. Dir I. KIRSH.

**Trans World Radio:** POB 64, Manzini; tel. 52781; telex 2196; fax 55333; f. 1974; religious broadcasts from five transmitters in 28 languages to southern, central and eastern Africa and to the Far East; Pres. THOMAS J. LOWELL.

### TELEVISION

**Swaziland Television Broadcasting Corporation:** POB A146, Mbabane; tel. 43036; telex 2138; fax 42093; f. 1978; state-owned; broadcasts seven hours daily in English; colour transmissions; Gen. Man. DAN S. DLAMINI.

## Finance

(cap. = capital; dep. = deposits; m. = million; res = reserves; br. = branch; amounts in emalangeni)

### BANKING

#### Central Bank

**Central Bank of Swaziland:** POB 546, Mbabane; tel. 43221; telex 2029; fax 42636; f. 1974; bank of issue; cap. and res 6.8m., dep. 281.6m. (Dec. 1994); Gov. JAMES MXUMALO; Dep. Gov. M. G. DLAMINI.

#### Commercial Banks

**Barclays Bank of Swaziland Ltd:** Allister Miller St, POB 667, Mbabane; tel. 42691; telex 2096; fax 45239; f. 1974; 40% state-owned; cap. and res 27.2m., dep. 342.1m. (Dec. 1993); Chair. DANIEL M. DLAMINI; Man. Dir MARK TAVERSHAM; 13 brs and agencies.

**Meridien BIAO Bank Swaziland Ltd:** Meridien BIAO House, West St, POB 261, Mbabane; tel. 45401; telex 2380; fax 44735; f. 1988; 10% state-owned; cap. and res 5.6m., dep. 11.9m. (Sept. 1991); Chair. EDWARD ROBERT SYDER; Man. Dir CHRISTOPHER EVANS; 4 brs.

**Standard Chartered Bank Swaziland Ltd** (United Kingdom): 21 Allister Miller St, POB 68, Mbabane; tel. 43351; telex 2220; fax 44060; f. 1974; 30% state-owned; cap. and res 14.4m., dep. 199.8m. (Dec. 1993); Chair. A. R. B. SHABANGU; Man. Dir P. V. DOCHERTY; 4 brs and 1 agency.

#### Development Banks

**Stanbic Bank Swaziland Ltd:** Stanbic House, 1st Floor, Swazi Plaza, POB A294, Mbabane; tel. 46587; telex 2216; fax 45899; f. 1988 as UnionBank of Swaziland Ltd, name changed 1994; cap. and res 21.8m., dep. 191.0m. (Dec. 1994); Man. Dir M. P. LUBBE; 4 brs.

**Swaziland Development and Savings Bank:** Engunwini, Allister Miller St, POB 336, Mbabane; tel. 42551; telex 2396; fax 41214; f. 1965; state-owned; cap. and res 25.3m., dep. 173.1m. (March 1993); Chair. T. M. J. ZWANE; Gen. Man. S. S. KUHLASE; 8 brs.

#### Financial Institution

**Swaziland National Provident Fund:** POB 1857, Manzini; tel. 53731; telex 3011; fax 54377; total assets 134m.

### STOCK EXCHANGE

**Swaziland Stockbrokers Ltd:** POB 2818, Mbabane; tel. 46163; fax 44132; f. 1993; CEO A. MCGUIRE.

### INSURANCE

Although the state-controlled Swaziland Royal Insurance Corporation (SRIC) operates as the country's sole authorized insurance company, cover in a number of areas not served by SRIC is available from several specialized insurers.

#### Insurance Companies

**Bowring & Minet:** Swazi Plaza, POB A32, Mbabane; tel. 42929; telex 2120; fax 45254.

**Swaziland Employee Benefit Consultants (Pty) Ltd:** POB 222, Mbabane; tel. 44776; telex 2101; fax 46413; specialized medical cover.

**Swaziland Insurance Brokers:** POB 222, Mbabane; tel. 43226; telex 2101; fax 46412; f. 1970; Man. Dir F. PETTIT.

**Swaziland Royal Insurance Corporation (SRIC):** Gilfillian St, POB 917, Mbabane; tel. 43231; telex 2043; fax 46415; 51% state-owned; sole auth. insurance co since 1974; Gen. Man. M. MKWANAZI.

**Tibiyo Insurance Brokers:** Swazi Plaza, POB A166, Mbabane; tel. 42010; telex 2170; fax 45035; Man. Dir C. FAUX.

#### Insurance Association

**Insurance Brokers' Association of Swaziland (IBAS):** Swazi Plaza, POB A32, Mbabane; tel. 42929; f. 1983; four mems.

## Trade and Industry

### DEVELOPMENT CORPORATIONS

**National Industrial Development Corporation of Swaziland (NIDCS):** POB 866, Mbabane; tel. 43391; telex 2052; fax 45619; f. 1971; state-owned; holding co for govt investments since 1987, when the majority of its assets were transferred to the Swaziland Industrial Development Co; Man. Dir P. K. THAMM.

**Small Enterprise Development Co (SEDCO):** POB A186, Mbabane; tel. 43046; telex 2130; fax 22723; govt development agency; supplies workshop space, training and expertise for 120 local entrepreneurs at seven sites throughout the country.

**Swaziland Industrial Development Co (SIDC):** Dhlan'Ubeka House, 5th Floor, cnr Tin and Walker Sts, POB 866, Mbabane; tel. 44010; telex 2052; fax 45619; f. 1986 to finance private-sector projects and to promote local and foreign investment; 34% state-owned; cap. E24.1m. (June 1994); Chair. M. E. FLETCHER; Gen. Man. P. K. THAMM.

   **Swaki (Pty) Ltd:** Liqhaga Bldg, 4th Floor, Nkoseluhlaza St, POB 1839, Manzini; tel. 52693; telex 2244; fax 52001; comprises a number of cos involved in manufacturing, services and the production and distribution of food (especially maize); jtly owned by SIDC and Kirsh Holdings.

**Tibiyo Takangwane** (Bowels of the Swazi Nation): POB 181, Kwaluseni; tel. 84390; telex 2116; fax 84399; f. 1968; national development agency, with investment interests in all sectors of the economy; participates in domestic and foreign jt investment ventures; total assets E260m. (1992); Gen. Man. A. T. DLAMINI.

### STATE AUTHORITIES

**National Agricultural Marketing Board:** POB 2801, Mbabane; tel. 84088.

**National Maize Corporation:** POB 158, Manzini; tel. 52261.

**Posts and Telecommunications Corporation:** POB 125, Mbabane; tel. 42341.

**Swaziland Citrus Board:** POB 343, Mbabane; tel. 44266; telex 2018; fax 43548.

**Swaziland Commercial Board:** POB 509, Mbabane; tel. 42930; Man. Dir J. M. D. FAKUDZE.

**Swaziland Cotton Board:** POB 230, Manzini; tel. 52775; Gen. Man. T. JELE.

**Swaziland Dairy Board:** POB 1789, Manzini; tel. 84411; fax 85313.

**Swaziland Electricity Board:** POB 258, Mbabane; tel. 42521.

**Swaziland Meat Industries Ltd:** POB 446, Manzini; tel. 84165; fax 84418; f. 1965; operates an abattoir and cannery at Matsapha to process meat for local and export markets; Gen. Man. P. PHILLIPS.

**Swaziland National Housing Board:** POB 798, Mbabane; tel. 45610; fax 45224.

**Swaziland Sugar Association:** POB 445, Mbabane; tel. 42646; telex 2031; fax 45005; Gen. Man. A. COLHOUN.

**Water Services Corporation:** POB 20, Mbabane; tel. 43161.

### CHAMBERS OF COMMERCE

**Sibakho Chamber of Commerce:** POB 2016, Manzini; tel. 54409.

**Swaziland Chamber of Commerce and Industry:** POB 72, Mbabane; tel. 44408; fax 45442; Sec. HARVEY BIRD.

### EMPLOYERS' ASSOCIATIONS

**The Building Contractors Association of Swaziland:** POB 2653, Mbabane; tel. 45566.

**Swaziland Association of Architects, Engineers and Surveyors:** Swazi Plaza, POB A387, Mbabane; tel. 42309.

**Swaziland Institute of Personnel and Training Managers:** c/o UNISWA, Private Bag, Kwaluseni; tel. 84545; fax 85276.

# SWAZILAND

### Employers' Federation

**Federation of Swaziland Employers:** POB 777, Mbabane; tel. 22768; fax 46107; f. 1964; 376 mems; Pres. R. SEAL; Exec. Dir E. HLOPHE.

### TRADE UNIONS

The following trade unions are currently recognized by the Ministry of Labour and Public Service:

The Association of Lecturers and Academic Personnel of the University of Swaziland, the Building and Construction Workers Union of Swaziland, Swaziland Agriculture and Plantation Workers' Union, Swaziland Commercial and Allied Workers' Union, Swaziland Conservation Workers' Union, Swaziland Electricity Supply, Maintenance and Allied Workers' Union, Swaziland Engineering, Metal and Allied Workers' Union, Swaziland Hotel, Catering and Allied Workers' Union, Swaziland Manufacturing and Allied Workers' Union, Swaziland Mining, Quarrying and Allied Workers' Union, Swaziland National Association of Civil Servants, Swaziland National Association of Teachers, Swaziland Post and Telecommunications Workers' Union, Swaziland Transport Workers' Union, Swaziland Union of Financial Institutions and Allied Workers, University of Swaziland Workers' Union, Workers Union of Swaziland Security Guards, Workers' Union of Town Councils.

### Trade Union Federation

**Swaziland Federation of Trade Unions (SFTU):** Mbabane; f. 1973; prin. trade union org. since mid-1980s; mems from public and private sectors, incl. agricultural workers; Pres. JAN SITHOLE.

### Staff Associations

Three staff associations exist for employees whose status lies between that of worker and that of management:

The Nyoni Yami Irrigation Scheme Staff Association, the Swazican Staff Association and the Swaziland Electricity Board Staff Association.

### CO-OPERATIVE ASSOCIATIONS

**Swaziland Central Co-operatives Union:** POB 551, Manzini; tel. 52787.

There are more than 123 co-operative associations, of which the most important is:

**Swaziland Co-operative Rice Co Ltd:** handles rice grown in Mbabane and Manzini areas.

### TRADE FAIR

**Swaziland International Trade Fair:** POB 877, Manzini; tel. 54242; telex 2232; fax 52324; annual 10-day event beginning in late August.

## Transport

Buses are the principal means of transport for many Swazis. Bus services are provided by private operators who are required to obtain annual permits for each route from the Road Transportation Board, which also regulates fares.

### RAILWAYS

The rail network, which totalled 294.4 km in 1991 provides a major transport link for imports and exports. The railways do not carry passengers. Railway lines connect with the South African ports of Richards Bay and Durban in the south, the South African town of Komatipoort in the north and the Mozambican port of Maputo in the east. Goods traffic is mainly in wood pulp, sugar, molasses, coal, citrus fruit and canned fruit.

**Swaziland Railway Board:** Swaziland Railway Bldg, POB 475, Johnstone St, Mbabane; tel. 42486; telex 2053; fax 45009; f. 1962; Chair. B. A. G. FITZPATRICK; CEO G. J. MAHLALELA.

### ROADS

In 1993 there were 2,960 km of roads, of which 804 km were bituminized. The rehabilitation of about 700 km of main and 600 km of district gravel-surfaced roads began in 1985, financed by World Bank and US loans totalling some E18m. In 1992 work commenced on the reconstruction of Swaziland's main road artery, connecting Mbabane to Manzini, via Matsapha.

**Ministry of Works and Construction:** POB 58, Mbabane; tel. 42321; telex 2104; fax 42364; Prin. Sec. EVART MADLOPHA; Sr Roads Engineer A. MANANA.

### SHIPPING

**Royal Swazi National Shipping Corporation Ltd:** POB 1915, Manzini; tel. 53788; telex 2065; fax 53820; f. 1980 to succeed Royal Swaziland Maritime Co; owns no ships, acting only as a freight agent; Gen. Man. M. S. DLAMINI.

### CIVIL AVIATION

Swaziland's only airport is at Matsapa, near Manzini, about 40 km from Mbabane.

**African International Airways (AIA):** POB 2117, Mbabane; tel. 43875; fax 43876; f. 1985; operates cargo services; Exec. T. M. LONGMORE.

**Air Swazi Cargo:** Dhlan'Ubeka House, Walker St, POB 2869, Mbabane; tel. 45575; telex 3026; fax 45003; charter services for freight to destinations in Africa and Europe; Man. BRIAN PARMENTER.

**Royal Swazi National Airways Corporation:** POB 939, Matsapa Airport, Manzini; tel. 84444; telex 2064; fax 85054; f. 1978; govt-owned; scheduled passenger and cargo services to destinations in Africa; also operates charter flights; Exec. Chair. Prince GABHENI DLAMINI; CEO Prince MATATAZELA DLAMINI.

## Tourism

Swaziland's attractions for tourists include game reserves and magnificent mountain scenery. In 1992 268,071 tourist arrivals were registered at hotels. The total number of visitors to Swaziland was 1,568,198. Revenue from the tourist sector totalled E93.9m. in 1993.

**Hotel and Tourism Association of Swaziland:** POB 462, Mbabane; tel. 42218.

**Ministry of Broadcasting, Information and Tourism:** POB 338, Mbabane; tel. 42761; fax 42774; Tourism Officer MDUDUZI MAGONGO.

# SWEDEN

## Introductory Survey

### Location, Climate, Language, Religion, Flag, Capital

The Kingdom of Sweden lies in north-western Europe, occupying about two-thirds of the Scandinavian peninsula. It is bordered by Finland to the north-east, and by Norway to the north-west and west. About 15% of Sweden's area lies north of the Arctic Circle. The Baltic Sea and the Gulf of Bothnia are to the east, the Skagerrak and Kattegat channels to the south-west. The country is relatively flat and is characterized by thousands of inland lakes and small coastal islands. There is a mountain range, the Kjölen mountains, in the north-west. Winters are cold and summers mild. In Stockholm the mean summer temperature is 18°C (64°F) and the mean winter temperature −3°C (27°F). The national language is Swedish, but there are Finnish and Lapp (Sámi) minorities (the latter numbering between 15,000 and 17,000), retaining their own languages. A majority of the inhabitants profess Christianity, and about 88% are adherents of the Evangelical Lutheran Church of Sweden. The national flag (proportions 8 by 5) is light blue with a yellow cross, the upright of the cross being to the left of centre. The capital is Stockholm.

### Recent History

Sweden has been a constitutional monarchy, traditionally neutral, since the early 19th century. During this time the country has not participated in any war or entered any military alliance. Norway, formerly united with Sweden, became independent in 1905. Sweden adopted parliamentary government in 1917, and universal adult suffrage was introduced in 1921. From 1932 until 1976, except for a short break in 1936, Sweden was governed by the Social Democratic Labour Party (Socialdemokratiska Arbetareparti—SAP), either alone or as the senior partner in coalitions (1936–45 and 1951–57). During those 44 years the country had only three Prime Ministers, all Social Democrats. Since the Second World War, Sweden has become an active member of many international organizations, including the UN (to which it has given military support), the Council of Europe and, from 1995, the European Union (EU).

Olof Palme succeeded Dr Tage Erlander as Prime Minister and leader of the SAP in October 1969. After a general election in September 1970, Palme formed a minority government. Under a constitutional reform, the Riksdag (Parliament) was reconstituted from January 1971, its two chambers being replaced by a unicameral assembly. King Gustaf VI Adolf, who had reigned since 1950, died in September 1973 and was succeeded by his grandson, Carl XVI Gustaf. A revised Constitution, effective from January 1975, ended the monarch's prerogative to appoint the Prime Minister: the Speaker of the Riksdag was to have this responsibility in future.

At the September 1976 election, dissatisfaction with high rates of taxation, necessary to maintain the advanced social welfare system which Sweden had developed, brought about the defeat of the SAP. Thorbjörn Fälldin, leader of the Centre Party (Centerpartiet—CP), formed a centre-right coalition in October. The wish of the CP to abandon Sweden's nuclear power programme caused serious controversy in June 1978, when an independent commission recommended its continued use as an energy source. This view was endorsed by the Liberals (Folkpartiet—FP) and Moderates (Moderata Samlingspartiet—MS), whose rejection of a proposal by Fälldin to submit the nuclear issue to a national referendum led to the resignation of the Government in October 1978. The FP formed a minority Government, led by Ola Ullsten. Following a general election in September 1979, Fälldin returned as Prime Minister of a coalition comprising members of the CP, MS and FP, with an overall parliamentary majority of only one seat. A referendum on the future of nuclear power was held in March 1980, and a narrow majority of the electorate approved a limited programme of nuclear reactor development, to be progressively eliminated by 2010 and replaced by alternative energy resources.

During 1980 the Government's economic policies came under attack, mainly because of the rising rate of inflation, and there was severe industrial strife. The MS, which disagreed with proposed tax reforms, left the coalition in May 1981. Fälldin was able to form a new minority Government with continued FP support, but once again there was disagreement within the Cabinet over economic policy, particularly concerning taxation, rising unemployment and the heavy budget deficit. At the next general election, held in September 1982, the SAP were returned to power, winning 45.6% of the votes (and 166 of the 349 seats in the Riksdag), but gaining an overall majority over the three non-socialist parties. In October Palme formed a minority Government, following an undertaking by the Communists, the Vänsterpartiet—Kommunisterna (VpK), who held 20 seats, that they would support the SAP. The new Government immediately devalued the krona by 16%. It was also planned to intensify negotiations for the creation of a nuclear-free zone in the Nordic area.

A general election was held in September 1985, in which Palme's Government was returned to power, with the support of the VpK, despite a financial scandal in 1983 involving the Minister of Justice. The SAP and the VpK together won 50.0% of the votes (securing 178 seats in the Riksdag), while the three main non-socialist parties won 48.0% (and the remaining 171 seats). The FP increased its share of seats in the Riksdag from 21 to 51, attracting voters from all of the other main parties. The Christian Democratic Party (Kristdemokratiska Samhällspartiet—KdS), having signed an electoral pact with the CP in 1984, also won its first parliamentary seat. Palme undertook to continue to follow his 'third way' economic policy, seeking to combat inflation and recession while avoiding both excessively high levels of public spending and reductions in social welfare benefits.

On 28 February 1986 Olof Palme was murdered by an unknown assailant in Stockholm. In March the Deputy Prime Minister, Ingvar Carlsson, took office as Prime Minister and was also appointed acting Chairman of the SAP, pending ratification by the National Congress in 1987. Carlsson retained Palme's Cabinet and declared that he would continue the policies of his predecessor. During 1986 and 1987 little progress was made towards discovering Palme's assassin, and considerable controversy surrounded the case, as disputes increased between the police and successive public prosecutors (officially in charge of the investigation). In October 1987 the Minister of Justice, Sten Wickbom, resigned after a convicted spy escaped from prison. He also acknowledged ultimate responsibility for the conduct of the inquiry into Palme's murder. In June 1988 his successor, Anna-Greta Leijon, admitted that she had authorized a private investigation into the murder. Leijon resigned when the minority Social Democratic Government seemed likely to lose a vote of 'no confidence' on the issue. In December a man with a history of mental illness and violent crime was arrested, and in June and July 1989 he was tried for the murder of Palme. He was convicted amid some controversy, only to be acquitted on appeal in October.

In March 1987 a parliamentary commission of inquiry was appointed to investigate the alleged complicity of the Government in sales of weapons to Middle Eastern countries, via Singapore, by Sweden's principal arms manufacturing company, Bofors AB, a subsidiary of Nobel Industries Sweden AB (contrary to Swedish law, which forbids the sale of weapons to nations engaged in war or to areas of military tension). Further allegations involving Bofors were made in April, when it was reported that a contract for supplying a field artillery system to the Indian Government, concluded in February, had been obtained by bribery. A report by Sweden's National Audit Bureau, presented in June, confirmed the existence of an agreement to pay commissions to unnamed persons, but it stated that there had been no violation of Swedish law. The investigation was abandoned in January 1988, on grounds of insufficient evidence, but in October 1989 a leading Indian newspaper published sections of the Swedish report that had hitherto remained undisclosed (because of legislation on banking secrecy), apparently confirming the existence of illegal payments to senior members of the Indian administration. Following a general election in India in November, the new Government, in January 1990, filed preliminary charges against three senior employees of Bofors. An investigation was also being conducted into the involvement of certain unidentified Indian officials, and in May the Swedish Government agreed to release its secret report. In January 1993 a Swiss court ordered the disclosure of information concerning Swiss bank accounts holding payments from Bofors, in connection with the Indian investigation.

Ecological concerns were heightened in 1988 by two disasters, both of which were attributed to the effects of pollutants: increase in the concentration of algae devastated the marine environment along the west coast, and this was followed by an outbreak of a virus that reduced the seal population of the North and Baltic Seas by up to two-thirds. At the general election in September the environmentalist Green Party (Miljöpartiet de Gröna—MpG) gained parliamentary representation for the first time, with 20 seats. The SAP lost three seats but remained in power with the continued support of the VpK, which had increased its number of seats by two to 21. The non-socialist opposition parties lost a considerable amount of support, with the KdS, no longer in an electoral alliance with the CP, losing its seat. The conservative MS, with 66 seats, remained the second-largest party in the Riksdag. In February 1990 the VpK (subsequently renamed the Left Party—VP) and the MpG refused to support the Government's proposed austerity measures, designed to combat rising inflation, a low rate of economic growth and industrial unrest. Carlsson therefore resigned, but, having secured support for a new and more moderate set of proposals, he formed another minority Government. The only significant changes in the Cabinet resulted from the resignation of the respected Minister of Finance, Kjell-Olof Feldt, who had previously expressed anxieties about the failure to introduce stringent austerity measures.

During 1990 the Swedish economy entered into recession, and in December the Riksdag approved a new austere economic programme, which was designed to reduce inflation and to restore confidence in the economy. The Government was forced to abandon the long-held belief that the commitment to full employment and the defence of the welfare state (supported by high levels of taxation and of public expenditure) should be overriding priorities. The measures included cuts of 15,000m. kronor in Government spending over the next three years, partial privatization of the state sector, including the telecommunications system and electricity network, and a new energy policy, which would postpone the phasing-out of nuclear power that had been planned to begin in 1995 and to be completed by 2010. In early 1991 the tax system was reformed, with reductions in income tax for all but the most highly paid, and a corresponding increase in the taxing of goods and services. In March changes in company law were proposed (to come into effect in July) to remove the legal barriers demarcating the activities of banks, finance houses and insurance companies; this signified a further step in the country's financial deregulation, bringing Sweden into line with general Western European practice.

These changes failed to increase the popularity of the SAP, and in the general election of September 1991 the party did not win enough seats to form a government, although it remained the largest party in the Riksdag, with 138 seats. The MS increased its representation to 80 seats, while the KdS and a recently-formed right-wing party, New Democracy (ND) won 26 and 25 seats respectively, at the expense of the FP and the CP; the MpG failed to secure 4% of the total votes, and thereby forfeited all its seats. Ingvar Carlsson resigned as Prime Minister, and in early October Carl Bildt, the leader of the MS (the largest non-socialist party in the legislature) was invited to form a government. He formed a coalition comprising members of four non-socialist parties—the MS, the CP, the FP and the KdS. Since these four parties, even in combination, still formed a minority in the Riksdag, they were obliged to rely on the ND for support in adopting legislation. Without delay, the new Government began to accelerate the deregulation of the economy that its Social Democratic predecessor had already begun. In November plans to make large long-term reductions in government spending were announced, together with proposals for the eventual privatization of 35 state-owned companies and the removal of restrictions on foreign majority ownership of Swedish enterprises. Bildt emphasized his Government's commitment to membership of the European Community (EC, now EU—see p. 143).

During 1992 the recession continued in Sweden. Although the Government's austerity measures succeeded in reducing inflation, the high level of the budgetary deficit was a cause of concern. In September speculation on the international currency markets caused a rapid outflow of capital. Initially the SAP agreed to co-operate with the Government in protecting the krona by giving its parliamentary support to a new programme of reductions in public spending, including further cuts in welfare payments, accompanied by increases in taxation: it was hoped that this would restore confidence in the economy and prevent any need for a devaluation of the currency. In November, however, the SAP refused to vote in favour of yet more proposals for reductions in expenditure, and a fresh outflow of capital forced the Government to allow the krona to 'float' in relation to other currencies, thereby effectively devaluing it by some 10%. In March 1993 the Government was defeated in the Riksdag when the ND refused to support budgetary proposals, but later in the same month the Government won a parliamentary vote of confidence, when the ND abstained from voting. In February 1994 the leader of the ND resigned; in March the party announced that it would no longer support the Government in the legislature, and voted against proposals for health-care reforms that included allowing the establishment of private hospitals and private medical practices.

At the general election, held on 18 September 1994, the SAP secured 45.3% of the votes cast, increasing its representation to 161 seats. The VP won 22 seats (compared to 16 in 1991) and the MpG won 18 seats. Although the MS maintained the level of support it gained at the previous election, the other parties in the coalition Government performed badly. Bildt resigned as Prime Minister, and in early October 1994 Ingvar Carlsson formed a minority Government, discounting a proposed coalition with the FP, whose leader, Bengt Westerberg, subsequently resigned. The results appeared to indicate a trend of increased support for parties opposed to Sweden's joining the EU. Despite opposition to EU membership within the SAP, Carlsson declared that a major objective of his Government would be to secure a mandate for Sweden to join the EU in the forthcoming national referendum (see below). He also emphasized the need for stringent economic measures to reduce unemployment, stabilize the budgetary deficit and safeguard welfare provisions. (It was widely held that reductions in welfare payments, introduced by the Bildt Government, had been a major factor in the defeat of the non-socialist coalition.) Economic austerity measures, proposed in November 1994 and January 1995, anticipated reductions in public expenditure of some 50,000m. kronor in the following four financial years. The measures were criticized as inadequate, however, by some economists, and a council of industrialists, convened by Carlsson to advise on national economic policy, urged the Government to take measures to stimulate the private sector in order to reduce unemployment. In April 1995 the Government reached an agreement with the CP to support further austerity measures, which included additional reductions in welfare provisions.

In March 1991 the Swedish and Danish Governments agreed to construct a 16-km combined bridge and tunnel for road and rail traffic, across the Öresund strait, between Malmö and Copenhagen (to be known as the Öresund Link). The plan aroused opposition in Sweden, on the grounds that the link might hinder the flow of water into the Baltic Sea, as well as increasing pollution by emissions from vehicles. In May 1994 a Swedish marine commission concluded that plans for the link did not provide sufficient guarantees to protect the flow of water into the Baltic. In the following month, however, the Swedish Government approved construction plans, prompting the resignation from the Government of the Minister of the Environment and leader of the CP, Olof Johansson. The link, which was rescheduled to open in 2000, was expected to cost an estimated US $3,300m., at 1990 prices.

The approaching completion of the single internal market of the EC caused much debate within Sweden on the future of relations with its main trading partner. The Government's policy, widely supported in the Riksdag, was to negotiate with the EC under the aegis of EFTA: negotiations on the creation of a free-trade area, the European Economic Area (EEA) were concluded by the EC and EFTA in 1991 (and ratified by the Riksdag in November 1992). The EEA came into being on 1

January 1994. In December 1990 the Riksdag approved a Government decision to apply to join the EC, and in July 1991 Sweden formally applied for membership. Negotiations on admission began in February 1993, when the Bildt Government declared that the country's tradition of neutrality would not prevent Sweden from participating fully in the common foreign and security policy of the EC. The negotiations were concluded in March 1994. Sweden obtained safeguards for its traditional policy of freedom of official information, and for its strict environmental standards, and won concessions on the maintenance of subsidies for agriculture in remote areas. A national referendum on membership was held on 13 November 1994, producing a 52.2% majority in favour of joining the EU. The Riksdag formally ratified membership in December, and Sweden's accession to the EU took effect from 1 January 1995. (At the same time Sweden withdrew from EFTA.) It was widely held that concern about the possible effects on the domestic economy of remaining outside the EU, together with fears regarding Sweden's ability to influence international affairs, such as the maintenance of effective environmental controls, had been major factors in the outcome of the referendum. Following the vote, the Carlsson Government reiterated that Sweden would retain its non-aligned policy within the EU and therefore remain outside NATO, although it would apply for observer status within Western European Union (see page 221). The Government also declared that Sweden would use its EU status to promote free trade and foster closer co-operation with the Baltic countries of Estonia, Latvia and Lithuania.

In 1981 a Soviet submarine was grounded on Swedish shores, and in subsequent years there were repeated allegations of unauthorized incursions by submarines into Swedish territorial waters. The USSR was believed to be responsible for most incidents, and this caused some tension in relations between the two countries. This was heightened by the nuclear accident at Chornobyl, in the USSR, in April 1986. In January 1988, however, a 19-year dispute over territorial rights in the Baltic Sea was settled by an accord that acknowledged Swedish control over 75% of the 13,500 sq km area in question. In February 1992 the Swedish Government announced that it would increase defence expenditure over the next five years, in response to the likelihood of instability in the former USSR, and that it would be willing to co-operate with other European countries on matters of security, in particular with Finland, Norway and the former Soviet Baltic states. In April 1995 a Russian trade official was arrested in Stockholm, accused of seeking to obtain secret documents relating to Sweden's military defence installations.

### Government

Sweden is a constitutional monarchy. The hereditary monarch is Head of State but has very limited formal prerogatives. Executive power rests with the Cabinet (Regeringen), which is responsible to the legislature (Riksdag). The unicameral Riksdag was introduced in January 1971. It has 349 members, elected by universal adult suffrage for four years (previously three), on the basis of proportional representation. The Prime Minister is nominated by the Speaker of the Riksdag and later confirmed in office by the whole House. The country is divided into 24 counties (Iän) and 288 municipal districts (Kommun): both counties and municipalities have popularly elected councils.

### Defence

In June 1994 Sweden maintained total armed forces of 64,000, including 36,600 conscripts. Military service for males (aged between 19 and 47) lasts between seven and 15 months in the army and navy, and between eight and 12 months in the air force. Basic training for women is voluntary. The army consisted of 43,500 men, of whom 27,000 were conscripts; the navy 9,000 men, including 4,100 conscripts, and the air force 11,500 men, including 5,500 conscripts. In addition, there were voluntary defence reservists totalling 729,000. The 1994/95 budget for defence was 40,000m. kronor (about 7% of total government expenditure).

### Economic Affairs

In 1993, according to estimates by the World Bank, Sweden's gross national product (GNP), measured at average 1991–93 prices, was US $216,294m., equivalent to $24,830 per head. During 1985–93, it was estimated, GNP per head increased, in real terms, at an average annual rate of 0.1%. Over the same period the population increased by an annual average of 0.6%. Sweden's gross domestic product (GDP) increased, in real terms, by an annual average of 2.2% in 1980–90: it contracted, however, by 1.1% in 1991, by 1.7% in 1992 and by 2.2% in 1993, but increased by an estimated 2.5% in 1994.

Agriculture (including hunting, forestry and fishing) contributed 2.3% of GDP in 1993, and employed 3.4% of the working civilian population. In 1992, according to the FAO, only 7% of Sweden's land area was utilized for agriculture, while an estimated 68% was covered by forest and woodland. The main agricultural products are dairy produce, meat, cereals and potatoes, primarily for domestic consumption. In 1993 forestry products (wood, pulp and paper) accounted for 16.3% of total merchandise exports. Agricultural production increased by an annual average of 0.6% in 1981–90, but declined by 14.2% in 1991 and by 7.9% in 1992. Output rose by 12.7% in 1993.

Industry (including mining, manufacturing, construction and power) provided 29.0% of GDP in 1993, and employed 25.4% of the working population. Industrial GDP increased by an annual average of 2.4% in 1980–89, but declined by 0.2% in 1990, by 3.9% in 1991 and by 0.8% in 1992.

Mining contributed 0.3% of GDP in 1993, and employed 0.3% of the working population. The principal product is iron ore, but there are also large reserves of uranium (some 15% of the world's total known reserves), copper, lead and zinc.

Manufacturing contributed 19.5% of GDP in 1993, and employed 18.3% of the working population. In 1990 the most important sectors (measured by total value of output) were transport equipment (13% of the total, chiefly comprising motor vehicles), foodstuffs, paper, machinery, metal products, wood products, chemicals, electrical goods and printing and publishing. Manufacturing GDP increased by an average of 2.3% per year in 1980–89, but declined by 0.7% in 1990, by 5.6% in 1991 and by 0.8% in 1992.

Energy is derived principally from hydroelectric power (which provided 52% of electricity generated in 1993) and nuclear power; Sweden has 12 nuclear reactors, which provided some 42% of electricity generated in 1993. Imports of hydrocarbon fuels accounted for an estimated 9.2% of total imports in 1993. Alternative sources of energy are also being developed, because of strict environmental legislation, the lack of potential for further hydroelectric projects and, primarily, the Riksdag's resolution to phase out nuclear power.

In 1993 Sweden recorded a merchandise trade surplus of US $7,707m., but there was a deficit of $1,835m. on the current account of the balance of payments. The EU dominates Swedish trade: in 1992 it provided 55.6% of imports and took 55.8% of exports, while members of the European Free Trade Association (EFTA) provided 16.4% of imports and took 17.4% of exports. In 1993 the principal single source of imports was Germany (17.9% of total imports), which was also the principal market for exports (14.4%). Other major individual trading partners include the United Kingdom, Norway, the USA, Denmark and Finland. The principal exports in 1993 were machinery and transport equipment (principally road vehicles and telecommunications equipment), wood, wood pulp, chemicals and paper. The principal imports were machinery and transport equipment, mineral fuels, foodstuffs, chemicals and other manufactures.

In the financial year ending 30 June 1994 there was a budgetary deficit of some 193,000m. kronor, and for 1994/95 a budget deficit of 161,000m. kronor (some 11% of GDP) was forecast by the Government. Sweden's total public debt at the end of 1993 was US $135,641m., of which foreign debt comprised $43,565m. The annual rate of inflation averaged 5.9% in 1985–93; consumer prices increased by an average of 4.6% in 1993, and by 2.2% in 1994. The average annual rate of unemployment increased from 4.8% in 1992 to 8.2% in 1993, and fell slightly, to 8.1%, in 1994.

Sweden is a member of the Nordic Council (see p. 187) and the Nordic Council of Ministers (see p. 188). Sweden and the EC concluded a free-trade agreement in 1972, and in January 1995 Sweden became a full member of the EU (as the EC had become) and withdrew from EFTA.

From the 1930s and 1940s until 1990–91 the so-called 'Swedish Model' operated in the economy, with a consensus between the Government, employers and the trade unions. The dominating principle was the maintenance of full employment, but during the late 1980s this became increasingly difficult to achieve, owing to a relatively high level of inflation, increasing labour costs and industrial unrest, and a low rate of economic growth (exemplified in the decline of the steel and shipbuilding industries). Austerity measures were introduced in 1990 and 1991 (see Recent History), and the transformation of the economy was accelerated after the formation, in October 1991, of a non-socialist Government, which promised further deregulation, reductions in taxation and in public spending, and the privatization of state enterprises. GDP contracted during 1991–93, and in 1993 and 1994 the Bildt Government concentrated on reducing a budgetary deficit that it regarded as unsustainable. In April 1993 the Government announced plans for a five-year programme of reductions in expenditure during the period 1994–98. The new SAP Government, formed in October 1994, continued the previous Government's policy of seeking to reduce the budgetary deficit: economic measures, announced in November 1994 and January 1995, provided for increased tax revenue and reductions in expenditure of some 50,000m. kronor during 1995–98. In the 1995/96 budget, proposed in January 1995, the Government announced that the principal aims of its economic policy would be to limit the budgetary deficit to 7% of GNP by 1998 and to stabilize total public debt (equivalent to some 90% of GDP in 1994) over the same period. The economy returned to growth in 1994, and in 1995 GDP was projected to increase by 2.5%–3.5%. Industrial production and export revenue were also expected to grow.

## Social Welfare

There is a highly advanced system of social security schemes covering medical care, sickness benefit, parental benefit and retirement pensions, administered through local authorities by the National Social Insurance Board (Riksförsäkringsverket). Jobless people are assisted primarily through unemployment benefit societies, organized by the trades unions. In 1993 Swedish hospitals provided a total of 49,207 beds, equivalent to one for every 178 inhabitants. In the same year there were an estimated 26,100 physicians working in the country. The budget for 1993/94 allocated 126,566m. kronor (23% of total expenditure) to health and social welfare.

## Education

Basic education, which is compulsory, extends for nine years, starting at the age of six or seven years, and is received at the comprehensive school (grundskolan). At the end of this period, a pupil may enter the integrated upper secondary school (gymnasieskolan). In accordance with new legislation being implemented between 1992 and 1995, courses at upper secondary schools last three years, and are organized into 16 nationally defined study programmes, comprising two university entrance programmes and 14 vocational programmes. In 1989 the number of children receiving primary or secondary education was equivalent to 95% of the school-age population. Enrolment at primary schools included 100% of children in the relevant age-group. There are 34 universities, university colleges and teacher-training colleges; other institutes of higher education are administered by local government. The budget for 1993/94 allocated 38,569m. kronor (7% of total expenditure) to education.

## Public Holidays

**1995:** 1 January (New Year's Day), 6 January (Epiphany), 14 April (Good Friday), 17 April (Easter Monday), 1 May (May Day), 25 May (Ascension Day), 5 June (Whit Monday), 24 June (Midsummer Holiday), 4 November (for All Saints' Day), 25 December (Christmas Day), 26 December (Saint Stephen's Day).

**1996:** 1 January (New Year's Day), 6 January (Epiphany), 6 April (Good Friday), 8 April (Easter Monday), 1 May (May Day), 16 May (Ascension Day), 27 May (Whit Monday), 22 June (Midsummer Holiday), 2 November (for All Saints' Day), 25 December (Christmas Day), 26 December (Saint Stephen's Day).

## Weights and Measures

The metric system is in force.

# Statistical Survey

Sources (unless otherwise stated): Statistics Sweden, 100 Karlavägen, 115 81 Stockholm; tel. (8) 783-40-00; Nordic Statistical Secretariat (Copenhagen), *Yearbook of Nordic Statistics.*

## Area and Population

### AREA, POPULATION AND DENSITY

| | |
|---|---:|
| Area (sq km) | |
| Land | 410,928 |
| Inland waters | 39,036 |
| Total | 449,964* |
| Population (census results)† | |
| 1 November 1985 | 8,360,178 |
| 1 November 1990 | |
| Males | 4,241,666 |
| Females | 4,344,241 |
| Total | 8,585,907 |
| Population (official estimates at 31 December)† | |
| 1991 | 8,644,119 |
| 1992 | 8,692,013 |
| 1993 | 8,745,109 |
| Density (per sq km) at 31 December 1993 | 19.4 |

* 173,732 sq miles.  † Population is *de jure*.

### POPULATION BY COUNTY (estimates, 31 December 1993)*

| | | | | |
|---|---:|---|---:|---|
| Stockholms län | 1,686,597 | Älvsborgs län | 447,650 |
| Uppsala län | 283,103 | Skaraborgs län | 279,413 |
| Södermanlands län | 259,259 | Värmlands län | 285,377 |
| Östergötlands län | 411,444 | Örebro län | 275,687 |
| Jönköpings län | 311,041 | Västmanlands län | 261,076 |
| Kronobergs län | 179,715 | Kopparbergs län | 290,699 |
| Kalmar län | 242,612 | Gävleborgs län | 289,747 |
| Gotlands län | 57,782 | Västernorrlands län | 260,737 |
| lekinge län | 151,909 | Jämtlands län | 136,140 |
| Kristianstads län | 293,392 | Västerbottens län | 258,263 |
| Malmöhus län | 800,409 | Norrbottens län | 267,159 |
| Hallands län | 264,759 | **Total** | **8,748,763** |
| Göteborg o. Bohus län | 754,793 | | |

* Provisional.

### PRINCIPAL TOWNS (estimated population at 31 December 1993)

| | | | |
|---|---:|---|---:|
| Stockholm (capital) | 693,103 | Sundsvall | 94,583 |
| Göteborg (Gothenburg) | 437,549 | Lund | 94,251 |
| Malmö | 237,531 | Eskilstuna | 89,863 |
| Uppsala | 178,071 | Gävle | 89,604 |
| Linköping | 128,689 | Halmstad | 82,145 |
| Örebro | 124,223 | Södertälje | 81,506 |
| Västerås | 121,656 | Karlstad | 77,850 |
| Norrköping | 121,097 | Skellefteå | 75,835 |
| Jönköping | 113,606 | Huddinge | 75,550 |
| Helsingborg | 111,917 | Kristianstad | 73,011 |
| Borås | 103,399 | Växjö | 71,431 |
| Umeå | 97,228 | Luleå | 69,819 |
| | | Botkyrka | 69,245 |

# SWEDEN

## BIRTHS, MARRIAGES AND DEATHS

|  | Registered live births | | Registered marriages | | Registered deaths | |
|---|---|---|---|---|---|---|
|  | Number | Rate (per 1,000) | Number | Rate (per 1,000) | Number | Rate (per 1,000) |
| 1985 | 98,463 | 11.8 | 38,297 | 4.6 | 94,032 | 11.3 |
| 1986 | 101,950 | 12.2 | 38,906 | 4.7 | 93,295 | 11.2 |
| 1987 | 104,699 | 12.4 | 41,223 | 4.9 | 93,307 | 11.1 |
| 1988 | 112,080 | 13.3 | 44,229 | 5.2 | 96,743 | 11.5 |
| 1989 | 116,023 | 13.6 | 108,919 | 12.8 | 92,110 | 10.9 |
| 1990 | 123,938 | 14.5 | 40,477 | 4.7 | 95,093 | 11.1 |
| 1991 | 123,737 | 14.4 | 36,836 | 4.3 | 95,202 | 11.0 |
| 1992 | 122,848 | 14.2 | 37,173 | 4.3 | 94,710 | 10.9 |
| 1993 | 117,998 | 13.5 | 34,005 | 3.9 | 97,008 | 11.1 |

**Expectation of life** (years at birth, 1993): males 75.5; females 80.8.

## IMMIGRATION AND EMIGRATION

|  | 1991 | 1992 | 1993 |
|---|---|---|---|
| Immigrants | 49,731 | 45,348 | 61,872 |
| Emigrants | 24,745 | 25,726 | 29,874 |

## ECONOMICALLY ACTIVE POPULATION
('000 persons aged 16 to 64 years)

|  | 1991 | 1992 | 1993* |
|---|---|---|---|
| Agriculture, forestry and fishing | 147 | 140 | 136 |
| Mining and quarrying | 12 | 11 | 11 |
| Manufacturing | 872 | 794 | 726 |
| Electricity, gas and water supply | 37 | 36 | 35 |
| Construction | 310 | 271 | 236 |
| Trade, restaurants and hotels | 620 | 601 | 567 |
| Transport, storage and communications | 313 | 300 | 277 |
| Finance, insurance, real estate and business services | 382 | 383 | 368 |
| Community, social and personal services† | 1,675 | 1,651 | 1,602 |
| Activities not adequately defined | 5 | 6 | 6 |
| **Total employed†** | 4,373 | 4,195 | 3,964 |
| Unemployed | 133 | 233 | 356 |
| **Total labour force** | 4,506 | 4,428 | 4,320 |
| Males | 2,345 | 2,305 | 2,244 |
| Females† | 2,160 | 2,123 | 2,076 |

* Figures are based on a revised method of survey, so are not strictly comparable with those for earlier years.
† Including members of the regular armed forces, but excluding persons on compulsory military service.

## Agriculture

### PRINCIPAL CROPS
('000 metric tons; holdings of more than 2 ha of arable land)

|  | 1991 | 1992 | 1993 |
|---|---|---|---|
| Wheat* | 2,243 | 1,406 | 1,746 |
| Rye† | 160 | 136 | 230 |
| Barley | 1,940 | 1,261 | 1,671 |
| Oats | 1,430 | 807 | 1,295 |
| Potatoes | 1,030 | 1,253 | 976 |
| Rapeseed | 290 | 284 | n.a. |

* Spring and winter wheat. † Winter rye.

## LIVESTOCK ('000 head at mid-year; holdings of more than 2 ha of arable land, or with large numbers of livestock)

|  | 1991 | 1992 | 1993 |
|---|---|---|---|
| Cattle | 1,707 | 1,773 | 1,803 |
| Sheep | 418 | 447 | 470 |
| Pigs | 2,201 | 2,109 | 2,101 |
| Poultry | 11,759 | 12,008 | 11,467 |

## LIVESTOCK PRODUCTS ('000 metric tons)

|  | 1991 | 1992 | 1993 |
|---|---|---|---|
| Beef and veal | 137 | 130 | 135* |
| Horse meat | 2 | 2 | 2* |
| Mutton and lamb | 4 | 5* | 5* |
| Pig meat | 268 | 278 | 295* |
| Cows' milk | 3,200 | 3,168 | 3,349* |
| Butter | 59.6 | 58.9 | 69.0* |
| Cheese | 115 | 116 | 115* |
| Hen eggs | 107 | 110 | 113† |

* Unofficial figure. † FAO estimate.
Source: FAO, *Production Yearbook*.

## Forestry

### ROUNDWOOD REMOVALS (estimates, million cubic metres)

|  | 1990/91 | 1991/92 | 1992/93 |
|---|---|---|---|
| Sawlogs | 22.4 | 24.3 | 25.0 |
| Pulpwood | 25.1 | 24.5 | 21.1 |
| Fuel wood | 3.0 | 3.0 | 3.8 |
| Other wood | 0.9 | 0.9 | 0.9 |

## Fishing

(landings in '000 metric tons)

|  | 1991 | 1992 | 1993 |
|---|---|---|---|
| Blue whiting (Poutassou) | 18.0 | 2.1 | 37.3 |
| Atlantic cod | 46.2 | 22.4 | 18.0 |
| Haddock | 1.0 | 2.0 | 1.3 |
| Saithe | 1.5 | 3.3 | 5.0 |
| Atlantic herring | 132.2 | 195.3 | 165.2 |
| Atlantic mackerel | 4.3 | 5.0 | 3.6 |
| European sprat | 17.3 | 59.3 | 96.9 |
| Other fishes | 11.0 | 12.7 | 9.1 |
| **Total fishes** | 231.6 | 302.1 | 336.3 |
| Northern prawn | 1.9 | 2.2 | 2.3 |
| Other crustaceans and molluscs | 1.4 | 0.9 | 1.0 |
| **Total catch** | 234.9 | 305.2 | 339.6 |

# SWEDEN

## Mining

('000 metric tons, unless otherwise indicated)

|  | 1989 | 1990 | 1991 |
|---|---|---|---|
| Crude petroleum* | 3 | 3 | n.a. |
| Iron ore† | 21,578 | 19,806 | 19,320 |
| Copper ore† | 276.6 | 296.3 | 332.6 |
| Tungsten ore (metric tons)*‡ | 180§ | — | — |
| Gold (kilograms)*‡ | 5,120§ | 5,000 | n.a. |
| Silver and lead ore† | 215.4 | 206.8 | 123.1 |
| Zinc ore† | 204.0 | 199.3 | 285.4 |

* Source: UN, *Industrial Statistics Yearbook*.
† Figures refer to gross weight. The estimated metal content (in '000 metric tons) was: Iron 13,455 in 1989, 12,382 in 1990, 13,046 in 1991; Silver 0.2 in 1989, 0.2 in 1990, 0.2 in 1991; Lead 82.9 in 1989, 84.2 in 1990, 87.0 in 1991; Zinc 168.0 in 1989, 159.9 in 1990, 157.5 in 1991; Copper 69.8 in 1989, 73.5 in 1990, 80.5 in 1991. Source: UN, *Industrial Statistics Yearbook*.
‡ Figures refer to metal content.
§ Provisional figure.

## Industry

**SELECTED PRODUCTS** ('000 metric tons, unless otherwise indicated)

|  | 1989 | 1990 | 1991 |
|---|---|---|---|
| Pig and sponge iron | 2,754 | 2,845 | 2,913 |
| Crude steel | 4,692 | 4,454 | 4,252 |
| Aluminium | 97.0 | 96.3 | 96.9 |
| Copper (refined) | 94.7 | 97.3 | 96.6 |
| Lead (refined) | 46.6 | 53.2 | 64.3 |
| Wool yarn | 0.3 | 0.2 | 0.2 |
| Wool fabrics | 0.5 | 0.4 | 0.2 |
| Cotton yarn | 4.3 | 4.9 | 4.2 |
| Cotton fabrics | 6.8 | 7.1 | 5.2 |
| Mechanical wood pulp | 3,000 | 2,953 | 2,709 |
| Chemical wood pulp | 7,055 | 6,677 | 6,768 |
| Newsprint | 2,165 | 2,273 | 2,063 |
| Other printing and writing paper | 1,690 | 1,655 | 1,793 |
| Other paper and paperboard | 4,508 | 4,491 | 4,493 |
| Cement | 2,430 | 2,475 | 2,395 |
| Bricks (million) | 83 | 84 | 78 |
| Dwellings completed (number) | 50,400 | 58,400 | 66,886 |
| Electricity (million kWh) | 139,415 | 141,713 | 142,579 |

**Electricity** (million kWh): 141,038 in 1992; 140,821 in 1993.

## Finance

**CURRENCY AND EXCHANGE RATES**

**Monetary Units**
100 öre = 1 Swedish krona (plural: kronor).

**Sterling and Dollar Equivalents** (31 December 1994)
£1 sterling = 11.631 kronor;
US $1 = 7.434 kronor;
1,000 Swedish kronor = £85.98 = $134.52.

**Average Exchange Rate** (kronor per US $)
1992  5.8238
1993  7.7834
1994  7.7160

**BUDGET** (voted estimates, million kronor, year ending 30 June)

| Revenue | 1991/92 | 1992/93 | 1993/94 |
|---|---|---|---|
| Taxes on income, capital gains and profits | 57,148 | 23,882 | 38,578 |
| Statutory social security fees | 85,423 | 81,060 | 54,332 |
| Taxes on property | 23,809 | 25,999 | 24,585 |
| Taxes on goods and services | 223,923 | 186,238 | 190,435 |
| Regional discount tax | 10,932 | 7,786 | — |
| **Total revenue from taxes** | 401,325 | 324,965 | 307,930 |
| Non-tax revenue | 54,796 | 43,365 | 28,236 |
| Capital revenue | 596 | 4,033 | 1 |
| Loan repayment | 7,108 | 8,795 | 6,115 |
| Computed revenue | 897 | 826 | 1,708 |
| **Total** | 464,632 | 381,984 | 343,990 |

| Expenditure | 1991/92 | 1992/93 | 1993/94 |
|---|---|---|---|
| Royal household and residences | 53 | 60 | 65 |
| Ministry of Justice | 7,128 | 17,857 | 19,193 |
| Ministry of Foreign Affairs | 15,427 | 17,535 | 16,702 |
| Ministry of Defence | 37,803 | 37,745 | 38,903 |
| Ministry of Health and Social Affairs | 125,706 | 131,013 | 126,566 |
| Ministry of Transport and Communications | 23,329 | 18,810 | 29,132 |
| Ministry of Finance | 28,797 | 84,061 | 97,238 |
| Ministry of Education and Cultural Affairs | 62,190 | 50,912 | 54,523 |
| Ministry of Agriculture | 10,273 | 7,730 | 7,009 |
| Ministry of Labour | 35,605 | 38,590 | 47,210 |
| Ministry of Housing and Physical Planning | 32,516 | 12,002 | — |
| Ministry of Industry | 6,368 | 4,295 | 4,289 |
| Ministry of Civil Service Affairs | 15,303 | 2,250 | 2,228 |
| Ministry of Environment and Natural Resources | 1,413 | 2,080 | 2,259 |
| Parliament and its agencies | 695 | 717 | 844 |
| Interest on national debt, etc. | 60,000 | 69,000 | 96,000 |
| Unforeseen expenditure | 1 | 1 | 1 |
| Estimated other expenditure | 7,500 | −12,500 | 7,500 |
| **Total** | 470,108 | 482,160 | 549,662 |

**INTERNATIONAL RESERVES** (US $million at 31 December)

|  | 1992 | 1993 | 1994 |
|---|---|---|---|
| Gold* | 292 | 292 | 308 |
| IMF special drawing rights | 45 | 58 | 68 |
| Reserve position in IMF | 621 | 620 | 659 |
| Foreign exchange | 21,959 | 18,372 | 22,527 |
| **Total** | 22,916 | 19,342 | 23,562 |

* Valued at SDR 35 per troy ounce.
Source: IMF, *International Financial Statistics*.

**MONEY SUPPLY** (million kronor at 31 December)

|  | 1992 | 1993 | 1994 |
|---|---|---|---|
| Currency outside banks | 64,300 | 67,050 | 68,810 |

Source: IMF, *International Financial Statistics*.

**COST OF LIVING** (Consumer Price Index. Base: 1980 = 100)

|  | 1991 | 1992 | 1993 |
|---|---|---|---|
| Food | 239.1 | 226.8 | 228.4 |
| Alcoholic drinks and tobacco | 238.8 | 242.2 | 267.6 |
| Housing, fuel and light | 249.9 | 268.6 | 283.9 |
| Clothing and footwear | 147.0 | 146.8 | 144.3 |
| Furniture and household utensils | 198.5 | 200.7 | 203.7 |
| Miscellaneous | 267.0 | 273.0 | 281.3 |
| **All items** | 227.2 | 232.4 | 243.2 |

## SWEDEN

### NATIONAL ACCOUNTS (million kronor at current prices)
#### National Income and Product

|  | 1991 | 1992 | 1993 |
|---|---|---|---|
| Compensation of employees | 895,127 | 883,597 | 858,021 |
| Operating surplus | 176,542 | 208,402 | 236,883 |
| **Domestic factor incomes** | 1,071,669 | 1,091,999 | 1,094,904 |
| Consumption of fixed capital | 191,562 | 193,291 | 202,944 |
| **Gross domestic product (GDP) at factor cost** | 1,263,231 | 1,285,290 | 1,297,848 |
| Indirect taxes | 256,806 | 235,067 | 225,632 |
| *Less* Subsidies | 72,710 | 78,634 | 81,299 |
| **GDP in purchasers' values** | 1,447,327 | 1,441,723 | 1,442,181 |
| Factor income received from abroad | 58,091 | } −53,036 | −57,014 |
| *Less* Factor income paid abroad | 99,529 | | |
| **Gross national product (GNP)** | 1,405,889 | 1,388,687 | 1,385,167 |
| *Less* Consumption of fixed capital | 191,562 | 193,291 | 202,944 |
| **National income in market prices** | 1,214,327 | 1,195,396 | 1,182,223 |
| Other current transfers from abroad | 30,700 | } −15,328 | −11,743 |
| *Less* Other current transfers paid abroad | 30,700 | | |
| **National disposable income** | 1,202,860 | 1,180,068 | 1,170,480 |

#### Expenditure on the Gross Domestic Product

|  | 1991 | 1992 | 1993 |
|---|---|---|---|
| Government final consumption expenditure | 394,394 | 402,508 | 403,504 |
| Private final consumption expenditure | 771,310 | 777,324 | 792,077 |
| Changes in stocks | −21,173 | −6,657 | −11,627 |
| Gross fixed capital formation | 280,371 | 244,603 | 205,631 |
| **Total domestic expenditure** | 1,424,902 | 1,417,778 | 1,389,585 |
| Exports of goods and services | 404,184 | 401,586 | 473,087 |
| *Less* Imports of goods and services | 381,759 | 377,641 | 420,491 |
| **GDP in purchasers' values** | 1,447,327 | 1,441,723 | 1,442,181 |

#### Gross Domestic Product by Economic Activity (at factor cost)

|  | 1991 | 1992 | 1993 |
|---|---|---|---|
| Agriculture, hunting, forestry and fishing | 33,369 | 32,330 | 31,668 |
| Mining and quarrying | 3,442 | 3,463 | 3,650 |
| Manufacturing | 257,456 | 247,622 | 265,638 |
| Electricity, gas and water | 41,482 | 43,678 | 44,238 |
| Construction | 95,832 | 89,646 | 81,000 |
| Trade, restaurants and hotels | 136,722 | 135,461 | 133,684 |
| Transport, storage and communications | 93,886 | 96,086 | 95,238 |
| Financing, insurance, real estate and business services | 282,448 | 299,485 | 337,684 |
| Community, social and personal services | 54,041 | 57,256 | 58,479 |
| Non-market services* | 308,169 | 313,848 | 310,936 |
| **Sub-total** | 1,306,847 | 1,318,875 | 1,362,215 |
| *Less* Imputed bank service charge | 61,709 | 46,647 | 65,125 |
| Statistical discrepancies and unallocated net indirect taxes | 18,093 | 13,062 | 758 |
| **Total** | 1,263,231 | 1,285,290 | 1,297,848 |

* Producers of government services and other non-market services.

### BALANCE OF PAYMENTS (US $ million)

|  | 1991 | 1992 | 1993 |
|---|---|---|---|
| Merchandise exports f.o.b. | 54,543 | 55,363 | 49,346 |
| Merchandise imports c.i.f. | −48,184 | −48,641 | −41,639 |
| **Trade balance** | 6,359 | 6,722 | 7,707 |
| Exports of services | 14,032 | 15,567 | 12,043 |
| Imports of services | −16,676 | −18,414 | −12,829 |
| Other income received | 10,187 | 9,756 | 8,579 |
| Other income paid | −16,501 | −18,688 | −15,580 |
| Private unrequited transfers (net) | −395 | −439 | −164 |
| Official unrequited transfers (net) | −1,653 | −2,174 | −1,591 |
| **Current balance** | −4,646 | −7,671 | −1,835 |
| Direct investment (net) | −929 | −938 | 314 |
| Portfolio investment (net) | 6,546 | 983 | 1,131 |
| Other capital (net) | −6,968 | 8,400 | 7,461 |
| Net errors and omissions | 5,958 | 6,234 | −4,961 |
| **Overall balance** | −40 | 7,008 | 2,110 |

Source: IMF, *International Financial Statistics*.

### OFFICIAL ASSISTANCE TO DEVELOPING COUNTRIES (US $million)

|  | 1991 | 1992 | 1993 |
|---|---|---|---|
| Bilateral assistance | 1,476.5 | 1,777.0 | 1,331.5 |
| Technical assistance | 204.0 | 527.1 | 351.9 |
| Grants (incl. capital project financing) | 1,265.5 | 1,238.5 | 955.3 |
| Loans and credits | 7.1 | 11.4 | 24.3 |
| Multilateral assistance | 639.9 | 682.5 | 437.0 |
| **Total official development assistance** | 2,116.4 | 2,459.5 | 1,768.5 |

## External Trade

### PRINCIPAL COMMODITIES (distribution by SITC, million kronor)

| Imports c.i.f. | 1991 | 1992 | 1993 |
|---|---|---|---|
| **Food and live animals** | 17,590 | 17,795 | 20,879 |
| Vegetables and fruit | 6,786 | 6,505 | 7,246 |
| **Crude materials (inedible) except fuels** | 10,040 | 10,364 | 10,989 |
| **Mineral fuels, lubricants, etc.** | 26,844 | 25,360 | 30,454 |
| Petroleum, petroleum products, etc. | 23,513 | 22,183 | 26,917 |
| Crude petroleum oils, etc. | 14,665 | 13,631 | 17,025 |
| Refined petroleum products | 8,457 | 8,195 | 9,457 |
| Motor spirit (petrol), etc. | 3,771 | 3,332 | 3,220 |
| Gas oils (distillate fuels) | 2,170 | 1,465 | 1,614 |
| Residual fuel oils (incl. partly refined petroleum) | 596 | 884 | 987 |
| **Chemicals and related products** | 30,726 | 30,618 | 38,123 |
| Plastics in primary form | 5,517 | 4,990 | 5,805 |
| **Basic manufactures** | 48,515 | 46,156 | 51,779 |
| Textile yarn, fabrics, etc. | 7,156 | 6,811 | 7,340 |
| Iron and steel | 9,222 | 9,156 | 10,790 |
| Flat-rolled products | 4,284 | 4,282 | 4,356 |
| Non-ferrous metals | 5,961 | 5,316 | 6,453 |
| Other metal manufactures | 9,638 | 9,154 | 10,270 |
| **Machinery and transport equipment** | 111,622 | 104,865 | 119,513 |
| Power-generating machinery and equipment | 7,201 | 7,369 | 8,931 |
| Office machines and automatic data-processing equipment | 15,215 | 14,643 | 17,291 |
| Telecommunications and recording apparatus | 9,844 | 9,101 | 11,124 |
| Road vehicles and parts* | 23,457 | 22,530 | 22,468 |
| Passenger motor cars (excl. buses) | 10,461 | 10,572 | 9,315 |
| Parts and accessories for motor vehicles* | 8,625 | 8,628 | 9,986 |

# SWEDEN

| Imports c.i.f. — *continued* | 1991 | 1992 | 1993 |
|---|---:|---:|---:|
| Other transport equipment | 8,929 | 6,377 | 5,957 |
|   Ships, boats and floating structures | 4,529 | 2,297 | 11,908 |
| **Miscellaneous manufactured articles** | 50,946 | 50,382 | 54,552 |
|   Articles of apparel and clothing accessories (excl. footwear) | 14,845 | 15,243 | 14,986 |
| **Total** (incl. others) | 301,291 | 290,929 | 332,195 |

* Excluding tyres, engines and electrical parts.

| Exports f.o.b. | 1991 | 1992 | 1993 |
|---|---:|---:|---:|
| **Food and live animals** | 5,776 | 5,384 | 5,996 |
| **Crude materials (inedible) except fuels** | 26,330 | 26,394 | 30,740 |
|   Cork and wood | 10,824 | 11,665 | 14,829 |
|     Simply worked wood (incl. railway sleepers) | 10,379 | 11,252 | 14,356 |
|       Sawn coniferous wood over 6mm thick | 10,053 | 10,944 | 13,992 |
|   Pulp and waste paper | 9,347 | 8,512 | 8,826 |
|     Soda or sulphate wood pulp (excl. dissolving grades) | 7,377 | 6,947 | n.a. |
|   Metalliferous ores and metal scrap | 6,958 | 6,658 | 7,080 |
|      | 4,311 | 4,545 | 5,355 |
|   Iron ore and concentrates | 2,356 | 2,683 | 3,286 |
| **Chemicals and related products** | 28,308 | 29,957 | 38,587 |
| **Basic manufactures** | 85,729 | 82,908 | 94,574 |
|   Paper, paperboard and manufactures | 37,918 | 36,353 | 39,682 |
|     Paper and paperboard | 33,300 | 31,596 | 34,330 |
|       Newsprint | 6,119 | 5,470 | 6,446 |
|       Kraft paper and paperboard | 8,570 | 8,419 | 8,808 |
|   Iron and steel | 19,246 | 18,501 | 22,347 |
|     Flat-rolled products | 9,011 | n.a. | n.a. |
|   Non-ferrous metals | 5,779 | 5,372 | 6,260 |
|   Other metal manufactures | 11,185 | 10,742 | n.a. |
| **Machinery and transport equipment** | 142,451 | 139,304 | 167,928 |
|   Power-generating machinery and equipment | 9,637 | 10,109 | 11,990 |
|   Mechanical handling equipment and parts | 5,939 | 5,579 | 6,451 |
|   Office machines and automatic data-processing equipment | 8,061 | 7,020 | 6,302 |
|   Telecommunications and recording apparatus | 15,351 | 15,523 | 22,441 |
|     Electrical line telephonic and telegraphic apparatus | 1,510 | 1,507 | 1,420 |
|   Road vehicles and parts* | 43,983 | 42,753 | 48,321 |
|     Passenger motor cars (excl. buses) | 17,739 | 19,957 | 23,256 |
|     Motor vehicles for goods transport (incl. special purpose vehicles) | 12,642 | 10,371 | 9,469 |
|       Goods vehicles | 12,452 | 10,167 | 9,167 |
|     Parts and accessories for motor vehicles* | 12,124 | 11,449 | 14,411 |
|   Other transport equipment | 5,383 | 6,062 | 10,669 |
|     Ships, boats and floating structures | 1,434 | 2,480 | 6,806 |
| **Miscellaneous manufactured articles** | 30,095 | 30,073 | 34,759 |
| **Total** (incl. others) | 332,779 | 326,031 | 388,245 |

* Excluding tyres, engines and electrical parts.

## PRINCIPAL TRADING PARTNERS* (million kronor)

| Imports c.i.f. | 1991 | 1992 | 1993 |
|---|---:|---:|---:|
| Austria | 4,148 | 3,937 | 4,321 |
| Belgium-Luxembourg | 9,711 | 10,262 | 11,503 |
| Denmark | 23,455 | 22,674 | 24,343 |
| Finland | 21,130 | 17,994 | 20,614 |
| France | 14,608 | 14,946 | 17,759 |
| Germany | 56,538 | 54,084 | 59,395 |
| Italy | 12,052 | 11,153 | 11,862 |
| Japan | 15,464 | 14,667 | 16,611 |
| Netherlands | 13,042 | 12,461 | 15,432 |
| Norway | 23,013 | 19,915 | 21,439 |
| Portugal | 4,168 | 4,007 | 3,573 |
| Switzerland | 5,563 | 5,529 | 6,738 |
| USSR (former) | 3,310 | 436 | 2 |
| United Kingdom | 25,041 | 25,010 | 31,275 |
| USA | 25,620 | 25,439 | 30,224 |
| **Total** (incl. others) | 301,291 | 290,929 | 332,195 |

| Exports f.o.b. | 1991 | 1992 | 1993 |
|---|---:|---:|---:|
| Australia | 3,363 | 4,139 | 5,079 |
| Austria | 4,579 | 4,930 | 5,277 |
| Belgium-Luxembourg | 12,632 | 13,844 | 16,144 |
| Canada | 4,159 | 3,672 | 4,417 |
| Denmark | 23,489 | 23,318 | 25,766 |
| Finland | 18,905 | 16,876 | 17,769 |
| France | 18,399 | 18,865 | 20,874 |
| Germany | 50,474 | 48,749 | 55,782 |
| Italy | 15,127 | 14,350 | 14,447 |
| Japan | 6,861 | 6,634 | 9,616 |
| Netherlands | 18,136 | 18,242 | 19,702 |
| Norway | 28,084 | 27,485 | 31,627 |
| Spain | 8,188 | 7,287 | 7,330 |
| Switzerland | 7,519 | 6,682 | 7,302 |
| USSR (former) | 2,308 | 278 | 2 |
| United Kingdom | 31,002 | 31,513 | 39,805 |
| USA | 26,731 | 26,899 | 32,612 |
| **Total** (incl. others) | 332,779 | 326,031 | 388,245 |

* Imports by country of origin: exports by country of destination.

# Transport

## RAILWAYS (traffic)

| | 1991 | 1992 | 1993 |
|---|---:|---:|---:|
| Passenger-kilometres (million)* | 5,745 | 5,583 | 5,975 |
| Freight ton-kilometres (million) | 18,815 | 18,609 | 17,337 |

* Excluding ferry boat traffic.

## ROAD TRAFFIC (motor vehicles in use at 31 December)

| | 1991 | 1992 | 1993 |
|---|---:|---:|---:|
| Passenger cars | 3,619,411 | 3,588,644 | 3,566,040 |
| Buses and coaches | 14,555 | 14,249 | 14,127 |
| Goods vehicles | 309,531 | 304,988 | 301,867 |
| Motorcycles* | 102,545 | 109,450 | 113,940 |

* At 30 June.

## SHIPPING

**Merchant Fleet** (Swedish vessels totalling 100 grt and over, displacement, '000 grt at 31 December)

| | 1991 | 1992 | 1993 |
|---|---:|---:|---:|
| Tankers | 1,094 | 1,020 | 610 |
| **Total** (incl. others) | 3,203 | 3,044 | 2,339 |

### International Sea-Borne Freight Traffic

|  | 1991 | 1992 | 1993 |
|---|---|---|---|
| Vessels entered ('000 grt) | 87,319 | 88,750 | 87,228 |
| Vessels cleared ('000 grt) | 89,032 | 90,873 | 87,510 |
| Goods loaded ('000 metric tons) | 45,533 | 46,871 | 48,223 |
| Goods unloaded ('000 metric tons) | 53,534 | 55,332 | 57,808 |

### CIVIL AVIATION ('000)

|  | 1990 | 1991 | 1992 |
|---|---|---|---|
| Kilometres flown | 120,361 | 107,151 | 105,766 |
| Passenger-kilometres | 9,118,152 | 8,162,346 | 8,077,690 |
| Cargo ton-kilometres | 185,597 | 175,723 | 168,580 |
| Mail ton-kilometres | 21,724 | 16,911 | 18,548 |

### Tourism*

|  | 1991 | 1992 | 1993† |
|---|---|---|---|
| Income from visitors (million kronor) | 17,962 | 19,250 | 22,322 |

* Since the introduction of the Scandinavian Passport Control Area, there are no figures available for total arrivals in Sweden.
† Provisional figure.

### Communications Media

|  | 1991 | 1992 | 1993 |
|---|---|---|---|
| Television licences | 3,331,000 | 3,327,000 | 3,332,000 |
| Book titles produced | 11,866 | 12,813 | 12,895 |
| Newspapers | 176 | 174 | 176 |
| Circulation | 4,834,000 | 4,833,000 | 4,678,000 |

## Education

(1993/94)

|  | Institutions | Teachers* | Students |
|---|---|---|---|
| Primary: Grade 1–6 | 4,826 | 90,234 | 600,392 |
| Secondary: Grade 7–9 |  |  | 293,540 |
| Integrated upper secondary schools | 600 | 29,539 | 313,728 |
| National higher education†: Teacher training | 37 | 25,100‡ | 192,600§ |
| Universities and specialized colleges |  |  |  |
| Municipal higher education | 34 | n.a. | 17,300 |
| People's colleges‖ | 132 | 3,534 | 18,500 |
| Municipal adult education | 427 | 6,713 | 140,650 |

* Full-time and part-time teachers and teachers on leave.
† From the autumn semester 1977 those colleges and professional schools traditionally regarded as of university level were reorganized with certain other categories of state-supported institutions and restructured as common integrated schools for higher education.
‡ Including research students giving a limited number of teaching lessons.
§ Autumn term 1992.
‖ Courses of at least 15 weeks.

# Directory

## The Constitution

The Swedish Constitution is based on four fundamental laws: the Instrument of Government (originally dating from 6 June 1809), the Act of Succession (1810), the Freedom of the Press Act (1949) and the Riksdag Act. Following partial reforms in 1968 and 1969, a new Instrument of Government and a new Riksdag Act were adopted in 1973 and 1974, and the revised Constitution, summarized below, came into force on 1 January 1975.

### GOVERNMENT

The Cabinet governs Sweden and is responsible to the Riksdag (Parliament). The Constitution of 1975 formalized the position of the Monarch relative to Cabinet and Parliament, and laid down rules on the selection and resignation of the Cabinet. In 1978 the Riksdag amended the constitutional law of succession to allow the first-born royal child, whether male or female, to be heir to the throne, with effect from 1980.

As head of state, the Monarch has representative and ceremonial duties only. The Monarch does not participate in the government of the country, which is conducted rather by the Cabinet at meetings not attended by the Monarch. Decisions of government do not require the Monarch's signature, and it is the Speaker of the Riksdag, and not the Monarch, who leads the procedure resulting in the formation of a new Government. Following consultations within the Riksdag, the Speaker nominates a candidate for Prime Minister. If not more than half of the total number of members of the Riksdag vote against the proposed candidate, he or she is approved. Failing this approval, the procedure has to be repeated. After four unsuccessful attempts to secure Riksdag approval of a candidate for the premiership, a new election to the Riksdag must be held within three months. A candidate for the premiership approved by the Riksdag nominates the other members of the Government.

The Prime Minister can be dismissed at his or her own request, by the Speaker of the Riksdag, or in the event of a vote of 'no confidence' in the Riksdag. Other ministers can be dismissed at their own request, by the Prime Minister or by a vote of 'no confidence'. If the Prime Minister should resign or die, all of the ministers in the Cabinet must resign. A Cabinet which is due to resign shall, however, remain in power until a new Prime Minister has been appointed.

A demand for a vote of 'no confidence' will be considered only if it is supported by 10% of the members of the Riksdag. A vote of 'no confidence' requires the support of more than half of the Riksdag members. If the Riksdag decides upon a vote of 'no confidence' the Cabinet can avoid resigning, if it calls for an extra general election within one week. The Riksdag may continue its business, or be summoned to convene, even after a decision has been made to hold new elections. A Riksdag session may, however, be terminated by a special decision of the Government. Existing terms of office do not expire until the new terms of office have begun.

### LEGISLATURE

The Riksdag is the prime representative of the Swedish people. It enacts laws, decides the amount and use of taxation and examines the Government's actions. The Riksdag at present contains 349 members, elected for four years.

In accordance with tradition, the work of the Swedish Riksdag is, to a great extent, carried on in a non-partisan atmosphere. This is largely the result of the thorough attention given to all questions by numerous standing committees elected by the Riksdag on a basis of proportional representation. Besides the Utrikesnämnden (Advisory Council on Foreign Affairs) and Special Committees, every Riksdag appoints from within the assembly a Constitution Committee, a Finance Committee, a Taxation Committee and at least 12 other committees.

The Constitution Committee has to examine the minutes of the Cabinet and deal with or initiate proposals concerning alterations of the fundamental laws and of laws regulating local government.

### ELECTORAL SYSTEM

In order that local and national government terms of office should coincide, the Constitution calls for local and general elections to be held on the same day. In both cases the term of office for the elected candidate is four years. Proportional representation was introduced in Sweden between the years 1906 and 1909, universal and equal suffrage by 1921. Under the provisions of legislation passed in 1976, all aliens resident in the country for three years are permitted to vote in local elections. The minimum voting age is 18 years. In allocating the 349 seats in the Riksdag, the seats are divided into two groups. The first group of 310 'constituency seats' is distributed among the constituencies according to the number of eligible voters, and within each constituency among the parties. The remaining 39 seats are distributed as 'adjustment seats'. First, it is calculated how many seats each party would have obtained if the whole country had been treated as a single constituency and if the distribution of seats had taken place according to a modified Lague method. From this figure is subtracted the number of 'constituency seats' received, the result being the number of 'compensatory seats' to be allocated to each party. These seats are filled by candidates nominated in the constituencies. There is a check to the emergence of small parties in that only parties which have received at least 4% of the total votes cast are entitled to a seat. However, any party which receives 12% or more of the votes in any constituency will be allowed to compete for a permanent seat in that constituency.

## The Government

### HEAD OF STATE

King Carl XVI Gustaf (succeeded to the throne 15 September 1973).

### THE CABINET
(June 1995)

**Prime Minister:** Ingvar Carlsson.
**Deputy Prime Minister and Minister for Equality Issues:** Mona Sahlin.
**Minister of Justice:** Laila Freivalds.
**Minister for Foreign Affairs:** Lena Hjelm-Wallén.
**Minister of Defence:** Thage G. Petersson.
**Minister of Health and Social Affairs:** Ingela Thalén.
**Minister of Transport and Communications:** Ines Uusmann.
**Minister of Finance:** Göran Persson.
**Minister of Education:** Carl Tham.
**Minister of Agriculture:** Margareta Winberg.
**Minister of Labour:** Anders Sundström.
**Minister of Industry and Commerce:** Sten Heckscher.
**Minister of Public Administration:** Marita Ulvskog.
**Minister of the Environment and Physical Planning:** Anna Lindh.
**Minister for Cultural Affairs:** Margot Wallström.
**Minister with special responsibility for Co-ordination:** Jan Nygren.
**Minister for International Development Co-operation:** Pierre Schori.
**Minister for Foreign Trade and European Union Affairs:** Mats Hellström.
**Deputy Minister of Health and Social Security:** Anna Hedborg.
**Minister for Schools and Adult Education:** Ylva Johansson.
**Minister with special responsibility for Refugee and Immigration Policy:** Leif Blomberg.
**Minister with special responsibility for Housing and Energy Policy:** Jorgen Andersson.

### MINISTRIES

**Cabinet Office:** Rosenbad 4, 103 33 Stockholm; tel. (8) 405-10-00; fax (8) 723-11-71.
**Ministry of Agriculture:** Drottninggt. 21, 103 33 Stockholm; tel. (8) 763-10-00; telex 15681; fax (8) 20-64-96.
**Ministry of Culture:** Jakobsgt. 26, 103 33 Stockholm; tel. (8) 763-10-00; telex 11461; fax (8) 21-68-13.
**Ministry of Defence:** Jakobsgt. 9, 103 33 Stockholm; tel. (8) 763-10-00; telex 17946; fax (8) 723-11-89.
**Ministry of Education:** Drottninggt. 16, 103 33 Stockholm; tel. (8) 763-10-00; telex 13284; fax (8) 723-11-92.
**Ministry of the Environment:** Tegelbacken 2, 103 33 Stockholm; tel. (8) 763-10-00; telex 15499; fax (8) 24-16-29.
**Ministry of Finance:** Drottninggt. 21, 103 33 Stockholm; tel. (8) 763-10-00; telex 11741; fax (8) 21-73-86.
**Ministry for Foreign Affairs:** Gustav Adolfstorg 1, POB 16121, 103 23 Stockholm; tel. (8) 786-60-00; telex 10590; fax (8) 723-11-76.
**Ministry of Health and Social Affairs:** Jakobsgt. 26, 103 33 Stockholm; tel. (8) 763-10-00; telex 11461; fax (8) 723-11-91.
**Ministry of Industry and Commerce:** Fredsgt. 8, 103 33 Stockholm; tel. (8) 763-10-00; telex 14180; fax (8) 411-36-16.
**Ministry of Justice:** Rosenbad 4, 103 33 Stockholm; tel. (8) 763-10-00; telex 17820; fax (8) 20-27-34.
**Ministry of Labour:** Drottninggt. 21, 103 33 Stockholm; tel. (8) 763-10-00; telex 12533; fax (8) 20-73-69.
**Ministry of Public Administration:** Fredsgt. 8, 103 33 Stockholm; tel. (8) 763-10-00; fax (8) 723-11-93.
**Ministry of Transport and Communications:** Jakobsgt. 26, 103 33 Stockholm; tel. (8) 763-10-00; telex 17328; fax (8) 11-89-43.

## Legislature

### RIKSDAG

**Speaker** (Talman): Ingegerd Troedsson.

**General Election, 18 September 1994**

|  | % of votes | Seats |
|---|---|---|
| Social Democratic Labour Party (SAP) | 45.3 | 161 |
| Moderate Party (MS) | 22.4 | 80 |
| Centre Party (CP) | 7.7 | 27 |
| Liberal Party (FP) | 7.2 | 26 |
| Left Party (VP) | 6.2 | 22 |
| Green Party (MpG) | 5.0 | 18 |
| Christian Democratic Party (KdS) | 4.1 | 15 |
| New Democracy (ND) | 1.2 | — |
| Others | 1.1 | — |
| **Total** | 100.0 | 349 |

## Political Organizations

**Centerpartiets Riksorganisation** (CP—Centre Party): Bergsgt. 7B, POB 22107, 104 22 Stockholm; tel. (8) 617-38-00; fax (8) 652-64-40; f. 1910 as an agrarian party; aims at social, environmental and progressive development and decentralization; Chair. Olof Johansson; Sec.-Gen. Åke Pettersson; 230,000 mems.

**Folkpartiet liberalerna** (FP—Liberal Party): POB 6508, 113 83 Stockholm; tel. (8) 674-16-00; telex 19545; fax (8) 673-25-91; f. 1902; advocates market-oriented economy; Chair. Maria Leissner; Sec.-Gen. Peter Örn.

**Kristdemokratiska Samhällspartiet** (KdS—Christian Democratic Party): Målargt. 7, POB 451, 101 29 Stockholm; tel. (8) 24-38-25; fax (8) 21-97-51; f. 1964 to promote emphasis on Christian values in political life; Chair. Alf Svensson; Sec.-Gen. Sven Persson; 29,000 mems.

**Miljöpartiet de Gröna** (MpG—Green Party): POB 16069, 103 22 Stockholm; tel. (8) 20-80-50; fax (8) 20-15-77; f. 1981; Co-Leaders Marianne Samuelsson, Birger Schlaug; approx. 8,000 mems.

**Moderata Samlingspartiet** (MS—Moderate Party): POB 1243, 111 82 Stockholm; tel. (8) 676-80-00; fax (8) 21-61-23; f. 1904; advocates liberal-conservative market-oriented economy; Chair. Carl Bildt; Sec. Gunnar Hökmark; 140,000 mems.

**Ny demokrati** (ND—New Democracy): Stockholm; tel. (8) 786-57-00; fax (8) 20-40-77; f. 1991; right-wing populist; Chair. Vivianne Franzén.

**Sveriges Socialdemokratiska Arbetareparti** (SAP—Swedish Social Democratic Labour Party): Sveavägen 68, 105 60 Stockholm; tel. (8) 700-26-00; fax (8) 21-93-31; f. 1889; egalitarian; Chair. Ingvar Carlsson; Sec.-Gen. Leif Linde; 259,800 mems.

SWEDEN — *Directory*

**Vänsterpartiet** (VP—Left Party): Kungsgt. 84, POB 12660, 112 93 Stockholm; tel. (8) 654-08-20; fax (8) 653-23-85; f. 1917 as Left Social Democratic Party of Sweden; affiliated to the Communists International 1919; renamed the Communist Party in 1921; renamed Left Party—Communists in 1967; renamed Left Party in 1990; policies based on the principles of Marxism, feminism and other theories; Chair. GUDRUN SCHYMAN; Sec. LARS OHLY.

## Diplomatic Representation

### EMBASSIES IN SWEDEN

**Albania:** Capellavägen 7, 181 32 Lidingö; tel. (8) 731-09-20; fax (8) 767-65-57; Ambassador: IDULZ ELMAZ KOUJARI.

**Algeria:** Danderydsgt. 3–5, POB 26027, 100 41 Stockholm; tel. (8) 679-91-30; telex 14734; fax (8) 611-49-57; Ambassador: MOURAD BENCHEIKH.

**Angola:** Hagagt. 1, POB 3199, 103 64 Stockholm; tel. (8) 24-28-90; fax (8) 34-31-27; Ambassador: JOSEFINA DIAKITÉ PITRA.

**Argentina:** Grevgt. 5, POB 14039, 104 40 Stockholm; tel. (8) 663-19-65; fax (8) 661-00-09; Ambassador: ATTILIO MOLTENI.

**Australia:** Sergelstorg 12, POB 7003, 103 86 Stockholm; tel. (8) 613-29-00; fax (8) 24-74-14; Ambassador: Dr ROBERT STUART MERRILLEES.

**Austria:** Kommendörsgt. 35, 114 58 Stockholm; tel. (8) 23-34-90; telex 10130; fax (8) 662-69-28; Ambassador: Dr FRANZ PARAK.

**Bangladesh:** Sturegt 6, 114 35 Stockholm; tel. (8) 679-95-55; fax (8) 611-98-17; Ambassador: GYASUDDIN A. CHOWDHURY.

**Belgium:** Villagt. 13A, POB 26114, 100 41 Stockholm; tel. (8) 411-89-58; telex 17405; fax (8) 10-64-43; Ambassador: CARLOS DE WEVER.

**Bolivia:** Södra Kungsvägen 60, 181 32 Lidingö, Stockholm; tel. (8) 731-58-30; fax (8) 767-63-11; Ambassador: (vacant).

**Bosnia and Herzegovina:** Birger Jarlsgt. 55, POB 7102, 111 45 Stockholm; tel. (8) 24-83-60; fax (8) 24-98-30; Ambassador: IZET SERDAREVIĆ.

**Botswana:** Tyrgt. 11, POB 26024, 100 41 Stockholm; tel. (8) 723-00-35; fax (8) 723-00-87; Ambassador: SEKGOMA T. KHAMA.

**Brazil:** Sturegt. 11, 114 36 Stockholm; tel. (8) 23-40-10; fax (8) 23-40-18; Ambassador: LUIZ FELIPE DE TEIXEIRA SOARES.

**Bulgaria:** Karlavägen 29, 114 31 Stockholm; tel. (8) 723-09-38; fax (8) 21-45-03; Ambassador: ANTOINETTE PRIMATAROVA-MILTCHEVA.

**Burundi:** 2nd Floor, Skeppsbron 8, 111 30 Stockholm; tel. (8) 21-96-95; fax (8) 21-53-35; Chargé d'affaires: JEAN RIGI.

**Canada:** 7th Floor, Tegelbacken 4, POB 16129, 103 23 Stockholm; tel. (8) 453-30-00; fax (8) 453-30; Ambassador: MICHAEL PHILLIPS.

**Chile:** 3rd Floor, Sturegt. 8, 114 35 Stockholm; tel. (8) 679-82-80; fax (8) 679-85-40; Ambassador: HUGO CUBILLOS.

**China, People's Republic:** Lidovägen 8, 115 25 Stockholm; tel. (8) 667-97-04; fax (8) 662-59-55; Ambassador: YANG GUIRONG.

**Colombia:** Östermalmsgt. 46, POB 5627, 114 86 Stockholm; tel. (8) 21-84-89; telex 16782; fax (8) 21-84-90; Ambassador: CLEMENCIA FORERO UCROS.

**Croatia:** 1st Floor, Birger Jarlsgt. 13, 111 45 Stockholm; tel. (8) 678-42-20; fax (8) 678-83-20; Ambassador: DAMIR PERINČIĆ.

**Cuba:** Karlavägen 49, 114 49 Stockholm; tel. (8) 663-08-50; telex 11910; fax (8) 661-14-18; Ambassador: NARCISO MARTÍN MORA DÍAZ.

**Cyprus:** Birger Jarlsgt. 37, POB 7649, 103 94 Stockholm; tel. (8) 24-50-08; fax (8) 24-45-18.

**Czech Republic:** Floragt. 13, POB 26156, 100 41 Stockholm; tel. (8) 24-81-53; fax (8) 411-28-40; Ambassador: VÁCLAV FRÝBERT.

**Denmark:** Jakobs Torg 1, POB 1638, 111 86 Stockholm; tel. (8) 23-18-60; telex 19625; fax (8) 791-72-20; Ambassador: G. ORTMANN.

**Dominican Republic:** 4th Floor, Sibyllegt. 13, POB 5584, 114 85 Stockholm; tel. (8) 667-46-11; Chargé d'affaires a.i.: ABIGAIL MEJÍA.

**Ecuador:** Engelbrektsgt. 13, POB 26095, 100 41 Stockholm; tel. (8) 679-60-43; telex 15141; fax (8) 611-55-93; Ambassador: HERNÁN GUARDERAS.

**Egypt:** Strandvägen 35, POB 14230, 104 40 Stockholm; tel. (8) 662-96-03; telex 17325; fax (8) 661-26-64; Ambassador: HAMDY NADA.

**Eritrea:** 1st Floor, Östermalmsgt. 34, POB 26068, 100 41 Stockholm; tel. (8) 20-14-70; fax (8) 20-66-06; Ambassador: TSEGGAI TESFAZION.

**Estonia:** 1st Floor, Storgt. 38, POB 14069, 104 40 Stockholm; tel. (8) 665-65-50; fax 662-99-80; Ambassador: MARGUS LAIDRE.

**Ethiopia:** Erik Dahlbergsallén 15, POB 10148, 100 55 Stockholm; tel. (8) 665-60-30; fax (8) 660-81-77; Ambassador: TEWOLDE GEBRU.

**Finland:** 6th Floor, Jakobsgt. 6, POB 7423, 103 91 Stockholm; tel. (8) 676-67-00; fax (8) 20-74-97; Ambassador: MATTI KALERVO KAHILUOTO.

**France:** Narvavägen 28, POB 10241, 100 55 Stockholm; tel. (8) 663-02-70; telex 10864; fax (8) 660-62-90; Ambassador: JOËLLE TIMSIT.

**Germany:** Skarpögt. 9, POB 27832, 115 93 Stockholm; tel. (8) 670-15-00; telex 19330; fax (8) 661-52-94; Ambassador: HARALD HOFMANN.

**Greece:** Riddargt. 60, 114 57 Stockholm; tel. (8) 660-88-60; fax (8) 660-54-70; Ambassador: EMMANUEL KALPADAKIS.

**Guatemala:** Wittstocksgt. 30, 115 27 Stockholm; tel. (8) 660-52-29; fax (8) 660-42-29; Ambassador: LARS H. PIRA.

**Hungary:** Strandvägen 74, POB 27162, 102 52 Stockholm; tel. (8) 661-67-62; fax (8) 660-29-59; Ambassador: LÁSZLÓ DESEÖ.

**Iceland:** Kommendörsgt. 35, 114 58 Stockholm; tel. (8) 662-40-16; telex 11921; fax (8) 660-74-23; Ambassador: SIGRÍÐUR ÁSDÍS SNÆVARR.

**India:** Adolf Fredriks Kyrkogt. 12, POB 1340, 111 83 Stockholm; tel. (8) 10-70-08; fax (8) 24-85-05; Ambassador: PARAMJIT SINGH SAHAI.

**Indonesia:** Singelbacken 12, 115 21 Stockholm; tel. (8) 663-54-70; fax (8) 660-98-32; Ambassador: H. I. JASIN.

**Iran:** Västra Yttringe Gård, Elfviksvägen, POB 6031, 181 06 Lidingö; tel. (8) 765-08-19; fax (8) 765-31-19; Ambassador: HOSSEIN PANAHIAZAR.

**Iraq:** Baldersgt. 6A, POB 26031, 100 41 Stockholm; tel. (8) 411-75-02; fax (8) 796-83-66; Chargé d'affaires a.i.: ABDUL RAZZAK M. SALIH.

**Ireland:** Östermalmsgt. 97, POB 10326, 100 55 Stockholm; tel. (8) 661-80-05; telex 11821; fax (8) 660-13-53; Ambassador: PAUL D. DEMPSEY.

**Israel:** Torstenssonsgt. 4, POB 14006, 104 40 Stockholm; tel. (8) 663-04-35; fax (8) 662-53-01; Ambassador: GIDEON BEN-AMI.

**Italy:** Oakhill, Djurgården, 115 21 Stockholm; tel. (8) 24-58-05; telex 10453; fax (8) 660-05-05; Ambassador: ONOFRIO SOLARI BOZZI.

**Japan:** Gärdesgt. 10, 115 27 Stockholm; tel. (8) 663-04-40; fax (8) 661-88-20; Ambassador: MATANO KAGECHIKA.

**Kenya:** 2nd Floor, Birger Jarlsgt. 37, POB 7694, 103 95 Stockholm; tel. (8) 21-83-00; fax (8) 20-92-61; Ambassador: AHMED IDHA SALIM.

**Korea, Democratic People's Republic:** Norra Kungsvägen 39, 181 31 Lidingö; tel. and fax (8) 767-38-36; telex 17193; Ambassador: RYOM KYONG SIK.

**Korea, Republic:** Laboratoriegt. 10, POB 27237, 115 27 Stockholm; tel. (8) 660-03-30; fax (8) 660-28-18; Ambassador: EUI-SOK CHAI.

**Kuwait:** POB 16421, 103 27 Stockholm; tel. (8) 450-99-80; fax (8) 450-99-55.

**Laos:** Hornsgt. 82B, POB 17113, 104 62 Stockholm; tel. (8) 668-51-22; fax (8) 669-21-76; Ambassador: THONESAY BODHISANE.

**Latvia:** Storgt. 38, POB 14085, 104 40 Stockholm; tel. (8) 667-34-00; fax (8) 661-93-55; Ambassador: IMANTS GROSS.

**Lebanon:** Kommendörsgt. 35, POB 10165, 100 55 Stockholm; tel. (8) 665-19-65; fax (8) 662-68-24; Ambassador: FOUAD SELIM AOUN.

**Libya** (People's Bureau): Valhallavägen 74, POB 10133, 100 55 Stockholm; tel. (8) 14-34-35; fax (8) 10-43-80; Ambassador: ABUGELA MUFTAH EL-HWEG.

**Lithuania:** Strandvägen 53, 115 23 Stockholm; tel. (8) 667-11-34; fax (8) 667-56-11; Ambassador: ROMUALDAS KALONAITIS.

**Macedonia, former Yugoslav republic:** Riddargt. 35, 114 57 Stockholm; tel. (8) 661-18-30; fax (8) 661-03-25.

**Malaysia:** Karlavägen 37, POB 26053, 100 41 Stockholm; tel. (8) 791-76-90; telex 13416; fax (8) 791-87-61; Ambassador: CHOO SIEW KIOH.

**Mexico:** Grevgt. 3, POB 14058, 104 40 Stockholm; tel. (8) 663-51-70; telex 10464; fax (8) 663-24-20; Ambassador: LORENZO VIGNAL.

**Morocco:** Kungsholmstorg 16, 112 21 Stockholm; tel. (8) 654-43-88; fax (8) 651-97-96; Ambassador: SAAD BADDOU.

**Mozambique:** Sturegt. 46, POB 5801, 102 48 Stockholm; tel. (8) 666-03-50; telex 10906; fax (8) 663-67-29; Ambassador: RUI BATAZAR DOS SANTOS ALVES.

**Namibia:** Luntmakargt. 86–88, POB 26042, 100 41 Stockholm; tel. (8) 612-77-88; fax (8) 612-66-55; Ambassador: TONATA L. ITENGE-EMVULA.

**Netherlands:** Götgt. 16A, POB 15048, 104 65 Stockholm; tel. (8) 24-71-80; telex 10541; fax (8) 702-96-83; Ambassador: Count LAMBERTUS DE MARCHANT ET D'ANSEMBOURG.

**Nicaragua:** 6th Floor, Sandhamnsgt. 40, 115 28 Stockholm; tel. (8) 667-18-57; fax (8) 662-41-60; Ambassador: PATRICIA DELGADO.

**Nigeria:** Tyrgt. 8, POB 628, 101 32 Stockholm; tel. (8) 24-63-90; fax (8) 24-63-98; Chargé d'affaires a.i.: JOSEPH OKEKE.

# SWEDEN

**Norway:** Strandvägen 113, POB 27829, 115 93 Stockholm; tel. (8) 665-63-40; telex 10112; fax (8) 782-98-99; Ambassador: KETIL BØRDE.

**Pakistan:** 14th Floor, Sergels Torg 12, 111 57 Stockholm; tel. (8) 20-33-00; fax (8) 24-92-33; Ambassador: ARSHAD SAMI KHAN.

**Panama:** Östermalmsgt. 59, POB 26146, 100 41 Stockholm; tel. (8) 662-65-35; fax (8) 663-04-07; Ambassador: RENÉ ORLANDO SINCLAIR ARAUZ.

**Peru:** Brunnsgt. 21B, 111 38 Stockholm; tel. (8) 411-00-19; telex 16855; fax (8) 20-55-92; Ambassador: JAIME STIGLICH.

**Philippines:** Skeppsbron 20, POB 2219, 103 15 Stockholm; tel. (8) 23-56-65; telex 16585; fax (8) 14-07-14; Ambassador: ROSARIO G. MANALO.

**Poland:** Karlavägen 35, 114 31 Stockholm; tel. (8) 411-41-32; telex 19847; fax (8) 10-10-69; Ambassador: BARBARA TUGE-ERECIŃSKA.

**Portugal:** 2nd Floor, Narvavägen 32, POB 27004, 102 51 Stockholm; tel. (8) 662-60-28; telex 10118; fax (8) 662-53-29; Ambassador: VASCO VALENTE.

**Romania:** Östermalmsgt. 36, POB 26043, 104 41 Stockholm; tel. (8) 10-86-03; telex 10166; fax (8) 10-28-52; Ambassador: NICOLAE I. IONESCU.

**Russia:** Gjörwellsgt. 31, 112 60 Stockholm; tel. (8) 13-04-41; fax (8) 618-27-03; Ambassador: OLEG GRINEVSKI.

**Saudi Arabia:** Sköldungagt. 5, POB 26073, 100 41 Stockholm; tel. (8) 23-88-00; telex 14330; fax (8) 796-99-56; Chargé d'affaires a.i.: MARWAN BASHIR AL-ROUME.

**Slovakia:** 3rd Floor, Arsenalsgt. 2, POB 7183, 103 88 Stockholm; tel. (8) 611-90-05; fax (8) 611-90-02; Ambassador: KLÁRA NOVOTNÁ.

**Slovenia:** 3rd Floor, Klarabergsgt. 33, 111 21 Stockholm; tel. (8) 21-89-21; fax (8) 723-01-75; Ambassador: IVO VAJGL.

**South Africa:** Linnégt. 76, 115 23 Stockholm; tel. (8) 24-39-50; fax (8) 660-71-36; Ambassador: IGNATIUS P. DE SWARDT.

**Spain:** Djurgårdsvägen 21, 115 21 Stockholm; tel. (8) 667-94-30; telex 17160; fax (8) 663-79-65; Ambassador: CAMILO BARCIA GARCÍA-VILLAMIL.

**Sri Lanka:** Strandvägen 39, POB 14053, 104 40 Stockholm; tel. (8) 663-65-23; telex 12338; fax (8) 660-00-89; Ambassador: ALFRED K. DAVID.

**Sudan:** Drottninggt. 81A, POB 45081, 104 30 Stockholm; tel. (8) 20-80-41; fax (8) 20-16-21; Ambassador: MOHAMED ZEIN EL-ABDEEN.

**Switzerland:** Birger Jarlsgt. 64, POB 26143, 100 41 Stockholm; tel. (8) 676-79-00; fax (8) 21-51-04; Ambassador: PAUL ANDRÉ RAMSEYER.

**Tanzania:** Oxtorgsgt. 2–4, POB 7255, 103 89 Stockholm; tel. (8) 24-48-70; telex 10514; fax (8) 10-98-15; Ambassador: WILSON KAMUHABWA TIBAIJUKA.

**Thailand:** Floragt. 3, POB 26220, 100 40 Stockholm; tel. (8) 791-73-40; telex 13769; fax (8) 791-73-51; Ambassador: SUCHINDA YONGSUNTHON.

**Tunisia:** Narvavägen 32, 115 22 Stockholm; tel. (8) 663-53-70; fax (8) 662-19-75; Ambassador: ABDELMAJID BAOUAB.

**Turkey:** Strandvägen 78, 115 27 Stockholm; tel. (8) 23-08-40; telex 17439; fax (8) 663-55-14; Ambassador: SOLMAZ UNAYDIN.

**Ukraine:** Markvardsgt. 5, 113 53 Stockholm; tel. (8) 612-75-66; fax (8) 15-79-42.

**United Kingdom:** Skarpögt. 6-8, POB 27819, 115 93 Stockholm; tel. (8) 671-90-00; telex 19340; fax (8) 662-99-89; Ambassador: ROGER BONE.

**USA:** Strandvägen 101, 115 89 Stockholm; tel. (8) 783-53-00; fax (8) 661-19-64; Ambassador: THOMAS L. SIEBERT.

**Uruguay:** Kommendörsgt. 35, POB 10114, 100 55 Stockholm; tel. (8) 660-31-96; telex 15361; fax (8) 665-31-66; Ambassador: RODOLFO OLAVARRÍA.

**Venezuela:** Engelbrektsgt. 35B, POB 26012, 100 41 Stockholm; tel. (8) 411-09-96; telex 12339; fax (8) 21-31-00; Ambassador: NELSON VALERA PARRA.

**Viet Nam:** Örby Slottsväg 26, 125 71 Älvsjö; tel. (8) 86-12-18; fax (8) 99-57-13; Ambassador: PHAM NGAC.

**Zambia:** Engelbrektsgt. 7, POB 26013, 100 41 Stockholm; tel. (8) 679-90-40; fax (8) 679-68-50; Ambassador: CLEMENT MUMBA MWANANSHIKU.

**Zimbabwe:** Kungsgt. 62, POB 7319, 103 90 Stockholm; tel. (8) 24-66-95; telex 15145; fax (8) 21-91-32; Ambassador: AMINA HUGHES.

# Judicial System

The judiciary and the executive are separate. Judges are appointed by the Government. A judge can be removed by an authority other than a court, but may, in such an event, request a judicial trial of the decision.

To supervise the courts in administrative matters, there is a central authority, the Domstolsverket, in Jönköping. This authority has no control over the judicial process, in which the court is independent even of the legislature and Government.

There are state officers who exercise control over the judiciary as well as the administrative authorities. The Justitiekansler (Chancellor of Justice or Attorney-General) and the four Justitieombudsmän supervise the courts and the general administration including the armed forces. The Justitiekansler performs his functions on behalf of the Government. The Justitieombudsmän are appointed by and act on behalf of the legislature.

**Justitiekansler:** J. HIRSCHFELDT.

## SUPREME COURT

The Supreme Court in Stockholm, consisting of 22 members, is the Court of Highest Instance. The Court works in three chambers, each of which is duly constituted of five members. Certain cases are decided by full session of the Court. There are also special divisions with three members (or, in simple cases, one member) which decide whether the Court is to consider a case.

**Chairman of the Supreme Court:** A. KNUTSSON.

## APPELLATE COURTS

The Court of Appeal, the Court of Second Instance, consists of a president, judges of appeal and associate judges of appeal. The work is apportioned between various divisions, each of which has five or six members. In criminal cases the bench consists of three professional judges and two lay assessors; in petty and civil cases there are three professional judges only. There are six Courts of Appeal.

**President of the Court of Appeal (Stockholm):** B. BLOM.

**President of the Court of Appeal (Jönköping):** C. A. PETRI.

**President of the Court of Appeal (Malmö):** B. BROOMÉ.

**President of the Court of Appeal (Göteborg):** O. LINDH.

**President of the Court of Appeal (Sundsvall):** H. WINBERG.

**President of the Court of Appeal (Umeå):** C.-I. SKARSTEDT.

## DISTRICT COURTS

The District Court acts as a Court of First Instance in both civil and criminal cases. There are about 100 District Courts. In criminal cases the court is composed of a presiding professional judge and three or, in serious cases, five lay assessors; in petty cases the court consists of the professional judge only. In civil cases the court is ordinarily composed of three professional judges; however, preparatory sessions are conducted by one professional judge. In family law cases, the court is composed of a professional judge and three lay assessors. The lay assessors are elected for a period of four years (during which they are on duty for about 10 days a year). They act as members of the bench and should consequently be distinguished from the jurors of other countries. In certain types of case technical experts may sit alongside the judges.

## ADMINISTRATIVE COURTS

In each of the 24 administrative districts of the country there is a County Administrative Court. This Court handles appeal cases concerning the assessment of social security and welfare. The bench ordinarily consists of a professional judge and three lay assessors, although in simple cases a professional judge may preside alone.

Appeals against decisions by the County Administrative Courts may be made to Administrative Courts of Appeal consisting of a president, judges of appeal and associate judges of appeal. The courts work in divisions, each of which normally has six members. The bench consists of at least three and not more than four judges. In certain cases there are, however, three professional judges and two lay assessors. There are four Administrative Courts of Appeal.

The Supreme Administrative Court of Sweden in Stockholm, consisting of 19 members, is the Court of Highest Instance in Administrative cases. The composition of the Court is governed by rules very similar to those that apply to the Supreme Court.

**Chairman of the Supreme Administrative Court:** G. WAHLGREN.

**President of the Administrative Court of Appeal (Stockholm):** R. LAURÉN.

**President of the Administrative Court of Appeal (Göteborg):** N. WENTZ.

**President of the Administrative Court of Appeal (Sundsvall):** B. ORRHEDE.

**President of the Administrative Court of Appeal (Jönköping):** J. FRANCKE.

SWEDEN                                                                                                    *Directory*

## SPECIAL COURTS

Special courts exist for certain categories of cases, e.g. fastighetsdomstolar (real estate courts) for cases concerning real estate.

## OMBUDSMEN

The post of Justitieombudsman was created in 1800 to supervise the manner in which judges, government officials and other civil servants observe the laws, and to prosecute those who act illegally, misuse their position or neglect their duties. The Ombudsman is allowed access to all documents and information and has the right to be present at the considerations of the courts and other authorities. Government ministers in Sweden are not subject to supervision by the Ombudsman. The term of office is four years.
**Ombudsmen:** CLAES EKLUNDH, GUNNEL NORELL SÖDERBLOM, JAN PENNLÖV, STINA WAHLSTRÖM.

# Religion

## CHRISTIANITY

**Sveriges Kristna Råd** (Christian Council of Sweden): Lästmakargt. 18, POB 1764, 111 87 Stockholm; tel. (8) 453-68-00; fax (8) 453-68-29; f. 1993 (replacing the Swedish Ecumenical Council); Gen. Sec. THORD-OVE THORDSON.

### Church of Sweden

**Svenska Kyrkan** (Church of Sweden): Of the Evangelical Lutheran faith. The Riksdag (Parliament) is responsible for legislation governing the Church, although many decision-making powers have been delegated to the Church's annual General Synod. The monarch must be a member of the Church. About 88% of the population are mems; 13 dioceses, 2,565 parishes, 3,249 active clergy (including missionaries in the mission fields); the Archbishop of Uppsala is head of the Church.
**Archbishop of Uppsala:** GUNNAR WEMAN, 751 70 Uppsala; tel. (18) 16-95-00; fax (18) 16-96-25.
**Evangeliska Fosterlands-Stiftelsen** (Swedish Evangelical Mission): von Bahrs väg 3, POB 23045, 750 23 Uppsala; tel. (18) 16-98-00; telex 76265; fax (18) 25-86-75; f. 1856; an independent mission organization within the Church of Sweden; about 23,000 mems; Chair. SVEN GUNNARSSON; Mission Dir BERTIL JOHANSSON.

### Other Protestant Churches

**Baptist Union of Sweden:** Ekensbergsvägen 128, 172 30 Sundbyberg; tel. (8) 629-85-00; fax (8) 29-31-73; 312 churches, 19,417 mems; Pres. INGVAR PAULSSON; Gen. Sec. Rev. BIRGIT KARLSSON.
**Eesti Evangeeliumi Luteri Usu Kirik** (Estonian Evangelical Lutheran Church): POB 45074, 104 30 Stockholm 45; tel. (8) 20-69-78; 15,200 mems; Archbishop KONRAD VEEM; Gen. Sec. ESMO RIDALA.
**Metodistkyrkan i Sverige** (United Methodist Church): Radmansgt. 69, 113 60 Stockholm; tel. (8) 31-55-70; fax (8) 31-55-79; f. 1868; 3,665 mems; Bishop HANS VÄXBY; Pres. of Conference Board ARNE ANGSTRÖM.
**Sjundedags Adventistsamfundet** (Seventh-day Adventists): POB 536, 101 30 Stockholm; tel. (8) 14-03-65; fax (8) 20-48-68; f. 1880; 3,300 mems; Pres. BERTIL WIKLANDER.
**Svenska Missionsförbundet** (Mission Covenant Church of Sweden): Tegnérgt. 8, POB 6302, 113 81 Stockholm; tel. (8) 15-18-30; telex 14275; fax (8) 15-87-57; f. 1878; 74,000 mems; Gen. Sec. and Pres. KRISTER ANDERSSON; Chair. of Board ELVER JONSSON.

### The Roman Catholic Church

For ecclesiastical purposes, Sweden comprises the single diocese of Stockholm, directly responsible to the Holy See. At 31 December 1993 there were 150,841 adherents in the country, representing 1.7% of the total population. The Bishop participates in the Scandinavian Episcopal Conference (based in Oslo, Norway).
**Bishop of Stockholm:** Most Rev. HUBERTUS BRANDENBURG, Götgt. 68, POB 4114, 102 62 Stockholm; tel. (8) 643-80-22; fax (8) 702-05-55.

### Other Denominations

Other Christian churches include the Pentecostal Movement (with 95,800 mems in 1991), the Orthodox Churches of the Greeks, Romanians, Russians, Serbians and Finnish (together numbering 100,400 mems in 1991), and the Salvation Army (26,600 mems).

## ISLAM

In 1991 there were some 73,000 Muslims in Sweden.
**Förenade Islamiska Församlingar i Sverge (FIFS):** Götgt. 103A, 116 62 Sockholm; tel. (8) 642-16-53; fax (8) 642-34-20.
**Islamiska Kulturcenterunionen i Sverige (IKUS):** POB 45245, 104 30 Stockholm; tel. (8) 15-98-88; fax (8) 15-68-88.

**Sveriges Muslimska Förbund (SMUF):** Götgt. 103A, 116 62 Stockholm; tel. (8) 643-10-04; fax (8) 642-34-20.

## JUDAISM

There are between 15,000 and 20,000 Jews living in Sweden. The largest Jewish community is in Stockholm.
**Jewish Community in Stockholm:** Wahrendorffsgt. 3B, POB 7427, 103 91 Stockholm; tel. (8) 679-29-00; fax (8) 611-24-13; about 5,000 mems; Chief Rabbi MORTON H. NARROWE.

## BAHÁ'Í FAITH

**National Spiritual Assembly:** Götavägen 22, 191 44 Sollentuna; tel. (8) 48-88-95.

# The Press

Press freedom in Sweden dates from a law of 1766. The 1949 Freedom of the Press Act, a fundamental law embodying the whole of the press legislation in the Constitution, guarantees the Press's right to print and disseminate ideas; protects those supplying information by forbidding editors to disclose sources under any circumstances; authorizes all public documents to be publicly available, official secrets being the only exception; and contains provision for defamation. Press offences are to be referred to common law, and all cases against the Press must be heard by jury.
  In 1916 the Press Council was founded. Lacking judicial status, it has powers to rehabilitate persons wronged by the Press who refuse to apply to courts of law. Its judgments are widely published and highly respected.
  In 1969 the office of Press Ombudsman was established to supervise adherence to ethical standards. Public complaints shall be directed to the Press Ombudsman, who is also entitled to act on his own initiative. He may dismiss a complaint if unfounded, or if the newspaper agrees to publish a retraction or rectification acceptable to the complainant. When he finds that the grievance is of a more serious nature, he will file a complaint with the Press Council, which will then publish a statement acquitting or criticizing the newspaper. The findings of the Council are published in the newspaper concerned.
  Since 1969, the Swedish Parliament has granted the newspapers several forms of press support. For the budget year 1993/94 the sum of the grants amounted to 500m. kronor.
  The 'non-socialist' press enjoys 64% of daily circulation, the 'non-political' 20%, and the 'socialist' 17%. Some papers are directly owned or operated by political parties or by the trade unions. Though these papers are party organs, in close contact with the party, each editor expresses a considerable measure of independence. The Trade Union Confederation owns *Aftonbladet*. Affiliated trade unions publish some 20 periodical organs, with 1.6m. total circulation, including *Metallarbetaren*.
  The dominating influence of the few major dailies is largely confined to Stockholm, the provinces having a strong Press of their own. The major dailies are: *Expressen*, *Dagens Nyheter*, *Aftonbladet*, *Svenska Dagbladet* (all Stockholm), *Göteborgs-Posten*, *iDag* (Göteborg), *Sydsvenska Dagbladet*, *Arbetet* (Malmö). In 1993 there were an estimated 100 daily newspapers with a combined circulation of 4.2m.
  The two principal magazine publishers in Sweden are the Bonnier group (also a large book publisher and the majority shareholder in the newspapers *Dagens Nyheter*, *Expressen* and *Sydsvenska Dagbladet*) and the Aller company. Four other companies produce most of the remainder of Sweden's magazine circulation. The most popular weekly periodicals include the family magazines *Året Runt*, *Hemmets Veckotidning* and *Hemmets Journal*, and the home and household magazine *ICA-Kuriren*. *Vi* caters for serious cultural and political discussion and *Bonniers Litterära Magasin* specializes in literary topics. In 1993 there were some 70 weekly newspapers in Sweden.

## PRINCIPAL NEWSPAPERS

Newspapers with a circulation exceeding 15,000 are listed below.

### Ängelholm

**Norvästra Skånes Tidningar:** 262 83 Ängelholm; tel. (431) 84-000; fax (431) 80-011; f. 1847; daily; Conservative; Chief Editor BENNIE OHLSSON; circ. 44,400 weekdays 44,400 Sundays.

### Bollnäs

**Ljusnan, Tidning för Hälsingland:** POB 1059, 821 12 Bollnäs; tel. (278) 27-500; telex 81003; fax (278) 27-518; f. 1912; morning; Liberal; Editor BÖRJE TIMERDAL; circ. 15,900.

### Borås

**Borås Tidning:** POB 224, 501 04 Borås; tel. (33) 17-80-00; fax (33) 10-14-36; f. 1826; morning; Conservative; Editor JAN ÖJMERTZ; circ. 55,700 weekdays, 56,000 Sundays.

SWEDEN

*Directory*

### Eksjö

**Smålands-Tidningen:** POB 261, 575 23 Eksjö; tel. (381) 13-200; fax (381) 17-145; f. 1899; morning; independent; Editor BENGT WENDLE; circ. 19,600.

### Eskilstuna

**Eskilstuna-Kuriren med Strengnäs Tidning:** POB 120, 631 02 Eskilstuna; tel. (16) 15-60-00; fax (16) 51-63-04; f. 1890; morning; Liberal; Editor JERKER NORIN; circ. 34,100.

**Folket:** POB 368, 631 05 Eskilstuna; tel. (16) 12-78-00; fax (16) 12-57-90; f. 1905; morning; Social Democrat; Editor ROLF SVENSSON; circ. 15,000.

### Falkenberg

**Hallands Nyheter:** 311 81 Falkenberg; tel. (346) 29-000; fax (346) 29-120; f. 1905; morning; Centre; Editor DORIS GUNNARSSON; circ. 31,100.

### Falun

**Dala-Demokraten:** POB 825, 791 29 Falun; tel. (23) 47-500; fax (23) 29-115; f. 1917; morning; Social Democrat; Editor VILLY BERGSTRÖM; circ. 27,400.

**Falu-Kuriren:** POB 265, 791 26 Falun; tel. (23) 93-500; telex 74029; fax (23) 12-073; f. 1894; morning; Liberal; Editor LENNART BENGTSSON; circ. 30,800.

### Gävle

**Arbetarbladet:** POB 287, 801 04 Gävle; tel. (26) 15-93-00; fax (26) 12-14-06; f. 1902; morning; Social Democrat; Editor KENNET LUTTI; circ. 28,800.

**Gefle Dagblad:** POB 367, 801 05 Gävle; tel. (26) 15-95-00; telex 81041; fax (26) 15-97-00; f. 1895; morning; Liberal; Editor ROBERT ROSÉN; circ. 31,200.

### Göteborg (Gothenburg)

**Göteborgs-Posten:** Polhemsplatsen 5, 405 02 Göteborg; tel. (31) 62-40-00; telex 21581; fax (31) 15-76-92; f. 1858; morning; Liberal; Publr and Editor PETER HJÖRNE; circ. 270,400 weekdays, 302,500 Sundays.

**iDag:** POB 417, 401 26 Göteborg; tel. (31) 63-90-00; telex 2505; fax (31) 52-74-13; f. 1990; evening; Liberal; also issued in Malmö; Editor BENGT HANSSON; circ. 153,500 weekdays, 218,500 Sundays.

### Halmstad

**Hallandsposten:** 301 81 Halmstad; tel. (35) 14-75-00; telex 38034; fax (35) 11-37-14; f. 1850; morning; Liberal; Editor SVERKER EMANUELSSON; circ. 32,900.

### Härnösand

**Nya Norrland:** POB 120, 871 23 Härnösand; tel. (611) 38-800; telex 71272; fax (611) 15-660; f. 1907; morning; Social Democrat; Chief Editor PER ÅHLSTRÖM; circ. 20,200.

**Västernorrlands Allehanda:** POB 208, 871 24 Härnösand; tel. (611) 15-000; telex 71023; fax (611) 23-163; f. 1874; morning; Conservative; Editor BO ÖSTMAN; circ. 15,800.

### Hässleholm

**Norra Skåne:** 281 81 Hässleholm; tel. (451) 14-200; telex 48073; fax (451) 12-622; f. 1899; morning; Centre; Editor YNGVE SUNESSON; circ. 24,400.

### Helsingborg

**Helsingborgs Dagblad:** POB 822, 251 08 Helsingborg; tel. (42) 17-50-00; fax (42) 17-50-01; f. 1867; morning; independent; Man. Editor E. JOENSSON; circ. 51,800 weekdays, 52,200 Sundays.

### Hudiksvall

**Hudiksvalls Tidning:** POB 1201, 824 15 Hudiksvall; tel. (650) 154-00; telex 71569; fax (650) 156-10; f. 1909; includes *Hälsinglands Tidning*; morning; Centre; Editor JÖRGEN BENGTSON; circ. 19,000.

### Jönköping

**Jönköpings-Posten/Smålands Allehanda:** 551 80 Jönköping; tel. (36) 30-40-50; telex 70140; fax (36) 12-61-11; f. 1865; morning; independent; Editor STIG FREDRIKSSON; circ. 44,700.

### Kalmar

**Barometern med Oskarshamns-Tidningen:** 391 88 Kalmar; tel. (480) 59-100; telex 43051; fax (480) 59-135; f. 1841; morning; Conservative; Editor ANDERS WENDELBERG; circ. 49,500.

### Karlskrona

**Blekinge Läns Tidning:** 371 89 Karlskrona; tel. (455) 77-000; fax (455) 13-765; f. 1869; morning; Liberal; Editor LENNART HJELMSTEDT; circ. 33,000.

**Sydöstra Sveriges Dagblad:** Landbrogt. 17, 371 88 Karlskrona; tel. (455) 19-000; telex 43004; fax (455) 12-403; f. 1903; morning; Social Democrat; Editor HÅKAN QUISTH; circ. 23,600.

### Karlstad

**Nya Wermlands-Tidningen:** POB 28, 651 02 Karlstad; tel. (54) 19-91-00; telex 66106; fax (54) 19-19-00; f. 1836; morning; Conservative; Editor STAFFAN ANDER; circ. 72,100.

**Värmlands Folkblad:** POB 67, 651 03 Karlstad; tel. (54) 19-05-00; telex 66067; fax (54) 15-16-59; f. 1918; morning; Social Democrat; Editor ROLF JANSSON; circ. 27,600.

### Köping

**Bärgslagsbladet och Arboga Tidning:** POB 120, 731 23 Köping; tel. (221) 18-400; fax (221) 10-214; f. 1890; morning; 5 a week; Liberal; Editor KARL ÖSTGREN; circ. 15,500.

### Kristianstad

**Kristianstadsbladet:** POB 537, 291 25 Kristianstad; tel. (44) 18-55-00; fax (44) 11-17-01; f. 1856; morning; Liberal; Man. Dir N. E. LARSSON; Editor C. NYBERG; circ. 32,300.

### Lidköping

**Nya Läns-Tidningen:** 531 81 Lidköping; tel. (510) 89-700; fax (510) 89-596; f. 1903; morning; 3 a week; Liberal; Editor LENNART HÖRLING; circ. 24,200.

### Linköping

**Östgöta Correspondenten:** 581 89 Linköping; tel. (13) 28-00-00; fax (13) 11-57-15; f. 1838; morning; Liberal; Editor ERNST KLEIN; circ. 66,400.

### Luleå

**Norrbottens-Kuriren:** 971 81 Luleå; tel. (920) 37-500; telex 80460; fax (920) 15-793; f. 1861; morning; Conservative; Editor PEO WÄRRING; circ. 31,700.

**Norrländska Socialdemokraten:** 971 83 Luleå; tel. (920) 36-000; telex 8301; fax (920) 89-210; f. 1919; morning; Social Democrat; Editor LENNART HÅKANSSON; circ. 42,800.

### Malmö

**Arbetet:** POB 125, 201 21 Malmö; tel. (40) 20-50-00; telex 32182; fax (40) 23-16-77; f. 1887; morning; Social Democrat; Editor ANDERS FERM; circ. 101,000 weekdays, 92,200 Sundays.

**iDag:** 205 26 Malmö; tel. (40) 28-16-00; telex 32337; fax (40) 93-92-24; f. 1990; evening; Liberal; Editor BENGT HANSSON; circ. 188,300 weekdays, 261,000 Sundays.

**Skånska Dagbladet:** Östergt. 11, POB 165, 201 21 Malmö; tel. (40) 738-00; telex 32800; fax (40) 97-47-70; f. 1888; morning; Centre; Editor JAN A. JOHANSSON; circ. 30,000 weekdays, 31,000 Sundays.

**Sydsvenska Dagbladet:** 205 05 Malmö; tel. (40) 28-12-00; telex 32318; fax (40) 93-54-75; f. 1848; morning; Liberal independent; Editor JAN WIFSTRAND; circ. 121,000 weekdays, 140,900 Sundays.

### Norrköping

**Norrköpings Tidningar:** 601 83 Norrköping; tel. (11) 20-00-00; telex 64051; fax (11) 20-01-40; f. 1758; morning; Conservative; Editor KARL-ÅKE BREDENBERG; circ. 51,000.

### Nyköping

**Södermanlands Nyheter:** 611 79 Nyköping; tel. (155) 76-700; fax (155) 21-62-51; f. 1893; morning; Centre; Editor LARS J. ERIKSSON; circ. 24,300.

### Örebro

**Nerikes Allehanda:** POB 1603, 701 16 Örebro; tel. (19) 15-50-00; fax (19) 10-52-90; f. 1843; morning; Liberal; Editor STIGBJÖRN BERGENSTEN; circ. 70,100.

### Örnsköldsvik

**Örnsköldsviks Allehanda:** POB 110, 891 23 Örnsköldsvik; tel. (660) 10-060; telex 6056; fax (660) 14-585; f. 1843; morning; Liberal; Editor JERRY ERIXON; circ. 22,000.

### Östersund

**Länstidningen:** 831 89 Östersund; tel. (63) 15-55-00; telex 44087; fax (63) 15-55-95; f. 1924; morning; Social Democrat; Editor PETER SWEDENMARK; circ. 29,300.

**Östersunds-Posten:** POB 720, 831 28 Östersund; tel. (63) 16-16-00; telex 44061; fax (63) 11-11-00; f. 1877; morning; Centre; Editor HÅKAN LARSSON; circ. 29,400.

### Piteå

**Piteå-Tidningen:** POB 193, 941 24 Piteå; tel. (911) 64-500; fax (911) 64-620; f. 1915; morning; Social Democrat; Editor LENNART LINDGREN; circ. 18,900.

SWEDEN                                                                                                          Directory

### Skara
**Skaraborgs Läns Tidning:** POB 214, 532 23 Skara; tel. (511) 13-010; telex 5028; fax (511) 18-815; f. 1884; morning; Liberal; Editor HANS MENZING; circ. 17,400.

### Skellefteå
**Norra Västerbotten:** POB 58, 931 21 Skellefteå; tel. (910) 14-000; telex 65072; fax (910) 56-513; f. 1910; morning; Liberal; Editor STIG ERICSSON; circ. 32,700.

### Skövde
**Skaraborgs Läns Allehanda:** POB 407, 541 28 Skövde; tel. (500) 46-75-00; fax (500) 48-05-82; f. 1884; morning; Conservative; Editor MÅNS JOHNSON; circ. 23,000.

### Södertälje
**Länstidningen:** POB 226, 151 23 Södertälje; tel. (8) 550-921-00; telex 10904; fax (8) 550-877-72; f. 1860; morning; 5 a week; Centre; Editor TORSTEN CARLSSON; circ. 17,800.

### Stockholm
**Aftonbladet:** 105 18 Stockholm; tel. (8) 725-20-00; telex 17138; fax (8) 600-01-77; f. 1830; evening; Social Democrat independent; Editors ROLF ALSING, TORBJÖRN LARSSON; circ. 358,933 weekdays, 462,435 Sundays.

**Dagen:** 105 36 Stockholm; tel. (8) 619-24-00; fax (8) 619-24-26; f. 1945; morning; 5 a week; Christian independent; Editor OLOF DJURFELDT; circ. 19,600.

**Dagens Industri:** POB 3177, 103 63 Stockholm; tel. (8) 736-50-00; telex 19373; fax (8) 789-88-67; f. 1976; 6 a week; business news; Editor HASSE OLSSON; circ. 91,700.

**Dagens Nyheter:** 105 15 Stockholm; tel. (8) 738-29-00; telex 10450; fax (8) 656-54-49; f. 1864; morning; independent; Chief Editor HANS BERGSTRÖM; circ. 379,700 weekdays, 429,600 Sundays.

**Expressen:** Gjörwellsgt. 30, 105 16 Stockholm; tel. (8) 738-30-00; fax (8) 738-33-40; f. 1945; evening; Liberal; Editor CHRISTINA JUTTERSTRÖM; circ. 451,000 weekdays, 550,000 Sundays.

**Svenska Dagbladet:** 105 17 Stockholm; tel. (8) 13-56-80; telex 17400; f. 1884; morning; Conservative; Chief Editor MATS SVEGFORS; circ. 203,100 weekdays, 217,000 Sundays.

### Sundsvall
**Sundsvalls Tidning:** 851 72 Sundsvall; tel. (60) 19-70-00; fax (60) 15-44-33; f. 1841; morning; Liberal; Editor KJELL CARNBRO; circ. 40,300 weekdays, 43,900 Sundays.

### Trollhättan
**Trollhättans Tidning:** POB 54, 461 22 Trollhättan; tel. (520) 12-670; fax (520) 10-439; f. 1906; morning; 5 a week; independent; Editor TORBJÖRN HÅKANSSON; circ. 15,800.

### Uddevalla
**Bohusläningen med Dals Dagblad:** 451 83 Uddevalla; tel. (522) 99-000; telex 42060; fax (522) 11-888; f. 1878; morning; Liberal; Editor ULF JOHANSSON; circ. 35,300.

### Umeå
**Västerbottens Folkblad:** POB 6104, 906 04 Umeå; tel. (90) 17-00-00; telex 54070; fax (90) 17-02-56; f. 1917; morning; Social Democrat; Editor LENNART ANDERSSON; circ. 20,400.

**Västerbottens-Kuriren:** 901 70 Umeå; tel. (90) 15-10-00; telex 54070; fax (90) 77-46-47; f. 1900; morning; Liberal; Editors OLOF KLEBERG, LARS WESTERLUND; circ. 45,500.

### Uppsala
**Upsala Nya Tidning:** POB 36, Danmarksgt. 28, 751 03 Uppsala; tel. (18) 17-00-00; telex 76035; fax (18) 12-95-07; f. 1890; morning; Liberal; Editor JÖRGEN ULLENHAG; circ. 65,400.

### Värnamo
**Värnamo Nyheter:** 331 84 Värnamo; tel. (370) 11-950; fax (370) 49-395; f. 1930; morning; 4 a week; independent; Editor SVEN LINDSTRÖM; circ. 25,300.

### Västerås
**Vestmanlands Läns Tidning:** POB 3, 721 03 Västerås; tel. (21) 19-90-00; fax (21) 19-91-38; f. 1831; morning; Liberal; Editor ANDERS H. PERS; circ. 50,000.

### Växjö
**Smålandsposten:** 351 70 Växjö; tel. (470) 77-05-00; fax (470) 39-270; f. 1866; morning; Conservative; Editor KJELL SVENSSON; circ. 42,400.

### Ystad
**Ystads Allehanda:** 271 81 Ystad; tel. (411) 64-500; telex 32341; fax (411) 13-955; f. 1873; morning; Liberal; Editor STAFFAN BJÖRNBERG; circ. 24,600.

## POPULAR PERIODICALS

**Allas Veckotidning:** Allers Förlag AB, 205 35 Malmö; tel. (40) 38-59-00; fax (40) 38-59-64; f. 1931; weekly; family; Chief Editor TINA JANSSON; circ. 173,500.

**Allers:** 251 85 Helsingborg; tel. (42) 17-35-00; fax (42) 17-35-68; f. 1877; weekly; family; Chief Editor CHRIS BERGENDORFF; circ. 263,700.

**Allt om Mat:** St. Goransgt. 57, POB 70452, 107 26 Stockholm; tel. (8) 736-37-00; telex 17473; fax (8) 651-57-90; f. 1970; monthly; food specialities; Chief Editor HAKAN LARSSON; circ. 123,500.

**Antik och Auktion:** POB 63, 272 01 Simrishamn; tel. (414) 13-770; fax (414) 13-455; f. 1978; monthly; antiques; Editor CHRISTIAN WOLLIN; circ. 52,300.

**Året Runt:** 105 44 Stockholm; tel. (8) 736-52-00; telex 10043; fax (8) 30-49-00; f. 1946; weekly; family; Editor ARNE WINERDAL; circ. 303,176.

**Det Bästa:** Reader's Digest AB, POB 25, 164 93 Kista; tel. (8) 752-03-60; fax (8) 703-99-29; f. 1943; monthly; family; Chief Editor ULLA-STINA ÖSTBERG; circ. 200,700.

**Bilsport:** POB 529, 371 23 Karlskrona; tel. (455) 33-53-25; telex 43165; fax (455) 31-17-15; f. 1962; fortnightly; motor-sport, cars; Chief Editor STIG L. SJÖBERG; circ. 53,700.

**Damernas Värld:** 105 44 Stockholm; tel. (8) 736-53-00; telex 10043; fax (8) 31-59-16; f. 1940; monthly; women's; Editor EVA BIRMANN; circ. 131,700.

**Datormagazin:** Bröderna Lindströms Förlag, 112 85 Stockholm; tel. (8) 692-01-40; fax (8) 650-97-05; f. 1985; 22 a year; computer games; Editor CHRISTER RINDEBLAD; circ. 38,000.

**Elle:** Saltmätargt. 7, 113 59 Stockholm; tel. (8) 736-14-00; fax (8) 32-19-30; f. 1988; monthly; women's; Editor EVA ABRAHAMSSON; circ. 58,994.

**Femina Månadens Magasin:** 251 85 Helsingborg; tel. (42) 17-35-00; telex 72273; fax (42) 17-36-82; f. 1981; monthly; women's; Editor STINA NORLING; circ. 114,000.

**Frida:** Annons Bolaget, POB 3161, 103 63 Stockholm; tel. (8) 736-55-00; fax (8) 32-04-40; fortnightly; for girls and young women aged 15–24; circ. 67,533.

**Hänt Extra:** POB 27704, 115 91 Stockholm; tel. (8) 679-46-00; telex 72273; fax (8) 679-46-77; f. 1986; weekly; family; Chief Editors JAN BARD, THORD SKÖLDEKRANS; circ. 125,600.

**Hänt i Veckan:** POB 27704, 115 91 Stockholm; tel. (8) 679-46-00; telex 72273; fax (8) 679-46-33; f. 1964; weekly; family; Chief Editor STEN HEDMAN; circ. 132,300.

**Hemmets Journal:** Hemmets Journal AB, 212 05 Malmö; tel. (40) 38-52-00; fax (40) 29-42-82; f. 1920; weekly; family; Chief Editor JANNE WALLES; circ. 283,000.

**Hemmets Veckotidning:** Allers Förlag AB, 205 35 Malmö; tel. (40) 38-59-00; fax (40) 38-59-14; f. 1929; weekly; family; Editor ULLA COCKE; circ. 268,000.

**Hus & Hem:** ICA Förlaget AB, Storagt. 41, 721 85 Västerås; tel. (21) 19-45-35; fax (21) 19-45-36; 10 a year; for house-owners; circ. 101,400.

**ICA Kuriren:** Storagt. 41, 721 85 Västerås; tel. (21) 19-40-00; fax (21) 19-41-36; f. 1942; weekly; home and household; Editor LENA BJÖRK; circ. 403,900.

**Kalle Anka & Co:** 212 05 Malmö; tel. (40) 38-53-30; fax (40) 93-70-04; f. 1948; weekly; comics; Editor UNN PRINTZ-PÅHLSSON; circ. 170,000.

**Kvällsstunden:** Lantmännens Tryckeriförening, POB 1080, 721 27 Västerås; tel. (21) 19-04-00; fax (21) 18-84-34; weekly; family magazine; Editor ÅKE LINDBERG; circ. 69,000.

**Må Bra:** POB 27710, 115 91 Stockholm; tel. (8) 679-46-00; fax (8) 667-34-39; f. 1978; monthly; health and nutrition; Chief Editor INGER RIDSTRÖM; circ. 84,000.

**MånadsJournalen:** 105 44 Stockholm; tel. (8) 736-53-00; telex 10043; fax (8) 32-78-40; f. 1980; monthly; cultural; Chief Editor STEFAN MEHR; circ. 53,400.

**Mitt Livs Novell:** POB 12857, 112 98 Stockholm; tel. (8) 654-23-00; fax (8) 651-01-88; f. 1964; fortnightly; romance; Chief Editor KARIN KRAUSZ; circ. 56,590.

**OKEJ:** POB 12547, 102 29 Stockholm; tel. (8) 692-01-20; fax (8) 650-86-25; f. 1980; fortnightly youth magazine; Editor SUSANNE GUVE; circ. 80,000.

**På TV:** Medviks TV-Förlag, POB 2155, 103 14 Stockholm; tel. (8) 791-19-40; fax (8) 20-27-22; f. 1990; weekly TV guide; Editor BERT WILLBORG; circ. 67,500.

SWEDEN                                                                                                                                                           *Directory*

**Premium Motor:** POB 6019, 175 06 Järfälla; tel. (8) 761-09-50; fax (8) 761-09-49; motoring; Editor STAFFAN SWEDENBORG; circ. 44,615.

**Privata Affärer:** Holländargt. 13, POB 3188, 103 63 Stockholm; tel. (8) 736-56-00; telex 17473; fax (8) 789-88-82; f. 1978; monthly; personal money management; Chief Editor ANDERS ANDERSSON; circ. 50,000.

**Röster i Radio/TV:** POB 27870, 115 93 Stockholm; tel. (8) 679-46-00; fax (8) 660-05-44; f. 1934; weekly; family magazine and programme guide to radio and television; Chief Editor HARRY STRAND; circ. 82,600.

**Sköna Hem & Allt i Hemmet:** 105 44 Stockholm; tel. (8) 736-53-00; fax (8) 33-74-11; f. 1979 (Sköna Hem), 1956 (Allt i Hemmet), merged 1992; monthly; interior decoration; Chief Editor BJÖRN VINGÅRD; circ. 104,600.

**Svensk Damtidning:** POB 27710, 115 91 Stockholm; tel. (8) 679-46-00; fax (8) 679-47-50; f. 1980; weekly; women's; Chief Editor KARIN LENMOR; circ. 132,000.

**Teknikens Värld:** POB 70452, 107 26 Stockholm; tel. (8) 736-37-00; fax (8) 791-72-10; f. 1947; fortnightly; motoring; Chief Editor CHRISTER GERLACH; circ. 58,500.

**Vår Bostad:** POB 12651, 112 93 Stockholm; tel. (8) 692-02-00; fax (8) 650-06-41; f. 1923; 11 a year; house and home; Editor OSTEN JOHANSSON; circ. 1,047,900.

**Vecko-Revyn:** POB 3161, 103 63 Stockholm; tel. (8) 736-55-00; fax (8) 32-04-40; f. 1935; weekly; young women's; Editor AMELIA ADAMO; circ. 104,400.

**Vi:** Annons Bolaget, POB 3161, 103 63 Stockholm; tel. (8) 736-55-00; fax (8) 32-04-40; weekly; environment, culture, holidays, for 18–39 age-group; circ. 78,300.

**Vi Bilägare:** POB 23800, 104 35 Stockholm; tel. (8) 736-12-00; fax (8) 736-12-49; f. 1930; fortnightly; auto, home and hobbies; Editor NILS-ERIC FRENDIN; circ. 218,000.

**Vi Föräldrar:** 105 44 Stockholm; tel. (8) 791-72-58; fax (8) 791-72-58; f. 1968; monthly; parents' magazine; Chief Editor MARIA HÖRNFELDT; circ. 75,000.

### SPECIALIST PERIODICALS

**Akademiker:** Annons Bolaget, POB 3161, 103 63 Stockholm; tel. (8) 736-55-00; fax (8) 32-04-40; quarterly magazine for academics; circ. 271,800.

**Aktuellt för Kontor:** POB 6903, 102 39 Stockholm; tel. (8) 31-00-07; fax (8) 31-00-11; f. 1964; 6 a year; management, electronic communications, stationery; Editor ALEXANDER SCARLAT; circ. 130,000.

**Aktuellt i POLITIKEN:** Sveavägen 68, 105 60 Stockholm; tel. (8) 700-26-00; fax (8) 11-65-42; weekly; social, political and cultural affairs; organ of Social Democratic Labour Party; circ. 55,000.

**Allt om Jakt & Vapen:** POB 70452, 107 26 Stockholm; tel. (8) 736-37-00; fax (8) 791-89-04; 11 a year; hunting; circ. 45,200.

**Arbetsledaren:** POB 12069, 102 22 Stockholm; tel. (8) 652-01-20; fax (8) 653-99-68; f. 1908; 10 a year; journal for foremen and supervisors; Editor INGRID ASKEBERG; circ. 87,400.

**Arbetsmiljö:** Maria Skolgt. 83, POB 17550, 118 91 Stockholm; tel. (8) 668-14-60; fax (8) 668-25-05; monthly; working environment; circ. 123,800.

**Barnen & Vi:** 107 88 Stockholm; tel. (8) 698-90-00; telex 11904; fax (8) 698-90-14; 7 a year; children's rights; circ. 138,000.

**Båtliv:** Martin Edén Reklam AB, POB 4070, 183 04 Täby; tel. (8) 756-28-06; fax (8) 756-83-28; 5 a year; for boat-owners and boat-club members; circ. 121,400.

**Bonniers Litterära Magasin:** Sveavägen 56, POB 3159, 103 63 Stockholm; tel. (8) 696-86-42; fax (8) 696-83-59; f. 1932; 6 a year; literary; Editor STEPHEN FARRAN-LEE.

**Byggnadsarbetaren:** 106 32 Stockholm; tel. (8) 728-48-00; fax (8) 728-49-80; f. 1949; 18 a year; building; Editor HÅKAN OLANDER; circ. 168,000.

**Dina Pengar:** POB 1712, 111 87 Stockholm; tel. (8) 23-66-20; fax (8) 10-34-75; 9 a year; finance; circ. 83,000.

**Focus:** POB 22107, 104 22 Stockholm; tel. (8) 652-64-40; fax (8) 617-38-00; f. 1929; 10 a year; organ of the Centre Party; Editor LENNART SVENSSON; circ. 113,400.

**Friluftsliv—i alla Väder:** POB 5019, 102 41 Stockholm; tel. (8) 679-60-60; fax (8) 611-55-22; 6 a year; outdoor sports; Editor PER GÖTHLIN; circ. 55,200.

**Handelsnytt:** POB 5074, 200 71 Malmö; tel. (40) 24-77-00; fax (40) 98-01-63; 11 a year; organ of the Union of Commercial Employees; circ. 177,400.

**HTF-Tidningen:** Vikingavägen 17D, 133 33 Saltsjöbaden; tel. (8) 717-98-41; fax (8) 717-50-04; 18 a year; organ of the Union of Commercial Salaried Employees; circ. 145,100.

**Hundsport:** POB 11141, 100 61 Stockholm; tel. (8) 642-37-20; fax (8) 641-00-62; monthly; for dog-owners; Editor TORSTEN WIDHOLM; circ. 109,000.

**Jaktmarker och Fiskevatten:** Västra Torggt. 18, 652 24 Karlstad; tel. (54) 10-03-70; fax (54) 10-09-83; 11 a year; hunting and fishing; circ. 68,929.

**Kommunalarbetaren:** POB 19034, 104 32 Stockholm; tel. (8) 728-28-00; fax (8) 30-61-42; 22 a year; organ of the Union of Municipal Workers; circ. 712,300.

**Kyrkans Tidning:** POB 342, 191 30 Sollentuna; tel. (8) 623-65-55; fax (8) 35-75-63; f. 1982; weekly; organ of the Church of Sweden; Man. Dir CLAES WAERN; Editor LARS B. STENSTRÖM; circ. 58,900.

**LAND-Lantbruksdelen/LAND-Familjetidningen:** Vasagt. 12, 105 33 Stockholm; tel. (8) 787-51-00; fax (8) 723-15-21; f. 1971; weekly; organ of the farmers' association; house, garden, cooking, hunting, travel; circ. 134,300 (Lantbruksdelen), 353,600 (Familjetidningen).

**Lärarnas Tidning:** POB 12239, 102 26 Stockholm; tel. (8) 737-65-00; fax (8) 737-65-69; 30 a year; for teachers; circ. 200,600.

**Medborgaren:** Lilla Nygt. 13, 111 28 Stockholm; tel. (8) 676-80-00; fax (8) 20-41-71; organ of the Moderate Party; f. 1915; 6 a year; Editors ANN-KARI EDENIUS, FOLKE SCHÖTT; circ. 77,000.

**Medlemstidningen Industrifacket:** POB 1120, 111 81 Stockholm; tel. (8) 786-85-00; monthly; organ of the Union of Factory Workers; circ. 122,000.

**Metallarbetaren:** POB 342, 101 24 Stockholm; tel. (8) 10-68-30; fax (8) 11-13-02; f. 1888; weekly; organ of Swedish Metal Workers' Union; Editor PER AHLSTRÖM; circ. 422,700.

**Motor:** POB 23142, 104 35 Stockholm; tel. (8) 690-38-00; fax (8) 690-38-22; monthly; cars and motoring; circ. 159,600.

**Motorföraren:** Fikja Backe 1-3, 145 84 Stockholm; tel. (8) 680-87-40; fax (8) 680-87-68; f. 1927; 10 a year; motoring and tourism; Editor KENNETH HAGBERG; circ. 82,500.

**Musiktidningen Musikomanen:** POB 6903, 102 39 Stockholm; tel. (8) 31-00-07; fax (8) 31-00-11; f. 1964; 6 a year; classical and modern music; circ. 90,000.

**Ny Teknik:** Klara Södrakyrkogt. 1, 106 12 Stockholm; tel. (8) 796-66-50; fax (8) 613-30-32; f. 1967; weekly; technical publication by the two largest engineering societies of Sweden; Editor-in-Chief LARS RUNDKVIST; circ. 131,100.

**PRO-Pensionären:** POB 3274, 103 65 Stockholm; tel. (8) 701-67-00; fax (8) 20-33-58; 10 a year; magazine for pensioners; circ. 294,400.

**SAF-Tidningen (Arbetsgivaren):** Blasieholmsgt. 4A, 103 30 Stockholm; tel. (8) 762-60-00; fax (8) 762-68-85; 40 a year; organ of the Employers' Confederation; circ. 60,000.

**SEKO-magasinet:** Barnhusgt. 10, POB 1102, 111 81 Stockholm; tel. (8) 791-41-00; fax (8) 21-16-94; f. 1955; 11 a year; organ of the National Union of Services and Communications Employees; Editor-in-Chief BJÖRN FORSBERG; circ. 197,000.

**SIA-Skogsindustriarbetaren:** Olof Palmesgt. 29[5], POB 1138, 111 81 Stockholm; tel. (8) 23-04-25; fax (8) 411-27-42; every 3 weeks; forestry; circ. 115,100.

**SIF-Tidningen:** Vikingavägen 17D, 133 33 Saltsjöbaden; tel. (8) 717-98-41; fax (8) 717-50-04; 19 a year; organ of the Union of Clerical and Technical Employees; circ. 328,000.

**Skog & Såg:** Såbi, Box 394, 551 15 Jönköping; tel. (36) 19-86-00; fax (36) 12-86-10; f. 1966; 4 a year; sawmills and forestry; Editor HENRIK ASPLUND; circ. 78,000.

**SKTF-Tidningen:** POB 7825, 103 97 Stockholm; tel. (8) 789-63-00; fax (8) 20-84-40; 20 a year; organ of the Union of Municipal Employees; circ. 185,100.

**Sunt Förnuft:** 114 95 Stockholm; tel. (8) 613-17-00; fax (8) 21-38-58; 8 a year; tax-payers' magazine; circ. 173,300.

**Svensk Bokhandel** (Journal of the Swedish Book Trade): Kungstensgt. 38, POB 6888, 113 86 Stockholm; tel. (8) 736-19-50; fax (8) 736-19-55; publ. by Swedish Publrs' Asscn, for book-sellers, publishers, antiquarians and librarians; Editor JAN-ERIK PETTERSSON; circ. 4,400.

**Svensk Golf:** POB 84, 182 11 Danderyd; tel. (8) 622-15-00; fax (8) 622-69-30; monthly; golf; circ. 220,000.

**Svensk Jakt:** POB 1, 163 21 Spånga; tel. (8) 795-33-00; fax (8) 761-20-15; f. 1862; 11 a year; for hunters and dog-breeders; circ. 175,800.

**Svensk Tennis:** ICA Förlaget AB, Storagt. 41, 721 85 Västerås; tel. (21) 19-40-00; fax (21) 19-42-21; f. 1991; 10 a year; for tennis players and spectators; Editor HANS MEJDEVI; circ. 85,100.

**Sveriges Natur:** POB 4625, 116 19 Stockholm; tel. (8) 702-65-00; fax (8) 702-27-02; 6 a year; nature; circ. 153,100.

SWEDEN
                                                                                                              *Directory*

**Transportarbetaren:** POB 714, 101 33 Stockholm; tel. (8) 723-77-00; fax (8) 723-00-76; 11 a year; organ of the Union of Transport Workers; Editor MARTIN VIREDIUS; circ. 68,300.

**Turist:** POB 27150, 102 25 Stockholm; tel. (8) 790-31-00; 6 a year; tourism and travel; Editor THELMA KIMSJÅO; circ. 260,000.

**Vårdfacket:** POB 3207, 103 64 Stockholm; tel. (8) 14-77-00; fortnightly; nursing and medical; circ. 111,400.

### NEWS AGENCIES

**Svenska Nyhetsbyrån** (Swedish Conservative Press Agency): Stora Nygt. 28, POB 1245, 111 82 Stockholm; tel. (8) 14-07-50; fax (8) 10-10-48; Pres. KJELL SVENSSON; Editor-in-Chief and Dir JÖRAN SVAHNSTRÖM.

**Svensk-Internationella Pressbyrån (SIP)** (Swedish-International Press Bureau): 131 84 Stockholm; tel. (8) 716-91-80; fax (8) 718-53-90; f. 1927; Man. STEFAN THORBERG; Editor-in-Chief BJÖRN F. HÖIJER.

**Tidningarnas Telegrambyrå** (Swedish News Agency): Kungsholmstorg 5, 105 12 Stockholm; tel. (8) 692-26-00; telex 19168; fax (8) 651-53-77; f. 1921; co-operative news agency, working in conjunction with Reuters, AFP, the 'Groupe 39' agencies, dpa and other telegraph agencies; Chair. ANDERS H. PERS; Gen. Man. ERIK NYLÉN.

#### Foreign Bureaux

**Agence France-Presse (AFP):** c/o Tidningarnas Telegrambyrå, Kungsholmstorg 5, 105 12 Stockholm; tel. (8) 651-01-60; fax (8) 650-82-28; Man. JEAN-LUC CHANDELIER.

**Agenzia Nazionale Stampa Associata (ANSA)** (Italy): Ynglingagt. 23, 113 47 Stockholm; tel. (8) 33-93-10; telex 17120; Man. GIACOMO OREGLIA.

**Associated Press (AP)** (USA): Sveavägen 17, POB 1726, 111 87 Stockholm; tel. (8) 411-12-44; fax (8) 21-24-71; Man. KEVIN COSTELLOE.

**Informatsionnoye Telegrafnoye Agentstvo Rossii-Telegrafnoye Agentstvo Suverennykh Stran (ITAR-TASS)** (Russia): Karlavägen 12, 114 31 Stockholm; tel. (8) 11-32-40; Man. NIKOLAI VOKOLOV.

**Kyodo Tsushin** (Japan): POB 2130, 145 56 Norsborg; tel. (0753) 83-215.

**United Press International (UPI)** (USA): c/o Burman, Rindögt. 26, 115 36 Stockholm; tel. (8) 663-21-52; fax (8) 663-21-52; Correspondent PÅL BURMAN.

**Xinhua (New China) News Agency** (People's Republic of China): Krokvägen 5, 181 33 Lidingö; tel. (8) 765-60-83; telex 11190; Man. LINFENG XIE.

### PRESS ASSOCIATIONS

**Precent** (Centre Party's Press Organization): POB 2033, 103 11 Stockholm; tel. (8) 786-48-84; fax (8) 24-30-04; f. 1929; Chief Editor JIMMY DOMINIUS; 33 mems.

**Svenska Journalistförbundet** (Swedish Union of Journalists): POB 1116, 111 81 Stockholm; tel. (8) 613-75-00; fax (8) 21-26-80; f. 1901; Pres. CLAES LEO LINDWALL; 16,500 mems.

**Svenska Tidningsutgivareföreningen** (Swedish Newspaper Publishers' Asscn): Kungsholmstorg 5, POB 22500, 104 22 Stockholm; tel. (8) 692-46-00; fax (8) 692-46-38; f. 1898; Man. Dir BARBRO FISCHERSTRÖM; 190 mems.

**Svenska Veckopressens Tidningsutgivareförening (VECTU)** (Swedish Magazine Publishers' Asscn): Kungsgt. 33, 111 56 Stockholm; tel. (8) 20-15-10; fax (8) 21-35-20; f. 1943; Man. Dir GUNVOR ENGSTRÖM.

**Sveriges Vänsterpressförening** (The Liberal Press Asscn): 901 70 Umeå; tel. (90) 15-10-00; fax (90) 11-46-47; f. 1905; Pres. OLOF KLEBERG; Sec. MATS OLOFSSON; approx. 145 mems.

## Publishers

At the beginning of 1994 there were about 200 professional publishers in Sweden. The five largest publishers—the Bonnier group, Wolfers Kluwer Sverige (including Norstedts), Natur och Kultur, Rabén & Sjögren and Bra Böcker—accounted for some 60% of total sales.

**Alfabeta Bokförlag AB:** POB 4284, 102 66 Stockholm; tel. (8) 714-93-53; fax (8) 643-24-31; fiction, psychology, biography, cinema, art, music, travel guides, children's books; Man. Dir DAG HERNRIED.

**Almqvist & Wiksell Förlag AB:** Hälsingegt. 49, POB 6411, 113 82 Stockholm; tel. (8) 690-92-00; fax (8) 690-93-00; f. 1972; languages, textbooks, teaching aids; Man. Dir LARS HONT.

**Bokförlaget Atlantis AB:** Sturegt. 24, 114 36 Stockholm; tel. (8) 783-04-40; fax (8) 661-72-85; f. 1977; fiction, non-fiction, art; Man. Dir KJELL PETERSON.

**Berghs Förlag AB:** Observatoriegt. 10, POB 45084, 104 30 Stockholm; tel. (8) 31-65-59; fax (8) 32-77-45; f. 1954; non-fiction for adults and children, picture books and fiction for children, craft books, popular science; Man. Dir CARL HAFSTRÖM.

**Bonnier Carlsen Bokförlag AB:** POB 1315, 111 83 Stockholm; tel. (8) 453-89-00; fax (8) 453-89-45; picture books, juvenile books, non-fiction, board books, comics; Man. Dir BODIL SJÖÖ.

**Bonnierförlagen AB:** Sveavägen 56, POB 3159, 103 63 Stockholm; tel. (8) 696-80-00; telex 14546; fax (8) 696-83-59; f. 1837; fiction, non-fiction, encyclopaedias, reference books, quality paperbacks; includes Albert Bonniers Förlag AB, Bokförlaget Bonnier Alba AB, Bonnier Lexikon AB, Bonnier Utbildning AB, Bokförlaget Forum AB, AB Wahlström & Widstrand; Chair. CARL-JOHAN BONNIER; Man. Dir PER-OLOV ATLE.

**Bokförlaget Bra Böcker:** Södra Vägen, 263 80 Höganäs; tel. (42) 33-90-00; fax (42) 33-05-04; f. 1965; Man. Dir ANDERS JANSON.

**Brombergs Bokförlag AB:** Industrigt. 4A, POB 12886, 112 98 Stockholm; tel. (8) 650-33-90; fax (8) 650-01-60; quality fiction, non-fiction; Man. Dir DOROTEA BROMBERG.

**Brutus Östlings Bokförlag Symposium:** Rönneholm 6, 240 36 Stehag.

**Carlsson Bokförlag AB:** Stora Nygt. 31, 111 27 Stockholm; tel. (8) 11-23-49; fax (8) 796-84-57; art, photography, ethnology, history, politics; Man. Dir TRYGVE CARLSSON.

**Dagens Nyheter Förlag:** 105 15 Stockholm; publishing division of *Dagens Nyheter* newspaper.

**Eriksson & Lindgren Bokförlag AB:** Hantverkagt. 87, POB 12085, 102 23 Stockholm; tel. (8) 652-32-27; fax (8) 652-32-26; f. 1990; Man. Dir MARIANNE ERIKSSON.

**Bokförlaget T. Fischer & Co.:** Norrlandsgt. 15, 111 43 Stockholm; tel. (8) 24-21-60; fax (8) 24-78-25; fiction, non-fiction; Man. Dir EVA NORLIN.

**Forum Publishers:** POB 14115, 104 41 Stockholm; tel. (8) 696-84-40; fax (8) 696-83-67; f. 1943; general fiction, non-fiction; Man. Dir BERTIL KÄLL.

**C. E. Fritzes AB:** 106 47 Stockholm; tel. (8) 690-90-90; fax (8) 690-90-70; f. 1837; Man. Dir CHRISTER BUNGE-MEYER.

**Gedins Förlag:** POB 5741, 114 87 Stockholm; tel. (8) 662-15-51; fax (8) 663-70-73; fiction, non-fiction, poetry, food, psychology, politics; Man. Dir PER I. GEDIN.

**AB Carl Gehrmans Musikförlag:** POB 6005, 102 31 Stockholm; tel. (8) 16-52-00; fax (8) 31-42-44; f. 1893; music; Pres. LARS LIDÉN; Man. Dir KETTIL SKARBY.

**ICA-förlaget AB:** 721 85 Västerås; tel. (21) 19-40-00; telex 40486; fax (21) 19-42-83; f. 1945; non-fiction, cookery, handicrafts, gardening, natural history, popular psychology, health, domestic animals, sports; Publr GÖRAN SUNEHAG; Man. Dir KJELL GUSTAFSSON.

**Informationsförlaget:** Sveavägen 61, POB 6884, 113 86 Stockholm; tel. (8) 34-09-15; fax (8) 31-39-03; f. 1979; publishers of books for companies and organizations on demand; trade books in non-fiction, reference, encyclopaedias, gastronomy, illustrated books; Man. Dir ULF HEIMDAHL.

**Liber Hermods AB:** Norra Vallgt. 100, 205 10 Malmö; tel. (40) 25-86-00; fax (8) 97-05-50; f. 1993; Man. Dir PER BERGKNUT.

**Liber Utbildning AB:** Hälsingegt. 49, POB 6440, 113 82 Stockholm; tel. (8) 690-93-50; fax (8) 690-94-57; f. 1993; Man. Dir ROLF ÖGREN.

**LTs förlag:** POB 14171, 104 41 Stockholm; tel. (8) 453-87-25; fax (8) 453-87-98; f. 1934; illustrated do-it-yourself books, agricultural textbooks for adult education; Man. Dir ROLF ELLNEBRAND.

**Abr. Lundquist Musikförlag AB:** POB 93, 182 11 Danderyd; tel. (8) 755-67-57; f. 1838; music; Man. Dir MONICA RUNDQVIST.

**Bokförlaget Natur och Kultur:** Karlavägen 31, POB 27323, 102 54 Stockholm; tel. (8) 453-86-00; fax (8) 453-87-90; f. 1922; textbooks, general literature, fiction; Man. Dir LARS GRAHN.

**Norstedts Förlag AB:** Norra Bankogränd 2, POB 2052, 103 12 Stockholm; tel. (8) 789-30-00; fax (8) 21-40-06; f. 1823; fiction, non-fiction, juvenile, practical handbooks, dictionaries and encyclopaedias; Man. Dir GUNNAR AHLSTRÖM.

**Bokförlaget Opal AB:** Tegelbergsvägen 31, POB 20113, 161 02 Bromma; tel. (8) 28-21-79; fax (8) 29-66-23; f. 1974; Man. Dir BENGT CHRISTELL.

**Ordfront Förlag AB:** Björngårdsgt. 15, POB 17506, 118 91 Stockholm; tel. (8) 644-93-90; fax (8) 702-01-43; fiction, history, politics, juvenile; Man. Dir DAN ISRAEL.

**AB Rabén & Sjögren Bokförlag:** Tegnérgt. 28, POB 45022, 104 30 Stockholm; tel. (8) 34-99-60; fax (8) 30-28-99; f. 1942; general, juvenile; also includes Bokförlaget Prisma AB (fiction, textbooks, reference books); Man. Dir KJELL BOHLUND.

**Rabén Prisma Bokförlag AB:** Drottninggt. 108, POB 45022, 104 30 Stockholm; tel. (8) 34-99-60; fax (8) 30-05-64; f. 1963; Man. Dir UNO PALMSTRÖM.

**Bokförlaget Semic AB:** Gjuteribacken 23, POB 1243, 172 25 Sundbyberg; tel. (8) 799-30-50; fax (8) 799-30-64; handbooks, calendars, comic magazines, juvenile; Pres. TORSTEN LARSSON.

**Stenströms Bokförlag AB:** Linnégt. 98, POB 27217, 102 53 Stockholm; tel. (8) 662-78-28; fax (8) 663-22-01; f. 1983; Man. Dir BENGT STENSTRÖM.

**Streiffert Förlag AB:** Karlavägen 71, POB 5334, 102 47 Stockholm; tel. (8) 661-58-80; fax (8) 783-04-33; f. 1990; Man. Dir BO STREIFFERT.

**Svenska Dagbladets Förlag AB:** 105 17 Stockholm; publishing division of *Svenska Dagbladet* newspaper.

**Bokförlags AB Tiden:** POB 45022, 104 30 Stockholm; tel. (8) 457-03-00; fax (8) 457-03-32; fiction, non-fiction, handbooks, illustrated books, paperbacks, juvenile; Man. Dir LARS HJALMARSON.

**AB Timbro:** POB 5234, 102 45 Stockholm; tel. (8) 670-35-00; fax (8) 660-27-09; economics, political science; Man. Dir MATS JOHANSSON.

**Bokförlaget Trevi AB:** POB 1140, 111 81 Stockholm; tel. (8) 696-85-71; fax (8) 696-83-78; fiction and non-fiction, practical handbooks; since 1991 an independent subsidiary of Bonnier; Man. Dir SOLVEIG NELLINGE.

**Verbum Förlag AB:** St Paulsgt. 2, POB 15169, 104 65 Stockholm; tel. (8) 743-65-00; fax (8) 641-45-85; f. 1911; theology, fiction, juvenile, music; Man. Dir LARS G. STÅHL.

**AB Wahlström & Widstrand:** Sturegt. 32, POB 5587, 114 85 Stockholm; tel. (8) 696-84-80; fax (8) 696-83-80; f. 1884; fiction, non-fiction, biography, history, science, paperbacks; Man. Dir JONAS MODIG.

**B. Wahlströms Bokförlag AB:** Warfvinges väg 30, POB 30022, 104 25 Stockholm; tel. (8) 619-86-00; fax (8) 618-97-61; fiction, non-fiction, juvenile, picture books, paperbacks; Man. Dir BERTIL WAHLSTRÖM.

**Wolfers Kluwer Sverige:** POB 6471, 113 82 Stockholm; tel. (8) 690-90-00; fax (8) 32-08-51; general and educational publishing; bookseller; Man. Dir BIRGITTA JOHANSSON-HEDBERG.

### PUBLISHERS' ASSOCIATIONS

**Föreningen Svenska Läromedelsproducenter** (Swedish Asscn of Publishers and Manufactures of Educational Material): Drottninggt. 97, 113 60 Stockholm; tel. (8) 736-19-40; fax (8) 736-19-44; f. 1973; Dir LENA WESTERBERG; 36 mems.

**Svenska Bokförläggareföreningen** (Swedish Publishers' Asscn): Drottninggt. 97, 113 60 Stockholm; tel. (8) 736-19-40; fax (8) 736-19-44; f. 1843; Chair. LASSE BERGSTRÖM; Dir KENTH MULDIN; 92 mems.

## Radio and Television

Until the end of 1992 public-service radio and television were organized within the state broadcasting corporation, Sveriges Radio AB, a public-service organization financed by licence fees; this operated two national television channels and three national radio channels, together with 24 local radio stations. On 1 January 1993 the state corporation was replaced by three independent companies, Sveriges Radio AB, Sveriges Television AB, and Sveriges Utbildningsradio AB, responsible for radio, television and educational radio and television respectively. The operations of these companies are regulated by law and by agreements with the Government. From 1 January 1994 the three companies came into the ownership of three foundations.

There are two public-service television channels (Kanal-1 and TV 2) and four public-service radio channels, one of which provides regional broadcasts in 25 areas of Sweden. The broadcasts are financed by licence fees. In 1991 the Government awarded the licence for a third terrestrial nationwide television channel to TV 4 (which is financed by advertising).

The construction of cable networks for the diffusion of satellite TV programmes began in 1984. In early 1994 an estimated 65% of households in Sweden had access to satellite transmissions. There are nine television channels transmitted by satellite and cable, directed at the Swedish audience: TV 3, Femman, TVb, TV21, Z-TV, and the film channels TV 1000, FilmMax, Filmnet Plus and Filmnet Movie.

Neighbourhood radio stations were introduced in 1979, and by 1994 there were 160 such stations. During 1993 and 1994 the Local Radio Authority licensed 81 private local radio stations (financed by advertising) in 35 areas of Sweden.

In 1993 there were 3,332,000 licensed TV receivers. An estimated 7,272,000 radio sets were in use in the same year.

**Sveriges Radio AB:** Oxenstiernsgt. 20, 105 10 Stockholm; tel. (8) 784-00-00; fax (8) 667-83-36; f. 1993; independent company responsible for national radio broadcasting; Man. Dir OVE JOANSON.

**Sveriges Television AB:** TH T2, 105 10 Stockholm; tel. (8) 784-00-00; fax (8) 784-15-00; f. 1993; independent company responsible for national television broadcasting; Man. Dir SAM NILSSON.

**Sveriges Utbildningsradio AB:** Tulegt. 7, 113 95 Stockholm; tel. (8) 784-00-00; fax (8) 660-32-63; f. 1993; independent company responsible for educational broadcasting on radio and television; Man. Dir LARS HANSSON.

**TV 3:** Skeppsbron 18, 103 11 Stockholm; tel. (8) 10-33-33; fax (8) 676-08-12; commercial satellite channel.

**TV 4:** Storängskroken 10, 115 79 Stockholm; tel. (8) 644-44-00; fax (8) 644-44-40; commercial terrestrial channel.

**IBRA Radio AB:** 105 36 Stockholm; tel. (8) 619-25-40; fax (8) 619-25-39; non-commercial private Christian company broadcasting to all continents; Pres. OWE LINDESKÄR; Dirs SUNE ELOFSON, GÖSTA ÅKERLUND.

## Finance

### BANKING

(cap. = capital; res = reserves; dep. = deposits; m. = million; brs = branches; amounts in kronor).

Following severe losses in the Swedish financial sector in 1990–92, the Government was obliged to intervene in 1992 to support Nordbanken, Gota Bank and the savings bank Forsta Sparbanken. In that year the Government established a Bank Support Authority (Bankstödsnämnden) to provide financial assistance for banks and credit institutions. Improved results were reported by many banks in 1993 and 1994. In 1993 there were 16 commercial banks with total assets of 1,116,792m. kronor.

#### Central Bank

**Sveriges Riksbank** (Swedish Central Bank): 103 37 Stockholm; tel. (8) 787-00-00; telex 19150; fax (8) 21-05-31; f. 1668; bank of issue; controlled by a board of eight delegates, seven of whom are appointed by the Riksdag and one, the Governor, by other board members; cap. 1,000m.; res fund 55,942m.; notes in circulation 76,442m. (Dec. 1994); Chair. KJELL-OLOF FELDT; Gov. URBAN BÄCKSTRÖM; Dep. Govs THOMAS FRANZEN, STEFAN INGVES

#### Commercial Banks

**Föreningsbanken:** Grev Turegt. 30, 114 91 Stockholm; tel. (8) 782-30-00; telex 10627; fax (8) 660-99-71; f. 1958 (as Jordbrukets Bank); cap. 1,305m., res 3,408m., dep. 65,325m. (Dec. 1993); Chair. THORBJÖRN FÄLLDIN; Pres. BO SÖDERBERG; 579 brs.

**JP Bank AB:** Klarabergsviadukten 70, 107 81 Stockholm; tel. (8) 700-47-00; telex 14439; fax (8) 411-06-86; f. 1874 as Jämtlands Folkbank; cap. 395m., dep. 1,526m. (Dec. 1993); Pres. BENGT LJUNGQVIST; Man. GÖRAN LARSSON.

**Nordbanken:** Smålandsgt. 17, 105 71 Stockholm; tel. (8) 614-70-00; telex 12399; fax (8) 20-08-46; f. 1974 as Post-och Kreditbanken by merger of Postbanken and Sveriges Kreditbank, renamed 1986 as PKbanken, which acquired Nordbanken in 1990 and changed name; 100% state-controlled; privatization expected to be undertaken in 1996; merged with Gota Bank in 1994; cap. 5,372m., res 8,138m., dep. 180,664m. (Dec. 1994); Chair. JACOB PALMSTIERNA; Chief Exec. HANS DALBORG; 345 brs, with access to 1,300 post offices.

**Östgöta Enskilda Bank:** Storgt. 23, POB 328, 581 03 Linköping; tel. (13) 11-65-00; fax (13) 11-65-24; cap. 701m., dep. 8,345m. (1993); in 1994 established three regional banks: Provinsbanken Halland (Halmstad), Provinsbanken Närke (Örebro), Provinsbanken Värmland (Karlstad); Chair. FREDRIK LUNDBERG; Pres. and CEO ULF LUNDAHL; 26 brs.

**Skandinaviska Enskilda Banken (S-E-Banken):** Kungsträdgårdsgt. 8, 106 40 Stockholm; tel. (8) 763-50-00; telex 16600; fax (8) 763-83-89; f. 1972 by merger of Skandinaviska Banken and Stockholm's Enskilda Bank; cap. 5,269m., res 18,059m., dep. 178,084m. (Dec. 1993); Chair. CURT G. OLSSON; Group Chief Exec. BJÖRN SVEDBERG; 320 brs and sub-brs.

**Svenska Handelsbanken:** Kungsträdgårdsgt. 2, 106 70 Stockholm; tel. (8) 701-10-00; fax (8) 611-50-71; f. 1871; cap. 22,771m., dep. 182,508m. (1994). Chair. TOM HEDELIUS; Pres. and CEO ARNE MÅRTENSSON; 485 brs.

**Swedbank (Sparbanken Sverige AB):** Brunkebergstorg 8, 105 34 Stockholm; tel. (8) 22-23-20; telex 12826; fax (8) 11-90-13; f. 1992 by merger of 11 largest Swedish savings banks; cap. 5,020m., res 11,480m., dep. 142,100m. (Dec. 1993); Chair. LEIF LEWIN; Pres. and CEO GÖRAN COLLERT.

SWEDEN                                                                                                                                                  *Directory*

### Banking Organizations

**Finansinspektionen** (Financial Supervisory Authority): POB 7831, 103 98 Stockholm; tel. (8) 787-80-00; fax (8) 24-13-35; f. 1991, by merger of Bankinspektionen (Bank Inspection Board, f. 1907) and Försäkringsinspektionen (Private Insurance Supervisory Service, f. 1904), for the supervision of commercial and savings banks, financial companies, insurance companies, insurance brokers, friendly societies, mortgage institutions, securities firms and unit trusts, the stock exchange and clearing functions, the securities registry centre and the information registry centre; Dir-Gen. CLAES NORGREN.

**Svenska Bankföreningen** (Swedish Bankers' Asscn): Regeringsgt. 42, POB 7603, 103 94 Stockholm; tel. (8) 453-44-00; fax (8) 796-93-95; f. 1880; Pres. BJÖRN SVEDBERG; Man. Dir ULLA LUNDQUIST; 29 mems.

### STOCK EXCHANGE

**Stockholm Stock Exchange Ltd**: Källargränd 2, POB 1256, 111 82 Stockholm; tel. (8) 613-88-00; telex 13551; fax (8) 10-81-10; f. 1863 under government charter; automated trading system introduced by 1990; from 1993 a limited company, owned by members and issuers; in 1993 formed joint securities trading system (Nordquote) with Danish, Finnish and Norwegian stock exchanges; in Feb. 1994 197 Swedish and 11 foreign companies were listed; Chair. INGEMAR ELIASSON; Pres. and CEO BENGT RYDÉN.

### INSURANCE

See also Finansinspektionen (under Banking Organizations above)

#### Principal Insurance Companies

**Folksam**: Bohusgt. 14, 106 60 Stockholm; tel. (8) 772-60-00; fax (8) 643-40-26; f. 1908; all branches of life and non-life insurance; Pres. and CEO HÅKAN TIDLUND.

**Länsförsäkringsbolagens AB**: Tegeluddsvägen 11–13, 106 50 Stockholm; tel. (8) 690-10-00; fax (8) 670-48-23; f. 1936; all branches of life and non-life insurance; Pres. and CEO JAN GUNNAR PERSSON.

**Skandia Group Försäkrings AB**: Sveavägen 44, 103 50 Stockholm; tel. (8) 788-10-00; telex 19347; fax (8) 10-31-74; f. 1855; all branches of life and non-life insurance; Pres. and CEO BJÖRN WOLRATH.

**Trygg-Hansa**: Flemminggt. 18, 106 26 Stockholm; tel. (8) 693-10-00; telex 19887; fax (8) 650-93-67; f. 1828; all branches of life and non-life insurance; Pres. and CEO LARS H. THUNELL.

**WASA Försäkring**: Hemvärnsgt. 9, 173 81 Stockholm; tel. (8) 635-35-00; fax (8) 635-51-51; f. 1987; all branches of life and non-life insurance; Pres. and CEO LARS ROSÉN.

#### Insurance Associations

**Svenska Försäkringsföreningen** (Swedish Insurance Society): Slöjdgt. 9, 115 87 Stockholm; tel. (8) 24-28-60; fax (8) 24-13-20; f. 1875 to promote sound development of the Swedish insurance business; Chair. ERLAND STRÖMBÄCK; Sec. ANDERS KLEVERMAN.

**Sveriges Försäkringsförbund** (Swedish Insurance Federation): POB 1436, 111 84 Stockholm; tel. (8) 783-71-50; fax (8) 723-03-08; Chair. BJÖRN WOLRATH; Man. Dir OLOV HERTZMAN.

## Trade and Industry

### TRADE COUNCIL

**Exportrådet** (Trade Council): Storgt. 19, POB 5513, 114 85 Stockholm; tel. (8) 783-85-00; telex 19620; fax (8) 662-90-93; f. 1972; Pres. TOM WACHTMEISTER; Man. Dir ULF DINKELSPIEL; 2,700 mems.

### CHAMBERS OF COMMERCE

**Handelskammaren i Jönköpings Län**: Elmiavägen, 554 54 Jönköping; tel. (36) 16-03-10; telex 70164; fax (36) 12-95-79; f. 1975; Pres. GUNNAR RANDHOLM; Sec. GÖRAN KINNANDER; 1,000 mems.

**Mellansvenska Handelskammaren**: POB 296, 801 04 Gävle; tel. (26) 10-54-30; fax (26) 14-38-72; f. 1907; Pres. INGVAR PETERSSON; Man. Dir ANDERS FRANCK; 535 mems.

**Norrbottens Handelskammare**: Storgt. 9, 972 38 Luleå; tel. (920) 122-10; fax (920) 94-857; f. 1904; Chair. STAFFAN PREUTZ; Dir. MONA BLOM.

**Handelskammaren för Örebro och Västmanlands Län**: POB 154, 701 43 Örebro; tel. (19) 611-22-23; telex 73152; fax (19) 11-77-50; f. 1907; Pres. EGON LINDEROTH; Sec. SVEN SVENSSON.

**Östsvenska Handelskammaren**: POB 1343, 600 43 Norrköping; tel. (11) 12-91-00; fax (11) 13-77-19; f. 1908.

**Stockholms Handelskammare**: V. Trädgårdsgt. 9, POB 16050, 103 21 Stockholm; tel. (8) 613-18-00; telex 15638; fax (8) 411-24-32; f. 1902; Pres. CARL ERIK HEDLUND; Dir PETER EGARDT.

**Sydsvenska Handelskammaren**: Skeppsbron 2, 211 20 Malmö; tel. (40) 73-550; telex 33388; fax (40) 11-86-09; f. 1905; Pres. HANS CAVALLI-BJÖRKMAN; Man. Dir STEN BENGTSSON; 3,050 mems.

**Västernorrlands och Jämtlands Läns Handelskammare**: Kyrkogt. 26, 852 52 Sundsvall; tel. (60) 17-18-80; telex 71263; fax (60) 486-40; f. 1913; Pres. ERIK EHN; Sec. PER-RICHARD MOLÉN; 348 mems.

**Västsvenska Handelskammaren**: POB 5253, 402 25 Göteborg; tel. (31) 83-59-00; telex 27430; fax (8) 83-59-36; f. 1661; Man. Dir STURE PERFJELL; about 2,250 mems.

**Västsvenska Handelskammaren Värmland**: Älvgt. 11, 652 25 Karlstad; tel. (54) 21-00-22; fax (54) 18-60-02; f. 1912; Pres. GÖRAN FRÖDIN; Sec. BJÖRN LJUNGDAHL; about 600 mems.

### INDUSTRIAL ASSOCIATIONS

**Sveriges Industriförbund** (Federation of Swedish Industries): Storgt. 19, POB 5501, 114 85 Stockholm; tel. (8) 783-80-00; fax (8) 662-35-95; f. 1910; the central organization of industrial and manufacturing firms; Chair. BERT-OLOF SVANHOLM; Man. Dir MAGNUS LEMMEL; consists of 16 trade associations; 6,000 mem. cos.

**Företagarnas Riksorganisation** (Federation of Private Enterprises): Vegagt. 14, 113 93 Stockholm; tel. (8) 610-17-00; fax (8) 33-10-20; f. 1990; Chair. ARNE JOHANSSON; Man. Dir CARL-JOHAN WESTHOLM; 60,000 mems.

**Grafiska Företagen** (Graphic Companies Federation): Blasieholmsgt. 4A, POB 16383, 103 27 Stockholm; tel. (8) 762-68-00; fax (8) 611-08-28; f. 1993 by merger of Grafiska Industriförbundet with Grafiska Arbetsgivareförbundet; Chair. BJÖRN BJURMAN; Man. Dir SVERKER ERLANDSON.

**Grossistförbundet Svensk Handel** (Federation of Swedish Commerce and Trade): Grevgt. 34, POB 5512, 114 85 Stockholm; tel. (8) 666-11-00; telex 19673; fax (8) 662-74-57; f. 1922; central organization for Swedish import trade; Pres. STURE LINDMARK; Dir Import Council BÖRJE RISINGGÅRD; 1,500 mems.

**Järnverksföreningen** (Ironworks Commercial Asscn): Kungsträdgårdsgt. 10, POB 1721, 111 87 Stockholm; f. 1889; Pres. DAN JOHANSSON; Sec. P. O. BOMAN; 35 mems.

**Jernkontoret** (Steel Producers Asscn): Kungsträdgårdsgt. 10, POB 1721, 111 87 Stockholm; tel. (8) 679-17-00; fax (8) 611-20-89; f. 1747; Man. Dir ORVAR NYQUIST.

**Skogsindustrierna** (Swedish Pulp and Paper Asscn): Storgt. 19, POB 5518, 114 85 Stockholm; tel. (8) 783-84-00; fax (8) 661-73-06; Chair. B. WERGENS; Dir-Gen. Dr JAN REMRÖD.

**Svensk Industriförening** (Swedish Small Industries Asscn): Torsgt. 2, POB 1133, 111 81 Stockholm; tel. (8) 23-63-00; f. 1941; Man. Dir SVEN LANGENIUS; 1,800 mems.

**Svenska Garveriidkareföreningen** (Swedish Tanners' Asscn): Blasieholmsgt. 5, POB 16105, 103 22 Stockholm; tel. (8) 762-60-00; telex 15051; fax (8) 762-69-48; f. 1901; Chair. GÖRAN TRUEDSON; Man. Dir PER BONDELID; 4 mems.

**Svenska Glasbruksföreningen** (Swedish Glass Manufacturers' Asscn): POB 5501, 114 85 Stockholm; tel. (8) 783-80-00; fax (8) 663-63-23; Chair. HERBERT FRITZSCHE; Man. Dir GEORG WERGEMAN.

**Svenska Kraftverksföreningen** (Swedish Power Asscn): Olof Palmesgt. 31, 101 53 Stockholm; tel. (8) 677-25-60; fax (8) 677-25-65; f. 1909; Pres. OLOF G. WIKSTRÖM; Man. Dir NILS ANDERSSON; 400 mems.

**Svenska Kvarnföreningen** (Swedish Flour Milling Asscn): St Goransgt. 160A, POB 30020, 104 25 Stockholm; tel. (8) 737-03-50; fax (8) 737-03-60; f. 1914; Chair. PER SORTE; Man. Dir ÅKE OLOFFSSON; 8 mems.

**Svenska Sågverks-och Trävaruexportföreningen** (Swedish Wood Exporters' Asscn): Villagt. 1, 114 32 Stockholm; tel. (8) 789-28-00; telex 13136; f. 1875; Pres. P. FREDELL; Man. Dir L. STRÄNGH; 350 mems.

**Svenska Skofabrikantföreningen** (Swedish Shoe Manufacturers' Asscn): c/o Arbesko-Gruppen AB, POB 1642, 701 16 Örebro; tel. (19) 30-66-00; fax (19) 30-66-50; f. 1910.

**Sveriges Handelsagenters Förbund** (Federation of Swedish Commercial Agents): POB 12705, 112 94 Stockholm; tel. (8) 654-09-75; fax (8) 650-35-17; f. 1914; Chair. BENGT LINDROTH; Man. Dir ANNA WIGARDT DUHS; 700 mems.

**Sveriges Kemiska Industrikontor (Kemikontoret)** (Asscn of Swedish Chemical Industries): Storgt. 19, POB 5501, 114 85 Stockholm; tel. (8) 783-80-00; telex 19990; fax (8) 663-63-23; f. 1917; Pres. GÖSTA WIKING; Man. Dir OWE FREDHOLM; 168 mems.

**Sveriges Köpmannaförbund** (Swedish Retail Federation): Kungsgt. 19, 105 61 Stockholm; tel. (8) 791-53-00; fax (8) 21-20-97; f. 1883; Chair. ROLF H. GARD; Man. Dir E. O. HOLM; 20,000 mems.

SWEDEN    Directory

**Swedish Textile and Clothing Industries' Asscn:** Storgt. 5, POB 5510, 114 85 Stockholm; tel. (8) 762-68-80; fax (8) 762-68-87; f. 1992 replacing fmr Textilrådet (Textile Manufacturers' Asscn, f. 1939); Man. Dir SVEN CELE.

### PRINCIPAL EMPLOYERS' ASSOCIATIONS
#### Central Organization

**Svenska Arbetsgivareföreningen (SAF)** (Swedish Employers' Confederation): Södra Blasieholmshamnen 4A, 103 30 Stockholm; tel. (8) 762-60-00; telex 19923; fax (8) 762-62-90; f. 1902; members are privately owned industrial and service enterprises; aims to create the best possible conditions for free enterprise and to safeguard the interests of the employers in questions concerning their relations with employees; comprises 34 employers' asscns with 42,000 mems; employing 1,200,000 people; Chair. of Board ULF LAURIN; Dir-Gen. GÖRAN TUNHAMMAR.

#### Branch Associations

**Allmänna Arbetsgivarförbundet** (General Group of the Swedish Employers' Confederation): POB 16105, 103 22 Stockholm; tel. (8) 762-69-00; fax (8) 762-69-48; f. 1921; Chair. GUNNAR NORDSTRÖM; Dir-Gen. GÖRAN TROGEN; 3,800 mems.

**ARBIO** (Forest and Agricultural Employers, Forest Industries, Wood Products Industry): Södra Blasieholmshamnen 4A, POB 16006, 103 21 Stockholm; tel. (8) 762-72-00; fax (8) 762-72-14; Chair. LENNART AHLGREN; Man. Dir JAN-PETER DUKER; 4,000 mems.

**Bageri-och Konditoriarbetsgivareförbundet** (Bakery and Confectionery Employers): Norrlandsgt. 31-33, 111 43 Stockholm; tel. (8) 762-60-00; fax (8) 20-79-94; f. 1954; Chair. HARALD JAHN; Man. Dir ULF GÖRAN LILJEBLADH; 720 mems.

**Biltrafikens Arbetsgivareförbund** (Road Transport Employers): Blasieholmsgt. 4A, 111 48 Stockholm; tel. (8) 762-60-00; fax (8) 611-46-99; Chair. REINHOLD ÖHMAN; Man. Dir GÖRAN LJUNGSTRÖM.

**Byggentreprenörerna** (Construction Federation): Narvavägen 12, POB 27308, 102 54 Stockholm; tel. (8) 665-35-00; fax (8) 662-97-00; f. 1919; Pres. TORSTEN ERIKSSON; Man. Dir BERT LILJA; 2,000 mem. cos.

**Byggnadsämnesförbundet** (Building Material Manufacturers Employers): POB 16105, 103 22 Stockholm; tel. (8) 762-60-00, fax (8) 762-69-48; Chair. ULF LINDEROTH; Man. Dir GUNNAR GÖTHBERG; 278 mem. cos.

**Elektriska Arbetsgivareföreningen** (Electrical Employers): POB 17537, 118 91 Stockholm; tel. (8) 616-04-00; fax (8) 668-86-17; Chair. GÖRAN AHLSTRÖM; Man. Dir BJÖRN TIBELL; 1,286 mem. cos.

**Förlags- och Medieförbundet** (Publishing and Media Companies): POB 16383, 103 27 Stockholm; tel. (8) 762-68-00; fax (8) 611-08-28; Chair. PER-OLOV ATLE.

**Försäkringsbranschens Arbetsgivareorganisation** (Insurance Employers): Stureplan 4, 114 35 Stockholm; tel. (8) 611-17-60; fax (8) 611-17-87; Chair. BJÖRN WOLRATH; Man. Dir ROLF HUGERT; 83 mem. cos.

**Gruvornas Arbetsgivareförbund** (Mine Owners): POB 1721, 111 87 Stockholm; tel. (8) 762-60-00; fax (8) 611-62-64; Pres. BENGT LÖFKVIST; Man. Dir BENGT HULDT; 20 mems with 6,500 employees.

**HAO-FÖRBUNDEN** (Commercial and Service Employers): Blasieholmsgt. 4B, POB 16371, 103 26 Stockholm; tel. (8) 762-77-00; fax (8) 678-69-33; Chair. LARS OTTERBECK; Man. Dir GUNNAR HÖGBERG; 11,500 mems with 192,000 employees.

**Livsmedelsbranschens Arbetsgivareförbund** (Food Producers): POB 16106, 103 22 Stockholm; tel. (8) 762-60-00; fax (8) 762-69-48; Chair. ALF LARSSON; Man. Dir GUNNAR GÖTHBERG; 385 mem. cos.

**Maskinentreprenörerna** (Earth Moving Contractors): POB 1609, 111 86 Stockholm; tel. (8) 762-70-65; fax (8) 655-85-41; Chair. ROLF GUNNARSSON; Man. Dir SVEN-OLA NILSSON; 3,669 mem. cos.

**Motorbranschens Arbetsgivareförbund** (Motor Trade Employers): Blasieholmsgt. 4A, POB 1621, 111 86 Stockholm; tel. (8) 762-60-00; telex 19923; fax (8) 611-46-99; Chair. GÖRAN GRERUP; Dir GÖRAN LJUNGSTRÖM; 2,330 mem. cos.

**Petroleumbranschens Arbetsgivareförbund** (Petroleum Industry Employers): Blasieholmsgt. 4A, POB 1621, 111 86 Stockholm; tel. (8) 762-60-00; telex 19923; fax (8) 611-46-99; f. 1936; Chair. JAN-OLOV ERICKSSON; Man. Dir GÖRAN LJUNGSTRÖM; 53 mem. cos.

**Plåtslageriernas Riksförbund** (Platers): Rosenlundsgt. 40, POB 17536, 118 91 Stockholm; tel. (8) 616-72-00; fax (8) 616-00-72; Chair. ÅKE NILSSON; Man. Dir DAN KRISTIANSEN; 808 mem. cos.

**Stål-och Metallförbundet** (Steel and Metal Industry Employers): POB 1721, 111 87 Stockholm; tel. (8) 762-60-00; fax (8) 611-62-64; Pres. GUNNAR BJÖRKLUND; Man. Dir BENGT HULDT; 203 mems with 46,500 employees.

**Stoppmöbelförbundet** (Upholstery Industry Employers): Storgt. 5, POB 5510, 114 85 Stockholm; tel. (8) 762-68-80; fax (8) 762-68-87; f. 1942; Pres. SVEN-HUGO SÖDERBERG; Man. Dir ANDERS SANDGREN; 50 mem. cos.

**Sveriges Hamn- och Stuveriförbund** (Ports and Stevedores): POB 1608, 111 86 Stockholm; tel. (8) 762-78-80; fax (8) 611-12-18; f. 1908; Chair. LARS-GUNNAR ALBÅGE; Man. Dir CLAES MANGNÄS; 51 mem. cos.

**Sveriges Kvarnyrkesförbund** (Flour Millers): Norrlandsgt. 31-33, 111 43 Stockholm; tel. (8) 762-60-00; fax (8) 20-79-94; f. 1909; Chair. PER SORTE; Man. Dir ULF GÖRAN LILJEBLADH; 14 mems.

**Sveriges Redareförening** (Swedish Shipowners' Asscn): see Shipping.

**Sveriges Verkstadsindustrier** (Engineering Industries): Storgt. 5, POB 5510, 114 85 Stockholm; tel. (8) 782-08-00; fax (8) 782-09-66; f. 1896; Pres. BERT-OLOF SVANHOLM; Man. Dir HEINRICH BLAUERT; 2,600 mems with 325,000 employees.

**Svets Mekaniska Arbetsgivareförbundet** (Welding Engineering): POB 1721, 111 87 Stockholm; tel. (8) 762-60-00; fax (8) 611-62-64; Pres. GUNNAR SKÖLD; Man. Dir BENGT HULDT; 431 mems with 4,000 employees.

**TEKOindustrierna** (Textile and Clothing Industries' Asscn): Storgt. 5, POB 5510, 114 85 Stockholm; tel. (8) 762-68-80; fax (8) 762-68-87; f. 1907; Chair. IVAN L. LUDVIGSON; Man. Dir ANDERS SANDGREN; 230 mems.

**VVS-Entreprenörernas Arbetsgivareförbund** (Heating, Plumbing, Refrigeration and Insulation Employers): Rosenlundsgt. 40, 118 91 Stockholm; tel. (8) 616-04-00; fax (8) 669-41-19; f. 1918; Chair. HÅKAN ÖSTLUND; Man. Dir CARL-GÖRAN WIVSTAM; 727 mems.

### TRADE UNIONS

The three principal trade union bodies are the Swedish Trade Union Confederation (LO), the Confederation of Professional Employees (TCO) and the Confederation of Professional Associations (SACO).

**Landsorganisationen i Sverige (LO)** (Swedish Trade Union Confederation): Barnhusgt.18, 105 53 Stockholm; tel. (8) 796-25-00; telex 19145; fax (8) 24-52-28; f. 1898; affiliated to ICFTU; Pres. BERTIL JONSSON; Sec. MARGARETA SVENSSON; 21 affiliated unions with a total membership of 2,230,490 (Dec. 1994).

Affiliated unions:

**Fastighetsanställdas Förbund** (Building Maintenance Workers): POB 70446, 107 25 Stockholm; tel. (8) 696-11-50; fax (8) 24-46-90; f. 1936; Chair. BARBRO PALMERLUND; 44,578 mems.

**Försäkringsanställdas Förbund** (Social Insurance Employees and Insurance Agents): POB 344, 101 26 Stockholm; tel. (8) 402-94-00; fax (8) 21-10-44; f. 1918; Chair. BÖRJE JOHANSSON; 19,925 mems.

**Grafiska Fackförbundet** (Graphic Workers): POB 1101, 111 81 Stockholm; tel. (8) 791-16-00; fax (8) 411-41-01; Pres. VALTER CARLSSON; Sec. GÖRAN SÖDERLUND; 42,933 mems.

**Handelsanställdas Förbund** (Commercial Employees): Stadiongt. 67, POB 5074, 200 71 Malmö; tel. (40) 24-77-00; telex 32838; fax (40) 98-01-57; f. 1906; Pres. KENTH PETTERSSON; 176,722 mems.

**Hotell-och Restauranganställdas Förbund** (Hotel and Restaurant Workers): POB 1143, 111 81 Stockholm; tel. (8) 781-02-00; fax (8) 21-71-18; Chair. SEINE SVENSK; 57,535 mems.

**Industrifacket** (Industrial Union): POB 1114, 111 81 Stockholm; tel. (8) 786-85-00; fax (8) 10-59-68; f. 1993 by merger of factory workers' and textile, garment and leather workers' unions; Chair. ARNE LÖKKEN; 109,617 mems.

**SEKO-Facket för Service och Kommunikation** (Services and Communications Employees): Barnhusgt. 6–10, POB 1105, 111 81 Stockholm; tel. (8) 791-41-00; telex 17989; fax (8) 21-89-53; f. 1970, present name since 1995; Chair. GUNNAR ERLANDSSON; 191,416 mems.

**Svenska Bleck-och Plåtslagareförbundet** (Sheet Metal Workers): POB 19015, 104 32 Stockholm; tel. (8) 34-09-45; fax (8) 32-91-85; f. 1893; Chair. KJELL WESTERLUND; 6,461 mems.

**Svenska Byggnadsarbetareförbundet** (Building Workers): POB 19013, 104 32 Stockholm; tel. (8) 728-48-00; fax (8) 34-50-51; Chair. OVE BENGTSBERG; 153,977 mems.

**Svenska Elektrikerförbundet** (Electricians): POB 1123, 111 81 Stockholm; tel. (8) 402-14-00; fax (8) 402-14-02; Pres. HANS SCHOUG; 29,757 mems.

**Svenska Kommunalarbetareförbundet** (Swedish Municipal Workers' Union): POB 19039, 104 32 Stockholm; tel. (8) 728-28-00; fax (8) 31-87-45; Pres. LILLEMOR ARVIDSSON; 661,381 mems.

**Svenska Lantarbetareförbundet** (Agricultural Workers): POB 1104, 111 81 Stockholm; tel. (8) 24-08-20; fax (8) 411-62-51; f. 1918; Pres. LEIF HAKANSSON; Sec. LENNART JOHANSSON; 16,536 mems.

SWEDEN	*Directory*

**Svenska Livsmedelsarbetareförbundet** (Food Workers): POB 1156, 111 81 Stockholm; tel. (8) 24-56-40; fax (8) 411-71-92; Chair. KJELL VARENBLAD; Sec. EVERT KAJHAMMAR; 62,266 mems.

**Svenska Målareförbundet** (Painters): POB 1113, 111 81 Stockholm; tel. (8) 23-25-80; fax (8) 791-00-09; f. 1887; Chair. KJELL JOHANSSON; 22,624 mems.

**Svenska Metallindustriarbetareförbundet** (Metal Workers): Olof Palmesgt. 11, 105 52 Stockholm; tel. (8) 786-80-00; fax (8) 24-86-74; f. 1888; Chair. GÖRAN JOHNSSON; 442,882 mems.

**Svenska Musikerförbundet** (Musicians): POB 43, 101 20 Stockholm; tel. (8) 674-05-00; fax (8) 16-80-20; f. 1994; Pres. ROLAND ALMLÉN; Sec. GÖRAN IVARSON; 6,900 mems.

**Svenska Pappersindustriarbetareförbundet** (Paper Workers): POB 1127, 111 81 Stockholm; tel. (8) 796-61-00; fax (8) 411-41-79; Chair. SUNE EKBÅGE; Sec. CLAES HELLGREN; 30,182 mems.

**Svenska Sjöfolksförbundet** (Seamen): Fjärde Långgt. 48, POB 31176, 400 32 Göteborg; tel. (31) 42-94-20; telex 21534; fax (31) 42-95-01; Chair. ANDERS LINDSTROM; Vice-Chair. BÖRJE PERSSON; 10,144 mems.

**Svenska Skogsarbetareförbundet** (Forest Workers): POB 903, 801 32 Gävle; tel. (26) 51-52-75; fax (26) 51-33-24; Chair. ÅKE PETTERSSON; Sec. SUNE BACK; 15,453 mems.

**Svenska Träindustriarbetareförbundet** (Wood Industry Workers): POB 1152, 111 81 Stockholm; tel. (8) 701-77-00; fax (8) 20-79-04; f. 1889; Chair. and Pres. GUNNAR A. KARLSSON; 61,789 mems.

**Svenska Transportarbetareförbundet** (Transport Workers): POB 714, 101 33 Stockholm; tel. (8) 723-77-00; fax (8) 24-03-91; Chair. HANS WAHLSTRÖM; 66,315 mems.

**SACO** (Confederation of Professional Asscns): POB 2206, Lilla Nygt. 14, 103 15 Stockholm; tel. (8) 613-48-00; fax (8) 24-77-01; f. 1947; 25 affiliated unions and professional organizations; Chair. ANDERS MILTON; 355,000 mems.

**Tjänstemännens Centralorganisation (TCO)** (Confederation of Professional Employees): Linnégt. 14, 114 94 Stockholm; tel. (8) 782-91-00; telex 19104; fax (8) 663-75-20; f. 1944; affiliated to ICFTU, European Trade Union Confed. and Council of Nordic Trade Unions; Pres. INGER OHLSSON; 20 affiliated unions with total membership of 1,308,482 (Dec. 1994), of which the following are the largest:

**Finansförbundet** (Bank Employees): Birger Jarlsgt. 31, POB 7375, 103 91 Stockholm; tel. (8) 614-03-00; fax (8) 611-38-98; Chair. ROLF BLOM; 47,669 mems.

**Handelstjänstemannaförbundet** (Commercial Salaried Employees): Franzengt. 5, POB 30102, 104 25 Stockholm; tel. (8) 737-80-00; fax (8) 618-22-45; Chair. LARS HELLMAN; 145,112 mems.

**Lärarförbundet** (Teachers): Segelbåtsvägen 15, POB 12229, 102 26 Stockholm; tel. (8) 737-65-00; fax (8) 656-94-15; Chair. CHRISTER ROMILSON; 202,053 mems.

**Statstjänstemannaförbundet** (Civil Servants): Sturegt. 15, POB 5308, 102 47 Stockholm; tel. (8) 790-51-00; fax (8) 24-29-24; Chair. LISBETH EKLUND; 117,349 mems.

**Svenska Hälso-och Sjukvårdens Tjänstemannaförbund** (Salaried Employees in the Health Service): Adolf Fredriks Kyrkogt. 11, POB 3260, 103 65 Stockholm; tel. (8) 14-77-00; fax (8) 11-42-29; Chair. EVA FERNVALL; 111,314 mems.

**Svenska Industritjänstemannaförbundet** (Clerical and Technical Employees in Industry): Olof Palmesgt. 17, 105 32 Stockholm; tel. (8) 789-70-00; fax (8) 791-77-90; Chair. BO HENNING; Gen. Sec. BENGT HANSSON; 311,678 mems.

**Sveriges Arbetsledareförbund (SALF)** (Supervisors): St Eriksgt. 26, POB 12069, 101 22 Stockholm; tel. (8) 652-01-20; fax (8) 650-34-93; Chair. BJÖRN BERGMAN; 83,938 mems.

**Sveriges Kommunaltjänstemannaförbund** (Local Government Officers): Kungsgt. 28A, POB 7825, 103 97 Stockholm; tel. (8) 789-63-00; fax (8) 21-52-44; Chair. STURE NORDH; 182,623 mems.

## LABOUR MARKET AGENCY

**Arbetsmarknadsstyrelsen (AMS)** (Labour Market Board): 171 99 Solna, Stockholm; tel. (8) 730-60-00; fax (8) 27-83-68; f. 1948; autonomous public agency, responsible for administration of Sweden's labour market; main aims: to provide social means for easing structural change in the economy, to organize labour market by balancing requirements of workers and employers, and to uphold commitment to concept of full employment; board mems appointed by govt, employers and trades unions; Dir GÖTE BERNHARDSSON.

## CO-OPERATIVE ASSOCIATION

**Kooperativa förbundet Group** (Co-operative Union and Wholesale Society): POB 15200, 104 65 Stockholm; tel. (8) 743-10-00; telex 19490; f. 1899; 140 co-operative retail societies with 2m. mems, 1,367 food stores, 140 restaurants, 309 supermarkets, 31 department stores, 23 hypermarkets, 14 furniture stores, 18 speciality stores, 17 factories, 2 joint production units, 18 variety stores, 9 travel agencies; total sales about 29,000m. kr (1985); Exec. Pres. LEIF LEWIN; 65,100 employees.

## STATE-OWNED INDUSTRIES

In October 1991 it was announced that 35 state-owned companies were to be sold to the private sector. In 1992 the Government decided to delay the privatization process, owing to Sweden's economic difficulties. In 1993 the defence group Celsius was sold (with the state retaining a 25% share), and in 1994 the pharmaceuticals and biotechnology company, Pharmacia AB, and the forestry company, AssiDöman, were privatized. By the end of April 1994 the Government had sold a majority shareholding in 18 companies.

**Apoteksbolaget AB:** Humlegardsgt. 20, 105 14 Stockholm; tel. (8) 666-70-00; telex 11553; fax (8) 666-75-15; f. 1970; two-thirds state-owned; pharmaceutical distribution, owns all pharmacies in Sweden; Chair. BERTIL DANIELSSON; Man. Dir ÅKE HALLMAN; 10,562 employees.

**Board of Civil Aviation:** see under Transport.

**SKDföretagen AB:** Jungfrudansen 21, POB 4040, 171 04 Solna; tel. (8) 705-80-00; fax (8) 27-91-25; f. 1969; partially privatized in 1994; 25% state-owned; management and data processing consultation; Pres. MATS HENTZEL; 1,500 employees.

**Statens Järnvägar:** see under Transport.

**AB Svelast:** POB 70349, 107 23 Stockholm; f. 1937; 100% state-owned; transport and distribution of goods; Man. Dir LEIF AXEN; 1,400 employees.

**Systembolaget AB:** Kungsträdgårdsgt. 14, 103 84 Stockholm; tel. (8) 789-35-00; fax (8) 789-35-02; f. 1955; 100% state-owned; monopoly of retail sale of wines, spirits and strong beers; Pres. GABRIEL ROMANUS; 2,694 employees.

**Telia AB:** Mårbackagt. 11, 123 86 Farsta; tel. (8) 713-10-00; fax (8) 713-33-33; f. 1993 (fmrly Swedish Telecom); 100% state-owned; owns and operates telecommunications networks and supplies equipment; CEO LARS BERG; 22,000 employees.

**Tidningstjänst AB:** Drottninggt. 70, 111 81 Stockholm; tel. (8) 21-44-41; fax (8) 21-05-40; f. 1969; 100% state-owned; distribution of newspapers and administration of state subsidies; Pres. OVE RAINER; Dir OLOF JONSSON; 2,487 employees.

**AB Tipstjänst:** 106 10 Stockholm; tel. (8) 757-77-00; telex 10789; f. 1934; 100% state-owned; monopoly of public betting on all sports except horse racing; Pres. WALTER SLUNGE; Man. Dir RICHARD FRIGREN; 780 employees.

**AB Trafikrestauranger:** POB 746, 101 35 Stockholm; tel. (8) 613-62-00; fax (8) 613-62-01; f. 1938; 100% state-owned; train and station catering; Chair. KARL-ERIK STRAND; Man. Dir PER JÖNSSON; 1,000 employees.

**Vattenfall AB:** 162 87 Stockholm; tel. (8) 739-50-00; telex 19653; fax (8) 37-01-70; f. 1909; became limited liability company in Jan. 1992; 100% state-owned; power generation and distribution; Pres. and CEO CARL-ERIK NYQUIST; 9,674 employees.

**Vin & Sprit AB:** POB 47319, 100 74 Stockholm; f. 1917; 100% state-owned; import, wholesale and export of wines and spirits; Chair. CLAES DAHLBACK; Man. EGON JACOBSSON; 850 employees.

## TRADE FAIR

**Malmö Trade Fair:** POB 19015, 200 73 Malmö; tel. (40) 80-030; telex 32256; fax (40) 19-25-20; f. 1919; international exhibition centre; Pres. LARS ROSENQVIST.

# Transport

## RAILWAYS

In 1993 there were 9,747 km of 1,435 mm gauge state railways and 1,137 km of private railways; 7,270 km of track was electrified. A railway line, linking Stockholm and Arlanda international airport was scheduled to open in 1998.

**Statens Järnvägar (SJ):** 105 50 Stockholm; tel. (8) 762-20-00; telex 19410; fax (8) 411-12-16; f. 1856; state-owned; Dir-Gen. STIG LARSSON; administers all state-owned railway track; the company also controls four ferry-boat lines with a total length of 164 km and 45,030 km of bus lines; 15,000 employees.

**BK Tag AB:** Brogardsgt., 57438 Vetlanda; tel. (383) 18-640; fax (383) 14-757; passenger services on six routes; Gen. Man. T. HULT; 667 km.

**Malmö-Limhamns Järnvägs AB:** POB 30022, 20061 Malmö; tel. (40) 36-16-90; fax (40) 16-27-80; Dir U. JOHANSSON; Traffic Man. K. HOLMBERG; 5 km of 1,435 mm gauge.

# SWEDEN

**TGOJ AB:** 631 92 Eskilstuna; tel. (16) 17-26-00; fax (16) 17-26-01; f. 1877; Chair. BERNT ANDERSSON; Pres. CURT BYLUND; 300 km of 1,435 mm gauge electrified railways.

## ROADS

At 31 December 1993 there were 134,920 km of roads: 14,587 km of main or national roads (including 1,061 km of motorways); 83,233 km of secondary or regional roads; and an estimated 37,100 km of other roads. In 1991 the Danish and Swedish Governments signed an agreement to provide a road-rail link between Malmö and Copenhagen (Denmark), across the 16-km Öresund strait. Construction of the link, initially delayed for environmental reasons, was scheduled to begin in 1996 and be completed by the year 2000.

## SHIPPING
### Principal Shipping Companies

**Argonaut AB:** Eriksbergsgt. 10, POB 5620, 114 86 Stockholm; tel. (8) 614-45-00; fax (8) 611-62-28; f. 1983; Pres. BJORN ERSMAN; 8 tankers totalling 2,430,000 dwt.

**B & N, Bylock & Nordsjöfrakt AB:** POB 102, 440 60 Skärhamn; tel. (304) 67-92-00; fax (304) 67-05-12; Man. Dir FOLKE PATRIKSSON; 50 vessels (reefers, roll-on roll-off, bulk).

**EffJohn International:** POB 29091, 100 52 Stockholm; tel. (8) 666-34-00; f. 1990 following merger of Effoa Finland Steamship Co. and Johnson Line (Sweden); passenger ferry operations. The EffJohn Group covers operations in the Baltic: Silja Line, SeaWind Line, Wasa Ferries, Sally Line, JBT, Svea Management; elsewhere in Europe: Sally Line UK; in USA: Commodore Cruise Line, Crown Cruise Line; 23 cruise vessels/ferries; Pres. HANS H. CHRISTNER.

**Ferm International Ship Management AB:** POB 39, 440 60 Skärhamn; tel. (304) 67-10-70; telex 2428; fax (304) 67-11-10; management company, operating specialized tanker services; Man. Dir ARNE HAMNÉN; 18 vessels totalling 1,512,536 dwt.

**Nordström & Thulin AB:** Skeppsbron 34–36, POB 1215, 111 82 Stockholm; tel. (8) 613-19-00; telex 17907; fax (8) 21-22-28; f. 1850; Man. Dir RONALD BERGMAN; 7 vessels totalling 780,000 dwt, 4 passenger ferries.

**Stena AB:** 405 19 Göteborg; tel. (31) 85-80-00; telex 2559; fax (31) 12-06-51; f. 1983 (Stena Line ferry service since 1962); in 1990 acquired Sealink (United Kingdom); Pres. BO LERENIUS; Man. Dir DAN S. OLSSON; 12 car and passenger ferries, 13 roll-on roll-off vessels, 2 super night ferries, 6 bulk carriers, 14 tankers.

**United Tankers AB:** POB 8806, 402 71 Göteborg; tel. (31) 779-30-00; telex 21060; fax (31) 779-30-12; f. 1990; specializes in transporting petroleum products, in north-west Europe and worldwide; Man. Dir BUSTER HULTMAN; 27 product tankers.

**Wallenius Lines:** Swedenborgsgt. 19, POB 17086, 104 62 Stockholm; f. 1934; tel. (8) 772-05-00; telex 19010; fax (8) 640-68-54; car and truck carriers; Pres. CHRISTER OLSSON; 29 vessels totalling 561,473 dwt.

### Associations

**Föreningen Sveriges Sjöfart och Sjöförsvar** (Swedish Maritime League): Kastellet, Kastellholmen, 111 49 Stockholm; tel. (8) 611-74-81; f. 1983 by merger of Swedish General Shipping Asscn and Swedish Navy League; Pres. K.-E. HALÉN; Gen. Sec. U. SAMUELSON; 2,000 mems.

**Sveriges Redareförening** (Swedish Shipowners' Asscn): Kungsportsavenyen 1, POB 53046, 400 14 Göteborg; tel. (31) 17-18-30; telex 27022; fax (31) 13-01-26; f. 1906; mem. of SAF (see above); Pres. BUSTER HULTMAN; Man. Dir HÅKAN GEZELIUS; mems 160 shipping companies with 253 ships (1995).

## CIVIL AVIATION

The main international airport is at Arlanda, connected by bus service to Stockholm, 42 km away. There are other international airports at Landvetter, 25 km from Göteborg, and at Sturup, 28 km from Malmö. There are regular flights between the main cities in Sweden. Many domestic flights operate from Bromma (Stockholm's city airport). Measures on the deregulation of civil aviation took effect in July 1992 and ended the virtual monopoly of domestic services previously held by the Scandinavian Airlines System.

**Board of Civil Aviation:** Vikboplan 11, 601 79 Norrköping; tel. (11) 19-20-00; telex 64250; f. 1923; state body; central government authority for matters concerning civil aviation; Dir-Gen. BENGT A. W. JOHANSSON; 3,035 employees.

**Scandinavian Airlines System (SAS):** Head Office: Frösundavik Allé 1, Bromma, 161 87 Stockholm; tel. (8) 797-00-00; telex 22263 (Denmark); fax (8) 85-87-41; f. 1946; the national carrier of Denmark, Norway and Sweden. It is a consortium owned two-sevenths by Danish Airlines (DDL), two-sevenths by Norwegian Airlines (DNL) and three-sevenths by Swedish Airlines (ABA). Each parent airline is a limited company owned 50% by government and 50% by private shareholders. The SAS group includes the consortium and the subsidiaries in which the consortium has a majority or otherwise controlling interest; the Board consists of two members from each of the parent companies and the chairmanship rotates among the three national chairmen on an annual basis. SAS absorbed Linjeflyg AB (domestic passenger, newspaper and postal services in Sweden) in January 1993. Chair. BO BERGGREN; Pres. and CEO JAN STENBERG.

> **AB Aerotransport:** POB 5571, 103 96 Stockholm; Chair. KRISTER WICKMAN; Pres. OLLE HEDBERG; Chair. Exec. Cttee CURT NICOLIN; Swedish partner of SAS.

**Air Operations of Europe:** Hammarbacken 4, 191 49 Sollentuna; tel. (8) 92-66-55; telex 10960; fax (8) 35-07-80; f. 1993; charter services; Man. Dir T. JOHANSSON.

**Holmstroem Air Hudiksvall AB:** Skogsta 41, 824 92 Hudiksvall; tel. (650) 24-285; fax (650) 24-224; f. 1993; Man. Dir SIEVERT ANDERSSON.

**Nordic East Airways:** POB 79, 190 45 Stockholm; tel. (8) 5936-2010; fax (8) 5936-1444; f. 1991; charter services; CEO GUNNAR OHLSSON.

**Swedair AB:** 195 87 Stockholm-Arlanda; tel. (8) 797-00-00; telex 19615; fax (8) 797-17-80; f. 1975 as result of merger of Svensk Flygtjanst and Crownair; passenger services to destinations within Scandinavia; Chair. and Pres. BENNY ZAKRISSON.

**Transwede Airways AB:** POB 135, 190 46 Stockholm-Arlanda; tel. (593) 65-000; telex 8126672; fax (593) 61-225; f. 1985; passenger services within Sweden and from Scandinavia to Europe and the Mediterranean; Chair. LARS FORSBERGH; Pres. LARS BERGVALL.

**West Air Sweden:** POB 82, 651 03 Karlstad; tel. (54) 18-00-10; telex 66310; fax (54) 18-44-10; f. 1963; Pres. OSKAR NILSSON.

# Tourism

Sweden offers a variety of landscape, from the mountains of the 'Midnight Sun', north of the Arctic Circle, to the white sandy beaches of the south. There are many lakes, waterfalls and forests, and Stockholm is famed for its beautiful situation and modern architecture. Most tourists come from the other Scandinavian countries and from Germany. In 1993 income from visitors totalled an estimated 22,322m. kronor.

**Image Sweden:** Stockholm; promotes Sweden internationally; Man. Dir JAN BRÄNNSTRÖM.

**Next Stop Sweden:** Stockholm; Swedish travel and tourism council; Pres. PER-JOHANN ORRBY.

**Styrelsen för Sverigebilden:** Biblioteksgt. 11, POB 7087, 103 87 Stockholm; tel. (8) 678-34-00; fax (8) 678-04-25.

**Svenska Turistföreningen** (Swedish Touring Club): Drottninggt. 31–33, POB 25, 101 20 Stockholm; tel. (8) 790-31-00; telex 17760; fax (8) 20-13-32; f. 1885; 323,000 mems; owns and operates mountain hotels, tourist stations, about 280 youth hostels and 420 guest ports; Pres. E. EHN; Sec.-Gen. INGEMAR LIMAN.

# SWITZERLAND

## Introductory Survey

**Location, Climate, Language, Religion, Flag, Capital**

The Swiss Confederation lies in central Europe, bounded to the north by Germany, to the east by Austria, to the south by Italy and to the west by France. The climate is generally temperate, but varies considerably with altitude and aspect. In Zürich the average temperature ranges from −1°C (30°F) in winter to 16°C (61°F) in summer. There are three official languages—German, French and Italian, spoken by 73.4%, 20.5% and 4.1% of resident Swiss nationals respectively in 1990. A fourth language, Raeto-Romansch, is spoken by 0.7%, mainly in parts of the canton of Graubünden (Grisons) in eastern Switzerland; other languages are spoken by the remaining 1.3% of the population. Including resident aliens, the linguistic proportions in 1990 were: German 63.6%, French 19.2%, Italian 7.6%. Most Swiss citizens profess Christianity: in 1990 47.3% were Protestants and 43.3% Roman Catholics. Of the total resident population in 1990, 40.0% were Protestants and 46.1% Roman Catholics. The Federal flag, which is square, consists of a white upright cross in the centre of a red ground. The capital is Bern (Berne).

**Recent History**

Switzerland, whose origins date back to 1291, has occupied its present area since its borders were fixed by treaty in 1815. At the same time, it was internationally recognized as a neutral country. Despite the strategic importance of Switzerland, its 'permanent neutrality' has never since been violated. The country has not entered any military alliances, and it avoided involvement in both World Wars. Executive authority is exercised on a collegial basis by the Federal Council (cabinet), with a President who serves, for only one year at a time, as 'the first among equals'. Owing to the restricted powers of the Federal Council, initiatives and referendums form the core of the political process. Switzerland is a confederation of 20 cantons and six half-cantons. In 1979 the mainly French-speaking region of Jura seceded from the predominantly German-speaking canton of Berne, becoming the first new canton to be established since 1815.

Despite the fact that Switzerland has long been the headquarters of many international organizations, the country has not yet joined the UN. However, Switzerland maintains a permanent observer at the UN and has joined the non-political UN specialized agencies. Following a proposal put forward by the Government for full membership, a referendum took place in 1986 at which 75.7% of voters rejected the proposal, although the Government had campaigned in its favour. The proportion of the electorate voting in the referendum, at 50.2%, represented a higher than average level of participation in the Swiss system of direct democracy. Switzerland was a founder member of the European Free Trade Association (EFTA—see p. 142) in 1960 and joined the Council of Europe (see p. 134) in 1963.

Switzerland began to emerge from its traditional isolation in the early 1990s. This was largely due to economic pressures resulting from the world recession, and the further integration of the European Community (EC, known as the European Union—EU—from November 1993, see p. 143), and to the overthrow of the communist governments of Eastern Europe. In May 1992 the Government's proposal for Switzerland to join the IMF and the World Bank was approved in a referendum. On the following day, the Federal Council announced that it was to present an immediate application for membership of the EC. During September and October 1992 the Swiss Parliament approved the necessary legislation to comply with an agreement, signed in May 1992, to create a free trade zone, the European Economic Area (see p. 142), encompassing both EC and EFTA member states. In a referendum on 6 December, however, the Swiss electorate voted against ratification of the agreement, by 16 cantons to seven. All the French-speaking cantons voted in favour of the agreement, while the Italian canton and German cantons (with the exception of Basel) voted against it. Nevertheless, the Government subsequently declared its intention to continue to pursue its application for membership of the EC. During 1993 Switzerland confined itself to seeking bilateral negotiations with the EC on issues of particular national interest, including transport and involvement in EC research programmes. In February 1994, however, in defiance of a government campaign, 52% of voters in a referendum approved a proposal to ban transit freight by road through Switzerland within 10 years (requiring its transportation by rail), in order to protect the Swiss Alps. This decision adversely affected Switzerland's relations with the EU and jeopardized future agreements on transport and other issues.

Since 1959 government posts have been divided between the members of the Social-Democratic Party, the Radical-Democratic Party, the Christian-Democratic People's Party and the Swiss People's Party. This coalition holds almost three-quarters of the seats in the National Council (the lower house of the Federal Assembly), and an even larger majority in the Council of States (the upper house). In a general election which took place in October 1975 the ruling coalition won 169 of the 200 seats in the National Council, and in October 1979 it retained this majority. The October 1983 election revealed a marginal erosion in support for the coalition, which secured 166 seats; the Radical-Democratic Party became the strongest single party, with 54 seats. Three seats were won by the Federation of Green Parties, which campaigned for environmental protection. (In May 1986 the Federation adopted the name of the Green Party of Switzerland.) During 1985 and 1986 significant gains were made at local elections in Geneva, Lausanne and Vaud by extreme nationalist parties, which advocated a stricter government policy on immigration. The general election to the National Council in October 1987 revealed a further slight decline in support for the coalition, which won 159 of the 200 seats. This was due to mounting support for environmentalist and socialist groups, prompted by public concern about nuclear safety, pollution of the River Rhine and the destruction of forest through 'acid rain'. The Green Party won nine seats, while the Progressive Swiss Organizations and the Green Alternative, which contested the election on a common platform, secured a further four seats. At the next elections to the National Council, held in October 1991, the ruling four-party coalition recorded a further decline in popular support, winning 149 of the 200 seats. The small Automobile Party, which had been founded in 1985 to defend motorists' rights and which had subsequently campaigned for restricted immigration, increased its representation in the Council to eight seats (an increase of six). The Green Party also increased its number of seats (to 14), maintaining its position as the fifth largest party in the Council.

The enfranchisement of women in federal elections was approved at a referendum in February 1971. However, the half-cantons of Appenzell Ausserrhoden and Appenzell Innerrhoden introduced female suffrage only in 1989 and 1990, respectively. In December 1983, during the selection of a new member of the Federal Council, the Federal Assembly rejected the official candidate of the Social-Democratic Party, a woman, and chose in preference a male replacement. As a result, the Government's long-standing stability was jeopardized when the Social-Democratic Party threatened to withdraw from the coalition (although they eventually voted to remain). In October 1984, however, the Assembly elected Switzerland's first woman cabinet minister (Dr Elisabeth Kopp, a leading member of the Radical-Democratic Party), who became Head of the Federal Department of Justice and Police. In December 1988 the Assembly elected Dr Kopp, by a large majority, to be Vice-President of the Swiss Confederation for 1989, concurrently with her other duties in the Federal Council. In the same month, however, she announced her resignation from her post as Head of the Federal Department of Justice and Police, following allegations that she had violated regulations concerning official secrecy by warning her husband of an impending investigation into the financial dealings of a company of which he was vice-chairman. In February 1989, following an official investigation of the case, Dr Kopp was replaced as Vice-President; in February 1990, however, she was finally acquitted by the Federal Supreme Court of violating official secrecy laws.

In January 1993 the Head of the Federal Department of Foreign Affairs, René Felber, resigned from the Federal Council. Under the terms of the coalition, Felber was to be replaced by another francophone member of the Social-Democratic Party. In March the official Social-Democratic candidate, Christiane Brunner, a trade union leader, was rejected by other members of the coalition in favour of a male candidate, Francis Matthey. Matthey, however, following pressure from within the party, refused to accept his election by the coalition. The Social-Democratic Party subsequently reconfirmed Brunner's candidacy but also presented a female candidate with similar political views, Ruth Dreifuss, a trade union activist. Following three rounds of voting, Dreifuss became the second woman to be elected to a ministerial position in Switzerland.

The commission that had investigated the allegations against Dr Kopp during 1989 (see above) subsequently revealed that the office of the Federal Public Prosecutor held about 900,000 secret files on some 200,000 Swiss citizens and foreigners. In March 1990 about 30,000 people demonstrated in Berne in protest at the existence of such files. The demonstration ended in rioting and street violence. The Government subsequently announced that it would commission a report on the activities of the security services and introduce new laws regulating state security; it also opened most of the files to public scrutiny. The completed report, which was published in June 1993, found that security service observation had been largely restricted to left-wing groups since 1945 and that security service personnel had at times behaved in an unprofessional manner.

During 1986 the Government introduced legislation which aimed to restrict the number of refugees who were to be granted political asylum in Switzerland. However, the new legislation was criticized by socialist, religious and humanitarian groups, and in April 1987 a national referendum on the issue was held. Of the 41.8% of the electorate who voted at the referendum, a substantial majority was in favour of the new restrictions. In a further national referendum, held in December 1988, 67% of voters rejected a proposal by a small extreme right-wing party to reduce by 300,000 the number of foreigners to be allowed to settle in Switzerland by the year 2003. In 1991 attacks on asylum-seekers' hostels (including incidents of arson) increased to 71, compared with a total of 27 in 1990. In March 1994, in an attempt to control increasing drugs-related crime (following allegations that immigrants trading in illicit drugs were exploiting the asylum laws to avoid extradition), the Government approved legislation restricting the rights of asylum-seekers and immigrants, which included provisions for their arrest and detention without trial for failure to possess the requisite identification documents; further strong measures against foreigners suspected of trafficking in illegal drugs were approved by national referendum in December. Civil rights groups accused the Government of yielding to popular xenophobic sentiment to divert attention from its failure to overcome the drugs problem. At the end of 1993 there were nearly 41,000 asylum-seekers in Switzerland, representing about 3% of the resident foreign population.

In November 1989 64.4% of voters in a referendum rejected a proposal to abolish the armed forces by the year 2000. The referendum, which had been instigated by the Group for Switzerland Without an Army (an alliance of socialist, pacifist, youth and ecological organizations), attracted an unusually high level of participation, almost 70% of the electorate. Following the referendum, the Head of the Federal Military (Defence) Department, Kaspar Villiger established a working party to examine proposals for reforms in the armed forces. In 1992 it was announced that the strength of the armed forces would be reduced by one-third by 1995. In June 1993 the Federal Assembly approved legislation that sought permission for Swiss forces to be included in future UN peace-keeping operations. However, at a referendum on the issue, which took place in June 1994, 57.3% of voters rejected the proposal.

Following the accident in April 1986 at the Chernobyl nuclear power station, in the former USSR, public concern about nuclear safety became a national issue in Switzerland. In June a large-scale anti-nuclear demonstration took place at Gösgen, the site of the largest of Switzerland's five nuclear power stations, and in the same month the Social-Democratic Party initiated a campaign to collect signatures for a referendum on the nuclear issue, and advocated the progressive elimination of the country's existing reactors, and the cancellation of any future nuclear projects. In March 1989 the Federal Assembly, after protracted debate, approved legislation to cancel the projected construction of a sixth nuclear power station, at Kaiseraugst (near Basel), and to provide compensation for the construction consortium. The decision followed increasing public disapproval of the project. In a referendum held in September 1990, a majority of voters rejected proposals to abandon the use of nuclear power, but approved a proposal for a 10-year moratorium on the construction of further nuclear power stations in Switzerland.

### Government

The Swiss Confederation, composed of 20 cantons and six half-cantons, has a republican federal Constitution. Legislative power is held by the bicameral Federal Assembly: the Council of States, with 46 members representing the cantons (two for each canton and one for each half-canton), elected for three to four years; and the National Council, with 200 members directly elected by universal adult suffrage for four years, on the basis of proportional representation. Executive power is held by the Federal Council, which has seven members elected for four years by a joint session of the Federal Assembly. The Assembly also elects one of the Federal Councillors to be President of the Confederation (Head of State) for one year at a time.

National policy is the prerogative of the Federal Government, but considerable power is vested in the cantons. Under the 1874 Constitution, the autonomous cantons hold all powers not specifically delegated to the federal authorities. The Swiss citizen shares three distinct allegiances—communal, cantonal and national. Direct participation is very important in communal government, and all adult Swiss residents may take part in the communal assemblies or referendums which decide upon local affairs. Each canton has its own written constitution, government and legislative assembly. The referendum, which can be on a communal, cantonal or national scale, further ensures the possibility of direct public participation in decision-making.

### Defence

National defence is based on compulsory military service. Switzerland maintains no standing army except for a small permanent personnel of commissioned and non-commissioned officers primarily concerned with training. Military service consists of 17 weeks' recruit training, followed by 'refresher' training of varying lengths, according to age. Service totals about one year between the ages of 20 and 50 years for a private. Each soldier keeps his equipment in his own home, and receives compulsory marksmanship training between periods of service. The total strength of the armed forces, when mobilized, is about 625,000. This number is to be reduced to 400,000 by 1995. The Confederation belongs to no international defence organizations, and the strategy of the army and air force is defensive. Defence expenditure for 1993 was budgeted at 5,753m. Swiss francs (14.2% of total expenditure).

### Economic Affairs

In 1993, according to estimates by the World Bank, Switzerland's gross national product (GNP), measured at average 1991–93 prices, was US $254,066m., equivalent to $36,410 per head. During 1985–93, it was estimated, GNP per head increased, in real terms, at an average annual rate of 0.7% per year. Over the same period the population increased by an annual average of 1.0%. Switzerland's gross domestic product (GDP) increased, in real terms, by an annual average of 2.1% in 1980–92, but fell by 0.3% in 1992 and by 0.9% in 1993. Real GDP rose by 2.1% in 1994.

Agriculture (including forestry and fishing) employed 5.6% of the working population in 1993, and provided an estimated 2.5% of GDP in 1990. The principal cash crops are sugar beet, potatoes and wheat. Dairy products, notably cheese, are also important. In terms of volume, agricultural production increased at an average rate of 0.5% per year during 1985–92; production declined by 3.0% in 1993, and by 2.1% in 1994.

Industry (including mining and quarrying, manufacturing, power and construction) employed 33.2% of the working population in 1993, and provided 34.5% of GDP in 1985. Industrial production increased at an average annual rate of 1.9% between 1980 and 1991.

Switzerland is not richly endowed with mineral deposits, and only rock salt and building materials are mined or quarried in significant quantities. In 1986 only 0.2% of the working population were employed in mining and quarrying.

In 1986 manufacturing employed 29.9% of the working population, and in 1985 the sector provided 25.0% of GDP. The most important branches are precision engineering, in particular clocks and watches (which provided 8.1% of export revenue in 1993), heavy engineering, machine-building, textiles, chocolate, chemicals and pharmaceuticals.

Energy is derived principally from hydroelectric and nuclear power and petroleum. In 1993 about 61% of total electricity output was provided by hydroelectric power, while petroleum and related products accounted for 59.5% of final energy consumption. In that year nuclear power (from five reactors with a total generating capacity of 2,985 MW) provided 37.1% of electricity. Imports of mineral fuels comprised 3.8% of the value of total imports in 1993.

Switzerland plays an important role as a centre of international finance, and Swiss markets account for a significant share of international financial transactions. The insurance sector is also highly developed, and Swiss companies are represented throughout the world. Switzerland also draws considerable revenue from tourism, both in summer and winter. In 1993 this was equivalent to nearly 14% of the value of merchandise exports.

In 1993 Switzerland recorded a visible trade surplus of US $2,237m., and there was a surplus of $16,696m. on the current account of the balance of payments. In 1993 the principal source of imports (32.6%) was Germany, which was also the principal market for exports (22.9%). In 1993 member states of the European Union (EU—known as the European Community until November 1993) accounted for some 72.6% of imports and 56.7% of exports, while fellow members of the European Free Trade Association (EFTA, see p. 142) accounted for 6.7% of imports and 6.3% of exports. In 1993 the principal exports were machinery, pharmaceutical and chemical products and clocks and watches and precision instruments. The principal imports were machinery, motor vehicles, agricultural and forestry products and pharmaceutical and chemical products.

In 1994 there was an estimated federal budgetary deficit of 5,100m. Swiss francs. The average annual rate of inflation was 3.2% in 1985–93; the rate was 3.3% in 1993 and 0.8% in 1994. Unemployment averaged 3.8% in 1994. Of all the major European countries, Switzerland has the highest percentage of foreign workers (28% of the working population in 1993).

Switzerland is a founder member of EFTA. Switzerland conducts a large proportion of its foreign trade with member countries of the EU and applied for membership of that organization (then the EC) in May 1992. In the same month Switzerland was admitted to membership of the IMF and the World Bank.

Political stability and peaceful industrial relations (Switzerland has the lowest reported incidence of strikes in the world), combined with traditionally low rates of inflation and unemployment, and Switzerland's reputation as a financial centre, have contributed to a high level of prosperity. In 1993, according to estimates by the World Bank, Switzerland's GNP per head was higher than that of any other country in the world. However, the introduction of a strict monetary policy in 1989, to counter an increase in inflation, contributed to a recession which began in 1991. Unemployment increased and the budgetary deficit was accentuated by an increase in social insurance payments and a decline in fiscal receipts. In order to increase revenue, a value-added tax at 6.5% was introduced at the beginning of 1995, replacing a turnover tax (which had placed Swiss manufacturers at a disadvantage by taxing both the goods that they produced and the machinery involved in production). Following the electorate's rejection of membership of the European Economic Area (see p. 142) in December 1992, Switzerland introduced measures to stimulate the economy through the elimination of anti-competitive practices (including cartels), the abolition of regulations that hinder commerce, and the simplification of immigration policy to facilitate the entry of skilled foreign workers. By 1995 inflation was low and an economic recovery was under way.

### Social Welfare

There is no national health service in Switzerland. From 1996 insurance against illness will be compulsory for all citizens; health insurance for persons on low incomes will be subsidized by both the Federal Government and canton governments. Old-age, widows', widowers' and invalids' insurance are also compulsory for all Swiss citizens. In addition, there are compulsory unemployment, accident and pension insurance schemes for all salaried employees. In 1992 Switzerland had 42,056 hospital beds (equivalent to one per 606 inhabitants) and 11,293 beds in psychiatric clinics. In the same year there were nearly 24,000 physicians working in the country. In the federal budget for 1993, 11,295m. Swiss francs (27.8% of total spending) was allocated to social welfare, while health received 167m. Swiss francs (0.4% of total expenditure). In addition, there are several social security schemes, with their own budgets.

### Education

Education is mainly under cantonal and communal control, with the result that there are 26 different systems in operation. Education has been compulsory for children between the ages of seven and 15 years since 1874, and in most cantons a further year of compulsory education is required. Primary education is from the age of seven to 13, after which, up to the age of 15 or 16, children attend one of two types of lower secondary school, according to ability. About 15% of 17-year-olds continue their studies at a higher secondary school (Gymnasium/Collège), and a leaving certificate (Matura/Maturité) from one of these is a prerequisite for entry to higher education. About 70% proceed to vocational training (trade and technical) for a period of two to four years. There are seven universities, two Federal Institutes of Technology (of university standing), an institute of economics, law, business and public administration, and 11 art and music colleges. Numerous private schools exist, and many foreign children receive part of their education in Switzerland. In the federal budget for 1993, 2,971m. francs (7.3% of total spending) was allocated to education and research. However, most public spending on education is by canton governments and communes.

### Public Holidays

**1995:** 1–2 January (New Year), 14 April (Good Friday), 17 April (Easter Monday), 1 May (Labour Day), 25 May (Ascension Day), 5 June (Whit Monday), 1 August (National Day), 25–26 December (Christmas).

**1996:** 1–2 January (New Year), 5 April (Good Friday), 8 April (Easter Monday), 1 May (Labour Day), 16 May (Ascension Day), 27 May (Whit Monday), 1 August (National Day), 25–26 December (Christmas).

In addition, various cantonal and local holidays are observed.

### Weights and Measures

The metric system is in force.

SWITZERLAND

# Statistical Survey

Source (unless otherwise stated): Federal Office of Statistics, 3003 Berne, Hallwylstr. 15; tel. (31) 618660; telex 32526; fax (31) 617856.

## Area and Population

### AREA, POPULATION AND DENSITY

| | |
|---|---:|
| Area (sq km) | 41,284* |
| Population (census results) | |
| 2 December 1980 | 6,365,960 |
| 4 December 1990 | |
| Males | 3,390,446 |
| Females | 3,483,241 |
| Total | 6,873,687 |
| Population (official estimates at 31 December) | |
| 1991 | 6,842,768 |
| 1992 | 6,907,959 |
| 1993 | 6,968,570 |
| Density (per sq km) at 31 December 1993 | 168.8 |

* 15,940 sq miles.

### LANGUAGES (%)

| | 1970 | 1980 | 1990 |
|---|---:|---:|---:|
| German | 64.9 | 65.0 | 63.6 |
| French | 18.1 | 18.4 | 19.2 |
| Italian | 11.9 | 9.8 | 7.6 |
| Raeto-Romansch | 0.8 | 0.8 | 0.6 |
| Others | 4.3 | 6.0 | 8.9 |

### CANTONS

| Canton | Area (sq km)* | Population (31 December 1993) Total | per sq km | Capital (with population, Dec. 1991) |
|---|---:|---:|---:|---|
| Zürich | 1,660.9 | 1,162,083 | 699.7 | Zürich (343,106) |
| Bern (Berne) | 5,932.4 | 956,617 | 161.3 | Berne (134,393) |
| Luzern (Lucerne) | 1,429.2 | 335,385 | 234.7 | Luzern (59,811) |
| Uri | 1,057.5 | 35,727 | 33.8 | Altdorf (8,200) |
| Schwyz | 851.6 | 118,528 | 139.2 | Schwyz (12,854) |
| Unterwalden | | | | |
| Obwalden | 480.7 | 30,837 | 64.2 | Sarnen (8,400) |
| Nidwalden | 241.5 | 35,393 | 146.6 | Stans (6,200) |
| Glarus | 680.6 | 39,138 | 57.5 | Glarus (5,700) |
| Zug (Zoug) | 207.1 | 88,583 | 427.7 | Zug (21,719) |
| Fribourg | 1,591.1 | 218,704 | 137.5 | Fribourg (34,200) |
| Solothurn (Soleure) | 790.6 | 236,389 | 299.0 | Solothurn (15,565) |
| Basel (Bâle) | | | | |
| Basel-Stadt (town) | 37.0 | 197,403 | 5,335.2 | Basel (172,768) |
| Basel-Landschaft (country) | 428.0 | 234,910 | 548.9 | Liestal (12,612) |
| Schaffhausen (Schaffhouse) | 298.2 | 73,588 | 246.8 | Schaffhausen (34,318) |
| Appenzell | | | | |
| Ausserrhoden | 242.8 | 54,087 | 222.8 | Herisau (16,002) |
| Innerrhoden | 172.5 | 14,680 | 85.1 | Appenzell (5,200) |
| St Gallen (Saint-Gall) | 1,950.6 | 436,967 | 224.0 | St Gallen (74,106) |
| Graubünden (Grisons) | 7,105.3 | 181,957 | 25.6 | Chur (30,284) |
| Aargau (Argovie) | 1,394.9 | 518,945 | 372.0 | Aarau (16,079) |
| Thurgau (Thurgovie) | 862.9 | 217,129 | 251.6 | Frauenfeld (16,908) |

### CANTONS — continued

| Canton | Area (sq km)* | Population (31 December 1993) Total | per sq km | Capital (with population, Dec. 1991) |
|---|---:|---:|---:|---|
| Ticino (Tessin) | 2,737.8 | 297,955 | 108.8 | Bellinzona (16,957) |
| Vaud | 2,822.4 | 596,736 | 211.4 | Lausanne (123,149) |
| Valais | 5,213.1 | 266,713 | 51.2 | Sion (25,622) |
| Neuchâtel | 716.7 | 163,884 | 228.7 | Neuchâtel (33,158) |
| Genève (Genf or Geneva) | 245.7 | 387,606 | 1,577.6 | Genève (167,697) |
| Jura | 836.5 | 68,626 | 82.0 | Delémont (11,652) |
| **Total** | 39,987.5 | 6,968,570 | 174.3 | — |

* Figures exclude lakes larger than 5 sq km (total area 1,289.5 sq km). Also excluded are special territories (total area 7.2 sq km).

### PRINCIPAL TOWNS (estimated population at 31 December 1993)

| | |
|---|---:|
| Bern (Berne, the capital) | 129,423 |
| Zürich (Zurich) | 343,045 |
| Basel (Bâle) | 176,220 |
| Genève (Genf or Geneva) | 171,744 |
| Lausanne | 117,153 |
| Winterthur (Winterthour) | 87,068 |
| St Gallen (Saint-Gall) | 72,391 |
| Luzern (Lucerne) | 59,920 |
| Biel (Bienne) | 51,823 |
| Thun (Thoune) | 38,695 |
| La Chaux-de-Fonds | 37,137 |
| Köniz | 36,511 |
| Schaffhausen (Schaffhouse) | 34,014 |
| Fribourg (Freiburg) | 32,693 |
| Neuchâtel (Neuenburg) | 31,709 |
| Chur (Coire) | 30,471 |

### BIRTHS, MARRIAGES AND DEATHS

| | Registered live births Number | Rate (per 1,000) | Registered marriages Number | Rate (per 1,000) | Registered deaths Number | Rate (per 1,000) |
|---|---:|---:|---:|---:|---:|---:|
| 1986 | 76,320 | 11.7 | 40,234 | 6.2 | 60,105 | 9.2 |
| 1987 | 76,505 | 11.7 | 40,063 | 6.6 | 59,511 | 9.1 |
| 1988 | 80,345 | 12.2 | 45,716 | 6.6 | 60,648 | 9.2 |
| 1989 | 81,180 | 12.2 | 45,066 | 6.8 | 60,882 | 9.2 |
| 1990 | 83,939 | 12.5 | 46,603 | 6.9 | 63,739 | 9.5 |
| 1991 | 86,200 | 12.7 | 47,567 | 7.0 | 62,634 | 9.2 |
| 1992 | 86,910 | 12.6 | 45,080 | 6.6 | 62,302 | 9.1 |
| 1993 | 83,762 | 12.1 | 43,257 | 6.2 | 62,512 | 9.0 |

**Expectation of life** (official estimates, years at birth, 1992/93): Males 74.7; females 81.4.

SWITZERLAND

## ECONOMICALLY ACTIVE POPULATION
(annual averages, '000 persons aged 15 years and over)

|  | 1991 | 1992 | 1993 |
|---|---|---|---|
| Agriculture, forestry and fishing | 197.2 | 194.0 | 191.4 |
| Mining and quarrying | | | |
| Manufacturing | 893.5 | 858.7 | 825.5 |
| Electricity, gas and water | | | |
| Construction | 332.0 | 319.8 | 299.7 |
| Trade, restaurants and hotels | 730.4 | 713.0 | 689.4 |
| Transport, storage and communications | 219.1 | 215.3 | 212.8 |
| Financing, insurance, real estate and business services | 383.4 | 374.3 | 371.7 |
| Community, social and personal services | 804.6 | 805.4 | 798.7 |
| **Total employed*** | **3,560.3** | **3,480.5** | **3,389.0** |
| Males | 2,197.6 | 2,151.4 | 2,095.4 |
| Females | 1,362.7 | 1,329.0 | 1,293.6 |

* Including foreigners ('000): 929.7 in 1991; 911.8 in 1992; 871.8 in 1993.

## Agriculture

### PRINCIPAL CROPS ('000 metric tons)

|  | 1991 | 1992 | 1993 |
|---|---|---|---|
| Wheat and spelt | 602 | 546 | 580 |
| Rye | 25 | 28 | 34 |
| Barley | 356 | 359 | 392 |
| Oats | 56 | 52 | 58 |
| Potatoes | 711 | 741 | 908 |
| Sugar beet | 896 | 907 | 976 |
| Apples | 145 | 433 | 243 |
| Pears | 81 | 163 | 106 |
| Plums | 10 | 22 | 7 |
| Grapes | 178 | 164 | 154 |

Source: FAO, *Production Yearbook*.

### LIVESTOCK ('000 head, year ending September)

|  | 1991 | 1992 | 1993 |
|---|---|---|---|
| Cattle | 1,829 | 1,783 | 1,745 |
| Horses | 49 | 52 | 54 |
| Pigs | 1,723 | 1,706 | 1,692 |
| Sheep | 409 | 415 | 424 |
| Goats | 65 | 58 | 57* |

* FAO estimate.

Poultry (million): 6 in 1991; 6 in 1992; 6 in 1993.

Source: FAO, *Production Yearbook*.

### LIVESTOCK PRODUCTS ('000 metric tons)

|  | 1991 | 1992 | 1993 |
|---|---|---|---|
| Beef and veal | 173 | 165 | 155 |
| Mutton and lamb | 5 | 6 | 6 |
| Pig meat | 265 | 264 | 260 |
| Poultry meat | 35 | 37 | 38 |
| Cows' milk | 3,917 | 3,873 | 3,927† |
| Goats' milk | 19 | 17 | 17 |
| Butter | 39.8 | 38.6 | 38.6* |
| Cheese | 136.6 | 134.6 | 134.6* |
| Poultry eggs | 36.4 | 37.9 | 37.5 |

* Unofficial figure.    † FAO estimate.

Source: FAO, *Production Yearbook*.

## Forestry

### ROUNDWOOD REMOVALS ('000 cubic metres, excluding bark)

|  | 1990 | 1991 | 1992 |
|---|---|---|---|
| Sawlogs, veneer logs and logs for sleepers | 4,488 | 2,987 | 2,917 |
| Pulpwood | 895 | 764 | 721 |
| Other industrial wood* | 70 | 70 | 70 |
| Fuel wood | 879 | 786 | 845 |
| **Total** | **6,332** | **4,607** | **4,553** |

* FAO estimates.

Source: FAO, *Yearbook of Forest Products*.

### SAWNWOOD PRODUCTION
('000 cubic metres, including railway sleepers)

|  | 1990 | 1991 | 1992 |
|---|---|---|---|
| Coniferous (softwood) | 1,783 | 1,555 | 1,413 |
| Broadleaved (hardwood) | 203 | 173 | 113 |
| **Total** | **1,985** | **1,727** | **1,525** |

Source: FAO, *Yearbook of Forest Products*.

## Fishing

('000 metric tons, live weight)

|  | 1990 | 1991 | 1992 |
|---|---|---|---|
| Total catch | 4.2 | 4.8 | 3.9 |

Source: FAO, *Yearbook of Fishery Statistics*.

## Industry

### SELECTED PRODUCTS
('000 metric tons, unless otherwise indicated)

|  | 1989 | 1990 | 1991 |
|---|---|---|---|
| Refined sugar | 134 | 146 | 129 |
| Cement | 5,461 | 5,206 | 4,716 |
| Cigars (million) | 242 | 230 | 205 |
| Cigarettes (million) | 28,059 | 31,771 | 32,943 |
| Gas (terajoules)* | 431 | 340 | 250 |
| Aluminium | 71.3 | 71.6 | 65.9 |
| Footwear ('000 pairs) | 4,285 | 4,039 | 3,353 |
| Woven woollen fabrics (million cu m)† | 8.8 | 9.5 | 9.8 |
| Flour (wheat) | 431 | 451 | 435 |
| Chocolate and chocolate products‡ | 104.2 | 108.9 | 111.5 |
| Wine ('000 hectolitres) | 1,100§ | 1,200 | 1,240 |

* Including Liechtenstein.
† Pure woollen fabrics only.
‡ Sales.
§ Estimate.

Source: UN, *Industrial Statistics Yearbook*.

**Watches** ('000 exported): 17,840 in 1984; 25,137 in 1985; 28,075 in 1986.

**Chalk** ('000 metric tons): 41 in 1984; 37 in 1985; 35 in 1986.

**New dwellings** (units completed): 37,597 in 1991; 35,422 in 1992; 34,580 in 1993.

**Wool yarn—pure and mixed** ('000 metric tons): 9.9 in 1990; 6.3 in 1991; 6.3 in 1992.

**Electric power** (million kWh): 56,078 in 1991; 57,348 in 1992; 59,313 in 1993.

# SWITZERLAND

*Statistical Survey*

# Finance

## CURRENCY AND EXCHANGE RATES

**Monetary Units:**
100 Rappen (centimes) = 1 Schweizer Franken (franc suisse) or Swiss franc.

**Sterling and Dollar Equivalents** (31 December 1994)
£1 sterling = 2.047 francs;
US $1 = 1.309 francs;
100 Swiss francs = £48.84 = $76.41.

**Average Exchange Rates** (Swiss francs per US $)
1992   1.4062
1993   1.4776
1994   1.3677

## FEDERAL BUDGET (million Swiss francs)

| Revenue | 1991 | 1992 | 1993 |
|---|---|---|---|
| Taxes on income and wealth | 12,887 | 14,269 | 11,993 |
| Taxes on consumption | 16,282 | 16,137 | 16,596 |
| Turnover tax | 10,006 | 9,817 | 9,381 |
| Tobacco tax | 972 | 980 | 1,167 |
| Customs duties | 1,212 | 1,221 | 1,166 |
| **Total** (incl. others) | 31,458 | 32,777 | 31,401 |

| Expenditure | 1991 | 1992 | 1993 |
|---|---|---|---|
| Foreign affairs | 1,788 | 2,133 | 2,070 |
| Defence | 6,202 | 6,249 | 5,753 |
| Education and research | 2,655 | 2,844 | 2,971 |
| Social welfare | 8,085 | 8,593 | 11,295 |
| Transport, environment and energy | 6,320 | 6,466 | 7,000 |
| Agriculture | 3,078 | 3,162 | 3,416 |
| Financial services | 4,586 | 5,564 | 5,245 |
| **Total** (incl. others) | 35,501 | 37,816 | 40,600 |

## INTERNATIONAL RESERVES (US $ million at 31 December)

|  | 1992 | 1993 | 1994 |
|---|---|---|---|
| Gold* | 8,176 | 8,046 | 9,077 |
| IMF special drawing rights | 16 | 155 | 236 |
| Reserve position in IMF | 799 | 830 | 939 |
| Foreign exchange | 32,440 | 31,650 | 33,554 |
| **Total** | 41,431 | 40,681 | 43,806 |

* Gold reserves have totalled 2,590.2 metric tons (83,275,000 troy oz) since 1976. The value in dollars is based on the Swiss national valuation, fixed at 4,595.74 francs per kg (142.95 francs per troy oz) since 1971.

Source: IMF, *International Financial Statistics*.

## MONEY SUPPLY (million Swiss francs at 31 December)*

|  | 1992 | 1993 | 1994 |
|---|---|---|---|
| Currency outside banks | 31,370 | 31,380 | 32,640 |
| Demand deposits at deposit money banks | 40,840 | 45,980 | 47,790 |
| Checking deposits at post office | 14,020 | 13,870 | 14,430 |
| **Total money** | 86,230 | 91,240 | 94,860 |

* Figures are rounded to the nearest 10 million francs.

Source: IMF, *International Financial Statistics*.

## COST OF LIVING (Consumer Price Index. Base: May 1993 = 100)

|  | 1991 | 1992 | 1993 |
|---|---|---|---|
| Foodstuffs | 99.6 | 99.8 | 99.6 |
| Clothing | 94.3 | 97.6 | 99.9 |
| Rent, heating and lighting | 89.8 | 94.9 | 99.3 |
| Transport and Communications | 89.9 | 94.2 | 99.2 |
| Health | 91.3 | 96.6 | 100.0 |
| Education, entertainment and culture | 92.2 | 95.9 | 99.9 |
| **All items** | 93.0 | 96.7 | 99.9 |

## NATIONAL ACCOUNTS (million Swiss francs at current prices)

### National Income and Product

|  | 1991 | 1992 | 1993 |
|---|---|---|---|
| Compensation of employees | 211,275 | 218,100 | 220,030 |
| Operating surplus | 70,000 | 70,225 | 71,325 |
| **Domestic factor incomes** | 281,275 | 288,325 | 291,355 |
| Consumption of fixed capital | 34,300 | 35,500 | 36,210 |
| **Gross domestic product (GDP) at factor cost** | 315,575 | 323,825 | 327,565 |
| Indirect taxes | 20,695 | 20,595 | 21,435 |
| *Less* Subsidies | 5,195 | 5,655 | 5,955 |
| **GDP in purchasers' values** | 331,075 | 338,765 | 343,045 |
| Factor income received from abroad | 29,285 | 27,715 | 29,195 |
| *Less* Factor income paid abroad | 14,970 | 14,285 | 15,110 |
| **Gross national product** | 345,390 | 352,195 | 357,130 |
| *Less* Consumption of fixed capital | 34,300 | 35,500 | 36,210 |
| **National income in market prices** | 311,090 | 316,695 | 320,920 |

### Expenditure on the Gross Domestic Product

|  | 1991 | 1992 | 1993 |
|---|---|---|---|
| Government final consumption expenditure | 46,640 | 49,320 | 49,725 |
| Private final consumption expenditure | 190,490 | 198,070 | 202,325 |
| Increase in stocks* | 4,545 | −980 | −3,190 |
| Gross fixed capital formation | 84,810 | 80,375 | 77,020 |
| **Total domestic expenditure** | 326,485 | 326,785 | 325,880 |
| Exports of goods and services | 116,720 | 122,170 | 124,995 |
| *Less* Imports of goods and services | 112,130 | 110,190 | 107,830 |
| **GDP in purchasers' values** | 331,075 | 338,765 | 343,045 |
| **GDP at constant 1980 prices** | 209,335 | 208,700 | 206,915 |

* Including statistical discrepancy.

## BALANCE OF PAYMENTS (US $ million)

|  | 1991 | 1992 | 1993 |
|---|---|---|---|
| Merchandise exports f.o.b. | 73,745 | 79,353 | 74,932 |
| Merchandise imports f.o.b. | −77,550 | −78,863 | −72,695 |
| **Trade balance** | −3,806 | 490 | 2,237 |
| Exports of services | 17,635 | 18,681 | 18,787 |
| Imports of services | −10,868 | −11,534 | −10,998 |
| Other income received | 29,345 | 28,293 | 26,201 |
| Other income paid | −19,361 | −18,743 | −16,671 |
| Private unrequited transfers (net) | −2,275 | −2,373 | −2,227 |
| Official unrequited transfers (net) | −346 | −624 | −633 |
| **Current balance** | 10,325 | 14,190 | 16,696 |
| Direct investment (net) | −3,363 | −4,422 | −5,730 |
| Portfolio investment (net) | −11,978 | −6,127 | −17,308 |
| Other capital (net) | 3,665 | −4,820 | 5,595 |
| Net errors and omissions | 2,322 | 5,599 | 1,157 |
| **Overall balance** | 970 | 4,420 | 411 |

Source: IMF, *International Financial Statistics*.

SWITZERLAND

# External Trade

*Note:* Swiss customs territory includes the Principality of Liechtenstein, the German enclave of Büssingen and the Italian commune of Campione, but excludes the free zone of the Samnaun Valley.

**PRINCIPAL COMMODITIES** (million Swiss francs)

| Imports c.i.f. | 1991 | 1992 | 1993 |
|---|---|---|---|
| Agricultural and forestry products | 8,111.5 | 7,979.1 | 7,869.4 |
| Mineral fuels | 4,358.6 | 3,897.6 | 3,440.3 |
| Textile yarn, fabrics, etc. | 2,820.9 | 2,766.6 | 2,579.7 |
| Clothing (excl. footwear) | 5,087.3 | 5,025.2 | 4,932.4 |
| Paper, paperboard and graphics | 3,810.2 | 3,819.0 | 3,667.0 |
| Articles of plastic | 2,056.2 | 2,091.9 | 2,077.0 |
| Chemical elements and unmoulded plastics | 4,780.0 | 4,838.5 | 4,558.7 |
| Pharmaceutical products | 2,390.0 | 2,970.0 | 3,589.1 |
| Building materials, ceramics, glass, etc. | 2,038.1 | 1,922.3 | 1,875.7 |
| Iron and steel | 1,981.2 | 1,836.0 | 1,692.4 |
| Metal products | 4,730.4 | 4,553.6 | 4,394.2 |
| Machinery (incl. electrical) | 18,882.2 | 18,224.3 | 17,979.7 |
| Passenger cars | 6,102.8 | 5,965.0 | 5,091.8 |
| Precision instruments | 2,904.4 | 3,038.3 | 2,841.1 |
| Jewellery | 1,761.1 | 1,570.6 | 1,907.9 |
| Home fittings and furnishings | 2,597.2 | 2,501.0 | 2,330.9 |
| **Total** (incl. others) | 95,031.8 | 92,330.4 | 89,829.7 |

| Exports f.o.b. | 1991 | 1992 | 1993 |
|---|---|---|---|
| Agricultural and forestry products | 3,157.9 | 3,360.3 | 3,425.9 |
| Textile yarn, fabrics etc. | 3,394.6 | 3,364.0 | 3,022.5 |
| Paper, paperboard and graphics | 2,213.6 | 2,270.8 | 2,157.2 |
| Leather, rubber and plastic products | 2,353.2 | 2,641.0 | 2,679.4 |
| Chemicals | 19,106.9 | 21,257.6 | 22,348.3 |
| Chemical elements and unmoulded plastics | 3,529.5 | 3,768.1 | 3,731.1 |
| Pharmaceutical products | 8,809.7 | 10,439.8 | 11,284.5 |
| Pigments | 2,156.3 | 2,355.6 | 2,603.3 |
| Metal products | 7,514.6 | 7,701.0 | 7,414.6 |
| Machinery (incl. electrical) | 25,223.3 | 25,392.4 | 24,808.7 |
| Transport equipment | 1,759.4 | 2,086.2 | 1,804.9 |
| Precision instruments | 4,833.0 | 4,946.2 | 4,869.9 |
| Clocks and watches | 6,852.1 | 7,369.3 | 7,588.8 |
| Jewellery | 1,812.9 | 1,974.6 | 2,650.0 |
| **Total** (incl. others) | 87,946.5 | 92,141.8 | 93,289.0 |

**PRINCIPAL TRADING PARTNERS** (million Swiss francs)*

| Imports c.i.f. | 1991 | 1992 | 1993 |
|---|---|---|---|
| Austria | 3,647.7 | 3,608.1 | 3,652.8 |
| Belgium-Luxembourg | 3,284.5 | 3,563.5 | 3,217.3 |
| China, People's Republic | 710.5 | 875.1 | 1,083.6 |
| Denmark | 950.3 | 1,016.7 | 1,001.5 |
| France | 10,347.2 | 9,987.4 | 9,813.6 |
| Germany | 31,133.6 | 30,879.9 | 29,247.7 |
| Italy | 9,490.8 | 9,987.4 | 8,784.5 |
| Japan | 4,127.9 | 3,982.3 | 3,469.5 |
| Netherlands | 3,899.4 | 4,114.8 | 4,051.6 |
| Spain | 1,234.0 | 1,260.3 | 1,230.2 |
| Sweden | 1,754.2 | 1,609.2 | 1,406.4 |
| United Kingdom | 5,260.2 | 5,335.6 | 6,487.7 |
| USA | 3,971.4 | 5,865.9 | 5,581.0 |
| **Total** (incl. others) | 95,031.8 | 92,330.4 | 89,829.7 |

| Exports f.o.b. | 1991 | 1992 | 1993 |
|---|---|---|---|
| Austria | 3,332.9 | 3,364.5 | 3,551.2 |
| Belgium-Luxembourg | 2,066.9 | 2,514.7 | 2,347.2 |
| China, People's Republic | 471.3 | 620.3 | 942.6 |
| Denmark | 978.3 | 1,027.8 | 982.0 |
| France | 8,465.4 | 8,726.2 | 8,503.5 |
| Germany | 20,907.5 | 21,592.7 | 21,400.7 |
| Hong Kong | 2,286.9 | 2,591.6 | 2,924.4 |
| Israel | 1,046.4 | 983.7 | 1,177.8 |
| Italy | 7,634.6 | 8,058.4 | 7,255.2 |
| Japan | 3,767.0 | 3,449.1 | 3,221.0 |
| Netherlands | 2,395.6 | 2,524.5 | 2,558.4 |
| Saudi Arabia | 964.0 | 1,092.8 | 1,491.3 |
| Singapore | 796.8 | 863.4 | 1,311.1 |
| Spain | 2,072.7 | 2,176.4 | 1,859.9 |
| Sweden | 1,285.6 | 1,339.8 | 1,280.9 |
| United Kingdom | 5,810.5 | 6,063.0 | 6,409.4 |
| USA | 7,153.1 | 7,786.5 | 8,212.1 |
| **Total** (incl. others) | 87,946.5 | 92,141.8 | 93,289.0 |

* Imports by country of production; exports by country of consumption.

# Transport

**RAILWAY TRAFFIC**

| | 1988 | 1989 | 1990 |
|---|---|---|---|
| Passengers ('000) | 520,400 | 521,400 | 528,800 |
| Passenger-kilometres (million) | 12,670 | 12,971 | 13,009 |
| Freight carried ('000 metric tons) | 48,493 | 51,069 | 53,023 |
| Freight ton-kilometres (million) | 7,938 | 8,627 | 8,862 |

**ROAD TRAFFIC** ('000 motor vehicles in use)

| | 1990 | 1991 |
|---|---|---|
| Private cars | 2,994 | 3,066 |
| Passenger transport vehicles | 7 | 7 |
| Goods transport vehicles | 252 | 258 |
| Agricultural and industrial vehicles | 210 | 213 |
| Motor cycles | 299 | 320 |
| **Total** | 3,809 | 3,913 |

Source: Federal Department of Transport.

**INLAND WATERWAYS**
(freight traffic at port of Basel, '000 metric tons)

| | 1987 | 1988 | 1989 |
|---|---|---|---|
| Goods loaded | 310.8 | 361.3 | 267.0 |
| Goods unloaded | 7,897.1 | 8,091.4 | 8,578.2 |

Source: Federal Department of Transport.

**CIVIL AVIATION** (Swiss airlines)

| | 1992 | 1993 | 1994 |
|---|---|---|---|
| Kilometres flown ('000) | 157,800 | 166,908 | 175,125 |
| Passenger-kilometres ('000) | 16,433,087 | 17,465,784 | 18,861,352 |
| Freight carried (metric tons) | 301,448 | 324,758 | 354,709 |
| Freight ton-kilometres ('000) | 1,111,156 | 1,285,839 | 1,459,805 |

Source: Federal Department of Transport.

## Tourism

**VISITORS BY ORIGIN** ('000 nights spent in hotels)

|  | 1991 | 1992 | 1993 |
|---|---|---|---|
| Belgium | 926 | 973 | 1,016 |
| France | 1,552 | 1,449 | 1,399 |
| Germany, Federal Republic | 7,251 | 7,125 | 7,311 |
| Italy | 1,422 | 1,411 | 1,092 |
| Netherlands | 920 | 908 | 926 |
| United Kingdom | 1,848 | 1,849 | 1,708 |
| USA | 1,579 | 1,891 | 1,811 |
| **Total** (incl. others) | 20,719 | 20,589 | 20,130 |

## Communications Media

|  | 1991 | 1992 | 1993 |
|---|---|---|---|
| Radio licences | 2,669,562 | 2,700,754 | n.a. |
| Television licences | 2,435,106 | 2,475,768 | n.a. |
| Books published (no. of titles) | 10,438 | 10,274 | 10,602 |
| Daily newspapers (number) | 103 | 99 | 96 |

**Telephones** (1986): 5,622,976 instruments in use.

## Education

(Students)

|  | 1990/91 | 1991/92 | 1992/93 |
|---|---|---|---|
| Primary | 404,154 | 414,129 | 420,089 |
| Secondary | 382,241 | 390,537 | 401,504 |
| Vocational | 221,319 | 209,927 | 200,317 |
| Higher | 137,492 | 143,192 | 146,288 |

# Directory

## The Constitution

The Constitution (summarized below) was adopted on 29 May 1874.

Switzerland is divided into federated cantons which have sovereign authority except where the Constitution defines limits to their powers or accords responsibility to the Federal authority. After a referendum in September 1978, the Constitution was amended to allow for the formation of the canton of Jura, increasing the number of cantons to 23 (three of these are subdivided and they are sometimes collectively referred to as the 26 states).

Principally, the Federal authority is responsible for civil, penal and commercial law, legislation concerning marriage, residence and settlement, export and import duties, defence, postal, telephone and telegraph services, the mint, forestry, hunting and fishing, hydro-electric power, the economy, railways, important roads and bridges, social insurance, and international affairs. Administration is largely in the hands of the cantons, and in the combined management of Federal authorities and cantons. The cantons derive their revenue from direct taxation. The Federal authority draws its revenue from direct and indirect taxation. The profits from Federal enterprises and customs duties are received by the Federal authorities.

### COMMUNES

Each of the more than 3,000 communes of Switzerland has local autonomy over such matters as public utilities and roads, and grants primary citizenship. Decisions are made by communal assemblies. The smallest communes have fewer than 20 inhabitants, the largest, Zürich, around 370,000.

### CANTONS

The 26 cantons and half-cantons of the Swiss Confederation each have their own constitution and their own method of choosing the members of the cantonal assembly and cantonal government and the States Councillors who represent them at the federal level. Five cantons, Glarus, Appenzell Ausserrhoden and Innerrhoden, Obwalden and Nidwalden, retain the Landsgemeinde, an assembly of all citizens of the canton held annually, as their decision-making authority. Elsewhere, democracy is less direct, the secret ballot and the referendum having replaced the mass assembly.

### FEDERAL ASSEMBLY

The Federal Assembly is the supreme governing body of the Confederation. It is composed of two bodies, the National Council and the Council of States, which deliberate separately. The 200 members of the National Council are elected directly, by proportional representation, every four years. The minimum age for voting and eligibility for election in the Confederation is 18 years. In 1971 women gained full political rights at federal level and in almost all the cantons (female suffrage had been introduced in all cantons by late 1990). The Council of States represents the cantons, each of which sends two councillors, elected by the people in various ways according to the cantonal constitutions. Legislative and fiscal measures must be accepted by both houses in order to be adopted, and the Federal Assembly supervises the army, the civil service and the application of the law, exercises the right of pardon and elects the Federal Supreme Court, the Federal Insurance Court, the General who commands the army in times of crisis, and the Federal Council.

### FEDERAL COUNCIL

Executive authority is vested in the Federal Council, whose seven members are each in charge of a Federal Department. Each year the Federal Assembly appoints the President and Vice-President of the Confederation from among the Federal Councillors. Generally, the Councillors are chosen from the members of the Federal Assembly for four years after every general election.

### REFERENDUMS AND INITIATIVES

Referendums are held on both cantonal and federal levels. In many cantons all legislation has to be accepted by a majority of the voters, and in some cantons major financial matters have to be submitted to the popular vote. In federal affairs the consent of a majority of the voters and of the cantons must be obtained for amendments to the Federal Constitution, for extraconstitutional emergency legislation and for the decision to join collective security organizations or international bodies, but referendums are optional for other legislation. A petition from 50,000 voters is needed to bring about a national referendum, which can accept or reject any legislation which has been passed by Parliament. The initiative gives voters in many cantons the right to propose a constitutional or legislative amendment and to demand a popular vote on it. A petition by 100,000 voters is needed to initiate a vote on an amendment to the Federal Constitution, but as federal laws cannot be proposed by means of an initiative, some constitutional amendments introduced in this manner concern relatively unimportant matters and participation of the voters is, on average, 40% to 45%. The initiative is also used by the political opposition to bring about changes in government policy.

SWITZERLAND

## The Government
(June 1995)

### FEDERAL COUNCIL

**President of the Swiss Confederation for 1995 and Head of Federal Military (Defence) Department:** KASPAR VILLIGER (Radical-Democratic Party).

**Vice-President and Head of Federal Department of Public Economy:** JEAN-PASCAL DELAMURAZ (Radical-Democratic Party).

**Head of Federal Department of Finance:** OTTO STICH (Social-Democratic Party).

**Head of Federal Department of Foreign Affairs:** FLAVIO COTTI (Christian-Democratic Party).

**Head of Federal Department of Home Affairs:** RUTH DREIFUSS (Social-Democratic Party).

**Head of Federal Department of Justice and Police:** ARNOLD KOLLER (Christian-Democratic Party).

**Head of Federal Department of Transport, Communications and Energy:** ADOLF OGI (Swiss People's Party).

**Chancellor of the Swiss Confederation:** FRANÇOIS COUCHEPIN.

### FEDERAL DEPARTMENTS

**Federal Chancellery:** Bundeshaus-West, 3003 Berne; tel. (31) 3222111; telex 911191; fax (31) 3223706.

**Federal Department of Finance:** Bernerhof, Bundesgasse 3, 3003 Berne; tel. (31) 3226111; telex 912868; fax (31) 3226187.

**Federal Department of Foreign Affairs:** Bundeshaus-West, 3003 Berne; tel. (31) 3222111; telex 911440; fax (31) 3223237.

**Federal Department of Home Affairs:** Bundeshaus, Inselgasse, 3003 Berne; tel. (31) 3229111; telex 912890; fax (31) 3228032.

**Federal Department of Justice and Police:** Bundeshaus-West, Bundesgasse, 3003 Berne; tel. (31) 3224111; telex 911199; fax (31) 3227901.

**Federal Department of Public Economy:** Bundeshaus-Ost, 3003 Berne; tel. (31) 3222111; fax (31) 3222056.

**Federal Department of Transport, Communications and Energy:** Bundeshaus-Nord, 3003 Berne; tel. (31) 3224111; fax (31) 3128901.

**Federal Military (Defence) Department:** Bundeshaus-Ost, 3003 Berne; tel. (31) 3241211; fax (31) 3123463.

## Legislature

### BUNDESVERSAMMLUNG/ASSEMBLÉE FÉDÉRALE
(Federal Assembly)

#### Nationalrat/Conseil National
(National Council)

**President:** CLAUDE FREY (1995).

**General Election, 20 October 1991**

| | Seats |
|---|---|
| Radical-Democratic Party | 44 |
| Social-Democratic Party | 43 |
| Christian-Democratic People's Party | 37 |
| Swiss People's Party | 25 |
| Green Party | 14 |
| Liberal Party | 10 |
| Automobile Party | 8 |
| Independent Alliance | 6 |
| Swiss Democrats | 5 |
| Evangelical People's Party | 3 |
| Workers' Party | 2 |
| Others | 3 |
| **Total** | **200** |

#### Ständerat/Conseil des Etats
(Council of States)

**President:** JEAN-FRANÇOIS LEUBA (1995).

**Elections, 1991** (Members are elected by canton; method and period of election differs from canton to canton)

| | Seats |
|---|---|
| Radical-Democratic Party | 18 |
| Christian-Democratic People's Party | 16 |
| Swiss People's Party | 4 |
| Social-Democratic Party | 3 |
| Liberal Party | 3 |
| Independent Alliance | 1 |
| Others | 1 |
| **Total** | **46** |

## Political Organizations

**Christlichdemokratische Volkspartei der Schweiz—Parti démocrate-chrétien suisse** (Christian-Democratic People's Party): Postfach 5835, Klaraweg 6, 3001 Berne; tel. (31) 3522364; fax (31) 3522430; f. 1912; policies are a Christian outlook on world affairs, federalism and Christian social reform by means of professional associations; non-sectarian; Pres. ANTON COTTIER; Gen. Sec. RAYMOND LORETAN; Leader of Parliamentary Group PETER HESS.

**Christlichsoziale Partei—Parti chrétien-social** (Christian-Socialist Party): Postfach 5775, 3001 Berne; tel. (31) 3702102; Sec. HEDY JAGER.

**Eidgenössisch-Demokratische Union—Union-Démocratique Fédérale** (Union of Federal Democrats): Postfach, 3607 Thun 7; tel. (33) 223637; fax (33) 223744; Pres. SCHERRER WERNER.

**Evangelische Volkspartei der Schweiz—Parti évangélique suisse** (Protestant People's Party): Josefstr. 32, 8023 Zürich; tel. (1) 2727100; fax (1) 2721437; f. 1919; Pres. OTTO ZWYGART; Sec. DANIEL REUTER.

**Frauen macht Politik** (Women in Politics): Postfach 9353, 8036 Zürich; tel. (1) 2424418; Secs BARBARA HUBER, CLAUDIA SCHÄTTI.

**Freiheits-Partei der Schweiz—Die Auto-Partei** (Automobile Party): Postfach 4622, Egerkingen; tel. (91) 612343; fax (91) 612608; f. 1985 to support motorists' rights; has subsequently campaigned for restricted immigration; Pres. JÜRG SCHERRER.

**Freisinnig-Demokratische Partei der Schweiz—Parti radical-démocratique suisse** (Radical-Democratic Party): Postfach 6136, 3001 Berne; tel. (31) 3113438; fax (31) 3121951; led the movement which gave rise to the Federative State and the Constitution of 1848; stands for the principle of a strong Federal power, while respecting the legitimate rights of the cantons and all the minorities; liberal-free democratic in tendency; Pres. FRANZ STEINEGGER; Sec. CHRISTIAN KAUTER; Leader of Parliamentary Group PASCAL COUCHEPIN.

**Grüne Alternative** (Green Alternative): an association of environmentalist groups.

**Grüne Partei der Schweiz—Parti écologiste suisse** (Green Party of Switzerland): Waisenhausplatz 21, 3011 Berne; tel. (31) 3126660; fax (31) 3126662; f. 1983; Pres. VERENA DIENER; Gen. Sec. BERNHARD PULVER; Leader of Parliamentary Group CÉCILE BÜHLMANN.

**Landesring der Unabhängigen—Alliance des Indépendants** (Independent Alliance): Gutenbergstr. 9, Postfach 7075, 3001 Berne; tel. (31) 3821636; fax (31) 3823695; f. 1936; 4,000 mems; opposition movement advocating the application of liberal, social and ecological principles to politics; Pres. MONIKA WEBER; Sec. RUDOLF HOFER; Leader of Parliamentary Group VERENA GRENDELMEIER.

**Lega dei Ticinesi** (Union of Ticino): CP 2311, 6901 Lugano; tel. (91) 513033; fax (91) 527492; Pres. GIULIANO BIGNASCA.

**Liberale Partei der Schweiz—Parti libéral suisse** (Liberal Party): Postfach 7107, Spitalgasse 32, 3001 Berne; tel. (31) 3229961; fax (31) 3125474; opposes centralizing tendencies; Pres. FRANÇOIS JEANNERET; Sec. PHILIPPE BOILLOD; Leader of Parliamentary Group JEAN-FRANÇOIS LEUBA.

**Partei der Arbeit der Schweiz—Parti suisse du travail** (Workers' Party): 25 rue du Vieux-Billard, CP 232, 1211 Geneva 8; tel. (22) 3281140; fax (22) 3296412; f. 1944 by members of the Communist Party and left-wing Socialists; aims at co-ordinating all left-wing elements in order to reorganize Switzerland on a socialist basis; Pres. JEAN SPIELMANN.

**Progressive Organisationen der Schweiz—Organisations progressistes suisses** (Progressive Swiss Organizations): Postfach 1461, Aarauerstr. 7, 4600 Olten; tel. (62) 266707; f. 1973; left-wing; Secs GEORGES DEGEN, EDUARD HAFNER.

# SWITZERLAND

**Schweizer Demokraten—Démocrates suisses** (Swiss Democrats): Postfach 8116, 3001 Berne; tel. (31) 3112774; fax (31) 3125632; formerly Nationale Aktion für Volk und Heimat—Action nationale; 6,000 mems; main objectives are preservation of the country's political independence and of individual freedom, protection of the environment, and a population policy restricting the number of immigrants; Pres. RUDOLF KELLER; Gen. Sec. ROBERT MEYER.

**Schweizerische Volkspartei—Union démocratique du centre** (Swiss People's Party): Brückfeldstr. 18, 3000 Berne 26; tel. (31) 3025858; fax (31) 3017585; f. 1971; Pres. HANS UHLMANN; Gen. Sec. MYRTHA WELTI (acting); Pres. HANS UHLMANN; Leader of Parliamentary Group THEO FISCHER.

**Sozialdemokratische Partei der Schweiz—Parti socialiste suisse** (Social-Democratic Party): Spitalgasse 34, 3001 Berne; tel. (31) 3110744; telex 912956; fax (31) 3115414; f. 1888; bases its policy on democratic socialism and collaborates with all political parties sharing the same principles. Its influence dates mainly from the introduction of proportional representation in 1919; 45,000 mems; Chair. PETER BODENMANN; Secs ANDRÉ DAGUET, HEIDI DENEYS, BARBARA GEISER, JEAN-FRANÇOIS STEIERT; Leader of Parliamentary Group URSULA MAUCH.

**Partito Socialista, sezione ticinese PSS** (Socialist Party): CP 2245, 6501 Bellinzona; tel. (92) 259462; fax (92) 259601; f. 1992; fmrly the Partito Socialista Unitario; Pres. JOHN NOSEDA.

## Diplomatic Representation

### EMBASSIES IN SWITZERLAND

**Albania:** Eigerstr. 46, 3007 Berne; tel. (31) 3720707; fax (31) 3724188; Ambassador: GAZMEND BESIM TURDIU.
**Algeria:** Willadingweg 74, 3006 Berne; tel. (31) 3526961; telex 912623; fax (31) 3526268; Ambassador: ABDELMALEK GUENAIZIA.
**Argentina:** Jubiläumsplatz 6, 3006 Berne; tel. (31) 3523565; telex 911286; fax (31) 3520519; Ambassador: SUSANA RUIZ CERUTTI.
**Austria:** Kirchenfeldstr. 28, 3005 Berne; tel. (31) 3510111; telex 911754; fax (31) 3515664; Ambassador: MARKUS LUTTEROTTI.
**Belarus:** Neuengasse 39, 3011 Berne; tel. (31) 3113800; fax (31) 310322; Ambassador: S. AGUZTSCU.
**Belgium:** Weststr. 6, 3005 Berne; tel. (31) 3510462; telex 912896; fax (31) 3525961; Ambassador: MARCEL HOULLEZ.
**Bosnia and Herzegovina:** Spitalgasse 32, 3011 Berne; tel. (31) 3123800; fax (31) 3123809; Ambassador: M. FILIPOVIĆ.
**Brazil:** Monbijoustr. 68, 3007 Berne, POB 30, 3000 Berne 23; tel. (31) 3718515; fax (31) 3710525; Ambassador: CARLOS EDUARDO DE AFFONSECA ALVES DE SOUZA.
**Bulgaria:** Bernastr. 2, 3005 Berne; tel. (31) 3511455; telex 911786; fax (31) 3510064; Ambassador: ELENA KIRTCHEVA.
**Cameroon:** Brunnadernrain 29, 3006 Berne; tel. (31) 3524737; telex 913356; Ambassador: FRANÇOIS-XAVIER NGOUBEYOU.
**Canada:** Kirchenfeldstr. 88, 3005 Berne; tel. (31) 3526381; fax (31) 3527315; Ambassador: RÉJEAN FRENETTE.
**Chile:** Eigerplatz 5, 12th Floor, 3007 Berne; tel. (31) 3710745; telex 912862; fax (31) 3720025; Ambassador: BENJAMIN CONCHA GAZMURI.
**China, People's Republic:** Kalcheggweg 10, 3006 Berne; tel. (31) 3527333; telex 912616; fax (31) 3514573; Ambassador: XIN FUTAN.
**Colombia:** Dufourstr. 47, 3005 Berne; tel. (31) 3511700; fax (31) 3527072; Ambassador: MANUEL JOSÉ CEPEDA ESPINOSA.
**Costa Rica:** Thunstr. 150E, 3074 Muri; tel. (31) 9526230; telex 911145; fax (31) 9526457; Ambassador: JANINA DEL VECCHIO UGALDE.
**Côte d'Ivoire:** Thormannstr. 51, 3005 Berne; tel. (31) 3511051; telex 912718; Ambassador: KOFFI KOUAMÉ.
**Croatia:** Gurtenweg 39, 3074 Muri; Ambassador: ZDENKO SKRABALO.
**Cuba:** Gesellschaftsstr. 8, 3012 Berne; tel. and fax (31) 3022111; telex 912621; Ambassador: MADELEINE TERAN RODRÍGUEZ.
**Czech Republic:** Muristr. 53, 3006 Berne; tel. (31) 3523645; fax (31) 3527502; Ambassador: RICHARD BELCREDI.
**Denmark:** Thunstr. 95, 3006 Berne; tel. (31) 3525011; telex 911933; fax (31) 3512395; Ambassador: JAN MARCUSSEN.
**Ecuador:** Helvetiastr. 19A, 3005 Berne; tel. (31) 3511755; telex 911476; fax (31) 3512771; Ambassador: MARCELO PEÑA DURRINI.
**Egypt:** Elfenauweg 61, 3006 Berne; tel. (31) 3528012; telex 912210; fax (31) 3520625; Ambassador: BAHER AS-SADEK.
**Finland:** Weltpoststr. 4, 3015 Berne; tel. (31) 3513031; telex 912023; fax (31) 3513001; Ambassador: HENRY SÖDERHOLM.
**France:** Schosshaldenstr. 46, 3006 Berne; tel. (31) 3522424; telex 912738; fax (31) 3520526; Ambassador: BERNARD GARCIA.
**Germany:** Willadingweg 83, 3006 Berne; tel. (31) 3594111; telex 911565; fax (31) 3594444; Ambassador: Dr EBERHARD HEYKEN.

**Ghana:** Belpstr. 11, 3000 Berne; tel. (31) 257852; telex 912993; fax (31) 3814941; Ambassador: BENJAMIN GODZI GODWYLL.
**Greece:** Jungfraustr. 3, 3005 Berne; tel. (31) 3521637; telex 912479; fax (31) 3520557; Ambassador: EMMANUEL GHIKAS.
**Holy See:** Thunstr. 60, 3006 Berne (Apostolic Nunciature); tel. (31) 3526040; fax (31) 3525064; Apostolic Nuncio: Most Rev. KARL-JOSEF RAUBER, Titular Archbishop of Iubaltiana.
**Hungary:** Muristr. 31, 3006 Berne; tel. (31) 3528572; fax (31) 3512001; Ambassador: PÁL GRESZNÁRYK.
**India:** Effingerstr. 45, 3008 Berne; tel. (31) 3823111; telex 911829; fax (31) 3822687; Ambassador: KIZHAKKE PIZHARATH BALAKRISHNAN.
**Indonesia:** Elfenauweg 51, 3006 Berne; tel. (31) 3520983; telex 911525; fax (31) 3515283; Ambassador: MACHMUD SUBARKAH.
**Iran:** Thunstr. 68, 3006 Berne; tel. (31) 3510801; telex 912779; fax (31) 3515652; Ambassador: MOHAMMAD REZA ALBORZI.
**Ireland:** Kirchenfeldstr. 68, 3005 Berne; tel. (31) 3521442; telex 912917; fax (31) 3521455; Ambassador: GEARÓID Ó CLÉRIGH.
**Israel:** Alpenstr. 32, 3006 Berne; tel. (31) 3511042; telex 912608; fax (31) 3527916; Ambassador: RAPHAËL GVIR.
**Italy:** Elfenstr. 14, 3006 Berne; tel. (31) 3524151; telex 912615; fax (31) 3511026; Ambassador: FRANCO FERRETTI.
**Japan:** Engerstr. 43, 3012 Berne; tel. (31) 3020811; telex 912653; fax (31) 3015325; Ambassador: YUSUSHI KUROKOCHI.
**Jordan:** Belpstr. 11, 3007 Berne; tel. (31) 3814146; telex 912945; fax (31) 3822119; Ambassador: MOHAMMAD SAEED ABOU NAWAR.
**Korea, Democratic People's Republic:** Pourtalèsstr. 43, 3074 Muri; tel. (31) 9516621; telex 912457; fax (31) 9515704; Ambassador: RI TCHEUL.
**Korea, Republic:** Kalcheggweg 38, 3006 Berne; tel. (31) 3511081; fax (31) 3512657; Ambassador: DAE-WAN KANG.
**Lebanon:** Thunstr. 10, 3074 Muri; tel. (31) 9512972; telex 912974; fax (31) 9518119; Ambassador: FOUAD AT-TURK.
**Libya:** Tavelweg 2, 3006 Berne; tel. (31) 3513076; telex 912996; fax (31) 3511325; Ambassador: SALAHEDDIN A. EL-MESALLATI.
**Liechtenstein:** Willadingweg 65, 3006 Berne; tel. (31) 3576411; fax (31) 3576415; Ambassador: Prince NICHOLAS OF LIECHTENSTEIN.
**Luxembourg:** Kramgasse 45, 3011 Berne; tel. (31) 3114732; telex 912554; fax (31) 3110019; Ambassador: PAUL PETERS.
**Mexico:** Bernastr. 57, 3005 Berne; tel. (31) 3511875; fax (31) 3513492; Ambassador: EZEQUIEL PADILLA COUTTOLENC.
**Monaco:** Junkerngasse 28, 3011 Berne; tel. (31) 3112858; fax (31) 3118696; Ambassador: (vacant).
**Morocco:** Helvetiastr. 42, 3005 Berne; tel. (31) 3510362; telex 912997; fax (31) 3510364; Ambassador: TAHAR NEJJAR.
**Netherlands:** Kollerweg 11, 3006 Berne; tel. (31) 3527063; telex 912739; fax (31) 3528735; Ambassador: W. SINNINGHE DAMSTÉ.
**Nigeria:** Zieglerstr. 45, 3007 Berne; tel. (31) 3820726; telex 912995; fax (31) 3821602; Chargé d'affaires a.i.: GODWIN A. AMEH.
**Norway:** Dufourstr. 29, 3005 Berne; tel. (31) 3524676; telex 912920; fax (31) 3515381; Ambassador: JAN GUNNAR JÖLLE.
**Pakistan:** Bernastr. 47, 3005 Berne; tel. (31) 3522992; telex 912856; fax (31) 3515440; Ambassador: M. ZIA ISPAHANI.
**Peru:** Thunstr. 36, 3005 Berne; tel. (31) 3518555; fax (31) 3324906; Ambassador: CÉSAR CASTILLO RAMÍREZ.
**Philippines:** Hallwylstr. 34, 3005 Berne; tel. (31) 3514211; fax (31) 3524341; Ambassador: TOMAS T. SYQUILA.
**Poland:** Elfenstr. 20A, 3006 Berne; tel. (31) 3520452; telex 912841; fax (31) 3523416; Ambassador: (vacant).
**Portugal:** Jungfraustr. 1, 3005 Berne; tel. (31) 3528329; telex 912837; fax (31) 3514432; Ambassador: FRANCISCO GRAINHA DO VALE.
**Romania:** Kirchenfeldstr. 78, 3005 Berne; tel. (31) 3523522; telex 912634; fax (31) 3526455; Ambassador: JOSIF BODA.
**Russia:** Brunnadernrain 37, 3006 Berne; tel. (31) 3520566; telex 911297; fax (31) 3525595; Ambassador: ANDREI I. STEPANOV.
**Saudi Arabia:** Kramburgstr. 12, 3006 Berne; tel. (31) 3521555; telex 912482; fax (31) 3514581; Ambassador: SAMIR SHIHABI.
**Senegal:** Monbijoustr. 10, 3011 Berne; tel. (31) 3821202; telex 3822994; fax (31) 3824795; Ambassador: IBRA DÉGUÈNE.
**Slovakia:** Thunstr. 99, 3006 Berne; tel. (31) 3523646; fax (31) 3514859; Ambassador: Prof. ÁBEL KRÁL.
**Slovenia:** Schwanengasse 9, 3011 Berne; tel. (31) 3124418; fax (31) 3124414; Ambassador: BORIS FRLEC.
**South Africa:** Jungfraustr. 1, 3005 Berne; tel. (31) 3522011; fax (31) 3521116; Ambassador: R. DIETRICHSEN.
**Spain:** Kalcheggweg 24, 3006 Berne; tel. (31) 3520412; telex 912360; fax (31) 3515229; Ambassador: FEDERICO GARAYALDE EMPARAN.

**Sweden:** Bundesgasse 26, 3001 Berne; tel. (31) 3120563; telex 911770; fax (31) 3121692; Ambassador: JAN MÅRTENSON.
**Thailand:** Eigerstr. 60, 3007 Berne; tel. (31) 3722281; telex 912445; fax (31) 3720757; Ambassador: DON PRAMUDWINAI.
**Tunisia:** Kirchenfeldstr. 63, 3005 Berne; tel. (31) 3528226; telex 912620; fax (31) 3510445; Ambassador: ISMAÏL LEJRI.
**Turkey:** Lombachweg 33, 3006 Berne; tel. (31) 3511691; telex 911879; fax (31) 3528819; Ambassador: RIZA TÜRMEN.
**Ukraine:** Feldeggweg 5, 3005 Berne; tel. (31) 3522316; fax (31) 3516416; Ambassador: OLEXANDRE SLIPTCHENKO.
**United Kingdom:** Thunstr. 50, 3000 Berne 15; tel. (31) 3525021; fax (31) 3520583; Ambassador: DAVID BEATTIE.
**USA:** Jubiläumsstr. 93, 3005 Berne; tel. (31) 3517011; telex 912603; fax (31) 3517344; Ambassador: LARRY LAWRENCE.
**Uruguay:** Kramgasse 63, 3011 Berne; tel. (31) 3122226; fax (31) 3112747; Ambassador: JORGE TALICE.
**Venezuela:** Morillonstr. 9, 3007 Berne; tel. (31) 3713282; telex 912797; fax (31) 3710424; Ambassador: JOSÉ F. SUCRE FIGARELLA.
**Yugoslavia:** Seminarstr. 5, 3006 Berne; tel. (31) 3526353; telex 912848; fax (31) 3514474; Chargé d'affaires a.i.: DRAGEN IGNJATIJEVIĆ.
**Zaire:** Sulgenheimweg 21, 3007 Berne; tel. (31) 3713538; telex 911431; Ambassador: NDEZE MATABARO.

## Judicial System

Switzerland has possessed a common Civil Code since 1912, but the Penal Code was only unified in 1942. Under the Code capital punishment was abolished by the few cantons which still retained it. The individual cantons continue to elect and maintain their own magistracy, and retain certain variations in procedure. The canton of Zürich, for example, has justices of the peace (Friedensrichter—normally one for each commune), District Courts (Bezirksgerichte), Labour Courts (Arbeitsgerichte), Courts for Tenancy Matters, an Appeal Court (Obergericht) with various specialized benches, a Cassation Court (Kassationsgericht), and, for the more important cases under penal law, a Jury Court (Geschworenengericht). Apart from military courts, there are only two Federal Judicial authorities, the Federal Supreme Court and the Federal Tribunal of Insurance.

### FEDERAL SUPREME COURT

The Federal Supreme Court sits at Lausanne. The Court is composed of 30 judges elected for a six-year term by the Federal Assembly. According to the Constitution any citizen eligible for election to the National Council can theoretically be elected Justice to the Court, but in practice only lawyers are considered for this office nowadays. All three official Swiss languages must be represented in the Court. The President of the Federal Supreme Court is elected by the Federal Assembly for a two-year term, with no possibility of re-election, from among the senior judges of the Court.

The Court is divided into six permanent branches or chambers, each of which has jurisdiction over cases pertaining to a specific subject, namely:

(a) two 'Public', i.e. Constitutional and Administrative Law Divisions, being composed of seven and six judges respectively.

(b) two Civil or Private Law Divisions of six judges each, which serve mainly as Courts of Appeal in civil matters.

(c) the Debt Execution and Bankruptcy Law Chamber of three judges (members of the Second Civil Law Division).

(d) the Criminal Law Division, the so-called Court of Cassation, which is composed of five judges and which mainly hears appeals in criminal law matters.

There are also four non-permanent divisions hearing exclusively cases which involve certain crimes against the Confederation, certain forms of terrorism, and other offences related to treason.

In 1993 the Court heard 2,215 constitutional law cases, and, in its capacity as the national court of appeal, 658 civil law cases, 836 criminal law cases and 964 administrative law cases.

### FEDERAL TRIBUNAL OF INSURANCE

The Tribunal was founded in 1918 and consists of seven members. It sits at Lucerne. Since 1969 it has been considered as the Court of Social Insurance (Sozialversicherungsabteilung, Cour des assurances sociales, Corte delle assicurazioni sociali) of the Federal Supreme Court.

## Religion

According to the 1990 census, the religious adherence per 1,000 of the population was as follows: Roman Catholic 461, Protestant 400, Old Catholic 2, Jewish 3, Muslim 22, other denominations (or without religion) 112.

### CHRISTIANITY
#### The Roman Catholic Church

For ecclesiastical purposes, Switzerland comprises six dioceses (one of which, Chur, includes the neighbouring Principality of Liechtenstein) and two territorial abbacies. All of the dioceses and abbacies are directly responsible to the Holy See.

**Bishops' Conference:** Secrétariat de la Conférence des Evêques Suisses, ave Moléson 21, 1700 Fribourg 6; tel. (37) 224794; fax (37) 224993; f. 1863; Pres. Mgr HENRI SALINA (Titular Bishop of Mons in Mauretania).

**Bishop of Basel:** (vacant), Bischöfliches Ordinariat, Baselstr. 58, 4501 Solothurn; tel. (65) 232811; fax (65) 235647.

**Bishop of Chur:** Mgr WOLFGANG HAAS, Bischöfliches Ordinariat, Hof 19, 7000 Chur; tel. (81) 222312; fax (81) 216140.

**Bishop of Lausanne, Geneva and Fribourg:** Mgr PIERRE MAMIE, 86 rue de Lausanne, BP 271, 1701 Fribourg; tel. (37) 221251; fax (37) 222129.

**Bishop of Lugano:** Mgr EUGENIO CORECCO, CP 2337, Via Borghetto 6, 6901 Lugano; tel. (91) 236081; fax (91) 236083.

**Bishop of St Gallen:** Mgr OTMAR MÄDER, Bischöfliches Ordinariat, Klosterhof 6B, 9000 St Gallen; tel. (71) 222096; fax (71) 225842.

**Bishop of Sion:** Cardinal HENRI SCHWERY, ave de la Tour 12, CP 2068, 1950 Sion 2; tel. (27) 231818; fax (27) 231836.

#### Old Catholic Church

**Christkatholische Kirche der Schweiz** (Old Catholic Church of Switzerland): Willadingweg 39, 3006 Berne; tel. (31) 3513530; fax (31) 3529560; f. 1874; 16,000 mems (1990); Pres. URS STOLZ; Bishop Rt Rev. HANS GERNY.

#### Protestant Churches

**Federation of Swiss Protestant Churches** (Schweizerischer Evangelischer Kirchenbund, Fédération des Eglises protestantes de la Suisse): Sulgenauweg 26, 3000 Berne 23; tel. (31) 3722511; fax (31) 3715418; f. 1920; comprises the 18 reformed churches of Aargau, Appenzell, Basel-Stadt, Basel-Land, Fribourg, Geneva, Glarus, Graubünden, Luzern, Neuchâtel, St Gallen, Schaffhausen, Solothurn, Tessin, Thurgau, Valais, Vaud, Zürich, the Synodalverband Berne-Jura, the Kirchenverband Zentralschweiz, the Eglise évangélique libre de Genève and the Evangelisch-methodistische Kirche, as well as the Swiss churches abroad; the executive organ is the Council of the Federation (Vorstand des Schweizerischen Evangelischen Kirchenbundes, Conseil de la Fédération): Pres. Rev. H. RUSTERHOLZ (Berne).

### JUDAISM

**Schweizerischer Israelitischer Gemeindebund/Fédération suisse des communautés israélites:** Gotthardstr. 65, 8002 Zürich; tel. (1) 2015583; fax (1) 2021672; Pres. ROLF BLOCH; Gen. Sec. MARTIN ROSENFELD.

### BAHÁ'Í FAITH

**Nationaler Geistiger Rat der Bahá'í der Schweiz/Assemblée spirituelle nationale des bahá'ís de Suisse:** Dufourstr. 13, 3005 Berne; tel. (31) 3521020; fax (31) 3524716; Chair. Dr AMIN KHAMSI; Sec. Dr JOHN PAUL VADER.

## The Press

Freedom of the Press in Switzerland is guaranteed by Article 55 of the amended 1874 Constitution, and the only formal restrictions on the press are the legal restraints concerned with abuses of this freedom. A federal law, enacted in 1968, protects the right of journalists to refuse, in administrative procedures, to reveal their sources of information, except in cases where the security of the state is involved.

The Swiss combination of a high literacy rate and a strong interest in local news, the political autonomy of communes and cantons, direct democracy, the federal constitutional structure and the coexistence of diverse languages and religions has tended to produce a decentralized press, fragmented into numerous local papers, often with very low circulations. In 1993 there were 96 daily newspapers, but only 12 had a circulation of over 50,000. The majority of newspapers are regional, even such high circulation ones as *Tages Anzeiger Zürich* and *Basler Zeitung* and national dailies such as *Neue Zürcher Zeitung*. About 67% of newspapers are printed in German, 25% in French, 6% in Italian and less than 2% in Raeto-Romansch. The presence of immigrant workers and the Swiss interest in foreign news has led to the

# SWITZERLAND

import of 100,000 copies of French, German, Italian and Spanish newspapers every day.

*Feuille d'Avis de Neuchâtel* (later renamed *L'Express*), dating from 1738, is the oldest Swiss paper. *Blick* (382,275) and *Tages Anzeiger Zürich* (280,000) have easily the largest circulations, followed by *Neue Zürcher Zeitung* (151,470), *Berner Zeitung* (121,887), *Basler Zeitung* (114,413) and *24 Heures* (96,131). The two most respected dailies are *Neue Zürcher Zeitung*, founded in 1780, and the French-language *Journal de Genève*, established nearly 50 years later. Both papers carry an exceptionally high proportion of foreign news, and have a large readership abroad.

## PRINCIPAL DAILIES

### Aarau
**Aargauer Tagblatt/Brugger Tagblatt/Freiämter Tagblatt:** Bahnhofstr. 39, 5001 Aarau; tel. (64) 266161; telex 981146; fax (64) 266376; liberal; circ. 56,433.

### Arbon
**Schweizer Bodensee-Zeitung:** Romanshornerstr. 36, 9320 Arbon; f. 1849; radical; circ. 17,000.

### Baden
**Badener Tagblatt:** Stadtturmstr. 19, 5400 Baden; tel. (56) 209222; telex 825000; fax (56) 222390; f. 1848; non-party; Publishers Dr O. Wanner, P. Wanner; circ. 44,641.

### Basel (Bâle)
**Basler Zeitung:** Hochbergerstr. 15, 4002 Basel; tel. (61) 661111; telex 962140; f. 1977; liberal; Editor H. P. Platz; circ. 114,413.

**Nordschweiz/Basler Volksblatt:** Petersgasse 34, 4001 Basel; telex 962604; Catholic; Publishers Cratander AG; circ. 13,000.

### Bellinzona
**La Regione:** Via Ghiringhelli 9, 6500 Bellinzona; tel. (92) 262252; fax (92) 263461; f. 1992; circ. 30,000.

### Berne (Bern)
**Berner Tagwacht:** Monbijoustr. 61, 3001 Berne; tel. (31) 456658; telex 912248; independent; circ. 10,029.

**Berner Zeitung:** Nordring, Postfach 1147, 3001 Berne; tel. (31) 414646; telex 33888; f. 1844; independent; Chief Editor Ronald Roggen; circ. 121,887.

**Der Bund:** Effingerstr. 1, 3001 Berne; tel. (31) 3851111; telex 912820; f. 1850; liberal; Chief Editor Dr Peter Ziegler; circ. 62,326.

### Bienne (Biel)
**Bieler Tagblatt/Seeländer Bote:** Freiestr. 9–13, 2501 Bienne; telex 934568; independent; Publisher W. Gassman; circ. 35,000.

**Journal du Jura/Tribune jurassienne:** 135 chaussée du Long-Champ, 2501 Bienne; tel. (32) 428242; fax (32) 428332; f. 1863; independent; Publisher W. Gassmann; circ. 16,420.

### Brig
**Walliser Bote:** Furkastr. 21, 3900 Brig; tel. (28) 232531; telex 473162; Catholic; Editor Pius Rieder; circ. 23,195.

### Buchs
**Werdenberger und Obertoggenburger:** Bahnhofstr. 14, 9470 Buchs; telex 855207; f. 1869; Liberal; circ. 10,247.

### La Chaux-de-Fonds
**L'impartial:** 14 rue Neuve, 2300 La Chaux-de-Fonds; tel. (39) 210210; fax (39) 210360; f. 1880; independent; circ. 29,418.

### Chur (Coire)
**Bündner Tagblatt:** Hartbertstr. 7, 7001 Chur; tel. (81) 221423; telex 851310; fax (81) 222309; f. 1852; independent; circ. 13,000.

**Bündner Zeitung:** Kasernenstr. 1, 7000 Chur; telex 851330; independent; Publisher Gasser AG; circ. 40,042.

### Delémont
**Le Quotidien Jurassien:** 6 route de Courroux, 2800 Delémont; tel. (66) 221751; fax (66) 226821; f. 1993; formed by a merger between *Le Démocrate* and *Le Pays*; independent; Editor M. Voisard; circ. 24,740.

### Dielsdorf
**Zürcher Unterländer:** Schulstr. 12, 8157 Dielsdorf; tel. (1) 8548282; fax (1) 8530690.

### Flawil
**Volksfreund/Wiler Zeitung/Gossauer Zeitung:** 9230 Flawil; independent; circ. 8,228.

### Frauenfeld
**Thurgauer Zeitung:** Promenadenstr. 16, 8500 Frauenfeld; tel. (54) 271111; telex 896383; f. 1798; independent; Publishers Huber & Co AG; circ. 25,334.

### Fribourg (Freiburg)
**Freiburger Nachrichten:** Bahnhofplatz 5, 1701 Fribourg; tel. (37) 814151; fax (37) 221446; Catholic; circ. 15,318.

### Geneva
**Geneva Post:** Geneva; f. 1994; English Language; Editor Harvey Morris.

**Journal de Genève:** 12 rue de Hesse, 1211 Geneva 11; tel. (22) 8198888; telex 422214; fax (22) 8198989; f. 1826; independent Liberal; Editor-in-Chief Jasmine Audemars; circ. 22,254.

**Tribune de Genève:** CP 5115, 1211 Geneva 11; tel. (22) 3224000; telex 422110; fax (22) 7810107; f. 1879; independent; morning; Editor Guy Mettan; circ. 62,000.

### Glarus
**Glarner Nachrichten:** 8750 Glarus; telex 875491; f. 1875; liberal; Publishers Tschudi & Co AG; circ. 17,199.

### Heerbrugg
**Der Rheintaler:** Auerstr. 17, 9435 Heerbrugg; tel. (71) 723503; fax (71) 723527; independent; Editor M. Löliger; circ. 11,688.

### Herisau
**Appenzeller Zeitung:** Kasernenstr. 64, 9100 Herisau; tel. (71) 513131; fax (71) 521424; Radical-Democrat; f. 1828; Publishers Schlapfer & Co SA; circ. 15,000.

### Lausanne
**Gazette de Lausanne:** 7 rue St Martin, 1003 Lausanne; tel. (21) 206161; telex 24634; f. 1798; Liberal-Democratic; morning; Chief Editor Jasmine Audemars; circ. 9,740.

**Le Matin:** 33 ave de la Gare, 1001 Lausanne; tel. (21) 494949; telex 454782; fax (21) 494110; f. 1862; independent; Editor Marcel A. Pasche; circ. 55,000, Sunday 160,000.

**Nouvelle Revue de Lausanne et du Pays de Vaud:** 15 ave Ruchonnet, 1003 Lausanne; tel. (21) 3400011; fax (21) 3400030; f. 1868; radical-democratic; circ. 9,500.

**24 heures:** 33 ave de la Gare, 1003 Lausanne; tel. (21) 494444; telex 24782; fax (21) 494110; f. 1762; independent; Editor Marcel A. Pasche; circ. 96,131.

### Liestal
**Basellandschaftliche Zeitung:** Schützenstr. 6, 4410 Liestal; telex 966012; f. 1832; Radical-Democratic; Publishers Ludin AG; circ. 18,230.

### Lucerne (Luzern)
**Luzerner Neuste Nachrichten:** Zürichstr. 5, 6002 Lucerne; tel. (41) 391515; telex 868133; f. 1896; independent; circ. 57,290.

**Luzerner Zeitung:** Maihofstr. 76, 6002 Lucerne; tel. (41) 395252; telex 865700; fax (41) 395383; circ. 76,600.

### Lugano
**Corriere del Ticino:** Ai Mulini, 6933 Muzzano; tel. (91) 583131; telex 844016; fax (91) 582779; f. 1891; independent; circ. 35,000.

**Giornale del Popolo:** Via San Gottardo 50, 6900 Lugano; tel. (91) 232271; telex 79112; fax (91) 232805; f. 1926; Catholic; circ. 22,085.

### Mels
**Der Sarganserländer:** Sarganserstr., 8887 Mels; telex 855785; Catholic; circ. 9,746.

### Montreux
**La Presse:** 22 ave des Planches, 1820 Montreux; tel. (21) 9634141; fax (21) 9633385; f. 1867; independent; circ. 22,216.

### Neuchâtel (Neuenburg)
**L'Express:** CP 561, 2001 Neuchâtel; telex 952542; fax (38) 250039; f. 1738; independent; circ. 31,710.

### Olten
**Oltner Tagblatt:** Ziegelfeldstr. 60, 4600 Olten; telex 981619; f. 1878; independent; circ. 14,313.

### St Gallen (St-Gall)
**Die Ostschweiz:** Oberer Graben 8, 9001 St Gallen; tel. (71) 308580; telex 77393; f. 1873; Catholic; circ. 25,407.

# SWITZERLAND

**St Galler Tagblatt:** Fürstenlandstr. 122, 9001 St Gallen; tel. (71) 297711; telex 77537; fax (71) 297476; f. 1839; Liberal; Editor-in-Chief JÜRG TOBLER; circ. 72,000.

## Schaffhausen (Schaffhouse)

**Schaffhauser Nachrichten:** Vordergasse 58, 8201 Schaffhausen; telex 897250; fax (53) 833401; f. 1861; Liberal; Publisher Dr MAX U. RAPOLD; circ. 23,773.

## Sion

**Nouvelliste et Feuille d'Avis du Valais:** 14 rue de l'Industrie, 1951 Sion; telex 472501; Catholic; Publishers Imprimerie Moderne SA; circ. 43,062.

## Solothurn

**Solothurner Zeitung:** Postfach 748, 4501 Solothurn; tel. (65) 247247; f. 1907; liberal; circ. 45,207.

## Spiez

**Berner Oberländer:** Seestr. 42, 3700 Spiez; tel. (33) 544444; fax (33) 547894; f. 1898; independent; Publishers G. MAURER AG; circ. 19,120.

## Stäfa

**Zürichsee-Zeitung:** Seestr. 86, 8712 Stäfa; tel. (1) 9285555; fax (1) 9285550; Radical-Democratic; Publisher and Editor-in-Chief Dr ULRICH E. GUT; circ. 30,000.

## Thun (Thoune)

**Thuner Tagblatt:** Rampenstr. 1, 3602 Thun; tel. (33) 228833; fax (33) 234867; independent; Dir FRITZ JUTZI; Editor-in-Chief RENÉ E. GYGAX; circ. 18,723.

## Uster

**Anzeiger von Uster:** Freiestr. 16, 8610 Uster; tel. (1) 9404747; telex 57484; f. 1846; independent; Publisher EUGEN WEILENMANN; circ. 9,211.

## Vevey

**Journal Riviera:** 5 rue du Simplon, 1800 Vevey; tel. (21) 9212158; telex 451236; fax (21) 9229865; independent; circ. 9,302.

## Wetzikon

**Zürcher Oberländer:** 8620 Wetzikon; tel. (1) 9333333; telex 875547; fax (1) 9323232; f. 1852; liberal; circ. 36,000.

## Winterthur (Winterthour)

**Der Landbote:** Garnmarkt 1, 8401 Winterthur; tel. (52) 2134051; telex 896417; fax (52) 2127518; f. 1836; independent; morning; Editor-in-Chief Dr RUDOLF GERBER; circ. 44,000.

## Yverdon

**Journal d'Yverdon:** 4 ave Haldimand, 1401 Yverdon; tel. (24) 231151; telex 457131; f. 1773; independent; circ. 9,101.

## Zofingen

**Zofinger Tagblatt:** Henzmannstr. 18, 4800 Zofingen; tel. (62) 509350; fax (62) 509419; f. 1872; liberal; Editor Dr PAUL EHINGER; circ. 16,777.

## Zürich

**Blick:** Dufourstr. 23, 8008 Zürich; tel. (1) 2596262; telex 817300; fax (1) 2622953; independent; Editor PETER BALSIGER; circ. 382,275.

**Neue Zürcher Zeitung:** Falkenstr. 11, Postfach, 8021 Zürich; tel. (1) 2581111; telex 817099; fax (1) 2521329; f. 1780; Independent-Liberal; Chief Editor Dr HUGO BÜTLER; Dir FRITZ HUBER; circ. 151,470.

**Tages Anzeiger Zürich:** Werdstr. 21, 8021 Zürich; tel. (1) 2484411; telex 812236; fax (1) 2484471; f. 1893; independent; Chief Editor R. DE WECK; circ. 280,500.

## PERIODICALS AND JOURNALS

**Allgemeine Schweizerische Militärzeitschrift:** Verlag Huber & Co AG, 8501 Frauenfeld; tel. (54) 223562; fax (54) 214977; f. 1834; monthly; Editor OTT CHARLES; circ. 34,000.

**Die Alpen:** Thorackerstr. 3, 3074 Muri; tel. (31) 9515787; fax (31) 9511570; monthly and quarterly; published by Schweizer Alpen-Club; circ. 77,000.

**Annabelle:** Baselstr. 30, 8048 Zürich; telex 814180; women's magazine; f. 1938; 2 a month; circ. 106,293.

**Auto:** Wasserwerkgasse 39, 3000 Berne 13; tel. (31) 3283111; fax (31) 3111734; published by the Automobile Club of Switzerland; 10 a year; circ. 70,431.

**Automobil Revue:** Nordring 4, 3001 Berne; tel. (31) 3323131; telex 912661; fax (31) 3327971; f. 1906; weekly published in German and French (Revue automobile); Editor HANS U. BUESCHI; circ. 80,000.

**Baukader Aktuelles Bauen:** Vogt-Schild AG, Postfach 748, 4501 Solothurn; tel. (65) 247247; fax (65) 247251; f. 1944; 10 a year; magazine for the construction industry; published by Imprimerie Vogt-Schild AG; circ. 15,000.

**Das Beste aus Reader's Digest:** Räffelstr. 11, 8021 Zürich; tel. (1) 4633833; telex 813231; Swiss German edition (circ. 250,314), Swiss French edition (circ. 83,451).

**Bilanz:** Edenstr. 20, 8021 Zürich; tel. (1) 2077221; telex 816765; fax (1) 2015916; f. 1977; review of the business world; circ. 60,000.

**Courrier neuchâtelois:** 4 rue de l'Etang, 2013 Colombier; tel. (38) 413265; fax (38) 411521; Wednesday; Editor RENÉ GESSLER; circ. 83,000.

**du:** Postfach, 8021 Zürich; tel. (1) 4046030; fax (1) 4046040; f. 1941; monthly art review; Editor Dr DIETER BACHMANN; circ. 28,700.

**Echo Illustré:** route de Meyrin 12, 1211 Geneva 7; tel. (22) 7349000; fax (22) 7340969; weekly; circ. 22,000.

**L'Eco dello Sport:** Via Industria, 6933 Muzzano; tel. (91) 575724; fax (91) 575750; circ. 7,132.

**Femme aujourd'hui:** 45A route des Acacias, CP 73, 1211 Geneva 25; tel. (22) 422646; fax (22) 429764; weekly; circ. 105,827.

**Finanz und Wirtschaft:** Weberstr. 8–10, Postfach 913, 8021 Zürich; tel. (1) 2411134; telex 812386; fax (1) 2911490; f. 1928; 2 a week; finance and economics; circ. 38,772.

**Glücks-Post:** Dufourstr. 23, 8008 Zürich; circ. 188,267.

**Graphis:** Dufourstr. 107, 8008 Zürich; tel. (1) 3838211; fax (1) 3831643; f. 1944; bi-monthly; graphic art and applied arts; published by Graphis Press Corporation; Editor B. MARTIN PEDERSEN; circ. 29,000.

**Handelszeitung:** Seestr. 37, 8027 Zürich; tel. (1) 2013500; telex 815517; fax (1) 2883565; f. 1862; financial, commercial and industrial weekly; Publisher Ralph Büchi; Chief Editor Dr KURT SPECK; circ. 37,540.

**L'Hebdo:** 3 Pont Bessières, 1005 Lausanne; tel. (21) 203611; fax (21) 203617; f. 1981; news magazine; Editor-in-Chief J. C. PECLET; circ. 60,000.

**L'Illustré:** Pont-Bessières 3, CP 3100, 1002 Lausanne; tel. (21) 3420808; fax (21) 3122784; f. 1921; weekly; Chief Editor JACQUES POGET; circ. 99,000.

**io Management Zeitschrift: Journal for Management and Industrial Engineering** (Management-Zeitschrift Industrielle Organisation/Revue Suisse pour l'organisation industrielle): Zürichbergstr. 18, 8028 Zürich; tel. (1) 2610800; telex 815065; fax (1) 2612468; f. 1932; monthly; organization, management, economics; published by Betriebswissenschaftliches Institut der Eidg. Technischen Hochschule (Institute of Management and Industrial Engineering affiliated to the Swiss Federal Institute of Technology); Editor Dr ROLAND MUELLER; circ. 14,000.

**Journal suisse d'horlogerie et de bijouterie:** 1093 La Conversion; tel. (21) 7911065; fax (21) 7914084; 6 a year; publ. in English as Swiss Watch and Jewelry Journal; circ. 20,000.

**Modeblatt:** Klausstr. 33, 8008 Zürich; tel. (1) 3837050; fax (1) 3834660; weekly; Publisher UELI STILLI; circ. 164,000.

**Museum Helveticum:** Schwabe & Co AG, Steinentorstr. 13, 4010 Basel; tel. (61) 2725523; fax (61) 2725573; f. 1944; quarterly; Swiss journal for classical philology, ancient history and classical archaeology; Editors Prof. M. BILLERBECK, Prof. A. GIOVANNINI, Prof. TH. GELZER, Prof. F. GRAF.

**Nebelspalter:** Pestalozzistr. 5, 9400 Rorschach; tel. (71) 414341; fax (71) 414313; f. 1875; satirical weekly; Editor IWAN RASCHLE; published by Verlag E. Löpfe-Benz AG; circ. 33,000.

**Opernwelt:** Postfach 369, 8053 Zürich; tel. (1) 4221653; telex 813575; fax (1) 3832859; f. 1960; opera monthly; published by Erhard Friedrich Verlag; Editor IMRE FABIAN; circ. 12,000.

**Orella:** Morgenstr. 6, 8036 Zürich; tel. (1) 2981220; fax (1) 2981277; monthly; fashion, handiwork; circ. 65,000.

**Plaisirs gastronomie:** 2013 Colombier; tel. (38) 411541; fax (38) 413179; 6 a year; gastronomy and tourism; Editor R. GESSLER; circ. 22,000.

**Politische Rundschau/Revue politique:** Postfach 6136, 3001 Berne; f. 1921; quarterly; Swiss and foreign politics, economics and culture; critical reviews (Radical); published by the Liberal-Democratic Party; circ. 2,500.

**PRO:** Im Morgental 35, 8126 Zürich; tel. (1) 9182728; f. 1951; monthly; Editor ANNEMARIE HERZOG.

**Rad-& Motor-Sport:** Industriestr. 47, POB 8152, Glattbrugg; tel. (1) 8100505; telex 823290; fax (1) 8101160; weekly; organ of Schweizerischer Radfahrer-und Motorfahrer Bund; Editor MORITZ H. MEYER; circ. 50,000.

SWITZERLAND

**Revue économique et sociale:** BFSH 1, 1015 Lausanne/Dorigny; tel. (21) 6915347; f. 1943; quarterly; Editors A. JENNY, K. NOSCHIS; circ. 1,400.

**Revue médicale de la suisse romande:** Edition et Publicité SA, 2 ave Bellefontaine, 1003 Lausanne; tel. (21) 3239866; fax (21) 3239737; f. 1880; monthly; Editor Dr E. C. BONARD; circ. 5,100.

**Revue militaire suisse:** CP 7, 1669 Albeuve; tel. (29) 81977; f. 1856; Editor-in-Chief Col. HERVÉ DE WECK.

**Revue suisse de zoologie:** Muséum d'Histoire Naturelle, CP 6434, 1211 Geneva 6; tel. (22) 7359130; fax (22) 7353445; f. 1893; quarterly; Dir V. MAHNERT.

**Schweizer Archiv für Neurologie und Psychiatrie** (Archives Suisses de Neurologie et de Psychiatrie): Verlag Baebler, Postfach 109, 3000 Berne 21; tel. (31) 3714552; fax (31) 3717040; f. 1917; 6 a year; published by Orell Füssli AG, Graphische Betriebe.

**Schweizer Familie:** Baslerstr. 30, Postfach, 8021 Zürich; tel. (1) 4046106; fax (1) 4046096; f. 1893; weekly; Editor ANDREAS DURISCH; circ. 217,900.

**Schweizer Illustrierte:** Dufourstr. 23, 8008 Zürich; fax (1) 2620442; f. 1911; illustrated weekly; circ. 206,493.

**Schweizer Jugend:** 5400 Baden; tel (56) 302200; fax (56) 302299; f. 1924; young people's fortnightly; circ. 42,700.

**Schweizer Monatshefte:** Vogelsangstr. 52, 8006 Zürich; political, economic and cultural monthly; Editors FRANÇOIS BONDY, ANTON KRÄTTLI.

**Der Schweizerische Beobachter:** Industriestr. 54, 8152 Glattbrugg; tel. (1) 8296111; fax (1) 8103791; f. 1927; 2 a month; Man. Dir HANNES HINNEN; circ. 407,669.

**Schweizerisches Handelsamtsblatt** (Feuille officielle suisse du commerce): Effingerstr. 3, 3001 Berne; tel. (31) 612221; f. 1883; commercial; published by Federal Dept of Foreign Trade; circ. 21,000.

**Schweizerische Medizinische Wochenschrift:** Schwabe & Co Ltd, Steinentorstr. 13, 4010 Basel; tel. (61) 2725523; fax (61) 2725573; f. 1870; weekly; Editors Dr R. KRAPF, Prof. R. RITZ, Prof. A. SCHAFFNER, Prof. P. W. STRAUB, Prof. R. A. STREULI, Prof. B. TRUNIGER, Prof. H. R. MARTI, Dr A. UEHLINGER; circ. 5,420.

**Schweizerische Technische Zeitschrift (STZ):** Rüdigerstr. 1, 8021 Zürich; tel. (1) 2078807; fax (1) 2078837; fortnightly; technical journal in German; circ. 18,000.

**Schweizerische Versicherungs-Zeitschrift** (Revue Suisse d'Assurances): Peter Lang AG, Jupiterstr. 15, 3000 Berne 15; tel. (31) 9402121; fax (31) 9402131; f. 1933; 6 a year; Editors Dr R. KÜNG, P. GMEINER, Prof. Dr B. VIRET; circ. 2,100.

**Schweizerische Zeitschrift für Psychologie** (Revue suisse de psychologie): Muesmattstr. 45, 3000 Berne 9; tel. (31) 6314046; fax (31) 6313606; f. 1942; quarterly; Editors Prof. Dr R. GRONER, Prof. Dr G. MUGNY.

**Ski:** Habegger Verlag, 4552 Derendingen; tel. (65) 411151; fax (65) 422632; f. 1968; 17 a year; German and French/Italian editions; Editor JOSEPH WEIBEL; circ. 111,002.

**Sport:** Edenstr. 20, 8021 Zürich; tel. (1) 2078383; telex 817695; fax (1) 2078888; f. 1920; weekly; Chief Editor HANS-RÜDI HOTTIGER; circ. 78,842.

**Swiss Review of World Affairs:** Postfach 660, 8021 Zürich; tel. (1) 2581111; telex 52157; fax (1) 2624029; monthly; published by Neue Zürcher Zeitung; circ. 2,500.

**TCS-Revue:** Alfred-Escher-Str. 38, 8027 Zürich; tel. (1) 2868613; fax (1) 2868637; official organ of the Zürich Touring Club; monthly; Chief Editor RETO CAVEGN; circ. 200,000.

**Tele:** Dufourstr. 23, 8008 Zürich; tel. (1) 2596111; telex 817214; fax (1) 2622706; f. 1967; radio and television weekly; Editor HANSULRICH INDERMAUR; circ. 284,831.

**Le Temps stratégique:** 33 ave de la Gare, 1000 Lausanne; tel. (22) 3282448; fax (22) 3212142; f. 1982; 6 a year; economic, social and political journal; Editor CLAUDE MONNIER.

**Textiles suisses:** ave de l'Avant-Poste 4, BP 1128, 1001 Lausanne; tel. (21) 3231824; telex 455425; fax (21) 3207337; f. 1926; professional export reviews for Swiss textiles; quarterly; published by the Swiss Office for Trade Promotion.

**Touring:** Maulbeerstr. 10, 3001 Berne; tel. (31) 3821626; fax (31) 3810226; f. 1935; fortnightly; German, French and Italian editions; Chief Editor BERNARD BICKEL; circ. 1,239,798.

**Trente Jours:** 23 Pré-du-Marché, 1004 Lausanne; tel. (21) 6473829; fax (21) 370280; f. 1949; Editor S. DE SENGER; circ. 400,060.

**TV 8:** 3 Pont Bessières, 1002 Lausanne; tel. (21) 3420880; fax (21) 4420881; weekly; circ. 53,000.

**VO Réalités:** 6 rue Pré-Jérôme, 1211 Geneva 4; tel. (22) 206335; telex 428270; f. 1944; Communist; circ. 8,000.

**Vox Romanica:** Langgassstr. 49, 3000 Berne; f. 1936; annual review of Romance linguistics and medieval literature.

**Weltwoche:** Edenstr. 20, 8021 Zürich; tel. (1) 2077311; telex 815503; fax (1) 2026127; f. 1933; weekly; independent; Editor-in-Chief JURG RAMSPECK; circ. 115,000.

**Werk, Bauen + Wohnen:** Vogelsangstr. 48, Postfach, 8033 Zürich; tel. (1) 3629566; fax (1) 3627032; f. 1913; monthly; architecture and art; circ. 9,000.

**Yakari:** 5400 Baden; tel. (56) 217383; fax (56) 217353; children's monthly; circ. 15,000.

## NEWS AGENCIES

**Schweizerische Depeschenagentur AG (SDA)** (Agence Télégraphique Suisse SA (ATS), Swiss News Agency): Länggassstr. 7, 3012 Berne; tel. (31) 3093333; telex 911500; fax (31) 3018538; f. 1894; agency for political and general news; Chief Editor BERNARD REIST.

### Foreign Bureaux

**Agence France-Presse (AFP):** Bureau C-14, Palais des Nations, 1211 Geneva 10; tel. (22) 7321120; telex 22210; fax (22) 7348292; Bureau Chief PHILIPPE DEBEUSSCHER.

**Agencia EFE** (Spain): Bureau 49, Palais des Nations, 1211 Geneva 10; tel. (22) 7336273; telex 22698; fax (22) 7332041; Man. PALOMA CABALLERO.

**Agenzia Nazionale Stampa Associata (ANSA)** (Italy): Salle de Presse 3, Palais des Nations, 1211 Geneva 10; tel. (22) 7334872; telex 414104; fax (22) 7345900; Bureau Chief MARIO MARTELLI.

**Allgemeiner Deutscher Nachrichtendienst (ADN)** (Germany): Bureau 53, Palais des Nations, 1211 Geneva 10; telex 28246; Correspondent HELMUT SCHULZ.

**Associated Press (AP)** (USA): Palais des Nations, 1211 Geneva 10; tel. (22) 7347222; telex 22127; Bureau Chief HANNS NEUERBOURG.

**Deutsche Presse-Agentur (dpa)** (Germany): Bureau 84, Palais des Nations, 1211 Geneva 10; tel. (22) 7315117; fax (22) 7332706; Bureau Chief Dr ARNO MAYER.

**Informatsionnoye Telegrafnoye Agentstvo Rossii—Telegrafnoye Agentstvo Suverennykh Stran (ITAR—TASS)** (Russia): Palais des Nations, Bureau 72, 1211 Geneva 10; tel. (22) 7343321; telex 4522830; fax (22) 7334888; Correspondent KONSTANTIN F. PRIBYTKOV.

**Inter Press Service (IPS)** (Italy): Bureau C504, Palais des Nations, 1211 Geneva 10; tel. (22) 7346011; telex 22442; fax (22) 7342430; Correspondent CHAKRAVARTHI RAGHAVAN.

**Jiji Tsushin-sha** (Japan): 54 chemin du Grand Puits, 1217 Meyrin/Geneva; tel. (22) 7341216; fax (22) 7335115; telex 23179; Man. TOKIHIKO KITAHARA.

**Kyodo Tsushin** (Japan): C521, Salle de Presse 1, Palais des Nations, 1211 Geneva 10; tel. (22) 7343856; telex 289390; fax (22) 7349669; Bureau Chief HIRO-TSUGU AIDA.

**Reuters** (UK): 1 rue de Jargonnant, 1207 Geneva; tel. (22) 7182020; telex 413387; fax (22) 7182697: Man. Dir JEAN-CLAUDE MARCHAND.

**United Press International (UPI)** (USA): Bureau 76, Palais des Nations, 1211 Geneva 10; tel. (22) 7341740; telex 22300; fax (22) 7341042; Bureau Chief MICHAEL HUGGINS.

**Xinhua (New China) News Agency** (People's Republic of China): 7 chemin des Préjins, 1218 Grand-Saconnex, Geneva; tel. (22) 983754; telex 22004; Correspondent REN ZHENDE.

## PRESS ASSOCIATIONS

**Association suisse des éditeurs de journaux et périodiques/Schweizerischer Verband der Zeitungs-und Zeitschriftenverleger** (Swiss Newspaper and Periodical Publishers' Asscn): Baumackerstr. 42, Postfach, 8050 Zürich; tel. (1) 3125015; fax (1) 3113132; f. 1899; Pres. Dr H. H. CONINX; Man. THOMAS KÄHR; 220 mems.

**Schweizer Verband der Journalistinnen und Journalisten/Fédération suisse des journalistes/Federazione svizzera giornalisti:** Postfach 316, Grand-Places 14A, 1701 Fribourg; tel. (37) 811200; fax (37) 231202; Pres. MARTIN EDLIN.

# Publishers

## FRENCH LANGUAGE PUBLISHING HOUSES

**L'Age d'Homme—La Cité:** 10 rue de Genève, BP 67, 1003 Lausanne 9; tel. (21) 3120095; fax (21) 3208440; f. 1966; fiction, biography, music, art, social science, science fiction, literary criticism; Man. Dir VLADIMIR DIMITRIJEVIC.

**Editions de l'Aire:** 15, rue de l'Union, BP 57, 1800 Vevey; tel. (21) 9236836; fax (21) 333011; Man. MICHEL MORET.

SWITZERLAND

**Editions de la Baconnière:** 19 ave du Collège, BP 185, 2017 Boudry; tel. (38) 421004; f. 1927; fine arts, history, folklore, travel, poetry, fiction, philosophy, literary studies, music, psychoanalysis; Dir MARIE-CHRISTINE HAUSER.

**La Bibliothèque des Arts:** 50 ave de Rumine, 1005 Lausanne; tel. (21) 3123667; art, culture; Dir FRANÇOISE DAULTE.

**Delachaux et Niestlé SA:** 79 route d'Oron, 1000 Lausanne 21; tel. (21) 6533044; fax (21) 6534095; f. 1861; natural history, psychology, pedagogy; Dir DAVID PERRET.

**Editions Delval SA:** 1774 Cousset; tel. (37) 613025; fax (37) 617141; pedagogy, psychology, sociology.

**Librairie Droz SA:** 11 rue Massot, BP 389, 1211 Geneva 12; tel. (22) 3466666; fax (22) 3472391; f. 1925; history, medieval literature, French literature, linguistics, social sciences, economics, archaeology; Dir ALAIN DUFOUR.

**Editions Edita SA:** 85 rue de Genève, 1000 Lausanne 9; tel. (21) 6251392; telex 450296; fax (21) 6254291; f. 1952; history, technical, art; Dir MICHEL FERLONI.

**Edito Georges Naef SA:** 33 quai Wilson, CP 54, 1211 Geneva 21; tel. (22) 7380502; telex 27168; fax (22) 7384224; f. 1986; childrens' books, health and beauty, history, languages and linguistics, psychology, reference books; Pres. GEORGES NAEF.

**Editions Eiselé SA:** 17 rue de Cossonay, CP 128, 1008 Prilly; tel. (21) 6256324; fax (21) 6256374; arts, education, popular science, textbooks.

**Elsevier Science SA:** 50 ave de la Gare, CP 564, 1001 Lausanne; tel. (21) 3207381; telex 450620; fax (21) 3235444; international research journals in natural sciences, engineering, materials, chemistry and technology; Dir H. FRANK.

**Editions d'En Bas:** BP 304, 1000 Lausanne 17; tel. (21) 233918; fax (21) 3123240; sociology, health, ecology, history; Dir MICHAEL GLARDON.

**Foetisch, Maurice et Pierre SA:** 6 rue de Bourg, 1002 Lausanne; tel (021) 239444; fax (21) 3115011; education and music; Dir JEAN-CLAUDE FOETISCH.

**Georg Editeur SA:** 46 chemin de la Mousse, 1225 Chêne-Bourg; tel. (22) 3481400; fax (22) 3482724; Dir H. WEISSENBACH.

**Pierre Gonin Editions d'Art:** 41 rue du Valentin 41, 1004 Lausanne; tel. (21) 3129996; f. 1926; art books.

**Editions du Grand-Pont:** 2 place Bel-Air, 1003 Lausanne; tel. (21) 3123222; fax (21) 3113222; f. 1971; general, art books and literature; Dir JEAN-PIERRE LAUBSCHER.

**Editions du Griffon:** 17 Faubourg du Lac, 2000 Neuchâtel; tel. (38) 252204; f. 1944; science, arts; Dir Dr MARCEL JORAY.

**Editions Ides et Calendes:** Evole 19, 2001 Neuchâtel; tel. (38) 253861; fax (38) 255880; f. 1941; art, literature, law; Dir ALAIN BOURET.

**La Joie de Lire:** 8 Cours des Bastions, 1205 Geneva; tel. (22) 3101480; fax (22) 3112779; juvenile.

**Editions Labor & Fides SA:** 1 rue Beauregard, 1204 Geneva; tel. (22) 3113290; fax (22) 7813051; f. 1924; theological and religious publications; Dir GABRIEL DE MONTMOLLIN.

**Livre Total SA:** 27 rue de la Borde, 1018 Lausanne; tel. (21) 6479772; fax (21) 6478831.

**Loisirs et Pédagogie SA:** en Budron B 12, 1052 Le Mont-sur-Lausanne; tel. (21) 653337; fax (21) 6535751; Dir PHILIPPE BURDEL.

**Médecine et Hygiène:** 78 ave de la Roseraie, CP 456, 1211 Geneva 4; tel. (22) 3469355; fax (22) 3475610; f. 1943; medicine, psychology, general science, university textbooks; Man. Dir P. Y. BALAVOINE.

**Editions Mon Village:** 1085 Vulliens; tel. (21) 9031363; f. 1956; Dir (vacant).

**Mondo SA:** 20 ave de Corsier, 1800 Vevey; tel. (21) 9241450; telex 452100; fax (21) 9217206; Dir ARSLAN ALAMIR.

**Noir sur Blanc SA:** Le Mottâ, 1147 Montricher; tel. (21) 8645931; fax (21) 8644026; f. 1986; literature.

**Editions Novos SA:** ave Nestlé 29, 1800 Vevey; tel. (21) 9227419; fax (21) 9214153; f. 1926; landscape books, calendars; Dir MAURICETTE JUVET.

**Olizane:** 11 Vieux-Grenadiers, 1205 Geneva; tel. (22) 3285252; telex 427460; fax (22) 3285796; f. 1981; travel, tourism, orientalism, photography; Dir MATTHIAS HUBER.

**Editions du Panorama:** BP 3511, 2500 Bienne 3; tel. (32) 236284; f. 1951; literature, languages and business; Dir PAUL THIERRIN.

**Editions Payot Lausanne:** Département d'Edipresse Livres SA, 33 ave de la Gare, 1001 Lausanne; tel. (21) 3495015; fax (21) 3495029; f. 1875; technical, textbooks, medicine, law, academic publications, popular science, art books, tourism, history, music, general non-fiction, Lausanne University publications; Dir JACQUES SCHERRER.

**Presses Polytechniques et Universitaires Romandes:** EPFL, 1015 Lausanne-Ecublens; tel. (21) 6932130; fax (21) 6934027; f. 1980; technical and scientific; Man. Dir CLAIRE-LISE DELACRAUSAZ.

**Editions Pro Schola:** 29 rue des Terreaux, POB 270, 1000 Lausanne 9; tel. (21) 3236655; fax (21) 3110229; f. 1928; education, language textbooks, audio-visual material; Dir JEAN BENEDICT.

**Editions du Randin SA:** 2-4 rue de Geneve, 1003 Lausanne; tel. and fax (21) 3290194; philosophy, psychology, sport.

**Editions Scriptar SA:** 1093 La Conversion; tel. (21) 7911065; fax (21) 7914084; f. 1946; watches and jewellery, gemmology; Dir. H. MARQUIS.

**Editions d'Art Albert Skira SA:** 89 route de Chêne, 1208 Geneva; tel. (22) 3495533; fax (22) 3495535; fine arts and literature; Dir JEAN-MICHEL SKIRA.

**Slatkine Reprints:** 5 rue des Chaudronniers, CP 765, 1211 Geneva 3; tel. (22) 7762551; fax (22) 7763527; Dir M.-E. SLATKINE.

**Tricorne:** 14 rue Lissignol, 1201 Geneva; tel. (22) 7388366; fax (22) 7319749; f. 1976; poetry, art, religion, psychology, mathematics; Dir SERGE KAPLUN.

**Editions Universitaires SA:** 42 blvd de Pérolles, 1700 Fribourg; tel. (37) 864311; fax (37) 864300; Man. Dir ANTON SCHERER.

**Institut Universitaire d'Etudes du Développement:** 24 rue Rothschild, 1211 Geneva 21; tel. (22) 7315940; fax (22) 7384416; f. 1961; educational; Dir JEAN-LUC MAURER.

**Editions 24 heures:** 33 ave de la Gare, 1001 Lausanne; tel. (21) 3495013; telex 455745; fax (21) 3495029; Dir J. SCHERRER.

**Editions Vivez Soleil SA:** 32 ave Petit-Senn, 1225 Chêne-Bourg; tel. (22) 492092; fax (22) 489680.

**Weber SA d'Editions:** 13 rue de Monthoux, 1211 Geneva 2; tel. (22) 7326450; fax (22) 7384305; f. 1951; art, architecture, photography; Dir MARCEL WEBER.

**Zoé:** 11 rue des Moraines, 1227 Carouge-Geneva; tel. (22) 420578; fax (22) 432964; Dir MARLYSE BACHMANN.

## GERMAN LANGUAGE PUBLISHING HOUSES

**Arche Verlag AG, Raabe + Vitali:** Hölderlinstr. 14, 8030 Zürich; tel. (1) 2522410; fax (1) 2611115; f. 1944; literature; Dirs ELISABETH RAABE, REGINA VITALI.

**Artemis Verlags AG:** Münstergasse 9, 8024 Zürich; tel. (1) 2521100; fax (1) 2624792; f. 1943; general science, philosophy, classics, poetry, juvenile, architecture, encyclopaedias, travel guides; Dir FRANZ EBNER.

**Atlantis Musikbuchverlag:** Klausstr. 10, 8008 Zürich; tel. (1) 3833622; fax (1) 3837620; f. 1976; history of music, dramatic and instrumental music; Dir MARTIN BRUGGER.

**Baufachverlag AG:** Schöneggstr. 102, Postfach 6721, 8953 Dietikon; f. 1970; building and architecture; Dir W. R. FELZMANN.

**Benteli Verlag:** Seftigenstr. 310, 3084 Waben, Berne; tel. (31) 9608484; fax (31) 9617414; f. 1908; philology, literature, belles-lettres, fine arts, photography, humour; Dir TILL SCHAAP.

**Benziger AG:** Kapuginerstr. 6, 4502 Solothurn; tel. (65) 238161; fax (65) 222931; f. 1792; theology, fiction, non-fiction; Pres. Dr T. AURELIO, G. ELBER.

**Birkhäuser Verlag AG:** Klosterberg 23, 4010 Basel; tel. (61) 2717400; fax (61) 2717666; scientific and technical books and periodicals; Man. Dir HANS-PETER THÜR.

**Cosmos Verlag:** Oberer Wehrliweg 5, 3074 Muri-Berne; tel. (31) 9516611; fax (31) 9516659; f. 1923; literature, local history, reference, children's; Dir RETO M. AEBERLI.

**Diogenes Verlag AG:** Sprecherstr. 8, 8032 Zürich; tel. (1) 2548511; telex 816383; fax (1) 2528407; f. 1953; fiction, graphic arts, children's books; Pres. DANIEL KEEL; Man. Dir RUDOLF C. BETTSCHART.

**Europa Verlag AG:** Rämistr. 5, 8001 Zürich; tel. (1) 2611629; fax (1) 2516081; f. 1933; politics, philosophy, history, biography, sociology, fiction; Dir MARLYS MOSER.

**Graphis Press Corpn:** Dufourstr. 107, 8008 Zürich; tel. (1) 3838211; fax (1) 3831643; f. 1944; *Graphis*, international two-monthly magazine for graphic and applied art, specialized books on visual art and graphic design; Dir B. MARTIN PEDERSEN.

**Hallwag:** Nordring 4, 3001 Berne; tel. (31) 3323131; telex 912661; fax (31) 3314133; f. 1912; publishers and printers; maps and guides, atlases, travel, current affairs, motor cars, wine, food, art, natural history, popular science and magazines; Pres. Dr JÜRGEN SCHAD.

**Huber, Hans AG, Buchhandlung und Verlag:** Länggassstr. 76, 3000 Berne 9; tel. (31) 3004500; telex 911886; fax (31) 3004590; f. 1927; medicine and psychology; Dir Dr G.-J. HOGREFE.

**Huber Verlag:** Promenadenstr. 16, Postfach 382, 8501 Frauenfeld; tel. (54) 271111; telex 896383; fax (54) 214410; f. 1809; economics, business, management, marketing, banking, computers, military,

SWITZERLAND

agriculture, art, history, philology, textbooks; Gen. Man. HEINZ JANSEN.

**Hüthig & Wepf Verlag:** Neugasse 29, 6301 Zug; tel. (42) 222454; fax (42) 218360; f. 1962; macromolecular chemistry and physics, polymers; Dirs HOLGER HÜTHIG.

**S. Karger AG:** Allschwilerstr. 10, Postfach, 4009 Basel; tel. (61) 3061111; telex 62652; fax (61) 3061234; f. 1890 in Berlin, 1937 in Basel; international medical journals, books on medicine, chemistry, psychology; Dir Dr THOMAS KARGER.

**Kümmerly & Frey Ltd:** Hallerstr. 6–10, 3001 Berne; tel. (31) 3015111; telex 32860; f. 1852; maps, geography; Dir WALTER FREY.

**Herbert Lang & CIE AG:** Münzgraben 2, 3000 Berne 7; tel. (31) 3118871; fax (31) 3123183; f. 1813 and re-formed 1921; scientific works; sellers of second-hand and rare books, agents for libraries throughout the world; Pres. CHRISTOPH LANG.

**Manesse Verlag:** Badergasse 9, 8001 Zürich; tel. (1) 2525551; fax (1) 2625347; f. 1944; world's classics (Manesse Bibliothek der Weltliteratur), poetry, history (Manesse Bibliothek der Weltgeschichte); Dir ANNE MARIE WELLS.

**Müller Rüschlikon Verlags AG:** Gewerbestr. 10, 6330 Cham; tel. (42) 443040; fax (42) 417115; f. 1936; non-fiction; Dir HANS-JÖRG DEGEN.

**Nagel & Kimche AG, Verlag:** Im Tiergarten 8, Postfach 1024, 8500 Frauenfeld; tel. (54) 222922; fax (54) 222926; f. 1983; belles-lettres, juvenile; Dir Dr RENATE NAGEL.

**Neptun Verlag AG:** Fidlerstr. 2, PF 171, 8272 Ermatingen; tel. (72) 642020; fax (72) 642023; f. 1946; travel books, children's books, contemporary history; Dir H. BERCHTOLD-MÜHLEMANN.

**Neue Zürcher Zeitung, Buchverlag:** Postfach, 8021 Zürich; tel. (1) 2581505; fax (1) 2581399; Man. WALTER KÖPFLI.

**Verlag Niggli AG:** Steinackerstr. 8, Postfach 135, 8583 Sulgen; tel. (72) 424666; f. 1950; art, architecture, typography; Gen. Man. Dr J. CHRISTOPH BÜRKLE.

**Novalis Verlag AG:** Steigstr. 59, 8200 Schaffhausen; tel. (53) 241245; fax (53) 833404; f. 1974; the arts, cultural and social sciences, education; Dir Dr MAX RAPOLD.

**Orell Füssli Verlag:** Postfach, 8036 Zürich; tel. (1) 4667711; telex 813021; fax (1) 4667412; f. 1519; art, history, children's picture books, law, school books; Gen. Man. MANFRED HIEFNER-HUG.

**Ott Verlag AG:** Länggasse 57, Postfach 802, 3600 Thun 7; tel. (33) 221622; fax (33) 222006; f. 1923; general non-fiction, mineralogy, military, sport, management and commerce; Dir HANS M. OTT.

**Verlag Pro Juventute/Atlantis Kinderbücher:** Seehofstr. 15, 8022 Zürich; tel. (1) 2520719; fax (1) 2522824; social science, children's literature; Man. INGRID RÖSLI.

**Reich Verlag AG:** Museggstr. 12, 6000 Lucerne 5; tel. (41) 513721; fax (41) 513227; f. 1974; 'terra magica' illustrated books; Man. ALFONS WÜEST.

**Friedrich Reinhardt AG:** Missionsstr. 36, Postfach 393, 4012 Basel; tel. (61) 2613390; telex 963755; f. 1900; belles-lettres, theology, periodicals; Dir Dr ERNST REINHARDT.

**Rentsch Verlag AG:** Dietzingerstr. 3, 8036 Zürich; tel. (1) 4667711; telex 813021; fax (1) 4667412; f. 1488; history, school books, pedagogy, psychology; Gen. Man. MANFRED HIEFNER-HUG.

**Rex-Verlag:** St Karliquai 12, 6000 Lucerne 5; tel. (41) 524719; fax (41) 524711; f. 1931; theology, pedagogics, fiction, juvenile; Dir MARKUS KAPPELER.

**Ringier AG:** Dufourstr. 23, 8008 Zürich; tel. (1) 2596111; telex 817202; fax (1) 2598623; f. 1831; newspapers, magazines, books; CEO OSCAR FREI.

**Sauerländer AG:** Laurenzvorstadt 89, 5001 Aarau; tel. (64) 268626; telex 981195; fax (64) 245780; f. 1807; juvenile, school books, textbooks, history, chemistry, periodicals (professional, trade, science); Dir HANS-CHRISTOF SAUERLÄNDER.

**Scherz Verlag AG:** Theaterplatz 4–6, 3000 Berne 7; tel. (31) 3117337; telex 911899; f. 1939; general fiction and non-fiction, crime thrillers, history, psychology and philosophy; Dir RUDOLF STREIT-SCHERZ.

**Schulthess Polygraphischer Verlag AG:** Zwingliplatz 2, 8022 Zürich; tel. (1) 2519336; fax (1) 2616394; f. 1791; legal, social science, university textbooks; Man. Dir WERNER STOCKER.

**Schwabe & Co AG:** Steinentorstr. 13, 4010 Basel; tel. (61) 2725523; fax (61) 2725573; f. 1488; medicine, art, history, philosophy; Propr Dr CHRISTIAN OVERSTOLZ; Dirs R. BIENZ, Dr U. BREITENSTEIN.

**Schweizer Spiegel Verlag:** Biberlinstr. 6, 8032 Zürich; tel. (1) 4221666; f. 1925; art, philosophy, psychology, poetry, education, general; Dir Dr P. HUGGLER.

**Schweizer Verlagshaus AG:** Klausstr. 10, 8008 Zürich; tel. (1) 3879134; telex 816414; f. 1907; fiction, non-fiction; Dirs Dr ARMIN MEYER, WALTER MEYER, FRITZ ROTHACHER.

*Directory*

**Verlag Stämpfli + Cie AG:** Hallerstr. 7–9, 3001 Berne; tel. (31) 3006311; fax (31) 3006688; f. 1799; law, economics, history, art; Man. Dir Dr RUDOLF STÄMPFLI.

**Theologischer Verlag und Buchhandlungen AG:** Räffelstr. 20, 8045 Zürich; tel. (1) 4617710; fax (1) 4615434; f. 1934; religion, theology; Dir WERNER BLUM.

**Walter Verlag AG:** Kapuzinerstr. 6, 4502 Solothurn; tel. (65) 238161; fax (65) 222931; f. 1916; psychology, religion, history of civilization, literature; Man. GUIDO ELBER.

**Weltwoche-ABC-Verlag:** Edenstr. 20, 8045 Zürich; tel. (1) 2078643; telex 58834; fax (1) 2078980; f. 1936; art and non-fiction; Man. Dir KATJA PFÄFFLI.

**Wepf & Co AG Verlag:** Eisengasse 5, 4001 Basel; tel. (61) 2616377; fax (61) 2613597; f. 1902; architecture, engineering, ethnology, geography, geology, mineralogy; Dir H. HERRMANN.

## PUBLISHERS' ASSOCIATIONS

**Association Suisse des Editeurs de Langue Française:** 2 ave Agassiz, 1001 Lausanne; tel. (21) 3197111; telex 455730; fax (21) 3197910; f. 1975; an association of publishers in the French-speaking part of Switzerland; Pres. HENRI WEISSENBACH; Sec.-Gen. P. SCHIBLI; 100 mems.

**Schweizerischer Buchhändler-und Verleger-Verband:** Baumackerstr. 42, 8050 Zürich; tel. (1) 3186400; fax (1) 3186462; f. 1849; an association of Swiss booksellers and publishers in the German-speaking part of Switzerland; Central Pres. Dr HANS FELIX GRYER; Dir EGON RÄZ; 980 mem. and affiliated firms.

# Radio and Television

In January 1992 there were 2,700,754 radio licences and 2,475,768 licenced television receivers in Switzerland.

In 1991 there were six medium-wave radio transmitters (including the three national ones at Beromünster, Sottens and Monte Ceneri), 511 VHF transmitters and 11 short-wave transmitters. Three different programmes each for German-, French-and Italian-speaking Switzerland, and regular programmes in Romansch are transmitted on medium-wave and VHF. Swiss Radio International broadcasts on short-wave in nine languages. The Swiss Wire Network Service, which broadcasts radio programmes on the telephone cable network of the PTT, comes under the same directorship as the short-wave service. It provides six programmes to around 250,000 subscribers. Paid advertising is forbidden on radio, except on private local radio stations.

In 1991 there were 1,397 television transmitters and boosters in operation. A complete TV programme service for each linguistic region and regular broadcasts in Romansch are provided on the 1st (VHF) channel. The 2nd and 3rd (UHF) channels are used in each linguistic region for transmitting programmes of the other two linguistic regions. Limited direct advertising (29 minutes on weekdays) is allowed.

**Société Suisse de Radiodiffusion et Télévision (SSR)** (Schweizerische Radio-und Fernsehgesellschaft (SRG), Società Svizzera di Radiotelevisione (SSR), Swiss Broadcasting Corporation (SBC): Giacomettistr. 3, 3000 Berne 15; tel. (31) 3509111; telex 911590; fax (31) 3509256; Pres. ERIC LEHMANN; Dir-Gen. ANTONIO RIVA; Sec.-Gen. BEAT DURRER.

The Swiss Broadcasting Corporation (SBC) is a private company which fulfils a public duty on the basis of a licence granted to it by the Swiss Federal Government. This gives the SBC the right to use the electrical and radio-electrical installations of the Swiss Postal, Telephone and Telegraphic Services (PTT) for public broadcasting of radio and television programmes. It specifies that the SBC is responsible for the programme services, whilst the PTT is responsible for all technical aspects of transmission. Receiver licence fees are collected by the PTT. The PTT takes 24.22% of the fee; the SBC 75.08% and the remaining 0.71% is allocated to local radio and television stations.

The SBC is composed of the following societies:

**Direction de la Radio-Télévision Suisse Romande (RTSR):** 6 ave de la Gare, 1001 Lausanne; tel. (21) 205911; telex 455825; fax (21) 237506; Dir of radio and TV JEAN-JACQUES DEMARTINES; Programme Dirs: Radio: GÉRALD SAPEY (RSR1), ESTHER JOUHET (RSR2), FRANÇOIS BENEDETTI (RSR3), Maison de la Radio, 1010 Lausanne; Television: GUILLAUME CHENEVIERE, 20 Quai Ernest Ansermet, 1211 Geneva 8; tel. (22) 293333; telex 427701.

**Radio und Fernsehen der deutschen und der rätoromanischen Schweiz (DRS):** Fernsehstr. 1–4, 8052 Zürich; Dirs: Radio: ANDREAS BLUM, Güterstr. 91, 4053 Basel; tel. (61) 343484; telex 963382; Television: PETER SCHELLENBERG, Fernsehstr. 1–4, 8052 Zürich; tel. (1) 3056611; telex 823823.

**Direzione della Radiotelevisione Svizzera di Lingua Italiana (RTSI):** 6903 Lugano-Besso; tel. (91) 585111; telex 844484;

# SWITZERLAND

fax (91) 585355; Dir of radio and television MARCO BLASER; TV Programme Dir DINO BALESTRA.

**Swiss Radio International:** Giacomettistr. 1, 3000 Berne 15; tel. (31) 3509222; telex 911538; fax (31) 3509569; programmes in French, German, Italian, Romansch, English, Spanish, Portuguese and Arabic, short-wave and via satellites Intelsat K, Astra and Intelsat VI. There are 12 short-wave transmitters situated at Schwarzenburg and Sottens (overseas), Lenk, Sarnen and Beromünster (Europe); relay stations in Gabon, the People's Rep. of China and Brazil; Dir ULRICH KÜNDIG.

## Finance

(cap. = capital; dep. = deposits; res = reserves; m. = million; brs = branches; all values are in Swiss francs)

### BANKING

Switzerland's neutrality during and since the First World War has helped to develop the reputation of the Swiss banks as a secure repository for foreign capital. A provision of the Swiss Banking Law of 1934 made it a penal offence for a bank to provide information about its clients without their explicit authorization, unless a court has ordered otherwise. When foreign authorities wish to investigate Swiss accounts, criminal charges must have been made in a foreign court and accepted as valid by Switzerland. The system of numbered accounts has also kept depositors' shares free from investigation. However, the abuse of bank secrecy by organized crime led Switzerland and the USA to sign a treaty in May 1973, under which the banking secrecy rules may be lifted in the case of common-law crime, but not for non-criminal tax evasion and anti-trust law infringements which are still immune from investigation.

An agreement concluded with the banks by the Swiss National Bank and the Swiss Bankers' Association in June 1977 led to stricter control of the Swiss banks' handling of foreign funds. The code made the opening of numbered accounts subject to closer scrutiny and checked the practice of banks actively encouraging the flow of foreign money into the country. The agreement was renewed and modified in 1982. In 1987, after the Swiss National Bank had decided no longer to be a party to the agreement, the code was adapted by the Swiss Bankers' Association into rules of professional conduct, and was again renewed and modified in 1992. In 1978, in view of the steady increase in Swiss banks' international business, the Federal Banking Commission was given greater supervisory powers. Banks were required for the first time to submit consolidated balance sheets to the Commission and new consolidation requirements forced banks to raise capital to between 6% and 8% of total liabilities. The capital requirement is now one of the highest in the world.

At the end of 1993 there were 4,027 bank branches (including 1,139 loan offices) in Switzerland, owned by 529 banks. The total assets of all banks operating in Switzerland at the end of 1993 was 1,219,335m. francs. Swiss banking is dominated by the 'Big Four Banks' (Union Bank of Switzerland, Swiss Bank Corporation, Crédit Suisse and Swiss Volksbank). About 50% of their share comes from foreign business. In March 1993 Crédit Suisse took over Swiss Volksbank, although Swiss Volkesbank continued to be represented throughout the country. Foreign banks have become increasingly important; in 1991 130 foreign-controlled banks and 16 branches of foreign banks held about 10% of all Swiss banking assets. At the end of 1993 there were 143 foreign-controlled banks and 13 branches of foreign banks in Switzerland.

The 28 canton banks are mostly financed and controlled by the cantons, and their activities are co-ordinated by the Association of Swiss Canton Banks. In 1991 they had 771 branches and controlled 20.5% of total banking assets.

### Central Bank

**Schweizerische Nationalbank/Banque nationale suisse** (Swiss National Bank): Börsenstr. 15, Postfach 4388, 8022 Zürich; tel. (1) 6313111; telex 812400; fax (1) 6313911; Bundesplatz 1, 3003 Berne; tel. (31) 3120211; telex 911310; fax (31) 3121953; f. 1907; head offices in Zürich and Berne; the object of the bank is to regulate the circulation of money, to facilitate payments transactions and to pursue a credit and monetary policy serving the general interest; Dept I (Zürich) is responsible for economic studies, statistics, legal matters, personnel and internal auditing; Dept II (Berne) issues notes, manages metal reserves, runs the main accounting section and banking transactions for the Federal Government; Dept III (Zürich) handles foreign exchange business and credits to the commercial banks in addition to giro and clearing functions. cap. 50m. frs, total assets 64,800m. frs (Dec. 1994); Pres. of Council JAKOB SCHÖNENBERGER; Gen. Mans Dr MARCUS LUSSER (Pres., Zürich), Dr HANS MEYER, JEAN ZWAHLEN; 8 brs.

### Canton Banks

There are 28 cantonal banks, of which the following are the largest:

**Aargauische Kantonalbank:** Bahnhofstr. 58, 5001 Aarau; tel. (64) 217721; telex 981200; fax (64) 217788; f. 1913; cap. 200m. frs, dep. 1,686m. frs (Dec. 1993); Pres. Dr WENDOLIN STUTZ; Dirs Dr WERNER BOLLETER, Dr J. N. BRÄNDLE, H. R. GLOOR; 6 brs.

**Banque de l'Etat de Fribourg:** Blvd de Pérolles 1, 1701 Fribourg; tel. (37) 207111; telex 942431; fax (37) 207507; f. 1892; cap. 70m. frs, dep. 1,222.7m. frs (Dec. 1993); Pres. CLAUDE SCHORDERET; 93 brs.

**Basler Kantonalbank:** Spiegelgasse 2, 4002 Basel; tel. (61) 2662121; telex 965959; fax (61) 2618434; f. 1899; cap. 210m. frs, dep. 3,925m. frs (Dec. 1994); Speaker Exec. Board WERNER SIGG; Sen. Vice-Pres. M. ARZNER, H. KUNZ, Dr U. ROHDE, P. WIRZ; 14 brs.

**Basellandschaftliche Kantonalbank:** Rheinstr. 7, 4410 Liestal; tel. (61) 9259111; telex 966166; fax (61) 9259317; f. 1864; cap. 220m. frs, dep. 3,244m. frs (Dec. 1993); Mans HANS FREY, PAUL NYFFELER, WERNER LÖW, Dr LUKAS SPIESS; 10 brs.

**Berner Kantonalbank:** 8 place Fédérale, 3001 Berne; tel. (31) 6661111; telex 911122; fax (31) 6666040; f. 1834; cap. 645m. frs, dep. 9,850m. frs (Dec. 1993); Gen. Mans M. GERBER, P. W. KAPPELER; Dr A. SUTER; 79 brs.

**Graubündner Kantonalbank:** Poststr. 2, 7002 Chur; tel. (81) 269111; telex 851122; fax (81) 226729; f. 1870; cap. 235m. frs, dep. 3,457m. frs (Dec. 1993); Mans U. GEBHARD, R. MONSCH, E. GASSER, Dr ULRICH IMMLER; 3 brs.

**Luzerner Kantonalbank:** Pilatusstr. 12, 6002 Lucerne; tel. (41) 292222; telex 862860; fax (41) 292901; f. 1850; cap. 490m. frs, dep. 6,918m. frs (Dec. 1993); Mans R. FREIMANN, F. GRÜTER, K. REICHMUTH, F. STUDER; 37 brs.

**St Gallische Kantonalbank:** St Leonhardstr. 25, Postfach 92, 9001 St Gallen; tel. (71) 203131; telex 881188; fax (71) 203232; f. 1868; cap. 465m. frs, dep. 6,335m. frs (Dec. 1993); Pres. R. SCHAAD; Gen. Mans J. C. MÜLLER, W. ALTHAUS, W. GABATHULER; 27 brs.

**Kantonalbank Schwyz:** Bahnhofstr. 3, 6430 Schwyz; tel. (43) 244111; telex 866047; fax (43) 217355; f. 1890; cap. 140m. frs, dep. 1,556m. frs (Dec. 1993); Pres. EUGEN DIETHELM; Man. Dr H. KOLLER; 10 brs.

**Thurgauer Kantonalbank:** Bankplatz 1, 8570 Weinfelden; tel. (72) 216111; telex 882323; fax (72) 216363; f. 1871; cap. 415m. frs, demand dep. 4,541m. frs (Dec. 1993); Pres. HEINZ MOLL; Man. H. MICHEL; 31 brs.

**Banca dello Stato del Cantone Ticino:** Viale H. Guisan 5, 6501 Bellinzona; tel. (92) 250277; telex 846481; fax (92) 264421; f. 1915; cap. 100m. frs, dep. 1,578m. frs (Dec. 1993); Man. Dr ROMANO MELLINI; 3 brs.

**Banque Cantonale du Valais:** 8 rue des Cèdres, 1951 Sion; tel. (27) 246111; telex 472518; fax (27) 246666; f. 1916; cap. 150m. frs, dep. 4,272m. frs (Dec. 1993); Man. JEAN-DANIEL PAPILLOUD; 120 brs.

**Banque Cantonale Vaudoise:** 14 place St François, 1002 Lausanne; tel. (21) 3171111; telex 454304; fax (21) 6421122; f. 1845; cap. 270m. frs, dep. 16,309m. frs (Dec. 1993); Gen. Man. J. TREYVAUD; 60 brs.

**Crédit Foncier Vaudois:** CP 77, 1000 Lausanne 9; tel. (21) 3416111; telex 454970; fax (21) 3416920; f. 1858; cap. 140m. frs (Dec. 1993), total assets 12,934m. frs (Dec. 1994); Pres. DANIEL SCHMUTZ; Gen. Man. JEAN-CLAUDE GRANGIER; Mans ANDRÉ JORDAN, JEAN-MARIE BRANDT; 63 brs.

**Zürcher Kantonalbank:** Bahnhofstr. 9, POB 8010, Zürich; tel. (1) 2201111; fax (1) 2111525; f. 1870; cap. 1,675m. frs, res 390m., total dep. 41,760m. frs (Dec. 1993); Gen. Mans P. HASENFRATZ, E. FRITSCHI, G. WEBER, U. NAEF, J. SCHWARZ; 164 brs.

### Commercial Banks (Selected List)

**Banca del Gottardo:** Viale S. Franscini 8, CP 2811, 6901 Lugano; tel. (91) 281111; telex 841051; fax (91) 239487; f. 1957; cap. 169m. frs, dep. 6,136m. frs, total assets 7,595m. frs (Dec. 1993); Pres. C. GENERALI; Gen. Man. FRANCESCO BOLGIANI.

**Bank Julius Bär & Co AG:** Bahnhofstr. 36, 8010 Zürich; tel. (1) 2285111; telex 812115; fax (1) 2112560; f. 1890; cap. 145m. frs, dep. 4,663m. frs (Dec. 1993); Chair. HANS J. BÄR.

**Bank Leu Ltd:** Bahnhofstr. 32, 8001 Zürich; tel. (1) 2191111; telex 812174; fax (1) 2193197; f. 1755; cap. 400m. frs, dep. 8,015m. frs (Dec. 1993); Chair. ERNST SCHNEIDER; Pres. PETER KÜPFER; Exec. Vice-Pres. GASTON GUEX, RETO DONATSCH, Dr WERNER FREY, WALTER FLUCK; 14 brs.

**Banque Paribas (Suisse) SA:** 2 place de Hollande, 1204 Geneva; tel. (22) 7877111; telex 422165; fax (22) 7878000; f. 1872; cap. 337.5m. frs, dep. 5,533m. frs (Dec. 1993); Chair. MICHEL FRANÇOIS-PONCET; Gen. Man. JEAN-PAUL RAMBAUD.

**Banque Privée Edmond de Rothschild SA:** 18 rue de Hesse, 1204 Geneva; tel. (22) 8189111; telex 422699; fax (22) 8189121; f. 1924;

# SWITZERLAND

cap. 45m. frs, dep. 936.0m. frs (Dec. 1993); Pres. Baron EDMOND DE ROTHSCHILD; Vice-Pres. and Gen. Man. CLAUDE MESSULAM.

**Banque Scandinave en Suisse:** 11 Cours de Rive, Geneva; tel. (22) 7873111; telex 413500; fax (22) 7353370; f. 1964; cap. 89.5m. frs, res 209.3m. frs (Dec. 1993); Chair. ANDRÉ DE PFYFFER; Gen. Man. PIERRE DEJARDIN-VERKINDER.

**BDL—Banco di Lugano:** Piazzetta San Carlo 1, 6901 Lugano; tel. (91) 208111; telex 841080; fax (91) 232631; f. 1947; cap. 50m. frs, dep. 3,157m. frs (Dec. 1994); Gen. Man. FRANCO MÜLLER.

**BSI—Banca della Svizzera Italiana:** Via Magatti 2, 6901 Lugano; tel. (91) 587111; telex 841020; fax (91) 587678; f. 1873; cap. 290m. frs, dep. 6,048m. frs (Dec. 1993); Chair. ALBERTO TOGNI; 23 brs in Switzerland.

**Coutts & Co AG:** Talstr. 59, 8022 Zürich; tel. (1) 2145111; telex 812816; fax (1) 2145396; f. 1930; cap. 110m. frs, dep. 2,302.3m. frs (Dec. 1993); Chair. Dr RETO F. DOMENICONI.

**Discount Bank and Trust Co:** 3 Quai de l'Ile, 1204 Geneva; tel. (22) 7053111; telex 422766; fax (22) 3101703; f. 1952 as Discount Bank (Overseas), name changed 1985; cap. 80m. frs, dep. 4,894m. frs (Dec. 1993); Chair. R. RECANATI.

**Migrosbank AG:** Seidengasse 12, 8023 Zürich; tel. (1) 2298111; telex 813464; fax (1) 2111244; f. 1957; cap. 340m. frs, dep. 2,812m. frs (Dec. 1993); Chair. J. KYBURZ; Exec. Vice Pres. E. HORT; Exec. Pres ALFRED ACHERMANN, F. JENNI, F. REICH, A. SCHWERZMANN.

**Neue Aargauer Bank:** Hauptstr. 1, 5200 Brugg; tel. (56) 327111; telex 825108; fax (56) 410991; f. 1989; cap. 175m. frs, dep. 3,446m. frs (Dec. 1993); Pres. Dr B. HUNZIKER; Gen. Man. GERHARD E. MEYER; 47 brs.

**Nordfinanz Bank Zürich:** Bahnhofstr. 1, 8022 Zürich; tel. (1) 2287111; telex 812147; fax (1) 2287447; f. 1964; cap. 67m. frs, dep. 3,901.7m. frs (Dec. 1993); Chair. PERTTI VOUTILAINEN.

**Schweizer Verband der Raiffeisenbanken/Union Suisse des Banques Raiffeisen:** Vadianstr. 17, 9001 St Gallen; tel. (71) 219111; telex 881350; fax (71) 219636; f. 1902; cap. 175m. frs, dep. 7,410m. frs (Dec. 1993); Pres. Dr MARIUS COTTIER; Gen. Man. Dr F. WALKER.

**Schweizerische Bankgesellschaft Union de Banques Suisses:** Bahnhofstr. 45, 8021 Zürich; tel. (1) 2341111; telex 813811; fax (1) 2356111; f. 1912; cap. 2,575m. frs, dep. 238,689m. frs, total assets 311,255m. frs (Dec. 1993); Chair. Dr N. SENN; Gen. Man. R. STUDER; 370 brs.

**Schweizerischer Bankverein Societe de Banques Suisses** (Swiss Bank Corporation): Aeschenplatz 6, 4002 Basel; tel. (61) 2882020; telex 962334; fax (61) 2884676; and Paradeplatz 6, 8022 Zürich; tel. (1) 2231111; telex 812581; fax (1) 4357606; f. 1872; cap. 3,772m. frs, total assets 206,968m. frs (Dec. 1993); Chair. WALTER FREHNER; Gen. Man. Dr G. BLUM; 278 brs.

**Schweizerische Hypotheken-und Handelsbank HYPOSWISS:** Bahnhofstr./Schützengasse 4, 8001 Zürich; tel. (1) 2143111; telex 812037; fax (1) 2115223; f. 1889; cap. 26m., total assets 833m. frs (Dec. 1993); Chair. Dr ANDREAS HENRICI; Gen. Man. ERNST RÜESCH.

**Schweizerische Kreditanstalt/Crédit Suisse:** 8070 Zürich; tel. (1) 3331111; telex 812412; fax (1) 3325555; f. 1856; cap. 2,146m. frs, dep. 139,493m. frs (Dec. 1993); Chair. RAINER E. GUT; 332 brs.

**Schweizerische Volksbank/Banque Populaire Suisse:** Weltpoststr. 5, 3015 Berne; tel. (31) 3587272; fax (31) 3587298; f. 1869; cap. 767m. frs, total assets 40,747m. frs (Dec. 1993); Chair. G. COTTI; Gen. Man. Dr K. WIDMER.

**Union Bancaire Privée:** 96–98 rue du Rhône, CP 1320, 1211 Geneva; tel. (22) 8192111; telex 415423; fax (22) 8192200; f. 1990; cap. 219m. frs, total assets 11,182m. frs (Dec. 1993); Pres. EDGAR DE PICCIOTTO.

**United Overseas Bank SA:** 11 quai des Bergues, 1201 Geneva 1; tel. (22) 9062111; telex 412100; fax (22) 7323002; f. 1961; cap. 105m. frs, dep 3,224m. frs (Dec. 1993); Chair. JÜRGEN SARRAZIN; Gen. Man. BERNARD FLEURY.

### Central Co-operative Credit Institution

**Coop Bank/Banque Coop:** Aeschenplatz 3, 4002 Basel; tel. (61) 2862121; telex 962290; fax (61) 2722521; f. 1927; fmrly Genossenschaftliche Zentralbank/Banque Centrale Coopérative; cap. 240m. frs, total assets 7,565m. frs (Dec. 1993); Chair. GERHARD METZ; Gen. Mans F. LEUENBERGER, H. WÄLTI, PAUL HUBER; 37 brs.

### Bankers' Organizations

**Association of Foreign Banks in Switzerland:** Asylstr. 81, 8030 Zürich; tel. (1) 2615440; fax (1) 2519152; Chair. C. GENERALI; Man. Dir M. C. SCHAEFER.

**Association Suisse des Banquiers/Schweizerische Bankiervereinigung** (Swiss Bankers Association): Wallstrasse 1, Postfach, 4002 Basel; tel. (61) 2716666; fax (61) 2716667; f. 1912; 5,499 mems; Chair. Dr GEORG F. KRAYER; Man. Dir J. P. CHAPUIS.

*Directory*

**Verband Schweizerischer Kantonalbanken/Union des Banques Cantonales Suisses** (Association of Swiss Cantonal Banks): Wallstr. 9, 4002 Basel; tel. (61) 2716666; fax (61) 2716667; f. 1907, permanent office established 1971; Man. CARLO MATI.

## STOCK EXCHANGES

**Basel Stock Exchange** (Börsenkammer des Kantons Basel-Stadt): Aeschenplatz 7, 4002 Basel; tel. (61) 2720555; telex 962524; fax (61) 2720626; f. 1876; 12 mems; Pres. Dr G. A. GUTH; Dir RENÉ KAUFMANN.

**Berne Stock Exchange** (Berner Börsenverein): Aarbergergasse 36, 3011 Berne; tel. (31) 3114042; fax (31) 3115309; f. 1884; 12 mems; Sec. JÜRG NIEDERHÄUSER.

**Effektenbörsenverein** (Zürich Stock Exchange): Selnaustr. 30, 8021 Zürich; tel. (1) 2292111; fax (1) 2292233; f. 1873; 24 mems; Pres. Dr J. FISCHER; Man. Dr R. T. MEIER.

## INSURANCE

**Allianz Continentale Allgemeine Versicherungs AG:** Seestr. 356, 8038 Zürich; tel. (1) 4889191; telex 817656; fax (1) 4823580; f. 1974; general; Pres. Dr PETER ALTHER.

**Allianz Continentale Lebensversicherungs AG:** Seestr. 356, 8038 Zürich; tel. (1) 4889191; telex 817656; fax (1) 4823580; f. 1964; life; Pres. Dr PETER ALTHER.

**Alpina Versicherungs-AG:** Seefeldstr. 123, 8034 Zürich; tel. (1) 3865151; telex 816302; f. 1923; Pres. FRITZ GERBER.

**Basler Versicherungs-Gesellschaft:** Aeschengraben 21, Postfach, 4002 Basel; tel. (61) 2858585; telex 756204; fax (61) 2857070; f. 1864; all classes, except life insurance; Chair. Dr ROBERT BAUMANN; Vice-Chair. GUY SARASIN.

**Basler Lebens-Versicherungs-Gesellschaft:** Aeschengraben 21, Postfach, 4002 Basel; tel. (61) 2858585; telex 756204; fax (61) 2857070; f. 1864; life, annuity; Chair. Dr ROBERT BAUMANN; Vice-Chair. GUY SARASIN.

**Berner Allgemeine Holdinggesellschaft:** Sulgeneckstr. 19, 3001 Berne; tel. (31) 3845111; fax (31) 3845300; f. 1909; Pres. Dr H. FLÜCKIGER.

**ELVIA-Life Swiss Life Insurance Company:** 2 ave du Bouchet, 1211 Geneva 28; tel. (22) 7344000; telex 27930; f. 1924; life; Pres. Dr HEINZ R. WUFFLI; Gen. Man. P. JUNGO.

**GAN Incendie Accidents, Compagnie Française d'Assurances et de Réassurances:** 70 ave C.-F. Ramuz, 1009 Pully-Lausanne; tel. (21) 7297121; fax (21) 7288076; Head Office, Paris; f. 1830; cap. 550m. frs.

**La Genevoise, Compagnie générale d'Assurances:** 16 ave Eugène-Pittard, 1211 Geneva 25; tel. (22) 7042424; telex 422478; fax (22) 7042704; f. 1950; cap. 10m. frs; Gen. Man. M. C. MEYER.

**La Genevoise, Compagnie d'Assurances sur la Vie:** 16 ave Eugène-Pittard, 1211 Geneva 25; tel. (22) 7042424; telex 422478; fax (22) 7042704; f. 1872; life; cap. 17m. frs; Gen. Man. M. C. MEYER.

**Lebensversicherungs-Gesellschaft:** Paulstr. 9, 8401 Winterthur; tel. (52) 2611111; telex 896120; fax (52) 853585; f. 1923; life; cap. 75m. frs; Chair. Dr P. SPÄLTI.

**Helvetia Schweizerische Versicherungsgesellschaft:** Dufourstr. 40, 9001 St Gallen; tel. (71) 265111; telex 884307; fax (71) 256376; f. 1861; fire, burglary, accident-liability, motor; Chair. Dr HANS-ULRICH BAUMBERGER; Gen. Man. E. WALSER.

**Neuchâteloise Assurances:** rue de Monruz 2, 2002 Neuchâtel; tel. (38) 235000; telex 754900; fax (38) 235555; f. 1869; Pres. YANN RICHTER; Gen. Man. CHARLES-EDOUARD LAMBELET.

**Pax, Schweizerische Lebensversicherungs-Gesellschaft:** Aeschenplatz 13, 4002 Basel; tel. (61) 2776666; telex 962922; fax (61) 2776456; f. 1876; life, health; Pres. Dr PIERRE L. VAN DER HAEGEN.

**Rentenanstalt, Swiss Life Insurance and Pension Company:** General Guisan-Quai 40, 8022 Zürich; tel. (1) 2843311; telex 815620; fax (1) 2842080; f. 1857; specializes in international employee benefit and pension plans; brs in Belgium, France, Germany, Italy, Luxembourg, Netherlands, Spain and UK; Chair. Dr GERHARD WINTERBERGER.

**Schweizerische Mobiliar:** Bundesgasse 35, 3001 Berne; tel. (31) 3896111; fax (31) 3896852; f. 1826; personal accident, sickness, fire and damage by the elements, glass breakage, machinery, construction work, interruption of business, epidemics, motor, travel, transport, third-party; Gen. Man. Dr WALTER BOSSHART.

**Schweizerische Rückversicherungs-Gesellschaft** (Swiss Re-insurance Co): Mythenquai 50/60, 8022 Zürich; tel. (1) 2852121; telex 815722; fax (1) 2852999; f. 1863; worldwide reinsurance; cap. 1,865m. frs; assets 10,519m. frs; Chair. ULRICH BREMI; CEO A. W. SAXER.

**Winterthur Schweizerische Versicherungs-Gesellschaft:** General Guisan-Str. 40, 8401 Winterthur; tel. (52) 2611111; telex 896232; fax (52) 2136620; f. 1875; Chair. Dr PETER SPÄLTI.

SWITZERLAND *Directory*

**Zenith Vie, Compagnie d'assurances sur la vie:** 70 ave C.-F. Ramuz, 1009 Pully-Lausanne; tel. (21) 7281356; telex 454096; fax (21) 7298420; f. 1987; life; cap. 20m. frs; Gen. Man. GILBERT SMADJA.

**Zurich Lebensversicherungs-Gesellschaft:** Austr. 46, 8036 Zürich; tel. (1) 4656565; fax (1) 4656444; f. 1922; life; CEO Dr GÜNTHER GOSE.

**Zürich Versicherungs-Gesellschaft:** Mythenquai 2, 8022 Zürich; tel. (1) 2052121; telex 815555; fax (1) 2013397; f. 1872; accident, sickness, liability, motor vehicles, aviation, boats, fire, loss of profits, burglary, water, glass, travel, valuables, machinery, general technical installations, computers, electronic office machinery, erection, contractors risks, performance bonds, fidelity, surety insurance, re-insurance of all classes; life, marine, goods in transit; CEO R. HÜPPI.

### Insurance Organization

**Schweizerischer Versicherungsverband** (Swiss Insurance Association): C. F. Meyer-Str. 14, 8022 Zürich; tel. (1) 2024826; fax (1) 2026672; f. 1901; Pres. (vacant); Secs P. GMEINER, B. ZELTNER; 71 mems.

## Trade and Industry

### PRINCIPAL CHAMBERS OF COMMERCE

**Aargauische Industrie-und Handelskammer:** Entfelderstr. 11, 5001 Aarau; tel. (64) 255577; Pres. HANS ERICH ROTH.

**Basler Handelskammer:** St Alban-Graben 8, 4001 Basel; tel. (61) 231888; fax (61) 236228; Pres. Dr GAUDENZ STAEHELIN; 670 mems.

**Bündner Handels-und Industrieverein:** Poststr. 43, 7002 Chur; tel. (81) 226306; fax (81) 220449; Pres. Dr CHASPER CAMPELL; Sec. MARCO ETTISBERGER.

**Camera di commercio dell'industria e dell'artigianato del Cantone Ticino:** Corso Elvezia 16, 6901 Lugano; tel. (91) 235031; fax (91) 220341; f. 1917; Pres. FRANCO AMBROSETTI; Dir CLAUDIO CAMPONOVO; 900 mems.

**Chambre fribourgeoise du commerce, de l'industrie et des services:** 37 route du Jura, 1706 Fribourg; tel. (37) 271220; fax (37) 271239; f. 1917; Pres. Dr HANS BLUMER.

**Chambre de commerce et d'industrie de Genève:** 4 blvd du Théâtre, 1211 Geneva 11; tel. (22) 8199111; fax (22) 8199100; f. 1865; Pres. IVAN PICTET; Dir PATRICK COIDAN; 1,600 mems.

**Chambre de commerce et d'industrie du Jura:** 2 chemin de la Perche, 2900 Porrentruy; tel. (66) 662465; fax (66) 664418; Pres. JACQUES SAUCY; Dir JEAN-FRÉDÉRIC GERBER.

**Chambre neuchâteloise du commerce et de l'industrie:** 4 rue de la Serre, 2001 Neuchâtel; tel. (38) 257541; fax (38) 247092; Pres. YANN RICHTER; Dir CLAUDE BERNOULLI.

**Chambre valaisanne de commerce** (Fédération économique du Valais): Bâtiment Grande Dixence, 2 rue de la Blancherie, 1951 Sion; tel. (27) 227575; fax (27) 229727; Pres. JEAN ACTIS; Dir PIERRE-NOËL JULEN; 492 mems.

**Chambre vaudoise du commerce et de l'industrie:** 47 ave d'Ouchy, 1000 Lausanne 13; tel. (21) 6177291; fax (21) 6177303; Pres. EDMOND HENRY; Dir JEAN-LUC STROHM; 1,700 mems.

**Glarner Handelskammer:** Spielhof 14A, 8750 Glarus; tel. (58) 611173; fax (58) 617435; Pres. Dr HEINZ KINDLIMANN; Sec. Dr KARLJÖRG LANDOLT.

**Handelskammer und Arbeitgebervereinigung Winterthur (HAW):** Hermannstr. 18, 8403 Winterthur; tel. (52) 2424955; fax (52) 2421424; Pres. Dr VICTOR BEGLINGER.

**Handels-und Industrieverein des Kantons Bern:** Gutenbergstr. 1, Postfach 5464, 3001 Berne; tel. (31) 261711; fax (31) 261715; Pres. VINZENZ LOSINGER.

**Industrie-und Handelskammer St Gallen-Appenzell:** Gallusstr. 16, 9001 St Gallen; tel. (71) 231515; fax (71) 224727; f. 1466; Pres. UELI FORSTER; 1,300 mems.

**Schweizerische Junge Wirtschaftskammer/Jeune Chambre économique suisse:** c/o Unirevisa, Spielhof 14A, 8750 Glarus; tel. (58) 617252; fax (58) 617435; Pres. MICHEL GUT; Sec. ROLAND SCHWARZMANN.

**Schweizerische Zentrale für Handelsförderung—Office suisse d'expansion commerciale (OSEC):** Stampfenbachstr. 85, 8035 Zürich; tel. (1) 3655151; telex 817272; fax (1) 3655221; and ave de l'Avant-Poste 4, 1001 Lausanne; tel. (21) 3203231; telex 455425; fax (21) 3207337; f. 1927; Pres. PHILIPPE LÉVY; Dir MARTIN MONSCH; 2,000 mems.

**Solothurnische Handelskammer:** Grabackerstr. 6, 4502 Solothurn; tel. (65) 222324; fax (65) 223693; Pres. Dr ROLF LEUENBERGER; Dir Dr HANS RUDOLF MEYER.

**Thurgauer Industrie-und Handelskammer:** Schützenstr. 23, Postfach, 8570 Weinfelden; tel. (72) 221919; fax (72) 226257; Pres. HANS ULRICH SCHMID.

**Zentralschweizerische Handelskammer:** Kapellplatz 2, 6002 Lucerne; tel. (41) 516865; fax (41) 515288; Pres. GERRY LEUMANN; Dir ALEX BRUCKERT; 560 mems.

**Zürcher Handelskammer:** Bleicherweg 5, Postfach 4031, 8022 Zürich; tel. (1) 2210742; fax (1) 2117615; Pres. Dr WALTER DIENER; Dir CHRISTIAN BOESCH; 1,475 mems.

### INDUSTRIAL ASSOCIATIONS AND EMPLOYERS' ORGANIZATIONS

#### Central Organizations

**Schweizerischer Bauernverband** (Union Suisse des Paysans, Lega svizzera dei contadini, Swiss Farmers' Union): Laurstr. 10, 5200 Brugg; tel. (56) 325111; fax (56) 415348; f. 1897; Pres. M. SANDOZ; Dir M. EHRLER; 90 sections.

**Schweizerischer Gewerbeverband** (Swiss Union of Small and Medium Enterprises): Schwarztorstr. 26, 3007 Berne; tel. (31) 3817785; f. 1879; Pres. HANS RUDOLF FRÜH; 270 sections.

**Schweizerischer Handels- und Industrie-Verein** (Swiss Federation of Commerce and Industry): Mainaustr. 49, Postfach 690, 8034 Zürich; tel. (1) 3822323; telex 813294; fax (1) 3822332; f. 1870; Pres. Dr ANDRES F. LEUENBERGER; Vice-Pres. Dr GUSTAV E. GRISARD; Exec. Dir Dr KURT MOSER; 118 sections.

**Zentralverband schweizerischer Arbeitgeber-Organisationen** (Federation of Swiss Employers' Organizations): Florastr. 44, 8034 Zürich; tel. (1) 3830758; fax (1) 3833980; f. 1908; Pres. Dr GUIDO RICHTERICH; Vice-Pres. MICHEL MAILLEFER; Dir Dr PETER HASLER; 71 mems.

#### Principal Regional Organizations

**Associazione Industrie Ticinesi:** Corso Elvezia 16, 6901 Lugano; tel. (91) 235041; fax (91) 234636; Pres. PIETRO SOMAINI; Sec.-Gen. Dr SANDRO LOMBARDI.

**Basler Volkswirtschaftsbund:** Aeschengraben 9, 4010 Basel; tel. (61) 7210240; fax (61) 2710243; Pres. Dr KURT STEUBER; Dir Dr G. TELEKI; 8,000 mems.

**Luzerner Industrie-Vereinigung:** Postfach 3142, Kapellplatz 2, 6002 Lucerne; tel. (41) 516889; Pres. ADOLF BÜRKLI; 109 mems.

**Union des associations patronales genevoises:** (Union of Employers' Associations in Geneva): 98 rue de Saint-Jean, 1211 Geneva 11; tel. (22) 7153111; fax (22) 7153213; Pres. RAYMOND EIGENMANN.

**Union des industriels valaisans:** CP 430, 1920 Martigny 1; tel. (26) 22867; Pres. WILLY GERTSCHEN; Sec. PASCAL COUCHEPIN.

**Verband industrieller Arbeitgeber von Bern und Umgebung:** Marktgasse 55, 3000 Berne 7; tel. (31) 3116151; fax (31) 3125087; f. 1919; employers' association for the Berne region; Pres. U. EMCH; Sec. Dr C. THOMANN; 170 mems.

**Verband Basellandschaftlicher Unternehmen:** Wasserturmplatz 2, 4410 Liestal; tel. (61) 9216620; employers' association for the Basel region; Pres. KURT J. SCHMID; Dir Dr P. JEGER.

**Vereinigung Zürcherischer Arbeitgeber-Organisationen:** Selnaunstr. 32, 8021 Zürich; tel. (1) 2292827; fax (1) 2292833; association of Zürich employers' organizations; Pres. THOMAS ISLER; Sec. D. SIGRIST.

#### Sectional Organizations

**Arbeitgeberverband der Schweizer Maschinenindustrie:** Kirchenweg 4, 8032 Zürich; tel. (1) 3844111; f. 1905; engineering and metal industry employers; Pres. M. C. CAPPIS; Dir Dr P. HASLER; 486 mems.

**Arbeitgeberverband Schweizerischer Papier-Industrieller:** Bergstr. 110, Postfach 134, 8030 Zürich; tel. (1) 2619747; fax (1) 2523882; paper manufacturers; Pres. H. P. MULLER; Dir A. GMÜR; 11 mems.

**Chocosuisse—Verband Schweizerischer Schokoladefabrikanten:** Münzgraben 6, 3000 Berne 7; tel. (31) 3116494; fax (31) 3122655; f. 1901; association of chocolate manufacturers; Dir D. KUSTER; 12 mems.

**Communauté de l'industrie suisse de la cigarette (CISC):** Pérolles 5, BP 212, Fribourg; tel. (37) 814121; fax (37) 226218; f. 1993; Pres. EDGAR OEHLER; Dir JEAN-CLAUDE BARDY; 7 mems.

**Convention Patronale de l'Industrie Horlogère Suisse:** 65 ave Léopold-Robert, 2301 La Chaux-de-Fonds; tel. (39) 211161; employers in watch-manufacturing; Pres. J. CAVADINI; Gen. Sec. J. GREDY; 12 mems.

**Fédération de l'Industrie Horlogère Suisse FH** (Federation of the Swiss Watch Industry): 6 rue d'Argent, 2501 Bienne; tel. (32) 280828; fax (32) 280880; f. 1876; Pres. F. HABERSAAT; Sec.-Gen. J. D. PASCHE; 500 mems.

**Föderation der Schweizerischen Nahrungsmittel-Industrie** (Federation of Swiss Foodstuffs Industry): Elfenstr. 19, 3000

Berne 16, Land Münzgraben 6, 3000 Berne 7; tel. (31) 3521188; fax (31) 3521185; foodstuffs; Sec. D. KUSTER; 216 mems.

**Gesamtverband der Schweizerischen Bekleidungsindustrie:** Gotthardstr. 61, Postfach 265, 8027 Zürich; tel. (1) 2027161; fax (1) 2020651; clothing industry; Pres. Dr J. SCHÖNENBERGER; Man. R. LANGENEGGER; 220 mems.

**Schweizerischer Baumeisterverband:** Weinbergstr. 49, 8035 Zürich 6; tel. (1) 2588111; fax (1) 2588335; f. 1897; building contractors; 4,600 mems.

**Schweizerische Gesellschaft für Chemische Industrie** (Swiss Society of Chemical Industries): Nordstr. 15, 8035 Zürich; tel. (1) 3681711; fax (1) 3681770; f. 1882; chemical industry; Pres. D. C. WAGNIÈRE; Dir Dr R. ULRICH; 254 mems.

**Schweizerischer Elektrotechnischer Verein (SEV)** (Swiss Electrotechnical Association): Seefeldstr. 301, 8008 Zürich; tel. (1) 3849111; telex 817431; fax (1) 4221426; f. 1889; Chair. R. BRÜDERLIN; Pres. Dr J. HEYNER; 1,830 mems.

**Schweizerischer Spenglermeister-und Installateur-Verband:** Auf der Mauer 11, 8001 Zürich; tel. (1) 2517400; fax (1) 2513228; f. 1891; metal goods; Pres. E. KULL; 3,500 mems.

**Schweizerischer Verband Grafischer Unternehmen:** Carmenstr. 6, Postfach 39, 8030 Zürich; tel. (1) 2521440; fax (1) 2521743; f.1869; printing industry; Pres. R. BALSIGER; Dir S. HEGNER; 1,256 mems.

**Schweizerischer Versicherungsverband:** (see under Insurance).

**Textilverband Schweiz:** Beethovenstr. 20, 8022 Zürich; tel. (1) 2015755; f. 1874; textiles; Pres. URS BAUMANN; Dir Dr A. HAFNER; 230 mems.

**Verband Schweizerischer Elektrizitätswerke:** Gerbergrasse 5, 8023 Zürich; tel. (1) 2115191; fax (1) 2210442; f. 1895; Pres. K. KÜFFER; Dir M. BREU.

**Verband der Schweizerischen Gasindustrie:** Grütlistr. 44, 8027 Zürich; tel. (1) 2883131; telex 58727; fax (1) 2021834; f. 1920; Pres. J. CAVADINI; Dir Dr Y. GENRE; 90 mems.

**Verband Schweizerischer Kreditbanken und Finanzierungsinstitute** (Association of Swiss Credit Banks and Finance Institutes): Stauffacherstr. 35, 8004 Zürich; tel. (1) 2427587; Pres. Dr LYDIA SAXER; Sec. Dr W. HAEFELIN.

**Verband der Schweizerischen Textil-Veredlungs-Industrie** (Swiss Textile Bleachers', Dyers' and Printers' Association): Beethovenstr. 20, 8002 Zürich; tel. (1) 2810990; fax (1) 2811001; f. 1941; Pres. M. HUGELSHOFER; Sec. H. PETERHANS; 15 mems.

**Verband der Schweizerischen Waren-und Kaufhäuser:** Holbeinstr. 22, 8032 Zürich; tel. (1) 2524040; fax (1) 2524097; retail trade; Pres. Dr K. HUG; Sec. R. KURTZ.

**Verband Schweizerische Ziegelindustrie** (Association of Swiss Heavy Clay Industry): Obstgartenstr. 28, 8035 Zürich; tel. (1) 3619650; fax (1) 3610205; f. 1874; Pres. P. KELLER; Dir Dr W. P. WELLER; 42 mems.

**Verband Zürcherischer Kreditinstitute:** Selnaustr. 32, 8021 Zürich; tel. (1) 2292829; fax (1) 2292833; f. 1902; asscn of Zürich credit institutes; Sec. D. SIGRIST.

**Verein Schweizerischer Maschinen-Industrieller** (Swiss Association of Machinery Manufacturers): Kirchenweg 4, 8032 Zürich; tel. (1) 3844844; fax (1) 3844848; f. 1883; Pres. Dr T. P. GASSER; Dir Dr M. ERB; 638 mems.

### TRADE UNIONS

**Schweizerischer Gewerkschaftsbund** (Swiss Federation of Trade Unions): Monbijoustr. 61, 3007 Berne; tel. (31) 3715666; fax (31) 3710837; f. 1880; the main organization of Swiss Trade Unions; affiliated to the International Confederation of Free Trade Unions; Pres. VASCO PEDRINA, CHRISTIANE BRUNNER; total affiliated membership 431,000.

The principal affiliated unions are:

**Gewerkschaft Bau und Industrie** (Building and Industry): Strassburgstr. 11, 8021 Zürich; tel. (1) 2951515; fax (1) 2951799; f. 1922; Pres. VASCO PEDRINA; 124,818 mems.

**Gewerkschaft Druck und Papier** (Print and Paper Workers): Monbijoustr. 33, 3011 Berne; tel. (31) 252248; fax (31) 263752; f. 1858; Pres. C. TIREFORT; 16,000 mems.

**Gewerkschaft Verkauf, Handel, Transport, Lebensmittel** (Workers in the Commerce, Transport and Food Industries): Birmensdorferstr. 67, 8036 Zürich; tel. (1) 2423576; f. 1904; Pres. PETER KÜNG; 28,000 mems.

**Schweizerischer Eisenbahnerverband** (Railwaymen): Steinerstr. 35, 3006 Berne; tel. (31) 3575757; f. 1919; Pres. CHARLY PASCHE; 60,200 mems.

**Schweizerischer Metall-und Uhrenarbeitnehmer-Verband** (Metal Workers and Watchmakers): Weltpoststr. 20, 3000 Berne 15; tel. (31) 435551; telex 912411; fax (31) 435501; f. 1888; Pres. A. TARABUSI; 112,000 mems.

**Schweizerischer Verband des Personals öffentlicher Dienste** (Public Services): Sonnenbergstr. 83, 8030 Zürich; tel. (1) 2519935; fax (1) 2514316; f. 1905; Pres. PETER KEIMER; Gen. Sec. Dr DORIS SCHUEPP; 42,000 mems.

**PTT-Union, Union Schweizerischer Post-, Telephon-und Telegraphenbeamter** (Swiss Post-, Telephone-and Telegraph-Functionaries): Oberdorfstr. 32, 3072 Ostermundigen; tel. (31) 9309211; fax (31) 9395262; f. 1891; Pres. DOMINIQUE BEUCHAT; Gen. Sec. HANS U. RUCHTI; 29,500 mems.

**Gewerkschaft Textil, Chemie, Papier** (Textile, Chemical, Paper Trade): Luisenstr. 29, 8031 Zürich 5; tel. (1) 2726911; f. 1904; Pres. HANS SCHÄPPI; 12,000 mems.

**Christlichnationaler Gewerkschaftsbund der Schweiz (CNG)** (Confederation of Christian Trade Unions): Hopfenweg 21, 3007 Berne; tel. (31) 3702111; fax (31) 3702109; f. 1907; Pres. H. FASEL; Sec B. KÖSTINGER; 106,267 mems.

The principal affiliated unions are:

**Christlicher Chemie-Textil-Bekleidungs-Papier-Personalverband** (Christian Chemical, Textile, Clothing, Paper and Staff Workers): Rotwandstr. 50, 8004 Zürich; Pres. J. ZUMSTEG; Secs J. FISCHER, J. BLEICHER; 6,630 mems.

**Christlicher Holz-und Bauarbeiterverband der Schweiz (CHB)** (Christian Building and Woodworkers): Zeughausstr. 39, 8004 Zürich; tel. (1) 2415442; f. 1901; Pres. ANTON SALZMANN; Secs A. ERNST, T. AMSLER, W. RINDLISBACHER, A. ZEHNDER; 44,153 mems.

**Christliche Gewerkschaft für Industrie, Handel und Gewerbe (CMV/FCOM)** (Christian Metalworkers): Lindstr. 39, 8410 Winterthur; tel. (52) 2680404; fax (52) 2680405; Pres. H. FASEL; 33,000 mems.

**Landesverband freier Schweizer Arbeitnehmer:** Badenerstr. 41, 8004 Zürich; tel. (1) 2410757; f. 1919; Pres. JAKOB ZÜST; Sec. ALFRED MEYER; 23,506 mems.

**Vereinigung schweizerischer Angestelltenverbände** (Salaried Employees): Badenerstr. 332, Postfach 1120, 8040 Zürich; tel. (1) 4912581; fax (1) 4010625; f. 1918; Pres. HANS-RUDOLF ENGGIST; 133,739 mems.

### TRADE FAIRS

**Basel Fair (MUBA):** 4021 Basel; tel. (61) 6862020; telex 962685; fax (61) 6862194; f. 1917; every March; Gen. Dir PHILIPPE LÉVY.

**National Fair:** Comptoir Suisse, Palais de Beaulieu, 1000 Lausanne 22; tel. (21) 6432111; telex 454044; fax (21) 6433711; f. 1920; every September.

**Swiss Agricultural and Dairy Farming Fair:** Olma Messen St Gallen, Splügenstr. 12, 9008 St Gallen; tel. (71) 260122; fax (71) 260101; f. 1943; Dir Dr RENÉ KÄPPELI; every October.

## Transport

### RAILWAYS

**Schweizerische Bundesbahnen (SBB)** (Chemins de fer fédéraux suisses): Hochschulstr. 6, 3030 Berne; tel. (31) 6801111; telex 991121; fax (31) 6804358; f. 1901; 2,998 km in 1992 (of which 2,985 km were electrified): Pres. J. KYBURZ; Gen. Man. Dr BENEDIKT WEIBEL.

There are altogether about 56 small private companies controlling private railways, chiefly along short mountain routes, with a total length of around 2,032 km. The following are among the principal private railways:

**Berner Alpenbahn-Gesellschaft:** Genfergasse 11, Postfach 2627, 3001 Berne; tel. (31) 221182; fax (31) 212481; f. 1906; 114 km; Thun-Spiez-Brigue, Thun-Interlaken, Moutier-Lengnau; boat services on the Lakes of Thun and Brienz; Man. M. JOSI.

**Bodensee-Toggenburg-Bahn (BT):** Bahnhofplatz 1A, Postfach 380, 9001 St Gallen; tel. (71) 231912; fax (71) 231952; f. 1904; 56 km; Romanshorn-St Gallen-Herisau-Nesslau-Neu St Johann; Man. W. DIETZ.

**Emmental-Burgdorf-Thun Railway:** 3401 Burgdorf; tel. (34) 223151; fax (34) 232248; 77 km; Gen. Man. Dr CH. KELLERHALS.

**Fribourg Railways (Chemins de fer fribourgeois):** 3 rue des Pilettes, 1701 Fribourg; tel. (37) 812161; fax (37) 223439; f. 1868; 99 km; Man. ANDRÉ GENOUD.

**Furka-Oberalp-Bahn:** Postfach 256, 3900 Brig; tel. (28) 228111; telex 473366; fax (28) 228103; f. 1915; Brig-Fiesch-Oberwald-Andermatt-Disentis and Andermatt-Göschenen; 101 km; Man. A. GASSER.

**Huttwil United Railways:** Bucherstr. 1-3, 3400 Burgdorf; tel. (34) 223151; fax (34) 232248; 64 km; Pres. Dr K. BABST; Man. Dir Dr CH. KELLERHALS.

# SWITZERLAND

**Jura Railways:** 1 rue Général-Voirol, 2710 Tavannes; tel. (32) 912745; f. 1944; 85 km; Porrentruy-Bonfol; La Chaux-de-Fonds-Glovelier; Tavannes-Noirmont; Pres. F. MERTENAT; Gen. Man. A. BOILLAT.

**Montreux-Oberland Bernois:** CP 1426, 1820 Montreux; tel. (21) 9645511; fax (21) 9646448; f. 1899; 75 km; Montreux-Château-d'Oex-Gstaad-Zweisimmen-Lenk i/S; Dir E. STYGER.

**Rhaetian Railway:** Bahnhofstr. 25, 7002 Chur; tel. (81) 219121; telex 993512; fax (81) 228501; f. 1889; 375 km; the most extensive of the privately-run railways; Dir S. FASCIATI.

**Ticino District Railways:** CP 1279, 6601 Locarno; tel. (93) 310031; telex 846169; fax (93) 315262; f. 1909; 19 km; Locarno-Camedo; Dir Ing. DIRK MEYER.

## ROADS

**Bundesamt für Strassenbau** (Office fédéral des routes): Monbijoustr. 40, 3003 Berne; tel. (31) 3229411; fax (31) 3719063; Dir KURT SUTER.

In 1993 Switzerland had 71,023 km of roads: 1,529 km of motorways (1,532.7 km in 1994), 18,297 km of other main roads and 51,197 km of secondary roads. The construction of a national network of approximately 1,855 km of motorways is scheduled for completion by 2010. At the beginning of 1994, 1,532.7 km of the network were in service. The road tunnel through the Saint Gotthard Pass, 17 km long and a European road link of paramount importance, was opened in 1980.

## INLAND WATERWAYS

The Swiss Rhine and Canal fleet numbered 161 vessels in 1994.

## SHIPPING

In 1994 Swiss shipping companies owned 20 ocean-going vessels with a displacement of around 402,368 grt. The principal shipping companies in Switzerland are:

**Hamburger Lloyd:** Lange Gasse 90, 4006 Basel; tel. (61) 6312233; Dir R. STRAUBHAAR; 7 ships.

**Keller Shipping Ltd:** Holbeinstr. 68, 4002 Basel; tel. (61) 2818686; telex 963751; fax (61) 224897; associated with Nautilus SA de Navigation Maritime, Transocéanique Suisse SA de Navigation; Pres. A. R. KELLER; 1 ship.

**Massoel SA:** 3 rue du Mont-Blanc, 1211 Geneva 1; tel. (22) 7151800; 3 ships.

**Mediterranean Shipping Co SA:** 18 chemin Rieu, 1208 Geneva; tel. (22) 3462822; fax (22) 3461336; Dir G. APONTE; 51 ships.

**Natural van Dam AG:** Westquaistr. 62, 4019 Basel; tel. (61) 6312233; Dir R. STRAUBHAAR; 7 ships.

**Schweizerische Reederei & Neptun AG:** Wiesendamm 4, 4019 Basel; tel. and fax (61) 6393466; Dir J. FENDT; 8 ships.

**Suisse-Atlantique, Société de Navigation Maritime SA:** 7 chemin Messidor, CP 4140, 1002 Lausanne; tel. (21) 3182201; telex 454101; fax (21) 3182279; world-wide tramping services; Pres. E. ANDRE; Dir G. TAILLARD and C. DIDAY; 13 ships; managers of:

    **Helica SA:** c/o Suisse-Atlantique, CP 4140, 1002 Lausanne; 6 ships of 194,347 grt.

    **Navemar SA:** 1 Grand' Places, 1700 Fribourg; 2 ships of 63,352 grt.

**Suisse-Outremer Reederei AG:** Winterthurerstr. 92, 8006 Zürich; tel. (1) 3634952; telex 817051; fax (1) 3628362; f. 1956; Man. Dir P. PREISIG.

**Vinalmar SA:** 7 rue du Mont-Blanc, 1211 Geneve 1; tel. (22) 9060431; 5 ships.

## CIVIL AVIATION

Switzerland's principal airports are situated at Zürich, Geneva and Basel-Mulhouse.

**Crossair:** 4002 Basel; tel. (61) 3252525; fax (61) 3253268; f. 1975; Swiss airline operating a network of regional and supplementary air transport services across Europe; Pres. MORITZ SUTER.

**Swissair** (Swiss Air Transport Co Ltd): 8058 Flughafen Zürich; tel. (1) 8121212; telex 825601; fax (1) 8108046; f. 1931; offices in all major cities of the world; services to Europe, the Middle East, North and South America, Africa and the Far East; Chair. HANNES GOETZ; Pres. OTTO LOEPFE.

# Tourism

Switzerland's principal attractions are the lakes and lake resorts and the mountains. Walking, mountaineering and winter sports are the chief pastimes. Receipts from tourism were an estimated 12,818m. francs in 1993, and overnight stays of visitors from abroad totalled 20.1m. in that year.

**Swiss National Tourist Office (SNTO):** Head Office: Bellariastr. 38, 8027 Zürich; tel. (1) 2881111; fax (1) 2881205; f. 1917; Dir MARCO HARTMANN; offices in most major cities of the world.

# SYRIA

## Introductory Survey

**Location, Climate, Language, Religion, Flag, Capital**

The Syrian Arab Republic lies in western Asia, with Turkey to the north, Iraq to the east and Jordan to the south. Lebanon and Israel are to the south-west. Syria has a coastline on the eastern shore of the Mediterranean Sea. Much of the country is mountainous and semi-desert. The coastal climate is one of hot summers and mild winters. The inland plateau and plains are dry but cold in winter. Average temperatures in Damascus are 2°C to 12°C (36°F to 54°F) in January and 18°C to 37°C (64°F to 99°F) in August. The national language is Arabic, with Kurdish a minority language. More than 80% of the population are Muslims (mostly Sunnis) but there is a substantial Christian minority of various sects. The national flag (proportions 2 by 1) has three equal horizontal stripes, of red, white and black, with two five-pointed green stars in the centre of the white stripe. The capital is Damascus.

**Recent History**

Syria was formerly part of Turkey's Ottoman Empire. Turkish forces were defeated in the First World War (1914–18) and Syria was occupied in 1920 by France, in accordance with a League of Nations mandate. Syrian nationalists proclaimed an independent republic in September 1941. French powers were transferred in January 1944, and full independence was achieved on 17 April 1946. In December 1949 Syria came under an army dictatorship, led by Brig. Adib Shishekly. He was elected President in July 1953 but was overthrown by another army coup in February 1954.

In February 1958 Syria merged with Egypt to form the United Arab Republic (UAR). In September 1961, following an army coup in Damascus, Syria seceded and formed the independent Syrian Arab Republic. In 1963 Maj.-Gen. Amin al-Hafiz formed a Government in which members of the Arab Socialist Renaissance (Baath) Party were predominant. In February 1966 the army deposed the Government of President al-Hafiz, replacing him with Dr Nur ed-Din al-Atasi. However, in November 1970, after a bloodless coup, the military (moderate) wing of the Baath Party seized power, led by Lt-Gen. Hafiz al-Assad, who was elected President in March 1971. In March 1972 the National Progressive Front (NPF), a grouping of the five main political parties, was formed under the leadership of President Assad.

From 1977 onwards, frequent assassinations of Alawites (a minority Islamic sect to which Assad belonged) indicated sectarian tension within Syrian society, and Assad attributed much of the opposition to the Muslim Brotherhood, a conservative Islamic group. In February 1982 an uprising in Hama, which was believed to be the work of the outlawed Muslim Brotherhood, was brutally suppressed. In November 1983 Assad suffered what was thought to be a heart attack. During his illness and, periodically, until March 1984, shows of military strength were staged by rivals to the succession, including Rifaat al-Assad, the President's brother. Ostensibly designed to ease Assad's workload following his illness, the appointment of three Vice-Presidents in March 1984 distributed power evenly between the President's potential successors, giving none the ascendancy. The army, Assad's guarantee of continued power, was still controlled by officers loyal to him.

President Assad was re-elected for a third seven-year term of office in February 1985. At a general election, held in February 1986, the Baath Party and other members of the NPF (excluding the Communist Party) obtained 151 of the 195 seats in the People's Assembly; the Communist Party (which contested the election independently of the NPF) won nine seats, and independent candidates 35.

In May 1986 the Government admitted that 144 people had been killed, and 149 injured, during a campaign of bombings in five Syrian towns, including Damascus, in April. A hitherto unknown Syrian group, with suspected pro-Iraqi, Islamic fundamentalist leanings, claimed responsibility for the campaign.

A major government reshuffle took place in November 1987, when, following the resignation of the Prime Minister, Abd ar-Rauf al-Kassem, Mahmoud az-Zoubi, the Speaker of the People's Assembly, was appointed Prime Minister. At elections to the People's Assembly (now expanded to 250 seats), held in May 1990, the Baath Party won 134 seats and other parties 32 seats, while 84 were reserved for independent candidates.

Increasing border tension between Syria and Israel was a major influence leading to the Six-Day War of June 1967, when Israel attacked its Arab neighbours as a reprisal for the closure of the Strait of Tiran by the UAR (Egypt). Israeli forces quickly made territorial gains, including the Golan Heights region of Syria, which remains under Israeli occupation. An uneasy truce lasted until October 1973, and all attempts by outside powers to arrange a peace settlement failed. War broke out again in October 1973, when Egyptian and Syrian forces launched simultaneous attacks on Israeli-held territory. On the Syrian front, there was fierce fighting in the Golan Heights area until a cease-fire was agreed after 18 days. In May 1974 the US Secretary of State, Dr Henry Kissinger, secured an agreement for the disengagement of forces. Israel formally annexed the Golan Heights in December 1981, hampering the chances of a negotiated final peace agreement.

Syria disapproved of the second interim Egyptian-Israeli Disengagement Agreement in September 1975, but agreed to acknowledge it as a *fait accompli* at the Arab summit conferences in Riyadh and Cairo in October 1976, in return for Egypt's acceptance of Syria's role in Lebanon. Syria had progressively intervened in the Lebanese civil war during 1976, finally providing the bulk of the 30,000-strong Arab Deterrent Force (ADF). Syria condemned President Sadat for Egypt's peace initiative with Israel in November and December 1977, the Camp David agreements between Egypt and Israel, signed in September 1978, and the subsequent peace treaty concluded between them.

The ADF, based in northern Lebanon, was unable to act when Israel invaded southern Lebanon in June 1982 and advanced to Beirut, trapping 14,000–15,000 troops of the Palestine Liberation Organization (PLO) and Syrian forces. In August these troops were evacuated under the supervision of a multinational peace-keeping force, and some 50,000 Syrian troops, deployed in the Beka'a valley and northern Lebanon, faced 25,000 Israelis in the south of the country, even though the mandate of the ADF had expired.

When protracted talks culminated in the signing on 17 May 1983 of an Israel-Lebanon peace agreement, formulated by the US Secretary of State, George Shultz, Syria rejected it, refused to withdraw its forces from Lebanon, and continued to supply the militias of the Lebanese Druze and Shi'ite factions in their fight against the Lebanese Government and the Christian Phalangists. At the same time Assad tried to unite Lebanese opposition leaders in a pro-Syrian 'national front' against the Government of President Amin Gemayel.

Syria supported a revolt which began in Lebanon's Beka'a valley in May 1983 against Yasser Arafat's leadership of the Palestine National Liberation Movement (Fatah). Syrian and rebel PLO forces finally trapped Arafat, the PLO Chairman, in the Lebanese port of Tripoli in November. After fierce fighting, Arafat and some 4,000 of his followers were permitted to leave Tripoli in December.

Although Israel withdrew its forces from Beirut to the Awali river in September 1983, Syria's troops remained entrenched in the north of Lebanon. The state of civil war existing in and around Beirut eventually compelled the evacuation of the multinational force in the first three months of 1984. In March President Gemayel capitulated to the influence of Syria in the affairs of Lebanon. He abrogated the 17 May agreement with Israel and reconvened the National Reconciliation Conference of the rival Lebanese factions (which had first met in Geneva in November 1983) in Lausanne, under pressure from Syria to agree constitutional reforms which would give the majority Muslim community of Lebanon greater representation in government. The National Reconciliation Conference failed to produce the results for which Syria had hoped, and it signalled the beginning of the disintegration of the Lebanese National

Salvation Front, comprised of leading Lebanese opponents of President Gemayel, which had been established, with Syrian backing, in July 1983.

At talks in April 1984, President Assad approved plans for a Lebanese government of national unity, put to him by President Gemayel, giving equal representation in the Cabinet to Muslims and Christians. Nabih Berri of the Shi'ite Amal militia and Walid Joumblatt, the Lebanese Druze leader (both of whom received financial support from Syria), were persuaded to participate in the new Government by President Assad, but inter-factional fighting continued in Beirut and Syria was repeatedly required to intervene.

A Syrian-sponsored security plan for Beirut was implemented at the beginning of July 1984, but met with only limited success. The extent of Syria's influence with its Lebanese allies came into question when even the threat of force failed to win Walid Joumblatt's unequivocal approval for an extension of the security plan to allow the Lebanese army into the Druze stronghold of the Chouf mountains. In September Syria arranged a truce to end fighting in Tripoli between the pro-Syrian Arab Democratic Party and the Sunni Muslim Tawheed Islami (Islamic Unification Movement). The Lebanese army entered the city in November, under the terms of an extended security plan, backed by Syria, to assert the authority of the Lebanese Government.

Syria approved Lebanese participation in talks with Israel to co-ordinate the departure of the Israeli Defence Force (IDF) from southern Lebanon with that of other security forces, in order to prevent an outbreak of civil violence. The Lebanese, under Syrian influence, wanted the UN Interim Force in Lebanon (UNIFIL) to police the Israel–Lebanon border (as it had been mandated to do in 1978), and the Lebanese army to deploy north of the Litani river, between the UNIFIL and Syrian forces in the Beka'a valley. Israel was not convinced of the competence of the Lebanese army, and wanted the UNIFIL to be deployed north of the Litani, while the Israeli-backed so-called 'South Lebanon Army' (SLA) patrolled the southern Lebanese border. In the absence of any agreement, Israel withdrew from the talks, and in January 1985 the Israeli Cabinet voted to effect a three-phased, unilateral withdrawal to the international border.

The final stage of the Israeli withdrawal was accomplished by early June 1985. Several hundred Israeli troops and advisers remained inside Lebanon to assist the SLA in policing a buffer zone, 10 km–20 km wide, along the Lebanese side of the international border, but Syria took advantage of the Israeli withdrawal to remove 10,000–12,000 troops from the Beka'a valley in July, leaving some 25,000 in position.

Heavy fighting took place in Muslim west Beirut in April 1985, between the Shi'ite Amal militia, allied with the Druze, and the Sunni Murabitoun militia and its Palestinian allies. This preceded renewed attempts by Syria, through its proxy, Amal, to prevent Yasser Arafat from re-establishing a power-base in Beirut. (Most of the estimated 5,000 PLO guerrillas who had returned to Lebanon after the Israeli withdrawal were thought to be loyal to Arafat.) An estimated 650 people died in the fighting before a fragile cease-fire agreement was reached in Damascus on 17 June.

One month of negotiations, under Syrian auspices, between the three main Lebanese militias, the Druze, Amal and the Lebanese Forces Christian militia (LF), which began in October 1985, led to the preparation of a draft accord for a politico-military settlement of the civil war. The agreement was finally signed by the three militia leaders on 28 December, in Damascus. The Shi'ite Hezbollah and the Sunni Murabitoun militias were not party to the agreement, and the Christian community was divided over it. President Gemayel, who had not been consulted during the drafting of the agreement, refused to endorse it. In January 1986 the LF came under the command of Samir Geagea, who opposed the agreement, effectively ending all hope that it could be implemented.

Leaders of the Muslim community in Lebanon met Syrian Government officials in Damascus and, on 14 June 1986, agreed to impose a cease-fire around the Palestinian refugee camps in Beirut, where fighting between Palestinian guerrillas and Shi'ite Amal militiamen had again developed into major clashes in May. The cease-fire agreement proved to be the first stage in a Syrian-sponsored peace plan for Muslim west Beirut. The Amal, Druze and Sunni militias were ordered to close their offices and to remain off the streets. Crucial to their co-operation was the deployment in Beirut in July, for the first time since 1982, of uniformed Syrian troops. The security plan was temporarily successful in its objective of curbing the activities of militias in west Beirut, but the plan (and Syria's active involvement in it) was strongly opposed in Christian east Beirut and was not extended to the predominantly Shi'ite southern suburbs, which contained the majority of the city's Palestinian refugees.

During February 1987 fierce fighting took place in west Beirut between Amal forces and an alliance of Druze, Murabitoun and Communist Party militias. Muslim leaders appealed to Syria to intervene to restore order and about 4,000 Syrian troops were deployed in west Beirut on 22 February. The Syrian force (which was soon increased to some 7,500 troops) succeeded in enforcing a cease-fire in the central and northern areas of west Beirut, but was not deployed in the southern suburbs. In September the Arafat wing of the PLO and Amal reached a comprehensive cease-fire agreement, which provided for the ending of the siege of the Palestinian refugee camps in Beirut, Tyre and Sidon, in return for a withdrawal of PLO forces from the positions overlooking Ain al-Hilweh, on the outskirts of Sidon, which they had captured from Amal in October and November 1986. However, neither measure was implemented, and differences concerning the withdrawal of Palestinian guerrillas led to renewed fighting around the disputed positions to the east of Sidon in mid-October. In January 1988, as a gesture of support for protests by Palestinians living in Israeli-occupied territories, Nabih Berri, the leader of Amal, announced the ending of Amal's siege of the Palestinian refugee camps in Beirut and southern Lebanon. On 21 January Syrian troops replaced Amal militiamen and soldiers of the sixth brigade of the Lebanese army in positions around the Beirut camps, and the 14-month siege of Rashidiyah camp, near Tyre, was ended. However, PLO guerrillas loyal to Yasser Arafat refused to withdraw from their positions overlooking Ain al-Hilweh. In April a reconciliation was reported to have taken place between President Assad and Yasser Arafat, when the two leaders held discussions for the first time since 1983. In May 1988 intense fighting took place between Amal and Hezbollah forces in the southern suburbs of Beirut. By late May Hezbollah had gained the advantage, and the intervention of Syrian troops was averted only by the opening of negotiations between Iranian and Syrian representatives, with the aim of facilitating a settlement between the two militias. Further talks in late May led to an agreement on the deployment of Syrian troops and Lebanese police in the suburbs, ending the hostilities.

The hostilities between Amal and Hezbollah had their roots in Syria's interest in the outcome of the Lebanese presidential elections, scheduled to be held in August 1988 (for a detailed account of the elections, see chapter on Lebanon). Syria's support for the candidacy of Sulaiman Franjiya (President of Lebanon between 1970 and 1976), and for Mikhail ad-Daher in September (after the election had been postponed for the first time), aroused the opposition of Lebanese Christian leaders, who objected to candidates imposed by foreign powers (i.e. the USA and Syria). Syria, in turn, refused to recognize the interim military government appointed by President Gemayel shortly before his term of office expired.

Syria, alone of all the Arab states, refused to recognize the independent Palestinian state (proclaimed at the 19th session of the Palestine National Council (PNC) in Algiers in November 1988), in accordance with its longstanding policy of preventing any other force in Lebanon from acquiring sufficient power to challenge Syrian interests. In March 1989 the Christian forces, commanded by Gen. Awn (the head of the Lebanese Government appointed by President Gemayel in September 1988), began an attempt to expel Syrian forces from Lebanon. This quickly developed into one of the most violent confrontations of the entire civil war. At an emergency summit meeting of Arab leaders in May 1989, the proposal (supported by Egypt, Iraq, Jordan and the PLO) that Syria should immediately withdraw its troops from Lebanon was abandoned, in response to Syrian opposition. However, Syria was restrained from using its overwhelming military superiority to impose its authority on 'Christian Lebanon' by the fear of provoking an Israeli intervention in support of Gen. Awn.

In October 1989 diplomacy undertaken by the Arab League resulted in the endorsement, by the Lebanese National Assembly, of a charter of national reconciliation (the Taif agreement) which envisaged a continuing role for the Syrian armed forces in Lebanon by stipulating that they should assist in the implementation of two security plans incorporated in the agreement, which included the constitutional amendments that Syria had long sought to effect in Lebanon. Following a meeting of the newly-formed Lebanese Cabinet in November 1989, it was announced that Gen. Awn had again been dismissed as Commander-in-Chief of the Lebanese army, and, in April 1990, Awn's position was weakened further by the LF's recognition of Elias Hrawi as President of Lebanon and by its acceptance of the Taif agreement and the role for Syria that it envisaged.

In October 1990 Gen. Awn was defeated in a joint operation launched by the Syrian and Lebanese armies. The defeat of Awn removed the major obstacle to the implementation of the provisions of the Taif agreement, which consolidated Syrian influence in Lebanon. Later in October the Lebanese Government began to put into effect the first of the two security plans contained in the Taif agreement (see chapter on Lebanon), ordering all militias to relinquish their positions to the Lebanese army. In May 1991 Syria and Lebanon signed a treaty of 'fraternity, co-operation and co-ordination' which was immediately denounced by Israel as a further step towards the formal transformation of Lebanon into a Syrian protectorate. Israel responded by deploying armed forces inside the 'buffer zone' in southern Lebanon, and the signing of the treaty was considered to have decreased the likelihood of its compliance with UN Security Council Resolution 425 (adopted in March 1978), which required the withdrawal of Israeli armed forces from southern Lebanon.

Although it failed to provide conclusive proof of Syrian involvement, the USA claimed that there was evidence of a link between Syria and the Palestinian terrorists who were responsible for bomb attacks in Europe in 1985 and 1986. President Assad denied that Syria was sponsoring terrorism, and refused to restrict the activities of Palestinian groups on Syrian territory. In November 1986 the United Kingdom and its partners in the EC (excluding Greece), and the USA and Canada, imposed limited diplomatic and economic sanctions against Syria. The Syrian Government persistently denied any involvement in international terrorism, and the EC, with the exception of the United Kingdom, lifted its ban on ministerial contacts with Syria in July 1987. Financial aid was resumed in September, although a ban on the sale of arms to Syria remained in force.

Syria's relationship with Iraq came under strain for some years in the 1970s, owing to rivalry between different wings of the Baath Party, in Damascus and Baghdad. Syria supported Iran in its war with Iraq, which began in September 1980. In November 1987 an extraordinary summit meeting of the League of Arab States, convened to discuss the Iran–Iraq War, produced a unanimous statement expressing solidarity with Iraq, condemning Iran for prolonging the war and for its occupation of Arab (i.e. Iraqi) territory. However, after the summit, Syria announced that a reconciliation with Iraq had not taken place, and that Syrian relations with Iran remained fundamentally unchanged. Syria had used its veto to prevent the adoption of an Iraqi proposal to readmit Egypt to membership of the League of Arab States, but it could not prevent the inclusion in the final communiqué of a clause permitting individual member nations to re-establish diplomatic relations with Egypt. Egypt's recognition of the newly-proclaimed Palestinian state in November 1988 gave fresh impetus to attempts to achieve a reconciliation between Egypt and Syria. These culminated in the restoration of diplomatic relations between Egypt and Syria in December 1989, and in the visit of President Muhammad Hosni Mubarak of Egypt to Damascus, the first such visit by an Egyptian head of state for more than 12 years.

In August 1990 Syria was eager to exploit the diplomatic opportunities arising from Iraq's invasion of Kuwait, earlier in the same month, and in particular to improve its relations with the USA. One major reason for this was Syria's evolving relations with the USSR. Syria signed a 20-year Treaty of Friendship and Co-operation with the USSR (a major source of military assistance) in October 1980. The continuing strength of Syrian-Soviet relations was confirmed in April 1990 by the visit of President Assad to Moscow. However, President Assad had criticized the programme of political liberalization being undertaken by the USSR, while the USSR had indicated its unwillingness to continue to underwrite Syria's attempt to achieve strategic parity with Israel.

Syria supported Egypt's efforts to co-ordinate an Arab response to Iraq's invasion of Kuwait, and agreed, at an emergency summit meeting held in Cairo in August 1990, to send troops to Saudi Arabia as part of a pan-Arab deterrent force, supporting the US effort to deter an Iraqi invasion of Saudi Arabia. Despite widespread popular support among Syria's Palestinian population for the Iraqi President, Saddam Hussain, Syria committed itself to the demand for an unconditional Iraqi withdrawal from Kuwait, and later in August the first contingent of Syrian troops was deployed in Saudi Arabia, joining a multinational force that was predominantly composed of US military personnel. In late November 1990 it became apparent that Syria's participation in the US-led multinational force was transforming its relations with the West, when diplomatic ties were restored between Syria and the United Kingdom.

In early 1991 the overwhelming military defeat of Iraq by the US-led multinational force placed Syria in a stronger position with regard to virtually all of its major regional concerns. Syria consolidated the improvement in relations with Egypt which had begun in December 1989, and laid the foundation for increased co-operation with Egypt in matters of regional security. In early March 1991 the Ministers of Foreign Affairs of the members of the Gulf Co-operation Council (Saudi Arabia, Kuwait, Qatar, Bahrain, the UAE and Oman) met the Egyptian and Syrian Ministers of Foreign Affairs in Damascus to discuss regional security issues. The formation of an Arab peace-keeping force, comprising mainly Egyptian and Syrian troops, was subsequently announced. (In early May, however, Egypt announced its decision to withdraw all of its forces from the Gulf region within three months, thus casting doubt on the future of joint Syrian-Egyptian security arrangements.) Most importantly, Syria's decision to ally itself, in opposition to Iraq, with the Western powers and the so-called 'moderate' Arab states led the USA to realize that it could no longer, as it had in the past, seek to exclude Syria from any role in the resolution of the Arab-Israeli conflict.

On 18 July 1991 President Assad agreed, for the first time (following a meeting with the US Secretary of State, James Baker), to participate in direct negotiations with Israel at a regional peace conference, for which the terms of reference would be a comprehensive peace settlement based on UN Security Council Resolutions 242 (of 1967) and 338 (1973). By agreeing to participate in a peace conference on the terms that the US Government had proposed, Syria decisively increased the diplomatic pressure on Israel to do likewise. On 4 August the Israeli Cabinet formally agreed to attend a peace conference on terms proposed by the USA and the USSR.

By May 1995—following an initial, 'symbolic' session of the conference held in Madrid, Spain, in October 1991, and attended by Israeli, Syrian, Egyptian, Lebanese and Palestinian-Jordanian delegations—a Syrian delegation had participated in 12 sessions of bilateral negotiations with an Israeli counterpart. By participating in the peace conference, Syria aimed to recover the Golan Heights, occupied by Israel since 1967; and to conclude a formal peace treaty with its principal regional rival. However, Syria emphasized that it was not prepared to achieve its national goals, by signing a separate peace agreement with Israel, at the expense of a comprehensive Middle Eastern peace settlement based on UN Security Council Resolutions 242 and 338. Initially, the Declaration of Principles on Palestinian Self-Rule in the Occupied Territories, signed by Israel and the PLO on 13 September 1993, drew a guarded response from Syria. Subsequently, however, President Assad indicated that he had serious reservations about the agreement, and that he regarded the secret negotiations between Israel and the PLO which had led to it as having weakened the united Arab position in the ongoing peace process with Israel. It appeared that Syria would not actively oppose the agreement, but there was no sign that it would cease to support those Palestinian factions, such as the Damascus-based Popular Front for the Liberation of Palestine—General Command, which had vowed to do so. Syria remained prepared to conclude a comprehensive peace settlement with Israel in return for a complete Israeli withdrawal from the Golan Heights, as it had been since the sixth round of bilateral negotiations with Israel; and was reported to fear that Israel might now view the terms of the Declaration of Principles concluded with the PLO as a model for an agreement with Syria on the Golan Heights (i.e. an exchange of only a partial withdrawal of Israeli armed forces from the Golan Heights for a comprehensive peace settlement).

In mid-January 1994 President Assad met the US President, Bill Clinton, in Geneva, Switzerland, his first such meeting with a US leader since 1977. The meeting was widely perceived as an attempt to give fresh impetus to the bilateral negotiations between Syria and Israel, and Assad was reported to have made detailed proposals regarding a peace settlement between the two countries. In late January a twelfth round of peace negotiations between Israeli, Jordanian, Syrian and Lebanese delegations commenced in Washington, DC. On 27 February, however, the Arab delegations temporarily withdrew from the negotiations in response to the murder, by a right-wing Jewish extremist, of some 50 Muslim worshippers in a mosque in Hebron on the West Bank. In early April President Assad met President Mubarak of Egypt in Cairo. There was speculation that the visit had been prompted by Syria's dissatisfaction at Egypt's support for the negotiations that were taking place between Israel and the PLO. In early May the official Syrian daily newspaper, *Ath-Thawra*, rejected the agreement between Israel and the PLO that provided for a limited Israeli withdrawal from the Occupied Territories, describing it as an obstacle to a comprehensive peace settlement. Throughout May the suspended negotiations between Syria and Israel were the target of US diplomacy, although few details of precisely how the USA sought to bring about their resumption were made public. It was reported in the Syrian press that President Assad might now be prepared to discuss a gradual withdrawal of Israeli armed forces from the Golan Heights. In early June Syria reacted warily to the signing by Jordan and Israel of so-called sub-agendas for future bilateral negotiations. Syria continued to adhere to the principle of a united Arab approach to negotiation with Israel, despite the various erosions of that position which had occurred in the wider peace process. In July and August the US Secretary of State, Warren Christopher, held further meetings with President Assad, and in September Israel published details of a plan for the partial withdrawal of its armed forces from the Golan Heights. The withdrawal was to be followed by a three-year period of normalization, after which the final point to which Israeli armed forces should withdraw was to be negotiated. However, Syria rejected the proposed partial withdrawal, although President Assad did make clear his willingness to achieve peace with Israel. In late October US President Clinton visited Damascus for talks with President Assad, in a further attempt to facilitate the resumption of talks between Syria and Israel. It was the first time in some 20 years that a US President had visited Syria. However, it was not until mid-March 1995—more than one year after their suspension—that talks between Syria and Israel finally resumed. Initially they involved only the Ambassador of each country to the USA, but were subsequently to include high-level Syrian and Israeli military delegations.

In the aftermath of Iraq's defeat by the US-led multinational force in February 1991 Syria was concerned that the USA might permit Israel to undermine, through military action, the implementation in Lebanon of the Taif agreement, which was being accelerated. The possibility of such military action arose from Syria's decision to allow Hezbollah fighters to continue to mount attacks on northern Israeli settlements, in the belief that only by continued coercion would Israel withdraw from occupied Arab territories. By the same token, the Israeli Government cited these attacks in justification of its refusal to comply with UN Security Council Resolution 425 and withdraw its forces from the southern Lebanese 'buffer zone'. In late March 1992 Syrian forces began to withdraw from Beirut, in preparation for their withdrawal to eastern Lebanon by September 1992 (in accordance with the Taif agreement). However, Syrian influence on Lebanese internal affairs remained pervasive and was regarded by some observers as having contributed to the resignation of the Lebanese Government on 6 May. The former Lebanese Prime Minister, Omar Karami, alleged that, had it not been for Lebanon's close relations with Syria, Western economic aid to Lebanon would have been more substantial, and the economic crisis that had led to his Government's resignation less severe. The decision of the Lebanese Government to hold elections to the National Assembly in August and September 1992, before the redeployment of Syrian armed forces to eastern Lebanon had taken place, attracted strong criticism both in Lebanon and abroad. Christian groups, Lebanese Maronites in particular, and Western Governments argued that the continued presence of the Syrian forces would prejudice the outcome of the elections. However, the Lebanese Government argued that its own army was still unable to guarantee the country's security in the absence of Syrian armed forces, and that the timetable for elections, as stipulated by the Taif agreement, should be observed. Syria claimed that the continued presence of its forces did not contravene the Taif agreement, which allowed for them to remain to assist the Lebanese Government until constitutional reforms had been fully implemented. There was no doubt, however, that the electoral process had been severely compromised in the eyes of Maronite Lebanese, and in many Maronite constituencies the participation of the electorate was very low. However, some Maronites adopted a more pragmatic approach, acknowledging Syria's domination of Lebanon as a *fait accompli*. In mid-1995 some 30,000 Syrian troops remained deployed in Lebanon.

There was speculation in late 1991 that President Assad was preparing to introduce a degree of liberalization into Syria's political system, which is widely regarded as one of the most autocratic in the world. In December it was announced that 2,864 political prisoners were to be released. In March 1992, in a speech to the People's Assembly, Assad indicated that new political parties might in future be established in Syria. However, he rejected the adoption by Syria of foreign democratic frameworks as unsuited to the country's level of economic development. In late June a reshuffle of the Council of Ministers took place, in which most senior ministers retained their portfolios. In January 1994 there was uncertainty as to Syria's future stability following the death, in a motor accident, of President Assad's eldest son, Basel, who had been expected to succeed his father as President. It was reported that the President's second son, Bashar, had been instructed to assume the role of his late brother in order to avoid a power struggle. In August senior government officials, including the Commander of the Special Forces, were removed from office in what was considered to be an attempt by Assad to consolidate his position and improve Syria's international standing. At elections to the People's Assembly held on 24 August, the ruling Baath Party and the parties allied to it in the National Progressive Front reinforced their dominance of Syrian affairs, winning 167 of the Assembly's total 250 seats. However, the participation of the electorate was reported to be only just over 50%. At the inaugural session of the new Assembly, on 14 November, the Prime Minister announced a programme of major economic reforms.

### Government

Under the 1973 Constitution, legislative power is vested in the unicameral People's Assembly, with 195 members (250 from May 1990) elected by universal adult suffrage. Executive power is vested in the President, elected by direct popular vote for a seven-year term. He governs with the assistance of an appointed Council of Ministers, led by the Prime Minister. Syria has 14 administrative districts (*mohafazat*).

### Defence

National service, which normally lasts 30 months, is compulsory for men. In June 1994 the regular armed forces totalled an estimated 408,000 men: an army of 300,000 (including 200,000 conscripts), an air defence command of 60,000, a navy of 8,000 and an air force of 40,000. In addition, Syria had active army reserves of 300,000, air force reserves of 92,000 and navy reserves of 8,000. Paramilitary forces comprise a gendarmerie of 8,000. It was estimated that 30,000 Syrian troops were deployed in Lebanon in mid-1994. Defence expenditure for 1994 was budgeted at £S8,700m. (US $778m.).

### Economic Affairs

In 1991, according to estimates by the World Bank, Syria's gross national product (GNP), measured at average 1989–91 prices, was US $14,607m., equivalent to $1,170 per head. During 1980–91, it was estimated, GNP increased, in real terms, at an average annual rate of 1.4%, although GNP per head declined by 2.1% per year. During 1985–93 the population increased by an annual average of 3.3%. Syria's gross domestic product (GDP) increased, in real terms, by an annual average of 3.5% in 1980–92, and by an estimated 4% in 1993.

Agriculture (including forestry and fishing) contributed an estimated 30.8% of GDP in 1993. About 23% of the working population were employed in agriculture in that year. The principal cash crops are cotton (which accounted for about 6% of export earnings in 1993) and fruit and vegetables. Agricultural production increased by an annual average of 2.1% in 1985–90. Output increased by 0.3% in 1991 and by 15.7% in 1992. It declined by 3.4% in 1993, but rose again, by 2.3%, in 1994.

Industry (including mining, manufacturing and power) contributed an estimated 14.1% (and construction 4.2%) of GDP in 1993. Industrial production (mining, manufacturing, electricity and water) increased by an annual average of 5.9% in 1980–92, and by about 2% in 1993. Of the total employed labour force (excluding foreign workers) in 1991, 14.5% were employed in industry, and a further 10.5% in construction.

Mining contributed an estimated 11.1% of GDP in 1992, and employed 0.2% of the working population (excluding foreign workers) in 1991. Crude petroleum is the major mineral export, accounting for almost 60% of total export earnings in 1993, and phosphates are also exported. Syria also has reserves of natural gas and iron ore. During 1980–91 the output of the mining sector increased at an average rate of 11.3% per year, and in 1992 by an estimated 9%.

Manufacturing contributed an estimated 4.2% of GDP in 1992, and employed 14.0% of the working population in 1991. During 1980–91 the output of the manufacturing sector increased at an average rate of 4.7% per year, and in 1992 it rose by an estimated 2%. In 1990 chemical, petroleum, coal, rubber and plastic products accounted for 29.2% of the total value of manufacturing output. Textiles, clothing, leather products and footwear contributed 23.8%, while food products, beverages and tobacco provided 28.3%.

Energy is derived principally from hydroelectric power and, to a lesser extent, petroleum. Imports of mineral fuels comprised 4.3% of the value of total imports in 1993.

In 1992 Syria recorded a visible trade surplus of US $159m. and there was a surplus of $55m. on the current account of the balance of payments. In 1993 there was a visible trade deficit of $322m. In that year the principal source of imports (10.2%) was Germany, while Italy was the principal market for exports (30.8%). Other major trading partners were France, Lebanon and Japan. The principal exports in 1993 were crude petroleum, textiles and vegetables and fruit, and the principal imports were machinery, base metals and manufactures, and transport equipment.

For 1995 the People's Assembly approved a draft budget which fixed expenditure at £S162,040m. and forecast revenue of £S125,718m. At the end of 1993 Syria's total external debt was US $19,975m., of which $16,234m. was long-term public debt. In that year the cost of servicing the debt was equivalent to 5.3% of the value of exports of goods and services. The average rate of inflation was 18.8% per year in 1980–93. The rate of inflation was 8.3% in the year to September 1994.

Syria is a member of the UN Economic and Social Commission for Western Asia (see p. 33), the Arab Fund for Economic and Social Development (see p. 237), the Arab Monetary Fund (see p. 237), the Council of Arab Economic Unity (see p. 133), the Islamic Development Bank (see p. 180) and the Organization of Arab Petroleum Exporting Countries (OAPEC) (see p. 207).

Among the problems that confronted the Syrian economy in 1995 were a trade deficit, inflationary pressure, declining consumer demand and rising unemployment. However, it was clear that economic reforms, introduced in recent years in order to lift restrictions on the private sector and establish a more market-oriented economy, had been successful. The private sector had become the main source of high economic growth and was likely to remain so in 1995, when it was planned to reform the banking sector, especially its dealings with potential investors in industry. In the long term, however, the success of the Syrian economy will depend on political factors: the conclusion of a comprehensive peace agreement with Israel; and, possibly, a degree of domestic political liberalization.

### Social Welfare

State hospitals provide free medical care for persons unable to afford private medical attention. In 1985 Syria had 195 hospital establishments, with a total of 11,891 beds. There were 8,593 physicians working in the country in 1987. Old-age pensions, and other benefits, are provided by law. The draft budget for 1992 envisaged expenditure of 1,103.1m. Syrian pounds (1.2% of total spending) on social welfare.

### Education

Primary education, which begins at six years of age and lasts for six years, is officially compulsory. In 1992 there were 2,573,181 pupils in primary education, equivalent to 97% of children in the relevant age-group. Secondary education, beginning at 12 years of age, lasts for a further six years, comprising two cycles of three years each. In 1992 there were 916,950 pupils in secondary education, equivalent to 44% of children in the relevant age-group.

There are agricultural and technical schools for vocational training, and higher education is provided by the universities of Damascus, Aleppo, Tishrin (the October University, in Latakia) and Homs (the Baath University, formerly the Homs Institute of Petroleum). There were some 170,000 students enrolled at the universities in 1995. The main language of instruction in schools is Arabic, but English and French are widely taught as second languages. In 1990, according to estimates by UNESCO, the average rate of adult illiteracy was 35.5% (males 21.7%; females 49.2%). The draft budget for 1992 allocated 7,594m. Syrian pounds (8.2% of total expenditure) to education.

### Public Holidays

**1995:** 1 January (New Year's Day), 3 March* (Id al-Fitr, end of Ramadan), 8 March (Revolution Day), 21–24 April (Greek Orthodox Easter), 10 May* (Id al-Adha, feast of the Sacrifice), 31 May* (Islamic New Year), 23 July (Egypt's Revolution Day), 9 August* (Mouloud, Birth of the Prophet), 1 September (Union of Syria, Egypt and Libya), 6 October (Beginning of October War), 16 November (National Day), 20 December* (Leilat al-Meiraj, ascension of Muhammad), 25 December (Christmas Day).

**1996:** 1 January (New Year's Day), 21 February* (Id al-Fitr, end of Ramadan), 8 March (Revolution Day), 12–15 April (Greek Orthodox Easter), 29 April* (Id al-Adha, feast of the Sacrifice), 19 May* (Islamic New Year), 23 July (Egypt's Revolution Day), 28 July* (Mouloud, Birth of the Prophet), 1 September (Union of Syria, Egypt and Libya), 6 October (Beginning of October War), 16 November (National Day), 8 December* (Leilat al-Meiraj, ascension of Muhammad), 25 December (Christmas Day).

* Islamic religious holidays may vary slightly from the dates given, depending on sightings of the moon.

### Weights and Measures

The metric system is in force.

# Statistical Survey

Source (unless otherwise stated): Central Bureau of Statistics, rue Abd al-Malek bin Marwah, Malki Quarter, Damascus; tel. (11) 335830; telex 411099.

## Area and Population

**AREA, POPULATION AND DENSITY**

| | |
|---|---:|
| Area (sq km) | |
| Land | 184,050 |
| Inland water | 1,130 |
| Total | 185,180* |
| Population (census results)† | |
| 8 September 1981 | 9,052,628 |
| 3 September 1994 | |
| Males | 7,005,385 |
| Females | 6,806,899 |
| Total | 13,812,284 |
| Density (per sq km) at 3 September 1994 | 74.6 |

* 71,498 sq miles.
† Including Palestinian refugees, numbering 193,000 at mid-1977.

**PRINCIPAL TOWNS** (estimated population at 30 June 1994)

| | | | |
|---|---:|---|---:|
| Damascus (capital) | 1,444,138 | Hama | 273,000 |
| Aleppo | 1,542,000 | Al-Kamishli | 165,242 |
| Homs | 558,000 | Rakka | 138,000 |
| Latakia | 303,000 | Deir ez-Zor | 133,000 |

**REGISTERED BIRTHS, MARRIAGES AND DEATHS**

| | Births | Marriages | Deaths |
|---|---:|---:|---:|
| 1987 | 478,136 | 102,626 | 51,581 |
| 1988 | 435,795 | 99,323 | 44,899 |
| 1989 | 421,733 | 102,557 | 45,481 |
| 1990 | 385,316 | 91,705 | 39,897 |

**Expectation of life** (years at birth, 1981): males 64.42; females 68.05
(Source: UN, *Demographic Yearbook*).

**ECONOMICALLY ACTIVE POPULATION**
(sample survey, persons aged 10 years and over, April 1991)*

| | Males | Females | Total |
|---|---:|---:|---:|
| Agriculture, hunting, forestry and fishing | 625,001 | 291,951 | 916,952 |
| Mining and quarrying | 6,651 | — | 6,651 |
| Manufacturing | 421,523 | 34,639 | 456,162 |
| Electricity, gas and water | 7,866 | 556 | 8,422 |
| Construction | 334,343 | 6,436 | 340,779 |
| Trade, restaurants and hotels | 368,955 | 9,295 | 378,250 |
| Transport, storage and communications | 158,358 | 8,607 | 166,965 |
| Financing, insurance, real estate and business services | 20,176 | 4,475 | 24,651 |
| Community, social and personal services | 767,428 | 183,676 | 951,104 |
| **Total employed** | 2,710,301 | 539,635 | 3,249,936 |
| Unemployed | 147,281 | 88,151 | 235,432 |
| **Total labour force** | 2,857,582 | 627,786 | 3,485,368 |

* Figures refer to Syrians only, excluding armed forces.
Source: ILO, *Year Book of Labour Statistics*.

## Agriculture

**PRINCIPAL CROPS** ('000 metric tons)

| | 1991 | 1992 | 1993 |
|---|---:|---:|---:|
| Wheat | 2,140 | 3,046 | 3,626 |
| Barley | 917 | 1,091 | 1,553 |
| Maize | 225 | 215 | 200 |
| Chick peas | 28 | 74 | 55 |
| Dry broad beans | 9 | 10 | 12* |
| Haricot beans | 2 | 9 | 8 |
| Lentils | 50 | 75 | 95 |
| Seed cotton | 555 | 689 | 639 |
| Tobacco | 16 | 24 | 10 |
| Sesame seed | 10 | 11 | 12 |
| Grapes | 487 | 462 | 354 |
| Olives | 226 | 519 | 325 |
| Apricots | 56 | 98 | 62 |
| Apples | 215 | 270 | 235 |
| Plums | 35 | 45 | 24 |
| Oranges | 202 | 154 | 233 |
| Almonds | 32 | 31 | 28 |
| Watermelons | 217 | 353 | 308 |
| Melons | 46 | 55 | 61 |
| Cucumbers | 143 | 158 | 160 |
| Squash | 113 | 136 | 116 |
| Sugar beet | 653 | 1,365 | 1,237 |
| Onions | 80 | 108 | 93 |
| Cabbages | 46 | 40 | 45* |
| Cauliflowers | 29 | 29 | 17 |
| Aubergines (Egg-plants) | 133 | 126 | 148 |
| Green peppers | 34 | 35 | 36 |
| Tomatoes | 428 | 481 | 395 |
| Potatoes | 452 | 413 | 396† |

* FAO estimate.   † Unofficial figure.
Source: FAO, *Production Yearbook*.

**LIVESTOCK** ('000 head, year ending September)

| | 1991 | 1992 | 1993* |
|---|---:|---:|---:|
| Cattle | 771 | 765 | 770 |
| Horses | 39 | 37 | 38 |
| Camels | 5 | 3 | 3 |
| Asses | 161 | 158 | 160 |
| Mules | 25 | 27 | 27 |
| Sheep | 15,194 | 14,665 | 16,000 |
| Goats | 963 | 951 | 950 |

Chickens (million): 15 in 1991; 18* in 1992; 18* in 1993.
* FAO estimate(s).
Source: FAO, *Production Yearbook*.

**LIVESTOCK PRODUCTS** ('000 metric tons)

| | 1991 | 1992 | 1993* |
|---|---:|---:|---:|
| Beef and veal | 33 | 29 | 30 |
| Mutton and lamb | 124 | 113 | 115 |
| Goat meat | 5 | 5 | 5 |
| Poultry meat | 68 | 90 | 92 |
| Cows' milk | 333 | 329 | 333 |
| Sheep's milk | 513 | 512 | 515 |
| Goats' milk | 58 | 62 | 64 |
| Butter and ghee | 16.2 | 16.0 | 17.0 |
| Cheese | 75.0 | 72.0 | 75.0 |
| Hen eggs† | 80.5 | 99.2 | 100.0 |
| Wool: | | | |
| greasy | 33.2 | 35.1 | 34.0 |
| clean | 17.0 | 18.0 | 18.0 |

* FAO estimates.   † Unofficial figures.
Source: FAO, *Production Yearbook*.

SYRIA

## Forestry

**ROUNDWOOD REMOVALS** ('000 cubic metres, excl. bark)

|  | 1990 | 1991 | 1992 |
|---|---|---|---|
| Sawlogs, veneer logs and logs for sleepers | 22 | 44 | 51 |
| Other industrial wood* | 19 | 19 | 19 |
| Fuel wood | 13 | 23 | 25 |
| **Total** | 54 | 86 | 95 |

* FAO estimates.

Sawnwood production ('000 cubic metres): 9 in 1980; 9 per year (FAO estimates) in 1981–92.

Source: FAO, *Yearbook of Forest Products*.

## Fishing

('000 metric tons, live weight)

|  | 1990 | 1991 | 1992* |
|---|---|---|---|
| Inland waters | 4.2 | 4.0 | 3.9 |
| Mediterranean sea | 1.6 | 1.5* | 1.5 |
| **Total catch** | 5.8 | 5.5* | 5.4 |

* FAO estimates.

Source: FAO, *Yearbook of Fishery Statistics*.

## Mining

('000 metric tons, unless otherwise indicated)

|  | 1990 | 1991 | 1992* |
|---|---|---|---|
| Crude petroleum ('000 cubic metres) | 23,474 | 27,276 | 29,763 |
| Phosphate rock | 1,633 | 1,469 | 1,265 |
| Salt (unrefined) | 127 | 74 | 84 |
| Natural asphalt | 71 | 67 | 72 |

* Figures are provisional.

Source: Central Bank of Syria, *Quarterly Bulletin*.

## Industry

**SELECTED PRODUCTS** ('000 metric tons, unless otherwise indicated)

|  | 1991 | 1992 | 1993 |
|---|---|---|---|
| Cotton yarn (pure) | 39 | 38 | 33 |
| Silk and cotton textiles | 28 | 26 | 29 |
| Woollen cloth (metric tons) | 616 | 498 | 660 |
| Cement | 2,843 | 3,246 | 3,667 |
| Glass and pottery products | 54 | 53 | 57 |
| Soap | 16 | 17 | 17 |
| Refined sugar | 179 | 178 | 183 |
| Margarine | 9 | 9 | 7 |
| Olive oil | 39 | 103 | 60 |
| Vegetable oil and fats | 28 | 29 | 22 |
| Cottonseed cake | 120 | 162 | 200 |
| Manufactured tobacco | 8 | 8 | 7 |
| Electricity (million kWh) | 11,249 | 11,626 | 11,709 |
| Refrigerators ('000) | 84.7 | 128.8 | 150.5 |
| Washing machines ('000) | 29.2 | 40.9 | 46.7 |
| Beer ('000 hectolitres) | 99 | 103 | 104 |
| Wine ('000 hectolitres) | 3 | 2.4 | 3 |
| Arak ('000 hectolitres) | 19 | 20 | 23 |

## Finance

**CURRENCY AND EXCHANGE RATES**

**Monetary Units**
100 piastres = 1 Syrian pound (£S).

**Sterling and Dollar Equivalents** (31 December 1994)
£1 sterling = £S17.562;
US $1 = £S11.225;
£S1,000 = £56.94 sterling = $89.09.

**Exchange Rate**
Between April 1976 and December 1987 the official mid-point rate was fixed at US $1 = £S3.925. On 1 January 1988 a new rate of $1 = £S11.225 was introduced. In addition to the official exchange rate, there is a promotion rate (applicable to most travel and tourism transactions) and a flexible rate.

**BUDGET** (estimates, £S million)

| Revenue | 1991 | 1992 | 1993 |
|---|---|---|---|
| Taxes and duties | 27,720.0 | 29,408.2 | 29,488.6 |
| Services, commutations and revenues from state properties and their public investments | 3,453.8 | 4,857.5 | 5,658.0 |
| Various revenues | 26,762.0 | 36,815.9 | 35,197.0 |
| Supply surplus | 13,078.1 | 16,126.8 | 18,504.5 |
| Exceptional revenues | 13,676.4 | 5,833.8 | 34,169.9 |
| **Total** | 84,690.3 | 93,042.2 | 123,018.0 |

| Expenditure | 1991 | 1992 | 1993 |
|---|---|---|---|
| Community, social and personal services | 64,120.8 | 63,330.4 | 71,816.7 |
| Agriculture, forestry and fishing | 7,912.9 | 10,192.8 | 12,229.8 |
| Mining and quarrying | 1,697.9 | 2,683.5 | 3,197.4 |
| Manufacturing | 2,020.5 | 3,953.6 | 10,941.2 |
| Electricity, gas and water | 3,020.3 | 4,934.2 | 12,671.0 |
| Building and construction | 289.2 | 911.2 | 203.9 |
| Trade | 867.5 | 1,226.5 | 1,470.7 |
| Transport, communications and storage | 3,156.2 | 3,920.8 | 8,097.0 |
| Finance, insurance and companies | 355.0 | 638.7 | 530.3 |
| Non-distributed funds | 1,250.0 | 1,250.0 | 1,850.0 |
| **Total** | 84,690.3 | 93,042.2 | 123,008.0 |

**CENTRAL BANK RESERVES** (US $ million at 31 December)

|  | 1986 | 1987 | 1988 |
|---|---|---|---|
| Gold* | 29 | 29 | 29 |
| Foreign exchange | 144 | 223 | 193 |
| **Total** | 173 | 252 | 222 |

* Valued at $35 per troy ounce.

Source: IMF, *International Financial Statistics*.

**MONEY SUPPLY** (£S million at 31 December)

|  | 1990 | 1991 | 1992 |
|---|---|---|---|
| Currency outside banks | 76,202.0 | 92,450.1 | 107,556.6 |
| Demand deposits at Central Bank | 6,627.0 | 11,840.5 | 21,227.2 |
| Demand deposits at commercial banks | 35,745.5 | 41,972.8 | 53,341.0 |
| **Total money** | 118,574.5 | 146,263.4 | 182,124.8 |

Source: Central Bank of Syria, *Quarterly Bulletin*.

# SYRIA

## COST OF LIVING
(Consumer Price Index for Damascus; base: 1980 = 100)

|  | 1990 | 1991 | 1992 |
|---|---|---|---|
| Food | 795.5 | 823.9 | 851.6 |
| Fuel and light | 493.7 | 544.7 | 766.8 |
| Clothing | 769.9 | 906.5 | 952.9 |
| Rent | 281.8 | 282.3 | 282.3 |
| **All items** (incl. others) | 715.4 | 770.2 | 843.5 |

Source: ILO, *Year Book of Labour Statistics*.

**1993:** Food 962.9; All items 942.5 (Source: UN, *Monthly Bulletin of Statistics*).

## NATIONAL ACCOUNTS (£S million at current prices)
### Expenditure on the Gross Domestic Product

|  | 1991 | 1992 | 1993* |
|---|---|---|---|
| Government final consumption expenditure | 47,582 | 53,588 | 57,459 |
| Private final consumption expenditure | 23,883 | 273,196 | 294,417 |
| Gross capital formation | 55,992 | 86,120 | 102,633 |
| **Total domestic expenditure** | 335,457 | 412,904 | 454,509 |
| Exports of goods and services | 76,038 | 97,577 | 113,985 |
| *Less* Imports of goods and services | 99,931 | 139,850 | 169,979 |
| **GDP in purchasers' values** | 311,564 | 370,631 | 398,515 |
| **GDP at constant 1985 prices** | 95,883 | 105,997 | 110,151 |

* Provisional figures.

### Gross Domestic Product by Economic Activity

|  | 1991 | 1992 | 1993* |
|---|---|---|---|
| Agriculture, hunting, forestry and fishing | 94,378 | 116,163 | 122,742 |
| Mining and quarrying | | | |
| Manufacturing | 56,856 | 53,152 | 56,348 |
| Electricity, gas and water | | | |
| Construction | 12,169 | 13,713 | 16,750 |
| Trade, restaurants and hotels | 67,003 | 95,407 | 101,294 |
| Transport, storage and communications | 30,696 | 34,513 | 38,565 |
| Finance, insurance, real estate and business services | 10,984 | 12,463 | 14,588 |
| Government services | 33,334 | 38,006 | 39,936 |
| Other community, social and personal services | 6,026 | 7,074 | 8,137 |
| Non-profit private services | 118 | 135 | 155 |
| **GDP in purchasers' values** | 311,564 | 370,631 | 398,515 |

* Provisional figures.

Source: Central Bank of Syria, *Quarterly Bulletin*.

## BALANCE OF PAYMENTS (US $ million)

|  | 1990 | 1991 | 1992 |
|---|---|---|---|
| Merchandise exports f.o.b. | 4,156 | 3,438 | 3,100 |
| Merchandise imports f.o.b. | −2,062 | −2,354 | −2,941 |
| **Trade balance** | 2,094 | 1,084 | 159 |
| Exports of services | 874 | 1,065 | 1,281 |
| Imports of services | −892 | −1,002 | −1,102 |
| Other income received | 45 | 65 | 69 |
| Other income paid | −831 | −1,096 | −1,214 |
| Private unrequited transfers (net) | 385 | 350 | 550 |
| Official unrequited transfers (net) | 88 | 234 | 313 |
| **Current balance** | 1,762 | 699 | 55 |
| Capital (net) | −1,836 | −515 | −50 |
| Net errors and omissions | 110 | −112 | 70 |
| **Overall balance** | 36 | 72 | 76 |

Source: IMF, *International Financial Statistics*.

# External Trade

## PRINCIPAL COMMODITIES (£S million)

| Imports c.i.f. | 1991 | 1992 | 1993 |
|---|---|---|---|
| Cotton textiles, other textile goods and silk | 2,421.2 | 2,941.5 | 3,920.6 |
| Mineral fuels and oils | 737.2 | 1,519.6 | 2,018.2 |
| Live animals, meat and canned meat | 2,932.9 | 1,384.5 | 1,413.1 |
| Vegetables and fruit | 766.4 | 291.6 | 338.4 |
| Sugar | 1,179.1 | 1,113.6 | 1,202.3 |
| Other foodstuffs | 5,042.5 | 4,213.0 | 4,810.5 |
| Machinery and apparatus | 4,631.0 | 6,989.5 | 9,960.0 |
| Base metals and manufactures | 3,323.9 | 5,776.0 | 6,355.3 |
| Chemicals and pharmaceutical products | 3,808.6 | 3,846.7 | 3,859.2 |
| Transport equipment | 2,034.7 | 5,153.6 | 5,797.1 |
| Paper and paper products | 899.1 | 734.7 | 817.4 |
| Wood and wood products | 298.5 | 562.0 | 746.1 |
| Resins, artificial rubber, etc. | 1,681.6 | 2,144.1 | 2,209.1 |
| **Total** (incl. others) | 30,794.4 | 39,178.3 | 46,468.9 |

| Exports f.o.b. | 1991 | 1992 | 1993 |
|---|---|---|---|
| Raw cotton | 1,920.8 | 1,912.0 | 1,955.8 |
| Textiles | 8,985.7 | 2,441.0 | 3,167.7 |
| Vegetables and fruit (fresh and prepared) | 2,388.1 | 2,615.0 | 3,154.0 |
| Live animals and meat | 1,391.6 | 1,305.0 | 1,052.3 |
| Lentils | 134.2 | 113.8 | 33.6 |
| Wool | 43.9 | 28.9 | 17.6 |
| Raw hides and leather | 109.4 | 194.2 | 243.2 |
| Phosphates | 394.4 | 488.0 | 172.8 |
| Crude petroleum | 17,217.8 | 20,773.5 | 21,007.2 |
| **Total** (incl. others) | 38,504.0 | 34,719.8 | 35,318.0 |

## PRINCIPAL TRADING PARTNERS (£S million)

| Imports c.i.f. | 1991 | 1992 | 1993 |
|---|---|---|---|
| Austria | 495.3 | 482.3 | 484.4 |
| Belgium | 1,062.6 | 1,240.7 | 1,566.8 |
| Bulgaria | 866.5 | 1,677.4 | 1,335.5 |
| China, People's Republic | 632.3 | 1,045.7 | 1,054.6 |
| Czechoslovakia | 377.1 | 620.6 | 712.5 |
| Egypt | 295.1 | 481.4 | 611.0 |
| France | 2,090.5 | 2,479.4 | 3,290.7 |
| Germany | 3,130.0 | 4,006.1 | 4,730.0 |
| Greece | 427.7 | 307.2 | 391.9 |
| Hungary | 286.4 | 357.3 | 513.3 |
| Iran | 16.9 | 135.4 | 215.3 |
| Italy | 2,257.1 | 3,208.4 | 3,818.2 |
| Japan | 1,403.8 | 3,899.6 | 3,798.4 |
| Lebanon | 330.4 | 519.4 | 733.4 |
| Netherlands | 793.3 | 1,137.2 | n.a. |
| Poland | 477.3 | 319.3 | 405.6 |
| Romania | 831.2 | 1,698.2 | 2,084.5 |
| Russia | 417.8 | 825.8 | 1,635.3 |
| Saudi Arabia | 411.6 | 465.1 | 530.5 |
| Spain | 552.3 | 443.3 | 610.1 |
| Sweden | 693.7 | 500.4 | 520.8 |
| Turkey | 2,851.7 | 2,431.8 | 2,519.4 |
| United Kingdom | 810.8 | 1,154.8 | 1,247.8 |
| USA | 2,907.8 | 2,397.1 | 2,992.7 |
| Yugoslavia | 672.2 | 230.6 | 171.8 |
| **Total** (incl. others) | 30,794.4 | 39,178.3 | 46,468.9 |

SYRIA

| Exports f.o.b. | 1991 | 1992 | 1993 |
|---|---|---|---|
| Bulgaria | 892.6 | 829.2 | 343.9 |
| France | 6,811.3 | 6,446.0 | 5,400.4 |
| Germany | 1,135.1 | 853.2 | 390.6 |
| Italy | 8,622.6 | 12,163.7 | 10,861.4 |
| Jordan | 768.4 | 581.7 | 820.6 |
| Kuwait | 188.3 | 692.1 | 629.0 |
| Lebanon | 3,695.2 | 4,516.3 | 3,717.8 |
| Netherlands | 627.8 | 244.9 | 579.4 |
| Romania | 677.3 | 378.0 | 252.8 |
| Russia | 7,259.6 | 534.0 | 984.0 |
| Saudi Arabia | 2,238.4 | 1,498.1 | 1,729.2 |
| Spain | 264.2 | 1,232.1 | 2,740.4 |
| Turkey | 1,036.4 | 482.0 | 761.8 |
| United Kingdom | 729.3 | 647.0 | 1,144.8 |
| USA | 208.5 | 273.6 | 674.6 |
| **Total** (incl. others) | 38,503.9 | 34,719.8 | 35,318.0 |

## Transport

**RAILWAYS** (traffic)

|  | 1988 | 1989 | 1990 |
|---|---|---|---|
| Passenger-km ('000) | 1,132,804 | 1,112,657 | 1,139,926 |
| Freight ('000 metric tons) | 5,992 | 5,341 | 5,236 |

**ROAD TRAFFIC** (motor vehicles in use)

|  | 1991 | 1992 | 1993 |
|---|---|---|---|
| Passenger cars | 113,347 | 111,906 | 125,807 |
| Buses and coaches | 13,549 | 16,100 | 23,972 |
| Lorries, trucks, etc. | 121,867 | 136,733 | 162,394 |
| Motor cycles | 82,165 | 85,473 | 80,533 |

**SHIPPING**

|  | 1991 | 1992 | 1993 |
|---|---|---|---|
| Vessels entered (number) | 2,446 | 2,836 | 3,316 |
| Cargo unloaded ('000 tons) | 4,968 | 5,676 | 5,086 |
| Cargo loaded ('000 tons) | 17,755 | 17,872 | 18,600 |

**CIVIL AVIATION** (traffic on scheduled services)

|  | 1989 | 1990 | 1991 |
|---|---|---|---|
| Kilometres flown (million) | 9 | 10 | 11 |
| Passengers carried ('000) | 456 | 613 | 661 |
| Passenger-km (million) | 797 | 1,105 | 1,136 |
| Freight ton-km (million) | 10 | 18 | 14 |

Source: UN, *Statistical Yearbook*.

## Tourism

**VISITOR ARRIVALS** ('000 visitors)

|  | 1991 | 1992 | 1993 |
|---|---|---|---|
| Jordanians, Lebanese and Iraqis | 923 | 982 | 1,119 |
| Other Arabs | 210 | 255 | 294 |
| Europeans | 54 | 68 | 79 |
| Asians | 340 | 357 | 322 |
| Others | 43 | 77 | 96 |
| **Total visitors** | 1,570 | 1,739 | 1,910 |

**Tourist Accommodation:** 30,249 tourist hotel beds (1993).

## Communications Media

|  | 1990 | 1991 | 1992 |
|---|---|---|---|
| Radio receivers ('000 in use) | 3,150 | 3,270 | 3,392 |
| Television receivers ('000 in use) | 740 | 770 | 810 |

Source: UNESCO, *Statistical Yearbook*.

## Education

|  | Teachers ||| Pupils |||
|---|---|---|---|---|---|---|
|  | 1990/91 | 1991/92 | 1992/93 | 1990/91 | 1991/92 | 1992/93 |
| Pre-primary | 3,122 | 3,257 | 3,922 | 83,552 | 86,006 | 90,439 |
| Primary | 97,811 | 102,617 | 106,164 | 2,452,086 | 2,539,081 | 2,573,181 |
| Secondary: |  |  |  |  |  |  |
| General | 44,875 | 46,218 | 47,889 | 847,783 | 849,530 | 845,631 |
| Vocational | 9,240 | 8,811 | 10,770 | 66,467 | 53,289 | 71,319 |

Source: UNESCO, *Statistical Yearbook*.

# Directory

## The Constitution

A new and permanent constitution was endorsed by 97.6% of the voters in a national referendum on 12 March 1973. The 157-article Constitution defines Syria as a 'Socialist popular democracy' with a 'pre-planned Socialist economy'. Under the new Constitution, Lt-Gen. al-Assad remained President, with the power to appoint and dismiss his Vice-President, Premier and government ministers, and also became Commander-in-Chief of the armed forces, Secretary-General of the Baath Socialist Party and President of the National Progressive Front. Legislative power is vested in the People's Assembly, with 250 members elected by universal adult suffrage (84 seats are reserved for independent candidates).

## The Government

### HEAD OF STATE

**President:** Lt-Gen. HAFIZ AL-ASSAD (elected 12 March 1971 for a seven-year term; re-elected 8 February 1978, 10 February 1985 and 2 December 1991).

**Vice-Presidents:** ABD AL-HALIM KHADDAM (responsible for Political and Foreign Affairs), RIFAAT AL-ASSAD (responsible for Military and National Security Affairs*), ZUHEIR MASHARKAH (responsible for Internal and Party Affairs).

* Reportedly resigned from all official posts in April 1988.

### COUNCIL OF MINISTERS
(June 1995)

**Prime Minister:** MAHMOUD AZ-ZOUBI.
**Deputy Prime Minister and Minister of Defence:** Gen. MUSTAFA TLASS.
**Deputy Prime Minister in charge of Public Services:** RASHID AKHTARINI.
**Deputy Prime Minister in charge of Economic Affairs:** SALIM YASSIN.
**Minister of Foreign Affairs:** FAROUK ASH-SHARA'.
**Minister of Information:** MUHAMMAD SALMAN.
**Minister of the Interior:** Dr MUHAMMAD HARBAH.
**Minister of Supply and Internal Trade:** NADIM AKKASH.
**Minister of Local Government:** YAHYA ABU ASALAH.
**Minister of Education:** GHASSAN HALABI.
**Minister of Higher Education:** Dr SALIHAH SANQAR.
**Minister of Electricity:** MUNIB ASAAD SAIM AL-DAHER.
**Minister of Culture:** Dr NAJAH AL-ATTAR.
**Minister of Transport:** Dr MUFID ABD AL-KARIM.
**Minister of Economy and Foreign Trade:** Dr MUHAMMAD AL-IMADI.
**Minister of Petroleum and Mineral Wealth:** Dr NADIR AN-NABULSI.
**Minister of Industry:** Dr AHMAD NIZAM AD-DIN.
**Minister of Finance:** KHALID AL-MAHAYNI.
**Minister of Housing and Utilities:** Eng. HUSAM AS-SAFADI.
**Minister of Justice:** Dr ABDULLAH TULBAH.
**Minister of Agriculture and Agrarian Reform:** ASSAD MUSTAFA.
**Minister of Irrigation, Public Works and Water Resources:** Eng. ABD AR-RAHMAN MADANI.
**Minister of Communications:** Eng. RADWAN MARTINI.
**Minister of Health:** Dr IYAD ASH-SHATTI.
**Minister of Construction:** MAJID IZZU RUHAYBANI.
**Minister of Awqaf (Islamic Endowments):** ABD AL-MAJID AT-TARABULSI.
**Minister of Tourism:** AMIN ABU ASH-SHAMAT.
**Minister of Labour and Social Affairs:** ALI KHALIL.
**Minister of State for Presidential Affairs:** WAHIB FADEL.
**Minister of State for Council of Ministers Affairs:** DANHU DAOUD.
**Minister of State for Planning Affairs:** Dr ABD AR-RAHIM SUBAYI.
**Minister of State for Environmental Affairs:** ABD AL-HAMID AL-MOUNAJJID.
**Minister of State for Foreign Affairs:** NASIR QADDOUR.
**Ministers of State:** Eng. YOUSUF AL-AHMAD, HUSSEIN HASSUN, NABIL MALLAH, Eng. HANNA MURAD.

### MINISTRIES

**Office of the President:** Damascus.
**Office of the Prime Minister:** Damascus.
**Ministry of Agriculture and Agrarian Reform:** 29 rue Ayar, Damascus; tel. (11) 113613.
**Ministry of Communications:** nr Majlis ash-Sha'ab, Damascus; telex 411993.
**Ministry of Economy and Foreign Trade:** Damascus; tel. (11) 113513; telex 411982.
**Ministry of Electricity:** BP 4900, 41 rue al-Jamhourieh, Damascus; tel. (11) 227981; telex 411256.
**Ministry of Finance:** POB 13136, Jule Jamal St, Damascus; tel. (11) 2239624; telex 411932; fax (11) 2224701.
**Ministry of Foreign Affairs:** Damascus; telex 411922.
**Ministry of Industry:** place Yousuf Ahmad, Damascus; tel. (11) 115647.
**Ministry of Information:** ave al-Mazzeh, Imm. Dar al-Baath, Damascus; tel. (11) 6664600.
**Ministry of Petroleum and Mineral Wealth:** rue Moutanabbi, Damascus; tel. (11) 116783; telex 411006.
**Ministry of Public Works and Water Resources:** rue Saadallah Jabri, Damascus.
**Ministry of Supply and Internal Trade:** opposite Majlis ash-Sha'ab, Damascus; tel. (11) 720604; telex 412908; fax (11) 2219803.
**Ministry of Tourism:** rue Victoria, Damascus; tel. (11) 2215916; telex 411672; fax (11) 2242636.
**Ministry of Transport:** BP 134, rue Abou Roumaneh, Damascus; tel. (11) 336801; telex 411994.

## Legislature

### MAJLIS ASH-SHA'AB
(People's Assembly)

**Speaker:** ABD AL-QADIR QADDURAH.

**Election, 24 August 1994**

| Party | Seats |
| --- | --- |
| Baath Party | 135 |
| Arab Socialist Unionist Party | 7 |
| Syrian Arab Socialist Union Party | 7 |
| Arab Socialist Party | 6 |
| Socialist Unionist Democratic Party | 4 |
| Communist Party | 8 |
| Independents | 83 |
| **Total** | **250** |

## Political Organizations

The **National Progressive Front**, headed by President Assad, was formed in March 1972 by the grouping of the following five parties:

**Arab Socialist Party:** Damascus; a breakaway socialist party; contested the 1994 election to the People's Assembly as two factions; Leader ABD AL-GHANI KANNOUT.

**Arab Socialist Unionist Party:** Damascus; Leader SAMI SOUFAN; Sec.-Gen. FAYIZ ISMAIL.

**Baath Arab Socialist Party:** National Command, BP 849, Damascus; Arab nationalist socialist party; f. 1947; result of merger of the Arab Revival (Baath) Movement (f. 1940) and the Arab Socialist Party (f. 1940); brs in most Arab countries; in power since 1963; supports creation of a unified Arab socialist society; Sec.-Gen. Pres. HAFIZ AL-ASSAD; Asst Sec.-Gen. ABDULLAH AL-AHMAR; Regional Asst Sec.-Gen. Dr SULEIMAN QADDAH; more than 800,000 mems in Syria.

**Communist Party of Syria:** Damascus; tel. (11) 448243; f. 1924; until 1943 part of joint Communist Party of Syria and Lebanon; Sixth Party Congress January 1987; contested the 1994 election to the People's Assembly as two factions; Sec.-Gen. YOUSUF FAISAL.

**Syrian Arab Socialist Union Party:** Damascus; tel. (11) 239305; Nasserite; Leader Dr JAMAL ATASI; Sec.-Gen. SAFWAN KOUDSI.

A sixth party, the **Socialist Unionist Democratic Party**, contested the elections held to the People's Assembly in May 1990 and August 1994 as a member of the National Progressive Front. There is also a **Marxist-Leninist Communist Action Party**, which regards itself as independent of all Arab regimes.

## Diplomatic Representation

### EMBASSIES IN SYRIA

**Afghanistan:** Immeuble Muhammad Amin Abd ar-Rabou, 2nd Floor, rue al-Bizan, West Malki; tel. (11) 713103; Ambassador: ABDUL JALIL PORSHOR.

**Algeria:** Raouda, Immeuble Noss, Damascus; telex 411344; Ambassador: SALEM BOUJOUMAA.

**Argentina:** BP 116, Raouda, rue Ziad ben Abi Soufian, Damascus; telex 411058; Ambassador: ANDRÉS GABRIEL CEUSTERMANS.

**Australia:** Immeuble Dakkak, 128A rue Farabi, East Villas, Mezzeh, Damascus; tel. (11) 6664317; telex 419132; fax (11) 8621195; Ambassador: PAUL ROBILLIARD.

**Austria:** BP 5634, Raouda, rue Chafik Mouayed, Immeuble Sabri Malki, Damascus; tel. (11) 3337528; telex 411389; fax (11) 3329232; Ambassador: Dr ROBERT KARAS.

**Belgium:** rue Ata Ayoubi, Immeuble Hachem, Damascus; tel. (11) 3332821; telex 411090; fax (11) 3330426; Ambassador: MICHEL LASTCHENKO.

**Brazil:** BP 2219, 76 rue Ata Ayoubi, Damascus; telex 411204; Ambassador: LUIZ CLAUDIO PEREIRA CARDOSA.

**Bulgaria:** 4 rue Chahbandar, Damascus; Ambassador: GEORGI YANKOV.

**Canada:** POB 3394, Lot 12, Autostrade Mezzeh, Damascus; tel. (11) 2236892; telex 412422; fax (11) 2228034; Ambassador: JOHN A. MCNEE.

**Chile:** BP 3561, 43 rue ar-Rachid, Damascus; tel. (11) 3338443; telex 411392; fax (11) 3331563; Chargé d'affaires a.i.: ALFREDO LABBÉ.

**China, People's Republic:** 83 rue Ata Ayoubi, Damascus; Ambassador: LI QINGYU.

**Cuba:** 40 rue ar-Rachid, Immeuble Oustwani and Charabati, Damascus; tel. (11) 3339624; telex 419155; fax (11) 3333802; Ambassador: ERNESTO GÓMEZ ABASCAL.

**Cyprus:** BP 3853, Abd al-Malek al-Marouan, Jaded ar-Rais, Abou Roumaneh, Damascus; tel. (11) 332804; telex 411411; Ambassador: NICOLAS MACRIS.

**Czech Republic:** place Abou al-Ala'a al-Maari, Damascus.

**Denmark:** BP 2244, Immeuble Patriarcat Grec-Catholique, rue Chekib Arslan, Abou Roumaneh, Damascus; tel. (11) 3331008; telex 419125; fax (11) 3337928; Ambassador: CHRISTIAN OLDENBURG.

**Egypt:** Damascus; Ambassador: MOUSTAFA ABD AL-AZIZ.

**Ethiopia:** Damascus; Ambassador: ABD AL-MONEM AHMAD.

**Finland:** BP 3893, Hawakir, Immeuble Yacoubian, West Malki, Damascus; tel. (11) 3338809; telex 411491; fax (11) 3734740; Ambassador: ARTO KURITTU.

**France:** BP 769, rue Ata Ayoubi, Damascus; tel. (11) 247992; telex 411013; Ambassador: JEAN-CLAUDE COUSSERAN.

**Germany:** BP 2237, 53 rue Ibrahim Hanano, Immeuble Kotob, Damascus; tel. (11) 3323800; telex 411065; fax (11) 3323812; Ambassador: THOMAS TRÖMEL.

**Greece:** 1 rue Farabi, Immeuble Tello, Mezzeh, Damascus; tel. (11) 244031; telex 411045; Ambassador: GEORGE CONSTANTIS.

**Holy See:** BP 2271, 82 rue Masr, Damascus (Apostolic Nunciature); tel. (11) 3332601; telex 412824; fax (11) 3327550; Apostolic Nuncio: Most Rev. PIER GIACOMO DE NICOLÒ, Titular Archbishop of Martana.

**Hungary:** BP 2607, 102 rue al-Fursan (Villas Eastern), al-Akram, Damascus; tel. (11) 3337966; telex 419151; fax (11) 6667917; Ambassador: LÁSZLÓ KÁDÁR.

**India:** 40/46 ave Adnan al-Malki, Immeuble Noueilati, Damascus; tel. (11) 718203; telex 411377; fax (11) 713294; Ambassador: R. N. MULYE.

**Indonesia:** 19 rue al-Amir Ezz ed-Din, Damascus; tel. (11) 3331238; telex 419188; fax (11) 3331485; Ambassador: WIDODO ATMOSUTIRTO.

**Iran:** Mezzeh Outostrade, nr ar-Razi Hospital, Damascus; telex 411041; Ambassador: Hojatoleslam MUHAMMAD HASSAN AKHTARI.

**Italy:** 82 ave al-Mansour, Damascus; Ambassador: RAFFAELE BERLENGHI.

**Japan:** 15 ave al-Jala'a, Damascus; tel. (11) 339421; telex 411042; Ambassador: RYUJI ONODERA.

**Jordan:** rue Abou Roumaneh, Damascus; telex 419161; Ambassador: ALI KHURAIS.

**Korea, Democratic People's Republic:** rue Fares al-Khouri-Jisr Tora, Damascus; Ambassador: PAK UI CHUN.

**Kuwait:** rue Ibrahim Hanano, Damascus; telex 419172; Ambassador: AHMAD ABD AL-AZIZ AL-JASSEM.

**Libya:** 36/37 Abou Roumaneh, Damascus; Head of People's Bureau: AHMAD ABD AS-SALAM BIN KHAYAL.

**Mauritania:** ave al-Jala'a, rue Karameh, Damascus; telex 411264; Ambassador: MUHAMMAD MAHMOUD OULD WEDDADY.

**Morocco:** Damascus; Ambassador: IDRIFF DHAHAQ.

**Netherlands:** POB 702, Immeuble Tello, rue al-Jalaa, Abou Roumaneh, Damascus; tel. (11) 3335119; telex 411032; fax (11) 3339369; Ambassador: R. H. MEYS.

**Oman:** Damascus.

**Pakistan:** BP 9284, rue al-Farabi, East Villat, Damascus; tel. (11) 662391; telex 412629; Ambassador: S. AZMAT HASSAN.

**Panama:** BP 2548, Malki, rue al-Bizm, Immeuble az-Zein, Apt 7, Damascus; tel. (11) 224743; telex 411918; Chargé d'affaires: CARLOS A. DE GRACIA.

**Poland:** BP 501, 21 rue Mehdi Ben Barakeh, Damascus; tel. (11) 333010; telex 412288; fax (11) 333010; Ambassador: KRZYSZTOF BALIŃSKI.

**Qatar:** BP 4188, Abou Roumaneh, place Madfa, Immeuble Allawi No. 20, Damascus; tel. (11) 336717; telex 411064; Ambassador: FAHD FAHD AL-KHATER.

**Romania:** BP 4454, rue Ibrahim Hanano No. 8, Damascus; tel. (11) 3327570; telex 411305; fax (11) 3327571; Ambassador: DORU PANA.

**Russia:** Boustan al-Kouzbari, rue d'Alep, Damascus; telex 411221; Ambassador: ALEKSANDR IVANOVICH ZOTOV.

**Saudi Arabia:** ave al-Jala'a, Damascus; telex 411906; Ambassador: ABDULLAH BIN SALEH AL-FADL.

**Slovakia:** POB 33115, place Mezza, East Villas, rue ash-Shafei, Damascus; tel. (11) 6669043; telex 412054; fax (11) 6616714; Chargé d'affaires a.i.: JOZEF MARHEFKA.

**Somalia:** ave Ata Ayoubi, Damascus; telex 419194; Ambassador: (vacant).

**Spain:** 81 ave al-Jala'a, Immeuble Sawaf, Damascus; telex 411253; Ambassador: JESÚS RIOSALIDO.

**Sudan:** Damascus; telex 411266.

**Sweden:** BP 4266, rue Chakib Arslan, Abou Roumaneh, Damascus; tel. (11) 3327261; telex 411339; fax (11) 3327749; Ambassador: STIG ELVEMAR.

**Switzerland:** Immeuble Chora, rue al-Mehdi ben Baraka, Damascus; tel. (11) 3311870; telex 411016; fax (11) 3321137; Ambassador: Dr KURT O. WYSS.

**Tunisia:** BP 4114, Villa Ouest, Jaddat Chafei, No. 6 Mezzeh, Damascus; tel. (11) 660356; telex 431302; Ambassador: MUHAMMAD CHERIF.

**Turkey:** 56–58 ave Ziad bin Abou Soufian, Damascus; tel. (11) 331370; Ambassador: ERHAN TUNÇEL.

**United Arab Emirates:** rue Raouda No. 62, Immeuble Housami, Damascus; telex 411213; Ambassador: SALIM RASHID AL-AQROUBI.

**United Kingdom:** POB 37, Damascus; tel. (11) 712561; telex 411049; fax (11) 713592; Ambassador: ADRIAN SINDALL.

**USA:** BP 29, rue al-Mansour 2, Damascus; tel. (11) 333052; telex 411919; fax (11) 718687; Ambassador: CHRISTOPHER W. S. ROSS.

**Venezuela:** BP 2403, Abou Roumaneh, Immeuble Tabbah, rue Zuheir Bin Abi Sulma, Damascus; tel. (11) 3335356; telex 411929; fax (11) 3333203; Ambassador: JOSÉ MIGUEL QUINTANA GUEVARA.

**Viet Nam:** 9 ave Malki, Damascus; tel. (11) 333008; Ambassador: LE THANH TAM.

**Yemen:** Abou Roumaneh, Charkassieh, Damascus; Ambassador: ABDULLAH HUSSAIN BARAKAT.

**Yugoslavia:** POB 739, ave al-Jala'a, Damascus; tel. (11) 336222; telex 412646; fax (11) 333690; Ambassador: RADMILO TROJANOVIĆ.

## Judicial System

The Courts of Law in Syria are principally divided into two juridical court systems: Courts of General Jurisdiction and Administrative Courts. Since 1973 the Supreme Constitutional Court (Damascus; tel. (11) 3331902) has been established as the paramount body of the Syrian judicial structure.

### THE SUPREME CONSTITUTIONAL COURT

This is the highest court in Syria. It has specific jurisdiction over: (i) judicial review of the constitutionality of laws and legislative decrees; (ii) investigation of charges relating to the legality of the election of members of the Majlis ash-Sha'ab (People's Assembly); (iii) trial of infractions committed by the President of the Republic

# SYRIA

in the exercise of his functions; (iv) resolution of positive and negative jurisdictional conflicts and determination of the competent court between the different juridical court systems, as well as other bodies exercising judicial competence. The Supreme Constitutional Court is composed of a Chief Justice and four Justices. They are appointed by decree of the President of the Republic for a renewable period of four years.

**Chief Justice:** NASRAT MOUNLA-HAYDAR.

## COURTS OF GENERAL JURISDICTION

The Courts of General Jurisdiction in Syria are divided into six categories: (i) The Court of Cassation; (ii) The Courts of Appeal; (iii) The Tribunals of First Instance; (iv) The Tribunals of Peace; (v) The Personal Status Courts; (vi) The Courts for Minors. Each of the above categories (except the Personal Status Courts) is divided into Civil, Penal and Criminal Chambers.

(i) **The Court of Cassation:** This is the highest court of general jurisdiction. Final judgments rendered by Courts of Appeal in penal and civil litigations may be petitioned to the Court of Cassation by the Defendant or the Public Prosecutor in penal and criminal litigations, and by any of the parties in interest in civil litigations, on grounds of defective application or interpretation of the law as stated in the challenged judgment, on grounds of irregularity of form or procedure, or violation of due process, and on grounds of defective reasoning of judgment rendered. The Court of Cassation is composed of a President, seven Vice-Presidents and 31 other Justices (Councillors).

(ii) **The Courts of Appeal:** Each court has geographical jurisdiction over one governorate (Mouhafazat). Each court is divided into Penal and Civil Chambers. There are Criminal Chambers which try felonies only. The Civil Chambers hear appeals filed against judgments rendered by the Tribunals of First Instance and the Tribunals of Peace. Each Court of Appeal is composed of a President and sufficient numbers of Vice-Presidents (Presidents of Chambers) and Superior Judges (Councillors). There are 54 Courts of Appeal.

(iii) **The Tribunals of First Instance:** In each governorate there are one or more Tribunals of First Instance, each of which is divided into several Chambers for penal and civil litigations. Each Chamber is composed of one judge. There are 72 Tribunals of First Instance.

(iv) **The Tribunals of Peace:** In the administrative centre of each governorate, and in each district, there are one or more Tribunals of Peace, which have jurisdiction over minor civil and penal litigations. There are 227 Tribunals of Peace.

(v) **Personal Status Courts:** These courts deal with marriage, divorce, etc. For Muslims each court consists of one judge, the 'Qadi Shari'i'. For Druzes there is one court consisting of one judge, the 'Qadi Mazhabi'. For non-Muslim communities there are courts for Roman Catholics, Orthodox believers, Protestants and Jews.

(vi) **Courts for Minors:** The constitution, officers, sessions, jurisdiction and competence of these courts are determined by a special law.

## PUBLIC PROSECUTION

Public prosecution is headed by the Attorney General, assisted by a number of Senior Deputy and Deputy Attorneys General, and a sufficient number of chief prosecutors, prosecutors and assistant prosecutors. Public prosecution is represented at all levels of the Courts of General Jurisdiction in all criminal and penal litigations and also in certain civil litigations as required by the law. Public prosecution controls and supervises enforcement of penal judgments.

## ADMINISTRATIVE COURTS SYSTEM

The Administrative Courts have jurisdiction over litigations involving the state or any of its governmental agencies. The Administrative Courts system is divided into two courts: the Administrative Courts and the Judicial Administrative Courts, of which the paramount body is the High Administrative Court.

## MILITARY COURTS

The Military Courts deal with criminal litigations against military personnel of all ranks and penal litigations against officers only. There are two military courts; one in Damascus, the other in Aleppo. Each court is composed of three military judges. There are other military courts, consisting of one judge, in every governorate, which deal with penal litigations against military personnel below the rank of officer. The different military judgments can be petitioned to the Court of Cassation.

# Religion

In religion the majority of Syrians follow a form of Islamic Sunni orthodoxy. There is also a considerable number of religious minorities: Shi'a Muslims; Ismaili Muslims; the Ismaili of the Salamiya district, whose spiritual head is the Aga Khan; a large number of Druzes, the Nusairis or Alawites of the Jebel Ansariyeh (a schism of the Shi'ite branch of Islam, to which President Assad belongs, who comprise about 11% of the population) and the Yezidis of the Jebel Sinjar, and a minority of Christians.

The Constitution states only that 'Islam shall be the religion of the head of the state'. The original draft of the 1973 Constitution made no reference to Islam at all, and this clause was inserted only as a compromise after public protest. The Syrian Constitution is thus unique among the constitutions of Arab states (excluding Lebanon) with a clear Muslim majority in not enshrining Islam as the religion of the state itself.

## ISLAM

**Grand Mufti:** AHMAD KUFTARO.

## CHRISTIANITY
### Orthodox Churches

**Greek Orthodox Patriarchate:** His Beatitude IGNATIUS HAZIM, Patriarch of Antioch and all the Orient; BP 9, Damascus; has jurisdiction over Syria, Lebanon, Iran and Iraq.

**Syrian Orthodox Patriarchate:** BP 914, Bab Touma, Damascus; tel. (11) 447036; Syrian Orthodox Patriarch: His Holiness IGNATIUS ZAKKA I IWAS, Patriarch of Antioch and All the East; the Syrian Orthodox Church includes one Catholicose (of the East), 30 Metropolitans and one Bishop, and has an estimated 3m. adherents throughout the world.

The Armenian Apostolic Church is also represented in Syria.

### The Roman Catholic Church

*Armenian Rite*

**Patriarchal Exarchate of Syria:** Exarcat Patriarcal Arménien Catholique, Bab Touma, Damascus; tel. (11) 5433438; represents the Patriarch of Cilicia (resident in Beirut, Lebanon); 3,500 adherents (31 December 1993); Exarch Patriarchal Mgr GEORGES TAYROYAN.

**Archdiocese of Aleppo:** Archevêché Arménien Catholique, BP 97, rue Tillel 121, Aleppo; tel. (21) 213946; 15,000 adherents (31 December 1993); Archbishop Mgr BOUTROS MARAYATI.

**Diocese of Kamichlié:** Evêché Arménien Catholique, BP 17, Al-Qamishli; tel. (531) 213946; fax (531) 235305; 6,300 adherents (31 December 1993); Bishop (vacant).

*Chaldean Rite*

**Diocese of Aleppo:** Evêché Chaldéen Catholique d'Alep, Soulémaniya; tel. (21) 441660; 15,000 adherents (31 December 1993); Bishop ANTOINE AUDO.

*Latin Rite*

**Apostolic Vicariate of Aleppo:** BP 327, 19 rue Antaki, Aleppo; tel. and fax (21) 210204; f. 1644; 10,500 adherents (31 December 1993); Vicar Apostolic ARMANDO BORTOLASO, Titular Bishop of Raphanea.

*Maronite Rite*

**Archdiocese of Aleppo:** Archevêché Maronite, BP 203, Aleppo; tel. (21) 248048; 3,625 adherents (31 December 1993); Archbishop Mgr PIERRE CALLAOS.

**Archdiocese of Damascus:** Archevêché Maronite, Bab Touma, Damascus; tel. (11) 5430129; 8,000 adherents (31 December 1993); Archbishop HAMID ANTOINE MOURANY.

**Diocese of Latakia:** Evêché Maronite, BP 161, rue Hamrat, Tartous; tel. (431) 223433; 27,000 adherents (31 December 1993); Bishop Mgr ANTOINE TORBEY.

*Melkite Rite*

**Melkite-Greek-Catholic Patriarchate:** BP 22249, Damascus, or POB 50076, Beirut, Lebanon; tel. (11) 5433129; fax (11) 5431266 (Damascus), or 413111 (Beirut); jurisdiction over 1.5m. Melkites throughout the world (including 166,500 in Syria); Patriarch of Antioch and all the East, of Alexandria and Jerusalem MAXIMOS V HAKIM. The Melkite Rite includes the patriarchal sees of Damascus, Cairo and Jerusalem and four other archdioceses in Syria; seven archdioceses in Lebanon; one in Jordan; one in Israel; and five Eparchies (in the USA, Brazil, Canada, Australia and Mexico).

**Archdiocese of Aleppo:** Archevêché Grec-Catholique, BP 146, Aleppo; tel. (21) 213218; Archbishop Mgr NÉOPHYTOS EDELBY.

**Archdiocese of Busra and Hauran:** Archevêché Grec-Catholique, Khabab, Hauran; tel. 13; Archbishop Mgr BOULOS NASSIF BORKHOCHE.

# SYRIA

**Archdiocese of Homs:** Archevêché Grec-Catholique, BP 1525, rue El-Bahri, Boustan ad-Diwan, Homs; tel. (31) 221587; Archbishop Mgr IBRAHIM NEHMÉ.

**Archdiocese of Latakia:** Archevêché Grec-Catholique, BP 151, Latakia; tel. 36077; Archbishop Mgr MICHEL YATIM.

*Syrian Rite*

**Archdiocese of Aleppo:** Archevêché Syrien Catholique, rue Azizié, Aleppo; tel. (21) 241200; Archbishop DENYS ANTOINE BEYLOUNI.

**Archdiocese of Damascus:** Archevêché Syrien Catholique, BP 2129, rue Bab Charki, Damascus; tel. (11) 432311; telex 411778; Archbishop Mgr EUSTACHE JOSEPH MOUNAYER.

**Archdiocese of Hassaké-Nisibi:** Archevêché Syrien Catholique, BP 6, Hasakeh; tel. (52) 220052; Archbishop JACQUES GEORGES HABIB HAFOURI.

**Archdiocese of Homs:** Archevêché Syrien Catholique, BP 368, rue Hamidieh, Homs; tel. (31) 221575; Archbishop Mgr BASILE MOUSSA DAOUD.

At 31 December 1993 the total number of adherents of the Syrian Rite within the jurisdiction of the four Syrian archbishops was 29,350.

### The Anglican Communion

Within the Episcopal Church in Jerusalem and the Middle East, Syria forms part of the diocese of Jerusalem (see the chapter on Israel).

### Protestant

**National Evangelical Synod of Syria and Lebanon:** POB 70890, Antelias, Lebanon; tel. 405490; f. 1920; 70,000 adherents (1993); Exec. Sec. Rev. Dr SALIM SAHIOUNY.

**Union of the Armenian Evangelical Churches in the Near East:** POB 110-377, Beirut, Lebanon; tel. 443547; fax 582191; f. 1846 in Turkey; comprises about 30 Armenian Evangelical Churches in Syria, Lebanon, Egypt, Cyprus, Greece, Iran and Turkey; 9,500 mems (1985); Moderator Rev. HOVHANNES KARJIAN; Sec. Rev. BARKEV APARTIAN.

# The Press

Since the Baath Arab Socialist Party came to power, the structure of the press has been modified according to socialist patterns. Most publications are published by organizations such as political, religious, or professional associations, trade unions, etc. and several are published by government ministries. Anyone wishing to establish a new paper or periodical must apply for a licence.

The major dailies are *Al-Baath* (the organ of the party), *Tishrin* and *Ath-Thawra* in Damascus, *Al-Jamahir al-Arabia* in Aleppo, and *Al-Fida'* in Hama.

### PRINCIPAL DAILIES

**Al-Baath** (Renaissance): BP 9389, Autostrade Mezzeh, Damascus; tel. (11) 664600; telex 419146; fax (11) 240099; f. 1946; morning; Arabic; organ of the Baath Arab Socialist Party; Gen. Dir and Chief Editor TURKI SAQR; circ. 65,000.

**Barq ash-Shimal** (The Syrian Telegraph): rue Aziziyah, Aleppo; morning; Arabic; Editor MAURICE DJANDJI; circ. 6,400.

**Al-Fida'** (Redemption): rue Kuwatly, Hama; morning; Arabic; political; publishing concession holder OSMAN ALOUINI; Editor A. AULWANI; circ. 4,000.

**Al-Jamahir al-Arabia** (The Arab People): Al-Wihdat Press, Printing and Publishing Organization, Aleppo; Arabic; political; Chief Editor MORTADA BAKACH; circ. 10,000.

**Al-Oroubat:** Al-Wihdat Press, Printing and Publishing Organization, Homs; morning; Arabic; published by Al-Wihdat Printing and Publishing Organization; circ. 5,000.

**Ash-Shabab** (Youth): rue at-Tawil, Aleppo; morning; Arabic; Editor MUHAMMAD TALAS; circ. 9,000.

**Syria Times:** Tishrin Foundation for Press and Publication, BP 5452, Corniche Meedan, Damascus; English; circ. 12,000.

**Ath-Thawra** (Revolution): Al-Wihdat Press, Printing and Publishing Organization, BP 2448, Damascus; morning; Arabic; political; circ. 55,000; Chief Editor M. KHAIR AL-WADI.

**Tishrin** (October): Tishrin Foundation for Press and Publication, BP 5452, Corniche Meedan, Damascus; tel. (11) 886900; telex 411916; Arabic; Chief Editor M. KHEIR WADI; circ. 70,000.

**Al-Wihdat** (Unity): Al-Wihdat Press, Printing and Publishing Organization, Latakia; Arabic; published by Al-Wihdat Press, Printing and Publishing Organization.

### WEEKLIES AND FORTNIGHTLIES

**Al-Ajoua'** (The Air): Compagnie de l'Aviation Arabe Syrienne, BP 417, Damascus; fortnightly; Arabic; aviation; Editor AHMAD ALLOUCHE.

**Al-Esbou ar-Riadi** (The Sports Week): ave Fardoss, Imm. Tibi, Damascus; weekly; Arabic; sports; Asst Dir and Editor HASRAN AL-BOUNNI; circ. 14,000.

**Al-Fursan** (The Cavalry): Damascus; Arabic; political magazine; Editor Major RIFAAT AL-ASSAD.

**Homs:** Homs; weekly; Arabic; literary; Publisher and Dir ADIB KABA; Editor PHILIPPE KABA.

**Jaysh ash-Sha'ab** (The People's Army): BP 3320, blvd Palestine, Damascus; f. 1946; fortnightly; Arabic; army magazine; published by the Political Department of the Syrian Army.

**Kifah al-Oummal al-Ishtiraki** (The Socialist Workers' Struggle): Fédération Générale des Syndicats des Ouvriers, rue Qanawat, Damascus; weekly; Arabic; labour; published by General Federation of Labour Unions; Editor SAID AL-HAMAMI.

**Al-Masirah** (Progress): Damascus; weekly; Arabic; political; published by Federation of Youth Organizations.

**Al-Maukef ar-Riadi:** Al-Wihdat Press, Printing and Publishing Organization, BP 2448, Damascus; weekly; Arabic; sports; published by Al-Wihdat Press, Printing and Publishing Organization; circ. 50,000.

**An-Nas** (The People): BP 926, Aleppo; f. 1953; weekly; Arabic; Publisher VICTOR KALOUS.

**Nidal al-Fellahin** (The Struggle of the Fellahin): FédérationGénérale des Laboureurs, BP 7152, Damascus; weekly; Arabic; peasant workers; Editor MANSOUR ABU AL-HOSN.

**Nidal ash-Sha'ab** (People's Struggle): Damascus; fortnightly; Arabic; published by the Communist Party of Syria.

**Ar-Riada** (Sport): BP 292, near Electricity Institute, Damascus; weekly; Arabic; sports; Dir NOUREDDINE RIAL; Publisher and Editor OURFANE UBARI.

**As-Sakafat al-Usbouiya** (Weekly Culture): BP 2570, Soukak as-Sakr, Damascus; weekly; Arabic; cultural; Publisher, Dir and Editor MADHAT AKKACHE.

**Al-Yanbu al-Jadid** (New Spring): Immeuble Al-Awkaf, Homs; weekly; Arabic; literary; Publisher, Dir and Editor MAMDOU AL-KOUSSEIR.

### OTHER PERIODICALS

**Ad-Dad:** rue Tital, Wakf al-Moiriné Bldg, Aleppo; monthly; Arabic; literary; Dir RIAD HALLAK; Publisher and Editor ABDALLAH YARKI HALLAK.

**Ecos:** BP 3320, Damascus; monthly review; Spanish.

**Al-Fikr al-Askari** (The Military Idea): BP 4259, blvd Palestine, Damascus; f. 1950; 6 a year; Arabic; official military review published by the Political Dept of the Syrian Army; Editor NAKHLE KALLAS.

**Flash:** BP 3320, Damascus; monthly review; English and French.

**Al-Irshad az-Zirai** (Agricultural Information): Ministry of Agriculture and Agrarian Reform, 29 rue Ayar, Damascus; tel. (11) 113613; 6 a year; Arabic; agriculture.

**Al-Jundi al-Arabi** (The Arab Soldier): BP 3320, blvd Palestine, Damascus; telex 411500; monthly; published by the Political Department of the Syrian Army.

**Al-Kalima** (The Word): Al-Kalima Association, Aleppo; monthly; Arabic; religious; Publisher and Editor FATHALLA SAKAL.

**Al-Kanoun** (The Law): Ministry of Justice, Damascus; monthly; Arabic; juridical.

**Al-Ma'arifa** (Knowledge): Ministry of Culture, Damascus; tel. (11) 331556; telex 411944; f. 1962; monthly; Arabic; literary; Editor ABD AL-KARIM NASIF; circ. 7,500.

**Al-Majalla al-Batriarquia** (The Magazine of the Patriarchate): Syrian Orthodox Patriarchate, BP 914, Damascus; tel. (11) 447036; f. 1962; monthly; Arabic; religious; Editor SAMIR ABDOH; circ. 11,000.

**Al-Majalla at-Tibbiya al-Arabiyya** (Arab Medical Magazine): rue al-Jala'a, Damascus; monthly; Arabic; published by Arab Medical Commission; Dir Dr SHAMS AD-DIN AL-JUNDI; Editor Dr ADNAN TAKRITI.

**Majallat Majma' al-Lughat al-Arabiyya bi-Dimashq** (Magazine of the Arab Language Academy of Damascus): Arab Academy of Damascus, BP 327, Damascus; tel. (11) 3713145; f. 1921; quarterly; Arabic; Islamic culture and Arabic literature, Arabic scientific and cultural terminology; Editor Dr SHAKER FAHAM; circ. 2,000.

**Al-Mawkif al-Arabi** (The Arab Situation): Ittihab al-Kuttab al-Arab, rue Murshid Khatir, Damascus; monthly; Arabic; literary.

**Monthly Survey of Arab Economics:** BP 2306, Damascus and POB 6068, Beirut; f. 1958; monthly; English and French editions; published by Centre d'Etudes et de Documentation Economiques, Financières et Sociales; Dir Dr CHAFIC AKHRAS.

**Al-Mouallem al-Arabi** (The Arab Teacher): Ministry of Education, Damascus; f. 1948; monthly; Arabic; educational and cultural.

**Al-Mouhandis al-Arabi** (The Arab Engineer): BP 2336, Immeuble Dar al-Mouhandisen, place Azme, Damascus; tel. (11) 214916; telex 411962; f. 1961; bi-monthly; Arabic; published by Inst. of Syrian Engineers; scientific and cultural; Dir Dr Eng. GHASSAN TAYARA; Editors Eng. ADNAN IBRAHIM and Dr Eng. AHMAD AL-GHAFARI; circ. 21,000.

**Al-Munadel** (The Militant): c/o BP 11512, Damascus; fax (11) 2126935; f. 1965; monthly; Arabic; magazine of Baath Arab Socialist Party; Dir Dr FAWWAZ SAYYAGH; circ. 100,000.

**Revue de la Presse Arabe:** 67 place Chahbandar, Damascus; f. 1948; French; 2 a week.

**Risalat al-Kimia** (Chemistry Report): BP 669, Immeuble al-Abid, Damascus; monthly; Arabic; scientific; Publisher, Dir and Editor HASSAN AS-SAKA.

**Saut al-Forat:** Deir ez-Zor; monthly; Arabic; literary; Publisher, Dir and Editor ABD AL-KADER AYACHE.

**Ash-Shourta** (The Police): Directorate of Public Affairs and Moral Guidance, Damascus; monthly; Arabic; juridical.

**Souriya al-Arabiyya** (Arab Syria): Ministry of Information, ave al-Mazzeh, Immeuble Dar al-Baath, Damascus; tel. (11) 660412; monthly; publicity; in four languages.

**Syrie et Monde Arabe:** BP 3550, place Chahbandar, Damascus; f. 1952; monthly; French and English; economic, statistical and political survey.

**At-Tamaddon al-Islami** (The Spreading of Islam): Darwichiyah, Damascus; tel. (11) 215120; telex 411258; f. 1932; monthly; Arabic; religious; published by At-Tamaddon al-Islami Association; Pres. of Asscn. MUHAMMAD ZAHIR KOUZBARI; Editor ADEL KOLTAKGY.

**At-Taqa Wattanmiya** (Energy and Expansion): BP 7748, rue al-Moutanabbi, Damascus; tel. (11) 233529; telex 411031; monthly; Arabic; published by the Syrian Petroleum Co.

**Al-Yakza** (The Awakening): Al-Yakza Association, BP 6677, rue Sisi, Aleppo; f. 1935; monthly; Arabic; literary social review of charitable institution; Dir HUSNI ABD AL-MASSIH; circ. 12,000.

**Az-Zira'a 2000** (Agriculture 2000): Ministry of Agriculture and Agrarian Reform, 29 rue Ayar, Damascus; tel. (11) 213613; telex 411643; f. 1985; monthly; Arabic; agriculture; circ. 12,000.

### PRESS AGENCIES

**Agence Arabe Syrienne d'Information:** Damascus; f. 1966; supplies bulletins on Syrian news to foreign news agencies; Dir-Gen. Dr SABIR FALHUT.

### Foreign Bureaux

**Agencia EFE** (Spain): Damascus; Correspondent ZACHARIAS SARME.

**Agence France-Presse (AFP):** BP 2400, Immeuble Adel Charaj, place du 17 avril, Damascus; tel. (11) 428253; telex 419173; Correspondent JOSEPH GHASI.

**Agenzia Nazionale Stampa Associata (ANSA)** (Italy): Hotel Méridien, BP 2712, Damascus; tel. (11) 233116; telex 411098; f. 1962; Correspondent ABDULLAH SAADEL.

**Allgemeiner Deutscher Nachrichtendienst (ADN)** (Germany): BP 844, Damascus; tel. (11) 332093; telex 411010; Correspondent FRANK HERRMANN.

**Associated Press (AP)** (USA): c/o Hotel Méridien, BP 2712, Damascus; tel. (11) 233116; telex 411196.

**Deutsche Presse-Agentur (dpa)** (Germany): c/o Hotel Méridien, BP 2712, Damascus; tel. (11) 332924; telex 411098.

Reuters (UK) is also represented in Syria.

## Publishers

**Arab Advertising Organization:** BP 2842-3034, 28 rue Moutanabbi, Damascus; tel. (11) 2225219; telex 411923; fax (11) 2220754; f. 1963; exclusive government establishment responsible for advertising; publishes *Directory of Commerce and Industry*, *Damascus International Fair Guide*, *Daily Bulletin of Official Tenders*; Dir-Gen. MUHAMMAD QATTAN.

**Damascus University Press:** Damascus; tel. (11) 2215100; telex 411971; fax (11) 2236010; arts, geography, education, history, engineering, medicine, law, sociology, economics, sciences, architecture, agriculture, school books.

**Office Arabe de Presse et de Documentation (OFA-Edition):** BP 3550, 67 place Chahbandar, Damascus; tel. (11) 4459166; telex 411613; fax (11) 4426021; f. 1964; numerous periodicals, monographs and surveys on political and economic affairs; Dir-Gen. SAMIR A. DARWICH. Has two affiliated branches, OFA-Business Consulting Centre (foreign company representation and services) and OFA-Renseignements Commerciaux (Commercial enquiries on firms and persons in Syria and Lebanon).

**The Political Administration Press:** BP 3320, blvd Palestine, Damascus; telex 411500; publishes *Al-Fikr al-Askari* (6 a year) and *Jaysh ash-Sha'ab* (fortnightly) and *Al-Jundi al-Arabi* (monthly).

**Syrian Documentation Papers:** BP 2712, Damascus; f. 1968; publishers of *Bibliography of the Middle East* (annual), *General Directory of the Press and Periodicals in the Arab World* (annual), and numerous publications on political, economic and social affairs and literature and legislative texts concerning Syria and the Arab world; Dir-Gen. LOUIS FARÉS.

**Al-Wihdat Press, Printing and Publishing Organization** (Institut al-Ouedha pour l'impression, édition et distribution): BP 2448, Dawar Kafr Soussat, Damascus; publishes *Al-Jamahir al-Arabia*, *Al-Ouroubat*, *Ath-Thawra*, *Al-Fida'* and *Al-Wihdat* (dailies), *al-Maukef ar-Riadi* (weekly) and other commercial publications.

## Radio and Television

In 1992 there were an estimated 3.4m. radio receivers and 810,000 television receivers in use.

**Directorate-General of Broadcasting and Television:** place Omayyad, Damascus; tel. (11) 720700; telex 411138; f. 1945; Dir-Gen. KHUDR OMRAN.

### RADIO

Broadcasts in Arabic, French, English, Russian, German, Spanish, Portuguese, Hebrew, Polish, Turkish, Bulgarian.

**Director of Radio:** SAFWAN GHANIM.

### TELEVISION

Services started in 1960.

**Director of Television:** M. ABD AS-SALAM HIJAB.

## Finance

(cap. = capital; res = reserves; dep. = deposits; m.= million; brs = branches; amounts in £S)

### BANKING
#### Central Bank

**Central Bank of Syria:** POB 2254, Altajrida al-Mughrabia Sq., Damascus; tel. (11) 2224800; telex 411910; fax (11) 2227109; f. 1956; cap. 10m., dep. 22,689m., total assets 46,202m. (June 1987); 9 brs; Gov. MUHAMMAD ASH-SHRAIF.

#### Other Banks

**Agricultural Bank:** BP 5325, rue Euphrates, Damascus; f. 1924; Dir-Gen. MAEN RISLAN; 55 brs.

**Commercial Bank of Syria:** BP 933, place Yousuf al-Azmeh, Damascus; tel. (11) 218890; telex 411002; fax (11) 2216975; f. 1967; govt-owned bank; cap. 191.8m., res 853.1m., dep. 151,996m. (Dec. 1992); 37 brs; Chair. and Gen. Man. MUHAMMAD RIYADH HAKIM.

**Industrial Bank:** BP 7578, 29 rue May, Damascus; tel. (11) 228200; f. 1959; nationalized bank providing finance for industry; cap. 100m.; 13 brs; Chair. ABD AL-QADIR OBEIDO.

**Popular Credit Bank:** BP 2841, rue Fardoss, Dar al-Mohandessin Blvd, 6th Floor, Damascus; tel. (11) 114260; f. 1967; government bank; provides loans to the services sector and is sole authorized issuer of savings certificates; cap. 25m., dep. 2,313m., res 42,765m. (Dec. 1984); 43 brs; Chair. and Gen. Man. MUHAMMAD HASSAN AL-HOUJJEIRI.

**Real Estate Bank:** BP 2337, rue al-Furat, Damascus; tel. (11) 218602; telex 419171; f. 1966; provides loans and grants for housing, schools, hospitals and hotel construction; cap. 515m.; 13 brs; Chair. and Gen. Man. MUHAMMAD A. MAKHLOUF.

### INSURANCE

**Syrian General Organization for Insurance:** BP 2279, rue Tajheez, Damascus; tel. (11) 2218430; telex 411003; fax (11) 2220494; f. 1953; auth. cap. 250m.; a nationalized company; operates throughout Syria; Chair. and Gen. Man. AMIN ABDULLAH.

# Trade and Industry

## CHAMBERS OF COMMERCE

**Federation of Syrian Chambers of Commerce:** POB 5909, Mousa Ben Nousair St, Damascus; tel. (11) 3337344; telex 411194; fax (11) 3331127; f. 1975; Chair. Dr RATEB ASH-SHALLAH.

**Aleppo Chamber of Commerce:** BP 1261, rue al-Moutanabbi, Aleppo; tel. (21) 38236; telex 331012; f. 1885; Pres. MUHAMMAD MAHROUSSEH; Sec. EUGENE GLORE; Dir ZEKI DAROUZI.

**Alkalamoun Chamber of Commerce:** POB 2507, Bucher A. Mawla St, Damascus; telex 411061; fax (11) 778394; Pres. M. SOUFAN.

**Damascus Chamber of Commerce:** BP 1040, rue Mou'awiah, Damascus; tel. (11) 211339; telex 411326; fax (11) 2225874; f. 1890; 18,000 mems.; Honorary Pres. BADR ED-DIN SHALLAH; Gen. Dir HISHAM AL-HAMWY.

**Hama Chamber of Commerce and Industry:** POB 147, rue al-Kouatly, Hama; tel. (11) 233304; telex 431046; fax (11) 223910; f. 1934; Pres. ABD AS-SALAM SABEH.

**Homs Chamber of Commerce and Industry:** BP 440, rue Abou al-Of, Homs; tel. 231000; telex 441025; fax (11) 224247; f. 1938; Pres. Eng. WALID TULIEMAT; Dir MUHAMMAD FARES AL-HUSAIMI.

**Latakia Chamber of Commerce:** rue al-Hurriyah, Latakia; Pres. JULE NASRI.

## CHAMBERS OF INDUSTRY

**Aleppo Chamber of Industry:** BP 1859, rue al-Moutanabbi, Aleppo; tel. (21) 339812; telex 331090; f. 1935; Pres. MUHAMMAD M. OUBARI; 7,000 mems.

**Damascus Chamber of Industry:** BP 1305, rue Harika Mou'awiah, Damascus; tel. (11) 2215042; telex 411289; fax (11) 2245981; Pres. Dr YEHYA AL-HINDI; Dir-Gen. Dr ABD AL-HAMID MALAKANI.

## EMPLOYERS' ORGANIZATIONS

**Fédération Générale à Damas:** Damascus; f. 1951; Dir TALAT TAGLUBI.

**Fédération de Damas:** Damascus; f. 1949.

**Fédération des Patrons et Industriels à Lattaquié:** Latakia; f. 1953.

## TRADE UNIONS

**Ittihad Naqabat al-'Ummal al-'Am fi Suriya** (General Federation of Labour Unions): POB 2351, rue Qanawat, Damascus; f. 1948; Chair. IZZ AD-DIN NASIR; Sec. MAHMOUD FAHURI.

## PETROLEUM

**Syrian Petroleum Company (SPC):** BP 2849, rue al-Moutanabbi, Damascus; tel. (11) 227007; telex 411031; f. 1958; state agency; holds the oil and gas concession for all Syria; exploits the Suweidiya, Karatchouk, Rumelan and Jbeisseh oilfields; also organizes exploring, production and marketing of oil and gas nationally; Dir-Gen. Dr Eng. ALI JEBRAN.

**Al-Furat Petroleum Company:** f. 1985; owned 50% by SPC and 50% by a foreign consortium of Pecten International, Royal Dutch/Shell and Deminex; exploits the ath-Thayyem, al-Asharah and al-Ward oilfields.

## STATE ENTERPRISES

Syrian industry is almost entirely controlled and run by the state. There are national organizations responsible to the appropriate ministry for the operation of all sectors of industry, of which the following are examples:

**Cotton Marketing Organization:** BP 729, rue Bab al-Faraj, Aleppo; tel. (21) 238486; telex 331210; fax (21) 218617; f. 1965; monopoly authority for purchase of seed cotton, ginning and sales of cotton lint; Pres. and Dir-Gen. ABD AS-SATTAR.

**General Organization for Phosphate and Mines (GECOPHAM):** BP 288, Homs; tel. 20405; telex 441000; production and export of phosphate rock.

**General Organization for the Exploitation and Development of the Euphrates Basin (GOEDEB):** Raqqa; telex 31004; Dir-Gen. Dr Eng. ABDO KASSEM.

**General Organization for the Textile Industries:** BP 620, rue Fardoss, Damascus; tel. (11) 116200; telex 411011; control and planning of the textile industry and supervision of textile manufacture; 13 subsidiary cos.

# Transport

## RAILWAYS

The present railway system totals 1,918 km of track (1990) and is composed of the following main lines: Meydan Ekbez (Turkish frontier)–Aleppo–Ar-Rai (166 km); Cobanbey (Turkish frontier)–Aleppo; Nassibin (Turkish frontier)–Jaroubieh (Iraq frontier) (81 km); Aleppo–Homs–Damascus (422 km); Homs–Akkari (Lebanese frontier)–Tartous–Latakia (110 km); Hama–M'hardeh (24 km); there are 1,686 km of normal gauge track (1,435 mm) and 232 km of narrow gauge track (1,050 mm), including the Hedjaz railway. A line from Latakia to Qamishliya, via Aleppo, (757 km) has been completed and is operating for passenger and goods traffic. Other new lines completed include an 180-km line from Homs to the phosphate mines at Khenefes and to Palmyra, a 19-km line from Hama to M'hardeh and a 42-km line from Tartous to Akkari. The line from Homs to Damascus (194 km) was opened in 1983, one from Damascus to Aleppo has also been completed, and an 80-km line from Tartous to Latakia is operating for passenger and goods traffic. A 170-km line from Deir ez-Zor to Abou Kemal, near the Iraqi border, is under construction.

**Syrian Railways:** BP 182, Aleppo; tel. (21) 213900; telex 331009; fax (21) 228480; f. 1897; Pres. of the Board of Administration and Dir-Gen. MUHAMMAD GHASSAN AL-KADDOUR.

**General Organization of the Hedjaz-Syrian Railway:** BP 134, place Hedjaz, Damascus; tel. (11) 215815; Gen. Man. Eng. A. ISMAIL; the Hedjaz Railway has 232 km of track (gauge 1,050 mm) in Syria; services operate between Damascus and Amman, and a branch line of about 24 km from Damascus to Katana was opened in 1977; in 1987 a study into the feasibility of reconstructing the historic railway to Medina, in collaboration with Jordan and Saudi Arabia, concluded that such a project would be financially viable only if the line were to be connected with European railway systems.

## ROADS

Arterial roads run across the country linking the north to the south and the Mediterranean to the eastern frontier. The main arterial networks are as follows: Sidon (Lebanon)–Quneitra–Suweidiya–Salkhad–Jordan border; Beirut (Lebanon)–Damascus–Khan Abu Chamat–Iraqi border–Baghdad; Tartous–Tell Kalakh–Homs–Palmyra; Banias–Hama–Salemie; Latakia–Aleppo–Rakka–Deir ez-Zor–Abou Kemal–Iraqi border; Tripoli (Lebanon)–Tartous–Banias–Latakia; Turkish border–Antakya; Amman (Jordan)–Dera'a–Damascus–Homs–Hama–Aleppo–Azaz (Turkish border); Quneitra–Damascus–Palmyra–Deir ez-Zor–Hassetche–Qamishliya.

At 31 December 1992 there were 850 km of motorways, 5,665 km of main, or national roads and 19,372 km of secondary, or regional roads.

**General Co for Roads:** BP 3143, Aleppo; tel. (21) 555406; telex 331403; f. 1975; Gen. Man. Eng. M. WALID EL-AJLANI.

## PIPELINES

The oil pipelines which cross Syrian territory are of great importance to the national economy, representing a considerable source of foreign exchange. Iraq halted the flow of oil through the pipeline between Kirkuk and Banias in April 1976, but it was resumed in February 1979. Syria closed the pipeline in April 1982, but it has since been used to pump output from the oilfield at ath-Thayyem, which came into operation in 1986, to the refinery at Homs, via a 92-km spur line. In May 1992 Syria was reported to be ready to enter into negotiations with Iraq and the UN regarding the use of the pipeline for exports of Iraqi petroleum.

Following the Iraqi Government's nationalization of the Iraq Petroleum Company, the Syrian Government nationalized the IPC's pipelines, pumping stations and other installations in Syria, setting up a new company to administer them:

**Syrian Company for Oil Transport (SCOT):** BP 13, Banias; tel. 22300; telex 441012; f. 1972; Dir-Gen. MUHAMMAD DOUBA.

## SHIPPING

Latakia is the principal port; it handled 5.88m. tons of goods in 1984. The other major ports are at Banias and Tartous. The amount of phosphates handled at Tartous doubled to 2.6m. tons in 1986.

**Syrian General Authority for Maritime Transport:** BP 730, 2 rue Argentina, Damascus; tel. (11) 226350; telex 411012.

**Ismail, A. M., Shipping Agency Ltd:** BP 74, rue du Port, Tartous; tel. 20543; operates a fleet of 1 tanker and 9 general cargo vessels; Man. Dir MAHMOUD ISMAIL.

**Sea Transport Agency:** BP 78, Kamilieh Quarter, Harbour St, Latakia; tel. 33964; telex 510044; operates 3 general cargo vessels; Gen. Man. WADIH M. NSEIR.

**Syrian Navigation Company:** BP 314, rue Baghdad, Latakia; tel. (41) 233778; telex 451028; fax (41) 235781; f. 1975; state-owned company operating 4 general cargo ships; Chair. and Man. Dir MUHAMMAD A. HAROUN.

**Syro-Jordanian Shipping Co:** BP 148, rue Port Said, Latakia; tel. 2316356; telex 451002; fax (11) 230250; f. 1976; operates 2 general cargo ships; transported 70,551 metric tons of goods in 1992; Chair. OSMAN LEBBADY.

**Tabalo, Muhammad Abd ar-Rahman:** BP 66, rue al-Mina, Tartous; tel. 20906; telex 470008; operates 4 general cargo vessels (1 refrigerated); Man. Dir ABDULLAH TABALO.

### CIVIL AVIATION

There is an international airport at Damascus, and the upgrading of Aleppo airport, to enable it to handle international traffic, is planned.

**Directorate-General of Civil Aviation:** place Nejmeh, Damascus; tel. (11) 331306; telex 411928.

**Syrian Arab Airlines (Syrianair):** BP 417, 5th Floor, Social Insurance Bldg, Jabri St, Damascus; tel. 232154; telex 411593; f. 1946, refounded 1961 to succeed Syrian Airways, after revocation of merger with Misrair; domestic passenger and cargo services (from Damascus, Aleppo, Latakia and Deir ez-Zor) and routes to Europe, the Middle East, North Africa and the Indian sub-continent; Chair. OMAR ALI REDA.

## Tourism

Syria's tourist attractions include a pleasant Mediterranean coastline, the mountains, the town bazaars and the antiquities of Damascus and Palmyra. A total of 1.9m. foreigners visited Syria in 1993.

**Ministry of Tourism:** rue Victoria, Damascus; tel. (11) 215916; telex 411672; f. 1972; Minister of Tourism AMIN ABU ASH-SHAMAT; Dir of Tourist Relations and Ministerial Adviser Mrs SAWSAN JOUZY.

**Middle East Tourism:** BP 201, rue Fardoss, Damascus; tel. (11) 211876; telex 411726; f. 1966; Pres. MUHAMMAD DADOUCHE; 7 brs.

# TAJIKISTAN

## Introductory Survey

**Location, Climate, Language, Religion, Flag, Capital**

The Republic of Tajikistan (formerly the Tajik Soviet Socialist Republic) is situated in the south-east of Central Asia. To the north and west it borders Uzbekistan, to the north-east Kyrgyzstan, to the east the People's Republic of China and to the south Afghanistan. The climate varies considerably according to altitude. The average temperature in January in Khojand (lowland) is −0.9°C (30.4°F); in July the average is 27.4°C (81.3°F). In the southern lowlands the temperature variation is somewhat more extreme. Precipitation is low in the valleys, in the range of 150–250 mm per year. In mountain areas winter temperatures can fall below −45°C (−51°F); the average January temperature in Murgab, in the mountains of south-east Gorny Badakhshan, is −19.6°C (−3.3°F). Levels of rainfall are very low in mountain regions and seldom exceed 60–80 mm per year. In 1989 Tajik replaced Russian as the official language of the republic. Tajik belongs to the south-west Iranian group of languages and is closely related to Farsi (Persian). Since 1940 the Cyrillic script has been used. The major religion is Islam. Most Tajiks and ethnic Uzbek residents follow the Sunni tradition, but the Pamiris are mostly of the Isma'ili sect. There are also representatives of the Russian Orthodox Church. There is a small Jewish community. The national flag (proportions 2 by 1) consists of four unequal horizontal stripes from top to bottom of red, white, green and red, with, on the obverse only, a crossed gold hammer and sickle below a gold-bordered red five-pointed star on the top red stripe, set near the hoist. The capital is Dushanbe.

**Recent History**

The Tajiks were probably a distinct ethnic group by about the eighth century AD. They were distinguished from their Turkic neighbours by their sedentary life-style and Iranian language. They formed several semi-independent territories under Uzbek suzerainty, but, as the Russian Empire expanded southwards in the 19th century, the northern Tajik principalities came under Russian rule. The southern regions were annexed by the expanding Emirate of Bukhara.

In 1918 the Bolsheviks established control over northern Tajikistan, which was incorporated into the Turkestan Autonomous Soviet Socialist Republic (ASSR), but did not conquer Dushanbe and the other territories subject to Bukhara until 1921. Opposition to Soviet rule was led by the *basmachis* (local guerrilla fighters) and foreign interventionists. Full Soviet control was not established in the remote south-east of Tajikistan until 1925. In 1924 the Tajik ASSR was established as a part of the Uzbek Soviet Socialist Republic (SSR), and on 2 January 1925 the south-east of Tajikistan was designated a Special Pamir Region (later renamed the Gorny Badakhshan Autonomous Region) within the Tajik ASSR. On 16 October 1929 the Tajik ASSR became a full Union Republic of the USSR (the Tajik SSR) and was slightly enlarged by the addition of the Khojand okrug (district) from the Uzbek SSR.

Soviet power brought economic and social benefits to Tajikistan, but living standards remained low. Cattle-breeding, the main occupation in the uplands, was severely disrupted by collectivization. During the repressions of the 1930s almost all Tajiks in the republican Government were removed and replaced by Russians, sent from Moscow.

During the 1970s there were reports of increased Islamic influence as well as violence towards non-indigenous nationalities. In 1978 there were reports of an anti-Russian riot, involving some 13,000 people, and after 1979 there were arrests of some activists opposed to Soviet intervention in Afghanistan.

As in other Central Asian republics of the USSR, the first manifestation of the policies of the Soviet leader, Mikhail Gorbachev, who came to power in 1985, was a campaign against corruption. Rakhmon Nabiyev, who had been First Secretary of the Communist Party of Tajikistan (CPT) since 1982, was replaced in late 1985 by Kakhar Makhkamov, who accused his predecessor of tolerating nepotism and corruption. Makhkamov was also openly critical of the economic situation in the republic, admitting that there were high levels of unemployment and that many people lived in poverty. Censorship was also relaxed and there was increased discussion of perceived injustices, such as alleged discrimination against Tajiks in Uzbekistan. In June 1989 there were violent confrontations between villagers on the border between Tajikistan and Kyrgyzstan, and there were discussions in the media about the fairness of the Uzbek–Tajik boundary.

Increased freedom of expression allowed discussion of Tajik culture and language, and greater interest in Iranian cultures in other countries. Links with Iran had been limited since the 1979 Iranian Revolution, but the pro-Soviet regime in Afghanistan developed cultural contacts with Tajikistan, and many Tajiks served in Afghanistan as interpreters. Tajik was declared the state language in 1989, and the teaching of the Arabic script (used by Tajiks prior to sovietization) was begun in schools.

In February 1990 rioting occurred in Dushanbe, after rumours that Armenian refugees were to be settled there. The scarcity of housing and work appeared to be the cause of the protests, which were directed against the CPT authorities. Demonstrators demanded democratic reforms as well as more radical economic reform. Violence broke out at a protest rally of about 3,000 people when demonstrators clashed with police, overturned cars and looted shops. A state of emergency was declared and a night-time curfew was imposed in Dushanbe. Makhkamov requested aid from the Soviet authorities, and some 5,000 troops of the USSR's Ministry of Internal Affairs were dispatched to the city. In conjunction with 'civilian militia' units, they suppressed the demonstrations; 22 people were reported dead and 565 injured.

The events of February 1990 prompted a more inflexible attitude towards political pluralism by the republic's leadership. The state of emergency was maintained during 1990, and two nascent opposition parties, Rastokhez (Rebirth), which had been involved in the February demonstrations, and the Democratic Party of Tajikistan (DPT), were refused official registration. In addition, the Islamic Renaissance Party (IRP) was refused permission to hold a founding congress in Dushanbe. All three groups, however, continued to attract popular support. In the elections to the Supreme Soviet (the republic's legislature), held in March, opposition politicians were refused permission to participate, and 94% of the elected deputies were members of the CPT.

In an apparent concession to growing Tajik nationalism, the Supreme Soviet adopted a declaration of sovereignty on 25 August 1990. Although the declaration emphasized the equality of all nationalities living in Tajikistan, the growth in Islamic influence, the rediscovery of the Tajiks' Iranian heritage and language and the uncertain political situation all contributed to an increase in emigration from the republic, mainly by Europeans and educated Tajiks. In November Makhkamov was elected to the new post of executive President of the republic by the Supreme Soviet. His only opponent was the former CPT leader, Rakhmon Nabiyev.

The Tajik Government, possibly anxious about increased Turkic dominance in Central Asia, displayed great enthusiasm for a new Union Treaty (effectively preserving the USSR), and Tajikistan was the first republic to declare its willingness to sign such a treaty. Tajiks voted overwhelmingly for the preservation of the USSR in the all-Union referendum in March 1991. According to official figures, 90.2% of eligible voters voted to preserve the USSR.

In August 1991, before the new Union Treaty could be signed, conservative leaders of the Communist Party of the Soviet Union and the Soviet security forces staged a *coup d'état* in Moscow. Makhkamov did not oppose the coup, and on 31 August, after the attempted coup had collapsed, he resigned as President. His resignation had been forced by mass demonstrations, which continued throughout much of September. They were organized by the three main opposition parties (the DPT, the IRP and Rastokhez). On 9 September, following the declarations of independence by neighbouring

Uzbekistan and Kyrgyzstan, the Tajik Supreme Soviet voted to proclaim Tajikistan an independent state, based on democratic principles and the rule of law. The name of the country was changed to the Republic of Tajikistan. This did not, however, satisfy the demonstrators, who demanded the dissolution of the CPT and new, multi-party elections. Kadriddin Aslonov, the Chairman of the Supreme Soviet and acting President, issued a decree which banned the CPT and nationalized its assets (earlier in September the CPT had reorganized as the Socialist Party of Tajikistan, but the original name was reinstated in January 1992). In response, the communist majority in the Supreme Soviet demanded Aslonov's resignation, declared a state of emergency in the republic and rescinded the prohibition of the CPT. Aslonov resigned and was replaced by the former CPT leader, Rakhmon Nabiyev. Nabiyev was, however, quickly obliged to make substantial concessions to the vociferous opposition, and in early October the Supreme Soviet rescinded the state of emergency, suspended the CPT and legalized the IRP, which had previously been banned under legislation that prohibited the formation of religious parties.

On 6 October 1991 Nabiyev resigned as acting President, in advance of the presidential election. There were seven candidates in the direct presidential election, which took place on 24 November. The main contenders were Nabiyev and Davlat Khudonazarov, the liberal Chairman of the USSR Cinematographers' Union, who was supported by the main opposition parties. Mostly as a result of strong support in rural areas, Nabiyev won 57% of the votes cast, compared with 30% for Khudonazarov. The latter claimed that there were electoral malpractices, but his complaints were not upheld and Nabiyev took office in early December. In early January 1992 a new Prime Minister, Akbar Mirzoyev, was appointed to head the Government. Meanwhile, in December 1991, Tajikistan had signed the declaration establishing the Commonwealth of Independent States (CIS), the successor body to the USSR (see below).

Anti-Government demonstrations began in Dushanbe in March 1992, initially prompted by President Nabiyev's dismissal of Mamadayez Navzhuvanov, the Minister of Internal Affairs, who was a prominent Badakhshani (Pamiri). Protests against his dismissal were led by the Pamiri group, Lale Badakhshon, which advocated greater autonomy for the Pamiri peoples of the Gorny Badakhshan Autonomous Region. They were joined by the other main opposition groups, Rastokhez, the IRP and the DPT, particularly after the arrest, in April, of Maksud Ikramov, the mayor of Dushanbe and an opposition sympathizer, on charges of abusing his authority. Demonstrators demanding the resignation of the President and the Government remained encamped in the centre of Dushanbe for nearly two months; in response the Government organized rival demonstrations, bringing supporters to the capital from Kulyab and even Leninabad. In late April members of the newly-formed national guard loyal to President Nabiyev opened fire on the demonstrators, killing at least eight people; in the first week of May the National Security Committee (NSC—formerly the KGB) allegedly distributed weapons to pro-communist supporters. The ensuing violent clashes then escalated into civil war. The fighting in Dushanbe ended when, in early May, Nabiyev negotiated a truce with opposition leaders and formed a new 'Government of National Reconciliation', in which eight of the 24 ministers were members of opposition parties; Mirzoyev retained the post of Prime Minister. The demonstrations ended in Dushanbe, but violent clashes erupted in Kulyab region, in the south of the country, between pro-communist Kulyabi forces, who opposed the President's compromise with the opposition, and members of Islamic and democratic groups.

Kulyab region and the northern, industrial Leninabad region were the main bases of support for President Nabiyev, while most members of Islamic and democratic groups were from the southern Kurgan-Tyube region and the Garm valley to the east of Dushanbe. In late May 1992 the conflict spread from Kulyab region into Kurgan-Tyube region, where a Kulyabi militia, the Tajik People's Front (TPF), led by Sangak Safarov (who had previously spent 23 years in prison for a variety of criminal offences), attempted to suppress the local forces of the informal Islamic/democratic coalition. The Kulyabis alleged that their opponents were receiving arms and assistance from Islamic groups in Afghanistan, and there were reports that Gulbuddin Hekmatyar, the leader of the Afghan *mujahidin* group, Hizb-i Islami, had established training camps in Afghanistan for Tajik fighters. The Islamic/democratic alliance, for its part, claimed that the ex-Soviet (Russian) garrisons were arming the pro-Government militias.

In late August 1992 several members of the DPT and Lale Badakhshon were killed by members of Kulyabi militias in the town of Kurgan-Tyube. A violent conflict ensued in the town, between local members of the opposition and Kulyabis, in which several hundred people were reported to have been killed. Meanwhile, in Dushanbe (where there had been little violence since May) anti-Government demonstrations resumed, and at the end of August demonstrators entered the presidential palace and took 30 officials hostage, although President Nabiyev succeeded in escaping into hiding. On 7 September, however, he was captured by opposition forces at Dushanbe airport, and was forced to announce his resignation. Akbarsho Iskandarov, the Chairman of the Supreme Soviet, temporarily assumed the responsibilities of Head of State, while the coalition Government remained in office. Mirzoyev also resigned and a Leninabad communist, Abdumalik Abdullojonov, was appointed as acting Prime Minister.

Iskandarov's administration, which had the support of all the main Islamic and democratic groups, had little influence outside the capital; much of the south of the country was under the control of Safarov's TPF militia, while some leaders of the northern Leninabad region (where there is a large Uzbek community) threatened to secede from Tajikistan if there was any attempt to introduce an Islamic state. In late October 1992 the Islamic/democratic alliance's control of Dushanbe itself was threatened, when forces led by Safarali Kenjayev, a former Chairman of the Supreme Soviet and a supporter of Nabiyev, entered the capital and attempted to seize power. Kenjayev briefly proclaimed himself Head of State, but his troops were forced to retreat outside the city by forces loyal to the regime. During the ensuing two months, however, Kenjayev's militias enforced a virtual economic blockade of the capital, resulting in shortages of foodstuffs and other goods in the city.

On 10 November 1992, having failed to achieve any success in ending the civil war, acting President Iskandarov and the Government resigned. Shortly afterwards the Tajik Supreme Soviet convened in Khojand (the capital of Leninabad region) to elect a new Government and to negotiate a cease-fire. The legislature abolished the office of President, and Imamali Sharipovich Rahmonov, a collective-farm chairman from Kulyab region, was appointed Chairman of the Supreme Soviet, a post now equivalent to Head of State. The Supreme Soviet elected a new Government, in which Abdumalik Abdullojonov retained the post of Prime Minister. However, all members of the opposition parties lost their portfolios, and the majority of the new ministers were Kulyabis or identified as sympathetic to ex-President Nabiyev. The Supreme Soviet also voted to combine Kurgan-Tyube and Kulyab regions into one administrative region, Hatlon, apparently in an attempt to ensure control of the south of the country by pro-communist forces from Kulyab.

In December 1992 forces loyal to the new Government, the TPF and Kulyabi/Hissarite militias, captured Dushanbe, hitherto under the control of the Popular Democratic Army (PDA), a newly-formed military coalition of Islamic and democratic groups. Hundreds of PDA fighters were reported to have been killed during the attack, and there were also reports of atrocities committed by the militias both in the capital and in the south, particularly against people from Garm and Gorny Badakhshan. It was to these areas, the mountains east of Dushanbe, that the opposition rebels fled. In February 1993 some of the insurgents in Garm attempted to declare an 'autonomous Islamic republic', but the Government had secured control of most of the country by March. The Government estimated that some 20,000 people had been killed during the civil war, while there were an estimated 600,000 people displaced by the fighting. Other estimates put the number of dead in the civil war and its immediate aftermath as high as 50,000 or even 100,000.

In December 1992 and January 1993 some 80,000 Tajiks fled to Afghanistan, after alleged reprisals against supporters of the democratic and Islamic forces, including executions of opposition members, and attacks on people from Garm by the Kulyabi militias. Such reports were denied by the Government and Kulyabi military leaders. Among those reported to have fled was the influential *kazi* (supreme judge) of Tajikistan,

Akbar Turajonzoda, the highest-ranking Muslim clergyman in the country and a senior member of the IRP, who was accused by the new Government of attempting to establish an Islamic state in Tajikistan. (In February 1993 he was replaced as spiritual leader of Tajikistan's Muslims by Fatkhullo Sharifov, who was given the title of *mufti*.)

In March 1993 the TPF leader, Sangak Safarov, was killed, apparently as a result of a brawl with one of his chief military commanders, and in April former President Nabiyev died of a heart attack.

Although the civil war effectively ended at the start of 1993, the continued insurgency of Islamic/democratic forces, notably from across the Afghan border (allegedly supported by Afghan *mujahidin*), continued to destabilize the country. With respect to the interior, government forces ended rebel resistance near Garm in March. In the same month 170 government troops were reported to have been killed during an offensive on Gorny Badakhshan, and fighting between government and rebel forces continued in that region. However, the Pamiri administration was forced in June to abandon claims for independence (contenting itself with assurances that government troops would not enter the autonomous region), in order to secure the supply of desperately-needed food along the crucial Dushanbe–Khorog road.

The communist Government effectively suspended press and broadcasting freedom in January and February 1993. In June the Supreme Court formally proscribed the IRP, Lale Badakhshon, Rastokhez and the DPT, leaving the CPT the only legal party in the country. Even the new parties established later in the year—the Party of Economic Freedom, the People's Democratic Party and the People's Party of Tajikistan—were founded or sponsored by members of the Government or its associates.

The main threat to the Government came from the potential for a factional dispute between the Leninabad élite and the newly-dominant Kulyab faction. In December 1993 Abdullojonov resigned from the premiership. This was perceived as a reverse for the Leninabad faction, although the new Chairman of the Council of Ministers (Prime Minister), Abdujalil Ahadovich Samadov, was also from Leninabad region. At the end of 1993 and in early 1994 Rahmonov, who had secured for his own office responsibility for the powerful Ministries of Defence and Internal Affairs and for the NSC (and, in February 1994, operational supervision of the broadcast media), began to show signs of compromise. When the new Government under Samadov was appointed in February 1994, Rahmonov announced that a priority would be the enactment of a new constitution and elections towards the end of the year. In early March Rahmonov announced that he was willing to negotiate with the Islamic/democratic opposition, and talks began in early April in Moscow, under the chairmanship of the UN and in the presence of the Russian Minister of Foreign Affairs, as well as representatives from Iran, Pakistan and the USA. The government delegation was led by the Minister of Labour and Employment, Shukurjon Zuhurov, while the opposition groups were represented by Ottakhon Latifi, the leader of the Moscow-based Co-ordinating Centre for the Democratic Forces of Tajikistan. The talks continued for two weeks and resulted in a protocol on the establishment of a joint commission on refugees. It was also agreed to hold further rounds of talks. On the ground, reconciliation was far from having been achieved: from March 1994 border incursions by Tajik guerrillas, with the alleged support of Afghan *mujahidin*, intensified, resulting in clashes with the CIS troops stationed on the frontier (see below). Many casualties were reported, particularly on the rebel side. There was also a renewal of insurgency in Gorny Badakhshan, with the number of armed anti-Government fighters within Tajikistan estimated at 4,000–5,000.

In June 1994 a further round of negotiations between representatives of the Government and the opposition took place in the Iranian capital, Teheran. Little progress was achieved, although both sides announced their support, in principle, for a cease-fire, and agreed to reconvene for further discussions. However, attacks by opposition forces on CIS and Tajik government troops patrolling the border with Afghanistan intensified in July and August, with many casualties reported on both sides. The continuing conflict along the Tajik–Afghan border was interpreted by some observers as being partly a battle for control of drugs-smuggling routes. Since gaining independence Tajikistan had become a major conduit for narcotics (chiefly opium) from Pakistan, Iran and Afghanistan to Russia and western Europe, and control of the trade was believed to be a major factor in the Tajik conflict. Much of the drugs trade was alleged to be under the control of Abulamon Ayumbekov (also known as Alex the Hunchback), who was murdered in December 1994.

In August 1994 the Government did not renew the state of emergency, which had been in effect since October 1992, claiming that greater political freedom would be permitted for the presidential election, which was scheduled to take place in September. In late August, however, the election was postponed until later in the year, apparently on the insistence of the Russian Minister of Foreign Affairs (who visited Dushanbe at the end of August), to allow time for opposition candidates to be included in the poll. In mid-September the DPT announced that it would participate in the election and that it had ended its two-year-old alliance with the IRP. Also in mid-September representatives of the Government and the Islamic and democratic opposition, meeting in Teheran, agreed to introduce a temporary cease-fire in the hostilities between the two sides. Nevertheless, in late September rebel forces launched a large-scale offensive in the district of Tavildara, to the east of Dushanbe, but their attack was repelled by government forces. The cease-fire eventually came into effect in late October, but it remained unclear to what extent the various armed bands based in Afghanistan were under the control of the IRP leadership.

Despite the DPT's initial decision to participate in the presidential election, when the poll eventually took place, on 6 November 1994, the only two candidates were Rahmonov, the incumbent Head of State (as Chairman of the Supreme Soviet), and Abdumalik Abdullojonov, currently Tajikistan's ambassador to Russia, who was strongly supported by the élite of Leninabad region. Some 85% of eligible voters were reported to have participated in the election. Rahmonov won the election with some 58% of the votes cast, while Abdullojonov gained the support of about 35% of voters. The result reflected the regional loyalties of the two candidates, Rahmonov (of the Kulyab clan) gaining most of his support in his home territories in the south of the country, while Abdullojonov received an overwhelming proportion of the votes in Leninabad and in Gorny Badakhshan. At the same time as the presidential election, a plebiscite was held on a new Constitution, which was approved by more than 90% of voters. Abdullojonov subsequently alleged that there had been large-scale irregularities in the voting, citing the unexpectedly high level of support for Rahmonov in Dushanbe, where Abdullojonov had expected to win a much higher number of votes. His criticisms were rejected by the Government, and Rahmonov was inaugurated as President in mid-November. In early December Rahmonov made a number of new appointments to the Council of Ministers, with Jamshed Karimov being appointed Chairman, and Mahmadsaid Ubaydulloyev being promoted to First Deputy Chairman.

In early February 1995 a fourth round of peace talks between government and opposition representatives opened in Almaty, Kazakhstan, but little progress was achieved. After the talks the IRP announced that it would not participate in parliamentary elections, scheduled for later in the month. Neither did the DPT participate, although its leader, Shodman Yusuf, was reported to have sought the legalization of the party to enable it to take part. (His increasingly moderate approach was criticized by more radical members of the party, and he was replaced as party leader in June.) In late February the newly-formed Party of Popular Unity and Accord (PPUA—led by Abdullojonov) also announced that it would not take part in the elections, after Abdullojonov's candidature had been disallowed by the electoral authorities. The Organization for Security and Co-operation in Europe (OSCE—see p. 198) refused to send observers to the elections, claiming that the electoral law was severely flawed.

Despite the opposition boycott, elections to the new Supreme Assembly took place on 26 February 1995. Although 350 candidates were reported to have contested the 181 seats, in some 40% of constituencies there was only one candidate. An estimated 84% of eligible voters participated in the poll. Most of those elected were reported to be state officials loyal to the President, but largely without party affiliation. The CPT was reported to have won some 60 seats, and its ally, the People's Party of Tajikistan, five seats. Despite the boycott of the elections by the PPUA, two representatives of the party were reported to have been elected to the legislature. A second round of voting was held on 12 March to decide 19 seats which had not been filled in the previous month. However, when the Supreme Assembly convened in early April, two seats reportedly remained vacant.

In early March 1995 the opposition announced a unilateral extension of the cease-fire for a further 50 days, but later in March there were further attacks on border posts on the Tajik–Afghan frontier. In early April there was a serious escalation of the conflict in the border zone, with a reported 34 border guards and 170 rebel troops killed during one week of fighting. In response, Russian aircraft were alleged to have bombed the Afghan town of Taloqan (reported to be the rebels' base in Afghanistan), killing some 125 civilians. (Russian official sources denied that the attack had taken place.) The opposition forces (comprising the IRP and Lale Badakhshon) claimed that they were responding to a large deployment of Tajik government troops and Russian border guards in Gorny Badakhshan, in violation of the cease-fire agreement. In mid-April talks opened between the Government and opposition groups in Moscow, but the opposition left the negotiations on the first day, dissatisfied with the Russian response to their demands for the withdrawal of troops from Gorny Badakhshan. Nevertheless, the talks were reconvened, and ended in late April with an agreement to extend the cease-fire, and to continue the talks in Almaty in May.

In mid-May 1995 President Rahmonov met Sayed Abdullo Nuri, the leader of the IRP, in Kabul, Afghanistan, for three days of talks. The negotiations resulted in an agreement to extend the cease-fire for a further three months. Subsequent talks between government and opposition delegations took place in late May in Almaty. Despite the agreement reached between Nuri and Rahmonov earlier in the month, the opposition delegation announced that it would not extend the cease-fire, apparently because government representatives had failed to agree to opposition demands for a limitation on the deployment of troops in Gorny Badakhshan. There was also disagreement concerning the opposition's demand for an assembly to be established to consider constitutional amendments. However, the two sides did agree to exchange prisoners. The IRP blamed the intervention of Russian officials in the negotiations for the failure of the talks: Russia claimed that progress was hampered by an unwillingness to compromise on the part of the opposition.

In October 1991 Tajikistan signed, with seven other (former) republics of the USSR, a treaty to establish an economic community, and on 21 December was one of the signatories of the Alma-Ata Declaration, by which the Commonwealth of Independent States (CIS—see p. 126) was established.

Tajikistan had already begun to develop relations outside the USSR in 1990 and 1991, notably with Iran, with which the Tajiks have strong ethnic and linguistic ties. However, the effective collapse of central authority in Tajikistan in 1992 severely hindered further development of foreign relations, although several states attempted to influence the progress of the country's civil war. Nevertheless, by 1995 Tajikistan had established diplomatic relations with more than 40 other states. Russian troops remained in Tajikistan following the demise of the USSR. These armed forces officially took a neutral stance during the civil war, but they were accused of covertly supporting the pro-communist forces. Following the communist victory in the capital in December 1992, Russian and Uzbek troops openly assisted pro-communist troops in quelling the opposition forces. The Uzbek leadership frequently expressed concern about the possibility of a victory for the Islamic/democratic alliance, and closed the Uzbek–Tajik border in mid-1992, ostensibly to prevent the unrest in Tajikistan from spreading to Uzbekistan. In March 1993 the Uzbek air force was involved in defeating rebels in Garm. Since the communist victory over the Islamic/democratic alliance, the Government has been increasingly dependent on Russia, both militarily and economically. In January 1993 Russia, Kazakhstan, Kyrgyzstan and Uzbekistan committed themselves in a collective security treaty to the defence of Tajikistan's southern frontiers, thus taking the Government's side in the continuing conflict on the Tajik–Afghan border. In practice, mainly Russian troops were responsible for repelling rebel fighters entering Tajikistan, with Russia defending the southern CIS border as if it were its own. In August Russia and the Central Asian states (excluding Turkmenistan, which initially refused any involvement in the Tajik conflict) signed an agreement establishing a CIS 'peace-keeping force' to police Tajikistan's border with Afghanistan. By December there were 25,000 troops in place: most of the units were from the Russian army, but there were also soldiers from Uzbekistan, Kazakhstan, Kyrgyzstan and Tajikistan itself. In August 1994 a further border security treaty was signed, by Russia, Tajikistan, Turkmenistan and Uzbekistan. Despite Russia's involvement in the Tajik civil conflict, it also sought to mediate between the Government and the opposition leadership in exile. During 1994–95 relations between the Russian authorities and President Rahmonov deteriorated, owing to disagreements regarding the approach of the Tajik Government to the peace negotiations and the inability of the two countries to agree on the terms of a possible monetary union (see below). Russia appeared increasingly eager to achieve a political settlement of the conflict as well as to reduce its military presence and economic expenditure in the country, particularly following the Russian military intervention in Chechnya.

In October 1994 Tajikistan and Uzbekistan signed a Co-operation Agreement, which envisaged greater co-ordination between the two countries, especially in the fields of foreign policy and security. However, in late 1994 and early 1995 relations between Rahmonov and Preident Karimov of Uzbekistan were reported to have worsened. Karimov criticized the stance of the Tajik Government in negotiations with the opposition as too inflexible, and in April 1995 he met for the first time with a leading IRP member, Akbar Turajonzoda. The Uzbek leadership was also reported to have criticized the treatment of the ethnic uzbek minority in Tajikistan, alleging that many ethnic Uzbeks had been replaced in their posts by Kulyabis.

Relations with Afghanistan were strained by the apparent inability of the Afghan Government to prevent *mujahidin* fighters and consignments of arms from crossing the frontier into Tajikistan. In July 1992 the Chairman of the Tajik legislature, Akbarsho Iskandarov, visited Afghanistan to request the Afghan Government to prevent further armaments from reaching Tajikistan; the Afghan Government denied that it was involved in the traffic of weapons, and it was widely believed that the main source of armaments was the renegade *mujahidin* leader, Gulbuddin Hekmatyar, over whom the Afghan Government held no authority. The election of a new, largely pro-communist Tajik Government in late 1992 further strained relations with Afghanistan, and in April 1993 the Tajik Government protested to the Afghan authorities about alleged incursions across the border by Afghans, apparently to assist the remaining rebel troops. In December the Afghan President, Burhannudin Rabbani, made an official visit to Tajikistan which resulted in the signature of a Tajik-Afghan friendship and co-operation treaty and agreements on economic co-operation and border security. A tripartite agreement was signed, together with the office of the UN High Commissioner for Refugees, on the safety of refugees returning to Tajikistan. Rabbani was, however, unable to exert control over the Afghan factions supporting the Tajik insurgents, and border incursions continued. In April 1995 Afghanistan protested strongly against alleged Russian attacks on rebel bases within Afghanistan, and continued to insist that there was no official support of rebel Tajik factions within the country.

Anti-Islamic groups in Tajikistan asserted that Iran was supplying armaments and other goods to Islamic elements in Tajikistan, but this was denied by the Iranian authorities, who admitted providing only cultural and humanitarian assistance. Following the defeat of the Islamic/democratic alliance at the end of 1992, the leadership of the IRP established itself in the Iranian capital, Teheran. Western countries gave tacit approval to Russia's support of the communist regime that took power in late 1992, probably because of fears that the opposition would transform Tajikistan into an Islamic state. However, in June 1993 the EC condemned the Tajik regime for its record of human rights abuses. In March 1994 the Tajik premier, Samadov, visited several western countries, in an attempt to persuade western business interests to invest in his country. However, the conduct of the presidential election in November 1994. and the parliamentary elections of February 1995 was strongly critized by the UN, the OSCE and several western countries.

## Government

Under the Constitution of November 1994, Tajikistan has a presidential system of government. The President is Head of State and also heads the executive branch of power. The President appoints a Prime Minister (or Chairman) to head the Government (Council of Ministers). Legislative power is vested in the 181-member Supreme Assembly. For administrative purposes, the country is divided into three regions (oblasts): Leninabad, in the north; Hatlan (formerly two regions of Kulyab and Kurgan-Tyube), in the south; and the autonomous region of Gorny Badakhshan. These regions are further subdivided into districts and towns. The city of Dushanbe has a separate status, and is administratively independent of the three regions.

## Defence

A Ministry of Defence was established in September 1992; in December it was announced that Tajikistan's future national armed forces would be formed on the basis of the Tajik People's Front and other paramilitary units supporting the Government. At mid-1994 there were estimated to be 2,000–3,000 armed personnel in the Tajik army, although military units had not yet been formed. There were also an estimated 12,000 forces of the Commonwealth of Independent States (CIS) based in Tajikistan (most of whom were from the Russian army). Defence expenditure for 1994 was estimated to be US $115m.

## Economic Affairs

In 1993, according to preliminary estimates by the World Bank, Tajikistan's gross national product (GNP), measured at average 1991–93 prices, was US $2,686m., equivalent to $470 per head (reportedly the lowest among all the former Soviet republics). During 1985–93, it was estimated, GNP per head declined, in real terms, by an average annual rate of 7.8%. During the same period the population increased by an annual average of 2.8%.

Despite the fact that only 7% of Tajikistan's land is arable (the remainder being largely mountainous), the Tajik economy is predominantly agricultural: in 1991 agriculture contributed 43.9% of net material product (NMP) and provided 44.6% of employment. The principal crop is cotton, followed in importance by grain, vegetables and fruit. Approximately 75% of the country's arable land is irrigated. In 1991 agricultural NMP decreased by 9.9%, compared with the previous year. Agricultural production was severely disrupted by the civil war in 1992–93, and there were frequent reports of shortages of foodstuffs in urban areas. In 1994 the value of production decreased by 3.2%, compared with 1993.

In 1991 industry and construction contributed 43.5% of NMP and provided 20.4% of employment. There is little heavy industry, except for mineral extraction, aluminium production and power generation. Light industry concentrates on food-processing, textiles and carpet-making. In 1991 industrial NMP declined by 4.2%, compared with 1990, and it was estimated that the volume of industrial production decreased by 40% between 1990 and 1993, as a result of disruption caused by the civil conflict. The value of industrial production declined sharply in 1994, by an estimated 31%, compared with 1993.

Tajikistan has considerable mineral deposits, including gold, aluminium, iron, lead, mercury and tin. Gold production amounted to 705 kg in 1992, but was expected to have decreased to 305 kg in 1993, owing to a shortage of diesel fuel. However, in late 1993 the opening of a new gold-mine in the west of the country was announced, which, it was hoped, would eventually provide 4m. metric tons of gold ore per year. There are deposits of coal as well as small reserves of petroleum and natural gas. However, Tajikistan relies heavily on imports of petroleum and gas and, owing to the collapse of the Soviet trading system and integrated economy and the disruptions caused by the civil war, there were widespread fuel shortages in 1992–93. The mountain river system is widely used for hydroelectric power generation (satisfying about 75% of domestic electricity requirements prior to the civil war). A new hydroelectric power station was being built at Rogun in early 1994, with assistance from Russia and Pakistan. Electric energy production decreased by 4% in 1994.

In 1992, according to World Bank figures, Tajikistan recorded a trade surplus of 5,760m. roubles (compared with a surplus of 33m. roubles in 1991). In the same year trade with other former Soviet republics accounted for 60% of total external trade (imports plus exports), although 55% of exports went to countries outside the former USSR. In 1994, by comparison, Western countries (principally the Netherlands, Switzerland, Belgium, the United Kingdom and the USA) accounted for 91% of Tajikistan's foreign trade. In that year the two main exports were aluminium (providing 73% of total export earnings) and cotton lint (25%). The principal imports were materials and machinery for aluminium plants (some 60% of the total), food products and consumer goods.

The 1994 budget projected a deficit of 175,100m. roubles. Tajikistan's total external debt was US $41.5m. at the end of 1993, of which $41.2m. was long-term public debt. In 1994 consumer prices increased by an estimated annual average of 240%. At the end of 1994 some 31,800 people were registered as unemployed.

In 1992 Tajikistan joined the Economic Co-operation Organization (ECO, see p. 238) and the European Bank for Reconstruction and Development (EBRD, see p. 140); it became a member of the IMF and the World Bank in 1993. Tajikistan has sought to promote closer economic integration among the member states of the Commonwealth of Independent States (CIS, see p. 126).

Already the poorest of the republics of the former USSR, during the early 1990s the Tajik economy was very seriously affected by the widespread disruption to the former Soviet trading system, caused by the collapse of the USSR, and by the civil war that broke out in 1992 (see Recent History). All economic sectors suffered badly: the EBRD estimated that gross domestic product (GDP) declined by 31% in 1992, and further in 1993, although by a smaller proportion. The communist Government that took power in late 1992 has been heavily subsidized by Russia and, to a lesser extent, Uzbekistan. In November 1993, suffering the effects of hyperinflation, the regime agreed to surrender control of monetary policy and government expenditure to the Central Bank of the Russian Federation, in order to gain membership of a new Russian 'rouble zone'. Russia granted Tajikistan a credit of US $100m. to facilitate its transfer to the 1993 Russian rouble, and the new currency was introduced in Tajikistan in early January 1994. However, during 1994 Russia appeared increasingly unwilling to assume the high level of expenditure that full monetary union between the two countries would entail, and showed reluctance to issue further currency for use by the Tajik Government. As a result, there was a severe shortage of currency for the payment of salaries in the country. In May 1995 Tajikistan introduced a new currency, the Tajik rouble, although the Tajik leadership continued to express a desire to achieve full monetary union with Russia. It was not clear initially to what extent the new currency would be financially supported by Russia, or by international organizations such as the IMF. By mid-1995 little progress had been made in economic reform in Tajikistan, although a programme of privatization was being implemented. Foreign investment was discouraged by the civil unrest, although in 1994–95 several Western companies formed joint ventures to exploit Tajikistan's large mineral reserves, especially gold. According to outside observers, Tajikistan's future economic development would most profitably be based on the country's as yet largely unexploited mineral reserves, as well as the established cotton industry.

## Social Welfare

In early 1992, in connection with the proposed transition to a market economy system and the expected social consequences thereof, the Tajik Government established an Employment Fund to provide unemployment benefits, which was to be almost entirely financed by employers' levies on salaries. Two further extrabudgetary funds, the Pension Fund and the Social Insurance Fund, were also in operation in 1992. In addition to the activities of the three extrabudgetary funds, the state budget for 1992 projected expenditure of 9,737m. roubles for social and cultural services (54.2% of total expenditure). In November 1992 the Government announced special social welfare measures to help victims of the country's civil war (including those who had been wounded or shell-shocked, lost their means of living, accommodation or property, and those who had been forced to become refugees).

In 1989 there were 105 hospital beds per 10,000 inhabitants.

## TAJIKISTAN

### Education

Education is controlled by the Ministry of Education and is fully funded by the State at all levels. The majority of pupils receive their education in Tajik (66.0% of pupils in general day schools in 1988); other languages in use include Uzbek (22.9%), Russian (9.7%), Kyrgyz (1.1%) and Turkmen (0.3%). Following the adoption of Tajik as the state language in 1989, pupils in Russian-language schools were to learn Tajik from the first to the 11th grades. Greater emphasis has been placed in the curriculum on Tajik language and literature, including classical Persian literature. In 1991 a new university was established in Khojand. In the previous year there were 10 institutes of higher education, with a total enrolment of 68,800 students. In 1989, according to census results, the average rate of adult illiteracy was only 2.3% (males 1.2%; females 3.4%).

### Weights and Measures

The metric system is in force.

# Statistical Survey

Principal sources: IMF, *Tajikistan, Economic Review*; World Bank, *Statistical Handbook: States of the Former USSR*.

## Area and Population

**AREA, POPULATION AND DENSITY**

| | |
|---|---:|
| Area (sq km) | 143,100* |
| Population (census results) | |
| 17 January 1979† | 3,806,220 |
| 12 January 1989† | |
| Males | 2,530,245 |
| Females | 2,562,358 |
| Total | 5,092,603 |
| Population (official estimates at mid-year) | |
| 1993 | 5,638,000 |
| 1994 | 5,751,000 |
| Density (per sq km) at mid-1994 | 40.2 |

\* 55,251 sq miles.
† Figures refer to *de jure* population. The *de facto* total at the 1989 census was 5,108,576.

**POPULATION BY NATIONALITY** (1989 census result)

| | % |
|---|---:|
| Tajik | 62.3 |
| Uzbek | 23.5 |
| Russian | 7.6 |
| Tatar | 1.4 |
| Others | 5.2 |
| **Total** | 100.0 |

**PRINCIPAL TOWNS** (estimated population at 1 January 1990)
Dushanbe (capital) 602,000; Khojand 163,000.

**BIRTHS, MARRIAGES AND DEATHS**

| | Registered live births | | Registered marriages | | Registered deaths | |
|---|---:|---:|---:|---:|---:|---:|
| | Number | Rate (per 1,000) | Number | Rate (per 1,000) | Number | Rate (per 1,000) |
| 1987 | 204,450 | 41.8 | 46,233 | 9.5 | 33,543 | 6.9 |
| 1988 | 201,864 | 40.1 | 46,933 | 9.3 | 35,334 | 7.0 |
| 1989 | 200,430 | 38.7 | 47,616 | 9.2 | 33,395 | 6.4 |

Source: UN, *Demographic Yearbook*.

**1993:** Registered live births 186,504, Rate (per 1,000) 33.1; Registered deaths 49,326, Rate (per 1,000) 8.7.
Source: UN, *Population and Vital Statistics Report*.

**Expectation of life** (years at birth, 1989): 69.4 (males 66.8; females 71.7) (Source: Goskomstat USSR).

**EMPLOYMENT** (annual averages, '000 persons)

| | 1989 | 1990 | 1991 |
|---|---:|---:|---:|
| Activities of the material sphere | 1,409 | 1,461 | 1,491 |
| Agriculture | 790 | 831 | 878 |
| Forestry | 2 | 2 | 3 |
| Industry* | 254 | 261 | 257 |
| Construction | 161 | 161 | 148 |
| Trade and catering† | 105 | 108 | 109 |
| Transport and communications‡ | 63 | 62 | 67 |
| Others | 34 | 37 | 33 |
| Activities of the non-material sphere | 464 | 473 | 478 |
| Transport and communications‡ | 27 | 27 | 26 |
| Housing and municipal services | 51 | 51 | 51 |
| Health care, social security, physical culture and sports | 101 | 104 | 106 |
| Education, culture and arts | 211 | 217 | 222 |
| Science, research and development | 30 | 29 | 26 |
| Government and finance | 45 | 46 | 47 |
| **Total employed** | 1,873 | 1,934 | 1,969 |

\* Comprising manufacturing (except printing and publishing), mining and quarrying, electricity, gas, water, logging and fishing.
† Including material and technical supply.
‡ Transport and communications servicing material production are included in activities of the material sphere. Other branches of the sector are considered to be non-material services.

## Agriculture

**PRINCIPAL CROPS** ('000 metric tons)

| | 1991 | 1992 | 1993 |
|---|---:|---:|---:|
| Wheat | 141 | 170 | 200* |
| Rice (paddy) | 24 | 20 | 20† |
| Barley | 47 | 42 | 40* |
| Maize | 60 | 32 | 30* |
| Other cereals | 11 | 14 | 13 |
| Potatoes | 181 | 167 | 100* |
| Pulses | 10† | 10 | 10† |
| Seed cotton | 828 | 410 | 580* |
| Cotton (lint) | 247 | 123* | 174* |
| Vegetables | 628 | 679 | 552 |
| Watermelons‡ | 200† | 136 | 150† |
| Grapes | 121 | 100 | 85† |
| Other fruits and berries | 177 | 181 | 135† |
| Tobacco (leaves) | 11 | 8† | 8† |

\* Unofficial figure.   † FAO estimate.
‡ Including melons, pumpkins and squash.
Source: FAO, *Production Yearbook*.

# TAJIKISTAN

## LIVESTOCK ('000 head at 1 January)

|         | 1991  | 1992   | 1993    |
|---------|-------|--------|---------|
| Horses  | 52    | 53*    | 53*     |
| Asses   | n.a.  | 36*    | 36*     |
| Cattle  | 1,352 | 1,266  | 1,159†  |
| Pigs    | 183   | 163    | 143†    |
| Sheep   | 2,462 | 2,620  | 2,550*  |
| Goats   | 830   | 780    | 760*    |
| Poultry | 8,000 | 6,000† | 5,000*  |

* FAO estimate.   † Unofficial figure.

Source: FAO, *Production Yearbook*.

## LIVESTOCK PRODUCTS ('000 metric tons)

|                | 1991  | 1992  | 1993  |
|----------------|-------|-------|-------|
| Beef and veal  | 48    | 39*   | 37*   |
| Mutton and lamb| 21    | 19†   | 18†   |
| Pig meat       | 6     | 5†    | 6*    |
| Poultry meat   | 10    | 8†    | 7†    |
| Cows' milk     | 557   | 475*  | 500*  |
| Goats' milk†   | 30    | 25    | 30    |
| Butter         | 5     | 4*    | 4*    |
| Cheese         | n.a.  | 7.0†  | 7.5†  |
| Hen eggs       | 25.2* | 18.0* | 16.0† |
| Wool:          |       |       |       |
| greasy         | 4.4   | 4.0†  | 3.0†  |
| scoured        | 2.7   | 2.4†  | 1.8†  |

* Unofficial figure.   † FAO estimate(s).

Source: FAO, *Production Yearbook*.

## Fishing

('000 metric tons, live weight)

|               | 1991 | 1992* |
|---------------|------|-------|
| Silver carp   | 2.0  | 2.0   |
| Hoven's carp  | 1.7  | 1.6   |
| Other fishes  | 0.2  | 0.3   |
| **Total catch** | 3.9 | 3.9  |

* FAO estimates.

Source: FAO, *Yearbook of Fishery Statistics*.

## Mining and Industry

**Production** (1989, unless otherwise stated): Coal 515,000 metric tons, Crude petroleum 190,000 tons, Natural gas 303 million cu m, Mineral fertilizers 88,100 tons, Domestic refrigerators 170,500, Copper cable (by copper weight) 16,200 tons, Technical lighting equipment 8.9 million roubles, Cotton yarn 129,000 tons, Woven cotton fabrics 125 million m, Knitted garments 13,200,000 (1986), Hosiery 36.1 million pairs (1986), Leather footwear 10.8 million pairs, Carpets and rugs 10.8 million sq m, Vegetable oil 93,200 tons, Tinned goods 374 million cans, Cement 1,111,000 tons, Reinforced concrete 1,169,000 cu m, Bricks 320.0 million, Electric energy 16,800 million kWh (1992).

# Finance

## CURRENCY AND EXCHANGE RATES

**Monetary Units**
100 kopeks = 1 rubl (ruble or rouble).

**Sterling and Dollar Equivalents** (31 December 1994)
£1 sterling = 5,006 roubles;
US $1 = 3,200 roubles;
10,000 roubles = £1.997 = $3.125.

**Average Exchange Rate** (roubles per US dollar)
1989   0.6274
1990   0.5856
1991   0.5819

Note: The figures for average exchange rates refer to official rates for the Soviet rouble. However, a multiple exchange rate system was in operation, with separate non-commercial and tourist rates. A commercial exchange rate was introduced on 1 November 1990, replacing the official rate for most transactions. The commercial rate (roubles per US dollar) was: 1.692 at 31 December 1990; 1.671 at 31 December 1991. Between November 1989 and April 1991 the tourist exchange rate valued the rouble at one-tenth of the official rate. In April 1991 this rate, renamed the 'special rate', was set at $1 = 27.6 roubles. It was subsequently adjusted. The average market exchange rate in 1991 was $1 = 31.2 roubles. Following the dissolution of the USSR in December 1991, Russia and several other former Soviet republics retained the rouble as their monetary unit. The average interbank market rate in 1992 was $1 = 222.1 Russian roubles. Tajikistan continued to use the old rouble when Russia withdrew all pre-1993 rouble notes in July 1993. By November the Tajik Government had agreed to the conditions of the Central Bank of the Russian Federation for readmission to a new 'rouble zone'. The new roubles were brought into circulation on 5–8 January 1994. However, in May 1995 Tajikistan introduced its own currency, the Tajik rouble, initially at an exchange rate of US $1 = 50 roubles. The exchange rates for the end of 1994 (see above) refer to market rates for the Russian rouble, then the legal tender in Tajikistan.

## STATE BUDGET (million Soviet/Russian roubles)

| Revenue                       | 1991  | 1992*  |
|-------------------------------|-------|--------|
| Turnover tax                  | 955   | —      |
| Tax on sales                  | 219   | —      |
| Value-added tax               | —     | 5,140  |
| Excises                       | —     | 5,070  |
| Enterprise profits tax        | 604   | 1,821  |
| Revaluation enterprise stocks | 393   | 2,263  |
| Income from privatizations    | —     | 1,363  |
| Personal income taxes         | 333   | 522    |
| Duties and local taxes        | 169   | 130    |
| Import and export taxes       | 2     | 233    |
| Land tax                      | 7     | 310    |
| Transfers from USSR budget    | 2,543 | —      |
| Balance from previous year    | 209   | —      |
| **Total** (incl. others)      | 5,457 | 16,875 |

| Expenditure                       | 1991  | 1992*  |
|-----------------------------------|-------|--------|
| Economy                           | 1,315 | 1,326  |
| Social and cultural services      | 3,138 | 9,737  |
| Science                           | 18    | 98     |
| Law enforcement                   | 49    | 4,159  |
| Authorities, agencies, courts     | 82    | 201    |
| Cabinet reserve fund              | —     | 170    |
| Other expenditure                 | 418   | 1,178  |
| Capital export union enterprises  | —     | 600    |
| Commonwealth of Independent States| —     | 500    |
| **Total**                         | 5,020 | 17,978 |

* Forecast.

## MONEY SUPPLY (million Soviet/Russian roubles at 31 December)

|                        | 1990  | 1991  |
|------------------------|-------|-------|
| Currency outside banks | 1,588 | 1,715 |

# TAJIKISTAN

## COST OF LIVING
(Index of consumer prices in state and co-operative sectors; base: previous year = 100)

|  | 1990 | 1991 | 1992 |
|---|---|---|---|
| Food (excl. alcohol) | 101.8 | 194.4 | 1,450.5 |
| Alcoholic beverages | 100.6 | 163.4 | 1,152.1 |
| Other products | 105.7 | 195.8 | 936.6 |
| **All items** | 104.0 | 193.0 | 1,153.9 |

## NATIONAL ACCOUNTS
**Net Material Product** (million Soviet/Russian roubles at current prices)

|  | 1989 | 1990 | 1991 |
|---|---|---|---|
| Agriculture | 1,793 | 2,015 | 4,622 |
| Forestry | 3 | 3 | 5 |
| Industry* | 1,284 | 1,503 | 3,228 |
| Construction | 738 | 772 | 1,353 |
| Transport and communications | 185 | 221 | 266 |
| Trade and catering† | 419 | 477 | 922 |
| Other activities of the material sphere | 396 | 500 | 143 |
| **Total** | 4,817 | 5,490 | 10,540 |

* Comprising manufacturing (except printing and publishing), mining and quarrying, electricity, gas, water, logging and fishing.
† Including material and technical supply.

# External Trade

**PRINCIPAL COMMODITIES** (million Soviet/Russian roubles)
**Trade with the Former USSR**

| Imports | 1990 | 1991 | 1992 |
|---|---|---|---|
| Industrial products | 3,035 | 2,960 | 23,142 |
| Petroleum and gas | 271 | 364 | 6,093 |
| Electricity | 71 | — | — |
| Iron and steel | 110 | 191 | 2,952 |
| Non-ferrous metallurgy | 193 | 79 | 524 |
| Chemical and petroleum products | 322 | 258 | 4,761 |
| Machinery and metalworking | 796 | 475 | 2,926 |
| Wood and paper products | 124 | 197 | 820 |
| Light industry | 558 | 574 | 2,777 |
| Food and beverages | 424 | 707 | 1,455 |
| Agricultural products (unprocessed) | 182 | 107 | 697 |
| Other commodities | 142 | — | — |
| **Total** | 3,359 | 3,067 | 23,839 |

| Exports | 1990 | 1991 | 1992 |
|---|---|---|---|
| Industrial products | 2,228 | 3,201 | 16,433 |
| Electricity | 63 | — | — |
| Non-ferrous metallurgy | 298 | 955 | 4,782 |
| Chemical and petroleum products | 119 | 72 | 787 |
| Machinery and metalworking | 228 | 486 | 4,661 |
| Construction materials | 29 | 181 | 225 |
| Light industry | 1,061 | 954 | 4,233 |
| Food and beverages | 405 | 491 | 1,091 |
| Agricultural products (unprocessed) | 92 | — | — |
| Other commodities | 59 | — | — |
| **Total** | 2,378 | 3,201 | 16,433 |

**Trade with Other Countries**

| Imports | 1990 | 1991 | 1992 |
|---|---|---|---|
| Industrial products | 687 | 475 | 257 |
| Non-ferrous metallurgy | 39 | — | — |
| Chemical and petroleum products | 57 | 1 | 10 |
| Machinery and metalworking | 113 | 2 | 13 |
| Light industry | 298 | 198 | 124 |
| Food and beverages | 151 | 272 | 95 |
| Agricultural products (unprocessed) | 81 | 126 | 6,790 |
| **Total** | 768 | 601 | 7,047 |

| Exports | 1990 | 1991 | 1992 |
|---|---|---|---|
| Industrial products | 304 | 500 | 20,213 |
| Non-ferrous metallurgy | 168 | 488 | 20,107 |
| Light industry | 126 | 2 | 76 |
| Agricultural products (unprocessed) | 4 | — | — |
| **Total** | 308 | 500 | 20,213 |

**PRINCIPAL TRADING PARTNERS** (million Soviet/Russian roubles)
**Trade with the Former USSR**

| Imports | 1991 | 1992 |
|---|---|---|
| Azerbaijan | 37 | 262 |
| Belarus | 61 | 662 |
| Georgia | 199 | 51 |
| Kazakhstan | 318 | 2,915 |
| Kyrgyzstan | 238 | 479 |
| Russia | 1,252 | 11,139 |
| Turkmenistan | 197 | 3,468 |
| Ukraine | 281 | 1,731 |
| Uzbekistan | 362 | 2,630 |
| **Total** (incl. others) | 3,066 | 23,839 |

| Exports | 1991 | 1992 |
|---|---|---|
| Armenia | 37 | 66 |
| Azerbaijan | 42 | 634 |
| Belarus | 109 | 680 |
| Kazakhstan | 417 | 2,411 |
| Kyrgyzstan | 61 | 381 |
| Russia | 1,831 | 7,813 |
| Turkmenistan | 96 | 705 |
| Ukraine | 249 | 1,927 |
| Uzbekistan | 244 | 1,470 |
| **Total** (incl. others) | 3,201 | 16,433 |

# Transport

**ROAD TRAFFIC** (motor vehicles in use at 31 December)

|  | 1990 | 1991 | 1992 |
|---|---|---|---|
| Passenger cars | 1,881 | 1,889 | 1,536 |
| Buses and coaches | 4,169 | 4,243 | 3,500 |
| Lorries and vans | 11,899 | 12,027 | 8,755 |

Source: IRF, *World Road Statistics*.

## Communications Media

|  | 1992 |
|---|---|
| Daily newspapers: | |
|   Titles | 9 |
|   Copies ('000) | 36,137 |
| Non-daily newspapers: | |
|   Titles | 110 |
|   Copies ('000) | 56,853 |
| Other periodicals: | |
|   Titles | 26 |
|   Copies ('000) | 18,841 |

Source: UNESCO, *Statistical Yearbook*.

**Telephones** ('000 main lines in use, 1991): 258 (Source: UN, *Statistical Yearbook*).

## Education

(1993)

|  | Institutions | Teachers | Students |
|---|---|---|---|
| Primary schools | n.a. | 25,000* | 570,300 |
| Secondary schools | 3,101† | 62,700 | 652,700 |
| Higher schools (incl. universities) | 10† | n.a. | 68,800‡ |

* 1992.  † 1989/90.  ‡ 1990.

Source: mainly UNESCO, *Statistical Yearbook*.

# Directory

## The Constitution

Tajikistan's Constitution entered into force on 6 November 1994, when it was approved by a majority of voters in a nation-wide plebiscite. It replaced the previous Soviet-style Constitution, adopted in 1978. The following is a summary of its main provisions:

### PRINCIPLES OF THE CONSTITUTIONAL SYSTEM

The Republic of Tajikistan is a sovereign, democratic, law-governed, secular and unitary state. The state language is Tajik, but Russian is accorded the status of a language of communication between nationalities.

Recognition, observance and protection of human and civil rights and freedoms is the obligation of the state. The people of Tajikistan are the expression of sovereignty and the sole source of power of the state, which they express through their elected representatives.

Tajikistan consists of Gorny Badakhshan Autonomous Region, regions, towns, districts, settlements and villages. The territory of the state is indivisible and inviolable. Agitation and actions aimed at disunity of the state are prohibited.

No ideology, including religious ideology, may be granted the status of a state ideology. Religious organizations are separate from the state and may not interfere in state affairs.

The Constitution of Tajikistan has supreme legal authority and its norms have direct application. Laws and other legal acts which run counter to the Constitution have no legal validity. The state, its bodies and officials are bound to observe the provisions of the Constitution.

Tajikistan will implement a peaceful policy, respecting the sovereignty and independence of other states of the world and will determine foreign relations on the basis of international norms. Agitation for war is prohibited.

The economy of Tajikistan is based on various forms of ownership. The state guarantees freedom of economic activity, entrepreneurship, equality of rights and the protection of all forms of ownership, including private ownership. Land and natural resources are under state ownership.

### FUNDAMENTAL DUTIES OF INDIVIDUALS AND CITIZENS

The freedoms and rights of individuals are protected by the Constitution, the laws of the republic and international documents to which Tajikistan is a signatory. The state guarantees the rights and freedoms of every person, regardless of nationality, race, sex, language, religious beliefs, political persuasion, social status, knowledge and property. Men and women have the same rights. Every person has the right to life. No one may be subjected to torture, punishment or inhuman treatment. No one may be arrested, kept in custody or exiled without a legal basis, and no one is adjudged guilty of a crime except by the sentence of a court in accordance with the law. Every person has the right freely to choose their place of residence, to leave the republic and return to it. Every person has the right to profess any religion individually or with others, or not to profess any, and to take part in religious ceremonies. Every citizen has the right to take part in political life and state administration; to elect and be elected from the age of 18; to join and leave political parties, trade unions and other associations; to take part in meetings, rallies or demonstrations. Every person is guaranteed freedom of speech. State censorship is prohibited.

Every person has the right: to ownership and inheritance; to work; to housing; to health care, provided free of charge by the state; to social security in old age, or in the event of sickness or disability. Every person has the right to education. Basic general education is compulsory.

A state of emergency is declared as a temporary measure to ensure the security of citizens and of the state in the instance of a direct threat to the freedom of citizens, the state's independence, its territorial integrity, or natural disasters. The period of a state of emergency is up to three months; it can be prolonged by the President of the Republic.

### THE SUPREME ASSEMBLY

The Supreme Assembly is the highest representative and legislative body of the republic. Its 181 members are elected for a five-year-term. Any citizen over the age of 25 may be elected to the Supreme Assembly.

The powers of the Supreme Assembly include: enactment and amendment of laws, and their annulment; interpretation of the Constitution and laws; determination of the basic direction of domestic and foreign policy; ratification of presidential decrees on the appointment and dismissal of the Chairman of the National Bank, the Chairman and members of the Constitutional Court, the Supreme Court and the Supreme Economic Court; ratification of the state budget; determining and altering the structure of administrative territorial units; ratification and annulment of international treaties; ratification of presidential decrees on a state of war and a state of emergency.

Laws are adopted by a majority of the deputies of the Supreme Assembly. If the President does not agree with the law, he may return it to the Supreme Assembly. If the Supreme Assembly once again approves the law, with at least a two-thirds majority, the President must sign it.

### THE PRESIDENT OF THE REPUBLIC

The President of the Republic is the Head of State and the head of the executive. The President is elected by the citizens of Tajikistan on the basis of universal, direct and equal suffrage for a five-year term. Any citizen who knows the state language and has lived on the territory of Tajikistan for the preceding 10 years may be nominated to the post of President of the Republic. A person may not be nominated to the office of President for more than two consecutive terms.

The President has the authority: to represent Tajikistan inside the country and in international relations; to establish or abolish ministries with the approval of the Supreme Assembly; to appoint or dismiss the Chairman (Prime Minister) and other members of the Council of Ministers and to propose them for approval to the Supreme Assembly; to appoint and dismiss chairmen of regions, towns and districts, and propose new appointments for approval to the relevant assemblies of people's deputies; to appoint and dismiss members of the Constitutional Court, the Supreme Court and the Supreme Economic Court (with the approval of the Supreme Assembly); to appoint and dismiss judges of lower courts; to sign laws; to lead the implementation of foreign policy and sign international treaties; to appoint diplomatic representatives

# TAJIKISTAN

abroad; to be Commander-in-Chief of the armed forces of Tajikistan; to declare a state of war or a state of emergency (with the approval of the Supreme Assembly).

In the event of the president's death, resignation, removal from office or inability to perform his duties, the duties of the President will be carried out by the Chairman of the Supreme Assembly until further presidential elections can be held. New elections must be held within three months of these circumstances. The President may be removed from office in the case of his committing a crime, by the decision of at least two-thirds of deputies of the Supreme Assembly, taking into account the decisions of the Constitutional Court.

### THE COUNCIL OF MINISTERS

The Council of Ministers consists of the Chairman (Prime Minister), the First Deputy Chairman, Deputy Chairmen, Ministers and Chairmen of State Committees. The Council of Ministers is responsible for implementation of laws and decrees of the Supreme Assembly and decrees and orders of the President. The Council of Ministers leaves office when a new President is elected.

### LOCAL GOVERNMENT

The local representative authority in regions, towns and districts is the assembly of people's deputies. Assemblies are elected for a five-year term. Local executive government is the responsibility of the President's representative: the chairman of the assembly of people's deputies, who is proposed by the President and approved by the relevant assembly. The Supreme Assembly may dissolve local representative bodies, if their actions do not conform to the Constitution and the law.

### THE GORNY BADAKHSHAN AUTONOMOUS REGION

The Gorny Badakhshan Autonomous Region is an integral and indivisible part of Tajikistan, the territory of which cannot be changed without the consent of the regional assembly of people's deputies.

### JUDICIARY

The judiciary is independent and protects the rights and freedoms of the individual, the interests of the state, organizations and institutions, and legality and justice. Judicial power is implemented by the Constitutional Court, the Supreme Court, the Supreme Economic Court, the Military Court, the Court of Gorny Badakhshan Autonomous Region, and courts of regions, the city of Dushanbe, towns and districts. The term of judges is five years. The creation of emergency courts is not permitted.

Judges are independent and are subordinate only to the Constitution and the law. Interference in their activity is not permitted.

### THE OFFICE OF THE PROCURATOR-GENERAL

The Procurator-General and procurators subordinate to him ensure the control and observance of laws within the framework of their authority in the territory of Tajikistan. The Procurator-General is responsible to the Supreme Assembly and the President, and is elected for a five-year term.

### PROCEDURES FOR INTRODUCING AMENDMENTS TO THE CONSTITUTION

Amendments and addenda to the Constitution are made by means of a referendum. A referendum takes place with the support of at least two-thirds of the people's deputies. The president, or at least one-third of the people's deputies, may submit amendments and addenda to the Constitution. The form of public administration, the territorial integrity and the democratic, law-governed and secular nature of the state are irrevocable.

## The Government

### HEAD OF STATE

**President of the Republic of Tajikistan:** IMAMALI SHARIPOVICH RAHMONOV (elected by popular vote on 6 November 1994).

### COUNCIL OF MINISTERS
(June 1995)

**Chairman (Prime Minister):** JAMSHED KARIMOV.
**First Deputy Chairman:** MAHMADSAID UBAYDULLOYEV.
**Deputy Chairmen:** BOZGUL DODKHUDOYEVA, JAMOLIDDIN MANSUROV, KADRIDDIN GHIYOSOV.
**Minister of Finance:** ANVAR MUZOFAROV.
**Minister of Industry:** SHAVKAT UMAROV.
**Minister of Construction:** ODIL OCHILOV.
**Minister of Grain Products:** BEKMUROD UROKOV.
**Minister of Transport:** FARIDDUN MUHIDDINOV.
**Minister of Culture and Information:** BOBOKHON MAHMADOV.
**Minister of Health:** ALAMKHON AHMEDOV.
**Minister of Environmental Protection and Water Resources:** SAYDULLO KHAYRULLOYEV.
**Minister of Security:** Maj.-Gen. SAYDAMIR ZUHUROV.
**Minister of Labour and Employment:** HIKMAT ESHMIRZOYEV.
**Minister of Communications:** IBRAHIM USMONOV.
**Minister of Defence:** Maj.-Gen. SHERALI KHAYRULLOYEV.
**Minister of Internal Affairs:** Maj.-Gen. YAKUB SALIMOV.
**Minister of Justice:** SHAVKAT ISMOILOV.
**Minister of Social Security:** ABDUSSATOR JABBOROV.
**Minister of the Economy and Foreign Economic Relations:** TUKHTABOY GAFAROV.
**Minister of Foreign Affairs:** TALBAK NAZAROV.
**Minister of Agriculture:** HABIBULLO TABAROV.

#### Chairmen of State Committees

**Chairman of State Committee for Construction and Architecture:** BAHAVADDIN ZUHURUDDINOV.
**Chairman of State Committee for Contracts and Trade:** HAKIM SOLIYEV.
**Chairman of State Committee for State Property:** MATLUBKHON S. DAVLYATOV.
**Chairman of State Committee for Youth, Sport and Tourism:** ZEBINISO RUSTAMOVA.
**Chairman of State Committee for Customs:** KH. HAMROKULOV.
**Chairman of State Committee for Statistics:** KHOLMAMED AZIMOV.
**Chairman of State Committee for Television and Radio:** IBRAHIM USMONOV.

### MINISTRIES

**Office of the Chairman of the Supreme Assembly:** Dushanbe.
**Secretariat of the Prime Minister:** Dushanbe; tel. (3772) 21-51-10.
**Ministry of Agriculture:** 734025 Dushanbe, Lenina 46; tel. (3772) 22-82-68.
**Ministry of Communications:** Dushanbe.
**Ministry of Construction:** Dushanbe.
**Ministry of Culture and Information:** 734018 Dushanbe, P. Karabayeva 17; tel. (3772) 33-58-84.
**Ministry of Defence:** Dushanbe.
**Ministry of the Economy and Foreign Economic Relations:** Dushanbe.
**Ministry of Education:** Dushanbe.
**Ministry of Environmental Protection and Water Resources:** Dushanbe.
**Ministry of Finance:** Dushanbe.
**Ministry of Foreign Affairs:** 734051 Dushanbe, Rudaki 42; tel. (3772) 21-18-08; telex 201137; fax (3772) 23-29-64.
**Ministry of Grain Products:** Dushanbe.
**Ministry of Health:** 734026 Dushanbe, I. Somoni 59; tel. (3772) 36-16-37.
**Ministry of Industry:** Dushanbe.
**Ministry of Internal Affairs:** Dushanbe.
**Ministry of Justice:** Dushanbe.
**Ministry of Labour and Employment:** Dushanbe.
**Ministry of Security:** Dushanbe.
**Ministry of Social Security:** Dushanbe.
**Ministry of Transport:** Dushanbe.

#### Principal State Committees

**State Committee for Construction and Architecture:** Dushanbe.
**State Committee for Contracts and Trade:** Dushanbe.
**State Committee for Customs:** Dushanbe.
**State Committee for State Property:** Dushanbe.
**State Committee for Statistics:** Dushanbe.
**State Committee for Television and Radio:** Dushanbe.
**State Committee for Youth, Sport and Tourism:** Dushanbe.

TAJIKISTAN                                                                                                              *Directory*

## President and Legislature

### PRESIDENT

A presidential election took place on 6 November 1994. There were two candidates, ABDUMALIK ABDULLOJONOV and IMAMALI RAHMONOV. RAHMONOV obtained 58.3% of the votes cast, while Abdullojonov received about 35%. RAHMONOV was inaugurated as President on 16 November.

### SUPREME ASSEMBLY

Elections to the new 181-member Supreme Assembly took place on 26 February and 12 March 1995. A total of 179 deputies took part in the Assembly's first session in April, one constituency having failed to return a deputy, and one deputy having been killed shortly after the elections. The majority of those elected had no overt party affiliation, but about 60 were reported to be members of the Communist Party of Tajikistan, five deputies were from the People's Party of Tajikistan, two from the Party of Popular Unity and Accord and one from the Tajikistan Party of Economic and Political Renewal.

**Chairman:** SAFARALI RAJABOV.
**First Deputy Chairman:** AMDULMAJID DOSTIYEV

## Political Organizations

**Communist Party of Tajikistan (CPT):** Dushanbe; f. 1924; only registered party until 1991; First Sec. of Cen. Cttee SHODI SHABDOLLOV.

**Party of Popular Unity and Accord (PPUA):** Dushanbe; f. 1994; represents interests of northern Tajikistan; Leader ABDUMALIK ABDULLOJONOV.

**People's Party of Tajikistan (PPT):** Dushanbe; f. 1993; pro-communist; Leader ABDULMAJID DOSTIYEV; c. 2,000 mems.

**Tajikistan Party of Economic and Political Renewal (TPEPR):** f. 1994; draws its support mainly from the emerging class of business executives; Leader MUKHTOR BOBOYEV.

The following parties were formally banned by the Supreme Court in June 1993:

**Democratic Party of Tajikistan (DPT):** in 1995 moved its headquarters from Teheran, Iran, to Moscow, Russia; f. 1990; secular nationalist and pro-Western; Chair. JUMABOY NIYAZOV, Dep. Chair. ABDUNABI SATORZODA; c. 15,000 mems (1991).

**Islamic Renaissance Party (IRP):** leadership believed to be based in Teheran, Iran; formally registered in 1991; br. of what was the Soviet IRP; formerly a moderate Islamic party; Leader SAYED ABDULLO NURI; First Dep. Leader Haji AKBAR TURAJONZODA; c. 10,000 mems (1990).

**Lale Badakhshon:** f. 1991; seeks greater autonomy for Gorny Badakhshan and the resident Pamiri peoples.

**Rastokhez** (Rebirth): f. 1990; nationalist-religious party favoured by intellectuals; Chair. TAKHIR ABDUZHABBOROV.

Many of the supporters of these parties maintained guerrilla warfare against the communist regime, often with the support of the Afghan *mujahidin*. The main opposition paramilitary grouping was known as **Defence of the Fatherland** (Najot-i Vatan; f. 1992 by MUHAMMED SHARIF HIMMATZODA, a leader of the IRP). An important role in the negotiations with the Government in 1994–95 was played by the Moscow-based opposition group **The Co-ordinating Centre for the Democratic Forces of Tajikistan** (leaders OTTAKHON LATIFI, KHUDOYBERDI KHOLEQNAZARZODA).

## Diplomatic Representation

### EMBASSIES IN TAJIKISTAN

**Afghanistan:** Dushanbe.
**China, People's Republic:** Dushanbe; Ambassador: XI ZHAOMING.
**Iran:** Dushanbe; Ambassador: ALI ASHRAF MOJTAHED-SHABESTARI.
**Pakistan:** 734001 Dushanbe, Hotel Tajikistan, 3rd Floor; tel. (3772) 27-52-12; telex 201134; fax (3772) 27-51-43; Chargé d'affaires a.i.: SYED HASAN JAVED.
**Russia:** Dushanbe; Ambassador: MECHISLAV SENKEVICH.
**Turkey:** 734001 Dushanbe, Hotel Tajikistan; tel. (3772) 27-53-05; telex 201220.
**USA:** Dushanbe, Ainii 39; tel. (3772) 24-82-33; Ambassador: R. GRANT SMITH (designate).

## Judicial System

**Chairman of the Supreme Court:** UBAIDULLO DAVLATOV.
**Procurator-General:** MUHMADNAZAR SOLIHOV.

## Religion

The majority of Tajiks are adherents of Islam and are mainly Sunnis (Hanafi school). Some of the Pamiri peoples, however, are Isma'ilis (followers of the Aga Khan), a Shi'ite sect. Under the Soviet regime the Muslims of Tajikistan were subject to the Muslim Board of Central Asia and a muftiate, both of which were based in Tashkent (Uzbekistan). The senior Muslim cleric in Tajikistan was the *kazi* (supreme judge). In late 1992 the incumbent, Haji Akbar Turajonzoda, fled to Afghanistan after the civil war. The new regime subsequently replaced him as the spiritual leader of Tajikistan's Muslims and established an independent muftiate. Most of the minority Christian population is Slav, the main denomination being the Russian Orthodox Church. There are some Protestant and other groups, notably a Baptist Church in Dushanbe.

**Chief Mufti:** FATKHULLO SHARIFOV, Dushanbe.

## The Press

In 1992, according to UNESCO, there were nine daily newspapers and 110 non-daily newspapers published in Tajikistan. There were also 26 periodicals published, with a total annual circulation of 18.8m. copies.

### PRINCIPAL NEWSPAPERS

**Adabiyet va sanat** (Literature and Art): Dushanbe, Ismail Somoni 8; tel. (3772) 24-57-39; f. 1959; weekly; organ of the Union of Writers and Ministry of Culture and Information; in Tajik; Editor A. KHAKIMOV.

**Bizness i Politika** (Business and Politics): Dushanbe.

**Djavononi Tochikiston** (Tajikistan Youth): Dushanbe; f. 1930; 5 a week; fmrly organ of the Cen. Cttee of the Leninist Young Communist League of Tajikistan; in Tajik; Editor O. FAKHRIEV.

**Narodnaya Gazeta:** Dushanbe; f. 1929; fmrly *Kommunist Tajikistana* (Tajik Communist), the organ of the Communist Party of Tajikistan; 5 a week; in Russian; Editor N. N. KUZMIN.

**Omuzgor** (Teacher): Dushanbe; f. 1932; weekly; organ of the Ministry of Education; in Tajik; Editor B. NASRIDDINOV.

**Posukh** (Answer): Dushanbe; f. 1995 by Ministry of Culture and Information and the Union of Journalists; weekly; Editor-in-Chief KURBONOV.

**Sadoi mardum** (The Voice of the People): Dushanbe; f. 1991; 5 a week; organ of the Supreme Assembly; in Tajik; Editor MIRZOMAHMUD MIRBOBOYEV.

**Tochikistoni** (Tajikistan): Dushanbe; f. 1925; 5 a week; fmrly organ of the Communist Party of Tajikistan; in Tajik; Editor M. MUHABBATSHOYEV.

### PRINCIPAL PERIODICALS

Monthly, unless otherwise indicated.

**Hajoti dehot** (Village Life): 734025 Dushanbe, Lenina 46; tel. (3772) 22-82-68; f. 1947; journal of the Ministry of Agriculture; in Tajik; Editor-in-Chief K. YA. AFZALI.

**Khorpushtak** (Hedgehog): Dushanbe; f. 1953; fortnightly; satirical; in Tajik.

**Mashal** (Torch): Dushanbe, Rudaki 33; tel. (3772) 24-83-17; f. 1952; fmrly journal of the Cen. Cttee of the Leninist Young Communist League and Republican Council of the Pioneer Organization of Tajikistan; juvenile fiction; in Tajik; Editor-in-Chief T. NIGOROVA; circ. 120,000.

**Pamir:** 734001 Dushanbe, Ismail Somoni 8; tel. (3772) 24-56-56; f. 1949; journal of the Union of Writers of Tajikistan; fiction; in Russian; Editor-in-Chief BORIS PSHENICHNY.

**Sadoi shark** (Voice of the East): 734001 Dushanbe, Ismail Somoni 8; tel. (3772) 24-56-79; f. 1924; journal of the Union of Writers; fiction; in Tajik; Editor-in-Chief (vacant).

**Selskaya zhizn** (Agriculture): Dushanbe; in Russian.

**Tochikiston** (Tajikistan): Dushanbe; f. 1938; social and political; in Tajik and Russian; Editor-in-Chief (vacant).

**Zanoni Tochikiston** (Women of Tajikistan): Dushanbe; f. 1954; popular; in Tajik; Editor-in-Chief M. KHAKIMOVA.

**Zdravookhraneniye Tajikistana** (Tajikistan Public Health System): 734026 Dushanbe, Ismail Somoni 59; tel. (3772) 36-16-37; f. 1933; 6 a year; journal of the Ministry of Health; medical research; in Russian; Editor-in-Chief AZAM T. PULATOV; circ. 7,000.

### NEWS AGENCY

**Khovar** (East): Dushanbe, Lenina 37; f. 1991 to replace TajikTA (Tajik Telegraph Agency); govt information agency; Dir NABI KARIMOV.

## Publishers

**Adib** (Literary Publishing House): Dushanbe, kuchai Ayni 126; f. 1987; juvenile and adult fiction; Dir K. MIRZOYEV.

**Irfon** (Light of Knowledge Publishing House): Dushanbe, kuchai Ayni 126; politics, science, economics and agriculture; Dir A. SANGINOV.

**Maorif** (Education Publishing House): Dushanbe, kuchai Ayni 126; educational; Dir A. GHAFUROV.

**Sarredaksiyai Ilmii Entsiklopediyai Tajik** (Tajik Scientific Encyclopaedia Publishing House): Dushanbe, kuchai Ayni 126; tel. (3772) 25-18-41; f. 1969; Editor-in-Chief J. AZIZQULOV.

## Radio and Television

The broadcast media are state-owned and under government control. The extent of this control was reinforced by a decree of February 1994, which placed the State TV-Radio Broadcasting Co of Tajikistan under the direct operational supervision of the Chairman of the legislature. The Government was also responsible for 'jamming' (blocking the signals) of the US broadcaster, Radio Liberty (based in Germany), during 1993. In the same year there were transmissions of a rebel opposition group, calling itself Voice of Free Tajikistan.

**State TV-Radio Broadcasting Co of Tajikistan:** 734025 Dushanbe, kuchai Chapayev 31.

**Tajik Radio:** 734025 Dushanbe, kuchai Chapayev 31; tel. (3772) 27-65-69; telex 201392; broadcasts in Russian, Tajik and Uzbek.

## Finance

### BANKING

In mid-1992 Tajikistan's banking system comprised the National Bank of Tajikistan, the Savings Bank (Sberbank), the Bank for Foreign Economic Activity (Vneshekonombank), three large banks (Promstroibank, Agroprombank and Tajikbankbusiness) which originated from former state banks, and three smaller commercial banks (all branches of Russian commercial banks). The National Bank of Tajikistan is the central bank of the country.

#### Central Bank

**National Bank of the Republic of Tajikistan:** 734024 Dushanbe, Rudaki 23/2; tel. (3772) 21-77-92; telex 201129; fax (3772) 21-25-02; f. 1991; Chair. MURODALI ALIMARDANOV; Dep. Chair. SHARIF RAKHIMOV.

#### Other Banks

**Bank for Foreign Economic Activity:** Dushanbe; fmrly br. of USSR Vneshekonombank; Chair. I. L. LALBEKOV.

**Orienbank—Tajik Joint Stock Commercial, Industrial and Construction Bank:** 734001 Dushanbe, Rudaki 95/1; tel. (3772) 21-09-20; telex 201136; fax (3772) 21-16-62; f. 1991; fmrly Promstroibank; cap. 5,709m. roubles, res 22,299m. roubles, dep. 537,323m. roubles (Jan. 1995); commercial bank (almost 18% of total lending in 1991); Pres. ABDULMUTALIB ABDUSATTAROV; Chair. BAHROM SIROGEV; 22 brs.

**Sberbank—Savings Bank:** Dushanbe; f. 1991; fmrly br. of all-Union Sberbank; licensed by presidential decree and not subject to the same controls as the commercial and trading banks.

**'Shark' Joint-Stock Commercial Agroindustrial Bank:** 734001 Dushanbe; Rudaki 95/1; tel. (3772) 21-16-00; telex 201131; fax (3772) 21-12-30; f. 1991; fmrly Agroprombank; cap. 17,400m. roubles, res 5,100m. roubles, dep 42,000m. roubles (Jan. 1995); Chair. M. S. KADIROV; 58 brs.

**Tajikbankbusiness:** Dushanbe; f. 1987 to assume commercial banking activities of the former Soviet Gosbank; second-largest bank in the country (some 37% of total lending in 1991).

In January 1994 the Council of Ministers resolved to form a development bank for Tajikistan, the State Bank for Development and Reconstruction, which was to be based in Dushanbe.

### COMMODITY EXCHANGES

**Tajik Republican Commodity Exchange—NAVRUZ:** 374001 Dushanbe, Orjonikidze 37; tel. (3772) 23-48-74; telex 116249; fax (3772) 27-03-91; f. 1991; Chair. SULEYMAN CHULEBAYEV.

**Vostok-Mercury Torgovy Dom:** 734026 Dushanbe, Lomonosova 162; tel. and fax (3772) 24-60-61; f. 1991; trades in a wide range of goods.

## Trade and Industry

### CHAMBER OF COMMERCE

**Chamber of Commerce and Industry:** 734012 Dushanbe, Mazayeva 21; tel. (3772) 27-95-19; Chair. KAMOL SUFIYEV.

### COMMERCIAL AND INDUSTRIAL ORGANIZATIONS

**National Association of Small- and Medium-Sized Businesses of Tajikistan:** Dushanbe; f. 1993, with govt support; independent org.

**Tajikvneshtorg:** 734051 Dushanbe, Lenina 42; tel. (3772) 23-29-03; co-ordinates foreign trade in a wide range of goods; Gen. Dir YU. G. GAYTSGORI.

**Tajikvneshtorg Industrial Association:** 734035 Dushanbe, POB 48, Rudaki 25; tel. (3772) 23-29-03; telex 201104; fax (3772) 22-81-20; f. 1988; co-ordinates trade with foreign countries in a wide range of goods; Pres. ABDURAKHMON MUKHTASHOV.

### TRADE UNIONS

**Council of Trade Unions of Tajikistan:** Dushanbe; confederation of the trade unions of the country.

## Transport

### RAILWAYS

There are few railways in Tajikistan, and those are lines linking the major centres of the country with the railway network of Uzbekistan. Thus, Khojand is connected to the Fergana valley lines, and the cotton-growing centre of Kurgan-Tyube is linked to Termez. A new line, between the town of Isfara, in Leninabad region, and Khavast, in Uzbekistan, was opened in 1995. The predominantly mountainous terrain makes the construction of a more extensive network unlikely.

### ROADS

At 31 December 1992 Tajikistan's road network totalled 32,752 km, including 18,243 km of main or national roads, 8,757 km of secondary or regional roads and 3,318 km of other roads. The principal highway of Tajikistan is the road that links the northern city of Khojand, across the Anzob Pass (3,372 m), with the capital, Dushanbe, carries on to the border town of Khorog (Gorny Badakhshan), before wending through the Pamir Mountains, north, to the Kyrgyz city of Osh, across the Akbaytal Pass (4,655 m). This arterial route exhibits problems common to much of the country's land transport: winter weather is likely to cause the road to be closed by snow for up to eight months of the year. There are also roads of a reasonable standard linking Dushanbe to the south-western cities of Kurgan-Tyube and Kulyab. In early 1994 Tajikistan and Pakistan discussed plans for a Dushanbe–Karachi highway.

### CIVIL AVIATION

The main international airport is at Dushanbe, although there is also a major airport at Khojand. The country is linked to cities in the Russian Federation and neighbouring Central Asian states. During the early 1990s, however, many flights, both domestic and international, were cancelled owing to the civil war or fuel shortages.

**TAL—Tajikistan Air Lines:** Dushanbe; f. 1993; joint venture between state airline co and British Airways; operates a total of 22 air routes, including to Saudi Arabia, Finland, Thailand, Egypt, Syria, Israel, Pakistan, India, Hungary, Turkey, Iran, Pakistan, the United Kingdom and the USA.

## Tourism

There was little tourism in Tajikistan even before the civil war of 1992. There is some spectacular mountain scenery, hitherto mainly visited by climbers, and, particularly in the Fergana valley, in the north of the country, there are sites of historical interest, notably the city of Khojand.

**State Committee for Youth, Sport and Tourism:** Dushanbe; Chair. ZEBINISO RUSTAMOVA.

# TANZANIA

## Introductory Survey

### Location, Climate, Language, Religion, Flag, Capital

The United Republic of Tanzania consists of Tanganyika, on the African mainland, and the nearby islands of Zanzibar and Pemba. Tanganyika lies on the east coast of Africa, bordered by Uganda and Kenya to the north, by Rwanda, Burundi and Zaire to the west, and by Zambia, Malawi and Mozambique to the south. Zanzibar and Pemba are in the Indian Ocean, about 40 km (25 miles) off the coast of Tanganyika, north of Dar es Salaam. The climate varies with altitude, ranging from tropical in Zanzibar and on the coast and plains to semi-temperate in the highlands. The official languages are Swahili and English, and there are numerous tribal languages. There are Muslim, Christian and Hindu communities. Many Africans follow traditional beliefs. The national flag (proportions 3 by 2) comprises two triangles, one of green (with its base at the hoist and its apex in the upper fly) and the other of blue (with its base in the fly and its apex at the lower hoist), separated by a broad, yellow-edged black diagonal stripe, from the lower hoist to the upper fly. The administrative functions of the capital are being transferred from Dar es Salaam to Dodoma.

### Recent History

Tanzania was formed in 1964 by a merger of the two independent states of Tanganyika and Zanzibar (see below).

Tanganyika became a German colony in 1884, and was later incorporated into German East Africa, which also included present-day Rwanda and Burundi. In 1918, at the end of the First World War, the German forces in the area surrendered, and Tanganyika was placed under a League of Nations mandate, with the United Kingdom as the administering power. In 1946 Tanganyika became a UN Trust Territory, still under British rule. Tanganyika's first general election was held in September 1958 and February 1959. A new Council of Ministers, including African members, was formed in July 1959. At the next election, in September 1960, the Tanganyika African National Union (TANU) won 70 of the 71 seats in the National Assembly. The party's leader, Dr Julius Nyerere, became Chief Minister. Internal self-government was achieved in May 1961, when Nyerere became Prime Minister. Tanganyika became independent, within the Commonwealth, on 9 December 1961, but Nyerere resigned as Prime Minister in January 1962, in order to devote himself to the direction of TANU. His successor as Prime Minister was Rashidi Kawawa. On 9 December 1962 Tanganyika became a republic, with Nyerere returning to power as the country's first President, having been elected in the previous month. Kawawa became Vice-President. Zanzibar (including the island of Pemba), a British protectorate since 1890, became an independent sultanate in December 1963. Following an armed uprising by the Afro-Shirazi Party in January 1964, the Sultan was deposed and a republic proclaimed. The new Government signed an Act of Union with Tanganyika in April 1964, thus creating the United Republic. The union was named Tanzania in October 1964 and a new Constitution was introduced in July 1965, which provided for a one-party state (although, until 1977, TANU and the Afro-Shirazi Party remained the respective official parties of mainland Tanzania and Zanzibar, and co-operated in affairs of state). Nyerere was re-elected President in 1965, 1970, 1975 and 1980.

In April 1972 Sheikh Abeid Karume, Chairman of the ruling Revolutionary Council of Zanzibar, nominated President of Zanzibar and First Vice-President of the United Republic, was assassinated. Aboud Jumbe, his successor, reorganized the Zanzibari Government in August 1972 by extending the powers of the Afro-Shirazi Party. Despite its incorporation in Tanzania, Zanzibar retained a separate administration which ruthlessly suppressed all opposition. A separate Constitution for Zanzibar was adopted in October 1979, providing for a popularly-elected President and a House of Representatives elected by delegates of the ruling party. The first elections to the 40-member Zanzibar House of Representatives were held in January 1980. In June of that year a coup plot against Jumbe was thwarted; Jumbe won an overwhelming majority at Zanzibar's first presidential elections, held in October. However, mounting dissatisfaction among Zanzibaris concerning the union with Tanganyika culminated in the resignation, in January 1984, of Jumbe and three of his ministers. In April Ali Hassan Mwinyi, a former Zanzibari Minister of Natural Resources and Tourism, was elected unopposed as President of Zanzibar, winning 87.5% of the votes cast. A new Constitution for Zanzibar came into force in January 1985, providing for the House of Representatives to be directly elected by universal adult suffrage.

In February 1977 TANU and the Afro-Shirazi Party were amalgamated to form Chama Cha Mapinduzi (CCM), the Revolutionary Party of Tanzania. In April the National Assembly approved a permanent Constitution for Tanzania; this provided for the election to the National Assembly of representatives from Zanzibar, in addition to those from the Tanzanian mainland. At presidential and general elections in October 1980 Nyerere was re-elected President of the United Republic. That about one-half of the elected members of the National Assembly, including several ministers, failed to retain their seats was interpreted as a protest by voters against commodity shortages and inefficient bureaucracy. In January 1983 several civilians and soldiers were arrested and charged with plotting a coup: in December 1985 nine of the accused were found guilty and sentenced to life imprisonment. Major changes to the Constitution were approved by the National Assembly in October 1984, limiting the President's powers and increasing those of the National Assembly.

President Nyerere retired in November 1985, and was succeeded by Ali Hassan Mwinyi (President of Zanzibar and Vice-President of Tanzania since April 1984), who, as the sole candidate, had won 96% of the votes cast at a presidential election in October. Elections to the National Assembly were held on the same day. Mwinyi appointed Joseph Warioba (previously Minister of Justice) as Prime Minister and First Vice-President. At presidential and legislative elections in Zanzibar, also held in October, Idris Abdul Wakil (formerly Speaker of the Zanzibar House of Representatives) was elected President of Zanzibar to replace Mwinyi; although the sole candidate, he received only 61% of the votes. Nyerere remained Chairman of the CCM.

In July 1986 Mwinyi declared an offensive against corruption and mismanagement within the CCM: in the following months several regional party officials and directors of parastatal bodies were dismissed or demoted, and in some cases expelled from the party. By late 1987 a division was apparent between 'conservative' socialists, who supported the CCM's traditional socialist ideology (as favoured by Nyerere), and 'pragmatists', who advocated a more liberal approach to government (as favoured by Mwinyi). It was thought that Nyerere's decision to accept renomination as Chairman of the CCM at this time, in spite of earlier announcements that he was to leave the post in 1987, reflected his desire to counter reformist influence in government: in October he was re-elected Chairman of the CCM by a huge majority at the party congress. In a cabinet reshuffle in December, however, Mwinyi dismissed three 'conservative' socialist ministers who had opposed his policies of economic liberalization.

In early 1988 tension began to increase in Zanzibar, reflecting underlying rivalries between the inhabitants of the main island and those of the smaller island of Pemba, between Zanzibar's African and Arab populations, and between advocates and opponents of the islands' unity with Tanganyika. In January President Wakil suspended the islands' Government, the Supreme Revolutionary Council, and assumed control of the armed forces from the office of his main rival, the Chief Minister, Seif Sharrif Hamad, following earlier claims by Wakil that a group of dissidents, including members of the Council, had been plotting the overthrow of his administration. When Wakil appointed a new Council later in that month, Hamad was among the five ministers dismissed. Omar Ali Juma, a senior government official, was appointed as the new Chief Minister. In May Hamad and six other party officials were expelled from the CCM for allegedly opposing the party's aims and endangering Tanzanian unity. In the same month some 4,000 Muslims rioted in Zanzibar. Restrictions were imposed on the Zanzibari press in September. In December about 4,000 troops were temporarily dispatched to Zanzibar from the mainland, as a preventive measure in response to reports that a coup was being planned against Wakil's Government.

In September 1989 Mwinyi assumed the defence and national service portfolio, and in March 1990 he dismissed seven cabinet ministers who had allegedly opposed plans for economic reform and presided over corrupt or irresponsible ministries. The President's position was further consolidated in August when, following the resignation of Nyerere, he was appointed Chairman of the CCM.

In October 1990 concurrent parliamentary and presidential elections were held in Zanzibar. Wakil did not stand for re-election as President of Zanzibar and Chairman of the Supreme Revolutionary Council; the sole presidential candidate, Dr Salmin Amour, was elected as Wakil's successor by 97.7% of the votes cast. Amour subsequently reappointed Juma as Chief Minister of Zanzibar. At the end of October parliamentary and presidential elections took place in Tanzania as a whole. In the parliamentary election, candidates contested 216 elective seats. Mwinyi, the sole candidate in the presidential election, was re-elected for a second term, taking 95.5% of the votes cast. Mwinyi promised further economic reforms. In November Mwinyi transferred Warioba to a lesser government post, replacing him as Prime Minister with John Malecela, previously the Tanzanian High Commissioner to the United Kingdom.

In December 1991 a presidential commission (which had been established in March to consider electoral reform) published recommendations for the establishment of a multi-party political system. In February 1992 proposed constitutional amendments to this effect were ratified by a special congress of the CCM, which stipulated that all new political organizations should command support in both Zanzibar and mainland Tanzania, and should be free of tribal, religious and racial bias, in order to protect national unity. In May the Constitutions of both the United Republic and Zanzibar were amended to enshrine a multi-party system. Several political organizations were officially registered from mid-1992; nevertheless, the Government continued to impose restrictions on opposition activities. In July four members of the newly-formed (unrecognized) Democratic Party (DP), including the organization's leader, the Rev. Christopher Mtikila, were arrested for staging an unauthorized public meeting. They were sentenced in the following month to terms of imprisonment, but in September their sentences were annulled by the High Court. In December Zanzibar unilaterally joined the Organization of the Islamic Conference (OIC, see p. 208), thereby precipitating controversy regarding the future of the Tanzanian union. A parliamentary commission, established to investigate the situation, reported in February 1993 that Zanzibar's membership of the OIC contravened the Constitution of the United Republic. Zanzibar withdrew from the OIC in August, and Malecela announced that the possibility of Tanzania's joining the organization would be investigated.

In January 1993 Mtikila and four DP supporters were detained and charged with sedition. In the same month security forces killed one person and wounded another while suppressing an opposition demonstration on Pemba. During April there were violent clashes between Islamic fundamentalists and the security forces; some 40 Muslims were arrested and charged with holding illegal demonstrations, and Sheikh Yahya Hussein, the leader of the Balukta Islamic movement, was charged with plotting against the Government. Balukta was outlawed later in the month, although charges against Hussein and several other defendants were withdrawn in June. Mtikila was detained and charged with sedition twice during September, and was again arrested in October, together with leaders of three authorized oppostition parties, and charged with unlawful assembly, intimidation and insulting the President and Government.

In August 1993 the National Assembly approved a motion proposing that a constitutional amendment be devised that would allow for the establishment of a separate government and legislature—mirroring the Zanzibar administrative structures—for Tanganyika. Among the most vociferous opponents of the reform was ex-President Nyerere, who warned that the creation of separate institutions for the mainland would undermine national unity. In November the Zanzibar authorities proposed that, in the event of the formation of a separate Tanganyika government, each element of the union (Zanzibar, Tanganyika and the central administration) be empowered to raise its own armed forces.

The continued influence of the CCM was exemplified in local polls and in parliamentary by-elections in 1993-94, at which candidates of the ruling party won convincing victories over opposition candidates. It was widely considered that divisions within recently-authorized parties might hinder the formation of a cohesive challenge to the CCM at the first full multi-party presidential and legislative elections, scheduled to take place in October 1995. Opposition parties also claimed that their supporters were frequently being harassed by the CCM. In mid-1993 opposition organizations in Zanzibar were reportedly promised increased access to the media. In October, none the less, some 30,000 opposition supporters staged a demonstration in Zanzibar to demand the right to hold authorized meetings. In the same month Amour imposed a ban on the formation of security forces by political parties.

In November 1994 some members of the international donor community reportedly threatened to withdraw aid to Tanzania unless the Government acted to eradicate alleged irregular activities by the Ministry of Finance. In early December Mwinyi responded to mounting pressure on the Government to regulate its affairs by reorganizing the Cabinet. Malecela was replaced as Prime Minister and First Vice-President by Cleopa Msuya, hitherto the Minister of Industry and Trade and previously Prime Minister during 1980-83; Jakaya Kikwete, previously Minister of Energy, Minerals and Water, was appointed Minister of Finance.

Tanzania's relations with Uganda and Kenya were uneasy throughout the 1970s, particularly after the dissolution of the East African Community (EAC) in 1977. Uganda briefly annexed the Kagera salient from Tanzania in November 1978. In early 1979 Tanzanian troops supported the Uganda National Liberation Front in the overthrow of President Amin, which was achieved in April. The Tanzania-Kenya border, closed since 1977, was reopened in November 1983, following an agreement on the distribution of the EAC's assets and liabilities. In the following month Tanzania and Kenya agreed to establish full diplomatic relations. The two countries reached agreement on a trade treaty and on the establishment of a joint co-operation commission in 1986. Tanzania pledged its support for the Museveni regime, which took power in Uganda in January of that year, and in November Tanzania began to send military instructors to Uganda to organize the training of Ugandan government troops. In November 1991 the Presidents of Tanzania, Kenya and Uganda met in Nairobi, Kenya, and declared their commitment to developing co-operation between the three countries in economic, political, cultural and security matters. In November 1993 the Presidents of the three countries signed an agreement establishing a permanent tripartite commission, with the aim of promoting mutual co-operation and economic development.

Tanzania gave active support to the Frente de Libertação de Moçambique (Frelimo) during the struggle that led to the independence of Mozambique in 1975, and the two countries subsequently co-operated closely on the basis of a common socialist ideology. Following the death of President Machel of that country in October 1986, Tanzania pledged military support to the Frelimo Government in its conflict with opposition guerrilla forces and agreed to station troops in Mozambique. In November 1988, however, all Tanzanian troops in Mozambique (then numbering 2,000-3,000) were withdrawn, reportedly owing to the Tanzanian Government's inability to pay the high costs incurred. In November 1987 it was reported that some 60,000 refugees had crossed from Mozambique into southern Tanzania, as a result of the unrest in Mozambique; by early 1994 there were an estimated 18,500 Mozambican refugees in Tanzania, of whom about one-fifth reportedly wished to remain in the country.

In August 1993, following a protracted mediation effort by the Mwinyi Government, a peace agreement was signed in the Tanzanian town of Arusha by the Rwandan authorities and the rebel Front patriotique rwandais. In April 1994, however, following the assassination of the Rwandan President, Juvénal Habyarimana, hundreds of thousands of Rwandans fled to Tanzania to escape the atrocities being perpetrated in their honmeland: in one 24-hour period in late April some 250,000 refugees were reported to have crossed the Rwanda-Tanzania

# TANZANIA

border. In May the Tanzanian authorities appealed for international emergency aid to assist in the care of the refugees, many of whom were sheltering in makeshift camps in the border region. (Earlier in the year Tanzania had appealed for assistance to offset severe domestic food shortages, resulting from drought, in the north and north-east.) In March 1995 Tanzania banned the admission of further refugees from both Rwanda and Burundi (where violent unrest had erupted in late 1994); some 750,000 Rwandan and Burundian refugees were reportedly sheltering in Tanzania in April 1995.

In November 1993 Tanzania revoked all economic sanctions against South Africa. In January 1994 the Tanzanian Government was reported to have suspended its links with the Pan-Africanist Congress, and to have banned that organization's armed wing, the Azanian People's Liberation Army, from launching attacks against South Africa from bases in Tanzania.

## Government

Under the provisions of the 1977 Constitution, with subsequent amendments, legislative power is held by the unicameral National Assembly, whose members serve for a term of five years. There is constitutional provision for both directly-elected members (chosen by universal suffrage) and nominated members (including five members elected by and from the Zanzibar House of Representatives). The number of directly-elected members exceeds the number of nominated members. The Electoral Commission may review and, if necessary, increase the number of constituencies before every general election. Executive power lies with the President, elected by popular vote for five years. The President must be at least 40 years of age and his mandate is limited to a maximum of two five-year terms. The President appoints two Vice-Presidents, one of whom is President of Zanzibar and the other Prime Minister of the Union. If the President comes from Tanganyika, the First Vice-President must represent Zanzibar, and vice versa. (In December 1994 a constitutional amendment was introduced whereby the President of Zanzibar would no longer also be a Vice-President of the Union Government; the amendment was to enter into effect following the next general election.) The President selects the Cabinet in consultation with the Prime Minister.

Zanzibar has its own administration for internal affairs, and the amended Zanzibar Constitution, which came into force in January 1985, provides for the President, elected by universal adult suffrage, to hold office for a maximum of two five-year terms, and for the House of Representatives, of 45–55 members, to be directly elected by universal adult suffrage. The President of Zanzibar appoints the Chief Minister, and the two co-operate in choosing the other members of the Supreme Revolutionary Council, which has a maximum of 20 members. A motion adopted by the National Assembly in August 1993 proposed the creation of separate administrative structures for Tanganyika.

In May 1992 the United Republic's Constitution was amended to legalize a multi-party political system.

## Defence

In June 1994 the total active armed forces numbered 49,600, of whom an estimated 45,000 were in the army, 1,000 in the navy and 3,600 in the air force. There are also paramilitary forces including a 1,400-strong Police Field Force and an 85,000-strong reservist Citizens' Militia. The estimated defence budget was 41,700m. shillings in 1994.

## Economic Affairs

In 1993, according to estimates by the World Bank, mainland Tanzania's gross national product (GNP), measured at average 1991–93 prices, was US $2,521m., equivalent to $100 per head. During 1985–93, it was estimated, GNP per head increased, in real terms, at an annual average rate of 1.4%. Over the same period the population of the country as a whole increased by an annual average of 3.0%. Mainland Tanzania's gross domestic product (GDP) increased, in real terms, by an annual average of 3.1% in 1980–92. The area's real GDP rose by 4.0% in 1993.

Agriculture (including forestry and fishing) contributed 61% of GDP in 1992, and employed an estimated 79.2% of the labour force in 1993. The principal cash crops are coffee (which provided 20.3% of export revenues in 1990), cotton (18.7%), tobacco, cloves (Zanzibar's most important export, cultivated on the island of Pemba), tea, cashew nuts, sisal, pyrethrum, coconuts, sugar and cardamom. Farmers have been encouraged to produce essential food crops, most importantly cassava and maize. A large proportion of agricultural output is produced by subsistence farmers. During 1980–92 mainland Tanzania's agricultural GDP increased by an annual average of 3.8%.

Industry (including mining, manufacturing, construction and power) contributed 12% of GDP in 1992, and employed an estimated 4.5% of the working population in 1980. During 1980–92 there was an average annual increase of 2.2% in mainland Tanzania's industrial GDP.

Mining provided only 1.2% of GDP in 1991. Diamonds, other gemstones (including rubies and sapphires), gold, petroleum, salt, phosphates, coal, gypsum, kaolin and tin are mined, and it is planned to exploit reserves of natural gas. Other mineral reserves include nickel, soda ash, iron ore and uranium, and exploration for petroleum is in progress.

Manufacturing contributed 5% of GDP in 1992. The most important manufacturing activities are food-processing, textile production, cigarette production and brewing. Pulp and paper, fertilizers, cement, clothing, footwear, tyres, batteries, pharmaceuticals, bricks and tiles and electrical goods are also produced, while other activities include oil-refining, metal-working, vehicle assembly and engineering. Manufacturing GDP increased by an annual average of 0.6% in 1980–92.

Energy is derived principally from hydroelectric power, which supplies more than 70% of Tanzania's electricity. Imports of mineral fuels accounted for 13% of imports in 1992.

Tourism is an important potential growth sector: earnings from tourism were US $147m. in 1993/94.

In 1993 Tanzania recorded a visible trade deficit of US $837.9m., and there was a deficit of $408.5m. on the current account of the balance of payments. In 1988 the principal source of imports was the United Kingdom, while the main market for exports was the Federal Republic of Germany. Japan is another important trading partner. The principal exports in 1990 were coffee beans, raw cotton, tobacco, cloves and tea. The principal imports were transport equipment, consumer goods, construction materials, and other industrial and intermediate goods.

For the financial year ending 30 June 1995 a budgetary deficit of 53,128m. shillings was forecast. At the end of 1993 Tanzania's external debt totalled US $7,522m., of which $6,734m. was long-term public debt. In that year the cost of debt-servicing was equivalent to 25.1% of the value of exports of goods and services. The rate of inflation averaged 25.8% per year in 1985–93; consumer prices increased by an annual average of 23.5% in 1993.

Tanzania is a member of the African Development Bank (see p. 102) and of the Southern African Development Community (see p. 219). In November 1993 Tanzania was among members of the Preferential Trade Area for Eastern and Southern African States (see p. 240) to sign a treaty providing for the establishment of a Common Market for Eastern and Southern Africa.

In terms of GNP per head, Tanzania is among the world's poorest countries. During the 1980s and early 1990s the economy suffered successive balance-of-payments deficits and shortages of foreign exchange with which to buy inputs for all sectors, while poor rates of tax collection undermined attempts to achieve a balanced budget. In addition, drought, intermittently-depressed commodity prices, and illegal mining and mineral smuggling adversely affected economic development. Since the mid-1980s the Government has adopted austerity measures recommended by the IMF, including devaluations of the currency, attempts at stringent budgetary controls and the easing of restrictions on foreign exchange. The liberalization of trade and of the banking sector is in progress, and, in its financial programme for the mid-1990s, the Government aims to encourage private investment in sectors hitherto controlled by the State. It is envisaged that some 400 state-owned enterprises could be sold, restructured or dissolved, of which 97 were scheduled for privatization in 1993–95; a parallel reform of the civil service envisages the loss of 50,000 jobs by the end of 1995. Despite recent rescheduling agreements, Tanzania's external debt remains high (at about 250% of annual GNP in late 1993), and donors have expressed concern at the relatively slow rate of reform—the necessity, in both 1992/93 and 1993/94, to introduce emergency measures in order to meet government spending obligations was attributed to poor fiscal policy.

# TANZANIA

## Social Welfare

The state-sponsored Rural Development Division exists to improve educational, labour and health conditions in small communities. The State operates hospitals and health centres, while Christian missions also provide medical care. In 1980 privately-owned medical facilities were nationalized. In 1984 Tanzania had 1,547 physicians and 9,711 midwives. In that year there were 149 hospitals and 239 health centres, with a total of 27,489 beds; by 1990 there were 173 hospitals and 276 health centres. Of total budgetary expenditure by the central Government in the financial year 1988/89, an estimated 5,509m. shillings (5.0%) was for health.

## Education

Education at primary level is provided free of charge. In secondary schools a government-stipulated fee is paid: from January 1995 this was 8,000 shillings per year for day pupils at state-owned schools and 50,000–60,000 shillings per year for day pupils at private schools. Villages and districts are encouraged to construct their own schools with government assistance. Almost all primary schools are government-owned. Universal primary education was introduced in 1977, and was made compulsory in 1978. Primary education begins at seven years of age and lasts for seven years. Secondary education, beginning at the age of 14, lasts for a further six years, comprising a first cycle of four years and a second of two years. As a proportion of the school-age population, total enrolment at primary and secondary schools rose from 22% in 1970 to 58% in 1981, but declined to the equivalent of 43% in 1992. Enrolment at primary schools in 1992 was equivalent to 68% of children in the relevant age-group (males 69%; females 67%). Secondary enrolment in that year was equivalent to only 5% of children in the appropriate age-group (males 6%; females 5%). The estimated rate of adult literacy rose from 33% in 1967 to 90.4% in 1986, as the result of adult literacy campaigns. There is a university at Dar es Salaam. Tanzania also has an agricultural university at Morogoro, and a number of vocational training centres and technical colleges. Education was allocated 4.0% of total recurrent budgetary expenditure by the central Government in 1991/92.

## Public Holidays

**1995:** 12 January (Zanzibar Revolution Day), 5 February (Chama Cha Mapinduzi Day), 3 March* (Id El Fitr, end of Ramadan), 14–17 April (Easter), 26 April (Union Day), 1 May (International Labour Day), 10 May* (Id El Haji, Feast of the Sacrifice), 7 July (Saba Saba Peasants' Day), 9 August* (Maulidi, Birth of the Prophet), 9 December (Independence Day), 25 December (Christmas).

**1996:** 12 January (Zanzibar Revolution Day), 5 February (Chama Cha Mapinduzi Day), 21 February* (Id El Fitr, end of Ramadan), 5–8 April (Easter), 26 April (Union Day), 29 April* (Id El Haji, Feast of the Sacrifice), 1 May (International Labour Day), 7 July (Saba Saba Peasants' Day), 28 July* (Maulidi, Birth of the Prophet), 9 December (Independence Day), 25 December (Christmas).

* These holidays are dependent on the Islamic lunar calendar and may vary by one or two days from the dates given.

## Weights and Measures

The metric system is in force.

# Statistical Survey

Source (unless otherwise stated): Bureau of Statistics, Dar es Salaam.

## Area and Population

### AREA, POPULATION AND DENSITY

| | |
|---|---:|
| Area (sq km) | 945,087* |
| **Population (census results)** | |
| 26 August 1978 | 17,512,611 |
| 28 August 1988† | |
| Males | 11,327,511 |
| Females | 11,846,825 |
| Total | 23,174,336 |
| **Population (official estimates at mid-year)** | |
| 1988 | 23,997,000 |
| 1989 | 24,802,000 |
| 1990 | 25,635,000‡ |
| Density (per sq km) at mid-1990 | 27.1 |

* 364,900 sq miles. Of this total, Tanzania mainland is 942,626 sq km (363,950 sq miles), and Zanzibar 2,461 sq km (950 sq miles).
† Figures are provisional. The revised total is 23,126,952.
‡ Tanzania mainland 24,972,000; Zanzibar 663,000.

### ETHNIC GROUPS
(private households, census of 26 August 1967)

| | | | | |
|---|---:|---|---:|---|
| African | 11,481,595 | Others | 839 | |
| Asian | 75,015 | Not stated | 159,042 | |
| Arabs | 29,775 | **Total** | 11,763,150 | |
| European | 16,884 | | | |

### REGIONS (population in 1978)

| | | | | |
|---|---:|---|---:|---|
| Arusha | 926,223 | Mtwara | 771,819 | |
| Dar es Salaam | 843,090 | Mwanza | 1,443,379 | |
| Dodoma | 972,005 | Pemba | 205,305 | |
| Iringa | 925,044 | Pwani (Coast) | 516,586 | |
| Kagera (Bukoba) | 1,009,000* | Rukwa | 451,897 | |
| Kigoma | 684,941 | Ruvuma | 561,575 | |
| Kilimanjaro | 902,437 | Shinyanga | 1,323,535 | |
| Lindi | 527,624 | Singida | 613,949 | |
| Mara | 723,827 | Tabora | 817,907 | |
| Mbeya | 1,079,864 | Tanga | 1,037,767 | |
| Morogoro | 939,264 | Zanzibar | 270,807 | |

* Estimate.

### PRINCIPAL TOWNS (estimated population at mid-1985)

| | | | |
|---|---:|---|---:|
| Dar es Salaam | 1,096,000 | Tanga | 172,000 |
| Mwanza | 252,000 | Zanzibar | 133,000 |
| Tabora | 214,000 | Dodoma | 85,000 |
| Mbeya | 194,000 | | |

Source: UN, *Demographic Yearbook*.

### BIRTHS AND DEATHS (UN estimates, annual averages)

| | 1975–80 | 1980–85 | 1985–90 |
|---|---:|---:|---:|
| Birth rate (per 1,000) | 47.5 | 47.5 | 47.9 |
| Death rate (per 1,000) | 16.4 | 15.0 | 14.4 |

**Expectation of life** (UN estimates, years at birth, 1985–90): 51.8 (males 50.1; females 53.5).

Source: UN, *World Population Prospects: The 1992 Revision*.

# TANZANIA

## ECONOMICALLY ACTIVE POPULATION (1967 census)

|  | Males | Females | Total |
|---|---|---|---|
| Agriculture, forestry, hunting and fishing | 2,549,688 | 2,666,805 | 5,216,493 |
| Mining and quarrying | 4,918 | 99 | 5,017 |
| Manufacturing | 85,659 | 13,205 | 98,864 |
| Construction | 32,755 | 318 | 33,073 |
| Electricity, gas, water and sanitary services | 5,704 | 158 | 5,862 |
| Commerce | 71,088 | 7,716 | 78,804 |
| Transport, storage and communications | 46,121 | 711 | 46,832 |
| Other services | 169,693 | 38,803 | 208,496 |
| Other activities (not adequately described) | 35,574 | 18,081 | 53,655 |
| **Total labour force** | 3,001,200 | 2,745,896 | 5,747,096 |

**1978 census:** Total labour force 7,845,105 (males 3,809,135; females 4,035,970) aged 5 years and over.

**Mid-1980** (ILO estimates, '000 persons): Agriculture etc. 8,140 (males 3,787, females 4,353); Industry 431 (males 353, females 78); Services 938 (males 630, females 308); Total 9,508 (males 4,769, females 4,739) (Source: ILO, *Economically Active Population Estimates and Projections, 1950–2025*).

**Mid-1993** (estimates in '000): Agriculture, etc. 10,688; Total labour force 13,495 (Source: FAO, *Production Yearbook*).

# Agriculture

## PRINCIPAL CROPS ('000 metric tons)

|  | 1991 | 1992 | 1993 |
|---|---|---|---|
| Wheat | 80 | 64 | 59* |
| Rice (paddy) | 625 | 371 | 631* |
| Maize | 2,332 | 2,226 | 2,824* |
| Millet | 200† | 263 | 221* |
| Sorghum | 550† | 587 | 707* |
| Potatoes† | 220 | 200 | 220 |
| Sweet potatoes | 291 | 257 | 260* |
| Cassava (Manioc) | 7,460 | 7,112 | 6,833* |
| Yams† | 10 | 9 | 10 |
| Dry beans† | 270 | 195 | 195 |
| Dry peas† | 24 | 16 | 16 |
| Chick-peas† | 24 | 16 | 16 |
| Other pulses† | 106 | 85 | 85 |
| Groundnuts (in shell)† | 70 | 65 | 70 |
| Sunflower seed | 30* | 30* | 30† |
| Sesame seed† | 24 | 23 | 24 |
| Cottonseed* | 166 | 142 | 109 |
| Coconuts† | 350 | 350 | 360 |
| Copra† | 31 | 31 | 32 |
| Palm kernels† | 6.2 | 6.2 | 6.3 |
| Onions (dry)† | 52 | 50 | 51 |
| Other vegetables† | 1,059 | 996 | 848 |
| Sugar cane† | 1,420 | 1,410 | 1,470 |
| Citrus fruits† | 36 | 34 | 35 |
| Mangoes† | 187 | 185 | 186 |
| Pineapples† | 72 | 70 | 72 |
| Bananas | 750 | 794* | 800* |
| Plantains | 750 | 794* | 800* |
| Other fruit | 262 | 256 | 261 |
| Cashew nuts | 29.9 | 40.1 | 37.0† |
| Coffee (green) | 46 | 56 | 59* |
| Tea (made) | 20 | 18* | 20* |
| Tobacco (leaves) | 17 | 17 | 24† |
| Sisal | 36 | 24* | 28† |
| Cotton (lint) | 85* | 73 | 56* |

\* Unofficial figure(s).  † FAO estimate(s).

Source: FAO, *Production Yearbook*.

## LIVESTOCK ('000 head, year ending September)

|  | 1991 | 1992 | 1993 |
|---|---|---|---|
| Cattle | 13,138 | 13,217* | 13,296 |
| Sheep | 3,556 | 3,706* | 3,828 |
| Goats | 8,814 | 9,073* | 9,373 |
| Pigs* | 330 | 330 | 335 |
| Asses† | 175 | 176 | 177 |

\* Unofficial figure(s).  † FAO estimates.

Chickens (FAO estimates, million): 23 in 1991; 25 in 1992; 27 in 1993.
Ducks (FAO estimates, million): 1 in 1991; 1 in 1992; 1 in 1993.

Source: FAO, *Production Yearbook*.

## LIVESTOCK PRODUCTS ('000 metric tons)

|  | 1991 | 1992 | 1993* |
|---|---|---|---|
| Beef and veal* | 197 | 199 | 200 |
| Mutton and lamb* | 10 | 10 | 11 |
| Goat meat* | 22 | 23 | 24 |
| Pig meat* | 9 | 9 | 9 |
| Poultry meat | 29 | 32 | 35 |
| Other meat | 13 | 13 | 12 |
| Cows' milk | 529 | 541 | 545 |
| Goats' milk* | 85 | 87 | 90 |
| Butter* | 4.6 | 4.6 | 4.8 |
| Hen eggs* | 45.1 | 50.1 | 50.1 |
| Other poultry eggs* | 1.4 | 1.5 | 1.5 |
| Honey* | 15.0 | 15.5 | 16.0 |
| Cattle hides* | 40.0 | 40.5 | 40.8 |
| Sheepskins* | 2.5 | 2.6 | 2.6 |
| Goatskins* | 4.6 | 4.8 | 4.9 |

\* FAO estimates.

Source: FAO, *Production Yearbook*.

# Forestry

## ROUNDWOOD REMOVALS
(FAO estimates, '000 cubic metres, excluding bark)

|  | 1990 | 1991 | 1992 |
|---|---|---|---|
| Sawlogs, veneer logs and logs for sleepers* | 317 | 317 | 317 |
| Pulpwood† | 145 | 145 | 145 |
| Other industrial wood | 1,509 | 1,554 | 1,599 |
| Fuel wood | 30,677 | 31,741 | 32,842 |
| **Total** | 32,648 | 33,757 | 34,903 |

\* Assumed to be unchanged since 1987.
† Assumed to be unchanged since 1988.

Source: FAO, *Yearbook of Forest Products*.

## SAWNWOOD PRODUCTION ('000 cubic metres)

|  | 1985 | 1986 | 1987 |
|---|---|---|---|
| Coniferous (softwood) | 53 | 76 | 85 |
| Broadleaved (hardwood) | 56 | 78 | 71 |
| **Total** | 109 | 154 | 156 |

**1988–92:** Annual production as in 1987 (FAO estimates).

Source: FAO, *Yearbook of Forest Products*.

TANZANIA

## Fishing

('000 metric tons, live weight)

|  | 1990 | 1991 | 1992 |
|---|---|---|---|
| Tilapias | 37.0 | 41.6 | 42.0 |
| Mouth-brooding cichlids | 12.8 | 13.3 | 13.5 |
| Torpedo-shaped catfishes | 15.2 | 11.4 | 12.0 |
| Other freshwater fishes (incl. unspecified) | 71.0 | 70.8 | 72.0 |
| Dagaas | 42.1 | 36.5 | 36.0 |
| Nile perch | 179.3 | 98.8 | 100.0 |
| Emperors | 7.9 | 11.6 | 11.5 |
| Other marine fishes (incl. unspecified) | 46.2 | 39.3 | 41.3 |
| Other marine animals | 2.6 | 3.5 | 3.3 |
| **Total catch** | **414.0** | **326.8** | **331.6** |
| Inland waters | 357.3 | 272.4 | 275.5 |
| Indian Ocean | 56.7 | 54.4 | 56.1 |

Source: FAO, *Yearbook of Fishery Statistics*.

## Mining

|  | 1989 | 1990 | 1991 |
|---|---|---|---|
| Diamonds ('000 carats) | 150* | 104* | 117 |
| Gold (kg) | 116* | 1,628* | 3,851 |
| Salt ('000 metric tons) | 20 | 20 | 64 |

* Estimates from the US Bureau of Mines.

Source: UN, *Industrial Statistics Yearbook*.

## Industry

### SELECTED PRODUCTS
('000 metric tons, unless otherwise indicated)

|  | 1989 | 1990 | 1991 |
|---|---|---|---|
| Canned meat | 34 | 26 | 12 |
| Salted, dried or smoked fish (metric tons)* | 65,000 | 65,000 | n.a. |
| Raw sugar* | 90 | 108 | 116 |
| Beer ('000 hectolitres) | 537 | 450 | 498 |
| Soft drinks ('000 hectolitres) | 520 | 934 | 669 |
| Footwear—excl. rubber ('000 pairs) | 445 | 459 | 328 |
| Cigarettes (million) | 2,845 | 3,742 | 3,870 |
| Cement | 595 | 300 | 1,022 |
| Cotton woven fabrics (million sq metres) | 46 | 46 | 38 |
| Jet fuel | 26 | 28 | 31 |
| Motor spirit—petrol | 80 | 85 | 95 |
| Kerosene | 38 | 37 | 37 |
| Distillate fuel oils | 151 | 150 | 162 |
| Residual fuel oils | 221 | 225 | 210 |
| Electric energy (million kWh) | 885 | 885 | 901 |

* Data from the FAO.

Source: UN, *Industrial Statistics Yearbook*.

## Finance

### CURRENCY AND EXCHANGE RATES

**Monetary Units**
100 cents = 1 Tanzanian shilling.

**Sterling and Dollar Equivalents** (31 December 1994)
£1 sterling = 818.94 Tanzanian shillings;
US $1 = 523.45 Tanzanian shillings;
1,000 Tanzanian shillings = £1.221 = $1.910.

**Average Exchange Rate** (Tanzanian shillings per US $)
1992   297.71
1993   405.27
1994   509.63

**BUDGET** (million shillings, year ending 30 June)*

| Revenue | 1986/87 | 1987/88 | 1988/89† |
|---|---|---|---|
| Tax revenue | 29,526 | 44,865 | 63,085 |
| Personal tax | 7,351 | 8,792 | 16,611 |
| Sales tax | 16,096 | 26,878 | 33,237 |
| Import duties | 4,067 | 6,483 | 8,478 |
| Export duties | — | — | |
| Other | 2,012 | 2,712 | 4,759 |
| Non-tax revenue | 4,973 | 10,585 | 8,704 |
| Parastatal dividends and interest and surplus transfers | 957 | 790 | n.a. |
| Import support | 3,112 | 8,850 | n.a. |
| Appropriation in aid | 65 | 75 | 225 |
| Other | 839 | 870 | n.a. |
| **Total** | **34,499** | **55,450** | **71,789** |

| Expenditure | 1986/87 | 1987/88 | 1988/89† |
|---|---|---|---|
| Public administration | 9,031 | 13,413 | 19,305 |
| Foreign affairs | 1,100 | 2,179 | 3,457 |
| Defence and security | 10,668 | 12,414 | 16,779 |
| Education | 3,191 | 3,990 | 6,338 |
| Health | 2,257 | 3,273 | 5,509 |
| Community services | 133 | 215 | 347 |
| Economic services |  |  |  |
| General administration and research | 1,282 | 1,896 | 860 |
| Agriculture, forestry, fishing and hunting | 3,198 | 3,880 | 6,037 |
| Mining, manufacturing and construction | 1,410 | 1,803 | 2,368 |
| Electricity and water | 1,000 | 1,434 | 2,486 |
| Roads and bridges | 1,473 | 2,148 | 2,710 |
| Transport and communications | 1,211 | 1,378 | 2,464 |
| **Total** (incl. others) | **49,722** | **73,298** | **111,221** |

* Figures refer to the Tanzania Government, excluding the revenue and expenditure of the separate Zanzibar Government.
† Provisional figures.

Source: Government Printer, *Economic Survey 1990*.

**1989/90** (million shillings): Revenue and loan repayments 97,867 (excl. grants received 27,664); Expenditure (incl. lending) 140,871.
**1990/91** (million shillings): Revenue and loan repayments 137,093 (excl. grants received 22,875); Expenditure (incl. lending) 207,292.
**1991/92** (million shillings): Revenue and loan repayments 173,566 (excl. grants received 32,798); Expenditure (incl. lending) 261,051.
**1992/93** (million shillings): Revenue and loan repayments 164,110 (excl. grants received 58,313); Expenditure (incl. lending) 336,015.
**1993/94** (million shillings): Revenue and loan repayments 242,444 (excl. grants received 106,790); Expenditure (incl. lending) 485,216.

Source: IMF, *International Financial Statistics*.

### INTERNATIONAL RESERVES
(Tanzania mainland, US $ million at 31 December)

|  | 1992 | 1993 | 1994 |
|---|---|---|---|
| Reserve position in IMF | 13.7 | 13.7 | 14.6 |
| Foreign exchange | 313.6 | 189.6 | 317.5 |
| **Total** | **327.3** | **203.3** | **332.1** |

Source: IMF, *International Financial Statistics*.

# TANZANIA

## MONEY SUPPLY
(Tanzania mainland, million shillings at 31 December)

|  | 1990 | 1992 | 1993 |
| --- | --- | --- | --- |
| Currency outside banks | 58,111 | 95,450 | 122,470 |
| Demand deposits at commercial banks | 51,716 | 90,420 | 115,410 |
| **Total money** | 109,827 | 185,870 | 237,880 |

Figures for 1991 are not available.
Sources: Bank of Tanzania, Dar es Salaam; IMF, *International Financial Statistics*.

## COST OF LIVING
(Consumer Price Index for Tanzania mainland; base: 1980 = 100)

|  | 1990 | 1991 | 1992 |
| --- | --- | --- | --- |
| Food | 1,209.4 | 1,481.7 | 1,798.1 |
| Fuel, light and water | 1,476.6 | 1,795.0 | 2,213.1 |
| Clothing | 1,338.4 | 1,614.0 | 1,980.0 |
| Rent | 283.3 | 344.1 | 403.0 |
| **All items** (incl. others) | 1,270.5 | 1,553.8 | 1,896.7 |

**1993:** Food 2,202.4; All items 2,341.9.
Source: ILO, *Year Book of Labour Statistics*.

## NATIONAL ACCOUNTS
(Tanzania mainland, million shillings at current prices)
**National Income and Product**

|  | 1989 | 1990 | 1991 |
| --- | --- | --- | --- |
| Compensation of employees | 40,470 | 53,554 | 59,278 |
| Operating surplus | 281,078 | 332,801 | 499,521 |
| **Domestic factor incomes** | 321,548 | 386,355 | 558,799 |
| Consumption of fixed capital | 13,957 | 14,364 | 14,737 |
| **Gross domestic product (GDP) at factor cost** | 335,505 | 400,719 | 573,536 |
| Indirect taxes | 72,283 | 95,608 | 117,821 |
| Less Subsidies | 1,246 | 1,328 | 936 |
| **GDP in purchasers' values** | 406,542 | 494,999 | 690,421 |
| Factor income received from abroad | 550 | 495 | 495 |
| Less Factor income paid abroad | 29,593 | 40,981 | 42,180 |
| **Gross national product (GNP)** | 377,499 | 454,513 | 648,736 |
| Less Consumption of fixed capital | 13,957 | 14,364 | 14,737 |
| **National income in market prices** | 363,542 | 440,149 | 633,999 |
| Other current transfers from abroad (net) | 93,510 | 135,271 | 190,481 |
| **National disposable income** | 457,052 | 575,420 | 824,480 |

Source: UN, *National Accounts Statistics*.

**Expenditure on the Gross Domestic Product**

|  | 1991 | 1992 | 1993 |
| --- | --- | --- | --- |
| Government final consumption expenditure | 71,027 | 85,531 | 95,110 |
| Private final consumption expenditure | 596,099 | 684,359 | 77,135 |
| Increase in stocks | 36,996 | 37,402 | 50,100 |
| Gross fixed capital formation | 231,430 | 305,076 | 487,195 |
| **Total domestic expenditure** | 935,532 | 1,112,368 | 709,540 |
| Exports of goods and services | 112,466 | 170,170 | 189,914 |
| Less Imports of goods and services | 350,330 | 475,202 | −56,553 |
| **GDP in purchasers' values** | 697,688 | 807,336 | 845,485* |
| **GDP at constant 1990 prices** | 524,847 | 543,741 | n.a. |

* Including statistical discrepancy.
Source: IMF, *International Financial Statistics*.

## Gross Domestic Product by Economic Activity
(at factor cost)

|  | 1989 | 1990 | 1991 |
| --- | --- | --- | --- |
| Agriculture, hunting, forestry and fishing | 207,059 | 233,804 | 358,693 |
| Mining and quarrying | 1,129 | 4,815 | 6,975 |
| Manufacturing | 15,197 | 18,301 | 20,680 |
| Electricity, gas and water | 4,842 | 7,438 | 8,395 |
| Construction | 9,720 | 12,650 | 14,416 |
| Trade, restaurants and hotels | 50,392 | 56,638 | 83,325 |
| Transport, storage and communications | 23,854 | 36,242 | 47,017 |
| Finance, insurance, real estate and business services | 19,187 | 24,123 | 28,757 |
| Community, social and personal services | 22,168 | 31,968 | 34,478 |
| **Sub-total** | 353,548 | 425,979 | 602,736 |
| Less Imputed bank service charge | 18,043 | 25,260 | 29,200 |
| **Total** | 335,505 | 400,719 | 573,536 |

Source: UN, *National Accounts Statistics*.

## BALANCE OF PAYMENTS (US $ million)

|  | 1991 | 1992 | 1993 |
| --- | --- | --- | --- |
| Merchandise exports f.o.b. | 362.2 | 400.7 | 462.0 |
| Merchandise imports f.o.b. | −1,284.7 | −1,313.6 | −1,299.9 |
| **Trade balance** | −922.5 | −912.9 | −837.9 |
| Exports of services | 142.1 | 147.4 | 270.9 |
| Imports of services | −308.1 | −336.1 | −413.0 |
| Other income received | 7.9 | 8.2 | 19.3 |
| Other income paid | −194.1 | −233.5 | −167.4 |
| Private unrequited transfers (net) | 269.2 | 325.0 | 193.2 |
| Government unrequited transfers (net) | 554.2 | 580.0 | 526.5 |
| **Current balance** | −451.3 | −421.9 | −408.5 |
| Direct investment (net) | — | 12.0 | 20.0 |
| Other capital (net) | 108.1 | 76.9 | 55.0 |
| Net errors and omissions | −20.2 | 44.6 | −18.6 |
| **Overall balance** | 363.4 | −288.4 | −352.1 |

Source: IMF, *International Financial Statistics*.

# External Trade

**PRINCIPAL COMMODITIES** (million shillings)

| Imports c.i.f. | 1985 | 1986 | 1987 |
| --- | --- | --- | --- |
| Consumer goods | 1,623 | 2,176 | 3,211 |
| Construction materials | 924 | 1,952 | 3,504 |
| Other intermediate goods | 5,679 | 10,087 | 17,637 |
| Transport equipment | 5,364 | 10,640 | 26,874 |
| Other industrial goods | 2,676 | 5,025 | 10,676 |
| **Total** | 16,966* | 29,880 | 61,902 |

* Including others.

**Total Imports** (million shillings): 80,828 in 1988; 176,357 in 1989; 265,964 in 1990; 335,934 in 1991; 449,480 in 1992; 446,713 in 1993. (Source: IMF, *International Financial Statistics*.)

| Exports f.o.b. | 1988 | 1989 | 1990 |
| --- | --- | --- | --- |
| Coffee beans | 8,482 | 11,452 | 16,074 |
| Raw cotton | 7,228 | 9,323 | 14,820 |
| Diamonds | 756 | 766 | 629 |
| Sisal | 376 | 501 | 638 |
| Cloves | 412 | 4,424 | 1,485 |
| Cashew nuts | 1,120 | 535 | 650 |
| Tea | 1,472 | 3,290 | 1,210 |
| Tobacco | 1,296 | 1,619 | 2,438 |
| **Total** (incl. others) | 33,946 | 53,387 | 79,055 |

Source: Government Printer, *Economic Survey 1990*.

# TANZANIA

## PRINCIPAL TRADING PARTNERS (US $'000)

| Imports | 1986 | 1987 | 1988 |
|---|---|---|---|
| Denmark | 29,156 | 45,463 | 70,875 |
| Germany, Federal Republic | 89,883 | 121,209 | 176,491 |
| Italy | 56,433 | 90,596 | 116,363 |
| Japan | 97,403 | 109,639 | 187,517 |
| Netherlands | 33,282 | 49,436 | 75,905 |
| Sweden | 26,771 | 28,754 | 46,443 |
| United Arab Emirates | 46,386 | 44,171 | 51,971 |
| United Kingdom | 101,388 | 141,671 | 258,631 |
| **Total** (incl. others) | 838,493 | 975,823 | 1,495,215 |

| Exports | 1986 | 1987 | 1988 |
|---|---|---|---|
| Finland | 29,102 | 30,501 | 13,884 |
| Germany, Federal Republic | 83,441 | 39,211 | 47,788 |
| India | 15,672 | 22,577 | 21,573 |
| Italy | 16,825 | 10,832 | 16,305 |
| Japan | 15,143 | 11,509 | 15,498 |
| Netherlands | 24,116 | 24,621 | 19,661 |
| Portugal | 8,631 | 8,741 | 13,605 |
| United Kingdom | 42,593 | 31,240 | 34,183 |
| **Total** (incl. others) | 344,826 | 309,928 | 337,106 |

Source: UN, *International Trade Statistics Yearbook*.

## Transport

### RAILWAYS (estimated traffic)

| | 1989 | 1990 | 1991 |
|---|---|---|---|
| Passenger-km (million) | 3,630 | 3,690 | 3,740 |
| Freight ton-km (million) | 1,420 | 1,470 | 1,490 |

Source: UN Economic Commission for Africa, *African Statistical Yearbook*.

### ROAD TRAFFIC (estimates, '000 motor vehicles in use)

| | 1989 | 1990 | 1991 |
|---|---|---|---|
| Passenger cars | 51 | 52 | 53 |
| Commercial vehicles | 33 | 34 | 34 |

Source: UN Economic Commission for Africa, *African Statistical Yearbook*.

### INTERNATIONAL SEA-BORNE SHIPPING
(estimated freight traffic, '000 metric tons)

| | 1988 | 1989 | 1990 |
|---|---|---|---|
| Goods loaded | 1,208 | 1,197 | 1,249 |
| Goods unloaded | 3,140 | 3,077 | 2,721 |

Source: Government Printer, *Economic Survey 1990*.

## CIVIL AVIATION (traffic on scheduled services)

| | 1990 | 1991 | 1992 |
|---|---|---|---|
| Kilometres flown (million) | 4 | 5 | 4 |
| Passengers carried ('000) | 292 | 290 | 216 |
| Passenger-km (million) | 215 | 284 | 174 |
| Total ton-km (million) | 21 | 30 | 18 |

Source: UN, *Statistical Yearbook*.

## Tourism

| | 1990 | 1991 | 1992 |
|---|---|---|---|
| Tourist arrivals ('000) | 153 | 187 | 202 |
| Tourist receipts (US $ million) | 65 | 95 | 120 |

Source: UN, *Statistical Yearbook*.

## Communications Media

| | 1990 | 1991 | 1992 |
|---|---|---|---|
| Radio receivers ('000 in use)* | 650 | 660 | 640 |
| Television receivers ('000 in use)* | 40 | 42 | 45 |
| Telephones ('000 main lines in use) | 73 | 75 | n.a. |
| Daily newspapers: Number | 3 | n.a. | 3 |
| Average circulation ('000 copies)* | 200 | n.a. | 220 |

* Estimates.

Sources: UNESCO, *Statistical Yearbook*; UN, *Statistical Yearbook*.

## Education
(1993, unless otherwise indicated)

| | Teachers | Pupils |
|---|---|---|
| Primary | 101,816 | 3,736,734 |
| General secondary | 9,568 | 180,899 |
| Teacher training colleges | 1,171 | 15,824 |
| Higher* | | |
|   Universities | 939 | 3,327 |
|   Other institutions | 267 | 1,927 |

* 1989 figures.

Sources: Ministry of Education and Culture, Dar es Salaam; UNESCO, *Statistical Yearbook*.

# Directory

## The Constitution

The United Republic of Tanzania was established on 26 April 1964, when Tanganyika and Zanzibar, hitherto separate independent countries, merged. An interim Constitution of 1965 was replaced, on 25 April 1977, by a permanent Constitution for the United Republic. In October 1979 the Revolutionary Council of Zanzibar adopted a separate Constitution, governing Zanzibar's internal administration, with provisions for a popularly-elected President and a House of Representatives elected by delegates of the then ruling party. A new Constitution for Zanzibar, which came into force in January 1985, provided for direct elections to the Zanzibar Parliament, the House of Representatives. The provisions below relate to the 1977 Constitution of the United Republic, as subsequently amended.

### GOVERNMENT

Legislative power is exercised by the Parliament of the United Republic, which is vested by the Constitution with complete sovereign power, and of which the present National Assembly is the legislative house. The Assembly also enacts all legislation concerning the mainland. Internal matters in Zanzibar are the exclusive jurisdiction of the Zanzibar executive, the Supreme Revolutionary Council of Zanzibar, and the Zanzibar legislature, the House of Representatives.

Note: It was envisaged that a constitutional amendment providing for a separate government and legislature for Tanganyika would be enacted in 1995.

#### National Assembly

The National Assembly comprises both directly-elected members (chosen by universal suffrage) and nominated members (including five members elected from the Zanzibar House of Representatives). The number of directly-elected members exceeds the number of nominated members. The Electoral Commission may review and, if necessary, increase the number of electoral constituencies before every general election. The National Assembly has a term of five years.

#### President

The President is the Head of State, Head of the Government and Commander-in-Chief of the Armed Forces. The President has no power to legislate without recourse to Parliament. The assent of the President is required before any bill passed by the National Assembly becomes law. Should the President withhold his assent and the bill be repassed by the National Assembly by a two-thirds majority, the President is required by law to give his assent within 21 days unless, before that time, he has dissolved the National Assembly, in which case he must stand for re-election.

To assist him in carrying out his functions, the President appoints two Vice-Presidents from the elected members of the National Assembly. If the President comes from the mainland, the First Vice-President must come from Zanzibar, and vice versa. One of the Vice-Presidents is President of Zanzibar and the other is Prime Minister of the Union, who leads government business in the Assembly.* The Vice-Presidents and ministers comprise the Cabinet, which is presided over by the President of the Republic. Ministers must be appointed from among the members of the National Assembly.

### JUDICIARY

The independence of the judges is secured by provisions which prevent their removal, except on account of misbehaviour or incapacity when they may be dismissed at the discretion of the President. The Constitution also makes provision for a Permanent Commission of Enquiry which has wide powers to investigate any abuses of authority.

### CONSTITUTIONAL AMENDMENTS

The Constitution can be amended by an act of the Parliament of the United Republic, when the proposed amendment is supported by the votes of not fewer than two-thirds of all the members of the Assembly.

* In December 1994 a constitutional amendment was introduced whereby the President of Zanzibar would no longer also be a Vice-President of the Union Government; the amendment was due to enter into effect following the next general election.

## The Government

### HEAD OF STATE

**President:** ALI HASSAN MWINYI (took office 5 November 1985; re-elected for second term 8 November 1990).

**First Vice-President:** CLEOPA DAVID MSUYA.

**Second Vice-President and President of Zanzibar:** Dr SALMIN AMOUR.

### CABINET
(June 1995)

**President and Commander-in-Chief of the Armed Forces, and Minister of Defence and National Service:** ALI HASSAN MWINYI.
**Prime Minister:** CLEOPA DAVID MSUYA.
**Minister of Home Affairs:** ERNEST NYANDA.
**Minister of Finance:** JAKAYA KIKWETE.
**Minister of Foreign Affairs:** JOSEPH CLEMENCE RWEGASIRA.
**Minister of Agriculture:** FREDERICK SUMAYE.
**Minister of Labour and Youth Development:** (vacant).
**Minister of Industry and Trade:** BASIL PESAMBILI MRAMBA
**Minister of Energy, Minerals and Water:** JACKSON MAKWETA.
**Minister of Education and Culture:** Prof. PHILOMEN SARUNGI.
**Minister of Health:** ZAKIA MEGHJI.
**Minister of Lands, Housing and Urban Development:** EDWARD LOWASSA.
**Minister of Information and Broadcasting:** PHILIP SANGOKA MARMO.
**Minister of Works, Communications and Transport:** NALAILA KIULA.
**Minister of Tourism, Natural Resources and Environment:** JUMA HAMAD UMAR.
**Minister of Science, Technology and Higher Education:** BENJAMIN MKAPA.
**Minister of Community Development, Women and Children:** ANNA MAKINDA.
**Minister of Justice and Constitutional Affairs:** SAMUEL SITTA.
**Ministers without Portfolio:** KIGUNGE NGOMBALE-MWIRU, JOHN SAMUEL MALECELA.

### MINISTRIES

All Dar es Salaam Ministries are to be transferred to Dodoma by 2005.

**Office of the President:** The State House, POB 9120, Dar es Salaam; tel. (51) 23261; telex 41192.
**Office of the Prime Minister and First Vice-President:** POB 980, Dodoma; tel. (61) 20511; telex 53159.
**Office of the Second Vice-President and President of Zanzibar:** POB 776, Zanzibar; tel. (54) 20511.
**Ministry of Agriculture:** POB 9192, Dar es Salaam; tel. (51) 27231.
**Ministry of Community Development, Women and Children:** Dar es Salaam.
**Ministry of Defence and National Service:** POB 9544, Dar es Salaam; tel. (51) 28291.
**Ministry of Education and Culture:** POB 9121, Dar es Salaam; tel. (51) 27211; telex 41742.
**Ministry of Energy, Minerals and Water:** POB 9153, Dar es Salaam; tel. (51) 31433.
**Ministry of Finance:** POB 9111, Dar es Salaam; tel. (51) 21271; telex 41329; fax (51) 38573.
**Ministry of Foreign Affairs:** POB 9000, Dar es Salaam; tel. (51) 21234; telex 41086.
**Ministry of Health:** POB 9083, Dar es Salaam; tel. (51) 20261.
**Ministry of Home Affairs:** POB 9223, Dar es Salaam; tel. (51) 27291; telex 41231.
**Ministry of Industry and Trade:** POB 9503, Dar es Salaam; tel. (51) 27251.
**Ministry of Information and Broadcasting:** Dar es Salaam.
**Ministry of Labour and Youth Development:** POB 2483, Dar es Salaam; tel. (51) 20781.

# TANZANIA

**Ministry of Lands, Housing and Urban Development:** POB 9372, Dar es Salaam; tel. (51) 27271.

**Ministry of Legal and Constitutional Affairs:** Dar es Salaam.

**Ministry of Science, Technology and Higher Education:** Dar es Salaam.

**Ministry of Tourism, Natural Resources and Environment:** Dar es Salaam.

**Ministry of Works, Communications and Transport:** POB 9423, Dar es Salaam; tel. (51) 23235; telex 41392.

## SUPREME REVOLUTIONARY COUNCIL OF ZANZIBAR
(May 1995)

**President and Chairman:** Dr Salmin Amour.

**Chief Minister:** Omar Ali Juma.

**Minister of Finance, Economic Affairs and Planning:** Amina Salim Ali.

**Minister of Agriculture, Natural Resources and Livestock:** Seif Rashid Seif.

**Minister of Trade, Industry and Marketing:** Aman Abeid Karume.

**Minister of Water, Works and Energy:** Isa Muhammad Isa.

**Minister of Communications and Transport:** Rufina Juma Mbaruk.

**Minister of Education:** Omar Ramadhan Mapuri.

**Minister of Health:** Ali Muhammad Shoka.

**Minister of Information, Culture, Tourism and Youth:** Sa'id Bakari Jecha.

# Legislature

## NATIONAL ASSEMBLY

At the National Assembly elections held on 28 October 1990 there were 216 elective seats. Of the total of 291 seats, the remainder were distributed as follows: 15 for women, 15 for representatives of the mass organizations of the Chama Cha Mapinduzi (Revolutionary Party of Tanzania), 15 for the President's nominees, 25 for Regional Commissioners, and five for members elected by the Zanzibar House of Representatives. The Constitution provides for the creation of new constituencies as necessary. The next general election to the National Assembly was scheduled to take place in 1995.

Note: In August 1993 the National Assembly adopted a motion that proposed the creation of a separate parliament for the mainland.

**Speaker:** Pius Msekwa.

## ZANZIBAR HOUSE OF REPRESENTATIVES

Under the provisions of the Constitution for Zanzibar, introduced in January 1985, the Zanzibar House of Representatives comprises 50 elected members, five regional commissioners, 10 presidential nominees and 10 members representing organizations affiliated to the CCM and women. The most recent general election was held on 21 October 1990.

**Speaker:** Ali Hamisi Abdallah.

# Political Organizations

During 1965–92 Tanzania was a one-party state. In 1992 the Constitution was amended to legalize a multi-party political system.

**Bismillah Party:** Pemba; seeks a referendum on the terms of the 1964 union of Zanzibar with mainland Tanzania.

**Chama Cha Demokrasia na Maendeleo (Chadema—Party for Democracy and Progress):** Plot No. 922/7, Block 186005, Kisutu St, POB 5330, Dar es Salaam; regd 1993; supports democracy and social development; Chair. Edwin I. M. Mtei; Sec.-Gen. Bob Nyanga Makani.

**Chama Cha Mapinduzi (CCM—Revolutionary Party of Tanzania):** Kuu St, POB 50, Dodoma; tel. (61) 2282; telex 53175; f. 1977 by merger of the mainland-based Tanganyika African National Union (TANU) with the Afro-Shirazi Party, which operated on Zanzibar and Pemba; sole legal party 1977–92; socialist orientation; Chair. Ali Hassan Mwinyi; Sec.-Gen. Lawrence Gama.

**Chama Cha Wananchi (CCW—Civic United Front):** Mtendeni St, Urban District, POB 3637, Zanzibar; f. 1992; Chair. James K. Mapalala; Sec.-Gen. Shaaban Khabis Mloo.

**Democratic Party (DP):** Dar es Salaam; unregistered; Leader Rev. Christopher Mtikila.

**Movement for Democratic Alternative (MDA):** Zanzibar; unregistered; seeks to review the terms of the 1964 union of Zanzibar with mainland Tanzania; supports democratic reform and political plurality and advocates the abolition of detention without trial and the removal of press censorship.

**National Convention for Construction and Reform (NCCR—Mageuzi):** Plot No. 48, Mchikichi St, Kariakoo Area, POB 5316, Dar es Salaam; f. 1992, regd 1993; Chair. Augustine Lyatonga Mrema; Sec.-Gen. Mahinja Bagenda.

**National League for Democracy (NLD):** Sinza D/73, POB 352, Dar es Salaam; regd 1993; Chair. Emmanuel J. E. Makaidi; Sec.-Gen. Michael E. A. Mhina.

**National Reconstruction Alliance (NRA):** House No. 4, Mvita St, Jangwani Ward, POB 16542, Dar es Salaam; regd 1993; Chair. Ulotu Abubakar Ulotu; Sec.-Gen. Salim R. Matinga.

**Popular National Party (PONA):** Plot 104, Songea St, Ilala, POB 21561, Dar es Salaam; regd 1993; Chair. Wilfrem R. Mwakitwange; Sec.-Gen. Nicolaus Mchaina.

**Pragmatic Democratic Alliance:** unregistered; Leader Munuo Mughuni.

**Republic Party:** f. 1992; Chair. N. N. Moe.

**Tanzania Democratic Alliance Party (TADEA):** Block 3, Plot No. 37, Buguruni Malapa, POB 63133, Dar es Salaam; regd 1993; Pres. Flora M. Kamoona; Sec.-Gen. John D. Lifa-Chipaka.

**Tanzania People's Party (TPP):** Mbezi Juu, Kawe, POB 60847, Dar es Salaam; regd 1993; Chair. Alec H. Che-Mponda; Sec.-Gen. Gravel Limo.

**United People's Democratic Party (UPDP):** Al Aziza Restaurant, Kokoni St, Narrow St, POB 3903, Zanzibar; regd 1993; Chair. Khalfani Ali Abdullah; Sec.-Gen. Ahmed M. Rashid.

**Union for Multi-Party Democracy of Tanzania (UMD):** 77 Tosheka St, Magomeni Mapiga, POB 41093, Dar es Salaam; regd 1993; Chair. Chief Abdalla Said Fundikira.

# Diplomatic Representation

## EMBASSIES AND HIGH COMMISSIONS IN TANZANIA

**Albania:** 93 Msese Rd, POB 1034, Kinondoni, Dar es Salaam; telex 41280; Ambassador: Mehdi Shaqiri.

**Algeria:** 34 Upanga Rd, POB 2963, Dar es Salaam; telex 41104; Ambassador: (vacant).

**Angola:** POB 20793, Dar es Salaam; tel. 26689; telex 41251; fax 32349; Ambassador: José Agostinho Neto.

**Belgium:** NIC Investment House, 7th Floor, Samora Machel Ave, POB 9210, Dar es Salaam; (51) tel. 46047; telex 41094; (51) fax 20604; Ambassador: Count M. Goblet d'Alviella.

**Brazil:** IPS Bldg, 9th Floor, POB 9654, Dar es Salaam; tel. (51) 21780; telex 41228; Ambassador: José Ferreira Lopes.

**Burundi:** Plot No. 10007, Lugalo Rd, POB 2752, Upanga, Dar es Salaam; tel. (51) 38608; telex 41340; Ambassador: Edouard Kadigiri.

**Canada:** 38 Mirambo St, POB 1022, Dar es Salaam; telex 41015; fax (51) 46005; High Commissioner: Patricia Marsden-Dole.

**China, People's Republic:** 2 Kajificheni Close at Toure Drive, POB 1649, Dar es Salaam; telex 41036; Ambassador: Sun Guotang.

**Cuba:** Plot No. 313, Lugalo Rd, POB 9282, Upanga, Dar es Salaam; telex 41245; Ambassador: A. Rolando Gallardo Fernández.

**Denmark:** Ghana Ave, POB 9171, Dar es Salaam; tel. (51) 46319; telex 41057; fax (51) 46312; Ambassador: Flemming Bjørk Pedersen.

**Egypt:** 24 Garden Ave, POB 1668, Dar es Salaam; tel. (51) 23372; telex 41173; Ambassador: Baher M. El-Sadek.

**Finland:** NIC Investment House, Samora Machel Ave, POB 2455, Dar es Salaam; tel. (51) 46324; telex 41066; fax (51) 46328; Ambassador: Ilari Rantakari.

**France:** Bagamoyo Rd, POB 2349, Dar es Salaam; tel. (51) 34961; telex 41006; Ambassador: Georges Rochiccioli.

**Germany:** NIC Investment House, Samora Ave, POB 9541, Dar es Salaam; tel. (51) 46334; telex 41003; fax (51) 46292; Ambassador: Dr Heinz Schneppen.

**Guinea:** 35 Haile Selassie Rd, POB 2969, Oyster Bay, Dar es Salaam; tel. (51) 68626; Ambassador: M. Bangoura.

**Holy See:** Msasani Peninsula, POB 480, Dar es Salaam (Apostolic Nunciature); tel. (51) 68403; fax (51) 40193; Apostolic Pro-Nuncio: Most Rev. Francisco-Javier Lozano, Titular Archbishop of Penafiel.

**Hungary:** 40 Bagamoyo Rd, POB 672, Dar es Salaam; tel. (51) 34762; telex 41428; Ambassador: János Zegnal.

**India:** NIC Investment House, Samora Ave, POB 2684, Dar es Salaam; tel. (51) 46341; telex 41335; fax (51) 46747; High Commissioner: Om Prakash Gupta.

**Indonesia:** 229 Upanga Rd, POB 572, Dar es Salaam; telex 41575; Ambassador: Hidayat Soemo.

**Iran:** Plot 685, Masengo Rd, POB 3802, West Upanga, Dar es Salaam; tel. (51) 34622; Ambassador: Abdul Ali Tavakkoli.

**Iraq:** 355 United Nations Rd, POB 5289, Dar es Salaam; tel. (51) 25728; telex 41193; Ambassador: Fawz Ali al-Bander.

**Italy:** Plot 316, Lugalo Rd, POB 2106, Dar es Salaam; tel. (51) 46353; telex 41062; fax (51) 46354; Ambassador: Torquato Cardilli.

**Japan:** 1018 Upanga Road, POB 2577, Dar es Salaam; tel. (51) 31215; telex 41065; Ambassador: Mitsuru Eguchi.

**Kenya:** NIC Investment House, Samora Machel Ave, POB 5231, Dar es Salaam; tel. (51) 31502; telex 41700; High Commissioner: Dickson I. Kathambana.

**Korea, Democratic People's Republic:** Plot 460B, United Nations Rd, POB 2690, Dar es Salaam; Ambassador: Chang Won Ok.

**Madagascar:** Magoret St, POB 5254, Dar es Salaam; tel. (51) 41761; telex 41291; Chargé d'affaires: Rahdray Desiré.

**Malawi:** IPS Bldg, POB 23168, Dar es Salaam; tel. (51) 37260; telex 41633; High Commissioner: L. B. Malunga.

**Mozambique:** Dar es Salaam; telex 41214; Ambassador: António C. F. Sumbana.

**Netherlands:** New ATC Town Terminal Bldg, cnr Ohio St and Garden Ave, POB 9534, Dar es Salaam; tel. (51) 46391; telex 41050; fax (51) 46189; Ambassador: J. J. Wijenberg.

**Nigeria:** 3 Bagamoyo Rd, POB 9214, Oyster Bay, Dar es Salaam; telex 41240; High Commissioner: Solomon A. Yisa.

**Norway:** Plot 160, Mirambo St, POB 2646, Dar es Salaam; tel. (51) 25195; telex 41221; fax (51) 46444; Ambassador: Arild Eik.

**Poland:** 63 Alykhan Rd, POB 2188, Dar es Salaam; tel. (51) 46294; telex 41022; fax (51) 46294; Chargé d'affaires: Kazimierz Tomaszewski.

**Romania:** Plot 11, Ocean Rd, POB 590, Dar es Salaam; Ambassador: (vacant).

**Russia:** Plot No. 73, Kenyatta Drive, POB 1905, Dar es Salaam; tel. (51) 66006; telex 41747; fax (51) 66818; Ambassador: Dr Kenesh N. Kulmatov.

**Rwanda:** Plot 32, Upanga Rd, POB 2918, Dar es Salaam; tel. (51) 30119; telex 41292; Ambassador: François Bararwerekana.

**Spain:** 99B Kinondoni Rd, POB 842, Dar es Salaam; tel. (51) 66936; telex 41589; Ambassador: (vacant).

**Sudan:** 'Albaraka', 64 Upanga Rd, POB 2266, Dar es Salaam; telex 41143; Ambassador: Charles de Wol.

**Sweden:** Extelcoms Bldg, 2nd Floor, Samora Machel Ave, POB 9274, Dar es Salaam; tel. (51) 23501; telex 41013; Ambassador: Thomas Palme.

**Switzerland:** 17 Kenyatta Drive, POB 2454, Dar es Salaam; tel. (51) 66008; telex 41322; fax (51) 66736; Ambassador: Jörg L. Kaufmann.

**Syria:** POB 2442, Dar es Salaam; tel. (51) 20568; telex 41339; Chargé d'affaires: Kanaan Hadid.

**United Kingdom:** Hifadhi House, Samora Machel Ave, POB 9200, Dar es Salaam; tel. (51) 29601; telex 41004; fax (51) 46301; High Commissioner: Alan E. Montgomery.

**USA:** Laibon Rd, POB 9123, Dar es Salaam; tel. (51) 66010; telex 41250; fax (51) 66701; Ambassador: Brady Anderson.

**Viet Nam:** 9 Ocean Rd, Dar es Salaam; Ambassador: Tran My.

**Yemen:** 353 United Nations Rd, POB 349, Dar es Salaam; tel. (51) 27891; Ambassador: Abubaker Saeed Ba-Abbad.

**Yugoslavia:** Plot 35/36, Upanga Rd, POB 2838, Dar es Salaam; tel. (51) 46377; telex 41749; Ambassador: (vacant).

**Zaire:** 438 Malik Rd, POB 975, Upanga, Dar es Salaam; telex 41407; Ambassador: Pelendo B. Mawe.

**Zambia:** Ohio St/City Drive Junction, POB 2525, Dar es Salaam; telex 41023; High Commissioner: John Kashonka Chitafu.

**Zimbabwe:** POB 20762, Dar es Salaam; tel. (51) 30455; telex 41386; High Commissioner: J. M. Shava.

# Judicial System

The Tanzanian Court of Appeal was established in September 1979 in succession to the former Court of Appeal for East Africa, which heard civil and criminal appeals from Kenya, Uganda and Tanzania.

People's Courts were established in Zanzibar in 1970. Magistrates are elected by the people and have two assistants each. Under the Zanzibar Constitution, which came into force in January 1985, defence lawyers and the right of appeal, abolished in 1970, were reintroduced.

**Permanent Commission of Enquiry:** POB 2643, Dar es Salaam; Chair. and Official Ombudsman A. L. S. Mhina; Sec. F. P. S. Malika.

**Court of Appeal:** Consists of the Chief Justice and four Judges of Appeal.

**Chief Justice of Tanzania:** Francis Nyalali.

**Chief Justice of Zanzibar:** Hamid Mahmoud Hamid.

**High Court:** Its headquarters are at Dar es Salaam but it holds regular sessions in all Regions. It consists of a Jaji Kiongozi and 29 Judges.

**Jaji Kiongozi:** Barnabas Samatta.

**District Courts:** These are situated in each district and are presided over by either a Resident Magistrate or District Magistrate. They have limited jurisdiction and there is a right of appeal to the High Court.

**Primary Courts:** These are established in every district and are presided over by Primary Court Magistrates. They have limited jurisdiction and there is a right of appeal to the District Courts and then to the High Court.

**Attorney-General:** Andrew Chenge.

**Director of Public Prosecutions:** Kulwa Massaba.

# Religion

### ISLAM

Islam is the religion of more than 97% of the population in Zanzibar and of about one-third of the mainland population. A large proportion of the Asian community is Isma'ili.

**Ismalia Provincial Church:** POB 460, Dar es Salaam.

**National Muslim Council of Tanzania:** POB 21422, Dar es Salaam; tel. (51) 34934; f. 1969; supervises Islamic affairs on the mainland only; Chair. Sheikh Hemed bin Juma bin Hemed; Exec. Sec. Alhaj Muhammad Mtulia.

**Supreme Muslim Council:** Zanzibar; f. 1991; supervises Islamic affairs in Zanzibar.

**Wakf and Trust Commission:** POB 4092, Zanzibar; tel. (51) 30853; f. 1980; Islamic affairs; Exec. Sec. Yusuf Abdulrahman Muhammad.

### CHRISTIANITY

In 1993 it was estimated that about one-half of the mainland population professed the Christian faith.

**Jumuiya ya Kikristo Tanzania** (Christian Council of Tanzania): Church House, POB 1454, Dodoma; tel. (61) 21204; fax (61) 24445; f. 1934; Chair. (acting) Most Rev. John Acland Ramadhani (Archbishop of the Anglican Church); Gen. Sec. Angetile Yesaya Musomba.

#### The Anglican Communion

Anglicans are adherents of the Church of the Province of Tanzania, comprising 16 dioceses. There were an estimated 647,000 members in 1985.

**Archbishop of the Province of Tanzania and Bishop of Zanzibar and Tanga:** Most Rev. John Ramadhani, POB 35, Korogwe.

**Provincial Secretary:** Rev. Mkunga Mtingele, POB 899, Dodoma; tel. (61) 21437; fax (61) 24265.

#### Greek Orthodox

**Archbishop of East Africa:** Nicademus of Irinoupoulis (resident in Nairobi, Kenya); jurisdiction covers Kenya, Uganda and Tanzania.

#### Lutheran

**Evangelical Lutheran Church in Tanzania:** POB 3033, Arusha; tel. (57) 8855; telex 42054; 1.5m. mems; Presiding Bishop Rt Rev. Dr Samson Mushemba (acting); Exec. Sec. Amani Mwenegoha.

#### The Roman Catholic Church

Tanzania comprises four archdioceses and 25 dioceses. There were an estimated 6,531,329 adherents at 31 December 1993.

**Tanzania Episcopal Conference:** Catholic Secretariat, Mansfield St, POB 2133, Dar es Salaam; tel. (51) 50309; telex 41989; f. 1980; Pres. Rt Rev. Justin Tetemu Samba, Bishop of Musoma.

**Archbishop of Dar es Salaam:** Most Rev. Polycarp Pengo, Archbishop's House, POB 167, Dar es Salaam; tel. (51) 22031; fax (51) 27729.

**Archbishop of Mwanza:** Most Rev. Anthony Mayala, Archbishop's House, POB 1421, Mwanza; tel. and fax (68) 41616.

TANZANIA

**Archbishop of Songea:** Most Rev. NORBERT WENDELIN MTEGA, Archbishop's House, POB 152, Songea; tel. (635) 2004; telex 40036; fax (635) 2593.

**Archbishop of Tabora:** Most Rev. MARIO EPIFANIO ABDALLAH MGULUNDE, Archbishop's House, Private Bag, PO Tabora; tel. (62) 2329; telex 47306; fax (62) 4000.

### Other Christian Churches

**Baptist Mission of Tanzania:** POB 9414, Dar es Salaam; tel. (51) 32298; telex 41014; f. 1956; Administrator BOYD PEARCE.

**Christian Missions in Many Lands (Tanzania):** German Branch; POB 34, Tunduru, Ruvuma Region; f. 1957; Gen. Sec. KARL-GERHARD WARTH.

**Moravian Church:** POB 377, Mbeya; 113,656 mems; Gen. Sec. Rev. SHADRACK MWAKASEGE.

**Pentecostal Church:** POB 34, Kahama.

**Presbyterian Church:** POB 2510, Dar es Salaam; tel. (51) 29075.

### BAHÁ'Í FAITH

**National Spiritual Assembly:** POB 585, Dar es Salaam; tel. (51) 21173; mems resident in 2,301 localities.

### OTHER RELIGIONS

There are some Hindu communities and followers of traditional beliefs.

# The Press

### NEWSPAPERS
#### Daily

**Daily News:** POB 9033, Dar es Salaam; tel. (51) 25318; telex 41071; f. 1972; govt-owned; publ. by Tanzania Standard (Newspapers) Ltd; Man. Editor CHARLES RAJABU; circ. 50,000.

**Kipanga:** POB 199, Zanzibar; Swahili; publ. by Information and Broadcasting Services.

**Uhuru:** POB 9221, Dar es Salaam; tel. (51) 64341; telex 41239; f. 1961; official publ. of CCM; Swahili; Man. Editor YAHYA BUZARAGI; circ. 100,000.

#### Weekly

**Business Times:** POB 71439, Dar es Salaam; weekly, independent; English; Editor F. RUHINDA; circ. 15,000.

**The Express:** POB 20588, Dar es Salaam; tel. (51) 25318; telex 41071; independent; English; Editor PASCAL SHIJA; circ. 20,000.

**Mzalendo:** POB 9221, Dar es Salaam; tel. (51) 64341; telex 41239; f. 1972; publ. by CCM; Swahili; Man. Editor YAHYA BUZARAGI; circ. 115,000.

**Sunday News:** POB 9033, Dar es Salaam; tel. (51) 29881; telex 41071; f. 1954; govt-owned; Man. Editor CHARLES RAJABU; circ. 60,000.

### PERIODICALS

**The African Review:** POB 35042, Dar es Salaam; tel. (51) 43500; 2 a year; journal of African politics, development and international affairs; publ. by the Dept of Political Science, Univ. of Dar es Salaam; Chief Editor Dr. C. GASARASI; circ. 1,000.

**Eastern African Law Review:** POB 35093, Dar es Salaam; tel. (51) 48336; f. 1967; 2 a year; Chief Editor Dr N. N. N. NDITI; circ. 1,000.

**Elimu Haina Mwisho:** POB 1986, Mwanza; monthly; circ. 45,000.

**Gazette of the United Republic:** POB 9142, Dar es Salaam; tel. (51) 31817; telex 41419; weekly; official announcements; Editor H. HAJI; circ. 6,000.

**Government Gazette:** POB 261, Zanzibar; f. 1964; official announcements; weekly.

**Habari za Washirika:** POB 2567, Dar es Salaam; tel. (51) 23346; telex 41809; monthly; publ. by Co-operative Union of Tanzania; Editor H. V. N. CHIBULUNJE; circ. 40,000.

**Jenga:** POB 2669, Dar es Salaam; tel. (51) 44419; telex 41068; fax (51) 44419; journal of the National Development Corpn; circ. 2,000.

**Kiongozi** (The Leader): POB 9400, Dar es Salaam; tel. (51) 29505; f. 1950; fortnightly; Swahili; Roman Catholic; Editor ROBERT MFUGALE; circ. 33,500.

**Kweupe:** POB 222, Zanzibar; weekly; Swahili; publ. by Information and Broadcasting Services.

**Mbioni:** POB 9193, Dar es Salaam; English; publ. monthly by the political education college, Kivukoni College; circ. 4,000.

**Mfanyakazi** (The Worker): POB 15359, Dar es Salaam; tel. (51) 26111; telex 41205; weekly; Swahili; trade union publ.; Editor HAMIDU NZOWA; circ. 100,000.

**Mlezi** (The Educator): POB 41, Peramiho; tel. 30; f. 1970; every 2 months; Editor Fr GEROLD RUPPER; circ. 19,200.

**Mwenge** (Firebrand): POB 1, Peramiho; tel. 30; f. 1937; monthly; Editor BALTASAR CHALE; circ. 33,000.

**Nchi Yetu** (Our Country): POB 9142, Dar es Salaam; tel. (51) 25375; telex 41419; f. 1964; govt publ.; monthly; Swahili; circ. 50,000.

**Nuru:** POB 1893, Zanzibar; tel. (54) 32353; fax (54) 33457; f. 1992; bi-monthly; official publ. of Zanzibari authorities; circ. 8,000.

**Safina:** POB 21422, Dar es Salaam; tel. (51) 34934; publ. by National Muslim Council of Tanzania; Editor YASSIN SADIK; circ. 10,000.

**Sauti Ya Jimbo:** POB 899, Dodoma; tel. (61) 21437; fax (61) 24265; quarterly; Swahili; Anglican diocesan, provincial and world church news.

**Sikiliza:** POB 635, Morogoro; tel. (56) 3338; fax (56) 4374; quarterly; Seventh-day Adventist; Editor G. H. MBWANA; circ. 100,000.

**Taamuli:** POB 35042, Dar es Salaam; tel. (51) 43500; 2 a year; journal of political science; publ. by the Dept of Political Science, Univ. of Dar es Salaam; circ. 1,000.

**Tanzania Education Journal:** POB 9211, Dar es Salaam; f. 1984; publ. by Institute of Education, Ministry of Education and Culture; three times a year; circ. 8,000.

**Tanzania Trade Currents:** POB 5402, Dar es Salaam; tel. (51) 27439; telex 41408; fax (51) 46240; bimonthly; publ. by Board of External Trade; circ. 2,000.

**Uhuru na Amani:** POB 3033, Arusha; tel. (57) 3221; telex 42054; bi-monthly; Swahili; publ. by Evangelical Lutheran Church in Tanzania; Editor ELIAS G. B. GOROI; circ. 15,000.

**Ukulima wa Kisasa (Modern Farming):** POB 2308, Dar es Salaam; tel. (51) 29047; telex 41246; f. 1955; monthly; Swahili; publ. by Ministry of Agriculture; Editor CLEOPHAS RWECHUNGURA; circ. 35,000.

**Wela:** POB 180, Dodoma; Swahili.

### NEWS AGENCIES

**SHIHATA:** 304 Nkomo Rd, POB 4755, Dar es Salaam; tel. (51) 29311; telex 41080; f. 1981; Dir ABDULLA NGORORO.

#### Foreign Bureaux

**Inter Press Service (IPS)** (Italy): 304 Nkomo Rd, POB 4755, Dar es Salaam; tel. (51) 29311; telex 41080; Chief Correspondent PAUL CHINTOWA.

**Rossiyskoye Informatsionnoye Agentstvo—Novosti (RIA—Novosti)** (Russia): POB 2271, Dar es Salaam; tel. (51) 23897; telex 41095; Dir ANATOLI TKACHENKO.

**Xinhua (New China) News Agency:** 72 Upanga Rd, POB 2682, Dar es Salaam; tel. (51) 23967; telex 41563; Correspondent HUAI CHENGBO.

Reuters (UK) is also represented in Tanzania.

# Publishers

**Central Tanganyika Press:** POB 1129, Dodoma; tel. (61) 24180; fax (61) 24565; f. 1954; religious; Man. Canon JAMES LIFA (acting).

**Dar es Salaam University Press:** POB 35182, Dar es Salaam; tel. (51) 43137; telex 41327; f. 1981; educational, academic and cultural books in Swahili and English; Dir Y. B. MJUNGU.

**Eastern Africa Publications Ltd:** POB 1002 Arusha; tel. (57) 3176; telex 42121; f. 1978; general and school textbooks; Gen. Man. ABDULLAH SAIWAAD.

**Inland Publishers:** POB 125, Mwanza; tel. (68) 40064; general non-fiction, religion, in Kiswahili and English; Dir Rev. S. M. MAGESA.

**Oxford University Press:** Maktaba Rd, POB 5299, Dar es Salaam; tel. (51) 29209; f. 1969; Man. LUCIUS M. THONYA.

**Pan-African Publishing Co. Ltd:** POB 4212, Dar es Salaam; tel. (51) 22380; f. 1977; Man. Dir. R. MAKHANGE.

**Tanzania Publishing House:** 47 Samora Machel Ave, POB 2138, Dar es Salaam; tel. (51) 32164; telex 41325; f. 1966; educational and general books in Swahili and English.

#### Government Publishing House

**Government Printer:** POB 9124, Dar es Salaam; tel. (51) 20291; telex 41631; Dir JONAS OFORO.

# TANZANIA

## Radio and Television

According to estimates by UNESCO, there were 640,000 radio receivers in use in Tanzania and 45,000 television receivers in use in Zanzibar in 1992. There is no television service on the mainland.

### RADIO

**Radio Tanzania:** POB 9191, Dar es Salaam; tel. (51) 38011; telex 41201; f. 1951; domestic services in Swahili; schools service in English and Swahili; external services in English and Afrikaans, and in vernacular languages of South Africa; Dir NKWABI NG'WANA-KILALA.

**Radio Tumaini** (Hope): POB 9330, Dar es Salaam; tel. (51) 31075; fax (51) 44935; broadcasts within Dar es Salaam; operated by the Roman Catholic Church; broadcasts on religious, social and economic issues; Dir Fr JEAN-FRANÇOIS GALTIER.

**The Voice of Tanzania Zanzibar:** POB 1178, Zanzibar; tel. (54) 31088; telex 57207; f. 1951; broadcasts in Swahili on three wavelengths; Dir YUSSEF OMAR SHUNDA.

### TELEVISION

**Television Zanzibar:** POB 314, Zanzibar; telex 57200; f. 1973; colour service; Dir JUMA SIMBA.

## Finance

(cap. = capital; dep. = deposits; res = reserves; m. = million; br. = branch; amounts in Tanzanian shillings)

### BANKING

Banks were nationalized in 1967. Efforts to liberalize the banking sector, in progress since 1992, resulted in the opening of Tanzania's first privately-owned banks in 1993–94.

#### Central Bank

**Bank of Tanzania:** 10 Mirambo St, POB 2939, Dar es Salaam; tel. (51) 46226; telex 41024; fax (51) 46037; f. 1966; bank of issue; cap. and res 19,612.2m., dep. 105,806 (June 1992); Gov. and Chair. Dr IDRIS RASHID; Dep. Gov. N. N. KITOMARI.

#### Principal Banks

**The Co-operative and Rural Development Bank (CRDB):** Azikiwe St, POB 268, Dar es Salaam; tel. (51) 46614; telex 41643; fax (51) 26518; f. 1984; provides commercial banking services and loans for rural development; 51% govt-owned, 30% owned by Co-operative Union of Tanzania Ltd (Washirika), 19% by Bank of Tanzania; cap. 1,493m. (June 1991), dep. 1,822m. (June 1987); restructuring in progress in 1993–94; Chair. and Man. Dir PHILIP A. MAGANI; Gen. Man. RABBIEL D. SWAI; 20 regional and 25 dist. offices, 8 brs.

**Meridien BIAO Bank Tanzania Ltd:** Sukari House, POB 72647, Dar es Salaam; tel. (51) 26251; telex 41415; fax (51) 44553; f. 1993; placed under control of Bank of Tanzania April 1995; cap. 1,000m. (Sept. 1993); Gen. Man. JOHN MONTGOMERY.

**The National Bank of Commerce (NBC):** NBC House, POB 1865, Dar es Salaam; tel. (51) 46100; telex 41581; fax (51) 46235; f. 1967; cap. 50,000m. (June 1992), dep. 233,484m. (June 1991); Man. Dir PAUL BOMANI; 179 brs, 23 agencies.

**People's Bank of Zanzibar Ltd (PBZ):** Gizenga St, POB 1173, Forodhani, Zanzibar; tel. (54) 31118; telex 57365; fax (54) 31121; f. 1966; controlled by Zanzibar Govt; cap. 16m. (June 1991); Chair. MOHAMED ABOUD; Gen. Man. N. S. NASSOR.

**Standard Chartered Tanzania Ltd:** 1st Floor, NIC Life House, cnr Sokoine Drive/Ohio St, Dar es Salaam; tel. (51) 44596; fax (51) 44594; f. 1992, activities commenced 1993; wholly owned by Standard Chartered PLC (United Kingdom); cap. 1,000m. (1993); Chair. and Man. Dir P. V. DOCHERTY.

**Tanzania Development Finance Co Ltd (TDFC):** TDFL Bldg, cnr Upanga Rd/Ohio St, POB 2478, Dar es Salaam; tel. (51) 25091; telex 41153; fax (51) 46145; f. 1962; owned by the Tanzania Investment Bank, govt agencies of the Netherlands and Germany, the Commonwealth Development Corpn and the European Investment Bank; cap. 380m. (Dec. 1992); Chair. F. M. KAZAURA; Gen. Man. H. K. SENKORO.

**Tanzania Housing Bank (THB):** POB 1723, Dar es Salaam; tel. (51) 31112; telex 41831; f. 1972; restructuring in progress in 1994; provides loans for residential and commercial projects; 52% govt-owned, 24% owned by National Insurance Corpn, 24% by National Provident Fund; cap. 400m., dep. 4,300m. (1992); Chair. DANIEL YONA; Gen. Man. TAIRO URASA; 21 brs, 1 agency.

**Tanzania Investment Bank (TIB):** Samora Machel Ave, POB 9373, Dar es Salaam; tel. (51) 28581; telex 41259; fax (51) 46934; f. 1970; provides finance and tech. assistance for economic development; 60% govt-owned, 30% owned by National Bank of Commerce, 10% by National Insurance Corpn; cap. 301m. (June 1992); Chair. IDDI SIMBA; Gen. Man. and CEO G. MWAIKAMBO.

**Tanzania Postal Bank (TPB):** Texco House, Pamba Rd, POB 9300, Dar es Salaam; tel. (51) 38212; telex 41663; fax (51) 32818; f. 1991; dep. 15,715.7m. (1994); Gen. Man. R. D. SWAI; 207 brs.

### INSURANCE

**National Insurance Corporation of Tanzania Ltd (NIC):** POB 9264, Dar es Salaam; tel. (51) 26561; telex 41146; f. 1963; nationalized 1967; all classes of insurance; Chair. IDO SIMBA; Man. Dir OCTAVIAN W. TEMU; 21 brs.

## Trade and Industry

### CHAMBERS OF COMMERCE

**Dar es Salaam Chamber of Commerce:** Kelvin House, Samora Machel Ave, POB 41, Dar es Salaam; tel. (51) 21893; telex 41628; Exec. Officer I. K. MKWAWA.

### TRADE, MARKETING AND PRODUCER ASSOCIATIONS AND BOARDS

**Board of External Trade (BET):** POB 5402, Dar es Salaam; tel. (51) 27439; telex 41408; fax (51) 46240; f. 1978; trade promotion, market research, marketing advisory and consultancy services, trade information, operational export promotion services; Dir-Gen. MBARUK K. MWANDORO.

**Board of Internal Trade (BIT):** POB 883, Dar es Salaam; tel. (51) 28301; telex 41082; f. 1967 as State Trading Corpn, reorg. 1973; state-owned; supervises seven national and 21 regional trading cos; distribution of general merchandise, agricultural and industrial machinery, pharmaceuticals, foodstuffs and textiles; shipping and other transport services; Dir-Gen. J. E. MAKOYE.

**Cashewnut Board of Tanzania:** POB 533, Mtwara; telex 56134; fax (59) 3536; Chair. Dr A. W. KHALID; Dir Gen. Maj Gen. R. L. MAKUNDA.

**Coffee Marketing Board of Tanzania:** POB 732, Moshi; telex 43088; Chair. W. KAPINGA; Gen. Man. A. M. RULEGURA.

**National Agricultural and Food Corporation (NAFCO):** POB 903, Dar es Salaam; telex 41295; produces and processes basic foods; Gen. Man. R. M. LINJEWILE.

**National Coconut Development Programme:** POB 6226, Dar es Salaam; tel. (51) 74834; fax 75549; f. 1979 to revive coconut industry; processing and marketing and projects including training, disease and pest control, smallholder and plantation development, breeding, agronomy trials; Project Co-ordinator P. L. KINYANA.

**National Milling Corporation (NMC):** POB 9502, Dar es Salaam; tel. (51) 860260; telex 41343; fax (51) 863817; f. 1968; stores and distributes basic foodstuffs, owns grain milling establishments and imports cereals as required; Chair. CRISPIN MOAPILA; Gen. Man. VINCENT M. SEMESI.

**National Textile Corporation:** POB 9531, Dar es Salaam; tel. (51) 26681; telex 41247; fax (51) 46899; f. 1974; holding corpn with 14 subsidiaries; production and marketing of yarn, fabrics, garments, agricultural bags and blankets; CEO S. H. NKYA.

**State Mining Corporation (STAMICO):** POB 4958, Dar es Salaam; tel. (51) 28781; telex 41354; fax (51) 30518; f. 1972; responsible for all mining and prospecting; Dir-Gen. AUGUSTINE Y. HANGI.

**State Motor Corporation:** POB 1307, Dar es Salaam; telex 41152; f. 1974 to control all activities of the motor trade; sole importer of cars, tractors and lorries; Gen. Man. H. H. IDDI.

**Sugar Development Corporation:** Dar es Salaam; tel. 46373; telex 41338; fax 30598; Gen. Man. GEORGE G. MBATI.

**Tanganyika Coffee Growers' Association Ltd:** POB 102, Moshi.

**Tanzania Cotton Lint and Seed Board:** POB 9161, Dar es Salaam; tel. (51) 46139; telex 41287; fax (51) 22564; f. 1984; regulates the marketing and export of cotton lint; Gen. Man. ANGELO K. MPUYA.

**Tanzania Pyrethrum Board:** POB 149, Iringa; f. 1960; Chair. Brig. LUHANGA; CEO P. B. G. HANGAYA.

**Tanzania Sisal Development Board:** Dar es Salaam; f. 1973 as the Tanzania Sisal Authority; co-ordinates the marketing of sisal; Chair. AUSTIN SHABA; Gen. Man. IBRAHIM KADUMA.

**Tanzania Tea Authority:** POB 2663, Dar es Salaam; tel. (51) 46700; telex 41130; fax (51) 23322; Chair. J. J. MUNGAI; Gen. Man. M. F. L. SHIRIMA.

**Tanzania Wood Industry Corporation:** POB 9160, Dar es Salaam; Gen. Man. E. M. MNZAVA.

# TANZANIA

**Tea Association of Tanzania:** POB 2177, Dar es Salaam; tel. (51) 22033; f. 1989; Chair. G. C. Theobald; Exec. Dir D. E. A. Mgwassa.

**Tobacco Authority of Tanzania:** POB 227, Morogoro; telex 55347; CEO J. N. Elinewinga; Gen. Man. Taki.

**Zanzibar State Trading Corporation:** POB 26, Zanzibar; tel. (54) 30271; telex 57208; fax (54) 31550; govt-controlled since 1964; sole exporter of cloves, clove stem oil, chillies, copra, copra cake, lime oil and lime juice; Gen. Man. Abdulrahman Rashid.

## DEVELOPMENT CORPORATIONS

**Capital Development Authority:** POB 1, Dodoma; tel. (61) 23310; telex 53177; f. 1973 to develop the new capital city of Dodoma; state-owned; Chair. Pius Msekwa; Dir-Gen. Thomas M. Mtei.

**Economic Development Commission:** POB 9242, Dar es Salaam; tel. (51) 29411; telex 41641; f. 1962 to plan national economic development; state-controlled.

**Investment Promotion Centre:** Dar es Salaam; Dir-Gen. Sir George Kahama.

**National Development Corporation:** POB 2669, Dar es Salaam; tel. (51) 46244; telex 41068; fax (51) 44419; f. 1965; state-owned; cap. 21.4m. sh.; promotes progress and expansion in production and investment; Man. Dir Prof. Simon Mbilinyi.

**Small Industries Development Organization (SIDO):** POB 2476, Dar es Salaam; tel. (51) 27691; telex 41123; f. 1973; promotes and assists development of small-scale industries in public, co-operative and private sectors, aims to increase rural industrialization and the involvement of women in small industries; Chair. J. E. F. Mhina; Dir-Gen. E. B. Toroka.

There are also development corporations for textiles and petroleum.

## TRADE UNIONS

Minimum wages are controlled by law and there is also compulsory arbitration under the Trades Disputes (Settlement) Act; strikes and lock-outs are illegal unless the statutory conciliation procedure has been followed.

**Union of Tanzania Workers (Juwata):** POB 15359, Dar es Salaam; tel. (51) 26111; telex 41205; f. 1978; Sec.-Gen. Joseph C. Rwegasira; Dep. Secs-Gen. C. Manyanda (Tanzania mainland), I. M. Issa (Zanzibar); 500,000 mems (1991); eight sections:

**Central and Local Government and Medical Workers' section:** Sec. R. Utukulu.

**Agricultural Workers' section:** Sec. G. P. Nyindo.

**Industrial and Mines Workers' section:** Sec. J. V. Mwambuma.

**Teachers' section:** Sec. W. Mwenura.

**Commerce and Construction section:** Sec. P. O. Olum.

**Domestic, Hotels and General Workers' section:** Sec. E. Kazoka.

**Communications and Transport Workers' section:** Sec. M. E. Kaluwa.

**Railway Workers' section:** Sec. C. Sammang' Ombe.

### Principal Unaffiliated Unions

**Organization of Tanzanian Trade Unions (OTTU):** Dar es Salaam; Sec.-Gen. Bruno Mpangal.

**Workers' Department of Chama Cha Mapinduzi:** POB 389, Vikokotoni, Zanzibar; f. 1965.

## CO-OPERATIVES

There are some 1,670 primary marketing societies under the aegis of about 20 regional co-operative unions. The Co-operative Union of Tanzania is the national organization to which all unions belong.

**Co-operative Union of Tanzania Ltd (Washirika):** POB 2567, Dar es Salaam; tel. (51) 23346; telex 41809; f. 1962; Sec.-Gen. D. Holela; 700,000 mems.

**Department of Co-operative Societies:** POB 1287, Zanzibar; tel. (54) 30747; telex 57311; f. 1952; encourages formation and development of co-operative societies in Zanzibar.

### Principal Societies

**Bukoba Co-operative Union Ltd:** POB 5, Bukoba; 74 affiliated societies; 75,000 mems.

**Kilimanjaro Native Corporation Union Ltd:** POB 3032, Moshi; tel. (55) 54410; telex 43014; fax (55) 54204; f. 1976; 88 registered co-operative societies.

**Nyanza Co-operative Union Ltd:** POB 9, Mwanza.

# Transport

## RAILWAYS

**Tanzania Railways Corporation (TRC):** POB 468, Dar es Salaam; tel. (51) 26241; telex 41308; f. 1977 after dissolution of East African Railways; operates 2,600 km of lines within Tanzania; also operates vessels on Lakes Victoria, Tanganyika and Malawi; a major restructuring scheme commenced in 1991 and was expected to be completed in 1995; Chair. J. V. Mwapachu; Dir-Gen. E. N. Makoi.

**Tanzania-Zambia Railway Authority (Tazara):** POB 2834, Dar es Salaam; tel. (51) 62191; telex 41097; fax (51) 62474; jtly owned and administered by the Tanzanian and Zambian Govts; 1,860-km railway link between Dar es Salaam and New Kapiri Mposhi, Zambia; opened in Oct. 1975; a 10-year rehabilitation programme, aided by the USA and EC (now EU) countries, began in 1985; plans to construct an additional line, linking Tanzania with the port of Mpulungu, on the Zambian shore of Lake Tanganyika, were announced in 1990; Chair. Richard Mariki; Gen. Man. A. S. Mweemba; Regional Man. (Tanzania) H. M. Teggisa; Regional Man. (Zambia) M. S. Banda.

## ROADS

In 1993 Tanzania had 88,000 km of classified roads, of which 10,270 km were primary roads and 17,730 km were secondary roads. About 4% of the network was paved in that year, and many roads are impassable in the wet season. A 1,930-km main road links Zambia and Tanzania, and there is a road link with Rwanda. A 10-year Integrated Roads Programme, funded by international donors and co-ordinated by the World Bank, commenced in 1991: its aim was to upgrade 70% of Tanzania's trunk roads and to construct 2,828 km of roads and 205 bridges, at an estimated cost of US $650m.

The island of Zanzibar has 619 km of roads, of which 442 km are bituminized, and Pemba has 363 km, of which 130 km are bituminized.

## INLAND WATERWAYS

Steamers connect with Kenya, Uganda, Zaire, Burundi, Zambia and Malawi. A joint shipping company was formed with Burundi in 1976 to operate services on Lake Tanganyika. A rail ferry service operates on Lake Victoria between Mwanza and Port Bell.

## SHIPPING

Tanzania's major harbours are at Dar es Salaam (eight deep-water berths for general cargo, three berths for container ships, eight anchorages, lighter wharf, one oil jetty for small oil tankers up to 36,000 tons, offshore mooring for super oil tankers up to 100,000 tons, one 30,000-ton automated grain terminal) and Mtwara (two deep-water berths). There are also ports at Tanga (seven anchorages and lighterage quay), Bagamoyo, Zanzibar and Pemba. Work on the first phase of a major modernization scheme for the port of Dar es Salaam commenced in 1985, and was expected to be completed in the early 1990s. The rehabilitation of the ports of Zanzibar and Pemba, begun in 1988, was completed in 1991.

**Tanzania Harbours Authority (THA):** POB 9184, Dar es Salaam; tel. (51) 21212; telex 41346; fax (51) 32066; Exec. Chair. J. K. Chande; Gen. Man. A. S. M. Janguo; 3 brs.

**National Shipping Agencies Co Ltd (NASACO):** POB 9082, Dar es Salaam; telex 41235; f. 1973; state-owned shipping co with which all foreign shipping lines are required to deal exclusively.

**Sinotaship (Chinese/Tanzanian Joint Shipping Line):** POB 696, Dar es Salaam; tel. (51) 46882; telex 41129; fax 46881; f. 1967; services between People's Republic of China, South East Asia, Eastern and Southern Africa, Red Sea and Mediterranean ports.

**Tanzania Coastal Shipping Line Ltd:** POB 9461, Dar es Salaam; tel. (51) 28907; telex 41124; fax (51) 46930; regular services to Tanzanian coastal ports; occasional special services to Zanzibar and Pemba; also tramp charter services to Kenya, Mozambique, the Persian (Arabian) Gulf, Indian Ocean islands and the Middle East; Gen. Man. A. S. Lutavi.

## CIVIL AVIATION

There are 53 airports and landing strips. The major international airport is at Dar es Salaam, 13 km from the city centre, and there are international airports at Kilimanjaro and Zanzibar.

**Air Tanzania Corporation:** Tancot House, City Drive, POB 543, Dar es Salaam; tel. (51) 38300; telex 41077; fax (51) 37191; f. 1977; operates an 18-point domestic network and international services to Africa, the Middle East and Europe; Chair. Bob N. Makani; Gen. Man. Sila Rwebangira.

**Air Zanzibar:** Zanzibar; f. 1990; operates charter services between Zanzibar and destinations in Tanzania, Kenya and Uganda.

**Alliance:** f. 1994; jtly owned by South African Airways, Air Tanzania Corpn, Uganda Airlines Corpn and the Tanzanian and Ugandan Govts; operates regional services and intercontinental services to Asia, the Middle East and Europe; Man. Dir Christo Roodt.

**New ACS Ltd:** Peugeot House, 36 Upanga Rd, POB 21236, Dar es Salaam; fax (51) 37017; operates domestic and regional services from Tanzania and Zaire; Dir MOHSIN RAHEMTULLAH.

## Tourism

Tanzania has set aside about one-third of its land for national parks and game and forest reserves. The country received an estimated 201,750 visitors in 1992, compared with 138,000 in 1987. Some 50,000 tourists visit Zanzibar each year. Revenue from tourism totalled US $147m. in 1993/94.

**Tanzania Tourist Board:** IPS Bldg, Maktaba St, POB 2485, Dar es Salaam; tel. (51) 27671; telex 41061; fax (51) 46780; state-owned; supervises the development and promotion of tourism; Man. Dir CREDO SINYANGWE.

**Tanzania Wildlife Corporation:** POB 1144, Arusha; tel. (57) 8830; telex 42080; fax (57) 8239; organizes safaris; also an exporter and dealer in live animals, birds and game-skin products; Gen. Man. M. A. NDOLANGA.

**Zanzibar Tourist Corporation:** POB 216, Zanzibar; tel. (54) 32344; telex 57144; fax (54) 33430; f. 1985; organizes tours and hotel services; Gen. Man. ALPHONCE KATEMA.

# THAILAND

## Introductory Survey

### Location, Climate, Language, Religion, Flag, Capital

The Kingdom of Thailand lies in South-East Asia. It is bordered to the west and north by Myanmar (Burma), to the north-east by Laos and to the south-east by Cambodia. Thailand extends southward, along the isthmus of Kra, to the Malay Peninsula, where it borders Malaysia. The isthmus, shared with Myanmar, gives Thailand a short coastline on the Indian Ocean, and the country also has a long Pacific coastline on the Gulf of Thailand. The climate is tropical and humid, with an average annual temperature of 29°C (85°F). There are three main seasons: hot, rainy and cool. Temperatures in Bangkok are generally between 20°C (68°F) and 35°C (95°F). The national language is Thai. There are small minorities of Chinese, Malays and indigenous hill peoples. The predominant religion is Buddhism, mainly of the Hinayana (Theravada) form. About 4% of the population, predominantly Malays, are Muslims, and there is also a Christian minority, mainly in Bangkok and the north. The national flag (proportions 3 by 2) has five horizontal stripes, of red, white, blue, white and red, the central blue stripe being twice as wide as each of the others. The capital is Bangkok.

### Recent History

Formerly known as Siam, Thailand took its present name in 1939. Under the leadership of Marshal Phibul Songkhram, Thailand entered the Second World War as an ally of Japan. Phibul was deposed in 1944, but returned to power in 1947 after a military coup. However, his influence declined during the 1950s, and in 1957 he was overthrown in a bloodless coup, led by Field Marshal Sarit Thanarat. Elections took place, but in 1958 martial law was declared and all political parties were dissolved. Sarit died in 1963 and was succeeded as Prime Minister by Gen. (later Field Marshal) Thanom Kittikachorn, who had served as Deputy Prime Minister since 1959. Thanom continued the combination of military authoritarianism and economic development instituted by his predecessor. A Constitution was introduced in 1968, and elections to a National Assembly took place in 1969, but in November 1971, following an increase in communist insurgency and internal political unrest, Thanom annulled the Constitution, dissolved the National Assembly and imposed martial law.

During 1972 there were frequent student demonstrations against the military regime, and in October 1973 the Government was forced to resign, after the army refused to use force to disperse student protesters, and King Bhumibol Adulyadej withdrew his support from the administration. An interim Government was formed under Dr Sanya Dharmasakti, the President of the Privy Council. In October 1974 a new Constitution, legalizing political parties, was promulgated, and in January 1975 elections were held to the new House of Representatives. A coalition Government was formed in February by Seni Pramoj, the leader of the Democratic Party (DP), but it was defeated by a vote of 'no confidence' in March 1975.

A new right-wing coalition Government, headed by the leader of the Social Action Party (SAP), Kukrit Pramoj (brother of Seni), was unable to maintain its unity, and Kukrit resigned in January 1976. After further general elections in April, a four-party coalition Government was formed, with Seni as Prime Minister. However, following violent student demonstrations in October, the Seni Government was dissolved, and a right-wing military junta, the National Administrative Reform Council (NARC), seized power. Martial law was declared, the 1974 Constitution was annulled, political parties were banned and strict press censorship was imposed. A new Constitution was promulgated, and a new Cabinet was announced, with Thanin Kraivixien, a Supreme Court judge, as Prime Minister.

Under the Thanin Government there was considerable repression of students and political activists. In October 1977 the Government was overthrown in a bloodless coup by a Revolutionary Council (later known as the National Policy Council—NPC) of military leaders, most of whom had been members of the NARC which had brought Thanin to power. The 1976 Constitution was abrogated, and the Secretary-General of the NPC (who was also the Supreme Commander of the Armed Forces), Gen. Kriangsak Chomanan, became Prime Minister. Many detainees were released, censorship was partially relaxed and the King nominated a National Assembly on the advice of the NPC. In December 1978 the National Assembly approved a new Constitution, and elections to a new House of Representatives were held in April 1979. Members of the Senate, however, were all nominated by the Prime Minister, and were almost all military officers. Kriangsak remained Prime Minister and formed a new Cabinet, after which the NPC was dissolved. However, Kriangsak resigned in March 1980, and was replaced by Gen. Prem Tinsulanonda, the Commander-in-Chief of the Army and the Minister of Defence. A new coalition Government, composed largely of centre-right politicians acceptable to the armed forces, was formed.

Although Prem's administration initially appeared to lack authority, it survived an abortive coup attempt in April 1981. In December of that year Prem effected a ministerial reshuffle, reincorporating members of the SAP (who had been excluded from the Government in March), in order to repulse a challenge from the new National Democracy Party (NDP), established by the former Prime Minister, Kriangsak. In April 1983 elections took place to the new House of Representatives. No single party won an overall majority, and a coalition Government was formed by the SAP, Prachakorn Thai, the DP and the NDP. Chart Thai, despite being the party with the largest number of seats, formed the opposition, and Prem was again appointed Prime Minister.

In September 1985 a group of military officers, dissatisfied with the decline of the role of the armed forces in politics, staged a coup attempt in Bangkok. Troops loyal to the Government quickly suppressed the revolt, but at least five people were killed and about 60 were injured during the fighting. The leader of the revolt, Col Manoon Roopkachorn (who had also led the coup attempt in 1981), fled the country, but 40 others, including Kriangsak, were put on trial in October, accused of inciting sedition and rebellion. Gen. Arthit Kamlang-ek, the Supreme Commander of the Armed Forces and Commander-in-Chief of the Army (who was believed to have been sympathetic to the aims of the coup leaders), was replaced in his posts by Gen. Chaovalit Yongchaiyut, hitherto the army Chief of Staff.

In September 1985 and January 1986 there were extensive changes in the Government, including the replacement of all members of the SAP, following the resignation of Kukrit as the party's leader, and the introduction of members of the Progress Party into the coalition. In May 1986, following a parliamentary defeat for the Government over proposed vehicle taxation, the House of Representatives was dissolved, 11 months before the expiry of its term. A general election for an enlarged legislature was held in July, when the DP won 100 of the 347 seats (compared with 56 of the 324 seats at the previous election). A coalition Government was formed, including members of the DP, Chart Thai, the SAP, Rassadorn and seven 'independent' ministers not belonging to the House of Representatives. Prem remained as Prime Minister.

In November 1987 a crisis arose concerning proposed legislation on copyright, which would have made illegal the previously uncontrolled counterfeiting of foreign manufactures and intellectual property (such as books and music recordings). In April 1988 dissident members of the DP voted to reject the copyright legislation, and 16 ministers belonging to the DP resigned, on the grounds that they had failed to maintain party unity. As a result, Prem asked the King to dissolve the House of Representatives, and new elections were held in July (two years before the expiry of the legislature's mandate). Internal disputes weakened support for the DP at the elections (25 dissidents had resigned in May), and Chart Thai gained the largest number of seats (87). Gen. Chatichai Choonhavan, the leader of Chart Thai, was appointed Prime Minister in early August, after Prem declined an invitation to remain in the post. A new Cabinet was formed, comprising members of six parties (Chart Thai, the DP, the SAP, Rassadorn, the United Democratic Party and the Muan Chon party).

Chatichai introduced reforms to encourage private enterprise and greater foreign investment, and also assumed an active role in foreign affairs. In an abrupt change of Thai policy, he sought to improve relations with Laos, Cambodia and Viet Nam, often without consulting the Minister of Foreign Affairs, Air Chief Marshal Siddhi Savetsila (leader of the SAP). In March 1989 a crisis within the coalition, caused by tension between Chatichai and Siddhi, was averted by discussions between senior members of Chart Thai and the SAP. In April Ruam Thai, the Community Action Party, the Prachachon Party and the Progressive Party merged to form an opposition grouping called Ekkaparb (Solidarity). Nine members of the Prachachon Party subsequently defected to Chart Thai, giving the ruling coalition control of 229 of the 357 seats in the House of Representatives.

Popular support for Chatichai declined towards the end of 1989. The Government's response to damage caused by a typhoon in November was widely perceived as inadequate and compounded allegations that Chatichai was preoccupied with foreign affairs to the detriment of domestic issues. In early 1990 the Government's public image was further damaged by corruption scandals and labour unrest. In March 1990 Chaovalit resigned as acting Supreme Commander of the Armed Forces; he also resigned as Commander-in-Chief of the Army, in which post he was succeeded by Gen. Suchinda Kraprayoon, hitherto his deputy.

Despite growing criticism of the administration, in July 1990 the House of Representatives overwhelmingly rejected a motion of 'no confidence' in the Government (sponsored by the opposition on the grounds of incompetence and corruption). In August, however, Chatichai reorganized the Cabinet, incorporating Puangchon Chao Thai (the party of the former Commander-in-Chief, Gen. Arthit Kamlang-ek) in the ruling coalition, and reducing the influence of the SAP, following the implication of many of its members in allegations of corruption. The inclusion of the Puangchon Chao Thai expanded the coalition's control to 246 of the 357 seats in the House.

In November 1990, in a further reorganization of the Government, Chatichai demoted the leader of the Muan Chon party, Chalerm Yubamrung, an outspoken critic of the armed forces, from his position as Minister to the Prime Minister's Office. The leadership of the armed forces had demanded Chalerm's dismissal, threatening unspecified intervention if government changes did not take place. In early December Chatichai resigned as Prime Minister; he was reappointed on the next day and subsequently formed a coalition Government comprising Chart Thai, Rassadorn, Puangchon Chao Thai and former opposition parties Prachakorn Thai and Ekkaparb. The DP, the SAP and the Muan Chon party were not included in the coalition, the composition of which provided Chatichai with reduced support (227 of the 357 seats) in the House of Representatives.

On 23 February 1991 Chatichai's Government was ousted in a bloodless military coup. Gen. Sunthorn Kongsompong, the Supreme Commander of the Armed Forces, assumed administrative power as the Chairman of the newly-created National Peace-keeping Council (NPC). The NPC was actually dominated by the effective head of the armed forces in Thailand, Gen. Suchinda Kraprayoon, who was appointed joint Deputy Chairman of the NPC together with the Commanders-in-Chief of the Air Force and Navy and the Director-General of the Police. The coup leaders cited government corruption and abuse of power to justify their action, and investigations were subsequently ordered into the activities of a number of prominent politicians. However, the coup was also widely believed to have been organized in response to the recent erosion of military influence under Chatichai.

Under the NPC, the Constitution was abrogated, the House of Representatives, the Senate and the Council of Ministers were dissolved, and martial law was imposed. The NPC won unprecedented royal approval, and in early March 1991 an interim Constitution, approved by the King, was published. Anand Panyarachun, a business executive and former diplomat, was appointed acting Prime Minister pending fresh elections. Anand appointed a predominantly civilian 35-member interim Cabinet, comprised mainly of respected technocrats and former ministers, and including only eight members of the armed forces. Chatichai and Arthit, who had been arrested at the time of the coup, were released after two weeks. The NPC appointed a 292-member National Legislative Assembly, which included 149 serving or former military personnel, as well as many civilians known to have connections with the armed forces.

In May 1991 martial law was repealed in most areas, and political activity was permitted to resume. The New Aspiration Party (NAP—formed in October 1990 by Gen. Chaovalit) gathered support as the traditional parties were in disarray, largely owing to investigations of corruption by the newly-created Assets Examination Committee. In June 1991 a new party, Samakkhi Tham, was created to compete with the NAP. It was sponsored by the Commander-in-Chief of the Air Force, Air Chief Marshal Kaset Rojananin, and led by Narong Wongwan, a former leader of Ekkaparb. In August Suchinda assumed, in addition to the post of Commander-in-Chief of the Army, the role of Supreme Commander of the Armed Forces, replacing Sunthorn, who remained Chairman of the NPC.

In November 1991 the Constitution Scrutiny Committee, which had been effectively nominated by the NPC, presented a draft Constitution to the National Legislative Assembly. Following public criticism of the draft (including a demonstration by 50,000 protesters in Bangkok), the document was amended to reduce the number of nominated senators from 360 (equal to the number of elected members of the House of Representatives) to 270, and to abolish provisions that allowed the Senate the right to participate in the selection of the Prime Minister. Opposition parties, including the NAP and Palang Dharma (led by the popular and influential Governor of Bangkok, Maj.-Gen. Chamlong Srimuang), continued to oppose the draft, claiming that it perpetuated the power of the NPC. Despite public criticism, the National Legislative Assembly approved the new Constitution in early December, but campaigners continued to express concern over certain provisional clauses (which were to remain in effect for four years), under which the NPC was to appoint the Prime Minister and the Senate, and regarding the Senate's right to vote jointly with the elected House on motions of 'no confidence', thus enabling the Senate to dismiss a government with the support of only 46 elected representatives.

The general election took place on 22 March 1992, when 2,185 candidates, representing 15 parties, contested the 360 seats; 59.2% of the electorate voted. Despite the establishment by Anand of an independent organization, Poll Watch, to monitor the elections, the practice of 'vote-buying' persisted in the poorer northern and north-eastern regions. Samakkhi Tham and Chart Thai secured the largest number of seats, 79 and 74 respectively. The NAP gained 72 seats and Palang Dharma won 41 seats, 32 of which were in Bangkok. On the day of the election the NPC appointed the 270 members of the Senate, 154 of whom were officers of the armed forces or police.

In late March 1992 it was announced that Narong Wongwan would lead a coalition government comprising his own party (Samakkhi Tham), Chart Thai, Prachakorn Thai, the SAP and Rassadorn, which together controlled 195 seats in the House of Representatives. US allegations of Narong's involvement in illicit drugs-trafficking, however, caused the nomination to be rescinded. In early April 1992 Suchinda was named as Prime Minister, despite his assurances before the election that he would not accept the post. He was replaced as Supreme Commander of the Armed Forces by Kaset and as Commander-in-Chief of the Army by his brother-in-law, Gen. Issarapong Noonpakdi, hitherto his deputy. Suchinda's accession to the premiership prompted an immediate popular protest by more than 50,000 demonstrators against the appointment of an unelected Prime Minister. Later in April Suchinda appointed eight other unelected members to a new Cabinet, retaining several technocrats from Anand's interim Government. The 49-member Council of Ministers also included three ministers who had been found guilty of 'possessing unusual wealth' by the Assets Examination Committee. Thus Suchinda's standing was damaged both by his failure to honour his pledge not to become Prime Minister and by the inclusion in the Government of the very politicians that the armed forces had overthrown on the grounds of corruption.

In early May 1992 Chamlong announced, at a rally attended by 100,000 demonstrators, that he would fast until death unless Suchinda resigned. The demonstrations continued uninterrupted for one week until the government parties agreed to amend the Constitution to prevent an unelected Prime Minister (including the incumbent Suchinda, who would have to resign) from taking office, and to limit the power of the unelected Senate. Chamlong abandoned his 'hunger strike' and temporarily suspended the demonstration. However, violent anti-Government demonstrations erupted in Bangkok when it appeared that the Government might renege on its commitments. The Government declared a state of emergency in Bangkok and neighbouring provinces, introducing a curfew and banning any large gatherings. Chamlong was arrested and more than 3,000 people were detained by security forces in a brutal attempt to suppress the riots, which continued for several days.

Following unprecedented intervention by King Bhumibol, Suchinda ordered the release of Chamlong, announced a general amnesty for those involved in the protests and pledged to introduce amendments to the Constitution. On 24 May 1992 Suchinda resigned, after failing to retain the support of the five coalition parties, which agreed to introduce a constitutional amendment preventing Suchinda's continued tenure of office as Prime Minister. On 10 June the National Assembly approved constitutional amendments, whereby the Prime Minister was required to be a member of the House of Representatives, the authority of the Senate was restricted and the President of the House of Representatives was to be the President of the National Assembly. On the same day the King, contrary to expectations, named Anand as Prime Minister. Anand appointed a politically neutral, unelected Cabinet, which included many of the figures from his previous administrations, and dissolved the National Assembly in preparation for a general election.

At the end of June 1992 the four parties that had opposed the military Government (the DP, the NAP, Palang Dharma and Ekkaparb) formed an alliance, the National Democratic Front (NDF), to contest the forthcoming elections. In July, in an effort to disassociate himself from the traditional coalition parties that had supported the Suchinda regime, Chatichai declined the leadership of Chart Thai and formed a new party, Chart Pattana, which quickly gained widespread support.

During June and July 1992 Anand introduced measures to curb the political power of the armed forces, reduce military control of state enterprises, and remove the authority of the armed forces to intervene in situations of social unrest. In early August, as part of a limited reorganization of the armed forces, Kaset and Issarapong were dismissed from their positions at the head of the armed forces and demoted to inactive posts. A more extensive military reshuffle took place in September. The new Commander-in-Chief of the Army, Gen. Wimol Wongwanit, pledged that the army would not interfere in politics during his period of command.

The general election took place on 13 September 1992, when 12 parties contested the 360 seats in the House of Representatives; 62.1% of the electorate voted. Poll Watch reported that 'vote-buying' and violence persisted, especially in the north-eastern region. The DP won the largest number of seats (79), while Chart Thai and Chart Pattana secured 77 and 60 seats respectively. The DP was able to form a coalition, with the NAP, Palang Dharma and Ekkaparb, which commanded 185 of the 360 seats. Despite its participation in the previous administration, the SAP (with 22 seats) was also subsequently invited to join the Government. On 23 September Chuan Leekpai, the leader of the DP, was formally approved as Prime Minister. Chamlong refused to accept a cabinet position, owing to Palang Dharma's disappointing performance in the election, although the party had increased its representation from 41 to 47 seats. Chuan declared his intention to eradicate corrupt practices, to decentralize government, to enhance rural development and to reduce the powers of the Senate.

Although Chuan's integrity as Prime Minister remained unquestioned, widespread dissatisfaction with his style of leadership began to emerge in early 1993. The SAP was openly critical of Chuan's alleged indecisiveness and slow progress in the implementation of national policy. The coalition was also adversely affected by the association of certain members of the Government with companies linked to major share price manipulation in 1992. In June 1993 Chuan's administration was threatened by two motions of 'no confidence' in the Cabinet, introduced by Chart Pattana and Chart Thai. The rejection of the motions by a considerable margin, however, consolidated the Government's position. In early September the SAP announced that it was to merge with four opposition parties, including Chart Pattana, under the leadership of Chatichai, while remaining in the ruling coalition. This appeared to be an attempt to secure the premiership for Chatichai, as the new SAP would command more seats than any other member of the coalition. However, four days after the merger plans were announced, the SAP was expelled from the Government. It was replaced by the Seritham Party, which controlled only eight seats, compared with 21 for the SAP, bringing the coalition's total representation to 193 seats. It was believed that the Seritham Party would constitute a better coalition partner than the SAP as its policies were closer to those of the Government. At the end of September a cabinet reorganization was implemented to replace former SAP ministers.

In August 1993 arsonists, believed to be members of the Muslim separatist grouping, the Pattani United Liberation Organization (PULO), set fire to 34 schools in the south of the country and subsequently ambushed a train. In the same month another separatist faction, the National Revolutionary Front, was reportedly responsible for an attack on a detachment of Thai army engineers in Yala province. Further bomb attacks took place in the south in early 1994.

In October 1993 Chaovalit, the Minister of the Interior and of Labour and Social Welfare in the ruling coalition, dismissed the Chief of Police, Sawat Amornwiwat, citing incompetence, insults to the Queen, and police involvement in the theft of royal Saudi jewels. In November motions of censure were introduced by the opposition in the House of Representatives against both Chaovalit and the Minister of Commerce, Uthai Phimchaichon, for wrongfully dismissing officials in their department. The opposition's attempt to force the resignation of the ministers and endanger the coalition failed, since both politicians received the maximum support from the coalition partners. Chuan subsequently requested Chaovalit, however, to investigate allegations of corruption involving his aides. (In April 1994 Sawat and six other senior police officers were charged with negligence and malfeasance in connection with the Saudi jewel theft.)

In January 1994 Palang Dharma initiated a campaign for decentralization through the introduction of elected provincial governors. Since decentralization was one of the ruling administrations stated policies, together with other democratic reforms of the Constitution, Palang Dharma succeeded in embarrassing its coalition partners. A parliamentary committee subsequently proposed 25 changes to the Constitution, eight of which were agreed by both the Government and the opposition. These amendments included the reduction of the appointed Senate from 270 to 120 members; a broader system for the selection of senators; lowering the voting age from 20 years to 18; and establishing an administrative court and a parliamentary ombudsman. Opposition leaders then campaigned for all 25 amendments to be passed at the proposed joint session of the Senate and the House of Representatives at the end of March. In the event, however, in an attempt to embarrass the Government and force its resignation, the opposition submitted their own amendments based on the pro-military 1978 Constitution, which excluded any reduction of the Senate and advocated a return to an appointed Prime Minister. With the support of the majority of senators (who were mostly appointees of the 1991 coup leaders), the opposition's amendments were approved at the first reading and were thus to be examined by a joint constitutional scrutiny committee, where the combined number of the Senate and opposition representatives exceeded that of the ruling coalition. On the following day the government motion to reduce the membership of the Senate was defeated. In April 1994 a further seven constitutional amendments submitted by the Government to the National Assembly were defeated and could thus not be considered by the constitutional scrutiny committee, which was expected to complete its deliberations towards the end of the year. Chuan announced that if the committee were to propose amendments that he considered undemocratic he would dissolve the National Assembly in preparation for elections.

In April 1994 Chamlong published the conditions of his entry to the Cabinet: the reorganization of the 10 ministerial portfolios held by Palang Dharma; his assumption of sole responsibility for mass transport in Bangkok; and the reorganization of the Bangkok bus service. Chuan insisted that Chamlong accept a cabinet position and then negotiate privately; Chamlong, however, announced that this proposal was unacceptable and abandoned his plans to enter the Cabinet.

In May 1994 Thanong Siripreechapong, a Chart Thai member of the House of Representatives, was indicted in the USA on charges of illicitly transporting about 49 tons of marijuana to the USA from Thailand between 1973 and 1987. This incident, and the suspected involvement of other members of the opposition in the narcotics trade, encouraged support for the ruling coalition.

In July 1994 the opposition sought to bring down the Government with a vote of 'no confidence' in four ministers, including the Minister of Foreign Affairs, Squadron Leader Prasong Soonsiri. The opposition attacked Prasong for allowing the US authorities to refuse a visa to the Deputy Chairman of Chart Thai, Vatana Asvahame, on the grounds of drugs-trafficking (the third such opposition representative about whom the US Government had made such allegations). The motion was defeated, however, when the Government successfully demonstrated that aspects of the charges were accurate.

In September 1994 Chamlong resumed the leadership of Palang Dharma in party elections, and subsequently persuaded the party executive committee to approve the replacement of all 11 of the party's cabinet members. In late October the appointments were confirmed in a cabinet reshuffle that incorporated 11 members of Palang Dharma as five full ministers and six deputy ministers (Chamlong was himself appointed Deputy Prime Minister), and three NAP members as one full minister and two deputy ministers. At Chamlong's instigation, a leading businessman, Thaksin Shinawatra, the Chairman of Thailand's largest telecommunications company, was appointed Minister of Foreign Affairs and a former president of the Bangkok Bank, Vichit Surapongchai, was appointed Minister of Transport and Communications. These appointments provoked strong protests within the divided Palang Dharma, which were led by Prasong, who opposed the selection of non-elected candidates and objected to Chamlong's authoritarian style of leadership.

At the end of November 1994 nine people, including a high-ranking police officer, were charged with the abduction and murder of the wife and son of a Thai jeweller who had been involved in receiving jewels stolen from Saudi Arabia (see above). Three other senior police officers were acquitted. (In September the national Chief of Police, Gen. Pratin Santiprabhob, had resigned, after another senior police officer, charged with involvement in the abduction, had implicated him in the affair.) Increasing frustration at the slow pace of the investigation prompted Saudi Arabia to refuse the issue of new visas to Thai migrant workers and to bar Saudi citizens from visiting Thailand. In late March 1995 the jeweller testified that a senior police officer had kidnapped and blackmailed him; this case exacerbated a growing public unease at malpratice and corruption in the police force.

In early December 1994 the NAP voted with the opposition against a proposed constitutional amendment that would provide for the election of sub-district (tambon) and village-level officials. The amendment, which would have effectively ended the tradition of 'jobs for life' for such officials, was, however, defeated. The decision by the NAP to vote against the amendment was thought to have stemmed from the fact that the NAP gained much of its support from local administrators. Having left the coalition Government, the NAP stated that it would not join the opposition. The defection left the governing coalition in a minority position in the House of Representatives, and not until Chart Pattana agreed to join the Government (in return for certain cabinet portfolios) could the Prime Minister be confident of maintaining a parliamentary majority. With the inclusion of Chart Pattana in the coalition, the Government increased its number of seats in the House of Representatives to 201. Shortly afterwards the King approved the removal of 12 ministers and deputy ministers from the Cabinet, many of whom were replaced with members of Chart Pattana. To pre-empt a vote of 'no confidence' in his office, the Minister of Agriculture had meanwhile resigned, in response to allegations that he had helped to manipulate a land reform programme to the benefit of wealthy landowners.

At the beginning of January 1995 a charter to amend the constitution was passed by the National Assembly in an almost unanimous vote. The amendments included: lowering the eligible voting age from 20 to 18 years (thereby increasing the number of voters by an estimated 2.25m. by 1996, when the next general election was due); ensuring equal rights for women in the law; reducing the number of representatives in the Senate to the equivalent of two-thirds of the membership of the House of Representatives (a reform that effectively restricted the influence of the military in the political process); banning cabinet members and senators from holding government concessions, directly or indirectly, and also requiring that ministers, members of the House of Representatives and Senators declare their financial assets; the establishment of an administrative court to adjudicate in cases against the State; the formation of an electoral commission within two years; and the appointment of five members of the House of Representatives to act as parliamentary ombudsmen. One immediate consequence of the amendments was the resignation of the Minister of Foreign Affairs, Thaksin Shinawatra, at the end of January, pre-empting the findings of a special constitutional tribunal established to adjudicate on his eligibility for the post: as Chairman of a large company, Thaksin had previously been involved in procuring government contracts.

Towards the end of February 1995 increasing dissension within the governing coalition led the opposition to demand a motion of 'no confidence' in the Government. The motion was passed when parliament reconvened in May, with Palang Dharma abstaining. Having failed to keep the coalition intact, Chuan was forced to dissolve the House of Representatives on 20 May and a general election was called for 2 July. In late May Thaksin Shinawatra reduced his personal holding in his company to less than 50%; he subsequently assumed the leadership of Palang Dharma, following the resignation of Chamlong. At the general election 12 parties contested 391 seats in the House of Representatives. Chart Thai won the largest number of seats (93), while the DP and the NAP won 86 and 56 seats, respectively. Chart Pattana secured 53 seats. The new Prime Minister, Banharn Silpa-Archa (the Secretary-General of Chart Thai), formed a six-party coalition government with the NAP, Palang Dharma, the SAP, Prachakorn Thai and Muan Chon.

During the late 1980s Thailand attempted to improve its traditionally poor relations with Laos and Cambodia. A border dispute in 1984 resulted in fighting between Thai and Laotian troops. Although Thai troops were withdrawn from the area in October of that year, subsequent attempts to solve the problem were unsuccessful. In 1987 a new dispute arose concerning another border area (see chapter on Laos). After three months of fighting, a cease-fire was effected in February 1988, and a joint committee to demarcate the entire common border was established in March 1989. Agreement was also reached on the repatriation of Laotian refugees. In March 1991, during a visit to Laos by Suchinda, Thailand and Laos agreed to withdraw their troops from the border area and to replace the border committee with a joint co-ordinating body which would promote bilateral trade and economic co-operation. In April 1994 the Friendship Bridge across the Mekong river between Thailand and Laos was formally opened, and towards the end of that year Thailand pledged to provide more aid to Laos for infrastructural and social development projects.

When he assumed the premiership in August 1988, Chatichai instigated an abrupt change in foreign policy towards Viet Nam and Cambodia. In November the Minister of Foreign Affairs, Siddhi, visited Viet Nam (the first such visit for 13 years). In January 1989 the Vietnamese-backed Prime Minister of the then Kampuchea, Hun Sen, visited Thailand. This represented a move away from the policy of the Association of South East Asian Nations (ASEAN, see p. 109), which had traditionally supported the coalition Government-in-exile of Democratic Kampuchea (see chapter on Cambodia). Two further visits by Hun Sen to Bangkok took place in 1989, as Thailand attempted, unsuccessfully, to negotiate a cease-fire between the four Cambodian factions, prior to the Vietnamese withdrawal in September (see chapter on Viet Nam). In November 1991 Thailand, the Supreme National Council of Cambodia and the office of the UN High Commissioner for Refugees signed an agreement on the repatriation of the 313,576 Cambodian refugees in Thailand; the programme was virtually completed by the end of March 1993.

In January 1993, despite its previous reluctance to do so, Thailand officially closed its border to trade with areas controlled by the communist Cambodian insurgent group, the Khmers Rouges, in compliance with UN sanctions against the movement. Nevertheless, violations of the embargo (mainly

# THAILAND

exports of logs and gems from Cambodia through Thailand) were widely reported during 1993. Accusations by representatives of the Cambodian Government that Thai complicity with the Khmers Rouges was undermining Cambodian attempts to end the insurgency were substantiated by reports from UN peace-keeping troops of members of the Thai armed forces providing transportation, medical care and other support for the Khmers Rouges. Official Thai government policy was to support the elected Government of Cambodia, but the armed forces controlled the border and were unwilling to jeopardize their lucrative business relations with the Khmers Rouges. In December 1993 a cache of 1,500 tons of Chinese-manufactured weapons, which were apparently being used to supply the Khmers Rouges, were discovered near Thailand's border with Cambodia. The armed forces declared that the arms had been under their control since the signing of the peace accords in October 1991, although it was reported that Cambodians were guarding the cache.

In January 1994 Chuan made an official visit to Cambodia (the first visit by a Thai premier) to improve bilateral relations, which had been adversely affected by the continuing allegations. During his visit, however, reports were published of Thai army trucks transporting the Khmers Rouges to the Cambodian border prior to an attack on villages in north-western Cambodia. In March, following the Cambodian Government's seizure of the Khmers Rouges headquarters at Pailin (which was recaptured in April), 25,000 Khmer Rouge supporters fled across the Thai border. The Thai armed forces immediately repatriated the refugees to territory under Khmers Rouges control, failing to comply with requests for access by international relief agencies and proposals by the Cambodian Government for returning them to areas under its control. Relief agencies suspected that the repatriation had been agreed between the Thai armed forces and the Khmers Rouges. In April Thailand responded to the Cambodian Government's declared intention to attack Khmers Rouges tanks on Thai territory by threatening military reprisals for incursions into Thai territory. Relations with Cambodia were further affected when 14 Thai workers were arrested in July on suspicion of complicity in an abortive coup in the Cambodian capital, Phnom-Penh. Although five of them were released shortly afterwards, the nine others were tried and sentenced to between three and five years each. The Cambodian leader of the failed coup was subsequently discovered in Bangkok, where the authorities arrested him. He was released in early 1995 and allowed by the Thai authorities to seek a third country of asylum, despite attempts by the Cambodian Government to have him extradited.

Following a military coup in Burma (now Myanmar) in September 1988, thousands of Burmese students fled to Thailand to avoid government reprisals. The human rights group, Amnesty International, subsequently accused the Thai Government of coercing the students to return (resulting in their arrest and, in some cases, execution). In 1990 Myanma soldiers achieved unprecedented success in attacks on the strongholds of ethnic minorities on the Thai–Myanma border, since they were able to launch offensives from inside Thailand. The attacks resulted in a new influx of Myanma students and members of rebel ethnic groups seeking refuge in Thailand. The Thai Government refused to recognize those fleeing from Myanmar as refugees or to offer them aid. The Thai Government was anxious not to jeopardize the preferential treatment that it received from the Myanma Government, which had recently granted many licences to Thai businesses for the exploitation of Myanmar's natural resources.

In 1992 Myanma forces intensified their attacks on rebel bases near the Thai border. In March the Myanma Government warned Thai armed forces to withdraw from nearby border areas, but later in the month Thai troops clashed with Myanma forces which had entered Thailand to attack a nearby rebel base. In early December King Bhumibol appealed for a peaceful agreement to end the tension caused by the continued occupation by Myanma forces of Hill 491 in Chumphan province. In accordance with a bilateral agreement signed shortly afterwards in Yangon, Myanmar, Myanma troops were withdrawn from the hill by late December. In February 1993 the two countries resolved to demarcate their common border. In April 1994 Thailand invited Myanmar to attend the annual ASEAN meeting of ministers responsible for foreign affairs in Bangkok, as a guest of the host country. In early 1995, however, relations with Myanmar were strained by the persistent

*Introductory Survey*

border incursions into Thailand by forces of the Myanma Government during their offensive to capture the headquarters of the Karen rebels at Manerplaw and, subsequently, at Kawmoora. Despite these incursions, the Thai Government sought to maintain good relations with Myanmar and continued with plans to construct a gas pipeline from the Gulf of Martaban, in the Andaman Sea, to Thailand.

During 1991, despite an unresolved fishing dispute, there was further improvement in relations between Thailand and Viet Nam. In October the Vietnamese premier, Vo Van Kiet, became the first senior Vietnamese official to visit Bangkok for 13 years. In January 1992 Anand attended a summit meeting in Hanoi, the Vietnamese capital. In February 1993 Viet Nam, Thailand, Laos and Cambodia signed a joint communique in Viet Nam, delineating the framework for resuming co-operation in the development of the Mekong river. Further discussions took place in Thailand in April. In April 1995 the four countries signed a co-operation agreement in Thailand governing the future sustainable development of the Mekong river basin. In March 1994 Chuan visited Viet Nam and announced his support for Viet Nam's application for membership of ASEAN. Thailand had, in the mean time, become a member of the Non-aligned Movement (see p. 249) in October 1993.

## Government

On 9 December 1991 a new Constitution was promulgated, which provided for a National Assembly (comprising an elected House of Representatives and an appointed Senate) and a Cabinet headed by a Prime Minister. On 10 June 1992 the National Assembly approved a constitutional amendment requiring the Prime Minister to be a member of the House of Representatives. On 4 January 1995 the National Assembly approved a constitutional charter, which provided for a number of amendments; these included lowering the voting age from 20 to 18 years and reducing the membership of the Senate to two-thirds of that of the House of Representatives.

## Defence

In June 1994 the Thai armed forces had an estimated total strength of 256,000: 150,000 in the army, 63,000 in the navy and 43,000 in the air force. Military service is compulsory for two years between the ages of 21 and 30. Paramilitary forces, including a volunteer irregular force, numbered an estimated 161,500 in mid-1994. In the 1994/95 budget, defence expenditure was an estimated 85,600m. baht.

## Economic Affairs

In 1993, according to estimates from the World Bank, Thailand's gross national product (GNP), measured at average 1991–93 prices, was US $120,235m., equivalent to $2,040 per head. During 1985–93, it was estimated, GNP per head increased, in real terms, at an average annual rate of 8.4%. During the same period the population increased by an annual average of 1.6%. Thailand's gross domestic product (GDP) increased, in real terms, by an annual average of 8.2% in 1980–92. In 1994 GDP grew by an estimated 8.5%.

Agriculture (including forestry, hunting and fishing) contributed an estimated 10% of GDP in 1993; 56.7% of the employed labour force were engaged in the sector in that year. Thailand's staple crop and principal agricultural export commodity is rice (which accounted for 4.2% of total export revenue in 1991). Other major crops include cassava (tapioca), rubber, sugar cane, maize and kenaf (a jute-like fibre). Timber was formerly a major source of export revenue, but a ban on uncontrolled logging was imposed in January 1989, following severe flooding as a result of deforestation; a reafforestation programme, initiated in the late 1980s, recommenced during 1993. Fisheries products (especially prawns, which constituted the sixth largest export commodity in 1990) and livestock (mainly buffaloes, cattle, pigs and poultry) are also important. During 1980–92 agricultural GDP increased by an annual average of 4.1%.

Industry (including mining, manufacturing, construction and power) provided an estimated 39.2% of GDP in 1993; 17.5% of the employed labour force were engaged in industrial activities in that year. During 1980–92 industrial GDP increased at an annual average rate of 10.1%.

Mining and quarrying contributed an estimated 1.5% of GDP in 1993: the sector engaged only 0.2% of the employed labour force in that year. Gemstones, notably diamonds, are the principal mineral export, accounting for 3.3% of total export revenue in 1991. Natural gas and, to a lesser extent, petroleum are also exploited. Tin, lignite, gypsum, tungsten, lead, antimony, manganese, copper, gold and zinc are also mined. A large deposit of potash was due for exploitation in the late 1990s and was expected to yield up to 2m. metric tons a year, making it the world's second largest potash mine.

Manufacturing provided an estimated 28.5% of GDP in 1993; 12.3% of the employed labour force were engaged in manufacturing activities in that year. Textiles and garments and electronics and electrical goods (particularly semiconductors) constitute Thailand's principal branches of manufacturing, accounting for 16.0% and 16.5%, respectively, of total export revenue in 1991. Other manufacturing industries include cement production, sugar and petroleum refining, and motor vehicle production. During 1980–92 manufacturing GDP increased by an annual average of 10.1%. In 1993 the manufacturing sector's share of export earnings was an estimated 80%.

Energy is derived principally from hydrocarbons. In 1991 there were estimated proven gas reserves of some 200,000 cu m. Lignite and hydroelectric power are also exploited. Solar and wind energy account for about 1% of electric power. Thailand remains, however, heavily dependent on imported petroleum. In early 1995 Thailand signed an agreement with Myanmar to import natural gas via a 400-km pipeline from the Gulf of Martaban. In 1994 demand for electricity in Thailand was an estimated 10,500 MW. In 1992 imports of mineral fuels and lubricants comprised 8.3% of the value of merchandise imports.

Services (including transport and communications, commerce, banking and finance, and hotels and catering) contributed an estimated 50.8% of GDP in 1993; 25.7% of the employed labour force were engaged in the services sector in that year. In 1993 tourism was the principal source of foreign exchange; an estimated 5.8m. tourists visited Thailand, and receipts from tourism totalled 127,802m. baht. During 1980–92 the GDP of the services sector expanded by an annual average of 8.1%.

In 1993 Thailand recorded a visible trade deficit of US $4,146m., and there was a deficit of $6,926m. on the current account of the balance of payments. In 1993 the principal source of imports (30.2%) was Japan; other major suppliers in that year were the USA, Singapore, Germany and Taiwan. The principal market for exports in 1993 was the USA (21.5%); other important purchasers were Japan and Singapore. The principal imports in 1991 were petroleum and petroleum products, non-electrical machinery, electrical machinery, chemicals, iron and steel. The principal exports were textiles and garments, electronic goods, rice, rubber, gemstones, cassava (tapioca) and sugar.

In the financial year ending September 1994 there was an estimated budgetary deficit of 25,000m. baht. Thailand's external debt totalled US $45,819m. at the end of 1993, of which $14,562m. was long-term public debt. In that year the cost of debt-servicing was equivalent to 18.6% of the value of exports of goods and services. The annual rate of inflation averaged 4.1% in 1985–93, and an estimated 5.1% in 1994. About 3.2% of the labour force were unemployed in 1993.

Thailand is a member of the Asian Development Bank (ADB, see p. 107), the Association of South East Asian Nations (ASEAN, see p. 109) and the Colombo Plan (see p. 238). In January 1993 the establishment of the ASEAN Free Trade Area, which was to be implemented over 15 years, commenced.

Thailand's rapid economic growth since the late 1980s has generated certain problems: inadequate infrastructural development (including a transport crisis in Bangkok); a shortage of highly-trained technical personnel; a widening deficit on the current account of the balance of payments; and an inequality of income distribution, owing to excessive centralization. In 1993 the economy recovered from the adverse effects of the political turmoil in 1991 and 1992, which had resulted in a decline in tourism and foreign investment and had delayed public investment and infrastructural projects. Inflation, which had remained low, despite the rapid rate of economic growth, began to rise in December 1993, following a large influx of foreign capital, which caused a reduction in interest rates, stimulating activity on the stock market. In late 1994 the Thai economy continued to display rapid growth, with exports of higher value-added manufactures increasingly substituting for the traditional exports. Towards the end of the year inflation began to rise again, prompting the Government to tighten monetary controls that had been introduced in 1993. The income disparity between rural and urban Thailand continued to increase during the year, however, and appeared likely to remain a serious problem in spite of government attempts to divert industry away from Bangkok into other provinces. Incentives were offered to industrial companies to relocate, in an attempt also to stem the mass movement of migrants to the cities in search of work, which, in Bangkok in particular, had already seriously burdened urban infrastructure and services.

### Social Welfare

Among the social services that are undertaken by the Department of Public Welfare are child welfare, family assistance, welfare for the aged, the disabled, the destitute and socially handicapped women, disaster relief, welfare and development programmes for the hill tribes and self-help land settlements. In 1982 Thailand had 408 hospitals and several thousand clinics. In 1984 there were 8,058 physicans and 54,012 nurses. The inability of Thailand's state hospitals to meet increasing demand led, in the 1980s and early 1990s, to the rapid growth of private hospital care. Estimated budgetary expenditure by the central Government in the financial year ending 30 September 1994 included 42,266m. baht (6.8% of total spending) for health and 22,330m. baht (3.6%) for social security and welfare.

### Education

Education is officially compulsory for six years, to be undertaken between seven and 15 years of age. In 1995 the Government announced that it would extend the period of compulsory education to nine years, beginning in 1996. Primary education begins at six years of age and lasts for six years. In 1992 total enrolment in primary education was equivalent to 97% of children in the relevant age-group. Secondary education, beginning at 12 years of age, also lasts for six years, divided into two equal cycles. In 1990 total secondary enrolment was equivalent to 33% of children in the relevant age-group (males 34%; females 32%). In the same year the total enrolment at primary and secondary schools was equivalent to 62% of all school-age children (males 63%; females 60%). There were 20 state universities (12 of which were in Bangkok) and 26 private universities and colleges in 1995. According to UNESCO estimates, the average rate of adult illiteracy in 1990 was 6.7% (males 4.4%; females 8.8%). Budgetary expenditure on education by the central Government was estimated at 122,553m. baht (19.6% of total spending) in the financial year 1993/94.

### Public Holidays

**1995:** 3 January (for New Year's Day), 14 February (Makhabuja*), 6 April (Chakri Day), 12–14 April (Songkran Festival), 1 May (Labour Day), 5 May (Coronation Day), 15 May (Visakhabuja*), May/June (Ploughing Ceremony), July (Asalhabuja*), 12 July (beginning of Buddhist Lent*), 14 August (for the Queen's Birthday), 23 October (Chulalongkorn Day), 5 December (King's Birthday), 11 December (for Constitution Day), 31 December (New Year's Eve).

**1996:** 1 January (New Year's Day), February (Makhabuja*), 6 April (Chakri Day), 13 April (Songkran Festival), 1 May (Labour Day), 5 May (Coronation Day), May/June (Visakhabuja*), May/June (Ploughing Ceremony), July (Asalhabuja*), July (beginning of Buddhist Lent*), 12 August (Queen's Birthday), 23 October (Chulalongkorn Day), 5 December (King's Birthday), 10 December (Constitution Day), 31 December (New Year's Eve).

* Regulated by the Buddhist lunar calendar.

### Weights and Measures

The metric system is in force, but a number of traditional measures are also used.

# Statistical Survey

Source (unless otherwise stated): National Statistical Office, Thanon Larn Luang, Bangkok 10100; tel. (2) 281-8606; fax (2) 281-3815.

## Area and Population

### AREA, POPULATION AND DENSITY

| | |
|---|---:|
| Area (sq km) | 513,115* |
| Population (census results)† | |
| 1 April 1980 | 44,824,540 |
| 1 April 1990 | |
| Males | 27,061,733 |
| Females | 27,486,797 |
| Total | 54,548,530 |
| Population (official estimates at 31 December) | |
| 1993 | 58,336,072 |
| 1994 | 59,095,419 |
| Density (per sq km) at 31 December 1994 | 115.2 |

* 198,115 sq miles.
† Excluding adjustment for underenumeration.

### PRINCIPAL TOWNS (population at 1990 census*)

| | |
|---|---:|
| Bangkok Metropolis†  | 5,876,000 |
| Nakhon Ratchasima | 278,000 |
| Songkhla | 243,000 |
| Nanthaburi | 233,000 |
| Khon-kaen | 206,000 |
| Chiang Mai | 167,000 |
| Nakhon Sauran | 152,000 |
| Ubon Ratchathani | 137,000 |
| Nakhon Si Thammarat | 112,000 |
| Saraburi | 107,000 |

* Preliminary figures.
† Formerly Bangkok and Thonburi.

Source: UN, *Demographic Yearbook*.

### BIRTHS, MARRIAGES AND DEATHS*

| | Registered live births | Rate (per 1,000) | Registered marriages | Rate (per 1,000) | Registered deaths | Rate (per 1,000) |
|---|---:|---:|---:|---:|---:|---:|
| 1985 | 973,624 | 18.8 | 343,134 | 6.7 | 225,088 | 4.4 |
| 1986 | 945,827 | 18.0 | 333,974 | 6.4 | 218,025 | 4.1 |
| 1987 | 884,043 | 16.5 | 373,637 | 7.0 | 232,968 | 4.3 |
| 1988 | 873,842 | 16.0 | 391,124 | 7.2 | 231,227 | 4.2 |
| 1989 | 905,837 | 16.3 | 406,134 | 7.4 | 246,570 | 4.4 |
| 1990 | 956,237 | 17.0 | 461,280 | 8.2 | 252,512 | 4.5 |
| 1991 | 960,556 | 17.0 | 449,913 | 7.9 | 264,350 | 4.7 |
| 1992 | 964,557 | 16.8 | 482,452 | 8.3 | 275,313 | 4.8 |

* Registration is incomplete. According to UN estimates, the average annual rates in 1980–85 were: Births 27.8 per 1,000; Deaths 8.0 per 1,000, and in 1985–90: Births 22.3 per 1,000; Deaths 7.0 per 1,000.

**1993:** 484,569 registered marriages (8.3 per 1,000).

Source: Ministry of Public Health, Ministry of the Interior, Thailand.

**Expectation of life** (official estimates, years at birth, 1985–86): Males 63.82; Females 68.85 (Source: UN, *Demographic Yearbook*).

### ECONOMICALLY ACTIVE POPULATION
('000 persons aged 13 years and over, August 1993)

| | |
|---|---:|
| Agriculture, forestry, hunting and fishing | 18,244.6 |
| Mining and quarrying | 57.3 |
| Manufacturing | 3,961.1 |
| Construction, repair and demolition | 1,474.9 |
| Electricity, gas, water and sanitary services | 144.8 |
| Commerce | 3,704.1 |
| Transport, storage and communications | 879.3 |
| Services | 3,667.9 |
| Activities not adequately described | 17.8 |
| **Total in employment** | **32,152.6** |

## Agriculture

### PRINCIPAL CROPS ('000 metric tons)

| | 1991 | 1992 | 1993 |
|---|---:|---:|---:|
| Rice (paddy) | 19,810 | 20,180 | 19,090 |
| Maize | 3,793 | 3,672 | 2,850* |
| Sorghum | 250 | 264* | 256 |
| Sweet potatoes† | 100 | 100 | 100 |
| Cassava (Manioc, Tapioca) | 20,356 | 19,767 | 19,610 |
| Dry beans | 305 | 250 | 310 |
| Soybeans | 436 | 435 | 480* |
| Groundnuts (in shell) | 157 | 146 | 159 |
| Cottonseed | 72 | 79 | 58 |
| Cotton (lint) | 43 | 30* | 25* |
| Coconuts | 1,379 | 1,379* | 1,379† |
| Copra† | 63 | 62 | 58 |
| Watermelons† | 390 | 392 | 395 |
| Sugar cane | 47,480 | 34,860 | 34,710* |
| Bananas† | 1,620 | 1,630 | 1,650 |
| Kenaf (Mesta) | 159 | 144 | 165 |
| Natural rubber | 1,152 | 1,531 | 1,500 |
| Pineapples | 1,931 | 2,438 | 2,674 |
| Onions (dry) | 207 | 210† | 220† |
| Tobacco (leaves)* | 70 | 96 | 95 |
| Castor beans | 28 | 30* | 32† |

* Unofficial figure(s).   † FAO estimate(s).

Source: FAO, *Production Yearbook*.

### LIVESTOCK ('000 head, year ending September)

| | 1991 | 1992 | 1993 |
|---|---:|---:|---:|
| Horses | 20 | 19 | 20 |
| Cattle | 5,631 | 5,815 | 7,190 |
| Buffaloes | 4,977 | 4,862 | 4,747 |
| Pigs | 4,859 | 4,655 | 4,800* |
| Sheep | 166 | 176 | 136 |
| Goats | 136 | 160 | 151 |

Chickens (million): 131 in 1991; 135 in 1992; 133 in 1993.
Ducks (million): 19 in 1991; 20 in 1992; 16* in 1993.

† Unofficial figure.

Source: FAO, *Production Yearbook*.

### LIVESTOCK PRODUCTS ('000 metric tons)

| | 1991 | 1992 | 1993 |
|---|---:|---:|---:|
| Beef and veal* | 210 | 191 | 240 |
| Buffalo meat* | 61 | 61 | 58 |
| Pig meat* | 340 | 342 | 351 |
| Poultry meat | 717 | 768 | 737 |
| Cows' milk | 142 | 177† | 145* |
| Buffalo milk* | 6 | 6 | 6 |
| Hen eggs* | 473.5 | 448.5 | 450.0 |
| Other poultry eggs* | 161.3 | 121.0 | 110.5 |
| Cattle and buffalo hides* | 49.2 | 53.2 | 54.9 |

* FAO estimate(s).
† Unofficial estimate.

Source: FAO, *Production Yearbook*.

# THAILAND

## Forestry

**ROUNDWOOD REMOVALS** ('000 cubic metres, excl. bark)

|  | 1990 | 1991 | 1992 |
|---|---|---|---|
| Sawlogs, veneer logs and logs for sleepers | 492 | 232 | 110 |
| Other industrial wood* | 2,558 | 2,592 | 2,626 |
| Fuel wood* | 33,948 | 34,393 | 34,855 |
| **Total** | 36,998 | 37,217 | 37,591 |

* FAO estimates.

Source: FAO, *Yearbook of Forest Products*.

**SAWNWOOD PRODUCTION**
('000 cubic metres, incl. railway sleepers)

|  | 1990 | 1991 | 1992 |
|---|---|---|---|
| **Total** | 1,170 | 939 | 1,077 |

Source: FAO, *Yearbook of Forest Products*.

## Fishing

('000 metric tons, live weight)

|  | 1990 | 1991 | 1992 |
|---|---|---|---|
| Inland waters | 231.0 | 258.7 | 233.0 |
| Indian Ocean | 448.8 | 678.7 | 722.6 |
| Pacific Ocean | 2,106.6 | 2,030.3 | 1,899.4 |
| **Total catch** | 2,786.4 | 2,967.7 | 2,855.0 |

Source: FAO, *Yearbook of Fishery Statistics*.

## Mining

(production in metric tons)

|  | 1991 | 1992 | 1993 |
|---|---|---|---|
| Tin concentrates* | 14,939 | 11,485 | 6,363 |
| Tungsten concentrates* | 441 | 178 | 203 |
| Lead concentrates* | 39,245 | 27,946 | 14,233 |
| Zinc ore* | 496,006 | 407,180 | 445,761 |
| Antimony ore* | 141 | 633 | 1,464 |
| Manganese ore* | 11,032 | n.a. | n.a. |
| Iron ore* | 240,075 | 427,242 | 208,939 |
| Gypsum | 7,169,390 | 7,111,109 | 7,454,806 |
| Lignite | 14,688,440 | 15,618,230 | 15,592,759 |
| Fluorite | 62,067 | 56,460 | 48,387 |
| Barytes | 113,534 | n.a. | n.a. |

* Figures refer to the gross weight of ores and concentrates. In 1991 the estimated metal content (in metric tons) was: Tin 10,900; Tungsten 300; Lead 15,700; Zinc 86,900; Manganese 5,000; Iron 139,000.

Source: Department of Mineral Resources.

## Industry

**SELECTED PRODUCTS**
('000 metric tons, unless otherwise indicated)

|  | 1989 | 1990 | 1991 |
|---|---|---|---|
| Raw sugar | 2,566 | 1,869 | 2,192 |
| Beer ('000 hectolitres) | 1,801 | 2,635 | 2,840 |
| Cigarettes (million) | 37,365 | 38,316 | 39,359 |
| Cotton yarn: pure | 124.1 | 133.1 | 123.7 |
| Non-cellulosic continuous filaments* | 62.7 | 69.9 | 87.7 |
| Tyres for road motor vehicles ('000) | 4,320 | 4,183 | 4,518 |
| Sulphuric acid | 64 | 72 | 82 |
| Hydrochloric acid | 112.6 | 122.1 | 174.8 |
| Caustic soda—100% | 144 | 158 | 194 |
| Liquefied petroleum gas | 481 | 741 | 1,000 |
| Naphtha | 180 | 190 | 195 |
| Motor spirit—petrol | 1,998 | 2,248 | 2,295 |
| Kerosene | 105 | 164 | 85 |
| Jet fuel | 1,336 | 2,120 | 1,503 |
| Fuel oils | 6,977 | 6,444 | 7,625 |
| Petroleum bitumen—asphalt | 178 | 198 | 210 |
| Cement | 15,042 | 18,040 | 19,210 |
| Crude steel† | 689 | 685 | n.a. |
| Tin—unwrought: primary (metric tons) | 14,571 | 15,512 | 11,255 |
| Passenger motor cars—assembly ('000) | 72 | 82 | 110 |
| Commercial motor vehicles—assembly ('000) | 155.1 | 236.2 | 202.0 |
| Electric energy (million kWh) | 39,106 | 46,175 | 52,486 |

* Data from the Fiber Economics Bureau, Inc (New York).
† Data from the US Bureau of Mines.

Source: UN, *Industrial Statistics Yearbook*.

**1992:** Raw sugar ('000 metric tons) 4,857; Beer ('000 hectolitres) 3,252; Cigarettes (million) 40,691; Tyres for road motor vehicles ('000) 88.0; Cement ('000 metric tons) 21,711; Crude steel ('000 metric tonnes) 975; Passenger motor cars—assembly ('000) 100.3; Commercial motor vehicles—assembly ('000) 223.7.

**1993:** Raw sugar ('000 metric tons) 3,650; Beer ('000 hectolitres) 4,153; Cigarettes (million) 42,043; Tyres for road motor vehicles ('000) 93.3; Cement ('000 metric tons) 21,711; Crude steel ('000 metric tons) 1,135; Passenger motor cars—assembly ('000) 144.0; Commercial motor vehicles—assembly ('000) 275.9.

Source: Bank of Thailand.

## Finance

**CURRENCY AND EXCHANGE RATES**

**Monetary Units**
100 satangs = 1 baht.

**Sterling and Dollar Equivalents** (31 December 1994)
£1 sterling = 39.25 baht;
US $1 = 25.09 baht;
1,000 baht = £25.48 = $39.86.

**Average Exchange Rate** (baht per US $)
1992   25.400
1993   25.319
1994   25.150

# THAILAND

## BUDGET (estimates, million baht, year ending 30 September)

| Revenue | 1991/92 | 1992/93 | 1993/94 |
|---|---|---|---|
| Taxation (net) | 416,308 | 468,796 | 524,458 |
| Direct taxes | 106,900 | 162,500 | 181,100 |
| Personal income taxes | 46,900 | 61,400 | 59,400 |
| Indirect taxes | 309,408 | 343,606 | 398,868 |
| Export-import duties | 103,020 | 92,550 | 109,800 |
| General sales taxes | 109,600 | 131,500 | 153,580 |
| Specific sales taxes | 90,738 | 113,771 | 128,896 |
| Licensing fees | 6,050 | 5,785 | 6,592 |
| Tax rebates of the Revenue Department | n.a. | −27,280 | −49,750 |
| Sales of assets and services | 13,817 | 18,763 | 18,113 |
| Income from state enterprises | 20,941 | 35,500 | 42,100 |
| Miscellaneous income | 9,334 | 11,341 | 15,329 |
| **Total** | 460,000 | 546,110 | 600,000 |

| Expenditure | 1991/92 | 1992/93 | 1993/94 |
|---|---|---|---|
| General public services | 20,887 | 26,128 | 28,414 |
| Defence | 70,572 | 80,330 | 86,695 |
| Public order and safety | 24,358 | 30,617 | 35,522 |
| Education | 85,473 | 108,070 | 122,553 |
| Health | 25,951 | 34,964 | 42,266 |
| Social security and welfare | 14,413 | 18,954 | 22,330 |
| Housing and community amenities | 11,978 | 22,302 | 30,135 |
| Fuel and energy | 1,402 | 1,407 | 1,987 |
| Agriculture, forestry, fishing and hunting | 48,389 | 57,343 | 70,150 |
| Transportation and communication | 43,260 | 61,482 | 69,557 |
| Other purposes | 113,718 | 118,403 | 115,392 |
| **Total** | 460,400 | 560,000 | 625,000 |

Source: Bureau of the Budget.

## INTERNATIONAL RESERVES (US $ million at 31 December)

| | 1992 | 1993 | 1994 |
|---|---|---|---|
| Gold* | 823 | 967 | 947 |
| IMF special drawing rights | 12 | 22 | 32 |
| Reserve position in IMF | 335 | 373 | 416 |
| Foreign exchange | 20,012 | 24,078 | 28,884 |
| **Total** | 21,182 | 25,440 | 30,279 |

* Revalued annually on the basis of the London market price.

Source: IMF, *International Financial Statistics*.

## MONEY SUPPLY (million baht at 31 December)

| | 1992 | 1993 | 1994 |
|---|---|---|---|
| Currency outside banks | 180,200 | 208,600 | 242,000 |
| Demand deposits held by public | 66,100 | 82,400 | 96,500 |
| **Total money** (incl. others) | 249,700 | 296,200 | 346,400 |

Source: IMF, *International Financial Statistics*.

## COST OF LIVING (Consumer Price Index. Base: 1986 = 100)

| | 1992 | 1993 | 1994 |
|---|---|---|---|
| Food | 140.5 | 143.5 | 155.6 |
| Housing | 119.8 | 122.6 | 129.2 |
| Clothing | 131.9 | 139.7 | 149.5 |
| **All items** (incl. others) | 130.8 | 135.1 | 143.8 |

Source: Department of Business Economics.

## NATIONAL ACCOUNTS (million baht at current prices)

### National Income and Product

| | 1991 | 1992 | 1993* |
|---|---|---|---|
| Compensation of employees | 628,463 | 745,342 | 855,327 |
| Operating surplus | 1,297,372 | 1,414,695 | 1,526,680 |
| **Domestic factor incomes** | 1,925,835 | 2,160,037 | 2,382,007 |
| Consumption of fixed capital | 234,394 | 284,951 | 340,910 |
| **Gross domestic product (GDP) at factor cost** | 2,160,229 | 2,444,988 | 2,722,917 |
| Indirect taxes, *less* subsidies | 359,389 | 388,289 | 438,457 |
| **GDP in purchasers' values** | 2,519,618 | 2,833,277 | 3,161,374 |
| Net factor income from abroad | −37,100 | −51,229 | −58,685 |
| **Gross national product** | 2,482,518 | 2,782,048 | 3,102,689 |
| *Less* Consumption of fixed capital | 234,394 | 284,951 | 340,910 |
| **National income in market prices** | 2,248,124 | 2,497,097 | 2,761,779 |

* Provisional.

### Expenditure on the Gross Domestic Product

| | 1991 | 1992 | 1993* |
|---|---|---|---|
| Government final consumption expenditure | 233,322 | 282,739 | 325,525 |
| Private final consumption expenditure | 1,383,669 | 1,540,283 | 1,714,681 |
| Increase in stocks | 20,696 | 10,024 | 3,357 |
| Gross fixed capital formation | 1,042,655 | 1,112,699 | 1,261,648 |
| Statistical discrepancy | 19,115 | 7,159 | −14,575 |
| **Total domestic expenditure** | 2,699,457 | 2,952,904 | 3,290,636 |
| Exports of goods and services | 885,795 | 1,028,391 | 1,169,839 |
| *Less* Imports of goods and services | 1,065,634 | 1,148,018 | 1,299,101 |
| **GDP in purchasers' values** | 2,519,618 | 2,833,277 | 3,161,374 |

* Provisional.

### Gross Domestic Product by Economic Activity

| | 1991 | 1992 | 1993* |
|---|---|---|---|
| Agriculture, forestry and fishing | 320,870 | 340,193 | 314,974 |
| Mining and quarrying | 38,903 | 41,759 | 46,538 |
| Manufacturing | 716,096 | 792,047 | 899,435 |
| Construction | 168,278 | 191,071 | 217,159 |
| Electricity and water | 53,461 | 65,518 | 77,294 |
| Transport and communications | 176,971 | 204,815 | 236,272 |
| Wholesale and retail trade, restaurants and hotels | 427,033 | 469,004 | 525,726 |
| Banking, insurance, real estate and business services | 205,801 | 259,191 | 313,584 |
| Community, social and personal services | 325,282 | 363,270 | 409,990 |
| Government services | 86,923 | 106,409 | 120,402 |
| **GDP in purchasers' values** | 2,519,618 | 2,833,277 | 3,161,374 |

* Provisional.

Source: Office of the National Economic and Social Development Board.

# THAILAND

*Statistical Survey*

## BALANCE OF PAYMENTS (US $ million)

|  | 1991 | 1992 | 1993 |
|---|---|---|---|
| Merchandise exports f.o.b. | 28,232 | 32,100 | 36,410 |
| Merchandise imports f.o.b. | −34,222 | −36,261 | −40,556 |
| **Trade balance** | **−5,989** | **−4,161** | **−4,146** |
| Exports of services | 7,270 | 8,561 | 10,102 |
| Imports of services | −7,834 | −9,671 | −11,547 |
| Other income received | 2,256 | 2,208 | 2,254 |
| Other income paid | −3,536 | −3,669 | −3,902 |
| Private unrequited transfers (net) | 163 | 323 | 281 |
| Official unrequited transfers (net) | 98 | 54 | 32 |
| **Current balance** | **−7,571** | **−6,355** | **−6,926** |
| Direct investment (net) | 1,847 | 1,969 | 1,493 |
| Portfolio investment (net) | −81 | 927 | 5,455 |
| Other capital (net) | 9,993 | 6,900 | 7,495 |
| Net errors and omissions | 431 | −517 | −347 |
| **Overall balance** | **4,618** | **2,924** | **7,170** |

Source: IMF, *International Financial Statistics*.

# External Trade

## PRINCIPAL COMMODITIES
(distribution by SITC, US $ million)

| Imports c.i.f. | 1990 | 1991 | 1992 |
|---|---|---|---|
| **Food and live animals** | 1,414.4 | 1,767.2 | 1,935.1 |
| Fish, crustaceans and molluscs | 769.6 | 1,011.5 | 890.6 |
| Fresh, chilled or frozen fish | 737.8 | 962.0 | 816.5 |
| Frozen fish (excl. fillets) | 722.3 | 938.2 | 775.2 |
| **Crude materials (inedible) except fuels** | 2,061.7 | 2,202.6 | 2,423.4 |
| Cork and wood | 541.1 | 631.1 | 723.0 |
| Textile fibres and waste | 638.5 | 765.1 | 742.1 |
| **Mineral fuels, lubricants, etc.** | 3,113.3 | 3,499.5 | 3,368.1 |
| Petroleum and petroleum products | 3,032.2 | 3,448.4 | 3,337.5 |
| Crude petroleum | 1,523.2 | 1,479.3 | 1,745.0 |
| Refined petroleum products | 1,476.5 | 1,927.6 | 1,536.5 |
| Gas oils | 849.9 | 1,095.7 | 695.8 |
| **Chemicals and related products** | 3,408.3 | 3,529.4 | 4,213.3 |
| Organic chemicals | 926.0 | 1,009.9 | 1,130.1 |
| Artificial resins, plastic materials, etc. | 766.7 | 757.9 | 915.7 |
| **Basic manufactures** | 7,023.3 | 8,728.5 | 8,269.9 |
| Textile yarn, fabrics, etc. | 898.3 | 1,000.3 | 1,209.7 |
| Non-metallic mineral manufactures | 1,441.8 | 2,444.1 | 1,071.2 |
| Pearls, precious and semi-precious stones, unworked or worked | 1,090.7 | 1,826.0 | 622.0 |
| Diamonds (excl. sorted industrial diamonds), unmounted | 689.7 | 784.4 | 463.8 |
| Iron and steel | 2,687.9 | 2,962.0 | 3,278.3 |
| Ingots and other primary forms | 732.3 | 827.5 | 949.0 |
| Bars, rods, angles, shapes and sections | 687.3 | 624.3 | 759.2 |
| Universals, plates and sheets | 1,074.7 | 1,301.1 | 1,327.5 |
| Non-ferrous metals | 694.3 | 752.2 | 798.8 |
| Other metal manufactures | 646.4 | 807.8 | 964.3 |
| **Machinery and transport equipment** | 13,687.0 | 14,881.5 | 17,020.1 |
| Power-generating machinery and equipment | 1,460.3 | 1,195.0 | 1,085.3 |
| Rotating electric plant and parts | 779.4 | 601.5 | 528.9 |

| Imports c.i.f. — *continued* | 1990 | 1991 | 1992 |
|---|---|---|---|
| Machinery specialized for particular industries | 2,292.0 | 2,676.3 | 2,456.0 |
| Textile and leather machinery and parts | 634.0 | 703.6 | 637.5 |
| General industrial machinery, equipment and parts | 1,627.8 | 2,387.9 | 2,385.6 |
| Heating and cooling equipment and parts | 363.4 | 787.8 | 572.4 |
| Office machines and automatic data-processing equipment | 1,114.4 | 1,301.1 | 1,619.8 |
| Parts and accessories for office machines, etc. | 882.5 | 987.8 | 1,200.5 |
| Telecommunications and sound equipment | 993.5 | 1,065.1 | 1,303.6 |
| Other electrical machinery, apparatus, etc. | 2,669.3 | 3,406.0 | 3,970.7 |
| Switchgear, etc., and parts | 441.8 | 655.8 | 749.9 |
| Thermionic valves, tubes, etc. | 1,312.6 | 1,588.6 | 1,899.5 |
| Road vehicles and parts | 2,316.9 | 2,011.2 | 2,481.1 |
| Passenger motor cars (excl. buses) | 397.3 | 472.3 | 935.5 |
| Parts and accessories for cars, buses, lorries, etc. | 1,567.7 | 1,110.2 | 1,036.5 |
| Other transport equipment | 750.6 | 192.3 | 1,149.6 |
| Aircraft, associated equipment and parts | 620.8 | 50.7 | 988.1 |
| **Miscellaneous manufactured articles** | 1,395.4 | 1,705.2 | 2,007.6 |
| **Total** (incl. others) | 33,371.4 | 37,588.3 | 40,686.8 |

| Exports f.o.b. | 1989 | 1990 | 1991 |
|---|---|---|---|
| **Food and live animals** | 6,730.3 | 6,495.0 | 7,510.9 |
| Meat and meat preparations | 247.6 | 314.2 | 435.8 |
| Fresh, chilled or frozen meat | 236.8 | 306.3 | 415.7 |
| Poultry meat | 236.2 | 303.3 | 412.9 |
| Fish, crustaceans and molluscs | 1,941.9 | 2,258.4 | 2,894.5 |
| Fresh, chilled, frozen, salted or dried crustaceans and molluscs | 923.1 | 1,060.8 | 1,354.7 |
| Prepared or preserved fish, crustaceans and molluscs | 848.2 | 993.1 | 1,188.1 |
| Prepared or preserved fish | 619.7 | 691.2 | 828.5 |
| Cereals and cereal preparations | 2,000.2 | 1,334.3 | 1,463.1 |
| Rice | 1,767.8 | 1,086.1 | 1,195.5 |
| Milled rice | 1,758.6 | 1,066.5 | 1,170.7 |
| Vegetables and fruit | 1,429.7 | 1,520.5 | 1,698.3 |
| Fresh or simply preserved vegetables | 935.8 | 900.3 | 885.5 |
| Preserved fruit and fruit preparations | 309.3 | 403.0 | 550.6 |
| Sugar, sugar preparations and honey | 786.0 | 749.0 | 653.8 |
| Sugar and honey | 777.6 | 739.6 | 638.8 |
| Raw sugar (solid) | 635.9 | 486.6 | 368.4 |
| **Crude materials (inedible) except fuels** | 1,425.2 | 1,314.7 | 1,415.5 |
| Crude rubber | 1,029.8 | 922.9 | 978.7 |
| Natural rubber | 1,027.8 | 921.4 | 977.6 |
| **Chemicals and related products** | 336.8 | 457.6 | 716.1 |
| **Basic manufactures** | 2,682.0 | 3,161.5 | 3,615.7 |
| Textile yarn, fabrics, etc. | 806.6 | 931.4 | 1,140.9 |
| Woven fabrics of man-made fibres | 284.5 | 334.7 | 420.1 |
| Non-metallic mineral manufactures | 829.4 | 1,078.1 | 1,192.2 |
| Pearls, precious and semi-precious stones, unworked or worked | 652.2 | 879.4 | 940.1 |
| Diamonds (excl. sorted industrial diamonds), unmounted | 184.8 | 304.3 | 407.4 |

# THAILAND

## Statistical Survey

| Exports f.o.b. — *continued* | 1989 | 1990 | 1991 |
|---|---|---|---|
| **Machinery and transport equipment** | 3,516.1 | 5,066.3 | 6,813.1 |
| General industrial machinery, equipment and parts | 276.4 | 417.0 | 598.5 |
| Office machines and automatic data-processing equipment | 1,067.5 | 1,562.4 | 1,954.3 |
| Automatic data-processing machines and units | 446.1 | 357.9 | 515.6 |
| Digital central storage units | 430.5 | 338.9 | 482.1 |
| Parts and accessories for office machines, etc. | 601.2 | 1,162.2 | 1,320.8 |
| Telecommunications and sound equipment | 539.8 | 1,057.0 | 1,553.5 |
| Television receivers | 71.9 | 253.8 | 466.2 |
| Colour television receivers | 71.1 | 253.2 | 465.3 |
| Other electrical machinery, apparatus, etc. | 1,315.4 | 1,605.1 | 2,077.5 |
| Thermionic valves, tubes, etc. | 725.8 | 901.0 | 1,122.0 |
| **Miscellaneous manufactured articles** | 4,903.6 | 6,009.1 | 7,579.9 |
| Furniture and parts | 263.1 | 309.6 | 412.2 |
| Clothing and accessories (excl. footwear) | 2,461.9 | 2,825.3 | 3,688.6 |
| Men's and boys' outer garments of non-knitted textile fabrics | 486.1 | 609.1 | 855.4 |
| Trousers, breeches, etc. | 242.5 | 309.5 | 473.4 |
| Women's, girls' and infants' outer garments of non-knitted textile fabrics | 739.7 | 813.4 | 1,035.6 |
| Knitted or crocheted outer garments and accessories (excl. gloves, stockings, etc.), non-elastic | 479.6 | 542.9 | 703.5 |
| Knitted or crocheted undergarments (incl. foundation garments of non-knitted fabrics) | 347.0 | 434.3 | 589.6 |
| Cotton undergarments, non-elastic | 214.6 | 290.8 | 408.5 |
| Footwear | 494.8 | 743.5 | 881.7 |
| Leather footwear | 335.4 | 560.8 | 686.9 |
| Baby carriages, toys, games and sporting goods | 318.2 | 462.4 | 571.8 |
| Children's toys, indoor games, etc. | 290.1 | 394.5 | 452.0 |
| Jewellery, goldsmiths' and silversmiths' wares, etc. | 517.6 | 565.3 | 561.4 |
| Jewellery of gold, silver or platinum-group metals (excl. watches and watch cases) and goldsmiths' or silversmiths' wares, incl. set gems | 469.8 | 510.4 | 504.8 |
| Articles of jewellery and parts, of precious metal or rolled precious metal | 466.8 | 504.7 | 494.2 |
| **Total** (incl. others) | 20,058.3 | 23,068.7 | 28,420.9 |

Source: UN, *International Trade Statistics Yearbook*.

## PRINCIPAL TRADING PARTNERS (million baht)

| Imports c.i.f. | 1992 | 1993 |
|---|---|---|
| Australia | 23,166.5 | 24,087.6 |
| Belgium | 9,498.7 | 13,303.9 |
| Brazil | 11,626.2 | 8,650.8 |
| Canada | 10,308.8 | 10,827.0 |
| China, People's Repub. | 30,979.1 | 27,609.8 |
| France | 23,962.0 | 23,220.8 |
| Germany | 54,961.0 | 62,847.7 |
| Hong Kong | 12,519.4 | 13,577.2 |
| India | 8,505.3 | 13,231.5 |
| Indonesia | 7,392.1 | 12,968.4 |
| Italy | 15,816.3 | 22,962.1 |
| Japan | 302,372.5 | 353,504.6 |
| Korea, Repub. | 45,352.8 | 49,315.9 |
| Malaysia | 40,526.5 | 42,384.5 |
| Netherlands | 10,863.5 | 10,203.6 |
| Russia | 8,331.5* | 15,698.5 |
| Saudi Arabia | 13,177.3 | 12,263.4 |
| Singapore | 75,438.0 | 75,188.0 |
| Sweden | 8,310.5 | 10,541.5 |
| Switzerland | 13,936.8 | 14,551.7 |
| Taiwan | 57,085.1 | 59,128.7 |
| United Arab Emirates | 8,024.9 | 11,318.6 |
| United Kingdom | 23,983.7 | 26,824.6 |
| USA | 121,218.0 | 136,047.0 |
| **Total** (incl. others) | 1,033,244.7 | 1,170,846.4 |

* Including imports from other countries of the former USSR.

| Exports f.o.b. | 1992 | 1993 |
|---|---|---|
| Australia | 13,333.5 | 12,958.2 |
| Belgium | 11,394.3 | 14,655.3 |
| Canada | 11,337.4 | 13,117.4 |
| China, People's Repub. | 9,800.8 | 13,636.3 |
| France | 18,770.4 | 19,553.3 |
| Germany | 36,255.3 | 37,458.2 |
| Hong Kong | 38,270.9 | 49,584.3 |
| Italy | 13,814.1 | 11,735.4 |
| Japan | 144,391.3 | 159,479.7 |
| Korea, Repub. | 13,542.8 | 11,683.3 |
| Malaysia | 21,375.4 | 26,323.2 |
| Netherlands | 35,661.8 | 29,286.3 |
| Poland | 9,262.8 | 11,057.9 |
| Saudi Arabia | 9,763.2 | 12,705.1 |
| Singapore | 71,684.7 | 112,844.9 |
| Taiwan | 15,705.4 | 18,692.6 |
| United Arab Emirates | 9,126.9 | 12,062.7 |
| United Kingdom | 29,757.7 | 30,083.4 |
| USA | 185,005.6 | 202,227.6 |
| **Total** (incl. others) | 824,643.3 | 940,862.6 |

Source: Department of Customs, Ministry of Finance.

# Transport

## RAILWAYS ('000)

| | 1991 | 1992 | 1993 |
|---|---|---|---|
| Passenger journeys | 86,906 | 87,769 | 87,183 |
| Passenger-km | 12,819,567 | 14,135,915 | 14,717,667 |
| Freight (ton-km) | 3,365,431 | 3,074,786 | 3,059,043 |
| Freight carried (metric tons) | 7,990 | 7,600 | 7,498 |

Source: The State Railway of Thailand.

## ROAD TRAFFIC (motor vehicles in use at 31 December)

| | 1991 | 1992 | 1993 |
|---|---|---|---|
| Passenger cars | 796,807 | 890,821 | 1,041,246 |
| Buses | 463,007 | 500,824 | 534,024 |
| Lorries and vans | 1,440,320 | 1,625,483 | 1,938,039 |
| Motor cycles | 5,521,391 | 6,307,800 | 7,260,665 |

Source: Department of Land Transport.

# THAILAND

## SHIPPING
Merchant Fleet (at 30 June)

|  | 1990 | 1991 | 1992 |
|---|---|---|---|
| Displacement ('000 grt) | 615 | 725 | 917 |

Source: UN, *Statistical Yearbook*.

### Freight Traffic
(Port of Bangkok)

|  | 1989 | 1990 | 1991 |
|---|---|---|---|
| Vessels entered: |  |  |  |
| Number* | 5,987 | 6,316 | 6,261 |
| Net registered tonnage† | 7,931,811 | 6,308,541 | 5,822,479 |
| Vessels cleared: |  |  |  |
| Number* | 5,856 | 6,320 | 6,157 |
| Net registered tonnage† | 11,843,150 | 15,085,534 | 17,282,502 |
| Cargo tons unloaded | 30,537,562 | 35,801,121 | 40,147,273 |
| Cargo tons loaded | 26,750,828 | 22,801,183 | 21,187,735 |

* In ballast and with cargo.  † In ballast.
Source: Department of Customs, Ministry of Finance.

### International Sea-borne Freight Traffic
('000 metric tons, all Thai ports)

|  | 1988 | 1989 | 1990 |
|---|---|---|---|
| Goods loaded | 26,126 | 28,437 | 29,854 |
| Goods unloaded | 26,586 | 29,059 | 30,057 |

Source: UN, *Monthly Bulletin of Statistics*.

## CIVIL AVIATION

|  | 1988 | 1989 | 1990 |
|---|---|---|---|
| Kilometres flown | 85,003,000 | 93,871,689 | 101,589,000 |
| Passengers carried |  |  |  |
| Number | 6,282,438 | 7,394,199 | 8,272,516 |
| Passenger-km ('000) | 16,742,348 | 18,876,972 | 19,869,143 |
| Freight carried |  |  |  |
| Tons | 157,964 | 165,502 | 199,399 |
| Ton-km ('000) | 589,064 | 626,497 | 799,267 |
| Mail carried |  |  |  |
| Tons | 7,636 | 8,893 | 9,287 |
| Ton-km ('000) | 33,576 | 39,104 | 39,070 |

Passenger-km ('000): 20,070,417 in 1991; 21,994,641 in 1992.
Source: Airport Authority of Thailand and the Department of Aviation.

## Tourism

|  | 1991 | 1992 | 1993 |
|---|---|---|---|
| Number of visitors | 5,086,899 | 5,136,443 | 5,760,533 |
| Receipts (million baht) | 100,004 | 123,135 | 127,802 |

Source: Tourism Authority of Thailand.

## Communications Media

|  | 1990 | 1991 | 1992 |
|---|---|---|---|
| Radio receivers ('000 in use) | 10,300 | 10,550 | 10,750 |
| Television receivers ('000 in use) | 6,250 | 6,300 | 6,400 |
| Book production: titles | 7,783 | 7,676 | 7,626 |
| Daily newspapers: |  |  |  |
| Number | 34 | n.a. | 35 |
| Circulation ('000) | 4,000 | n.a. | 4,150* |
| Non-daily newspapers (number) | 302 | n.a. | 302 |
| Other periodicals | 1,293 | n.a. | n.a. |
| Telephones (main lines in use) | 1,325,000 | 1,553,000 | n.a. |

Telephones (1992): 1,790,029 in use.
* Estimate.
Source: mainly UNESCO, *Statistical Yearbook*.

## Education
(1993)

|  | Institutions | Teachers | Students |
|---|---|---|---|
| Office of the National Primary Education Commission | 31,438 | 363,386 | 6,734,653 |
| Office of the Private Education Commission | 2,935 | 66,475 | 1,676,722 |
| Department of General Education | 2,087 | 105,540 | 2,095,533 |
| Bangkok Metropolitan Administration, Municipalities and Muang Pattaya | 909 | 23,931 | 515,444 |
| Vocational Education Department | 193 | 16,091 | 290,324 |
| Ministry of University Affairs* | 54 | 20,000 | 282,729 |
| Border Patrol Police | 166 | 1,060 | 18,409 |
| Department of Teacher Education | 61 | 6,496 | 99,442 |
| **Total** (incl. others) | 38,341 | 614,228 | 11,855,624 |

* Excluding Ramkhamhaeng University and Sukhothai Thammathirat Open University.
Source: Office of the Permanent Secretary, Ministry of Education.

# Directory

## The Constitution

A new Constitution was promulgated on 9 December 1991. It provided for the creation of a legislative body, the National Assembly, comprising an elected House of Representatives and an appointed Senate, and a Cabinet headed by a Prime Minister. In June 1992 constitutional amendments were adopted by the National Assembly, stipulating that the Prime Minister must be an elected member of the House of Representatives; restricting the power of the Senate to that of scrutiny or veto of draft legislation; and ensuring that the Speaker of the House of Representatives is the President of the National Assembly. A further set of constitutional amendments was adopted in January 1995 (see Recent History).

## The Government

### HEAD OF STATE

HM King BHUMIBOL ADULYADEJ (King RAMA IX); succeeded to the throne June 1946.

### PRIVY COUNCIL

Dr SANYA DHARMASAKTI (President).
Gen. (retd) PREM TINSULANONDA.
Dr PRAKOB HUTASINGH.
ARTHASIDHI SIDHISUNTHORN.
M. L. CHIRAYU NAVAWONGS.
Dr CHAOVANA NA SYLVANTA.
THANIN KRAIVIXIEN.
Prof. Dr KALYA ISRASENA.
CHITTI TINSABADH.
Rear-Adm. M. L. USNI PRAMOJ.
Air Vice-Marshal KAMTHON SINDHAVANANDA.
M. R. ADULKIT KITIYAKARA.
Air Chief Marshal SIDDHI SAVETSILA.
CHULANOPE SNIDVONGS.

### CABINET
(July 1995)

A coalition of Chart Thai, the New Aspiration Party (NAP), Palang Dharma, Social Action Party (SAP), Prachakorn Thai, Nam Thai and Muan Chon.

**Prime Minister and Minister of the Interior:** BANHARN SILPA-ARCHA (Chart Thai).
**Deputy Prime Ministers:** Air Chief Marshal SOMBUN RAHONG, Gen. CHAOVALIT YONGCHAIYUT (also **Minister of Defence**), Police Lt-Col THAKSIN SHINAWATRA, BUNPHAN KHAEWATTHANA, SAMAK SUNDARAVEJ, AMNUAT WIRAWAN.
**Ministers attached to the Prime Minister's Office:** PHONGPHON ADIREKSAN, RUANGWIT LIK, PIYANAT WATHACHARAPHON, PRASONG BUNPHONG, CHARAT PHUACHUAI, RAKKIAT SUTTHANA, PHOKHIN PHONLAKUN.
**Minister of Agriculture and Co-operatives:** MONTRI PONGPANICH.
**Minister of Commerce:** CHUCHIP HANSAWAT.
**Minister of Communications:** WANMUHAMATNO MATHA.
**Minister of Education:** SUKHAWIT RANDSITPHON.
**Minister of Finance:** SURAKIAT SATHIANTHAI.
**Minister of Foreign Affairs:** M.R. KASEMSAMOSON KASEMSI.
**Minister of Industry:** CHAIWUT SINSUWONG.
**Minister of Justice:** Police Capt. CHALOEM YUBAMRUNG.
**Minister of Labour and Social Welfare:** PHISAN MUNLASATSATHON.
**Minister of Public Health:** SANO THIANTHONG.
**Minister of Science, Technology and Environment:** YINGPHAN MANASIKAN.
**Minister of the State University Bureau:** BUNCHU TRITHONG.

The Cabinet also includes 23 deputy ministers.

### MINISTRIES

**Office of the Prime Minister:** Government House, Thanon Nakhon Pathom, Bangkok 10300; tel. (2) 280-3693; fax (2) 282-8792.
**Ministry of Agriculture and Co-operatives:** Thanon Ratchadamnoen Nok, Bangkok 10200; tel. (2) 281-5955.
**Ministry of Commerce:** Thanon Sanamchai, Bangkok 10200; tel. (2) 220-0855; telex 82389; fax (2) 226-3318.
**Ministry of Communications:** Thanon Ratchadamnoen Nok, Bangkok 10100; tel. (2) 281-3422; telex 70000; fax (2) 280-1714.
**Ministry of Defence:** Thanon Sanamchai, Bangkok 10200; tel. (2) 222-1121; fax (2) 226-3117.
**Ministry of Education:** Wang Chankasem, Thanon Ratchadamnoen Nok, Bangkok 10300; tel. (2) 281-7644.
**Ministry of Finance:** Thanon Phra Ram Hok, Bangkok 10400; tel. (2) 273-9021; telex 82823; fax (2) 273-9408.
**Ministry of Foreign Affairs:** Wang Saranrom, Bangkok 10200; tel. (2) 221-9171; telex 82698; fax (2) 225-6155.
**Ministry of Industry:** Thanon Phra Ram Hok, Bangkok 10400; tel. (2) 246-1137; telex 84375; fax (2) 246-8826.
**Ministry of the Interior:** Thanon Atsadang, Bangkok 10200; tel. (2) 222-1141.
**Ministry of Justice:** Thanon Ratchadapisek, Chatuchak, Bangkok 10900; tel. (2) 541-2300; fax (2) 541-2303.
**Ministry of Labour and Social Welfare:** Thanon Mitmaitri, Dindaeng, Huay Kwang, Bangkok 10400; tel. (2) 245-9525.
**Ministry of Public Health:** Wang Devaves, Thanon Samsen, Bangkok 10200; tel. (2) 282-2121; fax (2) 282-8488.
**Ministry of Science, Technology and Environment:** Thanon Phra Ram Hok, Phaya Thai, Bangkok 10400; tel. (2) 246-0064; telex 20838; fax (2) 246-8106.
**Ministry of the State University Bureau:** 328 Thanon Sri Ayudhya, Bangkok 10400; tel. (2) 246-0025; telex 72610; fax (2) 245-8636.

## Legislature

### NATIONAL ASSEMBLY
#### The Senate

**President:** MEECHAI RUCHUPAN.

A constitutional amendment was enacted in January 1995, limiting the membership of the Senate to two-thirds of that of the House of Representatives.

#### House of Representatives

**President and Speaker:** BOON-UA PRASERTSUWAN.

**General Election, 2 July 1995**

| Party | Seats |
|---|---|
| Chart Thai | 93 |
| Democrat Party | 86 |
| New Aspiration Party | 56 |
| Chart Pattana | 53 |
| Palang Dharma | 23 |
| Social Action Party | 23 |
| Prachakorn Thai | 18 |
| Nam Thai | 18 |
| Seritham Party | 10 |
| Ekkaparb | 8 |
| Muan Chon | 3 |
| **Total** | **391** |

## Political Organizations

**Chart Pattana** (National Development): Bangkok; f. 1992; Leader Gen. CHATICHAI CHOONHAVAN; Sec.-Gen. PRACHUAB CHAIYASARN.

**Chart Thai** (Thai Nation): Bangkok; tel. (2) 282-7054; f. 1981; right-wing; includes mems of fmr United Thai People's Party and fmr Samakkhi Tham (f. 1991); Sec.-Gen. BANHARN SILPA-ARCHA.

**Democrat Party (DP)** (Prachatipat): Bangkok; tel. (2) 270-0036; f. 1946; liberal; Leader CHUAN LEEKPAI; Sec.-Gen. Maj.-Gen. (retd) SANAN KAJORNPRASART.

**Ekkaparb** (Solidarity): Bangkok; tel. (2) 246-1881; f. 1989; opposition merger by the Community Action Party, the Prachachon Party, the Progressive Party and Ruam Thai; Leader UTHAI PHIMCHAICHON; Sec.-Gen. CHAIYOT SASOMSAP.

# THAILAND

**Lak Siam** (Siam Principle): Bangkok; f. 1994 by breakaway faction from Palang Dharma; Leader PHIRAPHONG THANOMPHONGPHAN.

**Muan Chon** (Mass Party): Bangkok; tel. (2) 424-0851; f. 1985; Leader CHALERM YUBAMRUNG; Sec.-Gen. SOPHON PETCHSAVANG.

**Nam Thai** (Leadership of Thailand): Bangkok; f. 1994; business-orientated; Leader AMNUAY WIRAWAN.

**New Aspiration Party (NAP):** Bangkok; tel. (2) 243-5000; f. 1990; Leader Gen. CHAOVALIT YONGCHAIYUT; Sec.-Gen. PHISAN MOONLASARTSATHORN.

**Palang Dharma (PD)** (Righteous Force): Bangkok; tel. (2) 246-7496; f. 1988; Leader THAKSIN SHINAWATRA; Sec.-Gen. WINAI SOMPONG.

**Prachakorn Thai** (Thai Citizens Party): Bangkok; tel. (2) 277-1194; f. 1981; right-wing; monarchist; Leader SAMAK SUNDARAVEJ; Sec.-Gen. KOSOL KRAIRERK.

**Puangchon Chao Thai** (Thai People's Party): Bangkok; tel. (2) 246-3692; f. 1981; Sec.-Gen. Maj.-Gen. BOONYONG WATTHANAPONG.

**Rassadorn** (Citizens' Party): Bangkok; tel. (2) 243-5002; f. 1981; conservative; Sec.-Gen. Gen. CHAIPAK SIRIWAT.

**Seritham Party** (Justice Freedom Party): Bangkok; f. 1992; Leader ARTHIT URAIRAT.

**Social Action Party (SAP)** (Kij Sangkhom): Bangkok 10300; tel. (2) 243-0100; fax (2) 243-3224; f. 1981; conservative; Leader MONTRI PONGPANICH.

Groupings in armed conflict with the Government include:

**National Revolutionary Front:** Yala; Muslim secessionists.

**Pattani United Liberation Organization (PULO):** advocates secession of the five southern provinces (Satun, Narathiwat, Yala, Pattani and Songkhla); Leader SIAMA-IL TAHNAM.

## Diplomatic Representation

### EMBASSIES IN THAILAND

**Argentina:** 20/85 Prommitr Villa, Soi 49/1, off Thanon Sukhumvit Soi 49, Bangkok 10110; tel. (2) 259-0401; telex 82762; fax (2) 259-0402; Ambassador: JESÚS FERNANDO TABOADA.

**Australia:** 37 Thanon Sathorn Tai, Bangkok 10120; tel. (2) 287-2680; fax (2) 287-2029; Ambassador: CAVAN HOGUE.

**Austria:** 14 Soi Nandha, off Soi Attakarnprasit, Thanon Sathorn Tai, Bangkok 10120; tel. (2) 287-3970; telex 82386; fax (2) 287-3925; Ambassador: Dr ERICH BINDER.

**Bangladesh:** 6-8 Charoenmitr, Soi 63 Thanon Sukhumvit, Bangkok; tel. (2) 391-8069; telex 82330; Ambassador: MOINUL HUSSAIN CHOUDHURY.

**Belgium:** 44 Soi Phya Phipat, off Thanon Silom, Bangkok 10500; tel. (2) 236-0150; telex 82563; fax (2) 236-7619; Ambassador: JEAN-MARIE NOIRFALISSE.

**Brazil:** 236 Soi Sarasin Thanon Ratchadamri, Lumpini-Patumwan, Bangkok 10330; tel. (2) 252-6023; telex 82742; fax (2) 254-2707; Ambassador: PAULO MONTEIRO LIMA.

**Brunei:** 154 Soi 14, Ekamai, Sukhumvit 63, Bangkok 10110; tel. (2) 391-5914; fax (2) 381-5921; Ambassador: Dato' Paduka Haji YAHYA BIN Haji HARRIS.

**Cambodia:** Bangkok; Ambassador: ROLAND ENG.

**Canada:** Boonmitr Bldg, 11th-12th Floors, 138 Thanon Silom, Bangkok 10500; tel. (2) 237-4126; fax (2) 236-6463; Ambassador: MANFRED G. VON NOSTITZ.

**Chile:** 15 Thanon Sukhumvit Soi 61, Sukhumvit Rd, Prakanong, Bangkok 10110; tel. (2) 391-8443; telex 84042; fax (2) 391-8380; Chargé d'affaires a.i.: MARIO SCHEGGIA.

**China, People's Republic:** 57 Thanon Rachadapisake, Bangkok; tel. (2) 245-7032; Ambassador: JIN GUIHUA.

**Czech Republic:** Silom Center Bldg, 21st Floor, Thanon Silom, Bangkok 10500; tel. (2) 236-2277; fax 236-5843; Ambassador: PAVEL FORT.

**Denmark:** 10 Soi Attakarn Prasit, Thanon Sathorn Tai, Bangkok 10120; tel. (2) 213-2021; telex 87304; fax (2) 213-1752; Ambassador: MOGENS KNUD ISAKSEN.

**Egypt:** 49 Soi Ruam Rudee, Thanon Ploenchit, Bangkok 10500; tel. (2) 253-0161; telex 82544; Ambassador: MOHAMED KHALIL AZAZI.

**Finland:** Amarin Tower, 16th Floor, 500 Thanon Ploenchit, Bangkok 10330; tel. (2) 256-9306; telex 82492; fax (2) 256-9310; Ambassador: EERO KALEVI SALOVAARA.

**France:** 35 Charoen Krung 36, Bangkok 10500; tel. (2) 266-8250; telex 82663; fax (2) 236-7973; Ambassador: JACQUES-ANTOINE RUMMELHARDT.

**Germany:** 9 Thanon Sathorn Tai, Bangkok 10120; tel. (2) 213-2331; telex 87348; fax (2) 287-1776; Ambassador: BERTHOLD VON PFETTEN-ARNBACH.

**Greece:** Thanakul Bldg, 3rd Floor, 99 Thanon Phra Ram IX, Bangkok 10310; tel. (2) 247-3551; fax (2) 246-7973; Ambassador: IOANNIS FOTOPOULOS.

**Holy See:** 217/1 Thanon Sathorn Tai, POB 12-178, Bangkok 10120 (Apostolic Nunciature); tel. (2) 212-5853; telex 20726; fax (2) 212-0932; Apostolic Nuncio: Most Rev. LUIGI BRESSAN (Titular Archbishop of Severiana).

**Hungary:** 28 Soi Sukchai, off Thanon Sukhumvit 42, Bangkok 10110; tel. (2) 391-2002; telex 82954; fax (2) 391-5250; Ambassador: ZOLTÁN SUDY.

**India:** 46 Soi Prasarnmitr, 23 Thanon Sukhumvit, Bangkok 10110; tel. (2) 258-0300; telex 82793; fax (2) 258-4627; Ambassador: RANJIT GUPTA.

**Indonesia:** 600-602 Thanon Phetchburi, Bangkok 10400; tel. (2) 252-3135; telex 82559; fax (2) 258-4627; Ambassador: Lt-Gen. I. GEDE AWETSARA.

**Iran:** 602 Thanon Sukhumvit, Bangkok 10110; tel. (2) 259-0611; telex 82684; fax (2) 259-3601; Ambassador: GHOLAMREZA YOUSEFI.

**Iraq:** 47 Thanon Pradipat, Samsen Nai, Phya Thai, Bangkok 10400; tel. (2) 278-5335; telex 82478; fax (2) 271-4218; Ambassador: MUNIR SHIBAB AHMED AL-BAYATI.

**Israel:** 31 Soi Lang Suan, Thanon Ploenchit, Bangkok 10330; tel. (2) 252-3131; telex 87322; fax (2) 254-5518; Ambassador: UZI MANOR.

**Italy:** 399 Thanon Nang Linchee, Bangkok 10120; tel. (2) 285-4090; telex 82523; fax (2) 285-4793; Ambassador: Dr LEOPOLDO G. M. FERRI DE LAZARA.

**Japan:** 1674 Thanon Phetchburi Tadmai, Bangkok 10130; tel. (2) 252-6151; telex 87302; fax (2) 253-4153; Ambassador: TAKASHI ONDA.

**Korea, Democratic People's Republic:** 314/1 Soi Viraya, Thanon Sri Ayuthaya, Bangkok 10400; tel. (2) 245-8369; telex 82123; fax (2) 318-6333; Ambassador: RI TO SOP.

**Korea, Republic:** 23 Thiam Ruammit, Huay Kwang, Thanon Samsen, Bangkok 10310; tel. (2) 247-7537; telex 82824; fax (2) 247-7535; Ambassador: TAK CHAE-HAN.

**Laos:** 193 Thanon Sathorn Tai, Bangkok 10120; tel. (2) 286-1232; telex 82192; fax (2) 287-3968; Ambassador: BOUNKEUT SANGSOMSAK.

**Malaysia:** 35 Thanon Sathorn Tai, Bangkok 10120; tel. (2) 286-1390; telex 87321; fax (2) 287-2348; Ambassador: Dato' ZAINAL ABIDIN ALIAS.

**Myanmar:** 132 Thanon Sathorn Nua, Bangkok 10500; tel. (2) 234-4698; telex 21467; fax (2) 236-6898; Ambassador: U TIN WINN.

**Nepal:** 189 Soi 71, Thanon Sukhumvit, Bangkok 10110; (2) 390-2280; telex 20216; fax (2) 381-2406; Ambassador: SUNDAR NATH BHATTARAI.

**Netherlands:** 106 Thanon Witthayu, Bangkok 10500; tel. (2) 254-7701; telex 82691; fax (2) 254-5579; Ambassador: G. A. M. WEHRY.

**New Zealand:** 93 Thanon Witthayu, Bangkok 10500; tel. (2) 251-8165; fax (2) 253-9045; Ambassador: PHILLIP GIBSON.

**Norway:** Bank of America Bldg, 1st Floor, 2/2 Thanon Witthayu, Bangkok 10330; tel. (2) 253-0290; telex 87309; fax (2) 256-0477; Ambassador: WILLY FREDRIKSEN.

**Pakistan:** 31 Soi Nana Nua (3), Thanon Sukhumvit, Bangkok 10110; tel. (2) 253-0288; telex 84774; fax (2) 253-0290; Ambassador: Maj.-Gen. RIAZ MAHMOUD.

**Philippines:** 760 Thanon Sukhumvit, Bangkok 10110; tel. (2) 259-0139; telex 34445; fax (2) 259-2809; Ambassador: ROSALINDA V. TIRONA.

**Poland:** Sriyukon Bldg, 84 Sukhumvit Soi 5, Bangkok 10110; tel. (2) 251-8891; telex 82074; fax (2) 381-2375; Ambassador: KRZYSZTOF SZUMSKI.

**Portugal:** 26 Bush Lane, Thanon Charoen Krung, Bangkok 10500; tel. (2) 234-2123; telex 82866; fax (2) 236-1954; Ambassador: SEBASTIÃO DE CASTELO-BRANCO.

**Romania:** 150 Soi Charoenporn 1, Thanon Pradipat, Bangkok 10400; tel. (2) 279-7902; telex 82872; fax (2) 279-7891; Ambassador: Dr IOAN VOICU.

**Russia:** 108 Thanon Sathorn Nua, Bangkok 10500; tel. (2) 234-9824; telex 21947; fax (2) 237-8488; Ambassador: OLEG V. BOSTORIN.

**Saudi Arabia:** Sathorn Thani Bldg, 10th Floor, 90 Thanon Sathorn Nua, Bangkok 10500; tel. (2) 237-1938; telex 87648; fax (2) 236-6442; Chargé d'affaires: MUHAMMAD SA'ID KHOJA.

**Singapore:** 129 Thanon Sathorn Tai, Bangkok 10500; tel. (2) 286-2111; telex 82930; fax (2) 287-2578; Ambassador: KWOK PUN WONG.

**Slovakia:** Bldg One, 12th Floor, 99/42 Thanon Witthayu, Pathumwan, Bangkok 10330; tel. (2) 256-6663; fax (2) 256-6141; Ambassador: (vacant).

**Spain:** Towers Bldg, 701-702, 73/1 Thanon Witthayu, Bangkok 10330; tel. (2) 252-6112; telex 82885; fax (2) 255-2388; Ambassador: CARLOS SPOTTORNO DIAZ-CARRO.

# THAILAND

**Sri Lanka:** 48/3 Soi 1, Thanon Sukhumvit, Bangkok 10500; tel. (2) 251-2788; telex 87019; Ambassador: H. C. GUNAWARDENA.
**Sweden:** Pacific Place, 20th Floor, 140 Thanon Sukhumvit, Bangkok 10110; tel. (2) 254-4954; telex 87114; fax (2) 254-4914; Ambassador: EVA HECKSCHER.
**Switzerland:** 35 Thanon Witthayu, POB 821, Bangkok 10501; tel. (2) 253-0156; telex 82687; fax (2) 255-4481; Ambassador: BLAISE GODET.
**Turkey:** 61/1 Soi Chatsan Thanon Suthisarn, Bangkok 10310; tel. (2) 274-7262; telex 82908; fax (2) 274-7261; Ambassador: IRFAN SARUHAN.
**United Kingdom:** Thanon Witthayu, Bangkok 10330; tel. (2) 253-0191; fax (2) 255-8619; Ambassador: CHRISTIAN ADAMS.
**USA:** 95 Thanon Witthayu, Bangkok 10330; tel. (2) 252-5040; fax (2) 254-2990; Ambassador (designate): WILLIAM ITOH.
**Viet Nam:** 83/1 Thanon Witthayu, Bangkok 10500; tel. (2) 251-7201; fax (2) 251-7201; Ambassador: NGUYEN TRUNG.
**Yugoslavia:** 28 Soi 61, Thanon Sukhumvit, Bangkok 10110; tel. (2) 391-9091; fax (2) 391-9090; Chargé d'affaires a.i.: BRANKO MARKOVIĆ.

## Judicial System

### SUPREME COURT

**Sarn Dika:** Thanon Ratchadamnoen Nai, Bangkok 10200; The final court of appeal in all civil, bankruptcy, labour, juvenile and criminal cases. Its quorum consists of three judges. However, the Court occasionally sits in plenary session to determine cases of exceptional importance or where there are reasons for reconsideration or overruling of its own precedents. The quorum, in such cases, is one-half of the total number of judges in the Supreme Court.
**President (Chief Justice):** PRAMARN CHANSUE.
**Vice-President:** CHOOSAK PANDITKUL.

### COURT OF APPEALS

**Sarn Uthorn:** Thanon Ratchadapisek Chatuchak, Bangkok 10900; Appellate jurisdiction in all civil, bankruptcy, juvenile and criminal matters; appeals from all the Courts of First Instance throughout the country, except the Central Labour Court, come to this Court. Two judges form a quorum.
**Chief Justice:** THAVORN TANTRAPORN.
**Deputy Chief Justices:** ATHAVIT VATHANAVINIG, THIEN YOONGTHONG, NEWET COMEPHONG, PINIV SHIMPALEE.

### COURTS OF FIRST INSTANCE

**Civil Court** (Sarn Pang): Ministry of Justice, Bangkok 10200; Court of first instance in civil and bankruptcy cases in Bangkok. Two judges form a quorum.
**Chief Justice:** SAKDA MOKKAMAKKUL.
**Criminal Court** (Sarn Aya): Thanon Ratchadapisek, Bangkok 10900; Court of first instance in criminal cases in Bangkok. Two judges form a quorum.
**Chief Justice:** PAITOON NATIPOH.
**Central Juvenile and Family Court** (Sarn Kadee Dek Lae Yaowachon): Thanon Rachini, Bangkok 10200; fax (2) 224-1546; Original jurisdiction over juvenile delinquency and matters affecting children and young persons. Two judges and two associate judges (one of whom must be a woman) form a quorum. There are courts in Bangkok, Songkla, Nakhon Ratchasima, Chiang Mai, Ubon Ratchathani and Rayong.
**Chief Justice:** PUNLOP PISITSUNGKAKARN.
**Central Labour Court** (Sarn Rang Ngan Klang): 404 Thanon Phra Ram IV, Bangkok 10500; Jurisdiction in labour cases throughout the country.
**Chief Justice:** SUTHEP KITSAWAT.
**Magistrates' Courts** (Sarn Kwaeng): Adjudicate in minor cases with minimum formality and expense. Judges sit singly.
**Provincial Courts** (Sarn Changwat): Exercise unlimited original jurisdiction in all civil and criminal matters, including bankruptcy, within its own district which is generally the province itself. Two judges form a quorum. At each of the five Provincial Courts in the south of Thailand (i.e. Pattani, Yala, Betong, Satun and Narathiwat) where the majority of the population are Muslims, there are two Dato Yutithum or Kadis (Muslim judges). A Kadi sits with two trial judges in order to administer Shari'a (Islamic) laws and usages in civil cases involving family and inheritance where all parties concerned are Muslims. Questions on Islamic laws and usages which are interpreted by a Kadi are final.
**Thon Buri Civil Court** (Sarn Pang Thon Buri): Civil jurisdiction over nine districts of metropolitan Bangkok.
**Thon Buri Criminal Court** (Sarn Aya Thon Buri): Criminal jurisdiction over nine districts of metropolitan Bangkok.

## Religion

Buddhism is the predominant religion, professed by more than 95% of Thailand's total population. About 4% of the population are Muslims, being ethnic Malays, mainly in the south. Most of the immigrant Chinese are Confucians. The Christians number about 305,000, of whom about 75% are Roman Catholic, mainly in Bangkok and northern Thailand. Brahmins, Hindus and Sikhs number about 85,000.

### BUDDHISM

**Sangha Supreme Council:** Bangkok; governing body of Thailand's 350,000 monks, novices and nuns.
**Supreme Patriarch of Thailand:** SOMDEJ PHRA YANSANGWARA.
**The Buddhist Association of Thailand:** 41 Thanon Phra Aditya, Bangkok 10200; tel. (2) 281-9563; f. 1934 under royal patronage; 4,183 mems; Pres. PRAPASANA AUYCHAI.

### CHRISTIANITY
#### The Roman Catholic Church

For ecclesiastical purposes, Thailand comprises two archdioceses and eight dioceses. At 31 December 1993 there were an estimated 243,409 adherents in the country, representing 0.4% of the population.
**Bishops' Conference of Thailand:** Praetham Bldg, 57 Trok Oriental, Bangrak, Bangkok 10500; tel. (2) 234-1730; fax (2) 237-5277; f. 1969; Pres. HE Cardinal MICHAEL MICHAI KITBUNCHU, Archbishop of Bangkok.
**Catholic Association of Thailand:** 57 Soi Burapa, Bangrak, Bangkok 10500; tel. (2) 233-2976.
**Archbishop of Bangkok:** HE Cardinal MICHAEL MICHAI KITBUNCHU, Assumption Cathedral, 40 Thanon Charoen Krung, Bangrak, Bangkok 10500; tel. (2) 233-8712; fax (2) 237-1033.
**Archbishop of Tharé and Nonseng:** Most Rev. LAWRENCE KHAI SAEN-PHON-ON, Archbishop's House, POB 6, Sakon Nakhon 47000; tel. (42) 711718; fax (42) 712023.

#### The Anglican Communion

Thailand is within the jurisdiction of the Anglican Bishop of Singapore (q.v.).

#### Other Christian Churches

**Baptist Church Foundation (Foreign Mission Board):** 90 Soi 2 Thanon Sukhumvit, Bangkok 10110; tel. (2) 252-7078; Mission Admin. TOM WILLIAMS, POB 832, Bangkok 10501.
**Church of Christ in Thailand:** 14 Thanon Pramuan, Bangkok 10500; tel. (2) 235-9499; fax (2) 238-3520; f. 1934; 55,670 communicants; Moderator Rev. SAMRAN KUANGWAEN; Gen. Sec. Rev. Dr SINT KIMHACHANDRA.

### ISLAM

**Office of the Chularajmontri:** 100 Soi Prom Pak, Thanon Sukhumvit, Bangkok 10110; Sheikh Al-Islam (Chularajmontri) Haji PRASERT MOHAMMED.

### BAHÁ'Í FAITH

**National Spiritual Assembly:** 77/1 Soi 4, Thanon Lang Suan, Bangkok 10330; tel. (2) 252-5355; fax (2) 254-4199; mems resident in 75 provinces.

## The Press

In January 1991 Decree 42 (a press censorship law which had been introduced in 1976, giving the Government arbitrary powers to suspend the publication of journals that might be regarded as a threat to national security) was repealed.

### DAILIES
#### Thai Language

**Baan Muang:** 1 Soi Pluem-Manee, Thanon Vibhavadi Rangsit, Bangkok; tel. (2) 513-0230; fax (2) 513-3106; Editor MANA PRAEBHAND; circ. 200,000.
**Daily Mirror:** 15/22 Thanon Lardprao 104, Bangkok; tel. (2) 538-0220; fax (2) 530-1826; f. 1978; Editor AMPORN BOONYA THISATHAM; circ. 100,000.

# THAILAND

**Daily News:** 1/4 Thanon Vibhavadi Rangsit, Bangkok; tel. (2) 579-0010; fax (2) 561-1343; f. 1964; Editor Pracha Hetrakul; circ. 650,000.

**Dao Siam:** 60 Mansion 4, Thanon Rajdamnern, Bangkok; tel. (2) 222-6001; fax (2) 222-6885; f. 1974; Editor Santi Untrakarn; circ. 120,000.

**Khao Panich** (Daily Trade News): 22/77 Thanon Ratchadapisek, Bangkok; tel. (2) 511-5066; Editor Samruane Sumphandharak; circ. 30,000.

**Krungthep Turakij Daily:** Nation Publishing Group Co Ltd, 44 Moo 10, Thanon Bangna-Trad, Bangna, Prakanong, Bangkok; tel. (2) 317-0042; fax (2) 317-1488; f. 1987; Publr and Group Editor Suthichai Yoon; Editor Adisak Limprungpatanakit; circ. 90,000.

**Matichon:** 12 Thanon Thedsaban Naruban, Prachanivate 1, Chatuchak, Bangkok; tel. (2) 580-0021; fax (2) 589-9112; f. 1978; Editor Wipa Sukkit; circ. 234,000.

**Naew Na** (Frontline): 96 Mooh 7, Thanon Vibhavadi Rangsit, Bangkok; tel. (2) 521-5120; fax (2) 552-3800; Editor Wanchai Wongmeechai; circ. 200,000.

**Siam Daily:** 192/8–9 Soi Vorapong, Thanon Visuthikasat, Bangkok; tel. (2) 281-7422; Editor Narong Charusophon.

**Siam Rath** (Siam Nation): 12 Mansion 6, Thanon Rajdamnern, Bangkok; tel. (2) 222-3629; fax (2) 224-1982; f. 1950; Editor Assiri Thammachot; circ. 120,000.

**Thai:** 423-425 Thanon Chao Khamrop, Bangkok; tel. (2) 223-3175; Editor Vichien Mana-Natheethoratham.

**Thai Rath:** 1 Thanon Vibhavadi Rangsit, Bangkok; tel. (2) 271-0217; telex 84207; fax (2) 271-4843; f. 1948; Editor Pithoon Sunthorn; circ. 800,000.

### English Language

**Bangkok Post:** Bangkok Post Bldg, 136 Soi Na Ranong, Klongtoey, Bangkok 10110; tel. (2) 240-3700; telex 84804; fax (2) 240-3666; f. 1946; morning; Editor Pichai Chuensukswadi; circ. 52,000.

**Business Day:** Bangkok; f. 1994; business news; Man. Editor Chatchai Yenbamroong.

**The Nation:** 44 Moo 10, Thanon Bangna-Trad, K.M. 4.5. Bangna, Phra Khanong, Bangkok 10260; tel. (2) 317-0420; fax (2) 317-1384; f. 1971; morning; Publr and Group Editor Suthichai Yoon; Editor Thepchai Yong; circ. 46,500.

### Chinese Language

**New Chinese Daily News:** 1022–1030 Thanon Charoen Krung, Talad-Noi, Bangkok; tel. (2) 234-6411; fax (2) 234-0684; Editor Pusadee Keetaworanart; circ. 72,000.

**Sing Sian Yit Pao Daily News:** 267 Thanon Charoen Krung, Bangkok 10100; tel. (2) 225-0070; telex 72306; fax (2) 225-4663; f. 1950; Editor Tawee Yodpetch; circ. 90,000.

**Sirinakorn:** 108 Thanon Suapa, Bangkok; tel. (2) 221-4182; f. 1959; Editor Prasert Vareves; circ. 80,000.

**Tong Hua Daily News:** 877/879 Thanon Charoen Krung, Talad-Noi, Bangkok; tel. (2) 236-9172; fax 238-5286; Editor Chart Payonithikarn; circ. 85,000.

**Universal Daily News:** 21/1 Thanon Charoen Krung, Bangkok; tel. (2) 226-0040; fax (2) 224-4745; Editor Yao Dte Wah; circ. 25,000.

## WEEKLIES
### Thai Language

**Bangkok Weekly:** 533–539 Thanon Sri Ayuthaya, Bangkok 10400; tel. (2) 245-6138; fax (2) 247-3410; Editor Vichit Rojanaprabha.

**Mathichon Weekly Review:** 12 Thanon Thedsaban Naruban, Prachanivate 1, Chatuchak, Bangkok; tel. (2) 580-0021; fax (2) 589-9112; Editor Ruangchai Sabnirand; circ. 150,000.

**Satri Sarn:** 83/35 Arkarntrithosthep 2, Thanon Prachathipatai, Bangkok 10300; tel. (2) 281-9136; f. 1948; women's magazine; Editor Nilawan Pintong.

**Siam Rath Weekly Review:** Mansion 6, Thanon Rajdamnern, Bangkok 10200; Editor Prachuab Thongurai.

**Skul Thai:** 58 Soi 36, Thanon Sukhumvit, Bangkok 10110; tel. (2) 258-5861; fax (2) 258-9130; Editor Santi Songsemsawas.

**Wattachak:** 88 Thanon Boromrajachonnee, Talingchan, Bangkok 10170; tel. (2) 434-0330; fax (2) 435-0900; Editor Praphan Boonyakiat; circ. 80,000.

### English Language

**Bangkok Post Weekly Review:** 136 Soi Na Ranong, off Thanon Sunthorn Kosa, Klongtoey, Bangkok 10110; tel. (2) 240-3700; telex 82833; fax (2) 240-3790; f. 1989; Editor Anussorn Thavisin; circ. 7,000.

**Business Times:** Thai Bldg, Thanon Phra Ram IV, Bangkok 10110.

## FORTNIGHTLIES
### Thai Language

**Dara Thai:** 9-9/1 Sriukson, Thanon Chuapleung, Thungmahamek Yannawa, Bangkok 10120; tel. (2) 249-1576; fax (2) 249-5415; f. 1954; television and entertainment; Editor Usa Bukkavesa; circ. 80,000.

**Dichan:** 1400 Thai Bldg, Thanon Phra Ram Si, Bangkok; tel. (2) 249-0351; fax (2) 249-9455; Editor Thipayawadee Pramoj Na Ayudhya.

**Lalana:** 44 Moo 10, Thanon Bangna-Trad, Bangna, Bangkok 10260; tel. (2) 317-1400; fax (2) 317-1409; f. 1972; Editor Nantawan Yoon; circ. 65,000.

## MONTHLIES

**Bangkok 30:** 139–41 Rimklongprapa Dusit, Bangkok 10800; tel. (2) 587-8029; fax (2) 586-9110; f. 1986; Thai; business; Publr Sonchai Limthongkul; Editor Boonsiri Namboonsri; circ. 65,000.

**Chao Krung:** 12 Mansion 6, Thanon Rajdamnern, Bangkok 10200; Thai; Editor Nopphorn Bunyarit.

**The Dharmachaksu** (Dharma-vision): Foundation of Mahamakut Rajavidyalaia, Thanon Phra Sumeru, Bangkok 10200; tel. 2828302; f. 1894; Thai; Buddhism and related subjects; Editor Wasin Indasara; circ. 5,000.

**Grand Prix:** 129–133 Rim Klong Prapa, Thanon Prachachuen, Bangkok 10800; tel. (2) 587-0101; fax (2) 587-6567; Editor Veera Junkajit; circ. 80,000.

**The Investor:** Pansak Bldg, 4th Floor, 138/1 Thanon Petchburi, Bangkok 10400; tel. (2) 282-8166; f. 1968; English language; business, industry, finance and economics; Editor Tos Patumsen; circ. 6,000.

**Kasikorn:** Dept of Agriculture, Bangkhen, Bangkok 10900; tel. (2) 579-5369; f. 1928; Thai; agriculture and agricultural research; Man. Vittaya Inman; Editor Udom Simaban.

**Look:** 1/54 Thanon Sukhumvit 30, Pra Khanong, Bangkok 10110; tel. (2) 258-1265; Editor Kanokwan Milindavanij.

**Look East:** 52/38 Soi Saladaeng 2, 12/F Silom Condominium, Thanon Silom, Bangkok 10500; tel. (2) 233-3401; fax (2) 236-6764; f. 1969; English; Editor Asha Sehgal; circ. 30,000.

**Motorcycle Magazine:** 4/133 Moo 2 Soi, Senachantira, Thanon Wat Ladpacao Bangkok, Bangkok 10200; tel. (2) 587-0101; fax (2) 587-6567; monthly; Publr Prachin Eamlamnow; circ. 70,000.

**Praew:** 413/27-36 Aroon Amarin, Bangkoknoi, Bangkok 10700; tel. (2) 424-2800; fax (2) 433-8792; women and fashion; Thai; Editor Supawadee Komaradat; circ. 120,000.

**Saen Sanuk:** 50 Soi Saeng Chan, Thanon Sukhumvit 42, Bangkok 10110; tel. (2) 392-0052; telex 20326; fax (2) 391-1486; English; Editor Somtawin Kongsawatkiat; circ. 85,000.

**Satawa Liang:** 689 Thanon Wang Burapa, Bangkok; Thai; Editor Thamrongsak Srichand.

**Villa Wina Magazine:** Chalerm Ketr Theatre Bldg, 3rd Floor, Bangkok; Thai; Editor Bhongsakdi Piamlap.

## NEWS AGENCIES
### Foreign Bureaux

**Agence France-Presse (AFP):** Panavongs Bldg, 104 Thanon Suriwong, POB 1567, Bangkok 10500; tel. (2) 236-6847; telex 82170; fax (2) 237-6748; Bureau Chief Charles Antoine Andrea de Nerciat.

**Agenzia Nazionale Stampa Associata (ANSA)** (Italy): 14/24 Soi Phanu Maphon, Thanon Chom Thong, 10150 Bangkok; tel. (2) 469-5648; Bureau Chief David Butler.

**Associated Press (AP)** (USA): Charn Issara Tower, 14th Floor, 942/51 Thanon Phra Ram IV, POB 775, Bangkok; tel. (2) 234-5553; telex 82606; Bureau Chief Denis D. Gray.

**Jiji Tsushin-sha (Jiji Press)** (Japan): Boonmitr Bldg, 8th Floor, 138 Thanon Silom, Bangkok; tel. (2) 236-8793; telex 82316; fax (2) 236-6800; Bureau Chief Junichi Ishikawa.

**Kyodo News Service** (Japan): U Chuliang Bldg, 2nd Floor, 968 Thanon Phra Ram IV, Bangkok 10500; tel. (2) 236-6822; telex 82562; Bureau Chief Yoshisuke Yasuo.

**Reuters** (UK): Maneeya Centre Bldg, 518/5 Thanon Ploenchit, 10330 Bangkok; tel. (2) 252-9950; telex 82636; Man. (Myanmar, Thailand and Indo-China) Graham D. Spencer.

**United Press International (UPI)** (USA): U Chuliang Bldg, 968 Thanon Phra Ram IV, Bangkok; tel. (2) 238-5244; telex 84614; Man. William Benholm Barnetson.

**Viet Nam News Agency (VNA):** 3/81 Soi Chokchai Ruamit, Bangkok; Bureau Chief Nguyen Vu Quang.

**Xinhua (New China) News Agency** (People's Republic of China): Room 407, Capital Mansion, 1371 Thanon Phahol Yotin, Bangkok; tel. (2) 278-3290; telex 82014; Correspondent Li Guo Tian.

THAILAND                                                                                                                                                                    *Directory*

### PRESS ASSOCIATIONS

**Confederation of Thai Journalists:** 538/1 Thanon Samsen, Dusit, Bangkok 10300; tel. (2) 241-4795; Pres. BANDHIT RAJAVATANADHANIN; Sec.-Gen. BUDDHA SRILERTCHAI.

**Press Association of Thailand:** 299 Thanon Ratchasima, Dusit, Bangkok 10300; tel. (2) 241-0766; f. 1941; Pres. PREECHA SAMAKKIDHAM.

There are also regional press organizations and journalists' organizations.

## Publishers

**Advance Media:** U Chuliang Bldg, 968 Thanon Phra Ram IV, Bangkok; Man. PRASERTSAK SIVASAHONG.

**Bhannakij Trading:** 34 Thanon Nakornsawan, Bangkok; tel. (2) 282-5520; Thai fiction, school textbooks; Man. SOMSAK TECHAKASHEM.

**Chalermnit Press:** 108 Thanon Sukhumvit Soi 53, Bangkok; tel. (2) 252-8759; f. 1957; dictionaries, history, literature, guides to Thai language, works on Thailand; Mans M. L. M. JUMSAI, Mrs JUMSAI.

**Dhamabuja:** 5/1-2 Thanon Asadang, Bangkok; religious; Man. VIROCHANA SIRI-ATH.

**Graphic Art Publishing:** 204/12-13 Thanon Surawong, Bangkok 10500; tel. (2) 233-0302; telex 20657; f. 1972; textbooks, science fiction, photography; CEO Mrs ANGKANA.

**Prae Pittaya Ltd:** POB 914, 716-718 Thanon Wang Burapa, Bangkok; tel. (2) 221-4283; general Thai books; Man. CHIT PRAEPANICH.

**Prapansarn:** Siam Sq., Soi 2, Thanon Phra Ram I, Bangkok; tel. (2) 251-2342; Thai pocket books; Man. Dir SUPHOL TAECHATADA.

**Ruamsarn (1977):** 1091/86 Thanon Petchburee 33, Bangkok 10400; tel. (2) 253-1489; fax (2) 253-7915; f. 1951; fiction, literature, philosophy, religion and textbooks; Man. T. PIYA.

**Ruang Silpa:** 663 Thanon Samsen Nai, Bangkok; Thai pocket books; Propr DHAMNOON RUANG SILPA.

**Sermvitr Barnakarn:** 222 Werng Nakorn Kasem, Bangkok; general Thai books; Man. PRAVIT SAMMAVONG.

**Suksapan Panit** (Business Organization of Teachers' Institute): Mansion 9, Thanon Rajdamnern, Bangkok 10200; telex 72031; f. 1950; general, textbooks, children's, pocket books; Pres. PANOM KAW KAMNERD.

**Suriayabarn Publishers:** 14 Thanon Pramuan, Bangkok 10500; tel. and fax (2) 236-1669; f. 1953; religion, children's, Thai culture; Man. Dir PISU ARKKAPIN.

**Thai Watana Panit:** 599 Thanon Maitrijit, Bangkok; tel. (2) 210111; children's, school textbooks.

**Watana Panit Printing and Publishing Co. Ltd:** 216-222 Thanon Bamrungmuang, Samanrat, Bangkok 10200; tel. 2221016; children's, school textbooks; Man. ROENGCHAI CHONGPIPATANASUK.

### PUBLISHERS' ASSOCIATION

**Publishers' and Booksellers' Association of Thailand:** 20 Rajprasong Trade Centre, Bangkok 10502; Pres. M. L. MANICH JUMSAI; Gen. Sec. Miss PLEARNPIT PRAEPANIT.

## Radio and Television

In 1992, according to UNESCO, there were an estimated 10.8m. radio receivers and 6.4m. television receivers in use.

### RADIO

**Radio Thailand (RTH):** National Broadcasting Services of Thailand, Government Public Relations Dept, 236 Thanon Vibhavadi Rangsit, Bangkok 10400; tel. (2) 277-9125; telex 72167; fax (2) 277-0122; f. 1930; govt-controlled; educational, entertainment, cultural and news programmes; operates 91 stations throughout Thailand; Dir of Radio Thailand BUNSUEB RUNGJAROEN.

**Home Service:** 13 stations in Bangkok and 85 affiliated stations in 49 provinces; operates three programmes; Dir SIRIPORN THONGKUMWONG.

**External Services:** f. 1928; in Thai, English, French, Vietnamese, Khmer, Japanese, Burmese, Lao, Malay, Chinese (Mandarin), German and Bengali; Dir AMPORN SAMOSORN.

**Ministry of Education Broadcasting Service:** Centre for Innovation and Technology, Ministry of Education, Bangkok; tel. (2) 246-0026; f. 1954; morning programmes for schools (Mon.–Fri.); afternoon and evening programmes for general public (daily); Dir of Centre PISAN SIWAYABRAHM.

**Pituksuntirad Radio Stations:** stations at Bangkok, Nakorn Rachasima, Chiangmai, Pitsanuloke and Songkla; programmes in Thai; Dir-Gen. PAITOON WAIJANYA.

**Voice of Free Asia:** Thanon Ratchadamnoen, POB 2-131, Bangkok 10200; tel. (2) 224-4904; fax (2) 226-1825; f. 1968; broadcasts in Thai, English, Lao, Khmer and Vietnamese; Dir of Broadcasting SINPAIBOON PATHANASOOTRA.

### TELEVISION

**Bangkok Broadcasting & TV Co Ltd (Channel 7):** 998/1 Soi Sirimitr, Phaholyothin, Talad Mawchid, POB 456, Bangkok 10900; tel. (2) 278-1255; telex 82730; fax (2) 270-1976; commercial.

**Bangkok Entertainment Co. Ltd (Channel 3):** 2259 Thanon Petchburi Tadmai, Bangkok 10310; tel. (2) 3145416; telex 82616; fax (2) 253-9978.

**The Mass Communication Organization of Thailand (Channel 9):** 222 Thanon Yaek Asok-Dindaeng, Bangkok 10300; tel. (2) 245-1844; telex 84577; fax (2) 245-1855; f. 1954 as Thai Television Co Ltd; colour service; Dir-Gen. SANGCHAI SUNTHORNWAT.

**The Royal Thai Army Television HSA-TV (Channel 5):** Thanon Phaholyothin, Sanam Pao, Bangkok 10400; tel. (2) 271-0060; telex 81080; fax (2) 270-1510; f. 1958; operates channels nation-wide; Dir-Gen. Gen. AREEYA UKOSKIT.

**Television of Thailand (Channel II):** National Broadcasting Services of Thailand, Public Relations Dept, Thanon Petchburi, Bangkok 10200; tel. (2) 314-4001; telex 72243; fax (2) 318-2991; operates 16 colour stations; Dir-Gen. SOMPONG VISUTTHIPAET

**TV Pool of Thailand:** c/o Royal Thai Army HSA-TV; established with the co-operation of all stations to present coverage of special events.

## Finance

(cap. = capital; p.u. = paid up; res = reserves; dep. = deposits; m. = million; brs = branches; amounts in baht)

### BANKING

The establishment of 'offshore' banking units by local and foreign banks was authorized by the Thai Government in September 1992. In March 1993 47 licences were granted to banks to begin 'offshore' operations. In 1995 the Bank of Thailand announced that it would license 14 new commercial banks to commence operating in 1996, seven of which would be foreign banks and the other seven Thai finance companies seeking to become banks.

#### Central Bank

**Bank of Thailand:** POB 154, 273 Thanon Samsen, Bangkhunprom, Bangkok 10200; tel. (2) 283-5353; telex 20139; fax (2) 280-0449; f. 1942; bank of issue; cap. p.u. 9,737m., dep. 324,538m. (1992); Gov. VIJIT SUPINIT; 3 brs.

#### Commercial Banks

**Bangkok Bank Public Co Ltd:** 333 Thanon Silom, Bangkok 10500; tel. (2) 231-3333; telex 82638; fax (2) 231-4742; f. 1944; cap. p.u. 10,000m., dep. 716,025m. (Dec. 1993); Chair. PRASIT KANCHANAWAT; Pres. CHARTSIRI SOPHONPANICH; 427 brs.

**Bangkok Bank of Commerce (Public) Co Ltd:** 99 Thanon Surasak, Bangkok 10500; tel. (2) 267-1900; telex 82525; fax (2) 234-2939; f. 1944; cap. p.u. 4,000m. (April 1994), dep. 98,428m. (Dec. 1993); Chair. M. R. KUKRIT PRAMOJ; Pres. KIRKKIAT JALICHANDRA; 165 brs.

**Bangkok Metropolitan Bank Public Co Ltd:** 2 Thanon Chalermkhet 4, Bangkok 10100; tel. (2) 223-0561; telex 82281; fax (2) 224-3768; f. 1950; cap. p.u. 6,751.5m., dep. 100,904.9m. (Dec. 1993); Chair. UDANE TEJAPAIBUL; Pres. VICHIEN TEJAPAIBUL; 114 brs.

**Bank of Asia Public Co Ltd:** 191 Thanon Sathorn Tai, Khet Yannawa, Bangkok 10120; tel. (2) 287-2211; telex 81185; fax (2) 287-2973; f. 1939; cap. p.u. 3,220m., dep. 64,639m. (Dec. 1993); Chair. Dr SNOH UNAKUL; Pres. CHULAKORN SINGHAKOWIN; 47 brs.

**Bank of Ayudhya Public Co Ltd:** 550 Thanon Ploenchit, POB 491, Bangkok 10330; tel. (2) 253-8601; telex 82334; fax (2) 208-2280; f. 1945; cap. p.u. 4,000m., dep. 183,861m. (Dec. 1993); Chair. ANANT TANGTATSWAS; Pres. KRIT RATANARAK; 279 brs.

**First Bangkok City Bank Public Co Ltd:** 20 Yukhon, 2 Suan Mali, Bangkok 10100; tel. (2) 223-0501; telex 84120; fax (2) 225-3037; f. 1934 as Thai Development Bank; cap. p.u. 7,200m., dep. 136,886m. (Dec. 1993); Chair. Gen. SITHI CHIRAROCHANA; Pres. UTHAI AKKARAPATTANAKOON; 64 brs.

**Krung Thai Bank Public Co Ltd** (State Commercial Bank of Thailand): 35 Thanon Sukhumvit, Bangkok 10110; tel. (2) 255-2222; telex 81179; fax (2) 256-8743; f. 1966; cap. 13,500m., dep.

# THAILAND

402,236m. (Dec. 1993); Chair. Dr ARAN THAMMANO; Pres. SIRIN NIMMANANAHAENINDA; 439 brs.

**Laem Thong Bank Public Co Ltd:** Chokechai Bldg, 690 Thanon Sukhumvit, POB 131, Bangkok 10110; tel. (2) 260-0090; telex 82989; fax (2) 260-5310; f. 1948; cap. p.u. 500m., dep. 17,889m. (Dec. 1993); Chair. Gen. SOM KATAPAN; Man. Dir GURDIST CHANSRICHAWLA; 22 brs.

**Nakornthon Bank Public Co Ltd:** 90 Thanon Sathorn Nua, POB 2731, Bangkok 10501; tel. (2) 233-2111; telex 82837; fax (2) 236-4226; f. 1933 as Wang Lee Bank Ltd, renamed 1985; cap. p.u. 962m., dep. 33,035m. (Dec. 1993); Chair. SUNTHORN HONGLADAROM; Pres. VORAWEE WANGLEE; 49 brs.

**Siam City Bank Public Co Ltd:** POB 488, 1101 Thanon Petchburi Tadmai, Bangkok 10400; tel. (2) 253-0200; telex 72032; fax (2) 253-1240; f. 1941; cap. p.u. 6,010m., dep. 116,416m. (Sept. 1993); Chair. CHALERM CHEO-SAKUL; Pres. SOM JATUSIPITAK; 172 brs.

**Siam Commercial Bank Public Co Ltd:** 1060 Thanon Petchburi, POB 15, Bangkok 10400; tel. (2) 256-1234; telex 82376; fax (2) 253-6697; f. 1906; cap. p.u. 3,800m., dep. 250,655m. (Dec. 1992); Chair. PRACHITR YOSSUNDARA; Pres. and CEO Dr OLARN CHAIPRAVAT; 211 brs.

**Thai Danu Bank Public Co Ltd:** 393 Thanon Silom, Bangkok 10500; tel. (2) 230-5000; telex 82959; fax (2) 236-7939; f. 1949; cap. p.u. 700m., dep. 47,544m. (Dec. 1993); Chair. PAKORN THAVISIN; Pres. PORNSANONG TUCHINDA; 76 brs.

**Thai Farmers Bank Public Co Ltd:** 400 Thanon Phahon Yothin, POB 1366, Bangkok 10400; tel. (2) 273-1199; telex 81159; fax (2) 271-4033; f. 1945; cap. p.u. 8,000m.; dep. 405,967m. (Dec. 1993); Pres. BANTHOON LAMSAM; Chair. BANYONG LAMSAM; 430 brs.

**Thai Military Bank Public Co Ltd:** 3000 Thanon Phahon Yothin, Bangkok 10900; tel. (2) 299-1111; telex 82324; fax (2) 273-7121; f. 1957; cap. p.u. 4,277m., dep. 176,451m. (Dec. 1993); Chair. Gen. (retd) PRAYUDH CHARUMANI; Pres. Gen. THANONG BIDAYA; 246 brs.

**Union Bank of Bangkok Ltd:** 1600 Thanon Petchburi Tadmai, POB 2114, Bangkok 10310; tel. (2) 253-0488; telex 82550; fax (2) 253-7428; f. 1949; cap. p.u. 750m., dep. 31,152m. (Dec. 1993); Chair. Gen. BANJURD CHOLVIJARN; Pres. PIYABUTR CHOLVIJARN; 94 brs.

## Foreign Banks

**Bank of America NT and SA** (USA): 2/2 Thanon Witthayu, POB 158, Bangkok 10330; tel. (2) 251-6333; telex 87329; fax (2) 253-1905; f. 1949; cap. p.u. 750m., dep. 1,526m. (Aug. 1993); Country Man. JAMES F. MCCABE.

**Bank of America (Asia) Ltd:** (Hong Kong): CP Tower Bldg, 4th Floor, 313 Thanon Silom, Bangkok 10500; tel. (2) 231-0320; telex 82941; fax (2) 231-0346; name changed from Security Pacific Asian Bank Ltd in 1993; cap. p.u. 300m., dep. 319m. (Aug. 1993); Man. ROBERT R. DAVIS.

**Bank of Tokyo Ltd** (Japan): Thaniya Bldg, 62 Thanon Silom, Bangkok 10500; tel. (2) 236-0119; telex 83100; fax (2) 266-3055; cap. p.u. 2,000m., dep. 10,701m. (Dec. 1993); Man. TAKUO OI.

**Banque Indosuez** (France): Kian Gwan Bldg, 142 Thanon Witthayu, POB 303, Bangkok 10330; tel. (2) 253-0106; telex 81156; fax (2) 253-3193; cap. p.u. 800m., dep. 2,500m. (Aug. 1993); Man. CHAKTIP NITIBHON.

**Bharat Overseas Bank Ltd** (India): AI Tower, 181/19 Thanon Suriwongse, Bangkok 10500; tel. (2) 236-9366; telex 82390; fax (2) 236-9349; f. 1974; cap. p.u. 180m., dep. 804m. (Aug. 1993); Man. M. DHANALAKSHMI NARAYANON.

**Chase Manhattan Bank, NA** (USA): Siam Centre, 965 Rama 1 Rd, Bangkok 10500; tel. (2) 252-1141; telex 82601; cap. p.u. 615m., dep. 2,720m. (Aug. 1993); Sr Vice-Pres. KENNETH L. WHITE.

**Citibank, NA** (USA): Panjapon Bldg, 127 Thanon Sathorn Tai, Bangkok 10120; tel. (2) 213-2441; telex 81063; fax (2) 287-2406; dep. 8,868m. (Aug. 1993); Man. DAVID L. HENDRIX.

**Deutsche Bank AG** (Germany): POB 1237, Thai Wah Tower, 21 Thanon Sathorn Tai, Bangkok 10120; tel. (2) 285-0021; telex 87949; fax (2) 285-0425; cap. p.u. 892m., dep. 4,065m. (Aug. 1993); Man. GERHARD HEIGL.

**Four Seas Bank Ltd** (Singapore): 231 Thanon Rajawongse, Bangkok 10100; tel. (2) 226-3780; telex 82191; fax (2) 224-4820; cap. p.u. 300m., dep. 368m. (Aug. 1993); Man. NG TANG CHYE.

**Hongkong and Shanghai Banking Corpn** (Hong Kong): 64 Thanon Silom, Bangkok 10500; tel. (2) 233-1904; telex 82932; fax (2) 236-7687; cap. p.u. 7,000m., dep. 4,909m. (Aug. 1993); Man. A. FLOCKHART.

**International Commercial Bank of China** (Taiwan): 36/12 P. S. Tower Asoke, 21 Sukhumvit, Klongtoey, Bangkok 10110; tel. (2) 259-2000; telex 87369; fax (2) 225-2439; cap. p.u. 320m., dep. 609m. (Aug. 1993); Man. SHUE-SHENG WANG.

**The Sakura Bank Ltd** (Japan): Boon-Mitr Bldg, 138 Thanon Silom, Bangkok 10500; tel. (2) 234-3841; telex 82828; fax (2) 236-8920;

*Directory*

cap. p.u. 2,200m., dep. 5,052m. (Aug. 1993); Man. MITSUTOSHI KOYAMA.

**Standard Chartered Bank** (UK): 946 Thanon Phra Ram IV, Bangkok 10330; tel. (2) 234-0821; telex 81163; fax (2) 236-9422; dep. 4,752m. (Aug. 1993); Man. E. IRVIN KNOX.

**United Malayan Banking Corpn Bhd** (Malaysia): 149 Thanon Suapa, POB 2149, Bangkok 10100; tel. (2) 221-9524; telex 81172; fax (2) 225-4027; Man. LAU CHAI CHOU.

### Development Finance Organizations

**Bank for Agriculture and Agricultural Co-operatives (BAAC):** 469 Thanon Nakorn Sawan, Dusit, Bangkok 10300; tel. (2) 280-0180; telex 72221; f. 1966 to provide credit for agriculture; cap. 5,036m., dep. 35,485m. (March 1991); Chair. TARIN NIMMANAHAEMINDA; Pres. SUWAN TRIPOL.

**Board of Investment (BOI):** 555 Thanon Viphavadee Rangsit, Bangkhen, Bangkok 10900; tel. (2) 270-1400; telex 72435; fax (2) 537-8177; f. 1958 to publicize investment potential and encourage economically and socially beneficial investments; Chair. The Prime Minister; Sec.-Gen. STAPORN KAVITANON.

**Export-Import Bank (Exim):** Bangkok; f. 1993; provides low-cost financing for exporters; CEO PRIDIYATHORN DEVAKUL.

**Government Housing Bank:** 212 Thanon Phra Ram IX, Huay Kwang, Bangkok 10310; tel. (2) 246-0303; telex 84474; fax (2) 246-1789; f. 1953 to provide housing finance; cap. 2,261.3m., assets 39,848.7m., dep. 30,539.1m. (June 1991); Chair. CHATU MONGOL SONAKUL; Man. SIDHIJAI TANPHIPHAT; 12 brs.

**Government Savings Bank:** 470 Thanon Phahonyothin, Samsennai, Bangkok 10400; tel. (2) 279-0060; telex 84115; fax (2) 271-1515; f. 1913; cap. 4,284.46m., dep. 59,561.47m. (Feb. 1986); Chair. PANDIT BUNYAPANA; Dir-Gen. VIBUL AUNSNUNTA; 483 brs.

**Industrial Finance Corpn of Thailand (IFCT):** 1770 Thanon Petchburi Tadmai, Bangkok 10310; tel. (2) 253-7111; telex 82163; fax (2) 253-9677; f. 1959 to assist in the establishment, expansion or modernization of industrial enterprises in the private sector; organizes pooling of funds and capital market development; makes medium- and long-term loans, complementary working capital loans, investment advisory services, underwriting shares and securities and guaranteeing loans; cap. p.u. 2,365.6m.; loans granted: 44,255.2m. on 3,024 projects (Dec. 1990); Chair. CHAVALIT THANACHANAN; Pres. ASWIN KONGSIRI.

**Small Industries Finance Office (SIFO):** 24 Mansion 5, Thanon Ratchadamnoen, Bangkok 10200; tel. (2) 224-1919; f. 1964 to provide finance for small-scale industries; cap. 154m. (1988); Chair. PISAL KONGSAMRAN; Man. VICHIEN OPASWATTANA.

### Bankers' Association

**Thai Bankers' Association:** Bangkok Insurance Bldg, 302 Thanon Silom, Bangkok 10500; tel. (2) 234-1140; Chair. BANYONG LAMSAM.

## STOCK EXCHANGE

**Stock Exchange of Thailand (SET):** Sinthon Bldg, 2nd Floor, 132 Thanon Witthayu, Bangkok 10330; tel. (2) 254-0960; fax (2) 254-3069; f. 1975; 44 mems; Pres. SERI CHINTANASERI; Chair. Prof. SANGVIAN INDARAVIJAYA.

**Securities and Exchange Commission:** Bangkok; f. 1992; supervises new share issues and trading in existing shares; Chair. Minister of Finance; Sec.-Gen. EKKAMOL KIRIWAT.

## INSURANCE

In 1991 there were 70 domestic insurance companies operating in Thailand (7 life, 52 non-life, 4 life and non-life, 6 health and 1 reinsurance). There were also 5 foreign companies (1 life, 4 non-life).

### Selected Domestic Insurance Companies

**Ayudhya Insurance Public Co Ltd:** Ploenchit Tower, 7th Floor, Thanon Ploenchit, Pathumwan, Bangkok 10330; tel. (2) 263-0335; fax (2) 263-0589; Chair. KRIT RATANARAK.

**Bangkok Insurance Public Co Ltd:** The Bangkok Insurance Bldg, 302 Thanon Silom, Bangkok 10500; tel. (2) 234-1155; telex 72230; fax (2) 236-6541; f. 1947; non-life; Chair. and Man. Dir CHAI SOPHONPANICH.

**Bangkok Union Insurance Public Co Ltd:** 175–177 Thanon Surawongse, Bangkok 10500; tel. (2) 233-6920; telex 82131; fax (2) 237-1856; f. 1929; non-life; Chair. PRACHAI LEOPHAIRATANA; Man. Dir MALINEE LEOPHAIRAT.

**China Insurance Co (Siam) Ltd:** 95 Thanon Suapa, Bangkok 10100; tel. (2) 221-4206; f. 1948; non-life; Chair. JAMES C. CHENG; Man. Dir FANG RONG-CHENG.

**INTERLIFE Co Ltd:** 364/29 Thanon Sri-Ayudhya, Samsen Nai District, Bangkok 10400; tel. (2) 245-2491; f. 1951; life; Chair. MANOCH KANCHANACHAYA; Acting Exec. Dir CHAISIT CHAIPHIBALSARISDI.

THAILAND — Directory

**International Assurance Co Ltd:** 488/7–9 Thanon Henri Dunant, Bangkok 10500; tel. (2) 251-8714; f. 1952; non-life, fire, marine, general; Chair. PICHAI KULAVANICH; Man. Dir SOMCHAI MAHASANTIPIYA.

**Ocean Insurance Co Ltd:** 163 Thanon Surawongse, Bangrak, Bangkok 10500; tel. (2) 234-8000; telex 72153; fax (2) 238-4157; f. 1949; life and non-life; Chair. KIRATI ASSAKUL; Man. Dir CHINNAWAT BULSUK.

**Paiboon Insurance Co Ltd:** Thanasap Bldg, 4th–5th Floors, 68/1 Thanon Silom, POB 1111, Bangkok 10500; tel. (2) 233-8960; telex 82353; f. 1927; non-life; Chair. ANUTHRA ASSAWANONDA; Pres. VANICH CHAIYAWAN.

**Siam Commercial Life Assurance Co Ltd:** 121 Thanon Viphavadee Rangsit, Phayatai, Bangkok 10400; tel. (2) 248-0850; fax (2) 248-0864; life; Chair. NARONG MAHANOND.

**South-East Insurance Co Ltd** (Arkanay Prakan Pai Co Ltd): South-East Insurance Bldg, 315 Thanon Silom, POB 2607, Bangkok 10500; tel. (2) 233-7080; telex 82343; f. 1946; life and non-life; Chair. PAYAP SRIKARNCHANA; Man. Dir ATHORN TITTIRANONDA.

**Syn Mun Kong Insurance Public Co Ltd:** 12/7–9 Thanon Plabplachai, Bangkok 10500; tel. (2) 223-2889; f. 1951; fire, automobile and personal accident; Chair. SUPASIT MAHAKUN; Man. Dir THANAVIT DUSADEESURAPOTE.

**Thai Commercial Insurance Public Co Ltd:** Sathorn Thani Bldg, 11th Floor, 90/27 Thanon Sathorn Nua, Bangrak, Bangkok 10500; tel. (2) 234-2345; fax (2) 236-5990; f. 1940; automobile, fire, marine and casualty; Chair. PHIPHAT POSHYANONDA; Man. Dir SURAJIT WANGLEE.

**Thai Health Insurance Co Ltd:** 123 Thanon Ratchadaphisek, Bangkok 10310; tel. (2) 246-9680; telex 82353; fax (2) 246-9806; f. 1979; Chair. APIRAK THAIPATANAKUL; Dir and Gen. Man. PRANEET VIRAKUL.

**Thai Insurance Public Co Ltd:** Lumpini Tower Bldg, 19th Floor, 1168/50-51 Thanon Phra Ram IV, Sathorn, Bangkok 10120; tel. (2) 679-7275; fax (2) 285-6300; f. 1938; non-life; Chair. PAKORN THAVISIN.

**Thai Life Insurance Co Ltd:** 123 Thanon Ratchadaphisek, Din-Daeng, Bangkok 10310; tel. (2) 247-0247; fax (2) 246-9946; f. 1942; life; Chair. VANICH CHAIYAWAN; Man. Dir APIRAK THAIPATANAGUL.

**Thai Prasit Insurance Co Ltd:** 295 Thanon Siphaya, Bangrak, Bangkok 10500; tel. (2) 235-3975; f. 1947; life, fire, marine, automobile and general; Chair. SURACHAN CHANSRICHAWLA; Man. Dir SUKHATHEP CHANSRICHAWLA.

**Thai Sethakit Life Assurance Public Co Ltd:** Sathorn Thani Bldg, 16th Floor, 90/42-43 Thanon Sathorn Nua, Bangkok 10500; tel. (2) 237-1175; fax (2) 236-7200; Chair. Prof. BUNCHANA ATTHAKOR; Chief Exec. KITTIPONG JINTAVARALUK.

**Wilson Insurance Co Ltd:** Bangkok Bank, Ratchawong Branch Bldg, 5th Floor, 245–249 Thanon Ratchawong, Bangkok 10100; tel. (2) 224-6405; fax (2) 225-1816; f. 1951; fire, marine, motor car, general; Chair. CHOTE SOPHONPANICH; Man. Dir VAJIRA HIRANSOMBOON.

### Associations

**General Insurance Association:** 223 Soi Ruamrudee, Thanon Witthayu, Bangkok 10330; tel. (2) 256-6032; fax (2) 256-6039; Man. BOONSERM PROMPIBALCHEEP.

**Thai Life Assurance Association:** 36/1 Soi Sapanku, Thanon Phra Ram IV, Bangkok 10120; tel. (2) 287-4596; fax (2) 679-7100; Pres. SOONTORN BOONSAI.

## Trade and Industry

### CHAMBER OF COMMERCE

**Thai Chamber of Commerce:** 150 Thanon Rajbopit, Bangkok 10200; tel. (2) 225-0086; fax (2) 225-3372; f. 1946; 2,000 mems, 10 assoc. mems (1993); Pres. PHOTIPONG LAMSAM.

### GOVERNMENT ORGANIZATIONS

**Central Sugar Marketing Centre:** Bangkok; f. 1981; responsible for domestic marketing and price stabilization.

**Communication Authority of Thailand:** Bangkok; responsible for the installation of new telephone lines and development of telecommunications; partial transfer to the private sector pending in 1995.

**Electricity Generating Authority of Thailand:** Bangkok; tel. (2) 423-0580; telex 72323; cap. 123,000m. baht (1989); established a subsidiary, the Electricity Generating Co (Egco), of which the Government began to transfer up to 50% to the private sector in 1994.

**Forest Industry Organization:** 76 Thanon Ratchadamnoen Nok, Bangkok 10200; tel. (2) 282-3243; fax (2) 282-5197; f. 1947; oversees all aspects of forestry and wood industries; Man. Col M. R. ADULDEJ CHAKRABANDHU.

**Metropolitan Waterworks Authority:** Bangkok; tel. (2) 574-0806; telex 85384; fax (2) 574-0840.

**National Economic and Social Development Board:** 962 Thanon Krung Kasem, Bangkok 10100; tel. (2) 282-1151; fax (2) 280-4085; economic planning agency; Sec.-Gen. PHISIT PAKKASEM.

**Office of the Cane and Sugar Board:** Ministry of Industry, Thanon Phra Ram VI, Ratchathewi, Bangkok 10400; tel. (2) 248-2147; fax (2) 246-0740.

**Petroleum Authority of Thailand (PTT):** 555 Thanon Vibhavadi Rangsit, Bangkok 10900; tel. (2) 537-2000; telex 87940; fax (2) 537-3498; f. 1978 through merger of the National Gas Organization of Thailand (NGOT) and the Oil Fuel Organization; activities relate to the development, exploitation, production and distribution of petroleum and gas; Chair. SIVAVONG CHANGKASIRI (acting); Gov. LUEN KRISNAKRI.

**Provincial Waterworks Authority:** 12 Thanon Chaengwattana, Laksi Donmuang, Bangkok 10210; tel. (2) 551-1020; telex 72080; fax (2) 552-1547; f. 1979; provides water supply systems except in Bangkok Metropolis; Gov. LERT CHAINARONG; Dep. Gov. WANCHAI CHOOPRASERT.

**Rubber Estate Organization:** Nabon Station, Nakhon Si Thammarat Province 80220; tel. (75) 411554; Man. Dir SUCHON DECHATIWONG NA-AYUDHYA.

**Telephone Organization of Thailand (TOT):** 89 Mooh 3, Thanon Chaengwattana, Donmuang, Bangkok 10210; tel. (2) 505-1112; partial transfer to the private sector pending in 1995; Man. Dir JUMPON HERABAT.

**Thai Oil:** Bangkok; petroleum-refining; sales US $1,594.2m. (1993); 1,018 employees.

**Thailand Tobacco Monopoly:** Ministry of Finance, Thanon Phra Ram IV, Bangkok 10400; telex 72438; fax (2) 255-4220.

### INDUSTRIAL AND TRADE ASSOCIATIONS

**Bangkok Rice Millers' Association:** 14/3 Thanon Sathorn Tai, Bangkok 10120; tel. (2) 286-8298.

**Board of Trade of Thailand:** 150 Thanon Rajbopit, Bangkok 10200; tel. (2) 221-0555; telex 84309; fax (2) 225-3995; f. 1955; mems: chambers of commerce, trade asscns, state enterprises and co-operative societies (large and medium-sized companies have associate membership); Chair. PHOTIPONG LAMSAM.

**The Federation of Thai Industries:** 394/14 Thanon Samsen, Tambol Wachira, Amphur Dusit, Bangkok 10300; tel. (2) 280-0951; telex 72202; fax (2) 280-0959; f. 1987, fmrly The Association of Thai Industries; 3,200 mems; Chair. Dr CHOKCHAI AKSARANAN.

**Mining Industry Council of Thailand:** 222/2 Soi, Thai Chamber of Commerce University, Thanon Vibhavadi Rangsit, Dindaeng, Huay Kwang, Bangkok 10400; tel. (2) 275-7684; fax (2) 275-7686; f. 1983; intermediary between govt organizations and private mining enterprises; Pres. DARMP TEWTHONG; Sec.-Gen. PUNYA ADULYAPICHIT.

**Rice Exporters' Association of Thailand:** 37 Soi Ngamdupli, Thanon Phra Ram IV, Bangkok 10120; tel. (2) 287-2674; fax (2) 287-2678; Chair. SMARN OPHASWONGSE.

**Rice Mill Association of Thailand:** 81–81/1 Thanon Yotha, Talat Noi, Bangkok 10100; tel. (2) 235-7863; Pres. NIPHON WONGTRAGARN.

**Sawmills Association:** 101 Thanon Amnuaysongkhram, Dusit, Bangkok 10300; tel. (2) 2434754; Pres. VITOON PONGPASIT.

**Thai Food Processors' Association:** 888/114 Mahatun Plaza Bldg, 11th Floor, Thanon Ploenchit, Bangkok 10330; tel. (2) 253-6791; fax (2) 255-1479.

**Thai Jute Association:** 1 Sivadol Bldg, 10th Floor, Rm 10, Thanon Convent, Silom, Bangrak, Bangkok 10500; tel. (2) 234-1438; fax (2) 234-1439.

**Thai Lac Association:** 66 Chalermkhetr 1, Bangkok 10100; tel. (2) 233-8331.

**Thai Maize and Produce Traders' Association:** 92/26–27 Sathorntane Bldg, Bangrak, Bangkok 10500; tel. (2) 236-8413; fax (2) 236-8413.

**Thai Pharmaceutical Manufacturers Association:** 1759/30 Soi Udomsub, Thanon Pinklao-Nakornchaisri, Bangkok 10700; tel. (2) 424-8588; telex 87278; fax (2) 433-6547; f. 1969; Pres. JARUROJNA DANKIETKONG.

**Thai Rubber Traders' Association:** 57 Thanon Rongmuang 5, Pathumwan, Bangkok 10500; tel. (2) 214-3420; Pres. SANG UDOMJARUMANCE.

**Thai Silk Association:** c/o Dept of Industrial Promotion, Thanon Phra Ram IV, Bangkok 10110; tel. (2) 390-0684.

**Thai Sugar Producers' Association:** Thai Ruam Toon Bldg, 794 Thanon Krung Kasem, Pomprap, Bangkok 10100; tel. (2) 282-2022; telex 82718; fax (2) 281-0342.

**Thai Sugar Manufacturing Association:** Kiatnakin Bldg, 4th Floor, 78 Captain Bush Lane, New Rd, Bangkok 10500; tel. (2) 233-4156; fax (2) 236-8438.

# THAILAND

**Thai Tapioca Trade Association:** Sathorn Thani Bldg, 20th Floor, 92/58 Thanon Sathorn Nua, Bangrak, Bangkok 10500; tel. (2) 234-4724; telex 20522; fax (2) 236-6084; Pres. SURASAK PICHETPONGSA.

**Thai Textile Manufacturing Association:** 454–460 Thanon Sukhumvit, Bangkok 101100; tel. (2) 258-2044; fax (2) 260-1525.

**Thai Timber Exporters' Association:** Ratchada Trade Centre, 4th Floor, 410/73-76 Thanon Ratchadaphisek, Bangkok 10310; tel. (2) 278-3229; fax (2) 259-0481.

**Timber Merchants' Association:** 4 Thanon Yen-Arkad, Thung-Mahamek, Yannawa, Bangkok 10120; tel. (2) 249-5565.

**Union Textile Merchants' Association:** 160 Sethi Bldg, 3rd Floor, Samphanthawong, Bangkok 10100; tel. (2) 222-3559; fax (2) 225-4454.

## CO-OPERATIVES

In 1992 there were 4m. members of co-operatives, including 1.6m. in agriculture.

## TRADE UNIONS

Under the Labour Relations Act (1975), a minimum of 10 employees are required in order to form a union; by the end of 1990 there were an estimated 642 such unions.

**Confederation of Thai Labour (CTL):** 25/20 Sukhumvit Rd, Viphavill Village, Tambol Paknam, Amphur Muang, Samutprakarn, Bangkok 10270; tel. (2) 756-5346; fax (2) 323-1074; represents 34 labour unions; Pres. AMPORN BANDASAK.

**Labour Congress of Thailand (LCT):** 420/393-394 Thippavan Village 1, Thanon Teparak, Amphur Muang, Samutprakarn, Bangkok 10270; tel. (2) 394-5385; f. 1978; represents 77 labour unions; Pres. SUVIT HATHONG.

**National Congress of Private Employees of Thailand (NPET):** 124/731 Revadee 1 Village, Tambol Talakwan, Amphur Muang, Nonthaburi, Bangkok 11000; tel. and fax (2) 588-4373; represents 3 labour unions: Pres. BANJONG PORNPATTANANIKOM.

**National Congress of Thai Labour (NCTL):** 364 Mu 1 Uar, Patthananivet Village, Thanon Sri Nakharin, Tambol Bangkaew, Amphur Bangpli, Samutprakarn, Bangkok 10540; tel. (2) 389-5134; fax (2) 385-5220; represents 171 unions; Pres. PANAS THAILUAN.

**National Free Labour Union Congress (NFLUC):** 277 Mu 3, Thanon Ratburana, Bangkok 10140; tel. (2) 427-6506; fax (2) 428-4543; represents 41 unions; Pres. ANUSSAKDI BOONYAPRANAI.

**National Labour Congress (NLC):** 539 Mu 3, Soi Ruampattana, Thanon Sukhumvit, Tambol Taiban, Amphur Muang, Samutprakarn, Bangkok 10270; tel. (2) 395-3055; fax (2) 702-1399; represents 39 labour unions; Pres. CHIN THAPPHLI.

**Thai Trade Union Congress (TTUC):** 420/393-394 Thippavan Village 1, Thanon Teparak, Tambol Samrong-nua, Amphur Muang, Samutprakarn, Bangkok 10270; tel. (2) 384-0438; fax (2) 384-0438; f. 1982; represents 172 unions; Pres. PANIT CHAROENPHAO.

**Thailand Council of Industrial Labour (TCIL):** 99 Mu 4, Thanon Sukhaphibarn 2, Khannayao, Bungkum, Bangkok; tel. (2) 517-0022; fax (2) 517-0628; represents 23 labour unions; Pres. SAMARN SRITHONG.

# Transport

**Metropolitan Rapid Transit Authority of Thailand:** Thanon Phaholyothin, Lad Yao, Bangkhen, Bangkok 10900; tel. (2) 579-5380; telex 72346; fax (2) 580-5984; responsible for the 60-km Mass Rapid Transit System in Bangkok comprising both road and rail links, work on which began in early 1995 and was due to be completed in 2001; Gov. SUKAVICH RANGSITPOL.

## RAILWAYS

Thailand has a railway network of 4,623 km, connecting Bangkok with Chiang Mai, Nong Khai, Ubon Ratchathani, Nam Tok and towns on the isthmus. In 1995 Thailand and Laos agreed to build a 30-km line linking Nong Khai province in Thailand with the Laotion capital of Vientiane.

**State Railway of Thailand:** Thanon Rong Muang, Pathumwan, Bangkok 10330; tel. (2) 220-4260; telex 72242; fax (2) 225-3801; f. 1897; 4,623 km of track in 1993; Chair. Dr PHISIT PAKKASEM; Gen. Man. SOMMAI TAMTHAI.

**Bangkok Transit System Corpn Ltd:** Alma Link Bldg, 9th Floor, 25 Soi Chidlom, Thanon Ploenchit, Lumpini, Bangkok 10330; fax (2) 255-8651; Pres. ANAT ARBHABHIRAMA.

## ROADS

The total length of the road network was 52,339 km in 1991, of which 171 km were motorways, 19,793 km were main roads and 32,546 km were secondary roads. The network expanded to 54,338 km in 1992, 89.7% of which was paved and to 59,903 km in 1993.

**Bangkok Mass Transit Authority (BMTA):** 131 Thanon Thiam Ruammit, Huai Khwang, Bangkok 10310; tel. (2) 251-6503; controls Bangkok's urban transport system; Chair. SAWARNG SRINILTA; Dir ANOTHAI UTENSUTE.

**Department of Highways:** Thanon Sri Ayudhaya, Bangkok 10400; tel. (2) 246-1122; Dir-Gen. SANAN SRIROONGROT.

**Department of Land Transport:** Thanon Phaholyothin, Bangkok 10900; tel. (2) 271-0120; Dir-Gen. SRIPORN KOMMAI.

**Express Transportation Organization of Thailand (ETO):** 485/1 Thanon Sri Ayudhaya, Bangkok 10400; tel. (2) 245-3231; telex 72053; f. 1947; Pres. AMARIT PANSIRI; Vice-Pres. NOPHARAT NERAMITMANSOOK.

## SHIPPING

There is an extensive network of canals, providing transport for bulk goods. The port of Bangkok is an important shipping junction for South-East Asia. A general cargo wharf was opened at Laem Chabang, 105 km south-east of Bangkok, in early 1991. Two further container wharves opened at the end of 1991.

**Harbour Department:** 1278 Thanon Yotha, Bangkok 10100; tel. (2) 223-1131; fax (2) 236-7248; Dir-Gen. SATHIEN VONGVICHIEN.

**Office of the Maritime Promotion Commission:** 19 Thanon Phra Atit, Bangkok 10200; tel. (2) 281-9367; f. 1979; Sec.-Gen. SACHEE SIRISON.

**Port Authority of Thailand:** 444 Thanon Tarua, Klongtoey, Bangkok 10110; tel. (2) 249-0399; telex 72311; fax (2) 249-0885; 37 berths at Bangkok Port, eight berths at Laem Chabang Port; Chair. Adm. PRACHET SIRIDEJ; Dir-Gen. ANUPARB SUNNANTA.

### Principal Shipping Companies

**CP Co Ltd:** Silom Bldg, 2nd Floor, 197/1 Thanon Silom, Bangkok 10500; tel. (2) 235-0240; telex 87345; services to Singapore; Chair. Rear-Adm. CHANO PHENJATI; Man. Dir PRAWAT HUTASINGH.

**Jutha Maritime Public Co Ltd:** Mano Tower 2nd Floor, 153 Soi 39, Thanon Sukhumvit, Bangkok 10110; tel. (2) 260-0050; telex 87366; fax (2) 259-9825; services between Thailand, Malaysia, Korea, Japan and Viet Nam; Chair. Rear-Adm. CHANO PHENJATI; Pres. CHANET PHENJATI.

**Siam United Services Public Co Ltd:** 30 Thanon Ratburana, Bangprakok, Ratburana, Bangkok 10140; tel. (2) 428-0029; telex 72110; fax (2) 427-6270; f. 1977; Chair. MONGKHOL SIMAROJ; Man. Dir CHAITAWAT SARAKUN.

**T. J. T. Services Co Ltd:** 501 Thavit Bldg, 61 Thanon Kasemras, Bangkok; tel. (2) 249-7264; telex 87218; Dir TAWATCHAI TANGJATROUNG.

**Thai International Maritime Enterprises Ltd:** Sarasin Bldg, 5th Floor, 14 Thanon Surasak, Bangkok 10500; tel. (2) 236-8835; telex 81176; services from Bangkok to Japan; Chair. and Man. Dir SUN SUNDISAMRIT.

**Thai Maritime Navigation Co Ltd:** Manorom Bldg, 15th Floor, 51 Thanon Phra Ram IV, Bangkok 10110; tel. (2) 249-0100; telex 87328; fax (2) 249-0108; services from Bangkok to Japan, the USA, Europe and ASEAN countries; Chair. Adm. HAN SAKULPANICH; Dir-Gen. ANUSAK INTHRAPHUVASAK.

**Thai Mercantile Marine Ltd:** Charn Issara Tower, 10th Floor, 942/144 Thanon Phra Ram IV, Bangkok 10500; tel. (2) 233-0926; telex 82924; fax (2) 236-7674; f. 1967; services between Japan and Thailand; Man. Dir SUTHIM TANPHAIBUL.

**Thai Overseas Line Ltd:** Sinthon Bldg, 7th Floor, 132 Thanon Witthayu, Bangkok 10500; tel. (2) 250-1460; telex 81161.

**Thai Petroleum Transports Co Ltd:** 355 Thanon Sunthornkosa, POB 2172, Klong Toey, Bangkok 10110; tel. (2) 249-0255; Chair. C. CHOWKWANYUN; Man. Capt. B. HAM.

**Unithai Line Public Co Ltd:** 25 Alma Link Bldg, 11th Floor, Soi Chidlom, Pathumwan, Bangkok 10330; tel. (2) 254-8400; telex 87984; fax (2) 255-1155; regular containerized/break-bulk services to Europe, Africa and Far East; also bulk shipping/chartering; Chair. M. L. JOENGJAN KAMBHU; Man. Dir KHONG CHAI SENG.

## CIVIL AVIATION

Bangkok, Chiang Mai, Hat Yai, Phuket and Surat Thani airports are of international standard. U-Tapao is an alternative airport. The airport at Chiang Rai was upgraded to international status in April 1992. In May 1991 plans were approved to build a new airport at Nong Ngu Hao, south-east of Bangkok, at an estimated cost of US $1,200m.

**Airports Authority of Thailand:** Bangkok International Airport, Thanon Vibhavadi Rangsit, Bangkok 10210; tel. (2) 535-1111; telex

## THAILAND

87424; fax (2) 531-5559; f. 1979; Man. Dir Air Marshal TAWORN KERDSIN.

**Department of Aviation:** 71 Soi Ngarmduplee, Thanon Phra Ram IV, Bangkok 10120; tel. (2) 287-0320; telex 72099; fax (2) 287-3139; f. 1963; Dir-Gen. ROUNGROJ SRIPRASERTSUK.

**Thai Airways International Public Co Ltd (THAI):** 89 Thanon Vibhavadi Rangsit, Bangkok 10900; tel. (2) 513-0121; telex 82890; fax (2) 513-5532; f. 1960; 93% govt-owned; shares listed in July 1991, began trading in July 1992; merged with Thai Airways Co in 1988; domestic services from Bangkok to 22 cities; international services to 51 destinations in 35 countries in Australasia, Europe, North America and Asia; Chair. AMARET SILA-ON; Pres. THAMNOON WANGLEE.

## Tourism

Thailand is a popular tourist destination, noted for its temples, palaces, pagodas and islands. In 1993 tourist arrivals increased to 5.8m. and receipts totalled 127,802m. baht.

**Tourism Authority of Thailand (TAT):** Head Office: 372 Thanon Bamrung Muang, Bangkok 10100; tel. (2) 226-0060; fax (2) 226-6227; f. 1960; Chair. SAVIT BHOTIVIHOK; Gov. SEREE WANGPAICHITR.

**Tourist Association of Northern Thailand:** Old Chiang Mai Cultural Centre, 185/3 Thanon Wualai, Chiang Mai 50000; tel. (53) 235097; Pres. Prof. PHOON-PHON ASANACHINTA.

# TOGO

## Introductory Survey

**Location, Climate, Language, Religion, Flag, Capital**

The Togolese Republic lies in West Africa, forming a narrow strip stretching north from a coastline of about 50 km (30 miles) on the Gulf of Guinea. It is bordered by Ghana to the west, by Benin to the east, and by Burkina Faso to the north. The climate in the coastal area is hot and humid, with an average annual temperature of 27°C (81°F), rainfall in this zone averages 875 mm (34.4 ins) per year, and is heaviest during May–October. Precipitation in the central region is heaviest in May–June and in October, and in the north, where the average annual temperature is 30°C (86°F), there is a rainy season from July–September. The official languages are French, Kabiye and Ewe. About one-half of the population follows animist beliefs, while about 35% are Christians and 15% Muslims. The national flag (approximate proportions 5 by 3) has five equal horizontal stripes, alternately green and yellow, with a square red canton, containing a five-pointed white star, in the upper hoist. The capital is Lomé.

**Recent History**

Togoland, of which modern Togo was formerly a part, became a German colony in 1894. Shortly after the outbreak of the First World War, the colony was occupied by French and British forces, who overthrew the German administration. After the war, Togoland was divided into zones of occupation, with France controlling the larger eastern section while the United Kingdom governed the west. French and British Togoland were each administered under a League of Nations mandate. The partition of Togoland split the homeland of the Ewe people, who inhabit the southern part of the territory, and this has been a continuing source of friction. After the Second World War, French and British Togoland became UN Trust Territories.

In May 1956 a UN-supervised plebiscite in British Togoland produced, despite Ewe opposition, majority support for a merger with the neighbouring territory of the Gold Coast, then a British colony, in an independent state. The region accordingly became part of Ghana (q.v.) in the following year. In October 1956, in another plebiscite, French Togoland voted to become an autonomous republic within the French Community. The new Togolese Republic had internal self-government until becoming fully independent on 27 April 1960.

Prior to independence Togo's foremost political parties were the Comité de l'unité togolaise (usually known as the Unité togolaise—UT), led by Sylvanus Olympio, and the Parti togolais du progrès (PTP), led by Nicolas Grunitzky, Olympio's brother-in-law. In 1956 Grunitzky became Prime Minister in the first autonomous Government, but in April 1958 a UN-supervised election was won by the UT. This brought to power Olympio, a campaigner for Ewe reunification, who became Prime Minister and led Togo to independence.

At elections in April 1961 Olympio became Togo's first President, elected (unopposed) for a seven-year term, while his UT party won all 51 seats in the Assemblée nationale after opposition candidates were disallowed. At the same time, a referendum approved a new Constitution. On 13 January 1963 the UT regime, which had become increasingly authoritarian, was overthrown by a military revolt, in which President Olympio was killed. At the request of the insurgents, Grunitzky returned from a period in exile and assumed the presidency on a provisional basis. A referendum in May 1963 approved another Constitution, confirmed Grunitzky as President (for a five-year term) and elected a new legislature from a single list of candidates, giving equal representation to the four main political parties, including Grunitzky's Union démocratique des peuples togolaises, which had replaced the PTP, and the UT. However, the new regime encountered opposition from UT supporters, who staged an unsuccessful coup attempt in November 1966.

Following a rift with the armed forces, President Grunitzky was deposed by a bloodless military coup on 13 January 1967, the fourth anniversary of Olympio's death. The Constitution was abrogated, and the Assemblée nationale was dissolved. The coup was led by Lt-Col (later Gen.) Etienne Gnassingbe Eyadéma, the Army Chief of Staff, who assumed the office of President in April. Political parties were banned, and the President ruled by decree. Eyadéma, a northerner and a member of the Kabiye ethnic group, had taken a prominent part in the 1963 rising and was reputedly Olympio's assassin. In November 1969 a new ruling party, the Rassemblement du peuple togolais (RPT), was founded, with Gen. Eyadéma as its President. In August 1970 a plot to overthrow Eyadéma was foiled, and several supporters of the late President Olympio were arrested.

A referendum, held in January 1972, produced a massive vote of support for Eyadéma. The President repeatedly announced his intention to return Togo to civilian rule, despite continuing public support for the army. At the RPT congress in November 1976 it was decided that the party's Political Bureau should take precedence over the Government. Comprehensive government changes in January 1977 left Eyadéma as the sole representative of the armed forces in the Council of Ministers.

In October 1977 a further coup plot was allegedly instigated by exiled supporters of the late President Olympio. A period of political tension followed, and in August 1979 a court in Lomé sentenced 10 men to death, eight of them *in absentia*. The sentences were subsequently repealed by Eyadéma.

In Togo's first elections for 16 years, held on 30 December 1979, Eyadéma (the sole candidate) was confirmed as President of the Republic for a seven-year term. At the same time a new Constitution (the first for more than 12 years) was overwhelmingly endorsed, while the list of 67 candidates for a single-party Assemblée nationale was approved by 96% of the votes cast. On 13 January 1980, the 13th anniversary of his accession to power, Eyadéma proclaimed the 'Third Republic'.

Eyadéma attempted to 'democratize' the electoral process by allowing a choice of RPT candidates to be presented at the legislative elections in March 1985, in which 77 seats were contested by 216 candidates. The RPT remained the only legal political party, but in May 1985 the Constitution was amended to allow deputies to the legislature to be elected by direct universal suffrage without first being proposed by the party.

During 1985 internal security was increased and arrests were made, following a series of bombings in Lomé and elsewhere (including attacks on government buildings and the RPT headquarters). The death in detention of one of those arrested prompted allegations of torture of political prisoners from international human rights organizations; the allegations were confirmed by French jurists who visited Togo in mid-1986. In July of that year nine people were arrested following the alleged discovery of a Libyan-backed 'international terrorist plot' in Lomé. Relations with neighbouring West African states were damaged following an abortive 'terrorist attack' on President Eyadéma's residence, the RPT headquarters and the national radio station in September of that year, during which 13 people died and 19 arrests were made. Accusations of support in the coup attempt (which were immediately denied) were levelled at the Governments of Ghana and Burkina Faso, and Togo's borders with Ghana were effectively closed until May 1987. Immediately following the attack, French troops were briefly deployed in Togo (in accordance with an unpublished 1963 defence pact between the two countries). Zairean troops also intervened in support of Eyadéma.

In December 1986 President Eyadéma was re-elected for a further seven-year term, reportedly obtaining 99.95% of the votes cast. In the same month 13 people were sentenced to death for complicity in the September coup attempt (the exiled opposition leader, Gilchrist Olympio, son of the former President, was sentenced *in absentia*). In October 1987 an official human rights commission, the Commission nationale des droits de l'homme (CNDH), was established, and it was announced that most of the death sentences imposed the previous December had been commuted.

In December 1989 two Togolese dissidents (who were allegedly members of an opposition movement, the Convention démocratique des peuples africains du Togo) were expelled from Côte d'Ivoire, after having reportedly been found in possession of tracts hostile to the Eyadéma Government. In late August 1990 13 people were arrested in Togo, on suspicion of a similar offence; 11 were later released, while two others, Logo Dossouvi and Doglo Agbelenko, remained in detention. An official inquiry was subsequently ordered to investigate allegations of the torture of the 13 detainees: the CNDH ruled that four of the detainees, including Dossouvi and Agbelenko, had been tortured while in custody. In early October Dossouvi and Agbelenko were each sentenced to five years' imprisonment. Violent demonstrations erupted in Lomé after supporters of the defendants were expelled from the trial. Protesters, who were demanding the release of Dossouvi and Agbelenko together with radical political reforms, attacked official property, and security forces were deployed in an attempt to restore calm: it was reported that four people were killed and more than 30 injured, while about 170 people (many of whom were foreigners) were arrested. Lawyers staged a 72-hour strike, in protest against the actions of the security forces, and prominent members of the legal profession denounced official allegations of an international plot to destabilize the Eyadéma administration. A presidential pardon that was announced in mid-October for Dossouvi and Agbelenko was followed by similar clemency measures for all those who had been detained during the unrest that had followed the trial.

Elections to the Assemblée nationale were held in March 1990, at which 230 candidates, all of whom declared their allegiance to the RPT, contested the legislature's 77 seats. In May a national council of the RPT considered the findings of five regional commissions that had been appointed in February to discuss the reform of the ruling party. Delegates unanimously rejected the possibility of the restitution of a multi-party system. However, greater freedom of expression, both nationally and within the RPT, was urged, and it was decided that proposals made by Eyadéma for the separation of the functions of the RPT and the State would be examined at a later date. In late July, during an official visit to the USA, Eyadéma indicated that Togo's political system would be reviewed at a congress of the RPT that was scheduled for December 1991.

In late October 1990 a commission was established to draft a new constitution, which would be submitted for approval in a national referendum in December 1991. Eyadéma instructed the commission to prepare a text that would permit an eventual transition to a multi-party political system. In the mean time, however, the Government reiterated its ban on political parties, at a time when several unofficial opposition movements were being formed. In late December the constitutional commission presented a draft document, which provided for the existence of a Prime Minister and of a Constitutional Council that would have jurisdiction over the constitutionality of legislation and guarantee an equitable separation of the powers of the organs of state; the existence of a plurality of political parties was also envisaged. In January 1991 Eyadéma announced an amnesty for all those (including exiles residing abroad) who had been implicated in political offences.

A boycott of classes by university students and secondary school pupils, in the first half of March 1991, provoked violent demonstrations that were ultimately to lead to the instigation of radical political reforms. Clashes between striking students and supporters of Eyadéma were dispersed by the security forces. The subsequent arrest of many young people prompted further protests (in defiance of an official ban on demonstrations): two protesters were reported to have been killed, following intervention by the security forces. Meanwhile, several opposition movements formed a co-ordinating organization, the Front des associations pour le renouveau (FAR), to campaign for the immediate introduction of a multi-party political system. Following a meeting between Eyadéma and the leader of the FAR, Maître Yao Agboyibo, an agreement was reached whereby Eyadéma consented to a general amnesty for all political dissidents (opposition movements asserted that the clemency measures that had been announced in January had not been implemented); moreover, political organizations would be legalized, and discussions would take place concerning the country's political evolution. In early April the trade union federation, the Confédération nationale des travailleurs du Togo (CNTT) announced its independence from the RPT.

In early April 1991 pupils of Catholic mission schools staged a demonstration in support of their teachers' demands for increases in remuneration. The protests were joined by other students, and two people were killed following intervention by the security forces. Two further deaths were reported at Kévé (to the north-west of Lomé), when a demonstration to demand Eyadéma's resignation was similarly dispersed. Violent protests subsequently erupted in Lomé; all educational establishments were closed, and a night-time curfew imposed. It was also reported that Togolese troops had been deployed along the border with Ghana, from where they had opened fire on Togolese nationals who were crossing into that country. The official endorsement, by the Assemblée nationale, of the legislation regarding the general amnesty and the legalization of political parties was overshadowed by the discovery of about 26 bodies in a lagoon in Lomé. Opposition groups' allegations that demonstrators had been beaten to death by the security forces, who had deposited the corpses in the lagoon, were denied by the Government, which later initiated an official inquiry into the deaths. The recovery of the bodies by demonstrators provoked further protests, at which the security forces again intervened. Eyadéma, fearing a civil conflict between the Kabiye and Ewe ethnic groups (the Government and armed forces were composed overwhelmingly of members of the first group, while opposition groups for the most part represented the Ewe people), appealed for national unity, and announced that a new constitution would be introduced within one year, and that legislative elections, in the context of a multi-party political system, would be organized. The curfew was ended in mid-April, and academic institutions generally reopened in early May.

In late April 1991 it was announced that the FAR was to be disbanded, to allow for the establishment of independent political parties. Agboyibo subsequently formed his own party, the Comité d'action pour le renouveau (CAR). Numerous other movements were accorded official status, and in early May 10 parties (including Agboyibo's CAR) announced the formation of a new 'umbrella' organization, the Front de l'opposition démocratique (FOD, later renamed the Coalition de l'opposition démocratique—COD), to co-ordinate the activities of opposition groups in preparation for the national meeting that was due to take place in mid-June.

In mid-May 1991 Eyadéma relinquished the defence portfolio to Maj.-Gen. Yao Mawulikplimi Amegi (hitherto Minister of the Interior and Security). In the same month representatives of the Government and the FOD disputed the status of the forthcoming meeting: the former designated it a 'national forum of dialogue', while the latter insisted that it should be a 'sovereign national conference' whose decisions would be legally enforceable. In early June the FOD organized a general strike, which was widely observed: violent incidents occurred when demonstrators confronted the security forces. The strike ended after six days, when the Government agreed that a 'national conference' should take place later in June, and should have the power to choose a transitional Prime Minister and to establish a transitional legislative body, in preparation for legislative and presidential elections. The conference eventually opened on 8 July, under the chairmanship of Philippe Kpodzro, then Bishop of Atakpamé: as many as 1,000 delegates attended, representing the organs of state, political parties, and religious and professional groups. The armed forces, although places were allocated to them, boycotted the conference. Gilchrist Olympio was allowed to return from exile to participate. When, early in the proceedings, participants adopted resolutions suspending the Constitution, dissolving the Assemblée nationale and giving the conference sovereign power, government representatives withdrew for one week, claiming that the conference had exceeded its mandate. Later in July the conference resolved to 'freeze' the assets of the RPT and of the CNTT. It also considered reports of atrocities and violations of human rights that had allegedly been committed by the security forces. In August the conference resolved to transfer most of the powers of the President to a Prime Minister, and to prevent Eyadéma from contesting future elections. This provoked criticism by members of the armed forces who supported Eyadéma, and, following allegations made at the conference that the Government was planning to assassinate leading opponents, Eyadéma announced the temporary suspension of the conference. In defiance of his decree, the conference proceeded to elect a Prime Minister, Joseph Kokou Koffigoh (a senior lawyer and President of an independent human rights organization, the Ligue togolaise des droits de l'homme—LTDH), to announce the dissolution of the RPT, and to form a transitional legislature, to be known as the Haut Conseil de la République (HCR). Eyadéma capitulated, signing a decree that proclaimed Koffigoh as transitional Prime Minister. On the same day the national conference concluded its deliberations. In early September Koffigoh announced the formation of a transitional Government, most of whose members had not previously held office: he himself assumed the defence portfolio.

During the first week of October 1991 members of the armed forces manifested their disapproval of the recent political developments by seizing control of the national broadcasting station and declaring the dissolution of the transitional Government, at the same time affirming their loyalty to Eyadéma and demanding that full executive powers should be restored to him. They returned to barracks on Eyadéma's orders, but a few days later troops attempted, unsuccessfully, to capture Koffigoh. Several people were reported to have been killed during demonstrations by civilians in support of Koffigoh; there was evidence that the traditional rivalry between the Ewe and Kabiye tribes had also contributed to the violence. (Three senior officers, regarded as close colleagues of Eyadéma, were arrested in November on charges of being implicated in the attempts to overthrow the transitional Government.) Later in October a new commission was established to draft a constitution, and Koffigoh confirmed that a constitutional referendum and elections would take place, as scheduled, in 1992. In late November 1991 unrest erupted anew after the HCR adopted legislation confirming the dissolution of the RPT. Troops again seized the broadcasting headquarters, and surrounded the Prime Minister's residence, demanding that Eyadéma nominate a new government and that the HCR be abolished. At least 20 people were killed in fighting between opponents and supporters of Eyadéma. In early December troops attacked the Prime Minister's residence and captured Koffigoh, killing several of his guards. Koffigoh, who had appealed unsuccessfully for French military support, agreed to form a new government. At the end of December the reconvened HCR adopted a programme of national reconciliation, restoring legal status to the RPT, and on the same day a new transitional 'Government of National Union' was announced. It comprised many of the members of the previous transitional administration, but also two close associates of Eyadéma: Yao Komlavi, who was appointed Minister of Territorial Administration and Security (equivalent to the post of Minister of the Interior and Security which he had previously occupied), and Aboudou Assouma, the new minister with responsibility for the armed forces.

In January 1992 an electoral schedule was announced, envisaging the conducting of a referendum on a new constitution and of local, legislative and presidential elections between April and June of that year. In March the Government approved the newly-drafted Constitution, and a census was begun for the purpose of establishing an electoral register. The announcement, in April, that the electoral schedule was to be delayed by one month provoked protests by the armed forces. In May the attempted assassination of Gilchrist Olympio, who was regarded as a potential presidential candidate, and the murder of another prominent member of the opposition, Dr Marc Attidépé (President of the Union togolaise pour la réconciliation and a member of the HCR), provoked widespread demonstrations and a three-day general strike. In late May the Council of Ministers abandoned the electoral timetable: the census, it was revealed, remained incomplete, the new electoral code had not yet been adopted by the HCR, and the draft Constitution was still under examination.

In July 1992 the HCR adopted the draft Constitution and an electoral code, and a new electoral timetable was announced, scheduling a referendum on the Constitution for the end of August. Also in July the Government was reorganized, following Koffigoh's dismissal of Assouma in June, and the resulting resignation of another minister. In early July the International Federation of Human Rights published a report (commissioned by the LTDH) on the attempted murder of Olympio, concluding that members of the armed forces had been responsible, and citing evidence that Eyadéma's son (a military officer) had been involved. Later in July Tavio Ayao Amorin, a member of the HCR and leader of the radical Parti pan-africain socialiste, was shot and fatally wounded. The Government's condemnation of his murder did not prevent demonstrations and a widely-observed general strike, organized by the recently-formed Collectif de l'opposition démocratique (COD-2), an alliance of some 25 political organizations and trade unions. In July and August representatives of the President and of eight major opposition parties met as a joint consultative committee to discuss security problems and electoral matters: they reached agreement on opposition access to the state-controlled media, and on the extension until 31 December of the transition period. In August equipment at the national centre for the processing of electoral data was damaged during an attack by unidentified armed men. The Government subsequently announced that the constitutional referendum was again to be postponed. Later in August the HCR approved the extension of the transition period to the end of the year. It also restored to Eyadéma several powers that he had been deprived of in 1991: he was empowered to preside over the Council of Ministers, and to represent the country abroad, and his agreement would henceforth be necessary in the appointment of members of the Government. At the same time, in an important concession to Eyadéma and his supporters, the draft Constitution was amended so that members of the armed forces would no longer have to resign their commissions before seeking election to public office.

The transitional Government was dissolved on 1 September 1992, and a new electoral schedule was announced: a referendum on the new Constitution was to take place later in September, local and legislative elections in October and November, and presidential elections in December. Later in September a new transitional Government was formed: Koffigoh remained as Prime Minister, and 10 parties were reportedly represented in the new administration—although the most influential ministries were allocated to members of the RPT. On 27 September the new Constitution was approved in a referendum by 98.11% of the votes cast. At the end of the month, however, it was announced that the elections were to be rescheduled yet again. In October eight opposition parties announced the formation of a 'Patriotic Front', to be led by Edem Kodjo (leader of the Union togolaise pour la démocratie—UTD) and Yao Agboyibo of the CAR. Later in October members of the armed forces entered a meeting of the HCR, holding some of its members hostage, and demanding that it authorize the reimbursement of contributions made to the RPT, whose assets had remained 'frozen' since 1991. Although Eyadéma stated that disciplinary measures would be taken against the men involved, the COD-2 successfully organized a general strike in protest at the incident. In November Koffigoh dismissed two ministers (both adherents of the RPT) for their conduct during the attack on the HCR, but his decision was overruled by Eyadéma. In the same month another general strike was organized by the COD-2 and independent trade unions, to support their demands for elections, the neutrality of the armed forces, the formation of a non-military 'peace force', and the bringing to justice of those responsible for the attacks on the HCR. The strike was widely observed, except in the north of Togo (where support for Eyadéma was strongest), and continued until mid-1993, causing considerable economic disruption.

In January 1993 Eyadéma dissolved the Government, but reappointed Koffigoh as Prime Minister. The President stated that he would appoint a new 'government of national unity', whose task would be to organize elections as soon as possible. His action provoked protests by the opposition parties, who claimed that, according to the Constitution, the HCR should appoint a Prime Minister since the transition period had now expired. In the same month two ministers representing the French and German Governments visited Togo to offer mediation in the political crisis. During their visit at least 20 people were killed when police opened fire on anti-Government protesters. Thousands of Togolese subsequently fled from Lomé, many crossing the borders into Benin and Ghana. In February discussions were organized in Colmar, France, by the French and German Governments, attended by representatives of Eyadéma, the RPT, Koffigoh, the HCR and the COD-2, but these failed when the presidential delegation left after one day. In the same month the French, German and US Governments announced the suspension of their programmes of aid to Togo. The formation of a new 'Crisis Government' was announced in February: eight new ministers were appointed (out of a total of 18), but supporters of Eyadéma retained the principal posts. The COD-2 declared that it now regarded Koffigoh as an obstacle to democratization, and in March COD-2 member parties, meeting in Benin, nominated a 'parallel' Prime Minister, Jean-Lucien Savi de Tové (the leader of the Parti des démocrates pour l'unité). In late March there was an armed attack on the military camp in Lomé where Eyadéma had his residence: more than 20 people were killed, including the deputy Chief of Staff of the Armed Forces, Col Kofi Tepe. The Government identified Tepe as the principal military organizer of the attack, but declared that it had been instigated by Gilchrist Olympio, with assistance from Ghana. Both Olympio and the Ghanaian Government denied the allegations.

In April 1993 a new electoral schedule was announced. As modified in May and again in June, it envisaged presidential elections in July and legislative elections in August. The RPT designated Eyadéma as its presidential candidate. In May the COD-2 declared that it would not take part in the elections, alleging that they would not be fairly conducted, and that opposition politicians had no guarantee of their safety during the electoral campaign. In June and July, however, discussions took place in Ouagadougou, Burkina Faso, between the Togolese Government and the COD-2, and in July they signed an agreement establishing 25 August as the date for the presidential election (with a second stage to be held on 8 September, should no candidate gain an absolute majority in the first round). The agreement stipulated that the Togolese armed forces should be confined to barracks during the election period, and that international military observers should be present to confirm this, while international civilian observers should also be present for the election. An independent, nine-member national electoral commission (NEC) was to be established, and was to include three members nominated by the opposition parties. The agreement also included the establishment of an international monitoring committee (comprising Burkinabè, French, German and US diplomats) to help organize the electoral process. Gilchrist Olympio, who had not returned to Togo since the attempt on his life in 1992, denounced the agreement, stating that the Government would retain too much control over the election, and that Togolese refugees abroad should be allowed to return home in safety before the poll. (By now the number of Togolese refugees in neighbouring countries—mostly in Ghana and Benin—was variously estimated at between 200,000 and 350,000.)

Later in July 1993 the COD-2 nominated Edem Kodjo, of the UTD, as its presidential candidate. In the same month, however, the opposition's lack of unity was demonstrated when two other candidates were nominated by parties affiliated to the COD-2: Yao Agboyibo of the CAR and Abou Djobo Boukari of Démocratie sociale togolaise. Olympio also announced his nomination as the presidential candidate of the Union des forces de changement (UFC), but in August the Supreme Court rejected his candidacy, on the grounds that he had not produced the requisite Togolese medical certificates. After intervention by the international monitoring committee, Olympio was invited to return to Togo to undergo a medical examination, but stated that he would not return until security conditions permitted the home-coming of all other Togolese exiles. The Prime Minster, Koffigoh (who had formed his own political party, the Coordination nationale des forces nouvelles, in June) expressed support for Eyadéma's re-election. During August Boukari withdrew from the election, claiming that the voters' registers contained some 500,000 fictitious names, and Kodjo and Agboyibo also announced their withdrawal, stating that preparations, including the display of voters' registers and the distribution of voting cards, were not sufficiently advanced. The chairman of the NEC himself admitted that false names were appearing on the voters' registers, and proposed a postponement. Teams of US and German observers withdrew shortly before the election took place; French observers remained, but concluded that the poll was not satisfactorily conducted. In the event only three candidates took part: Eyadéma and two little-known candidates, Adani Ifé Atakpamevi (of the Alliance togolaise pour la démocratie) and Jacques Amouzou (an independent). Only about 36% of the electorate voted in the election. Eyadéma was reported to have obtained 96.49% of the votes cast, while the other candidates won less than 2% each.

In September 1993 the COD-2 announced that it would only participate in the forthcoming legislative election if procedures were improved. The Government agreed to revise the suspect electoral registers. In November it announced that the election would take place in two stages in December and January, but both the NEC and the opposition parties declared that these dates were premature, and, after consulting the international monitoring committee, the Government agreed to postpone the first round of the election to 23 January 1994.

In early January 1994 an armed attack on Eyadéma's official residence was reported. As in March 1993, the Government alleged that the attack had been organized by Olympio, with Ghanaian support: this was denied both by Olympio and by the Ghanaian Government. A total of 67 people were officially reported to have died in the violence. It was claimed by the human rights oganization, Amnesty International, that at least 48 deaths took the form of summary executions by the armed forces. A UTD election candidate was accused by the Government of storing weapons for the attack. On the day after the disturbances the Government announced that the election would now take place on 6 February and 20 February 1994, rejecting requests by the CAR and the UTD for a further postponement.

In the legislative election of February 1994, 347 candidates contested 81 seats. Despite the murder of a newly-elected CAR candidate after the first round, and some incidents of violence at polling stations during the second round, international observers expressed themselves satisfied with the conduct of the election. The final result revealed a narrow victory for the opposition, with the CAR winning 36 seats and the UTD seven; the RPT obtained 35 seats and two smaller pro-Eyadéma parties won three. During March Eyadéma consulted the main opposition parties on the formation of a new government. In late March the CAR and the UTD reached an agreement on the terms of their alliance and jointly proposed the candidacy of Agboyibo for Prime Minister (a stipulation of the agreement was that the candidate for Prime Minister should be a member of the CAR). In rulings issued in late March and early April the Supreme Court declared the results of the legislative election invalid in three constituencies (in which the CAR had won two seats and the UTD one) and ordered by-elections. The CAR and the UTD refused to attend the new Assemblée nationale, in protest at the annulment. In April Eyadéma nominated Kodjo as Prime Minister. Kodjo accepted the appointment despite protest by the CAR that to do so was a violation of the agreement of March between the two parties. The CAR subsequently declared that it would not participate in an administration formed by Kodjo. Kodjo took office on 25 April, and expressed his priorities to be national reconciliation, the return of refugees, economic recovery, and the integration of the armed forces into democratic life. It was not until late May that he announced the formation of his Government, which comprised eight members of the RPT and other pro-Eyadéma parties, three members of the UTD, and eight independents. Shortly beforehand, the CAR had announced (in response to the postponement of the parliamentary by-elections) that it was to end its boycott of the Assemblée nationale.

In October 1994 the Government announced that an attempted terrorist attack on installations of the Office Togolais des Phosphates had been thwarted by the security forces. Reportedly, five heavily armed dissidents had infiltrated from Ghana with the intention of destroying a transformer at the phosphate mines in Hahotoé, some 50 km north-east of the capital. The group claimed to have been recruited by Togolese political exiles living in Ghana.

In November 1994 the CAR again suspended its participation in the Assemblée nationale, and indicated that it would return only when agreement had been reached with the Government on the conduct of the by-elections, ordered by the Supreme Court in April and due to be held on 27 November. The CAR's demands included the establishment of a joint electoral commission, the reinforcement of security measures and the entrustment of the electoral process to an independent body, such as the Constitutional Court. In the light of the dispute, on 25 November the by-elections were postponed. Later that month, in response to an invitation by the speaker of the Assemblée nationale to resume participation in the legislature, the CAR affirmed that it would return only when the Government had shown a commitment to reaching a general consensus on the organization of free and fair elections.

In December 1994 the Assemblée nationale adopted legislation granting a general amnesty to all those charged with political offences committed before 15 December 1994, including those alleged to have participated in attacks on the presidential residence in March 1993 and January 1994. The release of those held in detention for such offences began later in December.

In March 1995 the human rights organization, Amnesty International, expressed concern at the lack of effective measures for ensuring the observance of human rights in Togo, and criticized the absence of independent legal inquiry into abuses committed during the period of political transition in 1991–94. In the following month the CAR ended its boycott of the Assemblée nationale, following an agreement between the Government and the major opposition parties. The terms of the agreement provided for the Government and the legislative opposition to have equal representation on national, district and local electoral commissions.

Relations with neighbouring Ghana and Benin have frequently become strained, as both countries' borders with Togo have periodically been closed in an effort to combat smuggling and to curb political activity by exiles on both sides. In December 1984 security agreements were reached between Togo, Ghana, Benin and Nigeria, which included an extradition treaty and measures to reduce smuggling. Following the unrest in Togo in March and April 1991, the Ghanaian Government denied that it was supporting Togolese opposition movements. In October the Governments of Togo and Ghana signed an agreement on the free movement of goods and persons between the two countries. In January 1993 the Ghanaian Government criticized President Eyadéma and expressed fears of a breakdown in law and order in Togo. In March of that year, and again in January 1994, the Togo Government accused Ghana of supporting armed attacks on Eyadéma's residence (see above). About 6,000 Ghanaians were reported to have taken refuge in Togo in February 1994, as a result of ethnic conflict in north-east Ghana. By late 1994 relations with Ghana had improved considerably. In November full diplomatic relations, suspended since 1982, were formally resumed with the appointment of a Ghanaian ambassador to Togo. In the following month Togo's border with Ghana, which had been closed since January 1994, was reopened. In November 1994, following a visit by the President of Benin in the previous month, the Benin-Togo Border Demarcation Commission, which had been inactive since 1978, resumed its activities.

### Government

Under the terms of the Constitution that was approved in a national referendum on 27 September 1993, executive power is vested in the President of the Republic, who is directly elected, by universal adult suffrage, for a period of five years. The legislature is the unicameral Assemblée nationale, whose 81 members are also elected, by universal suffrage, for a five-year period. All elections take place in the context of a multi-party political system. The Prime Minister is appointed by the President from among the majority in the legislature, and the Prime Minister, in consultation with the President, nominates other ministers.

### Defence

In June 1994 Togo's armed forces officially numbered about 6,950 (army 6,500, air force 250, naval force 200). Paramilitary forces comprised a 750-strong gendarmerie. (At the time of the 1991 National Conference, several sources put the strength of the armed forces at 12,000.) Military service is by selective conscription and lasts for two years. Togo normally receives assistance with training and equipment from France; however, French military assistance was suspended in late 1992, in view of the political crisis in Togo, and only resumed in September 1994. The defence budget was estimated at 13,700m. francs CFA in 1993.

### Economic Affairs

In 1993, according to estimates by the World Bank, Togo's gross national product (GNP), measured at average 1991–93 prices, was US $1,325m., equivalent to $330 per head. During 1985–93, it was estimated, GNP per head declined, in real terms, at an average annual rate of 3.4%. Over the same period the population increased by an annual average of 3.6%. Togo's gross domestic product (GDP) increased, in real terms, by an average of 1.4% per year in 1980–92; GDP declined by 8.8% in 1992, and by 13.5% in 1993.

Agriculture (including forestry and fishing) contributed an estimated 48.6% of GDP in 1993. Some 68.5% of the working population were employed in the sector in that year. The principal cash crops are cotton (which contributed 21.9% of earnings from merchandise exports in 1991), cocoa and coffee. Togo has generally been self-sufficient in basic foodstuffs: the principal subsistence crops are yams, maize, cassava, millet and sorghum. Imports of livestock products and fish are necessary to satisfy domestic needs. A major reafforestation programme was in progress in the early 1990s. During 1980–92 agricultural GDP increased by an annual average of 4.9%.

Industry (including mining, manufacturing, construction and power) employed 9.2% of the working population in 1981, and contributed an estimated 17.9% of GDP in 1993. During 1980–92 industrial GDP increased by an annual average of only 1.1%, compared with growth of 7.7% per year in 1970–80.

Only 0.3% of the labour force were employed in the mining sector in 1981; in 1993, however, extractive activities contributed an estimated 3.9% of GDP. Togo has the world's richest reserves of first-grade calcium phosphates (exports of which provided 48.5% of total export earnings in 1991). Concerns regarding the high cadmium content of Togolese phosphate rock have prompted interest in the development of lower-grade carbon phosphates, which have a less significant cadmium content. Limestone and marble are also exploited. There are, in addition, deposits of iron ore, manganese, chromite and peat. Exploration for petroleum and uranium was in progress in the early 1990s. The GDP of the mining sector increased by an annual average of 3.4% in 1982–91.

Manufacturing contributed an estimated 7.0% of GDP in 1993. About 6% of the labour force were employed in the sector in 1981. Major companies are engaged notably in agro-industrial activities, the processing of phosphates, steel-rolling and in the production of cement. An industrial 'free zone' was inaugurated in Lomé in 1990: it was hoped to attract investment by local and foreign interests by offering certain (notably fiscal) advantages in return for guarantees regarding export levels and employment. Manufacturing GDP increased by an average of 2.5% per year in 1980–92.

Togo's dependence on imports of electrical energy from Ghana was reduced following the completion, in 1988, of a 65-MW hydroelectric installation (constructed in co-operation with Benin) at Nangbeto, on the Mono river. The development of similar plants was planned for the 1990s. Imports of fuels comprised 9.8% of the value of merchandise imports in 1991.

The services sector contributed an estimated 33.5% of GDP in 1993. Lomé has been of considerable importance as an entrepôt for the foreign trade of land-locked countries of the region. However, the political upheaval of the early 1990s has resulted in the diversion of a large part of this import-export activity to neighbouring Benin, and has also undermined the tourist industry (hitherto an important source of foreign exchange). The GDP of the services sector declined by an annual average of 0.7% in 1980–92.

In 1993 Togo recorded a visible trade deficit of US $33.9m., while there was a deficit of $98.4m. on the current account of the balance of payments. In 1991 the principal source of imports (33.1%) was France; other major suppliers were the Netherlands, Japan and the USA. The principal market for exports was Canada (which took 11.3% of Togo's exports in that year); other significant purchasers were Nigeria, Mexico, Spain and France. The principal exports in 1991 were calcium phosphates, ginned cotton, cocoa beans and green coffee. The principal imports in that year were machinery and transport equipment, basic manufactures (including cotton yarn and fabrics), food and live animals (especially cereals), chemicals, refined petroleum products and beverages and tobacco.

In 1993 there was an estimated budgetary deficit of 54,790m. francs CFA. Togo's total external debt was US $1,292m. at the end of 1993, of which $1,128m. was long-term public debt. In that year the cost of debt-servicing was equivalent to 8.5% of the value of exports of goods and services. Annual inflation averaged 0.6% in 1985–93. Some 4,076 people were registered as unemployed in 1985.

Togo is a member of the Economic Community of West African States (ECOWAS, see p. 138), of the West African organs of the Franc Zone (see p. 168), of the International Cocoa Organization (ICCO, see p. 235), of the International Coffee Organization (see p. 235) and of the Conseil de l'Entente (see p. 238).

Beginning in the late 1970s Togo experienced a severe decline in revenue from exports of its major commodities, and the cost of servicing a substantial external debt, incurred in support of ambitious economic expansion projects, became increasingly burdensome. Rigorous austerity measures (stipulated by the IMF as a condition of assistance) remained in force throughout the 1980s and early 1990s. Strict limits were imposed on expenditure in the public sector, the rehabilitation, liquidation or transfer to private ownership of unprofitable state-owned enterprises was undertaken, and the taxation system was revised. In addition, debt-relief concessions were obtained from bilateral and multilateral creditors. However, the political turmoil of the early 1990s had serious repercussions in all areas of the economy, and in late 1993 the Government estimated that losses arising from the nine-month general strike (of 1992–93) could amount to some 200,000m. francs CFA, exacerbating existing budgetary and balance-of-payments' difficulties. The disruption of economic activity was accompanied by a loss of external funding, as major donors, including France, Germany, the USA and the European Community (now European Union) withdrew assistance. In late 1994, however, following the devaluation of the CFA franc at the beginning of that year, the IMF approved a series of new credits (totalling US $95m.) in support of Togo's 1994–97 economic programme. Under the programme, tax reforms were to be reinforced, the tax administration strengthened and efforts made to expedite the privatization process. By March 1995 the majority of donor nations had resumed funding. In addition, France announced the cancellation of Togolese debt amounting to 400m. French francs. In February the Paris Club of creditor Governments proposed the cancellation of 67% of Togolese debt.

### Social Welfare

Medical services are provided by the State. In 1988 Togo had 268 physicians, 2,582 nurses, 348 midwives and 25 pharmacists. In that year there were 28 hospitals, with a total of 5,275 beds, and 348 health centres. Under the 1990 budget, an estimated 4,770m. francs CFA was to be allocated to the public health sector (5.2% of the total expenditure by the central Government), while 760m. francs CFA was for social security and welfare.

### Education

In 1990, according to UNESCO estimates, the adult illiteracy rate averaged 56.7% (males 43.6%; females 69.3%). Primary education, which begins at six years of age and lasts for six years, is (in theory) compulsory. Secondary education, beginning at the age of 12, lasts for a further seven years, comprising a first cycle of four years and a second of three years. In 1990 enrolment at primary schools included 76% of children in the relevent age-group (89% of boys; 62% of girls). In the same year secondary enrolment was equivalent to only 23% of the appropriate age-group (boys 35%; girls 12%). Proficiency in the two national languages, Ewe and Kabiye, is compulsory. Mission schools are important, educating almost one-half of all pupils. The Université du Bénin at Lomé had about 11,000 students in the mid-1990s, and scholarships to French universities are available. Budget estimates for 1990 allocated 21,384m. francs CFA to education (23.1% of total expenditure by the central Government).

### Public Holidays

**1995:** 1 January (New Year's Day), 13 January (Liberation Day, anniversary of the 1967 coup), 24 January (Day of Victory, anniversary of the failed attack at Sarakawa), 3 March* (Id al-Fitr, end of Ramadan), 17 April (Easter Monday), 24 April (Day of Victory), 27 April (Independence Day), 1 May (Labour Day), 10 May* (Tabaski, Feast of the Sacrifice), 25 May (Ascension Day), 5 June (Whit Monday), 15 August (Assumption), 24 September (anniversary of the failed attack on Lomé), 1 November (All Saints' Day), 25 December (Christmas).

**1996:** 1 January (New Year's Day), 13 January (Liberation Day, anniversary of the 1967 coup), 24 January (Day of Victory, anniversary of the failed attack at Sarakawa), 21 February* (Id al-Fitr, end of Ramadan), 8 April (Easter Monday), 24 April (Day of Victory), 27 April (Independence Day), 29 April* (Tabaski, Feast of the Sacrifice), 1 May (Labour Day), 16 May (Ascension Day), 27 May (Whit Monday), 15 August (Assumption), 24 September (anniversary of the failed attack on Lomé), 1 November (All Saints' Day), 25 December (Christmas).

* These holidays are dependent on the Islamic lunar calendar and may vary by one or two days from the dates given.

### Weights and Measures

The metric system is in force.

# Statistical Survey

Source (except where otherwise stated): Direction de la Statistique, BP 118, Lomé; tel. 21-22-87.

## Area and Population

### AREA, POPULATION AND DENSITY

| | |
|---|---|
| Area (sq km) | 56,785* |
| Population (census results) | |
| 1 March–30 April 1970 | 1,997,109 |
| 22 November 1981 | 2,705,250† |
| Population (official estimate at 31 January) | |
| 1988 | 3,296,000 |
| Density (per sq km) at 31 January 1988 | 58.0 |

* 21,925 sq miles.
† Provisional.

**Mid-year population** (UN estimates): 3,317,000 in 1988; 3,422,000 in 1989; 3,531,000 in 1990; 3,645,000 in 1991; 3,763,000 (66.3 per sq km) in 1992 (Source: UN, *World Population Prospects: The 1992 Revision*).

### PRINCIPAL TOWNS
(estimated population at 1 January 1977)

| | | | |
|---|---|---|---|
| Lomé (capital) | 229,400 | Tsevie | 15,900 |
| Sokodé | 33,500 | Aného | 13,300 |
| Palimé | 25,500 | Mango | 10,930* |
| Atakpamé | 21,800 | Bafilo | 10,100* |
| Bassari | 17,500 | Tabligbo | 5,120* |

* 1975 figure.

### BIRTHS AND DEATHS (UN estimates, annual averages)

| | 1975–80 | 1980–85 | 1985–90 |
|---|---|---|---|
| Birth rate (per 1,000) | 45.2 | 44.9 | 44.7 |
| Death rate (per 1,000) | 17.4 | 15.7 | 14.1 |

**Expectation of life** (UN estimates, years at birth, 1985–90): 53.0 (males 51.3; females 54.8).

Source: UN, *World Population Prospects: The 1992 Revision*.

# TOGO

## ECONOMICALLY ACTIVE POPULATION
(census of 22 November 1981)

|  | Males | Females | Total |
|---|---|---|---|
| Agriculture, hunting, forestry and fishing | 324,870 | 254,491 | 579,361 |
| Mining and quarrying | 2,781 | 91 | 2,872 |
| Manufacturing | 29,307 | 25,065 | 54,372 |
| Electricity, gas and water | 2,107 | 96 | 2,203 |
| Construction | 20,847 | 301 | 21,148 |
| Trade, restaurants and hotels | 17,427 | 87,415 | 104,842 |
| Transport, storage and communications | 20,337 | 529 | 20,866 |
| Financing, insurance, real estate and business services | 1,650 | 413 | 2,063 |
| Community, social and personal services | 50,750 | 12,859 | 63,609 |
| Activities not adequately defined | 14,607 | 6,346 | 20,953 |
| **Total employed** | 484,683 | 387,606 | 872,289 |
| Unemployed | 21,666 | 7,588 | 29,254 |
| **Total labour force** | 506,349 | 395,194 | 901,543 |

**Mid-1993** (estimates in '000): Agriculture, etc. 1,054; Total 1,538 (Source: FAO, *Production Yearbook*).

# Agriculture

**PRINCIPAL CROPS** ('000 metric tons)

|  | 1991 | 1992 | 1993 |
|---|---|---|---|
| Rice (paddy) | 40 | 26 | 33 |
| Maize | 230 | 290 | 393 |
| Millet and sorghum | 191 | 184 | 201 |
| Sweet potatoes | 2 | n.a. | 28 |
| Cassava (Manioc) | 511 | 480 | 389 |
| Yams | 376 | 393 | 529 |
| Taro (Coco yam) | 14 | 11 | 20 |
| Dry beans | 17 | 22 | 39 |
| Other pulses | 5 | 2 | 4 |
| Groundnuts (in shell) | 22 | 22 | 35 |
| Sesame seed* | 2 | 2 | 2 |
| Cottonseed* | 55 | 50 | 44 |
| Coconuts* | 14 | 14 | 14 |
| Copra* | 2 | 2 | 2 |
| Palm kernels* | 8 | 8 | 8 |
| Tomatoes* | 9 | 9 | 9 |
| Other vegetables* | 150 | 150 | 150 |
| Oranges* | 12 | 12 | 12 |
| Bananas* | 16 | 16 | 16 |
| Other fruit* | 20 | 20 | 20 |
| Coffee (green) | 26 | 27 | 28 |
| Cocoa beans | 5 | 4 | 7 |
| Tobacco (leaves) | 2† | 2* | 2* |
| Cotton (lint)† | 41 | 42 | 39 |

* FAO estimate(s).   † Unofficial figure(s).
Source: FAO, *Production Yearbook*.

**LIVESTOCK** ('000 head, year ending September)

|  | 1991 | 1992 | 1993 |
|---|---|---|---|
| Cattle | 247 | 246 | 246 |
| Sheep | 1,200 | 1,200 | 1,200 |
| Pigs | 709 | 800* | 850* |
| Goats | 1,900 | 1,900 | 1,900 |
| Horses* | 2 | 2 | 2 |
| Asses* | 3 | 3 | 3 |

Poultry (million): 7 in 1991; 7 in 1992; 7 in 1993.
* FAO estimate(s).
Source: FAO, *Production Yearbook*.

**LIVESTOCK PRODUCTS** (FAO estimates, '000 metric tons)

|  | 1991 | 1992 | 1993 |
|---|---|---|---|
| Beef and veal | 5 | 5 | 5 |
| Mutton and lamb | 3 | 3 | 3 |
| Goats' meat | 4 | 4 | 4 |
| Pig meat | 10 | 11 | 12 |
| Poultry meat | 8 | 8 | 8 |
| Cows' milk | 9 | 9 | 10 |
| Hen eggs | 5.8 | 6.0 | 6.3 |

Source: FAO, *Production Yearbook*.

# Forestry

**ROUNDWOOD REMOVALS** ('000 cubic metres, excluding bark)

|  | 1990 | 1991 | 1992 |
|---|---|---|---|
| Sawlogs, veneer logs and logs for sleepers | 12 | 8 | 7 |
| Other industrial wood* | 174 | 179 | 185 |
| Fuel wood | 718* | 1,048 | 1,072* |
| **Total** | 904 | 1,235 | 1,264 |

* FAO estimate(s).
Source: FAO, *Yearbook of Forest Products*.

# Fishing

('000 metric tons, live weight)

|  | 1990 | 1991 | 1992 |
|---|---|---|---|
| Tilapias | 4.0 | 4.0 | 4.5 |
| Other freshwater fishes | 0.9 | 0.9 | 1.0 |
| Sardinellas | 0.8 | 0.7 | 0.2 |
| European anchovy | 7.6 | 4.7 | 3.6 |
| Other clupeoids | 0.9 | 0.7 | 0.3 |
| Other marine fishes (incl. unspecified) | 1.6 | 1.5 | 1.2 |
| **Total catch** (incl. others) | 15.8 | 12.5 | 10.8 |

Source: FAO, *Yearbook of Fishery Statistics*.

# Mining

('000 metric tons)

|  | 1988 | 1989 | 1990 |
|---|---|---|---|
| Natural phosphates (gross weight) | 3,464 | 3,355 | 2,314 |

Source: UN, *Industrial Statistics Yearbook*.

# TOGO

## Industry

**SELECTED PRODUCTS**
('000 metric tons, unless otherwise indicated)

|  | 1985 | 1986 | 1987 |
|---|---|---|---|
| Salted, dried or smoked fish* | 3.7 | 2.7 | 3.6 |
| Wheat flour | 32 | 42 | 58 |
| Palm oil* | 14 | 14 | 14 |
| Beer ('000 hectolitres) | 423 | 464 | 452 |
| Soft drinks ('000 hectolitres) | 83 | 89 | 142 |
| Footwear—excl. rubber ('000 pairs) | 521† | 286 | 29 |
| Cement | 284 | 338† | 370 |
| Electric energy (million kWh) | 39 | 35 | 39 |

**1988** ('000 metric tons, unless otherwise indicated): Salted, dried or smoked fish 3.7*; Palm oil 14*; Footwear—excl. rubber ('000 pairs) 100; Cement 378; Electric energy (million kWh) 47.
**1989** ('000 metric tons, unless otherwise indicated): Salted, dried or smoked fish 3.8*; Palm oil 14*; Footwear—excl. rubber ('000 pairs) 100; Cement 389; Electric energy (million kWh) 38.
**1990** ('000 metric tons, unless otherwise indicated): Salted, dried or smoked fish 3.6; Palm oil 14*; Footwear—excl. rubber ('000 pairs) 100; Cement 400; Electric energy (million kWh) 59.
**1991** ('000 metric tons, unless otherwise indicated): Cement 399; Electric energy (million kWh) 60.

* Estimate(s) by the FAO.
† Provisional or estimated figure.

Source: mainly UN, *Industrial Statistics Yearbook*.

## Finance

**CURRENCY AND EXCHANGE RATES**

**Monetary Units**
100 centimes = 1 franc de la Communauté financière africaine (CFA).

**French Franc, Sterling and Dollar Equivalents**
(31 December 1994)
1 French franc = 100 francs CFA;
£1 sterling = 834.94 francs CFA;
US $1 = 533.68 francs CFA;
1,000 francs CFA = £1.198 = $1.874.

**Average Exchange Rate** (francs CFA per US $)
1992   264.69
1993   283.16
1994   555.20

Note: An exchange rate of 1 French franc = 50 francs CFA, established in 1948, remained in force until January 1994, when the CFA franc was devalued by 50%, with the exchange rate adjusted to 1 French franc = 100 francs CFA.

**BUDGET** (estimates, million francs CFA)

| Revenue | 1991 | 1992 | 1993 |
|---|---|---|---|
| Fiscal receipts | 68,850 | 54,820 | 30,850 |
| Taxes on income and profits | 22,550 | 20,680 | 7,250 |
| Individual taxes | 8,960 | 9,490 | 3,390 |
| Corporate and business taxes | 13,590 | 11,190 | 3,860 |
| Taxes on goods and services | 10,040 | 6,510 | 3,240 |
| Sales tax | 6,540 | 5,300 | 2,880 |
| Taxes on international trade and transactions | 32,310 | 25,280 | 13,480 |
| Import duties | 25,650 | 19,690 | 10,330 |
| Other current receipts | 10,040 | 17,770 | 7,370 |
| Property income | 2,070 | 10,530 | 1,170 |
| **Total** | **78,890** | **72,600** | **38,220** |

Source: IMF, *Togo—Recent Economic Developments*.

| Expenditure | 1988 | 1989 | 1990 |
|---|---|---|---|
| General public services | 19,684 | 22,472 | 23,495 |
| Defence | 12,834 | 13,354 | 13,817 |
| Public order and security | 1,864 | 2,373 | 2,438 |
| Education | 19,068 | 20,593 | 21,384 |
| Health | 4,758 | 4,492 | 4,770 |
| Social security and welfare | — | 634 | 760 |
| Housing and community services | — | 120 | 107 |
| Other community and social services | 2,188 | 2,257 | 2,403 |
| Economic services | 6,068 | 6,820 | 6,804 |
| Agriculture, forestry and fishing | 2,805 | 2,672 | 2,677 |
| Mining, manufacturing and construction | 149 | 322 | 324 |
| Transport and communications | 2,942 | 2,329 | 2,169 |
| Other economic services | 172 | 1,497 | 1,634 |
| Other purposes | 23,228 | 19,371 | 16,512 |
| Investment budget | 3,300 | 3,459 | 3,500 |
| Debt-repayment | 19,928 | 15,912 | 13,012 |
| **Total** | **89,692** | **92,486** | **92,490** |

Source: Banque centrale des états de l'Afrique de l'ouest.

**1991** (million francs CFA): Expenditure 114,990.
**1992** (estimate, million francs CFA): Expenditure 98,810.
**1993** (estimate, million francs CFA): Expenditure 93,010.
Source: IMF, *Togo—Recent Economic Developments*.

**CENTRAL BANK RESERVES**
(US $ million at 31 December)

|  | 1991 | 1992 | 1993 |
|---|---|---|---|
| Gold* | 4.4 | 4.3 | 4.7 |
| IMF special drawing rights | 0.4 | 0.3 | 0.1 |
| Reserve position | 0.4 | 0.3 | 0.3 |
| Foreign exchange | 364.1 | 271.9 | 155.9 |
| **Total** | **369.3** | **276.8** | **161.0** |

* Valued at market-related prices.

Source: IMF, *International Financial Statistics*.

**MONEY SUPPLY** ('000 million francs CFA at 31 December)

|  | 1991 | 1992 | 1993 |
|---|---|---|---|
| Currency outside banks | 36.29 | 22.34 | 10.72 |
| Demand deposits at deposit money banks | 41.19 | 34.14 | 35.13 |
| Checking deposits at post office | 1.00 | — | — |
| **Total money** | **78.48** | **56.48** | **45.96** |

Source: IMF, *International Financial Statistics*.

**COST OF LIVING**
(Consumer price index, Lomé. Base: 1963 = 100).

|  | 1989 | 1990 | 1991 |
|---|---|---|---|
| Food | 404.2 | 412.0 | 394.5 |
| Beverages | 335.6 | 333.3 | 356.4 |
| Household supplies and maintenance | 501.9 | 485.9 | 497.9 |
| Clothing | 622.6 | 637.3 | 707.9 |
| Housing | 368.0 | 351.8 | 353.0 |
| Services | 349.8 | 354.9 | 360.6 |
| **All items** (incl. others) | **419.1** | **423.4** | **425.4** |

Source: Banque centrale des états de l'Afrique de l'ouest.

# TOGO

*Statistical Survey*

## NATIONAL ACCOUNTS
(million francs CFA at current prices)

### Expenditure on the Gross Domestic Product

|  | 1991 | 1992 | 1993 |
| --- | --- | --- | --- |
| Government final consumption expenditure | 68,700 | 65,900 | 58,800 |
| Private final consumption expenditure | 334,400 | 334,500 | 303,300 |
| Increase in stocks | −3,400 | −7,800 | −18,700 |
| Gross fixed capital formation | 92,500 | 75,700 | 39,800 |
| **Total domestic expenditure** | 492,200 | 468,300 | 383,200 |
| Exports of goods and services | 151,200 | 119,500 | 79,900 |
| *Less* Imports of goods and services | 187,700 | 164,300 | 109,400 |
| **GDP in purchasers' values** | 455,500 | 423,600 | 353,800 |
| **GDP at constant 1978 prices** | 222,800 | 203,200 | 175,800 |

### Gross Domestic Product by Economic Activity

|  | 1991 | 1992* | 1993* |
| --- | --- | --- | --- |
| Agriculture, hunting, forestry and fishing | 148,400 | 160,100 | 171,800 |
| Mining and quarrying | 26,800 | 17,800 | 13,700 |
| Manufacturing | 47,400 | 42,600 | 24,700 |
| Electricity, gas and water | 20,500 | 20,400 | 19,600 |
| Construction | 13,700 | 13,800 | 5,500 |
| Trade, restaurants and hotels | 93,400 | 75,000 | 45,400 |
| Transport, storage and communications | 28,200 | 23,600 | 13,700 |
| Public administration and defence | 43,500 | 39,900 | 34,200 |
| Other services | 33,700 | 30,300 | 25,200 |
| **GDP in purchasers' values** | 455,500 | 423,600 | 353,800 |

* Estimates.

Source: IMF, *Togo—Recent Economic Developments*.

## BALANCE OF PAYMENTS (US $ million)

|  | 1991 | 1992 | 1993 |
| --- | --- | --- | --- |
| Merchandise exports f.o.b. | 393.1 | 322.3 | 214.7 |
| Merchandise imports f.o.b. | −452.3 | −417.8 | −248.6 |
| **Trade balance** | −59.2 | −95.6 | −33.9 |
| Exports of services | 142.9 | 129.2 | 68.6 |
| Imports of services | −213.0 | −203.3 | −135.6 |
| Other income received | 29.4 | 31.4 | 19.5 |
| Other income paid | −60.3 | −58.6 | −57.6 |
| Private unrequited transfers (net) | 14.2 | 8.7 | 9.5 |
| Official unrequited transfers (net) | 91.5 | 81.2 | 31.1 |
| **Current balance** | −54.6 | −106.9 | −98.4 |
| Capital (net) | 46.4 | 10.6 | −46.9 |
| Net errors and omissions | −33.7 | −62.1 | −42.2 |
| **Overall balance** | −41.9 | −158.5 | −187.5 |

Source: IMF, *International Financial Statistics*.

# External Trade

Source: UN, *International Trade Statistics Yearbook*.

## PRINCIPAL COMMODITIES (US $ million)

| Imports c.i.f. | 1989 | 1990 | 1991 |
| --- | --- | --- | --- |
| **Food and live animals** | 88.4 | 86.1 | 72.4 |
| Fish, crustaceans and molluscs | 14.3 | 15.3 | 16.6 |
| Fresh, chilled or frozen fish | 10.4 | 11.5 | 14.6 |
| Fish, frozen (excl. fillets) | 9.6 | 11.4 | 14.1 |
| Cereals and cereal preparations | 35.4 | 33.4 | 21.5 |
| Wheat (incl. spelt) and meslin, unmilled | 16.5 | 19.4 | 11.3 |
| Durum wheat, unmilled | 14.8 | 17.7 | 10.3 |
| Rice | 10.6 | 7.8 | 6.4 |
| Rice, semi-milled, milled | 10.4 | 7.7 | 6.4 |
| Sugar, sugar preparations and honey | 11.3 | 9.6 | 7.7 |
| Sugar and honey | 10.4 | 8.7 | 7.1 |
| Refined sugars, etc. | 10.2 | 8.6 | 2.3 |
| Miscellaneous edible products and preparations | 4.3 | 7.6 | 11.0 |
| Soups and broths | 0.7 | 3.8 | 9.1 |
| **Beverages and tobacco** | 25.2 | 35.5 | 25.2 |
| Tobacco and tobacco manufactures | 17.8 | 25.1 | 18.1 |
| Tobacco, manufactured | 17.8 | 24.9 | 17.9 |
| Cigarettes | 17.7 | 24.7 | 17.7 |
| **Crude material (inedible) except fuels** | 9.1 | 10.9 | 9.0 |
| **Mineral fuels, lubricants and related materials** | 29.0 | 48.1 | 43.6 |
| Petroleum, petroleum products and related materials | 28.7 | 47.7 | 43.3 |
| Petroleum products, refined | 28.3 | 45.9 | 42.7 |
| Motor spirit (gasoline) and other light oils | 11.6 | 19.3 | 42.6 |
| Motor spirit (gasoline), including aviation spirit | 11.6 | 19.3 | — |
| Other light petroleum oils | — | — | 42.6 |
| **Chemicals and related products** | 42.9 | 71.9 | 52.7 |
| Medicinal and pharmaceutical products | 15.4 | 30.0 | 21.0 |
| Medicaments | 14.1 | 25.4 | 19.7 |
| Medicaments containing antibiotics | 13.3 | 23.6 | 16.5 |
| Other chemical materials | 5.5 | 21.6 | 14.5 |
| Pesticides, disinfectants | 4.2 | 19.8 | 13.1 |
| Insecticides, for retail sale | 2.1 | 18.9 | 9.6 |
| **Basic manufactures** | 119.8 | 146.2 | 78.5 |
| Textile yarn, fabrics, etc. | 61.3 | 61.2 | 30.0 |
| Cotton fabrics, woven | 53.0 | 49.3 | 23.1 |
| Bleached and mercerized fabrics | 50.9 | 48.0 | 22.5 |
| Bleached cotton fabrics (containing 85% or more by weight of cotton) | 49.2 | 47.0 | 22.4 |
| Non-metallic mineral manufactures | 17.1 | 30.0 | 12.8 |
| Lime, cement and fabricated construction materials | 12.8 | 23.9 | 8.7 |
| Cement | 11.5 | 22.3 | 7.1 |
| Iron and steel | 12.6 | 16.4 | 8.6 |
| Other metal manufactures | 12.6 | 16.8 | 10.2 |
| **Machinery and transport equipment** | 118.8 | 131.2 | 125.5 |
| Power-generating machinery and equipment | 3.9 | 4.4 | 9.3 |
| Machinery specialized for particular industries | 20.0 | 13.0 | 14.5 |
| General industrial machinery, equipment and parts | 16.7 | 20.2 | 17.6 |
| Telecommunications and sound equipment | 11.4 | 11.8 | 16.7 |
| Other electrical machinery, apparatus, etc. | 17.1 | 18.0 | 16.8 |
| Road vehicles and parts | 39.8 | 49.6 | 41.4 |
| Passenger motor cars (excl. buses) | 14.3 | 19.5 | 14.5 |
| **Miscellaneous manufactured articles** | 29.5 | 40.4 | 28.6 |
| **Total** (incl. others) | 471.9 | 581.4 | 443.9 |

TOGO

*Statistical Survey*

| Exports f.o.b. | 1989 | 1990 | 1991 |
|---|---|---|---|
| **Food and live animals** | 47.6 | 57.3 | 43.6 |
| Cereals and cereal preparations | 8.8 | 17.3 | 9.2 |
| Flour of wheat or meslin | 7.4 | 12.3 | 6.8 |
| Coffee, tea, cocoa, spices, and manufactures thereof | 34.6 | 33.5 | 20.6 |
| Coffee (not roasted), coffee husks and skins | 22.1 | 17.8 | 9.1 |
| Cocoa beans, raw, roasted | 12.3 | 15.2 | 11.0 |
| **Crude materials (inedible) except fuels** | 173.2 | 178.9 | 186.6 |
| Textile fibres and waste | 39.4 | 55.7 | 60.4 |
| Cotton | 38.7 | 55.6 | 55.4 |
| Raw cotton (excl. linters) | 38.6 | 55.6 | 55.2 |
| Crude fertilizers and crude minerals | 130.6 | 119.6 | 124.7 |
| Natural calcium phosphates, etc | 130.4 | 119.1 | 122.8 |
| **Mineral fuels, lubricants and related materials** | — | 0.1 | 5.9 |
| Petroleum, petroleum products and related materials | — | — | 5.8 |
| Petroleum products, refined | — | — | 5.8 |
| Motor spirit (gasoline) and other light oils | — | — | 5.8 |
| Other light petroleum oils | — | — | 5.8 |
| **Basic manufactures** | 12.0 | 19.5 | 7.7 |
| Textile yarn, fabrics, etc. | 0.7 | 6.5 | 1.1 |
| Textile articles | 0.1 | 5.7 | 0.5 |
| Sacks and bags of textile materials | — | 5.7 | 0.5 |
| Non-metallic mineral manufactures | 5.2 | 7.0 | 3.0 |
| Lime, cement and fabricated construction materials | 5.2 | 6.9 | 3.0 |
| Cement | 5.1 | 6.9 | 3.0 |
| **Total** (incl. others) | 245.1 | 267.9 | 253.2 |

**PRINCIPAL TRADING PARTNERS** (US $ million)

| Imports c.i.f. | 1989 | 1990 | 1991 |
|---|---|---|---|
| Angola | 4.8 | 3.8 | 1.2 |
| Belgium-Luxembourg | 8.9 | 10.4 | 9.1 |
| Benin | 6.0 | 5.7 | 4.0 |
| Cameroon | 0.9 | 0.5 | 12.5 |
| Canada | 5.2 | 6.6 | 0.6 |
| China, People's Republic | 7.2 | 8.9 | 6.0 |
| Côte d'Ivoire | 12.1 | 46.9 | 16.8 |
| France | 139.6 | 177.2 | 146.9 |
| Gabon | 5.7 | 5.8 | 3.4 |
| Germany, Federal Republic | 36.1 | 35.0 | 18.5 |
| Ghana | 5.0 | 7.6 | 5.3 |
| Hong Kong | 10.0 | 14.9 | 10.9 |
| Italy | 14.4 | 13.3 | 14.0 |
| Japan | 19.9 | 25.0 | 29.7 |
| Netherlands | 55.5 | 52.7 | 33.5 |
| Nigeria | 8.0 | 13.1 | 12.8 |
| Norway | 1.0 | 7.7 | 3.6 |
| Senegal | 5.9 | 5.5 | 1.6 |
| Singapore | 7.3 | 7.4 | 5.6 |
| Spain | 13.5 | 9.6 | 4.9 |
| Switzerland-Liechtenstein | 2.5 | 3.1 | 5.3 |
| Thailand | 5.0 | 4.4 | 4.6 |
| United Kingdom | 20.0 | 21.8 | 16.3 |
| USA | 26.7 | 30.8 | 28.5 |
| **Total** (incl. others) | 471.9 | 581.3 | 443.9 |

| Exports f.o.b. | 1989 | 1990 | 1991 |
|---|---|---|---|
| Australia | 10.7 | 1.2 | — |
| Bangladesh | — | 5.7 | 0.5 |
| Belgium-Luxembourg | 4.3 | 5.9 | 2.1 |
| Benin | 7.1 | 5.7 | 5.1 |
| British Indian Ocean Territory | — | 3.2 | 4.6 |
| Burkina Faso | 5.7 | 8.8 | 5.7 |
| Canada | 30.6 | 33.4 | 28.7 |
| China, People's Republic | 0.9 | 0.2 | 4.6 |
| Denmark | 2.5 | 3.8 | 2.3 |
| France | 21.2 | 26.3 | 17.0 |
| Germany, Federal Republic | 3.4 | 10.0 | 7.1 |
| Ghana | 4.9 | 4.1 | 2.9 |
| Greece | 0.3 | 3.8 | 8.0 |
| Guinea | — | 3.7 | 0.2 |
| India | 8.0 | 14.1 | 6.5 |
| Indonesia | 1.8 | 2.2 | 4.1 |
| Italy | 18.4 | 14.2 | 10.4 |
| Mexico | 3.3 | 4.3 | 17.9 |
| Morocco | 3.0 | 2.5 | 1.7 |
| Netherlands | 15.3 | 8.8 | 2.2 |
| Niger | 2.8 | 3.6 | 3.3 |
| Nigeria | 6.1 | 8.8 | 19.4 |
| Philippines | 12.2 | 11.5 | 12.5 |
| Poland | 10.8 | 3.1 | 3.6 |
| Portugal | 9.1 | 14.6 | 4.0 |
| Singapore | 0.3 | 0.8 | 3.6 |
| Spain | 18.8 | 17.1 | 17.2 |
| Switzerland-Liechtenstein | 1.1 | 3.4 | 3.0 |
| Thailand | 3.0 | 1.7 | 9.3 |
| USSR | 4.9 | 12.6 | 10.4 |
| United Kingdom | 13.4 | 3.9 | 3.9 |
| USA | 0.3 | 3.0 | 0.2 |
| Yugoslavia | 2.6 | 1.2 | 0.9 |
| **Total** (incl. others) | 245.1 | 267.9 | 253.2 |

# Transport

**RAILWAYS** (estimated traffic)

| | 1989 | 1990 | 1991 |
|---|---|---|---|
| Passenger-km (million) | 124 | 129 | 132 |
| Freight (million ton-km) | 14 | 15 | 17 |

Source: UN Economic Commission for Africa, *African Statistical Yearbook*.

**ROAD TRAFFIC** (motor vehicles registered at 31 December)

| | 1986 | 1987 | 1988 |
|---|---|---|---|
| Passenger cars | 41,122 | 44,120 | 47,083 |
| Buses and coaches | 298 | 352 | 381 |
| Goods vehicles | 19,943 | 21,136 | 22,230 |
| Tractors (road) | 940 | 994 | 1,048 |
| Motor cycles and scooters | 25,400 | 27,483 | 29,179 |

Source: Banque centrale des états de l'Afrique de l'ouest.

**INTERNATIONAL SEA-BORNE SHIPPING**
(freight traffic, '000 metric tons)

| Port Lomé* | 1990 | 1991 | 1992 |
|---|---|---|---|
| Goods loaded | 180 | 162 | 178 |
| Goods unloaded | 1,157 | 1,050 | 1,114 |

* Excluding goods in transit.

Source: Banque centrale des états de l'Afrique de l'ouest.

| Port Kpémé | 1979 | 1980 | 1981 |
|---|---|---|---|
| Freight loaded* ('000 metric tons) | 2,990 | 2,895 | 2,200 |

* Phosphate from the OTP mines.

Source: *Statistiques douanières du Togo*.

TOGO

CIVIL AVIATION (traffic on scheduled services)*

|  | 1990 | 1991 | 1992 |
|---|---|---|---|
| Km flown (million) | 2 | 2 | 2 |
| Passengers carried ('000) | 76 | 66 | 66 |
| Passenger-km (million) | 232 | 207 | 201 |
| Total ton-km (million) | 39 | 36 | 34 |

* Including an apportionment of the traffic of Air Afrique.

Source: UN, *Statistical Yearbook*.

## Tourism

|  | 1990 | 1991 | 1992 |
|---|---|---|---|
| Tourist arrivals ('000) | 103 | 65 | 49 |
| Tourist receipts (US $ million) | 58 | 49 | 39 |

Source: UN, *Statistical Yearbook*.

## Communications Media

|  | 1990 | 1991 | 1992 |
|---|---|---|---|
| Radio receivers ('000 in use) | 745 | 770 | 795 |
| Television receivers ('000 in use) | 22 | 23 | 24 |
| Telephones ('000 main lines in use) | 11* | 11 | n.a. |
| Daily newspapers |  |  |  |
| Number | 1 | n.a. | 2 |
| Circulation ('000 copies) | 10 | n.a. | 12 |

* Estimate.

Sources: UNESCO, *Statistical Yearbook*; UN, *Statistical Yearbook*.

## Education

(1990, unless otherwise indicated)

|  | Institutions | Teachers | Males | Females | Total |
|---|---|---|---|---|---|
| Pre-primary | 252 | 383 | 5,540 | 5,409 | 10,949 |
| Primary | 2,494 | 11,105 | 396,320 | 255,642 | 651,962 |
| Secondary |  |  |  |  |  |
| General | n.a. | 4,231 | 87,548 | 29,605 | 117,153 |
| Vocational | n.a. | 261 | 6,231 | 2,161 | 8,392 |
| University level | n.a. | 276* | 6,702† | 1,030† | 7,732† |

* 1988 figure.   † 1989 figure.

Source: UNESCO, *Statistical Yearbook*.

# Directory

## The Constitution

The Constitution that was approved in a national referendum on 27 September 1993 defines the rights, freedoms and obligations of Togolese citizens, and defines the separation of powers among the executive, legislative and judicial organs of state.

Executive power is vested in the President of the Republic, who is elected, by direct universal adult suffrage, with a five-year mandate. The legislature, the Assemblée nationale, is similarly elected for a period of five years, its 81 members being directly elected by universal suffrage. The President of the Republic appoints a Prime Minister who is able to command a majority in the legislature, and the Prime Minister, in consultation with the President, appoints other government ministers. A Constitutional Court is designated as the highest court of jurisdiction in constitutional matters.

## The Government

### HEAD OF STATE

**President:** Gen. GNASSINGBE EYADÉMA (assumed power 13 January 1967; proclaimed President 14 April 1967; elected 30 December 1979; re-elected 21 December 1986 and 25 August 1993).

### COUNCIL OF MINISTERS
(June 1995)

**President:** Gen. GNASSINGBE EYADÉMA.
**Prime Minister:** EDEM KODJO.
**Minister of Justice and Keeper of the Seals:** KAGNI GABRIEL AKAKPOVIE.
**Minister of National Defence:** ALFA ABALO.
**Minister of Economy and Finance:** ELOME EMILE DADZIE.
**Minister of Foreign Affairs and Co-operation:** (vacant).
**Minister of the Interior and Decentralization:** KODJO SAGBO.
**Minister of Planning and Territorial Development:** YANDJA YENTCHABRE.
**Minister of National Education and Scientific Research:** Prof. KOMLAVI SEDDOH.
**Minister of Communications and Culture:** ATSUTSE AGBOBLI.
**Minister of Human Rights and Rehabilitation, in charge of Relations with the National Assembly:** DJOVI GALLY.
**Minister of Industry and State Enterprises:** FAYADOWA BOUKPESSI.
**Minister of Equipment:** TCHAMDJA ANDJO.
**Minister of Mines, Energy and Water Resources:** ANATO AGBOZOUHOUE.
**Minister of Rural Development, Environment and Tourism:** YAO DO FELLI.
**Minister of Trade, Price Control and Transport:** DEDEVI MICHÈLE EKUE.
**Minister of Health, Population and National Solidarity:** Prof. AFATSAO AMEDOME.
**Minister of Technical Education and Vocational Training:** BAMOUNI SOMOLOU STANISLAS BABA.
**Minister of Youth and Sports:** KOUAMI AGBOGBOLI IHOU.
**Secretary of State delegate to the Minister of the Interior and Decentralization, in charge of Security:** Col SEYI MEMENE.

### MINISTRIES

**Office of the President:** Palais Présidentiel, ave de la Marina, Lomé; tel. 21-27-01; telex 5201.
**Ministry of Communications and Culture:** Lomé.

TOGO
*Directory*

**Ministry of the Economy and Finance:** Ancien Palais, ave de la Marina, BP 387, Lomé; tel. 21-23-71; telex 5286; fax 21-76-02.

**Ministry of Employment, Labour, the Civil Service and Social Welfare:** angle ave de la Marina et rue Kpalimé, Lomé; tel. 21-26-53.

**Ministry of Equipment, Mines, Energy and Water Resources:** ave de Sarakawa, Lomé; tel. 21-38-01.

**Ministry of Foreign Affairs and Co-operation:** place du Monument aux Morts, Lomé; tel. 21-29-10; telex 5239.

**Ministry of Health, Population and National Solidarity:** rue Branly, Lomé; tel. 21-29-83.

**Ministry of Human Rights and Rehabilitation:** BP 1325, Lomé; tel. 21-30-53; fax 21-19-73.

**Ministry of Industry and State Enterprises:** BP 2748, Lomé; tel. 21-07-44; telex 5396.

**Ministry of the Interior and Decentralization:** rue Albert Sarraut, Lomé; tel. 21-23-19.

**Ministry of Justice:** ave de la Marina, rue Colonel de Roux, Lomé; tel. 21-26-53.

**Ministry of National Defence:** Lomé; tel. 21-28-91; telex 5321.

**Ministry of National Education and Scientific Research, Technical Education and Vocational Training:** Immeuble des Quatre Ministères, rue Colonel de Roux, Lomé; tel. 21-38-01; telex 5322.

**Ministry of Planning and Territorial Development:** Lomé; tel. 21-27-01; telex 5380.

**Ministry of Rural Development, Environment and Tourism:** ave de Sarakawa, Lomé; tel. 21-56-71.

**Ministry of Trade, Price Control and Transport:** rue de Commerce, Lomé; tel. 21-09-09.

**Ministry of Youth and Sports:** BP 3193, Lomé; tel. 21-23-52; telex 5103.

## President and Legislature

### PRESIDENT

**Presidential Election, 25 August 1993**

| Candidate | % of votes |
|---|---|
| Gen. Gnassingbe Eyadéma | 96.49 |
| Kwami Mensah Jacques Amouzou | 1.87 |
| Adani Ifé Atakpamevi | 1.64 |
| **Total** | **100.00** |

### ASSEMBLÉE NATIONALE

**Speaker:** Dahuku Pere (RPT).

**General Election, 6 and 20 February 1994**

| Party | Seats |
|---|---|
| Comité d'action pour le renouveau (CAR) | 36* |
| Rassemblement du peuple togolais (RPT) | 35 |
| Union togolaise pour la démocratie (UTD) | 7* |
| Union pour la justice et la démocratie (UJD) | 2 |
| Coordination nationale des forces nouvelles (CFN) | 1 |
| **Total** | **81** |

* The Supreme Court declared the election result invalid in two constituencies where the seats had been allocated to the CAR, and in one where the seat had been allocated to the UTD. By-elections were to be held in these constituencies at a later date.

## Political Organizations

Following the legalization of political parties in April 1991, numerous organizations obtained legal status. By mid-1993 63 parties were officially acknowledged. Of the parties in existence in mid-1995, among the most influential were:

**Alliance togolaise pour la démocratie (ATD):** Leader: Adani Ifé Atakpamevi.

**Comité d'action pour le renouveau (CAR):** Leader Me Yao Agboyibo.

**Convention démocratique des peuples africains (CDPA):** Leader Prof. Léopold Gnininvi.

**Démocratie sociale togolaise (DST):** linked to PDT; Leader Abou Djobo Boukari.

**Mouvement du 5 octobre (MO5):** radical group; Leader Bassirou Ayeva.

**Mouvement nationaliste de l'unité (MNU):** f. Oct. 1992; Gen. Sec. Koffitse Adzrako.

**Parti d'action pour la démocratie (PAD):** Leader Francis Ekoh.

**Parti démocratique togolais (PDT):** linked to DST; Leader Mba Kabassema.

**Parti des démocrates pour l'unité (PDU):** Leader Jean-Lucien Savi de Tové.

**Parti pour la démocratie et le renouveau (PDR):** Leader Zarifou Ayiva.

**Parti pan-africain socialiste (PPS):** radical; Leader Francis Agbobli.

**Rassemblement du peuple togolais (RPT):** place de l'Indépendance, BP 1208, Lomé; tel. 21-20-18; telex 5207; f. 1969; sole legal party 1969–91; Pres. Gen. Gnassingbe Eyadéma; Sec.-Gen. Vigniko Amedegnato.

**Union pour la démocratie et la solidarité (UDS):** Sec.-Gen. Antoine Foly.

**Union pour la justice at la démocratie (UJD):** pro-Eyadéma; Leader Lal Taxpandjan.

**Union des libéraux indépendants (ULD):** f. Nov. 1993 to succeed Union des démocrates pour le renouveau; Leader Kwami Mensah Jacques Amouzou.

**Union togolaise pour la démocratie (UTD):** Leader Edem Kodjo; Sec.-Gen. Adan Messan Ajavon.

**Union togolaise pour la réconciliation (UTR):** Leader Bawa Mankoubu.

Most of the above parties belonged to one or more of the following alliances, reported to be active in mid-1995:

**Collectif de l'opposition démocratique (COD-2):** f. 1992; alliance of about 26 political orgs and trade unions; incl. CAR, CDPA, PDU, PDR and UDS; Leader Antoine Foly (UDS).

**Comité de la résistance togolaise:** Paris, France; comprises c. 20 political orgs; Chair. Isidore Latizo; Sec.-Gen. Aurélio Amorin.

**Coordination nationale des forces nouvelles (CFN):** f. June 1993; comprises six political orgs and asscns; Pres. Me Joseph Kokou Koffigoh; Nat. Exec. Sec. Nicolas Nomedji.

**Groupe des démocrates sociaux pan-africains:** f. Dec. 1993; alliance of CDPA, PDR and PPS; Leader Prof. Léopold Gnininvi.

**Union des forces de changement:** comprises 20 parties; Leader Gilchrist Olympio.

## Diplomatic Representation

### EMBASSIES IN TOGO

**Belgium:** 165 rue Pelletier Caventou, BP 7643, Lomé; tel. 21-03-23; telex 5363; Ambassador: Pierre Vaesen.

**Brazil:** 119 rue de l'Ocam, BP 1356, Lomé; tel. 21-00-58; telex 5346; Chargé d'affaires a.i.: José Roberto Procopiak.

**China, People's Republic:** Tokoin-Ouest, BP 2690, Lomé; tel. 21-31-59; telex 5070; Ambassador: Zhou Xianjue.

**Egypt:** route d'Aného, BP 8, Lomé; tel. 21-24-43; telex 5310; Ambassador: Hussein el-Khazindar.

**France:** 51 rue du Golfe, BP 337, Lomé; tel. 21-25-71; telex 5202; Ambassador: Jean-Michel Gaussot.

**Gabon:** Tokoin Super-Taco, BP 9118, Lomé; tel. 21-47-76; telex 5307; Ambassador: Alain Maurice Mayombo.

**Germany:** Marina, route d'Aflao, BP 1175, Lomé; tel. 21-23-38; telex 5204; fax 22-18-88; Ambassador: Dr Reinald Steck.

**Ghana:** 8 rue Paulin Eklou, Tokoin-Ouest, BP 92, Lomé; tel. 21-31-94; fax 21-77-36; Ambassador: Nelson Kojo Dumevi.

**Israel:** 159 rue de l'OCAM, BP 61187, Lomé; tel. 21-79-58; telex 5424; fax 21-88-94; Ambassador: Jacob Topaz.

**Korea, Democratic People's Republic:** Tokoin-Est, Lomé; tel. 21-46-01; Ambassador: Pak Song Il.

**Libya:** blvd du 13 janvier, BP 4872, Lomé; tel. 21-40-63; telex 5288; Chargé d'affaires a.i.: Ahmed M. Abdulkafi.

**Nigeria:** 311 blvd du 13 janvier, BP 1189, Lomé; tel. 21-34-55; Ambassador: Vincent Okobi.

**USA:** angle rue Pelletier Caventou et rue Vauban, BP 852, Lomé; tel. 21-29-91; fax 21-79-52; Ambassador: Johnny Young.

**Zaire:** 325 blvd du 13 janvier, BP 102, Lomé; tel. 21-51-55; telex 5263; Ambassador: Lokoka Ikukele Bomolo.

## Judicial System

Justice is administered by the Cour Suprême (Supreme Court), two Cours d'Appel (Appeal Courts) and the Tribunaux de première instance, which hear civil, commercial and criminal cases. There is a labour tribunal and a tribunal for children's rights. In addition, there are two exceptional courts, the Cour de sûreté de l'Etat, which judges crimes against internal and external state security, and the Tribunal spécial chargé de la répression des détournements de deniers publics, which deals with cases of misuse of public funds. Under the Constitution adopted in September 1992, a Constitutional Court was to be established.

**Cour Suprême:** BP 906, Lomé; tel. 21-22-58; f. 1961; consists of four chambers; constitutional, judicial, administrative and auditing; Pres. EMMANUEL APEDO; Attorney-Gen. KOUAMI AMADOS-DJOKO.

## Religion

It is estimated that about 50% of the population follow traditional animist beliefs, some 35% are Christians (mainly Roman Catholics) and 15% are Muslims.

### CHRISTIANITY
#### The Roman Catholic Church

Togo comprises one archdiocese and six dioceses. At 31 December 1992 there were an estimated 856,489 adherents in the country, representing about 21.6% of the total population.

**Bishops' Conference:** Conférence Episcopale du Togo, 10 rue Maréchal Foch, BP 348, Lomé; tel. 21-22-72; f. 1979; Pres. Most Rev. PHILIPPE FANOKO KOSSI KPODZRO, Archbishop of Lomé.

**Archbishop of Lomé:** Most Rev. PHILIPPE FANOKO KOSSI KPODZRO, Archevêché, 10 rue Maréchal Foch, BP 348, Lomé; tel. 21-22-72.

#### Protestant Churches

There are about 170 mission centres, with a personnel of some 230, affiliated to European and American societies and administered by a Conseil Synodal, presided over by a moderator.

**Directorate of Protestant Churches:** 1 rue Maréchal Foch, BP 378, Lomé; Moderator Rev. Pastor AWUME (acting).

**Eglise Evangélique Presbyterienne du Togo:** 1 rue Tokmake, BP 2, Lomé; Moderator Rev. FATSEME AMIDU (acting).

### BAHÁ'Í FAITH

**National Spiritual Assembly:** BP 1659, Lomé; tel. 21-21-99; mems resident in 445 localities.

## The Press

### DAILIES

**Journal Officiel de la République du Togo:** EDITOGO, BP 891, Lomé; tel. 21-37-18; telex 5294.

**Togo-Presse:** EDITOGO, BP 891, Lomé; tel. 21-37-18; telex 5294; f. 1962; renamed *La Nouvelle Marche* 1979–91; daily; French, Kabiye and Ewe; political, economic and cultural; official govt publ.; Editor-in-Chief (vacant); circ. 15,000.

### PERIODICALS

**Bulletin de la Chambre de Commerce:** angle ave de la Présidence, BP 360, Lomé; tel. 21-70-65; telex 5023; fax 21-47-30; monthly; directory of commercial, industrial and agricultural activities.

**Bulletin d'Information de l'Agence Togolaise de Presse:** 35 rue Binger, Lomé; weekly; publ. by govt information service.

**Courrier du Golfe:** Lomé; f. 1990; independent.

**Espoir de la Nation Togolaise:** EDITOGO, BP 891, Lomé; tel. 21-37-18; telex 5294; monthly; Dir M. AWESSO; circ. 3,000.

**L'Eveil du Travailleur Togolais:** BP 163, Lomé; tel. 21-57-39; quarterly; Elrato; publ. by Confédération Nationale des Travailleurs du Togo; Chief Editor M. K. AGBEKA; circ. 5,000.

**Forum Hebdo:** Lomé; weekly; independent; Dir GABRIEL KOMI AGAH.

**Game su:** 19 ave de la Nouvelle Marche, BP 1247, Lomé; tel. 21-28-44; f. 1972; monthly; Ewe; publ. by Ministry of Health, Population and National Solidarity for the newly literate; circ. 6,000.

**La Parole:** Lomé; weekly; independent; Dir BERTIN KANGHI FOLY.

**Kpakpa Désenchanté:** Lomé; weekly; independent.

**Le Secteur Privé:** angle ave de la Présidence, BP 360, Lomé; tel. 21-70-65; telex 5023; fax 21-47-30; monthly; publ. by Chambre de Commerce, d'Agriculture et d'Industrie du Togo.

**Tev fema:** 19 ave de la Nouvelle Marche, BP 1247, Lomé; tel. 21-28-44; f. 1977; monthly; Kabiye; publ. by Ministry of Health, Population and National Solidarity; circ. 3,000.

**Togo-Dialogue:** EDITOGO, BP 891, Lomé; tel. 21-37-18; telex 5294; monthly; publ. by govt information service; circ. 5,000.

**Togo-Images:** BP 4869, Lomé; tel. 21-56-80; f. 1962; monthly series of wall posters depicting recent political, economic and cultural events in Togo; publ. by govt information service; Dir AKOBI BEDOU; circ. 5,000.

**La Tribune des Démocrates:** Lomé; weekly; independent; Editor MARTIN NBENOUGOU (imprisoned May 1994).

### NEWS AGENCIES

**Agence Togolaise de Presse (ATOP):** 35 rue des Media, BP 2327, Lomé; tel. 212507; telex 5320; f. 1975; Dir SESHIE SEYENA BIAVA.

#### Foreign Bureau

**Xinhua (New China) News Agency** (People's Republic of China): BP 2984, Lomé; tel. 21-39-20; telex 5273; Correspondent QIN DIANJIE.

## Publishers

**Centre Togolais de Communication Evangélique (CTCE):** 1 rue de Commerce, BP 378, Lomé; tel. 22-45-82; fax 21-29-67; Dir MARC K. ETSE.

**Editions Akpagnon:** BP 3531, Lomé; tel. 22-02-44; f. 1979; general literature; Man. Dir YVES-EMMANUEL DOGBÉ.

**Etablissement National des Editions du Togo (EDITOGO):** BP 891, Lomé; tel. 21-61-06; telex 5294; f. 1961; govt publishing house; general and educational; Pres. GBÉGNON AMEGBOH; Man. Dir KOKOU AMEDEGNATO.

**Nouvelles Editions Africaines du Togo (NEA TOGO):** 239 blvd du 13 janvier, BP 4862, Lomé; tel. 21-67-61; telex 5393; fax 22-10-03; general fiction and non-fiction; Man. Dir DOVI KAVEGUE.

## Radio and Television

In 1992, according to UNESCO, there were an estimated 795,000 radio receivers and 24,000 television receivers in use.

**Radiodiffusion du Togo (Internationale) — Radio Lomé:** BP 434, Lomé; tel. 21-24-93; telex 5320; fax 21-36-73; f. 1953; renamed Radiodiffusion-Télévision de la Nouvelle Marche 1979–91; state-controlled; radio programmes in French, English and vernacular languages; Dir BAWA SEMEDO.

**Radiodiffusion du Togo (Nationale):** BP 21, Kara; tel. 60-60-60; f. 1974 as Radiodiffusion Kara (Togo); state-controlled; radio programmes in French and vernacular languages; Dir M'BA KPENOUGOU.

**Radio Kara:** BP 21, Kara; tel. 60-60-60; Dir KODJOVI LE BLOND.

**Radio Liberté:** operated by the COD-2 opposition alliance, was reported to have commenced broadcasts in late 1992.

**Télévision Togolaise:** BP 3286, Lomé; tel. 21-53-57; telex 5320; fax 21-57-86; f. 1973; state-controlled; three stations; programmes in French and vernacular languages; Dir MARTIN AHIAVI.

## Finance

(cap. = capital; res = reserves; dep. = deposits; m. = million; br. = branch; amounts in francs CFA)

### BANKING
#### Central Bank

**Banque Centrale des Etats de l'Afrique de l'Ouest (BCEAO):** ave de Sarakawa, BP 120, Lomé; tel. 21-25-12; telex 5216; fax 21-76-02; headquarters in Dakar, Senegal; f. 1955; bank of issue and central bank for the seven states of the Union économique et monétaire ouest-africaine (UEMOA), comprising Benin, Burkina Faso, Côte d'Ivoire, Mali, Niger, Senegal and Togo; cap. and res 530,827m. (Sept. 1993); Gov. CHARLES KONAN BANNY; Dir in Togo YAO MESSAN AHO; br. at Kara.

#### Commercial Banks

**Banque Togolaise pour le Commerce et l'Industrie (BTCI):** 169 blvd du 13 janvier, BP 363, Lomé; tel. 21-46-41; telex 5221; fax 21-32-65; f. 1974; 24.8% owned by Société Financière pour les Pays d'Outre-mer, 23.8% by Banque Nationale de Paris, 21.0% by SNI & FA; cap. 1,700m. (Sept. 1992); Pres. DO FRANCK FIANYO; Man. Dir MAX KODJO OSSEYI; 8 brs.

**Ecobank—Togo:** 20 rue de Commerce, BP 3302, Lomé; tel. 21-72-14; telex 5440; fax 21-42-37; f. 1984, operations commenced 1988; 60% owned by Ecobank Transnational Inc (operating under the auspices of the Economic Community of West African States), 40% by Togolese private interests; cap. 750m., res 584m., dep. 10,862m. (Sept. 1993); Pres. YAO PALI TCHALLA; Man. Dir AMIN UDDIN.

**Meridien BIAO—Togo:** 13 rue de Commerce, BP 346, Lomé; tel. 21-32-86; telex 5218; fax 21-10-19; f. 1981, adopted present name in 1991; 60% owned by Meridien BIAO SA (Luxembourg), 40% by private Togolese interests; cap. 937.5m. (Sept. 1991); Pres. KOSSI R. PAASS; Man. Dir ALEXIS LAMSEH LOOKY; 6 brs.

**Société Interafricaine de Banques (SIAB):** route d'Aného, BP 4874, Lomé; tel. 21-28-30; telex 5301; fax 21-58-29; f. 1975; fmrly Banque Arabe Libyenne-Togolaise du Commerce Extérieur; 50% state-owned, 50% owned by Libyan Arab Foreign Bank; cap. 3,100m. (Sept. 1993); Pres. YENTCHABRE YANDJA; Man. Dir TAHER BUSHAALA.

**Union Togolaise de Banque (UTB):** 13 blvd du 13 janvier, BP 359, Lomé; tel. 21-64-11; telex 5215; fax 21-22-06; f. 1964; state-owned; cap. 2,000m. (Sept. 1992); Pres. Minister of the Economy and Finance; Dir-Gen. ALEXIS LAMSEH LOOKY; 9 brs.

### Development Banks

**Banque Togolaise de Développement (BTD):** angle rue des Nîmes et ave N. Grunitzky, BP 65, Lomé; tel. 21-36-41; telex 5282; fax 21-44-56; f. 1966; 43% state-owned, 20% owned by BCEAO, 20% by private Togolese interests; cap. 3,065m., res 870m., dep. 17,493m. (Sept. 1992); Pres. DÉDÉVI MICHÈLE EKUE; Man. Dir MENSAVI MENSAH; 8 brs.

**Société Nationale d'Investissement et Fonds Annexes (SNI & FA):** 11 ave du 24 janvier, BP 2682, Lomé; tel. 21-62-21; telex 5265; fax 21-62-25; f. 1971; state-owned; cap. 500m. (Sept. 1992); Pres. OGAMO BAGNAH; Man. Dir TANKPADJA LALLE.

### Bankers' Association

**Association Professionnelle des Banques et Etablissements Financiers du Togo:** Lomé.

### INSURANCE

**CICA—RE/Compagnie Commune de Réassurance des Etats Membres de la CICA:** ave du 24 janvier, BP 12410, Lomé; tel. 21-62-69; telex 5066; fax 21-49-64; regional reinsurance co grouping 12 west and central African states; cap. 600m.; Chair JACQUELINE OKILI; Gen. Man. DIGBEU KIPRE.

**Groupement Togolais d'Assurances (GTA):** route d'Atakpamé, BP 3298, Lomé; tel. 25-60-75; telex 5069; fax 25-26-78; f. 1974; 62.9% state-owned; cap. 100m.; all aspects of insurance and reinsurance; Pres. Minister of the Economy and Finance; Man. Dir KOSSI NAMBEA.

## Trade and Industry

### ECONOMIC AND SOCIAL COUNCIL

**Conseil Economique et Social:** Lomé; tel. 21-53-01; telex 5237; f. 1967; advisory body of 25 mems, comprising five trade unionists, five representatives of industry and commerce, five representatives of agriculture, five economists and sociologists, and five technologists; Pres. KOFFI GBODZIDI DJONDO.

### DEVELOPMENT AND MARKETING ORGANIZATIONS

Agricultural development is under the supervision of five regional development authorities, the Sociétés régionales d'aménagement et de développement.

**Caisse Française de Développement:** ave de Sarakawa, BP 33, Lomé; tel. 21-04-98; telex 5313; fax 21-79-32; f. 1992 to succeed the Caisse Centrale de Coopération Economique; Dir M. TYACK.

**Mission Française de Coopération:** BP 91, Lomé; telex 5413; fax 21-21-28; administers bilateral aid from France; Dir SUZANNE FAUCHEUX.

**Office de Développement et d'Exploitation des Forêts (ODEF):** 15 rue des Conseillers Municipaux, BP 334, Lomé; tel. 21-51-59; f. 1971; development and management of forest resources; Man. Dir KOFFI AGOGNO.

**Office National des Produits Vivriers (TOGOGRAIN):** 141 ave de la Libération, BP 3039, Lomé; tel. 21-59-55; telex 5220; development and marketing of staple food crops; Man. Dir M. WALLA.

**Office des Produits Agricoles du Togo (OPAT):** angle rue Branly et ave no. 3, BP 1334, Lomé; tel. 21-44-71; telex 5220; f. 1964; agricultural development, marketing and exports; Dir-Gen. AYENAM KPOWBIE.

**Office Togolais des Phosphates (OTP):** BP 3200, Lomé; tel. 21-22-28; telex 5287; f. 1974; cap. 15,000m. francs CFA; production and marketing of phosphates; Dir-Gen. EKUE LIKOU.

**Société d'Appui a la Filière Café-Cacao-Coton (SAFICC):** Lomé; f. 1992; development of coffee, cocoa and cotton production.

**Société Nationale de Commerce (SONACOM):** 29 blvd Circulaire, BP 3009, Lomé; tel. 21-31-18; telex 5281; f. 1972; cap. 2,000m. francs CFA; importer of staple foods; Dir-Gen. JEAN LADOUX.

**Société Togolaise du Coton (SOTOCO):** Lomé; f. 1974 to promote cotton cultivation.

### CHAMBER OF COMMERCE

**Chambre de Commerce, d'Agriculture et d'Industrie du Togo (CCAIT):** angle ave de la Présidence et ave Georges Pompidou, BP 360, Lomé; tel. 21-70-65; telex 5023; fax 21-47-30; f. 1921; Pres. ALEXIS LAMSEH LOOKY; Sec.-Gen. MICHEL KWAME MEYISSO.

### EMPLOYERS' ORGANIZATIONS

**Groupement Interprofessionnel des Entreprises du Togo (GITO):** BP 345, Lomé; Pres. CLARENCE OLYMPIO.

**Syndicat des Commerçants Importateurs et Exportateurs de la République Togolaise (SCIMPEXTO):** BP 345, Lomé; Pres. KODJO G. KENTZLER.

**Syndicat des Entrepreneurs de Travaux Publics, Bâtiments et Mines du Togo:** BP 1101, Lomé; Pres. CLARENCE OLYMPIO.

### TRADE UNIONS

**Collectif des Syndicats Indépendants (CSI):** Lomé; f. 1992 as 'umbrella' org. for three autonomous trade union confederations:

**Confédération Syndicale des Travailleurs du Togo (CSTT):** Lomé.

**Groupement Syndical Autonome (GSA):** Lomé.

**Union Nationale des Syndicats Indépendants du Togo (UNSIT):** Tokoin-Wuiti, BP 30082, Lomé; tel. 21-65-65; f. 1991; 17 affiliated unions.

**Confédération Nationale des Travailleurs du Togo (CNTT):** 160 blvd du 13 janvier, BP 163, Lomé; tel. 21-57-39; f. 1973; affiliated to RPT until April 1991; Sec.-Gen. DOUEVI TCHIVIAKOU.

## Transport

### RAILWAYS

**Société Nationale de Chemin de Fer Togolais (SNET):** BP 340, Lomé; tel. 21-43-01; telex 5178; f. 1905 as Chemin de Fer Togolais, restructured under present name in 1993; total length 537 km, incl. lines running inland from Lomé to Atakpamé and Blitta (280 km), and a coastal line, running through Lomé and Aného, which links with the Benin railway system, but which was closed to passenger traffic in 1988 (a service from Lomé to Palimé—119 km—has also been suspended); passengers carried: 630,000 in 1990, freight handled: 16,000 metric tons in 1990; Gen. Man. T. KPEKPASSI.

### ROADS

In 1993 there were some 7,545 km of roads, of which about one-quarter were paved. Principal roads run from Lomé to the borders of Ghana, Nigeria, Burkina Faso and Benin. In 1989 the EC agreed to provide more than 8,000m. francs CFA for the repair and maintenance of the road network.

**Africa Route International (ARI—La Gazelle):** km 9, route d'Atakpamé, BP 4730, Lomé; tel. 25-27-32; fax 29-09-93; f. 1991 as successor to 'privatized' Société Nationale de Transports Routiers; Pres. and Man. Dir BAWA S. MANKOUBI.

### SHIPPING

The major port, at Lomé, generally handles a substantial volume of transit trade for the land-locked countries of Mali, Niger and Burkina Faso, although the political crisis in Togo has resulted in the diversion of much of this trade to neighbouring Benin. Lomé handled about 1.5m. metric tons of goods (including transit trade) in 1992, compared with some 2m. tons in previous years. There is another port at Kpémé for the export of phosphates.

**Port Autonome de Lomé:** BP 1225, Lomé; tel. 27-47-42; telex 5243; fax 21-26-27; f. 1968; Pres. Ihoui Agboboli; Man. Dir Kodjo Agbejomé.

**Société Ouest-Africaine d'Entreprises Maritimes Togo (SOAEM-TOGO):** Zone Industrielle Portuaire, BP 3285, Lomé; tel. 21-07-20; telex 5207; fax 21-34-17; f. 1959; forwarding agents, warehousing, sea and road freight transport; Pres. Jean Fabry; Man. Dir John M. Aquereburu.

**Société Togolaise de Navigation Maritime (SOTONAM):** place des Quatre Etoiles, rond-point du Port, BP 4086, Lomé; tel. 21-51-73; telex 5285; fax 27-69-38; Man. Pakoum Kpema.

**SOCOPAO-Togo:** 18 rue du Commerce, BP 821, Lomé; tel. 21-55-88; telex 5205; fax 21-73-17; f. 1959; freight transport, shipping agents; Pres. Guy Mirabaud; Man. Dir Henri Chaulier.

**SORINCO-Marine:** 110 rue de l'OCAM, BP 2806, Lomé; tel. 21-56-94; freight transport, forwarding agents, warehousing, etc.; Man. Ahmed Edgar Collingwood Williams.

**Togolaise d'Armements et d'Agence de Lignes SA (TAAL):** 21 blvd du Mono, BP 9089, Lomé; tel. 22-02-43; telex 5329; fax 21-06-69; f. 1992; shipping agents, haulage management, crewing agency, forwarding agents; Pres. and Man. Dir Laurent Gbati Takassi-Kikpa.

## CIVIL AVIATION

There are international airports at Tokoin, near Lomé, and at Niamtougou. In addition, there are smaller airfields at Sokodé, Sansanné-Mango, Dapaong and Atakpamé.

**Air Afrique:** BP 111, Lomé; tel. 21-20-42; telex 5276; see under Côte d'Ivoire; Man. in Togo Raphaël Biam.

**Air Togo:** rue du Commerce, Lomé; tel. 21-33-10; f. 1963; cap. 5m. francs CFA; scheduled internal services; Man. Dir Amadou Isaac Ade.

**Peace Air Togo (PAT):** Lomé; internal services and services to Burkina Faso and Côte d'Ivoire; Man. Dir M. Djibom.

# Tourism

Some 49,000 tourists visited Togo in 1992, when receipts from tourism totalled US $39m. In 1990 there was a total of 119 hotels and guest houses, with 4,127 hotel beds.

**Direction des Professions Touristiques:** BP 1289, Lomé; tel. 21-56-62; telex 5007; Dir Gameli Ketomagnan.

# TONGA

## Introductory Survey

### Location, Climate, Language, Religion, Flag, Capital

The Kingdom of Tonga comprises 172 islands in the south-western Pacific Ocean, about 650 km (400 miles) east of Fiji. The Tonga (or Friendly) Islands are divided into three main groups: Vava'u, Ha'apai and Tongatapu. Only 36 of the islands are permanently inhabited. The climate is mild (16°–21°C or 61°–71°F) for most of the year, though usually hotter (27°C—81°F) in December and January. The languages are Tongan, which is a Polynesian language, and English. Tongans are predominantly Christians of the Wesleyan faith, although there are some Roman Catholics and Anglicans. The national flag (proportions 2 by 1) is red, with a rectangular white canton, containing a red cross, in the upper hoist. The capital is Nuku'alofa, on Tongatapu Island.

### Recent History

The foundations of the constitutional monarchy were laid in the 19th century. The kingdom was neutral until 1900, when it became a British Protected State. The treaty establishing the Protectorate was revised in 1958 and 1967, giving Tonga increasing control over its affairs. Queen Salote Tupou III came to the throne in 1918 and ruled Tonga until her death in December 1965. She was succeeded by her son, Prince Tupouto'a Tungi, who had been Prime Minister since 1949. He took the title of King Taufa'ahau Tupou IV and appointed his brother, Prince Fatafehi Tu'ipelehake, to be Prime Minister. Tonga achieved full independence, within the Commonwealth, on 4 June 1970.

Elections held in May 1981 resulted in an unexpected defeat for the People's Representatives group, and the new Assembly became dominated by traditionalist conservatives. In March 1982 the Minister of Finance, Mahe Tupouniua, resigned at the King's request after refusing to grant him travel funds above what had been allocated in the budget. Further elections to the Legislative Assembly took place in May 1984. In September 1985 the King declared his support for the French Government's programme of testing nuclear weapons in the South Pacific, on the grounds that it was in the broader interests of the Western alliance. However, he upheld his former statement of opposition to the tests at Mururoa Atoll in French Polynesia.

In October 1986, following lengthy talks held in Nuku'alofa, Tonga was one of a group of South Pacific island states to conclude a five-year fishing agreement with the USA, whereby the US tuna fleet was granted a licence to operate vessels within Tonga's exclusive economic zone (EEZ).

Following elections held in February 1987, six of the nine People's Representatives in the Legislative Assembly were replaced by newcomers, who were reported to include some of the Government's harshest critics.

In July 1988 the Supreme Court awarded $T26,500 in damages to 'Akilisi Pohiva, the editor of a local independent journal and one of the nine elected members of the Legislative Assembly. Pohiva had been required to leave his job in the Ministry of Education in 1985, after broadcasting on controversial issues, and subsequently sued the Government for unfair dismissal. The court ruling intensified opposition demands for the abolition of perceived feudal aspects within Tongan society.

In September 1989 the nine elected (commoner) members of the Legislative Assembly boycotted the Assembly, leaving it without a quorum, in protest at the absence of the Minister of Finance when they had wanted to question him about the proceeds of the Government's sale of Tongan passports to foreign nationals, a process which had been begun in 1983 as a means of acquiring revenue. Upon resuming their seats in the Assembly later in the month, the commoners introduced a motion demanding the reform of the Assembly to make it more accountable to the people. The motion proposed the creation of a more balanced legislature by increasing elected representation to 15 seats and reducing noble representation to three seats (the Cabinet's 12 members also sit in the Assembly). In March 1990 a group of Tongan conservatives submitted an electoral petition, alleging bribery and corruption against Pohiva, the leader of the reform-minded commoners, and his colleagues, who had been re-elected by substantial majorities in the February general election. (In July 1988 the King had indicated his opposition to majority rule, claiming that the monarchical Government reacted more quickly to the needs of the people than the Government of a parliamentary democracy.)

In October 1990 Pohiva initiated a court case against the Government, claiming that its controversial sale of passports to foreign citizens was unconstitutional and illegal. The passports were sold mainly in Hong Kong to citizens of the territory and of the People's Republic of China, for as much as US $30,000 each, allowing the purchasers, in theory, to avoid travel restrictions imposed on Chinese passport-holders. The sale aroused further concern when it was revealed that holders included Imelda Marcos, the widow of the former President of the Philippines, Ferdinand Marcos. In February 1991, however, a constitutional amendment to legalize the naturalization of the new passport-holders was adopted by an emergency session of the Legislative Assembly, and the case was therefore dismissed. In March a large demonstration was held in protest at the Government's actions, and a petition urging the King to invalidate the 426 passports in question, and to dismiss the Minister of Police (who was responsible for their sale), was presented by prominent commoners and church leaders. In the following month the Government admitted that Ferdinand Marcos and his family had been given Tongan passports as gifts, after his fall from power in 1986. The events that ensued from the sale of passports were widely viewed as indicative of the growing support for reform and for greater accountability in the government of the country.

In August 1991 the Prime Minister, Prince Fatafehi Tu'ipelehake, retired from office, owing to ill health, and was succeeded by the King's cousin, Baron Vaea, who had previously held the position of Minister of Labour, Commerce and Industries.

Plans by campaigners for democratic reform to establish a formal political organization were realized in November 1992, when the Pro-Democracy Movement was founded. The group, led by Fr Seluini 'Akau'ola (a Roman Catholic priest), organized a constitutional convention in the same month, at which options for the introduction of democratic reform were discussed. The Government, however, refused to recognize or to participate in the convention, prohibiting any publicity of the event and denying visas to invited speakers from abroad. Nevertheless, the pro-democracy reformists appeared to be enjoying increased public support, and, at elections in February 1993, won six of the nine People's Representative seats in the Legislative Assembly.

Despite continued resistance by the King to the development of a parliamentary democracy, in April 1993 Crown Prince Tupouto'a, the Minister of Foreign Affairs and Defence, stated that he favoured the establishment of a formal political structure (including the formation of political parties), although he remained critical of the apparent confrontational stance adopted by the reformists. However, Pohiva's position was undermined when, in December 1993 and February 1994, he lost two defamation cases in the Supeme Court, following the publication of allegations of fraudulent practice in his journal, *Kele'a*. In August 1994 Tonga's first political party was formed when the Pro-Democracy Movement launched its People's Party, under the chairmanship of a local businessman, Huliki Watab.

In March 1995 it was reported that the King had given an interview to a foreign journalist, in which he conceded that democracy and a fully-elected Government were inevitable prospects for the Kingdom. However, he subsequently denied the reports, claiming that his comments had been taken out of context, and stating that, although it was likely that the monarchy would relinquish more power in the future, elected representatives did not yet have sufficient experience or integrity to govern.

In May 1995 the Minister of Finance, Cecil Cocker, resigned from the Cabinet following allegations that he had sexually harassed three women while attending a regional conference in Auckland. Cocker received an official reprimand for his conduct from New Zealand's acting Prime Minister, Don McKinnon.

A friendship treaty that Tonga signed with the USA in July 1988 provided for the safe transit within Tongan waters of US ships capable of carrying nuclear weapons. Tonga was one of the few members of the South Pacific Forum not to have acceded to the South Pacific Nuclear-Free Zone Treaty. In June 1989 Tonga finally ratified the five-year fisheries treaty with the USA that had been concluded (provisionally) in 1986 (see above).

In September 1990 Tongasat, a Tongan telecommunications company founded earlier that year by Tongan citizens jointly with a US entrepreneur, laid claim to the last 16 satellite positions remaining in the earth's orbit that were suitable for trans-Pacific communications. Despite the protests of leading member nations of Intelsat (the international consortium responsible for most of the world's satellite services), the International Telecommunication Union was obliged to approve the claim, and Tongasat was subsequently granted six positions. In early 1992 an agreement allowing a US company to use two of these positions was signed, and was expected to earn Tonga an estimated $T10m. over five years. A dispute with Indonesia, concerning that country's use of satellite positions reserved by Tonga in 1990, was resolved by the signing of an agreement in December 1993. In May of the following year the two countries established diplomatic relations at ambassadorial level.

## Government

Tonga is a hereditary monarchy. The King is Head of State and Head of Government. He appoints, and presides over, the Privy Council which acts as the national Cabinet. Apart from the King, the Council includes 10 ministers, appointed for life and led by the Prime Minister, and the Governors of Ha'apai and Vava'u. The unicameral Legislative Assembly comprises the King and 30 members: the Privy Council, nine hereditary nobles (chosen by their peers) and nine representatives elected by all adult Tongan citizens. Elected members hold office for three years. There are no official political parties, although an opposition group was founded in late 1992 to campaign for democratic reform.

## Defence

Tonga has its own defence force, consisting of both regular and reserve units. Projected government expenditure on defence in the financial year 1989/90 was $T2,516,000 (4.9% of total budgetary expenditure).

## Economic Affairs

In 1993, according to estimates by the World Bank, Tonga's gross national product (GNP), measured at average 1991–93 prices, was US $150m., equivalent to US $1,610 per head. During 1985–93, it was estimated, GNP per head increased, in real terms, at an average annual rate of 1.5%. During the same period the population decreased by an annual average of 0.3%. Tonga's gross domestic product (GDP) increased, in real terms, by an estimated 1.4% in 1993 and by 6.7% in 1994.

Agriculture (including forestry and fishing) contributed 39.4% of GDP in 1992, and engaged 38.1% of the employed labour force in 1990. The principal cash crops are coconuts, vanilla and pumpkins, which normally form the major part of Tonga's exports. In 1991 exports of pumpkins provided 60.2% of total export earnings (compared with 16.4% in the previous year), and exports of vanilla beans 14.1%. Yams, taro, sweet potatoes, watermelons, tomatoes, cassava, lemons and limes, oranges, groundnuts and breadfruit are also cultivated as food crops, while the islanders keep pigs, goats, poultry and cattle. Food imports accounted for more than 21% of total import costs in 1991. In 1992 a US-funded study into the development of a fish-canning industry was undertaken, and proposals for a facility on the islands were being considered. Furthermore, the introduction of pearl farming to the islands and the cultivation of yam-beans as an export crop were among several proposals for diversification under discussion in the early 1990s.

Industry (including mining, manufacturing, construction and power) provided 11.0% of GDP in 1992 and engaged 20.6% of the employed labour force in 1990. Manufacturing contributed 5.4% of GDP in 1992, and employed 15.1% of the labour force in 1990. The most important industrial activities are the production of concrete blocks, small excavators, clothing, furniture, handicrafts, sports equipment (including small boats), brewing and coconut oil. There is also a factory for processing sandalwood. In mid-1993 companies from New Zealand, Canada and Taiwan expressed interest in prospecting for hydrocarbons in Tonga. In an attempt to reduce fuel imports (which accounted for about 16% of total import costs in 1991), a 2-MW wave-energy power plant was constructed in the early 1990s, and would, it was hoped, supply one-third of the islands' total electricity requirements when in full operation.

Tourism makes a significant contribution to the economy, and revenue from visitor arrivals by air was estimated at $T12.4m. in 1993. The trade, restaurants and hotels sector contributed 14.4% of GDP in 1992 and engaged 8.5% of the employed labour force in 1990. A 10-year development plan, introduced in the late 1980s, aimed to provide more hotel accommodation, and was expected to facilitate the expansion of the sector, as were improvements to Fua'amotu airport, completed in mid-1991.

In 1993 Tonga recorded a visible trade deficit of US $37.6m., while there was a surplus of US $4.1m. on the current account of the balance of payments. In 1991 the principal source of imports (29.6%) was New Zealand, while Japan was the principal market for exports (60.2%). Other major trading partners are Australia, Fiji and the USA. The principal exports in 1991 were pumpkins and vanilla beans. The principal imports were foodstuffs, basic manufactures, machinery and transport equipment and mineral fuels.

Exports of pumpkins to Japan provided Tonga with its first recorded trade surplus with that country in 1991. However, in early 1992 Japan demanded refunds for much of the produce, which was, Japan claimed, rotten or of poor quality. A decision to increase the quotas for exports of pumpkins was reversed in May 1993, following the intervention of the Minister of Labour, Commerce and Industry, who appealed for the industry to establish a reputation for good-quality produce before increasing its output. Demands by pumpkin farmers that export quotas be increased intensified following a record harvest of the crop in 1994. Exports of pumpkins to Japan earned some $T15m. in 1993.

In the financial year ending 30 June 1991 there was an estimated budgetary deficit of $T10.1m. (equivalent to 6.0% of GDP in that year). In the following year proposed expenditure totalled $T120.4m., and in 1992/93 the level increased by an estimated 5.9%. Tonga's total external public debt was US $44.2m. at the end of 1993, of which US $43.7m. was long-term public debt. In that year the cost of debt-servicing was equivalent to 3.3% of the total revenue from exports of goods and services. The annual rate of inflation averaged 8.5% in 1985–93, but only 1.1% in 1994. An estimated 4.2% of the labour force were unemployed in 1990.

Tonga is a member of the South Pacific Commission (see p. 215), the South Pacific Forum (see p. 217) and the UN's Economic and Social Commission for Asia and the Pacific (ESCAP—see p. 27).

During the late 1980s and early 1990s Tonga's economic development was adversely affected by inclement weather, inflationary pressures, a high level of unemployment, large-scale emigration and over-reliance on the agricultural sector. Diversifying sources of income and establishing an efficient source of energy, to enable a reduction in fuel imports, remained important issues for Tonga in the early 1990s. Among several controversial proposals, the possible establishment of a toxic waste disposal facility on the island of Niuafo'o was being discussed in late 1993. Meanwhile, it was revealed that a feasibility study was to be conducted into the prospect of building a petroleum refinery and power station on the islands. A trade delegation to Australia in mid-1993 sought to persuade business interests in the country to invest in various projects in Tonga, including coconut, vanilla and ginger processing, perfume production, the manufacture of garments, leather goods and bamboo furniture and the establishment of a small dairy. In addition, in December 1993 the King announced the conclusion of a joint-venture agreement between Tonga and the Provincial Government of Sarawak in Malaysia. The agreement provided for the settlement of Tongan workers on farms in the province, jointly owned by the Tongan and Sarawak Governments, where various crops (including taro, cassava, bananas, breadfruit and vanilla) would be produced for export.

### Social Welfare
In 1989 there were 15 hospitals and health centres, with a total of 361 beds, and 43 physicians working in the country. Of total projected expenditure by the Government in the financial year 1990/91, $T6,516,000 (6.6%) was for health, and a further $T750,000 (0.8%) for social security and welfare.

### Education
Free state education is compulsory for children between five and 14 years of age, while the Government and other Commonwealth countries offer scholarship schemes enabling students to go abroad for higher education. In 1992 there were 115 primary schools, with a total of 16,658 pupils, and there was a total of 13,318 pupils in secondary schools. There were also 10 technical and vocational colleges in 1990, with a total of 358 students in 1992, and one teacher-training college, with 226 students. In 1990 there were 230 Tongans studying overseas. Some degree courses are offered at the university division of 'Atenisi Institute. Projected government expenditure on education in 1990/91 was $T12,847,000 (13.0% of total budgetary expenditure).

### Public Holidays
**1995:** 1 January (New Year's Day), 14–17 April (Easter), 25 April (ANZAC Day), 4 May (HRH the Crown Prince's Birthday), 4 June (Independence Day), 4 July (HM the King's Birthday), 4 November (Constitution Day), 4 December (Tupou I Day), 25–26 December (Christmas Day and Boxing Day).
**1996:** 1 January (New Year's Day), 5–8 April (Easter), 25 April (ANZAC Day), 4 May (HRH the Crown Prince's Birthday), 4 June (Independence Day), 4 July (HM the King's Birthday), 4 November (Constitution Day), 4 December (Tupou I Day), 25–26 December (Christmas Day and Boxing Day).

### Weights and Measures
In 1980 Tonga adopted the metric system of weights and measures in place of the imperial system.

# Statistical Survey

Source (unless otherwise indicated): Tonga Government Department of Statistics, POB 149, Nuku'alofa; tel. 21966.

### AREA AND POPULATION
**Area:** 748 sq km (289 sq miles).
**Population:** 94,649 (47,611 males, 47,038 females) at census of 28 November 1986; 98,000 (official estimate) at mid-1993. *By group* (1986 census): Tongatapu 63,794; Vava'u 15,175; Ha'apai 8,919; 'Eua 4,393; Niuas 2,368.
**Density** (mid-1993): 131.0 per sq km.
**Principal Town:** Nuku'alofa (capital), population 21,383 at 1986 census.
**Births and Deaths** (1991): Live births 2,403 (birth rate 24.7 per 1,000); (1990) Deaths 484 (death rate 5.1 per 1,000).
**Expectation of Life** (World Bank estimate, years at birth, 1992): 68.
**Economically Active Population** (persons aged 10 years and over, July–September 1990): Agriculture, forestry and fishing 11,682; Mining and quarrying 48; Manufacturing 4,617; Electricity, gas and water 408; Construction 1,257; Trade, restaurants and hotels 2,597; Transport, storage and communications 1,821; Financing, insurance, real estate and business services 1,188; Community, social and personal services 7,051; Total employed 30,670 (males 20,955, females 9,717); Total unemployed 1,343 (males 481, females 862); Total labour force 32,013 (males 21,435, females 10,578). Source: ILO, *Year Book of Labour Statistics*.

The totals shown may differ from the sum of the component parts.

### AGRICULTURE, ETC.
**Principal Crops** (FAO estimates, metric tons, 1993): Coconuts 25,000; Yams 31,000; Taro 27,000; Sweet potatoes 14,000; Cassava 28,000; Copra 2,000; Vegetables and melons 8,000; Bananas 1,000; Oranges 3,000; Lemons and limes 3,000; Other fruits 6,000; Groundnuts (in shell) 1,000; Tomatoes 1,000. Source: FAO, *Production Yearbook*.
**Livestock** (FAO estimates, '000 head, year ending September 1993): Pigs 94; Horses 11; Cattle 10; Goats 16; Poultry 131 (1984). Source: FAO, *Production Yearbook*.
**Livestock Products** (FAO estimates, metric tons, 1993): Pigmeat 1,000; Hen eggs 260; Honey 16; Cattle and buffalo hides 40; Goatskins 5. Source: FAO, *Production Yearbook*.
**Forestry** (Roundwood removals, '000 cu m, excluding bark): 4 in 1985; 5 in 1986; 5 annually (FAO estimates) in 1987–92. Source: FAO, *Yearbook of Forest Products*.
**Fishing** (metric tons, live weight): Total catch 1,656 in 1990; 1,959 in 1991; 2,283 in 1992. Source: FAO, *Yearbook of Fishery Statistics*.

### FINANCE
**Currency and Exchange Rates:** 100 seniti (cents) = 1 pa'anga (Tongan dollar or $T). *Sterling and US Dollar Equivalents* (31 December 1994): £1 sterling = $T1.969; US $1 = $T1.258; $T100 = £50.79 = US $79.47. *Average Exchange Rate* (pa'anga per US $): 1.3471 in 1992; 1.3841 in 1993; 1.3202 in 1994. Note: Between November 1976 and February 1991 the pa'anga was officially at par with the Australian dollar.
**Budget** (estimates, '000 pa'anga, year ending 30 June 1991): *Revenue:* Taxation 33,718; Other current revenue 17,968; Total 51,686 (excl. grants received from abroad 51,530). *Expenditure:* General public services 26,282; Education 12,847; Health 6,516; Social security and welfare 750; Housing and community amenities 2,216; Economic affairs and services 50,563 (Agriculture, forestry, fishing and hunting 8,649, Transport and communications 22,992); Total 99,175 (excl. lending minus repayments 14,092). Source: IMF, *Government Finance Statistics Yearbook*.
*1991/92* (estimates, $T million): Recurrent expenditure 51.4; Development expenditure 69.0; Revenue 51.7.
**International Reserves** (US $ million at 31 December 1994): IMF special drawing rights 0.71; Reserve position in the IMF 1.76; Foreign exchange 32.19; Total 34.66. Source: IMF, *International Financial Statistics*.
**Money Supply** ('000 pa'anga at 31 December 1994): Currency outside banks 7,346; Demand deposits at deposit money banks 18,612; Total money 25,958. Source: IMF, *International Financial Statistics*.
**Cost of Living** (Consumer Price Index, excl. rent; base: 1990 = 100): 119.4 in 1992; 120.5 in 1993; 121.8 in 1994. Source: IMF, *International Financial Statistics*.
**Gross Domestic Product** (million pa'anga at current prices, year ending 30 June): 198.2 in 1992; 201.0 in 1993; 214.8 in 1994. Source: IMF, *International Financial Statistics*.
**Gross Domestic Product by Economic Activity** (provisional, '000 pa'anga at current prices, year ending 30 June 1992): Agriculture, forestry and fishing 59,431; Mining and quarrying 495; Manufacturing 8,140; Electricity, gas and water 1,861; Construction 6,131; Trade, restaurants and hotels 21,780; Transport, storage and communications 11,809; Finance, insurance, real estate and business services 11,472; Community, social and personal services 29,821; GDP at factor cost 150,940; Indirect taxes, *less* subsidies 26,028; *GDP in purchasers' values* 176,968. Source: UN, *Statistical Yearbook for Asia and the Pacific*.
**Balance of Payments** (US $ million, year ending 30 June 1993): Merchandise exports f.o.b. 11.90; Merchandise imports f.o.b. −49.50; *Trade balance* −37.60; Exports of services 16.20; Imports of services −19.09; Other income received 5.10; Other income paid −2.32; Private unrequited transfers (net) 34.93; Official unrequited transfers (net) 6.87; *Current balance* 4.10; Direct investment (net) 0.35; Portfolio investment (net) −0.10; Other capital (net) 3.02; Net errors and omissions 0.29; *Overall balance* 7.65. Source: IMF, *International Financial Statistics*.

### EXTERNAL TRADE
**Principal Commodities** ($T million, 1991): *Imports:* Food and live animals 16.5; Beverages and tobacco 3.1; Crude materials

# TONGA

*Statistical Survey, Directory*

(inedible) except fuels 3.6; Mineral fuels, lubricants, etc. 12.1; Chemicals 6.2; Basic manufactures 11.9; Machinery and transport equipment 14.6; Total (incl. others) 76.8. *Exports:* Pumpkins 12.4; Coconut oil 0.4; Vanilla beans 2.9; Re-exports 0.8; Total (incl. others) 20.6.

**1992** ($T million): *Imports:* 84.3; *Exports:* 16.6.

**1993** ($T million): *Imports:* 84.9; *Exports:* 23.4.

**Principal Trading Partners** ($T million, 1991): *Imports:* Australia 19.6; China (People's Republic) 1.4; Fiji 11.9; Hong Kong 1.2; Japan 6.9; New Zealand 22.7; Singapore 1.1; USA 7.0; Total (incl. others) 76.8. *Exports:* Australia 1.8; Japan 12.4; New Zealand 1.6; USA 2.7; Total (incl. others) 20.6.

## TRANSPORT

**Road Traffic** (vehicles in use, 1991): Commercial vehicles 3,100; Passenger cars 2,800. Source: UN, *Statistical Yearbook*.

**Shipping** (international traffic, '000 metric tons, 1990): Goods loaded 15; Goods unloaded 104. Source: UN, *Monthly Bulletin of Statistics*. **1991:** Vessels entered ('000 net registered tons) 1,950. Source: UN, *Statistical Yearbook*.

**Civil Aviation:** Aircraft arriving: 4,834 in 1987; 6,280 in 1988; 4,854 in 1989.

## TOURISM

**Visitors:** 31,876 in 1988; 31,584 in 1989; 38,823 in 1990.

## COMMUNICATIONS MEDIA

**Daily Newspapers** (1992): 1; estimated circulation 7,000*.

**Non-Daily Newspapers** (provisional, 1988): 2; estimated circulation 9,000*.

**Telephones** (provisional, '000 main lines, 1991): 5 in use†.

**Radio Receivers** (1992): 54,000 in use*.

**Television Receivers** (1992): 1,000 in use*.

* Source: UNESCO, *Statistical Yearbook*.
† Source: UN, *Statistical Yearbook*.

## EDUCATION

**Primary** (1992): 115 schools; 784 teachers; 16,658 pupils.

**General Secondary** (1990): 767 teachers; 13,318 pupils (1992).

**Technical and vocational** (1990): 4 government and 6 church colleges; 45 teachers; 358 students (1992).

**Teacher training** (1990): 20 teachers; 226 students (1992).

**Universities, etc.** (1985): 17 teachers; 85 students.

**Other Higher Education** (1985): 620 students.

Source: mainly UNESCO, *Statistical Yearbook*.

In 1990 230 students were studying overseas on government scholarships.

# Directory

## The Constitution

The Constitution of Tonga is based on that granted in 1875 by King George Tupou I. It provides for a government consisting of the Sovereign; a Privy Council, which is appointed by the Sovereign and consists of the Sovereign and the Cabinet; the Cabinet, which consists of a Prime Minister, a Deputy Prime Minister, eight other ministers and the Governors of Ha'apai and Vava'u; a Legislative Assembly and a Judiciary. Limited law-making power is vested in the Privy Council and any legislation passed by the Executive is subject to review by the Legislative Assembly. The unicameral Legislative Assembly comprises the King, the Cabinet, nine hereditary nobles (chosen by their peers) and nine representatives elected by all adult Tongan citizens. Elected members hold office for three years.

## The Government

**The Sovereign:** HM King TAUFA'AHAU TUPOU IV (succeeded to the throne 15 December 1965).

### CABINET
(June 1995)

**Prime Minister and Minister of Agriculture, Forestry and Fisheries, and Marine Affairs:** Baron VAEA of Houma.

**Deputy Prime Minister and Minister of Education, Civil Aviation and Works:** Dr SENIPISI LANGI KAVALIKU.

**Minister of Foreign Affairs and Defence:** HRH Crown Prince TUPOUTO'A.

**Minister of Finance, and of Labour, Commerce and Industries:** KINIKINILAU TUTOATASI FAKAFANUA.

**Minister of Police, Fire Services and Prisons:** GEORGE 'AKAU'OLA.

**Minister of Lands, Survey and Natural Resources:** Dr MA'AFU TUPOU.

**Minister of Health:** Dr SIONE TAPA.

**Attorney-General and Minister of Justice:** TEVITA P. TUPOU.

**Minister without Portfolio:** MA'AFU.

**Governor of Ha'apai:** FAKAFANUA.

**Governor of Vava'u:** TU'I'AFITU.

### MINISTRIES

**Office of the Prime Minister and Minister of Agriculture, Forestry and Fisheries, and Marine Affairs:** Nuku'alofa; tel. 21300; telex 66269; fax 23888.

**Office of the Deputy Prime Minister and Minister of Education, Civil Aviation and Works:** POB 61, Nuku'alofa; tel. 23511; fax 23866.

**Office of the Attorney-General and Minister of Justice:** POB 130, Nuku'alofa; tel. 21055; fax 23098.

**Office of the Minister of Finance:** Vuna Rd, POB 87, Nuku'alofa; tel. 23066; telex 66277; fax 21010.

**Office of the Minister of Foreign Affairs and Defence:** Nuku'alofa; tel. 23600; fax 23360.

**Office of the Minister of Health:** POB 59, Nuku'alofa; tel. 23200; fax 24291.

**Office of the Minister of Labour, Commerce and Industries:** POB 110, Nuku'alofa; tel. 23611; fax 23216.

**Office of the Minister of Lands, Survey and Natural Resources:** POB 5, Nuku'alofa; tel. 22655; telex 66269.

**Office of the Minister of Police, Fire Services and Prisons:** Nuku'alofa; tel. 23233; telex 66224.

## Legislative Assembly

The Legislative Assembly consists of the Speaker, the members of the Cabinet, nine nobles chosen by the 33 Nobles of Tonga, and nine representatives elected by all Tongans over 21 years of age. There are elections every three years, and the Assembly is required to meet at least once every year. The most recent election was in February 1993, when six of the nine elected representatives were members of the reformist Pro-Democracy Movement (which subsequently founded the People's Party—see below).

**Speaker and Chairman of the Legislative Assembly:** ESETA FUSITU'A.

## Political Organization

**People's Party:** Nuku'alofa; f. 1994 by members of the Pro-Democracy Movement; campaigns for democratic reform and increased parliamentary representation for the Tongan people; Chair HULIKI WATAB; Pres. VILIAMI FUKOFUKA; Vice-Pres. 'AKILISI POHIVA.

## Diplomatic Representation

### EMBASSY AND HIGH COMMISSIONS IN TONGA

**Australia:** Salote Rd, Nuku'alofa; tel. 23244; fax 23243; High Commissioner: JENNIFER E. RAWSON.

**China (Taiwan):** POB 842, Nuku'alofa; tel. 21766; fax 23726; Ambassador: HUGH O'YOUNG.

**New Zealand:** cnr Taufa'ahau and Salote Rds, POB 830, Nuku'alofa; tel. 23122; fax 23487; High Commissioner: NIGEL I. MOORE.

**United Kingdom:** Vuna Rd, POB 56, Nuku'alofa; tel. 21020; telex 66226; fax 24109; High Commissioner: ANDREW J. MORRIS.

## Judicial System

There are eight Magistrates' Courts, the Land Court, the Supreme Court and the Court of Appeal.

Appeal from the Magistrates' Courts is to the Supreme Court, and from the Supreme Court and Land Court to the Court of Appeal (except in certain matters relating to hereditary estates, where appeal lies to the Privy Council). The Chief Justice and Puisne Judge are resident in Tonga and are judges of the Supreme Court and Land Court. The Court of Appeal is presided over by the Chief Justice and consists of three judges from other Commonwealth countries. In the Supreme Court the accused in criminal cases, and either party in civil suits, may elect trial by jury. In the Land Court the judge sits with a Tongan assessor. Proceedings in the Magistrates' Courts are in Tongan, and in the Supreme Court and Court of Appeal in Tongan and English.

**Supreme Court:** POB 11, Nuku'alofa; tel. 23599; fax 24771.
**Chief Justice:** GORDON WARD.
**Puisne Judge:** JOHN LEWIS.
**Chief Magistrate:** GEORGE FIFITA.

## Religion

The Tongans are almost all Christians, and about 64% of the population belong to Methodist (Wesleyan) communities. There are also small numbers of Roman Catholics, Anglicans, Seventh-day Adventists and Latter-day Saints (Mormons). Fourteen churches are represented in total.

### CHRISTIANITY

**Kosilio 'ae Ngaahi Siasi 'i Tonga** (Tonga National Council of Churches): POB 1205, Nuku'alofa; tel. 21177; f. 1973; four mem. churches; Chair. Rev. SIMOTE M. VEA; Gen. Sec. LAITIA FIFITA.

#### The Anglican Communion

Tonga lies within the diocese of Polynesia, part of the Church of the Province of New Zealand. The Bishop of Polynesia is resident in Fiji.

**Archdeacon of Tonga and Samoa:** The Ven. SAM KOY, The Vicarage, POB 31, Nuku'alofa; tel. 22136.

#### The Roman Catholic Church

Tonga forms a single diocese, directly responsible to the Holy See. At 31 December 1993 there were an estimated 13,751 adherents in the country. The Bishop participates in the Catholic Bishops' Conference of the Pacific, based in Fiji.

**Bishop of Tonga:** Dr SOANE LILO FOLIAKI, Bishop's House, Toutaimana, POB 1, Nuku'alofa; tel. 23822; fax 23854.

#### Other Churches

**Church of Jesus Christ of Latter-day Saints (Mormon):** Mission Centre, POB 58, Nuku'alofa; tel. 21577; fax 21077; 21,000 mems; Pres. SAMISONI UASILAIA.

**Church of Tonga:** Nuku'alofa; f. 1928; a branch of Methodism; 6,912 mems; Pres. Rev. FINAV KATOANGA.

**Free Church of Tonga:** POB 23, Nuku'alofa; tel. 23966; fax 24458; f. 1885; 15,001 mems (1994); Pres. Rev. SEMISI FONUA; brs in Australia, New Zealand and USA.

**Free Wesleyan Church of Tonga (Koe Siasi Uesiliana Tau'ataina 'o Tonga):** POB 57, Nuku'alofa; tel. 23432; fax 24020; f. 1826; 36,500 mems; Pres. Rev. LOPETI TAUFA; Sec. Rev. Dr 'ALIFALETI MONE.

**Tokaikolo Christian Fellowship:** Nuku'alofa; f. 1978, as breakaway group from Free Wesleyan Church; 5,000 mems.

### BAHÁ'Í FAITH

**National Spiritual Assembly:** POB 133, Nuku'alofa; tel. 21568; fax 23120; mems resident in 156 localities.

## The Press

**Eva, Your Holiday Guide to Tonga:** POB 427, Nuku'alofa; tel. 23101; fax 23101; f. 1989; 6 a year; Editor PESI FONUA; circ. 4,000.
**Kele'a** (Conch Shell): POB 1567, Nuku'alofa; tel. 22233; f. 1986; 6 a year; independent news sheet; economic and political; Editor 'AKILISI POHIVA; circ. 4,500.
**Lali:** Nuku'alofa; f. 1994; monthly; English; national business magazine; Publr KALAFI MOALA.

**Matangi Tonga:** POB 427, Nuku'alofa; tel. 23101; fax 23101; f. 1986; 6 a year; national news magazine; Editor PESI FONUA; circ. 3,800.
**'Ofa ki Tonga:** POB 2055, Nuku'alofa; tel. 24190; monthly; newspaper of Tokaikolo Christian Fellowship; Editor Rev. LIUFAU VAILEA SAULALA.
**Taka-Trade:** POB 35, Nuku'alofa; tel. 24011; telex 66245; fax 22915; trade magazine; Editor TAKAFALAI BROWN.
**Taka-Travel:** POB 35, Nuku'alofa; tel. 24011; telex 66245; fax 22915; tourist newspaper; Editor WILL ILOLAHIA.
**Taumu'a Lelei:** POB 1, Nuku'alofa; tel. 23822; fax 23854; f. 1931; monthly; Roman Catholic; Editor (vacant).
**The Times of Tonga/Koe Taimi'o Tonga:** Nuku'alofa; f. 1989; weekly; English edition covers Pacific and world news, Tongan edition concentrates on local news; Publr KALAFI MOALA.
**Tohi Fanongonongo:** POB 57, Nuku'alofa; tel. 21623; monthly; Wesleyan; Editor Rev. SIMOTE VEA.
**Tonga Chronicle/Kalonikali Tonga:** POB 197, Nuku'alofa; tel. 21300; f. 1964; govt-sponsored; weekly; Editor PAUA MANU'ATU; circ. 6,000 (Tongan), 1,200 (English).
**Tonga Ngaue:** Nuku'alofa; f. 1990; independent newsletter; anti-reformist and pro-establishment; Editor TEVITA MANU FASI.

## Publisher

**Vava'u Press Ltd:** POB 427, Nuku'alofa; tel. 23101; fax 23101; f. 1980; books and magazines; Pres. PESI FONUA.

## Radio and Television

In 1992 there were an estimated 54,000 radio receivers and 1,000 television receivers in use. The introduction of a television service has been mooted since 1984. Oceania Broadcasting Inc started relaying US television programmes in 1991.

**Tonga Broadcasting Commission:** POB 36, Nuku'alofa; tel. 23555; telex 66225; fax 24417; f. 1961; independent statutory body; commercially-operated; programmes in Tongan and English; Man. S. TAVAKE FUSIMALOHI; CEO MALEKAMU PALU.

## Finance

(cap. = capital; res = reserves; dep. = deposits; m. = million; amounts in Tongan dollars)

### BANKING

**Australia and New Zealand Banking Group Ltd:** Cnr of Salote and Railway Rds, POB 910, Nuku'alofa; tel. 24944; telex 66288; fax 23870.

**Bank of Tonga:** POB 924, Nuku'alofa; tel. 23933; telex 66212; fax 23634; f. 1974; owned by Govt of Tonga (40%), Bank of Hawaii International (30%), and Westpac Banking Corpn (30%); cap. 3.0m. res 20.3m., dep. 68.9m. (Dec. 1993); Chair. PAUL J. FRIEND; Gen. Man. RICHARD F. CAMERON; 4 brs.

**Malaysian Borneo Finance Bank (MBF):** Nuku'alofa; 51% owned by Asian Capital Corpn, 25% owned by Crown Prince Tupouto'a.

**National Reserve Bank of Tonga:** Private Bag 25, Post Office, Nuku'alofa; tel. 24057; telex 66278; fax 24201; f. 1989 to assume central bank functions of Bank of Tonga; issues currency; manages exchange rates and international reserves; authorized cap. 2m.; Gov. SIOSIUA 'UTOIKAMANU.

**Tonga Development Bank:** Fatafehi Rd, POB 126, Nuku'alofa; tel. 23333; telex 66206; fax 22755; f. 1977; cap. 10.8m., dep. 2.9m. (Dec. 1991); Man. Dir PENISIMANI VEA; 4 brs.

## Trade and Industry

### DEVELOPMENT ORGANIZATIONS

**Tonga Investments Ltd:** POB 27, Nuku'alofa; tel. 21388; fax 21806; f. 1992 to replace Commodities Board; govt-owned; manages five subsidiary companies; Chair. Baron VAEA of Houma; Man. Dir ANTHONY WAYNE MADDEN.

**Tonga Association of Small Businesses:** Nuku'alofa; f. 1990 to cater for the needs of small businesses; Chair. SIMI SILAPELU.

### CO-OPERATIVES

In April 1990 there were 78 registered co-operative societies, including the first co-operative registered under the Agricultural Organization Act.

**Tonga Co-operative Federation Society:** Tungi Arcade, Nuku'alofa; telex 66253.

### TRADE UNIONS

**Squash Growers' Federation:** Nuku'alofa; f. 1995.

**Teachers' and Nurses' Association:** Nuku'alofa; Pres. FINAU TUTONE.

## Transport

### ROADS

There are about 198 km of all-weather metalled roads on Tongatapu, 74 km on Vava'u and 20 km on both Ha'apai and 'Eua. Total road length, including fair-weather-only dirt or coral roads, is some 386 km.

### SHIPPING

The chief ports are Nuku'alofa, on Tongatapu, and Neiafu, on Vava'u, with two smaller ports at Pangai and Niuatoputapu.

**Shipping Corporation of Polynesia Ltd:** Vuna Rd, POB 453, Nuku'alofa; tel. 21699; telex 66213; fax 22617; regular inter-islands passenger and cargo services; Chair. Baron VAEA of Houma; Gen. Man. Capt. VOLKER PAHL.

**Warner Pacific Line:** POB 93, Nuku'alofa; tel. 21088; telex 66219; services to American Samoa, Western Samoa, Australia and New Zealand; Man. Dir MA'AKE FAKA'OSIFOLAU.

### CIVIL AVIATION

Tonga is served by Fua'amotu Airport, 22 km from Nuku'alofa, and airstrips at Vava'u, Ha'apai, Niuatoputapu, Niuafo'ou and 'Eua.

**Royal Tongan Airlines:** Private Bag 9, Nuku'alofa; tel. 23660; fax 24056; f. 1985 as Friendly Islands Airways Ltd; govt-owned; operates international service to Auckland, New Zealand, Nadi, Fiji, Apia, Western Samoa, Sydney, Australia, and Los Angeles, USA and internal services to Fua'amotu, Ha'apai, Vava'u, 'Eua, Niuatoputapu and Niuafo'ou; Chair. Dr S. L. KAVALIKU; Gen. Man. GEOFF BOWMAKER.

## Tourism

Tonga's attractions include scenic beauty and a mild climate. There were 28,408 visitors to the islands in 1994, an increase of 11.3% compared with the previous year. Revenue from visitor arrivals by air in 1994 exceeded $T12m. Most tourists come from the USA, New Zealand or Australia. In 1991 there were a total of 564 hotel rooms in Tonga.

**Tonga Tourist Association:** Nuku'alofa; Pres. JOSEPH RAMANLAL.

**Tonga Visitors' Bureau:** Vuna Rd, POB 37, Nuku'alofa; tel. 21733; fax 22129; f. 1978; Dir SEMISI P. TAUMOEPEAU.

# TRINIDAD AND TOBAGO

## Introductory Survey

### Location, Climate, Language, Religion, Flag, Capital

The Republic of Trinidad and Tobago consists of Trinidad, the southernmost of the Caribbean islands, and Tobago, which is 32 km (20 miles) to the north-east. Trinidad, which accounts for 94% of the total area, lies just off the north coast of Venezuela, on the South American mainland, while the country's nearest neighbour to the north is Grenada. The climate is tropical, with a dry season from January to May. Rainfall averages 1,561 mm (61.5 ins) per year. Annual average daytime temperatures range between 32°C (90°F) and 21°C (70°F). The official and main language is English, but French, Spanish, Hindi and Chinese are also spoken. In 1990 some 40.3% of the population were Christians, mainly Roman Catholics (29.4%) and Anglicans (10.9%), while 23.8% were Hindus and 5.8% Muslims. The national flag (proportions 5 by 3) is deep red, divided by a white-edged black diagonal stripe from upper hoist to lower fly. The capital is Port of Spain, on the island of Trinidad.

### Recent History

Trinidad was first colonized by the Spanish in 1532, but was ceded to the British in 1802. Africans were transported to the island to work as slaves, but slavery was abolished in 1834. Shortage of labour led to the arrival of large numbers of Indian and Chinese immigrants, as indentured labourers, during the second half of the 19th century. In 1888 the island of Tobago, which had finally been ceded to the British in 1814, was joined with Trinidad as one political and administrative unit, and the territory remained a British colony until its independence on 31 August 1962.

The beginnings of modern politics emerged in the 1930s with the formation of a trade union movement. The first political party, the People's National Movement (PNM), was founded in 1956 by Dr Eric Williams. It campaigned successfully at the elections to the Legislative Council in September 1956, and Dr Williams became the colony's first Chief Minister in October. In 1958 the territory became a member of the newly-established Federation of the West Indies, and in the following year achieved full internal self-government, with Dr Williams as Premier. With the secession of Jamaica from the Federation in 1961, Trinidad and Tobago withdrew and the Federation collapsed. After independence, in 1962, Dr Williams was restyled Prime Minister, and the Governor became Governor-General. In 1967 Trinidad and Tobago became the first Commonwealth member of the Organization of American States (see p. 204).

In April 1970 the Government declared a state of emergency, following violent demonstrations, lasting several weeks, by supporters of 'Black Power', protesting against foreign influence in the country's economy and demanding solutions to the problem of unemployment, which was particularly severe among Trinidadians of African descent. On the day that the emergency was proclaimed, part of the Trinidad and Tobago Regiment (the country's army) mutinied. The mutiny collapsed after only three days, but some officers and soldiers who participated were subsequently sentenced to terms of imprisonment. At a general election in May 1971, the PNM won all 36 seats in the House of Representatives.

A new Constitution came into effect on 1 August 1976, making Trinidad and Tobago a republic, within the Commonwealth, and reducing the minimum voting age to 18 years. The first parliamentary elections of the republic were held in September, when the PNM won 24 of the 36 seats in the House of Representatives. The United Labour Front (ULF), a newly-formed party led by trade unionists, won 10 seats, while the Democratic Action Congress (DAC) won the two Tobago seats. The former Governor-General, Ellis Clarke, was sworn in as the country's first President in December 1976. A parliamentary resolution in 1977 to grant Tobago self-rule resulted, after long resistance from the Government, in the formation in 1980 of a Tobago House of Assembly, giving the island limited autonomy. Tobago was granted full internal self-government in January 1987.

Dr Williams, who had been Prime Minister since independence, died in March 1981, having consistently refused to nominate a successor. The President selected George Chambers, a deputy leader of the PNM and Minister of Agriculture, to assume the leadership *ad interim*. At a special convention of the PNM in May, Chambers was formally adopted as party leader and confirmed as Prime Minister. The PNM increased its majority in the House of Representatives by two seats in a general election in November. The ULF, the DAC and the Tapia House Movement, campaigning jointly as the Trinidad and Tobago National Alliance, succeeded in retaining only 10 seats. The newly-formed Organization for National Reconstruction (ONR), led by a former PNM minister, Karl Hudson-Phillips, emerged as the only serious threat to the PNM, gaining 22.3% of the total vote but no seats.

Co-operation between the four opposition parties increased, and, at local elections in August 1983, they combined to oppose the PNM. This new coalition, called the 'Accommodation', won 66 of the 120 council seats being contested. The PNM won the remaining 54, thus suffering its first electoral defeat since its foundation in 1956. In August 1984 the National Alliance and the ONR established a common front, to be known as the National Alliance for Reconstruction (NAR). At elections to the Tobago House of Assembly in November 1984, the DAC won a convincing victory, reducing the PNM's representation from four seats to one. In September 1985 A. N. R. Robinson, leader of the DAC and a former Deputy Prime Minister in the PNM Government, was elected leader of the NAR. In February 1986 the four parties merged to form one opposition party, still known as the NAR.

The stringent economic policies of the PNM Government undermined its public support and provoked labour unrest over wage restraint, notably in a bitter strike at Trinidad's petroleum refineries during May 1984. The next general election, held in December 1986, resulted in a decisive victory for the NAR, which received 66% of the total votes and won 33 of the 36 seats in the House of Representatives. A. N. R. Robinson was appointed Prime Minister. Chambers was among those members of the PNM who lost their seats, and in January 1987 Patrick Manning, the former Minister of Energy, was appointed leader of the parliamentary opposition. In March Noor Mohammed Hassanali, formerly a senior judge, took office as President, following the retirement of Ellis Clarke.

Although the NAR increased its majority of borough and county council seats at local elections held in Trinidad in September, the party experienced internal difficulties during 1987 and 1988. In June 1987 former members of the Tapia House Movement announced that they were to leave the NAR, and in November the Minister of Public Works and Settlements, formerly a member of the ULF, was dismissed from the Cabinet. In February 1988 more than 100 NAR members met to discuss the leadership of the alliance and the direction of its policies. Two cabinet ministers (including Basdeo Panday, the Minister of External Affairs) and one junior minister were subsequently dismissed from the Government. All three were former members of the ULF, which derived most of its support from the 'East' Indian community. Despite their accusations of racism against the NAR leadership, they were expelled from the party in October. In April 1989 Panday and the other dissidents announced the formation of a left-wing opposition party, the United National Congress (UNC). In July 1990 Panday was elected leader of the UNC at the party's first national assembly. In September President Hassanali confirmed Panday as the leader of the parliamentary opposition, replacing Manning. The UNC, with six seats in the House of Representatives, replaced the PNM, with only three seats, as the principal opposition party.

On 27 July 1990 members of the Jamaat al Muslimeen, a small Muslim group led by Yasin Abu Bakr, attempted to seize power from the Government. The rebels destroyed the capital's police headquarters and took control of the parliament building and the state television station. Some 45 people were taken hostage, including the Prime Minister, A. N. R. Robinson, and several cabinet ministers. The rebels demanded Robinson's resignation, elections within 90 days and an amnesty for those taking part in the attempted coup. On 28 July a state of emergency was declared and a curfew was imposed, following widespread looting in the capital by thousands taking advantage of the political crisis and consequent preoccupation of the police. On 31 July the Prime Minister, who had sustained gunshot wounds, was released from captivity by the rebels, on medical grounds. On 1 August the rebels surrendered unconditionally. An amnesty pardoning the rebels, signed by the President of the Senate, Joseph Emmanuel Carter, in his capacity as acting Head of State, was proclaimed invalid, on the grounds that it had been signed under duress. In mid-August Bakr and his followers were charged with treason, a capital offence. Some 30 people were killed and another 500 injured during the five-day attempted coup. In September, in the light of the failure of the security forces to prevent the attempted coup, the Minister of Justice and National Security, Selwyn Richardson, offered his resignation. The decision followed sustained demands by the opposition for him to do so; the Prime Minister, however, declined the offer.

In November 1991 the imprisoned Jamaat al Muslimeen rebels won an appeal to the Judicial Committee of the Privy Council in the United Kingdom (the final court of appeal for Trinidad and Tobago), which ruled that the validity of the presidential pardon issued during the attempted coup in July 1990 should be determined before the rebels were brought to trial, and that an application for their release should be heard by the High Court of Trinidad and Tobago immediately. On 30 June 1992 the High Court ruled that the pardon was valid, and ordered the immediate release of the 114 defendants. In mid-July the Government announced that it would pursue all legal means of appeal against the decision, which it deemed to be of great constitutional significance. In March 1993 delays in the payment of compensation to the rebels, for what the High Court ruled was their wrongful imprisonment, led Bakr to threaten 'action' against the Government, prompting fears of renewed violence by the rebels. In October the Court of Appeal ruled to uphold the decision of the High Court. In October 1994 the Judicial Committee of the Privy Council ruled to overturn the decisions of the High Court and the Court of Appeal, declaring the pardon invalid. As a result the Jamaat al Muslimeen would be unable to claim compensation for wrongful imprisonment. However, it was also ruled that to rearrest the rebels and try them for offences committed during the insurrection would constitute an abuse of legal process.

Widespread industrial discontent at the Government's continued refusal to meet public-sector union demands for payment of wage arrears, arising from the suspension in 1987 of a cost-of-living allowance, was reflected in a strike by teachers in February 1991. Further unrest occurred in the same month as sugar farmers went on strike in support of a demand for a 50% increase in the price paid to them by the state sugar company, Caroni, for sugar cane. In June labour leaders representing all of the country's affiliated and non-affiliated unions signed an agreement establishing a single unified trade union body, the National Trade Union Centre (NATUC).

General elections, held on 16 December 1991, resulted in a decisive victory for the PNM, which secured 45.1% of the votes and won 21 seats in the House of Representatives. The implementation of unpopular austerity measures was widely acknowledged as the main cause of the defeat of the ruling NAR, which lost all but two of its seats in the House. As a result of his party's defeat, A. N. R. Robinson resigned as leader of the NAR. A notable feature of the elections was the re-emergence of ethnic voting, with the vast majority of the votes divided between the Afro-Trinidadian-oriented PNM and the largely Indo-Trinidadian UNC, which secured 13 seats in the House of Representatives. On 17 December Patrick Manning was sworn in as Prime Minister, and on 20 December a new Cabinet was appointed. A promise made by the PNM in its election manifesto to settle the public-sector claim for salaries and allowances withheld during the austerity programme of the outgoing NAR Government was honoured in the budget submitted to Parliament in January 1992. However, the Government's continued failure to effect a settlement led to an intensification of industrial unrest during 1992. In February 1993 several thousand public-sector employees attended two consecutive demonstrations, organized by NATUC, to protest at the delay in payments and at the Government's plans for a restructuring of inefficient state enterprises involving some 2,600 redundancies. In early 1994 a government offer of a settlement of the public-sector claim, including options for payment in negotiable government bonds and paid holiday in lieu of salary arrears, was not favourably received by the unions. The majority of employees rejected the offer. In mid-1995 the Government introduced a new plan to settle the claim, involving the issue of bonds with tax credits. The Trinidad and Tobago Unified Teachers' Association was reported to have accepted the offer and it was expected that other unions would receive the offer favourably.

In mid-1992 British police detectives were engaged by the Government to investigate allegations, made by an assistant police commissioner, that an illegal drugs-trafficking cartel was operating within the islands' police force. In January 1993 the inquiry reported that, while there was no evidence of a single conspiracy to traffic drugs, corruption, including drugs-related activity, was prevalent at all levels of the police force. In February some 300 uniformed police officers staged an unprecedented demonstration outside Parliament in Port of Spain to protest at the appointment of British officers to five new high-ranking posts in the police force.

At elections to the Tobago House of Assembly, held on 7 December 1992, the NAR retained control, securing 11 seats, with the remaining elective seat won by the PNM. In July 1993 the Government and the Tobago House of Assembly agreed to begin discussions concerning the upgrading of Tobago's constitutional status. Measures under consideration by the legislature in 1994–95 included the establishment of an executive council on Tobago and the appointment of an independent senator to represent the island.

In August 1993 employees of the Trinidad and Tobago Electricity Commission staged demonstrations in protest at government plans for the privatization of the company. The protests were extended to strike action in September. In that month petroleum workers staged a half-day strike in protest against the restructuring of the sector. Industrial unrest continued throughout 1993–95, as unions opposed continuing government plans for the rationalization and privatization of unproductive public utilities.

Appeals for the restoration of capital punishment prompted by growing public concern at the increasing rate of murder and violent crime in Trinidad and Tobago gained considerable impetus in mid-August 1993 following the murder of the country's Prison Commissioner. Warrants issued shortly afterwards for the executions of two convicted murderers were suspended following protests by the human rights organization, Amnesty International.

In December 1993 members of the opposition UNC and NAR sought to discredit the Minister of Planning and Development, Lenny Saith, over his alleged involvement in a financial scandal. Saith denied that a substantial loan from the National Commercial Bank of Trinidad and Tobago to a property development company of which he had formerly been a director, had been cancelled following a merger involving the bank in August. In January 1994, following the resignation of the Minister of Trade, Industry and Tourism, Brian Kuei Tung, Manning conducted a reorganization of cabinet portfolios. A new Ministry of Social Development was created and the Ministry of Tourism was separated from that of Trade and Industry.

In July 1994 Trinidad and Tobago conducted its first execution since 1979. However, the condemned man, convicted murderer Glen Ashby, was hanged only minutes before a facsimile transmission from the Judicial Committee of the Privy Council in the United Kingdom was sent to the Court of Appeal in Trinidad granting a stay of execution. Reportedly, an undertaking had been given by the Attorney-General, Keith Sobion, that the execution would not be conducted until all applications for a stay had been exhausted. Ashby had been close to completing five years under sentence of death, a period which the Judicial Committee of the Privy Council had recommended, in a ruling in 1993, as meriting a commutation to life imprisonment on the grounds that a longer period amounted to 'cruel and inhuman punishment'. In the light of these events, in late July the Judicial Committee of the Privy Council issued a conservatory order whereby, in the case of two men due to be heard by the Trinidad Court of Appeal, should their execution be ordered, it could not be conducted until the case had been heard by the Judicial Committee of the Privy Council itself. This decision provoked protest from the Chief Justice of Trinidad and Tobago, who accused the Privy Council of pre-empting the Court of Appeal's exercise of its jurisdiction. Subsequently, the Government announced its intention to introduce legislation establishing the Court of Appeal as the final appeal court for criminal cases, pending regional agreement on a Caribbean appeal court. However, such legislation would require opposition support in order to amend the Constitution. (Legislation was introduced to the Senate in March 1995 but was withdrawn the following month for revision). At the end of July 1994 the UN Human Rights Committee denounced the execution of Ashby and announced that it was to pursue the case posthumously. (Trinidad and Tobago is a signatory to the UN International Covenant on Civil and Political Rights). In March 1995 an international jurists' inquiry into the Ashby case reported that the execution was illegal and that sufficient evidence existed to cite the Attorney-General, Keith Sobion, for contempt of court. However, the report was not binding on the Government of Trinidad and Tobago, and no action was taken.

In August 1994 Selby Wilson resigned as leader of the NAR, when the party's executive overruled his decision to withdraw from an agreement with the UNC to form an alliance, in opposition to the PNM, in order to contest a by-election to be held that month. Wilson had withdrawn from the agreement due to his own suspicions that the UNC were involved politically with the Jamaat al Muslimeen. The leader of the UNC, Basdeo Panday, denied any such involvement. In the same month, as part of an initiative introduced by Manning to curb increasing violent crime, the House of Representatives approved legislation preventing the granting of bail to repeat offenders with three or more convictions from a list of specified serious offences. The legislation raised concern that it might undermine civil rights. In May 1995 Manning conducted a reorganization of the Cabinet.

Import controls, imposed by Trinidad and Tobago during the early 1980s, had strained relations with Barbados and other members of the Caribbean Community and Common Market (CARICOM, see p. 114). This was aggravated in October 1983 by Chambers' decision not to support, or participate in, the US-led intervention in Grenada, resulting in the mutual withdrawal (until May 1985) of High Commissioners between Trinidad and Tobago and Barbados. However, a series of meetings between the ministers responsible for trade of the two countries during 1986 achieved significant reductions in trade restrictions. Relations with Antigua and Barbuda were affected in 1988 by a dispute over access for Trinidad and Tobago's national airline, BWIA, to the route between Antigua and London. The two Governments placed each other's goods under trade licence, but resolved the dispute in March, when all trade restrictions between the two countries were removed. In October 1988 CARICOM finally secured the implementation of a single internal market, with the removal of virtually all trade barriers within member countries.

In March 1990, following six months of negotiations, Trinidad and Tobago signed with Venezuela a joint declaration on maritime boundaries, under which Trinidad and Tobago's maritime boundary was to be extended from 200 nautical miles (370 km) to 350 nautical miles (648 km). The treaty was ratified in July 1991.

**Government**

Legislative power is vested in the bicameral Parliament, consisting of the Senate, with 31 members, and the House of Representatives, with 36 members. Representatives are elected for a five-year term by universal adult suffrage. The President is a constitutional Head of State, chosen by an electoral college of members of both the Senate and the House of Representatives. Members of the Senate are nominated by the President in consultation with, and on the advice of, the Prime Minister and the Leader of the Opposition. The Cabinet has effective control of the Government and is responsible to Parliament. Tobago Island was granted its own House of Assembly in 1980 and given full internal self-government in January 1987. The Tobago House of Assembly has 15 members, of whom 12 are elected. The remaining three are selected by the majority party.

**Defence**

In June 1994 the defence forces consisted of an army of 2,000 men, and a coastguard of 600, with nine patrol craft. Included in the coastguard is an air force of 50. There is also a paramilitary police force of 4,800 men. The defence budget for 1994 was TT $483.7m.

**Economic Affairs**

In 1993, according to estimates by the World Bank, Trinidad and Tobago's gross national product (GNP), measured at average 1991–93 prices, was US $4,776m., equivalent to $3,730 per head. During 1985–93, it was estimated, GNP per head decreased, in real terms, at an average annual rate of 2.7%. Over the same period, the population increased by an annual average of 1.3%. Trinidad and Tobago's gross domestic product (GDP) decreased, in real terms, by an annual average of 3.7% in 1980–92, and by 1.5% in 1993, before increasing by an estimated 4.7% in 1994.

Agriculture (including forestry, hunting and fishing) contributed 2.5% of GDP and employed 11.3% of the working population in 1993. The principal cash crops are sugar cane, coffee, cocoa and citrus fruits. The fishing sector is small-scale, but is an important local source of food. During 1980–92 agricultural GDP decreased by an annual average of 6.8%.

Industry (including mining and quarrying, manufacturing, construction and power) provided 41.7% of GDP and employed 26.4% of the working population in 1993. During 1980–92 industrial GDP decreased by an annual average of 6.6%.

Petroleum and asphalt, including mining and refining, provided 22.9% of GDP in 1993. Some 3.7% of the working population were employed in the mining sector in that year. The petroleum industry is the principal sector of Trinidad and Tobago's economy. In 1990 it accounted for 47% of government revenue, although by 1993 the proportion had been reduced to 15%, owing to declines in production and international prices. Trinidad has the world's largest deposits of natural asphalt. There are also substantial reserves of natural gas.

Manufacturing contributed 9.2% of GDP (excluding petroleum-refining) and employed 10.0% of the working population in 1993. In 1987 the principal branches (measured by value of output) were petroleum-refining (33% of the total), food products, iron and steel, beverages, chemicals, tobacco, paper, and printing and publishing. During 1980–92 manufacturing GDP decreased by an annual average of 8.7%.

Energy is derived principally from natural gas and petroleum. Locally-extracted natural gas generates most of Trinidad and Tobago's electricity supply, and is also used as fuel for the country's two petroleum refineries and several manufacturing plants. Imports of fuel products comprised 15.9% of the value of merchandise imports in 1993.

Tourism is the third largest source of foreign exchange, and more than 200,000 foreign visitors arrive annually. However, the majority of these are private or business visitors, and only about 10% stay in hotels. In the 1980s the Government initiated a revitalization of the tourist industry, improving airport and harbour facilities on Tobago, and promoting the construction of hotels.

In 1993 Trinidad and Tobago recorded a visible trade surplus of US $524.3m., and there was a surplus of US $101.6m. on the current account of the balance of payments. In 1992 the principal source of imports was the USA (41.4%); other major suppliers were Venezuela, the United Kingdom, Japan and Canada. The USA was also the principal market for exports (47.0%) in that year; other important purchasers were the Netherlands Antilles, Barbados, French Guiana, Guyana and Suriname. The principal exports in 1993 were mineral fuels and lubricants (especially petroleum and related products), chemicals and basic manufactures. The principal imports were machinery and transport equipment, basic manufactures, mineral fuels and lubricants and foodstuffs.

In 1993 there was an estimated budgetary surplus of TT $763.1m. At the end of 1993 Trinidad and Tobago's total external debt was US $2,137m., of which US $1,704m. was long-term public debt. In 1992 the cost of debt-servicing was equivalent to 27.7% of the value of exports of goods and services. The annual rate of inflation averaged 8.7% in 1985–93. Consumer prices increased by an average of 4.7% in the year to October 1994. An estimated 19.8% of the labour force were unemployed in late 1993.

Trinidad and Tobago is a member of the Caribbean Community and Common Market (CARICOM, see p. 114), the Inter-American Development Bank (IDB, see p. 170) and the Latin American Economic System (SELA, see p. 239). In March 1994 Trinidad and Tobago announced its intention to seek membership of the North American Free Trade Agreement (NAFTA, see p. 190).

Trinidad and Tobago's economy is largely based on its plentiful reserves of petroleum and natural gas. Following a decline

# TRINIDAD AND TOBAGO

*Introductory Survey, Statistical Survey*

in international petroleum prices in the early 1980s, and particularly in 1986, the Government sought successfully to diversify the economy by increasing manufacturing for export and by stimulating growth in the tourist industry. A depletion of international reserves, caused by high debt-service payments and the failure effectively to reduce public expenditure, caused the Government to devalue the currency in April 1993, through the introduction of a liberalized foreign exchange system. The devaluation, which was also aimed at encouraging foreign investment, was expected to increase the competitiveness of non-petroleum exports during 1994, which would offset the continuing decline in petroleum revenue resulting from a reduction in international prices and decreases in productivity. However, an upturn in the petroleum sector contributed to considerable GDP growth in 1994. Further growth in that sector was expected in 1995 and 1996, as a result of improved incentives for foreign investment and exploration. The transfer of state-owned enterprises to the private sector continued to help fund debt-service repayments in 1995, despite opposition by trade unions. In late 1994 Trinidad and Tobago signed a bilateral investment treaty and a bilateral intellectual property rights accord with the USA, thus strengthening economic links between the two countries and improving Trinidad and Tobago's eligibility for future membership of NAFTA. Plans were also under way in 1995 to develop the country into an 'offshore' financial centre, including proposed legislation providing for the establishment of a securities and exchange commission.

### Social Welfare

Old-age pensions are paid, and there is some unemployment relief. In 1993 there were 60 hospitals and nursing homes, with a total of 4,216 beds, and the country had 1,051 physicians. State medical services are free. In April 1972 the National Insurance System was inaugurated. The system is administered by an independent board, and its provisions are similar to those contained in the British system. Other social services include the provision of food stamps for the needy. Projected expenditure by the central Government in 1990 included TT $547.2m. (10.0% of total spending) on health.

### Education

Primary and secondary education is provided free of charge. Attendance at school is officially compulsory for children between five and 11 years of age. Primary education begins at the age of five and lasts for seven years. Secondary education, beginning at 12 years of age, lasts for up to five years, comprising a first cycle of three years and a second of two years. Entrance to secondary schools is determined by the Common Entrance Examination. Many schools are administered jointly by the State and religious bodies. In 1991 an estimated 89% of children in the relevant age-group were enrolled at primary schools (males 89%; females 90%). In that year enrolment at secondary schools was equivalent to 79% of children in the relevant age-group (males 78%; females 80%). In 1991 the total enrolment at primary and secondary schools was equivalent to 89% of the school-age population (males 89%; females 90%). The Trinidad campus of the University of the West Indies, at St Augustine, includes an engineering faculty. Other institutions of higher education are the Polytechnic Institute and the East Caribbean Farm Institute. The country has one teacher training college and three government-controlled technical institutes and vocational centres. In 1980 the adult illiteracy rate averaged 5.1% (males 3.5%; females 6.6%), and by 1990, according to UNESCO estimates, the rate had fallen to only 3.1% (males 2.0%; females 4.4%). Public expenditure on education in 1990 was TT $788m., representing 11.6% of total government spending.

### Public Holidays

**1995:** 1 January (New Year's Day), 27–28 February (Carnival), 3 March* (Id al-Fitr, end of Ramadan), 14–17 April (Easter), 5 June (Whit Monday), 15 June (Corpus Christi), 19 June (Labour Day), 1 August (Emancipation Day), 31 August (Independence Day), 24 September (Republic Day), October† (Divali), 25–26 December (Christmas).

**1996:** 1 January (New Year's Day), 19–20 February (Carnival), 21 February* (Id al-Fitr, end of Ramadan), 5–8 April (Easter), 27 May (Whit Monday), 6 June (Corpus Christi), 19 June (Labour Day), 1 August (Emancipation Day), 31 August (Independence Day), 24 September (Republic Day), October†(Divali), 25–26 December (Christmas).

* These holidays are dependent on the Islamic lunar calendar and may vary by one or two days from the dates given.
† Dependent on lunar sightings.

### Weights and Measures

The metric system is replacing the imperial system of weights and measures.

# Statistical Survey

Source (unless otherwise stated): Central Statistical Office, 35-41 Queen St, POB 98, Port of Spain; tel. 623-7069.

## Area and Population

### AREA, POPULATION AND DENSITY

| | |
|---|---:|
| Area (sq km) | 5,128* |
| Population (census results) | |
| 12 May 1980 | 1,079,791 |
| 2 May 1990† | |
| Males | 618,050 |
| Females | 616,338 |
| Total | 1,234,388 |
| Population (offical estimates at mid-year) | |
| 1992 | 1,252,000 |
| 1993 | 1,260,000 |
| Density (per sq km) at mid-1993 | 245.7 |

* 1,980 sq miles. Of the total area, Trinidad is 4,828 sq km (1,864 sq miles) and Tobago 300 sq km (116 sq miles).
† Figures are provisional.

### POPULATION BY ETHNIC GROUP
(1990 census, provisional*)

| | Males | Females | Total | % |
|---|---:|---:|---:|---:|
| African | 223,561 | 221,883 | 445,444 | 39.59 |
| Chinese | 2,317 | 1,997 | 4,314 | 0.38 |
| 'East' Indian | 226,967 | 226,102 | 453,069 | 40.27 |
| Lebanese | 493 | 441 | 934 | 0.08 |
| Mixed | 100,842 | 106,716 | 207,558 | 18.45 |
| White | 3,483 | 3,771 | 7,254 | 0.64 |
| Other | 886 | 838 | 1,724 | 0.15 |
| Unknown | 2,385 | 2,446 | 4,831 | 0.43 |
| **Total** | 560,934 | 564,194 | 1,125,128 | 100.00 |

* Excludes some institutional population and members of unenumerated households, totalling 44,444.

**Principal towns** (population at mid-1991): Port of Spain (capital) 51,076; San Fernando 30,115; Arima (borough) 29,483.

**Births and deaths** (1993): Registered live births 21,927 (birth rate 17.4 per 1,000); Registered deaths 8,191 (death rate 6.5 per 1,000).

**Expectation of life** (UN estimates, years at birth, 1985–90): 70.1 (males 67.7; females 72.7) (Source: UN, *World Population Prospects: The 1992 Revision*).

# TRINIDAD AND TOBAGO

## EMPLOYMENT
('000 persons aged 15 years and over, 1993)

|  | Males | Females | Total |
|---|---|---|---|
| Agriculture, forestry, hunting and fishing | 37.7 | 8.0 | 45.8 |
| Mining and quarrying | 13.1 | 1.9 | 15.0 |
| Manufacturing | 28.1 | 12.2 | 40.3 |
| Electricity, gas and water | 6.2 | 0.9 | 7.1 |
| Construction | 39.7 | 4.6 | 44.3 |
| Trade, restaurants and hotels | 35.5 | 35.6 | 71.1 |
| Transport and communications | 25.2 | 4.8 | 30.0 |
| Financing, insurance, real estate and business services | 15.4 | 12.5 | 27.9 |
| Community, social and personal services | 60.5 | 62.2 | 122.8 |
| Activities not adequately defined | 0.1 | 0.1 | 0.2 |
| **Total** | **261.8** | **142.8** | **404.5** |

Source: ILO, *Year Book of Labour Statistics*.

## Agriculture

### PRINCIPAL CROPS ('000 metric tons)

|  | 1991* | 1992 | 1993 |
|---|---|---|---|
| Sugar cane | 1,301 | 1,292 | 1,211 |
| Cocoa | 2 | 1 | 2 |
| Coffee (green) | 1 | — | 1 |
| Copra | 4 | 5 | 5 |
| Oranges | 8† | 1 | 4 |
| Grapefruit | 4† | 1 | 3 |
| Rice (paddy) | 15† | 22 | 16 |

* Source: FAO, *Production Yearbook*.   † FAO estimate.

### LIVESTOCK (FAO estimates, '000 head, year ending September)

|  | 1991 | 1992 | 1993 |
|---|---|---|---|
| Cattle | 60 | 55 | 55 |
| Buffaloes | 9 | 9 | 9 |
| Pigs | 54 | 54 | 48 |
| Sheep | 14 | 14 | 14 |
| Goats | 52 | 52 | 52 |

Poultry (FAO estimates, million): 11 in 1991; 11 in 1992; 12 in 1993.
Source: FAO, *Production Yearbook*.

### LIVESTOCK PRODUCTS ('000 metric tons)

|  | 1991* | 1992 | 1993 |
|---|---|---|---|
| Beef and veal | 1 | 1 | 1 |
| Pig meat | 2 | 2 | 2 |
| Poultry meat | 26 | 21 | 30 |
| Cows' milk | 12 | 10 | 9‡ |
| Poultry eggs† | 10 | 8 | 8 |

* Source: FAO, *Production Yearbook*.
† FAO estimates.
‡ Provisional.

## Forestry

### ROUNDWOOD REMOVALS ('000 cubic metres, excl. bark)

|  | 1990 | 1991 | 1992 |
|---|---|---|---|
| Sawlogs, veneer logs and logs for sleepers | 48 | 43 | 62 |
| Other industrial wood | 2* | 3 | 3 |
| Fuel wood* | 22 | 22 | 22 |
| **Total** | **72** | **68** | **87** |

* FAO estimate(s). Annual output of fuel wood is assumed to be unchanged since 1982.
Source: FAO, *Yearbook of Forest Products*.

### SAWNWOOD PRODUCTION
('000 cubic metres, incl. railway sleepers)

|  | 1990 | 1991 | 1992 |
|---|---|---|---|
| **Total** | 53 | 42 | 58 |

Source: FAO, *Yearbook of Forest Products*.

## Fishing
('000 metric tons, live weight)

|  | 1990 | 1991 | 1992* |
|---|---|---|---|
| Marine fishes | 0.8 | 1.8 | 2.0 |
| Shrimps and prawns | 7.6 | 10.4 | 13.0 |
| **Total catch** | **8.4** | **12.2** | **15.0** |

* FAO estimates.
Source: FAO, *Yearbook of Fishery Statistics*.

## Mining
('000 metric tons, unless otherwise indicated)

|  | 1989 | 1990 | 1991 |
|---|---|---|---|
| Crude petroleum | 7,714 | 7,863 | 7,442 |
| Natural gas (petajoules) | 194 | 215 | 221 |
| Natural asphalt | 30 | 23 | 25 |

Source: UN, *Industrial Statistics Yearbook*.
**Crude petroleum** (million metric tons): 7.2 in 1992.

## Industry

### SELECTED PRODUCTS
('000 metric tons, unless otherwise indicated)

|  | 1991 | 1992 | 1993 |
|---|---|---|---|
| Raw sugar | 100 | 110 | 105 |
| Rum ('000 proof gallons) | 3,137 | 3,612 | 3,390 |
| Beer and stout ('000 hectolitres) | 437 | 395 | 424 |
| Nitrogenous fertilizers | 2,466 | 2,362 | 2,292 |
| Aviation gasolene, jet fuels and kerosene | 715 | 528 | 577 |
| Motor spirit—petrol | 898 | 902 | 1,028 |
| Distillate fuel oils and residual fuel oils | 3,384 | 3,649 | 3,125 |
| Lubricating oils | 40 | 71 | 38 |
| Petroleum bitumen—asphalt | 21 | 19 | 19 |
| Cement | 486 | 482 | 527 |
| Refrigerators (number) | 12,557 | 10,006 | 2,956 |
| Gas cookers (number) | 17,519 | 21,261 | 18,356 |
| Radio receivers (number) | 2,712 | 3,088 | 3,845 |
| Television receivers (number) | 13,013 | 16,281 | 11,206 |
| Electric energy (million kWh) | 3,642 | 3,851 | 3,817 |

# TRINIDAD AND TOBAGO

# Finance

### CURRENCY AND EXCHANGE RATES
**Monetary Units**
100 cents = 1 Trinidad and Tobago dollar (TT $).

**Sterling and US Dollar Equivalents** (31 December 1994)
£1 sterling = TT $9.282;
US $1 = TT $5.933;
TT $1,000 = £107.73 = US $168.54.

**Exchange Rate**
Between August 1988 and April 1993 the official rate was fixed at US $1 = TT $4.250. Since April 1993 the rate has been market-determined. The average exchange rate (TT $ per US $) was: 5.351 in 1993; 5.925 in 1994.

### BUDGET (TT $ million)

| Revenue | 1991 | 1992 | 1993* |
|---|---|---|---|
| Direct taxes | 3,404.1 | 2,812.5 | 2,724.3 |
| Indirect taxes | 2,265.7 | 2,438.7 | 3,085.3 |
| Property and entrepreneurial income | 966.5 | 761.0 | 906.6 |
| Other recurrent revenue | 140.7 | 134.5 | 142.8 |
| Capital revenue (including borrowing) | 958.6 | 1,510.2 | 2,732.9 |
| **Total** | 7,735.6 | 7,656.9 | 9,591.9 |

| Expenditure | 1991 | 1992 | 1993* |
|---|---|---|---|
| Total recurrent expenditure | 6,943.6 | 6,227.4 | 6,869.1 |
| Personnel expenditure | 3,207.6 | 3,502.2 | 3.556.1 |
| Interest on public debt | 1,064.2 | 1,198.3 | 1,421.5 |
| Other recurrent expenditure | 2,671.8 | 1,526.9 | 1,891.5 |
| Total capital expenditure | 1,588.3 | 1,816.9 | 1,959.7 |
| Capital repayment and other debt charges | 703.2 | 1,029.4 | 1,163.4 |
| Other capital expenditure | 885.1 | 787.5 | 796.3 |
| **Total** | 8,531.9 | 8,044.3 | 8,828.8 |

* Revised estimates.

### INTERNATIONAL RESERVES (US $ million at 31 December)

| | 1991 | 1992 | 1993 |
|---|---|---|---|
| Gold* | 2.0 | 2.0 | 1.4 |
| IMF special drawing rights | 2.1 | 0.3 | 0.3 |
| Foreign exchange | 336.5 | 171.9 | 206.0 |
| **Total** | 340.6 | 174.2 | 207.7 |

* National valuation of gold reserves (54,000 troy oz in 1991 and 1992, 56,000 troy oz in 1993).
Source: IMF, *International Financial Statistics*.

### MONEY SUPPLY (TT $ million at 31 December)

| | 1991 | 1992 | 1993 |
|---|---|---|---|
| Currency outside banks | 747.8 | 698.2 | 707.4 |
| Demand deposits at commercial banks | 2,040.7 | 1,858.9 | 2,274.3 |
| **Total money** (incl. others) | 2,921.6 | 2,696.0 | 3,136.5 |

Source: IMF, *International Financial Statistics*.

### COST OF LIVING
(Consumer Price Index; base: 1980 = 100)

| | 1991 | 1992 | 1993 |
|---|---|---|---|
| Food | 441.1 | 479.6 | 570.3 |
| Fuel and light | 365.0 | 385.3 | 386.2 |
| Clothing | 185.3 | 184.4 | 182.4 |
| Rent | 166.1 | 166.5 | 168.2 |
| **All items** (incl. others) | 299.6 | 319.0 | 353.3 |

Source: ILO, *Year Book of Labour Statistics*.

### NATIONAL ACCOUNTS (TT $ million at current prices)
**Expenditure on the Gross Domestic Product**

| | 1990 | 1991 | 1992 |
|---|---|---|---|
| Government final consumption expenditure | 3,487.4 | 3,837.7 | 4,012.6 |
| Private final consumption expenditure | 11,428.3 | 13,739.5 | 13,102.2 |
| Increase in stocks | 4.9 | −20.0 | 92.6 |
| Gross fixed capital formation | 2,973.8 | 3,043.5 | 2,605.6 |
| **Total domestic expenditure** | 17,894.4 | 20,600.7 | 19,813.0 |
| Exports of goods and services | 9,770.7 | 9,332.2 | 9,161.3 |
| *Less* Imports of goods and services | 6,125.8 | 7,553.1 | 6,752.0 |
| **GDP in purchasers' values** | 21,539.3 | 22,379.8 | 22,222.3 |

**Gross Domestic Product by Economic Activity**

| | 1991 | 1992 | 1993 |
|---|---|---|---|
| Agriculture, hunting, forestry and fishing | 558.2 | 594.1 | 607.9 |
| Petroleum and asphalt, including mining and refining | 5,903.1 | 4,860.2 | 5,585.5 |
| Manufacturing | 2,062.7 | 2,107.7 | 2,274.6 |
| Electricity, water and construction | 2,133.3 | 2,281.5 | 2,320.1 |
| Distribution and restaurants | 2,954.2 | 3,107.0 | 3,523.5 |
| Transport, storage and communication | 1,936.6 | 2,074.7 | 2,281.3 |
| Other activities (incl. government activities) | 6,624.5 | 7,495.3 | 7,818.5 |
| **Sub-total** | 22,172.6 | 22,520.5 | 24,411.4 |
| *Less* Imputed bank service charge | 668.3 | 1,008.8 | 1,092.4 |
| Value-added tax | 1,054.5 | 968.6 | 1,280.8 |
| **GDP in purchaser's values** | 22,558.8 | 22,480.3 | 24,599.8 |

### BALANCE OF PAYMENTS (US $ million)

| | 1991 | 1992 | 1993 |
|---|---|---|---|
| Merchandise exports f.o.b. | 1,751.3 | 1,661.9 | 1,477.2 |
| Merchandise imports f.o.b. | −1,210.3 | −995.6 | −952.9 |
| **Trade balance** | 541.0 | 666.2 | 524.3 |
| Exports of services | 428.4 | 482.2 | 376.3 |
| Imports of services | −526.4 | −551.2 | −462.0 |
| Other income received | 48.6 | 29.8 | 40.2 |
| Other income paid | −498.7 | −488.6 | −370.4 |
| Private unrequited transfers (net) | −15.9 | −15.7 | −7.0 |
| Official unrequited transfers (net) | 2.1 | −0.4 | 0.2 |
| **Current balance** | −20.8 | 122.4 | 101.6 |
| Direct investment (net) | 169.3 | 177.9 | 379.2 |
| Other capital (net) | −396.2 | −332.1 | −280.4 |
| Net errors and omissions | −29.0 | −72.6 | −41.8 |
| **Overall balance** | −276.5 | −104.4 | 158.6 |

Source: IMF, *International Financial Statistics*.

# External Trade

### COMMODITY GROUPS (TT $ million)

| Imports c.i.f. | 1991 | 1992 | 1993 |
|---|---|---|---|
| Food and live animals | 895.1 | 896.7 | 938.9 |
| Crude materials (inedible) except fuels | 444.6 | 373.8 | 337.2 |
| Mineral fuels, lubricants, etc. | 1,038.6 | 549.0 | 1,189.0 |
| Chemicals | 892.2 | 769.2 | 827.3 |
| Basic manufactures | 1,359.8 | 1,226.8 | 1,238.9 |
| Machinery and transport equipment | 1,840.9 | 1,769.4 | 2,463.5 |
| Miscellaneous manufactured articles | 490.2 | 422.3 | 420.9 |
| **Total** (incl. others) | 7,084.8 | 6,096.5 | 7,495.3 |

# TRINIDAD AND TOBAGO

| Exports f.o.b. | 1991 | 1992 | 1993 |
|---|---|---|---|
| Food and live animals | 383.2 | 373.9 | 501.5 |
| Mineral fuels, lubricants, etc. | 5,506.5 | 5,099.3 | 5,070.0 |
| Chemicals | 1,425.1 | 1,216.6 | 1,483.0 |
| Basic manufactures | 786.4 | 865.0 | 1,108.8 |
| Machinery and transport equipment | 79.4 | 98.3 | 243.7 |
| Miscellaneous manufactured articles | 118.4 | 147.4 | 180.1 |
| **Total** (incl. others) | 8,436.4 | 7,943.0 | 8,800.9 |

## PRINCIPAL TRADING PARTNERS (US $ million)

| Imports c.i.f. | 1990 | 1991 | 1992 |
|---|---|---|---|
| Angola | 31.5 | — | — |
| Argentina | 14.5 | 10.2 | 8.6 |
| Barbados | 17.7 | 25.4 | 20.5 |
| Brazil | 51.9 | 63.3 | 49.5 |
| Canada | 73.5 | 81.8 | 73.8 |
| Colombia | 16.3 | 4.5 | 4.5 |
| France | 17.5 | 18.1 | 17.1 |
| Germany | 30.6 | 32.1 | 36.8 |
| Jamaica | 33.7 | 34.4 | 31.0 |
| Japan | 44.1 | 93.2 | 96.6 |
| Netherlands | 21.5 | 29.2 | 20.6 |
| Nigeria | 15.3 | 9.9 | 0.3 |
| Saint Vincent and the Grenadines | 83.8 | 4.8 | 5.4 |
| United Kingdom | 94.1 | 122.9 | 112.1 |
| USA | 511.2 | 645.6 | 593.5 |
| Venezuela | 94.2 | 234.9 | 139.1 |
| **Total** (incl. others) | 1,261.6 | 1,669.9 | 1,434.5 |

| Exports f.o.b. | 1990 | 1991 | 1992 |
|---|---|---|---|
| Barbados | 73.8 | 65.5 | 64.1 |
| Belgium-Luxembourg | 21.8 | 24.3 | 13.0 |
| Canada | 28.5 | 34.8 | 34.5 |
| Cuba | 37.8 | 4.5 | 12.0 |
| France | 22.2 | 26.1 | 34.8 |
| French Guiana | 42.3 | 53.4 | 48.2 |
| Grenada | 20.6 | 21.1 | 21.2 |
| Guadeloupe | 26.4 | 23.4 | 9.6 |
| Guyana | 27.3 | 30.4 | 42.3 |
| Italy | 28.7 | 36.4 | 2.4 |
| Jamaica | 56.2 | 41.7 | 30.9 |
| Japan | 16.1 | 25.3 | 19.3 |
| Netherlands | 20.6 | 36.9 | 10.0 |
| Netherlands Antilles | 62.7 | 64.9 | 87.6 |
| Saint Lucia | 26.6 | 28.9 | 29.6 |
| Suriname | 43.2 | 38.2 | 41.7 |
| United Kingdom | 58.8 | 44.1 | 32.0 |
| USA | 1,182.8 | 966.3 | 879.0 |
| Venezuela | 42.7 | 54.5 | 31.5 |
| **Total** (incl. others) | 2,080.4 | 1,984.7 | 1,868.9 |

## Transport

### ROAD TRAFFIC
(licensed vehicles at 31 December 1992)

| | |
|---|---|
| Passenger cars | 120,589 |
| Goods vehicles | 30,126 |
| Tractors (non-agricultural) | 5,112 |
| Motorcycles and scooters | 1,060 |

Total number of registered vehicles: 319,138 in 1990; 272,435 in 1991; 278,405 in 1992.

### SHIPPING
**International Sea-borne Freight Traffic**
(estimates, '000 metric tons)

| | 1988 | 1989 | 1990 |
|---|---|---|---|
| Goods loaded | 7,736 | 7,992 | 9,622 |
| Goods unloaded | 4,076 | 4,091 | 10,961 |

Source: UN, *Monthly Bulletin of Statistics*.

### CIVIL AVIATION (traffic on scheduled services)

| | 1990 | 1991 | 1992 |
|---|---|---|---|
| Kilometres flown (million) | 23 | 25 | 25 |
| Passengers carried ('000) | 1,285 | 1,345 | 1,354 |
| Passenger-km (million) | 2,726 | 3,129 | 3,077 |
| Total ton-km (million) | 308 | 351 | 346 |

Source: UN, *Statistical Yearbook*.

## Tourism

| | 1991 | 1992 | 1993 |
|---|---|---|---|
| Tourist arrivals | 220,206 | 234,759 | 248,815 |
| Tourist receipts (TT $ million) | 402.5 | 440.2 | 472.6 |

## Communications Media

| | 1990 | 1991 | 1992 |
|---|---|---|---|
| Radio receivers ('000 in use) | 600 | 615 | 625 |
| Television receivers ('000 in use) | 387 | 394 | 400 |
| Telephones ('000 main lines in use) | 174 | 176 | n.a. |
| Daily newspapers | | | |
| Number | 2 | n.a. | 4 |
| Average circulation ('000 copies) | 95 | n.a. | 175 |
| Non-daily newspapers | | | |
| Number | 5 | n.a. | n.a. |
| Average circulation ('000 copies) | 125 | n.a. | n.a. |

Source: UNESCO, *Statistical Yearbook*.

## Education
(1991/92)

| | Institutions | Teachers | Males | Females | Total |
|---|---|---|---|---|---|
| Pre-primary* | 792 | 830 | n.a. | n.a. | 20,408 |
| Primary† | 475 | 7,512 | 99,479 | 96,854 | 196,333 |
| Secondary | 101 | 4,844 | 48,543 | 48,710 | 97,253 |
| University and equivalent | 1 | 292 | 2,342 | 2,187 | 4,529 |

* Figures refer to 1990/91.
† Government-maintained and government-aided schools only.
Source: mainly UNESCO, *Statistical Yearbook*.

# Directory

## The Constitution

Trinidad and Tobago became a republic, within the Commonwealth, under a new Constitution on 1 August 1976. The Constitution provides for a President and a bicameral Parliament comprising a Senate and a House of Representatives. The President is elected by an Electoral College of members of both the Senate and the House of Representatives. The Senate consists of 31 members appointed by the President: 16 on the advice of the Prime Minister, six on the advice of the Leader of the Opposition and nine at the President's own discretion from among outstanding persons from economic, social or community organizations. The House of Representatives consists of 36 members who are elected by universal adult suffrage. The duration of a Parliament is five years. The Cabinet, presided over by the Prime Minister, is responsible for the general direction and control of the Government. It is collectively responsible to Parliament.

## The Government

### HEAD OF STATE
**President:** Noor Mohammed Hassanali (took office March 1987).

### THE CABINET
(June 1995)

**Prime Minister:** Patrick Manning.
**Minister of National Security:** John Eckstein.
**Minister of Energy:** Barry Barnes.
**Minister of Foreign Affairs and Public Information with responsibility for Public Administration:** Gordon Draper.
**Minister of Finance and of Tourism:** Wendell Mottley.
**Minister of Trade and Industry and Minister in the Ministry of Finance with responsibility for Investments:** Kenneth Valley.
**Minister of Agriculture, Land and Marine Resources:** Keith Rowley.
**Minister of Health:** Linda Baboolal.
**Minister of Education:** Augustus Ramrekersingh.
**Minister of Labour and Co-operatives:** Kenneth Collis.
**Minister of Planning and Development with responsibility for Science, Technology and Tertiary Education:** Lenny Saith.
**Minister of Social Development:** Russell Huggins.
**Minister of Community Development, Culture and Women's Affairs:** Joan Yuille-Williams.
**Minister of Public Utilities:** Ralph Maraj.
**Minister of Works and Transport and of Local Government:** Colm Imbert.
**Minister of Housing and Settlements:** Dr Vincent Lasse.
**Minister of Sport and Youth Affairs:** Jean Pierre.
**Minister in the Office of the Prime Minister and Minister of Consumer Affairs:** Camille Robinson-Regis.
**Attorney-General:** Keith Sobion.

### MINISTRIES

**Office of the President:** President's House, St Ann's; tel. 624-1261; fax 625-7950.
**Office of the Prime Minister:** Central Bank Tower, Eric Williams Plaza, Independence Sq., Port of Spain; tel. 623-3655; fax 627-3444.
**Central Administrative Services for Tobago:** Jerningham St, Scarborough; tel. 639-2652; fax 639-2505.
**Ministry of Agriculture, Land and Marine Resources:** St Clair Circle, Port of Spain; tel. 622-1221; fax 622-4246.
**Ministry of Community Development, Culture and Women's Affairs:** ALGICO Bldg, 8 Queen's Park East and Cnr Jerningham Ave, Port of Spain; tel. 623-7032; fax 625-3278.
**Ministry of Consumer Affairs:** Salvatori Bldg, Frederick St, Port of Spain; tel. 623-8841; fax 624-7727.
**Ministry of Education:** Alexandra St, St Clair, Port of Spain; tel. 622-2181; fax 625-5411.
**Ministry of Energy:** Level 9, Riverside Plaza, 3 Besson St, POB 96, Port of Spain; tel. 623-6708; telex 22715; fax 623-2726.
**Ministry of Finance:** Level 8, Financial Complex, Eric Williams Plaza, Independence Sq., Port of Spain; tel. 627-9700; telex 22450; fax 627-6108.
**Ministry of Foreign Affairs:** Knowsley Bldg, 1 Queen's Park West, Port of Spain; tel. 623-4116; telex 22321; fax 627-0571.
**Ministry of Health:** Cnr of Independence Square and Duncan St, Port of Spain; tel. 627-0010; fax 623-9528.
**Ministry of Housing and Settlements:** Sacred Heart Bldg, 16–18 Sackville St, Port of Spain; tel. 627-8378; fax 625-2793.
**Ministry of Labour and Co-operatives:** Level 11, Riverside Plaza, 3 Besson St, Port of Spain; tel. 623-4241; fax 624-4091.
**Ministry of Local Government:** Kent House, Long Circular Rd, Maraval, Port of Spain; tel. 628-1450; fax 625-2793.
**Ministry of National Security:** Knox St, Port of Spain; tel. 623-2441; fax 627-8044.
**Ministry of Planning and Development:** Level 14, Financial Complex, Eric Williams Plaza, Independence Sq., Port of Spain; tel. 627-8387; fax 627-6108.
**Ministry of Public Utilities:** Sacred Heart Bldg, 16–18 Sackville St, Port of Spain; tel. 627-4424; fax 625-7003.
**Ministry of Social Development:** Levels 1–4, Salvatori Bldg, Frederick St, Port of Spain; tel. 623-8841; fax 624-7727.
**Ministry of Sport and Youth Affairs:** Issa Nicholas Bldg, Cnr of Duke and Frederick Sts, Port of Spain; tel. 625-8874; fax 624-5505.
**Ministry of Tourism:** Level 15, Riverside Plaza, 3 Besson St, Port of Spain; tel. 623-2931; fax 627-8488.
**Ministry of Trade and Industry:** Level 15, Riverside Plaza, 3 Besson St, Port of Spain; tel. 623-2931; fax 627-8488.
**Ministry of Works and Transport:** 3 Edward St, Port of Spain; tel. 625-3292.
**Office of the Attorney-General:** WINSURE Bldg, 24–28 Richmond St, Port of Spain; tel. 623-7010; fax 624-3109.

## Legislature

### PARLIAMENT
**Senate**
**President:** Joseph Emmanuel Carter.

**House of Representatives**
**Speaker:** Occah Seapaul.

**Election, 16 December 1991**

| Party | % of Votes | Seats |
| --- | --- | --- |
| People's National Movement (PNM) | 45.1 | 21 |
| United National Congress (UNC) | 29.1 | 13 |
| National Alliance for Reconstruction (NAR) | 24.4 | 2 |
| National Joint Action Committee (NJAC) | 1.1 | — |
| Independents | 0.3 | — |

### TOBAGO HOUSE OF ASSEMBLY

The House is elected for a four-year term of office and consists of 12 elected members and three members selected by the majority party.
**Chairman:** Lennox Denoon.

**Election, 7 December 1992**

| Party | % of Votes | Seats |
| --- | --- | --- |
| National Alliance for Reconstruction | 91.7 | 11 |
| People's National Movement | 8.3 | 1 |

## Political Organizations

**Movement for Social Transformation:** Port of Spain; f. 1989; trade union-oriented; Leader: David Abdullah.

**Movement for Unity and Progress (MUP):** Port of Spain; f. 1994; Leader Hulsie Bhaggan.

**National Alliance for Reconstruction (NAR):** 71 Dundonald St, Port of Spain; tel. 627-6163; f. 1983 as a coalition of moderate opposition parties; reorganized as a unitary party, in February

# TRINIDAD AND TOBAGO

*Directory*

1986, merging the following parties: Democratic Action Congress (DAC), Organization for National Reconstruction (ONR), Tapia House Movement and United Labour Front (ULF); Leader JOSEPH TONEY (acting); Gen. Sec. JENNIFER U. JOHNSON.

**National Development Party (NDP):** Port of Spain; f. 1993; Leader CARSON CHARLES.

**National Joint Action Committee (NJAC):** 17A King St, Port of Spain; tel. 627-7136; left-wing grouping; contested its first election in 1981; Leader MAKANDAL DAAGA.

**National Vision Party (NVP):** Port of Spain; f. 1994; Leader YASIN ABU BAKR.

**People's National Movement (PNM):** 1 Tranquillity St, Port of Spain; tel. 625-1533; f. 1956; moderate nationalist party; Leader PATRICK MANNING; Chair. LENNY SAITH; Gen. Sec. MARTIN JOSEPH.

**Republic Party (RP):** Port of Spain; f. 1994; Leader NELLO MITCHELL.

**United National Congress (UNC):** Rienzi Complex, Southern Main Road, Couva; tel. 636-8145; f. 1989 by former ULF mems expelled from the NAR (see above); Leader BASDEO PANDAY; Chair WADE MARK; Gen. Sec. DAVE COWIE.

## Diplomatic Representation

### EMBASSIES AND HIGH COMMISSIONS IN TRINIDAD AND TOBAGO

**Brazil:** 18 Sweet Briar Rd, St Clair, POB 382, Port of Spain; tel. 622-5779; fax 622-4323; Ambassador: AGILDO SELLOS MOURA.

**Canada:** Huggins Bldg, 72–74 South Quay, POB 1246, Port of Spain; tel. 623-7254; telex 22429; fax 624-4016; High Commissioner: DILYS BUCKLEY-JONES.

**China, People's Republic:** 39 Alexandra St, St Clair, Port of Spain; tel. 622-6976; fax 622-7613; Ambassador: LU SHULI.

**Colombia:** 5 Rookery Nook, Maraval, Port of Spain; tel. 622-5904; Ambassador: ALVARO FORBES.

**France:** Tatil Bldg, 6th Floor, 11 Maraval Rd, Port of Spain; tel. 622-7446; fax 628-2632; Ambassador: PIERRE ARIOLA.

**Germany:** 7–9 Marli St, Newtown, POB 828, Port of Spain; tel. 628-1630; telex 22316; fax 628-5278; Ambassador: HOLGER EBERLE.

**Holy See:** 11 Mary St, St Clair, POB 854, Port of Spain: tel. 622-5009; telex 22500; fax 628-5457; Apostolic Pro-Nuncio: Most Rev. EUGENIO SBARBARO, Titular Archbishop of Tiddi.

**India:** 6 Victoria Ave, POB 530, Port of Spain; tel. 627-7480; telex 22514; fax 627-6985; High Commissioner: J. DODDAMANI.

**Jamaica:** 2 Newbold St, St Clair, Port of Spain; tel. 622-4995; telex 22234; fax 628-9180; High Commissioner: STAFFORD O. NEIL.

**Japan:** Barbados Mutual Bldg, 16 Queen's Park West, Port of Spain; tel. 622-6105; telex 22441; fax 622-0858; Ambassador: TAKESHI TSURUTA.

**Korea, Republic:** 61 Dundonald St, Albion Court, POB 1118, Port of Spain; tel. 627-6791; Ambassador: YOUNG-SHIK SONG.

**Netherlands:** Life of Barbados Bldg, 3rd Floor, 69–71 Edward St, POB 870, Port of Spain; tel. 625-1210; telex 22322; fax 625-1704; Ambassador: Jonkheer W. THEOPHILUS SIX.

**Nigeria:** 3 Maxwell-Phillip St, St Clair, Port of Spain; tel. 622-4002; telex 22390; fax 622-7162; High Commissioner: MOSES S. EIGBIRE.

**United Kingdom:** 19 St Clair Ave, St Clair, POB 778, Port of Spain; tel. 622-2748; fax 622-4555; High Commissioner: RICHARD A. NEILSON.

**USA:** 15 Queen's Park West, POB 752, Port of Spain; tel. 622-6371; fax 628-5464; Ambassador: BRIAN J. DONNELLY.

**Uruguay:** Tatil Bldg, Ground Floor, 11 Maraval Rd, Port of Spain; tel. 628-5696; fax 628-5695; Chargé d'affaires RODOLFO INVERNIZZI-ARENA (acting).

**Venezuela:** 16 Victoria Ave, POB 1300, Port of Spain; tel. 627-9821; telex 22268; fax 624-2508; Ambassador: FREDDY CHRISTIANS.

## Judicial System

**Supreme Court:** Knox St, Port of Spain; tel. 623-2417; fax 627-5477.

The Supreme Court of Judicature of Trinidad and Tobago consists of the High Court of Justice and the Court of Appeal. The High Court consists of the Chief Justice, who is, ex officio, a Judge of the High Court, and between six and 16 Puisne Judges. It has jurisdiction in civil and criminal cases.

The Court of Appeal consists of the Chief Justice, who is President, and six other Justices of Appeal.

Appeal lies to the Court of Appeal from all courts and to the Judicial Committee of the Privy Council in the United Kingdom.

**Chief Justice:** MICHAEL DE LA BASTIDE.

**Registrar (Supreme Court):** SHERMAN MCNICOLLS.

**Court of Appeal:** SATNARINE SHARMA, MUSTAPHA IBRAHIM, ROGER HAMEL-SMITH, LLOYD GOPEESINGH, ZAINOOL HOSEIN, JEAN PERMANAND.

**District Courts:** The Chief Magistrate, the Deputy Chief Magistrate, 13 Senior and 17 magistrates preside over the District Courts established in various parts of the country. In these Courts the work of the Petty Civil Courts (which have jurisdiction to try civil matters where the cause of action does not exceed $6,000) and the Court of Summary Jurisdiction is conducted.

**Chief Magistrate:** BEECHAM MAHARAJH, Nipdec House, Cipriani Blvd, Port of Spain; tel. 625-2781.

The Industrial Court and a Tax Appeal Board are superior courts of record.

**Industrial Court:** Pres. L. P. E. RAMCHAND.

**Tax Appeal Board:** Chair. MONICA BARNES.

**Attorney-General:** KEITH SOBION.

## Religion

In 1990 it was estimated that 29.4% of the population were members of the Roman Catholic Church, 10.9% Anglicans, 23.8% Hindus and 5.8% Muslims.

### CHRISTIANITY

**Christian Council of Trinidad and Tobago:** Hayes Court, 21 Maraval Rd, Port of Spain; f. 1967; church unity organization formed by the Roman Catholic, Anglican, Presbyterian, Methodist, African Methodist, Spiritual Baptist and Moravian Churches, the Church of Scotland and the Salvation Army, with the Ethiopian Orthodox Church and the Baptist Union as observers; Chair. Rev. CICELY ATHILL-HORSFORD.

#### The Anglican Communion

Anglicans are adherents of the Church in the Province of the West Indies, comprising eight dioceses. The Archbishop of the West Indies is the Bishop of the North Eastern Caribbean and Aruba (resident in Antigua).

**Bishop of Trinidad and Tobago:** The Rt Rev. RAWLE E. DOUGLIN, Hayes Court, 21 Maraval Rd, Port of Spain; tel. 622-7387; fax 628-1319.

#### Protestant Churches

**Presbyterian Church in Trinidad and Tobago:** POB 92, Paradise Hill, San Fernando; tel. 652-4829; f. 1868; Moderator Rt Rev. CYRIL PAUL; 45,000 mems.

**Baptist Union of Trinidad and Tobago:** High St, Princes Town; tel. 655-2291; f. 1816; Pres. Rev. BRIAN SKINNER; Gen. Sec. Rev. ANSLEM MARRICK.

#### The Roman Catholic Church

For ecclesiastical purposes, Trinidad and Tobago comprises the single archdiocese of Port of Spain. An estimated 32% of the population were adherents at 31 December 1993.

**Antilles Episcopal Conference:** 9A Gray St, Port of Spain; tel. 622-2932; fax 622-8255; f. 1975; 19 mems from the Caribbean region and Bermuda; Pres. Most Rev. KELVIN EDWARD FELIX, Archbishop of Castries (Saint Lucia).

**Archbishop of Port of Spain:** Most Rev. GORDON ANTHONY PANTIN, 27 Maraval Rd, Port of Spain; tel. 622-1103; fax 622-1165.

## The Press

### DAILIES

**Newsday:** 19–21 Chacon St, Port of Spain; tel. 623-4949; f. 1993; Gen. Man. DANIEL CHOKOLINGO; Editor-in-Chief THERESE MILLS.

**Trinidad Guardian:** POB 122, Port of Spain; tel. 623-8870; f. 1917; morning; independent; Editor CARL JACOBS; circ. 52,617.

**Trinidad and Tobago Express:** 35 Independence Sq., Port of Spain; tel. 623-1711; telex 22661; f. 1967; morning; Gen. Man. KEN GORDON; Editor KEITH SMITH; circ. 62,275.

### PERIODICALS

**Blast:** 5–6 Hingoo Lane, El Socorro, San Juan; tel. 674-4414; weekly; Editor ZAID MOHAMMED; circ. 22,000.

**The Bomb:** Southern Main Rd, Curepe; tel. 645-2744; weekly; Editor KIT ROXBURGH.

**Caribbean Affairs:** 93 Frederick St, Port of Spain; tel. 624-2477; fax 627-3013; f. 1988; every two months; business, political, social; Publr OWEN BAPTISTE.

# TRINIDAD AND TOBAGO

**Caribbean Herald:** Port of Spain; weekly.
**Caribbean Medical Journal:** 115 Abercromby St, Port of Spain; tel. 623-7246; quarterly; circ. 700.
**Catholic News:** 31 Independence Sq., Port of Spain; tel. 623-6093; fax 623-6093; f. 1892; weekly; Editor Fr MICHEL DE VERTEUIL; circ. 15,600.
**Chiao Sheng:** 10 Charlotte St, Port of Spain; weekly; Chinese.
**Naturalist:** 20 Collens Rd, Maraval, Port of Spain; tel. 622-3428; f. 1975; 9 a year; natural heritage and conservation in the Caribbean; Publr/Editor-in-Chief STEPHEN MOHAMMED; circ. 25,000.
**Quarterly Economic Report:** 35–41 Queen St, POB 98, Port of Spain; tel. 623-6495; f. 1950; quarterly; issued by the Central Statistical Office.
**Showtime:** Cnr 9th St and 9th Ave, Barataria; tel. 674-1692; weekly; Editor ANGELA MARTIN-HINDS; circ. 30,000.
**Sunday Express:** 35 Independence Sq., Port of Spain; tel. 623-1711; fax 627-1451; f. 1967; Editor LENNOX GRANT; circ. 60,000.
**Sunday Guardian:** POB 122, Port of Spain; tel. 623-8870; f. 1917; independent; morning; Editor MAXIE CUFFIE; circ. 68,000.
**Sunday Punch:** Cnr 9th St and 9th Ave, Barataria; tel. 674-1692; weekly; Editor ANTHONY ALEXIS; circ. 40,000.
**Tobago News:** Milford Rd, Scarborough; tel. 639-5565; f. 1985; weekly; Editor COMPTON DELPH.
**Trinidad and Tobago Gazette:** 2–4 Victoria Ave, Port of Spain; tel. 625-4139; weekly; official government paper; circ. 3,300.
**Trinidad and Tobago Mirror:** Cnr 9th St and 9th Ave, Barataria; tel. 674-1692; two a week; Editors KEN ALI, KEITH SHEPHERD; circ. 35,000.
**Tropical Agriculture:** Faculty of Agriculture, University of the West Indies, St Augustine; tel. 645-3640; telex 24520; fax 662-1182; f. 1924; journal of the Faculty of Agriculture (fmrly Imperial College of Tropical Agriculture); quarterly; Editor-in-Chief F. A. GUMBS.
**Weekend Heat:** Southern Main Rd, Curepe; tel. 645-2744; weekly; Editor STAN MORA.
**Woman's Weekly:** 93 Frederick St, Port of Spain; tel. 624-2477; fax 627-3013; f. 1994; weekly; circ. 20,000.

### NEWS AGENCIES

**Agencia EFE** (Spain): El Socorro Rd, Port of Spain; Correspondent ED WYNN BRANT.
**Associated Press (AP)** (USA): Television House, 11A Maraval Rd, Port of Spain; tel. 622-4141; Correspondent TONY FRASER.
**Caribbean News Agency (CANA)** (Barbados): Independence Sq., Port of Spain; tel. 623-5422; Correspondent DEBRA RANSOME.
**Inter Press Service (IPS)** (Italy): 3 Waterloo Rd, Carapichaima, Port of Spain; tel. 673-0227; Correspondent LINDSAY MACKOON.

## Publishers

**Caribbean Book Distributors Ltd:** 6 Eastern Main Rd, San Juan; tel. 674-4720; fax 674-0497.
**Caribbean Children's Press:** 1158 Debe Rd, Long Circular Rd, St James.
**Caribbean Educational Publishers:** 49 High St, San Fernando; tel. and fax 657-1012.
**Caribbean Publishing Co:** 44 Park St, POB 548, Port of Spain; tel. 623-4515.
**Charran Educational Publishers:** 64 Independence Sq., Port of Spain; tel. 625-3694.
**Columbus Publishers Ltd:** 64 Independence Sq., POB 140, Port of Spain; tel. 625-3695; industry, education, political science, sociology, anthropology, biography and textbooks; Chair. and Man. Dir P. A. HOADLEY.
**Key Publications:** Chancery Court, 13–15 St Vincent St, Port of Spain; tel. 623-1940; magazines and books; CEO ROY BOYKE.
**Longman Trinidad Ltd:** Cnr Macoya Rd and Churchill Roosevelt Highway, Trincity; tel. 662-9181; fax 662-9182; f. 1970; general; Dirs ROB FRANCIS, BRIAN DE LA ROSE; Man. Dir KEN JAIKARANSINGH.
**Paria Publishing Co Ltd:** 66 Woodford St, Newtown; tel. 622-4748; Dir GERRY BESSON.
**S. M. Publications:** 20 Collens Rd, Maraval; tel. 622-3428.
**Trinidad Publishing Co Ltd:** 22–24 St Vincent St, Port of Spain; tel. 623-8870; fax 625-7211; f. 1917; Man. Dir ALWIN S. CHOW.
**Trinidad and Tobago Educational Publishers Ltd:** 20 Henry St, Port of Spain; tel. 623-4523; telex 3000.
**University of the West Indies:** St Augustine; tel. 663-1334; telex 24520; fax 663-9684; f. 1960; academic books and periodicals; Principal Prof. G. M. RICHARDS.

**Vanguard Publishing Co Ltd:** 4A Lower Hillside, San Fernando; tel. 657-8548.

## Radio and Television

In 1992, according to UNESCO, there were an estimated 625,000 radio receivers and 400,000 television receivers in use.

### RADIO

**National Broadcasting Service (NBS Radio 610/Radio 100 FM Stereo):** Television House, 11A Maraval Rd, POB 665, Port of Spain; tel. 622-4141; telex 22222; fax 622-0344; f. 1957; AM and FM transmitters at Chaguanas, Cumberland Hill; government-owned; CEO LOUIS LEE SING; Programme Man. BRENDA DA SILVA; est. regular audience 650,000.
**Prime Radio Ltd:** 35-37 Independence Sq., Port of Spain; tel. 627-7463; fax 627-2721; commercial; Gen. Man. JULIAN RODGERS.
**Trinidad Broadcasting Co Ltd (Radio Trinidad** and **Radio Nine Five):** Broadcasting House, 11B Maraval Rd, POB 716, Port of Spain; tel. 622-1151; fax 622-2380; f. 1947; commercial; three programmes; Man. Dir GRENFELL KISSOON.

### TELEVISION

**CCN TV6:** 35 Independence Sq., Port of Spain; tel. 627-8806; fax 627-2721; f. 1991; owned by Caribbean Communications Network (CCN); CEO KEN GORDON; Gen. Man. BERNARD PANTIN.
**Trinidad & Tobago Television Co Ltd:** Television House, 11A Maraval Rd, POB 665, Port of Spain; tel. 622-4141; telex 22664; fax 622-0344; f. 1962; state-owned commercial station; Programme Man. AVION TAYLOR ROACH.

## Finance

(cap. = capital; dep. = deposits; res = reserves; m. = million; brs = branches; amounts in TT $)

### BANKING
#### Central Bank
**Central Bank of Trinidad and Tobago:** Central Bank Tower, Eric Williams Plaza, Independence Sq., POB 1250, Port of Spain; tel. 625-4835; telex 22532; fax 627-4696; f. 1964; cap. 30m., dep. 2,213m. (Dec. 1993); Gov. THOMAS AINSWORTH HAREWOOD.

#### Commercial Banks
**Bank of Commerce Trinidad and Tobago Ltd:** 72 Independence Sq., POB 69, Port of Spain; tel. 627-9325; telex 22227; fax 627-0904; f. 1979 to take over local branches of Canadian Imperial Bank of Commerce; cap. 40.8m., res 74.0m., dep. 1,414.2m. (Aug. 1994); Chair. RUPERT INDAR; Man. Dir RONALD HUGGINS; 17 brs.
**Bank of Nova Scotia, Trinidad and Tobago Ltd:** Scotia Centre, Cnr of Park and Richmond Sts, POB 621, Port of Spain; tel. 625-3566; telex 22241; fax 627-5278; cap. 39.9m., res 125.6m., dep. 1,619.8m. (Oct. 1993); Chair. C. E. RITCHIE; Man. Dir R. A. CHAN; 20 brs.
**Citibank (Trinidad and Tobago) Ltd:** 12 Queen's Park East, POB 1249, Port of Spain; tel. 625-1046; telex 22261; fax 624-8131; f. 1983; fmrly The United Bank of Trinidad and Tobago Ltd; name changed as above 1989; cap. 17.2m., res 11.3m., dep. 568.8m. (Dec. 1994); Chair. IAN E. DASENT; Man. Dir SURESH MAHARAJ; 2 brs.
**First Citizens Bank Ltd:** 50 St Vincent St, POB 718, Port of Spain; tel. 623-2576; telex 22584; fax 627-1969; f. 1993 as merger of National Commercial Bank of Trinidad and Tobago Ltd, Trinidad Co-operative Bank Ltd and Workers' Bank of Trinidad and Tobago; cap. 146.3m., res 83.9m., dep. 2,501.4m. (Sept. 1993); Chair. LEONARD WILLIAMS; Gen. Man. LARRY HOWAI; 24 brs.
**Republic Bank Ltd:** 11–17 Park St, POB 1153, Port of Spain; tel. 625-3611; telex 22223; fax 623-0371; f. 1837 as Colonial Bank; 1972 Barclays Bank; 1981 name changed as above; cap. 77.9m., res 302.8m., dep. 3,821.6m. (Sept. 1994); Chair. FRANK A. BARSOTTI; Man. Dir DUNBAR I. McINTYRE; 28 brs.
**Royal Bank of Trinidad and Tobago Ltd:** 3B Chancery Lane, POB 287, Port of Spain; tel. 623-4291; telex 22678; fax 625-3764; f. 1972 to take over local branches of Royal Bank of Canada; cap. 66.9m., res 199.5m., dep. 3,010.2m. (Sept. 1993); Chair. HERMAN P. URICH; Man. Dir PETER J. JULY; 20 brs.

#### Development Banks
**Agricultural Development Bank of Trinidad and Tobago:** 87 Henry St, POB 154, Port of Spain; tel. 623-6261; fax 624-3087; f. 1968; provides long-, medium- and short-term loans to farmers; Chair. DAVID W. H. KNOTT; Gen. Man. TERENCE O'NEIL LEWIS.

**Co-operative Development Bank of Trinidad and Tobago:** 153 Tragarete Rd, Port of Spain; tel. 622-3854; fax 622-6931; f. 1957; Pres. Dr DIANAND CHANDOOL; Gen. Man. MANCHAN SONACHANSINGH.

**Development Finance Ltd (DFC):** 8–10 Cipriani Blvd, POB 187, Port of Spain; tel. 623-4665; fax 624-3563; provides short- and long-term finance, and equity financing for projects in manufacturing, agro-industries, tourism and service enterprises; Gen. Man. GERARD PEMBERTON.

### INSURANCE

**American Life Insurance Co Ltd:** Pembroke St, Port of Spain; tel. 623-8891.

**Anchorage General Insurance Ltd:** 11–13 Milling Ave, Sea Lots, POB 283, Port of Spain; tel. 623-0868; telex 22280; fax 625-1243; f. 1979; general; Man. Dir ROBERT I. FERREIRA.

**Bankers Insurance Co of Trinidad and Tobago Ltd:** 177 Tragarete Rd, Port of Spain; tel. 622-4613; fax 628-6808.

**British-American Insurance:** 45 Tragarete Rd, Maraval; tel. 622-2913.

**Capital Insurance Ltd:** 38–42 Cipero St, San Fernando; tel. 657-8077; fax 652-7306; f. 1958; motor and fire insurance; total assets TT $60m.; 10 brs and 9 agencies.

**Caribbean Atlantic Life Insurance Co Trinidad and Tobago Ltd:** 95–97 Frederick St, POB 948, Port of Spain; tel. 623-4146; Gen. Man. ERIC NORMAN.

**Caribbean Commercial Insurance Co Ltd:** 19 Keate St, Port of Spain; tel. 625-4337; fax 624-6580.

**Caribbean Home Insurance Co Ltd:** 63 Park St, Port of Spain; tel. 625-4461; telex 22382; fax 625-5985; f. 1973; initial cap. 1m.; general and group life; Chair. W. SIDNEY KNOX; Man. Dir ROGER A. MACKENZIE.

**Colonial Life Insurance Co (Trinidad) Ltd:** Colonial Life Bldg, 29 St Vincent St, POB 443, Port of Spain; tel. 623-1421; fax 627-3821; f. 1936; Chair. L. A. DUPREY; Man. Dir A. C. MUSAIB-ALI.

**Goodwill General Insurance Co Ltd:** 88–90 Abercromby St, Port of Spain; tel. 623-4756; wholly owned subsidiary of Demerara Life Assurance Company of Trinidad and Tobago Ltd; Chair. BERTRAND H. DOYLE.

**Great Northern Insurance Co Ltd:** 29A Edward St, Port of Spain; tel. 625-1116.

**Gulf Insurance:** Woodford St, Port of Spain; tel. 622-5878.

**Guyana and Trinidad Mutual Fire Insurance:** 95–97 Queen St, Port of Spain; tel. 623-1525.

**Maritime General Insurance Co Ltd:** 3A Chancery Lane, Port of Spain; tel. 623-4207; fax 624-5261; f. 1978; property and casualty; CEO RICHARD ESPINET.

**Motor and General Insurance Co Ltd:** 17 Rust St, St Clair, Port of Spain; tel. 622-2637.

**Nationwide Insurance Co Ltd:** 24 Sackville St, Port of Spain; tel. 623-7123; Pres. BERT DUMAS.

**NEM (West Indies) Insurance Ltd:** 12 Abercromby St, Port of Spain; tel. 623-4741; fax 623-4320.

**New India Assurance Co (T & T) Ltd:** 22 St Vincent St, Port of Spain; tel. 623-1326; telex 22588; fax 625-0670.

**Presidential Insurance Co Ltd:** 54 Richmond St, Port of Spain; tel. 625-4788.

**Royal Caribbean Insurance Ltd:** 109 St Vincent St, Port of Spain; tel. 625-9980; fax 623-7895; f. 1977.

**Trinidad and Tobago Export Credit Insurance Co Ltd:** Mecalfab House, 92 Queen St, Port of Spain; tel. and fax 624-0028; Gen. Man. LENNOX OSBOURNE.

**Trinidad and Tobago Insurance Ltd (TATIL):** 11 Maraval Rd, POB 1004, Port of Spain; tel. 622-5351; fax 628-0035; Chair. M. K. MANSOOR; Man. Dir A. W. O'BRIEN.

**United Security Life Insurance Co Ltd:** 109 Abercromby St, Port of Spain; tel. 623-6155; telex 22589; Man. Dir R. A. SHEPPARD.

**West Indian National Insurance Co Ltd:** Winsure Bldg, 24–28 Richmond St, Port of Spain; tel. 623-1860; telex 3543; f. 1959; Man. Dir JOHN L. ACHAM.

**Western General Insurance Co Ltd:** 7 Victoria St, Port of Spain; tel. 623-5936; Man. Dir SANDRA VANAIK.

### INSURANCE ORGANIZATION

**National Insurance Board:** 2A Cipriani Blvd, POB 1195, Port of Spain; tel. 625-2171; fax 624-0276; f. 1971; statutory corporation; Chair. STEVE BIDESHI; Exec. Dir KELVIN URQUHART.

### STOCK EXCHANGE

**Trinidad and Tobago Stock Exchange:** 65 Independence Sq., Port of Spain; tel. 625-5108; telex 22532; fax 623-0089; f. 1981; 30 companies listed (Nov. 1991); Chair. ANDREW MCEACHRANE; Gen. Man. HUGH EDWARDS.

## Trade and Industry

### CHAMBER OF COMMERCE

**Trinidad and Tobago Chamber of Industry and Commerce (Inc):** Room 950–952, Hilton Hotel, POB 499, Port of Spain; tel. 624-6082; fax 627-4376; f. 1891; Pres. FRANK MOUTTET; Gen. Man. CARMENA BAIRD; 299 mems.

### EMPLOYERS' AND MANUFACTURERS' ASSOCIATIONS

**Agricultural Society of Trinidad and Tobago:** 2A Alexander St, Port of Spain; tel. 628-2486.

**Cocoa Planters' Association of Trinidad Ltd:** 23–25 Philipp St, POB 346, Port of Spain; tel. 625-1683; f. 1915; 75 mems; Pres. ROBERT C. MONTANO; Man. Dir IAN F. MCDONALD.

**CGA Ltd:** Eastern Main Rd, Laventille, POB 229, Port of Spain; tel. 623-5207; fax 623-2359; f. 1936; coconut growers' assoc.; 354 mems; CEO ROGER POON; Gen. Man. PETER TRABOULAY.

**Co-operative Citrus Growers' Association of Trinidad and Tobago Ltd:** Eastern Main Rd, POB 174, Laventille, Port of Spain; tel. 623-2255; fax 623-2487; f. 1932; 437 mems; Pres. J. MAHARAJ; Sec. N. WEEKES.

**Employers' Consultative Association:** 43 Dundonald St, POB 911, Port of Spain; tel. 625-4723; fax 625-4891; f. 1960; CEO EMRU MILLER; 12 mem. orgs.

**Managers' and Supervisors' Association of Trinidad and Tobago:** 30 Pembroke St, Port of Spain; tel. 627-5394; Pres. DONICIO ROBINSON; Gen. Sec. CARLISLE HOLDER.

**Pan Trinbago:** 75 Edward St, Port of Spain; tel. 623-4486; fax 625-6715; f. 1971; official body for Trinidad and Tobago steelbands; Pres. OWEN SERRETTE; Sec. RICHARD FORTEAU.

**Shipping Association of Trinidad and Tobago:** Mecalfab House, 4th Level, Suite 402, 92 Queen St, Port of Spain; tel. 623-8570; f. 1938; Pres. NOEL JENVEY ; Exec. Sec. S. JULUMSINGH.

**Sugar Association of the Caribbean:** 80 Abercromby St, Port of Spain; tel. 636-2847; fax 636-1259; f. 1942; promotes and protects sugar industry in the Caribbean; 6 mem. associations; Chair. Dr K. HARAKSINGH; Sec. J. DE LA BASTIDE.

**Sugar Manufacturers' Association Ltd of Trinidad and Tobago:** 80 Abercromby St, Port of Spain; tel. 623-6106; fax 623-6106; f. 1920; 2 mems; Chair. Dr KUSHA HARAKSINGH; Sec. S. PUJADAS.

**Trinidad and Tobago Businessmen's Association:** POB 322, Port of Spain; tel. 675-0848; fax 675-0848.

**Trinidad and Tobago Manufacturers' Association:** 8 Stanmore Ave, St Clair, POB 971, Port of Spain; tel. 623-1029; fax 623-1031; f. 1956; 250 mems; Pres. RICHARD LEWIS.

### STATE-OWNED CORPORATIONS

**Caribbean Food Corporation (CFC):** 30 Queen's Park West, POB 264, Port of Spain; tel. 622-5211; telex 3000; fax 622-4430; f. 1976; promotion of agricultural development; Man. Dir CLYDE PARRIS.

**Caribbean ISPAT Ltd (ISCOTT):** POB 476, Couva, Point Lisas; tel. 636-2211; telex 31254; fax 636-5696; fmrly Iron and Steel Co of Trinidad and Tobago Ltd; production of iron and steel wire and rods; Chair. M. L. MITTAL.

**CARIFLEX:** O'Meara Industrial Estate, O'Meara Rd, Arima; tel. 642-3482; fax 642-1266; f. 1971; manufacturer of stationery, folding cartons, labels; Dir HARRY SOOKNARINE.

**Caroni (1975) Ltd:** Brechin Castle, Couva; tel. 636-2311; telex 31361; fax 636-1259; sugar cane plantations and mills; producers of rum and other sugar by-products; Chair. Dr KUSHA HARAKSINGH; Gen. Man. J. R. WOTHERSPOON.

**Cocoa and Coffee Industry Board:** Salvatori Bldg, Rm 301, Frederick St, Port of Spain; tel. 625-0289; fax 627-4172; f. 1962; marketing of coffee and cocoa beans, regulation of cocoa and coffee industry; Man. KENT VILLAFANA.

**Federation Chemicals:** Port of Spain; fertilizer co, owned by Norsk Hydro.

**Food and Agriculture Corporation of Trinidad and Tobago Ltd:** Arena Rd, Port of Spain; tel. 673-1988; Chair. MOBARACK ALI AZIZ.

**National Feed Mill Ltd:** Lot 3A, Sea Lots, Port of Spain; tel. 623-1904; fax 623-0956; f. 1984; manufacture and sale of a wide range of livestock feeds; Chair. HUGH EASTMAN; Man. Dir CLYDE PARRIS.

**National Flour Mills Ltd:** Wrightson Rd, Port of Spain; tel. 625-2416; fax 625-4389; Chair. HUGH EASTMAN.

# TRINIDAD AND TOBAGO

**National Gas Company of Trinidad and Tobago Ltd:** Goodrich Bay Rd, Point Lisas, POB 1127, Port of Spain; tel. 636-4662; fax 679-2384; f. 1975; purchases, sells, compresses, transmits and distributes natural gas to local commercial and industrial companies; Chair. Prof. K. F. JULIEN; Man. Dir M. A. JONES.

**Petroleum Company of Trinidad and Tobago Ltd (PETROTRIN):** Petrotrin Administration Bldg, Pointe-à-Pierre; tel. 658-4220; telex 32367; fax 658-1315; f. 1993 following merger between Trinidad and Tobago Oil Company Ltd (TRINTOC) and Trinidad and Tobago Petroleum Company Ltd (TRINTOPEC); petroleum and gas exploration and production; operates refineries and a manufacturing complex, producing a variety of petroleum and petrochemical products; Chair. TREVOR BHOPSINGH.

**Polymer (Caribbean) Ltd:** 227 Western Main Rd, Cocorite, POB 1208, Port of Spain; tel. 628-7225; fax 628-0927; f. 1969; manufacture of packaging products, both rigid and flexible; Man. Dir STEPHEN SANTOS.

**Trinidad Cement Ltd:** Southern Main Rd, Claxton Bay; tel. 659-2381; fax 659-2540; f. 1954; manufacture and sale of Portland, sulphate-resisting and oil-well cement; Chair. SURASH MAHARAJ; Man. Dir YUSUFF OMAR.

**Trinidad and Tobago Electricity Commission (TTEC):** POB 121, 63 Frederick St, Port of Spain; tel. 623-2611; fax 623-7602; state electricity generating and distribution company; 51% govt-owned, 49% owned by Southern Electric Int./Amoco; Chair. ANDRÉ MONTEIL.

**Trinidad and Tobago Forest Products Ltd (TANTEAK):** Connector Rd, Carlsen Field, Chaguanas; tel. 665-0078; telex 3000; fax 665-6645; f. 1975; harvesting, processing and marketing of state plantation-grown teak and pine; privatization pending in 1995; Chair. RUSKIN PUNCH; Man. Dir CLARENCE BACCHUS.

**Trinidad and Tobago Marine Petroleum Company Ltd (TRINTOMAR):** Port of Spain; marine petroleum and natural-gas co; jointly owned by PETROTRIN and the National Gas Co of Trinidad and Tobago Ltd.

## DEVELOPMENT ORGANIZATIONS

**National Energy Corporation of Trinidad and Tobago Ltd:** Plipdeco House, Goodrich Bay Rd, Point Lisas; tel. 636-4662; telex 31344; fax 679-2384; f. 1979; Chair. MARTIN A. JONES; CEO M. A. JONES.

**National Housing Authority:** East End Foundry Bldg, 5–7 South Quay, POB 555, Port of Spain; tel. 627-8751; fax 625-3963; f. 1962; Chair. JACK BYNOE; Exec. Dir Dr KEITH BAILEY.

**Point Lisas Industrial Port Development Corporation Ltd (PLIPDECO):** Plipdeco House, Goodrich Bay Road, POB 191, Point Lisas, Couva; tel. 636-2706; fax 636-4008; f. 1966; deep-water port handling general cargo, liquid and dry bulk, to serve adjacent industrial estate which now includes iron and steel complex, fertilizer, methanol, urea and related downstream industries; Chair. PETER QUENTRAL THOMAS; CEO NEIL ROLINGSON.

**Tourism and Industry Development Company of Trinidad and Tobago (TIDCO):** Albion Court, 61 Dundonald St, Port of Spain; tel. 624-2953; fax 625-4755; f. 1994 to combine the functions of Industrial Development Corp. and Tourism Development Corp; Dir KIRK IFILL.

**Trinidad and Tobago Export Development Corporation:** Export House, 10–14 Philipps St, POB 582, Port of Spain; tel. 623-6022; telex 22646; fax 627-0050; encourages export-orientated projects from foreign investors; CEO OSCAR ALONSO.

## TRADE UNIONS

**The National Trade Union Centre (NATUC):** c/o NUGFW Complex, 145–147 Henry St, Port of Spain; tel. 623-4591; fax 625-7756; f. June 1991 as umbrella organization unifying entire trade-union movement, including former Trinidad and Tobago Labour Congress and Council of Progressive Trade Unions; Pres. ERROL K. MCLEOD (acting); Gen. Sec. SELWYN JOHN.

### Principal Affiliates

**Agricultural and General Workers' Union:** 178 Coffee St, San Fernando; f. 1981; Gen. Sec. HARRYLAL BEEPATH.

**All-Trinidad Sugar and General Workers' Trade Union (ATSGWTU):** Rienzi Complex, Exchange Village, Southern Main Rd, Couva; tel. 636-2354; fax 636-3372; f. 1937; Pres. BASDEO PANDAY; Gen. Sec. SAM MAHARAJ; 8,500 mems.

**Amalgamated Workers' Union:** 16 New St, Port of Spain; tel. 627-8993; f. 1953; Pres.-Gen. CYRIL LOPEZ; Sec. FLAVIUS NURSE; about 7,000 mems.

**Aviation, Communication and Allied Workers' Union:** 315 McConie St, Dinsley Village, Tacarigua; tel. 669-1762; f. 1982; Pres. PAUL HARRISON; Gen. Sec. MARTIN ELIGON.

**Bank and General Workers' Union:** 27 Borde St, Woodbrook, Port of Spain; tel. 627-3931; f. 1974; Pres. VINCENT CABRERA; Gen. Sec. CHRISTOPHER JACKSON-SMITH.

**Bank Employees' Union:** 7 Phillips St, Port of Spain; tel. 623-8641; fax 623-8639; Pres. CHRISTOPHER EUGENE; Gen. Sec. PATRICK RABATHALY.

**Communication, Transport and General Workers' Trade Union:** 14 Scott St, St Augustine; tel. 662-4977; f. 1954; Pres. MARTIN PACHECO; Gen. Sec. JENNIFER ROUSE.

**Communication Workers' Union:** 146 Henry St, Port of Spain; tel. 623-5588; f. 1953; Pres. ANTHONY FRITZ; Gen. Sec. LYLE TOWNSEND; about 2,100 mems.

**Movement for Social Transformation (MOTION):** f. 1990.

**National Farmers' and Workers' Union:** 25 Coffee St, San Fernando; tel. 652-4348; f. 1970; Pres. RAFFIQUE SHAH; Gen. Sec. DOOLIN NANKISSOOR.

**National Foodcrop Farmers' Association:** Boundary Rd, Aranjuez, San Juan; tel. 674-0853; f. 1974; Pres. RAGOONATH KEMRAGH; Gen. Sec. SELWYN SUKHU (acting).

**National Union of Domestic Employees:** 31 Eastern Main Rd, Laventille; Pres. CLOTHIL WALCOTT; Gen. Sec. SALISHA HOSEIN.

**National Union of Government and Federated Workers:** 145–147 Henry St, Port of Spain; tel. 623-4591; fax 625-7756; f. 1937; Pres. SELWYN JOHN; Gen. Sec. CECIL MCNEIL; about 20,000 mems.

**Oilfield Workers' Trade Union:** Paramount Bldg, 99A Circular Rd, San Fernando; tel. 652-2701; fax 652-7170; f. 1937; Pres. ERROL MCLEOD; Gen. Sec. DOODNATH MAHARAJ; 10,000 mems.

**Public Services Association:** 89–91 Abercromby St, POB 353, Port of Spain; tel. 623-7987; fax 627-2980; f. 1938; Pres. CLYDE WEATHERHEAD; Sec./Treas. JENNIFER BAPTISTE; about 15,000 mems.

**Seamen and Waterfront Workers' Trade Union:** 1D Wrightson Rd, Port of Spain; tel. 625-1182; f. 1937; Pres.-Gen. FRANCIS MUNGROO; Sec.-Gen. ROSS ALEXANDER; about 3,000 mems.

**Transport and Industrial Workers' Union of Trinidad and Tobago:** 114 Eastern Main St, Laventille, Port of Spain; tel. 623-4943; fax 623-2361; f. 1962; Pres. ALBERT ABERDEEN; Gen Sec. DESMOND O. BISHOP; about 5,000 mems.

**Trinidad Island-wide Rice Growers' Association:** 25 Coffee St, San Fernando; tel. 652-4348; f. 1974; Pres. CHAITRAM GAYA; Gen. Sec. PAUL T. BABOOLAL.

**Trinidad and Tobago Postmen's Union:** c/o General Post Office, Wrightson Rd, POB 692, Port of Spain; Pres. KENNETH SOOKOO; Gen. Sec. EVERALD SAMUEL.

**Trinidad and Tobago Unified Teachers' Association:** Cnr Fowler and Southern Main Rd, Curepe; tel. 645-2134; fax 662-1813; Pres. ANTHONY GARCIA; Gen. Sec. FRANK RAMNANAN.

**Union of Commercial and Industrial Workers:** 130–132 Henry St, Port of Spain; tel. 623-8381; f. 1951; Asst Sec. M. WILSON; about 1,500 mems.

# Transport

## RAILWAYS

The railway service was discontinued in 1968.

## ROADS

In 1985 there were 5,175 km (3,215 miles) of roads in Trinidad and Tobago, of which 1,950 km were main roads, and 50 km were motorway. In 1990 the total road network was some 8,000 km.

**Public Transport Service Corporation:** Railway Bldgs, South Quay, POB 391, Port of Spain; tel. 623-2341; telex 22801; fax 625-6502; f. 1965 to operate national bus services; Chair. MARTIN JOSEPH; Gen. Man. Dr TREVOR TOWNSEND; operates a fleet of 143 buses.

## SHIPPING

The chief ports are Port of Spain, Pointe-à-Pierre and Point Lisas in Trinidad and Scarborough in Tobago. Port of Spain and Scarborough each have a deep-water wharf. A special container berth, with two large overhead cranes, was built at Port of Spain, from where there are regular sailings to all parts of the world.

**Port Authority of Trinidad and Tobago:** Dock Rd, Port of Spain; tel. 625-4074; fax 627-2666; Chair. RONALD NURSE; Gen. Man. CLIVE R. W. SPENCER.

**Shipping Association of Trinidad and Tobago:** 1st level, Cruise Ship Complex, Wrightson Rd, Port of Spain; tel. 623-8570; fax 623-8570; Pres. NOEL JENVEY; Exec. Sec. S. JULUMSINGH.

**Shipping Corporation of Trinidad and Tobago (SCOTT):** 12th and 13th Floors, Central Bank Tower, Eric Williams Plaza, Independence Sq., POB 852, Port of Spain; tel. 623-6771; telex 22385; f. 1981; government-owned; freight services to/from United

Kingdom, USA and Canada; chartering and brokering; Chair. CARLYLE WILLIAMS.

**West Indies Shipping Corporation (WISCO):** 48–50 Sackville St, POB 448, Port of Spain; tel. 625-4334; telex 3422; owned by CARICOM govts; operates regional shipping service, including a service to Miami; Gen. Man. CHARLES PENNYCOOKE.

### CIVIL AVIATION

Piarco International Airport is situated 25.7 km (16 miles) southeast of Port of Spain and is used by numerous airlines. The first phase of a project to expand the airport began in 1994. There is a domestic service between Trinidad and Tobago. The runway at Tobago's Crown Point Airport has been extended to enable jet aircraft to use the airport.

**Air Caribbean:** 90 Independence Sq., POB 1021, Port of Spain; tel. 627-5109; fax 627-4519; f. 1993; operates scheduled passenger service between Trinidad and Tobago and charter service to destinations in southern Caribbean; Man. Dir Capt. ERIC MOWSER.

**BWIA—Trinidad and Tobago (BWIA International) Airways Corpn:** Administration Bldg, Golden Grove Rd, Piarco International Airport, POB 604, Port of Spain; tel. 669-3000; telex 25523; fax 664-3540; f. 1980 as merger of BWIA International (f. 1940) and Trinidad and Tobago Air Services (f. 1974); 51% owned by consortium headed by Acker Group (USA), 33.5% state-owned; operates scheduled passenger and cargo services linking destinations in the Caribbean region, North America and Europe; Chair. EDWARD ACKER; Pres. EDWARD WEGEL.

## Tourism

The climate and coastline attract visitors to Trinidad and Tobago. The latter island is generally believed to be the more beautiful and is less developed. The annual pre-Lenten carnival is a major attraction. In 1993 there were 248,815 foreign visitors, excluding cruise-ship passengers, when tourist receipts totalled TT $472.6m. In that year there were 2,159 hotel rooms.

**Tourism and Industry Development Company of Trinidad and Tobago (TIDCO):** (see Development Organizations).

**Trinidad and Tobago Hotel and Tourism Authority:** c/o Travel Center, Level 2, Uptown Mall, 44–58 Edward St, POB 243, Port of Spain; tel. and fax 624-3928; f. 1958; Pres. WINSTON BORRELL.

# TUNISIA

## Introductory Survey

**Location, Climate, Language, Religion, Flag, Capital**

The Republic of Tunisia lies in North Africa, bordered by Algeria to the west and by Libya to the south-east. To the north and east, Tunisia has a coastline on the Mediterranean Sea. The climate is temperate on the coast, with winter rain, but hot and dry inland. Temperatures in Tunis are generally between 6°C (43°F) and 33°C (91°F). The country's highest recorded temperature is 55°C (131°F). Average annual rainfall is up to 1,500 mm (60 ins) in the north, but less than 200 mm (8 ins) in the southern desert. The official language is Arabic, which is almost universally understood, and there is a small Berber-speaking minority. French is widely used as a second language. Islam is the state religion, and almost all of the inhabitants are Muslims. There are small minorities of Christians and Jews. The national flag (proportions 3 by 2) is red, with a white disc, containing a red crescent moon and a five-pointed red star, in the centre. The capital is Tunis.

**Recent History**

Until 1883, when Tunisia formally became a French protectorate, the country was a semi-independent monarchy, with the Bey of Tunis as Head of State. In the 1930s a campaign for independence from French rule began, led by the Néo-Destour (New Constitution) Party, founded in 1934 by Habib Bourguiba and a section of active former members of the Destour movement. France granted Tunisia internal self-government in September 1955 and full independence on 20 March 1956. Five days later elections were held for a Constitutional Assembly, which met in April and appointed Bourguiba as Prime Minister in a Government dominated by members of the Néo-Destour Party. In July 1957 the Assembly deposed the Bey, abolished the monarchy and established a republic, with Bourguiba as Head of State. A new Constitution was promulgated in June 1959. In the elections that followed in November Bourguiba was elected unopposed to the new office of President, and the Néo-Destour Party won all 90 seats in the new National Assembly.

Although a one-party system was not formally introduced in Tunisia, by 1964 the Néo-Destour Party had become the only legal political organization. In November of that year it was renamed the Parti Socialiste Destourien (PSD), and a moderate socialist economic programme was introduced, which began with the expropriation of foreign-owned lands in May 1964. However, attempts to introduce agricultural collectivization between 1964 and 1969, under the direction of Ahmad ben Salah, Minister of Finance and Planning, were abandoned in September 1969 because of resistance from the rural population. Ben Salah was dismissed, arrested and subsequently sentenced to 10 years' hard labour. He escaped in 1973 and fled to Europe, from where he organized the radical Mouvement de l'Unité Populaire (MUP). In 1970 Hedi Nouira, hitherto governor of the Tunisian Central Bank, was appointed Prime Minister. He began to reverse Ben Salah's socialist economic policies, with the introduction of liberal economic reforms in the sectors of industry and agriculture.

Liberalization of the economy was not accompanied by political reform, and the extensive powers of Nouira and Bourguiba were increasingly challenged by younger PSD members in the early 1970s. However, at the 1974 PSD Congress, Bourguiba reasserted his domination of Tunisian politics, when he was elected as President-for-Life of the PSD and Nouira was confirmed as Secretary-General. In March 1975, after approving the necessary amendments to the Constitution, the National Assembly elected Bourguiba President-for-Life of Tunisia. Political differences emerged concerning economic policy, and the previously loyal trade union movement, the Union Générale des Travailleurs Tunisiens (UGTT), led by Habib Achour (a former member of the PSD Political Bureau), began to assert its independence from the PSD. In January 1978, for the first time since independence, a 24-hour general strike took place, organized by the UGTT. In violent clashes between troops and strikers, at least 50 people were killed and many trade union leaders, including Achour, were arrested.

Achour was subsequently sentenced to 10 years' hard labour and a new Secretary-General of the UGTT, Tijani Abid, declared that the trade unions were now willing to co-operate with the Government.

In April 1980 Nouira resigned, owing to ill health, and was succeeded as Prime Minister and Secretary-General of the PSD by Muhammad Mzali (hitherto Minister of Education). Under Mzali, signs of greater political tolerance became apparent. The one-party system was ended in July 1981, when the Parti Communiste Tunisien (PCT), which had been proscribed in 1963, was granted legal status. The Government announced that any political group that gained more than 5% of the votes cast in the forthcoming legislative elections would also be officially recognized. Many of the UGTT leaders imprisoned after the 1978 disturbances were pardoned by Mzali, and Achour was again appointed Secretary-General of the UGTT. At the elections to the National Assembly of November 1981 the PSD and the UGTT formed an electoral alliance, the Front National, which received 94.6% of the total votes cast and won all 126 seats in the new Assembly. Opposition groups, such as the PCT, the MUP and the Mouvement des Démocrates Socialistes (MDS), complained of electoral malpractice. Since they all failed to register 5% of the vote, none of them was officially recognized. The MDS and the MUP were, however, eventually accorded official status in November 1983. The Government also encountered growing opposition from the illegal Mouvement de la Tendance Islamique (MTI), the strongest of the many Islamic fundamentalist groups established in Tunisia in the 1970s.

Widespread discontent with the political domination of the PSD and continuing economic problems resulted in outbreaks of rioting in January 1984, initially provoked by considerable increases in the prices of certain staple foodstuffs. The Government declared a state of emergency, and an estimated 100 people were killed in clashes between troops and demonstrators. Order was only restored when President Bourguiba personally rescinded the price increases. Later in 1984 a series of strikes in the public sector began, lasting until October 1985, when security forces occupied the headquarters of the UGTT and arrested many trade union leaders.

In early 1986 Bourguiba announced a series of ministerial changes, as a result of which ministers who were perceived to be supporters of Mzali were dismissed. In July Mzali was replaced as Prime Minister by Rachid Sfar (hitherto Minister of Finance), and was dismissed as Secretary-General of the PSD. Mzali subsequently fled to Algeria, and was sentenced *in absentia* to terms of imprisonment and hard labour for defamatory comments against Tunisian leaders and mismanagement of public funds. Elections to the National Assembly, in November 1986, were boycotted by all the opposition parties, with the result that the PSD, opposed only by 15 independent candidates, won all 125 seats. Official estimates of a high turn-out of voters (82.9%) were disputed by the opposition.

In 1986 and 1987 the Government acted vigorously to suppress Islamic fundamentalist groups in Tunisia. In July 1986 four Islamic fundamentalists were sentenced to death, and about 22 others were imprisoned, for a series of alleged offences. In early 1987 confrontation between Islamic fundamentalists and left-wing students at the University of Tunis resulted in many arrests. In March 1987 Tunisia severed diplomatic relations with Iran, accusing the Iranian Government of plotting to overthrow President Bourguiba and establish a pro-Iranian fundamentalist regime in Tunisia. More than 3,000 people were detained in connection with the alleged plot. There were further arrests of Islamic fundamentalists after a series of bomb explosions at tourist resorts in August. In September 90 Islamic fundamentalists were tried on charges of plotting against the Government. Despite criticism of the conduct of the trial by opposition and human rights groups, seven defendants were sentenced to death, while 69 received custodial sentences. However, only two death sentences were actually implemented.

During the second half of 1987 President Bourguiba's behaviour became increasingly erratic. In October he revoked several of his recent appointments of leading state officials, and dismissed Rachid Sfar from the premiership. Zine al-Abidine Ben Ali was appointed Prime Minister and Secretary-General of the PSD, while retaining the interior portfolio, which he had held since 1986. In November a disagreement between Bourguiba and Ben Ali was reported, apparently concerning the 90 Islamic fundamentalists tried in September. Bourguiba allegedly wanted them retried, with the aim of having the death sentence imposed on all 90 defendants.

On 7 November 1987 seven doctors declared that President Bourguiba was unfit to govern, owing to senility and ill health. In accordance with the Constitution, Ben Ali was sworn in as President. Hedi Baccouche (previously Minister of Social Affairs) was appointed Prime Minister, and a new Cabinet was announced, which excluded several close associates of Bourguiba. The new President announced plans to reform the Constitution and to permit greater political freedom. In the same month the Government permitted the publication of previously suspended opposition newspapers, and by early 1988 some 3,000 political and non-political detainees had been released. In February the PSD was renamed the Rassemblement Constitutionnel Démocratique (RCD), in order to reflect the new administration's commitment to democratic reform.

In April 1988 legislation was enacted by the National Assembly which instituted a multi-party system, and in July the Assembly approved a series of proposals to reform the Constitution. The office of President-for-Life was abolished, and the President was, henceforth, to be elected by universal suffrage every five years and limited to two consecutive terms of office. In the same month there was a significant reorganization of the Government, which included the dismissal of seven ministers who had served under Bourguiba. In September two additional opposition parties, the left-wing Rassemblement Socialiste Progressiste (RSP) and the liberal Parti Social pour le Progrès (PSP) were legalized. In November a further amnesty was announced, and the Government claimed that there were no longer any political prisoners in Tunisia, a total of 8,000 people having been released during the first year of Ben Ali's regime.

Ben Ali was nominated as the sole candidate (supported by all the officially-recognized parties) for the presidential election of 2 April 1989, and was duly elected President, receiving 99.3% of the votes cast. In legislative elections, the RCD won all 141 seats in the National Assembly, gaining some 80% of the votes cast. The fundamentalist MTI, now renamed Hizb an-Nahdah or the Parti de la Renaissance (whose candidates contested the election as independents, since the party was not officially recognized), won some 13% of the votes cast, but failed to win any seats under an electoral system that favoured the ruling party.

Also in April 1989 Ben Ali declared a general amnesty, restoring political and civil rights to 5,416 people who had been condemned by the previous regime. In September Ben Ali dismissed the Prime Minister, Hedi Baccouche, following a disagreement concerning the Government's economic policy, and appointed Hamed Karoui, the former Minister of Justice, in his place. In late 1989 an application for legal recognition by Hizb an-Nahdah was rejected by the authorities, resulting in violent anti-Government demonstrations in several universities by Islamic fundamentalists.

In May 1990, in response to complaints by opposition parties, the National Assembly approved a reformed electoral code, which introduced a system of partial proportional representation for forthcoming municipal elections. The winning party was to receive 50% of the seats, while the remainder were to be distributed among all the parties, according to the number of votes received by each one. However, the six legal opposition parties boycotted the elections, held on 10 June, on the grounds that they were neither free nor fair. Consequently, the RCD won control of all but one of the 245 municipal councils.

Following Iraq's invasion of Kuwait in August 1990, Ben Ali condemned Iraq, but subsequently expressed disapproval of the US-led multinational force deployed in the region of the Persian (Arabian) Gulf. His official criticism of Western intervention in the dispute was apparently influenced by the growing Arab nationalist support for Iraq within Tunisia. Evidence of this was the formation of a new political organization, the Comité National de Soutien à l'Irak, which comprised most opposition parties and professional associations. Disagreement over government policy regarding the Gulf crisis was the apparent cause of the replacement, in late August, of the Minister of Foreign Affairs, Ismaïl Khelil, by Habib Boulares (a prominent journalist and former Minister of Culture and Information). In September the Government announced that it would comply with the resolutions of the UN Security Council concerning Iraq, including the imposition of a trade embargo.

In November 1990 several members of an-Nahdah were arrested, following the discovery of explosives which were, it was alleged, to have been used by the group for terrorist activities, a claim denied by an-Nahdah. In late December senior officials of an-Nahdah were arrested, together with more than 100 other people, and accused of attempting to establish an Islamic state in Tunisia. The arrests provoked demonstrations by Islamic militants in January 1991, and in the same month thousands of Tunisians took part in pro-Iraqi demonstrations following the outbreak of war in the Gulf region between Iraq and the US-led multinational force. In February further demonstrations by Islamic activists were violently suppressed.

In March 1991 there was evidence of division within the ranks of the Islamists, when three senior officials of an-Nahdah who were still at liberty dissociated themselves from the acts of violence allegedly perpetrated by certain members of the organization. In particular they deplored a recent attack on the headquarters of the RCD, in which one person had been killed and several others injured. In May there were further demonstrations organized by Islamic fundamentalist groups, in which two students were killed during clashes with the security forces. Shortly afterwards, the Government announced that it had foiled a plot by members of an-Nahdah to seize power. More than 300 people, including about 100 members of the armed forces, were arrested. In June five an-Nahdah members were sentenced to death (two *in absentia*) for their part in the attack on the RCD headquarters.

In July 1991 the human rights organization, Amnesty International, stated that it had received more than 100 allegations of the torture of political detainees in Tunisia (most of whom were members or suspected members of an-Nahdah). In response, Ben Ali requested that a government human rights commission, formed in November 1990, should investigate the allegations. However, the Government persisted in its attempts to undermine Islamic fundamentalism, claiming in late September that it had thwarted a further conspiracy against the Government. Such disclosures were widely regarded with scepticism, and leaders of an-Nahdah vehemently denied involvement in any attempt to destabilize the country. In November clemency measures resulted in the release or reduction in the sentence of 1,070 detainees.

In late December 1991 Ben Ali announced that changes to the electoral system, to be formulated in consultation with opposition parties, would be implemented during 1992, with the aim of ensuring greater representation at the national level for parties other than the RCD. In December 1992 Ben Ali announced a revision of the electoral code, the most important feature of which was to be the introduction of partial proportional representation at legislative elections scheduled for March 1994. Further revisions of the press laws were also envisaged. However, this apparent willingness to co-operate with the legalized opposition was accompanied by further repression of the Islamic movement, with increased censorship of publications sympathetic to their cause, and the harassment of suspected fundamentalists. In February 1992 two an-Nahdah leaders, who were alleged to have been implicated in attempts to overthrow the Government, were sentenced to eight years' imprisonment for membership of an illegal organization.

In early March 1992 Amnesty International published a report which detailed the arrests of some 8,000 suspected an-Nahdah members over an 18-month period, and cited 200 cases of the torture and ill-treatment of detainees. It also claimed that at least seven fundamentalists had died while in custody. The Government initially denied the allegations, but later conceded that some violations of human rights had occurred and announced that such incidents would be investigated. In mid-March it was announced that human rights 'units' were to be established within the Ministries of Foreign Affairs, Justice and the Interior, although new restrictions were imposed on the activities of unofficial groups such as the Ligue Tunisienne des Droits de l'Homme (LTDH). In the same month (on the anniversary of independence) an amnesty was announced for more than 1,000 detainees. In mid-1992 the LTDH was officially dissolved by its leadership. This followed the enactment of legislation that effectively prohibited simultaneous membership of political parties and quasi-political associations such as the LTDH. The dissolution provoked criticism from the international community, but in March 1993 a ruling of a Tunis tribunal allowed the association to resume its activities. In July and August 1992 the trials were held in Tunis of 171 alleged members of an-Nahdah, and of 108 alleged members of the organization's military wing, who were all accused of conspiring to overthrow the Government. At the end of August 46 of the defendants were sentenced to life imprisonment, 16, including Rached Ghanouchi, the leader of an-Nahdah, *in absentia*. (In 1993 Ghanouchi was granted political asylum in the United Kingdom.) Lesser prison sentences of between one and 24 years were imposed on the remainder. At the beginning of October 1992 appeals on behalf of 265 of those convicted were rejected, and it was reported that a further 20 an-Nahdah sympathizers had been arrested and quantities of weapons and explosives seized in police raids. In June 1993 Amnesty International issued a report detailing widespread abuses of human rights in Tunisia, perpetrated in particular against female relatives of an-Nahdah members. The allegations were denied by government sources. A further Amnesty report, published in January 1994, claimed that thousands of suspected opponents of the Government had been arrested in the preceding three years, and that many had been tortured and imprisoned unjustly. The claims were expressly denied in a statement issued by the Tunisian Secretary of State responsible for Information, Fethi Houidi.

There were indications in 1993 of a revival of political activity, and in April the PCT, renamed the Mouvement de la Rénovation (MR), held a Congress. In June and August minor reorganizations of the Government were announced. At the RCD Congress, which took place at the end of July, Ben Ali was re-elected Chairman of the party; in early August a new, 13-member political bureau was announced, which included the Minister of Foreign Affairs, Habib Ben Yahia, and four other new members. In November Ben Ali announced that presidential and parliamentary elections were to take place on 20 March 1994. He had declared his candidacy for the presidency, which was supported not only by the RCD but also by most of the legal opposition parties, in the previous month. Moncef Marzouki, who had resigned his position as President of the LTDH, attempted to oppose Ben Ali in the presidential election but failed to gain the requisite support in the National Assembly. Shortly after the elections he was arrested and placed in detention on charges of defaming the judiciary. Marzouki was released from prison in mid-July; however, he was reported to have been prevented from leaving the country in December, and again in March 1995, when his passport was confiscated.

In January 1994 reforms to the electoral code were adopted by the National Assembly. Under the new system, designed to ensure opposition representation, 19 of the 163 seats in the enlarged National Assembly were to be allocated to opposition parties in proportion to their overall national vote. In March, prior to the elections, the Government imposed restrictions on the reporting and distribution of the international press. (In March 1995 the Government removed restrictions on the sale of two French newspapers, *Le Monde* and *Libération*.) In the presidential election, which took place concurrently with the legislative elections on 20 March 1994, Ben Ali was re-elected President, receiving 99.92% of the votes cast. In the legislative elections the RCD, which received 97.73% of the total votes cast, secured all 144 seats that were contested under a simple majority system. Of the 19 seats reserved for opposition candidates, the MDS gained 10, the MR four, the Union Démocratique Unioniste three and the Parti de l'Unité Populaire two. The rate of voter participation was officially estimated at 95.47%.

In April 1994 human rights groups criticized the detention of Hamma Hammani, the leader of the Parti des Ouvriers Communistes Tunisiens, who was sentenced to more than nine years' imprisonment for a variety of offences, including the formation of an illegal association. In August the London-based *al-Hayat* newspaper reported that a radical Islamic party, the Front Islamique du Salut (FIS—named after the Algerian Islamic organization), which advocates armed revolt in Tunisia, had been established under the leadership of Muhammad Ali el-Horani. In the same month President Ben Ali criticized the Governments of France, the United Kingdom and the USA for harbouring Islamic fundamentalists who threatened the stability of governments in North Africa and the Middle East.

In May and November 1994 President Ben Ali made minor alterations to the composition of the Government, and in January 1995 announced a major reorganization of the Council of Ministers. The new Government reflected the President's determination to secure economic growth, with the creation of Ministries of Economic Development, Industry and Trade, to replace the Ministry of National Economy. Abdallah Kallel, hitherto Minister of State and of the Interior, became Minister of State and Special Adviser to the President, in a transfer which signalled his retirement from active political life, due to ill health. At local elections held on 21 May the RCD won control of all municipal councils and received 99.86% of the votes cast. Independent candidates and members of five legal opposition parties, represented in 47 of the 257 constituencies, only won six of the 4,090 seats. The MDS complained of irregularities in the electoral procedure, including inadequate access for observers.

Relations with the other countries of the Maghreb improved considerably in the 1980s. A meeting between President Bourguiba and President Chadli of Algeria in March 1983 led to the drafting of the Maghreb Fraternity and Co-operation Treaty, which envisaged the eventual creation of a Greater Maghreb Union, and was signed by Mauritania in December 1983. Relations with Libya, however, deteriorated in August 1985, when it expelled some 30,000 Tunisian workers. In September Tunisia severed diplomatic relations with Libya, but they were restored in December 1987 following a resolution of the dispute concerning the expelled workers. In January 1988 Tunisia and Algeria held further discussions on the establishment of a greater Arab Maghreb, and in April border restrictions between Tunisia and Libya were removed, reflecting greatly improved relations between the two countries since the end of the Bourguiba regime. In February 1989, at a meeting of North African heads of state in Morocco, a treaty was concluded which proclaimed the Union of the Arab Maghreb (UMA, see p. 241), comprising Algeria, Libya, Mauritania, Morocco and Tunisia. The treaty envisaged the establishment of a council of heads of state; regular meetings of ministers responsible for foreign affairs; and, eventually, the free movement of goods, people, services and capital throughout the countries of the region.

The Ben Ali Government's preoccupation with a perceived fundamentalist threat severely strained its regional relations in the second half of 1991. The Tunisian Government accused Algeria of harbouring members of an-Nahdah, and of allowing them to conspire against the Tunisian Government from Algerian territory. The success of the fundamentalist Front Islamique du Salut (FIS) in the first round of legislative elections in Algeria in late December caused further concern in Tunisia. Meanwhile, in mid-October the Tunisian Government recalled its Ambassador to Sudan in protest against the support allegedly afforded to an-Nahdah members by the Sudanese authorities.

In 1982 President Bourguiba had permitted the Palestine Liberation Organization (PLO) to establish its headquarters near Tunis. In October 1985 Israeli aircraft attacked the PLO headquarters, and 72 people were reported to have been killed, including 12 Tunisians. US support for the right of Israel to retaliate (the attack was a reprisal for the murder of three Israeli citizens in Cyprus) severely strained relations between Tunisia and the USA. In April 1988 Abu Jihad, the military commander of the PLO, was assassinated at his home in Tunis. The Tunisian Government blamed Israel for the murder, and complained to the UN Security Council. Security provisions for PLO premises in Tunis were subsequently improved.

In January 1988 the Tunisian Government announced that diplomatic relations with Egypt, which had been severed in 1979, would be resumed. In March 1990 Ben Ali made the first visit to Cairo by a Tunisian President since 1965, and signed several agreements on bilateral co-operation between the two countries. In late September 1990 Tunisia and Iran restored diplomatic relations, which had been severed in 1987. Also in September a majority of members of the Arab League resolved to move the League's headquarters from Tunis (where it had been 'temporarily' established in 1979) to its original site in Cairo, Egypt. The Tunisian Government protested at the decision.

In January 1993 Tunisia assumed the annual presidency of the UMA. The Government made clear its determination to reactivate the process of Maghreb union, as well as dialogue with the European Community (EC, known as the European Union—EU—from 1 November 1993, see p. 143). However, according to a statement made by the Moroccan Minister of Foreign Affairs, Abd al-Latif Filali, in February 1993, following a meeting of the five UMA member states in Tunis, it had been decided to allow a 'pause' for reflection in the process of developing Maghreb union. Moreover, he noted that, of 15 agreements signed since the inauguration of the UMA in January 1989, none had yet been successfully implemented. In April 1994 at a meeting of the five UMA member states in Tunis, 11 agreements designed to improve co-operation and trade within the Maghreb were ratified; further meetings of UMA took place in 1994–95.

Throughout 1992 the Tunisian Government made efforts to negotiate a solution to the problem of the Lockerbie bombing suspects, whom Libya refused to release for trial (see chapter on Libya). In April 1993 President Ben Ali visited Libya and consulted with President Mubarak of Egypt in a further attempt to resolve the deadlock and bring an end to the economic sanctions imposed by the UN on Libya. Relations with Algeria improved appreciably after the second round of Algerian elections were suspended in January 1992, and Tunisia welcomed the appointment of Muhammad Boudiaf as Chairman of the High Council of State, as well as the suppression of the Islamic fundamentalist FIS. In February 1993 Boudiaf's successor, Ali Kafi, visited Tunis. During his stay he exchanged letters with President Ben Ali to ratify the official demarcation of the 1,000-km border between Tunisia and Algeria. This extended from the extreme south of Tunisia to the Mediterranean coast, and had been the subject of dispute between the two countries since Algerian independence. Ben Ali and Kafi also expressed their determination to work together to counter the threat of terrorism in the region. In mid-February 1995 six Tunisian border guards were reported to have been killed on the Tunisian–Algerian border in an attack which some believed to have been perpetrated by Algerian Islamic fundamentalists who objected to the Tunisian Government's alleged support for Algerian security forces. The Tunisian authorities denied the incident, and claimed that two guards had been killed and four wounded in a motoring accident.

The Tunisian Government welcomed the peace initiative in the Middle East and the signing of the PLO-Israeli Cairo agreement of May 1994 on implementing Palestinian self-rule in the Gaza Strip and in Jericho. In October the Tunisian Minister of Foreign Affairs, Habib Ben Yahia, and his Israeli counterpart, Shimon Peres, signalled the beginning of the normalization of relations between the two countries with the announcement of plans to establish interests offices in the Belgian embassies in Tel-Aviv and Tunis. The Tunisian Government subsequently announced its intention to install liaison offices in the Gaza Strip and Jericho; the office in the Gaza Strip opened in April 1995.

In June 1993 President Ben Ali, addressing the European Parliament in Strasbourg, advocated the establishment of a Euro-Maghreb Development Bank, which, by stimulating economic growth in North Africa, would alleviate illegal immigration into Europe. Negotiations between Tunisia and the EU, scheduled to be completed in mid-1995, aimed to finalize an association agreement that envisaged a closer political and commercial relationship between the two.

### Government

Under the 1959 Constitution, legislative power is held by the unicameral National Assembly, with 163 members who are elected by universal adult suffrage for a term of five years. (Of the 163 members, 144 are elected under a simple majority system, while 19 seats are reserved for the opposition under a system of proportional representation.) In 1988 a multi-party system was officially permitted by law. Executive power is held by the President, elected for five years by popular vote at the same time as the Assembly. The President, who is Head of State and Head of Government, appoints a Council of Ministers, headed by a Prime Minister, which is responsible to him. For local administration the country is divided into 18 governorates.

### Defence

In June 1994 total armed forces numbered 35,500 (including 26,400 conscripts), consisting of an army of 27,000, navy of 5,000 and an air force of 3,500. Paramilitary forces included a 10,000-strong national guard. Officer-training is undertaken in the USA and France as well as in Tunisia. The defence budget for 1994 was estimated at 563.2m. dinars.

### Economic Affairs

In 1993, according to estimates by the World Bank, Tunisia's gross national product (GNP), measured at average 1991–93 prices, was US $15,332m., equivalent to $1,780 per head. During 1985–93, it was estimated, GNP per head increased, in real terms, at an average annual rate of 2.2%. Over the same period, the population increased by an annual average of 2.1%. Tunisia's gross domestic product (GDP) increased, in real terms, by an annual average of 3.8% in 1980–92, by 2.1% in 1993 and by an estimated 4.4% in 1994.

Agriculture (including forestry and fishing) contributed 16% of GDP in 1993. In the same year an estimated 21.4% of the working population were employed in agriculture. The principal cereal crops are wheat and barley. Olives, citrus fruit and dates are grown for export, as well as for the domestic market, and in 1992 olive oil was the country's main agricultural export. However, Tunisia imports large quantities of dairy produce, cereals, meat and sugar. In 1980–92 agricultural GDP increased by an annual average of 3.8%.

Industry (including mining, manufacturing, construction and power) contributed 31% of GDP in 1992, and engaged 33.6% of the employed labour force in 1989. During 1980–92 industrial GDP increased by an annual average of 3.1%.

Mining and quarrying contributed 6.7% of GDP in 1991. In 1989 mining (with gas, electricity and water) employed 1.8% of the working population. In 1992 the principal mineral exports were petroleum (which accounted for 15% of total export earnings) and phosphates (fertilizers and phosphoric acids, 9.6%). At 1 January 1994 Tunisia's proven, published oil reserves were estimated at 1,700m. barrels, sufficient to maintain production (at 1993 levels) for a further 43.5 years. Iron, zinc and lead are also mined. In addition, Tunisia possesses large reserves of natural gas.

Manufacturing contributed 17% of GDP in 1992, and employed about 19.3% of the working population in 1989. Manufacturing is based on the processing of the country's principal agricultural and mineral products. Other important sectors include textiles, construction materials, machinery, chemicals, and paper and wood. Manufacturing GDP increased by an annual average of 6.3% in 1980–92.

Energy is derived principally from thermal installations, although Tunisia also possesses several hydroelectric plants. Imports of mineral fuels comprised 7.6% of the value of total imports in 1992. In early 1993 work began on the first phase of a 70m.-dinar project to link the Tunisian electricity grid to that of Libya.

Tourism represents an important source of revenue; receipts from tourism were estimated at 1,300m. dinars in 1994. The number of tourist arrivals totalled approximately 3.9m. in that year. In 1994 the number of tourist arrivals from Germany, France and the United Kingdom all increased, while those from Libya increased marginally, although the number had decreased by 53% since 1991.

In 1993 Tunisia recorded a visible trade deficit of US $2,068m., and a deficit of $912m. on the current account of the balance of payments. In 1992 the principal source of imports (25.5%) was France; other major suppliers were Italy, Germany, the USA and the Belgo-Luxembourg Economic Union. The principal market for exports (27.1%) was also France; other major purchasers were Italy and Germany. The member states of the European Community (EC, known as the European Union—EU—from 1 November 1993, see p. 143) accounted for around 77% of Tunisia's exports and 71% of its imports in 1992. In that year Tunisia's principal exports were crude petroleum, phosphates and fertilizers, clothing and accessories and olive oil. The principal imports were machinery, textiles, iron and steel and food and live animals.

In 1992 there was an estimated budgetary deficit of 349m. dinars (equivalent to 2.5% of GDP). At the end of 1993 Tunisia's total external debt was US $8,701m., of which $7,424m. was long-term public debt. In that year the cost of debt-servicing was equivalent to 20.2% of the value of exports of goods and services. The average annual rate of inflation was 6.7% in 1985–92, but declined to 4.0% in 1993, the lowest recorded level for 16 years, and increased only marginally in 1994, to 4.7%. An estimated 15.8% of the labour force were unemployed in 1992.

Tunisia is a member of the Arab Fund for Economic and Social Development (AFESD, see p. 237), the Arab Monetary Fund (see p. 237) and the Union of the Arab Maghreb (UMA, see p. 241). In April 1994 the UMA agreed to the establishment of a free-trade zone among the five member countries. Also in 1994 Tunisia entered negotiations with the EU, aimed at securing an association agreement that envisaged a 12-year transitional period during which the Tunisian economy would be more closely integrated with those of the member states of the EU. The agreement was due for completion in mid-1995.

In 1986, under a structural adjustment programme initiated under the auspices of the IMF, Tunisia introduced measures to liberalize trade, prices and investment and restructure the financial sector and public enterprises (including a privatization programme). These reforms succeeded in stimulating economic activity, controlling inflation and reducing the country's external debt, while strict austerity measures considerably reduced the budget deficit. In the early 1990s the economy expanded rapidly, although there was concern over the increasing trade deficit in 1993, which resulted from a rapid increase in imports, due to the reduction and rationalization of import duties (by 1993 86% of imports were free of duties), and a temporary deceleration in the growth of exports, due to an excess of olive oil (one of Tunisia's principal exports) on international markets. During 1993 the dinar became fully convertible on international currency markets, and in March 1994 a new foreign exchange was opened in Tunis. The 1994 budget provided for the completion of the removal of controls on prices (except for those subsidizing basic commodities) and on imports, and an increase in social expenditure to offset the adverse effects of economic reform. The association agreement negotiated with the EU in 1994–95 (see above) was expected to benefit Tunisia by giving the country greater access to EU funds and stimulating investment, albeit at the expense of exposing the agricultural and industrial sectors to increased competition from abroad. Real GDP growth of 6.3% was anticipated for 1995, as a result of augmented revenue from tourism and the export of manufactured and agricultural products, as well as the acceleration of the privatization programme. The Government's reliance on revenue from the agricultural sector remains precarious, however, as Tunisia is vulnerable both to drought and to fluctuations in olive oil quotas set by the EU.

### Social Welfare

A state system of social security provides benefits for sickness, maternity and old age. In 1985 Tunisia had 1,041 physicians, 499 dentists and 18,637 nurses, and there were 139 government hospitals (with 14,895 beds in 1984) and 1,196 clinics and health centres. Free health services are available to 70% of the population. Regional committees for social security care for the aged, needy and orphaned. Proposed administrative budget expenditure in 1992 included 290.9m. dinars for health. In 1991 the World Bank agreed to lend US $56m. for the reorganization of the 22 principal hospitals and the expansion of family-planning services.

### Education

Education is compulsory in Tunisia for a period of 11 years between the ages of six and 16. Primary education begins at six years of age and normally lasts for six years. Secondary education begins at the age of 12 and lasts for seven years, comprising a first cycle of three years and a second cycle of four years. In 1992 the total enrolment at primary and secondary schools, which are mostly state-run, was equivalent to 82% of the school-age population (87% of boys; 78% of girls). In 1993 an estimated 100% of children in the primary age-group (100% of boys; 97% of girls) were enrolled at primary schools, and in 1991 enrolment at secondary schools included 44% of children in the relevant age-group (47% of boys; 40% of girls). Arabic is the first language of instruction in primary and secondary schools, but French is also used. The University of Tunis was divided in 1988 to form separate institutions, one for the arts, the other for the sciences, and two new universities were opened in 1986, at Monastir and Sfax. Adult illiteracy averaged 62.0% (males 48.9%; females 75.2%) in 1975, but, according to UNESCO estimates, the rate declined to 34.7% (males 25.8%; females 43.7%) in 1990. Public expenditure on education was 770.7m. dinars (14.0% of total government spending) in 1994.

### Public Holidays

**1995:** 1 January (New Year's Day), 3 March* (Aid El Seghir, end of Ramadan), 20 March (Independence Day), 21 March (Youth Day), 9 April (Martyrs' Day), 1 May (Labour Day), 10 May* (Aid El Kebir, Feast of the Sacrifice), 25 July (Republic Day), 13 August (Women's Day), 15 October (Evacuation of Bizerta), 7 November (accession of President Ben Ali).

**1996:** 1 January (New Year's Day), 21 February* (Aid El Seghir, end of Ramadan), 20 March (Independence Day), 21 March (Youth Day), 9 April (Martyrs' Day), 29 April* (Aid El Kebir, Feast of the Sacrifice), 1 May (Labour Day), 25 July (Republic Day), 13 August (Women's Day), 15 October (Evacuation of Bizerta), 7 November (accession of President Ben Ali).

* Religious holidays, which are dependent on the Islamic lunar calendar, may differ by one or two days from the dates given.

### Weights and Measures

The metric system is in force.

# Statistical Survey

## Area and Population

### AREA, POPULATION AND DENSITY

| | |
|---|---:|
| Area (sq km) | |
|   Land | 154,530 |
|   Inland waters | 9,080 |
|   Total | 163,610* |
| Population (census results) | |
|   30 March 1984 | 6,966,173 |
|   20 April 1994 | |
|     Males | 4,447,341 |
|     Females | 4,338,023 |
|     Total | 8,785,364 |
| Population (official estimates at mid-year) | |
|   1991 | 8,253,000 |
|   1992 | 8,414,800 |
|   1993 | 8,572,200 |
| Density (per sq km) at April 1994 | 53.4 |

* 63,170 sq miles.

### PRINCIPAL COMMUNES (population at 1994 census)

| | | | |
|---|---:|---|---:|
| Tunis (capital) | 674,100 | Kairouan (Qairawan) | 102,600 |
| Sfax (Safaqis) | 230,900 | Gabès | 98,900 |
| Ariana | 152,700 | Bizerta (Bizerte) | 98,900 |
| Ettadhamen | 149,200 | Bardo | 72,700 |
| Sousse | 125,000 | Gafsa | 71,100 |

### BIRTHS, MARRIAGES AND DEATHS*

| | Registered live births | | Registered marriages | | Registered deaths | |
|---|---:|---:|---:|---:|---:|---:|
| | Number | Rate (per '000) | Number | Rate (per '000) | Number | Rate (per '000) |
| 1986 | 234,733 | 31.0 | 47,900 | 6.4 | 46,000 | 6.1 |
| 1987 | 224,169 | 29.3 | 49,452 | 6.5 | 45,500 | 5.9 |
| 1988 | 215,079 | 27.7 | 50,026 | 6.4 | 44,700 | 5.7 |
| 1989 | 199,459 | 25.2 | 55,163 | 7.0 | 44,600 | 5.6 |
| 1990 | 205,345 | 25.4 | 55,612 | 6.9 | 45,700 | 5.6 |
| 1991 | 207,455 | 25.2 | 59,010 | 7.2 | 46,300 | 5.6 |
| 1992 | 211,649 | 25.2 | 64,700 | 7.7 | 46,300 | 5.5 |
| 1993 | 206,800 | 24.1 | 54,200 | 6.3 | 49,400 | 5.8 |

* Birth registration is reported to be 100% complete. Death registration is estimated to be about 73% complete. UN estimates for average annual death rates are: 8.4 per 1,000 in 1980–85, 7.3 per 1,000 in 1985–90. UN estimates for average annual birth rates are: 33.7 per 1,000 in 1980–85, 31.1 per 1,000 in 1985–90.

Source: Institut National de la Statistique.

**Expectation of life** (UN estimates, years at birth, 1985–90): 65.6 (males 64.9; females 66.4) (Source: UN, *World Population Prospects: The 1992 Revision*).

### ECONOMICALLY ACTIVE POPULATION (sample survey, '000 persons aged 15 years and over, May–August 1989)

| | Males | Females | Total |
|---|---:|---:|---:|
| Agriculture, forestry and fishing | 422.2 | 87.5 | 509.7 |
| Manufacturing | 217.0 | 165.7 | 382.7 |
| Electricity, gas and water* | 33.5 | 1.7 | 35.2 |
| Construction | 244.8 | 2.8 | 247.6 |
| Trade, restaurants and hotels† | 301.9 | 26.7 | 328.6 |
| Community, social and personal services‡ | 347.2 | 97.1 | 444.3 |
| Activities not adequately defined | 26.2 | 4.5 | 30.7 |
| **Total employed** | 1,592.8 | 386.0 | 1,978.8 |
| Unemployed | 273.5 | 108.3 | 381.8 |
| **Total labour force** | 1,866.3 | 494.3 | 2,360.6 |

* Including mining and quarrying.
† Including financing, insurance, real estate and business services.
‡ Including transport, storage and communications.

Source: ILO, *Year Book of Labour Statistics*.

**Mid-1993** (estimates in '000): Agriculture, etc. 625; Total 2,917 (Source: FAO, *Production Yearbook*).

## Agriculture

### PRINCIPAL CROPS ('000 metric tons)

| | 1991 | 1992 | 1993 |
|---|---:|---:|---:|
| Wheat | 1,786 | 1,584 | 1,413 |
| Barley | 721 | 570 | 478 |
| Other cereals | 49 | 45 | 27 |
| Potatoes | 220 | 218 | 199 |
| Broad beans (dry) | 44 | 37 | 33 |
| Chick-peas | 23 | 30 | 27 |
| Olives | 1,325 | 630* | 800† |
| Tomatoes | 580 | 550 | 452 |
| Green peppers | 180 | 190 | 170 |
| Dry onions | 80 | 80 | 90 |
| Watermelons | 275 | 298 | 280 |
| Melons | 76 | 82 | 74 |
| Grapes | 95 | 97 | 108 |
| Dates | 75 | 76 | 90 |
| Sugar beet | 210 | 291 | 246 |
| Apples | 44 | 61 | 75 |
| Peaches and nectarines | 40 | 56 | 59 |
| Oranges | 117 | 98 | 156 |
| Tangerines, mandarins, clementines and satsumas | 41 | 28 | 41 |
| Lemons and limes | 14 | 18 | 17 |
| Grapefruit and pomelo | 53 | 41 | 57 |
| Apricots | 20 | 20 | 24 |
| Almonds | 40 | 45 | 47 |
| Tobacco (leaves) | 6 | 5 | 6 |

* Unofficial figure.  † FAO estimate.

Source: FAO, *Production Yearbook*.

### LIVESTOCK ('000 head, year ending September)

| | 1991 | 1992 | 1993 |
|---|---:|---:|---:|
| Horses* | 56 | 56 | 56 |
| Mules* | 79 | 80 | 81 |
| Asses* | 229 | 229 | 230 |
| Cattle | 631 | 636† | 659 |
| Camels* | 230 | 230 | 231 |
| Sheep | 6,290 | 6,400* | 7,110 |
| Goats | 1,313 | 1,350* | 1,417 |

Poultry (million): 41 in 1991; 38 in 1992; 39 in 1993.

* FAO estimate(s).  † Unofficial figure.

Source: FAO, *Production Yearbook*.

TUNISIA

**LIVESTOCK PRODUCTS** ('000 metric tons)

|  | 1991 | 1992 | 1993 |
|---|---|---|---|
| Beef and veal | 36 | 38 | 38 |
| Mutton and lamb | 35 | 35 | 35 |
| Poultry meat | 47 | 51 | 53 |
| Other meat | 15 | 14 | 15 |
| Cows' milk | 396 | 422 | 441 |
| Sheep's milk | 14 | 15 | 16 |
| Goats' milk | 12 | 12 | 13 |
| Poultry eggs | 55.3 | 53.3 | 53.7 |
| Wool: |  |  |  |
| greasy* | 12.3 | 12.4 | 12.7 |
| clean | 5.4 | 5.7 | 5.8* |
| Cattle hides* | 3.8 | 4.2 | 4.2 |
| Sheepskins* | 6.4 | 6.3 | 6.4 |

* FAO estimate(s).

Source: FAO, *Production Yearbook*.

## Forestry

**ROUNDWOOD REMOVALS** ('000 cu m, excluding bark)

|  | 1990 | 1991 | 1992 |
|---|---|---|---|
| Sawlogs, veneer logs and logs for sleepers | 15 | 17 | 6 |
| Pulpwood | 53 | 81 | 39 |
| Other industrial wood | 97 | 95 | 90 |
| Fuel wood* | 3,036 | 3,102 | 3,168 |
| **Total** | **3,201** | **3,295** | **3,303** |

* FAO estimates.

Source: FAO, *Yearbook of Forest Products*.

**SAWNWOOD PRODUCTION** ('000 cu m, including sleepers)

|  | 1990 | 1991 | 1992 |
|---|---|---|---|
| Coniferous (softwood) | 16 | 5 | 2 |
| Broadleaved (hardwood) | 1 | 12 | 4 |
| **Total** | **16** | **17** | **6** |

Source: FAO, *Yearbook of Forest Products*.

## Fishing

('000 metric tons, live weight)

|  | 1991 | 1992 | 1993 |
|---|---|---|---|
| Total catch | 87.6 | 89.0 | 85.0 |

Source: Commissariat Général à la Pêche.

## Mining

('000 metric tons, unless otherwise indicated)

|  | 1991 | 1992 | 1993 |
|---|---|---|---|
| Iron ore* | 295 | 291 | 299 |
| Lead concentrates* | 1.3 | 1.4 | 0.9 |
| Calcium phosphate | 6,352 | 6,335 | 5,476 |
| Zinc concentrates* | 9.4 | 4.1 | 2.4 |
| Crude petroleum | 5,191 | 5,195 | 4,650 |
| Natural gas (million cu m) | 387 | 402 | 366 |
| Salt (unrefined) | 441 | 460 | n.a. |

* Figures refer to the gross weight of ores and concentrates. The metal content (in '000 metric tons) was: Iron 153 in 1991; Lead 1.0 in 1991, 1.0 in 1992, 0.5 in 1993; Zinc 9.0 in 1991, 4.0 in 1992, 1.4 in 1993.

Source: Institut National de la Statistique.

## Industry

**SELECTED PRODUCTS** ('000 metric tons, unless otherwise indicated)

|  | 1991 | 1992 | 1993 |
|---|---|---|---|
| Superphosphates (16%) | 25.5 | 21.3 | 13.8 |
| Superphosphates (45%) | 713.6 | 786.6 | 641.8 |
| Phosphoric acid | 806.0 | 861.1 | 858.0 |
| Cement | 3,942 | 3,911 | 4,159 |
| Electric power—production by Société Tunisienne d'Electricité et de Gaz (million kWh) | 5,095.8 | 5,479.3 | 5,705.2 |
| Electric power—other producers (million kWh) | 604.7 | 658.8 | 607.6 |
| Beer ('000 hl) | 407 | 494 | 601 |
| Cigarettes (million) | 7,790 | 7,797 | 6,965 |
| Wine ('000 hl) | 425 | 333 | 344 |
| Olive oil | 165 | 280 | 135 |
| Semolina | 468.9 | 480.2 | 504.8 |
| Flour | 566.4 | 613.3 | 626.6 |
| Refined sugar | 60.8 | 68.7 | n.a. |
| Crude steel | 193 | 181.5 | 181.9 |
| Lime | 578 | 524 | 551 |
| Petrol | 269.9 | 289.3 | 289.3 |
| Kerosene | 149.9 | 153.1 | 146.8 |
| Diesel oil | 517.0 | 480.8 | 492.9 |
| Fuel oil | 506.4 | 419.5 | 449.3 |

Source: Institut National de la Statistique.

## Finance

**CURRENCY AND EXCHANGE RATES**

**Monetary Units**
1,000 millimes = 1 Tunisian dinar (TD).

**Sterling and Dollar Equivalents** (31 December 1994)
£1 sterling = 1.5507 dinars;
US $1 = 991.2 millimes;
100 Tunisian dinars = £64.49 = $100.89.

**Average Exchange Rate** (dinars per US $)
1992  0.8844
1993  1.0037
1994  1.0116

**BUDGET** (million dinars)*

| Revenue† | 1990 | 1991‡ | 1992§ |
|---|---|---|---|
| Taxation | 2,597.3 | 2,874.7 | 3,225.5 |
| Taxes on income, profits, etc. | 416.3 | 503.7 | 499.2 |
| Social security contributions | 439.2 | 426.3 | 488.9 |
| Taxes on property | 64.9 | 69.1 | 64.8 |
| Domestic taxes on goods and services | 646.3 | 786.7 | 935.5 |
| Sales taxes | 256.6 | 361.2 | 354.5 |
| Excises | 290.8 | 324.2 | 469.4 |
| Taxes on international trade | 931.7 | 986.9 | 1,123.9 |
| Import duties | 911.1 | 967.8 | 1,100.0 |
| Other current revenue | 723.7 | 604.9 | 721.7 |
| Property income | 630.9 | 482.6 | 603.2 |
| Capital revenue | 4.8 | 12.0 | 9.2 |
| **Total** | **3,325.8** | **3,491.6** | **3,956.4** |

# TUNISIA

## Statistical Survey

| Expenditure‖ | 1990 | 1991‡ | 1992§ |
|---|---|---|---|
| General public services | 694.6 | 736.7 | 852.0 |
| Defence | 217.7 | 224.2 | 236.7 |
| Public order and safety | 210.6 | 238.4 | 290.3 |
| Education | 637.4 | 702.3 | 770.7 |
| Health | 229.1 | 254.1 | 290.9 |
| Social security and welfare | 531.0 | 558.3 | 627.2 |
| Housing and community amenities | 71.0 | 176.4 | 191.7 |
| Recreational, cultural and religious affairs and services | 88.9 | 92.3 | 114.6 |
| Economic affairs and services | 1,039.1 | 980.9 | 989.1 |
|   Agriculture, forestry and fishing | 299.4 | 363.8 | 348.2 |
|   Mining (excl. fuel), manufacturing and construction | 120.3 | 97.7 | 46.3 |
|   Transport and communications | 103.0 | 92.1 | 103.6 |
| Other purposes | 358.8 | 416.0 | 451.0 |
| **Sub-total** | 4,078.2 | 4,379.7 | 4,814.2 |
| Adjustment to cash basis | −335.6 | −362.5 | −422.5 |
| **Total** | 3,742.6 | 4,017.2 | 4,391.7 |
| Current¶ | 2,923.4 | 3,176.0 | 3,478.7 |
| Capital | 819.2 | 841.2 | 913.0 |

\* Figures refer to the consolidated accounts of the central Government, including administrative agencies and social security funds. The data exclude the operations of economic and social agencies with their own budgets.
† Excluding grants from abroad (million dinars): 70.5 in 1990; 32.5 in 1991; 72.0 in 1992.
‡ Provisional figures.
§ Estimates.
‖ Excluding net lending (million dinars): 239.2 in 1990; 3.9 in 1991; −14.3 in 1992.
¶ Including interest payments (million dinars): 358.8 in 1990; 416.1 in 1991; 451.0 in 1992.

Source: IMF, *Government Finance Statistics Yearbook*.

### CENTRAL BANK RESERVES (US $ million at 31 December)

| | 1992 | 1993 | 1994 |
|---|---|---|---|
| Gold* | 4.6 | 4.2 | 4.4 |
| IMF special drawing rights | 12.1 | 1.8 | 2.7 |
| Reserve position in IMF | — | — | 0.1 |
| Foreign exchange | 839.9 | 852.0 | 1,458.8 |
| **Total** | 856.6 | 858.0 | 1,465.9 |

\* National valuation.

Source: IMF, *International Financial Statistics*.

### MONEY SUPPLY (million dinars at 31 December)

| | 1991 | 1992 | 1993 |
|---|---|---|---|
| Currency outside banks | 1,104 | 1,156 | 1,179 |
| Demand deposits at commercial banks | 1,437 | 1,555 | 1,676 |
| **Total money** (incl. others) | 2,697 | 2,894 | 2,998 |

Source: IMF, *International Financial Statistics*.

### COST OF LIVING (Consumer Price Index; base: 1980 = 100)

| | 1991 | 1992 | 1993 |
|---|---|---|---|
| Food | 244.6 | 255.0 | 261.9 |
| Fuel, light and water | 207.3 | 223.7 | 236.2 |
| Clothing | 249.5 | 268.3 | 286.1 |
| Rent | 163.2 | 176.7 | 190.5 |
| **All items** (incl. others) | 236.5 | 249.3 | 259.3 |

Source: ILO, *Year Book of Labour Statistics*.

**1994** (base: 1990 = 100): All items 124.7 (Source: IMF, *International Financial Statistics*).

### NATIONAL ACCOUNTS (million dinars at current prices)
**Expenditure on the Gross Domestic Product**

| | 1992 | 1993 | 1994 |
|---|---|---|---|
| Government final consumption expenditure | 2,168 | 2,380 | 2,641 |
| Private final consumption expenditure | 8,354 | 8,975 | 9,840 |
| Increase in stocks | 497 | 160 | 102 |
| Gross fixed capital formation | 3,634 | 4,168 | 4,658 |
| **Total domestic expenditure** | 14,653 | 15,683 | 17,241 |
| Exports of goods and services | 5,357 | 5,994 | 6,896 |
| *Less* Imports of goods and services | 6,256 | 6,989 | 8,003 |
| **GDP in purchasers' values** | 13,754 | 14,688 | 16,134 |
| **GDP at constant 1990 prices** | 12,110 | 12,365 | 12,906 |

Source: IMF, *International Financial Statistics*.

**Gross Domestic Product by Economic Activity**

| | 1989 | 1990 | 1991 |
|---|---|---|---|
| Agriculture | 1,261.3 | 1,757.4 | 2,135.2 |
| Mining and quarrying | 760.7 | 730.9 | 765.8 |
| Manufacturing | 1,655.4 | 1,829.4 | 2,049.4 |
| Electricity and water | 221.2 | 223.2 | 237.2 |
| Construction | 359.0 | 422.2 | 459.8 |
| Wholesale and retail trade | 1,927.2 | 2,215.2 | 2,411.7 |
| Transport, storage and communications | 694.1 | 762.0 | 832.2 |
| Hotels, cafés and restaurants | 526.9 | 557.4 | 428.6 |
| Government services | 1,260.1 | 1,360.6 | 1,532.0 |
| Other services | 48.2 | 52.7 | 59.4 |
| **Sub-total** | 8,714.1 | 9,911.0 | 10,911.3 |
| *Less* Imputed bank service charge | 263.0 | 326.3 | 357.9 |
| **GDP at factor cost** | 8,451.1 | 9,584.7 | 10,553.4 |
| Indirect taxes, *less* subsidies | 1,079.9 | 1,229.2 | 1,416.0 |
| **GDP in purchasers' values** | 9,531.0 | 10,813.9 | 11,969.4 |

Source: Institut National de la Statistique.

### BALANCE OF PAYMENTS (US $ million)

| | 1991 | 1992 | 1993 |
|---|---|---|---|
| Merchandise exports f.o.b. | 3,696 | 4,014 | 3,804 |
| Merchandise imports f.o.b. | −4,895 | −6,077 | −5,872 |
| **Trade balance** | −1,199 | −2,063 | −2,068 |
| Exports of services | 1,404 | 1,961 | 2,011 |
| Imports of services | −762 | −899 | −921 |
| Other income received | 69 | 122 | 127 |
| Other income paid | −686 | −744 | −767 |
| Private unrequited transfers (net) | 574 | 570 | 595 |
| Official unrequited transfers (net) | 131 | 88 | 112 |
| **Current balance** | −469 | −966 | −912 |
| Direct investment (net) | 122 | 364 | 239 |
| Portfolio investment (net) | 21 | 46 | 13 |
| Other capital (net) | 195 | 648 | 651 |
| Net errors and omissions | 77 | 5 | 16 |
| **Overall balance** | −55 | 97 | 7 |

Source: IMF, *International Financial Statistics*.

# TUNISIA

## External Trade

**PRINCIPAL COMMODITIES**
(distribution by SITC, US $ million)

| Imports c.i.f. | 1990 | 1991 | 1992 |
|---|---|---|---|
| **Food and live animals** | 473.5 | 304.8 | 404.7 |
| Cereals and cereal preparations | 220.4 | 107.9 | 145.4 |
| Wheat and meslin (unmilled) | 140.8 | 69.4 | 90.6 |
| **Crude materials (inedible) except fuels** | 420.8 | 358.5 | 380.9 |
| Crude fertilizers and crude minerals | 167.6 | 154.1 | 131.9 |
| Sulphur (excl. sublimed, precipitated or colloidal) | 137.1 | 126.2 | 101.4 |
| **Mineral fuels, lubricants, etc.** | 494.4 | 428.2 | 486.1 |
| Petroleum, petroleum products, etc. | 354.7 | 303.9 | 316.3 |
| Refined petroleum products | 290.0 | 280.5 | 271.1 |
| Motor spirit (gasoline) and other light oils | 288.3 | 278.5 | 268.7 |
| Gas (natural and manufactured) | 120.4 | 112.2 | 156.7 |
| Petroleum gases, etc., in the gaseous state | 90.8 | 31.8 | 125.3 |
| **Chemicals and related products** | 475.8 | 484.8 | 523.0 |
| Medicinal and pharmaceutical products | 124.5 | 136.4 | 149.5 |
| Medicaments (incl. veterinary) | 111.0 | 123.0 | 130.7 |
| Artificial resins, plastic materials, etc. | 114.9 | 116.9 | 123.4 |
| **Basic manufactures** | 1,494.6 | 1,456.0 | 1,961.3 |
| Textile yarn, fabrics, etc. | 789.2 | 824.8 | 998.5 |
| Textile yarn | 120.2 | 111.7 | 118.0 |
| Woven cotton fabrics* | 328.7 | 341.1 | 420.3 |
| Bleached and mercerized fabrics* | 309.3 | 316.2 | 390.5 |
| Woven fabrics of man-made fibres* | 186.9 | 208.1 | 265.9 |
| Iron and steel | 241.8 | 221.3 | 434.3 |
| Tubes, pipes and fittings | 39.3 | 58.3 | 236.0 |
| **Machinery and transport equipment** | 1,551.0 | 1,575.7 | 1,951.1 |
| Power-generating machinery and equipment | 109.9 | 121.9 | 134.4 |
| Machinery specialized for particular industries | 336.9 | 397.2 | 429.2 |
| Textile and leather machinery | 140.6 | 142.2 | 132.7 |
| General industrial machinery, equipment and parts | 294.3 | 297.3 | 325.5 |
| Telecommunications and sound equipment | 63.5 | 95.1 | 129.1 |
| Other electrical machinery, apparatus, etc. | 265.4 | 279.8 | 357.9 |
| Road vehicles and parts† | 303.8 | 211.2 | 287.9 |
| Other transport equipment† | 86.8 | 80.2 | 184.9 |
| **Miscellaneous manufactured articles** | 453.3 | 468.9 | 589.3 |
| Clothing and accessories (excl. footwear) | 190.7 | 208.2 | 250.6 |
| **Total** (incl. others) | 5,476.0 | 5,189.1 | 6,432.0 |

* Excluding narrow or special fabrics.
† Excluding tyres, engines and electrical parts.

| Exports f.o.b. | 1990 | 1991 | 1992 |
|---|---|---|---|
| **Food and live animals** | 234.4 | 216.1 | 213.8 |
| Fish, crustaceans and molluscs | 108.3 | 82.0 | 72.9 |
| Vegetables and fruit | 76.4 | 87.8 | 83.9 |
| **Crude materials (inedible) except fuels** | 82.5 | 63.2 | 73.3 |
| **Mineral fuels, lubricants, etc.** | 604.4 | 529.8 | 610.1 |
| Petroleum, petroleum products, etc. | 597.5 | 522.7 | 604.4 |
| Crude petroleum oils, etc. | 521.4 | 441.6 | 511.6 |
| Refined petroleum products | 76.1 | 81.1 | 92.8 |
| Motor spirit (gasoline) and other light oils | 76.1 | 81.1 | 92.8 |
| **Animal and vegetable oils, fats and waxes** | 121.2 | 290.9 | 158.5 |
| Fixed vegetable oils and fats | 121.2 | 290.7 | 158.4 |
| Olive oil | 121.2 | 290.7 | 158.4 |
| **Chemicals and related products** | 506.8 | 516.4 | 517.7 |
| Inorganic chemicals | 210.7 | 230.1 | 230.1 |
| Inorganic chemical elements, oxides and halogen salts | 140.5 | 170.8 | 164.2 |
| Inorganic acids and oxygen compounds of non-metals | 139.8 | 169.3 | 163.9 |
| Phosphorus pentoxide and phosphoric acids | 139.5 | 168.9 | 163.6 |
| Manufactured fertilizers | 259.4 | 239.6 | 236.4 |
| Phosphatic fertilizers | 245.5 | 230.8 | 225.2 |
| Superphosphates | 108.0 | 103.6 | 104.6 |
| **Basic manufactures** | 406.7 | 388.8 | 461.4 |
| Leather, leather manufactures and dressed furskins | 55.2 | 61.7 | 93.7 |
| Manufactures of leather, etc. | 50.2 | 59.1 | 91.3 |
| Parts of footwear (except metal and asbestos) | 49.6 | 58.3 | 90.7 |
| Textile yarn, fabrics, etc. | 111.7 | 100.9 | 121.3 |
| Non-metallic mineral manufactures | 118.3 | 83.8 | 101.8 |
| **Machinery and transport equipment** | 272.7 | 298.8 | 351.8 |
| Electrical machinery, apparatus, etc. | 189.9 | 219.4 | 275.7 |
| Equipment for distributing electricity | 58.6 | 65.3 | 117.4 |
| Insulated electric wire, cable, etc. | 58.6 | 65.2 | 117.3 |
| **Miscellaneous manufactured articles** | 1,240.0 | 1,347.2 | 1,616.4 |
| Clothing and accessories (excl. footwear) | 1,126.0 | 1,221.3 | 1,477.5 |
| Men's and boys' outer garments of non-knitted textile fabrics | 516.5 | 584.6 | 706.0 |
| Women's, girls' and infants' outer garments of non-knitted textile fabrics | 250.8 | 270.1 | 352.0 |
| Undergarments (excl. foundation garments) of non-knitted textile fabrics | 85.2 | 96.6 | 105.9 |
| Knitted or crocheted outer garments and accessories (excl. gloves, stockings, etc.), non-elastic | 144.7 | 133.6 | 146.5 |
| Knitted or crocheted undergarments (incl. foundation garments of non-knitted fabrics) | 100.4 | 102.9 | 129.3 |
| **Total** (incl. others) | 3,498.4 | 3,699.6 | 4,039.9 |

Source: UN, *International Trade Statistics Yearbook*.

TUNISIA
Statistical Survey

### PRINCIPAL TRADING PARTNERS (US $ '000)*

| Imports c.i.f. | 1990 | 1991 | 1992 |
|---|---|---|---|
| Algeria | 111,794 | 99,994 | 151,994 |
| Belgium-Luxembourg | 261,623 | 278,116 | 302,637 |
| Canada | 48,690 | 81,244 | 62,503 |
| France | 1,526,400 | 1,351,676 | 1,637,792 |
| Germany | 683,015 | 741,795 | 901,235 |
| Italy | 871,149 | 905,398 | 1,168,202 |
| Japan | 99,515 | 121,121 | 147,313 |
| Morocco | 47,798 | 67,400 | 74.370 |
| Netherlands | 143,473 | 112,108 | 142,316 |
| Poland | 54,466 | 46,839 | 67,824 |
| Russia | n.a. | n.a. | 82,847 |
| Spain | 169,551 | 160,057 | 213,548 |
| Sweden | 55,510 | 67,722 | 70,202 |
| Switzerland | 61,048 | 70,993 | 69,786 |
| USSR | 95,671 | 70,696 | — |
| United Kingdom | 92,329 | 92,176 | 113,840 |
| USA | 285,830 | 248,895 | 320,086 |
| **Total** (incl. others) | 5,471,095 | 5,184,856 | 6,425,382 |

| Exports f.o.b. | 1990 | 1991 | 1992 |
|---|---|---|---|
| Algeria | 81,080 | 78,683 | 97,800 |
| Belgium-Luxembourg | 244,707 | 231,190 | 278,905 |
| France | 931,685 | 933,943 | 1,093,979 |
| Germany | 528,227 | 607,527 | 685,971 |
| Greece | 15,211 | 23,235 | 84,199 |
| India | 43,288 | 68,098 | 75,508 |
| Iraq | 50,652 | 68 | 342 |
| Italy | 740,391 | 730,133 | 689,577 |
| Libya | 160,780 | 201,727 | 176,050 |
| Morocco | 23,561 | 26,777 | 46,059 |
| Netherlands | 89,012 | 99,618 | 103,418 |
| Spain | 91,922 | 135,718 | 110,816 |
| USSR | 43,701 | 41,199 | — |
| United Kingdom | 57,297 | 47,481 | 72,759 |
| **Total** (incl. others) | 3,498,273 | 3,699,503 | 4,039,731 |

* Imports by country of production; exports by country of last destination.

Source: UN, *International Trade Statistics Yearbook*.

## Transport

### RAILWAYS (traffic)

| | 1991 | 1992 | 1993 |
|---|---|---|---|
| Passenger-km (million) | 1,020 | 1,078 | 1,057 |
| Freight ton-km (million) | 1,813 | 2,015 | 2,012 |

Source: Ministère du Transport.

### ROAD TRAFFIC (motor vehicles in use at 31 December)

| | 1987 | 1988 | 1989 |
|---|---|---|---|
| Private cars | 281,201 | 292,673 | 320,101 |
| Buses | 8,446 | 8,986 | 9,453 |
| Commercial vehicles | 147,697 | 151,826 | 157,689 |
| Motor cycles | 12,247 | 12,290 | 12,472 |

Source: International Road Federation, *World Road Statistics*.

### SHIPPING
**Merchant Fleet** (vessels registered at 30 June)

| | Displacement ('000 gross reg. tons) | | |
|---|---|---|---|
| | 1990 | 1991 | 1992 |
| **Total** | 278 | 276 | 280 |

Source: UN, *Statistical Yearbook*.

### International Sea-borne Freight Traffic ('000 metric tons)

| | 1991 | 1992 | 1993 |
|---|---|---|---|
| Goods loaded* | 6,384 | 6,648 | 6,060 |
| Goods unloaded | 9,732 | 9,612 | 10,200 |

* Excluding Algerian crude petroleum loaded at La Skhirra.
Source: UN, *Monthly Bulletin of Statistics*.

### CIVIL AVIATION (traffic on scheduled services)

| | 1990 | 1991 | 1992 |
|---|---|---|---|
| Km flown (million) | 15 | 14 | 15 |
| Passengers carried ('000) | 1,313 | 1,201 | 1,250 |
| Passenger-km (million) | 1,502 | 1,407 | 1,673 |
| Total ton-km (million) | 154 | 144 | 168 |

Source: UN, *Statistical Yearbook*.

## Tourism

### FOREIGN TOURIST ARRIVALS BY NATIONALITY ('000)

| | 1992 | 1993 | 1994 |
|---|---|---|---|
| Algeria | 807.2 | 676.8 | 672.4 |
| Austria | 44.7 | 54.7 | 71.6 |
| Belgium | 64.1 | 73.6 | 78.1 |
| France | 357.1 | 447.8 | 484.8 |
| Germany | 649.3 | 711.8 | 852.5 |
| Italy | 224.0 | 241.8 | 229.8 |
| Libya | 635.6 | 538.4 | 543.9 |
| Netherlands | 66.1 | 66.9 | 80.3 |
| Scandinavia | 63.1 | 63.7 | 61.7 |
| Switzerland | 45.3 | 64.1 | 76.4 |
| United Kingdom | 202.8 | 245.8 | 267.2 |
| USA | 8.7 | 10.8 | 11.6 |
| **Total** (incl. others) | 3,539.9 | 3,655.6 | 3,855.5 |

Source: Ministère de l'Intérieur.

## Communications Media

| | 1990 | 1991 | 1992 |
|---|---|---|---|
| Radio receivers ('000 in use) | 1,600 | 1,640 | 1,680 |
| Television receivers ('000 in use) | 650 | 650 | 670 |
| Daily newspapers (number) | 6 | n.a. | 9 |
| Book production (titles)* | n.a. | 181 | 1,165 |

* Excluding pamphlets.
Telephones ('000 main lines in use): 277 in 1989; 303 in 1990; 337 in 1991.
Non-daily newspapers (1988): 9 (estimated circulation of 244,000 copies).
Sources: UNESCO, *Statistical Yearbook*; UN, *Statistical Yearbook*.

## Education

| | 1992/93 | 1993/94 | 1994/95 |
|---|---|---|---|
| Institutions | | | |
|   Primary | 4,044 | 4,164 | 4,286 |
|   Secondary | 625 | 655 | 712 |
| Teachers | | | |
|   Primary | 54,560 | 55,720 | 58,279 |
|   Secondary | 26,097 | 26,817 | 27,785 |
| Pupils | | | |
|   Primary | 1,432,112 | 1,467,411 | 1,472,844 |
|   Secondary | 567,381 | 605,935 | 662,222 |

Source: Ministère de l'Education et des Sciences.

# Directory

## The Constitution

A new Constitution for the Republic of Tunisia was promulgated on 1 June 1959 and amended on 12 July 1988. Its main provisions are summarized below:

### NATIONAL ASSEMBLY

Legislative power is exercised by the National Assembly, which is elected (at the same time as the President) every five years by direct universal suffrage. Every citizen who has had Tunisian nationality for at least five years and who has attained 20 years of age has the right to vote. The National Assembly shall hold two sessions every year, each session lasting not more than three months. Additional meetings may be held at the demand of the President or of a majority of the deputies.

### HEAD OF STATE

The President of the Republic is both Head of State and Head of the Executive. He must be not less than 40 years of age and not more than 70. The President is elected by universal suffrage for a five-year term which is renewable twice, consecutively. The President is also the Commander-in-Chief of the army and makes both civil and military appointments. The Government may be censured by the National Assembly, in which case the President may dismiss the Assembly and hold fresh elections. If censured by the new Assembly thus elected, the Government must resign. Should the presidency fall vacant for any reason before the end of a President's term of office, the President of the National Assembly shall take charge of affairs of the state for a period of 45 to 60 days. At the end of this period, a presidential election shall be organized. The President of the National Assembly shall not be eligible as a presidential candidate.

### COUNCIL OF STATE

Comprises two judicial bodies: an administrative body dealing with legal disputes between individuals and state or public bodies, and an audit office to verify the accounts of the state and submit reports.

### ECONOMIC AND SOCIAL COUNCIL

Deals with economic and social planning and studies projects submitted by the National Assembly. Members are grouped in seven categories representing various sections of the community.

## The Government

### HEAD OF STATE

**President:** ZINE AL-ABIDINE BEN ALI (took office on 7 November 1987; re-elected 2 April 1989 and 20 March 1994).

### THE CABINET
(June 1995)

**Prime Minister:** HAMED KAROUI.
**Minister of State and Special Adviser to the President:** ABDALLAH KALLEL.
**Minister of the Interior:** MUHAMMAD JEGHAM.
**Minister, Director of the Presidential Office:** MUHAMMAD JERI.
**Minister of Justice:** SADOK CHAABANE.
**Minister of Foreign Affairs:** HABIB BEN YAHIA.
**Minister of National Defence:** ABD AL-AZIZ BEN DHIA.
**Minister of Religious Affairs:** ALI CHEBBI.
**Minister of International Co-operation and Foreign Investment:** MUHAMMAD GHANNOUCHI.
**Minister of Finance:** NOURI ZORGATI.
**Minister of Economic Development:** MUSTAPHA NABLI.
**Minister of Industry:** SLAHEDDINE BOUGUERRA.
**Minister of Trade:** SLAHEDDINE BEN M'BAREK.
**Minister of Agriculture:** MUHAMMAD BEN REJEB.
**Minister of State Domains:** MUSTAPHA BOUAZIZ.
**Minister of Equipment and Housing:** ALI CHAOUCH.
**Minister of the Environment and Land Planning:** MUHAMMAD MEHDI MELIKA.
**Minister of Transport:** MONDHER ZENAIDI.
**Minister of Tourism and Handicrafts:** SLAHEDDINE MAAOUIA.
**Minister of Communications:** HABIB AMMAR.
**Minister of Education:** HATEM BEN OTHMANE.
**Minister of Higher Education:** DALY JAZI.
**Minister of Culture:** SALAH BACCARI.
**Minister of Public Health:** HEDI M'HENNI.
**Minister of Social Affairs:** SADOK RABAH.
**Minister of Professional Training and Employment:** MONCER ROUISSI.
**Minister of Children and Youth:** ABD AR-RAHIM ZOUARI.
**Secretary of State to the Interior Minister in charge of Security:** MUHAMMAD ALI GHANZAOUI.

### MINISTRIES

**Ministry of Agriculture:** 30 rue Alain Savery, Tunis; tel. 660-088; telex 13378.
**Ministry of Children and Youth:** 89 ave Hédi Chaker, Tunis; tel. 788-473; telex 14246.
**Ministry of Communications:** Tunis.
**Ministry of Culture:** place du Gouvernement, la Kasbah, 1008 Tunis; tel. 661-000; telex 12032; fax 567-019.
**Ministry of Economic Development:** 7 rue du Royaume d'Arabie Saoudite, 1035 Tunis; tel. 285-134; telex 14341.
**Ministry of Education:** place de la Kasbah, Tunis; tel. 660-088; telex 13004.
**Ministry of the Environment and Land Planning:** Tunis.
**Ministry of Equipment and Housing:** Cité Jardin, Tunis; tel. 680-088; telex 13565.
**Ministry of Finance:** place Alizouaui, Tunis; tel. 650-621; telex 51922.
**Ministry of Foreign Affairs:** place du Gouvernement, la Kasbah, Tunis; tel. 660-088; telex 13470.
**Ministry of the Interior:** ave Habib Bourguiba, Tunis; tel. 333-000; telex 13994.
**Ministry of International Co-operation and Foreign Investment:** 149 ave de la Liberté, 1002 Tunis; tel. 798-522; telex 18060; fax 799-069.
**Ministry of Justice:** ave Bab Benat, Tunis; tel. 660-088.
**Ministry of National Defence:** blvd Bab Menara, Tunis; tel. 260-244; telex 12580.
**Ministry of Public Health:** Bab Saadoun, 1030 Tunis; tel. 662-040; telex 15235; fax 567-100.
**Ministry of Religious Affairs:** Tunis.
**Ministry of Social Affairs:** blvd Farhat Hached, Tunis; tel. 660-088; telex 13711.
**Ministry of Tourism and Handicrafts:** ave Muhammad V, Tunis.
**Ministry of Transport:** 3 rue d'Angleterre, Tunis; tel. 660-088; telex 13040.

## President and Legislature

### PRESIDENT

At the presidential election, which took place on 20 March 1994, the sole candidate, Zine al-Abidine Ben Ali, was re-elected to the presidency with 2,987,375 votes, 99.92% of the votes cast.

# TUNISIA

## ASSEMBLÉE NATIONALE

**President:** HABIB BOULARES.

### Election, 20 March 1994

| Party | Votes | % | Seats |
|---|---|---|---|
| Rassemblement Constitutionnel Démocratique | 2,768,667 | 97.73 | 144 |
| Mouvement des Démocrates Socialistes | 30,660 | 1.08 | 10 |
| Mouvement de la Rénovation | 11,299 | 0.39 | 4 |
| Union Démocratique Unioniste | 9,152 | 0.32 | 3 |
| Parti de l'Unité Populaire | 8,391 | 0.30 | 2 |
| Parti Social pour le Progrès | 1,892 | 0.07 | 0 |
| Rassemblement Socialiste Progressiste | 1,749 | 0.06 | 0 |
| Independents | 1,061 | 0.04 | 0 |
| **Total** | **2,832,871*** | **100.00** | **163†** |

\* Excluding 8,686 spoilt ballot papers.
† Under the terms of an amendment to the electoral code adopted by the National Assembly in January 1994, 19 of the 163 seats in the National Assembly were reserved for candidates of opposition parties. These were allotted according to the proportion of votes received nationally by each party.

## Political Organizations

**Mouvement de l'Unité Populaire (MUP):** Tunis; supports radical reform; split into two factions, one led by AHMAD BEN SALAH, living in exile until 1988; the other became the Parti de l'Unité Populaire (see below). Co-ordinator BRAHIM HAYDER.

**Mouvement des Démocrates Socialistes (MDS):** Tunis; in favour of a pluralist political system; participated in 1981 election and was officially recognized in November 1983; Political Bureau of 14 mems, National Council of 60 mems, normally elected by the party Congress; Sec.-Gen. MUHAMMAD MOUADA.

**Mouvement de la Rénovation (MR):** Tunis; f. 1939; fmrly Parti Communiste Tunisien, name changed 1993; Sec.-Gen. MUHAMMAD HARMEL.

**Parti de la Renaissance—Hizb an-Nahdah:** Tunis; formerly Mouvement de la Tendance Islamique (banned in 1981); Leader RACHED GHANOUCHI; Sec.-Gen. Sheikh ABD AL-FATHA MOUROU.

**Parti des Ouvriers Communistes Tunisiens (POCT):** Tunis; illegal; Leader HAMMA HAMMANI.

**Parti Social pour le Progrès (PSP):** 3B rue Gandhi, Tunis; tel. 341-023; f. 1988; officially recognized September 1988; liberal; Sec.-Gen. MOUNIR BEJI.

**Parti de l'Unité Populaire (PUP):** 7 rue d'Autriche, 1002 Tunis; tel. 289-678; fax 796-031; broke away from MUP (see above); officially recognized November 1983; Leader MUHAMMAD BELHADJ AMOR.

**Rassemblement Constitutionnel Démocratique—RCD:** blvd 9 avril 1938, Tunis; f. 1934 as the Néo-Destour Party, following a split in the Destour (Constitution) Party; renamed Parti Socialiste Destourien in 1964; adopted present name in February 1988; moderate left-wing republican party, which achieved Tunisian independence; Political Bureau of 13 mems, and a Cen. Cttee of 200, elected by the party Congress; Chair. ZINE AL-ABIDINE BEN ALI; Vice-Chair. HAMED KAROUI; Sec.-Gen. CHEDLI NEFFATI.

**Rassemblement National Arabe:** Tunis; banned in 1981; Leader BASHIR ASSAD.

**Rassemblement Socialiste Progressiste (RSP):** Tunis; f. 1983, officially recognized September 1988; leftist; Sec.-Gen. NEJIB CHEBBI.

**Union Démocratique Unioniste (UDU):** Tunis; officially recognized November 1988; supports Arab unity; Sec.-Gen. ABDERRAH-MANE TLILI.

## Diplomatic Representation

### EMBASSIES IN TUNISIA

**Algeria:** 18 rue de Niger, Tunis; tel. 283-166; telex 13081; Ambassador: Dr MESSAOUD AIT CHAALAL.

**Argentina:** 10 rue al-Hassan et Houssaine, al-Menzah IV, 1004 Tunis; tel. 231-222; telex 13053; fax 750-050; Ambassador: MARCELO HUERGO.

**Austria:** 16 rue ibn Hamdiss, BP 23, al-Menzah, 1004 Tunis; tel. 751-091; telex 14586; fax 767-824; Ambassador: Dr KARL DIEM.

**Bahrain:** 72 rue Mouaouia ibn Abi Soufiane, al-Menzah 6, Tunis; tel. 231-811; telex 13733; Ambassador: JASSIM BUALLAY.

**Belgium:** 47 rue du 1er juin, BP 24, 1002 Tunis; tel. 781-655; telex 14342; fax 792-797; Ambassador: GUIDO COURTOIS.

**Brazil:** 37 ave d'Afrique, BP 64, al-Menzah V, 1004 Tunis; tel. 232-538; telex 14560; fax 750-367; Ambassador: LINDOLFO L. COLLOR.

**Bulgaria:** 5 rue Ryhane, Cité Mahragène, Tunis; tel. 796-182; telex 17289; fax 791-667; Ambassador: TCHAVDAR TCHERVENKOV.

**Canada:** 3 rue du Sénégal, Place d'Afrique, BP 31, Belvédère, 1002 Tunis; tel. 796-577; telex 25324; fax 792-371; Ambassador: MICHEL ROY.

**China, People's Republic:** 41 ave Jugurtha, Mutuellevilk, Tunis; tel. 282-090; telex 12221; Ambassador: WU CHUANFU.

**Côte d'Ivoire:** 84 ave Hédi Chaker, Tunis; tel. 283-878; telex 14353; Ambassador: COLLET PHILIPPE VIEIRA.

**Cuba:** 20 ave du Golfe Arabe, 1004 al-Menzah VIII, Tunis; tel. 712-844; telex 14080; fax 714-198; Ambassador: JORGE MANFUGAS-LAVIGNE.

**Czech Republic:** 98 rue de Palestine, BP 53, Belvédère, 1002 Tunis; tel. 280-486; telex 14466; fax 793-228.

**Denmark:** 5 rue de Mauritanie, BP 254, Belvédère, 1002 Tunis; tel. 792-600; telex 14352; fax 790-797; Ambassador: HERLUF HANSEN.

**Djibouti:** 5 rue Fatma al-Fahria, BP 71, Mutuelleville, Tunis; tel. 890-589; telex 13148; Ambassador: ALI ABDOU MUHAMMAD.

**Egypt:** Quartier Montplaisir, Routhi 6, Med V, Tunis; tel. 792-233; telex 13992; fax 794-389; Ambassador: ALI MAHER AS-SAYED.

**France:** place de l'Indépendance, Tunis; tel. 347-555; telex 15468; fax 354-388; Ambassador: JEAN-NOËL DE BOUILLANE DE LACOSTE.

**Germany:** 1 rue al-Hamra, Mutuelleville, Tunis; tel. 786-455; telex 15463; fax 788-242; Ambassador: Dr KARL HEINZ KUNZMANN.

**Greece:** 9 impasse Antelas, Nord Hilton, BP 151, Mahrajane, 1002, Tunis; tel. 288-411; telex 13742; fax 789-518; Ambassador: CONSTANTIN PREVEDOURAKIS.

**Hungary:** 12 rue Achtart, Nord-Hilton, Tunis; tel. 751-987; fax 750-620; Ambassador: LÁSZLÓ NIKICSER.

**India:** 4 place Didon, Notre Dame, Tunis; tel. 891-006; telex 18072; fax 783-394; Ambassador: NIGAM PRAKASH.

**Indonesia:** BP 63, al-Menzah, 1004 Tunis; tel. 797-188; telex 18173; fax 791-303; Ambassador: AMBIAR TAMALA.

**Iran:** 10 rue de Docteur Burnet, Belvédère, Tunis; tel. 285-305; telex 15138.

**Iraq:** ave Tahar B. Achour, route X2 m 10, Mutuelleville, Tunis; tel. 890-633; telex 12245; Ambassador: NOURI ISMAIL TOHA AL-WAYES.

**Italy:** 37 rue Gamal Abd an-Nasser, Tunis; tel. 341-811; telex 13501; fax 354-155; Ambassador: FRANCESCO CARUSO.

**Japan:** 10 rue Mahmoud al-Matri, BP 95, Belvédère, Tunis; tel. 285-937; telex 15456; Ambassador: YOSHIKAZU SUGITANI.

**Jordan:** 87 ave Jugurtha, Mutuelleville, Tunis; tel. 288-401; telex 13745; Ambassador: NABIH AN-NIMR.

**Korea, Republic:** 16 rue Caracalla, Notre Dame, 1002 Tunis; tel. 894-357; telex 15157; Ambassador: CHOI BONG-RHEUM.

**Kuwait:** 40 route Ariane, al-Menzah, Tunis; tel. 236-811; telex 12332; Ambassador: MEJREN AHMAD AL-HAMAD.

**Libya:** 48 bis rue du 1er juin, Tunis; tel. 236-666; telex 12275; Ambassador: ABD AL-ATTI OBEIDI.

**Mauritania:** 17 rue Fatma Ennechi, BP 62, al-Menzah, Tunis; tel. 234-935; telex 12234; Ambassador: MOHAMED LAMINE OULD YAHYA.

**Morocco:** 39 ave du 1er juin, Tunis; tel. 782-775; telex 14460; fax 787-103; Ambassador: ABD AL-HAKIM IRAQUI.

**Netherlands:** 6–8 rue Meycen, Belvédère, BP 47, 1082 Tunis; tel. 799-442; telex 15260; fax 785-557; Ambassador: R. J. MULDER.

**Norway:** 20 rue de la Kahéna, BP 9, 1082 Tunis; tel. 802-158; fax 801-944; Ambassador: KJELL ØSTREM.

**Pakistan:** 7 rue Ali ibn Abi Talib, BP 42, al-Menzah, Tunis; tel. 234-366; telex 14027; Ambassador: TARIQ KHAN.

**Poland:** 4 rue Sophonisbe, Notre Dame, Tunis; tel. 286-237; telex 14024; fax 795-118; Ambassador: JANUSZ FEKECZ.

**Portugal:** 2 rue Sufétula, Belvédère, 1002 Tunis; tel. 893-981; telex 18235; fax 791-008; Ambassador: CARLOS MILHEIRÃO.

**Qatar:** 2 Nahj al-Hakim Bourni, Belvédère, Tunis; tel. 285-600; telex 14131; Chargé d'affaires: MAJID AL-ALI.

**Romania:** 18 ave d'Afrique, al-Menzah V, Tunis; tel. 766-926; telex 15223; fax 767-695; Ambassador: GELU VOICAN VOICULESCU.

**Russia:** 1 el Manar, BP 48, Tunis; tel. 882-446; fax 882-478; Ambassador: BORIS ALEKSEYEVICH SHCHIBORIN.

**Saudi Arabia:** 16 rue d'Autriche, Belvédère, Tunis; tel. 281-295; telex 13562; Ambassador: Sheikh ABBAS FAIK GHAZZAOUI.

TUNISIA
*Directory*

**Senegal:** 122 ave de la Liberté, Tunis; tel. 282-544; telex 12477; Ambassador: Ibra Deguene Ka.

**Somalia:** 6 rue Hadramout, Mutuelleville, Tunis; tel. 289-505; telex 13480; Ambassador: Ahmad Abdallah Muhammad.

**Spain:** 22 ave Dr Ernest Conseil, Cité Jardin, Tunis; tel. 280-613; telex 13330; Ambassador: Fernando Arias Salgado.

**Sweden:** 87 ave Taieb Mhiri, 1002 Tunis; tel. 795-433; telex 15258; fax 788-894; Ambassador: John Hagard.

**Switzerland:** 10 rue ach-Chenkiti, BP 501, Mutuelleville, 1025 Tunis; tel. 281-917; telex 14922; fax 788-796; Ambassador: Dr Luciano Mordasini.

**Syria:** Cité al-Manor III, No. 119, Tunis; tel. 235-577; telex 13890; Ambassador: Omar as-Said.

**Turkey:** 30 ave d'Afrique, BP 134, al-Menzah 5, Tunis; tel. 750-668; fax 767-045; Ambassador: Altan Guven.

**United Arab Emirates:** 15 rue du 1er juin, Mutuelleville, Tunis; tel. 783-522; telex 12168; Ambassador: Hamad Salem al-Maqami.

**United Kingdom:** 5 place de la Victoire, Tunis; tel. 341-444; telex 14007; fax 354-877; Ambassador: Michael L. Tait.

**USA:** 144 ave de la Liberté, Tunis; tel. 782-566; fax 789-719; Ambassador: Mary Ann Casey.

**Venezuela:** 30 rue de Niger, 1002 Tunis; tel. 285-075; telex 15091; Ambassador: José Antonio Quijada Sánchez.

**Yemen:** rue Mouaouia ibn Soufiane, al-Menzah 6, Tunis; tel. 237-933; telex 13045; Ambassador: Salah Ali al-Achoual.

**Yugoslavia:** 4 rue de Libéria, Tunis; tel. 281-032; telex 18399; Ambassador: Nerkez Arifhodzić.

**Zaire:** 11 rue Tertullien, Notre Dame, Tunis; tel. 281-833; telex 12429; Ambassador: Mboladinga Katako.

## Judicial System

The **Cour de Cassation** in Tunis has three civil and one criminal sections. There are three **Cours d'Appel** at Tunis, Sousse and Sfax, and 13 **Cours de Première Instance**, each having three chambers, except the **Cour de Première Instance** at Tunis which has eight chambers. **Justices Cantonales** exist in 51 areas.

## Religion

The Constitution of 1956 recognizes Islam as the state religion, with the introduction of certain reforms, such as the abolition of polygamy. An estimated 7m., or 99% of the population, are Muslims. Minority religions include Jews (an estimated 2,000 adherents in 1993) and Christians. The Christian population comprises Roman Catholics, Greek Orthodox and French and English Protestants.

### ISLAM

**Grand Mufti of Tunisia:** Sheikh Muhammad Habir Belkhodja.

### CHRISTIANITY

**Reformed Church of Tunisia:** 36 rue Charles de Gaulle, 1,000 Tunis; f. 1880; c. 40 mems; Pastor Lee Dehoog.

**Roman Catholic Prelature:** 4 rue d'Alger, 1000 Tunis; tel. 335-225; fax 335-832; f. 1964; Prelate of Tunis Mgr Fouad Twal; 18,000 adherents (1995).

## The Press

### DAILIES

**L'Action:** 15 rue 2 Mars 1934, Tunis; tel. 264-899; telex 12163; f. 1932; French; organ of the Rassemblement Constitutionnel Démocratique (RCD); Dir Mustapha Masmoudi; circ. 50,000.

**Al-Amal** (Action): 15 rue 2 Mars 1934, Tunis; tel. 264-899; telex 12163; f. 1934; Arabic; organ of the RCD; Dir Hucine Maghrebi; circ. 50,000.

**La Presse de Tunisie:** 6 rue Ali Bach-Hamba, Tunis; tel. 341-066; telex 13880; fax 349-720; f. 1936; French; Dr Mahfouz Muhammad; circ. 40,000.

**As-Sabah** (The Morning): 4 rue Ali Bach-Hamba, Tunis; tel. 340-222; f. 1951; Arabic; Dir Habib Cheikhrouhou; circ. 50,000.

### PERIODICALS

**Al-Akhbar** (The News): 1 passage d'al-Houdaybiyah, Tunis; tel. 344-100; f. 1984; weekly; general; Dir Muhammad Ben Yousuf; circ. 50,000.

**Les Annonces:** 6 rue de Sparte, BP 1343, Tunis; tel. 350-177; telex 13206; fax 347-184; f. 1978; 2 a week; French/Arabic; Dir Muhammad Nejib Azouz; circ. 170,000.

**Al-Anouar at-Tounissia** (Tunisian Lights): 10 rue ach-Cham, 1002 Tunis; tel. 289-000; fax 289-357; f. 1981; weekly; general; Dir Slaheddine al-Amri; circ. 165,000.

**L'Avenir:** 26 rue Gamal Abd an-Nasser, BP 1200, Tunis; tel. 258-941; f. 1980; weekly; organ of Mouvement des Démocrates Socialistes.

**Al-Bayan** (The Manifesto): 103 ave de la Liberté, Tunis; tel. 780-366; telex 13982; weekly; general; Dir Hédi Jilani.

**Al-Biladi** (My Country): 15 rue 2 Mars 1934, Tunis; telex 12163; f. 1974; Arabic; political and general weekly for Tunisian workers abroad; Dir Hédi al-Ghali; circ. 90,000.

**Bulletin Mensuel de Statistique:** Institut National de la Statistique, BP 65, 70 rue ach-Cham, 1002 Tunis-Belvédère; monthly.

**Ach-Chourouk** (Sunrise): 10 rue ach-Cham, Tunis; tel 289-000; weekly; general; Dir Slaheddine al-Amri; circ. 110,000.

**Conjoncture:** 37 ave Khereddine Pacha, 1002 Tunis; tel. 784-223; fax 782-742; f. 1974; monthly; economic and financial surveys; Dir Hosni Toumi; circ. 5,000.

**Démocratie:** 118 rue de Yougoslavie, Tunis; f. 1978; monthly; French; organ of the Mouvement des Démocrates Socialistes; Dir Hassib Ben Ammar; circ. 5,000.

**Dialogue:** Maison du RCD, blvd 9 Avril 1938, Tunis; telex 12163; f. 1974; weekly; French; cultural and political organ of the RCD; Dir Naceur Bechekh; circ. 30,000.

**Etudiant Tunisien:** 11 rue d'Espagne, BP 286, Tunis; f. 1953; French and Arabic; Chief Editor Faouzi Aouam.

**Al-Fajr** (Dawn): Tunis; f. 1990; weekly; to become daily; Arabic; publ. of the Hizb an-Nahdah movement; Dir Hamadi Jebali (imprisoned Jan. 1991).

**Al-Falah:** rue Alain Savary, al-Khadra, 1003 Tunis; tel. 800-800; fax 797-292; weekly; political; Dir Abd al-Baki Bacha; Editor Yahia Amor; circ. 7,000.

**Al-Fikr** (Thought): 13 rue Dar al-Jel, BP 556, Tunis; tel. 260-237; f. 1955; monthly; Arabic; cultural review.

**Gazette Touristique:** rue 8601, 40, Zone Industrielle, La Charguia 2, 2035 Tunis; tel. 786-866; fax 794-891; f. 1971; monthly; French; tourism; Dir Tijani Haddad; circ. 5,000.

**L'Hebdo Touristique:** rue 8601, 40, Zone Industrielle, La Charguia 2, 2035 Tunis; tel. 786-866; fax 794-891; f. 1971; weekly; French; tourism; Dir Tijani Haddad; circ. 5,000.

**IBLA:** Institut des Belles Lettres Arabes, 12 rue Jemaa el-Haoua, 1008 Tunis Bab Menara, Tunis; tel. 560-133; fax 572-683; f. 1937; 2 a year; French; social and cultural review on Maghreb and Muslim-Arab affairs; Dir G. Demeerseman.

**Al-Idhaa wa Talvaza** (Radio and Television): 71 ave de la Liberté, Tunis; tel. 287-300; fax 781-058; f. 1956; fortnightly; Arabic language; broadcasting magazine; Dir Gen. Abd al-Hafidh Herguem; Editor Wahid Braham; circ. 10,000.

**Information Economique Africaine:** 16 rue de Rome, BP 61, 1015 Tunis; tel. 245-318; telex 14459; fax 353-172; f. 1970; monthly; Dir Muhammad Zerzeri.

**Irfane** (Children): 6 rue Mohammed Ali, Tunis; tel. 256-877; telex 12163; f. 1966; monthly; Arabic; publ. of the Tunisian Union of Youth Organizations; Dir-Gen. Khalid Abassi; circ. 100,000.

**Jeunesse Magazine:** 6 rue Mohammed Ali, Tunis; tel. 256-877; telex 12163; monthly; Arabic/French; Dir-Gen. Khalid Abassi; circ. 50,000.

**Journal Officiel de la République Tunisienne:** ave Farhat Hached, 2040 Radès; tel. 434-211; telex 14939; fax 434-234; f. 1860; the official gazette; French and Arabic editions published twice weekly by the Imprimerie Officielle (The State Press); Pres. and Dir-Gen. Romdhane Ben Mimoun; circ. 20,000.

**Al-Maoukif:** 6 rue de la Commission, Tunis; tel. 346-077; weekly; organ of the Rassemblement Socialiste Progressiste; Dir Ahmad Nejib Chabi.

**Al-Maraa** (The Woman): 56 blvd Bab Benat, Tunis; tel. 260-178; fax 567-131; f. 1961; monthly; Arabic/French; political, economic and social affairs; issued by the Union Nationale de la Femme Tunisienne; Dir Faiza Kefi; circ. 10,000.

**Le Mensuel:** 9 rue de Bassorah, 1002 Tunis; f. 1984; monthly; economic, social and cultural affairs.

**Al-Moussawar:** 10 rue ach-Cham, Tunis; tel. 289-000; fax 289-357; weekly; circ. 75,000.

**Outrouhat:** BP 492, 1049 Tunis; tel. 230-092; monthly; scientific; Dir Lotfi Ben Aissa.

**Ar-Rai** (Opinion): 118 rue de Yougoslavie, Tunis; tel. 242-251; f. 1977 by Mouvement des Démocrates Socialistes; weekly; opposition newspaper; Dir Hassib Ben Amar; circ. 20,000.

TUNISIA

**Réalités:** 85 rue de Palestine, Belvédère, BP 227, 1002 Tunis; tel. 788-313; fax 893-489; f. 1979; weekly; French/Arabic; Dir TAÏEB ZAHAR; circ. 25,000.

**At-Tariq al-Jadid** (New Road): 6 rue Metouia, Tunis; tel. 246-400; fax 350-748; f. 1981; organ of the Mouvement de la Rénovation; Editor MUHAMMAD HARHEL.

**Le Temps:** 4 rue Ali Bach-Hamba, Tunis; tel. 340-222; f. 1975; weekly; general news; French; Dir HABIB CHEIKHROUHOU; circ. 42,000.

**Tounes al-Khadra:** rue Alain Savary, 1003 Tunis; tel. 800-800; fax 797-292; f. 1976; monthly; agriculture; Dir ABD AL-BAKI BACHA; Editor GHARBI HAMOUDA; circ. 5,000.

**Tunis Hebdo:** 1 passage d'al-Houdaybiyah, Tunis; tel. 344-100; f. 1973; weekly; French; general and sport; Dir MUHAMMAD BEN YOUSUF; circ. 40,000.

### NEWS AGENCIES

**Tunis Afrique Presse (TAP):** 25 ave du 7 novembre, Tunis; telex 13400; f. 1961; Arab, French and English; Offices in Algiers, Rabat, Kuwait, Rome, Bonn, Paris and New York; weekly and monthly bulletins; Chair. and Gen. Man. RIDHA HAJRI.

### Foreign Bureaux

**Agence France-Presse (AFP):** 45 ave Habib Bourguiba, Tunis; tel. 337-896; telex 14628; fax 352-414; Chief MARC HUTTEN.

**Agencia EFE** (Spain): 126 rue de Yougoslavie, 1000 Tunis; tel. 331-497; fax 345-976; Chief MANUEL OSTOS.

**Agenzia Nazionale Stampa Associata (ANSA)** (Italy): 1 impasse des Vagues, Tunis; tel. 733-993; telex 12110; fax 733-888; Chief MANUELA FONTANA.

**Informatsionnoye Telegrafnoye Agentstvo Rossii—Telegrafnoye Agentstvo Suverennykh Stran (ITAR—TASS)** (Russia): 2 rue de Damas, Tunis; tel. 282-794; telex 12544; Chief VIKTOR LEBEDEV.

**Inter Press Service (IPS)** (Italy): 6 rue de Nablouss, 1001 Tunis; tel. 880-182; fax 337-809; f. 1976; Chief ABD AL-MAJID BEJAR.

**Reuters** (United Kingdom): BP 369, Belvédère, 1002 Tunis; tel. 787-711; telex 13933; fax 787-454; Chief (vacant).

**Rossiyskoye Informatsionnoye Agentstvo—Novosti (RIA—Novosti)** (Russia): 102 ave de la Liberté, Tunis; tel. 283-781; telex 15448; Chief NICOLAS SOLOGUBOVSKI.

**Tanjug** (Yugoslavia): 4 rue du Libéria, Tunis; Rep. SIME VUCKOVIĆ.

**Xinhua (New China) News Agency** (People's Republic of China): 6 rue Smyrne, Notre Dame, Tunis; tel. 281-308; telex 12127; Dir XIE BINYU.

## Publishers

**Addar al-Arabia Lil Kitab:** 4 rue Mohieddine El Klibi, al-Manar 2, BP 32, 2092 al-Manar 2, Tunis; tel. 888-255; telex 14966; fax 888-365; f. 1975; general literature, children's books, non-fiction; Dir-Gen. REBAH DEKHILI.

**Agence de Promotion de l'Industrie (API):** 63 rue de Syrie, Belvédère, 1002 Tunis; tel. 287-600; telex 14166; f. 1973; industrial investment; Man. Dir PACHA SLAHEDDINE.

**Bouslama Editions:** 15 ave de France, 1000 Tunis; tel. 243-745; telex 14230; fax 381-100; f. 1960; history, children's books; Man. Dir ALI BOUSLAMA.

**Ceres Productions:** 6 ave Abd ar-Rahman Azzam, BP 56, 1002 Tunis; tel. 782-033; fax 787-516; f. 1964; art books, literature, novels; Dir MUHAMMAD BEN SMAIL.

**Dar al-Amal:** rue 2 Mars 1934, Tunis; tel. 264-899; telex 12163; f. 1976; economics, sociology, politics; Man. Dir S. ZOGHLAMI.

**Dar al-Kitab:** 5 ave Bourguiba, 4000 Sousse; tel. 25097; f. 1950; literature, children's books, legal studies, foreign books; Pres. TAIEB KACEM; Dir FAYÇAL KACEM.

**Dar as-Sabah:** Centre Interurbain, BP 441, 1004 El Menzah, Tunis; tel. 717-222; fax 718-366; f. 1951; 200 mems; publishes daily and weekly papers which circulate throughout Tunisia, North Africa, France, Belgium, Luxembourg and Germany; Dir-Gen. MONCEF CHEIKHROUHOU.

**Imprimerie al-Manar:** 12 rue du Tribunal, BP 121, Tunis; tel. 260-641; telex 14894; fax 560-641; f. 1938; general, educational, Islam; Man. Dir HABIB M'HAMDI.

**Institut National de la Statistique:** 70 rue ach-Cham, BP 260, 1080 Tunis; publishes a variety of annuals, periodicals and papers concerned with the economic policy and development of Tunisia.

**Maison Tunisienne d'Edition:** rue de l'Oasis, El Menzah, Tunis; tel. 235-873; telex 12032; fax 353-992; f. 1966; all kinds of books, magazines, etc.; Dir ABDELAZIZ ACHOURI.

*Directory*

**An-Najah—Editions Hedi Ben Abd al-Gheni:** 11 ave de France, Tunis; tel. 246-886; Arab and French books, Koranic texts.

**Société d'Arts Graphiques, d'Edition et de Presse:** 15 rue 2 mars 1934, La Kasbah, Tunis; tel. 264-988; telex 13411; fax 569-736; f. 1974; prints and publishes daily papers, magazines, books, etc.; Chair. and Man. Dir HASSEN FERJANI.

**Société Tunisienne de Diffusion (STD):** 5 ave de Carthage, BP 440, Tunis; tel. 255-000; telex 12521; general and educational books, office supplies; Man. Dir SLAHEDDINE BEN HAMIDA.

**Sud Editions:** 3 ave Louis Braille, 1002 Tunis; tel. 785-179; telex 12363; fax 792-905; f. 1976; Arab literature, art and art history; Man. Dir M. MASMOUDI.

### Government Publishing House

**Imprimerie Officielle de la République Tunisienne:** ave Farhat Hached, 2040 Radès; tel. 434-211; telex 14939; fax 434-234; f. 1860; Man. Dir ROMDHANE BEN MIMOUN.

## Radio and Television

### RADIO

In 1992, according to UNESCO estimates, there were 1.68m. radio receivers and 670,000 television receivers in use.

**Radiodiffusion Télévision Tunisienne:** 71 ave de la Liberté, Tunis; tel. 287-300; telex 14365; government service; broadcasts in Arabic, French and Italian; stations at Gafsa, El-Kef, Monastir, Sfax and Tunis (two); Dir-Gen. ABDELHAFIDH HARGUEM.

### TELEVISION

Television was introduced in northern and central Tunisia in January 1966, and by 1972 transmission covered the country. A relay station to link up with European transmissions was built at al-Haouaria in 1967, and a second channel was introduced in 1983. In 1988 it was announced that the two channels would accept advertising.

## Finance

(cap. = capital; dep. = deposits; res = reserves; m. = million; brs = branches; amounts in dinars unless otherwise stated)

### BANKING
### Central Bank

**Banque Centrale de Tunisie:** 7 rue de la Monnaie, BP 369, Tunis; tel. 340-588; telex 15375; fax 340-615; f. 1958; cap. 6.0m., dep. 1,085.4m., res 42.6m., total assets 2,277.6m. (1990); Gov. ISMAIL KHELIL.

### Commercial Banks

**Alubaf International Bank:** 90–92 ave Hédi Chaker, BP 51, Belvédère, 1002 Tunis; tel. 783-500; telex 14971; fax 784-343; f. 1985; cap. US $10m., dep. $70.0m., res $2.6m., total assets 82.6m. (1992); Chair. MUHAMMAD ABDULJAWAD; Man. Dir PATRICK J. MASON.

**Arab Tunisian Bank:** 9 rue de la Monnaie, 1001 Tunis; tel. 351-155; telex 14205; fax 247-820; f. 1982; cap. 10m., dep. 287.6m., res 10m., total assets 400.5m. (1990); Pres., Dir-Gen. HAMMOUDA BELKHADJE; 14 brs.

**Banque Internationale Arabe de Tunisie:** 70–72 ave Habib Bourguiba, BP 520, 1080 Tunis; tel. 340-733; telex 15396; fax 340-680; f. 1976; cap. 20m., dep. 1,121.7m., res 19.95m., total assets 1,168.4m. (1991); Pres. MOKHTAR FAKHFAKH; Dir-Gen. HABIB FOURATI; 65 brs.

**Banque Nationale Agricole:** rue de la Monnaie, 1001 Tunis; tel. 791-000; telex 15436; fax 791-765; f. 1990 by merger of the Banque Nationale du Développement Agricole and the Banque Nationale de Tunisie; cap. 33m., dep. 2,044.2m., res 49.9m., total assets 2,551.7m. (1991); Pres. HABIB NIFAR; 71 brs.

**Banque du Sud:** 95 ave de la Liberté, Tunis; tel. 289-400; telex 13855; f. 1968; cap. 15m. (1990), dep. 396.1m., res 6m. (1989); Pres. MONCEF KAOUECH; Man. Dir ALLOUCH MILED; 65 brs.

**Banque de Tunisie:** 3 ave de France, BP 289, 1015 Tunis; tel. 259-999; telex 14070; fax 352-321; f. 1884; cap. 18m., dep. 482m., res 23m., total assets 833m. (1994); Pres. FAOUZI BEL KAHIA; 5 brs.

**Citibank N.A.:** 3 ave Jugurtha, BP 72, Belvédère, 1002 Tunis; tel. 790-066; telex 15139; fax 785-556; Gen. Man. BRADLEY LALONDE.

**Crédit Foncier et Commercial de Tunisie:** 13 ave de France, BP 52, 1000 Tunis; tel. 340-511; telex 14079; f. 1967; cap. 30m., res 18.1m., total assets 611.6m. (1993); Chair. and Pres. RACHID BEN YEDDER; Vice-Pres. and Gen. Man. AHMED EL KARM; 66 brs.

# TUNISIA

**Société Tunisienne de Banque;** rue Hedi Nouira, 1001 Tunis; tel. 340-477; telex 14135; fax 340-009; f. 1957; 29.5% govt-owned; cap. 50m., dep. 1,693m., res 29.3m., total assets 1,787.0m. (1993); Chair. and Gen. Man. ABDELLATIF JERIJINI; 109 brs.

**Union Bancaire pour le Commerce et l'Industrie:** 7–9 rue Gamal Abd an-Nasser, BP 829, 1000 Tunis; tel. 245-877; telex 14992; fax 346-737; f. 1961; cap. 15m., total assets 687m. (1992); affiliated to Banque Nationale de Paris Intercontinentale; Chair. ABD AS-SALAM BEN AYED; 28 brs and agencies.

**Union Internationale de Banques SA:** 65 ave Habib Bourguiba, BP 109, 1001 Tunis; tel. 347-000; telex 15397; fax 780-440; f. 1963 as a merging of Tunisian interests by the Société Tunisienne de Banque with Crédit Lyonnais (France) and other foreign banks, including Banca Commerciale Italiana; cap. 10m., dep. 503.9m., res 4.6m. (1988); Pres. and Gen. Man. MUHAMMAD BEN ZOUBIR; 43 brs.

### Merchant Bank

**International Maghreb Bank:** Tunis; f. 1995; auth. cap. 5m.; cap. p.u. 3m.; Chair MONCEF CHEIKH-ROUHOU; CEO ADEL DAJANI.

### Development Banks

**Banque Arabe Tuniso-Libyenne pour le Développement et le Commerce Extérieur:** 25 ave Kheireddine Pacha, BP 102, Belvédère, 1002 Tunis; tel. 781-500; telex 14938; fax 782-818; f. 1983; promotes trade and development projects between Tunisia and Libya, and provides funds for investment in poorer areas; cap. 53.7m., dep. 22.6m.; res. 17.6m. (1993); Pres., Chair. and Gen. Man. NOUREDDINE KOUBAA.

**Banque de Coopération du Maghreb Arabe:** ave Muhammad V, BP 46, Belvédère, 1002 Tunis; tel. 780-311; telex 15199; fax 781-056; f. 1981, began operations 1982; finances joint development projects between Tunisia and Algeria; cap. US $30m. (1988), res $1.8m. (1983); Chair. BABA AMMI HADJI; Dir-Gen. AÏSSA HIDOUSSI.

**Banque de Développement Economique de Tunisie (BDET):** 34 rue Hédi El Karray, El Menzah 1004, BP 48, 1080 Tunis; tel. 718-000; telex 14133; fax 713-744; f. 1959; main source of long term and equity finance for industrial and tourist enterprises; cap. 40m., dep. 585.9m., res 56.1m., total assets 690.4m. (1993); Pres. and Gen. Man. TIJANI CHELLI.

**Banque Tuniso-Koweïtienne de Développement:** ave Muhammad V, BP 49, 1001 Tunis; tel. 340-000; telex 14834; fax 346-106; f. 1981; provides long-term finance for development projects; cap. 100m. (1990); res 103.8m. (1985); Dir-Gen. ABD AL-GHAFFAR EZZEDDINE.

**Société Tuniso-Séoudienne d'Investissement et de Développement (STUSID):** 32 rue Hedi Kharray, BP 20, 1002 Tunis; tel. 718-233; telex 13594; fax 719-233; f. 1981; provides long-term finance for development projects; cap. 100m.; Chair. Dr MAHSOUN BAHJET JALAL; Pres. ABD AL-MAJID FRAJ.

### INSURANCE

**Caisse Tunisienne d'Assurances Mutuelles Agricoles:** 6 ave Habib Thameur, Tunis 1000; tel. 340-933; telex 12451; f. 1912; Pres. MOKTAR BELLAGHA; Dir-Gen. SLAHEDDINE FERCHIOU.

**Compagnie d'Assurances Tous Risques et de Réassurance (ASTREE):** 45 ave Kheireddine Pacha, BP 780, 1002 Tunis; tel. 792-211; telex 15149; fax 794-723; f. 1950; cap. 3m. dinars; Pres. and Dir-Gen. MUHAMMAD HACHICHA.

**Compagnie Tunisienne pour l'Assurance du Commerce Extérieur (COTUNACE):** ave Muhammad V/Montplaisir I, rue 8006, 1002 Tunis; tel. 783-000; telex 17373; fax 782-539; f. 1984; cap. 5m. dinars; 50 mem. cos; Pres. and Dir-Gen. TAOUFIK GAHBICHE.

**Lloyd Tunisien:** 7 ave de Carthage, 1000 Tunis; tel. 340-911; telex 13293; fax 340-909; f. 1945; fire, accident, liability, marine, life; cap. 1m. dinars; Chair. and Man. Dir M. ELTAIEF.

**Société Tunisienne de Réassurance (Tunis-Ré):** ave Muhammad V, 1002 Tunis; tel. 891-011; telex 18767; fax 789-656; f. 1981; all kinds of insurance and reinsurance; Pres., Dir-Gen. EZZEDDINE SOUAI.

## Trade and Industry

### CHAMBERS OF COMMERCE AND INDUSTRY

**Chambre de Commerce et d'Industrie de Tunis:** 1 rue des Entrepreneurs, 1000 Tunis; tel. 242-872; telex 14718; fax 354-744; f. 1888; 25 mems; Pres. YOUNES EL MENNAI.

**Chambre de Commerce et d'Industrie du Centre:** rue Chadli Khaznadar, Sousse; tel. (3) 25044; fax (3) 24227; f. 1895; 23 mems; Pres. KABOUDI MONCEF; Dir-Gen. SASSI FETHI.

**Chambre de Commerce et d'Industrie du Nord:** 46 rue ibn Khaldoun, 7000 Bizerte; tel. 431-044; telex 21086; fax 439-033; f. 1903; 5 mems; Pres. MOKHTAI NAAMAR; Sec.-Gen. MUHAMMAD LARBI ALMIA.

**Chambre de Commerce et d'Industrie de Sfax:** 127 rue Haffouz, BP 794, 3018 Sfax; tel. (4) 296-120; telex 40767; fax (4) 296-121; f. 1895; 25,000 mems; Dir IKRAM MAKIUS.

### STATE ENTERPRISES

**Compagnie des Phosphates de Gafsa (CPG):** Cité Bayech, Gafsa; tel. 22022; telex 60007; f. 1897; production and marketing of phosphates; Pres. MUHAMMAD AL-FADHEL KHELIL.

**Office des Céréales:** Ministry of Agriculture, 30 rue Alain Savery, Tunis; tel. 790-351; telex 14709; fax 789-573; f. 1962; responsible for the cereals industry; Chair. and Dir-Gen. A. SADDEM.

**Office National des Mines:** 24 rue 8601, Tunis; tel. 788-842; telex 15004; fax 794-016; f. 1963; mining of iron ores; research and study of mineral wealth; Pres. and Dir-Gen. ABD AR-RAHMAN TOUHAMI.

**Office National des Pêches (ONP):** Le Port, La Goulette, Tunis; tel. 275-093; telex 12388; marine and fishing authority; Dir-Gen. L. HALAB.

**Office des Terres Domaniales (OTD):** 43 rue d'Iran, Tunis; tel. 280-322; telex 13566; f. 1961; responsible for agricultural production and the management of state-owned lands; Dir BECHIR BEN SMAIL.

**Société Générale des Industries Textiles (SOGITEX):** Bir Kassaa, Ben Arous, Tunis; tel. 297-100; telex 12444; responsible for the textile industry; Chair. BECHIR SAIDANE.

**Société Tunisienne de l'Electricité et du Gaz (STEG):** 38 rue Kemal Atatürk, BP 190, 1080 Tunis; tel. 341-311; telex 14020; fax 349-981; f. 1962; responsible for generation of electricity and for production of natural gas; Pres. and Gen. Man. MONCEF BEN ABDALLAH; 36 branches.

### ECONOMIC AND COMMERCIAL ORGANIZATIONS

**Agence de Promotion de l'Industrie (API):** 63 rue de Syrie, 1002 Tunis; tel. 792-144; telex 14166; fax 792-144; f. 1987 by merger; co-ordinates industrial policy, undertakes feasibility studies, organizes industrial training and establishes industrial zones; overseas offices in Belgium, France, Germany, Italy, the United Kingdom, Sweden and the USA; Pres. and Dir-Gen. MUHAMMAD BEN KHALIFA.

**Centre de Promotion des Exportations (CEPEX):** 28 rue Ghandi, 1001 Tunis; tel. 350-341; telex 14716; fax 353-683; f. 1973; state export promotion organization; Pres. and Dir-Gen. HABIB DALDOUR.

**Office du Commerce de Tunisie (OCT):** 1 rue de Syrie, 1060 Tunis; tel. 682-901; telex 14177; Dir-Gen. MUHAMMAD AMOR.

**Union Nationale des Agriculteurs (UNA):** 6 ave Habib Thameur, 1000 Tunis; tel. 246-920; fax 349-843; f. 1955; Pres. BACHA ABD AL-BAKI.

**Union Tunisienne de l'Industrie, du Commerce et de l'Artisanat (UTICA):** 103 ave de la Liberté, Belvédère, 1002 Tunis; tel. 780-366; telex 18982 TN; fax 782-143; f. 1946; mems: 12 national federations and 150 syndical chambers at national levels; Pres. HEDI JILANI; First Sec.-Gen. ABDALLAH BEN MBAREK.

### TRADE AND OTHER UNIONS

**Union Générale des Etudiants de Tunisie (UGET):** 11 rue d'Espagne, Tunis; f. 1953; 600 mems; Pres. MEKKI FITOURI.

**Union Générale Tunisienne du Travail (UGTT):** 29 place Muhammad Ali, Tunis; f. 1946 by FARHAT HACHED; affiliated to ICFTU; mems 330,000 in 23 affiliated unions; 18-member executive bureau; Chair. HABIB TLIBA; Sec.-Gen. ISMAIL SAHBANI.

**Union Nationale de la Femme Tunisienne (UNFT):** 56 blvd Bab-Benat, Tunis; tel. 260-181; fax 567-131; f. 1956; 100,000 mems; Pres. FAIZA KEFI; Vice-Pres. RADHIA RIZA.

### TRADE FAIR

**Société Foire Internationale de Tunis SA:** BP 1, 2015 Le Kram Tunis; tel. 730-111; telex 15189; fax 730-666; f. 1990; Gen. Man. NEJIB BEN MILED.

## Transport

### RAILWAYS

In 1993 the total length of railways was 2,260 km. A total of 30.6m. passengers travelled by rail in Tunisia in 1992.

**Société du Métro Léger de Tunis (SMLT):** 6 rue Khartoum, BP 4, 1002 Tunis; tel. 780-100; telex 14072; fax 780-371; f. 1981; operates light railway system in and around Tunis (total length 31 km); Dir-Gen. HABIB ALLEGUE.

**Société Nationale des Chemins de Fer Tunisiens (SNCFT):** 67 ave Farhat Hached, Tunis; tel. 249-999; telex 14019; fax 344-045; f. 1956; state organization controlling all Tunisian railways; Pres. and Dir-Gen. MAHMOUD BEN FADHL.

## ROADS

In 1989 there were 29,183 km of roads. Of these, 52 km were motorways, 10,758 km main roads and 6,163 km secondary roads.

**Société Nationale des Transports (SNT):** 1 ave Habib Bourguiba, BP 660, 1001 Tunis; tel. 259-421; telex 15196; fax 342-727; f. 1963; operates 164 local bus routes with 817 buses; Chair. and Man. Dir Moncef Kafsi; Gen. Man. Hassine Hassani.

**Société Nationale de Transport Interurbain (SNTRI):** ave Muhammad V, BP 40, Belvédère, 1002 Tunis; tel. 784-433; telex 18335; fax 786-605; f. 1981; Dir-Gen. Ali Khalbous.

Hammamet and M'Saken each have two **Sociétés Régionales des Transports**, responsible for road transport (one for passengers and one for freight).

## SHIPPING

Tunisia has seven major ports: Tunis-La Goulette, Radès, Bizerta, Sousse, Sfax, Gabès and Zarzis. There is a special petroleum port at La Skhirra.

**Office des Ports Nationaux Tunisiens:** Bâtiment Administratif, Port de la Goulette, La Goulette, Tunis; tel. 735-300; telex 15386; fax 735-812; maritime port administration; Pres. and Dir-Gen. Hassine Hassani.

**Compagnie Tunisienne de Navigation SA:** 5 ave Dag Hammarskjoeld, BP 40, Tunis; tel. 333-925; telex 12475; fax 350-976; brs at Bizerta, Gabès, La Skhirra, La Goulette, Radès, Sfax and Sousse; Chair. C. Hajri.

**Gabès Chimie Transport:** 3 rue de Kenya, Belvédère, 1002 Tunis; tel. 283-174; telex 13323; fax 787-821; transportation of chemicals; fleet of 3 chemical tankers; Chair. Bounatirou Taoufik.

**Société Nationale Maritime Corse-Méditerranée:** 47 ave Farhat Hached, 1001 Tunis; tel. 338-222; telex 13078; fax 330-636.

## CIVIL AVIATION

There are international airports at Tunis-Carthage, Sfax, Djerba, Monastir, Tabarka, Habib Bourguiba, Thyna and Tozeur.

**Office des Ports Aériens:** BP 137, Aéroport International de Tunis-Carthage, Tunis; tel. 288-000; telex 13809; fax 781-460; air traffic control and airport administration; Pres. and Dir-Gen. Houcine Chouk.

**Air Liberté Tunisie:** Monastir; f. 1990; subsidiary of French airline Air Liberté; flights from Tunis, Djerba and Monastir airports to African countries, Scandinavia and other European countries; Chair. Aziz Miled; Man. Dir Slaheddine Kastalli.

**Tunis Air (Société Tunisienne de l'Air):** blvd 7 novembre, 2035 Tunis; tel. 700-100; telex 15283; fax 700-008; f. 1948; 84.9% government-owned; scheduled for privatization in 1995; flights to Africa, Europe and the Middle East; Pres. and Gen. Man. Tahar Hajali.

**Tunisavia (Société de Transports, Services et Travaux Aériens):** Immeuble Saadi Spric, Tour CD, 2080 L'Ariana, Tunis; tel. 717-793; telex 13121; fax 718-100; f. 1974; helicopter and charter operator.

# Tourism

The main tourist attractions are the magnificent sandy beaches, Moorish architecture and remains of the Roman Empire. Tunisia contains the site of the ancient Phoenician city of Carthage. Tourism, a principal source of foreign exchange, has expanded rapidly, following extensive government investment in hotels, improved roads and other facilities. The number of hotel beds increased from 71,529 in 1980 to 152,933 in 1994. In 1994 foreign tourist arrivals totalled 3.9m. (of whom some 2.4m. were European), while earnings from tourism in the same year increased to an estimated 1,300m. dinars.

**Office National du Tourisme Tunisien:** 1 ave Muhammad V, Tunis; tel. 341-077; telex 14381; fax 350997; f. 1958; Dir-Gen. Wahid Ibrahim.

# TURKEY

## Introductory Survey

**Location, Climate, Language, Religion, Flag, Capital**

The Republic of Turkey lies partly in south-eastern Europe and partly in western Asia. The European and Asian portions of the country (known, respectively, as Thrace and Anatolia) are separated by the Sea of Marmara, linking the Black Sea and the Aegean Sea. Turkey has an extensive coastline: on the Black Sea, to the north; on the Mediterranean Sea, to the south; and on the Aegean Sea, to the west. Most of Turkey lies in Asia, the vast Anatolian peninsula being bordered to the east by Armenia, Georgia, the Nakhichevan Autonomous Republic (part of Azerbaijan) and Iran, and to the south by Iraq and Syria. The smaller European part of the country is bordered to the west by Greece and Bulgaria. In the Asian interior the climate is one of great extremes, with hot dry summers and cold, snowy winters on the plateau. Temperatures in Ankara are generally between −4°C (25°F) and 30°C (86°F). On the Mediterranean coast it is more equable, with mild winters and warm summers. The principal language is Turkish, spoken by 90% of the population. About 7% speak Kurdish, mainly in the south-east. In 1928 the Arabic characters of the written Turkish language were superseded by Western-style script. Islam is the religion of 99% of the population. The national flag (proportions 3 by 2) is red, with a white crescent and a five-pointed white star to the left of centre. The capital is Ankara.

**Recent History**

Turkey was formerly a monarchy, ruled by a Sultan, with his capital in Constantinople (now Istanbul). At its zenith, the Turkish Empire, under the Osmanlı (Ottoman) dynasty, extended from the Persian (Arabian) Gulf to Morocco, including most Arab regions and south-eastern Europe. Following the dissolution of the Ottoman Empire after the First World War, political control of Turkey itself passed to the nationalist movement led by Mustafa Kemal, a distinguished army officer. On 23 April 1920, in defiance of the Sultan, a newly-elected assembly established a provisional Government, led by Kemal, in Ankara, then a minor provincial town. Kemal's forces waged war against the Greek army in 1920–22, forcing the Greeks to evacuate Smyrna (Izmir) and eastern Thrace (the European portion of Turkey). The new regime abolished the sultanate in November 1922 and declared Turkey a republic, with Ankara as its capital and Kemal as its first President, on 29 October 1923. The Ottoman caliphate (the former monarch's position as Islamic religious leader) was abolished in March 1924.

Kemal remained President of Turkey, with extensive dictatorial powers, until his death in November 1938. He vigorously pursued a radical programme of far-reaching reform and modernization, including the secularization of the state (in 1928), the abolition of Islamic courts and religious instruction in schools, the emancipation of women (enfranchised in 1934), the banning of polygamy, the development of industry, the introduction of a Latin alphabet, the adoption of the Gregorian (in place of the Islamic) calendar, and the encouragement of European culture and technology. Another westernizing reform was the introduction of surnames in 1934: Kemal assumed the name Atatürk ('Father of the Turks'). His autocratic regime attempted, with considerable success, to replace the country's Islamic traditions by the principles of republicanism, nationalism, populism and state control.

Following Atatürk's death, his Cumhuriyet Halk Partisi (CHP—Republican People's Party), the only authorized political grouping, remained in power under his close associate, İsmet İnönü, who had been Prime Minister in 1923–24 and from 1925 to 1937. İnönü was President from 1938 to 1950, and maintained Turkey's neutrality during most of the Second World War (Turkey declared war on Germany in February 1945). After the war, İnönü introduced some liberalization of the regime. The one-party system was ended in January 1946, when opposition leaders, including Celâl Bayar and Adnan Menderes, registered the Demokratik Parti (DP—Democratic Party). Numerous other parties were subsequently formed.

The DP won Turkey's first free election, in May 1950, and ruled for the next decade. Bayar became President, with Menderes as Prime Minister.

In May 1960 the Government was overthrown by a military coup, led by Gen. Cemal Gürsel, who assumed the presidency, claiming that the DP regime had betrayed Atatürk's principle of secularism. A series of coalition governments, mostly led by İnönü, held office from November 1961 until October 1965, when an election was won by the conservative Adalet Partisi (Justice Party), led by Süleyman Demirel, which appealed to supporters of the former DP. The Demirel Government remained in power until March 1971, when escalating student and labour unrest caused the armed forces to demand its resignation. 'Guided democracy', under military supervision, continued until October 1973, with a succession of right-wing 'non-party' administrations, martial law and the rigorous suppression of all left-wing activities.

The return to civilian rule began in April 1973, when the Grand National Assembly (the legislative body established in 1961) chose Adm. Fahri Korutürk as President, in preference to a candidate supported by the armed forces. Military participation in government was ended by an election in October 1973. No single party received sufficient support to form a government, and negotiations on the creation of a coalition continued until January 1974, when Bülent Ecevit, leader of the CHP (which had become a left-of-centre party), took office as Prime Minister, having negotiated a coalition with the Milli Selamet Partisi (MSP—National Salvation Party), a pro-Islamic right-wing group. Deteriorating relations with Greece were exacerbated by the Greek-backed coup in Cyprus (q.v.) in July 1974, when Turkey responded by dispatching troops, and occupying the northern part of the island, to protect the Turkish Cypriot population. Despite the failure of the coup, Turkish forces kept control of northern Cyprus, and the island remained effectively partitioned.

A long period of political instability was fostered by a succession of unsuccessful coalitions, headed by either Ecevit or Demirel, and prompted an escalation in political violence, mainly involving clashes between left-wing and right-wing groups. By September 1980 the violence was nearing the scale of civil war, with as many as 40 deaths each day.

On 12 September 1980 the armed forces, led by Gen. Kenan Evren, Chief of the General Staff, seized power in a bloodless coup, forming a five-member National Security Council (NSC) which appointed a mainly civilian Cabinet. Martial law was declared throughout the country. In December the NSC published a decree which provided the military regime with unlimited powers. During 1981–83 a campaign to eradicate all possible sources of political violence was undertaken. In April 1981 former politicians were banned from future political activities, and in October all political parties were disbanded.

The new Government succeeded in reducing the level of political violence in Turkey and in establishing law and order. However, the likelihood that this had been achieved only at the expense of human rights caused concern among Western governments: Turkey was banned from the Parliamentary Assembly of the Council of Europe (see p. 134), aid from the European Community (EC, now European Union—EU—see p. 143) was suspended, and fellow-members of NATO urged Turkey to return to democratic rule as soon as possible. In October 1981, a Consultative Assembly was established to draft a new constitution, which was approved by referendum in November 1982, despite widely-expressed objections that excessive powers were to be granted to the President, while judicial powers and the rights of trades unions and the press were to be curtailed. An appended 'temporary article' installed Evren as President for a seven-year term.

In May 1983 the NSC ended a 30-month ban and allowed political parties to be formed, subject to strict rules, in preparation for the first election to be held under the new Constitution. All the former political parties were to remain proscribed, and 723 former members of the Grand National Assembly and leading party officials were banned from political activity for up to 10 years. Followers of the former political parties regrouped under new names and with new leaders. Of the 15 new parties, however, only three were allowed to take part in the election: the Milliyetçi Demokrasi Partisi (MDP—Nationalist Democracy Party) and the Halkçı Partisi (HP—Populist Party), both of which had the tacit support of the NSC, and the conservative Anavatan Partisi (ANAP—Motherland Party), led by Turgut Özal, the former Deputy Prime Minister for Economic Affairs. In the general election of 6 November ANAP won 211 of the 400 seats in the unicameral National Assembly. Accordingly, Özal was appointed Prime Minister in December. Although this result suggested a decisive rejection of military rule, martial law was still in operation in almost one-half of the provinces a year after the election.

In November 1985 the HP and the Sosyal Demokrasi Partisi (Social Democratic Party), respectively the main opposition parties within and outside the National Assembly, merged to form the Sosyal Demokrat Halkçı Parti (SHP—Social Democratic Populist Party). However, the left-wing opposition was split as a result of the formation, a few days later, of the (Demokratik Sol Parti (DSP—Democratic Left Party) which drew support from the former CHP. The MDP voted to disband itself in May 1986. By-elections were held in 11 vacant seats in September. ANAP won six seats, while the Doğru Yol Partisi (DYP—True Path Party), with the unofficial backing of Demirel, had considerable success in winning four seats, but the SHP obtained only one seat. The DSP became a legitimate parliamentary group (i.e. it had more than 20 deputies in the National Assembly) when several deputies from the SHP defected and joined its ranks.

At a national referendum in September 1987, a narrow majority approved the repeal of the ban imposed on more than 200 politicians in 1981, which prohibited them from taking an active part in public life. This result enabled Ecevit to assume the leadership of the DSP, while Demirel was elected as leader of the DYP. In a general election, conducted on 29 November (the first free election in Turkey since the 1980 military coup, ANAP obtained 292 of the 450 seats in the enlarged National Assembly, while the SHP won 99 seats and the DYP won 59 seats. In December Özal formed a new, expanded Cabinet.

Following disappointing results for ANAP at local elections conducted in March 1989, Özal implemented an extensive cabinet reshuffle, which was aimed at restoring public confidence in the Government. In November Özal succeeded Evren as President, having secured the support of the simple majority required in a third round of voting by the National Assembly at the end of October. Özal unexpectedly appointed Yıldırım Akbulut, the Speaker of the National Assembly and a former Minister of the Interior, as Prime Minister.

In October 1990 the resignations of the Minister of Foreign Affairs, Ali Bozer, and the Minister of National Defence, Safa Giray (who were both members of a liberal movement within the ruling party), fuelled rumours of factional disaffection within ANAP. In December 1990 the Chief of Staff of the Armed Forces also resigned, suggesting (as had Bozer) that Özal's exclusive and self-promoting handling of the crisis in the Persian (Arabian) Gulf had prompted his decision to resign. Although Özal's visible and vociferous support for the UN's sanctions against Iraq (and for US initiatives in particular), following the forcible annexation of Kuwait by Iraq in August 1990, did much to enhance Turkey's international standing, political opponents accused the President of jeopardizing Turkey's position in the conflict unnecessarily.

At an ANAP party congress convened on 15 June 1991 Akbulut was defeated by former Minister of Foreign Affairs Mesut Yılmaz in a contest for the party leadership. The following day Akbulut resigned as Prime Minister, and on 17 June, in accordance with the Constitution, President Özal invited Yılmaz, the leader of the liberal faction within ANAP, to head a new administration. The appointment of Yılmaz to the premiership and the composition of a radically-altered Cabinet was widely interpreted as an attempt to balance the influence of the liberal and Islamic fundamentalist movements within the Government.

In a general election, held on 20 October, the DYP, under the leadership of Demirel, received an estimated 27.3% of the votes cast, narrowly defeating ANAP (with 23.9%) and the SHP (with 20.6%). Although the DYP failed to attract the level of support necessary for the formation of a single-party government, it was expected that Demirel would assume the premiership at the head of a coalition government. Following the election, the incumbent Cabinet tendered its resignation; in accordance with the Constitution, Demirel was afforded a 45-day post-election period in which to finalize the composition of a new administration. A new coalition Government, comprising 20 DYP ministers and 12 members of the SHP (who together accounted for 266 of the 450 newly-elected deputies in the National Assembly), was approved by the Assembly in late November. The deputy premiership was assigned to SHP party leader Erdal İnönü. The coalition's programme for political and economic reform included proposals for a new constitution, improvements in anti-terrorist legislation and matters of human rights, and increased levels of cultural recognition and of autonomy in local government for Kurds in Turkey. While international observers were impressed by Demirel's apparent commitment to human rights (the establishment of a separate Ministry of Human Rights, to be headed by an ethnic Kurd, was promptly announced), the formal adoption of amendments to the criminal procedure code, designed to discourage torture (including a proposed reduction in the length of periods of legitimate police detention), were impeded by a lack of consensus within the coalition Government, and the situation was exacerbated during 1992 by a succession of political defections from the SHP, which had reduced the representation of the coalition parties in the National Assembly to 229 by September. Although the DYP and the SHP had performed well at municipal elections conducted in early June (increasing their combined share of national support to 58%, compared with 48% in the October 1991 general election), the reactivation of the CHP in September (as a result of the introduction of more lenient guide-lines for the formation of political parties) threatened to undermine left-wing support for the Government.

At a special ANAP party conference, convened in December 1992, concern was expressed that right-wing extremism had become the dominant force behind the party leadership, prompting the emergence of a dissident, more conservative faction of the party. Some 70 deputies subsequently announced their intention to leave ANAP in order to form a new party, to be headed by President Özal. In April 1993, however, Özal died as a result of heart failure. On 16 May Süleyman Demirel was successfully elected to the presidency, with a simple majority in a third round of voting by the National Assembly. In early June Minister of State Tansu Çiller was elected to the DYP party leadership, and promptly assumed the premiership. Çiller (Turkey's first female Prime Minister) formed a new coalition Cabinet at the end of June, which consisted of the 12 SHP members of the previous Government but replaced 17 former DYP ministers—notably the Interior Minister İsmet Sezgin, who had also stood as a candidate for the DYP leadership, and other ministers loyal to Demirel.

In July 1993 Çiller secured a significant demonstration of support from the National Assembly when it endorsed the Government's economic programme. The new administration, however, was strained by a sharp escalation of violence resulting from the activities of the outlawed Kurdish Workers' Party (PKK) and the response of the Turkish security forces (see below). Çiller withdrew plans to extend cultural and educational rights to the Kurds, in response to opposition from Demirel, right-wing members of the DYP and military leaders, who in October effectively resisted a proposal to discuss the establishment of local autonomy for the Kurdish population in the south-east of the country. In December Çiller replaced five DYP ministers in order further to consolidate her personal support.

In early 1994 Çiller's political standing was adversely affected by a devaluation of the Turkish lira following a loss of confidence in the currency on the part of international credit agencies. The Governor of the Central Bank, who had been appointed by Çiller, resigned at the end of January, and poor economic figures revealed in February aroused opposition to the Prime Minister within the DYP. However, in municipal elections, conducted in late March, the DYP was unexpectedly successful, obtaining 24% of the national votes: Çiller was thus able to pursue her programme of economic austerity. None the less, expectations that the fundamentalist Refah Partisi (RP—Welfare Party) would gain political leverage in the elections were realized as the party obtained

18% of the votes and won overall control of Ankara, İstanbul and 20 other mayorships.

In July 1994 the Constitutional Court cancelled previous parliamentary decrees enabling the acceleration of the sale of state enterprises to private ownership, a key aspect of Çiller's economic programme. In October an attempt to introduce new privatization legislation revealed serious political differences within the coalition Government. Proposals for the democratization of the Constitution also provoked disagreements concerning the extent to which freedoms of expression and movement should be incorporated. Some SHP members threatened to withhold support for the privatization bill until assurances had been made that the reform measures would be implemented. In late November the National Assembly approved legislation enabling some 100 state enterprises to be transferred to the private sector. Thousands of workers participated in a demonstration in Ankara, organized by trade unions, to protest against the new law, despite the inclusion of provisions to compensate for any loss of employment. A few days later the Minister of Foreign Affairs, Mumtaz Soysal (who had unexpectedly entered the Government to replace Hikmet Çetin in a reorganization in July), resigned, owing to persistent differences with Çiller regarding foreign policy issues, the privatization legislation and, finally, a disagreement over the appointment of a new ministry official. Soysal was succeeded by Murat Karayalcin, who retained his position as Deputy Prime Minister.

Elections for 22 vacant Assembly seats, which were to have been held in December 1994, were rescheduled in November, following a ruling by the Constitutional Court that neccessitated the updating of electoral lists—in particular in the southeast of the country, where large-scale population displacement had occurred. The ruling marked a successful appeal by the RP, which was expected to benefit from the new registration of voters, against the Government. The elections (then due to be held on 25 December) were later postponed, in order to avoid polling in harsh winter conditions; however, no new date was determined.

In February 1995 a special conference of the SHP approved a proposal to integrate with the CHP (under the latter's name). Hikmet Çetin was duly elected leader of the enlarged party. The merger increased the Government's majority in the National Assembly, but prompted speculation as to whether the coalition would survive a renegotiation of conditions. An agreement to secure the future of the coalition administration was reached by Çiller and Çetin in March, and an extensive reorganization of the Government (in which Çetin became Deputy Prime Minister and Minister of State, while İnönü assumed the foreign affairs portfolio) was undertaken in order to accomodate the CHP.

In early June 1995 municipal elections were conducted in 34 towns. Çiller actively participated in the campaigning prior to the elections, which she depicted as a test of support for her position as leader of the DYP and for the Government's policies. Provisional results indicated that the DYP secured 39.1% of votes cast in the polls, while the CHP obtained 20.4% and the RP 17.2%.

During the 1980s trials of members of banned (mainly leftwing) political organizations continued, and allegations persisted, from internal and external sources, that torture of prisoners and other violations of human rights were still taking place. Although Turkey was readmitted to the Parliamentary Assembly of the Council of Europe in May 1984, the Assembly continued to advocate the establishment of full democracy and political freedom in the country. In July 1987 all martial law decrees were repealed when martial law was replaced with a state of emergency in several provinces. The Government's signing, in January 1988, of UN and Council of Europe agreements denouncing torture, however, met with a cynical response from both the domestic and international media. In July 1989, at the end of a seven-year trial, a military court sentenced seven left-wing extremists to death, 39 to life imprisonment and more than 300 to prison terms of up to 21 years, for activities dating back to the time of the 1980 military coup. Accusations of violations of human rights were reiterated, despite the Government's assertion that prison reforms would be implemented (raising the standards of Turkish prisons to match those of their Western counterparts), together with changes proposed by the Ministry of Justice to restrict the application of the death penalty. In November 1993 the human rights organization, Amnesty International, expressed concern at the approval given by the National Assembly of death sentences passed on 15 Kurdish separatists.

The Government was criticized by human rights groups in 1993 for its attempts to control the separatist violence, which included the closure of a pro-Kurdish newspaper and the detention of its staff journalists, the arrest in December of two journalists who were placed in a military gaol, following a televised discussion of national service, and the arrest of lawyers defending separatist militants. In March 1994 Western governments condemned the ending of the parliamentary immunity of several deputies of the pro-Kurdish Demokrasi Partisi (DEP—Democracy Party), including its leader, Hatip Dicle, who were arrested on leaving the refuge of the parliament building. Six members of parliament (among them an independent Kurdish deputy) were subsequently detained on charges of separatism. In June the Constitutional Court declared DEP to be an illegal movement, thus extending a detention order to all its deputies. The trial of the former deputies, imprisoned since March, commenced in August, attracting international media attention. In October members of the European Parliament suspended relations with Turkish deputies, in order to express their concern over the case. In December, having retracted the charges of treason, punishable by the death penalty, the Court imposed sentences of between three-and-a-half and 15 years, imprisonment on the defendants (as well as on the two DEP deputies who had not left the country and who had been arrested in July, following the Court's proscription of the party). The severity of the sentences was criticized by the EU, the US Government and human rights organizations.

A significant increase in outbreaks of urban terrorism in early 1990, coupled with a perceived increase in the influence of fundamentalist thought, led to widespread fears of a return to the extremist violence of the late 1970s. The increase in terrorist attacks by Islamic groups and left-wing groups, especially the Dev-Sol (Revolutionary Left), was exacerbated by the Government's stance in the Gulf Crisis (see below), and both factions unleashed a series of attacks against Western targets in Turkey, including US civilians, diplomatic missions and offices of several national airlines and banks in İstanbul and Ankara. The leader of Dev-Sol, Dursun Karatas, was detained in France, in September 1994, and diplomatic efforts began to ensure his extradition. Two weeks later a former Minister of Justice, Mehmet Topaç, was shot dead by Dev-Sol members in Ankara. In July 1993 some 36 people died in a fire started by Islamic fundamentalists who were protesting against a liberal cultural festival, organized by members of the secularist Alewi minority, that was being held in the eastern town of Sivas. The Cabinet, in an emergency meeting, responded to the renewed violence by imposing a curfew on Sivas and by dismissing the Director-General of the police force. Further serious violence occurred in March 1995, when militant Islamic fundamentalists opened fire on coffee houses in İstanbul associated with the Alewi sect. The incident provoked protests and clashes between the two groups, and subsequently, following allegations of violent repression of the unrest by the authorities, with the police. The civic disorder, which lasted several days, resulted in some 25 deaths.

In early April 1991 a draft anti-terrorism bill was approved by the National Assembly. Presented as a move towards greater liberalization and democratization, the bill contained provisions for the abolition of certain controversial articles of the penal code. The extent to which the bill would provide for greater democracy was, however, largely confused by the continued existence of separate laws reinforcing many of the articles abolished by the new legislation. By mid-April it was reported that some 5,000 political prisoners (of an estimated 250,000 detained since 1980) had already been released as a result of the new bill.

The opposition to Turkish rule by non-Turkish minorities within the country, particularly Kurds and Armenians, has been a long-standing source of tension. Armenian guerrilla groups responsible for a succession of terrorist attacks against Turkish officials overseas, perpetrated since the early 1970s, claim to be seeking revenge for the Turkish massacre of an estimated 1.5m. Armenians in 1915 and for the subsequent expulsion of Armenian survivors from their traditional territories in north-eastern Turkey, where a short-lived independent Armenian republic was violently suppressed by Turkish forces in 1920–21.

During the 1980s the Turkish authorities also encountered violent opposition from Kurdish secessionists. Despite the fact that there are an estimated 3m.-10m. Kurds in Turkey, they are not officially recognized as a separate ethnic group. In 1984 the outlawed PKK, which supports the creation of a Kurdish national homeland in Turkey, launched a violent guerrilla campaign against the Turkish authorities in the south-eastern provinces. The Government responded by arresting suspected Kurdish leaders, sending in more security forces, establishing local militia groups, and imposing martial law (and later states of emergency) in the troubled provinces. Violence continued to escalate, however, and in April and May 1990 clashes between rebel Kurds, security forces and civilians resulted in the deaths of 140 people, constituting the bloodiest period of the conflict since August 1984. In early 1991, in the context of the Kurdish uprising in Iraq, President Özal sought to alleviate mounting tension among Turkish Kurds by announcing the Government's decision to review existing legislation proscribing the use of languages other than Turkish and by allowing Kurds to celebrate openly the Kurdish new year for the first time. By mid-1991, however, a new wave of violence between the PKK guerrillas and the security forces had erupted in the south-eastern provinces. The conflict entered a new phase when in August and October 1991, and March 1992 (in retaliation for continuing cross-border attacks on Turkish troops), government fighter planes conducted numerous sorties into northern Iraq in order to attack suspected PKK bases there. In the course of these raids many civilians and refugees (including Iraqi Kurds) were reportedly killed, prompting international observers and relief workers publicly to call into question the integrity of the exercises. In October 1991 the Iraqi Government had lodged formal complaints with the UN, denouncing Turkish violations of Iraq's territorial integrity. In March 1992, in response to revelations that German-supplied armoured personnel vehicles had been used by Turkish security forces in attempts to suppress Kurdish insurgents, the German Government suspended all trade in arms with Turkey. A deterioration in relations between the two countries was exacerbated in April by the insistence of the German Government that a formal EC protest deploring Turkish antiinsurgency operations be drafted and delivered to Ankara.

Violence in the south-eastern provinces, resulting from ethnic tension, persisted into 1992, and, despite the stated commitment of the Demirel administration to foster new initiatives for improved relations with ethnic minorities, attempts to amend existing legislation so as to restrict the powers of the security forces were frustrated by lack of consensus within the ruling coalition. The armed response of the security forces to an escalation in violence in mid-1992 (together with the National Security Council's recommendation for a renewal of the state of emergency, dating from 1987, in several southern provinces) demonstrated no significant departure from anti-insurgency measures employed by the previous administration.

In late 1992 Turkish air and ground forces (in excess of 20,000 troops), conducted further attacks upon PKK bases inside northern Iraq, hoping to take advantage of losses inflicted on the Kurdish rebels by a simultaneous offensive, initiated by Iraqi Kurdish *peshmerga* forces in October, with the aim of forcing the PKK from Iraq. By mid-December most Turkish ground forces had been withdrawn from Iraqi territory, and in January 1993, the Turkish military offensive was redirected against PKK strongholds in south-eastern Turkey. Hopes that a negotiated resolution to the conflict might be achieved, following the unilateral declaration of a cease-fire by the PKK in March, were frustrated by renewed fighting in May. The conflict escalated dramatically in June, after the PKK announced that it would intensify its campaign. The bombing of several coastal resorts and of tourist attractions in central İstanbul confirmed the PKK's intention to disrupt the country's economy and attract international attention to the conflict. International concern increased in the second half of 1993, as foreign nationals were seized and held by the PKK.

In late June 1993 PKK activists and supporters conducted protests and attacked Turkish property throughout Europe. At the Turkish consulate in Munich, Germany, some 20 members of staff were briefly held hostage by the PKK, and in Bern, Switzerland, a Kurdish demonstrator outside the Turkish embassy was killed, allegedly shot by a member of the embassy staff. Diplomatic relations between Switzerland and Turkey subsequently deteriorated, owing to the refusal of the Turkish Government to withdraw the diplomatic immunity of the embassy staff, the transfer of the Turkish Ambassador, and the expulsion of the Swiss Ambassador to Turkey at the end of August. Following similar disturbances in November (in which the PKK denied participation), Germany and France declared a ban on all PKK activities on their territory.

In November 1993 the Government announced the creation of a 10,000-strong élite anti-terrorist force to counter the PKK fighters, in addition to the estimated 150,000–200,000 troops already positioned in the area of conflict. In early 1994 the security forces mounted an intensified offensive against the separatists, and conducted air attacks on suspected PKK strongholds in south-eastern Turkey and in northern Iraq. Reports that an estimated 6,000 Kurds were forcibly displaced into northern Iraq as a result of the destruction of their villages by security forces were denied by the Minister of Foreign Affairs. Further air offensives against Kurdish targets in northern Iraq were undertaken in August, while clashes between the PKK and security forces were reported in south-eastern Turkey. In late September the security forces initiated an operation in the eastern Munzur mountains, which included the burning of villages, in order to destroy PKK stores and supply routes. By October an estimated 5,130 people had been killed since the beginning of the year as a result of the conflict, of an official total of 13,000 since 1984. In November a Kurdish proposal for a cease-fire, accompanied by international mediation, to achieve a peaceful settlement to the conflict was rejected by the Government, which emphasized the success of its anti-terrorist campaign.

On 20 March 1995 a massive offensive involving 35,000 air and ground force troops, was initiated against PKK targets in northern Iraq. Turkish forces advanced some 40 km across the border, prompting protests from Iraq that the operation was a violation of its territorial sovereignty, as well as concern on the part of the USA and the EU that the military intervention must not be consolidated into a permanent occupation force. The Turkish Government insisted that the offensive was designed to destroy PKK base camps and to force the separatists from northern Iraq (necessary, it was claimed, since the PKK had taken advantage of a power vacuum in the region to become securely established). The UN assisted in the evacuation of several thousand Kurds from the northern Iraqi town of Zakho, amid reports of intimidation by the occupying Turkish troops. At the end of April Turkey announced the withdrawal of the majority of its troops, although 12,000 were to remain in the area. At the same time the Council of Europe, embodying the widespread condemnation by the international community of the continuing Turkish presence in northern Iraq, voted to suspend Turkey from the organization, with effect from 26 June, unless 'significant progress' had been made in the withdrawal of all Turkish troops. Earlier in April the PKK obtained permission to convene in the Netherlands, in an attempt to establish a Kurdish parliament-in-exile. Turkey recalled its Ambassador to that country in protest. In early May the Minister of Defence, Mehmet Golhan, announced the complete withdrawal of Turkish troops from northern Iraq. However, other reports from government members, including Çiller, indicated that some 3,000 troops remained in the region, although these were to be withdrawn later that month. At that time official figures stated that 555 Kurdish separatists and 58 Turkish soldiers had been killed as a result of the operation, while 13 separatists had been captured.

In August 1988 the Iraqi armed forces launched a major offensive against Kurdish separatists in northern Iraq. Thousands (an estimated 100,000–150,000 by early September) fled to the Turkish border, where, after initial hesitation, the Turkish Government opened the border to them on 'humanitarian grounds' and gave them asylum in makeshift camps. Following the Iraqi invasion of Kuwait in August 1990, the Turkish Government swiftly complied with UN proposals for economic sanctions against Iraq, and Turkey's border with Iraq was closed to all but essential supplies (and to all traffic in January 1991). Turkish nationals were evacuated from Iraq and Kuwait, and as many as 130,000 troops were redeployed along Turkey's border with Iraq. Despite the increase in the number of Turkish troops in the border region and the deployment of additional US and NATO aircraft in south-east Turkey in early 1991 (see below), President Özal continued to stress that Turkey had no intention of opening a second military front against Iraq and that Turkish forces would continue to guarantee Iraq's 'territorial integrity'.

In early March 1991 President Özal revealed that high-level talks had been conducted in Turkey between senior Turkish foreign ministry officials and the leaders of Kurdish groups within Iraq, during which Turkey had endorsed the notion of some form of autonomy for Iraqi Kurds within Iraqi territory. By the beginning of April, having suffered serious reversals at the hands of the Iraqi armed forces, more than 500,000 Iraqi refugees (mainly Kurds) were reported to be fleeing to the Turkish border. Although the Turkish Government formally announced the closure of the border, claiming that it was unable to accommodate such a large-scale exodus, by mid-April it was estimated that some 600,000 refugees (including 400,000 within Turkish borders) were encamped in the mountainous border region. Following intense international pressure, the Turkish authorities began to make provision for the removal of up to 20,000 of those refugees in greatest need of medical attention to better conditions at an existing camp at Silopi, inside Turkey. The Government insisted that such initiatives were merely temporary measures, and that the ultimate aim of the relief effort must be the complete repatriation of the Kurds. By mid-May it was estimated that some 200,000 refugees had returned to Iraq, while 89,000 remained in Turkey and a further 162,000 were still encamped on the Iraqi side of the border with Turkey.

Following the completion of the first phase of the international relief effort for the Kurdish refugees and the subsequent withdrawal of coalition forces, the Turkish Government agreed to the deployment in south-east Turkey of a 3,000-strong multinational 'rapid reaction force', which would respond to any further act of aggression by Iraq against the Kurds in the newly-created 'safe havens'. The force, to be jointly commanded by the USA and Turkey (the latter would reserve the right to veto attacks against Iraq launched from Turkish territory or airspace) would include a 1,000-strong Turkish battalion. In September 1991 the Government approved a 90-day extension for the presence, in south-east Turkey, of a small allied air-strike force; however, all allied ground forces were withdrawn in October. The Turkish authorities have continued to support the operation by granting six-month extensions of the mandate permitting the use of Turkish air bases for allied patrols of northern Iraq. In March 1995 the operation was suspended, on the initiative of the USA, owing to Turkey's military incursion into the region (see above).

Turkey has been a member of NATO since 1952, and is widely considered to have fulfilled a crucial role in NATO defence strategy in south-eastern Europe. The Turkish Government responded positively to requests from the USA for logistical aid, following the forcible annexation of Kuwait by Iraq in August 1990. September Turkey and the USA extended an agreement to allow the USA access to more than 25 military establishments, in return for military and economic aid, that had been initially signed in 1980, and renewed in 1987. In January 1991 it was reported that the Turkish Government had requested that the USA increase the number of US aircraft based in Turkey, which (together with aircraft from NATO's Allied Command Europe mobile force, which had been requested by the Government in December 1990) would constitute an effective deterrent to any possible Iraqi aggression while emphasizing NATO solidarity in the region. Two US-supplied Patriot air defence missile systems were also to be deployed at bases in southern Turkey. In mid-January 1991 a resolution to extend the war powers of the Government and effectively endorse the unrestricted use of Turkish air bases by coalition forces was agreed by the National Assembly. On the following day US aircraft embarked upon bombing missions into north-east Iraq from NATO bases inside south-east Turkey. In February and March the US Government announced substantial increases in military and economic aid to Turkey 1991–92. In September 1991 the 1980 defence and economic co-operation agreement was extended for a further year. In June 1992 it was announced that all US military personnel were to be withdrawn from the jointly-administered base at Sinop, near the Black Sea, by the end of 1993. Difficulties in Turkey's relations with the USA arose in 1994, following a decision by the US Congress to withhold a portion of military and economic aid (amounting to 25%, then reduced to 10%, of the total of US $453m.) in order to encourage greater respect for human rights in the Turkish Government's treatment of Kurdish separatists. In August Çiller rejected this conditional aid, insisting that Turkey's anti-terrorism campaign was a domestic matter.

Although Turkey and Greece are both members of NATO, long-standing disputes over sovereignty in the Aegean Sea and concerning Cyprus have strained relations between the two countries, and tension was exacerbated when Turkey granted recognition to the 'Turkish Republic of Northern Cyprus' ('TRNC'), proclaimed in November 1983 (see chapter on Cyprus). Turkey is the only country to have recognized the 'TRNC', and in May 1984 the two exchanged ambassadors. In April 1988 the Greek Prime Minister, Andreas Papandreou, officially accepted Turkey's status as an associate of the EC by signing the Protocol of Adaptation (consequent on Greece's accession to the EC) to the EC-Turkey Association Agreement, which the Greek Government had hitherto refused to do. In February 1990 relations deteriorated again, following violent clashes between Christians and the Muslim minority in western Thrace, in Greece. Throughout the early 1990s Turkey and Greece maintained strong support for their respective communities in Cyprus during the ongoing, but frequently interrupted, negotiations to resolve the issue. In August 1994 the Turkish Government supported the decision of the 'TRNC' Assembly to reject any solution based on a federal arrangement, and indicated Turkey's willingness to extend co-operation and integration with the 'TRNC'. Relations with Greece deteriorated during 1994, in particular owing to the issue of the demarcation of territorial waters in the Aegean Sea. Turkey insisted that it would retaliate against any expansion of territorial waters by Greece (as provided for under the terms of the UN Convention on the Law of the Sea—see p.34 that was scheduled to enter into force in mid-November). In the event, no action was taken by either country.

Two long-standing problems between Turkey and the EU have been the high number of Turkish workers within EU countries, and the quantity of textiles exported from Turkey to the EU. Aid from the (then) EC to Turkey was suspended following the 1980 military coup, and its full resumption was expected to depend on improved observance of human rights in Turkey. Greece has also demanded, as a further condition to its agreement to the release of EU aid to Turkey, the complete withdrawal of Turkish troops from Cyprus. In September 1986 Turkey was readmitted to associate membership of the EC, when the Turkish-EC Association Council (which was established in 1963, but had been suspended since the army coup in 1980) met for talks in Brussels, Belgium. Turkey, however, failed to gain access to the suspended EC aid and to extend the rights of Turkish workers in Europe. In April 1987 Turkey made a formal application to become a full member of the EC. In December 1989 the application was effectively rejected, at least until 1993, by the Commission of the European Communities. The Commission cited factors including Turkey's unsatisfactory human rights record, high rate of inflation, dependence upon the rural population and inadequate social security provisions as falling short of EC expectations. During informal discussions in 1993 representatives of the EC reiterated their concern at abuses of human rights in Turkey and the effective lack of progress in the political negotiations regarding Cyprus; however, they recognized the strategic importance of Turkey's role as a stable regional influence. The Turkish Government began to implement measures to construct a customs union with the EU, which was to become effective on 1 January 1995. Human rights issues remained a source of tension, and in December 1994 the Turkey-EU Association Council postponed the Customs Union agreement on these grounds. An attempt to conclude the agreement in January 1995 was unsuccessful, owing to opposition from the Greek Government. (The negotiations were complicated by Greek demands concerning EU relations with Cyprus.) In February Greece withdrew its veto on the Customs Union, having secured an arrangement whereby the EU would commence accession negotiations with Cyprus following the Union's 1996 intergovernmental conference. The agreement was signed in March 1995, and the Customs Union was scheduled to enter into force on 1 January 1996, subject to approval by the European Parliament.

Following the formal dissolution of the USSR in December 1991, the Turkish Government sought to further its political, economic and cultural influence in the central Asian region, in particular with the six Muslim states of the former Soviet

Union. In April 1992 Prime Minister Demirel undertook an official visit to several former Soviet republics, pledging aid of more than US $1,000m. in the form of credits for the purchase of Turkish goods and contracts. At the same time programmes broadcast by the Turkish national television company began to be relayed, by satellite, to the region. In June leaders of 11 nations, including Turkey, Greece, Albania and six former Soviet republics, established the Black Sea Economic Co-operation Group (see p. 238), and expressed their commitment to promoting greater co-operation with regard to transport, energy, information, communications and ecology. In December 1993 the Group, meeting in Bulgaria, agreed to establish a joint investment bank, the Black Sea Trade and Development Bank—to be based in Thessaloniki, Greece, with a Turkish presidency.

The Turkish Government's concern at the regional conflict between Armenia and Azerbaijan increased in mid-1993, when military losses and political and economic instability resulted in the overthrow of the Azeri President, Abulfaz Elchibay, who had promoted closer relations with Turkey. In September Turkey began to mobilize along the Armenian border, and demanded an unconditional withdrawal of Armenian forces from seized Azeri territory. Turkey has pursued a policy of support for the Azeri authorities, while promoting the need for peace in the region. The Turkish Government has promised to remove any obstructions to the provision of aid to, or the promotion of trade with, Armenia once a peaceful settlement to the Azeri–Armenian conflict has been concluded. In October 1994 a meeting of the Heads of State of Turkey, Azerbaijan, Turkmenistan, Uzbekistan, Kazakhstan and Kyrgyzstan took place in İstanbul, in an effort to develop and improve relations among the 'Turkic' republics.

In July 1994 an agreement was concluded with Russia on terms for the repayment of debt to Turkey, together with accords to increase co-operation in the fields of culture, science and health. Relations with Russia were, however, adversely affected in early 1995, owing to Turkey's criticism of the Russian authorities' suppression of the separatist movement in Chechnya, and Russia's insistence that weapons were reaching the conflict area via Turkey.

In the former Yugoslavia, Turkey has been strongly supportive of the Bosnian Muslims, and has endorsed the use of NATO air strikes against Serb targets and advocated the removal of the UN embargo on the sale of armaments to Bosnia and Herzegovina. In July 1994 Turkey initiated a series of tripartite meetings with the Ministers of Foreign Affairs of Croatia and of Bosnia and Herzegovina, during which a peace settlement based on the establishment of a Muslim-Croat federation was discussed. A contingent of some 1,500 Turkish troops was dispatched to the former Yugoslavia in mid-1994, to serve in the UN Protection Force and its successor operations (see p. 52 and Late Information).

## Government

Under the Constitution approved by referendum in November 1982, legislative power is vested in the unicameral National Assembly, with 400 deputies, who are elected by universal adult suffrage for a five-year term. Executive power is vested in the President, to be elected by the National Assembly for a seven-year term and empowered to appoint a Prime Minister and senior members of the judiciary, the Central Bank and broadcasting organizations; to dissolve the National Assembly; and to declare a state of emergency entailing rule by decree. An amendment, adopted in June 1987, increased the number of deputies in the National Assembly from 400 to 450.

For administrative purposes, Turkey comprises 74 provinces and 2,074 municipalities.

## Defence

Turkey joined the North Atlantic Treaty Organisation (NATO) in 1952. Military service in the army lasts for 18 months. The total strength of the active armed forces in June 1994 was 503,800 (including 410,200 conscripts), comprising an army of 393,000, a navy of 54,000 and an air force of 56,800. There was a gendarmerie numbering 70,000. Reserve forces totalled 952,300 in the armed forces and 50,000 in the gendarmerie. Defence expenditure for 1994 was budgeted at TL 93,453,000m.

## Economic Affairs

In 1993, according to estimates by the World Bank, Turkey's gross national product (GNP), measured at average 1991–93 prices, was US $126,330m., equivalent to $2,120 per head. During 1985–93, it was estimated, GNP per head increased, in real terms, at an average annual rate of 3.0%. Over the same period the population increased by an annual average of 2.1%. Turkey's gross domestic product (GDP) increased, in real terms, by an annual average of 4.9% in 1980–92.

Agriculture (including forestry and fishing) contributed 16.3% of GDP in 1994. About 43.6% of the employed population were engaged in agriculture in 1993. The country is self-sufficient in most basic foodstuffs, although some 605,000 metric tons of cereals were imported in 1992. The principal agricultural exports are cotton, tobacco, wheat, fruit and nuts. Other important crops are barley, sunflower and other oilseeds, maize, sugar beet, potatoes, tea and olives. The raising of sheep, goats, cattle and poultry is also an important branch of the economy. During 1980–92 agricultural GDP increased by an annual average of 2.8%.

Industry (including mining, manufacturing, construction and power) provided 31.3% of GDP in 1994, and engaged 22.2% of the employed population in 1993. During 1980–92 industrial GDP increased by an annual average of 5.8%.

Mining contributed 1.3% of GDP in 1994 and engaged 0.8% of the employed population in 1993. Chromium, copper and borax are the major mineral exports. Coal, petroleum, natural gas, bauxite, iron ore, manganese and sulphur are also mined.

Manufacturing contributed 20.1% of GDP in 1994. In 1993 15.0% of the employed population were engaged in the sector. The most important branches, measured by gross value of output, are textiles, food-processing, petroleum refineries, iron and steel, and industrial chemicals. In 1994 the textiles and clothing sector accounted for 30.5% of total export revenues. During 1980–92 manufacturing GDP increased by an annual average of 6.7%.

Energy is derived principally from thermal power plants (which account for around 70% of total energy generation), using petroleum, lignite and coal, and hydroelectric power. Total domestic output of crude petroleum and natural gas accounts for roughly 12% of the country's hydrocarbon requirements. Imports of crude petroleum comprised 10.5% of the value of total imports in 1994.

Tourism is one of Turkey's fastest growing sources of revenue. In 1994 revenues from around 6.7m. visitors to the country totalled US $4,321m. Remittances from Turkish workers abroad also make an important contribution to the economy, amounting to $2,664m. in 1994.

In 1994 Turkey recorded a visible trade deficit of US $4,216m., while there was a surplus of $2,631m. on the current account of the balance of payments. In 1994 the principal source of imports (15.7%) was Germany, which was also the principal market for exports (21.7%). Other major trading partners in 1994 were the USA, Italy, France, Saudi Arabia and the United Kingdom. The UN restrictions on trade with Iraq have overturned Turkey's previously strong trading relations with that country. Exports in 1994 were dominated by textiles and textile goods and iron and steel. In that year the principal imports were machinery, crude petroleum, iron and steel, transport vehicles and chemical products.

In 1992 there was a budgetary deficit of TL 47,328,000m. (equivalent to some 4.5% of GDP). Turkey's external debt at the end of 1993 was US $67,862m., of which $43,321m. was long-term public debt. In that year the cost of debt-servicing was equivalent to 28.3% of the value of exports of goods and services. The annual rate of inflation averaged 58.4% in 1985–93, and stood at 66.1% in 1993 and 106.3% in 1994. In 1993 unemployment was estimated at 7.9% of the labour force.

Turkey is a member of numerous international and regional organizations, including the Black Sea Economic Co-operation Group (see p. 238) and the Economic Co-operation Organization (ECO, see p. 238).

In spite of a rigorous economic plan adopted by Prime Minister Tansu Çiller, who took office in June 1993, figures released in February 1994 demonstrated that the budget deficit had doubled over the year and inflation remained high. In April, following a devaluation of the Turkish lira in January and a continuing sharp decline in the value of the currency, Çiller announced an austerity programme that included price rises of 80% on state-controlled products, a reduction of public-sector expenditure and an acceleration of 'privatizations' of state enterprises, in order to prevent long-term damage to Turkey's previously high rates of economic growth and foreign investment. This programme helped to restore international confidence in the Turkish economy and to secure an IMF stand-by loan, approved in July, of US $742m. Efforts to transfer many state enterprises to the private sector were to be promoted in 1995, following parliamentary approval, in November 1994, of new privatization legislation: the process was expected to generate revenue of $5,000m. in 1995. However, the legislation stipulates that this income may not be incorporated into the state budget, but must be transferred into funds to develop further the privatization process and to provide compensation for the predicted large-scale loss of employment. The 1995 budget envisaged a return to positive growth of the domestic economy (following a decline of an estimated 5.4% in 1994) and a reduction in the rate of inflation to 22.5% by the end of 1995 (although this figure was revised to 40% in March, as a result of discussions with IMF representatives). However, the management of the economy is likely to be afflicted by persisting negative elements, including a poor rate of tax collection and the internal war (costing an estimated $8,000m. each year), as well as by factors such as the vulnerability of the agricultural sector to adverse climatic conditions. In the long term, a major development project for south-east Anatolia, scheduled for completion in 2005 at an estimated cost of $11,000m., aims to increase Turkey's energy production by 70% and to irrigate 1.6m. ha of uncultivable or inadequately irrigated land, by constructing dams and hydroelectric plants on the Tigris and Euphrates rivers and their tributaries.

### Social Welfare

Social insurance for wage-earners is provided by the Workers' Social Insurance Institution of the Ministry of Labour and Social Security. In 1978 about 2.5m. workers and employees were covered by social insurance, including free medical care. In 1982 Turkey had 668 hospital establishments, with a total of 98,382 beds (equivalent to one for every 471 inhabitants), and in 1985 there were 36,427 physicians working in the country. Of total expenditure by the central Government in 1992, about TL 7,870,000m. (3.5%) was for health services, and a further TL 4,782,000m. (2.1%) for social security and welfare.

### Education

According to official estimates, the rate of adult illiteracy in 1984 averaged 25.8% (males 14.1%; females 37.5%); in 1990, according to census results, the rate was 20.8% (males 10.1%; females 31.5%). Education is compulsory for five years, to be undertaken between six and 14 years of age. All state education up to University or Higher Institute levels is co-educational and provided free of charge. The number of primary schools reached 49,974 in 1992/93, compared with 12,511 in 1950, and about 6.7m. children were receiving primary education, which lasts five years. In 1990 an estimated 99% of children in the relevant age-group were enrolled in primary schools. Secondary education, beginning at the age of 11, lasts for up to six years, comprising two equal cycles. The Middle School period lasts for three years, after which students may proceed to the Lycées for a further three years. In 1991 the total enrolment at primary and secondary schools was equivalent to 78% of the school-age population (boys 84%; girls 71%). A state examination must be passed by Lycée students wishing to proceed to a university or to an Institute of Higher Education. There were 1,385 Lycées in Turkey in 1988. By early 1994 the number of universities had increased from 19 in 1982 to 56. In 1992 expenditure on education by the central Government was about TL 45,114,000m. (20.0% of total spending).

### Public Holidays

**1995:** 1 January (New Year's Day), 3 March* (Şeker Bayram—End of Ramadan), 23 April (National Sovereignty and Children's Day), 10 May* (Kurban Bayram—Feast of the Sacrifice), 19 May (Commemoration of Atatürk and Youth and Sports Day), 30 August (Victory Day), 29 October (Republic Day).

**1996:** 1 January (New Year's Day), 21 February* (Şeker Bayram—End of Ramadan), 23 April (National Sovereignty and Children's Day), 29 April* (Kurban Bayram—Feast of the Sacrifice), 19 May (Commemoration of Atatürk and Youth and Sports Day), 30 August (Victory Day), 29 October (Republic Day).

* These holidays are dependent on the Islamic lunar calendar and may vary by one or two days from the dates given.

### Weights and Measures

The metric system is in force.

TURKEY

# Statistical Survey

Source (unless otherwise stated): Türkiye İş Bankası AS, Economic Research Dept, Atatürk Bul. 191, 06684 Kavaklıdere, Ankara; tel. (312) 4188096; telex 42082; fax (312) 4250750.

## Area and Population

### AREA, POPULATION AND DENSITY

| | |
|---|---|
| Area (sq km) | 779,452* |
| Population (census results) | |
| 20 October 1985 | |
| Males | 25,671,975 |
| Females | 24,992,483 |
| Total | 50,664,458 |
| 21 October 1990 | 56,473,035† |
| Population (official estimates at mid-year) | |
| 1992 | 58,584,000 |
| 1993 | 59,869,000 |
| 1994 | 61,183,000 |
| Density (per sq km) at mid-1994 | 78.5 |

* 300,948 sq miles. The total comprises Anatolia (Turkey in Asia or Asia Minor), with an area of 755,688 sq km (291,773 sq miles), and Thrace (Turkey in Europe), with an area of 23,764 sq km (9,175 sq miles).
† Comprising 50,497,586 in Anatolia and 5,975,449 in Thrace.

### PRINCIPAL TOWNS (population at 1990 census)

| | | | |
|---|---|---|---|
| Ankara (capital)* | 2,559,471 | Diyarbakir | 381,144 |
| İstanbul* | 6,620,241 | Antalya | 378,208 |
| İzmir (Smyrna)* | 1,757,414 | Samsun | 303,979 |
| Adana* | 916,150 | Malatya | 281,776 |
| Bursa | 834,576 | Şanlıurfa | 276,528 |
| Gaziantep | 603,434 | İzmit (Kocaeli) | 256,882 |
| Konya | 513,346 | Erzurum | 242,391 |
| Mersin (İçel) | 422,357 | Kahramanmaraş | 228,129 |
| Kayseri | 421,362 | Sivas | 221,512 |
| Eskişehir | 413,082 | | |

* Within municipal boundaries.

### BIRTHS AND DEATHS (UN estimates, annual averages)

| | 1975–80 | 1980–85 | 1985–90 |
|---|---|---|---|
| Birth rate (per 1,000) | 32.0 | 31.2 | 29.7 |
| Death rate (per 1,000) | 10.2 | 9.4 | 7.9 |

**Expectation of life** (UN estimates, years at birth, 1985–90): 65.3 (males 62.8; females 68.0).

Source: UN, *World Population Prospects: The 1992 Revision.*

### ECONOMICALLY ACTIVE POPULATION
(sample survey, persons aged 12 years and over, October 1993)

| | Males | Females | Total |
|---|---|---|---|
| Agriculture, hunting, forestry and fishing | 4,029,386 | 4,407,550 | 8,436,936 |
| Mining and quarrying | 148,505 | 2,081 | 150,586 |
| Manufacturing | 2,258,019 | 644,711 | 2,902,730 |
| Electricity, gas and water | 104,997 | 5,682 | 110,679 |
| Construction | 1,119,038 | 17,598 | 1,136,636 |
| Trade, restaurants and hotels | 2,290,396 | 186,409 | 2,476,805 |
| Transport, storage and communications | 891,511 | 62,626 | 954,137 |
| Financing, insurance, real estate and business services | 358,692 | 112,110 | 470,802 |
| Community, social and personal services | 2,146,956 | 551,647 | 2,698,603 |
| **Total employed** | 13,347,500 | 5,990,414 | 19,337,914 |
| Unemployed* | 1,191,472 | 467,316 | 1,658,788 |
| **Total labour force** | 14,538,972 | 6,457,730 | 20,996,702 |

* Including unemployed persons not previously employed.

Source: ILO, *Year Book of Labour Statistics.*

### WORKERS ABROAD ('000)

| | 1991 | 1992 | 1993 |
|---|---|---|---|
| Australia | 29 | 29 | 29 |
| Austria | 56 | 62 | 62 |
| Belgium | 23 | 23 | 23 |
| France | 98 | 112 | 112 |
| Germany | 696 | 740 | 742 |
| Libya | 10 | 10 | 13 |
| Netherlands | 89 | 89 | 89 |
| Saudi Arabia | 130 | 130 | 166 |
| Switzerland | 35 | 36 | 36 |
| **Total** (incl. others) | 1,235 | 1,300 | 1,329 |

### WORKERS' REMITTANCES FROM ABROAD (US $ million)

| | 1992 | 1993 | 1994 |
|---|---|---|---|
| Total | 3,074 | 2,963 | 2,664 |

## Agriculture

### PRINCIPAL CROPS (provisional figures, '000 metric tons)

| | 1992 | 1993 | 1994* |
|---|---|---|---|
| Wheat | 19,300 | 21,000 | 17,500 |
| Spelt | 18 | 16 | 14 |
| Rye | 230 | 235 | 195 |
| Barley | 6,900 | 7,500 | 7,000 |
| Oats | 240 | 245 | 230 |
| Maize | 2,225 | 2,500 | 1,850 |
| Millet | 4 | 4 | 4 |
| Rice (milled) | 225 | 225 | 200 |
| Dry beans | 200 | 200 | 180 |
| Chick peas | 770 | 740 | 650 |
| Lentils | 600 | 735 | 610 |
| Vetch | 174 | 195 | 175 |
| Broad beans (dry) | 68 | 65 | 52 |
| Potatoes | 4,600 | 4,650 | 4,350 |
| Onions (dry) | 1,700 | 1,650 | 1,800 |
| Garlic (dry) | 68 | 65 | 65 |
| Tomatoes | 6,400 | 6,150 | 6,350 |
| Cabbages (incl. black) | 698 | 697 | 699 |
| Melons and watermelons | 5,480 | 4,900 | 5,400 |
| Aubergines (Eggplants) | 740 | 750 | 810 |
| Apples | 2,100 | 2,080 | 2,095 |
| Grapes | 3,600 | 3,700 | 3,450 |
| Pears | 410 | 420 | 410 |
| Hazel-nuts (Filberts) | 520 | 305 | 490 |
| Sultanas | 120 | 180 | 176 |
| Figs (dried) | 35 | 45 | 46 |
| Walnuts | 120 | 115 | 120 |
| Pistachios (in shell) | 29 | 50 | 40 |
| Almonds | 47 | 48 | 47 |
| Chestnuts | 85 | 80 | 76 |
| Oranges | 820 | 840 | 920 |
| Lemons | 420 | 440 | 470 |
| Mandarins | 390 | 405 | 430 |
| Peaches | 370 | 370 | 375 |
| Plums | 190 | 200 | 204 |
| Apricots (incl. wild) | 320 | 230 | 400 |
| Cherries (incl. sour) | 155 | 245 | 250 |
| Cotton (lint) | 654 | 602 | 632 |
| Tobacco (leaves) | 334 | 324 | 242 |
| Sugar beet | 15,126 | 15,563 | 12,736 |
| Sesame seed | 34 | 30 | 34 |
| Sunflower seed | 950 | 815 | 740 |
| Olives | 750 | 550 | 1,400 |
| Olive oil | 100 | 50 | 168 |
| Tea (fresh leaves) | 731 | 579 | 654 |

* Figures are provisional.

# TURKEY

## LIVESTOCK ('000 head)

|  | 1991 | 1992 | 1993* |
|---|---|---|---|
| Cattle | 11,973 | 11,951 | 11,910 |
| Buffaloes | 336 | 352 | 316 |
| Camels | 2 | 2 | 2 |
| Pigs | 10 | 12 | 9 |
| Sheep | 40,433 | 39,416 | 37,541 |
| Goats | 10,764 | 10,454 | 10,133 |
| Horses | 496 | 483 | 450 |
| Mules | 192 | 181 | 172 |
| Asses | 944 | 895 | 841 |

Chickens (million): 139 in 1991; 153 in 1992; 178 in 1993.
Turkeys (million): 3 in 1991; 3 in 1992; 3 in 1993.

* Figures are provisional.

## LIVESTOCK PRODUCTS ('000 metric tons)

|  | 1991 | 1992 | 1993 |
|---|---|---|---|
| Beef and veal | 339 | 331* | 330† |
| Buffalo meat | 9 | 8 | 8† |
| Mutton and lamb | 303* | 302* | 301† |
| Goat meat* | 64 | 63 | 62 |
| Horse meat† | 3 | 3 | 3 |
| Poultry meat | 289 | 335 | 340 |
| Edible offals† | 115 | 88 | 85 |
| Cows' milk | 8,617 | 8,715 | 8,750† |
| Buffalo milk | 161 | 156 | 158† |
| Sheep milk | 1,127 | 1,089 | 1,050† |
| Goats' milk | 335 | 319 | 304† |
| Butter and ghee† | 116.4 | 116.5 | 116.2 |
| Cheese† | 140.8 | 138.7 | 138.3 |
| Hen eggs | 383.4 | 410.8 | 415.0† |
| Honey | 54.7 | 60.3 | 61.0† |
| Wool: |  |  |  |
| greasy | 44.7 | 43.5 | 43.2† |
| clean | 24.6 | 23.9 | 23.8† |
| Cattle and buffalo hides† | 41.5 | 39.7 | 39.7 |
| Sheep skins† | 65.2 | 65.0 | 64.7 |
| Goat skins† | 9.8 | 9.8 | 9.6 |

* Unofficial figure(s). † FAO estimate(s).

Source: FAO, mainly *Production Yearbook*.

## Forestry

### ROUNDWOOD REMOVALS ('000 cu m, excluding bark)

|  | 1990 | 1991 | 1992 |
|---|---|---|---|
| Sawlogs, veneer logs and logs for sleepers | 3,625 | 3,197 | 3,197 |
| Pulpwood* | 705 | 705 | 705 |
| Other industrial wood | 1,630* | 1,600 | 1,600* |
| Fuel wood | 9,796* | 9,750* | 9,750* |
| **Total** | 15,756 | 15,252 | 15,252 |

* FAO estimate(s). Annual output of pulpwood is assumed to be unchanged since 1987.

Source: FAO, *Yearbook of Forest Products*.

### SAWNWOOD PRODUCTION ('000 cu m, incl. railway sleepers)

|  | 1990 | 1991 | 1992 |
|---|---|---|---|
| Coniferous (softwood)* | 3,354 | 3,354 | 3,354 |
| Broadleaved (hardwood) | 1,569* | 1,574 | 1,574* |
| **Total** | 4,923* | 4,928 | 4,928* |

* FAO estimate(s). Annual output of coniferous sawnwood is assumed to be unchanged since 1984.

Source: FAO, *Yearbook of Forest Products*.

## Fishing

('000 metric tons, live weight)

|  | 1990 | 1991 | 1992 |
|---|---|---|---|
| Common carp | 17.0 | 15.3 | 15.8 |
| Whiting | 19.0 | 22.7 | 20.2 |
| Mullets | 22.4 | 28.3 | 27.4 |
| Bluefish | 9.5 | 12.3 | 9.7 |
| Atlantic horse mackerel | 14.2 | 9.3 | 8.9 |
| Mediterranean horse mackerel | 71.9 | 24.5 | 20.4 |
| European pilchard (sardine) | 18.8 | 30.3 | 29.8 |
| European anchovy | 74.0 | 90.6 | 174.6 |
| Atlantic bonito | 14.7 | 19.6 | 8.9 |
| Chub mackerel | 19.2 | 14.7 | 14.8 |
| Other fishes (incl. unspecified) | 56.4 | 65.4 | 82.3 |
| **Total fish** | 337.1 | 333.2 | 412.7 |
| Crustaceans | 7.7 | 2.1 | 3.7 |
| Molluscs | 38.9 | 26.9 | 35.7 |
| Frogs | n.a. | 1.3 | 1.7 |
| Jellyfishes | 1.1 | n.a. | 0.6 |
| **Total catch** | 384.8 | 363.5 | 454.3 |
| Inland waters | 41.7 | 44.2 | 49.6 |
| Mediterranean and Black Sea | 343.1 | 319.2 | 404.8 |

Source: FAO, *Yearbook of Fishery Statistics*.

## Mining

('000 metric tons)

|  | 1992 | 1993 | 1994 |
|---|---|---|---|
| Crude petroleum | 4,296 | 3,892 | 3,686 |
| Iron ore* | 5,450 | n.a. | 6,679 |
| Chromium ore* | 613 | n.a. | n.a. |
| Lignite† | 49,847 | 45,957 | 48,837 |
| Coal† | 4,918 | 2,722 | 2,917 |
| Copper (blister)† | 26 | 33 | 30 |

* Figures refer to the gross weight of ores.
† Production in the public sector only.

## Industry

### SELECTED PRODUCTS
('000 metric tons, unless otherwise indicated)

|  | 1991 | 1992 | 1993 |
|---|---|---|---|
| Paper* | 403 | 466 | 370 |
| Cotton yarn* | 47 | 47 | 44 |
| Woollen yarn* | 4 | 3.7 | 5.4 |
| Cotton fabrics (million metres)* | 178 | 177 | 147 |
| Woollen fabrics (million metres)* | 6.3 | 4 | 5.3 |
| Raki ('000 litres)* | 61,634 | 58,743 | 67,330 |
| Beer ('000 litres) | 418,719 | 484,348 | 552,406 |
| Cigarettes* | 72 | 70 | 75 |
| Pig iron | 4,594 | 4,508 | 4,355 |
| Cement | 26,261 | 28,607 | 31,311 |
| Sugar | 1,824 | 1,593 | 1,743 |
| Commercial fertilizers‡ | 6,321 | 7,710 | 7,108 |
| Electrolytic copper† | 21 | 7 | n.a. |
| Polyethylene* | 256 | 261 | 271 |
| Coke | 3,381 | 3,250 | 3,141 |
| Motor spirit (petrol) | 2,568 | 2,727 | 3,215 |
| Kerosene | 147 | 145 | 165 |
| Fuel oils | 8,697 | 8,664 | 8,705 |
| Hydroelectricity (million kWh) | 22,680 | 26,531 | 33,963 |
| Thermal electricity (million kWh) | 37,540 | 40,659 | 39,764 |

* Public sector only. † Private sector only.
‡ Excluding potassic fertilizers.

TURKEY

*Statistical Survey*

# Finance

## CURRENCY AND EXCHANGE RATES

**Monetary Units**
100 kuruş = 1 Turkish lira (TL) or pound.

**Sterling and Dollar Equivalents** (31 December 1994)
£1 sterling = 60,587 liras;
US $1 = 38,726 liras;
100,000 Turkish liras = £1.651 = $2.582.

**Average Exchange Rate** (liras per US $)
1992   6,872.4
1993  10,984.6
1994  29,608.7

## MONEY SUPPLY
(TL '000 million at 31 December)

|  | 1991 | 1992 | 1993 |
|---|---|---|---|
| Currency outside banks | 17,449 | 30,656 | 52,517 |
| Demand deposits at deposit money banks | 29,325 | 50,686 | 79,484 |

## GENERAL BUDGET (TL '000 million)*

| Revenue† | 1990 | 1991 | 1992 |
|---|---|---|---|
| Taxation | 45,431 | 78,734 | 141,797 |
| Taxes on income, profits, etc. | 23,246 | 40,419 | 70,134 |
| Taxes on property | 101 | 144 | 259 |
| Sales taxes | 12,371 | 22,832 | 42,088 |
| Excises | 957 | 3,357 | 9,147 |
| Other domestic taxes on goods and services | 3,924 | 4,952 | 8,203 |
| Import duties | 3,336 | 4,574 | 7,813 |
| Stamp taxes | 1,497 | 2,457 | 4,153 |
| Property income | 658 | 881 | 1,502 |
| Other current revenue | 7,586 | 10,488 | 32,268 |
| Capital revenue | 1,262 | 547 | 803 |
| **Total** | **54,937** | **90,650** | **176,370** |

| Expenditure‡ | 1990 | 1991 | 1992 |
|---|---|---|---|
| General public services | 17,215 | 34,192 | 65,563 |
| Defence | 7,966 | 13,783 | 25,558 |
| Education | 13,088 | 23,294 | 45,114 |
| Health | 2,437 | 3,934 | 7,870 |
| Social security and welfare | 1,445 | 2,661 | 4,782 |
| Housing and community amenities | 1,018 | 1,716 | 3,900 |
| Other community and social services | 507 | 787 | 1,554 |
| Economic services | 12,155 | 33,385 | 43,909 |
| Fuel and energy | 3,824 | 7,148 | 11,724 |
| Agriculture, forestry, fishing and hunting | 1,363 | 2,632 | 4,102 |
| Mining, manufacturing and construction | 607 | 1,503 | 1,437 |
| Transport and communications | 5,012 | 10,930 | 17,433 |
| Other purposes | 12,487 | 18,598 | 27,006 |
| **Total** | **68,318** | **132,350** | **225,256** |
| Current | 59,207 | 110,875 | 198,455 |
| Capital | 9,110 | 21,475 | 26,801 |

* Figures exclude the operations of central government units with their own budgets.
† Excluding grants received (TL '000 million): 1,636 in 1990; 8,434 in 1991; 1,700 in 1992.
‡ Excluding net lending (TL '000 million): 38 in 1990; 51 in 1991; 142 in 1992.

Source: IMF, *Government Finance Statistics Yearbook*.

## INTERNATIONAL RESERVES
(US $ million at 31 December)

|  | 1992 | 1993 | 1994 |
|---|---|---|---|
| Central bank: |  |  |  |
| Gold holding | 1,494 | 1,488 | 1,410 |
| Foreign exchange | 6,116 | 6,213 | 7,065 |
| Reserve holdings of other banks | 7,644 | 10,061 | 9,237 |
| **Total reserves** | **15,254** | **17,762** | **17,712** |

## COST OF LIVING
(Consumer Price Index for urban areas; base: 1987 = 100)

|  | 1992 | 1993 | 1994 |
|---|---|---|---|
| Food | 1,459.2 | 2,385.9 | 5,010.0 |
| Clothing | 1,505.1 | 2,504.7 | 5,130.2 |
| Household expenditures | 1,097.3 | 1,830.4 | 4,067.9 |
| Medical and personal care | 1,530.0 | 2,575.8 | 5,490.1 |
| Transport | 1,511.7 | 2,371.0 | 4,931.8 |
| Cultural and recreational expenditures | 1,272.3 | 2,207.2 | 4,478.1 |
| Dwelling expenditures* | 932.5 | 1,602.2 | 3,059.6 |
| **All items** | **1,283.1** | **2,131.2** | **4,395.9** |

* Rent is assumed to be fixed.

## NATIONAL ACCOUNTS (TL '000 million at current prices)
**Gross Domestic Product by Economic Activity**

|  | 1991 | 1992 | 1993 |
|---|---|---|---|
| Agriculture and livestock | 139,712 | 229,151 | 538,783 |
| Forestry and logging | 9,270 | 11,685 | 14,435 |
| Fishing | 4,363 | 7,520 | 24,331 |
| Mining and quarrying | 13,219 | 19,264 | 46,936 |
| Manufacturing | 188,751 | 326,642 | 713,852 |
| Electricity, gas and water | 27,616 | 49,575 | 108,088 |
| Construction | 69,679 | 122,261 | 241,117 |
| Wholesale and retail trade | 160,574 | 263,251 | 548,038 |
| Transport, storage and communications | 132,282 | 225,267 | 516,238 |
| Financial institutions | 38,560 | 67,938 | 94,133 |
| Ownership of dwellings | 35,775 | 56,880 | 105,096 |
| Other private services | 67,763 | 117,053 | 251,287 |
| Government services | 111,841 | 203,922 | 344,530 |
| **Gross domestic product at factor cost** | **999,405** | **1,700,409** | **3,546,864** |
| Indirect taxes | 118,486 | 221,551 | 425,965 |
| *Less* Subsidies | 24,523 | 29,354 | 89,001 |
| **GDP in purchasers' values** | **1,093,368** | **1,892,606** | **3,883,828** |
| Net factor income from abroad | 10,475 | 16,099 | 19,474 |
| **Gross national product** | **1,103,843** | **1,908,705** | **3,903,302** |

## BALANCE OF PAYMENTS (US $ million)

|  | 1992 | 1993 | 1994 |
|---|---|---|---|
| Merchandise exports f.o.b. | 14,891 | 15,611 | 18,390 |
| Merchandise imports f.o.b. | −23,082 | −29,771 | −22,606 |
| **Trade balance** | **−8,191** | **−14,160** | **−4,216** |
| Exports of services | 8,452 | 9,511 | 9,538 |
| Imports of services | −3,625 | −3,949 | −3,782 |
| Other income received | 1,999 | 2,277 | 2,153 |
| Other income paid | −3,637 | −3,880 | −4,154 |
| Private unrequited transfers (net) | 3,147 | 3,035 | 2,709 |
| Official unrequited transfers (net) | 912 | 733 | 383 |
| **Current balance** | **−943** | **−6,433** | **2,631** |
| Direct capital investment (net) | 779 | 622 | 559 |
| Portfolio investment (net) | 2,411 | 3,917 | 1,158 |
| Other capital (net) | 458 | 4,424 | −5,911 |
| Net errors and omissions | −1,221 | −2,222 | 1,769 |
| **Overall balance** | **1,484** | **308** | **206** |

# TURKEY

## External Trade

### PRINCIPAL COMMODITIES (US $ million)

| Imports (excl. grants) | 1992 | 1993 | 1994 |
|---|---|---|---|
| Crude petroleum | 2,632 | 2,550 | 2,432 |
| Iron and steel | 2,100 | 3,057 | 2,380 |
| Machinery | 5,886 | 7,236 | 5,586 |
| Transport vehicles | 2,222 | 4,012 | 2,137 |
| Chemical products | 1,463 | 1,636 | 1,313 |
| Plastic materials, natural and synthetic rubber | 986 | 1,161 | 1,009 |
| **Total** (incl. others) | 22,872 | 29,428 | 23,270 |

| Exports | 1992 | 1993 | 1994 |
|---|---|---|---|
| Fruits (dried) | 538 | 618 | 747 |
| Iron and steel | 1,549 | 1,991 | 2,352 |
| Cotton yarn and fabric, artificial and synthetic fibres, carpets, textile clothing and other textile goods | 5,156 | 5,452 | 5,518 |
| Tobacco (unprocessed leaves) | 309 | 396 | 395 |
| **Total** (incl. others) | 14,715 | 15,344 | 18,106 |

### PRINCIPAL TRADING PARTNERS (US $ million)

| Imports (excl. grants) | 1992 | 1993 | 1994 |
|---|---|---|---|
| Belgium-Luxembourg | 551 | 683 | 532 |
| France | 1,351 | 1,952 | 1,458 |
| Germany | 3,755 | 4,533 | 3,646 |
| Iran | 365 | 667 | 692 |
| Italy | 1,919 | 2,558 | 2,009 |
| Japan | 1,113 | 1,621 | 968 |
| Libya | 445 | 131 | 320 |
| Netherlands | 698 | 870 | 740 |
| Saudi Arabia | 1,665 | 1,500 | 1,229 |
| Switzerland | 688 | 651 | 473 |
| USSR* | 1,244 | 2,285 | 1,045 |
| United Kingdom | 1,187 | 1,546 | 1,170 |
| USA | 2,600 | 3,351 | 2,430 |
| **Total** (incl. others) | 22,872 | 29,428 | 23,270 |

| Exports | 1992 | 1993 | 1994 |
|---|---|---|---|
| Belgium-Luxembourg | 291 | 294 | 371 |
| France | 809 | 771 | 851 |
| Germany | 3,661 | 3,654 | 3,934 |
| Iran | 455 | 290 | 250 |
| Italy | 943 | 750 | 1,034 |
| Japan | 162 | 158 | 187 |
| Libya | 247 | 246 | 179 |
| Netherlands | 500 | 517 | 621 |
| Saudi Arabia | 486 | 652 | 609 |
| Spain | 298 | 195 | 232 |
| Switzerland | 223 | 216 | 239 |
| USSR* | 686 | 1,047 | 820 |
| United Kingdom | 796 | 835 | 889 |
| USA | 865 | 986 | 1,520 |
| **Total** (incl. others) | 14,715 | 15,344 | 18,106 |

* 1994 figures refer to Russia only.

## Transport

### RAILWAYS (traffic)

| | 1991 | 1992 | 1993 |
|---|---|---|---|
| Passenger journeys (million) | 133 | 131 | 146 |
| Freight (million metric tons) | 15 | 16 | 16 |

Source: Ministry of Transport and Communications.

### ROAD TRAFFIC (motor vehicles at 31 December)

| | 1991 | 1992 | 1993 |
|---|---|---|---|
| Passenger cars | 2,143,680 | 2,524,894 | 3,217,905 |
| Goods vehicles (incl. vans) | 868,857 | 949,214 | 861,005 |
| Buses and coaches | 83,519 | 93,668 | 106,662 |
| Tractors etc. | 794,651 | 826,308 | n.a. |
| Motorcycles and mopeds | 596,552 | 661,884 | n.a. |

Source: IRF, *World Road Statistics*.

### INTERNATIONAL SEA-BORNE SHIPPING*
(freight traffic, metric tons)

| | 1989 | 1990 | 1991 |
|---|---|---|---|
| Goods loaded | 115,965,257 | 118,176,339 | 134,422,786 |
| Goods unloaded | 62,936,036 | 65,503,301 | 69,194,966 |

* Excluding livestock.

Source: Turkish State Railways (TCDD).

### CIVIL AVIATION (Turkish Airlines)

| | 1990 | 1991 | 1992 |
|---|---|---|---|
| Number of passengers ('000) | 4,574 | 3,307 | 4,700 |
| Freight handled (metric tons)* | 56,662 | 35,000 | 51,494 |

* Cargo and mail.

Source: Turkish Airlines Annual Reports.

## Tourism

| | 1992 | 1993 | 1994 |
|---|---|---|---|
| Number of foreign arrivals ('000) | 7,076 | 6,501 | 6,668 |
| Receipts from foreign travel (million US $) | 3,639 | 3,959 | 4,321 |
| Expenditures for foreign travel (million US $) | 776 | 934 | 866 |

Source: Ministry of Tourism.

### TOURISTS BY COUNTRY OF ORIGIN ('000)

| Country | 1992 | 1993 | 1994 |
|---|---|---|---|
| France | 248 | 301 | 233 |
| Germany | 1,165 | 1,119 | 994 |
| Greece | 147 | 148 | 127 |
| Iran | 150 | 120 | 231 |
| Italy | 158 | 135 | 106 |
| Syria | 123 | 121 | 119 |
| United Kingdom | 315 | 442 | 568 |
| USA | 182 | 255 | 271 |
| Yugoslavia (former) | 156 | 170 | 119 |
| **Total** (incl. others) | 7,076 | 6,500 | 6,668 |

**TOURIST ACCOMMODATION** (registered by the Ministry of Tourism).
**1993:** 235,238 beds; **1994:** 314,184 beds.

TURKEY

## Communications Media

|  | 1990 | 1991 | 1992 |
|---|---|---|---|
| Radio receivers ('000 in use) | 9,000 | 9,200 | 9,425 |
| Television receivers ('000 in use) | 9,750 | 10,000 | 10,250 |
| Book production: titles | 6,291 | 6,365 | 6,549 |

**Daily newspapers** (1990): 399.

Source: UNESCO, *Statistical Yearbook*.

**Telephones** ('000 main lines in use): 6,893 in 1990; 8,152 in 1991 (Source UN, *Statistical Yearbook*).

## Education

(1992/93)

|  | Institutions | Teachers ('000) | Pupils ('000) |
|---|---|---|---|
| Primary | 49,974 | 236 | 6,708 |
| Secondary: |  |  |  |
| General | 8,700 | 125 | 3,234 |
| Technical and vocational | 3,083 | 62 | 1,066 |
| Higher (incl. academies, teacher training and other higher technical and vocational schools, universities) | 473 | 38 | 859 |

# Directory

## The Constitution

In October 1981 the National Security Council (NSC), which took power in September 1980, announced the formation of a Consultative Assembly to draft a new constitution, replacing that of 1961. The Assembly consisted of 40 members appointed directly by the NSC and 120 members chosen by the NSC from candidates put forward by the governors of the 74 provinces; all former politicians were excluded. The draft Constitution was approved by the Assembly in September 1982 and by a national referendum in November. Its main provisions are summarized below:

Legislative power is vested in the unicameral National Assembly, with 400 deputies, who are elected by universal adult suffrage for a five-year term. Executive power is vested in the President, to be elected by the National Assembly for a seven-year term and empowered to appoint a Prime Minister and senior members of the judiciary, the Central Bank and broadcasting organizations; to dissolve the National Assembly; and to declare a state of emergency entailing rule by decree. Strict controls on the powers of trades unions, the press and political parties were also included. An appended 'temporary article' automatically installed the incumbent President of the NSC as Head of State for a seven-year term, assisted by a Presidential Council comprising members of the NSC.

An amendment, adopted in June 1987, increased the number of deputies in the National Assembly from 400 to 450.

## The Government

### HEAD OF STATE

**President:** SÜLEYMAN DEMİREL (took office 16 May 1993).

### CABINET
(June 1995)

A coalition of the Doğru Yol Partisi (DYP) and the Cumhuriyet Halk Partisi (CHP).

**Prime Minister:** TANSU ÇİLLER (DYP).
**Deputy Prime Minister and Minister of State:** HİKMET ÇETİN (CHP).
**Minister of Justice:** MEHMET MOĞULTAY (CHP).
**Minister of National Defence:** MEHMET GÖLHAN (DYP).
**Minister of the Interior:** NAHİT MENTEŞE (DYP).
**Minister of Foreign Affairs:** ERDAL İNÖNÜ (CHP).
**Minister of Finance and Customs:** İSMET ATİLLA (DYP).
**Minister of Education:** NEVZAT AYAZ (DYP).
**Minister of Public Works and Housing:** ERMAN ŞAHİN (CHP).
**Minister of Health:** DOGAN BARAN (DYP).
**Minister of Transport and Communications:** ALI ŞEVKI EREK (DYP).
**Minister of Agriculture and Rural Affairs:** REFAİDDİN ŞAHİN (DYP).
**Minister of Forestry:** HASAN EKİNCİ (DYP).
**Minister of Labour and Social Security:** ZİYA HALÍS (CHP).
**Minister of Trade and Industry:** HASAN AKYOL (CHP).
**Minister of Energy and Natural Resources:** VEYSEL ATASOY (DYP).
**Minister of Culture:** İRFAN GÜRPINAR (CHP).
**Minister of Tourism:** İRFAN GÜRPINAR (CHP).
**Minister of the Environment:** RIZA AKÇALİ (DYP).
**Ministers of State:** NECMETTİN CEVEHERİ (DYP), YILDIRIM AKTUNA (DYP), ONUR KUMBARACIBAŞI (CHP), BEKİR SAMİ DACE (DYP), ALGAN HACALOĞLU (CHP), ESAT KIRATLIOĞLU (DYP), NAFİZ KURT (DYP), AYSEL BAYKAL (CHP), AYKON DOĞAN (DYP), ABDÜLKABİ ATAÇ (DYP), AYVAZ GOKDEMIR (DYP), ŞÜKRÜ ERDEM (DYP).

### MINISTRIES

**President's Office:** Cumhurbaşkanlığı Köşkü, Çankaya, Ankara; tel. (312) 4407212.

**Prime Minister's Office:** Başbakanlık, Bakanlıklar, Ankara; tel. (312) 4189056; fax (312) 4180476.

**Deputy Prime Minister's Office:** Başbakan yard. ve Devlet Bakanı, Bakanlıklar, Ankara; tel. (312) 4191621; fax (312) 4191547.

**Ministry of Agriculture and Rural Affairs:** Tarım ve Köy İşleri Bakanlığı, Bakanlıklar, Ankara; tel. (312) 4191677; fax (312) 4177168.

**Ministry of Culture:** Kültür Bakanlığı, Opera, Ankara; tel. (312) 3240322; fax (312) 3111431.

**Ministry of Energy and Natural Resources:** Enerji ve Tabii Kaynaklar Bakanlığı, Konya Yolu, Beştepe, Ankara; tel. (312) 2135330; fax (312) 2123816.

**Ministry of the Environment:** İstanbul Cad. 88, İskitler, Ankara; tel. (312) 3423900.

**Ministry of Finance:** Maliye Bakanlığı, Dikmen Cad., Ankara; tel. (312) 4250018; fax (312) 4250058.

**Ministry of Foreign Affairs:** Dişişleri Bakanlığı, Yeni Hizmet Binası, 06520 Balgat, Ankara; tel. (312) 2871665; fax (312) 2873869.

**Ministry of Forestry:** Orman Bakanlığı, Atatürk Bul., Bakanlıklar, Ankara; tel. (312) 4176000.

**Ministry of Health:** Sağlik Bakanlığı, Yenişehir, Ankara; tel. (312) 4312486; telex 42770; fax (312) 4339885.

**Ministry of the Interior:** Içişleri Bakanlığı, Bakanlıklar, Ankara; tel. (312) 4254080; fax (312) 4181795.

**Ministry of Justice:** Adalet Bakanlığı, 06100 Bakanlıklar, Ankara; tel. (312) 4191331; fax (312) 4173954.

**Ministry of Labour and Social Security:** Çalişma ve Sosyal Güvenlik Bakanlığı, Eskişehir Yolu 42, Emek, Ankara; tel. (312) 4170727; fax (312) 4179765.

**Ministry of National Defence:** Milli Savunma Bakanlığı, 06100 Ankara; tel. (312) 4254596; fax (312) 4184737.

**Ministry of National Education:** Milli Eğitim Bakanlığı, Ankara; tel. (312) 4255330; fax (312) 4177027.

TURKEY — *Directory*

**Ministry of Public Works and Housing:** Bayındırlık ve İskan Bakanlığı, Vekaletler Cad. 1, 06100 Ankara; tel. (312) 4255711; fax (312) 4180406.

**Ministry of Tourism:** Turizm Bakanlığı, İsmet İnönü Bul. 5, Bahçelievler, Ankara; tel. (312) 2128300; fax (312) 2136887.

**Ministry of Trade and Industry:** Sanayi ve Ticaret Bakanlığı, Tandoğan, Ankara; tel. (312) 4314866; fax (312) 2304251.

**Ministry of Transport and Communications:** Ulaştırma Bakanlığı, Sok. 5, Emek, Ankara; tel. (312) 2124416; fax (312) 2124930.

## Legislature

### NATIONAL ASSEMBLY

**Speaker:** HÜSAMETTİN CİNDORUK.

**General Election, 20 October 1991**

| Party | Seats |
| --- | --- |
| Doğru Yol Partisi (DYP) | 178 |
| Anavatan Partisi (ANAP) | 115 |
| Sosyal Demokrat Halkçı Parti (SHP) | 88* |
| Refah Partisi (RP) | 62† |
| Demokratik Sol Parti (DSP) | 7 |
| Total | 450 |

\* Including 22 seats for the Kurdish nationalist Halkın Emek Partisi (subsequently banned).
† Including 19 seats for the Milliyetçi Hareket Partisi (MÇP). Following the election, the MÇP's alliance with the RP was dissolved and the MÇP deputies announced their intention to serve as independents.

The emergence of several new political parties since 1992 has resulted in a redistribution of allegiances within the National Assembly. At mid-November 1994 the distribution of seats was the following: DYP 182; ANAP 96; SHP 49; RP 38; MÇP 16; Cumhuriyet Halk Partisi (CHP) 15; DSP 9; Büyük Birlik Partisi 7; Yeni Parti 3; Millet Partisi 2; Independents 11; vacant seats 22. The SHP merged with the CHP, under the latter's name, in February 1995.

## Political Organizations

All activities by political parties were banned by the National Security Council (NSC) on 12 September 1980, and all political parties were dissolved on 16 October 1981, prior to the formation of a Consultative Assembly. The most important parties which existed before that date were the Justice Party (Adalet Partisi), led by Süleyman Demirel, and the Republican People's Party (Cumhuriyet Halk Partisi—CHP), led by Bülent Ecevit.

From May 1983 new political parties were allowed to form, but their participation in the November general election was subject to strict rules: each had to have 30 party founders approved by the NSC and party organizations in at least 34 of the provinces, while candidates for the election were also subject to veto by the military rulers. Legislation enacted in March 1986 stipulated that a party must have organizations in at least 45 provinces, and in two-thirds of the districts in each of these provinces, in order to take part in an election. A political party is recognized by the Government as a legitimate parliamentary group only if it has at least 20 deputies in the National Assembly.

In mid-1992, following the adoption of more lenient guidelines for the formation of political parties (proposed by the new Demirel administration), several new parties were established, and the left-wing CHP, dissolved in 1981, was reactivated.

**Anavatan Partisi (ANAP)** (Motherland Party): 13 Cad. 3, Balgat, Ankara; tel. (312) 4468500; fax (312) 2865019; f. 1983; supports free-market economic system, moderate nationalist and conservative policies, rational social justice system, integration with the EEC, and closer ties with the Islamic world; merged with the Free Democratic Party (f. 1986) in December 1986; Chair. MESUT YILMAZ; Deputy Chair. EKREM PAKDEMİRLİ.

**Büyük Birlik Partisi (BBP)** (Grand Union Party): Tuna Cad. 28, Yenişehir, Ankara; tel. (312) 4413648; fax (312) 4355818; f. 1993; Chair. MUHSİN YAZICIOĞLU.

**Cumhuriyet Halk Partisi (CHP)** (Republican People's Party): Çevre Sok. 28, Ankara; tel. and fax (312) 4685969; f. 1923 by Kemal Atatürk, dissolved in 1981 and reactivated in 1992; merged with Sosyal Demokrat Halkçı Parti (Social Democratic Populist Party) in February 1995; left-wing; Leader HIKMET ÇETIN.

**Demokrasi ve Degisim Partisi (DDP)** (Democracy and Change Party): Ankara; f. 1995 by members of the proscribed Democracy Party and People's Labour Party; pro-Kurdish; Leader IBRAHIM AKSOY.

**Demokratik Sol Parti (DSP)** (Democratic Left Party): Fevzi Çakmak Cad. 17, Ankara; tel. (312) 2124950; fax (312) 2124188; f. 1985; centre-left; drawing support from members of the fmr Republican People's Party; Chair. BÜLENT ECEVİT.

**Doğru Yol Partisi (DYP)** (True Path Party): Akay Cad. 16, Ankara; tel. (312) 4172239; fax (312) 4185657; f. 1983; centre-right; replaced the Justice Party (f. 1961 and banned in 1981); Chair. TANSU ÇİLLER; Sec.-Gen. GÖKBERK ERGENEKON.

**Millet Partisi (MP)** (Nation Party): İstanbul Cad., Rizgarlı Mah. Gayret Sok. 2, Ankara; tel. (312) 3127626; fax (312) 3127651; f. 1992; Chair. AYKUT EDİPALİ.

**Milliyetçi Hareket Partisi (MÇP)** (Nationalist Movement Party): Strazburg Cad. 36, Sihhiye, Ankara; tel. (312) 3218700; fax (312) 2311424; f. 1983; fmrly the Conservative Party; Leader ALPASLAN TÜRKEŞ.

**Refah Partisi (RP)** (Welfare Party): Ziyabey Cad. 11, Sok. 24, Balgat, Ankara; tel. (312) 2873056; fax (312) 2877465; f. 1983; Islamic fundamentalist; opposes integration with the EU; supports closer ties with neighbouring Islamic states; Chair. Prof. NECMETTİN ERBAKAN.

**Yeni Demokrasi Hareket (YDH)** (New Democracy Movement): Ankara; f. 1994; independent political movement; supports a political solution to the Kurdish conflict and respect for human rights; Leader CEM BOYNER.

**Yeni Parti (YP)** (New Party): Rabat Sok. 27, Gaziosmanpaşa, Ankara; tel. (312) 4469254; fax (312) 4469579; f. 1993; Leader YUSUF BOZKURT ÖZAL.

The Workers' Party of Turkey and the Turkish Communist Party, both illegal, merged in 1988 to form the Türkiye Birleşik Komünist Partisi (Turkish United Communist Party).

## Diplomatic Representation

### EMBASSIES IN TURKEY

**Afghanistan:** Cinnah Cad. 88, 06551 Çankaya, Ankara; tel. (312) 4381121; telex 46769; fax (312) 4387745; Chargé d'affaires: MUHAMMAD SARWAR.

**Albania:** Nenehatun Cad. 89, 06700 Gaziosmanpaşa, Ankara; tel. (312) 4466527; fax (312) 4466528; Ambassador: SKENDER DRINI.

**Algeria:** Şehit Ersan Cad. 42, 06680 Çankaya, Ankara; tel. (312) 4278700; telex 42053; fax (312) 4268959; Ambassador: CHERIF DERBAL.

**Argentina:** Uğar Mumcu Cad. 60/3, 06700 Gaziosmanpaşa, Ankara; tel. (312) 4462061; telex 42373; fax (312) 4462063; Ambassador: ADOLFO OCTAVIANO SARACHO.

**Australia:** Nenehatun Cad. 83, 06680 Gaziosmanpaşa, Ankara; tel. (312) 4461180; telex 44284; fax (312) 4461188; Ambassador: DAVID WYKE EVANS.

**Austria:** Atatürk Bul. 189, Kavaklıdere, Ankara; tel. (312) 4342172; telex 42429; fax (312) 4189454; Ambassador: Dr JOHANN PLUTNER.

**Azerbaijan:** Cemal Nadir Sok. 20, Çelikler Apt, Çankaya, Ankara; tel. (312) 4412621; telex 46404; fax (312) 4412600; Ambassador: MEHMET ALIEV.

**Bangladesh:** Cinnah Cad., Çankaya, Ankara; tel. (312) 4392750; telex 46068; fax (312) 4392408; Ambassador: MAHMUDUL HASSAN.

**Belgium:** Nenehatun Cad. 109, Gaziosmanpaşa, Ankara; tel. (312) 4468247; telex 42258; fax (312) 4468251; Ambassador: ERIC KOBIA.

**Bosnia and Herzegovina:** Hafta Sok. 20, Ankara; tel. (312) 4464090; fax (312) 4466228; Ambassador: HAYRUDIN SOMUM.

**Brazil:** İran Cad. 47/1, Gaziosmanpaşa, Ankara; tel. (312) 4685320; telex 42657; fax (312) 4685324; Ambassador: LUIZ ANTÔNIO JARDIM GAGLIARDI.

**Bulgaria:** Atatürk Bul. 124, 06680 Kavaklıdere, Ankara; tel. (312) 4267455; fax (312) 4273178; Ambassador: BRANIMIR PETROV.

**Canada:** Nenehatun Cad. 75, 06700 Gaziosmanpaşa, Ankara; tel. (312) 4361275; telex 42369; fax (312) 4464437; Ambassador: PETER HANCOCK.

**Chile:** İran Cad. 45/2, Çankaya, Ankara; tel. (312) 4389444; telex 42755; fax (312) 4386145; Ambassador: FERNANDO CISTERNAS.

**China, People's Republic:** Gölgeli Sok. 34, 06700 Gaziosmanpaşa, Ankara; tel. (312) 4361453; telex 44532; fax (312) 4464248; Ambassador: HU CHANGLIN.

**Croatia:** Kelebek Sok. 15/A, Gaziosmanpaşa, Ankara; tel. (312) 4469460; fax (312) 4366212; Ambassador: H. BIŠČEVIĆ.

**Cuba:** Kuşkondu Sok. 7/1, Çankaya, Ankara; tel. and fax (312) 4394110; Ambassador: JORGE CASTRO BENÍTEZ.

# TURKEY — Directory

**Czech Republic:** Uğur Mumcu Cad. 100/3, 06770 Gaziosmanpaşa, Ankara; tel. (312) 4461244; telex 42380; fax (312) 4461245; Chargé d'affaires a.i.: Ilja Ulrich.

**Denmark:** Kırlangıç Sok. 42, 06700 Gaziosmanpaşa, Ankara; tel. (312) 4687760; telex 46385; fax (312) 4684559; Ambassador: Niels Helskov.

**Egypt:** Atatürk Bul. 126, 06680 Kavaklıdere, Ankara; tel. (312) 4261026; fax (312) 4270099; Ambassador: Mohammed Eldiwany.

**Finland:** Galip Dede Sok. 1/19, Farabi, 06680 Çankaya, Ankara; tel. (312) 4255921; telex 46737; fax (312) 4680072; Ambassador: Risto Kauppi.

**France:** Paris Cad. 70, 06540 Kavaklıdere, Ankara; tel. (312) 4681154; telex 42385; fax (312) 4679434; Ambassador: François Dopffer.

**Germany:** Atatürk Bul. 114, 06680 Kavaklıdere, Ankara; tel. (312) 4265465; telex 44394; fax (312) 4266959; Ambassador: (vacant).

**Greece:** Ziya ül-Rahman 9–11, 06610 Gaziosmanpaşa, Ankara; tel. (312) 4368860; telex 42146; fax (312) 4463191; Ambassador: Alexander Philon.

**Holy See:** Çukurça Mah. 2, Sok. 55, PK 33, 06552 Çankaya, Ankara (Apostolic Nunciature); tel. (4) 4390041; fax (312) 4402900; Apostolic Nuncio: Most Rev. Pier Luigi Celata, Titular Archbishop of Doclea.

**Hungary:** Gazi Mustafa Kemal Bul. 10, 06440 Kızılay, Ankara; tel. (312) 4258528; fax (312) 4188322; Ambassador: Dr István Vásáry.

**India:** Cinnah Cad. 77/A, 06680 Çankaya, Ankara; tel. (312) 4382195; telex 42561; fax (312) 4403429; Ambassador: K. Gajendra Singh.

**Indonesia:** Abdullah Cevdet Sok. 10, 06552 Çankaya, Ankara; tel. (312) 4382190; telex 43250; fax (312) 4382193; Ambassador: Sukarno Abdulrachman.

**Iran:** Tahran Cad. 10, Kavaklıdere, Ankara; tel. (312) 4274320; Ambassador: Mohammad Reza Bagheri.

**Iraq:** Turan Emeksiz Sok. 11, 06692 Gaziosmanpaşa, Ankara; tel. (312) 4266118; telex 42577; fax (312) 4684832; Ambassador: Danham Mejwel el-Tikriti.

**Israel:** Mahatma Gandhi Cad. 85, Gaziosmanpaşa, Ankara; tel. (312) 4463605; telex 42560; Chargé d'affaires: Uri Gordon.

**Italy:** Atatürk Bul. 118, Kavaklıdere, Ankara; tel. (312) 4265460; telex 42624; fax (312) 4265800; Ambassador: Dr Michelangelo Pisani Massamormile.

**Japan:** Reşit Galip Cad. 81, 06692 Gaziosmanpaşa, Ankara; tel. (312) 4460500; telex 42435; fax (312) 4371812; Ambassador: Yoichi Yamagushi.

**Jordan:** Cinnah Cad. 54/10, 06690 Çankaya, Ankara; tel. (312) 4402054; telex 43637; fax (312) 4404327; Ambassador: Saleh Kabariti.

**Kazakhstan:** Ebuzziya Tevfik Sok. 6, Çankaya, Ankara; tel. (312) 4412301; telex 46193; fax (312) 4412303; Ambassador: Kanat B. Saudabaev.

**Korea, Republic:** Cinnah Cad., Alaçam Sok. 5, 06690 Çankaya, Ankara; tel. (312) 4684822; telex 42680; fax (312) 4682279; Ambassador: Byung Woo Yu.

**Kuwait:** Reşit Galip Cad. 110, Gaziosmanpaşa, Ankara; tel. (312) 4450576; telex 43238; fax (312) 4466839; Chargé d'affaires: Abdul-Lateef Ali al-Mawnash.

**Kyrgyzstan:** Boyabat Sok. 11, Eren Apt, Gaziosmanpaşa, Ankara; tel. (312) 4468408; fax (312) 4468413.

**Lebanon:** Kızkulesi Sok. 44, Gaziosmanpaşa, Ankara; tel. (312) 4667487; telex 46063; fax (312) 4461023; Ambassador: Khalil al-Khalil.

**Libya:** Cinnah Cad. 60, 06690 Çankaya, Ankara; tel. (312) 4381110; telex 43270; fax (312) 4403862; Secretary of the People's Committee: Ahmed Abdulhamid el-Atrash.

**Macedonia, former Yugoslav republic:** Filistin Sok. 30/2, Gaziosmanpaşa, Ankara; tel. (312) 4469204; fax (312) 4469206.

**Malaysia:** Uğur Mumcu Cad. 6, 06700 Gaziosmanpaşa, Ankara; tel. (312) 4463547; telex 43616; fax (312) 4464130; Ambassador: H. A. Zaibedah.

**Mexico:** Çankaya Cad. 20/2, Çankaya, Ankara; tel. (312) 4413204; telex 42278; fax (312) 4413203; Ambassador: Raphael Steger Cataño.

**Moldova:** Gazi Osinan Pasa, Captan Pasa 49, Ankara; tel. (312) 4465527; fax (312) 4465816; Ambassador: Ion Botnaru.

**Morocco:** Reşit Galip Cad., Rabat Sok. 11, Gaziosmanpaşa, Ankara; tel. (312) 4376020; telex 42869; fax (312) 4468430; Ambassador: Mohamed Guedira.

**Netherlands:** Uğur Mumcu Cad. 16, 06700 Gaziosmanpaşa, Ankara; tel. (312) 4460470; telex 42612; fax (312) 4463358; Ambassador: Dr J. N. J. B. Horak.

**New Zealand:** İran Cad. 13/4, 06700 Kavaklıdere, Ankara; tel. (312) 4679054; fax (312) 4679013; Ambassador: Clive Pearson.

**Norway:** Kelebek Sok. 18, 06692 Gaziosmanpaşa, Ankara; tel. (312) 4379950; telex 42244; fax (312) 4376430; Ambassador: Nils Bølset.

**Oman:** Mahatma Gandhi Cad. 63, 06700 Gaziosmanpaşa; tel. (312) 4369691; telex 46507; fax (312) 4374445; Ambassador: Fakir bin Salim bin Farakh.

**Pakistan:** İran Cad. 37, 06700 Gaziosmanpaşa, Ankara; tel. (312) 4271410; fax (312) 4671023; Ambassador: Inam-ul Haque.

**Philippines:** Cayhane Sok. 24, Gaziosmanpaşa, Ankara; tel. (312) 4465831; fax (312) 4465733; Ambassador: Minerva Jean A. Falcon.

**Poland:** Atatürk Bul. 241, 06650 Ankara; tel. (312) 4261694; fax (312) 4273987; Ambassador: Wojciech Hensel.

**Portugal:** Kuleli Sok. 26, 06700 Gaziosmanpaşa, Ankara; tel. (312) 4461890; telex 46686; fax (312) 4461892; Ambassador: António Chrystêllo Tavares.

**Qatar:** Karaca Sok. 19, Gaziosmanpaşa, Ankara; tel. (312) 4411364; telex 46209; fax (312) 4411544; Ambassador: Saad Mohamed al-Kubais.

**Romania:** Bükreş Sok. 4, 06680 Çankaya, Ankara; tel. (312) 4271243; telex 42760; fax (312) 4271530; Ambassador: Alexandre Margaritescu.

**Russia:** Karyağdı Sok. 5, 06692 Çankaya, Ankara; tel. (312) 4392122; telex 46151; fax (312) 4383952; Ambassador: Vadim Igorevich Kuznetsov.

**Saudi Arabia:** Turan Emeksiz Sok. 6, Gaziosmanpaşa, Ankara; tel. (312) 4681540; telex 42456; fax (312) 4274886; Ambassador: Naji Mufti.

**Slovakia:** Atatürk Bul. 245, 06692 Kavaklıdere, Ankara; tel. (312) 4265887; fax (312) 4682689; Ambassador: Ján Szelepcsényi.

**South Africa:** Filistin Cad. 27, Gaziosmanpaşa, Ankara; tel. (312) 4464056; fax (312) 4466434; Ambassador: C. F. Jacobs.

**Spain:** Vali Dr. Reşit Sok. 6, 06680 Çankaya, Ankara; tel. (312) 4380392; telex 42551; fax (312) 4395170; Ambassador: Javier Villacieros.

**Sudan:** Zia Ül-Rahman Cad. 3/1, 06690 Çankaya, Ankara; tel. (312) 4461200; telex 46719; fax (312) 4467516; Ambassador: Omer Mohamed Shouna.

**Sweden:** Katip Çelebi Sok. 7, 06692 Kavaklıdere, Ankara; tel. (312) 4286735; telex 42230; fax (312) 4685020; Ambassador: Erik Cornell.

**Switzerland:** Atatürk Bul. 247, 06692 Kavaklıdere, Ankara; tel. (312) 4675555; telex 44161; fax (312) 4671199; Ambassador: André Faivet.

**Syria:** Abdullah Cevdet Sok. 7, 06680 Çankaya, Ankara; tel. (312) 4409657; telex 46688; fax (312) 4385609; Ambassador: Abdulaziz al-Rifa.

**Thailand:** Çankaya Cad. Kader Sok. 45/3, 06700 Gaziosmanpaşa, Ankara; tel. (312) 4673409; telex 46096; fax (312) 4386474; Ambassador: Santad Kiartitat.

**Tunisia:** Kuleli Sok. 12, 06700 Gaziosmanpaşa, Ankara; tel. (312) 4377720; telex 42215; fax (312) 4377100; Ambassador: Mohamed Megdiche.

**'Turkish Republic of Northern Cyprus':** Rabat Sok. 20, 06700 Gaziosmanpaşa, Ankara; tel. (312) 4376030; telex 42575; fax (312) 4465238; Ambassador: Nazif Borman.

**Turkmenistan:** Rabat Sok. 22, Gaziosmanpaşa, Ankara; tel. (312) 4468563; telex 46085; fax (312) 4468378.

**Ukraine:** Cemal Nadir Sok. 9, Çankaya, Ankara; tel. (312) 4399973; fax (312) 4406815; Ambassador: Igor M. Turyanskiy.

**United Arab Emirates:** Mahmut Yesari Sok. 10, 06680 Çankaya, Ankara; tel. (312) 4408410; telex 46044; fax (312) 4389854; Ambassador: Youssef Abdul Khalik Mohamed al-Ansari.

**United Kingdom:** Şehit Ersan Cad. 46/A, Çankaya, Ankara; tel. (312) 4274310; telex 42320; fax (312) 4683214; Ambassador: Sir Kieran Prendergast.

**USA:** Atatürk Bul. 110, Kavaklıdere, Ankara; tel. (312) 4686110; fax (312) 4670019; Ambassador: Marc Grossman.

**Uzbekistan:** Ahmet Rasim Sok. 14, 06550 Çankaya, Ankara; tel. (312) 4392740; telex 46028; fax (312) 4409222; Ambassador: Abdugafur Abdurahmanov.

**Venezuela:** Cinnah Cad. 78/2, Çankaya, Ankara; tel. (312) 4387135; telex 42453; fax (312) 4406619; Ambassador: Ramón Delgado.

**Yemen:** İlkadim Sok. 15, 06700 Gaziosmanpaşa, Ankara; tel. (312) 4379920; fax (312) 4461778; Ambassador: Ahmed Abdullah Abdulila.

# Judicial System

Until the foundation of the Turkish Republic, a large part of the Turkish civil law—the laws affecting the family, inheritance, property, obligations, etc.—was based on the Koran, and this holy law was administered by special religious (Shari'a) courts. The legal reform of 1926 was not only a process of secularization, but also a radical change of the legal system. The Swiss Civil Code and the Code of Obligation, the Italian Penal Code and the Neuchâtel (Cantonal) Code of Civil Procedure were adopted and modified to fit Turkish customs and traditions.

According to current Turkish law, the power of the judiciary is exercised by judicial (criminal), military and administrative courts. These courts render their verdicts in the first instance, while superior courts examine the verdict for subsequent rulings.

## SUPERIOR COURTS

**Constitutional Court:** Consists of 11 regular and four substitute members, appointed by the President. Reviews the constitutionality of laws, at the request of the President of the Republic, parliamentary groups of the governing party or of the main opposition party, or of one-fifth of the members of the National Assembly, and sits as a high council empowered to try senior members of state. The rulings of the Constitutional Court are final. Decisions of the Court are published immediately in the Official Gazette, and shall be binding on the legislative, executive, and judicial organs of the state.

**Court of Appeals:** The court of the last instance for reviewing the decisions and verdicts rendered by judicial courts. It has original and final jurisdiction in specific cases defined by law. Members are elected by the Supreme Council of Judges and Prosecutors.

**Council of State:** An administrative court of the first and last instance in matters not referred by law to other administrative courts, and an administrative court of the last instance in general. Hears and settles administrative disputes and expresses opinions on draft laws submitted by the Council of Ministers. Three-quarters of the members are appointed by the Supreme Council of Judges and Public Prosecutors, the remaining quarter is selected by the President of the Republic.

**Military Court of Appeals:** A court of the last instance to review decisions and verdicts rendered by military courts, and a court of first and last instance with jurisdiction over certain military persons, stipulated by law, with responsibility for the specific trials of these persons. Members are selected by the President of the Republic from nominations made by the Military Court of Appeals.

**Supreme Military Administrative Court:** A military court for the judicial control of administrative acts concerning military personnel. Members are selected by the President of the Republic from nominations made by the Court.

**Court of Jurisdictional Disputes:** Settles disputes among judicial, administrative and military courts arising from disagreements on jurisdictional matters and verdicts.

**The Court of Accounts:** A court charged with the auditing of all accounts of revenue, expenditure and government property, which renders rulings related to transactions and accounts of authorized bodies on behalf of the National Assembly.

**Supreme Council of Judges and Public Prosecutors:** The President of the Council shall be the Minister of Justice, and the Under-Secretary to the Minister of Justice shall serve as an *ex-officio* member of the Council. Three regular and three substitute members from the Court of Appeals, together with two regular and two substitute members of the Council of State, shall be appointed to the Supreme Council by the President of the Republic for a four-year term. Decides all personnel matters relating to judges and public prosecutors.

**Public Prosecutor:** The law shall make provision for the tenure of public prosecutors and attorneys of the Council of State and their functions. The Chief Prosecutor of the Republic, the Chief Attorney of the Council of State and the Chief Prosecutor of the Military Court of Appeals are subject to the provisions applicable to judges of higher courts.

**Military Trial:** Military trials are conducted by military and disciplinary courts. These courts are entitled to try the military offences of military personnel and those offences committed against military personnel or in military areas, or offences connected with military service and duties. Military courts may try non-military persons only for military offences prescribed by special laws.

# Religion

## ISLAM

More than 99% of the Turkish people are Muslims. However, Turkey is a secular state. Although Islam was stated to be the official religion in the Constitution of 1924, an amendment in 1928 removed this privilege. After 1950 subsequent governments have tried to re-establish links between religion and state affairs, but secularity was protected by the revolution of 1960, the 1980 coup and the 1982 Constitution.

**Diyanet İşleri Reisi** (Head of Religious Affairs in Turkey): Prof. Mustafa Sait Yazicioğlu.

## CHRISTIANITY

The town of Antioch (now Antakya) was one of the earliest strongholds of Christianity, and by the the 4th century had become a patriarchal see. Formerly in Syria, the town was incorporated in Turkey in 1939. Constantinople (now İstanbul) was also a patriarchal see, and by the 6th century the Patriarch of Constantinople was recognized as the Ecumenical Patriarch in the East. Gradual estrangement from Rome developed, leading to the final breach between the Catholic West and the Orthodox East, usually assigned to the year 1054.

In 1986 it was estimated that there were about 100,000 Christians in Turkey.

### The Orthodox Churches

**Armenian Patriarchate:** Ermeni Patrikliği, Şarapnel Sok. 20–22; 34480 Kumkapı, İstanbul; tel. (212) 5170970; fax (212) 5164833; f. 1461; 45,000 adherents (1989); Patriarch Karekin Bedros Kazandjian.

**Bulgarian Orthodox Church:** Bulgar Ortodoks Kilisesi, Halâskâr Gazi Cad. 319, Şişli, İstanbul; Rev. Archimandrite Ganco Çobanof.

**Greek Orthodox Church:** Rum Ortodoks Patrikhanesi, 34220 Fener-Haliç, İstanbul; tel. (212) 5319670; fax (212) 5349037; Archbishop of Constantinople (New Rome) and Ecumenical Patriarch Bartholomeo I.

### The Roman Catholic Church

At 31 December 1993 there were an estimated 27,084 adherents in the country.

**Bishops' Conference:** Conferenza Episcopale di Turchia, Ölçek Sok. 87, Harbiye, 80230 İstanbul; tel. (212) 2414552; fax (212) 2408801; f. 1978; Pres. Mgr Hovhannes Tcholakian (Archbishop of İstanbul).

*Armenian Rite*

**Patriarchate of Cilicia:** f. 1742; Patriarch Jean-Pierre XVIII Kasparian (resident in Beirut, Lebanon).

**Archbishopric of İstanbul:** Sakızağacı Cad. 31, PK 183, 80072 Beyoğlu, İstanbul; tel. (212) 2441258; fax (212) 2432364; f. 1830; two secular priests; 3,650 Catholics (1993); Archbishop Hovhannes Tcholakian.

*Byzantine Rite*

**Apostolic Exarchate of İstanbul:** Hamalbaşı Cad. 44, 80070 Beyoğlu, İstanbul; tel. (212) 2497104; f. 1861; one secular priest; 50 Catholics (1993); Vicar Delegate Rev. Archimandrite Thomas Varsamis.

**Bulgarian Catholic Church:** Bulgar Katolik Kilisesi, Eski Parmakkapı Sok. 15, Galata, İstanbul.

*Chaldean Rite*

**Archbishopric of Diyarbakır:** Hamalbaşı Cad. 48, PK 259, 80070 Beyoğlu, İstanbul; tel. (212) 2932713; fax (212) 2932064; six secular priests; 3,300 Catholics (1993); Archbishop Paul Karatas.

*Latin Rite*

**Metropolitan See of İzmir:** Church of St Polycarpe, Necatibey Cad. 2, PK 267, 35212 İzmir; tel. (232) 4848436; fax (232) 4845358; seven priests; 1,284 Catholics (1993); Archbishop of İzmir Giuseppe Germano Bernardini.

**Apostolic Vicariate of Anatolia:** Uray Cad. 85, PK 35, 33001 Mersin; tel. (324) 2320578; fax (324) 2320595; f. 1990; three secular priests, seven religious priests; 3,800 Catholics (1993); Vicar Apostolic Ruggero Franceschini, Titular Bishop of Sicilibba.

**Apostolic Vicariate of İstanbul:** Ölçek Sok. 83, 80230 Harbiye, İstanbul; tel. (212) 2480775; fax (212) 2408801; f. 1742; six secular priests, 27 religious priests; 15,000 Catholics (1993); Vicar Apostolic Louis Pelâtre, Titular Bishop of Sasima.

*Maronite Rite*

The Maronite Patriarch of Antioch is resident in Lebanon.

*Melkite Rite*

The Greek Melkite Patriarch of Antioch is resident in Damascus, Syria.

# TURKEY

*Syrian Rite*

The Syrian Catholic Patriarch of Antioch is resident in Beirut, Lebanon.

**Patriarchal Vicariate of Turkey:** Sarayarkası Sok. 15, PK 84, 80090 Ayazpaşa, İstanbul; tel. (212) 2432521; three secular priests, one religious priest; 2,100 Catholics (1993); Vicar Patriarchal Rev. YUSUF SAĞ.

### The Anglican Communion

Within the Church of England, Turkey forms part of the diocese of Gibraltar in Europe. The Bishop is resident in London, England.

**Archdeacon of the Aegean:** (acting) Canon JEREMY PEAKE, (resident in Vienna, Austria).

### JUDAISM

**Jewish Community of Turkey:** Türkiye Hahambaşılığı, Yemenici Sok. 23, Beyoğlu, 80050 Tünel, İstanbul; tel. (212) 2435166; fax (212) 2441980; Chief Rabbi DAVID ASSEO.

## The Press

Almost all İstanbul papers are also printed in Ankara and İzmir on the same day, and some in Adana. Among the most serious and influential papers are the dailies *Milliyet* and *Cumhuriyet*. The weekly *Gırgır* is noted for its political satire. The most popular dailies are the İstanbul papers *Sabah*, *Hürriyet*, *Milliyet*, *Yeni Günaydın* and *Zaman*; *Yeni Asır*, published in İzmir, is the best-selling quality daily of the Aegean region. There are numerous provincial newspapers with limited circulation.

### PRINCIPAL DAILIES

#### Adana

**Yeni Adana:** Abidinpaşa Cad. 56, Adana; tel. (322) 3511891; fax (322) 3593655; f. 1918; political; Propr ÇETİN REMZİ YÜREĞİR; Chief Editor AYTEN SENSALIVER; circ. 1,600.

#### Ankara

**Ankara Ticaret:** Rüzgârlı Sok. O. V. Han 2/6, Ankara; tel. (312) 4182832; telex 42308; f. 1954; commercial; Man. Editor NURAY TÜZMEN; Chief Editor MUAMMER SOLMAZ; circ. 1,351.

**Ankara Ulus:** Ankara; f. 1983; Propr ASIL NADİR.

**Belde:** Rüzgârlı Gayret Sok. 7/1, Ulus, Ankara; tel. (312) 3106820; f. 1968; Propr İLHAN İŞBİLEN; circ. 3,399.

**Ozgur Ulke:** Ankara; f. 1994; pro-Kurdish nationalist; proscribed by the government in February 1995; Editor-in-Chief BAKI KARADENIZ.

**Tasvir:** Ulus Meydanı, Ulus İş Hanı, Kat 4, Ankara; tel. (312) 4111241; f. 1960; conservative; Editor ENDER YOKDAR; circ. 3,055.

**Turkish Daily News:** Tunus Cad. 50/A-7, 06680 Kavaklıdere, Ankara; tel. (312) 4282957; fax 4278890; f. 1961; English language; Publisher İLHAN ÇEVİK; Editor-in-Chief İLNUR ÇEVİK; circ. 38,000.

**Türkiye Ticaret Sicili:** Karanfıl Sok. 56, Bakanlıklar, Ankara; f. 1957; commercial; Editor YALÇIN KAYA AYDOS.

**Vakit:** Konya Yolu 8km, 68 Balgat, Ankara; tel. (312) 2877906; f. 1978; Man. Editor NALİ ALAN; circ. 3,384.

**Yeni Tanin:** Rüzgârlı, Agâh Efendi Sok. Uçar Han, Kat 8/3, Ankara; f. 1964; political; Propr BURHANETTİN GÖĞEN; Man. Editor AHMET TEKEŞ; circ. 3,123.

**Yirmidört Saat:** Gazeteciler Cemiyeti Çevre Sok. 35, Çankaya, Ankara; tel. (312) 1682384; f. 1978; Propr BEYHAN CENKÇİ.

#### Eskişehir

**Milli İrade:** Siurihisar Cad. 31, Ekişehir; f. 1967; political; Propr ETEM KARACA; Editor ERKUT ÖZGENCİL.

#### İstanbul

**Apoyevmatini:** İstiklâl Cad., Suriye Pasajı 348, Beyoğlu, İstanbul; tel. (212) 2437635; f. 1925; Greek language; Publr Dr Y. A. ADAŞOĞLU; Editor İSTEFAN PAPADOPOULOS; circ. 1,200.

**Bugün:** Medya Plaza Basın Ekspres Yolu, 34540 Güneşli, İstanbul; tel. (212) 5504850; f. 1989; Propr ÖNAY BİLGİN; circ. 184,884.

**Cumhuriyet** (Republic): Türkocağı Cad. 39, 34334 Cağaloğlu, İstanbul; tel. (212) 5120505; telex 22246; fax (212) 5138595; f. 1924; morning; liberal; Editor-in-Chief ÖZGEN ACAR; Man. Editor İBRAHİM YILDIZ; circ. 72,000.

**Dünya** (World): 'Globus' Dünya Basinevi, 100 Yıl Mahallesi, 34440 Bağcilar, İstanbul; tel. (212) 6290808; telex 23822; fax (212) 6290305; f. 1952; morning; economic; Exec. Editor MUSTAFA MUTLU; circ. 50,000.

*Directory*

**Fotomaç:** Medya Plaza Basın Ekspres Yolu, 34540 Güneşli, İstanbul; tel. (212) 5504890; f. 1991; Propr SABAH YAYINCILIK.

**Günlük Ticaret:** Çemberlitaş Palas, Çemberlitaş, İstanbul; f. 1946; political; Editor SELİM BİLMEN; circ. 1,054.

**Hürriyet:** Kiregoeağı Merkii Evren Mah. Güneşli, İstanbul; tel. (212) 5500050; telex 22249; fax (212) 5503472; f. 1948; morning; independent political; Propr AYDIN DOĞAN; Chief Editor ERTUĞRUL ÖZKÖK; circ. 542,797.

**Jamanak:** İstiklâl Cad., Narmallı Yurdu, Beyoğlu, İstanbul; tel. (212) 2435639; f. 1908; Armenian; Editor HAGOP SİVASLIYAN; circ. 1,000.

**Meydan:** Prof. Kazım İsmail Gürkan Cad. 10, 34410 Cağaloğlu, İstanbul; tel. (212) 5194370; f. 1990; Propr REFİK ARAS.

**Milli Gazete:** Çayhane Sok. 1, 34040 Topkapı, İstanbul; tel. (212) 5674775; telex 23373; f. 1973; pro-Islamic; right-wing; Propr. HAZIM OKTAY BASER; Chief Editor HASAN KARAKAYA; circ. 24,496.

**Milliyet:** Nuruosmaniye Cad. 65, İstanbul; tel. (212) 5114410; telex 22884; fax (212) 5138742; f. 1950; morning; political; merged with *Hürriyet* in June 1994; Publr AYDIN DOĞAN; Editor-in-Chief UMUR TALU; monthly circ. 334,878.

**Nor Marmara:** İstiklâl Cad., Solakzade Sok. 5, PK 507, İstanbul; tel. (212) 2444736; f. 1940; Armenian language; Propr and Editor-in-Chief ROBER HADDELER; Gen. Man. ARİ HADDELER; circ. 2,200.

**Sabah** (Morning): Atakan Sok. 14, Mecideköy, İstanbul; tel. (212) 2752200; telex 26924; fax (212) 2752200; Propr DİNÇ BİLGİN; Editor ZAFER MUTLU; circ. 506,671.

**Tercüman:** Tercüman Tesisleri, Davutpaşa Cad. 115, Topkapı, İstanbul; tel. (212) 5779191; telex 22253; fax (212) 5671578; f. 1961; right-wing; Propr KEMAL ILICAK; Chief Editor ALTEMUR KİLİÇ; circ. 32,869.

**Turkiye:** Çatalçeşme Sok. 17, Cağaloğlu, İstanbul; tel. (212) 5139900; telex 22000; fax (212) 5209362; f. 1970; Man. Editor İSMAİL KAPAN; circ. 450,000.

**Yeni Günaydın:** Alayköşkü Cad., Eryılmaz Sok. 13, Cağaloğlu, İstanbul; tel. (212) 5285000; telex 22284; f. 1968; political; Propr HALDUN SİMAVİ; Chief Editor RAHMİ TURAN; circ. 300,000.

**Yeni Nesil** (New Generation): Sanayi Cad., Selvi Sok. 5, Yenibosna, Bakırköy, İstanbul; tel. (212) 5846261; telex 28620; fax (212) 5567289; f. 1970 as *Yeni Asya*; political; Propr MEHMET EMİN BİRİNCİ; Editor İHSAN ATASOY; monthly circ. 5,614.

**Zaman:** Cobancesme, Kalendar Sok. 21, Yenibosna, İstanbul; tel. (212) 5511477; fax (212) 5512822; f. 1962; morning; political, independent; Man. Editor ADEM KALAC; Chief Editor HALIT ESENDIR; circ. 210,000.

#### İzmir

**Rapor:** Gazi Osman Paşa Bul. 5, İzmir; tel. (232) 4254400; f. 1949; Owner DİNÇ BİLGİN; Man. Editor TANJU ATEŞER; circ. 9,000.

**Ticaret Gazetesi:** 1571 Sok. 16, 35110 Çınarlı, 35110 İzmir; tel. (232) 4619642; telex 52586; fax (232) 4619646; f. 1942; commercial news; Editor-in-Chief AHMET SUKÛTİ TÜKEL; Man. Editor CEMAL M. TÜKEL; circ. 5,009.

**Yeni Asır** (New Century): Gazi Osman Paşa Bul. 5, İzmir; tel. (232) 4252200; telex 53312; f. 1895; political; Propr DİNÇ BİLGİN; Editor-in-Chief CEMİL DEVRİM; monthly circ. 42,571.

#### Konya

**Yeni Konya:** Mevlâna Cad. 4, Konya; tel. (332) 2112594; f. 1945; political; Man. Editor M. NACİ GÜCÜYENER; Chief Editor ADİL GÜCÜYENER; monthly circ. 1,657.

**Yeni Meram:** Mevlâna Cad. 13, Sağlık Pasajı, Konya; tel. (332) 2112699; telex 48215; f. 1949; political; Propr M. YALÇIN BAHÇIVAN; Chief Editor YURDANUR ALPAY; monthly circ. 1,218.

### WEEKLIES

#### Ankara

**Bilim ve Teknik:** Bilim ve Teknik Dergisi Yazı İşleri Müdürlüğü, İstanbul, Cad. 88, İskitler, Ankara; tel. (312) 3419251; f. 1967; Propr Dr MEHMET ERGİN; Man. Editor FEYZULLAH AKBEN.

**EBA Briefing:** Bestekar Sok. 59/3, Kavaklıdere, Ankara; tel. (312) 4685376; telex 46836; fax (312) 4684114; f. 1975; publ. by Ekonomik Basın Ajansı (Economic Press Agency); political and economic survey; Publrs YAVUZ TOLUN, MELEK TOLUN.

**Ekonomi ve Politika:** Atatürk Bul. 199/A-45, Kavaklıdere, Ankara; f. 1966; economic and political; Publisher ZİYA TANSU.

**Türkiye İktisat Gazetesi:** Karanfil Sok. 56, 06582 Bakanlıklar, Ankara; tel. (312) 4184321; fax (312) 4183268; f. 1953; commercial; Chief Editor MEHMET SAĞLAM; circ. 11,500.

**Turkish Economic Gazette:** Atatürk Bul. 149, Bakanlıklar, Ankara; tel. (312) 4177700; telex 42343; publ. by UCCET.

**Turkish Probe:** Tunus Cad. 50/A-7, 06680 Kavaklıdere, Ankara; tel. (312) 4282956; fax (312) 4278890; English language; Publr A. ILHAN ÇEVIK; Editor-in-Chief ILNUR ÇEVIK; circ. 2,000.

### İstanbul

**Aktüel:** Medya Plaza Basın Ekspres Yolu, 34540 Güneşli, İstanbul; tel. (212) 5504870; f. 1991; Gen. Man. GÜLAY GÖKTÜRK; Man. Editor ALEV ER.

**Bayrak:** Çatalçeşme Sok. 50/5, 34410 Cağaloğlu, İstanbul; tel. (212) 5275575; fax (212) 5268363; f. 1970; political; Editor MEHMET GÜNGÖR; circ. 10,000.

**Doğan Kardeş:** Türbedar Sok. 22, Cağaloğlu, İstanbul; f. 1945; illustrated children's magazine; Editor ŞEVKET RADO; circ. 40,000.

**Ekonomik Panaroma:** Büyükdere Cad. Ali Kaya Sok. 8, 80720 Levent, İstanbul; tel. (212) 2696680; f. 1988; Gen. Man. AYDIN DEMIREL.

**Ekonomist:** Hürgüç Gazetecilik AŞ Hurriyet Tesisleri, Kireçocaği Mevkii, Evren Mah., Güneşli Köy, İstanbul; tel. (212) 5500050; f. 1991; Gen. Man. ADİL ÖZKOL.

**Gırgır:** Alayköşkü Cad., Çağaloğlu, İstanbul; tel. (212) 2285000; satirical; Propr and Editor OĞUZ ARAL; circ. 500,000.

**Hıbır:** İstanbul; satirical; circ. 250,000.

**Ikibine Doğru:** Nuruosmaniye Cad. 19/2 Cağaloğlu, İstanbul; f. 1987; Propr MEHMET SABUNCU; Man. Editor FERIT ILSEVER.

**İstanbul Ticaret:** İstanbul Chamber of Commerce, Gümüşpala Cad., PK 377, Eminönü, İstanbul; tel. (212) 5114150; telex 22682; f. 1958; commercial news; Publr YALIM EREZ.

**Nokta:** İstanbul; Editor ARDA USKAN; circ. 60,000.

**Tempo:** Hürgüç Gazetecilik AŞ Hürriyet Tesisleri, Güneşli, İstanbul; tel. (212) 5500081; f. 1987; Dir SEDAT SİMAVİ; Gen. Man. MEHMET Y. YILMAZ.

**Türk Dünyasi Araştirmalar Dergisi:** Hürgüç Gazetecilik AŞ Hurriyet Tesisleri, Güneşli, İstanbul; tel. (212) 5500081; Dir SEDAT SİMAVİ; Gen. Man. MEHMET Y. YILMAZ.

### İzmir

**Merhaba:** Cumhuriyet Bul. 238/3, İzmir; f. 1979; magazine; Editor ÜMIT ÇELIKER; circ. 90,000.

## PERIODICALS
### Ankara

**Adalet Dergisi:** Adalet Bakanlığı, Ankara; tel. (312) 4192199; f. 1909; legal journal publ. by the Ministry of Justice; Editor HÜSEYİN ERGÜL; circ. 3,500.

**Azerbaycan Türk Kültür Dergisi:** Vakıf İş Hani 324, Anafartalar, Ankara; f. 1949; literary and cultural periodical of Azerbaizhanian Turks; Editor Dr AHMET YAŞAT.

**Bayrak Dergisi:** Bestckar Sok. 44/5, Kavaklıdere, Ankara; f. 1964; Publr and Editor HAMİ KARTAY.

**Devlet Opera ve Balesi Genel Müdürlüğü:** Ankara; tel. (312) 3241476; telex 44401; fax (312) 3107248; f. 1949; state opera and ballet; Gen. Dir. RENGIM GOKMEN.

**Devlet Tiyatrosu:** Devlet Tiyatrosu Um. Md., Ankara; f. 1952; art, theatre.

**Eğitim ve Bilim:** Ziya Gökalp Cad. 48, Yenişehir, Ankara; tel. (312) 4313488; f. 1928; quarterly; education and science; publ. by the Turkish Educational Asscn (TED); Editor REFIK ÇÖLAŞAN; circ. 500.

**Elektrik Mühendisliği Mecmuası:** Gülden Sok. 2/A Güvenevler, Kavaklıdere, Ankara; f. 1954; publ. by the Chamber of Turkish Electrical Engineers; Pres. SEFA GÖMDENİZ.

**Halk Eğitimi:** Millî Eğitim Bakanlığı, Halk Eğitimi Genel Müdürlüğü, Ankara; f. 1966; publ. by the Ministry of Education.

**Karınca:** Türk Kooperatifçilik Kurumu, Mithatpaşa Cad. 38/A, 06420 Kızılay, Ankara; tel. (312) 4316125; fax (312) 4340646; f. 1934; monthly review publ. by the Turkish Co-operative Asscn; Editor Prof. Dr CELÂL ER; circ. 5,000.

**Maden Tetkik Arama Enstitüsü Dergisi:** İnönü Bul., Ankara; f. 1935; 2 a year; publ. by Mineral Research and Exploration Institute of Turkey; English Edition *Bulletin of the Mineral Research and Exploration Institute* (2 a year).

**Mimarlık** (Architecture): Konur Sok. 4, Kızılay, Ankara; tel. (312) 4173727; fax (312) 4180361; f. 1963; every 2 months; publ. by the Chamber of Architects of Turkey; Editor ASLI ÖZBAY; circ. 11,000.

**Mühendis ve Makina:** Sümer Sok. 36/7, 06640 Demirtepe, Ankara; tel. (312) 2301166; fax (312) 2313165; f. 1957; engineering; monthly; Publr Chamber of Mechanical Engineers; Propr MURAT ÖNDER; Editor OĞUZ ŞAHIN; circ. 30,000.

**Nûr** (the Light): Nuruosmaniye Cad., Sorkun Han 28/2, 34410, Cağaloğlu, İstanbul; tel. (212) 5277607; fax (212) 5208231; f. 1986; religion; Editor CEMAL UŞAK; circ. 10,000.

**Resmi Kararlar Dergisi:** Adalet Bakanlığı Eğitim Dairesi Başkanlığı, 06659 Bakanlıklar, Ankara; tel. (312) 4192199; fax (312) 4173954; f. 1966; legal; Editor AVNI ÖZENÇ; circ. 3,500.

**Teknik ve Uygulama:** Konur Sok. 4/4, 06442 Kızılay, Ankara; tel. (312) 4182374; f. 1986; engineering; every 2 months; publ. by the Chamber of Mechanical Engineers; Propr ISMET RIZA ÇEBI; Editor UĞUR DOĞAN; circ. 3,000.

**Türk Arkeoloji Dergisi** (General Directorate of Monuments and Museums): Kültür Bakanlığı, Anıtlar ve Müzeler Genel Müdürlüğü-II. Meclis Binası Ulus, Ankara; tel. (312) 3105363; fax (312) 3111417; archaeological.

**Türk Dili:** Türk Dil Kurumu, Atatürk Bul. 217, 06680 Kavaklıdere, Ankara; tel. (312) 4286100; fax (312) 4285288; f. 1951; monthly; Turkish literature and language; Editor Prof. Dr HASAN EREN.

**Turkey—Economic News Digest:** Karanfil Sok. 56, Ankara; f. 1960; Editor-in-Chief BEHZAT TANİR; Man. Editor SADIK BALKAN.

**Turkish Review:** Atatürk Bul. 203, 06688 Kavaklıdere, Ankara; tel. (312) 4671180; telex 42384; fax (312) 4682100; f. 1985; 4 a year; cultural, social and economic; English; publ. by the Directorate General of Press and Information; Chief Officers MURAT ERSACI, OSMAN ÜNTÜRK, NAZAN ERVE MINE CANPOLAT.

**Türkiye Bankacılık:** PK 121, Ankara; f. 1955; commercial; Publisher MUSTAFA ATALAY.

**Türkiye Bibliyografyası:** Milli Kütüphane Başkanlığı, 06490 Bahçelievler, Ankara; tel. (312) 2126200; fax (312) 2230451; f. 1934; monthly; Turkish national bibliography; publ. by the Bibliographical Centre of the Turkish National Library; Dir ORHAN DOĞAN.

**Türkiye Makaleler Bibliyografyası:** Milli Kütüphane Başkanlığı, 06490 Bahçelievler, Ankara; tel. (312) 2126200; fax (312) 2230451; f. 1952; monthly; Turkish articles, bibliography; publ. by the Bibliographical Centre of the Turkish National Library; Dir SEMA AKINCI.

### Bursa

**Tekstil ve Mühendis:** Elmasbahçeler Mah. Sabunevi Sok., Mühendisler İş Hanı 19, Kat. 2, 16230 Bursa; tel. (24) 538018; fax (24) 525514; textile engineering; every 2 months; publ. by the Chamber of Textile Engineers; Propr GÜNGÖR BAŞER; Editor ZIYA ÖZEK; circ. 4,000.

### İstanbul

**Archaeology and Art Magazine:** Hayriye Cad. 3/5 Çorlu Apt., Beyoğlu 80060, İstanbul; tel. (212) 2456838; fax (212) 2456877; f. 1978; quarterly; publ. by Archaeology and Art Publications; Publr and Editor NEZİH BAŞGELEN.

**İstanbul Key:** Halaskargazi Cad. 364, Şişli Meydanı, İstanbul; tel. (212) 2314631; telex 27800; f. 1989; publ. by Türk Turing, official travel agency of the Touring and Automobile Club of Turkey; Publr Prof. KEMAL KUTLU; Editor-in-Chief ÇELIK GÜLERSOY.

**İstanbul Ticaret Odası Mecmuası:** Gümüşpala Cad., PK 377, Eminönü, İstanbul; tel. (212) 5114150; telex 22682; f. 1884; quarterly; journal of the İstanbul Chamber of Commerce (ICOC); English; Editor-in-Chief CENGİZ ERSUN.

**Kulis:** Cağaloğlu Yokuşu 10/A, İstanbul; f. 1947; fortnightly arts magazine; Armenian; Publr HAGOP AYVAZ.

**Musiki Mecmuası:** PK 666, İstanbul; tel. (216) 3306299; fax (216) 3475273; f. 1948; monthly; music and musicology; Editor ETEM RUHI ÜNGÖR.

**Pirelli Mecmuası:** Büyükdere Cad. 117, Gayrettepe, İstanbul; tel. (212) 2663200; telex 26337; fax (212) 2726077; f. 1964; monthly; Publr Türk-Pirelli Lâstikleri AS; Editor UĞUR CANAL; circ. 24,500.

**Présence** (Aylık Dergi): Ölçek Sok. 82, 80230 Harbiye, İstanbul; tel. and fax (212) 2408801; f. 1986; 10 a year; publ. by the Apostolic Vicariate of İstanbul; Gen. Man. FUAT ÇÖLLÜ.

**Ruh ve Madde Dergisi** (Spirit and Matter): Ruh ve Madde Publications and Health Services Co., PK 9, 80072 Beyoğlu, İstanbul; tel. (212) 2431814; fax (212) 2526125; f. 1959; organ of the Foundation for Spreading the Knowledge to Unify Humanity; Editor ERGÜN ARIKDAL.

**Sevgi Dünyası** (World of Respect): Aydede Cad. 4/5, 80090 Taksim, İstanbul; tel. (212) 2504242; f. 1963; monthly; social, psychological and spiritual; Publr and Editor Dr REFET KAYSERİLİ OĞLU.

**Tıp Dünyası:** Ankara Cad. 31/51, Vakıf İş Hanı, Cağaloğlu, İstanbul; tel. (212) 5279611; f. 1927; monthly; organ of the Turkish Mental Health and Social Psychiatry Soc.; Editor Ord. Prof. Dr FAHREDDİN KERİM GÖKAY.

**Turkey:** Catalcesme Sok. 17, 34410 Cağaloğlu, İstanbul; tel. (212) 5110028; telex 22000; fax (212) 5135195; f. 1982; monthly; English language, economics; Editor MEHMET SOZTUTAN; circ. 80,000.

TURKEY
*Directory*

**Türkiye Turing ve Otomobil Kurumu Belleteni:** Halaskargazi Cad. 364, Şişli Meydanı, İstanbul; tel. (212) 2314631; f. 1930; quarterly; publ. by the Touring and Automobile Club of Turkey; Publr Prof. KEMAL KUTLU: Editor ÇELİK GÜLERSOY.

**Varlık:** Cağaloğlu Yokuşu 40/2, İstanbul; tel. (212) 5226924; fax (212) 5129528; f. 1933; monthly; literary; Editor FİLİZ NAYIR DENİZTEKİN.

### İzmir

**İzmir Ticaret Odası Dergisi:** Atatürk Cad. 126, İzmir; tel. (232) 4417777; telex 52331; fax (232) 4837853; f. 1927; every 2 months; publ. by Chamber of Commerce of İzmir; Sec.-Gen. Prof. İLTER AKAT: Man. ÜMİT ALEMDAROĞLU.

### Konya

**Çağrı Dergisi:** PK 99, Konya; f. 1957; monthly; literary; Editor FEYZİ HALICI.

## NEWS AGENCIES

**Akajans:** Tunus Cad. 28, Kat. 4, Bakanlıklar, Ankara; tel. (312) 4139720; Dir YAŞAR GÜNGÖR.

**Anatolian News Agency:** Hanımeli Sok. 7, Sıhhuye, Ankara; tel. (312) 2317000; telex 42088; fax (312) 2312174; f. 1920; Chair. ALİ AYDIN DUNDAR; Gen. Dir BEHİÇ EKŞİ.

**ANKA Ajansı:** Selanık Cad. 417/8, Kızılay, Ankara; tel. (312) 4172500; telex 42809; fax (312) 4180254; Dir-Gen. MÜŞERREF HEKİMOĞLU.

**EBA Ekonomik Basın Ajansı** (Economic Press Agency): Bestekar Sok. 59/3, Kavakıdere, 06680 Ankara; tel. (312) 4685376; telex 46836; fax (312) 4684114; f. 1969; private economic news service; Propr MELEK TOLUN; Editor YAVUZ TOLUN.

**Hürriyet Haber Ajansı:** Babıali Cad. 15–17 Kat. 3, 34360 Cağaloğlu, İstanbul; tel. (212) 5120000; telex 22249; fax (212) 5223155; f. 1963; Dir-Gen. HASAN YILMAER.

**IKA Haber Ajansı** (Economic and Commercial News Agency): Atatürk Bul. 199/A-45, Kavaklıdere, Ankara; tel. (312) 4267327; telex 42569; f. 1954; Dir ZİYA TANSU.

**Milha News Agency:** Nuruosmaniye Cad. 65, Cağaloğlu, İstanbul; tel. (212) 5114410; telex 22251; fax (212) 5283018.

**Ulusal Basın Ajansı (UBA):** Meşrutiyet Cad. 5/10, Ankara; Man. Editor OĞUZ SEREN.

### Foreign Bureaux

**Agence France-Presse (AFP):** Ahmet Rasik Sok. 10/1, 06550 Çankaya, Ankara; tel. (312) 4393550; telex 42399; fax (312) 4407815; Correspondent HERVÉ COUTURIER.

**Agenzia Nazionale Stampa Associata (ANSA)** (Italy): Sedat Simavı Sok. 30/5, Ankara; tel. (312) 4406084; telex 44337; fax (312) 4405029; Correspondent ROMANO DAMIANI.

**Associated Press (AP)** (USA): Tunus Cad. 87/3, Kavaklıdere, Ankara; tel. (312) 4282709; telex 42340; Correspondent EMEL ANIL.

**Bulgarska Telegrafna Agentsia (BTA)** (Bulgaria): Hatır Sok. 25/6, Gaziosmanpaşa, Ankara; tel. (312) 4273899; Correspondent LUBOMIR GABROVSKI.

**Deutsche Presse-Agentur (dpa)** (Germany): Yesil Yali Sok., Liman Apt 6/6 Yesilköy, İstanbul; tel. (212) 5738607; telex 44356; Correspondent BAHADETTIN GÜNGÖR.

**Informatsionnoye Telegrafnoye Agentstvo Rossii—Telegrafnoye Agentstvo Suverennykh Stran (ITAR—TASS)** (Russia): c/o Russian Embassy, Ankara; Correspondent SERGEY A. FEOKTISTOV.

**Reuters** (United Kingdom): Yavuz Sok. 5–7, Fulya, Mecidiyek oy, 80290 İstanbul; Bureau Chief KIM WATERS.

**United Press International (UPI)** (USA): Yerebatan Cad. 33, Cağaloğlu, İstanbul; tel. (212) 2285238; telex 22350; Correspondent İSMET İMSET.

**Xinhua (New China) News Agency** (People's Republic of China): Horasan Sok. 16/4, Gaziosmanpaşa, Ankara; tel. (312) 4361456; telex 46138; fax (312) 4465229; Correspondent WANG QIANG.

**Zhongguo Xinwen She** (China News Agency) (People's Republic of China): Nenehatun Cad. 88-2, Ata Apartmani, Gaziosmanpaşa, Ankara; tel. (312) 4362261; Correspondent CHANG CHILIANG.

AFP also has representatives in İstanbul and İzmir; AP is also represented in İstanbul.

## JOURNALISTS' ASSOCIATION

**Gazeteciler Cemiyeti:** Cağaloğlu, İstanbul; tel. (212) 5138300; telex 23508; fax (212) 5268046; f. 1946; Pres. NECMİ TANYOLAÇ; Sec. RIDVAN YELE.

## Publishers

**Altın Kitaplar Yayınevi Anonim ŞTİ:** Celal Ferdi Gökçay Sok., Nebioğlu Han, Kat. 1, Cağaloğlu, İstanbul; tel. (212) 5268012; telex 22627; fax (212) 5268011; f. 1959; fiction, non-fiction, biography, children's books, encyclopaedias, dictionaries; Publr FETHİ ULTURHAN BOZKURT; Chief Editor HÜSNÜ TEREK.

**Archaeology and Art Publs:** Hariye Cad. 3/5 Gorlu Apt., Beyoğlu, 80060 Istanbul; tel. (212) 2456838; fax (212) 2456877; classical, Byzantine and Turkish studies, art and archaeology, numismatics and ethnography books; Publr NEZİH BASGELEN.

**Ark Ticaret Ltd ŞTİ:** PK 137-35220, Merkez, İzmir; tel. (232) 2469550; f. 1962; import-export representation; imports technical books and exports all kinds of Turkish books, periodicals and newspapers; Gen. Man. ATILAN TÜMER.

**Cem Yayınevi:** İstanbul; f. 1964; novels, poetry, modern classics, cultural and historical books, children's books.

**Elif Kitabevi:** Sahaflar Çarşısı 4, Beyazıt, İstanbul; tel. (212) 5222096; f. 1956; all types of publications, especially historical, literary; political, drama and reference; old Ottoman and Turkish books and periodicals; Publr ARSLAN KAYNARDAĞ.

**Gelişim Yayınları AŞ:** Büyükdere Cad., Ali Kaya Sok., 80720 Levent, İstanbul; tel. (212) 2696680; telex 26510; f. 1974; encyclopaedias, magazines, reference and non-fiction; Man. ERCAN ARIKLI.

**Hürriyet Yayınları:** Cemal Nadir Sok. 7, Cağaloğlu, İstanbul; tel. (212) 2222038; telex 22276; fiction, history, classics, poetry, general reference books; Dir ÇETİN EMEÇ.

**Kanaat Kitabevi:** İlyas Bayar Halefi, Yakup Bayar, Ankara Cad. 133, İstanbul; f. 1896; textbooks, novels, dictionaries, posters, maps and atlases.

**Karacan Yayınları:** Köyaltı Mevki Oruç Reis Sok. 10, Yenibosna, Bakırköy, İstanbul; tel. (212) 5513038; f. 1980; literary books and magazines; Gen. Man. ALI NACI KARACAN.

**Öğretim Yayınevi:** Ankara Cad. 62/2, Sirkeci, İstanbul; f. 1959; English, French, German, Italian, Spanish and Dutch language courses, guides and dictionaries, phrase books for tourists; Dir İZİDOR KANT.

**Remzi Kitabevi AŞ:** Selvili Mescit Sok. 3, 34440 Cağaloğlu, İstanbul; tel. (212) 5220583; fax (212) 5229055; f. 1929; general and educational; Dirs EROL ERDURAN, ÖMER ERDURAN, AHMET ERDURAN.

**Türk Dil Kurumu** (Turkish Language Institute): Atatürk Bul. 217, 06680 Kavaklıdere, Ankara; tel. (312) 4268124; fax (312) 4285288; f. 1932; non-fiction, research, language; Pres. Prof. Dr AHMET B. ERCİLASUN.

**Varlık Yayınları:** Cağaloğlu Yokuşu 40/42, İstanbul; tel. (212) 5226924; fax (212) 5129528; f. 1946; fiction and non-fiction books; Dir FİLİZ NAYIR DENİZTEKİN.

### PUBLISHERS' ASSOCIATION

**Türkiye Yayıncılar Birliği Derneği** (The Publishers' Association of Turkey): Cağaloğlu Yokuşu, Edes Han 40/3, İstanbul; tel. 5125602; f. 1985; Pres. AYGÖREN DİRİM; Sec. ˇ

## Radio and Television

In July 1993 the Turkish National Assembly voted to abolish the state monopoly of radio and television services. New broadcasting legislation, which entered into force in April 1994, provided for the establishment of a Broadcasting Council, to be responsible for issuing licences, drafting regulations for cable and satellite transmissions and verifying the compliance of broadcasts with the 'public and national interest'. The legislation also limited foreign equity in companies to 20% and the proportion of advertising to 15% of daily broadcast time. In 1992, according to UNESCO, an estimated 9.4m. radio receivers and 10.3m. television receivers were in use.

**Türkiye Radyo Televizyon Kurumu (TRT)** (Turkish Radio-Television Corpn): Merkez Kutuphane, Oran, Ankara; tel. (312) 4900379; telex 43164; fax (312) 4901109; f. 1964; controls Turkish radio and television services; Dir-Gen. TAYFUN AKGUNER.

### RADIO

*Home Services:* There are four national radio-broadcasting networks and more than 50 local radio stations in Turkey. Head of Radio İSMAİL H. KÜLAHLI.

*Foreign Service* (Voice of Turkey); PK 333, 06443 Yenişehir, Ankara; tel. (312) 4353816; telex 42832; fax (312) 4353816; Man. Dir SAVAŞ MIRATLI.

**Ankara:** SW 250 kW (3), SW 500 kW (2). Fifteen daily shortwave transmissions in the following languages: Albanian, Arabic,

# TURKEY

*Directory*

Azerbaijanian Turkish, Bulgarian, Chinese, English, French, German, Greek, Hungarian, Persian, Romanian, Russian, Serbo-Croat, Turkish; Dir İSMAİL HAKKI TORAN.

There is also an educational radio service for schools and a station run by the Turkish State Meteorological Service. The American Forces have their own radio and television service.

### TELEVISION

A limited television service was set up in 1965, and regular broadcasts for Ankara began in 1968. In 1986 there were two national channels transmitting programmes every day, averaging 90 hours per week. A third national channel began broadcasting in 1989 and a fourth and fifth channel were providing reduced services by 1991. Head of Television BULENT VAROL; Dir. Ankara TV ATILLA ORAY.

## Finance

(cap. = capital; res = reserves; dep. = deposits; m. = million; brs = branches; amounts in Turkish liras unless otherwise stated)

The Central Bank of the Republic of Turkey was originally founded in 1930, and constituted in its present form in 1970. The central bank is the bank of issue and is also responsible for the execution of monetary and credit policies, the regulation of the foreign and domestic value of the Turkish lira jointly with the government, and the supervision of the credit system. In 1987 a decree was issued to bring the governorship of the Central Bank under direct government control.

There are 71 other banks operating in Turkey. Several banks were created by special laws to fulfil specialized services for particular industries. The Sümerbank directs the operation of a number of state-owned factories; Etibank operates primarily in the extractive industries and electric power industries; the Ziraat Bankası makes loans for agriculture; the Emlâk Bankası participates in industrial undertakings and the construction of all types of building.

The largest of the private sector Turkish banks is the Türkiye İş Bankası, which operates 808 branches.

There are several credit institutions in Turkey, including the Sınai Kalınma Bankası (Industrial Development Bank), which was founded in 1950, with the assistance of the World Bank, to encourage private investment in industry by acting as underwriter in the issue of share capital.

There are numerous co-operative organizations, including agricultural co-operatives in rural areas. There are also a number of savings institutions.

In 1990 the Turkish Government announced plans to establish a structure for offshore banking. A decree issued in October 1990 exempted foreign banks, operating in six designated free zones, from local banking obligations.

### BANKING

#### Central Bank

**Türkiye Cumhuriyet Merkez Bankası AŞ** (Central Bank of the Republic of Turkey): Head Office, İstiklal Cad. 10, 06100 Ulus, Ankara; tel. (312) 3103646; telex 44033; fax (312) 3107434; f. 1931; bank of issue; cap. 25,000.0m., res 2,854,621.5m., dep. 218,498,710.2m. (Dec. 1993); Gov. YAMAN TÖRÜNER; 22 brs.

#### State Banks

**Etibank Bankacılık A.O.:** Tunus Cad. 33, 06680 Kavaklıdere, Ankara; tel. (312) 4250277; fax (312) 4182938; f. 1935; cap. US $26m., dep. $506m. (Dec. 1994); Gen. Man. M. ZEKİ AKILLIOĞLU; 140 brs.

**İller Bankası** (Municipalities Bank): Atatürk Bul. 21, 06040 Ulus, Ankara; tel. (312) 3103141; telex 42724; fax (312) 3107459; f. 1933; cap. 530,999m.; res 23,207m., total assets 5,204,351m. (Dec. 1991); Gen. Man. SAYHAN BAYOĞLU; 1 br.

**Sümerbank AŞ:** Atatürk Bul. 70, 06440 Kızılay, Ankara; tel. (312) 4178545; telex 44098; fax (312) 4178379; f. 1933; cap. 850,000m., dep. 210,216m., total assets 1,328,484m. (Dec. 1993); Pres. RECEP ÖNAL; 49 brs.

**Türkiye Cumhuriyeti Ziraat Bankası** (Agricultural Bank of the Republic of Turkey): Atatürk Bul. 42, 06107 Ulus, Ankara; tel. (312) 3103750; telex 44004; fax (312) 3101135; f. 1863; cap. 6,197,420.0m., res 6,085,958.8m., dep. 157,066,113.7m. (Dec. 1993); in November 1983 took over three commercial banks (Hisarbank AŞ, İstanbul Bankası TAŞ and Ortadoğu İktisat Bankası TAŞ) following their liquidation; Chair. Dr ŞERİF COŞKUN ULUSOY; 1,279 brs.

**Türkiye Emlâk Bankası AŞ** (Real Estate Bank of Turkey): Büyükdere Cad., Maslak Meydanı 43/45, 80670 Levent, İstanbul; tel. (212) 2761610; telex 27780; fax (212) 2761659; f. 1988 as a merger of Anadolu Bankası AŞ and Türkiye Emlâk Kredi Bankası; absorbed Denizcilik Bankası TAŞ in 1992; cap. 2,190,224m., res 2,310,472m., dep. 52,110,216m. (Dec. 1993); Chair. Prof. AYOIN AYAYOIN; 429 brs.

**Türkiye Halk Bankası AŞ:** İlkiz Sok. 1, Sıhhiye, Ankara; tel. (312) 2317500; telex 44587; fax (312) 2295857; f. 1938; absorbed Turkiye Öğretmenler Bankası TAŞ in May 1992; cap. 923,314m., res 1,063,672m., dep. 19,362,744m. (Dec. 1992); Gen. Man. CIHAN PACACI; 782 brs.

**Türkiye İhracat Kredi Bankası AŞ (Türk Eximbank)** (Export Credit Bank of Turkey): Milli Müdafa Cad. 20, 06581 Bakanlıklar, Ankara; tel. (312) 4171300; telex 46106; fax (312) 4257896; f. 1964; fmrly Devlet Yatırım Bankası AŞ; cap. 575,510m., res 477,569m., total assets 24,770,808m. (Dec. 1993); extends credit to exporters, insures and guarantees export transactions; Pres. Dr AHMET ERTUĞRUL.

**Türkiye Kalkınma Bankası AŞ** (Development Bank of Turkey): İzmir Cad. 35, 06570 Kızılay, Ankara; tel. (312) 4179200; telex 43206; fax (312) 4183967; f. 1976, renamed in 1988 and in 1989 merged with Türkiye Cumhuriyeti Turizm Bankası AŞ; cap. 944,432m., res 59,140m., total assets 8,775,458m. (Dec. 1992); Chair. and Gen. Man. ÖZAL BAYSAL; 7 brs.

**Türkiye Vakıflar Bankası TAO** (Foundation Bank of Turkey): Atatürk Bul. 207, 06691 Kavaklıdere, Ankara; tel. (312) 4681160; telex 44428; fax (312) 4684541; f. 1954; cap. 1,000,000m., res 1,312,248m., dep. 44,046,492m. (Dec. 1993); Chair. FADİL ÜNVER; Gen. Man. YAŞAR YILMAZ ÖZEN; 326 brs.

#### Commercial Banks

**Akbank TAŞ:** Sabancı Center, 4 Levent, 80745 İstanbul; tel. (212) 2699041; telex 24134; fax (212) 2818188; f. 1948; cap. 4,000,000m., res 4,533,966m., dep. 85,973,127m. (Dec. 1994); Chair. NAİM TALU; Gen. Man. ÖZEN GÖKSEL; 500 brs.

**Bank Expres AŞ:** Kore Şehitleri Cad. 43, 80300 Zincirlikuyu, İstanbul; tel. (212) 2883838; telex 39511; fax (212) 2883867; f. 1992; cap 1,000,000m., dep. 5,774,471m., total assets 7,899,981m. (Dec. 1994); Chair AYHAN ŞAHENK; Pres. and CEO ACLAN ACAR; 10 brs.

**Demirbank TAŞ:** Büyükdere Cad. 122, Blok B, 80280 Esentepe, İstanbul; tel. (212) 2751900; telex 27368; fax (212) 2731988; f. 1953; cap. 500,000m., res 27,168m., dep. 6,714,000m. (Dec. 1993); Chair. NURİ CINGILLIOGLU; Gen. Man. SELAHATTIN SERBEST; 14 brs.

**Egebank AŞ:** Büyükdere Cad. 106, 80280 Esentepe, İstanbul; tel. (212) 2887400; telex 39491; fax (212) 2887316; f. 1928; cap. 500,000m., res 321,707m., dep. 4,349,631m. (Dec. 1993); Gen. Man. NACİ AYHAN; 33 brs.

**Eskişehir Bankası TAŞ (Esbank):** Meşrutiyet Cad. 141, 80050 Tepebaşı, İstanbul; tel. (212) 2517270; telex 24535; fax (212) 2434118; f. 1927; cap. p.u. 1,300,000m., res 56,752m., dep. 6,704,682m. (Dec. 1993); Chair. MESUT EREZ; Gen. Man. ÖZER GÜNEY; 40 brs.

**Finansbank AŞ:** Büyükdere Cad. 123, 80300 Mecidiyeköy, İstanbul; tel. (212) 2752450; telex 39280; fax (212) 2752496; f. 1987; cap. 1,000,000m., res 357,597m., dep. 3,627,659m. (Dec. 1994); Gen. Man. Dr ÖMER ARAS; 4 brs.

**İktisat Bankası TAŞ:** Büyükdere Cad. 165, 80504 Esentepe, İstanbul; tel. (212) 2747111; telex 27685; fax (212) 2747028; f. 1927; cap. 800,000m.; res 628,186m., dep. 10,897,974m. (Dec. 1993); Gen. Man. ALİ AYANLAR; 13 brs.

**Interbank (Uluslararası Endüstri ve Ticaret Bankası AŞ):** Büyükdere Cad. 108/C, 80496 Esentepe, İstanbul; tel. (212) 2742000; telex 26098; fax (212) 2721622; f. 1888; cap. 2,750,000m., res 1,453,000m., dep. 11,527,000m. (Dec. 1994); specializes in import and export financing; Chair. YILDIRIM AKTÜRK; CEO MELİH E. ARAZ; 12 brs.

**Koçbank AŞ:** Barbaros Bul. Mörbasan Sok. Koza İş Merkezi, Blok C, 80700 Beşiktaş, İstanbul; tel. (212) 2747777; telex 39069; fax (212) 2672987; f. 1986; cap. 1,000,000m., res 116,932m., dep. 2,472,521m. (Dec. 1993); Gen. Man. ENGİN AKÇAKOCA; 7 brs.

**Körfezbank AŞ** (United Turkish Gulf Bank): Büyükdere Cad., Doğuş Han 42–44, Kat 3–4, 80290 Mecidiyeköy, İstanbul; tel. (212) 2882000; telex 39714; fax (212) 2881217; f. 1988; cap. 250,000m., res 76,008m., dep. 4,291,074m. (Dec. 1993); Gen. Man. HALUK DAYIGİL; 4 brs.

**Marbank, Marmara Bankası AŞ:** Cumhuriyet Cad. 199, 80230 Elmadag, İstanbul; tel. (212) 2343406; telex 28259; fax (212) 2330358; f. 1988 as Netbank AŞ; cap. 400,000m., dep. 2,682,479m., total assets 10,761,155m. (Dec. 1993); Chair. ATILLA URAS; 11 brs.

**Pamukbank TAŞ:** Büyükdere Cad. 82, 80450 Gayrettepe, İstanbul; tel. (212) 2723484; telex 26959; fax (212) 2758217; f. 1955; cap.

# TURKEY

3,740,000m., dep. 72,858,370m. (Dec. 1994); Pres. CEMİL KÖKSAL; 155 brs.

**Şekerbank TAŞ:** Atatürk Bul. 171, 06442 Bakanlıklar, Ankara; tel. (312) 4179120; telex 42679; fax (312) 4254919; f. 1953; cap. 250,000.0m., res 395,852.5m., dep. 6,333,062.0m. (Dec. 1993); Gen. Man. HASAN BASRİ GÖKTAN; 183 brs.

**Toprakbank AŞ:** Büyükdere Cad. Nilüfer Han 103/1-5, 80300 Gayrettepe, İstanbul; tel. (212) 2884120; telex 27046; fax (212) 2882447; f. 1992; cap. 1,000,000m., dep. 8,289,691m., total assets 10,691,102m. (Dec. 1994); Gen. Man. MEVLÜT ASLANOĞLU; 68 brs.

**Türk Boston Bank AŞ:** Yıldız Posta Cad. 17, 80280 Esentepe, İstanbul; tel. (212) 2745222; telex 26537; fax (212) 2723348; cap. 200,000m., res 15,312m. (Dec. 1993); Gen. Man. IAN LEVACK; 1 br.

**Türk Dış Ticaret Bankası AŞ** (Turkish Foreign Trade Bank): Yıldız Posta Cad. 54, 80280 Gayrettepe, İstanbul; tel. (212) 2744280; telex 27992; fax (212) 2725278; f. 1964; cap. p.u. 400,000m., res 191,546m., dep. 12,072,029m. (Dec. 1993); Chair. ATILLA TAŞDEMİR; 21 brs.

**Türk Ekonomi Bankası AŞ:** Meclisi Mebusan Cad. 35, 80040 Fındıklı, İstanbul; tel. (212) 2512121; telex 25358; fax (212) 2496568; f. 1927; fmrly Kocaeli Bankası TAŞ; cap. 700,000m.; res 899,408m.; dep. 6,856,375m. (Dec. 1994); Chair ŞAHABETTİN BİLGİSU; Man. Dir. Dr AKIN AKBAYGİL; 10 brs.

**Türk Ticaret Bankası AŞ (Türkbank):** Yıldız Posta Cad. 2, 80280 Gayrettepe, İstanbul; tel. (212) 2885900; telex 22224; fax (212) 2886113; f. 1913; cap. 500,000m., res 1,065,538m., dep. 27,707,315m. (Dec. 1993); Chair. and Gen. Man. BEHZAT TUNCER; 345 brs.

**Türkiye Garanti Bankası AŞ:** Büyükdere Cad. 63, 80670 Maslak, İstanbul; tel. (212) 2855040; telex 27635; fax (212) 2854040; f. 1946; cap. 2,000,000m., res 318,220m., dep. 17,902,891m. (Dec. 1993); Chair. AYHAN ŞAHENK; Gen. Man. Y. AKIN ÖNGÖR; 238 brs.

**Türkiye İmar Bankası TAŞ:** Büyükdere Cad. Doğuş Han. 42-46, 80290 Mecidiyeköy, İstanbul; tel. (212) 2751190; telex 26592; fax (212) 2724720; f. 1928; cap. 107,500m., res 4,678m., dep. 2,783,382m. (Dec. 1991); Chair. KEMAL UZAN; Gen. Man. HİLMİ BAŞARAN; 4 brs.

**Türkiye İş Bankası AŞ (İşbank):** Atatürk Bul. 191, 06684 Kavaklıdere, Ankara; tel. (312) 4281140; telex 42082; fax (312) 4250750; f. 1924; cap. 1,936,326m., dep. 50,554,084m. (Dec. 1993); Chair. İLHAN EVLİYAOĞLU; CEO ÜNAL KORUKÇU; 808 brs.

**Türkiye Tütüncüler Bankası AŞ (Tütünbank):** Barbaros Bul. 121, 80700 Balmumcu-Beşiktaş, İstanbul; tel. (212) 2758400; telex 27130; fax (212) 2728314; f. 1924; cap. 420,000m., res 297,363m., dep. 10,750,944m. (Dec. 1993); Chair. SELÇUK YAŞAR; CEO and Man. Dir GAZİ ERCEL; 61 brs.

**Yapı ve Kredi Bankası AŞ:** Yapı Kredi Plaza, Blok A, Büyükdere Cad., 80620 Levent, İstanbul; tel. (212) 2801111; telex 24718; fax (212) 2801670; f. 1944; cap. 1,000,000m., dep. 19,737,604m. (Dec. 1992); Chair. RONA YIRCALI; CEO BURHAN KARAÇAM; 361 brs.

### Development and Investment Banks

**Park Yatırım Bankası AŞ:** Büyükdere Cad., Meşeli Sok. 9, Kat 4, 80620 Levent, İstanbul; tel. (212) 2814820; telex 27117; fax (212) 2780445; f. 1992; Chair. HASAN KARAMEHMET; Gen. Man. RIZA SUAT GÖKDEL.

**Sınai Yatırım ve Kredi Bankası AO** (Industrial Investment Credit Bank of Turkey): Barbaros Bul. Akdoğan Sok. 41-43, 80690 Beşiktaş, İstanbul; tel. (212) 2597414; telex 26263; fax (212) 2580405; f. 1963; cap. 108,086m., total assets 2,290,067m. (Dec. 1993); Chair. CAHİT KOCAÖMER; Gen. Man. Dr ORHAN ALTAN.

**Türkiye Sınai Kalkınma Bankası AŞ** (Industrial Development Bank of Turkey): PK 17 Karaköyi 80002 İstanbul; tel. (212) 2512792; telex 24344; fax (212) 2432975; f. 1950; cap. 420,000m.; res 165,203m.; dep. 11,372,200m. (Dec. 1993); Chair. Prof. MEMDUH YAŞA; Gen. Man. B. SAFA OCAK; 3 brs.

### Foreign Banks

**Arap Türk Bankası AŞ** (Arab Turkish Bank): Vali Konağı Cad. 10, PK 380-8223, 80220 Nişantaşı, İstanbul; tel. (212) 2250500; telex 26830; fax (212) 2250526; f. 1977; cap. 150,000m., res 1,351m., dep. 740,380m. (Dec. 1993); 48% owned by Libyan Arab Foreign Bank; Chair. YENAL CEVHERİOĞLU; Gen. Man. AYAD S. DAHAIM; 4 brs.

**Banca di Roma** (Italy): Tünel Cad. 18, 80000 Karaköy, İstanbul; tel. (212) 2510917; telex 25440; fax (212) 2496289; f. 1911; cap. 26,777m., res 5,868m. (Dec. 1992); Gen. Man. STEFANO GERMINI; 2 brs.

**Bank Mellat** (Iran): Büyükdere Cad. Binbirçiçek Sok. 1, PK 67, 80620 Levent, İstanbul; tel. (212) 2695820; telex 26502; fax (212) 2642895; f. 1982; cap. 29,602m., res 1,749m., dep. 72,550m. (Dec. 1992); Chair. and Gen. Man. AZIZ AKHOUNDI ASL; 2 brs.

**Chase Manhattan Bank, NA** (USA): Yıldız Posta Cad. 52/11, 80700 Esentepe, İstanbul; tel. (212) 2751280; telex 26625; fax (212) 2759932; f. 1984; cap. 30,000m., res 1,458m., dep. 72,340m. (Dec. 1991); Gen. Man. İSAK ANTİKA; 1 br.

**Citibank** (USA): Büyükdere Cad. 101, 80280 Esentepe, İstanbul; tel. (212) 2887700; telex 26277; fax (212) 2887760; f. 1981; cap. 207,537m., res 22,032m., dep. 302,100m. (March 1994); Gen. Man. ANJUM Z. IQBAL; 3 brs.

**Crédit Lyonnais** (France): Setüstü Haktan Han 45, Kat. 4, 80040 Kabataş, İstanbul; tel. (212) 2516300; telex 26836; fax (212) 2517724; f. 1988; cap. 45,663m., res 1,948m., dep. 6,646m. (Dec. 1992); Gen. Man. MICHEL MARTINOVITCH; 2 brs.

**Habib Bank Ltd** (Pakistan): Abide-i Hürriyet Cad. 12, PK 8, 80260 Şişli, İstanbul; tel. (212) 2460220; telex 27849; fax (212) 2340807; f. 1983; cap. 22,337m., res 775m., dep. 13,742m. (Dec. 1994); Gen. Man. ABDUL GHANI; 1 br.

**Holantse Bank Uni NV** (Netherlands): İnönü Cad. 15/17, 80090 Gümüşsuyu, İstanbul; tel. (212) 2938802; telex 24677; fax (212) 2492008; f. 1921; cap. 20,000m., res 1,359m., dep. 54,950m. (Dec. 1991); Gen. Man. ABRAM RUTGERS; 1 br.

**Indosuez EuroTürk Merchant Bank AŞ** (France): Yapı Kredi Plaza, Büyükdere Cad. 20-21, Blok C, Kat. 7, 80620 Levent, İstanbul; tel. (212) 2797070; telex 25117; fax (212) 2826301; f. 1986; cap. 38,400m., res 9,420m., dep. 109,893m. (Dec. 1992); Pres. ETIENNE DAVIGNON; 1 br.

**Midland Bank AŞ (England)** (UK): Cumhuriyet Cad. Elmadağ Han 8, 80200 Elmadağ, İstanbul; tel. (212) 2315560; telex 38385; fax (212) 2305300; f. 1990; cap. 30,000m., res 73,865m., dep. 163,072m. (Dec. 1994); Gen. Man. PIRAYE Y. ANTİKA; 1 br.

**Osmanlı Bankası AŞ** (Compagnie Financière Ottomane SA) (Luxembourg): Voyroda Cad. 35/37, PK 297, 80000 Karaköy, İstanbul; tel. (212) 2523000; telex 24193; fax (212) 2446471; f. 1893; cap. 450,000m., dep. 3,733,473m. (Dec 1993); Gen. Man. JEAN DE BOISGROLLIER; 63 brs.

**Saudi American Bank (SAMBA)** (Saudi Arabia): Cumhuriyet Cad. 233, PK 49, 80230 Harbiye, İstanbul; tel. (212) 2300284; telex 27224; fax (212) 2330201; f. 1985; cap. 10,000m., res 2,277m., dep. 73,079m. (Dec. 1991); Gen. Man. ZUBYR SOOMRO; 1 br.

**Société Générale SA** (France): Yapı Kredi Plaza, Büyükdere Cad., Blok B, Kat. 12, 80620 Levent, İstanbul; tel. (212) 2797051; telex 39454; fax (212) 2694574; f. 1990; cap. 31,340m., res 433m., dep. 44,447m. (Dec. 1991); Gen. Man. JEAN-PIERRE DUCROQUET; 1 br.

**Türk Sakura Bank AŞ:** Büyükdere Cad. 108/A, 80280 Esentepe, İstanbul; tel. (212) 2752930; telex 27718; fax (212) 2724270; f. 1985 as Chemical Mitsui Bank, adopted current name in 1992; cap. 124,500m., res 1,653m., dep. 94,863m. (Dec. 1993); Chair. NOBUAKI OGAWA; Gen. Man. NOBORU ONUMA; 2 brs.

**Turkish Bank AŞ ('TRNC'):** Valikonağı Cad. 7, 80200 Nişantaşı, İstanbul; tel. (212) 2250330; telex 27359; fax (212) 2250355; f. 1982; cap. 145,880m., res 11,916m., dep. 400,213m. (March 1994); Chair. TANJU ÖZYOL; 6 brs.

**WestLB (Europa) AG (Westdeutsche Landesbank)** (Germany): Nispetiye Cad. 38, 80630 Levent, İstanbul; tel. (212) 2792537; telex 26862; fax (212) 2802941; f. 1990; cap. 23,500m., res 1,512m., dep. 23,017m. (Dec. 1991); Gen. Man. GILLES LÉRAILLÉ; 2 brs.

### Banking Organization

**Banks' Association of Turkey:** Mithatpaşa Cad. 12, 06410 Yenişehir, Ankara; tel. (312) 4340160; telex 46771; fax (312) 4316679; f. 1958; Chair. Prof. Dr AYDIN AYAYDIN (acting); Sec.-Gen. ERHAN YAŞAR.

## STOCK EXCHANGE

**İstanbul Menkul Kıymetler Borsası (İMKB):** 80860 Istinye, İstanbul; tel. (212) 2982100; fax (212) 2982500; f. 1866; revived in 1986 after being dormant for about 60 years; 176 mems; Pres. TUNCAY ARTUN; Vice-Chairs ARIL SEREN, ALI İPEK, EMIN ALI GÜNDEZ, ABDULLAH AKYÜZ.

## INSURANCE

**Anadolu Sigorta TAŞ** (Anatolia Turkish Insurance Co): Rıhtım Cad. 57, PK 1845, 80330 Karaköy, İstanbul; tel. (212) 2516540; tel. (212) 2516540; telex 25407; fax (212) 242690; f. 1925; Chair. BURHAN KARAGÖZ; Gen. Man. AHMET YAVUZ.

**Ankara Sigorta TAŞ** (Ankara Insurance Co): Bankalar Cad. 80, 80020 Karaköy, İstanbul; tel. (212) 2521010; telex 24394; fax (212) 2524744; f. 1936; Chair. and Gen. Man. Dr SEBAHATTİN BEYAZ.

**Cigna-Sabancı Sigorta AŞ:** Barbaros Bul. 19, 80690 Beşiktaş, İstanbul; tel. (212) 2932963; telex 26085; fax (212) 2494790; f. 1964; fire, engineering, marine, accident; Chair. T. GÜNGÖR URAS.

**Destek Reasürans TAŞ:** Abdi İpekçi Cad. 75, 80200 Maçka, İstanbul; tel. (212) 2312832; telex 27748; fax (212) 2415704; f. 1945; reinsurance; Pres. SÜLEYMAN KAYA; Gen. Man. İBRAHİM YAYCIOĞLU.

TURKEY                                                                                                           *Directory*

**Doğan Sigorta AŞ:** Serdarı Ekrem Sok. 48, 80020 Kuledibi, İstanbul; tel. (212) 2516374; telex 25854; fax (212) 2516379; f. 1942; fire, marine, accident; Chair. T. GÜNGÖR URAS.

**Güven Sigorta TAŞ:** Bankalar Cad. 122–124, 80000 Karaköy, İstanbul; tel. (212) 2547900; telex 24336; fax (212) 2555888; f. 1924; Chair. ENVER AKOVA; Gen. Man. ENVER YALÇINKAYA.

**Halk Sigorta TAŞ:** Büyükdere Cad. 161, 80506 Zincirlikuyu, İstanbul; tel. (212) 2743940; telex 26438; fax (212) 2751668; f. 1944; Chair. HALUK CİLLOV; Gen. Man. ERHAN DUMANLI.

**Hür Sigorta AŞ:** Büyükdere Cad., Hür Han 15/A, 80260 Şişli, İstanbul; tel. (212) 2322010; telex 27501; fax (212) 2463673; Chair. BÜLENT SEMİLER; Gen. Man. GÜNER YALÇINER.

**İMTAŞ İttihadı Milli Sigorta TAŞ:** Büyükdere Cad. 116, 80300 Zincirlikuyu, İstanbul; tel. (212) 2747000; telex 26404; fax (212) 2720837; f. 1918; Chair. Prof. Dr ASAF SAVAŞ AKAT; Gen. Man. MUSTAFA AKAN.

**İstanbul Reasürans AŞ:** Halaskargazi Cad. 309, Kat. 4, 80260 Şişli, İstanbul; tel. (212) 2408070; telex 39014; fax (212) 2300464; f. 1979; Chair. CEMAL ZAGRA; Gen. Man. GÜLGÜN ÜNLÜOĞLU.

**Milli Reasürans TAŞ:** Teşvikiye Cad. 43–57, 80200 Teşvikiye, İstanbul; tel. (212) 2314730; telex 26472; fax (212) 2308608; f. 1929; Chair. ONUR ÖZBİLEN; Gen. Man. CAHİT NOMER.

**Şark Sigorta TAŞ:** Bağlarbaşı, Kısıklı Cad. 9, 81180 Altunizade, İstanbul; tel. (212) 3101250; telex 29739; fax (212) 3101349; f. 1923; Chair. M. RAHMİ KOÇ; Gen. Man. CEMAL ZAĞRA.

**Şeker Sigorta AŞ:** Meclisi Mebusan Cad. 87, Şeker Sigorta Hanı, PK 519, 80040 Fındıklı, İstanbul; tel. (212) 2514035; telex 24252; fax (212) 2491046; f. 1954; Chair. MEHMET SERT; Gen. Man. YURDAL SERT.

**Tam Sigorta AŞ:** İstanbul; f. 1964; all types of insurance except life; Chair. TURAN ÜLKER; Gen. Man. MEHMET NEZİR UCA.

**Türkiye Genel Sigorta AŞ:** Meclisi Mebusan Cad. 91, 80040 Salıpazarı, İstanbul; tel. (212) 2520010; telex 24453; fax (212) 2499651; f. 1948; Chair. MEHMET E. KARAMEHMET; Gen. Man. HULUSİ TAŞKIRAN.

## Trade and Industry

### DEVELOPMENT ORGANIZATIONS

**Turkish Atomic Energy Authority:** Prime Minister's Office, 06530 Ankara; tel. (312) 2875723; fax (312) 2878761; f. 1956; controls the development of peaceful uses of atomic energy; 11 mems; Pres. Prof. YALÇIN SANALAN; Sec.-Gen. EROL BARUTÇUGİL.

**Turkish Electricity Authority (Nuclear Power Plants Division):** İnönü Bul. 27, Bahçelievler, Ankara; tel. (312) 2229855; telex 42245; fax (312) 2138870; state enterprise to supervise the building and operation of nuclear power stations; attached to the Ministry of Energy and Natural Resources; Dir Dr AHMET KÜTÜKÇÜOĞLU.

### CHAMBERS OF COMMERCE AND INDUSTRY

**Union of Chambers of Commerce, Industry, Maritime Commerce and Commodity Exchanges of Turkey (UCCET):** 149 Atatürk Bul. 149, Bakanlıklar, Ankara; tel. (312) 4177700; telex 42343; fax (212) 4181002; f. 1952; represents 313 chambers and commodity exchanges; Pres. YALIM EREZ; Sec.-Gen. ŞEFİK TOKAT.

**İstanbul Chamber of Commerce (ICOC):** Ragip Gümüşpala Cad. 84,34378 Eminönü, İstanbul; tel (1) 5114150; telex 22682; fax (212) 5262197; f. 1882; more than 130,000 mems; Pres. ATALAY ŞAHİNOĞLU.

**İzmir Chamber of Commerce:** Atatürk Cad. 126, Alsancak, İzmir; tel. (232) 4417777; telex 52331; fax (232) 4837853; f. 1885; Pres. HALİT ŞARLAK.

### EMPLOYERS' ASSOCIATIONS

**Türk Sanayicileri ve İşadamları Derneği (TÜSİAD)** (Turkish Industrialists' and Businessmen's Association): Meşrutiyet Cad. 74, 80050 Tepebaşı, İstanbul; tel. (212) 2491131; telex 22318; fax (212) 2490913 f. 1971; 338 mems; Pres. HALİS KOMİLİ; Sec.-Gen. E. İHSAN ÖZOL.

**Türkiye İşveren Sendikaları Konfederasyonu (TİSK)** (Turkish Confederation of Employers' Associations): Meşrutiyet Cad. 1/4-5, 06650 Kızılay, Ankara; tel. (312) 4183217; telex 42122; fax (312) 4184473; f. 1962; represents (on national level) 18 employers' associations with 2,000 affiliated member employers or companies; official representative in labour relations; Pres. REFİK BAYDUR; Sec.-Gen. KUBİLAY ATASAYAR.

### TRADE UNIONS

#### Confederations

**DİSK (Türkiye Devrimci İşçi Sendikaları Konfederasyonu)** (Confederation of Progressive Trade Unions of Turkey): Merter Sitesi, Ahmet Kutsi Tecer Cad. Sendikalar Binası 12, Kat. 5, 34010 Merter, İstanbul; tel. (212) 5048083; fax (212) 5061079; member of ICFTU and ETUC; 30 affiliated unions; Pres. KEMAL NEBİOĞLU; Sec.-Gen. SÜLEYMAN ÇELEBİ.

**Türk-İş (Türkiye İşçi Sendikaları Konfederasyonu Genel Başkanlığı)** (Confederation of Turkish Trade Unions): Bayındır Sok. 10, Yenişehir, Ankara; tel. (312) 4333125; fax (312) 4336809; f. 1952; member of ICFTU, ETUC, ICFTU-APRO and OECD/TUAC; 32 national unions and federations with 1.7m. mems; Pres. BAYRAM MERAL; Gen. Sec. ŞEMSİ DENİZER.

#### Principal DISK Trade Unions

**Bank-Sen (Türkiye Devrimci Banka ve Sigorta İşçileri Sendikası):** Nakiye Elgun Sok. 117, Şişli, İstanbul; tel. (212) 2321000; fax (212) 2464112; Pres. HULUSİ KARLI; 11,800 mems.

**Basın-İş (Türkiye Basın İşçileri Sendikası)** (Press Workers' Union): İstanbul; f. 1964; Pres. YILMAZ ÖZDEMİR; Gen. Sec. DERVİŞ BOYOĞLU; 5,000 mems.

**Birlesik Metal-İs (Birlesik Metal İşçileri Sendikası):** Kirtasiyeci Sok. 21, 81300 Kadıköy, İstanbul; tel. (216) 3454703; fax (216) 3474598; Pres. ALİ RIZA İKİSİVRİ; 58,800 mems.

**Demiryol-İş (Türkiye Demiryolu İşçileri Sendikası)** (Railway Workers): Necatibey Cad., Sezenler Sok. 5, 06430 Yenişehir, Ankara; tel. (312) 2318029; fax (312) 2318032; f. 1952; Pres. ENVER TOÇOĞLU; Gen. Sec. NURETTİN GİRGİNER; 25,000 mems.

**Deri-İş (Türkiye Deri İşçileri Sendikası)** (Leather Industry): Ahmet Kutsi Tecer Cad. 12/6, Merter, İstanbul; tel. (212) 5048083; fax (212) 5061079; f. 1948; Pres. NUSRETTİN YILMAZ; Gen. Sec. ALİ SEL; 11,000 mems.

**Dev. Sağlık-İş (Türkiye Devrimci Sağlık İşçileri Sendikası)** (Health Employees): Oğuzhan Cad., Ahenk Apt. 39/8, Kat. 2, 34270 Fındıkzade, İstanbul; tel. (212) 5236190; fax (212) 5237647; f. 1961; Pres. DOĞAN HALİS; Gen. Sec. SABRİ TANYERİ; 15,000 mems.

**Genel-Iş (Türkiye Genel Hizmet İşçileri Sendikası)** (Municipal Workers): Çankırı Cad. 28, Kat 5-9, Ulus, Ankara; tel. (312) 3091547; fax (312) 3091046; f. 1983; Pres. İSMAİL HAKKI ÖNAL; Gen. Sec. ATILA ÖNGEL; 50,000 mems.

**Gıda-İş (Türkiye Gida Sanayii İşçileri Sendikası):** Ahmet Kutsi Tecer Cad. 12/3, Merter, İstanbul; tel. (212) 5757229; fax (212) 5753099; Pres. KEMAL NEBİOĞLU; 31,000 mems.

**Koop-Iş (Türkiye Kooperatif ve Büro İşçileri Sendikası)** (Cooperative and Office Workers): İzmir Cad. Fevzi Çadmak Sok. 15/11–12, Yenişehir, Ankara; tel. (312) 4300855; f. 1964; Pres. AHMET BALAMAN; Gen. Sec. AHMET GÜVEN; 29,000 mems.

**Limter-İş (Liman, Tersane Gemi Yapım Onarım İşçileri Sendikası)** (Harbour, Shipyard, Ship Building and Repairs): İcmeler Tren İstasyonu Yaru 12/1, Tuzla, İstanbul; tel. (216) 3955271; f. 1947; Pres. EMİR BABAKUŞ; Gen. Sec. ASKER ŞİT; 7,000 mems.

**Nakliyat-İş (Nakliye İşçileri Sendikası)** (Transportation Workers): Guraba Hüseyin Ağa Mah. Kakmacı Sok 10, Daire 11 Vatan Cad. Tranvay, Durağı Karşısı, Aksaray, İstanbul; tel. (212) 5332069; Pres. ŞEMSİ ERCAN; Gen. Sec. NEDİM FIRAT.

**OLEYIS (Türkiye Otel, Lokanta ve Eğlence Yerleri İşçileri Sendikası)** (Hotel, Restaurant and Places of Entertainment): Atatürk Bul. 57, Kızılay, Ankara; tel. (312) 4359680; fax (312) 4358654; f. 1947; Pres. ENVER ÖKTEM; Gen. Sec. TURAN UĞURLU; 25,000 mems.

**Petkim-İş (Türkiye Petrol, Kimya ve Lastik Sanayii İşçileri Sendikası):** İzmir Cad., Fevzi Çakmak Sok. 7/13, Ankara; tel. (312) 2300861; fax (312) 2299429; Pres. MUSTAFA KARADAYI; 18,000mems.

**Sosyal-Iş (Türkiye Sosyal Sigortalar, Eğitim, Büro, Ticaret Kooperatif Banka ve Güzet Sanatlar İşçileri Sendikası)** (Banking, Insurance and Trading): Necatibey Cad. Sezenler Sok. Lozan Apt. 2/14, Yenişehir, Ankara; tel. (312) 2318178; fax (312) 2294638; Pres. ÖZCAN KESGEÇ; Gen. Sec. H. BEDRİ DOĞANAY; 31,000 mems.

**Tekstil İşçileri Sendikası:** Ahmet Kutsi Tecer Cad. 12/1, Merter, İstanbul; tel. (212) 6429742; fax (212) 5044887; Pres. RIDVAN BUDAK; 45,000 mems.

**Tümka-İş (Türkiye Tüm Kağıt Selüloz Sanayii İşçileri Sendikası):** Gündoğdu Sok. 19/3, Merter, İstanbul; tel. (212) 5750843; Pres. SABRİ KAPLAN; 3,000 mems.

#### Other Principal Trade Unions

**Denizciler (Türkiye Denizciler Sendikası** (Seamen): Rıhtım Cad., Denizciler Sok. 7, Tophane, İstanbul; tel. (212) 2444838; f. 1959; Pres. EMİN KUL; Gen. Sec. MUSTAFA YÖNDEM; 12,000 mems.

**Findik-Is (Fiskobirlik İşçileri Sendikası)** (Hazelnut producers): Gazi Cad., Guven Pasajı 65/4, Giresun; tel. (51) 61950; fax (51) 62104; Pres. AKÇIN KOÇ; Gen. Sec. ERSAİT ŞEN.

**Hava-İş (Türkiye Sivil Havacılık Sendikası)** (Civil Aviation): İncirli Cad., Volkan Apt., 68/1 Bakırköy, İstanbul; tel. (212)

3063

## TURKEY

6601495; fax (212) 5719051; Pres. ATİLAY AYÇİN; Gen. Sec. ŞAFAK KURNAZ; 10,500 mems.

**Liman-İş (Türkiye Liman ve Kara Tahmil Tahliye İşçileri Sendikası)** (Longshoremen): Necatibey Cad., Sezenler Sok. 4, Kat. 5, Yenişehir, Ankara; tel. (312) 2317418; fax (312) 2302484; f. 1963; Pres. HASAN BİBER; Gen. Sec. RAİF KILIÇ; 5,000 mems.

**Şeker-İş (Türkiye Şeker Sanayii İşçileri Sendikası)** (Sugar Industry): Karanfil Sok. 59, Bakanlıklar, Ankara; tel. (312) 4184273; f. 1952; Pres. HİKMET ALCAN; Gen. Sec. ÖMER ÇELİK; 35,000 mems.

**Tarım-İş (Türkiye Orman, Topraksu, Tarım ve Tarım Sanayii İşçileri Sendikası)** (Agricultural Irrigation and Forestry Workers): Necatibey Cad. 22/9-12, Ankara Apt., Yenişehir, Ankara; tel. (312) 2317856; fax (312) 2298592; f. 1961; Pres. SABRİ ÖZDEŞ; Gen. Sec. ZEKİ KARA; 43,500 mems.

**Tekgıda-İş (Türkiye Tütün, Müskirat Gıda ve Yardımcı İşçileri Sendikası)** (Tobacco, Drink, Food and Allied Workers' Union of Turkey): 4 Levent Konaklar Sok., İstanbul; tel. (212) 2644996; fax (212) 2789534; f. 1952; Pres. ORHAN BALTA; Gen. Sec. HÜSEYİN KARAKOÇ; 176,000 mems.

**Teksif (Türkiye Tekstil, Örme ve Giyim Sanayii İşçileri Sendikası)** (Textile, Knitting and Clothing): Ziya Gökalp Cad. Aydoğmuş Sok. 1, Kurtuluş, Ankara; tel. (312) 4312170; fax (312) 4357826; f. 1951; Pres. ŞEVKET YILMAZ; Gen. Sec. ZEKİ POLAT; 120,000 mems.

**Tez-Koop-İş (Türkiye, Ticaret, Kooperatif, Eğitim, Büro ve Güzel Sanatlar İşçileri Sendikası)** (Commercial and Clerical Employees): Üç Yıldız Cad. 29, Subayevleri, Ayınlikevler, 06130 Ankara; tel. (312) 3183979; fax (312) 3183988; f. 1962; Pres. AHMET TAMER; Gen. Sec. ERTUĞRUL KAKMACI; 30,000 mems.

**Türk Harb-İş (Türkiye Harb Sanayii ve Yardımcı İşkolları İşçileri Sendikası)** (Defence Industry and Allied Workers): İnkılap Sok. 20, Kızılay, Ankara; tel. (312) 4175097; fax (312) 4171364; f. 1956; Pres. İZZET CETIN; Gen. Sec. NURI AYCICER; 35,000 mems.

**Türk-Metal (Türkiye Metal, Çelik, Mühimmat, Makina ve Metalden Mamul, Eşya ve Oto, Montaj ve Yardımcı İşçileri Sendikası)** (Auto, Metal and Allied Workers): Gazi Mustafa Kemal Bul., Akıncılar Sok. 14, Maltepe, Ankara; tel. (312) 2317940; fax (312) 2297714; f. 1963; Pres. MUSTAFA ÖZBEK; Gen. Sec. ÖZBEK KARAKUS; 123,000 mems.

**Yol-İş (Türkiye Yol, Yapı ve İnşaat İşçileri Sendikası)** (Road Construction and Building Workers' Unions): İstanbul Cad. 58, İskitler, Ankara; tel. (312) 3422240; fax (312) 3412705; f. 1963; Pres. BAYRAM MERAL; Gen. Sec. TEVFİK ÖZÇELİK; 170,000 mems.

### TRADE FAIR

**İzmir Enternasyonal Fuarı** (Izmir International Fair): Şair Eşref Bul. 50, 35230 Kültürpark, İzmir; tel. (232) 4821270; telex 53295; fax (232) 4254342; f. 1929; Pres. MUSTAFA H. BOYACIOGLU; Dir-Gen. DOĞON İŞLEYEN.

## Transport

### RAILWAYS

The total length of the railways operated within the national frontiers is 10,386 km (1994), of which 8,452 km are main lines, 1,093 km are electrified, and 1,359 km are signalled. A new direct rail link between Ankara and İstanbul, cutting the distance from 577 km to 416 km, is expected to be completed by the year 2000. There are direct rail links with Bulgaria to Iran and Syria. A light railway system for İstanbul, expected to total 109 km in length upon its completion, is currently under construction. In April 1990 work started on the construction of a new 14.6 km 'metro' transport system in Ankara, to be completed by 1994. An 8.5 km light rail route for the city is also under construction.

**Türkiye Cumhuriyeti Devlet Demiryolları İşletmesi Genel Müdürlüğü (TCDD)** (Turkish Republic State Railways): Genel Müdürlük, Talatpaşa Bul., 06330 Gar, Ankara; tel. (312) 3090515; telex 44390; fax (312) 3123215; f. 1924; operates all railways and connecting ports (see below) of the State Railway Administration, which acquired the status of a state economic enterprise in 1953, and a state economic establishment in 1984; 553 main-line diesel locomotives, 1,533 passenger coaches and 19,513 freight wagons; Chair. of Board and Gen. Dir TALAT GÜNSOY.

### ROADS

At 1 January 1994, 1,070 km of motorways were open to traffic and nearly 594 km of motorways were under construction; the total length of the highway network was 59,770 km and the total length of village roads was 308,000 km. In 1994 there were 56,466 km of roads in the maintenance programme with 48,149 km open all year and 8,327 km open, when possible, in winter.

**Bayındırlık ve İskan Bakanlığı Karayolları Genel Müdürlüğü** (General Directorate of Highways): KGM Sitesi, Yücetepe, 06100 Ankara; tel. (312) 4252343; fax (312) 4186996; f. 1950; Dir-Gen. DİNÇER YİĞİT.

### SHIPPING

At mid-1992 Turkey's merchant fleet comprised 920 vessels and had an aggregate displacement of 3.8m. gross tons.

General-purpose public ports are operated by two state economic enterprises. The ports of Bandırma, Derince, Haydarpaşa (İstanbul), İskenderun, İzmir, Mersin and Samsun, all of which are connected to the railway network, are operated by Turkish State Railways (TCDD) (see above), while the smaller ports of Antalya, Giresun, Hopa, Tekirdağ and Trabzon are operated by the Turkish Maritime Organization (TDI).

**Turkish Maritime Organization (TDI):** Genel Müdürlüğü, Karaköy, İstanbul; tel. (212) 2515000; telex 24895; fax (212) 2495391.

**Port of Bandırma:** TCDD Liman İşletme Müdürlüğü, Bandırma; tel. (266) 2234966; fax (266) 2236011; Port Man. HASAN KARAKUŞ; Harbour Master İBRAHİM YALKIRI.

**Port of Derince:** TCDD Liman İşletme Müdürlüğü, Derince; Port Man. ALİ ARİF AYTAÇ; Harbour Master HAYDAR DOĞAN.

**Port of Haydarpaşa (İstanbul):** TCDD Liman İşletme Müdürlüğü Haydarpaşa, İstanbul; tel. (212) 3379988; telex 29705; fax (212) 3451705; Port Man. LAMI TEKSÖZ; Harbour Master İSMAİL SAFAER.

**Port of İskenderun:** TCDD Liman İşletme Müdürlüğü, İskenderun; tel. (326) 6640047; telex 68109; fax (326) 6632424; Port Man. ABDULMUSA APAYDIN; Harbour Master CEVAT ÇOLAK.

**Port of İzmir:** TCDD Liman İşletme Müdürlüğü, İzmir; tel. (232) 4632252; fax (232) 4632248; Port Man. GÜNGÖR ERKAYA; Harbour Master MEHMET ONGEL.

**Port of Mersin:** TCDD Liman İşletme Müdürlüğü, Mersin; tel. (324) 2330687; telex 67279; fax (324) 2311350; Port Man. FAHRI SAYILI; Harbour Master H. TAŞKIN.

**Port of Samsun:** TCDD Liman İşletme Müdürlüğü, Samsun; tel. (362) 4357616; telex 82172; fax (362) 4317849; Port Man. SAFFET YAMAK; Harbour Master Capt. ARIF H. UZUNOĞLU.

**DB Deniz Nakliyatı TAŞ** (DB Turkish Cargo Lines): Meclisı Mebusan Cad. 151, 80104 Fındıklı, İstanbul; tel. (212) 2512696; telex 24125; fax (212) 2512696; f. 1955; regular liner services between Turkey and Mediterranean, Adriatic, Red Sea, Persian Gulf, Europe, Black Sea, US Atlantic, and Indian and Far East ports; Pres. TAHİR İLKER GÜLFİDAN; Chair. MUZAFFER AKKAYER; 31 general cargo ships, 4 roll-on, roll-off, 13 bulk/ore carriers, 6 tankers.

#### Private Companies

**Cerrahgil Denizcilik, Nakliyat ve Ticaret AŞ:** Abdi İpekçi Cad. 33, PK 108, 80200 Teşvikiye, İstanbul; tel. (212) 2324700; telex 39091; fax (212) 2310035; f. 1974; shipowners, bunker and paint suppliers, agents, charterers, brokers, traders; Asst Gen. Man. HAKAN GÜREZ; 5 vessels; 272,647 dwt (1995).

**Cerrahoğulları Umumi Nakliyat, Vapurculuk ve Ticaret AŞ:** Yıldız Posta Cad. 17, Kat. 4/5, 80280 Esentepe, İstanbul; tel. (212) 2749800; telex 26593; fax (212) 2668039; f. 1954; Pres. and Gen. Man. SAEED RABB CERRAHOĞLU; 2 vessels; 198,916 dwt.

**Genel Denizcilik Nakliyatı AŞ (Geden Line):** Meclisı Mebusan Cad. 91, Kat. 2/3, 80040 Salıpazarı, İstanbul; tel. (212) 2516700; telex 24248; fax (212) 2490479; f. 1975; shipowners, agents, brokers; Man. Dir ALTAN NADIMLI; 4 vessels; 122,786 dwt (1993).

**İstanbul Ship Management SA:** Rıhtım Cad. Zihni Han 28-30 Kat. 2, PK 390, 80030 Tophane, İstanbul; tel. (212) 2931950; telex 25805; fax (212) 2458024; f. 1993; Chair. AHMET ŞAHAP ÜNLÜ; Man. GÖKALP TUNCER; 3 vessels; 326,604 dwt.

**Kalkavan Denizcilik ve Ticaret AŞ:** Rıhtım Cad. Fatih İş Hanı 135, Kat. 4-5, 80060 Karaköy, İstanbul; tel. (212) 2525880; telex 25779; fax (212) 2445659; Pres. SEFER KALKAVAN; 10 vessels; 72,665 dwt.

**Koçtuğ Gemi İşletmeciliği ve Ticaret AŞ:** Bankalar Cad., Bozkurt Han Kat. 3, PK 884, 80000 Karaköy, İstanbul; tel. (212) 2513380; telex 24512; fax (212) 2515256; f. 1956; cargo services to and from Europe, North Africa and the USA; Pres. A. KOÇMAN; Gen. Man. M. LEBLEBİCİOĞLU; 4 general cargo vessels; 25,961 dwt.

**Marti Shipping and Trading Co:** Mechisi Mebusan Cad. 85, Orya Ishani Kat. 6, 80040 Salipazari, İstanbul; tel. (212) 2515500; telex 24051; fax (212) 2432567; Gen. Man. NECMETTIN OZGELIK; 9 bulk carriers; 896,658 dwt.

**Türkiye Denizcilik İşletmeleri Denizyolları İşletmesi Mudurlugu (TDI):** Meclisı Mebusan Cad. 68, 80040 Salıpazarı, İstanbul; tel. (212) 2521700; telex 25962; fax (212) 2515767; ferry company; Chair. KENAN ÖNER; Man. Dir BURHAN KÜLÜNK; 13 vessels; 14,218 dwt.

#### Shipping Associations

**SS Gemi Armatörleri Motorlu Taşıyıcılar Kooperatifi** (Turkish Shipowners' Asscn): Meclisı Mebusan Cad., Dursun Han, Kat. 7, No 89, Salıpazarı İstanbul; tel. (212) 2510945; telex 25553; fax (212) 2492786; f. 1960; Pres. GÜNDÜZ KAPTANOĞLU; Man. Dir A. GÖKSU; 699 vessels; 5,509,112 dwt (1993).

**Türk Armatörler Birliği** (Turkish Shipowners' Union): Meclisı Mebusan Cad. Dursun Han, Kat. 7 No. 89, Salıpazarı, İstanbul; tel. (212) 2453022; telex 25552; fax (212) 2492786; f. 1972; 460 mems; Pres. ŞADAN KALKAVAN; Co-ordinator ENVER ÖZYAZICI; 5,509,112 dwt (1993).

**Vapur Donatanları ve Acenteleri Derneği** (Turkish Shipowners' and Shipping Agents' Asscn): Mumhane Cad. Emek İş Hanı Kat. 3 No. 31, Karaköy, İstanbul; tel. (212) 2443294; f. 1902; worldwide agency service; Pres. Capt. M. LEBLEBİCİOĞLU; Man. Dir C. KAPLAN.

### CIVIL AVIATION

There are airports for scheduled international and internal flights at Atatürk (İstanbul), Esenboğa (Ankara), Adnan Menderes (Izmir and Trabzon), while international charter flights are handled by Adana, Dalaman and Antalya. Fifteen other airports handle internal flights only.

**Birgen Hava Yolları:** Cumhuriyet Cad., Efser Han 301/9, 80230 İstanbul; tel. (212) 2401150; telex 27988; fax (212) 2465711; f. 1989; scheduled and charter services; Chair. MUHİP İŞMEN; Gen. Man. ÇETİN BİRGEN.

**İstanbul Hava Yolları AŞ:** Firuzköy Yolu, Bağlar İçi Mevzii 26, 34850 Avcılar, İstanbul; tel. (212) 5092100; telex 21022; fax (212) 5936035; f. 1985; operates scheduled and charter services from major Turkish cities to European destinations; Gen. Man. SAFİ ERGİN.

**Onur Air:** Şenlikköy Catal Sok. 3, Florya, İstanbul; tel. (212) 6632300; fax (212) 6632314; f. 1992; scheduled and charter services; Gen. Man. SEVİNÇ PINAR.

**Pegasus Hava Taşımacılığı AŞ:** İstasyon Cad. 24, Kat. 1, Yeşilyurt, İstanbul; tel. (212) 6632934; telex 21117; fax (212) 5739627; f. 1990; charter services; Gen. Man. L. J. LOWTH.

**Türk Hava Yolları AŞ (THY):** (Turkish Airlines Inc.): Atatürk Hava Limanı, Yeşilköy, İstanbul; tel. (212) 6636300; telex 21198; fax (212) 6634744; f. 1933; majority state-owned; extensive internal network and flights to the Middle East, North Africa, the Far East, Central Asia, the USA and Europe; Chair. ERMAN YERDELEN; Pres. ATİLLA ÇELEBİ.

## Tourism

Visitors to Turkey are attracted by the climate, fine beaches and ancient monuments. Tourism is being stimulated by the Government, and the industry is expanding rapidly. In 1994 receipts from tourism reached a record US $4,321m., compared with $3,939m. in 1993, while the number of tourists increased slightly from 6.5m. in 1993 to 6.7m. in 1994.

**Ministry of Tourism:** İsmet İnönü Bul. 5, Bahçelievler, Ankara; tel. (312) 2128300; telex 42448; fax (312) 2128391; f. 1963; Dir-Gen. of Establishments MEVHİBE CAN; Dir-Gen. of Information FERMANİ UYGUN; Dir-Gen. GURKAN ERTAS.

# TURKMENISTAN

## Introductory Survey

### Location, Climate, Language, Religion, Flag, Capital

The Republic of Turkmenistan (or Turkmenia), formerly the Turkmen Soviet Socialist Republic, is situated in the south-west of Central Asia. It is bordered to the north by Uzbekistan, to the north-west by Kazakhstan, to the west by the Caspian Sea, to the south by Iran and to the south-east by Afghanistan. The climate is severely continental, with extremely hot summers and cold winters. The average temperature in January is −4°C (25°F), but winter temperatures can fall as low as −33°C (−27°F). In summer temperatures often reach 50°C (122°F) in the south-east Kara-Kum desert; the average temperature in July is 28°C (82°F). Precipitation is slight throughout much of the country: average annual rainfall ranges from only 80 mm (3.1 ins) in the north-west to about 300 mm (11.8 ins) in mountainous regions. In 1990 Turkmen was declared the official language of the republic. Turkmen is a member of the Southern Turkic group; in 1929 the traditional Arabic script was replaced by a Latin script, which was, in turn, replaced by the Cyrillic script in 1940. In 1993 it was announced that the republic would change to a Latin-based Turkish script by early 1996. Most of the population are Sunni Muslims. Islam in Turkmenistan has traditionally featured elements of Sufi mysticism and shamanism, and pilgrimages to local religious sites are reported to be common. The national flag (proportions 2 by 1) consists of three unequal vertical stripes, of green, maroon and green; the maroon stripe bears a vertical design of five different carpet patterns, while the green stripe nearest the fly has in its upper dexter corner five white five-pointed stars framed by a narrow white crescent moon. The capital is Ashgabat (Ashkhabad).

### Recent History

The Turkmen are descendants of the Oghuz tribes who migrated to Central Asia in about the 10th century AD. By the 15th century they had emerged as a distinct ethnic group, but were divided by tribal loyalties and territorial division between neighbouring powers. From the 15th to the 17th centuries the southern tribes were under Persian rule, while the north was under the suzerainty of the (Uzbek) Khanates of Khiva and Bukhara. In the early 18th century the Persians annexed Khivan and Bukharan territories, but Bukhara regained its power in the latter half of the century and retook Merv (now Mary) and deported its entire population to Bukhara. Meanwhile, the Russians had begun their expansion into Central Asia, and during the 19th century they gradually reduced the Khanates to the status of protectorates. In 1877 the Russians began a campaign against the Turkmen, which culminated in the battle of Gök Tepe, in 1881, at which some 20,000 Turkmen are estimated to have been killed. In 1895 the Russian conquest was confirmed by agreement with the British; the international boundary thus established divided some Turkmen under Russian rule from others in the British sphere of influence.

In 1917 the Bolsheviks attempted to take power in the region, but there was little support for them among the local population. An anti-Bolshevik Russian Provisional Government of Transcaspia was formed, and a Turkmen Congress was also established. Soviet forces were sent to Ashgabat (Ashkhabad), and a Turkestan Autonomous Soviet Socialist Republic, which included Transcaspia, was declared on 30 April 1918. In July, however, nationalists, aided by British forces, overthrew the Bolshevik Government and established an independent Government in Ashgabat, protected by a British garrison. After the British withdrew, however, the Government was soon overthrown, and by 1920 the Red Army, led by Gen. Frunze, was in control of Ashgabat. As part of the National Delimitation of Central Asia, the Turkmen Soviet Socialist Republic (SSR) was established on 27 October 1924. In May 1925 it became a constituent republic of the Union of Soviet Socialist Republics (USSR, established in December 1922). Political power in the republic became the preserve of the Communist Party of Turkmenistan (CPT).

Following the establishment of Soviet rule, resistance to Soviet forces continued for some years. The agricultural collectivization programme, which was begun in 1929 and entailed the forcible settlement of traditionally nomadic people in collective farms, provoked further military resistance; guerrilla warfare against Soviet power continued until 1936. In 1928 a campaign against the practice of religion in Turkmenistan was launched: almost all Islamic institutions were closed, including schools, courts and mosques. In 1917 an estimated 500 mosques were functioning in the region; by 1979 only four were still operating. In the early 1930s there was a campaign among the Turkmen intelligentsia for greater political autonomy for Turkmenistan. As a result, many Turkmen intellectuals were imprisoned or executed. The scope of the purges widened in the late 1930s to include government and CPT officials.

Despite the repressions, advances were made in the provision of social and health facilities among the Turkmen. Campaigns against illiteracy had a high rate of success, despite two changes in the written script of the Turkmen language. According to official figures, the level of literacy rose from 2.3% of the adult population in 1926 to 99% in 1970.

There was some small-scale industrialization of the republic in the 1930s, but after the early 1930s there was little development in the industrial sector. Agriculture was encouraged and irrigation extended, although with little regard for the possible ecological effects. Irrigation projects such as the Kara-Kum Canal, the largest such scheme in the USSR, enabled rapid development of cotton-growing, especially after 1945. However, the ecological consequences for the Aral Sea, to the north of the republic, were catastrophic.

The immigration of Russians into the urban areas of Turkmenistan, during and after the 1920s, gradually diminished the proportion of Turkmen in leading posts in the republic. In 1958 the First Secretary (leader) of the CPT, Babayev, proposed that Turkmen should occupy more leading positions. He was dismissed, together with many of his colleagues in government.

The major issues in Turkmenistan in the late 1980s were economic, environmental and cultural. Turkmenistan's position as a provider of raw materials (mainly natural gas and cotton) to more developed republics in the European parts of the USSR provoked strong criticism of the relationship between Turkmenistan and the all-Union authorities. The environmental and health hazards connected with over-intensive agriculture, notably the cultivation of cotton, were also widely discussed in the republican media. These issues, combined with those of language and history, all provoked dissatisfaction with the relationship with the USSR. However, the geographical remoteness of the republic and its poor level of communications with other parts of the USSR inhibited its involvement in the political changes occurring in other Soviet republics. Moreover, the lack of any history of a unified nation, together with the continuing tribal divisions, did not engender any mass movement for national autonomy, as occurred elsewhere.

In the absence of any significant democratic movement, the CPT dominated the republic's elections to the all-Union Congress of People's Deputies in Moscow in early 1989. In September of that year, however, Turkmen intellectuals met to form Agzybirlik, a 'popular front' organization concerned with the status of the Turkmen language, indigenous arts in the republic, environmental matters and economic issues. In the following month it was officially registered, albeit with some reluctance on the part of the authorities, and, after support for the movement increased, it was banned in January 1990. Nevertheless, Agzybirlik's founding congress took place in the following month. As a result of the official animosity towards the nascent democratic movement, only the CPT and its approved organizations were permitted to participate in elections to the republican Supreme Soviet (legislature) on 7 January, at which CPT members won the majority of the 175 seats. When the new Supreme Soviet convened, Saparmyrat

Niyazov, the First Secretary of the CPT since 1985, was elected Chairman of the Supreme Soviet, the highest government office in the republic.

Despite the continuing dominance of the CPT, some concessions were made to popular pressure. In May 1990 the Turkmen language officially became the state language, replacing Russian: Turkmenistan was the last of the Soviet republics to introduce such legislation. On 22 August the Turkmen Supreme Soviet adopted a declaration of sovereignty, which proclaimed the republic to be a zone free of nuclear and chemical weapons, and asserted the right of the republic to determine its own political and social system and to secede from the USSR. On 27 October Niyazov was elected, by direct ballot, to the new post of executive President of Turkmenistan. He was unopposed in the election and received 98.3% of the votes cast.

In late 1990 and early 1991 Turkmenistan participated in negotiations towards a new Union Treaty, which would redefine the status of the republics within the structure of the USSR. The underdeveloped state of the Turkmen economy, and the republic's dependence on the central Government for subsidies, ensured that the republic's leadership was one of the most enthusiastic proponents of the preservation of the USSR. At the all-Union referendum on the status of the USSR, in March 1991, 95.7% of all eligible voters in Turkmenistan approved the preservation of the USSR as a 'renewed federation', the highest proportion of any Soviet republic.

There was little response in Turkmenistan to the attempted coup in Moscow of August 1991. President Niyazov made no public announcements either opposing or supporting the self-proclaimed State Committee for the State of Emergency. However, opposition groups, including Agzybirlik, publicly opposed the coup, which led to the arrest of several of their leaders.

Following the failure of the coup attempt, Niyazov remained in power and announced that the CPT would be retained as the ruling party, unlike in other republics, where the communist parties had been suspended or dissolved; however, in December 1991 the CPT changed its name to the Democratic Party of Turkmenistan (DPT), with Niyazov as its Chairman. On 18 October Turkmenistan was among the signatories of the treaty establishing an economic community of eight republics. This was followed on 26 October by a national referendum at which, according to the official results, 94.1% of the electorate voted for independence. On the following day the Turkmen Supreme Soviet adopted a law on independence, declaring 27 October to be Independence Day. The name of the republic was changed from the Turkmen SSR to the Republic of Turkmenistan, and a new state emblem, flag and national anthem were adopted. In November the Turkmen leadership agreed to draft proposals for a new political union, the Union of Sovereign States. However, when this plan was superseded by the Commonwealth of Independent States (CIS, see p. 126), initially proposed by the three Slav republics, Turkmenistan indicated its wish to participate. On 21 December it became a signatory, with 10 other republics, of the Alma-Ata Declaration (see p. 127), by which the CIS was formally established; this decision was subsequently ratified by the Turkmen Supreme Soviet.

In the first half of 1992 Turkmenistan's state structures remained unchanged, with the DPT dominant both in the Council of Ministers and the Supreme Soviet—effectively the same position that the CPT had held during the Soviet period. However, ultimate power resided with Niyazov, in his capacity as President of the Republic and leader of the DPT. Although Niyazov reportedly continued to enjoy widespread popular support, there was criticism in some quarters of his increasingly authoritarian style of leadership, which involved the rigid control of the media, the restriction of opposition activity, and the promotion of a 'personality cult' of Niyazov. (It was reportedly the last ambition that prompted the resignation, in August, of the Minister of Foreign Affairs, Abdy Kuliyev.) The new Constitution, adopted on 18 May, further enhanced presidential authority, making Niyazov Head of Government (Prime Minister), in addition to his position as Head of State, and giving him certain legislative prerogatives. He was also to act concurrently as the Supreme Commander of the Armed Forces. In June Niyazov was re-elected, unopposed, to the presidency, receiving an estimated 99.5% of the votes cast in a direct ballot.

Certain other significant structural changes were introduced under the new Constitution. The Supreme Soviet was to be replaced as Turkmenistan's legislature by a 50-member Majlis (Assembly); however, until the expiry of its five-year term, the Supreme Soviet, as elected in 1990 (although renamed the Majlis), was to be retained as the republican legislature. A People's Council (Khalk Maslakhaty) was established as the 'supreme representative body of popular power'. The Council was to act only in a supervisory capacity, and it would not diminish the authority of the President or the Majlis; however, it was to debate and decide important political and economic issues, and would also be empowered to demand changes to the Constitution as well as to vote to express 'no confidence' in the President, if it found his actions to be at variance with the law. The Council was to comprise the 50 deputies of the Majlis in addition to 50 elected and 10 appointed representatives from the electoral districts of Turkmenistan (the former were directly elected in November–December 1992); it was also to include other prominent figures of Turkmen society, including the members of the Government and the Chairman of the Supreme Court, and was to be headed by the President. At its first session, in mid-December, the Council awarded Niyazov the rank of General, further enhancing his authority.

The presidential 'personality cult' was further strengthened during 1993, with numerous institutions, streets and public buildings being named after Niyazov—the Caspian Sea port of Krasnovodsk was renamed Turkmenbashi ('Head of the Turkmen', a recently-introduced mode of address for Niyazov). In November senior members of the DPT proposed that the presidential election scheduled for 1997 be cancelled and that Niyazov be made President for life. In the following month the Majlis voted to extend Niyazov's term of office until 2002, on the grounds that the republic's political and economic stability depended on the realization of Niyazov's '10 Years of Prosperity' programme of gradual reforms. The extension of Niyazov's presidency was endorsed by a reported 99.99% of the electorate in a referendum held on 15 January 1994. Although Turkmenistan remained for the mean time a one-party state, Niyazov indicated in late 1993 that a second party, the Peasants' Party, would eventually be permitted to register, as the first step towards a multi-party system.

Despite the result of the referendum of January 1994, elements of opposition to Niyazov were believed to be active in Turkmenistan. Other anti-Niyazov activists were based in exile, in other republics of the CIS, in particular the Russian Federation (where Abdy Kuliyev now led one branch of the opposition). In November two leading members of the Turkmen opposition in exile were arrested in Moscow by Russian security forces (allegedly acting at the behest of Niyazov). The Turkmen Government accused them of planning to assassinate Niyazov, and it urged the Russian authorities to extradite the suspects to Turkmenistan. However, following vocal protests by Russian human rights groups, the two men were released in December. In June 1995 the Turkmen Supreme Court sentenced two further opposition leaders to respective terms of 12 and 15 years' imprisonment in a labour colony, having found them guilty of involvement in the same alleged plot to overthrow Niyazov. The two had been detained by officers of the Uzbek security service in the Uzbek capital, Tashkent, in late 1994, and had subsequently been extradited to Turkmenistan.

Meanwhile, in December 1994, elections to the new, 50-member Majlis were held, officially with the participation of 99.8% of the registered electorate. It was reported that 49 of the 50 deputies had been elected unopposed (two candidates contested the remaining seat). The Majlis convened for the first time in late December. The overwhelming majority of the deputies were believed to be members of the DPT.

Following the adoption of the new Constitution in May 1992, there were fears that the rights of Turkmenistan's ethnic minorities (the largest two groups of which, Russians and Uzbeks, represented 10% and 9%, respectively, of the total population in the early 1990s) were in jeopardy, as the document stipulated that only ethnic Turkmen would be eligible for employment in state enterprises. Moreover, the Russian language was no longer to be used as the means of inter-ethnic communication (the status that it had held since 1990, when Turkmen replaced Russian as the official language). Nevertheless, during 1992 Turkmenistan did not experience inter-ethnic violence, such as occurred in other former republics of the USSR. The country also avoided religious conflict (unlike its close neighbour, Tajikistan). Although the population is predominantly Muslim, Turkmenistan's Constitution guarantees state secularism, a principle that has been strongly emphasized by President

Niyazov. However, this fact has not adversely affected relations with Turkmenistan's southern neighbour, Iran, which developed favourably during 1992. In that year a number of agreements on closer political, economic and cultural integration were signed (including an accord to construct a railway line between Iran and Turkmenistan). Turkmenistan also enjoys close relations with Turkey (which has been regarded as competing with Iran for political and economic influence in the region), not least owing to the Turkmen's ethnic and linguistic ties with the Turks. In late 1992 Turkmenistan and Turkey agreed in principle to co-operate on the construction of a pipeline to supply natural gas from Turkmenistan (its most valuable export commodity) to Europe via Iran and Turkey. Turkmenistan is a member, with both Iran and Turkey, of the Economic Co-operation Organization (ECO, see p. 238).

Concerning its membership of the CIS, Turkmenistan displayed an increasing opposition to any centralized structures within the organization, preferring to regard it as a 'consultative body'. Rather, during 1992 Turkmenistan concentrated on developing closer relations with the four other Central Asian republics of the CIS (Kazakhstan, Kyrgyzstan, Tajikistan and Uzbekistan), with which it held regular negotiations throughout the year. However, unlike Kazakhstan, Kyrgyzstan and Uzbekistan, Turkmenistan remained neutral regarding the civil war in Tajikistan (q.v.), and it did not contribute troops to the joint CIS peace-keeping forces in the region. At a summit meeting of the leaders of the CIS member states, held in Minsk, Belarus, in January 1993, Turkmenistan was one of three states not to sign a charter on closer political and economic integration. In May Turkmenistan was the only CIS member to refuse to sign a declaration of intent to establish an economic union; this, it was believed, was prompted by concern that Turkmenistan would be forced to sell natural gas to CIS countries at reduced prices. In December, however, Turkmenistan finally agreed to join the newly-realized CIS economic union.

In spite of Turkmenistan's somewhat equivocal attitude to CIS membership, the republic's relations with the Russian Federation (the leading CIS state) remained relatively cordial. In December 1993 the two countries signed an agreement granting dual citizenship to Turkmenistan's ethnic Russian population (the first such agreement between any of the former Soviet republics). It was also agreed that Russian border troops would be stationed on Turkmenistan's southern borders with Iran and Afghanistan.

### Government

Under the terms of the 1992 Constitution, the President of the Republic is directly elected, by universal adult suffrage, for five years, although in December 1993 the legislature voted to extend President Niyazov's mandate—due to expire in 1997—until 2002 (this was endorsed in a national referendum in January 1994). The President is both Head of State and Head of Government (Prime Minister in the Council of Ministers), holding executive power in conjunction with the Council of Ministers (which is appointed by the President), and is concurrently Supreme Commander of the Armed Forces. The supreme legislative body is the Majlis (Assembly), whose 50 members are directly elected for a term of five years. The deputies of the Majlis also sit on the People's Council (Khalk Maslakhaty), a supervisory organ which is described as the 'supreme representative body of popular power' and which also includes 50 directly-elected and 10 appointed representatives from all regions of Turkmenistan, the members of the Council of Ministers and other prominent figures, and is headed by the President of the Republic. For administrative purposes, Turkmenistan is divided into five regions (oblasts).

### Defence

In mid-1992 Turkmenistan began the establishment of national armed forces, based upon the former Soviet military units still stationed in the republic; under an agreement with the Russian Federation, Turkmenistan's nascent armed forces (numbering 28,000 in June 1994) were to be under joint Turkmen and Russian command for a transitional period of five to six years. However, in April 1995 the Russian Government reportedly stated that this agreement would not be ratified by Russia, as Turkmenistan had already completed the establishment of its armed forces. There is a small air force, and the Government also envisages the establishment of a navy; in 1993–95 Turkmenistan co-operated with Russia and Kazakhstan in the operation of the Caspian Sea Flotilla, another former Soviet force, based, under Russian command, at Astrakhan (Russia). In May 1994 Turkmenistan became the first Central Asian republic of the former USSR to join NATO's 'partnership for peace' programme (see p. 192). Military service is compulsory and lasts for 18 months. Projected defence expenditure for 1995 was 4,588m. Turkmen manats (some 7% of total budgetary expenditure).

### Economic Affairs

In 1992, according to preliminary estimates by the World Bank, Turkmenistan's gross national product (GNP) per head, measured at average 1990–92 prices, was US $1,380. During 1985-93, it was estimated, GNP per head declined, in real terms, by an annual average of 1.6%. Over the same period the population increased by an annual average of 2.5%. Turkmenistan's gross domestic product (GDP) declined by 5.3% in 1992, compared with the previous year. In 1993, according to estimates by the IMF, GDP increased by some 8%, compared with 1992.

Turkmenistan's economy is predominantly agricultural: in 1992 agriculture (including forestry) contributed an estimated 47.7% of net material product (NMP) and employed 44.2% of the working population. Although the Kara-Kum desert covers some 90% of the country's territory, widespread irrigation has enabled rapid agricultural development; in recent years, however, over-intensive cultivation of the principal crop, cotton, together with massive irrigation projects, have led to serious ecological damage. Other important crops include grain, vegetables and fruit (in particular grapes and melons), although the country remains heavily dependent on imports of foodstuffs. Livestock breeding (including the production of astrakhan and karakul wools) plays a central role in the sector. Silkworm breeding is also widespread. In 1991 agricultural NMP decreased by an estimated 1.6%, compared with the previous year.

Industry (including mining, manufacturing, construction and power) contributed an estimated 38.8% of NMP in 1992, when some 20% of the working population were employed in the sector. Industrial activity is chiefly associated with the extraction and processing of the country's mineral resources (predominantly natural gas and petroleum), energy generation and cotton-processing. In 1990 textile production accounted for some 36% of the value of total industrial production, while a further 30% was accounted for by the electricity-generating, chemical, gas and petroleum-processing industries. In 1992 industrial production declined by an estimated 16%, compared with 1991.

Turkmenistan is richly endowed with mineral resources, in particular natural gas and petroleum (reserves of which were estimated to be between 10,000,000m. and 15,000,000m. cu metres and 6,300m. metric tons, respectively, in 1993). In 1992 and 1993 Turkmenistan produced an annual average of about 63,000m. cu metres of natural gas, most of which was exported. Natural gas that is not exported is used domestically to fuel the country's thermal power stations; much of the energy thus produced is also exported. Petroleum is refined at two major refineries, at Turkmenbashi (Krasnovodsk) and Charjou. Turkmenistan also has large deposits of iodine-bromine, sodium sulphate and different types of salt.

Transport and communications services for industrial purposes form the major part of the services sector; with retailing and housing, they provide some 12% of employment. Non-industrial and consumer services are limited, and have declined sharply since 1990.

In 1992, according to official estimates, Turkmenistan recorded a visible surplus of US $1,139.9m. in combined inter-republican (former USSR) and other trade, and there was a surplus of $926.9m. on the current account of the balance of payments. In the late 1980s Turkmenistan's trade was conducted almost exclusively (about 95%) with other Soviet republics, but the proportion declined to an estimated 47% in 1992, as the country expanded trade with other partners. The principal imports in the early 1990s were machinery and metalwork, light industrial products and processed foods. The principal exports were light industrial products (mainly cotton yarn) and natural gas and petroleum. Exports of natural gas accounted for some 58% of total exports in 1992, and the proportion rose to an estimated 74% in the following year.

The 1995 budget projected a surplus of some 670m. Turkmen manats. At the end of 1993 Turkmenistan's total external debt was US $9.0m. Consumer prices increased by an annual average of 102.5% in 1991, by 492.9% in 1992 and by an estimated 1,150% in 1993. At mid-1992 some 40,000 people were officially registered as unemployed (about 2.5% of the labour force); however, unofficial sources estimated the rate to be much higher.

Turkmenistan became a member of the IMF and the World Bank in 1992. It also joined the European Bank for Reconstruction and Development (EBRD, see p. 140) as a 'Country of Operations' and, with five other former Soviet republics, the Economic Co-operation Organization (ECO, see p. 238). In 1994 Turkmenistan became a member of the Islamic Development Bank (IDB, see p. 180).

One of the poorest republics of the former USSR, Turkmenistan had experienced considerable economic decline even before the dissolution of the USSR in December 1991. The ensuing disruptions in inter-republican trade adversely affected Turkmenistan's industrial sector, which is heavily reliant on imported finished and intermediate goods. However, in 1991 and 1992 overall economic decline was less severe than in many other republics of the USSR, owing to an increase in petroleum- and cotton-processing (two of the mainstays of the Turkmen economy) as well as in the production of consumer goods in the former year, and to a relatively small agricultural decline and a strong performance in construction in the latter year. In 1993 there were indications of a significant economic recovery, which was attributed in large part to sustained exports of natural gas. Compared with other former USSR republics, the Turkmen Government initially adopted a cautious approach towards the implementation of market economic reforms, concerned that the population's living standards should not, as a consequence, deteriorate drastically. The 'privatization' of state property (to be effected in three stages) was commenced only in December 1993, considerably later than in other former Soviet republics. The initiation of the second stage of the 'privatization' programme was announced in November 1994.

Future economic development in Turkmenistan is expected to be based on exploitation of the country's enormous reserves of natural gas (of which it is the world's fourth largest producer) and petroleum, as well as other natural resources. In this connection the Government has sought to encourage foreign investment, and plans have been announced for the establishment of seven 'free' economic zones. However, at present Turkmenistan's exports of natural gas and petroleum flow through the former USSR's obsolescent pipeline system (which is controlled by the Russian Federation), and President Niyazov is exploring the possibility of two alternative routes—one to Europe, via Iran and Turkey, and the other to China and Japan—in order to lessen Turkmenistan's economic dependence on Russia.

Turkmenistan remained within the rouble area until November 1993, when a new national currency, the Turkmen manat, was introduced, thus facilitating Turkmenistan's full economic independence.

### Social Welfare

In 1990 the average life expectancy at birth was 66.4 years, the lowest of all the Soviet republics. In 1989 the rate of infant mortality reached 54.2 per 1,000 live births, the highest rate in the USSR. However, under-reporting of mortality rates is widespread and it is estimated that true figures may be 50%–100% higher than offically reported. A basic, state-funded health system was introduced under Soviet rule, but it was of low quality and was underfunded. The high levels of disease in Turkmenistan (among adults as well as children) are attributed to poor overall medical and sanitary conditions, and the critical state of the environment.

In the early 1990s, in order to counteract some of the adverse social consequences of the economic reforms taking place in Turkmenistan, the Government implemented extensive social protection measures (largely covered by the newly-established Pension Fund), which were of a more generous level than social welfare schemes in many other former Soviet republics. In April 1991 Turkmenistan introduced an unemployment compensation scheme, which was, however, terminated after only six months. In 1992, in view of an anticipated increase in the number of unemployed, the Government was considering the establishment of an employment fund, comparable to those introduced in other former republics of the USSR. From January 1993 supplies of electricity, gas and water were reportedly provided free of charge to the entire population. Free supplies of bread and flour were to be provided from 1996.

In the early 1990s there were 111 hospital beds per 10,000 inhabitants. The 1995 budget projected that some 5% of total spending would be allocated to health care and 5% to pensions and social benefits.

### Education

There were few educational establishments in pre-revolutionary Turkmenistan, but a state-funded education system was introduced under Soviet rule. Most school education is conducted in Turkmen (76.9% of all pupils at general day-schools in 1988), but there are also schools using Russian (16.0%), Uzbek (6.1%) and Kazakh (1.0%). Until the early 1990s most institutions of higher education used Russian, but there have been attempts to increase the provision of Turkmen-language courses. In 1989 8.3% of the population over 15 years of age had completed courses of higher education. In the early 1990s some 30% of schoolchildren in Turkmenistan reportedly studied in shifts, owing to inadequate staffing and facilities. The 1995 budget projected that 8% of total expenditure would be allocated to education.

### Weights and Measures

The metric system is in force.

TURKMENISTAN

# Statistical Survey

Principal sources (unless otherwise stated): IMF, *Turkmenistan, Economic Review*; World Bank, *Statistical Handbook: States of the Former USSR*.

## Area and Population

### AREA, POPULATION AND DENSITY

| | |
|---|---:|
| Area (sq km) | 488,100* |
| Population (census results)† | |
| 17 January 1979 | 2,764,748 |
| 12 January 1989 | |
| Males | 1,735,179 |
| Females | 1,787,538 |
| Total | 3,522,717 |
| Population (official estimates at 1 January) | |
| 1991 | 3,714,000 |
| 1993‡ | 4,254,000 |
| Density (per sq km) at 1 January 1993 | 8.7 |

* 188,456 sq miles.
† Figures refer to the *de jure* population. The *de facto* total at the 1989 census was 3,533,925.
‡ Figure for 1992 not available.

### POPULATION BY NATIONALITY
(official estimates at 1 January 1993)

| | Number | % |
|---|---:|---:|
| Turkmen | 3,118,000 | 73.3 |
| Russian | 419,000 | 9.8 |
| Uzbek | 382,000 | 9.0 |
| Kazakh | 87,000 | 2.0 |
| Tatar | 39,000 | 0.9 |
| Ukrainian | 34,000 | 0.8 |
| Azeri | 34,000 | 0.8 |
| Armenian | 32,000 | 0.8 |
| Belarusian | 9,000 | 0.2 |
| Others | 100,000 | 2.4 |
| **Total** | **4,254,000** | **100.0** |

**PRINCIPAL TOWNS** (estimated population at 1 January 1990)
Ashgabat (capital) 517,200*; Charjou 164,000; Tashauz 114,000.
* At 1 January 1993.

### BIRTHS, MARRIAGES AND DEATHS

| | Registered live births | | Registered marriages | | Registered deaths | |
|---|---:|---:|---:|---:|---:|---:|
| | Number | Rate (per 1,000) | Number | Rate (per 1,000) | Number | Rate (per 1,000) |
| 1987 | 126,787 | 37.2 | 31,484 | 9.2 | 26,802 | 7.9 |
| 1988 | 125,887 | 36.0 | 33,008 | 9.4 | 27,317 | 7.8 |
| 1989 | 124,992 | 34.9 | 34,890 | 9.8 | 27,609 | 7.7 |

Source: UN, *Demographic Yearbook*.

**Expectation of life** (official estimates, years at birth, 1989): 65.2 (males 61.8; females 68.4) (Source: Goskomstat USSR).

### EMPLOYMENT ('000 persons at 31 December)

| | 1990 | 1991 | 1992 |
|---|---:|---:|---:|
| Material sphere | 1,145.5 | 1,173.5 | 1,186.2 |
| Agriculture | 645.1 | 664.2 | 693.2 |
| Forestry | 1.7 | 2.1 | 2.0 |
| Industry* | 166.4 | 159.3 | 154.3 |
| Construction | 154.4 | 168.1 | 163.5 |
| Trade and catering† | 87.5 | 87.3 | 88.5 |
| Transport and communications‡ | 62.5 | 62.7 | 56.4 |
| Other activities | 27.9 | 29.8 | 28.3 |
| Non-material sphere | 396.8 | 397.3 | 386.7 |
| Transport and communications‡ | 29.5 | 29.7 | 27.7 |
| Housing and municipal services | 38.3 | 37.1 | 34.2 |
| Health care and social security | 86.4 | 86.5 | 82.1 |
| Education, culture and arts | 175.5 | 182.0 | 171.9 |
| Science, research and development | 28.3 | 23.1 | 21.0 |
| Other activities | 38.8 | 38.9 | 49.8 |
| **Total** | **1,542.3** | **1,570.8** | **1,572.9** |

* Comprising manufacturing (except printing and publishing), mining and quarrying, electricity, gas, water, logging and fishing.
† Including material and technical supply.
‡ Transport and communications servicing material production are included in activities of the material sphere. Other branches of the sector are considered to be non-material services.

## Agriculture

### PRINCIPAL CROPS ('000 metric tons)

| | 1991 | 1992 | 1993 |
|---|---:|---:|---:|
| Wheat | 206 | 368 | 500* |
| Rice (paddy) | 54 | 64 | 70† |
| Barley | 129 | 124 | 150* |
| Maize | 96 | 147 | 180* |
| Potatoes | 30 | 9 | 16 |
| Cottonseed | 710* | 822 | 737 |
| Cabbages | n.a. | 68* | 55* |
| Tomatoes | n.a. | 133* | 150* |
| Onions (dry) | n.a. | 71* | 98* |
| Grapes | 167 | 91 | 145 |
| Watermelons‡ | n.a. | 180 | 248 |
| Apples | } 56 { | 53* | 39† |
| Other fruits and berries | | 29* | 21† |
| Cotton (lint) | 430 | 307* | 450* |

* Unofficial figure.  † FAO estimate.
‡ Including melons, pumpkins and squash.
Source: FAO, *Production Yearbook*.

### LIVESTOCK ('000 head at 1 January)

| | 1991 | 1992 | 1993 |
|---|---:|---:|---:|
| Horses | 19 | 20* | 22* |
| Asses | n.a. | 26* | 26* |
| Camels | n.a. | 40* | 40* |
| Cattle | 800 | 777 | 711† |
| Pigs | 300 | 237 | 209† |
| Sheep | 5,280 | 5,380 | 5,405* |
| Goats | 220 | 220 | 224* |
| Chickens | 7,000† | 8,000† | 7,000* |

* FAO estimate.  † Unofficial figure.
Source: FAO, *Production Yearbook*.

# TURKMENISTAN

## LIVESTOCK PRODUCTS ('000 metric tons)

|  | 1991 | 1992 | 1993 |
|---|---|---|---|
| Beef and veal | 44 | 37* | 35* |
| Mutton and lamb | 30 | 30† | 30† |
| Goat meat | 6* | 4† | 4† |
| Pig meat | 9 | 6 | 8 |
| Poultry meat | 7 | 8* | 7† |
| Cows' milk | 458.2 | 400† | 400† |
| Butter | 4.3 | 4.0* | 4.0* |
| Hen eggs | 16.6* | 15.0* | 14.5† |
| Wool: |  |  |  |
| greasy | 16.3 | 17.0† | 18.0† |
| scoured | 9.8 | 10.2† | 10.8† |
| Sheepskins | n.a. | 20† | 20† |

* Unofficial figure.   † FAO estimate.
Source: FAO, *Production Yearbook*.

## Fishing

('000 metric tons, live weight)

|  | 1991 | 1992* |
|---|---|---|
| Freshwater fishes | 3.2 | 3.0 |
| Azov tyulka | 39.8 | 37.0 |
| **Total catch** (incl. others) | 43.0 | 40.0 |
| Inland waters | 43.0 | 40.0 |

* FAO estimates.
Source: FAO, *Yearbook of Fishery Statistics*.

## Mining

|  | 1992 | 1993 | 1994 |
|---|---|---|---|
| Crude petroleum ('000 metric tons) | 4,663 | 3,916 | 3,866 |
| Natural gas (million cu metres) | 60,071 | 65,213 | 35,636 |

## Industry

### SELECTED PRODUCTS
('000 metric tons, unless otherwise indicated)

|  | 1990 | 1991 | 1992 |
|---|---|---|---|
| Vegetable oil | 104.9 | 103.8 | 85.4 |
| Cotton yarn | 415.5 | 419.6 | 436.5 |
| Woven cotton fabrics ('000 sq m) | 29.0 | 28.2 | 29.1 |
| Carpets and rugs ('000 sq m) | 1,288 | 1,384 | 1,070 |
| Motor spirit (petrol) | 773.3 | 813.9 | 1,030.9 |
| Kerosene | 110.4 | 98.1 | 326.5 |
| Diesel oil | 1,572.5 | 2,236.1 | 1,942.3 |
| Mazout (heavy fuel oil) | 1,218.0 | 1,991.0 | 1,667.1 |
| Cement | 1,084.5 | 903.5 | 1,050.6 |
| Electric energy (million kWh) | 16,637 | 14,915 | 13,136 |

**1993** ('000 metric tons): Motor spirit (petrol) 730.6; Diesel oil 1,253.1; Mazout (heavy fuel oil) 1,262.1.
**1994** ('000 metric tons): Motor spirit (petrol) 741.0; Diesel oil 1,353.7; Mazout (heavy fuel oil) 1,214.6.

# Finance

## CURRENCY AND EXCHANGE RATES

**Monetary Units**
100 tenge = 1 Turkmen manat.

**Sterling and Dollar Equivalents** (31 December 1994)
£1 sterling = 15.645 manats;
US $1 = 10.000 manats (official rates);
1,000 Turkmen manats = £63.92 = $100.00.

Note: The Turkmen manat was introduced on 1 November 1993, replacing the Russian (formerly Soviet) rouble at a rate of 1 manat = 500 roubles. By the end of the year the rate was 600 roubles per manat. Based on the official rate of exchange, the average value of Soviet currency (roubles per US dollar) was: 0.6274 in 1989; 0.5856 in 1990; 0.5819 in 1991. However, a multiple exchange rate system was in operation, with separate non-commercial and tourist rates. A commercial exchange rate was introduced on 1 November 1990, replacing the official rate for most transactions. The commercial rate (roubles per US dollar) was: 1.692 at 31 December 1990; 1.671 at 31 December 1991. Between November 1989 and April 1991 the tourist exchange rate valued the rouble at one-tenth of the official rate. In April 1991 this rate, renamed the 'special rate', was set at $1 = 27.6 roubles. It was subsequently adjusted. The average market exchange rate in 1991 was $1 = 31.2 roubles. Following the dissolution of the USSR in December 1991, Russia and several other former Soviet republics retained the rouble as their monetary unit. The average interbank market rate in 1992 was $1 = 222.1 Russian roubles. Following the introduction of the Turkmen manat, a multiple exchange rate system was established. In December 1994, in addition to the official exchange rate (see above), there was a commercial rate of US $1 = 75 manats, while exchange offices traded foreign currency with the public at $1 = 220 manats (buying rate) or 230 manats (selling rate). Some of the figures in this Survey are still expressed in terms of roubles.

## BUDGET (million roubles)

| Revenue | 1990 | 1991 | 1992 |
|---|---|---|---|
| Taxation | 1,038 | 1,971 | 110,624 |
| Taxes on income and profits | 258 | 989 | 15,941 |
| Individual | 166 | 349 | 2,907 |
| Corporate | 92 | 640 | 13,034 |
| Domestic taxes on goods and services | 780 | 983 | 18,586 |
| Turnover tax | 780 | 669 | — |
| Sales tax | — | 314 | — |
| Value-added tax | — | — | 17,399 |
| Excises | — | — | 1,187 |
| Taxes on international trade | — | — | 76,097 |
| State duties and bonds | 54 | 43 | 274 |
| Funds from social security | 187 | — | — |
| Transfers from state-owned enterprises (formerly of the USSR) | 312 | — | — |
| Transfers from state-owned gas and cotton corporations | — | 1,551 | 18,253 |
| Other revenue | 917 | 1,515 | 8,659 |
| Transfers from the USSR | 728 | 1,409 | — |
| **Total** | 3,236 | 6,487 | 137,810 |
| Central government | 1,648 | 4,413 | 104,912 |
| Local government | 1,589 | 2,075 | 32,898 |

| Expenditure | 1990 | 1991 | 1992 |
|---|---|---|---|
| Financing of national economy | 1,848 | 2,302 | 60,234 |
| Social and cultural services | 1,162 | 3,355 | 25,806 |
| Education and science | 672 | 1,228 | 14,349 |
| Health care | 283 | 556 | 6,201 |
| Social security | 207 | 1,572 | 5,256 |
| Administration | 49 | 161 | 1,639 |
| Other purposes | 55 | 78 | 6,985 |
| **Total** | 3,114 | 5,896 | 94,656 |
| Central government | 1,597 | 3,822 | 65,288 |
| Local government | 1,517 | 2,074 | 29,368 |

## COST OF LIVING (Index of retail prices; base: previous year = 100)

|  | 1990 | 1991 | 1992 |
|---|---|---|---|
| All items | 104.2 | 202.5 | 592.9 |

# TURKMENISTAN

## NATIONAL ACCOUNTS

### Net Material Product by Economic Activity
(million roubles at current prices)

|  | 1990 | 1991 | 1992* |
|---|---|---|---|
| Agriculture and forestry | 2,548 | 5,680 | 44,260 |
| Industry† | 833 | 2,514 | 10,439 |
| Construction | 950 | 2,224 | 25,636 |
| Transport and communications | 451 | 815 | 5,469 |
| Other material services | 539 | 1,066 | 7,066 |
| **Total** | **5,321** | **12,299** | **92,870** |

* Excluding trade balance.
† Comprising manufacturing (except printing and publishing), mining and quarrying, electricity, gas, water, logging and fishing.

## BALANCE OF PAYMENTS (US $ million)

|  | 1990 | 1991 | 1992* |
|---|---|---|---|
| Merchandise exports f.o.b. | 304.3 | 1,237.7 | 2,148.9 |
| Merchandise imports f.o.b. | −582.1 | −648.2 | −1,009.0 |
| **Trade balance** | **−277.8** | **589.5** | **1,139.9** |
| Services (net) | −68.2 | −208.4 | −213.1 |
| Unrequited transfers (net) | 37.9 | 66.3 | — |
| **Current balance** | **−308.0** | **447.4** | **926.9** |
| Official financial credits | −44.0 | 21.0 | −215.2 |
| Private direct investment | — | — | 11.3 |
| Net errors and omissions | 34.3 | −46.6 | −830.9 |
| **Overall balance** | **−317.7** | **421.7** | **−107.9** |

* Estimates.

# External Trade

## PRINCIPAL COMMODITIES (million roubles)
### Trade with the Former USSR

| Imports f.o.b. | 1989 | 1990 | 1991* |
|---|---|---|---|
| Industrial products | 2,611 | 2,693 | 4,246 |
| Petroleum and gas | 100 | 79 | 125 |
| Iron and steel | 84 | 106 | 167 |
| Chemical and petroleum products | 209 | 203 | 320 |
| Machinery and metalworking | 949 | 959 | 1,509 |
| Wood and paper products | 125 | 97 | 152 |
| Light industry | 453 | 551 | 867 |
| Food and beverages | 478 | 445 | 700 |
| Agricultural products (unprocessed) | 34 | 132 | 208 |
| Other commodities | 99 | 98 | 154 |
| **Total** | **2,744** | **2,923** | **4,608** |

* Figures are provisional. The revised total is 5,636m. roubles.

| Exports f.o.b. | 1989 | 1990 | 1991* |
|---|---|---|---|
| Industrial products | 2,197 | 2,271 | 6,335 |
| Electricity | 70 | 67 | 152 |
| Petroleum and gas | 743 | 696 | 2,563 |
| Chemical and petroleum products | 152 | 147 | 400 |
| Light industry | 1,076 | 1,083 | 2,767 |
| Food and beverages | 85 | 206 | 300 |
| Agricultural products (unprocessed) | 128 | 124 | 370 |
| Other commodities | 93 | 74 | 80 |
| **Total** | **2,418** | **2,469** | **6,785** |

* Figures are provisional. The revised total is 6,731m. roubles.

### Trade with Other Countries

| Imports f.o.b. | 1989 | 1990 | 1991* |
|---|---|---|---|
| Industrial products | 539 | 625 | 811 |
| Iron and steel | 19 | 7 | 9 |
| Chemical and petroleum products | 21 | 27 | 35 |
| Machinery and metalworking | 93 | 120 | 155 |
| Wood and paper products | 12 | 9 | 12 |
| Light industry | 243 | 255 | 330 |
| Food and beverages | 144 | 185 | 240 |
| Agricultural products (unprocessed) | 51 | 60 | 78 |
| **Total** | **590** | **685** | **889** |

* Figures are provisional. The revised total is 1,302m. roubles.

| Exports f.o.b. | 1989 | 1990 | 1991* |
|---|---|---|---|
| Industrial products | 228 | 163 | 1,079 |
| Petroleum and gas | 2 | 9 | 445 |
| Chemical and petroleum products | 1 | 7 | 35 |
| Light industry | 223 | 139 | 576 |
| Food and beverages | 2 | 7 | 17 |
| Agricultural products (unprocessed) | 5 | 4 | 42 |
| Other commodities | 8 | 5 | — |
| **Total** | **241** | **172** | **1,121** |

* Figures are provisional. The revised total is 1,105m. roubles.

## PRINCIPAL TRADING PARTNERS
(million roubles)
### Trade with the Former USSR

| Imports f.o.b. | 1990 | 1991* | 1992* |
|---|---|---|---|
| Azerbaijan | n.a. | n.a. | 9,700 |
| Belarus | 105 | 165 | 4,700 |
| Kazakhstan | 117 | 184 | 3,600 |
| Kyrgyzstan | n.a. | n.a. | 1,600 |
| Russia | 1,222 | 1,925 | 40,200 |
| Tajikistan | n.a. | n.a. | 4,800 |
| Ukraine | 457 | 720 | 5,300 |
| Uzbekistan | 166 | 262 | 9,200 |
| **Total (incl. others)** | **2,927†** | **4,608†** | **89,800** |

* Figures are provisional. The revised total for 1991 is 5,636m. roubles.
† Including a statistical discrepancy (million roubles): 778 in 1990; 1,220 in 1991.

| Exports f.o.b. | 1990 | 1991* | 1992* |
|---|---|---|---|
| Armenia | n.a. | n.a. | 6,800 |
| Azerbaijan | n.a. | n.a. | 11,000 |
| Belarus | 51 | 140 | 2,600 |
| Georgia | n.a. | n.a. | 20,000 |
| Kazakhstan | 64 | 175 | 23,700 |
| Kyrgyzstan | n.a. | n.a. | 7,700 |
| Latvia | n.a. | n.a. | 2,400 |
| Moldova | n.a. | n.a. | 7,600 |
| Russia | 1,230 | 3,378 | 28,400 |
| Tajikistan | n.a. | n.a. | 10,700 |
| Ukraine | 183 | 502 | 47,800 |
| Uzbekistan | 686 | 1,884 | 24,000 |
| **Total (incl. others)** | **2,469†** | **6,785†** | **193,500** |

* Figures are provisional. The revised total for 1991 is 6,731m. roubles.
† Including a statistical discrepancy (million roubles): 198 in 1990; 547 in 1991.

TURKMENISTAN

## Communications Media

|  | 1989 | 1990 | 1991 |
|---|---|---|---|
| Telephones ('000 main lines in use) | . . | 210* | 220* | 237 |

* Estimate.
Source: UN, *Statistical Yearbook*.

**1992:** Book production (titles) 565, including 179 pamphlets; Book production ('000 copies) 6,604, including pamphlets 2,169 (Source: UNESCO, *Statistical Yearbook*).

## Education

(1984/85)

|  | Institutions | Students |
|---|---|---|
| Secondary schools | 1,900 | 800,000 |
| Secondary specialized schools. | 35 | 36,900 |
| Higher schools (incl. universities). | 9 | 38,900 |

**1990:** 41,800 students at higher schools. (Source: UNESCO, *Statistical Yearbook*).

# Directory

## The Constitution

A new Constitution was adopted on 18 May 1992, and included the following among its main provisions:

The President of the Republic is directly elected by universal adult suffrage for a five-year term. A President may hold office for a maximum of two terms. The President is not only Head of State, but also head of Government (Prime Minister in the Council of Ministers) and Supreme Commander of the Armed Forces. The President must ratify all parliamentary legislation and in certain circumstances may legislate by decree. The President appoints the Council of Ministers and chairs sessions of the Khalk Maslakhaty (People's Council).

Supreme legislative power resides with the 50-member Majlis, a unicameral parliament which is directly elected for a five-year term. Sovereignty, however, is vested in the people of Turkmenistan, and the supreme representative body of popular power is the Khalk Maslakhaty. This is described as a supervisory organ with no legislative or executive functions, but it is authorized to perform certain duties normally reserved to a legislature or constituent assembly. Not only does it debate and approve measures pertaining to the political and economic situation in the country, but it examines possible changes to the Constitution and may vote to express 'no confidence' in the President of the Republic, on grounds of unconstitutionality. The Khalk Maslakhaty is comprised of all the deputies of the Majlis, a further 50 elected and 10 appointed representatives from all districts of the country, the members of the Council of Ministers, the Chairmen of the Supreme Court and the Supreme Economic Court, the Procurator-General and the heads of local councils.

The Constitution, which defines Turkmenistan as a democratic state, also guarantees the independence of the judiciary and the basic human rights of the individual. The age of majority is 18 years (parliamentary deputies must be aged at least 21). Ethnic minorities are granted equality under the law, although Turkmen is the only official language.

Note: On 15 January 1994 a referendum confirmed President Saparmyrat Niyazov's exemption from the need to be re-elected in 1997.

## The Government

### HEAD OF STATE

**President of the Republic:** Gen. SAPARMYRAT A. NIYAZOV (directly elected 27 October 1990; re-elected 21 June 1992—a referendum on 15 January 1994 extended his term of office until 2002).

### COUNCIL OF MINISTERS
(July 1995)

**Prime Minister:** Gen. SAPARMYRAT A. NIYAZOV.
**Deputy Prime Minister and Minister of the Economy and Finance:** VALERY OTCHERTSOV.
**Deputy Prime Minister and Minister of Foreign Affairs:** BORIS SHIKHMYRADOV.
**Deputy Prime Minister and Minister of Internal Affairs:** GURBANMUKHAMMET KASYMOV.
**Deputy Prime Minister and Minister of State Property and Enterprise Support:** MATKARIM RAJAPOV.
**Deputy Prime Ministers:** ORAZGEDI AYDOGDYEV, MUKHAMMET ABALAKOV, REJEP SAPAROV, BATYR SARJAYEV, HAKIM ISHANOV, NAZAR SUYUNOV, REJEPMAMMET PUKHANOV, SPARGELDY MOTAYEV, KURBAN ORAZOV, PIRKULY ODEYEV, JUMAGELDY AMANSAKHATOV, ABAD S. IRZAYEVA.
**Minister of Agriculture, Food and the Processing Industries:** TAGANDURDY NURYEV.
**Minister of Agricultural Construction:** R. ABDYEV.
**Minister of the Building Materials Industry:** KHALMUKHAMMET ORAZSAKHATOV.
**Minister of Communications:** AMANMURAT JUMMYEV.
**Minister of Construction and Architecture:** ALLABERDY TEKAYEV.
**Minister of Consumer Goods:** BEGENCH NEPESOV.
**Minister of Culture and Tourism:** GELDYMYRAT NURMUKHAMMETOV.
**Minister of Defence:** Lt-Gen. DANATAR KOPEKOV.
**Minister of Education:** N. BAYRAMSAKHATOV.
**Minister of Forestry:** T. CHOREKLIYEV.
**Minister of Grain Products:** A. CHARYYAROV.
**Minister of Health:** (vacant).
**Minister of Justice:** TAGANDURDY KHALLYEV.
**Minister of Local Industry:** (vacant).
**Minister of Motor Transport:** SENAGULY RAKHMANOV.
**Minister of Natural Resources and Environmental Protection:** NURMAKHAMMET ASHIROV.
**Minister of Petroleum and Natural Gas:** AMANGELDY ESENOV.
**Minister of Social Security:** KHALYKBERDY ATAYEV.
**Minister of Trade and Resources:** KH. A. AGAKHANOV.
**Minister of Water Management:** (vacant).

#### Chairmen of State Committees

**Chairman of the State Committee for Fish Management:** GELDYKURBAN IBRAGIMOV.
**Chairman of the State Committee for Land Use, Land Organization and Land Reform:** A. NOBADOV.
**Chairman of the State Committee for Material-Technical Supply:** NURMUKHAMMET KHANAMOV.
**Chairman of the State Committee for National Security:** SAPARMYRAT SEYIDOV.
**Chairman of the State Committee for Preservation of State Secrets in the Press and Other Media:** KAKABAY ATAYEV.
**Chairman of the State Committee for Publishing, Printing and the Book Trade:** KH. DIVANKULIYEV.
**Chairman of the State Committee for Statistics:** BAYRAMKLYCH URAZOV.
**Chairman of the State Committee for the Supervision of Industrial Safety and Mining Inspection:** N. D. KLYCHEV.
**Chairman of the State Committee for the Supply of Petroleum Products:** A. S. KANAYEV.

### MINISTRIES

**Office of the President and the Council of Ministers:** Ashgabat.
**Ministry of Agriculture, Food and the Processing Industries:** Ashgabat.
**Ministry of Agricultural Construction:** Ashgabat.
**Ministry of the Building Materials Industry:** Ashgabat.

# TURKMENISTAN

**Ministry of the Building Materials Industry:** Ashgabat.
**Ministry of Communications:** Ashgabat.
**Ministry of Construction and Architecture:** Ashgabat.
**Ministry of Consumer Goods:** Ashgabat.
**Ministry of Culture and Tourism:** Ashgabat; tel. (3632) 25-35-60.
**Ministry of Defence:** Ashgabat, ul. Nurberdy Pomma 15; tel. (3632) 29-31-80.
**Ministry of the Economy and Finance:** Ashgabat.
**Ministry of Education:** Ashgabat, ul. Gyorogly 1.
**Ministry of Foreign Affairs:** Ashgabat, ul. Makhtumkuli 83; tel. (3632) 26-62-11; fax (3632) 25-35-83.
**Ministry of Forestry:** Ashgabat.
**Ministry of Grain Products:** Ashgabat.
**Ministry of Health:** Ashgabat, ul. Makhtumkuli 95; tel. (3632) 25-10-63; fax (3632) 25-50-32.
**Ministry of Internal Affairs:** Ashgabat, ul. Makhtumkuli 85; tel. (3632) 25-13-28.
**Ministry of Justice:** Ashgabat.
**Ministry of Local Industry:** Ashgabat.
**Ministry of Motor Transport:** Ashgabat.
**Ministry of Natural Resources and Environmental Protection:** Ashgabat.
**Ministry of Petroleum and Natural Gas:** Ashgabat.
**Ministry of Social Security:** 744007 Ashgabat, ul. Mollanepes 3; tel. (3632) 25-30-03.
**Ministry of State Property and Enterprise Support:** Ashgabat.
**Ministry of Trade and Resources:** Ashgabat.
**Ministry of Water Management:** Ashgabat.

All the principal state committees are also based in Ashgabat.

### KHALK MASLAKHATY (PEOPLE'S COUNCIL)

Under the Constitution of May 1992, the People's Council was established as the supreme representative body in the country. The People's Council is composed of all the Majlis deputies, 50 directly elected representatives and 10 appointed representatives from all regions of Turkmenistan, the members of the Council of Ministers, the Chairman of the Supreme Court, the Chairman of the Supreme Economic Court, the Procurator-General and the heads of the local councils. It is headed by the President of the Republic. Elections for the 50 regional representatives were held in November and December 1992; the Council convened for the first time later in December.

## Legislature

### MAJLIS (ASSEMBLY)

The Supreme Soviet of Turkmenistan, with 175 seats, was elected on 7 January 1990, for a term of five years, in elections contested only by the Communist Party of Turkmenistan (CPT) and its approved organizations. Under the Constitution of May 1992, the highest legislative body was to be a 50-member Majlis, directly elected for a term of five years. Until the expiry of its term, the former Supreme Soviet was to act as the Majlis. The first elections to the Majlis were held on 11 December 1994, officially with the participation of 99.8% of the registered electorate. It was reported that 49 of the 50 deputies were elected unopposed (two candidates contesting the remaining seat). The majority of those elected were believed to be members of the ruling party, the Democratic Party of Turkmenistan (the successor of the CPT). The Majlis convened for the first time in late December 1994. The deputies of the Majlis also form part of the Khalk Maslakhaty (see above).

**Chairman:** SAKHAT N. MYRADOV.
**Deputy Chairman:** ALEKSANDR D. DODONOV.

## Political Organizations

**Agzybirlik:** Ashgabat; f. 1989; popular front organization; denied official registration except from Oct. 1991 to Jan. 1992.
**Democratic Party of Turkmenistan:** 744014 Ashgabat 14, ul. Gogolya 28; tel. (3632) 25-12-12; name changed from Communist Party of Turkmenistan in 1991; Chair. Gen. SAPARMYRAT A. NIYAZOV; 116,000 mems (1991).
**Peasants' Party:** Ashgabat; f. 1993 by deputies of the agrarian faction in parliament; was considered likely to be registered in 1994.

There are several unregistered opposition groups, such as the Islamic Renaissance Party, which had been an all-Union Muslim party in the former USSR, and the remnants of another democratic party. The main opposition organization is Agzybirlik, although in early 1994 President Niyazov indicated that the Peasants' Party would be permitted registration in the near future. Other opposition elements are based in other republics of the CIS, in particular the Russian Federation. A leading opposition figure in exile is the former Minister of Foreign Affairs, Abdy Kuliyev (based in Moscow).

## Diplomatic Representation

### EMBASSIES IN TURKMENISTAN

**Iran:** Ashgabat; tel. (3632) 24-97-07; Ambassador: GHOLAMREZA BAQERI.
**Kazakhstan:** Ashgabat.
**Russia:** Ashgabat, pr. Saparmyrat Turkmenbashi 11; tel. (3632) 25-39-57; fax (3632) 29-84-66; Ambassador: VADIM CHEREPOV.
**Turkey:** Ashgabat, ul. Shevchenka 9; tel. (3632) 29-42-50; telex 228117.
**United Kingdom:** Ashgabat; Ambassador: NEIL HOOK (designate).
**USA:** Ashgabat, Yubilenaya Hotel; tel. (3632) 24-49-08; Ambassador: JOSEPH S. HULINGS, III.

## Judicial System

**Chairman of the Supreme Court:** N. M. YUSUPOV.
**Procurator-General:** V. M. VASILIUK.

## Religion

The majority of the population are adherents of Islam. In June 1991 the Turkmen Supreme Soviet adopted a Law on Freedom of Conscience and Religious Organizations.

### ISLAM

Turkmen are traditionally Sunni Muslims, but with elements of Sufism. Islam, the religion of the Turkmen for many centuries, was severely persecuted by the Soviet regime from the late 1920s. Until July 1989 Ashgabat was the only Central Asian capital without a functioning mosque. The Muslims of Turkmenistan are officially under the jurisdiction of the Muslim Board of Central Asia, based in Tashkent (Uzbekistan). The Board is represented in Turkmenistan by a kazi.

**Kazi of Turkmenistan:** NASRULLO IBADULLAYEV.

## The Press

In 1989, according to official statistics, 66 newspaper titles were published in Turkmenistan, including 49 published in Turkmen. There were 34 periodicals, including 16 in Turkmen. All publications are in Turkmen except where otherwise stated.

### PRINCIPAL NEWSPAPERS

**Edebiyat ve sungat** (Literature and Art): 744604 Ashgabat, ul. Atabayeva 20; tel. (3632) 5-30-34; f. 1958; weekly; publ. by the Ministry of Culture and Tourism and the Union of Writers of Turkmenistan; Editor HOJAMURAT GOCHMURADOV.
**Novcha:** Ashgabat, ul. Atabayeva 20; tel. (3632) 25-68-02; f. 1930; weekly; for children and teenagers; in Russian; Editor-in-Chief BABANIYAZ KAYUMOV.
**Turkmenskaya iskra** (Turkmen Spark): Ashgabat; f. 1924; 6 a week; organ of the Majlis and Council of Ministers; in Russian; Editor V. V. SLUSHNIK.
**Syyasy sokhbetdesh** (Political Symposium): 744014 Ashgabat 14, ul. Gogolya 28; tel. (3632) 25-12-12; weekly; organ of the Democratic Party of Turkmenistan; circ. 14,500.

### PRINCIPAL PERIODICALS

Monthly, unless otherwise indicated.
**Ashgabat:** 744000 Ashgabat, ul. Makhtumkuli 5; tel. (3632) 09-65-44; journal of the Union of Writers of Turkmenistan; popular; in Russian; Editor V. N. POU; circ. 6,000.
**Ovadan:** Ashgabat; f. 1952; for women; Editor A. B. SEITKULIYEVA.

# TURKMENISTAN

**Pioner** (Pioneer): Ashgabat; f. 1926; fmrly journal of the Republican Council of the Pioneer Organization of Turkmenistan; juvenile fiction; Editor A. RAKHMANOV.

**Politichesky sobesednik** (Political Symposium): 744014 Ashgabat 14, ul. Gogolya 28; tel. (3632) 25-12-12; 6 a year; in Russian; publ. by the Democratic Party of Turkmenistan; circ. 2,300.

**Sovet edebiyaty:** 744000 Ashgabat, ul. Makhtumkuli 5; tel. (3632) 5-14-33; journal of the Union of Writers of Turkmenistan; fiction and literary criticism.

**Tokmak** (Beetle): 744000 Ashgabat, ul. Atabayeva 20; tel. (3632) 25-10-39; f. 1925; satirical; Editor TACHMAMED JURDEKOV.

**Turkmenistanyn oba khozhalygy** (Agriculture of Turkmenistan): Ashgabat; f. 1957; journal of the Ministry of Agriculture, Food and the Processing Industries; Editor B. POLLIKOV.

## NEWS AGENCY

**Turkmen Press:** Ashgabat; Dir MYRAD KARANOV.

## Publishers

**Magaryf Publishing House:** Ashgabat; Dir N. ATAYEV.

**Turkmenistan Publishing House:** Ashgabat, ul. Gogolya 17A; f. 1965; politics and fiction; Dir A. M. JANMYRADOV.

**Ylym Publishing House:** 744000 Ashgabat, ul. Azady 59; tel. (3632) 29-04-84; f. 1952; desert development, science; Dir N.I. FAIZULAYEVA.

## Radio and Television

**National Television and Radio Co of Turkmenistan** (Turkmenistanin Milli Teleradiokompaniyasi): 744000 Ashgabat, ul. Makhtumkuli 89; Chair. ANAGELDY ORAZDURDIYEV.

**Turkmen Radio:** 744000 Ashgabat, ul. Makhtumkuli 89; tel. (3632) 25-15-15; telex 228125; fax (3632) 25-14-21; broadcasts local programmes and relays from Russia in Turkmen and Russian.

## Finance

### BANKING

Reforms in the financial system of the USSR were initiated in 1988 with the introduction of a two-tier banking system. Further restructuring of Turkmenistan's banking sector took place even before the attainment of full independence during 1991, after which time the republican State Bank was forced to become a full central bank. In November 1993 a Turkmen currency, the manat, was introduced, supported by the country's international reserves. In early 1995 there were reported to be some 20 commercial banks in operation in Turkmenistan. These included three banks with joint ownership and a branch of Bank Saderat Iran.

### Central Bank

**State Bank of Turkmenistan:** Ashgabat; central monetary authority, issuing bank and supervisory authority; Chair. of Bd A. B. BORJAKOV; 3 brs.

### Other Banks

**Agroprombank:** Ashgabat; f. 1989 as independent bank; specializes in agricultural sector; commercial bank.

**Industry and Construction Bank:** Ashgabat; f. 1989 as independent bank; specializes in industrial and construction sector; commercial bank.

**Republican Commercial Bank:** Ashgabat; f. 1989 as independent bank; fmrly the main commercial bank.

**Sberbank—Savings Bank:** Ashgabat; f. 1989 as independent bank; 50 brs (1992).

**State Bank for Foreign Economic Relations of Turkmenistan:** Ashgabat; f. 1991 as independent bank, from Soviet Vneshekonombank.

### COMMODITY EXCHANGE

**Turkmenistan Commodities Exchange:** Ashgabat; Chair. ILAMAN SHAYKHYYEV.

## Trade and Industry

### CHAMBER OF COMMERCE

**Chamber of Commerce and Industry:** 744000 Ashgabat, ul. Lakhuti 17; tel. (3632) 25-57-56; Chair. LIDIA N. OSIPOVA.

### SELECTED STATE-OWNED INDUSTRIAL ENTERPRISES

**Balkanneftekhimprom:** Ashgabat; f. 1992; petroleum and natural gas co; operates joint ventures with foreign cos.

**Turkmengas:** Ashgabat; official govt agency responsible for natural gas operations.

**Turkmenprod Aktsiyoner** (Turkmen Food Joint-Stock Co): Ashgabat; f. 1994; Dir NEDIRMAMMET ALOVOV.

### TRADE UNIONS

**Federation of Trade Unions of Turkmenistan:** Ashgabat.

## Transport

### RAILWAYS

The main rail line in the country runs from Turkmenbashi (Krasnovodsk), on the Caspian Sea, in the west, via Ashgabat, to Charjou in the east. From Charjou one line runs to the east, to the other Central Asian countries of the former USSR, while another runs north-west, via Uzbekistan and Kazakhstan, to join the rail network of the Russian Federation. In 1989 the total length of rail track in use was 2,120 km. In 1992 plans were approved for a rail link with Iran on the route Tejen–Sarakhs–Mashhad. From the Iranian town of Mashhad, the railway would be able to join the Iranian rail network and thus provide the possibility of rail travel between Turkmenistan and Istanbul (Turkey). The project was scheduled for completion in early 1996.

### ROADS

At 31 December 1989 there was a total of 22,600 km of roads, of which 17,800 km were hard-surfaced. In November 1991 a 600-km road was opened between Ashgabat and Tashauz.

### SHIPPING

Shipping services link Turkmenbashi (Krasnovodsk) with Baku (Azerbaijan) and the major Iranian ports on the Caspian Sea. The Amu-Dar'ya river is an important inland waterway.

#### Shipowning Company

**Middle-Asia Shipping Company:** 746100 Charjou, Flotilskaya ul. 8; Pres. N. B. BAZAROV.

### CIVIL AVIATION

Turkmenistan's international airport is at Ashgabat. A new terminal building was completed in late 1994, thus expanding the airport's capacity.

**National Civil Aviation Authority of Turkmenistan:** 744008 Ashgabat Airport; tel. (3632) 25-10-52; telex 228112; fax (3632) 25-44-02; f. 1992.

**Turkmenistan Airlines:** 744088 Ashgabat Airport; tel. (3632) 25-60-84; fax (3632) 29-07-24; operates under three divisions: Akhal Air Co, Khazar Air Co and Lebap Air Co; Dir ALEKSEY P. BOLDYREV.

## Tourism

Tourism is relatively undeveloped in Turkmenistan, owing to the harsh desert conditions and terrain (some 90% of the country is covered by the Kara-Kum desert). The most important tourist sights include the ruins of the 12th-century Seljuk capital at Merv (now Mary), the bazaar at Ashgabat and the hot sulphurous springs at Bacharden, at the foot of the Kopet Dagh mountains, on the border with Iran.

**Ministry of Culture and Tourism:** Ashgabat; tel. (3632) 25-35-60.

**Intourist:** Ashgabat, ul. Mala Bukharskaya 15.

# TUVALU

## Introductory Survey

### Location, Climate, Language, Religion, Flag, Capital

Tuvalu is a scattered group of nine small atolls (five of which enclose sizeable lagoons), extending about 560 km (350 miles) from north to south, in the western Pacific Ocean. Its nearest neighbours are Fiji to the south, Kiribati to the north and Solomon Islands to the west. The climate is warm and pleasant, with a mean annual temperature of 30°C (86°F), and there is very little seasonal variation. The average annual rainfall is about 3,000 mm (120 ins). The inhabitants speak Tuvaluan and English. Almost all of them profess Christianity, and about 98% are Protestants. The national flag (proportions 2 by 1) is light blue, with the United Kingdom flag as a rectangular canton in the upper hoist, occupying one-quarter of the area, and nine five-pointed yellow stars (arranged to symbolize a map of the archipelago) in the fly. However, a new flag was to be designed during 1995. The capital is on Funafuti atoll.

### Recent History

Tuvalu was formerly known as the Ellice (or Lagoon) Islands. Between about 1850 and 1875 many of the islanders were captured by slave-traders and this, together with European diseases, reduced the population from about 20,000 to 3,000. In 1877 the United Kingdom established the Western Pacific High Commission (WPHC), with its headquarters in Fiji, and the Ellice Islands, and other groups were placed under its jurisdiction. In 1892 a British protectorate was declared over the Ellice Islands, and the group was linked administratively with the Gilbert Islands to the north. In 1916 the United Kingdom annexed the protectorate, which was renamed the Gilbert and Ellice Islands Colony (GEIC). During the Japanese occupation of the Gilbert Islands in 1942–43, the administration of the GEIC was temporarily moved to Funafuti in the Ellice Islands. (For more details of the history of the GEIC, see the chapter on Kiribati.)

A series of advisory and legislative bodies prepared the GEIC for self-government. In May 1974 the last of these, the Legislative Council, was replaced by the House of Assembly, with 28 elected members (including eight Ellice Islanders) and three official members. A Chief Minister was elected by the House and chose between four and six other ministers, one of whom had to be from the Ellice Islands.

In January 1972 the appointment of a separate GEIC Governor, who assumed most of the functions previously exercised by the High Commissioner for the Western Pacific, increased the long-standing anxiety of the Ellice Islanders over their minority position as Polynesians in the colony, dominated by the Micronesians of the Gilbert Islands. In a referendum held in the Ellice Islands in August and September 1974, more than 90% of the voters favoured separate status for the group, and in October 1975 the Ellice Islands, under the old native name of Tuvalu ('eight standing together', which referred to the eight populated atolls), became a separate British dependency. The Deputy Governor of the GEIC took office as Her Majesty's Commissioner for Tuvalu. The eight Ellice representatives in the GEIC House of Assembly became the first elected members of the new Tuvalu House of Assembly. They elected one of their number, Toaripi Lauti, to be Chief Minister. Tuvalu was completely separated from the GEIC administration in January 1976. The remainder of the GEIC was renamed the Gilbert Islands and achieved independence, as Kiribati, in July 1979.

Tuvalu's first separate elections took place in August 1977, when the number of elective seats in the House of Assembly was increased to 12. An independence Constitution was finalized at a conference in London in February 1978. After five months of internal self-government, Tuvalu became independent on 1 October 1978, with Lauti as the first Prime Minister. The pre-independence House of Assembly was redesignated Parliament. Like Nauru, Tuvalu is a 'special member' of the Commonwealth, not represented at meetings of Heads of Government.

In 1983 the USA formally renounced its claim, dating from 1856, to the four southernmost atolls. Following elections to Parliament in September 1981, Lauti was replaced as Prime Minister by Dr Tomasi Puapua. Puapua was re-elected Prime Minister following the next legislative elections, which took place in September 1985.

In February 1986, in order to demonstrate its opposition to France's programme of testing nuclear weapons on Mururoa Atoll, in French Polynesia, the Puapua Government rejected an application by the French Government to send a warship to Tuvalu on a mission of goodwill. In the same month a nation-wide poll was conducted to establish public opinion as to whether Tuvalu should remain an independent constitutional monarchy, with the British monarch at its head, or became a republic. Only on one atoll did the community appear to be in favour of the adoption of republican status. In March Tupua (later Sir Tupua) Leupena, a former Speaker of Parliament, was appointed Governor-General, replacing Sir Penitala Teo, who had occupied the post since independence in 1978.

In September 1989 a general election took place. Although there are no official political parties in Tuvalu, supporters of Dr Puapua were reported to have been defeated in the election, and an opponent, Bikenibeu Paeniu (who had been appointed Minister for Community Services within the previous year), was elected Prime Minister. In October 1990 Toaripi Lauti succeeded Sir Tupua Leupena as Governor-General.

Legislation approved by Parliament in mid-1991, which sought to prohibit all new religions from the islands and to establish the Church of Tuvalu as the State Church, caused considerable controversy and extensive debate. A survey showed the population to be almost equally divided over the matter, although Paeniu firmly opposed the motion, describing it as incompatible with basic human rights.

In August 1991 the Government announced that it was to prepare a compensation claim against the United Kingdom for the allegedly poor condition of Tuvalu's economy and infrastructure at the time of the country's achievement of independence in 1979. Moreover, Tuvalu was to seek additional compensation for damage caused during the Second World War when the United Kingdom gave permission for the USA to build airstrips on the islands (some 40% of Funafuti is uninhabitable because of large pits created by US troops during the construction of an airstrip on the atoll). Relations with the United Kingdom deteriorated further in late 1992, following a meeting requested by the British Minister of State for Overseas Development, during which the financial policy of Paeniu's Government was harshly criticized. Paeniu defended his Government's policies, and stated that continued delays in the approval of aid projects from the United Kingdom meant that Tuvalu would not be seeking further development funds from the British Government.

In mid-1992 a member of Parliament for Funafuti proposed a motion to establish Tuvalu as a republic. it was subsequently reported, however, that (as in 1986) only one of the eight parliamentary constituencies supported the proposal.

At a general election held in September 1993, three of the 12 incumbent members of Parliament lost their seats. At elections to the premiership held in the same month, however, Paeniu and his challenger, Dr Tomasi Puapua (Prime Minister in 1981–89), received six votes each. When a second vote produced a similar result, the Governor-General dissolved Parliament, in accordance with the Constitution. Paeniu and his Cabinet remained in office until the holding of a further general election on 25 November. At elections to the premiership in the following month Kamuta Latasi defeated Paeniu by seven votes to five. Puapua, who had agreed not to challenge Paeniu in the contest in favour of supporting Latasi, was elected Speaker of Parliament.

In December 1994, in what was widely regarded as a significant rejection of its political links with the United Kingdom, the Tuvaluan Parliament voted to remove Britain's union flag from the Tuvalu national flag. A new design was to be selected by October 1995 from submissions to a national competition.

Speculation that the British monarch would be removed as Head of State intensified in the same month, following the appointment of a committee to review the Constitution. The three-member committee was to examine the procedure surrounding the appointment and removal of the Governor-General, and, particulartly, to consider the adoption of a republican system of government.

In May 1995 it was announced that the Australian Government had offered to assist with a project to rehabilitate Funafuti, at an estimated cost of $A3m. It was hoped that the reclamation of the affected areas (which cover some 40% of the total land area) would alleviate the increasingly serious problem of overcrowding on the atoll.

In October 1986 Tuvalu was one of a group of South Pacific island states to sign a five-year fishing agreement with the USA, whereby the US tuna-fishing fleet was granted a licence to operate within Tuvalu's exclusive economic zone. In 1989 a UN report on the 'greenhouse effect' (the heating of the earth's atmosphere as a result of pollution) listed Tuvalu as one of the island groups which would completely disappear beneath the sea in the 21st century, unless drastic action were taken. At the UN World Climate Conference, held in Geneva in November 1990, Paeniu expressed concern about the effects of climate change on Tuvalu. He appealed for urgent action by developed nations to combat the environmental changes caused by the 'greenhouse effect', which were believed to include a 10-fold increase in cyclone frequency (from two in 1940 to 21 in 1990), an increase in salinity in ground water and a considerable decrease in the average annual rainfall. The Government remained critical, however, of the inertia with which (it alleged) certain countries had reacted to its appeal for assistance, and in June 1993 Paeniu wrote to the leaders of the seven most important industrial nations (the so-called 'G-7'), expressing the Tuvaluan people's fears of physical and cultural extinction, and urging the heads of state not to ignore the warnings of climate scientists. The new Prime Minister, Kamuta Latasi, was similarly critical of the industrial world's apparent disregard for the plight of small island nations vulnerable to the effects of climate change, particularly when Tuvalu was struck by tidal waves in 1994 (believed to be the first experienced by the islands). During 1994 Latasi, who had stated that, in view of the threat to their islands, his main priority as Premier was to establish resettlement plans for Tuvaluans, tried unsuccessfully to secure approval for a relocation programme to other countries, including Australia and New Zealand.

### Government

Tuvalu is a constitutional monarchy. Executive authority is vested in the British sovereign, as Head of State, and is exercisable by her representative, the Governor-General, who is appointed on the recommendation of the Prime Minister and acts, in almost all cases, on the advice of the Cabinet. Legislative power is vested in the unicameral Parliament, with 12 members elected by universal adult suffrage for four years (subject to dissolution). The Cabinet is led by the Prime Minister, who is elected by and from the members of Parliament. On the Prime Minister's recommendation, other ministers are appointed by the Governor-General. The Cabinet is responsible to Parliament. Each of the inhabited atolls has its own elected Island Council which is responsible for local government.

### Economic Affairs

In 1987, according to estimates by the OECD, Tuvalu's gross national product (GNP), measured at current prices, was US $3m., equivalent to US $326 per head. Measured at current prices, Tuvalu's gross domestic product (GDP) per head was estimated at $A450 in 1986, increasing to $A479 in 1987. According to estimates by the Asian Development Bank (ADB), GDP increased by an annual average of some 9% in 1991 and 1992, and by 8.7% in 1993.

Agriculture (including fishing) is, with the exception of copra production, of a basic subsistence nature. Some 60% of Tuvaluans are engaged in subsistence farming. Coconuts (the source of copra) are the only cash crop. Pulaka, taro, papayas, the screw-pine (*Pandanus*) and bananas are cultivated as food crops. Livestock comprises pigs, poultry and goats. Honey is produced. Fish and other sea products are staple constituents of the islanders' diet. The sale of fishing licences to foreign fleets provides an important source of income, contributing some 17% of total recurrent revenue in 1990. Food imports accounted for 29.5% of total import costs in 1986.

Manufacturing is confined to the small-scale production of coconut-based products, soap and handicrafts. The sale of postage stamps made a significant contribution to the islands' income in the 1980s, accounting for 70% of export earnings in 1985, although, in subsequent years, receipts fell dramatically. An important source of revenue is provided by remittances from Tuvaluans working abroad, principally in the phosphate industry on Nauru. It was estimated that some 1,200 Tuvaluans were working overseas in the early 1990s, although many of these workers were expected to return to Tuvalu during the mid-1990s, as Nauruan phosphate reserves become exhausted. In 1990 revenue from this source was estimated to total some $A1.6m. Energy is derived principally from a power plant (fuelled by petroleum) and, on the outer islands, solar power. In 1986 mineral fuels accounted for almost 14% of total import costs.

The islands' remote situation and lack of amenities have hindered the development of a tourist industry. In 1989, however, plans for a national airline and the promotion of tourism were announced, and in 1992 the construction of a new runway to replace the grass landing strip at Funafuti was completed with a grant of $A30m. from the EC. A 17-room hotel, built with Taiwanese aid, was opened in 1994.

In 1986 Tuvalu recorded a visible trade deficit of US $2.8m. (compared with export revenues of US $15,000). The principal sources of imports in that year were Australia (40.6%) and New Zealand (10.9%). Copra was the sole domestic export. The principal imports were foodstuffs, basic manufactures, machinery and transport equipment and mineral fuels. In 1989 total export earnings were equivalent to only 1.5% of the value of imports.

In 1987 the Tuvalu Trust Fund was established, with assistance from New Zealand, Australia and the United Kingdom, to generate funding, through overseas investment, for development projects. In 1990 the Fund contributed 22.6% of total recurrent revenue and in early 1992 its value totalled some $A41.6m. However, dissatisfaction with British financial provision for Tuvalu led the Government to announce plans for a compensation claim to be brought against the United Kingdom in 1991 (see History). In 1989 there was (inclusive of budgetary aid) an estimated budgetary deficit of $A34,200. The 1991 budget envisaged expenditure of $A4.5m., with a deficit of some $A1m. However, a budgetary surplus of $A1.5m. was projected for 1993. The annual rate of inflation averaged 3.9% in 1985–93.

Tuvalu is a member of the South Pacific Commission (see p. 215) and the South Pacific Forum (see p. 217). In May 1993 the country was admitted to the ADB (see p. 107).

According to United Nations criteria, Tuvalu is one of the world's least developed nations. Its economic development has been adversely affected by inclement weather and inadequate infrastructure. Tuvalu's vulnerability to fluctuations in the price of copra on the international market, and its dependence on imports has resulted in a permanent visible trade deficit; it also remained reliant on foreign assistance for its development budget. Owing to a high rate of population growth and a drift from the outer islands to the capital, there is a serious problem of overcrowding on Funafuti. Various development projects, undertaken in the early 1990s, aimed to encourage diversification of agricultural production, and included schemes to manufacture beer from surplus honey, to develop the farming of seaweed and the manufacture of sweet biscuits. In August 1991 a seamount (an underwater mountain) was discovered east of Niulakita island in Tuvaluan waters. The discovery was thought to be important, owing to the possible presence of valuable minerals and pink coral, as well as deep-sea fish. In an attempt to diversify the country's sources of development assistance, the Prime Minister visited Japan in early 1995 for official discussions concerning the possible funding of projects in the islands.

### Social Welfare

In 1982 there were eight government hospitals, with a total of 72 beds, and in 1986 there were three physicians and 26 nurses working in the islands.

### Education

Education is provided by the Government, and is compulsory between the ages of seven and 15 years. In 1990 there were 12 primary schools, with a total of 72 teachers and 1,485 pupils. There were two secondary schools in 1991, with 31

TUVALU

teachers and 345 pupils in 1990. The only tertiary institution is a Maritime Training School at Amatuku on Funafuti. Further training or vocational courses are available in Fiji and Kiribati. The University of the South Pacific (based in Fiji) has an extension centre on Funafuti. A programme of major reforms in the education system in Tuvalu, begun in the early 1990s, resulted in the lengthening of primary schooling (from six to eight years) and a compulsory two years of secondary education, as well as the introduction of vocational, technical and commerce-related courses at the Maritime Training School. Total government expenditure on education in 1990 amounted to $A854,000, equivalent to 16.2% of total budgetary expenditure.

**Public Holidays**
**1995:** 1 January (New Year's Day), 6 March (Commonwealth Day), 14–17 April (Easter), 17 June (Queen's Official Birthday), 7 August (National Children's Day), 1–2 October (Tuvalu Day, anniversary of independence), 14 November (Prince of Wales's Birthday), 25 December (Christmas Day), 26 December (Boxing Day).
**1996:** 1 January (New Year's Day), 4 March (Commonwealth Day), 5–8 April (Easter), 15 June (Queen's Official Birthday), 5 August (National Children's Day), 1–2 October (Tuvalu Day, anniversary of independence), 14 November (Prince of Wales's Birthday), 25 December (Christmas Day), 26 December (Boxing Day).

# Statistical Survey

### AREA AND POPULATION

**Land Area:** 26 sq km (10 sq miles).

**Population:** 8,229 (males 3,902; females 4,327) at mini-census of June 1985; 9,043 at census of 1991. *By atoll* (1985 census): Funafuti 2,810; Vaitupu 1,231; Niutao 904; Nanumea 879; Nukufetau 694; Nanumaga 672; Nui 604; Nukulaelae 315; Niulakita 74.

**Density:** 348 per sq km (1991 census).

**Births and Deaths** (1990): Birth rate 25.0 per 1,000; Death rate 11.0 per 1,000. Source: UN, *Statistical Yearbook for Asia and the Pacific*.

**Economically Active Population:** In 1979 there were 936 people in paid employment, 50% of them in government service. In 1979 114 Tuvaluans were employed by the Nauru Phosphate Co, with a smaller number employed in Kiribati and about 255 on foreign ships.

### AGRICULTURE, ETC.

**Principal Crop** (FAO estimate, metric tons, 1993): Coconuts 2,000. Source: FAO, *Production Yearbook*.

**Livestock** (FAO estimate, '000 head, 1993): Pigs 13. Source: FAO, *Production Yearbook*.

**Livestock Products** (FAO estimates, metric tons, 1993): Hen eggs 12, Honey 1. Source: FAO, *Production Yearbook*.

**Fishing** (metric tons, live weight): Total catch 518 in 1990; 526 in 1991; 499 in 1992. Source: FAO, *Yearbook of Fishery Statistics*.

### FINANCE

**Currency and Exchange Rates:** Australian and Tuvaluan currencies are both in use. Australian currency: 100 cents = 1 Australian dollar ($A). *Sterling and US Dollar Equivalents* (31 December 1994): £1 sterling = $A2.017; US $1 = $A1.289; $A100 = £49.58 = US $77.57. *Average Exchange Rate* (US $ per Australian dollar): 0.7353 in 1992; 0.6801 in 1993; 0.7317 in 1994.

**Budget** (provisional, $A): *1988:* Total revenue 4,701,594 (British grant-in-aid 979,000, Tuvalu Trust Fund 800,000); Expenditure n.a. *1989:* Revenue (including grants) 5,372,973; Expenditure 5,407,173. *1990:* Expenditure 5,375,713.
*1991:* Expenditure 5,413,579 (Tuvalu Trust Fund 981,079).

**Development Budget** (provisional capital expenditure, $A '000, 1991): Australia 1,300; New Zealand 1,500; United Kingdom 1,500; Taiwan 2,340; European Development Fund 900; Japan 500; UNDP 900; France 250; USA 200; Total (incl. others) 10,077.

**Cost of Living** (Consumer Price Index for Funafuti; base: 1980 = 100): 192.7 in 1990; 205.1 in 1991; 192.8 in 1992. Source: ILO, *Year Book of Labour Statistics*.

### EXTERNAL TRADE

**Principal Commodities** (US $ '000, 1989): *Imports:* Food and live animals 1,514.6; Beverages and tobacco 201.6; Crude materials, inedible, except fuels 239.6; Mineral fuels, lubricants, etc. 660.7; Chemicals 369.1; Basic manufactures 1,001.3; Machinery and transport equipment 631.9; Miscellaneous manufactured articles 455.2; Total (incl. others) 5,170.3. *Exports:* Total 79.1.

**Principal Trading Partners** (US $ '000, 1986): *Imports:* Australia 1,154; Japan 85; New Zealand 310; United Kingdom 144; Total (incl. others) 2,841. *Exports:* Total 15.

Source: UN, *Statistical Yearbook for Asia and the Pacific*.

### TOURISM

**Tourist Arrivals:** 671 in 1990; 976 in 1991; 862 in 1992. Source: UN, *Statistical Yearbook*.

### COMMUNICATIONS MEDIA

**Non-Daily Newspapers** (1990): 1; estimated circulation 300.
**Radio Receivers** (1992): 3,000 in use.
Source: UN, *Statistical Yearbook*.

### EDUCATION

**Primary** (1990): 9 government schools, 3 church schools; 72 teachers; 1,485 pupils.

**General Secondary** (1990): 1 government school, 1 church school (1991); 31 teachers; 345 pupils.

In 1988 there were 13 kindergartens, three private primary schools, eight community training centres (mainly for the use of primary school leavers) and one maritime school for the training of 25 merchant seamen per year. Education reforms, begun in 1991, resulted in the closure of the largely unsuccessful community training centres and the expansion of the maritime school to offer vocational, technical and commerce-related courses.

# Directory

## The Constitution

A new Constitution came into effect at independence on 1 October 1978. Its main provisions are as follows:

The Constitution states that Tuvalu is a democratic sovereign state and that the Constitution is the Supreme Law. It guarantees protection of all fundamental rights and freedoms and provides for the determination of citizenship.

The British sovereign is represented by the Governor-General, who must be a citizen of Tuvalu and is appointed on the recommendation of the Prime Minister. The Prime Minister is elected by Parliament, and up to four other ministers are appointed by the Governor-General from among the members of Parliament, after consultation with the Prime Minister. The Cabinet, which is directly responsible to Parliament, consists of the Prime Minister and the other ministers, whose functions are to advise the Governor-General upon the government of Tuvalu. The Attorney-General is the principal legal adviser to the Government. Parliament is composed of 12 members directly elected by universal adult suffrage for four years, subject to dissolution, and is presided over by the Speaker (who is elected by the members). The Constitution also provides for the operation of a Judiciary (see Judicial System) and for an independent Public Service. Under a revised Constitution that took effect on 1 October 1986, the Governor-General no longer has the authority to reject the advice of the Government.

## The Government

**Head of State:** HM Queen ELIZABETH II.
**Governor-General:** TOARIPI LAUTI (took office 1 October 1990).

### CABINET
(June 1995)

**Prime Minister and Minister for Foreign Affairs and Economic Planning:** KAMUTA LATASI.
**Deputy Prime Minister and Minister for Home Affairs, Natural Resources and Rural Development:** OTINIEULU TAUSI.
**Minister for Health and Human Resources Development:** FAIMALAGA LUKU.
**Minister for Finance and Trade, Commerce and Public Corporations:** KOLOA TALAKE.
**Minister for Labour, Works and Communications:** HOUTI IELE.

### MINISTRIES
All ministries are in Vaiaku, Funafuti.

## Legislature

### PARLIAMENT

Parliament has 12 members who hold office for a term of up to four years. A general election was held on 2 September 1993. Following the legislature's failure to elect a Prime Minister, a further general election was held on 25 November. There are no political parties.

**Speaker:** Dr TOMASI PUAPUA.

## Diplomatic Representation

There are no embassies or high commissions in Tuvalu. The British Ambassador in Fiji is also accredited as High Commissioner to Tuvalu. Other Ambassadors or High Commissioners accredited to Tuvalu include the Australian, New Zealand, US, French and Japanese Ambassadors in Fiji.

## Judicial System

The Supreme Law is embodied in the Constitution. The High Court is the superior court of record, presided over by the Chief Justice, and has jurisdiction to consider appeals from judgments of the Magistrates' Courts and the Island Courts. Appeals from the High Court lie with the Court of Appeal in Fiji or, in the ultimate case, with the Judicial Committee of the Privy Council in the United Kingdom.

There are eight Island Courts with limited jurisdiction in criminal and civil cases.

## Religion

### CHRISTIANITY

**Church of Tuvalu (Ekalesia Tuvalu):** POB 2, Funafuti; tel. 755; telex 4800; f. 1861; autonomous since 1968; derived from the Congregationalist foundation of the London Missionary Society; some 98% of the population are adherents; Pres. Rev. MORIKAO KAUA; Gen. Sec. Rev. PUAFITU FAAALO.

**Roman Catholic Church:** Catholic Centre, POB 58, Funafuti; 91 adherents (31 December 1992); Superior Fr CAMILLE DESROSIERS.

Other churches with adherents in Tuvalu include the Church of Jesus Christ of Latter-day Saints (Mormons), the Jehovah's Witnesses, the New Apostolic Church and the Seventh-day Adventists.

### BAHÁ'Í FAITH

**National Spiritual Assembly:** POB 48, Funafuti; tel. 860; telex 4800; mems resident in 8 localities.

## The Press

**Tuvalu Echoes:** Broadcasting and Information Office, Vaiaku, Funafuti; tel. 731; fax 732; fortnightly; English; Editor RUBY BRUCE; circ. 250.

**Te Lama:** Ekalesia Kelisiano Tuvalu, POB 2, Funafuti; tel. 755; telex 4800; fax 755; monthly; religious; Pres. Rev. MORIKAO KAUA; Editor Rev. KITIONA TAUSI; circ. 1,000.

## Radio

In 1992 there were an estimated 3,000 radio receivers in use.

**Radio Tuvalu:** Broadcasting and Information Office, Vaiaku, Funafuti; f. 1975; tel. 731; telex 4800; fax 732; daily broadcasts in Tuvaluan and English, 43 hours per week; Chief Broadcasting and Information Officer PUSINELLI LAAFAI.

## Finance, Trade and Industry

**Department of Commerce:** POB 33, Funafuti; tel. 839.

**Development Bank of Tuvalu:** POB 9, Vaiaku, Funafuti; tel. 850; fax 850; f. 1993 to replace the Business Development Advisory Bureau.

**National Bank of Tuvalu:** POB 13, Vaiaku, Funafuti; tel. 802; telex 18102; fax 802; f. 1980; commercial bank; managed by Westpac Banking Corpn of Australia; Gen. Man. MICHAEL TANNER; brs on all atolls.

**National Fishing Corporation of Tuvalu (NAFICOT):** POB 93, Funafuti; tel. 724; fax 800; fishing vessel operators; seafood processing and marketing; agents for diesel engine spare parts, fishing supplies and marine electronics; Gen. Man. SEMU SOPOANGA TAAFAKI.

**Tuvalu Chamber of Commerce:** POB 17, Funafuti.

Retail trade is almost exclusively controlled by island co-operative societies, which are supplied by:

**Tuvalu Co-operative Society Ltd:** POB 17, Funafuti; tel. 724; telex 4800; fax 800; f. 1979 by amalgamation of the eight island socs; Gen. Man. MAATIA TOAFA; Co-operatives Officer MINUTE TAUPO.

## Transport

### ROADS

Funafuti has some impacted-coral roads; elsewhere, tracks exist.

### SHIPPING

There is a deep-water lagoon at the point of entry, Funafuti, and ships are able to enter the lagoon at Nukufetau. Irregular shipping services connect Tuvalu with Fiji and elsewhere. The Government operates an inter-island vessel.

TUVALU

### CIVIL AVIATION

There is a runway on Funafuti which was resurfaced with EC aid in 1992. Air Marshall Islands operates a twice-weekly service between Tarawa (Kiribati), Funafuti and Nadi (Fiji). Plans to create a national airline were announced in 1989.

## Tourism

In 1989 there was one hotel, with seven rooms, on Funafuti, which was enlarged to 17 rooms, with Taiwanese aid, and reopened in 1994. There were an estimated 862 tourist arrivals in 1992.

**Ministry of Commerce and Natural Resources** (responsible for tourism): Vaiaku, Funafuti; tel. 737.

# UGANDA

## Introductory Survey

**Location, Climate, Language, Religion, Flag, Capital**

The Republic of Uganda is a land-locked equatorial country in East Africa, bordered by Sudan to the north, Zaire to the west, Kenya to the east and Rwanda, Tanzania and Lake Victoria to the south. The climate is tropical, with temperatures, moderated by the altitude of the country, varying between 15°C and 30°C. The official language is English and there are many local languages, the most important of which is Luganda. More than 60% of the population follow Christian beliefs, while some 8% are Muslims. The national flag (proportions 3 by 2) has six horizontal stripes: black, gold, red, black, gold and red. In the centre is a white disc containing a crested crane. The capital is Kampala.

**Recent History**

Formerly a British protectorate, Uganda became an independent member of the Commonwealth on 9 October 1962. The Government was led by Dr Milton Obote, leader of the Uganda People's Congress (UPC) from 1960 and Prime Minister from April 1962. At independence the country comprised four regions, including the kingdom of Buganda, which had federal status. Exactly one year after independence Uganda became a republic, with Mutesa II, Kabaka (King) of Buganda, as first President. Executive power remained with the Cabinet. In February 1966 Dr Obote led a successful coup against the Kabaka, and in April he became executive President. In September 1967 a new Constitution was introduced, establishing a unitary republic, and Buganda was brought under the control of the central Government. After an assassination attempt on President Obote in December 1969 all opposition parties were banned.

President Obote was overthrown in January 1971 by the army, led by Maj.-Gen. (later Field Marshal) Idi Amin Dada, who assumed full executive powers and suspended political activity. The National Assembly was dissolved in February, when Amin declared himself Head of State, took over legislative powers and suspended parts of the 1967 Constitution. Obote took refuge in Tanzania. In August 1972 Amin, proclaiming an 'economic war' to free Uganda from foreign domination, undertook a mass expulsion of non-citizen Asians (who comprised the majority of the resident Asian population), thereby incurring widespread international condemnation.

Amin's regime was characterized by the ruthless elimination of suspected opponents, mass flights of refugees to neighbouring countries and periodic purges of the army (which, in turn, perpetrated numerous atrocities). In February 1977 the Anglican Archbishop of Uganda and two government ministers were murdered, arousing further world-wide indignation. Relations within the East African Community, comprising Uganda, Kenya and Tanzania, deteriorated during the 1970s. In February 1976 Amin claimed that large areas of western Kenya were historically part of Uganda, causing the temporary closure of the Kenya–Uganda border, and in November 1978 Uganda annexed the Kagera salient from Tanzania. In early 1979 an invasion force consisting of Tanzanian troops and the Uganda National Liberation Army (UNLA), formed by Ugandan exiles, gained control of the southern region of Uganda. Amin's forces capitulated, in spite of military aid and reinforcements from Libya, and in April a Tanzanian assault force entered Kampala. The remaining pro-Amin troops were defeated in June. Amin fled initially to Libya, and in 1980 found refuge in Saudi Arabia.

A provisional Government, the National Executive Council (NEC), was established in April 1979 from the ranks of the Uganda National Liberation Front (UNLF), a coalition of 18 previously exiled groups, with Dr Yusuf Lule, a former vice-chancellor of Makerere University, as President. When Lule attempted to reshuffle the NEC in June, opposition from within the UNLF forced his resignation. Lule was succeeded by Godfrey Binaisa (a former Attorney-General), who was, in turn, overthrown by the Military Commission of the UNLF in May 1980, after he had decided to allow only UNLF members to stand in parliamentary elections scheduled for December 1980 and attempted to reorganize the leadership of the UNLA. The December elections were contested by four parties and won by the UPC, with Obote, still the UPC's leader, becoming President for the second time. The defeated parties complained of gross electoral malpractice by UPC supporters.

From February 1981 the Obote Government was subject to constant attack from guerrilla groups operating inside the country. Hundreds of President Obote's opponents were subsequently detained, including Democratic Party (DP) members of the National Assembly, and several newspapers were banned. Following the withdrawal of Tanzanian troops in June, there were reports from the West Nile Region of further atrocities by Ugandan soldiers. In January 1982 the Uganda Popular Front was formed to co-ordinate, from abroad, the activities of the main opposition groups in exile, aiming to overthrow the Obote Government. These groups were the Uganda Freedom Movement (UFM), the Uganda National Rescue Front and the National Resistance Movement (NRM, led by Lule and his former Defence Minister, Yoweri Museveni). The NRM had a military wing, the National Resistance Army (NRA), which was led by Museveni. (Lule died in 1985, whereupon Museveni became sole leader of the NRM and NRA.) From 1982 thousands of Ugandans were reported to have fled to Sudan, Rwanda and Zaire, to escape fighting between guerrilla forces and UNLA troops. In March 1983, during a campaign by the UNLA to repel an NRA offensive, attacks on refugee camps resulted in the deaths of hundreds of civilians, and more than 100,000 people were displaced. The NRA denied involvement in the massacres.

In July 1985 President Obote was overthrown in a military coup, led by Brig. (later Lt-Gen.) Basilio Okello. Obote was subsequently granted political asylum by Zambia. In June 1985 a report by the human rights organization, Amnesty International, had alleged that the security forces had been responsible for the torture and murder of thousands of civilians under the Obote Government. A Military Council, headed by Lt-Gen. (later Gen.) Tito Okello, the Commander-in-Chief of the army, was established to govern the country, pending elections to be held one year later. In the following months, groups which had been in opposition to Obote, with the exception of the NRA and the NRM (see below), reached agreement with Okello, and occupied positions on the Military Council. An amnesty was declared for exiles who had supported Amin. Under the Okello Government, the UNLA continued to perpetrate atrocities.

In August 1985 the NRA, led by Museveni, entered into negotiations with the Government, with President Moi of Kenya acting as chairman, while conducting a simultaneous military campaign to overthrow Okello. During the following two months the NRA gained control of large areas of the country. In December the NRA and the Government signed a peace agreement, which granted the NRA seven seats on the Military Council. The terms of the accord were never implemented, however, and on 26 January 1986 the NRA took control of Kampala by force and dissolved the Military Council. Okello fled to Sudan. On 29 January Museveni was sworn in as President, and in February he announced the formation of a new Cabinet, comprising mainly members of the NRA and NRM, but also representatives of other political groups, including the DP, the UPC, the UFM, the Federal Democratic Movement (FEDEMO), and three members of the previous administration. A National Resistance Council (NRC) was formed to act in place of a legislature pending the introduction of a new constitution. All activity by political parties was banned in March, although political parties were not proscribed. At a summit meeting, in March, the heads of state of all the countries adjoining Uganda pledged their support for Museveni.

During 1986 the Museveni Government developed a system of resistance committees at local and district level. The responsibilities of the resistance committees included the maintenance of security and the elimination of corruption. In May and June two commissions of inquiry were appointed to investigate, respectively, allegations of government corruption and violations of human rights that had occurred since independence in 1962. As a result of an examination of the police force, more than 80% of its members were dishonourably dismissed in July 1986.

Initial attempts to integrate defeated rebel forces into the NRA were only partially successful, and guerrilla groups remained active in northern Uganda. An association of opposition groups, the Uganda People's Democratic Movement (UPDM), was formed in May 1986. In October 26 people were arrested and charged with treason. Among the accused were Andrew Kayiira, the Minister of Energy and leader of the UFM, and David Lwanga, the Minister of Environment Protection and leader of the FEDEMO. Although treason charges against eight of the accused, including Lwanga and Kayiira, were withdrawn in February 1987, the murder of Kayiira in March caused the UFM to withdraw its support from the coalition Government. Three of the accused were sentenced to death in March 1988.

In June 1987 the NRC offered an amnesty to rebels (except those accused of murder or rape). In August, however, the UPDM joined with a faction of the FEDEMO and another opposition group, the United National Front, to form an alliance which aimed to overthrow President Museveni. The most widespread source of disruption during 1987 was a rebellion that had arisen in northern and eastern Uganda in December 1986 by the 'Holy Spirit' movement, led by a religious leader, Alice Lakwena. The rebels initiated attacks against the NRA that were effectively suicidal; between December 1986 and November 1987 some 5,000 'Holy Spirit' fighters were reportedly killed. By December 1987 the rebellion had been suppressed, and Lakwena had escaped to Kenya. However, remaining members of the movement regrouped as the Lord's Resistance Army (LRA). In early 1988 the NRC extended the period of its amnesty to rebel groups: by mid-April it was reported that almost 30,000 rebels had surrendered to the Government. Many of these were integrated into the NRA. In October 24 people were arrested and charged with plotting against the Government. The problems of the Museveni Government at this time were compounded by the strain on resources that resulted from the repatriation of Ugandan refugees who had fled during the civil war. By early 1989 an estimated 350,000 refugees had returned from Sudan.

In February 1989 the first national election since 1980 was held. The NRC, which had previously comprised only members nominated by the President, was expanded from 98 to 278 members, to include 210 elected representatives. While 20 ministerial posts were reserved for nominated members of the NRC, 50 were allocated to elected members. As a result of these changes, 10 cabinet ministers and four deputy ministers lost their posts. In the same month Museveni appointed a constitutional commission to gauge public opinion on Uganda's political future and to draft a new constitution.

In October 1989 (despite opposition from the DP) the NRC approved draft legislation, submitted by the NRM, to prolong the Government's term of office by five years from January 1990, when its mandate had been due to expire: the NRM justified seeking to extend its rule by claiming that it required further time in which to prepare a new constitution, organize elections, eliminate continuing anti-Government guerrilla activity, improve the judiciary, police force and civil service and rehabilitate the country's infrastructure. In November Museveni replaced the Minister of State for Defence and the leadership of the NRA, reportedly as a measure to combat corruption and indiscipline in the armed forces. It was announced in January 1990 that several army officers and civilians had been charged with plotting to overthrow the Government. In March 1990 the NRM extended the national ban on party political activity (imposed in March 1986) for a further five years. In the following month the Minister of Culture, Youth and Sports, Brig. Moses Ali, was removed from his post and charged with plotting terrorist activities. (Ali was subsequently acquitted of this charge, but in January 1991 was found guilty of illegally possessing ammunition.) In July 1990 the leader of the UPDM, Eric Otema Allimadi, signed a peace accord with the Government; nevertheless, some members of the rebel organization reportedly did not take advantage of the Government's continuing amnesty. In January 1991 Samson Kisekka, the Prime Minister since 1986, was replaced by George Adyebo; Kisekka was appointed as Vice-President and Minister of Internal Affairs. In April Daniel Omara Atubo, the Minister of State for Foreign Affairs and Regional Co-operation, was arrested, together with two other members of the NRC, and charged with plotting to overthrow the Government; 15 other people (including further members of the NRC) were subsequently arrested on the same charge. During April the NRA initiated a campaign to eradicate continuing rebel activity in northern and eastern districts: by July it was reported that at least 1,500 guerrillas had been killed and more than 1,000 had been arrested. In May Museveni formally invited all former resident Asians, who had been expelled at the time of the Amin regime, to return, pledging the restitution of property expropriated under Amin's administration. A report by Amnesty International, released in December, accused the NRA of torturing and summarily executing prisoners during anti-insurgency operations against rebels. In October 1992 the Government launched a three-year programme to reduce the size of the NRA by about one-half, in response to pressure from the international donor community to reduce the exorbitant military budget.

In December 1992 negotiations on the restoration of the Bugandan monarchy commenced between President Museveni and Prince Ronald Muwenda Mutebi, the heir to the kingship, who had returned to Uganda from exile in 1987. In July 1993 the National Assembly adopted a constitutional amendment revoking the abolition of traditional rulers, as provided for under the 1967 Constitution. Restored traditional rulers would, however, have only ceremonial significance. Later that month Mutebi was enthroned as the Bugandan Kabaka (King) in a ceremony attended by Museveni. Two days earlier Patrick Olimi Kaboyo, the Ugandan Ambassador to Cuba, had been enthroned as King of Toro. Museveni, however, remained firmly opposed to the restoration of the kingdom of Ankole, although he was himself a member of the Ankole tribe. In defiance of Museveni's wishes, John Barigye was crowned King of Ankole in November 1993; Museveni subsequently declared the ceremony 'null and void'. In June 1994 Solomon Iguri Gafabusa was enthroned as King of Bunyoro.

At the end of December 1992 the Constitutional Commission presented its draft Constitution to the Government. In March 1993 President Museveni published the draft Constitution; the document (which was strongly opposed by the UPC and DP) provided for the proscription of party political activity for at least a further seven years and a continuation of 'non-party democracy', under the auspices of a national political movement to which all citizens would belong. In April the NRC passed legislation authorizing the establishment of a constituent assembly (see below).

In September 1993 nine army officers, who had been arrested on charges of treason between 1988 and 1990 and subsequently detained without trial, were released; the Government also agreed to review all death sentences that had been passed by army tribunals, declaring the latter to be 'illegal and incompetent'. In November former President Okello returned to Uganda (following his departure in 1986). Legislation adopted in 1991 had sanctioned his return and granted him the benefits of a former head of state.

In January 1994 the Ugandan National Democratic Alliance and the Ugandan Federal Army agreed to suspend their armed struggle, under the provisions of a government amnesty, and in March the surrender of senior members of the Rwenzururu Kingdom Freedom Movement in the south-west signified the end of a conflict that had begun following independence. In January the Government took part in negotiations with the rebel LRA. However, following the collapse of the discussions the LRA intensified guerrilla activities in northern Uganda. During 1994 the Government dispatched large numbers of security forces to the region, in an unsuccessful attempt to suppress the rebellion. In early 1994 Peter Otai, a former associate of Obote and the leader of the now-defunct Uganda People's Army, formed a new rebel group called the Uganda People's Freedom Movement.

At the elections to the 288-member Constituent Assembly, which took place on 28 March 1994, more than 1,500 candidates contested the 214 elective seats. Although the elections were conducted on a non-party basis, NRM members were believed to have secured the majority of votes in the centre, west and south-west of the country, whereas UPC and DP representatives, who advocated an immediate return to multi-party politics, secured the most seats in the north and east. The Constituent Assembly, which also comprised nominated representatives of the armed forces, political parties, trade unions, the youth and the disabled, was empowered to debate, amend and finally to enact the draft Constitution. Amendments to the draft required a two-thirds' majority of the Constituent Assembly; changes that received majority support but not the requisite two-thirds were to be submitted to a referendum. The new Constitution was due to be promulgated in June 1995, and legislative and presidential elections were scheduled to take place in December of that year.

In November 1994 Museveni reshuffled the Cabinet, replacing Adyebo as Prime Minister by Kintu Musoke, hitherto Minister of State for Security, and appointing Dr Speciosa Wandira Kazibwe, the Minister of Women's Affairs and Community Development, as Vice-President.

During 1987 Uganda's relations with neighbouring Kenya deteriorated, with the Museveni Government accusing Kenya of sheltering Ugandan rebels. In March the Kenyan authorities expelled hundreds of Ugandans. When, in October, Uganda stationed troops at the two countries' common border, Kenya threatened to retaliate with force against any attempts by Ugandan military personnel to cross the frontier in pursuit of rebels. In December clashes occurred between Kenyan and Ugandan security forces and the border was temporarily closed. In late December, following the intervention of the Organization of African Unity (see p. 200), discussions between the Heads of State of the two countries led to a resumption of normal traffic across the border. However, several incursions into Kenya by Ugandan troops were reported in 1988 and 1989. In February 1991 the Kenyan Government accused Uganda of plotting to invade Kenya; the Ugandan Government strongly denied the allegations. In November 1993 the Presidents of Uganda, Kenya and Tanzania met in Arusha, Tanzania, and established a permanent commission for co-operation between the three countries. During early 1995 Kenya protested strongly to the UN following the granting of refugee status in Uganda to an alleged Kenyan guerrilla leader; relations between Uganda and Kenya deteriorated further when Uganda covertly transferred the dissident to an undisclosed third country.

Tension also arose on the Uganda–Zaire border during 1988, owing to a number of attacks by Zairean troops on NRA units. During the late 1980s and early 1990s Sudanese troops reportedly made repeated incursions into Ugandan territory in pursuit of Sudanese rebels. In December 1989 Sudanese troops were reported to have crossed the Uganda–Sudan border and attacked a detachment of the NRA, and in October 1991, May 1992, December 1993 and January 1995 the Ugandan Government alleged that Sudanese aircraft had dropped bombs in northern Uganda. Relations between Uganda and Sudan deteriorated seriously in late 1994, when each Government accused the other of harbouring and supporting their respective outlawed guerrilla groups; in April 1994 Uganda severed diplomatic relations with Sudan, accusing several Sudanese diplomats of endangering Ugandan national security. In early 1992 nearly 80,000 Sudanese refugees fled to Uganda, followed by a further 50,000 in August 1993, owing to intense fighting between Sudanese rebels and government forces.

During the late 1980s an estimated 250,000 Rwandan refugees were sheltering in Uganda. Relations with Rwanda deteriorated in October 1990, following the infiltration of northern Rwanda by an invasion force of some 4,000 Rwandan rebels who had been based in Uganda and who were predominantly members of the NRA; their leader, Maj.-Gen. Fred Rwigyema (who was killed by the Rwandan armed forces), was a deputy commander of the NRA and a former Ugandan Deputy Minister of Defence. In November President Museveni dismissed all non-Ugandan members of the NRA. In February 1991 a conference on the Rwandan security situation, held in Dar es Salaam, Tanzania, was attended by President Museveni, President Habyarimana of Rwanda and by representatives of four other African states; an amnesty was agreed for all Rwandans who were exiled abroad, and the rebels were urged to observe a cease-fire. Nevertheless, the Uganda-based Rwandan rebels continued to operate in northern Rwanda during 1991–1993. In January 1992 the Presidents of Uganda, Rwanda and Tanzania met in Tanzania to discuss security on the Uganda–Rwanda border. In that month it was reported that 64,000 Ugandans residing near the two countries' common border had been displaced, owing to cross-border shelling by Rwandan troops. In August Uganda and Rwanda signed a security co-operation agreement, whereby each country was permitted to station a monitoring team in the other's territory.

### Government

Following the January 1986 coup, power was vested in a broad-based interim Government, headed by an executive President. A National Resistance Council (NRC) was formed to legislate by decree. In addition, resistance committees were formed at local and district level. Political activity was suspended, although political parties were not banned. National elections were held in February 1989. Representatives were elected directly to local-level resistance committees; these elected representatives to district-level resistance committees, and these, in turn, elected representatives to the NRC. The NRC was expanded from 98 members, all nominated by the President, to 278 members, of whom 68 were nominated by the President and 210 were elected. In October 1989 the NRC approved legislation prolonging the Government's term of office by five years from January 1990, when its mandate had been due to expire. A round of elections to local- and district-level resistance committees took place in February–March 1992. In March 1993 the Government published a draft Constitution. A Constituent Assembly was elected on 28 March 1994 to debate, amend and enact the draft Constitution. Upon completion of the Constituent Assembly's task, legislative and presidential elections were to be held.

### Defence

In June 1994 the National Resistance Army (NRA) was estimated to number 50,000 men. The size of the NRA was to be reduced to about 45,000 by the end of 1995. In October 1991 the police force numbered 16,890 men; the force was to be expanded to 30,000 members by 1994. Defence was allocated an estimated 105,100m. shillings by the central Government in 1994.

### Economic Affairs

In 1993, according to estimates by the World Bank, Uganda's gross national product (GNP), measured at average 1991–93 prices, was US $3,486m., equivalent to $190 per head. During 1985–93, it was estimated, GNP per head increased, in real terms, at an average annual rate of 1.9%. Over the same period, the population increased by an annual average of 3.2%. Uganda's gross domestic product (GDP) increased, in real terms, by an annual average of 5.1% in 1985–93; GDP grew by 4.0% in the financial year ending 30 June 1994.

Agriculture (including hunting, forestry and fishing) contributed 55.6% of GDP in 1993. About 79% of the labour force were employed in the sector in that year. The principal cash crops are coffee (which provided about 91% of export earnings in 1990), cotton, tea and maize. Tobacco, sugar cane, cocoa and horticultural produce are also cultivated. The main subsistence crops are plantains, cassava, sweet potatoes, millet, sorghum, maize, beans, groundnuts and rice. In addition, livestock (chiefly cattle, goats, sheep and poultry) are reared, and freshwater fishing is an important rural activity. During 1985–93 agricultural GDP increased by an annual average of 4.1%.

Industry (including mining, manufacturing, construction and power) contributed 11.8% of GDP in 1993, and employed 4.4% of the working population in 1980. During 1985–93 industrial GDP increased by an annual average of 9.7%.

Mining made a negligible contribution to GDP in 1989. The production of copper, formerly an important export, virtually ceased during the late 1970s; however, the Government announced in 1987 that funds were to be provided for the revival of the copper-mining industry. Apatite and limestone are mined, and there are also reserves of magnetite, tin, tungsten, beryllium, gold, bismuth, asbestos, graphite and tantalite.

Manufacturing contributed 4.9% of GDP in 1993. The most important manufacturing activities are the processing of agricultural commodities, brewing, vehicle assembly and the production of textiles, cement, soap, fertilizers, metal products, shoes, paints, matches and batteries. Manufacturing GDP increased by an annual average of 8.0% in 1985–93, and by 15.1% in 1993/94.

Energy is derived principally from hydroelectric power. Uganda exports hydroelectric power to Kenya. Imports of fuels accounted for 30% of the value of Uganda's merchandise imports in 1992.

In 1993 Uganda recorded a visible trade deficit of US $278.0m., and there was a deficit of $107.3m. on the current account of the balance of payments. In 1989 the principal sources of imports were Kenya, the United Kingdom and the Federal Republic of Germany, while the Netherlands, the USA and France were the main markets for exports. The principal export in 1990 was coffee. The main imports in 1979 were machinery and transport equipment.

In the financial year ending 30 June 1994 there was an estimated budgetary deficit equivalent to 11.3% of GDP. Uganda's external debt totalled US $3,056m. at the end of 1993, of which $2,617m. was long-term public debt. In that year the cost of debt-servicing was equivalent to 121.3% of the value of exports of goods and services. The rate of inflation averaged 78.5% annually in 1985–93. The average annual rate of inflation declined from 52.4% in 1992 to 6.1% in 1993, and was recorded at 9.8% in 1994.

Uganda is a member of the African Development Bank (see p. 102). In November 1993 it was among members of the Preferential Trade Area for Eastern and Southern African States (see p. 240) to sign a treaty establishing the Common Market for Eastern and Southern Africa.

Uganda's economic development was seriously retarded by the effects of the political unrest and the turbulent security situation which prevailed during the 1970s and early 1980s. Following its accession to power in 1986, the National Resistance Movement succeeded in winning the support of the international donor community for the rescheduling of debt repayments and for a Rehabilitation and Development Programme, which resulted in significant annual economic expansion in 1988–93, the reduction of inflation from 240% in 1986 to 6.1% in 1993 and the gradual accumulation of foreign exchange reserves. Under the programme, price controls were lifted, foreign exchange controls abolished, and the budget deficit significantly reduced. In the early 1990s donors drastically increased assistance to compensate for a deterioration in the balance of trade, caused by a sharp decline in international prices for coffee. Future increases in domestic and foreign investment are essential to reduce Uganda's significant dependence on aid. A programme to transfer state enterprises to the private sector, which began in 1991, had little effect on investment initially, as divestment was limited by the poor quality of the public companies; nevertheless, some 70 companies were due to be privatized during 1995–97. During 1993 increased revenue from coffee exports, high levels of aid and capital inflows from Asians returning from exile resulted in a significant appreciation of the shilling, which was detrimental to the competitiveness of exports and resulted in higher levels of imports, adversely affecting domestic products. A three-year economic reform programme (1994/95–1996/97), supported by the IMF, aimed to reorganize the tax collection system, to promote the diversification of exports and to improve the efficiency of the civil service, state enterprises (some of which were to be subsequently privatized) and the financial sector. In February 1995 international creditor Governments agreed to cancel some two-thirds of Uganda's bilateral government-guaranteed debt.

### Social Welfare

The health service was adversely affected by the departure of foreign personnel in 1972. Uganda had one physician for every 22,291 inhabitants in 1981, compared with one for every 15,050 in 1960. In 1981 Uganda had 485 hospital establishments, with a total of 19,782 beds. By the early 1990s the Acquired Immunodeficiency Syndrome (AIDS) virus had reached epidemic proportions in parts of Uganda. Health was allocated 9.9% of projected expenditure by the central Government in the budget for the financial year 1989/90.

### Education

Education is not compulsory. Most schools are sponsored by the Government, although a small proportion are sponsored by missions. All schools charge fees; however, the Government aims to introduce free primary school education by 1996. Primary education begins at six years of age and lasts for seven years. Secondary education, beginning at the age of 13, lasts for a further six years, comprising a first cycle of four years and a second of two years. In 1988 the number of pupils attending government-aided primary and secondary schools was equivalent to 53% of children in the relevant age-group. In 1994 there were 2,496,139 pupils enrolled at primary schools, and 244,248 pupils attending general secondary schools. In addition to Makerere University in Kampala there is a university of science and technology at Mbarara, and a small Islamic university is located at Mbale. In 1990 enrolment in tertiary education was equivalent to 1.1% of students in the relevant age-group (males 1.6%; females 0.6%). In 1991, according to census results, the average rate of adult illiteracy was 43.9% (males 31.8%; females 55.2%). Expenditure by the Ministry of Education in 1991 was 35,026m. shillings (15.0% of total government expenditure).

### Public Holidays

**1995:** 1 January (New Year's Day), 3 March* (Id al-Fitr, end of Ramadan), 14–17 April (Easter), 1 May (Labour Day), 10 May* (Id al-Adha, Feast of the Sacrifice), 3 June (Martyrs' Day), 9 October (Independence Day), 25 December (Christmas).

**1996:** 1 January (New Year's Day), 21 February* (Id al-Fitr, end of Ramadan), 5–8 April (Easter), 29 April* (Id al-Adha, Feast of the Sacrifice), 1 May (Labour Day), 3 June (Martyrs' Day), 9 October (Independence Day), 25 December (Christmas).

* These holidays are dependent on the Islamic lunar calendar and the exact dates may vary by one or two days from those given.

### Weights and Measures

The metric system is in force.

# Statistical Survey

Source (unless otherwise stated): Statistics Department, Ministry of Planning and Economic Development, Entebbe.

## Area and Population

### AREA, POPULATION AND DENSITY

| | |
|---|---:|
| Area (sq km) | |
| Land | 197,058 |
| Inland water | 44,081 |
| Total | 241,139* |
| Population (census results) | |
| 18 January 1980 | 12,636,179 |
| 12 January 1991 | |
| Males | 8,185,747 |
| Females | 8,485,958 |
| Total | 16,671,705 |
| Density (per sq km) at January 1991 | 69.1 |

* 93,104 sq miles. Source: Lands and Surveys Department.

### DISTRICTS (population at 1980 census)

| | | | | |
|---|---:|---|---:|---|
| Apac | 313,333 | Lira | 370,252 |
| Arua | 472,283 | Luwero | 412,474 |
| Bundibugyu | 112,216 | Masaka | 631,156 |
| Bushenyi | 524,669 | Masindi | 223,230 |
| Gulu | 270,085 | Mbale | 556,941 |
| Hoima | 294,301 | Mbarara | 688,153 |
| Iganga | 643,881 | Moroto | 188,641 |
| Jinja | 228,520 | Moyo | 106,492 |
| Kabale | 455,421 | Mpigi | 639,919 |
| Kabarole | 519,821 | Mubende | 510,260 |
| Kampala | 479,792 | Mukono | 634,275 |
| Kamuli | 349,549 | Nebbi | 233,000 |
| Kapchorwa | 73,967 | Rakai | 274,558 |
| Kasase | 277,697 | Rukungiri | 296,559 |
| Kitgum | 308,711 | Soroti | 476,629 |
| Kotido | 161,445 | Tororo | 668,410 |
| Kumi | 239,539 | | |

### PRINCIPAL TOWNS (population at 1969 census)

| | | | | |
|---|---:|---|---:|
| Kampala (capital) | 330,700 | Mbale | 23,544 |
| Jinja and Njeru | 52,509 | Entebbe | 21,096 |
| Bugembe planning area | 46,884 | Gulu | 18,170 |

**1980** (provisional census results): Kampala 458,423; Jinja 45,060; Masaka 29,123; Mbale 28,039; Mbarara 23,155; Gulu 14,958.

### BIRTHS AND DEATHS (UN estimates, annual averages)

| | 1975–80 | 1980–85 | 1985–90 |
|---|---:|---:|---:|
| Birth rate (per 1,000) | 50.3 | 48.6 | 50.5 |
| Death rate (per 1,000) | 17.6 | 17.9 | 19.5 |

**Expectation of life** (UN estimates, years at birth, 1985–90): 44.6 (males 43.2; females 46.1).

Source: UN, *World Population Prospects: The 1992 Revision*.

### ECONOMICALLY ACTIVE POPULATION
(ILO estimates, '000 persons at mid-1980)

| | Males | Females | Total |
|---|---:|---:|---:|
| Agriculture, etc. | 2,950 | 2,340 | 5,290 |
| Industry | 222 | 50 | 272 |
| Services | 353 | 247 | 600 |
| Total | 3,525 | 2,637 | 6,162 |

Source: ILO, *Economically Active Population Estimates and Projections, 1950–2025*.

**Mid-1993** (estimates in '000): Agriculture, etc. 6,611; Total 8,361 (Source: FAO, *Production Yearbook*).

### EMPLOYMENT ('000 employees at June each year)

| | 1976 | 1977 | 1978 |
|---|---:|---:|---:|
| Agriculture, forestry and fishing | 78.2 | 76.6 | 81.1 |
| Mining and quarrying | 4.1 | 4.1 | 3.6 |
| Manufacturing and electricity | 54.0 | 51.9 | 51.7 |
| Construction and water supply | 45.5 | 46.9 | 48.9 |
| Private commerce | 18.5 | 12.8 | 18.3 |
| Transport, storage and communications | 13.1 | 12.4 | 10.0 |
| Services* | 152.0 | 158.1 | 158.2 |
| Total | 365.4 | 362.8 | 371.8 |

* Including commerce of the public sector.

## Agriculture

### PRINCIPAL CROPS ('000 metric tons)

| | 1991 | 1992 | 1993 |
|---|---:|---:|---:|
| Wheat | 9 | 9 | 9 |
| Rice (paddy) | 61 | 68 | 71 |
| Maize | 567 | 706 | 681 |
| Millet | 576 | 634 | 652 |
| Sorghum | 363 | 375 | 382 |
| Potatoes | 254 | 268 | 270 |
| Sweet potatoes | 1,785 | 1,905 | 1,894 |
| Cassava (Manioc) | 3,229 | 2,892 | 3,982 |
| Beans (dry) | 383 | 402 | 441 |
| Other pulses | 109 | 110 | 115 |
| Soybeans | 59 | 53 | 71 |
| Groundnuts (in shell) | 144 | 147 | 150 |
| Sesame seed | 61 | 72 | 75 |
| Cottonseed* | 18 | 15 | 15 |
| Vegetables† | 415 | 400 | 413 |
| Sugar cane† | 845 | 880 | 1,010 |
| Bananas† | 570 | 560 | 570 |
| Plantains | 8,080 | 7,806 | 8,488 |
| Coffee (green) | 147 | 121 | 177* |
| Tea (made) | 9 | 10 | 12* |
| Tobacco (leaves) | 5 | 7 | 5 |
| Cotton (lint) | 8 | 7 | 7* |

* Unofficial figure(s). † FAO estimates.

Source: FAO, *Production Yearbook*.

### LIVESTOCK ('000 head, year ending September)

| | 1991 | 1992 | 1993 |
|---|---:|---:|---:|
| Cattle* | 5,000 | 5,100 | 5,200 |
| Sheep† | 1,380 | 1,560 | 1,760 |
| Goats† | 3,300 | 3,350 | 3,400 |
| Pigs* | 850 | 880 | 900 |
| Asses* | 17 | 17 | 17 |

* FAO estimates. † Unofficial figures.

Poultry (FAO estimates, million): 19 in 1991; 20 in 1992; 20 in 1993.

Source: FAO, *Production Yearbook*.

UGANDA

**LIVESTOCK PRODUCTS** (FAO estimates, '000 metric tons)

|  | 1991 | 1992 | 1993 |
|---|---|---|---|
| Beef and veal | 83 | 84 | 86 |
| Mutton and lamb | 7 | 8 | 9 |
| Goat meat | 14 | 14 | 14 |
| Pig meat | 46 | 48 | 49 |
| Poultry meat | 30 | 32 | 34 |
| Other meat | 17 | 17 | 16 |
| Cows' milk | 437 | 446 | 455 |
| Poultry eggs | 15.2 | 16.0 | 16.0 |
| Cattle hides | 11.6 | 11.8 | 12.0 |

Source: FAO, *Production Yearbook*.

## Forestry

**ROUNDWOOD REMOVALS**
(FAO estimates, '000 cubic metres, excluding bark)

|  | 1990 | 1991 | 1992 |
|---|---|---|---|
| Sawlogs, veneer logs and logs for sleepers* | 70 | 70 | 70 |
| Other industrial wood | 1,761 | 1,816 | 1,873 |
| Fuel wood | 12,320 | 12,705 | 13,103 |
| **Total** | 14,151 | 14,591 | 15,046 |

* Assumed to be unchanged since 1988.

Source: FAO, *Yearbook of Forest Products*.

**SAWNWOOD PRODUCTION**
('000 cubic metres)

|  | 1986* | 1987* | 1988 |
|---|---|---|---|
| Coniferous (softwood) | 7 | 7 | 8 |
| Broadleaved (hardwood) | 16 | 16 | 20 |
| **Total** | 23 | 23 | 28 |

* FAO estimates.

**1989–92:** Annual production as in 1988 (FAO estimates).

Source: FAO, *Yearbook of Forest Products*.

## Fishing

('000 metric tons, live weight)

|  | 1990 | 1991 | 1992 |
|---|---|---|---|
| Tilapias | 101.1 | 105.1* | 103.1 |
| African lungfishes | 4.2 | 4.4* | 4.3* |
| Characins | 6.1 | 6.3* | 6.2* |
| Naked catfishes | 4.0 | 4.1* | 4.0* |
| Torpedo-shaped catfishes | 4.4 | 4.6* | 4.5* |
| Other freshwater fishes | 5.2 | 5.4* | 5.3* |
| Nile perch | 120.3 | 125.1* | 122.7* |
| **Total catch** | 245.2 | 254.9 | 250.0* |

* FAO estimate.

Source: FAO, *Yearbook of Fishery Statistics*.

## Mining

(metric tons, unless otherwise indicated)

|  | 1989 | 1990 | 1991 |
|---|---|---|---|
| Tin concentrates* | 10 | 10 | 10 |
| Tungsten concentrates* | 4† | 4† | 4 |
| Salt—unrefined ('000 metric tons)‡ | 5 | 5 | 5 |

* Figures refer to the metal content of concentrates.
† Estimate.
‡ Data from the US Bureau of Mines.

Source: UN, *Industrial Statistics Yearbook*.

## Industry

**SELECTED PRODUCTS**
('000 metric tons, unless otherwise indicated)

|  | 1989 | 1990 | 1991 |
|---|---|---|---|
| Raw sugar | 16 | 29 | 46 |
| Beer ('000 hectolitres) | 195 | 194 | n.a. |
| Soft drinks ('000 hectolitres) | 179 | 243 | n.a. |
| Cigarettes (million) | 1,586 | 1,290 | 2,200 |
| Cement | 17 | 27 | 24* |
| Electric energy (million kWh) | 688 | 776 | 783 |

* Estimate.

Source: UN, *Industrial Statistics Yearbook*.

## Finance

**CURRENCY AND EXCHANGE RATES**

**Monetary Units**
100 cents = 1 new Uganda shilling.

**Sterling and Dollar Equivalents** (31 December 1994)
£1 sterling = 1,449.9 new Uganda shillings;
US $1 = 926.8 new Uganda shillings;
10,000 new Uganda shillings = £6,897 = $10.790.

**Average Exchange Rate** (new Uganda shillings per US $)
1992   1,133.8
1993   1,195.0
1994     979.4

Note: Between December 1985 and May 1987 the official exchange rate was fixed at US $1 = 1,400 shillings. In May 1987 a new shilling, equivalent to 100 of the former units, was introduced. At the same time, the currency was devalued by 76.7%, with the exchange rate set at $1 = 60 new shillings. Further devaluations were implemented in subsequent years. Some figures in this survey are still in terms of old shillings.

**GENERAL BUDGET***
(million old shillings, year ending 30 June)

| Revenue† | 1983/84 | 1984/85‡ | 1985/86‡ |
|---|---|---|---|
| Taxation | 88,424 | 162,092 | 284,374 |
| Taxes on income, profits, etc. | 6,245 | 9,762 | 15,632 |
| Corporate taxes | 5,925 | 8,875 | 14,319 |
| Domestic taxes on goods and services | 22,447 | 39,387 | 54,447 |
| Sales taxes | 17,679 | 31,873 | 42,230 |
| Excises | 3,484 | 5,554 | 9,726 |
| Taxes on international trade | 59,706 | 112,875 | 214,181 |
| Import duties | 9,234 | 14,293 | 17,640 |
| Export duties | 41,203 | 96,090 | 191,483 |
| Exchange profits | 7,831 | — | — |
| Freight charges | 1,348 | 2,492 | 5,058 |
| Other current revenue | 1,834 | | |
| Administrative fees, charges, etc. | 1,272 | — | — |
| **Total** | 90,258 | 162,092 | 284,374 |

# UGANDA

*Statistical Survey*

| Expenditure§ | 1983/84 | 1984/85‡ | 1985/86‡ |
|---|---|---|---|
| General public services | 26,826 | 53,986 | 99,066 |
| Defence | 19,229 | 35,919 | 120,443 |
| Education | 13,442 | 29,296 | 68,649 |
| Health | 2,908 | 7,968 | 10,917 |
| Social security and welfare | 1,811 | 3,572 | 9,673 |
| Housing | 1,408 | 2,661 | 3,506 |
| Other community and social services | 1,354 | 5,547 | 5,775 |
| Economic services | 9,893 | 24,376 | 67,548 |
|   Agriculture, forestry and fishing | 3,574 | 9,916 | 21,335 |
|   Mining, manufacturing and construction | 2,373 | 5,805 | 13,565 |
|   Transport and communications | 3,350 | 7,896 | 29,876 |
|   Roads | 2,562 | 7,020 | 28,265 |
| Other purposes | 25,864 | 59,127 | 71,732 |
| **Sub-total** | 102,735 | 222,452 | 457,309 |
| Settlement of outstanding arrears | 12,393 | 7,540 | — |
| **Total** | 115,128 | 229,992 | 457,309 |
| Current | 101,677 | 194,646 | 335,315 |
| Capital | 13,451 | 35,346 | 121,994 |

\* Figures represent a consolidation of Revenue and Development Accounts. The data exclude the operations of the Social Security Fund and other central government units with their own budgets.
† Excluding grants received (million old shillings): 3,500 in 1983/84; 4,800 in 1984/85; 38,444 in 1985/86.
‡ Provisional.
§ Excluding lending (million old shillings): 750 in 1983/84; 920 in 1984/85.

Source: IMF, *Government Finance Statistics Yearbook*.

**1986/87** (million new shillings): Revenue 5,005 (excluding grants 853); Expenditure 11,415.
**1987/88** (million new shillings): Revenue 22,262 (excluding grants 5,640); Expenditure 33,401.
**1988/89** (million new shillings): Revenue 46,719 (excluding grants 11,408); Expenditure 72,563.
**1989/90** (million new shillings): Revenue 86,459 (excluding grants 24,891); Expenditure 166,977 (excluding net lending 2,287).
**1990/91** (million new shillings): Revenue 136,808 (excluding grants 143,189); Expenditure 353,792 (excluding net lending 4,500).
**1991/92** (million new shillings): Revenue 187,901 (excluding grants 185,909); Expenditure 561,413 (excluding net lending 8,500).
**1992/93** (provisional, million new shillings): Revenue 287,112 (excluding grants 281,386); Expenditure 720,595 (excluding net lending 7,500).

Source: IMF, *International Financial Statistics*.

### INTERNATIONAL RESERVES (US $ million at 31 December)

| | 1992 | 1993 | 1994 |
|---|---|---|---|
| IMF special drawing rights | 9.0 | 0.1 | 3.1 |
| Foreign exchange | 85.4 | 146.3 | 318.1 |
| **Total** | 94.4 | 146.4 | 321.2 |

Source: IMF, *International Financial Statistics*.

### MONEY SUPPLY (million new shillings at 31 December)

| | 1991 | 1992 | 1993 |
|---|---|---|---|
| Currency outside banks | n.a. | 98,335 | 132,638 |
| Demand deposits at commercial banks | 78,626 | 107,676 | 126,757 |
| **Total money** (incl. others) | n.a. | 214,463 | 269,945 |

Source: IMF, *International Financial Statistics*.

### COST OF LIVING (Consumer Price Index for all households in Kampala; base: 1990 = 100)

| | 1991 | 1992 | 1993 |
|---|---|---|---|
| All items | 128 | 195 | 207 |

Source: IMF, *International Financial Statistics*.

### NATIONAL ACCOUNTS
(million new shillings at current prices)
**Gross Domestic Product by Economic Activity**

| | 1987 | 1988 | 1989 |
|---|---|---|---|
| Agriculture, hunting, forestry and fishing | 122,294 | 330,052 | 666,217 |
| Mining and quarrying | 34 | 35 | 37 |
| Manufacturing | 6,734 | 22,630 | 40,840 |
| Electricity, gas and water | 130 | 558 | 1,459 |
| Construction | 3,261 | 13,814 | 29,210 |
| Trade, restaurants and hotels | 18,977 | 61,829 | 122,680 |
| Transport, storage and communications | 5,812 | 14,700 | 39,919 |
| Finance, insurance, real estate and business services* | 4,975 | 14,509 | 27,212 |
| Community, social and personal services | 12,226 | 33,305 | 68,005 |
| **Total** | 174,443 | 491,432 | 995,579 |

\* After deducting imputed bank service charge.

Source: UN, *National Accounts Statistics*.

### BALANCE OF PAYMENTS (US $ million)

| | 1991 | 1992 | 1993 |
|---|---|---|---|
| Merchandise exports f.o.b. | 173.2 | 151.2 | 196.7 |
| Merchandise imports f.o.b. | −377.1 | −421.9 | −474.7 |
| **Trade balance** | −203.9 | −270.7 | −278.0 |
| Exports of services | 20.8 | 34.5 | 93.6 |
| Imports of services | −241.8 | −247.7 | −283.1 |
| Other income received | 2.8 | 4.1 | 6.4 |
| Other income paid | −76.7 | −88.3 | −71.2 |
| Private unrequited transfers (net) | 103.4 | 207.3 | 163.3 |
| Official unrequited transfers (net) | 225.6 | 261.2 | 261.7 |
| **Current balance** | −169.8 | −99.6 | −107.3 |
| Direct capital investment | 1.0 | 3.0 | 3.4 |
| Other capital (net) | 136.6 | 111.8 | 156.6 |
| Net errors and omissions | 0.6 | 9.0 | 5.5 |
| **Overall balance** | −31.7 | 24.2 | 58.1 |

Source: IMF, *International Financial Statistics*.

# External Trade

### PRINCIPAL COMMODITIES ('000 old shillings)

| Imports | 1977 | 1978 | 1979 |
|---|---|---|---|
| Paper and paper products | 25,994 | 35,822 | 27,773 |
| Cotton fabrics, other than grey | 2,520 | 2,669 | 2,261 |
| Iron and steel | 40,562 | 31,590 | 15,567 |
| Other metals and metal products | 78,151 | 84,642 | 57,221 |
| Machinery, incl. agricultural machinery | 58,771 } | 661,652 | 601,811 |
| Transport equipment | 227,025 } | | |
| **Total** (incl. others) | 1,460,939 | 1,470,261 | 1,244,314 |

**Total Imports c.i.f.** (million new shillings): 4,300 in 1986; 36,336 in 1987; 94,112 in 1988; 87,851 in 1989; 125,059 in 1990; 137,250 in 1991; 580,685 in 1992; 850,411 in 1994 (figure for 1993 not available) (Source: IMF, *International Financial Statistics*).

| Exports (incl. re-exports) | 1977 | 1978 | 1979 |
|---|---|---|---|
| Coffee, not roasted | 4,288,133 | 2,113,300 | 2,231,800 |
| Cotton, raw | 99,293 | 98,400 | 24,400 |
| Copper, unwrought | 23,658 | 18,000 | 9,400 |
| Tea | 105,136 | 20,900 | 12,200 |
| Hides, skins, etc. | 5,372 | 800 | 1,900 |
| **Total** (incl. others) | 4,592,399 | 2,317,200 | 2,306,600 |

**Total exports f.o.b.** (million new shillings): 6,100 in 1986 (Coffee 5,658); 13,684 in 1987 (Coffee 13,553); 29,070 in 1988 (Coffee 27,154); 55,674 in 1989 (Coffee 53,460); 64,653 in 1990 (Coffee 58,955); 146,661 in 1991; 159,387 in 1992; 213,846 in 1993; 393,960 in 1994 (Source: IMF, *International Financial Statistics*).

UGANDA

**PRINCIPAL TRADING PARTNERS** (US $ million)

| Imports | 1987 | 1988 | 1989 |
|---|---|---|---|
| Germany, Federal Republic | 48.7 | 34.3 | 53.1 |
| India | 27.8 | 32.6 | 38.1 |
| Italy | 65.0 | 35.3 | 23.0 |
| Japan | 36.0 | 28.0 | 30.7 |
| Kenya | 91.9 | 102.5 | 110.3 |
| United Kingdom | 69.4 | 69.1 | 70.6 |
| USA | 20.5 | 17.4 | 25.4 |

**Total imports c.i.f.** (US $ million): 555 in 1987; 544 in 1988; 390 in 1989; 293 in 1990; 197 in 1991; 516 in 1992 (Source: UN, *Monthly Bulletin of Statistics*).

| Exports | 1987 | 1988 | 1989 |
|---|---|---|---|
| France | 35.0 | 38.2 | 33.2 |
| Germany, Federal Republic | 17.6 | 23.6 | 24.4 |
| Italy | 11.5 | 16.4 | 17.2 |
| Japan | 16.1 | 9.2 | 9.4 |
| Netherlands | 28.2 | 39.1 | 40.5 |
| Spain | 30.2 | 30.4 | 27.0 |
| United Kingdom | 55.3 | 49.4 | 31.4 |
| USA | 77.7 | 56.5 | 39.6 |

**Total exports f.o.b.** (US $ million): 319 in 1987; 274 in 1988; 250 in 1989; 152 in 1990; 201 in 1991; 143 in 1992 (Source: UN, *Monthly Bulletin of Statistics*).

## Transport

**RAILWAYS** (traffic)

| | 1989 | 1990 | 1991 |
|---|---|---|---|
| Passenger-km (million) | 69 | 108 | 60 |
| Freight ton-km (million) | 90 | 103 | 139 |

Source: UN, *Statistical Yearbook*.

**ROAD TRAFFIC** (registered motor vehicles*)

| | 1978 | 1979 | 1980† |
|---|---|---|---|
| Heavy commercial vehicles | 5,812 | 3,216 | 3,500 |
| Pick-ups and vans | 5,101 | 3,336 | 3,500 |
| Minibuses etc. | 779 | 533 | 500 |
| Buses | 839 | 553 | 600 |
| Passenger cars | 15,757 | 11,279 | 11,000 |
| Motor cycles and scooters | 4,754 | 4,459 | 4,500 |

* Excluding government-owned vehicles.    † Estimates.

**1985** (vehicles in use at 31 December): Heavy commercial vehicles 4,659; Buses 987; Passenger cars 32,155; Motor cycles and scooters 4,809 (Source: International Road Federation, *World Road Statistics*).

**CIVIL AVIATION** (traffic on scheduled services)

| | 1990 |
|---|---|
| Kilometers flown (million) | 4 |
| Passengers carried ('000) | 116 |
| Passenger-km (million) | 278 |
| Total ton-km (million) | 47 |

Source: UN, *Statistical Yearbook*.

## Tourism

| | 1990 | 1991 | 1992 |
|---|---|---|---|
| Tourist arrivals ('000) | 69 | 69 | 50 |
| Tourist receipts (US $ million) | 10 | 15 | 10 |

Source: UN, *Statistical Yearbook*.

## Communications Media

| | 1990 | 1991 | 1992 |
|---|---|---|---|
| Radio receivers ('000 in use) | 1,900 | 1,975 | 2,040 |
| Television receivers ('000 in use) | 180 | 187 | 193 |
| Telephones ('000 main lines in use) | 28 | 29 | n.a. |
| Daily newspapers: | | | |
| Number | 2 | n.a. | 6 |
| Average circulation ('000 copies) | 30 | n.a. | 80* |

* Estimate.

Sources: UN, *Statistical Yearbook*; UNESCO, *Statistical Yearbook*.

## Education

(1994)

| | Teachers | Students |
|---|---|---|
| Primary | 102,126 | 2,496,139 |
| Secondary: | | |
| General | 16,245 | 244,248 |
| Vocational* | 826 | 12,552 |
| Primary teacher training colleges | 922 | 18,512 |
| Higher: | | |
| University | 941 | 8,966 |
| Other† | 1,018 | 15,174 |

* Technical schools and institutes.
† Includes secondary teacher training colleges.

Source: Ministry of Education and Sports, Kampala.

# Directory

## The Constitution

Following the military coup in July 1985, the 1967 Constitution was suspended, and all legislative and executive powers were vested in a Military Council, whose Chairman was Head of State. In January 1986 a further military coup established an executive Presidency, assisted by a cabinet of ministers and a legislative National Resistance Council (NRC), appointed by the President. In February 1989 national elections to an expanded NRC took place. In March 1993 the Government published a draft constitution. A Constituent Assembly (comprising 214 elected and 74 nominated members) was established to debate, amend and enact the draft Constitution; elections to this body took place in March 1994. Upon completion of the Constituent Assembly's task, legislative and presidential elections were to be held.

## The Government

### HEAD OF STATE

**President:** Lt-Gen. YOWERI KAGUTA MUSEVENI (took office 29 January 1986).

### THE CABINET
(June 1995)

**President and Minister of Defence:** Lt-Gen. YOWERI KAGUTA MUSEVENI.
**Vice-President and Minister of Women's Affairs and Community Development:** Dr SPECIOSA WANDIRA KAZIBWE.
**Prime Minister:** KINTU MUSOKE.
**First Deputy Prime Minister and National Political Commissar:** ERIYA KATEGAYA.
**Second Deputy Prime Minister and Minister of Public Service:** PAUL KAWANGA SSEMOGERERE.
**Third Deputy Prime Minister and Minister of Lands, Housing and Urban Development:** ERIC ADRIKO.
**Minister of Agriculture, Animal Industry and Fisheries:** VICTORIA SSEKITOLEKO.
**Minister of Education and Sports:** Maj. AMANYA MUSHEGA.
**Minister of Finance and Economic Planning:** JOSHUA MAYANJA-NKANGI.
**Minister of Foreign Affairs:** RUHAKANA RUGUNDA.
**Minister of Health:** Dr JAMES MAKUMBI.
**Minister of Information:** PAUL ETIANG.
**Minister of Internal Affairs:** CRISPUS KIYONGA.
**Minister of Justice and Attorney-General:** JOSEPH EKEMU.
**Minister of Labour and Social Welfare:** STEPHEN CHEBROT.
**Minister of Local Government:** BIDANDI SSALI.
**Minister of Natural Resources:** HENRY KAJURA.
**Minister of Tourism, Wildlife and Antiquities:** Brig. MOSES ALI.
**Minister of Trade and Industry:** RICHARD KAIJUKA.
**Minister of Works, Transport and Communications:** KIRUNDA KIVEJINJA.
**Minister without Portfolio:** JAMES WAPAKHABULO.

### MINISTRIES

**Office of the President:** Parliament Bldgs, POB 7108, Kampala; tel. 234881; telex 61389; fax 235459.
**Office of the Prime Minister:** POB 341, Kampala; tel. (41) 259518; telex 62001.
**Ministry of Agriculture, Animal Industry and Fisheries:** POB 102, Entebbe; tel. (42) 20752; telex 61287.
**Ministry of Defence:** Republic House, POB 3798, Kampala; tel. (41) 270331; telex 61023.
**Ministry of Education and Sports:** Crested Towers, POB 7063, Kampala; tel. (41) 234440; telex 61298.
**Ministry of Finance and Economic Planning:** POB 8147, Kampala; tel. (41) 234700; telex 61170; fax 234194.
**Ministry of Foreign Affairs:** POB 7048, Kampala; tel. (41) 258251; telex 61007; fax (41) 258722.
**Ministry of Health:** POB 8, Entebbe; tel. (42) 20201; telex 61373.
**Ministry of Information:** POB 7142, Kampala; tel. (41) 256888; telex 61373.
**Ministry of Internal Affairs:** POB 7191, Kampala; tel. (41) 231188; telex 61331.
**Ministry of Justice:** POB 7183, Kampala; tel. (41) 233219.
**Ministry of Labour and Social Welfare:** POB 7009, Kampala; tel. (41) 242837; telex 62167.
**Ministry of Lands, Housing and Urban Development:** POB 7122, Kampala; tel. (41) 242931; telex 61274.
**Ministry of Local Government:** POB 7037, Kampala; tel. (41) 241763; telex 61265; fax (41) 258127.
**Ministry of Natural Resources:** POB 7270, Kampala; tel. (41) 234995; telex 61098.
**Ministry of Public Service:** POB 7168, Kampala; tel. (41) 254881.
**Ministry of Tourism, Wildlife and Antiquities:** Parliament Ave, POB 4241, Kampala; tel. (41) 232971; telex 62218.
**Ministry of Trade and Industry:** POB 7103, Kampala; tel. (41) 258202; telex 61183.
**Ministry of Women's Affairs and Community Development:** POB 7136, Kampala; tel. (41) 254253.
**Ministry of Works, Transport and Communications:** POB 10, Entebbe; tel. (42) 20101; telex 61313; fax (42) 20135.

## Legislature

### NATIONAL RESISTANCE COUNCIL

The National Resistance Movement, which took office in January 1986, established a National Resistance Council (NRC), initially comprising 80 nominated members, to act as a legislative body. National elections were held on 11–28 February 1989, at which 210 members of an expanded NRC were elected by members of district-level Resistance Committees (themselves elected by local-level Resistance Committees, who were directly elected by universal adult suffrage). The remaining 68 seats in the NRC were reserved for candidates nominated by the President (to include 34 women and representatives of youth organizations and trades unions). Political parties were not allowed to participate in the election campaign. In October 1989 the NRC approved legislation extending the Government's term of office by five years from January 1990, when its mandate was to expire. The Constituent Assembly (see Constitution) extended further the NRM's term of office in November 1994. Legislative and presidential elections were due to take place in December 1995, following the adoption of a new constitution.

## Political Organizations

Political parties were ordered to suspend active operations, although not formally banned, in March 1986.

**Buganda Youth Movement:** f. 1994; seeks autonomy for Buganda; Leader STANLEY KATO.
**Conservative Party (CP):** f. 1979; Leader JOSHUA MAYANJA-NKANGI.
**Democratic Party (DP):** POB 7098, Kampala; tel. (41) 230244; f. 1954; main support in southern Uganda; seeks a multi-party system; Pres. PAUL SSEMOGERERE; Sec.-Gen. ROBERT KITARIKO.
**Federal Democratic Movement (FEDEMO):** Kampala.
**Forum for Multi-Party Democracy:** Kampala; Gen. Sec. JESSE MASHATTE.
**Movement for New Democracy in Uganda:** based in Zambia; f. 1994 to campaign for multi-party political system; Leader DAN OKELLO-OGWANG.
**National Resistance Movement (NRM):** f. to oppose the UPC Govt 1980–85, and also opposed the mil. Govt in power from July 1985 to Jan. 1986; its mil. wing, the National Resistance Army (NRA), led by Lt-Gen. YOWERI MUSEVENI, took power in Jan. 1986; Chair. Dr SAMSON KISEKKA.
**Nationalist Liberal Party:** Kampala; f. 1984 by a breakaway faction of the DP; Leader TIBERIO OKENY.
**Uganda Democratic Alliance:** opposes the NRM Govt; Leader APOLO KIRONDE.
**Uganda Freedom Movement (UFM):** Kampala; mainly Baganda support; withdrew from NRM coalition Govt in April 1987; Sec.-Gen. (vacant).
**Uganda Independence Revolutionary Movement:** f. 1989; opposes the NRM Govt; Chair. Maj. OKELLO KOLO.

# UGANDA

**Uganda Islamic Revolutionary Party (UIRP):** Kampala; f. 1993; Chair. IDRIS MUWONGE.

**Uganda National Unity Movement:** opposes the NRM Govt; Chair. Alhaji SULEIMAN SSALONGO.

**Uganda Patriotic Movement:** Kampala; f. 1980; Sec.-Gen. JABERI SSALI.

**Uganda People's Congress (UPC):** POB 1951, Kampala; f. 1960; socialist-based philosophy; ruling party 1962–71 and 1980–85, sole legal political party 1969–71; Chair. Alhaji BADRU WEGULO; Leader Dr MILTON OBOTE; Sec.-Gen. Dr LUWULIZA KIRUNDA.

**Ugandan People's Democratic Movement (UPDM):** seeks democratic reforms; support mainly from north and east of the country; includes mems of fmr govt armed forces; signed a peace accord with the Govt in 1990; Chair. ERIC OTEMA ALLIMADI; Sec.-Gen. EMMANUEL OTENG.

**Uganda Progressive Union (UPU):** Kampala; Chair. ALFRED BANYA.

The following organizations are in armed conflict with the Government:

**Lord's Resistance Army:** f. 1987; claims to be conducting a 'holy war' against the NRM Govt; forces number c. 800–1,000; Leader JOSEPH KONY.

**Uganda People's Freedom Movement (UPFM):** based in Tororo and Kenya; f. 1994 by mems of the fmr Uganda People's Army; Leader PETER OTAI.

## Diplomatic Representation

### EMBASSIES AND HIGH COMMISSIONS IN UGANDA

**Algeria:** POB 4025, Kampala; tel. (41) 232918; telex 61184; fax (41) 241015; Ambassador: RABAH SOUIBÈS.

**Burundi:** POB 4379, Kampala; tel. (41) 221697; telex 61076; Ambassador: GEORGES NTZEZIMANA.

**China, People's Republic:** POB 4106, Kampala; tel. (41) 236895; fax (41) 235087; Ambassador: XIE YOUKUN.

**Cuba:** POB 9226, Kampala; tel. (41) 233742; Chargé d'affaires: ANGEL NICHOLAS.

**Denmark:** Crusader House, 4th and 5th Floor, 3 Portal Ave, POB 11234, Kampala; tel. (41) 250926; telex 61560; fax (41) 254979; Ambassador: THOMAS SCHJERBECK.

**Egypt:** POB 4280, Kampala; tel. (41) 254525; telex 61122; fax (41) 232103; Ambassador: SAMIR ABDALLAH.

**France:** POB 7112, Kampala; tel. (41) 242120; telex 61079; fax (41) 241252; Ambassador: FRANÇOIS DESCOUEYTE.

**Germany:** 15 Philip Rd, POB 7016, Kampala; tel. (41) 256767; telex 61005; fax (41) 243136; Ambassador: CHRISTIAN NAKONZ.

**Holy See:** POB 7177, Kampala (Apostolic Nunciature); tel. (41) 221767; fax (41) 221774; Apostolic Pro-Nuncio: Most Rev. LUIS ROBLES DÍAZ, Titular Archbishop of Stephaniacum.

**India:** Bank of Baroda Bldg, 1st Floor, POB 7040, Kampala; tel. (41) 254943; telex 61161; fax (41) 254943; High Commissioner: N. N. DESAI.

**Italy:** POB 4646, Kampala; tel. (41) 241786; telex 61261; fax (41) 542678; Ambassador: ALESSIO CARISSIMO.

**Kenya:** POB 5220, Kampala; tel. (41) 267368; telex 61191; fax (41) 267369; High Commissioner: Brig. R. MUSONYE.

**Korea, Democratic People's Republic:** POB 3717, Kampala; tel. (41) 233667; telex 61017; Ambassador: CHON GYONG CHOL.

**Korea, Republic:** Baumann House, POB 3717, Kampala; tel. (41) 233667; telex 61017; Ambassador: JAE-KYU KIM.

**Libya:** POB 6079, Kampala; tel. (41) 244924; telex 61090; fax (41) 244969; Sec. of People's Bureau: ABU ALLAH ABDUL MULLAH.

**Nigeria:** 33 Nakasero Rd, POB 4338, Kampala; tel. (41) 233691; telex 61011; fax (41) 232543; High Commissioner: MAMMAN DAURA.

**Russia:** POB 7022, Kampala; tel. (41) 233676; telex 61518; Ambassador: STANISLAV NIKOLAYEVICH SEMENENKO.

**Rwanda:** POB 2468, Kampala; tel. (41) 244045; telex 61277; fax (41) 258547; Ambassador: CLAVER KANYARUSHOKI.

**Sudan:** POB 3200, Kampala; tel. (41) 243518; telex 61078; Ambassador: TAJ AL-SIRR ABBAS.

**Tanzania:** POB 5750, Kampala; tel. (41) 256756; telex 61062; High Commissioner: JOSHUA OPANGA.

**United Kingdom:** 10–12 Parliament Ave, POB 7070, Kampala; tel. (41) 257054; telex 61202; fax (41) 257304; High Commissioner: EDWARD CLAY.

**USA:** POB 7007, Kampala; tel. (41) 259795; Ambassador: MICHAEL SOUTHWICK.

**Zaire:** POB 4972, Kampala; tel. (41) 233777; telex 61284; Ambassador: NZAPA KENGO.

## Judicial System

**Courts of Judicature:** POB 7085, Kampala.

**The Supreme Court:** Mengo; hears appeals from the High Court.
  **Chief Justice:** SAMSON WILLIAM WAKO WAMBUZI.
  **Deputy Chief Justice:** S. T. MANYINDO.

**The High Court:** Kampala; tel. (41) 233422; has full criminal and civil jurisdiction over all persons and matters in the country. The High Court consists of the Principal Judge and 20 Puisne Judges.
  **Principal Judge:** J. H. NTAGOBA.

**Magistrates' Courts:** These are established under the Magistrates' Courts Act of 1970 and exercise limited jurisdiction in criminal and civil matters. The country is divided into magisterial areas, presided over by a Chief Magistrate. Under him there are three categories of Magistrates. The Magistrates preside alone over their courts. Appeals from the first category of Magistrates' Court lie directly to the High Court, while appeals from the second and third categories of Magistrates' Court lie to the Chief Magistrate's Court, and from there to the High Court.

## Religion

It is estimated that more than 60% of the population profess Christianity (with approximately equal numbers of Roman Catholics and Protestants). About 5% of the population are Muslims.

### CHRISTIANITY

#### The Anglican Communion

Anglicans are adherents of the Church of the Province of Uganda, comprising 21 dioceses. There are about 4m. adherents.

**Archbishop of Uganda and Bishop of Kampala:** Most Rev. LIVINGSTONE MPALANYI NKOYOYO, POB 14123, Kampala; tel. (41) 270218.

#### Greek Orthodox Church

**Archbishop of East Africa:** NICADEMUS OF IRINOUPOULIS (resident in Nairobi, Kenya); jurisidiction covers Kenya, Tanzania and Uganda.

#### The Roman Catholic Church

Uganda comprises one archdiocese and 15 dioceses. At 31 December 1993 there were an estimated 7,429,693 adherents.

**Uganda Episcopal Conference:** Uganda Catholic Secretariat, POB 2886, Kampala; tel. (41) 268157; fax (41) 268713; f. 1974; Pres. Rt Rev. PAUL KALANDA, Bishop of Fort Portal.

**Archbishop of Kampala:** Cardinal EMMANUEL WAMALA, Archbishop's House, POB 14125, Mengo, Kampala; tel. and fax (41) 245441.

### ISLAM

**The Uganda Muslim Supreme Council:** POB 3247, Kampala; Mufti of Uganda: IBRAHIM SAID LUWEMBA; Chief Kadi and Pres. of Council: HUSAYN RAJAB KAKOOZA.

### BAHÁ'Í FAITH

**National Spiritual Assembly:** POB 2662, Kampala; tel. (41) 540511; mems resident in 3,522 localities.

## The Press

### DAILY AND OTHER NEWSPAPERS

**The Citizen:** Kampala; official publ. of the Democratic Party; English; Editor JOHN KYEYUNE.

**The Economy:** POB 6787, Kampala; weekly; English; Editor ROLAND KAKOOZA.

**Financial Times:** Plot 17/19, Station Rd, POB 31399, Kampala; tel. (41) 245798; bi-weekly; English; Editor G. A. ONEGI OBEL.

**Focus:** POB 268, Kampala; tel. (41) 235086; telex 61284; fax (41) 242796; f. 1983; publ. by Islamic Information Service and Material Centre; 4 a week; English; Editor HAJJI KATENDE; circ. 12,000.

**Guide:** POB 5350, Kampala; tel. (41) 233486; fax (41) 268045; f. 1989; weekly; English; Editor-in-Chief A. A. KALIISA; circ. 30,000.

**The Monitor:** POB 12141; Kampala; tel. (41) 251353; fax (41) 251352; f. 1992; 3 a week; English; Editor-in-Chief WAFULA OGUTTU; Editor ONYANGO OBBO; circ. 34,000.

# UGANDA

**Mulengera:** POB 6787, Kampala; weekly; Luganda; Editor ROLAND KAKOOZA.

**Munnansi News Bulletin:** Kampala; f. 1980; weekly; English; owned by the Democratic Party; Editor ANTHONY SGEKWEYAMA.

**Munno:** POB 4027, Kampala; f. 1911; daily; Luganda; publ. by the Roman Catholic Church; Editor ANTHONY SSEKWEYAMA; circ. 7,000.

**New Vision:** POB 9815, Kampala; tel. (41) 235846; fax 235221; f. 1986; official govt newspaper; daily; English; Editor WILLIAM PIKE; circ. 37,000.

**Ngabo:** POB 9362, Kampala; tel. (41) 42637; telex 61236; f. 1979; daily; Luganda; Editor MAURICE SEKAWUNGU; circ. 7,000.

**The People:** Kampala; weekly; English; independent; Editor AMOS KAJOBA.

**The Star:** POB 9362, Kampala; tel. (41) 42637; telex 61236; f. 1980; revived 1984; daily; English; Editor SAMUEL KATWERE; circ. 5,000.

**Taifa Uganda Empya:** POB 1986, Kampala; tel. (41) 254652; telex 61064; f. 1953; daily; Luganda; Editor A. SEMBOGA; circ. 24,000.

**Weekly Topic:** POB 1725, Kampala; tel. (41) 233834; weekly; English; Editor JOHN WASSWA; circ. 13,000.

## PERIODICALS

**Eastern Africa Journal of Rural Development:** Dept of Agriculture, Makerere University, POB 7062, Kampala; 2 a year; circ. 800.

**Leadership:** POB 2522, Kampala; tel. (41) 221358; fax (41) 221576; f. 1956; 6 a year; English; Roman Catholic; circ. 7,400.

**Mkombozi:** c/o Ministry of Defence, Republic House, POB 3798, Kampala; tel. (41) 270331; telex 61023; f. 1982; military; Editor A. OPOLOTT.

**Musizi:** POB 4027, Mengo, Kampala; f. 1955; monthly; Luganda; Roman Catholic; Editor F. GITTA; circ. 30,000.

**Pearl of Africa:** POB 7142, Kampala; monthly; govt publ.

**Uganda Confidential:** Kampala; monthly; Editor TEDDY SSEZI-CHEEYE.

## NEWS AGENCIES

**Uganda News Agency (UNA):** POB 7142, Kampala; tel. (41) 32734; telex 61188; Dir (vacant); Editor-in-Chief F. A. OTAI.

### Foreign Bureaux

**Inter Press Service (IPS)** (Italy): Plot 2, Wilson Rd, POB 16514, Wandegeyn, Kampala; tel. (41) 245310; telex 61272; Correspondent DAVID MUSOKE.

**Rossiyskoye Informatsionnoye Agentstvo—Novosti (RIA-Novosti)** (Russia): POB 4412, Kampala; tel. (41) 232383; telex 62292; Correspondent Dr OLEG TETERIN.

**Xinhua (New China) News Agency** (People's Republic of China): Plot 25, Hill Drive, Kololo, POB 466, Kampala; tel. (41) 254951; telex 61189; Correspondent ZHANG YINGSHENG.

# Publishers

**Centenary Publishing House Ltd:** POB 2776, Kampala; tel. (41) 41599; f. 1977; religious (Anglican); Man. Dir Rev. SAM KAKIZA.

**Longman Uganda Ltd:** POB 3409, Kampala; tel. (41) 42940; f. 1965; Man. Dir M. K. L. MUTYABA.

**Uganda Publishing House Ltd:** Kampala; tel. (41) 59601; telex 61175; f. 1966; primary and secondary school textbooks; Man. Dir LABAN O. ERAPU.

### Government Publishing House

**Government Printer:** POB 33, Entebbe; telex 61336.

# Radio and Television

According to estimates by UNESCO, there were 2,040,000 radio receivers and 193,000 television receivers in use in 1992.

## RADIO

**Radio Uganda:** Ministry of Information, POB 7142, Kampala; tel. (41) 256888; telex 61084; f. 1954; state-controlled; broadcasts in 22 languages, including English, French, Arabic, Swahili and vernacular languages; Dir of Broadcasting JOHN C. SSERWADDA.

**Sanyu Radio:** Kampala; f. 1993; independent station broadcasting to Kampala and its environs.

## TELEVISION

**Sanyu Television:** Naguru; f. 1994; independent station broadcasting to Kampala and its environs.

**Uganda Television Service:** POB 4260, Kampala; tel. (41) 254461; telex 61084; f. 1962; state-controlled commercial service; programmes mainly in English, also in Swahili and Luganda; transmits over a radius of 320 km from Kampala; five relay stations have been built, others are under construction; Controller of Programmes FAUSTIN MISANVU.

# Finance

(cap. = capital; auth. = authorized; res = reserves; dep. = deposits; m. = million; brs = branches; amounts in new Uganda shillings unless otherwise indicated).

## BANKING

### Central Bank

**Bank of Uganda:** 37–43 Kampala Rd, POB 7120, Kampala; tel. (41) 258441; telex 61059; fax (41) 230878; f. 1966; bank of issue; auth. cap. 15,050m. (1994); Gov. CHARLES NYONYINTONO KIKONYOGO; Dep. Gov. EMMANUEL LULE; Gen. Man. ERIAB RUKYALEKERE.

### State Banks

**The Co-operative Bank Ltd:** 9 William St, POB 6863, Kampala; tel. (41) 258323; telex 61263; fax (41) 234578; f. 1970; cap. 153.0m., dep. 17,340m. old shillings (Dec. 1993); Gen. Man. GODFREY NSUBUGA.

**Uganda Commercial Bank:** Plot 12, Kampala Rd, POB 973, Kampala; tel. (41) 234710; telex 61073; fax (41) 259012; f. 1965; state-owned; cap. and res 27,174m., dep. 65,732m. (Sept. 1991); Chair. Dr EZERA SURUMA; 169 brs.

**Uganda Development Bank:** IPS Bldg, 14 Parliament Ave, POB 7210, Kampala; tel. (41) 230740; telex 61143; fax (41) 258571; f. 1972; state-owned; cap. 11m. (Dec. 1992); Man. Dir JOHN K. TWINOMUSINGUZI.

### Commercial Bank

**Nile Bank Ltd:** Spear House, Plot 22, Jinja Rd, POB 2834, Kampala; tel. (41) 231904; telex 61240; fax (41) 257779; f. 1988; dep. 15,200m. (Sept. 1993); private commercial bank; CEO Prof. EPHRAIM KAMUNTU.

### Development Bank

**East African Development Bank (EADB):** East African Development Bank Bldg, 4 Nile Ave, POB 7128, Kampala; tel. (41) 230021; telex 61074; fax (41) 259763; f. 1967; provides financial and tech. assistance to promote industrial development within Uganda, Kenya and Tanzania, whose Govts each hold 25.8% of the equity, the remaining 22.6% being shared by the African Development Bank, Barclays Bank, the Commercial Bank of Africa, Grindlays Bank, Standard Chartered Bank, Nordbanken of Sweden and a consortium of institutions in fmr Yugoslavia; regional offices in Nairobi and Dar es Salaam; Chair. E. TUMUSIIME-MUTEBILE; Dir-Gen. F. R. TIBEITA.

### Foreign Banks

**Bank of Baroda (Uganda) Ltd** (India): 18 Kampala Rd, POB 2971, Kampala; tel. (41) 233680; telex 61315; fax (41) 259467; f. 1969; 49% govt-owned; cap. and res 1,089m., dep. 35,482m. (Dec. 1994); Chair. and Man. Dir K. U. YAJNIK; 6 brs.

**Barclays Bank of Uganda Ltd** (United Kingdom): 16 Kampala Rd, POB 2971, Kampala; tel. (41) 232594; telex 61014; fax (41) 259467; f. 1969; 49% govt-owned; cap. and res 4,325m., dep. 45,946m. (Dec. 1993); Man. Dir C. J. MARTIN; 4 brs.

**Stanbic Bank Uganda Ltd:** 45 Kampala Rd, POB 7131, Kampala; tel. (41) 230811; telex 61018; fax (41) 231116; f. 1969 as Grindlays Bank International (Uganda) Ltd; 49% govt-owned; cap. 200m. (Sept. 1993); Chair. A. D. B. WRIGHT; Man. Dir A. B. MEARS.

**Standard Chartered Bank Uganda Ltd** (United Kingdom): 5 Speke Rd, POB 7111, Kampala; tel. (41) 258211; telex 61010; fax (41) 231473; f. 1969; cap. and res 760.0m., dep. 12,883.7m. (Dec. 1991); Chair. and Man. Dir L. E. A. BENTLEY.

**Tropical Africa Bank Ltd** (Libya): Plot 27, Kampala Rd, POB 7292, Kampala; tel. (41) 241408; telex 61286; fax (41) 232296; f. 1972 as Libyan Arab Uganda Bank for Foreign Trade and Development, adopted present name in 1994; 50% Govt-owned, 51% owned by Libyan Arab Foreign Bank; cap. 1,000m. (Jan. 1994); Chair. SULAIMAN SEMBAJJA; Gen. Man. ABD AL-GADER RAGHEI.

## STOCK EXCHANGE

**Kampala Stock Exchange:** Kampala; f. 1990; Chair. LEO BUGIRANGO.

## INSURANCE

**East Africa General Insurance Co Ltd:** 14 Kampala Rd, POB 1392, Kampala; telex 61378; life, fire, motor, marine and accident.

**National Insurance Corporation:** Plot 3, 3 Pilkington Rd, POB 7134, Kampala; tel. (41) 258001; telex 61222; fax (41) 259925; f. 1964; general; Man. Dir F. F. MAGEZI.

**Uganda American Insurance Co Ltd:** Kampala; telex 61101; f. 1970.

**Uganda Co-operative Insurance Ltd:** Plot 10, Bombo Rd, POB 6176, Kampala; tel. (41) 241826; fax (41) 258231; f. 1982; general.

## Trade and Industry

**Export and Import Licencing Division:** POB 7000, Kampala; tel. (41) 258795; telex 61085; f. 1987; advises importers and exporters and issues import and export licences; Prin. Commercial Officer JOHN MUHWEZI.

**Uganda Advisory Board of Trade:** POB 6877, Kampala; tel. (41) 33311; telex 61085; f. 1974; issues trade licences and service for exporters.

**Uganda Export Promotion Council:** POB 5045, Kampala; tel. (41) 259779; telex 61391; fax (41) 259779; f. 1983; provides market intelligence, organizes training, trade exhbns, etc.; Exec. Sec. HENRY NYAKOOJO.

**Uganda Investment Authority:** Investment Centre, Plot 28, Kampala Rd, POB 7418, Kampala; tel. (41) 251562; telex 61135; fax (41) 242903; f. 1991; promotes foreign and local investment, issues investment licences and provides investment incentives to priority industries; Exec. Dir G. W. RUBAGUMYA.

### CHAMBER OF COMMERCE

**Uganda National Chamber of Commerce and Industry:** Plot 17/19 Jinja Rd, POB 3809, Kampala; tel. (41) 258791; telex 61272; fax (41) 258793; Chair. BADRU BUNKEDDEKO; Sec. G. RUJOJO.

### DEVELOPMENT CORPORATIONS

**Agriculture and Livestock Development Fund:** f. 1976; provides loans to farmers.

**National Housing and Construction Corporation:** Crested Towers, POB 659, Kampala; tel. (41) 230311; telex 61156; fax (41) 258708; f. 1964; govt agent for building works, aims to improve living standards, principally by building residential housing; Chair. D. LUBEGA; Gen. Man. M. S. KASEKENDE.

**Ugandan Coffee Development Authority:** POB 7267, Kampala; tel. (41) 256940; telex 61412; fax (41) 256994; f. 1991; sets quality control standards, certifies coffee exports, maintains statistical data, advises Govt on local and world prices, promotes Ugandan coffee abroad, trains processors and quality controllers.

**Uganda Industrial Development Corporation Ltd (ULDC):** 9–11 Parliament Ave, POB 7042, Kampala; telex 61069; f. 1952; Chair. SAM RUTEGA.

### EMPLOYERS' ORGANIZATION

**Federation of Uganda Employers, Commerce and Industry:** POB 3820, Kampala; Chair. BRUNO ABALIWANO; Exec. Dir J. KASWARRA.

### MARKETING ORGANIZATIONS

**Coffee Marketing Board:** POB 7154, Kampala; tel. (41) 254051; telex 61157; fax (41) 230790; state-owned; purchases and exports coffee; Chair. and Man. Dir FRANCIS W. NAGIMESI.

**Lint Marketing Board:** POB 7018, Kampala; tel. (41) 232660; telex 61008; fax (41) 242426; state-owned; exporter of cotton lint; mfr of edible oil, soap and candles; Gen. Man. J. W. OBBO; Sec. G. KAKUBA.

**Produce Marketing Board:** POB 3705, Kampala; tel. (41) 236238; Gen. Man. ESTHER KAMPAMPARA.

**Uganda Coffee Development Authority:** POB 7154, Kampala; tel. (41) 230229; Man. Dir TRESS BUCYANAYANDI.

**Uganda Manufacturers' Association (UMA):** POB 6966, Kampala; tel. (41) 221034; fax (41) 220285; promotes mfr's interests; Chair. JAMES MULWANA.

**Uganda Tea Authority:** POB 4161, Kampala; tel. (41) 231003; telex 61120; state-owned; controls and co-ordinates activities of the tea industry; Gen. Man. MIRIA MARGARITA MUGABI.

### CO-OPERATIVE UNIONS

In 1993 there were 5,775 co-operative societies, grouped in 44 unions. There is at least one co-operative union in each administrative district.

**Uganda Co-operative Alliance:** Kampala; co-ordinating body for co-operative unions, of which the following are among the most important:

**Bugisu Co-operative Union Ltd:** Plot 2, Court Rd, Private Bag, Mbale; tel. (45) 2235; telex 66042; fax (45) 3565; f. 1954; processors and exporters of Bugisu arabica coffee; 226 mem. socs; Gen. Man. P. J. MUYIYI.

**East Mengo Growers' Co-operative Union Ltd:** POB 7092, Kampala; tel. (41) 241382; f. 1968; coffee, cotton, pineapples; 265 mem. socs; Chair. Y. KINALWA; Gen. Man. A. SSINGO.

**Kakumiro Growers' Co-operative Union:** POB 511, Kakumiro; processing of coffee and cotton; Sec. and Man. TIBIHWA-RUKEERA.

**Masaka Co-operative Union Ltd:** POB 284, Masaka; tel. (481) 20260; f. 1951; coffee, dairy farming, food processing, carpentry; 245 primary co-operative socs; Chair. J. M. KASOZI; Gen. Man. EDWARD C. SSERUUMA.

**Mubende District Co-operative Union:** coffee growers.

**Wamala Growers' Co-operative Union Ltd:** POB 99, Mityana; tel. 2036; f. 1968; coffee and cotton growers; 250 mem. socs; Gen. Man. HERBERT KIZITO.

**West Mengo Growers' Co-operative Union Ltd:** POB 7039, Kampala; tel. (41) 567511; f. 1948; cotton growing and buying, coffee buying and processing, maize milling; 250 mem. socs; Chair. H. E. KATABALWA MIIRO.

### TRADE UNIONS

**National Organization of Trade Unions (NOTU):** POB 2150, Kampala; tel. (41) 256295; f. 1973; Chair. E. KATURAMU; Sec.-Gen. MATHIAS MUKASA.

## Transport

The transport system was formerly mainly controlled by members of the Asian community, and deteriorated after their expulsion by President Amin in 1972. A reconstruction programme, assisted by foreign aid, is currently proceeding.

### RAILWAYS

In 1992 there were 1,241 km of 1000-mm-gauge track in operation. A programme to rehabilitate the railway network is under way.

**Uganda Railways Corporation:** Station Rd, POB 7150, Kampala; tel. (41) 254961; telex 61111; fax (41) 244405; formed after the dissolution of East African Railways in 1977; Man. Dir E. K. TUMUSUME.

### ROADS

In 1985 there was a total road network of 28,332 km, including 7,782 km of main roads and 18,508 km of secondary roads. About 22% of roads were paved. Under a US $150m. road rehabilitation project, which was launched in 1994, some 15 roads were to be improved by mid-1998.

### INLAND WATERWAYS

A rail wagon ferry service connecting Jinja with the Tanzanian port of Tanga, via Mwanza, was inaugurated in 1983, thus reducing Uganda's dependence on the Kenyan port of Mombasa. In 1986 the Uganda and Kenya Railways Corporations began the joint operation of Lake Victoria Marine Services, to ferry goods between the two countries via Lake Victoria.

### CIVIL AVIATION

The international airport is at Entebbe, on Lake Victoria, some 40 km from Kampala. In 1995 the airport was undergoing modernization. There are also several small airstrips.

**Alliance:** f. 1994; jtly owned by South African Airways, Air Tanzania Corpn, Uganda Airlines Corpn, the Ugandan and Tanzanian Govts and private investors; operates services to Africa, Europe, the Middle East and Asia; Man. Dir CHRISTO ROODT.

**Uganda Airlines Corporation:** Airways House, 6 Colville St, POB 5740, Kampala; tel. (41) 232990; telex 61239; fax (41) 257279; f. 1976; state-owned; scheduled cargo and passenger services to Africa and Europe; scheduled cargo and passenger domestic services; Chair. Dr EZRA SURUMA (acting); Gen. Man. BENEDICT MUTYABA.

## Tourism

Uganda's principal attractions for tourists are the forests, lakes and wildlife (including gorillas) and a good year-round climate. A programme to revive the tourist industry by building or improving hotels and creating new national parks was undertaken during the late 1980s. In 1993 visa requirements were abolished for visitors from a number of European, Asian and American countries in an effort to encourage tourism. An estimated 90,000 tourists reportedly visited Uganda in 1993/94 (compared with 12,786 in 1983). Revenue from tourism in 1992 was estimated at US $10m.

**Ministry of Tourism, Wildlife and Antiquities:** Parliament Ave, POB 4241, Kampala; tel. (41) 232971; telex 62218; provides some tourist information.

**Uganda Tourist Board:** Parliament Ave, POB 7211, Kampala; tel. (41) 242196; telex 61150; fax (41) 242188; promotes tourism and co-ordinates investment in the sector; Gen. Man. ELI K. KAGGANZI.

# UKRAINE

## Introductory Survey

### Location, Climate, Language, Religion, Flag, Capital

The Republic of Ukraine (formerly the Ukrainian Soviet Socialist Republic) is situated in east-central Europe. It is bordered by Poland, Slovakia, Hungary, Romania and Moldova to the west, by Belarus to the north and by the Russian Federation to the north-east and east. To the south lie the Black Sea and the Sea of Azov. The climate is temperate, especially in the south. The north and north-west share many of the continental climatic features of Poland or Belarus, but the Black Sea coast is noted for its mild winters. Droughts are not infrequent in southern areas. Average temperatures in Kiev range from −6.1°C (21°F) in January to 20.4°C (69°F) in July. Average annual rainfall in Kiev is 615 mm. The official state language is Ukrainian, an Eastern Slavonic language written in the Cyrillic script. Most of the population are adherents of Christianity, the major denominations being the Ukrainian Orthodox Church (Moscow Patriarchy), the Ukrainian Orthodox Church (Kievan Patriarchy) and the Roman Catholic Church (mostly Greek Catholics, followers of the Uniate or Eastern rite). There are also a number of Protestant churches, and small communities of Jews and Muslims. The national flag (proportions 3 by 2) has two equal horizontal stripes, of blue over yellow. The capital is Kiev (Kyiv).

### Recent History

The original Russian state, Kievan Rus, was based in what is now Ukraine, and is claimed as the precursor of Russia, Belarus and Ukraine. Following the fall of the Rus principalities, in the 13th and 14th centuries, during the Mongol invasions, the Ukrainians (sometimes known as Little Russians or Ruthenians) developed distinctively from the other Eastern Slavs, mainly under Polish and Lithuanian rulers. Ukrainians first entered the Russian Empire in 1654, when a Cossack state east of the Dniepr river sought Russian protection from Polish invasion. In 1667 Ukraine was divided: the regions east of the Dniepr became part of Russia, while Western Ukraine was annexed by Poland. Russia gained more Ukrainian lands as a result of subsequent partitions of Poland (1793 and 1795); the western regions were acquired by Austria.

When the Russian Empire collapsed, in 1917, Ukrainian nationalists set up a central Rada (council or soviet) in Kiev and demanded Ukrainian autonomy from the Provisional Government in Petrograd (St Petersburg). After the Bolshevik coup, in October 1917, the Rada proclaimed a Ukrainian People's Republic. Although they initially recognized the new republic, in December the Bolsheviks established a rival Government in Kharkiv (Kharkov), and by February 1918, after a two-month military offensive, almost the whole of Ukraine was occupied by Soviet forces. One month later, however, the Bolsheviks were forced to cede Ukraine to Germany, under the terms of the Treaty of Brest-Litovsk. Ukraine was the battleground for much of the fighting in the Civil War over the next two years, but in December 1920 a Ukrainian Soviet Socialist Republic (SSR) was established.

The Treaty of Riga, which formally ended the Soviet–Polish War in 1921, assigned Western Ukraine to Poland, Czechoslovakia and Romania, while eastern and central lands formed the Ukrainian SSR. The Ukrainian SSR was one of the founding members of the Union of Soviet Socialist Republics (USSR), in December 1922. The 1920s were a period of national development for Ukrainians: the use of the Ukrainian language was encouraged, literacy improved and the New Economic Policy (NEP) gave the peasants a certain measure of prosperity. However, the end of the NEP, in 1928, and the introduction of collectivization of agriculture, had severe consequences for the republic. Collectivization resulted in famine, in which an estimated 7m. Ukrainians died (although figures are disputed). The repressive policies of Stalin (who emerged as the Soviet leader in the late 1920s) were also particularly severe in Ukraine. The initial aim of Stalin's policies was to end the Ukrainian national revival, which had occurred in the 1920s. Advocates of the wider use of the Ukrainian language, or of greater autonomy for the republic, were labelled 'bourgeois nationalists' and arrested. By the late 1930s almost the entire Ukrainian cultural and political élite had been imprisoned, killed or exiled. Later the repressions widened to include people from all sectors of society.

The Second World War brought further suffering to Ukraine. Some 6m. Ukrainians are estimated to have died during the War and material losses were great. Soviet victory in the War did, however, unite the western and eastern areas of Ukraine, and in 1954 the territory was further expanded by the inclusion of Crimea (formerly part of the Russian Federation), whose Tatar inhabitants had been deported *en masse* to Soviet Central Asia, in 1944.

During the 1960s there was an increase in covert opposition to the regime, manifested in the production of independent publications, known as *samizdat* (self-publishing). In 1972, however, there was widespread repression of dissidents and a purge of the membership of the ruling Communist Party of Ukraine (CPU). In 1973 Petr Shelest, First Secretary (leader) of the CPU, who had been accused of tolerating dissent in the republic, was replaced by Vladimir Shcherbitsky, a loyal ally of the Soviet leader, Leonid Brezhnev. He remained in power until 1989.

The accession of Mikhail Gorbachev to the Soviet leadership, in 1985, had little initial effect in Ukraine. The reforms which he advocated were seldom implemented in Ukraine during Shcherbitsky's rule, despite the latter's avowed support for the concept of *perestroika* (restructuring). Dissidents were still harassed by the police, independent political and cultural groups were refused legal status, and the republican media remained under the strict control of the CPU.

On 26 April 1986 a serious explosion occurred at the Chornobyl nuclear power station, in northern Ukraine. Large amounts of radioactivity leaked into the atmosphere, but information on the accident and its consequences was strictly controlled by the authorities. Only after foreign scientists reported the unusually high levels of radiation in other European countries did Soviet officials admit the full extent of the damage. Thirty-one people were killed in the initial explosion and perhaps thousands more died from acute radiation sickness. A 50-km (30-mile) exclusion zone was created around Chornobyl, from which 135,000 people were evacuated, but other affected areas were not evacuated, and increased numbers of cancers and other related illnesses were reported throughout a large area. (In April 1995 it was reported that an estimated 125,000 people had died in Ukraine during 1988–94 from diseases contracted as a result of the disaster.)

Reaction to the secrecy surrounding the Chornobyl accident led to greater public support for opposition movements in Ukraine, which were also inspired by events elsewhere in the USSR, notably the success of the popular fronts (nationalist opposition groups) in the Baltic republics of Estonia, Latvia and Lithuania. In November 1988 the Ukrainian People's Movement for Restructuring (known as Rukh) was founded in the capital, Kiev, by a group of prominent writers and intellectuals. Despite official opposition, Rukh's manifesto was published in February 1989, and local branches were established throughout the republic. In 1989 the other major political force opposing the Government was the independent workers' movement, based in the mining communities of the Donbass area. Problems of housing, working conditions and food supply all contributed to a growing militancy, which produced 11 strikes in the first three months of the year.

Opposition also came from religious groups. The Ukrainian Catholic (Uniate) Church and the Ukrainian Autocephalous Orthodox Church began campaigns for official recognition in 1989. In May Ukrainian Catholics began a hunger strike in Moscow; in September 150,000 Catholics marched through Lviv (Lvov) demanding legalization; in late October Catholics took over the Church of the Transfiguration in Lviv and held public services. Legalization was eventually granted when Mikhail Gorbachev met Pope John Paul II in December.

The failure of Shcherbitsky to control the growing influence of Rukh, or to cope with the outbreak of worker unrest in mid-1989, led to his dismissal in September. Volodymyr Ivashko was elected as his replacement. Although the new leadership of the CPU began negotiations towards legalizing Rukh in late 1989, it was not registered until February 1990, after the date for nominations for the local and republican elections scheduled for 4 March. Nevertheless, candidates supported by the Democratic Bloc, a coalition of Rukh and other groups with similar aims, won 108 of the 450 seats in the Ukrainian Supreme Soviet (legislature). Independents supported by the Bloc won about 60 seats, giving the opposition parties up to 170 votes in the new Supreme Soviet, with an estimated 280 supporting the CPU leadership. The Bloc was particularly successful in western Ukraine and in urban areas (Rukh supporters took control of the city soviets of Lviv and Kiev), but performed poorly in the Russian-speaking communities of eastern Ukraine and in rural regions.

In June 1990 Ivashko was elected Chairman of the Supreme Soviet (the highest state post in the republic). In response to protests by deputies of the Democratic Bloc, who asserted that the Chairman of the Supreme Soviet should not also be the CPU leader, he resigned later in the month as First Secretary of the party and was replaced by his former deputy, Stanislav Hurenko. On 16 July the Ukrainian Supreme Soviet adopted a declaration of sovereignty, which asserted the right of Ukraine to have a national army and security forces, and proclaimed the supremacy of republican authority on the territory of the republic. Also in July Ivashko resigned as Chairman of the Supreme Soviet, after his appointment as Deputy General Secretary of the Communist Party of the Soviet Union (CPSU). The new Chairman of the Supreme Soviet was Leonid Kravchuk, hitherto Second Secretary of the CPU.

In October 1990 Vitaliy Masol was forced to resign as Chairman of the Council of Ministers after protest marches by up to 100,000 students in Kiev, some of whom were also on hunger strike. The Supreme Soviet also agreed to meet many of the students' political demands. In November Vitold Fokin was elected to succeed Masol. Fokin was seen as a compromise candidate who could unite the opposition and liberal communists behind a programme of economic reforms. Despite Rukh's support for independence, the Government participated in negotiations on a new union treaty and signed the protocol to a draft treaty in March 1991. The Government also agreed to conduct the all-Union referendum on the future of the USSR, but added an additional question to the ballot paper, asking voters if they agreed that Ukraine's 1990 declaration of sovereignty should form the basis for participation in a renewed federation. Of those eligible to vote, 84% participated in the referendum, 70% of whom approved Gorbachev's proposal to preserve the USSR as a 'renewed federation'. However, Ukraine's own question received greater support (80%), and an additional question in Western Ukraine (Lviv, Ternopil and Ivano-Frankivsk regions), which asked voters if they supported a fully independent Ukraine, gained the support of 90% of those voting.

Despite the apparent support for the preservation of some sort of union demonstrated in the March referendum, demands for full implementation of Ukraine's declaration of sovereignty increased during the next few months. Separatist parties such as the Ukrainian Republican Party and the Ukrainian Peasant Democratic Party advocated full independence, acquired by parliamentary means. More radical groups, many of which united in the Ukrainian Interparty Assembly, denied the legality of Ukraine's incorporation into the USSR and advocated the restoration of the Ukrainian People's Republic of 1918–19. Its parties did not recognize Soviet institutions; instead they recognized the Ukrainian government-in-exile, based in the USA. Meanwhile, within the CPU signs of growing differences emerged between the so-called 'national communists', led by Leonid Kravchuk, who supported moves towards greater independence, and the 'imperial communists', who remained committed to the USSR.

When the State Committee for the State of Emergency (SCSE) attempted to stage a *coup d'état* in Moscow, on 19 August 1991, there was an initially cautious response from the Ukrainian leadership. A declaration, which effectively denounced the SCSE, was adopted by the Presidium of the Ukrainian Supreme Soviet on 20 August, but opposition leaders protested that the leadership had been indecisive in its response. The collapse of the coup and the subsequent banning of the CPU led to significant changes in the politics of Ukraine. On 24 August the Supreme Soviet adopted a declaration of independence, pending confirmation by a referendum on 1 December, when direct presidential elections were also scheduled.

Despite his past record as a loyal communist official, Kravchuk's experience and support for Ukrainian independence ensured his election as President of the Republic on 1 December 1991. He was aided by the divided opposition, which nominated five candidates from the different factions. Kravchuk won 62% of the votes cast. His closest rival, with 23%, was Vyacheslav Chornovil, a former dissident and the leader of the radical Lviv regional council. The declaration of independence was overwhelmingly approved. Some 84% of the electorate took part in the referendum, of which 90% voted in favour of independence. The approval of the independence declaration was followed by measures aimed at consolidating independence, including the establishment of Ukrainian armed forces in early December and the formal adoption of new national symbols in early 1992. Kravchuk's victory in the presidential election divided the opposition, in particular Rukh, between those prepared to support Kravchuk and more radical groups who resented his past status as a CPU leader.

In June 1992 the Government narrowly avoided defeat in a vote of 'no confidence' in the Supreme Council (as the Supreme Soviet was now known), proposed by the New Ukraine group of deputies, which had been established in January to promote radical economic reforms. There was further criticism of Vitold Fokin and his Government in early July after the decision to free prices on foodstuffs (which had been excluded from the initial withdrawal of subsidies in January). The Government finally resigned in late September, after being heavily defeated in a second vote of 'no confidence', and in mid-October Leonid Kuchma, hitherto manager of a missiles factory, was appointed the new Prime Minister. The Supreme Council also approved a new Government, which included several members of Rukh and New Ukraine; advocates of market-orientated economic reform were appointed to the main ministries related to economic policy. Despite the appointment of the new, apparently reformist Government, radical student groups continued demonstrations which they had begun in early October. The demonstrators demanded immediate elections to the Supreme Council and the withdrawal of Ukraine from the Commonwealth of Independent States (CIS, which Ukraine and 10 other former Soviet republics had co-founded in December 1991, see below). Several students began a hunger strike when their demands were rejected by President Kravchuk, but the protests ended shortly afterwards, owing to divisions within the student movement.

In November 1992 the Supreme Council granted Prime Minister Kuchma special powers to rule by decree for a period of six months, in order to combat the worsening economic situation. He proposed an extensive programme of economic reform, including 'privatization', severe reductions in government expenditure and a strict policy against corruption. The Government's actions won widespread support from most centrist and right-wing political parties, but were strongly opposed by the Socialist Party of Ukraine (SPU), which had been formed from elements of the CPU, and other left-wing groups. The SPU and communist groups began a campaign in December to rescind the ban on the CPU, imposed in August 1991. In response, in February 1993 30 political parties and organizations, led by Rukh and the Congress of National Democratic Forces (CNDF), formed the Anti-Communist and Anti-Imperialist Front to campaign against the restoration of legal status to the CPU and in favour of the dissolution of the Supreme Council and the holding of new elections.

As the economic situation worsened, disputes concerning economic policy dominated domestic politics in early 1993. President Kravchuk's initial support for Prime Minister Kuchma appeared to have weakened by March, when Kravchuk strongly opposed the Government's budget proposals, criticizing in particular the effect on low-income families. Later in March Ihor Yukhnovsky, the First Deputy Prime Minister and a leading reformer, resigned, allegedly in response to the failure of President Kravchuk to support strong measures against corruption and the lack of support for government policies in the conservative-dominated Supreme Council. In the following month another key reformist in the Government, Viktor Pynzenyk, was divested of responsibility for economic reform, although he remained as a Deputy Prime Minister.

The growing conflict between the President, the Prime Minister and the Supreme Council culminated in a constitutional crisis in May 1993, when the Supreme Council, increasingly dissatisfied with the Government's economic austerity programme, refused to renew the special powers granted to Prime Minister Kuchma in November 1992. Kuchma offered to resign, and President Kravchuk requested special constitutional powers to enable him to head the Government himself. Although urged by the President to accept Kuchma's resignation, the legislature subsequently rejected it, apparently fearing that presidential rule would lessen the powers of the Supreme Council. The crisis deepened in June, when more than 2m. miners and factory workers, mainly in the Donbass region, joined a strike in protest against the declining standard of living and further sharp price increases. They also demanded a referendum of confidence in the President and in the Supreme Council; following the Council's acceptance of this demand, a plebiscite was scheduled for 26 September. A further concession was the appointment to the post of First Deputy Prime Minister of Yukhym Zvyahilsky, the Mayor of Donetsk, who reportedly enjoyed widespread popularity in the Donbass region.

The resignation, in August 1993, of Viktor Pynzenyk as Deputy Prime Minister, marked the departure from the Government of the last true advocate of Kuchma's economic reforms. In the following month Kuchma himself again tendered his resignation as Prime Minister, stating that the constant obstruction by the Supreme Council had made his reform programme impracticable. His resignation was this time accepted by the legislature. Yukhym Zvyahilsky was appointed to the vacant post, although after several days Kravchuk assumed direct control of the Government. The referendum that had been scheduled for 26 September was cancelled; instead, it was announced that early elections to a new Supreme Council would be held in March 1994. A new electoral law was duly approved by the legislature in November.

The elections to the new Supreme Council were held on 27 March 1994, with the unexpectedly high participation of some 76% of the electorate. However, in only 49 of the total 450 single-member constituencies did candidates secure more than 50% of the votes necessary for election. Thus a second round of voting was held, on 2–3 April and 9–10 April, with about 70% of the electorate participating. The result represented an overwhelming victory for communist and left-wing parties, as well as independent candidates. The CPU (which, pending the outcome of parliamentary discussions on its proposed relegalization, had been permitted to contest the elections) won the largest share of the seats (86). With its allied parties, the SPU and the Peasants' Party of Ukraine (which won 14 and 18 seats, respectively), the CPU was able to form the most powerful bloc in the Supreme Council, as had been the case in the outgoing parliament. However, the 170 seats won by candidates not declaring any party affiliation seemed likely to prove a decisive factor in the future workings of the Council. Rukh gained only 20 seats in the Council, with other moderate nationalist parties winning a combined total of 13. Liberal parties gained a representation of only nine seats; these included Kuchma's Inter-regional Bloc for Reform, which obtained five seats. The result of the election appeared to confirm the existence of a political division between eastern Ukraine (whose largely Russian population voted for left-wing, pro-Russian parties) and the west of the country (where moderate Ukrainian nationalist parties won the largest share of the votes). Nevertheless, 112 of the Council's seats remained unfilled, the contests for these seats having been declared invalid. Despite further rounds of voting, in July, August and November, 45 seats in the Council remained unfilled. In late May Oleksandr Moroz, the leader of the SPU, was elected Chairman of the Supreme Council.

In June 1994 Vitaliy Masol (the premier between 1987 and 1990) was elected to be the new Prime Minister. A minor government reshuffle followed at the end of the month, in which, *inter alia*, two Deputy Prime Ministers were removed from the Cabinet of Ministers. A direct presidential election, held on 26 June 1994 (with the participation of some 70% of the electorate), proved inconclusive, as none of the seven candidates secured the minimum 50% of the votes necessary for election. In a second round of voting, held on 10 July between the two most successful candidates in the first ballot, Kuchma was elected President, securing 52% of the votes cast, while Kravchuk gained 45%. The election result demonstrated the same distinct polarity in voting patterns that had been identifiable in the parliamentary elections of March: voters in eastern Ukraine largely supported Kuchma, who advocated closer economic and industrial ties with Russia and the CIS, while Kravchuk, who emphasized Ukraine's independence from Russia, secured a majority of the votes in western Ukraine. In October Pynzenyk was restored to the Cabinet of Ministers, as First Deputy Prime Minister with responsibility for economic reform. In the same month the Supreme Council voted to relegalize the CPU; owing to an alleged irregularity in the voting, however, a second ballot was held in November, when the majority of votes required to rescind the ban on the CPU was not achieved.

In March 1995 Masol resigned as Prime Minister, allegedly as a result of differences of opinion with President Kuchma over economic policy; he was replaced, in an acting capacity, by Yevhen Marchuk, hitherto Deputy Prime Minister and Chairman of the State Security Service. In April, however, the Supreme Council expressed a vote of 'no confidence' in the Cabinet of Ministers; the vote was not recognized by Kuchma. In late May, having repeatedly failed to persuade the Supreme Council to grant him broader executive powers, President Kuchma ordered a referendum of confidence in the President and the legislature to be held. The Supreme Council, fearing an outcome demonstrating widespread support for Kuchma, vetoed the President's decree, following which Kuchma revoked the Council's veto. Finally, in early June, the constitutional impasse appeared to have been resolved, when the President and the Supreme Council signed a 'constitutional agreement', according to which the proposed referendum was cancelled but Kuchma's presidential authority was strengthened. The agreement was to remain in force until the completion of the new Ukrainian Constitution (expected by late 1995), which would determine at last the division of state powers. Following the agreement, Kuchma confirmed that Marchuk would remain as Prime Minister; however, a major government reshuffle was initiated in July.

In May 1995, during a visit to Ukraine by President Clinton of the USA, President Kuchma announced that the Chornobyl nuclear power station was to be closed by the year 2000, although he stressed that financial aid would be required to construct a replacement energy source.

Although Ukraine did not experience the inter-ethnic violence that occurred in some other Soviet republics in the late 1980s and early 1990s, the ethnic diversity of the population caused serious political problems. In Crimea, which was part of the Russian Federation until 1954 and has a significant Russian majority (approximately 70% of the peninsula's population), there was considerable opposition to Ukrainian independence. The situation was further complicated by the desire of the Crimean Tatars to return to their homeland, from which they had been forcibly deported in 1944. In a referendum, on 20 January 1991, residents of Crimea voted to restore the region to the status of an autonomous republic. The decision, although it had no legal basis in existing Soviet law, was ratified by the Ukrainian legislature. The referendum was opposed by the Crimean Tatars, who claimed an exclusive right for the indigenous peoples to vote; they also opposed the movement for autonomy as led by the local Russian-dominated communist party, which, they claimed, sought to prevent 'Ukrainianization' and the influx of Tatars. Following the decision of the Russian Federation in January 1992 to re-examine the status of the transfer of Crimea to Ukraine in 1954, the Ukrainian parliament declared that this contravened a number of treaties, including one on the formation of the CIS. In February 1992 the Crimean Supreme Soviet voted to transform the region from an autonomous republic into the Republic of Crimea. Despite subsequent offers by the Ukrainian authorities for broader self-governing powers for Crimea, in May the Crimean legislature declared Crimea an independent state, also adopting a new Crimean Constitution, which confirmed the territory's independence. However, two weeks later, after the Ukrainian Supreme Council threatened to impose an economic blockade on Crimea as well as direct rule, the independence declaration was rescinded. In June the Ukrainian authorities confirmed Crimea's status as an autonomous republic. Meanwhile, relations between the local leadership and Crimean Tatars, some 250,000 of whom had returned to their homeland by late 1992, deteriorated steadily. In October a Tatar encampment was dispersed on the orders of the Crimean Government, and in response some 6,000 Tatars stormed the Crimean parliament building.

With the election of Yury Meshkov (an ethnic Russian and the leader of the Republican Party of Crimea) as President of Crimea in January 1994, it appeared likely that the region would renew moves towards sovereignty, as well as closer links with Russia. In response, the Ukrainian legislature approved constitutional amendments, according to which the Ukrainian President could nullify any measures taken by the Crimean authorities which he deemed to be illegal. In late March a referendum was held in Crimea, simultaneously with the nation-wide legislative elections; 70% of those voting in the referendum were in support of even broader autonomous powers for Crimea. The crisis deepened in May, when the Crimean parliament voted overwhelmingly to restore the suspended Crimean Constitution of May 1992, effectively a declaration of the peninsula's independence. This development was denounced by the Ukrainian Government, which ordered the Crimean legislature to rescind its decision within 10 days. By early June the crisis appeared to have been defused: delegations from the Ukrainian and Crimean parliaments met in Simferopol, the Crimean capital, where it was agreed that Crimea would continue to be subject to Ukrainian law.

In August 1994, the Crimean city of Sevastopol, base to the disputed former Soviet Black Sea Fleet, unilaterally declared itself to be part of the territory of the Russian Federation. Fears that increased tension between Ukraine and Russia might ensue were allayed by Russia's decision not to recognize the declaration. In September, following disputes over the drafting of a new Crimean Constitution, the Crimean legislature voted to restrict President Meshkov's executive authority, in response to which Meshkov suspended parliament. The crisis was apparently averted later in the month, when the Crimean parliament was reconvened. Meanwhile, the Ukrainian Supreme Council approved a constitutional amendment, permitting it to nullify legislation adopted by the Crimean parliament, which contravened the Ukrainian Constitution. In March 1995 the Ukrainian legislature voted to abolish both the Crimean Constitution of May 1992 and the Crimean presidency. In April President Kuchma announced that subsequent appointments to the Crimean leadership were to be subject to the consent of the Ukrainian President, and the Ukrainian Supreme Council debated draft legislation to dissolve the Crimean parliament. Later in the same month Kuchma declared illegal a decision by the Crimean parliament to hold a referendum in Crimea on the issue of the 1992 Constitution. However, the referendum, scheduled for late June 1995, did not, in fact, take place.

Other problems were experienced in the eastern Donbass region, where Russians were also dominant. Although there was no strong movement for secession, there was support for some autonomy for the region, with discussion on the reinstatement of the short-lived Donetsk-Kryvyi Rih (Krivoi Rog) Republic of 1918. In the western region of Transcarpathia, which had formed parts of Czechoslovakia and Hungary before the Second World War, the independence referendum of 1 December 1991 included a separate question on the introduction of autonomous status for the region. Demands for the establishment of a Transcarpathian Autonomous Republic have been made especially strongly by the Society of Carpathian Ruthenians (Rusyns), who consider themselves ethnically distinct from Ukrainians. In March 1992 they established the Subcarpathian Republican Party.

Following the approval of independence in the referendum of 1 December 1991, many states indicated that they would recognize Ukraine and establish diplomatic relations. Poland, Hungary and Canada were the first to do so; other states, including the USA, initially expressed reluctance to extend recognition until the Ukrainian Government could clarify its policies on nuclear weapons and on its ethnic minorities. Ukraine's cause was helped by its existing membership of the UN (granted after the Second World War, effectively to allow the USSR more voting rights).

The Ukrainian leadership was reluctant to sign any union agreement with the other former Soviet republics which might compromise its declaration of independence. Although Ukraine eventually signed a treaty to establish an economic community, on 6 November 1991, it refused to enter any new political union, such as the proposed Union of Sovereign States. Instead, on 8 December, in Minsk (Belarus), together with the leaders of the Russian Federation and Belarus, President Kravchuk agreed to establish the Commonwealth of Independent States (CIS, see p. 126), which would have very limited central powers. On 21 December 11 of the former republics of the USSR formally committed themselves to membership of the CIS. However, there were considerable difficulties over the details of the agreements, particularly in relation to the armed forces. Ukraine had reluctantly agreed to a unified command for those former Soviet forces that were termed 'strategic', but began establishing its own conventional armed forces. The major controversy between Ukraine and Russia concerned the status of the former Soviet Black Sea Fleet, based in Sevastopol in Crimea. In January 1992 both Ukraine and Russia claimed the fleet. Shortly afterwards, an initial agreement between Ukraine and Russia to divide the fleet was abrogated, owing to political pressure from nationalist groups in both countries. Although both states agreed in July to exercise joint control over the fleet for a transitional period of three years, subsequent negotiations between Presidents Yeltsin and Kravchuk over the eventual division of the fleet made no progress. The two Presidents met again in April 1994, following the seizure of one of the fleet's vessels by pro-Russian sailors, which had led to retaliation by Ukrainian army elements against Russian naval bases. When the crisis had been resolved, the two leaders agreed to new proposals for the eventual division of the fleet; the agreement, however, was abandoned shortly thereafter. In August the Ukrainian leadership reiterated its former proposal to divide the fleet, but to retain a joint base. The Russian parliament imposed a moratorium, however, in April 1995, on plans to divide the fleet. Nevertheless, in June a breakthrough appeared to have been reached, when Presidents Yeltsin and Kuchma agreed to the equal division of the fleet, with separate Ukrainian and Russian bases. The main Russian base was to be at Sevastopol, although the exact legal status of the city was left unresolved. It was widely believed that the agreement on the Black Sea Fleet would prepare the way for the signing of the long-delayed Russian-Ukrainian treaty of friendship and co-operation.

Relations with Russia were further undermined by disagreements on the future of the CIS, nuclear weapons and economic policy. Ukraine refused to sign the CIS charter on closer political and economic co-operation, agreed by seven other CIS members in January 1993, claiming that it was a threat to Ukraine's independent status. Fears for the security of Ukrainian statehood were also fuelled by the spread of pro-Russian sentiments among the predominantly Russian-populated areas of eastern Ukraine. Partly in response to continued tension in its relations with Russia, Ukraine delayed ratification of the first Strategic Arms Reduction Treaty (START I), according to which Ukraine was to transfer all nuclear weapons on its territory to Russia. Relations with the USA and other Western countries were damaged by Ukraine's apparent reluctance to ratify START I, although Ukraine insisted that it had no intention of remaining a nuclear state in the long term. Despite the fact that in May 1992 Ukraine had signed the Lisbon Protocol to START I (committing it to future ratification and implementation of the treaty), during 1993 it appeared that many deputies in the Supreme Council were intent on delaying ratification for as long a period as possible, in order to gain significant concessions, including economic assistance, from western countries. In January 1994, however, a trilateral agreement on the denuclearization of Ukraine was signed by Ukraine, Russia and the USA, and in November the Supreme Council voted to ratify the Treaty on the Non-Proliferation of Nuclear Weapons (see p. 68). In December President Kuchma formally signed the treaty after receiving detailed security guarantees from other nuclear states, including Russia and the USA, and START I entered into force. (The Supreme Council had voted to ratify START I in February 1994.) In March 1995 Kuchma announced that the transfer of the country's nuclear weapons to Russia would be completed by 1997.

## Government

Executive power is vested in the President and the Prime Minister, while legislative power is the prerogative of the 450-member Supreme Council. The President is elected by direct, popular vote for a mandate of five years. The President appoints the Prime Minister and the members of the Cabinet of Ministers, but all appointments must be approved by the Supreme Council. Ukraine is a unitary state, divided for administrative purposes into 24 regions, one autonomous republic (Crimea), and one metropolitan area (Kiev).

**Defence**

In December 1991 the Ukrainian Supreme Council adopted legislation which established independent Ukrainian armed forces. In June 1994 there were an estimated 517,000 active personnel in the Ukrainian armed forces, including 308,000 ground forces, 146,000 in the air force and air defence forces and an estimated 16,000 in the navy. There were an additional 66,000 paramilitary forces, of which 23,000 were serving in the National Guard and 43,000 in the border guard. Active personnel in other units numbered 47,000. Military service is compulsory for males over 18 years of age, for a period of 18 months. Projected defence expenditure for 1994 was 16,823,000m. karbovantsi.

Although Ukraine permitted the transfer of tactical nuclear weapons to Russian territory in 1992, it retains strategic nuclear weapons on its territory, consisting, in June 1994, of 156 intercontinental ballistic missiles and 42 nuclear-armed bombers. Under the terms of the Lisbon Protocol to the first Strategic Arms Reduction Treaty (START I), signed by Ukraine, Belarus and Kazakhstan in 1992, Ukraine is committed to the transfer of all nuclear weapons on its territory to the Russian Federation. Ukraine ratified START I in early 1994, and in December signed the Treaty on the Non-Proliferation of Nuclear Weapons (the Non-Proliferation Treaty—see p. 68). In the same year it also joined NATO's 'partnership for peace' programme (see p. 192).

**Economic Affairs**

In 1993, according to preliminary estimates by the World Bank, Ukraine's gross national product (GNP), measured at average 1991–93 prices, was US $99,677m., equivalent to $1,910 per head. During 1985–93, it was estimated, GNP per head declined, in real terms, at an average rate of 3.9% per year. Over the same period the population increased by an annual average of 0.3%. Gross domestic product (GDP) declined by 17%, in real terms, in 1993, compared with the previous year, and by a further 23% in 1994.

Agriculture (including fishing) contributed 22.5% of net material product (NMP) in 1992, and provided 20.8% of employment in 1993. Ukraine has large areas of extremely fertile land, forming part of the 'black earth' belt, and the country is self-sufficient in almost all aspects of agricultural production. The principal crops are grain, sugar beets, potatoes and other vegetables. Slightly more than 50% of agricultural activity is accounted for by animal husbandry. A programme to transfer state collective farms to private ownership was initiated in 1991, although by January 1995 only some 1.5m. ha of land had been affected. In 1994 agricultural production declined by 17%, compared with 1993.

Industry (including mining) contributed some 50.7% of NMP in 1992. In the following year the sector provided 30.0% of employment. Heavy industry dominates the sector, particularly metalworking, mechanical engineering, chemicals, and machinery products (including locomotives, railway equipment, tractors, motor cars and machine tools). Defence-related industrial activity, traditionally important, is currently being converted to non-military production. In 1994 industrial production declined by 28%, compared with 1993.

Ukraine has large deposits of coal (mainly in the huge Donbass coal basin) and high-grade iron ore, and there are also reserves of manganese, natural gas and petroleum. Although Ukraine is self-sufficient in coal, the economy's dependence on heavy industry necessitates substantial imports of other energy products (in particular petroleum and natural gas from Russia and Turkmenistan). Imports of mineral fuels comprised 52% of the value of total imports in 1994. Ukraine has five nuclear power stations, and in 1994 nuclear power accounted for an estimated 34% of electricity generation. However, following the accident at the Chornobyl station in 1986 (see Recent History), the viability of the country's nuclear power programme has been called into question. In 1994 some 60% of electricity generation was provided by thermal power stations, while hydro-electric stations supplied 6%.

In 1994 Ukraine recorded a trade surplus of US $114.7m. In that year the principal markets for exports were Russia (39%), Belarus, China and Moldova (each about 5%), and the USA and Switzerland (both about 3%). The principal sources of imports were Russia (59%), Turkmenistan (7%), Germany (6%), and Belarus and Switzerland (both about 3%). In 1990 the principal exports were machinery and metal goods, ferrous and non-ferrous materials, petrochemicals, coal, food, and consumer goods. The principal imports were machines and metal products, light industrial goods, chemicals, food, and energy requirements.

In 1994 there was a budgetary deficit of 109,000,000m. karbovantsi (9.6% of GDP), while the 1995 budget projected a deficit of 300,000,000m. karbovantsi (approximately 7.3% of GDP). In late 1991 Ukraine was assigned 16.4% (some US $10,000m.) of the former USSR's total external debt. At the beginning of 1995 Ukraine's external debt amounted to US $7,100m. The estimated average annual rate of inflation in 1992 was 1,210%, rising to 4,735% in 1993; in 1994 consumer prices increased by 842%, according to IMF sources, and by 501%, according to government sources. In early 1995 some 85,500 people were registered as unemployed (some 0.3% of the labour force), although a considerable number of people were believed to be working reduced hours or taking enforced unpaid leave from work.

Ukraine became a member of the IMF and the World Bank in 1992. It also joined the European Bank for Reconstruction and Development (see p. 140) as a 'Country of Operations'. In June 1994 Ukraine signed an agreement of partnership and co-operation with the EU.

As a result of the highly centralized structure of the USSR's economy, Ukraine, like other former Soviet republics following independence, had insufficient institutional infrastructure of its own necessary to administer its economic affairs effectively, let alone implement the planned transition to a market economic system. Economic development was further hampered by the extensive disruptions in the former Soviet trading system, as well as by disagreements between the Government, the legislature and President Kravchuk concerning the nature and extent of economic reform. Output declined in all sectors during 1991–93 and the economic crisis deepened, aggravated by the country's inability to secure all its energy requirements. In the latter year inflation increased drastically, and there were outbreaks of labour unrest.

In connection with the country's nascent market economic reform programme, legislation was adopted in early 1992 to permit the extensive privatization of state-owned property. Following the election of President Kuchma in July 1994, the reform programme was accelerated and extended after consultations with the IMF. The Government identified several key areas: price reform, the liberalization of regulations governing trade in order to strengthen export performance, a reduction in inflation to a monthly rate of 1% by the end of 1995, and a budgetary deficit for 1995 restricted to 7.3% of GDP. In addition, more than 30,000 enterprises were to be transferred to the private sector in 1995 (including some 8,000 large- and medium-sized companies), and it was proposed that 90% of agricultural land be eventually privatized. In April 1995 the IMF approved a loan of US $1,960m. to support the economic reform programme.

Concerned at the inflationary and other effects of remaining within the rouble area, the Government replaced the rouble, in November 1992, with a temporary coupon currency (karbovanets), which was due to be replaced by a permanent currency (the hryvnya) in the second half of 1995.

**Social Welfare**

During the Soviet period a comprehensive state-funded social welfare system was introduced. In 1991, with the progressive devolution of centralized Soviet power, followed by Ukraine's declaration of independence (in August), certain changes were made in the system. These included the creation of three extrabudgetary funds, the Pension Fund, the Social Insurance Fund and the Employment Fund, which were to administer most of Ukraine's social security activities, while an extensive programme of family allowances and compensation for price increases was to be directly financed by the state budget.

In 1995, according to the Ukrainian Health Centre, the average life expectancy at birth was 69 years, and the rate of infant mortality was 17.2 per 1,000 live births in 1992. In 1989 there were, respectively, 44 physicians and 135 hospital beds per 10,000 inhabitants. The compulsory retirement age in Ukraine is 55 years for women and 60 years for men; in the early 1990s about 25% of the population was in receipt of a pension. In 1993 central government expenditure on education, health and other social and cultural services was expected to amount to 2,634,000m. roubles (29% of the total budget expenditure).

# UKRAINE

## Education

The reversal of perceived 'Russification' of the education system was one of the principal demands of the opposition movements which emerged in the late 1980s. In the period 1980–88 the proportion of pupils who were taught in Russian increased from 44.5% to 51.8%, while the proportion taught in Ukrainian decreased from 54.6% to 47.5%. After Ukrainian was decreed the state language, in 1990, policies were adopted to ensure that all pupils were granted the opportunity of tuition in Ukrainian. In 1988 there was also tuition in Romanian (0.6% of all school pupils), Hungarian (0.3%) and a small number of pupils were taught in Polish. In the early 1990s there were significant changes to the curriculum, with more emphasis on Ukrainian history and literature. Some religious and private educational institutions were established in 1990–91, including a private university, the Kiev Mihyla Academy, which had been one of Europe's leading educational establishments before 1917. In 1991 there were 890,192 students in higher education (including those on evening and correspondence courses).

## Public Holidays

**1995:** 1–2 January (New Year's Day), 7 January (Christmas), 8 March (International Women's Day), 1–2 May (Spring and Labour Day), 9 May (Victory Day), 24 August (Ukrainian Independence Day).

**1996:** 1–2 January (New Year's Day), 7 January (Christmas), 8 March (International Women's Day), 1–2 May (Spring and Labour Day), 9 May (Victory Day), 24 August (Ukrainian Independence Day).

## Weights and Measures

The metric system is in force.

# Statistical Survey

Principal sources (unless otherwise stated): IMF, *Ukraine, Economic Review* and *International Financial Statistics: Supplement on Countries of the Former Soviet Union*; World Bank, *Statistical Handbook: States of the Former USSR*.

## Area and Population

### AREA, POPULATION AND DENSITY

| | |
|---|---:|
| Area (sq km) | 603,700* |
| Population (census results) | |
| 17 January 1979 | 49,754,642 |
| 12 January 1989† | |
| Males | 23,959,000 |
| Females | 27,745,000 |
| Total | 51,704,000 |
| Population (official estimates at 1 January) | |
| 1991 | 51,944,000 |
| 1992 | 52,057,000 |
| Density (per sq km) at 1 January 1992 | 86.2 |

* 233,090 sq miles.
† Figures are provisional. The revised total is 51,706,742.

### POPULATION BY NATIONALITY
(permanent inhabitants, census of 12 January 1989)

| | '000 | % |
|---|---:|---:|
| Ukrainian | 37,419.1 | 72.7 |
| Russian | 11,355.6 | 22.1 |
| Jewish | 486.3 | 0.9 |
| Belarusian | 440.0 | 0.9 |
| Moldovan | 324.5 | 0.6 |
| Bulgarian | 233.8 | 0.5 |
| Polish | 219.2 | 0.4 |
| Hungarian | 163.1 | 0.3 |
| Romanian | 134.8 | 0.3 |
| Greek | 98.6 | 0.2 |
| Tatar | 86.9 | 0.2 |
| Roma (Gypsy) | 47.9 | 0.1 |
| Crimean Tatar | 46.8 | 0.1 |
| Armenian | 38.6 | 0.1 |
| Others | 356.8 | 0.7 |
| **Total** | **51,452.0** | **100.0** |

### ADMINISTRATIVE DIVISIONS

| | Area ('000 sq km) | Population ('000, 1 Jan. 1991) | Density (per sq km) |
|---|---:|---:|---:|
| **Regions*** | | | |
| Cherkasy (Cherkassy) | 20.9 | 1,530.9 | 73.2 |
| Chernihiv (Chernigov) | 31.9 | 938.6 | 44.1 |
| Chernivtsi (Chernovtsy) | 8.1 | 1,405.8 | 115.6 |
| Dnipropetrovsk (Dnepropetrovsk) | 31.9 | 3,908.7 | 122.5 |
| Donetsk | 26.5 | 5,346.7 | 201.8 |
| Ivano-Frankivsk (Ivano-Frankovsk) | 13.9 | 1,442.9 | 103.8 |
| Kharkiv (Kharkov) | 31.4 | 3,194.8 | 101.7 |
| Kherson | 28.5 | 1,258.7 | 44.2 |
| Khmelnytskyi (Khmelnitsky) | 20.6 | 1,520.6 | 73.8 |
| Kyiv (Kiev)† | 28.9 | 4,589.8 | 158.8 |
| Kirovohrad (Kirovograd) | 24.6 | 1,245.3 | 50.6 |
| Luhansk (Lugansk) | 26.7 | 2,871.1 | 107.5 |
| Lviv (Lvov) | 21.8 | 2,764.4 | 126.8 |
| Mikolaiv (Nikolayev) | 24.6 | 1,342.4 | 54.6 |
| Odesa (Odessa) | 33.3 | 2,635.3 | 79.1 |
| Poltava | 28.8 | 1,756.9 | 61.0 |
| Rivne (Rovno) | 20.1 | 1,176.8 | 58.5 |
| Sumy | 23.8 | 1,430.2 | 60.1 |
| Ternopil (Ternopol) | 13.8 | 1,175.1 | 85.2 |
| Transcarpathia | 12.8 | 1,265.9 | 98.9 |
| Vinnytsia (Vinnitsa) | 26.5 | 1,914.4 | 72.2 |
| Volyn (Volin) | 20.2 | 1,069.0 | 52.9 |
| Zaporizhzhia (Zaporozhye) | 27.2 | 2,099.6 | 77.2 |
| Zhytomyr (Zhitomir) | 29.9 | 1,510.7 | 50.5 |
| **Republic** | | | |
| Crimea | 27.0 | 2,549.8 | 94.4 |
| **Total** | **603.7** | **51,944.4** | **86.0** |

* With the exception of Crimea and Transcarpathia, the names of regions are given in Ukrainian, with the Russian version in brackets where it differs.
† Combines Kyiv metropolitan area and Kyiv region, although they are administered separately.

# UKRAINE

## Statistical Survey

### PRINCIPAL TOWNS*
(estimated population at 1 January 1992)

| Town | Population | Town | Population |
|---|---|---|---|
| Kyiv (Kiev, capital) | 2,643,000 | Chernihiv (Chernigov) | 311,000 |
| Kharkiv (Kharkov) | 1,662,000 | Cherkasy (Cherkassy) | 308,000 |
| Dnipropetrovsk (Dnepropetrovsk) | 1,190,000 | Sumy | 305,000 |
| Donetsk | 1,121,000 | Zhytomyr (Zhitomir) | 299,000 |
| Odesa (Odessa) | 1,096,000 | Dniprodzerzhynsk (Dneprodzerzhinsk) | 286,000 |
| Zaporizhzhia (Zaporozhye) | 898,000 | Kirovohrad (Kirovograd) | 280,000 |
| Lviv (Lvov) | 807,000 | Chernivtsi (Chernovtsy) | 261,000 |
| Kryvyi Rih (Krivoi Rog) | 729,000 | Khemelnytskyi (Khmelnitsky) | 250,000 |
| Mariupol† | 523,000 | Kremenchug | 245,000 |
| Mikolaiv (Nikolayev) | 515,000 | Rivne (Rovno) | 244,000 |
| Luhansk (Lugansk)‡ | 505,000 | Ivano-Frankivsk (Ivano-Frankovsk) | 230,000 |
| Makayevka | 426,000 | Ternopil (Ternopol) | 225,000 |
| Vinnytsia (Vinnitsa) | 384,000 | Lutsk | 215,000 |
| Sevastopol | 371,000 | Bila Tserkva (Belaya Tserkov) | 209,000 |
| Kherson | 368,000 | Kramatorsk | 203,000 |
| Simferopol | 357,000 | | |
| Gorlovka | 336,000 | | |
| Poltava | 324,000 | | |

* As far as possible, the names of towns are given in transliterated Ukrainian, with the Russian version in brackets where it differs.
† Known as Zhdanov from 1948 to 1989.
‡ Known as Voroshilovgrad from 1935 to 1958 and from 1970 to 1989.

Source: UN, *Demographic Yearbook*.

### BIRTHS, MARRIAGES AND DEATHS (per 1,000)

| | Registered live births | | Registered marriages | | Registered deaths | |
|---|---|---|---|---|---|---|
| | Number | Rate (per 1,000) | Number | Rate (per 1,000) | Number | Rate (per 1,000) |
| 1988 | 744,056 | 14.5 | 455,770 | 8.9 | 600,725 | 11.7 |
| 1989 | 690,981 | 13.3 | 489,330 | 9.5 | 600,590 | 11.6 |
| 1990 | 657,202 | 12.7 | 482,753 | 9.3 | 629,602 | 12.1 |
| 1991 | 630,813 | 12.1 | 493,067 | 9.5 | 669,960 | 12.9 |
| 1992* | 500,233 | 9.6 | 344,433 | 6.6 | 570,900 | 11.0 |

* Provisional.

Source: UN, *Demographic Yearbook*.

**Expectation of Life** (years at birth, 1995): males 64; females 69 (Source: Ukrainian Health Centre).

### EMPLOYMENT (annual averages, '000 employees)

| | 1991 | 1992 | 1993 |
|---|---|---|---|
| Agriculture | 4,762 | 4,920 | 4,874 |
| Industry | 7,769 | 7,401 | 7,017 |
| Construction | 2,267 | 1,910 | 1,771 |
| Transport and communications | 1,774 | 1,623 | 1,604 |
| Trade and material services | 1,863 | 1,751 | 1,711 |
| Health and social services | 1,521 | 1,521 | 1,532 |
| Education and culture | 2,367 | 2,361 | 2,300 |
| Other activities | 2,654 | 2,498 | 2,618 |
| **Total** | **24,977** | **23,985** | **23,427** |

## Agriculture

### PRINCIPAL CROPS ('000 metric tons)

| | 1991 | 1992 | 1993 |
|---|---|---|---|
| Wheat | 21,155 | 19,507 | 21,831 |
| Barley | 8,047 | 10,106 | 13,550 |
| Maize | 4,747 | 2,851 | 3,786 |
| Rye | 982 | 1,158 | 1,180 |
| Oats | 945 | 1,246 | 1,479 |
| Millet | 338 | 226 | 294 |
| Other cereals | 494 | 454 | 605 |
| Potatoes | 14,550 | 20,277 | 21,009 |
| Dry peas | 1,782 | 2,776 | 2,731 |
| Sunflower seed | 2,448 | 2,127 | 2,075 |
| Cabbages | 1,299 | 1,221 | 1,273 |
| Tomatoes | 1,682 | 1,303 | 1,148 |
| Cucumbers and gherkins | 382 | 387 | 636 |
| Dry onions | 801 | 677 | 558 |
| Carrots | 322 | 322 | 414 |
| Watermelons, etc. | 766 | 246 | 314 |
| Grapes | 673 | 657 | 666 |
| Sugar beets | 36,168 | 28,783 | 33,717 |
| Apples | 798 | 1,148 | 1,774 |
| Pears | 118 | 199 | 233 |
| Plums | 256 | 250 | 224 |

Source: FAO, *Production Yearbook*.

### LIVESTOCK ('000 head at 1 January)

| | 1991 | 1992 | 1993 |
|---|---|---|---|
| Horses | 738 | 717 | 707 |
| Cattle | 24,623 | 23,728 | 22,457 |
| Pigs | 19,400 | 17,839 | 16,175 |
| Sheep | 7,332 | 7,259 | 6,597 |
| Goats | 523 | 570 | 640 |
| Poultry | 247,000 | 234,000 | 206,000 |

Source: FAO, *Production Yearbook*.

### LIVESTOCK PRODUCTS ('000 metric tons)

| | 1991 | 1992 | 1993 |
|---|---|---|---|
| Beef and veal | 1,878 | 1,656 | 1,275* |
| Mutton and lamb | 38 | 32 | 28† |
| Goat meat | 2 | 3 | 2† |
| Pig meat | 1,421 | 1,180 | 908* |
| Poultry meat | 654 | 498 | 384† |
| Cows' milk | 22,312 | 18,955 | 18,199 |
| Sheep's milk | 15 | 22 | 24 |
| Goats' milk | 82 | 137 | 154 |
| Butter | 376 | 303 | 311 |
| Poultry eggs | 913.8 | 776.2 | 679.1 |
| Hen eggs | 886.3 | 757.4 | 660.4 |
| Wool: | | | |
|   greasy | 26.6 | 23.1 | 21.1 |
|   scoured | 16.0 | 13.8 | 10.6 |

* Unofficial figure.   † FAO estimate.

Source: FAO, *Production Yearbook*.

UKRAINE                                                                                              *Statistical Survey*

## Fishing

('000 metric tons, live weight)

|  | 1991 | 1992 |
|---|---|---|
| Roaches | 10.4 | 7.5 |
| Azov tyulka | 19.1 | 6.7 |
| Alaska pollack | 9.2 | 5.7 |
| Southern blue whiting | 28.5 | 6.7 |
| Patagonian toothfish | 2.4 | 5.2 |
| Capelin | 4.5 | 6.3 |
| Chilean jack mackerel | 57.8 | 2.7 |
| Cape horse mackerel | 148.1 | 66.3 |
| Other jack and horse mackerels | 41.3 | 31.7 |
| Round sardinella | 55.2 | 29.9 |
| European pilchard | 165.4 | 139.1 |
| European sprat | 11.1 | 11.5 |
| European anchovy | 41.4 | 12.3 |
| Chub mackerel | 17.8 | 14.5 |
| Antarctic krill | 94.2 | 52.7 |
| Squids | 11.5 | 7.4 |
| **Total catch** (incl. others) | 789.2 | 453.9 |

Source: FAO, *Yearbook of Fishery Statistics*.

## Mining

('000 metric tons, unless otherwise indicated)

|  | 1988 | 1989 | 1990 |
|---|---|---|---|
| Hard coal | 181,800 | 180,200 | 155,532 |
| Brown coal (incl. lignite) | 9,900 |  | 9,280 |
| Crude petroleum* | 5,400 | 5,400 | 5,252 |
| Natural gas (million cu metres) | 32,400 | 30,800 | 28,082 |
| Iron ore: |  |  |  |
|   gross weight | 116,000 | n.a. | 104,982 |
|   metal content | 64,371 | 61,665 | 58,988 |
| Manganese ore† | n.a. | 2,279.5 | 2,208.3 |
| Magnesite | 855 | 851 | 828 |
| Chalk | 665 | 652 | 1,082 |
| Potash salts (crude) | 1,077 | 851 | 585 |
| Native sulphur | 2,556 | 2,407 | 2,118 |
| Salt (unrefined) | 8,186 | 8,338 | 8,309 |
| Gypsum (crude) | 1,030 | 1,034 | 1,014 |
| Peat: |  |  |  |
|   for fuel | 2,007 | 2,366 | 1,619 |
|   for agricultural use | 21,957 | 18,225 | 14,680 |

* Including gas condensates.
† Figures refer to the metal content of ore extracted.

Source: mainly UN, *Industrial Statistics Yearbook*.

**1991:** Coal 135.6m. metric tons; Crude petroleum 4.9m. metric tons; Natural gas 24,400m. cu m; Salt 8.4m. metric tons.
**1992:** Coal 133.6m. metric tons; Crude petroleum 4.5m. metric tons; Natural gas 20,900m. cu m.
**1993:** Coal 114.5m. metric tons; Natural gas 19,200m. cu m.
**1994:** Natural gas 18,300m. cu m.

## Industry

**SELECTED PRODUCTS**
('000 metric tons, unless otherwise indicated)

|  | 1988 | 1989 | 1990 |
|---|---|---|---|
| Margarine | 308.1 | 318.4 | 288.5 |
| Flour | 7,534 | 7,614 | 7,671 |
| Raw sugar* | 4,646 | 5,177 | 5,388 |
| Ethyl alcohol ('000 hectolitres) | 2,776 | 4,911 | 5,394 |
| Wine ('000 hectolitres) | 3,165 | 3,258 | 2,723 |
| Beer ('000 hectolitres) | 12,951 | 13,749 | 13,778 |
| Cigarettes (million) | 81,659 | 78,446 | 69,397 |
| Wool yarn: pure and mixed | 47.7 | 48.9 | 47.5 |
| Cotton yarn: pure and mixed | 160.5 | 161.8 | 157.1 |
| Flax yarn | 27.8 | 27.2 | 24.7 |
| Woven cotton fabrics (million sq metres) | 613 | 620 | 614 |
| Woven woollen fabrics (million sq metres) | 86.9 | 89.8 | 86.0 |
| Linen fabrics (million sq metres) | 107.3 | 109.0 | 102.4 |
| Footwear, excl. rubber ('000 pairs) | 190,583 | 193,673 | 196,466 |
| Paper | 343 | 353 | 369 |
| Hydrochloric acid | 270.5 | 279.3 | 273.7 |
| Sulphuric acid | 4,339 | 4,268 | 5,000 |
| Nitric acid | 214 | 244 | 229 |
| Phosphoric acid | 695 | 694 | 692 |
| Caustic soda (Sodium hydroxide) | 494 | 472 | 444 |
| Soda ash (Sodium carbonate) | 1,340 | 1,263 | 1,120 |
| Nitrogenous fertilizers (a)† | 3,635 | 3,275 | 3,022 |
| Phosphatic fertilizers (b)† | 1,725 | 1,695 | 1,648 |
| Potassic fertilizers (c)† | 203 | 170 | 143 |
| Rubber tyres ('000)‡ | 8,783 | 8,730 | 8,539 |
| Rubber footwear ('000 pairs) | 30,618 | 31,626 | 32,290 |
| Clay building bricks (million) | 6,792 | 7,118 | 7,241 |
| Quicklime | 8,929 | 8,931 | 8,677 |
| Cement | 23,533 | 23,416 | 22,729 |
| Pig-iron | 43,930 | 43,061 | 41,906 |
| Crude steel: |  |  |  |
|   for castings | 2,156 | 2,014 | 1,920 |
|   ingots | 54,282 | 52,772 | 50,702 |
| Tractors (number)§ | 130,705 | 115,913 | 106,221 |
| Household refrigerators ('000) | 843 | 882 | 903 |
| Household washing machines ('000) | 533 | 651 | 788 |
| Radio receivers ('000) | 432 | 574 | 778 |
| Television receivers ('000) | 3,434 | 3,572 | 3,774 |
| Passenger motor cars ('000) | 155 | 155 | 156 |
| Buses and motor coaches (number) | 14,834 | 14,561 | 12,713 |
| Lorries (number) | 29,789 | 28,111 | 27,680 |
| Motorcycles, scooters, etc. ('000) | 112 | 109 | 103 |
| Bicycles ('000) | 891 | 838 | 800 |
| Electric energy (million kWh) | 297,229 | 295,300 | 298,500 |

**1991:** Margarine 267,000 metric tons; Footwear 179m. pairs; Sulphuric acid 4.1m. metric tons; Caustic soda 443,000 metric tons; Cement 21.7m. metric tons; Tractors 90,100 units; Household refrigerators 873,000 units; Household washing machines 824,000 units; Radio receivers 880,000 units; Television receivers 3.6m. units; Passenger motor cars 156,000 units; Lorries 25,100 units; Motorcycles, scooters, etc. 101,000 units; Bicycles 812,000 units; Electric energy 278,700m. kWh.

* Production from home-grown sugar beet.
† Production of fertilizers is in terms of (a) nitrogen; (b) phosphoric acid; or (c) potassium oxide.
‡ Tyres for road motor vehicles.
§ Tractors of 10 horse-power and over, excluding industrial tractors and road tractors for tractor-trailer combinations.

Source: mainly UN, *Industrial Statistics Yearbook*.

**Electric energy:** 252,600m. kWh in 1992; 227,407m. kWh in 1993; 200,800m. kWh in 1994.

UKRAINE                                                                                                                    *Statistical Survey*

# Finance

## CURRENCY AND EXCHANGE RATES

**Monetary Units** (temporary)
A currency coupon, the karbovanets (plural: karbovantsi), is in use.

**Sterling and Dollar Equivalents** (31 December 1994)
£1 sterling = 211,207.5 karbovantsi;
US $1 = 135,000.0 karbovantsi;
1,000,000 karbovantsi = £4.735 = $7.407.

Note: Based on the official rate of exchange, the average value of the Soviet currency (roubles per US dollar) was: 0.6274 in 1989; 0.5856 in 1990; 0.5819 in 1991. However, a multiple exchange rate system was in operation, with separate non-commercial and tourist rates. A commercial exchange rate was introduced on 1 November 1990, replacing the official rate for most transactions. The commercial rate (roubles per US dollar) was: 1.692 at 31 December 1990; 1.671 at 31 December 1991. Between November 1989 and April 1991 the tourist exchange rate valued the rouble at one-tenth of the official rate. In April 1991 this rate, renamed the 'special rate', was set at $1 = 27.6 roubles. It was subsequently adjusted. Following the dissolution of the USSR in December 1991, Russia and several other former Soviet republics retained the rouble as their monetary unit. In November 1992 the rouble ceased to be legal tender in Ukraine, and was replaced (initially at par) by the karbovanets (see above) for a transitional period. However, some of the figures in this Survey are still in terms of roubles.

Since the introduction of the karbovanets, Ukraine has operated a system of multiple exchange rates. The National Bank of Ukraine's official exchange rate was US $1 = 637.7 karbovantsi at 31 December 1992 and $1 = 12,610 karbovantsi at 31 December 1993. Meanwhile, a separate auction rate was in operation: at the end of 1993 this stood at $1 = 25,000 karbovantsi. Ukraine has announced an intention to introduce its own permanent currency, the hryvnya, during 1995.

## BUDGET (million roubles)

| Revenue | 1991 | 1992 | 1993* |
|---|---|---|---|
| Taxation | 70,200 | 1,121,100 | 7,112,800 |
| Turnover tax | 27,800 | 485,000 | 1,995,200 |
| Excises | — | 59,400 | 808,100 |
| Profits tax on enterprises | 28,400 | 277,000 | 1,346,100 |
| Individual income tax | 9,300 | 148,400 | 554,800 |
| Chornobyl contribution† | 2,700 | 122,800 | 611,300 |
| Foreign-trade taxes | 900 | 7,200 | 1,005,600 |
| Other tax revenue | 1,100 | 21,200 | 791,700 |
| Non-tax revenue | 6,700 | 102,300 | 1,008,500 |
| **Total** | 76,900 | 1,223,400 | 8,121,300 |

| Expenditure | 1991 | 1992 | 1993* |
|---|---|---|---|
| Current expenditure by state budget | 99,800 | 1,831,200 | 8,405,200 |
| Social safety net | 50,200 | 361,700 | 1,849,700 |
| Subsidies | 38,400 | 234,900 | 1,145,700 |
| National economy | 13,100 | 597,200 | 1,326,400 |
| Education and health | } 29,300 | 431,500 | 2,276,900 |
| Other social and cultural services | | 39,200 | 357,100 |
| Science | — | 39,900 | 178,600 |
| Administration and justice | — | 75,400 | 575,500 |
| Defence | | 112,300 | 547,100 |
| Chornobyl disbursement† | 4,500 | 115,000 | 415,300 |
| Other current expenditure | 2,700 | 59,000 | 878,600 |
| Capital expenditure by state budget | 9,000 | 89,200 | 689,400 |
| **Total** | 108,800 | 1,920,400 | 9,094,600 |

* Projections.
† Relating to measures to relieve the effects of the accident at the Chornobyl nuclear power-station in April 1986.

## MONEY SUPPLY (million roubles at 31 December)

| | 1989 | 1990 | 1991 |
|---|---|---|---|
| Currency in circulation | 17,200 | 17,400 | 29,800 |
| Demand deposits at banks | 61,800 | 76,200 | 143,600 |
| **Total money** | 79,000 | 93,600 | 173,400 |

## COST OF LIVING
(Index of retail prices; base: previous year = 100)

| | 1989 | 1990 | 1991 |
|---|---|---|---|
| Food | 100.6 | 101.5 | 179.2 |
| Other commodities | 103.5 | 106.2 | 188.3 |
| **All items** | 102.2 | 104.2 | 184.2 |

## NATIONAL ACCOUNTS (million roubles at current prices)
**Net Material Product by Economic Activity**

| | 1990 | 1991 | 1992* |
|---|---|---|---|
| Agriculture and fishing | 35,800 | 67,800 | 852,100 |
| Industry and mining | 48,700 | 95,000 | 1,921,500 |
| Construction | 11,500 | 24,400 | 558,700 |
| Trade and catering | 6,500 | 13,000 | 160,700 |
| Transport and communications | 7,100 | 11,000 | 177,800 |
| Other activities of the material sphere | 8,400 | 13,100 | 119,900 |
| **Total** | 118,000 | 224,300 | 3,790,700 |

* Preliminary figures.

## BALANCE OF PAYMENTS (US $ million)

| | 1991 | 1992 | 1993 |
|---|---|---|---|
| Exports of goods and services | 50,496 | 11,707 | 16,400 |
| Imports of goods and services | −53,463 | −12,101 | −16,630 |
| Other income (net) | 0 | −5 | −45 |
| Current transfers (net) | 0 | 0 | 107 |
| **Current balance** | −2,967 | −399 | −168 |
| Long-term capital (net) | n.a. | 556 | 425 |
| Other capital (net) | n.a. | −61 | −160 |
| **Overall balance** | n.a. | 96 | 97 |

Source: World Bank, *Trends in Developing Economies*.

# External Trade

## PRINCIPAL COMMODITIES (million roubles)

| Imports | 1989 | 1990 |
|---|---|---|
| Petroleum and gas | 4,381 | 3,875 |
| Iron and steel | 2,893 | 2,679 |
| Non-ferrous metals | 2,188 | 2,136 |
| Chemicals and chemical products | 5,883 | 5,711 |
| Machine-building | 18,046 | 18,745 |
| Wood and paper products | 1,933 | 1,856 |
| Light industry | 9,694 | 9,738 |
| Food industry | 5,058 | 4,046 |
| Agricultural products (unprocessed) | 1,409 | 1,402 |
| **Total** (incl. others) | 54,540 | 54,059 |
| Foreign | 14,569 | 15,071 |
| Inter-republican (USSR) | 39,971 | 38,989 |

| Exports | 1989 | 1990 |
|---|---|---|
| Iron and steel | 8,088 | 7,619 |
| Non-ferrous metals | 965 | 914 |
| Chemicals and chemical products | 3,944 | 3,923 |
| Machine-building | 18,164 | 17,881 |
| Light industry | 2,674 | 2,326 |
| Food industry | 7,790 | 6,659 |
| Agricultural products (unprocessed) | 1,495 | 1,651 |
| **Total** (incl. others) | 48,062 | 45,606 |
| Foreign | 7,595 | 7,287 |
| Inter-republican (USSR) | 40,467 | 38,319 |

**1994** (US $ million): Imports 9,767.9; Exports 9,882.6.

UKRAINE

## Communications Media

|  | 1990 | 1991 | 1992 |
|---|---|---|---|
| Radio receivers ('000 in use) | 41,200 | 41,300 | 41,500 |
| Television receivers ('000 in use) | 16,950 | 17,100 | 17,300 |
| Book production*: |  |  |  |
| Titles | 7,046 | 5,857 | 4,410 |
| Copies ('000) | 170,476 | 136,417 | 128,471 |
| Daily newspapers: |  |  |  |
| Titles | 127 | n.a. | 90 |
| Circulation ('000) | 13,026 | n.a. | 6,083 |
| Non-daily newspapers: |  |  |  |
| Titles | 1,660 | n.a. | 1,605 |
| Circulation ('000) | 11,893 | n.a. | 18,194 |
| Other periodicals: |  |  |  |
| Titles | 185 | n.a. | 321 |
| Circulation ('000) | 9,957 | n.a. | 3,491 |

* Including pamphlets (1,878 titles and 53,874,000 copies in 1990; 1,506 titles and 36,634,000 copies in 1991; 860 titles and 25,639,000 copies in 1992).

Source: UNESCO, *Statistical Yearbook*.

## Education

(1992)

|  | Institutions | Teachers | Students |
|---|---|---|---|
| Pre-primary | 23,700 | 201,400 | 1,663,200 |
| Primary | 21,100 | 501,900 | 4,102,100 |
| General secondary |  |  | 2,737,200 |
| Specialized secondary |  |  |  |
| Teacher training | n.a. | n.a. | 22,600 |
| Vocational | n.a. | n.a. | 521,700 |
| Higher* | n.a. | 75,900† | 890,192† |

* Including evening and correspondence courses.
† 1991 figure.

Source: UNESCO, *Statistical Yearbook*.

# Directory

## Constitution

Ukraine's Constitution was adopted in 1978, and was modelled on the 1977 Constitution of the USSR. In the early 1990s significant amendments were made to the Constitution to reflect Ukraine's status as an independent, non-socialist state. In 1991 the institution of an executive presidency was introduced into the Constitution. A draft of a new constitution was prepared in 1992, but adoption of a new document was delayed by disagreements concerning the division of power, and notably the role of the President in any constitutional order. A further draft was published in October 1993. Following the election of a new legislature in 1994, discussions continued on the drafting of the new constitution (which was expected to be completed by late 1995).

## The Government

### HEAD OF STATE

**President:** LEONID D. KUCHMA (took office 19 July 1994).

### CABINET OF MINISTERS
(July 1995)

**Prime Minister:** YEVHEN K. MARCHUK.
**First Deputy Prime Minister:** PETRO LAZARENKO.
**First Deputy Prime Minister, responsible for Security Issues and Emergency Situations:** VASYL DURDYNETS.
**Deputy Prime Minister, responsible for Industrial Policy Issues:** ANATOLIY KINAKH.
**Deputy Prime Minister, responsible for Humanitarian Issues:** IVAN F. KURAS.
**Deputy Prime Minister, responsible for Agro-industrial Issues:** PETRO SABLUK.
**Deputy Prime Minister, responsible for Economic Issues:** ROMAN SHPEK.
**Minister of Defence:** VALERIY SHMAROV.
**Minister of Foreign Economic Relations and Trade:** SERHIY H. OSYKA.
**Minister of the Cabinet:** VALERIY P. PUSTOVOITENKO.
**Minister of the Interior:** YURIY KRAVCHENKO.
**Minister of Foreign Affairs:** HENNADIY UDOVENKO.
**Minister of the Economy:** VASYL HUREYEV.
**Minister of Culture:** (vacant).
**Minister of Health:** YEVHEN KOROLENKO.
**Minister of Communications:** (vacant).
**Minister of Forestry:** VALERIY I. SAMOPLAVSKY.

**Minister of Power and Electrification:** OLEKSIY SHEBERSTOV.
**Minister of Machine Building, Military-Industrial Complex and Conversion:** (vacant).
**Minister of Industry:** VALERIY MAZUR.
**Minister of Environmental Protection and Nuclear Safety:** YURIY I. KOSTENKO.
**Minister of Statistics:** MYKOLA BORYSENKO.
**Minister of Management of the Consequences of the Chornobyl Accident:** (vacant).
**Minister of Finance:** PETRO HERMANCHUK.
**Minister of Justice:** VOLODYMYR STRETOVYCH.
**Minister of Transport:** IVAN DANKEVYCH.
**Minister of Youth and Sports:** (vacant).
**Minister of Social Security:** ARKADIY V. YERSHOV.
**Minister of Labour:** (vacant).
**Minister of Education:** MYKHAILO Z. ZHUROVSKY.
**Minister of the Coal Industry:** VIKTOR POLTAVETS.
**Minister of National Minorities, Migration and Religious Issues:** (vacant).
**Minister of Food and Agriculture:** (vacant).
**Minister of Press and Information:** (vacant).
**Minister of Fisheries:** MYKOLA SHVEDENKO.

The following are *ex-officio* members of the Cabinet of Ministers:
**Governor of the National Bank:** VIKTOR YUSHCHENKO.
**Chairman of the Anti-Trust Committee:** (vacant).
**Chairman of the State Security Service:** VOLODYMYR RADCHENKO.
**Chairman of the State Property Fund:** YURIY I. YEHANUROV.

### MINISTRIES

**Cabinet of Ministers:** 252008 Kiev, vul. M. Hrushevskoho 12/2; tel. (44) 293-52-27.
**Ministry of the Coal Industry:** Kiev.
**Ministry of Communications:** 252001 Kiev, vul. Kreshchatik 22; tel. (44) 228-15-00; fax (44) 228-61-41.
**Ministry of Culture:** 252030 Kiev, vul. Ivana Franka 19; tel. (44) 224-49-11.
**Ministry of Defence:** 252005 Kiev, vul. Bankova 6; tel. (44) 226-26-56.
**Ministry of the Economy:** 252008 Kiev, vul. M. Hrushevskoho 12/2; tel. (44) 293-44-65.
**Ministry of Education:** 252135 Kiev, Peremohy pr. 10; tel. and fax (44) 216-10-49.

# UKRAINE

**Ministry of Environmental Protection and Nuclear Safety:** 252001 Kiev, vul. Kreshchatik 5; tel. (44) 228-06-44; fax (44) 229-83-83.

**Ministry of Finance:** 252008 Kiev, vul. M. Hrushevskoho 12/2; tel. (44) 293-53-63; fax (44) 293-21-78.

**Ministry of Fisheries:** Kiev.

**Ministry of Food and Agriculture:** 252001 Kiev, vul. Kreshchatik 24; tel. (44) 226-25-04; fax (44) 229-87-56.

**Ministry of Foreign Affairs:** 252018 Kiev, Mykhaylivska pl. 1; tel. (44) 21-28-33; fax (44) 226-31-69.

**Ministry of Foreign Economic Relations and Trade:** 252053 Kiev, Lvivska pl. 8; tel. (44) 226-27-33.

**Ministry of Forestry:** 252001 Kiev, vul. Kreshchatik 5; tel. (44) 226-32-53; fax (44) 228-77-94.

**Ministry of Health:** 252021 Kiev, vul. M. Hrushevskoho 7; tel. (44) 226-22-05; fax (44) 293-69-75.

**Ministry of Industry:** 253167 Kiev, vul. M. Paskovoy 15; tel. (44) 226-26-23.

**Ministry of the Interior:** 252024 Kiev, vul. Bohomoltsa 10; tel. (44) 291-18-30; fax (44) 291-31-82.

**Ministry of Justice:** 252030 Kiev, vul. M. Kotsyubynskoho 12; tel. (44) 226-24-16.

**Ministry of Labour:** 252004 Kiev, vul. Pushkinska 28; tel. (44) 224-63-47; fax (44) 224-59-05.

**Ministry of Machine Building, Military-Industrial Complex and Conversion:** Kiev, vul. Pushkinska 8; tel. (44) 291-50-53.

**Ministry of Management of the Consequences of the Chornobyl Accident:** 254655 Kiev, Lvivska pl. 8; tel. (44) 212-50-49; fax (44) 212-50-69.

**Ministry of National Minorities, Migration and Religious Issues:** 252021 Kiev, vul. Institutska 21/8; tel. (44) 293-53-35; fax (44) 293-35-31.

**Ministry of Power and Electrification:** 252001 Kiev, vul. Kreshchatik 30; tel. (44) 224-93-88.

**Ministry of Press and Information:** 252001 Kiev, vul. Prorizna 2; tel. and fax (44) 226-28-71.

**Ministry of Social Security:** 252053 Kiev, vul. Kudriavska 26/28; tel. (44) 226-24-01; fax (44) 212-25-35.

**Ministry of Statistics:** 252023 Kiev, vul. Shota Rustaveli 3; tel. (44) 226-20-21; telex 132368; fax (44) 227-42-66.

**Ministry of Transport:** 252113 Kiev, Peremohy pr. 57; tel. (44) 446-30-30.

**Ministry of Youth and Sports:** 252023 Kiev, vul. Esplanadna 42; tel. (44) 220-02-00; fax (44) 220-12-94.

**State Security Service:** 252003 Kiev, vul. Volodymyrska 33; tel. (44) 226-24-16.

# President and Legislature

## PRESIDENT

**Presidential Election, First Ballot, 26 June 1994**

| Candidate | Votes | % |
|---|---|---|
| Leonid M. Kravchuk | 9,977,766 | 37.68 |
| Leonid D. Kuchma | 8,274,806 | 31.25 |
| Oleksandr O. Moroz | 3,466,541 | 13.99 |
| Volodymyr T. Lanovy | 2,483,986 | 9.38 |
| Valeriy H. Babych | 644,263 | 2.43 |
| Ivan S. Pliusch | 321,686 | 1.22 |
| Petro M. Talanchuk | 143,361 | 0.54 |

**Second Ballot, 10 July 1994**

| Candidate | Votes | % |
|---|---|---|
| Leonid D. Kuchma | 14,017,684 | 52.14 |
| Leonid M. Kravchuk | 12,112,442 | 45.06 |

## VERKHOVNA RADA
(Supreme Council)

**General Election, 27 March, and 2–3 and 9–10 April 1994**

| Parties and groups | Seats |
|---|---|
| Communist Party of Ukraine | 86 |
| People's Movement of Ukraine (Rukh) | 20 |
| Peasants' Party of Ukraine | 18 |
| Socialist Party of Ukraine | 14 |
| Ukrainian Republican Party | 8 |
| Congress of Ukrainian Nationalists | 5 |
| Inter-regional Bloc for Reform | 5 |
| Others | 12 |
| Independent candidates | 170 |
| **Total** | **338*** |

*Subsequent rounds of voting were held in July, August and November 1994 to elect the 112 unfilled seats. However, only 67 seats were filled, and in mid-1995 the remaining 45 seats were reportedly still vacant.

**Supreme Council:** 252019 Kiev, vul. M. Hrushevskoho 5; tel. (44) 291-51-00.

**Chairman:** Oleksandr O. Moroz.

**Deputy Chairmen:** Oleksandr Tkachenko, Oleh Dyomin.

# Political Organizations

Until 1990 the only legal political party in Ukraine was the Communist Party of Ukraine (CPU), an integral part of the Communist Party of the Soviet Union. In 1988, however, a Ukrainian People's Movement for Restructuring (known as Rukh) was established to support greater democratization and freedom of speech, and several other political organizations were also founded. In 1990, after the CPU's constitutional monopoly was abolished, many new political parties were established. In 1992 several coalitions were formed, notably the Congress of National Democratic Forces, which unites conservative, nationalist parties, and New Ukraine, which has the support of centrist parties and many business executives. Rukh, which had been the main coalition of forces opposed to the CPU in 1988–91, became a political party (as the People's Movement of Ukraine) in 1993. By the beginning of 1994 both extreme left-wing and extreme right-wing parties had been formed in Ukraine, including the Ukrainian National Assembly and the National Fascist Party, and the extreme left-wing Socialist Party of Ukraine, which incorporated elements of the CPU. The CPU, which was banned after the coup attempt in Moscow in August 1991, was permitted to contest parliamentary elections in 1994, while a proposal for its reinstatement as a registered political organization was being considered by the Supreme Council. No final decision on the status of the CPU had been taken by mid-1995. The Inter-regional Bloc for Reform movement, which was closely associated with President Kuchma, was registered as a political party in 1994. Some 32 Ukrainian political parties were registered for the elections held to the Supreme Council in March and April 1994.

**All-Ukrainian Centrist Party of Civil Accord:** Kiev; f. 1993; 20,000 mems.

**Christian Democratic Party of Ukraine:** Kiev; democratic nationalist party; Leader Vitaliy Zhuravsky; 12,000 mems.

**Civic Congress of Ukraine:** Kiev; centrist; Leader Oleksandr Bazylyuk; 1,500 mems.

**Communist Party of Ukraine:** Kiev; banned in August 1991; discussions regarding its proposed reinstatement, begun in 1993, continued in 1995; Sec. Cen. Cttee Petro Symonenko; 120,000 mems.

**Congress of National Democratic Forces:** Kiev; f. 1992; alliance of 20 nationalist-conservative groups and parties; advocates a strong presidency, a unitary state, secession from the CIS, and a 'socially-just' market economy; Chair. Mykhailo Horyn; includes:

**Democratic Party of Ukraine:** Kiev; f. 1990; democratic nationalist party; opposes CIS membership, advocates national cultural and linguistic policies to support Ukrainian heritage; merger with the Ukrainian Republican Party proposed in 1994; Chair. Volodymyr Yavorisky; c. 5,000 mems.

**Ukrainian National Conservative Party:** Kiev; f. 1992 by merger of Ukrainian National Party and Ukrainian People's Democratic Party; radical nationalist party; Leader V. Radionov; 500 mems.

**Ukrainian Peasant Democratic Party:** Lviv, vul. 700-richya Lviva 63, kv. 712; tel. (322) 59-97-37; f. 1990; democratic nationalist party, advocates private farming, dissolution of collective farms; Chair. Serhiy Plachynda; 5,000 mems.

**Ukrainian Republican Party:** Kiev; f. 1990 as successor to Ukrainian Helsinki Union (f. 1988); democratic nationalist

# UKRAINE

party; advocates immediate departure from the CIS, consolidation of independence; merger with the Democratic Party of Ukraine proposed in 1994; Chair. MYKHAILO HORYN; c. 15,000 mems.

**Congress of Ukrainian Nationalists:** Kiev; radical nationalist party; Leader SLAVA STESTKO.

**Constitutional Democratic Party:** Kiev; centrist party; Leader V. ZOLOTAREV.

**Green Party of Ukraine:** 252024 Kiev, vul. Luteranska 24; tel. (44) 293-69-09; fax (44) 293-52-36; f. 1990 as political wing of environmental organization, Zeleny Svit (Green World—f. 1987); democratic nationalist party; Pres. VITALIY KONONOV; 3,000 mems (1993).

**Inter-regional Bloc for Reform:** Kiev; f. 1994; advocates political and economic reform, private ownership and a federal system of government; Chair. VOLODYMYR HRYNYOV.

**Labour Congress of Ukraine:** Kiev; centrist party; Leader A. MATVIYENKO; 2,000 mems.

**Liberal Democratic Party of Ukraine:** Kiev; democratic nationalist party; Leader V. KLYMCHUK; 1,000 mems.

**Liberal Party of Ukraine:** Kiev; centrist party; Leader OLEH SOSKIN; 10,000 mems.

**National Fascist Party:** Lviv; f. 1993; advocates supremacy of the Ukrainian nation and the extension of Ukrainian borders to the scale of Kievan Rus.

**New Ukraine:** Kiev; f. 1992; alliance of centrist parties and moderate left-wing groups; advocates radical economic reform and improvement of links with Russia and the CIS; Chair. VOLODYMYR FILENKO; c. 30,000 mems; includes:

**Party for Democratic Renewal of Ukraine:** 252034 Kiev, Proreznaya vul. 13, kv. 64; tel. (44) 229-29-68; fax (44) 224-23-12; f. 1990 as the Democratic Platform within the CPU; centrist party; advocates close economic links with Russia and the CIS, a market economy and privatization; Leader VOLODYMYR FILENKO; 2,500 mems.

**Organization of Ukrainian Nationalists:** Kiev; registered as a political party in 1993; radical nationalist; Leader MYKOLA PLAVYUK.

**Party of Free Peasants of Ukraine:** Kiev; democratic nationalist party; Leader V. HORDIYENKO; 4,500 mems.

**Party of Labour:** Kiev; centrist party; favours privatization; Chair. VALENTYN LANDYK; 10,000 mems.

**Party for the National Salvation of Ukraine:** Kiev; registered as a political party in 1993; centrist; Leader LEONID YERSHOV; 1,500 mems.

**Party of Slavic Unity:** Kiev; centrist party; Leader I. KARPENKO.

**Peasants' Party of Ukraine:** Kiev; f. 1992; centrist party; advocates retention of collective farm system, opposed to radical economic reform and land privatization; Leader SERHIY DOVHAN; 7,000 mems.

**People's Movement of Ukraine (Rukh):** Kiev; f. 1989 as popular front (Ukrainian People's Movement for Restructuring); registered as political party in 1993; democratic nationalist party; Leader VYACHESLAV CHORNOVIL; 62,000 full mems, 500,000 assoc. mems (1993).

**People's Party of Ukraine:** Kiev; centrist party; Leader L. TABURYANSKY; 3,671 mems.

**Social Democratic Party of Ukraine:** Kiev; f. 1995, by merger of the Ukrainian Party of Justice, the Party of Human Rights and the Social Democratic Party; advocates economic and political reform; centrist party; Chair. VASYL V. ONOPENKO.

**Socialist Party of Ukraine:** Kiev; f. 1991; formed as partial successor to CPU; advocates retention of large state role in the economy, stronger links with CIS, priority for workers in privatization; strongly anti-nationalist; Leader OLEKSANDRO MOROZ; c. 90,000 mems.

**State Independence of Ukraine:** Kiev; f. 1990; radical nationalist party; Leader ROMAN KOVAL.

**Ukrainian Conservative Republican Party:** Kiev; radical nationalist party; Leader STEPAN KHMARA; 3,000 mems.

**Ukrainian National Assembly:** Kiev; neo-fascist; Co-Leaders OLEH VITOVYCH, DMYTRO KORCHYNSKY; 10,000 mems.

**United Social Democratic Party of Ukraine:** Kiev; f. 1990; left-wing democratic party; advocates comprehensive social-welfare system, gradual approach to economic reform, and continued Ukrainian membership of the CIS; Leader OLEKSANDR ALIN; c. 1,000 mems.

### CRIMEAN POLITICAL ORGANIZATIONS

Like its Ukrainian counterpart, the Communist Party of Crimea was banned in August 1991. The following month, however, several local communist unions were established, which merged in June 1992 to form the Union of Communists of Crimea. On 18 June 1993 the Union was renamed the Communist Party of Crimea and was officially registered on 15 September. Several other powerful political interest groups emerged in 1993–94: various pro-Russian parties, including the Republican Party of Crimea, whose former leader, Yury Meshkov, won the Crimean presidential elections in January 1994; several parties promoting business interests, the most powerful of which was the Party for the Economic Renewal of Crimea; and Crimean Tatar movements. There were also centrist organizations, including the Democratic Party of Crimea. In July 1993 a law was passed by the Crimean Supreme Soviet, which stated that all-Ukrainian political parties would not be entitled to participate in the elections to the Crimean legislature (scheduled for 27 March 1994) unless they registered locally. The Ukrainian Civic Congress of Crimea was formed as a result of this legislation. The Ukrainian Republican Party and the Democratic Party of Ukraine did, nevertheless, have some support amongst the population of Crimea.

## Diplomatic Representation

### EMBASSIES IN UKRAINE

**Austria:** 252030 Kiev, vul. Ivana Franka 33; tel. (44) 220-57-59; fax (44) 227-54-65; Ambassador: Dr GEORG WEISS.

**Belarus:** 252011 Kiev, vul. Kutuzova 8; tel. (44) 294-82-12; fax (44) 294-80-06; Ambassador: VITALY KURASHIK.

**Belgium:** 252030 Kiev, vul. B. Khmelnitskoho 58; tel (044) 216-63-23; telex 131177; fax (44) 219-27-17; Ambassador: INGEBORG KRISTOFFERSEN.

**Bulgaria:** Kiev, vul. Hospitalna 1; tel. (44) 224-53-60; Ambassador: DIMITAR TSEROV.

**Canada:** 252034 Kiev, POB 200, Yaroslaviv val 31; tel. (44) 212-35-50; fax (44) 225-13-05; Ambassador: FRANÇOIS MATHYS.

**China, People's Republic:** Kiev, vul. Hospitalna 4, Hotel Rus; tel. (44) 227-84-02; Ambassador: ZHANG ZHEN.

**Croatia:** Kiev, vul. Artema 50/51; tel. (44) 216-58-62; fax (44) 244-69-43; Ambassador: DJURO VIDMAROVIĆ.

**Cuba:** 254053 Kiev, Bekhterevsky prov. 5; tel. (44) 216-32-29; fax (44) 244-66-33; Ambassador: SERGIO LÓPEZ BRIEL.

**Czech Republic:** 252034 Kiev, Yaroslaviv val 34; tel. (44) 212-21-10.

**Denmark:** 252034 Kiev, vul. Volodymyrska 45; tel. (44) 229-45-37; telex 131457; fax (44) 229-18-31; Ambassador: CHRISTIAN FABER-ROD.

**Estonia:** Kiev, Kutuzovsky pr. 8; tel. (44) 296-28-86; fax (44) 295-81-76; Chargé d'affaires a.i.: ANDREI BIROV.

**Finland:** Kiev, vul. Striletska 14; tel. (44) 228-70-47; fax (44) 228-20-32; Ambassador: ERIK ULFSTEDT.

**France:** Kiev, vul. Reytarska 39; tel. (44) 228-87-28; fax (44) 229-08-70; Ambassador: DOMINIQUE CHASSARD.

**Germany:** 252054 Kiev, vul. Chkalova 84; tel. (44) 216-67-94; fax (44) 216-92-33; Ambassador: Dr ALEXANDER ARNOT.

**Greece:** 252021 Kiev, vul. Lipska 5, Hotel Natsionalny; tel. (44) 291-88-75; fax (44) 291-54-68; Ambassador: VASSILIOS PATSIKAKIS.

**Holy See:** 250005 Kiev, vul. Chervonoarmiyska 96 (Apostolic Nunciature); tel. (44) 268-95-05; fax (44) 269-24-17; Apostolic Nuncio: Most Rev. ANTONIO FRANCO, Titular Bishop of Gallese.

**Hungary:** Kiev; Ambassador: ISTVÁN VARGA.

**India:** Kiev, Hotel Kiev; tel. (44) 227-88-60; Ambassador: S. T. DEVARE.

**Iran:** 252021 Kiev, vul. Lipska 5, Hotel Natsionalny; tel. (44) 291-88-69; fax (44) 291-54-68; Ambassador: BEHZAD MAZAHEVI.

**Israel:** Kiev, bul. Lesi Ukrainki 34; tel. (44) 295-62-16; fax (44) 294-97-48; Ambassador: ZVI MAGEN.

**Italy:** 252021 Kiev, vul. Sichnevoho povstannia 25; tel. (44) 290-72-44; telex 131462; fax (44) 290-51-62; Ambassador: VITTORIO SURDO.

**Japan:** 252021 Kiev, vul. Lipska 5, Hotel Natsionalny; tel. and fax (44) 291-88-72.

**Kazakhstan:** Kiev.

**Mongolia:** Kiev, vul. Kotsyubynskoho 3; tel. (44) 216-88-91; Ambassador: DASHNYAM YADMAAGIYN.

**Poland:** Kiev, Yaroslaviv val 12; tel. (44) 224-80-40; fax (44) 229-35-75; Ambassador: JERZY KOZAKIEWICZ.

**Romania:** 252030 Kiev, vul. Kotsyubynskoho 8; tel. (44) 224-52-61; fax (44) 225-20-25; Ambassador: ION BISTREANU.

**Russia:** 252021 Kiev, vul. Lipska 5, Hotel Natsionalny; tel. (44) 291-83-13; fax (44) 291-54-68; Ambassador: LEONID SMOLYAKOV.

# UKRAINE

**Slovakia:** 252034 Kiev, Yaroslaviv val 34; tel. (44) 229-79-22; fax (44) 212-32-71; Ambassador: Ambassador: Jozef Migaš.

**Spain:** Kiev, vul. Degtyarivska 38–41; tel. (44) 213-04-81; Ambassador: Eduardo Junco Bonet.

**Sweden:** 252021 Kiev, vul. Lipska 5, Hotel Natsionalny, Suite 1109; tel. (44) 291-89-19; fax (44) 291-62-33; Ambassador: Martin Hallqvist.

**Turkey:** 252021 Kiev, vul. Lipska 5, Hotel Natsionalny; tel. (44) 291-88-72; fax (44) 291-54-68; Ambassador: Acar Germen.

**Turkmenistan:** Kiev; Ambassador: Nedirhammed Alovov.

**United Kingdom:** 252025 Kiev, vul. Desyatinna 9; tel. (44) 228-05-04; telex 131429; fax (44) 228-39-72; Ambassador: Roy Reeve.

**USA:** Kiev, vul. Kotsyubynskoho 10; tel. (44) 244-73-44; fax (44) 244-73-51; Ambassador: William G. Miller.

## Judicial System

**Constitutional Court:** Kiev; Chair. (vacant).

**Supreme Court:** 252601 Kiev, vul. P. Orlika 4; tel. (44) 226-23-04; Chair. Vitaliy Boyko.

**Supreme Arbitration Court:** 252001 Kiev, vul. Kreshchatik 5; tel. (44) 226-32-39; fax (44) 228-70-42; f. 1991; Chief Justice Dmytro M. Prytyka.

**Procurator-General:** 252601 Kiev, vul. Riznitska 123/15; tel. (44) 226-20-27; Procurator-General Hennadiy Vasylyev (acting).

## Religion

### CHRISTIANITY

#### The Eastern Orthodox Church

Eastern Orthodoxy is the principal religious affiliation in Ukraine. Until 1990 all Orthodox churches were part of the Ukrainian exarchate of the Russian Orthodox Church. In that year the Russian Orthodox Church in Ukraine was renamed the Ukrainian Orthodox Church (UOC), partly to counter the growing influence of the Ukrainian Autocephalous Orthodox Church (UAOC). In the early 1990s there was considerable tension between the UOC and the UAOC over the issue of church property seized in 1930. A third Orthodox church was formed in June 1992, when Filaret, the disgraced former Metropolitan of Kiev, united with part of the UAOC to form the Kievan Patriarchate of the UOC, with himself as Patriarch. Patriarch Filaret had failed to secure canonical recognition for the Kievan Patriarchate of the UOC by January 1994.

**Ukrainian Autocephalous Orthodox Church:** Kiev; established in 1921 as part of the wider movement for Ukrainian autonomy, but forcibly incorporated into the Russian Orthodox Church in 1930; continued to operate clandestinely and among Ukrainian exiles; formally revived in Ukraine in 1990; Patriarch of Kiev and All Ukraine His Holiness Dmytro.

**Ukrainian Orthodox Church:** Kiev, Pechersk Monastery, Sichnevoho povstannia 21; tel. (44) 290-08-66; exarchate of the Russian Orthodox Church; owes allegiance to the Moscow Patriarchate; Metropolitan of Kiev Vladimir.

**Ukrainian Orthodox Church (Kievan Patriarchate):** Kiev; f. 1992; Patriarch of All Ukraine (vacant).

#### Roman Catholicism

Most Roman Catholics in Ukraine are adherents of the Byzantine Rite, the so-called Uniate ('Greek' Catholic) Church, which is based principally in Western Ukraine and Transcarpathia. In June 1992 there were 2,700 Uniate churches in Ukraine and 452 Roman Catholic churches of the Latin Rite. Ukraine comprises three archdioceses (including one each for Catholics of the Latin, Uniate and Armenian rites), nine dioceses (of which one is directly responsible to the Holy See) and one Apostolic Administration. At 31 December 1992 there were an estimated 7,357,847 adherents. Adherents of Latin-Rite Catholicism in Ukraine are predominantly ethnic Poles.

**Bishops' Conference:** 290008 Lviv, pl. Katedralna 1; tel. (322) 79-70-92; f. 1992; Pres. Most Rev. Marian Jaworski, Archbishop of Lviv.

**Armenian Catholic Church:** Lviv; Archbishop (vacant).

**Metropolitan See of Lviv (Latin Rite):** 290008 Lviv, pl. Katedralna 1; tel. (322) 72-56-82; Archbishop Marian Jaworski.

**Ukrainian Catholic (Uniate) Church:** 290000 Lviv, pl. Sviatoho Jura 5; tel. (322) 720-007; fax (322) 798-687; established in 1596 by the Union of Brest, which permitted Orthodox clergymen to retain the Eastern rite, but transferred their allegiance to the Pope; in 1946 at the Synod of Lvov (Lviv Sobor) the Uniates were forcibly integrated into the Russian Orthodox Church, but continued to function in an 'underground' capacity; Archbishop-Major of Lviv Cardinal Myroslav I. Lubachivsky.

### ISLAM

**Association of Independent Muslim Communities of Ukraine:** Donetsk; f. 1994; Chair. Rashid Bragin.

**Spiritual Administration of Muslims in Ukraine:** Kiev; Mufti Sheikh Ahmed Tamin.

## The Press

In 1992 there were 1,695 officially-registered newspaper titles published in Ukraine. There were also 321 periodicals.

The publications listed below are in Ukrainian, except where otherwise stated.

### PRINCIPAL NEWSPAPERS

**Demokratychna Ukraina** (Democratic Ukraine): 252047 Kiev, Peremohy pr. 50; tel. (44) 224-52-92; f. 1918; fmrly *Radyanska Ukraina* (Soviet Ukraine); 5 a week; independent; Editor Oleksandr Pobigai; circ. 311,300.

**Holos Ukrainy** (Voice of Ukraine): 252047 Kiev, vul. Nesterova 4; tel. (44) 441-88-23; fax (44) 224-72-54; organ of the Supreme Council; in Ukrainian and Russian; 5 a week; Editor Serhiy Pravdenko; circ. 448,000 (1992).

**Literaturna Ukraina:** 252601 Kiev, bul. Lesi Ukrainki 20; tel. (44) 296-36-39; f. 1927; weekly; organ of the Union of Writers of Ukraine; Editor Borys Rogoza; circ. 45,000 (1992).

**News from Ukraine:** 254107 Kiev, vul. O. Shmidta 35/37; f. 1964; weekly; publ. by the joint-stock co. News from Ukraine; in English; readership in 70 countries; Editor Volodymyr Kanash; circ. 20,000.

**Nezavizimost** (Independence): 252047 Kiev, Peremohy pr. 50; tel. (44) 441-85-78; fmrly *Komsomolskoe Znamya* (Komsomol Banner); independent; 2 a week; in Russian; Editor-in-Chief Volodymyr Kuleba.

**Pravda Ukrainy** (Ukrainian Pravda): 252047 Kiev, Peremohy pr. 50; tel. (44) 441-85-34; f. 1938; 5 a week; in Russian; Editor Oleksandr Gorobets; circ. 358,300.

**Rabochaya Gazeta/Robitnycha Hazeta** (Workers' Gazette): 252047 Kiev, Peremohy pr. 50; tel. (44) 224-33-01; fax (44) 446-02-98; f. 1957; 5 a week; publ. by the Cabinet of Ministers and Inter-regional Association of Manufacturers; editions in Russian and Ukrainian; Editor-in-Chief Evelina V. Babenko-Pivtoradni; circ. 176,000 (1993).

**Silski Visti** (Rural News): 252047 Kiev, Peremohy pr. 50; tel. (44) 441-83-33; fax (44) 446-93-71; f. 1920; 5 a week; Editor I. V. Spodarenko; circ. 550,000 (1992).

**Uryadovoiy Kuryer** (Official Courier): 252008 Kiev, vul. Sadova 1/14; tel. (44) 293-12-95; 5 a week; organ of the Cabinet of Ministers; Editor-in-Chief Mykhailo Soroka.

**Vecherniy Kyiv** (Evening Kiev): 252136 Kiev, vul. Marshala Hrechka 13; tel. (44) 434-61-09; fax (44) 443-96-09; f. 1919; 5 a week; Editor-in-Chief Vitaliy Karpenko; circ. 80,000–100,000.

**Za Vilnu Ukrainu:** 290000 Lviv, vul. Timiryazeva 3; tel. (322) 72-89-04; fax (322) 72-95-27; f. 1990; 5 a week; independent; Editor-in-Chief Bogdan Vovk; circ. 50,300 (1994).

### PRINCIPAL PERIODICALS

**Barvinok** (Periwinkle): 254119 Kiev, vul. Degtyarivska 38–44; tel. (44) 211-04-98; f. 1928; fortnightly; illustrated popular fiction for school-age children; in Ukrainian and Russian; Editor Vasyl Voronovich; circ. 150,000.

**Berezil** (March): 310002 Kharkiv, vul. Chernyshevskoho 59; tel. (572) 43-41-84; f. 1956; fmrly *Prapor*; monthly; publ. by the Prapor (Flag) Publishing House; journal of Union of Writers of Ukraine; fiction and socio-political articles; Editor-in-Chief Yuriy Stadnychenko; circ. 5,000.

**Dnipro** (The Dnieper River): 254119 Kiev, vul. Degtyarivska 38–44; tel. (44) 446-11-42; f. 1927; monthly; novels, short stories, essays, poetry; social and political topics; Editor Mykola Lukiv; circ. 71,900.

**Donbass** (The Donets Coal Basin): 340055 Donetsk, vul. Artema 80a; tel. (622) 93-82-26; f. 1923; monthly; journal of Union of Writers of Ukraine; fiction; in Ukrainian and Russian; circ. 20,000 (1991).

**Dzvin** (Bell): 290005 Lviv, vul. Vatutina 6; tel. (322) 72-36-20; f. 1940; monthly; publ. by the Kamenyar Publishing House; journal of Union of Writers of Ukraine; fiction; Editor Roman Fedoriv; circ. 152,500.

**Khronika 2,000—Nash Kray** (Chronicle 2,000—Our Land): 252001 Kiev, vul. M. Hrushevskoho 1d; tel. (44) 296-64-36; fax

# UKRAINE

(44) 228-88-62; f. 1992; Ukrainian cultural almanac; monthly; Editor-in-Chief YURIY BURYAK; circ. 15,000.

**Kiev:** 252025 Kiev, vul. Desyatinna 11; tel. (44) 229-02-80; f. 1983; monthly; publ. by the Ukrainsky Pysmennyk (Ukrainian Writer) Publishing House; journal of the Union of Writers of Ukraine and the Kiev Writers' Organization; fiction; Editor-in-Chief PETRO M. PEREBOINOS; circ. 39,600.

**Lel-revue:** 254119 Kiev, vul. Degtyarivska 38–44; tel. (44) 211-02-89; fax (44) 211-02-68; f. 1992; bimonthly; erotic fiction and arts; in Ukrainian, Russian, German and English; Editor-in-Chief SERHIY CHIRKOV; circ. 20,000.

**Lyudina i Svit** (Man and World): 254054 Kiev, vul. Observatorna; tel. (44) 216-78-17; f. 1960; monthly; popular scientific; religious; Editor-in-Chief MYKOLA RUBANETS; circ. 46,000.

**Malyatko** (Child): 254119 Kiev, vul. Degtyarivska 38–44; tel. (44) 213-98-91; f. 1960; monthly; illustrated; for pre-school children; Editor-in-Chief SVITLANA YEFIMENKO; circ. 180,000 (1994).

**Muzyka** (Music): 252001 Kiev, vul. Khreshchatik 48; tel. (44) 225-60-72; f. 1923; 6 a year; organ of the Ministry of Culture and the Musicians' Union of Ukraine; musical culture and aesthetics; Editor EDUARD YAVORSKY; circ. 8,200.

**Nauka ta Suspilstvo** (Science and Society): 252047 Kiev, Peremohy pr. 50; tel. (44) 441-88-10; f. 1923; monthly; journal of the Ukrainian Society Znannya (Knowledge); popular scientific; illustrated; Editor-in-Chief BORYS GICHKO; circ. 48,800.

**Obrazotvorche Mistetstvo** (Fine Arts): 254655 Kiev, vul. Artema 1–5; tel. (44) 212-02-86; f. 1935; 4 a year; publ. by the Artists' Union of Ukraine; fine arts; Editor-in-Chief MYKOLA MARYCHEVSKY; circ. 5,200.

**Odnoklassnik** (Classmate): 254119 Kiev, vul. Degtyarivska 38–44; tel. (44) 211-02-78; f. 1923; monthly; fiction; for teenagers; in Ukrainian and Russian; Editor-in-Chief SERHIY CHIRKOV; circ. 36,000 in Ukrainian, 19,000 in Russian.

**Perets** (Pepper): 252047 Kiev, Peremohy pr. 50; tel. (44) 441-82-14; f. 1927; fortnightly; publ. by the Presa Ukrainy (Press of Ukraine) Publishing House; satirical; Editor YURIY PROKOPENKO; circ. 1,946,900.

**Politika i Chas** (Politics and Time): 252025 Kiev, vul. Desyatinna 4–6; tel. (44) 229-75-73; f. 1992; monthly; organ of the Ministry of Foreign Affairs; international affairs and foreign relations of Ukraine; in Ukrainian and English; Editor-in-Chief L. S. BAYDAK; circ. 6,000.

**Raduga** (Rainbow): 252004 Kiev, vul. Pushkinska 32; tel. (44) 213-33-52; f. 1950; monthly; fiction and politics; in Russian; Editor YURIY KOVALSKY; circ. 51,140.

**Ranok** (Morning): 254119 Kiev, vul. Degtyarivska 38–44; tel. (44) 213-15-96; f. 1953; fortnightly; organ of the Liberal Party of Ukraine; for young people; social, political and fiction; Editor OLEKSANDR RUSHCHAK; circ. 105,000.

**Start** (Start): 254119 Kiev, vul. Degtyarivska 38–44; tel. (44) 224-71-20; f. 1922; monthly; sports news; Editor ANATOLIY CHALY; circ. 115,000.

**Ukraina** (Ukraine): 252047 Kiev, Peremohy pr. 50; tel. (44) 441-88-31; f. 1941; weekly; social and political life in Ukraine; illustrated; Editor-in-Chief OLEKSANDR KLIMCHUK; circ. 70,000.

**Ukrainsky Teatr** (Ukrainian Theatre): 252025 Kiev, vul. Velyka Zhytomyrska 6/2; tel. (44) 228-24-74; f. 1936; 6 a year; publ. by the Mistetstvo (Fine Art) Publishing House; journal of the Ministry of Culture and the Union of Theatrical Workers of Ukraine; Editor-in-Chief YURIY BOGDASHEVSKY; circ. 4,100.

**Visti z Ukrainy** (News from Ukraine): 252034 Kiev, vul. Zoloti Vorota 6; tel. (44) 228-56-42; fax (44) 228-04-28; f. 1960; weekly; aimed at Ukrainian diaspora; Editor VALERIY STETSENKO; circ. 50,000.

**Vitchizna** (Fatherland): 252021 Kiev, vul. M. Hrushevskoho 34; tel. (44) 293-28-51; f. 1933; monthly; publ. by the Ukrainsky Pysmennyk (Ukrainian Writer) Publishing House; journal of the Union of Writers of Ukraine; Ukrainian prose and poetry; Editor OLEKSANDR GLUSHKO; circ. 50,100.

**Vsesvit** (All the World): 252021 Kiev, vul. M. Hrushevskoho 34; tel. (44) 293-13-18; f. 1925; monthly; publ. by the Ukrainsky Pysmennyk (Ukrainian Writer) Publishing House; joint edition of the Union of Writers of Ukraine and the Ukrainian Peace Council; foreign fiction, critical works and reviews of foreign literature and art; Editor-in-Chief OLEG MIKITENKO; circ. 30,000.

**Zhinka** (Woman): 252047 Kiev, Peremohy pr. 50; tel. (44) 446-90-34; fax (44) 446-91-26; f. 1920; monthly; publ. by Presa Ukrainy (Press of Ukraine) Publishing House; social and political subjects; fiction; for women; Editor LIDIYA MAZUR; circ. 250,000.

## NEWS AGENCIES

**Respublika:** Kiev-140, POB 136, vul. Nyzhny val 23D; tel. (44) 417-13-32; independent press agency; Dir S. NABOKA.

**Rukh Press:** 252032 Kiev, Shevchenka bul. 37/122; tel. and fax (44) 244-64-00; affiliated to the Rukh political movement; f. 1989 as Rukh Inform, renamed 1990; issues information in Ukrainian and English; Dir DMYTRO PONAMARCHUK.

**Ukrainian National Information Agency (UKRINFORM):** 252601 Kiev, vul. Bohdana Khmelnytskoho 8/16; tel. (44) 226-32-30; telex 131210; fax (44) 229-24-39; official news agency, covering political, economic, diplomatic, cultural and sporting information; Dir VITALIY F. VOZIANOV.

**Ukrainian Press Agency:** Kiev, vul. Baumana 53/16; tel. (44) 221-55-07; fax (44) 221-55-07; independent news agency; Dir T. KUZIO.

### Foreign Bureaux

**Agenzia Nazionale Stampa Associata (ANSA)** (Italy): Kiev, Chitadelnaya 5–9, kv. 45; tel. (44) 290-21-38; fax (44) 290-21-38; Correspondent ALESSANDRO PARONE.

**Česká tisková kancelář (ČTK)** (Czech Republic): 252042 Kiev, vul. Ivana Kudri 41/22, kv. 49; tel. and fax (44) 295-91-61.

**Deutsche Presse-Agentur (dpa)** (Germany): 252001 Kiev, vul. Kreshchatik 29, kv. 32; tel. (44) 225-57-60.

**Magyar Távirati Iroda (MTI)** (Hungary): Kiev, vul. Ivana Franka 24A, kv. 8; Correspondent SÁNDOR MESTER.

**Reuters Ltd** (United Kingdom): Kiev, vul. Bohdana Khmelnytskoho 8/16, Office 112; tel. (44) 229-22-64; Chief Correspondent R. POPESKI.

## Publishers

In 1992 there were 4,410 book titles (including pamphlets and brochures) published in Ukraine (total circulation 128.5m.).

**Budivelnik** (Building): 254053 Kiev, Observatorna vul. 25; tel. (44) 212-10-90; f. 1947; books on building and architecture; in Ukrainian and Russian; Dir S. N. BALATSKY.

**Carpaty** (Carpathian Mountains): 294000 Ushhorod, Radyanska pl. 3; tel. (3122) 3-25-13; fiction and criticism; in Ukrainian and Russian; Dir V. I. DANKANICH.

**Dnipro** (The Dnieper River): 252601 Kiev, Volodymyrska vul. 42; tel. (44) 224-31-82; f. 1919; fiction, poetry and critical works; in Ukrainian and Russian; Dir TARAS I. SERGIYCHUK.

**Donbass** (The Donets Coal Basin): 340002 Donetsk, vul. Bohdana Khmelnytskoho 102; tel. (622) 93-25-84; fiction and criticism; in Ukrainian and Russian; Dir B. F. KRAVCHENKO.

**Kamenyar** (Stonecrusher): 290006 Lviv, vul. Pidvalna 3; tel. (322) 72-19-49; fiction and criticism; in Ukrainian; Dir M. V. NECHAY.

**Mayak** (Lighthouse): 270001 Odesa, vul. Zhukovskoho 14; tel. (482) 22-35-95; fiction and criticism; in Ukrainian and Russian; Dir D. A. BUKHANENKO.

**Mistetstvo** (Fine Art): 252034 Kiev, vul. Zolotovoritska 11; tel. (44) 225-53-92; fax (44) 229-05-64; f. 1932; fine art criticism, theatre and screen art, tourism, Ukrainian culture; in Ukrainian, Russian, English, French and German; Dir VALENTIN M. KUZMENKO.

**Molod** (Youth): 252119 Kiev, vul. Degtyarivska 38–44; tel. (44) 213-11-60; fax (44) 213-98-69; in Ukrainian; Dir A. I. DAVIDOV.

**Muzichna Ukraina** (Music of Ukraine): 252004 Kiev, Pushkinska vul. 32; tel. (44) 225-63-56; fax (44) 224-63-00; f. 1966; books on music; in Ukrainian; Dir N. P. LINNIK; Editor-in-Chief B. R. VERESHCHAGIN.

**Naukova Dumka** (Scientific Thought): 252601 Kiev, vul. Tereshchenkivska 3; tel. (44) 224-40-68; fax (44) 224-70-60; f. 1922; scientific books and periodicals in all branches of science; research monographs; in Ukrainian, Russian and English; Dir I. R. ALEXEYENKO.

**Osvita** (Education): 252053 Kiev, vul. Y. Kotsyubynskoho 5; tel. (44) 216-58-02; fax (44) 216-98-15; f. 1920; textbooks for secondary schools; Dir I. M. PODOLYUK.

**Politvidav Ukrainy** (Ukraine Political Publishing House): 254025 Kiev, vul. Desyatinna 4/6; tel. (44) 229-16-92; academic, reference and popular works; law, social and economic issues, religion; calendars, posters, etc.; in Ukrainian, Russian and other European languages; Dir G. F. NEMAZANY.

**Prapor** (Flag): 310002 Kharkiv, vul. Chubarya 11; tel. (572) 47-72-52; fmrly named Berezil (March); fiction and criticism; in Ukrainian and Russian; Dir A. M. KUMAKA.

**Sich** (Youth): 320070 Dnipropetrovsk, K. Marks pr. 60; tel. (562) 45-22-01; f. 1964; fiction, juvenile, socio-political, criticism; in Ukrainian, English, German, French and Russian; Dir V. A. SIROTA; Editor-in-Chief V. V. LEVCHENKO.

**Tavria:** 330000 Simferopol, vul. Gorkoho 5; tel. (652) 7-45-66; fiction and criticism; in Ukrainian and in Russian; Dir I. N. KLOSOVSKY.

# UKRAINE

**Tekhnika** (Technical Publishing House): 252601 Kiev, vul. Pushkinska 28/9; tel. (44) 228-22-43; f. 1930; industry and transport books, popular science, posters and booklets; in Ukrainian and Russian; Dir M. G. PISARENKO.

**Ukrainska Encyclopedia** (Ukrainian Encyclopedia): 252030 Kiev, vul. Bohdana Khmelnytskoho 51; tel. (44) 224-80-85; encyclopaedias, dictionaries and reference books; Dir A. V. KUDRITSKY.

**Ukrainsky Pysmennyk** (Ukrainian Writer): 252054 Kiev, vul. Chkalova 52; tel. (44) 216-25-92; f. 1933; publishing house of the Ukrainian Union of Writers; fiction; in Ukrainian; Dir V. P. SKOMAROVSKY.

**Urozhai** (Crop): 252035 Kiev, Yaroslaviv val 10; tel. (44) 245-11-96; f. 1925; books and journals about agriculture; Dir V. G. PRIKHODKO.

**Veselka** (Rainbow): 254055 Kiev, vul. Melnikova 63; tel. (44) 213-95-01; fax (44) 213-33-59; f. 1934; books for pre-school and school age children; in Ukrainian and foreign languages; Dir YAREMA HOYAN.

**Vyscha Shkola** (Higher School): 252054 Kiev, vul. Hoholivska 7; tel. (44) 216-33-05; f. 1968; educational, scientific, reference, etc.; Dir O. A. DOBROVOLSKY.

**Zdorovya** (Health Publishing House): 252601 Kiev, vul. Chkalova 65; tel. (44) 216-89-08; books on medicine, physical fitness and sport; in Ukrainian; Dir A. P. RODZIYEVSKY.

## Radio and Television

In 1992 there were a total of 17.3m. licensed television receivers and 41.5m. radio receivers in use.

**National Council for Television and Radio Broadcasting Issues** (Natsionalna Rada z Pytan Telebachennya i Radiomovlennya): Kiev; f. 1994; a state, extradepartmental body functioning in accordance with regulations approved by the Supreme Council.

**State Committee for Television and Radio** (Derzhteleradio): Kiev; f. 1995; Chair. ZYNOVIY KULYK; Deputy Chairs OLEKSANDR M. SAVENKO, VOLODYMYR P. REZNYKOV, VIKTOR P. ORKUSHA.

**Crimea (Krym) Television and Radio Company:** Simferopol; Pres. VALERIY ASTAKHOV.

## Finance

(cap. = capital; res = reserves; dep. = deposits; brs = branches; m. = million; amounts in karbovantsi

### BANKING
#### Central Bank

**National Bank of Ukraine:** 252007 Kiev, vul. Institutska 9; tel. (44) 293-38-22; telex 131251; fax (44) 293-16-98; Gov. VIKTOR YUSHCHENKO; Vice-Gov. Dr OLEKSANDR SAVCHENKO.

#### Other State Banks

**State Bank of Crimea:** Simferopol.

**UKREXIMBANK—Ukrainian Export-Import Bank:** 252001 Kiev, vul. Khreshchatik 8; tel. (44) 226-27-45; telex 131258; fax (44) 229-80-82; f. 1992; fmrly br. of USSR Vneshekonombank; deals with foreign firms, joint ventures and import-export associations; cap. 9,016.8m., res 395,498.4m., dep. 289,627.5m. (Jan. 1993); Chair. SERHIY O. YARMENKO; 10 brs.

#### Commercial Banks

In March 1995 there were 221 commercial banks in Ukraine.

**Commercial Bank for Development of Construction Materials Industry:** Kiev, vul. Artema 73; tel. (44) 211-39-13; telex 631266; fax (44) 216-75-95; cap. 1,000m., dep. 1,500m. (1993); Chair. of Bd V. I. GORBOVSKY; 2 brs.

**Inko Joint-Stock Bank:** 252021 Kiev, vul. Mechnikova 10; tel. (44) 432-45-66; fax (44) 294-87-90.

**Kiev Narodny Bank:** Kiev, vul. Sofiyevska 1; tel. (44) 228-74-51; telex 631334; fax (44) 229-35-55; f. 1989; cap. 496.8m. (Jan. 1993); Chair. of Bd VALERIY I. OHIYENKO; 4 brs.

**Kievcoopbank:** Kiev-5, vul. Anry Barbyusa 9; tel. (44) 268-32-04.

**Perkombank—Joint-Stock Commercial 'Personal Computer' Bank:** 254070 Kiev, vul. Sagaydachny 17; tel. (44) 291-86-20; telex 131420; fax (44) 291-86-60; f. 1990; cap. 12,000m., dep. 11,200m.; Chair. of Bd SERGEY P. BELY.

**Slaviansky Bank:** 330600 Zaporizhzhia, vul. Elektrozavodska; tel. (612) 52-13-25; fax (612) 52-13-80.

**Ukrinbank—Ukrainian Innovation Bank:** 252601 Kiev, vul. Institutska 12A; tel. (44) 228-76-37; telex 131320; fax (44) 229-02-75; f. 1989; long-term investment credits; commercial and foreign exchange transactions; cap. 109,000m.; Chair. YAROSLAV F. SOLTYS; 27 brs.

**Ukrlegbank—Commercial Bank for Development of Light Industry in Ukraine:** 252023 Kiev, vul. Esplanadnaya 8/10; tel. (44) 220-81-29; telex 631240; fax (44) 220-86-84.

**West-Ukrainian Commercial Bank:** 290017 Lviv, vul. Levitskoho 67; tel. (322) 75-05-51; telex 234199; fax (322) 75-05-71; f. 1990; cap. 66,986m., res 67,601m., dep. 19,323m. (April 1995); Pres. OLEKSANDR YA. DZHUBENKO; Chair. IVAN M. FESKIV; 15 brs.

**Zakhidkoopbank:** Ivano-Frankivsk; tel. (3422) 2-50-02; fax (3422) 2-38-82; f. 1990; cap. 500m., dep. 6,000m.; Dep. Chair. NELA POLITIKO; 6 brs.

#### Banking Association

**Association of Ukrainian Banks:** Kiev; fmrly Commercial Bank Asscn; Pres. OLEKSANDR SUHONYAKO.

### COMMODITY EXCHANGES

**Dnipropetrovsk Commodity Exchange:** 320006 Dnipropetrovsk, Turbinny spusk 3; tel. (562) 42-03-14; f. 1991; Gen. Man. VADIM KOMEKO.

**Kharkiv Commodity and Raw Materials Exchange:** 310022 Kharkiv, Office 307, Gosprom; tel. (572) 47-82-78; fax (572) 22-82-01; f. 1991; Chair. of Exchange Cttee ZAKHAR BRUK.

**Kiev Universal Commodity Exchange:** 252015 Kiev, vul. Leyptsihska 1A; tel. (44) 290-27-14; fax (44) 290-15-57; f. 1990; Pres. NIKOLAY DETOCHKA.

**Odesa Commodity Exchange:** 270114 Odesa, Chornomorskaya 140; tel. (482) 61-89-92; fax (482) 47-72-84; f. 1990; Gen. Man. NIKOLAY NIKOLISHEN.

**South Universal Commodity Exchange:** 327015 Mikolaiv, vul. Rabochaya 2A; tel. (510) 37-55-74; telex 272125; fax (510) 36-08-52; f. 1990; Gen. Dir NIKOLAY KOZHEMYAKIN.

### INSURANCE
#### State Insurance Company

**National Joint Stock Insurance Company—ORANTA:** 252021 Kiev, vul. M. Hrushevskoho 34/1; tel. (44) 293-45-16; fax (44) 293-15-84; state insurance grouping; inc. State Insurance Company of Ukraine; Head of Directorate S. P. HRUSHA.

#### Commercial Insurance Companies

**Inderzhstrakh:** Kiev; vul. Chekistiv 14/26; tel. (44) 212-29-19.

**Inkomrezerv:** Kiev, vul. Uritskoho 45; tel. (44) 244-09-80.

**OMETA Inster:** 254053 Kiev, vul. Artema 18; tel. (44) 244-69-72; fax (44) 212-38-58; Pres. V. SHEVCHENKO.

**Revival Insurance Company:** Kiev, vul. Kruhlouniversytetska 3; tel. (44) 224-71-50.

**ROSTOK Insurance Company:** Kiev, vul. Akademika Hlushkova 1, Pavilion 1; tel. (44) 261-75-55.

**SKAID Insurance Corporation:** Kiev, vul. Sofiyivska 9; tel. and fax (44) 228-05-22.

## Trade and Industry

### STATE PROPERTY AGENCY

**State Property Fund:** 252133 Kiev, vul. Kutuzova 18/9; tel. (44) 295-12-74; fax (44) 296-65-72; Chair. YURIY I. YEHANUROV.

### TRADE DIRECTORATE

**Chief Trade Directorate:** 252655 Kiev, Lvivska pl. 8; tel. (44) 226-27-33; f. 1993; a section of Ministry of Foreign Economic Relations and Trade.

### CHAMBERS OF COMMERCE

**Ukrainian Chamber of Commerce and Industry:** 254655 Kiev, vul. V. Zhytomyrska 33; tel. (44) 212-29-11; telex 131379; fax (44) 212-33-53; f. 1973; 20 brs; Chair. OLEKSIY P. MIKHAILICHENKO.

**Congress of Business Circles of Ukraine:** 252601 Kiev, vul. Prorizna 15; tel. (44) 228-64-81; fax (44) 229-52-84; Pres. VALERIY G. BABICH.

### FOREIGN TRADE ORGANIZATION

**Ukrimpex:** 252054 Kiev, vul. Vorovskoho 22; tel. (44) 216-21-74; telex 131384; fax (44) 216-29-96; f. 1987; imports and exports a wide range of goods; organizes joint ventures, exhibitions; provides consultancy and marketing expertise and business services; Dir-Gen. STANISLAV I. SOKOLENKO.

## TRADE UNIONS

**Federation of Trade Unions of Ukraine:** 252012 Kiev, Maydan Nezalezhnosti 2; tel. (44) 228-87-88; fax (44) 229-00-87; f. 1990; fmrly Ukrainian branch of General Confederation of Trade Unions of the USSR; affiliation of 41 br. trade unions and 26 regional trade union federations; Chair. OLEKSANDR M. STOYAN.

# Transport

### RAILWAYS

In 1993 there were 22,625 km of railway track in use, with lines linking most towns and cities in the republic. Kiev is linked by rail to all the other republics of the former USSR, and there are direct lines to Warsaw (Poland), Budapest (Hungary), Bucharest (Romania), Bratislava (Slovakia) and Berlin (Germany).

**State Railway Transport Administration:** 252034 Kiev, vul. Lysenka 6; tel. (44) 223-63-05; fax (44) 224-63-93; Dir-Gen. LEONID ZHELEZNIAK.

### ROADS

At 31 December 1993 there were 170,518 km of roads: 29,338 km of main or national roads; 1,808 km of motorways; 22,518 km of secondary or regional roads; and an estimated 116,854 km of other roads.

### INLAND WATERWAYS

In 1990 there were 4,400 km of navigable waterways. The Dnieper (Dnipro) river, which links Kiev, Cherkasy, Dnipropetrovsk and Zaporizhzhia with the Black Sea, is the most important route for river freight.

### SHIPPING

The main ports are Yalta and Yevpatoriya in Crimea, and Odesa. In addition to international shipping lines, there are services to the Russian ports of Novorossiysk and Sochi, and Batumi and Sukhumi in Georgia.

#### Shipping Companies

**Azov Shipping Company:** 341010 Mariupol, pr. Admirala Lunina 89; tel. (6292) 5-80-33; telex 115156; Pres. A. I. BANDURA.

**Black Sea Shipping Company (BLASCO):** 270026 Odesa, vul. Lastochkina 1; tel. (482) 25-21-60; telex 232248; Pres. PAVEL KUDYUKIN.

**Danube Shipping Company:** 272630 Izmail, pr. Suvorova 2; telex 232817; Pres. A. F. TEKHOV.

### CIVIL AVIATION

Ukraine has air links with cities throughout the former USSR and with major European, North American, Asian and African cities. The principal international airport is at Boryspil (Kiev).

#### National Airline

**Ukrainian International Airlines:** 252135 Kiev, Peremohy pr. 14; tel. (44) 221-81-35; fax (44) 216-79-94; f. 1992; scheduled services within Europe; Pres. VITALIY POTYOMSKY.

# Tourism

The Black Sea coast of Ukraine has several popular resorts, including Odesa and Yalta. The Crimean peninsula is a popular tourist centre in both summer and winter, owing to its temperate climate. Kiev and Odesa have important historical attractions. The tourist industry is little developed outside Kiev and the Black Sea resorts, and the number of hotels and other facilities is low. There were 650,000 foreign tourist arrivals in Ukraine in 1994, when revenue from tourism totalled US $189m.

**State Committee for Tourism:** 252034 Kiev, Yaroslaviv val 36; tel. (44) 212-42-15; telex 631443; fax (44) 224-81-59; Chair. VLADIMIR I. SKRINNIK.

# THE UNITED ARAB EMIRATES

## Introductory Survey

### Location, Climate, Language, Religion, Flag, Capital

The United Arab Emirates (UAE) lies in the east of the Arabian peninsula. It is bordered by Saudi Arabia to the west and south, and by Oman to the east. In the north the UAE has a short frontier with Qatar and a coastline of about 650 km (400 miles) on the southern shore of the Persian (Arabian) Gulf, separated by a detached portion of Omani territory from a small section of coast on the western shore of the Gulf of Oman. The climate is exceptionally hot in summer, with average maximum temperatures exceeding 40°C (104°F), and humidity is very high. Winter is mild, with temperatures ranging from 17°C (62.6°F) to 20°C (68°F). Average annual rainfall is very low: between 100mm (4 ins) and 200mm (8 ins). The official language is Arabic, spoken by almost all of the native population. Arabs are, however, outnumbered by non-Arab immigrants, mainly from India, Pakistan, Bangladesh and Iran. According to official estimates, UAE nationals represented about 25% of the total population in 1994. English is used as a second language in commerce. Most of the inhabitants are Muslims, mainly of the Sunni sect. The national flag (proportions 2 by 1) has three equal horizontal stripes, of green, white and black, with a vertical red stripe at the hoist. The capital is Abu Dhabi.

### Recent History

Prior to independence, the UAE was Trucial Oman, also known as the Trucial States, and the component sheikhdoms of the territory were under British protection. Although, from 1892, the United Kingdom assumed responsibility for the sheikhdoms' defence and external relations, they were otherwise autonomous and followed the traditional form of Arab monarchy, with each ruler having virtually absolute power over his subjects.

In 1952 a local body, the Trucial Council, comprising the rulers of the seven sheikhdoms, was established. The object of the Council was to encourage the adoption of common policies in administrative matters, possibly leading to a federation of the states. Petroleum, the basis of the area's modern prosperity, was first discovered in 1958, when deposits were located beneath the coastal waters of Abu Dhabi, the largest of the sheikhdoms. Onshore petroleum was found in Abu Dhabi in 1960. Commercial exploitation of petroleum began there in 1962, providing the state with greatly increased revenue. However, Sheikh Shakhbut bin Sultan an-Nahyan, the Ruler of Abu Dhabi since 1928, failed to use the income from petroleum royalties to develop his domain. As a result, the ruling family deposed Sheikh Shakhbut in August 1966, replacing him by his younger brother, Sheikh Zayed bin Sultan. Under the rule of Sheikh Zayed, Abu Dhabi was transformed by using its considerable income from the petroleum industry for public works and the provision of welfare services. Petroleum was discovered in neighbouring Dubai (the second largest of the Trucial States) in 1966. Production began there in 1969, and, using the resultant revenue, the sheikhdom also developed rapidly.

In January 1968 the United Kingdom announced its intention of withdrawing British military forces from the area by 1971. In March 1968 the Trucial States joined nearby Bahrain and Qatar, which were also under British protection, in what was named the Federation of Arab Emirates. It was intended that the Federation should become fully independent, but the interests of Bahrain and Qatar proved to be incompatible with those of the smaller sheikhdoms, and both seceded from the Federation in August 1971 to become separate independent states. In July six of the Trucial States (Abu Dhabi, Dubai, Sharjah, Umm al-Qaiwain, Ajman and Fujairah) had agreed on a federal Constitution for achieving independence as the United Arab Emirates (UAE). The United Kingdom accordingly terminated its special treaty relationship with the States, and the UAE became independent on 2 December 1971. The remaining sheikhdom, Ras al-Khaimah, joined the UAE in February 1972. At independence Sheikh Zayed of Abu Dhabi took office as the first President of the UAE. Sheikh Rashid bin Said al-Maktoum, the Ruler of Dubai since 1958, became Vice-President, while his eldest son, Sheikh Maktoum bin Rashid al-Maktoum (Crown Prince of Dubai), became Prime Minister in the Federal Council of Ministers. A 40-member consultative assembly, the Federal National Council, was also inaugurated.

In January 1972 the Ruler of Sharjah, Sheikh Khalid bin Muhammad al-Qasimi, was killed by rebels under the leadership of his cousin, Sheikh Saqr bin Sultan, who had been deposed as the sheikhdom's Ruler in June 1965. However, the rebels were defeated, and Sheikh Khalid was succeeded by his brother, Sheikh Sultan bin Muhammad al-Qasimi. Production of petroleum began in Sharjah in 1974, although output remains at a much lower level than that of Abu Dhabi or Dubai.

In August 1976 Sheikh Zayed, disappointed with progress towards centralization, reportedly announced that he was not prepared to accept another five-year term as President. In November, however, the highest federal authority, the Supreme Council of Rulers (comprising the Rulers of the seven emirates), re-elected him unanimously, following agreements granting the Federal Government greater control over defence, intelligence services, immigration, public security and border control.

Owing to a dispute over a senior appointment in February 1978, the forces of Dubai and Ras al-Khaimah refused to accept orders from the Federal Defence Force. Although Ras al-Khaimah later reintegrated with the Federal Defence Force, Dubai's armed forces effectively remained a separate entity. In March 1979 a 10-point memorandum from the National Council, containing proposals for increased unity, was rejected by Dubai, which, together with Ras al-Khaimah, boycotted a meeting of the Supreme Council. In April Sheikh Maktoum resigned as Prime Minister; he was replaced by his father, Sheikh Rashid, who formed a new Council of Ministers in July, while retaining the post of Vice-President. Although Sheikh Rashid's health was deteriorating, both he and Sheikh Zayed were re-elected to their posts by the Supreme Council in November 1981. (Sheikh Rashid had suffered a stroke which left him bedridden until his death in 1990.) Meanwhile, Sheikh Ahmad bin Rashid al-Mu'alla, the Ruler of Umm al-Qaiwain (the smallest of the seven emirates) since 1929, died in February 1981, and was succeeded by his son, Rashid. Sheikh Rashid bin Humaid an-Nuaimi, the Ruler of Ajman since 1928, died in September 1981, and was succeeded by his son, Humaid. By 1984 the worsening health of Sheikh Rashid of Dubai led to a transfer of power to his four sons, and, as a result, federal affairs were neglected, causing some general confusion in the internal affairs of the UAE.

In October 1986 the provisional Federal Constitution was renewed for a further five years, and Sheikh Zayed and Sheikh Rashid were unanimously re-elected to the posts of President, and Vice-President and Prime Minister, respectively.

An attempted coup took place in Sharjah in June 1987, when Sheikh Abd al-Aziz, a brother of Sheikh Sultan, announced (in his brother's absence), via the country's official news agency, the abdication of the Ruler, on the grounds that he had mismanaged the economy. The Supreme Council of Rulers intervened and endorsed Sheikh Sultan's claim to be the legitimate Ruler of Sharjah, and restored him to power. Sheikh Abd al-Aziz was given the title of Crown Prince and was granted a seat on the Supreme Council. In February 1990, however, Sheikh Sultan removed his brother from the post of Crown Prince and revoked his right to succeed him as Ruler. In July Sheikh Sultan appointed Sheikh Ahmad bin Muhammad al-Qasimi, the head of Sharjah's petroleum and mineral affairs office, as Deputy Ruler of Sharjah, although he was not given the title of Crown Prince.

In October 1990 (upon the death of his father) Sheikh Maktoum acceded to the positions of Ruler of Dubai and Vice-President and Prime Minister of the UAE. In November a reorganization of the Council of Ministers took place. The post of Minister of Foreign Affairs, unoccupied since 1982, was filled by the former Minister of State for Foreign Affairs, Rashid Abdullah an-Nuaimi. His former portfolio was subsequently assumed by the President's son, Sheikh Hamdan bin Zayed an-Nahyan, while another son, Sheikh Sultan bin Zayed an-Nahyan, was appointed Deputy Prime Minister. In October 1991 the Supreme Council confirmed Sheikh Zayed and Sheikh Maktoum as, respectively, President, and Vice-President and Prime Minister, each for a further five-year term. The Constitution was also renewed for a further period of five years.

In February 1994 Yousuf bin Omeir bin Yousuf, the Minister of Petroleum and Mineral Resources, resigned, citing personal reasons. He thus became the first minister to have resigned since the federation was established in 1971. In the same month Sheikh Zayed ordered that a wide range of crimes, including murder, theft, adultery and drugs offences, be tried in *Shari'a* (Islamic religious law) courts rather than in civil courts.

The UAE was a founder member of the Co-operation Council for the Arab States of the Gulf (generally known as the Gulf Co-operation Council—GCC, see p. 130) in May 1981. The GCC aims to achieve greater political and economic integration between Gulf countries, and, from 1983 onwards, the UAE took part in joint military exercises with the other member states.

Since the Arab-Israeli war of October 1973, in which it strongly supported the Arab cause, the UAE has contributed large sums of aid to Arab countries. Despite giving aid to Iraq in the Iran-Iraq war (1980-88), diplomatic relations with Iran were maintained, and the UAE offered to mediate between the two countries. In late 1983 Sheikh Zayed mediated between Iraq and Syria, and the UAE also participated in a GCC initiative to end conflict between rival Palestinian forces in the Lebanese port of Tripoli. The presence of mines (presumed to have been laid by Iran) off the UAE coast in 1987 persuaded the UAE Government to allow the use of its ports as a base for British and French minesweeping operations. From April 1988 the Mubarak oilfield, which belongs to the emirate of Sharjah, and is located 30 km off the coast of the UAE, was closed for a period of two months, following an attack on its installations by forces involved in the Iran-Iraq war.

In common with the other Arab states, the UAE condemned the 1979 Camp David agreements between Egypt and Israel, and diplomatic relations with Egypt were severed. Full diplomatic relations were restored in November 1987. Commercial links have since been fostered by the two countries.

In August 1990 Iraq's occupation of Kuwait provoked economic and political instability throughout the region. The UAE responded by supporting, with most Arab states, resistance to Iraqi aggression, and on 20 August the UAE ordered all nationals to join the armed forces for six weeks' military training. At the same time it was announced that foreign armed forces opposing the Iraqi invasion would be provided with military facilities in the Emirates. The British and French air forces were among those stationed in the UAE. In February 1991, after the outbreak of hostilities, four raids against Iraqi targets were undertaken by the UAE air force.

In 1991 the UAE became involved in a major international financial scandal, when, in July, the regulatory authorities in seven countries closed down (without warning) the operations of the Bank of Credit and Commerce International (BCCI), in which the Abu Dhabi ruling family and agencies had held a controlling interest (77%) since April 1990. The termination of the bank's activities followed the disclosure by an auditor's report, commissioned by the Bank of England, of systematic, large-scale fraud by BCCI authorities (perpetrated before April 1990). By the end of July 1991 BCCI's activities had been suspended in all 69 countries in which it had operated. Attempts to formulate a restructuring programme for the bank failed, and in February 1992 the bank's majority shareholders offered to pay a maximum of US $2,200m. into a fund to compensate BCCI creditors. By October the compensation plan, worth a total of $1,700m., had been approved by more than 90% of BCCI creditors. In that month the settlement received judicial authorization in Luxembourg (courts in the UK and the Cayman Islands—the other principal centres for the collapsed bank's activities—had already endorsed the plan). None the less, the compensation process was delayed in December, when three prominent creditors, who had objected to a clause that would require recipients of compensation to waive any further claims against Abu Dhabi in respect of the BCCI scandal, initiated appeal proceedings against the Luxembourg ruling.

The ruling was overturned in October 1993, and the BCCI's liquidators, Touche Ross, and the bank's majority shareholders were obliged to negotiate a new compensation agreement. In December the Abu Dhabi authorities instituted a civil action against 13 former executives of the bank, of whom 11 were in custody in the emirate at that time. At the conclusion of the trials in May 1994 all but one of the defendants were sentenced to terms of imprisonment ranging from three to 14 years. In February 1995 a compensation agreement worth a total of $1,800m. received judicial authorization in Luxembourg.

Conflict arose between the UAE and Iran in 1992 concerning the sovereignty of Abu Musa, an island situated between the states in the Persian (Arabian) Gulf. The island had been administered since 1991 under a joint agreement between Iran and Sharjah, in accordance with which an Iranian garrison was stationed on the island. In that year Iran had also seized the smaller neighbouring islands of Greater and Lesser Tumb. In April 1992 the Iranian garrison on Abu Musa was reported to have seized civilian installations on the island. There were further allegations that Iranian officials were attempting to force expatriate workers employed by the UAE to leave the island, preventing the entry of other expatriates, and increasing the number of Iranian nationals on the island. In September, in response to a GCC statement expressing support for the UAE in the dispute, the Iranian Government reiterated its claim to the three islands. Following Syrian mediation, delegations from the UAE and Iran met in Abu Dhabi at the end of the month, but negotiations collapsed on the following day. Indirect negotiations continued throughout October: the Iranian Government was reported to be prepared to negotiate over the administration of Abu Musa alone, and in November several expatriate residents were permitted to return to the island. At a GCC summit meeting in Abu Dhabi in December, however, it was demanded that Iran reverse the 'virtual annexation' of the islands. Reports in early 1993 suggested that tension between the two countries had eased, although no formal settlement of the sovereignty issue had been agreed. In April it was reported that all those who had been expelled from or refused entry to Abu Musa in 1992 had been permitted to return. In October 1993 President Zayed announced the introduction of a federal law standardizing the limits of the UAE's territorial waters to 10 nautical miles (18.5 km) off shore. This was in response to a similar announcement by the Iranian authorities. Despite the purported commitment of the Governments of the UAE and Iran to enter into direct negotiations during the following year, by late 1994 no significant progress had been made towards resolving the conflict, and in December the UAE announced its intention to refer the dispute to the International Court of Justice.

In May 1993 President Mubarak of Egypt visited Abu Dhabi for talks with Sheikh Zayed on subjects including the Middle East peace negotiations and the lack of progress made in establishing an Arab peace-keeping force as proposed in March 1991 in Damascus, Syria. In September 1993 the UAE welcomed the conclusion of an Israeli-Palestinian peace accord, and undertook to provide financial assistance to the Palestinians. In September 1994 the UAE, along with the other GCC member states, agreed to a partial removal of the Arab economic boycott of Israel. In mid-January 1995 the UAE signed a defence agreement with France which provided for 'consultations' in the event of aggression against or threats to UAE territory; in March a similar agreement was reportedly under negotiation with the United Kingdom.

### Government

The highest federal authority is the Supreme Council of Rulers, comprising the hereditary rulers of the seven emirates, each of whom is virtually an absolute monarch in his own domain. Decisions of the Supreme Council require the approval of at least five members, including the rulers of both Abu Dhabi and Dubai. From its seven members, the Supreme Council elects a President and a Vice-President. The President appoints the Prime Minister and the Federal Council of Ministers, responsible to the Supreme Council, to hold executive authority. The legislature is the Federal National Council, a consultative assembly (comprising 40 members appointed for two years by the emirates) which considers laws proposed by the Council of Ministers. There are no political parties.

## Defence

In June 1994 the armed forces totalled 61,500 men: an army of 57,000, an air force of 2,500 and a navy of 2,000. The Union Defence Force and the armed forces of Abu Dhabi, Dubai, Ras al-Khaimah and Sharjah were formally merged in 1976, although Abu Dhabi and Dubai still maintain a degree of independence. Military service is voluntary. The defence budget for 1994 was estimated at Dh 7,000m. (US $1,900m.).

## Economic Affairs

In 1993, according to estimates by the World Bank, the UAE's gross national product (GNP), measured at average 1991–93 prices, was US $38,720m., equivalent to $22,470 per head. During 1985–93, it was estimated, GNP per head increased, in real terms, at an average annual rate of 0.5%. Over the same period the population increased by an annual average of 3.2%. In 1994, according to official figures, about 75% of the population were non-UAE nationals. The UAE's gross domestic product (GDP) increased, in real terms, by an annual average of 0.3% in 1980–92, and registered growth of 2.9% in 1994.

Agriculture (including livestock and fishing) contributed an estimated 2.1% of GDP in 1993. In 1993 an estimated 2.1% of the economically active population were employed in the sector. The principal crops are dates, tomatoes and aubergines. Livestock-rearing and fishing are also important. During 1980–89 agricultural GDP increased by an annual average of 8.9%.

Industry (including mining, manufacturing, construction and power) contributed an estimated 57.4% of GDP in 1993. About 30.9% of the working population were engaged in industry in 1990. During 1980–89 industrial GDP declined by an annual average of 5.2%.

Mining and quarrying contributed an estimated 38.4% of GDP in 1993, and employed an estimated 1.5% of the working population in 1990. Petroleum production is the most important industry in the UAE, providing 60.1% of total exports in 1992. At 1 January 1994 the UAE's proven recoverable reserves of petroleum were 99,600m. barrels, representing 9.9% of world reserves. In 1992 it was reported that the UAE was to invest US $5,000m.–$6,000m. in an effort to increase the average daily production of crude petroleum by approximately 600,000 barrels by 1995. In 1993 UAE petroleum production averaged 2.2m. barrels per day. The UAE has large natural gas reserves, estimated at 5,335,000m. cu m in January 1992. Most petroleum and natural gas reserves are concentrated in Abu Dhabi. Dubai is the second largest producer of petroleum in the UAE.

The major heavy industries in the UAE are related to hydrocarbons. The most important products are residual fuel oils, liquefied petroleum gas and distillate fuel oils. There are two petroleum refineries in Abu Dhabi, and the emirate has 'downstream' interests abroad.

Non-oil manufacturing industry contributed an estimated 8.1% of GDP in 1993, and employed an estimated 9.2% of the working population in 1990. The most important sectors are aluminium, steel and chemicals.

Electric energy is generated by using the UAE's own petroleum and natural gas resources. In 1994 the total installed capacity of UAE power stations was 5,000 MW. A further 2,000 MW was expected to be installed by 2000 to meet rising demand.

In 1992 the UAE recorded an estimated visible trade surplus of Dh 21,800m., and there was an estimated surplus of Dh 9,700m. on the current account of the balance of payments. In 1991 the principal source of imports (15.6%) was Japan. Other important suppliers in that year were the USA, the United Kingdom, Germany and the Republic of Korea. Japan took 34.8% of the UAE's exports in 1982. The principal exports in 1988 were crude petroleum, natural gas, and re-exports, principally machinery and transport equipment. The principal imports in 1991 were machinery and transport equipment, basic manufactures, food and live animals, fuels and lubricants, and chemicals.

In the financial year ending 31 December 1994 a federal budgetary deficit of Dh 1,397m. was forecast, while budget estimates for 1995 envisaged a deficit of Dh 1,046m. The federal budget reflects only about one-half of the country's total public expenditure, as the individual emirates also have their own budgets for municipal expenditure and local projects. Abu Dhabi is the major contributor to the federal budget. Annual inflation averaged 1.1% in 1980–91, but official sources indicated that the rate had risen to 6.5% in mid-1994. Official sources estimated that about 93% of the work-force were non-UAE nationals in 1992.

The UAE is a member of the Co-operation Council for the Arab States of the Gulf (Gulf Co-operation Council—GCC, see p. 130) and the Council of Arab Economic Unity (see p. 133), both of which attempt to encourage regional economic co-operation and development; it also belongs to the Organization of Arab Petroleum Exporting Countries (OAPEC, see p. 207), and the Organization of the Petroleum Exporting Countries (OPEC, see p. 210). The UAE, and Abu Dhabi in particular, is a major aid donor. Abu Dhabi disburses loans through the Abu Dhabi Fund for Development (ADFD). In March 1994 the UAE became a contracting party to the General Agreement on Tariffs and Trade (GATT—to be superseded by the World Trade Organization—see p. 64).

Abu Dhabi and Dubai, the principal petroleum producers, dominate the economy of the UAE, while the northern emirates remain relatively undeveloped, and there is little co-ordination in the economic affairs of the emirates. The UAE has begun to promote foreign investment in the non-petroleum industry, and the advanced technology sector in particular, in an attempt to diversify the economy. The UAE is less dependent than other petroleum-producing countries on the hydrocarbons sector. Although in 1991 exports of petroleum and gas accounted for about 70% of total export earnings, the sector accounted for less than 50% of GDP in the early 1990s. Moreover, a degree of import-substitution in the manufacturing sector has meant that the UAE's reliance on imported goods has declined appreciably. Dubai is of particular importance as an entrepôt for regional trade. In late 1994 the Government introduced a uniform 4% import tariff, with the aim of doubling customs revenue, enhancing the competitiveness of local goods and slowing demand for imports, which had risen by 8.3% in Abu Dhabi and Dubai in that year. Similarly, a 50% increase in electricity charges, introduced in January 1995, was expected to yield significant additional government revenue, rationalize domestic use of electricity, and serve as a precedent for the gradual removal of all state subsidies. The Government's programme of privatization, announced in March 1994, proceeded at a cautious pace, partly due to the absence of a formal stock exchange, although the establishment of an exchange was reportedly under consideration in 1995.

## Social Welfare

Hospital treatment and medical care are provided free to nationals throughout the UAE, and grants are provided for those needing treatment at specialist centres abroad. The Government also operates a system of social welfare benefits. In 1990 the UAE had 42 hospital establishments (including nine private hospitals), with a total of 6,397 beds. In the same year there were 2,986 physicians working in official medical services, and the ratio of doctors per head of population was 1:1,619. Federal budget provisions for 1994 allocated Dh 2,250m. to health, representing 12.8% of total central government expenditure.

## Education

Primary education is compulsory, beginning at six years of age and lasting for six years. Secondary education, starting at the age of 12, also lasts for six years, comprising two equal cycles of three years. As a proportion of all school-age children, the total enrolment at primary and secondary schools was equivalent to 97% in 1992 (males 95%; females 98%), compared with only 61% in 1970. Secondary enrolment was equivalent to 64% of children in the relevant age-group in 1992 (males 61%; females 68%). Most of the teachers are from other Arab countries. In September 1988 four higher colleges of technology (two for male and two for female students) opened, admitting a total of 425 students, all of whom were citizens of the UAE. In 1992 9,793 students were enrolled at the university at al-Ain in Abu Dhabi. The university was being expanded to take 16,000 students by the year 2000. Many other students currently receive higher education abroad. Federal budget provisions for 1994 allocated Dh 2,770m. to education (15.7% of total expenditure by the central Government). Adult illiteracy averaged an estimated 46.5% (males 41.6%; females 61.9%) in 1975, but had decreased to 16.8% by 1993. A literacy and adult education programme is in operation. In January 1991 it was announced

# THE UNITED ARAB EMIRATES

that military education was to be a compulsory subject in all federal secondary schools from the 1991/92 academic year.

## Public Holidays

**1995:** 1 January (New Year's Day), 1 February* (first day of Ramadan), 3 March* (Id al-Fitr, end of Ramadan), 10 May* (Id al-Adha, Feast of the Sacrifice), 31 May* (Muharram, Islamic New Year), 6 August† (Accession of the Ruler of Abu Dhabi), 9 August* (Mouloud, Birth of Muhammad), 2 December (National Day), 20 December* (Leilat al-Meiraj, Ascension of Muhammad), 25 December (Christmas Day).

**1996:** 1 January (New Year's Day), 22 January* (first day of Ramadan), 21 February* (Id al-Fitr, end of Ramadan), 29 April* (Id al-Adha, Feast of the Sacrifice), 19 May* (Muharram, Islamic New Year), 28 July* (Mouloud, Birth of Muhammad), 6 August† (Accession of the Ruler of Abu Dhabi), 2 December (National Day), 8 December* (Leilat al-Meiraj, Ascension of Muhammad), 25 December (Christmas Day).

* Islamic religious holidays are dependent on sightings of the moon, and may vary slightly from the dates given.
† Applies only in Abu Dhabi.

## Weights and Measures

The imperial, metric and local systems are all in use.

# Statistical Survey

Source (unless otherwise indicated): Central Statistical Department, Ministry of Planning, POB 1134, Sharjah; tel. (6) 22704.

## Area and Population

### AREA, POPULATION AND DENSITY

| | |
|---|---:|
| Area (sq km) | 77,700* |
| Population (census results) | |
| 15 December 1980 | 1,042,099 |
| December 1985 | |
| Males | 1,052,577 |
| Females | 569,887 |
| Total | 1,622,464 |
| Population (official estimates)† | |
| 1991 | 1,908,800 |
| 1992 | 2,011,400 |
| 1993 | 2,083,100 |
| Density (per sq km) in 1993 | 26.8 |

* 30,000 sq miles.
† Source: Central Bank of the United Arab Emirates.

### POPULATION BY EMIRATE (1991, official estimates)

| | Area (sq km) | Population | Density (per sq km) |
|---|---:|---:|---:|
| Abu Dhabi | 67,350 | 798,000 | 11.8 |
| Dubai | 3,900 | 501,000 | 128.5 |
| Sharjah | 2,600 | 314,000 | 120.8 |
| Ras al-Khaimah | 1,700 | 130,000 | 76.5 |
| Ajman | 250 | 76,000 | 304.0 |
| Fujairah | 1,150 | 63,000 | 54.8 |
| Umm al-Qaiwain | 750 | 27,000 | 36.0 |
| Total | 77,700 | 1,909,000 | 24.6 |

### PRINCIPAL TOWNS (population at 1980 census)

| | | | |
|---|---:|---|---:|
| Dubai | 265,702 | Sharjah | 125,149 |
| Abu Dhabi (capital) | 242,975 | Al-Ain | 101,663 |

Source: UN, *Demographic Yearbook*.

### BIRTHS, MARRIAGES AND DEATHS

| | Registered live births | | Registered marriages | | Registered deaths | |
|---|---:|---:|---:|---:|---:|---:|
| | Number | Rate (per 1,000) | Number | Rate (per 1,000) | Number | Rate (per 1,000) |
| 1988 | 50,836 | n.a. | 9,282 | n.a. | 3,447 | n.a. |
| 1989 | 51,903 | 29.8 | 7,734 | 4.4 | 3,640 | 2.1 |
| 1990 | 52,264 | 28.3 | 7,357 | 4.0 | 3,938 | 2.1 |

**Expectation of life** (UN estimates, years at birth, 1985–90): 69.9 (males 68.6; females 72.9) (Source: UN, *World Population Prospects: The 1992 Revision*).

### EMPLOYMENT ('000 persons)

| | 1988 | 1989 | 1990* |
|---|---:|---:|---:|
| Agriculture, hunting, forestry and fishing | 39.5 | 42.6 | 43.1 |
| Mining and quarrying | 9.1 | 9.5 | 10.0 |
| Manufacturing | 61.1 | 61.8 | 63.4 |
| Electricity, gas and water | 19.8 | 20.2 | 20.6 |
| Construction | 110.0 | 114.2 | 119.2 |
| Trade, restaurants and hotels | 96.2 | 99.1 | 101.4 |
| Transport, storage and communications | 68.0 | 70.4 | 71.7 |
| Financing, insurance, real estate and business services | 17.5 | 18.4 | 18.8 |
| Community, social and personal services | 222.5 | 230.9 | 241.3 |
| **Total** | **643.7** | **667.1** | **689.5** |

* Estimates.

**Total employed:** 737,700 in 1991; 769,300 in 1992; 794,400 in 1993 (Source: Central Bank of the United Arab Emirates).

## Agriculture

### PRINCIPAL CROPS ('000 metric tons)

| | 1991 | 1992* | 1993* |
|---|---:|---:|---:|
| Cereals | 8 | 8 | 8 |
| Tomatoes | 82 | 85 | 90 |
| Cucumbers and gherkins | 10 | 12 | 15 |
| Aubergines | 56 | 60 | 61 |
| Green peppers | 12 | 13 | 14 |
| Watermelons | 4 | 5 | 5 |
| Melons | 3 | 3 | 3 |
| Dates | 173 | 175 | 176 |
| Tobacco (leaves) | 1 | 1 | 1 |

* FAO estimates.
Source: FAO, *Production Yearbook*.

### LIVESTOCK ('000 head, year ending September)

| | 1991 | 1992* | 1993* |
|---|---:|---:|---:|
| Cattle | 53 | 55 | 58 |
| Camels | 121 | 122 | 130 |
| Sheep | 272 | 275 | 277 |
| Goats | 703 | 720 | 747 |

* FAO estimates.

Poultry (FAO estimates, million): 7 in 1991; 7 in 1992; 7 in 1993.
Source: FAO, *Production Yearbook*.

# THE UNITED ARAB EMIRATES

## LIVESTOCK PRODUCTS ('000 metric tons)

|  | 1991 | 1992 | 1993 |
|---|---|---|---|
| Beef and veal* | 6 | 6 | 6 |
| Mutton and lamb* | 23 | 24 | 23 |
| Goat meat* | 5 | 5 | 5 |
| Poultry meat* | 15 | 15 | 16 |
| Cows' milk | 5 | 6* | 6* |
| Sheep's milk | 5 | 6* | 6* |
| Goats' milk | 16 | 17* | 18* |
| Hen eggs | 10.5† | 10.8* | 10.9* |

* FAO estimate(s).  † Unofficial figure.

Source: FAO, *Production Yearbook*.

## Fishing

('000 metric tons, live weight)

|  | 1990 | 1991 | 1992 |
|---|---|---|---|
| Fishes | 95.1 | 92.2 | 94.9 |
| Crustaceans and molluscs | 0.1 | 0.1 | 0.1 |
| **Total catch** | 95.1 | 92.3 | 95.0 |

Source: FAO, *Yearbook of Fishery Statistics*.

## Mining

('000 metric tons, unless otherwise indicated)

|  | 1989 | 1990 | 1991 |
|---|---|---|---|
| Crude petroleum | 89,265 | 101,959 | 114,769 |
| Natural gasoline* | 970 | 1,030 | 1,100 |
| Natural gas (petajoules) | 783 | 788 | 932 |

* Provisional or estimated figures.

Source: UN, *Industrial Statistics Yearbook*.

## Industry

### PETROLEUM PRODUCTS ('000 metric tons)

|  | 1989 | 1990 | 1991 |
|---|---|---|---|
| Jet fuels | 1,090 | 1,100 | 1,110 |
| Motor spirit (petrol) | 1,300 | 1,250 | 1,300 |
| Naphthas | 810 | 900 | 920 |
| Kerosene | 60 | 80 | 85 |
| Distillate fuel oils | 2,510 | 2,700 | 2,750 |
| Residual fuel oils | 2,620 | 2,800 | 2,900 |
| Liquefied petroleum gas: |  |  |  |
| from natural gas plants* | 2,360 | 2,470 | 2,500 |
| from petroleum refineries* | 200 | 240 | 256 |

* Provisional or estimated figures.

Source: UN, *Industrial Statistics Yearbook*.

### ELECTRIC ENERGY (million kWh)

|  | 1989 | 1990 | 1991 |
|---|---|---|---|
| Production | 13,270 | 13,590 | 13,790 |

Source: UN, *Industrial Statistics Yearbook*.

# Finance

## CURRENCY AND EXCHANGE RATES

**Monetary Units**
100 fils = 1 UAE dirham (Dh).

**Sterling and Dollar Equivalents** (31 December 1994)
£1 sterling = 5.743 dirhams;
US $1 = 3.671 dirhams;
100 UAE dirhams = £17.41 = $27.24.

**Exchange Rate**
The Central Bank's official rate has been fixed at US $1 = 3.671 dirhams since November 1980.

## GENERAL BUDGET (million UAE dirhams)*

| Revenue | 1987 | 1988 | 1989† |
|---|---|---|---|
| Taxation | 473 | 479 | 573 |
| Social security contributions | 38 | 41 | 42 |
| Domestic taxes on goods and services | 435 | 438 | 531 |
| Other current revenue | 2,288 | 1,438 | 766 |
| Capital revenue | 8 | 4 | 9 |
| Grants from other levels of government | 9,865 | 10,950 | 11,298 |
| **Total** | 12,634 | 12,871 | 12,646 |

| Expenditure | 1987 | 1988 | 1989† |
|---|---|---|---|
| General public services | 786 | 739 | 613 |
| Defence | 5,827 | 5,827 | 5,827 |
| Public order and safety | 1,713 | 1,697 | 1,789 |
| Education | 1,773 | 1,882 | 1,985 |
| Health | 912 | 919 | 916 |
| Social security and welfare | 423 | 420 | 420 |
| Housing and community amenities | 86 | 58 | 54 |
| Recreational, cultural and religious affairs and services | 352 | 353 | 357 |
| Economic affairs and services | 670 | 582 | 572 |
| Fuel and energy | 401 | 324 | 329 |
| Agriculture, forestry, fishing and hunting | 106 | 105 | 96 |
| Other purposes | 716 | 708 | 731 |
| **Total** | 13,258 | 13,185 | 13,264 |
| Current | 13,031 | 13,038 | 13,131 |
| Capital | 227 | 147 | 133 |

* Excluding the operations of the seven Emirate Governments.
† Provisional.

Source: IMF, *Government Finance Statistics Yearbook*.

**1990** (million dirhams): Revenue 15,251 (incl. grants 12,909); Expenditure 14,394.
**1991** (provisional, million dirhams): Revenue 14,621 (incl. grants 12,997); Expenditure 15,220.
**1992** (provisional, million dirhams): Revenue 16,717 (incl. grants 12,511); Expenditure 15,538.
**1993** (estimates, million dirhams): Revenue 15,900; Expenditure 17,630.
**1994** (estimates, million dirhams): Revenue 16,200; Expenditure 17,610 (Education 2,770, Health 2,250, Water and electricity 1,120).

## CENTRAL BANK RESERVES (US $ million at 31 December)

|  | 1992 | 1993 | 1994 |
|---|---|---|---|
| Gold* | 182.0 | 182.5 | 181.6 |
| IMF special drawing rights | 72.1 | 74.4 | 80.3 |
| Reserve position in IMF | 217.6 | 223.6 | 217.7 |
| Foreign exchange† | 5,422.1 | 5,805.7 | 6,360.8 |
| **Total** | 5,893.8 | 6,286.2 | 6,840.4 |

* Valued at US $228 per troy ounce.
† Figures exclude the Central Bank's foreign assets and accrued interest attributable to the governments of individual emirates.

Source: IMF, *International Financial Statistics*.

# THE UNITED ARAB EMIRATES

## Statistical Survey

**MONEY SUPPLY** (million UAE dirhams at 31 December)

|  | 1991 | 1992 | 1993 |
|---|---|---|---|
| Currency outside banks | 4,676 | 5,108 | 5,667 |
| Demand deposits at commercial banks | 8,336 | 9,873 | 12,507 |
| **Total money** | 13,012 | 14,981 | 18,174 |

Source: IMF, *International Financial Statistics*.

**NATIONAL ACCOUNTS** (million UAE dirhams at current prices)

**National Income and Product**

|  | 1988 | 1989 | 1990 |
|---|---|---|---|
| Compensation of employees | 25,226 | 26,769 | 27,996 |
| Operating surplus | 49,193 | 60,848 | 81,633 |
| **Domestic factor incomes** | 74,419 | 87,617 | 109,629 |
| Consumption of fixed capital | 14,382 | 15,127 | 16,078 |
| **Gross domestic product (GDP) at factor cost** | 88,801 | 102,744 | 125,707 |
| Indirect taxes, *less* subsidies | −1,695 | −1,768 | −1,699 |
| **GDP in purchasers' values** | 87,106 | 100,976 | 124,008 |
| Factor income from abroad | 9,940 | 10,600 | 10,900 |
| *Less* Factor income paid abroad | 9,690 | 10,178 | 12,200 |
| **Gross national product** | 87,356 | 101,398 | 122,708 |
| *Less* Consumption of fixed capital | 14,382 | 15,127 | 16,078 |
| **National income in market prices** | 72,974 | 86,271 | 106,630 |
| Other current transfers from abroad (net) | −1,040 | −744 | −11,000 |
| **National disposable income** | 71,934 | 85,527 | 95,630 |

Source: UN, *National Accounts Statistics*.

**Expenditure on the Gross Domestic Product**

|  | 1990* | 1991† | 1992† |
|---|---|---|---|
| Government final consumption expenditure | 20,100 | 21,350 | 23,380 |
| Private final consumption expenditure | 46,700 | 51,520 | 58,660 |
| Increase in stocks | 1,200 | 1,320 | 1,630 |
| Gross fixed capital formation | 24,100 | 25,200 | 27,250 |
| **Total domestic expenditure** | 92,100 | 99,390 | 110,920 |
| Exports of goods and services | 82,000 | 84,240 | 89,110 |
| *Less* Imports of goods and services | 50,600 | 59,440 | 72,700 |
| **GDP in purchasers' values** | 123,500 | 124,190 | 127,330 |

* Source: IMF, *International Financial Statistics*.
† Source: Ministry of Planning.

**Gross Domestic Product by Economic Activity** (at factor cost)

|  | 1991 | 1992 | 1993* |
|---|---|---|---|
| Agriculture, livestock and fishing | 2,563 | 2,730 | 2,838 |
| Mining and quarrying | 54,592 | 53,471 | 51,719 |
| Manufacturing | 9,770 | 9,942 | 10,891 |
| Electricity and water | 2,700 | 2,869 | 2,961 |
| Construction | 10,365 | 11,125 | 11,582 |
| Trade, restaurants and hotels | 11,943 | 13,020 | 13,382 |
| Transport, storage and communications | 6,711 | 7,167 | 7,390 |
| Finance, insurance and real estate | 12,928 | 14,611 | 15,139 |
| Government services | 13,634 | 14,376 | 14,881 |
| Other community, social and personal services | 2,689 | 2,931 | 3,107 |
| Domestic services of households | 551 | 605 | 638 |
| **Sub-total** | 128,446 | 132,847 | 134,528 |
| *Less* Imputed bank service charge | 2,182 | 2,684 | 2,868 |
| **Total** | 126,264 | 130,163 | 131,660 |

* Provisional figures.

Source: Central Bank of the United Arab Emirates.

**BALANCE OF PAYMENTS**
(estimates, million UAE dirhams)

|  | 1990 | 1991 | 1992 |
|---|---|---|---|
| Merchandise exports f.o.b. | 79,500 | 81,300 | 85,800 |
| Merchandise imports c.i.f. | 42,500 | 51,100 | 64,000 |
| **Trade balance** | 37,000 | 30,200 | 21,800 |
| Services and private transfers (net) | −7,000 | −7,200 | −9,400 |
| Official transfers (net) | −10,800 | −17,400 | −2,700 |
| **Current balance** | 19,200 | 5,600 | 9,700 |
| Capital (net) | −14,600 | −8,000 | −8,000 |
| Net errors and omissions | −5,600 | 7,580 | −2,390 |
| **Overall balance** | −1,000 | 5,180 | −690 |

Source: Central Bank of the United Arab Emirates.

# THE UNITED ARAB EMIRATES

*Statistical Survey*

## External Trade

**COMMODITY GROUPS** (million UAE dirhams; Abu Dhabi, Dubai and Sharjah)*

|  | Imports c.i.f.† 1990 | Imports c.i.f.† 1991 | National Exports‡ 1987 | National Exports‡ 1988 | Re-exports§ 1990 | Re-exports§ 1991 |
|---|---|---|---|---|---|---|
| Food and live animals | 1,919 | 1,664 | 86.7 | 70.1 | 467.0 | 605.8 |
| Beverages and tobacco | 131 | 131 | 27.5 | 50.3 | 10.4 | 31.8 |
| Crude materials (inedible) except fuels | 154 | 160 | 101.1 | 139.7 | 39.7 | 22.5 |
| Mineral fuels, lubricants, etc. | 119 | 138 | 138.2 | 120.2 | 10.0 | 10.9 |
| Animal and vegetable oils and fats | 35 | 81 | 1.6 | 2.6 | 4.3 | 5.3 |
| Chemicals | 1,027 | 1,088 | 81.1 | 92.7 | 82.9 | 110.5 |
| Basic manufactures | 2,091 | 2,642 | 978.6 | 1,251.0 | 374.7 | 581.5 |
| Machinery and transport equipment | 4,493 | 5,233 | 27.6 | 57.3 | 957.5 | 2,292.5 |
| Miscellaneous manufactured articles | 874 | 1,039 | 68.0 | 121.1 | 660.2 | 1,276.8 |
| Other commodities and transactions | 228 | 173 | 0.0 | 0.0 | 23.3 | 9.2 |
| **Total** | **11,071** | **12,349** | **1,510.3** | **1,905.1** | **2,629.9** | **4,946.9** |

\* Figures exclude inter-emirate trade. Also excluded is trade in gold and silver.
† Excluding transit trade, and not including Dubai (total imports 31,041.5m. dirhams in 1990, 38,111.3m. dirhams in 1991).
‡ Excluding crude petroleum, petroleum products and fertilizers.
§ Excluding Dubai (total re-exports 7,602.7m. dirhams in 1990, 7,525.5m. dirhams in 1991).
**Total Imports c.i.f.** (million dirhams): 42,500 in 1990; 51,100 in 1991; 64,328* in 1992; 72,495* in 1993; 80,400* in 1994.
**Petroleum Exports** (million dirhams): 54,500 in 1990; 52,700 in 1991; 51,600 in 1992.
**Total Exports and Re-exports f.o.b.** (million dirhams): 79,500 in 1990; 81,300 in 1991; 88,940* in 1992; 86,267* in 1993; 89,050* in 1994.
\* Figures from *Middle East Economic Digest*.
Source (unless otherwise indicated): Central Bank of the United Arab Emirates.

### PRINCIPAL TRADING PARTNERS

| Imports (million UAE dirhams)* | 1990 | 1991 |
|---|---|---|
| Australia | 809 | 944 |
| Bahrain | 487 | 416 |
| France | 1,507 | 2,249 |
| Germany, Fed. Rep. | 3,148 | 3,359 |
| Hong Kong | 438 | 473 |
| India | 1,696 | 2,310 |
| Indonesia | 525 | 953 |
| Iran | 620 | 804 |
| Italy | 1,916 | 2,032 |
| Japan | 5,988 | 7,863 |
| Korea, Republic | 1,852 | 2,325 |
| Malaysia | 675 | 930 |
| Netherlands | 926 | 1,055 |
| Pakistan | 494 | 526 |
| Qatar | 475 | 453 |
| Saudi Arabia | 1,525 | 1,328 |
| Singapore | 785 | 857 |
| Switzerland | 678 | 891 |
| Taiwan | 1,073 | 1,526 |
| Thailand | 1,152 | 1,318 |
| United Kingdom | 4,198 | 4,145 |
| USA | 3,851 | 4,984 |
| **Total** (incl. others) | **42,115** | **50,461** |

\* Figures refer to Abu Dhabi, Dubai and Sharjah.
Source: Central Bank of the United Arab Emirates, *Bulletin*.

| Exports (US $ million)† | 1980 | 1981 | 1982 |
|---|---|---|---|
| Australia | 201 | 240 | 292 |
| Brazil | 243 | 303 | 370 |
| France | 2,152 | 2,140 | 793 |
| Germany, Fed. Rep. | 1,120 | 774 | 227 |
| India | 420 | 607 | 384 |
| Italy | 575 | 728 | 470 |
| Japan | 7,697 | 7,631 | 5,858 |
| Netherlands Antilles | 944 | 698 | 315 |
| Pakistan | 286 | 394 | 373 |
| Saudi Arabia | 232 | 290 | 320 |
| United Kingdom | 712 | 388 | 355 |
| USA | 1,804 | 1,458 | 667 |
| **Total** (incl. others) | **21,618** | **21,238** | **16,837** |

† Figures refer to Abu Dhabi and Dubai.
Source: UN, *International Trade Statistics Yearbook*.

## Transport

**INTERNATIONAL SEA-BORNE SHIPPING**
(estimated freight traffic, '000 metric tons)

|  | 1988 | 1989 | 1990 |
|---|---|---|---|
| Goods loaded | 63,380 | 72,896 | 88,153 |
| Crude petroleum | 54,159 | 63,387 | 78,927 |
| Other cargo | 9,221 | 9,509 | 9,226 |
| Goods unloaded | 8,973 | 8,960 | 9,595 |

Source: UN, *Monthly Bulletin of Statistics*.

**CIVIL AVIATION** (traffic on scheduled services)*

|  | 1990 | 1991 | 1992 |
|---|---|---|---|
| Kilometres flown (million) | 31 | 34 | 50 |
| Passengers carried ('000) | 1,686 | 2,042 | 2,509 |
| Passenger-km (million) | 3,876 | 4,861 | 6,298 |
| Total ton-km (million) | 533 | 672 | 899 |

\* Figures include an apportionment (one-quarter) of the traffic of Gulf Air, a multinational airline with its headquarters in Bahrain.
Source: UN, *Statistical Yearbook*.

THE UNITED ARAB EMIRATES

*Statistical Survey, Directory*

## Communications Media

|  | 1990 | 1991 | 1992 |
|---|---|---|---|
| Radio receivers ('000 in use) | 515 | 530 | 545 |
| Television receivers ('000 in use) | 175 | 175 | 185 |
| Book production: |  |  |  |
| Titles* | 281 | n.a. | 302 |
| Copies ('000)* | 4,423 | n.a. | n.a. |

* Data refer only to school textbooks.

**Daily newspapers:** 8 (combined circulation 250,000 copies) in 1990; 11 in 1992.

Source: UNESCO, *Statistical Yearbook*.

**Telephones** ('000 main lines in use): 378 in 1989; 430 in 1990; 481 in 1991. Source: UN, *Statistical Yearbook*.

## Education

(1992)

|  | Teachers | Students Males | Females | Total |
|---|---|---|---|---|
| Pre-primary | 2,575 | 27,158 | 24,727 | 51,885 |
| Primary | 13,940 | 123,574 | 114,895 | 238,469 |
| Secondary |  |  |  |  |
| General | } 10,537 { | 62,887 | 65,756 | 128,643 |
| Vocational |  | 1,040 | — | 1,040 |
| University | 510 | 2,462 | 7,331 | 9,793 |

Source: UNESCO, *Statistical Yearbook*.

# Directory

## The Constitution

A provisional Constitution for the UAE took effect in December 1971. This laid the foundation for the federal structure of the Union of the seven emirates, previously known as the Trucial States.

The highest federal authority is the Supreme Council of Rulers, which comprises the rulers of the seven emirates. It elects the President and Vice-President from among its members. The President appoints a Prime Minister and a Council of Ministers. Proposals submitted to the Council require the approval of at least five of the Rulers, including those of Abu Dhabi and Dubai. The legislature is the Federal National Council, a consultative assembly comprising 40 members appointed by the emirates for a two-year term.

In July 1975 a committee was appointed to draft a permanent federal constitution, but the National Council decided in 1976 to extend the provisional document for five years. The provisional Constitution was extended for another five years in December 1981, and for further periods of five years in 1986 and 1991. In November 1976, however, the Supreme Council amended Article 142 of the provisional Constitution so that the authority to levy armed forces was placed exclusively under the control of the Federal Government.

## The Government

### HEAD OF STATE

**President:** Sheikh ZAYED BIN SULTAN AN-NAHYAN, Ruler of Abu Dhabi (took office as President of the UAE on 2 December 1971; re-elected 1976, 1981 and 1991).

**Vice-President:** Sheikh MAKTOUM BIN RASHID AL-MAKTOUM, Ruler of Dubai.

### SUPREME COUNCIL OF RULERS
(with each Ruler's date of accession)

**Ruler of Abu Dhabi:** Sheikh ZAYED BIN SULTAN AN-NAHYAN (1966).
**Ruler of Dubai:** Sheikh MAKTOUM BIN RASHID AL-MAKTOUM (1990).
**Ruler of Sharjah:** Sheikh SULTAN BIN MUHAMMAD AL-QASIMI (1972).
**Ruler of Ras al-Khaimah:** Sheikh SAQR BIN MUHAMMAD AL-QASIMI (1948).
**Ruler of Umm al-Qaiwain:** Sheikh RASHID BIN AHMAD AL-MU'ALLA (1981).
**Ruler of Ajman:** Sheikh HUMAID BIN RASHID AN-NUAIMI (1981).
**Ruler of Fujairah:** Sheikh HAMAD BIN MUHAMMAD ASH-SHARQI (1974).

### COUNCIL OF MINISTERS
(June 1995)

**Prime Minister:** Sheikh MAKTOUM BIN RASHID AL-MAKTOUM.
**Deputy Prime Minister:** Sheikh SULTAN BIN ZAYED AN-NAHYAN.
**Minister of the Interior:** Lt-Gen. MUHAMMAD SAID AL-BADI.
**Minister of Foreign Affairs:** RASHID ABDULLAH AN-NUAIMI.
**Minister of Finance and Industry:** Sheikh HAMDAN BIN RASHID AL-MAKTOUM.
**Minister of Defence:** Sheikh MUHAMMAD BIN RASHID AL-MAKTOUM.
**Minister of Economy and Commerce:** SAID GHOBASH.
**Minister of Information and Culture:** KHALFAN BIN MUHAMMAD AR-ROUMI.
**Minister of Communications:** MUHAMMAD SAID AL-MU'ALLA.
**Minister of Public Works and Housing and Acting Minister of Petroleum and Mineral Resources:** RAKAD BIN SALEM BIN RAKAD.
**Minister of Higher Education:** Sheikh NAHYAN BIN MUBARAK AN-NAHYAN.
**Minister of Education and Acting Minister of Health:** HAMAD ABD AR-RAHMAN AL-MADFA.
**Minister of Electricity and Water:** HUMAID NASSER AL-OWAIS.
**Minister of Labour and Social Affairs:** SAIF AL-JARWAN.
**Minister of Planning:** Sheikh HUMAID BIN AHMAD AL-MU'ALLA.
**Minister of Agriculture and Fisheries:** SAID MUHAMMAD AR-RAQABANI.
**Minister of Youth and Sports:** Sheikh FAISAL BIN KHALED BIN MUHAMMAD AL-QASIMI.
**Minister of Justice:** Dr ABDULLAH BIN OMRAN TARYAM.
**Minister of Islamic Affairs and Awqaf (Religious Endowments):** Sheikh MUHAMMAD BIN HASSAN AL-KHAZRAJI.
**Minister of State for Affairs of the Council of Ministers:** SAID AL-GHAITH.
**Minister of State for Supreme Council Affairs:** Sheikh MUHAMMAD BIN SAQR BIN MUHAMMAD AL-QASIMI.

### FEDERAL MINISTRIES

**Office of the Prime Minister:** POB 899, Abu Dhabi; tel. (2) 361555; telex 23245.
**Office of the Deputy Prime Minister:** POB 831, Abu Dhabi; tel. (2) 651881.
**Ministry of Agriculture and Fisheries:** POB 213, Abu Dhabi; tel. (2) 662781; fax (2) 654787.
**Ministry of Communications:** POB 900, Abu Dhabi; tel. (2) 651900; telex 22668; fax (2) 515133.
**Ministry of Defence:** POB 2838, Dubai; tel. (4) 532330; telex 45554; fax (4) 455033.
**Ministry of Economy and Commerce:** POB 901, Abu Dhabi; tel. (2) 215455; telex 22897; fax (2) 215339.
**Ministry of Education:** POB 295, Abu Dhabi; tel. (2) 213800; telex 22581; fax (2) 351164.
**Ministry of Electricity and Water:** POB 1672, Dubai; tel. (4) 690575; telex 46453; fax (4) 690064.
**Ministry of Finance and Industry:** POB 433, Abu Dhabi; tel. (2) 726200; telex 22937; fax (2) 773301.
**Ministry of Foreign Affairs:** POB 1, Abu Dhabi; tel. (2) 652200; telex 22217; fax (2) 653849.
**Ministry of Health:** POB 848, Abu Dhabi; tel. (2) 330000; telex 22678; fax (2) 212732.

# THE UNITED ARAB EMIRATES

**Ministry of Higher Education:** POB 15551, al-Ain; tel. (2) 669422; fax (2) 645277.

**Ministry of Information and Culture:** POB 17, Abu Dhabi; tel. (2) 453000; telex 22283; fax (2) 451155.

**Ministry of the Interior:** POB 398, Abu Dhabi; tel. (2) 447666; telex 22398; fax (2) 415688.

**Ministry of Islamic Affairs and Awqaf (Religious Endowments):** POB 2272, Abu Dhabi; tel. (2) 212300; fax (2) 316003.

**Ministry of Justice:** POB 753, Abu Dhabi; tel. (2) 652224; fax (2) 664944.

**Ministry of Labour and Social Affairs:** POB 809, Abu Dhabi; tel. (2) 651890; fax (2) 665889.

**Ministry of Petroleum and Mineral Resources:** POB 59, Abu Dhabi; tel. (2) 651810; telex 22544; fax (2) 663414.

**Ministry of Planning:** POB 904, Abu Dhabi; tel. (2) 211699; telex 22920; fax (2) 311375.

**Ministry of Public Works and Housing:** POB 878, Abu Dhabi; tel. (2) 651778; telex 23833; fax (2) 665598.

**Ministry of State for Affairs of the Council of Ministers:** POB 899, Abu Dhabi; tel. (2) 651113; telex 23245; fax (2) 652184.

**Ministry of State for Supreme Council Affairs:** POB 545, Abu Dhabi; tel. (2) 343921; fax (2) 344137.

**Ministry of Youth and Sports:** POB 539, Abu Dhabi; tel. (2) 393900; fax (2) 393919.

## Legislature

### FEDERAL NATIONAL COUNCIL

Formed under the provisional Constitution, the Council is composed of 40 members from the various emirates (8 each from Abu Dhabi and Dubai, 6 each from Sharjah and Ras al-Khaimah, and 4 each from Ajman, Fujairah and Umm al-Qaiwain). Each emirate appoints its own representatives separately. The Council studies laws proposed by the Council of Ministers and can reject them or suggest amendments.

**Speaker:** HILAL BIN AHMAD LOOTAH.

## Diplomatic Representation

### EMBASSIES IN THE UNITED ARAB EMIRATES

**Afghanistan:** POB 5687, Abu Dhabi; tel. (2) 661244; Chargé d'affaires: M. NOORULHUDA.

**Algeria:** POB 3070, Abu Dhabi; tel. (2) 448943; telex 23414; Ambassador: MUHAMMAD MELLOUH.

**Argentina:** POB 3325, Abu Dhabi; tel. (2) 436838; telex 23998; fax (2) 431392; Chargé d'affaires: ALFREDO C. BASCOU.

**Austria:** POB 3095, Abu Dhabi; tel. (2) 324103; telex 22675; Ambassador: Dr MARIUS CALLIGARIS.

**Bahrain:** POB 3376, Abu Dhabi; tel. (2) 312200; Ambassador: ISA MOHAMED AL-JAMEA.

**Bangladesh:** POB 2504, Abu Dhabi; tel. (2) 668375; telex 22201; Ambassador: ZIA-US-SHAMS CHOWDHURY.

**Belgium:** POB 3686, Abu Dhabi; tel. (2) 319449; telex 22860; fax (2) 319353; Ambassador: HENRY O. LOBERT.

**Belize:** POB 43432, Abu Dhabi; tel. (2) 333554; Ambassador: ELHAM S. FREIHA.

**Bosnia and Herzegovina:** Abu Dhabi; tel. (2) 785775; Chargé d'affaires: SALKO CANIK.

**Brazil:** POB 3027, Abu Dhabi; tel. (2) 665352; fax (2) 654559; Ambassador: CYRO ESPÍRITO SANTO CARDOSO.

**Brunei:** POB 5836, Abu Dhabi; tel. (2) 313739; Chargé d'affaires: Haji ADNAN BIN Haji ZAINAL.

**China, People's Republic:** POB 2741, Abu Dhabi; tel. (2) 434276; telex 23928; Ambassador: LIU BAOLAI.

**Croatia:** POB 41227, Abu Dhabi; tel. (2) 311700; fax (2) 338366; Ambassador: VANJA KALOGJERA.

**Czech Republic:** POB 27009, Abu Dhabi; tel. (2) 782800; fax (2) 795716; Chargé d'affaires: JOSEF BUZALKA.

**Denmark:** POB 46666, Abu Dhabi; tel. (2) 325900; telex 23677; fax (2) 351690; Ambassador: JENS OSTENFELD.

**Egypt:** POB 4026, Abu Dhabi; tel. (2) 445566; telex 22258; Ambassador: BAHAA ELDIN MOSTAFA REDA.

**Eritrea:** POB 2597, Abu Dhabi; tel. (2) 318388; fax (2) 346451; Ambassador: MOHAMED OMAR MAHMOUD.

**Finland:** POB 3634, Abu Dhabi; tel. (2) 328927; telex 23161; fax (2) 325063; Ambassador: PERTTI KAUKONEN.

**France:** POB 4014, Abu Dhabi; tel. (2) 435100; telex 22325; fax (2) 434158; Ambassador: JEAN-PAUL BARRE.

**Germany:** POB 2591, Abu Dhabi; tel. (2) 331630; telex 22202; fax (2) 323625; Ambassador: Dr HELMUT ARNDT.

**Greece:** POB 5483, Abu Dhabi; tel. (2) 654847; telex 24383; fax (2) 316815; Ambassador: SPYRIDON MORMORIS.

**Hungary:** POB 44450, Abu Dhabi; tel. (2) 660107; fax (2) 667877; Chargé d'affaires a.i.: CSABA KORÖSI.

**India:** POB 4090, Abu Dhabi; tel. (2) 664800; telex 22620; fax (2) 322403; Ambassador: MUTHAL MENON.

**Indonesia:** POB 7256, Abu Dhabi; tel. (2) 669233; telex 22253; fax (2) 653932; Ambassador: ABDULLAH FUAD RACHMAN.

**Iran:** POB 4080, Abu Dhabi; tel. (2) 447618; telex 22344; Ambassador: HASSAN AMINIAN.

**Italy:** POB 46752, Abu Dhabi; tel. (2) 435622; telex 23861; Ambassador: GIOVANNI FERRERO.

**Japan:** POB 2430, Abu Dhabi; tel. (2) 435969; telex 22270; Ambassador: SHIN WATANABE.

**Jordan:** POB 2787, Abu Dhabi; tel. (2) 447100; telex 24411; Ambassador: ABD AL-LATIF BAWAB.

**Kenya:** POB 3854, Abu Dhabi; tel. (2) 666300; telex 24244; Ambassador: MUDE DAE MUDE.

**Korea, Republic:** POB 3270, Abu Dhabi; tel. (2) 435337; telex 24237; fax (2) 435348; Ambassador: JUNG HO-KEUM.

**Kuwait:** POB 926, Abu Dhabi; tel. (2) 446888; telex 22804; fax (2) 444990; Ambassador: IBRAHIM AL-MANSOUR.

**Lebanon:** POB 4023, Abu Dhabi; tel. (2) 434722; telex 22206; Ambassador: GEORGES SIAM.

**Libya:** POB 5739, Abu Dhabi; tel. (2) 450030; Chargé d'affaires: ABDUL HAMID ALI SHAIKHY.

**Malaysia:** POB 3887, Abu Dhabi; tel. (2) 656698; telex 22630; fax (2) 656697; Ambassador: ZULKIFLY IBRAHIM BIN ABDUL RAHMAN.

**Mauritania:** POB 2714, Abu Dhabi; tel. (2) 462724; telex 22512; fax (2) 465772; Ambassador: TELMIDI OULD MOHAMED AMMAR.

**Morocco:** POB 4066, Abu Dhabi; tel. (2) 433963; telex 22549; fax (2) 313158; Ambassador: ABD EL-MANSOUR.

**Netherlands:** POB 46560, Abu Dhabi; tel. (2) 321920; telex 23610; Ambassador: RONALD MOLLINGER.

**Norway:** POB 47270, Abu Dhabi; tel. (2) 211221; Ambassador: KNUT SOLEM.

**Oman:** Al-Muharba Al-Jadid Al-Khaleej St, Villa 674, Abu Dhabi; tel. (2) 463333; fax (2) 464633; Ambassador: SULTAN AL-BUSAIDI.

**Pakistan:** POB 846, Abu Dhabi; tel. (2) 447800; telex 23003; Chargé d'affaires: ABDUL RAZZAK SOOMRO.

**Philippines:** POB 3215, Abu Dhabi; tel. (2) 345664; telex 23995; Ambassador: ROY V. SENERES.

**Poland:** Room 202, Khalidia Palace Hotel, Abu Dhabi; tel. (2) 465200; Chargé d'affaires: ANDRZEJ KAPISZEWSKI.

**Qatar:** Sudan St, Al-Minaseer, POB 3503, Abu Dhabi; tel. (2) 435900; telex 22664; Ambassador: ABDULLAH M. AL-UTHMAN.

**Romania:** POB 70416, Abu Dhabi; tel. (2) 666346; telex 23546; Ambassador: DUMITRU CHICAN.

**Russia:** POB 8211, Abu Dhabi; tel. (2) 721797; Ambassador: OLEG DERKOVSKY.

**Saudi Arabia:** POB 4057, Abu Dhabi; tel. (2) 445700; telex 22670; Ambassador: SALEH MOHAMMED AL-GHUFAILI.

**Slovakia:** POB 3382, Abu Dhabi; tel. (2) 321674; fax (2) 315839; Chargé d'affaires: DUSAN HORNIAK.

**Somalia:** POB 4155, Abu Dhabi; tel. (2) 669700; telex 22624; Ambassador: HUSSEIN MOHAMMED BULLALEH.

**South Africa:** Abu Dhabi; Chargé d'affaires: MOHAMED RAFIQ A. H. GANGAT.

**Spain:** POB 46474, Abu Dhabi; tel. (2) 213544; telex 23340; Ambassador: JAVIER NAVARRO IZQUIERDO.

**Sri Lanka:** POB 46534, Abu Dhabi; tel. (2) 666688; telex 23333; fax (2) 667921; Chargé d'affaires: TITUS MILTON KARUNATILAKE.

**Sudan:** POB 4027, Abu Dhabi; tel. (2) 666788; telex 22706; Chargé d'affaires: MOHIEDDIN SLAIM AHMED.

**Switzerland:** POB 46116, Abu Dhabi; tel. (2) 343636; telex 22824; fax (2) 216127; Ambassador: CHRISTIAN BLICKEN STORFER.

**Syria:** POB 4011, Abu Dhabi; tel. (2) 448768; telex 22729; fax (2) 449387; Ambassador: MUSTAFA OMRAN.

**Thailand:** POB 6677, Abu Dhabi; tel. (2) 211200; Ambassador: VICHIEN CHENSAVASDIJAI.

**Tunisia:** POB 4166, Abu Dhabi; tel. (2) 661331; telex 22370; Ambassador: ABDELKRIM MOUSSA.

THE UNITED ARAB EMIRATES
*Directory*

**Turkey:** POB 3204, Abu Dhabi; tel. (2) 655421; telex 23037; Ambassador: ALI ARSIN.
**Ukraine:** POB 45714; Abu Dhabi; tel. (2) 327586; fax (2) 327506; Ambassador: OLEH SEMENETS.
**United Kingdom:** POB 248, Abu Dhabi; tel. (2) 326600; telex 22234; fax (2) 341744; Ambassador: ANTHONY DAVID HARRIS.
**USA:** POB 4009, Abu Dhabi; tel. (2) 436691; fax (2) 435441; Ambassador: DAVID C. LITT.
**Yemen:** POB 2095, Abu Dhabi; tel. (2) 448454; telex 23600; Ambassador: Dr ABDULLAH HUSSAIN BARAKAT.

## Judicial System

The 95th article of the provisional Constitution of 1971 provided for the establishment of the Union Supreme Court and Union Primary Tribunals as the judicial organs of State.

The Union has exclusive legislative and executive jurisdiction over all matters that are concerned with the strengthening of the federation such as foreign affairs, defence and Union armed forces, security, finance, communications, traffic control, education, currency, measures, standards and weights, matters relating to nationality and emigration, Union information, etc.

President Sheikh Zayed signed the law establishing the new federal courts on 9 June 1978. The new law effectively transferred local judicial authorities into the jurisdiction of the federal system.

Primary tribunals in Abu Dhabi, Sharjah, Ajman and Fujairah are now primary federal tribunals, and primary tribunals in other towns in those emirates have become circuits of the primary federal tribunals.

The primary federal tribunal may sit in any of the capitals of the four emirates and have jurisdiction on all administrative disputes between the Union and individuals, whether the Union is plaintiff or defendant. Civil disputes between Union and individuals will be heard by primary federal tribunals in the defendant's place of normal residence.

The law requires that all judges take a constitutional oath before the Minister of Justice and that the courts apply the rules of *Shari'a* (Islamic religious law) and that no judgment contradicts the *Shari'a*. All employees of the old judiciaries will be transferred to the federal authority without loss of salary or seniority.

In February 1994 President Sheikh Zayed ordered that an extensive range of crimes, including murder, theft and adultery, be tried in *Shari'a* courts rather than in civil courts.

**Chief Shari'a Justice:** AHMAD ABD AL-AZIZ AL-MUBARAK.

## Religion

### ISLAM

Most of the inhabitants are Muslims of the Sunni sect. About 16% of the Muslims are Shi'ites.

### CHRISTIANITY

#### Roman Catholic Church

**Apostolic Vicariate of Arabia:** POB 54, Abu Dhabi; tel. (2) 461895; fax (2) 465177; responsible for a territory covering most of the Arabian peninsula (including Saudi Arabia, the UAE, Oman, Qatar, Bahrain and Yemen), containing an estimated 750,000 Catholics (31 December 1993); Vicar Apostolic Fr GIOVANNI BERNARDO GREMOLI, Titular Bishop of Masuccaba.

#### The Anglican Communion

Within the Episcopal Church in Jerusalem and the Middle East, the UAE forms part of the diocese of Cyprus and the Gulf. The Anglican congregations in the UAE are entirely expatriate. The Bishop in Cyprus and the Gulf resides in Cyprus.

**Archdeacon in the Gulf:** Ven. MICHAEL MANSBRIDGE, St Andrew's Church, POB 262, Abu Dhabi; tel. (2) 461631; fax (2) 465869.

## The Press

The Ministry of Information and Culture has placed a moratorium on new titles.

### Abu Dhabi

**Abu Dhabi Chamber of Commerce Review:** POB 662, Abu Dhabi; tel. (2) 214000; telex 22449; f. 1969; Arabic, some articles in English; monthly; circ. 16,500.

**Adh-Dhafra:** POB 4288, Abu Dhabi; tel. (2) 328103; Arabic; weekly; independent; publ. by Dar al-Wahdah.

**Emirates News:** POB 791, Abu Dhabi; tel. (2) 455555; telex 22763; fax (2) 453662; f. 1975; English; daily; publ. by Al-Ittihad Press, Publishing and Distribution Corpn; Chair. KHALFAN BIN MUHAMMAD AR-ROUMI; Man. Editor PETER HELLYER; circ. 15,000.

**Al-Fajr** (The Dawn): POB 505, Abu Dhabi; tel. (2) 478300; telex 22834; fax (2) 478436; Arabic; daily; Man. Editor OBEID AL-MAZROUI; circ. 23,800.

**Hiya** (She): POB 2488, Abu Dhabi; tel. (2) 478400; Arabic weekly for women; publ. by Dar al-Wahdah.

**Al-Ittihad** (Unity): POB 791, Abu Dhabi; tel. (2) 455555; telex 22984; f. 1972; Arabic; daily and weekly; publ. by Al-Ittihad Press, Publishing and Distribution Corpn; Man. Editor OBEID SULTAN; circ. 58,000 daily, 60,000 weekly.

**Khaleej Times:** POB 3082, Abu Dhabi; tel. (2) 336000; telex 23872; fax (2) 336424; daily; circ. 60,000.

**Majed:** POB 3558, Abu Dhabi; tel. (2) 451804; telex 22984; fax (2) 451455; Arabic; weekly; children's magazine; Man. Editor AHMAD OMAR; circ. 160,000.

**Ar-Riyada wa-Shabab** (Sport and Youth): POB 4230, Abu Dhabi; Arabic; weekly; general interest.

**UAE and Abu Dhabi Official Gazette:** POB 899, Abu Dhabi; Arabic; official reports and papers.

**UAE Press Service Daily News:** POB 2035, Abu Dhabi; tel. (2) 44292; f. 1973; English; daily; Editor RASHID AL-MAZROUI.

**Al-Wahdah** (Unity): POB 2488, Abu Dhabi; tel. (2) 478400; f. 1973; daily; independent; Man. Editor RASHID AWEIDHA; Gen. Man. KHALIFA AL-MASHWI; circ. 10,000.

**Zahrat al-Khaleej** (Splendour of the Gulf): POB 791, Abu Dhabi; tel. (2) 455555; fax (2) 451481; f. 1979; Arabic; weekly; publ. by Al-Ittihad Press, Publishing and Distribution Corpn; women's magazine; circ. 100,000.

### Dubai

**Akhbar Dubai** (Dubai News): Department of Information, Dubai Municipality, POB 1420, Dubai; f. 1965; Arabic; weekly.

**Al-Bayan** (The Official Report): POB 2710, Dubai; tel. (4) 444400; telex 47707; fax (4) 445973; f. 1980; owned by Dubai authorities; Arabic; daily; Editor-in-Chief Sheikh HASHER MAKTOUM; circ. 44,950.

**Dubai Annual Trade Review:** POB 516, Dubai; tel. (4) 531076; telex 47470; fax (4) 531959; English.

**Gulf News:** POB 6519, Dubai; tel. (4) 449139; telex 47030; fax (4) 441627; f. 1978; An-Nisr Publishing; English; daily; two weekly supplements, *Junior News* (Wednesday), *Gulf Weekly* (Thursday); Editor-in-Chief OBAID HUMAID AT-TAYER; Editor FRANCIS MATTHEW; circ. 79,250.

**Al-Jundi** (The Soldier): POB 2838, Dubai; tel. (4) 451516; telex 4554; fax (4) 455033; f. 1973; Arabic; monthly; military and cultural; Editor ISMAIL KHAMIS MUBARAK; circ. 4,000–7,000.

**Khaleej Times:** POB 11243; Dubai; tel. (4) 382400; telex 48620; fax (4) 383676; f. 1978; a Galadari enterprise; English; daily; free weekly supplement, *Weekend* (Friday); Exec. Editor KHALID A. H. ANSARI; Chief Editor ABD AL-LATIF GALADARI; circ. 70,000.

**Trade and Industry:** POB 1457, Dubai; tel. (4) 221181; telex 45997; fax (4) 211646; f. 1975; Arabic and English; monthly; publ. by Dubai Chamber of Commerce and Industry; circ. 17,500.

**What's On:** POB 2331; tel. (4) 824060; telex 48366; fax (4) 824436; Motivate Publishing; English; monthly; circ. 25,500.

### Ras al-Khaimah

**Akhbar Ras al-Khaimah** (Ras al-Khaimah News): POB 87, Ras al-Khaimah; Arabic; monthly; general interest.

**Ras al-Khaimah Chamber of Commerce Magazine:** POB 87, Ras al-Khaimah; f. 1970; Arabic and English; free monthly; Editor ZAKI H. SAQR.

**Ras al-Khaimah Magazine:** POB 200, Ras al-Khaimah; Arabic; monthly; commerce and trade; Chief Editor AHMAD AT-TADMORI.

### Sharjah

**Al-Azman al-Arabia** (Times of Arabia): POB 5823, Sharjah; tel. (6) 356034; telex 68674.

**Al-Khaleej** (The Gulf): POB 30, Sharjah; tel. (6) 598777; telex 68055; fax (6) 598547; f. 1970; Arabic; daily; political, independent; Editor GHASSAN TAHBOUB; circ. 60,000.

**Sawt al-Khaleej** (Voice of the Gulf): POB 1385, Sharjah; tel. (6) 358003; telex 68551.

**Ash-Sharooq** (Sunrise): POB 30, Sharjah; tel. (6) 598677; f. 1970; Arabic; weekly; general interest; Editor YOUSUF AL-HASSAN.

**At-Tijarah** (Commerce): Sharjah Chamber of Commerce and Industry, POB 580, Sharjah; tel. (6) 541444; telex 68205; fax (6) 541119; f. 1970; Arabic/English; monthly magazine; circ. 50,000; annual trade directory; circ. 100,000.

# THE UNITED ARAB EMIRATES

*Directory*

**UAE Digest:** POB 6872, Sharjah; tel. (6) 354633; telex 68715; fax (6) 354627; English; monthly; publ. by Universal Publishing; commerce and finance; Man. Dir Faraj Yassine; circ. 10,000.

### NEWS AGENCIES

**Emirates News Agency (WAM):** POB 3790, Abu Dhabi; tel. (2) 454545; telex 22979; f. 1977; operated by the Ministry of Information and Culture; Dir Ibrahim al-Abed.

### Foreign Bureaux

**Agenzia Nazionale Stampa Associata (ANSA)** (Italy): POB 44106, Abu Dhabi; tel. (2) 454545; telex 23823; Correspondent Muhammad Wadha.

**Inter Press Service (IPS)** (Italy): Airport Rd, near the Radio and Television Bldg., Abu Dhabi; tel. (2) 464200; telex 23823; fax (2) 454846; Correspondent (vacant).

**Reuters** (UK): POB 7872, Abu Dhabi; tel. (2) 328000; telex 24145; fax (2) 333380; Man. Jeremy Harris.

## Publishers

**Al-Ittihad Press, Publishing and Distribution Corpn:** POB 791, New Airport Rd, Abu Dhabi; tel. (2) 455555; telex 22984; fax (2) 451653; Chair. Khalfan bin Muhammad ar-Roumi.

**All Prints:** POB 857, Abu Dhabi; tel. (2) 338235; telex 22844; publishing and distribution; Partners Bushra Khayat, Tahseen S. Khayat.

**Motivate Publishing:** POB 2331, Dubai; tel. (4) 824060; telex 48366; fax (4) 824436; f. 1979; books and eight magazines; Dirs Obaid Humaid at-Tayer, Ian Fairservice.

## Radio and Television

In 1992, according to estimates by UNESCO, there were 545,000 radio receivers and 185,000 television receivers in use. Television stations take advertisements, as do Capital Radio (Abu Dhabi) and Dubai Radio.

**Abu Dhabi Radio:** POB 63, Abu Dhabi; tel. (2) 451000; telex 22557; fax (2) 451155; f. 1968; stations in Abu Dhabi, Dubai, Umm al-Qaiwain and Ras al-Khaimah, all broadcasting in Arabic over a wide area; Abu Dhabi also broadcasts in English, French, Bengali, Filipino and Urdu, Dubai in English and Ras al-Khaimah in Urdu; Dir-Gen. Abd al-Wahab Radwan.

**Capital Radio:** POB 63, Abu Dhabi; tel. (2) 451000; telex 22557; fax (2) 451155; English-language FM music and news station, operated by the Ministry of Information and Culture; Station Manager Aida Hamza.

**Dubai Radio and Colour Television:** POB 1695, Dubai; tel. (4) 370255; telex 45605; broadcasts domestic Arabic and European programmes; Chair. Sheikh Hasher Maktoum; Dir-Gen. Abd al-Ghafoor Said Ibrahim.

**Ras al-Khaimah Broadcasting Station:** POB 141, Ras al-Khaimah; tel. (7) 51151; two transmitters broadcast in Arabic and Urdu; Dir Sheikh Abd al-Aziz bin Humaid.

**Sharjah Broadcasting Station:** POB 155, Sharjah; broadcasts in Arabic and French.

**Umm al-Qaiwain Broadcasting Station:** POB 444, Umm al-Qaiwain; tel. (6) 666044; fax (6) 666055; f. 1978; broadcasts music and news in Arabic, Malayalam, Sinhala, Tagalog and Urdu; Gen. Man. Ali Jassem.

**UAE Radio and Television—Dubai:** POB 1695, Dubai; tel. (4) 370255; telex 45605; fax (4) 371079; broadcasts in Arabic and English to the USA, India and Pakistan, the Far East, Australia and New Zealand, Europe and North and East Africa; Chair. Sheikh Hashem Maktoum; Dir-Gen. Abd al-Ghaffour as-Said Ibrahim.

**UAE TV—Abu Dhabi:** POB 637, Abu Dhabi; tel. (2) 452000; telex 22557; fax (2) 451470; f. 1968; broadcasts programmes incorporating information, entertainment, religion, culture, news and politics; Dir-Gen. Ali Obaid.

**UAE Television—Sharjah:** POB 111, Sharjah; tel. (6) 361111; telex 68599; fax (6) 541755; f. 1989; broadcasts in Arabic and Urdu in the northern emirates; Executive Dir Muhammad Diab al-Musa.

## Finance

(cap. = capital; dep. = deposits; res = reserves; m. = million; brs = branches; amounts in dirhams, unless otherwise indicated)

### BANKING

In early 1994 the UAE's 19 domestic and 28 foreign banks had a combined local network of 326 branches, and Dh 155,000m. in assets.

### Central Bank

**Central Bank of the United Arab Emirates:** POB 854, Abu Dhabi; tel. (2) 652220; telex 22330; fax (2) 668483; f. 1973; acts as issuing authority for local currency; superseded UAE Currency Board December 1980; auth. cap. 300m.; total assets 21,073.1m. (1992); Chair. Muhammad Eid al-Muraikhi; Gov. Sultan Nasser as-Suwaidi.

### Principal Banks

**Abu Dhabi Commercial Bank (ADCB):** POB 939, Abu Dhabi; tel. (2) 720000; telex 22244; fax (2) 776499; f. 1985 by merger; cap. 1,250m., dep. 10,486m., res 368m., total assets 12,230m. (Dec. 1994); 65% government-owned, 35% owned by private investors; Chair. Fadhel Saeed al-Darmaki; CEO and Man. Dir Khalifa Hassan; 30 brs in UAE, 1 br. overseas.

**Arab Bank for Investment and Foreign Trade:** POB 46733, Abu Dhabi; tel. (2) 721900; telex 22455; fax (2) 777550; f. 1976; jointly owned by the UAE Govt, the Libyan Arab Foreign Bank and the Banque Extérieure d'Algérie; cap. 570m., dep. 2,285.0m., res 181.6m., total assets 3,046.4m. (Dec. 1994); Chair. Abd al-Hafid Zlitni; Gen. Man. Hadi M. Giteli; 2 brs in Abu Dhabi, and one each in Dubai and al-Ain.

**Bank of Sharjah Ltd:** POB 1394, Sharjah; tel. (6) 352111; telex 68039; fax (6) 350323; f. 1973; cap. 84.0m., dep. 666.6m., res 75.0m., total assets 845.7m. (1993); Chair. Ahmad an-Noman; Gen. Man. Varouj Nerguizian; br. in Abu Dhabi.

**Commercial Bank of Dubai Ltd:** POB 2668, Deira, Dubai; tel. (4) 523355; telex 49600; fax (4) 520444; f. 1969; cap. 220m., dep. 1,947.4m., res 157.9m., total assets 2,380.4m. (Dec. 1993); Chair. Ahmad Humaid at-Tayer; Sr Chief Exec. and Gen. Man. Omar Abd ar-Rahim Leyas; 9 brs.

**Dubai Islamic Bank PLC:** POB 1080, Deira, Dubai; tel. (4) 214888; telex 45889; fax (4) 237243; f. 1975; cap. 210m., dep. 4,709.7m., res 55.9m., total assets 5,605.0m. (1993); Chair. and Man. Dir Said Ahmad Lootah; 8 brs.

**Emirates Bank International Ltd (EBI):** POB 2923, Dubai; tel. (4) 256256; telex 46426; fax (4) 268005; f. 1977 by merger; the Govt of Dubai has an 80% share; cap. 450.2m., dep. 10,526.7m., res 934.6m., total assets 11,911.5m. (Dec. 1993); Chair. Ahmad Humaid at-Tayer; Gen. Man. David Berry; 9 brs in the UAE, 11 brs overseas.

**First Gulf Bank:** Al-Ittihad St, POB 414, Ajman; tel. (6) 423450; telex 69510; fax (6) 446503; f. 1979; cap. 120.0m., dep. 313.1m., res 88.2m., total assets 521.3m. (Dec. 1990); Chair. Rashid Oweidah; brs in Abu Dhabi and Sharjah.

**Investment Bank for Trade and Finance PLC (INVESTBANK):** Al-Borj Ave, POB 1885, Sharjah; tel. (6) 355391; telex 68576; fax (6) 546683; f. 1975; cap. 135.5m., dep. 1,426.1m., res 26.6m., total assets 1,588.2m. (Dec. 1993); Chair. Sheikh Saqr bin Muhammad al-Qasimi; Gen. Man. Afif N. Shehadeh; brs in Abu Dhabi, Dubai and al-Ain.

**Mashreq Bank Ltd:** POB 1250, Deira, Dubai; tel. (4) 229131; telex 45429; fax (4) 226061; f. 1967 as Bank of Oman; cap. 516.5m., dep. 9,196.4m., res 621.0m., total assets 11,035.4m. (1993); Chair. Saif Ahmad al-Ghurair; Pres. Abdullah Ahmad al-Ghurair; 25 brs in UAE; 13 brs overseas.

**Middle East Bank Ltd:** POB 5547, Deira, Dubai; tel. (4) 256256; telex 46074; fax (4) 255322; f. 1976; controlling interest held by EBI; cap. and res 258.0m., total assets 3,820.9m. (1989); Chair. Ahmad Humaid at-Tayer; Chief Gen. Man. Ibrahim Tahlak; 9 brs in UAE.

**National Bank of Abu Dhabi (NBAD):** POB 4, Abu Dhabi; tel. (2) 335262; telex 22266/7; fax (2) 336078; f. 1968; owned jointly by Abu Dhabi Investment Authority and UAE citizens; cap. 941.6m., dep. 20,690.8m., res 893.1m., total assets 23,016.8m. (Dec. 1993); Chair. Sheikh Muhammad Habroush as-Suwaidi; CEO John S. W. Coombs; 38 brs in UAE, 9 brs overseas.

**National Bank of Dubai Ltd:** POB 777, Dubai; tel. (4) 267000; telex 45421; fax (4) 268939; f. 1963; cap. 861.8m., dep. 19,638.6m., res 2,630.9m., total assets 23,177.0m. (Dec. 1993); Chair. Sultan Ali al-Owais; Gen. Man. D. F. McKenzie; 17 brs, 3 overseas.

**National Bank of Fujairah:** POB 887, Fujairah; tel. (9) 224518; telex 89050; fax (9) 224516; f. 1982; owned jointly by Govt of Fujairah (36.78%), Govt of Dubai (9.78%), and UAE citizens and cos (53.44%); cap. and res 399.3m., dep. 787m., total assets 1,322.2m. (1994); Chair. Sheikh Saleh bin Muhammad ash-Sharqi; Gen. Man. Michael J. Connor; brs in Abu Dhabi, Dubai, Fujairah and Dibba.

**National Bank of Ras al-Khaimah PSC:** POB 5300, Ras al-Khaimah; tel. (7) 221127; telex 99109; fax (7) 223238; f. 1976; cap. 129.8m., dep. 965.9m., res 67.9m., total assets 1,200.2m. (Dec. 1993); Chair. Sheikh Khalid bin Saqr al-Qasimi; Gen. Man. J. R. G. Parsons; 8 brs.

**National Bank of Sharjah:** POB 4, Sharjah; tel. (6) 547745; telex 68085; fax (6) 543483; f. 1976; commercial bank; cap. 260m., dep.

# THE UNITED ARAB EMIRATES

2,297.3m., res 142.5m., total assets 4,538.5m. (1988); Chair. AHMAD AN-NOMAN; CEO and Gen. Man. ALAN D. WHYTE; 8 brs.

**National Bank of Umm al-Qaiwain Ltd:** POB 800, Umm al-Qaiwain; tel. (6) 655225; telex 69733; fax (6) 655440; f. 1982; cap. 250.0m., dep. 714.7m., res 65.9m., total assets 1,123.4m. (1994); Chair. Sheikh SAUD BIN RASHID AL-MU'ALLA; Man. Dir and CEO Sheikh NASSER BIN RASHID AL-MU'ALLA; 9 brs.

**Union National Bank:** POB 3865, Abu Dhabi; tel. (2) 741600; telex 23693; fax (2) 786080; f. 1983; formerly Bank of Credit and Commerce (Emirates); cap. 352m., total assets 6,222.7m. (1989); Chair. Sheikh NAHYAN BIN MUBARAK AN-NAHYAN; CEO ANWER QAYUM SHER; Gen. Man. ALFRED CULLEN; 10 brs in Abu Dhabi, 5 brs in Dubai, and one each in al-Ain, Sharjah, Ras al-Khaimah and Fujairah.

**United Arab Bank:** POB 3562, Abu Dhabi; tel. (2) 325000; telex 22759; fax (2) 338361; f. 1975; affiliated to Société Générale, France; cap. 90.0m., dep. 945.7m., res 81.9m., total assets 1,142.3m. (1993); Chair. Sheikh FAISAL BIN SULTAN AL-QASIMI; Gen. Man. J. P. NEDELEC; 7 brs.

### Foreign Banks

**ABN AMRO Bank NV** (Netherlands): Faraj Bin Hamoodah Bldg, Sheikh Hamdan St, POB 2720, Abu Dhabi; tel. (2) 335400; telex 22401; fax (2) 330182; f. 1974; POB 2567, Deira, Dubai; tel. (4) 512233; telex 45610; fax (4) 511555; POB 1971, Sharjah; tel. (6) 355021; telex 68467; fax (6) 546036; Man. (Abu Dhabi) M.P.T. KLEIN.

**ANZ Grindlays Bank PLC** (UK): POB 241, Abu Dhabi; tel. (2) 330876; telex 22252; fax (2) 331767; POB 357, Sharjah; tel. (6) 359998; telex 68011; fax (6) 357046; POB 1100, al-Ain; tel. (3) 643400; telex 33531; fax (3) 645121; Gen. Man. ALAN COOPER.

**Arab Bank PLC** (Jordan): POB 875, Abu Dhabi; tel. (2) 334111; telex 24195; fax (2) 336433; f. 1970; POB 1650, Dubai; POB 130, Sharjah; POB 4971, Ras al-Khaimah; POB 300, Fujairah; POB 17, Ajman; Man. FATHI M. SKAIK; 8 local brs.

**Arab-African International Bank** (Egypt): POB 1049, Dubai; tel. (4) 223131; telex 45503; fax (4) 222257; f. 1970; POB 928, Abu Dhabi; tel. (2) 323400; telex 22587; fax (2) 216009; f. 1976; Chair. Dr FAHD AR-RASHID; Deputy Chair. and Man. Dir MUHAMMAD FARID.

**Bank of Baroda** (India): POB 2303, Abu Dhabi; tel. (2) 330244; telex 22391; fax (2) 335293; f. 1974; Sr Vice-Pres. J.K. SHAH; also brs in Deira (Dubai), Sharjah and Ras al-Khaimah.

**Bank Melli Iran:** Regional Office and Main Branch, POB 1894, Dubai; tel. (4) 268207; telex 46404; fax (4) 269157; f. 1969; Regional Dir AZIZ AZIMI NOBAR; brs in Dubai, Abu Dhabi, al-Ain, Sharjah, Fujairah and Ras al-Khaimah.

**Bank Saderat Iran:** POB 700, Abu Dhabi; tel. (2) 335155; telex 45456; fax (2) 325062; POB 4182, Dubai; also Sharjah, Ajman, Ras al-Khaimah, Fujairah and al-Ain; Man. NASER RAFAATI.

**Banque Banorabe** (France): POB 4370, Dubai; tel. (4) 284655; telex 45801; fax (4) 236260; POB 5803, Sharjah; tel. (6) 593361; telex 68512; fax (6) 596413; f. 1974; fmrly Banque de l'Orient Arabe et d'Outre Mer; Chair. and Gen. Man. Dr NAAMAN AZHARI; UAE Regional Man. BASSEM M. AL-ARISS.

**Banque du Caire** (Egypt): POB 533, Abu Dhabi; tel. (2) 328700; telex 22304; fax (2) 323881; POB 1502, Dubai; POB 254, Sharjah; POB 618, Ras al-Khaimah; Gulf Regional Man. FOUAD ABD AL-KHALEK TAHOON.

**Banque Indosuez** (France): POB 9256, Dubai; tel. (4) 314211; telex 45860; fax (4) 313201; f. 1975; POB 46786, Abu Dhabi; tel. (2) 338400; telex 22464; fax (2) 338581; f. 1981; UAE Regional Man. ALAIN DE TRUCHIS.

**Banque Libanaise pour le Commerce SA** (France): POB 4207, Dubai; tel. (4) 222291; telex 45671; fax (4) 279861; POB 854, Sharjah; POB 3771, Abu Dhabi; tel. (2) 320920; telex 22862; fax (2) 213851; POB 771, Ras al-Khaimah; UAE Regional Man. JEAN MAHER.

**Banque Paribas** (France): POB 2742, Abu Dhabi; tel. (2) 335560; telex 22331; fax (2) 215138; POB 7233, Dubai; tel. (4) 525929; telex 45755; fax (4) 521341; Gen. Man. (Abu Dhabi) PIERRE IMHOF; Gen. Man. (Dubai) GEORGES TABET.

**Barclays Bank PLC** (UK): POB 2734, Abu Dhabi; tel. (2) 335313; telex 22456; fax (2) 345815; POB 1891, Deira, Dubai; tel. (4) 283116; telex 45820; fax (4) 282788; POB 1953, Sharjah; tel. (6) 355288; telex 68100; fax (6) 543498; Man. D. G. C. THOMSON (Dubai).

**The British Bank of the Middle East (BBME)** (Jersey): POB 66, Dubai; tel. (4) 535000; telex 45424; fax (4) 531005; f. 1946; total assets £5,055m. sterling (1994); Exec. Dir DAVID HOWELLS; CEO ABDUL JALIL YOUSUF; 8 brs throughout UAE.

**Citibank NA** (USA): POB 749, Dubai; tel. (4) 522100; telex 45422; fax (4) 524942; f. 1963; POB 346, Sharjah; POB 999, Abu Dhabi; POB 294, Ras al-Khaimah; POB 1430, al-Ain; total assets 1,372.1m. (1988); Man. S. CRABTREE.

*Directory*

**First Interstate Bank of California** (USA): POB 6643, Abu Dhabi; tel. (2) 321897; telex 23496; fax (2) 330209; Vice-Pres. OSMAN MORAD.

**First National Bank of Chicago** (USA): POB 1655, Dubai; tel. (4) 226161; telex 45633; Vice-Pres. and Gen. Man. RICHARD L. KOLEHMAINEN.

**Habib Bank AG Zürich** (Switzerland): POB 2681, Abu Dhabi; tel. (2) 329157; telex 22205; fax (2) 351822; f. 1974; POB 1166, Sharjah; POB 3306, Dubai; POB 168, Ajman; POB 181, Umm al-Qaiwain; POB 767, Ras al-Khaimah; Joint Pres. H. M. HABIB; Vice-Pres. HATIM HUSAIN.

**Habib Bank Ltd** (Pakistan): POB 888, Dubai; tel. (4) 268514; telex 45430; fax (4) 267493; f. 1967; POB 897, Abu Dhabi; tel. (2) 333620; telex 22332; f. 1975; Vice-Pres. and Chief Man. (Dubai) MOHAMMAD A. BAQAR; Vice-Pres. and Chief Man. (Abu Dhabi) IZHAR JUNEJO; 6 other brs in UAE.

**Janata Bank** (Bangladesh): POB 2630, Abu Dhabi; tel. (2) 331400; telex 22402; fax (2) 348749; POB 3342, Dubai; CEO and Gen. Man. MUHAMMAD RUHUL AMIN; Man. K. M. SHAFIQUR RAHMAN; brs in al-Ain, Dubai and Sharjah.

**Lloyds Bank PLC** (UK): POB 3766, Dubai; tel. (4) 313005; telex 46450; fax (4) 313026; f. 1977; dep. 500.4m., total assets 1,431.3m. (1994); Regional Man. CHARLES J. NEIL.

**National Bank of Oman SAOG:** POB 3822, Abu Dhabi; tel. (2) 339543; telex 22866; fax (2) 216153; Man. MIRAJUDDIN AZIZ.

**Nilein Industrial Development Bank** (Sudan): POB 6013, Abu Dhabi; telex 22884; Man. ABDULLAH MAHMOUD AWAD.

**Royal Bank of Canada:** POB 3614, Dubai; tel. (4) 225226; telex 45926; fax (4) 215687; f. 1976; Man. A. POLLEY.

**Standard Chartered PLC** (UK): POB 240, Abu Dhabi; tel. (2) 330077; telex 22274; fax (2) 341511; POB 999, Dubai; tel. (4) 520455; telex 45431; fax (4) 526679; POB 5, Sharjah; tel. (6) 357788; telex 68245; fax (6) 546676; POB 1240, al-Ain; tel. (3) 641253; telex 34082; fax (3) 654824; Gen. Man. JAMES ALLHUSEN.

**United Bank Ltd** (Pakistan): POB 1000, Dubai; tel. (4) 223191; telex 45433; POB 237, Abu Dhabi; tel. (2) 338240; telex 22272; fax (2) 344090; f. 1959; Sr Vice-Pres. and Zonal Chief S. M. ASGHAR; 7 other brs in UAE.

### Bankers' Association

**United Arab Emirates Bankers' Association:** POB 44307, Abu Dhabi; tel. (2) 322541; telex 22781; fax (2) 324158; f. 1983.

### INSURANCE

**Abu Dhabi National Insurance Co (Adnic):** POB 839, Abu Dhabi; tel. (2) 343171; telex 22340; fax (2) 211358; f. 1972; subscribed 25% by the Government of Abu Dhabi and 75% by UAE nationals; all classes of insurance; Chair. and Gen. Man. KHALAF A. AL-OTAIBA.

**Al-Ahlia Insurance Co:** POB 128, Ras al-Khaimah; tel. (7) 721749; telex 47677; f. 1977; Gen. Man. T. A. SAID; 3 brs.

**Al-Ain Ahlia Insurance Co:** POB 3077, Abu Dhabi; tel. (2) 323551; telex 22352; fax (2) 323550; f. 1975; Chair. HAMIL AL-GAITH; Gen. Man. M. MAZHAR HAMADEH; brs in Dubai, Sharjah, Tarif and al-Ain.

**Dubai Insurance Co (S.A.D.):** POB 3027, Dubai; tel. (4) 693030; telex 45685; fax (4) 693727; f. 1970; Chair. MAJID AL-FUTTAIM; Gen. Man. FAROUK HUWAIDI.

**Sharjah Insurance and Reinsurance Co:** POB 792, Sharjah; tel. (6) 355090; telex 68060; fax (6) 352545; f. 1970; Gen. Man. ADIB S. ABED.

**Union Insurance Co:** Head Office: POB 460, Umm al-Qaiwain; tel. (6) 666223; POB 4623, Dubai; POB 3196, Abu Dhabi; Gen. Man. L. F. DOKOV.

# Trade and Industry

## CHAMBERS OF COMMERCE

**Federation of UAE Chambers of Commerce and Industry:** POB 3014, Abu Dhabi; tel. (2) 214144; telex 23883; fax (2) 339210; POB 8886, Dubai; tel. (4) 212977; telex 48752; fax (4) 235498; Pres. HASSAN ABDULLAH AN-NOMAN; Sec.-Gen. KHALIFA AL-JALLAFF.

**Abu Dhabi Chamber of Commerce and Industry:** POB 662, Abu Dhabi; tel. (2) 214000; telex 22499; fax (2) 215867; f. 1977; 7,000 mems; Pres. RAHMAN MUHAMMAD AL-MASOUD; Dir-Gen. TAHER MUSBEH AL-KINDI.

**Ajman Chamber of Commerce and Industry:** POB 662, Ajman; tel. (6) 422177; telex 69523; fax (6) 427591; f. 1977; Pres. HAMAD MUHAMMAD ABU SHIHAB; Dir-Gen. MUHAMMAD BIN ABDULLAH AL-HUMRANI.

**Dubai Chamber of Commerce and Industry:** POB 1457, Deira, Dubai; tel. (4) 221181; telex 45997; fax (4) 211646; f. 1965; 33,000 mems; Pres. SAID JUMA AN-NABOODAH; Dir-Gen. ABD AR-RAHMAN GHANEM AL-MUTAIWEE.

**Fujairah Chamber of Commerce, Industry and Agriculture:** POB 738, Fujairah; tel. (9) 222400; telex 89088; fax (9) 221464; Pres. SAIF SULTAN SAID; Dir-Gen. SHAHEEN ALI SHAHEEN.

**Ras al-Khaimah Chamber of Commerce, Industry and Agriculture:** POB 78, Ras al-Khaimah; tel. (7) 333511; telex 99140; fax (7) 330233; f. 1967; 5,220 mems; Pres. ALI ABDULLAH MUSABEH; Dir MUHAMMAD ALI AL-HARANKI.

**Sharjah Chamber of Commerce and Industry:** POB 580, Sharjah; tel. (6) 541444; telex 68205; fax (6) 541119; f. 1970; 23,000 mems; Chair. HASSAN ABDULLAH AN-NOMAN; Dir-Gen. SAID OBEID AL-JARWAN.

**Umm al-Qaiwain Chamber of Commerce and Industry:** POB 436, Umm al-Qaiwain; tel. (6) 656915; telex 69714; fax (6) 657056; Pres. ABDULLAH RASHID AL-KHARJI; Man. Dir SHAKIR AZ-ZAYANI.

## DEVELOPMENT ORGANIZATIONS

**Abu Dhabi Development Finance Corpn:** POB 30, Abu Dhabi; tel. (2) 22656; telex 820431; fax (2) 728890; purpose is to provide finance to the private sector; Deputy Man. Dir SAID MUHAMMAD.

**Abu Dhabi Fund for Development (ADFD):** POB 814; tel. (2) 725800; telex 22287; fax (2) 728890; f. 1971; purpose is to offer economic aid to other Arab states and other developing countries in support of their development; cap. 4,000m.; Chair. Sheikh KHALIFA BIN ZAYED AN-NAHYAN; Dir-Gen. KHALIFA MUHAMMAD AL-MUHAIRI.

**Abu Dhabi Investment Authority (ADIA):** POB 3600, Abu Dhabi; tel. (2) 213100; telex 22674; f. 1976; responsible for co-ordinating Abu Dhabi's investment policy; Chair. Sheikh KHALIFA BIN ZAYED AN-NAHYAN; Pres. Sheikh MUHAMMAD HABROUSH AS-SUWAIDI; 1 br. overseas.

**Abu Dhabi Investment Company (ADIC):** POB 46309, Abu Dhabi; tel. (2) 328200; telex 22968; fax (2) 212903; f. 1977; investment and merchant banking activities in the UAE and abroad; 90% owned by ADIA and 10% by National Bank of Abu Dhabi; total assets Dh 3,845m. (1991); Chair. HAREB MASOOD AD-DARMAKI; Gen. Man. HUMAID DARWISH AL-KATBI.

**Abu Dhabi Planning Department:** POB 12, Abu Dhabi; tel. (2) 727200; telex 23194; fax (2) 727749; f. 1974; supervises Abu Dhabi's Development Programme; Chair. MUSALLAM SAEED ABDULLAH AL-QUBAISI; Under-Sec. AHMED M. HILAL AL-MAZRUI.

**Emirates Industrial Bank:** POB 2722, Abu Dhabi; tel. (2) 339700; telex 23324; fax (2) 326397; f. 1982; offers low-cost loans to enterprises with at least 51% local ownership; 51% state-owned; cap. Dh 200m.; Chair. MUHAMMAD KHALFAN KHIRBASH; Gen. Man. MUHAMMAD ABD AL-BAKI MUHAMMAD.

**General Industry Corpn (GIC):** POB 4499, Abu Dhabi; tel. (2) 214900; telex 22938; fax (2) 325034; f. 1979; responsible for the promotion of non-petroleum-related industry; due for partial privatization in late 1995.

**International Petroleum Investment Company (IPIC):** POB 7528, Abu Dhabi; tel. (2) 336200; telex 22520; fax (2) 216045; f. 1984; cap. $200m.; state-owned venture to develop overseas investments in energy and energy-related projects; Chair. JOUAN SALEM ADH-DHAHIRI; Man. Dir KHALIFA MUHAMMAD ASH-SHAMSI.

**Sharjah Economic Development Corpn (SHEDCO):** POB 3458, Sharjah; tel. (6) 371212; telex 68789; industrial investment co; joint venture between Sharjah authorities and private sector; auth. cap. Dh 1,000m.; Gen. Man. J. T. PICKLES.

**United Arab Emirates Development Bank:** Abu Dhabi; tel. (2) 344986; telex 22427; f. 1974; participates in development of real estate, agriculture, fishery, livestock and light industries; cap. Dh 500m.; Gen. Man. MUHAMMAD SALEM AL-MELEHY.

## PRINCIPAL PETROLEUM CONCESSIONS

**Supreme Petroleum Council:** POB 26555, Abu Dhabi; tel. (2) 666000; telex 23300; fax (2) 661469; f. 1988; assumed authority and responsibility for the administration and supervision of all petroleum affairs in Abu Dhabi; Chair. Sheikh KHALIFA BIN ZAYED AN-NAHYAN; Sec.-Gen. SOHAIL FARES AL-MAZRUI.

### Abu Dhabi

**Abu Dhabi National Oil Co (ADNOC):** POB 898, Abu Dhabi; tel. (2) 6020000; telex 22215; fax (2) 722244; f. 1971; cap. Dh7,500m.; state company; deals in all phases of oil industry; owns two refineries: one on Umm an-Nar island and one at Ruwais; Habshan Gas Treatment Plant; a salt and chlorine plant; holds 60% participation in operations of ADMA-OPCO and ADCO, 88% of ZADCO and 88% of UDECO; has 100% control of Abu Dhabi National Oil Company for Oil Distribution (ADNOC-FOD), Abu Dhabi National Tanker Company (ADNATCO), National Drilling Co (NDC) and interests in numerous other companies, both in the UAE and overseas; ADNOC is operated by Supreme Petroleum Council, Chair. Sheikh KHALIFA BIN ZAYED AN-NAHYAN; Gen. Man. SOHAIL FARES AL-MAZRUI.

**Abu Dhabi Co for Onshore Oil Operations (ADCO):** POB 270, Abu Dhabi; tel. (2) 666100; telex 22222; fax (2) 669785; name changed from Abu Dhabi Petroleum Co Ltd (ADPC) in February 1979; shareholders are ADNOC (60%), British Petroleum, Shell and Total (9.5% each), Exxon and Mobil (4.75% each) and Partex (2%); average production (1990): 1.2m. b/d; Chair. SOHAIL FARES AL-MAZRUI; Gen. Man. DAVID WOODWARD.

**Abu Dhabi Drilling Chemicals and Products Ltd (ADDCAP):** POB 46121, Abu Dhabi; tel. (2) 730400; telex 23267; fax (2) 730725; f. 1975; manufacture and marketing of drilling chemicals and operation of an offshore supply marine base; ADNOC has a 75% share and NL Industries 25%; Chair. SOHAIL FARES AL-MAZRUI; Gen. Man. R. GONINON.

**Abu Dhabi Gas Industries Co (GASCO):** POB 665, Abu Dhabi; tel. (2) 651100; telex 22365; fax (2) 6047414; started production in 1981; recovers condensate and LPG from Asab, Bab and Bu Hasa fields for delivery to Ruwais natural gas liquids fractionation plant; capacity of 22,000 tons per day; ADNOC has a 68% share; Total, Shell Gas and Partex have a minority interest; Chair. YOUSUF BIN OMEIR BIN YOUSUF; Gen. Man. P. HILLAIREAUD.

**Abu Dhabi Gas Liquefaction Co (ADGAS):** POB 3500, Abu Dhabi; tel. (2) 333888; telex 22698; fax (2) 6065456; f. 1973; owned by ADNOC, 51%; the British Petroleum Co, $16\frac{1}{3}$%; Total, $8\frac{1}{6}$%; Mitsui and Co, $22\frac{1}{20}$%; Mitsui Liquefied Gas Co, $2\frac{9}{20}$%; operates LGSC and the LNG plant on Das Island, which was commissioned in 1977. The plant uses natural gas produced in association with oil from offshore fields and has a design capacity of approx. 2.3m. tons of LNG per year and 1.29m. tons of LPG per year. The liquefied gas is sold to the Tokyo Electric Power Co, Japan. Chair. ABDULLAH NASSER AS-SUWAIDI; Gen. Man. PETER CARR.

**Abu Dhabi Marine Operating Co (ADMA-OPCO):** POB 303, Abu Dhabi; tel. (2) 6060000; telex 22284; fax (2) 720099; operates a concession 60% owned by the Abu Dhabi National Oil Co, POB 898, Abu Dhabi and 40% by Abu Dhabi Marine Areas Ltd, Britannic House, Moor Lane, London, EC2Y 9BU, England (BP Co $14\frac{2}{3}$%; Japan Oil Development Co Ltd 12%; Total $13\frac{1}{3}$%). The concession lies in the Abu Dhabi offshore area and currently produces oil from Lower Zakum and Umm Shaif fields. ADMA-OPCO was created in 1977 as an operator for the concession. Production (1984): 67,884,769 barrels (8,955,721 metric tons); Chair. YOUSUF BIN OMEIR BIN YOUSUF; Gen. Man. MICHEL VIALLARD.

**Abu Dhabi National Oil Company for Distribution (ADNOC-FOD):** POB 4188, Abu Dhabi; tel. (2) 771300; telex 22358; fax (2) 722322; 100% owned by ADNOC; distributes petroleum products in Abu Dhabi; Chair. SOHAIL FARES AL-MAZRUI; Dir-Gen. ABDULLAH SAID AL-BADI.

**Abu Dhabi National Tanker Co (ADNATCO):** (see Shipping).

**Abu Dhabi Petroleum Ports Operating Co (ADPPOC):** POB 61, Abu Dhabi; tel. (2) 777300; telex 22209; fax (2) 763293; f. 1979; manages Jebel Dhanna, Ruwais, Das Island, Umm an-Nar and Zirku Island SPM terminal, Mubarraz; cap. Dh50m.; of which ADNOC has a 60% share and LAMNALCO Kuwait 40%; Chair. YOUSUF BIN OMEIR BIN YOUSUF; Gen. Man. T. E. DENNIS.

**The Liquefied Gas Shipping Co Ltd (LGSC):** POB 3500, Abu Dhabi; tel. (2) 333888; telex 22698; f. 1972; cap. $1m.; ADNOC holds 51% share, Mitsui 24.5%, Shell 16.3%, BP 8.2%; Gen. Man. Dr D. BROOKS.

**National Drilling Company (NDC):** POB 4017, Abu Dhabi; tel. (2) 316600; telex 22553; fax (2) 317045; drilling operations; Chair. RASHID SAIF AS-SUWAIDI; Gen. Man. MICHAEL MURPHY.

**National Marine Services Co (NMS):** (see Shipping).

**National Petroleum Construction Co Ltd (NPCC):** POB 2058, Abu Dhabi; tel. (2) 549000; telex 22638; fax (2) 549079; f. 1973; 'turnkey' construction and maintenance of offshore facilities for the petroleum and gas industries; cap. Dh 100m.; Chair. MUHAMMAD KHALIFA AL-KINDI; Gen. Man. FARID B. ASFOUR.

**Ruwais Fertilizers Industries Ltd (FERTIL):** POB 2288, Abu Dhabi; tel. (2) 6021111; telex 24205; fax (2) 728084; $66\frac{2}{3}$% owned by ADNOC and $33\frac{1}{3}$% by Total; began production of ammonia and urea in 1984; Chair. RASHID S. AS-SUWAIDI; Gen. Man. ABDUL HAKIM M. AS-SUWAIDI.

**Abu Dhabi Oil Co Ltd (Japan) (ADOC):** POB 630, Abu Dhabi; tel. (2) 661100; telex 22260; fax (2) 665965; consortium of Japanese oil companies, including Cosmo Oil, JNOC and Nippon Mining Co; holds offshore concession, extended by 1,582.5 sq km in 1979; export of oil from Mubarraz Island terminal began in June 1973, production 6,332,897 barrels (1985); Gen. Man. TOSHIO KUWAHARA.

**Amerada Hess Oil Corpn of Abu Dhabi (AHOC):** POB 2046, Abu Dhabi; tel. and fax (2) 779500; telex 22275; operates the Arzanah field; owned 41.25% by AHOC, 31.5% Pan Ocean, Bow Valley 2.5%, Syracuse Oil 7.5%, Wington Enterprises 4.75%, Neste Oy 10%, Sunningdale 2.5%; Gen. Man. M. MURPHY.

**Bunduq Oil Co:** POB 46015, Abu Dhabi; tel. (2) 213380; telex 23872; fax (2) 321794; f. 1975; production in al-Bunduq oilfield; Gen. Man. T. FUJIMURA.

**Neyrfor UAE:** POB 46135; Abu Dhabi; tel. (2) 371805.

**Total Abu al-Bukhoosh Oil Co Ltd:** POB 4058, Abu Dhabi; tel. (2) 785000; telex 22347; fax (2) 788477; owned by Total, operator of Abu al-Bukhoosh field; began production from the Abu al-Bukhoosh offshore field in July 1974; average production of 40,000 b/d in 1991; partner in the field is Amerada Hess Oil Corpn.

**Zakum Development Co (ZADCO):** POB 6808, Abu Dhabi; tel. (2) 661700; telex 22948; fax (2) 669448; joint venture between ADNOC (88%) and JODCO (12%); develop and produce from Upper Zakum, Umm ad-Dalkh and Satah fields on behalf of its owners; manages UDECO; Chair. SOHAIL FARES AL-MAZRUI; Gen. Man. I. NAHARA.

### Ajman

**Ajman National Oil Co (AJNOC):** POB 410, Ajman; tel. (6) 421218; f. 1983; 50% government-owned, 50% held by Canadian and private Arab interests.

### Dubai

**DUGAS (Dubai Natural Gas Company Ltd):** POB 4311, Dubai (Location: Jebel Ali); tel. (4) 46234; telex 45741; fax (4) 46118; wholly owned by Dubai authorities; Dep. Chair. and Dir MIRZA H. AS-SAYEGH.

**Dubai Petroleum Co (DPC):** POB 2222, Dubai; tel. (4) 442990; telex 45423; fax (4) 462200; holds offshore concession which began production in 1969; wholly owned by Dubai authorities; Pres. JOHN I. HORNING.

**Emirates General Petroleum Corpn (EGPC):** POB 9400, Dubai; tel. (4) 373300; telex 47980; fax (4) 373200; f. 1981; wholly owned by Ministry of Finance and Industry; distribution of petroleum.

**Emirates National Oil Co (ENOC):** Dubai; f. 1993; responsible for management of Dubai-owned companies in petroleum-marketing sector; Chair. Sheikh HAMDAN BIN RASHID AL-MAKTOUM.

**Emirates Petroleum Products Co (Pvt.) Ltd:** POB 5589, Dubai; tel. (4) 372131; telex 48342; fax (4) 375990; f. 1980; joint venture between Govt. of Dubai and Caltex Alkhaleej Marketing; sales of petroleum products, bunkering fuel and bitumen; Chair. Sheikh HAMDAN BIN RASHID AL-MAKTOUM.

**Sedco-Houston Oil Group:** POB 702, Dubai; tel. (4) 224141; telex 45469; holds onshore concession of over 400,000 ha as well as the offshore concession formerly held by Texas Pacific Oil; Pres. CARL F. THORNE.

### Sharjah

**Amoco Sharjah Oil Co:** POB 1191, Sharjah; telex 68685; holds onshore concession areas.

**Crescent Petroleum Co International:** POB 2222, Sharjah; tel. (6) 543000; telex 68015; fax (6) 542000; subsidiary of BGOI Inc; Chair. and CEO H. D. JAFAR.

**Meridian Oil N.L. Co:** POB 3943, Sharjah; tel. (6) 331388; telex 68577.

**Petroleum and Minaral Affairs Department:** POB 188, Sharjah; tel. (6) 541888; telex 68708; Dir ISMAIL A. WAHID.

**Sharjah Liquefied Petroleum Gas Co (SHALCO):** POB 787, Sharjah; tel. (6) 543666; telex 68799; fax (6) 548799; f. 1984; gas processing; 60% owned by Sharjah authorities, 25% Sharjah Amoco-Oil Co, 7.5% each Itochu Corp. and Tokyo Boeki of Japan; Gen. Man. SALEH ALI.

### Umm al-Qaiwain

**Petroleum and Mineral Affairs Department:** POB 9, Umm al-Qaiwain; tel. (6) 666034; Chair. Sheikh SULTAN BIN AHMAD AL-MU'ALLA.

## Transport

### ROADS

Roads are rapidly being developed in the United Arab Emirates, and Abu Dhabi and Dubai are linked by a good road which is dual carriageway for most of its length. This road forms part of a west coast route from Shaam, at the UAE border with the northern enclave of Oman, through Dubai and Abu Dhabi to Tarif. An east coast route links Dibba with Muscat. Other roads include the Abu Dhabi–al-Ain highway and roads linking Sharjah and Ras al-Khaimah, and Sharjah and Dhaid. An underwater tunnel links Dubai Town and Deira by dual carriageway and pedestrian subway. In 1993 there were more than 3,000 km of paved highways in the UAE.

### SHIPPING

Dubai has been the main commercial centre in the Gulf for many years. Abu Dhabi has also become an important port since the opening of the first section of its artificial harbour, Port Zayed. There are smaller ports in Sharjah, Fujairah, Ras al-Khaimah and Umm al-Qaiwain. Work on a dry-dock scheme for Dubai was completed in 1979. It possesses two docks capable of handling 500,000-ton tankers, seven repair berths and a third dock able to accommodate 1,000,000-ton tankers. In 1988 the Dubai port of Mina Jebel Ali, which has the largest man-made harbour in the world, contained 67 berths. Current modernization of Port Khalid in Sharjah was to double its berth capacity, and the two-berth port of Fujairah was opened in 1983.

**Abu Dhabi National Tanker Company (ADNATCO):** POB 2977, Abu Dhabi; tel. (2) 331800; telex 22747; fax (2) 322940; subsidiary company of ADNOC, operating owned and chartered tankships, and transporting crude petroleum, refined products and sulphur; Chair. KHALAF RASHID AL-OTEIBA; Gen. Man. BADER M. AS-SUWAIDI.

**Ahmad bin Rashid Port and Free Trade Zone:** POB 279, Umm al-Qaiwain; tel. (6) 655882; telex 69717; fax (6) 651552.

**Dubai Drydocks:** POB 8988, Dubai; tel. (4) 450626; telex 48838; fax (4) 450116; state-owned dry-docks with cleaning facilities, galvanizing plant, transport systems and facilities for maintenance and repair of ships of any size; Chief Exec. E. S. WARE.

**Dubai Ports Authority (DPA):** POB 17000, Dubai; tel. (4) 815000; telex 47398; fax (4) 816093; offers duty-free storage areas and facilities for loading and discharge of vessels; supervises ports of Mina Jebel Ali and Mina Rashid; handled more than 1.7m. containers in 1993; Chair. SULTAN AHMAD BIN SULAYEM; Exec. Dirs EDWARD BILKEY, DAVID GIBBONS.

**Fujairah Port:** POB 787, Fujairah; tel. (9) 228800; telex 89085; fax (9) 228811; f. 1982; offers facilities for handling full container, general cargo and 'roll on, roll off' traffic; Chair. Sheikh SALEH BIN MUHAMMAD ASH-SHARQI; Gen. Man. Capt. MOUSA MORAD.

**Jebel Ali Free Zone Authority (JAFZA):** POB 17000, Dubai; tel. (4) 815000; telex 47398; fax (4) 815001; the authority administers a 100 sq km zone, created by the Government of Dubai in 1985, which includes the 7,500-acre Jebel Ali port and industrial area offering 67 berths; offers facilities for handling container, bulk, general and liquid traffic; 'roll on, roll off' berths; 42,000 cu m capacity cold store; aluminium smelter; desalinization and power generating plants; by December 1994 735 companies had established business in the Free Zone; Rashid port and Jebel Ali port handled more than 25m. metric tons of cargo in 1994; Chair. SULTAN AHMAD BIN SULAYEM.

**Jebel Dhanna/Ruwais Petroleum Port:** c/o ADCO, POB 898, Abu Dhabi; tel. (2) 666100; telex 22222; fax (2) 669785; facilities include 5 tanker berths, export of crude petroleum, refined products, fertilizers, ammonia and sulphur; Terminal Superintendent J. B. SHEEHAN.

**Mina Zayed Port:** POB 422, Abu Dhabi; tel. (2) 730600; telex 22731; fax (2) 731023; facilities include 21 deep-water berths of up to 13 metres draft; 3 container gantry cranes of 40 tons capacity; specializes in container traffic, general and reefer cargoes; in 1993 Port Zayed handled 1.412m. metric tons of cargo; Chair. Sheikh SAID BIN ZAYED AN-NAHYAN; Dir MUBARAK AL-BU AINAIN.

**National Marine Services Co (NMS):** POB 7202, Abu Dhabi; tel. (2) 339800; telex 22965; fax (2) 211239; operate, charter and lease specialized offshore support vessels; cap. Dh 25m.; owned 60% by ADNOC and 40% by Jackson Marine Corporation USA; Chair. SOHAIL FARES AL-MAZRUI; Gen. Man. Capt. HASSAN A. SHAREEF.

**Ras al-Khaimah Port Services:** POB 5130, Ras al-Khaimah; tel. (7) 668444; telex 99280; fax (7) 668533; operate Mina Saqr port; govt-owned; Chair. Sheikh MUHAMMAD BIN SAQR AL-QASIMI; Man. Capt. HAZEM RAOUF ASSAD.

**Sharjah Ports and Customs Department:** POB 510, Sharjah; tel. (6) 281666; telex 68138; fax (6) 281425; the authority administers Port Khalid and Port Khor Fakkan and offers specialized facilities for container and 'roll on, roll off' traffic, reefer cargo and project and general cargo; in 1992 Port Khalid handled 37,400 20-ft equivalent units of containerized shipping, and Port Khor Fakkan 358,400 20-ft equivalent units; total cargo handled: 2.4m. metric tons; Chair. (Ports and Customs) Sheikh SAUD BIN KHALID AL-QASIMI; Dir-Gen. ABD AL-AZIZ SULAIMAN AS-SARKAL.

**Umm al-Qaiwain Port:** POB 225, Umm al-Qaiwain; tel. (6) 666126; telex 69611.

### CIVIL AVIATION

There are six international airports at Abu Dhabi, al-Ain (Abu Dhabi), Dubai, Fujairah and Ras al-Khaimah, and a smaller one at Sharjah, which forms part of Sharjah port, linking air, sea and overland transportation services. In 1988 900,000 passengers used

Sharjah international airport. In 1994 6.3m. passengers used Dubai international airport, and 3.1m. passed through Abu Dhabi airport.

**Civil Aviation Department:** POB 20, Abu Dhabi; tel. (2) 757500; telex 24406; responsible for all aspects of civil aviation; Chair. Hamdan bin Mubarak an-Nahyan.

**Abu Dhabi Aviation:** POB 2723, Abu Dhabi; tel. (2) 722733; telex 23409; Chair. Ali bin Khalfan adh-Dhahri; Gen. Man. Ali Said ash-Shamsi.

**Emirates Air Service:** POB 322, Abu Dhabi; tel. (2) 778222; telex 23056; fax (2) 770451; f. 1976 as Abu Dhabi Air Services; operates passenger and cargo charter flights within the UAE and to other destinations within the Gulf region; also operates contract flights for oil cos; wholly owned by Muhammad bin Masaood and Sons of Abu Dhabi; Pres. Abdullah Masaood; Man. Dir. C. O. Miller.

**Emirates (EK) Dubai:** POB 686, Dubai; tel. (4) 228151; telex 48085; fax (4) 214560; f. 1985; services to the Middle East, Europe and the Far East; owned by the Dubai authorities; in 1993/94 the airline carried 2.0m. passengers and 81,545 tons of freight; Chair. Sheikh Ahmad bin Said al-Maktoum; Man. Dir. Maurice Flanagan.

**Gulf Air Dubai:** Al Naboodah Bldg, al-Maktoum St, POB 4410, Dubai; tel. (4) 231700; f. 1950; serves 51 destinations world-wide.

**Gulf Air Co GSC (Gulf Air):** POB 5015, Sharjah; tel. (6) 356356; fax (6) 354354; f. 1950; jointly owned by Governments of Bahrain, Oman, Qatar and Abu Dhabi since 1974; flights world-wide; Pres. and Chief Exec. Salim bin Ali bin Nasser.

## Tourism

Tourism is an established industry in Sharjah, and plans are being implemented to foster tourism in other emirates, notably in Abu Dhabi (where a 'themed', 10 sq-km leisure complex, Lulu Island, is planned, at a cost of some US $2,500m.) and Dubai. In 1990 foreign visitors to the UAE totalled approximately 616,000.

**Dubai Information Department:** POB 1420, Dubai; Dir Omar Deesi.

**Ras al-Khaimah Information and Tourism Department:** POB 141, Ras al-Khaimah; tel. (7) 751151; Chair. Sheikh Abd al-Aziz bin Humaid al-Qassimi.

**Sharjah Department of Tourism:** POB 8, Sharjah; tel. (6) 581111; telex 68185; fax (6) 581167; f. 1980; Dir. Muhammad Saif al-Hajri.

# THE UNITED KINGDOM

# GREAT BRITAIN

## Introductory Survey

**Location, Climate, Language, Religion, Flag, Capital**

The United Kingdom of Great Britain and Northern Ireland lies in north-western Europe, occupying the major portion of the British Isles. The country's only land boundary is with the Republic of Ireland. Northern Ireland is a constitutionally distinct part of the United Kingdom (see subsequent chapter). Great Britain, consisting of one large island and a number of smaller ones, comprises England, Scotland to the north and Wales to the west. It is separated from the coast of western Europe by the English Channel to the south and by the North Sea to the east. The northern and western shores are washed by the Atlantic Ocean. Ireland lies to the west across the Irish Sea. The climate is generally temperate but variable. The average temperature is about 15°C (59°F) in summer and about 5°C (41°F) in winter. Average annual rainfall is 900 mm to 1,000 mm (35 in to 40 in). The language is English, but Welsh is spoken by about one-fifth of the Welsh population. The Church of England is the established church in England. Other large Christian denominations are Roman Catholicism, Methodism, the United Reformed Church and the Baptists. The national flag (proportions 2 by 1), known as the Union Jack, is a superimposition of the red cross of Saint George of England, the white saltire of Saint Andrew of Scotland and the red saltire of Ireland, all on a blue background. The capital is London.

**Recent History**

At the end of the Second World War, in 1945, the United Kingdom still ruled a vast overseas empire, and successive British Governments, in response both to nationalist aspirations and world pressure, gradually granted independence to the colonies. India and Pakistan became independent in 1947, and decolonization continued. By 1985 more than 30 other former British dependencies had achieved independence, nearly all of them becoming members of the Commonwealth (see p. 119). Although the Suez crisis of 1956 initiated a considerable decline in the international influence of the United Kingdom, British forces continued a nominal policing role 'East of Suez' until the early 1970s. Britain lost its dominant role in the Commonwealth, which became a free association of states, and by the end of the 1970s the country looked exclusively to the NATO alliance (see p. 191) and to the European Community (EC, now restructured as the European Union—EU—see p. 143) for its future security.

The Labour Party, led by Clement Attlee, gained a large majority of seats in the House of Commons in the general election of 1945 and a smaller one in 1950. Extensive social reforms were enacted, including the establishment of the National Health Service (NHS) and the nationalization of major industries and services. In 1951 a Conservative Government was formed by Winston Churchill, the wartime Prime Minister. The Conservatives remained in power for 13 years, led successively by Churchill, Sir Anthony Eden (1955–57), Harold Macmillan (1957–63) and Sir Alec Douglas-Home (1963–64). The election of 1964 gave a small parliamentary majority to the Labour Party, led by Harold Wilson. The Labour Party was re-elected in 1966, but in 1970 a Conservative Government, under Edward Heath, was returned.

After the general election of February 1974, Wilson formed a minority Government; in a further election, held in October, the Labour Party achieved a small majority in the House of Commons, although it secured less than 40% of the votes cast. In 1975 Heath was replaced as leader of the Conservative Party by Margaret Thatcher. Wilson resigned as Prime Minister in April 1976 and was succeeded by James Callaghan, hitherto the Secretary of State for Foreign and Commonwealth Affairs. The new Labour Government immediately encountered a serious monetary crisis, and, following a series of by-election defeats, became a minority Government again. In March 1977 the Government, modifying some of its policies, formed a pact with the Liberal Party, which had significantly increased its share of the vote in the 1974 elections but, without a system of proportional representation, held only 13 parliamentary seats. The pact ended in May 1978, with by-elections throughout the country showing a substantial loss of support for the Liberals.

In the general election of May 1979 the Conservative Party gained a parliamentary majority, with 43.9% of the votes, and formed a new government, under Thatcher, who became the United Kingdom's first woman Prime Minister. The Conservatives promised a policy of non-intervention in industry and the encouragement of private enterprise, while aiming to reduce public expenditure in central and local government. These policies proved to be controversial, owing to the austerity of certain economic measures, especially the severe reductions in spending on social and public services, and an accompanying increase in unemployment. The Government confronted the trade unions, introducing employment legislation which restricted their power.

Michael Foot was elected leader of the Labour Party in November 1980. The increasing prominence of extreme left-wing members caused serious rifts in the Labour Party, and in March 1981 four former ministers from the right wing of the party formed the Social Democratic Party (SDP). The SDP rapidly gained support, including that of other Labour Members of Parliament (MPs), and a political alliance was formed with the Liberals in 1981.

In April 1982 Argentine forces invaded the British dependency of the Falkland Islands. The successful military campaign to recover the islands by a British task force in June significantly increased the Government's popularity, despite rising unemployment and strict monetary control of the economy. In the general election of June 1983 the Conservative Party won a decisive victory, with a greatly increased majority in the House of Commons, despite a reduced share (42.4%) of the votes. The Labour Party won only 27.6% of the votes (compared with 36.9% in 1979) and suffered a significant reduction in its parliamentary representation. Although it received 25.4% of the votes, the SDP/Liberal Alliance won less than 4% of the seats. As a result of the Labour Party's defeat, Michael Foot resigned as the party's leader and was replaced by Neil Kinnock in October. With its large majority in the House of Commons, where it was faced by a divided opposition, the Conservative Government was able to command firm legislative support for its proposals, although it frequently had its measures rejected or amended by the non-elected House of Lords.

At an early general election in June 1987, the Conservative Party won 42.3% of the votes and an overall majority of 102 seats in the House of Commons (compared with 146 seats at the 1983 election). In July, following its third successive election defeat, the Labour Party announced a thorough review of its policies and subsequently modified its stance on several issues, including that of advocating unilateral nuclear disarmament (adopted in 1980). After their proportion of the total vote had fallen in the 1987 general election, the SDP/Liberal Alliance agreed in September to a merger, calling the new grouping the Social and Liberal Democrats (SLD), later to be known simply as the 'Liberal Democrats'. The party was formally launched in March 1988, under the joint leadership of David Steel (Liberal) and Robert Maclennan (SDP), but in July Paddy Ashdown (of the former Liberal Party) was elected sole leader of the SLD.

During the 1980s the Government significantly reduced the contribution of central government to the revenue of local authorities. Following the 1987 general election victory, the Conservatives introduced draft legislation proposing a new local tax, the community charge (popularly known as the 'poll tax'), to replace the existing system of domestic rates (charges on property collected by local authorities). The tax, which was payable at a uniform rate in each local authority by every resident over 18 years of age, came into force in Scotland in April 1989 and in England and Wales in April 1990. The introduction of the community charge contributed to considerable popular dissatisfaction with the Government in 1989, which was also caused by high levels of inflation and interest rates, proposed reforms to the NHS and the implementation of changes to the educational system. There were also divisions within the Government, chiefly concerning its policy on integration with the EC, which resulted, in October 1989, in the resignation of the Chancellor of the Exchequer, Nigel Lawson. In the ensuing cabinet reshuffle John Major became Chancellor of the Exchequer, while Douglas Hurd replaced Major as Secretary of State for Foreign and Commonwealth Affairs.

During March 1990 there were violent protests throughout England and Wales as local authorities set their community charges at higher levels than the Government had generally estimated. The protests culminated in a national rally in London, at the end of March, which ended in violent clashes between the police and demonstrators. The poor performance of Conservative Party candidates at local government elections in May 1990, at which the Labour Party achieved net gains of 300 seats, was widely attributed to popular disapproval of the community charge. In July, following a five-month review of the community charge, the Government announced there were to be no changes to the principle of the tax but that central Government would contribute a further £3,260m. to limit charges levied in 1991. In a further reverse for the Government, the Liberal Democrats achieved a significant by-election victory in October 1990, in a constituency with a previously large Conservative majority. Lack of support for the Government, contrasting with the high level of popularity enjoyed nationally by the Labour Party, raised the threat of a leadership challenge to Thatcher.

In early November 1990 Sir Geoffrey Howe resigned as the Lord President of the Council, Leader of the House of Commons and Deputy Prime Minister, in protest against Thatcher's overt hostility towards economic and political union within the EC. Howe subsequently criticized the Prime Minister in a personal statement to the House of Commons. On the following day Michael Heseltine announced that he would challenge Thatcher for the leadership of the Conservative Party, pledging the reform of the community charge and better prospects for the forthcoming general election. In the first ballot of the leadership election (conducted among Conservative MPs) Thatcher gained 204 votes, four less than the 15% margin required for outright victory. Although she initially announced her intention to contest the second ballot, Thatcher was subsequently persuaded to withdraw, and the contest was finally won by John Major, whose candidacy was formally endorsed by Thatcher.

On 28 November 1990 Major was officially appointed Prime Minister. In the ensuing cabinet reshuffle Norman Lamont, hitherto the Chief Secretary to the Treasury, was appointed Chancellor of the Exchequer, and Heseltine was awarded the environment portfolio, with the task of reforming the community charge. In March 1991 Heseltine announced the abolition of the community charge, and in April proposals for a new local tax, the 'council tax' (which was to be based on property values), were announced. (The relevant legislation was enacted in December, and took effect in April 1993.) However, continued concern about the restructuring of the NHS (implementation of which began in April 1991) and the effects (including a rapid increase in unemployment) of an economic recession, which had started in the latter half of 1990, resulted in Conservative losses of 850 seats at local council elections, which took place on 2 May.

Prior to contesting a general election in April 1992, the debate between the major parties focused on the issues of the economy, taxation, the NHS and education. The Labour Party presented an alternative budget, in an attempt to convince the electorate of its capability of governing the country. Opinion polls indicated that the party had sufficient popular support to secure its first election victory since 1974, albeit by a very narrow margin. However, on 9 April, contrary to all expectations, the Conservative Party was re-elected with an overall majority (although substantially reduced) in the House of Commons, which had been enlarged by one seat. It was the first occasion on which a party was elected to serve four consecutive terms since 1826. The Conservative Party obtained 336 seats and 41.9% of the votes cast (compared with 376 seats and 42.3% in 1987), the Labour Party 271 seats and 34.4% of the votes (229 seats and 30.9% in 1987), and the Liberal Democrats 21 seats and 17.9% of the votes (compared with 22 seats and 22.6% for the Liberal Party/SDP Alliance in 1987). It had been widely expected that the Conservatives would lose further seats at the election in Scotland, where a traditional lack of support for the party had been compounded by the early introduction of the community charge there in 1989. In the early 1990s opinion polls indicated that a substantial majority of Scots supported either devolution in Scotland or full independence from the United Kingdom. During the general election campaign the Labour Party advocated the establishment of a Scottish parliament with the power to raise taxes, a proposal largely supported by the Liberal Democrats, while the Conservative Party maintained its opposition to any form of devolution. At the general election, however, the Scottish National Party (SNP), which was committed to the establishment of an independent state of Scotland, lost one of its four parliamentary seats, although its share of the votes increased from 14% in 1987 to 21%. The Labour Party secured 49 of the 72 seats in Scotland, while the Conservative Party unexpectedly gained two, bringing its total to 11 seats (with 26% of the votes cast). Following the election, the Prime Minister effected a minor cabinet reshuffle, introducing five new ministers into the Cabinet, abolishing the Department of Energy and creating a new ministry, the Department of National Heritage. The new Government's parliamentary programme included further 'privatization' measures (including the transfer to the private sector of British Coal), the introduction of a national lottery to raise funds for charities, the arts, sport and the national heritage, and the implementation of the 'Citizen's Charter' (first announced in July 1991), which was to establish standards of performance for public services. In early May 1992 the Conservative Party consolidated its political dominance (with the Labour Party suffering substantial losses) by gaining control of seven councils and winning 308 seats overall at local council elections.

In April 1992, following the Labour Party's unexpected election defeat, Neil Kinnock and Roy Hattersley announced that they were to relinquish their positions as Leader and Deputy Leader of the party respectively. In the subsequent leadership poll John Smith was elected Leader of the party (and hence of the Opposition) by 91% of the party's electoral body, the largest ever mandate accorded a Labour leader. Margaret Beckett was elected his deputy. Smith expressed his support for reform of the relationship between the Labour Party and the trade unions, a policy that had been advocated by his predecessor. The annual party conference voted in late September to reduce the unions' voting share at the conference from 87% to 70%, with effect from 1993. In February Smith outlined proposals for further diminishing trade union influence on the party by basing election of party leaders and constituency candidates on a system of 'one-member, one-vote'. In spite of considerable opposition by the largest unions, the reform was narrowly approved at the party conference in September. In May 1994 John Smith died as a result of heart failure. Margaret Beckett succeeded as acting Leader and declared that in the forthcoming leadership poll the deputy leadership position could also be contested. In July Anthony (Tony) Blair, Labour's parliamentary spokesman on home affairs, was elected Leader, winning 57% of votes cast by the party's electoral college. John Prescott, who had also contested the leadership position (with Beckett as the third candidate), was elected Deputy Leader. The new leadership undertook to 'modernize' the party, in an attempt to increase its electoral appeal. Blair's initiative to abandon the party's commitment to the common ownership of the means of production (expressed in Clause IV of its constitution), which he announced at the party conference in October, provoked a much-publicized reassessment of the party's beliefs and became a test of support for the new leadership. In March 1995

Blair secured the support of the Party's National Executive Committee for a new text to replace Clause IV. Despite strong resistance by two large unions and left-wing party delegates, this constitutional draft was endorsed at a special party conference convened in April.

During 1992, as the economic recession continued, the newly-elected Government was subjected to increasing criticism of its economic policies, both from its political opponents and from industry. In September the weakness of the pound forced the Government to take drastic measures to attempt to maintain sterling's parity within the European Monetary System's exchange rate mechanism (ERM—see p. 160). These efforts, assisted by the German central bank, proved ineffective, however, and in the middle of the month the Government announced the pound's suspension from the ERM. The departure from the ERM was regarded as a major set-back for the Government, since participation in the mechanism had formed a central part of its economic policy.

In September 1992 David Mellor, the Secretary of State for National Heritage, was forced to resign following revelations about his private life.

The announcement, in mid-October 1992, that 31 of the country's 50 coal-mines were to be closed, and 30,000 miners made redundant, brought widespread outcry, and was regarded as particularly ill-judged in the context of inexorably rising unemployment. Opposition to the planned closures within the Conservative Party itself was so strong that the President of the Board of Trade, Michael Heseltine (responsible for energy policy), was obliged partially to reverse the decision.

Serious divisions in the Conservative Party over the provisions of the Treaty on European Union (the 'Maastricht Treaty', agreed by all EC member states at a summit meeting in December 1991—see p. 149) were exacerbated by the rejection of the Treaty by a Danish referendum in June 1992, and by the United Kingdom's departure from the ERM in September. While the Labour Party was largely in favour of the Treaty, it objected to the Government's refusal to adopt the 'Social Chapter' of the Treaty (which provided for the protection of workers' rights and for future joint EC social policy decisions). The Government's authority was threatened in early November when both Labour and 26 dissident Conservative MPs voted against a motion to proceed with draft legislation approving the Maastricht Treaty. Labour had attempted to turn the issue into one of lack of confidence in the Government, but the Government won by a margin of three votes, with the Liberal Democrats supporting the motion. In early May 1993 the Government announced that it would accept a Labour amendment to the legislation excluding the protocol on the Social Chapter (which permitted the United Kingdom's exemption from those provisions), in order to avert the prospect of a politically-damaging defeat in advance of county council elections and the first by-election since April 1992. In mid-May 1993 the draft legislation on the Maastricht Treaty completed its final stage through the House of Commons before being referred to the House of Lords, with the Government gaining a large majority as a result of a decision by Labour to abstain at this juncture. Majority support was secured in the House of Lords in July, in spite of fierce opposition by some Conservative 'rebels', including Baroness Thatcher (as she now was), and the abstention of Labour peers. A final crucial vote to ratify the Treaty, by adopting a motion on its Social Chapter, was conducted in the House of Commons in late July. The Labour Party's amendment, effectively blocking ratification, was defeated by one vote, having obtained the support of Conservative 'rebels'. Sufficient numbers of these dissident MPs opposed the Government to defeat its motion by 324 votes to 316, even though the Government had earlier secured the support of the Ulster Unionist Party (UUP). The Prime Minister introduced a confidence motion on the following day, and it was widely speculated that a government defeat would provoke Major into calling a general election. The threat to the future of the Government was sufficient to gain the support of 'rebel' MPs, and the motion was approved by a government majority of 40 votes. A few days later the High Court rejected an application that ratification of the Treaty would be illegal and unconstitutional, enabling the British Government to ratify the Maastricht Treaty in early August.

In presenting the 1993/94 budget in March 1993 the Chancellor of the Exchequer made controversial announcements that from 1994 value-added tax (VAT) of 8% would be imposed on domestic fuel bills (rising to 17.5%, consistent with the tax imposed on other goods and services, in 1995) and national insurance contributions would be increased by 1%. The Opposition fiercely attacked the Conservatives for reneging on pledges, made during its campaign for the 1992 general election, not to increase VAT or the level of national insurance contributions. On 6 May 1993 the Conservatives suffered a serious defeat at a by-election in Newbury, where the Liberal Democrats overturned a secure Conservative majority to win by a huge margin. In county council elections, held on the same day, the Conservatives lost overall control in 13 counties, and retained control in only one. The Liberal Democrats made considerable gains, increasing their number of county council seats by 473, but Labour emerged as the strongest party on the county councils, securing overall control in 14 counties, while the majority of councils were to be ruled by coalitions. In late May, under pressure from public opinion and the Conservative Party itself, the Prime Minister implemented a ministerial reorganization which involved the removal of Norman Lamont as Chancellor of the Exchequer. He was offered the environment portfolio, a demotion that he declined. Kenneth Clarke, hitherto Secretary of State for Home Affairs, was promoted to the position of Chancellor of the Exchequer, while Michael Howard (Secretary of State for the Environment) replaced Clarke at the Home Office. In a House of Commons speech following his resignation, Lamont criticized Major and questioned the authority of his policy-making and leadership. In June Michael Mates, a Minister of State at the Northern Ireland Office, resigned in response to mounting speculation in the national press, as well as from Conservative MPs, about his support for a businessman, Asil Nadir, who had fled the country in the previous month while under investigation by the Serious Fraud Office. The Conservative Party at that time was criticized by the Opposition over aspects of party financing, including receipt of a substantial donation from Nadir. At the end of July, following a divisive confrontation in Parliament over the Maastricht Treaty (see above), the Government was defeated at a by-election in Christchurch. The Liberal Democrat candidate won the seat, effectively causing the largest reduction in the Conservative vote ever recorded at a by-election. The election result was attributed to opposition to the imposition of VAT on domestic fuel, although the opposition parties had insisted that the poll signified a vote on the standing of the Prime Minister. Actions to appease the opposition to the plans for VAT were announced in November in the budget proposals for 1994/95, in the form of compensation measures for pensioners, disabled people and people on low incomes. The Chancellor of the Exchequer also announced a series of measures to raise revenue from taxation, in order to reduce the substantial borrowing requirement, which exposed the Government to a renewed claim by the Opposition, in early 1994, that the Conservative Party had reneged on its commitments to the electorate to reduce levels of taxation.

In November 1992 John Major announced the establishment of an independent judicial inquiry to investigate allegations of government complicity in the export to Iraq of equipment with potential military uses, in contravention of guidelines issued by the Foreign and Commonwealth Affairs Office in 1985. The inquiry, headed by Sir Richard Scott (a Lord Justice in the Court of Appeal), commenced public hearings in May 1993. Many serving and former senior civil servants, customs officials and ministers were questioned on their conduct relating to government export guidelines, the extent to which information was denied to Parliament and the use of Public Interest Immunity certificates to prevent the disclosure of documents concerning a machine tools manufacturer, Matrix Churchill, prior to the trial of that company's directors on charges of circumventing the guidelines. The inquiry revealed a high level of government involvement in breaching the export embargo of military-related trade to Iraq, although Major, who became the first serving Prime Minister to account for government policy in such an investigation, denied any knowledge of amendments to export guidelines. The preparation of Lord Justice Scott's final report was subject to a series of delays. In early June 1995 disclosures to the media of part of a draft copy intimated that the report was likely to be highly critical of the conduct of some senior members of Major's administration, prompting speculation concerning the impact of its publication, expected later in the year.

Government procedures underwent further investigation following the publication, in October 1993, of a report by the National Audit Office, stating that an unusually large amount of aid had been awarded by the British Government to finance a hydroelectric project in northern Malaysia, against the advice of senior aid officials. Disclosures in the national press of secret negotiations between Britain and Malaysia contributed to growing speculation that aid had been granted in order to secure defence contracts for British companies, a linkage that would be illegal under the Overseas Aid Acts. In February 1994 the controversy escalated when the Malaysian Prime Minister, Dr Mahathir Mohamad (angered by press coverage of the affair, which had included alleged reports that members of his Government had accepted bribes in return for awarding contracts), decreed a severe trade restriction against the participation of British companies in government projects. (The trade embargo was removed by the Malaysian Government in September.) The House of Commons Foreign Affairs Select Committee initiated an inquiry into the so-called Pergau Dam affair in March. A former Secretary of State for Defence, Lord Younger of Prestwick, admitted securing an agreement with the Malaysian Government with a commitment to provide aid worth 20% of all defence orders. The Committee subsequently learnt that John Major and the Secretary of State for Foreign Affairs, Douglas Hurd, had, in 1991, granted £234m. of aid for the construction of the hydroelectric dam, owing to a memorandum of understanding that Thatcher had signed with Dr Mahathir in 1988, on the basis of Lord Younger's earlier protocol agreement. In May 1994 Baroness Thatcher declined to appear before the Committee. The Committee's final report, which was published in July, criticized Lord Younger's conduct and the nature of the agreement. However, the report made no recommendations for future aid programmes. In November the High Court upheld a case, brought by the World Development Movement (a British-based pressure group), that Hurd's authorization of overseas aid for the dam project had been unlawful. In the following month the Government announced that the project would no longer be financed from the overseas aid budget, and revised the funding of three other aid projects, which had been approved on the basis of considerations other than their economic benefits.

In early 1994 two government ministers resigned their posts, and a Conservative MP died, amid critical publicity of their personal lives. The Government's agenda for greater individual responsibility and morality lost some credibility in the light of these events, and again it was widely speculated that Major's future was in jeopardy from a challenge by right-wing elements in the party. The Government's policy was further undermined by an independent auditor's provisional report into the activities of the Conservative-controlled council in the City of Westminster (a borough in Greater London). The report was highly critical of the council's alleged policy of selling houses to Conservative voters in order to secure electoral advantage for the party in marginal areas. A public hearing into the alleged misconduct of senior councillors and officials was initiated in October, and its findings were expected to be published in mid-1995.

In March 1994, despite Major's stated intention to unite the party and restore public confidence in the Government prior to forthcoming council and European elections, internal disputes emerged over the issue of Britain's voting rights within the European Union (see below), and the Prime Minister was criticized by members of his party for conceding these rights in the agreement that was concluded. In local council elections, conducted on 5 May, substantial losses were sustained by the Conservative Party. The Liberal Democrats achieved the largest net gain of seats among the parties, although the Labour Party won 42% of the votes cast. At elections for the European Parliament in June, the Conservative Party obtained 27.8% of the votes cast (its worst ever recorded electoral performance), which secured 18 seats (compared with its previous 34). The Labour Party won 44.2% of the votes and increased its representation in the European Parliament from 49 seats to 62. In five by-elections for the House of Commons, held concurrently, the Conservatives suffered a further loss of support, losing one seat to the Liberal Democrats, while the Labour Party retained the other constituencies with a significant increase in its percentage of the votes. However, at another by-election, held later in June (in the late John Smith's constituency), the Labour candidate only narrowly secured victory, having lost 19.2% of votes won in the 1992 general election to the SNP. In mid-July 1994 the Prime Minister undertook a reorganization of his Government. A long series of labour stoppages by railway employees began in June, in protest at a wage agreement for signalworkers. A settlement was reached in September.

From mid-1994 the Government's standing was adversely affected by criticism of a failure, by some of its members, to adhere to parliamentary rules and acceptable standards of public life. Intense media attention regarding this so-called political 'sleaze' focused on a range of allegations against several senior Conservative MPs, which included accepting payment to table questions in Parliament and receiving hospitality at the expense of a third party without having adequately declared the interest in the parliamentary register. In October, following the resignation of two ministers as a result of the allegations, Major announced the establishment of an inquiry into the standards of conduct of holders of public office, including arrangements relating to their financial and commercial activities. The commission of inquiry was to be chaired by a senior judge, Lord Nolan. In April 1995 two MPs were temporarily suspended from Parliament, on the recommendation of a House of Commons select committee, owing to their acceptance of payment to table questions, during an investigative report by journalists of a national newspaper. In the following month Lord Nolan issued his report, which included proposals for the establishment of an independent authority to investigate the conduct of MPs and for the enforced disclosure by MPs of earnings outside their parliamentary work, as part of measures to restore confidence in the legislature.

In November 1994 the Government decided to exclude from its forthcoming legislative programme proposals for the 'privatization' of the Post Office, owing to opposition within its party and concerns that the legislation would not be approved by Parliament. In that month parliamentary consideration of legislation to increase Britain's contribution to EU finances revealed persisting divisions within the Conservative Party with regard to the EU, and provoked criticism of Major's inability to maintain party unity. Following disclosures that the Government was presenting the bill as a vote of confidence in the administration, the legislation was approved by 330 votes to 303. Eight Conservative MPs, however, voted against the Government and were effectively outcast from the parliamentary party. One other MP voluntarily resigned the party whip. In early December these 'rebel' MPs contributed to a defeat of a government measure to implement the second stage of a proposed increase in VAT on domestic fuel (from 8% to 17.5%), forcing the Government to reconsider its 1995/96 budget. In a by-election later that month the Conservatives lost the seat to the Labour Party candidate, who gained 68.8% of the votes cast. In early 1995 divisions within the Conservative Party were manifested over various European issues, including a new EU fisheries agreement, EU immigration laws and the holding of a national referendum on further integration with the Union. However, in a parliamentary vote in early March, Major's administration gained a narrow margin of support for its policy on Europe. Later that month a more secure victory was achieved in a vote on the Government's policy on reform of the EU's common agricultural policy, as a result, in particular, of regaining the support of the UUP, which had earlier opposed the Government in protest at developments in the Northern Ireland peace process. In April, in an effort to enhance party unity and discipline in House of Commons votes, the eight 'rebel' MPs were readmitted into the parliamentary party.

In early April 1995 the Government suffered a political reverse at local elections held in Scotland, obtaining only 11% of the votes cast. The Labour Party, which had disclosed proposals for devolution in the event of its forming a government, won 47% of the votes, while the SNP secured 27%. In the following month, at local elections held in England and Wales, the Conservative Party, as had been widely anticipated, suffered a substantial loss of support, prompting speculation concerning a challenge to Major's leadership. Later in May the SNP won a seat from the Conservatives at a by-election, with 40% of the votes, which reduced the Government's majority in the House of Commons to 10 members. On 22 June Major resigned as leader of the Conservative Party, owing to apparent opposition within the party and mounting speculation of a challenge to his leadership, which, he claimed, was undermining his authority as Prime Minister as well as that of the Government. The Secretary of State for Wales, John Redwood, resigned from the Cabinet in order to challenge Major in the forthcoming leadership poll. In the ballot, which was held on 4 July, Major obtained 218 of the 329 votes of the parliamentary party (compared with Redwood's 89), thereby securing the majority necessary to prevent a second ballot; Major's victory was, moreover, widely deemed to be sufficient to forestall any further leadership contest prior to the next general election. On the following day the Prime Minister effected an extensive reorganization of the Government. A new position of First Secretary of State and Deputy Prime Minister was established in order to accommodate Michael Heseltine, hitherto President of the Board of Trade, while Malcolm Rifkind (previously Secretary of State for Defence) was awarded the foreign affairs portfolio—replacing Douglas Hurd, who had recently announced his retirement from the Cabinet. As a result of the reorganization, the Secretary of State for Education assumed, additionally, responsibility for employment.

In November 1993 the Government announced that a new criminal justice bill, which reflected its strict stance on law and order, was to be a core piece of legislation to be presented to the new session of Parliament. The bill contained controversial measures, including a proposal to abolish a suspect's right to silence while under interrogation or during court proceedings, and more extensive powers to detain young offenders. In February 1994 the Home Secretary, Michael Howard, adopted fundamental reforms to accompanying legislation on more centralized management of police authorities and magistrates courts, in response to cross-party criticism. In mid-1994 the House of Lords voted against several measures in the government-sponsored Criminal Justice and Public Order Bill, which delayed its enactment. Popular opposition to the proposed legislation, in particular to restrictions on public access and gatherings, provoked violent clashes between protestors and police when the bill received final parliamentary approval in October. In the following month Howard announced that legislation was to be introduced to establish a Criminal Cases Review Authority (having announced, earlier in the year, that the authority was to be delayed), with powers to initiate judicial inquiries and to refer cases back to the Court of Appeal. The creation of such an authority was among the recommendations of a report, published in July 1993, of the Royal Commission on Criminal Justice that had been established in 1991 in order to enhance public confidence in the judicial system amid mounting evidence of miscarriages of justice and false convictions. Successful appeals were conducted in 1991 to free those imprisoned for IRA bombings in Birmingham and Guildford in 1974. In May 1993 the police officers involved in the convictions of the so-called Guildford Four were acquitted of charges of falsifying evidence; in October the case against police officers charged with perverting justice for six people accused of the Birmingham bombing was dismised, owing to the intense publicity that had surrounded the release of the defendants and doubts that a fair trial could be conducted.

In the 1980s and early 1990s the Irish Republican Army (IRA) continued its campaign of violence and mounted frequent attacks against targets on the British mainland. In October 1984, during the annual conference of the Conservative Party in Brighton, the IRA attempted to assassinate Thatcher and the majority of her Cabinet by exploding a bomb in their hotel. All the members of the Government survived the attack. In an intensive bombing campaign on the British mainland between late 1989 and early 1991, the IRA initiated 20 attacks and caused 15 deaths. In February 1991 the IRA launched three improvised mortar bombs at the Prime Minister's residence, in which a meeting of several members of the Cabinet was taking place, causing structural damage but no injuries. Later in the month incendiary devices were detonated in two mainline railway stations in central London, killing one commuter and injuring many others. The IRA campaign intensified during 1991–92. In April 1992 a large bomb was exploded in the City of London, killing two people, injuring 70 and causing extensive damage to buildings in the financial area of the capital. During October 1992 15 explosive devices were detonated, including a bomb in a public house in central London, which caused the death of one man. In late March 1993 widespread public outrage was provoked by explosions in Warrington, in north-west England, which killed two children. Four other people were seriously injured. In late April the largest-ever IRA bomb on the mainland was exploded in the City of London, killing one man, injuring 36 others and causing damage estimated at £500m. In July a security cordon was formed around the City of London, which permitted police to stop and search vehicles passing through roadblocks at the eight access routes. Responsibility for countering the IRA's campaign was transferred from the police force to the intelligence unit, MI5, in order to increase the efficiency of the British State's campaign against terrorism. In late 1993 and early 1994 police made several large seizures of explosives, which the Government claimed to be evidence of improving anti-terrorist surveillance. During this period frequent discoveries of IRA devices and bomb alerts caused much disruption to public rail and underground travel. However, no major breach of security occurred until March 1994, when two mortar bombs, launched by the IRA on the day of a vote in the House of Commons on the renewal of anti-terrorism legislation, landed on a runway at Heathrow Airport, near London. Another mortar was found in a different area of the airport a few days later, but the attacks caused no injuries or structural damage. Despite a general decline in IRA activity in mid-1994, a large seizure of explosives in July and the discovery of several minor incendiary devices prompted concern of a continued terrorist presence on the mainland. However, in August the IRA declared a complete cessation of violence, as part of a peace process to achieve a political settlement in Northern Ireland. (For Northern Ireland, see subsequent chapter.)

The United Kingdom became a full member of the EC in January 1973. A referendum in 1975 endorsed British membership by a large majority. The first direct election of British representatives to the European Parliament took place in June 1979. During the 1980s the British Government demanded controls on spending by the EC, and particularly reform of the Common Agricultural Policy, and expressed scepticism regarding proposals for greater European economic unity, on the grounds that this was likely to entail a loss of national sovereignty. In October 1990, however, the United Kingdom joined the ERM. In December, at an EC summit meeting in Rome, the other members of the EC disregarded British objections, vehemently expressed by Thatcher, and established 1994 as the starting date for a new stage of economic and monetary union between EC members. Following Major's assumption of the British premiership, relations with individual members of the EC (particularly Germany) improved, and the Government adopted a more pragmatic approach towards European developments. Nevertheless, the British Government agreed to the terms of the Treaty on European Union (the Maastricht Treaty) only after several months of negotiations had produced substantial concessions for the United Kingdom. In particular, the United Kingdom's participation in the final stage of economic and monetary union (including the adoption of a single EC currency by the year 2000) was made optional; the 'Social Chapter', which provided for the protection of workers' rights, was agreed by the other 11 states in a protocol external to the main body of the Treaty; and the word 'federal' was removed from the Treaty's text. The Treaty did, however, commit the United Kingdom to a greater degree of co-operation on foreign policy and defence matters, albeit to a lesser extent than that desired by some other member states. The EC summit conference, held in Edinburgh, Scotland, in mid-December 1992, was the culmination of the United Kingdom's efforts to enable Denmark to hold a second referendum on the Treaty and to establish acceptable terms for future EC financing. Following the implementation of the Maastricht Treaty in November 1993 proposals to extend membership of the EU (as the EC had then become) to other European countries provoked concern on the part of the British Government over voting rights for larger countries within the EU's Council of Ministers. The Government, while under pressure from the anti-federalist faction within its party to resist proposed reforms to voting procedures, was accused by its partners of threatening the Union's enlargement. At the end of March 1994 the British Government accepted an agreement that would permit new members to join the EU, raise the number of votes required to veto legislation within the Council of Ministers to 27 (from 23), as initially proposed, but would allow legislation to be delayed by a grouping of states. It was agreed that the voting procedure would be reviewed at a proposed inter-governmental conference (IGC), due to be held in 1996. In June 1994, at a meeting of EU Heads of Government in Corfu, Major exercised the British veto in order to reject the proposed candidate for the presidency of the European Commission. His action was severely criticized by other members, in particular France and Germany. A candidate more widely acceptable to Union members was appointed in July. In December, despite objections on the part of the United Kingdom, EU ministers approved a new fisheries agreement, which permitted limited access for Spanish trawlers to an area of water around Ireland, with effect from 1 January 1996. British insistence that Spanish boats be entirely excluded from the Irish Sea and Bristol Channel was incorporated into the agreement. However, the accord remained deeply unpopular with British fishing communities, which advocated a withdrawal from the EU's Common Fisheries Policy. Confrontations between Spanish and British fishing vessels, which occurred in mid-1994 (over the enforcement of EU regulations on the size of fishing nets), were expected to recur at the start of the tuna fishing season in July 1995. In April a fishing dispute between Canada and Spain heightened tension between the United Kingdom and the EU, owing to the British Government's refusal to join the other member countries in issuing a formal protest against Canada. Britain's domestic political divisions regarding the EU, and frequent adjustments of the Government's policies to accommodate its different 'Euro' factions, were widely considered to be isolating Britain within the Union and undermining the country's role in preparations for the scheduled IGC.

During the 1980s the United Kingdom's traditionally strong diplomatic relationship with the USA was enhanced, owing largely to the close political and economic strategies shared by President Ronald Reagan and Thatcher. Following Iraq's forcible annexation of Kuwait in August 1990, the British Government promptly sent air and naval forces to the Persian (Arabian) Gulf region to support the USA in defending Saudi Arabia from potential Iraqi aggression. The British Government obtained broad support from Parliament and the public for the military escalation (including the deployment of ground forces in Saudi Arabia) and the subsequent engagement in hostilities against Iraq, under the auspices of the United Nations. A total of 42,000 British personnel were deployed in the Gulf region; 26 British soldiers died in the successful operation to liberate Kuwait in January–February 1991. In April British, US and French troops were sent to northern Iraq to protect refugee camps established under Major's proposal for 'safe havens' for Kurds, who were being persecuted by the Iraqi armed forces. In late August 1992 the USA, the United Kingdom, France and Russia announced that they were to establish a zone in southern Iraq from which aircraft were to be excluded, in order to protect the population of that region from attack by the Iraqi armed forces. In January 1993 British fighter aircraft participated in US-led attacks on military targets in Iraq, launched in response to renewed Iraqi incursions into Kuwait and obstruction of a UN investigation into a suspected Iraqi nuclear weapons programme (see chapter on Iraq).

During 1993-94 disagreements between the British Government and the US administration of President Bill Clinton arose regarding policy on the conflict in the former Yugoslavia, with Major strongly opposed to a removal of the embargo on the supply of armaments to Bosnia and Herzegovina, advocated by the USA, and the decision to grant a visa permitting the leader of Sinn Féin (the political representatives of the IRA) to visit the USA in February 1994. In March 1995 relations between Major and Clinton deteriorated sharply, following the latter's approval of a visit by prominent Sinn Féin members and the removal of the ban on Sinn Féin political fundraising in the USA. Major expressed his personal anger at the decision, which was taken at a time when the British Government was trying to extract a commitment from Sinn Féin on the decommissioning of IRA weapons. The tension was eased slightly when the two leaders expressed mutual support for their policies at a meeting in April.

The publication, in September 1988, of *The Satanic Verses* (by a British writer, Salman Rushdie), which contained allegedly offensive references to Islam, caused a deterioration in already hostile relations with Iran. In February 1989 Ayatollah Khomeini, the Iranian religious leader, announced a *fatwa* (edict) imposing a death sentence on Rushdie, and this was followed later in the month by the expulsion by the British Government of the Iranian chargé d'affaires in London, and in March by Iran's severing diplomatic relations. In September 1990 full diplomatic relations were restored between the two countries. Following a period of conciliation, relations between the United Kingdom and Iran suffered renewed setbacks in mid-1992 and in early 1993 the British Government declared that Iran's refusal to revoke the *fatwa* precluded normal relations with that country. In April 1994 the United Kingdom demanded that Iran desist from pursuing contacts with the IRA, although Iran denied having communicated with the organization. At the end of May the British Government ordered an Iranian official to leave the United Kingdom, and a British diplomat was subsequently expelled from Iran, amid allegations that representatives of the Iranian Government had forged correspondence purporting to be from members of the British Government, which was designed to discredit the United Kingdom's foreign policy in the former Yugoslavia.

In November 1991 the United Kingdom and the USA demanded that Libya extradite two intelligence agents who were alleged to be responsible for the explosion that destroyed a US passenger aircraft over Lockerbie, Scotland, in 1988, to be tried either in the United Kingdom or the USA. The Libyan Government denied any responsibility for the terrorist attack. In April 1992 Libya failed to extradite the accused men, in accordance with a UN Security Council resolution (adopted in the previous month), and a mandatory suspension of air links and an embargo on the sale of weapons to Libya were duly implemented.

In February 1990 diplomatic relations were renewed between the United Kingdom and Argentina. In January 1993 the Secretary of State for Foreign and Commonwealth Affairs visited Argentina: Douglas Hurd was the most senior British politician to have visited the country since the Falklands War. The visit represented a significant improvement in relations, although both sides continued to indicate that their respective claims to sovereignty over the Falkland Islands were not negotiable. Agreements for the co-operation of both Governments in the management and conservation of fish stocks in South Atlantic waters were signed in December 1992 and November 1993. In mid-1994 the extension of a fishing exclusion zone around the Islands, which the British Government claimed was necessary to conserve stocks of squid, was met with criticism from the Argentine authorities. The exploration of petroleum around the islands remained a potential source of tension between the two countries.

In September 1991 John Major became the first Western leader to visit the People's Republic of China since the massacre in Tiananmen Square, Beijing, in 1989 (see chapter on China). By 1993 there had been a substantial increase in trade between the two countries. However, disputes over political reforms in Hong Kong, in early 1994, were expected to have an adverse effect on the trading relationship. Note: See chapter on Hong Kong, p. 3227, for discussions between the United Kingdom and China on the future of Hong Kong.

Following the dismantling of the apartheid regime in South Africa, which was secured by democratic elections held in April 1994, the British Government expressed its readiness to renew its former close diplomatic and economic links with that country. In July an investment agreement was signed with the new South African administration to facilitate the implementation of development and business projects. In September John Major became the first British Prime Minister to visit South Africa for 34 years.

In mid-November 1992 the United Kingdom began dispatching troops to the former Yugoslav republic of Bosnia and Herzegovina, as part of the United Nations Protection Force (UNPROFOR—see Vol. I, p. 52). From 1993 the British Government has been involved in diplomatic efforts to achieve a peace settlement in Bosnia and Herzegovina. In August 1993 British military aircraft conducted an emergency evacuation of critically ill war-victims from hospitals in the Bosnian capital, Sarajevo, who were brought to Britain for treatment. In April 1995 the British contingent consisted of 3,380 troops. In May, however, the Government committed a further 6,000 troops to be sent to the region, following an escalation of hostilities. The additional troops were expected to assist the UN's existing humanitarian relief efforts and reinforce the peace-keeping mission. In April 1995 some 650 troops were dispatched to participate in an enlarged UN mission in Angola.

## Government

The United Kingdom is a constitutional monarchy. The Sovereign is the Head of State and the monarchy is hereditary.

# UNITED KINGDOM (GREAT BRITAIN)

*Introductory Survey*

Parliament consists of the House of Commons and the House of Lords. The 651 members of the Commons are elected for a maximum of five years by direct suffrage by all citizens of 18 years and over, using single-member constituencies. The House of Lords is composed of hereditary Peers of the Realm and Life Peers and Peeresses created by the Sovereign for outstanding public service. Legislation may be initiated in either House but it usually originates in the Commons. Each bill has three readings in the Commons and it is then passed to the House of Lords who may return it to the Commons with amendments or suggestions. The House of Lords may delay, but cannot prevent, any bill from becoming law once it has been passed by the Commons. Executive power is held by the Cabinet, headed by the Prime Minister. The Cabinet is responsible to the House of Commons.

## Defence

The United Kingdom is a member of the North Atlantic Treaty Organisation (NATO) and maintains a regular army. The total strength of the armed forces at June 1994, including women's services (17,650) and those enlisted outside Britain (7,200), was 254,300 (army 123,000 navy 55,600, air force 75,700). There is no compulsory military service. Britain possesses its own nuclear weapons. Defence expenditure for 1993 totalled £24,384m.

## Economic Affairs

In 1993, according to estimates by the World Bank, the United Kingdom's gross national product (GNP), measured at average 1991–93 prices, was US $1,042,700m., equivalent to $17,970 per head. During 1985–93, it was estimated, GNP per head increased, in real terms, at an average annual rate of 1.3%. Over the same period, the population increased by an annual average of 0.3%. The United Kingdom's gross domestic product (GDP) increased, in real terms, by an annual average of 2.7% in 1980–90, but declined by 2.0% in 1991 and by 0.5% in 1992.

Agriculture (including forestry and fishing) contributed 1.8% of GDP in 1993, and engaged 2.1% of the employed labour force (excluding Northen Ireland) in 1994. The principal crops include wheat, barley, potatoes and sugar beet. Livestock-rearing (particularly poultry and cattle) and animal products are important, as is fishing. Agricultural production increased by an annual average of 0.8% during 1983–92, but declined by 8.0% in 1993.

Industry (including mining, manufacturing, construction and power) contributed 30.5% of GDP in 1993, and engaged 26.1% of the employed labour force (excluding Northern Ireland) in 1994. Excluding the construction sector, industrial GDP increased, in real terms, by an annual average of 2.6% during 1983–90, but fell by 3.9% in 1991 and by 0.2% in 1992. Industrial GDP grew by 2% in 1993.

Mining (including petroleum and gas extraction) contributed 2.1% of GDP in 1993 and engaged 0.8% of the employed labour force in 1990. Coal, limestone, crude petroleum and natural gas are the principal minerals produced. In September 1994 there were 16 mines operating in the coal industry (compared with 170 mines in 1984). In 1994 a decline in the production of coal, which had decreased by 29% on output in 1993, was offset by substantial increases in production of North Sea petroleum and gas amounting to 27% and 8% respectively on 1993 levels. At the end of 1994 the Government approved the development of petroleum and gas reserves, which had been discovered in deep Atlantic waters west of the Shetland Islands. The GDP of the mining sector declined, in real terms, at an average rate of 3.1% per year during 1983–90, but increased by 2.1% in 1991, by 4.3% in 1992 and by 8.0% in 1993.

Manufacturing provided 20.8% of GDP in 1993. Excluding the manufacture of metals, mineral products and chemicals, the sector engaged 16% of the employed labour force in 1994. Measured by the value of output, the principal branches of manufacturing in 1990 were food products (accounting for 12.5% of the total), transport equipment (12.1%), non-electric machinery (11.3%), chemical products (11.0%) and metals and metal products (10.8%). In real terms, the GDP of the manufacturing sector increased by an annual average of 3.4% during 1983–90; it declined by 5.4% in 1991 and by 0.6% in 1992, but increased by 1.4% in 1993.

Energy is derived principally from coal and petroleum, although natural gas is increasingly favoured in preference to coal. Of the United Kingdom's total consumption of energy in 1993, 25.0% was derived from coal, 36.1% from petroleum, 10.6% from primary electricity (including nuclear power, hydroelectric power and imports) and 28.3% from natural gas. In 1992 mineral fuels accounted for about 5.6% of the value of total merchandise imports.

Services accounted for 67.7% of GDP in 1993 and engaged 76.0% of the employed labour force (excluding Northern Ireland) in 1994. The United Kingdom is an important international centre for business and financial services. In 1990 its foreign exchange markets had an estimated daily turnover of US $187,000m. Financial intermediation and other business services (including renting and real estate) contributed 23.5% of GDP in 1993. Receipts from tourism totalled £9,376m. in that year. Transport and communications are also important, and the sector contributed 8.1% of GDP in 1993.

In 1993 the United Kingdom recorded a visible trade deficit of £13,209m., and there was a deficit of £10,311m. on the current account of the balance of payments. In 1992 the principal source of imports (15.1%) and the principal market for exports (14.0%) was Germany. Other major trading partners include the USA, France, the Netherlands and Japan. The principal imports in 1992 were road vehicles, industrial and electrical machinery, automatic data-processing equipment, petroleum, paper, paperboard and manufactures and textiles. The principal exports were industrial and electrical machinery, automatic data-processing equipment, road vehicles and petroleum.

In 1993 there was a budgetary deficit of £44,484m. (equivalent to about 7.8% of GDP). At 31 March 1992 the foreign debt of the public sector was £36,504m. According to OECD figures, the annual rate of inflation averaged 5.7% in 1982–91; it decreased to 1.6% in 1993, but increased to 2.5% in 1994. The rate of unemployment averaged 10.5% of the labour force in 1993, and 9.6% in 1994.

The United Kingdom is a member of the European Union (EU—see p. 143) and joined the exchange rate mechanism (ERM) of the European Community's European Monetary System in October 1990; however, in September 1992 British membership of the ERM was suspended indefinitely. It is also a member of the Organisation for Economic Co-operation and Development (OECD—see p. 194).

Following a rapid growth in the economy in 1987–88, the rate of inflation began to accelerate, forcing the Government to institute a policy of more stringent monetary control and to increase interest rates in an attempt to slow inflation. In 1991 value-added tax (VAT) was increased by 2.5% (to 17.5%) in order to permit a reduction in the community charge. During 1979–91 the Government transferred 46 major businesses from the public to the private sector, reducing the state-owned sector of industry by about 65%. In mid-1990 the economy entered a recession: between June 1990 and June 1992 real GDP decreased by 4%, with a very high incidence of company liquidations, substantial reductions in investment and a rapid increase in unemployment. The Government greatly increased its public-sector borrowing requirement (PSBR) in 1992/93, as a result of a rise in social security payments and a decline in tax revenues (caused by the increase in unemployment and loss of revenue from businesses). In order to curb the PSBR, which rose to £46,000m. in 1993/94, the Government placed stringent controls on public expenditure and announced a series of measures to raise revenue from taxation, including an increase in national insurance contributions, reductions in tax relief and personal allowances, a tax on air travel and the imposition of VAT on domestic fuel bills. Further substantial reductions in public sector expenditure were incorporated into the budget for 1995/96, in order to restrict the PSBR to £21,500m. (from £34,400m. in 1994/95). The Government's medium-term financial strategy envisages eliminating the PSBR by 1998/99. A gradual reduction in unemployment and steady increases in industrial output stimulated expectations in 1993 that an economic recovery was entrenched. In 1994 growth in real GDP rose to 3.8%, the largest growth figure since 1988, which was stimulated by an increase in exports (in particular petroleum and chemicals) and invisible earnings. These also contributed to a marked reduction in the current account deficit of the balance of payments in that year. The rate of growth was expected to be maintained in 1995. However, there was concern that expansion of the domestic market would continue to be restrained by the impact of the wider taxation measures, rising interest rates (to counter inflationary pressures) and uncertainty regarding the employment market.

## Social Welfare

The National Insurance Scheme was started in 1948 and is administered by the Department of Social Security, through more than 400 local offices; the Department of Employment is the agency for administering unemployment benefit. The scheme is compulsory for most working people who are 16 years of age or over and under the minimum age of entitlement for a state retirement pension (which is 65 years for men, 60 for women). Employers and employees make earnings-related contributions. The scheme insures against loss of income due to unemployment, maternity and, in certain circumstances, to sickness, and provides retirement pensions and widows' benefits, maternity benefits, child and guardian allowances, and benefits for death and industrial injuries.

Child benefit is tax-free and payable for all children below 16 years of age, and below 19 years of age if the child is in full-time, non-advanced education. It can also continue for a short period for 16- and 17-year-old school-leavers waiting for youth training or work. One-parent families are usually entitled to an extra allowance (also tax-free) for their first or only child. Family credit is payable to families with at least one child, where at least one parent is working 16 hours or more per week, and where the family income is below a certain level. There are also provisions for disabled people and their attendants. Income support is available for people who are not in full-time work and whose resources are below a prescribed minimum level; the benefit is income-related. Housing Benefit Scheme is administered by local authorities and provides claimants with assistance to pay rent, while Council Tax Benefit Scheme, which became effective in April 1993, provides help with payment of the council tax.

The National Health Service (NHS) is a comprehensive health service, not based on an insurance scheme, which may be used by everyone who is ordinarily resident in the United Kingdom. Apart from charges (from which there are certain exemptions) for prescriptions and dental and ophthalmic treatment, the service is free. Most of the cost of the NHS is met from taxation; of the remainder, about 13% is made up from NHS contributions, while about 4% is made up from charges to patients. In 1993 England and Wales had 82,075 physicians, and in 1993/94 there were 237,083 hospital beds (one for every 217 inhabitants). In 1993 Scotland had 10,399 physicians employed by the NHS, and there were 46,731 hospital beds (one for every 110 inhabitants) in that year. In 1993 there were 30,100 general medical practitioners in England and Wales and 3,794 in Scotland. Public expenditure on health and social security in 1993/94 in the United Kingdom totalled £37,331m. and £81,640m. respectively.

## Education

Education is compulsory for all children from the commencement of the term following a pupil's fifth birthday until an appropriate school-leaving date related to the pupil's 16th birthday. Responsibility for education is substantially devolved: the Secretary of State for Education and Employment is responsible, in principle, for all aspects of education in England (the 109 local education authorities have substantial autonomy over the education system in their area) and for universities throughout Great Britain, while the Secretary of State for Wales is responsible for non-university education in Wales. The Secretaries of State for Scotland and Northern Ireland have full educational responsibilities, except for universities in the case of Scotland. Assessment of the quality of schools and further education colleges is undertaken in England by an inspectorate, the Office for Standards in Education (OFSTED), and in Wales by the Office of Her Majesty's Chief Inspector of Schools. Higher education institutions are subject to quality assurance procedures of the Higher Education Funding Councils (see below) and of the Higher Education Quality Council (HEQC).

Secondary education generally begins at the age of 11, although many areas have 'middle schools' for children aged eight to 12 years or nine to 13 years. In most areas, the state-maintained system of comprehensive schools prevails. Pupils are admitted to such schools without reference to ability. Some localities, however, retain a system of grammar and secondary modern schools, to which admission is determined through a test of ability. New legislation in 1988 provided for the establishment of City Technology Colleges (CTCs), to be funded by the central Government and private sponsors. These are non-fee-paying secondary schools for children aged 11 to 18 years and emphasize science and technology in their curricula. By September 1994 42 CTCs had been established. Until 1989 all state schools were financed primarily by local education authorities, but from September 1989 some state schools were directly funded by the Department for Education and Employment and became 'self-governing' schools (previously known as grant-maintained schools). By January 1993 there were 340 self-governing schools in England and Wales. Alongside the state system, there are independent schools which do not receive grants from public funds but are financed by fees and endowments; many of these schools are administered by charitable trusts and church organizations. Since 1981 the Government has offered assistance with the payment of fees for pupils of low-income families who have gained admission to selected independent schools which are of high academic calibre or which offer a specialized education to artistically gifted pupils.

Examinations for the single-system General Certificate of Secondary Education (GCSE) may be taken (usually at the age of 16) in as many subjects as a candidate wishes. In 1989 the Government implemented legislation introduced under the Education Reform Act (1988), which provided for a national curriculum and national testing of pupils aged seven, 11 and 14 years in state schools in England and Wales. In early 1994 the Government announced that reforms were to be made to the legislation, reducing the compulsory curriculum and the assessment programme, following dissatisfaction on the part of teachers, many of whom conducted an extensive boycott of the tests in the previous school year. The GCE Advanced Level is generally taken at the age of 18, in a few selected subjects, and serves as a qualification for entrance to higher education. An additional examination, Advanced Supplementary (AS) level, was introduced in 1987. The first examinations were held in 1989; the AS is intended to broaden the studies of pupils pursuing Advanced Level courses.

There were 472 institutions of further and higher education in England and Wales in 1992/93, providing vocational and academic courses, on a full-time, part-time and 'sandwich' basis (this figure includes teacher-training institutions). The decision to admit students is made by each university according to its own entrance requirements. The first degree course normally lasts three or four years and leads to a Bachelor of Arts or Sciences (BA or BSc) degree. One-year postgraduate and four-year undergraduate initial teacher training courses are provided at colleges, polytechnics and university departments of education. There are also some two-year Bachelor of Education (BEd) courses available in the subjects for which there is a shortage of teachers. Entrants to these courses may be admitted with a Business and Technician Education Council (BTEC) higher national award, Higher National Diploma (HND) level qualification or an advanced City and Guilds certificate and some relevant experience. Some two-year 'conversion' Postgraduate Certificate of Education (PGCE) courses are also available for intending secondary school teachers who wish to 'change subject' to teach a 'shortage' subject and whose initial degree is related to the intended teaching subject. In addition to the minimum requirements listed above, entrants to initial teacher training must have reached General Certificate of Secondary Education (GCSE) standard in mathematics and English.

In early 1993 there were 47 universities in Great Britain (39 in England and Wales and eight in Scotland), including the London and Manchester Business Schools, the privately-funded University of Buckingham and the Open University, which is funded directly by the Department for Education and Employment. Between the academic years 1988/89 and 1992/93 the number of students at these universities increased by 33%. The Open University provides degree courses by means of television, radio, correspondence and summer schools. No formal qualifications are required for entry to its courses. In early 1992 there were also 34 polytechnics in England and Wales, all of which had adopted the title 'university' by early 1993 (see below), and six equivalent institutions in Scotland. Polytechnics provide degree courses, as well as courses leading to vocational and professional qualifications.

Under the provisions of the Further and Higher Education Act (1992), polytechnics and equivalent institutions were granted the same status as universities and were to be permitted to adopt the title 'university'. Polytechnics were henceforth empowered to award their own degrees, a function previously performed by the Council for National Academic Awards. Universities and polytechnics, previously funded separately, were to be financed by a single Higher Education Funding Council for England, the Scottish Higher Education Funding Council or the Welsh Funding Council (Higher Education Division). The new legislation also removed further education and sixth-form colleges from the control of local education authorities, and these institutions were to be funded centrally by the (then) Department for Education (with effect from April 1993). The Department for Education and Employment has a general responsibility for the promotion of education, and for the training and supply of teachers. Public expenditure on education in 1993 totalled £33,885m.

### Public Holidays

**1995:** 2 January (for New Year's Day), 3 January* (Scotland only), 14 April* (Good Friday), 17 April† (Easter Monday), 1 May* (Scotland only), 8 May* (for May Day)‡, 29 May* (Spring Holiday), 7 August* (Summer Bank Holiday, Scotland only), 28 August† (Late Summer Holiday), 25 December (Christmas Day), 26 December* (Boxing Day).

**1996:** 1 January (New Year's Day), 2 January* (Scotland only), 5 April* (Good Friday), 8 April† (Easter Monday), 6 May* (for May Day), 27 May* (Spring Holiday), 5 August* (Summer Bank Holiday, Scotland only), 26 August† (Late Summer Holiday), 25 December (Christmas Day), 26 December* (Boxing Day).

* Bank Holidays but not national holidays in Scotland.
† Excluding Scotland.
‡ In 1995 the May Day bank holiday was to be held on the second Monday of the month in order to commemorate the 50th anniversary of VE (Victory in Europe) Day.

### Weights and Measures

The imperial system of weights and measures is in force; conversion to the metric system is in progress.

Weight:
  1 pound (lb) = 16 ounces (oz) = 453.59 grams.
  14 pounds = 1 stone = 6.35 kilograms.
  112 pounds = 1 hundredweight (cwt) = 50.8 kilograms.
  20 hundredweights = 1 ton = 1,016 kilograms.

Length:
  1 yard (yd) = 3 feet (ft) = 36 inches (in) = 0.9144 metre.
  1,760 yards = 1 mile = 1.609 kilometres.

Capacity:
  1 gallon = 4 quarts = 8 pints = 4.546 litres.

# Statistical Survey

Statistics refer to the United Kingdom unless otherwise indicated.

## Area and Population

### AREA, POPULATION AND DENSITY

| | |
|---|---|
| Area (sq km) | 241,752* |
| **Population usually resident (census results)** | |
| 5 April 1981 | 55,089,100 |
| 21 April 1991 | |
|   Males | 27,344,000 |
|   Females | 29,122,700 |
|   Total | 56,466,700 |
| **Population (official estimates at mid-year)** | |
| 1991 | 57,807,900 |
| 1992 | 58,006,500 |
| 1993 | 58,191,200 |
| Density (per sq km) at mid-1993 | 240.7 |

* 93,341 sq miles.
Source: Office of Population Censuses and Surveys.

### DISTRIBUTION OF POPULATION
(estimates, 30 June 1993)

| | Area (sq km) | Population ('000) | Density (per sq km) |
|---|---|---|---|
| Great Britain | 228,269 | 56,559.4 | 247.8 |
|   England | 130,423 | 48,532.7 | 372.1 |
|   Wales | 20,766 | 2,906.5 | 140.0 |
|   Scotland | 77,080 | 5,120.2 | 66.4 |
| Northern Ireland | 13,483 | 1,631.8 | 121.0 |
| **Total** | 241,752 | 58,191.2 | 240.7 |

Sources: Office of Population Censuses and Surveys; General Register Offices for Scotland and Northern Ireland.

**PRINCIPAL TOWNS*** (population estimates at mid-1993, '000)

| | | | |
|---|---|---|---|
| Greater London (capital) | 6,933.0 | Stockport | 291.4 |
| Birmingham | 1,012.4 | Leicester | 289.3 |
| Leeds | 724.5 | Newcastle upon Tyne | 285.3 |
| Glasgow | 681.5 | Nottingham | 282.6 |
| Sheffield | 531.9 | Kingston upon Hull | 267.9 |
| Bradford | 480.0 | Bolton | 264.9 |
| Liverpool | 477.0 | Walsall | 264.7 |
| Edinburgh | 441.6 | Plymouth | 259.0 |
| Manchester | 432.0 | Rotherham | 255.7 |
| Bristol | 397.6 | Stoke-on-Trent | 252.9 |
| Kirklees | 385.8 | Wolverhampton | 246.4 |
| Wirral | 334.1 | Salford | 229.3 |
| Wakefield | 317.5 | Derby | 228.6 |
| Wigan | 313.2 | Barnsley | 225.9 |
| Dudley | 311.5 | Tameside | 221.6 |
| Coventry | 304.1 | Oldham | 220.5 |
| Cardiff | 298.7 | Aberdeen | 218.2 |
| Sunderland | 297.8 | Trafford | 217.8 |
| Belfast | 296.7 | Southampton | 209.2 |
| Sefton | 294.3 | Rochdale | 206.8 |
| Sandwell | 294.2 | Gateshead | 202.9 |
| Doncaster | 292.7 | Renfrew | 201.2 |
| | | Solihull | 200.4 |

* Local authority areas after 1974 local government reorganization with populations greater than 200,000.

Sources: Office of Population Censuses and Surveys; General Register Offices for Scotland and Northern Ireland.

# UNITED KINGDOM (GREAT BRITAIN)

*Statistical Survey*

## ADMINISTRATIVE AREAS
(population estimates at mid-1993, '000)

### England
| | |
|---|---:|
| Greater London | 6,933.0 |

**Metropolitan Counties:**
| | |
|---|---:|
| Greater Manchester | 2,578.9 |
| Merseyside | 1,440.9 |
| South Yorkshire | 1,306.2 |
| Tyne and Wear | 1,137.9 |
| West Midlands | 2,633.7 |
| West Yorkshire | 2,101.6 |

**Non-Metropolitan Counties:**
| | |
|---|---:|
| Avon | 973.3 |
| Bedfordshire | 539.4 |
| Berkshire | 763.7 |
| Buckinghamshire | 651.7 |
| Cambridgeshire | 682.6 |
| Cheshire | 971.9 |
| Cleveland | 559.5 |
| Cornwall/Isles of Scilly | 477.0 |
| Cumbria | 490.2 |
| Derbyshire | 950.9 |
| Devon | 1,049.2 |
| Dorset | 667.5 |
| Durham | 607.5 |
| East Sussex | 722.2 |
| Essex | 1,560.3 |
| Gloucestershire | 543.9 |
| Hampshire | 1,593.7 |
| Hereford and Worcestershire | 694.8 |
| Hertfordshire | 999.7 |
| Humberside | 884.4 |
| Isle of Wight | 124.8 |
| Kent | 1,539.7 |
| Lancashire | 1,420.7 |
| Leicestershire | 910.3 |
| Lincolnshire | 601.4 |
| Norfolk | 765.1 |
| Northamptonshire | 591.9 |
| Northumberland | 307.2 |
| North Yorkshire | 721.8 |
| Nottinghamshire | 1,028.4 |
| Oxfordshire | 585.8 |
| Shropshire | 413.9 |
| Somerset | 474.1 |
| Staffordshire | 1,053.6 |
| Suffolk | 646.2 |
| Surrey | 1,037.9 |
| Warwickshire | 493.6 |
| West Sussex | 717.7 |
| Wiltshire | 583.0 |

### Wales
**Counties:**
| | |
|---|---:|
| Clwyd | 415.9 |
| Dyfed | 351.5 |
| Gwent | 450.3 |
| Gwynedd | 240.2 |
| Mid Glamorgan | 544.3 |
| Powys | 119.9 |
| South Glamorgan | 413.2 |
| West Glamorgan | 371.2 |

### Scotland
**Regions:**
| | |
|---|---:|
| Borders | 105.3 |
| Central | 272.9 |
| Dumfries and Galloway | 147.9 |
| Fife | 351.2 |
| Grampian | 528.1 |
| Highland | 206.9 |
| Lothian | 753.9 |
| Strathclyde | 2,286.8 |
| Tayside | 395.2 |

**Islands Area:**
| | |
|---|---:|
| Orkney | 19.8 |
| Shetland | 22.8 |
| Western Isles | 29.4 |

### Northern Ireland
**Districts:**
| | |
|---|---:|
| Antrim | 47.5 |
| Ards | 66.2 |
| Armagh | 52.4 |
| Ballymena | 57.0 |
| Ballymoney | 24.4 |
| Banbridge | 36.6 |
| Belfast | 296.7 |
| Carrickfergus | 34.5 |
| Castlereagh | 63.0 |
| Coleraine | 53.6 |
| Cookstown | 30.9 |
| Craigavon | 76.8 |
| Down | 60.5 |
| Dungannon | 46.2 |
| Fermanagh | 54.8 |
| Larne | 29.8 |
| Limavady | 30.3 |
| Lisburn | 104.1 |
| Londonderry | 100.5 |
| Magherafelt | 36.3 |
| Moyle | 14.7 |
| Newry and Mourne | 81.7 |
| Newtownabbey | 77.7 |
| North Down | 73.6 |
| Omagh | 46.3 |
| Strabane | 35.7 |

Sources: Office of Population Censuses and Surveys.

## BIRTHS, MARRIAGES AND DEATHS*

| | Registered live births | | Registered marriages | | Registered deaths | |
|---|---:|---:|---:|---:|---:|---:|
| | Number | Rate (per 1,000) | Number | Rate (per 1,000) | Number | Rate (per 1,000) |
| 1986 | 754,982 | 13.3 | 393,939 | 6.9 | 660,735 | 11.6 |
| 1987 | 775,617 | 13.6 | 397,937 | 7.0 | 644,342 | 11.3 |
| 1988 | 787,556 | 13.8 | 394,049 | 6.9 | 649,182 | 11.4 |
| 1989 | 777,285 | 13.6 | 392,042 | 6.8 | 657,733 | 11.5 |
| 1990 | 798,612 | 13.9 | 375,410 | 6.5 | 641,799 | 11.2 |
| 1991 | 792,506 | 13.7 | 349,739 | 6.0 | 646,181 | 11.2 |
| 1992 | 781,017 | 13.5 | 356,013 | 6.1 | 634,238 | 10.9 |
| 1993 | 761,713 | 13.1 | n.a. | n.a. | 658,000† | 11.3† |

* In England and Wales, figures for births are tabulated by year of occurence, while data concerning deaths and marriages refer to year of registration. All figures for Scotland and Northern Ireland are tabulated by year of registration.
† Provisional.

Source: Office of Population Censuses and Surveys.

**Expectation of life** (official estimates, years at birth, 1988–90): Males 72.7; Females 78.3 (Source: UN, *Demographic Yearbook*).

## IMMIGRATION AND EMIGRATION*

**Immigrants** ('000)

| Nationality and Country[1] | 1991 | 1992 | 1993 |
|---|---:|---:|---:|
| Commonwealth citizens | 183 | 151 | 139 |
|   EC[2] | 39 | 47 | 29 |
|   Commonwealth countries | 109 | 78 | 81 |
|     Australia | 30 | 20 | 24 |
|     Canada | 6 | 3 | 5 |
|     New Zealand | 10 | 9 | 7 |
|     African countries | 17 | 8 | 8 |
|     Bangladesh, India, Sri Lanka | 12 | 9 | 13 |
|     Pakistan | 12 | 8 | 7 |
|     Caribbean[3] | 3 | 2 | 2 |
|     Others | 20 | 18 | 16 |
|   Other foreign countries | 35 | 26 | 28 |
|     South Africa | 7 | 6 | 7 |
|     Latin America | 1 | 1 | 1 |
|     USA | 10 | 9 | 10 |
|     Others | 18 | 10 | 10 |
| Foreign citizens | 83 | 65 | 70 |
|   EC[2] | 32 | 22 | 21 |
|   Commonwealth countries | 4 | 4 | 1 |
|   Other foreign countries | 48 | 39 | 48 |
|     USA | 15 | 10 | 13 |
|     Others | 33 | 29 | 35 |
| **Total** | 267 | 216 | 209 |

# UNITED KINGDOM (GREAT BRITAIN)

## Emigrants ('000)

| Nationality and Country[1] | 1991 | 1992 | 1993 |
|---|---|---|---|
| Commonwealth citizens | 170 | 161 | 155 |
|   EC[2] | 47 | 43 | 42 |
|   Commonwealth countries | 85 | 71 | 77 |
|     Australia | 30 | 28 | 30 |
|     Canada | 14 | 6 | 8 |
|     New Zealand | 7 | 8 | 8 |
|     African countries | 5 | 7 | 6 |
|     Bangladesh, India, Sri Lanka | 5 | 3 | 4 |
|     Pakistan | 3 | 2 | 2 |
|     Caribbean[3] | 2 | 3 | 3 |
|     Others | 20 | 14 | 16 |
|   Other foreign countries | 38 | 47 | 36 |
|     South Africa | 6 | 3 | 2 |
|     Latin America | 2 | 2 | 1 |
|     USA | 14 | 17 | 17 |
|     Others | 17 | 25 | 16 |
| Foreign citizens | 68 | 66 | 57 |
|   EC[2] | 24 | 15 | 21 |
|   Commonwealth countries | 4 | 2 | 2 |
|   Other foreign countries | 40 | 49 | 35 |
|     USA | 18 | 19 | 16 |
|     Others | 22 | 30 | 19 |
| **Total** | **239** | **227** | **213** |

\* Figures are derived from a small sample of passengers and refer to long-term migration only, excluding all movements between the UK and the Republic of Ireland. Long-term migrants are defined as persons who have resided (or intend to reside) for one year or more in the UK and intend to reside (or have resided) outside the UK for one year or more.

[1] Figures refer to the country of immigrants' last permanent residence or emigrants' intended future residence.
[2] Figures for all years show the EC as it was constituted on 1 January 1992.
[3] Including Guyana and Belize.

Source: International Passenger Survey, Office of Population Censuses and Surveys.

## EMPLOYMENT ('000 persons, mid-year estimates)*

| | 1992 | 1993 | 1994 |
|---|---|---|---|
| Agriculture, forestry and fishing | 534 | 504 | 525 |
| Energy and water supply industries | 405 | 354 | 316 |
| Extraction of minerals and ores other than fuels; manufacture of metals, mineral products and chemicals | 651 | 628 | 601 |
| Metal goods, engineering and vehicles industries | 2,060 | 1,953 | 1,919 |
| Other manufacturing industries | 2,041 | 2,033 | 2,047 |
| Construction | 1,588 | 1,518 | 1,569 |
| Distribution, hotels and catering; repairs | 5,325 | 5,236 | 5,275 |
| Transport and communication | 1,466 | 1,419 | 1,374 |
| Banking, finance, insurance, business services and leasing | 3,058 | 3,076 | 3,108 |
| Other services | 7,414 | 7,469 | 7,494 |
| Work-related government training schemes† | 307 | 295 | 282 |
| Armed forces | 290 | 271 | 250 |
| **Total** | **25,137** | **24,756** | **24,759** |
| Males | 13,798 | 13,457 | 13,452 |
| Females | 11,340 | 11,300 | 11,307 |

\* Figures exclude Northern Ireland.
† Figures refer to persons who are receiving training or experience at a workplace but who do not have employment contracts.

Source: the former Department of Employment.

# Agriculture

## PRINCIPAL CROPS ('000 metric tons)

| | 1991 | 1992 | 1993 |
|---|---|---|---|
| Wheat | 14,363 | 14,092 | 12,753* |
| Barley | 7,627 | 7,366 | 6,013* |
| Oats | 523 | 504 | 477* |
| Rye | 49 | 37 | 30* |
| Potatoes | 6,267 | 7,802 | 7,065 |
| Sugar beet* | 7,673 | 9,300 | 8,988 |
| Beetroot | 99 | 86 | 94 |
| Carrots | 653 | 780 | 638 |
| Turnips and swedes | 169 | 171 | 173 |
| Parsnips | 58 | 85 | 79 |
| Dry onions | 251 | 259 | 346 |
| Leeks | 79 | 81 | 76 |
| Brussels sprouts | 111 | 111 | 117 |
| Cabbages, savoys, etc. | 661 | 609 | 660 |
| Cauliflowers | 345 | 360 | 352 |
| Beans, broad, runner and French | 63 | 60 | 68 |
| Green peas | 270 | 261 | 252 |
| Celery | 53 | 60 | 57 |
| Lettuce | 250 | 243 | 201 |
| Tomatoes | 137 | 139 | 134 |
| Cucumbers | 108 | 115 | 109 |
| Apples | 263 | 285 | 276 |
| Pears | 36 | 31 | 30 |
| Soft fruit | 97 | 103 | 95 |

\* Figure(s) from FAO, *Production Yearbook*.

Source: Central Statistical Office, *Annual Abstract of Statistics*.

## LIVESTOCK ON AGRICULTURAL HOLDINGS
('000 head at June)*

| | 1991 | 1992 | 1993 |
|---|---|---|---|
| Cattle | 11,866 | 11,804 | 11,751 |
| Sheep and lambs | 43,621 | 43,998 | 43,901 |
| Pigs | 7,596 | 7,609 | 7,756 |
| Chickens | 127,228 | 123,992 | n.a. |
| Ducks and geese | 2,191 | 2,347 | 2,553 |
| Turkeys† | 10,000 | 10,000 | 11,000 |

\* Figures include estimates for minor holdings in England and Wales.
† FAO estimates.

Source: Central Statistical Office, *Annual Abstract of Statistics*.

## LIVESTOCK PRODUCTS
('000 metric tons, unless otherwise indicated)

| | 1991 | 1992 | 1993 |
|---|---|---|---|
| Beef and veal[1] | 1,020 | 959 | 860 |
| Mutton and lamb[1] | 385 | 354 | 338 |
| Pork[1] | 778 | 781 | 810 |
| Bacon and ham[1] | 172 | n.a. | n.a. |
| Poultry meat[1] | 1,074 | 1,077 | 1,080 |
| Offal | 170 | 160 | 150 |
| Cows' milk (million litres)[2] | 13,664 | 13,525 | 13,576 |
| Butter | 112 | 98 | 109 |
| Cheese (incl. farmhouse) | 298 | 324 | 331 |
| Condensed milk[3] | 198 | 206 | 191 |
| Milk powder[4] | 224 | 186 | 193 |
| Cream[5] | 77 | 55 | 52 |
| Hen eggs | 633.8* | 626.7* | 623.6† |
| Wool (clean)* | 51.1 | 50.9 | 48.7 |

Cattle hides (FAO estimates, '000 metric tons): 101.0 in 1991; 93.8 in 1992; 96.3 in 1993.

\* FAO figure(s).
† Unofficial figure.

[1] Production of home-killed meat, including meat subsequently canned.
[2] Sold for food.
[3] Including condensed milk used in the manufacture of chocolate crumb.
[4] Including skimmed milk; excluding buttermilk and whey powder.
[5] Fresh and sterilized (including farm) cream.

Source: mainly Central Statistical Office, *Annual Abstract of Statistics*.

# UNITED KINGDOM (GREAT BRITAIN)

## Forestry

**ROUNDWOOD REMOVALS** ('000 cubic metres, excluding bark)

|  | 1990 | 1991 | 1992 |
|---|---|---|---|
| Sawlogs, veneer logs and logs for sleepers | 3,645 | 3,647 | 3,598 |
| Pulpwood | 2,270 | 2,245 | 2,245* |
| Other industrial wood | 210 | 230 | 230* |
| Fuel wood | 255 | 280 | 280* |
| Total | 6,380 | 6,402 | 6,353 |

* FAO estimate.

Source: FAO, *Yearbook of Forest Products*.

**SAWNWOOD PRODUCTION**
('000 cubic metres, including railway sleepers)

|  | 1990 | 1991 | 1992 |
|---|---|---|---|
| Coniferous (softwood) | 1,935 | 1,894 | 2,278 |
| Broadleaved (hardwood) | 336 | 347 | 170 |
| Total | 2,271 | 2,241 | 2,448 |

Source: FAO, *Yearbook of Forest Products*.

## Fishing*

**LANDINGS BY BRITISH VESSELS**
(Great Britain, '000 metric tons)

|  | 1991 | 1992 | 1993 |
|---|---|---|---|
| Marine ('wet') fish | 477.7 | 505.6 | 536.2 |
| Atlantic cod | 51.8 | 53.4 | 55.4 |
| Haddock | 46.2 | 46.4 | 75.1 |
| European plaice | 21.0 | 22.5 | 18.1 |
| Saithe (Coalfish) | 13.5 | 10.9 | 10.3 |
| Whiting | 38.4 | 39.1 | 40.4 |
| Atlantic herring | 92.4 | 88.8 | 87.2 |
| Atlantic mackerel† | 124.9 | 150.7 | 161.8 |
| Crustaceans, molluscs, etc. | 84.6 | 108.0 | 102.5 |
| Cockles | 20.4 | 32.1 | 21.4 |
| Nephrops (Norway lobster) | 25.1 | 24.8 | 28.4 |
| Total | 562.3 | 613.7 | 638.7 |

* Excluding fresh-water fish and seaweeds.
† Figures include transhipments (caught by British vessels but not landed at British ports).

Source: Central Statistical Office, *Annual Abstract of Statistics*.

## Mining and Quarrying

('000 metric tons, unless otherwise indicated)

|  | 1991 | 1992 | 1993 |
|---|---|---|---|
| Hard coal (incl. slurries) | 94,202 | 84,493 | 68,199 |
| Natural gas and petroleum: |  |  |  |
| Methane—colliery[1] | 86 | 78 | 69 |
| Methane—North Sea[1] | 50,525 | 51,387 | 60,493 |
| Crude petroleum | 86,832 | 89,184 | 93,950 |
| Condensates and others[2] | 4,428 | 5,067 | 6,136 |
| Iron ore[3] | 59 | 31 | 1 |
| China clay (sales) | 2,911 | 2,502[4] | 2,577[4] |
| Ball clay (sales) | 729 | 744 | 746 |
| Fireclay[5] | 867 | 572 | 479 |
| Fuller's earth (sales)[6] | 189 | 189 | 187 |
| Common clay and shale[5] | 13,038 | 12,155 | 10,891 |
| Slate[7] | 360 | 326 | 462 |
| Limestone | 94,861 | 89,399 | 93,727 |
| Dolomite | 19,454 | 18,539 | 17,985 |
| Chalk[5] | 10,317 | 9,171 | 9,076 |
| Chert and flint[5] | 5 | n.a. | n.a. |
| Sandstone[8] | 16,607 | 14,890 | 16,059 |
| Special sands | 4,201 | 3,615 | 3,587 |
| Common sand and gravel[9] | 106,364 | 98,912 | 100,017 |
| Igneous rock | 53,948 | 57,654[5] | 57,766[5] |
| Gypsum[10] | 2,500 | 2,500 | 2,500 |
| Rock salt | 1,635 | 1,400 | 1,200[10] |
| Salt from brine | 1,320 | 1,300 | 1,300[10] |
| Salt in brine[11] | 3,874 | 3,401 | 4,076 |
| Fluorspar | 78 | 76 | 70 |
| Barytes | 86 | 77 | 55 |
| Celestite | 2 | 2 | 2 |
| Talc | 11 | 5 | 5 |
| Sulphur[12] | 143 | 177 | 202 |
| Potash[13] | 825 | 883 | 925 |
| Tin (metric tons metal) | 2,326 | 2,044 | 2,232 |
| Lead (metric tons metal) | 241 | n.a. | n.a. |
| Copper (metric tons metal) | 294 | — | — |
| Zinc (metric tons metal) | 1,078 | n.a. | n.a. |
| Silver (metric tons metal) | 0.6 | — | — |

[1] Approximate oil equivalent: converted from original data at 425 therms = 1 metric ton.
[2] Includes ethane, propane and butane, in addition to condensates (pentane and hydrocarbons).
[3] Figures refer to gross weight. The estimated iron content is 22%.
[4] Dry weight.
[5] Excluding production in Northern Ireland.
[6] Estimates based on data from producing companies.
[7] Including waste used for constructional fill and powder and granules used in industry.
[8] Including grit and conglomerate.
[9] Including marine-dredged sand and gravel for both home consumption and export.
[10] Estimates.
[11] Used for purposes other than salt-making.
[12] Sulphur recovered from oil refineries.
[13] Marketable product (kc1).

Source: British Geological Survey.

UNITED KINGDOM (GREAT BRITAIN) — *Statistical Survey*

## Industry

**SELECTED PRODUCTS**
('000 metric tons, unless otherwise indicated)

| | 1991 | 1992 | 1993 |
|---|---|---|---|
| Wheat flour | 3,844 | 3,845 | 3,966 |
| Refined sugar[1] | 1,220 | 1,472 | 1,436 |
| Margarine and other table spreads | 467 | 498 | 448 |
| Crude seed and nut oil[2] | 597 | 636 | 659 |
| Beer ('000 hectolitres) | 59,552 | 57,616 | 56,756 |
| Cigarettes ('000 million) | 85.3 | 76.4 | 94.4 |
| Woven cotton fabrics (million metres) | 154 | 142 | 109 |
| Worsted yarn (million kg)[3] | 52.4 | 54.0 | 51.2 |
| Woven woollen fabrics (million sq metres)[4] | 72.1 | 71.8 | 70.4 |
| Man-made fibre continuous filaments | 92.6 | 93.8 | 86.6 |
| Man-made fibre staple and tow | 174.8 | 168.1 | 153.9 |
| Woven fabrics of man-made fibres (million metres)[5] | 232.2 | 230.1 | 222.0 |
| Leather footwear ('000 pairs)[6] | 39,149[7] | n.a. | n.a. |
| Other footwear—excl. rubber ('000 pairs)[6] | 39,930 | n.a. | n.a. |
| Newsprint* | 672† | 700† | n.a. |
| Other printing and writing paper | 1,478 | 1,583 | n.a. |
| Other paper and paperboard | 2,801 | 2,869 | n.a. |
| Synthetic rubber* | 273.8 | 253.0 | 220.4 |
| Rubber tyres—for cars, lorries, etc. ('000) | 28,544 | 30,408* | 29,256 |
| Sulphuric acid | 1,852.4 | n.a. | n.a. |
| Butane and propane[8] | 1,664 | 1,583 | 1,575 |
| Petroleum naphtha[8] | 2,515 | 3,040 | 2,696 |
| Motor spirit (petrol)[8] | 27,793 | 27,980 | 28,394 |
| Aviation turbine fuel[8] | 7,037 | 7,681 | 8,341 |
| Burning oil[8] | 2,446 | 2,450 | 2,707 |
| Diesel fuel and gas oil[8] | 26,057 | 25,650 | 27,361 |
| Fuel oil[8] | 13,205 | 12,388 | 13,183 |
| Lubricating oils[8] | 973 | 1,163 | 1,264 |
| Petroleum bitumen (asphalt)[8] | 2,302 | 2,336 | 2,450 |
| Coke | 7,703 | 6,868 | n.a. |
| Cement | 12,297 | 11,006 | n.a. |
| Pig-iron[9] | 12,062 | 11,679 | 11,579 |
| Crude steel (usable) | 16,474 | 16,212 | 16,625 |
| Aluminium—unwrought (metric tons) | 430,000 | 496,000 | 518,100 |
| Refined copper—unwrought (metric tons) | 70,100 | 42,100 | 46,500 |
| Refined lead—unwrought (metric tons)[10] | 311,000 | 346,800 | 363,800 |
| Zinc—unwrought: primary (metric tons) | 100,700 | 96,800 | 102,400 |
| Television receivers ('000) | 4,281 | n.a. | n.a. |
| Merchant vessels launched ('000 grt) | 152 | 172 | 205 |
| Passenger motor cars ('000) | 1,236.9 | 1,291.9 | 1,375.5 |
| Road goods vehicles ('000) | 204.6 | 237.1 | 184.2 |
| Construction: Permanent dwellings completed (number) | 190,970 | 178,733 | 182,261 |
| Electric energy (million kWh) | 322,811 | 320,961 | 323,030 |

[1] Production from home-grown sugar beet only.
[2] Including maize oil.
[3] Including all yarns spun on the worsted system.
[4] Deliveries of fabrics, except blankets, after undergoing finishing processes; fabrics woven from all yarns on the woollen and worsted systems.
[5] Including mixtures of man-made fibres and cotton.
[6] Manufacturers' sales.
[7] Excluding men's sandals.
[8] Refinery production only (excluding supplies from other sources).
[9] Including blast-furnace ferro-alloys.
[10] Excluding hard lead.
* Figure(s) from UN, *Monthly Bulletin of Statistics*.
† Provisional.

Source: mainly Central Statistical Office, *Annual Abstract of Statistics*.

## Finance

**CURRENCY AND EXCHANGE RATES**

**Monetary Units**
100 pence (pennies) = 1 pound sterling (£).

**Dollar Equivalents** (31 December 1994)
£1 sterling = US $1.5645;
US $1 = 63.92 pence.

**Average Exchange Rate** (US $ per pound sterling)
1992  1.7655
1993  1.5020
1994  1.5316

**BUDGET** (general government transactions, £ million)*

| Revenue | 1991 | 1992 | 1993 |
|---|---|---|---|
| Current receipts | 219,425 | 220,872 | 225,738 |
| Taxes on income | 75,021 | 73,755 | 73,070 |
| Taxes on expenditure | 85,416 | 87,506 | 91,361 |
| National insurance contributions, etc. | 36,373 | 37,220 | 38,503 |
| Community charge | 8,128 | 7,865 | 8,001 |
| Gross trading surpluses | −36 | 207 | 294 |
| Rents | 4,567 | 4,920 | 5,736 |
| Interest and dividends, etc. | 5,648 | 5,261 | 4,803 |
| Miscellaneous current transfers | 545 | 535 | 662 |
| Imputed charge for consumption of non-trading capital | 3,763 | 3,603 | 3,308 |
| Capital receipts | 3,558 | 2,921 | 2,627 |
| **Total** | 222,983 | 223,793 | 228,365 |

| Expenditure | 1991 | 1992 | 1993 |
|---|---|---|---|
| General public services | 11,517 | 12,786 | 12,633 |
| Finance and tax collection | 3,992 | 4,074 | 4,017 |
| External | 1,396 | 1,699 | 1,829 |
| Defence | 23,226 | 24,508 | 24,384 |
| Public order and safety | 12,923 | 13,774 | 14,979 |
| Police | 6,468 | 6,910 | 7,685 |
| Fire | 1,377 | 1,436 | 1,548 |
| Law courts | 3,251 | 3,604 | 4,120 |
| Prisons | 1,827 | 1,824 | 1,626 |
| Education | 29,355 | 31,925 | 33,885 |
| Health | 31,150 | 34,938 | 36,863 |
| Social security | 73,795 | 84,551 | 93,180 |
| Housing and community amenities | 8,650 | 10,249 | 10,939 |
| Housing | 5,960 | 6,091 | 6,406 |
| Recreational and cultural affairs | 3,914 | 3,838 | 3,705 |
| Fuel and energy | −3,054 | −627 | 954 |
| Agriculture, forestry and fishing | 2,737 | 2,930 | 3,930 |
| Mining and mineral resources, manufacturing and construction | 1,593 | 1,328 | 1,529 |
| Transport and communication | 6,717 | 6,402 | 6,838 |
| Other economic affairs and services | 4,352 | 4,573 | 4,977 |
| Other expenditure | 21,533 | 23,035 | 24,053 |
| Debt interest† | 16,993 | 17,118 | 18,446 |
| Non-trading capital consumption | 3,763 | 3,603 | 3,308 |
| **Total** | 228,408 | 254,210 | 272,849 |
| Current expenditure | 217,463 | 240,316 | 257,390 |
| Capital expenditure | 20,229 | 20,078 | 19,639 |
| Net lending | −351 | 1,400 | 1,197 |
| Public dividend capital, etc. | 1 | 1 | — |
| Company securities (net) | −8,934 | −7,585 | −5,377 |

* Consolidated accounts, covering current and capital transactions, of the central Government (all funds and accounts, including the National Insurance Funds) and local authorities.
† This item is omitted from the other categories of expenditure as it cannot be allocated satisfactorily under functional heads.

Source: Central Statistical Office, *United Kingdom National Accounts*.

# UNITED KINGDOM (GREAT BRITAIN)

*Statistical Survey*

## OFFICIAL RESERVES (US $ million at 31 December)*

|  | 1992 | 1993 | 1994 |
|---|---|---|---|
| Gold | 4,770 | 4,558 | 5,314 |
| IMF special drawing rights | 539 | 289 | 465 |
| Convertible currencies† | 34,338 | 36,210 | 36,223 |
| Reserve position in the IMF | 2,007 | 1,869 | 1,896 |
| **Total** | 41,654 | 42,926 | 43,898 |

* Reserves are revalued at 31 March each year.
† Including European currency units (ECUs) acquired from swaps with the European Monetary Co-operation Fund.

Source: Bank of England.

## CURRENCY IN CIRCULATION (£ million)

|  | 1992 | 1993 | 1994 |
|---|---|---|---|
| Annual averages: |  |  |  |
|   Bank of England notes* | 16,145 | 16,969 | 18,025 |
|   Scottish bank notes | 1,295 | 1,356 | 1,436 |
|   Northern Ireland bank notes | 453 | 529 | 596 |
|   **Total bank notes** | 17,893 | 18,854 | 20,057 |
|   Estimated coin* | 2,036 | 2,085 | 2,190 |
|   **Total outstanding** | 19,929 | 20,939 | 22,247 |
| of which: |  |  |  |
|   In public circulation† | 15,879 | 16,853 | 17,863 |
| At 31 December: |  |  |  |
|   Currency in public circulation† | 16,829 | 17,900 | 18,752 |

* Average of Wednesdays. Includes amounts held by Scottish and Northern Irish banks as backing for their own note issues.
† Outside banks and building societies.

Source: Bank of England.

## COST OF LIVING (General Index of Retail Prices, annual averages. Base: January 1987 = 100)

|  | 1992 | 1993 | 1994 |
|---|---|---|---|
| Food | 128.3 | 130.6 | 131.9 |
| Catering | 147.9 | 155.6 | 162.1 |
| Alcoholic drink | 148.1 | 154.7 | 158.5 |
| Tobacco | 144.2 | 156.4 | 168.2 |
| Housing | 159.6 | 151.0 | 156.0 |
| Fuel and light | 127.8 | 126.2 | 131.7 |
| Household goods | 126.5 | 128.0 | 128.4 |
| Household services | 137.0 | 141.9 | 142.0 |
| Clothing and footwear | 118.8 | 119.8 | 120.4 |
| Personal goods and services | 142.2 | 147.9 | 153.3 |
| Motoring expenditure | 138.7 | 144.7 | 149.7 |
| Fares and other travel costs | 143.9 | 151.4 | 155.4 |
| Leisure goods | 120.8 | 122.5 | 121.8 |
| Leisure services | 150.0 | 156.7 | 162.5 |
| **All items** | 138.5 | 140.7 | 144.1 |

Source: Central Statistical Office.

## NATIONAL ACCOUNTS (£ million at current prices)

### National Income and Product

|  | 1991 | 1992 | 1993 |
|---|---|---|---|
| Income from employment | 329,609 | 342,215 | 352,896 |
| Income from self-employment | 58,639 | 59,482 | 61,346 |
| Gross trading profits and surpluses | 60,592 | 62,762 | 77,106 |
| Rents | 44,707 | 49,193 | 52,872 |
| Imputed charge for consump-tion of non-trading capital | 4,363 | 4,207 | 3,942 |
| **Domestic factor incomes** | 497,910 | 517,859 | 548,162 |
| *Less* Stock appreciation | 2,010 | 1,832 | 2,359 |
| **Sub-total** | 495,900 | 516,027 | 545,803 |
| Residual error (net) | — | — | 317 |
| **Gross domestic product at factor cost** | 495,900 | 516,027 | 546,120 |
| Taxes on expenditure | 85,416 | 87,506 | 91,361 |
| *Less* Subsidies | 5,995 | 6,412 | 7,458 |
| **Gross domestic product at market prices** | 575,321 | 597,121 | 630,023 |
| Net property income from abroad | −217 | 4,293 | 3,062 |
| **Gross national product at market prices** | 575,104 | 601,414 | 633,085 |
| *Less* Capital consumption | 63,602 | 63,998 | 65,023 |
| **National income in market prices** | 511,502 | 537,416 | 568,062 |

Source: Central Statistical Office, *United Kingdom National Accounts*.

### Expenditure on the Gross Domestic Product

|  | 1991 | 1992 | 1993 |
|---|---|---|---|
| Private consumers' expenditure | 364,972 | 382,240 | 405,639 |
| Government consumption expenditure | 124,105 | 131,886 | 138,224 |
| Gross domestic fixed capital formation | 97,747 | 93,942 | 94,715 |
| Physical increase in stocks | −4,927 | −1,932 | −197 |
| **Total domestic expenditure** | 581,897 | 606,136 | 638,381 |
| Exports of goods and services | 134,234 | 140,477 | 157,999 |
| *Less* Imports of goods and services | 140,810 | 149,492 | 166,266 |
| **Sub-total** | 575,321 | 597,121 | 630,114 |
| Statistical discrepancy | — | — | −91 |
| **Gross domestic product at market prices** | 575,321 | 597,121 | 630,023 |

Source: Central Statistical Office, *United Kingdom National Accounts*.

# UNITED KINGDOM (GREAT BRITAIN)

## Gross Domestic Product by Economic Activity
(at factor cost)

|  | 1991 | 1992 | 1993 |
|---|---|---|---|
| Agriculture, hunting, forestry and fishing | 8,964 | 9,282 | 10,373 |
| Mining and quarrying (incl. petroleum and gas extraction) | 10,450 | 10,654 | 12,147 |
| Manufacturing | 108,834 | 111,644 | 118,294 |
| Electricity, gas and water supply | 13,388 | 13,339 | 13,994 |
| Construction | 31,470 | 29,760 | 29,221 |
| Wholesale and retail trade, hotels and restaurants, repairs | 71,558 | 74,536 | 78,348 |
| Transport, storage and communication | 42,051 | 43,905 | 46,263 |
| Financial intermediation, real estate, renting and business activities | 116,277 | 124,456 | 133,956 |
| Public administration, national defence and compulsory social security | 34,257 | 37,260 | 38,199 |
| Education, health and social work | 50,757 | 55,062 | 57,457 |
| Other services | 28,676 | 29,455 | 31,292 |
| **Sub-total** | 516,682 | 539,353 | 569,544 |
| Adjustment for financial services* | −20,782 | −23,326 | −23,741 |
| Residual error (net) | — | — | 317 |
| **Total** | 495,900 | 516,027 | 546,120 |

* Financial companies' net receipts of interest.

Source: Central Statistical Office, *United Kingdom National Accounts*.

## BALANCE OF PAYMENTS (£ million)

|  | 1991 | 1992 | 1993 |
|---|---|---|---|
| Merchandise exports f.o.b. | 103,413 | 107,343 | 121,414 |
| Merchandise imports f.o.b. | −113,697 | −120,447 | −134,623 |
| **Visible trade balance** | −10,284 | −13,104 | −13,209 |
| Exports of services: |  |  |  |
| General government | 457 | 398 | 434 |
| Private sector and public corporations: |  |  |  |
| Sea transport | 3,351 | 3,475 | 3,843 |
| Civil aviation | 4,039 | 4,448 | 5,075 |
| Travel | 7,168 | 7,890 | 8,951 |
| Financial and other services | 15,806 | 16,923 | 18,282 |
| **Total** | 30,821 | 33,134 | 36,585 |
| Imports of services: |  |  |  |
| General government | −2,808 | −2,546 | −2,332 |
| Private sector and public corporations: |  |  |  |
| Sea transport | −3,634 | −3,837 | −4,301 |
| Civil aviation | −4,423 | −4,969 | −5,529 |
| Travel | −9,834 | −11,244 | −12,257 |
| Financial and other services | −6,414 | −6,449 | −7,227 |
| **Total** | −27,113 | −29,045 | −31,643 |
| **Balance on services** | 3,708 | 4,089 | 4,942 |
| Interest, profits, dividends: |  |  |  |
| Receipts: government | 1,754 | 1,566 | 1,413 |
| Receipts: other | 75,207 | 67,598 | 72,628 |
| Payments: government | −2,565 | −3,137 | −3,281 |
| Payments: other | −74,610 | −61,737 | −67,697 |
| **Balance on interest, etc.** | −217 | 4,293 | 3,062 |
| Current transfers: |  |  |  |
| Receipts: government | 4,899 | 2,888 | 3,325 |
| Receipts: private | 1,900 | 1,975 | 2,050 |
| Payments: government | −5,982 | −7,722 | −8,161 |
| Payments: private | −2,200 | −2,250 | −2,320 |
| **Balance on transfers** | −1,383 | −5,109 | −5,106 |
| **'Invisible' balance** | 2,108 | 3,273 | 2,898 |
| **Current balance** | −8,176 | −9,831 | −10,311 |
| **Capital balance** | 11,298 | 1,962 | 9,015 |
| **Net errors and omissions** | −443 | 6,462 | 1,998 |
| **Changes in official reserves** | 2,679 | −1,407 | 702 |

Source: Central Statistical Office, *United Kingdom Balance of Payments*.

## GROSS PUBLIC EXPENDITURE ON OVERSEAS AID
(£ million, year ending 31 March)

|  | 1991/92 | 1992/93 | 1993/94 |
|---|---|---|---|
| ODA bilateral programmes | 1,074.8 | 1,126.9 | 1,156.4 |
| Project aid | 594.1 | 601.5 | 606.4 |
| Financial aid | 140.1 | 121.3 | 117.8 |
| Technical co-operation | 454.0 | 480.2 | 488.6 |
| Aid and trade provision | 101.2 | 93.0 | 84.7 |
| Programme aid | 119.0 | 138.4 | 122.1 |
| Emergency aid | 138.5 | 144.1 | 179.5 |
| Food aid | 47.7 | 37.5 | 40.8 |
| Disaster relief | 82.0 | 95.9 | 124.2 |
| Debt relief | 0.5 | 0.4 | 1.7 |
| Other technical co-operation | 61.5 | 74.6 | 87.1 |
| Official advances to CDC* | 60.0 | 75.0 | 75.0 |
| Other bilateral programmes | 163.0 | 303.6 | 223.1 |
| CDC* investment | 124.2 | 223.3 | 178.3 |
| **Total bilateral aid†** | 1,177.7 | 1,355.5 | 1,304.5 |
| ODA multilateral programmes | 819.1 | 935.9 | 954.6 |
| European Community | 413.4 | 464.4 | 510.0 |
| World Bank Group | 228.5 | 250.0 | 226.1 |
| International Monetary Fund | 1.5 | 10.0 | 20.0 |
| Regional development banks | 69.2 | 92.0 | 76.4 |
| UN agencies | 89.9 | 101.2 | 105.6 |
| Other multilateral programmes | 77.3 | 45.7 | 45.5 |
| European Community | 45.9 | 13.0 | 14.1 |
| UN agencies | 30.0 | 31.3 | 30.2 |
| **Total multilateral aid** | 896.4 | 981.6 | 1,000.1 |
| Administrative costs | 63.6 | 63.9 | 70.0 |
| **Total gross expenditure on aid** | 2,137.7 | 2,401.0 | 2,374.5 |

* Commonwealth Development Corporation.
† Excluding official advances to CDC.

Source: Overseas Development Administration.

# UNITED KINGDOM (GREAT BRITAIN)

*Statistical Survey*

## External Trade

Note: Figures include the Isle of Man and the Channel Islands.

**PRINCIPAL COMMODITIES** (distribution by SITC, £ million)

| Imports c.i.f. | 1990 | 1991 | 1992 |
|---|---|---|---|
| **Food and live animals** | 10,408.7 | 10,389.3 | 11,401.4 |
| Vegetables and fruit | 2,964.5 | 3,002.6 | 3,118.0 |
| **Crude materials (inedible) except fuels*** | 5,721.1 | 4,678.3 | 4,668.2 |
| **Mineral fuels, lubricants, etc.** | 7,864.5 | 7,510.7 | 7,014.1 |
| Petroleum, petroleum products, etc. | 6,285.1 | 5,773.6 | 5,326.6 |
| **Chemicals and related products** | 10,834.0 | 10,978.6 | 11,618.3 |
| Organic chemicals | 2,593.4 | 2,618.4 | 2,792.6 |
| **Basic manufactures*** | 21,902.4 | 20,519.9 | 20,670.4 |
| Paper, paperboard and manufactures | 4,014.3 | 3,868.4 | 3,801.3 |
| Textile yarn, fabrics, etc. | 3,936.1 | 3,738.0 | 3,940.5 |
| Non-metallic mineral manufactures* | 3,601.9 | 3,332.9 | 3,217.6 |
| Iron and steel | 2,683.4 | 2,620.2 | 2,513.7 |
| Non-ferrous metals | 3,003.3 | 2,557.9 | 2,589.7 |
| Other metal manufactures | 2,592.9 | 2,523.1 | 2,577.3 |
| **Machinery and transport equipment** | 47,160.9 | 43,101.6 | 47,317.0 |
| Power generating machinery and equipment | 3,518.4 | 3,345.5 | 3,611.8 |
| Machinery specialized for particular industries | 3,521.9 | 3,005.6 | 3,206.9 |
| Metalworking machinery | 993.4 | 860.7 | 800.5 |
| General industrial machinery, equipment and parts | 4,359.8 | 4,202.8 | 4,518.1 |
| Office machines and automatic data processing equipment | 7,715.0 | 7,586.5 | 8,360.9 |
| Telecommunications and sound equipment | 3,486.8 | 3,351.2 | 3,555.7 |
| Other electrical machinery, apparatus, etc. | 6,921.9 | 7,078.4 | 7,738.2 |
| Road vehicles and parts† | 12,594.2 | 10,227.2 | 12,118.5 |
| Other transport equipment† | 4,049.5 | 3,443.7 | 3,406.3 |
| **Miscellaneous manufactured articles** | 18,252.5 | 17,559.3 | 19,106.6 |
| Clothing and accessories (excl. footwear) | 3,904.1 | 4,128.5 | 4,477.9 |
| Professional, scientific and controlling instruments, etc. | 2,482.1 | 2,525.1 | 2,621.0 |
| **Total** (incl. others) | 126,086.1 | 118,786.0 | 125,866.8 |

* Sorted industrial diamonds, usually classified with natural abrasives (under 'crude materials'), are included with 'basic manufactures'.
† Excluding tyres, engines and electrical parts.

Source: Central Statistical Office, *Annual Abstract of Statistics*.

| Exports f.o.b. | 1990 | 1991 | 1992 |
|---|---|---|---|
| **Food and live animals** | 4,341.9 | 4,715.8 | 5,289.5 |
| **Beverages and tobacco** | 2,770.2 | 3,031.8 | 3,417.4 |
| Beverages | 2,112.8 | 2,251.7 | 2,447.7 |
| **Mineral fuels, lubricants, etc.** | 7,868.7 | 7,169.0 | 6,967.4 |
| Petroleum, petroleum products, etc. | 7,544.6 | 6,814.1 | 6,660.6 |
| **Chemicals and related products** | 13,181.6 | 13,788.6 | 14,976.3 |
| Organic chemicals | 3,351.6 | 3,468.4 | 3,699.2 |
| Medicinal and pharmaceutical products | 2,257.5 | 2,556.1 | 2,993.2 |
| **Basic manufactures*** | 15,821.6 | 15,581.1 | 15,482.3 |
| Textile yarn, fabrics, etc. | 2,447.0 | 2,349.0 | 2,457.4 |
| Non-metallic mineral manufactures* | 3,191.3 | 3,177.1 | 2,955.4 |
| Iron and steel | 3,036.0 | 3,011.3 | 3,004.4 |
| Other metal manufactures | 2,115.6 | 2,182.4 | 2,211.7 |
| **Machinery and transport equipment** | 41,850.6 | 43,627.1 | 44,420.1 |
| Power generating machinery and equipment | 5,250.7 | 5,073.1 | 5,536.6 |
| Machinery specialized for particular industries | 4,234.1 | 3,922.1 | 4,048.1 |
| General industrial machinery, equipment and parts | 4,545.7 | 4,520.6 | 4,579.5 |
| Office machines and automatic data processing equipment | 6,341.7 | 6,590.9 | 6,616.8 |
| Telecommunications and sound equipment | 2,685.5 | 2,942.8 | 2,857.8 |
| Other electrical machinery, apparatus, etc. | 5,648.2 | 5,709.7 | 6,354.5 |
| Road vehicles and parts† | 7,296.5 | 8,555.4 | 8,893.6 |
| Other transport equipment | 4,935.7 | 5,500.2 | 4,834.9 |
| **Miscellaneous manufactured articles** | 13,349.0 | 13,140.4 | 13,964.1 |
| Professional, scientific and controlling instruments, etc. | 2,945.2 | 2,992.7 | 3,077.2 |
| **Total** (incl. others) | 103,692.4 | 104,877.0 | 108,507.5 |

* Sorted industrial diamonds, usually classified with natural abrasives (under 'crude materials'), are included with 'basic manufactures'.
† Excluding tyres, engines and electrical parts.

Source: Central Statistical Office, *Annual Abstract of Statistics*.

**PRINCIPAL TRADING PARTNERS** (£ million)*

| Imports c.i.f. | 1990 | 1991 | 1992 |
|---|---|---|---|
| Belgium/Luxembourg | 5,732.0 | 5,472.5 | 5,741.1 |
| Canada | 2,207.7 | 1,923.1 | 1,897.0 |
| Denmark | 2,278.5 | 2,266.7 | 2,385.0 |
| Finland | 1,775.7 | 1,522.3 | 1,676.6 |
| France | 11,872.3 | 11,075.4 | 12,223.4 |
| Germany | 19,907.1 | 17,740.5 | 19,034.3 |
| Hong Kong | 1,972.1 | 2,147.6 | 2,397.4 |
| Ireland | 4,497.4 | 4,416.3 | 5,070.0 |
| Italy | 6,732.8 | 6,378.7 | 6,765.7 |
| Japan | 6,761.3 | 6,753.5 | 7,442.2 |
| Netherlands | 10,483.2 | 9,969.0 | 9,907.8 |
| Norway | 4,132.8 | 4,162.5 | 3,885.7 |
| Portugal | 1,176.2 | 1,043.3 | 2,939.0 |
| Spain (excl. Canary Is) | 2,870.7 | 2,627.7 | 1,170.8 |
| Sweden | 3,594.5 | 3,141.6 | 3,282.7 |
| Switzerland | 4,247.9 | 3,754.2 | 3,918.9 |
| Taiwan | 1,211.8 | 1,271.9 | 1,393.6 |
| USA | 14,352.7 | 13,692.5 | 13,714.0 |
| **Total** (incl. others) | 126,086.1 | 118,786.0 | 125,866.8 |

# UNITED KINGDOM (GREAT BRITAIN)

| Exports f.o.b. | 1990 | 1991 | 1992 |
|---|---|---|---|
| Australia | 1,632.9 | 1,355.7 | 1,376.7 |
| Belgium/Luxembourg | 5,649.4 | 5,873.3 | 5,715.1 |
| Canada | 1,906.4 | 1,700.6 | 1,583.9 |
| Denmark | 1,419.3 | 1,408.6 | 1,560.6 |
| France | 10,894.5 | 11,596.7 | 11,484.7 |
| Germany | 13,169.4 | 14,676.2 | 15,212.6 |
| Hong Kong | 1,238.0 | 1,387.4 | 1,613.0 |
| India | 1,264.2 | 1,107.4 | 945.5 |
| Ireland | 5,313.0 | 5,295.3 | 5,738.9 |
| Italy | 5,553.0 | 6,140.2 | 6,146.9 |
| Japan | 2,631.3 | 2,260.0 | 2,231.5 |
| Netherlands | 7,561.3 | 8,257.7 | 8,503.2 |
| Norway | 1,292.0 | 1,357.7 | 1,419.9 |
| Portugal | 1,031.8 | 1,085.1 | 1,164.1 |
| Saudi Arabia | 2,011.4 | 2,254.7 | 1,967.8 |
| Singapore | 1,040.7 | 1,018.4 | 1,145.3 |
| South Africa | 1,113.6 | 1,023.6 | 1,079.1 |
| Spain (excl. Canary Is) | 3,620.9 | 4,279.2 | 4,405.3 |
| Sweden | 2,712.3 | 2,471.2 | 2,439.0 |
| Switzerland | 2,358.9 | 2,104.7 | 1,844.6 |
| USA | 12,966.8 | 11,340.7 | 12,228.7 |
| **Total** (incl. others) | 103,692.4 | 104,877.0 | 108,507.5 |

* Imports by country of first consignment; exports by country of last consignment. The distribution by countries excludes trade (other than by parcel post) in items valued at less than £600. The value of such items (in £ million) was: Imports 778.1 in 1990, 743.3 in 1991, 784.5 in 1992; Exports 850.1 in 1990, 777.5 in 1991, 980.5 in 1992.

Source: Central Statistical Office, *Annual Abstract of Statistics*.

# Transport

### RAILWAYS (Great Britain)

|  | 1991/92 | 1992/93 | 1993/94 |
|---|---|---|---|
| British Rail: |  |  |  |
| Passenger journeys (million) | 741 | 745 | 713 |
| Passenger-kilometres (million) | 32,466 | 31,718 | 30,357 |
| Freight traffic (million metric tons) | 136 | 122 | 103 |
| Freight metric ton-kilometres (million) | 15,348 | 15,500 | 13,765 |
| London Transport: |  |  |  |
| Passenger journeys (million) | 751 | 728 | 735 |
| Passenger-kilometres (million) | 5,895 | 5,758 | 5,814 |

Source: Department of Transport.

### ROAD TRAFFIC
('000 licensed vehicles in Great Britain at 31 December)

|  | 1992 | 1993 | 1994 |
|---|---|---|---|
| Private motor cars* | 19,870 | 20,102 | 20,479 |
| Motor cycles, scooters and mopeds | 684 | 650 | 630 |
| Light goods vehicles† | 2,198 | 2,187 | 2,192 |
| Heavy goods vehicles | 432 | 428 | 434 |
| Public passenger vehicles | 107 | 107 | 107 |

* Including vans used privately.
† Goods vehicles less than 3,500 kg in weight (except farmers' and showmen's vehicles).

Source: Department of Transport.

### INTERNATIONAL SEA-BORNE SHIPPING
(freight traffic, '000 metric tons)

|  | 1990 | 1991 | 1992 |
|---|---|---|---|
| Goods imported | 174,195 | 173,202 | 176,599 |
| Goods exported* | 126,280 | 128,138 | 134,581 |

* Including re-exports.

Source: Department of Transport.

### CIVIL AVIATION (United Kingdom airlines*)
('000 metric ton-km, unless otherwise indicated)

|  | 1991 | 1992 | 1993 |
|---|---|---|---|
| All services: |  |  |  |
| Aircraft stage flights (number) | 568,122 | 601,500 | 601,620 |
| Aircraft-kilometres flown ('000) | 497,700 | 551,222 | 584,341 |
| Passengers carried ('000) | 34,592 | 38,242 | 40,099 |
| Passenger-kilometres flown (million) | 74,615 | 86,731 | 94,670 |
| Total cargo carried (metric tons) | 466,622 | 507,356 | 541,986 |
| Total metric ton-kilometres | 9,570,451 | 10,940,514 | 11,696,428 |
| Freight metric ton-kilometres | 2,379,915 | 2,644,104 | 2,919,591 |
| Mail metric ton-kilometres | 182,598 | 161,165 | 141,528 |
| Domestic services: |  |  |  |
| Aircraft stage flights (number) | 285,346 | 299,893 | 300,416 |
| Aircraft-kilometres flown ('000) | 86,026 | 91,699 | 93,518 |
| Passengers carried ('000) | 11,650 | 11,695 | 12,086 |
| Passenger-kilometres flown (million) | 4,664 | 4,728 | 4,934 |
| Total cargo carried (metric tons) | 37,739 | 35,420 | 30,660 |
| Total metric ton-kilometres | 396,484 | 401,127 | 47,299 |
| Freight metric ton-kilometres | 6,749 | 6,648 | 5,559 |
| Mail metric ton-kilometres | 7,403 | 7,066 | 6,528 |
| International services: |  |  |  |
| Aircraft stage flights (number) | 282,776 | 301,607 | 301,204 |
| Aircraft-kilometres flown ('000) | 411,674 | 459,523 | 490,823 |
| Passengers carried ('000) | 22,942 | 26,547 | 28,013 |
| Passenger-kilometres flown (million) | 69,952 | 82,003 | 89,736 |
| Total cargo carried (metric tons) | 428,883 | 471,936 | 511,326 |
| Total metric ton-kilometres | 9,173,967 | 10,539,387 | 11,649,129 |
| Freight metric ton-kilometres | 2,373,166 | 2,637,456 | 2,914,032 |
| Mail metric ton-kilometres | 175,195 | 154,099 | 135,000 |

* Excluding charter services.

Source: Civil Aviation Authority.

# Tourism

### FOREIGN VISITORS BY REGION OF ORIGIN ('000)

|  | 1991 | 1992 | 1993 |
|---|---|---|---|
| EC | 9,381 | 9,977 | 10,691 |
| Other Europe | 2,010 | 2,057 | 2,228 |
| North America | 2,867 | 3,377 | 3,402 |
| Other countries | 2,868 | 3,124 | 3,168 |
| **Total** | 17,125 | 18,535 | 19,488 |
| Total expenditure (£ million) | 7,386 | 7,891 | 9,376 |

Source: Central Statistical Office.

### VISITS BY COUNTRY OF PERMANENT RESIDENCE ('000)

|  | 1991 | 1992 | 1993 |
|---|---|---|---|
| Belgium/Luxembourg | 689 | 802 | 937 |
| France | 2,289 | 2,483 | 2,513 |
| Germany | 2,134 | 2,268 | 2,356 |
| Ireland | 1,314 | 1,416 | 1,554 |
| Italy | 722 | 784 | 793 |
| Netherlands | 1,118 | 996 | 1,213 |
| Scandinavia and Finland | 1,170 | 1,217 | 1,231 |
| Spain | 623 | 684 | 707 |
| Switzerland | 434 | 433 | 501 |
| Other Europe | 898 | 951 | 1,114 |
| USA | 2,320 | 2,748 | 2,815 |
| Canada | 547 | 629 | 587 |
| Japan | 458 | 554 | 491 |
| Australia/New Zealand | 577 | 620 | 585 |
| Southern Africa | 179 | 204 | 223 |
| Latin America | 200 | 234 | 216 |
| Middle East | 447 | 481 | 539 |
| Other countries | 1,006 | 1,030 | 1,113 |
| **Total** | 17,125 | 18,535 | 19,488 |

Source: Central Statistical Office.

UNITED KINGDOM (GREAT BRITAIN)  *Statistical Survey*

## Communications Media

|  | 1990 | 1991 | 1992 |
|---|---|---|---|
| Radio receivers ('000 in use) | 65,600 | 65,800 | 66,100 |
| Television receivers ('000 in use) | 24,900 | 25,000 | 25,100 |

**Book titles produced:** 86,573 (incl. 5,786 pamphlets) in 1992.
**Daily newspapers** (1992): 101 titles (estimated circulation 22,100,000 copies).
**Non-daily newspapers** (1988): 818 titles (average circulation 29,047,000 copies).
**Other periodicals:** 6,408 in 1984.
Source: UNESCO, *Statistical Yearbook*.
**Telephones:** 29,518,000 in use at 31 March 1984.

## Education

### ENGLAND AND WALES

|  | 1990/91 | 1991/92 | 1992/93 |
|---|---|---|---|
| Number of schools (January) | 29,312 | 29,070 | 28,856 |
| Teachers (January)[1]: |  |  |  |
| Maintained primary schools[2] | 189,715 | 191,570 | 193,153 |
| Maintained secondary schools | 198,703 | 199,368 | 200,052 |
| Other schools | 71,912 | 72,760 | 72,920 |
| **Total** | 460,330 | 463,698 | 466,125 |
| Full-time pupils (January): |  |  |  |
| Nursery schools[2] | 11,409 | 10,991 | 10,702 |
| Maintained primary schools[3,4] | 4,040,720 | 4,071,014 | 4,141,020 |
| Maintained secondary schools[4] | 3,038,481 | 3,094,781 | 3,157,232 |
| Special schools | 98,953 | 98,952 | 99,206 |
| Independent schools[5] | 558,160 | 558,256 | 549,840 |
| **Total** | 7,747,723 | 7,833,944 | 7,958,000 |
| Part-time pupils (January) | 350,547 | 364,858 | 376,672 |
| Further and higher education establishments[6] | 498 | 487 | 472 |
| Full-time students in further and higher education[6] | 760,728 | 886,269 | 993,390 |

[1] Full-time teachers and the full-time equivalent of part-time teachers.
[2] Including direct-grant nursery schools.
[3] Including centres for teaching English as a second language.
[4] Including middle schools deemed either primary or secondary and grant-maintained schools.
[5] Including City Technology Centres.
[6] At autumn term of academic years, including sandwich course students. Figures exclude universities (see below). All students on initial teacher-training courses at non-university establishments are included in statistics for further and higher education colleges following the reorganization of the former colleges of education.
Source: the former Department for Education.

### SCOTLAND

|  | 1991/92 | 1992/93 | 1993/94 |
|---|---|---|---|
| Education authority and grant-aided: |  |  |  |
| Schools: |  |  |  |
| Nursery | 680 | 705 | 758 |
| Primary | 2,365 | 2,348 | 2,342 |
| Secondary | 420 | 414 | 410 |
| Special | 339 | 341 | 334 |
| **Total** | 3,804 | 3,808 | 3,844 |
| Teachers:* |  |  |  |
| Nursery | 895 | 936 | 944 |
| Primary | 22,671 | 22,747 | 22,473 |
| Secondary | 23,868 | 24,041 | 24,326 |
| Special | 1,904 | 2,028 | 2,006 |
| **Total** | 49,338 | 49,752 | 49,749 |
| Pupils: |  |  |  |
| Nursery | 45,238 | 46,992 | 48,127 |
| Primary | 441,270 | 439,436 | 438,863 |
| Secondary | 296,992 | 303,645 | 311,833 |
| Special | 8,602 | 8,823 | 8,951 |
| **Total** | 792,102 | 798,896 | 807,774 |
| Further education establishments† | 63 | 60 | 60 |
| Full-time teachers in further education | 8,470 | 8,592 | 8,630 |
| Full-time students in further education‡ | 84,863 | 93,495 | 105,184 |

* Full-time teachers and the full-time equivalent of part-time.
† Vocational further education (day colleges and central institutions only).
‡ Full-time and 'sandwich' students on all courses, excluding those in universities.
Source: Scottish Office Education Department.

### UNIVERSITIES (Great Britain—academic years)*

|  | 1990/91 | 1991/92 | 1992/93 |
|---|---|---|---|
| Full-time teaching and research staff | 49,377 | 51,121 | 52,152 |
| Students taking university courses: |  |  |  |
| Full-time students | 352,574 | 382,416 | 414,814 |
| Part-time students | 51,944 | 59,034 | 67,436 |

* 45 universities, including the London and Manchester Business Schools, but excluding the privately-funded University of Buckingham and the Open University.
Source: the former Department for Education.

# Directory

## The Constitution

The United Kingdom is a constitutional monarchy. In the ninth century, when England was first united under a Saxon King, the monarchy was the only central power and the Constitution did not exist. Today, the Sovereign acts on the advice of her Ministers which she cannot, constitutionally, ignore; power, which has been at various times and in varying degrees in the hands of kings, feudal barons, ministers, councils and parliaments, or of particular groups or sections of society, is vested in the people as a whole, and the Sovereign is an essential part of the machinery of government which has gradually been devised to give expression to the popular will.

Both the powers of the Government and the functions of the Sovereign are determined by the Constitution, by the body of fundamental principles on which the State is governed and the methods, institutions and procedures which give them effect. But the United Kingdom has no written Constitution: there is no document, no one law or statute, to which reference can be made. The Constitution is an accumulation of convention, precedent and tradition which, although continually changing as the times change, is at any one moment binding and exact.

Some of the principles and many of the practices are secured by Statute, some are avowed by Declaration or Manifesto and many are incorporated in the Common Law. Magna Carta, in 1215, began the process by which the law of the land acquired a status of its own, independent of King and Parliament; the Bill of Rights of 1689 ended the long era of rivalry between Crown and Parliament and began the story of their co-operation; and the Reform Bill of 1832 dramatically broadened the basis of representative government and prepared the way for further changes. The Constitution is, above all, based on usage. It has been modified to match changing customs and to meet successive situations. Any one Parliament could, if it chose, revise or repeal every law and disown every convention that has constitutional significance. It could destroy the whole fabric of political and social existence, including its own; because, according to the Constitution, Parliament, which represents the people, is supreme. The work of one Parliament is not binding on its successors, except in so far as changes must be made by constitutional means. Parliament cannot disobey the law, but it can change it.

It would be impossible to enumerate the principles which are extant in the British Constitution. In constitutional as in legal practice, the way has been to admit the general principle in quite practical terms related to specific practical problems: the Habeas Corpus Act, for example, which establishes the principle of no imprisonment without trial, makes no mention of the principle itself but lays down in most concrete terms the punishments that shall be inflicted on a judge, or other law officer, if he fails to issue the Writ (commanding the prisoner to be brought before the court) when applied for. The principles of the Constitution and constitutional practice are in fact inherent in the Common Law on the one hand and in the structure, functions and procedures of the various instruments of government on the other: of the Crown, of Parliament, of the Privy Council, of the Government and the Cabinet and of the government departments.

### THE SOVEREIGN

The monarchy is hereditary, descending to the sons of the Sovereign in order of seniority or, if there are no sons, to the daughters.

The constitutional position of the Queen as head of the State, quite apart from her position as head of the Commonwealth, demands that she keep herself informed on all aspects of the life of her subjects, that she maintain absolute impartiality and that she should personally visit the different parts of her realm as often as it is possible for her to do so, but she has also quite specific functions, all exercised on ministerial advice: she summons, prorogues and dissolves Parliament; she must give Royal Assent to a Bill which has passed through both Houses of Parliament, before it becomes law; she is head of the judiciary (although the judiciary is now quite independent of the executive); she appoints all important state officials, including judges, officers of the forces and representatives abroad, and she confers honours and awards. Her formal consent is necessary before a Minister can take up office or a Cabinet be formed; and before a treaty may be concluded, war declared or peace made. These are some of the more essential functions. However, the Queen also has many residuary responsibilities, such as the guardianship of infants and persons of unsound mind, the creation of corporations, granting of printing rights for the Bible and Prayer Book and for state documents; and her signature and consent are necessary to many important state papers. Constitutional government cannot in fact be carried on without the Sovereign, so much so that provision has been made by Act of Parliament for the appointment of a Regent should the Sovereign be incapacitated or under age and for Counsellors of State to act in the temporary absence of the Queen.

### PARLIAMENT

The Queen in Parliament—the House of Commons and the House of Lords—is the supreme legislative authority in the United Kingdom. Under the Parliament Act of 1911 the maximum life of one Parliament was fixed at five years: if, that is, Parliament has not meanwhile been dissolved for any other reason, such as the fall of the Government, then a general election is at the end of five years necessary by law. During its lifetime, the power of Parliament is theoretically absolute; it can make or unmake any law. In practice, of course, it must take account of the electorate. Parliament is prorogued at intervals during its life, which therefore consists of a number of sessions; by present custom, a session has normally 160 sitting days and is divided into five periods: from November (when the session is opened) until Christmas (about 30 days), from January till Easter (50), from Easter till Whitsun (30), from Whitsun until the end of July (40) and 10 days in October.

The House of Commons has 651 members, each elected for one geographical constituency. The Speaker, who is elected by the members immediately a new parliament meets, presides. Members of Parliament may be elected either at a general election or at a by-election (held in the event of the death, resignation or expulsion of the sitting member) and in either case hold their seats during the life of the existing parliament. All British subjects who are more than 18 years of age (and subjects of any Commonwealth country and of the Republic of Ireland who are resident in the United Kingdom) have the vote unless legally barred (e.g. for insanity). Anyone who has the vote may stand as a candidate for election except clergymen of the Church of England, the established Churches of Scotland and Northern Ireland and the Roman Catholic Church, and certain officers of the Crown; civil servants must resign from the service if they wish to stand as a Member of Parliament.

There are over 1,200 peers who have the right to a seat in the House of Lords, including Princes of the Blood Royal (who, by tradition, take no part in the proceedings); hereditary peers of England and of the United Kingdom (peerages created since the Act of Union of England and Scotland of 1707 are all peerages of the United Kingdom); several Lords of Appeal in Ordinary (appointed for life to carry out the judicial duties of the House); Scottish peers; created life peers and life peeresses; and the two archbishops and the 24 senior bishops of the Church of England. All except the spiritual, judicial and life peerages are hereditary. The Lord Chancellor is the Speaker of the House. The 1963 Peerage Act made three main amendments to the Constitution: (1) An hereditary peerage may be disclaimed by the holder for the duration of his lifetime. The peerage can be reclaimed at his death by his heir, but he himself cannot reclaim it. (2) All Scottish peers, instead of only 16 representatives, and (3) peeresses in their own right, may take their seats in the House of Lords.

Members of Parliament whose views coincide form parties which agree in each case to support the policies put forward by their chosen leaders, and to present a common front on all important issues both in Parliament and to the electorate. This system evolved during the 17th and 18th centuries and is now essential to the working of the British Constitution. Under the party system, the Queen sends for the leader of the party which wins the majority of seats (although not necessarily of votes) at a general election and asks him or her to form a government. The party with the second largest number of seats forms the Opposition, which has quite specific functions. Members of other minority parties and independents may support the Government or Opposition as they choose. Each party has its own Whips, officials whose duty it is to arrange, (in consultation with the Whips of other parties), matters of procedure and organization; to ensure that members attend debates; and to muster for their party its maximum voting strength. In addition, each party has its own national and local organizations outside Parliament.

Parliamentary procedure, like the Constitution itself, is determined by rules, customs, forms and practices which have accumulated over many centuries. The Speaker is responsible for their application, and generally for controlling the course of business and debates in the house.

It is the duty of Parliament to make the laws which govern the life of the community, to appropriate the necessary funds for the various services of state and to criticize and control the Government. Parliament is also consulted before the ratification of certain international treaties and agreements.

Legislation may (with some exceptions) be initiated in either House and on either side of the House. In practice, most Public Bills are introduced into the House of Commons by the Government in power (the chief exceptions are Private Members' Bills) as the result of Cabinet decisions. Each Bill which is passed by the Commons at its third reading is sent to the House of Lords, who either accept it or return it to the Commons with suggested amendments. The Lords cannot in any instance prevent Bills passed by the Commons from becoming law: over Money Bills or Bills affecting the duration of Parliament they have no power at all, and by the Parliament Act of 1949 any other Bill passed by the Commons in two successive sessions may be presented for Royal Assent without the consent of the Lords, provided one year has elapsed between the date of the second reading in the Commons and the date of its final passing. In practice, the House of Lords is extremely unlikely to delay matters thus far, and its main function is to scrutinize the work of the Commons, to caution and suggest. Bills of a non-controversial kind are sometimes introduced initially in the House of Lords.

## THE PRIVY COUNCIL

The power of the Privy Council has declined with the development of the Cabinet and its main function today is to give effect to decisions made elsewhere. There are at present over 300 Privy Counsellors, including Cabinet Ministers (who are automatically created Privy Counsellors) and people who have reached eminence in some branch of public affairs. Meetings are presided over by the Queen, and the responsible minister is the Lord President of the Council, an office which, since 1600, has always been held by a member of the party in power, who is usually also a leading member of the Cabinet. The Privy Council is responsible for making Orders in Council, of which there are two kinds: those made in virtue of the Royal prerogative, e.g. the ratification of treaties, and those which are authorized by Act of Parliament and are, in fact, a form of delegated legislation. It has also various advisory functions which cover such subjects as scientific, industrial, medical and agricultural research. An important organ of the Privy Council is the Judicial Committee.

## HER MAJESTY'S GOVERNMENT

The Government is headed by the Prime Minister, who is also the leader of the party which holds the majority in the House of Commons. It includes ministers who are in charge of government departments and those who hold traditional offices which involve no special departmental duties; the Chancellor of the Exchequer and the Lord Chancellor, who are specially responsible for financial and economic, and legal affairs respectively; the law officers of the Crown (the Attorney-General and Solicitor-General, the Lord Advocate for Scotland and the Solicitor-General for Scotland); the Ministers of State, who are usually appointed to assist Ministers in charge of departments; and Parliamentary Secretaries and Under-Secretaries.

The cabinet system developed during the 18th century from the informal meetings of Privy Counsellors who were also ministers, and who formed a committee of manageable size which could take decisions far more quickly and simply than larger bodies. The Cabinet today has between 15–25 members at the discretion of the Prime Minister—its main duty is to formulate policy for submission to Parliament.

The doctrine of ministerial responsibility has also evolved gradually, but was generally accepted by the middle of the last century. Each Minister must take full responsibility, particularly in Parliament, for the work of his own department; if his department fails over any important matter, he will be expected to resign. Ministers also assume collective responsibility for the work of the Government and for any advice which it may offer to the Crown.

# The Government

## HEAD OF STATE

Her Majesty Queen ELIZABETH II (ELIZABETH ALEXANDRA MARY), succeeded to the throne 6 February 1952.

## THE MINISTRY
(July 1995)

### The Cabinet

**Prime Minister, First Lord of the Treasury and Minister for the Civil Service:** JOHN MAJOR.
**First Secretary of State and Deputy Prime Minister:** MICHAEL HESELTINE.
**Lord Chancellor:** Lord MACKAY OF CLASHFERN.
**Chancellor of the Exchequer:** KENNETH CLARKE.
**Secretary of State for the Home Department:** MICHAEL HOWARD.
**Secretary of State for Foreign and Commonwealth Affairs:** MALCOLM RIFKIND.
**President of the Board of Trade (Secretary of State for Trade and Industry):** IAN LANG.
**Lord President of the Council and Leader of the House of Commons:** ANTONY NEWTON.
**Secretary of State for the Environment (Minister for London):** JOHN GUMMER.
**Secretary of State for Social Security:** PETER LILLEY.
**Chief Secretary to the Treasury:** WILLIAM WALDEGRAVE.
**Secretary of State for Northern Ireland:** Sir PATRICK MAYHEW.
**Secretary of State for National Heritage:** VIRGINIA BOTTOMLEY.
**Secretary of State for Education and Employment:** GILLIAN SHEPHARD.
**Secretary of State for Defence:** MICHAEL PORTILLO.
**Minister without portfolio:** Dr BRIAN MAWHINNEY.
**Secretary of State for Health:** STEPHEN DORRELL.
**Lord Privy Seal and Leader of the House of Lords:** Viscount CRANBORNE.
**Secretary of State for Transport:** Sir GEORGE YOUNG.
**Minister of Agriculture, Fisheries and Food:** DOUGLAS HOGG.
**Secretary of State for Scotland:** MICHAEL FORSYTH.
**Chancellor of the Duchy of Lancaster (Minister of Public Service and Science):** ROGER FREEMAN.
**Secretary of State for Wales:** WILLIAM HAGUE.

### Law Officers

**Attorney-General:** Sir NICHOLAS LYELL.
**Lord Advocate:** Lord RODGER OF EARLSFERRY.
**Solicitor-General:** Sir DEREK SPENCER.
**Solicitor-General for Scotland:** DONALD MACKAY.

### Ministers not in the Cabinet

**Parliamentary Secretary to the Treasury:** ALASTAIR GOODLAD.
**Minister for Overseas Development:** Baroness CHALKER OF WALLASEY.
**Ministers of State, Foreign and Commonwealth Office:** Sir NICHOLAS BONSOR, JEREMY HANLEY, DAVID DAVIS.
**Ministers of State, Home Office:** ANN WIDDECOMBE, DAVID MACLEAN, Baroness BLATCH.
**Financial Secretary to the Treasury:** MICHAEL JACK.
**Paymaster-General:** DAVID HEATHCOAT-AMORY.
**Ministers of State, Department of Trade and Industry:** TIMOTHY EGGAR, Lord FRASER OF CARMYLLIE, ANTHONY NELSON.
**Minister of State, Department of Transport:** JOHN WATTS.
**Ministers of State, Ministry of Defence:** NICHOLAS SOAMES, JAMES ARBUTHNOT.
**Ministers of State, Department of the Environment:** DAVID CURRY, Earl FERRERS, ROBERT JONES.
**Ministers of State, Department of Social Security:** ALISTAIR BURT, Lord MACKAY OF ARDBRECKNISH.
**Minister of State, Scottish Office:** Lord JAMES DOUGLAS-HAMILTON.
**Ministers of State, Northern Ireland Office:** MICHAEL ANCRAM, Sir JOHN WHEELER.
**Ministers of State, Department for Education and Employment:** ERIC FORTH, Lord HENLEY.
**Minister of State, Department of Health (Minister for Health):** GERALD MALONE.
**Minister of State, Ministry of Agriculture, Fisheries and Food:** ANTONY BALDRY.
**Minister of State, Department of National Heritage:** IAIN SPROAT.

### MINISTRIES

**Prime Minister's Office:** 10 Downing St, London, SW1A 2AA; tel. (171) 270-3000.
**Office of the First Secretary of State and Deputy Prime Minister:** 68–72 Whitehall, London, SW1A 2AS; tel. (171) 270-1234.
**Ministry of Agriculture, Fisheries and Food:** Whitehall Place, London, SW1A 2HH; tel. (171) 270-3000; telex 889351; fax (171) 270-8125.

UNITED KINGDOM (GREAT BRITAIN)

**Office of the Chancellor of the Duchy of Lancaster (Office of Public Service and Science):** 70 Whitehall, London SW1A 2AS; tel. (171) 270-0400; fax (171) 270-0196.

**Ministry of Defence:** Main Bldg, Whitehall, London, SW1A 2HB; tel. (171) 218-9000.

**Department for Education and Employment:** Sanctuary Bldgs, Gt Smith St, London, SW1P 3BT; tel. (171) 925-5000; fax (171) 925-6000; and Caxton House, Tothill St, London, SW1H 9NF; tel. (171) 273-3000; telex 915564; fax (171) 273-5124.

**Department of the Environment:** 2 Marsham St, London, SW1P 3EB; tel. (171) 276-3000; telex 22221; fax (171) 276-0818.

**Foreign and Commonwealth Office:** King Charles St, London, SW1A 2AL; tel. (171) 270-1500; telex 297711; fax (171) 839-2417.

**Department of Health:** Richmond House, 79 Whitehall, London, SW1A 2NS; tel. (171) 210-3000.

**Home Office:** 50 Queen Anne's Gate, London, SW1H 9AT; tel. (171) 273-4000; telex 24986; fax (171) 273-2190.

**Lord Chancellor's Department:** Trevelyan House, 30 Great Peter St, London, SW1P 2BY; tel. (171) 210-8500; fax (171) 210-8549.

**Department of National Heritage:** 2–4 Cockspur St, London SW1Y 5DH; tel. (171) 211-6000; fax (171) 211-6210.

**Northern Ireland Office:** Whitehall, London, SW1A 2AZ; tel. (171) 210-3000. (See p. 3183 for office in Belfast.)

**Scottish Office:** Dover House, London, SW1A 2AU; tel. (171) 270-3000; fax (171) 270-6730. In Scotland: St Andrew's House, Regent Rd, Edinburgh EH1 3DG; tel. (131) 556-8400.

**Department of Social Security:** Richmond House, 79 Whitehall, London, SW1A 2NS; tel. (171) 210-3000.

**Department of Trade and Industry:** 1 Victoria St, London, SW1H 0ET; tel. (171) 215-5000; telex 8813148; fax (171) 828-3258.

**Department of Transport:** 2 Marsham St, London, SW1P 3EB; tel. (171) 276-3000; telex 22221; fax (171) 276-0818.

**Treasury:** Treasury Chambers, Parliament St, London, SW1P 3AG; tel. (171) 270-3000; telex 9413704; fax (171) 270-5653.

**Welsh Office:** Gwydyr House, Whitehall, London, SW1A 2ER; tel. (171) 270-3000. In Wales: Cathays Park, Cardiff, CF1 3NQ; tel. (1222) 825111; fax (1222) 823204.

## Legislature

### PARLIAMENT

#### House of Commons

**Speaker:** BETTY BOOTHROYD.

**Chairman of Ways and Means:** MICHAEL MORRIS.

**Leader of the House:** ANTONY NEWTON.

**General Election, 9 April 1992**

|  | Votes | % | Seats |
| --- | --- | --- | --- |
| Conservative Party | 14,092,235 | 41.9 | 336 |
| Labour Party | 11,562,717 | 34.4 | 271 |
| Social and Liberal Democrats | 6,002,809 | 17.9 | 20 |
| Scottish National Party | 629,555 | 1.9 | 3 |
| Plaid Cymru (Welsh National Party) | 154,390 | 0.5 | 4 |
| Ulster Unionists | 393,393* | 1.2 | 13† |
| Social Democratic and Labour Party | 184,445 | 0.5 | 4 |
| Others | 599,737 | 1.8 | — |
| Total | 33,619,281 | 100.0 | 651 |

* Including 271,049 votes for the Ulster Unionist Party, 103,039 votes for the Democratic Unionist Party, and 19,305 votes for the Ulster Popular Unionist Party.

† Ulster Unionist Party 9 seats, Democratic Unionist Party 3 seats, Ulster Popular Unionist Party 1 seat.

#### House of Lords
(May 1995)

**Lord High Chancellor:** Lord MACKAY OF CLASHFERN.

**Lord Chairman of Committees:** Lord BOSTON OF FAVERSHAM.

**Leader of the House:** Viscount CRANBORNE.

|  | Seats |
| --- | --- |
| Peers of the Blood Royal | 4 |
| Archbishops and Bishops | 26 |
| Dukes | 25 |
| Marquesses | 35 |
| Earls, Countesses | 175 |
| Viscounts | 106 |
| Barons, Baronesses | 829 |
| **Total** | **1,200*** |

The House of Lords comprised 772 hereditary peers and 402 life peers (the remaining 26 are Archbishops and Bishops).

* Including four minors, not entitled to attend the House.

## Political Organizations

**British National Party:** POB 117, Welling, Kent, DA16 3DW; tel. and fax (181) 316-4721; f. 1982 as a breakaway faction from the National Front; Leader JOHN TYNDALL.

**Communist Party of Britain:** 3 Ardleigh Rd, London, N1 4HS; tel. (171) 275-8162; fax (171) 249-9188; f. 1920, re-established 1988; militant Marxist-Leninist; Gen.-Sec. MIKE HICKS.

**Conservative and Unionist Party:** 32 Smith Sq., London, SW1P 3HH; tel. (171) 222-9000; telex 8814536; fax (171) 222-1135; f. 1870 as Conservative Central Office; aims to uphold the Crown and the Constitution; to build a sound economy based on freedom and enterprise; to encourage personal responsibility and a wider spread of ownership of property; to look after those most in need; to ensure respect for law and order; to improve educational standards and widen parents' choice; to strengthen Britain's defences, maintain its interests and increase its influence abroad, not least through commitment to the EC; allied with members of the European People's Party Group (Christian Democrats and Allies) in the European Parliament from May 1992; c. 500,000 mems (adherent on a local, rather than national, basis); Leader JOHN MAJOR; Chair. Dr BRIAN MAWHINNEY.

**Co-operative Party:** Victory House, 10-14 Leicester Sq., London, WC2H 7QH; tel. (171) 439-0123; fax (171) 439-3434; f. 1917; linked with the Co-operative Union Ltd, but has its own Annual Conference and National Executive Committee. Under an Agreement with the Labour Party it sponsors Labour and Co-operative candidates at local, UK and European parliamentary elections; protects the interests of the co-operative movement; seeks to extend co-operative enterprise and cares for the interests of the consumer; approx. 10,000 individual mems in 61 brs; 50 societies with approx. 7.75m. mems are affiliated; Chair. P. NURSE; Sec. Dr P. CLARKE.

**Democratic Left:** Cynthia St, London, N1; tel. (171) 278-4443; fax (171) 278-4425; f. 1920; fmrly the Communist Party of Great Britain; adopted present name 1991; aims to achieve a classless society, to be attained by democratic activity reflected in elections to a House of Commons on the basis of proportional representation; c. 1,600 mems (1993); Chair. MHAIRI STEWART; Co-Chairs JIM DOXFORD, MARIAN DARKE, DAVE PARKER; Sec. NINA TEMPLE.

**Green Party:** 1a Waterloo Rd, London, N19 5NJ; tel. (171) 272-4474; fax (171) 272-6653; f. 1973 as the Ecology Party; present name adopted in 1985; concerned with the protection of the environment, equality, human rights and peace; approx. 4,600 mems; Exec. Chair. JOHN MORRISSEY.

**Labour Party:** 144–152 Walworth Rd, London, SE17 1JT; tel. (171) 701-1234; telex 8811237; fax (171) 234-3417; f. 1900; a democratic socialist party affiliated to the Socialist International and the European Socialist Party whose central ideal is the brotherhood of man; rejects discrimination on grounds of race, colour or creed, stands for the right of all peoples to freedom, independence and self-government, pledges itself to support the UN Charter and to work for world disarmament; affirms the duty of richer nations to assist poorer ones, stands for social justice and the creation of a socialist community with a classless society and planned economy; stands for democracy in industry and the expansion of common ownership, the protection of all citizens from any exercise of arbitrary power; a member of the Socialist Group in the European Parliament since 1973; supports European economic and political union; 261,233 individual mems (1993), total individual and affiliated membership 5,287,271 (1990). Relations with the Trades Union Congress (TUC) and the co-operative movement are maintained through the National Council of Labour, representing the TUC General Council, the National Executive of the Labour Party (Chair. for 1994/95 GORDON COLLIN), the Parliamentary Labour Party (Chair. DOUGLAS HOYLE) and the Co-operative Union; Leader ANTHONY BLAIR; Gen. Sec. TOM SAWYER.

UNITED KINGDOM (GREAT BRITAIN)	*Directory*

**Liberal Democrats:** 4 Cowley St, London, SW1P 3NB; tel. (171) 222-7999; fax (171) 799-2170; f. 1988 following the merger of the Liberal Party (f. 1877) and the Social Democratic Party (f. 1981, disbanded 1990); c. 100,500 mems; Leader PADDY ASHDOWN; Pres. ROBERT MACLENNAN.

**Plaid Cymru (Welsh National Party):** 51 Cathedral Rd, Cardiff, CF1 9HD; tel. (1222) 231944; f. 1925; promotes Welsh interests and seeks national status for Wales; formed a parliamentary alliance with the SNP in April 1986; 10,000 mems; Pres. DAFYDD WIGLEY; Gen. Sec. KARL DAVIES.

**Revolutionary Communist Party (RCP):** BM RCP, London, WC1N 3XX; tel. (171) 278-9908; fax (171) 278-9844; f. 1981; Contact HELEN SIMONS.

**Scottish National Party (SNP):** 6 North Charlotte St, Edinburgh, EH2 4JH; tel. (131) 226-3661; fax (131) 226-7373; f. 1934; advocates independence for Scotland as a member of the EC and Scottish control of national resources; National Convener (Leader) ALEXANDER SALMOND; Pres. WINIFRED EWING; Nat. Sec. ALASDAIR MORGAN.

**Socialist Workers' Party (SWP):** POB 82, London, E3 3LH; tel. (171) 538-5821; fax (171) 538-0018; f. 1950; advocates workers' control through revolution, not reform; c. 9,000 mems; Chair. DUNCAN HALLAS.

## Diplomatic Representation

### EMBASSIES AND HIGH COMMISSIONS IN THE UNITED KINGDOM

**Afghanistan:** 31 Prince's Gate, London, SW7 1QQ; tel. (171) 589-8891; fax (171) 581-3452; Chargé d'affaires: AHMAD WALI MASUD.

**Albania:** 6 Wilton Court, 59 Eccleston Sq, London, SW1V 1PH; tel. (171) 976-5295; fax (171) 834-2508; Ambassador: PAVLI QESKU.

**Algeria:** 54 Holland Park, London, W11 3RS; tel. (171) 221-7800; fax (171) 221-0448; Ambassador: AMAR BENDJAMA.

**Angola:** 98 Park Lane, London, W1Y 3TA; tel. (171) 495-1752; telex 8813258; fax (171) 495-1635; Ambassador: ANTÓNIO DACOSTA FERNANDES.

**Antigua and Barbuda:** 15 Thayer St, London, W1M 5LD; tel. (171) 486-7073; telex 8814503; fax (171) 486-9970; High Commr: JAMES A. E. THOMAS.

**Argentina:** 53 Hans Place, London, SW1X 0LA; tel. (171) 584-6494; fax (171) 589-3106; Ambassador: ROGELIO PFIRTER.

**Armenia:** 25A Cheniston Gardens, London, W8 6TG; tel. (171) 938-5435; fax (171) 938-2595; Ambassador: Dr ARMEN SARKISSIAN.

**Australia:** Australia House, Strand, London, WC2B 4LA; tel. (171) 379-4334; telex 27565; fax (171) 240-5333; High Commr: Dr NEAL BLEWETT.

**Austria:** 18 Belgrave Mews West, London, SW1X 8HU; tel. (171) 235-3731; telex 28327; fax (171) 235-8025; Ambassador: DR GEORG HENNIG.

**Azerbaijan:** c/o Kensington Office Centre, London House, 19 Old Court Pl., London W8 4PL; tel. (171) 938-2222; fax (171) 937-8335; Ambassador: MAHMUD MAMED-KULIYEV.

**Bahamas:** 10 Chesterfield St, London, W1X 8AH; tel. (171) 408-4488; telex 892617; fax (171) 499-9937; High Commr: ARTHUR FOULKES.

**Bahrain:** 98 Gloucester Rd, London, SW7 4AU; tel. (171) 370-5132; telex 917829; fax (171) 370-7773; Ambassador: (vacant).

**Bangladesh:** 28 Queen's Gate, London, SW7 5JA; tel. (171) 584-0081; telex 918016; fax (171) 225-2130; High Commr: Dr A. F. M. YUSUF.

**Barbados:** 1 Great Russell St, London, WC1B 3JY; tel. (171) 631-4975; telex 262081; fax (171) 323-6872; High Commr: PETER SIMMONS.

**Belarus:** 1 St Stephen's Crescent, London, W2 5QT; tel. (171) 221-3941; fax (171) 221-3946; Ambassador: ULADZIMIR SHCHASNY.

**Belgium:** 103–105 Eaton Sq, London, SW1W 9AB; tel. (171) 235-5422; telex 22823; fax (171) 259-6213; Ambassador: Jonkheer PROSPER THUYSBAERT.

**Belize:** 10 Harcourt House, 19 Cavendish Sq., London, W1M 9AD; tel. (171) 499-9728; fax (171) 491-4139; High Commr: Dr URSULA H. BARROW.

**Bolivia:** 106 Eaton Sq., London, SW1W 9AD; tel. (171) 235-4248; telex 918885; fax (171) 235-1286; Ambassador: CARLOS MORALES-LANDIVAR.

**Bosnia and Herzegovina:** 40/41 Conduit St, London, W1R 9FB; tel. (171) 734-3758; fax (171) 734-3765; Chargé d'affaires: MUGDIM PASIĆ.

**Botswana:** 6 Stratford Place, London, W1N 9AE; tel. (171) 499-0031; telex 262897; fax (171) 495-8595; High Commr: ALFRED UYAPO MAJAYE DUBE.

**Brazil:** 32 Green St, London, W1Y 4AT; tel. (171) 499-0877; telex 261157; fax (171) 493-5105; Ambassador: RUBENS ANTÔNIO BARBOSA.

**Brunei:** 20 Belgrave Sq., London, SW1X 8PG; tel. (171) 581-0521; telex 888369; fax (171) 235-9717; High Commr: Dato KASSIM DAUD.

**Bulgaria:** 186–188 Queen's Gate, London, SW7 5HL; tel. (171) 584-9400; telex 25465; fax (171) 584-4948; Ambassador: STEFAN L. TAFROV.

**Cameroon:** 84 Holland Park, London, W11 3SB; tel. (171) 727-0771; telex 25176; fax (171) 792-9353; Ambassador: SAMUEL LIBOCK MBEI.

**Canada:** Macdonald House, 1 Grosvenor Sq., London, W1X 0AB; tel. (171) 258-6600; telex 261592; fax (171) 258-6333; High Commr: ROYCE H. FRITH.

**Chile:** 12 Devonshire St, London, W1N 2DS; tel. (171) 580-6392; telex 25970; fax (171) 436-5204; Ambassador: HERNÁN ERRÁZURIZ.

**China, People's Republic:** 49–51 Portland Pl., London, W1N 4JL; tel. (171) 636-9375; Ambassador: MA YUZHEN.

**Colombia:** Flat 3A, 3 Hans Crescent, London, SW1X 0LN; tel. (171) 589-9177; fax (171) 581-1829; Ambassador: NOEMÍ SANÍN POSADA DE RUBIO.

**Costa Rica:** Flat 1, 14 Lancaster Gate, London, W2 3LH; tel. (171) 706-8844; fax (171) 706-8655; Ambassador: JORGE BORBÓN ZELLER.

**Côte d'Ivoire:** 2 Upper Belgrave St, London, SW1X 8BJ; tel. (171) 235-6991; telex 23906; fax (171) 259-5439; Ambassador: GERVAIS ATTOUNGBRÉ.

**Croatia:** c/o 5th Floor, 18–21 Jermyn St, London, SW1Y 6HP; tel. (171) 434-2946; Ambassador: Dr ANTE ČIČIN-ŠAIN.

**Cuba:** 167 High Holborn, London, WC1V 6PA; tel. (171) 240-2488; telex 261094; fax (171) 836-2602; Chargé d'affaires a.i.: LUIS QUIRANTES.

**Cyprus:** 93 Park St, London, W1Y 4ET; tel. (171) 499-8272; fax (171) 491-0691; High Commr: ANGELOS ANGELIDES.

**Czech Republic:** 26 Kensington Palace Gardens, London, W8 4QY; tel. (171) 243-1115; telex 28276; fax (171) 727-9654; Ambassador: KAREL KÜHNL.

**Denmark:** 55 Sloane St, London, SW1X 9SR; tel. (171) 333-0200; telex 28103; fax (171) 333-0270; Ambassador: RUDOLPH THORNING-PETERSEN.

**Dominica:** 1 Collingham Gardens, London, SW5 0HW; tel. (171) 370-5194; telex 8813931; fax (171) 373-8743; High Commr: ASHWORTH ELWIN.

**Ecuador:** Flat 3B, 3 Hans Crescent, Knightsbridge, London, SW1X 0LS; tel. (171) 584-1367; telex 8811087; fax (171) 823-9701; Ambassador: PATRICIO MALDONADO.

**Egypt:** 26 South St, London, W1Y 8EL; tel. (171) 499-2401; telex 23650; fax (171) 355-3568; Ambassador: MOHAMED I. SHAKER.

**El Salvador:** 5 Great James St, London, WC1N 3DA; tel. (171) 430-2141; fax (171) 430-0484; Ambassador: ERNESTO TRIGUEROS ALCAINE.

**Estonia:** 16 Hyde Park Gate, London, SW7 5DG; tel. (171) 589-3428; fax (171) 589-3430; Chargé d'affaires: PEETER KAPTEN.

**Ethiopia:** 17 Prince's Gate, London, SW7 1PZ; tel. (171) 589-7212; telex 23681; Ambassador: Dr SOLOMON GIDADA.

**Fiji:** 34 Hyde Park Gate, London, SW7 5DN; tel. (171) 584-3661; fax (171) 584-2838; Ambassador: Brig.-Gen. Ratu EPELI NAILATIKAU.

**Finland:** 38 Chesham Pl., London, SW1W 8HW; tel. (171) 838-6200; telex 24786; fax (171) 235-3680; Ambassador: LEIF BLOMQVIST.

**France:** 58 Knightsbridge, London, SW1X 7JT; tel. (171) 201-1000; telex 261905; fax (171) 259-6498; Ambassador: JEAN GUÉGUINOU.

**Gabon:** 27 Elvaston Pl., London, SW7 5NL; tel. (171) 823-9986; telex 919418; fax (171) 584-0047; Chargé d'affaires: MICHEL MADOUNGOU.

**Gambia:** 57 Kensington Court, London, W8 5DG; tel. (171) 937-6316; telex 911857; fax (171) 937-9095; High Commr: HASSAN ALIEU GIBRIL.

**Germany:** 23 Belgrave Sq., London, SW1X 8PZ; tel. (171) 235-5033; fax (171) 235-0609; Ambassador: Dr JÜRGEN OESTERHELT.

**Ghana:** 104 Highgate Hill, London, N6 5HE; tel. (181) 342-8686; telex 28827; fax (181) 342-8566; High Commr: KENNETH DADZIE.

**Greece:** 1A Holland Park, London, W11 3TP; tel. (171) 229-3850; telex 266751; fax (171) 229-7221; Ambassador: ELIAS GOUNARIS.

**Grenada:** 1 Collingham Gardens, London, SW5 0AW; tel. (171) 373-7808; fax (171) 370-7040; High Commr: MAUREEN EMMANUEL (acting).

**Guatemala:** 13 Fawcett St, London, SW10 9HN; tel. (171) 351-3042; fax (171) 376-5708; Ambassador: EDMUNDO NANNE.

**Guyana:** 3 Palace Court, Bayswater Rd, London, W2 4LP; tel. (171) 229-7684; fax (171) 727-9809; High Commr: LALESHWAR K. N. SINGH.

**Holy See:** 54 Parkside, London, SW19 5NE (Apostolic Nunciature); tel. (181) 946-1410; fax (181) 947-2494; Apostolic Nuncio: Most Rev. LUIGI BARBARITO, Titular Archbishop of Fiorentino.

# UNITED KINGDOM (GREAT BRITAIN)

**Honduras:** 115 Gloucester Place, London, W1A 3PJ; tel. (171) 486-4880; fax (171) 486-4880; Ambassador: CELIA FRANCISCA DE CABAÑAS.

**Hungary:** 35 Eaton Place, London, SW1X 8BY; tel. (171) 235-4048; fax (171) 823-1348; Ambassador: TÁDÉ ALFÖLDY.

**Iceland:** 1 Eaton Terrace, London, SW1W 8EY; tel. (171) 730-5131; telex 918226; fax (171) 730-1683; Ambassador: BENEDIKT ÁSGEIRSSON.

**India:** India House, Aldwych, London, WC2B 4NA; tel. (171) 836-8484; fax (171) 836-4331; High Commr: Dr LAXMI MALL SINGHVI.

**Indonesia:** 38 Grosvenor Sq., London, W1X 9AD; tel. (171) 499-7661; telex 28284; fax (171) 491-4993; Ambassador: JUNUS EFFENDI HABIBIE.

**Iran:** 16 Prince's Gate, London, SW7 1PT; tel. (171) 225-3000; fax (171) 589-4440; Chargé d'affaires: GHOLAMREZA ANSARI.

**Iraq:** (see Jordan).

**Ireland:** 17 Grosvenor Pl., London, SW1X 7HR; tel. (171) 235-2171; telex 916104; fax (171) 245-6961; Ambassador: JOSEPH SMALL.

**Israel:** 2 Palace Green, Kensington, London, W8 4QB; tel. (171) 957-9500; fax (171) 957-9555; Ambassador: MOSHE RAVIV.

**Italy:** 14 Three Kings Yard, Davies St, London, W1Y 2EH; tel. (171) 629-8200; telex 23520; fax (171) 629-8200; Ambassador: Dr PAOLO GALLI.

**Jamaica:** 1–2 Prince Consort Rd, London, SW7 2BZ; tel. (171) 823-9911; telex 263304; fax (171) 589-5154; High Commr: DERICK HEAVEN.

**Japan:** 101–104 Piccadilly, London, W1V 9FN; tel. (171) 465-6500; fax (171) 491-9348; Ambassador: HIROAKI FUJII.

**Jordan:** 6 Upper Phillimore Gardens, London, W8 7HB; tel. (171) 937-3685; telex 919338; fax (171) 937-8795; Ambassador: FOUAD AYOUB; Iraqi Interests Section: 21 Queen's Gate, London, SW7 5JG; tel. (171) 584-7141; fax (171) 584-7716; Head of Section: ZUHAIR M. IBRAHIM.

**Kenya:** 45 Portland Place, London, W1N 4AS; tel. (171) 636-2371; telex 262551; fax (171) 323-6717; High Commr: JOSEPH K. ARAP RUTO.

**Korea, Republic:** 4 Palace Gate, London, W8 5NF; tel. (171) 581-0247; Ambassador: ROE CHANG-HEE.

**Kuwait:** 45–46 Queen's Gate, London, SW7; tel. (171) 589-4533; telex 261017; fax (171) 589-2978; Ambassador: KHALID AL-DUWAISAN.

**Latvia:** 45 Nottingham Pl., London, W1M 3FE; tel. (171) 312-0040; fax (171) 312-0042; Ambassador: JANIS LUSIS.

**Lebanon:** 15-21 Palace Gardens Mews, London, W8 4RA; tel. (171) 229-7265; telex 262048; fax (171) 243-1699; Ambassador: MAHMOUD HAMMOUD.

**Lesotho:** 7 Chesham Place, London, SW1 8HN; tel. (171) 235-5686; telex 262955; fax (171) 235-5023; High Commr: M. K. TSEKOA.

**Liberia:** 2 Pembridge Place, London, W2 4XB; tel. (171) 221-1036; telex 915463; Chargé d'affaires: ISHMAEL GRANT.

**Libya:** (see Saudi Arabia).

**Lithuania:** 17 Essex Villas, London, W8 7BP; tel. (171) 938-2481; fax (171) 938-3329; Ambassador: RAIMUNDAS RAJECKAS.

**Luxembourg:** 27 Wilton Crescent, London, SW1X 8SD; tel. (171) 235-6961; telex 28120; fax (171) 235-9734; Ambassador: JOSEPH WEYLAND.

**Macedonia, former Yugoslav republic:** 10 Harcourt House, 19A Cavendish Sq., London, W1M 9AD; tel. (171) 499-5152; fax (171) 499-2864; Ambassador: RISTO NIKOVSKI.

**Malawi:** 33 Grosvenor St, London, W1X 0DE; tel. (171) 491-4172; telex 263308; fax (171) 491-9916; High Commr: JAKE MUWAMBA.

**Malaysia:** 45 Belgrave Sq., London, SW1X 8QT; tel. (171) 235-8033; telex 262550; fax (171) 235-5161; High Commr: Dato KAMARUDDIN ABU.

**Malta:** 16 Kensington Sq., London, W8 5HH; tel. (171) 938-1712; fax (171) 937-0979; High Commr: SALV STELLINI.

**Mauritius:** 32–33 Elvaston Place, London, SW7 5NW; tel. (171) 581-0294; fax (171) 823-8437; High Commr: BABOORAM MAHADOO.

**Mexico:** 42 Hertford St, London, W1Y 7TF; tel. (171) 499-8586; fax (171) 495-4035; Ambassador: ANDRÉS ROZENTAL.

**Mongolia:** 7 Kensington Court, London, W8 5DL; tel. (171) 937-0150; telex 28849; fax (171) 937-1117; Ambassador: (vacant).

**Morocco:** 49 Queen's Gate Gardens, London, SW7 5NE; tel. (171) 581-5001; telex 28389; fax (171) 225-3862; Ambassador: KHALIL HADDAOUI.

**Mozambique:** 21 Fitzroy Sq., London, W1P 5HJ; tel. (171) 383-3800; fax (171) 383-3801; Ambassador: Lt-Gen. ARMANDO PANGUENE.

**Myanmar:** 19A Charles St, Berkeley Sq., London, W1X 8ER; tel. (171) 629-4486; telex 267609; fax (171) 629-4169; Ambassador: U HLA MAUNG.

**Namibia:** 6 Chandos St, London, W1M 0LQ; tel. (171) 636-6244; fax (171) 637-5694; High Commr: VEICCOH K. NGHIWETE.

**Nepal:** 12A Kensington Palace Gardens, London, W8 4QU; tel. (171) 229-1594; telex 261072; fax (171) 792-9861; Ambassador: SURYA PRASAD SHRESTHA.

**Netherlands:** 38 Hyde Park Gate, London, SW7 5DP; tel. (171) 584-5040; telex 28812; fax (171) 581-3450; Ambassador: JAN HERMAN VAN ROIJEN.

**New Zealand:** New Zealand House, Haymarket, London, SW1Y 4TQ; tel. (171) 930-8422; telex 24368; fax (171) 839-4580; High Commr: JOHN COLLINGE.

**Nicaragua:** 36 Upper Brook St, London, W1Y 1PE; tel. (171) 409-2536; fax (171) 409-2593; Ambassador: VERÓNICA LACAYO DE GÓMEZ.

**Nigeria:** Nigeria House, 9 Northumberland Ave, London, WC2N 5BX; tel. (171) 839-1244; telex 916814; fax (171) 839-8746; High Commr: Alhaji ABUBAKAR ALHAJI.

**Norway:** 25 Belgrave Sq., London, SW1X 8QD; tel. (171) 235-7151; telex 22321; fax (171) 245-6993; Ambassador: TOM VRAALSEN.

**Oman:** 167 Queen's Gate, London, SW7 5HE; tel. (171) 225-0001; telex 918775; fax (171) 589-2505; Ambassador: (vacant).

**Pakistan:** 35 Lowndes Sq., London, SW1X 9JN; tel. (171) 235-2044; telex 290226; fax (171) 416-8417; High Commr: WAJID SHAMSUL HASAN.

**Panama:** 48 Park St, London, W1Y 3PD; tel. (171) 493-4646; fax (171) 493-4333; Ambassador: AQUILINO BOYD DE LA GUARDIA.

**Papua New Guinea:** 3rd Floor, 14 Waterloo Place, London, SW1Y 4AR; tel. (171) 930-0922; telex 25827; fax (171) 930-0828; High Commr: KI NOEL LEVI.

**Paraguay:** Braemar Lodge, Cornwall Gardens, London, SW7 4AQ; tel. (171) 937-1253; fax (171) 937-5687; Chargé d'affaires a.i.: IGOR PANGRAZIO.

**Peru:** 52 Sloane St, London, SW1X 9SP; tel. (171) 235-1917; fax (171) 235-4463; Chargé d'affaires a.i.: MARÍA LANDAVERI.

**Philippines:** 9A Palace Green, Kensington, London, W8 4QE; tel. (171) 937-1600; fax (171) 937-2925; Ambassador: JESUS P. TAMBUNTING.

**Poland:** 47 Portland Place, London, W1N 3AG; tel. (171) 580-4324; telex 265691; fax (171) 323-4018; Ambassador: RYSZARD STEMPLOWSKI.

**Portugal:** 11 Belgrave Sq., London, SW1X 8PP; tel. (171) 235-5331; telex 28484; fax (171) 245-1287; Ambassador: ANTÓNIO LEAL DA COSTA LOBO.

**Qatar:** 1 South Audley St, London, W1Y 5DQ; tel. (171) 493-2200; telex 28469; fax (171) 235-7584; Ambassador: ALI M. JAIDAH.

**Romania:** Arundel House, 4 Palace Green, London, W8 4QD; tel. (171) 937-9666; telex 22232; fax (171) 937-8069; Ambassador: SERGIU CELAC.

**Russia:** 13 Kensington Palace Gardens, London, W8 4QX; tel. (171) 229-3628; telex 261420; fax (171) 727-8625; Ambassador: ANATOLY L. ADAMISHIN.

**Rwanda:** 42 Aylmer Rd, London, N2; Ambassador: GIDEON KAYINAMURA.

**Saint Christopher and Nevis:** 10 Kensington Court, London, W8 5DL; tel. (171) 937-9522; telex 913047; fax (171) 937-5514; High Commr: AUBREY HART.

**Saint Lucia:** 10 Kensington Court, London, W8 5DL; tel. (171) 937-9522; telex 913047; fax (171) 937-5514; High Commr: AUBREY HART.

**Saint Vincent and the Grenadines:** 10 Kensington Court, London, W8 5DL; tel. (171) 937-9522; telex 913047; fax (171) 937-5514; High Commr: AUBREY HART.

**Saudi Arabia:** 30 Charles St., London, W1X 7PM; tel. (171) 917-3000; fax (171) 917-3330; Ambassador: GHAZI ALGOSAIBI; Libyan Interests Section: c/o 119 Harley St, London, W1; tel. (171) 486-8387.

**Senegal:** 11 Phillimore Gardens, London, W8 7QG; tel. (171) 937-0925; telex 917119; fax (171) 937-8130; Ambassador: GABRIEL ALEXANDRE SAR.

**Seychelles:** Eros House, 2nd Floor, 111 Baker St, London, W1M 1FE; tel. (171) 224-1660; High Commr: JOHN PHILIP MASCARENHAS.

**Sierra Leone:** 33 Portland Place, London, W1N 3AG; tel. (171) 636-6483; High Commr: ALHAJI HAROUN BUHARI.

**Singapore:** 9 Wilton Crescent, London, SW1X 8SA; tel. (171) 235-8315; telex 262564; fax (171) 245-6583; High Commr: ABDUL AZIZ MAHMOOD.

**Slovakia:** 25 Kensington Palace Gardens, London, W8 4QY; tel. (171) 243-0803; fax (171) 727-5824; Ambassador: JÁN VILIKOVSKÝ.

**Slovenia:** Suite One, Cavendish Court, 11–15 Wigmore St, London, W1H 9LA; tel. (171) 495-7775; fax (171) 495-7776; Ambassador: MATJAŽ ŠINKOVEC.

# UNITED KINGDOM (GREAT BRITAIN)

**South Africa:** South Africa House, Trafalgar Sq., London, WC2N 5DP; tel. (171) 930-4488; telex 8952626; fax (171) 321-0835; High Commr: MENDI MSIMANG.
**Spain:** 24 Belgrave Sq., London, SW1A 8QA; tel. (171) 235-5555; telex 21110; fax (171) 259-5392; Ambassador: ALBERTO AZA ARIAS.
**Sri Lanka:** 13 Hyde Park Gardens, London, W2 2LU; tel. (171) 262-1841; telex 25844; fax (171) 262-7970; High Commr: SARATH K. WICKREMESINGHE.
**Sudan:** 3 Cleveland Row, St James's, London, SW1A 1DD; tel. (171) 839-8080; fax (171) 839-7560; Chargé d'affaires: ABDEL RAHMAN MOHAMED BAKHEIT.
**Swaziland:** 20 Buckingham Gate, London, SW1E 6LB; tel. (171) 630-6611; telex 28853; fax (171) 630-6564; High Commr: Rev. PERCY SIPHO MNGOMEZULU.
**Sweden:** 11 Montagu Pl., London, W1H 2AL; tel. (171) 724-2101; telex 28249; fax (171) 917-6477; Ambassador: LARS-ÅKE NILSSON.
**Switzerland:** 16–18 Montagu Pl., London, W1H 2BQ; tel. (171) 723-0701; telex 28212; fax (171) 724-7001; Ambassador: FRANÇOIS NORDMANN.
**Syria:** 8 Belgrave Sq., London, SW1X 8PH; tel. (171) 245-9012; fax (171) 235-4621; Ambassador: MOHAMMAD KHODOR.
**Tanzania:** 43 Hertford St, London, W1Y 8DB; tel. (171) 499-8951; telex 262504; fax (171) 491-9321; High Commr: Col ALI S. MCHUMO.
**Thailand:** 29–30 Queen's Gate, London, SW7 5JB; tel. (171) 589-2944; fax (171) 823-9695; Ambassador: VIDHYA RAYANANONDA.
**Tonga:** 36 Molyneaux St, London, W1H 6AB; tel. (171) 724-5828; High Commr: SIONE KITÉ.
**Trinidad and Tobago:** 42 Belgrave Sq., London, SW1X 8NT; tel. (171) 245-9351; telex 918910; fax (171) 823-1065; High Commr: RABINDRANATH PERMANAND.
**Tunisia:** 29 Prince's Gate, London, SW7 1QG; tel. (171) 584-8117; telex 23736; fax (171) 225-2884; Ambassador: MOHAMED LESSIR.
**Turkey:** 43 Belgrave Sq., London, SW1X 8PA; tel. (171) 393-0202; telex 884236; fax (171) 396-6666; Ambassador: ÖZDEM SANBACK.
**Uganda:** Uganda House, 58–59 Trafalgar Sq., London, WC2N 5DX; tel. (171) 839-5783; telex 915141; fax (171) 839-8925; High Commr: Prof. GEORGE KIRYA.
**Ukraine:** 78 Kensington Park Rd, London, W11 2PL; tel. (171) 727-6312; fax (171) 792-1708; Ambassador: Prof. SERGUI KOMISARENKO.
**United Arab Emirates:** 30 Prince's Gate, London, SW7 1PT; tel. (171) 581-1281; telex 918459; fax (171) 581-9616; Ambassador: EASA SALEH AL-GURG.
**USA:** 24–32 Grosvenor Sq., London, W1A 1AE; tel. (171) 499-9000; fax (171) 629-9124; Ambassador: Adm. WILLIAM J. CROWE, Jr.
**Uruguay:** 2nd Floor, 140 Brompton Rd, London, SW3 1HY; tel. (171) 584-8192; telex 264180; fax (171) 581-9585; Ambassador: JUAN ENRIQUE FISCHER.
**Uzbekistan:** 72 Wigmore St, London, W1H 9DL; tel. (171) 935-1899; fax (171) 935-9554; Chargé d'affaires: TIMUR SHARIFOVICH SAIDOV.
**Venezuela:** 1 Cromwell Rd, London, SW7 2HR; tel. (171) 584-4206; telex 264186; fax (171) 589-8887; Ambassador: Dr IGNACIO ARCAYA.
**Viet Nam:** 12–14 Victoria Rd, London, W8 5RD; tel. (171) 937-1912; telex 887361; fax (171) 937-6108; Ambassador: HUYNH NGOC AN.
**Yemen:** 57 Cromwell Rd, London, SW7 2ED; tel. (171) 584-6607; Ambassador: Dr HUSSEIN ABDULLAH AL-AMRI.
**Yugoslavia:** 5 Lexham Gardens, London, W8 5JJ; tel. (171) 370-6105; telex 928542; fax (171) 370-3838; Chargé d'affaires: RAJKO BOGOJEVIĆ.
**Zaire:** 26 Chesham Place, London, SW1X 8HH; tel. (171) 235-6137; telex 25651; fax (171) 235-9048; Chargé d'affaires: NSANGOLO IWULA.
**Zambia:** 2 Palace Gate, London, W8 5NG; tel. (171) 589-6655; telex 263544; fax (171) 581-1353; High Commr: LOVE MTESA.
**Zimbabwe:** Zimbabwe House, 429 Strand, London, WC2R 0SA; tel. (171) 836-7755; telex 262014; fax (171) 379-1167; High Commr: Dr NGONI TOGAREPI CHIDEYA.

## Judicial System

There are, historically, three sources of the law as administered in the law courts today: Statute Law, which is written law and consists mainly of Acts of Parliament, Common Law, which originated in ancient usage and has not been formally enacted, and Equity, which was the system evolved by the Lord Chancellor's court (Court of Chancery) to mitigate the strictness of some of the common law rules. The law of the European Community has now been added to these.

Scottish common and statute law differ in some respects from that current in the rest of the United Kingdom, owing to Scotland's retention of her own legal system under the Act of Union with England of 1707.

Three factors help to ensure a fair trial: the independence of judges, who, in the case of High Court Judges, are outside the control of the executive and can be removed from office only after an address from Parliament to the Sovereign (Circuit Judges can be removed by the Lord Chancellor); the participation of private citizens in all important criminal and some civil cases, in the form of a summoned jury of 12 persons, who judge, if necessary by a majority, the facts of a case, questions of law being decided by the judge; and the system of appeals to a higher court, including the Criminal and Civil Divisions of the Court of Appeal, and, thereafter, the House of Lords.

The Courts and Legal Services Act 1990 provided for radical change in the legal profession, including legislation permitting solicitors to appear in higher courts, and extensive reform of the civil courts, whereby the civil cases formerly heard in the High Court, could be transferred to the county courts.

### MAGISTRATES' COURTS OR PETTY SESSIONS

The criminal courts of lowest jurisdiction are presided over by Justices of the Peace, who are unpaid lay people appointed by the Lord Chancellor. They have power to try all non-indictable offences, and some of the less serious indictable offences, if the defendant agrees. The trial of nearly all criminal offences begins in the magistrates' court. Approximately 95% of all criminal offences are dealt with solely by magistrates' courts. In the vast majority of committals for trial in the Crown Court magistrates are not required to consider evidence.

In London and in certain other large towns there are a small number of professional salaried magistrates, known as metropolitan stipendiary magistrates in London and as stipendiary magistrates in the provinces, who sit alone, whereas lay justices normally sit in threes when acting judicially.

Youth Courts, composed of specially trained justices selected by the justices of each petty sessional division (in London, by the Lord Chancellor), have power to try most charges against children under 18 years. The general public is excluded and there are restrictions on newspaper reports of the proceedings.

Magistrates also have power to grant, renew, transfer or remove or order the forfeiture of licences for the sale of alcoholic drinks, and to control the structural design of premises where alcohol is sold for consumption on the premises. They also control the licensing of betting shops, and grant bookmakers' permits.

### COUNTY COURTS

A high proportion of civil actions are tried in these courts, which are presided over by a circuit judge, or, in some cases, a district judge, sitting alone. From 1 July 1991 county courts were granted unlimited jurisdiction.

### THE CROWN COURT

The Crown Court came into being on 1 January 1972, under the Courts Act 1971, replacing Quarter Sessions and Assizes, to deal with serious criminal cases where trial by jury is required. The Crown Court sits at various centres throughout England and Wales. Court centres have been administratively divided into three tiers. The most serious offences are tried at first and second tier centres presided over by High Court Judges, Circuit Judges or Recorders. Circuit Judges or Recorders preside over third tier centres, where the less serious offences are tried. The Crown Court for the City of London is the Central Criminal Court (the Old Bailey).

### HIGH COURT OF JUSTICE

Certain civil cases are heard in the three divisions of this court—Chancery, Queen's Bench and Family. The Chancery Division deals with litigation about property, patents, family trusts, companies, dissolution of partnerships and disputed estates. The Queen's Bench Division hears cases involving damage to property, personal injuries, etc. and also includes the Commercial and Admiralty Courts. The Family Division hears contested or complex divorce and separation cases and matters relating to children such as adoption, wardship or guardianship of minors.

#### Chancery Division

**President:** Lord MACKAY OF CLASHFERN (Lord High Chancellor).
**Judges:** Sir RICHARD RASHLEIGH FOLLIOTT SCOTT (Vice-Chancellor), Sir JEREMIAH LEROY HARMAN, Sir JOHN LEONARD KNOX, Sir DONALD KEITH RATTEE, Sir JOHN FRANK MUMMERY, Sir FRANCIS MURSELL FERRIS, Sir JOHN MURRAY CHADWICK, Sir JONATHAN FREDERIC PARKER, Sir JOHN EDMUND FREDERIC LINDSAY, Dame MARY HOWARTH ARDEN, Sir EDWARD CHRISTOPHER EVANS-LOMBE, Sir ROBERT (ROBIN) RAPHAEL HAYIM JACOB, Sir WILLIAM

# UNITED KINGDOM (GREAT BRITAIN)

Anthony Blackburne, Sir Gavin Anthony Lightman, Sir Robert Walker, Sir Robert John Anderson Carnwath, Sir Hugh Ian Lang Laddie.

### Queen's Bench Division
**Lord Chief Justice of England:** Lord Taylor of Gosforth (President).

**Judges:** Sir Ronald G. Waterhouse, Sir F. Maurice Drake, Sir Christopher J. S. French, Sir I. Charles R. McCullough, Sir Oliver B. Popplewell, Sir William A. Macpherson of Cluny, Sir Richard Howard Tucker, Sir Robert A. Gatehouse, Sir Patrick Neville Garland, Sir Michael John Turner, Sir John Downes Alliott, Sir Harry H. Ognall, Sir John A. D. Owen, Sir F. Humphrey Potts, Sir Richard G. Rougier, Sir Ian A. Kennedy, Sir Nicholas A. Phillips, Sir Stuart N. McKinnon, Sir Mark Howard Potter, Sir Henry Brooke, Sir T. Scott Baker, Sir Igor Judge, Sir Edwin Frank Jowitt, Sir Michael Morland, Sir G. Mark Waller, Sir Rodger John Buckley, Sir Anthony Brian Hidden, Sir John Michael Wright, Sir Charles B. K. Mantell, Sir John C. C. Blofeld, Sir Peter J. Cresswell, Sir Anthony T. K. May, Sir John G. M. Laws, Dame Ann Marian Ebsworth, Sir Simon L. Tuckey, Sir David N. R. Latham, Sir Christopher J. Holland, Sir John W. Kay, Sir Richard H. Curtis, Sir Stephen J. Sedley, Dame Janet H. Smith, Sir Anthony D. Colman, Sir Anthony P. Clarke, Sir John A. Dyson, Sir John Thayne Forbes, Sir Michael Alexander Geddes Sachs, Sir Stephen George Mitchell, Sir Rodger Bell, Sir Michael Guy Vicat Harrison, Sir Bernard Anthony Rix, Dame Anne Heather Steel, Sir William Marcus Gage, Sir Jonathan Hugh Mance, Sir Andrew Centlivres Longmore, Sir Thomas Richard Atkin Morison, Sir Richard Joseph Buxton, Sir David Wolfe Keene, Sir Andrew David Collins, Sir Maurice Ralph Kay, Sir (Frank) Brian Smedley, Sir Anthony Hooper, Sir Alexander Neil Logie Butterfield, Sir George Michael Newman.

### Family Division
**President:** Sir Stephen Brown.

**Judges:** Sir Edward James Holman, Sir Anthony B. Hollis, Sir Matthew Alexander Thorpe, Sir Edward Stephen Cazalet, Sir Robert Lionel Johnson, Sir Douglas Dunlop Brown, Dame Joyanne W. Bracewell, Sir Michael Bryan Connell, Sir Jan. P. Singer, Sir Nicholas A. R. Wilson, Sir Nicholas Peter Rathbone Wall, Sir Andrew T. H. Kirkwood, Sir Christopher Stuart Stuart-White, Dame Brenda Marjorie Hale, Sir Hugh Peter Derwyn Bennett, Sir (Edward) James Holman.

## COURT OF APPEAL
An appeal lies in civil cases to this court from County Courts and the High Court of Justice and in criminal cases from the Crown Courts. The Master of the Rolls is the effective head of the court.

### Ex-Officio Judges
**Lord High Chancellor:** Lord Mackay of Clashfern (President).
**Lord Chief Justice of England:** Lord Taylor of Gosforth.
**Master of the Rolls:** Sir Thomas Bingham.
**President of the Family Division:** Sir Stephen Brown.
**Vice-Chancellor:** Sir Richard Scott.

**Lords Justices of Appeal:** Sir Brian T. Neill, Sir Martin C. Nourse, Sir Iain D. L. Glidewell, Sir A. John Balcombe, Sir T. Patrick Russell, Dame Ann Elizabeth O. Butler-Sloss, Sir Murray Stuart-Smith, Sir Christopher S. T. J. T. Staughton, Sir Anthony J. D. McCowan, Sir A. Roy A. Beldam, Sir Andrew Leggatt, Sir Paul J. M. Kennedy, Sir David Hirst, Sir Simon Brown, Sir Anthony Evans, Sir Christopher Rose, Sir John Waite, Sir John Roch, Sir Peter Gibson, Sir John Stewart Hobhouse, Sir Denis Robert Maurice Henry, Sir Mark Oliver Saville, Sir Peter Julian Millett, Sir Swinton Barclays Thomas, Sir (Robert) Andrew Morritt, Sir Philip Howard Otton, Sir Robin Ernest Auld, Sir Malcolm Thomas Pill, Sir William Aldous, Sir Alan Hylton Ward, Sir Michael Hutchison, Sir Konrad Schiemann.

## HOUSE OF LORDS
In civil and criminal cases this is the final court of appeal.
**Lord High Chancellor:** Lord Mackay of Clashfern.

**Lords of Appeal in Ordinary:** Lord Keith of Kinkel, Lord Goff of Chieveley, Lord Jauncey of Tullichettle, Lord Browne-Wilkinson, Lord Mustill, Lord Slynn of Hadley, Lord Woolf, Lord Lloyd of Berwick, Lord Nolan, Lord Nicholls of Birkenhead, Lord Steyn, Lord Hoffmann.

## JUDICIAL COMMITTEE OF THE PRIVY COUNCIL
Final court of appeal for appeals from certain Commonwealth territories; also exercises domestic jurisdiction in ecclesiastical matters and appeals from disciplinary tribunals of certain professions.

# Scottish Judicial System

## CRIMINAL COURTS
Minor offences are dealt with in District courts.

### Sheriff Court
Most criminal actions, including all but the most serious offences, are tried in this court. Each of the six sheriffdoms of Scotland has a Sheriff Principal and a number of Sheriffs, who hear the cases.

### High Court of Justiciary
This is the supreme criminal court in Scotland: all the most serious cases are taken there. Appeal may be made to it from the Sheriff Court and from the District courts; there is, however, no further appeal to the House of Lords.

The 26 judges of this court are known as Lords Commissioners of Justiciary and are headed by the Lord Justice General and the Lord Justice Clerk. Apart from their criminal jurisdiction in this court, these judges are also judges of the Court of Session (see below) in civil cases. The Lord Justice General is also the President of the Court of Session.

## CIVIL COURTS
### Sheriff Court
This court hears civil as well as criminal cases, and in civil cases its jurisdiction is practically unlimited. It has concurrent jurisdiction with the Court of Session in divorce actions. Appeal may be made to the Court of Session or the Sheriff Principal.

### Court of Session
This is the supreme civil court in Scotland. It has an Inner House and an Outer House.

The Inner House has two divisions of equal standing, each consisting of four judges under the presidency of the Lord President and the Lord Justice Clerk respectively; it is mainly an appeal court, whence further appeal may be made to the House of Lords.

#### First Division
**Lord Justice General and President of the Court of Session:** Lord Hope of Craighead.
**Judges:** Lord Allanbridge, Lord Mayfield.

#### Second Division
**Lord Justice Clerk:** Lord Ross.
**Judges:** Lord Murray, Lord Davidson, Lord McCluskey, Lord Morison.

The Outer House deals with the major civil cases and divorce actions. The judges are those of the High Court of Justiciary, sitting in a civil capacity as judges of the Court of Session.

**Judges:** Lord Davidson*, Lord Sutherland, Lord Weir, Lord Clyde, Lord Cullen, Lord Prosser, Lord Kirkwood, Lord Coulsfield, Lord Milligan, Lord Caplan, Lord Cameron of Llochbroom, Lord Marnoch, Lord MacLean, Lord Penrose, Lord Osborne, Lord Abernethy Lord Johnston, Lord Gill.

* Chair. Scottish Law Commission.

# Religion

## CHRISTIANITY
**Council of Churches for Britain and Ireland:** Inter-Church House, 35–41 Lower Marsh, London SE1 7RL; tel. (171) 620-4444; fax (171) 928-0010; f. 1990, as successor to the British Council of Churches; co-ordinates the activities of member churches and organizations through four main church groupings; Pres Rev. Hugh Davidson, Myriel Davies, Most Rev. Dr John S. Habgood (life peer), Gillian Kingston, Rev. Io Smith, Cardinal Thomas Winning; Gen. Sec. Rev. John Reardon.

**Action of Churches Together in Scotland (ACTS):** Scottish Churches' House, Dunblane, Perthshire, FK15 0AJ; tel. (1786) 823588; fax (1786) 825844; aims to encourage and express unity of Christian Churches in Scotland; 14 mem. bodies; Chair. Very Rev. Prof. Robert Davidson; Gen. Sec. Rev. Maxwell Craig.

**The Irish Council of Churches:** Inter-Church Centre, 48 Elmwood Ave, Belfast, BT9 6AZ; tel. (1232) 663145; fax (1232) 381737; 8 mem. bodies; Pres. Rt Rev. J. H. Cooper; Gen. Sec. Dr David Stevens.

**Churches Together in England (CTE):** Inter-Church House, 35–41 Lower Marsh, London, SE1 7RL; tel. (171) 620-4444; fax (171) 928-5771; 22 mem. bodies; Pres. Most Rev. and Rt Hon. Dr George Carey, Rev. Kathleen Richardson, Cardinal Basil Hume, Rt Rev. Basil of Sergievo; Gen. Sec. Canon Martin Reardon.

# UNITED KINGDOM (GREAT BRITAIN)

**Churches Together in Wales (CYTUN):** fmrly the Council of Churches for Wales; 11 mem. bodies; Pres. Rev. DERWYN MORRIS JONES; Gen. Sec. Rev. NOEL A. DAVIES, 21 St Helen's Rd, Swansea, SA1 4AP; tel. (1792) 460876.

## The Anglican Communion

**The Church of England:** The Church of England is the Established Church, and as such acknowledges the authority of Parliament in matters in which secular authority is competent to exercise control. Queen Elizabeth I was declared 'supreme Governor on Earth' of the Church of England, and the Sovereign is consecrated to this office at coronation.

In England, there are two Provinces, Canterbury and York. The former contains 30, the latter 14, dioceses. Each Province has its ancient Convocations, the Upper and Lower House. By the Enabling Act the Constitution of the National Assembly of the Church of England ('Church Assembly') received statutory recognition in 1920, with power, subject to the control and authority of Parliament, of initiating legislation on all matters concerning the Church of England. Measures passed by the Assembly and approved by Parliament were submitted for the Royal Assent, having the force of Acts of Parliament.

In 1970, by the Synodical Government Measure (1969), the Church Assembly was reconstituted as the General Synod and was also given authority to exercise most of the functions of the Convocations. The House of Bishops consists of members of the Upper House of the Convocations (53 persons). The House of Clergy consists of the Lower Houses (a maximum of 259 persons). The House of Laity consists almost entirely of representatives of the dioceses elected by the deanery synods (a maximum of 258 persons).

In 1994 there were 1,485,513 people on the Church's electoral rolls.

The Archbishops and the 24 senior Bishops sit in the House of Lords.

**Archbishop of Canterbury, Primate of All England and Metropolitan:** Most Rev. GEORGE L. CAREY, Lambeth Palace, London, SE1 7JU; tel. (171) 928-8282; telex 915365; fax (171) 261-9836.

**Archbishop of York, Primate of England and Metropolitan:** Most Rev. Dr JOHN S. HABGOOD (life peer), (from August 1995) Dr DAVID M. HOPE, Bishopthorpe Palace, Bishopthorpe, York, YO2 1QE; tel. (1904) 707021; fax (1904) 709204.

**General Synod of the Church of England:** Church House, Great Smith St, London, SW1P 3NZ; tel. (171) 222-9011; fax (171) 799-2714; Sec.-Gen. PHILIP MAWER.

**The Church in Wales:** 39 Cathedral Rd, Cardiff, CF1 9XF; tel. (1222) 231638; fax (1222) 387835; the Province of Wales was created as a result of the Welsh Church Act of 1914, which took effect on 31 March 1920 and separated the four Welsh Dioceses from the Province of Canterbury. It is divided into six Dioceses served by 700 stipendiary clerics. The number of Easter communicants is approximately 100,000. The Church in Wales has an administrative governing body which is a legislative assembly composed of bishops, clergy and laity, and a representative body incorporated by Royal Charter, which holds and manages the property and central funds of the Church. Sec.-Gen. J. W. D. MCINTYRE; Clerical Sec. of the Governing Body Very Rev. D. G. LEWIS.

**Archbishop of Wales:** Most Rev. ALWYN RICE-JONES, Esgobty, St Asaph, Clwyd.

**The Scottish Episcopal Church:** 21 Grosvenor Cres., Edinburgh, EH12 5EE; tel. (131) 225-6357; fax (131) 346-7247; formerly the Established Church of Scotland, was disestablished and disendowed in 1689; is in full communion with all branches of the Anglican Communion; seven dioceses: Aberdeen and Orkney, Argyll and The Isles, Brechin, Edinburgh, Glasgow and Galloway, Moray, Ross and Caithness, and St Andrews, Dunkeld and Dunblane. There is a Bishop in each diocese; one of them is elected by the other Bishops as The Primus; Churches, mission stations, etc. 316, clergy 341, communicants 34,266; Sec.-Gen. to the General Synod JOHN SIMPSON.

**The Primus:** Most Rev. RICHARD HOLLOWAY (Bishop of Edinburgh), Diocesan Centre, Walpole House, Chester St, Edinburgh, EH3 7EN; tel. (131) 226-3359.

## The Roman Catholic Church

For ecclesiastical purposes Great Britain comprises seven archdioceses and 22 dioceses. At 31 December 1993 there were an estimated 4,164,796 adherents in England and Wales.

**Archbishop of Westminster:** HE Cardinal GEORGE BASIL HUME, Archbishop's House, Ambrosden Avenue, Westminster, London, SW1P 1QJ; tel. (171) 798-9033.

**Archbishop of Birmingham:** Most Rev. MAURICE COUVE DE MURVILLE, 8 Shadwell St, Birmingham, B4 6EY; tel. (121) 236-9090; fax (121) 212-0171.

**Archbishop of Liverpool:** Most Rev. DEREK WORLOCK, Archbishop's House, 87 Green Lane, Mossley Hill, Liverpool, L18 2EP; tel. (151) 722-2379.

**Archbishop of Southwark:** Most Rev. MICHAEL BOWEN, Archbishop's House, 150 St George's Rd, Southwark, London, SE1 6HX; tel. (171) 928-2495; fax (171) 928-7833.

**Archbishop of Cardiff:** Most Rev. JOHN A. WARD, Archbishop's House, 41–43 Cathedral Rd, Cardiff, South Glamorgan, CF1 9HD; tel. (1222) 220411; fax (1222) 345950.

At 31 December 1993 there were an estimated 766,451 adherents in Scotland.

**Archbishop of St Andrews and Edinburgh:** Most Rev. KEITH O'BRIEN, 106 White House Loan, Edinburgh, EH9 1BD; tel. (131) 452-8244; fax (131) 452-9153.

**Archbishop of Glasgow:** HE Cardinal THOMAS WINNING, Curial Offices, 196 Clyde St, Glasgow, G1 4JY; tel. (141) 226-5898; fax (141) 221-1962.

### Protestant Churches

**Free Church Federal Council:** 27 Tavistock Sq., London, WC1H 9HH; tel. (171) 387-8413; fax (171) 387-0150; central Council for the co-ordination of the work of the Free Churches throughout England and Wales; Moderator (1995–99) Rev. KATHLEEN M. RICHARDSON; Gen. Sec. Rev. DAVID STAPLE, (from April 1996) Rev. GEOFFREY H. ROPER.

**Baptist Union of Great Britain:** Baptist House, POB 44, 129 Broadway, Didcot, Oxfordshire, OX11 8RT; tel. (1235) 512077; fax (1235) 811537; f. 1813; the Baptist form of church government is congregational. Baptism by immersion of believers is practised. The Churches are grouped in associations, the majority of which belong to the Union; mems in British Isles (1994) 156,939; Pres. (1995/96) Rev. P. TONGEMON; Sec. Rev. D. R. COFFEY.

**The Church of Scotland:** 121 George St, Edinburgh, EH2 4YN; tel. (131) 225-5722; The National Church of Scotland was reformed in 1560, and became Presbyterian in doctrine and constitution. In 1921 'The Church of Scotland Act' was passed, by which the articles declaring the full spiritual freedom of the Church are recognized as lawful. In 1925 'The Church of Scotland (Property and Endowments) Act' became law, and made over to the Church of Scotland places of worship, manses and endowments in absolute property, vesting the future control of them in Trustees. The union of the Church of Scotland and the United Free Church was effected in 1929; Moderator of the General Assembly Rev. JAMES HARKNESS; Lord High Commr to the 1994 General Assembly Lady (MARION) FRASER; 838,659 mems (1988).

**Elim Pentecostal Church:** PO Box 38, Cheltenham, Glos., GL50 3HN; tel. (1242) 519904; fax (1242) 222279; f. 1915; c. 430 churches and 35,000 adherents in Great Britain; Gen. Superintendent Pastor I. W. LEWIS.

**The Free Church of Scotland:** The Mound, Edinburgh, EH1 2LS; tel. (131) 226-5286; fax (131) 220-0597; f. 1843; 180 congregations; Principal Clerk of Assembly Rev. Prof. JOHN L. MACKAY.

**Lutheran Church of Great Britain:** Lutheran Church House, 8 Collingham Gdns, London, SW5; tel. and fax (171) 373-1141; Chair. Very Rev. ROBERT PATKAI.

**The Methodist Church:** 1 Central Bldgs, Westminster, London, SW1H 9NH; tel. (171) 222-8010; fax (171) 233-1295; f. 1739 by Rev. John Wesley, a priest of the Church of England; the chief court of the Church is the Annual Conference, which consists of ministers and lay representatives. The Church throughout Great Britain is divided into 33 Districts, and these hold their Synod Meetings in the autumn and the spring. The Districts are divided into Circuits, which hold a Circuit Meeting twice a year, made up of representatives from the churches within the Circuit. There are also local church courts; 408,107 mems (1992); Pres. of the Methodist Conference (1995/96) Rev. BRIAN HOARE; Sec. of the Methodist Conference Rev. BRIAN E. BECK.

**Moravian Church:** 5 Muswell Hill, London, N16 3TJ; tel. (181) 883-3409; fax (181) 442-0112; Sec. Provincial Board Rev. M. J. MCOWAT.

**Presbyterian Church of Wales:** 53 Richmond Rd, Cardiff, CF2 3UP; tel. (1222) 494913; fax (1222) 464293; f. 1811; 971 churches, 117 full-time ministers; 56,500 mems (1994); Moderator of General Assembly Rev. IEUAN LLOYD; Gen. Sec. Rev. DAFYDD OWEN.

**The Religious Society of Friends (Quakers):** Friends House, Euston Rd, London, NW1 2BJ; tel. (171) 387-3601; fax (171) 388-1977; f. by George Fox, about the middle of the 17th century; the Quakers have 18,000 mems and 14,000 'attenders' in Great Britain; Recording Clerk (Sec.) DONALD H. D. SOUTHALL.

**Salvation Army:** PO Box 249, 101 Queen Victoria St, London, EC4P 4EP tel. (171) 236-5222; f. 1865; International Leader Gen. PAUL A. RADER.

**Scottish Congregational Church:** POB 189, Glasgow, G1 2BX; tel. (141) 332-7667; fax (141) 332-8463; Sec. Rev. ROBERT WATERS.

**Union of Welsh Independents;** 11 Heol Sant Helen, Swansea, West Glamorgan, SA1 4AL; tel. (1792) 652542; fax (1792) 650647; Sec. Rev. DERWYN JONES.

**The United Free Church of Scotland:** 11 Newton Place, Glasgow, G3 7PR; tel. (141) 332-3435; f. 1900; 72 congregations, 66 ministers and missionaries, 6,901 mems; Moderator of the General Assembly (1995) Rev. J. CREELMAN; Gen. Sec. Rev. J. O. FULTON.

**United Reformed Church:** 86 Tavistock Place, London, WC1H 9RT; tel. (171) 916-2020; fax (171) 916-2021; f. 1972 by union of the Congregational Church in England and Wales and the Presbyterian Church of England; joined by the Churches of Christ 1981; approx. 1,800 churches and 112,000 mems; Moderator Rev. JOHN P. REARDON; Gen. Sec. Rev. ANTHONY BURNHAM.

### Orthodox Churches

**Council of the Oriental Orthodox Churches:** The Armenian Vicarage, Iverna Gdns, London, W8 6BR; tel. (171) 937-0152; Sec. Rt Rev. YEGISHE GIZIRIAN.

**Greek Orthodox Church:** Thyateira House, 5 Craven Hill, London, W2 3EN; tel. (171) 723-4787; fax (171) 224-9301; Archbishop of Thyateira and Great Britain GREGORIOS.

**Russian Orthodox Patriarchal Church in Great Britain:** All Saints' Church, Ennismore Gdns, London, SW7 1NH; tel. (171) 584-0096; Archbishop ANTHONY OF SOUROZH.

### Other Christian Churches

**The Church of Christ, Scientist:** Christian Science Committee on Publication, 2 Elysium Gate, 126 New Kings Rd, London, SW6 4LZ; tel. (171) 371-0600; fax (171) 371-9204; f. 1879; The Mother Church, The First Church of Christ, Scientist, in Boston, Mass (USA); approx. 200 churches in Great Britain; District Man. for Great Britain and Ireland ALAN GRAYSON.

**Church of Jesus Christ of Latter-day Saints (Mormon):** Press Office, 751 Warwick Rd, Solihull, West Midlands, B91 3DQ; tel. (121) 711-2244; fax (121) 709-0180; f. 1830; c. 165,000 mems (1994); Area Pres. KENNETH JOHNSON.

**Jehovah's Witnesses:** Watch Tower House, The Ridgeway, London, NW7 1RN; tel. (181) 906-2211; fax (181) 906-3938; there were an estimated 120,000 Jehovah's Witnesses in the UK in 1990.

**Seventh-day Adventist Church:** Stanborough Park, Watford, Herts, WD2 6JP; tel. (1923) 672251; fax (1923) 893212; Sec. M. L. ANTHONY.

**The Spiritualists' National Union:** Redwoods, Stansted Hall, Stansted Mountfitchet, Essex, CM24 8UD; tel. (1279) 816363; fax (1279) 812034; f. in 1891 (and incorporated 1901) for the advancement of Spiritualism as a religion and a religious philosophy, it is a trust corporation officially recognized as the central and national body representing the Spiritualists of Great Britain; conducts the Arthur Findlay College of Psychic Science; 400 Spiritualist churches, societies and 20,000 individual mems; Pres. E. L. HATTON, 6 Broughton Rd, Wollescote, Stourbridge, DY9 0XP; Gen. Sec. C. S. COULSTON.

**Unitarian and Free Christian Churches:** Essex Hall, 1-6 Essex St, London, WC2R 3HY; tel. (171) 240-2384; fax (171) 240-3089; Gen. Sec. JEFFREY J. TEAGLE.

### ISLAM

The Muslim community in the United Kingdom, which is estimated to number over 1.5m., consists mainly of people from the Indian sub-continent and their British-born descendants. The chief concentrations of Muslims are in London, the Midlands, South Wales, Lancashire and Yorkshire. There are more than 314 mosques in the United Kingdom; the oldest is the Shah Jehan Mosque in Woking, Surrey.

**London Central Mosque Trust and Islamic Cultural Centre:** 146 Park Rd, London, NW8 7RG; tel. (171) 724-3363; Dir-Gen. Dr A. A. MUGHRAM AL-GHAMDI.

### SIKHISM

There are an estimated 400,000 Sikhs in the United Kingdom, who originally came from the Punjab region of the Indian sub-continent, although many are now British-born. Each gurdwara (temple) is independent, and there is no central national body.

**Sikh Missionary Society:** 10 Featherstone Rd, Southall, Middx, UB2 5AA; tel. (181) 574-1902; promotes Sikhism and provides information and free literature; Hon. Gen. Sec. TEJA SINGH.

### HINDUISM

There are an estimated 350,000 Hindus in the United Kingdom, with their own origins in India, East Africa and Sri Lanka, although many are now British by birth. Hindus in the United Kingdom are concentrated in London, the Midlands and Yorkshire.

### JUDAISM

The Jewish community in the United Kingdom is estimated to number 300,000.

**Chief Rabbi of the United Hebrew Congregations of the Commonwealth:** Rabbi Dr JONATHAN SACKS, Adler House, Tavistock Sq., London, WC1H 9HN; tel. (171) 387-1066; fax (171) 383-4920.

**Court of the Chief Rabbi (Beth Din):** Adler House, Tavistock Sq., London, WC1H 9HP; tel. (171) 387-5772; fax (171) 388-6666; Registrar Dr JEREMY PHILLIPS.

There is no comprehensive organization of synagogues covering the country as a whole. In London there are the following major synagogue organizations:

**Council of Reform and Liberal Rabbis:** Sternberg Centre for Judaism, 80 East End Rd, London, N3 2SY; tel. (181) 349-4731; f. 1968; its Chairman is elected every two years to represent and speak for Progressive Jewry, which does not recognize the authority of the Chief Rabbi of the United Hebrew Congregations; about 60 rabbis serving about 60 congregations in Great Britain and Ireland; Chair. Rabbi JACQUELINE TABICK.

**Federation of Synagogues:** 65 Watford Way, London, NW4 3AQ; tel. (181) 202-2263; fax (181) 203-0610; f. 1887; 30 constituent and affiliated synagogues with a total membership of about 12,000 families; Pres. A. J. COHEN.

**Spanish and Portuguese Jews' Congregation:** 2–4 Ashworth Rd, London, W9 1JY; tel. (171) 289-2573; fax (171) 289-2709; f. 1657; Pres. of the Bd of Elders E. J. N. NABARRO; Sec. Jo VELLEMAN.

**Union of Liberal and Progressive Synagogues:** The Montagu Centre, 21 Maple St, London, W1P 6DS; tel. (171) 580-1663; fax (171) 436-4184; f. 1902; 11,000 mems, 29 affiliated synagogues, 2 assoc. communities.

**Union of Orthodox Hebrew Congregations:** 40 Queen Elizabeth's Walk, London, N16 0HH; tel. (181) 802-6226; fax (181) 809-2610; f. 1926; over 6,000 mems; Rabbi JOSEPH DUNNER; Sec. J. R. CONRAD.

**United Synagogue:** Woburn House, Tavistock Sq., London, WC1H 0EZ; tel. (171) 387-4300; fax (171) 383-4934; f. 1870 by Act of Parliament; Pres. SEYMOUR G. SAIDEMAN; Chief Exec. JONATHAN M. LEW.

**West London Synagogue of British Jews:** 33 Seymour Place, London, W1H 6AT; tel. (171) 723-4404; f. 1840; c. 2,500 mems; Senior Rabbi HUGO GRYN; Exec. Dir MAURICE ROSS.

### BUDDHISM

The Buddhist community in the United Kingdom numbers about 25,000.

**The Buddhist Society:** 58 Eccleston Sq., London, SW1V 1PH; tel. (171) 834-5858; f. 1924; Gen. Sec. RONALD C. MADDOX.

### BAHÁ'Í FAITH

**National Spiritual Assembly of the Bahá'ís of the United Kingdom:** 27 Rutland Gate, London, SW7 1PD; tel. (171) 584-2566; fax (171) 584-9402; f. 1923; Sec.-Gen. HUGH C. ADAMSON; Chair. WENDI MOMEN.

# The Press

The United Kingdom has some of the highest circulation figures in the world for individual newspapers (*Daily Mirror* 2.5m., *The Sun* 4.1m., *News of the World* 4.6m.). In 1995 there were 14 national daily, 14 Sunday and 2,222 regional daily and weekly newspapers in the United Kingdom.

There is no law which specifies the operations of the press but several items of legislation bear directly on press activities. Although exact reporting of legal proceedings appearing at the time of trial is protected from later charges of defamation, the freedom to report cases is subject to certain restrictions as defined in the Judicial Proceedings Act of 1926, in the Children's and Young Persons' Act of 1933 and in the Criminal Justice Act 1967. The strict laws of contempt of court and of libel somewhat limit the scope of the press. Journalists are subject to the former if they publish material liable to interfere with a matter which is *sub judice*, but this law is qualified by the Administration of Justice Act of 1960 which declares an editor not guilty of contempt if, after taking reasonable care, he remained ignorant of the fact that proceedings were pending. The Scottish law of contempt is more severe than the English. Libel cases can involve the awarding of punitive damages against the press. The Defamation Act of 1952 lessened the possible repercussions of unintentional libel and made provision for the claim of fair comment by the defence.

The Official Secrets Act of 1911 prohibits the publication of secret information where this is judged not to be in the national interest. The Secretary of State for the Home Department is empowered to require a person with information about a violation

# UNITED KINGDOM (GREAT BRITAIN)

of the Act to disclose his source. Journalists have no exemption here. The publication of morally objectionable and harmful material is treated in the Children's and Young Persons' (Harmful Publications) Act of 1955 and in the Obscene Publications Act.

In recent years legislative measures have been taken to limit the excessive development of concentrations of newspaper ownership and the extent of the control by newspaper owners over other mass media such as the television. The Television Act of 1964 provided for intervention by the Postmaster-General or the Independent Broadcasting Authority where investments by newspaper owners in television companies are judged liable to lead to abuses. The Monopolies and Mergers Act of 1965 requires the written consent of the Department of Trade and Industry for the transfer of daily or weekly papers with an aggregate average of over 500,000 copies per day of publication. The Department's decision is based on the conclusions of the Monopolies Commission to which, with exception of cases of papers judged to be uneconomical and of papers with an average daily circulation of no more than 25,000 copies, all cases are referred for investigation.

The Press Complaints Commission, which replaced the Press Council in 1991, has an independent chairman and 16 members, drawn from the lay public and the press. It deals with complaints from the public and upholds a 18-point Code of Practice.

Among the most influential newspapers may be included: *The Times, The Guardian, The Independent, Daily Telegraph* and *Financial Times* (daily), *The Observer, The Independent on Sunday, The Sunday Times* and *Sunday Telegraph* (Sunday newspapers). Prominent among the popular press are: *Daily Mail, Daily Mirror, Daily Express* and *The Sun* (daily), *Sunday Mirror, News of the World* and *The People* (Sunday newspapers).

No important newspaper is directly owned by a political party. The great rate of news consumption has fostered the growth of large national groups or chains of papers controlled by a single organization or individual. The largest of these chains are as follows:

**Daily Mail and General Trust PLC:** Northcliffe House, 2 Derry St, London, W8 5TT; tel. (171) 938-6000; fax (171) 938-4626; controls through Associated Newspapers one national daily (*Daily Mail*), one national Sunday (*The Mail on Sunday*), one London daily (*Evening Standard*); through the Northcliffe Newspapers Group Ltd controls about 55 evening, morning and weekly papers, of which 26 are free newspapers; Group Chair. Viscount ROTHERMERE; Group Man. Dir C. J. F. SINCLAIR.

**Mirror Group Ltd:** 1 Canada Sq., Canary Wharf, London, E14 5AP; tel. (171) 293-3000; controls one national daily paper (*Daily Mirror*), two national Sunday papers (*The People, Sunday Mirror*) and two Scottish national papers (*Daily Record* and *Sunday Mail*); Chair. Sir ROBERT CLARK; Chief Exec. DAVID MONTGOMERY.

**News International PLC:** POB 495, Virginia St, London, E1 9XY; tel. (171) 782-6000; subsidiary cos: News Group Newspapers Ltd (controls *The Sun* and *News of the World*), Times Newspapers Ltd (controls *The Times* and *The Sunday Times*); Chair. RUPERT MURDOCH; Chief Exec. WILLIAM O'NEILL.

**Newspaper Publishing PLC:** 1 Canada Sq., Canary Wharf, London, E14 5DL; tel. (171) 293-2000; publishes one national daily, *The Independent*, and one national Sunday paper, *The Independent on Sunday*; Chair. ANDREAS WHITTAM SMITH; Man. Dir GRAHAM LUFF.

**Thomson Regional Newspapers Ltd:** 100 Avenue Rd, London, NW3 3HF; tel. (171) 393-7000; fax (171) 393-7472; subsidiary of The Thomson Corporation PLC; controls four morning papers, six evening papers, four Sunday papers, three weekly groups and 38 free newspapers; Chief Exec. STUART GARNER.

**United Newspapers PLC:** Ludgate House, 245 Blackfriars Rd, London, SE1 9UY; tel. (171) 921-5000; Propr of Express Newspapers PLC; publishes two national dailies (*Daily Express* and *Daily Star*), six provincial dailies, one national Sunday (*Sunday Express*), 131 provincial weekly papers (82 free), and 271 advertising periodicals, business and specialist consumer magazines and directories in the UK, the USA and the Far East; Chair. Lord STEVENS OF LUDGATE; Man. Dir GRAHAM WILSON.

## PRINCIPAL NATIONAL DAILIES

**Daily Express:** Ludgate House, 245 Blackfriars Rd, London, SE1 9UX; tel. (171) 928-8000; telex 21841; fax (171) 633-0244; f. 1900; Propr Express Newspapers Ltd; Editor Sir NICHOLAS LLOYD; circ. 1,292,888.

**Daily Mail:** 2 Derry St, Kensington, London, W8 5TT; tel. (171) 938-6000; telex 28301; fax (171) 938-4890; f. 1896, inc. *News Chronicle* 1960 and *Daily Sketch* 1971; Propr Associated Newspaper Holdings; Chair. Viscount ROTHERMERE; Editor-in-Chief PAUL DACRE; circ. 1,760,888.

**Daily Mirror:** 1 Canada Sq., Canary Wharf, London, E14 5AP; tel. (171) 293-3000; fax (171) 293-3758; f. 1903; Propr Mirror Group Newspapers Ltd; Editor COLIN MYLER; circ. 2,476,518.

**Daily Sport:** Marten House, 39–47 East Rd, London, N1 6AH; tel. (171) 251-2544; fax (171) 253-1653; f. 1988; Propr Sport Newspapers Ltd; Editor JEFFREY MCGOWAN.

**Daily Star:** Ludgate House, Blackfriars Rd, London, SE1 9UX; tel. (171) 928-8000; f. 1978; Propr Express Newspapers Ltd; Editor PHIL WALKER; circ. 782,378.

**Daily Telegraph:** 1 Canada Sq., Canary Wharf, London, E14 5AR; tel. (171) 538-5000; telex 22874; *Daily Telegraph* f. 1855, *Morning Post* f. 1772; amalgamated 1937; Propr The Telegraph PLC (Chair. CONRAD BLACK); Editor MAX HASTINGS; circ. 1,033,573.

**Financial Times:** Number One Southwark Bridge, London, SE1 9HL; tel. (171) 873-3000; telex 922186; fax (171) 407-5700; f. 1880; Propr Pearson PLC; Chair. FRANK BARLOW; Editor RICHARD LAMBERT; circ. 292,953.

**The Guardian:** 119 Farringdon Rd, London, EC1R 3ER; tel. (171) 278-2332; telex 8811746; fax (171) 837-2114; and 164 Deansgate, Manchester, M60 2RR; tel. (161) 832-7200; f. 1821; Propr Guardian Newspapers Ltd; Editor-in-Chief PETER J. PRESTON; Editor ALAN RUSBRIDGER; circ. 405,170.

**The Independent:** 1 Canada Sq., Canary Wharf, London, E14 5DL; tel. (171) 293-2000; f. 1986; Propr Newspaper Publishing PLC; Chair. LIAM HEALEY; Editor IAN HARGREAVES; circ. 287,347.

**Racing Post:** 120 Coombe Lane, Raynes Park, London, SW20 0BA; tel. (181) 879-3377; fax (181) 947-2652; f. 1986; covers national and international horse racing, greyhound racing, general sport and betting; Editor ALAN BYRNE; circ. 46,702.

**The Sporting Life:** 1 Canada Sq., Canary Wharf, London, E14 5AP; tel. (171) 293-3000; fax (171) 293-3758; f. 1859; Propr Mirror Group Ltd.; daily national sporting newspaper covering horse racing, greyhound racing and other betting sports; Editor TOM CLARKE; circ. 75,630.

**The Sun:** 1 Pennington St, Wapping, London, E1 9BD; tel. (171) 782-4000; telex 267827; f. 1921 as *Daily Herald*, present name since 1964; Propr News International PLC; Editor STUART HIGGINS; circ. 4,064,301.

**The Times:** 1 Pennington St, Wapping, London, E1 9XN; tel. (171) 782-5000; telex 262141; fax (171) 488-3242; f. 1785; Propr News International PLC; Editor PETER STOTHARD; circ. 614,311.

**Today:** 1 Virginia St, London, E1 9BS; tel. (171) 782-4600; telex 919925; f. 1986; Propr News International PLC; Editor RICHARD STOTT; circ. 594,121.

## LONDON EVENING DAILY

**Evening Standard:** 2 Derry St, Kensington, London, W8 5EE; tel. (171) 938-6000; telex 21909; f. 1827 merged with *Evening News* 1980; Monday–Friday; evening paper; Propr Associated Newspaper Holdings PLC; Editor STEWART STEVEN; circ. 518,789.

## PRINCIPAL PROVINCIAL DAILIES

### Aberdeen

**Evening Express:** Aberdeen Journals Ltd, POB 43, Lang Stracht, Mastrick, Aberdeen, AB9 8AF; tel. (1224) 690222; telex 73133; fax (1224) 699575; f. 1879; Editor R. J. WILLIAMSON; circ. 69,562.

**Press and Journal:** POB 43, Lang Stracht, Mastrick, Aberdeen, AB9 8AF; tel. (1224) 690222; fax (1224) 663575; f. 1748; morning; Propr Thomson Regional Newspapers Ltd; Editor DEREK TUCKER; circ. 107,965.

### Birmingham

**Birmingham Post:** 28 Colmore Circus, Queensway, Birmingham, B4 6AX; tel. (121) 236-3366; fax (121) 625-1105; f. 1857; Propr. Midland Independent Newspapers; morning; independent; Editor NIGEL HASTILOW.

**The Evening Mail:** 28 Colmore Circus, Queensway, Birmingham, B4 6AX; tel. (121) 236-3366; fax (121) 233-9087; f. 1870; Propr. Midland Independent Newspapers; evening; independent; Editor I. DOWELL.

**Sandwell Evening Mail:** 28 Colmore Circus, Queensway, Birmingham, B4 6AX; tel. (121) 236-3366; fax (121) 233-9087; f. 1975; Propr. Midland Independent Newspapers; Chief Exec. C. OAKLEY; Editor I. DOWELL.

### Bradford

**Telegraph & Argus:** Bradford and District Newspapers (Westminster Press Ltd), Hall Ings, Bradford, BD1 1JR; tel. (1274) 729511; f. 1868; evening; Editor PERRY AUSTIN-CLARKE; circ. 70,000.

### Brighton

**Evening Argus:** Argus House, Crowhurst Rd, Hollingbury, Brighton, BN1 8AR; tel. (1273) 544544; fax (1273) 566114; f. 1880; Editor CHRIS FOWLER; circ. 70,000.

## UNITED KINGDOM (GREAT BRITAIN)

### Bristol
**Evening Post:** Temple Way, Old Market, Bristol, BS99 7HD; tel. (117) 926-0080; f. 1932; inc. the *Evening World*; Propr Bristol United Press Ltd; independent; Editor A. KING; circ. (Mon.-Fri.) 104,317, (Sat.) 84,563.

**Western Daily Press:** Temple Way, Bristol, BS99 7HD; tel. (117) 926-0080; f. 1858; inc. *Bristol Times and Mirror*; Propr Bristol United Press Ltd; morning; independent; Man. Dir PAUL KEARNEY; Editor IAN BEALES; circ. 63,297.

### Cardiff
**South Wales Echo:** Thomson House, Havelock St, Cardiff, CF1 1WR; tel. (1222) 223333; fax (1222) 583624; f. 1884; evening; independent; Propr Thomson Regional Newspapers Ltd; Editor KEITH PERCH; circ. 85,000.

**The Western Mail:** Thomson House, Havelock St, Cardiff, CF1 1WR; tel. (1222) 223333; f. 1869; independent; Man. Dir MARK HAYSOM; Editor NEIL FOWLER; circ. 76,000.

### Coventry
**Coventry Evening Telegraph:** Corporation St, Coventry, CV1 1FP; tel. (1203) 633633; fax (1203) 550869; f. 1891 as *Midland Daily Telegraph*; Propr. Midland Independent Newspapers; independent; Editor DAN MASON; circ. (Mon.-Fri.) 85,882, (Sat.) 84,673.

### Darlington
**Northern Echo:** North of England Newspapers (Westminster Press Ltd), Priestgate, Darlington, Co Durham, DL1 1NF; tel. (1325) 381313; fax (1325) 380539; f. 1869; morning; independent; Editor DAVID FLINTHAM; circ. 80,000.

### Derby
**Derby Evening Telegraph:** Derby Daily Telegraph Ltd, Northcliffe House, Meadow Rd, Derby, DE1 2DW; tel. (1332) 291111; f. 1932 (inc. *Derby Daily Telegraph*, f. 1879, *Derby Daily Express*, f. 1884); Editor MIKE LOWE; circ. 81,275.

### Dundee
**Courier and Advertiser:** 80 Kingsway East, Dundee, DD4 8SL; tel. (1382) 223131; fax (1382) 454590; f. 1810; morning; Editor A. ARTHUR; circ. 105,957.

### Edinburgh
**Evening News:** 20 North Bridge, Edinburgh, EH1 1YT; tel. (131) 225-2468; telex 72255; fax (131) 225-7302; f. 1873; Propr Thomson Regional Newspapers Ltd; Editor HARRY ROULSTON; circ. 100,000.

**The Scotsman:** 20 North Bridge, Edinburgh, EH1 1YT; tel. (131) 225-2468; telex 72255; fax (131) 226-7420; f. 1817; morning; independent; Editor JAMES SEATON; circ. 85,543.

### Glasgow
**Daily Record:** 40 Anderston Quay, Glasgow, G3 8DA; tel. (141) 248-7000; telex 778277; fax (141) 242-3340; morning; independent; f. 1895; Propr Mirror Group Newspapers Ltd; Editor TERENCE QUINN; circ. 755,709.

**Glasgow Evening Times:** 195 Albion St, Glasgow, G1 1QP; tel. (141) 552-6255; fax (141) 553-1355; f. 1876; independent; Propr Caledonian Newspapers Ltd; Editor G. MCKECHNIE; circ. 160,000.

**The Herald:** 195 Albion St, Glasgow, G1 1QP; tel. (141) 552-6255; telex 779818; fax (141) 553-3576; f. 1783; morning; independent; Propr Caledonian Newspapers Ltd; Editor GEORGE MCKECHNIE; circ. 123,656.

**Scottish Daily Express:** Park House, Park Circus Place, Glasgow, G3 6AF; tel. (141) 332-9600; telex 778337; morning; regional edition of Daily Express; Propr United Newspapers PLC; circ. 155,000.

### Grimsby
**Grimsby Evening Telegraph:** 80 Cleethorpe Rd, Grimsby, South Humberside, DN31 3EH; tel. (1472) 359232; fax (1472) 358859; f. 1898; Editor PETER MOORE; circ. 72,934.

### Kingston upon Hull
**Hull Daily Mail:** POB 34, Blundell's Corner, Beverley Rd, Kingston upon Hull, HU3 1XS; tel. (1482) 327111; f. 1885; evening; Editor M. G. WOOD; circ. 93,000.

### Leeds
**Yorkshire Evening Post:** Wellington St, Leeds, LS1 1RF; tel. (113) 243-2701; telex 55425; fax (113) 244-3430; f. 1890; independent; Propr Yorkshire Post Newspapers Ltd; Editor C. H. BYE; circ. (Mon.-Fri.) 149,405, (Sat.) 134,879.

**Yorkshire Post:** POB 168, Wellington St, Leeds, LS1 1RF; tel. (113) 43-2701; telex 55425; fax (113) 44-3430; f. 1754; morning; Conservative; Propr Yorkshire Post Newspapers Ltd; Editor ANTHONY G. WATSON; circ. 82,500.

### Leicester
**Leicester Mercury:** St George St, Leicester, LE1 9FQ; tel. (116) 251-2512; fax (116) 253-0645; f. 1874; evening; Editor NICK CARTER; circ. 123,700.

### Liverpool
**Daily Post:** Liverpool Daily Post and Echo Ltd, POB 48, Old Hall St, Liverpool, L69 3EB; tel. (151) 227-2000; telex 629396; fax (151) 236-4682; f. 1855 (inc. *Liverpool Mercury*, f. 1811); morning; independent; Propr Trinity International Holdings; Editor KEITH ELY; circ. 77,500.

**Liverpool Echo:** Liverpool Daily Post and Echo Ltd, POB 48, Old Hall St, Liverpool, L69 3EB; tel. (151) 227-2000; f. 1879; evening; independent; Propr Trinity International Holdings; Editor JOHN GRIFFITH; circ. 207,013.

### Manchester
**Manchester Evening News:** 164 Deansgate, Manchester, M60 2RD; tel. (161) 832-7200; telex 668920; f. 1868; independent; Editor MICHAEL UNGER; circ. 320,000.

### Middlesbrough
**North Eastern Evening Gazette:** Borough Rd, Middlesbrough, Cleveland, TS1 3AZ; tel. (1642) 245401; f. 1869; Propr Thomson Regional Newspapers Ltd; Man. Dir S. J. BROWN; Editor RANALD ALLAN; circ. 69,128.

### Newcastle upon Tyne
**Evening Chronicle:** Thomson House, Groat Market, Newcastle upon Tyne, Tyne and Wear, NE99 1BO; tel. (191) 232-7500; f. 1885; independent; Propr Thomson Regional Newspapers Ltd; Editor NEIL BENSON; circ. (Mon.-Fri.) 136,104, (Sat.) 102,000.

**The Journal:** Thomson House, Groat Market, Newcastle upon Tyne, NE1 1ED; tel. (191) 232-7500; fax (191) 261-8869; f. 1832; morning; Editor WILLIAM BRADSHAW; circ. 60,000.

### Norwich
**Eastern Daily Press:** Prospect House, Rouen Rd, Norwich, NR1 1RE; tel. (1603) 628311; telex 975276; f. 1870; independent; Propr Eastern Counties Newspapers Ltd; Editor PETER FRANZEN; circ. 79,200.

### Nottingham
**Nottingham Evening Post:** T. Bailey Forman Ltd, POB 99, Nottingham, NG1 4AB; tel. (115) 948-2000; telex 377884; f. 1878; Editor BARRIE WILLIAMS; circ. 120,000.

### Plymouth
**Western Morning News:** 17 Brest Rd, Derriford Business Park, Plymouth, PL6 5AA; tel. (1752) 765500; f. 1860; Editor BARRIE WILLIAMS; circ. 57,923; companion evening paper, *Evening Herald*; Editor ALAN COOPER; circ. 59,553.

### Portsmouth
**The News:** The News Centre, Hilsea, Portsmouth, PO2 9SX; tel. (1705) 664488; fax (1705) 673363; f. 1877; evening; Editor GEOFF ELLIOTT; circ. 90,791.

### Preston
**Lancashire Evening Post:** Oliver's Place, Eastway, Fulwood, Preston, PR2 9ZA; tel. (1772) 254841; fax (1772) 880173; f. 1886; Editor PHILIP WELSH; circ. 70,000.

### Sheffield
**The Star:** York St, Sheffield, S1 1PU; tel. (114) 276-7676; fax (114) 272-5978; f. 1887; evening; independent; Propr United Provincial Newspapers PLC; Editor PETER CHARLTON; circ. (Mon.-Fri.) 100,370, (Sat.) 101,580.

### Southampton
**Southern Daily Echo:** 45 Above Bar, Southampton, SO9 7BA; tel. (1703) 634134; fax (1703) 630289; f. 1888; Editor P. FLEMING; circ. 68,036.

### Stoke-on-Trent
**Evening Sentinel:** Staffordshire Sentinel Newspapers Ltd, Sentinel House, Etruria, Stoke-on-Trent, ST1 5SS; tel. (1782) 289800; f. 1873; Editor SEAN DOOLEY; circ. 107,816.

### Sunderland
**Sunderland Echo:** Echo House, Pennywell, Sunderland, Tyne and Wear, SR4 9ER; tel. (191) 534-3011; fax (191) 534-3807; f. 1873; evening; Editor ANDY HUGHES; circ. 61,000.

UNITED KINGDOM (GREAT BRITAIN)                                                                     *Directory*

### Swansea

**South Wales Evening Post:** The Swansea Press Ltd, Adelaide St, Swansea, West Glamorgan, SA1 1QT; tel. (1792) 650841; fax (1792) 655386; f. 1930; Editor HUGH BERLYN; circ. 70,525.

### Telford

**Shropshire Star:** Ketley, Telford, Shropshire, TF1 4HU; tel. (1952) 242424; fax (1952) 254605; f. 1964; evening; Propr Shropshire Newspapers Ltd; Editor ANDY WRIGHT; circ. 94,727.

### Wolverhampton

**Express and Star:** 50 Queen St, Wolverhampton, West Midlands, WV1 3BU; tel. (1902) 313131; f. 1874; evening; Propr The Midland News Association Ltd; Editor W. WILSON; circ. 303,334.

## PRINCIPAL WEEKLY NEWSPAPERS

**The European:** 200 Gray's Inn Rd, London, WC1X 8NE; tel. (171) 418-7777; fax (171) 713-1840; Friday; Editor-in-Chief CHARLES GARSIDE.

**The Independent on Sunday:** 1 Canada Sq., Canary Wharf, London, E14 5DL; tel. (171) 293-2000; fax (171) 293-2435; f. 1990; Propr Newspaper Publishing PLC; Chief Exec. DAVID MONTGOMERY; Editor PETER WILBY; circ. 325,000.

**The Mail on Sunday:** Northcliffe House, 2 Derry St, London, W8 5TS; tel. (171) 938-6000; f. 1982; Propr Associated Newspaper Holdings; Editor JONATHAN HOLBOROW; circ. 1,990,000.

**News of the World:** 1 Virginia St, Wapping, London, E1 9XR; tel. (171) 782-4000; telex 262135; f. 1843; Propr News International PLC; independent; Sunday; Editor PIERS MORGAN; circ. 4,619,518.

**The Observer:** 119 Farringdon Rd, London, EC1R 3ER; tel. (171) 278-2332; f. 1791; acquisition by Guardian Newspapers Ltd approved in May 1993; independent; Sunday; Chief Exec. JIM MARKWICK; Editor-in-Chief PETER PRESTON; Editor ANDREW JASPAN; circ. 487,000.

**The People:** 1 Canada Sq., Canary Wharf, London, E14 5AP; tel. (171) 293-3000; telex 27286; fax (171) 293-3810; f. 1881; Propr Mirror Group Newspapers Ltd; independent; also edition aimed at Asian community; Editor BRIDGET ROWE; circ. 2,038,908.

**Scotland on Sunday:** 20 North Bridge, Edinburgh, EH1 1YT; tel. (131) 225-2468; fax (131) 220-2443; f. 1988; Editor BRIAN GROOM; circ. 87,936.

**Sunday Express:** Ludgate House, 245 Blackfriars Rd., London, SE1 9UX; tel. (171) 928-8000; telex 21841; fax (171) 620-1656; f. 1918; inc. *Sunday Despatch* 1961; independent; Propr Express Newspapers PLC; Editor BRIAN HITCHEN; circ. 1,719,627.

**Sunday Mail:** 40 Anderston Quay, Glasgow, G3 8DA; tel. (141) 248-7000; Propr Mirror Group Newspapers Ltd; Editor JIM CASSIDY; circ. 886,632.

**Sunday Mercury:** The Birmingham Post and Mail Ltd, 28 Colmore Circus, Queensway, Birmingham, B4 6AZ; tel. (121) 236-3366; telex 337552; f. 1918; Editor P. WHITEHOUSE; circ. 150,849.

**Sunday Mirror:** 1 Canada Sq., Canary Wharf, London, E14 5AP; tel. (171) 293-3000; fax (171) 822-3587; f. 1915; Propr Mirror Group Newspapers Ltd; independent; Editor TESSA HILTON; circ. 2,651,786.

**Sunday Post (Glasgow):** Courier Place, Dundee, DD1 9QJ; tel. (1382) 23131; telex 76380; fax (1382) 201064; Glasgow Office: 144 Port Dundas Rd; tel. (141) 332-9933; fax (141) 331-1595; f. 1920; Editor RUSSELL REID; circ. 1,226,555.

**Sunday Sport:** Marten House, 39–47 East Rd, London, N1 6AH; tel. (171) 251-2544; telex 269277; fax (171) 608-1979; f. 1986; Editor DOMINIC MOHAN; circ. 300,000.

**Sunday Sun:** Thomson House, Groat Market, Newcastle upon Tyne, NE1 1ED; tel. (191) 232-7500; fax (191) 232-2256; f. 1919; Propr Thomson Regional Newspapers Ltd; independent; north-east England; Editor CHRIS RUSHTON; circ. 127,702.

**Sunday Telegraph:** 1 Canada Sq., Canary Wharf, London, E14 5AR; tel. (171) 538-5000; telex 22874; fax (171) 513-2504; f. 1961; Propr The Telegraph PLC; Chair. CONRAD BLACK; Editor CHARLES MOORE; circ. 700,000.

**The Sunday Times:** 1 Pennington St, Wapping, London, E1 9XW; tel. (171) 782-5000; telex 262139; f. 1822; Propr News International PLC; Editor JOHN WITHEROW; circ. 1,272,591.

**Weekly News (Thomson's):** D. C. Thomson & Co Ltd, Albert Sq., Dundee, DD1 9QJ; tel. (1382) 23131; telex 76380; fax (1382) 201264; f. 1855; circ. 339,008.

## SELECTED PERIODICALS

### Arts and Literature

**Apollo Magazine:** 29 Chesham Place, London, SW1X 8HB; tel. (171) 235-1676; fax (171) 235-1673; f. 1925; monthly; fine and decorative art; Editor ROBIN SIMON.

**Architects' Journal:** EMAP Architecture, 33–39 Bowling Green Lane, London, EC1R 0DA; tel. (171) 837-1212; fax (171) 833-8072; f. 1895; Wednesday; Editor STEPHEN GREENBERG; circ. 19,500.

**Architectural Design Magazine:** Academy Group Ltd, 42 Leinster Gardens, London, W2 3AN; tel. (171) 402-2141; fax (171) 723-9540; f. 1930; six issues per year; architecture present and past; House Editor MAGGIE TOY; circ. 8,000.

**Architectural Review:** 33–35 Bowling Green Lane, London, EC1R 0DA; tel. (171) 837-1212; telex 299049; fax (171) 833-8072; f. 1896; monthly; Editor PETER DAVEY; circ. 20,003.

**Art and Design Magazine:** Academy Group Ltd, 42 Leinster Gardens, London, W2 3AN; tel. (171) 402-2141; fax (171) 723-9540; f. 1985; six issues per year; Editor NICOLA HODGES; circ. 6,000.

**The Artist:** c/o Caxton House, 63–65 High St, Tenterden, Kent, TN30 6BD; tel. (15806) 763673; fax (15806) 765411; f. 1931; monthly; Editor SALLY BULGIN.

**Art Review:** Starcity Ltd, 69 Faroe Rd, London, W14 0EL; tel. (171) 603-8533; fax (171) 603-5061; f. 1949; monthly; Editor DAVID LEE; circ. 5,000.

**BBC Music Magazine:** Room A1004, Woodlands, 80 Wood Lane, London, W12 0TT; tel. (181) 576-3283; fax (181) 576-3292; f. 1992; monthly; classical music; Editor FIONA MADDOCKS.

**Books Magazine:** 43 Museum St, London, WC1A 1LY; tel. (171) 404-0304; fax (171) 242-0762; f. 1955; every 2 months; literature and books of general interest; Editor RICHARD HALL.

**The Bookseller:** 12 Dyott St, London, WC1A 1DF; tel. (171) 836-8911; fax (171) 836-6381; f. 1858; incorporates *Bent's Literary Advertiser* (f. 1802); Friday; Propr J. Whitaker & Sons; Editor LOUIS BAUM; circ. 14,000.

**The Burlington Magazine:** 14–16 Dukes Rd, London, WC1H 9AD; tel. (171) 388-1228; fax (171) 388-1229; f. 1903; monthly; all forms of art, ancient and modern; Editor CAROLINE ELAM.

**Classic CD:** Future Publishing, Beauford Court, 30 Monmouth St, Bath, Avon, BA1 2BW; tel. (1225) 442244; fax (1225) 312228; f. 1990; Editor ROB AINSLEY; circ. 60,000.

**Dance & Dancers:** 214 Panther House, 38 Mount Pleasant, London, WC1X 0AP; tel. and fax (171) 837-2711; fax (171) 837-2755; f. 1950; monthly; ballet and modern dance; Editor JOHN PERCIVAL.

**Design:** Design Council, Haymarket House, 1 Oxendon St, London, SW1Y 4EE; tel. (171) 208-2121; fax (171) 839-6033; f. 1949; quarterly; all aspects of the design process, including design management and commissioning; Editor CARL GARDNER; circ. 15,000.

**Film Review:** Visual Imagination Ltd, PO Box 371, London, SW14; tel. (181) 875-1520; fax (181) 875-1588; f. 1954; monthly; international cinema and video; Editor DAVID RICHARDSON.

**Folklore:** The Folklore Society, University College London, Gower St, London, WC1E 6BT; tel. (171) 387-5894; f. 1878; 1 a year; Hon. Sec. Dr JULIETTE WOOD.

**Gramophone:** 177–179 Kenton Rd, Harrow, Middlesex, HA3 0HA; tel. (181) 907-4476; fax (181) 907-0073; f. 1923; monthly; Publr ANTHONY POLLARD; Editor JAMES JOLLY; circ. 65,941.

**Granta:** 2/3 Hanover Yard, Noel Rd, London, N1 8BE; tel. (171) 704-9776; fax (171) 704-0474; published in assoc. with Penguin Books UK Ltd; quarterly; Editor IAN JACK.

**Index on Censorship:** Writers and Scholars International Ltd, 33 Islington High St, London, N1 9LH; tel. (171) 278-2313; fax (171) 278-1878; f. 1972; six a year; concerned with freedom of expression throughout the world; Editor URSULA OWEN; circ. 12,000.

**Jazz Journal International:** Jazz Journal Ltd, 1–5 Clerkenwell Rd, London, EC1M 5PA; tel. (171) 608-1348; fax (171) 608-1292; f. 1948; monthly; Publr and Editor-in-Chief EDDIE COOK; circ. 11,000.

**The Journal of Philosophy and the Visual Arts:** Academy Group Ltd, 42 Leinster Gardens, London, W2 3AN; tel. (171) 402-2141; telex 896928; fax (171) 723-9540; 4 issues per subscription (irregular).

**Language Learning Journal:** Association for Language Learning, 150 Railway Terrace, Rugby, CV21 3HN; tel. (1788) 546443; fax (1788) 544149; f. 1990; 2 a year; Editor COLIN WRINGE; circ. 6,000.

**Library:** Oxford University Press, Pinkhill House, Southfield Rd, Eynsham, Oxford, OX8 1JJ; tel. (1865) 882283; fax (1865) 882890; f. 1893; quarterly; publ. by the Bibliographical Society; Editor M. C. DAVIES.

**Melody Maker:** IPC Magazines Ltd, 25th Floor, King's Reach Tower, Stamford St, London, SE1 9LS; tel. (171) 261-5463; fax (171) 260-6037; f. 1926; Tuesday; popular music; Editor ALLAN JONES; circ. 70,588.

**New Musical Express:** IPC Magazines Ltd, 25th Floor, King's Reach Tower, Stamford St, London, SE1 9LS; tel. (171) 261-5000; f. 1952; Wednesday; popular music; Editor STEVE SUTHERLAND; circ. 121,001.

UNITED KINGDOM (GREAT BRITAIN) *Directory*

**Opera:** 1A Mountgrove Rd, London, N5 2LU; tel. (171) 359-1037; fax (171) 354-2700; f. 1950; monthly; Editor RODNEY MILNES.

**Perspectives on Architecture:** 2 Hinde St, London, W1M 5RH; tel. (171) 224-1766; f. 1994; quarterly; Editor GILES WORSLEY.

**Plays and Players:** Second Floor, Northway House, 1379 High Rd, London, N12 8QX; tel. (181) 343-8515; fax (181) 343-9540; f. 1953; monthly; world theatre; Editor SANDRA RENNIE.

**Poetry Review:** 22 Betterton St, London, WC2H 9BU; tel. (171) 240-4810; fax (171) 240-4818; f. 1909; quarterly; Editor PETER FORBES; circ. 5,000.

**The Stage:** Stage House, 47 Bermondsey St, London, SE1 3XT; tel. (171) 403-1818; fax (171) 403-1418; f. 1880; Thursday; theatre, light entertainment, television, repertory; Editor BRIAN ATTWOOD; circ. 41,433.

**Sight and Sound:** British Film Institute, 21 Stephen Street, London, W1P 1PL; tel. (171) 255-1444; telex 27624; fax (171) 436-2327; f. 1932; monthly; international film review; Editor PHILIP DODD; circ. 40,000.

**The Times Literary Supplement:** Priory House, St John's Lane, London, EC1M 4BX; tel. (171) 253-3000; telex 24460; fax (171) 251-3424; f. 1902; Friday; weekly journal of literary criticism; Editor Sir FERDINAND MOUNT; circ. 27,200.

### Current Affairs and History

**Antiquity:** 85 Hills Rd, Cambridge, CB2 1PG; tel. (1223) 516271; fax (1223) 516272; f. 1927; quarterly; archaeological; Editor CHRISTOPHER CHIPPINDALE.

**The China Quarterly:** School of Oriental and African Studies, Thornhaugh Street, Russell Square, London, WC1H 0XG; tel. (171) 323-6129; telex 291829; fax (171) 580-6836; f. 1960; all aspects of contemporary China; Editor DAVID SHAMBAUGH; circ. 3,000.

**Classical Quarterly:** Journals Dept, Oxford University Press, Pinkhill House, Southfield Rd, Eynsham, Oxford, OX8 1JJ; tel. (1865) 56767; fax (1865) 882890; f. 1907; 2 a year; Editors Dr S. J. HEYWORTH, Dr P. C. MILLETT.

**Contemporary Review:** Cheam Business Centre, 14 Upper Mulgrave Rd, Cheam, Surrey, SM2 7AZ; tel. (181) 643-4846; fax (181) 241-7507; f. 1866; monthly; publ by Contemporary Review Co Ltd; politics, international affairs, social subjects, the arts; Editor Dr RICHARD MULLEN.

**English Historical Review:** Longman Group UK Ltd, Longman House, Burnt Mill, Harlow, Essex, CM20 2JE; tel. (1279) 26721; telex 81259; f. 1886; quarterly; learned articles and book reviews; Editors J. R. MADDICOTT, R. J. W. EVANS.

**History:** The Historical Association, 59A Kennington Park Rd, London, SE11 4JH; tel. (171) 735-3901; fax (171) 582-4989; f. 1912; 3 a year; Editor Prof. H. T. DICKINSON; circ. 4,000.

**History Today:** 20 Old Compton St, London, W1V 5PE; tel. (171) 439-8315; fax (171) 287-2592; f. 1951; monthly; illustrated general historical magazine; Editor GORDON MARSDEN; circ. 35,000.

**Illustrated London News:** 20 Upper Ground, London, SE1 9PF; tel. (171) 928-2111; fax (171) 620-1594; 6 a year; Editor-in-Chief JAMES BISHOP; circ. 53,970.

**International Affairs:** Royal Institute of International Affairs, Chatham House, 10 St James's Sq., London, SW1Y 4LE; tel. (171) 957-5700; fax (171) 957-5710; f. 1922; quarterly; publ. by Cambridge University Press; original articles, and reviews of publications on international affairs; Man. Editor CAROLINE BLACKER; circ. 6,800.

**Journal of Contemporary History:** 4 Devonshire St, London, W1N 2BH; tel. (171) 636-7247; fax (171) 436-6428; f. 1966; quarterly; publ. by Sage Publications Ltd; Editors WALTER LAQUEUR, GEORGE L. MOSSE, SEYMOUR DRESCHER, ARTHUR MARWICK.

**Keesing's Record of World Events:** Cartermill International Publishing, Maple House, 149 Tottenham Court Rd, London, W1P 9LL; tel. (171) 896-2424; fax (171) 896-2449; produced by CIRCA Research and Reference Information Ltd, 13–17 Sturton St, Cambridge, CB1 2SN; tel. (1223) 568017; fax (1223) 354643; f. 1931; monthly; subscription only; Editor ROGER EAST.

**Keesing's UK Record:** CIRCA Research and Reference Information Ltd, 13–17 Sturton St, Cambridge, CB1 2SN; tel. (1223) 568017; fax (1223) 354643; f. 1988; bi-monthly; factual account of British political, economic and social events; Editor ROBERT FRASER.

**London Gazette:** Room 418, HMSO Publications Centre, 51 Nine Elms Lane, London, SW8 5DR; tel. (171) 873-8300; f. 1665; 5 a week; the oldest existing world newspaper; government journal of official announcements.

**New Left Review:** 6 Meard St, London, W1V 3HR; tel. (171) 734-8830; fax (171) 734-0059; f. 1960; 6 a year; international politics, economics and culture; Editor ROBIN BLACKBURN.

**New Statesman and Society:** Foundation House, Perseverance Works, 38 Kingsland Rd, London, E2 8DQ; tel. (171) 739-3211; telex 28449; fax (171) 739-9307; f. 1988; weekly; politics and the arts; Editor STEVE PLATT; circ. 39,900.

**People in Power:** CIRCA Research and Reference Information Ltd, 13–17 Sturton St, Cambridge, CB1 2SN; tel. (1223) 568017; fax (1223) 354643; f. 1987; bi-monthly; Government listings.

**The Political Quarterly:** Blackwell Publishers Ltd, 108 Cowley Rd, Oxford, OX4 1JF; tel. (1865) 791100; fax (1865) 791347; f. 1930; 5 a year; Editors DAVID MARQUAND, ANTHONY WRIGHT; circ. 2,200.

**Race and Class:** The Institute of Race Relations, 2-6 Leeke St, London, WC1X 9HS; tel. (171) 837-0041; fax (171) 278-0623; f. 1959; quarterly; journal for black and Third World liberation; Editors A. SIVANANDAN

**The Spectator:** 56 Doughty St, London, WC1N 2LL; tel. (171) 405-1706; telex 27124; fax (171) 242-0603; f. 1828; Thursday; independent political and literary review; Editor DOMINIC LAWSON; circ. 36,137.

**Tribune:** 308 Gray's Inn Rd, London, WC1X 8DY; tel. (171) 278-0911; f. 1937; Friday; Labour's independent weekly; politics, current affairs, arts; Editor MARK SEDDON.

### Economics and Business

**Accountancy Age:** 32–34 Broadwick St, London, W1A 2HG; tel. (171) 439-4242; telex 23918; fax (171) 437-7001; f. 1969; weekly; Editor ROBERT OUTRAM; circ. 81,556.

**The Banker:** Pearson Professional, Maple House, 149 Tottenham Court Rd, London, W1P 9LL; tel. (171) 896-2525; telex 23700; fax (171) 896-2586; f. 1926; monthly; monetary and economic policy, international and domestic banking and finance, banking technology, country surveys; Editor STEPHEN TIMEWELL; circ. 15,000.

**Campaign:** Haymarket Publications Ltd, 30 Lancaster Gate, London, W2 3LY; tel. (171) 413-4036; telex 8954052; fax (171) 413-4507; f. 1968; advertising, marketing and media; Thursday; Editor DOMINIC MILLS; circ. 18,687.

**Computer Weekly:** Reed Business Publishing Ltd, Quadrant House, The Quadrant, Sutton, Surrey, SM2 5AS; tel. (181) 652-3122; fax (181) 652-4695; f. 1966; Thursday; Editor JOHN LAMB; circ. 113,737.

**Computing:** VNU Business Publications BV, VNU House, 32–34 Broadwick St, London, W1A 2HG; tel. (171) 316-9000; fax (171) 316-9003; f. 1973; Thursday; Editor JERRY SANDERS; circ. 116,000.

**Crops:** Reed Farmers Publishing, Quadrant House, The Quadrant, Sutton, Surrey, SM2 5AS; tel. (181) 652-4080; fax (181) 652-8928; f. 1984; fortnightly; Editor DEBBIE BEATON; circ. 34,000.

**Economic Journal:** University of York, Heslington, York, YO1 5DD; tel. (1904) 433575; fax (1904) 433433; f. 1891; publ. for the Royal Economic Society, Basil Blackwell; six a year; Editors J. D. HEY, M. J. ARTIS, R. E. BACKHOUSE, D. GREENAWAY, G. JUDGE, D. G. MAYES, D. M. G. NEWBERY, S. J. NICKELL, A. L. WINTERS.

**The Economist:** 25 St James's St, London, SW1A 1HG; tel. (171) 830-7000; telex 24344; f. 1843; 50% owned by the Financial Times, 50% by individual shareholders; Friday; Chair. DOMINIC CADBURY; Editor BILL EMMOTT; circ. 590,000.

**Euromoney:** Nestor House, Playhouse Yard, London, EC4V 5EX; tel. (171) 779-8888; telex 928726; fax (171) 779-8653; f. 1969; monthly; Editor GARRY EVANS; circ. 27,146.

**Farmers Weekly:** Reed Business Publishing, Quadrant House, The Quadrant, Sutton, Surrey, SM2 5AS; tel. (181) 652-4911; telex 892084; fax (181) 652-4005; f. 1934; Friday; Editor STEPHEN HOWE; circ. 97,273.

**Investors Chronicle:** Greystoke Place, Fetter Lane, London, EC4A 1ND; tel. (171) 405-6969; fax (171) 405-5276; f. as *Money Market Review* 1860; amalgamated with *Investors Chronicle* 1914; amalgamated with the *Stock Exchange Gazette* 1967; Friday; independent financial and economic review; Editor CERI JONES; circ. 56,000.

**Management Today:** 22 Lancaster Gate, London, W2 3LY; tel. (171) 413-4566; telex 8954052; fax (171) 413-4138; f. 1966; monthly; Editor CHARLES SKINNER; circ. 102,000.

**Sinclair User:** EMAP Business and Computer Publications, Priory Court, 30–32 Farringdon Lane, London, EC1R 3AU; tel. (171) 972-6700; fax (171) 972-6710; monthly; Sinclair computers; Editor GARTH SUMPTER; circ. 102,023.

**What Personal Computer:** Greater London House, Hampstead Rd, London, NW1 7QZ; tel. (171) 388-2430; fax (171) 383-5654; monthly; Editor GAIL ROBINSON; circ. 45,876.

### Education

**Higher Education Quarterly:** Blackwell Publishers Ltd, 108 Cowley Rd, Oxford, OX4 1JF; tel. (1865) 791100; telex 837022; fax (1865) 791347; f. 1946; Gen. Editor MICHAEL SHATTOCK.

**The Teacher:** Hamilton House, Mabledon Place, London, WC1H 9BD; tel. (171) 388-6191; fax (171) 387-8458; f. 1872; magazine

UNITED KINGDOM (GREAT BRITAIN) *Directory*

of the NUT; news, comments and articles on all aspects of education; eight times a year; Editor Mitch Howard; circ. 250,000.

**The Times Educational Supplement:** Admiral House, East Smithfield, London, E1; tel. (171) 253-3000; telex 24460; fax (171) 608-1599; f. 1910; Friday; Editor Patricia Rowan; circ. 126,000.

**The Times Higher Education Supplement:** Priory House, St John's Lane, London, EC1M 4BX; tel. (171) 253-3000; telex 24460; fax (171) 608-2349; f. 1971; Friday; Editor Auriol Stevens; circ. 19,333.

### Home, Fashion and General

**Arena:** Exmouth House, Pine St, London, EC1; tel. (171) 837-7270; fax (171) 837-3906; Editor Kathryn Flett; circ. 75,000.

**Bella:** H. Bauer Publishing Ltd, 2nd Floor, Shirley House, 25–27 Camden Rd, London, NW1 9LL; tel. (171) 284-0909; fax (171) 485-3774; f. 1987; weekly; fashion, beauty, health, cookery, handicrafts; Editor-in-Chief Jackie Highe; circ. 1,197,071.

**Best:** Gruner and Jahr (UK), Portland House, Stag Place, London, SW1E 5AU; tel. (171) 245-8700; f. 1987; weekly; women's interest; Editor Maire Fahey; circ. 564,233.

**Chat:** IPC Magazines Ltd, King's Reach Tower, Stamford St, London, SE1 9LS; tel. (171) 261-6565; fax (171) 261-6534; weekly; women's interest; Editor Terry Tavner; circ. 600,000.

**Company:** National Magazine House, 72 Broadwick St, London, W1V 2BP; tel. (171) 439-5000; telex 263879; fax (171) 437-6886; monthly; Editor Mandi Norwood; circ. 305,592.

**Cosmopolitan:** National Magazine House, 72 Broadwick St, London, W1V 2BP; tel. (171) 439-5000; telex 263879; fax (171) 439-5016; f. 1972; monthly; women's interest; Editor (vacant); circ. 456,000.

**Do It Yourself:** Link House, Dingwall Ave, Croydon, Surrey, CR9 2TA; tel. (181) 686-2599; fax (181) 781-1164; f. 1957; monthly; Editor John McGowan; circ. 42,000.

**Elle:** Emap Elan, 20 Orange St, London, WC2H 7ED; tel. (171) 957-8383; fax (171) 957-8400; f. 1985; monthly; women's interest; Editor Nicola Jeal.

**Esquire:** National Magazine House, 72 Broadwick St, London, W1V 2BP; tel. (171) 439-5000; telex 263879; fax (171) 439-5067; monthly; Editor Rosie Boycott; circ. 110,583.

**The Face:** Exmouth House, 3rd Floor, Block A, Pine St, London, EC1 0JL; tel. (171) 837-7270; fax (171) 837-3906; f. 1980; Editor Sheryl Garratt.

**Family Circle:** IPC Magazines Ltd, King's Reach Tower, Stamford St, London, SE1 9LS; tel. (171) 261-5000; telex 915748; fax (171) 261-5929; f. 1964; 13 a year; women's magazine; Editor Gilly Batterbee; circ. 310,000.

**Good Housekeeping:** National Magazine House, 72 Broadwick St, London, W1V 2BP; tel. (171) 439-5000; telex 263879; fax (171) 437-6886; f. 1922; monthly; Editor-in-Chief Sally O'Sullivan; circ. 518,534.

**GQ:** The Condé Nast Publications Ltd, Vogue House, Hanover Sq., London, W1R 0AD; tel. (171) 499-9080; telex 27338; fax (171) 495-1679; f. 1988; Editor Michael VerMeulen; circ. 109,235.

**Harpers & Queen:** National Magazine House, 72 Broadwick St, London, W1V 2BP; tel. (171) 439-5000; telex 263879; fax (171) 439-5506; f. 1929; Prprs National Magazine Co Ltd; monthly; international fashion, beauty, general features; Editor Fiona MacPherson; circ. 100,000.

**Hello!:** Hello! Ltd, Wellington House, 69–71 Upper Ground, London, SE1 9PQ; tel. (171) 334-7404; fax (171) 334-7412; Propr. HOLA S.A. (Spain); weekly; Editor Maggie Koumi; circ. 487,704.

**Homes and Gardens:** IPC Magazines Ltd, King's Reach Tower, Stamford St, London, SE1 9LS; tel. (171) 261-5000; telex 915748; fax (171) 261-6247; f. 1919; monthly; Editor Amanda Evans; circ. 183,000.

**House & Garden:** The Condé Nast Publications Ltd, Vogue House, Hanover Sq., London, W1R 0AD; tel. (171) 499-9080; fax (171) 629-2907; f. 1920; monthly; Editor Susan Crewe; circ. 159,942.

**Ideal Home:** IPC Magazines Ltd, King's Reach Tower, Stamford St, London, SE1 9LS; tel. (171) 261-5000; telex 915748; fax (171) 261-6697; f. 1920; monthly; Editor Terence Whelan; circ. 215,659.

**The Lady:** 39–40 Bedford St, London, WC2E 9ER; tel. (171) 379-4717; fax (171) 497-2137; f. 1885; Tuesday; Editor Arline Usden; circ. 63,461.

**Living Magazine:** IPC Magazines Ltd, King's Reach Tower, Stamford St, London, SE1 9LS; tel. (171) 261-5854; fax (171) 261-6892; f. 1967; monthly; women's magazine; Editor Sharon Brown; circ. 333,620.

**Me:** IPC Magazines Ltd, Elme House, 133 Long Acre, London, WC2E 9JD; tel. (171) 836-0519; fax (171) 497 2364; Editor Simon Geller; circ. 500,000.

**My Weekly:** D. C. Thomson & Co Ltd, 80 Kingsway East, Dundee, DD4 8SL; tel. (1382) 223131; telex 76380; fax (1382) 452491; f. 1910; Friday; women's interest; Editor Sandra Monks; circ. 607,065.

**New Woman:** Emap Elan, 20 Orange St, London, WC2H 7ED; tel. (171) 957-8383; fax (171) 957-8400; women's interest; Editor Gill Hudson; circ. 261,706.

**Options:** IPC Magazines Ltd, King's Reach Tower, Stamford St, London, SE1 9LS; tel. (171) 261-5000; fax (171) 261-7344; f. 1982; monthly; women's interest; Editor Maureen Rice; circ. 163,500.

**The People's Friend:** D. C. Thomson & Co Ltd, 80 Kingsway East, Dundee, DD4 8SL; tel. (1382) 462276; telex 76380; fax (1382) 452491; f. 1869; Wednesday; women's fiction, home, fashion, crafts, general; Editor Finclair Matieson; circ. 500,000.

**Prima:** Portland House, Stag Place, London, SW1E 5AU; tel. (171) 245-8700; fax (171) 630-5509; f. 1986 (English edition); seeks to cover over 100 topics of women's interest in every issue; Editor Sue James; circ. 700,027.

**Private Eye:** 6 Carlisle St, London, W1V 5RG; tel. (171) 437-4017; fax (171) 437-0705; f. 1961; fortnightly; satirical; Editor Ian Hislop; circ. 186,124.

**Reader's Digest:** Reader's Digest Association Ltd, (British Edition) Berkeley Square House, London, W1X 6AB; tel. (171) 629-8144; telex 264631; fax (171) 408-0748; f. 1938; monthly; Editor-in-Chief Russell Twisk; circ. 1,673,306.

**The Scots Magazine:** D. C. Thomson & Co. Ltd, 2 Albert Square, Dundee, DD1 9QI; tel. (1382) 223131; fax (1382) 222214; f. 1739; monthly; Scottish interest; circ. 75,565.

**She:** National Magazine House, 72 Broadwick St, London, W1V 2BP; tel. (171) 439-5000; telex 263879; fax (171) 439-5350; f. 1955; monthly; Editor Linda Kelsey; circ. 251,860.

**Smash Hits:** Mappin House, 4 Winsley St, London, W1N 7AP; tel. (171) 436-1516; fax (171) 636-5792; f. 1978; fortnightly; popular music; Editor Mark Frith; circ. 346,000.

**Take a Break:** Bauer Publishing Ltd, 3rd Floor, Shirley House, 25–27 Camden Rd, London, NW1 9LL; tel. (171) 284-0909; fax (171) 284-3778; Monday; Editor John Dale.

**Tatler:** The Condé Nast Publications Ltd, Vogue House, Hanover Sq., London, W1R 0AD; tel. (171) 499-9080; telex 27338; fax (171) 409-0451; f. 1709; 12 a year; Editor Jane Procter; circ. 80,373.

**Vanity Fair:** The Condé Nast Publications Ltd, Vogue House, Hanover Sq., London, W1R 0AD; tel. (171) 499-9080; telex 27338; fax (171) 499-4415; Editor E. Graydon Carter.

**Viz:** The Boat House, Crabtree Lane, London, SW6 6LU; tel. (171) 381-6007; fax (171) 381-3930; f. 1979; six a year; Editor Chris Donald; circ. 733,707.

**Vogue:** The Condé Nast Publications Ltd, Vogue House, Hanover Sq., London, W1R 0AD; tel. (171) 499-9080; telex 27338; fax (171) 493-1345; f. 1916; monthly; Editor Alexandra Shulman; circ. 181,000.

**The Voice:** Voice Group, 370 Coldharbour Lane, London, SW9 8PL; tel. (171) 737-7377; fax (171) 274-8994; f. 1982; Tuesday; black interest; Editor Winsome Cornish; circ. 51,318.

**Woman:** IPC Magazines Ltd, King's Reach Tower, Stamford St, London, SE1 9LS; tel. (171) 261-5000; fax (171) 261-5997; f. 1937; Monday; Editor Carole Russell; circ. 716,837.

**Woman and Home:** IPC Magazines Ltd, King's Reach Tower, Stamford St, London, SE1 9LS; tel. (171) 261-5000; f. 1926; monthly; Editor Orlando Murrin; circ. 435,000.

**Woman's Journal:** IPC Magazines Ltd, King's Reach Tower, Stamford St, London, SE1 9LS; tel. (171) 261-6220; telex 915748; fax (171) 261-7061; f. 1927; monthly; Editor-in-Chief Deirdre Vine; circ. 181,000.

**Woman's Own:** IPC Magazines Ltd, King's Reach Tower, Stamford St, London, SE1 9LS; tel. (171) 261-5474; telex 915748; fax (171) 261-5346; f. 1932; Tuesday; Editor Keith McNeill; circ. 795,000.

**Woman's Realm:** IPC Magazines Ltd, King's Reach Tower, Stamford St, London, SE1 9LS; tel. (171) 261-5000; telex 915748; fax (171) 261-5326; f. 1958; Friday; Editor Iris Burton; circ. 546,260.

**Woman's Weekly:** IPC Magazines Ltd, King's Reach Tower, Stamford St, London, SE1 9LS; tel. (171) 261-5000; telex 915748; f. 1911; Tuesday; Editor Olwen Rice; circ. 795,230.

### Law

**Law Quarterly Review:** Sweet & Maxwell, South Quay Plaza, 183 Marsh Wall, London, E14 9FT; tel. (171) 538-8686; telex 929089; fax (171) 538-8625; f. 1885; quarterly; Editor Prof. F. M. B. Reynolds.

**Law Society's Gazette:** 50–52 Chancery Lane, London, WC2A 1SX; tel. (171) 242-1222; telex 261203; fax (171) 831-0869; f. 1903; weekly; Editor Sheila Pratt; circ. 61,840.

UNITED KINGDOM (GREAT BRITAIN)  *Directory*

**Law Society's Guardian Gazette:** 50–52 Chancery Lane, London, WC2A 1SX; tel. (171) 242-1222; telex 261203; fax (171) 831-0869; f. 1972; publ. by the Law Society; monthly; Editor Sheila Pratt; circ. 79,091.

### Leisure Interests and Sport

**Autocar & Motor Magazine:** Haymarket Publishing Ltd, 38–42 Hampton Rd, Teddington, Middx, TW11 0JE; tel. (181) 943-5013; telex 8952440; fax (181) 943-5653; f. 1895; Wednesday; Editor Michael Harvey; circ. 84,159.

**Autosport:** Haymarket Specialist Motoring Magazines Ltd, 60 Waldegrave Rd, Teddington, Middx, TW11 8LG; tel. (181) 943-5000; telex 8952440; fax (181) 943-5922; f. 1950; Thursday; Editor Bruce Jones; circ. 55,000.

**Car:** EMAP National Publications Ltd, Bushfield House, Orton Centre, Peterborough, PE2 0UW; tel. (1733) 237111; fax (1733) 236940; f. 1965; monthly; Editor Gavin Green; circ. 132,248.

**Country Life:** IPC Magazines Ltd, King's Reach Tower, Stamford St, London, SE1 9LS; tel. (171) 261-7058; fax (171) 261-5139; f. 1897; Thursday; Editor Clive Aslet; circ. 42,000.

**The Countryman:** Sheep St, Burford, Oxford, OX18 4LH; tel. (199382) 2258; fax (199382) 2703; f. 1927; 6 a year; independent; Editor Christopher Hall; circ. 50,000.

**BBC Gardeners' World:** Redwood Publishing Ltd, 101 Bayham St, London, NW1 0AG; tel. (171) 331-3939; fax (171) 331-8162; f. 1991; monthly; Editor Adam Pasco; circ. 372,084.

**Hi-Fi News & Record Review:** Link House, Dingwall Ave, Croydon, Surrey, CR9 2TA; tel. (181) 686-2599; fax (181) 760-0973; f. 1956; monthly; all aspects of high quality sound reproduction, record reviews; Editor Steve Harris; circ. 24,014.

**Photo Answers:** EMAP Apex Publications, 5th Floor, Apex House, Oundle Rd, Peterborough, Cambridgeshire, PE2 9NP; tel. (1733) 898100; fax (1733) 894472; f. 1990; Editor Martyn Moore; circ. 44,368.

**Practical Photography:** Apex House, Oundle Rd, Peterborough, Cambridgeshire, PE2 9NP; tel. (1733) 898100; fax (1733) 898418; monthly; Editor William Cheung; circ. 110,295.

**Radio Times:** BBC Enterprises Ltd, Woodlands, 80 Wood Lane, London, W12 0TT; tel. (181) 576-3120; fax (181) 576-3160; f. 1923; weekly; programme guide to BBC, ITV, C4, satellite and radio broadcasts; Editor Nicholas Brett; circ. 1,574,000.

**Time Out:** Time Out House, 251 Tottenham Court Rd, London, W1P 0AB; tel. (171) 833-3000; fax (171) 813-6028; f. 1968; Wednesday; listings and reviews of events in London; Editor John Morrish; circ. 89,000.

**TV Times:** IPC Magazines Ltd, King's Reach Tower, Stamford St, London, SE1 9LS; tel. (171) 261-7000; fax (171) 261-7777; f. 1955; 13 editions weekly listing all BBC, ITV, C4 and satellite broadcasts; Editor Liz Murphy; circ. 1,015,141.

**What Car:** Haymarket Magazines Ltd, 38–42 Hampton Rd, Teddington, Middx, TW11 0JE; tel. (181) 943-5000; fax (181) 943-5959; f. 1973; Editor Mark Payton; circ. 127,500.

**What's On TV:** IPC Magazines Ltd, King's Reach Tower, Stamford St, London, SE1 9LS; tel. (171) 261-7769; fax (171) 261-7739; f. 1991; weekly; television programme guide and features; Editor Mike Hollingsworth.

### Medicine and Science

**Biochemical Journal:** 59 Portland Place, London, W1N 3AJ; tel. (171) 637-5873; fax (171) 323-1136; f. 1906; 2 a month; publ. by Portland Press on behalf of the Biochemical Society; Chair. Editorial Board A. J. Turner; Man. Editor R. C. Oliver.

**British Dental Journal:** Professional and Scientific Publications, BMA House, Tavistock Sq, London, WC1H 9JR; tel. (171) 387-4499; telex 265929; f. 1880; twice monthly; journal of the British Dental Asscn; Editor M. Grace; circ. 18,460.

**British Journal of Psychiatry:** 17 Belgrave Sq., London, SW1X 8PG; tel. (171) 235-8857; fax (171) 245-1231; monthly; original articles, reviews and correspondence; publ. by the Royal College of Psychiatrists; Editor Greg Wilkinson; circ. 12,500.

**British Journal of Psychology:** 13A Church Lane, East Finchley, London, N2 8DX; tel. (181) 444-1040; fax (181) 365-3413; f. 1904; quarterly; publ. by the British Psychological Society; Editor Prof. Vicki Bruce; circ. 2,900.

**British Journal of Sociology:** London School of Economics, Houghton St, London, WC2A 2AE; tel. (171) 955-7283; fax (171) 955-7405; f. 1950; quarterly; Editor Stephen Hill.

**British Medical Journal:** British Medical Asscn House, Tavistock Sq., London, WC1H 9JR; tel. (171) 387-4499; telex 265929; fax (171) 383-6418; f. 1840; Saturday; 10 overseas editions; Editor Prof. Richard Smith; circ. 112,000.

**The Ecologist:** Agriculture House, Bath Rd, Sturminster Newton, Dorset, DT10 1DU; tel. (1258) 473476; fax (1258) 473748; f. 1970; every 2 months; all aspects of ecology, the environment, etc.; Editors Nicholas Hildyard, Sarah Sexton; circ. 9,000.

**Flight International:** Reed Business Publishing, Quadrant House, The Quadrant, Sutton, Surrey, SM2 5AS; tel. (181) 652-3842; telex 892084; fax (181) 652-3840; f. 1909; Wednesday; Editor Allan Winn; circ. 60,000.

**The Geographical Magazine:** Bldg 3, Carriage Row, 203 Eversholt St, London, NW1 1BW; tel. (171) 391-8888; fax (171) 391-8835; f. 1935; monthly; Editor Lisa Sykes; circ. 25,700.

**Lancet:** 42 Bedford Sq., London, WC1B 3SL; tel. (171) 436-4981; telex 291785; fax (171) 436-7570; f. 1823; Saturday; medical; Man. Dir Stephen Bullock (acting); Editor Dr Robin Fox; circ. 49,500 world-wide.

**Nature:** Macmillan Magazines Ltd, Porters South, Crinan St, London, N1 9SQ; tel. (171) 833-4000; fax (171) 843-4596; f. 1869; Thursday; scientific; Editor Sir John Maddox; circ. 50,000.

**New Scientist:** IPC Holborn Publishing Group, King's Reach Tower, Stamford St, London, SE1 9LS; tel. (171) 261-5000; fax (171) 261-6464; f. 1956; Thursday; science and technology; Editor Alun Anderson; circ. 104,600.

**Nursing Times:** Macmillan Magazines Ltd, Porters South, Crinan St, London, N1 9SQ; tel. (171) 833-4000; fax (171) 843-4596; f. 1905; Wednesday; professional nursing journal; Editor John Gilbert; circ. 87,348.

**The Practitioner:** 30 Calderwood St, London, SE18 6QH; tel. (181) 855-7777; telex 896238; fax (181) 855-2406; f. 1868; 12 per year; medical journal for General Practitioners; Man. Editor Gavin Atkin; circ. 35,000.

### Religion and Philosophy

**Catholic Herald:** Herald House, Lambs Passage, Bunhill Row, London, EC1Y 8TQ; tel. (171) 588-3101; fax (171) 256-9728; f. 1888; Catholic weekly newspaper; Friday; Editor Cristina Odone; circ. 30,000.

**Christian Herald:** 96 Dominion Rd, Worthing, W. Sussex, BN14 8JP; tel. (1903) 821082; fax (1903) 821081; f. 1866; Saturday; Editor Bruce Hardy; circ. 20,000.

**Church Times:** 33 Upper St, London, N1 0PN; tel. (171) 359-4570; fax (171) 226-3073; f. 1863; Church of England news; Friday; Editor Paul Handley; circ. 38,035.

**Jewish Chronicle:** Jewish Chronicle Newspaper Ltd, 25 Furnival St, London, EC4A 1JT; tel. (171) 405-9252; fax (171) 405-9040; f. 1841; Friday; Editor Edward J. Temko; circ. approx. 50,000.

**Methodist Recorder:** 122 Golden Lane, London, EC1Y 0TL; tel. (171) 251-8414; fax (171) 608-3490; f. 1861; Thursday; Editor Michael Taylor; circ. 55,317.

**Mind:** Oxford University Press, Walton St, Oxford, OX2 6DP; tel. (1865) 56767; fax (1865) 267773; f. 1876; quarterly; philosophy; Editor Prof. Mark Sainsbury.

**New Blackfriars:** Blackfriars, Oxford, OX1 3LY; tel. (1865) 278414; fax (1865) 278403; f. 1920; monthly; religious and cultural; Editor Rev. Allan J. White.

**Philosophy:** Royal Institute of Philosophy, 14 Gordon Sq., London, WC1H 0AG; tel. (171) 387-4130; f. 1925; quarterly; Editor Renford Bambrough.

**The Universe:** 1st Floor, St James's Bldgs, Oxford St, Manchester, M1 6FP; tel. (161) 236-8856; fax (161) 236-8530; f. 1860; Sunday; illustrated Catholic newspaper and review; publ. by Gabriel Communications Ltd; Proprs The Catholic Media Trust; Editor Ann Knowles; circ. 95,000.

**Woman Alive:** 96 Dominion Rd, Worthing, West Sussex, BN14 8JP; tel. (1903) 821082; fax (1903) 821081; f. 1982; monthly; Editor Elizabeth Proctor; circ. 16,000.

### PRESS ORGANIZATION

**The Press Complaints Commission:** 1 Salisbury Sq., London, EC4Y 8AE; tel. (171) 353-1248; fax (171) 353-8355; f. 1991 to replace the Press Council, following the report of the Committee on Privacy and Related Matters; an independent organization established by the newspaper and magazine industry through the Press Standards Board of Finance to deal with complaints from the public about the contents and conduct of newspapers and magazines; the Commission has an independent chairman and 16 members, drawn from the lay public and the press. It upholds a 18-point Code of Practice, agreed by a committee of editors representing the newspaper and magazine industry. It aims to ensure that the British press maintains the highest professional standards, having regard to generally established press freedoms; Chair. Lord Wakeham; Dir Mark Bolland.

UNITED KINGDOM (GREAT BRITAIN) — *Directory*

## NEWS AGENCIES

**Associated Press Ltd:** Associated Press House, 12 Norwich St, London, EC4A 1BP; tel. (171) 353-1515; telex 262887; fax (171) 353-8118; f. 1931; British subsidiary of Associated Press of USA; delivers a world-wide foreign news and photographic service to Commonwealth and foreign papers; Chair. LOUIS D. BOCCARDI; Bureau Chief MYRON BELKIND.

**Press Association Ltd:** 85 Fleet St, London, EC4P 4BE; tel. (171) 353-7440; fax (171) 583-6082; f. 1868; national news agency of the United Kingdom and the Republic of Ireland; Chair. Sir RICHARD STOREY; Chief Exec. ROBERT SIMPSON; Editor PAUL POTTS; Gen. Man. COLIN WEBB.

**Reuters Holdings PLC:** 85 Fleet St, London, EC4P 4AJ; tel. (171) 250-1122; telex 23222; fax (171) 324-5400; f. 1851; world-wide news and information service by computer and teleprinter to business clients in 133 countries and media clients in 158 countries; Chair. Sir CHRISTOPHER HOGG; CEO PETER JOB; Man. Dir JOHN PARCELL.

**UK News:** St George St, Leicester, LE1 9FQ; tel. (116) 253-0022; fax (116) 251-2151; f. 1993 by Northcliffe Newspaper Group Ltd and Westminster Press Ltd; provides national and international news, sport and pictures to 33 British regional newspapers; serves local radio stations through Network News; Chair. CHRIS CARTER; Man. Dir ALEX LEYS.

**United Press International (UPI):** 408 Strand, London, WC2R 0NE; tel. (171) 333-0999; fax (171) 333-1690; supplies world-wide news and news-picture coverage to newspapers, radio and television stations throughout the world; Bureau Chief MICHAEL COLLINS; Business Man. MICHAEL RAWLINSON.

### Principal Foreign Bureaux

**Agence France-Presse (AFP):** 72–78 Fleet St, London, EC4Y 1HY; tel. (171) 353-7461; telex 28703; fax (171) 353-8359; Bureau Chief MONIQUE VILLA.

**Agencia EFE** (Spain): 5 Cavendish Sq., London, W1M 0DP; tel. (171) 636-5226; fax (171) 436-3562; Bureau Chief ALBERTO GARCÍA-MARRDER.

**Agenzia Nazionale Stampa Associata (ANSA)** (Italy): Essex House, 12–13 Essex St, London, WC2R 3AA; tel. (171) 240-5514; telex 25240; fax (171) 240-5518; Bureau Chief PIER ANTONIO LACQUA.

**ANGOP** (Angola): 270 Kilburn High Rd, London, NW6 2BY; tel. (171) 372-1000; telex 295813; Rep. ELIO GAMBOA.

**Australian Associated Press Pty Ltd (AAP):** 12 Norwich St, London, EC4A 1EJ; tel. (171) 353-0153; fax (171) 583-3563; Chief Correspondent DON WOOLFORD.

**Canadian Press News Agency:** Associated Press House, 12 Norwich St, London, EC4A 1EJ; tel. (171) 353-6355; telex 8812455; fax (171) 583-4238; Bureau Chief STEPHEN WARD.

**Central News Agency, Inc.** (Taiwan): First Floor, 14 Anson Rd, London, N7 0RD; tel. (171) 700-0087; fax (171) 700-0088.

**Česká tisková kancelář (ČTK)** (Czech Republic): 12 Elliot Sq., London, NW3 3SU; tel. (171) 483-1958; fax (171) 586-6377; Chief Correspondent IVAN KYTKA.

**Deutsche Presse-Agentur (dpa)** (Germany): 30 Old Queen St, London, SW1H 9HP; tel. (171) 233-2888; telex 215839; fax (171) 233-3534; Chief Correspondent EDGAR DENTER.

**Ghana News Agency:** 104 Highgate Hill, London, N6 5HE; tel. (181) 342-8891; telex 919569; fax (181) 342-8688; Bureau Chief EUGENE B. THOMPSON.

**Informatsionnoye Telegrafnoye Agentstvo Rossii—Telegrafnoye Agentstvo Suverennykh Stran (ITAR-TASS)** (Russia): Suite 12–20, Second Floor, Morley House, 314–320 Regent St, London, W1R 5AB; tel. (171) 580-5543; telex 24201; fax (171) 580-5547; Chief Correspondent N. PAKHOMOV.

**Inter Press Service (IPS)** (Italy): 44 Gray's Inn Rd, London, WC1X 8LR; tel. (171) 404-5730; Correspondent LUCY JOHNSON.

**Jiji Tsushin-sha (Jiji Press Ltd)** (Japan): International Press Centre, 76 Shoe Lane, London, EC4A 3JB; tel. (171) 936-2847; fax (171) 583-8353; Bureau Chief YOSHIYUKI DEN.

**Kyodo News Service** (Japan): Suite 119/130, North West Wing, Bush House, Aldwych, London, WC2B 4PJ; tel. (171) 438-4501; telex 21176; fax (171) 438-4511; Bureau Chief N. OSHIKA.

**Maghreb Arabe Presse** (Moroccan News Agency): Halton House, 65 Great Portland St, London, W1N 5DH; tel. (171) 436-0873; telex 262511; fax (171) 436-0260; Bureau Chief ALI BAHAIJOUB.

**Magyar Távirati Iroda (MTI)** (Hungary): 5 Marlborough St, London, SW1; tel. and fax (171) 732-6078; Correspondent RÓBERT KERTÓSZ.

**Rossiyskoye Informatsionnoye Agentstvo—Novosti (RIA—Novosti)** (Russia): 3 Rosary Gardens, London, SW7 4NW; tel. (171) 370-1873; telex 9419849; fax (171) 244-7875; Correspondent VICTOR ORLIK.

**Xinhua (New China) News Agency** (People's Republic of China): 8 Swiss Terrace, Belsize Rd, Swiss Cottage, London, NW6 4RR; tel. (171) 586-8271; telex 24400; fax (171) 722-8512; Chief Correspondent XUE YOUNGXIN.

## INSTITUTIONS

**Chartered Institute of Journalists:** 2 Dock Offices, Surrey Quays Rd, London, SE16 2XL; tel. (171) 252-1187; fax (171) 232-2302; f. 1884; Pres. DOMINICK HARROD; Gen. Sec CHRIS UNDERWOOD.

**Newspaper Press Fund:** Dickens House, 35 Wathen Rd, Dorking, Surrey, RH4 1JY; tel. (1306) 887511; f. 1864; Pres. Viscount ROTHERMERE; Sec. P. W. EVANS; 5,500 mems.

**Newspaper Publishers' Association:** 34 Southwark Bridge Rd, London, SE1 9EU; tel. (171) 928-6928; fax (171) 928-2067; f. 1906; comprises 8 national newspaper groups and 21 titles; Chair. Sir FRANK ROGERS; Dir DAVID POLLOCK.

**Newspaper Society:** Bloomsbury House, 74–77 Great Russell St, London, WC1B 3DA; tel. (171) 636-7014; fax (171) 631-5119; f. 1836; represents the regional and local press; Pres. GEOFFREY COPEMAN; Dir DUGAL NISBET-SMITH.

**Periodical Publishers' Association Ltd:** Imperial House, 15–19 Kingsway, London, WC2B 6UN; tel. (171) 379-6268; fax (171) 379-5661; f. 1913; Chair. JOHN MATTHEWS; Chief Exec. IAN LOCKS; 180 mems.

**Scottish Daily Newspaper Society:** Merchants House Bldg, 30 George Sq., Glasgow, G2 1EG; tel. (141) 248-2375; fax (141) 248-2362; f. 1915; Pres. ALAN SCOTT; Dir A. GRAHAME THOMSON.

**Scottish Newspaper Publishers' Association:** 48 Palmerston Place, Edinburgh, EH12 5DE; tel. (131) 220-4353; fax (131) 220-4344; Pres. P. COHEN; Dir J. B. RAEBURN.

(See also under Employers' Organizations and Trade Unions).

# Principal Publishers

Publishing firms in the United Kingdom are mainly located in London and many are members of large publishing groups, notably Reed Elsevier, Random Century, the Pearson Group and International Thomson Publishing Ltd. Fiction remains the largest category. The United Kingdom publishes more new titles every year than any other European country. In 1991 about 70,000 titles were issued.

### Government Publishing House

**Her Majesty's Stationery Office—HMSO:** St Crispins, Duke St, Norwich, NR3 1PD; tel. (1603) 622211; telex 97301; fax (1603) 696506; f. 1786; Dir of Publications C. N. SOUTHGATE.

**Academic Press Ltd:** 24–28 Oval Rd, London, NW1 7DX; tel. (171) 267-4466; fax (171) 485-4752; f. 1958; academic, medical, technical and scientific; a division of Harcourt Brace and Co; Man. Dir JAN VELTEROP.

**Academy Editions:** 42 Leinster Gardens, London, W2 3AN; tel. (171) 402-2141; fax (171) 723-9540; f. 1967; art, architecture, decorative arts, photography, design; publ. *Architectural Monographs, UIA Journal, Architectural Design, Art & Design* magazines and *Journal of Philosophy and the Visual Arts*; Dir JOHN STODDART.

**Addison-Wesley Longman:** Longman House, Burnt Mill, Harlow, Essex, CM20 2JE; tel. (1279) 426721; fax (1279) 431059; Propr Pearson; educational, English language teaching materals; Chief Exec. LARRY JONES.

**Edward Arnold (Publishers):** 338 Euston Rd, London, NW1 3BH; tel. (171) 873-6000; telex 957703; fax (171) 873-6325; f. 1890; imprint of Hodder Headline (see below); humanities, scientific, technical, medical; Man. Dir RICHARD STILEMAN.

**Ashgate Publishing Ltd:** Gower House, Croft Rd, Aldershot, Hants, GU11 3HR; tel. (1252) 331551; telex 317210; fax (1252) 344405; f. 1991; social sciences, arts and humanities; imprints: Avebury, Arena, Scolar Press, Variorum; Chair. N. FARROW.

**The Athlone Press:** 1 Park Drive, London, NW11 7SG; tel. (181) 458-0888; fax (181) 201-8115; f. 1950; philosophy, literature, history, economics; Japan and South-East Asia, etc.; Man. Dir DORIS SOUTHAM.

**Barrie & Jenkins:** Random House, 20 Vauxhall Bridge Rd, London, SW1V 2SA; tel. (171) 973-9710; fax (171) 233-6057; imprint of Random House Ltd; illustrated non-fiction; Chair. GAIL REBUCK; Man. Dir JULIAN SHUCKBURGH.

**Bartholomew:** 12 Duncan St, Edinburgh, EH9 1TA; tel. (131) 667-9341; fax (131) 662-4282; f. 1826; bought by News International PLC 1985; the cartographic division of Harper Collins; maps, atlases and guide books; Publr BARRY WINKLEMAN.

# UNITED KINGDOM (GREAT BRITAIN)

**B. T. Batsford Ltd:** 4 Fitzhardinge St, London, W1H 0AH; tel. (171) 486-8484; fax (171) 487-4296; f. 1843; crafts, hobbies, leisure, chess, architecture, building, horticulture, archaeology, costume, local history, academic, schools; Chief Exec. BOBBY COX.

**BBC Worldwide Publishing:** Woodlands, 80 Wood Lane, London, W12 0TT; tel. (181) 576-2000; telex 934678; fax (181) 749-0538; Dir NICK CHAPMAN.

**Berlitz Publishing Co Ltd:** Berlitz House, Peterly Rd, Oxford, OX4 2TX; tel. (1865) 747033; fax (1865) 779700; f. 1970; travel, languages, leisure; Publr JULIAN PARISH.

**A. & C. Black (Publishers) Ltd:** 35 Bedford Row, London, WC1R 4JH; tel. (171) 242-0946; fax (171) 831-8478; f. 1807; inc. Adlard Coles Nautical, Christopher Helm; children's and educational books, music, arts and crafts, drama, reference, sport, theatre, travel, sailing, ornithology; Chair. C. A. A. BLACK; Man. Dirs C. A. A. BLACK, J. COLEMAN.

**Blackie Academic and Professional:** Wester Cleddens Rd, Bishopbriggs, Glasgow, G64 2NZ; tel. (141) 762-2332; fax (141) 772-7524; f. 1809 as Blackie and Sons; Editorial Dir Dr A. GRAEME MACKINTOSH.

**Blackwell Publishers:** 108 Cowley Rd, Oxford, OX4 1JF; tel. (1865) 791100; telex 837022; fax (1865) 791347; f. 1921; academic, professional, business and finance books and journals; allied cos Polity Press, NCC Blackwell, Marston Book Services Ltd, Shakespeare Head Press; Man. Dir RENÉ OLIVIERI.

**Blackwell Science Ltd:** Osney Mead, Oxford, OX2 0EL; tel. (1865) 206206; fax (1865) 721205; f. 1939; medical, scientific, veterinary, technical, agricultural, botanical, ecological, geological, computer science; Chair. NIGEL BLACKWELL.

**Bloomsbury Publishing Plc:** 2 Soho Sq., London, W1V 6HB; tel. (171) 494-2111; fax (171) 434-0151; fiction, non-fiction, children's, music and reference; Chair. NIGEL NEWTON; Editorial Dirs LIZ CALDER, KATHY ROONEY, DAVID REYNOLDS.

**Boosey and Hawkes Music Publishers Ltd:** 295 Regent St, London, W1R 8JH; tel. (171) 580-2060; telex 8954613; fax (171) 436-5675; music, textbooks; Man. Dir R. A. FELL.

**Bowker-Saur Ltd:** Maypole House, Maypole Rd, East Grinstead, West Sussex, RH19 1HH; tel. (1342) 330100; fax (1342) 330191; part of Reed Reference Publishing; bibliographies and reference directories; Man. Dir CHARLES HALPIN.

**Marion Boyars Publishers Ltd:** 24 Lacy Rd, London, SW15 1NL; tel. (181) 788-9522; fax (181) 789-8122; fiction, plays, music, poetry, translations, literary criticism, sociology, ecology, political questions (Ideas in Progress Series); Dirs MARION BOYARS, ARTHUR BOYARS.

**British and Foreign Bible Society:** Bible House, Stonehill Green, Westlea, Swindon, Wilts., SN5 7DG; tel. (1793) 418100; fax (1793) 418118; f. 1804; Bibles, Testaments and scripture resource materials in many languages; Exec. Dir NEIL CROSBIE.

**Butterworth & Co (Publishers) Ltd:** Halsbury House, 35 Chancery Lane, London, WC2A 1EL; tel. (171) 400-2500; fax (171) 400-2842; f. 1818; a division of Reed International Books Ltd; law, tax, accountancy, banking books and journals; Chief Exec. NEVILLE CUSWORTH.

**Butterworth-Heinemann:** Linacre House, Jordan Hill, Oxford, OX2 8DP; tel. (1865) 310366; telex 83111; fax (1865) 310898; part of Reed Elsevier (UK) Ltd; imprints: Butterworth Architecture, Butterworth Medical, Butterworth Scientific, Digital Press, Focal Press, Made Simple, Heinemann Professional Publishing; Chair. RICHARD CHARKIN; Man. Dir DOUGLAS FOX.

**Calder Publications Ltd:** 9–15 Neal St, London, WC2H 9TU; tel. (171) 497-1741; f. 1950; fiction, plays, music, opera, European classics, translations, general books, social science, politics; Calderbooks, Platform Books, English National Opera guides, World in Crisis series; Man. Dir JOHN CALDER.

**Cambridge University Press:** The Edinburgh Bldg, Shaftesbury Rd, Cambridge, CB2 2RU; tel. (1223) 312393; telex 817256; fax (1223) 315052; f. 1534; academic and scientific monographs and textbooks, educational, English language teaching materials, microsoftware, bibles, prayer books and academic journals; incorporating Eyre and Spottiswoode Publishers Ltd; Chief Exec. ANTHONY K. WILSON.

**Jonathan Cape Ltd:** Random House, 20 Vauxhall Bridge Rd, London, SW1V 2SA; tel. (171) 973-9730; fax (171) 233-6117; f. 1921; imprint of Random House (UK) Ltd; general, biography, travel, belles-lettres, fiction; subsidiary imprint: The Bodley Head (biography, current affairs, humour); Publishing Dir DAN FRANKLIN.

**Carlton Books:** 20 St Anne's Court, London W1V 3AW; tel. (171) 734-7338; fax (171) 434-1196; f. 1992; Propr Carlton Communications PLC; Chief Exec. JONATHAN GOODMAN.

**Frank Cass & Co Ltd:** Newbury House, 890-900 Eastern Ave, Newbury Pk, Ilford, Essex, 1G2 7HH; tel. (181) 599-8866; fax (181) 599-0984; f. 1957; economics, economic and social history, politics, military studies, Soviet studies, development studies, business, sociology, slavery, African, Middle Eastern; reprints original studies, journals; Man. Dir FRANK CASS.

**Cassell PLC:** Wellington House, 125 Strand, London, WC2R 0BB; tel. (171) 420-5555; fax (171) 240-7261; f. 1848; imprints: Cassell Publishers Ltd, Cassell Educational Ltd, Geoffrey Chapman Publishers, Arms & Armour Press, Blandford Press, Mansell Publishing, Mowbray, New Orchard Editions, Studio Vista, Tycooly Publishing, Victor Gollancz Ltd, Ward Lock Ltd, Wisley Handbooks, H. F. & G. Witherby Ltd; Man. Dir P. J. STURROCK.

**Century:** Random House, 20 Vauxhall Bridge Rd, London, SW1V 2SA; tel. (171) 973-9670; telex 261212; fax (171) 233-6127; f. 1987; imprint of Random House (UK) Ltd; general, biography, travel, current affairs, fiction, memoirs, music, philosophy; Man. Dir SIMON KING.

**Chadwyck-Healey Ltd:** The Quorum, Barnwell Rd, Cambridge, CB5 8SW; tel. (1223) 215512; fax (1223) 215513; academic; Chair. Sir CHARLES CHADWYCK-HEALEY.

**Geoffrey Chapman:** Wellington House, 125 Strand, London, WC2R 0BB; tel. (171) 420-5555; fax (171) 240-7261; f. 1958; a division of Cassell PLC; liturgy, scripture, religious education, theology; Chair. P. J. STURROCK; Man. Dir STEPHEN BUTCHER.

**Chapman and Hall Ltd:** 2–6 Boundary Row, London, SE1 8HN; tel. (171) 865-0066; telex 290164; fax (171) 522-9632; f. 1830; also incorporating E. & F.N. Spon, Van Nostrand Reinhald (International), BMMR; imprints: Blackie Academic and Professional, Blueprint, H. K. Lewis and Co Ltd; scientific, technical, medical; Man. Dir DAVID INGLIS.

**Chatto and Windus, Ltd:** 20 Vauxhall Bridge Rd, London, SW1V 2SA; tel. (171) 973-9740; telex 299080; fax (171) 233-6123; imprint of Random House UK Ltd (see below); general, academic, poetry, biography, memoirs, cookery, crime, travel, politics, history, literary criticism, illustrated books, current affairs, psychology, and fiction; imprint: Hogarth Press; Publishing Dir JONATHAN BURNHAM.

**Churchill Livingstone:** Robert Stevenson House, 1–3 Baxter's Place, Leith Walk, Edinburgh, EH1 3AF; tel. (131) 556-2424; telex 262433; fax (131) 558-1278; f. 1863; medical division of Pearson Professional Ltd; medical science, dental, nursing books, allied health, medical and biomedical periodicals; Div. Man. Dir A. T. STEVENSON.

**James Clarke and Co Ltd:** POB 60, Cambridge, CB1 2NT; tel. (1223) 350865; telex 817114; fax (1223) 66951; f. 1859; religious, reference and academic; Man. Dir ADRIAN BRINK.

**Conran Octopus:** 37 Shelton St, London, WC2H 9HN; tel. (171) 240-6961; fax (171) 836-9951; illustrated reference books; imprint of Reed Consumer Books; Publishing Dir JOHN WALLACE.

**Constable and Co Ltd:** 3 The Lanchesters, 162 Fulham Palace Rd, London, W6 9ER; tel. (181) 741-3663; fax (181) 748-7562; all branches of literature; Chair. and Jt Man. Dir B. K. GLAZEBROOK; Publishing and Jt Man. Dir. ROBIN BAIRD-SMITH.

**Dartmouth Publishing Co. Ltd:** Gower House, Croft, Rd, Aldershot, Hants, GU11 3HR; tel. (1252) 331551; telex 317210; fax (1252) 344405; f. 1989; international relations and politics, management, law, philosophy; Chair. N. FARROW; Man. Dir J. IRWIN.

**Darton, Longman and Todd Ltd:** 1 Spencer Court, 140–142 Wandsworth High St, London, SW18 4JJ; tel. (181) 875-0155; fax (181) 875-0133; f. 1959; theology, spirituality, religious biography and history, Bibles; Sales and Marketing Dir M. SHEPPARD.

**David & Charles (Publishers) PLC:** Brunel House, Forde Close, Newton Abbot, Devon, TQ12 4PU; tel. (1626) 61121; telex 42904; fax (1626) 331367; f. 1960; general, trade and reference; imprint: Pevensey Press.

**J. M. Dent and Sons, Ltd:** Orion House, 5 Upper St Martin's Lane, London, WC2H 9EA; tel. (171) 240-3444; fax (171) 240-4823; f. 1888; imprint of Orion Publishing Group; publs Everyman titles, gardening, heritage, music, economics, sociology, psychology, law, history, popular reference, science; Dir HILARY LAURIE.

**André Deutsch Ltd:** 106 Great Russell St, London, WC1B 3LJ; tel. (171) 580-2746; fax (171) 631-3253; f. 1950; fiction, belles-lettres, biography, memoirs, cookery, poetry, humour, art, politics, history, travel, sport; Chair. TOM ROSENTHAL.

**Dorling Kindersley PLC:** 9 Henrietta St, London, WC2E 8PS; tel. (171) 836-5411; telex 8954527; fax (171) 836-7570; f. 1974; illustrated reference books; Chair. and Chief Exec. PETER KINDERSLEY.

**Gerald Duckworth and Co Ltd:** 48 Hoxton Sq., London, N1 6PB; tel. (171) 729-5986; fax (171) 729-0015; f. 1898; fiction, academic; Chair. STEPHEN HILL; Publr and Man. Dir ROBIN BAIRD-SMITH.

**Edinburgh University Press:** 22 George Sq., Edinburgh, EH8 9LF; tel. (131) 650-4218; telex 727442; fax (131) 662-0053; learned books and journals; Polygon Books imprint; Chair. DAVID MARTIN; Publisher VIVIAN BONE; Polygon Editor MARION SINCLAIR.

# UNITED KINGDOM (GREAT BRITAIN)

**Edward Elgar Publishing Ltd:** 8 Lansdown Place, Cheltenham, GL50 2HU; tel. (1242) 226934; fax (1242) 262111; f. 1986; economics and other social sciences; Chair. N. Farrow; Man. Dir E. Elgar.

**Elsevier Science Ltd:** The Boulevard, Langford Lane, Kidlington, Oxon., OX5 1GB; tel. (1865) 843000; fax (1865) 843010; Propr Reed Elsevier PLC; scientific, academic, engineering, architectural and technical books and journals; Man. Dir Michael Boswood.

**Encyclopaedia Britannica International, Ltd:** Carew House, Station Approach, Wallington, Surrey, SM6 0DA; tel. (181) 669-4355; fax (181) 773-3631; f. 1768; publs *Encyclopaedia Britannica, Britannica Book of the Year, Great Books of the Western World, Children's Britannica*; Man. Dir J. D. Adams.

**Europa Publications Ltd:** 18 Bedford Sq., London, WC1B 3JN; tel. (171) 580-8236; telex 21540; fax (171) 636-1664; f. 1926; international reference books, social and economic history and international affairs; Chair. Clive Martin; Man. Dir Patrick McGinley.

**Evans Brothers Ltd:** 2A Portman Mansions, Chiltern St, London, W1M 1LE; tel. (171) 935-7160; telex 8811713; fax (171) 487-5034; f. 1906; educational, children's, general and overseas books; Man. Dir S. T. Pawley.

**Faber and Faber Ltd:** 3 Queen Sq., London, WC1N 3AU; tel. (171) 465-0045; fax (171) 465-0034; f. 1929; art and architecture, biography, autobiography, children's, cookery, wine, economics, fiction, history, music, poetry; Faber Paperbacks; Chair. and Man. Dir Matthew Evans.

**The Folio Society Ltd:** 44 Eagle St, London, WC1R 4FS; tel. (171) 400-4200; fax (171) 400-4242; f. 1947; fine illustrated editions of fiction, history, biographies, drama and poetry; Editorial Dir Sue Bradbury.

**W. Foulsham & Co Ltd:** 837 Yeovil Rd, Slough, Berks, SL1 4JH; tel. (1753) 26769; telex 849041; fax (1753) 811409; f. 1819; art, educational, military, reference, technical, sports, games and pastimes, Foulsham-Sams Technical Books; Exec. Chair. R. Belasco.

**Fourth Estate Ltd:** 289 Westbourne Grove, London, W2 2QA; tel. (171) 727-8993; fax (171) 792-3176; f. 1984; general reference, current affairs; imprints: Blueprint Monographs, Fourth Estate Paperbacks, Guardian Books; Man. Dir Victoria Barnsley.

**Samuel French Ltd:** 52 Fitzroy St, London, W1P 6JR; tel. (171) 387-9373; fax (171) 387-2161; f. 1830; drama; Chair. Charles Van Nostrand; Man. Dir John Bedding.

**Gee and Co (Publishers) Ltd:** South Quay Plaza, 183 Marsh Wall, London, E14 9FS; tel. (171) 538-5386; fax (171) 538-8623; f. 1874; part of Professional Publishing Ltd (division of International Thomson Organisation); books and news letters on accountancy and financial management; Man. Dir Peter Lake.

**Robert Gibson and Sons, Glasgow, Ltd:** 17 Fitzroy Place, Glasgow, G3 7SF; tel. (141) 248-5674; f. 1883; educational and textbooks; Chair. R. D. C. Gibson.

**Ginn and Co Ltd:** Prebendal House, Parson's Fee, Aylesbury, Bucks., HP20 2QZ; tel. (1296) 394442; f. 1924; imprint of Reed Elsevier PLC; educational; Chair. S. Warshaw; Man. Dir Nigel Hall.

**Victor Gollancz Ltd:** Wellington House, 125 Strand, London, WC2R 0BB; tel. (171) 420-5555; fax (171) 240-7261; f. 1928; imprint of Cassell PLC (see above); fiction, crime and science fiction, biography, travel, politics, current affairs, architecture, music, bridge, children's books; Chair. P. J. Sturrock.

**Gower Publishing Ltd:** Gower House, Croft Rd, Aldershot, Hants., GU11 3HR; tel. (1252) 331551; telex 317210; fax (1252) 344405; f. 1967; business, management and human resource development; Chair. N. Farrow; Man. Dir C. Simpson.

**Gresham Books Ltd:** The Gresham Press, POB 61, Henley-on-Thames, Oxon. RG9 3LQ; tel. (1734) 403789; fax (1734) 403789; f. 1978; natural history, reprints, music, leisure, wood engraving, hymn books, naval and military; Chief Exec. M. V. Green.

**Guinness Publishing Ltd:** 33 London Rd, Enfield, Middx, EN2 6DJ; tel. (181) 367-4567; telex 23573; fax (181) 367-5912; f. 1954; reference, sport, music and general interest; Man. Dir Christopher Irwin.

**Robert Hale Ltd:** Clerkenwell House, 45–47 Clerkenwell Green, London, EC1R 0HT; tel. (171) 251-2661; fax (171) 490-4958; f. 1936; memoirs, biography, travel, sport, fiction, belles-lettres, general non-fiction; Man. Dir John Hale.

**Hamish Hamilton Ltd:** 27 Wrights Lane, London, W8 5TZ; tel. (171) 416-3100; telex 917181; fax (171) 416-3295; f. 1931; biography, history, politics, current affairs, international writing, fiction and children's books; holding co Pearson; Publishing Dir Andrew Franklin.

**Harcourt Brace and Co Ltd:** 24–28 Oval Rd, London, NW1 7DX; tel. (171) 264-4466; telex 25775; fax (171) 482-2293; academic, scientific and medical; Man. Dir William Barnett.

*Directory*

**Harlequin Mills and Boon Ltd:** Eton House, 18–24 Paradise Rd, Richmond, Surrey, TW9 1SR; tel. (181) 948-0444; fax (181) 288-2899; f. 1908; romantic fiction; Chair. J. T. Boon; Man. Dir A. Flynn.

**HarperCollins Publishers:** 77–85 Fulham Palace Rd, London, W6 8JB; tel. (181) 741-7070; telex 25611; fax (181) 307-4440; William Collins f. 1819; bought by News International 1989; fiction and non-fiction of all classes, including biographies, history, travel, nature, sport, art, children's, educational, classics, atlases, reference, religion; imprints: Armada, Bartholomew, Collins, Collins Bibles, Collins Cartographic, Collins Classics, Collins Crime, Collins Liturgical, Flamingo, Fount, HarperCollins, HarperCollins Audio, HarperCollins Paperbacks, HarperCollins Science Fiction and Fantasy, Invincible, Jets, Lions, Marshall Pickering, Nicholson, Pandora, Pandora Lions, Thorsons, Times Books, Tolkien, Tracks, Young Lions; Exec. Chair. and Publr E. Bell.

**The Harvill Press:** 84 Thornhill Rd, London, N1 1RD; tel. (171) 609-1119; fax (171) 609-2019; fiction; Editorial Dir Christopher MacLehose.

**Headline Book Publishing Ltd:** 338 Euston Rd, London, NW1 7BH; tel. (171) 873-6000; fax (171) 873-6124; imprint of Hodder Headlines PLC; fiction, history, humour, leisure, biography; Chair. Tim Hely Hutchinson; Man. Dir Sian Thomas.

**William Heinemann Ltd:** Michelin House, 81 Fulham Rd, London, SW3 6RB; tel. (171) 581-9393; telex 920191; fax (171) 589-8437; imprint of Reed Consumer Books; arts, biography, fiction, history, science, sports, travel; Publr Tom Weldon.

**Heinemann Educational:** Halley Court, Jordan Hill, Oxford, OX2 8EJ; tel. (1865) 311366; telex 837292; fax (1865) 310043; imprint of Reed Educational Publishing; educational textbooks for UK and abroad; Man. Dir Robert Osborne.

**Heinemann English Language Teaching:** Halley Court, Jordan Hill, Oxford, OX2 8EJ; imprint of Reed Educational Publishing; Man. Dir Mike Esplen.

**Hodder Headline PLC:** 338 Euston Rd, London, NW1 7BH; tel. (171) 873-6000; fax (171) 873-6124; f. 1993; imprints: Edward Arnold, Headline Book Publishing Ltd, Hodder and Stoughton Ltd; Group Chief Exec. Tim Hely Hutchinson.

**Hodder and Stoughton Ltd:** 338 Euston Rd, London, NW1 7BH; tel. (171) 873-6000; fax (171) 873-6124; f. 1868; imprints: Coronet, Knight, New English Library Ltd, Sceptre; general, biography, travel, religion, juvenile, fiction, current affairs, educational, academic and medical paperbacks; Man. Dir Martin Neild.

**IOP Publishing Ltd:** Techno House, Redcliffe Way, Bristol, BS1 6NX; tel. (117) 929-7481; telex 449149; fax (117) 929-4318; f. 1949; scientific and technical publishers; Operations Dir Dr K. Paulus.

**Jordan Publishing Ltd:** 21 St Thomas St, Bristol, BS1 6JS; tel. (117) 923-0600; telex 449119; fax (117) 925-0486; f. 1863; UK and international company formation, business administration, law; Man. Dir Richard Hudson.

**Michael Joseph Ltd:** 27 Wrights Lane, London, W8 5TZ; tel. (171) 416-3200; fax (171) 416-3293; f. 1936; imprints: Pelham Books Ltd; general, fiction; Propr Pearson; Publishing Dir Susan Watt.

**Richard Joseph Publishers Ltd:** Unit 2, Monks Walk, Farnham, Surrey, GU9 8HT; tel. (1252) 734347; fax (1252) 734307; reference and directories; Man. Dir Richard Joseph.

**Kelly's Directories:** Windsor Court, East Grinstead House, East Grinstead, West Sussex, RH19 1XA; tel. (1342) 326972; telex 95127; fax (1342) 326920; f. 1799; a division of Reed Information Services Ltd; directories and business reference books; Man. Dir K. Burton.

**Kenyon-Deane Ltd:** 10 Station Rd Industrial Estate, Malvern, Worcs., WR13 6RN; tel. (1684) 540154; f. 1971; incorporates Kenyon House Press, H. F. W. Deane Ltd; plays and drama textbooks, specialists in all-women plays and plays for young people; Man. Dir Leslie Smith.

**Kogan Page Ltd:** 120 Pentonville Rd, London, N1 9JN; tel. (171) 278-0433; telex 263088; fax (171) 837-6348; business, education, management, accountancy, textbooks, transport, careers, training, journals; Man. Dir Philip Kogan.

**Ladybird Books Ltd:** Beeches Rd, Loughborough, Leics., LE11 2NQ; tel. (1509) 268021; telex 341347; fax (1509) 234672; children's; Man. Dir Anthony Forbes Watson.

**Larousse PLC:** Elsley House, 24–30 Great Titchfield St, London, W1P 7AD; tel. (171) 631-0878; fax (171) 323-4694; English language and bilingual dictionaries, reference, children's books; imprints: Chambers, Larousse, Kingfisher; part of Groupe de la Cité; Chair. Daniel Grisewood; Man. Dir John Clement.

**Lawrence and Wishart Ltd:** 144a Old South Lambeth Rd, London, SW8 1XX; tel. (171) 820-9281; fax (171) 587-0469; f. 1936; politics, history, feminism, race, economics, Marxist theory, cultural studies; Man. Dir Sally Davison.

# UNITED KINGDOM (GREAT BRITAIN)

**Leicester University Press:** 25 Floral Street, London, WC2E 9DS; tel. (171) 240-9233; fax (171) 379-5553; f. 1951; a division of Pinter Publishers; academic books in the fields of history, archaeology, defence studies, international law, museum studies; Publr N. VII-NIKKA.

**Little, Brown and Co:** Brettenham House, Lancaster Place, London, WC2E 7EN; tel. (171) 911-8000; fax (171) 911-8100; subsidiary of Time-Warner Communications; paperbacks: Warner, Warner Futura, Abacus; hardback: Little, Brown; Little Brown Illustrated; Man. Dir PHILIPPA HARRISON.

**Liverpool University Press:** POB 147, Liverpool, L69 3BX; tel. (151) 794-2232; telex 627095; fax (151) 708-6502; f. 1901; general literature, education, social, political, economic and ancient history, geography, planning and environmental science, hispanic studies, archaeology, population studies, veterinary science, science fiction criticism series; Publr ROBIN BLOXSIDGE.

**Lund Humphries Publishers Ltd:** Park House, 1 Russell Gardens, London, NW11 9NN; tel. (181) 458-6314; fax (181) 905-5245; f. 1969; arts, graphic arts, architecture, scholarly, Arabic language; Dirs CLIVE BINGLEY, LIONEL LEVENTHAL.

**Lutterworth Press:** POB 60, Cambridge, CB1 2NT; tel. (1223) 350865; telex 817114; fax (1223) 66951; f. 1799; subsidiary of James Clarke & Co Ltd; the arts, crafts, biography, educational, environmental, history, theology, travel, sport, juvenile fiction and non-fiction; Man. Dir. ADRIAN BRINK.

**McGraw-Hill Book Co Europe:** McGraw-Hill House, Shoppenhangers Rd, Maidenhead, Berks., SL6 2QL; tel. (1628) 23432; telex 848484; fax (1628) 770224; technical, scientific, computer studies, professional reference, general and medical books; Man. Dir FRED PERKINS.

**Macmillan Education Ltd:** Houndmills, Basingstoke, Hants., RG21 2XS; tel. (256) 29242; telex 858493; fax (1256) 479985; a division of Macmillan Publishers Ltd; academic, reference and educational books; Chair. CHRISTOPHER PATERSON; Man. Dir CHRISTOPHER HARRISON.

**Macmillan General Books Ltd:** 18–21 Cavaye Pl., London, SW10 9PG; tel. (171) 373-6070; fax (171) 370-0746; fiction and non-fiction; imprints: Picador, Pan Paperbacks, Sidgwick and Jackson; Chair. A. R. SOAR; Man. Dir IAN CHAPMAN.

**The Macmillan Press Ltd:** Houndmills, Basingstoke, Hants., RG21 2XS; tel. (1256) 29242; fax (1256) 479476; academic, scientific and technical works and reference books, *Grove's Dictionaries of Music*; Chair. A. R. SOAR; Man. Dir D. J. G. KNIGHT.

**Macmillan Reference Books:** 18–21 Cavaye Pl., London, SW10 9PG; tel. (171) 373-6070; fax (171) 370-0746; general reference, dictionaries; a division of Macmillan Publishers Ltd; Publr JULIAN ASHBY.

**Manchester University Press:** Oxford Rd, Manchester, M13 9NR; tel. (161) 273-5539; telex 666517; fax (161) 274-3346; f. 1904; all branches of higher education, arts, science and social sciences; Publr FRANCIS BROOKE; Editorial Dir RICHARD PURSLOW.

**Medici Society Ltd:** 34–42 Pentonville Rd, London, N1 9HG; tel. (171) 837-7099; fax (171) 837-9152; f. 1908; art, children's books; Man. Dir P. A. MEATH BAKER.

**Methuen and Co Ltd:** Michelin House, 81 Fulham Rd, London, SW3 6RB; tel. (171) 581-9393; telex 920191; fax (171) 225-0933; f. 1889; imprint of Reed Consumer Books; literature, fiction, drama, humour, music; Publisher GEOFFREY STRACHAN.

**M-G Information Services Ltd:** Riverbank House, Angel Lane, Tonbridge, Kent, TN9 1SE; tel. (1732) 362666; telex 95132; fax (1732) 367301; reference and buyers' guides; Man. Dir MARK SIMPSON.

**Mitchell Beazley:** Michelin House, 81 Fulham Rd, London, SW3 6RB; tel. (171) 581-9393; fax (171) 584-8268; f. 1969; imprint of Reed Consumer Books; wine, travel, gardening, antiques, reference, astronomy, astrology, atlases, guides, interiors, sport and leisure; Publr ROBERT SNUGGS.

**John Murray:** 50 Albemarle St, London, W1X 4BD; tel. (171) 493-4361; fax (171) 499-1792; f. 1768; art, architecture, biography, autobiography, history, travel, crafts, decorative arts; secondary and self-teaching educational books; Chair. JOHN R. MURRAY.

**Nelson ELT:** 100 Avenue Rd, London, NW3 3HF; tel. (171) 722-3456; fax (171) 722-4600; English language teaching materials; Man. Dir GILES LEWIS.

**Thomas Nelson and Sons Ltd:** Nelson House, Mayfield Rd, Walton-on-Thames, Surrey, KT12 5PL; tel. (1932) 252211; fax (1932) 252497; f. 1798; Proprs International Thomson Organisation PLC; educational books for all ages up to further education level; Man. Dir ROD GAUVIN.

**New English Library:** 338 Euston Rd, London, NW1 3BH; tel. (171) 873-6000; fax (171) 873-6124; f. 1957; imprint of Hodder and Stoughton Ltd; publishers of NEL, NEL Hardcovers; Publr CLARE BRISTOW.

**James Nisbet and Co Ltd:** 78 Tilehouse St, Hitchin, Herts., SG5 2DY; tel. (1462) 438331; fax (1462) 431528; f. 1810; business management, educational; Chair. E. M. MACKENZIE-WOOD.

**Novello and Co Ltd:** 8/9 Frith St, London, W1V 5TZ; tel. (171) 434-0066; fax (171) 287-6329; music; Man. Dir ROBERT WISE.

**Oliver and Boyd:** Longman House, Burnt Mill, Harlow, Essex, CM20 2JE; tel. (1279) 426721; telex 81259; fax (1279) 431059; f. 1798; imprint of Longman Group Ltd; educational; Man. Dir JEFF ANDREW.

**Orion Publishing Group:** Orion House, 5 Upper St Martin's Lane, London, WC2H 9EA; tel. (171) 240-3444; fax (171) 240-4822; f. 1991; imprints: Orion, Phoenix, Millennium, Weidenfeld and Nicolson, J. M. Dent and Sons, Everyman; Chair. Sir JOHN CUCKNEY (life peer); Chief Exec. ANTHONY CHEETHAM.

**Pearson Professional Ltd:** Maple House, 149 Tottenham Court Rd, London, W1P 9LL; tel. (171) 896-2000; f. 1994 by amalgamation of business and professional publishing divisions of Financial Times Group and Longman Group; Chief Exec. PETER WARWICK.

**Peter Owen Ltd:** 73 Kenway Rd, London, SW5 0RE; tel. (171) 373-5628; fax (171) 373-6760; f. 1951; general publishers of fiction, autobiography, translations, etc.; publishers of books in the UNESCO series of Representative Works; Man. Dir PETER OWEN.

**Oxford University Press:** Walton St, Oxford, OX2 6DP; tel. (1865) 56767; telex 837330; fax (1865) 56646; f. *c*. 1478; Bibles, prayer books, *Oxford English Dictionary*, the *Dictionary of National Biography*, and many other dictionaries and books of reference, learned and general works from the humanities to the sciences, educational, electronic, music and children's books and audiovisual and English language teaching material; Sec. to the Delegates of the Press and Chief Exec. JAMES ARNOLD-BAKER.

**Pavilion Books Ltd:** 26 Upper Ground, London, SE1 9PD; tel. (171) 620-1666; fax (171) 620-1314; general; Man. Dir COLIN WEBB.

**Pelham Books Ltd:** 27 Wright's Lane, London, W8 5TZ; tel. (171) 416-3200; fax (171) 416-3293; f. 1961; imprint of Michael Joseph; *Pears Cyclopaedia*, *Junior Pears Encyclopaedia*, sport, practical, country; Publishing Dir SUSAN WATT.

**Penguin Books Ltd:** Bath Road, Harmondsworth, Middlesex, UB7 0DA; tel. (181) 899-4000; telex 933349; fax (181) 899-4099; f. 1936; holding co Pearson; paperback imprints: Penguin, Pelican, Puffin and Signet; reprints and original works of fiction and non-fiction including travel, biography, science and social studies, reference books, handbooks, plays, poetry, classics and children's books; hardback imprints: Hamish Hamilton, Michael Joseph, Viking, F. Warne and Blackie; Chair. and Chief Exec. P. MAYER; Man. Dir (UK) T. GLOVER.

**Phaidon Press Ltd:** Regent's Wharf, All Saints St, London, N1 9PA; tel. (171) 361-1000; applied decorative art, architecture, photography, performing arts and music, fine art; Chair. RICHARD SCHLAGMAN.

**George Philip Ltd:** Michelin House, 81 Fulham Rd, London, SW1 6RB; tel. (171) 581-9393; fax (171) 589-8419; imprint of Reed Elsevier (see below); maps, atlases, globes, books; Publr J. GAISFORD.

**Pitman Publishing:** 128 Long Acre, London, WC2E 9AN; tel. (171) 379-7383; telex 261367; fax (171) 240-5771; f. 1842; part of Longman Group UK Ltd; secretarial, business, management, professional, information technology books, magazines and computer software; Man. Dir R. BRISTOW.

**Pluto Publishing Ltd:** 345 Archway Rd, London, N6 5AA; tel. (181) 348-2724; fax (181) 348-9133; f. 1970; academic, scholarly, current affairs and reference; Man. Dir ROGER VAN ZWANENBERG.

**Random House UK Ltd:** Random House, 20 Vauxhall Bridge Rd, London, SW1V 2SA; tel. (171) 973-9000; telex 299080; fax (171) 233-6115; imprints: Arrow Books Ltd (imprint: Legend), Jonathan Cape, Century Publishing, Chatto & Windus (imprint: Hogarth Press), Hutchinson, Virago Press, Pimlico, Vintage, Bodley Head, Random House Children's, Julia MacRae Books, Red Fox, Ebury Press (imprints: Barrie & Jenkins, Condé Nast Books, Rider, Stanley Paul, Vermilion); Chair. and Chief Exec. GAIL REBUCK.

**Reed Information Services Ltd:** Windsor Court, East Grinstead House, East Grinstead, Sussex, RH19 1XE; tel. (1342) 326972; telex 91527; fax (1342) 315130; f. 1866; business directories; Chief Exec. R. J. E. DANGERFIELD.

**Reed International Books Ltd:** Michelin House, 81 Fulham Rd, London, SW3 6RB; tel. (171) 581-9393; telex 920191; fax (171) 589-8419; f. 1992; book publishing subsidiary of Reed Elsevier (UK) Ltd; Chair PAUL HAMLYN; Chief Exec. IAN IRVINE.
Incorporates the following main book-publishing divisions:

    **Butterworth and Co (Publishers) Ltd** (see above).

    **Reed Academic Publishing:** Linacre House, Jordan Hill, Oxford, OX2 8EJ; tel. (1865) 310898; Man. Dir DOUGLAS FOX.

    **Reed Consumer Books:** Michelin House, 81 Fulham Rd, London, SW3 6RB; tel. (171) 581-9393; fax (171) 225-9424; imprints:

# UNITED KINGDOM (GREAT BRITAIN)

Brimax Books, Conran Octopus, Hamlyn, Hamlyn Children's Reference Books, William Heinemann, Heinemann Young Books, Mammoth, Mandarin, Methuen, Methuen Children's Books, Minerva, Mitchell Beazley, Osprey, George Philip, Pitkin Pictorials, Secker and Warburg, Sinclair-Stevenson; Chief Exec. RICHARD CHARKIN.

**Reed Educational Publishing:** Halley Court, Jordan Hill, Oxford, OX2 8EJ; tel. (1865) 311366; fax (1865) 310043; imprints: Ginn & Co, Heinemann Educational, Heinemann English Language Teaching; Man. Dir WILLIAM SHEPHERD.

**Routledge:** 11 New Fetter Lane, London, EC4P 4EE; tel. (171) 583-9855; telex 263398; fax (171) 583-0701; f. 1988; formed from Routledge & Kegan Paul, Methuen Academic, Tavistock, Unwin Hyman Academic and Croom Helm; Proprs International Thompson Publishing Ltd; professional and academic; Man. Dir JANICE PRICE.

**Sage Publications Ltd:** 6 Bonhill St, London, EC2A 4PU; tel. (171) 374-0645; fax (171) 374-8741; f. 1971; academic and professional social science; Man Dir DAVID HILL.

**W. B. Saunders Co Ltd:** 24–28 Oval Rd, London, NW1 7DX; tel. (171) 267-4466; telex 25775; fax (171) 482-2293; f. 1900, inc. 1919; division of Harcourt Brace and Co; medical, veterinary and scientific; Editorial Dir SEAN DUGGAN.

**Schofield and Sims Ltd:** Dogley Mill, Fenay Bridge, Huddersfield, West Yorks., HD8 0NQ; tel. (1484) 607080; telex 51458; fax (1484) 606815; f. 1901; educational; Chair. JOHN S. NESBITT; Man. Dir J. STEPHEN PLATTS.

**SCM Press Ltd:** 26-30 Tottenham Rd, London, N1 4BZ; tel. (171) 249-7262; fax (171) 249-3776; f. 1929; religious, theological; Editor and Man. Dir JOHN BOWDEN.

**Scripture Union:** 130 City Rd, London, EC1V 2NJ; tel. (171) 782-0013; fax (171) 782-0014; f. 1867; Christian education; Worldwide Bible reading membership 2m. in 100 countries.

**Martin Secker and Warburg Ltd:** Michelin House, 81 Fulham Rd, London, SW3 6RB; tel. (171) 581-9393; telex 920191; fax (171) 225-9424; imprint of Reed Consumer Books; f. 1936; history, music, political, biography, art, criticism, science, plays, poetry, fiction; Publishing Dir MAX EILENBERG.

**Sheed and Ward Ltd:** 14 Coopers Row, London, EC3N 2BH; tel. (171) 702-9799; fax (171) 702-3583; f. 1926; theology, philosophy, church history and spiritual questions; mainly Catholic authors; Man. Dir M. T. REDFERN.

**Sidgwick and Jackson Ltd:** 18–20 Cavaye Pl., London, SW10 9PG; tel. (171) 373-6081; fax (171) 370-0746; f. 1908; art, archaeology, military history, rock music, biography, history, music, sport, business, money, cookery; Man. Dir W. ARMSTRONG.

**Simon and Schuster:** West Gdn Pl., Kendal St, London, W2 2AQ; tel. (171) 724-7577; fax (171) 402-0639; f. 1986; fiction, non-fiction, music, travel; imprints: Pocket Books, Touchstone; Man. Dir NICK WEBB.

**Sinclair-Stevenson Ltd:** Michelin House, 81 Fulham Road, London, SW3 6RB; tel. (171) 581-9393; fax (171) 225-0933; f. 1990; imprint of Reed Consumer Books; adult fiction and non-fiction; Man. Dir CHRISTOPHER SINCLAIR-STEVENSON.

**Society for Promoting Christian Knowledge:** Holy Trinity Church, Marylebone, London, NW1 4DU; tel. (171) 387-5282; fax (171) 388-2352; f. 1698; religious; imprints: SPCK, Triangle, Sheldon Press; Gen. Sec. PAUL CHANDLER.

**Souvenir Press Ltd:** 43 Great Russell St, London, WC1B 3PA; tel. (171) 580-9307; fax (171) 580-5064; general; Man. Dir E. HECHT.

**Stanfords Ltd:** 12–14 Long Acre, London, WC2E 9LP; tel. (171) 836-1321; telex 21667; fax (171) 836-0189; f. 1852; atlases, charts, globes, maps, travel books; Chair. P. N. GODFREY.

**Sweet and Maxwell Ltd:** South Quay Plaza, 183 Marsh Wall, London, E14 9FT; tel. (171) 538-8686; telex 929089; fax (171) 538-9508; f. 1799; imprints: Stevens and Sons Ltd, W. Green, ESC Publishing, the European Law Centre; holding co the Thomson Corporation; law books; Man. Dir STEPHEN HARRIS.

**Taylor and Francis Ltd:** 4 John St, London, WC1N 2ET; tel. (171) 400-3500; telex 858540; fax (171) 831-2035; f. 1798; academic, scholarly, scientific and technical; Hon. Pres. Sir NEVILL MOTT; Chair. ELNORA FERGUSON.

**Thames and Hudson Ltd:** 30–34 Bloomsbury St, London, WC1B 3QP; tel. (171) 636-5488; telex 25992; fax (171) 636-4799; art, archaeology, history, etc.; Chair. E. NEURATH; Man. Dir T. NEURATH.

**Stanley Thornes (Publishers) Ltd:** Ellenborough House, Wellington St, Cheltenham, GL50 1YD; tel. (1242) 228888; fax (1242) 221914; educational; imprint: Mary Glasgow Publications; Man. Dir DAVID J. SMITH.

**Thorsons:** 77–85 Fulham Palace Rd, London, W6 8JB; tel. (181) 741-7070; fax (181) 307-4440; Proprs Harper Collins Publishers Ltd; Man. Dir EILEEN CAMPBELL.

**Times Books Ltd:** 77–85 Fulham Palace Rd, Hammersmith, London, W6 8JB; tel. (181) 741-7070; telex 25611; fax (181) 307-4813; Proprs HarperCollins Publishers Ltd; atlases and general reference; Man. Dir ROBERT WILLIAMS.

**Times Mirror International Publishers Ltd:** Lynton House, 7–12 Tavistock Sq., London, WC1H 9LB; tel. (171) 388-7676; fax (171) 391-6555; medical, dental, veterinary and scientific texts and atlases; Editorial Vice-Pres. FIONA FOLEY.

**Transworld Publishers Ltd:** 61–63 Uxbridge Rd, London, W5 5SA; tel. (181) 579-2652; telex 267974; fax (181) 579-5479; imprints: Corgi Books, Bantam Books, Black Swan, Bantam Press, Partridge Press, Doubleday, Young Corgi, Picture Corgi, Freeway, Dell Yearling, Bantam Young Adult; all types of fiction and non-fiction; Man. Dir and Chief Exec. P. SCHERER.

**University of Wales Press:** 6 Gwennyth St, Cathays, Cardiff, CF2 4YD; tel. (1222) 231919; fax (1222) 230908; f. 1922; academic and educational (Welsh and English); Dir NED THOMAS.

**Usborne Publishing:** Usborne House, 83–85 Saffron Hill, London, EC1N 8RT; tel. (171) 430-2800; telex 8953598; fax (171) 430-1562; f. 1973; educational and children's literature; Man. Dir T. P. USBORNE.

**Viking:** 27 Wrights Lane, London, W8 5TZ; tel. (171) 416-3000; telex 917181; fax (171) 416-3099; hardcover imprint of Penguin Books; fiction, general non-fiction, biography, history, art, literature, science, popular culture; Publishing Dir CLARE ALEXANDER.

**Virago Press:** Random House, 20 Vauxhall Bridge Rd, London, SW1V 2SA; tel. (171) 973-9750; fax (171) 233-6123; f. 1973; imprint of Random House UK Ltd, fiction and non-fiction, all aspects of women's lives; Chair. K. GAVRON; Man. Dir HARRIET SPICER, Publishing Dir LENNIE GOODINGS.

**Virgin Publishing:** 332 Ladbroke Grove, London, W10 5AH; tel. (181) 968-7554; fax (181) 968-0929; W. H. Allen and Co. f. before 1800; general, popular culture, music, humour, biography, fiction, erotica; imprints: Virgin, Doctor Who, Black Lace and Nexus; Chair. ROBERT DEVEREUX; Man. Dir ROBERT SHREEVE.

**Ward Lock Ltd:** Wellington House, 125 Strand, London, WC2R 0BB; tel. (171) 420-5555; fax (171) 240-7261; f. 1854; Mrs Beeton, gardening, sports, equestrian, puzzles and quizzes, do-it-yourself, health; Man. Dir. P. J. STURROCK; Editorial Dir ALISON McWILLIAM.

**Frederick Warne (Publishers) Ltd:** 27 Wrights Lane, London, W8 5TZ; tel. (171) 416-3000; telex 917181; fax (171) 416-3199; f. 1865; a division of Penguin Books since 1983; classic illustrated children's books (including Beatrix Potter); Publisher SALLY FLOYER.

**George Weidenfeld and Nicolson Ltd:** Orion House, 5 Upper St Martin's Lane, London, WC2H 9EA; tel. (171) 240-3444; fax (171) 240-4822; f. 1947; imprint of Orion Publishing Group (see above); fiction and non-fiction covering wide range of subjects, biography, belles-lettres and art books; Chair. Lord WEIDENFELD.

**J. Whitaker and Sons Ltd:** 12 Dyott St, London, WC1A 1DF; tel. (171) 836-8911; fax (171) 836-2909; f. 1841; *Whitaker's Almanack, The Bookseller,* and book listings; Man. Dir SALLY WHITAKER.

**Wildwood House Ltd:** Gower House, Croft Rd, Aldershot, Hants., GU11 3HR; tel. (1252) 331551; telex 858001; fax (1252) 344405; f. 1972; imprint of Ashgate Publishing Ltd; business, general; Man. Dir C. SIMPSON.

**The Women's Press:** 34 Great Sutton St, London, EC1V 0DX; tel. (171) 251-3007; fax (171) 608-1938; f. 1978; feminist; Exec. Dirs KATHY GALE, MARY HEMMING.

**Zed Books Ltd:** 7 Cynthia Rd, London, N1 9JF; tel. (171) 837-4014; fax (171) 833-3960; academic, scholarly, current affairs; Editors ROBERT MOLTENO, LOUISE MURRAY.

**A. Zwemmer Ltd:** 26 Litchfield St, London, WC2H 9NJ; tel. (171) 240-4180; fax (171) 240-6975; f. 1921; architecture, visual arts, applied arts.

## PUBLISHERS' ORGANIZATIONS

**Book Development Council:** 19 Bedford Sq., London, WC1B 3HJ; tel. (171) 580-6321; fax (171) 636-5375; international division of the Publishers Association; Chair. SIMON WRATTEN; Dir IAN TAYLOR.

**Book Trust:** Book House, 45 East Hill, London, SW18 2QZ; tel. (181) 870-9055; fax (181) 874-4790; non-profit-making organization funded by voluntary donations and membership fees; f. 1945; originally f. 1925 as The National Book Council to extend the use and enjoyment of books; renamed Book Trust 1986; publishes annotated book lists; postal book information service; organizes book prizes, including the Booker Prize for Fiction; Young Book Trust inc. the Centre for Children's Books (reference collection of the current two years' children's books); Pres. Sir SIMON HORNBY; Chair. MARTYN GOFF; Chief Exec. BRIAN PERMAN.

**Publishers Association:** 19 Bedford Sq., London, WC1B 3HJ; tel. (171) 580-6321; telex 21792; fax (171) 636-5375; f. 1896; represents book and journal publishers in the UK and seeks to

UNITED KINGDOM (GREAT BRITAIN)  *Directory*

promote the sales of British books; Pres. Nick Chapman; Chief Exec. Clive Bradley; 180 mems.

**Scottish Publishers' Association:** Scottish Book Centre, 137 Dundee St, Edinburgh, EH11 1BG; tel. (131) 228-6866; fax (131) 228-3220; f. 1974; assists member publishers in the promotion and marketing of their books; administers Scottish Book Marketing Group; Chair. Stephanie Wolfe Murray; Dir Lorraine Fannin.

## Radio and Television

In 1992 there were an estimated 66.1m. radio receivers and 25.1m. television receivers in use.

**British Broadcasting Corporation (BBC):** Broadcasting House, London, W1A 1AA; tel. (171) 580-4468; telex 265781; f. 1922; operates under Royal Charter and a licence from the Home Department. It is financed by the television licence fees. Chair. Marmaduke Hussey; Dir-Gen. John Birt; Deputy Dir-Gen. Robert Phillis; Man. Dir. World Service Sam Younger; Man. Dir Network Television Will Wyatt; Man. Dir Regional Broadcasting Ronald Neil; Man. Dir Network Radio Elizabeth Forgan.

**Independent Television Commission (ITC):** 33 Foley St, London, W1P 7LB; tel. (171) 255-3000; fax (171) 306-7800; f. 1954 as the Independent Television Authority, renamed Independent Broadcasting Authority 1972 and Independent Television Commission 1990; public body responsible for licensing and regulating all commercially-funded television in the United Kingdom, including Independent Television (ITV-which was renamed Channel 3 from 1 Jan. 1993), Channel 4, the proposed Channel 5, cable and satellite services, public teletext and certain other text and data services; The ITC has a duty, under the Broadcasting Act of 1990, to ensure the variety and quality of programme services and to ensure that there is effective competition in the provision of such services. The ITC has the statutory powers to impose penalties on licensees if they do not comply with their licence conditions. In November 1993 government restrictions on mergers between ITV companies were relaxed.

In October 1991 the ITC, in accordance with the provisions of the Broadcasting Act of 1990, awarded the 16 licences that constituted the renamed Channel 3 (ITV). The franchises were allocated by a system of competitive tendering, although the ITC was empowered to select a company presenting a lower bid in 'exceptional circumstances'. The new licences came into force on 1 January 1993, when Channel 4 (q.v.) also became an ITC licensee. By the end of 1992 the ITC had also issued 27 non-domestic satellite and licensable programme service licences. In 1992 the ITC postponed the awarding of the licence to operate Channel 5, having rejected the sole application. New applications were submitted to the ITC in May 1995; the licence was expected to be awarded by November, with broadcasting scheduled to commence in January 1997. Chair. Sir George Russell; Chief Exec. David Glencross; Controller of Public Affairs Sarah Thane.

**Radio Authority:** Holbrook House, 14 Gt Queen St, London, WC2B 5DG; tel. (171) 430-2724; fax (171) 405-7064; f. 1991 to replace (with the ITC) the Independent Broadcasting Authority (IBA); regulatory body responsible for advertising and awarding licences to three new national commercial radio channels (INR-Independent National Radio) and new local radio stations. In August 1991 Classic FM was awarded the national franchise for INR-1, which began broadcasting in late 1992. In May 1992 Virgin Radio was awarded the franchise for INR-2, which began broadcasting in April 1993. The third national franchise was awarded in June 1994 to Talk Radio UK, which commenced broadcasts in February 1995. In 1992 there were about 90 licensed independent local radio contractors, providing about 120 services. Chair. Sir Peter Gibbings; Chief Exec. Peter Baldwin, (from July 1995) Anthony Stoller.

### RADIO

#### British Broadcasting Corporation

BBC Radio provides a service of five national networks throughout the United Kingdom, 33 local radio stations in England and the Channel Islands, Radio Scotland, Radio Wales, Radio Cymru, broadcasting in Welsh, and Radio Ulster.

Radio 1 broadcasts about 21 hours a day of rock and 'pop' music programmes; Controller Matthew Bannister.

Radio 2 provides 'middle of the road' music and light entertainment, and is the main channel for sports programmes; Controller Frances Line.

Radio 3 provides classical music, drama, talks and documentaries; Controller Nicholas Kenyon.

Radio 4 is the main channel for the coverage of news and current affairs and also provides a wide range of features, drama and discussions; Controller Michael Green.

Radio 5 Live began broadcasting in March 1994, replacing Radio 5. It provides a 24-hour service of news and sports programmes; Controller Jenny Abramsky.

**BBC World Service:** Bush House, Strand, London, WC2B 4PH; tel. (171) 240-3456; telex 265781; fax (171) 240-8760; the World Service in English is broadcast for 24 hours daily and directed to all areas of the world. In addition, there are special services to: the Far East (in Mandarin, Cantonese, Indonesian, Thai and Vietnamese); the Indian sub-continent (in Bengali, Burmese, Hindi, Nepali, Pashto, Persian, Sinhala, Tamil and Urdu); the Caucasus and Central Asia (in Azerbaijani, Uzbek and Russian); the Middle East and North Africa (in Arabic and French); Central, East, West and South Africa (in English, French, Hausa, Portuguese, Somali and Swahili); and the Western Hemisphere (in Portuguese for Brazil and Spanish for Latin America). Services in the following languages are transmitted for listeners in Europe: Albanian, Bulgarian, Croatian, Czech and Slovak, Finnish, French, German, Greek, Hungarian, Polish, Portuguese, Romanian, Russian, Serbian, Slovene and Turkish. A trilingual service, 'BBC for Europe', is broadcast in English, French and German. Man. Dir Sam Younger.

#### Independent National Radio

**Classic FM:** Academic House, 24–28 Oval Rd, London, NW1 7DQ; tel. (171) 284-3000; fax (171) 284-2835; began broadcasting September 1992; popular classical music; Chair. Sir Peter Michael; Chief Exec. John Spearman.

**Independent Radio News (IRN):** 200 Gray's Inn Rd, London, WC1X 8XZ; tel. (171) 430-4814; f. 1973; produced by ITN Radio; news agency for the independent local radio network; Man. Dir John Perkins.

**Talk Radio UK:** 76 Oxford St, London, W1M 0TR; tel. (171) 636-1089; began broadcasting February 1995; Chair. Sir David Nicholas; Man. Dir John Aumonier.

**Virgin Radio (Virgin 1215):** 1 Golden Square, London, W1R 4DJ; tel. (171) 434-1215; fax (171) 434-1197; began broadcasting April 1993; popular music; Programme Dir John Revell; Chief Exec. David Campbell.

### TELEVISION

**BBC Television:** Television Centre, Wood Lane, London, W12; tel. (181) 743-8000; operates two services, BBC-1 and BBC-2; both use the 625-line standard; Man. Dir Will Wyatt.

BBC-1: provides a coverage of over 99% of the population of the United Kingdom. Colour service began in 1969; a breakfast-time television service began in 1983; Controller BBC-1 Alan Yentob.

BBC-2: was opened in 1964, and is available to 99% of the population. Colour service began in 1967; Controller BBC-2 Michael Jackson.

**Channel Four Television Corp:** 124 Horseferry Rd, London, SW1P 2TX; tel. (171) 396-4444; f. 1980, began broadcasting 1982; national television service; available to 97% of the population; financed by advertising; in accordance with the Broadcasting Act (1990), Channel Four became a public corporation and ITC licensee, responsible for selling its own advertising, from January 1993; Chair. Sir Michael Bishop; Chief Exec. Michael Grade.

**S4C Welsh Fourth Channel Authority** (Awdurdod Sianel Pedwar Cymru): Parc Ty Glas, Llanishen, Cardiff, CF4 5DU; tel. (1222) 747444; fax (1222) 754444; f. 1982; television service for Wales; Chair. Ifan Prys Edwards; Chief Exec. Huw Jones.

#### Independent Television (ITV—Channel 3) Companies

**Independent Television Association Ltd (ITV):** ITV Network Centre, 200 Grays Inn Rd, London, WC1X 8HF; tel. (171) 843-8000; telex 262988; fax (171) 843-8158; f. 1956; from 1992 the central co-ordinating body for Channel 3 (ITV); the Assoc's Council comprises the Managing Directors of all 15 companies; Chief Exec. Andrew Quinn, (from November 1995) Marcus Plantin; Network Dir Marcus Plantin.

**Anglia Television Ltd:** Anglia House, Norwich, NR1 3JG; tel. (1603) 615151; telex 97424; fax (1603) 631032; 48 Leicester Sq., London, WC2H 7FB; tel. (171) 389-8555; East of England; acquired by MAI 1994; Chair. David McCall; Man. Dir Malcolm Wale.

**Border Television PLC:** Television Centre, Carlisle, CA1 3NT; tel. (1228) 25101; fax (1228) 41384; Borders and the Isle of Man; Chair. Melvyn Bragg; Man. Dir James L. Graham.

**Carlton Television Ltd:** 101 St Martin's Lane, London, WC2N 4AZ; tel. (171) 240-4000; fax (171) 240-4171; London area, Monday to Thursday, Friday to 5.15 p.m.; began broadcasting in January 1993 (replacing Thames Television Ltd); Chair. Nigel Walmsley; Man. Dir Paul Jackson.

**Central Broadcasting:** Central House, Broad St, Birmingham, B1 2JP; tel. (121) 643-9898; telex 338966; fax (121) 616-4766; East and West Midlands; merged with Carlton Television Ltd 1993; Chair. LESLIE HILL; Man. Dir ROD HENWOOD.

**Channel Television:** Television Centre, La Pouquelaye, St Helier, Jersey, JE2 3ZD; tel. (1534) 68999; fax (1534) 59446; St George's Place, St Peter Port, Guernsey; tel. (1481) 723451; fax (1481) 710739; Channel Islands; Chair. Maj. J. R. RILEY; Man. Dir J. P. HENWOOD.

**Good Morning TV (GMTV):** c/o London TV Centre, London, SE1 9LT; tel. (171) 827-7064; fax (171) 827-7001; nationwide breakfast-time service; began broadcasting in January 1993 (replacing TV-am PLC); Chair. NIGEL WALMSLEY; Man. Dir CHRISTOPHER STODDART.

**Grampian Television PLC:** Queen's Cross, Aberdeen, AB9 2XJ; tel. (1224) 646464; telex 73151; fax (1224) 635127; north Scotland; Chair. Dr CALUM A. MACLEOD; Deputy Chair. and Chief Exec. DONALD H. WATERS.

**Granada Television Ltd:** Granada TV Centre, Quay St, Manchester, M60 9EA; tel. and fax (161) 832-7211; telex 668859; north-west England; Chair. GERRARD (GERRY) ROBINSON; Chief Exec. CHARLES ALLEN.

**HTV Ltd:** Television Centre, Culverhouse Cross, Cardiff, CF5 6XJ; tel. (1222) 590590; telex 497703; The Television Centre, Bristol, BS4 3HG; tel. (117) 977-8366; fmrly Harlech Television; Wales and the West of England; Chair. LOUIS SHERWOOD; Chief Exec. CHRIS ROWLANDS.

**London Weekend Television Ltd (LWT):** The London Television Centre, Upper Ground, London, SE1 9LT; tel. (171) 620-1620; London area and the South East, 5.15 p.m. Friday to closedown on Sunday; Chief Exec. CHARLES ALLEN.

**Meridian Broadcasting Ltd:** Television Centre, Northam, Southampton, Hants, SO9 5HZ; tel. (1703) 222555; fax (1703) 335050; south and south-east England; began broadcasting in January 1993; Chief Exec. ROGER LAUGHTON.

**Scottish Television PLC:** Cowcaddens, Glasgow, G2 3PR; tel. (141) 332-9999; telex 77388; fax (141) 332-6982; f. 1957; central Scotland; Chair. WILLIAM BROWN; Man. Dir ANGUS (GUS) MACDONALD.

**Ulster Television PLC:** Havelock House, Ormeau Rd, Belfast, BT7 1EB; tel. (1232) 328122; telex 74654; fax (1232) 246695; f. 1959; Northern Ireland; Chair. JOHN B. MCGUCKIAN; Man. Dir J. DESMOND SMYTH.

**Westcountry Television Ltd:** Western Wood Way, Langage Science Park, Plymouth PL7 5BG; tel. (1752) 333333; south-west England; began broadcasting in January 1993; Chair. Sir JOHN BANHAM; Chief Exec. STEPHEN REDFARN.

**Yorkshire-Tyne Tees Holdings:** f. 1992 as result of merger between Yorkshire Television Ltd and Tyne Tees Television Ltd; Group Chair. GWYN WARD THOMAS.

**Yorkshire Television Ltd:** Television Centre, Leeds, LS3 1JS; tel. (113) 243-8283; telex 557232; fax (113) 244-5107; Television House, 32 Bedford Row, London, WC1R 4HE; tel. (171) 242-1666; Yorkshire; Chair. VICTOR WATSON; Man. Dir BRUCE GYNGELL.

**Tyne Tees Television Ltd:** Television Centre, City Rd, Newcastle upon Tyne, NE1 2AL; tel. (191) 261 0181; telex 53279; fax (191) 261-2302; Television House, 15 Bloomsbury Sq., London, WC1A 2LJ; tel. (171) 312-3700; f. 1959; north-east England; Chair. Sir RALPH CARR-ELLISON; Man. Dir JOHN CALVERT.

### Independent Television News

**Independent Television News (ITN):** 200 Gray's Inn Rd, London, WC1X 8XZ; tel. (171) 833-3000; telex 22101; f. 1955; Propr a consortium of Granada Group, Carlton Communications, Reuters Holdings, Anglia and Scottish Television; provides the main news programmes for all ITV areas and a news programme for Channel 4; became a profit-making company in 1993; Chair. GERRARD (GERRY) ROBINSON; Chief Exec. STEWART PURVIS.

### Satellite and Cable Broadcasting

There were almost 4m. satellite television receivers and 800,000 cable television subscribers in the United Kingdom in December 1994. The major satellite and cable television companies are listed below.

**BBC Worldwide Television:** Room AG200, Woodlands, 80 Wood Lane, London W12 0TT; tel. (181) 576-2974; fax (181) 576-2782; began broadcasting in 1991; BBC World, a 24-hour news and information channel, broadcasts to Europe, Africa, Asia (including a Japanese-language service to Japan), the Middle East (in Arabic) and New Zealand; a second channel, BBC Prime, broadcasts light entertainment for 24 hours daily to Europe; Man. Dir Dr JOHN THOMAS.

**British Sky Broadcasting:** 6 Centaurs Business Park, Grant Way; Isleworth, Middlesex, TW7 5QD; tel. (171) 705-3000; fax (171) 705-3030; f. 1990 by merger of British Satellite Broadcasting (BSB) and Sky TV PLC (a subsidiary of News International); 6-channel satellite service; Chair. GERRARD (GERRY) ROBINSON; CEO SAM CHISHOLM.

**Cable Communications Association:** 5th Floor, Artillery House, Artillery Row, London, SW1P 1RT; tel. (171) 222-2900; Chair. ALAN BATES; Dir-Gen. RICHARD WOOLLAM.

**Cable News Network Inc (CNN):** 19–22 Rathbone Place, London, W1P 1DF; tel. (171) 637-6800; fax (171) 637-6868; Bureau Chief DAVID FEINGOLD.

**Eurosport UK:** 55 Drury Lane, London, WC2B 5SQ; tel. (171) 468-7777; began broadcasting in 1989; Man. Dir J. KREMER.

**Live TV:** 1 Canada Sq., Canary Wharf, London, E14 5DJ; tel. (171) 293-3900; began broadcasting in June 1995; Dir DARRYL BURTON.

**MTV-Europe:** Hawley Cres., London, NW1 8TT; tel. (171) 284-7777; fax (171) 284-7788; popular music; Pres. WILLIAM ROEDY.

**UK Gold:** The Quadrangle, 180 Wardour St, London, W1V 4AE; tel. (171) 306-6100; fax (171) 306-6101; began broadcasting 1992; satellite and cable; Chair. DEREK LEWIS; Chief Exec. BRUCE STEINBERG.

### Advisory Body

**Broadcasting Standards Council:** 7 The Sanctuary, London, SW1P 3JS; tel. (171) 233-0544; fax (171) 233-0397; f. 1988, became a statutory body under the 1990 Broadcasting Act, with a remit to research and monitor broadcasting standards in the United Kingdom, with respect to the broadcast portrayal of violence, sexual conduct and matters of taste and decency; considers complaints from the public; produces a broadcasting Code of Practice; Chair. Lady HOWE OF ABERAVON; Dir COLIN SHAW.

## Finance

The United Kingdom's central bank is the Bank of England, which was established by Act of Parliament and Royal Charter in 1694 and nationalized under the Bank of England Act 1946. The Scottish and Northern Ireland banks issue their own notes but these are largely covered by holdings of Bank of England notes.

The Bank of England is responsible for advising the Government on the formulation of monetary policy and for its subsequent execution. It holds the main government accounts, acts as registrar of government stocks and as agent of the Government for a number of financial operations, including the management of the Exchange Equalization Account. It is also banker to a number of commercial banks. The London clearing banks maintain a substantial proportion of their total cash holdings in the form of balances at the Bank and these are used in the settlement of daily cheque and credit clearings.

The commercial banks may be divided into two broad categories: clearing banks and other banks.

The clearing banks are divided into the 10 clearing banks covering England and Wales, the three Scottish clearing banks and the four Northern Ireland banks. These banks play the main part in operating the money transmission system throughout the UK. At September 1991 these banks, together with other retail banks, held deposits totalling £443,932m.

The other banks comprise accepting houses (taking their name from their business of accepting bills of exchange for payment) and other UK-owned banks, overseas-owned banks and consortium banks. In 1992 there were 225 banks incorporated outside the UK represented in the London markets. The accepting houses and some of the UK-owned banks are specialists in bill finance, new issues and company finance.

Consortium banks have been formed in the UK by groups of banks, mostly from overseas, but including some British clearing banks. Initially they were set up to afford shareholders access to the Eurocurrency markets. More recently consortia have been formed as a means of combining institutions from similar geographical areas, when a London operation would be uneconomic for individual banks. Consortium banks are important participants in the major inter-bank markets in sterling and currency deposits and certificates of deposit.

The discount houses are a specialized group of institutions peculiar to London. They raise the greater part of their funds from within the banking sector. These funds are borrowed by the houses at call or short notice (thereby providing the lending banks with a highly liquid interest-bearing investment) and are used to purchase correspondingly liquid assets—mainly Treasury and commercial bills, short-dated government stocks, certificates of deposit, local authority debt, etc.

As a result of England's lead in international trade and finance during and after the industrial revolution, several countries tended to use sterling rather than their national currency for international trading transactions and maintained their central currency reserve in London. These countries pegged their currency exchange rate to the pound sterling when the gold standard was abandoned by the United Kingdom in 1931; the pound was

# UNITED KINGDOM (GREAT BRITAIN)

devalued by 30.5% in 1949, and by 14.3% in 1967. In June 1972 the pound was 'floated'. Since 1958 sterling has been, for non-residents, freely transferable and convertible into other currencies. In October 1990 the United Kingdom joined the Exchange Rate Mechanism (ERM) of the European Monetary System, although membership was suspended in September 1992 (see Vol. 1, p. 160). Sterling's departure from the ERM resulted in its effective devaluation by 15%. The United Kingdom's official reserves, comprising gold, convertible currencies and special drawing rights on the International Monetary Fund, are held in the Exchange Equalization Account operated since 1932 by the Bank of England as agent for the Treasury.

The London Gold Market operates under the auspices of the London Gold Market Bullion Association, which comprises 12 market-maker members and 50 ordinary members. The market engages in the trading, transporting, refining, melting, assaying and vaulting of gold. The unique feature of the London market is the 'fixing', which determines the price of gold on a twice-daily basis by matching orders from customers and markets throughout the world.

The building society movement is important both as a medium of savings (the largest in the UK) and for the finance of house purchase in a country where 68% (1990) of dwellings are owner-occupied. In 1993 there were 101 societies registered in the United Kingdom. The expansion of building societies into banking was a characteristic of the late 1980s.

National Savings are administered by the Department for National Savings and the Trustee Savings Banks. Through the Department for National Savings the Government administers the National Savings Bank 'investment' and 'ordinary' accounts, National Savings certificates, Premium bonds and other securities, all aimed primarily at the small saver. The outlets for these services are some 20,000 post offices in the UK.

There are certain institutions set up to provide finance for specific purposes; the more important of these are the 3i Group PLC (which provides investment capital to companies which do not have ready access to capital markets) and the Agricultural Mortgage Corporation (loans against mortgages on agricultural property).

The main capital market is the London Stock Exchange, and since October 1986 the volume of business transacted has greatly expanded with the introduction of the Stock Exchange Automated Quotations system (SEAQ), an electronic trading system which allows off-floor trading.

The UK has a highly developed insurance market, located primarily in London. Lloyd's, with its unique system of underwriting syndicates (of which there are about 230) has an international reputation for marine, aviation and reinsurance, as well as a significant share of the UK motor insurance market. Almost two-thirds of Lloyd's premium income comes from outside the United Kingdom through Lloyd's 219 accredited brokers. There are over 800 authorized insurance companies in the United Kingdom, dealing with life and general insurance, as well as international reinsurance.

## BANKING

(cap. = capital; p.u. = paid up; auth. = authorized; m. = million; dep. = deposits; res = reserves; subs. = subscribed; brs = branches)

The 1987 Banking Act replaced the Banking Act of 1979 under which a statutory framework for the supervision of the banking sector was established. The 1987 Act defines new criteria by which an institution can be authorized to accept deposits. The administrative authority for the Act is the Bank of England. In February 1992 the Bank of England recorded 518 authorized banking institutions in the United Kingdom.

### Central Bank

**Bank of England:** Threadneedle St, London, EC2R 8AH; tel. (171) 601-4444; telex 885001; inc. by Royal Charter in 1694, and nationalized by Act of Parliament on 1 March 1946; is the Government's banker and on its behalf manages the note issue and the National Debt; also the bankers' bank; mem. of the Clearing House; brs at Birmingham, Bristol, Leeds, Manchester, Newcastle upon Tyne, and agencies in Liverpool, Southampton and in Glasgow; capital stock amounting to £14.6m. is held by the Treasury; res £947.5m., public dep. £1,550.3m. (Feb. 1994); Gov. EDWARD (EDDIE) GEORGE; Chief Cashier GRAHAM KENTFIELD; Sec. J. R. E. FOOTMAN.

### Principal Banks Incorporated in Great Britain

**Abbey National PLC:** Abbey House, Baker St, London, NW1 6XL; tel. (171) 612-4000; f. 1944 as Abbey National Building Society; total assets £83,802m. (Dec. 1993); Chair. Lord TUGENDHAT; Chief Exec. PETER BIRCH; 678 brs.

**ANZ Grindlays Bank PLC:** Minerva House, POB 7, Montague Close, London, SE1 9DH; tel. (171) 378-2121; telex 885043; fax (171) 378-2310; f. 1863; wholly-owned susbsidiary of Australia and New Zealand Banking Group Ltd; cap. auth. £170m., cap. issued £155.8m., dep. £3,568.3m. (March 1993); Chair. Sir BRIAN SHAW; Sec. GARETH W. CAMPBELL.

**Bank of Scotland:** The Mound, Edinburgh, EH1 1YZ; tel. (131) 442-7777; telex 72275; fax (131) 243-5546; f. 1695; clearing bank; cap. p.u. £491.1m., dep. £23,437.5m., total assets £30,748.4m. (Feb. 1994); Gov. Sir BRUCE PATTULLO; Chief Gen. Man. PETER BURT; 320 brs.

**Barclays Bank PLC:** 54 Lombard St, London, EC3P 3AH; tel. (171) 626-1567; telex 887591; inc. 1896; clearing bank; principal operating co of Barclays PLC (group holding co); cap. £1,624m., res £3,688m., dep. £120,885m. (Dec. 1993); Group Chair. ANDREW BUXTON; Chief Exec. MARTIN TAYLOR; 3,500 brs in 76 countries.

**Clydesdale Bank PLC:** 30 St Vincent Place, Glasgow, G1 2HL; tel. (141) 248-7070; telex 77135; fax (141) 204-0828; f. 1838; wholly-owned by National Australia Bank Ltd; clearing bank; cap. 200m., dep. £4,626m. (Sept. 1993); Chair. Lord NICKSON; CEO FRANK CICUTTO; 314 brs.

**The Co-operative Bank PLC:** POB 101, 1 Balloon St, Manchester, M60 4EP; tel. (161) 832-3456; telex 667274; f. 1970; clearing bank; cap. auth. and issued £90m., dep. £3,153.1m. (Jan. 1994); Chair. TOM AGAR; Man. Dir. TERRY THOMAS; 110 brs.

**Coutts and Co:** 440 Strand, London, WC2R 0QS; tel. (171) 753-1000; telex 883421; fax (171) 753-1052; f. 1692; private clearing bank and asset management; parent co National Westminster Bank PLC; cap. £41.3m., res £62.8m., dep. £4,934.4m. (Dec. 1993); Chair. Sir EWEN FERGUSSON; Chief Exec. IAN FARNSWORTH, (from 1 July 1995) HERSCHER POST; 15 brs.

**Girobank PLC:** 10 Milk St, London, EC2V 8JH; tel. (171) 600-6020; telex 885700; fax (171) 726-0133; Bootle, Merseyside, G1R 0AA; tel. (151) 928-8181; telex 627271; f. 1968 as the Post Office Giro (a subsidiary of the Post Office); present name adopted 1985; a wholly-owned subsidiary of the Alliance and Leicester Building Society since 1990; became a clearing bank in 1983; cap. £22m., dep. £2,969.2m. (Dec. 1993); Chair. S. EVRAD; Man. Dir LEWIS EVANS; 9 brs.

**Lloyds Bank PLC:** 71 Lombard St, London, EC3P 3BS; tel. (171) 626-1500; telex 888301; f. 1765; clearing bank; issued share cap. £1,297m., res £2,252m. (Dec. 1994); Chair. Sir ROBIN IBBS; Chief Exec. Sir BRIAN PITMAN; 2,007 brs.

**Midland Bank PLC:** Poultry, London, EC2P 2BX; tel. (171) 260-8000; telex 888401; fax (171) 260-7065; f. 1836; from 1992 subsidiary of HSBC Holdings PLC; clearing bank; cap. p.u. £797m., dep. £58,225m. (Dec. 1994). Chair. Sir WILLIAM PURVES; Chief Exec. KEITH WHITSON; 1,740 brs.

**National Westminster Bank PLC:** 41 Lothbury, London, EC2P 2BP; tel. (171) 726-1000; telex 888388; f. 1968; clearing bank; share cap. £2,756m., dep. £118,656m. (Dec. 1993); Chair. Lord ALEXANDER OF WEEDON; Group Chief Exec. DEREK WANLESS; Sec. G. J. POVEY; 2,968 brs.

**NWS Bank PLC:** NWS House, City Rd, Chester, CH99 3AN; tel. (1244) 690000; telex 61493; fax (1244) 312067; f. 1942; wholly-owned subsidiary of Bank of Scotland; cap. £56.4m., res £168.9m., dep. £3,458.5m. (Dec. 1993); Chair. Prof. J. C. SHAW; Gen. Man. J. MERCER.

**The Royal Bank of Scotland PLC:** POB 31, 42 St Andrew Sq., Edinburgh, EH2 2YE; tel. (131) 556-8555; telex 72230; fax (131) 557-6565; f. 1985 as result of merger of Royal Bank of Scotland and Williams & Glyn's Bank. The Royal Bank of Scotland (est. by Royal Charter in 1727) merged with National Commercial Bank of Scotland in 1969. Williams & Glyn's Bank was result of merger of Glyn Mills & Co (est. 1835) and Williams Deacon's Bank (est. 1771); subsidiary of The Royal Bank of Scotland Group PLC; clearing bank; cap. issued £199.5m., res £1,697.5m., dep. £30,301.1m. (Sept. 1993); Chair. Lord YOUNGER OF PRESTWICK; Sec. KENNEDY FOSTER; 850 brs.

**Standard Chartered PLC:** 1 Aldermanbury Sq., London, EC2V 7SB; tel. (171) 280-7500; telex 885951; fax (171) 280-7156; f. 1853; formerly Standard Chartered Bank PLC, renamed 1985; holding co: Standard Chartered Bank; cap. £340m.; res. £957m., dep. £24,365m. (Dec. 1993); Chair. PATRICK GILLAM; Chief Exec. MALCOLM WILLIAMSON; 266 brs.

**TSB Group PLC:** 60 Lombard St, London, EC3V 9DN; tel. (171) 390-3980; fax (171) 398-3988; f. 1810 as Trustee Savings Banks; total assets £34,702m.; flotation Oct. 1986; Chair. Sir NICHOLAS GOODISON; Chief Exec. PETER ELLWOOD; more than 1,200 brs.

**TSB Bank PLC:** Victoria House, Victoria Sq., Birmingham, B1 1BZ; tel. (121) 600-6000; telex 945131; fax (121) 600-6444; f. 1973 as Central Trustee Savings Bank, later renamed TSB England and Wales PLC; cap. £1,263m., res £177m., dep. £21,438m. (Oct. 1993). Chair. Sir NICHOLAS GOODISON; Sec. L. H. W. MARCH; 1,380 brs.

UNITED KINGDOM (GREAT BRITAIN) *Directory*

**TSB Bank Scotland PLC:** POB 177, Henry Duncan House, 120 George St, Edinburgh, EH2 4TS; tel. (131) 225-4555; telex 727512; fax (131) 220-0240; f. 1983 following merger of four Scottish TSBs; cap. £75m., res £252.9m., dep. £2,780.4m. (Oct. 1993); Chair. GORDON ANDERSON; Chief Exec. ALASTAIR C. DEMPSTER; 270 brs.

**Yorkshire Bank PLC:** 56–58 Cheapside, London, EC2P 2BA; tel. (171) 248-1791; telex 888706; Regd Office: 20 Merrion Way, Leeds, LS2 8NZ; tel. (113) 247-2000; telex 420733; fax (113) 242-0733; f. 1859; wholly-owned by National Australia Bank Ltd; cap. £237m., res £27m. (Sept. 1993) Chair. Lord CLITHEROE; Chief Exec. D. T. GALLAGHER; 265 brs.

### Principal Merchant Banks

* Indicates members of the Accepting Houses Committee.

**Henry Ansbacher & Co Ltd:** 1 Mitre Sq., London, EC3A 5AN; tel. (171) 283-2500; telex 884580; fax (171) 626-0839; f. 1894; acquired by First National Bank of Southern Africa in 1992; cap. and res. £50.6m. (Sept. 1994); Chief Exec.. PETER SCAIFE.

**Banamex Investment Bank PLC:** Banamex House, 3 Creed Court, 5 Ludgate Hill, London, EC4M 7AA; tel. (171) 369-2900; f. 1974 as International Mexican Bank Ltd (Intermex); became wholly-owned subsidiary of Banco National de Mexico in 1994; cap. £40m. (Oct. 1994); Chair. ROBERTO HERNANDEZ; Man. Dir RAFAEL MANCERA.

**Barclays de Zoete Wedd Ltd:** Ebbgate House, 2 Swan Lane, London, EC4R 3TS; tel. (171) 623-2323; telex 8812124; fax (171) 623-6075; f. 1986; Chair. Sir PETER MIDDLETON; Chief Exec. DAVID BAND.

**\*Baring Brothers & Co Ltd:** 8 Bishopsgate, London, EC2N 4AE; tel. (171) 280-1000; telex 883622; fax (171) 283-2633; f. 1762; acquired by Internationale Nederlanden Groep in 1995; cap. £61.3m., res £177m., dep. £4,312m. (Dec. 1992); Co-Chair. MICHAEL MILES, ONNO VAN DEN BROEK.

**The British Linen Bank Ltd:** 4 Melville St, Edinburgh, EH3 7NZ; tel. (131) 453-1919; telex 727221; fax (131) 243-8393; 8 Frederick's Place, London, EC2R 8AT; tel. (171) 601-6840; telex 8952210; f. 1746; a wholly-owned subsidiary of Bank of Scotland; cap. p.u. £28m., dep. £828m. (Jan. 1994); Gov. W. C. C. MORRISON; Sec. JOHN W. ROBERTSON.

**\*Brown, Shipley & Co Ltd:** Founders Court, Lothbury, London, EC2R 7HE; tel. (171) 606-9833; telex 886704; f. 1810; acquired by Kredietbank SA Luxembourgeoise in 1992; cap. issued £23.4m., dep. £295m. (Dec. 1994); Chair. RICHARD MANSELL-JONES; Sec. A. H. EAGLE.

**Citibank Investment PLC:** 336 Strand, POB 242, London, WC2R 1HR; tel. (171) 836-1230; telex 299831; fax (171) 438-1090; f. 1972; cap. £323.3m., res £200.7m., dep. £2,977.0m.; Chair. E. W. BRUTSCHE; Sec. J. S. MITCHELL-HEWSON.

**\*Robert Fleming & Co Ltd:** 25 Copthall Ave, London, EC2R 7DR; tel. (171) 638-5858; telex 297451; fax (171) 588-7219; f. 1932; cap. £138m., dep. £2,664.4m. (March 1994); Chair. P. J. MANSER; Sec. C. A. LIONE.

**\*Guinness Mahon & Co Ltd:** POB 442, 32 St Mary at Hill, London, EC3P 3AJ; tel. (171) 623-9333; telex 884035; fax (171) 283-4811; f. 1836; subsidiary of Bank of Yokohama (Japan) Ltd; cap. £32.0m., res £0.6m., dep. £328.0m. (Dec. 1993); Chair. and Chief Exec. D. R. W. POTTER.

**\*Hambros Bank Ltd:** 41 Tower Hill, London, EC3N 4HA; tel. (171) 480-5000; telex 883851; f. 1839; principal subsidiary co of Hambros PLC; share cap. £143.8m., dep. £3,290.6m. (March 1994); Chair. and Chief Exec. Sir CHIPPENDALE KESWICK; Sec. P. L. PATRICK.

**\*Hill Samuel Bank Ltd:** 100 Wood St, London, EC2P 2AJ; tel. (171) 600-6000; telex 888822; fax (171) 726-4671; f. 1831; part of TSB Group; cap. issued £325.5m., dep. £2,233.8m. (Oct. 1993); Chair. JOHN R. SCLATER; Chief Exec. HUGH FREEDBERG.

**IBJ International PLC:** Bracken House, 1 Friday St, London, EC4M 9JA; tel. (171) 236-1090; telex 925621; fax (171) 236-0484; f. 1975; ultimate holding co The Industrial Bank of Japan Ltd; cap. £93.8m., res £40.2m., dep. £2,271.3m. (Dec. 1993); Chair, Y. KUROSAWA; Man. Dir and CEO T. TOBE.

**Leopold Joseph Holdings PLC:** 29 Gresham St, London, EC2V 7EA; tel. (171) 588-2323; telex 886454; fax (171) 726-0105; f. 1919; cap. auth. £7m., issued £5.3m., dep. £177m. (March 1994); Chair. ROBIN HERBERT; Chief Exec. MICHAEL QUICKE.

**\*Kleinwort Benson Ltd:** 20 Fenchurch St, London, EC3P 3DB; tel. (171) 623-8000; telex 888531; fax (171) 623-4069; f. Cuba 1792; wholly-owned subsidiary of Kleinwort Benson Group; share cap. £58m., res £361.4m., dep. £4,093.4m. (Dec. 1993); Chair. Lord ROCKLEY; Joint Chief Exec. DAVID CLEMENTI, Sir NICHOLAS REDMAYNE.

**\*Lazard Brothers & Co Ltd:** 21 Moorfields, London, EC2P 2HT; tel. (171) 588-2721; telex 886438; fax (171) 628-2485; f. 1919; cap. £30.7m., dep. £1,813.2m. (Dec. 1993); Chair. and Chief Exec. DAVID VEREY; Sec. A. EADY.

**\*Samuel Montagu & Co Ltd:** 10 Lower Thames St, London, EC3R 6AE; tel. (171) 260-9000; telex 887213; f. 1853; subsidiary of HSBC Holdings PLC; share cap. £112.3m., res £104.8m. (Dec. 1993); Chair. BERNARD ASHER; Chief Exec. CHRISTOPHER SHERIDAN.

**\*Morgan Grenfell & Co Ltd:** 23 Great Winchester St, London, EC2P 2AX; tel. (171) 588-4545; telex 8953511; fax (171) 826-6155; f. 1838; cap. p.u. £175m., res £169.9m., dep. £5,563.7m. (Dec. 1993); Chair. JOHN CRAVEN; Sec. R. P. ELLISTON.

**\*Rea Brothers Ltd:** Alderman's House, Alderman's Walk, London, EC2M 3XR; tel. (171) 623-1155; telex 886503; fax (171) 626-0130; f. 1919 as Rea, Warren and McLennan Ltd; subsidiary of Rea Brothers Group PLC; issued share cap. £10.4m., res £13.2m. (Dec. 1994); Chair. Sir JOHN HILL; Group Man. Dir R. W. PARSONS.

**Riggs A. P. Bank Ltd:** 21 Great Winchester St, London, EC2N 2HH; tel. (171) 588-7575; telex 888218; f. 1977 (formerly Anglo-Portuguese Colonial and Overseas Bank Ltd, f. 1919); wholly-owned subsidiary of The Riggs National Bank of Washington, DC; cap. p.u. £27m., res £2.9m., dep. £83.2m. (Dec. 1994); Chair. J. L. ALLBRITTON; Man. Dir T. A. LEX.

**\*N M Rothschild & Sons Limited:** New Court, St Swithin's Lane, London, EC4P 4DU; tel. (171) 280-5000; telex 888031; fax (171) 929-1643; f. 1804; cap. £50m., dep. £2,949.4m.; Chair. Sir EVELYN DE ROTHSCHILD.

**\*SBC Warburg:** 2 Finsbury Ave, London, EC2M 2PA; tel. (171) 860-1090; fax (171) 860-0901; f. 1934 as S. G. Warburg & Co; acquisition of S. G. Warburg Group by Swiss Bank Corporation completed in early July 1995; auth. cap. £150m., cap. issued £150m., res £298.3m., dep. £5,086m. (March 1993); Chair. Sir DAVID SCHOLEY; Chief Exec. MARCEL OSPER.

**\*J. Henry Schroder Wagg & Co Ltd:** 120 Cheapside, London, EC2V 6DS; tel. (171) 382-6000; telex 885029; fax (171) 382-3950; f. 1804; cap. £150m., res £118m., dep. £2,610m. (Dec. 1993); Chair. JEAN SOLANDT; Sec. A. M. GAULTER.

**\*Singer & Friedlander Ltd:** 21 New St, Bishopsgate, London, EC2M 4HR; tel. (171) 623-3000; telex 886977; fax (171) 623-2122; f. 1907; cap. £50m., res £89m., dep. £749m. (Dec. 1994); Chair. ANTHONY SOLOMONS; Chief Exec. JOHN HODSON; 11 brs.

**West Merchant Bank Ltd:** 33–36 Gracechurch St, London, EC3V 0AX; tel. (171) 623-8711; telex 884689; fax (171) 626-1610; f. 1947 as Standard Bank Finance and Development Corpn Ltd; renamed Chartered West LB Ltd 1989; present name adopted 1993; subsidiary of Westdeutsche Landesbank (Europa) AG; cap. £42.4m., res £10.7m., dep. £2,242.9m. (Dec. 1993); Chair. and Chief Exec. PATRICK MACDOUGALL.

### Consortium Banks

Joint ventures are recognized banks or licensed deposit-taking institutions which are registered in the United Kingdom and which have more than one bank among their principal shareholders, a majority of which are foreign.

**Anglo-Romanian Bank:** 42 Moorgate, London, EC2R 6EL; tel. (171) 588-4150; telex 886700; f. 1973; owned by Romanian Bank for Foreign Trade, Barclays PLC, Manufacturers Hanover; cap. £21.8m., dep. £46.4m. (Dec. 1993); Chair. PETER ARDRON.

**Saudi International Bank (Al-Bank Al-Saudi Al-Alami Ltd):** 1 Knightsbridge, London, SW1X 7XS; tel. (171) 259-3456; fax (171) 259-6060; f. 1975; cap. p.u. £127m., dep. £2,704.9m. (Dec. 1993); Chair. Sheikh ABDUL AZIZ AL-QURAISHI.

**UBAF Bank Ltd London:** 30 Gresham St, London, EC2V 7LP, tel. (171) 606-7777; telex 22961; fax (171) 600-3318; f. 1972; owned by UBIC Nederland BV (Netherlands), Midland Bank PLC (UK), Libyan Arab Foreign Bank (Libya), Bank Al-Maghrib (Morocco), Central Bank of Egypt, Banque Extérieure d'Algérie, Rafidain Bank (Iraq); share cap. £86.7m., loan cap. £29.4m., dep. £623.1m. (Dec. 1993); Chair. R. A. MISELLATI; Chief Exec. P. J. W. TAPLIN.

**United Bank of Kuwait:** 15 Baker St, London, W1M 2EB; tel. (171) 487-6500; telex 888441; fax (171) 487-6808; f. 1966; owned by 13 Kuwaiti banks; share cap. £110m., res £21m. (Dec. 1993); Chair. FAHAD MAZIAD AL-RAJAAN; Gen. Man. C. C. KEEN.

### Savings Organization

**Department for National Savings:** Headquarters: Charles House, 375 Kensington High St, London, W14 8SD; tel. (171) 605-9300.

National Savings Bank regional offices: Glasgow, G58 1SB; Durham, DH99 1NS; Blackpool, FY3 9YP; Lytham St Annes, Lancs., FY0 1YN; f. 1861; Dir of Savings DAVID BUTLER.

### Discount Houses

The following are members of the London Discount Market Association (see below):

**Alexanders Discount PLC:** Broadwalk House, 5 Appold St, London, EC2A 2DA; tel. (171) 588-1234; fax (171) 374-0350; f. 1810 as William Alexander and Co Ltd, name changed to Alexan-

3166

# UNITED KINGDOM (GREAT BRITAIN)

ders Discount Co Ltd 1919, as CL—Alexanders Discount PLC 1987, and as above 1989; merged with Jessel, Toynbee and Gillett 1985; acquired by Crédit Lyonnais 1987; cap. £19.8m., res £2m., dep. £1,650m. (Dec. 1993); Chair. Sir KENNETH COUZENS; Chief Exec. ROBIN MOSER.

**Cater Allen Ltd:** 20 Birchin Lane, London, EC3V 9DJ; tel. (171) 623-2070; telex 888553; f. 1981 by merger of Cater Ryder and Co Ltd (f. 1816) and Allen Harvey and Ross Ltd (f. 1888); owned by Cater Allen Holdings PLC; cap. £20m., dep. £2,982.5m. (April 1994); Chair. and Man. Dir J. C. BARCLAY.

**Clive Discount Co Ltd:** 9 Devonshire Sq., London, EC2M 4HP; tel. (171) 283-1401; telex 883431; fax (171) 548-4448; f. 1946; cap. auth. and p.u. £25.4m., dep. £1,578m. (Dec. 1994); Chair. J. R. STRANGFELD.

**Gerrard & National Holdings PLC:** 33 Lombard St, London, EC3V 9BQ; tel. (171) 623-9981; telex 883589; f. 1986; cap. p.u. £9.8m., dep. £2,864.0m. (April 1994); Chair. BRIAN WILLIAMSON.

**King & Shaxson Holdings PLC:** 52 Cornhill, London, EC3V 3PD; tel. (171) 623-5433; telex 888869; fax (171) 929-0075; f. 1933 following merger of King and Foa (f. 1886) and White and Shaxson (f. 1866); cap. £5.2m., res £2.7., dep. £1,176.1m. (April 1994); Chair. D. T. . PEARCE; Sec. D. E. MASON.

**Seccombe Marshall and Campion PLC:** 1 Angel Court, London, EC2R 7HQ; tel. (171) 600-4004; telex 269759; fax (171) 600-0076; f. 1922; wholly-owned subsidiary of Compagnie Parisienne de Réescompte; cap. £6.6m., dep. £581.3m. (Dec. 1993); Chair. P. J. POOLEY.

**Union PLC:** 39 Cornhill, London, EC3V 3NU; tel. (171) 623-1020; fax (171) 626-9069; f. 1885; fmrly the Union Discount Co; cap. issued £26.6m., res £16.3m., total assets £1,671.9m. (Dec. 1994); Chair. ROBIN A. E. HERBERT; Chief Exec. GEORGE BLUNDEN.

### Credit Institutions

**ECI Ventures:** Brettenham House, Lancaster Place, London, WC2E 7EN; tel. (171) 606-1000; f. 1976; advises and manages ECI Investments (£70m. Jersey Unit Trust), ECI International (£35m. Jersey Unit Trust, US Ltd Partnership and UK Ltd Partnership), ECI Eurofund (£30m. UK Ltd Partnerhip) and ECI Capital Partners (£57m. UK Ltd Partnership) to provide equity capital, mainly for unlisted companies; Man. Partner DAVID WANSBROUGH.

**3i Group PLC:** 91 Waterloo Rd, London, SE1 8XP; tel. (171) 928-3131; telex 917844; fax (171) 928-0058; f. 1945 as the Industrial and Commercial Finance Corpn Ltd by the English and Scottish clearing banks, renamed Finance for Industry PLC, renamed Investors in Industry Group PLC in 1983, and renamed as above in 1988; provides long-term and permanent finance, as well as commercial advice, to customers of all sizes; cap. £238.7m. (March 1994); Chair. Sir GEORGE RUSSELL; Chief Exec. EWEN MACPHERSON; Sec. P. C. BROWN.

### Banking and Finance Organizations

**British Bankers' Association:** 10 Lombard St, London, EC3V 9EL; tel. (171) 623-4001; fax (171) 283-7037; f. 1919; Pres. Sir NICHOLAS GOODISON; Dir-Gen. TIM SWEENEY.

**British Overseas and Commonwealth Banks Association:** 35 John St, London, WC1 2AT; tel. (171) 242-0311; fax (171) 430-0841; f. 1917; 30 mems; Chair. S. K. CHRISTENSEN; Hon. Sec. D. J. HILLBERY.

**The Chartered Institute of Bankers:** 10 Lombard St, London, EC3V 9AS; tel. (171) 623-3531; fax (171) 283-1510; f. 1879; professional bankers' association, 85,000 British and overseas mems; Pres. JOHN MELBOURN; Chief Exec. GAVIN SHREEVE.

**The Chartered Institute of Bankers in Scotland:** 19 Rutland Sq., Edinburgh, EH1 2DE; tel. (131) 229-9869; fax (131) 229-1852; f. 1875; professional examinations, courses and publications; approx. 14,000 mems; Chief Exec. Dr C. W. MUNN.

**Foreign Banks and Securities Houses Association:** 5 Laurence Pountney Lane, London, EC4R 0BS; tel. (171) 621-9557; fax (171) 220-7116; Chair. PETER BUERGER.

**London Discount Market Association:** 39 Cornhill, London, EC3V 3NU; tel. (171) 623-1020; fax (171) 220-7620; 8 mems; Chair. T. W. FELLOWES; Hon. Sec. R. J. VARDY.

**London Investment Banking Association:** 6 Frederick's Place, London, EC2R 8BT; tel. (171) 796-3606; mems c. 60 British and foreign banks and securities houses; Chair. P. J. MANSER; Dir-Gen. KIT FARROW.

## STOCK EXCHANGE

**The London Stock Exchange:** Old Broad St, London, EC2N 1HP; tel. (171) 797-1000; telex 886557; formed by amalgamation of the Stock Exchange (London, f. 1801), the other British Stock Exchanges, the Belfast Stock Exchange and the Irish Stock Exchange. The London Stock Exchange consists of two markets: a main market and a second-tier unlisted securities market, introduced in 1980, aimed at companies previously trading in over-the-counter markets. In February 1994 the London Stock Exchange had 405 member firms who may operate a variety of activities such as market making, broker dealing, inter-broker dealing and money broking. It is no longer necessary to be an individual member to conduct business in the London Stock Exchange. From March 1986 a change in the rules of the London Stock Exchange allowed foreign securities groups to become members while existing members were to be permitted to become 100% subsidiaries of outside institutions (such as banks) which had hitherto only been allowed stakes of up to 29.9% in member firms. Since October 1986 there have been major changes with the introduction of the Stock Exchange Automated Quotations system (SEAQ), an electronic trading system which allows off-floor trading and can accommodate some 10,000 terminals both within and without the Exchange. The old mandatory separation of the functions of brokers and jobbers and the system of fixed minimum commissions were then abolished. At March 1993 the total securities quoted on the Stock Exchange had a combined market value of £2,605,094m.; Chair. JOHN KEMP-WELCH; Chief Exec. MICHAEL LAWRENCE.

**Securities and Investments Board (SIB):** Gavrelle House, 2–14 Bunhill Row, London, EC1Y 8RA; tel. (171) 638-1240; fax (171) 382-5900; f. 1985; authorizes and regulates investment business, as required under the Financial Services Act (1986); maintains a central register of persons authorized to conduct investment business; Chair. ANDREW LARGE.

**Investment Management Regulatory Organisation Ltd (IMRO):** Broadwalk House, 6 Appold St, London, EC2A 2AA; tel. (171) 628-6022; Chair. CHARLES NUNNELEY; Chief Exec. PHILLIP THORPE.

**Personal Investment Authority (PIA):** 1 Canada Sq., Canary Wharf, London, E14 5AZ; tel. (171) 538-8860; fax (171) 895-8579; f. 1992, following a recommendation by the SIB, to replace the Financial Intermediaries, Managers and Brokers Regulatory Asscn (FIMBRA) and the Life Assurance and Unit Trust Regulatory Organization (LAUTRO); recognized by the SIB in July 1994; regulates firms conducting investment business with the private sector; all members of FIMBRA and LAUTRO were required to reapply to PIA; Chair. JOE PALMER; Chief Exec. COLETTE BOWE.

**Securities Institute:** Centurion House, 24 Monument St, London, EC3R 8AJ; tel. (171) 626-3191; fax (171) 626-3062; f. 1992; aims to promote professional standards and ethics in the securities industry; Chief Exec. TIM NICHOLSON.

**Securities and Futures Authority:** Cottons Centre, Cottons Lane, London, SE1 2QB; tel. (171) 378-9000.

## INSURANCE

**Lloyd's:** 1 Lime St, London, EC3M 7HA; tel. (171) 623-7100; telex 987321; fax (171) 626-2389; had its origins in the coffee house opened c. 1688 by Edward Lloyd and was incorporated by Act of Parliament (Lloyd's Acts 1871–1982); an international insurance market and Society of Underwriters, consisting of about 18,000 individual members grouped into syndicates who accept risks on the basis of personal and unlimited liability; business is effected through about 200 firms of accredited Lloyd's brokers who alone are permitted to place insurances either directly or by way of reinsurance, and three-quarters of the annual premium income (about £6,000m.) is from overseas business. The Lloyd's market is administered by the Corporation of Lloyd's through a 20-member Council, mostly elected by and from the underwriting membership. Lloyd's operates under a system of self-regulation, introduced by the Lloyd's Act of 1982. A regulatory board was established in October 1993. In early 1992 a series of proposals to substantially restructure Lloyd's was accepted by the Council. These included the granting of rights akin to those of shareholders to the individual members within the syndicates. From January 1994 companies were allowed to enter Lloyd's market on the basis of limited liability for the first time. Council Chair. DAVID ROWLAND; Chief Exec. PETER MIDDLETON.

### Principal Insurance Companies

**Abbey Life Assurance Co Ltd:** Abbey Life House, 80 Holdenhurst Rd, Bournemouth, Dorset, BH8 8AL; f. 1961; cap. p.u. £14m. (1984); Man. Dir ALAN J. FROST.

**Allied Dunbar Assurance PLC:** 9 Sackville St, London, W1X; tel. (171) 434-3211; subsidiary of BAT Industries; Chair. GEORGE GREENER; Chief Exec. SANDY LEITCH.

**AXA Equity & Law Life Assurance Society PLC:** Amersham Rd, High Wycombe, Bucks, HP13 5AL; tel. (1494) 463463; fax (1494) 461989; f. 1844; cap. auth. £1.2m.; Chair. Sir DOUGLAS WASS; Chief Exec. C. J. BROCKSON.

**Britannic Assurance PLC:** Moor Green, Moseley, Birmingham, B13 8QF; tel. (121) 449-4444; fax (121) 449-0456; f. 1866; cap.

# UNITED KINGDOM (GREAT BRITAIN)

auth. £12,063,500; Chair. M. A. H. WILLETT; Gen. Man. J. A. JEFFERSON; Gen. Man and Actuary B. H. SHAW.

**Clerical, Medical and General Life Assurance Society:** 15 St James's Sq., London, SW1Y 4LQ; tel. (171) 930-5474; telex 27432; fax (171) 321-1946; f. 1824; Mutual Society; Chair. MICHAEL HAMILTON; Actuary and Sec. SUSAN FOGARTY.

**Commercial Union PLC:** POB 420, St Helen's, 1 Undershaft, London, EC3P 3DQ; tel. (171) 283-7500; telex 887626; cap. auth. £198m.; Chair. N. H. BARING; Chief Exec. JOHN G. T. CARTER; 115 UK subsidiaries.

**Co-operative Insurance Society Ltd:** Miller St, Manchester, M60 0AL; tel. (161) 832-8686; telex 668621; fax (161) 837-4048; f. 1867; Chair. DAVID WISE; Chief Gen. Man. ALAN SNEDDON.

**Cornhill Insurance Co PLC:** 32 Cornhill, London, EC3V 3LJ; tel. (171) 626-5410; telex 884786; fax (171) 929-3562; f. 1905; Chair. Lord WALKER OF WORCESTER; Gen. Man. and Chief Exec. RAY TREEN.

**Eagle Star Insurance Co Ltd:** 60 St. Mary Axe, London, EC3A 8JQ; tel. (171) 929-1111; telex 914962; fax (171) 895-0497; f. 1904; subsidiary of BAT Industries; Chair. Dr GEORGE GREENER; Chief Exec. SANDY LEITCH.

**Ecclesiastical Insurance Office PLC:** Beaufort House, Brunswick Rd, Gloucester, GL1 1JZ; tel. (1452) 528533; telex 43646; fax (1452) 423557; f. 1887; Chair. C. ALAN McLINTOCK; Man. Dir B. V. DAY.

**Equitable Life Assurance Society:** City Place House, 55 Basinghall St, London, EC2D 5DR; tel. (171) 606-6611; f. 1762; Pres. Prof. JOHN R. SCLATER; Man. Dir and Actuary ROY RANSON.

**Friends' Provident Life Office:** Pixham End, Dorking, Surrey, RH4 1QA; tel. (1306) 740123; fax (1306) 740150; f. 1832; Chair. Lord JENKIN OF RODING; Man. Dir MICHAEL F. DOERR.

**General Accident Fire and Life Assurance Corpn PLC:** Pitheavlis, Perth, PH2 0NH; tel. (1738) 21202; telex 76237; fax (1738) 21843; f. 1885; cap. p.u. £54m.; Chair. Earl of AIRLIE; Group Chief Exec. W. N. ROBERTSON.

    **General Accident Life Assurance Ltd:** 2 Rougier St, York, YO1 1HR; tel. (1904) 628982; telex 57969; fax (1904) 611441; f. 1837; cap. p.u. £250,000; Chair. Earl of AIRLIE; Gen. Man. BILL JACK.

    **The Yorkshire Insurance Co Ltd:** 2 Rougier St, York, YO1 1HR; tel. (1904) 628982; telex 57969; fax (1904) 611441; f. 1824; cap. p.u. £2.2m.; Chair. and Gen. Man. W. N. ROBERTSON; Sec. R. A. WHITAKER.

**Guardian Royal Exchange Assurance PLC:** Royal Exchange, London, EC3V 3LS; tel. (171) 283-7101; fax (171) 621-2599; f. 1968; Principal UK subsidiary insurances cos: Atlas Assurance Co Ltd, Caledonian Insurance Co, GRE (UK) Ltd, GRE Linked Life Assurance Ltd, GRE Pensions Management Ltd, Guardian Assurance PLC, Royal Exchange Assurance, Guardian Direct Ltd; Other subsidiary cos: Aquis Securities PLC, Compass Securities Ltd, Guardian Royal Exchange Financial Management Ltd, Guardian Royal Exchange Unit Managers Ltd, The Metropolitan Trust plc; Chair. Lord HAMBRO; Sec. J. R. W. CLAYTON.

**Iron Trades Insurance Co Ltd:** 21–24 Grosvenor Place, London, SW1X 7JA; tel. (171) 235-6033; telex 21792; fax (171) 245-6308; f. 1990; commercial vehicle, commercial property, consequential loss, employers liability, engineering, fire and perils, glass, group health care, motor fleet, personal accident, office, private household, private motor car, public and products liability, shop, theft; Chair. G. H. SAMBROOK; Man. Dir ROGER PEEK.

**ITT London & Edinburgh Insurance Group Ltd:** The Warren, Worthing, W. Sussex, BN14 9QD; tel. (1903) 820820; telex 87412; f. 1894; cap. auth. £200m., p.u. £150m.; Chair. and Man. Dir W. STANWAY.

**Legal and General Assurance Society Ltd:** Temple Court, 11 Queen Victoria St, London, EC4N 4TP; tel. (171) 528-6200; fax (171) 528-6222; f. 1836; cap. auth. £100m.; Chair. D. J. PROSSER; Sec. T. A. F. SMITH.

    **Gresham Fire and Accident Insurance Society Ltd:** Temple Court, 11 Queen Victoria St, London, EC4N 4TP; tel. (171) 248-9678; telex 892971; f. 1910; cap. auth. £500,000; Chair. B. E. PALMER; Sec. V. S. AYER.

    **Legal and General Insurance Ltd:** Temple Court, 11 Queen Victoria St, London, EC4N 4TP; tel. (171) 528-6200; telex 892971; fax (171) 528-6222; f. 1946 as British Commonwealth Insurance Co; cap. auth. £3.5m.; Chair. E. CHRISTIE; Sec. T. A. F. SMITH.

**Life Association of Scotland Ltd:** 113 Dundas St, Edinburgh, EH3 5EB; tel. (131) 550-5000; telex 727344; fax (131) 550-5123; f. 1838; Chair. G. W. BURNET; Man. Dir R. R. T. BUCHANAN.

**Liverpool Victoria Friendly Society Ltd:** Victoria House, Southampton Row, London, WC1B 4DB; tel. (171) 405-4377; fax (171) 831-2216; f. 1843; Chair. ANDREW NOBLE; Sec. C. A. PETERS.

**London and Manchester Assurance Co Ltd:** Winslade Park, Exeter, EX5 1DS; tel. (1392) 444888; telex 42726; fax (1392) 410076; f. 1869; Chair. T. A. PYNE; Co Sec. A. R. SWINBURNE-JOHNSON.

**Mercantile and General Reinsurance Co PLC:** Moorfields House, Moorfields, London, EC2Y 9AL; tel. (171) 628-7070; telex 888748; fax (171) 588-4629; Man. Dir J. ENGESTRÖM.

**MGM Assurance (Marine and General Mutual Life Assurance Society):** MGM House, Heene Rd, Worthing, Sussex, BN11 2DY; tel. (1903) 204631; telex 87441; f. 1852; Chair. D. W. HARDY; Dir and Gen. Man. P. G. HEADEY.

**National Employers' Mutual General Insurance Association Ltd:** International House, 26–28 Creechurch Lane, London, EC3A 5AS; tel. (171) 283-2440; telex 886551; fax (171) 626-3984; f. 1914; Chair. P. H. DUNN; Man. Dir S. E. HALLOWELL.

**National Farmers' Union Mutual & Avon Group:** Tiddington Rd, Stratford upon Avon, Warwicks., CV37 7BJ; tel. (1789) 204211; telex 312346; fax (1789) 298992; f. 1910; Chair. ALUN EVANS; Man. Dir A. S. YOUNG.

**National Mutual Life Assurance Society:** The Priory, Hitchin, Herts, SG5 2DW; tel. (1462) 422422; telex 826226; fax (1462) 420010; f. 1830; life and pensions; Chair. NORMAN CHALMERS; Gen. Man. G. H. E. HILL.

**National Provident Institution:** National Provident House, Tunbridge Wells, Kent, TN1 2UE; tel. (1892) 515151; telex 886319; fax (1892) 705611; f. 1835; Chair. Lord REMNANT; Sec. S. J. O'BRIEN.

**The Norwich Union Group:** Surrey St, Norwich NR1 3NS; tel. (1603) 622200; telex 97388; fax (1603) 683659; Principal UK subsidiary insurance cos: Norwich Union Life Insurance Society, f.1808; Norwich Union Holdings PLC, f. 1981; Norwich Union Fire Insurance Society Ltd, f. 1797; Scottish Union and National Insurance Co; Chair. G. W. PAUL; Group Chief Exec. A. BRIDGEWATER; Gen. Man. and Sec. J. D. STANFORTH.

**The Orion Insurance Co PLC:** Orion House, Bouverie Rd West, Folkestone, Kent, CT20 2RW; tel. (1303) 850303; telex 965156; fax (1303) 850304; f. 1931; non-life insurance and reinsurance; cap. auth. £100m., issued £50m.; Chair. N. H. SMITH; Man. Dir A. L. VAN KOERT; Sec. D. J. HOPKIN.

**Pearl Assurance PLC:** The Pearl Centre, Lynch Wood, Peterborough, Cambridgeshire, PE2 6FY; tel. (1733) 470470; fax (1733) 472300; f. 1864; cap. auth. £2.55m.; Chair. and Man. Dir DAVID DAVIES.

**Provident Mutual Life Assurance Association:** POB 568, 25–31 Moorgate, London, EC2R 6BA; tel. (171) 628-3232; fax (171) 638-1840; f. 1840; Chair. Lord FARNHAM; Chief Exec. B. RICHARDSON.

**Provincial Insurance PLC:** Stramongate, Kendal, Cumbria, LA9 4BE; tel. (1539) 723415; fax (1539) 727112; London Office: 5/10 Bury St, London, EC3A 5AT; tel. (171) 929-4010; fax (171) 626-1631; f. 1903; Chair. CHARLES F. E. SHAKERLEY; Man. Dir MICHAEL HART.

**The Prudential Assurance Co Ltd:** 142 Holborn Bars, London, EC1N 2NH; tel. (171) 405-9222; telex 266431; fax (171) 548-3465; f. 1881; holding co: Prudential Corpn PLC; cap. auth. £120m.; Chair. Sir MARTIN JACOMB; Group Chief Exec. PETER DAVIS.

**Refuge Assurance PLC:** Refuge House, Alderley Rd, Wilmslow, Cheshire, SK9 1PF; tel. (1625) 535959; telex 667376; f. 1858; cap. auth. £1.25m.; Chair. J. CUDWORTH.

**Royal Insurance Holdings PLC:** 1 Cornhill, London, EC3V 3QR; tel. (171) 283-4300; telex 8955701; f. 1845; cap. auth. £155m.; cap. p.u. £120m.; Chair. ALLAN GORMLY; Group Chief Exec. RICHARD GAMBLE; principal subsidiary cos:

    **Royal Insurance (UK) Ltd:** New Hall Place, Liverpool, L69 3EN; tel. (151) 227-4422; Man. Dir P. J. SHARMAN.

    **Royal Life Holdings Ltd:** P.O.B. 30, New Hall Place, Old Hall St, Liverpool, L69 3HS; tel. (151) 239-3000; telex 628441; f. 1982; Man. Dir D. R. PARRY.

    **Royal Reinsurance Co Ltd:** 24B Lime St, London, EC3M 7ND; tel. (171) 623-2545; telex 885837; fax (171) 283-9500; f. 1978; general reinsurance; Man. Dir J. P. BARBER.

**Royal Liver Friendly Society:** Royal Liver Bldg, Liverpool, L3 1HT; tel. (151) 236-1451; fax (151) 236-2122; f. 1850; Chair. G. A. SCOTT; Sec. K. E. HAWKINS.

**Royal London Mutual Insurance Society Ltd:** Royal London House, Middleborough, Colchester, Essex, CO1 1RA; tel. (1206) 761761; f. 1861; Chair. M. J. PICKARD; Sec. S. D. FARMER.

**Scottish Amicable Life Assurance Society:** 150 St Vincent St, Glasgow, G2 5NQ; tel. (141) 248-2323; telex 77171; f. 1826; Chair. W. BROWN; Sec. J. C. MITCHELL.

**Scottish Life Assurance Co:** POB 54, 19 St Andrew Sq., Edinburgh, EH2 1YE; tel. (131) 225-2211; telex 72525; fax (131) 225-2586; f. 1881, re-inc. as a Mutual Company 1968; Chair. WILLIAM BERRY; Chief Gen. Man. G. M. MURRAY.

UNITED KINGDOM (GREAT BRITAIN) *Directory*

**The Scottish Mutual Assurance Society:** 109 St Vincent St, Glasgow, G2 5HN; tel. (141) 248-6321; telex 777145; fax (141) 221-1230; f. 1883; Chair. J. H. F. MACPHERSON; Chief Exec. F. D. PATRICK.

**The Scottish Provident Institution:** 6 St Andrew Sq., Edinburgh, EH2 2YA; tel. (131) 556-9181; fax (131) 558-2486; f. 1837; Chair. ANGUS PELHAM BURN; Man. Dir D. E. WOODS.

**Scottish Widows' Fund and Life Assurance Society:** 15 Dalkeith Rd, Edinburgh, EH16 5BU; tel. (131) 655-6000; telex 72654; fax (131) 662-4053; f. 1815; Chair. COLIN BLACK; Man. Dir M. D. ROSS.

**Standard Life Assurance Co:** 3 George St, Edinburgh, EH2 2XZ; tel. (131) 225-2552; telex 72539; f. 1825; Holborn Hall, Gray's Inn Rd, London, WC1X 8JD; tel. (171) 242-9700; f. 1825; assets £28,600m.; Chair. N. LESSELS; Man. Dir A. SCOTT BELL.

**Sun Alliance Group PLC:** 1 Bartholomew Lane, London, EC2N 2AB; tel. (171) 588-2345; telex 888310; cap. p.u. £197.8m.; principal subsidiary cos (all at same address) include Alliance Assurance Co Ltd (f. 1824; cap. p.u. £5.7m.), The London Assurance (f. 1720; cap. p.u. £4.2m.), Phoenix Assurance PLC (cap. p.u. $61.0m.), Sun Alliance & London Assurance Co Ltd (f. 1966; cap. p.u. $1m.), Sun Alliance and London Insurance PLC (f. 1959; cap. p.u. £49.3m.), Sun Alliance Insurance International Ltd (f. 1920; cap. p.u. £400m.), Sun Alliance Insurance Overseas Ltd (f. 1906; cap. p.u. £400m.), Sun Alliance Insurance U.K. Ltd (f. 1918; cap. p.u. $400m.), Sun Insurance Office Ltd (f. 1926; cap. p.u. £2.4m.); Chair. Sir CHRISTOPHER BENSON; Chief Exec. ROGER TAYLOR.

**Sun Life Assurance Society PLC:** Sun Life Court, St James Barton, Bristol, Avon; telex 449923; f. 1810; Chair. P. J. GRANT; Dep. Chair. Lord BANCROFT; Chief Gen. Man. LES BENSON

**Swiss Life (UK) PLC:** PO Box 127, Swiss Life House, 101 London Rd, Sevenoaks, Kent TN13 1BG; tel. (1732) 450161; fax (1732) 463801.

**Wesleyan Assurance Society:** Colmore Circus, Birmingham, B4 6AR; tel. (121) 200-3003; fax (121) 200-2971; f. 1841; assets exceed £1,400m.; Chair. Sir TIMOTHY HARFORD; Man. Dir L. D.MACLEAN.

**Zurich Municipal:** Zurich House, Stanhope Rd, Portsmouth, Hants, PO1 1DU; subsidiary of Zurich Insurance Co., Switzerland; f. 1872; took over a large part of business of Municipal Mutual Insurance Ltd, which ceased trading in 1992; Chief Exec. ROLF HÜPPI.

### Insurance Associations

**Associated Scottish Life Offices:** 40–44 Thistle St, Edinburgh, EH2 1EN; tel. (131) 220-4774; constituted 1841 as an Association of General Managers of Scottish Offices transacting life assurance business; 8 full mems; Chair. A. S. BELL; Sec. W. W. MAIR.

**Association of British Insurers:** 51 Gresham St, London, EC2V 7HQ; tel. (171) 600-3333; fax (171) 696-8999; f. 1985; principal trade association for insurance companies; protection, promotion, and advancement of the common interests of all classes of insurance business; c. 450 mems; Chair. ALLAN BRIDGEWATER; Dir-Gen. MARK BOLEAT.

**British Insurance and Investment Brokers' Association (BIIBA):** BIIBA House, 14 Bevis Marks, London, EC3A 7NT; tel. (171) 623-9043; Dir-Gen. (vacant).

**Chartered Insurance Institute:** 20 Aldermanbury, London, EC2V 7HY; tel. (171) 606-3835; fax (171) 726-0131; f. 1897; inc. 1912; approx. 68,000 mems; Pres. R. S. HILL; Dir-Gen. D. E. BLAND.

**Fire Protection Association:** 140 Aldersgate St, London, EC1A 4HX; tel. (171) 606-3757; (from Sept. 1995) Melrose Ave, Borehamwood, Herts., WD6 2BJ; tel. (181) 207-2345; fax (181) 207-6305; Dir. S. KIDD.

**Institute of London Underwriters:** 49 Leadenhall St, London, EC3A 2BE; tel. (171) 488-2424; telex 884165; f. 1884; Chair. LEONARD N. CAMPBELL; Chief Exec. ANTHONY J. FUNNELL.

**Insurance Institute of London:** 20 Aldermanbury, London, EC2V 7HY; tel. and fax (171) 600-1343; f. 1907; Pres. R. E. BROWN, (from October 1995) H. M. J. RITCHIE.

**Liverpool Underwriters' Association:** c/o Sun Alliance Insurance Group, Sun Alliance House, 30 Exchange St East, Liverpool, L2 3PX; tel. (151) 707-2233; fax (151) 236-1725; Chair. M. J. POPE.

**London Insurance and Reinsurance Market Association:** Third Floor, London Underwriting Centre, 3 Minster Court, London, EC3R 7DD; tel. (171) 617-4444; fax (171) 617-4440; Chair. C. H. D. DENNING; Chief Exec. MARIE-LOUISE ROSSI.

**Loss Prevention Council:** 140 Aldersgate St, London, EC1A 4HY; tel. (171) 606-1050; (from Sept. 1995) Melrose Ave, Borehamwood, Herts., WD6 2BJ; tel. (181) 207-2345; fax (181) 207-6303; Chair. PETER FOREMAN; Chief Exec. J. L. HILL.

### Advisory Body

**Personal Investment Authority:** see p. 3167.

### Associations of Actuaries

**Faculty of Actuaries:** 40–44 Thistle St., Edinburgh, EH2 1EN; tel. (131) 220-4555; fax (131) 220-2280; f. 1856; 906 Fellows; Pres. MALCOLM MURRAY; Sec. W. W. MAIR.

**Institute of Actuaries:** Staple Inn Hall, High Holborn, London, WC1V 7QJ; tel. (171) 242-0106; fax (171) 405-2482; f. 1848; Royal Charter 1884; 8,631 mems; Pres. CHRISTOPHER D. DAYKIN (1994–96); Sec.-Gen. ARTHUR TAIT.

## Trade and Industry

### CHAMBERS OF COMMERCE AND INDUSTRY

**Association of British Chambers of Commerce:** 9 Tufton St, London, SW1P 3QB; tel. (171) 222-1533; fax (171) 799-2202; f. 1860; in January 1993 subsumed National Chamber of Trade (f. 1897); 140 affiliated UK chambers, 10 British chambers of commerce in foreign countries and 17 trade associations; Pres. ROBIN BUSSELL; Dir-Gen. R. G. TAYLOR.

**DECTA:** St Nicholas House, St Nicholas Rd, Sutton, Surrey, SM1 1EL; tel. (181) 643-3311; telex 948116; fax (181) 643-8030; trade and enterprise development consultancy; Man. Dir RON HINSLEY.

**International Chamber of Commerce (ICC) United Kingdom:** 14–15 Belgrave Sq., London, SW1X 8PS; tel. (171) 823-2811; fax (171) 235-5447; f. 1920; British affiliate of the world business org.; Chair. PATRICK GILLAM; Dir R. C. I. BATE.

**London Chamber of Commerce and Industry:** Swan House, Queen St, London, EC4; tel. (171) 248-4444; telex 888941; fax (171) 489-0391; Pres. BRIAN HARRIS; Chief Exec. SIMON SPERRYN.

**London Enterprise Agency:** 4 Snow Hill, London, EC1A 2BS; tel. (171) 236-3000; a consortium of 21 major companies provides an advisory service to small firms; Chair. ROBIN HEAL.

### EMPLOYERS' ASSOCIATIONS

**British Retail Consortium:** Bedford House, 69–79 Fulham High St, London, SW6; tel. (171) 371-5185; fax (171) 371-0529; f. 1975; represents retailers; Dir-Gen. J. MAY.

**Confederation of British Industry (CBI):** Centre Point, 103 New Oxford St, London, WC1A 1DU; tel. (171) 379-7400; telex 21332; fax (171) 240-1578; f. 1965; acts as a national point of reference for all seeking views of industry and is recognized internationally as the representative organization of British industry and management. Advises the government on all aspects of policy affecting the interests of industry. Membership consists of more than 250,000 companies, directly or indirectly. Pres. Sir BRYAN NICHOLSON (1994–96); Dir-Gen. HOWARD DAVIES; Sec. MAURICE HUNT.

**Federation of Small Businesses:** 140 Lower Marsh, Westminster Bridge, London, SE1 7AE; tel. (171) 928-9272; fax (171) 401-2544; f. 1974; 58,000 mems; Dir STEPHEN ALAMBRITIS.

**Institute of Directors:** 116 Pall Mall, London, SW1Y 5ED; tel. (171) 839-1233; fax (171) 930-1949; f. 1903; 50,000 mems, including 15,000 overseas; Pres. Lord YOUNG OF GRAFFHAM; Dir-Gen. TIM MELVILLE-ROSS.

**Institute of Management:** 2 Savoy Court, Strand, London, WC2R 0EZ; tel. (171) 497-0580; fax (171) 497-0463; f. 1992 by amalgamation of British Institute of Management (f. 1947) and Institution of Industrial Managers (f. 1931); 70,000 individual mems; Chair. JAMES WATSON; Dir-Gen. ROGER D. YOUNG.

### EXPORT ORGANIZATIONS

**British Exporters Association:** 16 Dartmouth St, London, SW1H 9BL; tel. (171) 222-5419; Pres. Lord SELSDON; Dir H. W. BAILEY.

**Department of Trade and Industry:** Ashdown House, 123 Victoria St, London, SW1E 6RB; general enquiries; tel. (171) 215-5000; single European market; tel. (171) 200-1992; fax (171) 583-4900.

**Institute of Export:** 64 Clifton St, London, EC2A 4HB; tel. (171) 247-9812; fax (171) 377-5343; f. 1935 as a professional educational organization devoted to the development of British export trade and the interests of those associated with it; more than 6,000 mems; Pres. Earl of LIMERICK; Dir-Gen. I. J. CAMPBELL.

### CO-OPERATIVE ORGANIZATIONS

**Co-operative Union Ltd:** Holyoake House, Hanover St, Manchester, M60 0AS; tel. (161) 832-4300; fax (161) 831-7684; f. 1869; co-ordinates, informs and advises the 62 co-operative societies; Chief Exec. and Gen. Sec. D. L. WILKINSON.

**Co-operative Wholesale Society Ltd:** New Century House, Manchester, M60 4ES; tel. (161) 834-1212; fax (161) 834-4507; f. 1863; principal supplier to Co-op shops; Chair. LENNOX FYFE; Chief Exec. DAVID SKINNER; Sec. G. J. MELMOTH.

# UNITED KINGDOM (GREAT BRITAIN)

**National Association of Co-operative Officials:** Coronation House, Arndale Centre, Manchester, M4 2HW; tel. (161) 834-6029; Gen. Sec. L. W. EWING.

## PRINCIPAL INDUSTRIAL ORGANIZATIONS

**Aluminium Federation:** Broadway House, Calthorpe Rd, Five Ways, Birmingham, B15 1TN; tel. (121) 456-1103; fax (121) 456-2274; f. 1962; Pres. LEWIS GARFIELD; Sec.-Gen. Dr D. A. HARRIS.

**Association of the British Pharmaceutical Industry:** 12 Whitehall, London, SW1A 2DY; tel. (171) 930-3477; fax (171) 747-1411; f. 1930; Pres. Dr T. MEDINGER; Dir-Gen. Dr T. M. JONES.

**Association of Manufacturers of Domestic Electrical Appliances:** Leicester House, 8 Leicester St, London, WC2H 7AZ; tel. (171) 437-0678; fax (171) 494-1094; f. 1969; 130 mem. cos; Dir-Gen. PETER CARVER; Sec. J. A. JENNINGS.

**BFM Ltd:** 30 Harcourt St, London, W1H 2AA; tel. (171) 724-0851; merged in January 1993 with BFM Exhibitions and BFM Exports; represents furniture manufacturers; Chief Exec. ADRIAN HILL.

**Brewers and Licensed Retailers Association:** 42 Portman Sq., London, W1H 0BB; tel. (171) 486-4831; fax (171) 935-3991; f. 1904; 80 mems; Chair. Sir PAUL NICHOLSON; Dir. ROBIN SIMPSON.

**British Cable Makers' Confederation:** 56 Palace Rd, East Molesey, Surrey, KT8 9DW; tel. (181) 941-4079; fax (181) 783-0104; f. 1958; Pres. B. DAVIES; Sec.-Gen. C. G. G. RUDGE.

**British Carpet Manufacturers' Association:** 5 Portland Pl., London, W1N 3AA; tel. (171) 580-7155; fax (171) 580-4854; Pres. B. E. WILD; Exec. Dir. G. W. WILSON.

**British Cement Association:** Wexham Springs, Slough, SL3 6PL; tel. (1753) 662727; telex 848352; fax (1753) 660399; Chair. Sir GEORGE MOSELEY.

**British Ceramic Confederation:** Federation House, Station Rd, Stoke-on-Trent, Staffs., ST4 2SA; tel. (1782) 744631; fax (1782) 744102; f. 1919; 150 mems; Dir K. C. FARRELL; Sec. C. P. HALL.

**British Clothing Industry Association:** 5 Portland Pl., London, W1N 3AA; tel. (171) 636-7788; fax (171) 636-7515; f. 1980; Chair. JAMES MCADAM; Dir JOHN R. WILSON.

**British Footwear Manufacturers Federation:** Royalty House, 72 Dean St, London, W1V 5HB; tel. (171) 437-5573; fax (171) 494-1300; Dir-Gen. W. N. S. CALVERT.

**British Glass Manufacturers' Confederation:** Northumberland Rd, Sheffield, S10 2UA; tel. (1742) 686201; fax (1742) 681073; Company Sec. D. K. BARLOW.

**British Hospitality Association:** 40 Duke St, London, W1M 6HR; tel. (171) 499-6641; telex 296619; fax (171) 355-4596; f. 1907; Pres. ROCCO FORTE; Chief Exec. ROBIN LEES.

**British Non-Ferrous Metals Federation:** 10 Greenfield Crescent, Birmingham, B15 3AU; tel. (121) 456-3322; telex 339161; fax (121) 456-1394; Dir SIMON PAYTON.

**The British Precast Concrete Federation Ltd:** 60 Charles St, Leicester, LE1 1FB; tel. (116) 253-6161; fax (116) 251-4568; f. 1918; approx. 125 mems; Dir A. TYDEMAN; Sec. JOHN R. CARTER.

**British Printing Industries Federation:** 11 Bedford Row, London, WC1R 4DX; tel. (171) 242-6904; fax (171) 405-7784; f. 1900; 3,500 mems; Pres. NICHOLAS HUTTON; Dir-Gen. TOM MACHIN.

**British Ready Mixed Concrete Association:** The Bury, Church St, Chesham, Bucks, HP5 1JE; tel. (1494) 791050; fax (1494) 791140; Technical Dir T. A. HARRISON; Sec. K. WATSON.

**British Rubber Manufacturers' Association:** 90 Tottenham Court Rd, London, W1P 0BR; tel. (171) 580-2794; fax (171) 631-5471; f. 1968; Pres. D. G. POWELL; Dir W. R. POLLOCK.

**Building Employers Confederation:** 82 New Cavendish St, London, W1M 8AD; tel. (171) 580-5588; fax (171) 631-3872; f. 1878; 8,000 mems; Chair. JIM KANE; Dir-Gen. IAN DESLANDES.

**Dairy Industry Federation:** 19 Cornwall Terrace, London, NW1 4QP; tel. (171) 486-7244; telex 262027; fax (171) 487-4734; f. 1933; Pres. NEIL DAVIDSON; Dir-Gen. JOHN PRICE.

**Electrical Contractors' Association:** ESCA House, 34 Palace Court, London, W2 4HY; tel. (171) 229-1266; fax (171) 221-7344; f. 1901; Pres. (1995/96) J. R. HARROWER; Dir H. MCK. SIMPSON.

**Electricity Association Services Ltd:** 30 Millbank, London, SW1P 4RD; tel. (171) 344-5700; fax (171) 931-0356; f. 1990 as a trade asscn for the new electricity companies in England, Wales, Scotland and Northern Ireland, and to provide them with various services. Assoc. mems. include ESB Ireland, Jersey Electricity Co., States of Guernsey Electricity Board and Manx Electricity Authority; Chief Exec. P. E. G. DAUBENEY.

**Engineering Employers' Federation:** Broadway House, Tothill St, London, SW1H 9NQ; tel. (171) 222-7777; fax (171) 222-2782; f. 1896; 5,000 mems through 14 associations; Pres. NOEL DAVIES; Dir-Gen. GRAHAM MACKENZIE.

**Farmers' Union of Wales:** Llys Amaeth, Queen's Sq., Aberystwyth, Dyfed, SY23 2EA; tel. (1970) 612755; fax (1970) 624369; f. 1955; 14,000 mems; Pres. BOB PARRY; Sec. ROWLAND WILLIAMS.

**Federation of British Electrotechnical and Allied Manufacturers' Associations (BEAMA Ltd):** Westminster Tower, 3 Albert Embankment, London, SE1 7SL; tel. (171) 793-3000; fax (171) 793-3003; f. 1905 as British Electrical and Allied Manufacturers' Association Ltd, present name from 1983; 570 mems; Pres. Viscount WEIR; Dir-Gen. J. G. GADDES.

**Federation of Civil Engineering Contractors:** 6 Portugal St, London, WC2A 2HH; tel. (171) 404-4020; fax (171) 242-0256; f. 1919; Dir-Gen. JOHN HACKETT.

**Food and Drink Federation:** 6 Catherine St, London, WC2B 5JJ; tel. (171) 836-2460; telex 299388; fax (171) 836-0580; Pres. RICHARD GEORGE.

**Glass and Glazing Federation:** 44–48 Borough High St, London, SE1 1XB; tel. (171) 403-7177; fax (171) 357-7458; f. 1977; trade federation for the flat glass industry; Dir D. E. BALLARD; Deputy Dir and Nat. Sec. MICHAEL G. S. HILL.

**Incorporated National Association of British and Irish Millers Ltd:** 21 Arlington St, London, SW1A 1RN; tel. (171) 493-2521; telex 28878; fax (171) 493-6785; f. 1878; Dir-Gen. J. MURRAY; Sec. P. H. NEILL.

**Leather Producers' Association:** Leather Trade House, King's Park Rd, Moulton Park, Northampton, NN3 6JD; tel. (1604) 494131; fax (1604) 648220; f. 1919; Sec. JACK PURVIS.

**National Farmers' Union:** 22 Long Acre, London, WC2E 9LY; tel. (171) 331-7200; fax (171) 331-7382; f. 1908; Pres. Sir DAVID NAISH; Dir-Gen. DAVID EVANS.

**National Metal Trades Federation:** Fleming House, Renfrew St, Glasgow, G3 6TG; tel. (141) 332-0826; telex 779433; Sec. H. MACSHANNON.

**Producers Alliance for Cinema and Television (PACT) Ltd:** Gordon House, Greencoat Place, London, SW1P 1PH; tel. (171) 233-6000; fax (171) 233-8935; film and TV producers; represents 1,400 companies; Chief Exec. JOHN WOODWARD.

**Scottish Building Employers' Federation:** 13 Woodside Crescent, Glasgow, G3 7UP; tel. (141) 332-7144; fax (141) 331-1684; Pres. J. BIRNIE; Dir R. W. CAMPBELL.

**Scottish Textile Association:** 45 Moray Place, Edinburgh, EH3 6EQ; tel. (131) 225-3149; fax (131) 220-4942; present name since 1991; Chair. Sir RONALD MILLER; Chief Exec. KENNETH HARDY.

**Society of British Aerospace Companies Ltd:** 29 King St, St James's, London, SW1Y 6RD; tel. (171) 839-3231; telex 262274; fax (171) 930-3577; f. 1916; Pres. R. TURNER; Dir Sir BARRY DUXBURY.

**Society of Motor Manufacturers and Traders:** Forbes House, Halkin St, London, SW1X 7DS; tel. (171) 235-7000; fax (171) 235-7112; Pres. (1995/96) GEORGE SIMPSON.

**The Sugar Bureau:** Duncan House, Dolphin Sq., London, SW1V 3PW; tel. (171) 828-9465; fax (171) 821-5393; represents sugar companies in the UK, provides technical, educational and consumer information about sugar and health; Dir Dr R. C. COTTRELL.

**Timber Trade Federation:** Clareville House, 26–27 Oxendon St, London, SW1Y 4EL; tel. (171) 839-1891; fax (171) 930-0094; Pres. M. J. MEYER; Dir-Gen. P. G. HARRIS.

**United Kingdom Petroleum Industry Association:** 9 Kingsway, London, WC2B 6XH; tel. (171) 240-0289; fax (171) 379-3102; Pres. JOHN ORANGE; Dir-Gen. DAVID PARKER.

## TRADE UNIONS

### Central Organizations

**Trades Union Congress (TUC):** Congress House, 23–28 Great Russell St, London, WC1B 3LS; tel. (171) 636-4030; telex 268328; fax (171) 636-0632; f. 1868; a voluntary association of trade unions, the representatives of which meet annually to consider matters of common concern to their members. A General Council of 48 members is elected at the annual Congress to keep watch on all industrial movements, legislation affecting labour and all matters touching the interest of the trade union movement, with authority to promote common action on general questions and to assist trade unions in the work of organization. Through the General Council and its Executive Committee, the TUC campaigns on issues of concern to employees and provides services for affiliated unions. It also makes nominations to various bodies such as the Health and Safety Commission and the Advisory, Conciliation and Arbitration Service Council. In December 1994 68 unions, with a total membership of 7,298,262 were affiliated to the TUC. The TUC is affiliated to the International Confederation of Free Trade Unions and the European Trade Union Confederation, and nominates the British Workers' Delegate to the International Labour Organization; Pres. LEIF MILLS; Gen. Sec. JOHN MONKS.

# UNITED KINGDOM (GREAT BRITAIN)

**Scottish Trades Union Congress:** Middleton House, 16 Woodlands Terrace, Glasgow, G3 6DF; tel. (141) 332-4946; fax (141) 332-4649; f. 1897; 689,365 Scottish trade unionists affiliated through 49 trade unions and 27 trades councils (1994); Gen. Sec. CAMPBELL CHRISTIE.

**Wales Trades Union Council:** 1 Cathedral Rd, Cardiff; tel. (1222) 372345; fax (1222) 221940; f. 1973; Gen. Sec. DAVID JENKINS.

**General Federation of Trade Unions:** Central House, Upper Woburn Place, London, WC1H 0HY; tel. (171) 388-0852; fax (171) 383-0820; f. 1899 by the TUC; 32 affiliated organizations, with a total membership of 283,650; Sec. MICHAEL BRADLEY.

## Principal Trade Unions Affiliated to the TUC

(Includes all affiliated unions whose membership is in excess of 10,000)

**Amalgamated Engineering and Electrical Union (AEEU):** Hayes Court, West Common Rd, Bromley, Kent, BR2 7AU; tel. (181) 462-7755; fax (181) 462-4959; f. 1992 as a result of merger between Amalgamated Engineering Union (AEU) with Electrical, Electronic, Telecommunications and Plumbing Union (EETPU); Pres. NIGEL HARRIS (acting); Gen. Sec. PAUL GALLAGHER; 835,019 mems.

**Associated Society of Locomotive Engineers and Firemen (ASLEF):** 9 Arkwright Rd, London, NW3 6AB; tel. (171) 431-0275; fax (171) 794-6406; f. 1880; Gen. Sec. LEW ADAMS; 17,386 mems.

**Association of First Division Civil Servants:** 2 Caxton St, London, SW1H 0QH; tel. (171) 222-6242; fax (171) 222-5926; Pres. MARTIN BRIMMER; Gen. Sec. ELIZABETH SYMONS; 10,905 mems.

**Association of University Teachers (AUT):** United House, 9 Pembridge Rd, London, W11 3JY; tel. (171) 221-4370; fax (171) 727-6547; f. 1919; Pres. PETER BREEZE; Gen. Sec. DAVID TRIESMAN; 32,466 mems.

**Bakers, Food and Allied Workers' Union:** Stanborough House, Great North Rd, Stanborough, Welwyn Garden City, Herts., AL8 7TA; tel. (1707) 260150; fax (1707) 261570; f. 1861; Gen. Sec. JOSEPH MARINO; 32,222 mems.

**Banking, Insurance and Finance Union (BIFU):** Sheffield House, 1B Amity Grove, Raynes Park, London, SW20 0LG; tel. (181) 946-9151; fax (181) 879-7916; f. 1918 as Bank Officers Guild, present name from 1979; Pres. PETER SIMPSON; Gen. Sec. LEIF MILLS; 134,012 mems.

**British Actors' Equity Association:** Guild House, Upper St Martin's Lane, London, WC2H 9EG; tel. (171) 379-6000; fax (171) 379-7001; Gen. Sec. IAN MCGARRY; 41,592 mems.

**Broadcasting, Entertainment, Cinematograph and Theatre Union:** 111 Wardour St, London, W1V 4AY; tel. (171) 437-8506; fax (171) 437-8268; f. 1991 as a result of merger between Asscn. of Cinematograph, Television and Allied Technicians (f. 1933) and the Broadcasting and Entertainment Trades Alliance (f. 1984); Pres. TONY LENNON; Gen. Sec. ROGER BOLTON; 30,000 mems.

**Ceramic and Allied Trades Union:** Hillcrest House, Garth St, Hanley, Stoke-on-Trent, Staffs., ST1 2AB; tel. (1782) 272755; fax (1782) 284902; f. 1825; Gen. Sec. G. BAGNALL; 23,122 mems.

**Chartered Society of Physiotherapy:** 14 Bedford Row, London WC1R 4ED; tel. (171) 306-6666; fax (171) 306-6611; Gen. Sec. TOBY SIMON; 26,000 mems.

**Civil and Public Services Association:** 160 Falcon Rd, London, SW11 2LN; tel. (171) 924-2727; fax (171) 924-1847; f. 1903; Pres. MARION CHAMBERS; Gen. Sec. BARRY REAMSBOTTOM; 131,000 mems.

**Communication Managers' Association:** GMA House, Ruscombe Rd, Twyford, Reading, Berks., RG10 9JD; tel. (1734) 342300; fax (1734) 342087; formerly Post Office Management Staffs' Asscn; Pres. GEOFFREY THOMAS; Gen. Sec. T. L. DEEGAN; 15,474 mems.

**Communications Workers' Union:** CWU House, Crescent Lane, London, SW4 9RN; tel. (171) 622-9977; fax (171) 720-6853; and Greystoke House, 150 Brunswick Rd, London, W5 1AW; tel. (181) 998-2981; fax (181) 991-1410; f. 1995 by merger of the National Communications Union and the Union of Communication Workers; Gen. Secs ALAN JOHNSON, TONY YOUNG; 291,867 mems.

**Educational Institute of Scotland:** 46 Moray Place, Edinburgh, EH3 6BH; tel. (131) 225-6244; fax (131) 220-3151; Gen. Sec. RONALD A. SMITH; 49,371 mems.

**Engineers' and Managers' Association:** Flaxman House, Gogmore Lane, Chertsey, Surrey, KT16 9JS; tel. (1932) 564131; fax (1932) 567707; f. 1913; Gen. Sec. D. A. COOPER; 36,092 mems.

**Fire Brigades Union:** Bradley House, 68 Coombe Rd, Kingston upon Thames, Surrey, KT2 7AE; tel. (181) 541-1765; fax (181) 546-5187; f. 1918; Sec. KENNETH CAMERON; 50,706 mems.

**GMB:** 22-24 Worple Rd, Wimbledon, London, SW19 4DD; tel. (181) 947-3131; fax (181) 944-6552; f. 1982; Gen. Sec. JOHN EDMONDS; 830,743 mems.

**GMBTU Textiles Division:** Textile Union Centre, 5 Caton St, Rochdale, Lancs., OL16 1QJ; tel. (1706) 59551; Sec. R. G. MORROW; 13,000 mems.

**Graphical, Paper and Media Union:** 63-67 Bromham Rd, Bedford MK40 2AG; tel. (1234) 351521; fax (1234) 270580; f. 1991 as a result of merger between the National Graphical Association (1982) and the Society of Graphical and Allied Trades (SOGAT) '82; Pres. BRYN GRIFFITHS; Gen. Sec. TONY DUBBINS; 223,687 mems.

**Health Visitors' Association:** 50 Southwark St, London, SE1 1UN; tel. (171) 378-7255; fax (171) 407-3521; f. 1896; a section of Manufacturing, Science and Finance (MSF); Dir MARGARET BUTTIGIEG; 16,000 mems.

**Inland Revenue Staff Federation:** Douglas Houghton House, 231 Vauxhall Bridge Rd, London, SW1V 1EH; tel. (171) 834-8254; fax (171) 630-6258; f. 1936; Sec. CLIVE BROOKE; 59,000 mems.

**Institution of Professionals, Managers and Specialists:** 75-79 York Rd, London, SE1 7AQ; tel. (171) 928-9951; fax (171) 928-5996; f. 1919; Gen. Sec. BILL BRETT; 81,015 mems.

**Iron and Steel Trades Confederation:** Swinton House, 324 Gray's Inn Rd, London, WC1X 8DD; tel. (171) 837-6691; fax (171) 278-8378; f. 1917; Gen. Sec. D. K. BROOKMAN; 35,000 mems.

**Manufacturing, Science, Finance (MSF):** Park House, 64-66 Wandsworth Common North Side, London, SW18 2SH; tel. (181) 871-2100; fax (181) 877-1160; f. 1988 in a merger of the Association of Scientific, Technical and Managerial Staffs (ASTMS) and the Technical, Administrative and Supervisory Section (TASS) of the Amalgamated Engineering Union; Gen. Sec. ROGER LYONS; 516,000 mems.

**Musicians' Union:** 60-62 Clapham Rd, London, SW9 0JJ; tel. (171) 582-5566; fax (171) 582-9805; Gen. Sec. DENNIS SCARD; 35,591 mems.

**NATFHE—The University & College Lecturers' Union** (formerly National Association of Teachers in Further and Higher Education): 27 Britannia St, London, WC1X 9JP; tel. (171) 837-3636; fax (171) 837-4403; f. 1976; Gen. Sec. JOHN AKKER; 72,000 mems.

**National Association of Schoolmasters and Union of Women Teachers (NASUWT):** Hillscourt Education Centre, Rose Hill, Rednal, Birmingham, B45 8RS; tel. (121) 453-6150; fax (121) 453-7224; f. 1919, merged with UWT 1976; Gen. Sec. NIGEL DE GRUCHY; 213,000 mems.

**National Union of Civil and Public Servants:** New Bridgewater House, 5-13 Great Suffolk St, London, SE1 0NS; tel. (171) 928-9671; fax (171) 401-2693; f. 1988; Gen. Sec. JOHN SHELDON; 112,761 mems.

**National Union of Insurance Workers:** 27 Old Gloucester St, London, WC1N 3AF; tel. (171) 405-6798; fax (171) 404-8150; f. 1964; Pres. DEREK BARBER; Gen. Sec. KEN PERRY; 12,500 mems.

**National Union of Journalists (NUJ):** Acorn House, 314/320 Gray's Inn Rd, London, WC1X 8DP; tel. (171) 278-7916; telex 892384; fax (171) 837-8143; f. 1907; Sec.-Gen. JOHN FOSTER; 23,149 mems.

**National Union of Knitwear, Footwear and Apparel Trades:** The Grange, 108 Northampton Rd, Earls Barton, Northampton, NN6 0JH; tel. (116) 255-6703; fax (116) 254-4406; f. 1991; Pres. HELEN F. MCGRATH; Gen. Sec. PAUL GATES; 49,910 mems.

**National Union of Marine Aviation and Shipping Transport Officers (NUMAST):** Oceanair House, 750-760 High Rd, Leytonstone, London, E11 3BB; tel. (181) 989-6677; telex 892648; fax (181) 530-1015; f. 1936; Sec. BRIAN ORRELL; 18,332 mems.

**National Union of Mineworkers (NUM):** Miners' Offices, 2 Huddersfield Rd, Barnsley, S70 2LS; tel. (1226) 284006; fax (1226) 285486; Pres. ARTHUR SCARGILL; 18,227 mems.

**National Union of Rail, Maritime and Transport Workers (RMT):** Unity House, Euston Rd, London, NW1 2BL; tel. (171) 387-4771; fax (171) 387-4123; f. 1990 through merger of National Union of Railwaymen (f. 1872) and National Union of Seamen (f. 1887); Gen. Sec. JAMES KNAPP; 85,000 mems.

**National Union of Teachers (NUT):** Hamilton House, Mabledon Place, London, WC1H 9BD; tel. (171) 388-6191; fax (171) 387-8458; Pres. JOHN BILLS; Gen. Sec. DOUG McAVOY; 164,718 mems.

**Prison Officers' Association:** Cronin House, 245 Church St, London, N9 9HW; tel. (181) 803-0255; fax (181) 803-1761; Chair. J. BARTELL; Gen. Sec. D. M. EVANS; 29,077 mems.

**Society of Radiographers:** 14 Upper Wimpole St, London, W1M 8BN; tel. (171) 935-5726; fax (171) 487-3483; Gen. Sec. STEPHEN EVANS; 12,815 mems.

**Society of Telecom Executives:** 1 Park Rd, Teddington, Middlesex, TW11 0AR; tel. (181) 943-5181; telex 927162; fax (181) 943-2532; Gen. Sec. SIMON PETCH; 22,143 mems.

**Transport and General Workers' Union (TGWU):** Transport House, Smith Sq., London, SW1P 3JB; tel. (171) 828-7788; telex

## UNITED KINGDOM (GREAT BRITAIN)

919009; fax (171) 630-9463; Gen. Sec. WILLIAM MORRIS; 1,036,586 mems.

**Rural Agricultural and Allied Workers' National Trade Group (TGWU):** Transport House, 16 Palace St, London, SW1E 5JD; tel. (171) 828-7788; telex 919009; fax (171) 630-5861; Sec. BARRY LEATHWOOD; 35,000 mems.

**Transport and General Workers' Union Textile Trade Group:** National House, Sunbridge Rd, Bradford, W. Yorks., BD1 2QB; tel. (1274) 725642; fax (1274) 370282; Nat. Sec. PETER BOOTH; 30,000 mems.

**Transport Salaried Staffs' Association:** Walkden House, 10 Melton St, London, NW1 2EJ; tel. (171) 387-2101; fax (171) 383-0656; f. 1897; Pres. BRENDA HANKS; Gen. Sec. R. A. ROSSER; 38,492 mems.

**Union of Construction, Allied Trades and Technicians:** UCATT House, 177 Abbeville Rd, Clapham, London, SW4 9RL; tel. (171) 622-2362; fax (171) 740-4081; f. 1921; Pres. JOHN FLAVIN; Gen. Sec. GEORGE BRUMWELL; 135,878 mems.

**Union of Shop, Distributive and Allied Workers:** Oakley, 188 Wilmslow Rd, Fallowfield, Manchester, M14 6LJ; tel. (161) 224-2804; fax (161) 257-2566; Pres. AUDREY WISE; Gen. Sec. GARFIELD DAVIES; 316,491 mems.

**UNISON:** 1 Mabledon Pl., London, WC1H 9AJ; tel. (171) 388-2366; fax (171) 387-6692; f. 1993 through merger of Confederation of Health Service Employees (COHSE—f. 1910); National and Local Government Officers Asscn (NALGO—f. 1905) and National Union of Public Employees (NUPE—f. 1888); Pres MICKY BRYANT, BRENDA HUDSON, COLIN ROBINSON; Gen. Sec. ALAN JINKINSON; 1,457,726 mems.

**United Road Transport Union:** 76 High Lane, Manchester, M21 1FD; tel. (161) 881-6245; fax (161) 862-9127; f. 1890; Gen. Sec. DAVID HIGGINBOTTOM; 16,800 mems.

### Unions not affiliated to the TUC

**Association of Teachers and Lecturers:** 7 Northumberland St, London WC2N 5DA; tel. (171) 930-6441; fax (171) 930-1359; f. 1978; Gen. Sec. PETER SMITH; 161,000 mems.

**Union of Democratic Mineworkers (UDM):** Berry Hill, Mansfield, Notts, NG18 4JU; tel. (1623) 420140; f. 1986; Pres. and Gen. Sec. NEIL GREATREX; c. 7,000 mems.

### National Federations

**Confederation of Shipbuilding and Engineering Unions:** 140/142 Walworth Rd, London, SE17 1JW; tel. (171) 703-2215; 1,747,700 mems in 21 affiliated trade unions; Gen. Sec. ALAN ROBSON.

**Federation of Entertainment Unions:** 1 Highfield, Twyford, Hampshire, SO21 1QR; tel. and fax (1962) 713134; Sec. STEVE HARRIS.

**National Federation of Furniture Trade Unions:** 22–24 Worple Rd, London, SW19 4DD; tel. (181) 947-3131; fax (181) 944-6552; National Sec. COLIN A. CHRISTOPHER.

## NATIONALIZED INDUSTRIES

(Information about the British Railways Bd and London Regional Transport will be found in the section on Transport.

**AEA Technology:** Harwell, Oxfordshire, OX11 0RA; tel. (1235) 821111; telex 83135; fax (1235) 832591; f. 1954 as UK Atomic Energy Authority to take responsibility for UK research and development into all aspects of atomic energy; in 1990 adopted the trading name AEA Technology (since April 1994 this has referred to the Authority's commercial division, intended for eventual privatization); AEA Technology operates as a separate arm of the Authority (the other arm being UKAEA Government Division), and is a major international contract supplier of technological consultancy, research and development and engineering services to both industry and government. About 40% of its business is now for customers outside the nuclear industry, including the oil and gas, aerospace, defence, manufacturing and processing sectors. Key specialist areas include environmental protection, safety and reliability and the optimization of plant performance. These activities are conducted at sites at Risley (Cheshire), Windscale (Cumbria), Dounreay (Caithness), Harwell and Culham (Oxfordshire) and Winfrith (Dorset); Chair. Sir ANTHONY CLEAVER.

**The British Coal Corporation:** Hobart House, Grosvenor Place, London, SW1X 7AE; tel. (171) 235-2020; telex 882161; fax (171) 235-2020; established 1947 under the Coal Industry Nationalisation Act of 1946; powers to license coal operations and the ownership of British coal reserves was transferred to a new Coal Authority on 31 October 1994; the transfer to the private sector of all the Corporation's core mining activities was completed by December 1994; continues to act as a holding co for non-mining subsidiaries; Chair. J. NEIL CLARKE; Sec. P. L. HUTCHINSON.

**Nuclear Electric PLC:** Barnett Way, Barnwood, Gloucester, GL4 7RS; tel. (1452) 652855; fax (1452) 652750; responsible for all commercial nuclear power in England and Wales; Chair. JOHN COLLIER; Chief Exec. Dr ROBERT HAWLEY.

**The Post Office:** 5th Floor, 148 Old St, London, EC1V 9HQ; tel. (171) 250-2890; f. 1969 as a public corporation; established in 1981 as a separate corporation from telecommunications; provides Royal Mail postal services; Chair. MICHAEL HERON; Chief Exec. WILLIAM COCKBURN; Sec. D. SAVILL.

**Scottish Nuclear Ltd:** Peel Park, East Kilbride, G74 5PR; tel. (13552) 62626; fax (13552) 62000; responsible for operating nuclear power stations in Scotland; Chair. JAMES HANN; Chief Exec. Dr ROBIN JEFFREY.

## ADVISORY AND SUPERVISORY BODIES

**Advisory, Conciliation and Arbitration Service (ACAS):** 27 Wilton St, London, SW1X 7AZ; tel. (171) 210-3000; fax (171) 210-3708; f. 1974; an independent organization, under the management of a council comprising employers, trade union representatives and independent members, appointed by the Sec. of State for Employment. The service aims to promote good industrial relations in an impartial and confidential manner. ACAS provides collective conciliation, arbitration, mediation, advisory and information services, and conciliates in individual employment rights issues. Chair. JOHN HOUGHAM; Chief Conciliation Officer DEREK EVANS.

**Central Arbitration Committee:** 39 Grosvenor Place, London, SW1X 7BD; tel. (171) 210-3738; fax (171) 210-3708; f. 1976 as an independent body under the 1975 Employment Protection Act, in succession to Industrial Court/Industrial Arbitration Board; arbitrates on trade disputes; adjudicates on disclosure of information complaints; Chair. Prof. Sir JOHN WOOD.

**Employment Department (Training, Education and Enterprise Directorate):** Moorfoot, Sheffield, S1 4PQ; tel. (114) 275-3275; fax (114) 275-8316; f. 1973 as Manpower Services Commission; Dir-Gen. I. A. JOHNSTON.

**Forestry Commission:** 231 Corstorphine Rd, Edinburgh, EH12 7AT; tel. (131) 334-0303; fax (131) 334-3047; government department responsible for implementing forestry policy in Great Britain, particularly the sustainable management of existing forests and the encouragement and expansion of multi-purpose forestry; consists of (1) the Forestry Authority, which implements the Government's forestry policy within the framework of the Forestry Acts, administers the Woodland Grant Scheme, controls tree-felling through the issue of licences, administers plant health regulations to protect woodlands against tree-pests and diseases, and conducts research; and, (2) Forest Enterprise, responsible for the management of the national forests; scheduled to become operational as a 'next steps' executive agency as the Commission's commercial arm in mid- to late-1995 (Chief Exec. NEIL MCKERROW); Chair. Sir PETER HUTCHISON; Dir-Gen. T. R. CUTLER.

**Industrial Development Advisory Board:** Kingsgate House, 66–74 Victoria St, London, SW1E 6SW; tel. (171) 215-8180; fax (171) 215-2575; f. 1972 under Dept of Trade and Industry; Chair. Sir ANTHONY CLEAVER; Sec. A. WILKS.

**Monopolies and Mergers Commission:** New Court, 48 Carey St, London, WC2A 2JT; tel. (171) 324-1467; fax (171) 324-1400; f. 1948 as Monopolies and Restrictive Practices Commission; present name adopted 1973; investigates, and reports on, matters referred to it by the Sec. of State for Trade and Industry and by the Dir-Gen. of Fair Trading under the Fair Trading Act of 1973 and the Competition Act of 1980. Other references may be made under the Telecommunications Act of 1984, the Airports Act of 1986, the Gas Act of 1986, the Electricity Act of 1989, the Broadcasting Act of 1990, the Water Industry Act of 1991, the Railways Act of 1993; Chair. GRAEME ODGERS; Sec. A. J. NIEDUSZYNSKI.

**National Audit Office:** 157–197 Buckingham Palace Rd, London, SW1W 9SP; tel. (171) 798-7000; Comptroller and Auditor-General Sir JOHN BOURN.

**National Consumer Council:** 20 Grosvenor Gdns, London, SW1W 0DH; tel. (171) 730-3469; fax (171) 730-0191; f. 1975; 18 mems; Chair. Lady WILCOX; Dir RUTH EVANS.

**National Rivers Authority:** Eastbury House, 30–34 Albert Embankment, London, SE1 7TL; tel. (171) 820-0101; fax (171) 820-1603; f. 1989; regulates and promotes the use and conservation of the water environment in England and Wales; Chair. Lord CRICKHOWELL; Chief Exec. E. GALLAGHER.

**Office of Electricity Regulation (Offer):** Hagley House, Hagley Rd, Birmingham, B16 8QG; tel. (121) 456-2100; promotes competition in the generation and supply of electricity; protects consumer interests; Dir-Gen. of Electricity Supply Prof. STEPHEN LITTLECHILD.

**Office of Fair Trading:** Field House, Breams Bldgs, London, EC4A 1PR; tel. (171) 242-2858; telex 269009; fax (171) 269-8800; f.

1973; monitors consumer affairs, competition policy, consumer credit, estate agencies, etc.; Dir-Gen. JEFFREY PRESTON (acting).

**Office of Gas Supply (Ofgas):** Stockley House, 130 Wilton Rd, London, SW1V 1LQ; tel. (171) 828-0898; fax (171) 932-1600; f. 1986 as regulatory body to supervise the operations of the recently-privatized co, British Gas; has legal powers to protect consumer rights; Dir-Gen. CLARE SPOTTISWOODE.

**Office of Telecommunications (Oftel):** Export House, 50 Ludgate Hill, London, EC4M 7JJ; tel. (171) 634-8700; telex 883584; fax (171) 634-8943; f. 1984 under Telecommunications Act of 1984 as an independent regulatory body responsible for monitoring and enforcing telecommunications licences; protects consumer interests; Dir-Gen. DONALD CRUICKSHANK.

**Office of Water Services (Ofwat):** Centre City Tower, 7 Hill St, Birmingham, B5 4UA; tel. (121) 625-1300; economic regulatory body which supervises the performance of the recently-privatized water boards; protects consumer interests; Dir-Gen. of Water Services IAN BYATT.

**Rural Development Commission:** 141 Castle St, Salisbury, Wiltshire, SP1 3TP; tel. (722) 336255; fax (722) 332769; f. 1989; agency for economic and social development in rural areas; advises the Government principally on matters concerning job creation and the provision of essential services in rural areas; Chair. Lord SHUTTLEWORTH; Chief Exec. R. BUTT.

**Scottish Enterprise:** 120 Bothwell St, Glasgow, G2 7JP; tel. (141) 2700; telex 777600; fax (141) 221-3217; promotes business and industry in Scotland; Chair Prof. DONALD MACKAY.

**Sea Fish Industry Authority:** 18 Logie Mill, Logie Green Rd, Edinburgh, EH7 4HG; tel. (131) 558-3331; fax (131) 558-1442; f. 1981 from the White Fish Authority and the Herring Industry Board; markets UK fish products; administers grant schemes; conducts research; Chair. B. SKIPPER; Chief Exec. P. D. CHAPLIN.

**Welsh Development Agency:** Pearl House, Greyfriars Rd, Cardiff, CF1 3XX; tel. (1222) 222666; telex 497513; Chair. DAVID ROWE-BEDDOE; Chief Exec. BARRY HARTOP.

## Transport

### RAILWAYS

In 1993/94 British Rail operated 16,536 route km of railways and carried 713.2m. passengers and 103.3m. metric tons of freight. London Regional Transport operates the oldest and most extensive Underground railway in the world. In 1993/94 the Underground operated over 394 route km and carried 735m. passengers.

In July 1987 the Channel Tunnel Treaty was signed between the Governments of France and the United Kingdom, providing the constitutional basis for the construction of a cross-channel tunnel between the two countries, comprising a fixed link of two rail tunnels and one service tunnel, at an estimated cost of £4,700m. Of the total length of 31 miles, 23 miles are under the seabed. Construction began in 1987; the tunnel was opened in May 1994. Plans to construct a 68-mile fast rail link between the tunnel and London, estimated to cost £2,700m., are being developed; however, these are to be subject to parliamentary approval.

The Railways Act 1993 received royal assent in November 1993. The Act paved the way for the process of rail privatization, which will radically reform Britain's railways. A separate, government-owned company, Railtrack, was set up on 1 April 1994 to take responsibility for infrastructure (track, signals and stations). British Rail remains in control of all businesses (except Railtrack) until they transfer to the private sector. As a result of the 1993 Railways Act, 25 Train Operating Units (TOUs) came into being on 1 April 1994, and it is the principal objective of the Director of Passenger Rail Franchises to award franchises for the 25 TOUs as early as practicable. Railtrack, which will levy charges on train operators for track access, will also be transferred to the private sector in due course.

**British Railways Board:** POB 100, Euston House, 24 Eversholt St, London, NW1 1DZ; tel. (171) 928-5151; fax (171) 922-6944; Chair. and Chief Exec. JOHN WELSBY; Vice-Chair. CHRISTOPHER CAMPBELL.

**Railtrack PLC:** 40 Bernard St, London, WC1N 1BY; tel. (171) 344-7100; f. 1994; divided into 10 zones; Chair. ROBERT HORTON; Chief Exec. JOHN EDMONDS.

**Office of Passenger Rail Franchising:** 26 Old Queen St, London, SW1H 9HP; tel. (171) 799-8000; Dir of Passenger Rail Franchising ROGER SALMON.

#### Channel Tunnel

**Eurotunnel:** The Adelphi, John Adam St, London, WC2N 6JT; tel. (171) 747-6747; telex 915539; Anglo-French consortium; to design, finance and construct the Channel Tunnel under a concession granted for a period up to 2052; receives finance exclusively from the private sector, including international commercial banks; the Channel Tunnel was formally opened in May 1994; operates a service of road vehicle 'shuttle' trains and passenger and freight trains through the Channel Tunnel. Group Co-Chair. PATRICK PONSOLLE, Sir ALASTAIR MORTON; Group Chief Exec. GEORGES-CHRISTIAN CHAZOT.

**European Passenger Services:** EPS House, Waterloo Station, London, SE1 8SE; tel. (171) 922-4436; British operator of Eurostar, providing direct passenger rail services from London to Paris (seven a day) and from London to Brussels (five a day); services commenced in November 1994; Chair. JIM BUTLER; Man. Dir RICHARD EDGLEY.

#### Metropolitan Transport

**London Regional Transport (LRT):** 55 Broadway, London, SW1H 0BD; tel. (171) 222-5600; telex 893633; fax (171) 222-5719; f. 1933 as London Passenger Transport Board, present name since 1984; responsible for one of the world's largest urban passenger transport systems, consisting of rapid transit rail (the Underground, operated by a subsidiary company) and of bus services in London (operated under contract to LRT Buses); Chair. LRT PETER FORD; Man. Dir London Underground DENIS TUNNICLIFFE; Man. Dir London Buses CLIVE HODSON.

**Docklands Light Railway:** POB 154, London, E14 9QA; tel. (171) 538-0311; fax (171) 538-1508; opened Sep. 1987; in 1992 responsibility for the Railway was transferred from London Transport to the London Docklands Development Corporation; comprises a 26-station system bounded by Bank, Beckton, Stratford and Island Gardens (Isle of Dogs); Chair. Sir ANTHONY GILL; Man. Dir G. M. HUTCHINSON.

#### Association

**Railway Industry Association:** 6 Buckingham Gate, London, SW1E 6JP; tel. (171) 834-1426; Chair. R. A. HAINES; Dir D. R. GILLIAN.

### ROADS

Total road length in 1992 in Great Britain was 362,328 km (225,140 miles). In the same year there were 3,147 km (1,955 miles) of motorway.

Passenger traffic is handled by London Regional Transport, municipal companies, Passenger Transport Executives, private bus companies, the Scottish Bus Group, and private coach companies. Under The Transport Act 1985, 75% of local bus services were deregulated in October 1986.

**British Road Federation Ltd:** Pillar House, 194–202 Old Kent Rd, London, SE1 5TG; tel. (171) 703-9769; fax (171) 701-0029; f. 1932; mem. includes national organizations concerned with the construction and use of roads in Great Britain; Chair. V. THOMAS; Dir RICHARD DIMENT.

**NFC PLC:** 66 Chiltern St, London, W1M 1PR; tel. (171) 317-0123; fax (171) 224-2385; f. 1969 as the National Freight Corpn, a statutory body responsible to the Minister for Transport; became a limited company in 1980; bought by consortium of employees and former employees 1982; changed name from National Freight Consortium PLC 1989; Chair. Sir CHRISTOPHER BLAND; Chief Exec. GERALD MURPHY.

### INLAND WATERWAYS

There are some 3,200 km (2,000 miles) of inland waterways in Great Britain under the control of the British Waterways Board, varying from the river navigations and wide waterways accommodating commercial craft to canals taking small holiday craft.

**British Waterways:** Willow Grange, Church Rd, Watford, Herts. WD1 3QA; tel. (923) 226422; fax (923) 226081; f. 1963; Chair. BERNARD HENDERSON; Chief Exec. BRIAN DICE.

### SHIPPING

There are more than 400 ports in the United Kingdom, of which London, Milford Haven, the Tees and Hartlepool ports, the Forth ports, Grimsby and Immingham, Southampton, Sullom Voe, the Medway ports, Dover, Felixstowe and Liverpool are the largest (in terms of the tonnage of goods traffic handled). Twenty-two ports, including Southampton, Grimsby and Immingham, Hull and five ports in South Wales, are owned and administered by Associated British Ports. The majority of the other large ports are owned and operated by public trusts, including London, which is administered by the Port of London Authority, and Belfast, administered by the Belfast Harbour Commission. Under the Ports Act (1991), trust ports were permitted to become private, commercial enterprises. By May 1992, at least four major trust ports, including the Port of London Authority and the Medway Ports Authority, had been transferred to the private sector. Sullom Voe, Bristol and a number of smaller ports are under the control of

# UNITED KINGDOM (GREAT BRITAIN)

local authorities, and there are more than 100 ports owned and administered by statutory or private companies; of these, Felixstowe, Liverpool (owned by Mersey Docks and Harbour Company) and Manchester are the largest.

Britain is linked to the rest of Europe by an extensive passenger and vehicle ship ferry service. There are also hovercraft services to France for passengers and vehicles.

**Associated British Ports:** 150 Holborn, London, EC1N 2LR; tel. (171) 430-1177; telex 23913; fax (171) 430-1384; f. 1963; controls 22 UK ports; Chair. Sir KEITH STUART; Sec. H. REES.

**The Baltic Exchange Ltd:** St Mary Axe, London, EC3A 8BH; tel. (171) 623-5501; telex 8811373; fax (171) 369-1622; world market for chartering ships, also deals in commodities, chartering aircraft, buys and sells ships and aircraft; Chair. A. H. HARPER; Chief Exec. JAMES BUCKLEY.

**British Ports Association:** Africa House, Room 217, 64–78 Kingsway, London, WC2B 6AH; tel. (171) 242-1200; fax (171) 405-1069; promotes and protects the general interests of port authorities, comments on proposed legislation and policy matters; Dir D. WHITEHEAD.

**Port of London Authority:** Devon House, 58–60 St Katharine's Way, London, E1 9LB; tel. (171) 265-2656; Chair. Sir BRIAN SHAW.

## Principal Shipping Companies

**Associated Container Transportation (Services) Ltd:** Richmond House, Terminus Terrace, Southampton, SO9 1GG; tel. (1703) 634433; telex 477622; fax (1703) 330940; f. 1966; consortium owned by Blue Star Line Ltd, Cunard Steam-Ship Co PLC, Ellerman Lines PLC, Ben Line Steamers Ltd, The Charente Steam-Ship Co Ltd; Chair. A. R. C. B. COOKE; Sec. R. I. L. HOWLAND.

**Bibby Line Ltd:** 105 Duke St, Liverpool, L1 5JQ; tel. (151) 708-8000; telex 629241; fax (151) 794-1000; f. 1807; operates chemical carriers and shallow water accommodation units; Chair. S. P. SHERRARD.

**Blue Star Line Ltd:** Albion House, 20 Queen Elizabeth St, London, SE1 2LS; tel. (171) 407-2345; telex 888298; fax (171) 407-4636; f. 1911; Chair. E. H. VESTEY.

**Boyd Line Ltd:** Albert Dock, Hull, HU1 2DH; tel. (1482) 24024; telex 592333; fax (1482) 323737; Chair. and Man. Dir T. W. BOYD; 2 vessels.

**BP Oil UK Ltd:** BP House, Breakspear Way, Hemel Hempstead, Herts, HP2 4UL; tel. (1442) 225811; telex 826661; fax (1442) 225225; tanker services; Man. Dir J. R. W. ORANGE.

**BP Shipping Ltd:** BP House, Breakspear Way, Hemel Hempstead, Herts, HP2 4UL; tel. (1442) 232323; fax (1442) 225225; f. 1915; division of British Petroleum Ltd; Chief Exec. W. LUFF; 14 vessels.

**Caledonian MacBrayne Ltd:** The Ferry Terminal, Gourock, Strathclyde, PA19 1QP; tel. (1475) 650100; fax (1475) 637607; state-owned ferry co; extensive car and passenger services on Firth of Clyde and to Western Isles of Scotland; 31 roll-on/roll-off vessels; Chair. G. H. CROMBIE; Man. Dir C. S. PATERSON; 16 vessels.

**The China Navigation Co Ltd:** Swire House, 59 Buckingham Gate, London, SW1E 6AJ; tel. (171) 834-7717; telex 888800; fax (171) 630-0353; f. 1872; wholly-owned subsidiary of John Swire & Sons Ltd; diversified fleet operating throughout the Pacific; Chair. J. W. J. HUGHES-HALLETT; 14 vessels.

**Crescent Shipping Ltd;** Hays House, Otterham Quay Lane, Rainham, Kent, ME8 7UN; tel. (1634) 360077; telex 96276; fax (1634) 387500; Man. Dir M. HUTCHINSON; 27 vessels.

**The Cunard Steam-Ship Co PLC:** 1 Berkeley St, London, W1A 1BY; tel. (171) 499-9020; telex 21341; regd office: 30–35 Pall Mall, London, SW1Y 5LS; tel. (171) 930-4321; telex 295483; fax (171) 839-1837; f. 1878; Chair. NIGEL RICH; Sec. B. N. BARLOW; shipping subsidiaries: Cunard Line Ltd, Cunard Crusader World Travel Ltd, Cunard Cruise Ships Ltd, Cunard Sea Goddess Ltd.

**F. T. Everard & Sons Ltd:** 4 Elder St, London, E1 6DD; tel. (171) 247-8181; telex 887230; fax (171) 377-5562; forestry products service between Sweden and UK, tanker and dry cargo in Europe, the Mediterranean and the Baltic; 30 vessels.

**Furness Withy (Shipping) Ltd:** Furness House, 53 Brighton Rd, Redhill, Surrey, RH1 6YL; tel. (1737) 771122; telex 8950701; fax (1737) 775000; Chair. and Man. Dir J. E. KEVILLE; Gen. Man. W. E. KIRKBRIDE.

**Fyffes Group Ltd:** 12 York Gate, Regents Park, London, NW1 4QJ; tel. (171) 487-4472; fax (171) 224-0618; f. 1901; Chair. A. J. ELLIS; Sec. STEPHEN BAILEY.

**Geest Line:** POB 154, The Windward Terminal, Purbeck Water Ave, Southampton, SO15 1AJ; tel. (1703) 333388; fax (1703) 714050; Chair. MICHAEL DOWDALL.

**Gibson Gas Tankers Ltd:** 11 John's Place, Leith, Edinburgh, EH6 7EL; tel. (131) 554-4466; telex 727492; fax (131) 555-0310; f. 1966; Chair. and Man. Dir T. R. LOWRY; Dir W. H. G. MATHISON.

*Directory*

**Goulandris Bros Ltd:** 34A Queen Anne's Gate, London, SW1H 9AB; tel. (171) 222-5244; telex 915806; fax (171) 222-6817; tankers and bulk carriers; Man. Dir N. G. KAIRIS.

**Harrison Line Ltd:** Mersey Chambers, Covent Garden, Liverpool, L2 8UF; tel. (151) 236-5611; telex 628404; fax (151) 236-1200; f. 1853; liner shipping services to the Caribbean and east Africa; Chair. Sir THOMAS PILKINGTON.

**Holbud Ship Managment Ltd:** Hydery House, 66 Leman St, London, E1 8EU; tel. (171) 488-4901; telex 892002; fax (171) 265-0654; ship agents; Dir B. D. SABARWAL.

**London & Overseas Freighters (UK) Ltd:** 21 New Fetter Lane, London, EC4A 1EL; tel. (171) 583-5888; telex 22143; fax (171) 353-2872; shipping agents; Man. Dir NORRIS JACKSON.

**Mobil Shipping Co Ltd:** Mobil Court, 3 Clements Inn, London, WC2A 2EB; tel. (171) 412-4000; telex 8812411; fax (171) 430-2150; tanker services; Man. Dir J. R. ENSTON.

**North Sea Ferries Ltd:** King George Dock, Hedon Rd, Hull, HU9 5QA; tel. (1482) 795141; telex 592349; fax (1482) 712170; car and passenger services; Chair. G. D. S. DUNLOP; Man. Dir PETER VAN DER BRANDHOF.

**Ocean Group PLC:** Ocean House, The Ring, Bracknell, Berks, RG12 1AN; tel. (1344) 302000; fax (1344) 710031; Chair. P. I. MARSHALL; Chief Exec. J. M. ALLAN.

**Peninsular and Oriental Steam Navigation Co:** 79 Pall Mall, London, SW1Y 5EJ; tel. (171) 930-4343; telex 885551; fax (171) 925-0384; f. 1837; world-wide container and bulk shipping services; cruise and ferry operators; also engaged in non-shipping activities; Chair. and Chief Exec. Lord STERLING OF PLAISTOW; Man. Dir Sir BRUCE MACPHAIL.

**P & O Containers Ltd:** Beagle House, Braham St, London, E1 8EP; tel. (171) 488-1313; telex 883947; f. 1965; formerly Overseas Containers Ltd, wholly-owned subsidiary of the Peninsular and Oriental Steam Navigation Co.; transport container services between Europe and the USA, the Far East, Australia, southern and east Africa, the Middle East and the Indian sub-continent; and between the Far East, the Middle East and Australia; Chair. T. C. HARRIS.

**P & O European Ferries Ltd:** Channel House, Channel View Rd, Dover, Kent, CT17 9TJ; tel. (1304) 223000; telex 965104; fax (1304) 223223; wholly-owned subsidiary of the Peninsular and Oriental Steam Navigation Co; services to France, Spain, Belgium and the Netherlands from various ports in the UK; Chair. and Man. Dir G. D. S. DUNLOP.

**Ropner Shipping Services Ltd:** 140 Coniscliffe Rd, Darlington, Co Durham, DL3 7RP; tel. (1325) 462811; telex 58531; fax (1325) 489576; f. 1874; shipowners, managers, chartering brokers; Chair. J. V. ROPNER; Sec. A. THEAKSTON.

**Shell International Marine Ltd:** Shell Centre, London, SE1 7NA; tel. (171) 934-1234; telex 919651; provide freight services on behalf of, and act as marine consultants for, Shell International Petroleum Co Ltd; Man. Dir I. A. MCGRATH.

**Shell Tankers (UK) Ltd:** Shell Centre, London, SE1 7PQ; tel. (171) 934-1234; telex 919651; fax (171) 261-1061; owns and manages oil, gas and dry bulk vessels for the Royal Dutch/Shell Group, and provides management and consultancy services to bulk shipping industry; Chair. I. A. MCGRATH; Sec. M. HAMPSTEAD.

**Souter Shipping Ltd:** Clayton House, Regent Centre, Gosforth, Newcastle upon Tyne, NE3 3HW; tel. (191) 285-0621; telex 53186; bulk carriers, parcels tankers, conventional tankers; Man. Dir R. I. D. SOUTER.

**Stena Sealink Ltd:** Charter House, Park St, Ashford, Kent, TN24 8EX; tel. (1233) 647022; parent co Stena Line AB; services to Ireland, the Continent and various parts of the UK, services to France in conjunction with Société Nouvelle d'Armement Transmanche (SNAT); Man. Dir GARETH COOPER.

**Stephenson Clarke Shipping Ltd:** Eldon Court, Percy St, Newcastle-upon-Tyne, NE99 1TD; tel. (191) 232-2184; telex 53696; fax (191) 261-1156; f. 1730; Man. Dir G. WALKER.

**Texaco Overseas Tankship Ltd:** 1 Westferry Circus, Canary Wharf, London, E14 4HA; tel. (171) 719-3000; fax (171) 719-5148; Gen. Man. G. R. PENTECOST.

**Andrew Weir & Co Ltd:** Dexter Houe, 2 Royal Mint Court, London, EC3N 4XX; tel. (171) 265-0808; telex 887392; fax (171) 956-1178; f. 1885; shipowners, ship managers, intermodal transport operators, hotels, forestry and land, rubber dealers; Chair. Lord RUNCIMAN; Chief Exec. A. COOKE.

## Shipping Associations

**Chamber of Shipping Ltd:** Carthusian Court, 12 Carthusian St, London, EC1M 6EB; Pres. T. C. HARRIS (1995); Dir-Gen. Adm. Sir NICHOLAS HUNT.

UNITED KINGDOM (GREAT BRITAIN)

**Liverpool Steam Ship Owners' Association:** North Brocklebank Dock, Bootle, Liverpool L20 2DB; tel. (151) 933-4315; fax (151) 944-1540; Chair. J. E. Lenham.

**Passenger Shipping Asscn:** 9/10 Market Place, London, W1N 8HH; tel. (171) 436-2449; fax (171) 636-9206; formerly Ocean Travel Development (f. 1958); 50 mems; Chair. Eric Phippin; Dir and Sec. William Gibbons.

## CIVIL AVIATION

In addition to many international air services into and out of the country, an internal air network operates from 22 main commercial airports.

The principal airports are Heathrow, Gatwick and Stansted, serving London, and Luton, Manchester, and Glasgow, which in 1992 handled 45.2m., 20.0m., 2.4m., 2.0m., 12.1m. and 4.8m. passengers respectively. In March 1991 a new $400m. development was opened at Stansted, including a new terminal, cargo centre and rail link. Stansted now has a capacity of 8m. passengers a year. Heathrow and Gatwick are the world's two busiest airports. In March 1988 a new £250m. passenger terminal was opened at Gatwick to increase capacity to 25m. passengers a year. A new £30m. London City Airport, in the Docklands, opened in October 1987, providing domestic and international flights to and from city centres for business travellers. In March 1993 a second terminal was opened at Manchester Airport and the number of passengers handled there was expected to increase by 300% by 1998.

**BAA PLC:** 130 Wilton Rd, London, SW1V 1LQ; tel. (171) 834-9449; telex 919268; fax (171) 932-6699; f. 1966 as British Airports Authority; privatized in 1987; propr of Heathrow, Stansted, Gatwick, Southampton, Glasgow, Aberdeen and Edinburgh airports; Chair. Dr N. Brian Smith; Chief Exec. Sir John Egan.

**Civil Aviation Authority:** CAA House, 45–59 Kingsway, London, WC2B 6TE; tel. (171) 379-7311; telex 883092; f. 1972; responsible for economic and safety regulation of civil aviation; plans for the transfer to the private sector of National Air Traffic Services (provided jointly with Ministry of Defence) were announced in May 1994; Chair. Sir Christopher Chataway; Man. Dir Thomas Murphy.

### Principal Private Airlines

**Air 2000 Ltd:** First Choice House, London Rd, Crawley, W. Sussex, RH10 2GX; tel. (1293) 518966; telex 878434; fax (1293) 522927; f. 1986; wholly-owned subsidiary of First Choice Holidays; operates scheduled and charter flights to Mediterranean destinations and charter services to the USA, Canada, the Caribbean and Kenya; Chair. Errol Cossey; Man. Dir Ken Smith.

**Air UK:** Stansted House, London Stansted Airport, Stansted, Essex, CM24 1AE; tel. (1279) 660400; telex 817052; fax (1279) 660330; f. 1980 by amalgamation of British Island Airways, Air Anglia, Air Westward and Air Wales; serves 15 airports in the UK and Channel Islands, and 17 in Europe; Chair. Stephen Hanscombe; Man. Dir Andrew Gray.

**Airtours International:** Parkway Three, 300 Princess Rd, Manchester, M14 7LU; tel. (161) 232-6600; fax (161) 232-6610; charter passenger services to European and other Mediterranean and north African destinations; CEO Michael Lee.

**Britannia Airways:** London Luton Airport, Luton, Beds.; tel. (1582) 424155; telex 82239; fax (1582) 458594; f. 1962; propr Thomson Travel Group; acquired Orion Airways in 1988; charter and inclusive tour operations; services from 20 UK airports to more than 100 destinations; Man. Dir Roger Burnell.

**British Airways:** Speedbird House, POB 10, Heathrow Airport, Hounslow, Middx, TW6 2JA; tel. (181) 759-5511; telex 8813983; fax (181) 562-9930; f. 1972; operates extensive domestic, European and worldwide services, 677,000 unduplicated route km on scheduled services to 170 destinations in 77 countries; Chair. and Chief Exec. Sir Colin Marshall; Man. Dir Robert Ayling.

**British Midland:** Donington Hall, Castle Donington, Derby, DE74 2SB; tel. (1332) 854000; telex 371723; fax (1332) 854662; f. 1938; scheduled services within the UK and to Belgium, France, Germany, Ireland and the Netherlands; cargo and charter flights; Chair. Sir Michael Bishop; Man. Dir A. Reid.

**Caledonian Airways:** Caledonian House, Gatwick Airport, West Sussex, RH6 0LF; tel. (1293) 536321; telex 87542; fax (1293) 668353; f. 1988 as subsidiary of British Airways; acquired by Inspirations Ltd in 1995; operates charter passenger services to the USA, Canada, the Caribbean, Africa and the Far East; Man. Dir Clare Hollingsworth.

**Loganair Ltd:** St Andrews Drive, Glasgow Airport, Abbotsinch, Paisley, Renfrewshire, PA3 2TG; tel. (141) 889-1311; fax (141) 887-6020; f. 1962; a division of Airlines of Britain Holdings PLC; Scottish domestic services, and services within the United Kingdom and Ireland; Chair. Sir Michael Bishop; Man. Dir S. Grier.

**Monarch Airlines:** London Luton Airport, Luton, Beds, LU2 9NU; tel. (1582) 400000; telex 825624; fax (1582) 411000; f. 1967; scheduled and charter services to the Mediterranean, the Caribbean, Africa and the Far East; Man. Dirs D. D. McAngus, D. L. Bernstein.

**Virgin Atlantic Airways:** Ashdown House, High St, Crawley, West Sussex, RH10 1DQ; tel. (1293) 562345; telex 877077; fax (1293) 561721; f. 1984; operates services from London to seven destinations in the USA, and to Japan and Greece; Chair. Richard Branson; Man. Dirs Roy Gardner, Syd Pennington.

# Tourism

In 1993 there were 19.5m. arrivals by foreign visitors to the United Kingdom.

**British Tourist Authority:** Thames Tower, Black's Rd, London, W6 9EL; tel. (181) 846-9000; telex 21231; fax (181) 563-0302; Chair. Adele Biss; Chief Exec. Anthony Sell.

**English Tourist Board:** Thames Tower, Black's Rd, London, W6 9EL; tel. (181) 846-9000; telex 266975; fax (181) 563-0302; Chair. Adele Biss; Chief Exec. John East.

**Scottish Tourist Board:** 23 Ravelston Terrace, Edinburgh, EH4 3EU; tel. (131) 332-2433; telex 72272; fax (131) 343-1513; Chair. Ian D. Grant; Chief Exec. Derek D. Reid.

**Wales Tourist Board:** Brunel House, 2 Fitzalan Rd, Cardiff, CF2 1UY; tel. (1222) 499909; fax (1222) 485031; Chair. A. R. Lewis; Chief Exec. P. E. Loveluck.

**Northern Ireland Tourist Board:** see under Northern Ireland.

# NORTHERN IRELAND

## Introductory Survey

### Location, Climate, Language, Religion, Flag, Capital

Northern Ireland is situated in the north-east of Ireland and forms part of the United Kingdom of Great Britain and Northern Ireland. It comprises six of the nine counties in the Irish province of Ulster: Antrim, Armagh, Down, Fermanagh, Londonderry and Tyrone. The rest of the island comprises the Republic of Ireland. The climate is mild and free from extremes of temperature. The language is English. Almost all the inhabitants profess Christianity: about 58% are Protestants and 42% Roman Catholics. The flag is the union flag of the United Kingdom. The capital is Belfast.

### Recent History

The sectarian tension that has characterized Ireland's history began with the first major settlement by British Protestants, particularly Presbyterians from Scotland, in the 17th century. The main area of Protestant colonization in Ireland was the province of Ulster, comprising nine counties in the north-east of the island, in much of which Protestant supremacy was gradually established over the indigenous Roman Catholic population. In 1801, as a result of the Act of Union, Ireland became part of the new United Kingdom, but throughout the 19th century there were frequent demands for Irish independence, and an organized movement seeking Home Rule emerged. In the north, however, an Ulster Unionist Council was established in 1911, with Protestant support, to resist Irish nationalist demands and to campaign for the continuation of union with Great Britain.

The resentment of Irish nationalists culminated in 1916 with the Easter rising in Dublin. The rebellion was suppressed, but a clandestine organization, the Irish Republican Army (IRA), continued to wage a guerrilla campaign against the British administration in an attempt to force British withdrawal from Ireland. Faced with mounting popular support for independence, the British Government conceded to the demand for Home Rule, but only to a limited extent, since this was strongly opposed by Protestants in Ulster, who did not wish to become part of a Catholic-dominated all-Ireland state. The Government of Ireland Act (1920) provided for two parliaments in Ireland: one in Dublin, for 26 of the 32 counties, and one in Belfast, for the remaining six (mainly Protestant-populated) counties, which collectively became known as Northern Ireland and stayed within the United Kingdom. Although most of Ireland's political leaders initially rejected proposals for the division of the island, agreement was eventually reached on partition: in 1922 the 26 counties obtained dominion status as the Irish Free State, now the Republic of Ireland (see p. 1574).

With the support of the Protestant majority in Northern Ireland, the Unionists retained permanent control of the Belfast Parliament. The province was governed by a one-party administration, with an all-Unionist cabinet headed by a provincial Prime Minister. The British monarch was represented by a governor. Since the Catholics were not only effectively excluded from political power, but also suffered discrimination in civil matters, a state of tension continued.

During the late 1960s there emerged an active civil rights movement which sought to end the Catholics' grievances by non-violent means. However, Protestant extremists viewed the movement as a republican threat, and resorted to violence against Catholic activists. The IRA was originally a small element in the civil rights movement, but, after the increasingly serious disturbances of 1968–69, a breakaway group, calling itself the Provisional IRA, embarked on a campaign of violence with the aim of reuniting Ireland on its own terms. In April 1969 the Northern Ireland Government, faced by increasing disorder and acts of sabotage, requested that British army units be assigned to protect important installations. In August the British and Northern Ireland Governments agreed that all security forces in the province would be placed under British command. In March 1972, as a result of increased violence, the British Government assumed direct responsibility for law and order. Finding this unacceptable, the Northern Ireland Government resigned. The British Government prorogued the Northern Ireland Parliament and introduced direct rule from London, thus alienating many Protestants.

In 1973 new constitutional legislation abolished the office of Governor and the Northern Ireland Parliament, and provided for devolution of power to a Northern Ireland Assembly and an executive, while the United Kingdom was to retain responsibility for foreign affairs, defence and security. The 78-member Assembly was elected in June 1973, under a system of proportional representation employed in order to ensure that the Catholic minority obtained an equitable share of the seats. The Secretary of State for Northern Ireland appointed an executive comprising members of the Assembly from both communities and headed by Brian Faulkner, who had been Prime Minister of Northern Ireland between March 1971 and March 1972.

An important part of this new 'power-sharing' arrangement was the establishment of a limited role for the Irish Government in Northern Ireland's affairs. Accordingly, in December 1973, at Sunningdale (in southern England), the British and Irish Governments and the Northern Ireland Executive finalized an agreement to form a new body, the Council of Ireland (with members drawn from the Governments of Northern Ireland and the Republic), which would have a range of economic and cultural responsibilities in both parts of Ireland. However, the 'Sunningdale Agreement' and the new constitutional arrangements in Northern Ireland were rejected by many Protestants, and led, in 1974, to a general strike. A state of emergency was declared and the Executive was forced to resign. The Assembly was prorogued, and the province returned to direct rule by the British Government. The collapse of the Sunningdale Agreement led to a rise in popularity of the more extreme Democratic Unionist Party (DUP—founded in 1971, and led by Ian Paisley), which established itself as the main rival to the previously dominant Ulster Unionist Party (UUP—the 'official' Unionists).

Throughout the 1970s the Provisional IRA and the Irish National Liberation Army (INLA, which emerged in 1975) continued their terrorist attacks on both British military and civilian targets, while Protestant 'loyalist' paramilitary groups engaged in indiscriminate bombings and killings of Roman Catholics. Political status for prisoners claiming a political motive for their crime, introduced in 1972, was abolished in 1976. In 1981 a hunger strike by IRA and INLA members over conditions in the Maze prison, near Belfast, resulted in the self-inflicted deaths of 10 men before it was abandoned.

In 1982 the Secretary of State gained parliamentary assent to establish a new 78-member assembly which would monitor the activities of the Northern Ireland departments, and make proposals for legislation and constitutional reform. In the election to the Assembly in October the Ulster Unionists took the most seats; the predominantly Catholic Social Democratic and Labour Party (SDLP), advocating the reunification of Ireland by peaceful means, and Provisional Sinn Féin (the political wing of the Provisional IRA) won 14 and five seats respectively, but declined to take their places in the Assembly.

Discussions between the Governments of the United Kingdom and the Republic of Ireland in 1984–85 culminated in the signing of the Anglo-Irish Agreement in November 1985. The Agreement, which was subject to review after three years, established the Intergovernmental Conference, through which British and Irish ministers were to meet regularly to discuss political, security, legal and cross-border matters relating to Northern Ireland. While giving the Irish Government a formal consultative role in the affairs of Northern Ireland, the Agreement recognized that the constitutional status of Northern Ireland remained unchanged and would not be altered without the consent of a majority of the province's population. The Agreement had the support of the SDLP, and was approved by the Irish and British Parliaments. However, it was strongly opposed by most Unionist politicians, who organized mass demonstrations and violent protests against the agreement, and in November 15 Unionist MPs resigned their seats at Westminster. In the ensuing by-elections 14 Unionists were returned to Parliament, while one seat was won by the SDLP. The non-sectarian Alliance Party also opposed the Agreement, and its members boycotted meetings of the Northern Ireland Assembly from November 1985 onwards. In June 1986 the British Government responded by dissolving the Assembly, and leaving the date open for fresh elections, which had been due in October.

In February 1988 the Irish Government's disapproval of a decision, taken by the British Government in the previous month, not to prosecute officers of the Royal Ulster Constabulary (RUC—the Northern Ireland police force) who were alleged to have been implicated in a so-called 'shoot-to-kill' policy (killing suspected terrorists without previously attempting to apprehend them) in 1982 (which had resulted in the killing of six Republican sympathizers) led to the establishment of an inquiry. In June and July it was announced that, although no action was to be taken against the senior officers involved, 22 members from the lower ranks were to be subjected to disciplinary action. Disciplinary hearings were concluded in March 1989, when it was announced that 19 officers had been reprimanded, and charges against another officer withdrawn. Inquests into the deaths of the six men were subject to delays and legal disputes. Finally, in September 1994 the most recent inquest was suspended, owing to a High Court ruling in July denying access to the reports of the initial inquiries into the killings. In March 1988 the shooting of three leading members of the IRA by British forces in Gibraltar, allegedly to forestall a bomb attack against British troops there, resulted in a wave of violence and retaliatory killings in Belfast. In the same month five deaths at two IRA funerals provoked criticism of policing methods at public funerals.

The Provisional IRA's campaign of violence in Northern Ireland escalated during 1987; the murder of a senior judge in April prompted the British Government to announce that security would be intensified in the province. In 1988 IRA members conducted a successful campaign against British military targets, particularly in Western Europe. The British Government resisted pressure from Unionists for the reimposition of internment without trial (a policy introduced in 1971, but subsequently revoked as a result of international pressure), although more soldiers were killed in the first eight months of 1988 than in any similar period since 1979. In October 1988, however, the Government announced a ban on television and radio interviews with representatives of Sinn Féin and loyalist paramilitary groupings and also introduced legislation abolishing (in Northern Ireland only) the right whereby a defendant's silence could not be interpreted as evidence of guilt. In January 1994 the European Commission on Human Rights agreed that a case brought by a convicted member of the IRA, alleging that the legislation removed the right to a fair trial, would be considered by the European Court of Human Rights. Between late 1988 and early 1991 a series of terrorist attacks took place against British Army personnel and politicians in both mainland Britain and in continental Europe.

At a meeting of the Anglo-Irish Conference in September 1989 Irish ministers demanded a review of the Ulster Defence Regiment (UDR), the main security force in the province, following allegations that intelligence documents, containing information on IRA suspects, had been passed to loyalist paramilitary groups by the UDR. The controversy was provoked by claims by two paramilitary organizations that they had used intelligence information to target and murder members of the IRA. An inquiry into the alleged breaches of security was initiated by the British Government, and in May 1990 the inquiry confirmed that members of the UDR had passed information to paramilitary organizations, although it was emphasized that the practice was not widespread. As a result of the investigations, 94 people were arrested and 59 subsequently charged. Fresh evidence of collusion between the security forces and loyalist paramilitary organizations emerged during the case, heard in January 1992, of a member of the Ulster Defence Association (UDA) who was prosecuted as a result of the inquiry. The defendant, who was subsequently sentenced to 10 years' imprisonment on several charges of terrorist offences, continued to reveal his involvement with army intelligence. In August 1993 the inquiry into breaches of security reopened, at the request of the Director of Public Prosecutions, in order to investigate the latest claims of collusion and clarify the role of the security forces.

In April 1991 the major loyalist paramilitary groups announced a new combined command structure and their intention to implement a cease-fire to coincide with formal discussions on the future of Northern Ireland (see below). However, following the collapse of the negotiations in early July, the loyalist paramilitary groups announced an end to their cease-fire and in August there was an intensification of sectarian violence, which continued throughout the remainder of 1991. In January 1992 the IRA announced an escalation of its military activities in both Northern Ireland and in mainland Britain. The early part of 1992 was characterized by an increased level of murders, committed by both republicans and loyalists, with the vast majority of victims being civilians. In an attempt to contain the conflict, three additional army battalions were deployed in Northern Ireland, bringing the total number of soldiers there to its highest level since 1979. The period 1991–92 was notable for a significant increase in the number of killings by loyalist groups, mainly the UDA, using the name of Ulster Freedom Fighters (UFF) for its acts of violence, and the Ulster Volunteer Force (UVF). In mid-August 1992 the British Government announced the proscription of the UDA under the Emergency Provisions Act, a measure that was widely regarded as long overdue in the light of the UDA's paramilitary activities from the early 1970s onwards. In late August the death toll since the beginning of the conflict in 1969 rose above 3,000.

The controversy surrounding allegations of a 'shoot-to-kill' policy on the part of the security forces re-emerged in early February 1992, when the Director of Public Prosecutions directed that two members of the Royal Marines be prosecuted for the shooting of two men (one of whom was killed) at a road-block in 1990. Civil liberties groups, however, requested a review of the law on fatal shootings after the soldiers were acquitted, in December 1993, of all charges relating to the incident. In mid-February 1992 four members of the IRA were shot dead by undercover police officers, following a republican attack on a police station. In separate incidents in September and November members of the security forces shot dead two men, only one of whom belonged to the IRA. In November there were 13 British soldiers awaiting trial, charged variously with assault, attempted murder and murder. In May members of the Parachute Regiment assaulted a number of civilians in the largely nationalist town of Coalisland, County Tyrone, prompting the Irish Government to advocate the removal of the Regiment, which had previously been implicated in acts of brutality, from Northern Ireland. Charges were brought against six of the soldiers involved, but in May 1993 it was announced that the cases were to be abandoned, owing to a lack of evidence. In June a soldier, Private Lee Clegg, was convicted of the murder of a young woman in 1990 and sentenced to life imprisonment. An unsuccessful legal appeal by Clegg, in January 1995, attracted renewed interest in the case and in the issue of the accountability of British troops in Northern Ireland. In early July the decision by the British Government to release Clegg provoked civil unrest in republican areas of Northern Ireland and was severely criticized by members of Sinn Féin and a leading representative of the Roman Catholic Church.

In October 1989, at the party conference, the Conservative Party of Great Britain decided to organize in Northern Ireland, and in May 1990 the first candidate presented by the Conservative Party contested a by-election, but received little support. Conservative candidates stood in 11 constituencies in Northern Ireland in the general election to the British Parliament in April 1992. The party won no seats, taking only 5.7% of the votes cast. Nine seats were won by the UUP, four by the SDLP, three by the Democratic Unionist Party (DUP) and one by the Ulster Popular Unionist Party. Sinn Féin lost its seat in west Belfast (which had been held by the party's President, Gerry Adams, who had declined to take up his seat at Westminster) to the SDLP, apparently as a result of tactical voting on the part of Protestants in the constituency. District elections, held in mid-May 1993, were regarded as significant in terms of gauging public opinion on the future of the constitutional talks (see below). As such, the results were regarded as discouraging, with the extremist parties faring well, contrary to expectations: the DUP's share of the vote remained almost unchanged (17.1% in 1993, compared with 17.7% in 1989), while Sinn Fein's performance improved, with the party gaining eight new seats and increasing its share of the vote from 11.3% to 12.5%. However, the moderate Alliance Party also did well, gaining five new seats and increasing its proportion of the votes cast from 6.8% to 7.7%.

In the week following the local elections in May 1993 the IRA detonated four large bombs causing an estimated £22m. of damage. A campaign that seemed designed to inflict maximum structural damage, thus harming the local economy, continued into July when the town centre of Newtownards in Co Down was destroyed by an IRA bomb. Also in July loyalist paramilitaries led three days of violence and unrest, largely in protest at the increased security presence of the RUC in loyalist areas. Sectarian killings, which had persisted all year, intensified in October and were received with widespread condemnation. An IRA bomb explosion in a loyalist area of Belfast, which killed 10 people, provoked revenge attacks by loyalist forces, including the murder of seven people by a member of the UDA who opened fire in a bar in Co Londonderry. In early 1994 loyalist attacks on Sinn Féin offices and staff led to renewed allegations by the republican party of collusion between loyalist paramilitaries and the security forces. A period of increased terrorist violence occurred prior to the IRA's declaration of a cessation of military activity in August. Immediately following the announcement, loyalist paramilitaries conducted an indiscriminate killing in a Catholic area of Belfast. Later in September the UVF admitted detonating bombs close to Sinn Féin offices in Belfast and at a railway station in Dublin, which were condemned as attempts to disrupt the peace process. At the time of the loyalist cease-fire, announced in mid-October, 3,170 people had been killed as a result of the sectarian violence since 1969; of the 57 people killed in 1994 33 were victims of loyalist attacks, while 24 were republican killings. While the sectarian violence ceased, there was increasing concern at the number of severe 'disciplinary' beatings being carried out by the paramilitary groups on members of their own communities. As a result of progress in the peace negotiations, certain restrictions on Sinn Féin and loyalist representatives were removed, including, in September, the broadcasting ban which had been imposed in 1988, and, in October 1994, the exclusion orders preventing Sinn Féin leaders from visiting Britain.

Following the dissolution of the Northern Ireland Assembly in 1986, the different Unionist parties remained divided over possible alternative forms of government for Northern Ireland. Divisions within the nationalist community also persisted. Cross-party efforts to reach an agreement in 1988 and 1989 failed to achieve any results. In January 1990 the Secretary of State for Northern Ireland, Peter Brooke, launched an initiative to convene meetings between representatives from the major political parties in Northern Ireland and the British and Irish Governments to discuss devolution in Northern Ireland and the future of its relations with the Republic of Ireland. Sinn Féin were to be excluded from the talks because of their refusal to denounce the IRA's campaign of violence. Lengthy negotiations ensued, mainly concerned with the demands of the Unionist parties that elements of the Anglo-Irish agreement be suspended while the talks took place. In June Brooke announced plans for a three-tiered structure of interlocking talks: interparty talks in Northern Ireland; discussions involving the political parties in Northern Ireland and the Irish and British Governments; and talks between Ireland and the British Government. Eventually, a compromise having been reached on the status of the Anglo-Irish Conference during the talks and on the timing of the Irish Government's entry into the negotiations, bilateral discussions between the British Government and the DUP, the UUP, the SDLP and the Alliance Party began at the end of April 1991, during an 11-week hiatus in meetings of the Anglo-Irish Conference. In May, however, the first discussions between all the Northern Ireland parties and the Irish Government were delayed, owing to a dispute concerning the venue for subsequent meetings between the two sides. Brooke issued another effective ultimatum to all parties, stipulating that substantive discussions would take place in Belfast and confirming plans for an independent chairman. In mid-June all the parties approved the appointment as chairman of Sir Ninian Stephen, a former governor-general of Australia, thus enabling the immediate commencement of the first round of interparty discussions in Northern Ireland. However, the talks were suspended in early July, owing to the Unionists' refusal to continue negotiations if the next meeting of the Anglo-Irish Conference (scheduled for that month) took place. In February 1992 the Prime Minister, John Major, invited the leaders of the four Northern Irish parties involved in the interparty discussions to his residence in London and succeeded in persuading the four to recommence negotiations. Following the general election, held in April, the British and Irish Governments agreed, at a meeting of the Anglo-Irish Conference, to suspend further meetings of the Conference for three months, in order to allow the interparty negotiations to continue. Accordingly, the talks recommenced in late April. (Brooke had, by this time, been replaced as Secretary of State for Northern Ireland by Sir Patrick Mayhew.) In mid-June the Unionists agreed, for the first time, to a meeting to discuss the agenda for the second element of the talks, which were to involve the Irish Government in the process for the first time.

The second stage of negotiations formally began in early June 1992 in London and continued in Belfast until late July. When the second stage of talks reopened in Belfast, in early September, the principal point of contention was the Unionists' demand that Ireland hold a referendum on Articles 2 and 3 of its Constitution, which lay claim to the territory of Northern Ireland. The Irish Government, however, remained unwilling to make such a concession except as part of an overall settlement. The DUP left the talks over this issue, and boycotted the meeting in Dublin that was held later in the month. The UUP, however, attended the meeting: the first official Unionist visit to the Republic since 1922. With no progress made on the constitutional question, nor the subject of Ireland's role in the administration of Northern Ireland, the negotiations formally ended in early November, and the Anglo-Irish Conference was resumed. The failure of the talks encouraged the SDLP to initiate secret discussions with the Sinn Féin in early April 1993, while demands for a cessation of violence grew following the killing of two children by an IRA bomb in England in March. In April the British Government signalled that it was preparing firm proposals to provide the basis for future discussions: hitherto the Government had merely chaired the discussions between the parties involved. Attempts by the British and Irish Governments to recommence the negotiating process, following the local elections in mid-May, were threatened by the DUP's entrenched position regarding the Irish Constitution. At a meeting of the Anglo-Irish Conference in September 1993 both Governments agreed to renew efforts to recommence negotiations. A further meeting, that had been scheduled for the end of October, was cancelled following the explosion of an IRA bomb in a loyalist district of Belfast, killing 10 people. The Irish Government condemned the close relationship of Sinn Féin to those responsible for the attack and distanced itself from a peace initiative which Gerry Adams had negotiated with the SDLP leader, John Hume.

At the end of October 1993 Albert Reynolds, the Irish Prime Minister, and John Major issued a joint statement setting out the principles on which future negotiations were to be based. The statement emphasized the precondition that Sinn Féin permanently renounce violence before being admitted to the negotiations. In mid-December the Prime Ministers made a joint declaration, known as the 'Downing Street Declaration', which provided a specific framework for a peace settlement. The Declaration, which was widely supported by opposition parties in Britain and Ireland, referred to the possibility of a united Ireland and, for the first time in a joint statement, accepted the legitimacy of self-determination, while insisting on majority consent within Northern Ireland. In January 1994, in an apparently conciliatory approach to Sinn Féin's persistent requests for a 'clarification' of the Declaration, Dick Spring, the Irish Foreign Minister, and Sir Patrick Mayhew agreed to expand on this theme in public speeches, but declined to participate in direct meetings with Sinn Féin. Both Governments maintained pressure on the republican movement to offer a definitive response to the Declaration. However, at a meeting between Reynolds and Major, at the end of February, the leaders insisted that inter-party talks on Northern Ireland would resume, based on the principles of the Declaration, even without the participation of Sinn Féin or the DUP (which had already rejected the document). In March the UUP announced its opposition to re-opening the three-strand talks and condemned the Downing Street Declaration, which effectively removed any confidence of achieving an imminent peace settlement. In early April a 72-hour suspension of IRA violence was dismissed by the British Government as being insufficient to consider incorporating the republican movement into the peace process. In May the Government issued a written statement to Sinn Féin, clarifying 20 specific questions on the Downing Street Declaration. The communication marked a possible breakthrough in the peace process, although the Government insisted that it did not extend to negotiation. At a specially convened party conference, held in late July in Co Donegal, Ireland, Sinn Féin delegates rejected elements of the Declaration, in particular the commitment to the consent of the majority in Northern Ireland. The British and Irish Governments expressed their intention to pursue the peace process in spite of Sinn Féin's stance. Prior to this, however, Major and Reynolds had agreed to postpone a scheduled meeting to present a peace document, owing to disagreements on constitutional issues.

On 31 August 1994, following mounting speculation of a republican cease-fire, the IRA announced 'a complete cessation of violence' with effect from midnight that day. The announcement was widely welcomed, yet, while the Irish Government and the SDLP accepted that statement as a declaration of a permanent end to hostilities, the British Government insisted that the IRA should confirm that this was indeed the intention. On 13 October the Combined Loyalist Military Command of the loyalist paramilitary groups declared a suspension of military activity, which was effectively to be linked to that of the IRA. Although the loyalist announcement was welcomed as a means of stimulating efforts to complete a peace settlement, the Irish Government urged a substantitive response from the British to the IRA cease-fire, owing to fears that hardline republicans would advocate a return to violence in the absence of peace negotiations. Later that month Major announced new measures to reassert the peace process, including the removal of all security blocks on border roads, while adopting the 'working assumption' that the IRA cease-fire was permanent. In November the republican movement confirmed its commitment to the peace process, despite a sectarian murder conducted by a dissident IRA unit. The first public meeting between Sinn Féin and government officials was held in early December, marking the start of exploratory talks between the two sides. The political crisis in the Irish Republic (see Ireland, Vol. I) disrupted efforts to conclude a peace document. Negotiations, however, were pursued with the new administration. In February 1995 John Major and the Irish Prime Minister, John Bruton, presented a Framework Document, together with a separate British Government paper on a new Northern Ireland Assembly. The Framework Document reaffirmed the principles of the 'Downing Street Declaration', and included provisions for the co-operation and involvement of both Governments in the peace settlement, as well as guarantees of civil, political and human rights in the north and south of Ireland. In addition, the Document proposed the establishment of a cross-border body in which elected representatives of the Irish Parliament and a Northern Ireland Assembly might create and implement policy on issues agreed by the two Governments, in consultation with the Northern Irish parties. The proposals for the Northern Ireland Assembly envisaged a chamber of 90 members, elected for fixed terms of four or five years by a system of proportional representation. The Assembly was to enhance local accountability with wide legislative and executive responsibility (except, initially, over taxation or law and order), although it was to be monitored by a three-member elected panel as part of a series of measures to verify the impartiality of, and maintain confidence in, the institution. There was to be a committee system, comprised of Assembly members proportional to the distribution of party support within the chamber, to oversee the Northern Ireland governmental departments. Both Governments emphasized that the proposals were to form the basis of negotiations and public consideration, and any final agreement was to be subject to parliamentary approval and popular consent by means of a referendum.

Amid intense political scrutiny of the Framework Document, the first reduction of British forces in Northern Ireland was announced in March 1995, with the withdrawal of 400 troops, followed by a further 400 in April. Some 17,600 troops remained in Northern Ireland, although routine patrols of Belfast were terminated in March. In April fears of a persisting republican terrorist campaign, following the seizure of weapons destined for INLA groups in Northern Ireland, were allayed when the INLA revealed it had been observing a voluntary cease-fire since July 1994.

Despite a positive Sinn Féin response to the Framework Document, the issue of decommissioning IRA weapons remained the major obstacle to the opening of peace negotiations. The Government repeatedly objected to Sinn Féin's linking IRA decommissioning with the demilitarization of Northern Ireland. Having agreed that these would be discussed as separate issues, the first meeting between Sinn Féin representatives and a Minister of State for Northern Ireland, Michael Ancram, was convened in early May 1995, in Belfast. Later that month Sir Patrick Mayhew and Gerry Adams held their first meeting (the highest-level encounter of the two sides in 20 years) at an investment conference for Northern Ireland, held in Washington DC. While these ministerial talks were expected to continue, the Government insisted it would require evidence of progress on the decommissioning of paramilitary weapons before substantive political dialogue may begin.

In June 1995 a by-election to the House of Commons was won by Robert McCartney, standing as an independent United Kingdom Unionist candidate. The result, in which McCartney obtained 37.1% of the votes cast, was considered to be a significant reverse for the mainstream Unionist parties.

In December 1987 the Irish Government agreed to ratify the European Convention on the Suppression of Terrorism, which would facilitate the extradition of suspected IRA terrorists from the Irish Republic to the United Kingdom. Ratification was, however, accompanied by a provision that extradition was only to be granted subject to certification by the British Attorney-General that suspects against whom extradition warrants were issued (by the Irish Attorney-General) had a case to answer. In July 1988 the first Irishman was extradited from Ireland to the United Kingdom under the provisions of the European Convention: the defendant was, however, acquitted of charges of conspiracy to cause explosions in October 1991. In November the Irish Supreme Court upheld the extradition to the United Kingdom of one convicted member of the IRA, but overturned the extradition orders against two others (see chapter on Ireland).

In early February 1992 Ireland's President, Mary Robinson, met Peter Brooke in Belfast, thus becoming the first Irish Head of State to visit Northern Ireland in an official capacity. However, the Lord Mayor of Belfast refused to meet Robinson, objecting to Ireland's constitutional claim to the six counties of which Northern Ireland is composed.

In November 1988 the European Court of Human Rights ruled in favour of four men who were protesting against being detained without charge for more than four days, under the Prevention of Terrorism Act (which allows detention for up to seven days). In December the Government responded to the ruling by announcing a derogation from the European Convention for the Protection of Human Rights. In November 1991 the UN Committee Against Torture expressed concern over cases of alleged ill-treatment of terrorist suspects in detention and other abuses of human rights in Northern Ireland, which had been detailed in a report compiled by the human rights organization, Amnesty International.

### Government

After the collapse of the Northern Ireland Executive in May 1974, the Northern Ireland Act 1974 made the Secretary of State for Northern Ireland and his ministers answerable to Parliament at Westminster for the government of Northern Ireland, under a parliamentary order which is renewable annually. In October 1982 a 78-member Northern Ireland Assembly was elected, in accordance with the Northern Ireland Act 1982: its role was primarily consultative, pending the devolution of executive power. In November 1985, despite vigorous opposition by the Unionist parties, the Anglo-Irish Agreement was signed by the Prime Ministers of the United Kingdom and of the Republic of Ireland. The Agreement left the constitutional status of Northern Ireland unaltered, but gave the Republic of Ireland a consultative role in Northern Irish affairs, through an Intergovernmental Conference. In June 1986 the British Government announced the dissolution of the Northern Ireland Assembly, four months before the end of its four-year term, following a boycott of meetings by some members, in protest at the Anglo-Irish Agreement. In February 1989 a permanent joint consultative assembly, comprising 25 British and 25 Irish MPs, was established. It was, however, boycotted by the Unionist parties, because it resulted from the Anglo-Irish Agreement. The British Government continued to pursue its aim of establishing a devolved form of government in

Northern Ireland, acceptable to both sides of the community. A House of Commons select committee on Northern Ireland was established in March 1994.

Northern Ireland returns 17 members to the United Kingdom Parliament at Westminster.

**Defence**

All matters of defence come under the jurisdiction of the United Kingdom Parliament.

**Economic Affairs**

In 1993, according to official estimates, Northern Ireland's GDP amounted to £12,360m., and GDP per head amounted to £7,574.

Agriculture (including forestry and fishing) contributed an estimated 4.0% of GDP in 1993, and engaged 6.4% of the employed labour force in 1994. The principal crops include barley, potatoes and wheat. Livestock rearing (particularly poultry) and animal products are also important, as is fishing. According to the Department of Agriculture's Statistical Review, the volume of agricultural output decreased by 4% in 1989, while the value of gross output increased by 3.5% to reach £841m.

Industry (including mining, manufacturing, construction and power) contributed an estimated 25.9% of GDP in 1993, and engaged 24.0% of the employed labour force in 1994.

Mining contributed some 0.4% of GDP in 1993. The principal minerals are basalt, gritstone, limestone, and sand and gravel. Northern Ireland also possesses 1,200m. metric tons of recoverable reserves of lignite and two deposits of gold, but by the early 1990s neither mineral had been exploited.

Manufacturing contributed an estimated 18.6% of GDP in 1993, and engaged 19.8% of the employed labour force in 1990. Among the principal manufacturing sectors are food products, beverages and tobacco, textiles and clothing, and pharmaceuticals. Manufacturing production increased by an annual average of 2.9% over a seven-year period to mid-1990.

Energy is principally derived from petroleum and coal. In 1989 coal was used by 71% of domestic consumers for main heating. In March 1994 plans were made to construct a pipeline linking Northern Ireland to the natural gas transmission system on mainland Britain. The pipeline was to be completed in 1996. Northern Ireland is heavily reliant on imports of mineral fuels.

Services accounted for some 70.1% of GDP in 1993, and engaged 69.7% of the employed labour force in 1994. Financial and business services alone accounted for 17.1% of GDP.

Tourism represents a small but expanding sector of the economy, accounting for some 2% of GDP in 1993 and employing an estimated 1.6% of the working population. In 1992 and 1993 tourist arrivals totalled 1.25m. and 1.26m. respectively.

Trade in Northern Ireland is dependent on mainland Britain, which is both the principal market for exports and the main source of imports. Basic manufactures, especially textiles, and machinery and transport equipment are the main sources of export earnings. The principal import is petroleum.

For the financial year ending 31 March 1995 the budget was forecast to balance at £6,172m. (including a grant-in-aid of £2,146.6m. towards revenue). In 1993 public expenditure was equivalent to 46.9% of GDP. An estimated 12.7% of the labour force were unemployed in 1994.

For membership of economic groupings, see the preceding Great Britain chapter.

Northern Ireland's economy is closely linked to that of mainland Britain. However, GDP per head is substantially below that of the rest of the United Kingdom and unemployment, particularly the level of long-term unemployed, is traditionally higher than in any other region. Northern Ireland did not benefit fully from the effects of the rapid expansion of the British economy in the mid-1980s. However, it was less vulnerable to the adverse effects of the national recession in 1991–92, owing to the importance of the public sector (which provides about 40% of employment) and a high level of public funding from central Government (which amounts to some £3,300m. annually). The cessation of sectarian violence in 1994 created the prospect of expanding the economy in a peaceful environment, and generated considerable international interest in assisting the region to consolidate the peace. The tourist industry was expected to benefit from the political developments, and in 1995 Northern Ireland was to co-operate with Ireland to promote tourism on an all-island basis. The expansion of this sector, in addition to other business development, was expected to generate 15,000–30,000 new jobs. However, this was likely to be offset by job losses in security-related employment. In December 1994 a forum for international investment was held in Belfast, chaired by the Prime Minister, to stimulate foreign investment. A government industrial development programme has already been successful in attracting foreign companies by offering a series of incentives, as a result of which, since 1986, overseas investment has totalled £1,600m., creating 22,702 jobs in 265 projects. Foreign governments have supported peace and development in the region by contributing to an International Fund for Ireland, which totalled US $150m. at late 1994. The European Union, in addition to structural aid amounting to ECU 1,230m. for the period 1994–99, has approved ECU 300m. (approximately £236m.) for the development of deprived areas, and in February 1995 granted a further ECU 173.9m. (£137m.) to strengthen cross-border activity with Ireland.

**Social Welfare**

There is a comprehensive system of health and personal social services, similar to that in Great Britain. It is managed, on behalf of the Northern Ireland Department of Health and Social Services, by four Health and Social Services Boards and by the Central Services Agency. In 1990 Northern Ireland had 13,488 hospital beds, and there were 2,782 physicians and 727 dentists working in the region. Budget forecasts for 1994/95 allocated £1,544.0m. to health and personal social services and £1,675.4m. to social security (representing 25.0% and 27.1%, respectively, of total expenditure).

**Education**

Education is compulsory between the ages of five and 16 years, and is available free of charge in primary, secondary (intermediate) and special schools. Fees are payable in all grammar schools but the great majority of the pupils in their secondary departments receive non-fee-paying places on the basis of their performance in Transfer Procedure Tests. In 1993/94 a new examination system was to be introduced (replacing the Transfer Procedure Tests), whereby pupils were to be tested at the ages of eight, 11 and 14. Children receiving education in the preparatory departments of grammar schools are charged fees. Schools are divided largely on a sectarian basis, although integrated education is increasingly favoured. Northern Ireland has two main institutions of higher education: Queen's University of Belfast (QUB) and the University of Ulster (UU), formed in 1984, with campuses in Belfast, Coleraine, Jordanstown and Londonderry. Budget forecasts for 1994/95 allocated £1,317.1m. to education, libraries, science and the arts (21.3% of the total expenditure).

Teacher training is catered for by two general Colleges of Education, and by departments of education at the QUB and the UU.

**Public Holidays**

The main public holidays are the same as for Great Britain, with the addition of 17 March (St Patrick's Day) and 12 July (Battle of the Boyne).

**Weights and Measures**

The Imperial system of weights and measures is gradually being replaced by the metric system (see under Great Britain.)

# Statistical Survey

Source: Department of Finance & Personnel, 2nd Floor, The Arches Centre, 11-13 Bloomfield Ave, Belfast, BT5 5HD; tel. (1232) 520400; *Northern Ireland Annual Abstract of Statistics*.

## Area and Population

**AREA, POPULATION AND DENSITY**

| | |
|---|---:|
| Area (sq km) | 13,483* |
| Population (census results)† | |
| 5 April 1981 | 1,532,200 |
| 21 April 1991 | |
| Males | 769,000 |
| Females | 808,800 |
| Total | 1,577,800 |
| Population (official estimates at mid-year) | |
| 1991 | 1,601,400 |
| 1992 | 1,618,400 |
| 1993 | 1,631,800 |
| Density (per sq km) at mid-1993 | 121.0 |

\* 5,206 sq miles.
† Figures are rounded. The total at the 1991 census was 1,577,836.
**Capital:** Belfast, estimated population 287,100 at mid-1991.

**BIRTHS, MARRIAGES AND DEATHS**

| | Registered live births | | Registered marriages | | Registered deaths | |
|---|---:|---:|---:|---:|---:|---:|
| | Number | Rate (per 1,000) | Number | Rate (per 1,000) | Number | Rate (per 1,000) |
| 1991 | 26,265 | 16.4 | 9,221 | 5.8 | 15,096 | 9.4 |
| 1992 | 25,572 | 15.8 | 9,392 | 5.8 | 14,988 | 9.3 |
| 1993* | 24,909 | 15.3 | 9,060 | 5.6 | 15,633 | 9.6 |

\* Provisional figures.

**EMPLOYMENT** ('000 persons at June 1994)

| | |
|---|---:|
| Total civilian labour force[1] | 744.7 |
| Males | 432.6 |
| Females | 312.3 |
| Work-related training schemes | 15.8 |
| Self-employed persons | 82.2 |
| Total employees in employment | 550.7 |
| Total in civil employment[2] | 632.9 |
| Agriculture, forestry, fishing | 40.2 |
| Industry | 151.6 |
| Services | 441.2 |

[1] Includes persons temporarily laid off; claimant-based.
[2] Excluding HM Forces.

## Agriculture

**PRINCIPAL CROPS** ('000 metric tons)

| | 1991 | 1992 | 1993 |
|---|---:|---:|---:|
| Wheat | 39.6 | 40.6 | 37.3 |
| Barley | 165.8 | 169.8 | 138.1 |
| Oats | 11.6 | 13.5 | 9.4 |
| Potatoes | 335.1 | 317.0 | 256.7 |

**LIVESTOCK** ('000 head at June)

| | 1992 | 1993 | 1994 |
|---|---:|---:|---:|
| Cattle | 1,576 | 1,578 | 1,581 |
| Sheep | 2,657 | 2,611 | 2,531 |
| Pigs | 588 | 594 | 562 |
| Poultry | 12,302 | 13,382 | 13,642 |

## Fishing

(metric tons, live weight)

| | 1991 | 1992 | 1993 |
|---|---:|---:|---:|
| Herring | 3,862 | 4,038 | 3,634 |
| Mackerel | 1,040 | 19 | 227 |
| Prime* | 110 | 117 | 101 |
| Whiting | 3,279 | 3,196 | 3,385 |
| Other sea fish† | 7,083 | 7,352 | 7,062 |
| **Total fish** | 15,374 | 14,722 | 14,409 |
| Shell-fish | 9,041 | 8,140 | 7,194 |

\* Prime fish: turbot, brill, sole.
† Other sea fish: cod, dabs, haddock, hake, coalfish, skate, dogfish, pollack, sprats, roe, gurnard, conger eel, angler, ling, pout, megrims, plaice, witches, and other demersal fish.

## Mining and Quarrying

('000 metric tons)

| | 1991 | 1992 | 1993 |
|---|---:|---:|---:|
| Basalt | 7,787.1 | 9,024.0 | 8,557 |
| Grit | 3,678.8 | 3,304.0 | 3,959 |
| Limestone | 2,861.1 | 3,398.3 | 3,236 |
| Sand and gravel | 3,831.9 | 3,696.5 | 4,318 |

## Finance

**CURRENCY AND EXCHANGE RATES**

**Monetary Units**
100 pence (pennies) = 1 pound sterling (£).

**Dollar Equivalents** (31 December 1994)
£1 = US $1.5645;
US $1 = 63.92 pence.

**Average Exchange Rate** (US $ per pound)
1992    1.7655
1993    1.5020
1994    1.5316

# UNITED KINGDOM (NORTHERN IRELAND)

## BUDGET (£ million, year ending 31 March)

| Revenue | 1992/93 | 1993/94 | 1994/95* |
|---|---|---|---|
| Northern Ireland share of UK taxes (net) | 2,753.4† | 2,952.9 | 3,380.4 |
| Adjustment for previous years | −121.2 | 137.4 | — |
| Northern Ireland Office (grant-in-aid) | 2,185.0 | 2,391.6 | 2,146.6 |
| Regional and district rates | 206.5 | 203.1 | 350.0 |
| Interest on advances | 170.9 | 173.8 | 175.0 |
| Other receipts | 106.0 | 155.7 | 120.0 |
| **Total** | 5,300.6 | 6,014.5 | 6,172.0 |

* Forecast.     † Provisional figure.

| Expenditure | 1992/93 | 1993/94 | 1994/95* |
|---|---|---|---|
| Interest on borrowing | 174.8 | 185.4 | 185.0 |
| District rates | 136.5 | 145.3 | 160.0 |
| Supply services | 5,007.1 | 5,651.5 | 5,823.9 |
| of which: | | | |
| Agriculture, fisheries and forestry | 149.7 | 152.7 | 164.3 |
| Trade, industry, energy and employment | 394.6 | 455.4 | 427.5 |
| Roads, ports and transport | 178.4 | 184.0 | 183.5 |
| Housing | 194.5 | 194.5 | 187.8 |
| Other environmental services | 143.5 | 135.0 | 177.8 |
| Education, libraries, science and arts | 1,219.4 | 1,264.6 | 1,317.1 |
| Health and personal social services | 1,194.9 | 1,242.3 | 1,544.0 |
| Social security | 1,364.6 | 1,350.5 | 1,675.4† |
| **Total** (incl. others) | 5,319.6 | 5,983.3 | 6,171.9 |

* Forecast.
† Includes expenditure for the Social Security Agency.

## NATIONAL ACCOUNTS

**Gross Domestic Product by Economic Activity***
(£ million at current factor cost)

| | 1991 | 1992 | 1993† |
|---|---|---|---|
| Agriculture, forestry and fishing | 439 | 462 | 510 |
| Mining and quarrying | 42 | 42 | 48 |
| Manufacturing | 2,237 | 2,192 | 2,371 |
| Electricity, gas and water supply | 277 | 241 | 221 |
| Construction | 659 | 647 | 664 |
| Distribution, hotels and catering | 1,420 | 1,541 | 1,665 |
| Transport and communication | 612 | 638 | 691 |
| Financial and business services | 1,775 | 1,969 | 2,179 |
| Public administration and defence | 1,532 | 1,695 | 1,783 |
| Education and health services | 1,613 | 1,697 | 1,820 |
| Other services | 725 | 758 | 799 |
| **Sub-total** | 11,331 | 11,882 | 12,751 |
| Adjustment for financial services | −294 | −367 | −390 |
| **Total** | 11,037 | 11,515 | 12,360 |

* Gross domestic product is shown for each kind of activity after deducting stock appreciation.
† Provisional.

## Transport

**RAILWAYS** (year ending 31 March)

| | 1991/92 | 1992/93 | 1993/94 |
|---|---|---|---|
| Passenger journeys ('000) | 5,300 | 5,200 | 5,700 |

**ROAD TRAFFIC** (motor vehicles in use)

| | 1991 | 1992 | 1993 |
|---|---|---|---|
| Private cars | 498,471 | 516,194 | 515,185 |
| Goods vehicles | 18,901 | 19,601 | 20,074 |
| Buses and tramcars | 2,887 | 2,744 | 2,679 |
| Agricultural tractors, etc. | 7,199 | 6,892 | 7,201 |
| Motor cycles | 9,684 | 9,023 | 8,634 |
| Vehicles exempt from duty* | 21,176 | 23,858 | 32,552 |

* Vehicles used by the Royal Ulster Constabulary have been taxed since the force came under the Police Authority's control.

**CIVIL AVIATION** (flights in and out of Belfast International Airport)

| | 1991 | 1992 | 1993 |
|---|---|---|---|
| Passengers ('000) | 2,168 | 2,241 | 2,180 |
| Freight (metric tons) | 18,121 | 21,992 | 24,023 |

## Tourism

| | 1991 | 1992 | 1993 |
|---|---|---|---|
| Total number of visitors ('000) | 1,186 | 1,254 | 1,262 |
| From Great Britain | 650 | 726 | 704 |
| From the Republic of Ireland | 380 | 352 | 373 |
| From overseas | 156 | 176 | 185 |

## Communications Media

(at 31 March)

| | 1992 | 1993 | 1994 |
|---|---|---|---|
| Television licences | 319,610 | 337,036 | 347,624 |

Households with a telephone: 83% in 1993/94.

## Education

(1992/93)

| | Institutions | Students (Full-time) | Teachers (Full-time) |
|---|---|---|---|
| Primary* | 1,071 | 193,914 | 8,698 |
| Secondary | 164 | 145,512 | 9,583 |
| Special | 46 | 4,213 | 611 |
| Institutions of further education | 24 | 22,531 | 2,268 |
| Colleges of education | 2 | 1,324† | 135 |
| Universities | 2 | 18,499‡ | 1,536 |

* Includes nursery education and preparatory departments of grammar schools.
† Excludes full-time post-graduate students (56 in 1992/93).
‡ Excludes full-time post-graduate students.

# Directory

## The Constitution
(June 1995)

Following the prorogation of the Northern Ireland Parliament in 1972, responsibility for the Government of Northern Ireland rested with the Secretary of State for Northern Ireland. Direct rule continued until 1973, when the Northern Ireland Executive was established under the provisions of the Northern Ireland Constitution Act (1973). The Northern Ireland Executive assumed responsibility for the administration of Northern Ireland and was answerable to the Northern Ireland Assembly, elected in June 1973. The Executive collapsed in May 1974, and the Secretary of State resumed control of the Northern Ireland departments.

In October 1982 a new Northern Ireland assembly was elected under the provisions of the Northern Ireland Act 1982. Under the Act, the Assembly was eventually to resume legislative and executive functions, provided that it produced proposals for the resumption of its powers, deemed to be acceptable to the people of Northern Ireland by Parliament. In June 1986 the Assembly was dissolved, following its failure to produce satisfactory proposals.

In November 1985 the Anglo-Irish Agreement was signed by the Prime Ministers of the United Kingdom and the Republic of Ireland, leaving the status of Northern Ireland unaltered and confirming that the status of Northern Ireland would not be altered without the consent of a majority of its inhabitants. The Agreement provided for the establishment of an intergovernmental conference, through which the Government of the Republic of Ireland was permitted to make proposals on matters relating to Northern Irish affairs.

Northern Ireland returns 17 members to the United Kingdom Parliament at Westminster.

**Secretary of State for Northern Ireland** (responsible for political and constitutional matters, security policy and operations, broad economic questions and other major policy issues): Sir PATRICK MAYHEW.

**Minister of State** (responsible for the Department of Education (Northern Ireland), political development and community relations): MICHAEL ANCRAM.

**Minister of State** (responsible for security policy, the Department of Finance and Personnel and the Information Services): Sir JOHN WHEELER.

**Parliamentary Under-Secretaries of State** (responsible for the Department of Agriculture and the Department of Economic Development; spokesperson on all Northern Irish matters in the House of Lords): Baroness DENTON OF WAKEFIELD; (responsible for the Department of Health and Social Services, the Department of the Environment (Northern Ireland) and the 'Making Belfast Work' initiative): MALCOLM MOSS.

### NORTHERN IRELAND OFFICE AND ITS DEPARTMENTS

**Northern Ireland Office:** Stormont Castle, Belfast, BT4 3ST; tel. (1232) 520700.

**Department of Agriculture:** Dundonald House, Belfast, BT4 3SF; tel. (1232) 520100.

**Department of Economic Development:** Netherleigh, Massey Avenue, Belfast, BT4 2JP; tel. (1232) 529900.

**Department of Education:** Rathgael House, Balloo Rd, Bangor, Co Down, BT19 7PR; tel. (1247) 270077.

**Department of the Environment:** Clarence Court, Adelaide St, Belfast, BT2 8GB; tel. (1232) 540540.

**Department of Finance and Personnel:** Stormont, Belfast, BT4 3SW; tel. (1232) 520400.

**Department of Health and Social Services:** Dundonald House, Belfast, BT4 3SF; tel. (1232) 520520.

**Northern Ireland Civil Service:** Central Secretariat, Stormont Castle, Belfast, BT4 3ST; tel. (232) 520700; fax (1232) 528135.

## Political Organizations

**Alliance Party:** 88 University St, Belfast, BT7 1HE; tel. (1232) 324274; fax (1232) 333147; f. 1970; non-sectarian and non-doctrinaire party of the centre, attracting support from within both Catholic and Protestant sections of the community; 5,000 mems; Leader JOHN ALDERDICE; Gen. Sec. DAVID FORD.

**Conservative and Unionist Party:** (for headquarters in London, see Great Britain chapter) 13 Castle Street, Bangor, Co Down; f. 1870 as Conservative Central Office; organized in Northern Ireland since 1990.

**Democratic Unionist Party:** 91 Dundela Ave, Belfast, BT4 3BU; tel. (1232) 471155; fax (1232) 471797; f. 1971; right-wing anti-Republican Protestant party; Leader Rev. IAN R. K. PAISLEY; Chair. JAMES McCLURE; Sec. NIGEL DODDS.

**Progressive Unionist Party:** 200A Shankhill Rd, Belfast, BT13 0BJ; tel. (1232) 326233; loyalist party; Leader DAVID ERVINE.

**Sinn Féin** ('Ourselves Alone'): 51–55 Falls Rd, Belfast 12; tel. (1232) 323214; fax (1232) 231723; f. 1905; political wing of the Provisional IRA; seeks the reunification of Ireland by revolutionary means and the establishment of a 32-county democratic socialist state; engages in community politics; Pres. GERARD (GERRY) ADAMS.

**Social Democratic and Labour Party (SDLP):** Cranmore House, 611C Lisburn Road, Belfast, BT9 7GT; tel. (1232) 668100; fax (1232) 669009; f. 1970; radical, left-of-centre principles with a view to the eventual re-unification of Ireland by popular consent; Leader JOHN HUME.

**Ulster Democratic Party:** 12A Bridge St, Lisburn, Co. Anrim; tel. (1846) 667056; loyalist party; Leader GARY McMICHAEL.

**Ulster Popular Unionist Party:** 96 Seacliff Rd, Bangor, Co Down, BT20 5EZ; tel. (1247) 451690; f. 1980; aims to promote devolved government for Northern Ireland; Leader (vacant)..

**Ulster Unionist Party:** 3 Glengall St, Belfast, BT12 5AE; tel. (1232) 324601; fax (1232) 246738; f. 1905; governed Northern Ireland 1921–72; largest political party in Northern Ireland; supports parity and equality for Northern Ireland within the United Kingdom; Leader JAMES MOLYNEAUX; Gen. Sec. JIM WILSON.

**The Workers' Party:** 6 Springfield Rd, Belfast; tel. (1232) 228663; fax (1232) 333475; present name adopted 1978; democratic socialist party; aims to win state power for the working class and to establish a democratic, secular, socialist and unitary republic in Ireland; Chair. (Northern Ireland) TOM FRENCH; Gen. Sec. SEAN GARLAND.

The following paramilitary organizations are proscribed under Schedule 2 of the Emergency Provisions Act 1978: (nationalist) the Irish Republican Army, the Irish National Liberation Army, Cumann na mBan (women's section of the IRA), Fianna na hEireann (youth section of the IRA), Saor Eire and the Irish People's Liberation Organization; (loyalist) the Ulster Freedom Fighters, the Ulster Volunteer Force and the Red Hand Commandos. In August 1992 the loyalist Ulster Defence Association (UDA) was proscribed by the British Government.

## Judicial System

The judicial system of Northern Ireland, so far as the Supreme Court is concerned, is a miniature of the English system, and is based on the Judicature (Northern Ireland) Act 1978. It consists, as in England, of the High Court, the Court of Appeal, and the Crown Court (which has jurisdiction in criminal matters). The county court system corresponds to its English counterpart, but there is no system of pleadings, as is found in the English county court. There are also variations in jurisdiction levels. County court judges share with the judges of the High Court the exercise of the jurisdiction of the Crown Court. The jurisdiction of the Magistrates' Courts (Courts of Summary Jurisdiction) is exercised by a permanent judiciary of legally qualified resident magistrates.

**The Lord Chief Justice of Northern Ireland:** Sir BRIAN HUTTON.

### COURT OF APPEAL

**President:** The Lord Chief Justice of Northern Ireland.

**Judges:** Sir JOHN MACDERMOTT, Sir ROBERT CARSWELL, Sir MICHAEL NICHOLSON.

### HIGH COURT

**President:** The Lord Chief Justice of Northern Ireland.

**Judges:** Sir WILLIAM (LIAM) McCOLLUM; Sir ANTHONY CAMPBELL, Sir JOHN SHEIL, Sir BRIAN KERR, Sir JOHN PRINGLE, Sir MALACHY HIGGINS, Sir FREDERICK GIRVAN.

### COUNTY COURT

**Recorders:** Belfast: JAMES RUSSELL; Londonderry: JOHN MARTIN.

**Judges:** R. R. CHAMBERS, J. J. CURRAN, J. McKEE, G. P. H. GIBSON, A. R. HART, J. PETRIE, D. W. SMYTH, T. A. BURGESS, P. MARKEY.

UNITED KINGDOM (NORTHERN IRELAND)  *Directory*

# Religion

## CHRISTIANITY

The organization of the churches takes no account of the partition of the island of Ireland into two separate political entities. Thus the Republic of Ireland and Northern Ireland are subject to a unified jurisdiction for ecclesiastical purposes. The Roman Catholic and Church of Ireland Primates of All Ireland both have their seats in Northern Ireland, at Armagh, while Belfast is the headquarters of the Presbyterians and Methodists. In Northern Ireland the religious affiliations recorded at the 1991 census were:

| | |
|---|---:|
| Roman Catholic | 605,639 |
| Presbyterian | 336,891 |
| Church of Ireland | 279,280 |
| Methodist | 59,517 |
| Other denominations | 122,448 |
| None | 59,234 |
| Not stated | 114,827 |
| **Total** | **1,577,836** |

**Irish Council of Churches:** Inter-Church Centre, 48 Elmwood Ave, Belfast, BT9 6AZ; tel. (1232) 663145; f. 1922 (present name adopted 1966); eight mem. churches; Pres. Rt Rev. JOSEPH COOPER (Moravian Bishop); Gen. Sec. Dr DAVID STEVENS.

### The Roman Catholic Church

Ireland (including Northern Ireland) comprises four archdioceses and 22 dioceses. The dioceses of Down and Connor and Dromore are completely in Northern Ireland, while the archdiocese of Armagh and the dioceses of Derry and Clogher are partly in Northern Ireland and partly in the Republic of Ireland.

**Archbishop of Armagh and Primate of All Ireland:** HE Cardinal CAHAL BRENDAN DALY, Ara Coeli, Cathedral Rd, Armagh, BT61 7QY; tel. (1861) 522045; fax (1861) 526182.

### The Church of Ireland
(The Anglican Communion)

Ireland (including Northern Ireland) comprises two archdioceses and 10 dioceses.

**Archbishop of Armagh and Primate of All Ireland:** The Most Rev. Dr ROBERT EAMES (life peer), The See House, Cathedral Close, Armagh, BT61 7EE; tel. (1861) 522851.

### Protestant Churches

**Baptist Union of Ireland:** 117 Lisburn Rd, Belfast, BT9 7AF; tel. (1232) 663108; fax (1232) 663616; 108 churches; 95 ministers; 8,448 mems; Pres. S. J. CARSON; Sec. W. M. COLVILLE.

**Congregational Union of Ireland:** 38 Edgcumbe Gardens, Belfast, BT4 2EH; tel. (1232) 653140; Irish Union 1829; 26 churches; 37 ministers; 10,000 adherents; 25 Sunday Schools; Chair. B. AIKEN; Sec. Rev. M. COLES.

**Methodist Church in Ireland:** 1 Fountainville Ave, Belfast, BT9 6AN; tel. (1232) 324554; fax (1232) 239467; 234 churches; 196 ministers; 58,744 mems; Sec. Rev. EDMUND T. I. MAWHINNEY.

**Moravian Church in Ireland:** 158 Finaghy Rd South, Belfast, BT10 0DH; tel. (1232) 619755; f. 1749; Chair. of Conf. Rev. L. BROADBENT.

**Non-Subscribing Presbyterian Church of Ireland:** 102 Carrickfergus Rd, Larne. Co Antrim; tel. (1574) 272600; Clerk to Gen. Synod Rev. Dr JOHN W. NELSON.

**Presbyterian Church in Ireland:** Church House, Fisherwick Place, Belfast, BT1 6DW; tel. (1232) 322284; fax (1232) 248377; 559 churches; 617 ministers; 311,751 mems, 41,256 in Sunday Schools; Moderator of the General Assembly Rev. JOHN ROSS (from June 1995); Clerk of Assembly and General Sec. Rev. SAMUEL HUTCHINSON.

# The Press

## DAILIES

**Belfast Telegraph:** 124-144 Royal Ave, Belfast, BT1 1EB; tel. (1232) 321242; fax (1232) 242287; f. 1870; independent; evening; Proprs Thomson Organisation Ltd; Editor EDMUND CURRAN; circ. 130,987.

**Irish News:** 113-117 Donegall St, Belfast, BT1 2GE; tel. (1232) 322226; fax (1232) 337505; f. 1855; Irish nationalist; morning; Editor TOM COLLINS; circ. 44,162.

**News Letter:** 45-56 Boucher Crescent, Belfast, BT12 6QY; tel. (1232) 680000; fax (1232) 664412; f. 1737; pro-Union; morning; Editor GEOFF MARTIN; circ. 97,000.

## WEEKLIES

**An Phoblacht** (Republican News): 51-55 Falls Rd, Belfast; tel. (1232) 624421; fax (1232) 231723; weekly; party newspaper of Sinn Fein.

**Armagh Gazette:** Ulster Gazette (Armagh) Ltd, 56 Scotch St, Armagh, BT61 7DQ; tel. (1861) 522639; fax (1861) 527029; f. 1844; Thursday; Editorial Dir E. VILLIERS; Editor K. BUSHBY; circ. 11,114.

**Armagh Observer:** Observer Newspapers (NI) Ltd, Ann St, Dungannon, Co Tyrone; tel. (18687) 22557; fax (18687) 27334; f. 1930; Thursday; nationalist; Editor D. MALLON.

**Ballymena Guardian:** 83-85 Wellington St, Ballymena, Co Antrim; tel. (1266) 41228; f. 1970; Wednesday; Editor MAURICE O'NEILL; circ. 24,000.

**Ballymena Times:** 22 Ballymoney St, Ballymena, Co Antrim, BT43 6AD; tel. (1266) 653300; fax (1266) 41517; f. 1855; Wednesday; independent; mem. of Mortons Newspapers Ltd; Editor L. MACMULLAN; circ. 30,000.

**Banbridge Chronicle:** 14 Bridge St, Banbridge, Co Down; tel. (18206) 62322; fax (18206) 24397; f. 1870; Thursday; independent; Editor BRYAN HOOKS; circ. 7,866.

**Carrickfergus Advertiser and East Antrim Gazette:** 17 High St, Carrickfergus, Co Antrim, BT38 7AN; tel. and fax (19603) 63651; f. 1883; Wednesday; mem. of the Alpha Newspaper Group; Editor SANDRA CHAPMAN; circ. 5,000.

**Coleraine Chronicle:** 22 Railway Rd, Coleraine, Co Londonderry; tel. (1265) 43344; f. 1844; Thursday; Editor GRANT CAMERON; circ. 22,462.

**County Down Spectator:** 109 Main St, Bangor, Co Down, BT20 4AF; tel. (1247) 473861; f. 1904; Thursday; independent; Editor JOY BANNISTER; circ. 13,800.

**Derry Journal:** Buncrana Rd, Londonderry, BT48 8AA; tel. (1504) 265442; fax (1504) 262048; f. 1772; Tuesday and Friday; Editor P. MCART; circ. Tuesday 24,849, Friday 26,628.

**Down Recorder:** W. Y. Crichton & Co Ltd, 2-4 Church St, Downpatrick, Co Down, BT30 6EP; tel. (1396) 3711; fax (1396) 614624; f. 1836; Wednesday; Editor P. SYMINGTON; circ. 13,417.

**Dungannon Observer:** Observer Newspapers (NI) Ltd, Ann St, Dungannon, Co Tyrone; tel. (18687) 22557; fax (18687) 27334; f. 1930; Friday; nationalist; mem. of Observer Group of Weekly Newspapers; Editor D. MALLON.

**Fermanagh News:** Observer Newspapers (NI) Ltd, Ann St, Dungannon, Co Tyrone; tel. (18687) 22557; fax (18687) 27334; f. 1967; Saturday; nationalist; Editor D. MALLON.

**Impartial Reporter & Farmers' Journal:** 8-10 East Bridge St, Enniskillen, Co Fermanagh, BT74 7BT; tel. (1365) 324422; fax (1365) 325047; f. 1825; Thursday; independent; Editor DENZIL MCDANIEL; circ. 14,055.

**Londonderry Sentinel:** Suite 3, Spencer House, Spencer Rd, Londonderry, BT47 1AA; tel. (1504) 48889; f. 1829; Thursday; Editor J. H. CADDEN; circ. 14,100.

**Lurgan and Portadown Examiner:** Observer Newspapers (NI) Ltd, Ann St, Dungannon, Co Tyrone; tel. (18687) 22557; fax (18687) 27334; f. 1930; Saturday; nationalist; Editor D. MALLON.

**Mid-Ulster Mail:** 52 Oldtown St, Cookstown, Co Tyrone, BT80 8BB; tel. (16487) 62288; fax (16487) 64295; f. 1891; Thursday; Chair. J. S. MORTON; Editor GARY MCDONALD; circ. 12,824.

**Mid-Ulster Observer:** Observer Newspapers (NI) Ltd, Ann St, Dungannon, Co Tyrone; tel. (18687) 22557; fax (18687) 27334; f. 1952; Wednesday; Nationalist; Editor D. MALLON.

**Mourne Observer and Co Down News:** The Roundabout, Castlewellan Rd, Newcastle, Co Down, BT33 0JX; tel. (13967) 22666; fax (13967) 24566; f. 1949; Wednesday; independent; Man. Dir and Editor D. J. HAWTHORNE; circ. 13,394.

**Newry Reporter, Down, Armagh and Louth Times:** 4 Margaret St, Newry, Co Down; tel. (1693) 67633; fax (1693) 63157; f. 1867; Thursday; independent; Editor DONAL O'DONNELL; circ. 14,500.

**Newtownards Chronicle:** 25 Frances St, Newtownards, Co Down, BT23 3DT; tel. (1247) 813333; fax (1247) 820087; f. 1873; Thursday; independent; Editor JOHN SAVAGE; circ. 11,641.

**Newtownards Spectator:** 109 Main St, Bangor, Co Down; tel. (1247) 270270; fax (1247) 271544; f. 1904; Thursday; independent; Editor PAUL FLOWERS; circ. 11,893.

**North West Echo:** Suite 3, Spencer House, Spencer Rd, Londonderry, BT47 1AA; tel. (1504) 42226; f. 1991; Tuesday; Editor J. H. CADDEN; circ. 30,150.

**Northern Constitution:** 22 Railway Rd, Coleraine, Co Londonderry, BT52 1PD; tel. (1265) 43344; fax (1265) 43606; f. 1875; Friday; independent; Editor GRANT CAMERON; circ. 8,790.

**Outlook:** Castle St, Rathfriland, Co Down, BT34 5NH; tel. (18206) 30202; fax (18206) 31022; f. 1939; Thursday; independent; Editor KEN PURDY; circ. 9,500.

**Portadown Times** (incorporating **Craigavon News**): 14 Church St, Portadown, Co Armagh, BT62 3LN; tel. (1762) 336111; fax (1762) 350203; f. 1859; Friday; Editor David Armstrong; circ. 13,000.

**Strabane Chronicle:** 10 John St, Omagh, Co Tyrone, BT78 1DT; tel. (1662) 243444; fax (1662) 242206; Proprs North-West of Ireland Printing and Publishing Co Ltd; Thursday.

**Strabane Weekly News:** 25–27 High St, Omagh, Co Tyrone, BT78 1BD; tel. (1662) 242721; f. 1908; Friday; Unionist; Editor Wesley Atchison; circ. 2,284.

**Sunday News:** 51–67 Donegall St, Belfast, BT1 2GB; tel. (1232) 244441; telex 74407; fax (1232) 230715; f. 1965; independent; Editor Chris Harbinson; circ. 21,299.

**Tyrone Constitution:** 25–27 High St, Omagh, Co Tyrone, BT78 1BD; tel. (1662) 242721; f. 1844; Thursday; Unionist; Editor Wesley Atchison; circ. 10,210.

**Tyrone Courier and Dungannon News:** 58 Scotch St, Dungannon, BT70 1BD; tel. (18687) 22271; f. 1880; Wednesday; Editor R. G. Montgomery; circ. 13,662.

**Ulster Herald:** 10 John St, Omagh, Co Tyrone, BT78 1DT; tel. (1662) 243444; fax (1662) 242206; f. 1901; Proprs North-West of Ireland Printing and Publishing Co Ltd; Thursday; nationalist; Editor E. J. Quigley.

**Ulster Star:** Morton Newspapers Ltd, 21–35 Windsor Ave, Lurgan, Co Armagh; tel. (17622) 326161; f. 1957; Friday; Unionist; Editor David Fletcher; circ. 13,407.

### Association

**Associated Northern Ireland Newspapers:** c/o W. Trimble Ltd, 8–10 East Bridge St, Enniskillen, Co Fermanagh, BT74 7BT; tel. (1365) 324422; fax (1365) 325047; Chair. N. Armstrong; Sec. J. McVey.

## Radio and Television

### STATE BROADCASTING

**British Broadcasting Corporation (BBC):** Broadcasting House, 22–27 Ormeau Ave, Belfast, BT2 8HQ; tel. (1232) 338000; telex 265781; fax (1232) 338800; National Gov. for Northern Ireland Sir Kenneth Bloomfield; Controller BBC, Northern Ireland Robin Walsh.

#### Radio

Northern Ireland relays the five national BBC radio programmes broadcast throughout the United Kingdom and two regional services, BBC Radio Ulster and BBC Radio Foyle in the north-west.

#### Television

The BBC has two colour TV studios in Belfast and a full-scale colour outside broadcast unit. A wide range of programmes is made for broadcasting in Northern Ireland, and for the BBC-1 and BBC-2 UK networks. The BBC has 44 television transmitting stations and 11 radio transmitting stations in Northern Ireland.

The main television transmitters at Divis, Limavady, Brougher Mountain and Londonderry serve most of Northern Ireland on BBC-1 and BBC-2 625-line colour television.

### COMMERCIAL BROADCASTING

**Independent Television Commission (ITC):** Head Office: Foley St, London, W1P 7LB; tel. (171) 255-3000; Chief Exec. David Glencross; Royston House, 34 Upper Queen St, Belfast, BT1 6HG; tel. (1232) 248733; Officer for Northern Ireland Don Anderson.

**Cool FM:** POB 974, Belfast, BT1 1RT; tel. (1247) 817181; fax (1247) 814974; f. 1990; independent music radio station; Chair. J. T. Donnelly; Man. Dir. G. D. Sloan.

**Downtown Radio:** Newtownards, Co Down, BT23 4ES; tel. (1247) 815555; fax (1247) 818913; f. 1976; independent local radio station; Chair. J. T. Donnelly; Man. Dir G. D. Sloan.

**Ulster Television PLC:** Havelock House, Ormeau Rd, Belfast, BT7 1EB; tel. (1232) 328122; fax (1232) 246695; started transmission 1959; Chair. John B. McGuckian; Man. Dir J. Desmond Smyth.

## Finance

(cap. = capital; auth. = authorized; p.u. = paid up; res = reserves; dep. = deposits; m. = million; br.(s) = branch(es))

### BANKS

**AIB Group Northern Ireland PLC:** First Trust Centre, 92 Ann St, Belfast, BT1 3HH; tel. (1232) 325599; fax (1232) 321754; subsidiary of Allied Irish Banks; cap. £20m., dep £563.7m. (Dec. 1993); Chair. William Carson; Sec. Eugene McErlean.

**Bank of Ireland:** Belfast Office: 54 Donegall Place, Belfast, BT1 5BX; tel. (1232) 234334; telex 74663; Head Office: Lower Baggot St, Dublin 2; London Office: 36 Queen St, EC4R 1BN; f. 1783; cap. IR£487.0m., dep. IR£12,829.3m. (March 1994); mem. of Associate Banks; Gov. Howard Kilroy; Chief Exec. Patrick J. Molloy; Gen. Man. (Northern Ireland) D. P. Murphy; 45 brs (Northern Ireland).

**Northern Bank Ltd:** POB 183, 12–15 Donegall Sq. West, Belfast, BT1 6JS; tel. (1232) 245277; telex 747674; fax (1232) 893214; f. 1824; owned by National Australia Bank; cap. auth. £100m., dep. £1,895m. (1993); Chair. Sir Desmond Lorimer; Chief Exec. John Wright; Sec. N. C. Beattie; 108 brs.

**Northern Bank Executor and Trustee Co Ltd:** POB 183, Donegall Sq. West, Belfast, BT2 7EB; tel. (1232) 245277; fax (1232) 241790; f. 1960; owned by the Northern Bank Ltd; cap. auth. £500,000, issued £200,000 (Dec. 1987); Gen. Man. W. J. McClelland; Sec. N. C. Beattie.

**Northern Bank Development Corpn Ltd:** POB 183, Donegall Sq. West, Belfast, BT2 7EB; tel. (1232) 245277; fax (1232) 893413; f. 1971; cap. auth. £10m., p.u. £9m. (1988); Chair. J. R. Wright; Man. J. D. Walmsley; Sec. N. C. Beattie.

**Ulster Bank Ltd:** 47 Donegall Place, POB 232, Belfast, BT1 5AU; tel. (1232) 244744; telex 747334; fax (1232) 898588; f. 1836; mem. of National Westminster Group; cap. p.u. £105.0m., dep. £5,522.6m. (Dec. 1994); Chair. Sir George Quigley; Chief Exec. Ronnie Kells; 181 brs.

### Banking Association

**Northern Ireland Bankers' Asscn:** Stokes House, 17–25 College Sq. East, Belfast BT1 6DE; tel. (1232) 327551; fax (1232) 331449; Chair. D. E. Harvey; Sec. J. N. Simpson (acting).

### STOCK EXCHANGE

**Stock Exchange:** 10 High St, Belfast BT1 2BP; tel. (1232) 321094; fax (1232) 328149; Head Office: London; see under Great Britain.

## Trade and Industry

**Confederation of British Industry (CBI):** Fanum House, 108 Great Victoria St, Belfast, BT2 7PD; tel. (1232) 326658; fax (1232) 245915; Dir Nigel Smyth.

**Foyle Development Organization:** c/o Guildhall, Londonderry; tel. (1504) 365151; f. 1979 by Derry city council; agency for industrial development, representing management, labour and city council interests.

**Industrial Development Board for Northern Ireland:** IDB House, Chichester St, Belfast, BT1 4JX; tel. (1232) 233233; telex 747025; fax (1232) 231328; f. 1982 to replace the Northern Ireland Development Agency and the Industrial Development Organisation; to promote, encourage and support industry and create new investment in Northern Ireland; Chair. John B. McGuckian; Chief Exec. F. McCann (acting).

**LEDU** (Northern Ireland Small Business Agency): LEDU House, Upper Galwally, Belfast, BT8 4TB; tel. (1232) 491031; fax (1232) 691432; f. 1971, as the Local Enterprise Development Unit, to encourage enterprise and stimulate competitiveness of businesses within defined markets; concentrates on small businesses (usually with fewer than 50 employees) with export potential in manufacturing and certain service areas; Chair. P. McWilliams; Chief Exec. Chris Buckland.

**Northern Ireland Certification for Trade Unions and Employers' Associations:** 16th floor, Windsor House, 9–15 Bedford St, Belfast, BT2 YNU; tel. (1232) 237773.

**Northern Ireland Chamber of Commerce and Industry:** Chamber of Commerce House, 22 Great Victoria St, Belfast, BT2 7BJ; tel. (1232) 244113; fax (1232) 247024; f. 1783; Pres. D. Galway; Dir R. J. Stringer; 900 mems.

**Northern Ireland Chamber of Trade:** POB 444, Belfast, BT1 1DY; tel. (1232) 230444; Sec. J. Roberts.

**Northern Ireland Economic Council:** Bulloch House, 2 Linenhall St, Belfast, BT2 8BA; tel. (1232) 232125; fax (1232) 331250; f. 1977; monitors economic policy and advises the Secretary of State on regional economic development; 15 mems representing trade union, employer, and independent interests; Chair. Sir George Quigley.

### EMPLOYERS' ASSOCIATIONS

**Belfast Shipbuilders' Asscn:** c/o Harland and Wolff Holdings PLC, Queen's Island, Belfast, BT3 9DU; tel. (1232) 458456; telex 74396; fax (1232) 732880; f. 1989.

**Construction Employers' Federation Ltd:** 143 Malone Rd, Belfast, BT9 6SU; tel. (1232) 661711; fax (1232) 666323; f. 1945; Dir G. Burnison.

# UNITED KINGDOM (NORTHERN IRELAND)

**Electrical Contractors' Asscn** (Ireland Regional Office): 17 Farm Lodge Drive, Upper Rd, Greenisland, Carrickfergus, Co Antrim, BT38 8XN; tel. (1232) 854553; fax (1232) 851528; Reg. Officer I. BROWNLEES.

**Engineering Employers' Federation, NI Asscn:** 2 Greenwood Ave, Belfast, BT4 3JJ; tel. (1232) 672490; fax (1232) 658571; f. 1866; Dir PETER BLOCH.

**Northern Ireland Textiles and Apparel Association:** 5C The Square, Hillsborough, BT26 6AG; tel. (1846) 689999; fax (1846) 689968; f. 1993; Chair. T. MCCARTNEY; Dir D. MORGAN; 70 mems.

**Northern Ireland Trade Asscns Ltd:** 10 Arthur St, Belfast, BT1 4GD; tel. (1232) 323274; fax (1232) 439364; Secretariat to 14 Trade Asscns; Dir HAMILTON MARTIN.

**Ulster Chemists' Asscn:** 73 University St, Belfast, BT7 1HL; tel. (1232) 320787; fax (1232) 313737.

**Ulster Farmers' Union:** Dunedin, 475 Antrim Rd, Belfast, BT15 3DA; tel. (1232) 370222; fax (1232) 370739; f. 1918; Pres. HUGH LINEHAN; Dir Gen. A. MACLAUGHLIN; 11,800 mems.

## TRADE UNIONS

The organization of trade unions in Northern Ireland is a similar system to that in Great Britain. Below are some of the major organizations in Northern Ireland, some of which are affiliated to corresponding unions in Great Britain and the Republic of Ireland. Many of the large unions in Great Britain are represented by branches in Northern Ireland. Membership figures are for Northern Ireland only.

**Irish Congress of Trade Unions (NI Committee):** 3 Wellington Park, Belfast, BT9 6DJ; tel. (1232) 681726; fax (1232) 682126; NI Officer T. CARLIN; Gen. Sec. PETER CASSELLS.

**Amalgamated Transport and General Workers' Union:** Transport House, 102 High St, Belfast, BT1 2DL; tel. (1232) 232381; fax (1232) 240133; Irish Regional Sec. J. FREEMAN; 40,537 mems.

**Amalgamated Engineering and Electrical Union, AEU Section:** AEEU House, 26–34 Antrim Rd, Belfast, BT15 2AA; tel. (1232) 743271; fax (1232) 745810; f. 1992 as a result of merger between Amalgamated Engineering Union and Electrical, Electronics, Telecommunications and Plumbing Union; Divisional Sec. P. WILLIAMSON; 12,000 mems.

**Amalgamated Engineering and Electrical Union, EETPU Section:** AEEU House, 26–34 Antrim Rd, Belfast, BT15 2AA; tel. (1232) 740244; fax (1232) 748156; Nat. Officer W. J. KIRKWOOD; 7,200 mems.

**Confederation of Shipbuilding and Engineering Unions:** AEU House, 26–34 Antrim Rd, Belfast, BT15 2AA; tel. (1232) 743271; fax (1232) 745810; District Sec. P. WILLIAMSON.

**General, Municipal, Boilermakers and Allied Trades Union:** 3/4 Donegall Quay, Belfast, BT1 3EA; tel. (1232) 312111; fax (1232) 312333; Regional Official MARTIN DUMMIGAN; 27,001 mems.

**Irish National Teachers' Organization:** 23 College Gardens, Belfast, BT9 6BS (headquarters in Dublin); tel. (1232) 381455; fax (1232) 662803; f. 1868; Northern Sec. F. BUNTING; 5,300 mems.

**Manufacturing, Science and Finance Union:** 545 Antrim Rd, Belfast, BT15 2AA; tel. (1232) 370551; fax (1232) 370687; Regional Officer J. BOWERS; 10,000 mems.

**National Federation of Building Trade Operatives:** Irish Regional Sec. in Dublin, Branch Secs in the principal Northern Ireland towns.

**Northern Ireland Public Service Alliance:** Harkin House, 54 Wellington Park, Belfast, BT9 6DP; tel. (1232) 661831; fax (1232) 665847; Gen. Sec. J. MCCUSKER; 36,000 mems.

**Services Industrial Professional Technical Union:** 3 Antrim Rd, Belfast, BT15 2BE; tel. (1232) 314000; fax (1232) 314040; Gen. Sec. TOM GARRY; Regional Sec. ROBERT BRADY; 7,001 members.

**Ulster Teachers' Union:** 94 Malone Rd, Belfast, BT9 5HP; tel. (1232) 662216; fax (1232) 663055; f. 1919; Gen. Sec. DAVID ALLEN; Asst Gen. Sec. RAY CALVIN; Field Officer AVRIL CHATTERLEY; 5,000 mems.

**Union of Communication Workers:** 22 Croob Park, Ballynahinch, Co Down, BT24 8BB; Irish Rep. I. BURROWS; 2,698 mems.

**Union of Construction, Allied Trades and Technicians:** 78–81 May St, Belfast, BT9 6JL; tel. (1232) 322366; Regional Sec. J. CROOKS; 5,142 mems.

**Union of Shop, Distributive and Allied Workers:** 40 Wellington Park, Belfast, BT9 6DN; tel. (1232) 663773; fax (1232) 662133; Area Organizers A. WHITE, ROBERT GOURLEY, E. J. O'NEILL; 6,635 mems.

**UNISON:** 523 Antrim Rd, Belfast, BT15 3BS; tel. (1232) 770813; fax (1232) 779772; f. 1993 by amalgamation of Confederation of Health Service Employees (COHSE), Nat. and Local Government Officers Asscn (NALGO) and Nat. Union of Public Employees (NUPE); Regional Sec. INEZ MCCORMACK; 32,000 mems.

# Transport

In 1988 plans were announced for the improvement of Northern Ireland's transport infrastructure, at a projected cost of £200m. The programme, due for completion by the end of 1993, included the development of ports and major improvements to airports, roads and railways.

### RAILWAYS

**Northern Ireland Railways Co Ltd:** Central Station, East Bridge St, Belfast, BT1 3PB; tel. (1232) 899400; fax (1232) 899401; f. 1967; subsidiary of Northern Ireland Transport Holding Co; operates rail services for passenger traffic over 336 km and for freight traffic over 268 km of railway track; Chief Exec. J. W. AIKEN (acting).

### ROADS

In 1992 there were 24,218 km (15,049 miles) of roads of all classes including 113 km (70 miles) of motorway. At the end of 1985 there were 1,478 licensed road freight operators.

**Northern Ireland Transport Holding Co:** Chamber of Commerce House, 22 Great Victoria St, Belfast, BT2 7LX; tel. (1232) 243456; fax (1232) 333845; publicly-owned; three subsidiaries.

**Citybus Ltd:** Milewater Rd, Belfast, BT3 9BG; tel. (1232) 351201; telex 747802; fax (1232) 351474; responsible for operating municipal transport in the City of Belfast.

**Ulsterbus Ltd:** Milewater Rd, Belfast, BT3 9BG; tel. (1232) 351201; telex 747802; fax (1232) 351473; responsible for almost all bus transport in Northern Ireland, except Belfast city; services into the Republic of Ireland; assoc. co Flexibus Ltd (minibus contract hire).

### SHIPPING

There are regular freight services from Belfast, Warrenpoint and Larne to ports in Great Britain and Europe; freight services also operate from Londonderry and Coleraine. Passenger services operate daily between Belfast and Stranraer, between Larne and Stranraer, and between Larne and Cairnryan. With major financial assistance from the EC, Northern Ireland ports are implementing a major programme of modernization. At the port of Belfast two 'roll on, roll off' terminals and a large container terminal are now operational. The port of Londonderry has been transferred to a new location at Lishally with 200 m of quay completed by February 1993. The port of Larne is modernizing a 'roll on, roll off' terminal.

**B.G. Freightline:** c/o T.R. Shipping Services, Victoria Terminal 3, West Bank Rd, Belfast, BT3 9JL; tel. (1232) 777968; fax (1232) 773822; container service to Rotterdam.

**Belfast Freight Ferries Ltd:** Victoria Terminal 1, Dargan Rd, Belfast, BT3 9LJ; tel. (1232) 770112; fax (1232) 781217; roll-on, roll-off service to Heysham; Chair. ANGUS FRASER.

**Coastal Container Line Ltd:** Coastal House, Victoria Terminal 3, West Bank Rd, Belfast, BT3 9JL; tel. (1232) 371371; fax (1232) 371333; container service to Liverpool.

**Dragon Shipping Line Ltd:** York Dock Terminal, Dufferin Rd, Belfast, BT3 9AA; tel. (1232) 351313; fax (1232) 351521; container service to Swansea.

**Heyn Group Ltd:** Head Line Bldgs, 10 Victoria St, Belfast, BT1 3GP; tel. (1232) 230581; telex 74534; fax (1232) 231367; parent co of the Ulster Steamship Co Ltd; Man. Dir M. W. S. MACLARAN.

**John Kelly Ltd:** 23 Station St, Belfast, BT3 9DA; tel. (1232) 459566; telex 74644; fax (1232) 738628; f. 1840; coal and petroleum distributors, shipping agent; Chair. B. S. HARTISS; Man. Dir M. WOODS.

**Merchant Ferries Ltd:** Ferry Terminal, the Docks, Warrenpoint, Co Down; tel. (16937) 53639; fax (16937) 752616; roll-on, roll-off freight services to Fleetwood and Heysham.

**Norse Irish Ferries:** Victoria Terminal 2, West Bank Rd, Belfast, BT3 9JN; tel. (1232) 779090; fax (1232) 775520; roll-on, roll-off freight, car and passenger services to Liverpool.

**P & O European Ferries (Felixstowe) Ltd:** The Harbour, Larne, Co Antrim, BT40 1AQ; tel. (1574) 272201 (freight), (1574) 274321 (passenger); telex 74528 (freight), 747322 (passenger); fax (1574) 272477 (freight), (1574) 270949 (passenger); subsidiary of P & O Group; Port Man. A. P. WILSON.

**Pandoro Ltd:** Larne Harbour, Larne, Co Antrim, BT40 1AX; tel. (1574) 260511; telex 74536; fax (1574) 273454; roll-on, roll-off freight services twice daily to Fleetwood and daily to Ardrossan; Man. GRAHAM MCCULLOUGH.

**Stena Sealink Ltd:** Group Travel and Short Breaks Department, Sea Terminal, Larne, Co Antrim, BT40 1AW; tel. (1574) 272774; fax (1574) 272704; roll-on, roll-off car and passenger services Larne–Stranraer.

### CIVIL AVIATION

Belfast International Airport at Aldergrove handled 2.2m. passengers and 24,000 metric tons of freight during 1993. There are daily scheduled flights to one destination in Europe and 9 in Great Britain; and regular charter flights to cities in Europe and North America. There are also direct services from Belfast City Airport at Sydenham to 19 destinations in Great Britain. In 1993 Belfast City Airport handled 846,000 passengers. From City of Derry Airport, in Co Londonderry, there are direct services to Glasgow and Manchester. In 1993 City of Derry Airport handled 31,000 passengers.

**Belfast International Airport Ltd:** Belfast International Airport, Belfast, BT29 4AB; tel. (1849) 422888; telex 747980; fax (1849) 452096; f. 1961 as Northern Ireland Airports Ltd; transferred to private ownership in 1994; Man. Dir JIM DORNAN.

## Tourism

Tourist attractions include unspoilt beaches, the Giant's Causeway, in Co Antrim, the Mourne mountains, in Co Down, and a range of new indoor attractions developed with assistance from EU funds. There were about 1.26m. visitors to Northern Ireland in 1993. The total was expected to increase markedly with the prospect of a sustained peace.

**Northern Ireland Tourist Board:** St. Anne's Court, 59 North Street, Belfast, BT1 1NB; tel. (1232) 231221; fax (1232) 240960; Chair. Lord RATHCAVAN; Chief Exec. I. G. HENDERSON.

# UNITED KINGDOM CROWN DEPENDENCIES

The Isle of Man and the Channel Islands lie off shore from the United Kingdom but are not integral parts of the country. They are dependencies of the British Crown and have considerable self-government in internal affairs.

## THE ISLE OF MAN

### Introduction

The Isle of Man lies in the Irish Sea between the Cumbrian coast of England and Northern Ireland. It is a dependency of the Crown and does not form part of the United Kingdom. It has its own legislative assembly and legal and administrative systems, its laws depending for their validity on Orders made by the Queen in Council. Her Majesty's Government in the United Kingdom is responsible for the defence and international relations of the island, and the Crown is ultimately responsible for its good government. However, control of direct taxation is exercised by the Manx Government and, although most rates of indirect taxation are the same on the island as in the United Kingdom, there is some divergence of rates. The capital is Douglas. In addition to the British public holidays, the Isle of Man also celebrates 5 July (Tynwald Day).

### Statistical Survey

Source: Economic Affairs Division, Government Offices, Illiam Dhone House, 2 Circular Rd, Douglas, IM1 1PQ; tel. (1624) 685743; fax (1624) 685747.

#### AREA, POPULATION AND DENSITY

**Area:** 572 sq km (221 sq miles).
**Population:** (census, 14–15 April 1991): 69,788 (males 33,693, females 36,095). *Principal towns* (1991): Douglas (capital) 22,214, Onchan 8,483, Ramsey 6,496, Peel 3,829, Castletown 3,152.
**Density** (per sq km, 1991): 122.0.
**Births and Deaths** (1994): Live births 883 (birth rate 12.7 per 1,000); Deaths 902 (death rate 12.9 per 1,000).
**Employment** (14–15 April 1991): 31,829 (males 18,262, females 13,567); Manufacturing 3,348, Construction 3,404, Transport and communication 2,012, Retail distribution 2,993, Banking and finance 2,425, Professional and scientific services 5,438, Public administration 2,144.

#### AGRICULTURE, ETC.

**Crops** (area in acres, 1994): Cereals and vegetables 12,481, Grass 65,866, Rough grazing 36,587.
**Livestock** (1994): Cattle 32,510, Sheep 161,380, Pigs 4,571, Poultry 53,557.
**Fishing:** *Amount landed* (metric tons, 1994): Scallops 645; Queen Scallops 3,005; *Value of landings* (1993): Scallops £638,554; Queen Scallops £1,707,764; Total first hand sale value of all landings: £2,892,285.

#### FINANCE

**Currency and Exchange Rates:** 100 pence = 1 pound sterling (£).
*Dollar Equivalents* (31 December 1994): £1 = US $1.5645; US $1 = 63.92 pence.
Note: United Kingdom coins and notes are also legal tender.
**Budget:** (projections, year ending 31 March 1996): *Revenue* (major items) Customs duties £100.4m., Income tax £101.1m.; *Expenditure* (major items) Social security £93.8m., Health services £45.3m., Education £43.0m.

#### TRANSPORT

**Road Traffic** (vehicles in use, 1993/94): Private 42,433, Engineering 313, Goods 4,440, Agricultural 1,066, Hackney 751, Public service 266, Motorcycles, scooters and tricycles 2,859.
**Shipping** (1994): Passenger arrivals 244,633.
**Civil Aviation** (1994): Passengers 268,654. (1993): Freight unloaded 3,022 metric tons; freight loaded 712 metric tons.

#### TOURISM

**Tourist Arrivals** (May–September 1994): Passenger arrivals by air 132,693, Passenger arrivals by sea 177,524, Total 310,217.

#### COMMUNICATIONS MEDIA

**Telephone Connections** (1995): 41,000.
**Television Licences** (1995): 23,600.

#### EDUCATION

**Primary** (1994): 32 schools, 4,078 students.
**Secondary** (1994): 5 schools, 4,559 students.
**College** (1994): 1.

### Directory
### The Constitution

The legislature is Tynwald, comprising two branches, the Legislative Council and the House of Keys, sitting together as one body, but voting separately on all questions except in certain eventualities. The House of Keys has 24 members elected by adult suffrage for five years. The Legislative Council is composed of a President, the Lord Bishop of Sodor and Man, the Attorney-General and eight members elected by the House of Keys. The Head of State of the Isle of Man is the British monarch. The Lieutenant-Governor, who is the Crown's personal representative on the island, is appointed by the Head of State for a five year term.

### The Government
(June 1995)

#### HEAD OF STATE

**Lord of Mann:** HM Queen Elizabeth II.
**Lieutenant-Governor:** Air Marshal Sir Laurence Jones.

#### COUNCIL OF MINISTERS

**Chief Minister:** Miles R. Walker.

#### GOVERNMENT OFFICES

**Isle of Man Government:** Bucks Rd, Douglas; tel. (1624) 685685; fax (1624) 685747.

### Legislature

#### TYNWALD

**President:** Sir Charles Kerruísh.

#### Legislative Council (Upper House)

**President of the Council:** Sir Charles Kerruísh.
**Lord Bishop of Sodor and Man:** Rt Rev. Noel Debroy Jones.
**Attorney-General:** John Michael Kerruísh.
**Members appointed by the House of Keys:** G. H. Waft, E. J. Mann, D. K. K. Delaney, J. N. Radcliffe, B. Barton, A. C. Luft, E. G. Lowey, C. M. Christian.
**Clerk:** T. A. Bawden.

# UK CROWN DEPENDENCIES (ISLE OF MAN)

### House of Keys (Lower House)
**Speaker:** James Crookall Cain.
**Secretary:** Prof. T. St. J. N. Bates.

The House of Keys consists of 24 members, elected by adult suffrage—eight for Douglas, two for Ramsey, one each for Peel and Castletown, and 12 for rural districts. The last general election was held in November 1991. There are no political parties as such on the Isle of Man.

## Judicial System

The Isle of Man is, for legal purposes, an autonomous sovereign country under the British Crown, with its own legislature and its own independent judiciary administering its own common or customary and statute law. The law of the Isle of Man is, in most essential matters, the same as the law of England and general principles of equity administered by the English Courts are followed by the Courts of the Isle of Man unless they conflict with established local precedents. Her Majesty's High Court of Justice of the Isle of Man is based upon the English system but modified and simplified to meet local conditions. Justices of the Peace are appointed by the Lord Chancellor of England usually on the nomination of the Lieutenant-Governor. The Deemsters (see below), the High Bailiff, the Mayor of Douglas, and the Chairmen of the Town and Village Commissioners are ex-officio JPs. The Manx Court of Appeal consists of the Deemsters and the Judge of Appeal.

**First Deemster and Clerk of the Rolls:** J. W. Corrin.
**Second Deemster:** T. W. Cain.
**Judge of Appeal:** B. A. Hytner.

## Religion

### CHRISTIANITY

#### The Church of England
The Isle of Man forms the diocese of Sodor and Man, comprising 27 parishes. The parish church at Peel was designated a cathedral in 1980.
**Lord Bishop of Sodor and Man:** Rt Rev. Noel Debroy Jones, Bishop's House, Quarterbridge Rd, Douglas, IM2 3RF; tel. (1624) 622108; fax (1624) 672890.

#### Roman Catholic Church
The deanery of the Isle of Man is part of the archdiocese of Liverpool. There are eight Catholic churches on the island.
**Dean of the Isle of Man:** Very Rev. Canon Brendan Alger, St Mary of the Isle, Douglas, IM1 3EG; tel. (1624) 675509.

#### Other Churches
There are also congregations of the following denominations: Baptist, Congregational, Independent Methodist, Methodist, Presbyterian, Elim Pentecostal, and Society of Friends; also Christian Science, Jehovah's Witnesses and the Church of Jesus Christ of Latter-day Saints.
There are small Jewish and Muslim communities on the island.

## The Press

**Isle of Man Courier:** Publishing House, Peel Rd, Douglas, IM1 5PZ; tel. (1624) 623451; fax (1624) 661041; f. 1884; weekly; Editor Lionel Cowin; circ. 30,000.

**Isle of Man Examiner:** Publishing House, Peel Rd, Douglas, IM1 5PZ; tel. (1624) 623451; fax (1624) 661041; f. 1880; weekly; Editor Lionel Cowin; circ. 15,000.

**The Manx Independent:** Publishing House, Peel Rd, Douglas, IM1 5PZ; tel. (1624) 623451; fax (1624) 611149; f. 1987; Tuesday and Friday; Editor Lionel Cowin; circ. 9,000.

**Manx Life:** 14 Douglas St, Peel, IM5 1BA; tel. (1624) 843882; f. 1971; monthly; Editor Ian Faulds; circ. 3,500.

**Manx Post:** Ballafodda Farm, Ballabeg, Arbory; tel. (1624) 823355.

**Manx Tails Magazine:** Spring Valley Industrial Estate, Douglas, IM2 2QS; tel. (1624) 662066; fax (1624) 625623.

**Peel City Guardian:** 14 Douglas St, Peel, IM5 1BA; tel. (1624) 843882; f. 1882; fortnightly on Saturday; Editor Ian Faulds; circ. 6,000.

**Ramsey Chronicle:** 14 Douglas St, Peel, IM5 1BA; tel. (1624) 842160; f. 1986; fortnightly on Saturday; Editor Ian Faulds; circ. 3,000.

## Publishers

**American Connection Ltd:** Willesden, Main Rd, Baldrine, IM4 7HB; tel. (1624) 861641.

**Amulree Publications:** Glen Rd, Laxey, IM4 7AJ; tel. (1624) 862238.

**Electrochemical Publications Ltd:** Asahi House, Church Rd, Port Erin, IM99 8HD; tel. (1624) 834941.

**Executive Publications:** Spring Valley Industrial Estate, Braddan, Douglas; tel. (1624) 662066; fax (1624) 625623.

**Grove Publishing Co:** The Ballacrosha, Ballaugh; tel. (1624) 897355.

**Imagination Ltd:** Willesden, Main Road, Baldrine, IM4 7HB; tel. (1624) 861638.

**Lily Publications (I.O.M.) Ltd:** Portland House, Station Road, Ballasalla, IM9 2AE; tel. (1624) 823848.

**Mannin Media Ltd:** Spring Valley Industrial Estate, Braddan, IM2 2QS; tel. (1624) 611315; fax (1624) 661655.

**Mansk-Svenska Publishing Co. Ltd:** 17 North View, Peel, IM5 1DQ; tel. (1624) 842855; children's, fiction, history, genealogy, reference; Man. Dir G. V. C. Young.

**Media Action:** 2/3 Station Shops, Peel Rd, Douglas, IM1 4LW; tel. and fax (1624) 611100.

**Pines Press:** The Pines, Ballein, Maughold, Laxey, IM7 1HJ; tel. (1624) 862030.

**Technical Reference Publications Ltd:** Asahi House, 10 Church Rd, Port Erin, IM99 8HD; tel. (1624) 834941.

**Trafalgar Press Ltd:** 14 Douglas St, Peel, IM5 1BA; tel. (1624) 843102.

**Wela Publications:** Asahi House, Church Rd, Port Erin, IM99 8HD; tel. (1624) 834941.

## Radio and Television

**Isle of Man Communications Commission:** Homefield, 88 Woodbourne Rd, Douglas, IM2 3AP; tel. (1624) 677022; fax (1624) 621298; appointed by the Isle of Man Government to represent the Island's interests in all matters of radio and television; Chair. of Comm. R. K. Corkill; Dir B. R. Waddington; Chair. of Radio Manx Ltd W. A. Wilcocks.

**Manx Radio:** POB 1368, Broadcasting House, Douglas, IM99 1SW; tel. (1624) 661066; fax (1624) 661411; commercial station operated (by agreement with the Isle of Man Government) by Radio Manx Ltd; Man. Dir Stewart Watterson.

The Isle of Man also receives television programmes from the BBC and from the Independent Television Network (Border Television).

## Finance

**Isle of Man Government Financial Supervision Commission:** POB 58, 1–4 Goldie Terrace, Upper Church St, Douglas, IM99 1DT; tel. (1624) 624487; fax (1624) 629342; responsible for the licensing, authorization and supervision of banks, building societies, investment businesses and collective investment schemes; Chief Exec. J. E. Noakes.

**Treasury:** Government Offices, Buck's Rd, Douglas, IM1 3PU; tel. (1624) 685586; fax (1624) 685662; Minister D. J. Gelling; Chief Financial Officer J. A. Cashen; Commercial Devt Officer M. J. Gates.

### BANKS
(cap. = capital; res = reserves; dep. = deposits; m. = million; brs = branches)

Total bank deposits in the Isle of Man were £12,148m. in 1994, and there were 59 licensed banks. In May 1989 it was announced that foreign banks were to be allowed to establish subsidiaries in the Isle of Man, subject to strict supervision.

**AIB Bank (Isle of Man) Ltd:** POB 186, 10 Finch Rd, Douglas, IM99 1QE; tel. (1624) 624315; telex 628782; fax (1624) 673447; f. 1977; cap and res £63.6m. (Dec. 1994); Mans W. C. P. Hudson, S. K. Dowling.

**Alliance & Leicester (IOM) Ltd:** 10–12 Prospect Hill, Douglas, IM99 1RY; tel. (1624) 663566; fax (1624) 663577; Man. A. V. Lodge.

**Allied Dunbar Bank International Ltd:** Lord St, Douglas, IM99 1ET; tel. (1624) 661551; telex 629784; fax (1624) 662183; Man. Ian Crawford.

**Anglo Irish Bank Corpn (IOM) PLC:** St. James's Chambers, 65 Athol St, Douglas, IM1 1JE; tel. (1624) 625508; Man. Dir G. Drake.

**Bank of Bermuda (IOM) Ltd:** 12/13 Hill Street, Douglas, IM1 1JE; tel. (1624) 623446; Man. Dir T. A. Barnham.

# UK CROWN DEPENDENCIES (ISLE OF MAN)

**Bank of Ireland (IOM) Ltd:** Christian Rd, Douglas, IM1 2SD; tel. (1624) 661102; telex 628270; fax (1624) 662786; Man. Dir M. J. ENNIS.

**Bank of Scotland (Isle of Man) Ltd:** POB 19, Prospect Hill, Douglas IM99 1AT; tel. (1624) 623074; telex 629677; fax (1624) 625677; f. 1976; cap. £5m.; Man. Dir B. HOLT.

**Barclays Bank PLC:** POB 9, Barclays House, Victoria St, Douglas, IM99 1AJ; tel. (1624) 682000; telex 418139; fax (1624) 682040; private banking and international services; Man. E. SHALLCROSS; 6 brs.

**Barclays Finance Co (IOM) Ltd:** POB 9, Barclays House, Victoria St, Douglas, IM99 1AJ; tel. (1624) 682266; telex 418139; fax (1624) 682126; cap. and res £13.5m.; Man. P. COX.

**Barclay's Private Bank and Trust (Isle of Man) Ltd:** POB 48, Queen Victoria House, Victoria St, Douglas, IM99 1DF; tel. (1624) 673514; telex 629587; fax (1624) 620905; Dir C. JONES.

**Bradford & Bingley (Isle of Man) Ltd:** 30 Ridgeway St, Douglas, IM1 1TA; tel. (1624) 661868; fax (1624) 661962; cap. and res £16m.; Gen. Man. PAUL HUTCHINSON.

**Britannia International Ltd:** Britannia House, Victoria St, Douglas, IM99 1SD; tel. (1624) 628512; fax (1624) 661015; Man. Dir D. H. FULTON.

**Caymanx Trust Co Ltd:** 34 Athol St, Douglas, IM1 1RD; tel. (1624) 672320; Man. Dir I. CALLOW.

**Celtic Bank Ltd:** POB 114, Lord St, Douglas, IM99 1JW; tel. (1624) 622856; fax (1624) 620926; f. 1977; issued cap. £6.8m., res £1.1m.; Man. Dir. R. G. DANIELSON.

**Conister Trust Ltd:** POB 17, Conister House, 16–18 Finch Rd, Douglas, IM99 1AR; tel. (1624) 674455; fax (1624) 624278; f. 1935; Man. Dir E. J. THORN.

**Coutts & Co. (Isle of Man) Ltd:** Coutts House, Summerhill Rd, Onchan, Douglas, IM99 1DU; tel. (1624) 632222; Man. Dir C. TUMMON.

**Duncan Lawrie (IOM) Ltd:** 14/15 Mount Havelock, Douglas IM1 2QG; tel. (1624) 620770; telex 627724; fax (1624) 676315; Chair. N. J. G. SHARP; Man. Dir B. DUTTON.

**Habib European Bank Ltd:** St James's House, Market St, Douglas, IM1 2PQ; tel. (1624) 622554; telex 629263; fax (1624) 627135; Ass. Vice-Pres. L. A. SHAIKH.

**Isle of Man Bank Ltd:** POB 13, 2 Athol St, Douglas IM99 1AN; tel. (1624) 637100; telex 627071; f. 1865; cap. issued £7.5m., dep. £1,260m. (Dec. 1993); bankers to Isle of Man Government; mem. of the National Westminster Group; Chair. W. L. B. STOTT; Gen. Man. T. W. N. WALSH; 15 brs.

**Leeds Overseas Ltd:** POB 30, Douglas, IM99 1TA; tel. (1624) 612323; Man. Dir P. G. MCQUILLEN.

**Lloyds Bank Finance (Isle of Man) Ltd:** Peveril Bldgs, Peveril Sq., Douglas, IM99 1SS; tel. (1624) 625614; telex 629820; Man. and Dir J. CORLETT.

**Lloyds Bank PLC:** Victory House, Prospect Hill, Douglas, IM99 1AH; tel. (1624) 625614; fax (1624) 626033; Island Man. P. NIVEN; 3 brs.

**Lloyds Private Banking (Isle of Man) Ltd:** Peveril Bldg, Peveril Sq., Douglas, IM99 1SS; tel. (1624) 625614; telex 626110; fax (1624) 676289; Dir and Man. R. S. HETHERINGTON.

**Lombard Bank (Isle of Man) Ltd:** Hillary House, 30–38 Prospect Hill, Douglas, IM99 1NF; tel. (1624) 629595; cap. £5m., dep. £142m. (Sept. 1990); Man. L. F. RENSHAW.

**MeesPierson (Isle of Man) Ltd:** POB 156, Pierson House, 18–20 North Quay, Douglas, IM99 1NR; tel. (1624) 688300; telex 626159; fax (1624) 688334; Chief Exec. E. GILMORE.

**Meghraj Bank (IOM) Ltd:** POB 3, Meghraj Centre, Upper Church St, Douglas, IM99 1AE; tel. (1624) 620848; telex 627594; fax (1624) 677318; Dir D. MOORHOUSE.

**Midland Bank PLC:** 10 Victoria St, Douglas, IM99 1AU; tel. (1624) 623051; telex 628037; Area Man. C. J. TUNLEY; 2 brs.

**Midland Bank Trust Corpn (Isle of Man) Ltd:** Celtic House, Victoria St, Douglas, IM99 1BU; tel. (1624) 684800; Man. Dir M. S. WALSH.

**N. & P. Overseas Ltd:** POB 150, 56 Strand St, Douglas, IM99 1NH; tel. (1624) 662244; fax (1624) 662482; Man. Dir D. A. SIDDALL.

**National Westminster Bank PLC:** 1 Prospect Hill, Douglas, IM99 1AQ; tel. (1624) 629292; telex 627959; fax (1624) 620187; Chief Man. R. BRERETON.

**Nationwide Overseas Ltd:** POB 217, 45–51 Athol St, Douglas, IM99 1RN; tel. (1624) 663494; Operations Dir J. S. BINGHAM.

**Northern Bank (IOM) Ltd:** POB 113, 49 Victoria St, Douglas, IM99 1JN; tel. (1624) 624152; fax (1624) 627508; merchant bank; mem. of National Australia Bank Group; Man. R. I. MONTGOMERY.

**Rea Brothers (IOM) Ltd:** POB 203, 29 Athol St, Douglas, IM99 1RB; tel. (1624) 629696; telex 627752; fax (1624) 622039; f. 1976; merchant bank; cap. and res £1.9m., dep. £31.1m.; Man. Dir W. A. HAMILTON-TURNER.

**Robert Fleming (IOM) Ltd:** 3 Mount Pleasant, Douglas, IM1 2PU; tel. (1624) 661880; telex 628482; Dir N. OWEN.

**Royal Bank of Canada (IOM) Ltd:** 60–62 Athol St, Douglas, IM99 1RX; tel. (1624) 629521; Man. Dir T. D. WYNN.

**The Royal Bank of Scotland (IOM) Ltd:** Victory House, Prospect Hill, Douglas, IM99 1NJ; tel. (1624) 629111; telex 628214; Chair. C. G. PEARSON; Dir and Man. A. E. BARBER.

**The Royal Bank of Scotland PLC:** Victory House, Prospect Hill, Douglas, IM99 1NJ; tel. (1624) 629111; Regional Man. A. E. BARBER.

**Singer & Friedlander (Isle of Man) Ltd:** S & F House, 12–14 Ridgeway St, Douglas, IM99 1QB; tel. (1624) 623235; telex 627936; fax (1624) 620257; f. 1971; merchant bank; cap. £5m., dep. £77.3m.; Dir and Man. D. A. C. LEVER.

**Standard Bank (IOM) Ltd:** POB 43, 64 Athol St, Douglas, IM99 1BZ; tel. (1624) 623916; telex 628665; fax (1624) 623970; cap. £4m.; Man. Dir K. J. FODEN.

**Standard Bank Investment Corporation (Isle of Man) Ltd:** POB 220, Exchange House, 54–58 Athol St, Douglas, IM99 1BB; tel. (1624) 662522; Man. J. R. HALL.

**TSB Bank PLC:** 78 Strand St, Douglas, IM99 1AB; tel. (1624) 673755; fax (1624) 624203; Sr Branch Man. R. CHRISTIAN; 3 brs.

**Tyndall Bank International Ltd:** POB 62, Tyndall House, Kensington Rd, Douglas, IM99 1DZ; tel. (1624) 629201; telex 628732; fax (1624) 620200; Man. Dir D. ROBBIE.

**Ulster Bank (IOM) Ltd:** 45 Victoria St, Douglas; tel. (1624) 672211; telex 628797; fax (1624) 661276; f. 1979; Chair. T. N. WALSH; Man. D. J. MCCAULEY.

### 'Offshore' Banks

**Clydesdale Bank PLC:** POB 113, Victoria St, Douglas, IM86 1PX; tel. (1624) 672592; fax (1624) 663312; Man. R. I. MONTGOMERY.

**Coutts & Co (IOM) Ltd:** Coutts House, Summerhill Rd, Onchan, Douglas, IM3 1RB; tel. (1624) 632222; Man. M. LAMBE.

**The Derbyshire (Isle of Man) Ltd:** Celtic House, Victoria St, Douglas, IM99 1LR; tel. (1624) 663432; Man. Dir M. S. WALSH.

**First Trust Bank (IOM) Ltd:** 10 Finch Rd, Douglas, IM99 1SF; tel. (1624) 661567; Man. G. R. LEE.

**Jardine Fleming Bank (Isle of Man) Ltd:** 5 Mount Pleasant, Douglas, IM1 2PU; tel. (1624) 661880; Man. Dir N. W. S. OWEN.

**Jardine Fleming & Co Ltd:** as Jardine Fleming Bank Ltd.

**National Irish Bank Ltd:** POB 113, 49 Victoria St, Douglas, IM86 1PX; tel. (1624) 628314; Man. R. I. MONTGOMERY.

### Restricted Banks

**Britannia International Ltd:** 8 Victoria St, Douglas, IM99 1SD; tel. (1624) 628512; Man. Dir D. H. FULTON.

**Commercial and Development Bank Ltd:** POB 28, Lord St, Douglas, IM99 1BE; tel. (1624) 663300; fax (1624) 663359; Man. Dir R. G. DANIELSON.

**Irish Permanent (IOM) Ltd:** St James's Chambers, 64A Athol St, Douglas; tel. (1624) 676726; Man. Dir PHILIP MURRAY.

**Merrill Lynch Bank and Trust Co (Cayman) Ltd:** Atlantic House, Circular Rd, Douglas, IM1 1QW; tel. (1624) 688600; Man. N. ORDERS.

## INSURANCE

There were 154 authorized insurance companies in the Isle of Man in 1994, including:

**Albany International Assurance Ltd:** St Mary's, The Parade, Castletown, IM9 1RJ; tel. (1624) 823262.

**CMI Insurance Co Ltd:** Clerical Medical House, Victoria Rd, Douglas, IM99 1LT; tel. (1624) 625599.

**Eagle Star (International Life) Ltd:** Eagle Star House, 45–51 Athol St, Douglas, IM99 1PW; tel. (1624) 662266; telex 628775; fax (1624) 662038.

**Equity and Law International Life Assurance Co Ltd:** Victory House, Prospect Hill, Douglas, IM1 1QP; tel. (1624) 677877; fax (1624) 672700.

**Hansard International Ltd:** POB 192, Anglo International House, Bank Hill, North Quay, Douglas, IM99 1QL; tel. (1624) 688000; fax (1624) 625133.

**Isle of Man Assurance Ltd:** IOMA House, Prospect Hill, Douglas, IM99 1PU; tel. (1624) 624141; fax (1624) 622500; Man. Dir R. N. S. BIGLAND.

**Prudential Assurance Co Ltd:** 19–21 Circular Rd, Douglas; tel. (1624) 675393; fax (1624) 6626060.

**Royal Insurance Service Co (IOM) Ltd:** 19 Athol St, Douglas, IM99 1BF; tel. (1624) 673446; fax (1624) 663864; Man. DAVID STACEY.

**Royal Life Insurance International Ltd:** Royal Court, Castletown, IM9 1RA; tel. (1624) 821212; telex 627848; fax (1624) 824405; Man. Dir RODERICK HAIRE.

**Royal Skandia Life Assurance Ltd:** Skandia House, Finch Rd, Douglas, IM99 1NY; tel. (1624) 611611; telex 626111; fax (1624) 611715.

**Safe Assurance Ltd:** Scarab House, 15 St Georges St, Douglas, IM1 1AJ; tel. (1624) 663435; fax (1624) 663424.

**Scottish Provident International Life Assurance Ltd:** Clinch's House, Lord St, Douglas, IM1 4LN; tel. (1624) 677446; fax (1624) 677336; f. 1991; Dirs C. S. FAIRCLOUGH, P. L. TOWERS.

**Tower Insurance Co Ltd:** POB 27, Atlantic House, 4–8 Circular Rd, Douglas, IM99 1BF; tel. (1624) 673446; telex 627056; fax (1624) 663864; Dir DAVID STACEY.

### Insurance Association

**Insurance Authority:** S & F House, 12–14 Ridgeway St, Douglas, IM1 1EN; tel. (1624) 685695; fax (1624) 663346; Chief Exec. Dr W. J. HASTINGS.

## Trade and Industry

### Chamber of Commerce

**Isle of Man Chamber of Commerce:** 17 Drinkwater St, Douglas, IM1 1PP; tel. (1624) 674941; fax (1624) 663367; associated organizations are the Castletown Chamber of Trade and Commerce, Ramsey Chamber of Trade and Commerce, Peel Chamber of Trade and Tourism, Laxey Traders' Association, Onchan Traders' Association and Port Erin Traders' Association; 450 mems.

### Trade Unions

In 1991 the Trade Union Act was approved by Tynwald, providing for the registration of trade unions. Although trade unions had been active previously on the Isle of Man, they had not received legal recognition.

**Isle of Man Fisherman's Association Ltd:** Association Bldg, Station Place, Peel, IM5 1AT; tel. (1624) 842144; fax (1624) 844395.

**Manx Democratic Workers' Union:** 41 Peveril Rd, Willaston, Douglas, IM2 6JH; tel. (1624) 628634; f. 1986; Chair. JOHN CORRIS.

**Manx National Farmers' Union:** The Old School House, Cronkbourne Village, Tromode, IM4 4QH; tel. (1624) 674191.

**Transport and General Workers' Union:** 25 Fort St, Douglas, IM1 2LJ; tel. (1624) 621156; District Sec. J. B. MOFFATT.

**Unison Health Care:** 16 Patrick St, Peel, IM5 1BR; tel. and fax (1624) 843377.

## Transport

### RAILWAYS

**Isle of Man Railways:** Strathallan Crescent, Douglas, IM2 4NR; tel. (1624) 663366; fax (1624) 663637; 27 km (17 miles) of electric track; also 25 km (16 miles) of steam railway track, and Snaefell Mountain Railway (16½ km of electric track); Chief Exec. R. H. SMITH.

### ROADS

There are over 640 km (400 miles) of country roads, excluding streets and roads in the four towns; about one-half are main roads. Some roads form the course for the International TT races.

**Dept of Transport:** Sea Terminal, Douglas, IM1 2RF; tel. (1624) 686600; telex 629335; fax (1624) 686677; Chief Exec. N. R. COOIL.

**Isle of Man Transport:** Strathallan Crescent, Douglas, IM2 4NR; tel. (1624) 663366; fax (1624) 663637; operates local bus services; Chief Exec. R. H. SMITH.

### SHIPPING

**Isle of Man Steam Packet Co Ltd:** PO Box 5, Douglas, IM99 1AF; tel. (1624) 623344; telex 629414; fax (1624) 620233; f. 1830; daily services operate all the year round between Heysham and Douglas; during the summer there are frequent services between Douglas and Dublin, Douglas and Ardrossan, Douglas and Belfast, Douglas and Fleetwood and Douglas and Liverpool; Chair. JUAN KELLY; Man. Dir DAVID DIXON; fleet of 2 passenger/car ferries, 1 roll-on/roll-off passenger/freight ferry and 1 freight roll-on/roll-off vessel.

**Laxey Towing Co Ltd;** Unit 24, South Quay Industrial Estate, Douglas, IM1 5AT; tel. (1624) 623556; fax (1624) 611695; f. 1978; bulk carriers, towing services and salvage; Man. Dir. Capt. S. P. CARTER.

**Mezeron Ltd:** East Quay, Ramsey, IM8 1BG; tel. (1624) 812302; fax (1624) 815613; telex 629250; f. 1983; cargo services; Man. Dir N. A. LEECE.

**Ramsey Steamship Co Ltd:** 13 North Quay, Douglas, IM1 4LE; tel. (1624) 673557; telex 627279; fax (1624) 620460; f. 1913; cargo services; Sec. and Man. A. G. KENNISH.

### CIVIL AVIATION

**Island Aviation and Travel Ltd:** Ronaldsway Airport, Ballasalla, IM9 2AD; tel. (1624) 824300; fax (1624) 824946; provides special charter and executive aviation services, runs air-ambulance services.

**Jersey European Airways:** Ronaldsway Airport, Ballasalla, IM9 2AS; tel. (1624) 824354; daily services, operating all year round, to Blackpool and Belfast City airports.

**Manx Airlines Ltd:** Ronaldsway Airport, Ballasalla, IM9 2JE; tel. (1624) 826000; telex 629683; fax (1624) 826001; f. 1982 by British Midland Airways and Air UK; scheduled passenger and freight services throughout the UK and Ireland, and to Brussels and Paris; Chair. Sir MICHAEL BISHOP; Man. Dir T. R. P. LIDDIARD.

## Tourism

**Dept of Tourism and Leisure, Tourism Division:** Sea Terminal Buildings, Douglas, IM1 2RG; tel. (1624) 686801; fax (1624) 686800; responsibilities of tourist board, also operates modern and vintage transport systems, a Victorian theatre and an indoor and outdoor sport and leisure complex; f. 1896; CEO T. P. TOOHEY.

# THE CHANNEL ISLANDS

## Introduction

The Channel Islands lie off the north-west coast of France and are the only portions of the Duchy of Normandy now belonging to the Crown of England, to which they have been attached since 1106. They do not, however, form part of the United Kingdom. The islands have their own legislative assemblies and legal and administrative systems, their laws depending for their validity on Orders made by the Queen in Council. Her Majesty's Government in the United Kingdom is responsible for the defence and international relations of the islands, and the Crown is ultimately responsible for their good government.

Exports are protected by British tariff barriers. The citizens of the Channel Islands enjoy tax sovereignty and imports are free of British purchase tax. Income tax is low. Jersey and Guernsey, especially the former, are being developed as finance centres, and Jersey's commercial laws have encouraged the founding of several merchant banks, mainly subsidiaries of London banks, which benefit the economy, otherwise largely based on tourism and agriculture.

In addition to the British public holidays, the Channel Islands also celebrate 9 May (Liberation Day).

# JERSEY

Jersey, the largest of the Channel Islands, is situated to the south-east of Guernsey, from which it is separated by 27 km (17 miles) of sea. The official language of Jersey is English (since 1960), although French is still used in the courts. The state and civil flag is white with a red saltire and coat of arms bearing three yellow lions and surmounted by a yellow crown. The capital is St Helier.

## Statistical Survey

Source: States Greffe, States of Jersey; tel. (1534) 603000.

### AREA, POPULATION AND DENSITY
**Area:** 116.2 sq km (144.8 sq miles).
**Population** (estimate, 1993): 84,082.
**Density** (per sq km, 1993): 725.
**Births and Deaths** (1994): Live births 1,210; Deaths 841.

### AGRICULTURE
There are 66 sq km (25.5 sq miles) of land under cultivation and 0.5 sq km under glasshouses. The principal crops are potatoes, cauliflowers and tomatoes. Dairy and cattle farming are important activities.

### FINANCE
**Currency and Exchange Rates:** 100 pence = 1 pound sterling (£).
*Dollar Equivalents* (31 December 1994): £1 = US $1.5645; US $1 = 63.92 pence.
Note: United Kingdom coins and notes are also legal tender.
**Budget** (£ million, 1995, estimates): Revenue 407.8; Expenditure 378.3.

### EXTERNAL TRADE
**Exports** (£ '000, 1989): Agricultural products 34,444.

### TRANSPORT
**Road Traffic** (vehicles registered at December 1994): Auto cycles and scooters 1,169, Motor cycles 3,831, Private cars 58,491 (incl. taxis and hire cars), Buses and minibuses 53, Tractors 2,400, Vans 5,806, Lorries and trucks 3,303, Coaches 760, Others 960.
**Shipping** (1994): *Vessels using St Helier port:* Commercial vessel arrivals 4,730, Passenger arrivals 440,840.
**Civil Aviation** (1994): Aircraft movements 82,023, Total passengers carried 1,740,991.

## Directory

### The Constitution

The Lieutenant-Governor and Commander-in-Chief of Jersey is the personal representative of the Sovereign, the Commander of the Armed Forces of the Crown, and the channel of communication between the Crown and the Insular Government. He is appointed by the Crown, and is entitled to sit and speak in the Assembly of the States of Jersey, but not to vote. He has a veto on certain forms of legislation.

The Bailiff is appointed by the Crown, and is President both of the Assembly of the States (the insular legislature) and the Royal Court of Jersey. In the States, he has a right of dissent, and a casting vote.

The Deputy Bailiff is appointed by the Crown and, when authorized by the Bailiff to do so, he may discharge any function appertaining to the office of Bailiff.

The government of the island is conducted by Committees appointed by the States. The States consist of 12 Senators (elected for six years, six retiring every third year), 12 Constables (triennial), and 29 Deputies (triennial). They are elected by universal suffrage. The Dean of Jersey, the Attorney-General and Solicitor-General are appointed by the Crown and are entitled to sit and speak in the States, but not to vote. Permanent laws passed by the States require the sanction of Her Majesty in Council, but Triennial Regulations do not.

### The Government
(July 1995)

**Lieutenant-Governor and C-in-C Jersey:** Gen. Sir MICHAEL WILKES.
**Secretary to the Lieutenant-Governor and ADC:** Commdr D. M. L. BRAYBROOKE.
**Bailiff:** FRANCIS CHARLES HAMON.
**Deputy Bailiff:** PHILIP MARTIN BAILHACHE.
**Dean of Jersey:** Very Rev. JOHN SEAFORD.
**Attorney-General:** MICHAEL CAMERON ST JOHN BIRT.
**Solicitor-General:** STEPHANIE CLAIRE NICOLLE.
**Greffier of the States:** GEOFFREY HENRY CHARLES COPPOCK.

### Judicial System

Justice is administered in Jersey by the Royal Court, which consists of the Bailiff or Deputy Bailiff and 12 Jurats elected by an Electoral College. There is a court of Appeal which consists of the Bailiff (or Deputy Bailiff) and two Judges, selected from a panel appointed by the Crown. A final appeal lies to the Privy Council in certain cases.

A Stipendiary Magistrate deals with minor civil and criminal cases. He also acts as an Examining Magistrate in criminal matters.

### Religion

#### CHRISTIANITY
#### The Church of England

The Church of England is the established church. The Deanery of Jersey is an Ecclesiastical Peculiar, governed by its own canons, the Dean being the Ordinary of the Island; it is attached to the diocese of Winchester for episcopal purposes.

**Dean of Jersey:** Very Rev. JOHN SEAFORD, The Deanery, David Place, St Helier, JE2 4TE; tel. (1534) 20001; fax (1534) 617488.

#### The Roman Catholic Church

The diocese of Portsmouth includes the Channel Islands and part of southern England. The Episcopal Vicar for the Channel Islands resides at St Peter Port, Guernsey. In Jersey there are 12 Roman Catholic churches, including St Mary and St Peter's, Wellington Rd (English), and St Thomas, Val Plaisant, St Helier (French).

### Other Christian Churches

The Baptist, Congregational New Church, Methodist and Presbyterian churches are also represented.

## The Press

**Jersey Evening Post:** POB 582, JE4 8XQ; tel. (1534) 611611; fax (1534) 611622; f. 1890; independent; progressive; Editor C. BRIGHT; Man. Dir M. J. BISSON; circ. 24,053.

**Jersey Weekly Post:** POB 582, JE4 8XQ; tel. (1534) 611611; fax (1534) 611622; Thursday; Editor C. BRIGHT; circ. 1,800.

## Publishers

**Anson & Co Ltd:** 8 Vine St, Royal Square, St Helier, JE2 4WB; tel. (1534) 22572; fax (1534) 23439.

**Ashton & Denton Publishing Co (CI) Ltd:** 3 Burlington House, St Saviour's Rd, St Helier, JE2 4LA; tel. (1534) 35461; fax (1534) 75805; f. 1957; local history, holiday guides, financial; Man. Dir A. MACKENZIE.

**Neville Spearman (Jersey) Ltd:** Normandy House, POB 75, St Helier; occult, metaphysical, unorthodox; Dirs N. ARMSTRONG, M. J. ARMSTRONG.

## Radio and Television

Programmes are received from the British Broadcasting Corporation (BBC) and the Independent Television Commission in England, and also from France. A new local radio station, Channel 103 FM, began broadcasting in 1992.

**BBC:** Radio and Television (see Great Britain).

**BBC Radio Jersey:** Broadcasting House, Rouge Bouillon, St Helier; tel. (1534) 870000; fax (1534) 32569; f. 1982; broadcasts 40–45 hours a week; Station Man. ROBERT BUFTON; News Editor MIKE VIBERT.

**Independent Television Commission:** Television programmes are transmitted through the following company:

**Channel Television:** Television Centre, La Pouquelaye, St Helier, JE1 3ZD; tel. (1534) 68999; fax (1534) 59446; f. 1962; daily transmissions; Chair. Maj. J. R. RILEY; Man. Dir J. P. HENWOOD.

## Finance

(cap. = capital; auth. = authorized; m. = million; dep. = deposits; res = reserves; br./brs = branch(es).)

### BANKS

In 1993 total bank deposits in Jersey were £52,900m. in 71 financial institutions.

#### British Clearing Banks

The banks listed below are branches of British banks, and details concerning directors, capital, etc. of the parent bank will be found under the appropriate section in the pages dealing with Great Britain.

**Barclays Bank PLC:** POB 8, 13 Library Place, St Helier; tel. (1534) 878511; fax (1534) 58662; Jersey Man. M.SCRIVEN; 4 brs.

**Lloyds Bank PLC:** 11 Bath St, St Helier, JE4 8RB; tel. (1534) 284000; telex 888301; fax (1534) 284406; Island Dir D. J. WATKINS; 4 brs.

**Midland Bank PLC:** POB 14, 2 Hill St, St Helier; tel. (1534) 606606; telex 4192122; Man. J. C. TIBBO; 4 brs.

**National Westminster Bank PLC:** POB 11, 23 Broad St, St Helier; tel. (1534) 282828; fax (1534) 35315; Man. P. TAYLOR; 6 brs.

**Royal Bank of Scotland PLC:** POB 64, 71 Bath St, St Helier, JE4 8PJ; tel. (1534) 285200; telex 4192385; fax (1534) 285222; Regional Man. D. RIGBY.

#### Other Banks

**ABN AMRO Bank N.V.:** 8 Hill St, St Helier; tel. (1534) 66640; fax (1534) 59041; Man. A. H. A. GOLDBERG.

**ABN AMRO Trust Company (Jersey) Ltd:** 8 Hill St, St Helier; tel. (1534) 66640; telex 4192082; fax (1534) 35552; Man. Dir J. C. W. VAN BURG.

**AIB Bank (CI) Ltd:** POB 468, AIB House, Grenville St, St Helier; tel. (1534) 883000; fax (1534) 31245; f. 1981; cap. £2.5m., res £50m. (Dec. 1993); Man. Dir J. F. LYNES.

**Ansbacher (Jersey) Ltd:** 7–11 Britannia Place, Bath St, St Helier; tel. (1534) 504504; telex 4192190; fax (1534) 504575; f. 1984 as Westpac Banking Corpn (Jersey) Ltd; acquired by Henry Ansbacher Group 1995; Man. Dir R. D. ELLIS.

**ANZ Grindlays Bank (Jersey) Ltd:** POB 80, West House, Wests Centre, Peter St, St Helier; tel. (1534) 874248; telex 4192062; f. 1969; subsidiary of ANZ Grindlays Bank PLC, London; cap. and res £60m., dep. £850m.; Chair. B. R. LE MARQUAND; Man. Dir I. F. PETERKIN.

**Abbey National Treasury International Ltd:** Abbey National House, Ingouville Place, St Helier, JE4 8XG; tel. (1534) 58815; fax (1534) 21615; Man. P. DONNE DAVIS.

**BHF-Bank (Jersey) Ltd:** 6 West's Centre, St Helier; tel. (1534) 790448; fax (1534) 879246; cap. DM 7.5m., dep. 161.8m. (Dec. 1993).

**Bank of America (Jersey) Ltd:** POB 193, 11 Esplanade, St Helier; tel. (1534) 875471; fax (1534) 30062; Man. R. G. GAUTIER.

**Bank of India:** 37 New St, St Helier, JE2 3RA; tel. (1534) 873788; telex 4192107; fax (1534) 68640; Man. A. D. RAJMOHAN.

**Bank of Ireland (Jersey) Ltd:** POB 416, Don Rd, St Helier; tel. (1534) 23451; fax (1534) 37916; cap. £1.5m., res £14.6m. (March 1993); Man. M. T. GERAGHTY.

**Bank of Scotland:** Eagle House, 4 Don Rd, St Helier; tel. (1534) 38855.

**Bank of Scotland (Jersey) Ltd:** Eagle House, 4 Don Rd, St Helier; tel. (1534) 59399; fax (1534) 38633; Man. I. MENZIES.

**Bank of Wales (Jersey) Ltd:** 31 Broad St, St Helier, JE4 8NZ; tel. (1534) 873364; telex 4192101; fax (1534) 69038; cap. £1m., dep. £64.7m. (Feb. 1994); Man. A. K. HEWITT.

**Banque Bruxelles Lambert (Jersey) Ltd:** Huguenot House, 28 La Motte St, St Helier, JE2 4SZ; tel. (1534) 880888; telex 4192336; fax (1534) 873367; Man. K. MACKENZIE.

**Banque Nationale de Paris, SA:** POB 158, BNP House, Anley St, St Helier, JE4 8RD; tel. (1534) 66777; telex 4192352; Man. D. J. ORMSBY.

**Barclays Bank Finance Co (Jersey) Ltd:** POB 191, 29–31 Esplanade, St Helier, JE4 8RN; tel. (1534) 877990; telex 4192037; cap. and res £53m. (1994); Man. P. S. BUNTING.

**Barclays Private Bank and Trust Ltd:** POB 82, 39–41 Broad St, St Helier; tel. (1534) 873741; telex 4192066; fax (1534) 72737; Man. Dir W. KAY.

**Bilbao Vizcaya Bank (Jersey) Ltd:** 2 Mulcaster St, St Helier, JE2 3NJ; tel. (1534) 22600; telex 419042; fax (1534) 34649; cap. £6.5m., res £25.7m. (Dec. 1993); Man. M. LOPEZ.

**Cantrade Private Bank Switzerland (CI) Ltd:** POB 350, Cantrade House, 24 Union St, St Helier, JE4 8UJ; tel. and fax (1534) 611200; telex 4192127; f. 1979; subsidiary of Union Bank of Switzerland; cap. and res £30.5m. (Dec. 1994); Man. Dir J. G. BAERLOCHER.

**Cater Allen Bank (Jersey) Ltd:** 23 Commercial St, St Helier; tel. (1534) 877106; fax (1534) 38577; cap. £2m., res £5m., dep. £297.2m; Man. A. M. HAIRE.

**Chase Bank & Trust Co (CI) Ltd:** POB 127, Chase House, Grenville St, St Helier; tel. (1534) 626262; fax (1534) 626300; cap. US $3m., dep. US $3,101m. (Dec. 1993); Chair. T. TODMAN.

**Chase Manhattan Bank N.A.:** POB 127, Chase House, Grenville St, St Helier, JE4 8QH; tel. (1534) 626262; fax (1534) 626301; Man. Dir J. S. BUB.

**Citibank (Channel Islands) Ltd:** 38 The Esplanade, St Helier; tel. (1534) 608000; fax (1534) 608290; dep. US $748.2m. (Dec. 1993); Man. Dir RONALD MITCHELL.

**Citicorp Banking Corporation Jersey:** 38 The Esplanade, St Helier, JE4 8QB; tel. (1534) 608000; fax (1534) 608290; Man. RONALD MITCHELL.

**Coutts and Co (Jersey) Ltd:** POB 6, 23/25 Broad St, St Helier, JE4 8ND; tel. (1534) 282345; telex 4192077; fax (1534) 282400; Man. Dir G. B. H. TRIBE.

**Girobank PLC:** POB 106, Mont Millais, St Helier; tel. (1534) 26262; fax (1534) 873690; Man. M. BOLEAT.

**HSBC Private Bank (Jersey) Ltd:** POB 88, 1 Grenville St, St Helier, JE4 9PF; tel. (1534) 606500; telex 4192254; fax (1534) 606504; Exec. Dir P. N. POLES.

**Hambros Bank (Jersey) Ltd:** POB 78, 13 Broad St, St Helier; tel (1534) 878577; telex 4192241; fax (1534) 871913; f. 1967; subsidiary of Hambros Bank Ltd, London; cap. £29.9m., dep. £608.5m. (March 1993); Chair. C. E. HAMBRO; Man. Dir B. CURTIS.

**Hill Samuel Bank (Jersey) Ltd:** POB 63, 7 Bond St, St Helier; tel. (1534) 604604; fax (1534) 604608; f. 1961; merchant bank;

ultimate parent bank TSB; cap. and res £11.65m., dep. £330.23m. (Oct. 1994); Man. Dir E. Le Rossignol.

**Hyposwiss:** POB 492, 24 Union St, St Helier, JE4 8WX; tel. (1534) 611340; telex 4192099; fax (1534) 615073; investment banking.

**Kleinwort Benson (Jersey) Ltd:** POB 76, Kleinwort Benson House, Wests Centre, St Helier, JE4 8PQ; tel. (1534) 613000; telex 4192284; fax (1534) 878908; f. 1962; subsidiary of Kleinwort Benson Group PLC, London; cap. and res £23m., dep. £454.7m. (Dec. 1993); Man. Dir R. F. Robins.

**Lazard Brothers & Co, (Jersey) Ltd:** Lazard House, 2-6 Church St, St Helier, JE4 8QD; tel. (1534) 620620; telex 4192154; fax (1534) 620621; f. 1970; merchant bankers; subsidiary of Lazard Bros & Co, London; cap. issued £2m.; Chair. A. L. Blakesley; Man. Dir P. R. Williams.

**Lloyds Bank Finance (Jersey) Ltd:** 4 Bond St, St Helier; tel. (1534) 284100; telex 4192071; fax (1534) 284481; Man. John Mair.

**Lloyds Bank International (Jersey) Ltd:** Commercial House, Commercial St, St Helier; tel. (1534) 22271; fax (1534) 27380; Man. S. P. Harvey.

**Lombard Banking (Jersey) Ltd:** POB 554, 39 La Motte St, St Helier; tel. (1534) 27511; fax (1534) 38099; cap. £8m., res. £19.5m., dep. £573.4m.; Man. Dir C. Lee.

**Midland Bank International Finance Corporation Ltd:** POB 26, 28–34 Hill St, St Helier, JE4 8NR; tel. (1534) 606000; telex 4192098; fax (1534) 606016; cap. £1.3m., res. £50.9m. (Dec. 1993); Man. Dir P. G. Hickman.

**Morgan Grenfell (CI) Ltd:** POB 727, 12 Dumaresq St, St Helier; tel. (1534) 66711; telex 4192007; f. 1972; cap. £15m.; Chair. P. E. Smith; Man. Dir J. C. Boothman.

**Royal Bank of Canada (Jersey) Ltd:** 19–21 Broad St, St Helier; tel. (1534) 27441; fax (1534) 32513; cap. £3.5m., dep. £497.9m. (Aug. 1993); Man. M. J. Lagopoulos.

**Royal Bank of Scotland (Jersey) Ltd:** 71 Bath St, St Helier; tel. (1534) 285500; fax (1534) 285555; Man. P. Shirreffe.

**Standard Bank Investment Corporation (Jersey) Ltd:** POB 583, 1 Waverley Place, St Helier, JE4 8XR; tel. (1534) 67557; telex 4192105; fax (1534) 505949; f. 1977; fmrly Brown Shipley (Jersey); cap. and res £9.6m.; Chair. and Man. Dir D. J. Berkeley.

**Standard Chartered Bank (CI) Ltd:** POB 89, Conway St, St Helier; tel. (1534) 507000; telex 4192013; fax (1534) 507111; f. 1966; cap. £3.6m., res £26.4m., dep. £1,163.2m. (Dec. 1993); Chair. Sir Ronald Leach; Man. C. Dickinson.

**Swiss Bank Corporation (Jersey) Ltd:** 40 Esplanade, St Helier, JE4 8NW; tel. (1534) 506500; telex 4192288; fax (1534) 506501; merchant bank; Man. Dir Duncan Baxter.

**TSB Bank Channel Islands Ltd:** 25 New St, St Helier, JE4 8RG; tel. (1534) 503000; telex 4192164; fax (1534) 503047; total funds £1,192m. (Oct. 1994); Chief Exec. M. J. E. Chambers; 5 brs in Jersey, 4 brs in Guernsey, 1 br in Alderney.

**S. G. Warburg & Co (Jersey) Ltd:** Forum House, Grenville St, St Helier, JE4 8RL; tel. (1534) 600600; fax (1534) 600687; f. 1963 (present name from 1976); cap. £3m.; Man. D. Ferguson.

### INSURANCE

**Jersey Mutual Insurance Soc., Inc:** 74 Halkett Place, St Helier, JE1 1BT; tel. (1534) 34246; fax (1534) 33381; f. 1869; fire; Man. Dir J. E. Gready; Sec. R. H. Bayliss.

## Trade and Industry

**Chamber of Commerce:** 19 Royal Sq., St Helier, JE2 4WA; tel. (1534) 24536; fax (1534) 34942; f. 1768; Pres. P. J. B. Pitcher; Chief Exec. J. M. Snell; 700 mems.

## Transport

### SHIPPING

The harbour of St Helier has 1,400 m of cargo working quays, with 10 berths in dredged portion (2.29 m) and eight drying berths. Range of tide 2.7 m–12.2 m. Unloading facilities include 14 electric cranes of 3 to 30 tons, two Scotch Derricks of 32 tons and 35 tons and two 15-ton mobile cranes.

**British Channel Island Ferries:** Terminal Bldg, Elizabeth Harbour, St Helier; tel. (1534) 38300; fax (1534) 58722; a daily passenger service is run between Jersey and Poole from April to November; freight services between Jersey and Poole throughout the year; Man. I. Taylor.

**Condor Jersey Ltd:** POB 25, Elizabeth Terminal and Albert Quay, St Helier; tel. (1534) 607080; fax (1534) 280767; head office in Guernsey.

### CIVIL AVIATION

The States of Jersey Airport is at St Peter, Jersey. The following airlines serve Jersey: Aer Lingus, Air UK, Aurigny Air Services, British Airways, British Midland, British Caledonian, Brymon Airways, Jersey European Airways (see below).

#### Airline

**Jersey European Airways:** States Airport, St Peter; tel. (1534) 45661; telex 4192166; f. 1983; services between Jersey and Guernsey, London, Exeter, Blackpool, Bristol, Leeds/Bradford, Birmingham, the Isle of Man, Belfast and Dinard.

## Tourism

In 1993 a total of 683,700 tourists stayed in Jersey (compared with 701,000 in 1992). Tourist expenditure was £243m. in 1992.

**Jersey Tourism Committee:** Liberation Square, St Helier, JE1 1BB; tel. (1534) 500700; fax (1534) 500899; Pres. Richard Joseph Shenton; CEO Sheila Henwood.

# GUERNSEY

The civil flag of Guernsey is white, bearing a red cross of St George, with a yellow couped cross superimposed on the cross. The capital is St Peter Port. English is the language in common use, but the Norman *patois* may be heard in the rural parishes. Dependencies of Guernsey are Alderney, Brechou, Great Sark, Little Sark, Herm, Jethou and Lihou.

## Statistical Survey

(including Herm and Jethou)

Source: Office of the Lieutenant-Governor, Guernsey; tel. (1481) 726666.

### AREA, POPULATION AND DENSITY

**Area:** 65 sq km (25.1 sq miles).
**Population** (census, 1991): 58,867 (males 28,297; females 30,570).
**Density** (per sq km, 1991): 905.6.
**Births and Deaths** (1994): Live births 695; Deaths 592.

### AGRICULTURE

The principal crops are tomatoes and flowers, much of which is grown under glass. About 21.6 km (8.4 sq miles) are cultivated.

### FINANCE

**Currency and Exchange Rates:** 100 pence = 1 pound sterling (£). *Coins:* 1, 2, 5, 10, 20 and 50 pence; £1 and £2. *Notes:* £1, £5, £10 and £20. *Dollar Equivalents* (31 December 1994): £1 = US $1.5645; US $1 = 63.92 pence.

Note: United Kingdom coins and notes are also legal tender.

**Budget** (£ '000, 1993): *Revenue:* General revenue income (including Alderney): 158,659; *Expenditure:* General revenue expenditure (including Alderney): 148,953.

### EXTERNAL TRADE

**Principal Commodities:** *Imports* (1993): Coal 19,502 metric tons, Petrol and oil 152,223,000 litres. *Exports* (1993, £ million): Light industry 40, Total flowers 25, Total vegetables 5.

### TRANSPORT

**Road Traffic** (vehicles registered, 1994): Cars 33,037, Motorcycles 3,013, Commercial vehicles 7,522.

**Shipping** (1994): Passenger arrivals 326,048.

**Civil Aviation** (1994): Passenger arrivals 790,592.

# Directory

## The Constitution

The Lieutenant-Governor and Commander-in-Chief of Guernsey is the personal representative of the Sovereign and the channel of communication between the Crown and the Insular Government. He is appointed by the Crown. He is entitled to sit and speak in the Assembly of the States, but not to vote.

The Bailiff is appointed by the Crown and is President both of the Assembly of the States (the insular legislature) and of the Royal Court of Guernsey and has a casting vote.

The government of the island is conducted by committees appointed by the States.

The States of Deliberation is composed of the following members:

(a) The Bailiff, who is President ex-officio.

(b) The 12 Conseillers elected by popular franchise.

(c) HM Procureur (Attorney-General) and HM Comptroller (Solicitor-General) Law Officers of the Crown, who are appointed by the Crown. They are entitled to sit in the States and to speak, but not to vote.

(d) The 33 People's Deputies elected by popular franchise.

(e) The 10 Douzaine Representatives elected by their respective Parochial Douzaines.

(f) The two Alderney Representatives elected by the States of Alderney.

Projets de Loi (Permanent Laws) require the sanction of Her Majesty in Council.

The function of the States of Election is to elect persons to the offices of Jurat and Conseiller. It is composed of the following members:

(a) The Bailiff (President ex-officio).

(b) The 12 Jurats or 'Jures-Justiciers'.

(c) The 12 Conseillers.

(d) The 10 Rectors of the Parishes.

(e) HM Procureur and HM Comptroller.

(f) The 33 People's Deputies.

(g) The 34 Douzaine Representatives.

Meetings of the States and of the Royal Court, formerly conducted in French, are now conducted in English, but the proceedings in both are begun and ended in French.

## The Government

(June 1995)

**Lieutenant-Governor and Commander-in-Chief of the Bailiwick of Guernsey:** Vice-Admiral Sir JOHN COWARD.

**Secretary and ADC to the Lieutenant-Governor:** Capt. D. P. L. HODGETTS.

**Bailiff of Guernsey:** Sir GRAHAM DOREY.

**Deputy Bailiff:** DE VIC G. CAREY.

**HM Procureur (Attorney-General):** A. CHRISTOPHER K. DAY.

**HM Comptroller (Solicitor-General):** GEOFFREY R. ROWLAND.

**States Supervisor:** M. BROWN.

## Judicial System

Justice is administered in Guernsey by the Royal Court, which consists of the Bailiff and the 12 Jurats. The Royal Court also deals with a wide variety of non-contentious matters. A Stipendiary Magistrate deals with minor civil and criminal cases. The Guernsey Court of Appeal deals with appeals from the Royal Court.

## Religion

### CHRISTIANITY

#### The Church of England

The Church of England in Guernsey is the established church. The Deanery includes the islands of Alderney, Sark, Herm and Jethou; it forms part of the diocese of Winchester.

**Dean of Guernsey:** Very Rev. JEFFERY FENWICK (until Oct. 1995), The Deanery, St Peter Port, GY1 1BZ; tel. (1481) 720036.

#### The Roman Catholic Church

The diocese of Portsmouth includes the Channel Islands and part of southern England. In Guernsey there are five Roman Catholic churches, of which the senior is St Joseph and St Mary, Cordier Hill, St Peter Port.

**Catholic Dean of Guernsey:** Canon GERARD HETHERINGTON, St Peter Port; tel. (1481) 720196.

#### Other Christian Churches

The Presbyterian Church and the Church of Scotland are represented by St Andrew's Church, The Grange, St Peter Port. The Baptist, Congregational, Elim and Methodist Churches are also represented in the island.

## The Press

**Guernsey Evening Press and Star:** The Guernsey Press Co, POB 57, Braye Rd, Vale; tel. (1481) 45866; fax (1481) 48972; f. 1897; independent; Editor G. INGROUILLE; circ. 15,840.

**Guernsey Weekly Press:** The Guernsey Press Co, POB 57, Braye Rd, Vale; tel. (1481) 45866; fax (1481) 48972; f. 1902; independent; Thursday; Editor G. INGROUILLE.

## Publisher

**Toucan Press:** Saravia, rue des Monts, St Sampson; tel. (1481) 722434; f. 1850; archaeology, history, Thomas Hardy, Channel Islands; Man. Dir G. STEVENS COX.

## Radio and Television

Programmes are received from the British Broadcasting Corporation (BBC) and the Independent Television Commission in England, and also from France.

### RADIO

**BBC Radio Guernsey:** Commerce House, St Peter Port; tel. (1481) 728977; fax (1481) 713557; f. 1982; Man. BOB LLOYD-SMITH.

**Island FM:** 12, Westerbrook, St Sampson's; tel. (1481) 42000; fax (1481) 49676.

### TELEVISION

**Channel Television:** Television Centre, St George's Place, St Peter Port; tel. (1481) 723451; fax (1481) 710739; Man. ROGER BOWNS. (See also under Jersey).

## Finance

(cap.=capital; dep.=deposits; res=reserves; br./brs=branch(es).

### BANKS

In 1993 total bank deposits in Guernsey were £37,482m. in 75 financial institutions.

**Director-General of Banking:** JOHN ROPER.

**Guernsey Financial Services Commission:** Valley House, Hirzel St, St Peter Port; regulates financial and insurance activities.

#### British Clearing Banks

**Barclays Bank PLC:** POB 41, 6–8 High St, St Peter Port; tel. (1481) 723176; telex 4191671; Man. K. GREGSON; 4 brs.

**Lloyds Bank PLC:** Smith St, St Peter Port; tel. (1481) 725131; telex 4191454; fax (1481) 712427; Island Dir A. FORD; also The Bridge, St Sampsons; sub-brs. at St Martin's and Alderney.

**Midland Bank PLC:** POB 31, St Peter Port; tel. (1481) 717717; telex 4191617; Man. G. J. DAVIES; 5 brs.

**National Westminster Bank PLC:** 35 High St, St Peter Port; tel. (1481) 726851; Chief Man. P. MARCHANT.

#### Other Banks

**ANZ Bank (Guernsey) Ltd:** POB 153, St Peter Port; tel. (1481) 726771; telex 4191663; fax (1481) 727851; f. 1973; cap. £1m., res £8.8m. (Sept. 1993); Man. Dir B. J. HUMAN.

**Bank Julius Baer (Guernsey) Ltd:** POB 87, Frances House, Sir William Place, St Peter Port; tel. (1481) 726618; telex 4191129; fax (1481) 728813.

**Bank of Bermuda (Guernsey) Ltd:** POB 208, Bermuda House, St Julian's Ave, St Peter Port, GY1 3NF; tel. (1481) 707000; telex 4191502; fax (1481) 726987; f. 1973; cap. £10m., res £4.8m. (June 1993); Man. Dir JAMES D. MCCULLOCH.

**Banque Belge (Guernsey) Ltd:** POB 125, Banque Belge House, St Julian's Avenue, St Peter Port; tel. (1481) 726614; telex 4191188; fax (1481) 711553; f. 1984; cap. £2.1m., res £9.4m. (Dec. 1993); Dir and Gen. Man. ROGER S. BAILEY.

# UK CROWN DEPENDENCIES (CHANNEL ISLANDS) — Guernsey

**Banque Paribas Suisse (Guernsey) Ltd:** POB 224, La Plaiderie House, St Peter Port; tel. (1481) 712171; telex 4191403; fax (1481) 712172; f. 1987.

**Barclays Finance Co (Guernsey) Ltd:** POB 269, Cambria House, New St, St Peter Port; tel. (1481) 723223; telex 4191629; Man. Dir W. ALLAN.

**Barclays Private Bank and Trust Ltd:** POB 184, Barclaytrust House, Les Echelons, South Esplanade, St Peter Port; tel. (1481) 724706; fax (1481) 728376; Chief Man. S. K. OLIPHANT.

**Baring Brothers (Guernsey) Ltd:** POB 71, Arnold House, St Julian's Ave, St Peter Port; tel. (1481) 726541; telex 4191606; fax (1481) 720132; cap. £25.6m., dep. £528.3m. (Dec. 1994); Chair. P. P. WALSH; Man. Dir T. K. ENGLISH.

**CIBC Bank and Trust Co (CI) Ltd:** CIBC House, rue du Pré, St Peter Port; tel. (1481) 710151; telex 4191594; fax (1481) 711670; subsidiary of Canadian Imperial Bank of Commerce; Man. Dir KEITH S. BETTS.

**Chemical Bank (Guernsey) Ltd:** Albert House, South Esplanade, St Peter Port; tel. (1481) 723961; telex 4191415; fax (1481) 726734; fmrly Manufacturers Hanover Bank (Guernsey) Ltd, merged with Chemical Bank and Howard de Walden Ltd June 1992; cap. US $2m., res $19.1m. (Dec. 1993); Dir RICHARD B. DE LA RUE.

**Coutts and Co (Guernsey) Ltd:** POB 16, 35 High St, St Peter Port; tel. (1481) 726101; telex 4191608; fax (1481) 728272.

**Crédit Suisse (Guernsey) Ltd:** POB 368, Helvetia Court, South Esplanade, St Peter Port; tel. (1481) 719000; fax (1481) 724676; f. 1986; cap. £3m., res £19.6m. (Dec. 1993); Man. Dir ROLAND HURNI-GOSMAN.

**Guinness Mahon (Guernsey) Ltd:** POB 188, La Vieille Cour, St Peter Port; tel. (1481) 723506; telex 4191482; fax (1481) 720844; f. 1977; wholly-owned subsidiary of Guinness Mahon & Co Ltd, London; cap. £2m., res £3.6m. (Dec. 1994); Chair. P. M. HILL; Man. Dir C. P. GOODWIN.

**Hambros Bank (Guernsey) Ltd:** POB 6, Hambro House, St Julian's Ave, St Peter Port; tel. (1481) 726521; telex 4191110; f. 1967 (present name from 1978); merchant bankers; wholly-owned subsidiary of Hambros Bank Ltd; called-up share capital £2.5m., dep. £441.9m. (March 1994); Chair. C. E. HAMBRO; Man. Dir R. A. OLLIVER.

**Hanson Bank Ltd:** POB 252, Hirzel House, Smith St, St Peter Port; tel. (1481) 723055; telex 4191426; fax (1481) 715910; f. 1975; cap. £1m., dep. £70m.; Chair. L. A. MOSS; Sec. R. K. PLEASANT; 1 br.

**International Bank and Trust Co (Guernsey) Ltd:** POB 79, La Plaiderie House, St Peter Port; tel. (1481) 726421; telex 4191524; f. 1971; merchant bankers; cap. £4m., res £4.8m. (Sept. 1993); wholly-owned subsidiary of Henry Ansbacher & Co Ltd, London; Chair. J. M. BUTTON; Man. Dir L. C. MORGAN.

**Italian International Bank (Channel Islands) Ltd:** St Julian's Court, St Julian's Ave, St Peter Port; tel. (1481) 723776; telex 4191529; fax (1481) 712345; f. 1973; cap. £1m., res £5.1m. (Dec. 1993); Man. Dir A. P. WILLS; Banking Man. C. N. MANNING.

**Leopold Joseph & Sons (Guernsey) Ltd:** POB 244, Albert House, South Esplanade, St Peter Port; tel. (1481) 712771; telex 4191505; fax (1481) 727025; f. 1972; private bankers; wholly-owned indirect subsidiary of Leopold Joseph & Sons Ltd, London; cap. and res £7.3m., dep. £127m. (March 1995); Chair. and Chief Exec. T. HENDERSON; Dirs A. W. GUILLE, C. J. WAKEFIELD.

**Kleinwort Benson (Guernsey) Ltd:** POB 44, The Grange, St Peter Port; tel. (1481) 727111; telex 4191316; fax (1481) 728317; f. 1963; merchant bankers; cap. £1m. (Dec. 1992), dep. £450.6m. (Dec. 1994); Chair. D. HINSHAW.

**Lazard Bros & Co (Guernsey) Ltd:** POB 275, Lazard House, 1 St Julian's Ave, St. Peter Port; tel. (1481) 710461; telex 4191643; fax (1481) 726709; f. 1984; merchant bankers; subsidiary of Lazard Bros & Co Ltd, London; cap. £2m., res £7.8m. (Dec. 1993); Man. Dir R. E. ALCOCK.

**Lloyds Bank International (Guernsey) Ltd:** POB 136, Sarnia House, Le Truchot, St Peter Port; tel. (1481) 726761; telex 4191514; fax (1481) 727416; cap. £2m., res £24.2m. (Dec. 1993); Man. Dir D. S. COPPERWAITE.

**Mees-Pierson (CI) Ltd:** POB 253, Bordage House, Le Bordage, St Peter Port; tel. (1481) 708708; telex 4191164; cap. £1m.

**Midland Bank Trustee (Guernsey) Ltd:** POB 156, 22 Smith St, St Peter Port; tel. (1481) 717717; telex 4191586; f. 1968 (fmrly Midland Bank Trust Corpn (Guernsey) Ltd, present name 1994); wholly-owned subsidiary of HSBC Private Banking (CI) (CI); cap. £350,000; Chair. T. O'BRIEN; Man. Dir G. MORRISSEY.

**National Westminster Bank Finance (CI) Ltd:** POB 272, National Westminster House, Le Truchot, St Peter Port; tel. (1481) 726486; Man. C. J. C. WHALLEY.

**Rea Bros (Guernsey) Ltd:** POB 116, Commerce House, Les Banques, St Peter Port; tel. (1481) 726014; telex 4191388; fax (1481) 727645; f. 1965; subsidiary of Rea Bros Ltd, London; cap. £1m., dep. £151.6m. (Dec. 1993); Gen. Man. K. M. PRATT.

**Republic National Bank of New York (Guernsey) Ltd:** rue du Pré, St Peter Port; tel. (1481) 710901; fax (1481) 711824; cap. US $21.6m., res $161.9m. (Dec. 1993); Chair. ANDREW PUCHER.

**N. M. Rothschild & Sons (CI) Ltd:** POB 58, St Julian's Court, St Julian's Ave, St Peter Port; tel. (1481) 713713; telex 4191507; fax (1481) 727705; f. 1967; subsidiary of N. M. Rothschild & Sons Ltd, London; cap. £5m., dep. £818m. (March 1994); Chair. DAVID SULLIVAN; Man. Dir CHARLES TRACY.

**Royal Bank of Canada (Channel Islands) Ltd:** POB 48, Canada Court, St Peter Port; tel. (1481) 723021; telex 4191527; fax (1481) 723524; f. 1973; wholly-owned subsidiary of Royal Bank of Canada; cap. £5m., res £28.6m. (Oct. 1993); Chair. A. A. WEBB; Man. Dir T. J. BETLEY.

**Royal Bank of Scotland (Guernsey) Ltd:** St Andrews House, Le Bordage, St Peter Port; tel. (1481) 710051; fax (1481) 728628; cap. £2m., res £13.7m., dep. £412.3m. (Sept. 1993); Chair. C. G. PEARSON.

### INSURANCE

There were 204 insurance companies with offices in Guernsey in 1992.

**Britannic Assurance PLC:** 7 Berthelot St, St Peter Port, GY1 1JS; tel. (1481) 720907.

**Commercial Union Assurance:** 10 Lefebvre St, St Peter Port, GY1 2PE; tel. (1481) 723308.

**Eagle Star Life Assurance Co Ltd:** POB 155, Valley House, Hirzel St, St Peter Port; tel. (1481) 726277; fax (1481) 712697.

**Eagle Star Trust Co (Guernsey) Ltd:** POB 155, Block F, Hirzel Court, St Peter Port, GY1 4ET; tel. (1481) 726277; fax (1481) 726196.

**General Accident Fire & Life Assurance Corpn Ltd:** St Julian's Ave, St Peter Port; tel. (1481) 724224.

**Insurance Corpn of the Channel Islands Ltd:** POB 160, Dixcart House, Sir William Place, St Peters Port; tel. (1481) 713322; telex 4191497; subsidiary of Royal Insurance (UK) Ltd.

**The Islands' Insurance Co Ltd:** Invicta House, Candie Rd, St Peter Port; tel. (1481) 710731.

**Norwich Union Insurance Group:** Hirzel Court, St Peter Port; tel. (1481) 724864.

**Pearl Assurance Co Ltd:** 23 The Pollet, St Peter Port; tel. (1481) 720612.

**Polygon Insurance Co Ltd:** POB 225, Helvetia Court, Les Echelons, St Peter Port; tel. (1481) 716000; telex 4191521; fax (1481) 728452.

**Prudential Assurance Co Ltd:** La Tonnelle House, Les Banques, St Sampsons; tel. (1481) 721953; fax (1481) 713003.

**Refuge Assurance PLC:** Palma, Green Lane, St Peter Port; tel. (1481) 722466.

**Royal Liver Friendly Society:** The Albany, South Esplanade, St Peter Port; tel. (1481) 720459.

**Royal London Mutual Insurance Society:** 21 Saumarez Street, St Peter Port; tel. (1481) 723194.

**Sun Alliance & London Insurance Group:** Hirzel Court, St Peter Port; tel. (1481) 723984; fax (1481) 729217.

**Sun Alliance International Life Assurance Co Ltd:** POB 77, Phoenix House, New St, St Peter Port; tel. (1481) 714108; telex 4191174; fax (1481) 712424.

**United Friendly Insurance Co Ltd:** Block A5, Hirzel Court, St Peter Port, tel. (1481) 723858.

## Trade and Industry

**Guernsey Chamber of Commerce:** States Arcade, Market St, St Peter Port; tel. (1481) 727483; fax (1481) 710755; f. 1808; Pres. R. MAHY.

## Transport

### SHIPPING

**Commodore Ferries Ltd:** POB 10, Commodore House, Bulwer Ave, St Sampsons; tel. (1481) 46841; fax (1481) 49543; regular ro-ro freight services between Portsmouth, Guernsey, Jersey and St Malo; Man. Dir J. VIDAMOUR.

**Condor Ltd:** New Jetty, White Rock, St Peter Port; tel. (1481) 726121; fax (1481) 712555; f. 1964; regular passenger service operating between the Channel Islands and St Malo, and between the Channel Islands and Weymouth; Man. Dir D. P. NORMAN.

UK CROWN DEPENDENCIES (CHANNEL ISLANDS)

### CIVIL AVIATION

**Aurigny Air Services:** Grande Rue, St Martins; tel. (1481) 35311; telex 4191156; fax (1481) 37041; f. 1968; services from Guernsey to Alderney, Jersey, Southampton, Cherbourg, Dinard.

Guernsey is also served by the following airlines: Air UK, British Midland, Brymon Airways, Jersey European Airways, Loganair, NLM City Hopper.

## Tourism

A total of 363,000 tourists visited Guernsey during 1993.

**Guernsey Tourist Board:** POB 23, St Peter Port; tel. (1481) 726611; fax (1481) 721246; Dir of Tourism C. D. BROCK.

# ISLANDS OF THE BAILIWICK OF GUERNSEY

## Alderney

The area of Alderney is 7.9 sq km (3.1 sq miles) and in 1985 the population was about 2,000. The principal town is St Anne's.

The President is the civic head of Alderney and has precedence on the island over all persons except the Lieutenant-Governor of Guernsey, and the Bailiff of Guernsey or his representative. He presides over meetings of the States of Alderney, which are responsible for the administration of the Island with the exception of police, public health and education, which are administered by the States of Guernsey. The States consist of 12 members who, with the President, hold office for three years and are elected by universal suffrage of residents.

**President of the States:** G. BARON.
**Clerk of the States:** D. V. JENKINS.
**Clerk of the Court:** A. JOHNSON.

### PUBLISHER

**Ampersand Press (CI) Ltd:** 39 Victoria St; tel. (1481) 823462.

### BANKS

**Lloyds Bank PLC:** Victoria St; tel. (1481) 822136; fax (1481) 822702.
**Midland Bank PLC:** Victoria St; tel. (1481) 822293; Man. J. P. LEE.
**National Westminster Bank PLC:** 13 Victoria St; tel. (1481) 822681.
**TSB Channel Islands Ltd:** 17 Victoria St; tel. (1481) 822340.

### TRANSPORT

**Alderney Shipping Co Ltd:** White Rock, Guernsey; tel. (1481) 724810; telex 4191549; fax (1481) 712081.
**Alderney Railway:** POB 75, Alderney; Gen. Man. B. C. NIGHTINGALE.
**Aurigny Air Services:** Alderney; tel. (1481) 822804; fax (1481) 823670; f. 1968; services to Guernsey, Jersey, Southampton, Bournemouth, Dinard and Cherbourg; Customer Services Dir M. McCORMICK.

## Sark

The area of the island is 5.5 sq km (2.1 sq miles) and in 1984 the population was 420.

The Seigneur of Sark is the hereditary civic head of the island and thereby entitled to certain privileges. The Seigneur is a member of the Chief Pleas of Sark, the island's parliament, and has a suspensory veto on its ordinances. The Seigneur has the right, subject to the approval of the Lieutenant-Governor of Guernsey, to appoint the Seneschal of Sark, who is President of the Chief Pleas and Chairman of the Seneschal's Court, which is the local Court of Justice.

**Seigneur of Sark:** J. M. BEAUMONT.
**Seneschal:** L. P. DE CARTERET.
**Greffier:** J. P. HAMON.
**Sark Committee Office:** rue Lucas; tel. (1481) 832118.

### BANKS

**Midland Bank PLC:** rue Lucas; tel. (1481) 832080; Man. J. P. LEE.
**National Westminster Bank PLC:** tel. (1481) 832090.

### TRANSPORT

No motor vehicles are permitted apart from a small number of tractors. In summer a daily boat service runs between Guernsey and Sark, and in winter a limited service is provided. There are two harbours on the island.

**Isle of Sark Shipping Co Ltd:** The White Rock, St Peter Port, Guernsey; tel. (1481) 724059; telex 4191549; fax (1481) 712081; operates daily services to and from Sark via Guernsey.

### TOURISM

**Sark Tourism:** Information Centre; tel. (1481) 832345; fax (1481) 832483.

## Herm

Herm is leased by the States of Guernsey to a tenant who is obliged by contract to carry out some of the day-to-day administration of Herm on behalf of the States. The island has an area of 2.0 sq km (0.8 sq miles).

**Tenant:** Major A. G. WOOD.
**Herm Island Administration Office:** tel. (Herm) 22377.

### TRANSPORT

There are daily boat services between Guernsey and Herm, provided by the following companies:

**Herm Ferry Launches:** Picquet House, St Peter Port, Guernsey; tel. (1481) 34678.
**Trident Charter Co:** Weighbridge, St Peter Port, Guernsey; tel. (1481) 21379.

## Jethou

Jethou has an area of 0.2 sq km (0.07 sq mile) and is leased by the Crown to a tenant who has no official functions.

## Brechou and Lihou

Brechou (measuring 1.2 km by 0.5 km) and Lihou (area 0.2 sq km) are leased by the Crown.

# BRITISH DEPENDENT TERRITORIES

## ANGUILLA

### Introductory Survey

**Location, Climate, Language, Religion, Flag, Capital**

Anguilla, a coralline island, is the most northerly of the Leeward Islands, lying 113 km (70 miles) to the north-west of Saint Christopher (St Kitts) and 8 km (5 miles) to the north of St Maarten/St Martin. Also included in the Territory are the island of Sombrero, 48 km (30 miles) north of Anguilla, and several other uninhabited small islands. The climate is sub-tropical, the heat and humidity being tempered by the trade winds. Temperatures average 27°C (80°F) and mean annual rainfall is 914 mm (36 ins). English is the official language. Many Christian churches are represented, the principal denominations being the Anglican and Methodist Churches. The flag (proportions 5 by 3 on land, 2 by 1 at sea) has a dark blue field with the Union flag in the upper hoist corner and, in the centre of the fly, a white shield bearing three orange circling dolphins above a light blue base. The capital is The Valley.

**Recent History**

Anguilla, previously inhabited by Arawaks and Caribs, was a British colony from 1650 until 1967. From 1825 the island became increasingly associated with Saint Christopher (St Kitts) for administrative purposes (also see chapter on Saint Christopher and Nevis). The inhabitants of Anguilla petitioned for separate status in 1875 and 1958. In February 1967, however, St Christopher-Nevis-Anguilla assumed the status of a State in Association with the United Kingdom, as did four other former British colonies in the Eastern Caribbean. These Associated States became independent internally, while the British Government retained responsibility for external affairs and defence.

In May 1967 the Anguillans, under the leadership of Ronald Webster, a local businessman and head of the only political party, the People's Progressive Party (PPP), repudiated government from Saint Christopher. After attempts to repair the breach between Saint Christopher and Anguilla had failed, British security forces were landed in Anguilla in March 1969 to install a British Commissioner. Members of London's Metropolitan Police Force remained on the island until the Anguilla Police Force was established in 1972. In July 1971 the British Parliament approved the Anguilla Act, one clause of which provided that, should Saint Christopher-Nevis-Anguilla decide to end its associated status, Anguilla could be separated from the other islands. In August the British Government's Anguilla Administration Order 1971 determined that the British Commissioner would continue to be responsible for the direct administration of the island, with the co-operation of a local elected council. The terms of this Order were superseded by the introduction of a new Constitution in February 1976. Anguilla formally separated from Saint Christopher-Nevis-Anguilla on 19 December 1980, assuming the status of British Dependent Territory. In accordance with the terms of the British Government's Anguilla Constitution Order of 1982, a new Constitution came into operation in Anguilla on 1 April 1982.

Elections to the legislature were held in March 1976, and Webster was appointed Chief Minister. In February 1977, following his defeat on a motion of confidence, he was replaced by Emile Gumbs as Chief Minister and as leader of the PPP (renamed the Anguilla National Alliance—ANA—in 1980). Webster was returned to power, at the head of the recently-formed Anguilla United Party (AUP), at a general election in May 1980. The dismissal of the Minister of Agriculture in May 1981 led to serious divisions within the Government, and the resignation in sympathy of another minister precipitated the collapse of Webster's administration. Webster subsequently formed a new political party, the Anguilla People's Party (APP), which won five of the seven seats in a general election in June. An early general election in March 1984 resulted in a conclusive defeat for the APP, including the loss of Webster's own seat. Gumbs became Chief Minister, and pursued a policy of revitalizing the island's economy, mainly through tourism and attracting foreign investment. Webster resigned from the leadership of the APP, which was renamed the Anguilla Democratic Party (ADP).

The majority of the population expressed no desire for independence, but the new Government appealed for wider powers for the Executive Council, and for more aid and investment from the United Kingdom in the island's economy and infrastructure. In October 1985 the Governor appointed a committee to review the Constitution, in response to an earlier unanimous request from the House of Assembly for modifications in the island's Constitution, particularly concerning the status of women and of persons born overseas of Anguillan parents. The amendments, which provided for the appointment of a Deputy Governor and designated international financial affairs (the 'offshore' banking sector) as the Governor's responsibility, came into effect in May 1990. Alan Hoole, a former Attorney-General, was subsequently appointed Deputy Governor.

Gumbs remained Chief Minister following a general election in February 1989. The ANA won only three seats in the House of Assembly but was supported by the independent member, Osbourne Fleming, who retained his cabinet portfolio. The ADP secured one seat and the revived AUP won two, although Webster, who had reassumed the leadership of the party, failed to be elected.

In May 1991 the British Government abolished capital punishment for the crime of murder in Anguilla (as well as in several other British Dependent Territories). The announcement by the Governor in late 1991 that a number of professionals from overseas were to be appointed to help in the management of the island's administration provoked widespread criticism, both from Anguillans resident in the Territory and from those abroad. In August 1992 Alan Shave assumed office as Governor of Anguilla (replacing Brian Canty).

A general election in March 1994 failed to produce a clear majority for any one party, and a coalition was subsequently formed by the ADP and the AUP, which had each won two seats and, respectively, secured 31.2% and 11.4% of total votes cast. The ANA, under the leadership of Eric Reid, won two seats with 35.7% of the vote, while the remaining seat was secured by Fleming. A newly-formed party, Anguillans for Good Government (whose candidates included Webster), failed to win any seats, despite attaining 11.6% of total votes cast. The AUP leader, Hubert Hughes, was subsequently appointed Chief Minister, replacing Sir Emile Gumbs (as he had become).

In one of his first public interviews in his capacity as Chief Minister in May 1994, Hughes expressed dissatisfaction with the British Government, which, he claimed, had ceased to fund development projects on the island, and he stated that he might seek Anguilla's independence from the United Kingdom, possibly by placing the island under UN administration. The appointment of one of the nominated members of the House of Assembly in that month led to a dispute between the Governor and Hughes: the latter strongly disapproved of the nomination of David Carty, a leading member of the ANA who had failed to win a parliamentary seat in March, and alleged that Shave had not consulted him regarding the appointment, a charge strenuously denied by the Governor.

### Government

The Constitution vests executive power in a Governor, appointed by the British monarch. The Governor is responsible for external affairs, international financial affairs, defence and internal security. In most other matters the Governor acts on the advice of the Executive Council, led by the Chief Minister. Legislative power is held by the House of Assembly, comprising 11 members: two *ex officio*, two nominated by the Governor, and seven elected for five years by universal adult suffrage. The Executive Council is responsible to the House.

### Economic Affairs

In 1993, according to official figures, the gross domestic product (GDP) of Anguilla, at factor cost, was, EC $139.4m.; in that year real GDP increased by 7.7%, and in the following year by 6.5%. Between 1984 and 1992 the population increased at an average rate of 3.2% per year. In addition, there are a great many Anguillans living abroad (in 1988, it was estimated, there were more than 4,000 in the US Virgin Islands and some 10,000 in the United Kingdom).

Agriculture (including fishing) contributed only 2.6% of GDP in 1991, reflecting a decrease of 27.1% in output from the sector compared with the previous year. However, agricultural production increased by 30.7% in 1992, before decreasing by 8.8% in 1993. The agricultural sector engaged 4.2% of the employed labour force in 1992. Smallholders grow vegetables and fruit for domestic consumption; the principal crops are pigeon peas, sweet potatoes and maize. An increase in crop production in the late 1980s and early 1990s was attributed, in part, to the reintroduction of okra, as well as to increased levels of rainfall. Livestock-rearing traditionally supplies significant export earnings, but the principal productive sector is the fishing industry (which is also a major employer). In 1987 lobsters accounted for some 64% of the value of merchandise exports, and fish for a further 35.6%. In 1991 fish accounted for some 20% of total exports.

Industry, which accounted for 21.5% of GDP in 1991 and engaged 23.7% of the employed labour force in 1992, is traditionally based on salt production and shipbuilding. Output in the mining and quarrying sector, which employed only 0.2% of the working population in 1992, increased by 16.7% in 1993, mainly owing to increased demand for sand and stone from the construction industry. It contracted by 15.2%, however, in the following year. Anguilla's principal mineral product is salt. The manufacturing sector, accounting for 3.2% of employment in 1992, consists almost entirely of boat-building and fisheries processing; output increased by some 4.5% in 1993. The construction industry, which engaged 18.3% of the employed labour force in 1992, accounted for 18.3% of GDP in 1991. Output in the sector increased by 16.3% in 1992, before decreasing by 14.9% in 1993. Most energy needs are met by imported hydrocarbon fuels.

Tourism is increasingly the dominant industry of the economy, and is a catalyst for growth in other areas, providing some 37.8% of GDP in 1992. Revenue from hotels and restaurants alone increased by 17.4% in 1993. In that year tourist expenditure totalled some EC $43.3m. The USA provided 62.3% of visitors in 1991.

In 1993 Anguilla recorded a trade deficit of EC $89.7m., and a deficit on the current account of the balance of payments of EC $26.5m. The trade deficit was partly offset by receipts from the 'invisibles' sector: tourism, financial services, remittances from Anguillans abroad and official assistance. The principal sources of imports are the USA and Puerto Rico, Trinidad and Tobago and the European Union (EU), mainly the United Kingdom. The principal markets for exports are the US Virgin Islands, Puerto Rico and St Maarten/St Martin. The main commodity exports are lobsters, fish, livestock and salt. Imports, upon which Anguilla is highly dependent, consist of foodstuffs, construction materials, manufactures, machinery and transport equipment.

In 1993 a current budgetary surplus of EC $2.0m. was recorded. Anguilla's external public debt totalled US $1.64m. in 1990. The average annual rate of inflation was 3.9% in 1985–92; consumer prices increased by an average of 2.4% in 1992. An estimated 7.2% of the labour force were unemployed in 1993 (compared with 26% in 1985).

In April 1987 Anguilla became the eighth member of the Eastern Caribbean Central Bank (see pp. 116 and 2609). As a dependency of the United Kingdom, Anguilla has the status of Overseas Territory in association with the EU (see p. 143).

Since its reversion to dependency on the United Kingdom, as a separate unit, the island has developed its limited resources. The traditional industries of shipbuilding and salt production remain, but have declined in relative importance. The fishing industry, particularly the catch of lobsters, expanded during the 1980s and early 1990s, helped by the growth of tourism, both locally and regionally. Tourism has become the dominant industry. During the late 1980s and early 1990s hotel-building and the Government's programme of infrastructure development caused a high level of activity in the construction industry. Between 1981 and 1988, deposits at 'offshore' banks by non-residents increased by an annual average of 90%, and at the beginning of 1990 there were 45 'offshore' banks registered in Anguilla. During 1990, however, following a review of the sector, the licences of 30 banks were withdrawn, and more stringent regulations governing the operations of 'offshore' banks were introduced. Furthermore, in an attempt to prevent the abuse of the sector by criminal organizations, particularly drugs-traffickers, an international operation, involving the establishment of a 'fake' bank on Anguilla, was carried out. The operation led to the seizure of some US $40m. in illegal funds and the arrest of more than 90 people in 1994. Both tourism and the international banking sector have apparently benefited from the perceived stability of dependent status. In late 1993 the British Government granted Anguilla £10.5m. in capital aid and technical assistance, to be used to implement a programme of economic measures aimed at improving the Territory's potential for self-sufficiency.

### Social Welfare

In 1992 Anguilla had one cottage hospital, with 24 beds, and there were five government medical officers. In addition, there were two private medical surgeries, with resident general practitioners. A new 36-bed hospital was opened in October 1993. A social security scheme was introduced in 1982, and a health insurance scheme for public servants was introduced in November 1993. Government expenditure on health in the budget for 1992 was EC $5.0m., representing 12% of total expenditure.

### Education

Education is free and compulsory between the ages of five and 16 years. There are six government primary schools and one government secondary school. A 'comprehensive' secondary school education system was introduced in September 1986. Post-secondary education is undertaken abroad. Government expenditure on education in the budget for 1991 was EC $4.8m., equivalent to 17% of total expenditure.

### Public Holidays

**1995:** 1 January (New Year's Day), 14 April (Good Friday), 17 April (Easter Monday), 1 May (Labour Day), 30 May (Anguilla Day), 5 June (Whit Monday), 17 June (Queen's Official Birthday), 7 August (August Monday), 10 August (August Thursday), 11 August (Constitution Day), 19 December (Separation Day), 25–26 December (Christmas).

**1996:** 1 January (New Year's Day), 5 April (Good Friday), 8 April (Easter Monday), 6 May (Labour Day), 27 May (Whit Monday), 30 May (Anguilla Day), 15 June (Queen's Official Birthday), 5 August (August Monday), 8 August (August Thursday), 9 August (Constitution Day), 19 December (Separation Day), 26–27 December (for Christmas).

### Weights and Measures

The metric system has been adopted, although imperial weights and measures are also used.

## Statistical Survey

Source: Government of Anguilla, The Secretariat, The Valley; tel. 497-2451; telex 9313; fax 497-3389.

### AREA AND POPULATION

**Area** (sq km): 96 (Anguilla 91, Sombrero 5).

**Population:** 8,960 (males 4,473; females 4,487) at census of 14 April 1992.

**Density** (April 1992): 93.3 per sq km.

**Principal Town** (population at 1992 census): The Valley (capital) 595.

**Births, Marriages and Deaths** (registrations, 1993): 169 live births (birth rate 18.4 per 1,000); (1991) 154 marriages (marriage rate 17.1 per 1,000); 59 deaths (death rate 6.4 per 1,000).

**Economically Active Population** (population aged 14 years and over, 1992 census): Agriculture, hunting, forestry and fishing 175; Mining and quarrying 7; Manufacturing 131; Electricity, gas and water 86; Construction 754; Trade, restaurants and hotels 1,441; Transport, storage and communications 326; Financing, insurance, real estate and business services 214; Community, social and personal services 969; Activities not adequately defined 19; *Total employed* 4,122 (males 2,397, females 1,725); Unemployed 324 (males 156, females 168); *Total labour force* 4,446 (males 2,553, females 1,893). Source: ILO, *Year Book of Labour Statistics*.

### AGRICULTURE, ETC.

**Livestock** (1979): EC $210,000 (exports).

**Fishing** (metric tons, 1991): Lobsters 49; Conch 5; Other fish 270.

### MINING

**Exports** (1979): Salt EC $661,000.

### FINANCE

**Currency and Exchange Rates:** 100 cents = 1 East Caribbean dollar (EC $). *Sterling and US Dollar Equivalents* (31 December 1994): £1 sterling = EC $4.224; US $1 = EC $2.700; EC $100 = £23.67 = US $37.04. *Exchange Rate:* Fixed at US $1 = EC $2.70 since July 1976.

**Budget** (EC $ million, 1993): *Recurrent revenue* Tax revenue 23.4; Non-tax revenue 13.2; Total 36.6. *Recurrent expenditure* Total 34.6 (Wages and salaries 16.3, Other goods and services 17.3, Pensions 0.7, Interest payments 0.3). Source: Eastern Caribbean Central Bank, *Annual Report*.

**Cost of Living** (Consumer Price Index; twelve months ending 30 November; base: 1985 = 100): 121.73 in 1990; 127.35 in 1991; 130.35 in 1992.

**Gross Domestic Product by Economic Activity** (EC $ million at current prices, 1991): Agriculture, hunting, forestry and fishing 3.9; Mining and quarrying 1.2; Manufacturing 1.0; Electricity, gas and water 2.5; Construction 27.1; Trade, restaurants and hotels 54.2; Transport, storage and communications 18.1; Finance, insurance, real estate and business services 18.9; Community, social and personal services 2.3; Government services 18.5; *Sub-total* 147.7; *Less* Imputed bank service charge 12.4; *GDP at factor cost* 135.3.

**Balance of Payments** (EC $ million, 1993): Merchandise exports f.o.b. 2.8; Merchandise imports c.i.f. −92.5; *Trade balance* −89.7; Balance of services 41.3; Transfers 21.8; *Current balance* −26.5; Capital account 29.4; *Overall balance* 2.9. Source: Eastern Caribbean Central Bank, *Annual Report*.

### TRANSPORT

**Road Traffic** (1992): 4,620 registered motor vehicles.

### TOURISM

**Visitor arrivals:** 90,575 in 1991; 93,180 in 1992; 111,350 (Excursionists 73,692, Stop-overs 37,658) in 1993.

### COMMUNICATIONS MEDIA

**Radio Receivers** (estimate, 1992): 2,000 in use.
**Telephones** (1992): 3,053 exchange lines in use.

### EDUCATION

**Institutions** (1992): Pre-primary centres 9; State primary schools 6; State secondary school 1; **Total pupils** (1992): 2,404.

# Directory

## The Constitution

The Constitution which was established in 1976 accorded Anguilla the status of a British Dependent Territory. It formally became a separate dependency on 19 December 1980, and is administered under the Anguilla Constitution Orders of 1982 and 1990. The British monarch is represented locally by a Governor, who presides over the Executive Council and the House of Assembly. The Governor is responsible for defence, external affairs (including international financial affairs), internal security (including the police), the public service, the judiciary and the audit. The Governor appoints a Deputy Governor. On matters relating to internal security, the public service and the appointment of an acting governor or deputy governor, the Governor is required to consult the Chief Minister. The Executive Council consists of the Chief Minister and not more than three other ministers (appointed by the Governor from the elected members of the legislative House of Assembly) and two *ex-officio* members (the Deputy Governor and the Attorney-General). The House of Assembly is elected for a maximum term of five years by universal adult suffrage and consists of seven elected members, two *ex-officio* members (the Deputy Governor and the Attorney-General) and two nominated members who are appointed by the Governor, one upon the advice of the Chief Minister, and one after consultations with the Chief Minister and the Leader of the Opposition. The House elects a Speaker and a Deputy Speaker.

The Governor may order the dissolution of the House of Assembly if a resolution of 'no confidence' is passed in the Government, and elections must be held within two months of the dissolution.

The Constitution provides for an Anguilla Belonger Commission, which determines cases of whether a person can be 'regarded as belonging to Anguilla' (i.e. having 'belonger' status). A belonger is someone of Anguillan birth or parentage, someone who has married a belonger, or someone who is a citizen of the British Dependent Territories from Anguilla (by birth, parentage, adoption or naturalization). The Commission may grant belonger status to those who have been domiciled and ordinarily resident in Anguilla for not less than 15 years.

## The Government

**Governor:** ALAN W. SHAVE (assumed office 14 August 1992).

### EXECUTIVE COUNCIL
(June 1995)

**Chief Minister and Minister of Home Affairs, Tourism, Agriculture and Fisheries:** HUBERT HUGHES.
**Minister of Finance and Economic Development:** VICTOR BANKS.
**Minister of Education, Health, Social Services and Lands:** EDISON BAIRD.
**Minister of Communications, Public Utilities and Works:** ALBERT HUGHES.
**Attorney-General:** KURT DEFREITAS.
**Deputy Governor:** HENRY MCCRORY.

### MINISTRIES

**Office of the Governor:** Government House, The Valley; tel. 497-2622; telex 9351; fax 497-3151.
**Office of the Chief Minister:** The Secretariat, The Valley; tel. 497-2518; telex 9313; fax 497-3389.

All ministries are based in The Valley, mostly at the Secretariat (tel. 497-2451).

## Legislature

### HOUSE OF ASSEMBLY

**Election, 16 March 1994**

| Party | Seats |
|---|---|
| Anguilla Democratic Party | 2 |
| Anguilla National Alliance | 2 |
| Anguilla United Party | 2 |
| Independent | 1 |

There are also two *ex-officio* members and two nominated members.

**Clerk to House of Assembly:** MAJORIE CONNOR.

## Political Organizations

**Anguilla Democratic Party (ADP):** The Valley; f. 1981 as Anguilla People's Party; name changed 1984; Leader VICTOR BANKS.
**Anguillans for Good Government:** The Valley; Leader RONALD WEBSTER.
**Anguilla National Alliance (ANA):** The Valley; f. 1980 by reconstitution of People's Progressive Party; Leader ERIC REID.
**Anguilla United Party (AUP):** The Valley; f. 1979, revived 1984; Leader HUBERT HUGHES.
**Party for Anguilla's Culturation and Economy (PACE):** The Valley; Leader CUTHWIN LAKE.

## Judicial System

Justice is administered by the High Court, Court of Appeal and Magistrates' Courts. During the High Court sitting, the Eastern Caribbean Supreme Court provides Anguilla with a judge.

## Religion

### CHRISTIANITY

#### The Anglican Communion

Anglicans in Anguilla are adherents of the Church in the Province of the West Indies, comprising nine dioceses. Anguilla forms part of the diocese of the North Eastern Caribbean and Aruba. The Bishop, who is also Archbishop of the Province, resides in St John's, Antigua.

**Anglican Church:** St Mary's, The Valley.

#### The Roman Catholic Church

The diocese of St John's-Basseterre, suffragan to the archdiocese of Castries (Saint Lucia), includes Anguilla, Antigua and Barbuda, the British Virgin Islands, Montserrat and Saint Christopher and Nevis. The Bishop resides in St John's, Antigua.

**Roman Catholic Church:** St Gerard's, The Valley; tel. 497-2405.

#### Protestant Churches

**Methodist Church:** South Hill; Minister (vacant).

The Seventh-day Adventist, Baptist, Church of God, Pentecostal, Apostolic Faith and Jehovah's Witnesses Churches and sects are also represented.

## The Press

**Anguilla Life Magazine:** Caribbean Commercial Centre, POB 109, The Valley; tel. 497-3080; fax 497-2501; quarterly; circ. 10,000.
**Official Gazette:** The Valley; tel. 497-2451; monthly; government news-sheet.

## Radio

There were an estimated 2,000 radio receivers in use in 1992.

**Caribbean Beacon Radio:** POB 690, The Valley; tel. 497-4340; fax 497-4311; (Head Office: POB 7008, Columbus, Ga 31908, USA); f. 1981; privately owned and operated; religious and commercial; broadcasts 24 hours daily; Pres. Dr Gene Scott; CEO Kevin Mooney.

**Radio Anguilla:** The Valley; tel. 497-2218; fax 497-5432; f. 1969; owned and operated by the Govt of Anguilla since 1976; 250,000 listeners throughout the north-eastern Caribbean; broadcasts 17 hours daily; Dir of Information and Broadcasting Nat Hodge; News Editor Wycliffe Richardson.

**ZJF FM:** The Valley; tel. 497-3157; f. 1989; commercial.

## Finance

(cap. = capital; dep. = deposits; res = reserves; m. = million; amounts in EC dollars)

The Eastern Caribbean Central Bank (see p. 116), based in Saint Christopher, and of which Anguilla became a member in April 1987, is the central issuing and monetary authority for the Territory.

### BANKING

**Bank of Nova Scotia** (Canada): POB 250, George Hill; tel. 497-3331; telex 9333; fax 497-3344; Man. David Bodden.

**Barclays Bank PLC** (UK): POB 140, The Valley; tel. 497-2301; telex 9310; fax 497-2980; Man. J. O. Espejo.

**Caribbean Commercial Bank (Anguilla) Ltd:** POB 23, The Valley; tel. 497-2571; telex 9306; fax 497-3570; Man. P. Bryan.

**National Bank of Anguilla Ltd:** POB 44, The Valley; tel. 497-2101; telex 9305; fax 497-3310; f. 1985; cap. 1.5m., res 4.9m., dep. 58.0m. (Mar. 1991); Chair. Clive D. Carty; Gen. Man. Selwyn F. Horsford.

There are 'offshore', foreign banks based on the island, but most are not authorized to operate in Anguilla. There is a financial complex known as the Caribbean Commercial Centre in The Valley.

**Anguilla Offshore Financial Centre:** The Valley; tel. 497-5881; fax 497-5872.

### TRUST COMPANIES

**Anguilla Trust Co Ltd:** POB 244, The Valley; tel. 497-2587; telex 9336.

**Hansa Bank and Trust Co Ltd:** POB 213, The Valley; tel. 497-3800.

### INSURANCE

**Anguilla Mutual Assurance Co Ltd:** The Valley; tel. 497-2246.

**Anguilla National Insurance Co Ltd:** Airport Rd, POB 44, The Valley; tel. 497-5280; fax 497-3870.

**British American Insurance Co Ltd:** Old Factory Complex, POB 148; tel. 497-2653.

**D-3 Enterprises:** POB 14, The Valley; tel. 497-3525; fax 497-3526.

**Gulf Insurance Ltd:** Blowing Point; tel. 497-6613.

**Malliouhana Insurance:** Caribbean Commercial Centre, POB 492, The Valley; tel. 497-3712; fax 497-3710.

**Nagico Insurance:** POB 79, The Valley; tel. 497-2976; fax 497-3155.

**National Caribbean Insurance Co Ltd:** Caribbean Commercial Centre, POB 323, The Valley; tel. 497-2865; fax 497-3783.

**North Islands Insurance Agency Ltd:** Caribbean Commercial Centre, POB 164, The Valley; tel. 497-2144; telex 9325; fax 497-3880.

## Trade and Industry

**Anguilla Chamber of Commerce:** POB 321, The Valley; tel. 497-2701; fax 497-5858; Exec. Dir Paula Mack; Pres. Sutcliffe Hodge.

**Anguilla Development Board:** The Valley; tel. 497-3690; fax 497-2959.

**Anguilla Register of Companies:** The Valley; tel. 497-3881; fax 497-5872.

## Transport

### ROADS

Anguilla has 140 km (87 miles) of roads, of which 100 km (62 miles) are tarred. A total of EC $5.3m. was spent on road construction and improvement projects in 1992.

### SHIPPING

The principal port of entry is Sandy Ground on Road Bay. There is a daily ferry service between Blowing Point and Marigot (St Martin).

### CIVIL AVIATION

Wallblake Airport, 3.2 km (2 miles) from The Valley, has a bitumen-surfaced runway with a length of 1,100m (3,600 ft). Air taxi and charter services are provided by:

**Air Anguilla:** POB 110, The Valley; tel. 497-2643; fax 497-2982; scheduled services to St Thomas, St Maarten/St Martin, Saint Christopher and Beef Island (British Virgin Islands); Pres. Restormel Franklin.

**American Eagle:** POB 659, Wallblake Airport; tel. 497-3131; operates a scheduled flight from Puerto Rico.

**Tyden Air:** Wallblake Airport; tel. 497-2719; fax 497-3079; charter company servicing whole Caribbean.

LIAT and Carib Aviation (Antigua and Barbuda), Air St Martin, Air St Kitts and WINAIR (Netherlands Antilles) operate charter flights and scheduled services to St Maarten/St Martin, the British and US Virgin Islands and Saint Christopher.

## Tourism

Anguilla's sandy beaches and unspoilt natural beauty attract tourists and also day visitors from neighbouring St Maarten/St Martin. In 1992 tourist arrivals totalled 93,180 and increased by 19.5%, to 111,350, in the following year. There were 978 hotel rooms on the island in 1993. Earnings from the tourist industry totalled EC $43.3m. in 1993.

**Anguilla Tourist Board:** POB 1388, The Valley; tel. 497-2759; fax 497-3091.

**Anguilla Hotel and Tourism Association:** The Valley; tel. 497-2944; fax 497-3091.

# BERMUDA

## Introductory Survey

**Location, Climate, Language, Religion, Flag, Capital**

The Bermudas or Somers Islands are an isolated archipelago, comprising about 150 islands, in the Atlantic Ocean, about 917 km (570 miles) off the coast of South Carolina, USA. Ten of the islands are linked by bridges and causeways to form the principal mainland. The climate is mild and humid. Temperatures are generally between 8°C (46°F) and 32°C (90°F), with an average annual rainfall of 1,470 mm (58 ins). The official language is English, but there is a small community of Portuguese speakers. Most of the inhabitants profess Christianity, and numerous denominations are represented, the principal one being the Anglican Church. The flag (proportions 2 by 1) is the British 'Red Ensign' (this usage being unique among the British colonies), with, in the fly, the colony's badge: a seated red lion holding a shield (with a gold baroque border), which depicts the wreck off Bermuda of the ship of the first settlers. The capital is Hamilton.

**Recent History**

Discovered by Spanish navigators in the early 16th century, Bermuda was first settled by the British from 1609. It has had a representative assembly since 1620 (and thus claims one of the oldest parliaments in the world), and became a British crown colony in 1684. Bermuda was granted internal self-government by the Constitution introduced in 1968, although the British Government retains responsibility in certain matters. Various amendments to the 1968 Constitution were made in 1973, the most important being the establishment of the Governor's Council, through which the Governor exercises responsibility for external affairs, defence, internal security and the police. In 1974 the Government Leader was restyled Premier and the Executive Council became the Cabinet.

The first general election under the new Constitution, which took place in May 1968 against a background of rioting and racial tension (some 60% of the population are of African origin, the rest mostly of European extraction), was won by the United Bermuda Party (UBP), a moderate, multi-racial party whose policies were based on racial co-operation and continued support for dependent status. The underlying racial tensions were emphasized in 1972 and 1973 by shooting incidents which resulted in the deaths of the Governor, the Commissioner of Police and three others. In December 1977 the Governor's assassin and another convicted murderer were executed, and further rioting and arson ensued. A state of emergency was declared, and British troops were flown to Bermuda to restore order.

At the general election of May 1976, the UBP was returned to power with a decreased majority, winning 26 of the 40 seats in the House of Assembly. The remaining seats were won by the mainly black, left-wing Progressive Labour Party (PLP), which campaigned for independence and received 46% of the vote. In August 1977 Sir John Sharpe, Premier and leader of the UBP since December 1975, resigned both posts and was succeeded by David Gibbons, the Minister of Finance.

In February 1978 a Royal Commission was established to investigate the causes of racial violence, and in August the Commission published a report which suggested the redrawing of constituency boundaries to improve the PLP's prospects for winning seats. Despite this, the UBP won the December 1980 election with a narrow majority, securing 22 seats in the House of Assembly. Gibbons resigned as Premier and UBP leader in January 1982, although retaining the finance portfolio, and was succeeded by John Swan, the Minister of Home Affairs. At a general election in February 1983, the UBP gained a further four seats in the House of Assembly. Internal divisions within the PLP led to the expulsion from the party of four PLP members of the House of Assembly. The four members, after sitting as independents, formed a new centre party, the National Liberal Party (NLP), in August 1985. In October Swan called an early general election, hoping to take advantage of the divided opposition. The UBP was decisively returned to power, securing 31 of the 40 seats in the House of Assembly, while the PLP retained only seven seats and the NLP won two. Following a general election in February 1989, the UBP remained in power, but with a reduced representation in the House of Assembly of only 23 seats. By contrast, the PLP increased its representation to 15 seats.

Constitutional amendments, introduced in 1979, included provision for closer consultation between the Premier and the Leader of the Opposition on the appointment of members of the Public Service Commission and the Boundaries Commission, and on the appointment of the Chief Justice. The 1978 Royal Commission recommended early independence for Bermuda, but the majority of the population at that time seemed to oppose such a policy. Swan had declared himself in favour of eventual independence for the colony, but only with the support of the Bermudian people.

It was announced in April 1992 that Lord Waddington (former leader of the British House of Lords) was to replace Sir Desmond Langley as Governor. He assumed office in August.

During 1992 and 1993 the Government attracted international criticism for its refusal to amend legislation criminalizing homosexual activities. However, in May 1994 legislation was approved in the House of Assembly, by 22 votes to 16, to legalize homosexual acts between consenting adults (with 18 years as the age of consent). The bill's sponsor, John Stubbs, a founder member of the UBP, died shortly after the historic vote.

At a general election on 5 October 1993 (the first to be held since the voting age was lowered from 21 to 18 years in 1990), the UBP was returned to power, winning 22 seats in the House of Assembly, while the PLP secured 18. In February 1994 legislation providing for the organization of a referendum on independence for Bermuda was approved by 20 votes to 18 in the House of Assembly. The debate on independence was believed to have intensified as a result of the announcement in late 1993 that British and US forces would close their facilities and withdraw permanently from the island by April 1995 and September 1995 respectively. However, an opinion poll, conducted in early 1994, indicated that a significant majority of Bermudians favoured the retention of dependent status. The PLP, which is a strong advocate of independence for Bermuda, consistently opposed the organization of a referendum on the subject, believieving that the independence issue should be determined by a general election. In May 1994 a PLP motion to reject a proposed government inquiry into the possibilities for independence was approved by 18 votes to 17 in the House of Assembly, effectively halting further progress towards a referendum. However, the debate continued, and in October a government delegation travelled to London for official discussions on the subject. Further legislation regarding the proposed referendum was narrowly approved in March 1995, and it was subsequently announced that a vote would be held on 15 August. The PLP stated that it would encourage its supporters to boycott the poll, which would require not only a majority of votes, but also the approval of 40% of eligible voters in order to achieve a pro-independence result.

**Government**

Bermuda is a crown colony of the United Kingdom, with a wide measure of internal self-government. The British monarch is represented by an appointed Governor, responsible for external affairs, defence and internal security. The bicameral legislature comprises the Senate (11 nominated members) and the House of Assembly, with 40 members elected for five years by universal adult suffrage. The Governor appoints the majority leader in the House as Premier, and the latter nominates other ministers. The Cabinet is responsible to the legislature. For the purposes of local government, the island has long been divided into nine parishes (originally known as 'tribes', except for the 'public land' of St George's, the capital until 1815). The town of St George's and the city of Hamilton constitute the two municipalities of the Territory.

**Defence**

The local defence force is the Bermuda Regiment, with a strength of some 700 men and women in 1993. The US Armed Forces (USAF), which lease 2.3 sq miles (6 sq km) or some 11% of Bermuda's land area, maintain a military base in the Territory. In November 1993, however, it was announced that this facility was to be closed and all forces withdrawn by September 1995. The British military base on Bermuda closed in April 1995.

**Economic Affairs**

In 1993 Bermuda's gross domestic product (GDP) was estimated to be US $1,698m., equivalent to US $28,200 per head, one of the highest levels in the world. GDP decreased, in real terms, by an estimated 6.0% during 1990–93, but was expected to increase by up to 3% in 1994. The population increased by an annual average of 1.3% in 1985–93.

Agriculture (including forestry and fishing) engaged only 1.2% of the employed labour force in 1993, and the sector makes a minimal contribution to GDP. The principal crops in that year were potatoes, tomatoes, carrots, broccoli, cauliflower, bananas and cabbage. Flowers are grown for export. Other vegetables and fruit are also grown, but Bermuda remains very dependent upon food imports, which accounted for more than 16% of total imports in 1990. Livestock-rearing includes cattle and goats (both mainly for dairy purposes), pigs and poultry. There is a small fishing industry, again mainly for domestic consumption.

Industry (including manufacturing, construction and public utilities) contributed about 10.2% of GDP in 1993 and engaged 10.2% of the employed labour force in that year. The main activities include ship repairs, boat-building and the manufacture of paints and pharmaceuticals. The principal industrial sector is construction (in which 5.2% of the employed labour force were engaged in 1993). Most of Bermuda's water is provided by privately-collected rainfall. Energy requirements are met mainly by the import of mineral fuels (8.6% of total imports in 1990).

Bermuda is overwhelmingly a service economy, the traditional principal sector being tourism. In 1992, despite the growth of financial services, it was estimated that tourism still accounted for some 40% of foreign exchange earnings and 32.1% of GDP. In 1992 some 17.8% of the employed labour force worked in restaurants and hotels, but tourism is estimated to account for some 60% of all employment, directly and indirectly. The sector earned an estimated B $504.5m. in 1994. The total number of tourists, particularly of cruise-ship passengers, is strictly controlled, in order to maintain Bermuda's environment and its market for wealthier visitors. Most tourists come from the USA (86.3% in 1993).

There is a significant commercial and 'offshore' financial sector, and Bermuda is one of the world's leading insurance markets. It was estimated that, in 1992, the entire sector accounted for some 42.6% of foreign exchange earnings and contributed 30.0% of GDP. About 15.5% of the employed labour force were engaged directly in the finance, insurance, real estate and business sectors in 1992. There were 7,578 exempted companies registered in Bermuda at the end of 1993. Another important source of income is the 'free-flag' registration of shipping, giving Bermuda the fifth-largest such fleet in the world in 1993.

Bermuda is almost entirely dependent upon imports, has very few commodity exports and, therefore, consistently records a large visible trade deficit (B $426.8m. in 1992). Receipts from the service industries normally ensure a surplus on the current account of the balance of payments (B $22m. in 1991). The USA is the principal source of imports (66% of total imports in 1992) and the principal market for exports (62% in that year). Other important trading partners include the United Kingdom, Canada and Japan. The main exports are rum, flowers (orchids), medicinal and pharmaceutical products (which accounted for 82% of total exports in 1992) and the re-export of petroleum products. The principal imports are machinery, transport equipment and other manufactured articles, and food.

In the financial year ending 31 March 1993 Bermuda recorded a budgetary deficit of B $25.7m. (equivalent to 1.5% of GDP). The average annual rate of inflation was 4.3% in 1985–93. The rate decreased to 3.0% in 1994. Unemployment, which had been negligible in previous years, was estimated to have increased to some 6% at the time of the 1991 census. In late 1993 there were 7,299 foreign professional workers registered in the Territory.

Bermuda, the oldest colony of the United Kingdom, has the status of Overseas Territory in association with the EU and has also been granted Designated Territory status by the British Government (this allows Bermudian-based funds and unit trusts access to the British market). Bermuda's financial services also benefit from a special tax treaty with the USA.

Bermudians enjoy a high standard of living. The high density of population, however, has given rise to environmental concerns and local disquiet at the cost of property. Since 1972, no new hotels have been built. Proximity to the USA and the parity of the US and Bermuda dollars help both tourist and financial industries and Bermuda's dependent status remains a perceived contributor to political stability and financial integrity. The maintenance of the service economy is fundamental to Bermuda, which has to import 80% of its food requirements and all of its energy requirements, and exports products to the value of some 10% of imports. Plans for new legislation to permit stricter control of 'offshore' financial operations were discussed in the early 1990s: concern had been expressed that existing laws made no provision for cases involving the diversion of illicit funds from drugs-trafficking. The Territory's important insurance industry experienced a period of rapid expansion in 1993. Bermuda's economy was expected to be adversely affected by the closure of a Canadian naval communications base in 1993 and of the US naval air station, as well as the withdrawal of British forces in 1995. The combined facilities contributed an estimated US $54.5m. to the economy in 1992 (equivalent to 3.2% of GDP) and directly employed 136 Bermudians. Concern was expressed in 1995 that debate surrounding the impending referendum on independence (see Recent History) would result in the polarization of political opinion in Bermuda, and thus affect the Territory's reputation for political stability, which has apparently contributed to the success of the financial sector.

### Social Welfare

A wide range of welfare work is undertaken by the Department of Health and the Department of Social Services, as well as by a number of voluntary organizations (many of which specialize in treating the increasing incidence of problems related to drugs-abuse).

Almost all employees are registered under the Government's contributory pension scheme, and the 1970 Hospital Insurance Act made hospital insurance available for all. It also provided for free hospital care for children and subsidized rates for the elderly. In 1993 Bermuda had three hospital establishments, a general hospital with 224 beds, a geriatric hospital with 102 beds and a hospital for the mentally ill with 160 beds. In that year there were 59 physicians, 27 dentists and 50 nurses operating in the Territory. In 1989/90 government expenditure on health, social services and housing in the financial year (B $60.9m.) was equivalent to 22% of total expenditure. In 1992/93 it accounted for 21.1% of total expenditure.

### Education

There is free compulsory education in government schools between the ages of five and 16 years, and a number of scholarships are awarded for higher education and teacher training. There are also seven private secondary schools which charge fees. The Bermuda College, founded in 1972, accepts students over the age of 16, and is the only post-secondary educational institution. Extramural degree courses are available through Queen's University, Canada, and Indiana and Maryland Universities, USA. In 1970 adult illiteracy was only 1.6%. In 1989/90 government expenditure on education (B $43.7m.) accounted for 15.9% of total expenditure and in 1991/92 it represented 14.2% of expenditure.

### Public Holidays

**1995:** 1 January (New Year's Day), 14 April (Good Friday), 24 May (Bermuda Day), 19 June (Queen's Official Birthday), 27 July (Cup Match), 28 July (Somers' Day), 4 September (Labour Day), 11 November (Remembrance Day), 25–26 December (Christmas).

**1996:** 1 January (New Year's Day), 5 April (Good Friday), 24 May (Bermuda Day), 17 June (Queen's Official Birthday), 25 July (Cup Match), 26 July (Somers' Day), 2 September (Labour Day), 11 November (Remembrance Day), 25–26 December (Christmas).

### Weights and Measures

The metric system has been widely adopted but imperial and US weights and measures are both used in certain fields.

## Statistical Survey

Source: Department of Information Services, Global House, 43 Church St, Hamilton HM 12; tel. 292-6384; fax 295-5267.

### AREA AND POPULATION

**Area:** 53 sq km (20.59 sq miles).

**Population** (excluding visitors): 58,460 (males 28,345; females 30,115) at census of 20 May 1991; 59,549 (official estimate) at 31 December 1993; *Principal towns* (population at 1991 census): Hamilton 1,100; St George's 1,648.

**Density** (31 December 1993): 1,124 per sq km.

**Births, Marriages and Deaths** (1993): 901 live births; 871 marriages; 452 deaths.

**Expectation of Life** (years at birth, 1980): Males 68.8; females 76.3. Source: UN, *Demographic Yearbook*.

**Employment** (excluding unpaid family workers, August 1992): Agriculture, fishing and quarrying 502; Manufacturing 1,076; Electricity, gas and water 507; Construction 1,832; Wholesale and retail trade 4,859; Restaurants and hotels 6,003; Transport, storage and communications 2,346; Finance and insurance 2,591; Real estate and business services 2,639; Community, social and personal services 9,289; International bodies 2,006; Total 33,650 (males 17,120; females 16,530).

### AGRICULTURE, ETC.

**Principal Crops** ('000 lb, 1993): Potatoes 440; Carrots 225; Broccoli 102; Cauliflower 82; Lettuce 6; Cabbage 190; Tomatoes 212; Bananas 70.

**Livestock:** (1993) Cattle 500; Goats 1,000; Pigs 400; Poultry 20,000; Beehives 350.

**Livestock Products** (1993): Cows' and goats' milk 1,492,830 quarts; Animal meat 141 carcasses; Hen eggs 1.3m.; Honey n.a.

**Fishing** (metric tons, live weight): 463 in 1990; 428 in 1991; 432 in 1992. Source: FAO, *Yearbook of Fishery Statistics*.

## INDUSTRY

**Electric Energy** (production, million kWh): 466 in 1989; 490 in 1990; 513 in 1991. Source: UN, *Industrial Statistics Yearbook*.

## FINANCE

**Currency and Exchange Rates:** 100 cents = 1 Bermuda dollar (B $). *Sterling and US Dollar equivalents* (31 December 1994): £1 sterling = B $1.5645; US $1 = B $1.000; B $100 = £63.92 = US $100.00. *Exchange Rate:* The Bermuda dollar is at par with the US dollar. Note: US and Canadian currencies are also accepted.

**Budget** (estimates, B $ million, 1993/94): Total revenue 352.5; Total expenditure 331.8.
*1994/95:* Total revenue B $395m.
*1995/96:* Total revenue B $426m.

**Cost of Living** (Consumer Price Index; base: 1980 = 100): 185.3 in 1991; 190.3 in 1992; 195.1 in 1993. Source: ILO, *Year Book of Labour Statistics*.

**Expenditure on the Gross Domestic Product** (B $ million, year ending 31 March 1992): Government final consumption expenditure 216.6; Private final consumption expenditure 1,165.7; Gross capital formation 180.3; *Total domestic expenditure* 1,562.6; Exports of goods and services 960.4; *Less* Imports of goods and services 882.1; *GDP in purchasers' values* 1,640.9. Source: UN, *National Accounts Statistics*.

**Balance of Payments** (B $ million, 1991): Payments (gross) 1,025 (Imports 456); Receipts (gross) 1,010 (Tourism 454, International companies 334); *Current balance* net 22.

## EXTERNAL TRADE

**Principal Commodities** (B $ '000, 1990): *Imports:* Food and live animals 86,862; Beverages and tobacco 34,294; Crude materials (inedible) except fuels 4,698; Mineral fuels and lubricants 46,651; Chemicals 53,821; Basic manufactures 74,054; Machinery and transport equipment 109,165; Miscellaneous manufactured articles 129,515; Total (incl. others) 540,631. *Exports:* Medicinal and pharmaceutical products 48,774; Total (incl. others) 59,730.

**Principal Trading Partners** (B $ '000, 1992): *Imports:* Canada 20,198; Japan 26,664; Switzerland 17,121; United Kingdom 34,544; USA 336,391; Venezuela 18,637; Total (incl. others) 511,136. *Exports:* Canada 3,415; Italy 4,990; United Kingdom 17,350; USA 52,529; Total (incl. others) 84,256.

*1991* (B $ million): Imports 463.7; Exports 48.7.

Source: UN, *International Trade Statistics Yearbook*.

## TRANSPORT

**Road Traffic** (vehicles in use, 1992): Motor and auxiliary cycles 19,884; Private cars 19,712; Goods vehicles 3,389; Public service vehicles 770; Trailers 357; Forces vehicles 353; Miscellaneous 151.

**Shipping:** *Ship arrivals* (1992): Yachts 1,078; Passenger and cargo 355; Naval supplies 65; Total (incl. others) 1,604. *International Shipping Register:* (1992) 94 Commercial ships (3,139,164 grt); (1991) 317 Yachts (30,289 grt). *Fishing vessels* (registered, 1988): 209; *International freight traffic*\* ('000 metric tons, 1990): Goods loaded 130; Goods unloaded 470.

\* Source: UN, *Monthly Bulletin of Statistics*.

**Civil Aviation** (1992): Aircraft arrivals 5,101; passengers 487,195; air cargo 5,568,118 kg; air mail 667,669 kg.

## TOURISM

**Visitor Arrivals:** 506,237 (131,006 cruise-ship passengers) in 1992; 566,454 in 1993; 588,788 (172,865 cruise-ship passengers) in 1994.

## COMMUNICATIONS MEDIA

**Radio Receivers** (1992): 78,000 in use\*.
**Television Receivers** (1992): 57,000 in use\*.
**Telephones** (1987): 56,270 in use.
**Daily Newspapers** (1993): 1 (estimated circulation 17,500).
**Non-Daily Newspapers** (1990): 1 (estimated circulation 35,000)\*.

\* Source: UNESCO, *Statistical Yearbook*.

## EDUCATION

**Pre-primary** (1993): 13 schools; 37 teachers (public education only); 469 pupils.
**Special** (1992): 5 schools; 33 teachers; 163 pupils.
**Primary** (1992): 18 schools; 277 teachers; 4,309 pupils.
**General Secondary** (1992): 14 schools (incl. 2 denominational, 1 USAF and 3 other private schools); 236 teachers; 9,819 pupils.
**Higher** (1992): 1 institution; 594 students.

Source: mainly UNESCO, *Statistical Yearbook*.

# Directory
## The Constitution

The Constitution, introduced on 8 June 1968 and amended in 1973 and 1979, contains provisions relating to the protection of fundamental rights and freedoms of the individual; the powers and duties of the Governor; the composition, powers and procedure of the Legislature; the Cabinet; the judiciary; the public service and finance.

The British monarch is represented by an appointed Governor, who retains responsibility for external affairs, defence, internal security and the police.

The Legislature consists of the monarch, the Senate and the House of Assembly. Three members of the Senate are appointed at the Governor's discretion, five on the advice of the Government leader and three on the advice of the Opposition leader. The Senate elects a President and Vice-President. The House of Assembly, consisting of 40 members elected under universal adult franchise from 20 constituencies, elects a Speaker and a Deputy Speaker, and sits for a five-year term.

The Cabinet consists of the Premier and at least six other members of the Legislature. The Governor appoints the majority leader in the House of Assembly as Premier, who in turn nominates the other members of the Cabinet. They are assigned responsibilities for government departments and other business and, in some cases, are assisted by Permanent Cabinet Secretaries.

The Cabinet is presided over by the Premier. The Governor's Council enables the Governor to consult with the Premier and two other members of the Cabinet nominated by the Premier on matters for which the Governor has responsibility. The Secretary to the Cabinet, who heads the public service, acts as secretary to the Governor's Council.

Voters must be British subjects aged 18 years or over (lowered from 21 years in 1990), and, if not possessing Bermudian status, must have been registered as electors on 1 May 1976. Candidates for election must qualify as electors, and must possess Bermudian status.

## The Government

**Governor and Commander-in-Chief:** Lord WADDINGTON (assumed office 25 August 1992).
**Deputy Governor:** PETER WILLIS.

### CABINET
(June 1995)

**Premier:** Sir JOHN W. SWAN.
**Deputy Premier and Minister of the Labour and Home Affairs:** IRVING PEARMAN.
**Minister of Finance:** Dr DAVID J. SAUL.
**Minister of Tourism:** CLARENCE V. JIM WOOLRIDGE.
**Minister of the Environment:** GERALD D. E. SIMONS.
**Minister of Health, Social Serivces and Housing:** QUINTON L. EDNESS.
**Minister of Education:** Dr CLARENCE R. TERCEIRA.
**Minister of Youth, Sport and Recreation:** PAMELA F. GORDON.
**Minister of Human Affairs and Information:** JEROME DILL.
**Minister of Community and Cultural Affairs:** WAYNE L. FURBERT.
**Minister of Works and Engineering:** LEONARD O. GIBBONS.
**Minister of Transport:** MAXWELL BURGESS.
**Minister of Management and Technology:** Dr E. GRANT GIBBONS.

### MINISTRIES

**Office of the Governor:** Government House, 11 Langton Hill, Pembroke, HM 13; tel. 292-3600; telex 3202; fax 295-3823.
**Office of the Premier:** Cabinet Bldg, 105 Front St, Hamilton HM 12; tel. 292-5501; fax 292-8397.
**Ministry of Community and Cultural Affairs:** Old Fire Station Bldg, 81 Court St, Hamilton HM 12; tel. 292-1681; fax 292-2474.
**Ministry of Education:** POB HM 1185, Hamilton HM EX; tel. 236-6904; fax 236-4006.
**Ministry of the Environment:** Government Administration Bldg, 30 Parliament St, Hamilton HM 12; tel. 295-5151; fax 292-2349.

BRITISH DEPENDENT TERRITORIES                                                                                                  *Bermuda*

**Ministry of Finance:** Government Administration Bldg, 30 Parliament St, Hamilton HM 12; tel. 295-5151; telex 3609; fax 295-8152.
**Ministry of Health, Social Services and Housing:** Old Hospital Bldg, 7 Point Finger Rd, Paget DV 04; tel. 236-0224; fax 236-3971.
**Ministry of Human Affairs and Information Services:** Mechanics Bldg, 3rd Floor, 12 Church St, POB HM 2552, Hamilton HM 11; tel. 296-0609; fax 296-0616.
**Ministry of Labour and Home Affairs:** Government Administration Bldg, 30 Parliament St, Hamilton HM 12; tel. 295-5151; telex 3775; fax 295-4780.
**Ministry of Management and Technology:** Cabinet Bldg, 105 Front St, Hamilton HM12; tel. 292-5501; fax 296-0435.
**Ministry of Tourism:** Global House, 43 Church St, Hamilton HM 12; tel. 292-0023; telex 3243; fax 292-7537.
**Ministry of Transport:** Global House, 43 Church St, Hamilton HM 12; tel. 295-3130; fax 295-1013.
**Ministry of Works and Engineering:** Post Office Bldg, 56 Church St, POB 525, Hamilton HM 12; tel. 295-5151; fax 295-0170.
**Ministry of Youth, Sport and Recreation:** Old Fire Station Bldg, 81 Court St, Hamilton HM 12; tel. 295-0855; fax 295-6292.

## Legislature

### SENATE

**President:** ALBERT S. JACKSON.
There are 11 nominated members.

### HOUSE OF ASSEMBLY

**Speaker:** ERNEST D. DECOUTO.
There are 40 elected members.
**Clerk to the Legislature:** JAMES SMITH, The Legislature, Hamilton.

**General Election, 5 October 1993**

| Party | Seats |
| --- | --- |
| United Bermuda Party | 22 |
| Progressive Labour Party | 18 |

## Political Organizations

**National Liberal Party (NLP):** POB HM 1794, Hamilton HM HX; tel. 292-8587; f. 1985; Leader GILBERT DARRELL; Chair. GRAEME OUTERBRIDGE.
**Progressive Labour Party (PLP):** Court St, POB HM 1367, Hamilton HM FX; tel. 292-2264; fax 295-2933; f. 1963; advocates the 'Bermudianization' of the economy, more equitable taxation, a more developed system of welfare and immediate preparation for independence; Leader FREDERICK WADE; Chair. IRA P. PHILIP.
**United Bermuda Party (UBP):** Central Office, 87 John F. Burrows Bldg, Chancery Lane, POB HM 715, Hamilton HM CX; tel. 295-0729; f. 1964; policy of participatory democracy, supporting system of free enterprise; Leader Sir JOHN W. SWAN; Chair. GARY R. PITMAN.

## Judicial System

**Chief Justice:** AUSTIN WARD.
**President of the Court of Appeal:** Sir DENYS ROBERTS.
**Registrar of Supreme Court and Court of Appeal:** NORMA WADE.
**Attorney-General:** ELLIOTT MOTTLEY.
**Solicitor-General:** BARRIE MEADE.

The Court of Appeal was established in 1964, with powers and jurisdiction of equivalent courts in other parts of the Commonwealth. The Supreme Court has jurisdiction over all serious criminal matters and has unlimited civil jurisdiction. The Court also hears civil and criminal appeals from the Magistrates' Courts. The three Magistrates' Courts have jurisdiction over all petty offences, and have a limited civil jurisdiction.

## Religion

### CHRISTIANITY

Many Christian denominations are represented in Bermuda, the major ones being Anglican and Episcopal, African Methodist, Roman Catholic, Wesleyan Methodist, Presbyterian, Seventh-day Adventist, Baptist and Pentecostal.

### The Anglican Communion

The Anglican Church of Bermuda consists of a single, extra-provincial diocese, directly under the metropolitan jurisdiction of the Archbishop of Canterbury, the Primate of All England. There are about 23,000 Anglicans and Episcopalians in Bermuda.
**Bishop of Bermuda:** Rt Rev. WILLIAM DOWN, Bishop's Lodge, POB HM 769, Hamilton HM CX; tel. 292-2967; fax 292-5421.

### The Roman Catholic Church

Bermuda forms a single diocese, suffragan to the archdiocese of Kingston in Jamaica. At 31 December 1993 there were an estimated 9,980 adherents in the Territory. The Bishop participates in the Antilles Episcopal Conference (currently based in Port of Spain, Trinidad and Tobago).
**Bishop of Hamilton in Bermuda:** BRIAN LEO HENNESSY, St Theresa's Cathedral, 2 Astwood Rd, POB HM 1191, Hamilton HM EX; tel. 236-7740; fax 236-7224.

### Protestant Churches

**Baptist Church:** Emmanuel Baptist Church, 35 Dundonald St, Hamilton HM 10; tel. 295-6555; Minister DANIEL STANLEY.
**Wesley Methodist Church:** 41 Church St, POB HM 346, Hamilton HM BX; tel. 292-0418; fax 295-9460.

## The Press

**Bermuda Magazine:** POB HM 2032, Hamilton HM HX; tel. 292-7279; f. 1990; quarterly; Editor-in-Chief CHARLES BARCLAY.
**The Bermuda Sun:** 41 Victoria St, POB HM 1241, Hamilton HM FX; tel. 295-3902; fax 292-5597; f. 1964; weekly; official government gazette; Editor TOM VESEY; circ. 15,500.
**The Bermuda Times:** 9 Burnaby St, Hamilton; tel. 292-2596; f. 1987; weekly community newsletter; Chair. Dr EWART F. BROWN.
**The Bermudian:** Addendum Lane, POB HM 283, Hamilton HM AX; tel. 295-0695; fax 295-8616; f. 1930; monthly; pictorial and resort magazine; Editor KEVIN STEVENSON; circ. 14,000.
**The Mid-Ocean News:** Par-la-Ville Rd, POB HM 1025, Hamilton HM DX; tel. 295-5881; f. 1911; weekly with *TV Guide*; Editor TIM HODGSON; Gen. Man. KEITH JENSEN; circ. 14,500.
**The Royal Gazette:** Par-la-Ville Rd, POB HM 1025, Hamilton HM DX; tel. 295-5881; f. 1828; morning daily; Editor DAVID L. WHITE; Gen. Man. KEITH JENSEN; circ. 17,500.
**The Worker's Voice:** 49 Union Sq., Hamilton HM12; tel. 292-0044; fax 295-7992; fortnightly; organ of the Bermuda Industrial Union; Editor B. B. BALL.

## Radio and Television

In 1992 there were an estimated 78,000 radio receivers and 57,000 television receivers in use.
**Bermuda Broadcasting Company:** POB HM 452, Hamilton HM BX; tel. 295-2828; fax 295-4282; f. 1982 as merger of ZBM (f. 1943) and ZFB (f. 1962); operates 4 radio stations and 2 TV stations (Channels 9 and 7); CEO RICK RICHARDSON; Programme Dir JANNELL FORD.
**DeFontes Broadcasting Co Ltd—VSB:** POB HM 1450, Hamilton HM 5; tel. 295-1450; fax 295-1658; f. 1981 as St George's Broadcasting Co; commercial; 4 radio stations, 1 television station; Pres. KENNETH DEFONTES; Man. DUDLEY E. BROWNE.
**Bermuda Cablevision:** 2 Cavendish Rd, Hamilton; tel. 292-5544; f. 1988; 45 channels; Pres. DAVID LINES.

## Finance

(cap. = capital; dep. = deposits; res = reserves; m. = million; br. = branch; amounts in Bermuda dollars)

### BANKING
#### Central Bank

**Bermuda Monetary Authority:** Sofia Bldg, 48 Church St, POB HM 2447, Hamilton HM 12; tel. 295-5278; telex 3567; fax 292-7471; f. 1969; central issuing and monetary authority; cap. 9.0m., res 8.2m., dep. 0.4m. (Dec. 1993); Chair. MANSFIELD H. BROCK Jnr; Gen. Man. MALCOLM E. WILLIAMS.

#### Commercial Banks

**Bank of Bermuda Ltd:** 6 Front St, Hamilton HM 11; tel. 295-4000; telex 3212; fax 295-7093; f. 1889; cap. 18.6m., res 142.1m., dep. 6,847.8m. (June 1994); Chair. ELDON H. TRIMINGHAM; Pres. and CEO CHARLES VAUGHAN-JOHNSON; 6 domestic brs, 14 overseas brs.

BRITISH DEPENDENT TERRITORIES                                                                                                         *Bermuda*

**Bank of N. T. Butterfield & Son Ltd:** 65 Front St, POB HM 195, Hamilton HM AX; tel. 295-1111; fax 292-4365; f. 1858; inc. 1904; cap. 52.8m., res 164.6m., dep. 3,039.8m. (June 1993); Chair. Sir DAVID GIBBONS; Pres. and CEO J. MICHAEL COLLIER; 5 brs.

**Bermuda Commercial Bank Ltd:** Bermuda Commercial Bank Bldg, 44 Church St, POB HM 1748, Hamilton HM GX; tel. 295-5678; telex 3336; fax 295-8091; f. 1969; 32%-owned by First Curaçao International Bank NV; cap. 3.4m., res 6.9m., dep. 201.3m. (Sept. 1993); Pres. JOHN DEUSS; Man. Dir AUDETTE EXEL.

### INSURANCE

Bermuda had a total of 1,791 registered insurance companies in 1992, the majority of which are subsidiaries of foreign insurance companies, or owned by foreign industrial or financial concerns. Many of them have offices on the island.

**Ace Ltd:** Ace Bldg, 30 Woodbourne Ave, POB HM 1015, Hamilton HM DX; tel. 292-5200; fax 295-5221.

**Argus Insurance Co Ltd:** Argus Insurance Bldg, 12 Wesley St, POB HM 1064, Hamilton HM EX; tel. 295-2021; telex 3342; fax 292-6763.

**Paumanock Insurance Co Ltd:** POB HM 2267, Hamilton HM JX; tel. 292-2404; fax 292-2648.

## Trade and Industry

**Bermuda Chamber of Commerce:** 50 Front St, POB HM 655, Hamilton HM CX; tel. 295-4201; fax 292-5779; f. 1905; Pres. LOUIS MOWBRAY; Exec. Vice-Pres. CAROLYN MELLO; 700 mems.

**Bermuda International Business Association:** Hamilton; Chair. CUMMINGS ZUILL.

**Bermuda Small Business Development Corpn:** POB HM 637, Hamilton HM CX; tel. 292-5570; f. 1980; funded jointly by the Government and private banks; guarantees loans to small businesses; assets $500,000; Dir MICHELLE KHALDUN.

### EMPLOYERS' ASSOCIATIONS

**Bermuda Employers' Council:** 304 Bermuda Mechanics Bldg, Hamilton; tel. 295-5070; f. 1960; advisory body on labour relations; Pres. DENNIS TUCKER; Exec. Dir MALCOLM DIXON; 300 mems.

**Construction Association of Bermuda:** POB HM 238, Hamilton HM AX; tel. 292-5920; fax 292-5864; f. 1968; Pres. D. EXELL; Hon. Sec. L. MARSHALL; 33 mems.

**Hotel Employers of Bermuda:** c/o Bermuda Hotel Association, 'Carmel', 61 King St, Hamilton HM 19; tel. 295-2127; fax 292-6671; f. 1968; Pres. ROGER BORSINK; Vice-Pres. WILLIAM GRIFFITH; 18 mems.

### TRADE UNIONS

There are nine registered trade unions, the principal ones being:

**Amalgamated Bermuda Union of Teachers:** POB HM 726, Hamilton HM CX; tel. 292-6515; fax 292-0697; f. 1963; Pres. MICHAEL A. CHARLES; 640 mems.

**Bermuda Federation of Musicians and Variety Artists:** Reid St, POB HM 6, Hamilton HM AX; tel. 291-0138; Sec.-Gen. LLOYD H. L. SIMMONS; 318 mems.

**Bermuda Industrial Union:** 49 Union Sq., Hamilton HM 12; tel. 292-0044; fax 295-5992; f. 1946; Pres. OTTIWELL SIMMONS; Gen. Sec. HELENA BURGESS; 5,202 mems.

**Bermuda Public Services Association:** POB HM 763, Hamilton HM CX; tel. 292-6985; fax 292-1149; re-formed 1961; Pres. LELEATH BAILEY; Gen. Sec. EUGENE BLAKENEY; 2,500 mems.

## Transport

### ROADS

There are some 240 km (150 miles) of well-surfaced roads, with almost 6 km (4 miles) reserved for cyclists and pedestrians. Each Bermudian household is permitted only one passenger vehicle, and visitors may only hire mopeds, to limit traffic congestion.

### SHIPPING

The chief port of Bermuda is Hamilton, with a secondary port at St George's. Both are used by freight and cruise ships. An administrative board, the Ports Authority, co-ordinates the capital development of all ports in Bermuda and regulates the berthing, anchoring and mooring of all ships and boats within the ports.

There is a 'free' port, Freeport, on Ireland Island, which is administered by the Public Works Department of the Bermuda Government, but the management of the Freeport commercial docks is conducted on its behalf by the Marine and Ports Services Department. The docks in Hamilton and St George's are operated by the municipal authorities.

Bermuda is a free-flag nation, and, at January 1993, the shipping register comprised 106 commercial ships totalling 3,494,439 grt and 330 yachts totalling 32,238 grt (the fifth-largest free-flag merchant fleet in the world).

**Department of Marine and Ports Services:** POB HM 180, Hamilton HM AX; tel. 295-6575; telex 3505; fax 295-3718; Dir of Marine and Ports Services RONALD D. ROSS; Deputy Dir and Habour Master MICHAEL DOLDING.

**Bermuda Registry of Shipping:** POB HM 1628, Hamilton HM GX; tel. 295-7251; telex 3505; fax 295-3718.

#### Principal Shipping Companies

**A. M. Services Ltd:** 10 Queen St, Hamilton HM 11; tel. 295-0850; fax 292-3704.

**Atlantic Marine Limited Partnership:** Richmond House, 12 Par-la-Ville Rd, POB HM 2089, Hamilton HM HX; tel. 295-0614; telex 3658; fax 292-1549; f. 1970; Gen. Man. BRUCE LUCAS.

**Bermuda International Shipping Ltd:** 35 Church St, Hamilton HM 12; tel. 295-4176; fax 292-4823.

**Container Ship Management Ltd:** 14 Par-la-Ville Rd, Hamilton HM JX; tel. 295-1624; fax 295-3781.

**Gearbulk Holding Ltd:** Par-la-Ville Place, 14 Par-la-Ville Rd, Hamilton HM JX; tel. 295-2184; fax 295-2234.

**Globe Forwarding Co:** 32 Parliament St, Hamilton; tel. 292-3218; fax 295-3502.

**Gotaas-Larsen Shipping Corpn:** Perry Bldg, Church St, Hamilton; tel. 295-3457; telex 3641; liquefied petroleum gas, liquefied natural gas, product/chemical and crude oil carriers; Man. Dir A. CLAUSEN.

**Red Rose Ltd:** Clarendon House, Church St, Hamilton; Pres. FRANK MUTCH; Sec. ALAN L. BROWN.

**Shell Bermuda (Overseas) Ltd:** Shell House, Ferry Reach, POB 2, St George's 1.

**World-Wide Shipping Managers Ltd:** Clarendon House, 2 Church St, Hamilton HM 5.

Principal non-Bermudian lines calling at Bermuda: All America, Atlantic Lines, Bermuda Express Service, Cunard, Flagships Inc, Independent Gulf, Pacific Steam Navigation Co and Saguenay.

### CIVIL AVIATION

The only airfield is the US Naval Air Station, Bermuda. All civil aircraft are handled under the jurisdiction of the Department of Civil Aviation, and must have a licence from the US Navy before using the airfield. In November 1993 it was announced that US forces would withdraw from the island by September 1995, and thereafter the airport would be operated by the Bermudian Government.

**Department of Civil Aviation:** Bermuda Air Terminal, 2 Kindley Field Rd, St George's GE CX; tel. 293-1640; telex 3248; fax 293-2417; responsible for all civil aviation matters; Dir of Civil Aviation HERMAN G. TUCKER (acting).

## Tourism

Tourism is the principal industry of Bermuda and is government-sponsored. The great attractions of the islands are the climate, scenery, and facilities for outdoor entertainment of all types. In 1994 a total of 588,788 tourists (including 172,865 cruise-ship passengers) visited Bermuda. The industry earned B $504.5m. in 1993, when there were 4,236 hotel rooms. The majority of visitors are from the USA.

**Department of Tourism:** Global House, 43 Church St, Hamilton HM 12; tel. 292-0023; fax 292-7537; Dir of Tourism GARY L. PHILLIPS.

**Bermuda Hotel Association:** 'Carmel', 61 King St, Hamilton HM 19; tel. 295-2127; fax 292-6671; Chair. J. CHRISTOPHER ASTWOOD; Pres. STEPHEN BARKER; Pres.-Elect DENNIS TUCKER; 45 mem. hotels.

# THE BRITISH ANTARCTIC TERRITORY

The British Antarctic Territory lies within the Antarctic Treaty area (i.e. south of latitude 60° S). The Territory, created a British colony on 3 March 1962, consists of all islands and territories south of latitude 60° S, between longitudes 20° and 80° W, and includes the South Orkney Islands, the South Shetland Islands, the Antarctic Peninsula and areas south and east of the Weddell Sea. With the island of South Georgia and the South Sandwich Islands (now forming a separate territory, q.v.), this area had been constituted by the United Kingdom as the Falkland Islands Dependencies in 1908.

**Area:** Land covers about 1,710,000 sq km (660,000 sq miles).

**Population:** There is no permanent population, but scientists and support personnel (59 in the Antarctic winter of 1992) staff the British Antarctic Survey stations.

**Commissioner:** ANTHONY LONGRIGG (South Atlantic and Antarctic Dept, Foreign and Commonwealth Office, Whitehall, London SW1A 2AP, England; tel. (171) 270-3000).

**British Antarctic Survey:** High Cross, Madingley Rd, Cambridge, CB3 0ET, England; tel. (1223) 251400; telex 817725; fax (1223) 362616; f. 1962 to replace Falkland Islands Dependencies Survey; responsible for almost all British scientific activities in Antarctica; operates two ice-strengthened ocean-going vessels, four de Havilland Twin Otter and one Dash-7 aircraft; the Survey's total expenditure for 1993/94 was £21.9m.; Dir Dr R. BARRY HEYWOOD.

### SURVEY STATIONS

|  | Latitude | Longitude |
|---|---|---|
| Damoy Point (summer only) | 64° 49' S | 63° 32' W |
| Faraday | 65° 15' S | 64° 16' W |
| Fossil Bluff (summer only) | 71° 20' S | 68° 17' W |
| Halley | 75° 35' S | 26° 44' W |
| Rothera | 67° 34' S | 68° 07' W |
| Signy | 60° 43' S | 45° 36' W |

# THE BRITISH INDIAN OCEAN TERRITORY (BIOT)

The British Indian Ocean Territory (BIOT) was formed in November 1965, through the amalgamation of the former Seychelles islands of Aldabra, Desroches and Farquhar with the Chagos Archipelago, a group of islands 1,930 km north-east of Mauritius, and previously administered by the governor of Mauritius. Aldabra, Desroches and Farquhar were ceded to Seychelles when that country was granted independence in June 1976. Since then BIOT has comprised only the Chagos Archipelago, including the coral atoll Diego Garcia, with a total land area of 60 sq km (23 sq miles), together with a surrounding area of some 54,400 sq km (21,000 sq miles) of ocean.

BIOT was established to meet British and US defence requirements in the Indian Ocean. Previously, the principal economic functions of the islands were fishing and the production of copra: the islands, together with the coconut plantations, were owned by a private company. After the purchase of the islands by the British crown in 1967, the plantations ceased to operate, and the population were offered the choice of resettlement in Mauritius or in the Seychelles. The majority (which numbered about 1,200) went to Mauritius, the resettlement taking place during 1969–73, prior to the construction of the military facility. Mauritius subsequently campaigned for the immediate return of the Territory, and received support from the Organization of African Unity and India. The election victory of the Mouvement Militant Mauricien in 1982 led to an intensification of these demands. Mauritius supported the former island population in a protracted dispute with the United Kingdom over compensation for those displaced, which ended in 1982 when the British government agreed to an *ex gratia* payment of £4m. In early 1984, however, it was reported that people who had been displaced from Diego Garcia were seeking $6m. from the US government to finance their resettlement in Mauritius. The US administration declined to accept any financial responsibility for the population.

A 1966 agreement between the United Kingdom and the USA provides for BIOT to be used by both countries over an initial period of 50 years, with the option of extending this for a further 20 years. The United Kingdom undertook to cede the Chagos Archipelago to Mauritius when it was no longer required for defence purposes. All US activities in BIOT are conducted in consultation with the British Government. Originally the US military presence was limited to a communications centre on Diego Garcia. In 1972, however, construction of a naval support facility was begun, apparently in response to the expansion of the Soviet maritime presence in the Indian Ocean. This plan was expanded in 1974, the agreement being formalized by an 'exchange of notes' in 1976, and again following Soviet military intervention in Afghanistan in December 1979. Facilities on Diego Garcia include a communications centre, a runway with a length of 3,650 m, anchorage, refuelling and various ancillary services. During the 1980s the US government undertook a programme of expansion and improvement of the naval support facility which was to include a space-tracking station. In August 1987 the US navy began to use Diego Garcia as a facility for minesweeping helicopters taking part in operations in the Persian (Arabian) Gulf. Following Iraq's invasion of Kuwait in August 1990, Diego Garcia was used as a base for US B-52 aircraft, which were deployed in the Gulf region.

In January 1988 Mauritius renewed its campaign to regain sovereignty over the Chagos Archipelago, and reiterated its support for a 'zone of peace' in the Indian Ocean. In November 1989, following an incident in which a military aircraft belonging to the US air force accidentally bombed a US naval vessel near Diego Garcia, a demonstration was held outside the US embassy in Mauritius, demanding the withdrawal of foreign military forces from the area. The Mauritius Government announced that it would draw the attention of the UN Security Council to the dangers that it perceived in the execution of US military air exercises. However, the US assistant secretary of state for african affairs reiterated during an official visit to Mauritius, in the same month, that the US would maintain its military presence in the Indian Ocean.

In January 1994 arrangements were agreed for the establishment of a joint British-Mauritius fisheries commission to promote and co-ordinate conservation and scientific research within the territorial waters of BIOT. In May the Mauritius Ministers of Foreign Affairs and Fisheries paid a two-day official visit to the Chagos Archipelago.

The civil administration of BIOT is the responsibility of a non-resident commissioner in the foreign and commonwealth office in London, represented on Diego Garcia by a royal naval commander and a small British naval presence. A chief justice, a senior magistrate and a principal legal adviser (who performs the functions of an attorney-general) are resident in the United Kingdom.

**Land Area:** about 60 sq km.

**Population:** There are no permanent inhabitants. In 1991 there were about 1,200 US and British military personnel and 1,700 civilian contractors in the Territory.

**Currency:** The pound sterling and the US dollar are both used.

**Commissioner:** DAVID MACLENNAN, Head of African Dept (Equatorial), Foreign and Commonwealth Office, King Charles St, London, SW1A 2AH, England; tel. (171) 270-3000.

**Administrator:** DAVID SMITH, African Dept (Equatorial), Foreign and Commonwealth Office, King Charles St, London, SW1A 2AH, England; tel. (171) 270-3000.

**Commissioner's Representative:** Commdr N. J. P. WRAITH, RN, Diego Garcia, c/o BFPO Ships; telex 938 6903.

# THE BRITISH VIRGIN ISLANDS

## Introductory Survey

**Location, Climate, Language, Religion, Flag, Capital**

The British Virgin Islands consist of more than 60 islands and cays, of which only 16 are inhabited. The islands, most of which are mountainous and of volcanic origin (the only exception of any size is the coralline island of Anegada), lie at the northern end of the Leeward Islands, about 100 km (62 miles) to the east of Puerto Rico and adjoining the United States Virgin Islands. The climate is sub-tropical but extremes of heat are relieved by the trade winds. The average annual rainfall is 1,000 mm (39 ins). The official language is English. Most of the inhabitants profess Christianity. The flag is the British 'Blue Ensign', with the Territory's badge (a green shield, with a white-clad virgin and 12 oil lamps, above a scroll bearing the motto 'vigilate') in the fly. The capital, Road Town, is situated on the island of Tortola.

**Recent History**

Previously peopled by Caribs, and named by the navigator Christopher Colombus after St Ursula and her 11,000 fellow-martyrs, the islands were settled by buccaneers and the Dutch, but were finally annexed by the British in 1672. In 1872 they became part of the British colony of the Leeward Islands, which was administered under a federal system. The federation was dissolved in July 1956, but the Governor of the Leeward Islands continued to administer the British Virgin Islands until 1960, when direct responsibility was assumed by an appointed Administrator (restyled Governor in 1971). Unlike the other Leeward Islands, the British Virgin Islands did not join the Federation of the West Indies (1958–62), preferring to develop its links with the US Virgin Islands.

A new Constitution was introduced in April 1967, when H. Lavity Stoutt became the islands' first Chief Minister. He was later replaced by Willard Wheatley. At an election in September 1975 Stoutt's Virgin Islands Party (VIP) and the United Party (UP) each won three of the seven elective seats on the Legislative Council. The balance of power was held by Wheatley, sitting as an independent member, and he continued in office, with Stoutt as Deputy Chief Minister.

An amended Constitution took effect in June 1977, giving more extensive internal self-government; some electoral changes were also made (see Constitution, below). In the first election to the enlarged Legislative Council to take place under the new Constitution, in November 1979, independent candidates won five of the nine elective seats, with the VIP winning the remainder. Stoutt secured enough support to be reinstated as Chief Minister. In the November 1983 election the VIP and the UP each secured four seats. The one successful independent candidate, Cyril Romney, became Chief Minister and formed a coalition Government with members of the UP.

In August 1986 the Legislative Council was dissolved by the Governor, six days before a scheduled council debate on a motion of 'no confidence' against Romney (who had allegedly been involved with a company under investigation by the British police and the US Department of Justice's Drug Enforcement Administration—DEA). At a general election in September the VIP won five of the nine elective seats, with the UP and independent candidates (including Romney) taking two seats each. Stoutt was appointed Chief Minister.

The Deputy Chief Minister, Omar Hodge, was dismissed from the Executive Council in March 1988, following an official inquiry into allegations of financial malpractice (he continued to protest his innocence, and won a libel suit in January 1990). Hodge was replaced by Ralph O'Neal, formerly leader of the UP, who joined the VIP. In March 1989 Hodge formed a new political party, the Independent People's Movement (IPM), together with the Director of Tourism, who complained of a lack of government support for the industry.

At a general election in November 1990 the VIP increased its majority to six seats, while the IPM gained one seat and independent candidates secured two; the UP lost both its seats. Stoutt retained the post of Chief Minister.

The principal concern of the Stoutt administration in the early 1990s was the trade in, and increasing local use of, illicit drugs. Meanwhile, the British Government was considering ways to improve the islands' air and sea defences against the illegal drugs trade, and was encouraging the introduction of legislation that would permit the confiscation of the assets of convicted traffickers. Similarly, in late 1990 the Stoutt administration introduced legislation to impose more stringent regulations governing the 'offshore' financial sector, while plans to review immigration policy were under discussion, in an attempt to reduce the number of illegal immigrants entering the Territory. Both areas had previously been considered to be insufficiently protected from exploitation by traffickers seeking to introduce illicit drugs into the islands or to divert funds from their sale through the financial sector. In December 1991 the DEA paid the Government of the British Virgin Islands US $0.6m. and in May 1992 a further US $1.8m. in assets confiscated from drugs-traffickers convicted in the USA.

In October 1991 Peter Alfred Penfold was appointed Governor of the Territory.

In May 1993 Cyril Romney resigned as leader of the Opposition in the Legislative Council and was replaced by another independent member, Walwyn Brewley. In August the British Government appointed three commissioners to review the Territory's Constitution at the request of the Legislative Council. Proposed changes included the introduction of direct elections for the position of Chief Minister, the enlargement of the Legislative Council and the adoption of a bill of rights. The British Government's decision in early 1994 to accept the commission's proposal to enlarge the Legislative Council to 13 seats (by the creation of four seats representing the Territory 'at large') was strongly criticized by Stoutt. His opposition to the changes intensified in July, when he failed to obtain a deferral of the decision in order that the Legislative Council could debate the issue.

At elections to the newly-enlarged legislature on 20 February 1995 the VIP won six seats, the UP and the Concerned Citizens' Movement (CCM—formerly IPM) each secured two seats and independent candidates won three seats. One of the successful independents, Alvin Christopher, subsequently gave his support to the VIP, thus providing the party with the majority required to form a Government. Stoutt retained the post of Chief Minister, and Christopher was appointed Minister of Communications, Works and Public Utilities in the new Government.

In May 1995 the Deputy Chief Minister, Ralph O'Neal, was appointed acting Chief Minister, following the sudden death of Stoutt.

In the early 1990s concern was expressed over possible environmental damage, particularly to the coral reefs, as a result of exploitation by the tourist industry.

**Government**

Under the provisions of the 1977 Constitution, the Governor is appointed by the British monarch and is responsible for external affairs, defence and internal security. The Governor is also Chairman of the Executive Council, which comprises five other members. The Legislative Council comprises 15 members: a Speaker, one *ex-officio* member, and 13 members elected by universal adult suffrage.

**Economic Affairs**

In 1991, according to official figures, the British Virgin Islands recorded a gross domestic product (GDP), at current prices, of US $175m. and GDP per head of US $10,479. In 1992 GDP grew by an estimated 2.5%, a slightly smaller increase than in previous years, owing largely to a decrease in tourist arrivals. It was forecast that GDP would increase by some 4% in 1995.

Agriculture (including forestry and fishing) contributed 3.4% of GDP in 1989, and engaged 1.8% of those in paid employment in 1987. The infertility of the soil limits the cultivation of crops, which mainly consist of fruit and vegetables, for domestic consumption or export to the US Virgin Islands, and some sugar cane (for the production of rum). The fishing industry caters for local consumption and export, and provides a sporting activity for tourists.

Industry (including mining, manufacturing, construction and public utilities) accounted for 13.6% of GDP in 1989 and engaged 16.0% of the employed labour force in 1987. The mining sector is small, consisting of the extraction of materials for the construction industry and of some salt. There are residual reserves of copper, gold and silver. Manufacturing, which provided 3.0% of GDP in 1989, consists mainly of light industry; there is one rum distillery, some plants for the preparation of construction materials and some small-scale industries. A water desalination plant began operations on Virgin Gorda in February 1994 and another was to be opened later in the year. Construction activity accounted for 6.7% of GDP in 1989. Most energy requirements must be imported (petroleum products accounted for an estimated 5.3% of total imports in 1987).

Services, primarily tourism and financial services, constitute the principal economic sector of the British Virgin Islands, contributing 83.0% of GDP in 1989. The tourist industry earned some US $109.4m. in 1992, and employed one-third of the working population, directly or indirectly. The British Virgin Islands is the largest 'bareboat' chartering centre in the Caribbean, and in 1987 some 62% of stop-over visitors were catered for by the charter-yacht sub-sector. Nevertheless, in 1989 the restaurants and hotels sector contributed 27.9% of GDP. Most visitors come from the USA (61.7% of total stop-over arrivals in 1987).

Financial services expanded as a result of legislative measures adopted in 1984, and also benefited from political disturbances in Panama in 1988 and 1989 and political uncertainty in Hong Kong in the early 1990s. In 1990 the 'offshore' sector contributed an estimated US $7.2m. in revenue, and in 1987 4.4% of the employed labour force were engaged in the financial and business sector. The business sector contributed 22.0% of GDP in 1989. Revenue from the registration of new companies earned more than US $16m. in 1992. There were more than 130,000 international businesses registered in the islands at the end of 1994.

In 1990 the British Virgin Islands recorded a trade deficit of US $127.5m. (exports were worth some 2.6% of imports). The trade deficit is normally offset by receipts from tourism, development aid, remittances from islanders working abroad (many in the US Virgin Islands) and, increasingly, from the 'offshore' financial sector. The principal sources of imports (most of the islands' requirements must be imported) are the USA and, especially, its dependencies of Puerto Rico and the US Virgin Islands, and also the United Kingdom. The principal market for the limited amount of exports is the US Virgin Islands and Puerto Rico; rum is exported principally to the USA. Machinery and transport equipment are the main import, and fresh fish, fruit and vegetables, rum, sand and gravel the main exports.

In the financial year ending 30 June 1995 there was an estimated budget surplus of some US $8m., excluding capital expenditure for which the British Virgin Islands receive aid. British budgetary support ceased in 1977, but the United Kingdom grants development aid (£800,000 in 1988). External debt totalled US $35.0m. at the end of 1992. The average annual rate of inflation was 3.8% in 1985–92; consumer prices increased by an average of 3.2% in 1992. Unemployment is negligible, with the people of the Territory enjoying privileged access to the US Virgin Islands, where employment has generally been plentiful.

The British Virgin Islands became an associate member of the Caribbean Community and Common Market (CARICOM, see p. 114) in 1991; it is a member of CARICOM's Caribbean Development Bank (see p. 116) and an associate member of the Organisation of Eastern Caribbean States (see p. 116). In economic affairs the Territory has close affiliations with the neighbouring US Virgin Islands, and uses US currency. As a dependency of the United Kingdom, the islands have the status of Overseas Territory in association with the European Union (see p. 143).

The British Virgin Islands receive assistance for capital development projects, but the recurrent budget habitually operates with a small surplus. In 1991 the Government announced that it was to invest the budgetary surplus in several capital projects, including improvements to the islands' port and airport facilities and the construction of a community college and a central administration complex. A commission was also established to encourage film production on the islands. In terms of government revenue and employment, the Territory benefited during the 1980s from the expansion of the 'offshore' financial sector. An information exchange agreement with the USA (signed in 1987, but specifically excluding the investigation of tax evasion) provides some protection against the use of the islands for the processing of profits of the illegal drugs trade. Under the terms of further regulations, introduced in 1990 and 1991, all 'offshore' companies were required to hold a licence, and their operations were liable to be overseen by an inspector. Legislation aimed at attracting more insurance companies to the islands was approved in late 1994, and further incentives were expected to be introduced in 1995. The Government is also anxious to expand the tourist industry (which was suffering from the effects of recession in 1991 and 1992), while preventing damage to the environment or a decline in the islands' reputation as a centre for visitors of above-average wealth.

## Social Welfare

In 1989 the islands had one hospital with a total of 50 beds (there is also a private, 8-bed hospital specializing in cosmetic surgery), and in 1987 there were 11 physicians and two dentists. There are also nine health centres and one senior citizens' home. Estimated expenditure on medical services was US $5.7m. in 1991. Public assistance is provided for needy persons.

## Education

Primary education is free and universal. Secondary education is also free. In 1989 there were four private or denominational and 15 state primary schools, one comprehensive High School and three other secondary schools. In 1993 3,401 pupils were enrolled in all primary and pre-primary schools, while 1,247 were enrolled in secondary education. Higher education is available at the University of the Virgin Islands (St Thomas, US Virgin Islands) and elsewhere in the Caribbean, in North America and in the United Kingdom. In 1970 only 1.7% of the adult population had received no schooling; illiteracy is negligible. Estimated expenditure on education in 1991 was US $6.1m., or 12.0% of budgetary expenditure.

## Public Holidays

**1995:** 1 January (New Year's Day), 6 March (Commonwealth Day), 14 April (Good Friday), 17 April (Easter Monday), 5 June (Whit Monday), 12 June (Queen's Official Birthday), 1 July (Territory Day), 7–9 August (August Monday, Tuesday and Wednesday), 21 October (Saint Ursula's Day), 14 November (Prince of Wales' Birthday), 25–26 December (Christmas).

**1996:** 1 January (New Year's Day), 4 March (Commonwealth Day), 5 April (Good Friday), 8 April (Easter Monday), 27 May (Whit Monday), 10 June (Queen's Official Birthday), 1 July (Territory Day), 5–7 August (August Monday, Tuesday and Wednesday), 21 October (Saint Ursula's Day), 14 November (Prince of Wales' Birthday), 25–26 December (Christmas).

## Weights and Measures

The imperial system is used.

# Statistical Survey

Sources: Deputy Governor's Office, Tortola; OECS Economic Affairs Secretariat, *Statistical Digest*.

### AREA AND POPULATION

**Area:** 153 sq km (59 sq miles). *Principal islands* (sq km): Tortola 54.4; Anegada 38.8; Virgin Gorda 21.4; Jost Van Dyke 9.1.

**Population:** 16,644 (males 8,570; females 8,074) at census of 12 May 1991; *By island* (1980): Tortola 9,119; Virgin Gorda 1,412; Anegada 164; Jost Van Dyke 134; Other islands 156; (1991) Tortola 13,568.

**Density** (1991): 108.8 per sq km.

**Principal Town:** Road Town (capital), population 2,500 (estimate, 1987).

**Births, Marriages and Deaths** (registrations, 1989): 244 live births (birth rate 19.5 per 1,000); (1988) 176 marriages (marriage rate 14.2 per 1,000); 77 deaths (death rate 6.1 per 1,000). Source: UN, *Demographic Yearbook*.

**Employment** (1987): Agriculture, hunting, forestry and fishing 118; Mining and quarrying 17; Manufacturing 365; Electricity, gas and water 154; Construction 515; Trade, restaurants and hotels 605; Transport, storage and communications 430; Financing, insurance, real estate and business services 292; Community, social and personal services 4,071; Total 6,567 (males 3,732, females 2,835). Figures exclude own-account workers and unpaid family workers. Source: ILO, *Year Book of Labour Statistics*.

**Total employed:** 8,534 in 1989; 8,625 in 1990.

### AGRICULTURE, ETC.

**Fishing** (metric tons, live weight): Total catch 1,377 in 1990; 1,400 in 1991; 1,400 (FAO estimate—Marine fishes 1,200, Crustaceans 200) in 1992. Source: FAO, *Yearbook of Fishery Statistics*.

### INDUSTRY

**Electric Energy** (production, million kWh): 44 in 1989; 45 in 1990; 45 in 1991. Source: UN, *Industrial Statistics Yearbook*.

### FINANCE

**Currency and Exchange Rate:** United States currency is used: 100 cents = 1 US dollar ($). *Sterling Equivalent* (31 December 1994): £1 sterling = US $1.5645; US $100 = £63.92.

**Budget** (estimates, $ million, 1993/94): Recurrent revenue $77.1m.; Recurrent expenditure $76.4m. *1994/95:* Recurrent expenditure $99.1m.

**Cost of Living** (Consumer Price Index for Road Town; base: 1980 = 100): 152.1 in 1990; 161.9 in 1991; 167.0 in 1992. Source: ILO, *Year Book of Labour Statistics*.

**Gross Domestic Product** ($ million in current prices): 117 in 1987; 131 in 1988; 156 in 1989. Source: UN, *National Accounts Statistics*.

**Gross Domestic Product by Economic Activity** ($ million at current factor cost, 1989): Agriculture, hunting, forestry and fishing 4.8; Mining and quarrying 0.3; Manufacturing 4.3; Electricity, gas and water 5.2; Construction 9.5; Trade, restaurants and hotels 39.5; Transport, storage and communications 21.3; Finance, insurance, real estate and business services 31.2; Community, social and personal services 6.5; Government services 19.0; Sub-total 141.5; *Less* Imputed bank service charge 9.0; Indirect taxes *less* subsidies 23.8; GDP in purchasers' values 156.2. Source: UN, *National Accounts Statistics*.

### EXTERNAL TRADE

**Principal Commodities** ($ '000, 1982): *Imports c.i.f.*: Food and live animals 12,336; Mineral fuels, lubricants, etc. 6,179 (refined petroleum products 5,789); Basic manufactures 6,641; Machinery 5,695; Transport equipment 13,626 (ships and boats 10,987); Miscellaneous manufactured articles 5,033; Total (incl. others) 58,546. *Exports f.o.b.*: Fish and fish preparations 262; Alcoholic beverages 700; Machinery and transport equipment 128; Total (incl. others) 1,241. Source: UN, *International Trade Statistics Yearbook*.

**1990** (provisional, $ million): Imports 130.9; Exports 3.4.

**Principal Trading Partners** ($ '000, 1982): *Imports c.i.f.* (by country of purchase): Netherlands Antilles 5,229; United Kingdom 4,194; USA and Puerto Rico 38,165; US Virgin Islands 7,384; Total (incl. others) 58,546. *Exports f.o.b.* (by country of consumption): USA and Puerto Rico 716; US Virgin Islands 422; Total (incl. others) 1,241. Source: UN, *International Trade Statistics Yearbook*.

### TRANSPORT

**Road Traffic** (motor vehicles registered): 2,539 in 1985; 3,719 in 1986; 3,860 in 1987.

**Shipping:** *International Freight Traffic* ('000 metric tons, 1990): Goods loaded 2; Goods unloaded 55. Source: UN, *Monthly Bulletin of Statistics*. *Cargo Ship Arrivals* (1988): 1,139.

**Civil Aviation** (aircraft arrivals): 8,972 in 1985; 9,854 in 1986.

### TOURISM

**Tourist Arrivals:** 317,670 in 1990; 287,718 in 1991; 269,399 (100,497 stop-overs, 87,551 cruise-ship passengers, 81,351 excursionists) in 1992.

### COMMUNICATIONS MEDIA

**Radio Receivers** (1992): 9,000 in use*.
**Television Receivers** (1992): 4,000 in use*.
**Telephones** (1985): 4,000 in use†.
**Non-Daily Newspapers** (1990): 2 (estimated circulation 4,000)*.

* Source: UNESCO, *Statistical Yearbook*.
† Source: UN, *Statistical Yearbook*.

### EDUCATION

**Pre-primary** (1984): 8 schools; 15 teachers; 174 pupils.
**Primary** (incl. pre-primary, 1987/88): 27 schools; 104 teachers; 2,710 pupils (1990).
**Secondary** (1987/88): 4 schools; 81 teachers; 1,247 pupils (1993).

## Directory

## The Constitution

The British Virgin Islands have had a representative assembly since 1774. The present Constitution took effect from June 1977. Under its terms, the Governor is responsible for defence and internal security, external affairs, terms and conditions of service of public officers, and the administration of the Courts. The Governor also possesses reserved legislative powers in respect of legislation necessary in the interests of his special responsibilities. There is an Executive Council, with the Governor as Chairman, one *ex-officio* member (the Attorney-General), the Chief Minister (appointed by the Governor from among the elected members of the Legislative Council) who has responsibility for finance, and three other ministers (appointed by the Governor on the advice of the Chief Minister); and a Legislative Council consisting of a Speaker, chosen from outside the Council, one *ex-officio* member (the Attorney-General) and 13 elected members (nine members from one-member electoral districts and four members representing the Territory 'at large').

The division of the islands into nine electoral districts, instead of seven, came into effect at the November 1979 general election. The four 'at large' seats were introduced at the February 1995 general election. The minimum voting age was lowered from 21 years to 18 years.

## The Government

**Governor:** DAVID MACKILLIGIN (assumed office June 1995).

### EXECUTIVE COUNCIL
(June 1995)

**Chairman:** The Governor.
**Chief Minister and Minister of Finance:** RALPH O'NEAL (acting).
**Deputy Chief Minister and Minister for Health, Education and Welfare:** (vacant).
**Minister for Communications, Works and Public Utilities:** ALVIN CHRISTOPHER.
**Minister for Natural Resources and Labour:** OLIVER CILLS.
**Attorney-General:** DONALD TROTMAN.

### MINISTRIES

**Office of the Governor:** Government House, Tortola; tel. 42345; telex 7984; fax 45582.
**Office of the Chief Minister:** Road Town, Tortola; tel. 43701; fax 44435.
**Ministry of Communications and Works and Public Utilities:** Road Town, Tortola; tel. 43701.
**Ministry of Finance:** Road Town, Tortola; tel. 43701.
**Ministry of Health, Education and Welfare:** Road Town, Tortola; tel. 43701.
**Ministry of Natural Resources and Labour:** Road Town, Tortola; tel. 43701.

All ministries are based in Road Town, Tortola, mainly at the Central Administration Building (fax 44435).

### LEGISLATIVE COUNCIL

**Speaker:** KEITH FLAX.
**Clerk:** ALLINGTON HODGE.

**General Election, 20 February 1995**

| Party | % of votes | Seats |
| --- | --- | --- |
| Virgin Islands Party | 31.9 | 6 |
| Concerned Citizens' Movement | 14.2 | 2 |
| United Party | 16.5 | 2 |
| Independent | 37.5 | 3 |

## Political Organizations

**Concerned Citizens' Movement (CCM):** Road Town, Tortola; f. 1994 as successor to Independent People's Movement; Leaders OMAR HODGE, WALWYN BREWLEY.

**United Party (UP):** Road Town, Tortola; Chair. ROY PICKERING; Leader CONRAD MADURO.

**Virgin Islands Party (VIP):** Road Town, Tortola; Leader (vacant).

## Judicial System

Justice is administered by the Eastern Caribbean Supreme Court, based in Saint Lucia, which consists of two divisions: The High Court of Justice and The Court of Appeal. There is a resident Puisne Judge on the islands. There are also a Magistrate's Court, a Juvenile Court and a Court of Summary Jurisdiction.

**Puisne Judge:** SYLVIA BERTRAND.
**Registrar General:** SYDNEY C. JACOBS, Courts of Justice, Road Town, Tortola.

## Religion

### CHRISTIANITY

#### The Roman Catholic Church

The diocese of St John's-Basseterre, suffragan to the archdiocese of Castries (Saint Lucia), includes Anguilla, Antigua and Barbuda, the British Virgin Islands, Montserrat and Saint Christopher and Nevis. The Bishop is resident in St John's, Antigua.

### The Anglican Communion

The British and US Virgin Islands form a single, missionary diocese of the Episcopal Church of the United States of America. The Bishop of the Virgin Islands is resident on St Thomas in the US Virgin Islands.

### Protestant Churches

Various Protestant denominations are represented, principally the Methodist Church. Others include the Seventh-day Adventist, Church of God and Baptist Churches.

## The Press

**The BVI Beacon:** POB 3030, Road Town, Tortola; tel. 43767; fax 46267; f. 1984; weekly; Editor LINNELL M. ABBOTT; circ. 3,000.

**The Island Sun:** POB 21, Road Town, Tortola; tel. 42476; fax 44540; f. 1962; weekly; Editor VERNON PICKERING; circ. 2,500.

**The Welcome:** POB 133, Road Town, Tortola; tel. 42413; fax 44413; f. 1971; every 2 months; general, tourist information; Publr PAUL BACKSHALL; Editor CLAUDIA COLLI; annual circ. 138,000.

## Radio and Television

In 1992, according to UNESCO, there were an estimated 9,000 radio receivers and 4,000 television receivers in use.

### RADIO

**Caribbean Broadcasting System:** POB 3059, Road Town, Tortola; tel. 44990; commercial; Gen. Man. ALVIN KORNGOLD.

**Virgin Islands Broadcasting Ltd—Radio ZBVI:** Baughers Bay, POB 78, Road Town, Tortola; tel. 42430; fax 41139; f. 1965; commercial; 10,000 watts with stand-by transmitting facilities of 1,000 watts; Man. Dir MERITT HERBERT.

Two FM radio stations began broadcasting in 1988.

### TELEVISION

**BVI Cable TV:** Fishlock Rd, POB 694, Road Town, Tortola; tel. 53205; telex 7972; programmes from US Virgin Islands and Puerto Rico; 12 stations; Man. Dir TODD KLINDWORTH.

**Television West Indies Ltd—ZBTV:** Broadcast Peak, Chawell, POB 34, Tortola; tel. 43332; commercial.

## Finance

### BANKING

#### Commercial Banks

**Bank of Nova Scotia** (Canada): Wickhams Cay 1, POB 434, Road Town, Tortola; tel. 42526; telex 7951; fax 44657; f. 1967; Man. L. WRIGHT.

**Barclays Bank PLC** (United Kingdom): Wickhams Cay 1, POB 70, Road Town, Tortola; tel. 42171; telex 7928; fax 44315; f. 1965; Man. FRANK GRIFFITHS; br. on Virgin Gorda.

**Chase Manhattan Bank, NA** (USA): Wickhams Cay 1, POB 435, Road Town, Tortola; tel. 42662; telex 7935; fax 43863; f. 1968; Man. MARGUERITE D. HODGE.

**CoreStates First Pennsylvania Bank** (USA): Wickhams Cay 1, POB 67, Road Town, Tortola; tel. 42117; telex 7970; fax 45294; f. 1961; Man. AUDLEY MADURO.

Commercial banking facilities in St Thomas and St Croix, US Virgin Islands, are also available.

#### Development Bank

**Development Bank of the British Virgin Islands:** Wickhams Cay 1, POB 275, Road Town, Tortola; tel. 43737; fax 43119.

### INSURANCE

Several US and other foreign companies have agents in the British Virgin Islands.

## Transport

### ROADS

There are about 113 km (70 miles) of motorable roads, and in 1987 there were 3,860 licensed motor vehicles.

### SHIPPING

There are two direct steamship services, one from the United Kingdom and one from the USA. Motor launches maintain daily mail and passenger services with St Thomas and St John, US Virgin Islands. A new cruise-ship pier, built at a cost of US $6.9m. with assistance from the Caribbean Development Bank, was opened in Road Town in November 1994.

**Ports and Marine Services:** Road Town, Tortola; tel. 43435; ports authority; Dir Capt. B. SALLAH.

### CIVIL AVIATION

Beef Island Airport, about 16 km (10 miles) from Road Town, is capable of receiving 48-seat turbo-prop aircraft. In early 1993 studies were being carried out to investigate the possibility of upgrading the runway on Beef Island. There are small airstrips on Virgin Gorda and Anegada.

**Director of Civil Aviation:** M. CREQUE; tel. 43701.

**Atlantic Air BVI Ltd:** Beef Island, POB 85, Road Town, Tortola; tel. 52001; fax 51741; f. 1971; national airline; internal services and external flights to Puerto Rico, and other destinations in the Eastern Caribbean; Pres. ELIHU RHYMER; Controller EDISON O'NEAL.

## Tourism

The main attraction of the islands is their tranquillity and clear waters, which provide excellent facilities for sailing, fishing, diving and other water sports. In 1992 there were an estimated 1,121 hotel rooms in the islands. There are also many charter yachts offering overnight accommodation. There were 269,399 visitors in 1992 (compared with visitors in 1991). Some 265 cruise ships called at the islands in 1994. Receipts from tourism were estimated at US $109.4m. in 1992.

**British Virgin Islands Tourist Board:** Waterfront Drive, POB 134, Road Town, Tortola; tel. 43134; fax 43866; Chair. ELIHU RHYMER; Dir RUSSELL HARRIGAN.

**British Virgin Islands Hotel and Commerce Association:** POB 376, Road Town, Tortola; tel. 43514; fax 46179; f. 1986; Chair. PAUL BACKSHALL; Exec. Dir NADINE BATTLE.

# THE CAYMAN ISLANDS

## Introductory Survey

### Location, Climate, Language, Religion, Flag, Capital

The Cayman Islands lie about 290 km (180 miles) west-north-west of Jamaica and consist of three main islands: Grand Cayman and, to the north-east, Little Cayman and Cayman Brac. The climate is tropical but is tempered by the trade winds, with a cool season between November and March, when temperatures average 24°C (75°F). Mean annual rainfall is 1,524 mm (60 ins). The official language is English. Many Christian churches are represented. The flag is the British 'Blue Ensign', with the islands' coat of arms (a golden lion on a red background above three stars in green, representing the three main islands, superimposed on wavy lines of blue and white, the shield surmounted by a torse of white and blue bearing a yellow pineapple behind a green turtle, and with the motto 'He hath founded it upon the seas' on a scroll beneath) on a white roundel in the fly. The capital is George Town, on the island of Grand Cayman.

### Recent History

The Cayman Islands came under acknowledged British rule in 1670 and were settled mainly from Jamaica and by privateers and buccaneers. The islands of Little Cayman and Cayman Brac were permanently settled only in 1833, and until 1877 there was no administrative connection between them and Grand Cayman. A representative assembly first sat in 1832. The islands formed a dependency of Jamaica until 1959, and the Governor of Jamaica held responsibility for the Cayman Islands until Jamaican independence in 1962, when a separate administrator was appointed (the title was changed to that of Governor in 1971). The 1959 Constitution was revised in 1972, 1992 and 1994 (see below).

For many years there have been no formal political parties on the islands, despite the emergence of a nascent party political system during the 1960s with the formation, in 1961, of the National Democratic Party (NDP), as part of a campaign for self-government. The Christian Democratic Party was formed as a conservative opposition. Both parties disappeared within a few years despite the electoral success of the NDP, largely owing to the system of gubernatorial nomination to the Executive Council. In the 1970s elections for the 12 elective seats in the Legislative Assembly came to be contested by 'teams' of candidates, as well as by independents. Two such teams were formed, Progress and Dignity (the more conservative) and Unity, but all candidates were committed to augmenting the economic success of the Caymans, and favoured continued dependent status. There are no plans for independence, and the majority of the population wish to maintain the islands' links with the United Kingdom.

At elections in November 1980 the Unity team, led by Jim Bodden, took eight of the 12 seats. In the November 1984 elections opposition independents won nine seats, aided by public disquiet at the rapid growth of the immigrant work force, and the implications of the recent US challenges to the Cayman Islands' bank secrecy laws. In 1987 the Legislative Assembly successfully sought stricter regulations of status and residency for those able to participate in elections, in an attempt to protect the political rights of native Caymanians (in view of the very large immigrant population). At a general election in November 1988 seven of the existing members were returned, and five new members were elected. Prior to the election the teams had regrouped into more informal coalitions, indicating the primacy of personal over 'party' affiliations.

In July 1990 the Legislative Assembly approved proposals that the legislature's finance committee should become a committee of the whole house (including the non-elected members of the Executive Council, who are obliged to vote in accordance with the wishes of the Council's elected members). As the Executive Council did not command an overall majority of the elected members of the legislature, the finance committee had hitherto been able to exert considerable influence over economic policy, and had frequently effected changes to budget proposals. However, opposition members claimed that the reform would mean that the Government would henceforth be guaranteed absolute control over the formulation of economic policies. In the same month the Legislative Assembly approved proposals to review the Constitution, and in January 1991 the British Government sent two commissioners to the Territory to discuss possible amendments. The implementation of most recommendations, including the appointment of a Chief Minister, was postponed pending a general election to be held in 1992. One of the amendments, however, which involved increasing the number of elective seats in the Legislative Assembly to 15, was adopted in March 1992. The proposed reforms had prompted the formation, in August 1991, of the Territory's first political organization since the 1960s, the Progressive Democratic Party (PDP). During 1992 the organization developed into a coalition, including members from all three islands, and was renamed the National Team. At the general election of 18 November 1992 National Team members secured 12 of the elective seats in the Legislative Assembly, while independent candidates won the remaining three. The three elected members of the Executive Council who stood for re-election were defeated, while the fourth did not contest the seat. The new Government opted to revoke the provisions in the Constitution for a Chief Minister; however, it decided to introduce a ministerial system and to create a fifth ministerial portfolio. The amendments took effect on 1 February 1994. In November of that year James Ryan was appointed Chief Secretary, following the retirement of Lemuel Hurlston.

Drugs-related crime continued to be a serious problem in the early 1990s, when an estimated 75% of all thefts and burglaries in the islands were attributed, directly or indirectly, to the drugs trade. The Mutual Legal Assistance Treaty (signed in 1986, and ratified by the US Senate in 1990) between the Cayman Islands and the USA provides for the mutual exchange of information for use in combating crime (particularly drugs-trafficking and the diversion of funds gained illegally from the drugs trade).

In May 1991 the British Government abolished capital punishment for the crime of murder in five of the Dependent Territories of the United Kingdom, including the Cayman Islands.

The increase in surveillance of Cuba's north coast during mid-1994, in an attempt to restrict the illegal migration of Cuban nationals to the USA, resulted in the arrival of large numbers of Cubans in the Cayman Islands. By September more than 1,000 such migrants had arrived in the islands, placing severe pressure on the Territory's resources, particularly its 240-strong police force. Appeals by the Governor for assistance from the US Government in dealing with the crisis resulted in an agreement to transfer up to 900 of the migrants to the US base at Guantánamo on Cuba. Relocation was carried out during the first half of 1995, while some 40 of the Cubans in temporary accommodation in the Cayman Islands were granted political refugee status.

From January 1990 the United Kingdom declared that the territorial waters of the Cayman Islands were to be extended from three to 12 nautical miles from the coast.

### Government

Under the revised Constitution of 1994, the Governor, who is appointed by the British monarch, is responsible for external affairs, defence, internal security and the public service. The Governor is Chairman of the Executive Council, comprising three members appointed by the Governor and five members elected by the Legislative Assembly. The Legislative Assembly comprises three official members and 15 members elected by universal adult suffrage for a period of four years.

### Defence

The United Kingdom is responsible for the defence of the Cayman Islands.

### Economic Affairs

In 1992, according to official figures, the gross domestic product (GDP) of the Cayman Islands, at current prices, was US $783.6m., equivalent to US $27,480 per head. Between 1987 and 1991 the Cayman Islands' GDP increased, in real terms, by an annual average of 9.3%.

Agriculture (which employed only 1.4% of the labour force and contributed less than 1% of GDP in 1991) is limited by infertile soil, low rainfall and high labour costs. The principal crops are citrus fruits and bananas, and some other produce for local consumption. Livestock-rearing consists of beef cattle, poultry (mainly for eggs) and pigs. The traditional activity of turtle-hunting has virtually disappeared; the turtle farm (the only commercial one in the world) now produces mainly for domestic consumption (and serves as a research centre), following the imposition of US restrictions on the trade in turtle products in 1979. There is some fishing, mainly for lobster and shrimp.

Industry, employing 19.4% of the labour force and providing 14.0% of GDP in 1991, consists mainly of construction and related manufacturing, some food-processing and tourist-related light industries. The construction sector contributed 8.9% of GDP in 1991, while manufacturing activities accounted for only 1.5% of the total in that year. Energy requirements are satisfied by the import of hydrocarbon fuels (9.9% of total imports in 1993).

Service industries dominate the Caymanian economy, accounting for 79.1% of employment and 85.6% of GDP in 1991. The tourist industry is the principal economic activity, and in 1991 accounted for 22.9% of GDP and employed, directly and indirectly, some 50% of the working population. The industry earned an estimated US $446m. in 1994. Most visitors are from the USA (77% in 1994). The Cayman Islands is the largest 'offshore' financial centre in the world. In 1993 the financial services sector employed some 8% of the working population, and in 1994 generated some CI $24.5m. in government fees.

In 1993 the Cayman Islands recorded a trade deficit of CI $239.3m. (commodity exports were only 0.7% of the value of total imports). Receipts from tourism (in 1994 tourist expenditure totalled US $326.4m.) and the financial sector, remittances and capital inflows normally offset the trade deficit. The principal source of imports is the USA (which provided some 77% of total imports in 1993), which is also one of the principal markets for exports (37.0% in 1992). Other major trading partners in 1993 included the United Kingdom, Japan and the Netherlands Antilles (which received 15.5% of total exports in that year). The principal exports in the 1980s were meat (mainly turtle meat, the export of which was subsequently banned under international treaty) and chemical products (in the late 1980s and early 1990s second-hand cars were a significant export). The principal imports are machinery and transport equipment (25.8% of total imports in 1991), manufactured articles (17.9%), foodstuffs (18.9%) and mineral fuels (10.1%).

In 1993 the Cayman Islands recorded an overall budgetary surplus of CI $2.9m. A surplus of CI $0.2m. was forecast for 1995. Capital development aid from the United Kingdom ceased in 1982. At the end of 1993 the public debt stood at CI $27.6m. The average annual rate of inflation was 4.6% in 1984–93 and stood at 3.1% in 1994. During the 1980s unemployment was negligible, and immigrant labour comprised more than 40% of the working population. By late 1993, however, some 7.1% of the labour force were unemployed.

The United Kingdom is responsible for the external affairs of the Cayman Islands, and the dependency has the status of Overseas Territory in association with the European Union. The Cayman Islands has observer status in the Caribbean Community and Common Market (CARICOM, see p. 114), and is a member of CARICOM's Caribbean Development Bank (see p. 116).

Both the principal economic sectors, 'offshore' finance and tourism, benefit from the Cayman Islands' political stability, good communications and infrastructure, and extensive development. Many companies relocated to the islands from Panama as a result of the instability there in the late 1980s. The financial sector enhanced its reputation for integrity and reliability by an information exchange treaty with the USA, concluded in 1987 and ratified in 1990. The sector continued to expand during the early 1990s. In March 1994 legislation was passed providing for a reduction in the registration fee for 'offshore' companies, in an attempt to compete with cheaper financial centres. Tourism is also expanding, and in 1987 the Government limited the number of cruise ships allowed to call at the islands to three per day, in an attempt to control the increasing number of visitors. However, the use of larger ships has resulted in a continued growth in tourist arrivals. A proposal in mid-1994 to provide new mooring positions for cruise ships off the north-west point of Grand Cayman aroused strong opposition from the Chamber of Commerce, environmentalists and watersports associations, because of the damage that this would necessarily cause to the coral reef. Economic success has caused an increase in the real estate and construction industries, and required large-scale immigration of labour. In October 1989, according to official census figures, only 67% of the resident population of the islands were Caymanian (compared with 79% in 1980).

### Social Welfare

In 1994 Grand Cayman and Cayman Brac had one hospital each, with 52 beds (and a geriatric unit with eight beds) and 18 beds respectively and there were 20 physicians (and 26 in private practice). There are four district health centres and a clinic on Little Cayman. Of total expenditure by the central Government in 1994, CI $6.0m. (4.0%) was for health services, and CI $8.3m. (5.5%) for social welfare. Some CI $15.1m. (8.4% of total expenditure) was allocted for health services in 1995. There is no system of state pensions or free health services on the islands, but children are entitled to free medical and dental care, and a number of welfare services are provided by private charities and service clubs. The establishment of a national health insurance scheme was under consideration in 1994.

### Education

Schooling is compulsory for children between the ages of five and 15 years. It is provided free in 10 government-run primary schools, and there are also three state secondary schools, as well as six church-sponsored schools (five of which offer secondary as well as primary education). Primary education, from five years of age, lasts for six years. Secondary education is for seven years. Government expenditure on education in 1994 was CI $31.5m. (20.9% of total spending). Some CI $17.7m. (9.9% of total expenditure) was allocated for education in 1995.

### Public Holidays

**1995:** 2 January (for New Year's Day), 1 March (Ash Wednesday), 14 April (Good Friday), 17 April (Easter Monday), 15 May (Discovery Day), 12 June (Queen's Official Birthday), 3 July (Constitution Day), 13 November (Remembrance Day), 25–26 December (Christmas).

**1996:** 1 January (New Year's Day), 21 February (Ash Wednesday), 5 April (Good Friday), 8 April (Easter Monday), 20 May (Discovery Day), 17 June (Queen's Official Birthday), 1 July (Constitution Day), 11 November (Remembrance Day), 25–27 December (Christmas).

### Weights and Measures

The imperial system is in use.

## Statistical Survey

Source: Government Information Services, Broadcasting House, Grand Cayman; tel. 949-8092; fax 949-8092.

### AREA AND POPULATION

**Area:** 259 sq km (100 sq miles). The main island of Grand Cayman is about 197 sq km (76 sq miles), about one-half of which is swamp.

**Population:** 25,355 (males 12,372; females 12,983) at census of 5 October 1989; 30,000 (official estimate) at 31 December 1992. *By island* (1989): Grand Cayman 23,881; Cayman Brac 1,441; Little Cayman 33.

**Density** (1992): 115.8 per sq km.

**Principal Towns** (population at census of 1989): George Town (capital) 12,921; West Bay 5,632; Bodden Town 3,407.

**Births, Marriages and Deaths** (1993): 527 live births (birth rate 17.3 per 1,000); 245 marriages (marriage rate 8.0 per 1,000); 133 deaths (death rate 3.9 per 1,000).

**Economically Active Population** (sample survey, persons aged 15 years and over, October 1991): Agriculture, hunting, forestry and fishing 240; Manufacturing 225; Electricity, gas and water 310; Construction 2,680; Trade, restaurants and hotels 5,055; Transport, storage and communications 1,215; Financing, insurance, real estate and business services 2,780; Community, social and personal services 4,060; Total labour force 16,565 (males 8,540, females 8,025). Figures exclude persons seeking work for the first time, totalling 180 (males 105, females 75), but include other unemployed persons, totalling 810 (males 345, females 465). Source: ILO, *Year Book of Labour Statistics*. **October 1993** (sample survey): Total labour force 16,815 (males 8,180, females 8,635).

### AGRICULTURE, ETC.

**Livestock** (1994): 1,664 head of cattle; 5,000 chickens; 430 goats; 483 pigs.

**Fishing** (incl. flag of convenience vessels: metric tons, live weight): Total catch 837 (FAO estimate) in 1990; 825 in 1991; 825 in 1992. Source: FAO, *Yearbook of Fishery Statistics*.

### INDUSTRY

**Electric Energy** (production, million kWh): 234 in 1991; 242 in 1992; 256 in 1993.

### FINANCE

**Currency and Exchange Rates:** 100 cents = 1 Cayman Islands dollar (CI $). *Sterling and US Dollar Equivalents* (31 December 1994): £1 sterling = CI $1.2985; US $1 = 83.0 CI cents; CI $100 = £77.01 = US $120.48. *Exchange rate:* Fixed at US $1 = 83.0 CI cents.

**Budget** (CI $ million, 1994): *Revenue:* Tax revenue 135.3 (Taxes on goods and services 49.1, Import duties 75.8); Other current revenue 22.5; Total 157.8. *Expenditure:* General public services 60.4; Protective services 17.1; Education 31.5; Health 6.0; Social welfare 8.3; Tourism 14.2; Agriculture 1.6; Housing, construction and planning 1.9; Transport and communications 9.9; Total 150.9.

**Cost of Living** (Consumer Price Index; base: 1984 = 100): 144.8 in 1991; 146.9 in 1992; 150.4 in 1993.

**Gross Domestic Product** (CI $ million in current prices): 653.1 in 1992; 701.5 in 1993; 761.6 in 1994.

**Gross Domestic Product by Economic Activity** (CI $ million in current prices, 1991): Primary industries 5; Manufacturing 9; Electricity, gas and water 19; Construction 54; Trade, restaurants and hotels 138; Transport, storage and communications 65; Finance, insurance, real estate and business services 210; Community, social and personal services 42; Government services 63; Statistical discrepancy 1; Sub-total 606; Import duties *less* imputed bank service charge 11; GDP in purchasers' values 617.

### EXTERNAL TRADE

**Principal Commodities** (US $ million, 1991): *Imports c.i.f.*: Food and live animals 50.5; Beverages and tobacco 13.0; Mineral fuels, lubricants, etc. 26.9; Chemicals 15.7; Basic manufactures 34.7; Machinery and transport equipment 69.1; Miscellaneous manufactured articles 47.8; Total (incl. others) 267.4. *Exports f.o.b.*: Total 2.9.

**Principal Trading Partners** (US $ million, 1991): *Imports c.i.f.*: Japan 8.2; Netherlands Antilles 27.0; United Kingdom 10.4; USA 201.4; Total (incl. others) 267.4. *Exports f.o.b.*: USA 0.6; Total (incl. others) 2.9.

Source: UN, *International Trade Statistics Yearbook*.

**1991:** *Total imports* CI $278.4m.; *Total exports* CI $3.7m.
**1992:** *Total imports* CI $261.1m.; *Total exports* CI $1.8m.

### TRANSPORT

**Road Traffic** (1994): Motor vehicles registered 15,864.

**Shipping:** *International Freight Traffic\** ('000 metric tons, 1990): Goods loaded 735; Goods unloaded 736. *Cargo Vessels* (1993): Vessels 15, Calls at port 243. *Registered Shipping* (George Town, December 1993): 181.

*Source: UN, *Monthly Bulletin of Statistics*.

### TOURISM

**Visitor Arrivals:** 908,618 in 1992; 892,992 in 1993; 940,878 (Stopovers 341,491, Cruise-ship passengers 599,387) in 1994.

### COMMUNICATIONS MEDIA

**Radio Receivers:** 28,200 in use in 1992*.
**Television Receivers:** 6,000 in use in 1992*.
**Telephones:** 19,755 in use in 1992.
**Daily Newspapers:** 1 (estimated circulation 8,000) in 1993.
* Source: UNESCO, *Statistical Yearbook*.

### EDUCATION

**Institutions** (Sept. 1993): 10 state primary schools (with 1,646 pupils); 6 private primary and secondary schools (1,503 pupils); 3 state high schools (1,330 pupils); 1 community college; 1 private college (487 pupils).

# Directory

## The Constitution

The Constitution of 1959 was revised in 1972, 1992 and 1994. Under its terms, the Governor is responsible for defence and internal security, external affairs, and the public service. The Executive Council comprises the Chief Secretary, the Financial Secretary, the Attorney-General and five other members elected by the Legislative Assembly from their own number. The office of Administrative Secretary was abolished in April 1992 and replaced by the re-established post of Chief Secretary. There are 15 elected members of the Legislative Assembly (elected by direct, universal adult suffrage for a term of four years) and three official members appointed by the Governor. The Speaker presides over the Assembly. The United Kingdom retains full control over foreign affairs.

## The Government

**Governor:** MICHAEL E. J. GORE (assumed office 14 September 1992); to be succeeded by JOHN OWEN in September 1995.

### EXECUTIVE COUNCIL
(June 1995)

**Chairman:** The Governor.

**Official Members:**
  **Chief Secretary:** JAMES RYAN.
  **Attorney-General:** RICHARD COLES.
  **Financial Secretary:** GEORGE MCCARTHY.

**Elected Members:**
THOMAS C. JEFFERSON (Aviation, Commerce, Tourism and Environment).
ANTHONY EDEN (Health, Drug-Abuse Prevention and Rehabilitation).
JOHN B. MCLEAN (Agriculture, Communications and Works).
TRUMAN M. BODDEN (Education, Planning and Aviation).
MCKEEVA BUSH (Community Development, Sports, Youth Affairs and Culture).

### LEGISLATIVE ASSEMBLY

**Members:** The Chief Secretary, the Financial Secretary, the Attorney-General, and 15 elected members. The most recent general election to the Assembly was on 18 November 1992. There are no formal political parties (apart from the National Team, formed in 1992 to oppose aspects of the draft constitution) and personalities tend to be more important. In February 1991 a Speaker was elected to preside over the Assembly (despite provision for such a post in the Constitution, the functions of the Speaker had hitherto been assumed by the Governor).

**Speaker:** SYBIL MCLAUGHLIN.
**Clerk:** G. MYRIE.

### GOVERNMENT OFFICE

**Office of the Governor:** Government Administration Bldg, Grand Cayman; tel. 949-7900; fax 949-7544.

## Political Organization

There have been no formal political parties in the Cayman Islands since the 1960s. However, an organization was established in 1992 to express opposition to the constitutional amendments under review in that year:

**National Team:** Grand Cayman; f. 1992; Leader THOMAS C. JEFFERSON.

## Judicial System

There is a Grand Court of the Islands (with Supreme Court status), two Summary Courts, a Juvenile Court and a Coroner's Court. The Grand Court, which sits six times a year, has jurisdiction in all civil matters, admiralty matters, and in felonies and indictable misdemeanours. Appeals lie to the Court of Appeal of the Cayman Islands and beyond that to the Privy Council in the United Kingdom. The Summary Courts deal with criminal and civil matters (up to a certain limit defined by law) and appeals lie to the Grand Court.

**Chief Justice:** GEORGE HARRE.
**Solicitor-General:** MICHAEL MARSDEN.
**Registrar of the Grand Court of the Islands:** DELENE M. BODDEN, Court's Office, George Town, Grand Cayman; tel. 949-4296; telex 4260; fax 949-9856.

## Religion

### CHRISTIANITY

The oldest-established denominations are (on Grand Cayman) the United Church of Jamaica and Grand Cayman (Presbyterian), and (on Cayman Brac) the Baptist Church. Anglicans are adherents of the Church in the Province of the West Indies (Grand Cayman forms part of the diocese of Jamaica). Within the Roman Catholic Church, the Cayman Islands forms part of the archdiocese of Kingston in Jamaica. Other denominations include the Church of God, Church of God (Full Gospel), Church of Christ, Seventh-day Adventist, Wesleyan Holiness and Church of God (Universal).

## The Press

**Chamber of Commerce Newsletter:** POB 1000, George Town, Grand Cayman; tel. 949-8090; fax 949-0220; Man. WILL PINEAU; circ. 1,500.

**The Daily Caymanian Compass:** POB 1365, Grand Cayman; tel. 949-5111; fax 949-7033; f. 1965; 5 a week; Publr BRIAN UZZELL; circ. 9,500.

**The Executive:** George Town, Grand Cayman; tel. 949-8710; fax 949-0538; quarterly; Editor RYHAAN SHAH.

**The New Caymanian:** POB 1139, George Town, Grand Cayman; tel. 949-7414; fax 949-0036; weekly; Publr and Editor-in-Chief PETER JACKSON.

**Newstar:** POB 173, George Town, Grand Cayman; tel. 949-8710; fax 949-0538; monthly; Man. Editor RYHAAN SHAH; Editor DAVID MARTINS.

## Publishers

**Caribbean Publishing Co (Cayman) Ltd:** Paddington Place, Suite 306, POB 688, George Town, Grand Cayman; tel. 949-7027; fax 949-8366; f. 1978.

**Cayman Free Press Ltd:** POB 1365, Crewe Rd, George Town, Grand Cayman; tel. 949-5111; fax 949-7033.

**Cayman Publishing Co:** POB 173, George Town, Grand Cayman; tel. 949-8710; fax 949-0538.

**Progressive Publications Ltd:** Economy Printers Bldg, POB 764, George Town, Grand Cayman; tel. 949-5780.

## Radio and Television

In 1992, according to UNESCO, there were an estimated 28,200 radio receivers in use. There are two local television stations, and an estimated 6,000 television receivers were in use in 1992.

**Radio Cayman:** POB 1110, George Town, Grand Cayman; tel. 949-7799; telex 4260; fax 949-6536; started full-time broadcasting 1976; govt-owned commercial radio station; service in English; Dir LOXLEY E. M. BANKS.

**Radio ICCI-FM:** International College of the Cayman Islands, Newlands, Grand Cayman; tel. 947-1100; f. 1973; educational and cultural; Pres. Dr ELSA M. CUMMINGS.

**Radio Z99.9 FM:** POB 30110; tel. 945-1166; fax 945-1006; Gen. Man. RANDY MERREN.

**Cayman International Television Network (CITN):** George Town, Grand Cayman; f. 1992; 24 hrs daily; local and international news and US entertainment; 10-channel cable service of international programmes by subscription; Mans COLIN WILSON, JOANNE WILSON.

**Cayman Television Service (CTN):** George Town, Grand Cayman; f. 1993; 24 hrs daily; local and international news from a regional perspective; Mans COLIN WILSON, JOANNE WILSON.

## Finance

Banking facilities are provided by commercial banks. The islands have become an important centre for offshore companies and trusts. At the end of 1994 there were more than 30,000 companies and 561 banks (including 47 of the world's 50 largest banks) and trust companies registered in the Cayman Islands, with 78 of the latter maintaining a physical presence on the islands. The number of insurance companies registered increased from 65 in 1986 to 389 in 1994. The islands are well-known as a tax haven because of the absence of any form of direct taxation.

**Department of Finance and Development:** Govt Bldg, George Town, Grand Cayman; tel. 949-7900; telex 4260; fax 949-7544; the Financial Secretary is responsible, to the Governor, for supervision of the financial services sector.

**Inspector of Financial Services:** JENNIFER DILBERT.

**Deputy Inspector of Financial Services (Insurance):** JOHN DARWOOD.

**Deputy Inspector of Financial Services (Banking):** ANDREW MCNAB.

### PRINCIPAL BANKS AND TRUST COMPANIES

**AALL Trust and Banking Corpn Ltd:** AALL Bldg, POB 1166, Grand Cayman; tel. 949-5588; fax 949-8265; Man. Dir KEVIN DOYLE.

**Ansbacher (Cayman) Ltd:** POB 887, George Town, Grand Cayman; tel. 949-8655; telex 4305; fax 949-7946; Man. Dir FRASER JENNINGS.

**Banco Português do Atlântico:** POB 30124, Grand Cayman; tel. 949-8322; fax 949-7243; Gen. Man. ALVARO CORTES.

**Bank of America National Trust and Savings Association:** POB 1078, Grand Cayman; tel. 949-4088; telex 4306; Man. Dir DANIEL R. HAASE.

**Bank America Trust and Banking Corpn Ltd:** POB 1092, Anchorage Centre, Grand Cayman; tel. 949-7888; telex 4234; fax 949-7883; Man. Dir DANIEL R. HAASE.

**Bank of Butterfield International (Cayman) Ltd:** Fort St, POB 705, Grand Cayman; tel. 949-7055; telex 4263; fax 949-7004; f. 1967; acquired Washington International Bank and Trust Ltd in 1989; Man. Dir NICHOLAS J. DUGGAN.

**Bank of Nova Scotia:** Cardinall Ave, POB 689, George Town, Grand Cayman; tel. 949-7666; telex 4330; fax 949-0020; also runs trust company; Man. C. D. I. MCKIE.

**Bank of Novia Scotia Trust Company (Cayman) Ltd:** POB 501; tel. 949-2001.

**Barclays Bank PLC:** Cardinall Ave, POB 68, Grand Cayman; tel. 949-7300; telex 4219; fax 949-7179; one sub-br. at Cayman Brac; Man. ALEXANDER WOOD.

**Barclays Finance Corporation of the Cayman Islands Ltd:** POB 1321, Grand Cayman; tel. 949-4310.

**Barclays Private Bank and Trust (Cayman) Ltd:** POB 487, Grand Cayman; tel. 949-7128.

**Bermuda Trust (Cayman) Ltd:** POB 513, Grand Cayman; tel. 949-9898; fax 949-7959; f. 1968 as Arawak Trust Co; became subsidiary of Bank of Bermuda in 1988; bank and trust services; Chair. ELDON TRIMINGHAM; Man. Dir STANLEY WRIGHT; Gen. Man. RICHARD RICH.

**British American Bank Ltd:** POB 914, George Town, Grand Cayman; tel. 949-5774; telex 4265; fax 949-6064; Pres. and CEO LEONARD EBANKS.

**CIBC Bank and Trust Co (Cayman) Ltd:** POB 695, Grand Cayman; tel. 949-8666; telex 4222; fax 949-7904; f. 1967; subsidiary of Canadian Imperial Bank of Commerce; Man. Dir PETER H. LARDER.

**Caledonian Bank and Trust Ltd:** POB 1043, Grand Cayman; tel. 949-0050; Man. Dir DAVID SARGISON.

**Cayman International Trust Co Ltd:** POB 500, Grand Cayman; banking, trustee, company management services; mem. Ansbacher Int. Trust Group; tel. 949-4653; telex 4247; fax 949-7946; Man. Dir JOHN BRYAN BOTHWELL; Gen. Man. J. HENNING.

**Cayman National Bank and Trust Co Ltd:** West Wind Bldg, POB 1097, Grand Cayman; tel. 949-4655; telex 4313; fax 949-7506; f. 1974; Chair. BENSON O. EBANKS, Jnr; Pres. PETER A. TOMKINS.

**Coutts and Co (Cayman) Ltd:** POB 707, West Bay Rd, Grand Cayman; tel. 947-4777; telex 4217; fax 947-4799; fmrly Nat West International Trust Corpn (Cayman) Ltd; Man. Dir C. N. FISH.

**First Cayman Bank Ltd:** West Bay Rd, POB 1113, Grand Cayman; tel. 949-5266; telex 4347; fax 949-5398; f. 1978.

**IBJ Schroder Bank and Trust Co:** West Wind Bldg, POB 1040, Grand Cayman; tel. 949-5566; Man. ROGER HEALY.

**Julius Baer Trust Co (Cayman) Ltd:** POB 1100, Grand Cayman; tel. 949-7212; Man. Dir C. A. ROWLANDSON.

**Lloyds Bank International (Cayman) Ltd:** POB 857, Grand Cayman; tel. 949-7854; fax 949-0090; Man. ROGER C. BARKER.

**Mees Pierson (Cayman) Ltd:** POB 2003, Grand Cayman; tel. 949-7942; telex 4498; fax 949-8340; Man. Dir PETER DE RUIJTER.

**Mercury Bank and Trust Ltd:** POB 1040, Grand Cayman; tel. 949-0800; Man. VOLKER MERGENTHALER.

**Merrill Lynch Bank and Trust Co (Cayman) Ltd:** POB 694, Grand Cayman; tel. 949-8206; fax 949-8895.

**Midland Bank Trust Corporation (Cayman) Ltd:** POB 1109, Grand Cayman; tel. 949-7755; fax 949-7634.

**Morgan Grenfell (Cayman) Ltd:** POB 1984, Grand Cayman; tel. 949-8244; fax 949-8178; Man. Dir RAYMOND APSEY.

**Royal Bank of Canada:** Cardinall Ave, POB 245, Grand Cayman; tel. 949-4600; telex 4244; fax 949-7396; Man. HARRY C. CHISHOLM.

**Royal Bank of Canada Trust Co (Cayman) Ltd:** POB 245; tel. 949-9107; fax 949-5777.

**Swiss Bank & Trust Corpn Ltd:** POB 852, Grand Cayman; tel. 949-7344; telex 4252; fax 949-7308; Dir and Pres. J. KAUFMANN.

### INSURANCE

Several foreign companies have agents in the islands. There were 26 domestic and 361 'offshore' companies registered at the end of 1994. Local companies include the following:

**British Caymanian Insurance Co Ltd:** Elizabethan Sq., POB 74, Grand Cayman; tel. 949-8699; fax 949-8411.

**Cayman General Insurance Co Ltd:** Zephyr House, POB 2171, George Town, Grand Cayman; tel. 949-7028; fax 949-7457.

**Global Life Assurance Co Ltd:** Global House, POB 1087, Grand Cayman; tel. 949-8211; fax 949-8262.

## Trade and Industry

**Cayman Islands Chamber of Commerce:** Harbour Centre Bldg, POB 1000, George Town, Grand Cayman; tel. 949-8090; fax 949-0220; f. 1965; Pres. ROY MCTAGGART; Man. WILL PINEAU; 600 local mems.

**Agricultural and Industrial Development Board:** Elizabethan Sq., George Town, Grand Cayman; tel. 949-5277; development loans organization; Gen. Man. ANGELA MILLER.

**Labour Office:** Tower Bldg, 4th Floor; tel. 949-7999; fax 949-8487; Dir DALE BANKS.

The Cayman Islands have had a labour law since 1942, but only three trade unions have been registered.

## Transport

### ROADS

There are some 406 km (252 miles) of motorable roads, of which 304 km (189 miles) are surfaced with tarmac. The road network connects all districts on Grand Cayman and Cayman Brac (which has 76 km (47 miles) of motorable road), and there are 27 miles of motorable road on Little Cayman (of which about 11 miles are paved). There were 15,864 licensed motor vehicles in 1994.

### SHIPPING

George Town is the principal port and a new port facility was opened in July 1977. Cruise liners, container ships and smaller cargo vessels ply between the Cayman Islands, Florida, Jamaica and Costa Rica. The port of Cayman Brac is Creek; there are limited facilities on Little Cayman.

**Port Authority of the Cayman Islands:** Harbour Drive, POB 1358, George Town, Grand Cayman; tel. 949-2055; fax 949-5820; Dir E. BUSH.

**Marine Survey Section:** Tower Bldg, Grand Cayman; tel. 949-8831; fax 949-8849.

**Kirk Line:** POB 1372, George Town, Grand Cayman; tel. 949-4977; fax 949-8402.

**Thompson Shipping Co Ltd:** POB 188, George Town, Grand Cayman; tel. 949-8044; fax 949-8349; f. 1977.

**World-Wide Shipping Group Ltd:** Cayman International Trust Bldg, Albert Panton St, George Town, Grand Cayman.

### CIVIL AVIATION

There are two international airports in the Territory, Owen Roberts International Airport, 3.5 km (2 miles) from George Town, and Gerard Smith Airport on Cayman Brac. Both are capable of handling jet aircraft. There is an airstrip on Little Cayman, which can cater for light aircraft.

**Civil Aviation Authority:** Beacon House, POB 277, George Town, Grand Cayman; tel. 949-7811; telex 4458; fax 949-0761; f. 1987; Dir SHELDON HISLOP.

**Cayman Airways Ltd:** POB 1101, George Town, Grand Cayman; tel. 949-8200; telex 4272; fax 949-7607; f. 1968; wholly govt-owned since 1977; operates local services and scheduled flights to Jamaica and the USA; Chair. LEONARD EBANKS; Man. Dir RAY WILSON.

The islands are also served by scheduled carriers: Northwest Airlines Inc., American Airlines, Air Jamaica, British Airways and Caledonian Airlines. Islenas Airlines operates a weekly flight to and from Honduras.

## Tourism

The Cayman Islands are a major tourist destination, the majority of visitors coming from North America. The beaches and opportunities for diving in the offshore reefs form the main attraction for most tourists. Major celebrations include Pirates' Week in October and the costume festivals on Grand Cayman (Batabano), at the end of April, and, one week later, on Cayman Brac (Brach-anal). In 1993 there were an estimated 1,844 hotel rooms, and in 1994 there were 341,491 overnight and 599,387 cruise visitors. The tourist industry earned an estimated US $446m. in 1994.

**Cayman Islands Department of Tourism:** Cricket Sq., POB 67, George Town, Grand Cayman; tel. 949-0623; fax 949-4053; f. 1965; Dir ANGELA MARTINS.

**Cayman Islands Hotel and Condominium Association (CIHCA):** West Bay Rd, POB 1367, George Town; tel. 947-4057; fax 947-4143; Pres. LISSA ADAM; Sec. L. EBANKS.

**Sister Islands Tourism Association:** Stake Bay, POB 187, Cayman Brac; tel. and fax 948-1345.

BRITISH DEPENDENT TERRITORIES

*The Falkland Islands*

# THE FALKLAND ISLANDS

## Introductory Survey

**Location, Climate, Language, Religion, Flag, Capital**

The Falkland Islands, comprising two large islands and about 200 smaller ones, are in the south-western Atlantic Ocean, about 770 km (480 miles) north-east of Cape Horn, South America. The climate is generally cool, with strong winds (mainly westerly) throughout the year. The mean annual temperature is 6°C (42°F), while average annual rainfall is 635 mm (25 in). The language is English. Most of the inhabitants profess Christianity, with several denominations represented. The flag is the British 'Blue Ensign', with the colony's coat of arms (a shield showing a white and violet ram standing in green grass, on a blue background, above a sailing ship bearing red crosses on its pennants and five six-pointed stars on its central sail, on three white horizontal wavy lines, with the motto 'Desire the Right' on a scroll beneath) on a white disc in the centre of the fly. The capital is Stanley, on East Falkland Island.

**Recent History**

The first recorded landing on the islands was made from a British ship in 1690, when the group was named after Viscount Falkland, then Treasurer of the Royal Navy. French sailors named the islands 'Les Malouines' (after their home port of Saint-Malo), from which the Spanish name 'Islas Malvinas' is derived. A French settlement was established in 1764 on the island of East Falkland, but in 1767 France relinquished its rights to the territory to Spain, which then ruled the adjacent regions of South America. Meanwhile, a British expedition annexed West Falkland in 1765, and a garrison was established. The British settlement, formed in 1765–66, was recognized by Spain in 1771 but withdrawn in 1774. The Spanish garrison was withdrawn in 1811.

When the United Provinces of the River Plate (now Argentina) gained independence from Spain in 1816, the Falkland Islands had no permanent inhabitants, although they provided temporary bases for sealing and whaling activities by British and US vessels. In 1820 an Argentine ship was sent to the islands to proclaim Argentine sovereignty as successor to Spain. An Argentine settlement was founded in 1826 but most of its occupants were expelled by a US warship in 1831. The remaining Argentinians were expelled by a British expedition in 1832, and British sovereignty was established in 1833.

The islands became a Crown Colony of the United Kingdom, administered by a British-appointed Governor. However, Argentina did not relinquish its claim, and negotiations to resolve the dispute began in 1966 at the instigation of the UN. The inhabitants of the islands, nearly all British by descent, consistently expressed their desire to remain under British sovereignty.

After routine talks between delegations of the British and Argentine Governments in New York in February 1982, the Argentine Foreign Ministry announced that it would seek other means to resolve the dispute. Rumours of a possible invasion had begun in the Argentine press in January, and Argentina's military regime took advantage of a British protest at the presence of a group of Argentine scrap merchants, who had made an unauthorized landing on South Georgia (q.v.) in March and had raised an Argentine flag, to invade the Falkland Islands on 2 April. A small contingent of British marines was overwhelmed, the British Governor, Rex (later Sir Rex) Hunt, was expelled and an Argentine military governorship was established. Although the Argentine Government promised to respect the rights of the islanders, some property was damaged, stolen or destroyed, and livestock was lost. The USA and the UN attempted (unsuccessfully) to mediate, in an effort to prevent military escalation. British forces, which had been dispatched to the islands immediately after the Argentine invasion, recaptured South Georgia on 25 April. The Argentine forces on the Falklands formally surrendered on 14 June, after a conflict in the course of which about 750 Argentine, 255 British and three Falklanders' lives were lost.

The Governor returned to the islands as Civil Commissioner on 25 June, and Britain established a 'protection zone' around the islands, extending 150 nautical miles (278 km) offshore, as well as a garrison of about 4,000 troops, in accordance with the Government's 'Fortress Falklands' policy. The British Government began an investigation into the possibilities of developing the islands' economy, and in November 1982 agreed to grant the Falkland Islanders full British citizenship. In November 1983 the post of Chief Executive of the Falkland Islands Government was created, in combination with the executive vice-chairmanship of the newly-formed Falkland Islands Development Corporation. The Civil Commissioner, Sir Rex Hunt, retired in September 1985, whereupon a new Governor was appointed.

The issue of the sovereignty of the Falkland Islands remained a major impediment to the normalization of relations between Argentina and the United Kingdom. The Argentine Government refused to agree to a formal declaration that hostilities were ended until the United Kingdom agreed to participate in negotiations over sovereignty, while the United Kingdom refused to negotiate until Argentina had formally ended hostilities.

Following the return to civilian rule in Argentina in December 1983, the newly-elected President, Dr Raúl Alfonsín, stated his Government's desire to seek a negotiated settlement to the dispute over the Falkland Islands. He offered to provide, in exchange for the transfer of the islands to Argentina, a special statute within the Constitution, which would guarantee the interests of the islanders. In October 1984 the Argentine Government removed restrictions on British companies and interests in Argentina as a possible prelude to resuming negotiations.

The British Government's refusal to discuss the issue of sovereignty, and its insistence on the paramountcy of the Falkland Islanders' wishes, were reflected in the new Constitution for the Falklands, which was approved by the islands' Legislative Council in January 1985. Under the Constitution, the islanders' right to self-determination was guaranteed. The Argentine Government claimed that the document represented a further obstacle to the negotiation of a peaceful solution to the dispute.

The number of British troops stationed on the islands was reduced, following the opening, in May 1985, of a new military airport at Mount Pleasant, about 30 km south-east of Stanley, allowing access to wide-bodied jet aircraft and thus enabling rapid reinforcement of the garrison, if necessary. In July the British Government ended its ban on Argentine imports, which had been in force since 1982, as an indication of its willingness to restore normal economic and commercial relations. In October elections took place on the Falklands for a new Legislative Council. In the same month, South Georgia and the South Sandwich Islands (see separate section) ceased to be dependencies of the Falkland Islands, although the Governor of the Falkland Islands was to be (*ex officio*) Commissioner for the territories.

In 1986 parliamentary delegations from the United Kingdom and Argentina conducted exploratory talks. However, the British Government remained intransigent on the issue of the sovereignty of the islands. In early 1986 Argentina's continued claim to the naval 'protection zone' was manifested in attacks on foreign fishing vessels by Argentine gunboats. In October of that year Britain unilaterally declared a fisheries conservation and management zone extending 150 nautical miles (278 km) around the islands, with effect from 1 February 1987, to prevent the overfishing of the waters. The imposition of this zone, whose radius coincided with that of the naval protection zone, was condemned by the majority of UN members, as was Britain's rejection, in November 1986, of an offer by Argentina to declare a formal end to hostilities in exchange for the abolition of the protection zone. In April 1988 discussions took place in Guatemala City between members of the Argentine Congress and the British Parliament on bilateral relations and the Falklands issue.

The resignation, in June 1989, of three members of the Legislative Council, in protest against a proposed agricultural grants scheme, prompted the dissolution of the legislative body. In the ensuing parliamentary elections, which were held in October, eight independent candidates, all of whom vigorously opposed the notion of renewed links, at any level, with Argentina, defeated 10 other candidates to take all the elective seats. Three representatives of a recently-formed political organization, the Desire the Right Party (DRP), which advocated a policy of limited *rapprochement* with Argentina, received little support.

In August 1992 William Fullerton was succeeded as Governor by David Tatham.

On 14 October 1993 25 independent candidates contested elections to the eight elective seats of the Legislative Council. The successful candidates (elected to represent the two four-member constituencies of Camp and Stanley) had all expressed a reluctance to develop closer contacts with Argentina as long as the Argentine Government continued to claim sovereignty over the islands.

Beginning in 1982 the UN General Assembly voted annually, by an overwhelming majority, in favour of the resumption of negotiations between Argentina and the United Kingdom. The British Government, however, consistently declined to engage in such dialogue. However, relations between Argentina and the

United Kingdom improved, following the election, in May 1989, of a new Argentine President, Carlos Saúl Menem. Following his accession to power, Menem stated that his country would be willing temporarily to suspend its demand that the issue of the sovereignty of the Falkland Islands be discussed, in the interests of the restoration of full diplomatic and commercial relations with the United Kingdom. In October a meeting of representatives from Argentina and the United Kingdom, which took place in Madrid (Spain), culminated in the formal cessation of all hostilities, and the re-establishment of diplomatic relations at consular level. Restrictions on Argentine merchant vessels with regard to the naval protection zone around the Falkland Islands were also eased. In the following month, however, the United Kingdom announced that it was to increase the extent of its territorial waters around the islands from three to 12 nautical miles, in spite of protests from the Argentine authorities. In February 1990 Argentina and the United Kingdom conducted further negotiations in Madrid, as a result of which the two parties re-established full diplomatic relations. It was also announced that the naval protection zone around the Falkland Islands was to be modified in March, and that mutually-agreed military procedures, that would ensure the security of the region, would take effect. In mid-July 1993, in view of a sustained improvement in bilateral relations, the further reduction of military restrictions around the islands was announced by both Governments.

Following successful negotiations between Argentina and the United Kingdom in Madrid in November 1990, an agreement regarding the protection and conservation of the South Atlantic fishing area was finally announced. By the terms of the new agreement, a temporary ban on fishing (to be enforced, through co-operation, by both countries) was to be extended to an area incorporating an additional 50-mile (93-km) semicircular region to the east of the islands, beyond the existing 150-mile fishing zone, and would become effective from 26 December 1990. (The agreement was subsequently renewed in December 1991 and 1992.) The two sides also agreed to establish a South Atlantic Fisheries Commission, which was to meet at least twice in every year that the ban remained in place, in order to discuss fishing activity and conservation in the region. Throughout 1990 the Falkland Islands Government had appealed to the British Government to exercise its legal right under international law to extend the 150-mile fisheries conservation and management zone to 200 miles (370 km), claiming that over-fishing of the previously well-stocked waters just beyond the 150-mile limit by vessels from Taiwan and the Republic of Korea (ignoring voluntary restraints on fishing in the area which had been previously agreed) had seriously depleted stocks and posed a threat to the islands' lucrative squid-fishing industry (see Economic Affairs).

In January 1993, during a five-day visit to the region, undertaken by the British Secretary of State for Foreign and Commonwealth Affairs, Douglas Hurd, Falkland Islanders reiterated concerns that the Argentine Government's decision, announced earlier in the month, to commence the sale of fishing licences for the region (effectively breaking the islands' monopoly), would seriously undermine the islands' economic future, and could result in further significant depletion of stocks. The British Government's decision, taken in May, to extend from 12 to 200 nautical miles its territorial jurisdiction in the waters surrounding South Georgia and the South Sandwich Islands, was interpreted as a direct response to this threat. In December 1993 the Argentine Government indicated its acceptance of the UK's proposed extension of fishing rights around the Falkland Islands from 150 to 200 miles, in order to allow the islanders to fulfil an annual squid-fishing quota of 150,000 metric tons (effective from January 1994), a figure established in consultation with Argentine authorities in November. The Argentine quota was agreed at 220,000 tons (compared with an estimated catch of 130,000 tons in 1992).

In November 1991 the Governments of both Argentina and the United Kingdom claimed rights of exploration and exploitation of the seabed and the sub-soil of the continental shelf around the Falkland Islands (which are believed to be rich in petroleum reserves). In April 1992 the Falkland Islands Government invited tenders for seismic reports of the region. However, in order to preserve recent improvements in bilateral relations with Argentina, advanced exploration in the area would not be undertaken prior to the successful negotiation of an exploration agreement between the British and Argentine authorities. In early December 1993 the British Geological Survey reported that preliminary seismic investigations indicated deposits in excess of those located in British North Sea oilfields. Attempts to conclude a bilateral agreement on the exploitation of the islands' petroleum reserves were further complicated in August 1994 by the British Government's unilateral decision to extend its fisheries conservation zone north of the islands, and thereby to annex a small but lucrative fishing ground (not previously protected by British or Argentine legislation) which was being plundered, at regular intervals, by foreign fishing vessels.

### Government
Administration is conducted by the appointed Governor (who is the personal representative of the British monarch), aided by the Executive Council, comprising two *ex-officio* members and three members elected by the Legislative Council. The Legislative Council is composed of two *ex-officio* members and eight elected members. Voting is by universal adult suffrage.

### Defence
In June 1994 there were approximately 1,700 British troops stationed on the islands. The total cost of the conflict in 1982 and of building and maintaining a garrison for four years was estimated at £2,560m. The current annual cost of maintaining the garrison is approximately £60m. Further defence spending between 1985 and 1988 was put at £1,700m. Defence expenditure on the islands in 1987/88 was estimated to be £292m., compared with £684m. in 1984/85. There is a Falkland Islands Defence Force, composed of islanders.

### Economic Affairs
Most of the agricultural land on the Falkland Islands is devoted to the rearing of sheep. However, the land is poor and up to six acres are required to support one animal. In 1989 exports of wool were valued at more than £4m. In March 1992 sheep farmers on the islands announced plans to establish a stud flock of 650 imported Tasmanian sheep (at a cost of £260,000), in order to improve the quality of wool produced. Some vegetables are produced, and there are small dairy herds. From 1987, when a licensing system was introduced for foreign vessels fishing within a 150-nautical-mile conservation and management zone (see Recent History), the economy was diversified and the islands' annual income increased considerably. Revenue from the sale of licences totalled £25m. in 1991 but declined to £23m. in 1994, following the Argentine Government's commencement of the sale of fishing licences. In the late 1980s about one-third of the world's total catch of *Illex* and *Loligo* squid was derived from this fishing zone. However, over-fishing in the area surrounding the conservation zone had a detrimental effect on stocks of fish in the islands' waters, and in 1989 the Government was obliged to call an early halt to the exploitation of *Loligo* squid; a similar moratorium with regard to *Illex* squid was necessary in the 1990 season. Further diversification of the agriculture sector (particularly in the context of the collapse of the international wool market in 1990), including the development of fishing activities in inland waters and the construction of a hydroponic market garden, was envisaged for the early 1990s.

Manufacturing activity on the islands reflects the predominance of the agricultural sector: a wool mill on West Falkland produces garments and knitting kits for export; some fish-processing also takes place.

The Falkland Islands are heavily dependent on imports of all fuels, except peat. Important reserves of petroleum are known to exist off shore, but their exploitation has, hitherto, been impeded by the uncertain political situation and by technical difficulties. In late 1989, however, it was reported that several companies had expressed an interest in studying both the offshore deposits and those on shore in the Lafonia region of East Falkland.

The Falkland Islands Development Corporation (FIDC) was established in 1983 to oversee the islands' economic development on behalf of the Government. The Falkland Islands Company was a major landowner and employer until early 1991, when the Falklands Islands Government purchased its land; in the late 1980s the company had controlled about one-third of land area and wool production and employed about one-fifth of the working population.

During the 1980s the Government of the Falkland Islands sought to promote the development of the tourism sector. The sale of postage stamps and coins represents a significant source of income; in 1984 the value of sales of the former was estimated at £900,000, while the value of sales of the latter was put at £315,000.

In 1992 the islands recorded a trade deficit of £11,500,260. Wool, most of which is purchased by the United Kingdom, is the islands' only significant export. The principal imports are fuel, provisions, alcoholic beverages, building materials and clothing.

Ordinary budget estimates for the financial year 1993/94 envisaged revenue of £28,409,210 and expenditure of £19,005,190. The annual rate of inflation averaged 6.4% in 1984–88 and 4.1% in 1990–93. There is a significant shortage of local labour on the islands.

In December 1982 the British Government announced that it was to invest a total of £31m., over a period of six years, in the development of the Falkland Islands' economy, in accordance with the recommendations of a revised economic survey of the islands that had been conducted by Lord Shackleton (the original 'Shackleton report' had been commissioned in 1975). Since 1982 the economy of the Falkland Islands has enjoyed a period of strong and sustained growth, notably since the introduction of the fisheries licensing scheme. However, the demands of reconciling profitability with conservation have exemplified the need for a revision of the licensing system, and for the further diversification of the economy. The restoration of diplomatic relations between Argentina and the United Kingdom, in early 1990, was expected to facilitate an eventual increase in Argentine participation in the Falkland Islands' economic activites. However, the extent to which the population of the islands will accommodate such intervention remains uncertain.

### Social Welfare

Old-age pensions and child allowances are provided, and charitable relief is administered by the Medical Department. Medical care, which is funded by a 1.5% levy on income, is provided free of charge. A joint civilian-military hospital (with 28 beds) was opened at Stanley in 1987. In 1993/94 there were six registered medical practitioners, one dentist, 15 registered nurses/midwives and eight locally-trained nurses. The total budget of the Medical Department for 1993/94 was estimated at £1,965,420.

### Education

Education is compulsory, and is provided free of charge, for children between the ages of five and 15 years. Facilities are available for further study beyond the statutory school-leaving age. In 1994 133 pupils were instructed by 12 teachers at the primary school in Stanley, while 149 pupils received instruction from 17 teachers at the new secondary school in the capital. In 1991, a further 63 pupils received education in rural districts. Total expenditure on education and training was estimated at £2,152,230 for 1992/93.

### Public Holidays

**1995:** 2 January (for New Year's Day), 14 April (Good Friday), 21 April (HM the Queen's Birthday), 14 June (Liberation Day), 5 October (Bank Holiday), 8 December (Anniversary of the Battle of the Falkland Islands in 1914), 25–29 December (Christmas).
**1996:** 1 January (New Year's Day), 5 April (Good Friday), 21 April (HM the Queen's Birthday), 14 June (Liberation Day), 5 October (Bank Holiday), 8 December (Anniversary of the Battle of the Falkland Islands in 1914), 25–29 December (Christmas).

### Weights and Measures

Both the imperial and metric systems are in general use.

## Statistical Survey

Source: The Treasury of the Falkland Islands Government, Stanley.

### AREA, POPULATION AND DENSITY

**Area:** approx. 12,173 sq km (4,700 sq miles): East Falkland and adjacent islands 6,760 sq km (2,610 sq miles); West Falkland and adjacent islands 5,413 sq km (2,090 sq miles).
**Population:** 2,050 (males 1,095; females 955) at census of 5 March 1991. *Principal town:* Stanley (capital), population 1,329 (1989).
**Density** (1991): 0.17 per sq km.
**Births and Deaths** (1993): Live births 31; Deaths 33.
**Economically Active Population** (persons aged 15 years and over, 1991 census): 1,132 (males 734; females 398). Source: ILO, *Year Book of Labour Statistics*.

### AGRICULTURE

**Livestock** (1992/93): Sheep 721,252; Cattle 4,875; Horses 1,412.
**Wool** (metric tons, 1993): 2,521 greasy; 1,645 clean.

### FINANCE

**Currency and Exchange Rates:** 100 pence (pennies) = 1 Falkland Islands pound (FI £). *Sterling and US Dollar Equivalents* (31 December 1994): £1 sterling = FI £1.0000; US $1 = 63.92 pence; FI £100 = £100.00 sterling = $156.45.
**Budget** (1993/94 estimates): Ordinary Revenue £28,409,210; Ordinary Expenditure £19,005,190.
**Cost of Living** (Retail Price Index, excl. rent, for Stanley; base: 1990 = 100): 104.8 in 1991; 111.7 in 1992; 112.8 in 1993. Source: ILO, *Year Book of Labour Statistics*.

### EXTERNAL TRADE

**1992:** *Imports:* £14,555,762, *Exports:* £3,055,502.
Wool is the principal export. Trade is mainly with the United Kingdom.

### TRANSPORT

**Shipping** (1989): 1,833 ships (displacement 1,282,631 tons) entered and cleared.

### EDUCATION

**1994** (Stanley): *Primary:* Teachers 12; Pupils 133, *Secondary:* Teachers 17; Pupils 149.

## Directory
### The Constitution

The present Constitution of the Falkland Islands came into force on 3 October 1985 (replacing that of 1977). The Governor, who is the personal representative of the British monarch, is advised by the Executive Council, comprising six members: the Governor (presiding), three members elected by the Legislative Council, and two *ex-officio* members, the Chief Executive and the Financial Secretary of the Falkland Islands Government, who are non-voting. The Legislative Council is composed of eight elected members and the same two (non-voting) *ex-officio* members. One of the principal features of the Constitution is the reference in the preamble to the islander's right to self-determination. The separate post of Chief Executive (responsible to the Governor) was created in 1983. The electoral principle was introduced, on the basis of universal adult suffrage, in 1949. The minimum voting age was lowered from 21 years to 18 years in 1977.

### The Government
(June 1995)

**Governor:** David E. Tatham (took office August 1992).
**Chief Executive of the Falkland Islands Government:** Andrew Gurr.
**Government Secretary:** Craig S. M. Shelton.
**Financial Secretary:** Derek F. Howatt.
**Attorney General:** D. G. Lang.
**Military Commander:** Air Commodore P. G. Johnson.

#### EXECUTIVE COUNCIL
The Council consists of six members (see Constitution, above).

#### LEGISLATIVE COUNCIL
Comprises the Governor, two *ex-officio* (non-voting) members and eight elected members.

#### GOVERNMENT OFFICES
**Office of the Governor:** Government House, Stanley; tel. 27433; fax 27434.
**Office of the Secretary:** Secretariat, Stanley; tel. 27242; fax 27212.

### Political Organization

**Desire the Right Party (DRP):** f. 1988; promotes and supports community self-reliance and favours a limited *rapprochement* with Argentina; 100 mems.

### Judicial System

The judicial system of the Falkland Islands is administered by the Supreme Court (presided over by the non-resident Chief Justice), the Magistrate's Court (presided over by the Senior Magistrate) and the Court of Summary Jurisdiction. The Court of Appeal for the Territory sits in England and appeals therefrom may be heard by the Judicial Committee of the Privy Council.

**Chief Justice of the Supreme Court:** Sir Dermot Renn Davis.
**Acting Judge of the Supreme Court and Senior Magistrate:** A. S. Jones.
**Registrar:** Mrs B. Greenland.

#### FALKLAND ISLANDS COURT OF APPEAL
**President:** Sir Lionel Brett.
**Registrar:** Michael J. Elks.

## Religion

### CHRISTIANITY

The Anglican Communion, the Roman Catholic Church and the United Free Church predominate. Also represented are the Evangelist Church, Jehovah's Witnesses, the Lutheran Church, Seventh-day Adventists and the Baháʼí faith.

#### The Anglican Communion
**Bishop of the Falkland Islands:** Most Rev. GEORGE CAREY, Archbishop of Canterbury (Lambeth Palace, London, SE1 7JU, England; tel. (171) 928-8282).
**Rector:** Rev. Canon STEPHEN PALMER, The Deanery, Christ Church Cathedral, Stanley; tel. 21100; fax 21842.

#### The Roman Catholic Church
**Prefect Apostolic of the Falkland Islands:** Rev. Fr ANTON AGREITER, St Mary's Presbytery, Ross Rd, Stanley; tel. 21204; fax 22242; f. 1764; about 549 adherents.

## The Press

**The Falkland Islands Gazette:** Stanley; tel. 27242; fax 27212; government publication.
**Falkland Islands News Network:** Stanley; tel. 21182; relays news daily via fax; Man. JUAN BROCK; publishes:
  **Teaberry Express:** Stanley; tel 21182; weekly.
**Penguin News:** Ross Rd, Stanley; tel. 22684: fax 22238; f. 1979; weekly; publicly-supported newspaper; Man. Editor JOHN A. T. FOWLER; circ. 1,000.

## Radio

There is a government-operated broadcasting station at Port Stanley. Transmissions are on 550 kHz. A VHF transmitter broadcasts on 90, 90.7, 98.5 and 100 mHz. In 1989 Cable and Wireless PLC installed a £5.4m. digital telecommunications network covering the entire Falkland Islands. The Government contributed to the cost of the new system, which provides international services as well as a new domestic network. In 1992, according to UNESCO, there were an estimated 1,000 radio receivers in use.
**Falkland Islands Broadcasting Station (FIBS):** Broadcasting Studios, Stanley; tel. 27277; fax 27279; 24-hour service, financed by local Government in association with SSVC of London, England; broadcasts in English; Broadcasting Officer PATRICK J. WATTS; Assistant Producer WENDY TEGGART.
**British Forces Broadcasting Service:** BFBS Falkland Islands, Mt Pleasant, BFPO 655; tel. 32179; fax 32193; Senior Engineer: STEVE BROWN.

## Finance

### BANK
**Standard Chartered Bank PLC:** Box 166, Ross Rd, Stanley; tel. 21352; telex 2422; fax 21219; branch opened in 1983; Man. N. BLACK.

### INSURANCE
The British Commercial Union, Royal Insurance and Norman Tremellen companies maintain agencies in Stanley.
**Consultancy Services (Falkland Islands) Ltd:** 44 John St, Stanley; tel. 22666; fax 22639; Man. A. IRVINE.

## Trade and Industry

**Falkland Islands Development Corporation (FIDC):** Stanley; tel. 27211; fax 27210; f. 1983; Chair. ANDREW GURR; Gen. Man. MICHAEL VICTOR SUMMERS.

**Falkland Islands Co Ltd:** Crozier Place, Stanley; tel. 27600; telex 2418; fax 27603; f. 1851; a subsidiary of Anglo-United PLC, offered for sale in early 1992; the largest trading company; retailing, insurance and fishing agents; operates as agent for Lloyd's of London and general shipping concerns; building contractors and hoteliers; Man. TERENCE G. SPRUCE.

### EMPLOYERS' ASSOCIATION
**Sheep Owners' Association:** Fitzroy Rd, Stanley; association for sheep-station owners; telex 2418; fax 27603.

### TRADE UNION
**Falkland Islands General Employees Union:** Ross Rd, Stanley; tel. 21151; f. 1943; general union; affiliated to ICFTU; Chair. J. F. SIMPSON; Gen. Sec. J. L. BROCK; 300 mems.

### CO-OPERATIVE SOCIETY
**Stanley Co-operative Society:** Stanley; f. 1952; open to all members of the public; Man. N. THON.

## Transport

### ROADS
There are 27 km (17 miles) of made-up road in and around Stanley. There are 54 km (34 miles) of all-weather road linking Stanley and the Mount Pleasant airport. Road links to Stanley were being improved in the early 1990s, with several new roads under construction. Elsewhere, settlements are linked by tracks, which are passable by land-rover or motor cycle except in the most severe weather conditions.

### SHIPPING
There is a ship on charter to the Falkland Islands Company which makes the round trip to the United Kingdom four or five times a year, carrying cargo. A floating deep-water jetty was completed in 1984. The Ministry of Defence charters ships, which sail for the Falkland Islands once every three weeks. There are irregular cargo services between the islands and southern Chile and Uruguay.
**Stanley Port Authority:** c/o Department of Fisheries, Stanley; tel. 27260; telex 2426; fax 27265; Harbour Master J. CLARK.

#### Private Companies
**Byron Marine Ltd:** Stanley; tel. 22245.
**São Rafael Fishing Co Ltd:** Stanley; 1 fishing vessel, 1,444 dwt.
**Sulivan Shipping Services Ltd:** Stanley; tel. 22626; telex 2430; fax 22625.

### CIVIL AVIATION
There are airports at Stanley and Mount Pleasant; the latter has a runway of 2,590 m, and is capable of receiving wide-bodied jet aircraft. A Chilean airline, Aerovías DAP, operates a regular air link between the Falkland Islands and the South American mainland, with a fortnightly/weekly service to the Chilean port of Punta Arenas. In addition, the British Royal Air Force operates two weekly flights from the United Kingdom to Mount Pleasant. In April 1992 a Uruguayan airline, Air Atlantic, was authorized to establish two weekly air links between Brussels and Stanley via Montevideo and the Argentine airport at Ezeiza.
**Falkland Islands Government Air Service (FIGAS):** Stanley Airport, Stanley; tel. 27219; fax 27309; f. 1948 to provide social, medical and postal services between the settlements and Stanley; aerial surveillance for Fishery Department since 1990; Gen. Man. V. R. STEEN.

## Tourism

Approximately 1,000 tourists visit the islands each year. Birdwatching and hiking are popular tourist activities. The Falkland Islands Development Corporation plans to develop the sector, in order to generate £500,000 per year from tourism.
**Falkland Islands Tourist Board:** Airport Rd, Stanley; tel. 22215; fax 22619; Rep. CHERILYN KING.

# GIBRALTAR

## Introductory Survey

**Location, Climate, Language, Religion, Flag**

The City of Gibraltar lies in southern Europe. The territory consists of a narrow peninsula running southwards from the south-west coast of Spain, to which it is connected by an isthmus. About 8 km (5 miles) across the bay, to the west, lies the Spanish port of Algeciras, while 32 km (20 miles) to the south, across the Strait of Gibraltar, is Morocco. The Mediterranean Sea lies to the east. The climate is temperate, and snow or frost are extremely rare. The mean minimum and maximum temperatures during the winter are 12°C (54°F) and 18°C (65°F) respectively, and during the summer they are 12°C (54°F) and 29°C (85°F) respectively; the average annual rainfall is 890 mm (35 ins). The official language is English, although most of the population are bilingual in English and Spanish. In 1991 76.9% of the population were Roman Catholic, 6.9% Muslim, 6.9% Church of England and 2.3% Jewish. The flag (proportions 2 by 1) bears the arms of Gibraltar (a red castle with a pendant golden key) on a background, the upper two-thirds of which are white and the lower one-third red.

**Recent History**

Since the Second World War, this British dependency has undergone considerable social and economic progress, through intensive development of the medical, educational, housing and social security services, and by the expansion of business and the encouragement of tourism. Partial self-government was granted in 1964 and Gibraltar has exercised control over most internal matters since 1969.

The Spanish Government lays claim to Gibraltar as a part of its territory, while the United Kingdom maintains that the Treaty of Utrecht (1713) granted sovereignty over Gibraltar to the United Kingdom in perpetuity (with the stipulation that, if the United Kingdom relinquished the colony, it would be returned to Spain). In 1963 the Spanish Government began a campaign, through the UN, for the cession of Gibraltar to Spain. It also introduced a programme of restrictions against Gibraltar, culminating in the closure of the frontier in 1969, the withdrawal of the Spanish labour force, and the severing of transport and communication links with Spain.

In pursuance of a UN resolution stating that the interests of the people of Gibraltar should be taken into account, the United Kingdom conducted a referendum in the territory in September 1967, in which the overwhelming majority voted in favour of retaining British sovereignty. This was followed by the drafting of a new Constitution, promulgated in 1969, in which the British Government gave an undertaking never to enter into arrangements whereby the people of Gibraltar would pass under the sovereignty of another state against their freely and democratically expressed wishes. Gibraltar joined the European Community (EC, now European Union—EU—see p. 143) with the United Kingdom in 1973, under the provisions of the Treaty of Rome that relate to European territories for whose external relations a member state is responsible.

Spain's increasingly flexible attitude towards Gibraltar became apparent during talks held between Spanish and British ministers in November 1977, which, for the first time, included representatives of the Gibraltar Government as part of the British delegation. Telephone links with Spain were restored at the end of 1977. In December 1979 Spain requested new negotiations, and at meetings in April 1980 it was agreed, in principle, to reopen the frontier by June. However, the reopening was delayed by the Spanish Government's insistence that Spanish workers in Gibraltar should be allowed equal status with nationals of EC countries. In October the British Parliament granted Gibraltarians the right to retain full British citizenship. Negotiations for the full opening of the frontier continued in 1982, but a change of attitudes in both countries, following the war between the United Kingdom and Argentina over the sovereignty of the Falkland Islands (see chapter on the Falkland Islands), resulted in an indefinite postponement. In December Spain reopened the border to pedestrians of Spanish nationality and to British subjects resident in Gibraltar.

In a general election held in January 1984, the Gibraltar Labour Party—Association for the Advancement of Civil Rights (GLP—AACR), led by Sir Joshua Hassan, retained a majority of one seat in the House of Assembly. The Gibraltar Socialist Labour Party (GSLP), led by Joseph Bossano, secured the remaining seven seats, replacing the Democratic Party of British Gibraltar as the opposition party in the House of Assembly. (Under the terms of the Constitution, the party with the largest share of the vote obtains a maximum of eight seats in the House of Assembly.)

In November 1984 the British and Spanish Governments reached an agreement to provide equality of rights for Spaniards in Gibraltar and for Gibraltarians in Spain; to allow free movement for all traffic between Gibraltar and Spain; and to conduct negotiations on the future of the territory, including (for the first time) discussions on sovereignty. Border restrictions were finally ended in February 1985, and negotiations took place between representatives of the British and Spanish Governments to improve cross-border co-operation, especially in tourism and civil aviation. In December, however, Spanish proposals for an interim settlement of the territory's future were rejected by the British Government as unacceptable since they implied the eventual automatic cession of Gibraltar to Spain. Subsequent discussions concerning principally Spain's demands for access to the Gibraltar airport (which, according to the Spanish Government, was situated on land not covered by the terms of the Treaty of Utrecht) were inconclusive, owing to the Gibraltar Government's continued insistence that the airport remain exclusively under the control of the British and Gibraltar authorities. In December 1987 negotiators concluded an agreement that recommended increased co-operation between Spain and Gibraltar in the area of transport, in particular the joint administration of Gibraltar's airport, which would exempt passengers travelling to and from Spain from Gibraltar frontier controls. It was announced that Gibraltar's inclusion in an EC directive concerning air transport regulation was subject to the Gibraltar Government's approval of the Anglo-Spanish agreement. However, Gibraltar's House of Assembly subsequently rejected the agreement, on the grounds that it would represent an infringement of British sovereignty, and voted unanimously to contest Gibraltar's exclusion from the EC directive. The Spanish Government announced that, if Gibraltar continued to reject the agreement, it would consider the construction of its own airport on the Spanish side of the border.

In December 1987 Hassan resigned from his posts as Chief Minister and leader of the ruling GLP—AACR. Adolfo Canepa, the Deputy Chief Minister, succeeded him in both posts. In a general election, which took place in March 1988, the GSLP received 58.2% of the votes cast, thereby obtaining eight seats in the House of Assembly, and the GLP—AACR received 29.3% of the vote, securing seven seats. The newly-formed Independent Democratic Party contested the election for the first time, but failed to win any parliamentary seats. Joe Bossano replaced Adolfo Canepa as Chief Minister, at the head of Gibraltar's first socialist Government. Following his electoral victory, Bossano announced that he would not participate in Anglo-Spanish negotiations regarding the issue of sovereignty, on the grounds that increased political integration within the EC (which Spain had joined in January 1986) would, in his view, eventually guarantee local autonomy.

In March 1988 three unarmed members of the Irish Republican Army (IRA), suspected of planning an attack on British forces, were killed by British security personnel in Gibraltar. In October a majority verdict of lawful killing was announced, following an inquest by the Gibraltar coroner, at which seven members of the British Army's Special Air Service (SAS) Regiment gave evidence anonymously, testifying that the killings were unpremeditated. In May 1989, however, Spanish officials claimed that, contrary to the account of the events given by the British Government, there had been sufficient opportunity for the British authorities to arrest and question the suspects. The incident contributed to widespread disquiet at the presence of British armed forces on Gibraltar.

In January 1989, in an unprecedented gesture of co-operation between Gibraltar and Spain, Bossano met the mayor of La Línea, the Spanish town bordering Gibraltar, and offered to assist in financing an economic revival in the region. In February 1990 the British and Spanish Governments agreed to contest a legal action that was to be brought by Gibraltar in the European Court of Justice against Gibraltar's exclusion from measures adopted to liberalize European air transport, which prevented the territory from expanding its air links with Europe. The decision to contest the action was considered to be a further attempt by the United Kingdom to persuade Gibraltar to co-operate with Spain. In March 1991 the United Kingdom withdrew the majority of British army personnel from Gibraltar, although the Royal Navy and Royal Air Force detachments remained.

In May 1991 the Spanish Prime Minister made an official visit to the United Kingdom, and was reported to have proposed a plan for joint sovereignty over Gibraltar, whereby the dependency would become effectively autonomous, with the British and Spanish monarchs as joint heads of state. Although it represented a significant concession by the Spanish Government (which had hitherto demanded full sovereignty over Gibraltar), the plan was rejected by the Gibraltar Government in July. In August reports emerged of proposals by the Gibraltar Government, whereby Gibraltar was to attain independence, while responsibility for defence and foreign affairs were to be transferred to the EC. However, the Spanish Government announced that the proposed agreement had not been formally presented for consideration, and was not a subject of negotiation. At the EC summit meeting at Maastricht in December, Spain continued to refuse to recognize Gibraltar's status as a member of the EC, and remained determined to exclude it from the External Frontiers Convention, which was designed to strengthen common controls on entry into countries belonging to the EC. The Spanish Government opposed the designation of Gibraltar as a point of entry into member countries of the EC, unless Spanish officials were permitted to monitor arrivals at Gibraltar airport, in accordance with the 1987 agreement.

In a general election, which took place on 16 January 1992, the GSLP, which received 73.3% of the vote, retained eight seats in the House of Assembly, and Bossano was returned for a second term as Chief Minister. The Gibraltar Social Democrats, an organization founded in 1989 which supported Gibraltar's participation in Anglo-Spanish negotiations, obtained 20.2% of the vote and secured the remaining seven seats. A newly-formed political association, the Gibraltar National Party, and an independent candidate, who was a member of the GLP—AACR, also contested the election, but failed to win any seats. In February, prior to discussions with British ministers in London, Bossano announced to the House of Assembly that Gibraltar was to attempt to obtain a revision of the 1969 Constitution, with the aim of achieving self-determination within four years. Bossano proposed that responsibility for Gibraltar's defence and foreign affairs be transferred to the EC, and that the United Kingdom retain formal sovereignty over Gibraltar, which would otherwise be self-governing. The proposed agreement was widely regarded as an attempt to amend the Treaty of Utrecht, which Bossano had previously criticized as archaic, without direct contravention of its provisions. The British Government, however, announced that it would not consider granting independence to Gibraltar, unless the Spanish Government was prepared to accept the agreement, and excluded the possibility of formal negotiations on the issue. In March it was announced that the Royal Air Force detachment stationed in Gibraltar was to be withdrawn.

In May 1992 Spain announced that it would continue to exclude Gibraltar from the EC External Frontiers Convention, unless there was progress in the Anglo-Spanish negotiations regarding the restoration of Spain's sovereignty over Gibraltar. Later in May it was reported that an agreement between Spain and the United Kingdom concerning the administration of the Gibraltar airport was envisaged, whereby Gibraltar would continue to maintain border controls at the airport, while the Spanish authorities would also monitor arrivals, probably from an observation base within the Spanish border. Later that year, however, further Anglo-Spanish negotiations, which were due to take place in November, were postponed, while the continued failure to reach an agreement on the issue of the administration of Gibraltar airport prevented the ratification of the External Frontiers Convention. In September Bossano announced that the Governments of Gibraltar and the Falkland Islands were to co-operate in political and economic matters.

In January 1993 Gibraltar citizens formally protested, after increasingly stringent monitoring of vehicles by Spanish customs officials resulted in severe delays at the border with Spain. In March an official meeting between the British Secretary of State for Foreign and Commonwealth Affairs, Douglas Hurd, and the Spanish Minister of Foreign Affairs, Javier Solana Madariaga, achieved little progress; it was agreed, however, that contacts between British and Spanish officials were to be maintained. In May, however, the Gibraltar Government announced that it was to contest a decision by the European Court of Justice (see above) that would permit Spain to construct and administer a second terminal at the airport. In early 1994 Bossano accused the British Government of subordinating the interests of Gibraltar to the promotion of harmonious relations with Spain, and demanded a renegotiation of the 1987 agreement.

In September 1994 the Gibraltar Government began to come under pressure both from the UK and Spain to implement EU legislation governing customs procedures and the regulation of the banking and financial services sectors. It was alleged by Spain and Britain, but strongly denied by the Gibraltar Government, that substantial flows of capital from international drugs-trafficking were passing through the territory, and that insufficient action was being taken by Gibraltar to curtail the smuggling (for transhipment through Spain) of drugs and tobacco from Morocco. The imposition in October of stringent border inspections by Spain, leading to lengthy delays in commercial and visitor traffic, prompted a protest by the British Government, and the border checks were eased in December following an undertaking by the UK to renew its efforts to secure Gibraltar's compliance with EU regulations.

Spain reimposed frontier controls in March 1995 and was again criticized by the British Government. In May, however, it emerged that the Gibraltar Government had brought into effect only about one-quarter of the relevant EU directives, and Gibraltar was warned by the British Government that substantial progress must be made by late June. Bossano, however, declared that the Gibraltar Parliament had the sole right to interpret EU legislation as it saw fit, and that any interference by the United Kingdom would be challenged in the British courts. In early July, following an indication by the British Government that it was contemplating the suspension of the 1969 Constitution and the imposition of direct rule, the Gibraltar administration introduced emergency legislation to bring the territory's financial services sector into compliance with EU requirements. Bossano sought, however, to delay the implementation of these measures until similar regulations had been made applicable to all other British Dependent Territories.

### Government

Gibraltar is a British Crown Colony. The British monarch is represented by the Governor, who is the executive authority. The Governor is advised by the Gibraltar Council, which comprises four ex-officio members and five elected members of the House of Assembly. The Council of Ministers is presided over by the Chief Minister. The Council of Ministers is responsible for domestic affairs, excluding defence and internal security. The Gibraltar House of Assembly comprises the Speaker (who is appointed by the Governor), two *ex-officio* members, and 15 members who are elected for a four-year term. The party that receives the largest share of the vote at a general election is restricted to a maximum of eight seats in the Assembly.

### Defence

There is a local defence force, the Gibraltar Regiment, which, following the abolition of conscription, was reorganized as a predominantly volunteer reserve unit (comprising 400 members in June 1993). In June 1993 British army personnel stationed in Gibraltar numbered 100, while the Royal Navy and Royal Marines detachment numbered 800.

### Economic Affairs

In 1992/93 Gibraltar's gross national product (GNP), measured at current prices, was £284.6m., equivalent to £10,461 per head. Gibraltar's population was 28,051 in 1993. According to government sources, the economy expanded, in real terms, by about 19% in 1990/91.

Gibraltar lacks agricultural land and natural resources, and the territory is dependent on imports of foodstuffs and fuels. Foodstuffs accounted for 12.0% of total imports in 1989.

The industrial sector (including manufacturing, construction and power) employed 26.5% of the working population in 1993.

Manufacturing employed 3.6% of the working population in 1993. The most important sectors are ship-building and ship-repairs, and small-scale domestic manufacturing (mainly bottling, coffee-processing, pottery and handicrafts).

Gibraltar is dependent on imported petroleum for its energy supplies. Mineral fuels (excluding petroleum products) comprised 18.7% of the value of total imports in 1989.

Tourism and banking make a significant contribution to the economy. In 1993 revenue from tourism was estimated at £79m. In that year the financial sector employed 11% of the working population. Some Spanish banks have established offices in Gibraltar, encouraging the growth of the territory as an 'offshore' banking centre, while the absence of taxes for non-residents has also encouraged the use of Gibraltar as a financial centre. The value of bank deposits increased by more than 550% in the period 1987–93.

In 1993 Gibraltar recorded a visible trade deficit of £205.3m. In that year the principal source of imports was the United Kingdom (53.4%). Other major trading partners included Spain, Denmark and the Netherlands. The principal imports in 1989 were mineral fuels, manufactured goods and foodstuffs. The principal re-exports in that year were petroleum products, manufactured goods and wines, spirits, malt and tobacco.

In 1994/95 there was an estimated budgetary deficit of £3,407,000. The annual rate of inflation averaged 7.5% in 1991, 6.8% in 1992, 4.9% in 1993 and 0.8% in 1994. In September 1992 an estimated 11% of the labour force were unemployed.

Gibraltar joined the European Community (EC—now European Union, see p. 143) with the United Kingdom in 1973.

The Gibraltar economy is based on revenue from the British defence forces, tourism, shipping, and banking and finance, and is dependent on development aid from the United Kingdom. In 1988 the Bossano Government declared its aim to develop Gibraltar as an 'offshore' financial centre, to stimulate private investment, and to promote the tourism sector. A project to build a new financial and administrative centre on land reclaimed from the sea was initiated in 1990. In mid-1990 a Financial Services Commission was appointed to regulate financial activities in Gibraltar. In 1994, following the reduction in British military personnel in Gibraltar, revenue from the British defence forces (which had accounted for some 60% of the economy in 1985) contributed only 10% to total government revenue. In late 1991 the Government initiated the construction of a tunnel linking the two sides of the territory, which was designed to promote investment through infrastructural development and the creation of new land from tunnelled rock. In 1994 the Gibraltar Government came under concerted pressure both from Spain and the British Government to implement EU directives governing the conduct of 'offshore' financial activities (see Recent History).

### Social Welfare

The social security system consists of two contributory schemes, covering insurance against industrial diseases and injuries received during employment. Social insurance arrangements provide short-term benefits such as maternity and death grants and unemployment benefit. In 1994 Gibraltar had two hospitals, with a total of 244 beds, and there were 32 physicians working in the territory.

### Education

Education is compulsory between the ages of five and 15 years, and is provided free in government schools. There are two nursery schools, 12 primary schools, one Service school (administered by the Ministry of Defence for the children of military personnel) and two comprehensive schools—one for boys and one for girls. Scholarships for students in higher education are provided by both government and private sources. There is also one college providing technical and vocational training, and a special school for handicapped children.

### Public Holidays

**1995:** 1 January (New Year's Day), 13 March (Commonwealth Day), 14 April (Good Friday), 17 April (Easter Monday), 1 May (May Day), 29 May (Spring Bank Holiday), 14 June (Queen's Official Birthday), 28 August (Late Summer Bank Holiday), 25–26 December (for Christmas).

**1996:** 1 January (New Year's Day), 11 March (Commonwealth Day), 5 April (Good Friday), 8 April (Easter Monday), 1 May (May Day), 27 May (Spring Bank Holiday), 12 June (Queen's Official Birthday), 26 August (Late Summer Bank Holiday), 25–26 December (for Christmas).

### Weights and Measures

Imperial weights and measures are in use, but the metric system is gradually being introduced.

## Statistical Survey

Source (unless otherwise stated) General Division, No 6 Convent Place, Gibraltar; tel. 70071; telex 2223; fax 74524.

### AREA AND POPULATION

**Area:** 6.5 sq km (2.5 sq miles).

**Population** (1993): 28,051: 20,275 Gibraltarians; 4,465 other British; 3,311 non-British. Figures exclude visitors and transients.

**Births, Marriages and Deaths** (1993): Live births 518; marriages 758; deaths 275. Figures exclude members of the armed forces.

**Employment** (April 1993): Manufacturing 493; Construction 2,095; Electricity and water 275; Trade, restaurants and hotels 2,503; Community, social and personal services 7,129; Total (incl. others) 12,499 (males 8,951; females 3,548). Figures cover only non-agricultural activities, excluding mining and quarrying.

### FINANCE

**Currency and Exchange Rates:** 100 pence (pennies) = 1 Gibraltar pound (G£). *Sterling and Dollar Equivalents* (31 December 1994): £1 sterling = G£1.0000; US $1 = 63.92 pence; G£100 = £100.00 sterling = $156.45. *Note:* The Gibraltar pound is at par with sterling.

**Budget** (G£'000, 1992/93, estimates): *Revenue:* Income tax 42,900; General rates 9,600; Total (incl. Import duties and others) 72,800. *Expenditure:* Education and sport 11,100; Electricity undertaking 4,600; Police 5,600; Trade and industry 6,000; Housing 3,900; Fire service 1,800; Consolidated fund charges 24,900; Total (incl. others) 51,100.

**Cost of Living** (Index of Retail Prices; base: 1981 = 100): 173.8 in 1991; 185.7 in 1992; 194.8 in 1993.

### EXTERNAL TRADE

**Principal Commodities** (G£'000, 1989): *Imports* (excl. petroleum products): Foodstuffs 24,054, Manufactured goods 31,318, Fuels 37,491, Wines, spirits, malt, tobacco 23,087; Total (incl. others) 200,493. *Re-exports:* Wines, spirits, malt, tobacco 12,935, Petroleum products 34,228, Manufactured goods 28,975; Total (incl. others) 76,138. **1991** (G£ '000): Imports (excl. petroleum products) 219,121; Re-exports (excl. petroleum products) 12,900. **1992** (G£'000): Imports (excl. petroleum products) 262,200; Re-exports (excl. petroleum products) 35,400.

**Principal Trading Partner** (G£'000, 1993): *Imports* (excl. petroleum products): United Kingdom 102,583; Total (incl. others) 267,592.

### TRANSPORT

**Road Traffic** (registered motor vehicles, 1994): Cars and taxis 18,404, Commercial vehicles 1,064, Motor cycles 6,343.

**Shipping** (1994): Tonnage entered ('000 grt) 64,800; Vessels cleared 4,026.

**Civil Aviation** (1993): Passenger arrivals 91,300; Passenger departures 93,300; Freight loaded 74.0 metric tons; Freight unloaded 597.0 metric tons. Figures exclude military passengers and freight.

### TOURISM

**Visitor Arrivals** (1993): 4,279,995.

### COMMUNICATIONS MEDIA

**Radio and Television Licences** (1993): 7,447.

**Daily Newspapers** (1994): 1.

**Telephones** (1994): 19,356.

### EDUCATION

**Primary** (1994): 12 schools, 2,759 pupils.

**Secondary** (1994): 2 schools, 1,890 pupils.

Total teaching staff at primary and secondary schools (1994): 291.

**Technical and Vocational** (1994): 1 college, 262 full-time students, 24 teachers.

# Directory

## The Constitution

Gibraltar is a Crown Colony, and the supreme authority is vested in the Governor and Commander-in-Chief, who is the representative of the British monarch. Relations with the British Government are maintained through the Foreign and Commonwealth Office.

Gibraltar controls the majority of its domestic affairs, while the United Kingdom is responsible for matters of external affairs, defence and internal security. Following the referendum of 10 September 1967 (in which the people of Gibraltar voted in favour of retaining British sovereignty), a new Constitution was published on 30 May 1969 and came into immediate effect. The Constitution contains a code of human rights and provides for its enforcement by the Supreme Court of Gibraltar. The other main provisions are as follows:

### BRITISH SOVEREIGNTY

The Preamble to the Gibraltar Constitution Order contains assurances that Gibraltar will remain part of the dominions of the British Crown (unless these provisions are amended by further legislation adopted by the British Parliament), and that the United Kingdom will never enter into arrangements under which the people of Gibraltar would pass under the sovereignty of another State against their freely and democratically expressed wishes.

### THE GOVERNOR AND COMMANDER-IN-CHIEF

As a representative of the British monarch, the Governor and Commander-in-Chief is responsible for matters which directly relate to external affairs, defence and internal security and certain other matters not specifically defined as domestic matters. The Governor is also head of the executive and administers Gibraltar, acting generally on the advice of the Gibraltar Council. In exceptional circumstances, the Governor has special powers to refuse any advice from the Gibraltar Council which, in the Governor's opinion, may not be in the interests of maintaining financial and economic stability. The Governor's formal assent, on behalf of the Crown, is required for all legislation. In some cases, the prior concurrence of the Crown, conveyed through the Secretary of State for Foreign and Commonwealth Affairs, is also required. The Crown may, through the Governor and Commander-in-Chief, disband the House of Assembly, introduce direct rule and enact legislation for the 'peace, order and good government of Gibraltar'.

### THE GIBRALTAR COUNCIL

The Council consists of the Deputy Governor, the Land Forces Commander, the Attorney-General, the Financial and Development Secretary, *ex officio*, the Chief Minister, who is appointed by the Governor as the elected member of the House of Assembly most likely to command the confidence of the other elected members, and four other ministers designated by the Governor after consultation with the Chief Minister. The Council advises the Governor, who usually acts on its advice.

### COUNCIL OF MINISTERS

The Council of Ministers comprises the Chief Minister and between four and eight other ministers appointed from the elected members of the Assembly by the Governor, in consultation with the Chief Minister. It is presided over by the Chief Minister and deals with domestic matters which have been defined as such by the Constitution. Individual ministers may be given responsibility for specific business. Heads of Departments and other government officials appear before it when required.

### HOUSE OF ASSEMBLY

The House of Assembly is composed of the Speaker, 15 elected members and two *ex-officio* members (the Attorney-General and the Financial and Development Secretary). The Financial and Development Secretary is appointed by the British Government, and is constitutionally responsible for Gibraltar's economy. The Speaker is appointed by the Governor, after consultation with the Chief Minister and the Leader of the Opposition.

The normal term of the House of Assembly is four years. Elections are open to all adult British subjects and citizens of the Republic of Ireland who have been ordinarily resident in Gibraltar for a continuous period of six months prior to the date for registration as an elector. The minimum voting age is 18 years. The system of proportional representation, which was formerly used for elections to the Legislative Council, has been abandoned in favour of a new system, whereby each elector may vote for a maximum of eight candidates, and the party with the largest share of the vote is restricted to a maximum of eight seats.

The elected members of the House of Assembly elect the Mayor from among their number, and he carries out ceremonial and representational functions on behalf of the City of Gibraltar.

## The Government

(June 1995)

**Governor and Commander-in-Chief:** Field Marshal Sir JOHN CHAPPLE (took office April 1993).

### GIBRALTAR COUNCIL

**President:** The Governor.

**Ex-Officio Members:** A. CARTER (Deputy Governor), Rear-Adm. J. T. SANDERS (Land Forces Commander), E. MONTADO (Acting Financial and Development Secretary).

Note: The Attorney-General is also an *ex-officio* member.

**Elected Members:** JOSEPH J. BOSSANO, JOE PILCHER, MICHAEL FEETHAM, JOSEPH BALDACHINO, JUAN CARLOS PÉREZ.

### COUNCIL OF MINISTERS

**Chief Minister, with responsibility for Information:** JOSEPH J. BOSSANO.

**Deputy Chief Minister and Minister for the Environment and Tourism:** JOE PILCHER.

**Minister for Trade and Industry:** MICHAEL FEETHAM.

**Minister for Government Services:** JUAN CARLOS PÉREZ.

**Minister for Social Services:** ROBERT MOR.

**Minister for Employment and Training:** JOSEPH BALDACHINO.

**Minister for Medical Services and Sport:** MARY MONTEGRIFFO.

**Minister for Education, Culture and Youth Affairs:** JOSEPH MOSS.

### GOVERNMENT OFFICE

**Office of the Governor:** The Convent; tel. 54201; fax 54586.

## Legislature

### HOUSE OF ASSEMBLY

**Speaker:** Maj. ROBERT J. PELIZA.

**General Election, 16 January 1992**

| Party | % of votes cast | Seats |
|---|---|---|
| Gibraltar Socialist Labour Party | 73.3 | 8 |
| Gibraltar Social Democrats | 20.2 | 7 |
| Gibraltar National Party | 4.7 | — |
| Independent | 2.0 | — |
| Total | 100.0 | 15 |

In addition to the 15 elected members, the House of Assembly has an appointed Speaker and two *ex-officio* members (the Attorney-General and the Financial and Development Secretary).

## Political Organizations

**Gibraltar Labour Party—Association for the Advancement of Civil Rights (GLP—AACR):** inactive since 1988; Leader ADOLFO J. CANEPA; Gen. Sec. JOHN PIRIS.

**Gibraltar National Party (GNP):** f. 1991; supports self-determination for Gibraltar; Leader Dr JOSEPH GARCÍA.

**Gibraltar Self-Determination Movement:** Chair. DENNIS MATTHEWS.

**Gibraltar Social Democrats (GSD):** Haven Court, 5 Library Ramp; tel. and fax 77888; f. 1989; official opposition party; supports the participation of Gibraltar in Anglo-Spanish negotiations; Leader PETER R. CARUANA.

**Gibraltar Socialist Labour Party (GSLP):** 42 Merlot House, The Vineyards; tel. 42359; f. 1976; holds a majority of seats in the House of Assembly; advocates self-determination for Gibraltar; Leader JOSEPH J. BOSSANO; Chair. ERNEST COLLADO; Gen. Sec. JOE VICTORY.

## Judicial System

### COURT OF APPEAL
**President:** JOHN FIELDSEND.
**Justices of Appeal:** Sir DERMOT RENN DAVIS, Sir ALAN HUGGINS, RORY O'CONNOR.

### SUPREME COURT
**Chief Justice:** ALISTER KNELLER.
**Additional Justice:** GILES HARWOOD.

### COURT OF FIRST INSTANCE
**Judge:** FELIX E. PIZZARELLO.

### MAGISTRATES' COURT
**Stipendiary Magistrate:** FELIX E. PIZZARELLO.

## Religion

In 1991 76.9% of the population were Roman Catholic, 6.9% Muslim, 6.9% Church of England and 2.3% Jewish.

### CHRISTIANITY
#### The Roman Catholic Church
Gibraltar forms a single diocese, directly responsible to the Holy See. At 31 December 1993 there were an estimated 23,000 adherents in the territory.
**Bishop of Gibraltar:** Rt Rev. BERNARD DEVLIN, Bishop's House, 215 Main St; tel. 76688.

#### The Church of England
The diocese of Gibraltar in Europe, founded in 1980, has jurisdiction over the whole of continental Europe, Turkey and Morocco.
**Bishop of Gibraltar in Europe:** Rt Rev. JOHN HIND, 14 Tufton St, London, SWIP 3QZ, England; tel. (171) 976 8001; fax (171) 976 8002; in Gibraltar: Cathedral of the Holy Trinity, Cathedral Sq., Main St; tel. 75745.

#### Other Christian Churches
**Church of Scotland** (St Andrew's Presbyterian): Governor's Parade; tel. 77040; f. 1800; Minister Rev. JAMES MURDOCK ROGERS, St Andrew's Manse, 29 Scud Hill; 50 mems.
**Methodist Church:** Rev. P. A. MEARS, Wesley House, 297 Main St; tel. 77491; f. 1769; 80 mems.

### JUDAISM
**Jewish Community:** Managing Board, 10 Bomb House Lane, POB 318; tel. 72606; fax 40487; Pres. D. BENAIM; Hon. Sec. L. J. ATTIAS; 600 mems.

## The Press

**Gibraltar Chronicle:** 2 Library Gardens; tel. 78589; fax 79927; f. 1801; daily; English; Man. Editor F. CANTOS; circ. 6,000.
**Gibraltar Gazette:** f. 1949; publ. by Government Secretariat; tel. 70071; telex 2223; fax 74524; Thursday; circ. 375.
**Panorama:** 93–95 Irish Town; tel. 79797; f. 1975; weekly; English; independent; Editor JOE GARCÍA; circ. 3,500.
**The People:** POB 593; tel. 72867; weekly; English with Spanish section; Editor JOSEPH VICTORY; circ. 1,800.
**Vox:** POB 306, 38 Engineer Lane; tel. 77414; fax 72531; f. 1955; weekly; English, with Spanish section; Editor E. J. CAMPELLO; circ. 1,500.

## Radio and Television

In 1993 there were 7,447 combined radio and television licences.
**Gibraltar Broadcasting Corporation (GBC):** Broadcasting House, 18 South Barracks Rd; tel. 79760; fax 78673; f. 1963; responsible for television broadcasting; Gen. Man. G. J. VALARINO.

### RADIO
**GBC-Radio (Radio Gibraltar):** 24 hours daily in English and Spanish, including commercial broadcasting. In addition to local programmes, BBC transcripts and relays are used. Transmissions in VHF Stereo on 91.3, 92.6., 100.5 MHz and 206m.

### TELEVISION
**GBC-TV:** operates in English for 24 hours daily; GBC and BBC programmes are transmitted.

## Finance

(cap. = capital; res = reserves; dep. = deposits; m. = million; brs = branches; amounts in G£)

### BANKING
There were 28 banks operating in Gibraltar in 1991. In 1990 the Financial Services Commission was established to regulate financial activities. The following are among the principal banks licensed to conduct both domestic and 'offshore' transactions:
**ABN AMRO Bank (Gibraltar) Ltd:** 2–6 Main St, POB 100; tel. 79220; telex 2234; fax 78512; f. 1964; subsidiary of ABN AMRO Bank NV (the Netherlands); cap. and res 3.5m., dep. 118.5m. (Dec. 1993); Chair. V. DUMAS; Man. Dir J. M. J. HUISMAN.
**Banco Bilbao Vizcaya (Gibraltar) Ltd:** 260–262 Main St; tel. 77796; telex 2153; fax 77621; Man. JOAQUÍN SANCHO GARCÍA.
**Banco Bilbao Vizcaya International (Gibraltar) Ltd:** Hadfield House, 3rd Floor, Library St; tel. 79420; telex 2212; fax 73870; Man. JOSÉ NAVARRO.
**Banco Central Hispano Americano SA:** Abco Arcade, Suite 14, 30–38 Main St; tel. 74199; telex 2154; fax 74174; Man. CARLOS DE LAS ALTAS PUMARINO.
**Banco Español de Credito SA:** 114–116 Main St; tel. 76518; telex 2362; fax 73947; Man. MANUEL FRANCIS ROCCA.
**Banque Indosuez** (France): 206–210 Main St, POB 26; tel. 75090; telex 2216; fax 79618; f. 1875; Man. (Gibraltar) J. L. TAVARES.
**Barclays Bank PLC:** 84–90 Main St, POB 187; tel. 78565; telex 2231; fax 42987; Chief Man. J. J. FERRO; 3 brs.
**Hambros Bank (Gibraltar) Ltd:** Hambro House, 32 Line Wall Rd, POB 375; tel. 74850; telex 2251; fax 79037; est. 1981; cap and res 7.5m., dep. 69.5m. (March 1994); Chair. D. J. THOMASON; Man. Dir D. C. FARROW.
**Jyske Bank (Gibraltar) Ltd:** 76 Main St, POB 143; tel. 72782; telex 2215; fax 72732; cap. and res 26.7m., dep. 135.7m. (1994); Chair. P. M. POULSEN; Man. Dir J. C. B. LAURITZEN.
**Lloyds Bank International Private Banking:** 323 Main St; tel. 77373; telex 2108; fax 70023; Sr Man. A. D. LANGSTON.
**National Westminster Bank PLC:** Natwest House, 57–63 Line Wall Rd, POB 707; tel. 77737; fax 74557; f. 1988; Chief Man. STEVEN ZYBERT.
**Royal Bank of Scotland (Gibraltar) Ltd:** 1 Corral Rd; tel. 73200; telex 2124; fax 70152; Man. K. M. BLIGHT.

#### 'Offshore' Banks
**Abbey National (Gibraltar) Ltd:** 237–239 Main St; tel. 76090; telex 2158; fax 72028; Man. Dir JOHN ANDERSON.
**Crédit Suisse (Gibraltar) Ltd:** Neptune House, Marina Bay; tel. 78399; telex 2144; fax 76027; f. 1987; Man. Dir C. W. ROBINSON.
**Gibraltar Private Bank Ltd:** International Commercial Centre, Suites 10/1–10/2, Main St; tel. 73350; telex 2141; fax 73475; Man. SERGE METTRAUX.
**Hispano Commerzbank (Gibraltar) Ltd:** Don House, 30–38 Main St; tel. 74199; telex 2152; fax 74174; f. 1991; cap. and res 5.4m., dep. 38m. (Dec. 1993); Chair. BALDOMERO FALCONES.
**Republic National Bank of New York:** Neptune House, POB 557, Marina Bay; tel. 79374; telex 2291; fax 75684; f. 1986; cap. and res 184.9m., dep. 1,805m. (Dec. 1994); Chair. ANDREW PUCHER; Gen. Man. MARTIN PIETROFORTE.

#### Savings Bank
**Gibraltar Government Savings Bank:** Gibraltar Post Office, 104 Main St; tel. 75624; telex 2223; fax 72476; f. 1882; deposits guaranteed by the Govt; dep. 89.5m. (March 1992); Minister for Govt Services JUAN CARLOS PÉREZ; Dir of Postal Services S. BENSADON.

### INSURANCE
**Eurolife Assurance (International) Ltd:** 30 Rosia Rd, POB 43; tel. 73495; fax 76394; Man. A. SMITH.
**Norwich Union Fire Insurance Society (Gibraltar) Ltd:** Regal House, 3 Queensway, POB 45; tel. 79520; telex 2369; fax 70942; f. 1984; cap. 800,000; Man. Dir PAUL SAVIGNON.
Many insurance companies have agencies in Gibraltar.

## Trade and Industry

The Trade Unions and Trades Disputes Ordinance of 1947 provides for the compulsory registration of trade unions (both employers' and employees' organizations), and for the appointment of the Registrar of Trade Unions.

At 31 December 1991 there were 16 registered unions (total membership 7,602). Of these, eight, including the Chamber of Commerce, were employers' associations, and eight were unions of employees. Two of the employees' unions are branches of UK unions.

**Registrar of Trade Unions:** Directorate of Labour and Social Security, 23 John Mackintosh Sq.

### CHAMBER OF COMMERCE

**Gibraltar Chamber of Commerce:** 30–38 Main St, POB 29; tel. 78376; fax 78403; f. 1882; Pres. C. E. ISOLA; Sec. T. NICHOLS; 300 mems.

### EMPLOYERS' ASSOCIATIONS

**Association of Gibraltar Travel Agents:** tel. 76070; telex 2211; f. 1962; Hon. Sec. A. PARODY; 14 mems.

**Gibraltar Hotel Association:** c/o Caleta Palace; tel. 76508; f. 1960; Pres. B. CALLAGHAN; 7 mems.

**Gibraltar Licensed Victuallers' Association:** c/o Winston's Restaurant, 4 Cornwall's Parade; tel. 42675; f. 1976; Chair. M. OTON; 100 mems.

**Gibraltar Motor Traders' Association:** POB 167; tel. 79004; telex 2251; f. 1961; Gen. Sec. G. BASSADONE; 6 mems.

**Gibraltar Shipping Association:** 47 Irish Town, POB 9; tel. 78646; telex 2220; fax 77838; f. 1957; Sec. P. L. IMOSSI; 10 mems.

**Hindu Merchants' Association:** POB 82; tel. 73521; fax 79895; f. 1964; Pres. H. K. BUDHRANI; Hon. Sec. R. G. MELVANI; 125 mems.

### PRINCIPAL TRADE UNIONS

**Gibraltar Taxi Association:** 19 Waterport Wharf; tel. 70027; fax 76986; f. 1957; Pres. LOGAN YOUNG; Sec. AGUSTÍN GALIA; 110 mems.

**Transport & General Workers' Union (UK) (Gibraltar District):** tel. 74185; fax 75617; f. 1924; Dist. Officer JOSÉ NETTO; 4,664 mems.

**Gibraltar Trades Council:** POB 279; tel. 76930; comprises unions representing 60% of the working population; affiliated to the UK Trades Union Congress; Pres. S. LINARES.

Affiliated unions:

**Gibraltar Teachers' Association:** 40 Town Range; tel. 76308; f. 1962; Pres. S. LINARES; Sec. Y. WRIGHT; 290 mems.

**Government General & Clerical Association/Institution of Professionals, Managers and Specialists (UK) (Gibraltar):** 7 Hargrave's Ramp, POB 279; tel. 76930; f. 1967; Pres. Ms M. C. PECINO; Br. Sec. Ms E. M. SURREY; c. 600 mems.

## Transport

There are no railways in Gibraltar.

### ROADS

**Support Services Department:** Highways and Sewers Division, British Lines Depot; tel. 77506; telex 2223; fax 42659; responsible for the maintenance of all public highways. There are 12.9 km of such roads in the City, and a total road length of 49.9 km, incl. 6.8 km of footpaths.

### SHIPPING

The Strait of Gibraltar is a principal ocean route between the Mediterranean and Black Sea areas and the rest of the world.

Gibraltar is used by many long-distance liners, and has dry dock facilities and a commercial ship-repair yard. Tax concessions are available to ship-owners who register their ships at Gibraltar. At 31 December 1994 1,202 vessels, with an aggregate tonnage of 600,000 grt, of which 30 were merchant vessels, were registered at Gibraltar.

**Kvaerner Gibraltar Ltd:** Main Wharf Rd, The Dockyard; tel. 40354; fax 42022; Man. Dir GUNNAR SKJELBRED.

**M. H. Bland & Co Ltd:** POB 554, Cloister Bldg, Market Lane; tel. 75009; telex 2211; fax 71608; f. 1810; ship agents, salvage and towage contractors; Chair. JOHN G. GAGGERO.

### CIVIL AVIATION

**Gibraltar Civil Aviation Advisory Board:** Air Terminal, Winston Churchill Ave; tel. 73026; fax 73925; Sec. JOHN GONCALVES.

## Tourism

Gibraltar's tourist attractions include its climate, beaches, and a variety of amenities. Following the reopening of the border with Spain in February 1985, the resumption of traffic by day-visitors contributed to the expansion of the tourist industry. Revenue from tourism totalled £70m. in 1992. In that year 4,276,171 tourists (including day-trippers) visited Gibraltar. There are an estimated 2,000 hotel beds in Gibraltar.

**Gibraltar National Tourist Board:** Head Office: POB 303, Cathedral Square; tel. 79336; fax 70029; Man. Dir J. V. VIALE.

# HONG KONG

## Introductory Survey

### Location, Climate, Language, Religion, Flag, Capital

The Territory of Hong Kong lies in east Asia, off the south coast of the People's Republic of China, and consists of the island of Hong Kong, Stonecutters Island, the Kowloon Peninsula and the New Territories, which are partly on the mainland. The climate is sunny and dry in winter, and hot and humid in summer. The average annual rainfall is 2,160 mm (85 in), of which about three-quarters falls between June and August. The official languages are English and Chinese: Cantonese is spoken by the majority of the Chinese community, and Putonghua (Mandarin) is widely understood. The main religion is Buddhism. Confucianism, Islam, Hinduism and Daoism are also practised, and there are about 500,000 Christians. The flag is the British 'Blue Ensign', with Hong Kong's coat of arms, on a white disc, in the fly. The capital is Victoria.

### Recent History

Hong Kong Island was ceded to the United Kingdom under the terms of the Treaty of Nanking (Nanjing) in 1842. The Kowloon Peninsula was acquired by the convention of Peking (Beijing) in 1860. The New Territories were leased from China in 1898 for a period of 99 years. From the establishment of the People's Republic in 1949, the Chinese Government asserted that the 'unequal' treaties giving Britain control over Hong Kong were no longer valid.

Japanese forces invaded Hong Kong in December 1941, forcing the British administration to surrender. In August 1945, at the end of the Second World War, the territory was recaptured by British forces. Colonial rule was restored, with a British military administration until May 1946. With the restoration of civilian rule, the territory was again administered in accordance with the 1917 Constitution, which vested full powers in the British-appointed Governor. In 1946 the returning Governor promised a greater measure of self-government but, after the communist revolution in China in 1949, plans for constitutional reform were abandoned. Thus, unlike most other British colonies, Hong Kong did not proceed, through stages, to democratic rule. The essential features of the colonial regime remained unaltered until 1985, when, following the Sino-British Joint Declaration (see below), the first changes were introduced into the administrative system. Prior to 1985, the Executive and Legislative Councils consisted entirely of nominated members, including many civil servants in the colonial administration. There were, however, direct elections for one-half of the seats on the Urban Council, responsible for public health and other amenities, but participation was low: in the 1983 elections only about 7% of the eligible voters took part.

During the 20th century, Hong Kong has received many refugees from China. Between 1949 and 1964 an estimated 1m. refugees crossed from the People's Republic of China to Hong Kong. The influx of Chinese into an already crowded territory put serious strains on Hong Kong's housing and other social services. None the less, the population has continued to grow rapidly. More than 460,000 Chinese immigrants arrived, many of them illegally, between 1975 and 1980. Strict measures, introduced in October 1980, reduced the continuous flow of refugees from China (at one time averaging 150 per day), but the number of legal immigrants remained at a high level—more than 50,000 per year in 1980 and 1981, although by 1984 the figure had declined to around 27,700.

In 1981–82 a new problem arose with the arrival of Vietnamese refugees: by January 1987 there were 8,254 in Hong Kong, of whom 62% had spent more than three years living in camps, and refugees continued to arrive in increasing numbers. The Hong Kong authorities, meanwhile, exerted pressure on the British Government to end its policy of granting first asylum to the refugees. In response, legislation was introduced in June 1988 to distinguish between political refugees and 'economic migrants'. The latter were to be denied refugee status, and in October the British and Vietnamese Governments agreed terms for their voluntary repatriation. In March 1989 the first group of co-operative 'economic migrants' flew back to Viet Nam.

More than 18,000 Vietnamese arrived in Hong Kong between June 1988 and May 1989, despite the extremely unpleasant conditions in the detention camps where they were confined on arrival, and the restricting of the definition of refugee status, while the relative paucity of those who agreed to return to Viet Nam (totalling 1,225 by February 1990) caused the British Government to claim that the policy of voluntary repatriation was not effective. In May 1989 some 56,000 Vietnamese were being accommodated in Hong Kong's detention camps. After the British Government had failed on a number of occasions, particularly through the UN, to gain general international endorsement for a policy of compulsory repatriation (which, it was claimed, would discourage further large-scale immigration), the Vietnamese Government announced in December 1989 that an agreement had been concluded between the United Kingdom and Viet Nam on a programme of 'involuntary' repatriation. Under the agreement, 'economic migrants' could be returned to Viet Nam against their will, on condition that no physical force were used. Before dawn on the next day, and without prior warning, a group of 51 Vietnamese were removed from one of the camps and repatriated to Viet Nam. There were reports that physical force had been used in the operation, and violent disturbances broke out in many of the camps. The programme of involuntary repatriation was halted, in anticipation of a meeting in January 1990 of the UN steering committee for the Comprehensive Plan of Action on Indochinese refugees. The 29-nation committee failed to agree upon a policy, the USA and Viet Nam each adhering to the principle of a moratorium on involuntary repatriation, in order to allow more time to persuade 'economic migrants' to return voluntarily. By May 1990, no further cases of the repatriation of Vietnamese against their will had been reported. At an international conference held in that month, Hong Kong and the member countries of ASEAN threatened to refuse asylum to Vietnamese refugees altogether, unless the USA and Viet Nam gave approval to the policy of involuntary repatriation. In September Hong Kong, Viet Nam and the United Kingdom reached an agreement, supported by the UNHCR, to allow the repatriation of a new category of refugees—those who were not volunteering to return but who had indicated that they would not actively resist repatriation. By mid-1991, however, very few refugees had returned to Viet Nam, and the number of those arriving in Hong Kong had increased considerably. By June more than 60,000 Vietnamese were accommodated in permanent camps. In October, following protracted negotiations, it was announced that Viet Nam had agreed to the mandatory repatriation of refugees from Hong Kong. The first forcible deportation (mainly of recent arrivals) under the agreement was carried out in November 1991. Tension in the camps continued, and in February 1992 23 refugees were burned to death and almost 130 were injured in rioting at one of the detention centres. In May 1992 the United Kingdom and Viet Nam signed an agreement providing for the forcible repatriation of all economic migrants. The first deportees under this agreement were returned to Viet Nam in June. By the end of 1994 the refugee camp population had been reduced to 24,757. During that year new arrivals of Vietnamese migrants totalled only 363. Demonstrations and riots in the camps continued intermittently. Almost 200 people were injured during clashes in May 1995, when security officers attempted to transfer 1,500 inmates from a detention centre to a transit camp. Although the Government had aimed to close all camps by 1996, the fulfilment of this target appeared increasingly unlikely.

Following a visit to Hong Kong by the British Prime Minister in September 1982, talks between the United Kingdom and China were held at diplomatic level about the territory's future status. In 1984 the United Kingdom conceded that in mid-1997, upon the expiry of the lease on the New Territories, China would regain sovereignty over the whole of Hong Kong. In September 1984 British and Chinese representatives met in Beijing and initialled a legally-binding agreement, the Sino-British Joint Declaration, containing detailed assurances on the future of Hong Kong. China guaranteed the continuation of the territory's capitalist economy and life-style for 50 years after 1997. The territory, as a special administrative zone of the People's Republic, would be designated 'Hong Kong, China', and would continue to enjoy a high degree of autonomy, except in matters of defence and foreign affairs. It was agreed that Hong Kong would retain its identity as a free port and separate customs territory, and its citizens would be guaranteed freedom of speech, of assembly, of association, of travel and of religious belief. In December 1984, after being approved by the National People's Congress (Chinese legislature) and the British Parliament, the agreement was signed in Beijing by the British and Chinese Prime Ministers, and in May 1985 the two Governments exchanged documents ratifying the agreement. A Joint Liaison Group (JLG), comprising British and Chinese representatives, was established to monitor the provisions of the agreement, and this group held its first meeting in July 1985. A 58-member Basic Law Drafting Committee (BLDC) was formed in Beijing in June, with the aim of drawing up a new Basic Law (Constitution) for Hong Kong, in accordance with Article 31 of the Chinese Constitution, which provides for special administrative regions within the People's Republic. The BLDC included 23 representatives from Hong Kong itself.

A special office, which had been established in Hong Kong to assess the views of the people of the territory, reported that the majority of the population accepted the terms of the Joint Declaration, but the sensitive issue of the future nationality of Hong Kong residents proved controversial. The 1981 British Nationality Act had already caused alarm in the territory, where the reclassification of 2.3m. citizens was seen as a downgrading of their status. As holders of Hong Kong residents' permits, they have no citizenship status under British law. Following the approval of the Hong Kong agreement, the British Government announced a new form of nationality, to be effective from 1997, designated 'British National (Overseas)', which would not be transferable to descendants and would confer no right of abode in the United Kingdom.

In view of the eventual change of administration, a number of new measures were introduced into Hong Kong's internal legislative system. In September 1985 indirect elections were held for 24 new members of an expanded Legislative Council, to replace the former appointees and government officials. The status of the Governor and the Executive Council was not affected by the changes. The turn-out for the elections was low (less than 1% of the total population was eligible to vote, and only 35% of these participated). In March 1986 municipal elections were held for the urban and regional councils, which were thus, for the first time, wholly directly-elected.

In December 1986 the Governor, Sir Edward Youde, died unexpectedly while on a visit to Beijing. The new Governor, Sir David Wilson (who had played a prominent part in the Sino-British negotiations on the territory's future), formally assumed office in April 1987. In May the Hong Kong Government published proposals regarding the development of representative government during the final decade of British rule. Among the options that it proposed was the introduction, in 1988, of direct elections to the Legislative Council, based upon universal adult franchise. In spite of the disapproval of the Chinese Government with regard to the introduction of direct elections before the new Constitution was promulgated in 1990, a survey was held in 1987 to assess the reaction of the public to the proposals. A majority was found to be in favour of the introduction of direct elections before 1990. In February 1988 the Hong Kong Government published a policy document on the development of representative government; the principal proposal was the introduction, in 1991, of 10 (subsequently increased) directly-elected members of the Legislative Council.

In April 1988 the first draft of the Basic Law for Hong Kong was published, and a Basic Law Consultative Committee (BLCC) was established in Hong Kong, initially with 176 members, to collect public comments on its provisions, over a five-month period; the draft was to be debated by the Legislative Council and by the Parliament of the United Kingdom, but no referendum was to be held in Hong Kong, and final approval of the Basic Law rested with the National People's Congress of China. The draft offered five options for the election of a chief executive, either by universal suffrage (with candidates nominated by the Legislative Council or by a special committee) or by various forms of electoral college. Four options were presented regarding the composition of the future Legislative Council, involving election by different combinations of universal suffrage, electoral colleges and professional organizations: none of these options, however, proposed that the Council should be entirely elected by universal suffrage. Although the legislature would be empowered to impeach the chief executive for wrongdoing, the Chinese Government would have final responsibility for his removal. Critics of the draft Basic Law complained that it failed to offer democratic representation or to guarantee basic human rights; they argued that Hong Kong's autonomy was not clearly defined, and would be threatened by the fact that power to interpret those parts of the Basic Law relating to defence, foreign affairs and China's 'executive acts' would be granted to the National People's Congress in Beijing and not to the Hong Kong judiciary.

In November 1988 the UN Commission on Human Rights criticized the British attitude to the transfer of Hong Kong, with particular reference to the lack of direct elections. A second draft of the Basic Law was approved by China's National People's Congress in February 1989. It ignored all five options previously proposed for the election of a chief executive. The chief executive would be chosen by an electoral college for the first three terms of office, after which a referendum would be held to decide whether the chief executive should be elected by universal suffrage. In May there were massive demonstrations in Hong Kong in support of the anti-Government protests taking place in China. In the same month, two Hong Kong members of the BLDC resigned in protest at the imposition of martial law in China. They also resigned from the BLCC, which then announced that it was suspending work on the territory's post-1997 Constitution. In June, following the killing of thousands of protesters by the Chinese armed forces in Tiananmen Square in Beijing, further demonstrations and a general strike took place in Hong Kong, expressing the inhabitants' revulsion at the massacres and their doubts as to whether the Basic Law would, in practice, be honoured by the Chinese Government after 1997. The British Government refused to consider renegotiating the Sino-British Joint Declaration, but, in response to demands that the British nationality laws should be changed to allow Hong Kong residents the right to settle in the United Kingdom after 1997, it announced in December 1989 that the British Parliament would be asked to enact legislation enabling as many as 50,000 Hong Kong residents (chosen on a 'points system', which was expected to favour leading civil servants, business executives and professional workers), and an estimated 175,000 dependants, to be given the right of abode in the United Kingdom. The measure was intended to 'maintain confidence' in the colony during the transition to Chinese sovereignty, by stemming the emigration of skilled personnel (42,000 Hong Kong residents having left the colony in 1989). The announcement received a cautious welcome from the Hong Kong authorities. However, the proposals angered the Chinese Government, which feared they would have a potentially destabilizing effect. China warned prospective applicants that their British nationality would not be recognized by the Chinese Government after 1997. There were also widespread popular protests in Hong Kong itself over the unfairness of a scheme which was perceived as élitist. The bill containing the measures received approval at its second reading in the United Kingdom House of Commons in April 1990. (It was estimated that a record 66,000 Hong Kong residents left the colony in 1992, the number of emigrants declining to 53,000 in 1993, before rising to 62,000 in 1994.)

Among other recommendations made by the parliamentary select committee were the introduction of a Bill of Rights for Hong Kong and an increase in the number of seats subject to direct election in the Hong Kong Legislative Council, to one-half of the total in 1991, leading to full direct elections in 1995. A draft Bill of Rights, based on the UN International Covenant on Civil and Political Rights, was published by the Hong Kong Government in March 1990. The draft was criticized in principle because its provisions would have been subordinate, in the case of conflict, to the provisions of the Basic Law. Nevertheless, the Bill of Rights entered into law in June 1991, its enactment immediately being deemed unnecessary by the Government of China. In the same month thousands of Hong Kong citizens attended rallies to commemorate the second anniversary of the Tiananmen Square killings in Beijing, provoking minor clashes between demonstrators and the police.

China's National People's Congress approved a final draft of the Basic Law for Hong Kong in April 1990; seven members of the BLDC had earlier voted against the draft at the committee's final session in February. In the approved version of the Basic Law, 24 of the 60 seats in the Legislative Council would be subject to direct election in 1999, and 30 seats in 2003; a referendum, to be held after 2007, would consult public opinion on the future composition of the Council, although the ultimate authority to make any changes would rest with China's National People's Congress. The British Government had agreed to co-operate with these measures by offering 18 seats for direct election in 1991 and 20 seats in 1995. Under the Basic Law, the Chief Executive of the Hong Kong Special Administrative Region (SAR), as the territory was to be designated in 1997, would initially be elected for a five-year term by a special 800-member election committee, whose composition was not specified; a referendum was to be held during the third term of office in order to help to determine whether the post should be subject to a general election. However, no person with the right of residence in another country would be permitted to hold an important government post. Particular concern was expressed over a clause in the Law which would 'prohibit political organizations and groups in the Hong Kong SAR from establishing contacts with foreign political organizations or groups.' The British Government and the Hong Kong authorities expressed disappointment that the Basic Law did not allow the development of democratic government at a more rapid pace.

Relations between Hong Kong and China were adversely affected in October 1989 by the territory's announcement that the HMS *Tamar* naval base would be relocated from its prime position in order to free the site for commercial development. China wished to inherit the base, and the issue became a subject of negotiation. In May 1993, however, the base was relocated to Stonecutters Island.

In October 1989 the Governor announced plans to construct a new international airport off the island of Lantau, together with extensive new port facilities in the west of the harbour and massive infrastructural development, at a projected cost (at 1989 prices) of HK $127,000m. The airport was expected to be completed by 1997/98. China, however, expressed serious concern about the high cost of the ambitious project, thus leading to fears that difficulties in raising the necessary finances might be encountered. By the beginning of 1991 relations between China and Hong Kong had deteriorated considerably, with several members of the Chinese Government claiming the right to be consulted about all major new projects undertaken in the colony before 1997. In January 1991 Hong Kong officials visited Beijing to discuss the details of the proposed project. The talks broke down, however, when Chinese officials demanded that Hong Kong postpone the project until China and the United Kingdom had reached some agreement as to how it should proceed. The Government of Hong Kong rejected China's demands, reasserted its responsibility for governing the territory until 1997 and stated that work on the project would go ahead. It agreed, however, that China should be kept informed about the project, and later in the month tension was eased somewhat following talks in Beijing between Chinese and Hong Kong government officials, although China continued to express its fears that the scheme would drastically deplete the colony's public funds. In July 1991, following the holding of several rounds of senior-level negotiations, China and the United Kingdom reached agreement on a memorandum of understanding permitting the airport project to proceed, subject to certain conditions. China, however, subsequently raised objections to the revised costs and financing arrangements (see below). Discussions were suspended in October 1992. Upon their resumption in June 1993, China approved plans for the construction of a third cross-harbour road tunnel, to link the airport with the central business district and to be funded by the private sector. In November 1994, the cost of the entire project now having reached HK $158,000m., the United Kingdom and China signed an accord relating to the overall financing arrangements for the airport and for its railway link. Public debt was to be limited to HK $23,000m. A detailed agreement was reached in June 1995.

In April 1990, meanwhile, liberal groups formed Hong Kong's first formal political party, the United Democrats of Hong Kong (UDHK), with Martin Lee as its Chairman. The party subsequently became the main opposition to the conservatives, and achieved considerable success in local elections in March and May 1991. In November 1990 it had been announced that less than one-half of Hong Kong's eligible voters had registered to vote in elections for 18 seats in the Legislative Council, which were due to be held in September 1991 and which were to be the territory's first direct legislative elections. Of the 18 seats open to election by universal suffrage, 17 were won by members of the UDHK and like-minded liberal and independent candidates. Only 39% of registered electors, however, were reported to have voted. Following their victory, the UDHK urged the Governor to consider liberal candidates when selecting his direct appointees to the Legislative Council. The Governor, however, resisted this pressure, appointing only one of the UDHK's 20 suggested candidates. Changes in the membership of the Executive Council were announced in October, liberal citizens again being excluded by the Governor. The UDHK suffered a set-back in August 1992 when, at a Legislative Council by-election arising from the death of a member, their candidate was defeated.

In September 1991 the Sino-British JLG announced the future composition of the Hong Kong Court of Appeal, which in 1993 was to assume the function hitherto performed by the British Privy Council in London. Local lawyers, however, denounced the proposed membership, arguing that the new body would lack independence and flexibility. In December the Legislative Council voted overwhelmingly to reject the proposed composition of the Court.

Sir David Wilson was to retire in 1992. Months of speculation over the Governor's replacement were ended in April, with the appointment of Christopher Patten, hitherto Chairman of the Conservative Party in the United Kingdom, who took office in July 1992. In the following month the new Governor held discussions with Zhou Nan, director of the Xinhua News Agency and China's most senior representative in Hong Kong. In October Patten announced ambitious plans for democratic reform in the territory. Immediate changes included the separation of the Executive Council from the Legislative Council. The former was reorganized to include prominent lawyers and academics. At the 1995 elections to the latter, the number of directly-elected members was to be increased to the maximum permissible of 20; the franchise for the existing 21 'functional constituencies', representing occupational and professional groups, was to be widened and nine additional constituencies were to be established, in order to encompass all categories of workers. Various social and economic reforms were also announced. In the same month the new Governor paid his first visit to China.

The proposed electoral changes were denounced by China as a contravention of the Basic Law and of the 1984 Joint Declaration.

Although Patten's programme received the general support of the Legislative Council, many conservative business leaders were opposed to the proposals. In November 1992, following Hong Kong's announcement that it was to proceed with the next stage of preparations for the construction of the airport (without, as yet, the Chinese Government's agreement to the revised financing of the project), China threatened to cancel, in 1997, all commercial contracts, leases and agreements between the Hong Kong Government and the private sector that had been signed without its full approval. The dispute continued in early 1993, China's criticism of the territory's Governor becoming increasingly acrimonious. In February China announced plans to establish a 'second stove', or alternative administration for Hong Kong, if the Governor's proposed reforms were implemented. In April, however, the impasse was broken when the United Kingdom and China agreed to resume negotiations. No details of the discussions, which began in Beijing later that month, were revealed. In July the 57-member Preliminary Working Committee (PWC), established to study issues relating to the transfer of sovereignty in 1997 and chaired by the Chinese Minister of Foreign Affairs, held its inaugural meeting in Beijing. Negotiations between the United Kingdom and China continued intermittently throughout the year. In December, however, no progress having been made, proposed electoral reforms were submitted to the Legislative Council. The Governor's decision to proceed unilaterally was denounced by China, which declared that it would regard as null and void any laws enacted in Hong Kong.

In January 1994, during a visit to London for consultations, Patten urged China to resume negotiations. In the following month the Legislative Council approved the first stage, which included the lowering of the voting age from 21 to 18 years, of the reform programme. China confirmed that all recently-elected bodies would be disbanded in 1997. The second stage was presented to the Legislative Council in March. Relations with China deteriorated further in April, upon the publication of a British parliamentary report endorsing Patten's democratic reforms. In the same month the UDHK and Meeting Point, a smaller party, announced their intention to merge and form the Democratic Party of Hong Kong. In April the trial in camera of a Beijing journalist (who worked for a respected Hong Kong newspaper) on imprecise charges of 'stealing state secrets' and his subsequent severe prison sentence aroused widespread concern in the territory over future press freedom. Hundreds of journalists took part in a protest march through the streets of Hong Kong.

In June 1994, in an unprecedented development that reflected growing unease with Patten's style of government, the Legislative Council passed a motion of censure formally rebuking the Governor for refusing to permit a debate on an amendment to the budget. Nevertheless, at the end of the month the Legislative Council approved further constitutional reforms, entailing an increase in the number of its directly-elected members and an extension of the franchise. Despite China's strong opposition to these reforms, shortly afterwards the People's Republic and the United Kingdom concluded an agreement on the transfer of defence sites, some of which were to be retained for military purposes and upgraded prior to 1997, while others were to be released for redevelopment. At the end of August, following the issuing of a report by the PWC in the previous month, the Standing Committee of the National People's Congress in Beijing approved a decision on the abolition, in 1997, of the current political structure of Hong Kong. The Legislative Council was to be replaced by a new body. In September, during a visit to the territory, the British Secretary of State for Foreign and Commonwealth Affairs was accused by members of the Legislative Council of failing to give adequate support to Hong Kong, and was urged to permit the establishment of an independent commission to protect human rights in the territory after 1997.

In September 1994 at elections to the 18 District Boards, the first to be held on a fully democratic basis, 75 of the 346 seats were won by the Democratic Party of Hong Kong. The pro-Beijing Democratic Alliance for the Betterment of Hong Kong (DAB) won 37 seats, the progressive Association for Democracy and People's Livelihood (ADPL) 29 seats, and the pro-Beijing Liberal Party and Liberal Democratic Foundation 18 seats and 11 seats respectively. Independent candidates secured 167 seats. The level of voter participation was a record 33.1%.

In early October 1994 the Governor of Hong Kong offered his full co-operation with China during the 1,000 remaining days of British sovereignty. In December the director of the State Council's Hong Kong and Macau Affairs Office and secretary-general of the PWC, Lu Ping, formally confirmed that the Legislative Council would be disbanded in 1997. The territory's future Chief Executive and senior officials were to be nominated in 1996.

A new dispute with China, this time relating to the personal files of Hong Kong civil servants, arose in January 1995. China's demand for immediate access to these confidential files, ostensibly for the purposes of verifying integrity and of determining nationality (and thus eligibility for senior posts), was rejected by the Governor.

In February 1995 China announced that it was to play an active part in the forthcoming municipal elections. Elections for the 32 seats on the Urban Council and the 27 seats on the Regional Council took place in March. The Democratic Party of Hong Kong took 23 seats, the DAB eight seats and the ADPL also eight seats. Fewer than 26% of those eligible voted in the polls. In the same month Donald Tsang was nominated as Financial Secretary, his predecessor, along with other expatriate senior officials, having been requested to take early retirement in order to make way for a local civil servant.

Following a redrafting of the legislation, in June 1995 the United Kingdom and China reached agreement on the establishment of the Court of Final Appeal, which was to replace the Privy Council in London. Contrary to the Governor's original wishes, this new body would not now be constituted until after the transfer of sovereignty in mid-1997. In July 1995 a motion of 'no confidence' in the Governor was defeated at the Legislative Council.

**Government**

Until 30 June 1997 Hong Kong will continue to be administered by a British-appointed Governor, who presides over an Executive Council, with three *ex-officio* members and up to 12 appointed members. In mid-1995 the Legislative Council consisted of 60 members: 18 directly elected by universal suffrage in nine double-member geographical constituencies; 21 elected by limited franchise in 15 'functional constituencies', each representing an occupational or professional group; and 21 (including the Vice-President and three ex-officio members) appointed by the Governor. At the September 1995 elections, the number of directly-elected members was to be increased to 20 (see above).

**Defence**

The British army, navy and air force are all represented in Hong Kong under the overall command of the Commander British Forces, who advises the Governor on matters affecting the security of Hong Kong. In June 1994 the total strength of the British armed forces was 1,900. The army numbered 1,400 (including some remaining Gurkhas). The Royal Hong Kong Regiment (which was to be disbanded in September 1995) consisted of 1,200 reserves. The navy/marines comprised 525 members, of whom 275 were locally enlisted, and there were 12 patrol boats operating. The Royal Air Force numbered 250. In 1990 a new police unit, which was established in 1988, began to take over the army's role of guarding Hong Kong's border against illegal immigrants from the mainland. This transfer of responsibility was completed in 1992. Owing to the reductions in British forces, in April 1994 the 500-strong Hong Kong Logistic Support Regiment was established. Projected expenditure on internal security in 1994/95 totalled HK $15,533m. In 1997 China was expected to station several thousand troops in Hong Kong.

**Economic Affairs**

In 1993, according to estimates by the World Bank, Hong Kong's gross domestic product (GDP), measured at average 1991–93 prices, was US $104,731m., equivalent to US $17,860 per head. During 1985–93, it was estimated, GDP per head increased, in real terms, at an average annual rate of 5.3%. Over the same period, the population increased by an annual average of 0.9%. GDP was officially estimated to have risen by 5.8% in 1993 and by 5.5% in 1994, a similar level of growth being forecast for 1995.

Agriculture and fishing together employed only 0.6% of the working population in 1994, and contributed an estimated 0.2% of GDP in 1993. Crop production is largely restricted to flowers, vegetables and some fruit and nuts, while pigs and poultry are the principal livestock. Hong Kong relies heavily on imports for its food.

Industry (including mining, manufacturing, construction and power) provided an estimated 17.3% of GDP in 1993. In 1994 the sector employed almost 28.0% of the working population.

Manufacturing employed 19.6% of the working population in 1994, and contributed an estimated 10.6% of GDP in 1993. Measured by the value of output, the principal branches of manufacturing are textiles and clothing, plastic products, metal products and electrical machinery (particularly radio and television sets).

The services sector plays an important role in the economy, accounting for 82.5% of GDP in 1993. The value of Hong Kong's invisible exports (financial services, tourism, shipping, etc.) was HK $246,846m. in 1994. Revenue from tourism (excluding expenditure by visitors from the People's Republic of China) was HK $64,300m. in 1994, when more than 9.3m. people visited the territory. Hong Kong banking and mercantile houses have branches throughout the region, and the territory is regarded as a major financial centre, owing partly to the existence of an excellent international telecommunications network and to the absence of restrictions on capital inflows.

In 1994 Hong Kong recorded a visible trade deficit of HK $80,696m. Imports amounted to HK $1,250,709m., while domestic exports and re-exports together totalled HK $1,170,013m. Re-exports constituted 81.0% of total exports in 1994. The principal sources of Hong Kong's imports in 1994 were the People's Republic of China (37.6%) and Japan (15.6%); the principal markets for exports (including re-exports) were the People's Republic of China (32.8%) and the USA (23.2%). Other major trading partners included Taiwan, Germany and Singapore. In 1994 the principal domestic exports were textiles, clothing, electrical machinery, data-processing equipment and telecommunications and sound recording apparatus. The principal imports were foodstuffs, chemicals, textiles, machinery, transport equipment, and other manufactured articles.

Following 11 consecutive years of surplus, the 1995/96 budget envisaged a deficit of HK $2,600m. The annual rate of inflation averaged 8.1% in 1985–93, declining from 8.5% in 1993 to 8.1% in 1994. An estimated 2.8% of the labour force were unemployed, according to seasonally-adjusted figures for the quarter ending March 1995. The shortage of skilled labour continued.

Hong Kong is a member of the Asian Development Bank (ADB, see p. 107) and an associate member of the UN's Economic and Social Commission for Asia and the Pacific (ESCAP, see p. 27). The territory became a member of Asia-Pacific Economic Co-operation (APEC, see p. 106) in late 1991, and was to remain so after 1997.

The scheduled surrender of Hong Kong to the People's Republic of China in mid-1997 has had a destabilizing influence on the territory's economy, and led to an exodus of skilled personnel. In October 1989 approval was given for major infrastructural improvements in Hong Kong, which included the expansion of port facilities, the construction of a new airport off the island of Lantau, and the building of a road/rail suspension bridge to connect Lantau with the mainland. The high cost of the project provoked strong criticism from the Chinese Government, which feared that it would be burdened with massive foreign debts after 1997 as a result of the ambitious undertaking. In 1994–95 Hong Kong's financial markets continued to be intermittently affected by political and other uncertainties. Between January and December 1994 the stock-market index decreased by 31%, its worst performance since 1982. Furthermore, the territory's competitiveness continued to decline, owing to sharp increases in labour costs and property prices, leading many companies (mainly in the manufacturing sector but also businesses such as data-processing) to relocate operations to southern China and elsewhere. In 1995 the visible trade balance continued to deteriorate. Rising interest rates were expected to curb economic growth and to reduce consumption.

**Social Welfare**

Social welfare is administered by the Social Welfare Department. Expansion of social welfare services in the 1990s was to continue in accordance with the objectives formulated in the 1991 White Paper on social welfare. The establishment of a government-administered pension scheme for the elderly was proposed in 1994. Resettlement of refugees from mainland China is also undertaken by the Government. In December 1994 there were 7,670 registered physicians, 33,664 nurses (not all resident and working in Hong Kong) and 27,572 hospital beds in the territory. In 1994/95 budgetary expenditure on health services and social welfare was projected at HK $18,921m. and HK $11,026m. respectively.

**Education**

In September 1994 180,109 children attended kindergarten. Full-time education is compulsory between the ages of six and 15. Primary education has been free in all government schools and in nearly all aided schools since 1971 and junior secondary education since 1978. There are three main types of secondary school: grammar, technical and pre-vocational. The four government-run teacher-training colleges merged to form the Hong Kong Institute of Education in 1994. There are seven government-funded technical institutes. In 1987 almost all children aged six to 11 years attended primary schools, while 97% of those aged 12 to 14 years received junior secondary education, and 76% of those aged 15 to 16 years received senior secondary education. In September 1994 the six universities and Lingnan College had a combined enrolment of 49,969 full-time and 22,184 part-time students. The Open Learning Institute of Hong Kong, founded in 1989, had 18,400 students in October 1994. Budgetary expenditure (capital and recurrent) on education was estimated at HK $29,219m. in the financial year 1994/95.

**Public Holidays**

**1995:** 2 January (first weekday in January), 31 January–2 February (Chinese New Year), 5 April (Ching Ming), 14–17 April (Easter), 2 June (Tuen Ng, Dragon Boat Festival), 17–19 June (for Queen's Official Birthday), 26 August (last Saturday in August),

BRITISH DEPENDENT TERRITORIES                                                                                                             Hong Kong

28 August (Liberation Day), 9 September (Chinese Mid-Autumn Festival), 1 November (Chung Yeung Festival), 25–26 December (Christmas).

**1996:** 1 January (first weekday in January), 19–21 February (Chinese New Year), 4 April (Ching Ming), 5–8 April (Easter), 15–17 June (for Queen's Official Birthday), 20 June (Tuen Ng, Dragon Boat Festival), 24 August (Saturday in August), 26 August (Liberation Day), 28 September (the day following Chinese Mid-Autumn Festival), 21 October (the day following Chung Yeung Festival), 25–26 December (Christmas).

**Weights and Measures**

The metric system is in force. Chinese units include: tsün (37.147 mm), chek or ch'ih (37.147 cm); kan or catty (604.8 grams), tam or picul (60.479 kg).

# Statistical Survey

Source: Census and Statistics Department, Wanchai Tower, 12 Harbour Rd, Hong Kong; tel. 25824736; fax 28021101.

## Area and Population

**AREA, POPULATION AND DENSITY**

| | |
|---|---:|
| Land area (sq km) | 1,084* |
| Population (census results)† | |
| 11 March 1986 | 5,495,488 |
| 15 March 1991 | |
| Males | 2,900,344 |
| Females | 2,773,770 |
| Total | 5,674,114 |
| Population (official estimates at mid-year)‡ | |
| 1992 | 5,757,900 |
| 1993 | 5,878,100 |
| 1994 | 6,034,000 |
| Density (per sq km) at mid-1994 | 5,790‡ |

* 419 sq miles.
† All residents on the census date, including those who were temporarily absent from Hong Kong.
‡ Excluding Vietnamese migrants. For density, the marine population and the surface areas of reservoirs are also excluded.

**DISTRIBUTION OF RESIDENT POPULATION**
(1991 census)

| Hong Kong Island | Kowloon and New Kowloon | Marine | New Territories |
|---:|---:|---:|---:|
| 1,250,993 | 2,030,683 | 17,620 | 2,374,818 |

**BIRTHS, MARRIAGES AND DEATHS***

| | Known live births | | Registered marriages | | Known deaths | |
|---|---:|---:|---:|---:|---:|---:|
| | Number | Rate (per '000) | Number | Rate (per '000) | Number | Rate (per '000) |
| 1987† | 69,958 | 12.6 | 48,561 | 8.7 | 26,916 | 4.8 |
| 1988† | 75,412 | 13.4 | 45,238 | 8.1 | 27,659 | 4.9 |
| 1989† | 69,621 | 12.3 | 43,947 | 7.8 | 28,745 | 5.1 |
| 1990† | 67,731 | 12.0 | 47,168 | 8.3 | 29,136 | 5.2 |
| 1991 | 68,281 | 12.0 | 42,568 | 7.5 | 28,429 | 5.0 |
| 1992 | 70,949 | 12.3 | 45,702 | 7.9 | 30,550 | 5.3 |
| 1993 | 70,451 | 12.0 | 41,681 | 7.1 | 30,571 | 5.2 |
| 1994‡ | 71,762 | 11.9 | 38,264 | 6.3 | 29,552 | 4.9 |

* Excluding Vietnamese migrants.
† Figures revised on the basis of the 1991 census results.
‡ Provisional figures.

**Expectation of life** (years at birth, 1994): Males 75.4; Females 81.0.

**ECONOMICALLY ACTIVE POPULATION**
(1994, persons aged 15 years and over)*

| | Employed | Unemployed |
|---|---:|---:|
| Agriculture and fishing | 18,100 | — |
| Mining and quarrying | 300 | 100 |
| Manufacturing | 570,200 | 14,900 |
| Electricity, gas and water | 19,300 | 200 |
| Construction | 225,600 | 6,500 |
| Trade, restaurants and hotels | 839,300 | 16,500 |
| Transport, storage and communications | 347,200 | 4,500 |
| Financing, insurance, real estate and business services | 331,100 | 3,400 |
| Community, social and personal services | 564,100 | 4,000 |
| Activities not adequately defined | 100 | — |
| Unemployed without previous job | — | 7,200 |
| **Total labour force** | **2,915,400** | **57,200** |

* Figures may not add up to the total of the component parts, owing to rounding.

Source: General Household Survey.

## Agriculture

**PRINCIPAL CROPS**

| | 1992 | 1993 | 1994 |
|---|---:|---:|---:|
| Field crops* (metric tons) | 540 | 670 | 710 |
| Vegetables† (metric tons) | 95,000 | 91,000 | 89,000 |
| Fresh fruit and nuts (metric tons) | 2,730 | 4,150 | 5,340 |
| Flowers (HK $'000) | 156,646 | 117,369 | 163,352 |

* Includes yam, millet, groundnut, soybean, sugar cane, sweet potato and water chestnut.
† Fresh, frozen or preserved.

**LIVESTOCK** (estimates—head)

| | 1992 | 1993 | 1994 |
|---|---:|---:|---:|
| Cattle | 2,660 | 2,450 | 1,790 |
| Water buffaloes | 80 | 90 | 150 |
| Pigs | 104,150 | 96,900 | 106,700 |
| Goats | 260 | 460 | 280 |
| Chickens | 4,005,800 | 3,916,600 | 3,512,100 |
| Ducks | 213,900 | 229,200 | 102,600 |
| Quail | 145,500 | 97,100 | 48,000 |
| Pigeons (pairs) | 673,400 | 470,900 | 358,100 |

Source: Agriculture and Fisheries Department.

BRITISH DEPENDENT TERRITORIES                                                            *Hong Kong*

## Fishing*

('000 metric tons, live weight)

|  | 1992 | 1993 | 1994 |
|---|---|---|---|
| Inland waters: |  |  |  |
| Freshwater fish | 5.4 | 5.8 | 5.5 |
| Pacific Ocean: |  |  |  |
| Marine fish | 192.6 | 191.3 | 184.1 |
| Crustaceans | 12.7 | 9.9 | 9.5 |
| Molluscs | 14.8 | 16.9 | 17.4 |
| **Total catch** | 225.5 | 223.9 | 216.5 |

* Including estimated quantities landed directly from Hong Kong vessels in Chinese ports.

## Industry

### SELECTED PRODUCTS
('000 metric tons, unless otherwise indicated)

|  | 1990 | 1991 | 1992 |
|---|---|---|---|
| Crude groundnut oil | 21 | 18 | 20 |
| Uncooked macaroni and noodle products | 83 | 78 | 73 |
| Soft drinks ('000 hectolitres) | 3,277 | 3,305 | 2,984 |
| Cigarettes (million) | 23,132 | 32,721 | 36,513 |
| Cotton yarn (pure and mixed) | 194.8 | 178.0 | 179.8 |
| Cotton woven fabrics (million sq m) | 818 | 753 | 807 |
| Knitted sweaters ('000) | 170,445 | 182,154 | 159,606 |
| Men's and boys' jackets ('000) | 16,444 | 17,556 | 21,130 |
| Men's and boys' trousers ('000) | 93,653 | 94,004 | 120,099 |
| Women's and girls' blouses ('000) | 246,406 | 247,855 | 220,638 |
| Women's and girls' dresses ('000) | 9,184 | 18,892 | 11,788 |
| Women's and girls' skirts, slacks and shorts ('000) | 143,134 | 152,739 | 116,824 |
| Men's and boys' shirts ('000) | 173,282 | 171,615 | 148,344 |
| Footwear (excl. rubber—'000 pairs) | 73,496 | 25,301 | 8,433 |
| Telephones ('000) | 11,268 | 5,323 | 5,949 |
| Watches ('000) | 186,743 | 202,202 | n.a. |
| Electric energy (million kWh)† | 28,938 | 31,807 | 34,914 |

**1993:** Cotton yarn (pure and mixed) 166,043 metric tons; Cotton woven fabrics 755 million sq m; Electric energy 36,394 million kWh†.

* Figure includes mineral water.
† Source: Hong Kong Energy Statistics.
Source: Census and Statistics Department, Hong Kong.

## Finance

### CURRENCY AND EXCHANGE RATES
**Monetary Units**
100 cents = 1 Hong Kong dollar (HK $).

**Sterling and US Dollar Equivalents** (31 December 1994)
£1 sterling = HK $12.105;
US $1 = HK $7.737;
HK $1,000 = £82.61 = US $129.25.

**Average Exchange Rate** (US cents per HK $)
1992   12.92
1993   12.93
1994   12.94

**COST OF LIVING** (Consumer price index.* Base: October 1989–September 1990 = 100)

|  | 1992 | 1993 | 1994 |
|---|---|---|---|
| Foodstuffs | 124.1 | 133.1 | 141.6 |
| Housing | 131.7 | 148.3 | 164.9 |
| Fuel and light | 115.7 | 120.1 | 124.3 |
| Alcoholic drinks and tobacco | 159.6 | 176.3 | 186.1 |
| Clothing and footwear | 117.6 | 126.5 | 137.7 |
| Durable goods | 107.0 | 109.4 | 112.4 |
| Miscellaneous goods | 116.0 | 123.9 | 132.3 |
| Transport and vehicles | 124.5 | 134.8 | 147.4 |
| Services | 129.7 | 142.1 | 158.8 |
| **All items** | 125.2 | 135.9 | 146.9 |

* The index covers about 50% of households. The monthly expenditure was between HK $2,500 and HK $9,999 in 1989–90.

**BUDGET** (HK $ million, year ending 31 March)

| Revenue | 1992/93 | 1993/94 | 1994/95* |
|---|---|---|---|
| Direct taxes: |  |  |  |
| Earnings and profits tax | 55,061 | 65,439 | 74,700 |
| Estate duty | 1,025 | 1,186 | 1,300 |
| Indirect taxes: |  |  |  |
| Duties on petroleum products, beverages, tobacco and cosmetics | 7,216 | 7,113 | 7,837 |
| General rates (property tax) | 4,423 | 4,461 | 5,155 |
| Motor vehicle taxes | 4,940 | 4,192 | 4,429 |
| Royalties and concessions | 1,136 | 1,379 | 1,686 |
| Others | 23,012 | 30,020 | 22,844 |
| Fines, forfeitures and penalties | 892 | 1,123 | 1,459 |
| Receipts from properties and investments | 1,821 | 2,265 | 1,994 |
| Reimbursements and contributions | 3,798 | 3,755 | 4,065 |
| Operating revenue from utilities: |  |  |  |
| Airport and air services | 2,373 | 2,841 | 3,017 |
| Postal services | 2,428 | 2,611 | 2,796 |
| Water | 1,911 | 2,255 | 2,268 |
| Others | 462 | 290 | 302 |
| Fees and charges | 8,015 | 8,627 | 9,747 |
| Interest receipts (operating revenue) | 1,767 | 3,387 | 4,570 |
| Capital Works Reserve Fund (land sales and interest) | 8,957 | 19,112 | 19,323 |
| Capital Investment Fund | 2,368 | 2,764 | 2,763 |
| Loan funds | 686 | 823 | 900 |
| Other capital revenue | 501 | 2,956 | 2,405 |
| Net borrowing | 2,519 | 3 | — |
| **Total government revenue** | 135,311 | 166,602 | 173,561 |

## BRITISH DEPENDENT TERRITORIES

| Expenditure† | 1992/93 | 1993/94 | 1994/95* |
|---|---|---|---|
| Economic affairs and services | 7,563 | 12,447 | 8,045 |
| Internal security | 13,488 | 14,209 | 15,533 |
| Immigration | 1,207 | 1,358 | 1,541 |
| Other security services | 1,590 | 1,755 | 2,052 |
| Social welfare | 7,299 | 9,170 | 11,026 |
| Health services | 13,636 | 18,457 | 18,921 |
| Education | 22,158 | 25,409 | 29,219 |
| Environmental services | 3,129 | 3,134 | 4,614 |
| Recreation, culture and amenities | 5,929 | 7,204 | 8,324 |
| Other community and external affairs | 1,044 | 1,122 | 1,264 |
| Transport | 5,927 | 9,013 | 10,773 |
| Land and buildings | 7,933 | 9,738 | 11,782 |
| Water supply | 3,624 | 4,300 | 5,030 |
| Support | 16,034 | 21,284 | 21,961 |
| Housing | 12,932 | 16,607 | 20,767 |
| **Total** | 123,493 | 155,207 | 170,852 |
| Recurrent | 91,258 | 105,255 | 122,103 |
| Capital | 32,235 | 49,952 | 48,749 |

\* Estimates.

† Figures refer to consolidated expenditure by the public sector. Of the total, government expenditure, after deducting grants, debt repayments and equity injections, was (in HK $ million): 104,971 in 1992/93; 134,004 in 1993/94; 144,801 (estimate) in 1994/95. Expenditure by other public-sector bodies (in HK $ million) was: 18,522 in 1992/93; 21,203 in 1993/94; 26,051 (estimate) in 1994/95.

**MONEY SUPPLY** (HK $ million at 31 December)

| | 1992 | 1993 | 1994 |
|---|---|---|---|
| Currency outside banks | 52,172 | 63,354 | 67,783 |
| Demand deposits at licensed banks | 103,385 | 124,255 | 117,554 |
| **Total money** | 155,557 | 187,608 | 185,337 |

**NATIONAL ACCOUNTS**
(HK $ million at current market prices)

**Expenditure on the Gross Domestic Product**

| | 1992 | 1993* | 1994* |
|---|---|---|---|
| Government final consumption expenditure | 64,070 | 72,335 | 83,246 |
| Private final consumption expenditure | 451,670 | 515,312 | 600,040 |
| Change in stocks | 8,187 | 2,040 | 19,880 |
| Gross domestic fixed capital formation | 213,808 | 246,472 | 297,478 |
| **Total domestic expenditure** | 737,735 | 836,159 | 1,000,644 |
| Exports of goods and services | 1,114,304 | 1,263,697 | 1,416,859 |
| *Less* Imports of goods and services | 1,072,704 | 1,202,261 | 1,398,275 |
| **GDP at current market prices** | 779,335 | 897,595 | 1,019,228 |
| **GDP at constant (1990) market prices** | 650,347 | 688,344 | 726,177 |

\* Revised estimates.

## Hong Kong

**Gross Domestic Product by Economic Activity**

| | 1991 | 1992 | 1993* |
|---|---|---|---|
| Agriculture and fishing | 1,441 | 1,468 | 1,612 |
| Mining and quarrying | 222 | 205 | 198 |
| Manufacturing | 97,223 | 99,764 | 94,294 |
| Electricity, gas and water | 13,521 | 15,637 | 17,588 |
| Construction | 34,659 | 37,337 | 41,534 |
| Wholesale, retail and import/export trades, restaurants and hotels | 163,284 | 190,760 | 219,115 |
| Transport, storage and communication | 60,604 | 71,227 | 81,805 |
| Financing, insurance, real estate and business services | 143,296 | 178,923 | 212,681 |
| Community, social and personal services | 94,293 | 110,703 | 126,649 |
| Ownership of premises | 68,873 | 80,941 | 93,925 |
| **Sub-total** | 667,416 | 786,965 | 889,401 |
| *Less* Imputed bank service charges | 45,902 | 54,846 | 63,015 |
| **GDP at factor cost** | 631,514 | 732,120 | 826,386 |
| Indirect taxes, *less* subsidies | 36,323 | 48,777 | 53,278 |
| **GDP in purchasers' values** | 667,837 | 780,897 | 879,664 |

\* Revised estimates.

# External Trade

**PRINCIPAL COMMODITIES** (HK $ million, excl. gold)

| Imports | 1992 | 1993 | 1994 |
|---|---|---|---|
| **Food and live animals** | 43,469 | 43,235 | 50,776 |
| **Chemicals and related products** | 67,627 | 66,836 | 84,122 |
| Plastic in primary forms | 21,119 | 20,563 | 28,438 |
| **Basic manufactures** | 207,778 | 220,253 | 259,536 |
| Textile yarn, fabrics, made-up articles, etc. | 101,322 | 98,895 | 118,205 |
| Non-metallic mineral manufactures | 29,335 | 33,431 | 39,790 |
| **Machinery and transport equipment** | 307,002 | 377,482 | 443,633 |
| Telecommunications and sound recording and reproducing apparatus and equipment | 75,629 | 93,346 | 120,621 |
| Electrical machinery, apparatus and appliances n.e.s., and electrical parts thereof | 95,434 | 116,357 | 138,881 |
| Road vehicles | 33,653 | 50,466 | 51,419 |
| **Miscellaneous manufactured articles** | 265,599 | 303,058 | 337,549 |
| Clothing (excl. footwear) | 80,078 | 91,325 | 96,277 |
| Photographic apparatus, equipment and supplies, optical goods, watches and clocks | 45,860 | 48,661 | 54,314 |
| **Total** (incl. others) | 955,295 | 1,072,597 | 1,250,709 |

# BRITISH DEPENDENT TERRITORIES

*Hong Kong*

| Domestic exports | 1992 | 1993 | 1994 |
|---|---|---|---|
| **Chemicals and related products** | 7,686 | 7,765 | 8,418 |
| **Basic manufactures** | 28,316 | 28,009 | 26,455 |
| Textile yarn, fabrics, made-up articles, etc. | 17,226 | 16,180 | 15,038 |
| **Machinery and transport equipment** | 61,437 | 61,697 | 62,211 |
| Office machines and automatic data-processing equipment | 20,530 | 17,247 | 17,623 |
| Telecommunications and sound recording and reproducing apparatus and equipment | 12,983 | 13,278 | 11,622 |
| Other electrical machinery, apparatus, etc. | 20,138 | 22,668 | 24,815 |
| **Miscellaneous manufactured articles** | 122,526 | 112,342 | 112,472 |
| Clothing (excl. footwear) | 77,156 | 71,857 | 73,086 |
| Photographic apparatus, equipment and supplies, optical goods, watches and clocks | 18,879 | 16,053 | 16,207 |
| **Total** (incl. others) | 234,123 | 223,027 | 222,092 |

| Re-exports | 1992 | 1993 | 1994 |
|---|---|---|---|
| **Chemicals and related products** | 43,860 | 45,330 | 56,731 |
| Plastic in primary forms | 14,218 | 14,845 | 20,771 |
| **Basic manufactures** | 129,123 | 143,321 | 165,653 |
| Textile yarn, fabrics, made-up articles, etc. | 67,744 | 70,556 | 82,145 |
| Non-metallic mineral manufactures | 14,440 | 16,127 | 18,779 |
| **Machinery and transport equipment** | 191,624 | 258,455 | 304,789 |
| Office machines and automatic data-processing equipment | 21,994 | 28,756 | 37,050 |
| Telecommunications and sound recording and reproducing apparatus and equipment | 55,763 | 74,082 | 99,552 |
| Electric machinery, apparatus and appliances n.e.s., and electrical parts thereof | 53,746 | 69,141 | 83,767 |
| **Miscellaneous manufactured articles** | 277,427 | 326,656 | 361,579 |
| Clothing (excl. footwear) | 78,095 | 90,574 | 92,335 |
| Footwear | 35,327 | 47,226 | 53,269 |
| **Total** (incl. others) | 690,829 | 823,224 | 947,921 |

**PRINCIPAL TRADING PARTNERS** (HK $ million, excl. gold)

| Imports | 1992 | 1993 | 1994 |
|---|---|---|---|
| China, People's Repub. | 354,348 | 402,161 | 470,876 |
| France | 11,138 | 14,804 | 15,361 |
| Germany | 21,911 | 24,918 | 28,660 |
| Italy | 14,825 | 17,880 | 22,778 |
| Japan | 166,191 | 178,034 | 195,036 |
| Korea, Repub. | 44,155 | 48,220 | 57,551 |
| Malaysia | 12,825 | 15,855 | 20,147 |
| Singapore | 39,087 | 47,835 | 61,968 |
| Switzerland | 12,343 | 12,236 | 14,836 |
| Taiwan | 87,019 | 93,968 | 107,310 |
| Thailand | 11,811 | 13,015 | 17,196 |
| United Kingdom | 19,221 | 21,438 | 25,405 |
| USA | 70,594 | 79,419 | 89,343 |
| **Total** (incl. others) | 995,295 | 1,072,597 | 1,250,709 |

| Domestic exports | 1992 | 1993 | 1994 |
|---|---|---|---|
| Australia | 2,733 | 2,339 | 2,565 |
| Canada | 5,018 | 4,734 | 4,173 |
| China, People's Repub. | 61,959 | 63,367 | 61,009 |
| France | 3,164 | 2,707 | 2,813 |
| Germany | 15,956 | 13,969 | 12,811 |
| Japan | 10,997 | 9,677 | 10,455 |
| Malaysia | 2,500 | 2,569 | 2,813 |
| Netherlands | 4,878 | 4,520 | 4,775 |
| Philippines | 2,378 | 2,264 | 2,912 |
| Singapore | 10,360 | 11,344 | 12,225 |
| Taiwan | 6,500 | 6,261 | 6,076 |
| Thailand | 2,228 | 2,046 | 2,524 |
| United Kingdom | 12,541 | 10,771 | 10,292 |
| USA | 64,600 | 60,292 | 61,419 |
| **Total** (incl. others) | 234,123 | 223,027 | 222,092 |

| Re-exports | 1992 | 1993 | 1994 |
|---|---|---|---|
| Australia | 10,100 | 11,425 | 13,877 |
| Canada | 11,101 | 12,656 | 14,199 |
| China, People's Repub. | 212,105 | 274,561 | 322,835 |
| France | 11,039 | 12,864 | 13,671 |
| Germany | 33,103 | 40,798 | 41,617 |
| Italy | 10,663 | 9,969 | 11,028 |
| Japan | 37,465 | 44,156 | 54,745 |
| Korea, Repub. | 13,588 | 15,538 | 16,483 |
| Macau | 8,721 | 9,750 | 10,748 |
| Netherlands | 9,781 | 11,977 | 13,542 |
| Philippines | 6,200 | 8,072 | 11,524 |
| Singapore | 13,866 | 17,143 | 20,346 |
| Taiwan | 26,156 | 21,910 | 22,416 |
| United Kingdom | 20,591 | 24,536 | 27,318 |
| USA | 148,500 | 180,349 | 210,077 |
| **Total** (incl. others) | 690,829 | 823,224 | 947,921 |

## Transport

**RAILWAYS** (traffic)

|  | 1992 | 1993 | 1994 |
|---|---|---|---|
| Passenger-kilometres ('000) | 3,120,543 | 3,268,646 | 3,497,396 |
| Freight ton-kilometres ('000) |  |  |  |
|   Incoming traffic | 49,070 | 39,239 | 35,695 |
|   Outgoing traffic | 12,002 | 11,915 | 11,256 |

**ROAD TRAFFIC** (registered motor vehicles at 31 December)

|  | 1992 | 1993 | 1994 |
|---|---|---|---|
| Private cars | 265,755 | 291,913 | 311,929 |
| Private buses | 240 | 266 | 285 |
| Public buses | 8,207 | 8,618 | 9,007 |
| Private light buses | 2,525 | 2,564 | 2,589 |
| Public light buses | 4,349 | 4,350 | 4,350 |
| Taxis | 17,720 | 17,758 | 18,111 |
| Goods vehicles | 140,755 | 144,093 | 141,876 |
| Motor cycles | 24,871 | 26,768 | 28,372 |
| Crown vehicles (excl. vehicles of HM Forces) | 6,780 | 7,155 | 7,478 |
| **Total** (incl. others) | 471,221 | 503,509 | 524,021 |

Note: Figures do not include tramcars.

BRITISH DEPENDENT TERRITORIES

Hong Kong

## SHIPPING (1994)

|  | Ocean-going Vessels | River Vessels |
|---|---|---|
| Vessels entered (number) | 36,721 | 155,260 |
| Tonnage entered ('000 nrt) | 161,834 | 39,975 |
| Passengers landed ('000) | 10,333* | — |
| Passengers embarked ('000) | 10,578* | — |
| Cargo tons landed ('000 metric tons) | 76,672 | 10,600† |
| Cargo tons loaded ('000 metric tons) | 34,274 | 10,100† |

* Includes river vessels.  † 1993 figure.

Note: Figures on ocean-going vessels are based on the Shipping Statistics System established by the Census and Statistics Department, whereas figures on river vessels are provided by the Marine Department.

Merchant shipping fleet ('000 grt at 31 December 1994): 8.0m.

## CIVIL AVIATION

|  | 1992 | 1993 | 1994 |
|---|---|---|---|
| Passengers: |  |  |  |
| Arrivals | 8,439,237 | 9,339,250 | 9,889,567 |
| Departures | 8,624,415 | 9,492,264 | 1,002,784 |
| Freight (in metric tons): |  |  |  |
| Arrivals | 422,620 | 512,534 | 605,782 |
| Departures | 534,288 | 626,556 | 686,722 |

## Tourism

### VISITOR ARRIVALS BY COUNTRY OF RESIDENCE

|  | 1992 | 1993 | 1994 |
|---|---|---|---|
| Australia | 261,182 | 264,722 | 267,158 |
| Canada | 180,231 | 189,432 | 185,290 |
| France | 128,497 | 138,569 | 138,920 |
| Germany | 172,200 | 219,706 | 236,384 |
| India | 80,022 | 78,911 | 80,099 |
| Indonesia | 160,896 | 174,346 | 176,014 |
| Japan | 1,324,399 | 1,280,905 | 1,440,632 |
| Malaysia | 232,910 | 234,127 | 202,181 |
| Philippines | 229,567 | 236,363 | 249,698 |
| Singapore | 283,229 | 289,717 | 270,585 |
| Taiwan | 1,640,032 | 1,777,310 | 1,665,330 |
| Thailand | 319,663 | 293,495 | 285,041 |
| United Kingdom | 314,231 | 339,162 | 379,577 |
| USA | 694,290 | 755,666 | 776,039 |
| **Total** (incl. others)* | 8,010,524 | 8,937,500 | 9,331,156 |

* Includes visitors from the People's Republic of China (1.7m. in 1993); 1.9m. in 1994.

## Communications Media

|  | 1991 | 1992 | 1993 |
|---|---|---|---|
| Telephones* | 3,455,000 | 3,649,000 | 3,854,000 |
| Periodicals | 603 | 598 | 663 |
| Newspapers | 64 | 66 | 76 |

* Estimates.

**1994:** Telephones (estimate): 4,047,000.
**1992:** Radio receivers in use: 3,875,000; Television receivers in use: 1,630,000 (Source: UNESCO, *Statistical Yearbook*).

## Education

(Pupils, at September)

|  | 1992 | 1993 | 1994 |
|---|---|---|---|
| Kindergarten | 189,730 | 187,549 | 180,109 |
| Primary | 501,625 | 465,061 | 476,847 |
| Secondary and matriculation | 461,460 | 472,200 | 471,121 |
| Approved post-secondary colleges | 3,070 | 2,787 | 2,712 |
| Teacher training |  |  |  |
| Full-time | 2,211 | 2,315 | 2,721 |
| Part-time* | 1,529 | 1,257 | 1,226 |
| Special education | 8,257 | 8,279 | 8,065 |
| Technical institutes |  |  |  |
| Full-time | 12,717 | 12,640 | 13,652 |
| Part-time | 37,336 | 35,452 | 34,121 |
| Technical colleges |  |  |  |
| Full-time | n.a. | n.a. | 3,257 |
| Part-time | n.a. | n.a. | 6,090 |
| Universities and Lingnan College |  |  |  |
| Full-time | 42,966 | 46,596 | 49,969 |
| Part-time | 25,823 | 23,585 | 22,184 |
| Adult education and others | 88,011 | 84,823 | 94,657 |

* Enrolment in short courses excluded.

# Directory

## The Constitution

The Government of Hong Kong, which consists of the Governor (representing the British monarch), the Executive Council and the Legislative Council, is constituted under the authority of Letters Patent and Royal Instructions. The Executive Council is composed entirely of non-elected members.

The Executive Council is consulted by the Governor on all important administrative questions. In addition to three *ex-officio* members, there are up to 12 appointed members, including one official member.

The Legislative Council, which advises on and approves the enactment of the territory's laws and approves all expenditure from public funds, consists of 60 members (see below). It meets in public to scrutinize all government expenditure proposals; two subcommittees deal with public works capital expenditure, and with government staff increases.

## The Government

**Governor:** CHRISTOPHER FRANCIS PATTEN (assumed office 9 July 1992).

### EXECUTIVE COUNCIL
(June 1995)

**President:** The Governor.
**Ex-Officio Members:**
  **Chief Secretary:** ANSON CHAN.
  **Financial Secretary:** Sir HAMISH MACLEOD (DONALD TSANG from September 1995).
  **Attorney General:** JEREMY F. MATHEWS.

# BRITISH DEPENDENT TERRITORIES
*Hong Kong*

**Appointed Members:**
Baroness DUNN (to retire July 1995)
JOHN GRAY
ROSANNA WONG YICK-MING
MICHAEL SZE CHO-CHEUNG (Secretary for the Civil Service)
DENIS CHANG KHEN-LEE
Prof. EDWARD CHEN KWAN-YIU
Dr RAYMOND CH'IEN KUO-FUNG
ANDREW LI KWOK-NANG
Prof. FELICE LIEH MAK
TUNG CHEE-HWA.

### LEGISLATIVE COUNCIL

In mid-1995 the Legislative Council comprised 60 members: 18 directly elected by universal suffrage in nine double-member geographical constituencies; 21 elected by limited franchise in 15 'functional constituencies', each representing an occupational or professional group; and 21 (including three *ex-officio* members) appointed by the Governor. At the elections of September 1991, of the 18 seats open (for the first time) to direct election, 12 were won by the United Democrats of Hong Kong, most of the remaining seats being taken by liberal and progressive independent candidates. At the September 1995 elections, the number of directly-elected members was to be increased to the maximum permissible of 20; the franchise for the existing 21 'functional constituencies' was to be widened, and nine additional constituencies were to be established.

**President:** Sir JOHN SWAINE.

**Ex-Officio Members:** The Chief Secretary, the Attorney General, the Financial Secretary.

### GOVERNMENT OFFICES

**Office of the Governor:** Government House, Upper Albert Rd, Hong Kong; tel. 25232031; telex 73380; fax 28101592.

**Government Secretariat:** Central Government Offices, Lower Albert Rd, Hong Kong; tel. 28102717; telex 73380; fax 28457895.

**Government Information Services:** Beaconsfield House, Queen's Rd, Central; tel. 28428777; fax 28459078.

## Political Organizations

After the signing of the Sino-British Joint Declaration in 1984, numerous associations advocating immediate democratic reforms for Hong Kong were formed.

**Association for Democracy and People's Livelihood (ADPL):** Room 1104, Sun Beam Commercial Bldg, 469–471 Nathan Rd, Kowloon; tel. 27822699; fax 27823137; advocates democracy; Sec LEE YIU-KWAN.

**Democratic Alliance for the Betterment of Hong Kong (DAB):** China Overseas Bldg, 24/F, 2/F, 139 Hennessy Rd, Wanchai; tel. 25280136; fax 25284339; f. 1992; pro-Beijing; Chair. TSANG YOK-SING; Sec.-Gen. CHENG KAI-NAM.

**Democratic Party of Hong Kong:** Room 401/413, Central Government Offices, West Wing, 11 Ice House St, Central; tel. 25372471; fax 23978998; f. 1994 by merger of United Democrats of Hong Kong (UDHK—declared a formal political party in 1990) and Meeting Point; liberal grouping; advocates democracy; Chair. MARTIN LEE; Sec.-Gen. LAW CHI-KWONG.

**Hong Kong Democratic Foundation:** GPOB 12287; tel. 28696443; fax 28696318; advocates democracy; Chair. PATRICK SHIU.

**Hong Kong Progressive Alliance:** Hong Kong; tel. 25262316; fax 28450127; f. 1994; advocates close relationship with the People's Republic of China; 52-mem. organizing cttee drawn from business and professional community; Spokesman AMBROSE LAU.

**Liberal Democratic Foundation (LDF):** Hong Kong; pro-Beijing.

**Liberal Party:** Shun Ho Tower, 2/F, 24–30 Ice House St, Central; tel. 28696833; fax 28453671; f. 1993 by mems of Co-operative Resources Centre (CRC); business-oriented; pro-Beijing; Leader ALLEN LEE PENG-FEI.

**New Hong Kong Alliance:** 4/F, 14–15 Wo On Lane, Central; fax 28691110; pro-China.

The **Chinese Communist Party** (based in the People's Republic) and the **Kuomintang** (Nationalist Party of China, based in Taiwan) also maintain organizations.

## Judicial System

The Supreme Court consists of a Court of Appeal and of a High Court. The High Court of Justice has unlimited jurisdiction in civil and criminal cases, the District Court having limited jurisdiction. Appeals from these courts lie to the Court of Appeal, presided over by the Chief Justice or a Vice-President of the Court of Appeal with one or two Justices of Appeal. Appeals from Magistrates' Courts are heard by a High Court judge.

Beyond the Court of Appeal, further appeal lies to the Judicial Committee of the Privy Council in London. This was to be replaced by a local Court of Final Appeal, pursuant to the Joint Declaration.

### SUPREME COURT

**Chief Justice:** Sir TI-LIANG YANG.

**Justices of Appeal:** W. J. SILKE, N. P. POWER, R. G. PENLINGTON, N. MACDOUGALL, G. P. NAZARETH, H. LITTON, K. BOKHARY, J. B. MORTIMER, G. M. GODFREY, B. T. M. LIU, S. H. MAYO.

**High Court Judges:** E. DE B. BEWLEY, J. J. RHIND, B. L. JONES, M. K. C. WONG, R. A. W. SEARS, N. J. BARNETT, J. M. DUFFY, T. J. RYAN, M. SAIED, N. KAPLAN, T. M. GALL, B. R. KEITH, D. J. LEONARD, A. S. C. LEONG, K. H. WOO, P. CHAN, F. STOCK, J. CHAN, A. G. ROGERS, M. S. MOORE, D. YAM, W. WAUNG, C. SEAGROATT.

### OTHER COURTS

**District Courts:** There are 29 District Judges.

**Magistrates' Courts:** There are 71 Magistrates, sitting in 10 magistracies.

## Religion

The Chinese population is predominantly Buddhist. In 1994 the number of active Buddhists was estimated at between 650,000 and 700,000. Confucianism and Daoism are widely practised. The three religions are frequently found in the same temple. In 1990 there were more than 500,000 Christians, approximately 50,000 Muslims, 12,000 Hindus, 1,000 Jews and 3,000 Sikhs. The Bahá'í faith and Zoroastrianism are also represented.

### BUDDHISM

**Hong Kong Buddhist Association:** 1/F, 338 Lockhart Rd; tel. 25749371; fax 28340789; Pres. Ven. KOK KWONG.

### CHRISTIANITY

**Hong Kong Christian Council:** 9/F, 33 Granville Rd, Kowloon; tel. 23687141; fax 27242131; f. 1954; 18 mem. orgs; Chair. SIMON SIT; Gen. Sec. Rev. Dr MAN-KING TSO.

#### The Anglican Communion

**Bishop of Hong Kong and Macau:** Rt Rev. PETER K. K. KWONG, Bishop's House, 1 Lower Albert Rd; tel. 25265355; telex 62822; fax 25212199.

#### The Lutheran Church

**Evangelical Lutheran Church of Hong Kong:** 50A Waterloo Rd, Kowloon; tel. 23885847; fax 23887539; 12,400 mems; Pres. Rev. KOY YING-KWEI.

#### The Roman Catholic Church

For ecclesiastical purposes, Hong Kong forms a single diocese, nominally suffragan to the archdiocese of Canton (Guangzhou), China. In 1994 there were an estimated 254,140 adherents in the territory, representing about 5% of the total population.

**Bishop of Hong Kong:** Cardinal JOHN BAPTIST WU CHENG-CHUNG, Catholic Diocese Centre, 16 Caine Rd; tel. 25241633; fax 25218737.

## The Press

Hong Kong has a thriving press, with, after Japan, the highest newspaper readership in Asia. In 1994, according to government figures, there were 76 newspapers, including 43 Chinese-language and seven English-language dailies, and 663 periodicals. In March 1987 the Legislative Council approved proposals to abolish the Government's hitherto extensive powers over the local media.

### PRINCIPAL DAILY NEWSPAPERS

#### English Language

**Asian Wall Street Journal:** GPO Box 9825; tel. 25737121; telex 83828; fax 28345291; f. 1976; business; Editor URBAN C. LEHNER; circ. 43,729.

**Eastern Express:** Oriental Press Centre, Wang Tai Rd, Kowloon Bay, Kowloon; tel. 27071111; fax 27071122; f. 1994; Editor MICHAEL CHUGANI; circ. 60,000.

**Hong Kong Standard:** Sing Tao Bldg, 4/F, 1 Wang Kwong Rd, Kowloon Bay, Kowloon; tel. 27982798; fax 27953009; f. 1949; Editor-in-Chief DAVID C. T. WONG; circ. 55,000.

**International Herald Tribune** (Asian Edn): 7/F, 50 Gloucester Rd; tel. 28613073; telex 61170; Correspondent KEVIN MURPHY.

BRITISH DEPENDENT TERRITORIES                                                                                                        Hong Kong

**South China Morning Post:** Tong Chong St, POB 47; tel. 25652222; telex 86008; fax 28111278; f. 1903; Editor-in-Chief David Armstrong; circ. 110,000.

**Target Financial Service:** Wah Tao Bldg, 4/F, 42 Wood Rd, Wanchai; tel. 25730379; fax 28381597; f. 1972; financial news, commentary, politics, property, litigations, etc.

### Chinese Language

**Apple Daily:** Hong Kong; f. 1995; Publr Jimmy Lai.

**Ching Pao:** 3/F, 141 Queen's Rd East; tel. 25273836; f. 1956; Editor Mok Kong; circ. 120,000.

**Express News:** Aik San Factory Bldg, 13/F, 14 Westlands Rd, Quarry Bay; tel. 25653535; fax 25650396; f. 1963; Chief Editor Peter Chiu; circ. 90,000.

**Hong Kong Daily News:** All Flats, Hong Kong Industrial Bldg, 17/F, 444 Des Voeux Rd West; tel. 28160261; telex 83567; fax 28171114; f. 1958; morning; Man. Dir Simon Lung; Chief Editor K. P. Fung; circ. 101,815.

**Hong Kong Economic Journal:** North Point Industrial Bldg, 22/F, 499 King's Rd; tel. 28567567; fax 28111070; circ. 70,000.

**Hong Kong Economic Times:** Kodak House, 6/F, Block 2, 321 Java Rd, North Point; tel. 25654288; fax 28111926; f. 1988; Publr and Chief Editor Lawrence Fung; circ. 62,000.

**Hong Kong Sheung Po** (Hong Kong Commercial Daily): 499 King's Rd, North Point; tel. 25640788; f. 1952; morning; Editor-in-Chief H. Cheung; circ. 110,000.

**Hsin Wan Pao** (New Evening Post): 342 Hennessy Rd; tel. 25757181; telex 72859; f. 1950; Editor-in-Chief Chao Tse-lung; circ. 90,000.

**Ming Pao:** Ming Pao Bldg, 9/F, 651 King's Rd, North Point; tel. 25653111; telex 80788; fax 28110599; f. 1959; morning; Chief Editor C. C. Tung; circ. 120,000.

**Oriental Daily News:** Oriental Press Centre, Wang Tai Rd, Kowloon Bay, Kowloon; tel. 27953333; telex 39888; fax 27953322; Publr C. K. Ma; Editor-in-Chief Ma Chung-pak; circ. 600,000.

**Seng Weng Evening News:** 5/F, 198 Tsat Tse Mui Rd; tel. 25637523; f. 1957; Editor Wong Long-Chau; circ. 60,000.

**Sing Pao Daily News:** Sing Pao Bldg, 101 King's Rd, North Point; tel. 25702201; telex 60587; fax 28072013; f. 1939; morning; Chief Editor Hon Chung-suen; circ. 229,250.

**Sing Tao Daily:** Sing Tao Bldg, 3/F, 1 Wang Kwong Rd, Kowloon Bay, Kowloon; tel. 27982323; telex 40347; fax 27953022; f. 1938; morning; Editor-in-Chief Luk Kam Wing; circ. 60,000.

**Sing Tao Wan Pao:** Sing Tao Bldg, 3/F, 1 Wang Kwong Rd, Kowloon; tel. 27982323; telex 40347; fax 27950856; f. 1938; evening; Editor Daniel Lee; circ. 122,000.

**Ta Kung Pao:** 342 Hennessy Rd; tel. 25757181; telex 72859; fax 28345174; f. 1902; morning; supports People's Republic of China; Editor T. S. Tsang; circ. 150,000.

**Tin Tin Yat Pao:** 6/F, 633–635 King's Rd, Jademan Centre, North Point; tel. 25652652; fax 25658036; f. 1960; Chief Editor To Shing; circ. 199,258.

**Wen Wei Po:** 197–199 Wanchai Rd; tel. 25722211; fax 25720441; f. 1948; morning; communist; Editor-in-Chief Liu Zai-ming; circ. 180,000.

## SELECTED PERIODICALS
### English Language

**Asia Magazine:** Morning Post Bldg, Tong Chong St, Quarry Bay, POB 34; tel. 25652515; telex 89131; fax 25655608; f. 1961; Sunday supplement for English language newspapers; Editor Peter Cordingley; circ. 660,000.

**Asian Business:** c/o Far East Trade Press Ltd, Block C, 10/F, Seaview Estate, 2–8 Watson Rd, North Point; tel. 25668381; fax 25080255; monthly; Publr and Editor-in-Chief Jack Maisano; circ. 100,000.

**Asian Medical News:** Pacific Plaza, 8/F, 410 Des Voeux Rd West; tel. 25595888; fax 25596910; f. 1979; Chief Editor John Fox; circ. 28,050.

**Asian Oil and Gas:** Publications Ltd, 14/F, 200 Lockhart Rd; tel. 25111301; fax 25074620; f. 1980; monthly; oil industry trade journal; Editor Andrew Burns; circ. 6,211.

**Asian Profile:** Asian Research Service, GPO Box 2232; tel. 25707227; telex 63899; fax 25128050; f. 1973; 6 a year; multi-disciplinary study of Asian affairs.

**Asiaweek:** Citicorp Centre, 34/F, 18 Whitfield Rd, Causeway Bay; tel. 25082688; telex 83540; fax 25710916; f. 1975; Asian news weekly; Man. Editor Ann Morrison; circ. 100,000.

**Business Traveller Asia/Pacific:** Tung Sun Commercial Bldg, 13/F, 200 Lockhart Rd, Wanchai; tel. 25119317; telex 62107; fax 25196846; f. 1982; consumer business travel; 12 a year; Editor and Publr Vijay K. Verghese; circ. 23,000.

**Executive Magazine:** Executive Media Ltd, 3/F Hollywood Centre, 233 Hollywood Rd; tel. 28155221; fax 28542794; f. 1979; monthly; Publr Joan Howley; Chief Exec. Editor Gerald Delilkhan; circ. 18,225.

**Far East Business:** POB 9765; tel. 25721116; telex 66381; fax 28650844; f. 1967; business, government and industry; 12 a year; Editor Lewis H. Young; circ. 70,000.

**Far Eastern Economic Review:** Citicorp Centre, 25/F, 18 Whitfield Rd, Causeway Bay, GPO Box 160; tel. 25084381; telex 75297; fax 25031530; f. 1946; weekly; Editor and Publr L. Gordon Crovitz; circ. 76,000.

**Hong Kong Electronics:** Office Tower, Convention Plaza, 38/F, 1 Harbour Rd; tel. 25844333; telex 73595; fax 28240249; f. 1985; quarterly; publ. by the Hong Kong Trade Development Council; circ. 40,000.

**Hong Kong Enterprise:** Office Tower, Convention Plaza, 38/F, 1 Harbour Rd; tel. 25844333; telex 73595; fax 28240249; f. 1967; monthly; also 2 a year in Chinese; publ. by the Hong Kong Trade Development Council; Editor Saul Lockhart; circ. 70,000.

**Hong Kong Government Gazette:** Govt Printing Dept, Cornwall House, Taikoo Trading Estate, 28 Tong Chong St, Quarry Bay; tel. 25649500; weekly.

**Hong Kong Household:** Office Tower, Convention Plaza, 38/F, 1 Harbour Rd; tel. 25844333; telex 73595; fax 28240249; f. 1983; publ. by the Hong Kong Trade Development Council; household and hardware products; 2 a year; Editor Saul Lockhart; circ. 30,000.

**Hong Kong Industrialist:** Federation of Hong Kong Industries, Hankow Centre, 4/F, 5–15 Hankow Rd, Tsimshatsui, Kowloon; tel. 27323188; telex 30101; fax 27213494; monthly; publ. by the Federation of Hong Kong Industries; Editor Sally Hopkins; circ. 7,000.

**Hong Kong Trader:** Office Tower, Convention Plaza, 38/F, 1 Harbour Rd; tel. 25844333; telex 73595; fax 28240249; f. 1983; publ. by the Hong Kong Trade Development Council; trade, economics, financial and general business news; monthly; Editor T. S. Tan; circ. 52,000.

**Official Hong Kong Guide:** Wilson House, 3/F, 19–27 Wyndham St, Central; tel. 25215392; telex 74523; fax 25218638; f. 1982; monthly; information on sightseeing, shopping, dining, etc. for overseas visitors; Editor-in-Chief Derek Davies; circ. 9,300.

**Orientations:** 200 Lockhart Rd, 14/F; tel. 25111368; telex 62107; fax 25074620; f. 1970; monthly; arts of East Asia, the Indian subcontinent and South-East Asia; Publr and Editorial Dir Elizabeth Knight.

**Reader's Digest (Asia Edn):** 3 Ah Kung Ngam Village Rd, Shaukiwan; tel. 28845643; telex 74700; fax 25689024; f. 1963; general topics; monthly; Editor-in-Chief Janie Couch; circ. 277,000.

**Sunday Examiner:** Catholic Diocese Centre, 11/F, 16 Caine Rd; tel. 25220487; fax 25213095; f. 1946; religious; weekly; Editor Fr John J. Casey; circ. 2,300.

**Sunday Morning Post Magazine:** South China Morning Post Bldg, Tong Chong St, Quarry Bay; tel. 25652515; telex 89131; fax 25655608; f. 1989; weekly; fashion, travel, food, etc.; Editor Ann Quon; circ. 80,000.

**Target Intelligence Report:** Wah Tao Bldg, 4/F, 42 Wood Rd, Wanchai; tel. 25730379; fax 28381597; f. 1972; weekly; financial analysis, investigations, surveys, food, wine and car reviews, etc.; Editor D. E. Kibble; circ. 120,000.

**Textile Asia:** c/o Business Press Ltd, California Tower, 11/F, 30–32 D'Aguilar St, GPO Box 185, Central; tel. 25233744; telex 60275; fax 28106966; f. 1970; monthly; textile and clothing industry; Publr and Editor-in-Chief Kayser W. Sung; circ. 16,200.

**Tradefinance Asia:** 16/F, 2 Wellington St; telex 84247; monthly; Editor Richard Tourret.

**Travel Business Analyst:** GPO Box 12761; tel. 25072310; telex 62107; fax 25074620; f. 1982; travel trade; monthly; Editor Murray Bailey.

### Chinese Language

**Affairs Weekly:** Professional Bldg, 4/F, 19–23 Tung Lo Wan Rd; tel. 28950801; fax 25767842; f. 1980; general interest; Editor Wong Wai Man; circ. 130,000.

**Cheng Ming Monthly:** Hennessy Rd, POB 20370; tel. 25740664; Chief Editor Wan Fai.

**City Magazine:** Hang Seng Bldg, 7/F, 200 Hennessy Rd, Wanchai; tel. 28931393; telex 84289; fax 28388761; f. 1976; monthly; fashion, wine, cars, society, etc.; Publr John K. C. Chan; Chief Editor Peter Wong; circ. 30,000.

**Contemporary Monthly:** Unit 705, Westlands Centre, 20 Westlands Rd, Quarry Bay; tel. 25638122; fax 25632984; f. 1989; monthly; current affairs; 'China-watch'; Editor-in-Chief CHING CHEONG; circ. 50,000.

**Disc Jockey:** Fuk Keung Ind. Bldg, B2, 14/F, 66–68 Tong Mei Rd, Taikoktsui, Kowloon; tel. 23905461; fax 27893869; f. 1990; monthly; music; Publr VINCENT LEUNG; circ. 32,000.

**Eastweek:** Oriental Press Centre, Wang Tai Rd, Kowloon Bay, Kowloon; tel. 27951111; fax 27952299; f. 1992; weekly; general interest; Chair. C. K. MA; circ. 162,000.

**Economic Digest:** 7C Lockhart Rd, Wanchai; tel. 25748797; fax 28383395; f. 1981; weekly; financial news, stocks, etc.; Chief Editor TERENCE LEUNG; circ. 42,000.

**Elegance So-En:** Cheung Kong Bldg, 10/F, 661 King's Rd, Quarry Bay; tel. 25651313; telex 84289; fax 25658217; f. 1977; monthly; for working women; Chief Editor LAU TIN MAY; circ. 75,000.

**Fresh Weekly:** 7/F, Jademan Centre, 633–635 King's Rd, North Point; tel. 25657883; fax 25659958; f. 1980; entertainment, fashion, etc.; Publr TONG WONG; circ. 80,000.

**Kung Kao Po** (Catholic Chinese Weekly): 11/F, 16 Caine Rd; tel. 25220487; fax 25213095; f. 1928; religious; weekly; Editor-in-Chief Fr JAMES WAN.

**Lisa's Kitchen Bi-Weekly:** Fuk Keung Ind. Bldg, B2, 14/F, 66–68 Tong Mei Rd, Taikoktsui, Kowloon; tel. 23910668; fax 27893869; f. 1984; recipes; Publr VINCENT LEUNG; circ. 50,000.

**Metropolitan Weekly:** Toppan Bldg, Rm 1008, 10/F, 22A Westlands Rd, Quarry Bay; tel. 28113811; fax 28113822; f. 1983; weekly; entertainment, social news; Chief Editor CHARLES YOU; circ. 130,000.

**Ming Pao Monthly:** 5/F, 651 King's Rd, North Point; tel. 25653175; telex 80788; fax 28809310; Chief Editor POON YIU MING.

**Motor Magazine:** Flat D, 1/F, Prospect Mansion, 66–72 Paterson St, Causeway Bay; tel. 28822230; telex 49505; fax 28823949; f. 1990; Publr and Editor-in-Chief KENNETH LI; circ. 32,000.

**Next Magazine:** Westlands Centre, 10/F, 20 Westlands Rd, Quarry Bay; tel. 28119686; fax 28113862; f. 1989; weekly; news, business, lifestyle, entertainment; Editor-in-Chief LEUNG TIN WAI; circ. 180,000.

**The Nineties Monthly:** Going Fine Ltd, Flats A & B, 1/F, Southward Mansion, 3 Lau Li St, Causeway Bay; tel. 28873997; fax 28873897; f. 1970; Editor LEE YEE; circ. 20,000.

**Open Magazine:** Hennessy Rd, POB 20558; tel. 28939197; fax 28935591; f. 1990; monthly; Chief Editor KAM CHONG; circ. 15,000.

**Oriental Sunday:** Oriental Press Centre, Wang Tai Rd, Kowloon Bay, Kowloon; tel. 27951111; fax 27952299; f. 1991; weekly; leisure magazine; Chair. C. K. MA; circ. 120,000.

**Reader's Digest (Chinese Edn):** Reader's Digest Association Far East Ltd, 3 Ah Kung Ngam Village Rd, Shaukiwan; tel. 28845596; fax 25671479; f. 1965; monthly; Editor-in-Chief ANNIE CHENG; circ. 300,000.

**Today's Living:** Flat D, 1/F, Prospect Mansion, 66–72 Paterson St, Causeway Bay; tel. 28822230; telex 49505; fax 28823949; f. 1987; monthly; interior design; Publr and Editor-in-Chief KENNETH LI; circ. 35,000.

**TV Week:** 1 Leighton Rd; tel. 28319111; telex 62770; fax 28346717; f. 1967; weekly; official guide of HK-TVB; Publr JEANNETTE CHEUNG; circ. 58,985.

**Yazhou Zhoukan:** Block A, Ming Pao Industrial Centre, 15/F, 18 Ka Yip St, Chai Wan; tel. 25155358; telex 83540; fax 25059662; f. 1987; global Chinese news weekly; Man. Editor YAU LOP-POON; circ. 93,000.

**Young Generation:** Jademan Centre, 7/F, 633–635 King's Rd, North Point; tel. 25657883; fax 25659958; biweekly; fashion and beauty; Publr TONY WONG; circ. 52,579.

**Young Girl Magazine:** Fuk Keung Ind. Bldg, B2, 14/F, 66–68 Tong Mei Rd, Taikoktsui, Kowloon; tel. 23910668; fax 27893869; f. 1987; biweekly; Publr VINCENT LEUNG; circ. 65,000.

**Yuk Long TV Weekly:** Jademan Centre, 7/F, 633–635 King's Rd, North Point; tel. 25657883; fax 25659958; f. 1977; entertainment, fashion, etc.; Publr TONY WONG; circ. 82,508.

### NEWS AGENCIES

**International News Service:** 2E Cheong Shing Mansion, 33–39 Wing Hing St, Causeway Bay; tel. 25665668; Rep. AU KIT MING.

#### Foreign Bureaux

**Agence France-Presse (AFP):** Telecom House, Room 1840, 18/F, 3 Gloucester Rd, Wanchai, GPO Box 5613; tel. 28020224; telex 73415; fax 28027292; Regional Dir YVAN CHEMLA.

**Agencia EFE** (Spain): Telecom House, Room 126A, 12/F, 3 Gloucester Rd, Wanchai; tel. 28020785; fax 28024261; Chief Correspondent JOSEP BOSCH.

**Agenzia Nazionale Stampa Associata (ANSA)** (Italy): 12 Broadwood Rd; tel. 28956712; fax 25764527; Correspondent LAURENT BALLOUHEY.

**Associated Press (AP)** (USA): 1282 New Mercury House, Waterfront Rd; tel. 25274324; telex 73265; Bureau Chief ROBERT LIU.

**Central News Agency (CNA) Inc** (Taiwan): 60 Tanner Rd, 8/F-A, North Point; tel. 25277885; fax 28656810; Bureau Chief CONRAD LU.

**Jiji Tsushin-Sha** (Japan): Room 1811, Hutchinson House, 10 Harcourt Rd; tel. 25237112; telex 73295; fax 28459013; Correspondent NOBUO KAMIYAMA.

**Kyodo News Service** (Japan): 7A Shun-ho Tower, 24–30 Ice House St, Central; tel. 25249750; telex 76499; Correspondents TAKASHI OKADA, DUNCAN FREEMAN.

**Reuters Asia Ltd** (United Kingdom): Gloucester Tower, 5F, 11 Pedder St, Central; tel. 258436363; telex 73310; Bureau Man. GEOFF WEETMAN.

**United Press International (UPI)** (USA): 1287 Telecom House, 3 Gloucester Rd, POB 5692; tel. 28020221; telex 73418; fax 28024972; Vice-Pres. (Asia) ARNOLD ZEITLIN; Editor (Asia) PAUL H. ANDERSON.

**Xinhua (New China) News Agency** (People's Republic of China): 387 Queen's Rd East, Wanchai; tel. 28314126; telex 73383; Dir ZHOU NAN.

### PRESS ASSOCIATIONS

**Chinese Language Press Institute:** Hong Kong; tel. 25616211.

**Hong Kong Chinese Press Association:** 3/F, 48 Gage St; tel. 25439477.

**Hong Kong Journalists Association:** POB 11726; tel. 25910692; fax 25727329; f. 1968; 650 mems; Chair. TONG KAM-PIU.

**Newspaper Society of Hong Kong:** POB 47; tel. 25490882; fax 25594238; f. 1954; 27 mems and 4 assoc. mems; Chair. SHUM CHOI-SANG.

## Publishers

**Asian Research Service:** GPO Box 2232; tel. 25707227; telex 63899; fax 25128050; f. 1972; geography, maps, atlases, monographs on Asian studies and journals; authorized agent for China National Publishing Industry Trading Corporation; Dir NELSON LEUNG.

**Business Press Ltd:** California Tower, 11/F, 30–32 D'Aguilar St, GPO Box 185, Central; tel. 25233744; telex 60275; fax 28106966; f. 1970; textile magazine; Man. Dir KAYSER W. SUNG.

**Chinese University Press:** Chinese University of Hong Kong, Sha Tin, New Territories; tel. 26096508; fax 26036692; f. 1977; studies on China and Hong Kong and other academic works; Dir PAUL S. L. WONG.

**Commercial Press (Hong Kong) Ltd:** Kiu Ying Bldg, 2D Finnie St, Quarry Bay; tel. 25651371; telex 86564; fax 25645277; f. 1897; trade books, dictionaries, textbooks, Chinese classics, art, etc.; Man. Dir and Chief Editor CHAN MAN HUNG.

**Excerpta Medica Asia Ltd:** 8/F, 67 Wyndham St; tel. 25243118; telex 71866; fax 28100687; f. 1980; sponsored medical publications, abstracts, journals etc.

**Far East Trade Press Ltd:** Seaview Estate, Block C, 10/F, 2–8 Watson Rd, North Point; tel. 25668381; fax 25080255; trade magazines and directories; Gen. Man. JACK MAISANO.

**Hong Kong University Press:** University of Hong Kong, 139 Pokfulam Rd; tel. 25502703; telex 71919; fax 28750734; f. 1956; Publr BARBARA CLARKE; Man. Editor DENNIS CHEUNG.

**Ling Kee Publishing Co Ltd:** Zung Fu Industrial Bldg, 1067 King's Rd, Quarry Bay; tel. 25616151; fax 28111980; f. 1956; educational and reference; Chair. B. L. AU; Man. Dir K. W. AU.

**Oxford University Press (HK) Ltd:** Warwick House, 18/F, 979 King's Rd, Taikoo Place, Quarry Bay; tel. 25163222; fax 25658491; f. 1961; school textbooks, reference, academic and general works relating to Hong Kong and China; Regional Dir A. F. D. SCOTT.

#### Government Publishing House

**Government Information Services:** see p. 3236.

### PUBLISHERS' ASSOCIATIONS

**Hong Kong Publishers' and Distributors' Association:** National Bldg, 4/F, 240–246 Nathan Rd, Kowloon; tel. 23674412.

**Society of Hong Kong Publishers:** c/o Wendy Hughes Ltd, Henan Bldg, 23/F, 90 Jaffe Rd, Wanchai; tel. 28654007; fax 28652559.

## Radio and Television

In 1992 it was estimated that there were 3,875,000 radio receivers and 1,630,000 television receivers in use.

**Radio Television Hong Kong:** Broadcasting House, 30 Broadcast Drive, POB 70200, Kowloon Central PO; tel. 23396300; telex 45568;

fax 23380279; f. 1928; govt-sponsored; 24-hour service in English and Chinese on seven radio channels; television division produces drama, documentary and public affairs programmes; also operates an educational service for transmission by two local commercial stations; Dir M. Y. Cheung.

### RADIO

**British Forces Broadcasting Service:** BFPO 1; tel. 24838000; telex 34513; fax 24885455; f. 1971; broadcasts in English and Nepali on two channels; Gen. Man. David Raven; Nepali Network Dir Kishorkumar Gurung; English Programme Organizer Jamie Gordon.

**Hong Kong Commercial Broadcasting Co Ltd:** GPO Box 3000; tel. 23365111; fax 23380021; f. 1959; broadcasts in English and Chinese on three radio frequencies; Chair. and Man. Dir George Ho; Dir and Gen. Man. Winnie Yu.

**Metro Radio:** Site 11, Basement 1, Whampoa Gardens, Hunghom, Kowloon; tel. 23649333; fax 23646577; f. 1991; broadcasts on three channels in English, Cantonese and Mandarin; Gen. Man. Craig B. Quick.

### TELEVISION

**Asia Television Ltd (ATV):** Television House, 81 Broadcast Drive, Kowloon; tel. 23387123; telex 44680; fax 23384347; f. 1973; operates two commercial television services (English and Chinese) and produces television programmes; Dir and CEO Lim Por Yen.

**Television Broadcasts Ltd (TVB):** TV City, Clearwater Bay Rd, Kowloon; tel. 27194828; telex 43596; fax 23581337; f. 1967; operates Chinese and English language services; two colour networks; Exec. Chair. Sir Run Run Shaw.

#### Satellite and Cable Television

**Satellite Television Asian Region—Star TV:** Hutchison House, 12/F, 10 Harcourt Rd, Central; tel. 25321888; fax 25244093; f. 1990; 24-hour satellite news, sport and entertainment broadcasts in English, Mandarin and Cantonese; free regional service on five channels reaching 53 countries (397,537 homes in Hong Kong); Man. Dir Gary Davey.

**Wharf Cable Ltd:** c/o Ocean Centre, 16/F, Harbour City, Canton Rd, Kowloon; f. 1993; 24-hour subscription service of news, sport and entertainment initially on 16 channels; carries BBC World Service Television; Chair. Peter Woo; Man. Dir Stephen Ng.

## Finance

(cap. = capital; res = reserves; dep. = deposits; m. = million; brs = branches; amounts in Hong Kong dollars unless otherwise stated)

### BANKING

In December 1994 there were 180 licensed banks, of which 32 were locally incorporated, operating in Hong Kong. There were also 63 restricted licence banks (formerly known as licensed deposit-taking companies), 137 deposit-taking companies, and 157 foreign banks' representative offices.

**Hong Kong Monetary Authority (HKMA):** 30/F, 3 Garden Rd, Central; tel. 28788196; telex 64282; fax 28788214; f. 1993 by merger of Office of the Commissioner of Banking and Office of the Exchange Fund; supervises licensed banks, restricted licence banks and deposit-taking cos in Hong Kong as well as their overseas brs and representative offices; CEO Joseph Yam; Deputy CEO (Banking) D. T. R. Carse; Exec. Dir (Banking Supervision) A. S. Cheok.

#### Banks of Issue

**Bank of China** (People's Repub. of China): 1 Garden Rd, Central; tel. 28266888; telex 73772; fax 28105963; f. 1917; Gen. Man. Zhou Zhenxing; 35 brs; became third bank of issue in May 1994.

**Hongkong and Shanghai Banking Corpn Ltd:** 1 Queen's Rd, Central; tel. 28221111; telex 73201; fax 28101112; f. 1865; cap. 16,254m., res 31,268m., dep. 986,093m. (Dec. 1993); Chair. and Chief Exec. John M. Gray; more than 1,400 offices world-wide.

**Standard Chartered Bank:** Standard Chartered Bank Bldg, 4–4A Des Voeux Rd, Central; tel. 28211333; telex 73230; fax 28100651; f. 1853; Area Gen. Man. (Hong Kong and China) Ian Wilson; 115 brs.

#### Other Commercial Banks

**Bank of East Asia Ltd:** GPOB 31, 10 Des Voeux Rd, Central; tel. 28423200; telex 73017; fax 28459333; inc in Hong Kong in 1918; cap. 1,447m., res 4,136m., dep. etc. 65,927m. (Dec. 1993); Chair. F. W. Li; Dir and Chief Exec. David K. P. Li; 66 brs in Hong Kong and 12 overseas brs.

**Chekiang First Bank Ltd:** Chekiang First Bank Bldg, 60 Gloucester Rd; tel. 29221222; telex 73686; fax 28669133; f. 1950; cap. 200m., res 867m., dep. 18,739m. (Dec. 1993); Chair. James Z. M. Kung; 14 brs.

**Commercial Bank of Hong Kong Ltd:** 120 Des Voeux Rd, Central; tel. 25419222; telex 73085; fax 25410009; f. 1934; cap. 400.0m., res 188.0m., dep. 5,973.8m. (Dec. 1993); Chair. and CEO Robin Y. H. Chan; Vice-Chair. and Exec. Dir John C. C. Cheung; 15 brs.

**Dao Heng Bank Ltd:** Wu Chung House, 32–35/F, 213 Queen's Rd East; tel. 28315000; telex 73345; fax 28916683; f. 1921; cap. and res 1,597.9m., dep. etc. 29,697.5m. (June 1993); Chair. Quek Leng Chan; CEOs Kwek Leng Hai, Werner Max Michael Makowski; 47 brs.

**Hang Seng Bank Ltd:** 83 Des Voeux Rd, Central; tel. 28255111; telex 73311; fax 28459301; f. 1933; cap. and res 35,547m., dep. 264,588m. (Dec. 1994); Chair. Sir Quo-Wei Lee; Man. Dir and CEO A. S. K. Au; 135 brs.

**Hongkong Chinese Bank Ltd:** Lippo Centre, 89 Queensway; tel. 28676833; telex 73749; fax 28459221; f. 1954; cap. 573m., res 356.9m., dep. 10,748.5m. (Dec. 1993); Chair. Mochtar Riady; Man. Dir T. C. Chang; 16 brs.

**International Bank of Asia Ltd:** 38 Des Voeux Rd, Central; tel. 28426222; telex 63394; fax 28101483; f. 1982 as Sun Hung Kai Bank Ltd, name changed 1986; subsidiary of Arab Banking Corpn; cap. 636m., res 480m., dep. 8,989m. (Dec. 1993); Chair. Sheikh Ali Jarrah al-Sabah; Man. Dir and CEO M. M. Murad; 20 brs.

**Jian Sing Bank Ltd:** 99–105 Des Voeux Rd, Central; tel. 25410088; telex 65712; fax 25411115; f. 1964; cap. 246m., dep. 2,702m. (Dec. 1993); Chair. David S. Y. Wong; 2 brs.

**Kwong On Bank Ltd:** 137–141 Queen's Rd, Central; tel. 28153636; telex 73359; fax 28506129; f. 1938, inc 1954; cap. 600m., res 950m., dep. 14,813m. (Dec. 1993); Chair. Ronald Leung Ding-bong; Sr Man. Dir Kenneth T. M. Leung; 30 brs.

**Liu Chong Hing Bank Ltd:** POB 2535, 24 Des Voeux Rd, Central; tel. 28417417; telex 75700; fax 25218060; f. 1948; cap. 150m., res. 2,223.4m., dep. 13,614.9m. (Dec. 1993); Chair. Liu Lit-for; Man. Dir Liu Lit-man; 30 brs.

**Nanyang Commercial Bank Ltd:** 151 Des Voeux Rd, Central; tel. 28520888; telex 73412; fax 28153333; f. 1949; cap. p.u. 600m., res 2,380m., dep. 45,557.96m. (Dec. 1992); Chair. Shu Tse Wong; 41 brs, 5 brs overseas.

**Overseas Trust Bank Ltd:** OTB Bldg, 160 Gloucester Rd; tel. 25756657; telex 74545; fax 25727535; f. 1955; under govt control 1985–93; cap. 2,333.1m., res 2,188.1m., dep. 14,523.8m. (June 1993); acquired by Dao Heng Bank in 1993; Chair. Quek Leng Chan; 42 brs in Hong Kong, 6 brs overseas.

**Shanghai Commercial Bank Ltd:** 12 Queen's Rd, Central; tel. 28415415; telex 73390; fax 28104623; f. 1950; cap. US $128.2m., res US $515.3m., dep. US $4,497.1m. (1994); Chair. and Man. Dir Pao-chu Shih; Gen. Man. John Kam-pak Yan; 38 brs.

**Union Bank of Hong Kong Ltd:** Union Bank Tower, 122–126 Queen's Rd, Central; tel. 25343333; telex 73264; fax 28051166; f. 1964; cap. 474.1m., res 667.2m., dep. 11,345.0m. (Dec. 1994); Chair. Jiang Bo; 20 brs.

**Wing Lung Bank Ltd:** 45 Des Voeux Rd, Central; tel. 28268333; telex 73360; fax 28100592; f. 1933; cap. 806m. (April 1995); res 1,334m., dep. 27,680m. (Dec. 1994); Chair. Michael Po-ko Wu; Exec. Dir and Gen. Man. Che-shum Chung; 29 brs.

**Wing On Bank Ltd:** Dah Sing Financial Centre, 36/F, 108 Gloucester Rd; tel. 25078866; telex 74024; fax 25985052; f. 1931; cap. 350m., total assets 3,200m. (Dec. 1993); Chair. David S. Y. Wong; CEO Ronald Carstairs; 1 br.

#### Principal Foreign Banks

**ABN-AMRO Bank NV** (Netherlands): Edinburgh Tower, 3–4/F, POB 61, 15 Queen's Rd, Central; tel. 28429211; telex 73453; fax 28459049; Gen. Man. L. H. Steffen; 9 brs.

**American Express Bank Ltd** (USA): One Pacific Place, 35/F, 88 Queensway; tel. 28440688; telex 73675; fax 28453637; Exec. Dir and Regional Head John Filmeridis; 6 brs.

**Bangkok Bank Public Co Ltd** (Thailand): 28 Des Voeux Rd, Central; tel. 28016688; telex 73679; fax 28105679; Gen. Man. Phallobh Sopitpongstorn; 3 brs.

**Bank of America (Asia) Ltd** (USA): 17/F, 979 King's Rd; tel. 25972888; telex 73471; fax 25972500; Chair. Ressel Fok; Pres. and CEO James E. Hulihan.

**Bank of Communications** (People's Repub. of China): 20 Pedder St, Central; tel. 28419611; telex 73409; fax 28106993; Gen. Man. Fang Liankui; 29 brs.

**Bank of India:** Ruttonjee House, 2/F, 11 Duddell St, Central; tel. 25240186; telex 75646; fax 28106149; Dep. Gen. Man. S. K. Puri; 2 brs.

**Bank Negara Indonesia (Persero):** Far East Finance Centre, 16 Harcourt Rd, Central; tel. 25299871; telex 73624; fax 258656500; Gen. Man. Amien Mastur; 2 brs.

# BRITISH DEPENDENT TERRITORIES
*Hong Kong*

**Bank of Scotland:** Jardine House, 11/F, Connaught Rd, Central; tel. 25212155; telex 73435; fax 28459007; Senior Man. A. R. ION; 1 br.

**Bank of Tokyo Ltd** (Japan): Far East Finance Centre, 1/F, 16 Harcourt Rd, Central; tel. 28627888; telex 73252; fax 28652006; Dir and Gen. Man. H. IMAI; 7 brs.

**Bank of Yokohama Ltd** (Japan): Edinburgh Tower, 36/F, 15 Queen's Rd, Central; tel. 25236041; telex 63061; fax 28459022; Gen. Man. SUSUMU YAMADA; 1 br.

**Banque Indosuez** (France): One Exchange Square, 42–45/F, Central; tel. 28489000; telex 73766; fax 28681406; Man. PHILIPPE DESGRANGES; 3 brs.

**Banque Nationale de Paris** (France): Central Bldg, 23 Queen's Rd, Central; tel. 25218218; telex 73442; fax 28106252; f. 1966; Chief Exec. Man. PHILIPPE COTTUS; 6 brs.

**Banque Worms** (France): Central Plaza, 39/F, 18 Harbour Rd, Wanchai; tel. 28028382; telex 60139; fax 28028065; Gen. Man. ANTOINE FOSSORIER; 1 br.

**Barclays Bank PLC** (UK): United Centre, 11/F, 95 Queensway, POB 9716; tel. 28261888; telex 75144; fax 28450223; f. 1973; Regional CEO Asia H. R. PERCY.

**Belgian Bank** (Belgium): Belgian House, 28–32/F, 77–79 Gloucester Rd, Wanchai; tel. 28230566; telex 73207; fmrly Generale Bank Overseas; Man. Dir GEORGES LEGROS; 20 brs.

**Chase Manhattan Bank, NA** (USA): World Trade Centre, 280 Gloucester Rd, Causeway Bay; tel. 28375111; telex 83830; fax 28375099; Sen. Vice-Pres. JAMES B. BREW; 9 brs.

**China and South Sea Bank Ltd** (People's Repub. of China): 22–26 Bonham Strand East; tel. 25429429; telex 73384; fax 25418242; Gen. Man. L. S. NG; 19 brs.

**China State Bank Ltd** (People's Repub. of China): 39–41 Des Voeux Rd, Central; tel. 28419333; telex 73410; Gen. Man. GUAN CHANG YI; 19 brs.

**Chung Khiaw Bank Ltd** (Singapore): Edinburgh Tower, Room 2508, 25/F, The Landmark, 15 Queen's Rd, Central; tel. 25326888; telex 75103; fax 28684598; Man. LIEW CHAN HARN; 2 brs.

**Citibank, NA** (USA): Citicorp Tower, 40–50/F, Citibank Plaza, 3 Garden Rd, Central; tel. 28078211; telex 73243; 27 brs.

**Commerzbank AG** (Germany): Hong Kong Club Bldg, 21/F, 3A Chater Rd, Central; tel. 28429666; fax 28681414; 1 br.

**Crédit Lyonnais** (France): Three Exchange Square, 25/F, 8 Connaught Place, Central, POB 9757; tel. 28267333; telex 76390; fax 28101270; 1 br.

**Dai-Ichi Kangyo Bank Ltd** (Japan): Gloucester Tower, 31/F, 11 Pedder St, Central; tel. 25266591; telex 60489; fax 28681421; Gen. Man. JIRO HANEDA; 1 br.

**Deutsche Bank (Asia) AG** (Germany): New World Tower, 16–18 Queen's Rd, Central, POB 3193; tel. 28430400; telex 73498; fax 28459056; Gen. Mans Dr MICHAEL THOMAS, REINER RUSCH; 2 brs.

**Equitable Banking Corpn** (Philippines): 4 Duddell St; tel. 28680323; telex 73382; fax 28100050; Sen. Vice-Pres. CHARLES GO; 1 br.

**Indian Overseas Bank:** PB 182, Ruttonjee House, 3/F, 11 Duddel St; tel. 25227157; telex 74795; fax 28451549; 2 brs.

**Kincheng Banking Corpn** (People's Repub. of China): Asia Standard Tower, G/F, 59–65 Queen's Rd, Central; tel. 28430222; telex 73405; fax 28450116; f. 1917; Gen. Man. SUN HUNG-KAY; 27 brs.

**Korea Exchange Bank** (Repub. of Korea): Far East Finance Centre, 32/F, 16 Harcourt Rd; tel. 25201221; telex 73459; fax 28612379; f. 1977; Gen. Man. KIM SUH-BONG; 3 brs.

**Kwangtung Provincial Bank** (People's Repub. of China): 1–3/F, 13–14 Connaught Rd, Central; tel. 28410410; telex 83654; fax 28459302; Gen. Man. ZHENG BAILIN; 26 brs.

**Malayan Banking Berhad** (Malaysia): 505 Worldwide House, 19 Des Voeux Rd, Central; tel. 25225529; telex 60907; fax 28106013; Man. JEFFERY LAM PAU WAN; 1 br.

**Mitsubishi Bank Ltd** (Japan): Tower I, Admiralty Centre, 14/F, 18 Harcourt Rd; tel. 28236666; telex 74357; fax 28610794; Gen. Man. TAKAO WADA; 3 brs.

**National Bank of Pakistan:** Central Bldg, Room 324, Queen's Rd, Central; tel. 25217321; telex 75137; fax 28451703; Vice-Pres. MOHAMMAD AKRAM BUTT; 2 brs.

**National Commercial Bank Ltd** (People's Repub. of China): 1–3 Wyndham St, Central; tel. 28432888; telex 83491; fax 28104634; Gen. Man. S. M. CUI; 22 brs.

**National Westminster Bank PLC** (UK): St George's Building, 5/F, 2 Ice House St, Central; tel. 25257325; telex 60111; fax 258104103; Man. Dir D. GUEST; 1 br.

**Oversea-Chinese Banking Corpn Ltd** (Singapore): Edinburgh Tower, 6/F, The Landmark, 15 Queen's Rd, Central; tel. 28682086; telex 73417; fax 28453439; Man. NA WU BENG; 3 brs.

**Overseas Union Bank Ltd** (Singapore): Edinburgh Tower, 5/F, 15 Queen's Rd, Central; tel. 25211521; telex 73258; fax 28105506; Vice-Pres. and Gen. Man. KWIK SAM AIK; 3 brs.

**Philippine National Bank:** Wing's Bldg, 2/F, 110–116 Queen's Rd, Central; tel. 25439555; telex 73019; fax 25416645; Senior Vice-Pres. and Gen. Man. FRANCISCO S. MAGSAJO, Jr; 1 br.

**Royal Bank of Canada:** Gloucester Tower, 18/F, 11 Pedder St, Central; tel. 28430888; telex 60884; fax 28685802; Vice-Pres. T. P. GIBBS; 1 br.

**Sanwa Bank Ltd** (Japan): Fairmont House, 8 Cotton Tree Drive, Central; tel. 28433888; telex 73423; fax 28400730; Gen. Man. Y. KIDA; 6 brs.

**Sin Hua Bank Ltd** (People's Repub. of China): 134–136 Des Voeux Rd, Central; tel. 28536388; telex 73416; fax 28542596; f. 1914; Gen. Man. and Exec. Dir MA CHING HUA; 41 brs.

**Sumitomo Bank Ltd** (Japan): 2601 Edinburgh Tower, 15 Queen's Rd, Central; tel. 28421700; telex 73343; fax 28106452; Gen. Man. TOSIO MORIKAWA; 3 brs.

**Toyo Trust and Banking Co Ltd** (Japan): Gloucester Tower, 15/F, 11 Pedder St; tel. 25265657; telex 85198; fax 28459247; Gen. Man. SHUNICHI FURUHATA; 1 br.

**United Overseas Bank Ltd** (Singapore): 54–58 Des Voeux Rd, Central; tel. 28425666; telex 74581; fax 28105773; Sen. Vice-Pres. and CEO ROBERT CHAN TZE LEUNG; 4 brs.

**Yien Yieh Commercial Bank Ltd** (People's Repub. of China): 242–252 Des Voeux Rd, Central; tel. 25411601; telex 83542; fax 28581577; Gen. Man. PAN JAW LING; 21 sub-brs.

### Banking Associations

**The Chinese Banks' Association:** South China Bldg, 5/F, 1–3 Wyndham St, Central; tel. 25224789; fax 28775102; 34 mems; Chair. Bank of East Asia (represented by DAVID K. P. LI).

**The Hong Kong Association of Banks:** GPO Box 11391; tel. 25211169; fax 28685035; f. 1981 to succeed The Exchange Banks' Asscn of Hong Kong; all licensed banks in Hong Kong are required by law to be mems of this statutory body, whose function is to represent and further the interests of the banking sector; Chair. Standard Chartered Bank (represented by IAN R. WILSON); Sec. PAUL R. LOWNDES.

## STOCK EXCHANGE

**The Stock Exchange of Hong Kong Ltd:** Exchange Sq., Tower 1 & 2; tel. 25221122; telex 86839; fax 28104475; f. 1986 by unification of four fmr exchanges; 680 mems.; Chair. EDGAR CHENG WAI-KIN; CEO PAUL CHOW.

## FUTURES EXCHANGE

**Hong Kong Futures Exchange Ltd:** Asia Pacific Finance Tower, Suite 605–608, 6/F, Citibank Plaza, 3 Garden Rd; tel. 28429333; fax 28452043; Chair. LEONG KA-CHAI; CEO IVERS RILEY.

## SUPERVISORY BODY

**Securities and Futures Commission (SFC):** Edinburgh Tower, 12/F, The Landmark, 15 Queen's Rd, Central; tel. 28409222; telex 61919; fax 28459553; f. 1989 to supervise the stock and futures markets; Chair. ANTHONY NEOH.

## INSURANCE

In December 1993 there were 229 insurance companies, including 125 overseas companies, authorized to transact insurance business in Hong Kong. The following are among the principal companies:

**Asia Insurance Co Ltd:** World-Wide House, 16/F, 19 Des Voeux Rd, Central; tel. 28677988; telex 74542; fax 28100218; Man. Dir SEBASTIAN LAU KI CHIT.

**Lombard General Insurance Ltd:** Natwest Tower, 25F, Times Square, 1 Matheson St, Causeway Bay; tel. 25096888; telex 69795; fax 25062221; Man. Dir KENNETH T. W. KWOK.

**Mercantile and General Reinsurance Co PLC:** 13C On Hing Bldg, 1 On Hing Terrace, Central; tel. 28106160; telex 74062; fax 25217353; Man. J. C. D. LONG-PRICE.

**Ming An Insurance Co (HK) Ltd:** International Bldg, 14 and 11/F, 141 Des Voeux Rd, Central; tel. 28151551; telex 74172; fax 25416567; Dir and Gen. Man. Y. W. SIU.

**National Mutual Asia Ltd:** 151 Gloucester Rd, Wanchai; tel. 25191111; fax 25984965; life assurance; Chair. Sir DAVID AKERS-JONES.

**New Zealand Insurance Co Ltd:** World Trade Centre, 36/F, Causeway Bay; tel. 28940555; telex 75609; fax 28950426; Gen. Man. MICHAEL HANNAN.

**Prudential Assurance Co Ltd:** Bank of East Asia Bldg, 18/F, 10 Des Voeux Rd, Central; tel. 25252367; telex 65399; fax 28104903; Gen. Man. DENIS WILKINSON.

**South British Insurance Co Ltd:** World Trade Centre, 36/F, Causeway Bay; tel. 28940666; telex 75609; fax 28950426; Regional Dir P. C. TSAO; Gen. Man. M. C. HANNAN.

**Summit Insurance (Asia) Ltd:** Shanghai Industrial Investment Bldg, 22–24/F, 48–62 Hennessy Rd; tel. 28238238; telex 65188; fax 28652395; Dir and Gen. Man. PETER FONG.

**Sun Alliance and London Insurance plc:** Dina House, 3/F, Ruttonjee Centre, 11 Duddell St; tel. 28107383; telex 80139; fax 28450389.

**Taikoo Royal Insurance Co Ltd:** Swire House, 3/F, Chater Rd, Central; tel. 28469333; fax 28101007; Dir ANDREW LEUNG.

**Willis Faber (Far East) Ltd:** 5108 Central Plaza, 18 Harbour Rd, Wanchai; tel. 28270111; telex 85240; fax 28270966; Man. Dir PETER W. A. HOGG.

**Winterthur Swiss Insurance:** Dah Sing Financial Centre, 19/F, 108 Gloucester Rd, Wanchai; tel. 25986282; fax 25985838.

### Insurance Associations

**General Insurance Council of Hong Kong:** Malaysia Bldg, 21/F, 50 Gloucester Rd, Wanchai; tel. 25201868; fax 25201967; Chair. MALCOLM R. CLARKE.

**Hong Kong Federation of Insurers (HKFI):** Malaysia Bldg, 21/F, 50 Gloucester Rd, Wanchai; tel. 25201868; fax 25201967; Chair. ALEX WONG.

**Insurance Institute of Hong Kong:** GPOB 6747; fax 28345862; f. 1967; Pres. ALEX CHAN.

**Life Insurance Council of Hong Kong:** First Pacific Bank Centre, 9/F, 56 Gloucester Rd, Wanchai; tel. 25201868; fax 25201967; 47 mems; Chair. VICTOR APPS; Exec. Dir LOUISA FONG.

## Trade and Industry

**Trade Department:** Trade Department Tower, 700 Nathan Rd, Kowloon; tel. 27897555; telex 45126; fax 27892491; Dir-Gen. J. A. MILLER.

**Industry Department:** Ocean Centre, 14/F, 5 Canton Rd, Kowloon; tel. 27372208; telex 50151; fax 27304633; Dir-Gen. DENISE YUE.

### CHAMBERS OF COMMERCE

**Chinese Chamber of Commerce, Kowloon:** 2/F, 8–10 Nga Tsin Long Rd, Kowloon; tel. 23822309; 252 mems; Chair. YEUNG CHOR-HANG.

**Chinese General Chamber of Commerce:** 24 Connaught Rd, Central; tel. 25256385; telex 89854; fax 28452610; f. 1900; 6,000 mems; Chair. Dr TSANG HIN-CHI.

**Hong Kong General Chamber of Commerce:** United Centre, 22/F, 95 Queensway, POB 852; tel. 25299229; telex 83535; fax 25279843; f. 1861; 3,600 mems; Chair. WILLIAM FUNG; Dir I. A. CHRISTIE.

**Hong Kong Junior Chamber of Commerce:** 1/F, 60 Bonham Strand, East, Sheung Wan; tel. 25438913; fax 25436271; f. 1950; 1,278 mems; Pres. DANIEL CHAM; Sec.-Gen. HELEN YU.

**Kowloon Chamber of Commerce:** KCC Bldg, 3/F, 2 Liberty Ave, Homantin, Kowloon; tel. 27600393; telex 32624; fax 27610166; 1,739 mems; Chair. TONG KWOK-WAH; Exec. Dir CHENG PO-WO.

### EXTERNAL TRADE ORGANIZATIONS

**Hong Kong Chinese Importers' and Exporters' Association:** Champion Bldg, 7–8/F, 287–291 Des Voeux Rd, Central; tel. 25448474; fax 25444677; 2,846 mems; Pres. HUI CHEUNG-CHING.

**Hong Kong Exporters' Association:** Room 825, Star House, 3 Salisbury Rd, Tsimshatsui, Kowloon; tel. 27309851; telex 57905; fax 27301869; f. 1955; 300 mems comprising leading merchants and manufacturing exporters; Chair. LOUIS K. C. WONG; Sen. Exec. Officer CATHERINE FUNG.

**Hong Kong Trade Development Council:** Office Tower, Convention Plaza, 39/F, 1 Harbour Rd, Wanchai; tel. 25844333; telex 73595; fax 28240249; f. 1966; Chair. Dr VICTOR K. FUNG; Exec. Dir FRANCIS LO.

### INDUSTRIAL ORGANIZATIONS

**Hong Kong Productivity Council:** HKPC Bldg, 78 Tat Chee Ave, Yau Yat Chuen, Kowloon Tong, Kowloon; tel. 27885678; telex 32842; fax 27885900; f. 1967 to promote increased productivity of industry and to encourage optimum utilization of resources; council of 23 mems appointed by the Government, representing management, labour, academic and professional interests, and govt depts associated with productivity matters; Chair. KENNETH FANG; Exec. Dir THOMAS S. K. CHAN.

**Chinese Manufacturers' Association of Hong Kong:** CMA Bldg, 64–66 Connaught Rd, Central; tel. 25428600; telex 63526; fax 25414541; f. 1934 to promote and protect industrial and trading interests; operates testing and certification laboratories; 3,700 mems; Pres. HERBERT H. Y. LIANG; Exec. Sec. FRANCIS T. M. LAU.

**Employers' Federation of Hong Kong:** United Centre, Unit C3, 12/F, 95 Queensway; tel. 25280536; fax 28655285; f. 1947; 280 mems; Chair. MARK LEESE; Sec. MAY CHOW.

**Federation of Hong Kong Garment Manufacturers:** 4/F, 25 Kimberley Rd, Tsimshatsui, Kowloon; tel. 27211383; fax 23111062; 250 mems; Pres. ERNEST M. K. KWAN; Sec.-Gen. ANTHONY K. K. TANG.

**Federation of Hong Kong Industries (FKHI):** Hankow Centre, 4/F, 5–15 Hankow Rd, Tsimshatsui, Kowloon; tel. 27323188; telex 30101; fax 27213494; f. 1960; 1,706 mems; Chair. Dr RAYMOND K. F. CH'IEN.

**Federation of Hong Kong Watch Trades and Industries Ltd:** Room 604, Peter Bldg, 58–62 Queen's Rd, Central; tel. 25233232; fax 28684485; f. 1947; 770 mems; Chair. DANIEL CHAN CHING YAN.

**Hong Kong Electronic Industries Association Ltd:** Room 208–9, HK Ind. & Tech. Centre, 72 Tat Chee Ave, Kowloon; tel. 27788328; fax 27882200.

**Hong Kong Factory Owners' Association:** Wing Wong Bldg, 11/F, 557–559 Nathan Rd, Kowloon; tel. 23882372; fax 23857184; 528 mems; Pres. HWANG JEN.

**Hong Kong Garment Manufacturers Association:** East Ocean Centre, 2/F, 98 Granville Rd, Tsimshatsui East, Kowloon; tel. 23673392; fax 27217537; 34 mems; Chair. HARRY N. S. LEE; Exec. Sec. JUSTIN YUE.

**Hong Kong Jade and Stone Manufacturers' Association:** Hang Lung House, 16/F, 184–192 Queen's Rd, Central; tel. 25430543; fax 28150164; f. 1965; 118 mems; Chair. HUNG-YOU FONG.

**Hong Kong Jewelry Manufacturers' Association:** Unit 5, 1/F, Hunghom Sq., 37–39 Ma Tau Wai Rd, Kowloon; tel. 27663002; fax 23623647; 160 mems; Chair. EDDIE CHEUNG.

**Hong Kong Knitwear Exporters and Manufacturers Association:** 3/F, Clothing Industry Training Authority, Kowloon Bay Training Centre, 63 Tai Yip St, Kowloon; tel. 27552621; fax 27565672; 110 mems; Chair. WILLIE LIN; Exec. Sec. SHIRLEY LIU.

**Hong Kong and Kowloon Footwear Manufacturers' Association:** Kam Fung Bldg, 3/F, Flat D, 8 Cleverly St, Sheung Wan; tel. 25414499; 102 mems; Chair. LEE CHI-NAM.

**Hong Kong Optical Manufacturers' Association:** 2/F, 11 Fa Yuen St, Kowloon; tel. 23326505; fax 27705786; 98 mems; Pres. HARVEY W. FUNG.

**Hong Kong Plastics Manufacturers Association:** 1/F, Flat B, Fu Yuen, 39–49 Wanchai Rd; tel. 25742230; fax 25742843; 120 mems; Pres. KENNETH TING.

**Hong Kong Printers Association:** 1/F, 48–50 Johnston Rd, Wanchai; tel. 25275050; fax 28610463; f. 1939; 428 mems; Chair. YIP YU BUN.

**Hong Kong Rubber and Footwear Manufacturers' Association:** Block A, 2/F, 185 Prince Edward Rd, Kowloon; tel. 23812297; fax 23976927; 220 mems; Chair. TONY CHAU MUN; Sec. WENDY LAI.

**Hong Kong Sze Yap Commercial and Industrial Association:** Hang Lung House, 1/F, 184–192 Queen's Rd, Central; tel. 25438095; fax 25449495; 1,089 mems; Chair. KWAN WONG CHAU.

**Hong Kong Toys Council:** Hankow Centre, 4/F, 5–15 Hankow Rd, Tsimshatsui, Kowloon; tel. 27323188; telex 30101; fax 27213494; 190 mems; Chair. DENNIS H. S. TING.

**Hong Kong Watch Manufacturers' Association:** Yu Wing Bldg, 3F/11F, Unit A, 64–66 Wellington St, Central; tel. 25225238; fax 28106614; 599 mems; Pres. EDDIE W. H. LEUNG.

**Textile Council of Hong Kong Ltd:** 3/F, 63 Tai Yip St, Kowloon Bay, Kowloon; tel. 23052893; fax 23052493; 31 mems; Chair. KENNETH FANG; Exec. Dir KENNETH YEUNG.

### CO-OPERATIVES
(socs = societies; feds = federations; mems = membership; cap. = paid-up share capital in Hong Kong dollars)

**Registrar of Co-operatives:** c/o Director of Agriculture and Fisheries, 393 Canton Rd, Kowloon; tel. 27332211; fax 23113731; 342 socs, 21,357 mems, cap. 2,010,645 (March 1994).

#### Co-operative Societies

**Agricultural Credit:** socs 3, mems 114, cap. 81,170.

**Agricultural Thrift and Loan:** soc. 1, mems 45, cap. 620.

**Apartment Owners:** soc. 1, mems 60, cap. 6,000.

**Better Living:** socs 27, mems 2,363, cap. 58,530.

**Consumers:** socs 10, mems 3,080, cap. 48,125.

**Farmers' Irrigation:** soc. 1, mems 37, cap. 185.

**Federation of Co-operative Building Societies:** fed. 1, mem.-socs 127, cap. 12,700.

# BRITISH DEPENDENT TERRITORIES

*Hong Kong*

**Federation of Fisheries' Societies:** feds 4, mem.-socs 42, cap. 4,525.

**Federation of Pig Raising Societies:** fed. 1, mem.-socs 17, cap. 48,125.

**Federation of Vegetable Marketing Societies:** fed. 1, mem.-socs 26, cap. 5,200.

**Fishermen's Credit:** socs 47, mems 747, cap. 10,955.

**Fishermen's Credit and Housing:** socs 2, mems 38, cap. 270.

**Housing:** socs 197, mems 4,951, cap. 1,316,500.

**Pig Raising:** socs 16, mems 924, cap. 309,165.

**Salaried Workers' Thrift and Loan:** soc. 1, mems 480, cap. 19,080.

**Vegetable Marketing:** socs 29, mems 8,306, cap. 89,495.

There were also 69 Credit Unions in 1994.

## DEVELOPMENT CORPORATIONS

**Hong Kong Housing Authority:** 33 Fat Kwong St, Homantin, Kowloon; tel. 27615002; fax 27621110; f. 1973; plans, builds and manages public housing; Chair. ROSANNA WONG YICK-MING; CEO and Dir of Housing T. FUNG.

**Kadoorie Agricultural Aid Association:** c/o Director of Agriculture and Fisheries, Canton Rd Govt Offices, Kowloon; tel. 27332211; fax 23113731; f. 1951; assists farmers in capital construction by technical direction and by donations of livestock, trees, plants, seeds, fertilizers, cement, road and building materials, farming equipment, etc.

**Kadoorie Agricultural Aid Loan Fund:** c/o Director of Agriculture and Fisheries, Canton Rd Govt Offices, Kowloon; tel. 27332211; fax 23113731; f. 1954; in conjunction with the Hong Kong govt, provides low-interest loans to assist farmers in the development of projects; HK $5,120,000 was loaned in 1994/95.

**J. E. Joseph Trust Fund:** c/o Director of Agriculture and Fisheries, Canton Rd Govt Offices, Kowloon; tel. 27332211; fax 23113731; f. 1954; grants credit facilities to farmers; HK $1,121,000 was loaned in 1994/95.

## TRADE UNIONS

In December 1994 there were 548 trade unions in Hong Kong. The 506 employees' unions had 545,800 members, the 26 employers' associations had 2,500 members, and the 16 mixed organizations had 14,600 members.

**Hong Kong and Kowloon Trades Union Council (TUC):** Labour Bldg, 11 Chang Sha St, Kowloon; tel. 23845150; telex 36866; f. 1949; 65 affiliated unions, mostly covering the catering and building trades; 30,600 mems; supports the Republic of China (Taiwan); affiliated to ICFTU; Officer-in-Charge WONG YIU KAM.

**Hong Kong Confederation of Trade Unions:** 2/F, 101–107 Portland St, Kowloon; tel. 27708668; fax 27707388; registered Feb. 1990; 28 affiliated independent unions, 78,500 mems.

**Hong Kong Federation of Trade Unions (FTU):** 7/F, 50 Ma Tau Chung Rd, Tokwawan, Kowloon; tel. 27120231; fax 27608477; f. 1948; 91 member unions, mostly concentrated in the civil service, shipyards, public transport, textile mills, construction, department stores, printing and public utilities; supports the People's Republic of China; membership: 200,300; Chair. CHENG YIU-TONG; Pres. LEE CHARK-TIM; Gen. Sec. CHAN JIK-KWEI.

Also active are the **Federation of Hong Kong and Kowloon Labour Unions** (23 affliated unions with 19,400 mems) and the **Joint Organisation of Unions—Hong Kong** (16 affiliated unions 9,000 mems).

# Transport

**Transport Department:** Immigration Tower, 41/F, 7 Gloucester Rd, Wanchai; tel. 28295258; fax 28240433; Transport Commr LILY YAM KWAN PUI-YING.

## RAILWAYS

**Mass Transit Railway Corporation (MTRC):** Chevalier Commercial Centre, 17/F, 8 Wang Hoi Rd, Kowloon Bay, GPO Box 9916; tel. 27512111; telex 56257; fax 27988822; f. 1975; network of 43 km and 38 stations; the first section of the underground railway system opened in October 1979; a 15.6-km line from Kwun Tong to Central opened in February 1980; a 10.5-km Tsuen Wan extension opened in May 1982; the first section of the 12.5-km Island Line opened in May 1985; the second section opened in May 1986; in August 1989 a second harbour crossing between Cha Kwo Ling and Quarry Bay, known as the Eastern Harbour Crossing, commenced operation, adding 4.6 km to the railway system; Chair. and Chief Exec. H. T. MATHERS.

**Kowloon–Canton Railway:** KCR House, Sha Tin, New Territories; tel. 26069333; telex 51666; fax 26951168; operated by the Kowloon–Canton Railway Corpn, a public statutory body f. 1983 and wholly owned by the Hong Kong Govt; the line is 34 km long and runs from the terminus at Hung Hom to the Chinese frontier at Lo Wu; through passenger services to China, suspended in 1949, were resumed in 1979; the electrification and double-tracking of the entire length and redevelopment of all stations has been completed, and full electric train service came into operation in 1983; in 1988 a light railway network serving Tuen Mun and Yuen Long in the western New Territories was opened; Chair. and CEO KEVIN HYDE.

## TRAMWAYS

**Hong Kong Tramways Ltd:** Whitty Street Tram Depot, Connaught Rd West, Western District; tel. 25598918; telex 73591; fax 28583697; f. 1904; operates six routes and 161 double-deck trams between Kennedy Town and Shaukeiwan; Operations Man. A. T. LEECH.

## ROADS

In December 1994 there were 1,661 km of roads, 419 km on Hong Kong Island, 395 km in Kowloon and 847 km in the New Territories. Almost all of them are concrete or asphalt surfaced. Owing to the hilly terrain, and the density of building development, the scope for substantial increase in the road network is limited.

The 123-km Hong Kong–Guangzhou section of the Hong Kong–Macau highway was completed in 1994.

## FERRIES

Conventional ferries, hydrofoils and jetfoils operate between Hong Kong and Macau. There is also an extensive network of private ferry services to outlying districts. In 1988 the China Ferry Terminal was opened in order to deal with the growth of passenger traffic between Hong Kong and China.

**Hongkong and Yaumati Ferry Co Ltd:** Central Harbour Services Pier, 1/F, Pier Rd, Central; tel. 25423081; telex 83140; fax 25423958; 15 passenger, one vehicular ferry service across the harbour and to outlying districts; also operates hoverferry services between Hong Kong, Whampoa and Shekou and catamaran service to Macau; Pres. and CEO PETER M. K. WONG.

**'Star' Ferry Co Ltd:** Kowloon Point Pier, Tsimshatsui, Kowloon; tel. 27388480; fax 23114395; f. 1899; operates 12 passenger ferries between the Kowloon Peninsula and Central, the main business district of Hong Kong; between Central and Hung Hom; and between Tsimshatsui and Wanchai; Man. WILLIAM CHOW.

## SHIPPING

Hong Kong is one of the world's largest shipping centres. Hong Kong was a British port of registry until the inauguration of a new and independent shipping register in December 1990. At the end of 1994 the register comprised a fleet of 592 vessels, totalling 8m. grt.

**Hong Kong Government Marine Department:** Harbour Bldg, 22/F, 38 Pier Rd, Central, GPO Box 4155; tel. 28523001; telex 64553; fax 25449241; Dir of Marine A. C. PYRKE.

### Shipping Companies

**Anglo-Eastern Ship Management Ltd:** Dominion Centre, 20/F, 43–59A Queen's Rd East, Hennessy Rd, POB 20587; tel. 28636111; telex 75478; fax 28612419; Chair. J. SAVARYS; Man. Dir K. P. MCGUINNESS.

**Chung Gai Ship Management Co Ltd:** Admiralty Centre Tower 1, 31/F, 18 Harcourt Rd; tel. 25295541; telex 73556; fax 28656206; Chair. S. KODA; Man. Dir K. ICHIHARA.

**Fairmont Shipping (HK) Ltd:** Fairmont House, 21/F, 8 Cotton Tree Drive; tel. 25218338; telex 75228; fax 28104560; Man. CHARLES LEUNG.

**Far East Enterprising Co (HK) Ltd:** China Resources Bldg, 18–19/F, 26 Harbour Rd, Wanchai; tel. 28283668; telex 73333; fax 28275584; f. 1949; shipping, chartering, broking; Gen. Man. WEI KUAN.

**Gulfeast Shipmanagement Ltd:** Great Eagle Centre, 9/F, 23 Harbour Rd, Wanchai; tel. 28313344; telex 86204; Finance Dir A. T. MIRMOHAMMADI.

**Hong Kong Borneo Shipping Co Ltd:** 815 International Bldg, 141 Des Voeux Rd, Central; tel. 25413797; telex 74135; fax 28153473; Pres. Datuk LAI FOOK KIM.

**Island Navigation Corpn International Ltd:** Harbour Centre, 29/F, 25 Harbour Rd, Wanchai; tel. 28333222; telex 73108; fax 28270001; Man. Dir C. C. TUNG.

**Jardine Ship Management Ltd:** Jardine Engineering House, 11/F, 260 King's Rd, North Point; tel. 28074101; telex 74570; fax 28073351; Gen. Man. Capt. PAUL UNDERHILL.

**Oak Maritime (Hong Kong) Inc Ltd:** Room 3201-3, NatWest Tower, Times Square, 1 Matheson St, Causeway Bay; tel. 25063866;

telex 73005; fax 25063563; Chair. Steve G. K. Hsu; Man. Dir F. C. P. Tsai.

**Ocean Tramping Co Ltd:** Hongkong Shipping Centre, 24–29/F, 167 Connaught Rd West; tel. 25892888; telex 73462; fax 25461041; Chair. Z. M. Gao.

**Orient Overseas Container Line Ltd:** Harbour Centre, 31/F, 25 Harbour Rd, Wanchai; tel. 28333888; telex 73490; fax 28389779; Chair. C. H. Tung.

**P & O Asia:** Suite 4801, One Exchange Square; f. 1992; Exec. Dir Ian Mullen.

**Teh-Hu Cargocean Management Co Ltd:** Belgian House, 7/F, 77–79 Gloucester Rd; tel. 25275424; telex 73458; fax 28610642; f. 1974; Man. Dir K. W. Lo.

**Wah Kwong Shipping Agency Co Ltd:** Shanghai Industrial Investment Bldg, 26/F, 48–62 Hennessy Rd, POB 483; tel. 25279227; telex 73430; fax 28656544; Chair. Tsong-yea Chao.

**Wah Tung Shipping Agency Co Ltd:** China Resources Bldg, Rooms 2101–5, 21/F, 26 Harbour Rd, Wanchai; tel. 28272818; telex 89410; fax 28275361.

**Wallem & Co Ltd:** Hopewell Centre, 48/F, 183 Queen's Rd East; tel. 25283911; telex 73217; fax 25297451; Chair. Michael J. Steele; Man. Dir Aswin K. Atre.

**Worldwide Shipping Agency Ltd:** Wheelock House, 6–7/F, 20 Pedder St; tel. 28423888; telex 73247; fax 28100617; Man. J. Wong.

### Associations

**Hong Kong Cargo-Vessel Traders' Association:** 2/F, 21–23 Man Wai Bldg, Ferry Point, Kowloon; tel. 23847102; fax 27820342; 978 mems; Chair. Pang Yiu-son.

**Hong Kong Shipowners' Association:** Queen's Centre, 12/F, 58–64 Queen's Rd East, Wanchai; tel. 25200206; telex 89157; fax 28651582; 203 mems; Chair. Peter Cowling.

**Hong Kong Shippers' Council:** Wu Chung House, 31/F, 213 Queen's Rd East; tel. 28340010; fax 28919787; mems: 15 trade asscns, 50 individual cos; Chair. Chan Wing-kee.

### CIVIL AVIATION

Hong Kong's international airport (Kai Tak) is served by 60 international airlines. Its runway, which extends 3,390m. into Kowloon Bay, can accommodate all types of conventional wide-bodied and supersonic aircraft. The planned construction of a new international airport, on the island of Chek Lap Kok, near Lantau Island, was announced in 1989. The new airport is to be commissioned in 1997/98, initially with one runway and the capacity to handle 35m. passengers and 1.5m. metric tons of cargo per year. A helicopter link with Macau was established in 1990.

**Civil Aviation Department:** Queensway Government Offices, 46/F, 66 Queensway; tel. 28674332; telex 61361; fax 28690093; Dir P. K. N. Lok.

**Air Hong Kong (AHK) Ltd:** Block 2, Tien Chu Centre, 2/F, 1E Mok Cheong St, Kowloon; tel. 27618588; telex 37625; fax 27618586; f. 1986; cargo carrier; Chief Operating Officer Stanley H. C. Hui; Gen. Man. Richard A. K. Cater.

**Cathay Pacific Airways Ltd:** Swire House, 9 Connaught Rd, Central; tel. 27475000; telex 82345; fax 2810563; f. 1946; services to more than 40 major cities in the Far East, Middle East, North America, Europe, South Africa, Australia and New Zealand; Chair. Peter D. A. Sutch; Man. Dir Rod Eddington.

**Hong Kong Dragon Airlines Ltd (Dragonair):** Devon House, 22/F, Taikoo Place, 979 King's Rd, Quarry Bay; tel. 25901328; telex 45936; fax 25901333; f. 1985; scheduled and charter flights to 14 cities in China, scheduled services to Phuket (Thailand), Hiroshima and Sendai (Japan), Phnom-Penh (Cambodia), Dhaka (Bangladesh) and Kota Kinabalu (Malaysia); Chair. K. P. Chao; Chief Operating Officer Philip N. L. Chen.

## Tourism

Tourism is a major source of foreign exchange, and (excluding spending by visitors from the People's Republic of China) contributed revenue of HK $64,300m. in 1994. More than 9.3m. people (including 1.9m. from the People's Republic of China) visited Hong Kong in 1994. The number of hotel rooms available totalled 33,490 in December 1994.

**Hong Kong Tourist Association:** Citicorp Centre, 9–11/F, 18 Whitfield Rd, North Point, POB 2597; tel. 28017111; fax 28104877; f. 1957; co-ordinates and promotes the tourist industry; has govt support and financial assistance; 11 mems of the Board represent the Govt, the private sector and the tourism industry; Chair. Martin G. Barrow; Exec. Dir Amy Chan.

# MONTSERRAT

## Introductory Survey

### Location, Climate, Language, Religion, Flag, Capital

Montserrat is one of the Leeward Islands in the West Indies. A mountainous, volcanic island, it lies about 55 km (35 miles) north of Basse-Terre, Guadeloupe, and about 43 km (27 miles) south west of Antigua. The climate is generally warm, with a mean maximum temperature of 30°C (86°F) and a mean minimum of 23°C (73°F), but the island is fanned by sea breezes for most of the year. The average annual rainfall is about 1,475 mm (58 ins), although there is more rain in the central and western areas. English is the official language. Many Christian churches are represented, but the principal denominations are the Anglican, Roman Catholic and Methodist Churches. The flag is the British 'Blue Ensign', with the island's badge (a shield depicting a woman dressed in green holding a harp and a cross) on a white roundel in the fly. The capital is Plymouth.

### Recent History

Montserrat was first settled by the British (initially Roman Catholic exiles) in 1632, by which time the few original Carib inhabitants had disappeared. It formed part of the federal colony of the Leeward Islands from 1871 until 1956, when the federation was dissolved and the presidency of Montserrat became a separate colony. Montserrat participated in the short-lived Federation of the West Indies (1958–62) and, from 1960, the island had its own Administrator (the title was changed to that of Governor in 1971). The Constitution (see below) came into force in 1960.

The first priority of successive legislatures has been to improve infrastructure and maintain a healthy economy. Between 1952 and 1970 island politics were dominated by William Bramble. His son, Austin Bramble, leader of the Progressive Democratic Party (PDP), opposed and succeeded him as Chief Minister. In November 1978 the People's Liberation Movement (PLM) won all seven elective seats in the Legislative Council, and the PLM's leader, John Osborne, became Chief Minister. In the general election of February 1983 the PLM was returned to government with five seats. The remainder were won by the PDP, whose commitment to development projects, agriculture and education complemented those of the PLM.

Discussions on the possible formation of an opposition alliance between the PDP and the National Development Party (NDP—formed by business interests and former members of the PDP) were finally abandoned in July 1987. Against a divided opposition, the PLM won four of the seven elective seats in the Legislative Council at an early general election in August of that year. The NDP won two seats, and the PDP one (Bramble lost his seat and announced his retirement from politics). Osborne was returned to office as Chief Minister. In August 1989 an NDP member of the Legislative Council resigned from the party to become an independent.

Osborne was an advocate of independence from the United Kingdom, despite the apparent lack of popular support for this policy. A referendum on the issue was planned for 1990, but the devastation caused by Hurricane Hugo in September 1989, meant that any plans for independence were postponed. Furthermore, the Osborne Government and the British authorities were embarrassed by controversy over the hitherto lucrative 'offshore' financial sector. In early 1989 the Governor's office announced that serious allegations against certain banks (involving the processing of illegal funds from a variety of criminal activities) were being investigated by the British police. Registration was suspended, several people were charged with criminal offences and, at the end of 1989, most banking licences were revoked. The Montserrat Government agreed to introduce recommended provisions for the regulation of the financial sector, but Osborne objected strongly to a proposed amendment to the Constitution which transferred responsibility for the sector from the Chief Minister to the Governor. Agreement on the new constitutional provisions was reached in December 1989, when Osborne acknowledged that 'offshore' finance was part of the British Government's responsibility for external affairs.

In October 1990 a dispute arose between the Chief Minister and his deputy, Benjamin Chalmers, who was reported to have accused Osborne of dishonesty in his relations with the Executive Council. Noel Tuitt, the Minister of Agriculture, Trade, Lands and Housing, was also accused of contriving to destabilize Osborne, a charge which he denied. Allegations of corruption continued in 1991, and in June an inquiry was undertaken by the British police to investigate the possible involvement of members of the Executive Council in the 1989 banking scandal, as well as in fraudulent land transfers.

The resignation of Benjamin Chalmers in September 1991, following a further dispute with Osborne, resulted in the loss of the Government's majority in the Legislative Council. This prompted an early election in the following month, when the National Progressive Party (NPP), which had been formed only two months prior to the election, secured four seats. The PLM and the NDP retained one seat each, while the remaining seat was won by an independent candidate. The leader of the NPP, Reuben Meade, became Chief Minister.

In December 1991 the Legislative Council approved legislation allowing the re-establishment of a comprehensive 'offshore' financial centre. The new regulations were reported to be considerably more stringent than those in force prior to 1989. However, more than 90% of the island's 'offshore' and commercial banks were closed down, following investigations by British inspectors in mid-1992.

In February 1993 John Osborne and Noel Tuitt were acquitted on charges of corruption and conspiracy, following their arrest in July of the previous year, for allegedly soliciting funds from a US businessman in exchange for a land licence. In June 1993 David Taylor was replaced as Governor by Frank Savage.

In March 1994 Meade dismissed the Deputy Chief Minister and Minister of Communications, Works and Sport, David Brandt, accusing him of failing to express adequate support for the Government. He was replaced by the opposition member, Noel Tuitt.

In May 1991 the British Government abolished the death penalty for the crime of murder in five of its Dependent Territories, including Montserrat.

### Government

Under the provisions of the 1960 Constitution and subsequent legislation, the Governor is appointed by the British monarch and is responsible for defence, external affairs and internal security. The Governor is President of the seven-member Executive Council. The Legislative Council comprises 12 members: a Speaker, two official members, two nominated and seven elected by universal adult suffrage.

### Economic Affairs

In 1992, according to official figures, Montserrat's gross domestic product (GDP) was estimated to be EC $145.1m. (US $53.7m.). In that year, it was estimated, GDP increased by 1.3%, in real terms, but declined by 0.3% in the following year. GDP per head was reported to be equivalent to US $4,846 in 1993. In 1985–90 it was estimated that GDP increased by an annual average of 10%.

Agriculture (including forestry and fishing) contributed 4.3% of GDP in 1987, and engaged 5.6% of the employed labour force in 1992. Subsistence agriculture is important and a policy of import substitution was being undertaken in the mid-1990s. The principal crops are white potatoes and onions for export and domestic consumption, and sea-island cotton. The cultivation of grapes for export began in the early 1990s. Livestock farming is an important activity, particularly cattle (which contribute to exports), goats, sheep and poultry. Output in the sector increased by 14.0% in 1993. About 24% of the land area is covered by forests, and these are being developed for the prevention of soil erosion and the ecologically-balanced exploitation of timber. Montserrat's fisheries are under-exploited, owing to the absence of a sheltered harbour.

Industry (including mining, manufacturing, construction and public utilities) engaged some 30.9% of the employed labour force in 1987. Manufacturing contributed 3.7% of GDP in 1993, engaged 5.6% of the employed labour force (together with mining) in 1992 and accounted for about 70% of exports in the early 1990s. Output in the sector increased by 2.4% in 1993, following serious declines in the previous three years. Light industries comprise the processing of agricultural produce (especially cotton and tropical fruits), as well as spring-water bottling and the manufacture of garments and plastic bags. In 1993 a factory producing jams and jellies began operations. The principal activity is the assembly of electrical components, which accounted for 60% of export earnings in 1986. Construction, the most important of the industrial sectors, contributed 10.1% of GDP in 1993 and employed 17.5% of the working population in 1988. The sector enjoyed further growth in the early 1990s, owing to reconstruction programmes in response to the devastation caused by Hurricane Hugo in 1989.

# BRITISH DEPENDENT TERRITORIES
## Montserrat

Energy requirements are dependent upon the import of hydrocarbon fuels (8.3% of total imports in 1987).

Service industries dominate the economy. The development of telecommunications has enabled Montserrat to become a data-processing centre, and there is a computer centre of regional significance. Financial services, which expanded in the late 1980s and provided an important source of government revenue, contracted severely in 1989 and 1990, owing to a banking scandal. Despite legislation introduced in late 1991, which aimed to encourage renewed financial activity on the island, 319 of a total of 343 banks were closed in mid-1992, following an investigation into their operations (see Recent History). The principal industry is tourism, which earned an estimated EC $40m. in 1993. Output from the hotel and restaurant sector increased by 28.1% in 1993, and engaged 5.2% of the employed labour force in 1992. The traditional tourist visitors are less significant than the so-called 'villa' tourists, members of the large community of retired expatriates. Most of the visitors and villa-owners are from North America.

In 1993 Montserrat recorded a visible trade deficit of EC $59.3m. (total exports were 9.3% of the value of imports). Persistent trade deficits are normally offset by earnings from the service sector: mainly tourist receipts and net transfers (EC $45.4m. in 1990 in remittances from Montserratians abroad and the income of foreign retired people). There was an estimated deficit on the current account of the balance of payments of EC $6.5m. in 1993, compared with a deficit of EC $28.0m. the previous year. The principal trading partner is the USA (31.0% of imports and 90.4% of domestic exports in 1987). Other trading partners include the United Kingdom, Canada and, of the OECS and CARICOM nations, Antigua and Barbuda and Saint Christopher and Nevis. Electrical components, especially light fittings, are the most important of the few exports. Food imports constituted 16.0% of total imports in 1988; the principal imports are machinery and transport equipment.

In the financial year ending 31 March 1994 there was a projected budgetary surplus of EC $0.9m. on recurrent items. The capital budget is funded almost entirely by overseas aid, notably from the United Kingdom and Canada. Montserrat's total external public debt was US $10.2m. at the end of 1994, equivalent to 17% of GDP. The average annual rate of inflation increased to 6.9% in 1990 and 9.2% in 1991, but declined to 2.8% and 2.9% in 1992 and 1993 respectively. Unemployment was estimated at some 6% of the labour force in 1992.

Montserrat is a member of the Caribbean Community and Common Market (CARICOM, see p. 114), the Organisation of Eastern Caribbean States (OECS, see p. 116) and, as a dependency of the United Kingdom, has the status of Overseas Territory in association with the European Union.

Montserrat's relative prosperity is dependent upon tourism and other services. However, despite the approval of legislation in late 1991, intended to improve the reputation of the 'offshore' financial sector (which virtually collapsed following investigations in 1989), a further inquiry in 1992 resulted in the closure of more than 90% of the island's banks. Montserrat is already an important communications, technological and media centre for the region, and its generally very high standard of infrastructure is also of benefit to tourism and light industries (the main exporters). However, Hurricane Hugo devastated the island in September 1989, forestalling further progress for at least two years. The resulting environmental damage was enormous, and economic activity in the early 1990s was dominated by an extensive recovery programme. In January 1994 the Government announced a five-year tourism plan, which would include the creation of a tourist board to promote Montserrat as a holiday destination, as well as measures to preserve its reputation as a centre for visitors of above-average wealth.

### Social Welfare
There is a general hospital, which had 67 beds in 1988, and 12 health centres. In the same year there were seven physicians on the island. Free dental treatment is provided for children, pregnant mothers and the elderly. The Government operates a social security scheme.

### Education
Education, beginning at five years of age, is compulsory up to the age of 14. In 1990 there were 13 primary schools, including 10 government schools. Secondary education begins at 12 years of age, and comprises a first cycle of five years and a second, two-year cycle. In 1989 there was one government secondary school and one private secondary school. In addition there are 10 nursery schools, sponsored by a government-financed organization, while the Technical College provides vocational and technical training for school-leavers. A 'comprehensive' secondary school education system was introduced in September 1986. There is an extra-mural department of the University of the West Indies in Plymouth (with some 216 students in 1989).

### Public Holidays
**1995:** 1 January (New Year's Day), 17 March (St Patrick's Day), 14 April (Good Friday), 17 April (Easter Monday), 1 May (Labour Day), 5 June (Whit Monday), 12 June (Queen's Official Birthday), 7 August (August Monday), 23 November (Liberation Day), 25–26 December (Christmas), 31 December (Festival Day).

**1996:** 1 January (New Year's Day), 17 March (St Patrick's Day), 5 April (Good Friday), 8 April (Easter Monday), 6 May (Labour Day), 27 May (Whit Monday), 10 June (Queen's Official Birthday), 5 August (August Monday), 23 November (Liberation Day), 25–26 December (Christmas), 31 December (Festival Day).

### Weights and Measures
The imperial system is in use but the metric system is being introduced.

## Statistical Survey
Sources (unless otherwise stated): Office of the Chief Minister, POB 292, Plymouth; tel. 491-2444; fax 491-2367; Eastern Caribbean Central Bank, POB 89, Basseterre, Saint Christopher; OECS Economic Affairs Secretariat, *Statistical Digest*.

### AREA AND POPULATION
**Area:** 102 sq km (39.5 sq miles).
**Population:** 11,606 (males 5,582; females 6,024) at census of 12 May 1980; 10,639 (official estimate) in 1992.
**Density** (1992): 104.3 per sq km.
**Principal Town:** Plymouth (capital), population 1,478 at 1980 census.
**Births and Deaths** (1986): 200 live births (birth rate 16.8 per 1,000); 123 deaths (death rate 10.3 per 1,000).
**Employment** (1992): Agriculture, forestry and fishing 298; Mining and manufacturing 254; Electricity, gas and water 68; Wholesale and retail trade 1,666; Restaurants and hotels 234; Transport and communication 417; Finance, insurance and business services 242; Public defence 390; Other community, social and personal services 952; Total 4,521. Source: *The Commonwealth Yearbook*.

### AGRICULTURE, ETC.
**Livestock** (estimates, 1993): Cattle 10,000*; Donkeys and asses 200 (1988); Pigs 1,000*; Sheep 5,000*; Goats 7,000*; Poultry 50,500 (1988).
* Source: FAO, *Production Yearbook*.
**Livestock Products** (FAO estimates, metric tons, 1993): Beef and veal 1,000; Hen eggs 63. Source: FAO, *Production Yearbook*.
**Fishing** (metric tons, live weight): Total catch 150 in 1990; 101 in 1991; 115 in 1992. Source: FAO, *Yearbook of Fishery Statistics*.

### INDUSTRY
**Electric Energy** (production, million kWh): 14 in 1989; 14 in 1990; 15 in 1991. Source: UN, *Industrial Statistics Yearbook*.

### FINANCE
**Currency and Exchange Rates:** 100 cents = 1 East Caribbean dollar (EC $). *Sterling and US Dollar equivalents* (31 December 1994): £1 sterling = EC $4.224; US $1 = EC $2.700; EC $100 = £23.67 = US $37.04. *Exchange Rate:* Fixed at US $1 = EC $2.70 since July 1976.
**Budget** (estimates, EC $ million, 1993/94): Recurrent revenue 38.8 (Tax revenue 34.7); Recurrent expenditure 37.9 (Wages and salaries 24.4, Goods and services 11.2); Capital expenditure 20.5. Source: Eastern Caribbean Central Bank, *Annual Report*.
**Cost of Living** (consumer price index; base: Sept. 1982 = 100): 115.8 in 1986; 120.1 in 1987; 124.4 in 1988.
**Gross Domestic Product** (EC $ million at current factor cost): 114.1 in 1986; 129.0 in 1987; 146.3 in 1988.
**Balance of Payments** (EC $ million, 1993): Merchandise exports f.o.b. 6.1; Merchandise imports c.i.f. −65.4; *Trade balance* −59.3; Travel (net) 37.8; Other services −20.4; Transfers (net) 35.5; *Current balance* −6.5; Capital account 5.4; *Overall balance* −1.1. Source: Eastern Caribbean Central Bank, *Annual Report*.

### EXTERNAL TRADE
1993 (provisional, EC $ million): *Imports:* 74.0; *Exports:* 1.62.

### TOURISM
**Visitor Arrivals:** 23,160 (16,510 stop-overs, 5,564 cruise-ship passengers, 1,086 excursionists) in 1992; 21,763 in 1993; 23,613 in 1994.

## TRANSPORT

**Road Traffic** (vehicles in use, 1990): Passenger cars 1,823; Goods vehicles 54; Public service vehicles 4; Motor cycles 21; Miscellaneous 806.

**Shipping** *International freight traffic*\*, ('000 metric tons, 1990): Goods loaded 6; Goods unloaded 49. *Ship Arrivals* (1988): Cargo vessels 734; Cruise ships 47.

\* Source: UN, *Monthly Bulletin of Statistics*.

**Civil Aviation** (1985): Aircraft arrivals 4,422; passengers 25,380; air cargo 132.4 metric tons.

## COMMUNICATIONS MEDIA

**Radio Receivers** (estimate, 1992): 6,000 in use\*.
**Television Receivers** (estimate, 1992): 2,000 in use\*.
**Telephones** (estimate, 1990): 3,000 exchange lines in use.
**Non-Daily Newspapers** (1990): 2 (estimated circulation 2,000)\*.

\* Source: UNESCO, *Statistical Yearbook*.

## EDUCATION

**Institutions** (1989): 10 pre-primary schools (with 330 pupils); 13 primary schools in 1990 (with 1,403 pupils); 1 comprehensive secondary school (900 pupils); 1 private secondary school (21 students in 1985); 1 technical college (41 students).

Source: *The Commonwealth Yearbook*.

# Directory

## The Constitution

The present Constitution came into force on 19 December 1989 and made few amendments to the constitutional order established in 1960. The Constitution now guarantees the fundamental rights and freedoms of the individual and grants the Territory the right of self-determination. Montserrat is governed by a Governor and has its own Executive and Legislative Councils. The Governor retains responsibility for defence, external affairs (including international financial affairs) and internal security. The Executive Council consists of the Governor as President, the Chief Minister and three other Ministers, the Attorney-General and the Financial Secretary. The Legislative Council consists of the Speaker (chosen from outside the Council), seven elected, two official and two nominated members.

## The Government

**Governor:** FRANK SAVAGE (appointed February 1993).

### EXECUTIVE COUNCIL
(June 1995)

**President:** The Governor.

**Official Members:**
  **Attorney-General:** GERTEL THOM.
  **Financial Secretary:** C. T. JOHN.

**Chief Minister and Minister of Finance and Economic Development:** REUBEN T. MEADE.

**Deputy Chief Minister and Minister of Communications, Works and Sports:** NOEL TUITT.

**Minister of Education, Health and Community Services:** LAZELLE HOWES.

**Minister of Agriculture, Trade and Environment:** CHARLES KIRNON.

**Clerk to the Executive Council:** VERONICA LEE.

### MINISTRIES

**Office of the Governor:** Peebles St, Plymouth; tel. 491-2409; fax 491-4553.
**Office of the Chief Minister:** Government Headquarters, POB 292, Plymouth; tel. 491-2444; telex 5720; fax 491-2367.
**Ministry of Agriculture, Trade and Environment:** The Grove, Plymouth; tel. 491-2546; fax 491-7275.
**Ministry of Communications, Works and Sports:** Lovers Lane, Upper Dagenham; tel. 491-2521; fax 491-4534.
**Ministry of Education, Health and Community Services:** Parliament St, Plymouth; tel. 491-2541; fax 491-6941.
**Ministry of Finance and Economic Development:** POB 292, tel. 491-2066; fax 491-4632.

### LEGISLATIVE COUNCIL

**Speaker:** Dr HOWARD A. FERGUS.

**Election, 8 August 1991**

| Party | Seats |
|---|---|
| National Progressive Party (NPP) | 4 |
| People's Liberation Movement (PLM) | 1 |
| National Development Party (NDP) | 1 |
| Independent | 1 |

There are also two *ex-officio* members (the Attorney-General and the Financial Secretary), and two nominated members.

## Political Organizations

**National Development Party (NDP):** Wapping, Plymouth; tel. 491-3600; f. 1984; centre-right; Chair. DAVE FENTON; Leader BERTRAND B. OSBORNE.
**National Progressive Party (NPP):** POB 280, Plymouth; tel. 491-2444; f. 1991; Leader REUBEN T. MEADE.
**People's Liberation Movement (PLM):** Plymouth; centrist; Leader JOHN A. OSBORNE.
**Progressive Democratic Party (PDP):** Plymouth; f. 1970; centrist; Leader EUSTACE DYER.

## Judicial System

Justice is administered by the Eastern Caribbean Supreme Court (based in Saint Lucia), the Court of Summary Jurisdiction and the Magistrate's Court.

**Puisne Judge (Montserrat Circuit):** NEVILLE L. SMITH.
**Magistrate:** ANNA B. RYAN, The Court House, Parliament St, Plymouth.
**Registrar:** EULALIE GREENAWAY, The Court House, Parliament St, Plymouth.

## Religion

### CHRISTIANITY

**The Montserrat Christian Council:** Plymouth; tel. 491-2813.

#### The Anglican Communion

Anglicans are adherents of the Church in the Province of the West Indies, comprising eight dioceses. Montserrat forms part of the diocese of the North Eastern Caribbean and Aruba. The Bishop, who is also Archbishop of the Province, is resident in St John's, Antigua.

#### The Roman Catholic Church

Montserrat forms part of the diocese of St John's-Basseterre, suffragan to the archdiocese of Castries (Saint Lucia). The Bishop is resident in St John's, Antigua.

#### Other Christian Churches

There are Baptist, Methodist, Pentecostal and Seventh-day Adventist churches and other places of worship on the island.

## The Press

**The Montserrat Reporter:** Parliament St, Plymouth; tel. 491-3600; fax 491-2052; weekly on Fridays; circ. 2,000.
**The Montserrat Times:** POB 28, Plymouth; tel. 491-2501; fax 491-6069; weekly on Fridays; circ. 1,000.

## Radio and Television

There are three radio stations in Montserrat, and television services can also be obtained from Saint Christopher and Nevis, Puerto Rico, and from Antigua (ABS). In 1992, according to UNESCO, there were an estimated 6,000 radio receivers and 2,000 television receivers in use.

### RADIO

**Radio Montserrat—ZJB:** POB 51, Plymouth; tel. 491-2885; telex 5720; fax 491-9250; f. 1952, first broadcast 1957; govt station; Station Man. ROSE WILLOCK.
**Radio Antilles:** Church Rd, POB 35/930, Montserrat; tel. 491-2755; telex 5717; f. 1963; in 1989 the Govt of Montserrat, on behalf of the OECS, acquired the station; has one of the most powerful transmitters in the region; commercial; regional; broad-

casts in English and French; Chair. Dr H. Fellhauer; Man. Dir Kristian Knaack.

**Gem Radio Network:** Marina Drive, POB 488, Plymouth; tel. 3601; fax 2505; f. 1984; commercial; Station Man. Kevin Lewis; Man. Dir Kenneth Lee.

### TELEVISION

**Antilles Television Ltd:** Richmond Hill, POB 342, Plymouth; tel. 491-2226; telex 5734; fax 491-4511; 2 channels for region; Gen. Man. Karney Osborne; Technical Dir Z. A. Joseph.

**Cable Television of Montserrat Ltd:** Church Rd, POB 447, Plymouth; tel. 491-2507; fax 491-3081; Man. Sylvia White.

**Montserrat Television Foundation:** 35 Church Rd, POB 447, Plymouth; tel. 491-7767; fax 491-3081.

## Finance

The Eastern Caribbean Central Bank (see p. 116), based in Saint Christopher, is the central issuing and monetary authority for Montserrat.

**Financial Services Centre:** POB 292, Plymouth; tel. 491-2444; fax 491-2367.

### BANKING

**Bank of Montserrat:** Parliament St, POB 10, Plymouth; tel. 491-3843; telex 5740; fax 491-3189; CEO H. Fenton.

**Barclays Bank PLC:** Church Rd, POB 131, Plymouth; tel. 491-2501; telex 5718; fax 491-3801; Man. D. A. Pinard.

**Government Savings Bank:** Plymouth; 1978 depositors (March 1994).

**Royal Bank of Canada:** Parliament St, Plymouth; tel. 491-2426; telex 5713; fax 491-3991; Man. J. R. Gilbert.

## Trade and Industry

**Montserrat Chamber of Commerce and Industry:** Marine Drive, POB 384, Plymouth; tel. 491-3640; fax 491-4660; refounded 1971; 39 company mems, 32 individual mems; Pres. H. Fenton; Sec./Treas. J. A. Allen.

**Montserrat Sea Island Cotton Co Ltd:** POB 95, Plymouth; tel. 491-2236; telex 5720; f. 1980; grows, spins, dyes and hand-weaves West Indian sea-island cotton goods.

### TRADE UNIONS

**Montserrat Allied Workers' Union (MAWU):** Dagenham, Plymouth; tel. 491-2919; f. 1973; private-sector employees; Pres. Charles (Nick) Ryan; 1,000 mems.

**Montserrat Seamen's and Waterfront Workers' Union:** John St, Plymouth; tel. 491-6335; fax 491-6335; f. 1980; Sec.-Gen. Chedmond Browne; 100 mems.

**Montserrat Union of Teachers:** POB 460, Plymouth; f. 1981; Pres. Joseph H. Meade; 120 mems.

## Transport

### ROADS

Montserrat has an extensive and well-constructed road network. There are 203 km (126 miles) of good surfaced main roads, 24 km (15 miles) of secondary unsurfaced roads and 42 km (26 miles) of rough tracks. A road linking Blackburne Airport and St John's was completed in 1983, running along the east coast. There were 2,708 registered vehicles in use in 1990.

### SHIPPING

Plymouth is the main port. Improvements to the port were delayed by hurricane damage in 1989, which destroyed the jetty. An expanded facility was reopened in June 1993. There were plans for a 'safe' harbour to be created at Carr's Bay, in the north of the island.

Regular trans-shipment steamship services are provided by Harrison Line and Nedlloyd Line. The Bermuth Line and the West Indies Shipping Service link Montserrat with Miami, USA and with neighbouring territories. A high-speed ferry service operates regular services between Montserrat and Antigua, Guadeloupe and Dominica.

**Port Authority of Montserrat:** Plymouth; tel. 491-2791; fax 491-8063.

**Montserrat Shipping Services:** Plymouth; tel. 491-2513; fax 491-6657.

### CIVIL AVIATION

The main airport is Blackburne at Trants, 13 km (8 miles) from Plymouth. A project to expand the airport at a cost of US $8m. was to be undertaken in 1995. Montserrat is a shareholder in the regional airline, LIAT (based in Antigua and Barbuda), which operates six flights daily to Antigua, and regular services to Nevis, Saint Christopher (St Kitts), Guadeloupe and Sint Maarten.

**Montserrat Airways Ltd:** Plymouth; tel. 491-6494; fax 491-6205; charter services.

**Montserrat Aviation Services Ltd:** Lower George St, POB 257, Plymouth; tel. 491-2533; telex 5716; f. 1981; ceased operating its own flights in 1988; handling agent.

## Tourism

Montserrat's principal attractions for tourists are its mountainous and lush scenery, and its quiet atmosphere. Known as the 'Emerald Isle of the Caribbean', Montserrat is noted for its Irish connections and for its range of flora and fauna. In 1994 there were 23,613 tourist arrivals (35% from Caribbean countries, 31% from the USA, 14% from the United Kingdom and 7% from Canada). In 1992 it was estimated that some 43% of visitors were Montserrat nationals residing overseas. In 1993 earnings from the sector amounted to some EC $40m.

**Montserrat Tourist Board:** Marine Drive, POB 7, Plymouth; tel. 491-2230; fax 491-7430; f. 1961; Chair. Hensey Fenton; Dir of Tourism Leona Midgette.

# PITCAIRN ISLANDS

The Pitcairn Islands consist of Pitcairn Island and three uninhabited islands, Henderson, Ducie and Oeno. Pitcairn, situated at 25°04′ S, and 130°06′ W, and about midway between Panama and New Zealand, has an area of 4.5 sq km (1.75 sq miles) and had a population of 55 in December 1993.

Discovered in 1767 and first settled by the British in 1790, Pitcairn officially became a British settlement in 1887. In 1893 a parliamentary form of government was adopted, and in 1898 responsibility for administration was assumed by the High Commissioner for the Western Pacific. Pitcairn came under the jurisdiction of the Governor of Fiji in 1952, and, from 1970 onwards, of the British High Commissioner in New Zealand acting as Governor, in consultation with an Island Council, presided over by the Island Magistrate (who is elected triennially) and comprising one ex-officio member (the Island Secretary), five elected and three nominated members. In 1987 the British High Commissioner in Fiji, acting on behalf of Pitcairn, the United Kingdom's last remaining dependency in the South Pacific, joined representatives of the USA, France, New Zealand and six South Pacific island states in signing the South Pacific Regional Environment Protection Convention, the main aim of which is to prevent the dumping of nuclear waste in the region.

The economy is based on subsistence gardening, fishing, handicrafts and the sale of postage stamps. A steady decline in the population, due mainly to emigration to New Zealand, is the island's main problem. In 1992 an exclusive economic zone (EEZ), designated in 1980 and extending 370 km (200 nautical miles) off shore, was officially declared. Development projects have been focused on harbour improvements, power supplies, telecommunications and road-building. A reafforestation scheme, begun in 1963, concentrated on the planting of miro trees, which provide a rosewood suitable for handicrafts. Pitcairn's first radio-telephone link was established in 1985, and a modern telecommunications unit was installed in 1992. In 1987 the Governor of the islands signed a one-year fishing agreement with Japan, whereby the Japan Tuna Fisheries Co-operative Association was granted a licence to operate vessels within Pitcairn's EEZ. The agreement was subsequently renewed, but lapsed in 1990.

In 1989 uninhabited Henderson Island was included on the UNESCO 'World Heritage List'. The island, 168 km (104 miles) east-north-east of Pitcairn, is to be preserved as a bird sanctuary. There are five species of bird unique to the island: the flightless rail or Henderson chicken, the green Henderson fruit dove, the Henderson crake, the Henderson warbler and the Henderson lorikeet. However, in 1994 scientists studying the island claimed that its unique flora and fauna were threatened by the accidental introduction of foreign plant species by visitors and by an increase in the rat population.

There is no taxation (except for small licensing fees on guns and vehicles), and government revenue is derived from philatelic sales (one-half of current revenue in 1992/93), and from interest earned on investments. In 1993/94 revenue totalled $NZ1.09m. and expenditure $NZ1.08m. Capital assistance is received from the United Kingdom. New Zealand currency is used.

In early 1992 it was reported that significant mineral deposits, formed by underwater volcanoes, had been discovered within the islands' EEZ. The minerals, which were believed to include manganese, iron, copper, zinc, silver and gold, could (if exploited) dramatically affect the Territory's economy.

In April 1993, during an official visit to Pitcairn, the Governor was presented with a document expressing dissatisfaction with British policy towards the islands, and raising the question of a transfer of sovereignty. Improved relations with France provoked speculation that an arrangement might be established with the French Government, concerning the future administration of the Territory.

A minor diplomatic incident arose between New Zealand and the United Kingdom in late 1994, when a former employee of the Governor's office (based in New Zealand) brought a case of unfair dismissal before New Zealand's Employment Court. The court's ruling, however, was declared invalid at an appeal brought by the Governor's office, which ruled that the employee was subject to British law and therefore the case could be heard only by a British court.

## Statistical Survey

Source: Office of the Governor of Pitcairn, Henderson, Ducie and Oeno Islands, c/o British Consulate-General, Private Bag 92014, Auckland, New Zealand.

### AREA AND POPULATION

**Area:** 35.5 sq km. *By island:* Pitcairn 4.35 sq km; Henderson 30.0 sq km; Oeno is less than 1 sq km and Ducie is smaller.

**Population** (at 31 December): 66 in 1991; 54 in 1992; 55 in 1993.

**Density** (Pitcairn only, 1993): 13 per sq km.

**Employment** (able-bodied men, 1993): 14.

### FINANCE

**Currency and Exchange Rates:** 100 cents = 1 Pitcairn dollar. The Pitcairn dollar is at par with the New Zealand dollar ($NZ). New Zealand currency is usually used (see p. 2245).

**Budget** ($NZ, 1993/94): Revenue 1,087,500; Expenditure 1,079,000.

### TRANSPORT

**Road Traffic** (motor vehicles, 1993): Motor cycles 37 (two-wheeled 4, three-wheeled 22, four-wheeled 11); Tractors 2; Passenger car 1; Bulldozer 1.

**Shipping:** *Local vessels* (communally-owned open surf boats, 1993): 2. *International Shipping Arrivals* (visits by passing vessels, 1992): Ships 39; Yachts 32.

## Directory

### The Constitution and Government

Pitcairn is a British settlement under the British Settlements Act 1887, although the islanders reckon their recognition as a colony from 1838, when a British naval captain instituted a Constitution with universal adult suffrage and a code of law. That system served as the basis of the 1904 reformed Constitution and the wider reforms of 1940, effected by Order in Council. The Constitution of 1940 provides for a Governor of Pitcairn, Henderson, Ducie and Oeno Islands (who, since 1970, is concurrently the British High Commissioner in New Zealand), representing the British monarch. An Island Magistrate is elected every three years to preside over the Island Court (which has limited jurisdiction) and the Island Council. The Local Government Ordinance 1964 constituted an Island Council of 10 members: in addition to the Island Magistrate, five members are elected annually; three are nominated for terms of one year (the Governor appoints two of these members at his own discretion); and the Island Secretary is an *ex-officio* member. Liaison between the Governor and the Island Council is conducted by a Commissioner, usually based in the Office of the British Consulate-General in Auckland, New Zealand.

Customary land tenure provides for a system of family ownership (based upon the original division of land in the 18th century). Alienation to foreigners is not forbidden by law, but in practice this is difficult. There is no taxation, and public works are performed by the community.

**Governor of Pitcairn, Henderson, Ducie and Oeno Islands:** ROBERT J. ALSTON (British High Commissioner in New Zealand—took office August 1994).

**Office of the Governor of Pitcairn, Henderson, Ducie and Oeno Islands:** c/o British High Commission, 44 Hill St, POB 1812, Wellington, New Zealand; tel. (4) 472-6049; fax (4) 471-1974.

#### ISLAND COUNCIL
(June 1995)

**Island Magistrate:** JAY WARREN.

**Island Secretary** (*ex officio*): OLIVE CHRISTIAN.

**Chairman of Internal Committee:** DAVE BROWN.

**Other Members:** Meralda Warren, Brian Young, Carol Warren, Betty Christian, Dennis Christian, Pippa Foley, Pastor Mark Ellmoos.

Elections to the Island Council take place each December. Meetings are held at the Court House in Adamstown (which last served in its judicial capacity in 1968).

**Office of the Island Secretary:** The Square, Adamstown.

## Religion

### CHRISTIANITY

Since 1887 many of the islanders have been adherents of the Seventh-day Adventist Church.

**Pastor:** Mark Ellmoos, SDA Church, The Square, POB 24, Adamstown; tel. 872-144-5372; fax 872-144-5373.

## The Press

**Pitcairn Miscellany:** monthly four-page mimeographed news sheet; f. 1959 and edited by the Education Officer; circulation was about 1,550 in 1994.

## Finance, Trade and Industry

There are no formal banking facilities. A co-operative trading store was established in 1967. Industry consists of handicrafts.

## Transport

### ROADS

There are approximately 6.4 km (4 miles) each of dirt road suitable for four-wheeled vehicles and of dirt track suitable for two-wheeled vehicles. In 1993 there were four conventional motor cycles, 22 three-wheelers and 11 four-wheeled motor cycles, one motor car and two tractors; traditional wheelbarrows are used occasionally.

### SHIPPING

No passenger ships have called regularly since 1968, and sea communications are restricted to cargo vessels operating between New Zealand and Panama, which make scheduled calls at Pitcairn four times a year, as well as a number of unscheduled calls. There are also occasional visits by private yachts. Bounty Bay, near Adamstown, is the only possible landing site, and there are no docking facilities. In 1993 the jetty derrick was refitted with an hydraulic system. The islanders have two open surf boats.

# ST HELENA AND DEPENDENCIES

## St Helena

St Helena lies in the South Atlantic Ocean, about 1,930 km (1,200 miles) from the south-west coast of Africa. Governed by the British East India Company from 1673, the island was brought under the direct control of the British Crown in 1834. The present Constitution came into force in 1989 (see below). At general elections held in September 1976, the St Helena Progressive Party, advocating the retention of close economic links with the United Kingdom, gained 11 of the 12 elective seats in the Legislative Council. The election was contested by the St Helena Labour Party, which opposed dependence on economic aid. A similar result was obtained in the November 1980 elections, although both parties were reported to be inactive. General elections, again on a non-partisan basis, were held in 1984. Formal political activity has remained dormant. In October 1981 the Governor announced the establishment of a constitutional commission to review the island's Constitution. The commission reported in 1983 that it was unable to find any proposal for constitutional change that would command the support of the majority of the islanders. In 1988, however, the Government obtained the introduction of a formal constitution to replace the Order in Council and Royal Instructions under which St Helena had been governed since 1967. The Constitution entered into force on 1 January 1989.

The economy depends on development aid, provided by the British Government. In 1990/91 St Helena received £11.7m. in British aid. This comprised a budgetary subvention of £3.6m., a shipping subsidy of £2.8m., development aid of £1.4m., technical co-operation finance of £2.0m. and £2.0m. for a replacement ship.

The island's main economic activities are fishing, the rearing of livestock, and handicrafts. In 1993 exports of fish (which, apart from a small quantity of coffee, is the only commodity exported) totalled 16 metric tons (compared with 27.2 tons in 1985) and export earnings from this source amounted to £183,514. Timber production is being developed. However, a large proportion of the labour force is forced to seek employment overseas, particularly on Ascension. In September 1993 792 St Helenians were working on Ascension.

St Helena is of interest to naturalists for its rare flora and fauna. The island has about 40 species of flora that are unknown anywhere else in the world.

## Statistical Survey

### AREA AND POPULATION

**Area:** 122 sq km (47 sq miles).

**Population:** 5,147 (males 2,514; females 2,633) at census of 31 October 1976; 5,644 (males 2,769; females 2,875) at census of 22 February 1987.

**Density:** 46.3 per sq km (1987 census).

**Principal town:** Jamestown (capital), population 1,413 (1987 census).

**Births and Deaths** (1993): Registered live births 69; Registered deaths 58.

**Employment:** 2,516 (1,607 males, 909 females) at census of 22 February 1987; 2,416 in April 1991.

### AGRICULTURE, ETC.

**Livestock** (1991): Cattle 989; Sheep 1,364; Pigs 657; Goats 1,197; Donkeys 306; Poultry 8,513.

**Fishing** (metric tons, live weight, including Ascension and Tristan da Cunha): Total catch 802 in 1990; 626 in 1991; 651 in 1992. Figures include catches of rock lobster from Tristan da Cunha during the 12 months ending 30 April of the year stated. Source: FAO, *Yearbook of Fishery Statistics*.

### FINANCE

**Currency and Exchange Rate:** 100 pence (pennies) = 1 St Helena pound (£). *Sterling and Dollar Equivalents* (31 December 1994): £1 sterling = St Helena £1; US $1 = 63.92 pence; £100 = $156.45. *Average Exchange Rate* (US $ per £): 1.7655 in 1992; 1.5020 in 1993; 1.5316 in 1994. Note: The St Helena pound is at par with the pound sterling.

**Budget** (1991/92): *Revenue* £4,385,000 (including budgetary aid of £3,424,000); *Expenditure* £7,013,000.

**Cost of Living** (Consumer Price Index; base: November 1987 = 100): 108.8 in 1989; 111.1 in 1990; 116.6 in 1991.

### EXTERNAL TRADE

**Principal Commodities:** *Imports* (1990/91): £5,774,351 (including food and drink £1,154,568, tobacco £107,273, motor spirits and fuel oils £423,824, animal feed £123,403, building materials £477,298, motor vehicles and parts £355,562, electrical equipment, other machinery and parts £757,090); *Exports* (1990/91): fish £183,514; coffee n.a. Trade is mainly with the United Kingdom and South Africa.

### TRANSPORT

**Road Traffic** (1990): 1,484 vehicles in use.

**Shipping** (1991): Vessels entered 132.

### EDUCATION

**Primary** (1987): 8 schools; 32 teachers; 675 pupils.

**Secondary** (1987): 4 schools; 74 teachers; 513 pupils.

## Directory

### The Constitution

The St Helena Constitution Order 1988, which entered into force on 1 January 1989, replaced the Order in Council and Royal Instructions of 1 January 1967. Executive and legislative authority is reserved to the British Crown, but is ordinarily exercised by others in accordance with provisions of the Constitution. The Constitution provides for the office of Governor and Commander-in-Chief of St Helena and its dependencies (Ascension Island and Tristan da Cunha). The Legislative Council for St Helena consists of the Speaker, three *ex-officio* members (the Chief Secretary, the Financial Secretary and the Attorney-General) and 12 elected members; the Executive Council is presided over by the Governor and consists of the above *ex-officio* members and five of the elected members of the Legislative Council. The elected members of the legislature choose from among themselves those who will also be members of the Executive Council. Although a member of both the Legislative Council and the Executive Council, the Attorney-General does not vote on either. Members of the legislature provide the Chairmen and a majority of the members of the various Council Committees. Executive and legislative functions for the dependencies are exercised by the Governor.

### The Government

(June 1995)

**Governor and Commander-in-Chief:** David Smallman.

**Chief Secretary:** J. Perrott.

**Financial Secretary:** R. Perrott.

**Chairmen of Council Committees:**

    **Agriculture and Natural Resources:** P. Peters.

    **Public Works and Services:** E. Benjamin.

    **Public Health:** J. Musk.

    **Social Welfare:** I. George.

    **Education:** R. Pridham.

    **Finance:** R. Perrott.

#### GOVERNMENT OFFICE

**Office of the Governor:** Plantation House; tel. 2555; telex 202; fax 2598.

## Political Organizations

There are no political parties in St Helena. Elections to the Legislative Council, the latest of which took place in July 1993, are conducted on a non-partisan basis.

## Judicial System

There are four Courts on St Helena: the Supreme Court, the Magistrate's Court, the Small Debts Court and the Juvenile Court. Provision exists for the St Helena Court of Appeal, which can sit in Jamestown or London.
**Chief Justice:** Sir JOHN FARLEY SPRY (non-resident).
**Attorney-General:** DAVID JEREMIAH.
**Magistrate:** J. BEEDON.

## Religion

The majority of the population belongs to the Anglican Communion.

### CHRISTIANITY
#### The Anglican Communion

Anglicans are adherents of the Church of the Province of Southern Africa, comprising 22 dioceses. The Metropolitan of the Province is the Archbishop of Cape Town, South Africa. St Helena forms a single diocese.
**Bishop of St Helena:** Rt Rev. JOHN RUSTON, Bishopsholme, POB 62, St Helena; tel. 4471; fax 4330; diocese f. 1859; has jurisdiction over the islands of St Helena and Ascension.

#### The Roman Catholic Church

The Church is represented in St Helena, Ascension and Tristan da Cunha by a Mission, established in August 1986.
**Superior:** Rev. Fr ANTON AGREITER (also Prefect Apostolic of the Falkland Islands), Sacred Heart Church, Jamestown; tel. and fax 2535; Vicar Delegate Rev. Fr JOSEPH WHELAN; visits Tristan da Cunha once a year, and Ascension several times a year; 60 mems.

#### Other Christian Churches

Jehovah's Witnesses and the Seventh-day Adventist Church are also active on the island.

## The Press

**St Helena News:** Broadway House, Jamestown; tel. 2612; telex 4202; fax 2802; f. 1986; govt-sponsored weekly; Editor NICOLA DILLON; circ. 1,500.

## Radio and Television

There were an estimated 2,500 radio receivers in use in 1990. A satellite television link came into operation in July 1994.
**Government Broadcasting Service:** Information Office, Broadway House, Jamestown; tel. 4669; telex 2202; fax 4542; 73 hours weekly; Information Officer NICOLA DILLON; Station Man. ANTHONY D. LEO.

## Finance

### BANK
**Government Savings Bank:** Jamestown; tel. 2291; telex 4202; total deposits (31 March 1991): £4,178,072.

### INSURANCE
**Alliance Assurance Co Ltd:** Agents: Solomon & Co (St Helena) PLC, Jamestown; tel. 2380; telex 4204; fax 2423.

## Trade and Industry

### CHAMBER OF COMMERCE
**St Helena Chamber of Commerce:** Jamestown.

### CO-OPERATIVE
**St Helena Growers' Co-operative Society:** Jamestown; vegetable marketing and suppliers of agricultural tools, seeds and animal feeding products; 25 mems (1982); Chair. L. LAWRENCE; Sec. and Man. M. BENJAMIN.

### TRADE UNION
**St Helena General Workers' Union:** Market St, Jamestown; 175 mems (1988); Gen. Sec. E. BENJAMIN.

## Transport

There are no railways or airfields in St Helena.

### ROADS
In 1990 there were 98 km of bitumen-sealed roads, and a further 20 km of earth roads, which can be used by motor vehicles only in dry weather. All roads have steep gradients and sharp bends.

### SHIPPING
**St Helena Line Ltd:** Jamestown; mailing address: The Shipyard, Porthleven, Helston, Cornwall, TR13 9JA, England; tel. (1326) 563434; telex 46564; fax (1326) 564347; operates services to and from the United Kingdom six times a year, calling at the Canary Islands, Ascension Island and Capetown, South Africa, and at Tristan da Cunha once a year; commenced operation of a scheduled service with one passenger/cargo ship in 1978; this vessel was replaced by the RMS *St Helena* in 1990; Man. Dir ANDREW BELL.

# Ascension

Ascension lies in the South Atlantic Ocean, 1,131 km (703 miles) north-west of St Helena, of which it is a dependency. The island is an important communications centre, being a major relay station for the cables between South Africa and Europe. Under an agreement with the British Government, US forces occupy Wideawake Airfield, which is used as a tracking station for guided missiles. Ascension has no indigenous population, being inhabited solely by British military personnel, *émigré* workers from St Helena and expatriate personnel of the BBC, Cable and Wireless PLC and the US military base. Ascension does not raise its own finance; the costs of administering the island are borne collectively by the user organizations. Facilities on Ascension underwent rapid development in 1982 to serve as a major staging post for British vessels and aircraft on their way to the Falkland Islands (q.v.), and the island has continued to provide a key link in British supply lines to the South Atlantic.
**Area:** 88 sq km (34 sq miles).
**Population** (excluding British military personnel, September 1993): 1,112 (St Helenians 792, UK nationals 164, US nationals 156).

**Production** (1992/93): Vegetables 14,863 lb; Pork 13,488 lb; Mutton and lamb 2,296 lb.

**Budget** (estimates for year ending 31 March 1994): Revenue £335,185; Expenditure £554,748.

**Government:** The Government of St Helena is represented by an Administrator.

**Administrator:** BRIAN N. CONNELLY, The Residency, Ascension; tel. 6311; telex 3214; fax 6152.

**Magistrate:** BRIAN N. CONNELLY.

**Justices of the Peace:** R. A. LAWRENCE, A. GEORGE, S. A. YOUDE, G. F. THOMAS, S. N. BOWERS.

**Religion:** Ascension forms part of the Anglican diocese of St Helena; some of the inhabitants are Roman Catholics.

**Transport** (1994): *Road vehicles:* 1,049. *Shipping:* ships entered and cleared 96. The St Helena Line Ltd (q.v.) serves the island with a two-monthly passenger/cargo service between Cardiff, in the United Kingdom, and Cape Town, in South Africa.

# Tristan da Cunha

The island of Tristan da Cunha lies in the South Atlantic Ocean, 2,400 km (1,500 miles) west of Cape Town, South Africa. It comes under the jurisdiction of St Helena, 2,100 km (1,300 miles) to the north-east. Also in the group are Inaccessible Island, 32 km (20 miles) west of Tristan; the three Nightingale Islands, 32 km (20 miles) south; and Gough Island (Diego Alvarez), 350 km (220 miles) south. Tristan da Cunha was evacuated in 1961, after volcanic eruptions, but was resettled in 1963. The entire working population is employed by the Government or by Tristan Investments Ltd (a subsidiary of the South Atlantic Islands Development Corporation), which operates a plant for processing the catch of Tristan rock lobster (crayfish). The catch is exported to the USA, France and Japan. The island's major source of revenue derives from a royalty from Tristan Investments Ltd for the crayfishing concession, supplemented by income from the sale of postage stamps and other philatelic items, and handicrafts. Budget estimates for 1992/93 projected a surplus of £6,575. Development aid from the United Kingdom ceased in 1980; since then the island has financed its own projects.

**Area:** Tristan da Cunha 98 sq km (38 sq miles); Inaccessible Island 10 sq km (4 sq miles); Nightingale Island 2 sq km (¾ sq mile); Gough Island 91 sq km (35 sq miles).

**Population** (December 1993): 300 (including 5 expatriates) on Tristan; there is a small weather station on Gough Island, staffed, under agreement, by personnel employed by the South African Government.

**Fishing** (catch, metric tons, year ending 30 April): Tristan da Cunha rock lobster 451 in 1989/90; 426 in 1990/91; 361 in 1991/92. Source: FAO, *Yearbook of Fishery Statistics*.

**Budget:** (estimates for 1992/93) Revenue £743,477; Expenditure £736,902.

**Government:** The Administrator, representing the British Government, is aided by a council of eight elected members (of whom at least one must be a woman) and three appointed members, which has advisory powers in legislative and executive functions. The Council's advisory functions in executive matters are performed through small committees of the Council dealing with the separate branches of administration. The most recent election was held in May 1991.

**Administrator:** PHILIP H. JOHNSON, The Residency, Tristan da Cunha; tel. 5424; telex 5434; fax 5435.

**Legal System:** The Administrator is also the Magistrate.

**Religion:** Adherents of the Anglican church predominate on Tristan da Cunha, which is within the Church of the Province of Southern Africa, and is under the jurisdiction of the Archbishop of Cape Town, South Africa. There is also a small number of Roman Catholics.

# SOUTH GEORGIA AND THE SOUTH SANDWICH ISLANDS

South Georgia, an island of 3,592 sq km (1,387 sq miles), lies in the South Atlantic Ocean, about 1,300 km (800 miles) east-south-east of the Falkland Islands. The South Sandwich Islands, which have an area of 311 sq km (120 sq miles), lie about 750 km (470 miles) south-east of South Georgia.

The United Kingdom annexed South Georgia and the South Sandwich Islands in 1775. With a segment of the Antarctic mainland and other nearby islands (now the British Antarctic Territory), they were constituted as the Falkland Islands Dependencies in 1908. Argentina made formal claim to South Georgia in 1927, and to the South Sandwich Islands in 1948. In 1955 the United Kingdom unilaterally submitted the dispute over sovereignty to the International Court of Justice (based in the Netherlands), which decided not to hear the application in view of Argentina's refusal to submit to the Court's jurisdiction. South Georgia was the site of a British Antarctic Survey base (staffed by 22 scientists and support personnel) until it was invaded in April 1982 by Argentine forces, who occupied the island until its recapture by British forces three weeks later. The South Sandwich Islands were uninhabited until the occupation of Southern Thule in December 1976 by about 50 Argentines, reported to be scientists. Argentine personnel remained until removed by British forces in June 1982.

Under the provisions of the South Georgia and South Sandwich Islands Order of 1985, the islands ceased to be governed as dependencies of the Falkland Islands on 3 October 1985. The Governor of the Falkland Islands is, *ex officio,* Commissioner for the territory.

In May 1993, in response to the Argentine Government's decision to commence the sale of fishing licences for the region's waters, the British Government announced an extension, from 12 to 200 nautical miles (370 km), of its territorial jurisdiction in the waters surrounding the islands, in order to conserve crucial fishing stocks.

**Commissioner:** David E. Tatham (Stanley, Falkland Islands).

**Assistant Commissioner:** Craig S. M. Shelton (Stanley, Falkland Islands).

# THE TURKS AND CAICOS ISLANDS

## Introductory Survey

**Location, Climate, Language, Religion, Flag, Capital**

The Turks and Caicos Islands consist of more than 30 low-lying islands forming the south-eastern end of the Bahamas chain of islands, and lying about 145 km (90 miles) north of Haiti. Eight islands are inhabited: Grand Turk and Salt Cay (both in the smaller Turks group to the east of the Caicos), South Caicos, Middle (Grand) Caicos, North Caicos, Providenciales (Provo), Pine Cay and Parrot Cay. The climate is warm throughout the year but tempered by constant trade winds. The average annual temperature is 27°C (82°F) and rainfall ranges from 530mm (21 ins) in the eastern islands to 1,000mm (40 ins) in the west. The official language is English, though some Creole is spoken by Haitian immigrants. Many Christian churches are represented, the largest denomination being the Baptist Union (25.5% of the population at the census of May 1990). The flag is the British 'Blue Ensign', with the shield from the islands' coat of arms, bearing a shell, a lobster and a cactus, in the fly. The capital is Cockburn Town, on Grand Turk island.

**Recent History**

The Turks and Caicos Islands were first settled by Amerindian peoples. It has been claimed that the first landing in the Americas by the navigator, Christopher Columbus, was actually on Grand Turk and not in the neighbouring Bahamas. The islands were then inhabited by privateers, and were settled from Bermuda and by exiled 'Loyalists' from the former British colonies in North America. A Jamaican dependency from 1874 to 1959, the Turks and Caicos Islands became a separate colony in 1962, following Jamaican independence. After an administrative association with the Bahamas, the islands received their own Governor in 1972. The first elections under the present Constitution took place in 1976, and were won by the pro-independence People's Democratic Movement (PDM). In 1980 an agreement was made with the United Kingdom whereby, if the governing PDM won the 1980 elections, the islands would receive independence and a payment of £12m. However, lacking the leadership of J. A. G. S. McCartney, the Chief Minister, (who had been killed in an aircraft accident in May 1980), the PDM lost the election in November to the Progressive National Party (PNP), which is committed to continued dependent status. At the next general election, in May 1984, the PNP, led by the Chief Minister, Norman Saunders, won eight of the 11 elective seats.

In March 1985 the Chief Minister, the Minister for Development and Commerce and a PNP member of the Legislative Council were arrested in Miami, Florida, on charges involving illicit drugs and violations of the US Travel Act. All three men were subsequently convicted and imprisoned (with Saunders receiving an eight-year sentence). Saunders resigned and was replaced as Chief Minister by Nathaniel Francis, hitherto the Minister of Public Works and Utilities. Emily Saunders won the by-election for her husband's constituency in December, and PNP candidates were returned unopposed in the other two vacant seats, thus maintaining the number of seats in the Legislative Council held by the PNP.

In April 1986 a commission of inquiry was appointed to investigate allegations of arson and administrative malpractice, following the destruction by fire of a government building in December 1985. The commission's report, published in July 1986, concluded that Francis and two of his ministers were unfit for ministerial office, accusing them of unconstitutional behaviour and ministerial malpractice; all three ministers subsequently resigned. Two members of the PDM were also accused of criminality and deemed to be unfit for public office. In the same month the Government was dissolved by the Governor, and the Executive Council was replaced by an interim advisory council, comprising the Governor and four members of the former Executive Council. A constitutional commission was appointed in September to review the islands' future government. In July 1987 a deportation order was served on Terence Donegan, Attorney-General from 1980–82, after a commission of inquiry revealed that he had committed 'various acts of misfeasance' while in public office.

Three of the four members of the Advisory Council resigned from the PNP in February 1987 and subsequently formed a new party, the National Democratic Alliance. All four members resigned from the Council in May, to enable the appointment of a new Council that would be more representative of the balance of parties in the Legislative Council.

A general election, preceding the return to ministerial rule, took place in March 1988, the British Government having accepted the principal recommendations of the constitutional commission in March 1987. Under a new multi-member system of representation (see Constitution, below), the PDM won 11 of the 13 seats on the Legislative Council, and the PNP won the remaining two. Oswald O. Skippings, the leader of the PDM, was appointed Chief Minister. The new Constitution strengthened the reserve powers of the Governor, but otherwise the form of government was similar to the provisions of the 1976 Constitution.

In May 1991 the British Government abolished capital punishment for the crime of murder in five British Dependent Territories, including the Turks and Caicos Islands. A general election took place in April of that year, at which the PNP secured eight seats, defeating the PDM (which won the remaining five). Skippings was replaced as Chief Minister by Washington Misick, the leader of the PNP.

Following his expulsion from the PDM, the former Minister of Social Services, Wendal Swann, founded a new party in 1993, the United Democratic Party (UDP).

At a general election in January 1995 the PDM secured eight seats, while the PNP won four. Norman Saunders, who had failed to secure nomination as a candidate for the PNP, won his seat as an independent. The UDP fielded three candidates but failed to win a seat. The PDM's victory was largely attributed to widespread popular discontent with the previous Government's policies of economic austerity, which included severe reductions in the number of public service employees.

An agreement was signed in September 1986 with the USA, giving US investigators into drugs-trafficking access to banking information in the islands.

**Government**

Under the provisions of the 1976 Constitution (amended in 1988), executive power is vested in the Governor, appointed by the British monarch. The Governor is responsible for external affairs, internal security, defence and the appointment of public officers. The Governor is President of the Executive Council, which comprises eight members: three *ex officio* and five appointed by the Governor from among the elected members of the Legislative Council. The Legislative Council comprises the Speaker, three nominated members, the *ex-officio* members of the Executive Council and 13 members elected by universal adult suffrage.

**Economic Affairs**

The Turks and Caicos Islands, according to official figures, had a gross domestic product (GDP) of some US $78.8m. in 1992, equivalent to an estimated $6,252 per head. In 1987–91 real GDP increased by an annual average of 8.2%, and in 1993 by an estimated 2%.

Agriculture is not practised on any significant scale in the Turks Islands or on South Caicos (the most populous island of the Territory). The other islands of the Caicos group grow some beans, maize and a few fruits and vegetables. There is some livestock-rearing, but the islands' principal natural resource is fisheries (traditionally based on South Caicos, but now also on Providenciales), which account for almost all commodity exports, the principal species caught being the spiny lobster (exports of which earned some $3.1m. in 1992) and the conch (which earned $1.0m. in that year). Conchs are now being developed commercially (on the largest conch farm in the world), and there is potential for larger-scale fishing.

Industrial activity consists mainly of construction (especially for the tourist industry) and fish-processing. Salt produced by solar evaporation was the principal export until 1964; however, by the early 1990s the activity had virtually ceased. Dredging of a new harbour between South and East Caicos is likely to yield valuable aragonite sea-sand. The islands are dependent upon the import of mineral fuels to satisfy energy requirements.

The principal economic sector is the service industry. This is dominated by tourism, the development of which was concentrated on the island of Providenciales (or Provo—in the Caicos group) during the 1980s. The market is for wealthier visitors, most of whom come from the USA. An 'offshore' financial sector was encouraged in the 1980s, and new, regulatory legislation was ratified at the end of 1989. In mid-1994 there were some 13,798 companies registered in the islands, with more than 70% classified as foreign or exempt. Banks and insurance companies are also being encouraged.

In 1991 the Turks and Caicos Islands recorded a trade deficit of $35.4m. (exports were 11.1% of the value of imports). This deficit is normally offset by receipts from tourism, aid from the United Kingdom and revenue from the 'offshore' financial sector. The USA is the principal trading partner, but some trade is conducted with the United Kingdom and with neighbouring nations.

In the financial year ending 31 March 1994 the Government estimated a recurrent budgetary deficit of $4.1m., following six previous modest overall surpluses. British budgetary support ended in March 1989, although development grants remain vital. The total public debt was reduced to $1.4m. by March 1990. The rate of inflation, which stood at about 5% in 1990, is dependent upon the movement of prices in the USA, the Territory's principal trading partner, and the currency of which it uses. Unemployment increased to an estimated 12% in 1990. A large number of Turks and Caicos 'belongers' have emigrated, many to the Bahamas, especially in search of skilled labour (there is no tertiary education in the Territory).

The Turks and Caicos Islands, as a dependency of the United Kingdom, have the status of Overseas Territory in association with the European Union. The Territory is also a member of the Caribbean Development Bank (see p. 116).

After the political scandals of 1986–88 (see Recent History), the Government successfully eliminated the need for British budgetary support, but benefited from the continued high level of capital aid. Infrastructural development has been encouraged, following the British Government's acceptance that economic (and political) stability depended upon the expansion of tourism, as recommended by an official report. Economic progress, however, seems to be dependent on the rehabilitation of the Territory's administrative reputation. New financial regulations were introduced in 1989, and the Government has adopted measures against the trade in illicit drugs. A five-year development programme, initiated in 1991, aimed to achieve annual average economic growth of 15%, as well as self-sufficiency in the recurrent budget.

**Social Welfare**

In 1990 there was a cottage hospital of 24 beds on Grand Turk, and 10 health clinics on the other main islands. In the same year there were eight doctors and two dentists on the islands.

**Education**

Primary education, beginning at seven years of age and lasting seven years, is compulsory, and is provided free of charge in government schools. Secondary education, from the age of 14, lasts for five years, and is also free. In 1990 there were 14 government primary schools, two private primary schools, one private secondary school and four government secondary schools. Expenditure on education in 1985 was US $1.4m., or 11.2% of total government spending.

**Public Holidays**

**1995:** 1 January (New Year's Day), 6 March (Commonwealth Day), 14 April (Good Friday), 17 April (Easter Monday), 15 May (National Heroes' Day), 6 June (J.A.G.S. McCartney Memorial Day), 12 June (Queen's Official Birthday), 1 August (Emancipation Day), 22 September (National Youth Day), 9 October (for Columbus Day), 24 October (International Human Rights Day), 25–26 December (Christmas).

**1996:** 1 January (New Year's Day), 4 March (Commonwealth Day), 5 April (Good Friday), 8 April (Easter Monday), 13 May (National Heroes' Day), 6 June (J.A.G.S. McCartney Memorial Day), 10 June (Queen's Official Birthday), 1 August (Emancipation Day), 20 September (National Youth Day), 7 October (for Columbus Day), 24 October (International Human Rights Day), 25–26 December (Christmas).

**Weights and Measures**

The imperial system is in use.

## Statistical Survey

Source: Chief Secretary's Office, Grand Turk; tel. 946-2300; telex 8212; fax 946-2886.

### AREA AND POPULATION

**Area:** 430 sq km (166 sq miles).
**Population:** 7,435 (males 3,602; females 3,833) at census of 12 May 1980; 12,350 at census of 31 May 1990. *By island* (1980): Grand Turk 3,098; South Caicos 1,380; Middle Caicos 396; North Caicos 1,278; Salt Cay 284; Providenciales 977 (1990): Grand Turk 3,761; Providenciales 5,586.

**Density:** 28.7 per sq km (at census of 1990).
**Principal Towns:** Cockburn Town (capital, on Grand Turk), population 2,500 (estimate, 1987); Cockburn Harbour (South Caicos), population 1,000.
**Births and Deaths** (registrations, 1990): Live births 240; Deaths 37.
**Economically Active Population** (1990 census): 4,848 (males 2,306; females 2,542).

### AGRICULTURE, ETC.

**Fishing** (metric tons, live weight): Total catch 1,041 in 1990; 1,220 in 1991; 1,293 (Fishes 400, Stromboid conchs 441, Caribbean spiny lobster 452) in 1992. Source: FAO, *Yearbook of Fishery Statistics*.

### INDUSTRY

**Electric Energy** (production, million kWh): 5 in 1989; 5 in 1990; 5 in 1991. Source: UN, *Industrial Statistics Yearbook*.

### FINANCE

**Currency and Exchange Rate:** United States currency is used: 100 cents = 1 US dollar ($). *Sterling Equivalent* (31 December 1994): £1 sterling = US $1.5645; $100 = £63.92.
**Budget** (estimates, $ million, 1989/90): *Revenue:* Recurrent 16.0 (Import duties 9.0, Company registrations 2.2, Fees and sales (non-tax) 3.7); Capital 23.9 (British development aid 23.8). *Expenditure:* Recurrent 20.0 (Wages and salaries 10.7); Capital 23.9. *1990/91* (estimates, $ million): Recurrent revenue 26.1; Recurrent expenditure 26.0. *1992/93* (estimates, $ million): Recurrent revenue 28.2.; Recurrent expenditure 23.4. *1993/94* (estimates, $ million): Recurrent revenue 26.0; Recurrent expenditure 30.1.

### EXTERNAL TRADE

**1991** ($ million): *Imports:* 39.8. *Exports:* 4.4.

### TRANSPORT

**Road Traffic** (1984): 1,563 registered motor vehicles.
**Shipping** (international freight traffic, estimates in '000 metric tons, 1990): Goods loaded 135; Goods unloaded 149. Source: UN, *Monthly Bulletin of Statistics*.

### TOURISM

**Tourist Arrivals:** 54,616 in 1991; 52,300 (approximate) in 1992; 67,303 in 1993.

### COMMUNICATIONS MEDIA

**Radio Receivers** (1992): 7,000 in use*.
**Telephones** (1985): 1,446 in use.
**Non-Daily Newspapers** (1990): 1; (estimated circulation 10,000)*.
* Source: UNESCO, *Statistical Yearbook*.

### EDUCATION

**1990:** 14 government primary schools; 2 private primary schools; 1,494 primary pupils (1994); 4 government secondary schools (with 1,133 pupils in 1994); 1 private secondary school.

## Directory

## The Constitution

The Order in Council of July 1986 enabled the Governor to suspend the ministerial form of government, for which the Constitution of 1976 made provision. Ministerial government was restored in March 1988, following amendments to the Constitution, recommended by a constitutional commission.

The revised Constitution of 1988 provides for an Executive Council and a Legislative Council. Executive authority is vested in the British monarch and is exercised by the Governor (the monarch's appointed representative), who also holds responsibility for external affairs, internal security, defence, the appointment of any person to any public office and the suspension and termination of appointment of any public officer.

The Executive Council comprises: three *ex-officio* members (the Financial Secretary, the Chief Secretary and the Attorney-General); a Chief Minister (appointed by the Governor) who is, in the judgement of the Governor, the leader of that political party represented in the Legislative Council which commands the support of a majority of the elected members of the Council; and four other ministers, appointed by the Governor, on the advice of the Chief Minister. The Executive Council is presided over by the Governor.

The Legislative Council consists of the Speaker, the three *ex-officio* members of the Executive Council, 13 members elected by residents aged 18 and over, and three nominated members (appointed by the Governor, one on the advice of the Chief Minister, one on the advice of the Leader of the Opposition and one at the Governor's discretion).

For the purposes of elections to the Legislative Council, the islands are divided into five electoral districts. In 1988 and 1991 a multiple voting system was used, whereby three districts elected three members each, while the remaining five districts each elected two members. However, in the 1995 election a single-member constituency system was used.

## The Government

**Governor:** Martin Bourke (appointed June 1993).

### EXECUTIVE COUNCIL
(June 1995)

**President:** The Governor.

**Ex-Officio Members:**
   **Financial Secretary:** Austin Robinson.
   **Attorney-General:** Glen Gatland.
   **Chief Secretary:** Paul Fabian.

**Chief Minister and Minister of Finance, Development and Commerce:** Derek Taylor.

**Deputy Chief Minister and Minister of Works, Labour and Immigration:** Samuel Harvey.

**Minister of Transport, Communications, Tourism, Information and CARICOM Affairs:** Oswald O. Skippings.

**Minister of Education, Health, Youth and Sports:** Clarence Selver.

**Minister of Natural Resources, Planning, Environment and Heritage:** Steven Rigby.

**Minister of Agriculture and Fisheries, Social Welfare and Local Government:** Hilly Ewing.

### GOVERNMENT OFFICES

**Office of the Governor:** Government House, Waterloo, Grand Turk; tel. 946-2309; fax 946-2903.

**Office of the Chief Minister:** Government Compound, Grand Turk; tel. 946-2801; fax 946-2777.

**Chief Secretary's Office:** Government Secretariat, Grand Turk; tel. 946-2702; telex 8212; fax 946-2886.

**Office of the Permanent Secretary:** Finance Department, South Base, Grand Turk; tel. 946-2935; fax 946-2557.

### LEGISLATIVE COUNCIL

**Speaker:** Emily Saunders.

**Election, 31 January 1995**

| Party | Seats |
| --- | --- |
| People's Democratic Movement | 8 |
| Progressive National Party | 4 |
| Independent | 1 |
| Total | 13 |

There are three *ex-officio* members (the Chief Secretary, the Financial Secretary and the Attorney-General).

## Political Organizations

**National Democratic Alliance:** Grand Turk; f. 1986; Leader Ariel Misick.

**People's Democratic Movement (PDM):** POB 38, Grand Turk; favours internal self-government and eventual independence; Leader Derek H. Taylor.

**Progressive National Party (PNP):** Grand Turk; against independence; Chair. Tom Lightbourne; Leader Washington Misick.

**Turks and Caicos United Party:** Grand Turk; f. 1985; Leader Glenn Evans-Clarke.

**United Democratic Party:** Grand Turk; f. 1993; Leader Wendal Swann.

## Judicial System

Justice is administered by the Supreme Court of the islands, presided over by the Chief Justice. Following the suspension of the Constitution in 1986, an inquiry recommended that the Chief Justice should reside in the Territory. There is a Magistrate resident on Grand Turk, who also acts as Judge of the Supreme Court.

The Court of Appeal held its first sitting in February 1995. Previously the islands had shared a court of appeal in Nassau, Bahamas. In certain cases, appeals are made to the Judicial Committee of the Privy Council (based in the United Kingdom).

**Chief Justice:** Sir Frederic Gladstone Smith.

**Magistrate:** M. Jackson.

## Religion

### CHRISTIANITY

**The Anglican Communion**

Within the Church in the Province of the West Indies, the Turks and Caicos Islands form part of the diocese of Nassau and the Bahamas. The Bishop is resident in Nassau, Bahamas. According to census results, there were 1,465 adherents in 1990.

**The Roman Catholic Church**

The Bishop of Nassau, Bahamas (suffragan to the archdiocese of Kingston in Jamaica), has jurisdiction in the Turks and Caicos Islands, as Superior of the Mission to the Territory (founded in June 1984).

**Catholic Mission:** Cockburn Town, Grand Turk; churches on Grand Turk and on Providenciales; 132 adherents in 1990 (according to census results); Superior: Bishop of Nassau.

**Protestant Churches**

The Baptist, Methodist, Church of God and Seventh-day Adventist faiths are represented on the islands.

**Baptist Union of the Turks and Caicos Islands:** South Caicos; tel. 946-3220; 3,153 adherents in 1990 (according to census results); Pres. (vacant).

**Methodist Church:** Stubbs Rd, Cockburn Town, Grand Turk; tel. 946-2351; 1,238 adherents in 1990 (according to census results).

## The Press

**Conch News:** Mission Folly, POB 17, Grand Turk; tel. 946-2923; weekly.

**Times of the Islands Magazine:** Caribbean Place, POB 234, Providenciales; tel. 946-4788; fax 946-4703; f. 1988; quarterly; circ. 7,000.

**Turks and Caicos Current:** POB 173, Grand Turk; tel. 946-2131; telex 8256; every 2 months.

**Turks and Caicos News:** Central Sq., Providenciales; tel. 946-4664; telex 8256; fax 946-4661; weekly.

## Radio and Television

In 1992 there were an estimated 7,000 radio receivers in use.

**Coral Radio:** Butterfield Sq., Providenciales; tel. 946-4496; commercial; 24 hrs; Station Man. Bob Cooper.

**Radio Providenciales:** Leeward Highway, POB 32, Providenciales; tel. 946-4496; fax 946-4108; commercial.

**Radio Turks and Caicos (RTC):** POB 69, Grand Turk; tel. 946-2041; telex 8212; fax 946-2777; govt-owned; commercial; broadcasts 105 hrs weekly; Man. Lynette Smith.

**Turks and Caicos Beacon Ltd:** North End, South Caicos; tel. 946-3311; commercial.

**Vic Radio:** Butterfield Sq., Providenciales; tel. 946-4496.

**WPRT Radio:** Leeward Highway, Providenciales; tel. 946-4267; commercial; Station Man. Peter Stubbs.

Television programmes are available from a cabled network, and broadcasts from the Bahamas can be received in the islands.

**WIV Cable TV:** BWI Arcade, Providenciales; tel. 946-4273.

## Finance

**Financial Services Commission:** Post Office Bldg, Front St, Grand Turk; tel. 946-2791; fax 946-2821; regulates local and 'offshore' financial sector; in 1993 there were 10,959 cos registered; Superintendent John D. K. Lawrence.

## BANKING

**Bank of Nova Scotia** (Canada): Harbour House, Front St, Cockburn Town, POB 132, Grand Turk; tel. 946-2506; telex 8247; fax 946-2667; Man. J. E. ALDER; br. on Providenciales.

**Barclays Bank (International) PLC** (United Kingdom): POB 61, Cockburn Town, Grand Turk; tel. 946-2831; telex 8214; fax 946-2695; Man. S. J. S. LIGHTBOURNE; 3 brs.

**Bordier International Bank and Trust Ltd:** Caribbean Place, POB 5, Providenciales; tel. 946-4535; telex 8428; fax 946-4540; Man. ELISE HARTSHORN.

**Turks and Caicos Banking Co Ltd:** Harbour House, Front St, POB 123, Grand Turk; tel. 946-2368; telex 8226; fax 946-2365; f. 1980; cap. $2.7m., dep. $9.7m.; Man. Dir ANTON FAESSLER.

## INSURANCE

**Turks and Caicos Islands National Insurance Board:** Church Folly, POB 250, Grand Turk; tel. 946-1048; fax 946-1362.

Several foreign (mainly US and British) companies have offices in the Turks and Caicos islands. Some 1,491 insurance companies were registered at the end of 1993.

## Trade and Industry

**Chamber of Commerce:** POB 148, Grand Turk; tel. 946-2368; Pres. ANTON FAESSLER.

**General Trading Company (Turks and Caicos) Ltd:** PMBI, Cockburn Town, Grand Turk; tel. 946-2464; telex 8234; fax 946-2799; shipping agents, importers, air freight handlers; wholesale distributor of petroleum products, wines and spirits.

**Turks Islands Importers Ltd (TIMCO):** Front St, POB 72, Grand Turk; tel. 946-2480; fax 946-2481; f. 1952; agents for Lloyds of London, importers and distributors of food, beer, liquor, building materials, hardware and appliances; Dir H. E. MAGNUS.

### DEVELOPMENT ORGANIZATION

**Turks and Caicos Islands Investment Agency:** Hibiscus Sq., Pond St, POB 105, Grand Turk; tel. 946-2058; fax 946-1464; f. 1984 as Development Board of the Turks and Caicos Islands; statutory body; development finance for private sector; promotion and management of internal investment.

### TRADE UNION

**St George's Industrial Trade Union:** Cockburn Harbour; Sec. ELIZA BASDEN; 250 mems.

## Transport

### ROADS

There are 121 km (75 miles) of road in the islands, of which 24 km (15 miles), on Grand Turk, South Caicos and Providenciales, are tarmac.

### SHIPPING

There are regular freight services from Miami, Florida. The main sea ports are Grand Turk, Providenciales, Salt Cay and Cockburn Harbour on South Caicos. Harbour facilities on South Caicos and Providenciales are being improved, and there are plans for a new port on North Caicos.

**Caicos Maritime (BWI) Ltd:** Barclays Bank Bldg, Providenciales; tel. 946-4400; telex 8431.

**Ocean Research and Recovery Ltd:** The Mariner, POB 64, Providenciales; tel. 946-4109; fax 946-4939.

**Seacair Ltd:** Churchill Bldg, POB 170, Grand Turk; tel. 946-2591; fax 946-2226.

**Seacorp Shipping Ltd:** Grand Turk; tel. 946-2226; fax 946-2226.

**Southeast and Caribbean Shipping Co Ltd:** Churchill Bldg, Front St, POB 103, Grand Turk; tel. 946-2355.

**Turks and Caicos National Shipping and Development Co Ltd:** Front St, POB 103, Grand Turk; tel. 946-2194.

**Vulcan Shipping Co Ltd:** Churchill Bldg, Front St, POB 4, Grand Turk; tel. 946-2355.

### CIVIL AVIATION

There are international airfields on Grand Turk, South Caicos, North Caicos and Providenciales, the last being the most important; there are also landing strips on Middle Caicos, Pine Cay, Parrot Cay and Salt Cay.

**Department of Civil Aviation:** Off Waterloo Rd, Grand Turk; tel. 946-2137.

**Caicos Caribbean Airlines:** South Caicos; tel. 946-3283; fax 946-3377; freight to Miami.

**Flamingo Air Services Ltd:** Grand Turk Int. Airport, POB 162, Grand Turk; tel. 946-2109; fax 946-2188.

**Turks Air Ltd:** Grand Turk Int. Airport, Grand Turk; tel. 946-4205; fax 946-4504; (Head Office: POB 523158, Miami, Florida, USA; tel. 871-1433; fax 871-1622); twice-weekly cargo service to and from Miami; Grand Turk Local Agent CRIS NEWTON.

**Turks and Caicos National Airlines (1983) Ltd:** POB 12, Grand Turk; tel. 946-2082; telex 8520; fax 946-2081; f. 1976 as Air Turks and Caicos, privatized 1983; scheduled inter-island service, and international services to Haiti, the Dominican Republic and the Bahamas; charter flights; Gen. Man. JAMES BASSETT; Chief Pilot Capt. STANLEY JHAGROO.

## Tourism

The islands' main tourist attractions are the numerous unspoilt beaches, and the opportunities for diving. Hotel accommodation is available on Grand Turk, Salt Cay, South Caicos, Pine Cay and Providenciales. In 1993 there were 67,303 tourist arrivals (an increase of almost 30% compared with the previous year) and 1,079 hotel rooms. Revenue from the sector in 1989 totalled US $3.4m.

**Turks and Caicos Islands Tourist Board:** Pond St, POB 128, Grand Turk; tel. 946-2321; fax 946-2733.

**Turks and Caicos Hotel Association:** Third Turtle Inn, Providenciales; tel. 946-4230.

# THE UNITED STATES OF AMERICA

## Introductory Survey

**Location, Climate, Language, Religion, Flag, Capital**

The United States of America comprises mainly the North American continent between Canada and Mexico. Alaska, to the north-west of Canada, and Hawaii, in the central Pacific Ocean, are two of the 50 States of the USA. There is considerable climatic variation, with mean annual average temperatures ranging from 29°C (77°F) in Florida to −13.3°C (10°F) in Alaska. Annual rainfall averages 735 mm (29 in), ranging from 1,640 mm (64.6 in) in Alabama to 106 mm (4.2 in) in Nevada. Much of Texas, New Mexico, Arizona, Nevada and Utah is desert. The language is English, although there are significant Spanish-speaking minorities. Christianity is the predominant religion. The national flag (proportions 19 by 10) has 13 alternating stripes (seven red and six white) with a dark blue rectangular canton, containing 50 white five-pointed stars, in the upper hoist. The capital is Washington, DC.

**Recent History**

The threat of communist advances in Asia led the USA to provide most of the support required by UN forces in the Korean War of 1950–53 and to its subsequent military involvement, beginning in 1961, in South Viet Nam. Following President Kennedy's assassination in 1963, the scale of US military operations in Indo-China was increased by his successor, Lyndon Johnson. The growing unpopularity of the war and the transfer of the presidency in 1969 to Richard Nixon, a Republican, who was re-elected in 1972, resulted in 1973 in the withdrawal of US troops from Viet Nam. A series of scandals involving the presidency and senior administration officials on charges of corruption and obstruction of justice, known as the 'Watergate' affair, eventually led to Nixon's resignation in August 1974 and his replacement by the Vice-President, Gerald Ford.

In November 1976 Jimmy Carter, a Democrat, was elected President. The new administration took the initiative on several foreign policy issues, including attempts to solve the impasse in the Middle East, which culminated in the signing in 1979 of a peace treaty between Egypt and Israel. In 1978 the USA severed formal links with Taiwan and established diplomatic relations with the People's Republic of China. Domestically, economic recession and inflation preoccupied the Carter administration, and the President's management of the economy was a decisive factor in his defeat by the Republican candidate, Ronald Reagan, in the 1980 presidential election.

The conservative orientation of the Reagan administration was expressed domestically in a programme aimed at transferring to the individual states the financial responsibility for many federal social programmes, while expanding expenditure on defence. Despite problems of severe economic recession and high unemployment, the Republicans retained their previous level of congressional representation in the November 1982 elections. With the resumption of economic growth in 1983, and its strong resurgence through 1984, unemployment and inflation fell, and in November Reagan was re-elected for a further four-year term, securing the largest majority of electoral votes in US history.

In foreign affairs, the Reagan administrations generally pursued a firmly anti-communist line, notably in their active support of right-wing regimes in Latin America, where the US military occupation of Grenada in November 1983 attracted considerable international criticism, and in Africa and the Middle East. Generally friendly relations were, however, maintained with the People's Republic of China. Relations with the USSR pursued an uneven course. The change of leadership in the USSR in November 1982 was followed by a period of deterioration in contacts between the two countries.

Negotiations, held in Geneva, between the USA and the USSR on the reduction of medium-range missiles proved unsuccessful and were terminated by the USSR in November 1983. Formal disarmament talks, which coincided with the assumption of leadership in the USSR by Mikhail Gorbachev, were eventually resumed in Geneva in March 1985. Their subsequent course, as well as that of US–Soviet relations generally, was overshadowed by President Reagan's pursuit of his Strategic Defense Initiative (SDI). Initiated in 1983, this advanced-technology research programme aimed to create a space-based system of defences against nuclear attack. The Reagan Government consistently refused to negotiate the termination of SDI, although it offered to share these research findings with the USSR, which viewed the programme as a potential source of arms escalation and a first step in the militarization of space.

In November 1985 Reagan and Gorbachev held a summit meeting in Geneva. While no agreements were reached on major arms control issues, the talks established a cordial framework of relations between the two leaders. Agreements were concluded on a number of other matters, including the prohibition of the manufacture and stockpiling of chemical weapons, the sharing of research on the sun as an energy source, and the resumption of US–Soviet cultural exchanges, which were sharply curtailed by the US Government following Soviet military intervention in Afghanistan in 1979.

During 1985 and 1986, US foreign policy continued to focus on the support of anti-communist activism in areas experiencing political and military unrest. In May 1985 a trade embargo was imposed against Nicaragua, although the President experienced difficulties in securing congressional funds on a regular basis for the support of the Nicaraguan Contras (anti-government insurgents). In Africa, the Reagan administration provided support for guerrilla forces opposing the Angolan Government, which was continued despite the 1988 accord reached by Angola, Cuba and South Africa over Namibian independence, in which the USA acted as an unofficial mediator and which provided for the withdrawal of Cuban troops from Angola. In 1985 President Reagan opposed the imposition of economic sanctions against the South African Government, but in 1986 his veto was overturned by Congress.

During the Reagan administration the USA adopted a forceful stance (generally welcomed by other Western governments) on international air and sea terrorism. However, a ban on trade with Libya, which President Reagan alleged to be promoting terrorist activity, received little support from other Western countries in 1985. In March 1986 US and Libyan forces came into armed conflict during the course of US naval manoeuvres in the Gulf of Sirte. In April, following a terrorist outrage against US military personnel in West Berlin, President Reagan ordered the selective bombing of government offices and military installations in Tripoli and Benghazi. Direct US military involvement in the Middle East, which had been minimized since its withdrawal in 1984 from peace-keeping operations in Lebanon, was reactivated in July 1987, when Reagan agreed to a request by Kuwait to provide military protection for its petroleum tankers in the Persian (Arabian) Gulf, following attacks on them by Iran. Subsequent incidents in the Gulf brought the USA and Iran into armed confrontations. In April 1988 the USA was a signatory, with the USSR, Afghanistan and Pakistan, of an agreement for the phased withdrawal of Soviet troops from Afghanistan, which was completed in February 1989.

Negotiations on the issue of arms control were maintained between the USA and the USSR during 1986. In October Reagan and Gorbachev met for a two-day summit conference in Reykjavík, Iceland. The meeting made some headway in delineating long-range nuclear weapon limitations and verification procedures, but achieved little progress overall because of Reagan's refusal to scale down the US commitment to SDI research. In November the USA abandoned the weapon deployment limits set by the 1979 Strategic Arms Limitation Treaty (SALT II), which, although never ratified by Congress, had been informally observed by both the USA and the USSR. In March 1987, however, the US Government responded favourably to an indication by the USSR that it was willing to expedite an agreement to eliminate medium-range nuclear missiles from Europe by 1992.

These discussions, which were subsequently extended to include short-range nuclear weaponry, resulted, in September 1987, in an agreement in principle on terms under which both countries would eliminate all stocks of medium- and short-range nuclear missiles. The resultant Intermediate Nuclear Forces (INF) treaty, the first to terminate an entire class of offensive nuclear weapon, was formally signed by Reagan and Gorbachev at a summit meeting held in Washington, DC, in December. The two leaders also agreed to pursue negotiations towards a new Strategic Arms Reduction Treaty (START) to reduce long-range nuclear weaponry by up to 50%, and a further summit conference took place in Moscow in May-June 1988 at which the INF treaty was ratified and activated. Some initial progress was made towards finalizing terms for START. The USSR, however, continued to oppose the further advancement of SDI, whose future had become increasingly conjectural: the US Congress proved reluctant to allocate its high funding requirements, and during 1988 and 1989 expressed doubts about the feasibility of the project's goals. The USSR, while maintaining its objections to SDI, agreed in February 1990 to exclude it from the ambit of negotiations on START.

In November 1986 details were disclosed, in the press, of covert foreign policy operations by senior members of the Reagan administration in relation to US contacts with the Government of Iran. The ensuing scandal, known as the 'Irangate' or 'Iran-Contra' affair, developed into a major political embarrassment, bringing into question the credibility and competence of the President. Subsequent investigations by an independent commission, and by the US Congress, concluded that secret arms sales had been made to the Government of Iran, in return for an undertaking by Iran to help to secure the release of US hostages held by pro-Iranian Islamic groups in Lebanon, and that Reagan had been misled by officials of the Central Intelligence Agency (CIA) and the National Security Council (NSC) into authorizing the arms transactions, and bypassing the required congressional consultative procedures. It was also determined that considerable evidence existed to support allegations that between $10m. and $30m., derived from the arms sales, had been secretly diverted into bank accounts held by the Nicaraguan Contra rebels. Reagan, who accepted full personal responsibility for the 'Iran-Contra' affair, was exonerated of any deliberate attempt to misrepresent his role in the events. The closing months of Reagan's presidency were clouded by further political embarrassments, which included the resignation of the Attorney-General, who had been under judicial investigation for alleged ethical conflicts arising from his personal business interests.

The competence and integrity of the Reagan administration formed a major theme of the 1988 presidential election campaign of the Democratic candidate, Michael Dukakis. Vice-President George Bush, the Republican nominee, who based his campaign on Reagan's record of management of the economy and conduct of foreign affairs, was elected to the presidency, although the Senate and House of Representatives both retained Democratic majorities. The initial months of the Bush administration were dominated by concern over the formulation of effective measures to contain the federal budget deficit, and over the future course of arms reduction negotiations with the USSR. In June 1989, following an agreement to resume START discussions, President Bush proposed the initiation of new negotiations aimed at achieving substantial reductions in NATO and Warsaw Pact countries' conventional ground forces in Europe. In September the USA and USSR finalized agreements on the monitoring of chemical weapons and procedures for the verification of limits on strategic forces and nuclear tests. A summit meeting between Bush and Gorbachev followed at Valletta, Malta, in December, where further progress was made on proposals for the eventual total elimination of chemical weapons. This meeting, which was declared by both leaders to have marked the opening of a new era in US-Soviet relations, examined prospects for new agreements by the mid-1990s for reductions of 50% in nuclear strategic arms, together with substantial reductions in the size of conventional forces based in Europe. In addition to disarmament issues, the two leaders discussed developments in Eastern Europe (see below), confirmed the termination of US aid to the Nicaraguan Contras, and proposed the strengthening of US-Soviet bilateral trade.

The withdrawal by the USSR in late 1989 and early 1990 from the exercise of direct political influence on the internal affairs of the countries of Eastern Europe was accompanied by a further improvement in US-Soviet relations, and by the implementation of programmes of US economic aid for several of the former Soviet 'client' states. In September 1990 the USA and USSR, with France and the United Kingdom, the other powers that occupied Germany at the end of the Second World War, formally agreed terms for the unification of the two post-war German states, which took effect in the following month. US-Soviet relations came under some strain, however, following the assertion by Lithuania of independence from the Soviet Union and subsequent Soviet measures to blockade the Lithuanian economy. This issue was included in discussions at a second summit meeting between Bush and Gorbachev, held in May-June in Washington, DC, at which the two leaders expressed confidence that further arms limitation agreements would be finalized during 1990. A trade accord favouring Soviet economic interests was signed, although its implementation by the US Government was made subject to a liberalization of Soviet emigration laws. In July the USA, together with the world's six largest industrial democracies, agreed to provide the USSR with economic and technical assistance in undertaking a change-over to a market economy. In the same month, a summit meeting of NATO members proposed that the USSR and the other members of the Warsaw Pact alliance join in a formal declaration that the two military groupings were no longer adversaries and would refrain from the threat or use of force. This initiative was followed in November by the signing in Paris, by members of NATO and the Warsaw Pact, of a Treaty on Conventional Armed Forces in Europe (CFE), which provided for bilateral limits to be placed on the number of non-nuclear weapons sited between the Atlantic Ocean and the Ural Mountains. Immediately following the signing of the CFE Treaty, Presidents Bush and Gorbachev were present at a meeting of the Conference on Security and Co-operation in Europe (CSCE), at which the USA, the USSR and 32 other countries signed a charter declaring the end of the post-war era of confrontation and division in Europe. The signatories also undertook to conduct their future relations on the basis of 'respect and co-operation'. The charter provided for the establishment of a CSCE secretariat and the convening of regular bi-annual meetings of heads of state and government, with effect from 1992. A further meeting of the CFE Treaty signatories, to begin negotiations on specific weapon reductions, was held in February 1991. Although US-Soviet relations maintained a generally cordial tone during 1990 and early 1991, there was disquiet in the USA over President Gorbachev's opposition to independence movements in Estonia and Latvia, as well as Lithuania, together with wider unease that many of Gorbachev's earlier reforms remained vulnerable to political change and unrest within the USSR.

In September 1989 President Bush outlined the terms of a federal programme aimed at combating drug abuse, which in recent years had become a serious social problem in the USA. The initiative received co-operation from the governments of Bolivia, Colombia and Peru, but the activities of drugs-traffickers operating from Panama, allegedly with the collusion of the regime controlled by Gen. Manuel Noriega (who was sought for trial in the USA on drugs-trafficking charges), had been unaffected by US sanctions, in operation since 1988. In September 1989 the USA broke off diplomatic relations with Panama, and in the following month an internal coup attempt, carried out with non-military US support, was suppressed by the Panamanian authorities. On 20 December, following incidents involving US personnel, the USA sent in 23,000 troops with the stated objectives of protecting US residents in Panama, safeguarding the Panama Canal, restoring democratic government and bringing Noriega to face trial in the USA. The invasion, which was condemned by the UN Security Council, installed an elected government and eventually apprehended Noriega, after some delay, in January 1990. US troops were withdrawn in February, and relations with Panama were normalized in April. In Nicaragua the departure of the Sandinista government, as the result of a general election held in February 1990, was followed by the resumption of cordial relations with the US Government.

During 1990 the Bush administration pursued domestic policy reforms in a number of areas, particularly in education and banking, although considerable delay was encountered in obtaining congressional approval for the federal budget, in which tax increases formed an unpopular part of measures aimed at containing persistently heavy deficits. President

Bush's political prestige, however, was considerably enhanced by his management of the US involvement in an unexpected conflict in the Middle East.

Following the invasion of Kuwait by Iraqi forces on 2 August 1990, and the subsequent annexation of that country by Iraq, the US Government assumed a leading international role in the implementation of political, economic and military measures to bring about an Iraqi withdrawal. The imposition of mandatory economic sanctions against Iraq by the UN Security Council on 6 August was quickly followed by 'Operation Desert Shield', in which US combat troops and aircraft were dispatched to Saudi Arabia, at that country's request, to secure its borders against a possible attack by Iraq. Tensions were heightened in mid-August by Iraq's detention of Western nationals resident in Kuwait and Iraq, and the harassment of Western diplomatic personnel in Kuwait. An offer, subsequently repeated, by President Saddam Hussain of Iraq to link withdrawal from Kuwait with a resolution of other outstanding Middle Eastern problems, was rejected, and in late August the UN Security Council endorsed the use of military action to enforce its economic sanctions. Despite intense diplomatic activity, in which the USSR was prominent, the crisis deepened. On 9 September Presidents Bush and Gorbachev held an emergency summit meeting in Helsinki, Finland, and jointly demanded an Iraqi withdrawal, although the USSR expressed reluctance to support military operations by the UN. In late September the UN Security Council intensified its economic measures against Iraq. However, the ineffectiveness both of economic sanctions and of diplomatic negotiation had become evident by late November, and the USSR gave its assent to the use of force against Iraq, although it did not participate in the multinational force that was now arrayed in the Gulf region and included, under US command, air, sea and ground forces from the United Kingdom, France, Italy, Egypt, Morocco, Kuwait and the other Arab Gulf states. Jordan, which was active throughout the crisis in seeking to promote a negotiated settlement, was perceived by the US Government as sympathetic to Iraq, and US financial aid programmes to that country were suspended.

On 29 November 1990 the UN Security Council authorized the use of 'all necessary means' to force Iraq to withdraw from Kuwait, unless it did so by 15 January 1991. By early January, US troop deployment in the Gulf region exceeded 430,000 ground troops, together with 1,300 fighter and support aircraft, 2,000 tanks and 55 warships. An unsuccessful meeting between the US Secretary of State and the Iraqi Minister of Foreign Affairs, on 9 January, was followed, three days later, by the US Congress's adoption of motions authorizing President Bush to initiate armed action against Iraq, and on 17 January 'Operation Desert Storm' was launched, with massive air and missile attacks against Iraqi positions, both in Iraq and Kuwait. (For a detailed account of military operations, see Recent History of Iraq, p. 1556.) In the course of the conflict, more than 110,000 attacking air missions were flown over Kuwait and Iraq by multinational air forces, while naval support operations were conducted from the Gulf. In the following weeks, severe damage was inflicted on Iraqi military and economic targets, while counter-attacks by its air force, and attempts to draw Israel into the conflict by launching missile attacks on population centres, proved ineffective. A ground offensive by the multinational force was launched on 23–24 February, and Iraqi positions were quickly overrun. Hostilities were suspended on 28 February. The Government of Iraq accepted cease-fire terms on 3 March, leaving the multinational forces in control of Kuwait, together with an area of southern Iraq, comprising about 15% of that country's total national territory. Troop withdrawals from the occupied area of Iraq commenced in March, with the remaining US troops evacuated in early May, to be replaced by a UN peace-keeping force.

Following the conclusion of hostilities, in which 148 US troops died in combat, internal rebellions broke out within Iraq by groups opposed to President Saddam Hussain. The severity with which these were suppressed, particularly in the northern region among the Kurdish ethnic group, and the subsequent flight of refugees into neighbouring areas of Turkey and Iran, prompted large-scale international relief operations, as well as widespread criticism of the US Government for its refusal to support the anti-government insurgents and to take action to depose Saddam Hussain. In May 1991 the USA responded by airlifting troops to northern Iraq to establish 'safe' enclaves, to which Kurdish refugees were encouraged to return. The US military continued to monitor events in these Kurdish areas from operational bases in Turkey.

In the period following the Gulf War, the US Government actively pursued initiatives to convene a regional conference, under joint US and Soviet sponsorship, to seek a permanent solution to the wider problems of the Middle East. In early August 1991 the US Secretary of State, James Baker, obtained the agreement of Egypt, Israel, Jordan, Lebanon and Syria to take part in such a conference, the opening session of which was convened in Madrid, Spain, in October. Successive negotiating sessions failed to make any substantive progress, and traditionally close relations between Israel and the USA subsequently came under strain, following pressure by the US Government on Israel to suspend the construction of Jewish settlements in occupied territories, pending the eventual outcome of the peace negotiations.

During the second half of 1991 concern at the implications of economic dislocation and political unrest within the USSR was the dominant preoccupation of US foreign policy. In June President Bush offered the USSR guarantees of up to $1,500m. in loans for grain purchases, together with assistance in restructuring the Soviet food distribution system. In the following month Presidents Bush and Gorbachev met at an international economic conference in London, when further assistance was promised by the leaders of the major industrial democracies. In late July the USA and USSR signed START, providing for a 30% reduction in long-range nuclear weapons over a seven-year period. Further moves towards bilateral disarmament followed in September, when the USA announced that it was to begin the phased elimination of sea and air tactical nuclear weapons in Europe and Asia; in October the USSR offered to reduce its holdings of nuclear weapons to below the levels agreed in START.

The advancing prospect of the political dissolution of the USSR prompted President Bush, on a visit to the Ukraine in August 1991, to promise US support for Soviet republics pursuing policies of democratic and economic reform. In September the newly-independent Baltic republics were granted modest economic aid, and in the same month the USA and USSR discontinued military assistance to rival guerrilla factions in Afghanistan. Worsening economic conditions within the USSR during December led the US Government to provide an additional $100m. in humanitarian aid, and airlifts of food by military aircraft to Russian cities.

In December 1991, following the replacement of the USSR by the Commonwealth of Independent States (CIS) comprising 11 of the republics of the former Soviet Union, the independence of each republic was recognized by the USA, although diplomatic relations were initially established with only five republics, on the grounds that the remainder had yet to achieve acceptable standards of democratic practices and human rights guarantees. In January 1992 a meeting was held between President Bush and President Yeltsin of Russia, the dominant republic within the CIS. President Bush expressed concern that effective measures should be taken by the Russian Government to ensure that the nuclear weapons and related technical expertise of the former USSR did not become available to countries not in possession of nuclear weapons capability, or to nations in the Middle East or to the Democratic People's Republic of Korea. At a subsequent meeting held in February, the Russian leader assured President Bush that immediate safeguards were in force, and that all short-range nuclear warheads would be moved into Russia from sites in other CIS republics by July 1992. President Yeltsin also proposed that the USA and Russia should share in the joint future development of the SDI project (see above), and further reductions in nuclear arsenals were agreed by the two leaders. In the following months the USA continued to assist Russia and the other CIS members to achieve political and economic integration within the international community, and actively supported an application by Russia to join the International Monetary Fund. In May 1992 the US Government announced that it would participate in a multinational aid programme for Russia of $24,000m. Concern remained, however, at the potential global dangers if Russian controls on nuclear weapons movements should prove ineffective.

At a summit meeting held between Presidents Bush and Yeltsin in June 1992 in Washington, DC, agreement was reached on further substantial reductions in nuclear arms, under which, by the year 2003, total holdings of nuclear warheads would be reduced to less than one-half of the quotas contained in START. Agreements covering other areas of co-operation, including the encouragement of US private-sector investment in Russia, arrangements for mutual assistance in the event of accidents in space, and the outline of a joint ballistic missiles protection system, were also signed.

In its relations with the former communist countries in Europe, the USA augmented its commitment to the CSCE with economic support, and promoted the membership of former members of the Warsaw Pact in the North Atlantic Co-operation Council, an offshoot of NATO. Contacts were also revived between the USA and Viet Nam, and in May 1992 there was a partial relaxation of a 19-year trade embargo. Relations with Iraq remained tense following the discovery, made in November 1991 by UN representatives, that President Saddam Hussain's regime was seeking to conceal its continuing development of nuclear weapons capability. In November 1991 the US Government indicated that it had not excluded the possibility of military intervention in Libya to secure the extradition for trial in Britain of two Libyan nationals accused of complicity in the bombing of a US passenger aircraft, with heavy loss of life, in December 1988.

Following the conclusion of the Gulf War in early 1991, Bush's political popularity began to decline sharply, amid growing public perception that the Government was assigning greater priority to foreign affairs than to addressing the problems of the US economy, which had been in recession since early 1989. Criticism was also directed at the administration's alleged neglect of other domestic issues, particularly in the areas of social welfare, medical costs and health care, and the increasingly interrelated issues of urban poverty and civil rights. In 1990 Bush vetoed legislation providing financial compensation for those victimized by discrimination in employment, although a compromise version was eventually approved in November 1991. In April 1992 serious rioting broke out in Los Angeles and spread briefly to several other cities. The underlying causes of the disorders were widely ascribed to the worsening economic and social plight of the impoverished urban black minority. An outbreak of rioting in New York in July prompted a congressional proposal to provide $27,000m. in long-term urban aid, but this plan was vetoed by President Bush, following the November elections, on the grounds that it would be adverse to the interests of small businesses and urban workers, and would violate fiscal discipline.

The 1992 presidential election campaign, in which Bush was opposed by Bill Clinton, a Democrat state governor, and Ross Perot, a populist independent, was dominated by domestic social and economic issues. The problems of health care, urban crime and the legal status of abortion were major topics of debate, although Bush's record of economic management, particularly in relation to the persistence of federal budget deficits, provided the major line of attack by the opposing candidates. The perception of the electorate that the Bush presidency had neglected urgent domestic problems in its concentration on foreign affairs proved to be the decisive factor in the election: the turn-out of voters, at 55.2%, was the highest at any presidential election since 1968, and gave a decisive majority, of 43.0% to 37.4%, to Bill Clinton. Perot, whose campaign had concentrated on the question of federal deficit spending, obtained almost 19% of the popular vote.

Foreign relations remained in the forefront of the final months of the Bush administration. In July 1992 contention arose between the Government of Iraq and the UN over the rights of UN observers to inspect Iraqi nuclear facilities, and in the following month the US Government sought to limit internal military operations by the Iraqi Government by imposing an air exclusion zone south of latitude 32°N. This was followed, in January 1993, by the US air force's participation in selective bombings of Iraqi missile sites. In December 1992 relations with the People's Republic of China, which had been strained since 1989 by the Chinese Government's persistent suppression of political dissent, were revived by the removal of a US embargo on sales of military equipment. In the same month President Bush launched 'Operation Restore Hope', under which 24,000 US troops were sent to Somalia, as part of an international force under US command, to protect shipments of food aid and to assist in the restoration of civil order.

Shortly before the transfer of the presidency to Bill Clinton in January 1993, Presidents Bush and Yeltsin met in Moscow to sign a second Nuclear Arms Reduction Treaty (START II), which provided for the elimination by 2003 of almost 75% of all US and CIS-held nuclear warheads. The implementation, however, of START I and START II cannot begin until Belarus, Kazakhstan and Ukraine, the other former republics of the USSR which hold stocks of nuclear weapons, have endorsed START I. By June 1994 only Ukraine had not granted such ratification, although in March the Ukrainian Government accepted an offer of increased aid from the USA to cover the cost of dismantling its nuclear weapons. In May 1993 President Clinton announced the termination of SDI.

The initial preoccupation of the Clinton administration was with the formulation of an economic recovery plan, aimed at achieving reductions of $500,000m., over a five-year period, in the federal budget deficit by means of increased taxation and economies in the cost of government, rather than by reduced levels of federal spending. Military expenditure was a particular area in which economies were proposed, while additional spending was planned for infrastructural projects and measures to stimulate economic activity. A major restructuring of the US health care system was also planned, and a commission to formulate proposals was placed under the chairmanship of President Clinton's wife. Certain aspects of the economic recovery plan, particularly those relating to higher income tax and a new energy tax, encountered initial opposition in the Democrat-controlled Congress, but were eventually approved, in a modified form, by the House of Representatives in May 1993. Approval by the Senate, following further amendments, took place in late June. By mid-1993, however, the President's initial popularity had fallen sharply, owing in part to perceptions of indecisiveness by Clinton in formulating effective policies. There was also widespread criticism of the competence of some of his appointees and advisers.

In April 1993 President Clinton met President Yeltsin at a summit conference held in Vancouver, Canada, at which the USA undertook to provide Russia with $1,600m. of emergency short-term aid in technical assistance, food and medical supplies. In the following month the USA transferred command of operations in Somalia to the UN, although about 4,000 US troops remained until the termination of the peace-keeping operation in March 1994. In the Middle East the Clinton administration renewed the initiatives taken by President Bush in promoting a settlement between the Arab states and Israel (see below). In late June 1993 the US Government launched a missile attack against the headquarters of Iraqi military intelligence in Baghdad, in retaliation for an alleged plot by Iraq to assassinate ex-President Bush in Kuwait in April.

By mid-1993 the crisis in former Yugoslavia had assumed increased importance as a foreign policy issue, leading to disagreements between the USA and the Western European powers, which opposed US proposals to launch direct air strikes against military positions held by Bosnian Serbs. The US administration, while avoiding any direct military commitment, gave its support, through NATO, to peace-keeping operations in Bosnia and Herzegovina. President Clinton was unsuccessful, however, in efforts to secure the removal of the international embargo on arms sales to the Bosnian Muslims. In June 1994 the US Government associated itself with proposals by the EU countries for the tripartite partition of Bosnia and Herzegovina.

Although President Clinton chose not to pursue an initiative in August 1993 by Cuba to normalize its economic and diplomatic relations with the USA, renewed efforts were made to restore to power Fr Jean-Bertrand Aristide, the first democratically elected President of Haiti, who had taken refuge in the USA following his overthrow by a military junta in 1991. An economic embargo imposed by the OAS (see p. 204), together with implied threats of military intervention by the US Government, had failed to displace the military regime, and conditions within Haiti had led large numbers of refugees to seek asylum in the USA, many of whom were forcibly repatriated by the US authorities. In June 1994, following the imposition in the previous month of international sanctions against Haiti by the UN Security Council, President Clinton announced that all commercial and financial transactions with Haiti were being suspended. In September, following a diplomatic mission led by former President Carter, a UN-sponsored multinational force, composed almost entirely of US troops, arrived in Haiti with the agreement of the military junta, which relinquished power in October. US troops were withdrawn from the UN force in March 1995.

During 1993 the US Government continued to foster efforts to promote a general resolution of tensions in the Middle East. With US assistance, but as a direct result of secret diplomatic mediation by Norway, the Palestine Liberation Organization (PLO) and the Government of Israel signed an agreement providing for Palestinian self-government in the Occupied Territories and for mutual recognition by Israel and the PLO. Implementation of this agreement was proceeding in mid-1995. In January 1994, following a meeting held in Geneva, Switzerland, between Clinton and President Assad of Syria, negotiations were initiated for a settlement between Israel and Syria.

Political and economic contacts with Russia continued on a cordial level, with the two countries adopting a co-operative stance in many areas of foreign policy. In February 1994 the US Government lifted its embargo on trade with Viet Nam, which had been in force since 1975. The establishment of full diplomatic relations with Viet Nam was announced in July 1995. Relations with the People's Republic of China improved in mid-1994, following a controversial decision by Clinton to extend enhanced trading privileges to that country until June 1995, despite China's continued suppression of free political debate. Little progress, however, was made in the resolution of the persistently adverse US balance of trade with Japan, despite an agreement between the two countries in July 1993 to implement measures to reduce the trade deficit. In March 1994 the US Government assumed reserve powers to impose high retaliatory tariffs on Japanese imports; following protracted and inconclusive negotiations to resolve the disagreement, the US Government announced that a tariff of 100% was to be levied on certain Japanese motor vehicles in June 1995. However, an agreement between the two Governments, under which Japan was to afford increased access to US motor vehicle parts, was finalized a few hours before the trade sanctions were due to take effect.

In March 1994 the USA extended its ban on nuclear testing until September 1995. The prevention of nuclear proliferation, which has remained a prime objective of US foreign policy, led in 1993 and early 1994 to a serious confrontation between the USA and the Democratic People's Republic of Korea (DPRK). In March 1993 the DPRK, which is a signatory of the Nuclear Non-proliferation Treaty and is subject, by virtue of its membership of the IAEA (see p. 66), to the monitoring of its nuclear installations, refused to grant the IAEA inspectorate full access to its nuclear power facility. It cited as its reasons the existence of joint military exercises between the Republic of Korea and the USA and 'unjust acts' by the IAEA. The US Government stated that it had reason to suspect that the DPRK had been diverting nuclear plant material for the development of atomic weapons. In July Clinton visited the Republic of Korea, and warned the DPRK that any use of nuclear weapons by them would mean the end of their country. He reiterated that the USA would maintain its military presence in the Republic of Korea. Despite increasing international pressure (from which the People's Republic of China remained aloof), and attempts at mediation by the UN, the DPRK repeatedly asserted its refusal to comply with the treaty's inspection requirements. The crisis steadily worsened during early 1994, and in June the US Government, after seeking unsuccessfully to offer the DPRK economic aid, investment and diplomatic recognition, began to seek support for the imposition of UN economic sanctions. Later in the same month, following a visit to the DPRK by ex-President Carter (acting as an unofficial representative of the Government), the DPRK agreed to a temporary suspension of its nuclear programme, pending formal discussions with the US Government. These meetings were convened in July. Negotiations aimed at improving relations between the USA and the DPRK, and at fostering a political settlement between the DPRK and the Republic of Korea, were continuing in 1995. It was reported in June that the Governments of the USA and the DPRK had reached an effective agreement on measures to curtail the nuclear programme of the DPRK.

In September 1993 the President announced his proposals for the reform of health care, under which universal coverage was to be available for medical and hospital care. The plan, which was estimated to cost $350,000m. over a seven-year period, was opposed by the American Medical Association, the private health insurance sector and by many employers, who, under its provisions, were to be responsible for 80% of employees' insurance premiums. Congressional opposition to the plan, however, resulted in substantial amendments to the Clinton proposals, and to the effective removal of provisions for federal subsidies. Subsequent efforts to formulate compromise legislation were eventually abandoned in September 1994.

During 1993 and 1994 the personal integrity of both the President and his wife was challenged by accusations of financial irregularities in their alleged involvement in a savings bank and property development company that collapsed in 1989, during Clinton's tenure as Governor of Arkansas. These allegations, which were strenuously denied by the Clintons, were made the subject of official investigations, which remained unresolved in mid-1995. Related allegations of involvement in the affair, however, resulted in the resignations of five senior presidential appointees during 1993 and 1994, and proved politically damaging to Clinton. In October 1994 a sixth official, the Secretary of Agriculture, resigned following accusations of unethical financial dealings during Clinton's state governorship.

The collapse of plans for health care reform, together with increasing public concern about the domestic economy and the effectiveness of Clinton's policies on social issues (notably in the areas of welfare expenditure, law enforcement, and the protection of traditional social values), led in 1994 to a sharp rise in support for the conservative doctrines of politicians representing the right wing of the Republican Party. At congressional elections held in November, the Republicans gained control both of the Senate (for the first time since 1986) and the House of Representatives (which had been controlled by the Democrats since 1954). At state level, the Democrats lost 11 governorships to Republican candidates.

The new congressional leadership declared its intention of implementing a 'Contract with America', which encompassed a range of measures aimed at narrowing the range of federal social programmes, reducing taxation and balancing the federal budget by the year 2002. In its social policies, the 'Contract' proposed substantial reductions in welfare programmes and the transfer to state governments of responsibilities for many federally-funded services. President Clinton, in an attempt to reach a consensus with the Republicans, proposed a 'New Covenant', promoting increased individual responsibility, less involvement by federal government, and agreeing to co-operate in an overhaul of the welfare system.

In February 1995, however, clear divisions began to emerge between the President and Congress, when Clinton threatened to veto foreign policy legislation on the grounds that it violated the President's constitutional prerogatives in foreign relations and defence. Attempts to legislate for a mandatory balanced budget were defeated in Congress, as was a proposal to impose limits on the tenure of members of the Senate and House of Representatives. An important agreement was reached, however, under which the President obtained the right to veto individual provisions in fiscal legislation without being obliged to reject the entire bill. By mid-1995, however, no agreement had been reached on the provisions of the 1995/96 federal budget.

The interlinked issues of political terrorism and the private possession of firearms (which is constitutionally guaranteed) came to the fore in April 1995, when 167 lives were lost in the terrorist bombing of a federal building in Oklahoma City. Initial investigations suggested the complicity of paramilitary groups whose supporters accuse the federal government of conducting a conspiracy to deprive them of individual and constitutional freedoms.

In foreign affairs, the Clinton administration has continued to support economic reform in Russia and the successor states of the former USSR, with particular emphasis on fostering the change-over from defence to consumer production. The US Government has, however, expressed disapproval of the scale of Russian military operations in Chechnya, and in May 1995 the Clinton administration was refused Russian co-operation in its ban on US trade and investment in Iran, in retaliation for that country's alleged involvement in international terrorism. The reluctance of the Clinton administration to participate directly in UN military operations in Bosnia and Herzegovina was modified in June 1995 with a statement by Clinton that US ground troops would be sent to Bosnia in 'emergency'

# THE UNITED STATES OF AMERICA

circumstances on a 'limited basis' if required to assist in the redeployment of existing UN forces, or to participate in monitoring an eventual peace settlement. In the same month, the President renewed enhanced trading privileges for China for a further year. The US Government has remained unwilling to restore relations with Cuba, with which a crisis over mass immigrant migrations arose in August 1994. In January 1995 the USA led an international financial consortium to provide substantial loan guarantees to resolve a major financial crisis in Mexico. In the previous month President Clinton proposed the formation by 2006 of a 'Free Trade Area of the Americas', comprising 34 countries of the Western Hemisphere.

## Government

The USA is a federal republic. Each of the 50 constituent states and the District of Columbia exercises a measure of internal self-government. Defence, foreign affairs, coinage, posts, the higher levels of justice, and internal security are the responsibility of the federal government. The President is head of the executive and is elected for a four-year term by a college of representatives elected directly from each state. The President appoints the other members of the executive, subject to the consent of the Senate. The Congress is the seat of legislative power and consists of the Senate (100 members) and the House of Representatives (435 members). Two senators are chosen by direct election in each state, to serve a six-year term, and one-third of the membership is renewable every two years. Representatives are elected by direct and universal suffrage for a two-year term. The number of representatives of each state in Congress is determined by the size of the state's population. Ultimate judicial power is vested in the Supreme Court, which has the power to disallow legislation and to overturn executive actions which it deems unconstitutional.

## Defence

In June 1994 US armed forces totalled 1,650,500: army 559,900, air force 433,800, navy 482,800 and 174,000 marine corps. There are also active reservists numbering 1,839,400. Military conscription ended in 1973. The Strategic Air Command and Polaris nuclear submarines are equipped with nuclear weapons. The USA is a member of the NATO alliance. Defence expenditure for 1993/94 totalled $281,563m., and proposed expenditure for 1994/95 was $271,600m. (some 17.6% of total federal budgetary expenditure).

## Economic Affairs

In 1993, according to estimates by the World Bank, the USA's gross national product (GNP), measured at average 1991–93 prices, was US $6,387,686m., equivalent to $24,750 per head. During 1985–93, it was estimated, GNP per head increased, in real terms, at an average annual rate of 1.2%. Over the same period, the population increased by an annual average of 0.9%. The USA's gross domestic product (GDP) increased, in real terms, by an average of 2.6% per year in 1980–90, but declined by 1.2% in 1991. Real GDP rose by 3.3% in 1992, by 3.1% in 1993 and by 4.1% in 1994.

Agriculture (including forestry and fishing) contributed 1.9% of GDP in 1991. About 2.9% of the working population were employed in this sector in 1994. The principal crops are hay, potatoes, sugar beet and citrus fruit, which, together with cereals, cotton and tobacco, are important export crops. The principal livestock are cattle, pigs and poultry. The agricultural sector provided 7.0% of total exports in 1992. Agricultural production declined at an average annual rate of 3.9% in 1985–88, but increased by 8.1% in 1989 and by 3.1% in 1990. It fell by 0.4% in 1991, but rose by 8.5% in 1992, but declined by 8.4% in 1993.

Industry (including mining, manufacturing, construction and utilities) provided 26.2% of GDP in 1991, and employed 24.0% of the working population in 1994. Industrial output (excluding construction) rose at an average annual rate of 2.7% during 1980–90, but fell by 1.9% in 1991. Production increased by 1.5% in 1992, by 2.1% in 1993 and by 6.1% in 1994.

Mining and quarrying contributed 1.6% of GDP in 1991, and employed 0.5% of the working population in 1994. The USA's principal mineral deposits are of petroleum, natural gas, coal, copper, iron, silver and uranium. The mining sector accounted for 2.1% of total exports in 1992. The output of the sector declined at an average annual rate of 0.8% during 1980–91.

*Introductory Survey*

Manufacturing contributed 17.8% of GDP in 1991, and employed 16.2% of the working population in 1994. In 1991 the principal branches (measured by value of output) were transport equipment (13.5% of the total), food products (12.0%), chemical products (10.6%), machinery, electrical goods, petroleum refineries, printing and publishing and metal products. Manufacturing provided 90.9% of total exports in 1992. The output of the sector increased at an average annual rate of 3.3% during 1980–90, but declined by about 2% in 1991.

Energy is derived principally from domestic and imported hydrocarbons. In 1992 imports of petroleum amounted to 9.5% of total import costs. In 1993 nuclear power provided 21.2% of the total electricity supply.

Services provided 71.9% of GDP in 1991 and 73.1% of total employment in 1994. The combined GDP of all service sectors rose, in real terms, at an average rate of 3.0% per year during 1980–90, but by only 0.9% in 1991.

In 1994 the USA recorded a visible trade deficit of $166,364m. (excluding military trasnactions), and there was a deficit of $155,673m. on the current account of the balance of payments. The USA's principal export market and main source of imports in 1992 was Canada, with which a free trade agreement came into force in January 1989, providing for the progressive elimination, over a 10-year period, of virtually all trade tariffs between the two countries. In 1992 Canada accounted for 20.2% of total US exports and 18.5% of total imports. Japan was the second-largest trading partner (providing 18.3% of US imports in 1992), but the imbalance in its trade with the USA (Japan accounted for 10.7% of the USA's exports in 1992) has been a source of friction between the two countries in recent years. Other major trading partners include Mexico, the United Kingdom, Germany and other members of the European Union (EU). In 1992 machinery and transport equipment constituted the principal category of exports (accounting for 48.1% of the total) and of imports (43.6%).

In the financial year ending 30 September 1994 there was an estimated federal budget deficit of $203,169m. (3.4% of GDP). The annual rate of inflation averaged 3.7% in 1980–90, increasing to 5.4% in 1990, and declining to 4.2% in 1991, 3.0% per year in 1992 and 1993 and 2.6% in 1994. The rate of unemployment averaged 5.5% of the labour force in 1990, 6.7% in 1991, 7.4% in 1992 and 6.8% in 1993. In 1994 the unemployment rate averaged 6.1%.

During the 1980s the growth in the US trade deficit, together with a rising trend in federal government expenditure (particularly in the sphere of defence), led to increasing levels of indebtedness. The USA is the world's leading debtor, with the Federal Government's foreign debt reaching $653,900m. at 30 September 1994. The depreciation of the US dollar in relation to other major world currencies led to an increase in foreign acquisitions of US assets, which created disquiet in US business circles. At the end of 1993 an estimated $2,926,162m. of US assets were foreign-owned, compared with $2,370,427m. of US-owned assets overseas. The persistently adverse balance-of-payments position has revived the question of trade protectionism, particularly in relation to imports of advanced-technology and electronic equipment from Japan, Taiwan and the Republic of Korea, and of agricultural produce from the EU. Following the 1989 trade agreement with Canada, the US Government undertook discussions with Mexico, aimed at the eventual conclusion of a full North American Free Trade Agreement (NAFTA, see p. 190), covering an area with a population of more than 360m. These negotiations, which began formally in June 1991, were concluded in December 1992 with the signing of an agreement. Following legislative ratification in December 1993, NAFTA arrangements, under which tariffs were to be eliminated over a 15-year period, entered into operation in January 1994.

## Social Welfare

Provision of welfare and medical services is being progressively standardized and extended by federal legislation. Despite opposition from the medical profession, there is now available a far more comprehensive scheme of publicly-funded medical care. Provision by employers of health insurance for employees is mandatory. In 1992 the USA had 653,062 registered physicians (39.1 per 10,000 of population). In 1986 there were 6,841 hospitals, with 1,283,000 beds (one for every 188 people). Of total expenditure by the Federal Government in the financial year 1993/94, $251,869m. (17.2%) was for health, and a further $533,601m. (36.5%) for social security and welfare. Spending on health and social welfare at state and local government level in 1990/91 was about $208,075m. (19.6% of total state and local government expenditure).

### Education

Education is primarily the responsibility of state and local governments, but some federal funds are available to help meet special needs at primary, secondary and higher education levels. Public education is free in every state from elementary school through high school. The period of compulsory education varies among states, but most states require attendance between the ages of seven and 16 years. At the beginning of the 1992/93 academic year there were 27.9m. pupils enrolled in public primary schools and 14.8m. in public secondary schools. Private school enrolment was approximately 4.2m. at primary level and about 1.2m. at secondary level. There were more than 3,600 two-year and four-year universities and colleges, with a total enrolment of about 14.5m. students at the beginning of the 1992/93 academic year. Federal government expenditure on educational programmes administered by the US Department of Education totalled approximately $31,500m. in 1992/93. Spending on education by all levels of government in 1990/91 was $329,494m. (13.8% of total public expenditure).

### Public Holidays*

**1995:** 1 January (New Year's Day), 16 January (Martin Luther King Day), 20 February (Presidents' Day), 29 May (Memorial Day), 4 July (Independence Day), 4 September (Labor Day), 9 October (Columbus Day), 11 November (Veterans' Day), 23 November (Thanksgiving Day), 25 December (Christmas Day).

**1996:** 1 January (New Year's Day), 15 January (Martin Luther King Day), 19 February (Presidents' Day), 27 May (Memorial Day), 4 July (Independence Day), 2 September (Labor Day), 14 October (Columbus Day), 11 November (Veterans' Day), 28 November (Thanksgiving Day), 25 December (Christmas Day).

* Federal legal public holidays are designated by presidential proclamation or congressional enactment, but need not be observed in individual states, which have legal jurisdiction over their public holidays.

### Weights and Measures

With certain exceptions, the imperial system is in force. One US billion equals 1,000 million; one US cwt equals 100 lb; long ton equals 2,240 lb; short ton equals 2,000 lb. A policy of gradual voluntary conversion to the metric system is being encouraged.

# Statistical Survey

## Area and Population

Source (unless otherwise stated): Statistical Information Office, Population Division, Bureau of the Census, US Department of Commerce, Washington, DC 20233-0001.

### AREA, POPULATION AND DENSITY

| | |
|---|---:|
| Area (sq km) | 9,809,155* |
| Population (census results)† | |
| 1 April 1980 | 226,545,805 |
| 1 April 1990 | |
| Males | 121,239,418 |
| Females | 127,470,455 |
| Total | 248,709,873 |
| Population (official estimates at mid-year)‡ | |
| 1992 | 255,028,000 |
| 1993 | 257,783,000 |
| 1994 | 260,341,000 |
| Density (per sq km) at mid-1994 | 26.5 |

* This is the official US equivalent of 3,787,319 sq miles, assuming a conversion factor of 1 sq mile = 2.59 sq km, a rounded version of the internationally accepted standard of 1 sq mile = 2.5899881 sq km.
† Excluding adjustment for underenumeration.
‡ Estimates of the resident population, based on 1990 census results (excluding adjustment for underenumeration).

**RACES** (1990 census)

| | Male | Female | Total | % |
|---|---:|---:|---:|---:|
| White | 97,475,880 | 102,210,190 | 199,686,070 | 80.29 |
| Black | 14,170,151 | 15,815,909 | 29,986,060 | 12.06 |
| Asian and Pacific Islanders | 3,558,038 | 3,715,624 | 7,273,662 | 2.92 |
| American Indian, Eskimo and Aleut | 967,186 | 992,048 | 1,959,234 | 0.79 |
| Others | 5,068,163 | 4,736,684 | 9,804,847 | 3.94 |
| **Total** | 121,239,418 | 127,470,455 | 248,709,873 | 100.00 |

# THE UNITED STATES OF AMERICA

*Statistical Survey*

## STATES

| State | Gross Area (Land and water) (sq km) | Resident population* mid-1993 estimates ('000) |
|---|---|---|
| Alabama | 135,775 | 4,219 |
| Alaska | 1,700,138 | 606 |
| Arizona | 295,276 | 4,075 |
| Arkansas | 137,742 | 2,453 |
| California | 424,002 | 31,431 |
| Colorado | 269,618 | 3,656 |
| Connecticut | 14,358 | 3,275 |
| Delaware | 6,448 | 706 |
| District of Columbia | 177 | 570 |
| Florida | 170,314 | 13,953 |
| Georgia | 153,952 | 7,055 |
| Hawaii | 28,313 | 1,179 |
| Idaho | 216,456 | 1,133 |
| Illinois | 150,007 | 11,752 |
| Indiana | 94,328 | 5,752 |
| Iowa | 145,754 | 2,829 |
| Kansas | 213,111 | 2,554 |
| Kentucky | 104,665 | 3,827 |
| Louisiana | 134,275 | 4,315 |
| Maine | 91,653 | 1,240 |
| Maryland | 32,134 | 5,006 |
| Massachusetts | 27,337 | 6,041 |
| Michigan | 250,465 | 9,496 |
| Minnesota | 225,182 | 4,567 |
| Mississippi | 125,443 | 2,669 |
| Missouri | 180,546 | 5,278 |
| Montana | 380,850 | 856 |
| Nebraska | 200,358 | 1,623 |
| Nevada | 286,367 | 1,457 |
| New Hampshire | 24,219 | 1,137 |
| New Jersey | 22,590 | 7,904 |
| New Mexico | 314,939 | 1,654 |
| New York | 141,080 | 18,169 |
| North Carolina | 139,397 | 7,070 |
| North Dakota | 183,123 | 638 |
| Ohio | 116,103 | 11,102 |
| Oklahoma | 181,048 | 3,258 |
| Oregon | 254,819 | 3,086 |
| Pennsylvania | 119,291 | 12,052 |
| Rhode Island | 4,002 | 997 |
| South Carolina | 82,902 | 3,664 |
| South Dakota | 199,744 | 721 |
| Tennessee | 109,158 | 5,175 |
| Texas | 695,676 | 18,378 |
| Utah | 219,902 | 1,908 |
| Vermont | 24,903 | 580 |
| Virginia | 110,792 | 6,552 |
| Washington | 184,672 | 5,343 |
| West Virginia | 62,759 | 1,822 |
| Wisconsin | 169,643 | 5,082 |
| Wyoming | 253,349 | 476 |
| **Total** | 9,809,155 | 260,341 |

* Includes armed forces residing in each State.

## PRINCIPAL CITIES (estimated population at mid-1992)

| | | | | |
|---|---|---|---|---|
| New York | 7,311,966 | | New Orleans | 489,595 |
| Los Angeles | 3,489,779 | | Denver | 483,852 |
| Chicago | 2,768,483 | | Fort Worth | 454,430 |
| Houston | 1,690,180 | | Oklahoma City | 453,995 |
| Philadelphia | 1,552,572 | | Portland, OR | 445,458 |
| San Diego | 1,148,851 | | Long Beach, CA | 438,771 |
| Dallas | 1,022,497 | | Kansas City, MO | 431,553 |
| Phoenix | 1,012,230 | | Virginia Beach, VA | 417,061 |
| Detroit | 1,012,110 | | Charlotte | 416,294 |
| San Antonio | 966,437 | | Tucson | 415,079 |
| San Jose | 801,331 | | Albuquerque | 398,492 |
| Indianapolis | 746,538 | | Atlanta | 394,848 |
| San Francisco | 728,921 | | St Louis | 383,733 |
| Baltimore | 726,096 | | Sacramento | 382,816 |
| Jacksonville | 661,177 | | Fresno | 376,130 |
| Columbus, OH | 642,987 | | Tulsa | 375,307 |
| Milwaukee | 617,043 | | Oakland | 373,219 |
| Memphis | 610,275 | | Honolulu | 371,320 |
| Washington, DC (capital) | 585,221 | | Miami | 367,016 |
| Boston | 551,675 | | Pittsburgh | 366,852 |
| El Paso | 543,813 | | Cincinnati | 364,278 |
| Seattle | 519,598 | | Minneapolis | 362,696 |
| Cleveland | 502,539 | | Omaha | 339,671 |
| Nashville-Davidson | 495,012 | | Toledo | 329,325 |
| Austin | 492,329 | | Buffalo | 323,284 |
| | | | Wichita | 311,746 |

## BIRTHS, MARRIAGES, DEATHS

| | Registered live births | | Registered marriages | | Registered deaths | |
|---|---|---|---|---|---|---|
| | Number ('000) | Rate (per 1,000) | Number ('000) | Rate (per 1,000) | Number ('000) | Rate (per 1,000) |
| 1986 | 3,731 | 15.5 | 2,400 | 10.0 | 2,099 | 8.7 |
| 1987 | 3,829 | 15.7 | 2,421 | 9.9 | 2,127 | 8.7 |
| 1988 | 3,913 | 15.9 | 2,389 | 9.7 | 2,171 | 8.8 |
| 1989 | 4,021 | 16.2 | 2,404 | 9.7 | 2,155 | 8.7 |
| 1990 | 4,179 | 16.7 | 2,448 | 9.8 | 2,162 | 8.6 |
| 1991 | 4,111 | 16.3 | 2,371 | 9.4 | 2,165 | 8.6 |
| 1992 | 4,084 | 16.0 | 2,362 | 9.3 | 2,177 | 8.5 |
| 1993 | 4,039 | 15.7 | 2,353 | 9.2 | 2,268 | 8.8 |

**Expectation of life** (years at birth, 1993): males 72.1; females 78.9.

Source: National Center for Health Statistics, US Department of Health and Human Services.

# THE UNITED STATES OF AMERICA

*Statistical Survey*

**IMMIGRATION** (year ending 30 September)

| Country of last permanent residence | 1991 | 1992 | 1993 |
|---|---|---|---|
| All countries* | 1,827,167 | 973,977 | 904,292 |
| Europe | 153,234 | 145,392 | 165,711 |
| Austria | 589 | 701 | 1,880 |
| France | 2,450 | 3,288 | 3,959 |
| Germany | 6,509 | 9,888 | 9,965 |
| Greece | 2,079 | 1,858 | 2,460 |
| Ireland (excl. N. Ireland) | 4,767 | 12,226 | 13,396 |
| Italy | 2,619 | 2,592 | 3,899 |
| Netherlands | 1,283 | 1,586 | 1,542 |
| Poland | 19,199 | 25,504 | 27,288 |
| Portugal | 4,524 | 2,748 | 2,075 |
| Romania | 8,096 | 6,500 | 4,517 |
| Spain | 1,849 | 1,631 | 1,791 |
| Sweden | 1,080 | 1,463 | 1,540 |
| Switzerland | 696 | 1,023 | 1,263 |
| USSR (former) | 56,980 | 43,614 | 59,949 |
| United Kingdom | 13,909 | 20,148 | 20,422 |
| Yugoslavia | 2,713 | 2,604 | 2,781 |
| Asia | 358,533 | 356,955 | 345,525 |
| Cambodia | 3,251 | 2,573 | 450 |
| China (incl. Taiwan) | 46,229 | 55,251 | 73,532 |
| Hong Kong | 10,427 | 10,452 | 14,026 |
| India | 45,064 | 36,755 | 38,653 |
| Iran | 19,569 | 13,233 | 8,908 |
| Korea, Repub. | 26,518 | 19,359 | 17,320 |
| Laos | 9,950 | 8,696 | 2,831 |
| Philippines | 63,596 | 61,022 | 63,406 |
| Thailand | 7,397 | 7,090 | 36,205 |
| Viet Nam | 55,307 | 77,735 | 31,894 |
| North and South America | 1,401,468 | 496,913 | 361,476 |
| Argentina | 3,889 | 3,877 | 2,972 |
| Brazil | 8,133 | 4,755 | 4,759 |
| Canada | 13,504 | 15,205 | 23,898 |
| Colombia | 19,702 | 13,201 | 12,597 |
| Cuba | 10,349 | 11,791 | 12,976 |
| Dominican Repub. | 41,405 | 41,969 | 45,464 |
| Ecuador | 9,958 | 7,286 | 7,400 |
| El Salvador | 47,351 | 26,191 | 26,794 |
| Guatemala | 25,527 | 10,521 | 11,990 |
| Guyana | 11,666 | 9,064 | 7,809 |
| Haiti | 47,527 | 11,002 | 9,899 |
| Jamaica | 23,828 | 18,915 | 16,761 |
| Mexico | 946,167 | 213,802 | 126,642 |
| Panama | 4,204 | 2,845 | 3,088 |
| Peru | 16,237 | 9,868 | 10,302 |
| Trinidad and Tobago | 8,407 | 7,008 | 6,577 |
| Africa | 36,179 | 27,086 | 25,532 |
| Australia and New Zealand | 2,471 | 3,205 | 4,454 |
| Other Oceania | 3,765 | 1,964 | 1,690 |
| Not specified | 70 | 18 | 4 |

* Figures include previously illegal aliens granted permanent resident status: 1,123,162 in 1991; 163,342 in 1992; 24,278 in 1993.

Source: Immigration and Naturalization Service, US Department of Justice.

**ECONOMICALLY ACTIVE POPULATION**
(annual averages, '000 persons aged 16 and over)

|  | 1992 | 1993 | 1994 |
|---|---|---|---|
| Agriculture, forestry and fisheries | 3,379 | 3,257 | 3,586 |
| Mining | 664 | 669 | 669 |
| Manufacturing | 19,972 | 19,557 | 20,157 |
| Electricity, gas and water | 1,618 | 1,597 | 1,545 |
| Construction | 7,013 | 7,220 | 7,493 |
| Wholesale and retail trade | 24,354 | 24,769 | 25,699 |
| Transport, storage and communications | 6,627 | 6,884 | 7,147 |
| Finance, insurance and real estate | 7,764 | 7,962 | 8,141 |
| Private households | 1,127 | 1,114 | 976 |
| Business and repair services | 6,553 | 6,838 | 7,304 |
| Personal services | 3,273 | 3,329 | 3,363 |
| Medical services (incl. hospitals) | 10,271 | 10,553 | 10,588 |
| Educational services | 9,201 | 9,485 | 9,703 |
| Other private services | 10,161 | 10,315 | 10,874 |
| Public administration | 5,620 | 5,756 | 5,814 |
| **Civilian employment** | 117,598 | 119,306 | 123,060 |
| Resident armed forces | 1,566 | 1,485 | 1,413 |
| **Total employment** | 119,164 | 120,791 | 124,473 |
| Unemployed | 9,384 | 8,734 | 7,996 |
| **Total labour force** | 128,548 | 129,525 | 132,469 |

Source: Bureau of Labor Statistics, US Department of Labor.

# Agriculture

**PRINCIPAL CROPS** (production in harvest units*)

|  | 1992 | 1993 | 1994 |
|---|---|---|---|
| Maize (Corn) (million bushels)† | 9,477 | 6,336 | 10,103 |
| Wheat (million bushels) | 2,467 | 2,396 | 2,321 |
| Oats (million bushels) | 294 | 207 | 230 |
| Barley (million bushels) | 455 | 398 | 375 |
| Rice (million lb) | 17,966 | 15,611 | 19,778 |
| Sorghum (million bushels)† | 875 | 534 | 655 |
| Cotton lint (million bales) | 16.2 | 16.1 | 19.7 |
| Cottonseed ('000 short tons) | 6,230 | 6,343 | 7,669 |
| Hay ('000 short tons) | 146,903 | 146,799 | 150,124 |
| Dry beans (million lb) | 2,262 | 2,191 | 2,919 |
| Soybeans (million bushels) | 2,190 | 1,871 | 2,558 |
| Potatoes (million lb) | 42,537 | 42,869 | 45,934 |
| Tobacco (million lb) | 1,722 | 1,614 | 1,593 |
| Peanuts (million lb) | 4,284 | 3,392 | 4,265 |
| Sugar beet ('000 short tons) | 29,143 | 26,249 | 32,008 |
| Rye (million bushels) | 11.4 | 10.3 | 11.1 |
| Apples (million lb) | 10,578.5 | 10,715.8 | 10,909.3 |
| Peaches (million lb) | 2,659.0 | 2,652.9 | 2,506.5 |
| Pears ('000 tons) | 926.1 | 949.3 | 1,036.2 |
| Grapes ('000 tons) | 6,051.9 | 6,026.2 | 5,927.6 |
| Oranges and tangerines‡ ('000 boxes) | 215,850 | 261,610 | 246,650 |
| Grapefruit‡ ('000 boxes) | 55,265 | 68,375 | 64,900 |
| Lemons‡ ('000 boxes) | 20,200 | 24,800 | 25,900 |

* A bushel is equal to 56 lb (25.4 kg) for maize; 60 lb (27.2 kg) for wheat and soybeans; 32 lb (14.5 kg) for oats; 48 lb (21.8 kg) for barley. A bale of cotton is 500 lb (226.8 kg) gross, 480 lb (217.7 kg) net.
† Figures relate to crops harvested for grain only.
‡ Production during season ending in year stated.

**LIVESTOCK** ('000 head at 1 January)

|  | 1993 | 1994* | 1995* |
|---|---|---|---|
| Cattle | 99,175 | 100,988 | 103,265 |
| Pigs† | 58,202 | 57,904 | 59,612 |
| Sheep | 10,201 | 9,742 | 8,895 |
| Chickens† | 371,483 | 379,640 | 383,779 |

* Preliminary.
† At 1 December of the preceding year.

# THE UNITED STATES OF AMERICA

**LIVESTOCK PRODUCTS** (million lb)

|  | 1991 | 1992 | 1993 |
|---|---|---|---|
| Beef | 22,917 | 23,086 | 23,049 |
| Veal | 306 | 311 | 286 |
| Lamb and mutton | 362 | 349 | 337 |
| Pork | 16,000 | 17,233 | 17,087 |
| Eggs (million) | 69,465 | 70,749 | 71,936 |

Source (for all Agriculture tables): Agricultural Statistics Board, US Department of Agriculture, Washington, DC 20250-2000.

## Forestry

**ROUNDWOOD REMOVALS** (million cu feet)

|  | 1988 | 1989* | 1990* |
|---|---|---|---|
| Industrial | 15,680 | 15,625 | 15,165 |
| Coniferous (soft wood) | 11,520 | 11,440 | 11,015 |
| Broadleaved (hard wood) | 4,160 | 4,185 | 4,150 |
| Fuel wood | 3,300 | 3,395 | 2,930 |
| **Total** | 18,980 | 19,020 | 18,095 |

* Preliminary.

**LUMBER PRODUCTION**
(sawnwood and railway sleepers, million board feet)

|  | 1990 | 1991 | 1992* |
|---|---|---|---|
| Soft wood | 35,791 | 33,161 | 34,118 |
| Hard wood | 10,704 | 10,213 | 11,176 |
| **Total** | 46,495 | 43,374 | 45,294 |

* Preliminary.

Source (for all Forestry tables): Forest Service, US Department of Agriculture, Washington, DC 20090-6090.

## Fishing*

(million lb, live weight)

|  | 1991 | 1992 | 1993 |
|---|---|---|---|
| Atlantic cod | 92.6 | 61.3 | 52.0 |
| Pacific cod | 553.7 | 550.5 | 482.8 |
| Flounders | 405.0 | 645.8 | 599.1 |
| Pacific hake | 56.0 | 123.7 | 310.2 |
| Halibut | 66.3 | 68.6 | 63.1 |
| Atlantic herring | 134.2 | 123.0 | 109.6 |
| Pacific herring | 123.1 | 159.1 | 106.6 |
| Pacific mackerel | 63.3 | 41.9 | 24.1 |
| Atlantic menhaden | 876.4 | 690.1 | 766.8 |
| Gulf menhaden | 1,214.1 | 954.3 | 1,216.5 |
| Alaska pollock | 2,855.3 | 2,952.1 | 3,258.0 |
| Rockfishes | 97.5 | 125.1 | 120.7 |
| Sablefish | 83.6 | 75.5 | 77.5 |
| Chum (Keta) salmon | 76.2 | 90.4 | 90.4 |
| Pink (Humpback) salmon | 362.8 | 203.7 | 343.1 |
| Red (Sockeye) salmon | 268.8 | 346.6 | 394.9 |
| Silver (Coho) salmon | 55.4 | 57.3 | 41.0 |
| Skipjack tuna | 391.5 | 9.3 | 11.5 |
| Yellowfin tuna | 105.6 | 23.6 | 18.2 |
| Whiting | 36.5 | 35.9 | 35.7 |
| **Total fish** (incl. others) | 8,645.0 | 8,174.2 | 8,999.0 |
| Clams | 134.2 | 142.4 | 147.8 |
| Crabs | 650.0 | 624.3 | 604.4 |
| Lobsters | 70.4 | 60.7 | 62.6 |
| Oysters | 31.9 | 36.2 | 33.6 |
| Scallops | 40.0 | 33.9 | 18.6 |
| Shrimps | 320.1 | 337.8 | 292.9 |
| Squids | 139.6 | 111.4 | 162.4 |
| Other shellfish, etc. | 110.1 | 115.5 | 145.5 |
| **Total catch** | 10,141.3 | 9,637.3 | 10,446.9 |

* Figures refer to the total catch (excl. weight of mollusc shells) by US flag vessels, wherever landed.

Source: National Marine Fisheries Service, US Department of Commerce.

## Mining

('000 metric tons, unless otherwise indicated)

|  | 1992 | 1993 | 1993* |
|---|---|---|---|
| Phosphate rock | 46,965 | 35,494 | 41,000 |
| Sulphur | 2,320 | 1,904 | 2,700 |
| Gypsum | 14,759 | 15,812 | 17.300 |
| Lead | 407 | 362 | 365 |
| Zinc | 523 | 488 | 540 |
| Copper | 1,760 | 1,800 | 1,840 |
| Gold ('000 troy oz) | 10,610 | 10,642 | 10,610 |
| Silver (metric tons) | 1,804 | 1,645 | 1,400 |
| Molybdenum (metric tons) | 49,725 | 36,803 | 40,000 |

* Provisional.

Source: Bureau of Mines, US Department of the Interior.

Coal (million short tons): 997.5 (bituminous and lignite 994.1, anthracite 3.5) in 1992; 412.6 in 1993.
Crude petroleum (million metric tons): 412.6 in 1992; 402.8 in 1993.
Iron ore ('000 metric tons, usable ore): 55,600 in 1992; 55,700 in 1993; 40 in 1993; 57,000 in 1994 (the average iron content is about 63%).
Bauxite (estimates, '000 metric tons): 45 in 1992; 40 in 1993.
Uranium (metric tons): 1,808 in 1992; 1,192 in 1993.
Natural gas (petajoules): 19,379.3 in 1992; 20,042.5 in 1993.

# THE UNITED STATES OF AMERICA

## Industry

**PRINCIPAL MANUFACTURES** (value added—$ million)

|  | 1990 | 1991 | 1992 |
|---|---|---|---|
| Food and kindred products | 140,972.8 | 145,336.0 | 156,843.4 |
| Beverages | 4,118.2 | 3,814.8 | 29,065.0 |
| Tobacco products | 22,561.3 | 24,484.4 | 27,167.1 |
| Textile mill products | 26,541.6 | 26,925.0 | 29,862.1 |
| Apparel and other textile products | 33,034.0 | 33,432.1 | 36,357.0 |
| Lumber and wood products | 28,597.2 | 26,994.9 | 33,352.4 |
| Furniture and fixtures | 21,644.7 | 20,668.9 | 22,820.8 |
| Paper and allied products | 59,823.3 | 58,280.7 | 59,992.7 |
| Printing and publishing | 103,179.0 | 103,770.8 | 113,244.3 |
| Newspapers | 26,559.6 | 26,092.7 | 27,263.6 |
| Chemicals and allied products | 153,032.4 | 154,792.6 | 165,134.8 |
| Petroleum and coal products | 27,214.1 | 24,023.6 | 23,792.7 |
| Petroleum refining | 22,822.0 | 19,795.7 | 19,103.9 |
| Rubber and plastic products | 49,889.0 | 50,295.3 | 58,477.0 |
| Leather and products | 4,586.6 | 4,292.9 | 4,516.7 |
| Stone, clay and glass products | 34,140.2 | 31,839.2 | 34,577.8 |
| Primary metal industries | 53,366.6 | 46,604.9 | 51,816.4 |
| Iron and steel foundries | 6,691.5 | 6,193.9 | 6,915.9 |
| Non-ferrous rolling and drawing | 11,832.5 | 10,955.5 | 12,123.9 |
| Fabricated metal products | 79,951.9 | 76,669.6 | 83,870.8 |
| Structural metal products | 19,934.5 | 19,313.1 | 21,403.1 |
| Machinery, excluding electrical | 132,165.8 | 124,235.3 | 132,143.6 |
| Construction | 13,928.0 | 12,530.7 | 12,668.3 |
| Metalworking | 16,515.6 | 15,514.5 | 16,508.4 |
| General industrial | 16,811.0 | 16,832.4 | 17,953.6 |
| Electronic and other electric equipment | 106,983.9 | 106,669.0 | 121,949.6 |
| Household appliances | 7,835.9 | 7,412.7 | 7,816.5 |
| Communications equipment | 22,349.7 | 21,286.3 | 26,992.8 |
| Transport equipment | 146,916.3 | 151,978.5 | 161,058.4 |
| Motor vehicles | 69,648.7 | 73,332.6 | 80,524.5 |
| Aircraft and parts | 44,903.2 | 49,046.3 | 49,279.1 |
| Instruments and related products | 81,665.6 | 82,535.9 | 89,805.8 |
| Miscellaneous manufactures, incl. ordnance | 20,095.6 | 19,999.0 | 22,009.7 |

Source: Bureau of the Census, US Department of Commerce, *Annual Survey of Manufactures*.

## Finance

### CURRENCY AND EXCHANGE RATES

**Monetary Units**
100 cents = 1 United States dollar ($).

**Sterling Equivalents** (31 December 1994)
£1 sterling = US $1.5645;
US $100 = £63.92.

**FEDERAL BUDGET** ($ million, year ending 30 September)

| Revenue* | 1994 | 1995† | 1996† |
|---|---|---|---|
| Individual income taxes | 543,055 | 588,460 | 623,372 |
| Corporation income taxes | 140,385 | 150,864 | 157,449 |
| Social insurance taxes and contributions | 461,475 | 484,409 | 509,315 |
| Excise taxes | 55,225 | 57,600 | 57,194 |
| Estate and gift taxes | 15,225 | 15,587 | 16,760 |
| Customs duties and fees | 20,099 | 20,913 | 22,332 |
| Miscellaneous receipts | 22,282 | 28,581 | 29,034 |
| **Total** | **1,257,745** | **1,346,414** | **1,415,456** |

| Expenditure‡ | 1994 | 1995† | 1996† |
|---|---|---|---|
| National defence | 281,563 | 271,600 | 261,424 |
| International affairs | 17,083 | 18,713 | 16,735 |
| General science, space research and technology | 16,227 | 16,977 | 16,851 |
| Energy | 5,219 | 4,589 | 4,369 |
| Natural resources and environment | 21,064 | 21,891 | 21,839 |
| Agriculture | 15,121 | 14,401 | 13,552 |
| Commerce and housing credit | −5,121 | −11,958 | −7,553 |
| Transportation | 38,134 | 39,154 | 38,639 |
| Community and regional development | 10,454 | 12,598 | 12,815 |
| Education, training, employment and social services | 46,307 | 56,065 | 57,173 |
| Health | 107,122 | 115,098 | 124,002 |
| Medicare | 144,747 | 157,288 | 177,824 |
| Income security | 214,036 | 223,006 | 233,153 |
| Social security | 319,565 | 336,149 | 354,548 |
| Veterans' benefits and services | 37,642 | 38,392 | 38,092 |
| Administration of justice | 15,256 | 17,631 | 19,732 |
| General government | 11,312 | 14,493 | 14,580 |
| Net interest | 202,957 | 234,224 | 257,001 |
| Allowances | — | — | −224 |
| Undistributed offsetting receipts | −37,772 | −41,392 | −42,424 |
| **Total** | **1,460,914** | **1,538,920** | **1,612,128** |

* Including off-budget receipts.
† Estimates at February 1995.
‡ Including off-budget federal entities and programmes.

Source: Office of Management and Budget, Executive Office of the President.

**STATE AND LOCAL GOVERNMENT FINANCES**
($ million, year ending 30 June)

| Revenue | 1989/90 | 1990/91 |
|---|---|---|
| From Federal Government | 136,802 | 154,099 |
| From State and Local Governments | 895,313 | 926,763 |
| General Revenue from own sources | 712,700 | 748,108 |
| Taxes | 501,619 | 525,355 |
| Property | 155,613 | 167,999 |
| Sales and gross receipts | 177,885 | 185,570 |
| Individual income | 105,640 | 109,341 |
| Corporation income | 23,566 | 22,242 |
| Other | 38,915 | 40,202 |
| Charges and miscellaneous | 211,081 | 222,753 |
| Utility and liquor stores | 58,642 | 60,736 |
| Insurance Trust Revenue | 123,970 | 117,919 |
| Unemployment compensation | 18,441 | 18,025 |
| Employee retirement | 94,268 | 87,206 |
| Other | 11,262 | 12,688 |
| **Total** | **1,032,115** | **1,080,862** |

# THE UNITED STATES OF AMERICA

| Expenditure | 1989/90 | 1990/91 |
|---|---|---|
| General Expenditure | 834,818 | 908,108 |
| Education | 288,148 | 309,302 |
| Local schools | 202,009 | 217,643 |
| Institutions of higher education | 73,418 | 78,749 |
| Other | 12,720 | 12,911 |
| Libraries | 4,102 | 4,442 |
| Public welfare | 110,518 | 130,402 |
| Hospitals | 50,412 | 54,404 |
| Health | 24,223 | 26,706 |
| Social insurance administration | 3,014 | 3,250 |
| Veterans' services | 152 | 157 |
| Highways | 61,057 | 64,937 |
| Other transportation | 9,571 | 10,473 |
| General public buildings | 5,643 | 6,051 |
| Housing and urban renewal | 15,479 | 16,648 |
| Police | 30,577 | 32,772 |
| Fire | 13,186 | 13,796 |
| Correction | 24,635 | 27,356 |
| Protective inspection | 5,570 | 6,008 |
| Parks and recreation | 14,326 | 15,930 |
| Sewerage and sanitation | 28,453 | 31,014 |
| Natural resources | 12,330 | 12,575 |
| General control | 22,976 | 25,415 |
| Financial administration | 16,217 | 16,995 |
| Interest on General Debt | 49,739 | 52,234 |
| Other and unallocable | 44,490 | 47,242 |
| Utility and liquor stores | 77,801 | 81,004 |
| Insurance Trust Expenditure | 63,321 | 74,159 |
| Unemployment compensation | 16,499 | 22,135 |
| Employee retirement | 38,355 | 42,121 |
| Other | 8,467 | 9,902 |
| **Total** | 975,940 | 1,063,270 |

Source: Economics and Statistics Administration, US Department of Commerce, *Government Finances*, Series GF-91 No. 5.

## CURRENCY AND COIN IN CIRCULATION*
($ million at 31 March)

| | 1992 | 1993 | 1994 |
|---|---|---|---|
| Total | 303,215 | 332,823 | 371,466 |

* Currency outside Treasury and Federal Reserve banks, including currency held by commercial banks.

Source: Financial Management Service, US Department of the Treasury.

**COST OF LIVING** (Consumer Price Index for all urban consumers, average of monthly figures. Base: 1982–84 = 100)

| | 1992 | 1993 | 1994 |
|---|---|---|---|
| Food and beverages | 138.7 | 141.6 | 144.9 |
| Housing | 137.5 | 141.2 | 144.8 |
| Rent | 146.9 | 150.3 | 154.0 |
| House ownership | 155.3 | 160.2 | 165.5 |
| Fuel and other utilities | 117.8 | 121.3 | 122.8 |
| Furnishings and maintenance | 118.0 | 119.3 | 121.0 |
| Clothes and upkeep | 131.9 | 133.7 | 133.4 |
| Transport | 126.5 | 130.4 | 134.3 |
| Medical care | 190.1 | 201.4 | 211.0 |
| Entertainment | 142.3 | 145.8 | 150.1 |
| Other goods and services | 183.3 | 192.9 | 198.5 |
| **All items** | 140.3 | 144.5 | 148.2 |

Source: Bureau of Labor Statistics, US Department of Labor.

## NATIONAL ACCOUNTS
($ '000 million at current prices)
**National Income and Product** (provisional)

| | 1990 | 1991 | 1992 |
|---|---|---|---|
| Compensation of employees | 3,313.5 | 3,418.5 | 3,597.2 |
| Operating surplus | 1,065.1 | 1,064.0 | 1,112.8 |
| **Domestic factor incomes** | 4,378.6 | 4,482.5 | 4,710.0 |
| Consumption of fixed capital | 687.5 | 714.7 | 749.1 |
| Statistical discrepancy | 7.8 | 9.6 | 23.6 |
| **Gross domestic product (GDP) at factor cost** | 5,073.9 | 5,206.8 | 5,482.7 |
| Indirect taxes | 444.0 | 476.6 | 502.8 |
| Less Subsidies | 28.3 | 28.9 | 32.1 |
| **GDP in purchasers' values** | 5,489.6 | 5,654.4 | 5,953.3 |
| Factor income received from abroad | 168.6 | 146.1 | 129.2 |
| Less Factor income paid abroad | 138.6 | 122.7 | 111.7 |
| **Gross national product (GNP)** | 5,519.6 | 5,677.8 | 5,970.8 |
| Less Consumption of fixed capital | 687.5 | 714.7 | 749.1 |
| **National income in market prices** | 4,832.1 | 4,963.1 | 5,221.5 |
| Other current transfers received from abroad | 9.2 | 47.2 | 6.2 |
| Less Other current transfers paid abroad | 38.1 | 35.8 | 39.2 |
| **National disposable income** | 4,803.2 | 4,974.5 | 5,188.7 |

Source: Bureau of Economic Analysis, US Department of Commerce.

**Expenditure on the Gross Domestic Product**

| | 1992 | 1993 | 1994 |
|---|---|---|---|
| Government final consumption expenditure | 974.7 | 993.3 | 1,014.5 |
| Private final consumption expenditure | 4,136.9 | 4,378.2 | 4,628.4 |
| Increase in stocks | 3.0 | 15.4 | 52.2 |
| Gross fixed capital formation | 935.9 | 1,021.7 | 1,141.5 |
| **Total domestic expenditure** | 6,050.5 | 6,408.5 | 6,836.6 |
| Exports of goods and services | 638.1 | 659.1 | 718.7 |
| Less Imports of goods and services | 668.4 | 724.3 | 816.9 |
| **GDP in purchasers' values** | 6,020.2 | 6,343.3 | 6,738.4 |
| **GDP at constant 1990 prices** | 5,637.5 | 5,813.2 | 6,050.4 |

Source: IMF, *International Financial Statistics*.

**Gross Domestic Product by Economic Activity** (provisional)*

| | 1989 | 1990 | 1991 |
|---|---|---|---|
| Agriculture, hunting, forestry and fishing | 106.4 | 113.6 | 110.3 |
| Mining and quarrying | 85.7 | 104.5 | 93.2 |
| Manufacturing | 1,012.3 | 1,032.1 | 1,034.1 |
| Electricity, gas and water | 155.2 | 158.3 | 171.0 |
| Construction | 239.1 | 243.3 | 226.6 |
| Trade, restaurants and hotels | 843.8 | 868.5 | 897.7 |
| Transport, storage and communications | 310.9 | 325.6 | 337.8 |
| Finance, insurance, real estate and business services | 943.1 | 999.7 | 1,057.5 |
| Government enterprises | 78.8 | 83.5 | 91.5 |
| Government services | 621.6 | 667.5 | 706.6 |
| Other community, social and personal services | 956.6 | 1,048.1 | 1,098.0 |
| **Sub-total** | 5,353.4 | 5,644.7 | 5,824.2 |
| Import duties | 17.5 | 17.5 | 16.9 |
| Statistical discrepancy† | 1.1 | 7.8 | 9.6 |
| Less Imputed bank service charge | 167.4 | 180.3 | 196.2 |
| **GDP in purchasers' values** | 5,204.6 | 5,489.6 | 5,654.4 |

* The distribution is based on the US Standard Industrial Classification, which differs from the ISIC. The contribution of the various industries excludes the activities of government enterprises, listed separately.
† Referring to an adjustment to the consumption of fixed capital.

Source: UN, *National Accounts Statistics*.

# THE UNITED STATES OF AMERICA

*Statistical Survey*

**BALANCE OF PAYMENTS** ($ million)

|  | 1993 Credit | 1993 Debit | 1993 Net | 1994 Credit | 1994 Debit | 1994 Net |
|---|---|---|---|---|---|---|
| Merchandise trade (free alongside ship) | 456,866 | 589,441 | −132,575 | 502,729 | 669,093 | −166,364 |
| Military transactions | 11,413 | 12,176 | −763 | 10,845 | 10,577 | 268 |
| Travel and transport | 97,322 | 76,482 | 20,840 | 102,385 | 81,335 | 21,050 |
| Investment income | 113,856 | 109,910 | 3,946 | 134,855 | 150,036 | −15,181 |
| Royalties and licence fees | 20,398 | 4,840 | 15,558 | 22,823 | 5,926 | 16,897 |
| Other private services | 54,870 | 32,119 | 22,751 | 58,453 | 34,791 | 23,662 |
| Other government services | 808 | 2,344 | −1,536 | 782 | 2,663 | −1,881 |
| **Total goods, services and income** | 755,533 | 827,312 | −71,779 | 832,871 | 954,422 | −121,551 |
| Government grants (net) | — | 14,620 | −14,620 | — | 14,532 | −14,532 |
| Other government transfers (net) | — | 3,785 | −3,785 | — | 4,246 | −4,246 |
| Private transfers (net) | — | 13,712 | −13,712 | — | 15,343 | −15,343 |
| **Current balance** (net) | — | 103,896 | −103,896 | — | 155,673 | −155,673 |
| US Government capital (net) | 1,360 | — | 1,360 | 2,236 | — | 2,236 |
| Direct private investments | 21,366 | 57,870 | −36,504 | 60,071 | 58,422 | −1,649 |
| US Treasury securities (net)* | 24,849 | — | 24,849 | 32,925 | — | 32,925 |
| Other securities | 80,068 | 119,983 | −39,915 | 58,562 | 60,621 | −2,059 |
| Other capital (net) | 64,374 | — | 64,374 | 112,432 | — | 112,432 |
| Statistical discrepancy | 21,096 | — | 21,096 | — | 33,255 | −33,255 |
| **Capital balance** (net) | 35,260 | — | 35,260 | 113,929 | — | 113,929 |
| **Overall balance** | — | 68,636 | 68,636 | — | 41,744 | −41,744 |

* Excluding foreign official assets.
Note: Details may not add to totals because of rounding.
Source: Bureau of Economic Analysis, US Department of Commerce.

**INTERNATIONAL INVESTMENTS** ($ million at 31 December)

|  | 1991 | 1992 | 1993* |
|---|---|---|---|
| US assets abroad: |  |  |  |
| US official reserve assets† | 159,223 | 147,435 | 164,945 |
| Gold† | 92,561 | 87,168 | 102,556 |
| SDRs† | 11,240 | 8,503 | 9,039 |
| Reserve position in the IMF† | 9,488 | 11,759 | 11,818 |
| Foreign currencies† | 45,934 | 40,005 | 41,532 |
| US Government assets, other than official reserve assets | 78,984 | 80,635 | 80,882 |
| US loans and other long-term assets‡ | 77,426 | 79,011 | 78,987 |
| US foreign currency holdings and US short-term assets | 1,558 | 1,624 | 1,895 |
| US private assets: |  |  |  |
| Direct investments abroad | 650,591 | 668,181 | 716,163 |
| Foreign securities | 301,493 | 331,445 | 518,481 |
| US claims on unaffiliated foreigners reported by US non-banking concerns | 256,295 | 253,870 | 254,502 |
| US claims reported by US banks, n.i.e. | 690,402 | 668,023 | 635,454 |
| Foreign assets in the USA: |  |  |  |
| Foreign official assets in the USA | 401,487 | 442,943 | 516,874 |
| US Government securities | 315,932 | 335,695 | 388,528 |
| Other US Government liabilities§ | 18,419 | 20,991 | 22,657 |
| US liabilities reported by US banks, n.i.e. | 38,396 | 54,967 | 69,633 |
| Other foreign official assets | 28,740 | 31,290 | 36,056 |
| Other foreign assets in the USA: |  |  |  |
| Direct investments in the USA | 491,877 | 497,059 | 516,724 |
| US Treasury securities | 189,506 | 224,835 | 254,082 |
| US securities other than US Treasury securities | 559,180 | 620,972 | 733,172 |
| US liabilities to unaffiliated foreigners reported by US non-banking concerns | 208,908 | 220,692 | 233,299 |
| US liabilities reported by US banks, n.i.e. | 635,571 | 651,031 | 672,011 |

* Preliminary.
† US holdings of special drawing rights and the reserve position include changes in the SDR based on changes in a weighted average of exchange rates for selected national currencies.
‡ Also includes paid-in capital subscription to international financial institutions and outstanding amounts of miscellaneous claims that have been settled through international agreements to be payable to the US Government over periods in excess of one year. Excludes World War I debts that are not being serviced.
§ Includes, primarily, US Government liabilities associated with military sales contracts and other transactions arranged with or through foreign official agencies.
Source: Bureau of Economic Analysis, US Department of Commerce.

THE UNITED STATES OF AMERICA  *Statistical Survey*

## INTERNATIONAL INVESTMENT INCOME, BY AREA ($ million)

| Area and type of investment | 1993 Receipts | 1993 Payments | 1994 Receipts | 1994 Payments |
|---|---|---|---|---|
| Total, all areas | 113,856 | 109,910 | 134,855 | 150,036 |
| Direct | 57,515 | 5,110 | 66,585 | 25,188 |
| Other private | 51,272 | 63,239 | 64,232 | 77,829 |
| US Government | 5,070 | 41,561 | 4,038 | 47,019 |
| Canada | 10,312 | 4,197 | 13,324 | 7,682 |
| Direct | 4,005 | −35 | 5,351 | 2,691 |
| Other private | 6,293 | 2,721 | 7,968 | 3,024 |
| US Government | 13 | 1,511 | 5 | 1,967 |
| Latin America and Other Western Hemisphere | 27,213 | 19,065 | 32,620 | 26,159 |
| Direct | 14,496 | −286 | 15,991 | 1,033 |
| Other private | 12,061 | 14,846 | 16,236 | 19,871 |
| US Government | 656 | 4,505 | 393 | 5,255 |
| Western Europe | 46,051 | 58,663 | 54,356 | 77,015 |
| Direct | 24,371 | 9,193 | 28,425 | 19,277 |
| Other private | 19,659 | 33,274 | 24,356 | 39,996 |
| US Government | 2,021 | 16,196 | 1,575 | 17,742 |
| Japan | 5,831 | 12,758 | 6,868 | 21,026 |
| Direct | 1,782 | −2,319 | 3,015 | 2,412 |
| Other private | 3,444 | 5,120 | 3,424 | 5,919 |
| US Government | 605 | 9,957 | 429 | 12,695 |
| Other Countries* | 24,450 | 15,227 | 27,686 | 18,154 |
| Direct | 12,860 | −1,443 | 13,803 | −225 |
| Other private | 9,815 | 7,278 | 12,248 | 9,019 |
| US Government | 1,775 | 9,392 | 1,636 | 9,360 |

* Including international organizations and unallocated transactions.
Source: Bureau of Economic Analysis, US Department of Commerce.

## FOREIGN AID ($ million)

| | 1991 | 1992 | 1993* |
|---|---|---|---|
| International Organizations | 1,498 | 1,419 | 1,132 |
| AfDB | — | 9 | — |
| AfDF | 78 | 131 | 103 |
| ADB | 146 | 86 | 50 |
| EBRD | 36 | 99 | 33 |
| IDB | 74 | 128 | 65 |
| Inter-American Investment Corpn | — | 12 | — |
| IBRD | 72 | 94 | 59 |
| IDA | 1,051 | 835 | 782 |
| IFC | 40 | 25 | 38 |
| Military and Non-Military Assistance | −33,281 | 15,535 | 14,644 |
| Western Europe | −5,862 | 155 | 210 |
| Germany | −6,117 | — | −1 |
| Portugal | 44 | 159 | 51 |
| Spain | −76 | −104 | −114 |
| United Kingdom | −113 | −115 | −118 |
| Eastern Europe | 854 | 622 | 2,081 |
| Armenia | — | 18 | 51 |
| Belarus | — | 25 | 74 |
| Georgia | — | 2 | 63 |
| Kyrgyzstan | — | 1 | 59 |
| Poland | 646 | 31 | 20 |
| Russia | — | 96 | 1,855 |
| Ukraine | — | 8 | 66 |
| Former USSR (regional) | — | 59 | 252 |
| Unspecified | 135 | 230 | 179 |
| Near East and South Asia | −24,589 | 7,339 | 6,944 |
| Bangladesh | 188 | 146 | 91 |
| Egypt | 2,508 | 2,538 | 2,733 |
| Greece | −181 | 389 | 184 |
| India | 100 | 43 | 33 |
| Iraq | 336 | 9 | 2 |
| Israel | 2,029 | 4,746 | 2,886 |
| Jordan | 67 | 121 | 113 |
| Kuwait | −13,550 | −2 | — |
| Pakistan | 346 | 120 | −39 |
| Saudi Arabia | −13,913 | −1,328 | — |
| Sri Lanka | 109 | 53 | 34 |
| Turkey | 865 | 259 | 592 |
| United Arab Emirates | −3,709 | — | — |

| — continued | 1991 | 1992 | 1993* |
|---|---|---|---|
| Africa | 1,485 | 1,538 | 1,657 |
| Cameroon | 57 | 42 | 23 |
| Côte d'Ivoire | 58 | 46 | 22 |
| Ethiopia | 123 | 80 | 107 |
| Kenya | 88 | 82 | 78 |
| Liberia | 64 | 30 | 29 |
| Malawi | 51 | 45 | 41 |
| Morocco | 98 | 26 | −18 |
| Mozambique | 89 | 67 | 70 |
| Somalia | 11 | 323 | 502 |
| South Africa | 28 | 44 | 66 |
| Sudan | 113 | 21 | 35 |
| Uganda | 39 | 23 | 54 |
| Zambia | 50 | 76 | 52 |
| Zimbabwe | 28 | 67 | 28 |
| Far East and Pacific | −8,991 | 812 | −2 |
| China, People's Repub. | 55 | 31 | 14 |
| Indonesia | 23 | 82 | −64 |
| Japan | −9,377 | −30 | −1 |
| Korea, Repub. | −331 | −132 | −431 |
| Marshall Islands | 52 | 63 | 24 |
| Micronesia | 107 | 108 | 45 |
| Palau | 20 | 34 | 83 |
| Philippines | 391 | 528 | 129 |
| Thailand | 49 | 43 | 84 |
| Americas | 1,977 | 2,352 | 529 |
| Argentina | 87 | 90 | 79 |
| Bolivia | 197 | 181 | 112 |
| Brazil | −21 | 409 | −188 |
| Chile | −40 | −53 | −33 |
| Colombia | 19 | −75 | −227 |
| Costa Rica | 63 | 24 | 13 |
| Dominican Repub. | 25 | 3 | 161 |
| El Salvador | 308 | 290 | 215 |
| Guatemala | 82 | 107 | 74 |
| Haiti | 69 | 47 | 49 |
| Honduras | 194 | 127 | 85 |
| Jamaica | 111 | 84 | 57 |
| Mexico | 38 | −110 | −161 |
| Nicaragua | 396 | 206 | 24 |
| Panama | 153 | 193 | 49 |
| Peru | 139 | 644 | 93 |
| Other International Organizations and Unspecified Areas | 1,844 | 2,295 | 2,505 |

* Preliminary.
Source: Bureau of Economic Analysis, US Department of Commerce.

## THE UNITED STATES OF AMERICA

# External Trade

The customs territory of the USA includes Puerto Rico and the US Virgin Islands. Figures exclude trade with other US possessions.

**PRINCIPAL COMMODITIES** (distribution by SITC, $ million)

| Imports f.o.b.* | 1991 | 1992 |
|---|---|---|
| **Food and live animals** | 21,936 | 22,645 |
| Fish (not marine mammals), crustaceans, molluscs, etc., and preparations | 5,638 | 5,657 |
| Vegetables and fruit | 5,391 | 5,698 |
| Coffee, tea, cocoa, spices and preparations | 3,347 | 3,212 |
| **Beverages and tobacco** | 4,819 | 5,380 |
| Beverages | 3,609 | 4,072 |
| **Crude materials, inedible, except fuels** | 13,036 | 13,968 |
| Cork and wood | 3,057 | 3,970 |
| Metalliferous ores and metal scrap | 3,561 | 3,323 |
| **Mineral fuels, lubricants, etc.** | 54,056 | 55,028 |
| Petroleum, petroleum products, etc. | 49,762 | 50,357 |
| Gas (natural and manufactured) | 3,497 | 3,662 |
| **Animal and vegetable oils, fats and waxes** | 850 | 1,074 |
| **Chemicals and related products** | 24,131 | 27,684 |
| Chemical elements and compounds | 11,429 | 12,666 |
| Organic chemicals | 8,133 | 9,366 |
| Inorganic chemicals | 3,296 | 3,300 |
| Medicinal and pharmaceutical products | 3,047 | 3,812 |
| **Basic manufactures** | 57,340 | 60,371 |
| Rubber manufactures | 3,334 | 3,729 |
| Paper, paperboard and manufactures | 8,021 | 7,998 |
| Textile yarn, fabrics, etc. | 6,981 | 7,840 |
| Non-metallic mineral manufactures | 9,678 | 10,170 |
| Iron and steel | 9,333 | 9,317 |
| Non-ferrous metals | 8,430 | 8,501 |
| Other metal manufactures | 8,834 | 9,496 |
| **Machinery and transport equipment** | 210,364 | 231,975 |
| Non-electric machinery | 73,079 | 82,821 |
| Power-generating machinery and equipment | 14,195 | 15,910 |
| Machinery specialized for particular industries | 10,864 | 11,826 |
| Metalworking machinery | 3,605 | 3,170 |
| General industrial machinery, equipment and parts | 14,396 | 15,522 |
| Office machines and automatic data-processing machines | 30,019 | 36,393 |
| Electrical machinery, apparatus, etc. | 58,513 | 65,547 |
| Telecommunications and sound equipment | 23,446 | 25,819 |
| Transport equipment | 78,773 | 83,607 |
| Road vehicles (incl. air-cushion vehicles) and parts† | 70,576 | 75,252 |
| Motor cars and other motor vehicles for passengers (excl. buses) | 45,722 | 46,894 |
| Motor vehicles for goods transport, etc. | 8,207 | 9,619 |
| Parts and accessories for cars, buses, lorries, etc.† | 14,418 | 16,193 |
| Aircraft and spacecraft and parts† | 7,393 | 7,406 |
| **Miscellaneous manufactured articles** | 83,332 | 95,009 |
| Furniture and parts; bedding, mattresses, etc. | 4,936 | 5,505 |
| Clothing and accessories (excl. footwear) | 26,202 | 31,242 |
| Footwear | 9,554 | 10,165 |
| Professional, scientific and controlling instruments, etc. | 6,733 | 7,604 |
| Photographic apparatus, etc., optical goods, watches and clocks | 7,469 | 7,921 |
| **Other commodities and transactions** | 17,266 | 19,217 |
| **Total** | 487,129 | 532,352 |

* Figures are provisional. The revised totals (in $'000 million) are: 488.45 in 1991; 532.67 in 1992 (Source: IMF, *International Financial Statistics*).

† Excluding tyres, engines and electrical parts.

**Total imports f.o.b.** ($'000 million): 580.51 in 1993; 663.83 in 1994 (Source: IMF, *International Financial Statistics*).

| Exports f.o.b. | 1991 | 1992* |
|---|---|---|
| **Food and live animals** | 30,489 | 33,793 |
| Meat and meat preparations | 3,653 | 4,228 |
| Fish (not marine mammals), crustaceans, molluscs, etc., and preparations | 3,181 | 3,486 |
| Cereals and cereal preparations | 10,927 | 12,206 |
| Vegetables and fruit | 5,908 | 6,265 |
| Animal feeding-stuff (excl. unmilled cereals) | 3,281 | 3,635 |
| **Beverages and tobacco** | 6,839 | 7,143 |
| Tobacco and tobacco manufactures | 6,028 | 6,177 |
| **Crude materials, inedible, except fuels** | 25,832 | 25,727 |
| Oil seeds and oleaginous fruits | 4,320 | 4,804 |
| Cork and wood | 5,131 | 5,331 |
| Pulp and waste paper | 3,627 | 3,874 |
| Textile fibres (excl. wool tops, etc.) and their wastes | 3,704 | 3,114 |
| Metalliferous ores and metal scrap | 4,163 | 3,603 |
| **Mineral fuels, lubricants, etc.** | 12,287 | 11,198 |
| Coal, coke and briquettes | 4,781 | 4,326 |
| Petroleum, petroleum products, etc. | 6,770 | 6,066 |
| **Animal and vegetable oils, fats and waxes** | 1,151 | 1,453 |
| **Chemicals and related products** | 43,428 | 44,722 |
| Chemical elements and compounds | 15,185 | 15,399 |
| Organic chemicals | 11,044 | 11,141 |
| Inorganic chemicals | 4,141 | 4,258 |
| Medicinal and pharmaceutical products | 4,679 | 5,446 |
| Plastics in primary forms | 7,560 | 7,203 |
| **Basic manufactures** | 37,778 | 38,173 |
| Paper, paperboard and manufactures | 6,034 | 6,393 |
| Textile yarn, fabrics, etc. | 5,610 | 5,889 |
| Non-metallic mineral manufactures | 4,720 | 4,864 |
| Iron and steel | 4,457 | 3,856 |
| Non-ferrous metals | 5,822 | 5,075 |
| Other metal manufactures | 6,700 | 7,264 |
| **Machinery and transport equipment** | 200,089 | 215,017 |
| Non-electric machinery | 84,393 | 88,708 |
| Power-generating machinery and equipment | 17,368 | 18,454 |
| Machinery specialized for particular industries | 17,192 | 17,245 |
| General industrial machinery, equipment and parts | 17,567 | 18,876 |
| Office machines and automatic data-processing machines | 29,461 | 30,983 |
| Electrical machinery, apparatus, etc. | 45,376 | 49,751 |
| Telecommunications and sound equipment | 10,896 | 12,327 |
| Transport equipment | 70,321 | 76,558 |
| Road vehicles (incl. air-cushion vehicles) and parts† | 33,133 | 37,946 |
| Motor cars and other motor vehicles for passengers (excl. buses) | 12,277 | 14,892 |
| Motor vehicles for goods transport, etc. | 4,039 | 3,550 |
| Parts and accessories for cars, buses, lorries, etc.† | 14,799 | 17,038 |
| Aircraft and spacecraft and parts† | 35,483 | 36,594 |
| **Miscellaneous manufactured articles** | 46,730 | 51,276 |
| Clothing and accessories (excl. footwear) | 3,316 | 4,211 |
| Professional, scientific and controlling instruments, etc. | 14,062 | 14,944 |
| Photographic apparatus, etc., optical goods, watches and clocks | 4,247 | 4,338 |
| **Other commodities and transactions** | 17,106 | 18,969 |
| Non-monetary gold (excl. gold ores and concentrates) | 3,337 | 4,092 |
| **Total** | 421,730 | 447,471 |

* Figures are provisional. The revised total is $448,163 million (Source: UN, *Monthly Bulletin of Statistics*).

† Excluding tyres, engines and electrical parts.

**Total exports f.o.b.** ($ million): 464,773 in 1993; 512,670 in 1994 (Source: UN, *Monthly Bulletin of Statistics*).

# THE UNITED STATES OF AMERICA

## PRINCIPAL TRADING PARTNERS
($ million)

| Imports f.o.b. | 1990 | 1991* | 1992* |
|---|---|---|---|
| Australia | 4,447 | 3,988 | 3,692 |
| Belgium | 4,585† | 3,929 | 4,479 |
| Brazil | 7,898 | 6,717 | 7,611 |
| Canada | 91,380 | 91,064 | 98,497 |
| China, People's Repub. | 15,237 | 18,969 | 25,729 |
| Colombia | 3,168 | 2,736 | 2,849 |
| France | 13,153 | 13,333 | 14,811 |
| Germany | 28,162‡ | 26,136 | 28,829 |
| Hong Kong | 9,622 | 9,279 | 9,799 |
| India | 3,197 | 3,192 | 3,781 |
| Indonesia | 3,341 | 3,241 | 4,527 |
| Israel | 3,313 | 3,484 | 3,812 |
| Italy | 12,751 | 11,764 | 12,300 |
| Japan | 89,684 | 91,511 | 97,181 |
| Korea, Repub. | 18,485 | 17,019 | 16,691 |
| Malaysia | 5,272 | 6,102 | 8,294 |
| Mexico | 30,157 | 31,130 | 35,189 |
| Netherlands | 4,952 | 4,811 | 5,287 |
| Nigeria | 5,982 | 5,168 | 5,074 |
| Philippines | 3,384 | 3,471 | 4,358 |
| Saudi Arabia | 10,021 | 10,900 | 10,367 |
| Singapore | 9,800 | 9,957 | 11,318 |
| Spain | 3,311 | 2,848 | 3,001 |
| Sweden | 4,937 | 4,525 | 4,716 |
| Switzerland | 5,587 | 5,576 | 5,643 |
| Taiwan | 22,666 | 23,023 | 24,601 |
| Thailand | 5,289 | 6,122 | 7,528 |
| United Kingdom | 20,188 | 18,413 | 20,152 |
| Venezuela | 9,480 | 8,179 | 8,168 |
| **Total** (incl. others) | 495,310 | 487,129 | 532,498 |

| Exports f.o.b. | 1990 | 1991 | 1992* |
|---|---|---|---|
| Australia | 8,538 | 8,404 | 8,913 |
| Belgium | 10,451† | 10,572 | 9,779 |
| Brazil | 5,048 | 6,148 | 5,740 |
| Canada | 83,674 | 85,150 | 90,562 |
| China, People's Repub. | 4,806 | 6,278 | 7,470 |
| Colombia | 2,029 | 1,952 | 3,282 |
| France | 13,665 | 15,346 | 14,575 |
| Germany | 18,760‡ | 21,302 | 21,236 |
| Hong Kong | 6,817 | 8,137 | 9,069 |
| Indonesia | 1,897 | 1,891 | 2,778 |
| Israel | 3,203 | 3,911 | 4,074 |
| Italy | 7,992 | 8,570 | 8,698 |
| Japan | 48,580 | 48,125 | 47,764 |
| Korea, Repub. | 14,404 | 15,505 | 14,630 |
| Malaysia | 3,425 | 3,900 | 4,396 |
| Mexico | 28,279 | 33,277 | 40,598 |
| Netherlands | 13,022 | 13,511 | 13,740 |
| Philippines | 2,471 | 2,264 | 2,753 |
| Saudi Arabia | 4,049 | 6,557 | 7,163 |
| Singapore | 8,023 | 8,804 | 9,624 |
| Spain | 5,213 | 5,474 | 5,487 |
| Sweden | 3,405 | 3,286 | 2,844 |
| Switzerland | 4,943 | 5,557 | 4,536 |
| Taiwan | 11,491 | 13,182 | 15,205 |
| Thailand | 2,995 | 3,753 | 3,982 |
| United Kingdom | 23,490 | 22,046 | 22,808 |
| Venezuela | 3,108 | 4,656 | 5,438 |
| **Total** (incl. others) | 393,592 | 421,730 | 448,156 |

* Figures are provisional.
† Including trade with Luxembourg.
‡ Excluding trade with the former German Democratic Republic.
Source: Bureau of the Census, US Department of Commerce.

# Transport

## RAILWAYS

|  | 1991 | 1992 | 1993 |
|---|---|---|---|
| Passengers carried (million) | 340 | 335 | 344 |
| Passenger-miles (million) | 13,617 | 13,138 | 13,138 |
| Freight revenue ($ million)* | 26,949 | 27,508 | 27,991 |
| Passenger revenue ($ million)* | 94 | 90 | 83 |

* Excluding Amtrak.

## ROAD TRAFFIC
('000 motor vehicles registered at 31 December)

|  | 1991 | 1992 | 1993 |
|---|---|---|---|
| Passenger cars and taxis | 142,955 | 144,213 | 146,314 |
| Buses and coaches | 631 | 645 | 654 |
| Goods vehicles | 44,785 | 45,504 | 47,095 |
| Motor cycles | 4,177 | 4,065 | 3,978 |

## INLAND WATERWAYS (freight traffic in million ton-miles)

|  | 1991 | 1992 | 1993 |
|---|---|---|---|
| Coastal waterways | 450,000 | 502,311 | 448,404 |
| Lake waterways | 53,000 | 55,785 | 56,438 |
| Internal waterways | 286,000 | 297,639 | 283,894 |
| Local waterways | 1,200 | 950 | 922 |
| **Total** | 790,200 | 856,685 | 789,658 |

## OCEAN SHIPPING
### Sea-going Merchant Vessels

|  | 1991 | 1992 | 1993 |
|---|---|---|---|
| Number of vessels |  |  |  |
| Combination passengers/cargo | 10 | 11 | 12 |
| Freighters | 359 | 349 | 321 |
| Bulk carriers | 24 | 23 | 21 |
| Tankers | 226 | 220 | 210 |
| **Total** | 619 | 603 | 564 |
| Displacement ('000 gross tons) |  |  |  |
| Combination passengers/cargo | 92 | 97 | 104 |
| Freighters | 7,154 | 7,191 | 7,205 |
| Bulk carriers | 1,014 | 991 | 949 |
| Tankers | 14,253 | 14,162 | 13,048 |
| **Total** | 22,513 | 22,461 | 21,126 |

### Vessels Entered and Cleared in Foreign Trade in all Ports

|  | 1991 | 1992 | 1993 |
|---|---|---|---|
| Entered |  |  |  |
| Number | 57,245 | 55,056 | 54,834 |
| Displacement ('000 net tons) | 515,819 | 515,428 | 514,926 |
| Cleared |  |  |  |
| Number | 55,100 | 54,127 | 53,637 |
| Displacement ('000 net tons) | 520,717 | 519,066 | 518,534 |

## CIVIL AVIATION
### Scheduled Air Carriers (million)

|  | 1991 | 1992 | 1993 |
|---|---|---|---|
| Passengers | 412 | 432 | 443 |
| Passenger-miles | 332,566 | 347,931 | 354,177 |
| Freight ton-miles | 4,946 | 5,284 | 5,458 |
| Mail ton-miles | 1,412 | 1,573 | 1,673 |

Source (for all Transport tables): US Department of Transportation, Bureau of Transportation Statistics.

# THE UNITED STATES OF AMERICA

## Tourism

**FOREIGN VISITORS BY COUNTRY OF NATIONALITY**
('000)

|  | 1992 | 1993 | 1994* |
|---|---|---|---|
| Canada | 18,598 | 17,293 | 14,715 |
| France | 795 | 845 | 853 |
| Germany | 1,692 | 1,827 | 1,704 |
| Japan | 3,653 | 3,543 | 4,056 |
| Mexico | 10,872 | 9,824 | 11,500 |
| United Kingdom | 2,824 | 2,999 | 3,017 |
| **Total** (incl. others) | 47,261 | 45,779 | 45,715 |
| Tourist receipts ($ million)† | 54,284 | 57,621 | 57,165 |

* Provisional.   † Excluding transportation.

Source: Office of Research, US Travel and Tourism Administration, US Department of Commerce.

## Communications Media

|  | 1990 | 1991 | 1992 |
|---|---|---|---|
| Radio receivers ('000 in use)* | 529,000 | 534,800 | 540,500 |
| Television receivers ('000 in use)* | 203,000 | 205,500 | 208,000 |
| Books published (titles)† | 46,738 | 48,146 | 49,276 |
| Daily newspapers‡ | 1,611 | 1,586 | n.a. |
| Newspaper circulation ('000)‡ | 62,328 | 60,700 | n.a. |

* Estimates.
† Figures cover only the commercial production of the book trade (other than pamphlets), excluding government publications, university theses and other non-trade book production.
‡ Figures relate to English language dailies only.

Sources: John A. Volpe National Transportation Systems Center, US Department of Transportation; UNESCO, *Statistical Yearbook*.

## Education

(1993/94*)

|  | Teaching staff ('000) | Pupils/Students ('000) |
|---|---|---|
| Primary† | 1,753 | 32,577‡ |
| Public | 1,491 | 28,297 |
| Private | 262 | 4,280 |
| Secondary† | 1,088 | 16,348 |
| Public | 984 | 15,157 |
| Private | 104 | 1,191 |
| Universities and colleges | 890§ | 14,589‖ |
| Public | 627 | 11,408 |
| Private | 263 | 3,181 |

* Estimates.
† Includes teachers and enrolments in local public school systems and in most private schools. Excludes sub-collegiate departments of institutions of higher education, residential schools for exceptional children, and federal schools. Also excludes pre-primary teachers in schools without a first grade. Teachers are reported in full-time equivalents.
‡ Includes most kindergarten and some nursery school enrolment. Excludes pre-primary enrolment in schools that do not offer first grade.
§ Includes full-time and part-time faculty with the rank of instructor or above in universities, other four-year colleges and two-year colleges.
‖ Includes full-time and part-time students enrolled in degree-credit and non-degree-credit courses in universities, other four-year colleges and two-year colleges.

Source: National Center for Education Statistics, US Department of Education.

# Directory

## The Constitution

Adopted 4 March 1789.

### PREAMBLE

We, the people of the United States, in order to form a more perfect Union, establish justice, insure domestic tranquillity, provide for the common defence, promote the general welfare, and secure the blessings of liberty to ourselves and our posterity, do ordain and establish this Constitution for the United States of America.

### ARTICLE I

**Section 1**

All legislative powers herein granted shall be vested in a Congress of the United States, which shall consist of a Senate and House of Representatives.

**Section 2**

1. The House of Representatives shall be composed of members chosen every second year by the people of the several States and the electors in each State shall have the qualifications requisite for electors of the most numerous branch of the State Legislature.

2. No person shall be a Representative who shall not have attained to the age of 25 years and been seven years a citizen of the United States and who shall not, when elected, be an inhabitant of that State in which he shall be chosen.

3. Representatives and direct taxes shall be apportioned among the several States which may be included within this Union according to their respective numbers, which shall be determined by adding to the whole number of free persons, including those bound to service for a term of years, and excluding Indians not taxed, three-fifths of all other persons. The actual enumeration shall be made within three years after the first meeting of the Congress of the United States, and within every subsequent term of 10 years, in such manner as they shall by law direct. The number of Representatives shall not exceed one for every 30,000, but each State shall have at least one Representative; and until such enumeration shall be made, the State of New Hampshire shall be entitled to choose 3; Massachusetts 8; Rhode Island and Providence Plantations 1; Connecticut 5; New York 6; New Jersey 4; Pennsylvania 8; Delaware 1; Maryland 6; Virginia 10; North Carolina 5; South Carolina 5; and Georgia 3.*

4. When vacancies happen in the representation from any State, the Executive Authority thereof shall issue writs of election to fill such vacancies.

5. The House of Representatives shall choose their Speaker and other officers and shall have the sole power of impeachment.

**Section 3**

1. The Senate of the United States shall be composed of two Senators from each State, chosen by the Legislature thereof, for six years; and each Senator shall have one vote.

2. Immediately after they shall be assembled in consequence of the first election, they shall be divided as equally as may be into three classes. The seats of the Senators of the first class shall be vacated at the expiration of the second year, of the second class at the expiration of the fourth year, and of the third class at the

* See Amendment XIV.

expiration of the sixth year, so that one-third may be chosen every second year, and if vacancies happen by resignation or otherwise, during the recess of the Legislature or of any State, the Executive therefore may make temporary appointment until the next meeting of the Legislature, which shall then fill such vacancies.

3. No person shall be a Senator who shall not have attained to the age of 30 years, and been nine years a citizen of the United States, and who shall not, when elected, be an inhabitant of that State for which he shall be chosen.

4. The Vice-President of the United States shall be President of the Senate, but shall have no vote unless they be equally divided.

5. The Senate shall choose their other officers, and also a President *pro tempore*, in the absence of the Vice-President, or when he shall exercise the office of the President of the United States.

6. The Senate shall have the sole power to try all impeachments. When sitting for that purpose, they shall be on oath or affirmation. When the President of the United States is tried, the Chief Justice shall preside; and no person shall be convicted without the concurrence of two-thirds of the members present.

7. Judgment of case of impeachment shall not extend further than to removal from office, and disqualification to hold and enjoy any office of honour, trust, or profit under the United States; but the party convicted shall nevertheless be liable and subject to indictment, trial, judgment, and punishment, according to law.

### Section 4

1. The times, places and manner of holding elections for Senators and Representatives shall be prescribed in each State by the Legislature thereof; but the Congress may at any time by law make or alter such regulations, except as to places of choosing Senators.

2. The Congress shall assemble at least once in every year, and such meeting shall be on the first Monday in December, unless they shall by law appoint a different day.

### Section 5

1. Each House shall be the judge of the elections, returns, and qualifications of its own members, and a majority of each shall constitute a quorum to do business; but a smaller number may adjourn from day to day, and may be authorized to compel the attendance of absent members in such manner and under such penalties as each House may provide.

2. Each House may determine the rules of its proceedings, punish its members for disorderly behaviour, and with the concurrence of two-thirds, expel a member.

3. Each House shall keep a journal of its proceedings, and from time to time publish the same, excepting such parts as may in their judgment require secrecy; and the yeas and nays of the members of either House on any question shall, at the desire of one-fifth of those present, be entered on the journal.

4. Neither House, during the session of Congress shall, without the consent of the other, adjourn for more than three days, nor to any other place than that in which the two Houses shall be sitting.

### Section 6

1. The Senators and Representatives shall receive a compensation for their services to be ascertained by law, and paid out of the Treasury of the United States. They shall in all cases, except treason, felony, and breach of the peace, be privileged from arrest during their attendance at the session of their respective Houses, and in going to and returning from the same; and for any speech or debate in either House they shall not be questioned in any other place.

2. No Senator or Representative shall, during the time for which he was elected, be appointed to any civil office under the authority of the United States which shall have been created, or the emoluments whereof shall have been increased during such time; and no person holding any office under the United States shall be a member of either House during his continuance in office.

### Section 7

1. All bills for raising revenue shall originate in the House of Representatives, but the Senate may propose or concur with amendments, as on other bills.

2. Every bill which shall have passed the House of Representatives and the Senate shall, before it becomes a law, be presented to the President of the United States; if he approve, he shall sign it, but if not he shall return it, with his objections to that House in which it shall have originated, who shall enter the objections at large on their journal and proceed to reconsider it. If after such reconsideration two-thirds of that House shall agree to pass the bill, it shall be sent, together with the objections, to the other House, by which it shall likewise be reconsidered; and if approved by two-thirds of that House it shall become a law. But in such cases the votes of both Houses shall be determined by yeas and nays, and the names of the persons voting for and against the bill be entered on the journal of each House respectively. If any bill shall not be returned by the President within 10 days (Sundays excepted) after it shall have been presented to him the same shall be a law in like manner as if he had signed it, unless the Congress by their adjournment prevent its return; in which case it shall not be a law.

3. Every order, resolution, or vote to which the concurrence of the Senate and House of Representatives may be necessary (except on a question of adjournment) shall be presented to the President of the United States, and before the same shall take effect shall be approved by him, or being disapproved by him shall be repassed by two-thirds of the Senate and the House of Representatives, according to the rules and limitations prescribed in the case of a bill.

### Section 8

1. The Congress shall have power:

To lay and collect taxes, duties, imposts, and excises, to pay the debts and provide for the common defence and general welfare of the United States; but all duties, imposts, and excises shall be uniform throughout the United States.

2. To borrow money on the credit of the United States.

3. To regulate commerce with foreign nations; and among the several States and with the Indian tribes.

4. To establish a uniform rule of naturalization and uniform laws on the subject of bankruptcies throughout the United States.

5. To coin money, regulate the value thereof, and of foreign coin, and fix the standard of weights and measures.

6. To provide for the punishment of counterfeiting the securities and current coin of the United States.

7. To establish post-offices and post-roads.

8. To promote the progress of science and useful arts by securing for limited times to authors and inventors the exclusive rights to their respective writings and discoveries.

9. To constitute tribunals inferior to the Supreme Court.

10. To define and punish piracies and felonies committed on the high seas, and offences against the law of nations.

11. To declare war, grant letters of marque and reprisal, and make rules concerning captures on land and water.

12. To raise and support armies, but no appropriation of money to that use shall be for a longer term than two years.

13. To provide and maintain a navy.

14. To make rules for the government and regulation of the land and naval forces.

15. To provide for calling forth the militia to execute the laws of the Union, suppress insurrections, and repel invasions.

16. To provide for organizing, arming and disciplining the militia, and for governing such part of them as may be employed in the service of the United States, reserving to the States respectively the appointment of the officers, and the authority of training the militia according to the discipline prescribed by Congress.

17. To exercise exclusive legislation in all cases whatsoever over such district (not exceeding 10 miles square) as may, by cession of particular States and the acceptance of Congress, become the seat of Government of the United States and to exercise like authority over all places purchased by the consent of the Legislature of the State in which the same shall be, for the erection of forts, magazines, arsenals, dry-docks, and other needful buildings.

18. To make all laws which shall be necessary and proper for carrying into execution the foregoing powers and all other powers vested by this Constitution in the Government of the United States, or in any department or officer thereof.

### Section 9

1. The migration or importation of such persons as any of the States now existing shall think proper to admit shall not be prohibited by the Congress prior to the year 1808, but a tax or duty may be imposed on such importations, not exceeding 10 dollars for each person.

2. The privilege of the writ of habeas corpus shall not be suspended, unless when in cases of rebellion or invasion the public safety may require it.

3. No bill or attainder or *ex post facto* law shall be passed.

4. No capitation or other direct tax shall be laid, unless in proportion to the census or enumeration hereinbefore directed to be taken.

5. No tax or duty shall be laid on articles exported from any State.

6. No preference shall be given by any regulation of commerce or revenue to the ports of one State over those of another, nor shall

vessels bound to or from one State be obliged to enter, clear, or pay duties to another.

7. No money shall be drawn from the Treasury but in consequence of appropriations made by law; and a regular statement and account of the receipts and expenditures of all public money shall be published from time to time.

8. No title of nobility shall be granted by the United States. And no person holding any office of profit or trust under them shall, without the consent of the Congress, accept of any present, emolument, office, or title of any kind whatever from any king, prince, or foreign state.

**Section 10**

1. No State shall enter into any treaty, alliance or confederation, grant letters of marque and reprisal, coin money, emit bills of credit, make anything but gold and silver coin a tender in payment of debts, pass any bill of attainder, *ex post facto* law, or law impairing the obligation of contracts, or grant any title of nobility.

2. No State shall, without the consent of the Congress, lay any impost or duties on imports or exports, except what may be absolutely necessary for executing its inspection laws, and the net produce of all duties and imposts, laid by any State on imports or exports, shall be for the use of the Treasury of the United States; and all such laws shall be subject to the revision and control of the Congress.

3. No State shall, without the consent of Congress, lay any duty of tonnage, keep troops or ships of war in time of peace, enter into agreement or compact with another State, or with a foreign power, or engage in war, unless actually invaded, or in such imminent danger as will not admit of delay.

## ARTICLE II

**Section 1**

1. The Executive power shall be vested in a President of the United States of America. He shall hold his office during the term of four years, and, together with the Vice-President chosen for the same term, be elected as follows:

2. Each State shall appoint, in such manner as the Legislature thereof may direct, a number of electors equal to the whole number of Senators and Representatives to which the State may be entitled in the Congress; but no Senator or Representative or person holding an office of trust or profit under the United States shall be appointed an elector.

3. The electors shall meet in their respective States and vote by ballot for two persons, of whom one at least shall not be an inhabitant of the same State with themselves. And they shall make a list of all the persons voted for, and of the number of votes for each, which list they shall sign and certify and transmit, sealed, to the seat of the Government of the United States, directed to the President of the Senate. The President of the Senate shall, in the presence of the Senate and House of Representatives, open all the certificates, and the votes shall then be counted. The person having the greatest number of votes shall be the President, if such number be a majority of the whole number of electors appointed, and if there be more than one who have such a majority, and have an equal number of votes, then the House of Representatives shall immediately choose by ballot one of them for President; and if no person have a majority, then from the five highest on the list the said House shall in like manner choose the President. But in choosing the President, the vote shall be taken by States, the representation from each State having one vote. A quorum, for this purpose, shall consist of a member or members from two-thirds of the States, and a majority of all the States shall be necessary to a choice. In every case, after the choice of the President, the person having the greatest number of votes of the electors shall be the Vice-President. But if there should remain two or more who have equal votes, the Senate shall choose from them by ballot the Vice-President.*

4. The Congress may determine the time of choosing the electors and the day on which they shall give their votes, which day shall be the same throughout the United States.

5. No person except a natural born citizen, or a citizen of the United States, at the time of the adoption of the Constitution, shall be eligible to the office of President; neither shall any person be eligible to that office who shall not have attained to the age of 35 years and been 14 years a resident within the United States.

6. In case of the removal of the President from office, or of his death, resignation, or inability to discharge the powers and duties of the said office, the same shall devolve on the Vice-President, and the Congress may by law provide for the case of removal, death, resignation, or inability, both of the President and Vice-President, declaring what officer shall then act as President, and such officer shall act accordingly until the disability be removed or a President shall be elected.†

7. The President shall, at stated times, receive for his services a compensation which shall neither be increased nor diminished during the period for which he shall have been elected, and he shall not receive within that period any other emolument from the United States, or any of them.

8. Before he enter on the execution of his office he shall take the following oath or affirmation:

'I do solemnly swear (or affirm) that I will faithfully execute the office of President of the United States, and will, to the best of my ability, preserve, protect, and defend the Constitution of the United States.'

**Section 2**

1. The President shall be Commander-in-Chief of the Army and Navy of the United States, and of the militia of the several States when called into the actual service of the United States; he may require the opinion, in writing, of the principal officer in each of the executive departments upon any subject relating to the duties of their respective offices, and he shall have the power to grant reprieves and pardons for offences against the United States except in cases of impeachment.

2. He shall have power by and with the advice and consent of the Senate to make treaties, provided two-thirds of the Senators present concur; and he shall nominate and by and with the advice and consent of the Senate shall appoint ambassadors, other public ministers and consuls, judges of the Supreme Court, and all other officers of the United States whose appointments are not herein otherwise provided for, and which shall be established by law; but the Congress may by law vest the appointment of such inferior officers as they think proper in the President alone, in the courts of law, or in the heads of departments.

3. The President shall have power to fill up all vacancies that may happen during the recess of the Senate by granting commissions, which shall expire at the end of their next session.

**Section 3**

He shall from time to time give to the Congress information of the state of the Union, and recommend to their consideration such measures as he shall judge necessary and expedient; he may, on extraordinary occasions, convene both Houses, or either of them, and in case of disagreement between them with respect to the time of adjournment, he may adjourn them to such time as he shall think proper; he shall receive ambassadors and other public ministers; he shall take care that the laws be faithfully executed, and shall commission all the officers of the United States.

**Section 4**

The President, Vice-President, and all civil officers of the United States shall be removed from office on impeachment for conviction of treason, bribery or other high crimes and misdemeanours.

## ARTICLE III

**Section 1**

The judicial power of the United States shall be vested in one Supreme Court, and in such inferior courts as the Congress may from time to time ordain and establish. The judges, both of the Supreme and inferior courts, shall hold their offices during good behaviour, and shall at stated times receive for their services a compensation which shall not be diminished during their continuance in office.

**Section 2**

1. The judicial power shall extend to all cases in law and equity arising under this Constitution, the laws of the United States, and treaties made, or which shall be made, under their authority; to all cases affecting ambassadors, other public ministers and consuls; to all cases of admiralty and maritime jurisdiction; to controversies to which the United States shall be a party; to controversies between two or more States, between a State and citizens of another State, between citizens of different States, between citizens of the same State claiming lands under grants of different States, and between a State, or the citizens thereof, and foreign States, citizens, or subjects.

2. In all cases affecting ambassadors, other public ministers, and consuls, and those in which a State shall be party, the Supreme Court shall have original jurisdiction. In all the other cases before mentioned the Supreme Court shall have appellate jurisdiction both as to law and fact, with such exceptions and under such regulations as the Congress shall make.

---

* This clause is superseded by Amendment XII.

† This clause is amended by Amendments XX and XXV.

3. The trial of all crimes, except in cases of impeachment, shall be by jury, and such trials shall be held in the State where the said crimes shall have been committed; but when not committed within any State the trial shall be at such place or places as the Congress may by law have directed.

**Section 3**

1. Treason against the United States shall consist only in levying war against them, or in adhering to their enemies, giving them aid and comfort. No person shall be convicted of treason unless on the testimony of two witnesses to the same overt act, or on confession in open court.

2. The Congress shall have power to declare the punishment of treason, but no attainder of treason shall work corruption of blood, or forfeiture except during the life of the person attained.

### ARTICLE IV

**Section 1**

Full faith and credit shall be given in each State to the public acts, records, and judicial proceedings of every other State. And the Congress may by general laws prescribe the manner in which such acts, records, and proceedings shall be proved, and the effect thereof.

**Section 2**

1. The citizens of each State shall be entitled to all privileges and immunities of citizens in the several States.

2. A person charged in any State with treason, felony, or other crime, who shall flee from justice, and be found in another State, shall, on demand of the Executive authority of the State from which he fled, be delivered up, to be removed to the State having jurisdiction of the crime.

3. No person held to service or labour in one State, under the laws thereof, escaping into another shall in consequence of any law or regulation therein, be discharged from such service or labour, but shall be delivered up on claim of the party to whom such service or labour may be due.

**Section 3**

1. New States may be admitted by the Congress into this Union; but no new State shall be formed or erected within the jurisdiction of any other State, nor any State be formed by the junction of two or more States, or parts of States, without the consent of the Legislatures of the States concerned, as well as of the Congress.

2. The Congress shall have the power to dispose of and make all needful rules and regulations respecting the territory or other property belonging to the United States; and nothing in this Constitution shall be so construed as to prejudice any claims of the United States, or of any particular State.

**Section 4**

The United States shall guarantee to every State in this Union a Republican form of government, and shall protect each of them against invasion, and on application of the Legislature, or of the Executive (when the Legislature cannot be convened) against domestic violence.

### ARTICLE V

The Congress, whenever two-thirds of both Houses shall deem it necessary, shall propose amendments to this Constitution, or, on the application of the Legislature of two-thirds of the several States, shall call a convention for proposing amendments, which in either case, shall be valid to all intents and purposes, as part of this Constitution, when ratified by the Legislature of three-fourths of the several States, or by conventions in three-fourths thereof, as the one or the other mode of ratification may be proposed by the Congress, provided that no amendment which may be made prior to the year 1808 shall in any manner affect the first and fourth clauses in the Ninth Section of the First Article; and that no State, without its consent, shall be deprived of its equal suffrage in the Senate.

### ARTICLE VI

1. All debts contracted and engagements entered into before the adoption of this Constitution shall be as valid against the United States under this Constitution as under the Confederation.

2. This Constitution and the laws of the United States which shall be made in pursuance thereof and all treaties made, or which shall be made, under the authority of the United States, shall be the supreme law of the land, and the judges in every State shall be bound thereby, anything in the Constitution or laws of any State to the contrary notwithstanding.

3. The Senators and Representatives before mentioned, and the members of the several State Legislatures, and all executives and judicial officers, both of the United States and of the several States, shall be bound by oath or affirmation to support this Constitution; but no religious test shall ever be required as a qualification to any office or public trust under the United States.

### ARTICLE VII

The ratification of the Conventions of nine States shall be sufficient for the establishment of this Constitution between the States so ratifying the same.

## Amendments to the Constitution

Ten Original Amendments, in force 15 December 1791:

### AMENDMENT I

Congress shall make no law respecting an establishment of religion, or prohibiting the free exercise thereof; or abridging the freedom of speech or of the Press; or the right of the people peaceably to assemble and to petition the Government for a redress of grievances.

### AMENDMENT II

A well-regulated militia being necessary to the security of a free State, the right of the people to keep and bear arms shall not be infringed.

### AMENDMENT III

No soldier shall, in time of peace, be quartered in any house without the consent of the owner, nor in time of war but in a manner to be prescribed by law.

### AMENDMENT IV

The right of the people to be secure in their persons, houses, papers, and effects, against unreasonable searches and seizures, shall not be violated, and no warrants shall issue but upon probable cause, supported by oath or affirmation, and particularly describing the place to be searched, and the persons or things to be seized.

### AMENDMENT V

No person shall be held to answer for a capital or other infamous crime unless on a presentment or indictment of a Grand Jury, except in cases arising in the land or naval forces, or in the militia, when in actual service, in time of war or public danger; nor shall any person be subject for the same offense to be twice put in jeopardy of life or limb; nor shall be compelled in any criminal case to be a witness against himself, nor be deprived of life, liberty, or property, without due process of law; nor shall private property be taken for public use without just compensation.

### AMENDMENT VI

In all criminal prosecutions, the accused shall enjoy the right to a speedy and public trial, by an impartial jury of the State and district wherein the crime shall have been committed, which districts shall have been previously ascertained by law, and to be informed of the nature and cause of the accusation; to be confronted with the witnesses against him; to have compulsory process for obtaining witnesses in his favour, and to have the assistance of counsel for his defense.

### AMENDMENT VII

In suits at common law, where the value in controversy shall exceed 20 dollars, the right of trial by jury shall be preserved, and no fact tried by a jury shall be otherwise re-examined in any court of the United States than according to the rules of the common law.

### AMENDMENT VIII

Excessive bail shall not be required, nor excessive fines imposed, nor cruel and unusual punishments inflicted.

### AMENDMENT IX

The enumeration in the Constitution of certain rights shall not be construed to deny or disparage others retained by the people.

### AMENDMENT X

The powers not delegated to the United States by the Constitution, nor prohibited by it to the States, are reserved to the States respectively, or to the people.

Subsequent Amendments:

## AMENDMENT XI
(became part of the Constitution February 1795)

The judicial power of the United States shall not be construed to extend to any suit in law or equity, commenced or prosecuted against one of the United States, by citizens of another State, or by citizens or subjects of any foreign State.

## AMENDMENT XII
(ratified June 1804)

The Electors shall meet in their respective States, and vote by ballot for President and Vice-President, one of whom at least shall not be an inhabitant of the same State with themselves; they shall name in their ballots the person voted for as President, and in distinct ballots the person voted for as Vice-President; and they shall make distinct list of all persons voted for as President, and of all persons voted for as Vice-President, and of the number of votes for each, which list they shall sign and certify, and transmit, sealed, to the seat of the Government of the United States, directed to the President of the Senate; the President of the Senate shall, in the presence of the Senate and House of Representatives, open all the certificates and the votes shall then be counted; the person having the greatest number of votes for President shall be the President, if such number be a majority of the whole number of Electors appointed; and if no person have such majority, then from the persons having the highest number, not exceeding three, on the list of those voted for as President, the House of Representatives shall choose immediately, by ballot, the President. But in choosing the President, the votes shall be taken by States, the representation from each State having one vote; a quorum for this purpose shall consist of a member or members from two-thirds of the States, and a majority of all the States shall be necessary to a choice. And if the House of Representatives shall not choose a President, whenever the right of choice shall devolve upon them, before the fourth day of March next following, then the Vice-President shall act as President, as in the case of the death or other constitutional disability of the President. The person having the greatest number of votes as Vice-President shall be the Vice-President if such number be a majority of the whole number of Electors appointed, and if no person have a majority, then, from the two highest numbers on the list the Senate shall choose the Vice-President; a quorum for the purpose shall consist of two-thirds of the whole number of Senators, and a majority of the whole number shall be necessary to a choice. But no person constitutionally ineligible to the office of President shall be eligible to that of Vice-President of the United States.

## AMENDMENT XIII
(ratified December 1865)

1. Neither slavery nor involuntary servitude, except as a punishment for crime whereof the party shall have been duly convicted, shall exist within the United States, or any place subject to their jurisdiction.

2. Congress shall have the power to enforce this article by appropriate legislation.

## AMENDMENT XIV
(ratified July 1868)

1. All persons born or naturalized in the United States, and subject to the jurisdiction thereof, are citizens of the United States and of the State wherein they reside. No State shall make or enforce any law which shall abridge the privileges or immunities of citizens of the United States, nor shall any State deprive any person of life, liberty, or property without due process of law, nor deny to any person within its jurisdiction the equal protection of the laws.

2. Representatives shall be apportioned among the several States according to their respective numbers, counting the whole number of persons in each State excluding Indians not taxed. But when the right to vote at any election for the choice of Electors for President and Vice-President of the United States, Representatives in Congress, the executive and judicial officers of a State, or the members of the Legislature thereof, is denied to any of the male inhabitants of such State, being 21 years of age, and citizens of the United States, or in any way abridged, except for participation in rebellion, or other crime, the basis of representation therein shall be reduced in the proportion which the number of such male citizens shall bear to the whole number of male citizens 21 years of age in such State.

3. No person shall be a Senator or Representative in Congress, or Elector of President and Vice-President or hold any office, civil or military, under the United States, or under any State, who, having previously taken an oath as member of Congress or as an officer of the United States, or as a member of any State Legislature, or as an executive or judicial officer of any State, to support the Constitution of the United States, shall have engaged in insurrection or rebellion against the same, or given aid and comfort to the enemies thereof. But Congress may, by vote of two-thirds of each House, remove such disability.

4. The validity of the public debt of the United States, authorized by law, including debts incurred for payment of pensions and bounties for services in suppressing insurrection and rebellion, shall not be questioned. But neither the United States nor any State shall assume or pay any debt or obligation incurred in aid of insurrection or rebellion against the United States, or any claim for the loss or emancipation of any slave; but all such debts, obligations, and claims shall be held illegal and void.

5. The Congress shall have power to enforce by appropriate legislation the provisions of this article.

## AMENDMENT XV
(ratified March 1870)

1. The right of the citizens of the United States to vote shall not be denied or abridged by the United States or by any State on account of race, colour, or previous condition of servitude.

2. The Congress shall have power to enforce the provisions of this article by appropriate legislation.

## AMENDMENT XVI
(ratified February 1913)

The Congress shall have power to lay and collect taxes on incomes, from whatever sources derived, without apportionment among the several States, and without regard to any census or enumeration.

## AMENDMENT XVII
(ratified May 1913)

1. The Senate of the United States shall be composed of two Senators from each State, elected by the people thereof, for six years; and each Senator shall have one vote. The electors in each State shall have the qualifications requisite for electors of the most numerous branch of the State Legislature.

2. When vacancies happen in the representation of any State in the Senate, the executive authority of such State shall issue writs of election to fill such vacancies: Provided that the Legislature of any State may empower the Executive thereof to make temporary appointment until the people fill the vacancies by election as the Legislature may direct.

3. This amendment shall not be so construed as to affect the election or term of any Senator chosen before it becomes valid as part of the Constitution.

## AMENDMENT XVIII
(ratified January 1919*)

1. After one year from the ratification of this article the manufacture, sale, or transportation of intoxicating liquors within, the importation thereof into, or the exportation thereof from the United States, and all territory subject to the jurisdiction thereof for beverage purposes is hereby prohibited.

2. The Congress and the several States shall have concurrent power to enforce this article by appropriate legislation.

3. This article shall be inoperative unless it shall have been ratified as an amendment to the Constitution by the Legislatures of the several States, as provided in the Constitution, within seven years from the date of the submission hereof to the States by the Congress.

## AMENDMENT XIX
(ratified August 1920)

1. The right of citizens of the United States to vote shall not be denied or abridged by the United States or by any State on account of sex.

2. Congress shall have power, by appropriate legislation to enforce the provisions of this article.

## AMENDMENT XX
(ratified January 1933)

**Section 1**

The terms of the President and Vice-President shall end at noon on the 20th day of January, and the terms of Senators and Representatives at noon on the third day of January, of the years in which such terms would have ended if this article had not been ratified; and the terms of their successors shall then begin.

**Section 2**

The Congress shall assemble at least once in every year, and such meetings shall begin at noon on the third day of January, unless they shall by law appoint a different day.

---

* Repealed by Amendment XXI.

# THE UNITED STATES OF AMERICA

### Section 3
If, at the time fixed for the beginning of the term of the President, the President elect shall have died, the Vice-President elect shall become President. If a President shall not have been chosen before the time fixed for the beginning of his term, or if the President elect shall have failed to qualify, then the Vice-President elect shall act as President until a President shall have qualified; and the Congress may by law provide for the case wherein neither a President elect nor a Vice-President elect shall have qualified, declaring who shall then act as President, or the manner in which one who is to act shall be selected, and such person shall act accordingly until a President or Vice-President shall have qualified.

### Section 4
The Congress may by law provide for the case of the death of any of the persons from whom the House of Representatives may choose a President whenever the right of choice shall have devolved upon them, and for the case of the death of any of the persons from whom the Senate may choose a Vice-President whenever the right of choice shall have devolved upon them.

### Section 5
Sections 1 and 2 shall take effect on the 15th day of October following the ratification of this article.

### Section 6
This article shall be inoperative unless it shall have been ratified as an amendment to the Constitution by the legislature of three-fourths of the several States within seven years from the date of its submission.

## AMENDMENT XXI
(ratified December 1933)

### Section 1
The 18th article of amendment to the Constitution of the United States is hereby repealed.

### Section 2
The transportation or importation into any State, Territory or Possession of the United States for delivery or use therein of intoxicating liquors, in violation of the laws thereof, is hereby prohibited.

### Section 3
This article shall be inoperative unless it shall have been ratified as an amendment to the Constitution by conventions in the several States, as provided in the Constitution, within seven years from the date of the submission hereof to the States by the Congress.

## AMENDMENT XXII
(ratified February 1951)

No person shall be elected to the office of President more than twice, and no person who has held the office of President, or acted as President, for more than two years of a term to which some other person was elected President shall be elected to the office of President more than once. But this article shall not apply to any person holding the office of President when this Article was proposed by Congress, and shall not prevent any person who may be holding the office of President, or acting as President, during the term within which this Article becomes operative from holding the office of President or acting as President during the remainder of such term.

## AMENDMENT XXIII
(ratified March 1961)

### Section 1
The District constituting the seat of Government of the United States shall appoint in such manner as the Congress may direct:
A number of electors of President and Vice-President equal to the whole number of Senators and Representatives in Congress to which the District would be entitled if it were a State, but in no event more than the least populous State; they shall be in addition to those appointed by the States, but they shall be considered, for the purposes of the election of President and Vice-President, to be electors appointed by a State; and they shall meet in the District and perform such duties as provided by the 12th article of amendment.

### Section 2
The Congress shall have power to enforce this article by appropriate legislation.

## AMENDMENT XXIV
(ratified January 1964)

### Section 1
The right of citizens of the United States to vote in any primary or other election for President or Vice-President, for electors for President or Vice-President, or for Senator or Representative in Congress, shall not be denied or abridged by the United States or any State by reason of failure to pay any poll tax or other tax.

### Section 2
The Congress shall have power to enforce this article by appropriate legislation.

## AMENDMENT XXV
(ratified February 1967)

### Section 1
In the case of the removal of the President from office or of his death or resignation, the Vice-President shall become President.

### Section 2
Whenever there is a vacancy in the office of the Vice-President, the President shall nominate a Vice-President who shall take office upon confirmation by a majority vote of both Houses of Congress.

### Section 3
Whenever the President transmits to the President *pro tempore* of the Senate and the Speaker of the House of Representatives his written declaration that he is unable to discharge the powers and duties of his office, and until he transmits to them a written declaration to the contrary, such powers and duties shall be discharged by the Vice-President as Acting President.

### Section 4
Whenever the Vice-President and a majority of either the principal officers of the executive departments or of such other body as Congress may by law provide, transmit to the President *pro tempore* of the Senate and the Speaker of the House of Representatives their written declaration that the President is unable to discharge the powers and duties of his office, the Vice-President shall immediately assume the powers and duties of the office as Acting President.
Thereafter, when the President transmits to the President *pro tempore* of the Senate and the Speaker of the House of Representatives his written declaration that no inability exists, he shall resume the powers and duties of his office unless the Vice-President and a majority of either the principal officers of the executive department or of such other body as Congress may by law provide, transmit within four days to the President *pro tempore* of the Senate and the Speaker of the House of Representatives their written declaration that the President is unable to discharge the powers and duties of his office. Thereupon Congress shall decide the issue, assembling within 48 hours for that purpose if not in session. If the Congress, within 21 days after receipt of the latter written declaration, or, if Congress is not in session, within 21 days after Congress is required to assemble, determines by two-thirds vote of both Houses that the President is unable to discharge the powers and duties of his office, the Vice-President shall continue to discharge the same as Acting President; otherwise, the President shall resume the powers and duties of his office.

## AMENDMENT XXVI
(ratified July 1971)

### Section 1
The right of citizens of the United States, who are 18 years of age or older, to vote shall not be denied or abridged by the United States or by any State on account of age.

### Section 2
The Congress shall have power to enforce this article by appropriate legislation.

## AMENDMENT XXVII
(ratified May 1992)

No law, varying the compensation for the services of the Senators and Representatives, shall take effect, until an election of Representatives shall have intervened.

By Article IV, Section 3 of the Constitution, implemented by vote of Congress and referendum in the territory concerned, Alaska was admitted into the United States on 3 January 1959, and Hawaii on 21 August 1959.

THE UNITED STATES OF AMERICA                                                                                                      *Directory*

# The Executive

### HEAD OF STATE
**President:** BILL CLINTON (took office 20 January 1993).
**Vice-President:** ALBERT A. GORE, Jr.

### THE CABINET
(June 1995)

**Secretary of State:** WARREN M. CHRISTOPHER.
**Secretary of the Treasury:** ROBERT E. RUBIN.
**Secretary of Defense:** WILLIAM J. PERRY.
**Attorney-General:** JANET RENO.
**Secretary of the Interior:** BRUCE E. BABBITT.
**Secretary of Agriculture:** DANIEL R. GLICKMAN.
**Secretary of Commerce:** RONALD H. BROWN.
**Secretary of Labor:** ROBERT B. REICH.
**Secretary of Health and Human Services:** DONNA SHALALA.
**Secretary of Housing and Urban Development:** HENRY G. CISNEROS.
**Secretary of Transportation:** FEDERICO F. PEÑA.
**Secretary of Energy:** HAZEL R. O'LEARY.
**Secretary of Education:** RICHARD W. RILEY.
**Secretary of Veterans Affairs:** JESSE BROWN.

### Officials with Cabinet Rank
**Director of the Office of Management and Budget:** ALICE M. RIVLIN.
**US Trade Representative:** MICKEY KANTOR.

### GOVERNMENT DEPARTMENTS

**Department of Agriculture:** 14th St and Independence Ave, SW, Washington, DC 20250-0001; tel. (202) 447-2791; fax (202) 447-5340; f. 1889.
**Department of Commerce:** 14th St and Constitution Ave, NW, Washington, DC 20230-0001; tel. (202) 377-2000; fax (202) 377-5270; f. 1913.
**Department of Defense:** The Pentagon, Washington, DC 20310-0001; tel. (202) 545-6700; fax (202) 697-1656; f. 1947.
**Department of Education:** 400 Maryland Ave, SW, Washington, DC 20202-0001; tel. (202) 401-1576; fax (202) 401-3130; f. 1979.
**Department of Energy:** James Forrestal Bldg, 1000 Independence Ave, SW, Washington, DC 20585-0001; tel. (202) 586-5000; fax (202) 586-6783; f. 1977.
**Department of Health and Human Services:** 200 Independence Ave, SW, Washington, DC 20201-0001; tel. (202) 690-7000; fax (202) 690-7203; f. 1980.
**Department of Housing and Urban Development:** 451 7th St, SW, Washington, DC 20410-0001; tel. (202) 708-1112; fax (202) 708-0299; f. 1965.
**Department of the Interior:** 18th and C Sts, NW, Washington, DC 20240-0001; tel. (202) 343-1100; f. 1849.
**Department of Justice:** 10th St and Constitution Ave, NW, Washington, DC 20530-0001; tel. (202) 633-2000; fax (202) 633-1678; f. 1870.
**Department of Labor:** 200 Constitution Ave, NW, Washington, DC 20210-0001; tel. (202) 219-6411; fax (202) 219-6354; f. 1913.
**Department of State:** 2201 C St, NW, Washington, DC 20520-0001; tel. (202) 647-4000; fax (202) 632-5854; f. 1789.
**Department of Transportation:** 400 7th St, SW, Washington, DC 20590-0001; tel. (202) 366-4000; f. 1967.
**Department of the Treasury:** 1500 Pennsylvania Ave, NW, Washington, DC 20220-0001; tel (202) 566-2000; fax (202) 566-8066; f. 1789.
**Department of Veterans Affairs:** 810 Vermont Ave, NW, Washington, DC 20420-0001; tel. (202) 233-4010; fax (202) 376-5517; f. 1989.

### EXECUTIVE OFFICE OF THE PRESIDENT

**The White House Office:** 1600 Pennsylvania Ave, Washington, DC 20500-0001; tel. (202) 456–1414; co-ordinates activities relating to the President's immediate office; White House Chief of Staff LEON E. PANETTA.
**Council of Economic Advisers:** Old Executive Office Bldg, 17th St and Pennsylvania Ave, NW, Washington, DC 20500-0001; tel. (202) 395-5042; Chair. JOSEPH E. STIGLITZ.
**Domestic Policy Council:** Old Executive Office Bldg, 1600 Pennsylvania Ave, NW, Washington, DC 20500-0001; tel. (202) 456-6515; fax (202) 456-2883; Dep. Asst to the President (Domestic Policy Council) CAROL H. RASCOW.
**National Economic Council:** Executive Office Bldg, Washington, DC 20503; Dir LAURA TYSON.
**National Security Council:** Executive Office Bldg, 1600 Pennsylvania Ave, NW, Washington, DC 20500-0001; tel. (202) 456-1414; Asst to the Pres. for Nat. Security Affairs W. ANTHONY LAKE.
**Office of Administration:** 725 17th St, NW, Room 480, Washington, DC 20503; tel. (202) 395-6963; fax (202) 395-7279; Dir PATSY L. THOMASSON.
**Office of Federal Procurement Policy:** Executive Office Bldg, Washington, DC 20503; tel. (202) 395-5802.
**Office of Management and Budget:** 725 17th St, NW Washington, DC 20503-0001; tel. (202) 395-3000; fax (202) 456-2883; Dir ALICE M. RIVLIN.
**Office of National Drug Control Policy:** Old Executive Office Bldg, 17th St and Pennsylvania Ave, NW, Washington, DC 20506; Dir LEE P. BROWN.
**Office of Science and Technology Policy:** Old Executive Office Bldg, Room 424, 17th St and Pennsylvania Ave, NW, Washington, DC, 20500-0001; tel. (202) 456-7116; fax (202) 456-6021; Dir Dr JOHN H. GIBBONS.
**Office of the United States Trade Representative:** 600 17th St, NW, Washington, DC 20506-0001; tel. (202) 395-3230; fax (202) 395-3911; US Trade Rep. MICKEY KANTOR.

**United States Mission to the United Nations:** 799 United Nations Plaza, New York, NY 10017; US Rep. to the United Nations MADELEINE K. ALBRIGHT.

**Presidential Election, 3 November 1992**

|  | Popular votes | % of Popular votes | Electoral College votes |
|---|---|---|---|
| BILL CLINTON (Democrat) | 44,908,254 | 42.95 | 370 |
| GEORGE BUSH (Republican) | 39,102,343 | 37.40 | 168 |
| ROSS PEROT (Independent) | 19,741,065 | 18.88 | — |
| Others | 801,074 | 0.77 | — |
| Total | 104,552,736 | 100.00 | 538 |

# Legislature

### CONGRESS
#### Senate
(June 1995)

The Senate comprises 100 members. Senators' terms are for six years, one-third of the Senate being elected every two years.
**President of the Senate:** Vice-President ALBERT A. GORE, Jr.
**President Pro Tempore:** STROM THURMOND.
 **Republicans:** 54 seats
 **Democrats:** 46 seats
**Majority Leader:** ROBERT J. DOLE.
**Minority Leader:** THOMAS A. DASCHLE.

#### Members
With political party and year in which term expires, on 3 January in all cases.

**Alabama**
| | | |
|---|---|---|
| HOWELL T. HEFLIN | Dem. | 1997 |
| RICHARD C. SHELBY | Rep. | 1999 |

**Alaska**
| | | |
|---|---|---|
| TED STEVENS | Rep. | 1997 |
| FRANK H. MURKOWSKI | Rep. | 1999 |

**Arizona**
| | | |
|---|---|---|
| JOHN MCCAIN, III | Rep. | 1999 |
| JON KYL | Rep. | 2001 |

**Arkansas**
| | | |
|---|---|---|
| DAVID H. PRYOR | Dem. | 1997 |
| DALE BUMPERS | Dem. | 1999 |

**California**
| | | |
|---|---|---|
| BARBARA BOXER | Dem. | 1999 |
| DIANNE FEINSTEIN | Dem. | 2001 |

# THE UNITED STATES OF AMERICA — Directory

**Colorado**
| | | |
|---|---|---|
| Hank Brown | Rep. | 1997 |
| Ben Nighthorse Campbell | Rep. | 1999 |

**Connecticut**
| | | |
|---|---|---|
| Christopher J. Dodd | Dem. | 1999 |
| Joseph I. Lieberman | Dem. | 2001 |

**Delaware**
| | | |
|---|---|---|
| Joseph R. Biden, Jr | Dem. | 1997 |
| William V. Roth, Jr | Rep. | 2001 |

**Florida**
| | | |
|---|---|---|
| D. Robert Graham | Dem. | 1999 |
| Connie Mack | Rep. | 2001 |

**Georgia**
| | | |
|---|---|---|
| Sam Nunn | Dem. | 1997 |
| Paul Coverdell | Rep. | 1999 |

**Hawaii**
| | | |
|---|---|---|
| Daniel K. Inouye | Dem. | 1999 |
| Daniel K. Akaka | Dem. | 2001 |

**Idaho**
| | | |
|---|---|---|
| Larry E. Craig | Rep. | 1997 |
| Dirk Kempthorne | Rep. | 1999 |

**Illinois**
| | | |
|---|---|---|
| Paul Simon | Dem. | 1997 |
| Carol Moseley Braun | Dem. | 1999 |

**Indiana**
| | | |
|---|---|---|
| Daniel R. Coats | Rep. | 1999 |
| Richard G. Lugar | Rep. | 2001 |

**Iowa**
| | | |
|---|---|---|
| Tom Harkin | Dem. | 1997 |
| Charles E. Grassley | Rep. | 1999 |

**Kansas**
| | | |
|---|---|---|
| Nancy Landon Kassebaum | Rep. | 1997 |
| Robert J. Dole | Rep. | 1999 |

**Kentucky**
| | | |
|---|---|---|
| A. Mitchell McConnell | Rep. | 1997 |
| Wendell H. Ford | Dem. | 1999 |

**Louisiana**
| | | |
|---|---|---|
| J. Bennett Johnston | Dem. | 1997 |
| John B. Breaux | Dem. | 1999 |

**Maine**
| | | |
|---|---|---|
| William S. Cohen | Rep. | 1997 |
| Olympia J. Snowe | Rep. | 2001 |

**Maryland**
| | | |
|---|---|---|
| Barbara A. Mikulski | Dem. | 1999 |
| Paul S. Sarbanes | Dem. | 2001 |

**Massachusetts**
| | | |
|---|---|---|
| John F. Kerry | Dem. | 1997 |
| Edward M. Kennedy | Dem. | 2001 |

**Michigan**
| | | |
|---|---|---|
| Carl Levin | Dem. | 1997 |
| Spencer Abraham | Rep. | 2001 |

**Minnesota**
| | | |
|---|---|---|
| Paul D. Wellstone | Dem. | 1997 |
| Rod Grams | Rep. | 2001 |

**Mississippi**
| | | |
|---|---|---|
| Thad Cochran | Rep. | 1997 |
| Trent Lott | Rep. | 2001 |

**Missouri**
| | | |
|---|---|---|
| Christopher S. Bond | Rep. | 1999 |
| John Ashcroft | Rep. | 2001 |

**Montana**
| | | |
|---|---|---|
| Max Baucus | Dem. | 1997 |
| Conrad Burns | Rep. | 2001 |

**Nebraska**
| | | |
|---|---|---|
| J. James Exon | Dem. | 1997 |
| Bob Kerrey | Dem. | 2001 |

**Nevada**
| | | |
|---|---|---|
| Harry M. Reid | Dem. | 1999 |
| Richard H. Bryan | Dem. | 2001 |

**New Hampshire**
| | | |
|---|---|---|
| Robert C. Smith | Rep. | 1997 |
| Judd Gregg | Rep. | 1999 |

**New Jersey**
| | | |
|---|---|---|
| Bill Bradley | Dem. | 1997 |
| Frank R. Lautenburg | Dem. | 2001 |

**New Mexico**
| | | |
|---|---|---|
| Pete V. Domenici | Rep. | 1997 |
| Jeff Bingaman | Dem. | 2001 |

**New York**
| | | |
|---|---|---|
| Alfonse M. D'Amato | Rep. | 1999 |
| Daniel P. Moynihan | Dem. | 2001 |

**North Carolina**
| | | |
|---|---|---|
| Jesse A. Helms | Rep. | 1997 |
| Lauch Faircloth | Rep. | 1999 |

**North Dakota**
| | | |
|---|---|---|
| Byron L. Dorgan | Dem. | 1999 |
| Kent Conrad | Dem. | 2001 |

**Ohio**
| | | |
|---|---|---|
| John H. Glenn, Jr | Dem. | 1999 |
| Mike DeWine | Rep. | 2001 |

**Oklahoma**
| | | |
|---|---|---|
| James M. Inhofe | Rep. | 1997 |
| Don Nickles | Rep. | 1999 |

**Oregon**
| | | |
|---|---|---|
| Mark O. Hatfield | Rep. | 1997 |
| Robert W. Packwood | Rep. | 1999 |

**Pennsylvania**
| | | |
|---|---|---|
| Arlen Specter | Rep. | 1999 |
| Rick Santorum | Rep. | 2001 |

**Rhode Island**
| | | |
|---|---|---|
| Claiborne Pell | Dem. | 1997 |
| John H. Chafee | Rep. | 2001 |

**South Carolina**
| | | |
|---|---|---|
| Strom Thurmond | Rep. | 1997 |
| Ernest F. Hollings | Dem. | 1999 |

**South Dakota**
| | | |
|---|---|---|
| Larry Pressler | Rep. | 1997 |
| Thomas A. Daschle | Dem. | 1999 |

**Tennessee**
| | | |
|---|---|---|
| Fred Thompson | Rep. | 1997 |
| Bill Frist | Rep. | 2001 |

**Texas**
| | | |
|---|---|---|
| Phil Gramm | Rep. | 1997 |
| Kay Bailey Hutchison | Rep. | 2001 |

**Utah**
| | | |
|---|---|---|
| Robert F. Bennett | Rep. | 1999 |
| Orrin G. Hatch | Rep. | 2001 |

**Vermont**
| | | |
|---|---|---|
| Patrick J. Leahy | Dem. | 1999 |
| James M. Jeffords | Rep. | 2001 |

**Virginia**
| | | |
|---|---|---|
| John W. Warner | Rep. | 1997 |
| Charles S. Robb | Dem. | 2001 |

**Washington**
| | | |
|---|---|---|
| Patty Murray | Dem. | 1999 |
| Slade Gorton | Rep. | 2001 |

## THE UNITED STATES OF AMERICA

**West Virginia**

| John D. Rockefeller, IV | Dem. | 1997 |
| Robert C. Byrd | Dem. | 2001 |

**Wisconsin**

| Russell D. Feingold | Dem. | 1999 |
| Herbert H. Kohl | Dem. | 2001 |

**Wyoming**

| Alan K. Simpson | Rep. | 1997 |
| Craig Thomas | Rep. | 2001 |

### House of Representatives
(July 1995)

A new House of Representatives, comprising 435 members, is elected every two years.

**Speaker:** Newt Gingrich.

  **Republicans:** 232 seats

  **Democrats:** 202 seats

  **Independent:** 1 seat

**Majority Leader:** Richard K. Armey.

**Minority Leader:** Richard A. Gephardt.

## Independent Agencies

**ACTION:** 1100 Vermont Ave, NW, Washington, DC 20525-0001; tel. (202) 606-4880; fax (202) 606-4928; f. 1971; Dir John Seal (acting).

**Administrative Conference of the United States:** 2120 L St, NW, Washington, DC 20037-1568; tel. (202) 254-7020; f. 1964; Chair. Thomasina V. Rogers.

**African Development Foundation:** 1400 Eye St, NW, 10th Floor, Washington, DC 20005; tel. (202) 673-3916; telex 6711367; fax (202) 673-3810; Pres. Gregory Robeson Smith.

**American Battle Monuments Commission:** 20 Massachusetts Ave, NW, Washington, DC 20314-0001; tel. (202) 761-0533; fax (202) 761-1375; f. 1923; Chair. Gen. (retd) Frederick F. Woerner.

**Appalachian Regional Commission:** 1666 Connecticut Ave, NW, Washington, DC 20235; tel. (202) 673-7968; fax (202) 673-7930; f. 1965; Fed. Co-Chair. Jacqueline Phillips, States' Co-Chair. (vacant)

**Board for International Broadcasting:** 1201 Connecticut Ave, Suite 400, NW, Washington, DC 20036; tel. (202) 254-8040; fax (202) 254-3929; f. 1973; Chair. Daniel A. Mica.

**Central Intelligence Agency:** Washington, DC 20505; tel. (703) 351-7676; f. 1947; Dir John M. Deutch.

**Commission on Civil Rights:** 624 9th St, NW, Washington, DC 20425; tel. (202) 376-7700; f. 1957; Chair. Mary Frances Berry.

**Commission of Fine Arts:** 441 F St, NW, Washington, DC 20001; tel. (202) 566-1066; f. 1910; Chair. J. Carter Brown.

**Commodity Futures Trading Commission:** 2033 K St, NW, Washington, DC 20581; tel. (202) 254-6387; fax (202) 254-6265; f. 1974; Chair. Mary L. Schapiro.

**Consumer Product Safety Commission:** East-West Towers, 4330 East-West Hwy, Bethesda, MD 20814; tel. (301) 504-0444; f. 1972; Chair. Ann Brown.

**Environmental Protection Agency:** 401 M St, SW, Washington, DC 20460; tel. (202) 382-4700; telex 892757; fax (202) 382-7886; f. 1970; Admin. Carol M. Browner.

**Equal Employment Opportunity Commission:** 1801 L St, NW, Washington, DC 20507; tel. (202) 634-6922; fax (202) 634-7332; f. 1965; Chair. Tony E. Gallegos (acting).

**Export-Import Bank of the United States:** see Finance—Banking.

**Farm Credit Administration:** 1501 Farm Credit Drive, McLean, VA 22102–5090; tel. (703) 883-4000; Chair. Billy Ross Brown.

**Federal Communications Commission:** see Radio and Television.

**Federal Deposit Insurance Corporation:** 550 17th St, NW, Washington, DC 20429-0001; tel. (202) 393-8400; fax (202) 347-2773; f. 1933; Chair. Ricki Helfer.

**Federal Election Commission:** 999 E St, NW, Washington, DC 20463-0001; tel. (202) 291-3440; fax (202) 219-3880; f. 1971; Chair. Trevor Potter.

**Federal Emergency Management Agency:** 500 C St, SW, Washington, DC 20472-0001; tel. (202) 646-2500; fax (202) 646-2531; f. 1979; Dir James Lee.

**Federal Housing Finance Board:** 1777 F St, NW, Washington, DC 20006; tel. (202) 408-2938; fax (202) 408-1435; Chair. (vacant).

**Federal Labor Relations Authority:** 607 14th St, NW, Washington, DC 20424-0001; tel. (202) 482-6500; fax (202) 482-6635; f. 1978; Chair. Phyllis N. Segal.

**Federal Maritime Commission:** see Transport—Ocean Shipping.

**Federal Mediation and Conciliation Service:** 2100 K St, NW, Washington, DC 20427-0001; tel. (202) 653-5290; f. 1947; Dir Joan Calhoun Weils.

**Federal Reserve System:** see Finance—Banking.

**Federal Retirement Thrift Investment Board:** 1250 H St, NW, Washington, DC 20005; tel. (202) 523-5660; Chair. James H. Atkins (acting).

**Federal Trade Commission:** Pennsylvania Ave at 6th St, NW, Washington, DC 20580-0001; tel. (202) 326-3650; f. 1914; Chair. Janet D. Steiger.

**General Accounting Office:** 441 G St, NW, Washington, DC 20548-0001; tel. (202) 275-5481; telex 710-8229273; fax (202) 275-4021; Comptroller-Gen. of the US Charles A. Bowsher.

**General Services Administration:** 18th and F Sts, NW, Room 6137, Washington, DC 20405-0001; tel. (202) 501-0800; fax (202) 219-1243; f. 1949; Admin. Roger W. Johnson.

**Government Printing Office:** see Publishers.

**Inter-American Foundation:** 901 North Stuart St, Arlington, VA 22203; tel. (703) 841-3800; telex 247008; fax (703) 841-0973; f. 1969; Pres. George A. Evans.

**Interstate Commerce Commission:** see Transport.

**Library of Congress:** 10 First St, SE, Washington, DC 20540; tel. (202) 707-5000; telex 710-8220185; fax (202) 707-5844; f. 1800; Librarian James H. Billington.

**Merit Systems Protection Board:** 1120 Vermont Ave, NW, Washington, DC 20419; tel. (202) 653-7101; fax (202) 653-5793; f. 1883; Chair. Benjamin L. Erdreich.

**National Aeronautics and Space Administration:** 600 Independence Ave, SW, Washington, DC 20546-0001; tel. (202) 453-1000; fax (202) 755-9234; f. 1958; Admin. (vacant).

**National Archives and Records Administration:** Pennsylvania Ave at 7th St, NW, Washington, DC 20408; tel. (202) 501-5130; fax (202) 501-5244; f. 1934; Archivist Trudy H. Peterson (acting).

**National Capital Planning Commission:** 801 Pennsylvania Ave, NW, Suite 301, Washington, DC 20576-0001; tel. (202) 724-0174; fax (202) 724-0195; f. 1952; Chair. Harvey B. Gantt.

**National Credit Union Administration:** 1775 Duke St, Alexandria, VA 22314-3428; tel. (703) 518-6300; fax (703) 518-6319; f. 1970; Chair. Norman E. D'Amours.

**National Endowment for the Arts:** 1100 Pennsylvania Ave, NW, Room 802, Washington, DC 20506-0001; tel. (202) 682-5400; fax (202) 682-5798; f. 1965; Chair. Jane Alexander.

**National Endowment for the Humanities:** 1100 Pennsylvania Ave, NW, Room 402, Washington, DC 20506; tel. (202) 606-8400; f. 1965; Chair. Dr Sheldon Hackney.

**National Labor Relations Board:** 1099 14th St, NW, Washington, DC 20570; tel. (202) 254-9392; fax (202) 254-6781; f. 1935; Chair. William B. Gould, IV.

**National Mediation Board:** 1301 K St, NW, Suite 250, Washington, DC 20572; tel. (202) 523-5335; f. 1934; Chair. Ernest W. DuBester.

**National Science Foundation:** 4201 Wilson Blvd, Arlington, VA 22230; tel. (202) 357-9498; fax (202) 357-7745; f. 1950; Dir James J. Dunderstadt.

**National Transportation Safety Board:** see Transport.

**Nuclear Regulatory Commission:** 1717 H St, NW, Washington, DC 20555; tel. (202) 492-7000; Chair. Ivan Selin.

**Occupational Safety and Health Review Commission:** 1120 20th St, NW, Washington, DC 20036; tel. (202) 634-7943; f. 1970; Chair. Stuart E. Weisberg, Jr.

**Office of Personnel Management:** 1900 E St, NW, Washington, DC 20415-0001; tel. (202) 632-9594; telex 4931447; f. 1979; Dir James B. King.

**Overseas Private Investment Corporation:** 1615 M St, NW, Washington, DC 20527; tel. (202) 457-7001; f. 1971; Pres. and CEO Ruth Harkin.

**Panama Canal Commission:** International Sq., 1825 I St, NW, Suite 1050, Washington, DC 20006-5402; tel. (202) 634-6441; f. 1979; Chair. Robert R. McMillan.

**Peace Corps:** 1990 K St, NW, Washington, DC 20526-0001; tel. (202) 606-3010; f. 1961; Dir (vacant).

**Pennsylvania Avenue Development Corporation:** 1331 Pennsylvania Ave, NW, Suite 1220 North, Washington, DC 20004-1703; tel. (202) 724-9091; fax (202) 724-0246; f. 1972; Chair. Richard A. Hauser.

THE UNITED STATES OF AMERICA

**Pension Benefit Guaranty Corporation:** 2020 K St, NW, Washington, DC 20006-1860; tel. (202) 778-8800; fax (202) 778-8819; f. 1974; Exec. Dir JAMES B. LOCKHART.

**Postal Rate Commission:** 1333 H St, NW, Washington, DC 20268; tel. (202) 789-6800; fax (202) 789-6861; f. 1970; Chair. EDWARD J. GLEIMAN.

**Railroad Retirement Board:** 844 Rush St, Room 804, Chicago, IL 60611; tel. (312) 751-4500; fax (312) 751-4923; f. 1935; Chair. GLEN L. BOWER.

**Resolution Trust Corporation:** 801 17th St, NW, Washington, DC 20434-0001; tel. (202) 416-6940; f. 1989; Chair. JOHN E. RYAN.

**Securities and Exchange Commission:** see Finance—Principal Stock Exchanges.

**Selective Service System:** 1515 Wilson Blvd, Arlington, VA 22209-2425; tel. (703) 235-2555; fax (703) 235-2212; f. 1940; Dir GIL CORONADO.

**Small Business Administration:** 409 Third St, SW, Washington, DC 20416; tel. (202) 205-7561; f. 1953; Admin. PHILIP LADER.

**Smithsonian Institution:** Smithsonian Institution Bldg, 1000 Jefferson Drive, SW, Washington, DC 20560-0001; tel. (202) 357-2700; fax (202) 786-2515; f. 1846; Sec. I. MICHAEL HEYMAN.

**Tennessee Valley Authority:** 400 West Summit Hill Drive, Knoxville, TN 37902-1499; tel. (615) 632-2101; f. 1933; Chair. CRAVEN CROWELL.

**Thrift Depositor Protection Oversight Board:** 808 17th St, NW, Washington, DC 20232; Chair. LLOYD BENTSEN.

**United States Arms Control and Disarmament Agency:** 320 21st St, NW, Washington, DC 20451-0001; tel. (202) 647-8677; fax (202) 647-6721; f. 1961; Dir JOHN HOLUM.

**United States Information Agency:** 301 Fourth St, SW, Washington, DC 20547; tel. (202) 619-4742; f. 1953; Dir JOSEPH DUFFEY.

**United States International Development Co-operation Agency:** 320 21st St, NW, Washington, DC 20523; tel. (202) 647-9620; f. 1979; Dir JAMES H. MICHEL (acting).

**United States International Trade Commission:** 500 E St, SW, Washington, DC 20436-0001; tel. (202) 205-2000; fax (202) 205-2798; f. 1916; Chair. PETER S. WATSON.

**United States Postal Service:** 475 L'Enfant Plaza, SW, Washington, DC 20260-0001; tel. (202) 268-2000; fax (202) 245-5791; f. 1970; Postmaster-Gen. MARVIN T. RUNYON.

## State Governments

(with expiration date of Governors' current term of office; legislatures at mid-1994)

**Alabama**
Governor: FOB JAMES, Jr; Rep.; Jan. 1999.
Senate: Dem. 27, Rep. 8.
House: Dem. 82, Rep. 23.

**Alaska**
Governor: TONY KNOWLES; Dem.; Dec. 1998.
Senate: Dem. 10, Rep. 10.
House: Dem. 20, Rep. 18, other 2.

**Arizona**
Governor: J. FIFE SYMINGTON, III; Rep.; Jan. 1999.
Senate: Dem. 12, Rep. 18.
House: Dem. 25, Rep. 35.

**Arkansas**
Governor: JIM GUY TUCKER; Dem.; Jan. 1999.
Senate: Dem. 30, Rep. 5.
House: Dem. 88, Rep. 11, Ind. 1.

**California**
Governor: PETE WILSON; Rep.; Jan. 1999.
Senate: Dem. 22, Rep. 15, Ind. 2, 1 vacancy.
Assembly: Dem. 47, Rep. 33.

**Colorado**
Governor: ROY ROMER; Dem.; Jan. 1999.
Senate: Dem. 16, Rep. 19.
House: Dem. 31, Rep. 34.

**Connecticut**
Governor: JOHN G. ROWLAND; Rep.; Jan. 1999.
Senate: Dem. 19, Rep. 17.
House: Dem. 86, Rep. 65.

*Directory*

**Delaware**
Governor: THOMAS R. CARPER; Dem.; Jan. 1997.
Senate: Dem. 14, Rep. 7.
House: Dem. 18, Rep. 23.

**Florida**
Governor: LAWTON CHILES; Dem.; Jan. 1999.
Senate: Dem. 20, Rep. 20.
House: Dem. 71, Rep. 49.

**Georgia**
Governor: ZELL MILLER; Dem.; Jan. 1999.
Senate: Dem. 38, Rep. 17, 1 vacancy.
House: Dem. 128, Rep. 51, 1 vacancy.

**Hawaii**
Governor: BEN CAYETANO; Dem.; Dec. 1998.
Senate: Dem. 22, Rep. 3.
House: Dem. 47, Rep. 4.

**Idaho**
Governor: PHIL BATT; Rep.; Jan. 1999.
Senate: Dem. 12, Rep. 23.
House: Dem. 20, Rep. 50.

**Illinois**
Governor: JIM EDGAR; Rep.; Jan. 1999.
Senate: Dem. 27, Rep. 32.
House: Dem. 67, Rep. 51.

**Indiana**
Governor: EVAN BAYH; Dem.; Jan. 1997.
Senate: Dem. 22, Rep. 28.
House: Dem. 55, Rep. 45.

**Iowa**
Governor: TERRY E. BRANSTAD; Rep.; Jan. 1999.
Senate: Dem. 27, Rep. 23.
House: Dem. 49, Rep. 51.

**Kansas**
Governor: BILL GRAVES; Rep.; Jan. 1999.
Senate: Dem. 13, Rep. 27.
House: Dem. 59, Rep. 66.

**Kentucky**
Governor: BRERETON C. JONES; Dem.; Dec. 1999.
Senate: Dem. 23, Rep. 14.
House: Dem. 71, Rep. 29.

**Louisiana**
Governor: EDWIN W. EDWARDS; Dem.; May 1996.
Senate: Dem. 33, Rep. 6.
House: Dem. 86, Rep. 17, Ind. 11, 1 vacancy.

**Maine**
Governor: ANGUS KING; Ind., Jan. 1999.
Senate: Dem. 20, Rep. 15.
House: Dem. 90, Rep. 61.

**Maryland**
Governor: PARRIS GLENDENING; Dem.; Jan. 1999.
Senate: Dem. 38, Rep. 9.
House: Dem. 117, Rep. 24.

**Massachusetts**
Governor: WILLIAM F. WELD; Rep.; Jan. 1999.
Senate: Dem. 31, Rep. 9.
House: Dem. 124, Rep. 35, Ind. 1.

**Michigan**
Governor: JOHN ENGLER; Rep.; Jan. 1999.
Senate: Dem. 15, Rep. 22, 1 vacancy.
House: Dem. 55, Rep. 55.

**Minnesota**
Governor: ARNE H. CARLSON; Ind. Rep.; Jan. 1999.
Senate: Dem. Farm. Lab. 45, Ind. Rep. 22.
House: Dem. Farm. Lab. 85, Ind. Rep. 49.

**Mississippi**
Governor: KIRK FORDICE; Rep.; Jan. 1996.
Senate: Dem. 37, Rep. 15.
House: Dem. 90, Rep. 30, Ind. 2.

# THE UNITED STATES OF AMERICA

### Missouri
Governor: MEL CARNAHAN; Dem.; Jan. 1997.
Senate: Dem. 19, Rep. 14, 1 vacancy.
House: Dem. 95, Rep. 67, 1 vacancy.

### Montana
Governor: MARC RACICOT; Rep.; Jan. 1997.
Senate: Dem. 30, Rep. 20.
House: Dem. 46, Rep. 53, 1 vacancy.

### Nebraska
Governor: BEN NELSON; Dem.; Jan. 1999.
Legislature: unicameral body comprising 49 members elected on a non-partisan ballot and classed as senators.

### Nevada
Governor: ROBERT MILLER; Dem.; Jan. 1999.
Senate: Dem. 10, Rep. 11.
Assembly: Dem. 29, Rep. 13.

### New Hampshire
Governor: STEVE MERRILL; Rep.; Jan. 1997.
Senate: Dem. 11, Rep. 13.
House: Dem. 137, Rep. 257, Ind. and other 5, 1 vacancy.

### New Jersey
Governor: CHRISTINE TODD WHITMAN; Rep.; Jan. 1998.
Senate: Dem. 13, Rep. 27.
Assembly: Dem. 27, Rep. 53.

### New Mexico
Governor: GARY JOHNSON; Rep.; Jan. 1999.
Senate: Dem. 26, Rep. 15, Ind. 1.
House: Dem. 53, Rep. 17.

### New York
Governor: GEORGE E. PATAKI; Rep.; Jan. 1999.
Senate: Dem. 26, Rep. 35.
Assembly: Dem. 102, Rep. 48.

### North Carolina
Governor: JAMES B. HUNT, Jr; Dem.; Jan. 1997.
Senate: Dem. 39, Rep. 11.
House: Dem. 78, Rep. 42.

### North Dakota
Governor: EDWARD T. SCHAFER; Rep.; Jan. 1997.
Senate: Dem. 25, Rep. 24.
House: Dem. 33, Rep. 65.

### Ohio
Governor: GEORGE V. VOINOVICH; Rep.; Jan. 1999.
Senate: Dem. 13, Rep. 20.
House: Dem. 53, Rep. 46.

### Oklahoma
Governor: FRANK KEATING; Rep.; Jan. 1999.
Senate: Dem. 37, Rep. 11.
House: Dem. 68, Rep. 33.

### Oregon
Governor: JOHN KITZHABER; Dem.; Jan. 1999.
Senate: Dem. 16, Rep. 14.
House: Dem. 32, Rep. 28.

### Pennsylvania
Governor: THOMAS RIDGE; Rep.; Jan. 1999.
Senate: Dem. 26, Rep. 24.
House: Dem. 102, Rep. 101.

### Rhode Island
Governor: LINCOLN C. ALMOND; Rep.; Jan. 1999.
Senate: Dem. 39, Rep. 11.
House: Dem. 85, Rep. 15.

### South Carolina
Governor: DAVID BEASLEY; Rep.; Jan. 1999.
Senate: Dem. 30, Rep. 16.
House: Dem. 73, Rep. 50, Ind. 1.

### South Dakota
Governor: WILLAM J. JANKLOW; Rep.; Jan. 1999.
Senate: Dem. 20, Rep. 15.
House: Dem. 29, Rep. 41.

### Tennessee
Governor: DON SUNDQUIST; Rep.; Jan. 1999.
Senate: Dem. 19, Rep. 14.
House: Dem. 63, Rep. 36.

### Texas
Governor: GEORGE W. BUSH; Rep.; Jan. 1999.
Senate: Dem. 18, Rep. 13.
House: Dem. 92, Rep. 58.

### Utah
Governor: MICHAEL O. LEAVITT; Rep.; Jan. 1997.
Senate: Dem. 11, Rep. 18.
House: Dem. 26, Rep. 49.

### Vermont
Governor: HOWARD DEAN; Dem.; Jan. 1997.
Senate: Dem. 14, Rep. 16.
House: Dem. 87, Rep. 59, Progressive Coalition 2, Ind. 2.

### Virginia
Governor: GEORGE F. ALLEN; Rep.; Jan. 1998.
Senate: Dem. 22, Rep. 18.
House: Dem. 58, Rep. 41, Ind. 1.

### Washington
Governor: MIKE LOWRY; Dem.; Jan. 1997.
Senate: Dem. 28, Rep. 21.
House: Dem. 65, Rep. 33.

### West Virginia
Governor: GASTON CAPERTON; Dem.; Jan. 1997.
Senate: Dem. 32, Rep. 2.
House: Dem. 79, Rep. 21.

### Wisconsin
Governor: TOMMY G. THOMPSON; Rep.; Jan. 1999.
Senate: Dem. 16, Rep. 17.
Assembly: Dem. 52, Rep. 47.

### Wyoming
Governor: JIM GERINGER; Rep.; Jan. 1999.
Senate: Dem. 10, Rep. 20.
House: Dem. 19, Rep. 45.

## Political Organizations

**Communist Party USA:** 235 West 23rd St, 7th Floor, New York, NY 10011; tel. (212) 989-4994; fax (212) 229-1713; f. 1919; Chair. GUS HALL.

**Conservative Caucus:** 450 Maple Ave East, Vienna, VA 22180; tel. (703) 938-9626; fax (703) 281-4108; f. 1974; Dir HOWARD PHILLIPS.

**Democratic National Committee:** 430 South Capitol St, SE, Washington, DC 20003; tel. (202) 863-8000; fax (202) 863-8140; f. 1848; Nat. Chair. DONALD F. FOWLER; Gen. Chair. CHRISTOPHER DODD; Sec. KATHLEEN M. VICK; Treas. ROBERT MATSUI.

**The Greens/Green Party USA:** POB 30208, Kansas City, MO 64112; tel. (816) 931-9366; f. 1984; 15 regional groups.

**International Green Party:** 516 East Central, Lombard, IL 60148; f. 1973 to promote ecological issues; 500,000 mems; Chair. RANDALL TOLER.

**Libertarian Party:** 1528 Pennsylvania Ave, SE, Washington, DC 20003; tel. (202) 543-1988; fax (202) 546-6094; f. 1971; Chair. MARY T. GINGELL; Nat. Dir D. NICK DUNBAR.

**Populist Party of America:** POB 1992, Ford City, PA 16226; f. 1891, revived 1987; nationalist philosophy; Chair. DONALD B. WASSALL.

**Prohibition National Committee:** POB 2635, Denver, CO 80201; tel. (303) 572-0646; f. 1869; opposes the manufacture and sale of alcoholic drinks; opposes abortion, drug abuse and euthanasia; Nat. Chair. EARL F. DODGE; Nat. Sec. MARGARET L. STORMS.

**Republican National Committee:** 310 First St, SE, Washington, DC 20003; tel. (202) 863-8500; fax (202) 863-8820; f. 1854; Chair. HALEY BARBOUR; Sec. NELDA BARTON; Treas. WILLIAM J. MCMANUS.

**Social Democrats, USA:** 815 15th St, NW, Washington, DC 20005; tel. (202) 638-1515; fax (202) 347-5585; f. 1972 to succeed Socialist Party est. in 1901; Pres. DONALD SLAIMAN; Exec. Dir RITA FREEDMAN.

**Socialist Labor Party:** 111 West Evelyn Ave, Suite 209, Sunnyvale, CA 94086-6140; tel. (408) 245-2047; fax (408) 245-2049; f. 1877; Nat. Sec. ROBERT BILLS.

**Socialist Party USA:** 516 West 25th St, Suite 404, New York, NY 10001-5525; tel. (212) 691-0776; fax (212) 691-0776; f. 1901; Nat. Co-Chair. DAVID MCREYNOLDS, KARI FISHER; Nat. Sec. ANN ROSENHAFT.

THE UNITED STATES OF AMERICA

**Socialist Workers Party:** 406 West St, New York, NY 10014; tel. (212) 242-5530; f. 1938; Nat. Sec. JACK BARNES.

## Diplomatic Representation

### EMBASSIES IN THE UNITED STATES

**Afghanistan:** 2341 Wyoming Ave, NW, Washington, DC 20008; tel. (202) 234-3770; telex 248206; fax (202) 328-3516; Chargé d'affaires a.i.: YAR MOHAMMAD MOHABBAT.

**Albania:** 1511 K St, NW, Suite 1010, Washington, DC 20005; tel. (202) 223-4942; fax (202) 628-7342; Ambassador: LUBLIN DILJA.

**Algeria:** 2118 Kalorama Rd, NW, Washington, DC 20008; tel. (202) 265-2800; telex 892443; fax (202) 667-2174; Ambassador: Hadj OSMANE BENCHERIF.

**Angola:** 1899 L St, NW, Suite 400, Washington, DC 20036; tel. (202) 785-1156; fax (202) 785-1258; Ambassador: JOSÉ PATRICIO.

**Antigua and Barbuda:** 3216 New Mexico Ave, NW, Suite 4M, Washington, DC 20866; tel. (202) 362-5122; telex 8221130; fax (202) 362-5225; Ambassador: Dr PATRICK LEWIS.

**Argentina:** 1600 New Hampshire Ave, NW, Washington, DC 20009; tel. (202) 939-6400; fax (202) 332-3171; Ambassador: RAÚL GRANILLO OCAMPO.

**Armenia:** 1660 L St, NW, 11th Floor, Washington, DC 20036; tel. (202) 628-5766; fax (202) 628-5769; Ambassador: ROUBEN SHUGARIAN.

**Australia:** 1601 Massachusetts Ave, NW, Washington, DC 20036; tel. (202) 797-3000; fax (202) 797-3168; Ambassador: Dr DONALD RUSSELL.

**Austria:** 3524 International Court, NW, Washington, DC 20008-3035; tel. (202) 895-6700; telex 440010; fax (202) 895-6750; Ambassador: HELMUT TUERK.

**Azerbaijan:** 927 15th St, NW, Suite 700, Washington, DC 20005; tel. (202) 842-0001; fax (202) 842-0004; Ambassador: HAFIZ PASHAYEV.

**Bahamas:** 2220 Massachusetts Ave, NW, Washington, DC 20008; tel. (202) 319-2660; fax (202) 319-2668; Ambassador: TIMOTHY DONALDSON.

**Bahrain:** 3502 International Drive, NW, Washington, DC 20008; tel. (202) 342-0741; Ambassador: ABDUL GHAFFAR ABDULLA.

**Bangladesh:** 2201 Wisconsin Ave, NW, Washington, DC 20007; tel. (202) 342-8372; fax (202) 333-4971; Ambassador: HUMAYUN KABIR.

**Barbados:** 2144 Wyoming Ave, NW, Washington, DC 20008; tel. (202) 939-9200; telex 64343; fax (202) 332-7467; Ambassador: COURTNEY N. M. BLACKMAN.

**Belarus:** 1619 New Hampshire Ave, NW, Washington, DC 20009; tel. (202) 986-1604; fax (202) 986-1805; Ambassador: SERGUEI MARTYNOV.

**Belgium:** 3330 Garfield St, NW, Washington, DC 20008; tel. (202) 333-6900; telex 440139; fax (202) 333-3079; Ambassador: ANDRÉ ADAM.

**Belize:** 2535 Massachusetts Ave, NW, Washington, DC 20008; tel. (202) 332-9636; telex 140997; fax (202) 332-6888; Ambassador: DEAN LINDO.

**Benin:** 2737 Cathedral Ave, NW, Washington, DC 20008; tel. (202) 232-6656; telex 64155; fax (202) 265-1996; Ambassador: LUCIEN TONOUKOUIN.

**Bolivia:** 3014 Massachusetts Ave, NW, Washington, DC 20008; tel. (202) 483-4410; telex 440049; fax (202) 328-3712; Ambassador: ANDRÉS PETRICEVIC R.

**Bosnia and Herzegovina:** 1707 L St, NW, Suite 760, Washington, DC 20036; tel. (202) 833-3612; fax (202) 833-2061; Ambassador: SVEN ALKALAJ.

**Botswana:** 3400 International Drive, NW, Suite 7M, Washington, DC 20008; tel. (202) 244-4990; fax (202) 244-4164; Ambassador: BOTSWELETSE SEBELE.

**Brazil:** 3006 Massachusetts Ave, NW, Washington, DC 20008; tel. (202) 745-2700; fax (212) 745-2827; Ambassador: PAULO-TARSO FLECHA DE LIMA.

**Brunei:** 2600 Virginia Ave, NW, Suite 300, Washington, DC 20037; tel. (202) 342-0159; telex 904081; fax (202) 342-0158; Ambassador: Haji JAYA BIN ABDUL LATIF.

**Bulgaria:** 1621 22nd St, NW, Washington, DC 20008; tel. (202) 387-7969; fax (202) 234-7973; Ambassador: SNEJANA BOTOUCHAROVA.

**Burkina Faso:** 2340 Massachusetts Ave, NW, Washington, DC 20008; tel. (202) 332-5577; telex 440399; fax (202) 265-1996; Ambassador: GAËTAN R. OUÉDRAOGO.

**Burundi:** 2233 Wisconsin Ave, NW, Suite 212, Washington, DC 20007; tel. (202) 342-2574; Ambassador: SEVERIN NTAHOMVUKIYE.

**Cameroon:** 2349 Massachusetts Ave, NW, Washington, DC 20008; tel. (202) 265-8790; Ambassador: JEROME MENDOUGA.

**Canada:** 501 Pennsylvania Ave, NW, Washington, DC 20001; tel. (202) 682-1740; telex 89664; fax (202) 682-7726; Ambassador: RAYMOND CHRÉTIEN.

**Cape Verde:** 3415 Massachusetts Ave, NW, Washington, DC 20007; tel. (202) 965-6820; fax (202) 965-1207; Ambassador: CORENTINO VIRGILLIO SANTOS.

**Central African Republic:** 1618 22nd St, NW, Washington, DC 20008; tel. (202) 483-7800; fax (202) 332-9893; Ambassador: HENRY KOBA.

**Chad:** 2002 R St, NW, Washington, DC 20009; tel. (202) 462-4009; fax (202) 265-1937; Ambassador: AHMAT MAHAMAT-SALEH.

**Chile:** 1732 Massachusetts Ave, NW, Washington, DC 20036; tel. (202) 785-1746; fax (202) 887-5579; Ambassador: JOHN BIEHL.

**China, People's Republic:** 2300 Connecticut Ave, NW, Washington, DC 20008; tel. (202) 328-2500; fax (202) 232-7855; Ambassador: LI DAOYU.

**Colombia:** 2118 Leroy Place, NW, Washington, DC 20008; tel. (202) 387-8338; fax (202) 232-8643; Ambassador: CARLOS LLERAS.

**Comoros:** 336 East 45th St, 2nd Floor, New York, NY 10017; tel. (212) 972-8010; fax (212) 983-4712; Ambassador: (vacant).

**Congo:** 4891 Colorado Ave, NW, Washington, DC 20011; tel. (202) 726-0825; fax (202) 726-1860; Ambassador: PIERRE BOUSSOUKOU-BOUMBA.

**Costa Rica:** 2114 S St, NW, Washington, DC 20008; tel. (202) 234-2945; fax (202) 265-4795; Ambassador: SONIA PICADO.

**Côte d'Ivoire:** 2424 Massachusetts Ave, NW, Washington, DC 20008; tel. (202) 797-0300; telex 64364; fax (202) 387-6381; Ambassador: KOFFI MOÏSE KOUMOUÉ.

**Croatia:** 2343 Massachussetts Ave, NW, Washington, DC 20008; tel. (202) 588-5899; fax (202) 588-8936; Ambassador: PETAR ŠARČEVIĆ.

**Cuba:** 'Interests section' in the Embassy of Switzerland, 2630 16th St, NW, Washington, DC 20009; tel. (202) 797-8518; fax (202) 797-8521; Counselor: ALFONSO FRAGA PÉREZ.

**Cyprus:** 2211 R St, NW, Washington, DC 20008; tel. (202) 462-5772; telex 440596; fax (202) 483-6710; Ambassador: ANDREW JACOVIDES.

**Czech Republic:** 3900 Spring of Freedom St, NW, Washington, DC 20008; tel. (202) 363-6315; fax (202) 966-8540; Ambassador: MICHAEL ZANTOVSKY.

**Denmark:** 3200 Whitehaven St, NW, Washington, DC 20008-3683; tel. (202) 234-4300; telex 440081; fax (202) 328-1470; Ambassador: PETER DYVIG.

**Djibouti:** 1156 15th St, NW, Suite 515, Washington, DC 20005; tel. (202) 331-0270; telex 4490085; fax (202) 331-0302; Ambassador: ROBLÉ OLHAYE.

**Dominican Republic:** 1715 22nd St, NW, Washington, DC 20008; tel. (202) 332-6280; fax (202) 265-8057; Ambassador: JOSÉ DEL CARMEN ARIZA.

**Ecuador:** 2535 15th St, NW, Washington, DC 20009; tel. (202) 234-7200; fax (202) 667-3482; Ambassador: Dr EDGAR TERÁN TERÁN.

**Egypt:** 3521 International Court, NW, Washington, DC 20008; tel. (202) 895-5400; fax (202) 244-4319; Ambassador: AHMED MAHER EL-SAYED.

**El Salvador:** 2308 California St, NW, Washington, DC 20008; tel. (202) 265-9671; Ambassador: ANA CRISTINA SOL.

**Equatorial Guinea:** 57 Magnolia Ave, Mount Vernon, NY 10553; tel. (914) 738-9584; fax (914) 667-6838; Chargé d'affaires a.i.: TEODORO BIYOGO NSUE.

**Eritrea:** 910 17th St, NW, Suite 400, Washington, DC 20006; tel. (202) 429-1991; fax (202) 429-9004; Ambassador: AMDEMICAEL KAHSAI.

**Estonia:** 1030 15th St, NW, Suite 1000, Washington, DC 20005; tel. (202) 789-0320; fax (202) 789-0471; Ambassador: TOOMAS ILVES.

**Ethiopia:** 2134 Kalorama Rd, NW, Washington, DC 20008; tel. (202) 234-2281; fax (202) 328-7950; Ambassador: BERHANE GEBRE-CHRISTOS.

**Fiji:** 2233 Wisconsin Ave, NW, Suite 240, Washington, DC 20007; tel. (202) 337-8320; telex 4971930; fax (202) 337-1996; Ambassador: PITA KEWA NACUVA.

**Finland:** 3301 Massachusetts Ave, NW, Washington, DC 20008; tel. (202) 298-5800; telex 248268; fax (202) 298-5801; Ambassador: JUKKA VALTASAARI.

**France:** 4101 Reservoir Rd, NW, Washington, DC 20007; tel. (202) 944-6000; fax (202) 944-6072; Ambassador: JACQUES ANDRÉANI.

**Gabon:** 2233 Wisconsin Ave, NW, Suite 200, Washington, DC 20007; tel. (202) 797-1000; Ambassador: PAUL BOUNDOUKOU-LATHA.

# THE UNITED STATES OF AMERICA

**Gambia:** 1155 15th St, NW, Suite 1000, Washington, DC 20005; tel. (202) 785-1399; fax (202) 785-1430; Chargé d'affaires a.i.: AMINATTA DIBBA.

**Georgia:** 1511 K St, NW, Suite 424, Washington, DC 20005; tel. (202) 393-6060; Ambassador: TEDO DJAPARIDZE.

**Germany:** 4645 Reservoir Rd, NW, Washington, DC 20007-1998; tel. (202) 298-4000; telex 248321; fax (202) 298-4249; Ambassador: JÜRGEN CHROBOG.

**Ghana:** 3512 International Drive, NW, Washington, DC 20008; tel. (202) 686-4520; telex 64539; fax (202) 686-4527; Ambassador: EKWOW SPIO-GARBRAH.

**Greece:** 2221 Massachusetts Ave, NW, Washington, DC 20008; tel. (202) 939-5800; fax (202) 939-5824; Ambassador: LOUCAS TSILAS.

**Grenada:** 1701 New Hampshire Ave, NW, Washington, DC 20009; tel. (202) 265-2561; Ambassador: DENNETH MODESTE.

**Guatemala:** 2220 R St, NW, Washington, DC 20008; tel. (202) 745-4952; fax (202) 745-1908; Ambassador: EDMOND MULET.

**Guinea:** 2112 Leroy Place, NW, Washington, DC 20008; tel. (202) 483-9420; telex 49606982; fax (202) 483-8688; Ambassador: El-Hadj BOUBACAR BARRY.

**Guinea-Bissau:** 918 16th St, NW, Mezzanine Suite, Washington, DC 20006; tel. (202) 872-4222; fax (202) 872-4226; Ambassador: ALFREDO LOPES CABRAL.

**Guyana:** 2490 Tracy Place, NW, Washington, DC 20008; tel. (202) 265-6900; telex 64170; fax (202) 232-1297; Ambassador: Dr ODEEN ISHMAEL.

**Haiti:** 2311 Massachusetts Ave, NW, Washington, DC 20008; tel. (202) 332-4090; telex 440202; fax (202) 745-7215; Ambassador: JEAN CASIMIR.

**Holy See:** 3339 Massachusetts Ave, NW, Washington, DC 20008; tel. (202) 333-7121; telex 440117; fax (202) 337-4036; Apostolic Pro-Nuncio: Most Rev. AGOSTINO CACCIAVILLAN, Titular Archbishop of Amiterno.

**Honduras:** 3007 Tilden St, NW, Washington, DC 20008; tel. (202) 966-7702; fax (202) 966-9751; Ambassador: ROBERTO FLORES BERMÚDEZ.

**Hungary:** 3910 Shoemaker St, NW, Washington, DC 20008; tel. (202) 362-6730; fax (202) 966-8135; Ambassador: GYÖRGY BÁNLAKI.

**Iceland:** 1156 15th St, NW, Washington, DC 20005; tel. (202) 265-6653; fax (202) 265-6656; Ambassador: EINAR BENEDIKTSSON.

**India:** 2107 Massachusetts Ave, NW, Washington, DC 20008; tel. (202) 939-7000; fax (202) 939-7027; Ambassador: SIDDHARTHA RAY.

**Indonesia:** 2020 Massachusetts Ave, NW, Washington, DC 20036; tel. (202) 775-5200; fax (202) 775-5365; Ambassador: ARIFIN MOHAMAD SIREGAR.

**Iran:** 'Interests section' in the Embassy of Pakistan, 2209 Wisconsin Ave, NW, Washington DC 20007; tel. (202) 965-4990.

**Iraq:** 'Interests section' in the Embassy of Algeria, 1801 P St, NW, Washington, DC 20036; tel. (202) 483-7500; fax (202) 462-5066; Third Secretary: SATIE A. M. AL-TAI.

**Ireland:** 2234 Massachusetts Ave, NW, Washington, DC 20008; tel. (202) 462-3939; telex 64160; fax (202) 232-5993; Ambassador: DERMOT GALLAGHER.

**Israel:** 3514 International Drive, NW, Washington, DC 20008; tel. (202) 364-5500; fax (202) 364-5610; Ambassador: ITAMAR RABINOVICH.

**Italy:** 1601 Fuller St, NW, Washington, DC 20009; tel. (202) 328-5500; telex 64461; fax (202) 462-3605; Ambassador: BORIS BIANCHERI.

**Jamaica:** 1520 New Hampshire Ave, NW, Washington, DC 20006; tel. (202) 452-0660; telex 64352; fax (202) 452-0081; Ambassador: Dr RICHARD BERNAL.

**Japan:** 2520 Massachusetts Ave, NW, Washington, DC 20008-2869; tel. (202) 939-6700; telex 904017; fax (202) 328-2187; Ambassador: TAKAKAZU KURIYAMA.

**Jordan:** 3504 International Drive, NW, Washington, DC 20008; tel. (202) 966-2664; telex 64113; fax (202) 966-3110; Ambassador: FAYEZ TARAWNEH.

**Kazakhstan:** 3421 Massachusetts Ave, NW, Washington, DC 20008; tel. (202) 233-4504; fax (202) 233-4509; Ambassador: TOULEOUTAI S. SOULEIMENOV.

**Kenya:** 2249 R St, NW, Washington, DC 20008; tel. (202) 387-6101; Ambassador: BENJAMIN KIPKORIR.

**Korea, Republic:** 2450 Massachusetts Ave, NW, Washington, DC 20008; tel. (202) 939-5600; fax (202) 797-0595; Ambassador: KUN WOO PARK.

**Kuwait:** 2940 Tilden St, NW, Washington, DC 20008; tel. (202) 966-0702; fax (202) 966-0517; Ambassador: Dr MOHAMMED SABAH AS-SALIM AS-SABAH.

**Kyrgyzstan:** 1511 K St, NW, Suite 705, Washington, DC 20005; tel. (202) 347-3732; fax (202) 347-3718; Chargé d'affaires a.i.: ALMAS CHUKIN.

**Laos:** 222 S St, NW, Washington, DC 20008; tel. (202) 332-6416; telex 904061; fax (202) 332-4923; Ambassador: HIEM PHOMMACHANH.

**Latvia:** 4325 17th St, NW, Washington, DC 20011; tel. (202) 726-8213; fax (202) 726-6785; Ambassador: OJARS KALNINS.

**Lebanon:** 2560 28th St, NW, Washington, DC 20008; tel. (202) 939-6300; fax (202) 939-6324; Ambassador: RIAD TABBARAH.

**Lesotho:** 2511 Massachusetts Ave, NW, Washington, DC 20008; tel. (202) 797-5533; fax (202) 234-6815; Ambassador: Dr EUNICE M. BULANE.

**Liberia:** 5201 16th St, NW, Washington, DC 20011; tel. (202) 723-0437; Chargé d'affaires a.i.: T. H. KONAH BLACKETT.

**Lithuania:** 2622 16th St, NW, Washington, DC 20009; tel. (202) 234-5860; fax (202) 328-0466; Ambassador: ALFONSAS EIDINTAS.

**Luxembourg:** 2200 Massachusetts Ave, NW, Washington, DC 20008; tel. (202) 265-4171; telex 64130; fax (202) 328-8270; Ambassador: ALPHONSE BERNS.

**Madagascar:** 2374 Massachusetts Ave, NW, Washington, DC 20008; tel. (202) 265-5525; Ambassador: PIERROT RAJAONARIVELO.

**Malawi:** 2408 Massachusetts Ave, NW, Washington, DC 20008; tel. (202) 797-1007; fax (202) 265-0976; Ambassador: W. CHOKANI.

**Malaysia:** 2401 Massachusetts Ave, NW, Washington, DC 20008; tel. (202) 328-2700; telex 440119; fax (202) 483-7661; Ambassador: Dato MOHAMED ABDUL MAJID.

**Mali:** 2130 R St, NW, Washington, DC 20008; tel. (202) 332-2249; Ambassador: SIRAGATOU CISSÉ.

**Malta:** 2017 Connecticut Ave, NW, Washington, DC 20008; tel. (202) 462-3611; fax (202) 387-5470; Ambassador: Dr ALBERT BORG OLIVIER DE PUGET.

**Marshall Islands:** 2433 Massachusetts Ave, NW, Washington, DC 20008; tel. (202) 234-5414; fax (202) 232-3236; Ambassador: WILFRED KENDALL.

**Mauritania:** 2129 Leroy Place, NW, Washington, DC 20008; tel. (202) 232-5700; Ambassador: ISMAIL OULD IYAHI.

**Mauritius:** 4301 Connecticut Ave, NW, Suite 441, Washington, DC 20008; tel. (202) 244-1491; telex 64362; fax (202) 966-0983; Ambassador: ANUND NEEWOOR.

**Mexico:** 1911 Pennsylvania Ave, NW, Washington, DC 20006; tel. (202) 728-1600; telex 248459; fax (202) 234-7739; Ambassador: JESÚS SILVIA HERZOG.

**Micronesia:** 1725 N St, NW, Washington, DC 20036; tel. (202) 223-4383; fax (202) 223-4391; Ambassador: JESSE MAREHALAU.

**Moldova:** 1511 K St, NW, Suite 329, Washington, DC 20005; tel. (202) 783-3012; fax (202) 783-3342; Ambassador: NICOLAE TĂU.

**Mongolia:** 2833 M St, NW, Washington, DC 20007; tel. (202) 333-7117; fax (202) 298-9227; Ambassador: LUVSANDORJ DAWAGIV.

**Morocco:** 1601 21st St, NW, Washington, DC 20009; tel. (202) 462-7979; telex 248378; fax (202) 265-0161; Ambassador: MOHAMED BENAISSA.

**Mozambique:** 1990 M St, NW, Suite 570, Washington, DC 20036; tel. (202) 293-7146; telex 248530; fax (202) 835-0245; Ambassador: ESPERANÇA MATAVELE.

**Myanmar:** 2300 S St, NW, Washington, DC 20008; tel. (202) 332-9044; telex 248310; fax (202) 332-9046; Ambassador: U THAUNG.

**Namibia:** 1605 New Hampshire Ave, NW, Washington, DC 20009; tel. (202) 986-0540; fax (202) 986-0443; Ambassador: TULIAMENI KALOMOH.

**Nepal:** 2131 Leroy Place, NW, Washington, DC 20008; tel. (202) 667-4550; telex 440085; fax (202) 667-5534; Ambassador: BUSUDEV PRASAD DHUNGNA.

**Netherlands:** 4200 Linnean Ave, NW, Washington, DC 20008; tel. (202) 244-5300; fax (202) 362-3430; Ambassador: ADRIAAN JACOBOVITS DE SZEGED.

**New Zealand:** 37 Observatory Circle, NW, Washington, DC 20008; tel. (202) 328-4800; fax (202) 667-5227; Ambassador: JOHN WOOD.

**Nicaragua:** 1627 New Hampshire Ave, NW, Washington, DC 20009; tel. (202) 939-6570; fax (202) 939-6542; Ambassador: ROBERTO MAYORGA-CORTES.

**Niger:** 2204 R St, NW, Washington, DC 20008; tel. (202) 483-4224; fax (202) 483-3169; Ambassador: ADAMOU SEYDOU.

**Nigeria:** 1333 16th St, NW, Washington, DC 20036; tel. (202) 986-8400; Ambassador: ZUBAIR KAZAURE.

**Norway:** 2720 34th St, NW, Washington, DC 20008; tel. (202) 333-6000; telex 892374; fax (202) 337-0870; Ambassador: KJELD VIBE.

**Oman:** 2535 Belmont Rd, NW, Washington, DC 20008; tel. (202) 387-1980; telex 440267; fax (202) 745-4933; Ambassador: ABDULLA MOHAMED AQEEL AL-DHAHAB.

# THE UNITED STATES OF AMERICA

**Pakistan:** 2315 Massachusetts Ave, NW, Washington, DC 20008; tel. (202) 939-6200; fax (202) 387-0484; Ambassador: Dr Maleeha Lodhi.

**Panama:** 2862 McGill Terrace, NW, Washington, DC 20008; tel. (202) 483-1407; telex 64371; fax (202) 483-8413; Ambassador: Ricardo Arias.

**Papua New Guinea:** 1615 New Hampshire Ave, NW, 3rd Floor, Washington, DC 20009; tel. (202) 745-3680; fax (202) 745-3679; Ambassador: Kepas Isimel Watangia.

**Paraguay:** 2400 Massachusetts Ave, NW, Washington, DC 20008; tel. (202) 483-6960; fax (202) 234-4508; Ambassador: Jorge G. Prieto.

**Peru:** 1700 Massachusetts Ave, NW, Washington, DC 20036; tel. (202) 833-9860; telex 197675; fax (202) 659-8124; Ambassador: Ricardo V. Luna.

**Philippines:** 1600 Massachusetts Ave, NW, Washington, DC 20036-2274; tel. (202) 467-9300; telex 440059; fax (202) 328-7614; Ambassador: Raul Ch. Rabe.

**Poland:** 2640 16th St, NW, Washington, DC 20009; tel. (202) 234-3800; fax (202) 328-6271; Ambassador: Jerzy Kozminski.

**Portugal:** 2125 Kalorama Rd, NW, Washington, DC 20008; tel. (202) 328-8610; fax (202) 462-3726; Ambassador: Fernando Andresen Guimarães.

**Qatar:** 600 New Hampshire Ave, NW, Suite 1180, Washington, DC 20037; tel. (202) 338-0111; Ambassador: Sheikh Abdulrahman bin Saud al-Thani.

**Romania:** 1607 23rd St, NW, Washington, DC 20008; tel. (202) 332-4848; fax (202) 232-4748; Ambassador: (vacant).

**Russia:** 2650 Wisconsin Ave, NW, Washington, DC 20007; tel. (202) 298-5700; fax (202) 298-5735; Yuli M. Vorontsov.

**Rwanda:** 1714 New Hampshire Ave, NW, Washington, DC 20009; tel. (202) 232-2882; telex 248505; fax (202) 232-4544; Chargé d'affaires a.i.: Joseph W. Mutaboba.

**Saint Christopher and Nevis:** 2100 M St, NW, Suite 608, Washington DC 20037; tel. (202) 833-3550; fax (202) 833-3553; Ambassador: Erstein Edwards.

**Saint Lucia:** 3216 New Mexico Ave, NW, Washington, DC 20016; tel. (202) 364-6792; fax (202) 364-6728; Ambassador: Dr Joseph Edmunds.

**Saint Vincent and the Grenadines:** 1717 Massachusetts Ave, NW, Suite 102, Washington, DC 20036; tel. (202) 462-7806; fax (202) 462-7807; Ambassador: Kingsley Layne.

**Saudi Arabia:** 601 New Hampshire Ave, NW, Washington, DC 20037; tel. (202) 342-3800; telex 440132; Ambassador: Prince Bandar bin Sultan.

**Senegal:** 2112 Wyoming Ave, NW, Washington, DC 20008; tel. (202) 234-0540; fax (202) 352-6315; Ambassador: Mamadou Seck.

**Seychelles:** 820 Second Ave, Suite 900F, New York, NY 10017; tel. (212) 687-9766; telex 220032; fax (212) 922-9177; Ambassador: Marc Marengo.

**Sierra Leone:** 1701 19th St, NW, Washington, DC 20009; tel. (202) 939-9261; Counselor: William B. Wright.

**Singapore:** 3501 International Place, NW, Washington, DC 20008; tel. (202) 537-3100; fax (202) 537-0876; Ambassador: S. R. Nathan.

**Slovakia:** 2201 Wisconsin Ave, NW, Suite 250, Washington, DC 20007; tel. (202) 965-5160; fax (202) 965-5166; Ambassador: Branislav Lichardus.

**Slovenia:** 1525 New Hampshire Ave, NW, Washington, DC 20036; tel. (201) 667-5363; fax (202) 667-4563; Ambassador: Dr Ernest Petrič.

**South Africa:** 3051 Massachusetts Ave, NW, Washington, DC 20008; tel. (202) 232-4400; telex 248364; fax (202) 265-1607; Ambassador: Franklin Sonn.

**Spain:** 2700 15th St, NW, Washington, DC 20009; tel. (202) 265-0190; telex 64125; fax (202) 332-5451; Ambassador: Jaime de Ojeda.

**Sri Lanka:** 2148 Wyoming Ave, NW, Washington, DC 20008; tel. (202) 483-4025; telex 49616790; fax (202) 232-7181; Ambassador: J. C. B. Dhanapala.

**Suriname:** 4301 Connecticut Ave, NW, Suite 108, Washington, DC 20008; tel. (202) 244-7488; telex 892656; fax (202) 244-5878; Ambassador: Willem Udenhout.

**Swaziland:** 3400 International Drive, NW, Washington, DC 20008; tel. (202) 362-6683; fax (202) 244-8059; Ambassador: Mary M. Kanya.

**Sweden:** 1501 M St, NW, Washington, DC 20005; tel. (202) 467-2600; fax (202) 467-2699; Ambassador: Carl Henrik Sihver Liljegren.

**Switzerland:** 2900 Cathedral Ave, NW, Washington, DC 20008; tel. (202) 745-7900; telex 440055; fax (202) 387-2564; Ambassador: Carlo Jagmetti.

**Syria:** 2215 Wyoming Ave, NW, Washington, DC 20008; tel. (202) 232-6313; fax (202) 234-9548; Ambassador: Walid al-Moualem.

**Tanzania:** 2139 R St, NW, Washington, DC 20008; tel. (202) 939-6125; telex 64213; fax (202) 797-7408; Ambassador: Charles Nyirabu.

**Thailand:** 1024 Wisconsin Ave, NW, Washington, DC 20007; tel. (202) 944-3600; fax (202) 944-3611; Ambassador: Manaspas Xuto.

**Togo:** 2208 Massachusetts Ave, NW, Washington, DC 20008; tel. (202) 234-4212; fax (202) 232-3190; Ambassador: Kossivi Osseyi.

**Trinidad and Tobago:** 1708 Massachusetts Ave, NW, Washington, DC 20036; tel. (202) 467-6490; fax (202) 785-3130; Ambassador: Corinne McKnight.

**Tunisia:** 1515 Massachusetts Ave, NW, Washington, DC 20005; tel. (202) 862-1850; fax (202) 862-1858; Ambassador: Azouz Ennifar.

**Turkey:** 1714 Massachusetts Ave, NW, Washington, DC 20036; tel. (202) 659-8200; Ambassador: Nuzhet Kandemir.

**Turkmenistan:** 1511 K St, NW, Suite 412, Washington, DC 20005; tel. (202) 737-4800; fax (202) 737-1152; Ambassador: Halil Ugur.

**Uganda:** 5911 16th St, NW, Washington, DC 20011; tel. (202) 726-7100; fax (202) 726-1727; Ambassador: Stephen Katenta-Apuli.

**Ukraine:** 3350 M St, NW, Washington, DC 20007; tel. (202) 333-0606; fax (202) 333-0817; Ambassador: Yuriy Shcherbak.

**United Arab Emirates:** 3000 K St, NW, Suite 600, Washington, DC 20007; tel. (202) 338-6500; Ambassador: Mohammad bin Hussein al-Shaali.

**United Kingdom:** 3100 Massachusetts Ave, NW, Washington, DC 20008; tel. (202) 462-1340; telex 64224; fax (202) 898-4255; Ambassador: Sir John Kerr (designate).

**Uruguay:** 1918 F St, NW, Washington, DC 20006; tel. (202) 331-1313; fax (202) 331-8142; Ambassador: Dr Eduardo MacGillycuddy.

**Uzbekistan:** 1511 K St, NW, Suite 619, Washington, DC 20005; tel. (202) 638-4266; Ambassador: Fatikh Teshabaev.

**Venezuela:** 1099 30th St, NW, Washington, DC 20007; tel. (202) 342-2214; Ambassador: Pedro Luis Echeverría.

**Western Samoa:** 820 Second Ave, Suite 800, New York, NY 10017; tel. (212) 599-6196; fax (212) 599-0797; Ambassador: Tuiloma Slade.

**Yemen:** 2600 Virginia Ave, NW, Suite 705, Washington, DC 20037; tel. (202) 965-4760; telex 897027; fax (202) 337-2017; Ambassador: Mohsin Alaini.

**Yugoslavia:** 2410 California Ave, NW, Washington, DC 20008; tel. (202) 462-6566; fax (202) 797-9663; Chargé d'affaires a.i.: Zoran Popović.

**Zaire:** 1800 New Hampshire Ave, NW, Washington, DC 20009; tel. (202) 234-7690; Ambassador: Manata Tatanene.

**Zambia:** 2419 Massachusetts Ave, NW, Washington, DC 20008; tel. (202) 265-9717; fax (202) 332-0826; Ambassador: Dunstan Kamana.

**Zimbabwe:** 1608 New Hampshire Ave, NW, Washington, DC 20009; tel. (202) 332-7100; telex 248402; fax (202) 483-9326; Ambassador: Amos Midzi.

## Judicial System

Each state has a judicial system structured similarly to the Federal system, with a Supreme Court and subsidiary courts, to deal with cases arising under State Law. These courts have jurisdiction in most criminal and civil actions. Each state has its own bar association of lawyers and its own legal code.

### SUPREME COURT OF THE UNITED STATES
(Supreme Court Bldg, 1 First St, NE, Washington, DC 20543; tel. (202) 479-3000; fax (202) 479-3036)

The Supreme Court is the only Federal Court established by the Constitution. It is the highest court in the nation, comprising a Chief Justice and eight Associate Justices. Appointments, which are for life or until voluntary retirement, are made by the President, subject to confirmation by the US Senate.

**Chief Justice:** William H. Rehnquist (appointed Associate Justice 1971, Chief Justice 1986).

**Associate Justices:** John Paul Stevens (1975), Sandra Day O'Connor (1981), Antonin Scalia (1986), Anthony M. Kennedy (1988), David H. Souter (1990), Clarence Thomas (1991), Ruth Bader Ginsburg (1993), Stephen G. Breyer (1994).

### US COURTS OF APPEAL
(Administrative Office of the US Courts, Washington, DC 20544; tel (202) 273-2777)

The USA is divided into 12 judicial circuits, in each of which there is one Court of Appeals. The Court of Appeals for the Federal Circuit has nation-wide specialized jurisdiction.

THE UNITED STATES OF AMERICA

Federal Courts hear cases involving federal law, cases involving participants from more than one state, crimes committed in more than one state and civil or corporate cases that cross state lines. Federal District Courts, of which there are 94, are the courts of first instance for most federal suits.

**Federal Circuit:** Glenn L. Archer, Jr, (Chief Judge), Helen W. Nies, Giles S. Rich, Pauline Newman, H. Robert Mayer, Paul R. Michel, S. Jay Plager, Alan D. Lourie, Raymond C. Clevenger, III, Randall R. Rader, Alvin A. Schall, William C. Bryson.

**District of Columbia Circuit:** Harry T. Edwards (Chief Judge), Patricia M. Wald, Laurence H. Silberman, James L. Buckley, Stephen F. Williams, Douglas H. Ginsburg, David B. Sentelle, Karen LeCraft Henderson, A. Raymond Randolph, Judith W. Rogers, David S. Tatel.

**First Circuit** (Maine, Massachusetts, New Hampshire, Rhode Island, Puerto Rico): Juan R. Torruella, (Chief Judge), Bruce M. Selya, Conrad K. Cyr, Michael Boudin, Norman H. Stahl.

**Second Circuit** (Connecticut, New York, Vermont): Jon O. Newman (Chief Judge), Amalya Lyle Kearse, Ralph K. Winter, Jr, Roger J. Miner, Frank X. Altimari, J. Daniel Mahoney, John M. Walker, Jr, Joseph M. McLaughlin, Dennis G. Jacobs, Pierre N. Leval, Guido Calabresi, Jose A. Cabranes, Fred I. Parker.

**Third Circuit** (Delaware, New Jersey, Pennsylvania, Virgin Islands): Dolores Korman Sloviter (Chief Judge), Edward R. Becker, Walter K. Stapleton, Carol Los Mansmann, Morton I. Greenberg, William D. Hutchinson, Anthony J. Scirica, Robert E. Cowen, Richard L. Nygaard, Samuel A. Alito, Jr, Jane R. Roth, Timothy K. Lewis, Theodore A. McKee, H. Lee Sarokin.

**Fourth Circuit** (Maryland, North Carolina, South Carolina, Virginia, West Virginia): Sam J. Ervin, III (Chief Judge), Donald Stuart Russell, H. Emory Widener, Jr, Kenneth K. Hall, Francis D. Murnaghan, Jr, J. Harvie Wilkinson, III, William W. Wilkins, Jr, Paul V. Niemayer, Clyde H. Hamilton, J. Michael Luttig, Karen J. Williams, M. Blaine Michael, Diana Gribbon Motz.

**Fifth Circuit** (Louisiana, Mississippi, Texas): Henry A. Politz (Chief Judge), Carolyn Dineen King, William D. Garwood, E. Grady Jolly, Patrick E. Higginbotham, W. Eugene Davis, Edith Hollan Jones, Jerry E. Smith, John M. Duhe, Jr, Rhesa H. Barksdale, Jacques L. Wiener, Jr, Emilio M. Garza, Harold R. DeMoss, Jr, Fortunato P. Benavides, Carl E. Stewart, Robert M. Parker.

**Sixth Circuit** (Kentucky, Michigan, Ohio, Tennessee): Gilbert S. Merritt (Chief Judge), Cornelia G. Kennedy, Boyce F. Martin, Jr, H. Ted Milburn, David A. Nelson, James L. Ryan, Danny J. Boggs, Alan E. Norris, Robert F. Suhrheinrich, Eugene E. Siler, Jr, Alice M. Batchelder, Martha Craig Daughtrey.

**Seventh Circuit** (Illinois, Indiana, Wisconsin): Richard A. Posner (Chief Judge), Walter J. Cummings, John L. Coffey, Joel M. Flaum, Frank H. Easterbrook, Kenneth F. Ripple, Daniel A. Manion, Michael S. Kanne, Ilana Diamond Rovner.

**Eighth Circuit** (Arkansas, Iowa, Minnesota, Missouri, Nebraska, North Dakota, South Dakota): Richard S. Arnold (Chief Judge), Theodore McMillan, George G. Fagg, Pasco M. Bowman, II, Roger L. Woolman, Frank J. Magill, C. Arlen Beam, James B. Loken, David R. Hansen, Morris S. Arnold, Diana E. Murphy.

**Ninth Circuit** (Alaska, Arizona, California, Guam, Hawaii, Idaho, Montana, Nevada, Northern Mariana Islands, Oregon, Washington): J. Clifford Wallace (Chief Judge), James R. Browning, Procter Hug, Jr, Mary M. Schroeder, Betty B. Fletcher, Harry Pregerson, Cecil F. Poole, William C. Canby, Jr, Stephen Reinhardt, Robert B. Beezer, Cynthia H. Hall, Charles E. Wiggins, Melvin Brunetti, Alex Kozinski, John T. Noonan, Jr, David R. Thompson, Dairmuid F. O'Scannlain, Edward Leavy, Stephen S. Trott, Ferdinand F. Fernandez, Pamela Ann Rymer, Thomas G. Nelson, Andrew J. Kleinfeld, Michael D. Hawkins.

**Tenth Circuit** (Colorado, Kansas, New Mexico, Oklahoma, Utah, Wyoming): Stephanie K. Seymour (Chief Judge), John P. Moore, Stephen H. Anderson, Deanell R. Tacha, Bobby R. Baldock, Wade Brorby, David M. Ebel, Paul J. Kelly, Jr, Robert H. Henry.

**Eleventh Circuit** (Alabama, Florida, Georgia): Gerald B. Tjoflat (Chief Judge), Phyllis A. Kravitch, Joseph W. Hatchett, R. Lanier Anderson, III, J. L. Edmonson, Emmett R. Cox, Stanley F. Birch, Jr, Joel F. Dubina, Susan H. Black, Edward E. Carnes, Rosemary Barkett.

### UNITED STATES COURT OF FEDERAL CLAIMS
(717 Madison Place, NW, Washington, DC 20005; tel. (202) 219-9657)

**Judges:** Loren A. Smith (Chief Judge), James F. Merow, John P. Wiese, Robert J. Yock, Reginald W. Gibson, Lawrence S. Margolis, Christine O. C. Miller, Moody R. Tidwell, III, Marian Blank Horn, Eric G. Bruggink, Bohdan A. Futey, Wilkes C. Robinson, Roger B. Andewelt, James T. Turner, Robert H. Hodges Jr., Diane G. Weinstein.

### US COURT OF INTERNATIONAL TRADE
(1 Federal Plaza, New York, NY 10007; tel. (212) 264-2814)

**Judges:** Dominick L. DiCarlo (Chief Judge), Gregory W. Carman, Jane A. Restani, Thomas J. Aquilino, Jr, Nicholas Tsoucalas, R. Kenton Musgrave, Richard W. Goldberg.

# Religion

Christianity is the predominant religion. The largest single denomination is the Roman Catholic Church. Other major groups in terms of membership are the Baptist, Methodist, Lutheran and Orthodox churches. Numerous other beliefs are represented, the largest in terms of adherents being Judaism, Islam and Buddhism.

## CHRISTIANITY

**National Council of the Churches of Christ in the USA:** 475 Riverside Drive, New York, NY 10115-0050; tel. (212) 870-2227; fax (212) 870-2030; telex 234579; f. 1950; an ecumenical agency of 32 Protestant and Orthodox denominations, whose mems number c. 50m.; conducts more than 60 interdenominational programmes; Pres. Rev. Dr Gordon Sommers; Gen. Sec. Rev. Joan B. Campbell.

### The Anglican Communion

**The Episcopal Church in the USA:** 815 Second Ave, New York, NY 10017-4564; tel. (212) 867-8400; telex 4909957001; f. 1789; 7,367 churches; 2.5m. mems (1993 estimate); Presiding Bishop and Pres. Exec. Council Rt Rev. Edmond Lee Browning; Exec. Officer Gen. Convention and Sec. Exec. Council Rev. Donald A. Nickerson, Jr.

### The Baptist Church

Members (1993 estimate): 36.4m., in 19 bodies, of which the following have the greatest number of members:

**American Baptist Association:** 4605 North State Line Ave, Texarkana, TX 75503-2916; tel. (903) 792-2783; f. 1905; 1,705 churches; 250,000 mems; Recording Clerk W. E. Norris.

**American Baptist Churches in the USA:** POB 851, Valley Forge, PA 19482-0851; tel. (215) 768-2000; fax (215) 768-2275; f. 1907; 5,845 churches; 1.5m. mems; Pres. Rev. Dr James A. Scott; Gen. Sec. Rev. Dr Daniel E. Weiss.

**Conservative Baptist Association of America:** POB 66, Wheaton, IL 60189; tel. (708) 260-3800; fax (708) 653-5387; f. 1947; 1,084 churches; 200,000 mems; Gen. Dir Dr Dennis N. Baker.

**General Association of Regular Baptist Churches:** 1300 North Meacham Rd, Schaumburg, IL 60173-4888; tel. (708) 843-1600; fax (708) 843-3757; 1,472 churches; 160,000 mems; Chair. Rev. Richard Christen; Nat. Rep. Dr Mark Jackson.

**National Baptist Convention, USA:** 1700 Baptist World Center Drive, Nashville, TN 37207-4948; tel. (615) 228-6292; fax (615) 226-5935; f. 1880; 33,000 churches; 8.2m. mems; Pres. Rev. T. J. Jemison; Gen. Sec. W. Franklyn Richardson.

**Southern Baptist Convention:** 901 Commerce St, Nashville, TN 37203-3629; tel. (615) 244-2355; fax (615) 742-8919; f. 1845; 38,401 churches; 15.4m. mems; Pres. Rev. Jim Henry; Pres. Exec. Cttee Dr Morris H. Chapman.

### The Lutheran Church

Members (1993 estimate): 8.4m., in 13 bodies, of which the following have the greatest number of members:

**Evangelical Lutheran Church in America:** 8765 West Higgins Rd, Chicago, IL 60631; tel. (312) 380-2700; telex 4900009321; fax (312) 380-1465; f. 1988 by merger; 11,120 churches; 5.2m. mems; Bishop Rev. Dr Herbert W. Chilstrom; Sec. Rev. Dr Lowell G. Almen.

**Lutheran Church—Missouri Synod:** 1333 South Kirkwood Rd, St Louis, MO 63122-7295; tel. (314) 965-9000; telex 434452; f. 1847; 5,991 churches; 2.6m. mems; Pres. Dr Alvin L. Barry; Sec. Dr Walter L. Rosin.

### The Methodist Church

Members (1993 estimate): 13.7m. in 12 bodies, of which the following have the greatest number of members:

**African Methodist Episcopal Church:** POB 19039, East Germantown Station, Philadelphia, PA 19138; tel. (215) 877-8330; f. 1816; 8,000 churches, 3.5m. mems; Sr Bishop John H. Adams; Gen. Sec. Dr O. U. Infill, Sr.

**African Methodist Episcopal Zion Church:** 8605 Caswell Court, Raleigh, NC 27612; f. 1796; 3,000 churches; 1.2m. mems; Sr Bishop William Milton Smith; Sec. Bd of Bishops John Henry Miller, Sr.

**The United Methodist Church:** 204 North Newlin St Veedersburg, IN 47987; f. 1968 by merger; 37,100 pastoral charges (in USA); Sec. Gen. Conf. Carolyn M. Marshall.

# THE UNITED STATES OF AMERICA

### The Orthodox Churches
Members (1993 estimate): 3.4m. in 16 bodies, of which the following have the greatest number of members:

**Antiochian Orthodox Christian Archdiocese of North America (Greek Orthodox Patriarchate of Antioch and all the East):** 358 Mountain Rd, Englewood, NJ 07631-3798; tel. (201) 871-1355; fax (201) 871-7954; f. 1895; 192 churches; 350,000 mems; Primate Metropolitan PHILIP (SALIBA)..

**Armenian Church of America:** Eastern Diocese, 630 Second Ave, New York, NY 10016; tel. (212) 686-0710; fax (212) 779-3558; Western Diocese, 1201 North Vine St, Hollywood, CA 90038; tel. (213) 466-5265; fax (213) 466-7612; f. 1889; 72 churches; 414,000 mems; Primate (Eastern Diocese) Bishop KHAJAG BARSAMIAN; Primate (Western Diocese) Archbishop VATCHE HOVSEPIAN.

**Coptic Orthodox Church:** 427 West Side Ave, Jersey City, NJ 07304; 85 churches; 180,000 mems; Archpriest Fr GABRIEL ABDEL-SAYED.

**Greek Orthodox Archdiocese of North and South America:** 8–10 East 79th St, New York, NY 10021-0191; tel. (212) 570-3500; fax (212) 861-8060; inc. 1922; 555 churches; 1.5m. mems; Primate Archbishop IAKOVOS; Chancellor Very Rev. GERMANOS STAVROPOULOS.

**Orthodox Church in America:** POB 675, Syosset, NY 11791; tel. (516) 922-0550; f. 1794; fmrly Russian Orthodox Greek Catholic Church of North America; 700 churches; 600,000 mems; Primate Metropolitan THEODOSIUS; Chancellor Archpriest ROBERT S. KONDRATICK.

The Albanian, Assyrian, Bulgarian, Carpatho-Russian, Romanian, Russian, Serbian, Syrian and Ukrainian Orthodox Churches are also represented.

### The Presbyterian Church
Members (1993 estimate): 4.2m. in eight bodies, of which the following have the greatest number of members:

**Presbyterian Church in America:** 1852 Century Place, Atlanta, GA 40345-4305; tel. (404) 320-3366; fax (404) 329-1275; f. 1973; 1,280 churches; 250,600 mems; Moderator WILLIAM S. BARKER, III; Stated Clerk Dr PAUL R. GILCHRIST.

**Presbyterian Church (USA):** 100 Witherspoon St, Louisville, KY 40202-1396; tel. (502) 569-5000; telex 405139; fax (502) 569-5018; f. 1984 by merger; 11,456 churches; 3.8m. mems; Moderator Rev. JOAN SALMON CAMPBELL; Stated Clerk Rev. JAMES E. ANDREWS.

### The Roman Catholic Church
In 1993 there were 19,863 parishes in 155 dioceses and 33 archdioceses; 59.2m. mems.

**National Conference of Catholic Bishops:** 3211 Fourth St, NE, Washington, DC 20017; tel. (202) 541-3193; Pres. Cardinal WILLIAM H. KEELER (Archbishop of Baltimore); Gen. Sec. Mgr ROBERT N. LYNCH.

#### Archbishops
**Anchorage:** FRANCIS T. HURLEY.
**Atlanta:** JOHN F. DONOGHUE.
**Baltimore:** Cardinal WILLIAM H. KEELER.
**Boston:** Cardinal BERNARD F. LAW.
**Chicago:** Cardinal JOSEPH L. BERNARDIN.
**Cincinnati:** DANIEL E. PILARCZYK.
**Denver:** JAMES F. STAFFORD.
**Detroit:** Cardinal ADAM J. MAIDA.
**Dubuque:** DANIEL W. KUCERA.
**Hartford:** DANIEL A. CRONIN.
**Indianapolis:** DANIEL M. BUECHLEIN.
**Kansas City in Kansas:** JAMES P. KELEHER.
**Los Angeles:** Cardinal ROGER M. MAHONY.
**Louisville:** THOMAS C. KELLY.
**Miami:** JOHN C. FAVALORA.
**Milwaukee:** REMBERT G. WEAKLAND.
**Mobile:** OSCAR H. LIPSCOMB.
**Newark:** THEODORE E. MCCARRICK.
**New Orleans:** FRANCIS B. SCHULTE.
**New York:** Cardinal JOHN J. O'CONNOR.
**Oklahoma City:** EUSEBIUS J. BELTRAN.
**Omaha:** ELDEN F. CURTISS.
**Philadelphia:** Cardinal ANTHONY J. BEVILACQUA, STEPHEN SULYK (Ukrainian, Byzantine Rite).
**Pittsburgh:** JUDSON M. PROCYK (Ruthenian, Byzantine Rite).
**Portland in Oregon:** WILLIAM J. LEVADA.
**Saint Louis:** JUSTIN F. RIGALI.
**Saint Paul and Minneapolis:** JOHN R. ROACH.
**San Antonio:** PATRICK F. FLORES.
**San Francisco:** JOHN R. QUINN.
**Santa Fe:** MICHAEL J. SHEEHAN.
**Seattle:** THOMAS J. MURPHY.
**Washington:** Cardinal JAMES A. HICKEY.

### Other Christian Churches
**Assemblies of God:** 1445 Boonville Ave, Springfield, MO 65802-1894; tel. (417) 862-2781; telex 436442; fax (417) 863-6614; f. 1914; 11,764 churches; 2.2m. mems; Gen. Supt THOMAS E. TRASK; Gen. Sec. GEORGE O. WOOD.

**Christian Church (Disciples of Christ):** 130 East Washington St, POB 1986, Indianapolis, IN 46206; tel. (317) 635-3100; telex 3413193; fax (317) 635-3700; f. 1809; 4,069 congregations; 1.0m. mems; Gen. Minister and Pres. Dr RICHARD L. HAMM.

**Christian Reformed Church in North America:** 2850 Kalamazoo Ave, SE, Grand Rapids, MI 49560; tel. (616) 246-0744; fax (616) 246-0834; f. 1857; 739 churches; 225,000 mems (USA and Canada); Gen. Sec. Dr DAVID H. ENGLEHARD.

**Church of Christ, Scientist:** 175 Huntington Ave, Boston, MA 02115; tel. (617) 450-2000; fax (617) 450-3325; f. 1879; 2,500 congregations world-wide; Pres. RUTH E. JENKS; Clerk OLGA M. CHAFFEE.

**Church of Jesus Christ of Latter-day Saints (Mormon):** 47 East South Temple St, Salt Lake City, UT 84150-0001; tel. (801) 240-1000; telex 381556; fax (801) 240-2033; f. 1830; 9,654 wards and branches (congregations); 4.4m. mems; Pres. GORDON B. HINCKLEY.

**Church of the Nazarene:** 6401 The Paseo, Kansas City, MO 64131-1284; tel. (816) 333-7000; fax (816) 361-4983; f. 1908; 11,118 churches; 1.1m. mems; Gen. Sec. JACK STONE.

**Friends United Meeting:** 101 Quaker Hill Drive, Richmond, IN 47374; tel. (317) 962-7573; fax (317) 966-1293; f. 1902; 55,000 mems; Presiding Clerk HAROLD SMUCK; Gen. Sec. JOHAN MAURER.

**Mariavite Old Catholic Church—Province of North America:** 2803 Tenth St, Wyandotte, MI 48192-4994; tel. (313) 281-3082; f. 1930; 158 churches; c. 357,000 mems; Prime Bishop Most Rev. Archbishop Dr ROBERT R. J. M. ZABOROWSKI.

**Reformed Church in America, General Synod:** 475 Riverside Drive, New York, NY 10115-0101; tel. (212) 870-3071; fax (212) 870-3071; fax (212) 870-2499; f. 1628; 960 churches; 318,000 mems; Pres. Rev. HAROLD KORVER; Gen. Sec. Rev. WESLEY GRANBERG-MICHAELSON.

**Seventh-day Adventists:** 12501 Old Columbia Pike, Silver Spring, MD 20904-6600; tel. (301) 680-6000; fax (301) 680-6090; f. 1863; 4,261 churches; 749,000 mems (in USA and Canada); Pres. ROBERT S. FOLKENBERG; Sec. G. RALPH THOMPSON.

**United Church of Christ:** 700 Prospect Ave, Cleveland, OH 44115; tel. (216) 736-2100; fax (216) 736-2120; f. 1957 by merger; 6,225 churches; 1.5m. mems; Moderator VICTOR MELENDEZ; Pres. Rev. PAUL SHERRY; Sec. EDITH A. GUFFEY.

**United Pentecostal Church International:** 8855 Dunn Rd, Hazelwood, MO 63042-2212; tel. (314) 837-7300; fax (314) 837-4503; f. 1945; 3,720 churches; 500,000 mems; (USA and Canada); Gen. Supt Rev. NATHANIEL A. URSHAN.

## BAHÁ'Í FAITH
**National Spiritual Assembly:** 536 Sheridan Rd, Wilmette, IL 60091; tel. (708) 869-9039; fax (708) 869-0247; f. 1844 in Persia; c. 120,000 mems residing in over 7,000 localities; Chair. JAMES NELSON; Sec.-Gen. Dr ROBERT C. HENDERSON.

## BUDDHISM
**Buddhist Churches of America:** 1710 Octavia St, San Francisco, CA 94109-4341; tel. (415) 776-5600; fax (415) 771-6293; f. 1899; Hongwanji-ha Jodo Shinshu denomination; 100,000 mems; Leader Bishop SEIGEN H. YAMAOKA.

## ISLAM
There are an estimated 4.0m. Muslims in the USA, of whom African-American Muslims are believed to number 1.3m.

**Council of Masajid of United States (CMUS):** 99 Woodview Drive, Old Bridge, NJ 08857; tel. (908) 679-8617; fax (908) 679-1260; f. 1978; educational agency representing 650 local groups; Pres. DAWUD ASSAD.

**Federation of Islamic Associations in the US and Canada:** 25351 Five Mile and Aubery Rd, Redford Township, MI 48239; tel. (313) 534-3295; fax (313) 534-1474; f. 1951; co-ordinating agency for 45 affiliated orgs; Gen. Sec. NIHAD HAMED.

# THE UNITED STATES OF AMERICA
*Directory*

**Islamic Center of New York:** 1711 Third Ave, New York, NY 10029-7303; tel. (212) 722-5234; f. 1966; Imam and Dir Dr MUHAMMAD SALEM AGWA.

**Islamic Mission of America:** 143 State St, Brooklyn, NY 11201; tel. (718) 875-6607; f. 1938; maintains an educational and training inst.; 15,000 mems; Chair. MOHAMED KABBAJ.

### JUDAISM

There are an estimated 5.9m. Jews in the USA.

**American Jewish Congress:** 15 East 84th St, New York, NY 10028-0407; tel. (212) 879-4500; f. 1918; Exec. Dir HENRY SIEGMAN; 50,000 mems.

**Central Conference of American Rabbis:** 192 Lexington Ave, New York, NY 10016-6823; tel. (212) 684-4990; fax (212) 689-1649; f. 1889; Reform; Pres. Rabbi SHELDON ZIMMERMAN; Exec. Vice-Pres. Rabbi JOSEPH B. GLASER; 1,650 mems.

**The Rabbinical Assembly:** 3080 Broadway, New York, NY 10027-4650; tel. (212) 678-8060; fax (212) 749-9166; f. 1901; Pres. Rabbi ALAN SILVERSTEIN; Exec. Vice-Pres. Rabbi JOEL H. MEYERS; 1,500 mems.

**The Synagogue Council of America:** 327 Lexington Ave, New York, NY 10016-2606; tel. (212) 686-8670; f. 1926; a co-ordinating agency for Orthodox, Conservative and Reform bodies; 6 mems; Pres. Rabbi JEROME K. DAVIDSON; Exec. Vice-Pres. Rabbi HENRY D. MICHELMAN.

**Union of American Hebrew Congregations:** 838 Fifth Ave, New York, NY 10021-7046; tel. (212) 249-0100; f. 1873; Reform; Pres. Rabbi ALEXANDER M. SCHINDLER; Sr Vice-Pres. Rabbi DANIEL B. SYME; 855 affiliated congregations representing c. 1.3m. mems.

**Union of Orthodox Jewish Congregations of America:** 333 Seventh Ave, 18th Floor, New York, NY 10001; tel. (212) 563-4000; f. 1898; Pres. Dr MANDELL GANCHROW; Exec. Vice-Pres. Rabbi PINCHAS STOLPER; 1,200 affiliated congregations representing c. 1m. mems.

**United Synagogue of Conservative Judaism:** 155 Fifth Ave, New York, NY 10010-6802; tel. (212) 533-7800; f. 1913; Pres. ALAN ADES; Exec. Vice-Pres. Rabbi JEROME EPSTEIN; 800 affiliated congregations in North America representing c. 2m. mems.

### SIKHISM

There are an estimated 250,000 Sikhs in North America.

**International Sikh Organization:** 2025 Eye St, NW, Suite 922, Washington, DC 20006; tel. (202) 833-3262; fax (202) 452-9161; Pres. Dr GURMIT SINGH AULAKH.

# The Press

The USA publishes more newspapers and periodicals than any other country. Most dailies give a greater emphasis to local news because of the strong interest in local and regional affairs and the decentralized structure of many government services. These factors, together with the distribution problem inherent in the size of the country, are responsible for the lack of national newspapers. Daily newspapers are published in 1,513 US cities, and almost every small town has its own journal. In 1993 almost 115m. people, representing 61.7% of the adult population, read a daily newspaper.

Most influential and highly respected among the few newspapers with a national readership are the *New York Times* (which introduced a national edition in 1980), the *Washington Post*, *Los Angeles Times* and *The Wall Street Journal* (the financial and news daily with editions in New York City, California, Illinois and Texas, and a European and an Asian edition). In 1982 the first national general interest newspaper, *USA Today*, was introduced by Gannett. An international edition was launched in 1984.

At the end of 1993, 43 daily newspapers had circulations of over 250,000 copies. Among the largest of these, in order of daily circulation, were *The Wall Street Journal*, *USA Today*, *The New York Times*, *Los Angeles Times*, *The Washington Post*, *New York Daily News*, *Newsday*, *Chicago Tribune*, *The Detroit Free Press* and the *San Francisco Chronicle*.

At the end of 1993 there were 1,556 English language daily newspapers (621 morning, 956 evening, including 21 'all-day' newspapers) with a total circulation of 59,815,032 copies per day. The Sunday edition is an important and distinctive feature of US newspaper publishing; many Sunday newspapers run to over 300 pages. At the end of 1993 there were 889 Sunday newspapers with a total circulation of 62,643,679. In December 1993 there were 7,437 weekly papers with a total circulation of 56,734,526.

The famous tradition of press freedom in the USA is grounded in the First Amendment to the Constitution which declares that 'Congress shall make no law . . . abridging the freedom of speech or of the Press . . .' and confirmed in the legislations of many states which prohibit any kind of legal restriction on the dissemination of news.

Legislation affecting the Press is both state and federal. A source of controversy between the Press and the courts has been the threat of the encroachment by judicial decrees on the area of courtroom and criminal trial coverage. In 1972 the Supreme Court ruled that journalists were not entitled to refuse to give evidence before grand juries on information they have received confidentially. Since then the frequent issuing of subpoenas to journalists and the jailing of several reporters for refusing to disclose sources has led to many 'shield' bills being put before Congress and state legislatures calling for immunity for journalists from both federal and state jurisdiction.

In recent years, increased production costs have subjected the industry to considerable economic strain, resulting in mergers and take-overs, a great decline in competition between dailies in the same city, and the appearance of inter-city dailies catering for two or more adjoining centres. A consequence of these trends has been the steady growth of newspaper groups or chains. In 1992 the 20 largest groups, in terms of circulation, published 519 daily newspapers, accounting for almost 60% of US daily newspaper circulation.

The following are among the principal daily newspaper groups:

**Dow Jones & Co Inc:** World Financial Center, New York, NY 10281; tel. (212) 416-2000; telex 422221; fax (212) 416-3478; Chair. and CEO PETER R. KANN; Pres. and Chief Operating Officer KENNETH L. BURENGA; 22 daily newspapers, including *The Wall Street Journal*; also operates domestic and international news wires and provides radio and television news reports.

**Gannett Co Inc:** 1000 Wilson Blvd, 10th Floor, Arlington, VA 22229-0001; tel. (703) 276-5800; fax (703) 558-3813; f. 1906; Chair., Pres. and CEO JOHN J. CURLEY; largest US newspaper group in terms of total circulation; 83 daily newspapers, including *USA Today* and *The Detroit News*.

**Hearst Corpn:** Hearst Magazine Bldg, 959 Eighth Ave, New York, NY 10019; tel. (212) 649-2000; fax (212) 765-4037; Pres. and CEO FRANK A. BENNACK, Jr; 12 daily newspapers, including *San Francisco Examiner*.

**Knight-Ridder Inc:** One Herald Plaza, Miami, FL 33132-1693; tel. (305) 376-3800; fax (305) 376-3876; Chair. JAMES K. BATTEN; Pres. and CEO P. ANTHONY RIDDER; 28 daily newspapers.

**Newhouse Newspapers:** Court and Plains Sts, Newark, NJ 07101; Pres. DONALD E. NEWHOUSE; 26 daily newspapers.

**E. W. Scripps Co:** POB 5380, Cincinnati, OH 45201-5380; tel. (513) 977-3000; fax (513) 977-3721; Chair. and CEO LAWRENCE A. LESER; Pres. WILLIAM R, BURLEIGH; 18 daily newspapers.

**Thomson Newspapers Inc:** 3150 Des Plaines Ave, Des Plaines, IL 60018; Chair. of Board KENNETH R. THOMSON; Pres. ST CLAIR MCCABE; 109 daily newspapers.

**Times Mirror Co:** Times Mirror Sq., Los Angeles, CA 90053; tel. (213) 237-3700; fax (213) 237-3800; f. 1884; Chair., Pres. and CEO MARK H. WILLES; 11 daily newspapers, including *Los Angeles Times*, *Newsday* and *Baltimore Sun*.

**Tribune Co:** 435 North Michigan Ave, Chicago, IL 60611; tel. (312) 222-9100; fax (312) 222-0499; Pres. JOHN MADIGAN; six daily newspapers, including *Chicago Tribune*.

### PRINCIPAL DAILY AND SUNDAY NEWSPAPERS

In general, only newspapers with circulations exceeding 50,000 are included, except in Wyoming, where the newspaper with the largest circulation is listed.

(M = morning; E = evening; D = all day; S = Sunday; Publr = Publisher)

#### Alabama

**Birmingham News:** 2200 North Fourth Ave, POB 2553, Birmingham, AL 35202-2553; tel. (205) 325-2222; fax (205) 325-3246; f. 1888; Publr V. H. HANSON, II; Editor JAMES E. JACOBSON; circ. 163,000 (E), 209,000 (S).

**Huntsville Times:** 2317 Memorial Pkwy, Huntsville, AL 35801-5623; tel. (205) 532-4000; fax (205) 532-4420; f. 1910; Publr BOB LUDWIG, Editor JOE DISTELHEIM; circ. 60,000 (D), 85,000 (S).

**Mobile Register** (M) f. 1813, **Mobile Press-Register** (S): 304 Government St, POB 2488, Mobile, AL 36630; tel. (334) 433-1551; fax (334) 434-8662; Publr HOWARD BRONSON; Editor STAN TINER; circ. 69,000 (M), 117,000 (S).

**Montgomery Advertiser:** 200 Washington Ave, POB 1000, Montgomery, AL 36101-1000; tel. (334) 262-1611; fax (334) 261-1501; f. 1828; Publr RICHARD H. AMBERG, Jr; Editor WILLIAM BROWN; circ. 62,000 (M), 78,000 (S).

**Post-Herald:** POB 2553, Birmingham, AL 35202; tel. (205) 325-2214; f. 1887; Editor JAMES H. DENLEY; Ind; circ. 62,000 (M).

THE UNITED STATES OF AMERICA                                                                                                                    *Directory*

### Alaska
**Anchorage News:** POB 149001, Anchorage, AK 99514-9001; tel. (907) 257-4200; fax (907) 258-2157; f. 1946; Publr FULLER A. COWELL; Editor HOWARD WEAVER; circ. 74,000 (M), 94,000 (S).

### Arizona
**Arizona Daily Star** (MS) f. 1877, Ind., **Tucson Citizen** (E) f. 1870, Ind.-Rep.: 4850 South Park Ave, POB 26807, Tucson, AZ 85726-6807; tel. (520) 573-4400; fax (520) 573-4107 (Star); tel. (520) 573-4560; fax (520) 573-4569 (Citizen); Publrs MICHAEL E. PULITZER (Star), DONALD HATFIELD (Citizen); circ. 101,000 (M), 51,000 (E), 185,000 (S).
**Arizona Republic** (MS) f. 1890, **Phoenix Gazette** (e) f. 1880: 120 East Van Buren St, POB 1950, Phoenix, AZ 85001; tel. (602) 271-7300; telex 9510604; fax (602) 271-7363; Publr LOUIS A. WEIL, III; Man. Editor JOHN OPPEDAHL; circ. 390,000 (M), 80,000 (E), 607,000 (S).

### Arkansas
**Democrat Gazette:** 112 West 3rd St, POB 1821, Little Rock, AR 72201; tel. (501) 371-3994; fax (501) 371-3778; Publr WILLIAM T. MALONE; Exec. Editor GRIFFIN SMITH, Jr; circ. 125,000 (M), 222,000 (S).

### California
**Bakersfield Californian:** POB 440, Bakersfield, CA 93302-0440; tel. (805) 395-7500; fax (805) 395-7519; f. 1866; Publr HARRELL FRITTS; Exec. Editor (vacant); circ. 77,000 (M), 92,000 (S).
**Fresno Bee:** 1626 E St, Fresno, CA 93786; tel. (209) 441-6111; fax (209) 441-6436; f. 1922; Publr GARY B. PRUITT; Exec. Editor BEVERLY KEES; circ. 153,000 (M), 191,000 (S).
**Investor's Business Daily:** 12655 Beatrice Ave, Los Angeles, CA 90066; tel. (310) 448-6000; fax (310) 577-7350; f. 1984; Publr W. SCOTT O'NEIL; Editor WESLEY F. MANN; circ. 176,000 (M).
**Los Angeles Times:** Times Mirror Co, Times Mirror Sq., Los Angeles, CA 90053; tel. (213) 237-5000; fax (213) 237-4712; f. 1881; Publr and CEO RICHARD T. SCHLOSBERG, III; Pres. and Chief Operating Officer DONALD F. WRIGHT; Editor and Exec. Vice-Pres. C. SHELBY COFFEY, III; circ. 1,105,000 (D), 1,502,000 (S).
**Modesto Bee:** POB 1325 H St, Modesto, CA 95354; tel. (209) 578-2351; fax (209) 578-2207; f. 1884; Editor SANDERS LAMONT; circ. 85,000 (M), 92,000 (S).
**Oakland Tribune:** 66 Jack London Sq., Oakland, CA 94607; tel. (510) 208-6313; fax (510) 208-6305; f. 1874; Editor ROBERT C. MAYNARD; circ. 77,000 (M), 75,000 (S).
**Orange County Register:** 625 North Grand Ave, POB 11626, Santa Ana, CA 92701; tel. (714) 835-1234; fax (714) 542-5037; Publr. R. D. THRESHIE, Jr; Editor TONNIE KATZ; circ. 354,000 (D), 416,000 (S).
**Press-Democrat:** 427 Mendocino Ave, Santa Rosa, CA 95402; tel. (707) 546-2020; fax (707) 546-7538; Publr MICHAEL PARMAN; Exec. Editor BRUCE KYSE; circ. 98,000 (M), 103,000 (S).
**Press-Telegram:** 604 Pine Ave, Long Beach, CA 90844-0001; tel. (310) 435-1161; fax (310) 437-7892; Pres. and Publr RICK SADOWSKI; Exec. Editor JIM CRUTCHFIELD; circ. 124,000 (D), 142,000 (S).
**Sacramento Bee:** 2100 Q St, POB 15779, Sacramento, CA 95852; tel. (916) 321-1475; fax (916) 321-1306; f. 1857; Exec. Editor GREGORY FAVRE; circ. 278,000 (M), 349,000 (S).
**San Bernardino County Sun:** 399 North D St, San Bernardino, CA 92401; tel. (714) 889-9666; fax (714) 381-3976; f. 1873; Publr BROOKS JOHNSON; Editor ARNOLD GARSON; circ. 87,000 (M), 100,000 (S).
**San Diego Union–Tribune:** POB 191, San Diego, CA 92112-4106; tel. (619) 299-3131; fax (619) 293-1896; f. 1868; Publr HELEN K. COPLEY; Editor GERALD L. WARREN; circ. 407,000 (M), 461,000 (S).
**San Francisco Chronicle:** 901 Mission St, San Francisco, CA 94103; tel. (415) 777-1111; fax (415) 512-8196; f. 1865; Publr and Editor RICHARD T. THIERIOT; circ. 570,000 (M), 704,000 (S).
**San Francisco Examiner:** 110 Fifth St, San Francisco, CA 94103; tel. (415) 777-5700; fax (415) 243-8058; f. 1865; Publr and Editor WILLIAM R. HEARST, III; circ. 138,000 (E), 704,000 (S).
**San Jose Mercury News:** 750 Ridder Park Drive, San Jose, CA 95190; tel. (408) 920-5000; fax (408) 288-8060; Publr LARRY JINKS; Exec. Editor ROBERT INGLE; circ. 285,000 (M), 345,000 (S).
**Stockton Record:** 530 East Market St, POB 900, Stockton, CA 95201; tel. (209) 943-6397; fax (209) 943-6565; f. 1895; Publr VIRGIL SMITH; Editor BETTY LIDDICK; circ. 54,000 (M), 60,000 (S).

### Colorado
**Denver Post:** 1560 Broadway, Denver, CO 80202; tel. (303) 820-1010; fax (303) 820-1406; f. 1895; Publr RYAN MCKIBBEN; Editor NEIL WESTERGAARD; circ. 287,000 (M), 440,000 (S).
**Gazette Telegraph:** 30 South Prospect, Colorado Springs, CO 80903; tel. (719) 632-5511; fax (719) 636-0202; f. 1872; Publr CHRIS ANDERSON; Editor JOHN STEPLETON; circ. 122,000 (M), 117,000 (S).
**Rocky Mountain News:** 400 West Colfax Ave, Denver, CO 80204; tel. (303) 892-5000; fax (303) 892-5081; f. 1859; Publr LARRY STRUTTON; Editor JAY AMBROSE; circ. 344,000 (M), 459,000 (S).

### Connecticut
**Connecticut Post:** 410 State St, Bridgeport, CT 06604; tel. (203) 333-0161; fax (203) 366-3373; f. 1883; Publr DUDLEY THOMAS; Editor RICK SAYERS; circ. 75,000 (M), 93,000 (S).
**Hartford Courant:** 285 Broad St, Hartford, CT 06115; tel. (203) 241-6200; fax (203) 241-3865; f. 1764; Editor MICHAEL J. DAVIES; circ. 232,000 (M), 321,000 (S).
**New Haven Register:** Long Wharf, 40 Sargent Drive, New Haven, CT 06511; tel. (203) 789-5200; fax (203) 865-7894; f. 1812; CEO WILLIAM RUSH; Editor DAVID BUTLER; circ. 101,000 (M), 127,000 (S).

### Delaware
**News–Journal:** 950 West Basin Rd, POB 15505, New Castle, DE 19720; tel. (302) 324-2617; fax (302) 324-5518; Publr SAL DE VIVO; Editor J. DONALD BRANDT; circ. 119,000 (M), 140,000 (S).

### District of Columbia
**Washington Post:** 1150 15th St, NW, Washington, DC 20071; tel. (202) 334-6000; f. 1877; Publr DONALD E. GRAHAM; Exec. Editor LEONARD DOWNIE, Jr; Man. Editor ROBERT KAISER; circ. 852,000 (M), 1,163,000 (S).
**Washington Times:** 3600 New York Ave, NE, Washington, DC 20002; tel. (202) 636-3000; fax (202) 529-2471; f. 1982; Man. Editor WESLEY PRUDEN; circ. 90,000 (M), 65,000 (S).

### Florida
**Diario Las Américas:** 2900 NW 39th St, Miami, FL 33142; tel. (305) 633-3341; fax (305) 635-7668; f. 1953; Publr and Editor HORACIO AGUIRRE; circ. 66,000 (M), 70,000 (S).
**Florida Times-Union:** POB 1949, Jacksonville, FL 32231; tel. (904) 359-4111; fax (904) 359-4400; f. 1864; Publr CARL N. CANNON; Exec. Editor FREDERICK W. HARTMANN; circ. 182,000 (M), 257,000 (S).
**Miami Herald:** One Herald Plaza, Miami, FL 33132-1693; tel. (305) 350-2111; fax (305) 376-2287; f. 1910; Publr DAVID LAWRENCE; Exec. Editor DOUGLAS CLIFTON; circ. 407,000 (M), 533,000 (S).
**Orlando Sentinel:** 633 North Orange Ave, Orlando, FL 32801-1349; tel. (407) 420-5000; fax (407) 420-5661; f. 1876; Publr HAROLD R. LIFVENDAHL; Man. Editor JANE HEALY; circ. 278,000 (D), 400,000 (S).
**Palm Beach Post:** 2751 South Dixie Highway, West Palm Beach, FL 33405; tel. (407) 820-4100; f. 1916; Publr TOM GIUFFRIDA; Editor EDWARD M. SEARS; circ. 180,000 (M), 220,000 (S).
**Pensacola News Journal:** One News-Journal Plaza, Pensacola, FL 32501; tel. (904) 435-8500; fax (904) 435-8633; f. 1889; Publr KENNETH W. ANDREWS; Exec. Editor ANNE SAUL; circ. 62,000 (M), 84,000 (S).
**Sarasota Herald Tribune:** 801 South Tamiami Trail, Sarasota, FL 34236; tel. (813) 953-7755; fax (813) 957-5235; f. 1925; Publr J. E. GRUBBS; Editor WALDO PROFFITT; circ. 126,000 (M), 158,000 (S).
**St Petersburg Times:** 490 First Ave South, POB 1121, St Petersburg, FL 33731; tel. (813) 893-8111; telex 523413; fax (813) 893-8675; f. 1896; Pres., Editor and CEO ANDREW BARNES; circ. 379,000 (M), 471,000 (S).
**Sun-Sentinel:** 200 East Las Olas, Fort Lauderdale, FL 33301-2293; tel. (305) 761-4000; fax (305) 356-4559; f. 1960; Publr BYRON C. CAMPBELL; Editor GENE CRYER; circ. 282,000 (M), 383,000 (S).
**Tampa Tribune:** 202 South Parker St, POB 191, Tampa, FL 33601; tel. (813) 259-7711; fax (813) 259-7676; f. 1893; Publr JACK BUTCHER; Editor H. DOYLE HARVILL; circ. 276,000 (M), 376,000 (S).

### Georgia
**Atlanta Constitution** (M) f. 1868, **Atlanta Journal** (e) f. 1883, **Atlanta Journal-Constitution** (s): 72 Marietta St, NW, Atlanta, GA 30303; tel. (404) 526-5151; fax (404) 526-5746; Publr DENNIS BERRY; Editor RON MARTIN; circ. 310,000 (M), 140,000 (E), 723,000 (S).
**Augusta Chronicle** (M) f. 1785, **Chronicle-Herald** (s): 725 Broad St, POB 1928, Augusta, GA 30913; tel. (706) 724-0851; Publr W. S. MORRIS, III; Exec. Editor DENNIS SODOMKA; circ. 75,000 (M), 103,000 (S).
**Macon Telegraph:** 120 Broadway, 4167, Macon, GA 31201-3444; tel. (912) 744-4200; fax (912) 744-4269; f. 1826; Publr ED OLSON; Editor RICK THOMAS; circ. 77,000 (M), 106,000 (S).
**Savannah Morning News:** 111 West Bay St, POB 1088, Savannah, GA 31402; tel. (912) 236-9511; f. 1850; Publr DON HARWOOD; Exec. Editor WALLACE M. DAVIS, Jr; circ. 56,000 (M), 82,000 (S).

### Hawaii
**Honolulu Advertiser** (M) f. 1856, **Honolulu Star-Bulletin** (E) f. 1912, **Honolulu Star-Bulletin & Advertiser** (S) f. 1962: 605

THE UNITED STATES OF AMERICA                                                                                              *Directory*

Kapiolani Blvd, POB 3110, Honolulu, HI 96802; tel. (808) 525-8000; fax (808) 525-8037; Editors GERRY KEIR (Advertiser), JOHN FLANAGAN (Star-Bulletin); circ. 107,000 (M), 82,000 (E), 197,000 (S).

### Idaho

**Idaho Statesman:** 1200 North Curtis Rd, POB 40, Boise, ID 83707; tel. (208) 377-6200; fax (208) 377-6309; f. 1864; Publr GORDON R. BLACK; Editor BILL STEINAUER; circ. 64,000 (M), 86,000 (S).

### Illinois

**Bloomington Pantagraph:** 301 West Washington, Bloomington, IL 61701; tel. (309) 829-9411; fax (309) 829-9104; f. 1837; Publr JOHN R. GOLDRICK; Exec. Editor FRED KARDON; circ. 51,000 (M), 56,000 (S).

**Chicago Sun-Times:** 401 North Wabash Ave, Chicago, IL 60611; tel. (312) 321-3000; fax (312) 321-3084; f. 1948; Publr SAM MCKEEL; Editor DENNIS A. BRITTON; circ. 524,000 (M), 517,000 (S).

**Chicago Tribune:** 435 North Michigan Ave, Chicago, IL 60611; tel. (312) 222-3232; fax (312) 222-3736; f. 1847; Publr JOHN W. MADIGAN; Editor JACK FULLER; circ. 697,000 (M), 1,111,000 (S).

**Daily Herald:** POB 280, Arlington Heights, IL 60006; tel. (708) 870-3600; fax (708) 398-0172; f. 1872; Editor JIM SLUSHER; circ. 124,000 (M), 120,000 (S).

**Journal Star:** 1 News Plaza, Peoria, IL 61643; tel. (309) 686-3000; fax (309) 686-3025; f. 1855; Publr JOHN T. MCCONNELL; Editor JACK BRIMEYER; circ. 81,000 (M), 108,000 (S).

**Rockford Register Star:** 99 East State St, Rockford, IL 61104; tel. (815) 987-1302; fax (815) 962-6578; f. 1888; Publr MARY P. STIER; Exec. Editor LINDA G. CUNNINGHAM; circ. 78,000 (M), 90,000 (S).

**State Journal-Register:** One Copley Plaza, POB 219, Springfield, IL 62705-0219; tel. (217) 788-1300; fax (217) 788-1372; f. 1831; Publr JOHN P. CLARKE; Editor J. STEPHEN FAGAN; circ. 67,000 (M), 77,000 (S).

### Indiana

**Evansville Courier:** 300 Walnut St, Evansville, IN 47713; tel. (812) 424-7711; fax (812) 422-8196; f. 1845; Publr and Editor THOMAS W. TULEY; circ. 63,000 (M), 119,000 (S).

**Indianapolis Star** (MS) f. 1903, **Indianapolis News** (e) f. 1869: 307 North Pennsylvania St, Indianapolis, IN 46204; tel. (317) 633-1240; fax (317) 633-1174; Publr EUGENE S. PULLIAM; Editors JOHN H. LYST (Star), RUSSELL B. PULLIAM (News); circ. 231,000 (M), 93,000 (E), 411,000 (S).

**Journal-Gazette:** 600 West Main St, Fort Wayne, IN 46802; tel. (219) 461-8333; fax (219) 461-8648; f. 1863; Publr RICHARD G. INSKEEP; Editor CRAIG KLUGMAN; circ. 62,000 (M), 137,000 (S).

**News-Sentinel:** 600 West Main St, Fort Wayne, IN 46802; tel. (219) 461-8439; fax (219) 461-8649; f. 1833; Publr (vacant); Editor JOSEPH A. WEILER; circ. 54,000 (E).

**Post-Tribune:** 1065 Broadway, Gary, IN 46402; tel. (219) 881-3000; fax (219) 881-3232; f. 1909; Publr FRED MOTT, Jr; Exec. Editor BETTY WELLS; circ. 72,000 (M), 83,000 (S).

**South Bend Tribune:** 225 West Colfax Ave, South Bend, IN 46626; tel. (219) 235-6161; fax (219) 236-1765; f. 1872; Publr and Editor JOHN J. MCGANN; circ. 87,000 (E), 123,000 (S).

### Iowa

**Cedar Rapids Gazette:** 500 Third Ave SE, POB 5201, Cedar Rapids, IA 52406; tel. (319) 398-8211; fax (319) 398-5846; f. 1883; Publr and Editor J. F. HLADKY, III; Man. Editor MARK BOWDEN; circ. 71,000 (M), 85,000 (S).

**Des Moines Register:** 715 Locust St, POB 957, Des Moines, IA 50304; tel. (515) 284-8000; fax (515) 284-8103; f. 1849; Publr CHARLES C. EDWARDS, Jr; Editor GENEVA OVERHOLSER; circ. 185,000 (M), 319,000 (S).

**Quad–City Times:** 500 East Third St, POB 3828, Davenport, IA 52808; tel. (319) 383-2200; fax (319) 383-2433; f. 1855; Publr ROBERT A. FUSIE; Editor DANIEL K. HAYES; circ. 54,000 (D), 85,000 (S).

**Sioux City Journal:** 515 Pavonia St, Sioux City, IA 51102; tel. (712) 279-5026; fax (712) 279-5059; f. 1864; Publr D. A. KRENZ; Editor LARRY MYHRE; circ. 50,000 (M).

### Kansas

**Topeka Capital-Journal:** 616 SE Jefferson St, Topeka, KS 66607-1120; tel. (913) 295-1111; fax (913) 295-1230; Publr and Editor PETER W. STAUFFER; circ. 66,000 (M), 74,000 (S).

**Wichita Eagle:** 825 East Douglas St, Wichita, KS 67202; tel. (316) 268-6000; fax (316) 268-6609; f. 1872; Publr REID ASHE; Editor W. DAVIS MERRITT, Jr; circ. 115,000 (M), 191,000 (S).

### Kentucky

**Courier-Journal:** 525 West Broadway, Louisville, KY 40201; tel. (502) 582-4011; fax (502) 582-4075; Publr EDWARD MANASSAH; Editor DAVID V. HAWPE; circ. 240,000 (M), 330,000 (S).

**Lexington Herald-Leader:** 100 Midland Ave, Lexington, KY 40508; tel. (606) 231-3100; fax (606) 254-9738; f. 1860; Publr LEWIS OWENS; Editor TIMOTHY M. KELLY; circ. 85,000 (M), 167,000 (S).

### Louisiana

**Advocate:** 525 Lafayette St, Baton Rouge, LA 70802-5494; tel. (504) 383-1111; fax (504) 388-0129; f. 1925; Publr and Editor DOUGLAS L. MANSHIP; circ. 101,000 (M), 139,000 (S).

**The Times:** 222 Lake St, Shreveport, LA 71101; tel. (318) 459-3200; fax (318) 459-3301; f. 1872; Publr RICHARD STONE; Editor TERRY EBERLE; circ. 83,000 (M), 104,000 (S).

**Times-Picayune:** 3800 Howard Ave, New Orleans, LA 70140; tel. (504) 826-3300; fax (504) 826-3007; f. 1880; Publr ASHTON PHELPS, Jr; Editor JIM AMOSS; circ. 267,000 (D), 324,000 (S).

### Maine

**Bangor Daily News:** 491 Main St, POB 1329, Bangor, ME 04402-1329; tel. (207) 990-8000; fax (207) 941-0885; f. 1834; Publr and Editor RICHARD J. WARREN; circ. 72,000 (M).

**Portland Press Herald** (M) f. 1862, **Maine Sunday Telegram** (S) f. 1887: 390 Congress St, POB 1460, Portland, ME 04101; tel. (207) 780-9000; fax (207) 780-9499; Publr JEAN GANNETT HAWLEY; Exec. Editor LOUIS URENECK; circ. 75,000 (M), 145,000 (S).

### Maryland

**Baltimore Sun:** 501 North Calvert St, Baltimore, MD 21278-0001; tel. (410) 332-6300; fax (410) 332-6670; f. 1837; Publr MARY JUNCK; Man. Editors JAMES I. HOUCK, JOHN M. LEMMON; circ. 348,000 (M), 492,000 (S).

### Massachusetts

**Boston Globe:** POB 2378, Boston, MA 02107-2378; tel. (617) 929-2000; fax (617) 929-3192; f. 1872; Publr WILLIAM O. TAYLOR; Editor MATTHEW V. STORIN; circ. 517,000 (M), 798,000 (S).

**Boston Herald:** One Herald Sq., Boston, MA 02106; tel. (617) 426-3000; fax (617) 426-1896; f. 1825; Publr PATRICK PURCELL; Editor ANDREW F. COSTELLO, Jr; circ. 328,000 (M), 223,000 (S).

**The Enterprise:** 60 Main St, POB 1450, Brockton, MA 02403; tel. (508) 586-6200; fax (508) 586-7903; f. 1880; Publr C. M. FULLER; Exec. Editor BRUCE P. SMITH; circ. 51,000 (E), 64,000 (S).

**Christian Science Monitor:** 1 Norway St, Boston, MA 02115-3122; tel. (617) 450-2312; f. 1908; Mon.–Fri.; Editor DAVID COOK; circ. 95,000 (M).

**Lowell Sun:** 15 Kearney Sq., POB 1477, Lowell, MA 01853; tel. (508) 458-7100; fax (508) 970-4800; f. 1878; Pres. JOHN H. COSTELLO, Sr; Editor JOHN H. COSTELLO, Jr; circ. 55,000 (E), 57,000 (S).

**Patriot Ledger:** 400 Crown Colony Drive, Quincy, MA 02169; tel. (617) 786-7000; fax (617) 786-7298; f. 1837; Publr K. PRESCOTT LOW; Editor WILLIAM B. KETTER; circ. 87,000 (E).

**Springfield Union–News** (M) f. 1864, **Sunday Republican** f. 1824, 1860 Main St, Springfield, MA 01101; tel. (413) 788-1000; fax (413) 788-1301; Publr DAVID STARR; Editor ARNOLD S. FRIEDMAN; circ. 108,000 (D), 157,000 (S).

**Worcester Telegram & Gazette:** 20 Franklin St, POB 15012, Worcester, MA 01613-0012; tel. (508) 793-9100; fax (508) 793-9281; Publr PETER E. THERIOT; Exec. Man. Editor JOHN P. WIDDISON; circ. 111,000 (D), 143,000 (S).

### Michigan

**Detroit Free Press:** 321 West Lafayette Blvd, Detroit, MI 48231; tel. (313) 222-6400; fax (313) 678-5981; f. 1831; Publr NEAL SHINE; Editor JOE H. STROUD; circ. 552,000 (M), 1,173,000 (S).

**Detroit News:** 615 West Lafayette Blvd, Detroit, MI 48226; tel. (313) 222-6400; fax (313) 222-2335; f. 1873; Publr LOIUS A. WEILL, II; Exec. Editor ROBERT H. GILES; circ. 910,000 (M), 1,173,000 (S).

**Flint Journal:** 200 East First St, Flint, MI 48502; tel. (313) 766-6100; fax (313) 767-7518; f. 1876; Publr DANNY R. GAYDOU; Editor TOM LINDLEY; circ. 102,000 (E), 124,000 (S).

**Grand Rapids Press:** 155 Michigan St, NW, Grand Rapids, MI 49503; tel. (616) 459-1567; f. 1892; Editor MICHAEL S. LLOYD; circ. 141,000 (E), 179,000 (S).

**Kalamazoo Gazette:** 401 South Burdick St, Kalamazoo, MI 49007; tel. (616) 345-3511; fax (616) 345-0583; f. 1883; Publr DANIEL M. RYAN; Editor JAMES R. MOSBY, Jr; circ. 64,000 (E), 82,000 (S).

**Lansing State Journal:** 120 East Lenawee St, Lansing, MI 48919; tel. (517) 377-1000; fax (517) 377-1298; f. 1855; Publr W. CURTIS RIDDLE; Editor ZACK BINKLEY; circ. 71,000 (E), 96,000 (S).

**Oakland Press:** 48 West Huron St, POB 9, Pontiac, MI 48342; tel. (313) 332-8181; fax (313) 332-8294; f. 1843; Publr BRUCE H. MCINTYRE; Editor WILLIAM THOMAS; circ. 72,000 (E), 81,000 (S).

**Saginaw News:** 203 South Washington Ave, Saginaw, MI 48607-1283; tel. (517) 752-7171; fax (517) 752-3115; f. 1859; Publr REX THATCHER; Editor PAUL CHAFFEE; circ. 57,000 (E), 67,000 (S).

## THE UNITED STATES OF AMERICA — Directory

### Minnesota
**Star Tribune:** 425 Portland Ave, Minneapolis, MN 55488; tel. (612) 673-4000; fax (612) 673-4359; f. 1867; Publr JOEL KRAMER; Exec. Editor TIM J. MCGUIRE; circ. 413,000 (M), 689,000 (S).

**St Paul Pioneer Press:** 345 Cedar St, St Paul, MN 55101; tel. (612) 222-5011; fax (612) 228-5500; f. 1849; Publr PETER RIDDER; Exec. Editor WALKER LUNDY; circ. 211,000 (D), 276,000 (S).

### Mississippi
**Clarion-Ledger:** 311 East Pearl St, POB 40, Jackson, MS 39205; tel. (601) 961-7000; fax (601) 961-7047; Publr ROBERT E. ROBBINS; Editor JOHN JOHNSON; circ. 112,000 (E), 130,000 (S).

### Missouri
**Kansas City Star:** 1729 Grand Blvd, Kansas City, MO 64108; tel. (816) 234-4280; fax (816) 234-4926; f. 1880; Publr ROBERT C. WOODWORTH; Editor ART BRISBANE; circ. 294,000 (M), 434,000 (S).

**St Louis Post-Dispatch:** 900 North Tucker Blvd, St Louis, MO 63101; tel. (314) 340-8000; fax (314) 240-3050; f. 1878; Publr NICHOLAS G. PENNIMAN, IV; Editor WILLIAM F. WOO; circ. 344,000 (M), 563,000 (S).

### Montana
**Billings Gazette:** POB 36300, Billings, MT 59107; tel. (406) 657-1200; fax (406) 657-1345; f. 1885; Publr WAYNE SCHILE; Editor RICHARD J. WESNICK; circ. 54,000 (M), 63,000 (S).

### Nebraska
**Omaha World-Herald:** 1334 Dodge St, Omaha, NE 68102-1122; tel. (402) 444-1000; fax (402) 345-0183; f. 1885; Editor G. WOODSON HOWE; circ. 233,000 (E), 292,000 (S).

### Nevada
**Las Vegas Review-Journal:** 1111 West Bonanza, Las Vegas, NV 89106; tel. (702) 383-0211; f. 1908; Publr SHERMAN FREDERICK; Editor TRUDY PATTERSON; circ. 144,000 (E), 215,000 (S).

**Reno Gazette Journal:** POB 22000, Reno, NV 89520-2000; tel. (702) 788-6397; fax (702) 788-6438; f. 1870; Publr SUE CLARK-JACKSON; Editor WARD BUSHEE; circ. 66,000 (M), 84,000 (S).

### New Hampshire
**Union Leader** (M) f. 1863, **New Hampshire Sunday News** f. 1946: POB 9555, Manchester, NH 03108; tel. (603) 668-4321; fax (603) 668-0382; Publr Mrs NACKEY SCRIPPS LOEB; Editor-in-Chief JOSEPH W. MCQUAID; circ. 68,000 (M), 99,000 (S).

### New Jersey
**Asbury Park Press:** 3601 Highway 66, POB 1550, Neptune, NJ 07754-1550; tel. (908) 922-6000; fax (908) 922-4818; f. 1879; Publr and Editor E. DONALD LASS; circ. 163,000 (M), 231,000 (S).

**Courier-News:** 1201 Highway 22 West, POB 6600, Bridgewater, NJ 08807; tel. (908) 722-8800; fax (914) 694-5018; f. 1884; Publr HENRY FREEMAN; Editor CAROL A. HUNTER; circ. 50,000 (E).

**Courier-Post:** 301 Cuthbert Blvd, Cherry Hill, NJ 08002; tel. (609) 663-6000; fax (609) 663-2831; f. 1875; Publr ROBERT T. COLLINS; Exec. Editor EVERETT S. LANDERS; circ. 88,000 (M), 101,000 (S).

**Home News:** 35 Kennedy Blvd, POB 551, New Brunswick, NJ 08901; tel. (908) 246-5500; fax (908) 246-5518; f. 1879; Publr JOSEPH FONTANA; Editor RICHARD HUGHES; circ. 54,000 (E), 62,000 (S).

**Jersey Journal:** 30 Journal Sq., Jersey City, NJ 07306; tel. (201) 653-1000; fax (201) 653-1414; f. 1867; Editor STEVEN NEWHOUSE; circ. 57,000 (E).

**The Record:** 150 River St, Hackensack, NJ 07601; tel. (201) 646-4000; fax (201) 646-4251; f. 1895; Pres. VIVIEN WAIXEL; Editor GLENN RITT; circ. 160,000 (M), 225,000 (S).

**Star-Ledger:** Star-Ledger Plaza, Newark, NJ 07102; tel. (201) 877-4141; fax (201) 643-7248; f. 1917; Publr MARTIN BARTNER; Editor MORT PYE; circ. 463,000 (M), 697,000 (S).

**The Times:** 500 Perry St, Trenton, NJ 08605; tel. (609) 396-3232; fax (609) 396-3633; f. 1882; Publr RICHARD BILOTTI; Exec. Editor BRIAN S. MALONE; circ. 84,000 (M), 96,000 (S).

**Trentonian:** 600 Perry St, Trenton, NJ 08602; tel. (609) 989-7800; fax (609) 393-6072; f. 1946; Publr EDWARD L. HOFFMAN; Editor EMIL G. SLABODA; circ. 76,000 (M), 60,000 (S).

### New Mexico
**Albuquerque Journal:** 7777 Jefferson NE, Albuquerque, NM 87109; tel. (505) 823-3393; fax (505) 823-3369; f. 1880; Publr T. H. LANG; Editor JERRY CRAWFORD; circ. 118,000 (M), 168,000 (S).

### New York
**Albany Times Union:** News Plaza, POB 15000, Albany, NY 12212; tel. (518) 454-5694; fax (518) 454-5514; f. 1856; Publr TIMOTHY WHITE; Editor HARRY M. ROSENFELD; circ. 101,000 (M), 162,000 (S).

**The Buffalo News:** 1 News Plaza, POB 100, Buffalo, NY 14240; tel. (716) 849-3434; fax (716) 849-3409; f. 1880; Publr STANFORD LIPSEY; Editor MURRAY B. LIGHT; circ. 310,000 (M), 388,000 (S).

**Daily Gazette:** POB 1090, Schenectady, NY 12301-1090; tel. (518) 374-4141; fax (518) 395-3089; f. 1894; Editor JOHN E. N. HUME, III; circ. 58,000 (M), 62,000 (S).

**Democrat and Chronicle** (MS) f. 1833, **Rochester Times-Union** (E) f. 1826: 55 Exchange Blvd, Rochester, NY 14614-2001; tel. (716) 232-7100; fax (716) 258-2487; Publr DAVID J. MACK; Editor J. KEITH MOYER; circ. 141,000 (M), 64,000 (E), 258,000 (S).

**Newsday:** 235 Pinelawn, Melville, NY 11747; tel. (516) 843-2020; f. 1940; Publr RAYMOND A. JANSEN; Editor ANTHONY MARRO; circ. 694,000 (D), 827,000 (S).

**Post-Standard** (M) f. 1829, **Herald-Journal** (E) f. 1877: Clinton Sq., POB 4915, Syracuse, NY 13221; tel. (315) 470-0011; fax (315) 470-3081; Publr STEPHEN A. ROGERS; Editor (Post-Standard) MICHAEL J. CONNOR, (Herald-Journal) TIMOTHY BUNN; circ. 87,000 (M), 83,000 (E).

**Press & Sun-Bulletin:** Vestal Pkwy East, Binghamton, NY 13902; tel. (607) 798-0261; fax (607) 798-0261; Publr BERNIE GRIFFIN; Exec. Editor LOU BRANCACCIO; circ. 70,000 (M), 91,000 (S).

**Times Herald-Record** (M), **Record** (S): 40 Mulberry St, Middletown, NY 10940; tel. (914) 343-2181; fax (914) 343-2170; f. 1956; Publr JOHN M. SZEFC; Editor GARY GROSSMAN; circ. 86,000 (M), 102,000 (S).

**USA Today:** 1 Gannett Drive, White Plains, NY 10604; tel. (914) 694-9300; fax (914) 694-5018; f. 1982; Publr TOM CURLEY; Editor DAVID MAZZARELLA; circ. 1,429,000 (M).

### New York City
**New York Daily News:** 220 East 42nd St, New York, NY 10017; tel. (212) 210-2100; fax (212) 210-2049; f. 1919; Co-Publrs MORTIMER B. ZUCKERMAN, FRED DRASNER; Editor-in-Chief MARTIN DUNN; circ. 753,000 (M), 931,000 (S).

**New York Post:** 210 South St, New York, NY 10002; tel. (212) 815-8000; fax (212) 349-2511; f. 1801; Publr MARTIN SINGERMAN; Editor KEN CHANDLER; circ. 405,000 (M).

**New York Times:** 229 West 43rd St, New York, NY 10036; tel. (212) 556-1234; f. 1851; Publr ARTHUR OCHS SULZBERGER, Jr; Exec. Editor JOSEPH LELYVELD; circ. 1,115,000 (M), 1,762,000 (S).

**Staten Island Advance:** 950 Fingerboard Rd, Staten Island, New York, NY 10305; tel. (718) 981-1234; f. 1886; Publr RICHARD E. DIAMOND; Editor BRIAN J. LALINE; circ. 78,000 (E), 95,000 (S).

**Wall Street Journal:** 420 Lexington Ave, New York, NY 10170; tel. (212) 808-6600; fax (212) 808-6898; f. 1889; Publr PETER R. KANN; Editor ROBERT BARTLEY; circ. 1,780,000 (M).

### North Carolina
**Charlotte Observer:** 600 South Tryon St, POB 32188, Charlotte, NC 28020; tel. (704) 358-5000; fax (704) 358-5036; f. 1886; Publr ROLFE NEILL; Editor RICH OPPEL; circ. 236,000 (M), 305,000 (S).

**Greensboro News and Record:** 200 East Market St, POB 20848, Greensboro, NC 27420-0848; tel. (919) 373-7000; fax (919) 373-7043; f. 1905; Publr CARL MAGNUM, Jr; Exec. Editor BEN BOWERS; circ. 110,000 (M), 129,000 (S).

**News and Observer:** 215 South McDowell St, POB 191, Raleigh, NC 27602; tel. (919) 829-4500; fax (919) 829-4529; Publr FRANK DANIELS, Jr; Editor FRANK DANIELS, III; circ. 167,000 (M), 200,000 (S).

**Winston-Salem Journal:** POB 3159, Winston-Salem, NC 27102-3159; tel. (919) 727-7211; fax (919) 727-7315; Publr JOE DOSTER; Man. Editor JOE GOODMAN; circ. 91,000 (M), 104,000 (S).

### North Dakota
**The Forum:** POB 2020, Fargo, ND 58107; tel. (701) 235-7311; fax (701) 241-5487; f. 1878; Publr WILLIAM C. MARCIL; Editor JOSEPH DILL; circ. 56,000 (D), 71,000 (S).

### Ohio
**Akron Beacon Journal:** POB 640, Akron, OH 44309-0640; tel. (216) 996-3000; fax (216) 996-3053; f. 1839; Publr JOHN DOTSON, Jr; Editor DALE ALLEN; circ. 158,000 (M), 226,000 (S).

**Canton Repository:** 500 Market Ave South, Canton, OH 44711-9901; tel. (216) 454-5611; fax (216) 454-5745; f. 1815; Publr JAMES MCKEARNEY; Editor MICHAEL E. HANKE; circ. 63,000 (E), 81,000 (S).

**Cincinnati Enquirer:** 312 Elm St, Cincinnati, OH 45202; tel. (513) 721-2700; fax (513) 768-8330; f. 1841; Publr HARRY M. WHIPPLE; Editor GEORGE R. BLAKE; circ. 205,000 (M), 357,000 (S).

**Cincinnati Post:** 125 East Court St, Cincinnati, OH 45202; tel. (513) 352-2000; fax (513) 621-3962; f. 1881; Editor PAUL F. KNUE; circ. 93,000 (E).

**Cleveland Plain Dealer:** 1801 Superior Ave, Cleveland, OH 44114; tel. (216) 344-4500; fax (216) 999-6355; f. 1842; Publr and Editor THOMAS VAIL; circ. 404,000 (M), 548,000 (S).

# THE UNITED STATES OF AMERICA

*Directory*

**Columbus Dispatch:** 34 South Third St, Columbus, OH 43215; tel. (614) 461-5000; fax (614) 461-7580; Publr JOHN F. WOLFE; Editor ROBERT B. SMITH; circ. 264,000 (M), 405,000 (S).

**Dayton Daily News** (D), **Dayton Journal Herald** (S): 45 South Ludlow St, Dayton, OH 45402; tel. (513) 225-2335; fax (513) 225-2489; Publr BRAD TILSON; Editor MAX JENNINGS; circ. 169,000 (D), 225,000 (S).

**Toledo Blade:** 541 North Superior St, Toledo, OH 43660; tel. (419) 245-6000; fax (419) 245-6439; f. 1835; Editor THOMAS WALTON; circ. 152,000 (E), 207,000 (S).

**The Vindicator:** Vindicator Sq., POB 780, Youngstown, OH 44501-0780; tel. (216) 747-1471; fax (216) 747-0712; Publr BETTY H. BROWN JAGNOW; Editor PAUL C. JAGNOW; circ. 89,000 (E), 135,000 (S).

## Oklahoma

**Daily Oklahoman:** 9000 North Broadway, Oklahoma City, OK 73125; tel. (405) 475-3311; f. 1894; Pres., Publr EDWARD L. GAYLORD; Editor ED KELLY; circ. 232,000 (M), 335,000 (S).

**Tulsa Tribune:** 315 South Boulder Ave, POB 1770, Tulsa, OK 74102; tel. (918) 581-8400; fax (918) 584-1037; f. 1904; Publr JENKIN L. JONES; Editor JENK JONES, Jr.; circ. 67,000 (E).

**Tulsa World:** 315 South Boulder Ave, POB 1770, Tulsa, OK 74102; tel. (918) 581-8300; f. 1906; Publr ROBERT E. LORDON; Exec. Editor JOE WORLEY; circ. 175,000 (M), 245,000 (S).

## Oregon

**The Oregonian:** 1320 SW Broadway, Portland, OR 97201; tel. (503) 221-8327; fax (503) 294-8413; f. 1850; Publr FRED A. STICKEL; Editor WILLIAM HILLIARD; circ. 349,000 (M), 446,000 (S).

**The Register-Guard:** 975 High St, POB 10188, Eugene, OR 97401; tel. and fax (503) 485-1234; f. 1867; Publr and Editor ALTON F. BAKER, III; circ. 76,000 (M), 80,000 (S).

**Statesman Journal:** POB 13009, Salem, OR 97309; tel. (503) 399-6611; fax (503) 399-6808; f. 1851; Publr SARAH M. BENTLEY; Exec. Editor WILLIAM FLORENCE; circ. 60,000 (M), 72,000 (S).

## Pennsylvania

**Bucks County Courier Times:** 8400 Route 13, Levittown, PA 19057-5198; tel. (215) 949-4151; fax (215) 949-4114; f. 1954; Editor TIMOTHY J. BIRCH; circ. 71,000 (M), 77,000 (S).

**Johnstown Tribune–Democrat:** 425 Locust St, Johnstown, PA 15901; tel. (814) 532-5150; fax (814) 539-1409; f. 1853; Publr PAMELA MAYER; Editor BRIAN L. LONG; circ. 50,000 (M), 56,000 (S).

**Lancaster New Era** (E) f. 1877, **Sunday News** f. 1923: 8 West King St, POB 1328, Lancaster, PA 17608-1328; tel. (717) 291-8600; fax (717) 399-6507; Editor MELVIN W. WILLIAMS; circ. 52,000 (E), 105,000 (S).

**Morning Call** f. 1883, **Call Chronicle** (s) f. 1921: 101 North 6th St, Allentown, PA 18105; tel. (215) 820-6646; fax (215) 820-6617; Publr GARY K. SHORTS; Exec. Editor LAWRENCE H. HYMANS; circ. 137,000 (M), 189,000 (S).

**Patriot-News:** 812 Market St, POB 2265, Harrisburg, PA 17101; tel. (717) 255-8100; fax (717) 255-8456; f. 1854; Publr RAYMOND L. GOVER; Man. Editor CLEMENT J. SWEET; circ. 106,000 (M), 178,000 (S).

**Philadelphia Inquirer** (MS) f. 1829, **Philadelphia Daily News** (E) f. 1925: 400 North Broad St, Philadelphia, PA 19130; tel. (215) 854-2000; fax (215) 854-4794; Editors MAXWELL KING (Inquirer), ZACHARY STALBERG (Daily News); circ. 486,000 (M), 199,000 (E), 947,000 (S).

**Pittsburgh Post-Gazette:** 34 Blvd of the Allies, Pittsburgh, PA 15222; tel. (412) 263-1100; fax (412) 263-2014; f. 1786; Publrs JOHN R. BLOCK, WILLIAM BLOCK, Jr; Editor JOHN G. CRAIG, Jr; circ. 251,000 (M), 455,000 (S).

## Rhode Island

**Providence Journal–Bulletin:** 75 Fountain St, Providence, RI 02902-9985; tel. (401) 277-7847; fax (401) 277-7461; f. 1863; Publr STEPHEN HAMBLETT; Exec. Editor JAMES WYMAN; circ. 190,000 (D), 265,000 (S).

## South Carolina

**Greenville News** (M) f. 1874, **News-Piedmont** (s) f. 1874: 305 South Main St, POB 1688, Greenville, SC 29602-1688; tel. (803) 298-4487; fax (803) 298-4001; Publr STEVEN BRANDT; Editor THOMAS HUTCHINSON; circ. 97,000 (M), 145,000 (S).

**The Post and Courier:** 134 Columbus St, Charleston, SC 29403-4800; tel. (803) 577-7111; fax (803) 853-5673; f. 1803; Publr IVAN V. ANDERSON, Jr; Editor LARRY TARLETON; circ. 112,000 (M), 122,000 (S).

**The State:** POB 1333, Columbia, SC 29202; tel. (803) 771-6161; fax (803) 771-8430; f. 1891; Publr FRANK M. MCCOMAS; Exec. Editor GIL THELEN; circ. 134,000 (M), 170,000 (S).

## South Dakota

**Argus Leader:** 200 South Minnesota Ave, POB 5034, Sioux Falls, SD 57117-5034; tel. (605) 331-2200; fax (605) 331-2371; f. 1881; Publr LARRY FULLER; Editor RICHARD SOMERVILLE; circ. 51,000 (M), 75,000 (S).

## Tennessee

**Chattanooga Press:** 400 East 11th St, POB 1447, Chattanooga, TN 37401-1447; tel. (615) 756-6900; fax (615) 757-6383; f. 1888; Publr and Editor ROY MCDONALD; circ. 51,000 (E), 110,000 (S).

**The Commercial Appeal:** 495 Union Ave, Memphis, TN 38103; tel. (901) 529-2211; fax (901) 529-2522; f. 1841; Gen. Man. JOSEPH R. WILLIAMS; Editor LIONEL LINDER; circ. 187,000 (M), 284,000 (S).

**Knoxville News-Sentinel:** 208 West Church Ave, POB 59038, Knoxville, TN 37902-9038; tel. (615) 523-3131; fax (615) 521-5126; f. 1886; Editor HARRY MOSKOS; circ. 126,000 (M), 184,000 (S).

**Nashville Banner:** 1100 Broadway, Nashville, TN 37203; tel. (615) 259-8800; fax (615) 259-8890; f. 1876; Publr IRBY C. SIMPKINS, Jr; Editor EDWARD JONES; circ. 56,000 (E).

**The Tennessean:** 1100 Broadway, Nashville, TN 37203; tel. (615) 259-8333; fax (615) 259-8820; f. 1812; Publr JOHN SEIGENTHALER; circ. 147,000 (M), 286,000 (S).

## Texas

**Austin American-Statesman:** POB 670, Austin, TX 78767; tel. (512) 445-3745; fax (512) 445-3800; f. 1871; Publr ROGER KINTZEL; Editor MAGGIE BALOUGH; circ. 178,000 (M), 236,000 (S).

**Beaumont Enterprise:** 380 Main St, POB 3071, Beaumont, TX 77704; tel. (409) 833-3311; fax (409) 838-2857; f. 1889; Publr GEORGE B. IRISH; Editor BEN HANSEN; circ. 67,000 (M), 84,000 (S).

**Corpus Christi Caller-Times:** 820 Lower North Broadway, POB 9136, Corpus Christi, TX 78469; tel. (512) 884-2011; fax (512) 886-3732; f. 1883; Publr STEPHEN W. SULLIVAN; Exec. Editor DAVID A. HOUSE; Ind.; circ. 69,000 (M), 98,000 (S).

**Dallas Morning News:** POB 665237, Dallas, TX 75265; tel. (214) 977-8222; fax (214) 977-8638; f. 1885; Publr and Editor BURL OSBORNE; circ. 536,000 (M), 828,000 (S).

**El Paso Times:** 300 North Campbell, El Paso, TX 79901-1470; tel. (915) 546-6260; fax (915) 546-6404; f. 1881; Publr and Editor TOM FENTON; circ. 61,000 (M), 97,000 (S).

**Fort Worth Star-Telegram:** 400 West Seventh St, Fort Worth, TX 76102; tel. (817) 390-7400; fax (817) 390-7831; f. 1895; Publr RICHARD L. CONNOR; Exec. Editor MIKE BLACKMAN; circ. 256,000 (D), 353,000 (S).

**Houston Chronicle:** 801 Texas Ave, Houston, TX 77002; tel. (281) 220-7171; fax (281) 220-6677; f. 1901; Publr RICHARD J. V. JOHNSON; Editor JACK LOFTIS; circ. 412,000 (M), 607,000 (S).

**Lubbock Avalanche-Journal:** Eighth St and Ave J, POB 491, Lubbock, TX 79408; tel. (806) 762-8844; fax (806) 744-9603; f. 1922; Publr. DAVID C. SHARP; Editor BURLE PETTIT; circ. 68,000 (M), 77,000 (S).

**San Antonio Express-News:** POB 2171, San Antonio, TX 78297-2171; tel. (512) 225-7411; fax (512) 225-8351; f. 1864; Publr W. LAWRENCE WALKER, Jr; Exec. Editor JIM MOSS; circ. 239,000 (M), 407,000 (S).

**Waco Tribune-Herald:** 900 Franklin Ave, Waco, TX 76701; tel. (817) 767-5757; fax (817) 763-6115; f. 1911; Publr RAYMOND R. PREDDY; Editor BOB LOTT; circ. 44,000 (M), 59,000 (S).

## Utah

**Deseret News:** 30 East First St South, POB 1257, Salt Lake City, UT 84110; tel. (801) 237-2100; fax (801) 237-2121; f. 1850; Pres. and Publr WILLIAM JAMES MORTIMER; Man. Editor DON WOODWARD; circ. 65,000 (E), 69,000 (S).

**Salt Lake Tribune:** 143 South Main St, POB 867, Salt Lake City, UT 84111; tel. (801) 237-2045; fax (801) 521-9418; f. 1871; Publr JERRY O'BRIEN; Editor JAMES SHELLEDY; circ. 124,000 (M), 159,000 (S).

**Standard-Examiner:** 455 23rd St, POB 951, Ogden, UT 84402; tel. (801) 625-4200; fax (801) 625-4508; f. 1888; Editor RANDY HATCH; circ. 60,000 (E), 61,000 (S).

## Vermont

**Burlington Free Press:** 191 College St, Burlington, VT 05401; tel. (802) 863-3441; fax (802) 862-5622; f. 1827; Publr JAMES CAREY; Editor JENNIFER CARROLL; circ. 54,000 (M), 66,000 (S).

## Virginia

**Daily Press:** POB 746, Newport News, VA 23607; tel. (804) 247-4600; fax (804) 245-8618; f. 1896; Publr JOSEPH D. CANTRELL; Editor JACK DAVIS; circ. 104,000 (M), 125,000 (S).

**Richmond Times-Dispatch:** 333 East Grace St, POB 85333, Richmond, VA 23293; tel. (804) 649-6000; fax (804) 775-8059; f. 1850;

# THE UNITED STATES OF AMERICA

*Directory*

Publr J. STEWART BRYAN, III; Man. Editor LOUISE C. SEALS; circ. 214,000 (D), 260,000 (S).

**Roanoke Times & World-News:** POB 2491, Roanoke, VA 24010; tel. (703) 981-3100; fax (703) 981-3171; Publr WALTER RUGABER; Exec. Editor FORREST M. LANDON; circ. 115,000 (M), 127,000 (S).

**Virginian–Pilot** (MS) f. 1865, **Ledger-Star** (E) f. 1876: 150 West Brambleton Ave, Norfolk, VA 23510; tel. (804) 446-2030; fax (804) 626-1375; Publrs ROBERT BENSON (Ledger Star), FRANK BATTEN, Jr (Virginian-Pilot); Editor SANDRA ROWE; circ. 165,000 (M), 50,000 (E), 239,000 (S).

## Washington

**The Herald:** Grand and California Sts, POB 930, Everett, WA 98206; tel. (360) 339-3000; fax (360) 339-3049; f. 1891; Publr LARRY HANSON; Exec. Editor STAN STRICK; circ. 53,000 (E), 64,000 (S).

**News Tribune:** POB 11000, Tacoma, WA 98411; tel. (206) 597-8742; fax (206) 597-8266; f. 1883; Publr KELSO GILLENWATER; Editor JOHN D. KOMEN; circ. 126,000 (M), 143,000 (S).

**Seattle Post-Intelligencer:** 101 Elliott Ave West, POB 1909, Seattle, WA 98119; tel. (206) 448-8000; fax (206) 448-8166; f. 1863; Publr VIRGIL FASSIO; Editor MARJI RUIZ; circ. 203,000 (M), 504,000 (S).

**Seattle Times:** POB 70, Seattle, WA 98111; tel. (206) 464-2111; fax (206) 464-2261; f. 1886; Publr FRANK A. BLETHEN; Editor MICHAEL R. FANCHER; circ. 231,000 (E), 504,000 (S).

**Spokesman-Review:** 999 West Riverside, POB 2160, Spokane, WA 99210; tel. (509) 459-5000; fax (509) 459-5234; f. 1883; Publr W. H. COWLES, III; Editor CHRISTOPHER PECK; Ind.; circ. 124,000 (M), 156,000 (S).

## West Virginia

**Charleston Daily Mail:** 1001 Virginia St East, Charleston, WV 25331; tel. (304) 348-5140; fax (304) 348-4847; Publr TERRY HORNE; Editor DAVID GREENFIELD; circ. 100,000 (E), 106,000 (S).

## Wisconsin

**Green Bay Press-Gazette:** 435 East Walnut St, POB 19430, Green Bay, WI 54307-9430; tel. (414) 435-4411; fax (414) 431-8499; f. 1915; Publr W. T. NUSBAUM; Editor JOHN D. GIBSON; circ. 61,000 (E), 88,000 (S).

**Milwaukee Journal:** POB 371, Milwaukee, WI 53201; tel. (414) 224-2000; fax (414) 224-2049; f. 1882; Editor SIG GISSLER; circ. 225,000 (E), 489,000 (S).

**Milwaukee Sentinel:** POB 371, Milwaukee, WI 53201; tel. (414) 224-2000; fax (414) 224-2049; f. 1837; Editor KEITH SPORE; circ. 171,000 (M).

**Post-Crescent:** POB 59, Appleton, WI 54912; tel. (414) 733-4411; fax (414) 733-1945; f. 1920; Publr DONALD KAMPFER; Editor MICHAEL WALTER; circ. 61,000 (E), 76,000 (S).

**Wisconsin State Journal:** 1901 Fish Hatchery Rd, POB 8058, Madison, WI 53708; tel. (608) 252-6100; fax (608) 252-6119; f. 1839; Publr JAMES E. BURGESS; Editor FRANK DENTON; circ. 86,000 (M), 168,000 (S).

## Wyoming

**Star-Tribune:** POB 80, Casper, WY 82602; tel. (307) 266-0500; fax (307) 266-0501; f. 1891; Publr ROBIN HURLESS; Editor ANNE MACKINNON; circ. 34,000 (M), 38,000 (S).

## SELECTED PERIODICALS

(Q = quarterly; M = monthly; F = fortnightly; W = weekly)

**American Heritage:** 60 Fifth Ave, New York, NY 10011-8890; tel. (212) 206-5500; fax (212) 620-2332; f. 1954; Editor RICHARD F. SNOW; circ. 304,000 (8 a year).

**American Historical Review:** 914 Atwater, Indiana University, Bloomington, IN 47405; tel. (812) 855-7609; fax (812) 855-5827; f. 1895; Editor DAVID L. RANSEL; circ. 19,000 (5 a year).

**American Hunter:** c/o National Rifle Asscn, 11250 Waples Mill Rd, Fairfax, VA 22030; tel. (703) 267-1300; fax (703) 267-3971; f. 1973; Editor THOMAS FULGHAM; circ. 1,500,000 (M).

**American Journal of Psychiatry:** American Psychiatric Asscn, 1400 K St, NW, Washington, DC 20005; tel. (202) 682-6020; fax (202) 682-6016; Editor Dr NANCY C. ANDREASEN; circ. 47,000 (M).

**American Legion Magazine:** 700 North Pennsylvania St, POB 1055, Indianapolis, IN 46206-1055; tel. (317) 635-8411; f. 1919; organ of the American Legion; Publr DANIEL WHEELER; circ. 2,900,000 (M).

**American Motorcyclist:** POB 6114, Westerville, OH 43081-6114; tel. (614) 891-2425; fax (614) 891-5012; f. 1947; Exec. Editor GREG HARRISON; circ. 165,000 (M).

**American Political Science Review:** 1527 New Hampshire Ave, NW, Washington, DC 20036; tel. (202) 483-2512; fax (202) 483-2657; f. 1906; Editor G. BINGHAM POWELL; circ. 15,000 (Q).

**American Teacher:** 555 New Jersey Ave, NW, Washington, DC 20001-2079; tel. (202) 879-4430; fax (202) 783-2014; f. 1916; Editor TRISH GORMAN; circ. 654,000 (8 a year).

**Architectural Record:** 1221 Ave of the Americas, New York, NY 10020-1001; tel. (212) 512-4686; fax (212) 512-4256; f. 1891; Editor STEPHEN KLIMENT; circ. 70,000 (14 a year).

**Aviation Week and Space Technology:** 1221 Ave of the Americas, 42nd Floor, New York, NY 10020-1001; tel. (212) 512-4116; fax (212) 512-6068; f. 1916; Editor-in-Chief DONALD E. FINK, Jr; circ. 141,000 (W).

**Barron's National Business & Financial Weekly:** 200 Liberty St, New York, NY 10281; tel. (212) 416-2700; fax (212) 416-2829; f. 1921; Editor JAMES P. MEAGHER; circ. 269,000 (W).

**Better Homes and Gardens:** 1716 Locust St, Des Moines, IA 50309-3023; tel. (515) 284-3000; fax (515) 284-3684; f. 1922; Editor JEAN LEMMON; circ. 7,600,000 (M).

**Better Living:** 80 Central Park West, Suite 16B, New York, NY 10023; tel. (212) 581-2000; f. 1980; Editor JOSEPH QUEENAN; circ. 200,000 (Q).

**Boating Magazine:** 1633 Broadway, New York, NY 10019; tel. (212) 767-5800; fax (212) 486-4216; f. 1956; Editor JOHN OWENS; circ. 195,000 (M).

**Bon Appetit:** 6300 Wilshire Blvd, 10th Floor, Los Angeles, CA 90048; tel. (213) 965-3600; telex 901-3212437; fax (213) 930-2369; f. 1955; Editor-in-Chief WILLIAM J. GARRY; circ. 1,295,000 (M).

**Boys' Life:** 1325 West Walnut Hill Lane, POB 152079, Irving, TX 75015-2079; tel. (214) 580-2366; fax (214) 580-2079; f. 1912; Man. Editor J. D. OWEN; circ. 1,300,000 (M).

**Bride's:** 140 East 45th St, New York, NY 10017-3704; tel. (212) 880-8800; fax (212) 880-6689; f. 1934; Editor MILLIE BRATTEN; circ. 324,000 (6 a year).

**Broadcasting & Cable:** 1705 De Sales St, NW, Washington, DC 20036-4405; tel. (202) 659-2340; fax (202) 429-0651; f. 1931; Editor DON WEST; circ. 34,000 (W).

**Business Week/World Wide:** 1221 Ave of the Americas, New York, NY 10020-1001; tel. (212) 512-4686; fax (212) 512-4256; f. 1929; Editor-in-Chief STEPHEN B. SHEPARD; circ. 884,000 (W).

**Capper's:** 1503 SW 42nd St, Topeka, KS 66609-1265; tel. (913) 274-4346; fax (913) 274-4305; f. 1879; Editor NANCY PEAVLER; circ. 370,000 (F).

**Car and Driver:** 2002 Hogback Rd, Ann Arbor, MI 48105-9795; tel. (313) 971-3600; fax (313) 971-9188; f. 1955; Editor-in-Chief CSABA CSERE; circ. 1,100,000 (M).

**Catholic Digest:** POB 64090, St Paul, MN 55164-0090; tel. (612) 962-6725; fax (612) 962-6755; f. 1936; Editor RICHARD REECE; circ. 540,000 (M).

**Chemical and Engineering News:** American Chemical Society, 1155 16th St, NW, Washington, DC 20036-4800; tel. (202) 872-4570; fax (202) 872-4574; f. 1923; Editor MIKE HEYLIN; circ. 130,000 (W).

**Child Life:** 1100 Waterway Blvd, POB 567, Indianapolis, IN 46206; tel. (317) 636-8881; fax (317) 684-8094; f. 1921; Editor LISE HOFFMAN; circ. 80,000 (8 a year).

**Christianity Today:** 465 Gundersen Drive, Carol Stream, IL 60188-2498; tel. (708) 260-6200; fax (708) 260-0014; f. 1956; Exec. Editor DAVID NEFF; circ. 180,000 (14 a year).

**Civil Engineering:** 345 East 47th St, 16th Floor, New York, NY 10017-2330; tel. (212) 705-7754; fax (212) 705-7712; f. 1930; Editor VIRGINIA FAIRWEATHER; circ. 100,000 (M).

**Congressional Digest:** 3231 P St, NW, Washington, DC 20007; tel. (202) 333-7332; fax (202) 625-6670; f. 1921; Editor SARAH ORRICK; (10 a year).

**Consumer Reports:** 101 Truman Ave, Yonkers, NY 10703-1057; tel. (914) 378-2000; fax (914) 378-2904; f. 1936; Editor EILEEN DENVER; circ. 4,600,000 (M).

**Consumers Digest:** 5705 North Lincoln Ave, Chicago, IL 60659-4774; tel. (312) 275-3590; fax (312) 275-7273; f. 1959; Editor JOHN MANOS; circ. 925,000 (6 a year).

**Cosmopolitan:** 224 West 57th St, New York, NY 10019-3203; tel. (212) 649-3700; fax (212) 757-6792; f. 1886; women's; Editor HELEN GURLEY BROWN; circ. 2,627,000 (M).

**Country Living:** 224 West 57th St, New York, NY 10019-3203; tel. (212) 649-3700; fax (212) 757-6792; f. 1978; Editor RACHEL NEWMAN; circ. 1,977,000 (M).

**CQ Researcher:** 1414 22nd St, NW, Washington, DC 20037; tel. (202) 887-8500; fax (202) 728-1862; f. 1945; publ. by Congressional Quarterly Inc; politics and government; Editor SANDRA STENCEL; circ. 5,000 (W).

# THE UNITED STATES OF AMERICA

**Cumulative Book Index:** The H. W. Wilson Co, 950 University Ave, Bronx, NY 10452; tel. (718) 588-8400; fax (718) 590-1617; f. 1898; Editor Nancy Wong; circ. 6,000 (M).

**Ebony:** 820 South Michigan Ave, Chicago, IL 60605; tel. (312) 322-9200; fax (212) 322-9375; f. 1945; news and illustrated; Exec. Editor Herbert Nipson; circ. 1,940,000 (M).

**Editor & Publisher—The Fourth Estate:** 11 West 19th St, New York, NY 10011-4234; tel. (212) 675-4380; fax (212) 691-7287; f. 1884; Man. Editor John P. Consoli; circ. 25,000 (W).

**Elks Magazine:** 425 West Diversey Pkwy, Chicago, IL 60614-6196; tel. (312) 528-4500; f. 1922; Exec. Editor Fred D. Oakes; circ. 1,346,000 (M).

**Ellery Queen's Mystery Magazine:** 1540 Broadway, 15th Floor, New York, NY 10036; f. 1941; Editor Janet Hutchings; circ. 251,000 (M).

**Entertainment Weekly:** Time-Life Bldg, Rockefeller Center, New York, NY 10019; tel. (212) 522-4158; fax (212) 522-0074; f. 1990; Editor-in-Chief Jason McManus; circ. 600,000.

**Esquire:** 250 West 55th St, New York, NY 10019-3203; tel. (212) 469-4020; f. 1933; Editor-in-Chief Edward Kosner; circ. 737,000 (M).

**Essence:** 1500 Broadway, 6th Floor, New York, NY 10036-4071; tel. (212) 642-0600; fax (212) 921-5173; f. 1970; Editor-in-Chief Susan L. Taylor; circ. 1,000,000 (M).

**Family Circle:** 110 Fifth Ave, New York, NY 10011-5699; tel. (212) 463-1000; fax (212) 463-1553; f. 1932; Editor Jacqueline Leo; circ. 5,114,000 (every 3 weeks).

**Family Handyman:** 7900 International Drive, Suite 950, Minneapolis, MN 55425-1510; tel. (612) 851-8640; fax (612) 854-8620; f. 1951; Editor Gary Havens; circ. 1,151,000 (10 a year).

**Farm Journal:** 230 West Washington Sq., Philadelphia, PA 19106-0000; tel. (215) 829-4700; fax (215) 829-4803; f. 1877; Editor Earl Ainsworth; circ. 840,000 (M).

**Field & Stream:** 2 Park Ave, New York, NY 10016-5601; tel. (212) 779-5000; fax (212) 725-3836; f. 1895; Editor Duncan Barnes; circ. 2,016,000 (M).

**Flower and Garden Magazine:** 700 West 47th St, Suite 310, Kansas City, MO 64112; tel. (816) 531-5730; fax (816) 531-3873; f. 1957; Exec. Editor Kay M. Olson; circ. 631,000 (6 a year).

**Forbes:** 60 Fifth Ave, New York, NY 10011-8802; tel. (212) 620-2200; fax (212) 620-2417; f. 1917; Editor James W. Michaels; circ. 770,000 (F).

**Foreign Affairs:** 58 East 68th St, New York, NY 10021-5987; tel. (212) 734-0400; fax (212) 861-2759; f. 1922; Editor David Kellogg; circ. 102,000 (6 a year).

**Fortune:** 1271 Ave of the Americas, New York, NY 10020; tel. (212) 522-1212; fax (212) 765-2699; f. 1930; Man. Editor John Huey; circ. 911,000 (F).

**Glamour:** 350 Madison Ave, New York, NY 10017-3704; tel. (212) 880-8800; fax (212) 880-8331; f. 1939; Editor Jack Kliger; circ. 2,081,000 (M).

**Golf Digest:** 5520 Park Ave, POB 0395, Trumbull, CT 06611-0395; tel. (203) 373-7000; fax (203) 373-7033; f. 1950; Editor Jerry Tarde; circ. 1,462,000 (M).

**Golf Magazine:** 2 Park Ave, New York, NY 10016-5601; f. 1959; tel. (212) 779-5000; fax (212) 779-5522; Editor-in-Chief George Peper; circ. 1,250,000 (M).

**Good Housekeeping:** 959 Eighth Ave, New York, NY 10019-5203; tel. (212) 649-2000; fax (212) 977-9824; f. 1885; Editor (vacant); circ. 5,163,000 (M).

**Gourmet—The Magazine of Good Living:** 560 Lexington Ave, New York, NY 10022; tel. (212) 880-2788; f. 1941; Editor Gail Zweigonthal; circ. 889,000 (M).

**Grit:** 1503 SW 42nd St, Topeka, KS 66609-1214; f. 1882; Editor Michael Rafferty; circ. 561,000 (W).

**Harper's Bazaar:** 1700 Broadway, New York, NY 10019-5970; tel. (212) 903-5000; fax (212) 262-1701; Editor-in-Chief Elizabeth Tilberis; circ. 738,000 (M).

**Harper's Magazine:** 666 Broadway, New York, NY 10012-2317; tel. (212) 614-6500; fax (212) 228-5889; f. 1850; Editor Lewis H. Lapham; circ. 217,000 (M).

**Harvard Business Review:** 1554 South Sepulveda, Suite 209, Los Angeles, CA 90025; tel. (310) 575-5610; fax (310) 575-5615; f. 1922; Editor Rosabeth Moss Kanter; circ. 213,000 (6 a year).

**Highlights for Children:** 803 Church St, Honesdale, PA 18431; tel. (717) 253-1080; fax (717) 253-0179; f. 1946; Editor Kent L. Brown Jr; circ. 3,000,000 (M).

**Home Mechanix:** 2 Park Ave, New York, NY 10016-5601; tel. (212) 779-5000; fax (212) 779-5465; f. 1928; Editor Michael Chotiner; circ. 1,025,000 (M).

**Hot Rod Magazine:** 8490 Sunset Blvd, Los Angeles, CA 90069-1946; tel. (310) 854-2320; fax (310) 854-1700; f. 1948; Editor Jeff Smith; circ. 785,000 (M).

**House Beautiful:** 1700 Broadway, New York, NY 10019-5970; tel. (212) 903-5000; fax (212) 262-7101; f. 1896; Editor Jo Ann Barwick; circ. 1,009,000 (M).

**Industry Week:** 1100 Superior Ave, Cleveland, OH 44114-2518; tel. (216) 696-7000; fax (216) 696-7670; f. 1882; Editor-in-Chief John R. Brandt; circ. 233,000 (F).

**Jet:** 820 South Michigan Ave, Chicago, IL 60605-2190; tel. (312) 322-9200; fax (312) 322-0918; f. 1951; Exec. Editor Robert Johnson; circ. 969,000 (W).

**Journal of Accountancy:** Harborside Financial Center, Plaza III, Jersey City, NJ 07311; tel. (201) 938-3292; fax (201) 938-3303; f. 1905; Editor Colleen Katz; circ. 328,000 (M).

**Journal of the American Medical Association (JAMA):** 515 North State St, Chicago, IL 60610-4319; tel. (312) 464-2400; fax (312) 464-4184; f. 1883; Editor Dr George D. Lundberg; circ. 349,000 (W).

**Journal of Family and Consumer Sciences:** American Asscn of Family and Consumer Sciences, 1555 King St, Alexandria, VA 22314; tel. (703) 706-4600; fax (703) 706-4663; f. 1909; Editor Harriet K. Light; circ. 25,000 (Q).

**Junior Scholastic:** 555 Broadway, New York, NY 10012; tel. (212) 343-6295; fax (212) 343-6333; f. 1937; Editor Lee Baier; circ. 600,000 (F).

**Kiplinger's Personal Finance Magazine:** 1729 H St, NW, Washington, DC 20006-3904; tel. (202) 887-6400; fax (202) 331-1206; f. 1947; personal finance and consumer matters; Editor Ted Miller; circ. 1,100,000 (M).

**Ladies' Home Journal:** 100 Park Ave, New York, NY 10017-5599; tel. (212) 953-7070; fax (212) 351-3650; f. 1883; Editor-in-Chief Myrna Blyth; circ. 5,002,000 (M).

**Life Magazine:** 1271 Ave of the Americas, New York, NY 10020-1393; tel. (212) 522-1212; f. 1936; Editor Daniel Okrent; circ. 1,500,000 (M).

**Lion Magazine:** 300 22nd St, Oak Brook, IL 60521; tel. (708) 571-5466; fax (708) 571-8890; f. 1918; business and professional; Editor Robert Kleinfelder; circ. 600,000 (M).

**Mademoiselle:** 350 Madison Ave, New York, NY 10017-3704; tel. (212) 880-8800; fax (212) 880-8289; f. 1935; Editor Elizabeth Crow; circ. 1,219,000 (M).

**Management Review:** American Management Asscn, 135 West 50th St, 15th Floor, New York, NY 10020-1201; tel. (212) 903-8393; fax (212) 903-8083; f. 1917; Man. Editor Martha H. Peak; circ. 67,000 (M).

**Materials Engineering:** 1100 Superior Ave, Cleveland, OH 44114; tel. (216) 696-7000; telex 4218245; fax (216) 696-0177; f. 1929; Editor Margaret Hunt; circ. 50,000 (M).

**McCall's Magazine:** 110 Fifth Ave, New York, NY 10011; tel. (212) 463-1000; fax (212) 463-1403; f. 1876; women's; Editor Sally Koslow; circ. 4,600,000 (M).

**Metropolitan Home:** 1633 Broadway, New York, NY 10019; tel. (212) 767-5800; fax (212) 486-4216; f. 1969; Editor-in-Chief Donna Warner; circ. 710,000 (M).

**Money:** 1271 Ave of the Americas, New York, NY 10020-1301; tel. (212) 522-1212; fax (212) 522-0907; f. 1972; Man. Editor Frank Lalli; circ. 1,915,000 (M).

**Motor Trend:** 6420 Wilshire Blvd, Los Angeles, CA 90048; tel. (310) 854-2222; fax (310) 854-2355; f. 1949; Editor Mike Anson; circ. 933,000 (M).

**Motorland:** 150 Van Ness Ave, San Francisco, CA 94102-5208; tel. (415) 565-2451; fax (415) 552-5825; f. 1917; Editor Lynn Ferrin; circ. 2,070,000 (6 a year).

**The Nation:** 72 Fifth Ave, New York, NY 10011-8046; tel. (212) 242-8400; fax (212) 463-9712; f. 1865; Editor Katrina Vanden Heuvel; politics and the arts; circ. 100,000 (W).

**Nation's Business:** US Chamber of Commerce, 1615 H St, NW, Washington, DC 20062-2000; tel. (202) 463-5650; fax (202) 887-3437; f. 1912; Editor Robert T. Gray; circ. 861,000 (M).

**National Enquirer:** 600 South East Coast Ave, Lantana, FL 33462; tel. (407) 586-1111; fax (407) 510-1777; f. 1926; Editor Iain Calder; circ. 4,381,000 (W).

**National Geographic Magazine:** National Geographic Society, 17th and M Sts, NW, Washington, DC 20036-4701; tel. (202) 857-7000; fax (202) 775-6141; f. 1888; Editor William Allen; circ. 9,921,000 (M).

**National Review:** 150 East 35th St, New York, NY 10016-4196; tel. (212) 679-7330; fax (212) 696-0309; f. 1955; Editor John O'Sullivan, Jr; circ. 221,000 (F).

# THE UNITED STATES OF AMERICA

**New Republic:** 1220 19th St, NW, Suite 600, Washington, DC 20036-2474; tel. (202) 331-7494; fax (202) 331-0275; f. 1914; Editor ANDREW SULLIVAN; circ. 94,000 (W).

**New York Magazine:** 755 Second Ave, New York, NY 10017-5998; tel. (212) 880-0700; fax (212) 682-3883; f. 1968; Editor EDWARD KOSNER; circ. 434,000 (W).

**New York Review of Books:** 250 West 57th St, New York, NY 10107-0171; tel. (212) 757-8070; fax (212) 333-5374; f. 1963; Editors ROBERT SILVERS, BARBARA EPSTEIN; circ. 120,000 (F).

**The New Yorker:** 20 West 43rd St, New York, NY 10036-7448; tel. (212) 840-3800; fax (212) 536-5735; f. 1925; Editor TINA BROWN; circ. 800,000 (W).

**Newsweek:** 251 West 57th St, New York, NY 10019; tel. (212) 445-4000; fax (212) 445-5068; f. 1933; Editor-in-Chief RICHARD M. SMITH; circ. 3,156,000 (W).

**Omni:** 324 West Wendover Ave, Suite 205, Greensboro, NC 27408; f. 1978; Editor KEITH FERRELL; circ. 700,000 (M).

**Organic Gardening:** 33 East Minor St, Emmaus, PA 18098; tel. (610) 967-8650; fax (610) 967-8181; f. 1942; Editor MIKE MCGRATH; circ. 735,000 (M).

**Outdoor Life:** 2 Park Ave, New York, NY 10016-5601; tel. (212) 779-5000; fax (212) 779-5470; f. 1898; Editor VIN T. SPARANO; circ. 1,512,000 (M).

**Parents' Magazine:** 685 Third Ave, 3rd Floor, New York, NY 10017-4052; tel. (212) 878-8700; fax (212) 986-2656; f. 1926; Editor-in-Chief ANN PLESHETTE MURPHY; circ. 1,776,000 (M).

**Partisan Review:** 236 Bay State Rd, Boston, MA 02215; tel. (617) 353-4260; fax (617) 353-7444; f. 1934; Editor-in-Chief WILLIAM PHILLIPS; circ. 8,000 (Q).

**Penthouse:** 277 Park Ave, 4th Floor, New York, NY 10172-0003; tel. (212) 702-6000; telex 237128; fax (212) 702-6262; f. 1969; Publr and Editor BOB GUCCIONE; circ. 1,502,000 (M).

**People Weekly:** Time-Life Bldg, Rockefeller Center, New York, NY 10020; tel. (212) 522-1212; fax (212) 522-1863; f. 1974; Editor PATRICIA RYAN; circ. 3,447,000 (W).

**Playboy:** 680 North Lake Shore Drive, Chicago, IL 60611-4402; tel. (312) 751-8000; fax (312) 751-2818; f. 1953; men's; Editor-in-Chief HUGH M. HEFNER; circ. 3,403,000 (M).

**Political Science Quarterly:** 475 Riverside Drive, Suite 1274, New York, NY 10115-1274; tel. (212) 870-2506; fax (212) 870-2202; f. 1886; Editor DEMETRIOS CARALEY; circ. 8,000 (Q).

**Popular Mechanics:** 224 West 57th St, New York, NY 10019-3203; tel. (212) 649-3700; fax (212) 757-6792; f. 1902; Editor JOE OLDHAM; circ. 1,657,000 (M).

**Popular Photography:** 1633 Broadway, New York, NY 10019; tel. (212) 767-5800; fax (212) 486-4216; f. 1937; Editor JASON SCHNEIDER; circ. 652,000 (M).

**Popular Science:** 2 Park Ave, New York, NY 10016; tel. (212) 779-5000; fax (212) 481-8062; f. 1872; Editor-in-Chief FRED ABATEMARCO; circ. 1,808,000 (M).

**Prevention:** 33 East Minor St, Emmaus, PA 18098-0001; tel. (215) 967-8650; fax (215) 967-8181; f. 1950; Editor MARK BRICKLIN; circ. 3,221,000 (M).

**Progressive Architecture:** 600 Summer St, POB 1361, Stamford, CT 06904; tel. (203) 348-7531; fax (203) 348-4023; f. 1920; Editor JOHN MORRIS DIXON; circ. 55,000 (M).

**Progressive Farmer:** 2100 Lakeshore Drive, POB 2581, Birmingham, AL 35202; tel. (205) 877-6000; fax (205) 877-6700; f. 1886; Editor TOM CURL; circ. 276,000 (M).

**Publishers Weekly:** 249 West 17th St, New York NY 10011-5399; tel. (212) 463-6758; fax (212) 463-6631; f. 1872; Editor NORA RAWLINSON; circ. 38,000 (W).

**QST:** American Radio Relay League, 225 Main St, Newington, CT 06111-1494; tel. (203) 666-1541; fax (203) 665-7531; f. 1915; Editor MARK WILSON; circ. 164,000 (M).

**Reader's Digest:** Reader's Digest Rd, Pleasantville, NY 10570-7000; tel. (914) 238-1000; fax (914) 238-4559; f. 1922; Editor JOHN DONOGHUE; circ. 16,262,000 (M).

**Redbook Magazine:** 224 West 57th St, 6th Floor, New York, NY 10019-3203; tel. (212) 649-3331; fax (212) 581-7805; f. 1903; Editor-in-Chief ELLEN LEVINE; circ. 3,345,000 (M).

**Road & Track:** 1499 Monrovia Ave, Newport Beach, CA 92663-2752; tel. (714) 720-5300; fax (714) 631-2757; f. 1947; Editor THOMAS L. BRYANT; circ. 740,000 (M).

**Rolling Stone:** 1290 Ave of the Americas, New York, NY 10104; tel. (212) 484-1616; fax (212) 767-8209; f. 1967; Exec. Editor ROBERT B. WALLACE; circ. 1,237,000 (F).

**The Rotarian:** Rotary International, One Rotary Center, 1560 Sherman Ave, Evanston, IL 60201-3698; tel. (708) 866-3000; telex 724465; fax (708) 866-9732; f. 1911; Editor W. L. WHITE; circ. 523,000 (M).

**Saturday Evening Post:** 1100 Waterway Blvd, Indianapolis, IN 46202-2174; tel. (317) 636-8881; fax (317) 637-0126; f. 1821; Editor CORY J. SERVASS; circ. 460,000 (6 a year).

**School and Community:** Missouri State Teachers Asscn, POB 458, Columbia, MO 65205-0458; tel. (314) 442-3127; fax (314) 443-5079; f. 1915; Editor LETHA ALBRIGHT; circ. 32,000 (Q).

**Science:** 1333 H St, NW, Washington, DC 20005-4792; tel. (202) 326-6500; fax (202) 682-0816; f. 1880; publ. by the American Asscn for the Advancement of Science; Editor DANIEL E. KOSHLAND, Jr; circ. 153,000 (W).

**Science News:** 1719 N St, NW, Washington, DC 20036-2890; tel. (202) 785-2255; fax (202) 659-0365; f. 1921; Editor PATRICK YOUNG; circ. 237,000 (W).

**Scientific American:** 415 Madison Ave, New York, NY 10017-1179; tel. (212) 754-0550; fax (212) 335-6245; f. 1845; Editor JOHN RENNIE; circ. 633,000 (M).

**Scouting Magazine:** 1325 West Walnut Hill Lane, POB 152079, Irving, TX 75015-2079; tel. (214) 580-2355; fax (214) 580-2079; f. 1913; Editor ERNEST DOCLAR; circ. 1,032,000 (6 a year).

**SELF Magazine:** 350 Madison Ave, New York, NY 10017-3704; tel. (212) 880-8800; fax (212) 880-8331; f. 1979; Editor-in-Chief ALEXANDRA PENNEY; circ. 1,314,000 (M).

**Seventeen:** 850 Third Ave, New York, NY 10022; tel. (212) 407-9700; fax (212) 935-4237; f. 1944; Editor-in-Chief MIDGE RICHARDSON; circ. 1,941,000 (M).

**Smithsonian Magazine:** 900 Jefferson Drive, Washington, DC 20560-0001; tel. (202) 786-2900; f. 1970; Editor DON MOSER; circ. 2,302,000 (M).

**Soap Opera Digest:** 45 West 25th St, New York, NY 10010-2754; tel. (212) 645-2100; fax (212) 645-0683; f. 1975; Editor LYNN LEAHEY; circ. 1,500,000 (F).

**Southern Living:** 2100 Lakeshore Drive, Birmingham, AL 35209-6721; tel. (205) 877-6000; fax (205) 877-6700; f. 1966; Editor JOHN ALEX FLOYD, Jr; circ. 2,300,000 (M).

**Special Libraries:** Special Libraries Asscn, 1700 18th St, NW, Washington, DC 20009-2508; tel. (202) 234-4700; fax (202) 265-9317; f. 1909; Editor GAIL REPSHER; circ. 16,000 (Q).

**Sport Magazine:** 6420 Wilshire Blvd, Los Angeles, CA 90048; tel. (310) 854-2222; fax (310) 854-2355; f. 1946; Editor CAM BENTY; circ. 792,000 (M).

**Sporting News:** 1212 North Lindbergh Blvd, St Louis, MO 63132-1704; tel. (314) 997-7111; f. 1886; Editor TOM BARNRIDGE; circ. 725,000 (W).

**Sports Illustrated:** Time-Life Bldg, Rockefeller Center, New York, NY 10019-0001; tel. (212) 522-4158; fax (212) 522-0074; f. 1954; Editor MARK MALVOY; circ. 3,357,000 (W).

**Star:** 660 White Plains Rd, Tarrytown, NY 10591; tel. (914) 332-5000; fax (914) 332-5000; f. 1974; Editor RICHARD KAPLAN; circ. 2,752,000 (W).

**Sunset Magazine:** 85 Willow Rd, Menlo Park, CA 94025-3600; tel. (415) 321-3600; fax (415) 321-0551; f. 1898; Editor WILLIAM MARKEN; circ. 1,442,000 (M).

**'TEEN:** 6420 Wilshire Blvd, Los Angeles, CA 90048; tel. (310) 854-2222; fax (310) 854-2355; f. 1957; Editor ROXIE CAMRON; circ. 1,171,000 (M).

**Time:** Time-Life Bldg, Rockefeller Center, New York, NY 10020-1393; tel. (212) 522-1212; fax (212) 522-1863; f. 1923; Editor HENRY MULLER; circ. 4,104,000 (W).

**Travel/Holiday:** 28 West 23rd St, New York, NY 10010-5204; tel. (212) 366-8800; fax (212) 366-8899; f. 1901; Editor MARGARET STAATS SIMMONS; circ. 599,000 (M).

**Travel & Leisure:** 1120 Ave of the Americas, 10th Floor, New York, NY 10036-6770; tel. (212) 382-5600; fax (212) 768-1568; f. 1971; Editor-in-Chief NANCY NOVOGRAD; circ. 900,000 (M).

**True Story:** 233 Park Ave South, 6th Floor, New York, NY 10003; tel. (212) 979-4860; fax (212) 979-7431; f. 1919; Editor SUE WEINER; circ. 825,000 (M).

**TV Guide:** 1211 Ave of the Americas, New York, NY 10036; tel. (212) 852-7500; f. 1953; Editor ANTHEA DISNEY; circ. 14,123,000 (W).

**US:** 1290 Ave of the Americas, New York, NY 10104-0002; tel. (212) 484-1616; fax (212) 767-8209; f. 1977; Editor JANN S. WENNER; circ. 1,040,000 (F).

**US News & World Report:** 2400 N St, NW, Washington, DC 20037-1196; tel. (202) 955-2000; fax (202) 955-2049; f. 1933; Editor MERRILL MCLOUGHLIN; circ. 2,281,000 (W).

**Vanity Fair:** 350 Madison Ave, New York, NY 10017; tel. (212) 880-8800; fax (212) 880-8289; f. 1983; Editor GRAYDON CARTER; circ. 1,340,000 (M).

# THE UNITED STATES OF AMERICA
*Directory*

**Variety:** 475 Park Ave South, New York, NY 10016-6999; tel. (212) 689-3600; telex 126335; fax (212) 545-5400; f. 1905; Editor Peter Bart; circ. 30,000 (w).

**VFW Magazine:** 406 West 34th St, Kansas City, MO 64111-2700; tel. (816) 756-3390; fax (816) 968-1169; f. 1912; Editor Richard K. Kolb; circ. 2,037,000 (11 a year).

**Village Voice:** 36 Cooper Sq., New York, NY 10003; tel. (212) 475-3300; fax (212) 475-8944; f. 1955; Editor Jon Z. Larsen; circ. 136,000 (w).

**Vogue:** 350 Madison Ave, New York, NY 10017-3799; tel. (212) 880-8800; fax (212) 880-8331; f. 1892; Editor Anna Wintour; circ. 1,250,000 (M).

**Weight Watchers Magazine:** 360 Lexington Ave, New York, NY 10017-6547; tel. (212) 370-0644; fax (212) 687-4398; f. 1968; Editor Lee Haiken; circ. 1,020,000 (M).

**Workbasket:** 700 West 47th St, Suite 310, Kansas City, MO 64112; tel. (816) 531-5730; fax (816) 531-3873; f. 1935; Exec. Editor Kay M. Olson; circ. 752,000 (6 a year).

**Working Woman Magazine:** 230 Park Ave, New York, NY 10169-0005; tel. (212) 551-9500; fax (212) 599-4763; f. 1976; Editor Lynn Povich; circ. 750,000 (M).

**Yale Review:** 208243 Yale Station, New Haven, CT 06520; tel. (203) 432-0499; f. 1911; Editor J. D. McClatchy; circ. 6,000 (Q).

**Yankee Magazine:** POB 520, Dublin, NH 03444-0520; tel. (603) 563-8111; fax (603) 563-8252; f. 1935; Editor Judson D. Hale; circ. 713,000 (M).

## NEWS AGENCIES

**Associated Press (AP):** 50 Rockefeller Plaza, New York, NY 10020-1666; tel. (212) 621-1500; f. 1848; Pres. and CEO Louis D. Boccardi; Vice-Pres. and Dir of World Services Claude E. Erbsen; c. 1,700 newspaper mems in the US, 6,000 broadcast mems and over 8,500 subscribers abroad.

**Feature News Service:** 2330 South Brentwood Blvd, St Louis, MO 63144-2096; tel. (314) 961-9827; fax (314) 961-2300; f. 1924; feature services to 87 weekly newspapers; Pres. Martha F. Stroud.

**Jewish Telegraphic Agency (JTA):** 330 Seventh Ave, 11th Floor, New York NY 10001-5010; tel. (212) 643-1890; fax (212) 643-8498; world-wide coverage of Jewish news; offices in Washington, DC, Paris and Jerusalem; Editor Mark Joffe.

**Religion News Service:** 1101 Connecticut Ave, NW, Suite 350, Washington, DC 20036; tel. (202) 463-8777; fax (202) 463-0033; Editor John Connell.

**Singer Media Corpn:** Seaview Business Park, 1030 Calle Cordillera, Unit 106, San Clemente, CA 92673; tel. (714) 498-7227; fax (714) 498-2162; f. 1940; includes OPS-Oceanic Press Service; news and features services and book excerpts to 100 publs in 20 countries; Chair., Pres. and Editor Kurt Singer.

**United Media (UM):** 200 Madison Ave, 4th Floor, New York, NY 10016; tel. (212) 293-8606; fax (212) 293-8616; f. 1978; includes United Feature Syndicate (UFS) and Newspaper Enterprise Asscn (NEA); news features; Pres. and CEO Douglas R. Stern; Editorial Dir Diana Loevy.

**United Press International (UPI):** 1400 I St, NW, Washington, DC 20005; tel. (202) 898-8000; fax (202) 898-8057; f. 1907; CEO L. Brewster Jackson; Exec. Editor Raphael Callis; serves c. 3,000 news outlets world-wide.

### Foreign Bureaux

**Agence France-Presse (AFP):** 1612 K St, NW, Suite 400, Washington, DC 20006; tel. (202) 293-9380; telex 248465; fax (202) 861-8524; Bureau Chief Pierre Lesourd; also office in New York.

**Allgemeiner Deutscher Nachrichtendienst (ADN)** (Germany): UN Secretariat Bldg, Room 482, UN Plaza, New York, NY 10017; tel. (212) 421-5876; fax (212) 832-5140; Bureau Chief Andreas Lindner.

**Agenzia Nazionale Stampa Associata (ANSA)** (Italy): National Press Bldg, Suite 1285, Washington, DC 20045; tel. (202) 628-3317; fax (202) 638-1792; Bureau Chief Bruno Marolo; also offices in New York and San Francisco.

**Central News Agency (CNA)** (Taiwan): 1173 National Press Bldg, Washington, DC 20045; tel. (202) 628-2738; fax (202) 637-6788; Bureau Chief Rock Jo-shui Leng; also offices in New York and San Francisco.

**Česká tisková kancelář (ČTK)** (Czech Republic): 40 River Rd, Roosevelt Island, NY 10044; tel. (212) 888-2992; fax (212) 888-3067.

**Deutsche Presse-Agentur (dpa)** (Germany): National Press Bldg, Suite 969, Washington, DC 20045; tel. (202) 783-5097; telex 197984; fax (202) 783-4116; Bureau Chief Herbert Winkler; also office in New York.

**Informatsionnoye Telegrafnoye Agentstvo Rossii—Telegrafnoye Agentstvo Suverennykh Stran (ITAR—TASS)** (Russia): 50 Rockefeller Plaza, Suite 501, New York, NY 10020-1696; tel. (212) 245-4250; telex 223346; fax (212) 245-4258; Regional Man. Yuri Romantsov; also offices in Washington, DC, and San Francisco.

**Inter Press Service (IPS)** (Italy): POB 462, Grand Central Station, New York, NY 10017; tel. (212) 751-3255; telex 175600; fax (212) 371-9020; Dir Marco Napoli; also office in Washington, DC.

**Jiji Press** (Japan): 120 West 45th St, 14th Floor, New York, NY 10036; tel. (212) 575-5830; fax (212) 764-3950; f. 1945; Chief Rep. Suguru Sasaki; also offices in Washington, DC, Los Angeles, San Francisco and Chicago.

**Kyodo Tsushin** (Japan): National Press Bldg, Suite 400, Washington, DC 20045; tel. (202) 347-5767; fax (202) 393-2342; Bureau Chief Mikio Haruna; also offices in New York and Los Angeles.

**Magyar Távirati Iroda (MTI)** (Hungary): 8515 Farrell Drive, Chevy Chase, MD 20815; tel. (301) 565-2221; fax (301) 589-6907; Correspondent Péter Rácz.

**Reuters** (United Kingdom): 1333 H St, NW, Suite 410, Washington, DC 20005; tel. (202) 898-8300; fax (202) 898-8383; Editor Robert Doherty; also offices in New York, Chicago, San Francisco and five other cities.

**Tlačová agentúra Slovenskej republiky (TASR)** (Slovakia): 4501 Connecticut Ave, Apt 713, NW, Washington, DC 20008; tel. (202) 686-4710; fax (202) 537-0584; f. 1992; Chief Officer Otakar Kořinek.

**Xinhua (New China) News Agency** (People's Republic of China): 40-35 72nd St, Woodside, NY 11377; tel. (718) 335-8388; fax (718) 335-8778; Bureau Dir Zhaolong Xia; also office in Washington, DC.

Agencia EFE (Spain), PAP (Poland), RIA—Novosti (Russia), Canadian Press, Ghana News Agency and Prensa Latina (Cuba) are also represented.

## NATIONAL ASSOCIATIONS

**American Business Press:** 675 Third Ave, Suite 415, New York, NY 10017; tel. (212) 661-6360; fax (212) 370-0736; f. 1965; 717 mems; Sr Vice-Pres. Terilyn McGovern.

**American Society of Magazine Editors:** 919 Third Ave, New York, NY 10022; tel. (212) 872-3700; fax (212) 888-4217; Exec. Dir Marlene Kahan; 700 mems.

**American Society of Newspaper Editors:** POB 4090, Reston, VA 22090-1700; tel. (703) 648-1144; fax (703) 476-6125; f. 1922; 900 mems; Pres. William B. Ketter.

**Audit Bureau of Circulations:** 900 North Meacham Rd, Schaumburg, IL 60173; tel. (708) 605-0909; fax (708) 605-0483; Chair. Hugh F. Dow; Pres. and Man. Dir M. David Keil; 5,000 mems.

**Council of Literary Magazines and Presses (CLMP):** 154 Christopher St, Suite 3c, New York, NY 10014-2839; tel. (212) 741-9110; fax (212) 741-9112; f. 1967; provides services to non-commercial US literary magazines and presses; Exec. Dir Jim Sitter; 450 mems.

**Magazine Publishers of America:** 919 Third Ave, New York, NY 10022; tel. (212) 872-3700; fax (212) 888-4217; f. 1919; Pres. Donald D. Kummerfeld; Chair. William T. Kerr; 327 mems.

**Media Credit Association:** 919 Third Ave, New York, NY 10022; tel. (212) 872-3700; fax (212) 888-4623; f. 1903; Vice-Pres. James E. Van Meter; 800 mems.

**National Newspaper Association:** 1525 Wilson Blvd, Arlington, VA 22209; tel. (703) 907-7900; fax (703) 907-7901; f. 1885; CEO Tonda F. Rush; 4,200 mems.

**Newspaper Association of America:** The Newspaper Center, 11600 Sunrise Valley Drive, Reston, VA 22091; tel. (703) 648-1000; fax (703) 620-4557; f. 1992 as successor to American Newspaper Publishers Asscn (ANPA); Chair. Uzal H. Martz, Jr; Pres. and CEO Cathleen P. Black; c.1,500 mems in USA and Canada accounting for over 80% of US daily newspaper circulation.

**The Newspaper Guild:** 8611 2nd Ave, Silver Springs, MD 20910; tel. (301) 585-2990; fax (301) 585-0668; f. 1933; affil. to AFL-CIO, Canadian Labour Congress, Int. Fed. of Journalists; Pres. Charles Dale; 31,000 mems.

**Periodical & Book Association of America Inc:** 120 East 34th St, Suite 7k, New York, NY 10016; tel. (212) 689-4952; fax (212) 545-8328; Exec. Dir Michael Morse; 75 mems.

# Publishers

**Abaris Books Inc:** 70 New Canaan Ave, Norwalk, CT 06896; tel. (203) 938-1655; fax (203) 938-4017; f. 1973; Publr Anthony S. Kaufmann; academic and trade illustrated and fine arts reference.

**Abbeville Publishing Group:** 488 Madison Ave, 23rd-24th Floors, New York, NY 10022; tel. (212) 888-1969; telex 428141; fax (212)

# THE UNITED STATES OF AMERICA

644-5085; f. 1977; Pres. and Publr ROBERT E. ABRAMS; fine arts and illustrated books.

**Abingdon Press:** POB 801, Nashville, TN 37202-0801; tel. (615) 749-6000; f. 1789; Editorial Dir NEIL M. ALEXANDER; religious, general.

**Harry N. Abrams, Inc:** 100 Fifth Ave, New York, NY 10011; tel. (212) 206-7715; fax (212) 645-8437; Pres., CEO and Editor-in-Chief PAUL GOTTLIEB; art, architecture, natural history, popular culture.

**Academic Press, Inc:** 525 B St, Suite 1900, San Diego, CA 92101-4495; tel. (619) 231-0926; telex 568364; fax (619) 699-6320; f. 1942; division of Harcourt Brace & Co; Pres. PIETER S. H. BOLMAN; medical, scientific and technical books and journals.

**Addison-Wesley Publishing Co Inc:** One Jacob Way, Reading, MA 01867-3999; tel. (617) 944-3700; telex 949416; fax (617) 944-9338;; Chair. and CEO WARREN R. STONE; educational and professional.

**Andrews & McMeel:** 4900 Main St, Kansas City, MO 64112; tel. (816) 932-6700; fax (816) 932-6706; Pres. THOMAS N. THORNTON; humour, general trade.

**Jason Aronson, Inc:** 230 Livingston St, Northvale, NJ 07647; tel. (201) 767-4093; fax (201) 767-4330; f. 1965; Pres. JASON ARONSON; psychiatry, psychoanalysis and behavioural sciences; Judaica.

**Augsburg Fortress, Publishers:** 426 South Fifth St, POB 1209, Minneapolis, MN 55440; tel. (612) 330-3300; fax (612) 330-3455; f. 1890; Pres. MARVIN ROLOFF (acting); religious.

**August House Inc, Publishers:** POB 3223, Little Rock, AR 72203; tel. (501) 372-5450; fax (501) 372-5579; f. 1979; Pres. TED PARKHURST; fiction, folklore, children's.

**Avery Publishing Group, Inc:** 120 Old Broadway, Garden City Park, NY 11040; tel. (516) 741-2155; fax (516) 742-1892; Pres. RUDY SHUR; college textbooks, trade books specializing in childbirth, child care, military science, health, cookery, art, fantasy.

**Avon Books:** 1350 Ave of the Americas, New York, NY 10019; tel. (212) 261-6800; fax (212) 261-6895; f. 1941; Pres. and CEO HOWARD KAMINSKY; reprints and originals.

**Baker Book House:** POB 6287, Grand Rapids, MI 49516; tel. (616) 676-9185; fax (616) 676-9573; f. 1939; Pres. RICHARD BAKER; religious (Protestant).

**Ballantine/Del Rey/Fawcett/Ivy Books:** 201 East 50th St, New York, NY 10022; tel. (212) 752-2713; fax (212) 572-4912; division of Random House Inc; Pres. LINDA GREY; fiction, non-fiction, paperbacks and reprints.

**Bantam Doubleday Dell Publishing Group:** 1540 Broadway, New York, NY 10036; tel. (212) 354-6500; telex 237992; fax (212) 782-9597; f. 1945; Pres. JACK HOEFT; general fiction and non-fiction.

**Barron's Educational Series, Inc:** 250 Wireless Blvd, Hauppauge, NY 11788; tel. (516) 434-3311; fax (516) 434-3723; f. 1941; Pres. MANUEL H. BARRON; general non-fiction, educational, juvenile.

**Beacon Press:** 25 Beacon St, Boston, MA 02108; tel. (617) 742-2110; fax (617) 723-3097; f. 1854; Dir WENDY J. STROTHMAN; world affairs, religion, general non-fiction.

**Matthew Bender and Co Inc:** 11 Penn Plaza, New York, NY 10001; tel. (212) 967-7707; fax (518) 462-3788; f. 1887; Pres. ALEX SANN; legal, accountancy, insurance and banking texts and treatises.

**The Benjamin/Cummings Publishing Co, Inc:** 390 Bridge Pkwy, Redwood City, CA 94065; tel. (415) 594-4400; fax (415) 594-4456; division of Addison-Wesley Publishing Co; Pres. SALLY ELLIOTT; life, physical and health sciences, mathematics, computer science, general science.

**Berkley Publishing Group:** 200 Madison Ave, New York, NY 10016; tel. (212) 951-8800; telex 422386; fax (212) 213-6706; division of the Putnam Berkley Group Inc; Pres. DAVID SHANKS; paperback.

**The Borgo Press:** POB 2845, San Bernardino, CA 92406; tel. (909) 884-5813; fax (909) 888-4942; f. 1975; Publrs ROBERT REGINALD, MARY A. BURGESS; academic and scholarly.

**R. R. Bowker Co:** 121 Chanlon Rd, New Providence, NJ 07974; tel. (908) 464-6800; fax (908) 464-3553; f. 1872; Pres. IRA SIEGEL; reference, bibliographies.

**Braille Inc:** 184 Seapit Rd, POB 457, East Falmouth, MA 02536-0457; tel. (508) 540-0800; fax (508) 548-6116; f. 1971; Pres. JOAN B. ROSE; fiction, non-fiction, mathematics, science, educational and computer materials in Braille transcription.

**George Braziller, Inc:** 60 Madison Ave, New York, NY 10010; tel. (212) 889-0909; fax (212) 689-5405; f. 1955; Publr GEORGE BRAZILLER; fiction and non-fiction, fine arts.

**Brookings Institution:** 1775 Massachusetts Ave, NW, Washington, DC 20036; tel. (202) 797-6000; fax (202) 797-6004; f. 1927; Dir of Publs ROBERT L. FAHERTY; economics, government, foreign policy.

*Directory*

**Burgess International Group Inc:** 7110 Ohms Lane, Edina, MN 55439-2143; tel. (612) 831-1344; fax (612) 831-3167; f. 1925; Pres. BERNARD BREY; college textbooks and manuals.

**Cambridge University Press:** 40 West 20th St, New York, NY 10011-4211; tel. (212) 924-3900; fax (212) 691-3239; Dir ALAN WINTER; scholarly and academic, textbooks.

**Carol Publishing Group:** 600 Madison Ave, New York, NY 10022; tel. (212) 486-2200; fax (212) 486-2231; f. 1989; Publr STEVEN SCHRAGIS; general fiction and non-fiction, university textbooks.

**The Catholic University of America Press:** 620 Michigan Ave, NE, Washington, DC 20064; tel. (202) 319-5052; fax (202) 319-5802; f. 1939; Dir DAVID J. MCGONAGLE; scholarly.

**The Caxton Printers, Ltd:** 312 Main St, Caldwell, ID 83605; tel. (208) 459-7421; fax (208) 459-7450; f. 1903; Pres. GORDON GIPSON; Western Americana.

**Childrens Press:** 5440 North Cumberland Ave, Chicago, IL 60656-1494; tel. (312) 693-0800; telex 2215226; fax (312) 693-0574; f. 1944; Exec. Vice-Pres. HOWARD FAGERBERG; juvenile educational.

**Churchill Livingstone Inc:** 650 Ave of the Americas, New York, NY 10011; tel. (212) 206-5000; telex 662266; fax (212) 727-7808; division of Longman Publishing Group; Pres. and CEO TONI M. TRACY; medical.

**Columbia University Press:** 562 West 113th St, New York, NY 10025; tel. (212) 316-7100; fax (212) 316-7169; f. 1893; Pres. JOHN D. MOORE; trade, educational, scientific, reference.

**Concordia Publishing House:** 3558 South Jefferson Ave, St Louis, MO 63118; tel. (314) 268-1000; fax (314) 268-1329; f. 1869; Pres. JOHN W. GERBER; religious (Protestant), fiction, music.

**Congressional Quarterly Books:** 1414 22nd St, NW, Washington, DC 20037; tel. (202) 887-8500; fax (202) 728-1863; f. 1945; Pres. ANDREW BARNES; business, education and government; directories.

**Cornell University Press:** Sage House, 512 East State St, POB 250, Ithaca, NY 14851; tel. (607) 277-2338; fax (607) 277-2374; f. 1869; Dir JOHN G. ACKERMAN; scholarly, non-fiction.

**Creative Education, Inc:** 123 South Broad St, POB 227, Mankato, MN 56001; tel. (507) 388-6273; fax (507) 388-2746; f. 1932; Pres. TOM PETERSON; juvenile.

**Crossroad Publishing Co:** 370 Lexington Ave, New York, NY 10017; tel. (212) 532-3650; fax (212) 532-4922; f. 1980; Pres. and CEO GWENDOLIN HERDER; religion, psychology.

**Da Capo Press Inc:** 233 Spring St, New York, NY 10013; tel. (212) 620-8000; telex 421139; fax (212) 463-0742; f. 1964; division of Plenum Publishing Corpn; Pres. MARTIN E. TASH; trade and scholarly.

**F. A. Davis Co:** 1915 Arch St, Philadelphia, PA 19103; tel. (215) 568-2270; telex 834837; fax (215) 568-5065; f. 1879; Chair. ROBERT H. CRAVEN; medical, nursing and allied health textbooks.

**DAW Books, Inc:** 375 Hudson St, New York, NY 10014-3658; tel. (212) 366-2096; telex 236109; fax (212) 366-2090; f. 1971; Publrs ELIZABETH R. WOLLHEIM, SHEILA E. GILBERT; science fiction, fantasy.

**John De Graff, Inc:** Clinton Corners, NY 12514; tel. (914) 266-5800; f. 1951; Pres. JOHN G. DE GRAFF; pleasure boating.

**Marcel Dekker, Inc:** 270 Madison Ave, New York, NY 10016; tel. (212) 696-9000; telex 421419; fax (212) 685-4540; f. 1963; Pres. and CEO MARCEL DEKKER; textbooks and reference.

**Devin-Adair Publishers:** 6 North Water St, Greenwich, CT 06830; tel. (203) 531-7755; f. 1911; Publr CLAUDE HARMON; general non-fiction, nature, health, conservative politics, revisionist history, gardening, cookery, photography, Irish interest.

**Doubleday:** 1540 Broadway, New York, NY 10036; tel. (212) 354-6500; fax (212) 302-7985; f. 1897; division of Bantam Doubleday Dell Publishing Group; Pres. and Publr ARLENE FRIEDMAN; general fiction and non-fiction.

**Dover Publications, Inc:** 31 East Second St, Mineola, NY 11501; tel. (516) 294-7000; telex 127731; fax (516) 742-6953; f. 1941; Pres. HAYWARD CIRKER; trade, reprints, scientific, classics, language, arts and crafts.

**Drama Book Publishers:** 260 Fifth Ave, New York, NY 10001; tel. (212) 725-5377; fax (212) 725-8506; f. 1967; Pres. and Editor-in-Chief RALPH PINE; performing arts.

**Dufour Editions, Inc:** POB 7, Chester Springs, PA 19425-0007; tel. (215) 458-5005; fax (215) 458-7103; f. 1946; Pres. CHRISTOPHER MAY; literary, poetry, fiction, humanities, music, history.

**Duke University Press:** Box 90660, Durham, NC 27708-0660; tel. (919) 687-3600; fax (919) 688-4574; f. 1921; Exec. Dir STANLEY FISH; scholarly.

**Duquesne University Press:** 600 Forbes Ave, Pittsburgh, PA 15282; tel. (412) 396-6610; fax (412) 396-5780; f. 1927; Dir JOHN DOWDS; scholarly.

**Ediciones Universal:** 3090 Eighth St, Miami, FL 33135; tel. (305) 642-3234; telex 6811258; fax (305) 642-7978; f. 1965; Man. JUAN MANUEL SALVAT; Spanish language fiction and non-fiction.

# THE UNITED STATES OF AMERICA

**Elsevier Science Publishing Co, Inc:** 655 Ave of the Americas, New York, NY 10010; tel. (212) 989-5800; telex 420643; fax (212) 633-3965; f. 1962; Pres. RONALD H. SCHLOSSER; scientific, medical, technical journals and books.

**Encyclopaedia Britannica, Inc:** 310 South Michigan Ave, Chicago, IL 60604; tel. (312) 347-7000; telex 2213243; fax (312) 347-7135; f. 1768; Chair. and CEO ROBERT P. GWINN; encyclopedias, reference.

**M. Evans & Co, Inc:** 216 East 49th St, New York, NY 10017; tel. (212) 688-2810; fax (212) 486-4544; f. 1960; Pres. GEORGE C. DE KAY; adult and juvenile fiction and non-fiction.

**Facts on File Inc:** 460 Park Ave South, New York, NY 10016; tel. (212) 683-2244; telex 238552; fax (212) 213-4578; f. 1940; Publr MARTIN GREENWALD; non-fiction, reference.

**Farrar, Straus & Giroux, Inc:** 19 Union Sq. West, New York, NY 10003; tel. (212) 741-6900; fax (212) 633-9385; f. 1946; Pres. and CEO ROGER W. STRAUS; general, new writing.

**J. G. Ferguson Publishing Co:** 200 West Madison St, 3rd Floor, Chicago, IL 60606; tel. (312) 580-5480; fax (312) 580-4948; f. 1940; Pres. STEWART W. LAPHAM; reference.

**Fodor's Travel Publications Inc:** 201 East 50th St, New York, NY 10022; tel. (212) 572-8784; telex 126575; fax (212) 572-2248; division of Random House Inc; Pres. and Publr KRISTINA PETERSON; travel guides.

**Fordham University Press:** University Box L, Bronx, NY 10458-5172; tel. (718) 817-4780; fax (718) 817-4785; f. 1907; Dir SAVERIO PROCARIO; scholarly.

**Fortress Press:** 426 South Fifth St, POB 1209, Minneapolis, MN 55440; tel. (612) 330-3300; fax (612) 330-3455; f. 1855; Pres. GARY AAMODT; religious (Lutheran).

**W. H. Freeman & Co, Publishers:** 41 Madison Ave, New York, NY 10010; tel. (212) 576-9400; telex 12326; fax (212) 481-1891; f. 1946; Pres. ROBERT L. BIEWEN; textbooks, science, mathematics.

**Samuel French, Inc:** 45 West 25th St, New York, NY 10010; tel. (212) 206-8990; fax (212) 206-1429; f. 1830; Man. Dir CHARLES R. VAN NOSTRAND; plays.

**Funk & Wagnalls:** 1 International Blvd, Suite 444, Mahwah, NJ 07495-0017; tel. (201) 529-6900; fax (201) 529-6920; f. 1876; Pres. and CEO GEORGE PHILIPS; encyclopedias, general reference.

**Futura Publishing Co Inc:** 135 Bedford Rd, POB 418, Armonk, NY 10504-0418; tel. (914) 273-1014; fax (914) 273-1015; f. 1970; Chair. STEVEN E. KORN; medical and scientific.

**Gale Research Inc:** 835 Penobscot, Detroit, MI 48226; tel. (313) 961-2242; telex 810-2217086; fax (313) 961-6083; f. 1954; Pres. and CEO KEITH M. LASSNER; reference.

**Garland Publishing Inc:** 717 Fifth Ave, New York, NY 10022; tel. (212) 751-7447; fax (212) 308-9399; f. 1969; Chair. ELIZABETH B. BORDEN; reference, college textbooks, paperbacks.

**Bernard Geis Associates:** 500 Fifth Ave, Suite 3600, New York, NY 10110; tel. (212) 730-4730; fax (212) 730-4464; f. 1958; Pres. BERNARD GEIS; general fiction and non-fiction.

**Genealogical Publishing Co:** 1001 North Calvert St, Baltimore, MD 21202; tel. (410) 837-8271; fax (410) 752-8492; f. 1959; Editor-in-Chief MICHAEL TEPPER; genealogy, immigration studies, heraldry, local history.

**The K. S. Giniger Co, Inc:** 250 West 57th St, Suite 519, New York, NY 10107; tel. (212) 570-7499; fax (212) 369-6692; f. 1965; Pres. KENNETH S. GINIGER; general non-fiction.

**Warren H. Green, Inc:** 8356 Olive Blvd, St Louis, MO 63132; tel. (314) 991-1335; fax (314) 997-1788; f. 1966; Pres. JOYCE R. GREEN; medical, science, technology, philosophy.

**Greenwood Publishing Group:** 88 Post Rd West, POB 5007, Westport, CT 06881; tel. (203) 226-3571; fax (203) 222-1502; f. 1967; Pres. ROBERT HAGELSTEIN; business reference and non-fiction.

**Grove/Atlantic:** 841 Broadway, New York, NY 10003-4793; tel. (212) 614-7850; fax (212) 614-7886; Pres. MORGAN ENTREKIN; fiction and non-fiction.

**Gulf Publishing Co, Book/Software/Video Division:** POB 2608, Houston, TX 77252-2608; tel. (713) 529-4301; telex 275418; fax (713) 520-4438; f. 1916; Vice-Pres. and Dir CLAYTON A. UMBACH, Jr; texts and computer software on chemical and mechanical, engineering, petroleum, business, construction, videotape training.

**Hammond Inc:** 515 Valley St, Maplewood, NJ 07040; tel. (201) 763-6000; fax (201) 763-7658; f. 1900; Chair. CALEB D. HAMMOND; Pres. and CEO C. DEAN HAMMOND, III; maps, cartography, atlases.

**Harcourt Brace & Co:** 525 B St, Suite 1900, San Diego, CA 92101; tel. (619) 231-6616; telex 181726; f. 1919; Pres. and CEO RICHARD MORGAN; fiction, textbooks, general.

**HarperCollins Publishers:** 10 East 53rd St, New York, NY 10022; tel. (212) 207-7000; telex 62501; fax (212) 207-7759; f. 1817; Pres. and CEO GEORGE CRAIG; fiction, non-fiction, reference, religious, children's, general.

**Harvard University Press:** 79 Garden St, Cambridge, MA 02138; tel. (617) 495-2600; fax (617) 495-5898; f. 1913; Dir WILLIAM P. SISLER; scholarly and trade.

**Hastings House, Book Publishers:** 141 Halstead Ave, Mamaroneck, NY 10543; tel. (914) 835-4005; fax (914) 835-1037; f. 1936; Pres. HY STEIRMAN; communication arts, consumer affairs, media, travel, cookery, history.

**D. C. Heath & Co:** 125 Spring St, Lexington, MA 02173; tel. (617) 860-1340; fax (617) 860-1508; f. 1885; Pres. LOREN KORTE; textbooks.

**Lawrence Hill Books:** 611 Broadway, Suite 530, New York, NY 11238; tel. (212) 260-0576; fax (212) 260-0853; f. 1972; Publr SHIRLEY A. CLOYES; African and African-American studies, women's studies, Middle East, contemporary issues, politics.

**Hill and Wang:** 19 Union Sq. West, New York, NY 10003; tel. (212) 741-6900; telex 667428; fax (212) 633-9385; division of Farrar, Straus & Giroux, Inc; Publr ELIZABETH SIFTON; general, drama, history.

**Holiday House Inc:** 425 Madison Ave, New York, NY 10017; tel. (212) 688-0085; fax (212) 421-6134; f. 1935; Pres. JOHN H. BRIGGS, Jr; juvenile.

**Holloway House Publishing Co:** 8060 Melrose Ave, Los Angeles, CA 90046; tel. (213) 653-8060; fax (213) 655-9452; f. 1960; Pres. RALPH WEINSTOCK; Black, Hispanic and American Indian literature, games and gambling.

**Holmes & Meier Publishers, Inc:** 30 Irving Place, New York, NY 10003; tel. (212) 254-4100; fax (212) 254-4104; f. 1969; Man. Dir MIRIAM H. HOLMES; history, political science, area studies, general non-fiction, foreign literature in translation and scholarly.

**Hoover Institution Press:** Stanford University, Stanford, CA 94305-6010; tel. (415) 723-3373; telex 348402; fax (415) 723-1687; f. 1962; Exec. Editor PATRICIA A. BAKER; scholarly.

**Houghton Mifflin Co:** 222 Berkeley St, Boston, MA 02116; tel. (617) 351-5000; telex 4430255; fax (617) 227-5409; f. 1832; Chair. and CEO NADER F. DAREHSHORI; general and educational.

**Indiana University Press:** 601 North Morton, Bloomington, IN 47404-3797; tel. (812) 855-4203; telex 272279; fax (812) 855-7931; f. 1950; Dir JOHN GALLMAN; trade and scholarly non-fiction.

**International Universities Press, Inc:** 59 Boston Post Rd, Madison, CT 06443-1524; tel. (203) 245-4000; telex 282986; fax (203) 245-0775; f. 1943; Pres. MARTIN V. AZARIAN; psychology, psychiatry, medicine, social sciences and journals.

**Iowa State University Press:** 2121 South State Ave, Ames, IA 50010; tel. (515) 292-0140; fax (515) 292-3348; f. 1924; Dir LINDA SPETH; scholarly non-fiction, textbooks, reference.

**Richard D. Irwin, Inc:** 1333 Burr Ridge Pkwy, Burr Ridge, IL 60521; tel. (708) 789-4000; fax (708) 789-6938; f. 1933; Pres. and CEO JEFFREY SUND; economics, business.

**Jewish Publication Society:** 1930 Chestnut St, Philadelphia, PA 19103-4599; tel. (215) 564-5925; fax (215) 564-6640; f. 1888; Pres. D. WALTER COHEN.

**Johns Hopkins University Press:** 2715 North Charles St, Baltimore, MD 21218-4319; tel. (410) 516-6900; fax (410) 516-6968; f. 1878; Dir JACK G. GOELLNER; social and physical sciences, humanities, health sciences, economics, literary criticism, history.

**Jossey-Bass, Inc, Publishers:** 350 Sansome St, San Francisco, CA 94104; tel. (415) 433-1740; fax (415) 433-0499; f. 1966; Pres. and CEO LYNN LUCKOW; scholarly, professional, social and behavioural sciences, education, management, health, public administration.

**Augustus M. Kelley, Publishers:** POB 1048, Fairfield, NJ 07004-1048; tel. (212) 685-7202; fax (212) 685-7202; f. 1947; Editor FREDERICK S. CHEESMAN; reprints of economic classics.

**Kendall/Hunt Publishing Co:** 4050 Westmark Drive, Dubuque, IA 52002; tel. (319) 589-1000; fax (319) 589-1114; f. 1944; Pres. RONALD R. MALONE; educational.

**Kluwer Academic Publishers:** 101 Philip Drive, Norwell, MA 02061; tel. (617) 871-6600; telex 200190; fax (617) 871-6528; f. 1978; Pres. H. A. PABBRUWE; scientific, technical, medical, scholarly and professional books and journals.

**Alfred A. Knopf, Inc:** 201 East 50th St, New York, NY 10022; tel. (212) 751-2600; fax (212) 572-2593; f. 1915; division of Random House Inc; Pres. and Editor-in-Chief SONNY MEHTA; fiction, textbooks, general literature.

**Krieger Publishing Co:** POB 9542, Melbourne, FL 32902-9542; tel. (407) 724-9542; fax (407) 951-3671; f. 1970; Pres. DONALD E. KRIEGER; scientific and technical originals and reprints.

**J. B. Lippincott Co:** 227 East Washington Sq., Philadelphia, PA 19106; tel. (215) 238-4200; telex 834566; fax (215) 238-4227; f.

1792; Pres. and CEO Dr ALAN M. EDELSON; medical, dental, veterinary.

**Little, Brown and Co, Inc:** 34 Beacon St, Boston, MA 02108; tel. (617) 227-0730; fax (617) 227-4633; f. 1837; Pres. and CEO CHARLES E. HAYWARD; fiction, biography, history, current affairs, general trade, children's, medical, law, photography, art.

**Longman Publishing Group:** 10 Bank St, White Plains, NY 10606; tel. (914) 993-5000; fax (914) 997-8115; f. 1973; division of Addison-Wesley Publishing Co; Vice-Pres. FRANK DE MELLO; educational, trade, scientific, engineering, and language teaching materials.

**Lothrop, Lee and Shepard Books:** 1350 Ave of the Americas, New York, NY 10019; tel. (212) 261-6500; telex 224063; fax (212) 261-6648; f. 1859; division of William Morrow & Co Inc; Editor-in-Chief SUSAN PEARSON; juveniles.

**Loyola University Press:** 3441 North Ashland Ave, Chicago, IL 60657; tel. (312) 281-1818; fax (312) 281-0555; f. 1912; Dir GEORGE A. LANE.

**McGraw-Hill, Inc:** 1221 Ave of the Americas, New York, NY 10020; tel. (212) 512-2000; telex 127960; fax (212) 512-2821; f. 1888; Chair., CEO and Pres. JOSEPH L. DIONNE; publishing and information services for business, industry, government and the professions.

**Macmillan Publishing Co:** 866 Third Ave, New York, NY 10022; tel. (212) 702-2000; telex 225252; fax (212) 605-3099; division of Macmillan, Inc; Chair., Pres. and CEO DAVID H. SHAFFER; scientific, technical, medical, reference, education.

**Meredith Books:** 1716 Locust St, Des Moines, IA 50309-3023; tel. (515) 284-3000; fax (515) 284-2514; f. 1902; Editor BETTY RICE; trade.

**Merriam-Webster Inc:** 47 Federal St, Springfield, MA 01102; tel. (413) 734-3134; telex 981608; fax (413) 731-5979; f. 1831; division of Encyclopaedia Britannica Inc; Pres. JOSEPH J. ESPOSITO; dictionaries, reference.

**Michigan State University Press:** 1405 South Harrison Rd, Suite 25, East Lansing, MI 48823-5202; tel. (517) 355-9543; fax (517) 432-2611; f. 1947; Dir FRED C. BOHM; scholarly trade.

**The MIT Press:** 55 Hayward St, Cambridge, MA 02142; tel. (617) 253-5646; telex 921473; fax (617) 258-6779; f. 1932; Dir FRANK URBANOWSKI; computer sciences, architecture, design, linguistics, economics, philosophy, general science, neuroscience, environmental studies and cognitive science.

**Moody Press:** 820 North LaSalle Drive, Chicago, IL 60610; tel. (312) 329-2101; fax (312) 329-2144; f. 1894; Man. GREG THORNTON; religious.

**William Morrow & Co Inc:** 1350 Ave of the Americas, New York, NY 10019; tel. (212) 261-6500; telex 224063; fax (212) 261-6595; f. 1926; Pres. and CEO ALLEN MARCHIONI; fiction, non-fiction, juveniles.

**Mosby—Year Book Inc:** 11830 Westline Industrial Drive, St Louis, MO 63146; tel. (314) 872-8370; telex 442402; fax (314) 432-1380; CEO JOHN F. DILL; medical, dental and nursing education, biosciences, physical education, social sciences.

**National Academy Press:** 2101 Constitution Ave, NW, Lockbox 285, Washington, DC 20055; tel. (202) 334-3313; telex 248664; fax (202) 334-2451; f. 1863; division of National Academy of Sciences; Dir SCOTT LUBECK; scientific and technical, academic, catalogues.

**National Education Association Professional Library:** 1201 16th St, NW, Washington, DC 20036; tel. (202) 822-7252; fax (202) 822-7206; f. 1857; Exec. Dir DON CAMERON; professional.

**National Learning Corpn:** 212 Michael Drive, Syosset, NY 11791; tel. (516) 921-8888; fax (516) 921-8743; f. 1967; Pres. MICHAEL P. RUDMAN; professional and vocational study guides.

**National Textbook Co:** 4255 West Touhy Ave, Lincolnwood, IL 60646; tel. (312) 679-5500; telex 2230736; fax (312) 679-2494; f. 1962; Pres. S. WILLIAM PATTIS; elementary, secondary and university textbooks.

**Thomas Nelson Inc:** Nelson Place at Elm Hill Pike, Nashville, TN 37214; tel. (615) 889-9000; telex 4990852; fax (615) 391-5225; f. 1961; Pres. SAM MOORE; bibles, religious (Roman Catholic), juveniles, trade.

**Nelson-Hall Publishers:** 111 North Canal St, Chicago, IL 60606; tel. (312) 930-9446; fax (312) 930-5903; f. 1909; Pres. and Publr STEPHEN A. FERRARA; general interest non-fiction and educational.

**New Directions Publishing Corpn:** 80 Eighth Ave, New York, NY 10011; tel. (212) 255-0230; fax (212) 255-0231; f. 1936; Pres. and Publr JAMES LAUGHLIN; modern literature, poetry, criticism, belles-lettres.

**New York University Press:** 70 Washington Sq. South, New York, NY 10012; tel. (212) 998-2575; telex 235128; fax (212) 995-3833; f. 1916; Dir COLIN H. JONES; Man. Editor DESPINA GIMBEL; scholarly, non-fiction, general.

**Northwestern University Press:** 625 Colfax St, Evanston, IL 60208-4210; tel. (708) 491-5313; fax (708) 491-8150; f. 1958; Dir NICHOLAS WEIR-WILLIAMS; scholarly and trade.

**W. W. Norton & Co Inc:** 500 Fifth Ave, New York, NY 10110; tel. (212) 354-5500; telex 220014; fax (212) 869-0856; f. 1923; Pres. W. DRAKE MCFEELY; general fiction and non-fiction, college textbooks, paperbacks.

**NOVA Publications:** 1324 Kurtz Rd, McLean, VA 22101; tel. (703) 356-1151; fax (703) 356-1152; f. 1993; Publr ARNOLD C. DUPUY; military history, political science, Russian and Middle Eastern studies.

**Oceana Publications Inc:** 75 Main St, Dobbs Ferry, NY 10522; tel. (914) 693-5956; fax (914) 693-0402; f. 1957; Pres. DAVID R. COHEN; international law and trade.

**Octagon Books:** 171 Madison Ave, New York, NY 10016; tel. (212) 685-4371; fax (212) 779-9338; f. 1983; Pres. and Editor-in-Chief GEORGE BLAGOWIDOW; scholarly reprints.

**Ohio State University Press:** 1070 Carmack Rd, Columbus, OH 43210; tel. (614) 292-6930; f. 1957; Dir PETER JOHN GIVLER; general scholarly non-fiction.

**Ohio University Press:** Scott Quadrangle 220, Ohio University, Athens, OH 45701; tel. (614) 593-1155; fax (614) 593-4536; f. 1964; Dir DUANE SCHNEIDER.

**Open Court Publishing Co:** 315 Fifth St, Peru, IL 61354; tel. (815) 223-2520; telex 6731015; fax (815) 223-1350; f. 1887; Publr M. BLOUKE CARUS; general non-fiction.

**Orbis Books:** POB 308, Maryknoll, NY 10545-0308; tel. (914) 941-7636; fax (914) 945-0670; f. 1970; Exec. Dir ROBERT GORMLEY; theology, religion and social concerns.

**Oxford University Press Inc:** 200 Madison Ave, New York, NY 10016; tel. (212) 679-7300; telex 130479; fax (212) 725-2972; f. 1896; Pres. EDWARD W. BARRY; non-fiction, trade, religious, reference, bibles, college textbooks, medical, music.

**Paladin Press:** POB 1307, Boulder, CO 80306; tel. (303) 443-7250; telex 364412; fax (303) 442-8741; f. 1970; Chair. and Pres. PEDER C. LUND; military science and history.

**Pantheon Books/Schocken Books:** 201 East 50th St, New York, NY 10022; tel. (212) 572-2404; telex 126575; fax (212) 572-6030; division of Random House Inc; Vice-Pres. and Exec. Editor ERROLL MCDONALD; fiction, non-fiction, history, philosophy, art, illustrated editions.

**Paragon House:** 370 Lexington Ave, New York, NY 10017; tel. (212) 953-5950; fax (212) 953-5940; f. 1982; Dir MICHAEL GIAMPAOLI; general trade non-fiction, university texts, reference, monographs.

**Penguin USA:** 375 Hudson St, New York, NY 10014; tel. (212) 366-2000; telex 236109; fax (212) 366-2666; f. 1925; Pres. JOHN F. MOORE; fiction, non-fiction and juvenile.

**Pennsylvania State University Press:** 820 North University Drive, University Park, PA 16802; tel. (814) 865-1327; fax (814) 863-1408; f. 1956; Dir SANFORD G. THATCHER; scholarly.

**Pergamon Press Inc:** 660 White Plains Rd, Tarrytown, NY 10591-5153; affiliate of Elsevier Science Publishing; tel. (914) 524-9200; telex 137328; fax (914) 333-2444; f. 1952; Man. Dir MICHAEL BOSWOOD; reference, textbooks, encyclopedias.

**Philosophical Library, Inc:** POB 1789, New York, NY 10010; tel. (212) 886-1873; f. 1941; Pres. and Dir ROSE MORSE RUNES; educational, reference, scholarly non-fiction.

**Plenum Publishing Corpn:** 233 Spring St, New York, NY 10013; tel. (212) 620-8000; telex 421139; fax (212) 463-0742; Chair. and Pres. MARTIN E. TASH; scientific and technical books and journals, dictionaries, translations and medical.

**Clarkson Potter Publishers:** 201 East 50th St, New York, NY 10022; tel. (212) 572-6165; telex 126575; fax (212) 572-6181; f. 1959; division of Random House Inc; Pres. MICHELLE SIDRANE; general.

**Praeger Publishers, Inc:** 88 Post Rd West, POB 5007, Greenwich, CT 06881; tel. (203) 226-3571; fax (203) 222-1502; f. 1950; Vice-Pres. RONALD D. CHAMBERS; general non-fiction, reference, scholarly, academic.

**Princeton University Press:** 41 William St, Princeton, NJ 08540; tel. (609) 258-4900; telex 6852306; fax (609) 258-6305; f. 1905; Dir WALTER H. LIPPINCOTT, Jr; Editor-in-Chief EMILY WILKINSON; scholarly.

**The Putnam Berkley Group Inc:** 200 Madison Ave, New York, NY 10016; tel. (212) 951-8400; telex 422386; fax (212) 213-6706; f. 1838; Pres. and CEO PHYLLIS GRANN; general.

**Raintree/Steck-Vaughn Publishers:** 8701 North Mopac Expressway, Suite 200, Austin, TX 78759; tel. (512) 343-8227; fax (512) 343-6854; f. 1991; Man. Dir JUDY SOMMER; juvenile fiction and non-fiction, library and trade paperbacks.

**Rand McNally & Co:** POB 7600, Chicago, IL 60680; tel. (708) 329-8100; f. 1856; Pres. ANDREW MCNALLY, IV; maps, atlases, travel guides.

# THE UNITED STATES OF AMERICA

**Random House Inc:** 201 East 50th St, New York, NY 10022; tel. (212) 751-2600; telex 126575; fax (212) 572-8700; f. 1925; Chair., Pres. and CEO ALBERTO VITALE; originals, reprints, paperbacks, juvenile, series, textbooks.

**Raven Press:** 1185 Ave of the Americas, New York, NY 10036; tel. (212) 930-9500; telex 640073; fax (212) 869-3495; f. 1964; Pres. MARY M. ROGERS; books and journals in medicine, psychiatry, psychology and science.

**Reader's Digest Association, Inc:** Reader's Digest Rd, Pleasantville, NY 10570-7000; tel. (914) 238-1000; telex 421171; fax (914) 238-4559; Chair. and CEO GEORGE V. GRUNE; reference and non-fiction.

**Rizzoli International Publications Inc:** 300 Park Ave South, New York, NY 10010-5399; tel. (212) 387-3400; fax (212) 387-3535; f. 1975; Pres., CEO and Publr GIANFRANCO MONACELLI; fine arts, performing arts, architecture.

**Rutgers University Press:** 109 Church St, New Brunswick, NJ 08901; tel. (908) 932-7762; fax (908) 932-7039; Dir STEPHEN MAIKOWSKI (acting); scholarly and regional.

**William H. Sadlier Inc:** 9 Pine St, New York, NY 10005; tel. (212) 227-2120; fax (212) 312-6080; f. 1832; Pres. WILLIAM S. DINGER; textbooks.

**St Martin's Press Inc:** 175 Fifth Ave, New York, NY 10010; tel. (212) 674-5151; fax (212) 420-9314; f. 1952; Chair. and CEO THOMAS J. MCCORMACK; general, scholarly, college textbooks, reference.

**Howard W. Sams & Co Inc, Publishers:** 201 West 103rd St, Indianapolis, IN 46290; tel. (317) 581-3500; fax (317) 581-3550; Pres. SCOTT FLANDERS; textbooks, computers, scientific and technical.

**W. B. Saunders Co:** The Curtis Center, Independence Sq. West, Philadelphia, PA 19106; tel. (215) 238-7800; telex 173146; fax (215) 238-7883; f. 1888; division of Harcourt, Brace & Co; Pres. and CEO LEWIS REINES; medical, dental and allied health sciences textbooks.

**Scarecrow Press, Inc:** 52 Liberty St, Metuchen, NJ 08840; tel. (908) 548-8600; fax (908) 548-5767; f. 1950; division of Grolier, Inc; Pres. ALBERT W. DAUB; reference, textbooks, library science.

**Scholastic, Inc:** 730 Broadway, New York, NY 10003; tel. (212) 505-3000; telex 5812057; fax (212) 505-3377; f. 1920; Chair., Pres. and CEO M. RICHARD ROBINSON; children's periodicals, textbooks, educational materials.

**Scott Foresman:** 1900 East Lake Ave, Glenview, IL 60025; tel. (708) 729-3000; telex 729371; fax (708) 729-3065; f. 1896; Pres. KATE NYQUIST; educational.

**Shoe String Press Inc:** 2 Linsley St, POB 657, North Haven, CT 06473; tel. (203) 239-2702; fax (203) 239-2568; f. 1952; Pres. and Editorial Dir DIANTHA THORPE, scholarly and general non-fiction.

**Silhouette Books:** 300 East 42nd St, New York, NY 10017; tel. (212) 682-6080; telex 966697; fax (212) 682-4539; f. 1979; Pres. and CEO BRIAN HICKEY; romantic fiction.

**Simon & Schuster, Inc:** 1230 Ave of the Americas, New York, NY 10020; tel. (212) 698-7000; telex 6720471; fax (212) 698-7007; f. 1924; Chair. and CEO JONATHAN NEWCOMB; trade, juvenile, reference, educational, elementary and secondary school textbooks, business and professional.

**Slavica Publishers Inc:** POB 14388, Columbus, OH 43214-0388; tel. (614) 268-4002; f. 1966; Pres. and Editor CHARLES GRIBBLE; textbooks and scholarly works in Slavic and Eastern European languages.

**Peter Smith Publisher, Inc:** 5 Lexington Ave, Magnolia, MA 01930; tel. (508) 525-3562; fax (508) 525-3674; Pres. MARY ANN LASH; reprints.

**Smithmark Publishers Inc:** Raritan Plaza III, Fieldcrest Ave, Edison, NJ 08837; tel. (212) 532-6600; fax (212) 683-5768; f. 1978; Chair. and CEO HARVEY S. MARKOWITZ; fiction and non-fiction.

**Smithsonian Institution Press:** 470 L'Enfant Plaza, Room 7100, Washington, DC 20560; tel. (202) 287-3738; telex 264729; fax (202) 287-3184; f. 1848; Dir DANIEL H. GOODWIN (acting); history, science, art, anthropology, aviation, reference.

**Southern Illinois University Press:** POB 3697, Carbondale, IL 62902-3697; tel. (618) 453-2281; fax (618) 453-1221; f. 1953; Dir JOHN F. STETTER; scholarly non-fiction.

**Springer-Verlag New York, Inc:** 175 Fifth Ave, 19th Floor, New York, NY 10010; tel. (212) 460-1500; telex 232235; fax (212) 473-6272; Pres. and CEO HANS-ULRICH DANIEL; scientific, technical and medical.

**Standard Educational Corpn:** 200 West Madison St, Chicago, IL 60606; tel. (312) 346-7440; telex 724451; fax (312) 580-7215; f. 1909; Pres. PETER EWING; encyclopedias, children's.

**Stanford University Press:** Stanford, CA 94305; tel. (415) 723-9434; fax (415) 725-3457; f. 1925; Dir NORRIS POPE; scholarly.

**State University of New York Press:** State University Plaza, Albany, NY 12246; tel. (518) 472-5000; fax (518) 472-5038; f. 1966; Dir LOIS G. PATTON (acting); scholarly.

**Steck-Vaughn Co:** POB 26015, Austin, TX 78755; tel. (512) 343-8227; fax (512) 795-3397; f. 1936; Pres. and CEO ROY MAYERS; educational.

**Sterling Publishing Co, Inc:** 387 Park Ave South, New York, NY 10016-8810; tel. (212) 532-7160; fax (212) 213-2495; f. 1949; Chair. and CEO BURTON H. HOBSON; non-fiction, reference, textbooks.

**Summy-Birchard Inc:** 15800 NW 48th Ave, Miami, FL 33014; tel. (305) 620-1500; fax (305) 621-1094; f. 1876; Editor JUDI GOWE; educational music methods and texts.

**Syracuse University Press:** 1600 Jamesville Ave, Syracuse, NY 13244-5160; tel. (315) 443-5534; fax (315) 443-5545; f. 1943; Dir ROBERT A. MANDEL; scholarly.

**Tahrike Tarsile Qur'ān, Inc:** POB 731115, Elmhurst, NY 11373-0115; tel. (718) 446-6472; fax (718) 446-4370; f. 1978; Pres. AUNALI KHALFAN; Qur'ān and Islamic religious texts.

**Taplinger Publishing Co Inc:** POB 1324, New York, NY 10185; tel. (201) 432-3257; fax (201) 432-3708; f. 1955; Pres. LOUIS STRICK; general fiction and non-fiction.

**Charles C Thomas, Publisher:** 2600 South First St, Springfield, IL 62794-9265; tel. (217) 789-8980; fax (217) 789-9130; f. 1927; Pres. PAYNE E. L. THOMAS; textbooks and reference on education, medicine, psychology and criminology.

**Time-Life Books Inc:** 777 Duke St, Alexandria, VA 22314; tel. (703) 838-7000; telex 899162; fax (703) 838-7225; f. 1961; Pres. and CEO and Chair. JOHN M. FAHEY; general non-fiction.

**Times Books:** 201 East 50th St, New York, NY 10022; tel. (212) 572-8100; telex 126575; fax (212) 940-7464; f. 1959; division of Random House Inc; Publr PETER OSNOS; general trade non-fiction.

**Charles E. Tuttle Co, Inc:** POB 410, Rutland, VT 05701-0410; tel. (802) 773-8930; fax (802) 773-6993; f. 1832; Pres. PETER ACKROYD; the Far East, particularly Japan, languages, art, Americana, culture, juveniles.

**United Nations Publications:** Sales Section, Room DC2-0853, New York, NY 10017; tel. (212) 963-8302; fax (212) 963-3489; f. 1946; Chief of Section SUSANNA H. JOHNSTON; world and national economies, international trade, social questions, human rights, international law.

**Universe Publishing:** 300 Park Ave South, New York, NY 10010; tel. (212) 387-3400; fax (212) 387-3644; f. 1956; division of Rizzoli International Publications; Publr CHARLES MIERS; children's calendars, record books.

**University of Alabama Press:** POB 870380, Tuscaloosa, AL 35487-0380; tel. (205) 348-5180; fax (205) 348-9201; f. 1945; Dir MALCOLM M. MACDONALD; scholarly non-fiction.

**University of Alaska Press:** Gruening Bldg, 1st Floor, POB 756240, Fairbanks, AK 99775-6240; tel. (907) 474-6389; f. 1967; Dir CLAUS-M. NASKE; scholarly, regional, non-fiction.

**University of Arizona Press:** 1230 North Park Ave, Suite 102, Tucson, AZ 85719; tel. (602) 621-1441; telex 187167; fax (602) 621-8899; f. 1959; Dir STEPHEN COX; scholarly, popular, regional, non-fiction.

**University of Arkansas Press:** Fayetteville, AR 72701; tel. (501) 575-3246; fax (501) 575-6044; f. 1980; Dir MILLER WILLIAMS; general humanities, literature, regional studies, natural history.

**University of California Press:** 2120 Berkeley Way, Berkeley, CA 94720; tel. (510) 642-4247; telex 2959492; fax (510) 643-7127; f. 1893; Dir JAMES H. CLARK; academic, scholarly.

**University of Chicago Press:** 5801 Ellis Ave, Chicago, IL 60637; tel. (312) 702-7700; fax (312) 702-9756; f. 1891; Dir MORRIS PHILIPSON; scholarly books and journals, general.

**University of Georgia Press:** 330 Research Drive, Athens, GA 30602-4901; tel. (706) 369-6130; fax (706) 369-6131; f. 1939; Dir MALCOLM CALL; academic, scholarly, poetry, short fiction, literary trade.

**University of Hawaii Press:** 2840 Kolowalu St, Honolulu, HI 96822; tel. (808) 956-8257; telex 7238409; fax (808) 988-6052; f. 1947; Dir WILLIAM H. HAMILTON; Asian, Pacific and Hawaiian studies.

**University of Idaho Press:** 16 Brink Hall, Moscow, ID 83844-1107; tel. (208) 885-5939; fax (208) 885-9059; f. 1972; Dir PEGGY PACE; scholarly, regional studies, natural history, native American studies.

**University of Illinois Press:** 1325 South Oak St, Champaign, IL 61820-6903; tel. (217) 333-0950; fax (217) 244-8082; f. 1918; Dir RICHARD L. WENTWORTH; scholarly, poetry and short fiction.

**University of Massachusetts Press:** POB 429, Amherst, MA 01004-0429; tel. (413) 545-2217; fax (413) 545-1226; f. 1964; Dir BRUCE G. WILCOX; scholarly non-fiction.

THE UNITED STATES OF AMERICA                                                                                    *Directory*

**University of Michigan Press:** 839 Greene St, POB 1104, Ann Arbor, MI 48106; tel. (313) 764-4392; fax (313) 936-0456; f. 1930; Dir COLIN DAY; academic, textbooks, paperbacks.

**University of Minnesota Press:** 111 Third Ave South, Suite 290, Minneapolis, MN 55401-5250; tel. (612) 627-1970; fax (612) 627-1980; f. 1927; Dir LISA FREEMAN; scholarly, textbooks, general.

**University of Missouri Press:** 2910 LeMone Blvd, Columbia, MO 65201; tel. (314) 882-7641; fax (314) 884-4498; Dir BEVERLY JARRETT.

**University of Nebraska Press:** 312 North 14th St, Lincoln, NE 68588-0484; tel. (402) 472-3581; telex 484340; fax (402) 472-0308; f. 1941; Dir WILLIS G. REGIER; general scholarly non-fiction, regional history.

**University of New Mexico Press:** 1720 Lomas Blvd, NE, Albuquerque, NM 87131-1591; tel. (505) 277-2346; fax (505) 277-9270; f. 1929; Dir ELIZABETH C. HADAS; scholarly, regional studies.

**University of North Carolina Press:** POB 2288, Chapel Hill, NC 27515-2288; tel. (919) 966-3561; fax (919) 966-3829; f. 1922; Dir KATE D. TORREY; biographical, regional, scholarly non-fiction.

**University of Notre Dame Press:** Notre Dame, IN 46556; tel. (219) 631-6346; telex 953008; fax (219) 631-8148; f. 1949; Dir JAMES R. LANGFORD; humanities and social sciences.

**University of Oklahoma Press:** 1005 Asp Ave, Norman, OK 73019-0445; tel. (405) 325-5111; fax (405) 325-4000; f. 1928; Dir GEORGE W. BAUER; scholarly, regional.

**University of Pennsylvania Press:** Blockley Hall, 418 Service Drive, Philadelphia, PA 19104; tel. (215) 898-6261; telex 6700328; fax (215) 898-0404; Dir TIMOTHY R. CLANCY (acting); scholarly.

**University of Pittsburgh Press:** 127 North Bellefield Ave, Pittsburgh, PA 15260; tel. (412) 624-4111; fax (412) 624-4110; f. 1936; Dir CYNTHIA MILLER; scholarly.

**University of South Carolina Press:** 1716 College St, Columbia, SC 29208; tel. (803) 777-5243; fax (803) 777-0160; Dir CATHERINE FRY; scholarly, regional studies.

**University of South Dakota Press:** 414 East Clark St, Vermillion, SD 57069-2390; tel. (605) 677-5401; fax (605) 677-5583; f. 1962; Dir GILBERT M. FRENCH; scholarly.

**University of Tennessee Press:** 293 Communications Bldg, Knoxville, TN 37996-0325; tel. (615) 974-3321; fax (615) 974-3724; f. 1940; Editor MEREDITH MORRIS-BABB; scholarly and regional non-fiction.

**University of Texas Press:** POB 7819, Austin, TX 78713-7819; tel. (512) 471-7233; fax (512) 320-0668; f. 1950; Dir JOANNA HITCHCOCK; general scholarly non-fiction.

**University of Utah Press:** 101 University Services Bldg, Salt Lake City, UT 84112; tel. (801) 581-6771; fax (801) 581-3365; f. 1949; Dir JEFFREY L. GRATHWOHL; scholarly, trade, regional studies.

**University of Washington Press:** POB 50096, Seattle, WA 98145-5096; tel. (206) 543-4050; fax (206) 543-3932; f. 1920; Dir DONALD R. ELLEGOOD; general, scholarly, non-fiction, reprints.

**University of Wisconsin Press:** 114 North Murray St, Madison, WI 53715-1199; tel. (608) 262-2782; fax (608) 262-7560; f. 1936; Dir ALLEN N. FITCHEN; scholarly non-fiction.

**University Press of America Inc:** 4720 Boston Way, Lanham, MD 20706; tel. (301) 459-3366; fax (301) 459-2118; f. 1974; Pres. RAYMOND FELLERS; scholarly.

**University Press of Florida:** 15 NW 15th St, Gainesville, FL 32611; tel. (904) 392-1351; fax (904) 392-7302; f. 1945; Dir KEN SCOTT; general, scholarly, regional.

**University Press of Kansas:** 2501 West 15th St, Lawrence, KS 66049; tel. (913) 864-4154; fax (913) 864-4586; f. 1946; Dir FRED M. WOODWARD; scholarly.

**University Press of Kentucky:** 663 South Limestone St, Lexington, KY 40508-4008; tel. (606) 257-2951; fax (606) 257-2984; f. 1943; Dir KENNETH CHERRY; Editor NANCY G. HOLMES; scholarly, regional.

**University Press of Mississippi:** 3825 Ridgewood Rd, Jackson, MS 39211; tel. (601) 982-6205; fax (601) 982-6217; f. 1970; Dir RICHARD ABEL; scholarly, non-fiction, regional.

**University Press of New England:** 23 South Main St, Hanover, NH 03755-2048; tel. (603) 643-7100; fax (603) 643-1540; f. 1970; Dir THOMAS L. MCFARLAND; general scholarly.

**University Press of Virginia:** POB 3608, University Station, Charlottesville, VA 22903; tel. (804) 924-3468; fax (804) 982-2655; f. 1963; Dir NANCY C. ESSIG; general scholarly non-fiction, literary criticism, women's studies, political science, African studies.

**Vanderbilt University Press:** POB 1813, Station B, Nashville, TN 37235; tel. (615) 322-3585; fax (615) 343-8823; Dir CHARLES BACKUS.

**Van Nostrand Reinhold:** 115 Fifth Ave, 4th Floor, New York, NY 10003-1085; tel. (212) 254-3232; fax (212) 254-9499; f. 1980; Pres. BRIAN D. HEER; textbooks, reference.

**Warner Books Inc:** 1271 Ave of the Americas, New York, NY 10020; tel. (212) 522-7200; telex 237283; fax (212) 522-7991; f. 1961; Pres. LAURENCE J. KIRSHBAUM; fiction and non-fiction reprints and originals.

**Franklin Watts:** 95 Madison Ave, New York, NY 10016; tel. (212) 951-2650; fax (212) 689-7803; f. 1942; division of Grolier Inc; Publr JOHN W. SELFRIDGE; juvenile non-fiction.

**Wayne State University Press:** Leonard N. Simons Bldg, 5959 Woodward Ave, Detroit, MI 48202; tel. (313) 577-4600; fax (313) 577-6131; f. 1941; Dir ARTHUR EVANS.

**Western Publishing Co, Inc:** 1220 Mound Ave, Racine, WI 53404; tel. (414) 633-2431; fax (414) 631-5035; f. 1907; Pres. FRANK P. DIPRIMA; juvenile, general.

**Westminster John Knox Press:** 100 Witherspoon St, Louisville, KY 40202-1396; tel. (502) 569-5043; fax (502) 569-5018; f. 1938; Pres. and Publr DAVIS PERKINS; religious (Presbyterian) and scholarly.

**Westview Press Inc:** 5500 Central Ave, Boulder, CO 80301; tel. (303) 444-3541; telex 239479; fax (303) 449-3356; Publr MATTHEW HELD; scholarly, scientific.

**John Wiley and Sons, Inc:** 605 Third Ave, New York, NY 10158; tel. (212) 850-6000; telex 127063; fax (212) 850-6088; f. 1807; Pres. and CEO CHARLES R. ELLIS; scientific, technical, medical and social science.

**Williams & Wilkins:** 428 East Preston St, Baltimore, MD 21202; tel. (301) 528-4000; telex 87669; fax (301) 528-8597; f. 1890; Pres. SARA A. FINNEGAN; medical, dental, veterinary, scientific.

**H. W. Wilson Co:** 950 University Ave, Bronx, NY 10452; tel. (718) 588-8400; telex 4990003; fax (718) 538-2716; f. 1898; Pres. LEO M. WEINS; book and periodical indices, reference.

**Yale University Press:** 92A Yale Station, New Haven, CT 06520; tel. (203) 432-0960; telex 963531; fax (203) 432-0948; f. 1908; Dir JOHN G. RYDEN; scholarly.

### Government Publishing House

**Government Printing Office:** 732 North Capitol St, NW, Washington, DC 20401; tel. (202) 512-2034; fax (202) 512-1347; Public Printer MICHAEL F. DIMARIO.

### ORGANIZATIONS AND ASSOCIATIONS

**American Booksellers Association (ABA):** 828 White Plains Rd, Tarrytown, NY 10591; tel. (914) 591-2665; fax (914) 631-8391; f. 1900; 8,000 mems; Exec. Dir BERNARD E. RATH.

**American Medical Publishers' Association:** c/o Jill G. Rudansky, 14 Fort Hill Rd, Huntington, NY 11743; tel. (516) 423-0075; fax (516) 423-0075; f. 1960; 61 mems; Pres. MARY K. COWELL.

**Association of American Publishers, Inc (AAP):** 71 Fifth Ave, New York, NY 10003-3004; tel. (212) 255-0200; fax (212) 255-7007; f. 1970; 220 mems; Pres. NICHOLAS A. VELIOTES.

**Association of American University Presses (AAUP):** 584 Broadway, Suite 410, New York, NY 10012; tel. (212) 941-6610; fax (212) 941-6618; f. 1937; 116 mems; Exec. Dir PETER C. GRENQUIST.

**The Children's Book Council, Inc:** 568 Broadway, New York, NY 10012; tel. (212) 966-1990; fax (212) 966-2073; 75 mems; Pres. PAULA QUINT.

**Copyright Society of the USA:** 1133 Ave of the Americas, New York, NY 10036; tel. (212) 354-6401; fax (212) 354-2847; f. 1953; 850 mems; Pres. ROGER ZISSO.

**National Association of Independent Publishers:** POB 430, Highland City, FL 33846-0430; tel. and fax (813) 648-4420; f. 1985; 500 mems; Exec. Dir BETSY A. LAMPE.

**Publishers Marketing Association (PMA):** 2401 Pacific Coast Highway, Suite 102, Hermosa Beach, CA 90254; tel. (310) 372-2732; fax (310) 374-3342; 2,300 mems; Exec. Dir JAN NATHAN.

## Radio and Television

**Federal Communications Commission (FCC):** 1919 M St, NW, Washington, DC 20554; tel. (202) 632-7000; fax (202) 653-5402; f. 1934; regulates inter-state and foreign communication by radio, wire and cable; Chair. JAMES H. QUELLO.

### RADIO

In 1986 there were 3,969 licensed FM radio stations, 1,272 licensed educational FM radio stations, 4,887 licensed AM stations and almost 50 radio programme networks. In 1992 there were an estimated 540.5m. radio receivers in use.

#### Commercial Networks

**American Broadcasting Companies Radio Networks (ABC/SMN):** 125 West End Ave, New York, NY 10023-6298; tel. (212)

# THE UNITED STATES OF AMERICA

456-1000; f. 1986; Pres ROBERT F. CALLAHAN, Jr; serves more than 3,400 radio stations broadcasting seven full service line networks.

**Chancellor Broadcasting Network (CBC Radio Network):** Union Plaza Hotel, One Main St, Las Vegas, NV 89101; tel. (702) 798-1798; fax (702) 798-2922; Pres. DAVID PAPANDREA; syndicated radio broadcasts to 75 affiliated stations throughout North America.

**Columbia Broadcasting System Radio Networks (CBS):** 51 West 52nd St, New York, NY 10019-6165; tel. (212) 975-4321; telex 232068; fax (212) 975-1519; Pres. NANCY C. WIDMANN; 22 owned radio stations, 440 affiliated network stations.

**Mutual Broadcasting System Inc (MBS):** 1755 South Jefferson Davis Highway, 12th Floor, Arlington, VA 22202-3587; tel. (703) 413-8000; telex 4979269; fax (703) 413-8445; f. 1934; Pres. JACK B. CLEMENTS; over 900 affiliated stations.

**National Black Network:** 463 Seventh Ave, 6th Floor, New York, NY 10018; tel. (212) 714-1000; Chair. SYDNEY L. SMALL; Pres. GEORGE R. EDWARDS; 145 affiliated stations.

**National Broadcasting Co, Inc (NBC):** 30 Rockefeller Plaza, New York, NY 10112-0100; tel. (212) 664-4444; fax (212) 765-1478; f. 1926; Pres. and CEO ROBERT C. WRIGHT; Pres. NBC Radio Network WILLIAM J. BATTISON; 8 owned stations, 206 affiliated stations.

### Non-Commercial

**American Public Radio:** 100 North Sixth St, Suite 900A, St Paul, MN 55403; tel. (612) 338-5000; fax (612) 330-9222; Pres. and CEO STEPHEN SAYLER; serves 393 public radio stations via satellite.

**National Public Radio:** 2025 M St, NW, Washington, DC 20036; tel. (202) 822-2300; fax (202) 822-2329; Chair. DALE OUTZ; Pres. DOUGLAS J. BENNET; private non-profit corpn providing programmes and support facilities to more than 460 mem. stations in 48 States, District of Columbia and Puerto Rico; satellite service to Europe commenced in Nov. 1993.

### External Radio Services

**ABC International Development:** 77 West 66th St, 21st Floor, New York, NY 10023; tel. (212) 456-7628; fax (212) 456-7635; division of Capital Cities/ABC Video Enterprises; Vice-Pres. (Operations) MIKE DUBESTER; 50 stations in Latin America, Japan, Australia, Canada and elsewhere.

**Armed Forces Radio and Television Service Broadcast Center (AFRTS-BC):** 10888 La Tuna Canyon Rd, Los Angeles, CA 91352-2098; tel. (818) 504-1201; fax (818) 504-1234; operated by the US Dept of Defense; Commdr Capt. C. L. HANEY, USN; Dir. of Programming GERALD M. FRY; provides radio and TV programming in English by satellite and mail for exclusive use by US mil. personnel and their families overseas; c. 750 outlets in more than 130 countries, US territories and aboard US Navy ships-at-sea.

**Radio Free Europe/Radio Liberty:** 1201 Connecticut Ave, NW, Washington, DC 20036; tel. (202) 457-6900; fax (202) 457-6959; f. 1950; financed by the federal govt; merger with Voice of America pending in 1995; Pres. KEVIN KLOSE; Dirs A. ROSS JOHNSON (RFE Div.), S. ENDERS WIMBUSH (Radio Liberty Div.); broadcasts from Prague, Czech Republic to Central and Eastern Europe c. 1,000 hours weekly in 21 languages.

**Radio Station KGEI Inc/The Voice of Friendship:** 1406 Radio Rd, Redwood City, CA 94065; tel. (415) 591-7374; fax (415) 591-0233; f. 1939; owned and operated by Far East Broadcasting Co Inc; Pres. BILL TARTER; Station Man. DEAN BRUBAKER; short-wave broadcasts in Spanish.

**Voice of America:** 300 Independence Ave, SW, Washington, DC 20547; tel. (202) 485-8075; f. 1942; govt-controlled; merger with Radio Free Europe/Radio Liberty pending in 1995; Dir GEOFFREY COWAN; broadcasts in 47 languages to all areas of the world.

## TELEVISION

In 1991 there were 1,594 commercial television stations.

In May 1994 there were an estimated 94.2m. households owning one or more television receivers.

In May 1994 there were an estimated 59.3m. households receiving commercial cable TV. There were 46 national cable networks in operation in 1987.

### Commercial Networks
(see Radio Section for full addresses)

**American Television & Communications Corpn (ATC):** 300 First Stamford Place, Stamford, CT 06902; tel. (203) 328-0600; Chair. and CEO JOSEPH J. COLLINS; Pres. JAMES H. DOOLITTLE; cable television system servicing c. 4.1m. subscribers.

**Capital Cities/American Broadcasting Companies, Inc:** 77 West 66th Street, New York, NY 10023; tel. (212) 456-7777; fax (212) 887-7168; Pres. and CEO THOMAS MURPHY (acting); Pres. ABC-TV Network DAVID WESTIN; 8 owned and 208 affiliated stations.

*Directory*

**Columbia Broadcasting System Inc:** 51 West 52nd St, New York, NY 10019; tel. (212) 975-4321; Chair., Pres. and CEO LAURENCE A. TISCH; 6 owned and operated, and over 200 affiliated, stations.

**Fox Television Network:** 205 East 67th St, New York, NY 10021; tel. (212) 452-5555; Chair and CEO CHASE CAREY.

**Multimedia Cablevision Inc:** 701 East Douglas, POB 3027, Wichita, KS 67201; tel. (316) 262-4270; fax (316) 262-2309; Chair. and CEO DONALD SBARRA; cable television system serving more than 355,000 subscribers.

**National Broadcasting Co, Inc:** 30 Rockefeller Plaza, New York, NY 10112; tel. (212) 664-4444; Pres. and CEO ROBERT WRIGHT; 5 owned and 214 affiliated stations.

**Turner Network Television (TNT):** One CNN Center, POB 105366, Atlanta, GA 30348-5366; tel. (404) 827-1647; fax (404) 827-1190; Chair. R. E. TURNER, III; Pres. SCOTT SASSA; operates Cable News Network (CNN), an all-news cable television network using satellite facilities.

**USA Network (Cable):** 1230 Ave of the Americas, 18th Floor, New York, NY 10020; tel. (212) 408-9100; fax (212) 408-3600; Pres. and CEO KAY KOPLOVITZ; cable television network with 10,100 affiliates serving c. 59m. homes.

### Non-Commercial

**Metromedia, Inc:** 205 East 67th St, New York, NY 10021; tel. (212) 734-1000; Chair., Pres. and CEO JOHN W. KLUGE.

**Public Broadcasting Service (PBS):** 1320 Braddock Place, Alexandria, VA 22314-1698; tel. (703) 739-5000; fax (703) 739-0775; non-profit-making; financed by private subscriptions and federal govt funds; provides programming to 346 independent non-commercial TV stations; Pres. and CEO BRUCE CHRISTENSEN.

### Associations

**National Association of Broadcasters (NAB):** 1771 N St, NW, Washington, DC 20036; tel. (202) 429-5300; telex 350085; fax (202) 429-5343; f. 1922; Pres. and CEO EDWARD O. FRITTS; trade asscn of radio and TV stations and networks; 7,500 mems.

**National Cable Television Association (NCTA):** 1724 Massachusetts Ave, NW, Washington, DC 20036-1905; tel. (202) 775-3550; fax (202) 775-3695; f. 1952; Pres. and CEO S. DECKER ANSTROM; c. 3,000 mems.

# Finance

## BANKING

### Commercial Banking System

The US banking system is the largest and, in many respects, the most comprehensive and sophisticated in the world. Banking has, however, been largely subject to state rather than federal jurisdiction, and this has created a structure very different from that in other advanced industrial countries. In general, no bank may open branches or acquire subsidiaries in states other than that in which it is based, although in June 1985 the US Supreme Court ruled that federal legislation prohibiting interstate banks does not preclude state governments from permitting regional interstate banking. A number of such mergers have followed, although some states continue to restrict banks to a single branch, or to operating only in certain counties of the state. Federal anti-trust laws also limit mergers of banks within a state. The effect of these measures has been to preserve the independence of a very large number of banks: 11,927 in 1992. Nevertheless, the dominant banks are the main banks in the big industrial states; of the 10 largest in 1992, five were based in New York and two in California. The influence of these banks, however, has been increasingly challenged by the formation of several groupings of regional banks. Federal legislation permitting the operation of interstate branch banking networks was pending in 1995.

During the late 1980s there was a severe loss of confidence in the banking system, and many small banks became insolvent after the failure of investments or the withdrawal of deposits by investors. The Federal Deposit Insurance Corporation, a government-sponsored body which insures deposits in banks and acts as receiver for national and state banks that have been placed in receivership, was obliged to provide assistance for a large number of institutions. These bank failures, which numbered only 10 annually between 1979–81, rose steadily in the 1980s, reaching a record of 221 institutions in 1988. These insolvencies have, however, since declined each year, to 122 in 1992. Many banks, meanwhile, have expanded their 'fee income' activities (such as sales of mutual fund investments) to offset declines in customer borrowing, particularly from the industrial and commercial sectors.

The possession of bank accounts and the use of banking facilities are perhaps more widespread among all regions and social groups

3304

# THE UNITED STATES OF AMERICA

in the USA than in any other country. This has influenced the formulation of monetary theory and policy, as bank credit has become a more important factor than currency supply in the regulation of the economy. The use of current accounts and credit cards is so common that many authorities claim that the USA can be regarded as effectively a cashless society.

### Bank Holding Companies

Since 1956 bank holding companies, corporations that control one or more banks in the USA, have become significant elements in the banking system. At the end of 1989 there were 5,837 bank holding companies in the USA. These organizations control commercial banks which at the end of 1989 held 93.4% of the total assets of insured commercial banks in the USA.

### Banking Activities Overseas

From the mid-1960s, the leading banks rapidly expanded their overseas interests. At the end of 1960 there were only eight US banks operating foreign branches, mostly in Latin America and the Far East. The main factors behind this expansion were the geographical limitations imposed by law at home; the rapid expansion of US business interests abroad; the faster economic growth of certain foreign markets; and finally the profitability of the 'Eurodollar' capital markets. The expansion in the overseas activities of US banks reached a high point in 1984. Subsequently declining levels of profitability in this area have resulted in the closure of some overseas offices, although the aggregate total of assets held has continued to rise. At 31 December 1992 (the most recent date for which this data is available), US banks were operating 775 branches and 713 subsidiaries in foreign countries, representing about $332,125m. and $206,273m., respectively, in terms of total assets held.

In 1981 the Federal Reserve Board sanctioned the establishment of domestic International Banking Facilities (IBF), permitting commercial banks within the US (including US branches and agencies of foreign banks) to transact certain types of foreign deposit and loan business free of reserve requirements and, in most cases, state income tax liability.

### Federal Reserve System

(20th St and Constitution Ave, NW, Washington, DC 20551; tel. (202) 452-3462; fax (202) 452-3819)

The Federal Reserve System, founded in 1913, comprises the Board of Governors, the Federal Open Market Committee, the Federal Advisory Council, the Consumer Advisory Council, the Thrift Institutions Advisory Council, and the 12 Federal Reserve Banks with 25 branches.

The Board of Governors is composed of seven members appointed by the President of the United States with the advice and consent of the Senate.

The Reserve Banks are empowered to issue Federal Reserve notes fully secured by the following assets, alone or in any combination: (i) Gold certificates; (ii) US Government and agency securities; (iii) Other eligible assets as described by statute; and (iv) Special Drawing Rights certificates. The Reserve Banks may discount paper for depository institutions and make properly secured advances to depository institutions. Federal Reserve Banks were established by Congress as the operating arms of the nation's central banking system. Many of the services performed by this network for depository institutions and for the government are similar to services performed by banks and thrifts for business customers and individuals. Reserve Banks hold the cash reserves of depository institutions and make loans to them. They move currency and coin into and out of circulation, and collect and process millions of cheques each day. They provide banking services for the Treasury, issue and redeem government securities, and act in other ways as fiscal agent for the US Government. The Banks also take part in the primary responsibility of the Federal Reserve System, the setting of monetary policy, through participation on the Federal Open Market Committee.

At the end of 1993, 4,281 of the nation's 10,922 Federal and State-chartered banks, accounting for 72% of total bank deposits in the USA, were members of the Federal Reserve System. All National Banks, of which there were 3,315 in 1993, are required to be members of the Federal Reserve System.

The Comptroller of the Currency (see below) has primary supervisory authority over all federally chartered banks, and the banking supervisors of the States have similar jurisdiction over banks organized under State laws. State member banks are examined by the Federal Reserve.

#### Board of Governors

**Chairman:** ALAN GREENSPAN.

**Vice-Chairman:** ALAN S. BLINDER.

**Governors:** EDWARD W. KELLEY, Jr, LAWRENCE B. LINDSEY, SUSAN M. PHILLIPS, JANET L. YELLEN, one vacancy.

**Secretary of the Board:** WILLIAM W. WILES.

#### Federal Reserve Banks

| | Chairman | President |
|---|---|---|
| Boston | JEROME H. GROSSMAN | CATHY E. MINEHAN |
| New York | MAURICE R. GREENBERG | WILLIAM J. MCDONOUGH |
| Philadelphia | JAMES M. MEAD | EDWARD G. BOEHNE |
| Cleveland | A. WILLIAM REYNOLDS | JERRY L. JORDAN |
| Richmond | HENRY J. FAISON | J. ALFRED BROADDUS, Jr |
| Atlanta | LEO BENATAR | ROBERT P. FORRESTAL |
| Chicago | ROBERT M. HEALEY | MICHAEL H. MOSKOW |
| St Louis | ROBERT H. QUENON | THOMAS C. MELZER |
| Minneapolis | GERALD A. RAVENHORST | GARY H. STERN |
| Kansas City | HERMAN CAIN | THOMAS M. HOENIG |
| Dallas | CECE SMITH | ROBERT D. MCTEER, Jr |
| San Francisco | JUDITH M. RUNSTAD | ROBERT T. PARRY |

#### Comptroller of the Currency

(250 E St, SW, Washington, DC 20219; tel. (202) 874-5000)

The Comptroller of the Currency has supervisory control over all federally chartered banks (the national banks), comprising less than one-third of the banks but holding almost 60% of the assets in the US banking system.

**Comptroller:** EUGENE A. LUDWIG.

#### Principal Commercial Banks

In general, only banks with a minimum of $2,000m. deposits are listed. In states where no such bank exists, that with the largest deposits is listed.

(cap. = total capital and reserves; dep. = deposits;
m. = million; amounts in US dollars)

##### Alabama

**AmSouth Bank NA:** POB 11007, Birmingham, AL 35288; tel. (205) 326-5120; telex 596150; fax (205) 326-5682; f. 1873; cap. 758m., dep. 6,497.2m. (June 1994); Chair. and CEO JOHN W. WOODS.

**Compass Bank:** 15 South 20th St, POB 10566, Birmingham, AL 35296; tel. (205) 933-3000; telex 593004; fax (205) 933-3996; f. 1964; cap. 362.6m., dep. 3,677.3 (Dec. 1993); Chair. and CEO D. PAUL JONES, Jr.

**First Alabama Bank:** 417 North 20th St, POB 10247, Birmingham, AL 35202; tel. (205) 326-7281; telex 596159; fax (205) 326-7440; f. 1928; cap. 487.4m., dep. 5,267.1m. (Dec. 1990); Chair., Pres. and CEO J. STANLEY MACKIN.

**Southtrust Bank of Alabama NA:** 420 North 20th St, POB 2554, Birmingham, AL 35290; tel. (205) 254-5000; telex 59837; fax (205) 254-5656; f. 1887; cap. 339.3m., dep. 3,158m. (Dec. 1993); Chair., Pres. and CEO JULIAN W. BANTON.

##### Alaska

**National Bank of Alaska:** 301 West Northern Lights Blvd, Anchorage, AK 99503; tel. (907) 276-1132; telex 25226; fax (907) 265-2141; f. 1916; cap. 234.4m., dep. 1,606.1m. (Dec. 1993); Chair. EDWARD B. RASMUSON; Pres. RICHARD STRUTZ.

##### Arizona

**Bank of America Arizona:** 101 North First Ave, Phoenix, AZ 85003; tel. (602) 262-2000; telex 187140; fax (602) 253-2855; f. 1902; cap. 1,144m., dep. 7,310.6m. (March 1994); Pres. KATHY MUNRO; CEO DAVID S. HANNA.

**Bank One, Arizona NA:** POB 71, Phoenix, AZ 85001; tel. (602) 221-2900; telex 187102; fax (602) 261-1598; f. 1899; cap. 709.3m., dep. 10,860.5m. (June 1994); Chair. and CEO RICHARD J. LEHMANN; Pres. JOHN WESTMAN.

**First Interstate Bank of Arizona NA:** First Interstate Plaza, 100 West Washington, POB 53456, Phoenix, AZ 85072-3456; tel. (602) 528-1000; telex 187103; fax (602) 528-6570; f. 1877; cap. 470.5m., dep. 6,611.1m. (Dec. 1993); Chair., Pres. and CEO WILLIAM S. RANDALL.

##### Arkansas

**Union National Bank of Arkansas:** 124 West Capitol Ave, Little Rock, AR 72201; tel. (501) 378-4000; telex 284794; fax (501) 375-8823; f. 1934; cap. 41.3m., dep. 430.2m. (Dec. 1986); Chair. H. HALL MCADAMS, II; CEO HERBERT H. MCADAMS.

##### California

**Bank of America National Trust and Savings Asscn:** Bank of America Center, 555 California St, San Francisco, CA 94104; f. 1904; tel. (415) 622-3456; telex 67652; fax (415) 675-8170; cap. 15,904m., dep. 106,369m. (Dec. 1993); Chair., Pres. and CEO RICHARD M. ROSENBERG.

**Bank of California, NA:** 400 California St, San Francisco, CA 94104; tel. (415) 765-0400; telex 184942; fax (415) 981-3761; f.

1864; cap. 619.6m., dep. 4,913.5m. (Dec. 1993); Chair., Pres. and CEO HIROO NOZAWA.

**Bank of the West:** 180 Montgomery St, San Francisco, CA 94104; tel. (415) 765-4800; telex 278607; fax (415) 434-3470; f. 1874; cap. 364.3m., dep. 3,159.5m. (Dec. 1993); Chair. ROBERT A. FUHRMAN; Pres. DON J. MCGRATH; CEO MICHEL LARROUILH.

**City National Bank:** 400 North Roxbury Drive, Beverly Hills, CA 90210; tel. (310) 550-5400; telex 677653; fax (310) 623-1163; f. 1953; cap. 281.3m., dep. 3,664.2m. (Dec. 1991); Chair. BRAM GOLDSMITH; Pres. GEORGE H. BENTER, Jr.

**First Interstate Bank of California:** 707 Wilshire Blvd, Los Angeles, CA 90017; tel. (213) 614-5129; telex 674421; fax (213) 614-2323; f. 1905; cap. 1,439.9m., dep. 16,130.6m. (Dec. 1991); Chair., Pres. and CEO BRUCE G. WILLISON.

**Sumitomo Bank of California:** 320 California St, San Francisco, CA 94104; tel. (415) 445-8000; telex 470075; fax (415) 445-3952; f. 1953; cap. 544.1m., dep. 4,401.4m. (Dec. 1993); Pres. TADAICHI IKAGAWA.

**Union Bank:** 350 California St, San Francisco, CA 94104; tel. (415) 705-7000; telex 6717763; fax (415) 445-7146; f. 1883; cap. 1,621.9m., dep. 12,554.4m. (Dec. 1993); Chair. TAMOTSU YAMAGUCHI; Pres. and CEO TAISUKE SHIMIZU.

**Wells Fargo Bank NA:** 420 Montgomery St, San Francisco, CA 94163; tel. (415) 396-0123; telex 184904; fax (415) 397-6634; f. 1852; cap. 1,115.3m. (Dec. 1983), dep. 36,462.6m. (Dec. 1989); Chair. and CEO (vacant); Pres. PAUL HAZEN.

### Colorado

**Colorado National Bank:** 1515 Arapahoe St, POB 5548, Denver, CO 80217; tel. (303) 585-5000; telex 168141; fax (303) 585-7346; f. 1862; cap. 628.1m., dep. 6,197.2m. (Dec. 1993); Chair. ROBERT MALONE; Pres. DANIEL YOHANNES.

### Connecticut

**Fleet Bank NA:** One Constitution Plaza, Hartford, CT 06115; tel. (203) 244-5000; telex 144203; fax (617) 346-1958; f. 1991; cap. 603.1m., dep. 6,050m. (Dec. 1993); Pres. and Chair. FREDERICK C. COPELAND, Jr.

**Shawmut Bank Connecticut, NA:** 777 Main St, Hartford, CT 06115; tel. (203) 728-2000; telex 221086; fax (203) 722-9378; f. 1792; cap. 1,131.6m., dep. 414.6m. (Dec. 1993); Chair. and CEO JOEL B. ALVORD; Pres. EILEEN S. KRAUS.

**Union Trust Co:** 300 Main St, Stamford, CT 06904-0700; tel. (203) 348-2611; telex 4750327; fax (203) 348-5583; f. 1969; cap. 165m., dep. 2,963.4m. (Dec. 1991); Chair. and CEO FRANK J. KUGLER, Jr; Pres. GEORGE R. KABUREK.

### Delaware

**Bank of Delaware:** 222 Delaware Ave, POB 791, Wilmington, DE 19899; tel. (302) 429-1011; telex 5106662280; fax (302) 429-1206; f. 1952; cap. 147.8m., dep. 1,781m. (Dec. 1991); Chair., Pres. and CEO CALVERT A. MORGAN, Jr.

### District of Columbia

**American Security Bank NA:** 1501 Pennsylvania Ave, NW, Washington, DC 20013; tel. (202) 624-4000; telex 197721; fax (202) 605-8113; f. 1889, reorg. as NationsBank NA in 1994; cap. 320.5m., dep. 2,576.4m. (Dec. 1992); Chair. and CEO FRANK P. BRAMBLE; Pres. WALTER R. FATZINGER, Jr.

**Riggs National Bank of Washington, DC:** 1503 Pennsylvania Ave, NW, Washington, DC 20005; tel. (202) 835-6000; telex 248363; fax (202) 624-1642; f. 1896; cap. 310.7m., dep. 4,201.8m. (March 1992); Chair. JOE L. ALLBRITTON; Pres. FRED BOLLERER.

### Florida

**Barnett Bank of South Florida, NA:** 800 Brickell Ave, POB 010429, Miami, FL 33101-0429; tel; (305) 350-7122; telex 519542; fax (305) 825-1419; f. 1877; cap. 206m., dep. 3,566.3m. (Dec. 1985); Chair. and Pres. WILLIAM R. MYERS; CEO LEE HANNA.

**First Florida Bank, NA:** POB 31265, Tampa, FL 33631-3265; tel. (813) 224-1111; telex 052812; f. 1883; cap. 395.3m., dep. 4,631.6m. (Dec. 1989); Pres. D. L. MURPHY.

**First Union National Bank of Florida:** First Union Financial Center, 200 South Biscayne Blvd, Miami, FL 33131; tel. (305) 789-6900; telex 6811519; fax (305) 789-6930; f. 1908; cap. 1,933.6m., dep. 21,834.6m. (Dec. 1991); Chair. and CEO BYRON HODNETT.

**NationsBank of Florida NA:** 400 North Ashley St, POB 31590, Tampa, FL 33602; tel. (813) 224-5151; telex 6815308; fax (813) 224-5581; f. 1983; cap. 1,138.9m., dep. 15,171m. (Dec. 1993); CEO HUGH L. MCCOLL, Jr.

**SunBank/Miami NA:** One SE Third Ave, POB 523527, Miami, FL 33131; tel. (305) 592-0800; telex 6734609; fax (305) 789-7336; f. 1964; cap. 203.1m., dep. 2,069.5m. (Dec. 1993); Chair. and CEO ROBERT COORDS; Pres. CARL MENTZER.

### Georgia

**Bank South, NA:** 55 Marietta St, Atlanta, GA 30303; tel. (404) 529-4111; telex 542753; fax (404) 529-4698; f. 1910; cap. 199.2m., dep. 2,911.2m. (June 1991); Chair. and CEO PATRICK FLINN.

**NationsBank of Georgia NA:** NationsBank Plaza, 600 Peachtree St, NE, Atlanta, GA 30308; tel. (404) 581-2121; telex 6733667; fax (404) 581-5061; f. 1887; cap. 1,023.8m., dep. 8,852.4m. (Dec. 1993); CEO HUGH L. MCCOLL, Jr.

**Trust Company Bank:** One Park Place, NE, Atlanta, GA 30303; tel. (404) 588-8707; telex 542210; fax (404) 588-8129; cap. 1,156.7m., dep. 5,612.7m. (Dec. 1993); Chair. EDWARD P. GOULD; Pres. ROBERT R. LONG.

**Wachovia Bank of Georgia NA:** 191 Peachtree St, POB 4155, Atlanta, GA 30303; tel. (404) 332-5000; telex 542553; fax (404) 332-5735; f. 1865; cap. 849.7m., dep. 6,541.5m. (June 1993); Chair. G. JOSEPH PRENDERGAST; Pres. and CEO D. GARY THOMPSON.

### Hawaii

**Bank of Hawaii:** 111 South King St, Honolulu, HI 96813; tel. (808) 537-8111; telex 7430134; f. 1897; cap. 766.4m., dep. 6,330m. (Dec. 1993); Chair. and CEO LAWRENCE M. JOHNSON; Pres. RICHARD DAHL.

**First Hawaiian Bank:** 1132 Bishop St, POB 3200, Honolulu, HI 96813; tel. (808) 525-7000; telex 7238329; fax (808) 525-8753; f. 1929; cap. 586.3m., dep. 4,257.9m. (June 1994); Chair. and CEO WALTER A. DODS, Jr; Pres. JOHN K. TSUI.

### Idaho

**West One Bank, Idaho, NA:** 101 South Capitol Blvd, POB 8247, Boise, ID 83733; tel. (208) 383-7000; telex 262542; fax (208) 383-7563; f. 1891; cap. 249.3m., dep. 2,779m. (Dec. 1992); Chair. DANIEL R. NELSON; Pres. and CEO ROBERT LANE.

### Illinois

**American National Bank and Trust Co of Chicago:** 33 North LaSalle St, Chicago, IL 60690; tel. (312) 661-5000; telex 6733816; fax (312) 661-6417; f. 1928; cap. 488.3m., dep. 4,530.9m. (Dec. 1993); Chair. LEO F. MULLIN; Pres. and CEO ALAN F. DELP.

**Continental Bank NA:** 231 South LaSalle St, Chicago, IL 60697; tel. (312) 828-2345; telex 253412; fax (312) 828-3820; f. 1857; cap. 2,018m., dep. 13,873m. (June 1993); Chair. and CEO (vacant).

**First National Bank of Chicago:** One First National Plaza, Chicago, IL 60670; tel. (312) 732-4000; telex 4330253; fax (312) 732-1176; f. 1863; cap. 3,916.8m., dep. 23,852.5m. (June 1994); Chair. and CEO RICHARD L. THOMAS; Pres. LEO F. MULLIN.

**Harris Trust and Savings Bank:** 111 West Monroe St, Chicago, IL 60603; tel. (312) 461-2121; telex 824164; fax (312) 461-7142; f. 1882; cap. 734.5m., dep. 6,457.4m. (Dec. 1993); Chair. and CEO B. KENNETH WEST.

**LaSalle National Bank:** 120 South LaSalle St, Chicago, IL 60603; tel. (312) 443-2000; telex 190393; fax (312) 443-2819; f. 1927; cap. 735.8m., dep. 6,309.6m. (June 1994); Chair. ROBERT K. WILMOUTH; Pres. and CEO NORMAN BOBINS.

**Northern Trust Co:** 50 South LaSalle St, Chicago, IL 60675; tel. (312) 630-6000; telex 253236; fax (312) 444-5244; f. 1889; cap. 723.8m., dep. 7,769.4m. (Dec. 1993); Chair. DAVID W. FOX.

### Indiana

**Bank One, Indianapolis, NA:** 111 Monument Circle, Indianapolis, IN 46277-0188; tel. (317) 321-3000; telex 027324; fax (317) 321-7965; f. 1839; cap. 513.9m., dep. 3,875.9m. (Dec. 1993); Pres. and CEO JOSEPH D. BARNETTE, Jr.

**National City Bank, Indiana:** 101 West Washington St, Indianapolis, IN 46255; tel. (317) 267-8851; telex 244038; fax (317) 267-7152; f. 1865; cap. 399m., dep. 3,694.1m. (June 1994); Chair. OTTO N. FRENZEL, III; Pres. and CEO VINCENT A. DIGIROLAMO.

**NDB Bank NA:** 1 Indiana Sq., Indianapolis, IN 46266; tel. (317) 266-6000; telex 205615; fax (317) 266-6379; f. 1834; cap. 912m., dep. 8,037.9m. (Dec. 1993); Chair. THOMAS M. MILLER; Pres. ANDREW J. PAINE, Jr.

### Iowa

**Norwest Bank Iowa, NA:** POB 837, Des Moines, IA 50304; tel. (515) 245-3146; telex 1561793; fax (515) 245-3139; f. 1929; cap. 426.3m., dep. 3,989.5m. (Dec. 1993); Chair. and CEO H. LYNN HORAK; Pres. DARRYL D. HANSEN.

### Kansas

**Bank IV Kansas, NA:** POB 4, Wichita, KS 67201; tel. (316) 261-4444; telex 6734510; fax (316) 261-2243; f. 1887; cap. 356.5m., dep. 3,691.6m. (Dec. 1993); Chair. and Pres. K. GORDON GREER.

# THE UNITED STATES OF AMERICA

### Kentucky
**Citizens Fidelity Bank and Trust Co:** Citizens Plaza, Fifth and Jefferson Sts, Louisville, KY 40296; tel. (502) 581-3250; telex 204136; fax (502) 581-2302; f. 1944; cap. 360.9m., dep. 3,260.3m. (Dec. 1991); CEO Daniel C. Ulmer, Jr.

**Liberty National Bank and Trust Co:** POB 32500, Louisville, KY 40232; tel. (502) 566-2297; telex 204359; fax (502) 566-2200; f. 1935; cap. 275.2m., dep. 2,780.5m. (Dec. 1993); Chair. and CEO Malcolm B. Chancey, Jr.

**National City Bank, Kentucky:** 3700 First National Tower, 101 South Fifth St, Louisville, KY 40202; tel. (502) 581-4200; telex 6842090; fax (502) 581-7909; f. 1863; cap. 484.4m., dep. 3,843.2m. (June 1994); Chair. Morton Boyd; Pres. Leonard V. Hardin.

### Louisiana
**First National Bank of Commerce:** 210 Baronne St, POB 60279, New Orleans, LA 70160; tel. (504) 561-1371; telex 58321; fax (504) 561-7082; f. 1933; cap. 307.2m., dep. 3,268.5m. (Dec. 1993); Chair. and CEO Howard C. Gaines; Pres. Ashton J. Ryan, Jr.

**Hibernia National Bank:** 313 Carondelet St, New Orleans, LA 70130; tel. (504) 533-5552; telex 6734628; fax (504) 533-5739; f. 1933; cap. 389.8m., dep. 4,199.9m. (June 1994); Chair. Robert H. Boh; Pres. Stephen A. Hansel.

**Whitney National Bank:** 228 St Charles Ave, New Orleans, LA 70130; tel. (504) 586-7272; telex 58393; fax (504) 586-7383; f. 1883; cap. 259m., dep. 2,505m. (Dec. 1993); Chair. and CEO William L. Marks.

### Maine
**Fleet Bank of Maine:** One City Center, POB 9791, Portland, ME 04104; tel. (207) 874-5000; telex 144203; fax (617) 573-5397; f. 1991; cap. 227m., dep. 2,164m. (Dec. 1993); Pres. and Chair. Anne Szostak.

### Maryland
**First National Bank of Maryland:** 25 South Charles St, Baltimore, MD 21201; tel. (410) 244-4000; telex 6849150; fax (410) 539-4594; f. 1806; cap. 528.2m., dep. 6,086.1m. (Dec. 1993); Chair. Jeremiah E. Casey; Pres. and CEO Charles W. Cole, Jr.

**NationsBank of Maryland NA:** 6610 Rockledge Drive, Bethesda, MD 20817; tel. (301) 270-5000; telex 6733667; f. 1951, reorg. by Merger in 1994; cap. 256.4m., dep. 3,260.8m. (March 1993); CEO Hugh L. McColl, Jr.

**Signet/Maryland:** 7 St Paul St, POB 1077, Baltimore, MD 21203; tel. (410) 332-5000; telex 6716670; fax (410) 752-7357; f. 1930; cap. 214.1m., dep. 2,297.6m. (June 1994); Pres. Kenneth H. Trout.

### Massachusetts
**Bank of Boston:** 100 Federal St, POB 2016, Boston, MA 02106-2016; tel. (617) 434-2200; telex 940581; fax (617) 434-3661; f. 1784; cap. 2,071.9m., dep. 20,627.6m. (Dec. 1993); Chair. and CEO Ira S. Stepanian.

**Fleet Bank of Massachusetts NA:** 75 State St, Boston, MA 02109; tel. (617) 742-4000; telex 144203; fax (617) 346-1958; f. 1991; cap. 578.1m., dep. 6,262.6m. (Dec. 1993); Chair. Leo R. Breitman; Pres. John P. Hamill.

**Shawmut Bank NA:** 1 Federal St, Boston, MA 02211; tel. (617) 292-2000; telex 6817133; fax (617) 556-4694; f. 1836; cap. 1,024.3m., dep. 7,485.7m. (Dec. 1993); Chair. and CEO Joel B. Alvord; Pres. Allen W. Sanborn.

**State Street Bank and Trust Co:** 225 Franklin St, POB 470, Boston, MA 02102; tel. (617) 786-3000; telex 200139; fax (617) 654-3759; f. 1792; cap. 1,164.3m., dep. 14,845.2m. (June 1994); Chair. and CEO Marshall N. Carter.

### Michigan
**Comerica Bank:** 211 West Fort St, POB 64858, Detroit, MI 48264; tel. (313) 222-3300; telex 235245; fax (313) 222-9449; f. 1849; cap. 2,030.1m., dep. 16,695m. (Dec. 1993); Chair., Pres. and CEO Eugene A. Miller.

**First of America Bank—Southeast Michigan NA:** 400 Renaissance Center, Suite 2600, Detroit, MI 48243; tel. (313) 396-4440; telex 170310; fax (313) 396-4498; f. 1949; cap. 274.7m., dep. 3,512.9m. (Dec. 1993); Pres. and CEO Richard R. Spears.

**NBD Bank NA:** Woodward at Fort, Detroit, MI 48232; tel. (313) 225-1000; telex 4320060; fax (313) 225-2371; f. 1933; cap. 1,755.9m., dep. 18,400.2m. (June 1994); Chair. Verne G. Istock; Pres. Thomas H. Jeffs, II.

### Minnesota
**First Bank NA:** First Bank Place, Minneapolis, MN 55480; tel. (612) 973-1111; telex 192179; fax (612) 973-0838; f. 1929; cap. 1,489.9m., dep. 12,309.9m. (Dec. 1993); Chair., Pres. and CEO John F. Grundhofer.

**Norwest Bank Minnesota NA:** Norwest Center, Sixth St and Marquette Ave, Minneapolis, MN 55479; tel. (612) 667-8110; telex 822008; fax (612) 667-5185; f. 1872; cap. 1,220.8m., dep. 8,728.8m. (Dec. 1993); Pres. and CEO James R. Campbell.

### Mississippi
**Deposit Guaranty National Bank:** 1 Deposit Guaranty Plaza, Jackson, MS 39201; tel. (601) 354-8553; telex 585431; fax (601) 968-4767; f. 1925; cap. 429.9m., dep. 3,997m. (Dec. 1994); Chair. E. B. Robinson, Jr; Pres. Howard McMillan, Jr.

### Missouri
**Boatmen's First National Bank of Kansas City:** POB 419038, Kansas City, MO 64183; tel. (816) 221-2800; telex 42246; fax (816) 691-7930; f. 1886; cap. 304.2m., dep. 2,823.8m. (Dec. 1994); Chair., Pres. and CEO William C. Nelson.

**Boatmen's National Bank of St Louis:** One Boatmen's Plaza, 800 Market St, St Louis, MO 63101; tel. (314) 466-6000; telex 6734242; fax (314) 466-6353; f. 1847; cap. 652.3m., dep. 7,913.8m. (Dec. 1992); Chair. Samuel B. Hayes, III; Pres. and CEO John Morton, III.

**Mercantile Bank of St Louis NA:** One Mercantile Tower, Seventh and Washington Sts, POB 524, St Louis, MO 63166; tel. (314) 425-3770; telex 6841103; fax (314) 425-8075; f. 1855; cap. 1,068.2m., dep. 9,053.8m. (Dec. 1994); Chair. Thomas H. Jacobsen.

### Montana
**First Interstate Bank of Montana NA:** 2 Main St, POB 7130, Kalispell, MT 59901; tel. (406) 752-5001; f. 1891; cap. 30m., dep. 216m. (Dec. 1992); Chair. James Curran; Pres. Dean A. Nelson.

### Nebraska
**First National Bank of Omaha:** 1 First National Center, Omaha, NE 68103; tel. (402) 341-0500; telex 484410; f. 1857; cap. 163.6m., dep. 1,919m. (June 1993); Chair. F. P. Giltner; Pres. B. R. Lauritzen.

### Nevada
**First Interstate Bank of Nevada NA:** 3800 Howard Hughes Pkwy, POB 98588, Las Vegas, NV 89193-8588; tel. (702) 385-8011; telex 3957099; f. 1902; cap. 219.8m., dep. 2,969.1m. (Dec. 1991); Chair. and CEO Donald D. Snyder.

### New Hampshire
**Fleet Bank—NH:** One Indian Head Plaza, Nashua, NH 03060; tel. (603) 594-5000; telex 144203; fax (617) 346-1958; f. 1989; cap. 137.7m., dep. 1,312.5m. (Dec. 1993); Chair. Dean T. Holt; Pres. Michael D. Whitney.

### New Jersey
**Citizens First National Bank of New Jersey:** 208 Harristown Rd, Glen Rock, NJ 07452; tel. (201) 445-3400; telex 178460; fax (201) 670-2049; f. 1899; cap. 92.9m., dep. 2,362.4m. (Dec. 1991); Chair. and CEO Allan D. Nichols.

**Constellation Bank NA:** 68 Broad St, Elizabeth, NJ 07207; tel. (908) 855-2600; telex 6716459; fax (908) 750-9643; f. 1812; cap. 141.4m., dep. 2,231.8m. (March 1993); Pres. and CEO George R. Zoffinger.

**First Fidelity Bank NA:** 550 Broad St, Newark, NJ 07102; tel. (201) 565-3200; telex 235989; fax (201) 565-6945; f. 1812; cap. 593.5m., dep. 7,209.8m. (Dec. 1986); Chair. Anthony P. Terracciano; Pres. and CEO Leslie E. Goodman.

**Midlantic National Bank:** Metro Park Plaza, POB 600, Edison, NJ 08818; tel. (201) 321-8000; telex 138490; fax (201) 494-6093; f. 1804; cap. 366.6m., dep. 4,658.3m. (Dec. 1988); Chair. R. Van Buren; Pres. D. P. McDonald.

**United Jersey Bank:** 210 Main St, Hackensack, NJ 07602; tel. (201) 646-5240; telex 134352; f. 1903; cap. 506.5m., dep. 5,220m. (March 1994); Chair. and Pres. T. Joseph Semrod.

### New Mexico
**Sunwest Bank of Albuquerque NA:** 303 Roma St, NW, POB 25500, Albuquerque, NM 87125-0500; tel. (505) 765-2211; telex 660430; fax (505) 764-4165; f. 1924; cap. 155.9m., dep. 1,604.3m. (June 1994); Chair. Ike Kalangis.

### New York
**American Express Bank Ltd:** American Express Tower, World Financial Center, POB 740, New York, NY 10008; tel. (212) 298-5000; telex 62297; fax (212) 619-9731; f. 1919; cap. 755m., dep. 10,185m. (Dec. 1993); Chair., Pres. and CEO Steven D. Goldstein.

**Bank Leumi Trust Co of New York:** 579 Fifth Ave, New York, NY 10017; tel. (212) 382-4000; telex 177766; fax (212) 226-5628; f. 1968; cap. 119.6m., dep. 2,238.2m. (June 1992); Pres. Richard Kane; Chair. David Friedmann; CEO Zalman Segal.

**Bank of New York:** 48 Wall St, New York, NY 10286; tel. (212) 495-1784; telex 62763; fax (212) 495-1239; f. 1784; cap. 3,950.6m.,

# THE UNITED STATES OF AMERICA

dep. 27,716.6m. (Dec. 1993); Chair. and CEO J. CARTER BACOT; Pres. ALAN R. GRIFFITH.

**Bank of Tokyo Trust Co:** 1251 Ave of the Americas, New York, NY 10020; tel. (212) 782-4000; telex 420742; f. 1955; cap. 775.5m., dep. 5,308.5m. (Dec. 1993); Chair. SHIN NAKAHARA; Pres. SACHIO KOHJIMA.

**Bankers' Trust Co:** 280 Park Ave, New York, NY 10017; tel. (212) 250-2500; telex 233121; fax (212) 250-4029; f. 1903; cap. 3,019m., dep. 25,194m. (Dec. 1992); Chair. and CEO CHARLES S. SANFORD, Jr (until 1996).

**Chase Manhattan Bank, NA:** One Chase Manhattan Plaza, New York, NY 10081; tel. (212) 552-2222; telex 232163; fax (212) 552-3875; f. 1955; cap. 9,476m., dep. 65,609m. (Dec. 1993); Chair. and CEO THOMAS G. LABRECQUE; Pres. (vacant).

**Chemical Bank:** 270 Park Ave, New York, NY 10017; tel. (212) 270-6000; telex 222271; fax (212) 755-1126; f. 1824; cap. 12,387m., dep. 76,462m. (Dec. 1993); Chair. and CEO WALTER V. SHIPLEY; Pres. EDWARD D. MILLER.

**Citibank NA:** 399 Park Ave, New York, NY 10022; tel. (212) 559-1000; telex 347; fax (212) 223-2681; f. 1812; cap. 11,148m., dep. 122,962m. (Dec. 1993); Chair. and CEO JOHN S. REED.

**European American Bank:** EAB Plaza, Long Island, NY 11555; tel. (516) 296-5000; telex 177603; fax (516) 296-6034; f. 1950; cap. 391.3m., dep. 4,659m. (Dec. 1993); Chair. HARRISON F. TEMPEST.

**Fleet Bank:** 300 Broad Hollow Rd, Melville, NY 11747; tel. (516) 547-8000; telex 144203; fax (617) 346-1958; f. 1887; cap. 173.4m., dep. 2,263.9m. (Dec. 1993); Pres. and Chair. THOMAS A. DOHERTY.

**Fleet Bank of New York:** 69 State St, Albany, NY 12201; tel. (518) 447-4100; telex 144203; fax (617) 346-1958; f. 1803; cap. 827.5m., dep. 7,561.3m. (Dec. 1993); Chair. ROBERT F. MACFARLAND; Pres. ERLAND KAILBOURNE.

**Key Bank of New York:** 66 South Pearl St, Albany, NY 12207; tel. (518) 486-3500; telex 6716404; fax (518) 486-8773; f. 1825; cap.1,121.6m., dep. 11,226.7m. (Dec. 1994); Pres. and CEO JAMES P. MENZIES.

**Manufacturers' and Traders' Trust Co—M & T Bank:** One M & T Plaza, Buffalo, NY 14240; tel. (716) 842-4200; telex 91347; f. 1856; cap. 569.7m., dep. 6,143.3m. (Dec. 1993); Chair. and CEO ROBERT G. WILMERS.

**Marine Midland Bank:** One Marine Midland Center, Buffalo, NY 14240; tel. (716) 841-2424; telex 62822; fax (212) 658-1460; f. 1976; cap. 1,541.6m., dep. 13,380.7m. (Dec. 1993); Pres. and CEO JAMES H. CLEAVE.

**Morgan Guaranty Trust Co of New York:** 60 Wall St, New York, NY 10260; tel. (212) 483-2323; telex 232194; fax (212) 233-2623; f. 1838; cap. 10,195m., dep. 45,404m. (June 1994); Chair and CEO DOUGLAS A. WARNER, III.

**Republic National Bank of New York:** 452 Fifth Ave, New York, NY 10018; tel. (212) 525-5000; telex 234967; fax (212) 930-6258; f. 1966; cap. 2,028.9m., dep. 19,141.5 (June 1994); Chair. WALTER H. WEINER; Pres. DOV C. SCHLEIN.

**United States Trust Co of New York:** 114 West 47th St, New York, NY 10036-1532; tel. (212) 852-1000; telex 420003; fax (212) 995-5642; f. 1853; cap. 185m., dep. 2,251m. (June 1993); Chair. and CEO H. MARSHALL SCHWARZ; Pres. JEFFREY S. MAURER.

## North Carolina

**First Union National Bank of North Carolina:** One First Union Center, Charlotte, NC 28288; tel. (704) 374-6161; telex 572422; fax (704) 374-3420; f. 1908; cap. 1,694.4m., dep. 17,264.9m. (Dec. 1993); Chair. and CEO EDWARD E. CRUTCHFIELD, Jr.

**NationsBank, NA:** 100 North Tryon St, Charlotte, NC 28255-0001; tel. (704) 386-5000; telex 669965; fax (704) 386-0645; f. 1960; cap. 8,651m., dep. 91,113m. (Dec. 1993); CEO HUGH L. MCCOLL, Jr.

**Wachovia Bank of North Carolina NA:** 301 North Main St, POB 3099, Winston-Salem, NC 27150; tel. (910) 770-5000; telex 440585; fax (910) 770-5931; f. 1866; cap. 1,456.6m., dep. 11,383.3m. (Dec. 1993); Chair. L. M. BAKER Jr; Pres. and CEO J. WALTER MCDOWELL.

## Ohio

**Bank One, Columbus, NA:** 100 East Broad St, Columbus, OH 43271-0214; tel. (614) 248-5830; telex 4949515; fax (614) 248-5649; f. 1868; cap. 485.8m., dep. 4,450.8m. (Dec. 1993); Chair. and CEO MICHAEL J. MCMENNAMIN.

**Bank One, Dayton, NA:** Kettering Tower, Dayton, OH 45401; tel. (513) 449-8600; telex 433074; fax (513) 449-8703; f. 1857; cap. 220.9m., dep. 2,362.4m. (Dec. 1991); Chair. and CEO DONALD H. KASLE; Pres. CHARLES W. HELD.

**Fifth Third Bank:** 38 Fountain Sq. Plaza, Cincinnati, OH 45263; tel. (513) 579-5300; telex 214567; fax (513) 579-4185; f. 1927; cap. 1,399m., dep. 10,631m. (Dec. 1994); Chair. (vacant); Pres. and CEO GEORGE A. SCHAEFER, Jr.

**Huntington National Bank:** Huntington Center, Columbus, OH 43287; tel. (614) 480-4930; telex 245475; fax (614) 480-3761; f. 1866; cap. 766.3m., dep. 6,935m. (Dec. 1994); Chair. FRANK WOBST.

**National City Bank:** 1900 East 9th St, Cleveland, OH 44114; tel. (216) 575-2943; telex 212537; fax (216) 575-9263; f. 1845; cap. 610.8m., dep. 5,940.8m. (June 1994); Chair. DAVID A. DABERKO; Pres. WILLIAM E. MACDONALD, III.

**National City Bank, Columbus:** 155 East Broad St, Columbus, OH 43251; tel. (614) 463-7528; telex 246610; fax (614) 463-6919; f. 1888; cap. 381m., dep. 4,508.6m. (Dec. 1994); Pres. GARY A. GLASER.

**PNC Bank, Ohio, NA:** 201 East Fifth St, Cincinnati, OH 45202; tel. (513) 651-8562; telex 214187; fax (513) 651-8058; f. 1862; cap. 334.1m., dep. 2,466.2m. (June 1994); Pres. and CEO RALPH S. MICHAEL.

**Society National Bank:** 127 Public Sq., Cleveland, OH 44114; tel. (216) 689-3000; telex 985517; fax (216) 689-3683; f. 1849; cap. 1,868.1m., dep. 18,658m. (Dec. 1992); Chair. and CEO ROBERT W. GILLESPIE.

**Star Bank NA:** POB 1038, Cincinnati, OH 45201; tel. (513) 632-4130; telex 170346; fax (513) 632-4888; f. 1863; cap. 376.7m., dep. 4,010m. (March 1993); Chair. OLIVER W. WADDELL.

## Oklahoma

**Bank of Oklahoma NA:** Bank of Oklahoma Tower, POB 2300, Tulsa, OK 74192; tel. (918) 588-6030; telex 261707; fax (918) 588-6026; f. 1933; cap. 188.4m., dep. 2,431m. (Dec. 1993); Chair. and CEO GEORGE B. KAISER; Pres. STANLEY A. LYBARGER.

## Oregon

**First Interstate Bank of Oregon NA:** 1300 SW Fifth Ave, POB 3131, Portland, OR 97208; tel. (503) 225-2501; telex 6734324; fax (503) 225-4698; f. 1865; cap. 396m., dep. 5,323.4m. (Dec. 1993); Chair. and CEO JAMES J. CURRAN.

**United States National Bank of Oregon:** 321 SW Sixth Ave, Portland, OR 97204; tel. (503) 275-6111; telex 360540; fax (503) 275-5132; f. 1891; cap. 1,014.6m., dep. 7,579m. (Dec. 1993); Chair. and CEO ROGER BREEZLEY; Pres. JOHN ESKILDSEN.

## Pennsylvania

**Continental Bank:** Main and Swede Sts, Norristown, PA 19401; tel. (215) 564-7000; telex 4761112; fax (215) 564-7491; f. 1965; cap. 238.4m., dep. 3,174.6m. (Dec. 1988); Chair. ROY T. PERAINO; Pres. and CEO RICHARD C. RISHEL.

**CoreStates First Pennsylvania Bank:** Centre Sq., 15th and Market Sts, Philadelphia, PA 19102; tel. (215) 973-3100; telex 4990118; fax (215) 786-5979; f. 1782; cap. 343m., dep. 4,328.3m. (June 1988); Pres. ROSEMARIE B. GRECO.

**Equibank:** 2 Oliver Plaza, Pittsburgh, PA 15222; tel. (412) 288-5000; telex 4423037; fax (412) 288-5111; f. 1871; cap. 150.8m., dep. 2,556.2m. (June 1992); Chair., Pres. and CEO GARY W. FIEDLER.

**First Fidelity Bank NA:** Broad and Walnut Sts, Philadelphia, PA 19109; tel. (215) 985-6000; telex 0834480; fax (215) 499-8025; f. 1866; cap. 482.6m., dep. 6,857.9m. (Dec. 1987); Pres. and CEO ROLAND K. BULLARD, II.

**Hamilton Bank:** 100 North Queen St, Lancaster, PA 17604; tel. (717) 291-3304; telex 848416; fax (717) 569-8731; f. 1970; cap. 214m., dep. 2,445.2m. (Dec. 1990); Chair., Pres. and CEO DONALD M. COOPER.

**Mellon Bank, NA:** One Mellon Bank Center, Pittsburgh, PA 15258-0001; tel. (412) 234-5000; telex 199103; fax (412) 234-4025; f. 1869; cap. 2,892.7m., dep. 24,550.8m. (Dec. 1992); Chair., Pres. and CEO FRANK V. CAHOUET.

**Meridian Bank:** 35 North Sixth St, POB 1102, Reading, PA 19603; tel. (215) 655-2500; telex 173003; fax (215) 655-2428; f. 1901; cap. 1,138.1m., dep. 10,065.9m. (Dec. 1993); Chair. and CEO SAMUEL A. MCCULLOUGH; Pres. EZEKIEL S. KETCHUM.

**Philadelphia National Bank:** Broad and Chestnut Sts, POB 7618, Philadelphia, PA 19101; tel. (215) 973-3100; telex 845297; fax (215) 973-2605; f. 1803; cap. 1,314.6m., dep. 13,424.9m. (Dec. 1993); Chair. TERRENCE A. LARSEN; Pres. and CEO FRANK E. REED.

**PNC Bank, NA:** Pittsburgh National Bldg, Pittsburgh, PA 15265; tel. (412) 762-2000; telex 866533; fax (412) 762-5022; f. 1864; cap. 2,877.1m., dep. 21,806.3m. (March 1994); Chair. JAMES E. ROHR; Pres. and CEO BRUCE E. ROBBINS.

## Rhode Island

**Fleet National Bank:** 111 Westminster St, Providence, RI 02903; tel. (401) 278-6000; telex 144203; fax (617) 346-1958; f. 1791; cap. 720.9m., dep. 5,611.6m. (Dec. 1993); Chair. RICHARD A. HIGGINBOTHAM; Pres. THOMAS J. SKALA.

# THE UNITED STATES OF AMERICA

**Rhode Island Hospital Trust National Bank:** 1 Hospital Trust Plaza, Providence, RI 02903; tel. (401) 278-8000; telex 4430090; fax (401) 278-8079; f. 1867; cap. 232m., dep. 2,902m. (Dec. 1992); Chair. FRED C. LOHRUM.

### South Carolina

**NationsBank of South Carolina NA:** 1301 Gervais St, Columbia, SC 29202; tel. (803) 765-8011; telex 669965; f. 1874; cap. 741.1m., dep. 4,872.2m. (Dec. 1993); CEO HUGH L. MCCOLL, Jr.

**Wachovia Bank of South Carolina:** 1426 Main St, Columbia, SC 29226; tel. (803) 765-3000; telex 205807; fax (803) 765-3892; f. 1834; cap. 469m., dep. 4,860.6m. (Dec. 1993); Pres. and CEO ANTHONY L. FURR.

### South Dakota

**Norwest Bank South Dakota, NA:** 101 North Phillips Ave, Sioux Falls, SD 57117; tel. (605) 339-7300; fax (605) 333-4815; f. 1935; cap. 176.9m., dep. 2,056.5m. (Dec. 1993); Pres. GARY G. OLSON.

### Tennessee

**First American National Bank:** First American Center, Nashville, TN 37237; tel. (615) 748-2821; telex 6823023; fax (615) 748-2485; f. 1883; cap. 617m., dep. 5,861m. (Dec. 1994); Chair. DENNIS C. BOTTORF; Pres. DALE W. POLLEY.

**First Tennessee Bank NA, Memphis:** 165 Madison Ave, POB 84, Memphis, TN 38101; tel. (901) 523-4433; telex 6828099; fax (901) 523-4438; f. 1864; cap. 748.8m., dep. 7,688.4m. (Dec. 1994); Chair. RONALD TERRY; Pres. and CEO RALPH HORN.

**NationsBank of Tennessee, NA:** One NationsBank Plaza, Nashville, TN 37219; tel. (615) 749-3333; telex 6733667; fax (615) 749-4640; f. 1916; cap. 402.6m., dep. 4,272.2m. (Dec. 1993); CEO HUGH L. MCCOLL, Jr.

### Texas

**Frost National Bank:** 100 West Houston St, POB 1600, San Antonio, TX 78296; tel. (210) 220-4011; telex 4108711155; f. 1899; cap. 235.2m., dep. 2,923.9m. (Dec. 1993); Chair. and CEO T. C. FROST.

**NationsBank of Texas NA:** 901 Main St, Dallas, TX 75202; tel. (214) 508-6262; telex 6829317; fax (214) 508-3937; f. 1988; cap. 2,569.5m., dep. 24,560.8m. (Dec. 1993); CEO HUGH L. MCCOLL, Jr.

**Texas Commerce Bank NA:** 712 Main St, Houston, TX 77002; tel. (281) 236-4865; telex 166350; fax (281) 236-4402; f. 1964; cap. 1,694.8m., dep. 17,276.3m. (Dec. 1993); Chair. and CEO MARC J. SHAPIRO; Pres. ALAN R. BUCKWALTER.

### Utah

**First Security Bank of Utah:** 41 East 100 South, Salt Lake City, UT 84111; tel. (801) 246-6000; telex 3789450; fax (801) 246-5992; f. 1881; cap. 433.2m., dep. 3,712.9m. (Dec. 1994); Chair. and Pres. SCOTT NELSON.

### Vermont

**Howard Bank:** 111 Main St, Burlington, VT 05402; tel. (802) 658-1010; telex 954649; fax (802) 860-5437; f. 1870; cap. 45m., dep. 470m. (Sept. 1991); Chair. RICHARD MALLARY; Pres. JOSEPH L. BOUTIN.

### Virginia

**Central Fidelity Bank NA:** 1021 East Carey St, POB 27602, Richmond, VA 23261; tel. (804) 697-6858; telex 240518; fax (804) 697-6869; f. 1865; cap. 594.6m., dep. 6,714.9m. (June 1993); Pres. and CEO LEWIS N. MILLER, Jr.

**Crestar Bank:** 919 East Main St, POB 26665, Richmond, VA 23219; tel. (804) 782-7416; telex 6734275; fax (804) 782-7324; f. 1865; cap. 792.7m., dep. 8,201.8m. (June 1993); Chair. and CEO RICHARD G. TILGHMAN; Pres. JAMES M. WELLS, III.

**NationsBank of Virginia NA:** 12th and Main Sts, POB 27025, Richmond, VA 23261; tel. (804) 553-5000; telex 6733667; fax (804) 788-2525; f. 1963; cap. 898.3m., dep. 9,380m. (Dec. 1993); CEO HUGH L. MCCOLL, Jr.

**Signet Bank/Virginia:** 7 North Eighth St, Richmond, VA 23219; tel. (804) 747-2000; telex 6716670; fax (410) 752-7357; f. 1922; cap. 585.5m., dep. 4,920m. (June 1994); Chair. and CEO ROBERT M. FREEMAN; Pres. MALCOLM S. MCDONALD.

### Washington (State)

**First Interstate Bank of Washington:** First Interstate Center, 999 Third Ave, POB 160, Seattle, WA 98104; tel. (206) 292-3323; telex 160550; fax (206) 343-8254; f. 1885; cap. 412m., dep. 3,199m. (Dec. 1993); CEO GARY R. SEVERSON.

**Key Bank of Washington:** POB 90, Seattle, WA 98111-0090; tel. (206) 684-6000; telex 140616; fax (206) 684-6238; f. 1905; cap. 545.4m., dep. 5,658.3m. (March 1993).

**Seattle–First National Bank:** 701 Fifth Ave, POB 3586, Seattle, WA 98124; tel. (206) 358-3000; telex 3730000; fax (206) 358-3771; f. 1870; cap. 1,549.2m., dep. 12,359m. (Dec. 1992); Chair. and CEO JOHN RINDLAUB.

### West Virginia

**One Valley Bank NA:** One Valley Sq., POB 1793, Charleston, WV 25326; tel. (304) 348-7000; telex 9301816; f. 1867; cap. 30.7m., dep. 366.6m. (Sept. 1983); Chair. ROBERT F. BARONNER.

### Wisconsin

**Bank One, Milwaukee, NA:** 111 East Wisconsin Ave, Milwaukee, WI 53202; tel. (414) 765-3000; telex 19115; fax (414) 765-0553; f. 1930; cap. 212.9m., dep. 2,162.8m. (Dec. 1990); Chair. and CEO FREDERICK L. CULLEN; Pres. and CEO RONALD C. BALDWIN.

**Firstar Bank Milwaukee NA:** 777 East Wisconsin Ave, Milwaukee, WI 53202; tel. (414) 765-5705; telex 6734217; fax (414) 765-6207; f. 1863; cap. 398.6m., dep. 4,095.1m. (Dec. 1993); Chair. and CEO CHRIS M. BAUER.

### Wyoming

**First Interstate Bank of Commerce:** 4 South Main St, POB 2007, Sheridan, WY 82801; tel. (307) 674-7411; f. 1889; cap. 19.7m., dep. 269.8m. (Dec. 1991); Pres E. GARDING, R. J. PASCO.

### Co-operative Bank

**CoBank, ACB:** POB 5110, Denver, CO 80217; tel. (303) 740-4000; telex 3720469; fax (303) 740-4002; f. 1933; provides loan finance and domestic and international banking services for agricultural and farmer-owned co-operatives; total assets $13,863m. (Dec. 1994); CEO DOUG S. SIMS; Pres. JAMES A. PIERSON.

### Trade Bank

**Export-Import Bank of the United States:** 811 Vermont Ave, NW, Washington, DC 20571; tel. (202) 566-8990; telex 248460; fax (202) 566-7524; f. 1934, independent agency since 1945; capital subscribed by the US Treasury; finances and facilitates US external trade, guarantees payment to US foreign traders and banks, extends credit to foreign governmental and private concerns; dep. $8,470.5m. (Sept. 1992); Chair. and Pres. KENNETH BRODY.

## BANKING ASSOCIATIONS

There is a State Bankers Association in each state.

**American Bankers Association:** 1120 Connecticut Ave, NW, Washington, DC 20036; tel. (202) 663-5000; telex 892787; fax (202) 828-4532; f. 1875; Exec. Vice-Pres. DONALD G. OGILVIE; 9,000 mem. banks.

**America's Community Bankers:** 900 19th St, NW, Suite 400, Washington, DC 20006; tel. (202) 857-3100; fax (202) 296-8716; f. 1992; Pres. PAUL A. SCHOSBERG; 2,000 mems.

**Bank Administration Institute:** 1 North Franklin St, Chicago, IL 60606; tel. (312) 533-4600; Pres. RONALD G. BURKE; 8,000 mems.

**Independent Bankers Association of America:** One Thomas Circle, NW, Suite 950, Washington, DC 20005; tel. (202) 659-8111; f. 1930; Exec. Vice-Pres. KENNETH A. GUENTHER; 6,000 banks.

**Mortgage Bankers Association of America:** 1125 15th St, NW, Washington, DC 20005; tel. (202) 861-6500; f. 1914; Exec. Vice-Pres. WARREN LASKO; 2,700 mems.

## PRINCIPAL STOCK EXCHANGES

**Securities and Exchange Commission:** 450 Fifth St, NW, Washington, DC 20549; tel. (202) 942-0100; fax (202) 942-9646; f. 1934; federal govt agency which administers the federal securities laws; Chair. ARTHUR LEVITT, Jr.

**American Stock Exchange:** 86 Trinity Place, New York, NY 10006; tel. (212) 306-1000; telex 129297; fax (212) 306-1152; f. 1849; Chair. RICHARD F. SYRON; mems: 661 regular, 160 associate, 203 option principal, 13 limited trading permit holders.

**Boston Stock Exchange Inc:** One Boston Place, Boston, MA 02108; tel. (617) 723-9500; fax (617) 723-2474; f. 1834; Chair. and CEO WILLIAM G. MORTON, Jr; 190 mems.

**Chicago Stock Exchange:** 440 South LaSalle St, Chicago, IL 60605; f. 1882; Chair. ERWIN E. SHULZE; Pres. and CEO HOMER J. LIVINGSTON, Jr; 446 mems.

**New York Stock Exchange Inc:** 11 Wall St, New York, NY 10005; tel. (212) 656-3000; telex 710-5815464; fax (212) 656-5646; f. 1792; Chair. and CEO RICHARD A. GRASSO; 1,366 mems.

**Pacific Stock Exchange, Inc:** 301 Pine St, San Francisco, CA 94104; tel. (415) 393-4000; telex 203025; fax (415) 393-4202; f. 1882; Chair., Pres. and CEO LEOPOLD KORINS; 551 mems.

# THE UNITED STATES OF AMERICA

**Philadelphia Stock Exchange Inc:** Stock Exchange Bldg, 1900 Market St, Philadelphia, PA 19103; tel. (215) 496-5000; fax (215) 496-6729; f. 1790; Chair. JOHN J. WALLACE; Pres. and CEO NICHOLAS A. GIORDANO; 505 mems.

## INSURANCE

### Principal Companies

**Acacia Mutual Life Insurance Co:** 51 Louisiana Ave, NW, Washington, DC 20001-2176; tel. (202) 628-4506; f. 1869; Chair., Pres. and CEO CHARLES T. NASON.

**Aetna Life and Casualty Co:** 151 Farmington Ave, Hartford, CT 06156-0001; tel. (203) 273-0123; f. 1853; Chair. and CEO RONALD E. COMPTON; Pres. (vacant).

**Allstate Life Insurance Co:** Allstate Plaza, Northbrook, IL 60062-6299; tel. (312) 402-5000; f. 1931; CEO WAYNE E. HEDIEN.

**American Mutual Life Insurance Co:** Liberty Bldg, 418 Sixth Ave, Des Moines, IA 50309-2499; tel. (515) 280-1331; f. 1897; Pres. W. R. ENGEL.

**American National Insurance Co:** One Moody Plaza, Galveston, TX 77550-7999; tel. (409) 763-4661; f. 1905; Chair. R. L. MOODY; Pres. and CEO O. C. CLAY.

**American United Life Insurance Co:** One American Sq., Indianapolis, IN 46204-1925; tel. (317) 263-1877; f. 1877; Chair., Pres. and CEO JERRY D. SEMLER.

**Baltimore Life Insurance Co:** 10075 Red Run Blvd, Owings Mills, MD 21117-6050; tel. (410) 581-6600; f. 1882; Chair. and CEO J. E. BLAIR, Jr; Pres. L. J. PEARSON.

**Bankers' Life & Casualty Co:** 4444 West Lawrence Ave, Chicago, IL 60630-4501; tel. (312) 777-7000; f. 1880; Chair. and CEO R. T. SHAW; Pres. J. W. GARDINER.

**Berkshire Life Insurance Co:** 700 South St, Pittsfield, MA 01201-8212; tel. (413) 499-4321; f. 1851; Pres. and CEO ALBERT C. CORNELIO.

**Business Men's Assurance Co of America:** BMA Tower, 1 Penn Valley Park, POB 419458, Kansas City, MO 64141; tel. (816) 753-8000; f. 1909; Chair. and CEO GIORGIO BALZER; Pres. J. W. SAYLER, Jr.

**Central Life Assurance Co:** 611 Fifth Ave, Des Moines, IA 50309-1633; tel. (515) 283-2371; f. 1896; Chair. and CEO R. K. BROOKS.

**CIGNA Insurance Co:** 1600 Arch St, Philadelphia, PA 19103-2029; tel. (215) 523-4000; f. 1982 by merger; Chair. and CEO ROBERT D. KILPATRICK; Pres. and CEO WILSON H. TAYLOR.

**Combined Insurance Co of America:** 123 North Wacker Drive, Chicago, IL 60606; tel. (312) 275-8000; f. 1949; Chair. and CEO P. G. RYAN.

**Commercial Union Insurance Companies:** One Beacon St, Boston, MA 02108-3106; tel. (617) 725-6000; f. 1861; Chair. and CEO KENNETH J. DUFFY.

**Commonwealth Life Insurance Co:** POB 32800, Louisville, KY 40232; tel. (502) 587-7371; f. 1904; Chair., Pres. and CEO THOMAS H. SCHNICK.

**Connecticut Mutual Life Insurance Co:** 140 Garden St, Hartford, CT 06154-0001; tel. (203) 727-6500; f. 1846; Chair. and CEO DENIS F. MULLANE.

**Continental American Life Insurance Co:** 300 Continental Drive, Newark, DE 19713-4399; tel. (302) 454-5000; fax (302) 731-1101; f. 1907; Chair. WILLIAM G. COPELAND; Pres. and CEO JOHN T. UNIPAN.

**Continental Assurance Co/Continental Casualty Co:** CNA Plaza, 333 South Wabash Ave, Chicago, IL 60685-0001; tel. (312) 822-5000; Chair. and Pres. E. J. NOHA.

**The Continental Insurance Co:** 180 Maiden Lane, New York, NY 10038-4925; tel. (212) 440-3000; f. 1853; Chair. and CEO J. P. MASCOTTE.

**Country Life Insurance Co:** 1701 Towanda Ave, Bloomington, IL 61701-2040; tel. (309) 557-2111; f. 1925; Pres. JOHN WHITE, Jr.

**Equitable of Iowa Companies:** 699 Walnut St, 20th Floor, Des Moines, IA 50309-3929; tel. (515) 282-1335; f. 1867; Chair. and CEO F. S. HUBBELL.

**Equitable Life Assurance Society of the US:** 787 Seventh Ave, New York, NY 10019-6018; tel. (212) 554-1234; f. 1859; Chair. and CEO JOSEPH J. CARTER; Pres. JOSEPH J. MELLONE.

**Farmers Group Inc:** 4680 Wilshire Blvd, Los Angeles, CA 90010-3807; tel. (213) 930-3200; Chair., Pres. and CEO LEO E. DENLEA, Jr.

**Federal Insurance Co:** POB 1615, Warren, NJ 07061; tel. (908) 580-2000; CEO DEAN R. O'HARE.

**Fidelity and Guaranty Life Insurance Co:** POB 1137, Baltimore, MD 21203; tel. (301) 547-3000; CEO IHOR HRON.

**Franklin Life Insurance Co:** 1 Franklin Sq., Springfield, IL 62713; tel. (217) 528-2011; f. 1884; Chair. W. J. ALLEY; Pres. and CEO HOWARD C. HUMPHREY.

**General American Life Insurance Co:** POB 396, St Louis, MO 63166; tel. (314) 231-1700; f. 1933; Chair., Pres. and CEO H. EDWIN TRUSHEIM.

**Great Southern Life Insurance Co:** 500 North Akard St, Dallas, TX 75201-3320; tel. (214) 954-7111; f. 1909; Chair. ROBERT T. SHAW; Pres. JOHN W. GARDINER.

**Guarantee Mutual Life Co:** Guarantee Centre, 8801 Indian Hills Drive, Omaha, NE 68114-4069; tel. (402) 390-7300; f. 1901; Pres. R. D. BATES.

**The Guardian Life Insurance Co of America:** 201 Park Ave South, New York, NY 10003-1605; tel. (212) 598-8000; f. 1860; Chair. and CEO ARTHUR V. FERRARA; Pres. JOSEPH D. SARGENT.

**Gulf Insurance Co:** 4600 Fuller Drive, Dallas, TX 75038-6511; tel. (214) 650-2800; fax (214) 650-0924; f. 1925; Pres. and CEO D. W. BANNISTER.

**Gulf Life Insurance Co:** 1301 Gulf Life Drive, Jacksonville, FL 32207-9048; tel. (904) 390-7000; f. 1911; Pres. and CEO R. O. PURCIFULL.

**Hanover Insurance Co:** 100 North Parkway, Worcester, MA 01605; tel. (508) 853-7200; f. 1973; Chair. JOHN F. O'BRIEN; Pres. and CEO T. J. RUPLEY.

**Home Beneficial Life Insurance Co:** 3901 West Broad St, Richmond, VA 23230-3913; tel. (804) 358-8431; f. 1899; Chair., Pres. and CEO R. W. WILTSHIRE.

**The Home Insurance Co:** 59 Maiden Lane, New York, NY 10038-4540; tel. (212) 530-7000; f. 1853; Pres. JAMES J. MEENAGHAN.

**Home Life Insurance Co:** 75 Wall St, New York, NY 10005-2833; tel. (212) 428-2000; f. 1860; Pres. and CEO WILLIAM WALLACE.

**Indianapolis Life Insurance Co:** 2960 North Meridian St, Indianapolis, IN 46208-4789; tel. (317) 927-6500; f. 1905; Pres. and CEO EUGENE M. BUSCHE.

**Integon Corpn:** 500 West Fifth St, Winston-Salem, NC 27152-0001; tel. (919) 770-2000; f. 1920; Pres. JAMES T. LAMBIE.

**John Hancock Mutual Life Insurance Co:** POB 111, Boston, MA 02117; tel. (617) 572-6000; CEO E. JAMES MORTON.

**Kansas City Life Insurance Co:** 3520 Broadway, Kansas City, MO 64141-6139; tel. (816) 753-7000; f. 1895; Chair. and Pres. JOSEPH R. BIXBY.

**Lamar Life Insurance Co:** 317 East Capitol St, Jackson, MS 39201-3405; tel. (601) 949-3100; f. 1906; Pres. JACK P. DEAN.

**Liberty Life Insurance Co:** Liberty Life Bldg, 2000 Wade Hampton Blvd, Greenville, SC 29615; tel. (803) 268-8111; fax (803) 292-4411; f. 1905; Chair. W. HAYNE HIPP; Pres. RALPH L. OGDEN.

**Liberty Mutual Fire Insurance Co:** 175 Berkeley St, Boston, MA 02117-0140; tel. (617) 357-9500; Chair. and CEO GARY L. COUNTRYMAN.

**Liberty National Life Insurance Co:** 2001 Third Ave South, Birmingham, AL 35233-2186; tel. (205) 325-2722; f. 1900; Chair. R. K. RICHEY; Pres. C. B. HUDSON.

**Life Insurance Co of Georgia:** 5780 Powers Ferry Rd, NW, Atlanta, GA 30327-4390; tel. (404) 980-5100; f. 1891; Chair. LYNN H. JOHNSTON; CEO DAVID A. STONECIPHER.

**Life Insurance Co of Virginia:** POB 27601, Richmond, VA 23261; tel. (703) 281-6000; f. 1871; CEO PAUL RUTLEDGE.

**Lincoln National Life Insurance Co:** 1300 South Clinton St, Fort Wayne, IN 46802-3506; tel. (219) 455-2000; telex 232673; f. 1905; Pres. and CEO IAN M. ROLLAND.

**Manhattan Life Insurance Co:** 111 West 57th St, New York, NY 10019-2211; tel. (212) 484-9300; f. 1850; Chair. and CEO D. M. FORDYCE.

**Massachusetts Mutual Life Insurance Co:** 1295 State St, Springfield, MA 01111-0001; tel. (413) 788-8411; f. 1851; Chair. WILLIAM J. CLARK; Pres. and CEO THOMAS B. WHEELER.

**Metropolitan Life Insurance Co:** 1 Madison Ave, New York, NY 10010-3681; tel. (212) 578-2211; f. 1868; Chair. and CEO ROBERT SCHWARTZ.

**Minnesota Mutual Life Insurance Co:** 400 North Robert St, St Paul, MN 55101-2015; tel. (612) 298-3500; f. 1880; Chair., Pres. and CEO COLEMAN BLOOMFIELD.

**Monarch Life Insurance Co:** 1 Monarch Place, Springfield, MA 01144-1001; tel. (413) 784-2000; fax (413) 784-7294; f. 1901; CEO ROGER T. SERVISON.

**Mutual Life Insurance Co of New York (MONY):** 1740 Broadway, New York, NY 10019; tel. (212) 708-2000; f. 1842; Chair. and CEO JAMES B. FARLEY.

**Mutual of Omaha Insurance Co:** Mutual of Omaha Plaza, Omaha, NE 68175-0001; tel. (402) 342-7600; f. 1909; Chair. and CEO THOMAS J. SKUTT; Pres. JOHN W. WEEKLY.

**National Home Life Assurance Co:** 20 Moores Rd, Frazer, PA 19355; tel. (215) 648-5000; CEO DONALD D. KENNEDY, Jr.

THE UNITED STATES OF AMERICA                                                                                              *Directory*

**Nationwide Mutual Insurance Co:** One Nationwide Plaza, Columbus, OH 43215-2239; tel. (614) 249-7111; f. 1925; CEO JOHN E. FISHER.

**New York Life Insurance Co:** 51 Madison Ave, New York, NY 10010-1603; tel. (212) 576-7000; f. 1845; CEO HARRY G. HOHN.

**Niagara Fire Insurance Co:** 180 Maiden Lane, New York, NY 10038-4925; tel. (212) 440-3000; f. 1850; Chair. J. P. MASCOTTE.

**Northwestern Mutual Life Insurance Co:** 720 East Wisconsin Ave, Milwaukee, WI 53202-4703; tel. (414) 271-1444; f. 1857; Pres. and CEO JAMES D. ERICSON.

**Northwestern National Life Insurance Co:** 20 South Washington Ave, Minneapolis, MN 55401-1908; tel. (612) 372-5432; telex 4310138; f. 1885; CEO JOHN E. PEARSON.

**The Ohio National Life Insurance Co:** 237 William Howard Taft Rd, Cincinnati, OH 45219-2679; tel. (513) 861-3600; f. 1909; CEO BARNEY L. WARNEMUNDE.

**Old Line Life Insurance Co of America:** 707 North 11th St, Milwaukee, WI 53233-2399; tel. (414) 271-2820; f. 1910; Pres. and CEO JAMES A. GRIFFIN.

**Pacific Mutual Life Insurance Co:** 700 Newport Center Drive, Newport Beach, CA 92660-6397; tel. (714) 640-3011; telex 910-5961376; f. 1868; Pres. and CEO THOMAS C. SUTTON.

**The Paul Revere Life Insurance Co:** 18 Chestnut St, Worcester, MA 01608-1528; tel. (508) 799-4441; f. 1930; Pres. CHARLES E. SOULE, Jr.

**Penn Mutual Life Insurance Co:** 530 Walnut St, Philadelphia, PA 19172-0001; tel. (215) 956-8000; fax (215) 956-8347; f. 1847; Chair. JOHN E. TAIT.

**Philadelphia Life Insurance Co:** 500 North Akard St, Dallas, TX 75201-3320; tel. (214) 954-7111; f. 1906; Pres. and CEO R. M. HOWE.

**Phoenix Mutual Life Insurance Co:** One American Row, Hartford, CT 06115-2520; tel. (203) 275-5000; f. 1851; Chair. and CEO JOHN GUMMERE.

**Protective Life Insurance Co:** 2801 Highway 280 South, Birmingham, AL 35223-2488; tel. (205) 879-9230; telex 810-7333592; f. 1907; Chair. WILLIAM J. RUSHTON, III.

**Provident Life and Accident Insurance Co of America:** Fountain Sq., Chattanooga, TN 37402-1389; tel. (615) 755-1011; f. 1887; Pres. and CEO WINSTON W. WALKER.

**Provident Mutual Life Insurance Co of Philadelphia:** 1600 Market St, Philadelphia, PA 19101-7378; tel. (215) 636-5000; f. 1865; Chair. JOHN A. MILLER; Pres. and CEO L. J. ROWELL, Jr.

**The Prudential Insurance Co of America:** 751 Broad St, Newark, NJ 07102-3714; tel. (201) 877-6000; f. 1875; Chair. and CEO ARTHUR F. RYAN; Pres. RONALD D. BARBARO.

**Reliance Insurance Group:** 55 East 52nd St, New York, NY 10055; tel. (212) 909-1100; f. 1817; Chair. and CEO S. P. STEINBERG.

**SAFECO Corpn:** Safeco Plaza, Seattle, WA 98185-0001; tel. (206) 545-5000; f. 1929; tel. (206) 545-5000; Chair. and CEO R. M. TRAFTON; Pres. BRUCE MAINES.

**St Paul Fire and Marine Insurance Co:** 385 Washington St, St Paul, MN 55102-1396; tel. (612) 221-7911; telex 297082; f. 1853; Chair. and CEO DOUGLAS W. LEATHERDALE.

**Southwestern Life Insurance Co:** 500 North Akard St, Dallas, TX 75201-3320; tel. (214) 954-7111; f. 1903; Pres. THOMAS J. BROPHY.

**Standard Insurance Co:** 1100 SW Sixth Ave, Portland, OR 97204-1093; tel. (503) 248-2700; fax (503) 796-7935; f. 1906; Chair. and CEO BENJAMIN R. WHITELEY.

**State Farm Life Insurance Co:** One State Farm Plaza, Bloomington, IL 61710-0001; tel. (309) 766-2311; f. 1929; Chair. MARVIN D. BOWER; Pres. EDWARD B. RUST, Jr.

**State Farm Mutual Automobile Insurance Co:** One State Farm Plaza, Bloomington, IL 61710-0001; tel. (309) 766-2311; f. 1922; Pres. EDWARD B. RUST, Jr.

**State Life Insurance Co:** 141 East Washington St, Indianapolis, IN 46204-3649; tel. (317) 681-5300; f. 1894; Chair. and Pres. ARTHUR L. BRYANT.

**State Mutual Companies:** 440 Lincoln St, Worcester, MA 01605-1978; tel. (508) 855-1000; fax (508) 853-6332; f. 1844; Pres. and CEO JOHN F. O'BRIEN.

**Transamerica Occidental Life Insurance Co:** 1150 South Olive St, Los Angeles, CA 90015-2290; tel. (213) 742-2111; telex 3422111; f. 1906; Chair., Pres. and CEO DAVID R. CARPENTER.

**Travelers Insurance Co:** One Tower Sq., Hartford, CT 06183-0001; tel. (203) 277-0111; f. 1893; Chair. THOMAS H. MCABOY; Pres. and CEO RICHARD W. MCLAUGHLIN.

**Unigard Security Insurance Co:** 1215 Fourth Ave, Seattle, WA 98161; tel. (206) 292-7861; fax (206) 292-7867; f. 1901; Pres. PAUL SWEENEY.

**Union Central Life Insurance Co:** POB 179, Cincinnati, OH 45201-0179; tel. (513) 595-2200; f. 1867; Pres. and CEO C. C. HINCKLEY.

**United Insurance Co of America:** One East Wacker Drive, Chicago, IL 60601-1883; tel. (312) 661-4500; f. 1955; Pres. RICHARD C. VIE; Chair. J. V. JEROME.

**United of Omaha Life Insurance Co:** Mutual of Omaha Plaza, Omaha, NE 68175-0001; tel. (402) 342-7600; f. 1926; Chair. and CEO T. J. SKUTT; Pres. JOHN W. WEEKLY.

**United States Fidelity & Guaranty Co:** 100 Light St, Baltimore, MD 21202-1036; tel. (301) 547-3000; telex 87538; f. 1896; Chair. and CEO JACK MOSELEY; Pres. PAUL SCHEEL.

**UNUM Life Insurance Co:** 2211 Congress St, Portland, ME 04122-0001; tel. (207) 770-2211; f. 1848; Pres., Chair and CEO JAMES F. ORR, III.

**USLICO Corpn:** POB 3700, Arlington, VA 22203; tel. (703) 875-3600; CEO C. V. GIUFFRA.

**Washington National Corpn:** 1630 Chicago Ave, Evanston, IL 60201-4584; tel. (312) 570-5500; f. 1911; Chair. and CEO ROBERT PATIN.

**Western National Life Insurance Co:** POB 871, Amarillo, TX 79167; tel. (806) 378-3400; CEO J. K. CLAYTON.

**Western & Southern Life Insurance Co:** 400 Broadway, Cincinnati, OH 45202-3341; tel. (513) 629-1800; f. 1888; Chair. and CEO W. J. WILLIAMS.

**Wisconsin National Life Insurance Co:** 220 Washington Ave, Oshkosh, WI 54901-5030; tel. (414) 235-0800; f. 1908; Pres. A. DEAN ARGANBRIGHT.

### INSURANCE ORGANIZATIONS

**American Council of Life Insurance:** 1001 Pennsylvania Ave, NW, Washington, DC 20004-2599; tel. (202) 624-2000; fax (202) 624-2319; f. 1976; 606 mem. cos; Pres. CARROLL A. CAMPBELL, Jr.

**American Institute of Marine Underwriters:** 14 Wall St, 21st Floor, New York, NY 10005-2145; tel. (212) 233-0550; fax (212) 227-5102; f. 1898; 105 mems; Pres. WALTER M. CRAMER.

**American Insurance Association:** 1130 Connecticut Ave, NW, Washington, DC 20036; tel. (202) 828-7100; fax (202) 293-1219; f. 1964; 250 mems; Chair. DOUGLAS W. LEATHERDALE; Pres. ROBERT E. VAGLEY.

**Casualty Actuarial Society:** 1100 North Glebe Rd, Suite 600, Arlington, VA 22201; tel. (703) 276-3100; fax (703) 3108; f. 1914; 2,400 mems; Pres. Exec. Dir JAMES H. TINSLEY.

**Life Insurance Marketing and Research Association, Inc:** POB 208, Hartford, CT 06141; tel. (203) 677-0033; telex 643952; fax (203) 678-0187; f. 1916; 290 mems; Pres. and CEO JOHN C. SCULLY.

**Life Office Management Association:** 5770 Powers Ferry Rd, NW, Atlanta, GA 30327-4308; tel. (404) 951-1770; fax (404) 984-0441; f. 1924; 878 mem. cos; Chair. WILLIAM E. BRADFORD; Pres. LYNN G. MERRITT.

**National Association of Life Underwriters:** 1922 F St, NW, Washington, DC 20006-4387; tel. (202) 331-6000; fax (202) 331-2179; 1,000 mems; CEO WILLIAM V. REGAN, III.

**National Association of Mutual Insurance Companies:** 3601 Vincennes Rd, POB 68700, Indianapolis, IN 46268-0700; tel. (317) 875-5250; fax (317) 879-8408; 1,240 mems; Pres. LARRY L. FORRESTER.

**Reinsurance Association of America:** 1301 Pennsylvania Ave, NW, Suite 900, Washington, DC 20004; tel. (202) 638-3690; fax (202) 638-0936; f. 1969; 27 mems; Pres. FRANKLIN W. NUTTER.

## Trade and Industry

### CHAMBER OF COMMERCE

**Chamber of Commerce of the USA:** 1615 H St, NW, Washington, DC 20062-2000; tel. (202) 659-6000; fax (202) 463-5836; f. 1912; mems: c. 215,000 cos, professional asscns and chambers of commerce; Pres. RICHARD L. LESHER.

### EMPLOYERS' ORGANIZATIONS

#### Chemicals

**American Institute of Chemists:** 7315 Wisconsin Ave, Bethesda, MD 20814; tel. (301) 652-2447; f. 1923; 4,000 mems; Exec. Dir D. A. H. ROETHEL.

**Chemical Manufacturers Association:** 2501 M St, NW, Washington, DC 20037-1306; tel. (202) 887-1100; telex 89617; fax (202) 887-1237; f. 1872; 175 mems; Pres. and CEO FREDERICK L. WEBBER; Sec. JOHN P. CONNELLY.

# THE UNITED STATES OF AMERICA
*Directory*

**Drug, Chemical and Allied Trades Association, Inc:** 2 Roosevelt Ave, 3rd Floor, Syosset, NY 11791; tel. (516) 496-3317; fax (516) 496-2231; f. 1890; c. 500 mems; Exec. Dir. RICHARD J. LERMAN.

**The Fertilizer Institute:** 501 Second St, NE, Washington, DC 20002-4916; tel. (202) 675-8250; f. 1955; 300 mems; Pres. GARY D. MYERS.

**National Association of Retail Druggists/ (NARD-Pharmacies):** 205 Daingerfield Rd, Alexandria, VA 22314; tel. (703) 683-8200; fax (703) 683-3619; f. 1898; 30,000 mems; Exec. Vice-Pres. CHARLES M. WEST.

**Pharmaceutical Manufacturers Association:** 1100 15th St, NW, Suite 900, Washington, DC 20005-1797; tel. (202) 835-3400; telex 8229494; f. 1958; 87 mems; Pres. GERALD J. MOSSINGHOFF.

**Soap and Detergent Association:** 475 Park Ave South, New York, NY 10016; tel. (212) 725-1262; fax (212) 213-0685; f. 1926; 145 mems; Pres. GERALD R. PFLUG.

## Construction
(see also Electricity, and Engineering and Machinery)

**Associated Builders and Contractors (ABC):** 1300 North 17th St, Rosslyn, VA 22209; tel. (703) 812-2000; fax (202) 347-1121; f. 1950; 19,000 mems; Exec. Vice-Pres. DANIEL J. BENNET.

**Associated General Contractors of America:** 1957 E St, NW, Washington, DC 20006-5107; tel. (202) 393-2040; fax (202) 393-2040, Ext. 204; f. 1918; 32,500 mems; Exec. Vice-Pres. HUBERT BEATTY.

**Associated Specialty Contractors:** 3 Bethesda Metro Center, Suite 1100, Bethesda, MD 20814-5372; tel. (301) 657-3110; fax (301) 215-4500; f. 1950; 8 mem. asscns; Pres. DANIEL G. WALTER.

**Construction Specifications Institute:** 601 Madison St, Alexandria, VA 22314-1791; tel. (703) 684-0300; f. 1948; 17,300 mems; Exec. Dir GREG BALESTERO.

**Mechanical Contractors Association of America, Inc:** 1385 Piccard Drive, Rockville, MD 20850-4329; tel. (301) 869-5800; fax (301) 990-9690; f. 1889; 1,300 mems; Exec. Vice-Pres. JAMES R. NOBLE.

**National Association of Plumbing-Heating-Cooling Contractors:** 180 South Washington St, POB 6808, Falls Church, VA 22046-2040; tel. (703) 237-8100; fax (703) 327-7442; f. 1883; 5,100 mems; CEO ALLEN INLOW.

**Tile Council of America:** POB 326, Princeton, NJ 08542-0326, tel. (609) 921-7050; fax (609) 452-7255; f. 1944; 29 mems; Exec. Dir ROBERT J. KLEINHANS.

## Electricity
(see also Construction, and Engineering and Machinery)

**Edison Electric Institute:** 701 Pennsylvania Ave, NW, Washington, DC 20004-2696; tel. (202) 508-5000; telex 8220132; fax (202) 508-5360; f. 1933; mems: 208 investor-owned electric utility cos; 31 int. affiliates; Pres. THOMAS R. KUHN.

**Electronic Industries Association:** 2500 Wilson Blvd, Arlington, VA 22201-3438; tel. (703) 907-7500; fax (703) 907-7501; f. 1924; over 1,200 mems; Pres. P. F. MCCLOSKEY.

**Institute of Electrical and Electronics Engineers:** 345 East 47th St, New York, NY 10017; tel. (212) 705-7900; f. 1963; 274,000 mems; Gen. Man. ERIC HERZ.

**National Association of Electrical Distributors:** 45 Danbury Rd, Wilton, CT 06897; tel. (203) 834-1908; f. 1908; 2,900 mems; Pres. RICHARD A. COLDRICK.

**National Electrical Contractors Association:** 3 Bethesda Metro Center, Bethesda, MD 20814-5372; tel. (301) 657-3110; fax (301) 215-4500; f. 1901; 4,200 mems; Exec. Vice-Pres. JOHN M. GRAU.

**National Electrical Manufacturers Association:** 2101 L St, NW, Washington, DC 20037-1581; tel. (202) 457-8400; telex 904077; fax (202) 457-8468; f. 1926; 650 mems; Pres. MALCOLM E. O'HAGAN.

## Engineering and Machinery
(see also Electricity and Construction)

**Air-Conditioning and Refrigeration Institute:** 4301 North Fairfax Drive, Suite 425, Arlington, VA 22203; tel. (703) 524-8800; telex 892351; fax (703) 528-3816; f. 1953; 190 mems; Pres. A. W. BRASWELL.

**American Consulting Engineers Council:** 1015 15th St, NW, Washington, DC 20005-2670; tel. (202) 347-7474; f. 1973; 5,200 mems; Exec. Vice-Pres. HOWARD MESSNER.

**American Institute of Chemical Engineers:** 345 East 47th St, 11th Floor, New York, NY 10017-2330; tel. (212) 705-7338; f. 1908; 57,000 mems; Exec. Dir RICHARD EMMERT.

**American Institute of Mining, Metallurgical and Petroleum Engineers, Inc:** 345 East 47th St, 14th Floor, New York, NY 10017-2330; tel. (212) 705-7695; f. 1871; four constituent socs representing 79,000 mems; Exec. Dir ROBERT H. MARCRUM.

**American Railway Engineering Association:** 50 F St, NW, Suite 7702, Washington, DC 20001; tel. (202) 639-2190; telex 892352; fax (202) 639-2183; f. 1899; 4,000 mems; Exec. Dir L. T. CERNY.

**American Society of Civil Engineers:** c/o Kelly Cunningham, 1015 15th St, NW, Suite 600, Washington, DC 20005; tel. (212) 705-7496; telex 422847; fax (212) 980-4681; f. 1852; 110,000 mems; Exec. Dir EDWARD O. PFRANG.

**American Society of Heating, Refrigerating and Air Conditioning Engineers:** 1791 Tullie Circle, NE, Atlanta, GA 30329-2398; tel. (404) 636-8400; telex 705343; fax (404) 321-5478; f. 1895; 55,000 mems; Exec. Dir FRANK M. CODA.

**American Society of Mechanical Engineers:** 345 East 47th St, New York, NY 10017-2385; tel. (212) 705-7722; telex 5815267; f. 1880; 125,000 mems; Exec. Dir Dr DAVID BELDEN.

**American Society of Naval Engineers Inc:** 1452 Duke St, Alexandria, VA 22314-3403; tel. (703) 836-6727; fax (703) 836-7491; f. 1888; 8,000 mems; Exec. Dir Capt. (retd) CHARLES J. SMITH.

**Association for Manufacturing Technology:** 7901 Westpark Drive, McLean, VA 22102-4269; tel. (703) 893-2900; telex 353819; fax (703) 893-1151; f. 1902; 300 mems; Pres. ALBERT W. MOORE.

**Society of Automotive Engineers/SAE (Automotive):** 400 Commonwealth Drive, Warrendale, PA 15096-0001; tel. (412) 776-4841; telex 866355; f. 1905; 64,000 mems; Exec. Vice-Pres. MAX E. RUMBAUGH, Jr.

**Society of Naval Architects and Marine Engineers:** 601 Pavonia Ave, Suite 400, Jersey City, NJ 07306-2907; tel. (201) 798-4800; fax (201) 798-4975; f. 1893; 10,000 mems; Exec. Dir FRANCIS M. CAGLIARI.

## Food

**American Meat Institute:** POB 3556, Washington, DC 20007; tel. (703) 841-2400; telex 5270938; fax (703) 527-0938; f. 1906; 1,175 mems; Pres. J. PATRICK BOYLE.

**DFA of California:** 303 Brokaw Rd, POB 270A, Santa Clara, CA 95052; tel. (408) 727-9302; fax (408) 970-3833; f. 1908; 42 mems; Pres. FRANK A. MOSEBAR.

**Distilled Spirits Council of the US, Inc (DISCUS):** 1250 I St, NW, Suite 900, Washington, DC 20005-3998; tel. (202) 628-3544; fax (202) 682-8888; f. 1973; 21 active mems and 34 affiliates; Pres. and CEO F. A. MEISTER.

**Food Marketing Institute:** 800 Connecticut Ave, NW, Washington, DC 20006-2701; tel. (202) 452-8444; telex 892722; fax (202) 429-4519; f. 1977; 1,500 mems; Pres. TIMOTHY M. HAMMONDS.

**Grocery Manufacturers of America, Inc:** 1010 Wisconsin Ave, NW, Suite 900, Washington, DC 20007-3603; tel. (202) 337-9400; fax (202) 337-4508; f. 1908; 130 mems; Pres. and CEO C. MANLY MOLPUS.

**Millers' National Federation:** 600 Maryland Ave, SW, Suite 305-W, Washington, DC 20024; tel. (202) 484-2000; f. 1902; c. 50 mems, accounting for 90% of flour produced in the USA; Pres. ROY M. HENWOOD.

**National-American Wholesale Grocers' Association:** 201 Park Washington Court, Falls Church, VA 22046; tel. (703) 532-9400; fax (703) 538-4673; f. 1906; 320 mems; Pres. JOHN R. BLOCK.

**National Confectioners Association of the US:** 7900 Westpark Drive, Suite A-320, McLean, VA 22102-0000; tel. (703) 790-5750; fax (703) 790-5752; f. 1884; 340 mems; Pres. RICHARD T. O'CONNELL.

**National Dairy Council:** 10255 West Higgins Rd, Suite 900, Rosemont, IL 60018-5616; tel. (708) 803-2000; f. 1915; 24 mems; CEO THOMAS GALLAGHER.

**National Food Brokers Association:** 2100 Reston Pkwy, Suite 400, Reston, VA 22091-1208; tel. (703) 758-7790; fax (703) 758-7787; f. 1904; 1,400 corporate and 40,000 individual mems; Pres. and CEO ROBERT C. SCHWARZE.

**National Grain Trade Council:** 1300 L St, NW, Suite 925, Washington, DC 20005; tel. (202) 842-0400; fax (202) 682-4033; f. 1930; 64 mems; Pres. ROBERT PETERSEN.

**National Live Stock and Meat Board:** 444 North Michigan Ave, Chicago, IL 60611-3978; tel. (312) 467-5520; f. 1922; Pres. JOHN L. HUSTON.

**National Soft Drink Association:** 1101 16th St, NW, Washington, DC 20036-4803; tel. (202) 463-6732; telex 510-1004811; fax (202) 463-6178; f. 1919; 1,700 mems; Pres. WILLIAM L. BALL, III.

**National Sugar Brokers Association:** 90 West St, Suite 706, New York, NY 10006; tel. (212) 349-6063; fax (212) 233-6815; f. 1903; 100 mems; Exec. Sec. GWEN CODY.

**United Fresh Fruit and Vegetable Association:** 727 North Washington St, Alexandria, VA 22314; tel. (703) 836-3410; fax (703) 836-2049; f. 1904; 2,100 mems; Pres. and CEO TOM E. STENZEL.

## Iron and Steel

**American Hardware Manufacturers Association:** 801 North Plaza Drive, Schaumburg, IL 60173-4977; tel. (708) 605-1025; fax

(708) 605-1093; f. 1901; 1,000 mems; Pres. and CEO WILLIAM P. FARRELL.

**American Iron and Steel Institute:** 1101 17th St, NW, Washington, DC 20036-4700; tel. (202) 463-6573; f. 1908; 1,200 mems; Pres. ANDREW G. SHARKEY, III.

**Steel Founders' Society of America (SFSA):** 455 State St, Des Plaines, IL 60016; tel. (708) 299-9160; fax (708) 299-3105; f. 1902; 75 mems; Exec. Vice-Pres. RAYMOND W. MONROE.

### Leather

**Footwear Industries of America:** 1420 K St, NW, Suite 600, Washington, DC 20005; tel. (202) 789-1420; f. 1869; 150 mems; Pres. FAWN EVENSON.

**Leather Apparel Association:** 19 West 21st St, Suite 403, New York, NY 10010; tel. (212) 924-8895; fax (212) 727-1218; f. 1990; 93 mems; Dir LILI KASDAN.

**Leather Industries of America:** 1000 Thomas Jefferson St, NW, Suite 515, Washington, DC 20007-3835; tel. (202) 342-8086; fax (202) 342-9063; f. 1917; 250 mems; Pres. CHARLES S. MYERS.

**Luggage and Leather Goods Manufacturers of America:** 350 Fifth Ave, Suite 2624, New York, NY 10118-0110; tel. (212) 695-2340; fax (212) 643-8021; f. 1938; 240 mems; Exec. Vice-Pres. ROBERT K. ERMATINGER.

### Lumber
(see also Paper)

**American Forest and Paper Association:** 1250 Connecticut Ave, NW, Suite 200, Washington, DC 20036-2615; tel. (202) 463-2455; fax (202) 463-2461; f. 1932; 850 mems; Pres. REDD CARANEY.

**American Plywood Association:** POB 11700, Tacoma, WA 98411-0700; tel. (206) 565-6600; fax (206) 565-7265; 124 mems; Pres. D. L. ROGOWAY.

**American Pulpwood Association:** 1025 Vermont Ave, NW, Suite 1020, Washington, DC 20005; tel. (202) 347-2900; fax (202) 783-2685; f. 1934; 4,000 mems; Pres. R. LEWIS.

**National Lumber and Building Material Dealers Association:** 40 Ivy St, SE, Washington, DC 20003; tel. (202) 547-2230; f. 1915; 23 mems; Exec. Vice-Pres. HARLAN W. HUMMEL.

**National Wooden Pallet and Container Association:** 1800 North Kent St, Suite 911, Arlington, VA 22209-2109; tel. (703) 527-7667; fax (703) 527-7717; f. 1967; 354 mems; Exec. Vice-Pres. JOHN J. HEALY.

**Southern Forest Products Association:** POB 641700, Kenner, LA 70064; tel. (504) 443-4464; fax (504) 443-6612; f. 1915; 220 mems; Pres. KARL W. LINDBERG.

**Western Forest Industries Association:** 1500 SW Taylor, Portland, OR 97205; tel. (503) 224-5455; fax (503) 224-0592; f. 1947; 125 mems; Pres. DAVID A. FORD.

**Wood Products Manufacturers Association:** 175 State Rd East, Westminster, MA 01473; tel. (508) 874-5445; fax (508) 874-9946; f. 1929; 460 mems; Exec. Dir ALBERT J. BIBEAU.

### Metals

**Aluminum Association, Inc:** 900 19th St, NW, Suite 300, Washington, DC 20006-2168; tel. (202) 862-5104; telex 8221129; fax (202) 862-5164; f. 1933; 80 mems; Pres. DAVID N. PARKER.

**American Mining Congress:** 1920 N St, NW, Suite 300, Washington, DC 20036-1662; tel. (202) 861-2800; telex 8220126; fax (202) 861-7535; f. 1897; 400 mems; Pres. JOHN A. KNEBEL.

**ASM International:** Materials Park, OH 44073; tel. (216) 338-5151; fax (216) 338-4634; f. 1913 as American Soc. for Metals; 50,000 mems; Man. Dir EDWARD L. LANGER.

**Copper and Brass Fabricators Council Inc:** 1050 17th St, NW, Suite 440, Washington, DC 20036; tel. (202) 833-8575; f. 1964; Pres. JOSEPH L. MAYER.

**Copper Development Association Inc:** 260 Madison Ave, New York, NY 10016; tel. (212) 251-7200; fax (212) 251-7234; f. 1963; 65 mems; Pres. ROBERT M. PAYNE.

**Gold Institute:** 1112 16th St, NW, Suite 240, Washington, DC 20036; tel. (202) 835-0185; fax (202) 835-0155; f. 1976; 89 mems; Pres. JOHN H. LUTLEY.

**Lead Industries Association:** 295 Madison Ave, New York, NY 10017-6304; tel. (212) 578-4750; fax (212) 684-7714; f. 1928; 52 mems; Exec. Dir J. F. SMITH.

**Manufacturing Jewelers and Silversmiths of America, Inc:** One State St, 6th Floor, Providence, RI 02908; tel. (401) 274-3840; fax (401) 274-0265; f. 1903; 2,300 mems; Pres. MATTHEW RUNCI.

**Metal Powder Industries Federation:** 105 College Rd East, 1st Floor, Princeton, NJ 08540-6692; tel. (609) 452-7700; telex 6852516; fax (609) 987-8523; f. 1944; 250 corporate mems; Exec. Dir DONALD G. WHITE.

**Mining and Metallurgical Society of America:** 9 Escalle Lane, Larkspur, CA 94939; tel. (415) 924-7441; fax (415) 924-7463; f. 1908; 340 mems; Exec. Dir ROBERT M. CRUM.

**Silver Institute:** 1112 16th St, NW, Suite 240, Washington, DC 20036; tel. (202) 835-0185; fax (202) 835-0155; f. 1971; 53 mems; Exec. Dir JOHN H. LUTLEY.

### Paper
(see also Lumber)

**American Forest and Paper Association:** 1250 Connecticut Ave, NW, 2nd Floor, Washington, DC 20036; tel. (202) 463-2455; fax (202) 463-2461; f. 1964; 550 mems; Pres. REDD CARANEY.

**National Paper Trade Association, Inc:** 111 Great Neck Rd, Great Neck NY 11021; tel. (516) 829-3070; fax (516) 829-3074; f. 1903; 1,800 mems; Pres. JOHN J. BUCKLEY.

**Paperboard Packaging Council:** 1101 Vermont Ave, NW, Suite 411, Washington, DC 20005; tel. (202) 289-4100; fax (202) 289-4243; f. 1964; Pres. JOHN A. MCINTYRE.

### Petroleum and Fuel

**American Gas Association:** 1515 Wilson Blvd, Arlington, VA 22209; tel. (703) 841-8400; fax (703) 841-8406; f. 1918; 4,175 mems; Pres. MICHAEL BALY, III.

**American Petroleum Institute:** 1220 L St NW, Washington, DC 20005; tel. (202) 682-8000; telex 8229586; fax (202) 682-8232; f. 1919; 300 corporate mems; Chair. K. T. DERR; Pres. CHARLES J. DIBONA.

**Coal Exporters' Association of the US, Inc:** 1130 17th St, NW, Washington, DC 20036; tel. (202) 463-2639; fax (202) 833-9636; f. 1945; 35 mems; Exec. Dir MOYA PHELLEPS.

**Independent Petroleum Association of America:** 1101 16th St, NW, Washington, DC 20036; tel. (201) 857-4722; fax (202) 857-4799; f. 1929; 6,000 mems; Pres. DENISE BADE.

**National Mining Association:** 1130 17th St, NW, Washington, DC 20036; tel. (202) 463-2625; f. 1995 by merger; 395 mems; Pres. RICHARD L. LAWSON.

**National Petroleum Refiners Association:** 1899 L St, NW, Suite 1000, Washington, DC 20036; tel. (202) 457-0480; fax (202) 457-0486; f. 1902; 420 mems; Pres. URVAN R. STERNFELS.

**Western States Petroleum Association:** 509 North Brand Blvd, Suite 1400, Glendale, CA 91203-1925; tel. (818) 545-4105; fax (818) 545-0954; f. 1907; 60 mems; Exec. Dir DOUGLAS F. HENDERSON.

### Printing and Publishing
(see also Publishers)

**Binding Industries of America:** 70 East Lake St, Chicago, IL 60601-5907; tel. (312) 372-7606; fax (312) 704-5025; f. 1955; 340 mems; Exec. Dir JAMES R. NIESEN.

**Book Manufacturers' Institute Inc:** 45 William St, Suite 245, Wellesley, MA 02181-4007; tel. (617) 239-0013; fax (617) 239-0106; f. 1920; 90 mems; Exec. Vice-Pres. STEPHEN P. SNYDER.

**National Association of Printers & Lithographers:** 780 Palisade Ave, Teaneck, NJ 07666-3129; tel. (201) 342-7000; fax (201) 692-0286; 3,700 mems; Pres. I. GREGG VAN WERT.

**Printing Industries of America, Inc:** 100 Daingerfield Rd, Alexandria, VA 22314; tel. (703) 519-8100; fax (703) 548-3227; f. 1887; 14,000 mems; Pres. RAY ROPER.

### Public Utilities

**American Public Gas Association:** 11094-D Lee Highway, Suite 102, Fairfax, VA 22030; tel. (703) 352-3890; fax (703) 352-1271; f. 1961; 430 mems; Dir ROBERT S. CAVE.

**American Public Power Association:** 2301 M St, NW, 3rd Floor, Washington, DC 20037-1484; tel. (202) 467-2900; fax (202) 467-2910; f. 1940; 1,750 mems; Exec. Dir LARRY HOBART.

**American Public Works Association:** 106 West 11th St, Suite 1800, Kansas City, MO 64105-1806; tel. (816) 472-6100; fax (816) 472-1610; f. 1894; 28,000 mems; Exec. Dir WILLIAM J. BERTERA.

**American Water Works Association:** 6666 West Quincy Ave, Denver, CO 80235-3098; tel. (303) 794-7711; telex 450895; fax (303) 794-7310; f. 1881; 53,000 mems; Exec. Dir JOHN B. MANNION.

### Rubber

**Rubber Manufacturers Association:** 1400 K St, NW, Suite 900, Washington, DC 20005-2043; tel. (202) 682-4800; telex 892666; fax (202) 682-4854; f. 1915; 156 mems; Pres. THOMAS E. COLE.

**Rubber Trade Association of North America, Inc:** 220 Maple Ave, POB 196, Rockville Centre, NY 11571-0196; tel. (516) 536-7228; fax (516) 536-2251; f. 1914; 39 mems; Sec. F. B. FINLEY.

### Stone, Clay and Glass Products

**Glass Association of North America:** 3310 SW Harrison St, Topeka, KS 66611-2279; Tel. (913) 266-7013; f. 1949; 125 mems; Exec. Vice-Pres. WILLIAM J. BIRCH.

# THE UNITED STATES OF AMERICA

**National Aggregates Association:** 900 Spring St, Silver Spring, MD 20910; tel. (301) 587-1400; fax (301) 585-4219; f. 1911; 500 mems; Pres. VINCENT P. AHEARN, Jr.

**National Glass Association:** 8200 Greensboro Drive, Suite 302, McLean, VA 22102-3881; tel. (703) 442-4890; fax (703) 442-0630; f. 1948; 4,400 mems.; Pres. and CEO PHILIP J. JAMES.

**National Stone Association:** 1415 Elliot Place, NW, Washington, DC 20007; tel. (202) 342-1100; fax (202) 342-0702; f. 1985; 575 mems; Pres. ROBERT G. BARTLETT.

## Textiles

**American Apparel Manufacturers Association:** 2500 Wilson Blvd, Suite 301, Arlington, VA 22201; tel. (703) 524-1864; fax (703) 522-6741; f. 1962; 815 mems; Pres. G. STEWART BOSWELL.

**American Fiber Manufacturers Association Inc:** 1150 17th St, NW, Suite 310, Washington, DC 20036; tel. (202) 296-6508; fax (202) 296-3052; 17 mems; Pres. PAUL T. O'DAY.

**American Textile Manufacturers Institute, Inc:** 1801 K St, NW, Suite 900, Washington, DC 20006-1301; tel. (202) 862-0500; fax (202) 862-0570; f. 1949; 250 mems; Exec. Vice-Pres. CARLOS MOORE.

**Apparel Retailers of America:** 2011 Eye St, NW, Washington, DC 20006-1833; tel. (202) 347-1932; fax (202) 457-0386; f. 1916; 1,200 mems; Exec. Dir DOUGLAS W. WIEGAND.

**The Custom Tailors and Designers Association of America, Inc:** 17 East 45th St, New York, NY 10017; tel. (212) 661-1960; f. 1881; 350 mems; Exec. Dir IRMA B. LIPKIN.

**Knitted Textile Association:** 386 Park Ave South, Suite 901, New York, NY 10016; tel. (212) 689-3807; fax (212) 889-6160; f. 1965; 140 mems; Exec. Dir DAVID HERRICK.

**Knitwear Employers Association:** 75 Livingston St, Brooklyn, NY 11201; tel. (718) 875-2300; f. 1959; 40 mems.

**National Knitwear and Sportswear Association:** 386 Park Ave South, New York, NY 10016; tel. (212) 683-7520; telex 239801; fax (212) 532-0766; f. 1918; 600 mems; Exec. Dir SETH M. BODNER.

**Northern Textile Association:** 230 Congress St, Boston, MA 02110; tel. (617) 542-8220; fax (617) 542-2199; f. 1854; 300 mems; Pres. KARL SPILHAUS.

**United Infants' and Children's Wear Association Inc:** 1328 Broadway, Suite 814, New York, NY 10001; tel. (212) 244-2953; f. 1933; 50 mems; Pres. ALAN D. LUBELL.

**Wool Manufacturers Council:** 230 Congress St, Boston, MA 02110; tel. (617) 542-8220; fax (617) 542-2199; f. 1956; 30 mems; Chair. JOHN P. BISHOP.

## Transport

**Aerospace Industries Association of America, Inc:** 1250 Eye St, NW, Suite 1100, Washington, DC 20005; tel. (202) 371-8400; fax (202) 371-8470; f. 1919; 50 mems; Pres. DON FUQUA.

**Air Transport Association of America:** see Civil Aviation—Association.

**American Automobile Manufacturers Association:** 1401 H St, NW, Suite 900, Washington, DC 20005; tel. (202) 326-5500; fax (202) 326-5567; f. 1913; 7 mems; Pres. ANDREW CARD.

**American Bureau of Shipping:** see Ocean Shipping—Associations.

**American Bus Association:** 1100 New York Ave, NW, Suite 1050, Washington, DC 20005-2934; tel. (202) 842-1645; fax (202) 842-0850; f. 1926; 3,000 mems; Pres. and CEO GEORGE T. SNYDER, Jr.

**American Institute of Merchant Shipping:** see Ocean Shipping—Associations.

**American Public Transit Association:** 1201 New York Ave, NW, Suite 400, Washington, DC 20005-3917; tel. (202) 898-4000; fax (202) 898-4070; f. 1974; 1,000 mems; Exec. Vice-Pres. JACK R. GILSTRAP.

**American Short Line Railroad Association:** see Principal Railways—Associations.

**American Trucking Associations:** 2200 Mill Rd, Alexandria, VA 22314-4654; tel. (703) 838-1700; fax (703) 684-5720; f. 1933; 4,100 mems; Pres. and CEO THOMAS J. DONOHUE.

**Association of American Railroads:** see Principal Railways—Associations.

**National Automobile Dealers Association:** 8400 Westpark Drive, McLean, VA 22102-3522; tel. (703) 821-7407; fax (703) 821-7075; f. 1917; 19,000 mems; Exec. Vice-Pres. FRANK E. MCCARTHY.

**Shipbuilders Council of America:** 4301 North Fairfax Drive, Suite 330, Arlington, VA 22203; tel. (703) 276-1700; fax (703) 276-1707; f. 1920; 70 mems; Pres. JOHN J. STOCKER.

## Miscellaneous

**American Advertising Federation:** 1101 Vermont Ave, NW, Suite 500, Washington, DC 20005; tel. (202) 898-0089; fax (202) 898-0159; f. 1967; 52,000 mems; Pres. WALLIE SNYDER.

**American Association of Exporters and Importers:** 11 West 42nd St, 30th Floor, New York, NY 10036-8002; tel. (212) 944-2230; fax (212) 382-2606; f. 1921; 1,200 mems; Pres. EUGENE J. MILOSH.

**American Farm Bureau Federation:** 225 West Touhy Ave, Park Ridge, IL 60068-4202; tel. (312) 399-5700; fax (312) 399-5896; f. 1919; 4.4m. mems; Pres. DEAN R. KLECKNER.

**American Management Association:** 135 West 50th St, New York, NY 10020-1201; tel. (212) 586-8100; fax (212) 903-8168; f. 1923; 70,000 corporate and individual mems; Pres. and CEO DAVID FAGIANO.

**American Marketing Association:** 250 South Wacker Drive, Suite 200, Chicago, IL 60606-5834; tel. (312) 648-0536; fax (312) 993-7542; 53,000 mems; Chief Operating Officer DENNIS JORGENSEN.

**American Society of Association Executives:** 1575 Eye St, NW, Washington, DC 20005-1168; tel. (202) 626-2723; fax (202) 371-8825; f. 1920; 21,000 mems; Pres. R. WILLIAM TAYLOR.

**Farmers Educational and Cooperative Union of America (National Farmers Union):** 10065 East Harvard Ave, Denver, CO 80231-5964; tel. (303) 337-5500; fax (303) 368-1390; f. 1902; 250,000 mems; Pres. LELAND SWENSON.

**Motion Picture Association of America, Inc:** 1600 Eye St, NW, Washington, DC 20006; tel. (202) 293-1966; fax (202) 452-9823; f. 1922; 9 mems; Pres. JACK J. VALENTI.

**National Association of Manufacturers:** 1331 Pennsylvania Ave, NW, Suite 1500-N, Washington, DC 20004-1790; tel. (202) 637-3000; fax (202) 637-3182; f. 1895; 13,500 mems; Pres. JERRY J. JASINOWSKI.

**National Association of Purchasing Management:** 2055 East Centennial Circle, POB 22160, Tempe, AZ 85285-2160; tel. (602) 752-6276; fax (602) 752-7890; f. 1915; 36,000 mems; Exec. Vice-Pres. R. JERRY BAKER.

**National Association of Realtors:** 430 North Michigan Ave, Suite 500, Chicago, IL 60611-4087; tel. (312) 329-8200; fax (312) 329-8576; f. 1908; 805,000 mems; Exec. Vice-Pres. ALMON R. SMITH.

**National Cooperative Business Association:** 1401 New York Ave, NW, Suite 1100, Washington, DC 20005-2160; tel. (202) 638-6222; fax (202) 638-1374; f. 1916; 350 mems; Pres. and CEO RUSSELL C. NOTAR.

**National Farmers Organization:** 2505 Elwood Drive, Ames, IA 50010-2000; tel. (515) 292-2000; fax (515) 292-7106; f. 1955; Pres. RAYMOND A. OLSON.

**National Retail Federation:** 325 7th St, NW, Suite 1000, Washington, DC 20004; tel. (202) 783-7941; fax (202) 737-2849; f. 1911; 55,000 mems; Pres. TRACY MULLIN.

**Tobacco Institute:** 1875 Eye St, NW, Suite 800, Washington, DC 20006-5470; tel. (202) 457-4800; fax (202) 457-9350; f. 1958; 11 mems; Pres. SAMUEL CHILCOTE.

### TRADE UNIONS

In 1985 there were 175 trade unions, of which 93 were affiliated to the American Federation of Labor and Congress of Industrial Organizations (AFL-CIO). In 1991 there were approximately 16.6m. union members in the USA, representing 16.1% of the civilian labour force.

Many trade unions based in the USA have members throughout North America. Almost 37% of Canada's trade union members belong to unions having headquarters in the USA.

**American Federation of Labor and Congress of Industrial Organizations (AFL-CIO):** 815 16th St, NW, Washington, DC 20006; tel. (202) 637-5000; fax (202) 637-5058; f. 1955; Pres. THOMAS DONAHUE (designate); Sec.-Treas. (vacant); 90 affiliated unions with total membership of 13.3m. (1994).

### AFL-CIO Affiliates
(with 50,000 members and over)

**Associated Actors and Artistes of America:** 165 West 46th St, New York, NY 10036; tel. (212) 869-0358; fax (212) 869-1746; f. 1919; Pres. THEODORE BIKEL; International Exec. Sec. JOHN C. HALL, Jr; mems: 9 nat. unions representing 220,000 mems (1990).

**Aluminum, Brick and Glass Workers International Union:** 3362 Hollenberg Drive, Bridgeton, MO 63044; tel. (314) 739-6142; fax (314) 739-1216; f. 1982; Pres. ERNIE J. LABAFF; 51,800 mems (1991).

**Automobile, Aerospace and Agricultural Implement Workers of America, United:** 8000 East Jefferson Ave, Detroit, MI 48214; tel. (313) 926-5000; fax (313) 832-6016; f. 1935; Pres. OWEN F. BIEBER; Sec.-Treas. BILL CASSTEVENS; 1m. mems (1991).

**Bakery, Confectionery and Tobacco Workers' International Union:** 10401 Connecticut Ave, Kensington, MD 20895; tel. (301) 933-8600; f. 1886; Pres. FRANK HURT; Sec.-Treas. GENE MCDONALD; 135,000 mems (1992).

# THE UNITED STATES OF AMERICA

**Boilermakers, Iron Ship Builders, Blacksmiths, Forgers and Helpers, International Brotherhood of:** 753 State Ave, Suite 570, Kansas City, KS 66101; tel. (913) 371-2640; fax (913) 371-5335; f. 1880; Pres. CHARLES W. JONES; Sec.-Treas. JERRY Z. WILLBURN; 95,000 mems (1991).

**Bricklayers and Allied Craftsmen, International Union of:** 815 15th St, NW, Washington, DC 20005; tel. (202) 783-3788; fax (202) 393-0219; f. 1865; Pres. JOHN T. JOYCE; Sec.-Treas. L. GERALD CARLISLE; 106,000 mems (1991).

**Bridge, Structural and Ornamental Iron Workers, International Association of:** 1750 New York Ave, NW, Suite 400, Washington, DC 20006; tel. (202) 383-4810; fax (202) 638-4856; f. 1896; Pres. JAKE WEST; Gen. Sec. LEROY E. WORLEY; 130,000 mems (1993).

**Carpenters and Joiners of America, United Brotherhood of:** 101 Constitution Ave, NW, Washington, DC 20001; tel. (202) 546-6206; fax (202) 543-5724; f. 1881; Pres. SIGURD LUCASSEN; Sec. JAMES T. PATTERSON; 500,000 mems (1993).

**International Chemical Workers' Union:** 1655 West Market St, Akron, OH 44313; tel. (216) 867-2444; fax (216) 867-0544; f. 1944; Pres. FRANK D. MARTINO; Sec.-Treas. E. ROBERT MARLOW; 50,000 mems (1991).

**Civil Service Employees Association, Inc:** 143 Washington Ave, Albany, NY 12210; tel. (518) 434-0191; fax (518) 436-0398; f. 1910; Pres. DANNY DONOHUE; 220,000 mems (1990).

**Amalgamated Clothing and Textile Workers Union:** 15 Union Sq. West, New York, NY 10003; tel. (212) 242-0700; fax (212) 255-7230; f. 1976; Pres. JACK SHEINKMAN; Sec.-Treas. ARTHUR LOEVY; 273,000 mems (1991).

**Communications Workers of America:** 501 Third St, NW, Washington, DC 20001; tel. (202) 434-1100; fax (202) 434-1279; f. 1939; Pres. MORTON BAHR; Sec.-Treas. BARBARA J. EASTERLING; 700,000 mems (1992).

**Electrical Workers, International Brotherhood of:** 1125 15th St, NW, Washington, DC 20005; tel. (202) 833-7000; fax (202) 467-6316; f. 1891; Pres. J. J. BARRY; Sec. JACK F. MOORE; 900,000 mems (1991).

**Electronic, Electrical, Technical, Salaried, Machine and Furniture Workers, International Union of (IUE):** 1126 16th St, NW, Washington, DC 20036; tel. (202) 296-1200; fax (202) 785-4563; f. 1949; Pres. WILLIAM H. BYWATER; Sec.-Treas. EDWARD FIRE; 160,000 mems (1991).

**Fire Fighters, International Association of:** 1750 New York Ave, NW, Washington, DC 20006-5395; tel. (202) 737-8484; f. 1918; Pres. ALFRED K. WHITEHEAD; Sec.-Treas. VINCENT J. BOLLON; 195,000 mems (1991).

**United Food and Commercial Workers International Union:** 1775 K St, NW, Washington, DC 20006; tel. (202) 223-3111; f. 1979; Int. Pres. DOUGLAS H. DORITY; Int. Sec.-Treas. JERRY MENAPACE; 1.3m. mems (1991).

**Glass Molders, Pottery, Plastics & Allied Workers International Union, AFL-CIO, CLC:** 608 East Baltimore Pike, POB 607, Media, PA 19063; tel. (215) 565-5051; f. 1842; Pres. FRANK W. CARTER; Sec.-Treas. JAMES H. RANKIN; 90,000 mems (1991).

**Government Employees, American Federation of:** 80 F St, NW, Washington, DC, 20001; tel. (202) 737-8700; fax (202) 639-6441; f. 1932; Nat. Pres. JOHN N. STURDIVANT; Nat. Sec.-Treas. BOBBY L. HARNAGE; 172,000 mems (1991).

**Graphic Communications International Union:** 1900 L St, NW, Washington, DC 20036; tel. (202) 462-1400; fax (202) 331-9516; f. 1983; Pres. JAMES J. NORTON; Sec.-Treas. GUY DEVITO; 183,000 mems (1991).

**Hotel Employees & Restaurant Employees International Union:** 1219 28th St, NW, Washington, DC 20007; tel. (202) 393-4373; fax (202) 333-0468; f. 1891; Pres. EDWARD T. HENLEY; Sec.-Treas. HERMAN LEAVITT; 330,000 mems (1991).

**Allied Industrial Workers of America, International Union:** 1475, Nashville, TN 37202-1475, POB; f. 1935; Int. Pres. NICK SERRAGLIO; Sec.-Treas. KEITH R. KIRCHNER; 50,00 mems (1993).

**Laborers' International Union of North America:** 905 16th St, NW, Washington, DC 20006; tel. (202) 737-8320; fax (202) 867-0544; f. 1903; Pres. ARTHUR A. COIA; Gen. Sec.-Treas. JAMES J. NORWOOD; 500,000 mems (1991).

**Ladies' Garment Workers' Union, International:** 1710 Broadway, New York, NY 10019; tel. (212) 265-7000; f. 1900; Pres. JAY MAZUR; 175,000 mems (1991).

**Letter Carriers, National Association of:** 100 Indiana Ave, NW, Washington, DC 20001; tel. (202) 393-4695; fax (202) 737-1540; f. 1889; Pres. VINCENT R. SOMBROTTO; Sec.-Treas. WILLIAM R. YATES; 311,000 mems (1991).

**International Longshoremen's Association:** 17 Battery Place, Room 1530, New York, NY 10004; tel. (212) 425-1200; f. 1892; Pres. JOHN BOWERS; Sec.-Treas. HARRY R. HASSELGREN; 77,000 mems (1991).

**Longshoremen's and Warehousemen's Union, International:** 1188 Franklin St, San Francisco, CA 94109; tel. (415) 775-0533; f. 1937; Pres. DAVID ARIAN; Sec.-Treas. CURTIS MCCLAIN; 55,000 mems (1991).

**Machinists and Aerospace Workers, International Association of:** 9000 Machinists Place, Upper Marboro, MD 20772; tel. (301) 967-4500; f. 1888; Int. Pres. GEORGE J. KOURPIAS; Gen. Sec.-Treas. TOM DUCY; 827,000 mems (1991).

**Maintenance of Way Employes, Brotherhood of:** 26555 Evergreen Rd, Suite 200, Southfield, MI 48076-4225; tel. (810) 948-1010; fax (810) 948-7150; f. 1887; Pres. MAC A. FLEMING; Sec.-Treas. WILIAM E. LARUE; 75,000 mems (1991).

**Musicians of the United States and Canada, American Federation of:** 1501 Broadway, Suite 600, New York, NY 10036; tel. (212) 869-1330; fax (212) 764-6134; f. 1896; Pres. MARK TULLY MASSAGLI; Sec.-Treas. STEPHEN R. SPRAGUE; 206,000 mems (1991).

**Office and Professional Employees International Union:** 265 West 14th St, Suite 610, New York, NY 10011; tel. (212) 675-3210; telex 3202918; fax (212) 727-3466; f. 1945; Int. Pres. JOHN KELLY; Sec.-Treas. GILLES BEAUREGARD; 135,000 mems (1991).

**Oil, Chemical and Atomic Workers International Union, (AFL-CIO):** POB 281200, Denver, CO 80228-8200; tel. (303) 987-2229; fax (303) 987-1967; f. 1918; Pres. ROBERT E. WAGES; Sec.-Treas. ANTHONY MAZZOCCHI; 100,000 mems (1991).

**Operating Engineers, International Union of:** 1125 17th St, NW, Washington, DC 20036; tel. (202) 429-9100; fax (202) 429-0316; f. 1896; Gen. Pres. FRANK HANLEY; 375,000 mems (1991).

**Painters and Allied Trades, International Brotherhood of:** 1750 New York Ave, NW, Washington, DC 20006; tel. (202) 637-0720; f. 1887; Gen. Pres. A. L. MONROE; Sec.-Treas. ROBERT PETERSDORF; 149,000 mems (1991).

**Paperworkers International Union, United:** POB 1475, Nashville, TN 37202; tel. (615) 834-8590; fax (615) 834-7741; f. 1884; Pres. WAYNE E. GLENN; Sec.-Treas. NICHOLAS C. VRATARIC; 230,000 mems (1991).

**Journeymen and Apprentices of the Plumbing and Pipe Fitting Industry of the United States and Canada, United Association of:** POB 37800, Washington, DC 20013; tel. (202) 628-5823; fax (202) 628-5024; f. 1889; Pres. MARVIN J. BOEDE; Sec.-Treas. MARION A. LEE; 325,000 mems (1991).

**Plasterers' and Cement Masons' International Association of the USA and Canada, Operative:** 1125 17th St, NW, Washington, DC 20036; tel. (202) 393-6569; fax (202) 393-2514; Gen. Pres. DOMINIC A. MARTELL; 65,000 mems (1991).

**Postal Workers Union, American:** 1300 L St, NW, Washington, DC 20005; tel. (202) 842-4200; fax (202) 842-8530; f. 1971; Pres. MORRIS BILLER; Sec.-Treas. DOUGLAS C. HOLBROOK; 330,000 mems (1991).

**Retail, Wholesale and Department Store Union:** 30 East 29th St, New York, NY 10016; tel. (212) 684-5300; fax (212) 779-2809; f. 1937; Pres. LENORE MILLER; Sec.-Treas. GUY DICKINSON; 140,000 mems (1993).

**United Rubber, Cork, Linoleum and Plastic Workers of America:** 570 White Pond Drive, Akron, OH 44320; tel. (216) 869-0320; fax (216) 869-5627; f. 1935; Pres. KENNETH L. COSS; Sec.-Treas. GLENN ELLISON; 100,000 mems (1991).

**Screen Actors Guild:** 5757 Wilshire Blvd, Los Angeles, CA 90036; tel. (213) 954-1600; fax (213) 549-6656; f. 1933; Pres. BARRY GORDON; Nat. Exec. Dir KEN ORSATTI; 78,000 mems (1993).

**Seafarers International Union of North America:** 5201 Auth Way, Camp Springs, MD 20746; tel. (301) 899-0675; fax (301) 899-7355; f. 1938; Pres. MICHAEL SACCO; Sec.-Treas. JOHN FAY; 85,000 mems (1991).

**Service Employees' International Union (SEIU):** 1313 L St, NW, Washington, DC 20005; tel. (202) 898-3200; fax (202) 898-3403; f. 1921; Pres. JOHN J. SWEENEY; Sec.-Treas. RICHARD W. CORDTZ; 1.1m. mems (1995).

**Sheet Metal Workers' International Association:** 1750 New York Ave, NW, Washington, DC 20006; tel. (202) 783-5880; fax (202) 662-0894; f. 1888; Gen. Pres. ARTHUR MOORE; Sec.-Treas. MICHAEL J. SULLIVAN; 150,000 mems (1991).

**State, County and Municipal Employees, American Federation of:** 1625 L St, NW, Washington, DC 20036; tel. (202) 429-1000; telex 892376; fax (202) 429-1293; f. 1936; Pres. GERALD W. MCENTEE; Sec.-Treas. WILLIAM LUCY; 1.3m. mems (1995).

**United Steelworkers of America:** 5 Gateway Center, Pittsburgh, PA 15222; tel. (412) 562-2400; fax (412) 562-2445; f. 1936; Int. Pres. LYNN R. WILLIAMS; Sec. EDGAR L. BALL; 750,000 mems (1991).

**Teachers, American Federation of:** 555 New Jersey Ave, NW, Washington, DC 20001; tel. (202) 879-4400; telex 8220009; fax (202) 879-4545; f. 1916; Pres. ALBERT SHANKER; Sec.-Treas. EDWARD J. MCELROY; 800,000 mems (1992).

# THE UNITED STATES OF AMERICA

**Teamsters, International Brotherhood of:** 25 Louisiana Ave, NW, Washington, DC 20001; tel. (202) 624-6800; f. 1903; Pres. RONALD CAREY; Gen. Sec.-Treas. TOM SEVER; 1.6m. mems (1991).

**Television and Radio Artists, American Federation of:** 260 Madison Ave, 7th Floor, New York, NY 10016-2401; tel. (212) 532-0800; fax (212) 921-8454; f. 1937; Exec. Dir BRUCE A. YORK; 67,000 mems (1991).

**Theatrical Stage Employees and Moving Picture Machine Operators of the US and Canada, International Alliance of:** 1515 Broadway, Suite 601, New York, NY 10036; tel. (212) 730-1770; fax (212) 921-7699; f. 1893; Pres. THOMAS C. SHORT; Sec.-Treas. MICHAEL W. PROSCIA; 61,000 mems (1991).

**Amalgamated Transit Union:** 5025 Wisconsin Ave, NW, Washington, DC 20016; tel. (202) 537-1645; fax (202) 244-7824; f. 1892; Int. Pres. JOHN W. ROWLAND; 165,000 mems (1991).

**Transport Workers Union of America:** 80 West End Ave, New York, NY 10023; tel. (212) 873-6000; f. 1934; Int. Pres. JOHN E. LAWE; Sec.-Treas. GEORGE LEITZ; 100,000 mems (1991).

**Transportation Communications International Union:** 3 Research Place, Rockville, MD 20850; tel. (301) 948-4910; fax (301) 330-7661; f. 1899; Pres. ROBERT A. SCARDELLETTI; Sec.-Treas. D. A. BOBO; 128,000 mems (1991).

**Utility Workers Union of America AFL-CIO:** 815 16th St, NW, Room 605, Washington, DC 20006; tel. (202) 347-8105; fax (202) 347-4872; f. 1945; Pres. MARSHALL M. HICKS; Sec.-Treas. JOHN M. WALSH; 55,000 mems (1993).

### Independent Unions
(with 50,000 members and over)

**National Education Association of the United States:** 1201 16th St, NW, Washington, DC 20036; tel. (202) 833-4000; fax (202) 822-7974; f. 1857; Pres. KEITH GEIGER; Exec. Dir DON CAMERON; 2m. mems (1991).

**National Federation of Federal Employees:** 1016 16th St, NW, Suite 300, Washington, DC 20036; tel. (202) 862-4400; fax (202) 862-4432; f. 1917; Pres. SHEILA K. VELAZCO; Sec.-Treas. ABRAHAM ORLOFSKY; 60,000 mems (1991).

**International Brotherhood of Locomotive Engineers:** 1370 Ontario Ave, Mezzanine, Cleveland, OH 44113-1702; tel. (216) 241-2630; fax (216) 241-6516; f. 1863; Pres. RONALD P. MCLAUGHLIN; Gen. Sec.-Treas. JOHN D. RINEHART; 55,000 mems (1991).

**United Mine Workers of America, International Union:** 900 15th St, NW, Washington, DC 20005; tel. (202) 842-7200; f. 1890; Int. Pres. RICHARD TRUMKA; Sec.-Treas. JERRY D. JONES; 186,000 mems (1993).

**American Nurses Association:** 600 Maryland Ave, SW, Suite 100 West, Washington, DC 20024-2571; tel. (202) 651-7000; fax (202) 651-7001; f. 1896; Pres. VIRGINIA TROTTER BETTS; Exec. Dir GERALDINE MARULLO; 53 constituent state asscns comprising 210,000 mems (1994).

**National Fraternal Order of Police:** 1410 Donelson Pike, A17, Nashville, TN 37217-2933; Nat. Pres. DEWEY STOKES; Nat. Sec. CHARLES R. ORMS; 225,000 mems (1991).

**National Alliance of Postal and Federal Employees:** 1628 11th St, NW, Washington, DC 20001; tel. (202) 939-6325; fax (202) 939-6389; f. 1913; Nat. Pres. ROBERT L. WHITE; 90,000 mems (1990).

**National Rural Letter Carriers' Association:** 1630 Duke St, 4th Floor, Alexandria, VA 22314-3465; tel. (703) 684-5545; f. 1903; Pres. SCOTTIE B. HICKS; 87,000 mems (1995).

**United Transportation Union:** 14600 Detroit Ave, Cleveland, OH 44107-4250; tel. (216) 228-9400; fax (216) 228-5755; f. 1969; Pres. FRED A. HARDIN; Sec.-Treas. THOMAS J. MCGUIRE; 100,000 mems (1991).

**Treasury Employees Union, National:** 901 E St, NW, Suite 600, Washington, DC 20004; tel. (202) 783-4444; fax (202) 783-4085; f. 1938; Nat. Pres. ROBERT M. TOBIAS; 140,000 mems (1991).

## Transport

**Federal Railroad Administration:** US Dept of Transportation, 400 Seventh St, SW, Washington, DC 20590; tel. (202) 366-4000; (202) 366-7009; formulates federal railway policies and administers and enforces safety regulations; Admin. JOLENE M. MOLITORIS.

**Interstate Commerce Commission:** 12th St and Constitution Ave, NW, Washington, DC 20423-0001; tel. (202) 927-7600; fax (202) 927-5984; f. 1887; federal body with regulatory authority over domestic surface common carriers; jurisdiction extends over rail, inland waterways and motorized traffic; Chair. LINDA J. MORGAN.

**National Transportation Safety Board:** 490 L'Enfant Plaza East, SW, Washington, DC 20594; tel. (202) 382-6600; fax (202) 382-6715; f. 1975; seeks to ensure that all types of transportation in the USA are conducted safely; carries out studies and accident investigations; Chair. C. W. VOGT.

### PRINCIPAL RAILWAYS

**Alaska Railroad Corpn:** POB 107500, Anchorage, AK 99510-7500; tel. (907) 265-2468; fax (907) 258-1456; f. 1912; independent corpn owned by the State of Alaska; year-round freight service and summer passenger service; Pres. and CEO ROBERT S. HATFIELD, Jr; 846 track-km.

**Amtrak (National Railroad Passenger Corpn):** 60 Massachusetts Ave, NE, Washington, DC 20002; tel. (202) 906-3000; fax (202) 906-3865; f. 1970; govt-funded public corpn operating inter-city passenger services over 38,000 track-km in 43 states; Chair. and Pres. THOMAS DOWNS.

**Atchison, Topeka and Sante Fe Railway:** 1700 East Golf Rd, Schaumburg, IL 60173-5860; tel. (708) 995-6000; fax (312) 995-6219; Chair. R. D. KREBS; Pres. M. R. HAVERTY; 14,078 track-km.

**Burlington Northern Railroad Co:** 777 Main St, Fort Worth, TX 76102; tel. (817) 878-2000; Pres. and CEO GERALD GRINSTEIN; 37,348 track-km.

**Chicago and North Western Transportation Co:** 165 North Canal, Chicago, IL 60606; tel. (312) 559-7000; fax (312) 559-6495; Chair., Pres. and CEO R. W. SCHMIEGE; 8,995 track-km.

**Conrail (Consolidated Rail Corpn):** 2001 Market St, Philadelphia, PA 19101-1401; tel. (215) 209-2000; fax (215) 209-1338; f. 1975 by federal govt merger of six bankrupt freight carriers in the midwest and north-east regions; returned to private-sector ownership in 1987; Chair., Pres. and CEO JAMES A. HAGEN; 20,434 track-km.

**CSX Transportation Inc (Rail Transport):** 500 Water St, Jacksonville, FL 32202, tel. (904) 359-3100; fax (904) 359-1899; f. 1980 by merger; Pres. and CEO ALVIN R. CARPENTER; 30,248 track-km.

**Guilford Transportation Industries—Rail Division:** Iron Horse Park, North Billerica, MA 01862; tel. (508) 663-1030; telex 951864; fax (508) 663-1199; Chair., Pres. and CEO D. A. FINK; 3,516 track-km.

**Illinois Central Railroad:** 455 Cityfront Plaza Drive, Chicago, IL 60611; tel. (312) 755-7500; fax (312) 755-7839; f. 1851; Chair. and CEO E. L. MOYERS; 4,452 track-km.

**Kansas City Southern Railway Co:** 114 West 11th St, Kansas City, MO 64105; tel. (816) 556-0303; telex 42327; fax (816) 556-0297; Chair. L. H. ROWLAND; Pres. G. W. EDWARDS; 2,561 track-km.

**Long Island Rail Road Co:** Jamaica Station, Jamaica, NY 11435; tel. (212) 990-7400; fax (212) 990-8212; f. 1834; Pres. C. HOPPE; 435 track-km.

**Norfolk Southern Corpn:** NS Tower, Three Commercial Place, Norfolk, VA 23510-2191; tel. (804) 629-2600; fax (804) 629-2822; f. 1894; Chair., Pres. and CEO D. R. GOODE; 23,691 track-km.

**Southern Pacific Lines:** One Market Plaza, San Francisco, CA 94105; tel. (415) 541-1000; fax (415) 541-1929; Chair. P. F. ANSCHUTZ; Pres. and CEO E. L. MOYERS; 37,475 track-km.

**Union Pacific Railroad Co:** 1416 Dodge St, Omaha NE 68179; tel. (402) 271-5000; telex 484491; fax (402) 271-5572; f. 1897; division of Union Pacific Corpn; Chair. and CEO DREW LEWIS; Pres. RICHARD DAVIDSON; 35,208 track-km.

### Associations

**American Short Line Railroad Association:** 1120 G St, NW, Suite 520, Washington, DC 20005; tel. (202) 628-4500; fax (202) 628-6430; f. 1913; Pres. WILLIAM E. LOFTUS; 630 mems.

**Association of American Railroads:** 50 F St, NW, Washington, DC 20001; tel. (202) 639-2100; telex 62899732; fax (202) 639-2986; f. 1934; Pres. and CEO WILLIAM DEMPSEY; 71 mems, representing virtually all major railroads in the USA, Canada and Mexico.

### ROADS

In 1992 there were 6,227,859 km of roads, of which 86,818 km were motorways and 654,052 km were other main or national roads. In 1992 an estimated 58.8% of all roads were paved.

**Federal Highway Administration:** US Dept of Transportation, 400 Seventh St, SW, Washington, DC 20590; tel. (202) 366-0650; fax (202) 366-7239; implements federal highway policy and promotes road safety; Admin. RODNEY E. SLATER.

### INLAND WATERWAYS

**St Lawrence Seaway Corpn:** US Dept of Transportation, POB 44090, Washington, DC 20026-4090; tel. (202) 366-0091; responsible for the international maintenance of sections of the St Lawrence Seaway within the territorial limits of the USA.

THE UNITED STATES OF AMERICA *Directory*

### Principal Companies

**American Commercial Lines:** CSX Corpn, One James Center, POB C-32222, Richmond, VA 23261; tel. (804) 782-1400; operates barge services along c. 24,000 km of the Mississippi and Ohio rivers and tributaries to the Gulf Intracoastal Waterway; Pres. and CEO H. JOSEPH BOBIZEN, Jr; fleet of 2,400 barges and 96 towboats.

**American Steamship Co:** 3200 Marine Midland Center, Buffalo, NY 14203; tel. (716) 854-7644; fax (716) 854-7473; f. 1907; Pres. and CEO NED A. SMITH; 17 self-unloading cargo vessels on the Great Lakes.

**Erie Sand and Gravel, Inc:** Foot of Sassafras St, POB 179, Erie, PA 16512; tel. (814) 453-6721; Pres. S. E. SMITH, Jr; 2 vessels.

**Great Lakes Dredge & Dock Co:** 2122 York Rd, Oak Brook, IL 60521; tel. (708) 574-3000; fax (708) 574-2909; f. 1890; dredging, marine construction and reclamation; operates tugboats, drillboats, carfloats, barges and dredges; Man. (International Business) WILLIAM HANNUM; 149 vessels.

**Inland Lakes Management, Inc:** POB 646, Alpena, MI 49707; tel. (517) 354-2232; Pres. JAMES W. GASKELL; 7 vessels.

**Interlake Steamship Co:** 629 Euclid Ave, Suite 400, Cleveland, OH 44114; tel. (216) 694-4008; Man. J. O. GREENWOOD; 11 vessels.

**Oglebay Norton Co Marine Transportation Division:** 1100 Superior Ave, Cleveland, OH 44114-2598; tel. (216) 861-3300; fax (216) 861-2863; services on the Great Lakes; Chair. and Pres. R. THOMAS GREEN, Jr; 13 vessels.

**United States Steel Great Lakes Fleet, Inc:** Missabe Bldg, Room 400, Duluth, MN 55802; tel. (218) 723-2460; telex 5610050; Pres. W. B. BUHRMANN; 10 vessels.

### Associations

**American Waterways Operators:** 1600 Wilson Blvd, Suite 1000, Arlington, VA 22209; tel. (703) 841-9300; fax (703) 841-0389; f. 1944; 305 mems; Pres. THOMAS A. ALLEGRETTI.

**Lake Carriers' Association:** 915 Rockefeller Bldg, Cleveland, OH 44113-1383; tel. (216) 621-1107; fax (216) 241-8262; f. 1892; 14 mem cos; Pres. GEORGE J. RYAN.

**National Waterways Conference:** 1130 17th St, NW, Suite 200, Washington, DC 20036; tel. (202) 296-4415; fax (202) 835-3861; f. 1960; 500 mems; Pres. HARRY N. COOK.

## OCEAN SHIPPING

**Federal Maritime Commission:** 800 North Capitol St, NW, Washington, DC 20573; tel. (202) 523-5725; fax (202) 523-3782; f. 1961 to regulate the waterborne foreign and domestic offshore commerce of the USA; comprises 5 mems; Chair. WILLIAM D. HATHAWAY.

**Maritime Administration:** US Dept of Transportation, Nasif Bldg, 400 Seventh St, SW, Washington, DC 20590; tel. (202) 366-5807; concerned with promoting the US Merchant Marine; also administers subsidy programme to ship operators; Admin. ALBERT HERBERGER.

### Principal Ports

The three largest ports in the USA, in terms of traffic handled, are the Port of South Louisiana (New Orleans), handling 199.7m. tons in 1992, Houston (137.7m. tons) and New York (115.3m. tons). Many other large ports serve each coast, 29 of them handling between 20m. and 127m. tons of traffic annually. The deepening of channels and locks on the St Lawrence–Great Lakes Waterway, allowing the passage of large ocean-going vessels, has increased the importance of the Great Lakes ports, of which the largest, Duluth-Superior, handled more than 39.3m. tons in 1992.

### Principal Companies

**Alcoa Steamship Co, Inc:** 1501 Alcoa Bldg, Pittsburgh, PA 15219; tel. (412) 553-2545; telex 232777; fax (412) 553-2624; bulk services world-wide; Pres. R. S. HOSPODAR; 5 vessels.

**American President Lines Ltd:** 1111 Broadway, Oakland, CA 94607; tel. (510) 272-8000; telex 335478; fax (510) 272-7220; f. 1929; serves east and west coasts of North America, Mexico, Caribbean Basin, Middle East and Far East; Pres. and CEO J. HAYASHI; 19 vessels.

**Amoco Corpn:** 200 East Randolph Drive, POB 5910-A, Chicago, IL 60601; tel. (312) 856-6111; telex 190219; fax (312) 856-2460; Pres. C. D. PHILLIPS.

**Central Gulf Lines, Inc:** 650 Poydras St, Suite 1700, POB 53366, New Orleans, LA 70153; tel. (504) 529-5461; telex 587435; fax (504) 529-5745; Chair. N. W. JOHNSEN; Pres. E .F. JOHNSEN; 14 vessels.

**Chevron Shipping Co:** 555 Market St, Suite 1740, San Francisco, CA 94105-2870; tel. (415) 894-7700; telex 470074; fax (415) 894-4583; world-wide tanker services; Pres. THOMAS R. MOORE; 37 tankers.

**Colonial Marine Industries, Inc:** 26 East Bryan St, POB 9981, Savannah, GA 31412; tel. (912) 233-7000; telex 49615623; fax (912) 232-8216; Exec. Vice-Pres. THOMAS MCGOLDRICK; 7 vessels.

**Coscol Marine Corpn:** 9 Greenway Plaza, Houston, TX 77046; tel. (713) 877-3370; telex 49616712; fax (713) 877-3433; Pres. EDWARD W. KNUTSEN; 6 tankers.

**Crowley Maritime Corpn:** 155 Grand Ave, Oakland, CA 94612; tel. (510) 251-7500; telex 6771521; fax (510) 251-7625; f. 1895; Chair., Pres. and CEO T. B. CROWLEY; 10 vessels.

**Energy Transportation Corpn:** 1185 Ave of the Americas, 24th Floor, New York, NY 10036; tel. (212) 642-9800; telex 824298; fax (212) 642-9890; Pres. K. C. CHEN; 8 vessels.

**Falcon Carriers, Inc:** 1010 Lamar St, Suite 1400, Houston, TX 77002; tel. (713) 951-9551; fax (713) 951-9552; Chair. KATHERINE WEI; Pres. H. REED WASOON; Man. Dir Capt. JOSEPH CECIRE; 5 vessels.

**Farrell Lines Inc:** 1 Whitehall St, New York, NY 10004; tel. (212) 440-4200; telex 420187; f. 1926; regular mail and freight services from US Atlantic to west Africa and Mediterranean; Chair. and CEO GEORGE F. LOWMAN; Pres. RICHARD GRONDA.

**Keystone Shipping Co:** 313 Chestnut St, Philadelphia, PA 19106; tel. (215) 928-2800; telex 845327; fax (215) 928-2825; Pres. A. B. KURZ; 17 vessels.

**Lasco Shipping Co:** 3200 NW Yeon Ave, POB 10047, Portland, OR 97210; tel. (503) 227-7447; telex 289875; fax (503) 323-2794; Pres. K. LEWIS; 17 vessels.

**Lykes Bros Steamship Co Inc:** 111 East Madison, POB 31244, Tampa, FL 33631-3244; Orleans, LA 70130; tel. (813) 276-4600; f. 1900; routes from US Gulf and Atlantic ports to United Kingdom and northern Europe, Mediterranean, west coast of South America, Africa and the Far East; also Great Lakes to Mediterranean; Chair., Pres. and CEO THOMPSON LYKES RANKIN; 19 vessels.

**Maritime Overseas Corpn:** 43 West 42nd St, New York, NY 10036; tel. (212) 953-4100; telex 420347; manages over 60 tankers and dry bulk carriers.

**Matson Navigation Co:** 333 Market St, POB 7452, San Francisco, CA 94120; tel. (415) 957-4000; fax (415) 957-4559; f. 1901; container and other freight services between US west coast and Hawaii; container leasing world-wide; Chair. R. J. PFEIFFER; Pres. C. B. MULHOLLAND.

**Mobil Oil Corpn:** 3225 Gallows Rd, Fairfax, VA 22037; tel. (703) 846-1520; telex 64299; fax (703) 846-3180; Chair. and CEO L. A. NOTO; 29 vessels.

**OMI Corpn:** 90 Park Ave, New York, NY 10016-1302; tel. (212) 986-1960; telex 224060; fax (212) 297-2100; Chair. M. KLEBANOFF; Pres. and CEO J. GOLDSTEIN; 45 vessels.

**Sea-Land Service, Inc:** 150 Allen Rd, POB 2555, Elizabeth, NJ 07207; tel. (908) 558-6000; largest US-flag container shipping co; 68 vessels providing containerized services to 80 ports in 70 countries; Pres. and CEO JOHN P. CLANCEY.

**SeaRiver Maritime, Inc:** POB 1512, Houston, TX 77251-1512; tel. (713) 758-5000; fax (713) 758-5091; Pres. A. ELMER; 12 tankers.

**Stolt Parcel Tankers Inc:** Stolt-Nielsen Bldg, 8 Sound Shore Drive, POB 2300, Greenwich, CT 06836; tel. (203) 625-9400; telex 179101; fax (203) 661-7695; Chair. J. STOLT-NIELSEN, Jr; Pres. S. A. COOPERMAN; 63 tankers.

**Sun Transport Inc:** Delaware Ave and Green St, POB 1078, Marcus Hook, PA 19061; tel. (610) 859-1004; fax (610) 859-1016; Gen. Man. JAMES L. FIDLER; Man. Ship Operations Capt. H. L. ELLWANGER; 2 vessels.

**Waterman Steamship Corpn:** 120 Wall St, New York, NY 10005; tel. (212) 747-8550; telex 235949; fax (212) 747-8588; f. 1919; services to the Middle East and South-East Asia; Chair. C. S. WALSH; Pres. E. P. WALSH; 6 vessels.

### Associations

**American Bureau of Shipping:** 2 World Trade Center, 106th Floor, New York, NY 10048; tel. (212) 839-5000; telex 232099; fax (212) 839-5130; f. 1862; Chair. FRANK J. IAROSSI; Pres. ROBERT D. SOMERVILLE; 565 mems.

**American Institute of Merchant Shipping:** 1000 16th St, NW, Suite 511, Washington, DC 20036; tel. (202) 775-4399; fax (202) 659-3795; f. 1969; Pres. ERNEST J. CORRADO; 23 mems; represents owners and operators of US-flag tankers, bulk carriers, container vessels and barges.

**Federation of American Controlled Shipping:** 50 Broadway, Suite 3400, New York, NY 10004; tel. (212) 344-1483; fax (212) 943-0798; f. 1958; Chair. PHILIP J. LOREE; Exec. Sec. VIOLET EFRON; 16 mems.

# THE UNITED STATES OF AMERICA

## CIVIL AVIATION

**Federal Aviation Administration:** US Dept of Transportation, 800 Independence Ave, SW, Washington, DC 20591; tel. (202) 267-3484; fax (202) 267-5039; f. 1958; promotes safety in the air, regulates air commerce and assists in development of an effective national airport system; Admin. DAVID R. HINSON.

### Principal Scheduled Companies

**American Airlines Inc:** POB 619616, MD 5616, Dallas/Fort Worth Airport, TX 75261-9616; tel. (817) 967-1234; telex 791651; fax (817) 967-4044; f. 1934; coast-to-coast domestic routes and services to Canada, Hawaii, Mexico, the Caribbean, South America, Europe and the Far East; Chair., Pres. and CEO ROBERT L. CRANDALL.

**Continental Airlines Inc:** 2929 Allen Pkwy, POB 4607, Houston, TX 77019; tel. (713) 834-5000; telex 790275; fax (713) 523-4085; f. 1934; serves 90 US destinations and 56 points in Mexico, Canada, Europe and the Far East; Pres. and CEO GORDON BETHUNE.

**Delta Air Lines Inc:** Hartsfield Atlanta International Airport, Atlanta, GA 30320-6001; tel. (404) 765-2600; telex 542316; fax (404) 715-5876; f. 1929; Chair., Pres. and CEO RONALD W. ALLEN; domestic and international services to 208 cities in 32 countries.

**Flying Tiger Line:** 7401 World Way West, Los Angeles, CA 90009; telex 674496; f. 1945; world's largest air cargo carrier; scheduled services and charters serving North America, Asia, Australia, the Middle East and Europe; Pres. JEFFREY RODEK.

**Hawaiian Airlines Inc:** POB 30008, Honolulu International Airport, Honolulu, HI 96820; tel. (808) 525-5511; telex 7430075; fax (808) 525-3299; f. 1929; Pres. and CEO BRUCE NOBLES; inter-island, US mainland and South Pacific services.

**Northwest Airlines, Inc:** 5101 Northwest Drive, St Paul, MN 55111-3034; tel. (612) 726-2331; telex 297024; fax (612) 726-6599; f. 1926; Chair. ALFRED A. CHECCHI; Pres. and CEO JOHN DASBURG; coast-to-coast domestic routes and services to Canada, Europe and the Far East.

**Trans World Airlines Inc (TWA):** 515 North 6th St, St Louis, MO 63101; tel. (314) 589-3000; telex 217711; fax (314) 589-3268; f. 1925; Chair. and CEO JOHN C. CAHILL; Pres. and CEO JEFFREY C. ERICKSON; domestic and international services.

**United Airlines Inc:** 1200 East Algonquin Rd, Elk Grove Township, IL 60007; tel. (708) 952-4000; telex 275362; fax (708) 952-4081; f. 1934; Chair. and CEO GERALD GREENWALD; Pres. JOHN C. POPE; domestic services from coast to coast, and Hawaii; international services to Canada, Europe and the Far East.

**USAir, Inc:** 2345 Crystal Drive, Arlington, VA 22227; tel. (703) 418-7000; f. 1939; Chair. and CEO SETH E. SCHOFIELD; Pres. FRANK L. SALIZZONI; scheduled passenger services to 98 points in the USA and 3 in Canada.

### Association

**Air Transport Association of America:** 1301 Pennsylvania Ave, NW, Suite 1100, Washington, DC 20004-1707; tel. (202) 626-4000; fax (202) 626-4181; f. 1936; Pres. CAROL HALLETT; mems: 20 US airlines; 2 foreign-flag assoc. mems.

## Tourism

**American Society of Travel Agents Inc:** 1101 King St, Alexandria, VA 22314; tel. (703) 739-2782; telex 7607718; fax (703) 684-8319; f. 1931; Pres. and CEO EARLENE CAUSEY; Exec. Vice-Pres. DICK KNODT; 21,000 mems.

**United States Travel and Tourism Administration:** US Dept of Commerce, Room 1865, Washington, DC 20230; tel. (202) 377-0136; fax (202) 377-8887; f. 1961; fed. agency promoting US tourist industry; also collects and analyses data on tourism.

# UNITED STATES COMMONWEALTH TERRITORIES

There are two US Commonwealth Territories, the Northern Mariana Islands, in the Pacific Ocean, and Puerto Rico, in the Caribbean Sea. A Commonwealth is a self-governing incorporated territory that is an integral part of, and in full political union with, the USA.

## THE NORTHERN MARIANA ISLANDS

### Introductory Survey

**Location, Climate, Language, Religion, Flag, Capital**

The Commonwealth of the Northern Mariana Islands comprises 16 islands (all the Marianas except Guam) in the western Pacific Ocean, about 5,300 km (3,300 miles) west of Honolulu (Hawaii). The temperature normally ranges between 24°C (75°F) and 30°C (86°F) in June–November, but is generally cooler and drier from December to May. The average annual rainfall is about 2,000 mm (79 ins). English, Chamorro and Carolinian are the official languages. The population is predominantly Christian, mainly Roman Catholic. The national flag of the United States of America (q.v.) is used by the Northern Mariana Islands. Six islands, including the three largest (Saipan, Tinian and Rota), are inhabited; the principal settlement and the administrative centre are on Saipan.

**Recent History**

The islands which comprise the Northern Mariana Islands were first sighted by Europeans during the 1520s, and were claimed for Spain in 1565. They were sold to Germany in 1899, but control was transferred to Japan, which had taken the islands from Germany in 1914, by the League of Nations in 1921. The USA captured Saipan and Tinian from the Japanese after fierce fighting in 1944, and the Northern Mariana Islands became a part of the Trust Territory of the Pacific Islands in 1947. (See chapter on the Marshall Islands.)

In June 1975 the Northern Mariana Islands voted for separate status as a US Commonwealth Territory, and in March 1976 President Ford signed the Northern Marianas Commonwealth Covenant. In October 1977 President Carter approved the Constitution of the Northern Mariana Islands, which provided that, from January 1978, the former Marianas District was internally self-governing. In December 1977 elections took place for a bicameral legislature, a Governor and a Lieutenant-Governor. In July 1984 it was reported that the US President, Ronald Reagan, had signed a proclamation giving residents of the Northern Mariana Islands a broad range of civil and political rights in the USA, including equal employment opportunities within the federal government, civil service and armed forces. The Northern Marianas were formally admitted to US Commonwealth status in November 1986, after the ending of the Trusteeship in the Territory. At the same time a proclamation, issued by President Reagan, conferred US citizenship on the islands' residents.

At elections in November 1989 Republicans retained control of the governorship and ousted a Democrat from the position of Washington Representative. Larry Guerrero was elected Governor after Pedro Tenorio had decided to stand down. Democrat candidates, however, won a majority of seats in the House of Representatives.

In December 1990 the UN Security Council voted to end the Trusteeship of the Northern Marianas, as well as that of two other Pacific Trust Territories. Although the decision to terminate the relationship had been taken in 1986, voting had been delayed, owing to apprehension of a Soviet veto in the Security Council. Guerrero, however, opposed the termination and had requested that the vote be postponed. The new relationship would, he argued, leave the islands subject to US law while remaining unrepresented in the US Congress; moreover, several important sovereignty issues (such as local control of marine resources) would remain unresolved.

At elections to the House of Representatives (which had been enlarged by three seats) in November 1991 Republicans regained a majority. Similarly, the party increased the number of its senators to eight. At elections to the House of Representatives in November 1993 Republican candidates retained a majority of seats. However, in the gubernatorial election a Democrat, Froilan Tenorio, was successful, obtaining 5,197 votes, compared with the incumbent Guerrero's 4,144 votes. Similarly, a Democratic candidate, Jesus Borja, was elected as Lieutenant-Governor, while Juan Babauta remained as Washington Representative. The newly-elected Tenorio stated that his priorities as Governor included the equalization of the minimum wage in the islands with that of the mainland, and the abolition of assumed privileges for government employees.

In January 1995 the minimum wage was increased by 12.2%, in accordance with the Governor's stated objectives; however, five days later Tenorio signed legislation that effectively reversed the decision. This prompted several members of the House of Representatives to demand that the US Federal Bureau of Investigations (FBI) conduct an investigation into the incident and the allegations of bribery surrounding the Governor's actions. The Territory's reputation deteriorated further in April when the Government of the Philippines introduced a ban on its nationals accepting unskilled employment in the islands, because of persistent reports of abuse and exploitation of immigrant workers. Meanwhile, the US Congress announced that it was to allocate US $7m. towards the enforcement of the islands' labour and immigration laws, following the publication of a report in late 1994, which alleged the repeated violations of these regulations, as well as widespread corruption among immigration officials and business leaders.

**Government**

Legislative authority is vested in the Northern Marianas Commonwealth Legislature, a bicameral body consisting of the Senate and the House of Representatives. There are nine senators, elected for two-year terms, and 18 members of the House of Representatives, elected for two-year terms. Executive authority is vested in the Governor, who is elected by popular vote.

**Defence**

The USA is responsible for the defence of the Northern Marianas.

**Economic Affairs**

The economy of the Northern Marianas is dominated by the services sector, particularly tourism. The Commonwealth's gross national product (GNP) was estimated to be US $512m. in the year ending 30 September 1989.

Agriculture is concentrated in smallholdings, important crops being coconuts, breadfruit, tomatoes and melons. Cattle-ranching was established on Tinian during the 1960s. Vegetables, beef and pork are important exports. In 1987 sales of agricultural commodities declined to a total value of US $0.6m. (compared with US $1.4m. in 1986), owing to a typhoon and the reinfestation of the melon fly. The principal manufacturing activity is the garment industry, which grew rapidly after its establishment in the mid-1980s to become the islands' chief export sector. Manufacturers benefit from US regulations that permit duty-free and quota-free imports from the Commonwealth. Garment exports to the USA earned an estimated US $279m. in 1992. Other small-scale industries include handicrafts and the processing of fish and copra. The manufacturing sector engaged 13.3% of the employed labour force in 1992. The most important industry, however, is tourism, which, together with its related activities, contributes some 50% of gross domestic product (GDP) and employs some 45% of the paid labour force. Large-scale investment from predominantly Japanese sources resulted in a threefold increase in hotel rooms between 1982 and 1989, and a similar increase in tourist arrivals. (The construction industry, one of the principal beneficiaries of this growth, engaged 18.1% of the paid labour force in 1992.) The signing of a new aviation agreement with Japan in 1990 further improved air links with the country, which provided 73% of the islands' visitors in 1991. Tourist arrivals increased by more than 25% in 1990, compared with 1989, and by a further 1.8% in the following year. In 1993 a total of 536,263 tourists visited the islands.

Rapid economic expansion in the 1980s led to a shortage of local labour and an increase in non-resident alien workers. However, owing to the resulting excess of immigrant workers (whose numbers increased by 655% between 1980 and 1989 and exceeded the permanent population by the early 1990s), wages remained relatively low, and there were widespread complaints of poor working conditions. In response to increasing concern over the alleged exploitation of foreign workers in the islands' garment factories, the House of Representatives approved legislation gradually to increase the minimum wage to parity with the mainland level by 2000 (see above).

The Northern Marianas are very dependent on imports, the value of which totalled US $385.3m. in 1991 (an increase of 16% compared with the previous year). In that year there was a trade deficit of US $126.9m. The annual rate of inflation averaged 7.1% in 1980–93.

Under the Covenant between the Commonwealth of the Northern Mariana Islands and the USA, the islands received a second seven-year development grant of US $228m. (55% for capital development projects) in 1985. Budget estimates predicted total revenue of US $150.4m. in the financial year ending 30 September 1992, of which the Covenant Fund accounted for 6.8% and local revenue some 93%.

The main restraint on development is the need to expand the islands' infrastructure, coupled with the problem of a labour shortage and the dependence on foreign workers. The islands benefit from their political association with the USA and their relative proximity to Japan. However, controversy surrounding the constitutionality of certain land-leasing arrangements with several important Japanese investors threatened to damage relations with Japan in late 1993. The Territory is a member of the South Pacific Commission (see p. 215) and an associate member of the UN Economic and Social Commission for Asia and the Pacific (ESCAP—see p. 27).

### Social Welfare

In 1981 the Trust Territory of the Pacific Islands (including the Northern Mariana Islands, Palau and the Federated States of Micronesia) had nine hospitals, with a total of 629 beds, and there were 55 physicians working in the islands.

### Education

School attendance is compulsory from six to 16 years of age. In 1993/94 there were 17 public and 11 private primary and secondary schools, with a total enrolment of 10,239 pupils. There was one college of further education.

### Public Holidays

**1995:** 1 January (New Year's Day), 3 January (Commonwealth Day), 13 February (for George Washington's Birthday), 22 May (Memorial Day), 4 July (US Independence Day), 4 September (Labor Day), 23 November (Thanksgiving Day), 25 December (Christmas Day).

**1996:** 1 January (New Year's Day), 3 January (Commonwealth Day), 12 February (for George Washington's Birthday), 20 May (Memorial Day), 4 July (US Independence Day), 2 September (Labor Day), 21 November (Thanksgiving Day), 25 December (Christmas Day).

### Weights and Measures

With certain exceptions, the imperial system is in force. One US cwt equals 100 lb; one long ton equals 2,240 lb; one short ton equals 2,000 lb. A policy of gradual voluntary conversion to the metric system is being encouraged by the Federal Government.

## Statistical Survey

*Source (unless otherwise indicated): Business Reference and Investment Guide to the Commonwealth of the Northern Mariana Islands.*

### AREA AND POPULATION

**Area:** 457 sq km (176.5 sq miles). *By island:* Saipan 120 sq km (46.5 sq miles); Tinian 102 sq km (39.2 sq miles); Rota 85 sq km (32.8 sq miles); Pagan 48 sq km (18.6 sq miles); Anatahan 32 sq km (12.5 sq miles); Agrihan 30 sq km (11.4 sq miles).

**Population:** 52,900 at the census of 1992. *By island:* Saipan 47,786; Rota 2,561; Tinian 2,511; Northern Islands 42.

**Density** (1992 census): 115.8 per sq km (299.7 per sq mile).

**Births and Deaths** (1992): 1,511 live births (birth rate 28.6 per 1,000); 157 deaths (death rate 3.0 per 1,000).

**Employment** (household survey, 1992): Agriculture, hunting, forestry and fishing 664; Mining 13; Manufacturing 4,086; Construction 5,543; Trade 4,902; Transport, storage and communication 2,028; Financing, insurance and real estate 674; Public administration 3,940; Other services 8,762; Total 30,613 (males 18,109; females 12,504).

### AGRICULTURE, ETC.

**Fishing** (metric tons, live weight): Total catch 141 in 1992; 135 in 1993. Source: Department of Natural Resources, Fish and Wildlife Division.

### FINANCE

**Currency and Exchange Rates:** 100 cents = 1 United States dollar (US $). *Sterling Equivalents* (31 December 1994): £1 sterling = US $1.5645; US $100 = £63.92.

**Budget** (estimates, US $ million, year ending 30 September): *1989:* Local revenue 67.7; Expenditure 80. *1991:* Total Revenue 138.4 (Covenant grants 11, Federal grants 17.9, Local revenue 109.6). *1992:* Total Revenue 150.4 (Covenant grants 10.3, Local revenue 141.0). *1993:* Total Revenue 138.0.

**Cost of Living** (Consumer Price Index; base: 1980=100): 214.9 in 1991; 232.9 in 1992; 243.1 in 1993.

**Gross National Product** (US $ million in current prices, year ending 30 September): 512 in 1989.

### EXTERNAL TRADE

**Imports:** (f.o.b., US $ million, 1987): Food items 23.1; Construction materials (incl. fixtures) 39.9; Automobiles (incl. parts) 11.9; Beverages (other than dairy products and fruit juices) 7.5; Petroleum products 21.5; Clothing 1.8; Tobacco products 3.3; All other items 40.3; Total 149.3.

*1988* (US $ million): *Total imports* 218.6; *Total exports* 134.8.
*1989* (US $ million): *Total imports* 304.8; *Total exports* 149.4.
*1990* (US $ million): *Total imports* 333.2; *Total exports* 198.4.
*1991* (US $ million): *Total imports* 385.3; *Total exports* 258.4.

Source: UN, *Statistical Yearbook for Asia and the Pacific.*

### TRANSPORT

**International Sea-borne Shipping** (freight traffic, '000 short tons, 1987): Goods loaded 33.2; Goods unloaded 205.3.

**Civil Aviation** (Saipan Int. Airport, 1993): 21,555 aircraft landings; 590,857 boarding passengers. Source: Commonwealth Ports Authority.

### TOURISM

**1991:** Visitor arrivals 424,458 (Japan 308,395, USA and Guam 72,916); Hotel rooms 2,950.
**1992:** Visitor arrivals 488,330; Hotel rooms 2,852.
**1993:** Visitor arrivals 536,263; Hotel rooms 3,189.

### COMMUNICATIONS MEDIA

**Radio Receivers** (estimate, 1987): 15,350 in use.
**Television Receivers** (estimate, 1993): 10,650 in use.
**Telephones** (1993): 13,618.

### EDUCATION

**Primary and Secondary** (1993/94): 28 schools (17 state, 11 private); 451 teachers; 10,239 students.

**Higher** (1993/94): 1 college; 3,051 students.

## Directory

## The Government

(June 1995)

**Governor:** Froilan Tenorio (took office 9 January 1994).
**Lieutenant-Governor:** Jesus C. Borja.
**Resident Representative in Washington, DC:** Juan N. Babauta.

### GOVERNMENT OFFICES

**Government Headquarters:** Caller Box 10007, Capitol Hill, Saipan, MP 96950; tel. 322-5091; fax 322-5102.

**Office of the Resident Representative to the USA, Commonwealth of the Northern Mariana Islands:** 2121 R St, NW, Washington, DC 20008; tel. (202) 673-5869; fax (202) 673-5873; the Commonwealth Govt also has liaison offices in Hawaii and Guam.

**Department of the Interior, Office of Territorial and International Affairs (OTIA):** Field Office of the OTIA, Dept of the Interior, POB 2622, Saipan, MP 96950; tel. 234-8861; fax 234-

## Legislature

Legislative authority is vested in the Northern Marianas Commonwealth Legislature, a bicameral body consisting of the Senate and the House of Representatives. There are nine senators, elected for two-year terms, and 18 members of the House of Representatives, elected for two-year terms. The most recent elections were held in November 1993, at which the Republicans and the Democrats each won three seats in the Senate, while the Republicans took 10 seats in the House of Representatives, the Democrats six and independent candidates two.

**Senate President:** JUAN DEMAPAN.
**Speaker of the House:** DIEGO BENAVENTE.
**Commonwealth Legislature:** Capitol Hill, Saipan, MP 96950; tel. 664-5643.

## Political Organizations

**Democratic Party:** Caller Box AAA-A10, Capitol Hill, Saipan, MP 96950; tel. 234-7497; fax 233-0641; Chair. Dr CARLOS S. CAMACHO.
**Republican Party:** c/o Commonwealth Legislature, Capitol Hill, Saipan MP 96950; Chair. BENIGNO R. FITIAL.

## Judicial System

The judicial system in the Commonwealth of the Northern Mariana Islands (CNMI) consists of the Superior Court, the Commonwealth Supreme Court (which considers appeals from the Superior Court) and the Federal District Court. Under the Covenant, federal law applies in the Commonwealth, apart from the following exceptions: the CNMI is not part of the US Customs Territory; the federal minimum wage provisions do not apply; federal immigration laws do not apply; and, the CNMI may enact its own taxation laws.

## Religion

The population is predominantly Christian, mainly Roman Catholic. There are small communities of Episcopalians (Anglicans—under the jurisdiction of the Bishop of Hawaii, in the USA) and Protestants.

### CHRISTIANITY
#### The Roman Catholic Church

The Northern Mariana Islands comprise the single diocese of Chalan Kanoa, suffragan to the archdiocese of Agaña (Guam). The Bishop participates in the Catholic Bishops' Conference of the Pacific, based in Fiji. At 31 December 1993 there were 50,697 adherents in the Northern Mariana Islands, including temporary residents.

**Bishop of Chalan Kanoa:** Most Rev. TOMAS AGUON CAMACHO, Bishop's House, Chalan Kanoa, POB 745, Saipan, MP 96950; tel. 234-3000; fax 235-3002.

## The Press

The weekly *Focus on the Commonwealth* is published in Guam, but distributed solely in the Northern Mariana Islands.

**Marianas Observer:** POB 2119, Saipan, MP 96950; tel. 233-3955; weekly; Gen. Man. SYLVESTER IGUEL; circ. 2,000.
**Marianas Review:** POB 1074, Saipan, MP 96950; tel. 234-7160; f. 1979 as *The Commonwealth Examiner*; weekly; English and Chamorro; independent; Publr LUIS BENAVENTE; Editor RUTH L. TIGHE; circ. 1,700.
**Marianas Variety News and Views:** POB 231, Saipan, MP 96950; tel. 234-6341; fax 234-9271; Mon.–Fri.; English and Chamorro; independent; Mans ABED YOUNIS, PAZ YOUNIS; circ. 3,000.
**Micronesian Investment Quarterly:** Saipan, MP 96950; quarterly; Editor ROGER G. STILLWELL.
**Pacific Daily News** (Saipan bureau): POB 822, Saipan, MP 96950; tel. 234-6423; fax 234-5986; Publr LEE WAVER; circ. 5,000.
**Pacific Star:** POB 5815 CHRB, Saipan, MP 96950; tel. 235-3449; weekly; Operational Man. NICK LEGASPI; circ. 3,000.
**Pacifica:** POB 2143, Saipan, MP 96950; monthly; Editor MIKE MALONE.
**Saipan Tribune:** POB 5305, Saipan, MP 96950; tel. 233-8742; fax 233-3733; 2 a week; Editor-in-Chief MARK M. BROADHURST; Publr REX I. PALACIOS; circ. 3,500.

## Radio and Television

There were an estimated 15,350 radio receivers in 1987 and some 10,650 television receivers (incl. in hotels) in use in 1993.

### RADIO

**Inter-Island Communications Inc:** POB 914, Saipan, MP 96950; tel. 234-7239; f. 1984; commercial; station KCNM-AM, or KZMI-FM in stereo; Gen. Man. HANS W. MICKELSON.
**Far East Broadcasting Co:** POB 209, Saipan, MP 96950; tel. 322-9088; fax 322-3060; non-commercial religious broadcasts; Dir CHRIS R. SLABAUGH.
   **KSAI-AM:** fax 322-3060; f. 1978; local service; Programme Dir PATRICK MURPHY.
   **KFBS-SW:** tel. 322-9088; international broadcasts in Chinese, Indonesian, Russian; Chief Engineer ROBERT SPRINGER.
**Station KHBI-SW:** POB 1837, Saipan, MP 96950; tel. 234-6515; fax 234-5452; fmrly KYOI; non-commercial station owned by the *Christian Science Monitor* (USA); Gen. Man. DOMINGO VILLAR.
**Station KPXP:** POB 415, Saipan, MP 96950; tel. 235-7996; fax 235-7998; f. 1981; Gen. Man. REX SORENSON.
**Station KRSI:** POB 413, Saipan, MP 96950; Gen. Man. PATRICK WILLIAMS.

### TELEVISION

**Tropic Isles Cable TV Corpn:** POB 1015, Saipan, MP 96950; tel. 234-7350; fax 234-9828; 33-channel commercial station, with 5 pay channels, broadcasting 24 hours a day; US programmes and local and international news; 5,000 subscribers; Gen. Man. FRED LORD.
**KMCV-TV:** POB 1298, Saipan, MP 96950; tel. 235-6365; fax 235-0965; f. 1992; 41-channel commercial station, with 5 pay channels, broadcasting 24 hours a day; US programmes and local and international news; 5,650 subscribers; Gen. Man. KEN TRIPP.

## Finance

### BANKING

**Bank of Guam** (USA): POB 678, Saipan, MP 96950; tel. 233-5001; fax 233-5003; Gen. Man. JAMES LYNN; brs on Tinian and Rota.
**Bank of Hawaii** (USA): Nauru Bldg, POB 566, Saipan, MP 96950; tel. 234-6673; telex 783621; fax 234-3478; Gen. Man. DAVID BUEHLER.
**Bank of Saipan:** POB 690, Saipan, MP 96950; tel. 234-6260; telex 783682; fax 234-7582; Gen. Man. JUAN TORRES.
**City Trust Bank:** San Jose, POB 1867, Saipan, MP 96950; tel. 234-7773; fax 234-8664; Gen. Man. MARIA LOURDES JOHNSON.
**Development Bank:** Wakins Bldg, Gualo Rai, Saipan, MP 96950; tel. 234-7145; funds capital improvement projects and private enterprises.
**First Savings and Loan Asscn of America** (USA): Beach Rd, Susupe, POB 324, Saipan, MP 96950; tel. 234-6617; Man. SUZIE WILLIAMS.
**Guam Savings and Loan Bank:** POB 3201, Saipan, MP 96950; tel. 233-2265; fax 233-2227; Gen. Man. GLEN PEREZ.
**Union Bank:** Oleai Centre, Beach Rd, Chalan Laulau, POB 1053, Saipan, MP 96950; tel. 234-6559; fax 234-7438; Gen. Man. KEN KATO.

There were three 'offshore' banks licensed, but not operating, in 1988.

### INSURANCE

**Associated Insurance Underwriters of the Pacific Inc:** POB 1369, Saipan, MP 96950; tel. 234-7222; fax 234-5367; Gen. Man. MAGGIE GEORGE.
**JTS Insurance Co Inc:** POB 2119, Saipan, MP 96950; tel. 234-8808; fax 234-6778; Gen. Man. TOM CANTOS.
**Marianas Insurance Co Ltd:** POB 2505, Saipan, MP 96950; tel. 234-5019; fax 234-5093; Gen. Man. ROSALIA S. CABRERA.
**Mitsui Marine and Fire Insurance Co Ltd:** POB 267, Saipan, MP 96950; tel. 234-2811; fax 234-5462; Man. Dir GEOFFREY BLANE.
**Moylan's Insurance Underwriters (Int.) Inc:** POB 658, Saipan, MP 96950; tel. 234-6442; telex 783610; fax 234-8641.
**The New Zealand Insurance Co Ltd (Microl Corporation):** POB 267, Saipan, MP 96950; tel. 234-2811; fax 234-5462; Man. Dir GEOFFREY BLANE.
**Pacifica Insurance Underwriters Inc:** POB 168, Saipan, MP 96950; tel. 234-6267; fax 234-5880; Pres. NORMAN T. TENORIO.
**Primerica Financial Services:** POB 964, Saipan, MP 96950; tel. 235-2912; fax 235-7910; Gen. Man. JOHN SABLAN.

**Staywell:** POB 2050, Saipan, MP 96950; tel. 235-4260; fax 235-4263; Gen. Man. LARRY LAVEQUE.

## Trade and Industry

### CHAMBER OF COMMERCE

**Saipan Chamber of Commerce:** Chalan Kanoa, POB 806, Saipan, MP 96950; tel. 233-7150; fax 234-7151; Pres. KIMBERLY CLASS; Co-ordinator OLIVE STEWART.

### GOVERNMENT CORPORATIONS

**Commonwealth Development Authority:** Wakins Bldg, Gualo Rai, Saipan, MP 96950; tel. 234-7145; foreign sales corpn and govt lending institution; invests Federal funds available under the Covenant.

**Commonwealth Utilities Corpn:** POB 1220, Saipan, MP 96950; tel. 322-4033; fax 322-4323.

**Marianas Public Land Corpn:** POB 380, Saipan, MP 96950; tel. 322-6914; manages public land, which constitutes 73% of total land area in the Commonwealth (38% on Saipan).

### TRADE UNION AND CO-OPERATIVES

**International Brotherhood of Electrical Workers:** c/o Micronesian Telecommunications Corpn, Saipan, MP 96950; Local 1357 of Hawaii branch of US trade union based in Washington, DC.

The Mariana Islands Co-operative Association, Rota Producers and Tinian Producers Associations operate in the islands.

## Transport

### RAILWAYS

There have been no railways operating in the islands since the Japanese sugar industry railway, on Saipan, ceased operations in the Second World War.

### ROADS

In 1991 there were 494 km (307 miles) of roads on the islands, 320 km (199 miles) of which are on Saipan. First grade roads constitute 135 km (84 miles) of the total, 99 km (62 miles) being on Saipan. There is no public transport, apart from a school bus system.

### SHIPPING

The main harbour of the Northern Mariana Islands is on Saipan. There are also two major harbours on Rota and one on Tinian.

Several shipping lines link Saipan, direct or via Guam, with ports in Japan, Asia, the Philippines, the USA and other territories in the Pacific.

**Commonwealth Ports Authority:** Saipan Int. Airport, POB 1055, Saipan, MP 96950; tel. 234-8315; fax 234-5962.

**Saipan Shipping Co Inc. (Saiship):** Saiship Bldg, Charlie Dock, POB 8, Saipan, MP 96950; tel. 322-9706; telex 783619; fax 322-3183; weekly barge service between Guam, Saipan and Tinian; monthly services to Japan and Micronesia.

### CIVIL AVIATION

Air services are centred on the main international airport, Isley Field, on Saipan. There are also airports on Rota and Tinian.

**Air Micronesia Inc:** POB 298, Saipan, MP 96950; tel. 646-0230; telex 721140; fax 646-6821; f. 1966; owned by Pacific Micronesia Corpn; internal services and, internationally, to Hawaii (USA), the US Pacific territories of Johnston Atoll, Palau, the Marshall Islands and the Federated States of Micronesia, and to the Philippines, Australia, Papua New Guinea, the Republic of Korea, Taiwan and Japan; Pres. GEORGE A. WARDE; Gen. Man. DANIEL H. PURSE.

**Air Mike Express:** Saipan Int. Airport, Saipan, MP 96950; f. 1989; jointly-owned with Continental Airlines; services to Rota and Guam.

**Freedom Air:** POB 239, Saipan, MP 96950; tel. 288-5001; services to Rota, Tinian and Guam; Gen. Man. JOAQUIN FLORES.

**Pacific Island Aviation:** POB 318, Saipan, MP 96950; tel. 234-3600; fax 234-3604; services to Rota, Tinian and Guam; repair station; flight instruction; Gen. Man. JAMES STOWELL.

## Tourism

Tourism is the most important industry in the Northern Mariana Islands. Most of the islands' hotels are Japanese-owned, and in 1991 73% of tourists came from Japan. The islands received a total of 536,263 visitors in 1993 (an increase of some 9.8% on the figure for 1992), in which year there were 3,189 hotel rooms. The islands of Asuncion, Guguan, Maug, Managaha, Sariguan and Uracas (Farallon de Pajaros) are maintained as uninhabited preserves. Visitors are mainly attracted by the white, sandy beaches and the excellent diving conditions. There is also interest in the *Latte* or *Taga* stones (mainly on Tinian), pillars carved from the rock by the ancient Chamorros, and relics from the Second World War.

**Marianas Visitors Bureau:** POB 861, Saipan, MP 96950; tel. 234-8325; fax 234-3596; f. 1976; responsible for the promotion and development of tourism in the Northern Mariana Islands; Man. Dir BENNET T. SEMAN.

# PUERTO RICO

## Introductory Survey

### Location, Climate, Language, Religion, Flag, Capital

The Commonwealth of Puerto Rico comprises the main island of Puerto Rico, together with the small offshore islands of Vieques and Culebra and numerous smaller islets, lying about 80 km (50 miles) east of Hispaniola (Haiti and the Dominican Republic) in the Caribbean Sea. The climate is maritime-tropical, with an average annual temperature of 24°C (75°F) and a normal range between 17°C (63°F) and 36°C (97°F). The official languages are Spanish and English. Christianity is the dominant religion, and about 81% of the population are Roman Catholics. The flag (proportions 5 by 3) has five alternating red and white horizontal stripes of equal width, with a blue triangle, in the centre of which is a five-pointed white star, at the hoist. The capital is San Juan.

### Recent History

Puerto Rico, also known as Borinquen (after the original Arawak Indian name Boriquen), was ruled by Spain from 1509 until 1898, when it was ceded to the USA at the conclusion of the Spanish–American war, and administered as an 'unincorporated territory' of the USA. In 1917 Puerto Ricans were granted US citizenship, and in 1947 Puerto Rico was given the right to elect its own Governor. A Constitution, promulgated in 1952, assigned Puerto Rico the status of a self-governing 'Commonwealth', or 'Estado Libre Asociado', in its relation to the USA.

The Partido Popular Democrático (PPD) held a majority in both chambers of the legislature from 1944 until 1968, when, following a split within the party, the Partido Nuevo Progresista (PNP), an advocate of statehood, won the governorship and legislative control. This followed a plebiscite in 1967, when 60.5% of voters had ratified a continuation of Commonwealth status in preference to independence (0.6%) or incorporation as a State of the USA (38.9%). In the general elections of 1972 the PPD, under the leadership of Rafael Hernández Colón, regained the governorship and legislative control from the PNP, only to lose them again in 1976. The victorious PNP was led by Carlos Romero Barceló, who became Governor in January 1977.

Romero Barceló, who had promised a referendum on statehood if re-elected for a further term in 1980, abandoned this plan following the election, in which he defeated former Governor Hernández Colón by a margin of only 3,500 votes in a poll of 1.6m., and the opposition PPD gained control of both houses of the legislature. During 1981 eight cabinet secretaries and numerous senior government officials resigned, evidencing dissension within the PNP and dissatisfaction with Romero Barceló's leadership. In February 1983 these divisions became more distinct. The Vice-President of the party, Angel Viera Martínez, refused to support Romero Barceló as a candidate for re-election as Governor and also asked him to relinquish his presidency of the PNP. Romero Barceló's supporters countered by removing Viera Martínez from his position as PNP leader in the House of Representatives, and forcing his resignation from the party. The other potential PNP candidate for the gubernatorial nomination, Hernán Padilla Ramírez, the Mayor of San Juan, left the PNP and formed a new party, the Partido de Renovación Puertorriqueño (PRP).

The 1984 gubernatorial election, in which Romero Barceló, Hernández Colón, Padilla Ramírez and Fernando Martín García of the pro-independence Partido Independentista Puertorriqueño (PIP) were candidates, was contested mainly on economic issues. There were, however, damaging allegations of corruption within the Romero Barceló administration. Hernández Colón won the election by 50,000 votes, with the PPD retaining substantial majorities in both legislative chambers. In September 1985 Romero Barceló was succeeded as leader of the PNP by Baltasar Corrada del Río.

Gubernatorial elections, held in November 1988, resulted in the re-election of Hernández Colón, who obtained 48.7% of the popular vote, compared with 45.8% for Corrada del Río and 5.5% for Rubén Barrios Martínez of the PIP. Electoral participation was unusually high, at almost 90%.

The question of eventual independence for Puerto Rico has been a politically sensitive issue for over 50 years. With the PPD supporting the continuation and enhancement of Commonwealth status and the PNP advocating Puerto Rico's inclusion as a State of the USA, mainstream party encouragement of independence aims has come mainly from the PIP and other left-wing groups. There are two small, and occasionally violent, terrorist factions, the Ejército Popular Boricua (Macheteros), which operates in Puerto Rico, and the Fuerzas Armadas de Liberación Nacional (FALN), functioning principally on the US mainland.

The debate on the island's constitutional future has continued to dominate Puerto Rican political life in recent years. In the 1988 election campaign, Corrada del Río, whose campaign was endorsed by the successful US presidential candidate, George Bush, advocated the admission of Puerto Rico as the 51st State of the USA, while Hernández Colón reiterated the traditional PPD policy of 'maximum autonomy' for Puerto Rico 'within a permanent union with the USA'. President Bush's open support of the statehood option was criticized by Hernández Colón and the PPD. In January 1989 Hernández Colón promised that a further plebiscite would be held to ascertain popular feeling on Puerto Rico's future status. Although it was initially planned to hold the referendum in June 1991, in February the proposed legislation to make its result binding on the US Government failed to secure sufficient support in the US Senate to allow it to proceed to full consideration by the US Congress.

In December 1991 the PPD Government organized a referendum on a proposal to adopt a charter of 'democratic rights', which included guarantees of US citizenship regardless of future change in Puerto Rico's constitutional status, and the maintenance of Spanish as the official language. The proposed charter was rejected by a margin of 53% to 45%. This result was widely interpreted as an indication that the majority of voters wished to retain Puerto Rico's Commonwealth status. Hernández Colón, who reiterated that a plebiscite on independence would take place at an unspecified future date, announced in January 1992 that he would not seek re-election in the gubernatorial election in November, and in the following month resigned as leader of the PPD. His successor as party leader, Victoria Muñoz Mendoza, was defeated in the gubernatorial election, held in November, by the PNP candidate, Pedro Rosselló, by a margin of 49.9% of the popular vote to 45.9% for the PPD. The leadership of the PPD subsequently passed to a former President of the Senate, Héctor Luis Acevedo.

Rosselló, who took office in January 1993, announced that a further referendum on Puerto Rico's future constitutional status would be held during the year. The Government proceeded with legislation rescinding the removal, in 1991, of English as an official language of the island. The referendum, which took place in November 1993, resulted in a 48% vote favouring the retention of Commonwealth status, with 46% of voters supporting accession to statehood and 4% advocating full independence.

### Government

Executive power is vested in the Governor, elected for a four-year term by universal adult suffrage. The Governor is assisted by the appointed Cabinet of 17 Secretaries. Legislative power is held by the bicameral Legislative Assembly, comprising the Senate (with 27 members) and the House of Representatives (53 members). The members of both chambers are elected by direct vote for four-year terms. The Resident Commissioner, also elected for a four-year term, represents Puerto Rico in the US House of Representatives, but is permitted to vote only in committees of the House. Puerto Ricans are citizens of the USA, but those resident in Puerto Rico, while eligible to participate in national party primary elections, may not vote in presidential elections.

### Defence

The USA is responsible for the defence of Puerto Rico. The US Navy maintains a base in eastern Puerto Rico, which includes large sections of the island of Vieques. Puerto Rico has a paramilitary National Guard numbering about 11,000, which is funded mainly by the US Department of Defense.

### Economic Affairs

In 1993, according to estimates by the World Bank, Puerto Rico's gross national product (GNP), measured at average 1991–93 prices, was US $25,317m., equivalent to $7,020 per head. In 1985–93, it was estimated, GNP per head increased, in real terms, at an average rate of 1.8% per year. The population increased by an annual average of 0.8% over the same period. Puerto Rico's gross domestic product (GDP) increased, in real terms, at an average rate of 3.8% per year between 1980/81 and 1992/93, and by an estimated 3.5% in 1993/94.

In the year ending 30 June 1994 agriculture, forestry and fishing contributed an estimated 1.4% of GDP and employed 3.4% of the working population. Dairy produce and other livestock products are the mainstays of the agricultural sector. The principal crops are sugar cane, coffee, pineapples, tropical plants and coconuts. Cocoa cultivation has been successfully introduced, and measures to improve agricultural land use have included the replanting of some sugar-growing areas with rice and the cultivation of plantain trees over large areas of unproductive hill land. Commercial fishing is practised on a small scale. The GDP of the agricultural sector increased, in real terms, at an average rate of 2.1% per year between 1980/81 and 1990/91. It declined by about 6% in 1991/92 and remained stagnant in 1992/93.

Industry (including manufacturing, construction and mining) employed 21.8% of the working population and provided an estimated 43.2% of GDP in 1993/94. Industrial GDP increased, in real terms, at an average annual rate of 2.9% between 1980/81 and 1990/91. It rose by 2.1% in 1991/92 and by 3.2% in 1992/93. Puerto Rico has no commercially exploitable mineral resources, although deposits of copper and nickel have been identified.

Manufacturing is the main source of income, accounting for an estimated 41.0% of GDP and employing 16.4% of the working population in 1993/94. The principal branch of manufacturing in 1990/91, based on contribution to GDP, was chemical products (accounting for 47.0% of the total sector), mainly drugs and medicines. Other important products were electrical machinery (11.3%), beverages and professional goods. The GDP of the manufacturing sector increased, in real terms, by 2.9% per year between 1980/81 and 1990/91, by 2.2% in 1991/92 and by 3.4% in 1992/93.

Tourism is of increasing importance. In 1993/94 tourist arrivals were estimated at a record 4,022,600 visitors, attracting revenue totalling $1,670m. Visitors from the US mainland comprise more than one-half of the total.

US federal aid programmes are of central importance to the Puerto Rican economy, and in the early 1990s federal welfare transfers exceeded $3,800m. annually. In addition, the island received $1,300m. in disaster relief in respect of 'Hurricane Hugo', which widely disrupted the island's economy in late 1989 and for much of 1990. In 1993/94 Puerto Rico recorded a visible trade surplus of $4,265m., but there was a deficit of $3,334m. on the current account of the balance of payments. The mainland USA is the island's dominant trading partner, providing 67.2% of Puerto Rico's recorded imports and absorbing 87.4% of its recorded exports in 1993/94. Japan, the United Kingdom, the Dominican Republic and the US Virgin Islands are also significant in Puerto Rico's foreign trade. The principal category of recorded exports in 1993/94 was chemical products (accounting for 46.7% of the total), mainly drugs and pharmaceutical preparations. Other major exports were processed food and electrical machinery. The main imports were also chemical products, electrical machinery and food.

The annual inflation rate averaged 2.9% in 1985–93. Consumer prices increased by an average of 2.8% in 1993 and by 3.6% in 1994. Puerto Rico is very densely populated, and unemployment has been a persistent problem. Assisted by the growth in the tourist industry, however, the average rate progressively declined from 21.8% of the labour force in 1985 to 14.1% in 1990. The unemployment rate rose to 16.0% in 1991, and to 16.6% in 1992, increasing to 17.0% in 1993.

Puerto Rico holds associate status in the UN Economic Commission for Latin America and the Caribbean (ECLAC—see p. 29) and has observer status in the Caribbean Community and Common Market (CARICOM—see p. 114). Puerto Rico declined to accept associate status in the Association of Caribbean States (ACS), formed in 1994, on the grounds of opposition by the US Government to the inclusion of Cuba.

Puerto Rico's economic growth has been inhibited by the lack of an adequate infrastructure. Government programmes of industrial and taxation incentives, aimed at attracting US and foreign investors and encouraging domestic reinvestment of profits and long-term capital investment, have generated growth in the manufacturing and services sectors. However, the extent of US federal government support has been under review since 1994 as part of the programme by President Clinton to reduce the US budget deficit.

### Social Welfare

Puerto Rico is covered by most provisions of the US federal social security programme, and more than 25% of the 1989/90 Commonwealth budget was allocated to public housing and welfare. In addition to federal benefits, there is a local programme covering health, accidents, disability and unemployment. There were 4,057 practising physicians in 1980, and in 1985 Puerto Rico had 69 hospitals, with a total of 10,900 beds.

### Education

The public education system is centrally administered by the Department of Education. Education is compulsory for children between six and 16 years of age. In the academic year 1989/90 there were 651,225 pupils attending public day schools. The 12-year curriculum, beginning at five years of age, is subdivided into six grades of elementary school, three years at junior high school and three years at senior high school. Vocational schools at the high school level and kindergartens also form part of the public education system. Instruction is conducted in Spanish, but English is a required subject at all levels. In 1989/90 more than 20% of the Commonwealth budget was allocated to education. In 1985 there were 1,782 public day schools, 818 private elementary and secondary schools and 69 public and private institutions of higher education. The State University system consists of three principal campuses and six regional colleges. In 1980 the average rate of adult illiteracy was 10.9% (males 10.3%; females 11.5%).

### Public Holidays

**1995:** 1 January (New Year), 6 January (Epiphany), 9 January (Birthday of Eugenio María de Hostos), 16 January (Martin Luther King Day), 20 February (Presidents' Day), 22 March (Emancipation of the Slaves), 14 April (Good Friday), 17 April (for Birthday of José de Diego), 29 May (Memorial Day), 24 June (Feast of St John the Baptist), 4 July (US Independence Day), 17 July (Birthday of Luis Muñoz Rivera), 24 July (Birthday of José Celso Barbosa), 25 July (Constitution Day), 4 September (Labor Day), 9 October (Columbus Day), 11 November (Veterans' Day), 20 November (for Discovery of Puerto Rico Day), 23 November (US Thanksgiving Day), 25 December (Christmas Day).

**1996:** 1 January (New Year), 6 January (Epiphany), 9 January (Birthday of Eugenio María de Hostos), 15 January (Martin Luther King Day), 19 February (Presidents' Day), 22 March (Emancipation of the Slaves), 5 April (Good Friday), 16 April (Birthday of José de Diego), 27 May (Memorial Day), 24 June (Feast of St John the Baptist), 4 July (US Independence Day), 17 July (Birthday of Luis Muñoz Rivera), 24 July (Birthday of José Celso Barbosa), 25 July (Constitution Day), 2 September (Labor Day), 14 October (Columbus Day), 11 November (Veterans' Day), 19 November (Discovery of Puerto Rico Day), 28 November (US Thanksgiving Day), 25 December (Christmas Day).

### Weights and Measures

The US system is officially in force. Some old Spanish weights and measures, as well as the metric system, are used in local commerce.

# Statistical Survey

Source (unless otherwise stated): Puerto Rico Planning Board, San Juan, 00940-9985.

## Area and Population

### AREA, POPULATION AND DENSITY

| | |
|---|---:|
| Area (sq km) | 8,959* |
| Population (census results) | |
| 1 April 1980 | |
|   Males | 1,556,727 |
|   Females | 1,639,793 |
|   Total | 3,196,520 |
| 1 April 1990 | 3,522,039 |
| Population (official estimates at mid-year) | |
| 1992 | 3,580,000 |
| 1993 | 3,622,000 |
| 1994 | 3,685,000 |
| Density (per sq km) at mid-1994 | 411.3 |

* 3,459 sq miles.

### PRINCIPAL TOWNS (population at 1990 census)

| | | | | |
|---|---:|---|---|---:|
| San Juan (capital) | 437,745 | | Caguas | 133,447 |
| Bayamón | 220,262 | | Mayagüez | 100,371 |
| Ponce | 187,749 | | Arecibo | 93,385 |
| Carolina | 177,806 | | Guaynabo | 92,886 |

### BIRTHS, MARRIAGES AND DEATHS

| | Registered live births | | Registered marriages | | Registered deaths | |
|---|---:|---:|---:|---:|---:|---:|
| | Number | Rate (per 1,000) | Number | Rate (per 1,000) | Number | Rate (per 1,000) |
| 1989 | 66,692 | 19.1 | 31,642 | 9.0 | 25,987 | 7.3 |
| 1990 | 66,555 | 18.9 | 33,080 | 9.4 | 26,148 | 7.4 |
| 1991 | 64,516 | 18.2 | 33,222 | 9.4 | 26,328 | 7.4 |
| 1992 | 64,481 | 18.0 | 33,911* | 9.4* | 27,397 | 7.7 |
| 1993* | 65,000 | 18.0 | n.a. | n.a. | 28,000 | 7.9 |
| 1994* | 66,000 | 17.9 | n.a. | n.a. | 29,000 | 7.9 |

* Provisional.

### ECONOMICALLY ACTIVE POPULATION
('000 persons aged 16 years and over)

| | 1991/92 | 1992/93 | 1993/94* |
|---|---:|---:|---:|
| Agriculture, forestry and fishing | 34 | 34 | 34 |
| Manufacturing | 164 | 168 | 166 |
| Electricity, gas and water | 16 | 16 | 16 |
| Construction | 55 | 58 | 54 |
| Trade | 193 | 201 | 201 |
| Government | 219 | 217 | 224 |
| Other | 296 | 305 | 316 |
| **Total employed** | 977 | 999 | 1,011 |
| Unemployed | 193 | 202 | 192 |
| **Total labour force** | 1,170 | 1,201 | 1,201 |

* Preliminary.

## Agriculture

### PRINCIPAL CROPS

| | 1989 | 1990 | 1991* |
|---|---:|---:|---:|
| Sugar (raw) ('000 tons) | 91.3 | 68.1 | 73.9 |
| Coffee ('000 cwt) | 320.0 | 285.0 | 280.0 |
| Tobacco ('000 cwt) | 1.3 | 0.2 | n.a. |
| Pineapples (tons) | 54.0 | 51.6 | 65.6 |

* Preliminary.

### LIVESTOCK (at January each year)

| | 1988 | 1989 | 1990 |
|---|---:|---:|---:|
| Cattle | 559,187 | 585,581 | 614,857 |
| Pigs | 194,554 | 198,938 | 205,814 |
| Chickens | 10,819,639 | 10,352,936 | 11,021,163 |

## Fishing

(metric tons, live weight)

| | 1990 | 1991 | 1992 |
|---|---:|---:|---:|
| Fishes | 1,692 | 1,893 | 1,419 |
| Crustaceans | 251 | 288 | 223 |
| Molluscs | 121 | 110 | 79 |
| **Total catch** | 2,064 | 2,291 | 1,721 |

Source: FAO, *Yearbook of Fishery Statistics*.

## Industry

### SELECTED PRODUCTS

| | 1989 | 1990 | 1991* |
|---|---:|---:|---:|
| Molasses ('000 gallons) | 6,547 | 4,687 | 5,236 |
| Distilled spirits ('000 proof gallons) | 28,252 | 26,276 | 32,239 |
| Beer ('000 proof gallons) | 13,867 | 16,583 | 11,039 |
| Cement ('000 barrels of 94 lb) | 29,469 | 30,598 | 30,383 |
| Electricity (million kWh) | 14,675 | 14,794 | 15,487 |

* Preliminary.

## Finance

### CURRENCY AND EXCHANGE RATES

**Monetary Units**
United States currency: 100 cents = 1 US dollar (US $).

**Sterling Equivalent** (31 December 1994)
£1 sterling = US $1.5645; US $100 = £63.92.

# UNITED STATES COMMONWEALTH TERRITORIES

*Puerto Rico*

**BUDGET** (US $ million, year ending 30 June)

| Revenue | 1992/93 | 1993/94* |
|---|---|---|
| Taxation | 3,649 | 4,235 |
|   Income taxes | 2,412 | 2,873 |
|   Property taxes | 80 | 66 |
|   Excise taxes | 1,099 | 1,236 |
|   Licences | 56 | 57 |
| Intergovernmental transfers | 2,123 | 2,198 |
| Other receipts | 324 | 450 |
| **Total** | 6,095 | 6,882 |

| Expenditure | 1989/90 |
|---|---|
| General government | 318 |
| Public safety | 542 |
| Health | 219 |
| Public housing and welfare | 1,606 |
| Education | 1,270 |
| Economic development | 678 |
| Aid to municipalities | 246 |
| Lottery prizes | 316 |
| Capital outlays | 504 |
| Debt service | 564 |
| **Total** | 6,263 |

*Provisional.
Source: Department of the Treasury, Commonwealth of Puerto Rico.

**COST OF LIVING** (Consumer Price Index; base: 1980 = 100)

| | 1991 | 1992 | 1993 |
|---|---|---|---|
| Food | 149.1 | 157.0 | 167.3 |
| Fuel and light | 151.8 | 149.0 | 149.1 |
| Rent | 111.9 | 115.4 | 119.3 |
| Clothing | 108.6 | 104.6 | 103.0 |
| **All items** (incl. others) | 139.5 | 143.0 | 147.0 |

Source: ILO, *Year Book of Labour Statistics*.

**NATIONAL ACCOUNTS**
(US $ million at current prices, year ending 30 June)
**Expenditure on the Gross Domestic Product**

| | 1991/92 | 1992/93 | 1993/94* |
|---|---|---|---|
| Government final consumption expenditure | 4,805.2 | 5,087.5 | 5,332.5 |
| Private final consumption expenditure | 21,398.4 | 22,721.1 | 23,912.8 |
| Increase in stocks | 309.4 | 429.9 | 346.0 |
| Gross fixed capital formation | 5,042.29 | 5,544.7 | 5,869.7 |
| **Total domestic expenditure** | 31,555.2 | 33,783.2 | 35,461.0 |
| Exports of goods and services<br>*Less* Imports of goods and services | 3,075.2 | 3,064.3 | 3,803.8 |
| **GDP in purchasers' values** | 34,630.4 | 36,847.5 | 39,264.8 |
| **GDP at constant 1954 prices** | 7,079.3 | 7,356.2 | 7,616.5 |

* Preliminary.

**Gross Domestic Product by Economic Activity**

| | 1991/92 | 1992/93 | 1993/94* |
|---|---|---|---|
| Agriculture | 420.0 | 408.0 | 411.2 |
| Manufacturing | 14,183.0 | 15,238.5 | 16,308.9 |
| Construction and mining | 798.3 | 836.4 | 850.1 |
| Transportation and public utilities | 2,830.4 | 2,994.8 | 3,092.5 |
| Trade | 4,990.2 | 5,343.7 | 5,675.8 |
| Finance, insurance and real estate | 4,595.9 | 4,791.4 | 5,085.2 |
| Services | 3,582.2 | 3,926.5 | 4,249.3 |
| Government | 3,672.0 | 3,881.3 | 4,071.2 |
| **Sub-total†** | 35,069.8 | 37,417.7 | 39,740.4 |
| Statistical discrepancy | −439.4 | −570.2 | −475.6 |
| **Total** | 34,630.4 | 36,847.5 | 39,264.8 |

* Preliminary. † Including adjustment.

**BALANCE OF PAYMENTS**
(US $ million, year ending 30 June)

| | 1991/92 | 1992/93 | 1993/94* |
|---|---|---|---|
| Merchandise exports f.o.b. | 22,506.3 | 22,028.0 | 23,753.5 |
| Merchandise imports f.o.b. | −19,150.1 | −18,442.2 | −19,488.8 |
| **Trade balance** | 3,356.2 | 3,585.8 | 4,264.7 |
| Investment income received | 1,100.5 | 1,097.7 | 1,036.5 |
| Investment income paid | −12,586.1 | −13,3269.4 | −14,373.1 |
| Services and other income (net) | 148.4 | 137.1 | 257.4 |
| Unrequited transfers (net) | 4,770.0 | 5,306.0 | 5,682.6 |
| Net interest of Commonwealth and municipal governments | −158.9 | −189.5 | −202.3 |
| **Current balance** | −3,370.1 | −3,432.3 | −3,334.1 |

* Provisional.

## External Trade*

**PRINCIPAL COMMODITIES** (US $ million)

| Imports | 1991/92 | 1992/93 | 1993/94 |
|---|---|---|---|
| Mining products | 595.4 | 573.0 | 501.5 |
| Manufacturing products | 14,486.2 | 15,491.6 | 15,720.9 |
|   Food | 2,028.4 | 2,020.7 | 2,000.3 |
|   Clothing and textiles | 761.8 | 733.3 | 707.8 |
|   Wood, wood products and furniture | 318.2 | 362.0 | 355.0 |
|   Paper, printing and publishing | 525.5 | 501.6 | 476.3 |
|   Chemical products | 3,462.1 | 3,688.8 | 3,109.3 |
|     Drugs and pharmaceutical preparations | 2,066.0 | 2,244.6 | 1,500.9 |
|   Petroleum refining and related products | 1,047.8 | 1,027.3 | 890.1 |
|   Rubber and plastic products | 642.1 | 589.0 | 596.7 |
|   Primary metal products | 382.2 | 373.0 | 357.7 |
|   Fabricated metal products | 336.4 | 367.6 | 349.7 |
|   Machinery, except electrical | 1,020.8 | 1,013.9 | 1,128.4 |
|     Electronic computers | 361.8 | 282.1 | 330.0 |
|   Electrical machinery | 1,467.1 | 1,852.8 | 2,441.4 |
|   Transport equipment | 916.7 | 1,227.8 | 1,490.2 |
|   Professional and scientific instruments | 632.9 | 747.4 | 691.9 |
| **Total** (incl. others) | 15,387.3 | 16,385.9 | 16,654.2 |

| Exports | 1991/92 | 1992/93 | 1993/94 |
|---|---|---|---|
| Manufacturing products | 20,877.2 | 19,657.0 | 21,576.8 |
|   Food | 3,006.3 | 3,016.6 | 2,902.4 |
|   Fish | 412.1 | 446.8 | 361.6 |
|   Clothing and textiles | 826.2 | 877.7 | 838.8 |
|   Chemical products | 9,169.8 | 8,532.2 | 10,168.3 |
|     Drugs and pharmaceutical preparations | 7,255.5 | 6,420.0 | 7,987.7 |
|   Machinery, except electrical | 2,667.6 | 1,909.7 | 1,938.7 |
|     Electronic computers | 2,356.5 | 1,583.5 | 1,619.8 |
|   Electrical machines | 1,770.5 | 1,976.3 | 2,265.2 |
|   Professional and scientific instruments | 1,706.9 | 1,608.5 | 1,690.4 |
| **Total** (incl. others) | 21,051.2 | 19,790.7 | 21,752.6 |

* Figures refer to recorded transactions only. Adjusted totals (US $ million): Imports f.o.b. 19,150.1 in 1991/92; 18,442.2 in 1992/93; 19,488.8† in 1993/94. Exports f.o.b. 22,506.3 in 1991/92; 22,028.0 in 1992/93; 23,753.5† in 1993/94.
† Provisional figures.

UNITED STATES COMMONWEALTH TERRITORIES

*Puerto Rico*

**PRINCIPAL TRADING PARTNERS** (US $'000)

|  | 1989/90 Imports | 1989/90 Exports | 1990/91 Imports | 1990/91 Exports |
|---|---|---|---|---|
| Bahamas | 279,119 | 17,850 | 349,908 | 5,349 |
| Brazil | 134,711 | 20,475 | 129,424 | 28,701 |
| Dominican Repub. | 309,134 | 387,597 | 320,470 | 446,055 |
| Ecuador | 135,761 | 1,255 | 91,173 | 1,013 |
| France | 91,410 | 106,425 | 81,508 | 89,615 |
| Japan | 507,504 | 32,063 | 505,125 | 66,723 |
| Netherlands | 46,053 | 131,212 | 48,498 | 170,611 |
| Netherlands Antilles | 63,493 | 86,610 | 67,706 | 65,235 |
| Trinidad and Tobago | 29,000 | 54,759 | 34,802 | 56,968 |
| United Kingdom | 155,476 | 152,964 | 142,394 | 172,134 |
| USA | 10,801,208 | 16,780,492 | 10,739,205 | 18,484,375 |
| US Virgin Islands | 9,276 | 272,694 | 30,370 | 270,717 |
| Venezuela | 687,113 | 71,788 | 893,479 | 38,903 |
| **Total** (incl. others) | 15,721,624 | 19,305,398 | 15,904,281 | 21,322,973 |

## Transport

**ROAD TRAFFIC** (vehicles in use)

|  | 1987/88 | 1988/89 | 1989/90 |
|---|---|---|---|
| Cars |  |  |  |
| Private | 1,322,069 | 1,289,873 | 1,305,074 |
| For hire | 14,814 | 11,033 | 10,513 |
| Trucks |  |  |  |
| Private | 15,790 | 13,273 | 12,577 |
| For hire | 4,131 | 3,933 | 3,283 |
| Light trucks | 176,583 | 174,277 | 189,705 |
| Other vehicles | 75,155 | 74,930 | 60,929 |
| **Total** | 1,608,542 | 1,567,319 | 1,582,081 |

**SHIPPING** (year ending 30 June)

|  | 1985/86 | 1986/87 | 1987/88 |
|---|---|---|---|
| Passengers arriving | 29,559 | 59,089 | 33,737 |
| Passengers departing | 33,683 | 63,987 | 35,627 |
| Cruise visitors | 448,973 | 584,429 | 723,724 |

**1988/89:** Cruise visitors: 777,405.
**1989/90:** Cruise visitors: 866,090.
**1990/91:** Cruise visitors: 891,348.

**CIVIL AVIATION** (year ending 30 June)

|  | 1988/89 | 1989/90 | 1990/91 |
|---|---|---|---|
| Passengers arriving | 4,064,762 | 4,282,324 | 4,245,137 |
| Passengers departing | 4,072,828 | 4,297,521 | 4,262,154 |
| Freight (tons)* | 173,126 | 208,586 | 222,172 |

* Handled by the Luis Muñoz Marín International Airport.

## Tourism

(year ending 30 June)

|  | 1991/92 | 1992/93 | 1993/94* |
|---|---|---|---|
| Total visitors ('000)† | 3,730.0 | 3,869.0 | 4,022.6 |
| From USA‡ | 1,839.2 | 1,994.7 | 2,117.1 |
| From other countries‡ | 786.9 | 830.5 | 896.0 |
| Expenditure ($ million) | 1,452.7 | 1,563.1 | 1,670.0 |

* Preliminary.
† Includes cruise-ship visitors.
‡ Excludes cruise-ship visitors.

## Communications Media

|  | 1990 | 1991 | 1992 |
|---|---|---|---|
| Radio receivers ('000 in use) | 2,510 | 2,540 | 2,565 |
| Television receivers ('000 in use) | 930 | 942 | 952 |
| Telephones ('000 main lines in use)* | 991 | 1,030 | n.a. |
| Daily newspapers: |  |  |  |
| Number | 3 | n.a. | 3 |
| Average circulation ('000 copies) | 456 | n.a. | 507 |

Non-daily newspapers (estimates, 1988): 4 titles (average circulation 106,000 copies).
* Data refer to switched access lines of the Puerto Rico Telephone Co.
Sources: UNESCO, *Statistical Yearbook*; UN, *Statistical Yearbook*.

## Education

|  | 1987/88 | 1988/89 | 1989/90 |
|---|---|---|---|
| Total number of students | 951,188 | 955,662 | 953,140 |
| Public day schools | 666,255 | 661,576 | 651,225 |
| Private schools (accredited)* | 129,220 | 137,183 | 145,768 |
| University of Puerto Rico† | 56,904 | 56,993 | 55,626 |
| Private colleges and universities | 98,809 | 99,910 | 100,521 |
| Number of teachers‡ | 32,733 | 33,357 | 33,427 |

* Includes public and private accredited schools not administered by the Department of Education.
† Includes all university level students.
‡ School teachers only.

# Directory

## The Constitution

### RELATIONSHIP WITH THE USA

On 3 July 1950 the Congress of the United States of America adopted Public Law No. 600, which was to allow 'the people of Puerto Rico to organize a government pursuant to a constitution of their own adoption'. This Law was submitted to the voters of Puerto Rico in a referendum and was accepted in the summer of 1951. A new Constitution was drafted in which Puerto Rico was styled as a commonwealth, or estado libre asociado, 'a state which is free of superior authority in the management of its own local affairs', though it remained in association with the USA. This Constitution, with its amendments and resolutions, was ratified by the people of Puerto Rico on 3 March 1952, and by the Congress of the USA on 3 July 1952; and the Commonwealth of Puerto Rico was established on 25 July 1952.

Under the terms of the political and economic union between the USA and Puerto Rico, US citizens in Puerto Rico enjoy the same privileges and immunities as if Puerto Rico were a member state of the Union. Puerto Rican citizens are citizens of the USA and may freely enter and leave that country.

The Congress of the USA has no control of, and may not intervene in, the internal affairs of Puerto Rico.

Puerto Rico is exempted from the tax laws of the USA. While it has no representation in the US Congress, the Puerto Rican Resident Commissioner to the USA, directly elected for a four-year term, enjoys the privileges of membership, without voting, of the House of Representatives of the US Congress.

There are no customs duties between the USA and Puerto Rico. Foreign products entering Puerto Rico—with the single exception of coffee, which is subject to customs duty in Puerto Rico, but not in the USA—pay the same customs duties as would be paid on their entry into the USA.

The US social security system is extended to Puerto Rico except for unemployment insurance provisions. Laws providing for economic co-operation between the Federal Government and the States of the Union for the construction of roads, schools, public health services and similar purposes are extended to Puerto Rico. Such joint programmes are administered by the Commonwealth Government.

Amendments to the Constitution are not subject to approval by the US Congress, provided that they are consistent with the US Federal Constitution, the Federal Relations Act defining federal relations with Puerto Rico, and Public Law No. 600. Subject to these limitations, the Constitution may be amended by a two-thirds vote of the Puerto Rican Legislature and by the subsequent majority approval of the electorate.

### BILL OF RIGHTS

No discrimination shall be made on account of race, colour, sex, birth, social origin or condition, or political or religious ideas. Suffrage shall be direct, equal and universal for all over the age of 18. Public property and funds shall not be used to support schools other than State schools. The death penalty shall not exist. The rights of the individual, of the family and of property are guaranteed. The Constitution establishes trial by jury in all cases of felony, as well as the right of habeas corpus. Every person is to receive free elementary and secondary education. Social protection is to be afforded to the old, the disabled, the sick and the unemployed.

### THE LEGISLATURE

The Legislative Assembly consists of two chambers, whose members are elected by direct vote for a four-year term. The Senate is composed of 27 members, the House of Representatives of 53 members. Senators must be over 30 years of age, and Representatives over 25 years of age. The Constitution guarantees the minority parties additional representation in the Legislature, which may fluctuate from one quarter to one third of the seats in each House.

The Senate elects a President and the House of Representatives a Speaker from their respective members. The sessions of each house are public. A majority of the total number of members of each house constitutes a quorum. Either house can initiate legislation, although bills for raising revenue must originate in the House of Representatives. Once passed by both Houses, a bill is submitted to the Governor, who can either sign it into law or return it, with his reasons for refusal, within 10 days. If it is returned, the Houses may pass it again by a two-thirds majority, in which case the Governor must accept it.

The House of Representatives, or the Senate, can impeach one of its members for treason, bribery, other felonies and 'misdemeanours involving moral turpitude'. A two-thirds majority is necessary before an indictment may be brought. The cases are tried by the Senate. If a Representative or Senator is declared guilty, he is deprived of his office and becomes punishable by law.

### THE EXECUTIVE

The Governor, who must be at least 35 years of age, is elected by direct suffrage and serves for four years. Responsible for the execution of laws, the Governor is Commander-in-Chief of the militia and has the power to proclaim martial law. At the beginning of every regular session of the Assembly, in January, the Governor presents a report on the state of the treasury, and on proposed expenditure. The Governor chooses the Secretaries of Departments, subject to the approval of the Legislative Assembly. These are led by the Secretary of State, who replaces the Governor at need.

### LOCAL GOVERNMENT

The island is divided into 78 municipal districts for the purposes of local administration. The municipalities comprise both urban areas and the surrounding neighbourhood. They are governed by a mayor and a municipal assembly, both elected for a four-year term.

## The Government

### HEAD OF STATE

**Governor:** PEDRO ROSSELLÓ (inaugurated 2 January 1993).

### EXECUTIVE
(June 1995)

**Governor:** PEDRO ROSSELLÓ.
**Secretary of State:** BALTASAR CORRADA DEL RÍO.
**Secretary of Justice:** PEDRO PIERLUISI.
**Secretary of the Treasury:** MANUEL DÍAZ SALDAÑA.
**Secretary of Education:** VÍCTOR FAJARDO.
**Secretary of Labor and Human Resources:** CÉSAR ALMODÓVAR MARCHANI.
**Secretary of Transportation and Public Works:** CARLOS PESQUERA MORALES.
**Secretary of Health:** Dr CARMEN FELICIANO.
**Secretary of Agriculture:** NEFTALÍ SOTO.
**Secretary of Housing:** CARLOS VIVONI.
**Secretary of Natural and Environmental Resources:** PEDRO GELABERT.
**Secretary of Drug Addiction Services:** ASTRID OYOLA DE BENÍTEZ.
**Secretary of Consumer Affairs:** IVÁN AYALA CÁDIZ.
**Secretary of Recreation and Sports:** MARIMER OLAZAGASTI.
**Secretary of Economic Development and Commerce:** LUIS FORTUÑO.
**Secretary of Social Services:** CARMEN RODRÍGUEZ RIVERA.
**Secetary of the Governorship:** ALVARO CIFUENTES.

**Resident Commissioner in Washington:** CARLOS ROMERO BARCELÓ.

### GOVERNMENT OFFICES

**Office of the Governor:** La Fortaleza, POB 82, PR 00901; tel. (809) 721-7000: fax (809) 721-7483.
**Department of Agriculture:** POB 10163, San Juan, PR 00908-1163; tel. (809) 721-2120; fax (809) 723-9747.
**Department of Consumer Affairs:** POB 41059, San Juan, PR 00940-1059; tel. (809) 722-7555; fax (809) 726-6576.
**Department of Drug Addiction Services:** POB 21414, Río Piedras, San Juan, PR 00928; tel. (809) 763-7575.
**Department of Economic Development and Commerce:** POB 4435, San Juan, PR 00902-4435; tel. (809) 721-2400; fax (809) 725-4417.
**Department of Education:** POB 190759, San Juan, PR 00919; tel. (809) 758-4949; fax (809) 250-0275.
**Department of Health:** POB 70184, San Juan, PR 00936; tel. (809) 766-1616.
**Department of Housing:** POB 21365, San Juan, PR 00928-1365; tel. (809) 274-2004; fax (809) 758-9263.
**Department of Justice:** POB 192, San Juan, PR 00902; tel. (809) 724-4700; fax (809) 725-6144.

UNITED STATES COMMONWEALTH TERRITORIES                                    Puerto Rico

**Department of Labor and Human Resources:** 505 Muñoz Rivera Ave, San Juan, PR 00918; tel. (809) 754-5353; fax (809) 753-9550.

**Department of Natural and Environmental Resources:** POB 5887, Puerta de Tierra, San Juan, PR 00906; tel. (809) 724-8774.

**Department of Recreation and Sports:** POB 3207, San Juan, PR 00904; tel. (809) 721-2800.

**Department of Social Services:** POB 11398, Santurce, San Juan, PR 00910; tel. (809) 722-7400.

**Department of State:** POB 3271, San Juan, PR 00902-3271; tel. (809) 722-2121; fax (809) 725-7303.

**Department of Transportation:** POB 41269, San Juan, PR 00940; tel. (809) 722-2929; fax (809) 728-8963.

**Department of the Treasury:** POB 4515, San Juan, PR 009012; tel. (809) 721-2020; fax (809) 723-6213.

**Gubernatorial Election, 3 November 1992**

| Candidate | Votes | % |
| --- | --- | --- |
| Pedro Rosselló (PNP) | 919,029 | 49.9 |
| Victoria Muñoz Mendoza (PPD) | 845,372 | 45.9 |
| Fernando Martín (PIP) | 76,357 | 4.1 |
| Total | 1,840,758 | 100.0 |

## Legislature

### LEGISLATIVE ASSEMBLY
#### Senate
(27 members)

**President of the Senate:** Roberto Rexach Benítez.

**Election, 3 November 1992**

| Party | Seats |
| --- | --- |
| PNP | 20 |
| PPD | 6 |
| PIP | 1 |

#### House of Representatives
(53 members)

**Speaker of the House:** Zaída Hernández.

**Election, 3 November 1992**

| Party | Seats |
| --- | --- |
| PNP | 36 |
| PPD | 16 |
| PIP | 1 |

## Political Organizations

**National Republican Party of Puerto Rico:** POB 366108, San Juan, PR 00936-6108; tel. (809) 793-4040; Chair. Luis A. Ferre.

**Partido Comunista Puertorriqueño (PCP)** (Puerto Rican Communist Party): f. 1934; advocates full independence and severance of ties with the USA.

**Partido Independentista Puertorriqueño (PIP)** (Puerto Rican Independence Party): 963 F. D. Roosevelt Ave, Hato Rey, San Juan PR 00918; f. 1946; moderate left-wing; seeks immediate independence for Puerto Rico as a socialist-democratic republic; c. 60,000 mems; Leader Rubén Barríos Martínez.

**Partido Nuevo Progresista (PNP)** (New Progressive Party): San Juan; f. 1967; advocates eventual admission of Puerto Rico as a federated state of the USA; c. 225,000 mems; Pres. Pedro Rosselló; Sec.-Gen. Marcos Morell.

**Partido Popular Democrático (PPD)** (Popular Democratic Party): 403 Ponce de León Ave, POB 5788, Puerta de Tierra, San Juan, PR 00906; telex 0601; f. 1938; liberal; advocates social reform; supports continuation and improvement of the present Commonwealth status of Puerto Rico; c. 660,000 mems; Pres. and Leader Héctor Luis Acevedo.

**Partido Socialista Puertorriqueño (PSP)** (Puerto Rican Socialist Party): 256 Padre Colón St, Río Piedras, San Juan, PR 00925; f. 1971; seeks the establishment of an independent socialist republic; c. 6,000 mems; Pres. and Leader Carlos Gallisá.

**Puerto Rico Democratic Party:** POB 5788, San Juan, PR 00906; tel. (809) 722-4952; Exec. Dir Dr Richard Machado.

The Fuerzas Armadas de Liberación Nacional Puertorriqueña (FALN) (Puerto Rican National Liberation Armed Forces) and the Ejército Popular Boricua (Macheteros, Leader Filiberto Ojeda Ríos), which seek to attain independence through non-electoral means, are not incorporated or registered as political parties.

## Judicial System

The Judiciary is vested in the Supreme Court and other courts as may be established by law. The Supreme Court is composed of the Chief Justice and six Associate Justices, appointed by the Governor with the consent of the Senate. The lower Judiciary consists of Superior and District Courts and Municipal Justices equally appointed.

There is also a US Federal District Court, whose judges and attorney are appointed by the President of the United States.

### SUPREME COURT OF PUERTO RICO
(POB 2392, Puerta de Tierra, San Juan, PR 00902-2392; tel. (809) 724-3551; fax (809) 725-4910)

**Chief Justice:** José A. Andréu García.

**Justices:** Federico Hernández Denton, Myriam Naveira de Rodón, Antonio S. Negrón García, Francisco Rebollo López, Rafael Alonso Alonso, Jaime B. Fuster Berlingeri.

### US FEDERAL DISTRICT COURT FOR PUERTO RICO
(San Juan PR 0018)

**Judges:** Carmen Consuelo Cerezo, (Chief Judge), Raymond L. Acosta, Héctor M. Laffitte, Jaime Pieras, Jr, Gilberto Gierbolini Ortiz, José A. Fusté, Juan M. Pérez-Giménez.

**US District Attorney for Puerto Rico:** Guillermo Hill (acting).

## Religion

About 81% of the population belonged to the Roman Catholic Church at the end of 1990. The Protestant churches active in Puerto Rico include the Episcopalian, Baptist, Presbyterian, Methodist, Seventh-day Adventist, Lutheran, Mennonite, Salvation Army and Christian Science. There is a small Jewish community.

### CHRISTIANITY
#### The Roman Catholic Church

Puerto Rico comprises one archdiocese and four dioceses. At 31 December 1993 there were an estimated 2,914,000 adherents.

**Bishops' Conference of Puerto Rico:** POB 40682, San Juan, PR 00940-0682; tel. (809) 728-1650; fax (809) 728-1654; f. 1967; Pres. Rt Rev. Iñaki Mallona Txertudi, Bishop of Arecibo.

**Archbishop of San Juan de Puerto Rico:** Cardinal Luis Aponte Martínez, Arzobispado, Apdo S-1967, Calle San Jorge 201, Santurce, San Juan, PR 00902; tel. (809) 727-7373; fax (809) 841-1778.

#### Other Christian Churches

**Episcopal Church of Puerto Rico:** POB 902, Saint Just Station, St Just, PR 00978; tel. (809) 761-9800; fax (809) 761-0320; diocese of the Episcopal Church in the USA, part of the Anglican Communion; Bishop Rt Rev. David Andrés Alvarez.

**Evangelical Council of Puerto Rico:** Calle El Roble 54, Apdo 21343, Río Piedras, San Juan, PR 00928; tel. (809) 765-6030; fax (809) 765-5977; f. 1954; 6 mem. churches; Pres. Rev. Harry del Valle; Exec. Sec. Rev. Moisés Rosa-Ramos.

### BAHÁ'Í FAITH

**Spiritual Assembly:** POB 11603, Santurce, San Juan, PR 00910-2703; tel. (809) 721-6584; fax (809) 722-8099.

### JUDAISM

**Jewish Community Center:** 903 Ponce de León Ave, Santurce, San Juan, PR 00907; tel. (809) 724-4157; f. 1953; conservative congregation with 250 families; Rabbi Alejandro B. Felch.

There is also a reform congregation with 60 families.

## The Press

Puerto Rico has high readership figures for its few newspapers and magazines, as well as for mainland US periodicals. Several newspapers have large additional readerships among the immigrant communities in New York.

### DAILIES
(m = morning; s = Sunday)

**El Nuevo Día:** 404 Ponce de León Ave, POB S-297, San Juan, PR 00902; tel. (809) 793-7070; telex 3252305; fax (809) 793-8850;

f. 1970; Publr and Editor Antonio Luis Ferre; circ. 229,000 (M), 223,000 (S).

**The San Juan Star:** POB 364187, San Juan, PR 00936-4187; tel. (809) 793-7152; fax (809) 783-5788; f. 1959; English; Publr Adolfo Comas Bacardi; Editor Scott Ware; circ. 35,000 (M), 37,000 (S).

**El Vocero de Puerto Rico:** 206 Ponce de León Ave, POB 3831, San Juan, PR 00902-3831; tel. (809) 721-2300; fax (809) 725-8422; f. 1974; Publr and Editor Gaspar Roca; circ 259,000 (M).

### PERIODICALS

**Buena Salud:** 1700 Fernández Juncos Ave, San Juan, PR 00909; tel. (809) 728-7325; f. 1990; monthly; Editor Ivonne Longueira; circ. 59,000.

**Caribbean Business:** 1700 Fernández Juncos Ave, San Juan, PR 00909; tel. (809) 728-3000; telex 380239; fax (809) 728-7325; f. 1973; weekly; business and finance; Man. Editor Manuel A. Casiano Jr; circ. 47,000.

**Educación:** c/o Dept of Education, POB 190759, Hato Rey Station, San Juan, PR 00919; f. 1960; 2 a year; Spanish; Editor José Galarza Rodríguez; circ. 28,000.

**Imagen:** 1700 Fernández Juncos Ave, Stop 25, San Juan, PR 00909-2999; tel. (809) 728-4545; fax (809) 728-7325; f. 1986; monthly; women's interest; Editor Norma Borges; circ. 83,000.

**Industrial Puerto Rico:** 721 Hernández St, Miramar Towers, Santurce, San Juan, PR 00907; bi-monthly; English; industry and business; circ. 5,000.

**Qué Pasa:** POB 4435, Old San Juan Station, San Juan, PR 00905; tel. (809) 721-2400; fax (809) 721-3878; f. 1948; quarterly; English; publ. by Puerto Rico Tourism Co; official tourist guide; Editor Kathryn Robinson; circ. 180,000.

**Revista Colegio de Abogados de Puerto Rico:** POB 1900, San Juan, PR 00902; tel. (809) 721-3358; fax (809) 725-0330; f. 1914; quarterly; Spanish; law; Editor Dr Carmelo Delgado-Cintrón; circ. 9,000.

**Revista del Instituto de Cultura Puertorriqueña:** POB 4184, San Juan, PR 00902-4184; tel. (809) 725-7515; f. 1958; quarterly; Spanish; arts, literature, history, theatre, Puerto Rican culture; Editor Alberto Arroyo Gómez; circ. 1,000.

**La Torre:** POB 23322, UPR Station, San Juan, PR 00931-3322; tel. (809) 758-0148; fax (809) 753-9116; f. 1953; publ. by University of Puerto Rico; quarterly; literary criticism and linguistics; Editor Dr Arturo Echavarría; circ. 1,000.

**Vea:** POB 190240, San Juan, PR 00919-0240; tel. (809) 721-0095; fax (809) 725-1940; f. 1969; weekly; Spanish; TV and Cable-TV programmes; Editor Enrique Pizzi; circ. 88,000.

**El Visitante:** POB 41305, Minillas Station, San Juan, PR 00940-1305; tel. (809) 728-3710; f. 1975; weekly; publ. by the Puerto Rican Conference of Roman Catholic Bishops; Dir Aníbal Colón Rosado; Editor Rev. Efraín Zabala; circ. 60,000.

### FOREIGN NEWS BUREAUX

**Agencia EFE** (Spain): Cobian's Plaza, Suite 214, Santurce, PR 00910; tel. (809) 723-6023; fax (809) 725-8651; Dir Elías García.

**Associated Press (AP)** (USA): POB 5829, Puerta de Tierra, San Juan, PR 00906; tel. (809) 722-7575; telex 0480; fax (809) 721-5922; Chief Kernan R. Turner.

**United Press International (UPI)** (USA): POB 9655, Santurce, San Juan, PR 00908; tel. (809) 725-4460; Bureau Chief Virgilio Espetia.

## Publishers

**Ediciones Huracán Inc:** González 1002, Río Piedras, San Juan, PR 00925; tel. (809) 763-7407; fax (809) 763-7407; f. 1975; textbooks, literature, social studies, history; Dir Carmen Rivera-Izcoa.

**Editorial Académica, Inc:** 67 Santa Anastacia St, El Vigía, Río Piedras, PR 00926; tel. (809) 760-3879; f. 1988; regional history, politics, government, educational materials, fiction; Dir Fidelio Calderón.

**Editorial Biblioteca de Autores Puertorriqueños:** POB 582, San Juan, PR 00902.

**Editorial Club de la Prensa:** POB 4692, San Juan, PR 00905; travel, fiction, folklore, essays.

**Editorial Coquí:** POB 21992, UPR Station, San Juan, PR 00931.

**Editorial Cordillera, Inc:** Calle Mexico 17, Cond. Centrum Plaza, Local A Comm., Hato Rey, San Juan, PR 00917; tel. (809) 767-6188; fax (809) 767-8646; f. 1962; Pres. Héctor Serrano; Treas. Isaac Serrano.

**Editorial Cultural Inc:** POB 21056, Río Piedras, San Juan, PR 00928; tel. (809) 765-9767; f. 1949; general literature; Dir Francisco M. Vázquez.

**Editorial Edil, Inc:** POB 23088, UPR Station, Río Piedras, PR 00931; tel. (809) 753-9381; fax (809) 250-1407; f. 1967; university texts, literature, technical and official publs; Dir Norberto Lugo Ramírez.

**Editorial Instituto de Cultura Puertorriqueña:** POB 4184, San Juan, PR 00905; tel. (809) 723-2115; telex 9686; f. 1955; general literature, history, poetry, music, textbooks; Man. Dir Marta Aponte Alsina.

**University of Puerto Rico Press (EDUPR):** POB 23322, UPR Station, Río Piedras, San Juan, PR 00931-3322; tel. (809) 250-0435; fax (809) 753-9116; f. 1932; general literature, children's literature, law, philosophy, science, educational; Dir José Ramón de la Torre (acting).

### Government Publishing House

**División Editorial Departamento de Instrucción Pública:** Avda Teniente César González, esq. Calaf, Urb. Tres. Monjitas, Hato Rey, San Juan, PR 00917; Dir Adrián Santos Tirado.

## Radio and Television

There were 118 radio stations and 15 television stations operating in 1995. The only non-commercial stations are the radio station and the two television stations operated by the Puerto Rico Department of Education. The US Armed Forces also operate a radio station and three television channels. All television services are in colour. There were an estimated 4.5m. radio receivers and 915,000 television receivers in use in 1995.

**Asociación de Radiodifusores de Puerto Rico** (Puerto Rican Radio Broadcasters' Asscn): Cobian's Plaza 414, 1607 Ponce de León Ave, Santurce, San Juan, PR 00912; tel. (809) 724-8150; fax (809) 722-2667; f. 1947; 112 mems; Pres. Huberto Biaggi; Exec. Dir José A. Ribas Dominicci.

**Broadcasters' Association of Puerto Rico:** POB Q, Hato Rey, San Juan, PR 00919; 49 mems; Pres. Héctor Reichard.

## Finance

(cap. = capital; res = reserves; dep. = deposits; brs = branches; amounts in US dollars)

### BANKING
#### Government Bank

**Government Development Bank for Puerto Rico:** POB 42001, Minillas Station, San Juan, PR 00940-2001; tel. (809) 729-6000; telex 3857265; fax (809) 721-1143; f. 1942; an independent govt agency; acts as fiscal (borrowing) agent to the Commonwealth Govt and its public corpns and provides long- and medium-term loans to private businesses; also acts as clearing agency for Puerto Rico's commercial banks; cap. and res 845.9m., dep. 4,940.6m. (June 1993); Chair. Manuel Díaz Saldaña; Pres. Marcos Rodríguez-Ema.

#### Commercial Banks

**Banco Popular:** 209 Muñoz Rivera Ave, POB 362708, Hato Rey, San Juan, PR 00936; tel. (809)765-9800; telex 3450033; fax (809) 754-7803; f. 1893; cap. and res 425.8m., dep. 4,926.3m. (Dec. 1989); Chair. Rafael Carrión, Jr; Pres. and CEO Richard L. Carrión; 160 brs.

**Banco Santander Puerto Rico:** 207 Ponce de León Ave, Hato Rey, San Juan, PR 00918; tel. (809) 759-7070; telex 3450062; fax (809) 763-1366; f. 1976; cap. and res 374.6m., dep. 2,489.1m. (Dec. 1993); Chair., Pres. and CEO Benito Cantalapiedra; 53 brs.

**Banco de la Vivienda:** POB 345, Hato Rey, San Juan, PR 00919; tel. (809) 765-2537; f. 1961; housing bank and finance agency; helps low-income families to purchase houses; cap. and res 44m. (June 1989); Pres. Carmen S. Melero; 7 brs.

**Central Hispano–Puerto Rico:** 221 Ponce de León Ave, POB 366270, Hato Rey, San Juan, PR 00917; tel. (809) 250-2578; telex 3453090; fax (809) 250-2578; f. 1977; cap. and res 194.6m., dep. 1,647.6m. (Dec. 1992); Pres. Antonio C. Campos; 21 brs.

**Roig Commercial Bank:** Carreras and Georgetti Sts, POB 457, Humacao, PR 00661; tel. (809) 852-1010; telex 3450624; fax (809) 850-5555; f. 1922; cap. and res 52m., dep. 623.8m. (Dec. 1994); Chair. J. Adalberto Roig; Pres. J. Adalberto Roig, Jr; 25 brs.

**Royal Bank of Canada:** Royal Bank Centre, 225 Ponce de León Ave, POB 819, Hato Rey, PR 00919; tel. (809) 250-3900; telex 3450465; fax (809) 230-3971; f. 1927; cap. and res 34m., dep. 471.5m. (Oct. 1991); Regional Rep. R.W. Brydon; 17 brs.

**Scotiabank de Puerto Rico:** Plaza Scotiabank, 273 Ponce de León Ave, POB 2230, Hato Rey, San Juan, PR 00917; tel. (809) 758-8989; telex 3450130; fax (809) 766-7879; f. 1979; cap. and res 91.7m., dep.

511.8m. (Sept. 1993); Chair. D. F. Babensee; Pres. I. A. Méndez; 10 brs.

### Savings Banks

**First Federal Savings Bank:** First Federal Bldg, 1519 Ponce de León Ave, POB 9146, Santurce, PR 00908; tel. (809) 729-8200; fax (809) 729-8254; f. 1948; dep. 1,383m., total assets 1,895m. (Sept. 1991); Pres. Angel Alvarez-Pérez; 30 brs.

**Oriental Federal Savings Bank:** 2 Hoya y Hernández, POB 1952, Humacao, PR 00792; tel. (809) 852-0378; fax (809) 850-8280; Chair., Pres. and CEO José Enrique Fernández.

**Ponce Federal Bank, FSB:** Villa esq. Concordia, POB 1024, Ponce, PR 00733; tel. (809) 844-8100; fax (809) 848-5380; f. 1958; total assets 1,197.4m. (Sept. 1991); Pres. and CEO Hans H. Hertell; 19 brs.

**R & G Federal Savings Bank:** POB 2510, Guaynabo, PR 00970; tel. (809) 766-6677; fax (809) 766-8175; Chair., Pres. and CEO Víctor J. Galán.

### US Banks in Puerto Rico

**Bank of Boston:** Royal Bank Center, Main Floor, 255 Ponce de León Ave, POB 70101, Hato Rey, San Juan, PR 00918; tel. (809) 756-8080; telex 3450740; fax (809) 765-5540; Vice-Pres. and Gen. Man. Luiz de Campos Salles; 3 brs.

**Chase Manhattan Bank NA:** 254 Muñoz Rivera Ave, San Juan, PR 00936; tel. (809) 753-3400; telex 9076; Man. Dir and Gen. Man. Robert C. Dávila; 1 br.

**Citibank NA:** Citibank Drive, POB 364106, San Juan, PR 00926-9631; tel. (809) 753-5555; fax (809) 766-3880; Gen. Man. Horacio Igust; 7 brs.

### SAVINGS AND LOAN ASSOCIATIONS

**Caguas Central Federal Savings of Puerto Rico:** POB 7199, Caguas, PR 00626; tel. (809) 783-3370; f. 1959; assets 800m.; Pres. Lorenzo Muñoz Franco.

**United Federal Savings and Loan Association of Puerto Rico:** POB 2647, San Juan, PR 00936; f. 1957; cap. and res 151.4m., assets 164.1m.; Pres. Guillermo S. Marqués; 8 brs.

**Westernbank Puerto Rico:** 19 West McKinley St, Mayagüez, PR 00680; tel. (809) 834-8000; fax (809) 831-5958; cap. 60m., dep. 680m. (1992); Chair. and CEO Lic. Frank C. Stipes; 31 brs.

### Banking Organization

**Asociación de Bancos de Puerto Rico:** Popular Center Bldg, Suite 1014, 209 Muñoz Rivera Ave, San Juan, PR 00918; tel. (809) 753-8630; Pres. Juan A. Net; Exec. Vice-Pres. Arturo L. Carrión.

### INSURANCE

**American Income Life Insurance Co:** Banco Cooperativo Bldg, 236 Ponce de León Ave, POB 4164, Hato Rey, San Juan PR 00917; tel. (809) 766-7753; fax (809) 7321; Gen. Man. Joseph Carn, Sr.

**Atlantic Southern Insurance Co:** POB 362889, San Juan, PR 00936-2889; tel. (809) 767-9750; fax (809) 764-4707; f. 1945; Chair. R.D. Williams; Pres. Ramón L. Galanes.

**Caribbean American Life Assurance Co:** Scotiabank Plaza, Suite 350, POB 195167, Hato Rey, San Juan PR 00919; tel. (809) 250-6470; fax (809) 250-7680; Pres. Harry Lewis.

**Cooperativa de Seguros Multiples de Puerto Rico:** POB 3846, San Juan, PR 00936; general insurance; Pres. Edwin Quiñones Suárez.

**La Cruz Azul de Puerto Rico:** Road 1, Río Piedras, POB 366068, San Juan, PR 00936-6068; tel. (809) 272-9898; telex 0365256; fax (809) 751-5545; health; Exec. Dir José Julián Alvarez.

**General Accident Life Assurance Co of Puerto Rico:** POB 363786, San Juan, PR 00936-3786; tel. (809) 758-4888; fax (809) 766-1985; Pres. Hermes Vargas.

**Pan American Life Insurance Co:** POB 364865, San Juan, PR 00907-4865; tel. (809) 724-6075; fax (809) 722-0253; Gen. Man. Felipe Pía.

**Puerto Rican–American Insurance Co:** POB 70333, San Juan, PR 00936-8333; tel. (809) 250-6500; telex 3450352; fax (809) 250-5380; f. 1920; total assets 119.9m. (1993); Chair. and CEO Rafael A. Roca; Pres. Rodolfo E. Criscuolo.

**Security National Life Insurance Co:** POB 193309, Hato Rey, PR 00919; tel. (809) 753-6161; fax (809) 758-7409; Pres. Carlos Fernández.

There are numerous agents, representing Puerto Rican, US and foreign companies.

## Trade and Industry

### CHAMBERS OF COMMERCE

**Chamber of Commerce of Puerto Rico:** Chamber of Commerce Bldgs, Tetuán 100, POB S-3789, San Juan, PR 00902-3789; tel. (809) 721-6060; fax (809) 723-1891; f. 1913; 1,600 mems; Pres. Frank Unanue.

**Chamber of Commerce of Bayamón:** POB 2007, Bayamón, PR 00619; tel. (809) 786-4320; 350 mems; Pres. Iván A. Marrero; Exec. Sec. Angelica B. de Remírez.

**Chamber of Commerce of Ponce and the South of Puerto Rico:** POB 7455, Ponce, PR 00732-7455; tel. (809) 844-4000; fax (809) 844-4705; f. 1885; 450 mems; Pres. Gennaro Dessy; Exec. Dir Vivien Mattei.

**Chamber of Commerce of Río Piedras:** 1057 Ponce de León Ave, San Juan, PR 00923; f. 1960; 300 mems; Pres. Neftalí González Pérez.

**Chamber of Commerce of the West of Puerto Rico Inc:** POB 9, Mayagüez, PR 00681; tel. (809) 832-3749; fax (809) 832-3250; f. 1962; c. 300 mems; Pres. Dr Miguel Santiago Meléndez.

**Official Chamber of Commerce of Spain:** POB 894, San Juan, PR 00902; tel. (809) 725-5178; fax (809) 724-0527; f. 1966; promotes Spanish goods; provides information for Spanish exporters and Puerto Rican importers; 300 mems; Pres. Manuel García; Gen. Sec. Antonio Trujilo.

### DEVELOPMENT ORGANIZATION

**Commonwealth of Puerto Rico Economic Development Administration—EDA:** POB 362350, San Juan, PR 00936-2350; 355 Roosevelt Ave, Hato Rey, San Juan, PR 00918; tel. (809) 758-4747; fax (809) 764-1415; public agency responsible, with its subsidiary the Puerto Rico Industrial Development Co (PRIDCO), for the govt-sponsored industrial development programme; Admin. Clifford Myatt.

### PROFESSIONAL, INDUSTRIAL AND COMMERCIAL ASSOCIATIONS

**Home Builders' Association of Puerto Rico:** 1605 Ponce de León Ave, Condominium San Martin, Santurce, San Juan, PR 00909; tel. (809) 723-0279; 150 mems; Pres. Franklin D. López; Exec. Dir Wanda I. Navajas.

**Puerto Rico Bar Association:** POB 1900, San Juan, PR 00902; tel. (809) 721-3358; fax (809) 725-0330; f. 1840; 8,954 mems; Dir Mady Pacheco-García de la Noceda.

**Puerto Rico Farm Bureau:** Cond. San Martín, 4°, Ponce de León 1605, Pda 23, Santurce, San Juan, PR 00909; f. 1925; over 8,000 mems; Pres. Antonio Alvarez.

**Puerto Rico Institute of Engineers and Surveyors:** GPO Box 3845, San Juan, PR 00936-3845; tel. (809) 758-2250; fax (809) 758-7639; f. 1938; 7,000 mems; Pres. Miguel A. Roa Vargas.

**Puerto Rico Manufacturers' Association:** POB 192410, San Juan, PR 00919-2410; tel. (809) 759-9445; fax (809) 756-7670.

**Puerto Rico Medical Association:** POB 9387, San Juan, PR 00908-9387; tel. (809) 721-6969; fax (809) 722-1191; f. 1902; 3,000 mems; Pres. Dr Adalberto Mendoza-Vallejo.

**Puerto Rico Teachers' Association:** POB 1088, Hato Rey, San Juan, PR 00919; f. 1911; 23,115 mems; Pres. José Eligio Vélez; Exec. Sec. Agustín García Estrada.

**Puerto Rico United Retailers Center:** POB 190127, San Juan, PR 00919-0127; tel. (809) 759-8405; f. 1891; 18,000 mems; Pres. Carlos M. Declet.

#### Co-operatives

**Cooperativa de Cafeteros de Puerto Rico** (Coffee Growers' Co-operative): Bo. Cuatro Calles, POB 1511, Ponce, PR 00731; f. 1924; 4,080 mems; Chair. Diez Urrutia; Gen. Man. and Sec. Ramiro L. Colón, Jr.

**Co-operative League of Puerto Rico:** POB 360707, San Juan, PR 00936-0707; f. 1948; tel. (809) 764-2727; fax (809) 250-6093; 295 mems; Pres. Carlos J. Acevedo Rivera; Exec. Dir Norberto Falcón Morales.

### TRADE UNIONS

**American Federation of Labor-Congress of Industrial Organizations (AFL-CIO):** San Juan; c. 60,000 mems; Regional Dir Agustín Benítez.

**Central Puertorriqueña de Trabajadores (CPT):** POB 364084, San Juan, PR 00936-4084; tel. (809) 781-6649; fax (809) 792-0030; f. 1982; Pres. Federico Torres Montalvo.

**Confederación General de Trabajadores de Puerto Rico:** 620 San Antonio St, San Juan, PR 00907; f. 1939; Pres. Francisco Colón Gordiany; 35,000 mems.

**Federación del Trabajo de Puerto Rico (AFL-CIO):** POB S-1648, San Juan, PR 00903; tel. (809) 722-4012; f. 1952; Pres. Hipólito Marcano; Sec.-Treas. Clifford W. Depin; 200,000 mems.

**Puerto Rico Industrial Workers' Union, Inc:** POB 22014, UPR Station, San Juan, PR 00931; Pres. David Muñoz Hernández.

**Sindicato Empleados de Equipo Pesado, Construcción y Ramas Anexas de Puerto Rico, Inc** (Construction and Allied Trades Union): Calle Hicaco 95–Urb. Milaville, Río Piedras, San Juan, PR 00926; f. 1954; Pres. Jesús M. Agosto; 950 mems.

**Sindicato de Obreros Unidos del Sur de Puerto Rico** (United Workers' Union of South Puerto Rico): POB 106, Salinas, PR 00751; f. 1961; Pres. José Caraballo; 52,000 mems.

**Unión General de Trabajadores de Puerto Rico:** Apdo 29247, Estación de Infantería, Río Piedras, San Juan, PR 00929; tel. (809) 751-5350; fax (809) 751-7604; f. 1965; Pres. Juan G. Eliza-Colón; Sec.-Treas. Osvaldo Romero-Pizarro.

**Unión de Trabajadores de la Industría Eléctrica y Riego de Puerto Rico:** POB 13068, Santurce, San Juan, PR 00908; tel. (809) 721-1700; telex 4060; Pres. Herminio Martínez Rodríguez; Sec.-Treas. Rafael Ortega; 6,000 mems.

## Transport

### RAILWAYS

There are no passenger railways in Puerto Rico.

**Ponce and Guayama Railway:** Aguirre, PR 00608; tel. (809) 853-3810; owned by the Corporación Azucarera de Puerto Rico; transports sugar cane over 96 km of track route; Exec. Dir A. Martínez; Gen. Supt J. Rodríguez.

### ROADS

The system of paved roads totalled 9,351 km (5,812 miles) in 1982. A modern highway system links all cities and towns along the coast and cross-country. A highways authority oversees the design and construction of roads, highways and bridges.

### SHIPPING

There are nine major ports in the island, the principal ones being San Juan, Ponce and Mayagüez. Other ports include Guayama, Guayanilla, Guánica, Yabucoa, Aguirre, Aguadilla, Fajardo, Arecibo, Humacao and Arroyo. San Juan, one of the finest and longest all-weather natural harbours in the Caribbean, is the main port of entry for foodstuffs and raw materials and for shipping finished industrial products. In 1992 it handled 14.3m. tons of cargo. Passenger traffic is limited to tourist cruise vessels, which brought an estimated 1.0m. visitors to Puerto Rico in 1992/93.

**Puerto Rico Ports Authority:** POB 362829, San Juan, PR 00936-2829; tel. (809) 729-8805; fax (809) 722-7867; manages and administers all ports and airports; Exec. Dir Dr Herman Sulsona.

#### Agents for Foreign Lines

**Antilles Shipping Corporation:** POB 3827, San Juan, PR 00904; f. 1955; agents for over 50 cos in liners, tankers, barges and cruise ships; Pres. Hans Heitkonig; Vice-Pres. Hans Meijer.

**Caribe Shipping Co, Inc:** POB 3267, San Juan, PR 00902-3267; tel. (809) 724-5800; telex 3450275; fax (809) 722-7665; f. 1942; agents for numerous shipping cos, cruise lines and cargo ships; Pres. José A. Oller, Jr.

**Celta Inc, Naviera:** 555 Independencia St, Hato Rey, PR 00918; tel. (809) 765-6605; fax (809) 765-8041.

**Fred Imbert, Inc:** POB 4424, San Juan, PR 00905; agents for Belfran Line, Fabre Line, French Line, Horn Line, Kawasaki Kisen Kaisha Ltd, Suriname Navigation Co Ltd.

**H & A Trading Co, Inc:** Edificio Caribe, Calle Palmeras, Esq. San Jeronimo, 10 piso, Puerta de Tierra, San Juan, PR 00901; tel. (809) 722-7594; telex 2873; fax (809) 721-2260.

**Intermar Shipping Inc:** POB 3408, San Juan, PR 00904.

**International Shipping Agency, Inc:** Pier 11, Fernández Juncos Ave, POB 2748, Puerta de Tierra, San Juan, PR 00902; tel. (809) 721-4355; telex 3252405; fax (809) 721-4343; f. 1966; agents for NYK Lines, Sea Barge Agency, DSR/Stinnes West Indies Services and other lines; also stevedoring and terminal operations; Pres. David R. Segarra, Jr.

**Puerto Rico Line, Inc:** POB 5434, San Juan, PR 00906; tel. (809) 724-8070; telex 3252849; fax (809) 721-0699.

**San Juan Mercantile Corporation:** POB 4352, San Juan, PR 00905; f. 1923; agents for: Seaboard Shipping Co, 'K' Line, Paal Wilson, Westship International Inc, The East Asiatic Co Inc, Continental Line, Montemar SA.

**Universal Shipping Corporation:** POB 737, San Juan, PR 00902.

#### CIVIL AVIATION

The principal airports are at San Juan (Carolina), Ponce, Mayagüez and Aguadilla.

## Tourism

An estimated 4,022,600 tourists visited Puerto Rico in 1993/94, when revenue from this source was estimated at $1,670m. More than 52% of tourists were from the USA.

**Commonwealth of Puerto Rico Tourism Co:** POB 4435, Old San Juan Station, San Juan, PR 00904; tel. (809) 721-2400; fax (809) 725-4417; Exec. Dir Miguel A. Domenech.

# UNITED STATES EXTERNAL TERRITORIES

The External or Unincorporated Territories of the USA comprise the Pacific Territories of American Samoa and Guam, the Caribbean Territory of the US Virgin Islands, and a number of smaller islands.

## AMERICAN SAMOA

### Introductory Survey

**Location, Climate, Language, Religion, Flag, Capital**

American Samoa comprises the seven islands of Tutuila, Tau, Olosega, Ofu, Aunuu, Rose and Swain's. They lie in the southern central Pacific Ocean, along latitude 14°S at about longitude 170°W, about 3,700 km (2,300 miles) south-west of Hawaii. The temperature normally ranges between 21°C (70°F) and 32°C (90°F), and the average annual rainfall is 5,000 mm (197 ins), the greatest precipitation occurring between December and March. English and Samoan, a Polynesian language, are spoken. The population is largely Christian, more than 50% being members of the Christian Congregational Church. The flag has a dark blue field, on which is superimposed a red-edged white triangle (with its apex at the hoist and its base at the outer edge of the flag), containing an eagle, representing the USA, grasping in its talons a yellow *fue* (staff) and *uatogi* (club), Samoan symbols of sovereignty. The capital is Pago Pago, on Tutuila (the officially designated seat of government is the village of Fagatogo).

**Recent History**

The Samoan islands were first visited by Europeans in the 1700s, but it was not until 1830 that missionaries from the London Missionary Society settled there. In 1878 the Kingdom of Samoa, then an independent state, gave the USA the right to establish a naval base at Pago Pago. The United Kingdom and Germany were also interested in the islands, but the United Kingdom withdrew in 1899, leaving the western islands for Germany to govern. The chiefs of the eastern islands ceded their lands to the USA in 1904, and the islands officially became an Unincorporated Territory of the USA in 1922.

Until 1978 American Samoa was administered by a Governor, appointed by the US Government, and a legislature comprising the Senate and the House of Representatives. In November 1977 the first gubernatorial elections took place and, in January 1978, Peter Coleman was inaugurated as Governor, with Tufele Li'a as Lieutenant-Governor. Both were re-elected for a second term in November 1980, after three years in office instead of four, to allow synchronization with US elections in 1980. At elections in November 1984, A. P. Lutali was elected Governor and Faleomavaega Eni Hunkin was elected Lieutenant-Governor. The High Court of American Samoa had ruled earlier that Coleman was ineligible to stand for a third successive term as Governor, because a law restricted tenure by any individual to two successive terms. In July 1988 the Territory's delegate to the US House of Representatives, Fofō Sunia, announced that he would not seek re-election, as he was then the subject of official investigation for alleged financial mismanagement. In October he was sentenced to a period of between five and 15 months in prison for fraud. Eni Hunkin replaced Sunia as delegate in November. At gubernatorial elections, which took place in November, Coleman was elected Governor for a third term, while Galea'i Poumele replaced Hunkin as Lieutenant-Governor.

In mid-1986 the Governments of American Samoa and Western Samoa signed a Memorandum of Understanding, under which a permanent committee was to be established to ensure mutual development in such areas as tourism, transport and fishing.

In October 1986 a constitutional convention completed a comprehensive rewriting of the American Samoan Constitution. The draft revision, which at mid-1995 had yet to be ratified by the US Congress, included provisions relating to the promotion of local business interests, environmental protection and the development of non-nuclear energy, impeachment procedures and the expansion of the Senate, the House of Representatives and the High Court, together with the introduction of trial by jury and the creation of a land titles court. However, the revised Constitution maintained the current system of election by Matai (chiefs), whereby commoners and women are excluded from voting.

Cyclone Ofa struck American Samoa in February 1990, causing considerable damage. Further damage to crops and infrastructure occurred when Cyclone Val hit the islands in December 1991.

At gubernatorial elections in November 1992 Peter Coleman was defeated by A. P. Lutali, who secured 52.4% of the vote, compared with Coleman's 35.7%.

At elections to the House of Representatives in November 1994 about one-third of those members who sought re-election was defeated. Faleomavaega Eni Hunkin was re-elected as non-voting delegate.

In late 1994 and early 1995 American Samoa was one of a number of Pacific islands to express concern at the proposed passage through their waters of regular shipments of plutonium, *en route* from Europe to Japan.

**Government**

Executive power is vested in the Governor, who is elected by popular vote and has authority which extends to all operations within the Territory of American Samoa. He has the power of veto with respect to legislation approved by the Fono (Legislature). The Fono consists of the Senate and the House of Representatives, with a President and a Speaker presiding over their respective divisions. The Senate is composed of 18 members, elected, according to Samoan custom, from local chiefs, or Matai, for a term of four years. The House of Representatives consists of 20 members who are elected by popular vote for a term of two years, and a non-voting delegate from Swain's Island. The Fono meets twice a year, in January and July, for not more than 45 days, and at such special sessions as the Governor may call. The Governor has the authority to appoint heads of government departments with the approval of the Fono. Local government is carried out by indigenous officials.

**Defence**

The USA is responsible for the defence of American Samoa.

**Economic Affairs**

In 1985, according to estimates by the World Bank, the Territory's gross national product (GNP), measured at average 1983–85 prices, was about US $190m., equivalent to US $5,410 per head. Between 1973 and 1985, it was estimated, GNP increased, in real terms, at an average rate of 1.7% per year, with real GNP per head rising by only 0.1% per year. In 1985–92 the population increased by an annual average of 1.5%. An estimated 85,000 American Samoans live on the US mainland or Hawaii.

Agricultural production provides little surplus for export. Major crops are coconuts, bananas, taro, pineapples, yams and breadfruit. Local fisheries are at subsistence level, but tuna-canning plants at Pago Pago process fish from US, Taiwanese and South Korean vessels, and canned tuna constituted 96.6% of exports in 1989, when export earnings totalled US $307.5m. and expenditure on imports was US $168.7m. Fish-canning engaged more than 42% of the employed labour force in the early 1990s. Other activities include meat-canning, handicrafts, dairy farming and the manufacture of soap, perfume and alcoholic beverages. In early 1995 it was announced that seven new manufacturing installations were to be established in the islands by the end of the year. The factories, which were expected to create employment for 5,000 people, were to manufacture a range of products, including sausages, watches and paper cartons. The tourist industry is developing slowly, and earned some US $10m. in 1990. The designation of a national park in late 1993, comprising 3,200 ha of native forests and coral reefs, was expected to assist the growth of the industry. The average annual rate of inflation was 4.5% in 1985–91. An estimated 10.1% of the total labour force were unemployed in 1989.

American Samoa is a member of the South Pacific Commission (see p. 215), and is an associate member of the UN Economic and Social Commission for Asia and the Pacific (ESCAP—see p. 27).

# UNITED STATES EXTERNAL TERRITORIES

*American Samoa*

In late 1989 American Samoa experienced a severe financial crisis. At the end of September 1989 the budgetary deficit was US $7.5m. In February 1990 the Governor imposed pay cuts on 3,800 government workers and introduced the emergency 'freezing' of local prices. At the end of the year the budgetary deficit was estimated to have reached US $17.7m. Continued economic difficulties prompted the Fono to approve legislation in late 1991 to reduce planned expenditure in the budget for the following year by more than US $2m. to about US $127m. In September 1992 the Territory's total debt amounted to some US $60m.

The issue of wage levels caused considerable controversy in late 1990, when the Government came under pressure to review the minimum wage structure. American Samoa remained the only part of the USA in which a lower standard minimum wage applies. The situation has been largely attributed to the presence of the two tuna-canning plants on the islands, which employ almost half of the labour force, and consequently exert substantial influence over the setting of wage levels. In April 1991, while the minimum wage on the US mainland increased by some 12%, it was announced that the rate in American Samoa was to remain unchanged (leaving the Territory's minimum wage level some 50% below that of the mainland). The American Samoan Government, however, was strongly opposed to an increase proposed in the US Congress in late 1991, arguing that, with higher costs, the Territory's tuna-canning industry would be unable to compete with other parts of the world. Following the election of a new Governor in November 1992, further measures aimed at reducing budgetary expenditure were introduced. These included severe reductions in the number of government employees, who totalled some 5,400 in early 1993. A further reduction of 20% in government employees was to take place in early 1995. A state of disaster was declared in mid-1993 following the outbreak of taro-leaf blight in the islands, and some US $0.2m. was allocated by the Government for a spraying campaign to combat the disease. By the end of the year reports indicated that spraying had effectively confined the disease to the eastern and western areas of Tutuila.

### Social Welfare
In 1981 American Samoa had 157 hospital beds, and in 1984 there were 25 physicians and 18 nurses working in the Territory. Expenditure on health and welfare in 1988/89 amounted to US $19.7m., or 16.4% of total government expenditure.

### Education
Education is officially compulsory for 12 years between six and 18 years of age. Primary education begins at six years of age and lasts for eight years. Secondary education, beginning at the age of 14, lasts for a further four years. In 1991 there were 92 pre-primary schools, with 2,694 pupils, 30 primary schools, with 7,884 pupils, and eight secondary schools (in 1989), with 3,643 pupils. There is also a community college of further education, with 1,011 students in 1989. Expenditure on education and culture in 1988/89 was US $30.4m., or 25.3% of total government expenditure.

### Public Holidays
**1995:** 1 January (New Year's Day), 13 February (for George Washington's Birthday), 17 April (Flag Day, commemorating the first raising of the US flag in American Samoa), 22 May (Memorial Day), 4 July (US Independence Day), 3 September (Labor Day), 23 November (Thanksgiving Day), 25 December (Christmas Day).
**1996:** 1 January (New Year's Day), 12 February (for George Washington's Birthday), 17 April (Flag Day, commemorating the first raising of the US flag in American Samoa), 20 May (Memorial Day), 4 July (US Independence Day), 3 September (Labor Day), 21 November (Thanksgiving Day), 25 December (Christmas Day).

### Weights and Measures
With certain exceptions, the imperial system is in force. One US cwt equals 100 lb; one long ton equals 2,240 lb; one short ton equals 2,000 lb. A policy of gradual voluntary conversion to the metric system is being encouraged by the Federal Government.

## Statistical Survey

Source (unless otherwise indicated): Research and Statistics Division, Economic Development Planning Office: *American Samoa Statistical Digest*.

### AREA AND POPULATION
**Area:** 194.8 sq km (76.1 sq miles).
**Population:** 32,297 (males 16,384; females 15,913) at census of 1 April 1980; 46,773 at census of 1 April 1990; 53,000 (official estimate) at mid-1993. *By island* (1980): Tutuila 30,124 (Western District 41%, Eastern District 59%); Manu'a District (Ta'u, Olosega and Ofu islands) 1,732; Aunu'u 414; Swain's Island (Olohenga) 27.
**Density** (1993): 272.1 per sq km.
**Capital:** Pago Pago (population 3,075 at 1980 census).
**Births, Marriages and Deaths** (1992): Registered live births 1,817 (birth rate 35.7 per 1,000); (1989) Registered marriages 317 (marriage rate 7.0 per 1,000); Registered deaths 217 (death rate 4.3 per 1,000).
**Employment** (provisional, 1989): Tuna canneries 4,418; Government 4,299; Others 3,711; Unemployed 1,392; Total labour force 13,820.

### AGRICULTURE, ETC.
**Principal Crops** (FAO estimates, metric tons, 1993): Coconuts 5,000; Taro 2,000; Bananas 1,000. Source: FAO, *Production Yearbook*.
**Livestock** (1980): Pigs 5,899; Poultry 23,581; Cattle 88; Horses, mules and colts 105. *1993:* Pigs 11,000 (FAO estimate).
**Fishing** (metric tons, live weight): Total catch 42 in 1990; 45 in 1991; 45 (FAO estimate) in 1992. Source: FAO, *Yearbook of Fishery Statistics*.

### MINING
**Production** (1981): Pumice and pumicite 2,500 metric tons (estimate by US Bureau of Mines).

### INDUSTRY
**Production** (1988): Tinned fish 109,800 metric tons; Electric energy 90 million kWh (1991). Source: UN, *Industrial Statistics Yearbook*.

### FINANCE
**Currency and Exchange Rates:** United States currency is used. For details, see section on the Northern Mariana Islands.
**Budget** (US $ million, year ending Sept. 1989): *Revenue:* Local taxation 26.6; Permits, fees and services 8.8; Territorial govt enterprises 24.2; Federal funds 52.2 (Dept of the Interior operating grant 20.6); Total (incl. others) 112.6. *Expenditure:* General govt 16.4; Public works 10.0; Health and welfare 19.7; Education and culture 30.4; Govt enterprises 22.7; Total (incl. others) 120.1.
**Cost of Living** (Consumer Price Index, excluding rent; base: Oct.–Dec. 1982 = 100): 120.3 in 1989; 129.6 in 1990; 135.3 in 1991.

### EXTERNAL TRADE
**Principal Commodities** (provisional, US $ million, year ending Sept. 1989): *Imports:* Food, beverages and tobacco 38.0; Mineral fuels 26.9; Building materials 15.1 (Treated timber 2.6); Textiles and clothing 5.8; Machinery and transport equipment 19.6 (Motor vehicles 7.1); Miscellaneous manufactured items 63.1 (Metalware (for canning) 14.0); Total (incl. others) 168.7. *Exports:* Canned tuna 297.0; Pet food 10.4; Fresh fish 0.05; Aluminium 0.08; Total 307.5.
**Principal Trading Partners** (US $ million, 1989): *Imports:* Australia 16.5; Fiji 6.0; Hong Kong 2.4; Japan 14.6; Republic of Korea 4.7; New Zealand 12.1; Taiwan 1.7; USA 105.7; Western Samoa 1.7; Total (incl. others) 168.7. *Exports:* Total 307.5 (almost entirely to the USA).

### TRANSPORT
**Road Traffic** (govt and registered motor vehicles): 4,310 in 1987; 4,527 in 1988; 5,079 (Private cars, etc. 4,139) in 1989.
**International Sea-borne Shipping** (estimated freight traffic, '000 metric tons, 1990): Goods loaded 380; Goods unloaded 733. Source: UN, *Monthly Bulletin of Statistics*.
**Civil Aviation** (Pago Pago Int. Airport, 1989): Flights 11,032; Passengers 158,609 (Boarding 69,578, Disembarking 71,437, Transit 17,594); Freight and mail (metric tons) 1,052 (Loaded 726, Unloaded 326).

### TOURISM
**Tourist Arrivals:** 7,026 in 1987; 10,129 in 1988; 8,366 (New Zealand 2,256; USA 3,538) in 1989.

### COMMUNICATIONS MEDIA
**Non-Daily Newspapers** (1990): 2; estimated circulation 5,000*.
**Radio Receivers** (1992): 50,000* in use.
**Television Receivers** (1992): 11,000* in use.
**Telephones** (1989): 8,276 in use; 165 facsimile (fax) subscribers.
* Source: UNESCO, *Statistical Yearbook*.

## EDUCATION

**Pre-primary** (1991): 92 schools; 123 teachers; 2,694 pupils.
**Primary** (1991): 30 schools; 524 teachers; 7,884 pupils.
**Secondary** (1991): 8 high schools (2 private) (1989); 266 teachers; 3,643 pupils.
**Higher** (1989): American Samoa Community College 1,011 students; 76 students receive specialist education at one institution.

Source: mainly UNESCO, *Statistical Yearbook*.

# Directory
## The Constitution

American Samoa is an unincorporated territory of the USA. Therefore not all the provisions of the US Constitution apply. As an unorganized territory it has not been provided with an organic act by Congress. Instead the US Secretary of the Interior, on behalf of the President, has plenary authority over the territory and enabled the people of American Samoa to draft their own Constitution.

According to the 1967 Constitution, executive power is vested in the Governor, whose authority extends to all operations within the territory of American Samoa. The Governor has veto power with respect to bills passed by the Fono (Legislature). The Fono consists of the Senate and the House of Representatives, with a President and a Speaker presiding over their respective divisions. The Senate is composed of 18 members, elected, according to Samoan custom, from local chiefs, or Matai, for a term of four years. The House of Representatives consists of 20 members who are elected by popular vote for a term of two years, and a non-voting delegate from Swain's Island. The Fono meets twice a year, in January and July, for not more than 45 days and at such special sessions as the Governor may call. The Governor has the authority to appoint heads of government departments with the approval of the Fono. Local government is carried out by indigenous officials. In August 1976 a referendum on the popular election of a Governor and a Lieutenant-Governor resulted in an affirmative vote. The first gubernatorial elections took place on 8 November 1977 and the second occurred in November 1980; subsequent elections were to take place every four years.

American Samoa sends one non-voting delegate to the US House of Representatives, who is popularly elected every two years.

## The Government
(June 1995)

**Governor:** A. P. LUTALI (elected November 1992).
**Lieutenant-Governor:** TAUESE SUNIA.

### GOVERNMENT OFFICES

**Governor's Office:** Pago Pago, AS 96799; tel. 633-4116; telex 782501; fax 633-2269.
**Department of the Interior, Office of Territorial and International Affairs (OTIA):** Field Office of the OTIA, Dept of the Interior, POB 3809, Pago Pago, AS 96799; tel. 633-2800; fax 633-2415; Field Representative DALE JONES.
**Office of the Representative to the Government of American Samoa:** Office of the Govt of American Samoa, Suite 3315A, 300 Ala Moana Blvd, Honolulu, HI 96850, USA; tel. (808) 545-7451; fax (808) 537-2837; federal liaison officer; Representative TIVA AGA.

## Legislature
### FONO
#### Senate

The Senate has 18 members, elected, according to Samoan custom, from local chiefs, or Matai, for a term of four years.
**President:** LETULI TOLOA.

#### House of Representatives

The House has 20 members who are elected by popular vote for a term of two years, and a non-voting delegate from Swain's Island.
**Speaker:** TUANAITAU F. TUIA.

### CONGRESS

Since 1980 American Samoa has been able to elect, for a two-year term, a delegate to the Federal Congress, who may vote in committee but not on the floor of the House of Representatives. Elections took place in November 1994.
**Delegate of American Samoa:** ENI F. H. FALEOMAVAEGA, US House of Representatives, 413 Cannon House Office Bldg, Washington, DC 20515, USA; tel. (202) 225-8577.

## Judicial System

The judicial system of American Samoa consists of the High Court, presided over by the Chief Justice and assisted by Associate Justices (all appointed by the Secretary of the Interior), and a local judiciary in the District and Village Courts. The judges for these local courts are appointed by the Governor, subject to confirmation by the Senate of the Fono. The High Court consists of three Divisions: Appellate, Trial, and Land and Titles. The Appellate Division has limited original jurisdiction and hears appeals from the Trial Division, the Land and Titles Division and from the District Court when it has operated as a court of record. The Trial Division has general jurisdiction over all cases. The Land and Titles Division hears cases involving land or Matai titles.

The District Court hears preliminary felony proceedings, misdemeanours, infractions (traffic and health), civil claims less than US $3,000, small claims, Uniform Reciprocal Enforcement of Support cases, and *de novo* trials from Village Courts. The Village Courts hear matters arising under village regulations and local customs.

**Chief Justice:** MICHAEL KRUSE.
**Associate Justice:** LYLE L. RICHMOND.
**High Court:** Office of the Chief Justice, High Court, Pago Pago, AS 96799; tel. 633-1261.
**Judge of the District Court:** MALAETASI TOGAFAU, Pago Pago, AS 96799; tel. 633-4131.
**Judge of the Village Court:** FAISIOTA TAUANU'U, Pago Pago, AS 96799; tel. 633-1102.

## Religion

The population is largely Christian, more than 50% being members of the Congregational Christian Church and about 20% being Roman Catholics.

### CHRISTIANITY

**American Samoa Council of Christian Churches:** c/o CCCAS Offices, POB 1637, Pago Pago, AS 96799; f. 1985; six mem. churches; Pres. Cardinal PIO TAOFINU'U (Roman Catholic Archbishop of Samoa-Apia and Tokelau); Gen. Sec. Rev. ENOKA L. ALESANA (Congregational Christian Church in American Samoa).

#### The Roman Catholic Church

American Samoa comprises the single diocese of Samoa-Pago Pago, suffragan to the archdiocese of Samoa-Apia and Tokelau. At 31 December 1993 there were an estimated 9,100 adherents in the Territory. The Bishop participates in the Catholic Bishops' Conference of the Pacific, based in Fiji.
**Bishop of Samoa-Pago Pago:** Rt Rev. JOHN QUINN WEITZEL, Diocesan Pastoral Center, POB 596, Fatuoaiga, Pago Pago, AS 96799; tel. 699-1402; fax 699-1459.

#### The Anglican Communion

American Samoa is within the diocese of Polynesia, part of the Church of the Province of New Zealand. The Bishop of Polynesia is resident in Fiji.

#### Protestant Churches

**Congregational Christian Church in American Samoa (CCCAS):** POB 1637, Pago Pago, AS 96799; 34,000 mems (22,000 in American Samoa) in 1985.

Other active Protestant groups include the Baptist Church, the Christian Church of Jesus Christ, the Methodist Church, Assemblies of God, Church of the Nazarene and Seventh-day Adventists. The Church of Jesus Christ of Latter-day Saints (Mormon) is also represented.

## The Press

**News Bulletin:** Office of Public Information, American Samoa Government, Utulei; tel. 633-5490; daily (Mon.–Fri.); English; non-commercial; Editor PHILIP SWETT; circ. 1,800.
**Samoa Journal and Advertiser:** POB 3986, Pago Pago, AS 96799; tel. 633-2399; weekly; English and Samoan; Editor MICHAEL STARK; circ. 3,000.

**Samoa News:** POB 909, Pago Pago, AS 96799; tel. 633-5599; fax 633-4864; 3 a week; English and Samoan; Publr Lewis Wolman; circ. 4,500.

## Radio and Television

In 1992 there were an estimated 50,000 radio receivers and 11,000 television receivers in use.

### RADIO

**WVUV:** POB 2567, Pago Pago, AS 96799; tel. 633-1648; fmr govt-administered station leased to Radio Samoa Ltd in 1975; commercial; English and Samoan; 24 hours a day; Man. Vincent Iuli.

### TELEVISION

**KVZK:** Office of Public Information, Pago Pago, AS 96799; tel. 633-4191; telex 782519; fax 633-1044; f. 1964; govt-owned; non-commercial; English and Samoan; broadcasts 18 hours daily on three channels; Gen. Man. Fulifuli Taveuveli; Technical Dir Robert Blauvelt.

## Finance

(cap. = capital; dep. = deposits; m. = million; amounts in US dollars)

### BANKING

#### Commercial Banks

**Amerika Samoa Bank:** POB 3790, Pago Pago, AS 96799; tel. 633-5053; telex 782587; fax 633-5057; f. 1979; cap. 6.7m., dep. 46.7m. (Dec. 1994); Pres. and CEO Harold P. Fielding.

**Bank of Hawaii** (USA): POB 69, Pago Pago, AS 96799; tel. 633-4226; telex 782504; fax 633-2918; f. 1897; total assets 12,674.6m. (Mar. 1993); Man. Brent A. Schwenke.

#### Development Bank

**Development Bank of American Samoa:** POB 9, Pago Pago, AS 96799; tel. 633-4031; fax 633-1163; f. 1969; govt-owned and non-profit-making; cap. 6.4m. (1989); Chair. Eugene G. C. H. Reid; Pres. Manutafea E. Meredith.

### INSURANCE

**American International Underwriters (South Pacific) Ltd:** Pago Pago, AS 96799; tel. 633-4845; telex 782524.

**National Pacific Insurance Ltd:** Lumana'i Bldg, POB 1386, Pago Pago, AS 96799; tel. 633-4266; f. 1977; Man. Arnie C. Carter.

**Oxford Pacific Insurance Management:** POB 1420, Pago Pago, AS 96799; tel. 633-4990; fax 633-2721; f. 1977; represents major international property and life insurance cos; Pres. Bob Batson; Gen. Man. Rick Petri.

## Trade and Industry

### DEVELOPMENT ORGANIZATIONS

**American Samoa Development Corporation:** Pago Pago, AS 96799; tel. 633-4241; telex 782511; f. 1962; financed by private Samoan interests.

**Office of Economic Development Planning:** Territorial Planning Commission, Pago Pago, AS 96799; tel. 633-5155; fax 633-4195; Chair. (Territorial Planning Office) Laautuilevanu Tue; Dir Alfonso P. Galea'i.

## Transport

### ROADS

There are about 150 km (93 miles) of paved and 200 km (124 miles) of secondary roads. Non-scheduled commercial buses operate a service over 350 km (217 miles) of main and secondary roads.

### SHIPPING

There are various passenger and cargo services from the US Pacific coast, Japan, Australia (mainly Sydney) and New Zealand, that call at Pago Pago. The Pacific Forum Line, Pacific Navigation of Tonga, Farrell Lines, Kyowa Line, General Steamship Corpn, Warner Pacific Line, Polynesian Shipping Services and Pacific Islands Transport Line are among the shipping companies which operate regular cargo services to American Samoa. Inter-island boats provide frequent services between Western and American Samoa.

### CIVIL AVIATION

There is an international airport at Tafuna, 11 km (7 miles) from Pago Pago, and smaller airstrips on the islands of Ta'u and Ofu.

**Samoa Air:** Tafuna Int. Airport, Pago Pago, AS 96799; f. 1986; operates service between Pago Pago and Western Samoa, Tonga and Niue; Pres. and Chair. James Porter.

## Tourism

The tourist industry is encouraged by the Government, but suffers from the cost and paucity of air services linking American Samoa with its main sources of custom, particularly the USA. Pago Pago is an important mid-Pacific stop-over for large passenger aircraft; of the 84,816 international arrivals in 1989, only 8,366 were tourists (19.6% of the total were visiting relatives, 13.3% were business visitors and 44.2% were returning residents). The industry earned an estimated US $10m. in 1990. A national park comprising native forests and coral reefs (designated in late 1993) was to be promoted as a tourist attraction.

**Office of Tourism:** Convention Center, Pago Pago, AS 96799; tel. 633-1091; fax 633-1094.

# GUAM

## Introductory Survey

### Location, Climate, Language, Religion, Flag, Capital

Guam is the southernmost and largest of the Mariana Islands, situated about 2,170 km (1,350 miles) south of Tokyo (Japan) and 5,300 km (3,300 miles) west of Honolulu (Hawaii). The temperature normally ranges between 24°C (75°F) and 30°C (86°F) in June–November, but is generally cooler and drier from December to May. The average annual rainfall is about 2,000 mm (79 ins). English is the official language, but Japanese and Chamorro, the local language, are also spoken. The principal religion is Christianity, about 90% of the population being Roman Catholics. The national flag of the United States of America (q.v.) is used by Guam. The capital is Agaña.

### Recent History

Members of a Spanish expedition, under the Portuguese navigator Fernão Magalhães (Ferdinand Magellan), were the first Europeans to discover Guam, visiting the island in 1521, during a voyage that accomplished the first circumnavigation of the globe. The island was claimed by Spain in 1565, and the first Jesuit missionaries arrived three years later. The native Micronesian population is estimated to have fallen from 100,000 in 1521 to fewer than 5,000 in 1741, owing largely to a combination of aggression by the Spaniards and exposure to imported diseases. The intermarrying of Micronesians, Spaniards and Filipinos resulted in the people now called Chamorros. Guam was ceded to the USA after the Spanish–American War of 1898, but was invaded by Japan in 1941. Fierce fighting took place before the island was recaptured by US forces in 1944.

Guam became an Unincorporated Territory of the USA, under the jurisdiction of the US Department of the Interior, in 1950. In 1970 the island elected its first Governor, and in 1972 a new law gave Guam one Delegate to the US House of Representatives. The Delegate may vote in committee but not on the floor of the House. In September 1976 an island-wide referendum decided that Guam should maintain close ties with the USA, but that negotiations should be held to improve the island's status. In a further referendum, in 1982, in which only 38% of eligible voters participated, the status of a Commonwealth, in association with the USA, was the most favoured of six options, supported by 48% of the votes cast. In August 1987, in a referendum on the provisions of a draft law aimed at conferring the status of Commonwealth on the Territory, voters approved the central proposal, while rejecting articles empowering the Guam Government to restrict immigration and granting the indigenous Chamorro people the right to determine the island's future political status. In a further referendum in November 1987 both outstanding provisions were approved. Negotiations between the Guam Commission for Self Determination, led by the Republican Governor, Joseph Ada, and the USA continued throughout 1988 and 1989, and the draft Guam Commonwealth Act was discussed in Washington, DC, in February 1990. In 1992 the proposed change of status received further support from certain sectors of the business community (see Economic Affairs). As well as demands for greater autonomy, the Commission raised the issue of military bases on the island, particularly the Guam Naval Air Station, which Ada requested should be returned to civilian use. In December 1993 a US Government representative visited Guam for further discussions on the Commonwealth Act, and concluded that legislation proposing a change of status for the Territory could be presented to the US Congress by late 1994.

In February 1987 the former Governor of Guam, Ricardo Bordallo, was found guilty of charges of bribery, extortion and conspiracy to obstruct justice. Despite Bordallo's claim that his prosecution by the authorities had been prompted by political motives, he was sentenced to 30 years' imprisonment (later reduced to nine years) in April. In November Bordallo's wife, Madeleine, was elected to replace him in the Guam Legislature, and in October 1988 Bordallo won an appeal and his sentence was cancelled. Bordallo was liable for imprisonment in the USA on charges of obstruction and attempting to influence witnesses, but he committed suicide at the end of January 1990. Madeleine Bordallo was the Democratic candidate for Governor in November 1990, when Ada was re-elected. Concurrent elections to the Guam Legislature resulted in a Democratic majority of one seat.

In early 1990 the unanimous approval by the Legislature of a law that made abortion illegal under any circumstances caused considerable controversy; after being reported to the American Civil Liberties Union, the legislation was ruled unconstitutional by the district court. However, despite continued pressure from the anti-abortion lobby and the largely Roman Catholic members of the Legislature, an appeal against the district court's ruling was finally rejected by the US Supreme Court in April 1992.

In June 1990 legislation before the US Congress, supported by the Guamanian Delegate and a Hawaiian representative, introduced proposals to include Wake Island (an atoll territory of the USA) within the Territory of Guam. The Marshall Islands (then a US Associated State), opposed the suggestion.

Guam was declared a disaster zone after being struck by Typhoon Omar in August 1992. The typhoon left some 5,000 people homeless and caused damage estimated at US $100m. In August 1993 a severe earthquake caused damage estimated at more than $250m.

At legislative elections in November 1992 the Democrats increased their representation to 14 seats, while the Republicans secured only seven. Robert Underwood was elected as the new Democratic Delegate to the US House of Representatives, replacing the Republican, Ben Blaz.

The issue of immigration re-emerged in early 1993, when a pressure group campaigning for the rights of indigenous people, 'Chamoru Nation', appealed for stricter controls to be introduced. Members of the group expressed concern that the increased numbers of immigrants entering Guam would threaten the Chamorro culture and the political and social stability of the island.

In January 1994 the US Congress approved legislation providing for the transfer of 3,200 acres of land on Guam from federal to local control. This was a significant achievement for the Government of Guam, which had campaigned consistently for the return of 27,000 acres (some 20% of Guam's total area), appropriated by US military forces after the Second World War. Chamorro rights activists, however, opposed the move, claiming that land should not be transferred to the Government of the Territory, but rather to the original landowners.

At gubernatorial elections in November 1994 the Democrat, Carl Gutierrez, defeated his Republican opponent, Tommy Tanaka, winning 54.6% of total votes cast, while Madeleine Bordallo was elected to the position of Lieutenant-Governor (defeating the Republican Doris Flores Brooks). Legislative elections held concurrently also resulted in a Democratic majority, with candidates of the party securing 13 seats, while the Republicans won eight. Robert Underwood was re-elected unopposed as Delegate to the US House of Representatives.

In March 1995 it was announced that the centrally-located US naval air station of Brewer Field was to be returned to civilian use. The Government of Guam planned to incorporate the station into the adjacent Guam International Airport.

### Government

Guam is governed under the Organic Act of Guam of 1950, which gave the island statutory local power of self-government and made its inhabitants citizens of the United States, although they are not permitted to vote in national elections. Guam's non-voting Delegate to the US House of Representatives is elected every two years. Executive power is vested in the civilian Governor, who is elected by popular vote every four years. The Government has 48 executive departments, whose heads are appointed by the Governor with the consent of the Guam Legislature. The Legislature consists of 21 members elected by popular vote every two years. It is empowered to enact legislation on local matters, including taxation and fiscal appropriations.

### Defence

Guam is an important strategic military base for the USA, with about 2,450 members of the Air Force and 4,600 naval personnel stationed there in mid-1994. In April 1992 it had been reported that the USA was to expand its military installations on the island considerably to compensate for the closure of a major naval base in the Philippines, despite continued requests by the Governor that the bases be returned to civilian use. However, the US naval air station, Brewer Field, was returned to the Government of Guam for civilian use in early 1995

### Economic Affairs

In 1985, according to estimates by the World Bank, Guam's gross national product (GNP), measured at average 1983–85 prices, was about US $670m., equivalent to US $5,470 per head. Between 1973 and 1985, it was estimated, GNP declined, in real terms, at an average rate of 3.0% per year, with real GNP per head falling by 4.5% per year. GNP per head declined by 6.7% in 1985. In 1985–93 the population increased by an annual average of 2.0%.

Crops on the island, including water-melons, maize, sweet potatoes, cassava, bananas, breadfruit, coconuts and sugar cane, are grown mainly for local consumption. In 1990 production of fruit and vegetables totalled 5.6m. lb (about 2,500 metric tons). Livestock reared includes pigs, cattle and poultry. The fishing industry expanded greatly during the late 1980s, and in 1988 there were 79 vessels operating from Guam, mainly Japanese, Korean and Taiwanese, fishing in the waters of the Federated States of Micronesia.

Industrial enterprises, including a petroleum refinery and textile and garment firms, were established in the early 1970s and revitalized in the 1980s, in addition to existing smaller-scale manufacturing of soft drinks, confectionery and watches. Boat-building is also a commercial activity on Guam. Manufacturing industries engaged 4.3% of the private-sector employed labour force in 1992. Guam is a duty-free port and an important distribution point for goods destined for Micronesia. Re-exports constitute a high proportion of Guam's exports, major commodities being petroleum and petroleum products, iron and steel scrap, and eggs. In March 1984, however, the Territory's petroleum refinery was closed for an indefinite period, after the US Government, a principal customer, had decided to buy cheaper fuel for its military base on Guam from refineries in Singapore. In 1983 the value of exports was US $39.2m., while imports amounted to $636.1m. Total exports were valued at $86.1m. in 1992. Japan provided an estimated 80% of total imports in the early 1990s.

The Government has attempted to diversify Guam's economy by attracting increased foreign investment, principally from Asian manufacturers. In 1993 some 784,018 tourists, of whom about 70% were Japanese, visited the island (compared with 407,100 in 1986). In 1988 annual tourist expenditure was estimated at more than US $450m., providing about 33% of gross domestic product (GDP); more than 10% of government revenue was derived from this source. The construction industry has been one of the principal beneficiaries of growth in tourism, and engaged 24.6% of the private-sector employed labour force in 1992. Guam's unemployment rate, which at 1.9% in 1990 constituted the lowest figure in the USA, increased slightly to 2.2% at the end of 1991, and to 6.6% in late 1993. The average annual rate of inflation was 8.2% in 1985–93; consumer prices increased by an annual average of 8.3% in 1993. Revenue from US military installations on Guam accounted for 12% of GDP in 1988. Budget proposals for 1991 envisaged total expenditure of US $527m. and revenue of US $655m. Considerable interest in establishing an 'offshore' financial centre on Guam was expressed in 1992. The development of such a centre, however, was dependent upon Guam's achievement of commonwealth status, which would allow the introduction of new tax laws. The Territory was severely affected by a series of natural disasters in the early 1990s (including a typhoon in August 1992 and an earthquake in August 1993), which resulted in infrastructural damage, a pronounced decline in tourist arrivals and therefore a significant loss of revenue.

### Social Welfare

Guam had four hospitals, with a total of 223 beds, in 1979, and there were 147 physicians and 394 nurses working in the Territory in 1986.

### Education

School attendance is compulsory from six to 16 years of age. There were 25 public elementary schools, six junior high and five senior high schools, as well as a number of private schools operating on the island in 1993. The University of Guam had 2,385 enrolled students in 1991/92; there is also a community college as well as two private business colleges. In 1990 the rate of adult illiteracy was 1.0%. Government expenditure on education (excluding higher education) was US $60,200 in 1985.

### Public Holidays

**1995:** 1 January (New Year's Day), 13 February (for George Washington's Birthday), 6 March (Guam Discovery Day), 22 May (Memorial Day), 4 July (US Independence Day), 4 September (Labor Day), 23 November (Thanksgiving Day), 25 December (Christmas Day).

**1996:** 1 January (New Year's Day), 12 February (for George Washington's Birthday), 4 March (Guam Discovery Day), 20 May (Memorial Day), 4 July (US Independence Day), 2 September (Labor Day), 21 November (Thanksgiving Day), 25 December (Christmas Day).

### Weights and Measures

With certain exceptions, the imperial system is in force. One US cwt equals 100 lb; one long ton equals 2,240 lb; one short ton equals 2,000 lb. A policy of gradual voluntary conversion to the metric system is being encouraged by the Federal Government.

## Statistical Survey

Sources (unless otherwise stated): Department of Commerce, Government of Guam, 590 South Marine Drive, 601 GITC Bldg, Tamuning, GU 96911; United States Department of the Interior, Office of the Secretary, Washington, DC 20240, USA.

### AREA AND POPULATION

**Area:** 549 sq km (212 sq miles).

**Population:** 105,979 (males 55,321, females 50,658) at census of 1 April 1980; 133,152 (males 70,945, females 62,207) at census of 1 April 1990; 143,000 (official estimate) at mid-1993. Figures include members of the armed forces and their dependants (estimated at 21,500 in 1980 and at 21,193 in 1990).

**Density** (1993): 260.5 per sq km.

**Principal Towns:** Agaña (capital), population 1,139 at 1990 census; Tamuning (commercial centre); Dededo.

**Births, Marriages and Deaths** (1992): 4,196 live births (birth rate 30.1 per 1,000); (1989) 1,371 marriages (marriage rate 10.5 per 1,000); 584 deaths (death rate 4.2 per 1,000).

**Expectation of Life** (World Bank estimate, years at birth, 1992): 72.

**Employment** (payroll employees at June 1992): Agriculture 460; Construction 12,280; Manufacturing 2,170; Transportation and utilities 4,150; Trade 14,700; Finance, insurance and real estate 2,790; Services 13,440; *Total Private Sector* 49,990; Federal government 7,430; Territorial government 11,260; *Total Public Sector* 18,690.

### AGRICULTURE, ETC.

**Agriculture:** Production (1990): Fruit and vegetables 5,564,000 lb; Poultry eggs 369,000 dozen; Pork 215,000 lb; Beef 11,000 lb; Poultry 90,000 lb.

**Fishing** (metric tons, live weight): Total catch 706 in 1990; 751 in 1991; 728 in 1992. Source: FAO, *Yearbook of Fishery Statistics*.

### INDUSTRY

**Electric Energy** (million kWh): 800 per year in 1987–91. Source: UN, *Industrial Statistics Yearbook*.

### FINANCE

**Currency and Exchange Rates:** US currency is used. For details, see section on the Northern Mariana Islands.

**Budget** (1991, US $ million): Expenditure 527; Revenue 655.

**Cost of Living** (Consumer Price Index; base: 1980 = 100): 233.2 in 1991; 256.9 in 1992; 278.3 in 1993. Source: ILO, *Year Book of Labour Statistics*.

**Gross Domestic Product** (provisional, US $ '000 at current market prices): 180,627 in 1984; 266,170 in 1985; 406,365 in 1986.

### EXTERNAL TRADE

**Principal Commodities** (US $ million, 1992): *Exports:* Food and live animals 41.7; Beverages and tobacco 0.4; Crude materials, inedible, except fuels 16.6; Mineral fuels, lubricants and related materials 0.6; Animal and vegetable oils and fats 1.1; Chemicals 0.6; Basic manufactures 0.3; Machinery and transport equipment 3.3; Miscellaneous manufactured articles 19.6; Total (incl. others) 86.1. Source: UN, *Statistical Yearbook for Asia and the Pacific*.

**Principal Trading Partners** (US $ million, 1983): *Imports:* Hong Kong 18.8; Japan 121.7; Philippines 7.9; Taiwan 11.6; USA 143.2; Total (incl. others) 636.1. *Exports:* Hong Kong 0.8; Japan 1.9; Trust Territory of the Pacific Islands 24.6; USA 9.8; Total (incl. others) 39.2.

### TRANSPORT

**Road Traffic** (govt and registered motor vehicles): 75,327 in 1986; 78,321 (Private cars, etc. 55,854) in 1987; 89,860 in 1989.

**International Sea-borne Shipping** (estimated freight traffic, '000 metric tons, 1991): Goods loaded 195.1; Goods unloaded 1,524.1; Goods transhipped 314.7.

**Air Cargo** ('000 lb): 65,382 in 1991.

### TOURISM

**Foreign Visitor Arrivals:** 737,300 (approx.) in 1991; 876,742 in 1992; 784,018 in 1993.

## COMMUNICATIONS MEDIA

**Radio Receivers** (1992): 195,000 in use.
**Television Receivers** (1992): 920,000 in use.
**Daily Newspapers** (1992): 1 (estimated circulation 25,000).
**Non-daily Newspapers** (1988): 4 (estimated circulation 26,000).
Source: UNESCO, *Statistical Yearbook*.

## EDUCATION

**Institutions** (public schools only, 1993): Elementary 25; Junior high 6; Senior high 5; Business colleges (private) 2; Guam Community College; University of Guam.
**Teachers** (public schools only, 1991/92): Elementary 827; Secondary 392.
**Enrolment** (1991/92, unless otherwise indicated): Elementary 18,852 (Public 16,452); Junior high 7,966 (Public 6,460); Senior high 6,159 (Public 4,926); Guam Community College 1,095 (1989/90); University of Guam 2,385.

# Directory

## The Constitution

Guam is governed under the Organic Act of Guam of 1950, which gave the island statutory local power of self-government and made its inhabitants citizens of the United States, although they cannot vote in presidential elections. Their Delegate to the US House of Representatives is elected every two years. Executive power is vested in the civilian Governor and the Lieutenant-Governor, first elected, by popular vote, in 1970. Elections for the governorship occur every four years. The Government has 48 executive departments, whose heads are appointed by the Governor with the consent of the Guam Legislature. The Legislature consists of 21 members elected by popular vote every two years (members are known as Senators). It is empowered to pass laws on local matters, including taxation and fiscal appropriations.

## The Government
(June 1995)

**Governor:** CARL T. C. GUTIERREZ (Democrat—took office 1 March 1995).
**Lieutenant-Governor:** MADELEINE Z. BORDALLO.

### GOVERNMENT OFFICES

Government offices are located throughout the island.
**Office of the Governor:** POB 2950, Adelup, Agaña, GU 96910; tel. 475-9201; fax 477-4826.
**Department of the Interior, Office of Territorial and International Affairs (OTIA):** OTIA Field Office, Post Office BJ, Agaña, GU 96910; tel. 472-7319; fax 472-7474; Field Representative TONY PALOMO.
**Department of Agriculture:** PDN Bldg, Suite 407, 238 Archbishop Flores St, Agaña, GU 96910.
**Department of Commerce:** GITC Bldg, Suite 601, 590 South Marine Drive, Tamuning, GU 96911; tel. 646-6931; fax 646-7242.
**Department of Labor:** PDN Bldg, Suite 1003D, 238 Archbishop Flores St, Agaña, GU 96910.
**Department of Revenue and Taxation:** 855 West Marine Drive, Agaña, GU 96910; tel. 477-5107; fax 472-2643.
**Department of the Treasury:** PDN Bldg, Suite 404, 238 Archbishop Flores St, Agaña, GU 96910.

## Legislature

### GUAM LEGISLATURE

The Guam Legislature has 21 members, directly elected by popular vote for a two-year term. Elections took place in November 1994, when the Democratic Party won 13 seats and the Republican Party eight.
**Speaker:** JOE T. SAN AGUSTIN.

### CONGRESS

Guam elects a Delegate to the House of Representatives. An election was held in November 1994, when the Democratic candidate, Robert Underwood was re-elected as Delegate unopposed.

**Delegate:** ROBERT UNDERWOOD, US House of Representatives, 1130 Longworth House Office Bldg, Washington, DC 20515, USA; tel. (202) 225-1188; fax (202) 225-0086.

## Judicial System

**District Court of Guam:** PDN Bldg, 238 Archbishop Flores St, Agaña, GU 96910. Judge appointed by the President of the USA. The court has the jurisdiction of a Federal district court and of a bankruptcy court of the United States in all cases arising under the laws of the United States. Appeals may be made to the Court of Appeals for the Ninth Circuit and to the Supreme Court of the United States.
**Presiding Judge:** CRISTOBAL C. DUENAS.
**Superior Court of Guam:** Judges are appointed by the Governor of Guam for an initial eight-year term and are thereafter elected by popular vote. The Superior Court has jurisdiction over cases arising in Guam other than those heard in the District Court.
**Presiding Judge:** ALBERTO C. LAMORENA III.
There are also Probate, Traffic, Domestic, Juvenile and Small Claims Courts.

## Religion

About 90% of the population are Roman Catholic, but there are also members of the Episcopal (Anglican) Church, the Baptist churches and the Seventh-day Adventist Church. There are small communities of Muslims, Buddhists and Jews.

### CHRISTIANITY

#### The Roman Catholic Church

Guam comprises the single archdiocese of Agaña. The Archbishop participates in the Catholic Bishops' Conference of the Pacific, based in Fiji, and the Federation of Catholic Bishops' Conferences of Oceania, based in New Zealand.
At 31 December 1993 there were 122,263 adherents in Guam.
**Archbishop of Agaña:** Most Rev. ANTHONY SABLAN APURON, Chancery Office, POB 125, Cuesta San Ramón 26, Agaña, GU 96910; tel. 472-6116; fax 477-3519.

### BAHÁ'Í FAITH

**National Spiritual Assembly:** POB 20280, Guam Main Facility, Agaña, GU 96921; tel. 828-8639; fax 828-8112; mems resident in 19 localities in Guam and 10 localities in the Northern Mariana Islands.

## The Press

### NEWSPAPERS AND PERIODICALS

**Drive Guam:** POB 3191, Agaña, GU 96910; tel. 649-0883; f. 1991; quarterly; Publr STEPHEN V. NYGARD; circ. 30,000.
**Guam Business News:** POB 3191, Agaña, GU 96910; tel. 649-0883; fax 649-8883; f. 1983; monthly; Publr STEPHEN V. NYGARD; Editor ALISON RUSSELL; circ. 2,500.
**Guam Tribune:** POB EG, Agaña, GU 96910; tel. 646-5871; telex 6184; fax 646-6702; Tue. and Fri.; Publr MARK PANGILINAN; Man. Editor ROBERT TEODOSIO.
**Pacific Daily News** and **Sunday News:** POB DN, Agaña, GU 96910; tel. 477-9712; fax 472-1512; f. 1944; Publr LEE P. WEBBER; Man. Editor MARGARET SIZEMORE; circ. 24,184 (weekdays), 23,107 (Sunday).
**The Pacific Voice:** POB 2553, Agaña, GU 96910; f. 1950; Sunday; Roman Catholic; Gen. Man. BERNARD L. URBIZTANDO; Editor Rev. Fr BRIGIDO U. ARROYO; circ. 6,500.
**TV Guam Magazine:** 237 Mamis St, Tamuning, GU 96911; tel. 646-4030; fax 646-7445; f. 1973; weekly; Editor DAVE FURLONG; circ. 15,000.

### NEWS AGENCY

**United Press International (UPI)** (USA): POB 1617, Agaña, GU 96910; tel. 632-1138; Correspondent DICK WILLIAMS.

## Radio and Television

In 1992 there were an estimated 195,000 radio receivers and an estimated 92,000 television receivers in use.

### RADIO

**K-Stereo:** POB 20249, Guam Main Facility, Barrigada, GU 96921; tel. 477-9448; fax 477-6411; operates on FM 24 hours a day; Pres. EDWARD H. POPPE; Gen. Man. FRANCES W. POPPE.

## UNITED STATES EXTERNAL TERRITORIES

**KGUM/KZGZ:** POB GM, Agaña, GU 96910; tel. 477-5700; fax 477-3982; Chair. and CEO REX SORENSEN; Pres. JON ANDERSON.

**KOKU:** 530 West O'Brien Drive, Agaña, GU 96910; tel. 477-5658; fax 472-7663; operates on FM 24 hours a day; Pres. LEE M. HOLMES; Gen. Man. ERNIE A. GALITO.

**Radio Guam (KUAM):** POB 368, Agaña, GU 96910; tel. 637-5826; fax 637-9865; f. 1954; operates on AM and FM 24 hours a day; Pres. PAUL M. CALVO; Gen. Man. JON M. DENIGHT.

**Trans World Radio Pacific (TWR):** 1868 Halsey Drive, Asan, GU 96922; tel. 477-9701; fax 477-2838; f. 1975; broadcasts religious programmes on one medium-wave station covering Guam and nearby islands, and operates four short-wave transmitters reaching most of Asia, Africa and the Pacific; Pres. THOMAS LOWELL; Station Dir ED STORTRO.

### TELEVISION

**Guam Cable TV:** 530 West O'Brien Drive, Agaña, GU 96910; tel. 477-7815; telex 6296; f. 1968; Pres. LEE M. HOLMES; Gen. Man. HARRISON O. FLORA.

**KGTF—TV:** POB 21449 Guam Main Facility, Agaña, GU 96921; tel. 734-2207; fax 5483; f. 1970; cultural, public service and educational programmes; Gen. Man. JOE TIGHE; Technical Dir EDMOND CHEUNG.

**.KUAM—TV:** POB 368, Agaña, GU 96910; tel. 637-5826; fax 637-9865; f. 1956; operates colour service; Pres. JON M. DENIGHT; Station Man. TOM BLAZ.

## Finance

(m. = million; brs = branches; amounts in US dollars)

### BANKING

#### Commercial Banks

**Allied Banking Corpn** (Philippines): POB CT, Agaña, GU 96910; tel. 646-9143; fax 649-5002; Man. NOEL L. CRUZ; 1 br.

**Bank of Guam:** POB BW, Agaña, GU 96910; tel. 472-8865; telex 6280; fax 477-8687; total assets 600m. (1992); Pres. and CEO ANTHONY A. LEON GUERRERO; Chair. JESUS S. LEON GUERRERO; 16 brs.

**Bank of Hawaii** (USA): POB BH, Agaña, GU 96910; tel. 477-9781; telex 6104; fax 477-1019; Vice-Pres. RODNEY KIMURA; 3 brs.

**Bank of the Orient** (USA): POB EI, Agaña, GU 96910; tel. 477-9067; telex 6421; Vice-Pres. and Man. JOSEPH M. GOLDEN; 1 br.

**California Overseas Bank** (USA): POB GP, Agaña, GU 96910; tel. 477-9761; telex 6244; Man. JOSEPH DEL ROSARIO; 1 br.

**Citibank NA** (USA): POB FF, Agaña, GU 96910; tel. 477-2484; fax 477-9441; Vice-Pres. JOE SORIANO; 2 brs.

**Citizens Security Bank (Guam) Inc:** POB EQ, Agaña, GU 96910; tel. 472-1161; fax 472-1177; Pres. and CEO DANIEL L. WEBB.

**First Commercial Bank** (Taiwan): POB 2461, Agaña, GU 96910; tel. 472-6864; telex 6325; fax 477-8921; Gen. Man. BING CHANG HSU; 1 br.

**First Hawaiian Bank** (USA): POB AD, Agaña, GU 96910; tel. 477-7851; telex 6153; Vice-Pres. and Man. (Agaña) JOHN K. LEE; 2 brs.

**First Savings and Loan Association of America:** POB 21959, Guam Main Facility, GU 96921; tel. 632-0331; fax 632-0407; total assets 165m.; Pres. ZENY H. SANTOS; 4 brs.

**Guam Savings and Loan Association:** 151 Aspinall Ave, POB 2888, Agaña, GU 96910; tel. 472-8160; fax 477-1483; Pres. PHILIP J. FLORES; Exec. Vice-Pres. and CEO MARK O. FISH; 5 brs.

**Hongkong and Shanghai Banking Corpn Ltd** (Hong Kong): POB 27C, Agaña, GU 96910; tel. 646-3757; telex 6309; fax 646-3767; Man. DAVID P. D. LEIGHTON; 1 br.

**Metropolitan Bank and Trust Co** (USA): GCIC Bldg, 414 West Soledad Ave, Agaña, GU 96910; tel. 477-9554; telex 6460; fax 472-6012; Man. ESMERALDA S. J. CAPIRAL.

**Oceanic Bank** (USA): 1088 West Marine Drive, Suite 115A, Micronesia Mall, Dededo, GU 96912; tel. 637-1037; telex 6626; fax 637-2295; Man. ALEX D. B. LIM; 1 br.

**Pacific Financial Corpn:** POB AT, Agaña, GU 96910; tel. 649-5109; fax 646-1249; Pres. and Gen. Man. EDUARDO G. CAMACHO.

**Union Bank** (USA): POB 7809, Tamuning, GU 96911; tel. 477-8811; telex 6305; fax 472-3284; Man. KINJI SUZUKI; 2 brs.

### CHAMBER OF COMMERCE

**Guam Chamber of Commerce:** 173 Aspinall Ave, Suite 102, Ada Plaza Center, POB 283, Agaña, GU 96910; tel. 472-6311; fax 472-6202; Pres. ELOISE R. BAZA; Chair. OVIDIO R. A. CALVO.

## Trade and Industry

### DEVELOPMENT ORGANIZATION

**Guam Economic Development Authority (GEDA):** Guam International Trade Center Bldg, Suite 909, 590 South Marine Drive, Tamuning, GU 96911; tel. 649-4141; fax 649-4146; f 1965; Chief Economic Planner KIMBLEY S. A. LUJAN.

### EMPLOYERS' ORGANIZATION

**Guam Employers' Council:** Old Afia Bldg, Suite 202, 2nd Floor, 148 Aspinall Ave, Agaña, GU 96910; tel. 472-6736; f. 1966; private, non-profit asscn providing management development training and advice on personnel law and labour relations; annual wage, benefit and practices survey; Exec. Dir E. L. GIBSON.

### TRADE UNIONS

Many workers belong to trade unions based in the USA such as the American Federation of Government Employees and the American Postal Workers' Union. About 4,000 of the island's working population of 65,380 (in 1991) belong to unions.

**Guam Federation of Teachers (GFT):** Local 1581, POB 2301, Agaña, GU 96910; tel. 734-4391; fax 734-8085; f. 1965; affiliate of American Federation of Teachers; Pres. PAT PEXA; Vice-Pres. VERNON DAVIS; 4,000 mems.

## Transport

### ROADS

There are 674 km of modern all-weather roads.

### SHIPPING

**Ambyth, Shipping and Trading:** 1026 Cabras Highway Suite 205, Piti, GU 96925; tel. 477-8200; telex 6405; fax 472-1264; agents for all types of vessels and charter brokers; Vice-Pres. GREGORY R. DAVID.

**Atkins, Kroll Inc:** 443 South Marine Drive, Tamuning, GU 96911; tel. 646-1866; telex 6105; f. 1914; Pres. ALBERT P. WERNER.

**Island Shipping Lines:** Agaña, GU 96910; f. 1985; services to the Federated States of Micronesia.

**Maritime Agencies of the Pacific Ltd:** Suite 101, 1026 Cabras Highway, Piti, GU 96925; tel. 477-8500; telex 6101; fax 477-5726; f. 1976; agents for fishing vessels, cargo, dry products and construction materials; Pres. ROBERT E. HAHN.

**Pacific Navigation System:** POB 7, Agaña, GU 96910; f. 1946; Pres. KENNETH T. JONES, Jr.

**Tucor Services Inc:** POB 6128, Tamuning, GU 96931; tel. 646-6947; fax 646-6945; general agents for numerous dry cargo, passenger and steamship cos; Vice-Pres. ROY G. ADKERSON.

Monthly cargo services are operated by Kyowa Line vessels, calling at Guam en route from Hong Kong, Taiwan, the Republic of Korea and Japan to various Pacific islands, by Daiwa Line vessels, linking Guam with Japan and Pacific islands including Fiji, New Caledonia and American and Western Samoa, by Micronesia Transport Line, en route from Sydney (Australia), Palau and Yap to Saipan, Chuuk and Pohnpei, by American President Lines, en route from California to Japan, by Sea-Land Services from the West Coast of the USA via Honolulu and by Austfreight Services (NZ) from New Zealand every two months.

### CIVIL AVIATION

Guam is served by Air Nauru, Hawaiian Airlines (USA), Japan Airlines, All Nippon Airways (Japan), Northwest Orient Airlines (USA), Philippine Airlines and several air taxi operators.

**Guam Marianas Air:** Int. Airport, Agaña, GU 96910.

## Tourism

Tourism is an important industry on Guam, which received a total of 737,260 visitors in 1991, 876,742 in 1992 and 784,018 in 1993. In 1984, in an attempt to encourage tourism, the US Congress approved legislation whereby Guam was permitted to waive the standard US visa requirement for tourists. Most of Guam's hotels are situated in, or near to, Tumon, where amenities for entertainment are well-developed. There were an estimated 6,675 hotel rooms on Guam in 1993. About 70% of tourists come from Japan.

**Guam Visitors Bureau:** 401 Pale San Vitores Rd, Tumon, POB 3520, Agaña, GU 96911; tel. 646-5278; fax 646-8861; Gen. Man. MICHAEL D. CARLSON (acting).

# THE UNITED STATES VIRGIN ISLANDS

## Introductory Survey

### Location, Climate, Language, Religion, Flag, Capital

The Territory consists of three main inhabited islands (St Croix, St Thomas and St John) and about 50 smaller islands, mostly uninhabited. They are situated at the eastern end of the Greater Antilles, about 64 km (40 miles) east of Puerto Rico in the Caribbean Sea. The climate is tropical, although tempered by the prevailing easterly trade winds. The temperature averages 26°C (79°F), with little variation between winter and summer. The humidity is low for the tropics. English is the official language, but Spanish and Creole are also widely used. The people of the US Virgin Islands are predominantly of African descent. There is a strong religious tradition, and most of the inhabitants are Christians, mainly Protestants. The flag (proportions 3 by 2) is white, with a modified version of the US coat of arms (an eagle holding an olive branch in one foot and a sheaf of arrows in the other, with a shield, comprising a small horizontal blue panel above vertical red and white stripes, superimposed), between the letters V and I, in the centre. The capital is Charlotte Amalie, on the island of St Thomas.

### Recent History

The Virgin Islands, originally inhabited by Carib and Arawak Indians, were discovered by Europeans in 1493. The group subsequently passed through English, French, and Dutch control, before the western islands of St Thomas and St John, colonized by Denmark after 1670, and St Croix, purchased from France in 1733, became the Danish West Indies. In 1917 these islands, which are strategically placed in relation to the Panama Canal, were sold for US $25m. by Denmark to the USA. They now form an unincorporated territory of the USA. Residents of the US Virgin Islands are US citizens, but cannot vote in presidential elections, if resident in the islands. The US Virgin Islands is represented by the US House of Representatives by one popularly-elected Delegate, who is permitted to vote only in committees of the House.

The inhabitants of the islands were granted a measure of self-government by the Organic Act, as revised in 1954, which created the elected 15-member Senate. Since 1970, executive authority has been vested in the elected Governor and Lieutenant-Governor. In the first gubernatorial election, in 1970, the Republican incumbent, Melvin Evans, retained office. In 1974 Cyril E. King, leader of the Independent Citizens Movement (a breakaway faction of the Democratic Party), was elected Governor. On King's death in 1978, the former Lieutenant-Governor, Juan Luis, was elected Governor. He was returned to power in the 1982 election. The governorship passed to the Democratic Party with the election of Alexander Farrelly in 1986. Farrelly was re-elected Governor in 1990, and in the 1994 elections was succeeded by another Democrat, Dr Roy Schneider.

Since 1954 there have been five attempts to redraft the Constitution to give the US Virgin Islands greater autonomy. Each draft has, however, been rejected by a referendum. The US Government has expressed the view that it would welcome reform, if approved by the residents, as long as it were economically feasible and did not affect US national security. A non-binding referendum on the islands' future status, which was to take place in November 1989, was postponed following the disruption caused by 'Hurricane Hugo' (see Economic Affairs). Voting, which eventually took place in October 1993, produced support of 80.3% for retaining the islands' existing status, with 14.2% favouring full integration with the USA and 4.8% advocating the termination of US sovereignty. The result of the referendum was, however, invalidated by the low turn-out: only 27.4% of registered voters took part, falling short of the 50% participation required for the referendum to be valid.

### Economic Affairs

According to estimates by the Territorial Government, the islands' gross national product (GNP) in 1987 was US $1,246m., equivalent to $8,717 per head, or about 56.3% of the US mainland average.

Most of the land is unsuitable for large-scale cultivation, but tax incentives have encouraged the growing of vegetables, fruit and sorghum, which are produced for local consumption.

The islands are heavily dependent on links with the US mainland. More than 90% of trade is conducted with Puerto Rico and the USA. There are no known natural resources, and, because of limited land space and other factors, the islands are unable to produce sufficient food to satisfy local consumption. Most goods are imported, mainly from the mainland USA.

Tourism, which is estimated to account for more than 60% of gross domestic product (GDP), is the mainstay of the islands' income and employment, and provides the major source of direct and indirect revenue for the trade, transportation and services sectors. The emphasis is on the visiting cruise-ship business, and the advantages of duty-free products for American visitors.

St Croix has one of the world's largest petroleum refineries, with a capacity of 550,000 barrels per day (b/d). Since 1981, however, it has been operating at reduced levels of throughput. An alumina processing plant, closed down in 1985, was acquired in 1989 by commodity trading interests. It was intended to rehabilitate the plant, which has an annual throughput capacity of 700,000 metric tons, and alumina shipments to the USA and Europe were to begin in 1990. Efforts have been made to introduce labour-intensive and non-polluting manufacturing industries. Rum is an important product. This industry, however, was expected to encounter increased competition from Mexico as a result of the North American Free Trade Agreement (NAFTA, see p.190), which entered into operation in January 1994.

Since the early 1960s the population has increased dramatically. This inflow has included people from neighbouring Caribbean countries, together with wealthy white settlers from the US mainland, attracted by the climate and the low taxes. At the 1990 census, between 30% and 35% of the population originated from other Caribbean islands, and 13% from the mainland USA.

Owing to the islands' heavy reliance on imported goods, local prices and inflation are higher than on the mainland, and the islands' economy, in contrast to that of the USA, remained in recession for most of the 1980s. The rate of unemployment averaged 8.2% of the labour force in 1983, but, with a revival in tourism, it declined to 3.0% in 1987. In 1989 the tourist industry was affected by a prolonged strike by employees of the principal US airline operating in the Caribbean. The unemployment rate in that year was 3.7%. 'Hurricane Hugo', which struck the islands in September 1989, was estimated to have caused $1,000m. in property damage. Work on rebuilding, however, temporarily revitalized employment in the construction sector, where the demand for labour rose to between two and three times normal levels. Expenditure by the US Government on recovery measures was expected to exceed $580m. The rate of unemployment fell to 2.8% in 1990, but rose to 6.2% in March 1994.

### Social Welfare

In 1989 the islands had 252 hospital beds and approximately 130 physicians in practice. Hospitals and clinics are operated by the Government and governed by a Hospital Board.

### Education

Education is compulsory up to the age of 16 years. It generally comprises eight years at primary school and four years at secondary school. In 1990 there were 28,691 elementary and secondary students at public and private schools, and 1,762 public school teachers. The University of the Virgin Islands, with campuses on St Thomas and St Croix, had 924 full-time and 1,792 part-time undergraduate students in 1992.

### Public Holidays

**1995:** 1 January (New Year's Day), 6 January (Three Kings' Day), 16 January (Martin Luther King Day), 20 February (Presidents' Day), 31 March (Transfer Day), 14–17 April (Easter), 29 May (Memorial Day), 19 June (Organic Act Day), 3 July (Danish West Indies Emancipation Day), 4 July (US Independence Day), 24 July (Hurricane Supplication Day), 4 September (Labor Day), 9 October (Columbus Day and Puerto Rico Friendship Day), 18 October (Virgin Islands Thanksgiving Day), 1 November (D. Hamilton Jackson Day), 11 November (Veterans' Day), 23 November (US Thanksgiving Day), 25–26 December (Christmas).

**1996:** 1 January (New Year's Day), 6 January (Three Kings' Day), 15 January (Martin Luther King Day), 19 February (Presidents' Day), 31 March (Transfer Day), 5–9 April (Easter), 27 May (Memorial Day), 19 June (Organic Act Day), 3 July (Danish West Indies Emancipation Day), 4 July (US Independence Day), 24 July (Hurricane Supplication Day), 2 September (Labor Day), 14 October (Columbus Day and Puerto Rico Friendship Day), 16 October (Virgin Islands Thanksgiving Day), 1 November (D. Hamilton Jackson Day), 11 November (Veterans' Day), 28 November (US Thanksgiving Day), 25–26 December (Christmas).

UNITED STATES EXTERNAL TERRITORIES

## Statistical Survey

Source: Office of Public Relations, Office of the Governor, Charlotte Amalie, St Thomas, VI 00802; tel. (809) 774-0294; fax (809) 774-4988.

### AREA AND POPULATION

**Area:** 347.1 sq km (134 sq miles): St Croix 215 sq km (83 sq miles); St Thomas 80.3 sq km (31 sq miles); St John 51.8 sq km (20 sq miles).
**Population:** 96,569 (males 46,204; females 50,365) at census of 1 April 1980; 101,809 (males 49,210; females 52,599) at census of 1 April 1990. *Distribution by island* (1990 census): St Croix 50,139, St Thomas 48,166, St John 3,504.
**Capital:** Charlotte Amalie (population 12,331 at 1990 census).
**Births and Deaths** (1993): Registered live births 2,529; Registered deaths 569. Source: UN, *Population and Vital Statistics Report*.
**Economically Active Population** (persons aged 16 years and over, 1990 census): Agriculture, hunting, forestry and fishing 576; Mining and quarrying 30; Manufacturing 2,916; Electricity, gas and water 731; Construction 5,712; Trade, restaurants and hotels 10,343; Transport, storage and communications 3,715; Financing, insurance, real estate and business services 3,631; Community, social and personal services 12,883; Activities not adequately defined 6,906; Total labour force 47,443 (males 24,762; females 22,681). Source: ILO, *Year Book of Labour Statistics*.

### AGRICULTURE, ETC

**Livestock** (1987): Cattle 3,672; Sheep 2,889; Pigs 2,404; Goats 4,035; Chickens 18,345.
**Fishing** (metric tons, live weight): Total catch 793 in 1989; 684 in 1990; 880 in 1991. Source: FAO, *Yearbook of Fishery Statistics*.

### INDUSTRY

**Production** ('000 metric tons, unless otherwise indicated, 1992): Jet fuels 1,465; Motor spirit (petrol) 2,085; Kerosene 32; Distillate fuel oils 2,735; Residual fuel oils 3,785; Liquefied petroleum gas 190 (estimate); Electric energy 1,020 million kWh (net production). Source: UN, *Industrial Commodity Statistics Yearbook*.

### FINANCE

**Currency and Exchange Rates:** 100 cents = 1 United States dollar (US $). *Sterling Equivalent* (31 December 1994): £1 sterling = US $1.5643; $100 = £63.92.
**Budget** (US $ million, 1990, estimates): Revenue 364.4; Expenditure 364.4.

### EXTERNAL TRADE

**Total** (US $ million, 1992): *Imports*: 2,200; *Exports*: 1,800. The main import is crude petroleum, while the principal exports are refined petroleum products.

### TRANSPORT

**Road Traffic** (registered motor vehicles, 1990): 59,682.
**Shipping** (1989): Cruise-ship arrivals 1,106; Passenger arrivals 1,062,500.
**Civil Aviation** (1989): Passenger arrivals 664,200.

### TOURISM

**Foreign Visitors** ('000 arrivals, excl. cruise-ship passengers): 463 in 1990; 470 in 1991; 487 in 1992. Source: UN, *Statistical Yearbook*.

### COMMUNICATIONS MEDIA*

**Radio Receivers** (1992): 105,000 in use.
**Television Receivers** (1992): 65,000 in use.
**Telephones** (1991): 51,000 main lines in use.
**Daily Newspapers** (1992): 2 titles (combined average circulation 22,000 copies).
**Non-daily Newspapers** (estimates, 1988): 2 titles (combined average circulation 4,000 copies).

* Sources: UNESCO, *Statistical Yearbook*; UN, *Statistical Yearbook*.

### EDUCATION

**Elementary** (public schools, 1990): 760 teachers; 12,412 students.
**Secondary** (public schools, 1990): 541 teachers; 9,263 students.
In 1990 there were also 44 private schools, with 7,016 students. In 1992 the University of the Virgin Islands had an enrolment of 924 full-time and 1,792 part-time undergraduate students.

*The United States Virgin Islands*

## Directory
### The Constitution

The Government of the US Virgin Islands is organized under the provisions of the Organic Act of the Virgin Islands, passed by the Congress of the United States in 1936 and revised in 1954. Subsequent amendments provided for the popular election of the Governor and Lieutenant-Governor of the Virgin Islands in 1970, and, since 1973, for representation in the US House of Representatives by a popularly-elected Delegate. The Delegate has voting powers only in committees of the House. Executive power is vested in the Governor, who is elected for a term of four years by universal adult suffrage and who appoints, with the advice and consent of the Legislature, the heads of the executive departments. The Governor may also appoint administrative assistants as his representatives on St John and St Croix. Legislative power is vested in the Legislature of the Virgin Islands, a unicameral body composed of 15 Senators, elected by popular vote. Legislation is subject to the approval of the Governor. All residents of the islands, who are citizens of the United States and at least 18 years of age, have the right to vote in local elections but not in national elections. In 1976 the Virgin Islands were granted the right to draft their own constitution, subject to the approval of the US President and Congress. A Constitution permitting a degree of autonomy was drawn up in 1978 and gained the necessary approval, but was then rejected by the people of the Virgin Islands in a referendum in March 1979. A fourth draft, providing for greater autonomy than the 1978 draft, was rejected in a referendum in November 1981.

### The Government
(June 1995)

**Governor:** Dr Roy L. Schneider.
**Lieutenant-Governor:** Kenneth E. Mapp.
**Regional Audit Manager:** Arnold Van Beverhoudt.
**Administrators for St Croix:** Ohanio Harris (Frederiksted), Alexander Petersen (Christiansted), Ruth Bermudez-Cruz (Mid-Island).
**Administrator for St John:** James Dalmida.
**Administrator for St Thomas:** Levron Sarauw, Sr.
**President of the Senate:** Almando Liburd.
**Secretary of the Senate:** Allison Petrus.
**US Virgin Islands Delegate to the US Congress:** Victor O. Frazer.

#### GOVERNMENT DEPARTMENTS

The Executive Departments (headed by Commissioners) are as follows: Economic Development and Agriculture, Education, Finance, Health, Housing, Parks and Recreation, Human Services, Justice (Attorney-General), Labor, Licensing and Consumer Affairs, Planning and Natural Resources, Property and Procurement, Public Works, and Police.

**Office of the Governor:** Government House, 21–22 Kongens Gade, Charlotte Amalie, St Thomas, VI 00802; tel. (809) 774-0001; telex 0060; fax (809) 774-4988.
**Office of the Lieutenant-Governor:** Government Hill, 18 Kongens Gade, St Thomas, VI 00802; tel. (809) 774-2991; fax (809) 774-1361.
**Department of Agriculture and Tourism:** 81 AB Kronprindsens Gade, POB 6400, St Thomas, VI 00801; tel. (809) 774-8784; fax (809) 774-4390.
**Department of Finance:** 76 Kronprindsens Gade, St Thomas, VI 00801; tel. (809) 774-1553.
**Department of Labor:** 35A–54AB Kronprindsens Gade, POB 2608, St Thomas, VI 00801; tel. (809) 774-3700.

### Legislature

The Senate comprises 15 members, elected for a term of two years. The most recent general election was held in November 1994.
**President of the Senate:** Almando Liburd.

### Political Organizations

**Democratic Party of the Virgin Islands:** POB 3739, Charlotte Amalie, St Thomas, VI 00801; tel. (809) 774-3130; affiliated to the Democratic Party in the USA; Chair. Marylyn A. Stapleton.
**Independent Citizens Movement:** Charlotte Amalie, St Thomas, VI 00801; Chair. Virdin C. Brown.

**Republican Party of the Virgin Islands:** Charlotte Amalie, St Thomas, VI 00801; tel. (809) 776-7660; affiliated to the Republican Party in the USA; Chair. SHERON E. HODGE; Exec. Dir KRIM BALLENTINE.

## Judicial System

**US Federal District Court of the Virgin Islands:** Federal Bldg and US Courthouse, 5500 Veteran's Drive, St Thomas, VI 00802; tel. (809) 774-0640; jurisdiction in civil, criminal and federal actions; the judges are appointed by the President of the United States with the advice and consent of the Senate.
**Judges:** THOMAS K. MOORE (Chief Judge), RAYMOND L. FINCH.
**Territorial Court of the Virgin Islands:** Alexander A. Farrelly Justice Center, POB 70, St Thomas, VI 00802; tel. (809) 774-6680; jurisdiction in violations of police and executive regulations, in criminal cases and civil actions involving not more than $200,000, in domestic and juvenile matters concurrently with the US Federal District Court; judges are appointed by the Governor.
**Judges:** VERNE A. HODGE (Chief Judge), ISHMAEL MEYERS, ALPHONSO ANDREWS, MARIA CABRET, IVE A. SWAN, SOROYA DIASE, BRENDA HOLLAR, PATRICIA STEELE.

## Religion

The population is mainly Christian. The main churches with followings in the islands are the Roman Catholic (with an estimated 30,000 adherents in 1990), Episcopalian, Lutheran, Methodist, Moravian and Seventh-day Adventist. There is also a small Jewish community.

### CHRISTIANITY
#### The Roman Catholic Church

The US Virgin Islands comprise a single diocese, suffragan to the archdiocese of Washington, DC, USA. At 31 December 1993 there were an estimated 33,000 adherents in the territory
**Bishop of St Thomas:** Mgr ELLIOTT G. THOMAS, Bishop's Residence, POB 1825, 68 Kronprindsens Gade, St Thomas, VI 00803; tel. (809) 774-3166; fax (809) 774-5816.

#### The Episcopal Church
**Bishop of the Virgin Islands:** Rt Rev. E. DON TAYLOR, Assistant Bishop of New York, 1047 Amsterdam Ave, New York, NY 10025; tel. (212) 316-7400; fax (212) 932-7354.

## The Press

**The Business Journal:** 4000 Taarnberg, POB 1298, St Thomas, VI 00804; f. 1986; fortnightly; independent; Editor JEAN ETSINGER; circ. 2,000.
**Pride Magazine:** 22A Norre Gade, POB 7908, St Thomas, VI 00801; tel. (809) 776-4106; f. 1983; monthly; Editor JUDITH WILLIAMS; circ. 4,000.
**St Croix Avis:** La Grande Princesse, Christiansted, St Croix, VI 00820; tel. (809) 773-2300; f. 1944; morning; independent; Editor RENA BROADHURST-KNIGHT; circ. 10,000.
**Tradewinds:** POB 1500, Cruz Bay, St John 00831; tel. (809) 776-6496; f. 1972; fortnightly; Editor THOMAS C. OAT; circ. 2,000.
**Virgin Islands Daily News:** 49 and 52A Estate Thomas, POB 7760, Charlotte Amalie, St Thomas, VI 00801; tel. (809) 774-8772; fax (809) 776-0740; f. 1930; morning; CEO RON DILLMAN; Publr and Editor ARIEL MELCHIOR, Jr; circ. 16,000.

## Radio and Television

In 1992, according to UNESCO, there were an estimated 105,000 radio receivers and 65,000 television receivers in use.

### RADIO
**WAVI—FM:** POB 25016, Gallows Bay Station, St Croix, VI 00824; tel. (809) 773-3693; commercial; Gen. Man. DOUG HARRIS.
**WGOD:** Crown Mountain, POB 5012, St Thomas, VI 00803; tel. (809) 774-4498; fax (809) 776-0877; commercial; Gen. Man. PETER RICHARDSON.
**WIYC—FM:** 5A Caret Bay, POB 5234, St Thomas, VI 00801; tel. (809) 775-2104; commercial; Gen. Man. LANCE DEBOCK.
**WJKC—FM:** Caravelle Arcade, Suite V2, Christiansted, St Croix, VI 00820; tel. (809) 773-0995; commercial; Gen. Man. JONATHAN COHEN.
**WRRA:** Frederiksted, POB 277, St Croix, VI 00841; tel. (809) 772-1290; commercial; Gen. Man. ENRIQUE RODRIGUEZ.

**WSTA:** Sub Base, POB 1340, St Thomas, VI 00801; tel. (809) 774-1340; fax (809) 776-1316; commercial; Gen. Man. LEN STEIN.
**WTBN—FM:** Havensight Executive Towers, 19 Estate Thomas, Suite 103, St Thomas, VI 00802; tel. (809) 776-2610; commercial; Gen. Man. WINTHROP MADURO.
**WVGN—FM:** 1D Havensight, Wells Bldg, St Thomas, VI 00802; tel. (809) 776-1556; commercial; Gen. Man. SANDY WHEELER.
**WVWI (Thousand Islands Corpn):** Franklin Bldg, 3rd Floor, POB 5678, St Thomas, VI 00803; tel. (809) 776-1000; fax (809) 776-5357; f. 1962; commercial; Pres. and Gen. Man. R. E. NOBLE.

### TELEVISION
**Caribbean Communications Corpn:** One Beltjen Place, St Thomas, VI 00802-6735; tel. (809) 776-2150; fax (809) 774-5029; f. 1966; cable service, 67 channels; Pres. RANDOLPH H. KNIGHT.
**St Croix, VI Cable TV:** Heron Commercial Park, POB 5968, Sunny Isle, St Croix, VI 00823; f. 1981; 32 channels; Gen. Man. JACK WHITE.
**WSVI—TV:** Sunny Isle, POB 8ABC, Christiansted, St Croix, VI 00823; tel. (809) 778-5008; fax (809) 778-5011; f. 1965; one channel and one translator; Gen. Man. BARAKAT SALEH.
**WTJX—TV (Public Television Service):** Barbel Plaza, POB 7879, St Thomas, VI 00801; tel. (809) 774-6255; fax (809) 774-7092; one channel; Gen. Man. CALVIN BASTIAN.

## Finance

### BANKING
**Banco Popular de Puerto Rico:** Church St, Christiansted, St Croix, VI 00820; tel. (809) 773-0077; 6 brs.
**Bank of Nova Scotia** (Canada): 214c Altona and Welgunst, POB 420, Charlotte Amalie, St Thomas, VI 00804; tel. (809) 774-0037; telex 3472072; fax (809) 776-5997; Man. R. HAINES; 9 brs.
**Barclays Bank PLC** (UK): POB 6880, St Thomas, VI 00804; tel. (809) 776-5080; telex 0057; fax (809) 776-5922; Man. JOHN INGRAM.
**Chase Manhattan Bank, NA** (USA): Waterfront, Charlotte Amalie, St Thomas, VI 00801; tel. (809) 776-2222; telex 3472110; brs in St Croix and St John; Gen. Man. WARREN BEER.
**Citibank, NA** (USA): Veterans Drive, Charlotte Amalie, St Thomas, VI 00801; tel. (809) 774-4800; telex 2252; Vice-Pres. ALBERT MALAVE.
**CoreStates First Pennsylvania Bank NA** (USA): 12 King St, Christiansted, St Croix, VI 00821; tel. (809) 773-0440; Pres. PAUL LODGEK; br. in Frederiksted.
**First Federal Savings Bank:** Veterans Drive, St Thomas, VI; tel. (809) 774-2022; fax (809) 776-1313; Man. ALFRED LESLIE; br. in St Croix.
**First Virgin Islands Federal Savings Bank:** 50 Kronprindsens Gade, Charlotte Amalie, St Thomas, VI 00803; tel. (809) 776-9494; Pres. AL GRAF.

### INSURANCE
A number of mainland US companies have agencies in the Virgin Islands.

## Trade and Industry

### CHAMBERS OF COMMERCE
**St Croix Chamber of Commerce:** POB 4369, Kingshill, St Croix, VI 00851; tel. (809) 773-1435; f. 1925; 450 mems; Exec. Dir RACHEL HAINES.
**St Thomas–St John Chamber of Commerce:** 6–7 Main St, POB 324, St Thomas, VI 00804; tel. (809) 776-0010; Exec. Dir JOSEPH F. AUBAIN.

## Transport

### ROADS
There are good roads on St Thomas and St Croix; the roads on all three main islands were improved during the 1980s. The islands' road network totals approximately 855.5 km (531.6 miles).

### SHIPPING
**Virgin Islands Port Authority:** POB 1707, St Thomas, VI 00803; tel. (809) 774-1629; fax (809) 774-0025; also at POB 1134, St Croix, VI 00821; tel. (809) 778-1012; fax (809) 778-1033; f. 1968; semi-autonomous govt agency; maintains, operates and develops marine and aviation facilities; Exec. Dir GORDON FINCH.

Cruise ships and cargo vessels of Carnival Lines, Costa, Cunard Renaissance, Royal Caribbean, Windstar Cruises, Consolidated

# UNITED STATES EXTERNAL TERRITORIES

*The United States Virgin Islands, Other Territories*

Freight, Island Express, Lady Romney Shipping & Trading, Tropical Shipping and others call at the Virgin Islands. The bulk of cargo traffic is handled at a container port on St Croix. A ferry service provides frequent daily connections between St Thomas and St John and between St Thomas and Tortola (British Virgin Islands).

## CIVIL AVIATION

There are airports on St Thomas and St Croix, and an airfield on St John. Seaplane services link the three islands. The runways at Cyril E. King Airport, St Thomas, and Alexander Hamilton Airport, St Croix, can accommodate intercontinental flights.

## Tourism

The islands have a well developed tourist infrastructure, offering excellent facilities for fishing, yachting and other aquatic sports. A National Park covers about two-thirds of St John. There were about 5,500 hotel rooms in 1993, when an estimated 1.9m. tourists (including 1.2m. cruise-ship passengers) visited the islands. Tourist expenditure in that year was estimated at $800m.

**Hotel Association of St Croix:** POB 3869, Christiansted, St Croix, VI 00820; tel. (809) 773-7117.

**Hotel Association of St Thomas–St John:** POB 2300, St Thomas, VI 00803; tel. (809) 774-6835.

# OTHER TERRITORIES

**Baker and Howland Islands:** in the Central Pacific Ocean, about 2,575 km (1,600 miles) south-west of Honolulu, Hawaii; comprises two low-lying coral atolls without lagoons; uninhabited. Both islands were mined for guano in the late 19th century. Settlements, known as Meyerton (on Baker) and Itascatown (on Howland), were established by the USA in 1935, but were evacuated during the Second World War, owing to Japanese air attacks. The islands are national wildlife refuges and since 1974 have been administered by the US Fish and Wildlife Service. In 1990 legislation before Congress proposed that the islands be included within the boundaries of the State of Hawaii. Permission to land is required from the US Fish and Wildlife Service, Refuge Complex Office, POB 50167, Honolulu, HI 96850, USA.

**Jarvis Island:** in the Central Pacific Ocean, about 2,090 km (1,300 miles) south of Hawaii; a low-lying coral island; uninhabited. A settlement, known as Millersville, was established by the USA in 1935, but was evacuated during the Second World War. Legislation before Congress in 1990 proposed that the island be included within the State of Hawaii. The island is a national wildlife refuge and has been administered by the US Fish and Wildlife Service since 1974 (address as above).

**Johnston Atoll:** in the Pacific Ocean, about 1,319 km (820 miles) west-south-west of Honolulu, Hawaii; comprises Johnston Island (population 327 in 1980), Sand Island (uninhabited) and two man-made islands, North (Akua) and East (Hikina); area 2.6 sq km (1 sq mile). In 1983 plans were announced to build a chemical weapons disposal facility on the atoll. There was concern in the Pacific region in late 1989, when the US Government agreed to remove artillery shells containing more than 400 tons of nerve gas from the Federal Republic of Germany, and destroy them on Johnston Island. In late 1991, following expressions of protest to the US Government by the South Pacific Forum nations (see p. 217), together with many environmental groups, a team of scientists visited the chemical disposal facility to monitor the safety and environmental impact of its activities. In January 1995, following a series of fires and accidental chemical releases during the previous year, the US army announced that it was to seek an extension to the 30 August 1995 deadline, the date by which the 400,000 weapons stored on the island were due to be destroyed. A facility capable of performing atmospheric tests of nuclear weapons remains operational on the atoll. A hurricane that struck Johnston Island in August 1994 forced the evacuation of 1,105 civilian and military personnel and resulted in damage estimated at some US$15m. Johnston Atoll has been designated a Naval Defense Sea Area and Airspace Reservation, and is closed to public access. Johnston Atoll is administered by the Commander, Johnston Atoll (FCDNA), APO San Francisco, CA 96035.

**Kingman Reef:** in the Pacific Ocean, about 1,500km (925 miles) south-west of Hawaii; comprises a reef and shoal measuring about 8 km (5 miles) by 15 km (9.5 miles). Kingman Reef has been designated a Naval Defense Sea Area and Airspace Reservation, and is closed to public access. Legislation before Congress in 1990 proposed the inclusion of Kingman Reef within the boundaries of the State of Hawaii. It is administered by the US Department of Defense, Department of the Navy, The Pentagon, Washington, DC 20350; tel. (202) 695-0965.

**Midway Island:** in the northern Pacific Ocean, about 1,850 km (1,150 miles) north-west of Hawaii; a coral atoll, comprising Sand Island, Eastern Island and several small islets within the reef; area about 5 sq km (2 sq miles); population 2,200 in 1983 (although this declined in subsequent years); forms part of a Naval Defense Sea Area, to which unauthorized access is forbidden. Legislation before Congress in 1990 proposed the inclusion of the Territory within the State of Hawaii. The islands are administered by the US Department of Defense, Department of the Navy, The Pentagon, Washington, DC 20350; tel. (202) 695-0965.

**Palmyra:** in the Pacific Ocean, about 1,600 km (1,000 miles) south of Honolulu, Hawaii; comprises some 50 low-lying islets; area 100 ha; uninhabited; privately-owned. Since 1961 the Territory has been administered by the US Department of the Interior. In 1990 legislation before Congress proposed the inclusion of Palmyra within the boundaries of the State of Hawaii. Permission to land on the islands is required from the owners, principally Leslie, Dudley and Ainlie Fullard-Leo of Hawaii, USA.

**Wake Island:** in the Pacific Ocean, about 2,060 km (1,280 miles) east of Guam; a coral atoll comprising the three islets of Wake, Wilkes and Peale; area less than 8 sq km (3 sq miles); population estimated to be almost 2,000 in 1988. Legislation before Congress in 1990 proposed the inclusion of the islands within the Territory of Guam. However, the Republic of the Marshall Islands, some 500 km (310 miles) south of Wake, exerted its own claim to the atoll, known as Enenkio to the Micronesians, which is a site of great importance for the islands' traditional chiefly rituals. Since 1972 the group has been administered by the US Department of Defense, Department of the Air Force, The Pentagon, Washington, DC 20380; tel. (202) 694-8010.

# URUGUAY

## Introductory Survey

### Location, Climate, Language, Religion, Flag, Capital

The Eastern Republic of Uruguay lies on the south-east coast of South America, with Brazil to the north and Argentina to the west. The climate is temperate, with an average winter temperature of 14°C–16°C (57°F–61°F) and an average summer temperature of 21°C–28°C (70°F–82°F). The language is Spanish. There is no state religion but Roman Catholicism is predominant. The national flag (proportions 3 by 2) has nine horizontal stripes (five white and four blue, alternating), with a square white canton, containing a yellow sun with sixteen alternating straight and wavy rays, in the upper hoist. The capital is Montevideo.

### Recent History

Since independence from Spain, gained in 1825, Uruguay's political life has been dominated by two parties: the Colorados ('reds' or Liberals) and the Blancos ('whites' or Conservatives, subsequently also known as the Partido Nacional). Their rivalry resulted in frequent outbreaks of civil war in the 19th century: the names derive from the flags of the civil war of 1836. From 1880 to 1958 the governing Partido Colorado was led by the Batlle family. Owing to the progressive policies of José Batlle y Ordóñez, Colorado President from 1903 to 1907 and 1911 to 1915, Uruguay became the first welfare state in Latin America. Between 1951 and 1966 the presidency was in abeyance, being replaced by a collective leadership.

In December 1967 Jorge Pacheco Areco assumed the presidency. His period in office was notable for massive increases in the cost of living, labour unrest and the spectacular exploits of the Tupamaro urban guerrilla movement. A presidential election was held in November 1971, and the official Colorado candidate, Juan María Bordaberry Arocena, was declared the winner, taking office in March 1972. The army took complete control of the campaign against the Tupamaros, and by the end of 1973 had crushed the movement. Military intervention in civilian affairs led, in 1973, to the closure of the Congreso (Congress) and its replacement by an appointed 25-member Council of State (subsequently increased to 35 members). The Partido Comunista and other left-wing groups were banned; repressive measures, including strict press censorship, continued. In September 1974 army officers were placed in control of the major state-owned enterprises.

President Bordaberry was deposed by the army in June 1976 because of his refusal to countenance any return, however gradual, to constitutional rule. In July the recently formed Council of the Nation elected Dr Aparicio Méndez Manfredini to the presidency for five years. Despite the Government's announcement that there would be a return to democracy, persecution of political figures continued, and the number of political prisoners held in 1976 was thought to have reached 6,000. Although the decision taken by the USA in 1979 to restore a fraction of its former military aid to Uruguay was governed by an easing of repression, the Red Cross reported in 1981 that some 1,100 political prisoners were still being detained.

President Méndez introduced several constitutional amendments, known as Institutional Acts, to consolidate the internal situation and to create a 'new order'. By 1980 severe economic problems made the army anxious to return executive responsibility to civilian politicians. A new constitution, by which the armed forces would continue to be involved in all matters of national security, was drafted and submitted to a plebiscite in November 1980, but was rejected by 57.8% of voters. The military leadership was therefore forced to amend the draft document in consultation with leaders of the recognized political parties, and, in September 1981, a retired army general, Gregorio Alvarez Armellino, was appointed by the Joint Council of the Armed Forces to serve as President during the transition period to full civilian government.

The Government's reluctance to permit greater public freedom and to improve observance of human rights caused serious unrest throughout 1983. Popular discontent was further aroused by the rapid deterioration of the Uruguayan economy and the effect of events in Argentina. In August the Government suspended all public political activity and reserved the right to impose a new constitution without consultation, insisting, however, that the original electoral timetable would be maintained. The political opposition responded by threatening to boycott the elections and by uniting with the proscribed opposition parties to hold a national day of protest. In September the first organized labour protest for 10 years was supported by 500,000 workers.

Political agitation increased during 1984, and the Government threatened to postpone the elections, planned for 25 November 1984, unless the political parties agreed to its proposals for constitutional reform. Political tension increased in June, following the return from exile and the subsequent arrest of Ferreira Aldunate, the proposed presidential candidate of the Partido Nacional. Talks between the Government, the Partido Colorado and the Unión Cívica (a Christian democratic party) resumed in July. The parties obtained several important concessions from the Government, including the right to engage in political activity. In August, encouraged by the Government's commitment to the restoration of the democratic process, the parties (with the exception of the Partido Nacional) agreed to the Government's proposals, including a transitional set of laws and the formation of the Consejo Nacional de Seguridad (National Security Council). The Government confirmed that elections would take place, and all restrictions on political activity were withdrawn.

At the elections in November 1984 the Partido Colorado, led by Dr Julio María Sanguinetti Cairolo, secured a narrow victory over the opposition. In February 1985 the military regime relinquished power, one month earlier than originally planned. President Sanguinetti was inaugurated on 1 March, as was a Government of national unity, including representatives of the other parties. At the same time various outlawed organizations, including the Partido Comunista, were legalized. All political prisoners were released under an amnesty law later in the same month.

The new Government's most pressing concern was Uruguay's economic recession. However, attempts to arrest the economic decline were hampered by frequent industrial stoppages. In August 1985 the Government began discussions with trade union leaders and representatives of the business sector but, following another series of strikes, the Government unilaterally suspended negotiations. Discussions were resumed in September. In 1986 and 1987 further strikes were staged by public-sector employees in protest against government economic policy and reductions in planned budgetary expenditure; they also demanded wage increases.

A major political issue in 1986 was the investigation into alleged violations of human rights by the armed forces during the military dictatorship. In August the Government proposed legislation that would offer an amnesty for all military and police personnel accused of this type of crime, in accordance with a pact made with the armed forces that human rights trials would not take place. In October this draft legislation was rejected by opposition parties, but in December a revised law (the 'punto final') was approved, which, while its sponsors insisted that it was not an amnesty law, brought an end to current military trials and made Sanguinetti responsible for any further investigations. There was widespread opposition to the new law, particularly from left-wing political parties, trade unions and student groups. In February 1987 a campaign was initiated to organize a petition containing at least 550,000 signatures, or 25% of the registered electorate in Uruguay, in order to force a referendum on the issue. (A clause in the 1966 Constitution stipulates that, if such a petition is successfully produced, a referendum must be held within 60 days.) The campaign was supported principally by human rights groups, trade unions and the centre-left coalition, the Frente Amplio. By late 1988 the required number of signatures had been collected, and a referendum took place in April 1989, at which a total of 52.57% of the votes were cast in favour of maintaining the amnesty law. All political parties agreed to respect the result of the referendum.

Industrial unrest, which had re-emerged earlier in 1989 in response to price increases, intensified as the presidential and legislative elections approached. In October the trade union confederation, the Plenario Intersindical de Trabajadores—Convención Nacional de Trabajadores (PIT—CNT), organized two 24-hour general strikes, in support of a teachers' pay dispute and to protest against the conditions that had been stipulated by the World Bank upon granting a new structural adjustment loan (which were expected to result in widespread redundancies in the services sector). The presidential and legislative elections, in November 1989, resulted in victory (for the first time since 1962) for the Partido Nacional. In the presidential election, Luis Alberto Lacalle, the party's main candidate (the Uruguayan electoral code permits each party to present more than one candidate), received 37% of the votes, while his closest rival, Jorge Batlle Ibáñez of the Partido Colorado, received 30%. However, the Partido Nacional failed to obtain a working majority in the Congreso, thus compelling the President-elect to seek support from a wider political base. Immediately before taking office, in March 1990, he announced the conclusion of an agreement, the 'coincidencia nacional', between the two principal parties, whereby the Partido Colorado undertook to support proposed legislation on economic reform, in return for the appointment of four of its members to the Council of Ministers. The coalition Government was committed to renegotiating the foreign debt, transferring state-owned companies to the private sector, reducing government expenditure and encouraging foreign investment.

Labour unrest intensified during the early 1990s. The trade union confederation organized a series of general strikes in support of demands for wage increases and in opposition to government austerity measures and plans for the transfer to private ownership of state-owned companies. The unions claimed that, by allowing foreign-owned multinational organizations to gain control of important state services, the Government would be placing Uruguay's sovereignty in jeopardy.

Opposition from within the coalition Government to the planned 'privatization' of state enterprises became apparent in May 1991, when former President Sanguinetti, the leader of the Foro Batllista faction of the Partido Colorado, withdrew his support from the Government, thus forcing the resignation of the faction's single representative in the Council of Ministers, the Minister of Public Health, Alfredo Solari Damonte. Reservations about the 'privatization' bill were also expressed by elements of the Partido Nacional. In late September, none the less, the legislation was narrowly approved by the Congreso. In response, the opposition Frente Amplio, with the support of another political organization, Nuevo Espacio, and the trade unions, proposed to conduct a campaign to overrule the legislature by way of a referendum. By mid-February 1992 the procedures required under the Constitution that would allow the organization of a petition had been fulfilled.

In late January 1992, partly in response to mounting pressure from within the Partido Nacional for the dismissal of the Minister of Economy and Finance, Enrique Braga Silva, President Lacalle sought the resignation of the Council of Ministers. The Vice-President, Dr Gonzalo Aguirre Ramírez, had been among those who had openly criticized the Government's economic policies. In addition, the Batllismo Radical faction of the Partido Colorado, led by Jorge Batlle, withdrew its single minister from the Government. In early February Lacalle appointed a new Council of Ministers, replacing Braga and two other ministers.

In January 1992 the PIT—CNT organized a 24-hour general strike, in protest against the violent eviction by police of workers from a factory in Montevideo. The workers, who had been made redundant, had been occupying the building while unions attempted to negotiate with the company's management. In May 1992 a further strike was organized by the trade union confederation in opposition to government proposals for the reform of the social security sector. (The proposals were later rejected by the legislature.) Industrial unrest in the public sector intensified in the second half of 1992, owing primarily to the Government's refusal to grant wage increases in line with inflation. In November, however, following a four-day strike by the police, the Government was forced to concede wage increases of up to 50% to the security forces. Encouraged by this concession, transport and public health workers immediately initiated strikes in support of demands for wage increases. Industrial action continued throughout 1993. In March the PIT—CNT organized a 24-hour general strike in support of teachers' and public health workers' wage claims, and in May it called a further 24-hour stoppage in protest at the Government's programme of austerity. Further strikes were organized by the trade union confederation in June in support of demands for wage increases and a revision of government economic policy. In the same month construction workers' unions staged a 24-hour national strike. In June the PIT—CNT organized a general strike (the ninth since Lacalle took office in March 1990), in protest at the Government's introduction, in the previous month, of a series of further economic adjustment measures, which were designed to attain economic targets determined in consultation with the IMF. In August the PIT—CNT organized a 36-hour general strike, in support of pay demands by construction workers and in protest at declining living standards, owing to sustained high levels of inflation. The protest was joined by agricultural unions, which had earlier encouraged their members to suspend payment of taxes, in protest at government agricultural policy.

In early May 1992 President Lacalle summoned the political leaders of all the major parties to discuss the defence of the democratic process, following two bomb explosions and a series of threatened bomb attacks in late April and early May. A right-wing terrorist group that claimed responsibility for the explosions was said to have links with the armed forces.

In October 1992, in a special poll, some 30% of the electorate voted for a full referendum to be held on the partial amendment of the Government's 'privatization' legislation. (An earlier poll, held in July, had failed to gain the support of 25% of the electorate, which was required to conduct a referendum.) At the referendum, on 13 December, 71.6% of voters supported the proposal for a partial repeal of the legislation. The vote was also widely recognized as a vote of censure against Lacalle's economic policy, and in particular his determination to keep public sector wage increases to a minimum. While the result of the referendum did not affect all divestments planned by the Government, it was considered to be a serious reverse and served to undermine confidence in government economic policy. However, Lacalle indicated that he would continue to pursue the 'privatization' programme.

In January 1993 Lacalle implemented a reorganization of the Council of Ministers, but made no attempt to reconstruct the coalition with the Partido Colorado. (The 'coincidencia nacional', agreed in 1990, had failed to ensure the Government a majority in the legislature on key economic reforms.) In the same month Lacalle conducted consultations with opposition factions in an attempt to assess the viability of his policies in his remaining two years in office.

In March 1993 Lacalle's failure to accede to demands for the dismissal of the Minister of Economy and Finance, Ignacio de Posadas, and for a change in economic policy, led to the withdrawal of legislative support by two influential factions of the Partido Nacional, the Movimiento Nacional de Rocha—Corriente Popular Nacionalista, led by Carlos Julio Pereyra, and Renovación y Victoria, led by the Vice-President, Dr Gonzalo Aguirre Ramírez. Consequently, the Minister of Public Works and Transport, Wilson Santiago Elso Goñi, a member of the Movimiento Nacional de Rocha, presented his resignation. He was replaced by a member of Lacalle's own Consejo Nacional Herrerista faction, Juan Carlos Raffo.

In June 1993 revelations implicating members of the Uruguayan armed forces in the abduction of a former employee of the Chilean secret service, Eugenio Berríos Sagredo, had serious political repercussions for the Government, creating diplomatic tension between Uruguay and Chile, and prompting concern at the Government's lack of control over the armed forces. Reportedly, Berríos, who was to give testimony in Chile at various legal proceedings concerning alleged human rights violations which took place during the period of military rule in that country, had been abducted and transferred via Argentina to Uruguay by units of the armed forces of the three countries acting in secret co-operation. In Uruguay Berríos had escaped detention but had been returned to his captors by a local police chief, Col (retd) Ramón Rivas. Rivas's subsequent dismissal by the Ministry of the Interior for his involvement in the affair provoked criticism from senior military leaders, and a confrontation occurred when the Commander-in-Chief of the Armed Forces, Lt-Gen. Juan Modesto Rebollo, attempted to assume responsibility for the actions of all his subordinates implicated in the affair. Following conciliatory discussions between Lacalle and the military leadership, it was agreed that those charged with involvement in the abduction were to be tried by military tribunal rather than by the civilian courts. Lacalle was obliged to relieve the head of army intelligence, Gen. Mario Aguerrondo, of his position (although he was purportedly a close associate of the President); Aguerrondo was subsequently appointed director of a military academy. In August, however, it emerged that Aguerrondo had been responsible for planting an illicit electronic listening device in the office of a senior military official. Rebollo was dismissed for demanding that Lacalle force Aguerrondo into retirement. Lacalle did, however, subsequently remove Aguerrondo from his post and also dismissed the Minister of National Defence, Mariano Romeo Brito Cecchi, for his involvement in the internal espionage, in order to avoid a motion of censure by the Senate.

In October 1993, following the resignation of Dr Ramón P. Díaz as President of the Central Bank, Lacalle conducted a reorganization of the Council of Ministers, in an attempt to improve the Government's economic performance. In the following month Juan Andrés Ramírez resigned as Minister of the Interior in order to pursue nomination for the forthcoming presidential election, which, concurrently with the legislative elections, was due on 27 November 1994. In May 1994 the two members of the Partido Colorado remaining in the Council of Ministers, Eduardo Ache (responsible for industry, energy and mining) and José Villar Gómez (responsible for tourism), resigned, in order to participate in election campaigning. They were replaced by Miguel Galán and Mario Amestoy, respectively, both of whom were members of the Partido Nacional.

In June 1994 Congress adopted legislation providing for a partial reform of the Constitution, subject to approval in a plebiscite to be held in August. The legislation included amendments providing for a reform of electoral procedure in order to allow voters to split their ballot between different parties for national and local posts. However, other amendments contained in the legislation proposed changes to the state pension and social security system, and provoked suspicion amongst Uruguay's pensioners, who comprised a significant percentage of the country's voters; consequently the plebiscite resulted in a rejection of the legislation.

On 24 August 1994 violent confrontations between the security forces and demonstrators outside a hospital in the capital resulted in the death of two civilians. The demonstrators were protesting against the extradition, to Spain, of three suspected members of the Basque separatist organization Euskadi ta Askatasuna (ETA). The three were being treated in the hospital following a 14-day period on hunger strike. Despite the protest, they were repatriated on 25 August. On that day the PIT—CNT organized a 24-hour general strike in protest at the events of the previous day and to demand the resignation of the Minister of the Interior. On the following day the Government expelled Jon Idígoras, a member of the Spanish Congress of Deputies and a leader of Herri Batasuna (considered to be ETA's political wing), for allegedly contributing to the climate of violence surrounding the extradition issue.

In October 1994 Vice-President Aguirre announced his withdrawal from the forthcoming presidential election, following a claim by former President Sanguinetti that Aguirre's candidacy was in violation of the Constitution, which stated that anyone holding presidential office within three months of a presidential election was not eligible to contest it; Aguirre had been acting President during Lacalle's absence abroad in September. Despite rejecting this interpretation of the Constitution, Aguirre withdrew in order to prevent any controversy from affecting the electoral process. It was widely believed that Sanguinetti's intervention was a retaliatory action prompted by an earlier request by the Partido Nacional that the Electoral Commission annul the candidacy of a member of the Partido Colorado for the mayorship of Montevideo. In that month it was announced that two plebiscites would be conducted concurrently with the forthcoming presidential and legislative elections, due to be held in late November. The plebiscites concerned education and social security. The education proposal, which was promoted by the teachers' unions, sought to devote 27% of the national budget allocated to education. The social security proposal, which was promoted by pensioners' organizations, sought the repeal of social security legislation enacted during the Lacalle administration.

The presidential and legislative elections of 27 November 1994 were notable for the emergence of a third political force to rival the traditional powers of the Partido Nacional and the Partido Colorado. The Encuentro Progresista — a predominantly left-wing alliance principally comprising the parties of the Frente Amplio, as well as dissidents of the Partido Nacional and other minor parties — secured 30.8% of the votes, while the Partido Nacional obtained 31.4% and the Partido Colorado won a narrow victory with 32.5% of the vote. The leading presidential candidate of the Partido Colorado, Dr Julio María Sanguinetti Cairolo, was subsequently pronounced President-elect (to be inaugurated in March 1995 for his second term in office) and indicated that he would seek to appoint a broadly-based council of ministers in order to ensure legislative support for his administration. The two plebiscites held concurrently with the presidential and legislative elections resulted in the rejection of the education proposal. Conversely, the proposal concerning the repeal of social security legislation enacted under the Lacalle administration was approved. However, there was widespread recognition amongst the major political parties that the social security system required prompt and substantial modification, and a resolution of the issue was later identified by the Sanguinetti administration as its main priority.

In early 1995, following talks with opposition parties, the Partido Colorado established a 'governability pact' with the Partido Nacional providing for a coalition Government. In February Sanguinetti announced the appointment of the Council of Ministers, allocating six portfolios to members of the Partido Colorado, four to the Partido Nacional, one to the Unión Cívica, and one to the Partido por el Gobierno del Pueblo (Lista 99), which had contested the elections in alliance with Sanguinetti's Foro Batllista faction of the Partido Colorado, and whose leader, Hugo Batalla, had been elected as Sanguinetti's Vice-President. The Encuentro Progresista remained in opposition to the Government, but the principal member of the alliance, the Frente Amplio, was reported to have given an undertaking to co-operate with the new administration in return for government consideration of its views when determining social policy. Later that month the major political parties began negotiations regarding the reform of the electoral process.

In March 1991 the Presidents and Ministers of Foreign Affairs of Argentina, Brazil, Paraguay and Uruguay met in Paraguay, where they signed a formal agreement creating a common market of the 'Southern Cone' countries, the Mercado Común del Sur (MERCOSUR, see p. 240). The agreement allowed for the dismantling of trade barriers between the four countries, and entered full operation in 1995. In February 1992 President Lacalle announced the creation of a 'special cabinet', charged with overseeing the restructuring of Uruguay's industrial sector to ensure that it would be competitive in MERCOSUR.

In May 1991 Uruguay and the USA signed an agreement facilitating joint investigations into the diversion of illicit proceeds from drugs-trafficking in Uruguay. The accord, which came in response to an acknowledged increase in such 'money-laundering' activities in Uruguay's 'offshore' banking system, permitted more rapid access to suspect accounts.

### Government

Uruguay is a republic comprising 19 departments. Under the 1966 Constitution, executive power is held by the President, who is directly elected by universal adult suffrage for a term of five years. The President is assisted by the Vice-President and the appointed Council of Ministers. Legislative power is vested in the bicameral Congreso, comprising the Senate and the Chamber of Representatives, also directly elected for five years. The President, the Vice-President, the Senators (who number 31, including the Vice-President, who is automatically allocated a seat as President of the Senate) and the 99 Deputies are elected nationally.

### Defence

In June 1994 the armed forces consisted of 25,600 volunteers between the ages of 18 and 45, who contract for one or two years of service. There was an army of 17,200, a navy of 5,400 and an air force of 3,000. There were also paramilitary forces of 1,200. Government expenditure on defence in 1994 was budgeted at an estimated 1,000m. pesos uruguayos.

## Economic Affairs

In 1993, according to estimates by the World Bank, Uruguay's gross national product (GNP), measured at average 1991–93 prices, was US $12,314m., equivalent to $3,910 per head. During 1985–93, it was estimated, GNP per head increased, in real terms, at an average annual rate of 3.0%. Over the same period the population increased by an annual average of 0.6%. Uruguay's gross domestic product (GDP) increased, in real terms, by an annual average of 1.0% in 1980–92, by 1.5% in 1993 and by an estimated 4.0% in 1994.

According to preliminary figures, agriculture (including forestry and fishing) contributed 9.3% of GDP in 1991. Some 13.0% of the working population were employed in the sector in 1993. The principal crops are rice, sugar (both cane and beet), wheat, potatoes, barley, sorghum and maize. Livestock-rearing, particularly sheep and cattle, is traditionally Uruguay's major economic activity. Exports of live animals, animal products, skins and hides provided 36.1% of export revenue in 1992. During 1980–92 agricultural GDP increased by an annual average of 0.7%.

Industry (including mining, manufacturing, construction and power) contributed 30.2% of GDP in 1991, and employed 25.5% of the working population in 1985. During 1980–92 industrial GDP increased by an annual average of 0.2%.

Mining and quarrying contributed an estimated 0.2% of GDP in 1991. Uruguay has no mineral reserves of any economic significance, and, apart from the small-scale extraction of building materials and iron ore, there is little mining activity.

Manufacturing is the largest sector of the Uruguayan economy, accounting for 23.8% of GDP in 1991, and employing 18.3% of the working population in 1985. Measured by the value of output, the principal branches of manufacturing in 1988 were food products (accounting for 26.4% of the total), textiles and clothing, petroleum and coal products, chemicals, beverages, transport equipment and leather products. During 1980–92 manufacturing GDP increased by an annual average of 0.5%.

Energy is derived principally from hydroelectric power and mineral fuels. Uruguay is a net exporter of electric energy. Imports of fuel products comprised 18% of the value of merchandise imports in 1990.

Tourism is a significant source of foreign exchange, earning US $381.3m. (equivalent to 23.6% of merchandise exports) in 1992.

In 1993 Uruguay recorded a visible trade deficit of US $386.7m., and there was a deficit of $226.8m. on the current account of the balance of payments. In 1992 the principal source of imports was Brazil (24.8%); other major suppliers were Argentina, the USA, Japan and Germany. Brazil was also the principal market for exports (17.5%) in that year; other major recipients were Argentina, the USA and Germany. The main exports in 1992 were textiles, live animals and animal products, hides and skins, and vegetable products. The principal imports in that year were machinery and appliances, transport equipment, chemical products and mineral products.

In 1991 there was a budgetary surplus of 184,000m. new pesos, equivalent to 0.9% of GDP. At the end of 1993 Uruguay's total external debt was US $7,259m., of which $4,629m. was long-term public debt. In that year the cost of debt-servicing was equivalent to 48.8% of the value of exports of goods and services. The average annual rate of inflation was 74.8% in 1985–93. Consumer prices increased by an average of 44.7% in 1994. An estimated 8.0% of the labour force were unemployed in 1994.

Uruguay is a member of the Inter-American Development Bank (IDB, see p. 170), of the Latin American Integration Association (Asociación Latinoamericana de Integración—ALADI, see p. 181), of the Latin American Economic System (Sistema Económica Latinoamericano—SELA, see p. 239) and of the Mercado Común del Sur (MERCOSUR, see p. 240).

In March 1990 the Government initiated an IMF-approved programme of austerity, which sought to reduce rampant inflation and to restrict the substantial budgetary deficit. President Lacalle's policy of keeping public-sector pay increases below inflation, in conjunction with plans to reduce the overstaffed state sector, resulted in intensified strike action in 1992 and early 1993, with attendant disruption to the economy. The social security sector continued to exacerbate public-sector debt, owing to the Government's failure to secure sufficient legislative support to reform the sector. Government attempts to increase revenue by implementing a programme of 'privatization' of state enterprises suffered a reverse in late 1992, when a referendum forced changes limiting the 'privatization' law. A new currency, the peso uruguayo, came into circulation in March 1993. Austerity measures, designed to reduce public spending and combat inflation, were announced in March and June, including reductions in investment expenditure and increases in taxation and public utility tariffs. A decline in competitiveness, especially in the manufacturing sector (owing, in part, to the gradual reduction of trading restrictions within MERCOSUR, resulted in an exceptionally high trade deficit in 1993. In March 1995 the newly-elected Sanguinetti administration identified its main priorities to be the reform of the social security sector (which accounted for as much as 37% of budget expenditure) and a reduction of the fiscal deficit (which was equivalent to almost 3% of GDP). In that month the Government announced a programme of austerity measures aimed at curbing the fiscal deficit, including increases in taxation and reductions in public spending.

## Social Welfare

Uruguay is noted for its advanced scheme of social welfare, which covers professional accidents, industrial diseases, sickness, unemployment, disability, old age, maternity and child welfare. The social welfare system is financed by contributions from workers, employers and the Government. The pension age is low (30 years' service, sometimes less); social charges payable by companies, however, are high, reaching 79% for the construction industry. There are also laws governing the protection of minors and women in employment, insurance against suspension from work, annual licences, redundancy payments, etc. Grants for families are provided by the Family Subsidies Fund. Of total expenditure by the central Government in 1991, 275m. pesos uruguayos (4.8%) was for health services, and a further 2,993m. pesos uruguayos (52.2%) for social security and welfare. A major restructuring of the social security sector was identified as the main priority of the Government in 1995. In 1986 Uruguay had 69 government-administered hospitals, with 5,756 physicians.

## Education

All education, including university tuition, is provided free of charge. Education is officially compulsory for six years between six and 14 years of age. Primary education begins at the age of six and lasts for six years. Secondary education, beginning at 12 years of age, lasts for a further six years, comprising two cycles of three years each. In 1992 the total enrolment at primary and secondary schools was equivalent to 95% of the school-age population. In that year primary enrolment included an estimated 93% of children in the relevant age-group (males 93%; females 94%), while secondary enrolment was equivalent to 83% of the population in the appropriate age-group. The programmes of instruction are the same in both public and private schools, and private schools are subject to certain state controls. In 1985 adult illiteracy averaged 5.0% (males 5.6%; females 4.5%), decreasing to an estimated 3.8% in 1990 (males 3.4%; females 4.1%). There are two universities. Public expenditure on education in 1992 was 959m. pesos uruguayos (15.4% of total government spending).

## Public Holidays

**1995:** 1 January (New Year's Day), 6 January (Epiphany), 19 April (Landing of the 33 Patriots), 1 May (Labour Day), 18 May (Battle of Las Piedras), 19 June (Birth of General Artigas), 18 July (Constitution Day), 25 August (National Independence Day), 12 October (Discovery of America), 2 November (All Souls' Day), 8 December (Blessing of the Waters), 25 December (Christmas Day).

**1996:** 1 January (New Year's Day), 6 January (Epiphany), 19 April (Landing of the 33 Patriots), 1 May (Labour Day), 18 May (Battle of Las Piedras), 19 June (Birth of General Artigas), 18 July (Constitution Day), 25 August (National Independence Day), 12 October (Discovery of America), 2 November (All Souls' Day), 8 December (Blessing of the Waters), 25 December (Christmas Day).

Many businesses close during Carnival week (27 February–3 March 1995 and 19–23 February 1996) and Tourist week (Easter).

## Weights and Measures

The metric system is in force.

URUGUAY

# Statistical Survey

Sources (unless otherwise stated): CENCI-Uruguay, Misiones 1361, Casilla 1510, Montevideo; tel. (2) 954578; Banco Central del Uruguay, Avda Juan P. Fabini, esq. Florida, Montevideo; tel. (2) 917117; telex 26659; fax (2) 921634; Cámara Nacional de Comercio, Misiones 1400, Casilla 1000, Montevideo; tel. (2) 961277; telex 6996.

## Area and Population

### AREA, POPULATION AND DENSITY*

| | |
|---|---:|
| Area (sq km) Total | 176,215† |
| Population (census results) | |
| 21 May 1975 | 2,788,429 |
| 23 October 1985 | |
| Males | 1,439,021 |
| Females | 1,516,220 |
| Total | 2,955,241 |
| Population (official estimates at mid-year) | |
| 1991 | 3,112,000 |
| 1992 | 3,131,000 |
| 1993 | 3,149,000‡ |
| Density (per sq km) at mid-1993 | 17.9 |

* Census results exclude, and estimates include, adjustment for underenumeration, estimated at 2.6% at 1985 census.
† 68,037 sq miles.
‡ Preliminary figure.

### PRINCIPAL TOWNS (population at 1985 census)

| | | | | |
|---|---:|---|---|---:|
| Montevideo (capital) | 1,251,647 | Rivera | . | 57,316 |
| Salto | 80,823 | Melo | . | 42,615 |
| Paysandú | 76,191 | Tacuarembó | . | 40,513 |
| Las Piedras | 58,288 | Mercedes | . | 36,702 |
| | | Minas | . | 34,661 |

### BIRTHS, MARRIAGES AND DEATHS

| | Registered live births* | | Registered marriages | | Registered deaths | |
|---|---:|---:|---:|---:|---:|---:|
| | Number | Rate (per 1,000) | Number | Rate (per 1,000) | Number | Rate (per 1,000) |
| 1987 | 53,368 | 17.5 | 22,728 | 7.5 | 29,885 | 9.8 |
| 1988 | 55,798 | 18.2 | 21,528 | 7.0 | 30,912 | 10.1 |
| 1989 | 55,324 | 18.0 | 22,684 | 7.4 | 29,629 | 9.6 |
| 1990 | 56,013 | 18.1 | 20,084 | 6.5 | 30,225 | 9.8 |
| 1991 | 54,754 | 17.6 | n.a. | n.a. | 29,784 | 9.6 |

* Data are tabulated by year of registration rather than by year of occurrence.

Source: UN, mainly *Demographic Yearbook*.

**1992** (provisional): Live births 54,186 (birth rate 17.3 per 1,000).

**Expectation of life** (UN estimates, years at birth, 1985–90): 72.0 (males 68.9; females 75.3) (Source: UN, *World Population Prospects: The 1992 Revision*).

### ECONOMICALLY ACTIVE POPULATION (ISIC Major Divisions, persons aged 12 years and over, 1985 census*)

| | Males | Females | Total |
|---|---:|---:|---:|
| Agriculture, hunting, forestry and fishing | 155,801 | 14,382 | 170,183 |
| Mining and quarrying | 1,711 | 60 | 1,771 |
| Manufacturing | 142,134 | 72,811 | 214,945 |
| Electricity, gas and water | 14,632 | 2,745 | 17,377 |
| Construction | 63,509 | 876 | 64,385 |
| Trade, restaurants and hotels | 92,734 | 46,508 | 139,242 |
| Transport, storage and communications | 51,425 | 7,864 | 59,289 |
| Financing, insurance, real estate and business services | 28,324 | 14,364 | 42,688 |
| Community, social and personal services† | 169,749 | 199,511 | 369,260 |
| Activities not adequately defined | 55,510 | 24,369 | 79,879 |
| **Total** | **785,944** | **390,864** | **1,176,808** |

* Figures exclude 17,789 persons (10,415 males; 7,374 females) seeking their first job but include about 60,000 other unemployed.
† Including armed forces, totalling 28,500 (27,600 males; 900 females).

**Mid-1993** (estimates in '000): Agriculture, etc. 160; Total 1,230 (Source: FAO, *Production Yearbook*).

## Agriculture

### PRINCIPAL CROPS ('000 metric tons)

| | 1991 | 1992 | 1993 |
|---|---:|---:|---:|
| Wheat | 188 | 341 | 300 |
| Maize | 124 | 116 | 128 |
| Barley | 138 | 307 | 140 |
| Oats | 35 | 37 | 35 |
| Sorghum | 136 | 137 | 130 |
| Rice (paddy) | 522 | 600 | 700 |
| Potatoes | 196 | 155 | 170* |
| Sugar cane | 583 | 545 | 350 |
| Sugar beet | 156 | 156 | 40* |
| Sunflower seed | 57 | 62 | 52 |
| Linseed | 6 | 6 | 9* |

* FAO estimate.

Source: FAO, *Production Yearbook*.

### LIVESTOCK ('000 head, year ending September)

| | 1991 | 1992 | 1993 |
|---|---:|---:|---:|
| Cattle | 8,889 | 9,508 | 10,093 |
| Sheep | 25,986 | 25,941 | 25,702† |
| Pigs* | 215 | 220 | 223 |
| Horses* | 470 | 475 | 477 |

* FAO estimates.   † Unofficial figure.

Poultry (FAO estimates, million): 9 in 1991; 9 in 1992; 9 in 1993.

Source: FAO, *Production Yearbook*.

# URUGUAY

## LIVESTOCK PRODUCTS ('000 metric tons)

|  | 1991 | 1992 | 1993 |
|---|---|---|---|
| Beef and veal | 350 | 360 | 317 |
| Mutton and lamb* | 63 | 64 | 72 |
| Pigmeat | 22 | 22 | 23* |
| Poultry meat† | 30 | 30 | 31 |
| Cows' milk | 1,032 | 1,101 | 1,171 |
| Poultry eggs | 22.1* | 22.2† | 22.4† |
| Wool (greasy) | 93.6 | 83.9 | 81.0 |
| Wool (scoured) | 56.5* | 50.7* | 49.4 |
| Cattle hides† | 46.0 | 49.2 | 42.1 |
| Sheepskins† | 21.9 | 22.5 | 24.2 |

* Unofficial figure(s).  † FAO estimate(s).

Source: FAO, *Production Yearbook*.

## Forestry

### ROUNDWOOD REMOVALS ('000 cubic metres)

|  | 1990 | 1991 | 1992 |
|---|---|---|---|
| Sawlogs, veneer logs and logs for sleepers | 670 | 600 | 784 |
| Pulpwood | 127 | 214 | 217 |
| Other industrial wood | 45 | 43 | 42 |
| Fuel wood | 2,935 | 3,021 | 3,038 |
| **Total** | 3,777 | 3,878 | 4,081 |

Source: FAO, *Yearbook of Forest Products*.

### SAWNWOOD PRODUCTION
('000 cubic metres, incl. railway sleepers)

|  | 1990 | 1991 | 1992 |
|---|---|---|---|
| Coniferous (softwood) | 77 | 67 | 84 |
| Broadleaved (hardwood) | 152 | 138 | 185 |
| **Total** | 229 | 205 | 269 |

Source: FAO, *Yearbook of Forest Products*.

## Fishing

('000 metric tons, live weight)

|  | 1990 | 1991 | 1992 |
|---|---|---|---|
| **Total catch*** | 90.8 | 143.7 | 125.7 |

* Excluding seals, recorded by number and not weight. The catch of South American fur seals was: 5,439 in 1990; 5,375 in 1991; 102 in 1992 (Source: FAO, *Yearbook of Fishery Statistics*).

## Industry

### SELECTED PRODUCTS
('000 metric tons, unless otherwise indicated)

|  | 1989 | 1990 | 1991 |
|---|---|---|---|
| Raw sugar* | 80 | 80 | 70 |
| Wine ('000 hectolitres)* | 850 | 900 | 800 |
| Cigarettes (million) | 3,900 | 3,900 | 3,900 |
| Jet fuels | 29 | 24 | 35 |
| Motor spirit (petrol) | 193 | 197 | 237 |
| Kerosene | 49 | 50 | 56 |
| Distillate fuel oils | 330 | 390 | 413 |
| Residual fuel oils | 404 | 367 | 322 |
| Cement | 465† | 469 | 458 |
| Electric energy (million kWh) | 5,749 | 7,443 | 7,017 |

* FAO estimates.  † Provisional figure.

Source: UN, *Industrial Statistics Yearbook*.

## Finance

### CURRENCY AND EXCHANGE RATES

**Monetary Units**
100 centésimos = 1 peso uruguayo.

**Sterling and Dollar Equivalents** (31 December 1994)
£1 sterling = 8.785 pesos;
US $1 = 5.615 pesos;
100 pesos uruguayos = £11.38 = $17.81.

**Average Exchange Rate** (pesos per US $)
1992  3.0270
1993  3.9484
1994  5.0529

Note: On 1 March 1993 a new currency, the peso uruguayo (equivalent to 1,000 former new pesos), was introduced.

### BUDGET (million pesos uruguayos)*

| Revenue | 1989 | 1990 | 1991 |
|---|---|---|---|
| Taxation† | 1,079 | 2,461 | 5,510 |
| Taxes on income, profits, etc. | 82 | 175 | 337 |
| Individual taxes | 29 | 66 | 136 |
| Corporate taxes | 46 | 96 | 183 |
| Social security contributions | 331 | 699 | 1,713 |
| Taxes on property | 56 | 137 | 259 |
| Domestic taxes on goods and services | 503 | 932 | 2,025 |
| Value-added tax | 337 | 582 | 1,274 |
| Excises | 153 | 329 | 683 |
| Taxes on international trade | 106 | 254 | 472 |
| Import duties | 83 | 200 | 393 |
| Export duties | 5 | 14 | 12 |
| Exchange taxes | 18 | 40 | 67 |
| Other taxes | 78 | 171 | 373 |
| Tax refunds | −71 | −96 | −139 |
| Other current revenue | 58 | 132 | 238 |
| Property income | 14 | 38 | 93 |
| Administrative fees, charges, etc. | 28 | 48 | 100 |
| Capital revenue | 5 | 5 | 20 |
| **Total** | 1,142 | 2,598 | 5,768 |

| Expenditure‡ | 1989 | 1990 | 1991 |
|---|---|---|---|
| General public services | 153 | 310 | 716 |
| Defence | 114 | 233 | 363 |
| Education | 98 | 187 | 376 |
| Health | 62 | 114 | 275 |
| Social security and welfare | 641 | 1,274 | 2,993 |
| Housing and community amenities | 1 | 2 | 9 |
| Other community and social services | 7 | 14 | 21 |
| Economic services | 114 | 222 | 425 |
| Agriculture, forestry and fishing | 17 | 38 | 93 |
| Transport and communications | 84 | 154 | 268 |
| Other purposes | 145 | 206 | 552 |
| **Sub-total** | 1,334 | 2,563 | 5,730 |
| *Less* Government contribution as employer | 42 | 24 | 179 |
| **Total** | 1,292 | 2,539 | 5,550 |
| Current§ | 1,185 | 2,353 | 5,227 |
| Capital | 107 | 186 | 323 |

* Figures represent the consolidated accounts of the central Government, comprising the General Budget, the Directorate General of Social Security and three other social security funds.
† Including adjustments to a cash basis (million pesos uruguayos): −6 in 1989; 189 in 1990; 471 in 1991.
‡ Excluding net lending (million pesos uruguayos): 11 in 1989; 23 in 1990; 34 in 1991.
§ Including interest payments (million pesos uruguayos): 104 in 1989; 206 in 1990; 395 in 1991.

Source: IMF, *Government Finance Statistics Yearbook*.

# URUGUAY

## INTERNATIONAL RESERVES
(US $ million at 31 December)

|  | 1992 | 1993 | 1994 |
|---|---|---|---|
| Gold* | 541 | 454 | 497 |
| Reserve position in the IMF | 21 | 21 | 22 |
| Foreign exchange | 488 | 737 | 946 |
| **Total** | 1,050 | 1,212 | 1,465 |

* Source: Banco Central del Uruguay; gold valued at $267 per troy ounce in 1992, at $292 per ounce in 1993 and at $306 per ounce in 1994.

Source: IMF, *International Financial Statistics*.

## MONEY SUPPLY (million pesos uruguayos at 31 December)

|  | 1992 | 1993 | 1994 |
|---|---|---|---|
| Currency outside banks | 1,426.0 | 2,312.8 | 3,313.8 |
| Demand deposits at commercial banks | 1,148.1 | 1,735.4 | 2,349.0 |
| **Total money** (incl. others) | 2,583.3 | 4,073.9 | 5,677.6 |

Source: IMF, *International Financial Statistics*.

## COST OF LIVING
(Consumer Price Index for Montevideo, average of monthly figures. Base: December 1985 = 100)

|  | 1992 | 1993 | 1994 |
|---|---|---|---|
| Food | 4,425.2 | 6,698.2 | 9,417.4 |
| Clothing | 5,278.8 | 7,635.9 | 10,421.7 |
| Housing | 4,326.6 | 6,995.4 | 10,905.5 |
| Miscellaneous | 5,397.5 | 8,118.3 | 11,551.8 |
| **All items** | 4,709.5 | 7,257.2 | 10,504.2 |

## NATIONAL ACCOUNTS
(million pesos uruguayos at current prices)

### Composition of the Gross National Product

|  | 1989 | 1990* | 1991* |
|---|---|---|---|
| Compensation of employees | 1,943.0 | 3,880.9 | 8,397.4 |
| Operating surplus } Consumption of fixed capital } | 2,163.5 | 4,126.5 | 7,139.4 |
| **Gross domestic product (GDP) at factor cost** | 4,106.5 | 8,007.4 | 15,536.8 |
| Indirect taxes, *less* subsidies | 732.9 | 1,690.7 | 3,598.7 |
| **GDP in purchasers' values** | 4,839.4 | 9,698.1 | 19,135.5 |
| Net factor income from abroad | −211.6 | −377.1 | −470.2 |
| **Gross national product** | 4,627.8 | 932.1 | 18,665.3 |

* Preliminary.

Source: UN, *National Accounts Statistics*.

### Expenditure on the Gross Domestic Product

|  | 1991 | 1992 | 1993 |
|---|---|---|---|
| Government final consumption expenditure | 2,731.1 | 4,523.1 | 7,299.4 |
| Private final consumption expenditure | 14,164.3 | 25,650.9 | 37,114.9 |
| Increase in stocks | 317.5 | 237.9 | 713.9 |
| Gross fixed capital formation | 2,418.0 | 4,634.0 | 7,382.2 |
| **Total domestic expenditure** | 19,630.9 | 35,045.9 | 52,510.4 |
| Exports of goods and services | 4,678.9 | 7,907.7 | 10,494.5 |
| *Less* Imports of goods and services | 4,038.5 | 7,608.0 | 11,108.0 |
| **GDP in purchasers' values** | 20,271.3 | 35,345.6 | 51,896.9 |
| **GDP at constant 1990 prices** | 10,098.3 | 10,879.3 | 11,041.3 |

Source: IMF, *International Financial Statistics*.

## Gross Domestic Product by Economic Activity

|  | 1989 | 1990* | 1991* |
|---|---|---|---|
| Agriculture | 592.5 | 1,091.4 | 1,794.6 |
| Fishing | 12.9 | 22.8 | 75.6 |
| Mining and quarrying | 10.3 | 17.0 | 34.6 |
| Manufacturing | 1,267.2 | 2,544.3 | 4,812.5 |
| Electricity, gas and water | 112.7 | 274.9 | 535.7 |
| Construction | 183.5 | 302.4 | 726.4 |
| Commerce | 578.2 | 1,181.4 | 2,391.1 |
| Transport, storage and communications | 318.3 | 631.0 | 1,219.9 |
| Finance and insurance | 597.5 | 1,282.6 | 2,406.9 |
| Real estate | 571.1 | 1,183.0 | 2,554.7 |
| Government services | 474.7 | 899.5 | 1,683.8 |
| Other community, social and personal services | 407.5 | 867.3 | 1,971.2 |
| **Sub-total** | 5,126.2 | 10,297.7 | 20,206.9 |
| Import duties | 179.5 | 409.5 | 823.8 |
| *Less* Imputed bank service charge | 466.4 | 1,009.2 | 1,895.2 |
| **GDP in purchasers' values** | 4,839.3 | 9,698.0 | 19,135.5 |

* Preliminary.

## BALANCE OF PAYMENTS (US $ million)

|  | 1991 | 1992 | 1993 |
|---|---|---|---|
| Merchandise exports f.o.b. | 1,604.7 | 1,801.4 | 1,731.6 |
| Merchandise imports f.o.b. | −1,543.7 | −1,923.2 | −2,118.3 |
| **Trade balance** | 61.0 | −121.8 | −386.7 |
| Exports of services | 596.2 | 830.3 | 916.8 |
| Imports of services | −422.5 | −558.8 | −640.6 |
| Other income received | 234.7 | 225.0 | 249.7 |
| Other income paid | −467.1 | −412.1 | −390.8 |
| Official unrequited transfers (net) | 40.1 | 28.6 | 24.8 |
| **Current balance** | 42.4 | −8.8 | −226.8 |
| Direct investment (net) | — | — | 75.8 |
| Portfolio investment (net) | 109.4 | 229.1 | 158.3 |
| Other capital (net) | −538.6 | −320.6 | −39.6 |
| Net errors and omissions | 468.8 | 238.3 | 220.8 |
| **Overall balance** | 82.0 | 138.0 | 188.5 |

Source: IMF, *International Financial Statistics*.

# External Trade

## PRINCIPAL COMMODITIES (US $ '000)

| Imports c.i.f. | 1990 | 1991 | 1992 |
|---|---|---|---|
| Vegetable products | 57,080 | 62,816 | 103,654 |
| Foodstuffs, beverages and tobacco | 30,335 | 49,295 | 74,060 |
| Mineral products | 223,737 | 265,357 | 215,960 |
| Chemical products | 219,126 | 231,630 | 252,168 |
| Synthetic plastic, resins and rubber | 114,560 | 119,853 | 136,130 |
| Raw materials for paper production and paper products | 33,813 | 47,634 | 50,710 |
| Textiles and textile products | 65,735 | 87,474 | 103,774 |
| Base metals and products | 80,032 | 84,401 | 104,775 |
| Machinery and appliances | 253,497 | 345,932 | 363,066 |
| Transport equipment | 139,984 | 183,674 | 310,191 |
| **Total** (incl. others) | 1,342,932 | 1,636,491 | 1,915,945 |

| Exports f.o.b. | 1990 | 1991 | 1992 |
|---|---|---|---|
| Live animals and animal products | 422,298 | 375,860 | 377,377 |
| Vegetable products | 192,208 | 207,425 | 180,933 |
| Foodstuffs, beverages and tobacco | 66,513 | 70,573 | 76,817 |
| Synthetic plastics, resins and rubber | 49,563 | 43,177 | 73,447 |
| Hides, skins, leather products, etc. | 234,325 | 216,571 | 207,106 |
| Textiles and textile products | 486,812 | 430,666 | 461,434 |
| **Total** (incl. others) | 1,692,927 | 1,604,724 | 1,616,989 |

URUGUAY

## PRINCIPAL TRADING PARTNERS (US $ '000)

| Imports | 1990 | 1991 | 1992 |
|---|---|---|---|
| Argentina | 218,210 | 271,317 | 345,819 |
| Brazil | 329,080 | 372,637 | 474,870 |
| Chile | 20,343 | 25,788 | 33,809 |
| France | 41,560 | 51,324 | 60,969 |
| Germany, Federal Republic | 91,632 | 75,368 | 90,579* |
| Italy | 49,665 | 45,640 | 68,609 |
| Japan | 44,920 | 58,543 | 100,219 |
| Mexico | 49,972 | 28,953 | 37,860 |
| Nigeria | 9,771 | 83,211 | 35,988 |
| Spain | 23,503 | 28,796 | 32,154 |
| Switzerland | 23,204 | 26,362 | 27,807 |
| United Kingdom | 41,880 | 37,281 | 38,678 |
| USA | 138,556 | 151,314 | 185,679 |
| Venezuela | 7,545 | 35,220 | 23,935 |
| **Total** (incl. others) | 1,342,932 | 1,636,491 | 1,915,945 |

* Figure includes the former German Democratic Republic.

| Exports | 1990 | 1991 | 1992 |
|---|---|---|---|
| Argentina | 82,403 | 163,088 | 248,776 |
| Brazil | 502,021 | 383,978 | 283,122 |
| Chile | 16,613 | 22,220 | 49,308 |
| France | 52,080 | 41,133 | 37,968 |
| German Democratic Republic | 1,203 | 21 | } 131,794 |
| Germany, Federal Republic | 130,989 | 136,431 | |
| Iran | 35,238 | 8,136 | 14,900 |
| Israel | 27,751 | 37,102 | 38,178 |
| Italy | 74,732 | 61,646 | 74,697 |
| Japan | 21,019 | 19,914 | 20,151 |
| Netherlands | 55,440 | 47,760 | 53,290 |
| Spain | 13,636 | 14,480 | 24,232 |
| USSR | 88,296 | 50,149 | 2,884 |
| United Kingdom | 70,868 | 59,477 | 65,627 |
| USA | 158,335 | 156,463 | 171,113 |
| **Total** (incl. others) | 1,692,927 | 1,604,724 | 1,616,989 |

## Transport

**RAILWAYS** (traffic)

| | 1985 | 1986 | 1987 |
|---|---|---|---|
| Passenger-km (million) | 240.8 | 195.6 | 140.5 |
| Freight ton-km (million) | 174.2 | 199.1 | 209.0 |

Freight ton-km (million): 213 in 1988; 243 in 1989; 204 in 1990; 203 in 1991 (Source: UN, *Statistical Yearbook*). Note: Passenger services ceased in 1988.

**ROAD TRAFFIC** (motor vehicles in use at 31 December)

| | 1988 |
|---|---|
| Passenger cars and station wagons | 346,706 |
| Buses and coaches | 4,323 |
| Goods vehicles | 42,522 |
| Taxis | 3,506 |
| Motorcycles | 214,535 |

**1989** ('000): Passenger cars 360.3; Commercial vehicles 50.2. **1990** ('000): Passenger cars 379.6; Commercial vehicles 49.9. **1991** ('000): Passenger cars 389.6; Commercial vehicles 48.6. (Source: UN, *Statistical Yearbook*).

**SHIPPING**
**Merchant Fleet** (gross registered tons at 30 June)

| | 1990 | 1991 | 1992 |
|---|---|---|---|
| Oil tankers | 47,000 | 47,000 | 46,000 |
| Total | 104,000 | 105,000 | 127,000 |

Source: UN, *Statistical Yearbook*.

*Statistical Survey*

**International Sea-borne Shipping***
(freight traffic, '000 metric tons)

| | 1988 | 1989 | 1990 |
|---|---|---|---|
| Goods loaded | 670 | 680 | 710 |
| Goods unloaded | 1,415 | 1,395 | 1,450 |

* Port of Montevideo only.
Source: UN, *Monthly Bulletin of Statistics*.

**CIVIL AVIATION** (traffic on scheduled services)

| | 1986 | 1987 | 1990* |
|---|---|---|---|
| Kilometres flown (million) | 5 | 5 | 5 |
| Passengers carried ('000) | 341 | 351 | 318 |
| Passenger-km (million) | 459 | 459 | 471 |
| Freight ton-km (million) | 3 | 2 | 3 |

* Figures for 1988 and 1989 are not available.
Source: UN, *Statistical Yearbook*.

## Communications Media

| | 1990 | 1991 | 1992 |
|---|---|---|---|
| Radio receivers ('000 in use)* | 1,865 | 1,880 | 1,890 |
| Television receivers ('000 in use)* | 720 | 720 | 725 |
| Telephones ('000 main lines in use) | 415 | 451 | n.a. |
| Daily newspapers | | | |
| Number | 30 | n.a. | 32 |
| Average circulation ('000 copies)* | 720 | n.a. | 750 |
| Book production (titles) | n.a. | 1,143 | n.a. |

* Estimates.
Sources: UNESCO, *Statistical Yearbook*; UN, *Statistical Yearbook*.

## Tourism

| | 1990 | 1991 | 1992 |
|---|---|---|---|
| Number of tourists ('000) | 1,267 | 1,509 | 1,801 |
| Foreign exchange receipts (US $ '000) | 261,800 | 332,500 | 381,300 |

## Education

(1992)

| | | | Students | | |
|---|---|---|---|---|---|
| | Institutions | Teachers | Males | Females | Total |
| Pre-primary | 1,567 | 2,400 | 34,256 | 33,792 | 68,048 |
| Primary | 2,419 | 16,376 | 173,698 | 164,322 | 338,020 |
| Secondary | | | | | |
| General | 281* | n.a. | n.a. | n.a. | 227,060 |
| Vocational | n.a. | n.a. | 23,836 | 21,726 | 45,562 |
| Tertiary | | | | | |
| University and equivalent institutions | n.a. | 6,442 | n.a. | n.a. | 56,760 |
| Other higher | n.a. | n.a. | n.a. | n.a. | 11,467 |

* Figure refers to 1988.
Source: mainly UNESCO, *Statistical Yearbook*.

URUGUAY

# Directory

## The Constitution

The present Constitution of Uruguay was ratified by plebiscite, on 27 November 1966, when the country voted to return to the presidential form of government after 15 years of 'collegiate' government. The main points of the Constitution are as follows:

### General Provisions

Uruguay shall have a democratic republican form of government, sovereignty being exercised directly by the Electoral Body in cases of election, by initiative or by referendum, and indirectly by representative powers established by the Constitution, according to the rules set out therein.

There shall be freedom of religion; there is no state religion; property shall be inviolable; there shall be freedom of thought. Anyone may enter Uruguay. There are two forms of citizenship: natural, being persons born in Uruguay or of Uruguayan parents, and legal, being people established in Uruguay with at least three years' residence in the case of those with family, and five years' for those without family. Every citizen has the right and obligation to vote.

### Legislature

Legislative power is vested in the Congreso (Congress or General Assembly), made up of two houses, which may act separately or together according to the dispositions of the Constitution. It elects in joint session the members of the Supreme Court of Justice, of the Electoral Court, Tribunals, Administrative Litigation and the Accounts Tribunal.

Elections for both houses, the President and the Vice-President and the departmental governments shall take place every five years on the last Sunday in November; sessions of the Assembly begin on 15 March each year and last until 15 December (15 October in election years, in which case the new Congreso takes office on 15 February). Extraordinary sessions can be called only in case of extreme urgency.

### Chamber of Representatives

The Chamber of Representatives has 99 members elected by direct suffrage by the people according to the system of proportional representation, with at least two representatives to each Department. The number of representatives can be altered by law by a two-thirds' majority in both houses. Their term of office is five years and they must be over 25 and natural citizens or legal citizens with five years' exercise of their citizenship. The members have the right to bring accusations against any member of the Government or judiciary for violation of the Constitution or any other serious offence.

### Senate

The Senate is made up of 31 members, including the Vice-President, who sits as President of the Senate, and 30 members elected directly by the people by proportional representation on the same lists as the representatives, for a term of five years. They must be natural citizens or legal citizens with seven years' exercise of their rights, and be over 30 years of age. The Senate is responsible for hearing any cases brought by the representatives and can deprive a guilty person of a post by a two-thirds' majority.

### The Executive

Executive power is exercised by the President and the Council of Ministers. There shall be a Vice-President, who shall also be President of the Congreso and of the Senate. The President and Vice-President are elected by simple majority of the people by means of the system of double simultaneous vote, and remain in office for five years. They must be over 35 and natural citizens of Uruguay.

The Council of Ministers is made up of the office holders in the ministries or their deputies, and is responsible for all acts of government and administration. It is presided over by the President of the Republic, who has a vote.

### The Judiciary

Judicial Power shall be exercised by the Supreme Court of five members and by Tribunals and local courts; members of the Supreme Court must be over 40, natural citizens, or legal citizens with 10 years' exercise and 25 years' residence, and must be lawyers of 10 years' standing, eight of them in public or fiscal ministry or judicature. Members serve for 10 years and can be re-elected after a break of five years. The Court nominates all other judges and judicial officials.

## The Government

### HEAD OF STATE

**President:** Dr JULIO MARÍA SANGUINETTI CAIROLO (took office 1 March 1995).
**Vice-President:** Dr HUGO BATALLA.

### COUNCIL OF MINISTERS
(June 1995)

**Minister of the Interior:** Dr DIDIER OPERTI.
**Minister of Foreign Affairs:** ALVARO RAMOS.
**Minister of National Defence:** Dr RAÚL ITURRIA.
**Minister of Economy and Finance:** LUIS MOSCA.
**Minister of Industry, Energy and Mining:** FEDERICO SLINGER.
**Minister of Livestock, Agriculture and Fishing:** CARLOS GASPARRI.
**Minister of Public Works and Transport:** LUCIO CÁCERES.
**Minister of Labour and Social Security:** Dra ANALÍA PIÑEYRÚA.
**Minister of Tourism:** BENITO STERN.
**Minister of Education and Culture:** SAMUEL LICHTENSZTEJN.
**Minister of Public Health:** Dr ALFREDO SOLARI.
**Minister of Housing, Territorial Regulation and the Environment:** JUAN CHIRUCHI.
**Minister in the Office of the President and Director of the Office of Planning and Budgetary Affairs:** ARIEL DAVRIEUX
**Secretary to the Presidency:** Dr ELIAS BLUTH.

### MINISTRIES

**Office of the President:** Casa de Gobierno, Edif. Libertad, Avda Luis Alberto de Herrera 3350, esq. Avda José Pedro Varela, Montevideo; tel. (2) 472110; fax (2) 809397.
**Ministry of Economy and Finance:** Colonia 1089, 3°, Montevideo; tel. (2) 921017; telex 6269; fax (2) 921277.
**Ministry of Education and Culture:** Reconquista 535, Montevideo; tel. (2) 950103; telex 23133; fax (2) 962632.
**Ministry of Foreign Affairs:** 18 de Julio 1205, Montevideo; tel. (2) 921007; telex 22074; fax (2) 921327.
**Ministry of Housing, Territorial Regulation and the Environment:** Zabala 1427, Montevideo; tel. (2) 950211; fax (2) 962914.
**Ministry of Industry, Energy and Mining:** Rincón 747, Montevideo; tel. (2) 900231; telex 22072; fax (2) 921245.
**Ministry of the Interior:** Mercedes 993, Montevideo; tel. (2) 989024; telex 22045; fax (2) 920716.
**Ministry of Labour and Social Security:** Juncal 1511, 4°, Montevideo; tel. (2) 962681; telex 23211; fax (2) 963767.
**Ministry of Livestock, Agriculture and Fishing:** Avda Constituyente 1476, Montevideo; tel. (2) 404155; telex 937; fax (2) 499623.
**Ministry of National Defence:** Edif. General Artígas, 8 de Octubre 2628, Montevideo; tel. (2) 809707; telex 23317; fax (2) 809397.
**Ministry of Public Health:** 18 de Julio 1892, Montevideo; tel. (2) 400101; fax (2) 488676.
**Ministry of Public Works and Transport:** Rincón 561, Montevideo; tel. (2) 957386; telex 22057; fax (2) 962883.
**Ministry of Tourism:** Avda Libertador Brig.-General Lavalleja 1409, 2° y 4°–6°, Montevideo; tel. (2) 989105; fax (2) 921624.

## President and Legislature

### PRESIDENT

**Election, 27 November 1994**

| Candidate | Votes | %* |
|---|---|---|
| Dr JULIO MARÍA SANGUINETTI CAIROLO (Partido Colorado) | 656,428 | 32.5 |
| ALBERTO VOLONTÉ (Partido Nacional) | 633,364 | 31.4 |
| TABARÉ VÁZQUEZ (Encuentro Progresista) | 603,188 | 30.8 |
| RAFAEL MICHELINI (Nuevo Espacio) | 101,286 | 5.1 |
| Others | n.a. | 0.2 |

* Percentages are approximate.

Note: Parties may present more than one presidential candidate. The leading candidate in each party assumes the total number of votes for candidates in that party.

URUGUAY

## CONGRESO
### Senate
Election, 27 November 1994

| Party | Seats |
| --- | --- |
| Partido Colorado | 11 |
| Partido Nacional | 10 |
| Encuentro Progresista | 9 |
| Nuevo Espacio | 1 |
| **Total** | **31** |

### Chamber of Representatives
Election, 27 November 1994

| Party | Seats |
| --- | --- |
| Partido Colorado | 32 |
| Partido Nacional | 31 |
| Encuentro Progresista | 31 |
| Nuevo Espacio | 5 |
| **Total** | **99** |

### CONSEJO NACIONAL DE SEGURIDAD
(National Security Council)

Temporary regulations, appended to the 1966 Constitution in August 1984, stipulated that, following the transfer of power to a new civilian government in March 1985, the Consejo Nacional de Seguridad would be composed of nine members, including the Ministers of the Interior, Foreign Affairs and National Defence and the three Commanders-in-Chief of the armed forces. The Council would convene by presidential request and would act as an advisory body to the President.

## Political Organizations

**Alianza Libertadora Nacionalista:** Montevideo; extreme rightwing; Leader OSVALDO MARTÍNEZ JAUME.

**Frente Amplio:** Colonia 1367, 2°, Montevideo; f. 1971; left-wing grouping; Leader Gen. LÍBER SEREGNI MOSQUERA; members include:

    **Frente Izquierda de Liberación (FIDEL):** Montevideo; f. 1962; Socialist; Leader ADOLFO AGUIRRE GONZÁLEZ.

    **Grupo Pregón:** Montevideo; left-wing Liberal party; Leaders SERGIO PREVITALI, ENRIQUE MORAS.

    **Movimiento de Acción Nacionalista (MAN):** Montevideo; left-wing nationalist organization; Leader JOSÉ DURÁN MATOS.

    **Movimiento Blanco Popular y Progresista (MBPP):** Montevideo; moderate left-wing; Leader A. FRANCISCO RODRÍGUEZ CAMUSSO.

    **Movimiento de Liberación Nacional (MLN)—Tupamaros:** Montevideo; f. 1962; radical socialist; between 1962 and 1973 the MLN, operating under its popular name of the **Tupamaros**, conducted a campaign of urban guerrilla warfare until it was defeated by the armed forces by the end of 1973; following the return to civilian rule, in 1985, the MLN announced its decision to abandon its armed struggle; legally recognized in May 1989; Sec.-Gen. JOSÉ MÚJICA.

    **Movimiento 26 de Marzo:** Durazno 1118, Montevideo; tel. (2) 911584; telex 23112; f. 1971; socialist; Pres. EDUARDO RUBIO; Sec.-Gen. FERNANDO VAZQUES.

    **Partido Comunista:** Río Negro 1525, Montevideo; tel. (2) 917171; fax (2) 911050; f. 1920; Sec.-Gen. MARINA ARISMENDI; 42,000 mems (est.).

    **Partido de Democracia Avanzada:** Montevideo; communist.

    **Partido Socialista del Uruguay:** Casa del Pueblo Soriano 1218, Montevideo; tel. (2) 913344; fax (2) 419466; f. 1910; Pres. JOSÉ PEDRO CARDOSO; Sec.-Gen. REINALDO GARGANO.

**Nuevo Espacio:** Montevideo; f. 1989 by parties withdrawing from the Frente Amplio; moderate left-wing; Leader RAFAEL MICHELINI; members include:

    **Partido Demócrata Cristiano (PDC):** fmrly Unión Cívica del Uruguay; f. 1962; Pres. JUAN GUILLERMO YOUNG; Sec.-Gen. CARLOS VASSALLO.

    **Partido por el Gobierno del Pueblo (Lista 99):** Calle Ejido 1480, Montevideo; tel. (2) 987194; f. 1962; left-wing; Leader RAFAEL MICHELINI

**Unión Cívica:** Río Branco 1486, Montevideo; tel. (2) 905535; f. 1912; recognized Christian Democrat faction which split from the Partido Demócrata Cristiano in 1980.

**Partido Azul (PA):** Paul Harris 1722, Casilla 11500, Montevideo; tel. and fax (2) 616327; f. 1993; Leader Dr ROBERTO CANESSA; Gen. Sec. Ing. ARMANDO VAL.

**Partido Colorado:** Andrés Martínez Trueba 1271, Montevideo; tel. (2) 490180; f. 1836; Sec.-Gen. JORGE BATLLE IBÁÑEZ; Leader JOSÉ LUIS BATLLE; factions include:

    **Batllismo Radical:** leader JORGE BATLLE IBÁÑEZ.

    **Cruzada 94:** Leader PABLO MIUOR.

    **Foro Batllista:** Leader Dr JULIO MARÍA SANGUINETTI CAIROLO.

    **Unión Colorada y Batllista (Pachequista):** right-wing; Leader JORGE PACHECO ARECO.

**Partido Justiciero:** Montevideo; extreme right-wing; Leader BOLÍVAR ESPÍNDOLA.

**Partido Nacional (Blanco):** Juan Carlos Gómez 1384, Montevideo; tel. (2) 903355; f. 1836; Leader CARLOS ALFREDO CAT VIDAL; Sec.-Gen. ALBERTO ZUMARÁN; tendencies within the party include:

    **Consejo Nacional Herrerista:** Leaders LUIS ALBERTO LACALLE, FRANCISCO UBILLES.

    **Divisa Blanca:** conservative; Leader EDUARDO PONS ETCHEVERRY.

    **Movimiento Nacional de Rocha—Corriente Popular Nacionalista:** Leaders CARLOS JULIO PEREYRA, JUAN PIVEL DEVOTO.

    **Partido Nacional—Barrán.**

    **Renovación y Victoria:** Leader Dr GONZALO AGUIRRE RAMÍREZ.

    **Sector por la Patria:** Leader ALBERTO ZUMARÁN.

**Partido del Sol:** 18 de Julio 1235, Montevideo; tel. (2) 901616; fax (2) 906739; ecologist, pacifist; Leader HOMERO MIERES.

**Partido de los Trabajadores:** Convención 1196, esq. Canelones, Montevideo; tel. (2) 982624; f. 1980; extreme left-wing; Leader JUAN VITAL ANDRADE.

**Partido Verde Etoecologista (PVE):** Montevideo; ecologist; Leader RODOLFO TÁLICE.

## Diplomatic Representation

### EMBASSIES IN URUGUAY

**Argentina:** Cuareim 1470, Montevideo; tel. (2) 928166; fax (2) 928172; Ambassador: Dra ALICIA MARTÍNEZ RÍOS.

**Belgium:** Leyenda Patria 2880, 4°, Montevideo; tel. (2) 701571; telex 22612; Ambassador: ROGER TYBERGHEIN.

**Bolivia:** Río Branco 1320, 4°, Of. 401, Montevideo; Chargé d'affaires: ANA MARÍA SILES DE REGULES.

**Brazil:** Artígas 1328, Casilla 11300, Montevideo; tel. (2) 772119; telex 22576; fax (2) 772086; Ambassador: RENATO PRADO GUIMARÃES.

**Bulgaria:** Rambla Mahatma Gandhi 647, 5°, Casilla 502, Montevideo; Ambassador: DIMITUR MARKOV MARCHEVSKI.

**Chile:** Andes 1365, 2°, Montevideo; telex 6418; Ambassador: JUAN GUILLERMO TORO DÁVILA.

**China, People's Republic:** Montevideo; Ambassador: XIE RUMAO.

**Colombia:** Juncal 1305, 18°, Montevideo; telex 6587; Ambassador: Dr SANTIAGO SALAZAR SANTOS.

**Costa Rica:** José Martí 3295, Apt 102, Casilla 12242, Montevideo; tel. (2) 783645; fax (2) 789714; Ambassador: JUAN W. VALENZUELA C.

**Cuba:** Artígas 1125, Montevideo; tel. (2) 416512; telex 23031; fax (2) 482140; Ambassador: MANUEL AGUILERA DE LA PAZ.

**Czech Republic:** Luis B. Cavia 2996, Casilla 12262, Montevideo; tel. (2) 787808.

**Dominican Republic:** Plaza Independencia 838, 5°, Of. 31, Montevideo; Ambassador: Dr JESÚS MARÍA HERNÁNDEZ SÁNCHEZ.

**Ecuador:** Colonia 993, 3°, Montevideo; tel. (2) 921028; telex 26998; Ambassador: EDUARDO CABEZAS MOLINA.

**Egypt:** Avda Brasil 2663, Montevideo; tel. (2) 781553; telex 22391; fax (2) 780977; Ambassador: FAROUK EL-HOFY.

**El Salvador:** Buxareo 1117, Casilla 203, Montevideo; tel. (2) 794831; telex 23095; fax (2) 798718; Ambassador: MARION VON ZITZEWITZ.

**France:** Avda Uruguay 853, Casilla 290, Montevideo; tel. (2) 920077; telex 6986; fax (2) 923711; Ambassador: PIERRE CHARASSE.

**Germany:** La Cumparsita 1435, Casilla 20014, Montevideo; tel. (2) 925222; telex 23764; fax (2) 923422; Ambassador: Dr LUDGER BUERSTEDDE.

**Guatemala:** España 2921, Casilla 301, Montevideo; tel. (2) 782104; Ambassador: Dr JUAN ALFREDO RENDÓN MALDONADO.

**Holy See:** Artígas 1270, Casilla 1503, Montevideo (Apostolic Nunciature); tel. (2) 772016; telex 26670; fax (2) 772209; Apostolic Nuncio: Most Rev. FRANCESCO DE NITTIS, Titular Archbishop of Tunes.

**Honduras:** Pagola 3306/501, Casilla 338, Montevideo; telex 22629; Ambassador: Dr HERNÁN ANTONIO BERMÚDEZ AGUILAR.

# URUGUAY

**Hungary:** Dr Prudencio de Pena 2469, Montevideo; tel. (2) 786173; telex 23232; Ambassador: Dr BÉLA SZABÓ.

**Israel:** Artígas 1585, Montevideo; tel. (2) 404164; telex 26497; Ambassador: AVRAHAM TOLEDO.

**Italy:** José B. Lamas 2857, Casilla 268, Montevideo; tel. (2) 785316; telex 22077; Ambassador: Dr TOMMASO DE VERGOTTINI.

**Japan:** Artígas 953, Montevideo; tel. (2) 487645; telex 23807; fax (2) 487980; Ambassador: KATSUHIKO TSUNODA.

**Korea, Republic:** Jaime Zudáñez 2836, Apt 1001, Casilla 12135, 11300 Montevideo; tel. (2) 709996; telex 22343; Ambassador: PARK TAE-JIN.

**Lebanon:** Rivera 2278, Montevideo; tel. (2) 486365; telex 22257; Ambassador: RIAD KANTAR.

**Mexico:** Andes 1365, 7°, Montevideo; tel. (2) 920791; telex 23178; fax (2) 921232; Ambassador: IGNACIO VILLASEÑOR.

**Netherlands:** Leyenda Patria 2880, 2°, Casilla 1519, Montevideo; telex 22273; Ambassador: C. J. VREEDENBURGH.

**Nicaragua:** Rambla República del Perú 1139, Montevideo; Chargé d'affaires a.i.: MARIO DUARTE ZAMORA.

**Panama:** Rambla Mahatma Gandhi 509, Casilla 404, Montevideo; Ambassador: ALEXIS CABRERA QUINTERO.

**Paraguay:** Artígas 1256, Montevideo; tel. (2) 772138; telex 6440; fax (2) 783682; Ambassador: BENITO PEREIRA SAGUIER.

**Peru:** Soriano 1124, Casilla 126, Montevideo; tel. (2) 921194; telex 26985; fax (2) 921194; Ambassador: JORGE DEL CAMPO VIDAL.

**Poland:** Jorge Canning 2389, Casilla 1538, Montevideo; tel. (2) 801313; telex 26447; fax (2) 473389; Ambassador: Dr RYSZARD SCHNEPF.

**Portugal:** Avda Dr Francisco Soca 1128, Apdo 701, 11300 Montevideo; tel. (2) 784061; telex 22318; Ambassador: Dr MANUEL BARREIROS MARTINS.

**Romania:** Ing. Federico Abadie 2940, Casilla 102, Montevideo; telex 23766; Chargé d'affaires: ANTON DONCIU.

**Russia:** España 2741, Montevideo; tel. (2) 781884; fax (2) 786597; Ambassador: BORIS V. GOLOVIN.

**South Africa:** Prudencio de Pena 2483, Montevideo; Ambassador: VAUGHAN C. R. DEWING.

**Spain:** Avda Brasil 2786, Montevideo; tel. (2) 786010; telex 22439; Ambassador: RICARDO PEIDRO CONDE.

**Switzerland:** Ing. Federico Abadie 2936/40, 11300 Montevideo; tel. (2) 704315; telex 23175; fax (2) 715031; Ambassador: JÖRG LAURENZ KAUFMANN.

**United Kingdom:** Marco Bruto 1073, Casilla 16024, 11300 Montevideo; tel. (2) 623650; fax (2) 627815; Ambassador: R. A. M. HENDRIE.

**USA:** Lauro Muller 1776, Montevideo; tel. (2) 236061; fax (2) 488611; Ambassador: THOMAS DODD.

**Venezuela:** Avda Manuel Albo 2675, Montevideo; tel. (2) 472788; telex 23035; fax (2) 472785; Ambassador: Dr GERMÁN LAIRET U.

**Yugoslavia:** España 2697, Montevideo; Ambassador: LJUBISA JEREMIĆ.

## Judicial System

The Court of Justice is made up of five members appointed at the suggestion of the executive, for a period of five years. It has original jurisdiction in constitutional, international and admiralty cases, and hears appeals from the appellate courts, of which there are seven, each with three judges.

Cases involving the functioning of the State administration are heard in the ordinary Administrative Courts, and in the Supreme Administrative Court which consists of five members appointed in the same way as members of the Court of Justice.

In Montevideo there are 19 civil courts, 10 criminal and correctional courts, 19 courts presided over by justices of the peace, three juvenile courts, three labour courts and courts for government and other cases. Each departmental capital, and some other cities, has a departmental court; each of the 224 judicial divisions has a justice of the peace.

The administration of justice became free of charge in 1980, with the placing of attorneys-at-law in all courts to assist those unable to pay for the services of a lawyer.

**Supreme Court of Justice:** Gutiérrez Ruiz 1310, 11100 Montevideo; tel. (2) 901041; fax (2) 923549.

**Court of Justice:** Ibicuy 1310, Montevideo.

**Supreme Administrative Tribunal:** Mercedes 961, Montevideo; tel. (2) 908047.

**President of the Supreme Court of Justice:** Dr LUIS TONELLO.

## Religion

Under the Constitution, the Church and the State were declared separate and toleration for all forms of worship was proclaimed. Roman Catholicism predominates.

### CHRISTIANITY

**Federación de Iglesias Evangélicas del Uruguay:** 8 de Octubre 3324, 11600 Montevideo; tel. (2) 472002; f. 1956; eight mem. churches; Pres. BASILIO ERDELYI; Sec. EDITH MOYEIKO.

#### The Roman Catholic Church

Uruguay comprises one archdiocese and nine dioceses. At 31 December 1993 there were an estimated 2,552,300 adherents in the country, representing about 78% of the total population.

**Bishops' Conference:** Conferencia Episcopal Uruguaya, Avda Uruguay 1319, 11100 Montevideo; tel. (2) 981975; fax (2) 911802; f. 1972; Pres. Rt Rev. ORLANDO ROMERO CABRERA, Bishop of Canelones.

**Archbishop of Montevideo:** Most Rev. JOSÉ GOTTARDI CRISTELLI, Arzobispado, Calle Treinta y Tres 1368, Casilla 356, 11000 Montevideo; tel. (2) 958127; fax (2) 958926.

#### The Anglican Communion

Uruguay is the newest diocese in the Province of the Southern Cone of America, having been established in 1988. The Presiding Bishop of the Iglesia Anglicana del Cono Sur de América, is the Bishop of Chile.

**Bishop of Uruguay:** Rt Rev. HAROLD WILLIAM GODFREY, Centro Diocesano Reconquista 522, Casilla 6108, 11000 Montevideo; tel. (2) 959627; fax (2) 962519.

#### Other Churches

**Baptist Evangelical Convention of Uruguay:** Avda Agraciada 3452, Montevideo; tel. (2) 394846; Pres: Rev. LEMUEL LARROSA.

**Iglesia Adventista** (Adventist Church): Castro 167, Montevideo; f. 1901; 4,000 mems; Principal officers Dr GUILLERMO DURÁN, Dr ALEXIS PIRO.

**Iglesia Evangélica Metodista en el Uruguay** (Evangelical Methodist Church in Uruguay): Estero Bellaco 2678, 11600 Montevideo; tel. (2) 800984; fax (2) 472181; f. 1876; 910 mems (1992); Pres. BEATRIZ FERRARI.

**Iglesia Evangélica Valdense** (Waldensian Evangelical Church): Avda 8 de Octubre 3037, 11600 Montevideo; tel. (2) 801093; f. 1952; 15,000 mems; Pastor CARLOS DELMONTE.

**Primera Iglesia Bautista** (First Baptist Church): Dr D. Fernández Crespo 1741, Casilla 5051, Montevideo; tel. (2) 498744; fax (2) 928155; f. 1911; 619 mems; Pastor LEMUEL J. LARROSA.

Other denominations active in Uruguay include the Iglesia Evangélica del Río de la Plata and the Iglesia Evangélica Menonita (Evangelical Mennonite Church).

### BAHÁ'Í FAITH

**National Spiritual Assembly of the Bahá'ís:** Joaquín Requena 1090, 11800 Montevideo; tel. (2) 489850; f. 1938; mems resident in 110 localities.

## The Press

### DAILIES

#### Montevideo

**El Día:** Avda 18 de Julio, Montevideo; independent; Dir ENRIQUE TARIGÓ.

**El Diario:** Río Negro 1028, Montevideo; tel. (2) 920348; telex 26654; fax (2) 921326; f. 1923; evening; independent; Editor Dr SALVADOR ALABÁN DEMARE; circ. 80,000.

**El Diario Español:** Cerrito 551–555, Apdo 899, Montevideo; f. 1905; morning (except Monday); newspaper of the Spanish community; Editor CARLOS REINANTE; circ. 20,000.

**Diario Oficial:** Florida 1178, Montevideo; f. 1905; morning; publishes laws, official decrees, parliamentary debates, judicial decisions and legal transactions; Dir Sra ZAIN NASSIF DE ZARUMBE.

**Gaceta Comercial:** Juncal 1391, 11000 Montevideo; tel. (2) 965618; fax (2) 962596; f. 1916; morning (Mon.–Fri.); Dir MILTON SANS; Editor PABLO SANS; circ. 4,500.

**La Hora Popular:** Yatay 1446 casi Marcelino Sosa, Montevideo; tel. (2) 205002; telex 23130; f. 1984; morning; left-wing; Dir VÍCTOR ROSSI; circ. 30,000.

**La Mañana:** Río Negro 1028, Montevideo; tel. (2) 920348; telex 26654; fax (2) 921326; f. 1917; Colorado; Editor Dr SALVADOR ALABÁN DEMARE; circ. 40,000.

URUGUAY

**Mundocolor:** Cuareim 1287, Montevideo; f. 1976; evening (except Sunday); Dir Daniel Herrera Lussich; circ. 4,500.

**El País:** Michelini 1287, Montevideo; tel. (2) 912175; f. 1918; morning; supports Partido Nacional; Editor Martín Aguirre; circ. 130,000.

**Ultimas Noticias:** Paysandú 1179, Montevideo; tel. (2) 920452; fax (2) 920034; f. 1981; evening (except Sunday); owned by Impresora Polo Ltd; Publr Julián Safi; circ. 25,000.

### Florida

**El Heraldo:** Independencia 824, Casilla 94000, Florida; tel (352) 2229; fax (352) 4546; f. 1919; evening (except Sunday); independent; Dir Alvaro Riva Rey; circ. 1,800.

### Minas

**La Unión:** Florencio Sánchez 569, Minas; tel. (442) 2065; f. 1877; evening (except Sunday); Dir Edgar Martínez Lucero; Editor Washington Guadalupe Pereira; circ. 2,650.

### Paysandú

**El Telégrafo:** 18 de Julio 1027, Paysandú; f. 1910; morning; independent; Dir Fernando M. Baccaro; circ. 10,000.

### Salto

**Tribuna Salteña:** Joaquín Suárez 71, Salto; f. 1906; morning; Dir Modesto Llantada Fabini; circ. 3,000.

## PERIODICALS
### Montevideo

**Aquí:** Zabala 1322, Esc. 102, Montevideo; weekly; supports the Frente Amplio; Dir Francisco José O'Honelli.

**Boletín Comercial:** Colón 1580, Montevideo; f. 1935; monthly; Dir Antonio Benvenuto; circ. 2,500.

**Brecha:** Avda Uruguay 844, 11100 Montevideo; tel. (2) 916723; telex 23779; fax (2) 920388; f. 1985; weekly; politics, current affairs; circ. 14,500.

**Búsqueda:** Avda Uruguay 1146, Montevideo; tel. (2) 921300; fax (2) 922036; f. 1972; weekly; independent; politics and economics; Dir Danilo Arbilla Frachia; circ. 21,000.

**Charoná:** Gutiérrez Ruiz 1276, Esc. 201, Montevideo; f. 1968; tel. (2) 986665; f. 1968; fortnightly; children's; Dir Sergio Boffano; circ. 25,000.

**Colorín Colorado:** Dalmiro Costa 4482, Montevideo; f. 1980; monthly; children's; Dir Sara Minster de Murninkas; circ. 3,000.

**Crónicas Económicas:** Avda Libertador Brig.-General Lavalleja, Montevideo; f. 1981; weekly; independent; economics; Dirs Julio Ariel Franco, Walter Hugo Pagés, Jorge Estellano.

**La Democracia:** Colonia 1308, Montevideo; f. 1981; weekly; organ of the Partido Nacional; Editor Alberto Zumarán; circ. 17,000.

**La Gaceta Militar Naval:** Montevideo; monthly.

**Indice Industrial-Anuario de la Industria Uruguaya:** Sarandí 456, Montevideo; tel. (2) 951963; f. 1957; annually; Dir W. M. Trias; circ. 6,000.

**Jaque:** Montevideo; f. 1983; weekly; politics, current affairs; Dir Manuel Flores Silva.

**Judicatura:** Avda Libertador Brig.-General Lavalleja 1464, Montevideo; f. 1975; monthly; jurisprudence; Dirs Dr Eduardo Brito del Pino, Dr Nelson Nicoliello, Dra Jacinta Balbela de Delgue; circ. 5,000.

**La Justicia Uruguaya:** 25 de Mayo 555, Montevideo; tel. (2) 957587; fax (2) 959721; f. 1940; weekly; jurisprudence; Dir Oscar Arias Barbe; circ. 3,000.

**La Juventud:** Durazno 1118, Montevideo; tel. (2) 911584; telex 23112; weekly; supports the Movimiento 26 de Marzo.

**Marketing Directo:** Duvimioso Terra 1157, Casilla 11200, Montevideo; tel. (2) 412174; fax 487221; f. 1988; monthly; Dir Edgardo Martínez Zimarioff; circ. 9,500.

**Mate Amargo:** Montevideo; f. 1986; magazine of the Movimiento de Liberación Nacional; circ. 22,500.

**Opción:** J. Barrios Amorín 1531, Casilla 102, Montevideo; f. 1981; weekly; Dir Francisco José Ottonelli; circ. 15,000.

**Patatín y Patatán:** Florida 1472, Esc. 2, Montevideo; f. 1977; weekly; children's; Dir Juan José Ravaioli; circ. 3,000.

**La Propaganda Rural:** Arenal Grande 1341, Montevideo; f. 1902; monthly; cattle, agriculture and industry; Dirs Oscar Martín, Alberto R. Conde; circ. 5,000.

**Revista Militar y Naval:** 25 de Mayo 279, Montevideo; military.

## PRESS ASSOCIATIONS

**Asociación de Diarios del Uruguay:** Río Negro 1308, 6°, Montevideo; f. 1922; Pres. Batlle T. Barbato.

**Asociación de la Prensa Uruguaya:** Avda Uruguay 1255, Montevideo; tel. and fax (2) 913695; f. 1944; Pres. Gustavo Aguirre.

### PRESS AGENCIES
#### Foreign Bureaux

**Agence France-Presse (AFP):** Colonia 1479, 9°, Montevideo; tel. (2) 403191; telex 749; Chief Jupiter Puyo.

**Agencia EFE** (Spain): Maldonado 1359, Montevideo; tel. (2) 981301; Bureau Chief Manuel Cabrera Santonja.

**Agenzia Nazionale Stampa Associata (ANSA)** (Italy): Florida 1400, Montevideo; tel. (2) 911032; telex 23838; fax (2) 981950; Bureau Chief Juan Atella.

**Associated Press (AP)** (USA): Cuareim 1283, 4°, Casilla 674, Montevideo; tel. (2) 910940; Correspondent Daniel Gianelli.

**Deutsche Presse-Agentur (dpa)** (Germany): Avda 18 de Julio 994, 4°, Of. A, Montevideo; tel. (2) 906201; telex 26396; fax (2) 922662; Correspondent Luis Alberto Zenga.

**Inter Press Service (IPS)** (Italy): Juan Carlos Gómez 1445, Esc. 102, Montevideo; tel. (2) 964397; fax (2) 963598; Dir Mario Lubetkin.

**Reuters** (United Kingdom): Florida 1408, 4°, Of. 304, Casilla 1154, Montevideo; tel. (2) 920336; telex 23179.

**Prensa Latina** (Cuba): Avda Francisco Soca 1263, Casilla 202, esq. Pres. Gestido y Bartolito Mitre, Montevideo; tel. (2) 792955; telex 23086; Correspondent Manuel Villar Burchard.

**United Press International (UPI)** (USA): Avda 18 de Julio 1224, 2°, Montevideo; Chief Carlos Díaz.

## Publishers

**Editorial Arca SRL:** Andes 1118, Montevideo; tel. (2) 924468; fax (2) 930188; f. 1963; general literature, social science and history; Man. Dir Claudio Rama.

**Ediciones de la Banda Oriental:** Montevideo; general literature; Man. Dir H. Raviolo.

**Barreiro y Ramos, SA:** 25 de Mayo 604, Casilla 15, 11000 Montevideo; tel. (2) 950150; fax (2) 962358; f. 1871; general; Man. Dir Gastón Barreiro Zorrilla.

**Casa del Estudiante:** Eduardo Acevedo 1422, Montevideo; literature; Man. Oscar Torres.

**CENCI—Uruguay** (Centro de Estadísticas Nacionales y Comercio Internacional): Misiones 1361, Casilla 1510, Montevideo; tel. (2) 952930; fax (2) 954578; f. 1956; economics, statistics; Dirs Cristina Z. de Vertesi, Kenneth Brunner.

**Editorial Ciencias:** Duvimioso Terra 1461, Montevideo; medicine.

**Librería Delta Editorial:** Avda Italia 2817, Montevideo; f. 1960; medicine, biological sciences; Man. Dir A. Breitfeld.

**Editorial y Librería Jurídica Amalio M. Fernández SRL:** 25 de Mayo 477, B°, Of. 2, Montevideo; tel. (2) 951782; fax (2) 951782; f. 1951; law and sociology; Man. Dir Amalio M. Fernández.

**Fundación de Cultura Universitaria:** 25 de Mayo 568, Casilla 1155, 11000 Montevideo; tel. (2) 961152; fax (2) 952549; f. 1968; law and social sciences; Man. Dir Carlos H. Fuques.

**Hemisferio Sur:** Buenos Aires 335, Casilla 1755, Montevideo; tel. (2) 964515; fax (2) 964520; f. 1951; agronomy and veterinary science.

**Editorial Idea:** Brandzén 2245, Montevideo; law; Dir Dr Guillermo Vezcovi.

**Editorial Kapelusz:** Avda Uruguay 1331, Montevideo; educational.

**Editorial Medina SRL:** Gaboto 1521, Montevideo; tel. (2) 44100; f. 1933; general; Pres. Marcos Medina Vidal.

**A. Monteverde & Cía, SA:** 25 de Mayo 577, Casilla 371, Montevideo; tel. (2) 959019; f. 1879; educational; Man. Dir Héctor Mussini.

**Mosca Hnos:** 18 de Julio 1578, Montevideo; tel. (2) 493141; telex 22203; f. 1888; general; Man. Dir Raúl Santiago Mosca.

**Editorial Nuestra Tierra:** Cerrito 566, Casilla 1603, Montevideo; tel. (2) 957528; fax (2) 957528; f. 1968; general; Man. Dir Daniel Aljanati.

**Librería Selecta Editorial:** Guayabo 1865, 11200 Montevideo; tel. (2) 486989; fax (2) 486831; f. 1950; academic books; Dir Fernando Masa.

### ASSOCIATION

**Cámara Uruguaya del Libro:** Juan D. Jackson 1118, Montevideo; tel. (2) 415732; fax (2) 411860; f. 1944; Pres. Vicente Porcelli; Man. Ana Cristina Rodríguez de Iglesias.

URUGUAY

## Radio and Television

In 1992, according to UNESCO, there were an estimated 1,890,000 radio receivers and 725,000 television receivers in use.

**Administración Nacional de Telecomunicaciones (ANTEL):** Avda Daniel Fernández Crespo 1534, Montevideo; tel. (2) 404585; telex 22208; fax (2) 486071; f. 1974; govt-owned; Pres. ROSARIO MEDERO; Vice-Pres. Dr JUAN DE LA CRUZ SILVEIRA ZAVALA.

**Asociación Nacional de Broadcasters Uruguayos (ANDEBU):** Calle Yí 1264, Montevideo; tel. (2) 900053; telex 843; f. 1933; 101 mems; Pres. RAÚL FONTAINA; Sec.-Gen. Dr RAFAEL INCHAUSTI.

**Dirección Nacional de Comunicaciones:** Artígas 1520, Casilla 927, Montevideo; tel. (2) 773662; telex 23213; fax (2) 773591; f. 1984; Dir Dr JUAN JOSÉ CAMELO.

### RADIO

In 1994 there were 25 medium- and short-wave radio stations and 10 FM stations in the Montevideo area. There were another 76 radio stations outside the capital.

**Radio El Espectador:** Río Branco 1483, 11100 Montevideo; commercial; Dir LUIS DE MARÍA.

### TELEVISION

**Monte Carlo TV Color:** Paraguay 2253, Casilla 5019, Montevideo; tel. (2) 944591; telex 23052; fax (2) 942001; f. 1961; Dir HUGO ROMAY SALVO.

**SAETA TV—Canal 10:** Dr Lorenzo Carnelli 1234, Montevideo; tel. (2) 402120; fax (2) 409771; f. 1956; Pres. JORGE DE FEO.

**SODRE—Servicio Oficial de Difusión Radiotelevisión y Espectáculos:** Artígas 2552, Montevideo; tel. (2) 806448; telex 26602; Dir VICTOR BJÖRGAN.

**Teledoce Televisora Color—Canal 12:** Enriqueta Compte y Riqué 1276, Montevideo; tel. (2) 235856; telex 22403; f. 1962; Pres. EDUARDO SCHECK; Gen. Man. HORACIO SCHECK.

In 1994 there were 22 television stations outside the capital.

## Finance

### BANKING

(cap. = capital; res = reserves; dep. = deposits; m. = million; amounts in new pesos, unless otherwise indicated)

#### State Banks

**Banco Central del Uruguay:** Avda Juan P. Fabini, esq. Florida, Casilla 1467, Montevideo; tel. (2) 917117; telex 26659; fax (2) 921634; f. 1967; note-issuing bank, also controls private banking; Pres. ENRIQUE BRAGA SILVA; Gen. Man. JUAN OLASCOAGA.

**Banco Hipotecario del Uruguay:** Avda Fernández Crespo 1508, Montevideo; f. 1892; State Mortgage Bank; in 1977 assumed responsibility for housing projects in Uruguay; Pres. PEDRO W. CERSÓSIMO.

**Banco de la República Oriental del Uruguay:** Calle Cerrito 351 y Zabala, Montevideo; tel. (2) 950157; telex 26990; fax (2) 963708; f. 1896; a state institution; cap. and res 2,699,349m., dep. 8,625,614m. (Dec. 1992); Pres. ENRIQUE BRAGA; 106 brs.

**Banco de Seguros del Estado:** Avda Agraciada y Mercedes, Montevideo; tel. (2) 981114; telex 398398; f. 1911; Pres. Dr GABRIEL GIAMPIETRO BORROS; Gen. Man. ALFREDO SCELZA; 18 brs.

#### Principal Commercial Banks

**Banco Comercial:** Cerrito 400, Casilla 34, Montevideo; tel. (2) 960541; telex 26911; fax (2) 953569; f. 1857; 'privatized' in Oct. 1990; cap. and res US $397.6m., dep. $3,246.8m. (Dec. 1994); Pres. Dr ARMANDO M. BRAUN ESTRUGAMON; Vice-Pres. CARLOS ROHM CONTE; 46 brs.

**Banco de Crédito:** Avda 18 de Julio 1451, Montevideo; tel. (2) 404141; telex 26257; fax (2) 961324; f. 1908; cap. 47,573m., res 28,304m., dep. 1,242,538m. (Dec. 1993); Pres. CHARLES M. HAM; Gen. Man. OSCAR RICO; 28 brs.

**Banco Exterior SA—Uruguay:** Rincón 493, Casilla 914, 11000 Montevideo; tel. (2) 960042; telex 22315; fax (2) 961089; f. 1982; cap. 26,043m., res 5,347m., dep. 654,478m. (Dec. 1993); Pres. IÑIGO DE LA SOTA GALDIZ; Gen. Man. RAPHAEL SÁNCHEZ GARRÓS; 21 brs.

**Banco La Caja Obrera:** 25 de Mayo 500, Montevideo; tel. (2) 954114; telex 26613; fax (2) 950051; f. 1905; taken over by Banco de la República Oriental del Uruguay in 1987; cap. 18,000m., res 23,832m., dep. 570,980m. (Dec. 1991); Pres. JAIME M. BARDECIO; Vice-Pres. ROBERTO PÉREZ TARRAT; 32 brs.

**Banco de Montevideo:** Misiones 1399, Casilla 612, Montevideo; tel. (2) 1881; telex 23775; fax (2) 960952; f. 1941; cap. 25,000m., res 112,996m., dep. 1,728,465m., (Dec. 1994); Pres. Dr JORGE ECHEVERRÍA LEÚNDA; Gen. Man. ERIC SIMON; 7 brs.

**Banco Pan de Azúcar:** Rincón 518/528, Casilla 1891, Montevideo; tel. (2) 960925; telex 26652; fax 961493; f. 1945; cap. and res 1,651m., dep. 29,057m. (Dec. 1985); Pres. ENRIQUE A. RADMILOVICH; Exec. Vice-Pres. EMILIO BERRIEL GARRIDO; 18 brs.

**Banco Real del Uruguay, SA:** Julio Herrera y Obes 1365, 1°, Casilla 964, Montevideo; tel. (2) 920376; telex 26915; fax (2) 921510; f. 1962; cap. 3,525m., dep. 653,333m. (Dec. 1993); Pres. ENIO ALVES VIEIRA; Vice-Pres. CELIO TUNHOLI; 6 brs.

**Banco Santander** (Spain): 18 de Julio 1271, Montevideo; tel. (2) 905406; telex 26931; fax (2) 963685; Vice-Pres. MIGUEL ESTRUGO SANTAEUGENIA; Dir JORGE JOURDÁN PEYRONEL; 28 brs.

**Banco Surinvest SA:** Rincón 530, 1100 Montevideo; tel. (2) 960177; telex 26982; fax (2) 960241; f. 1981 as Surinvest Casa Bancaria, name changed as above 1991; cap. 2,431m., res 30,334m., dep. 183,131m. (Dec. 1992); Chair. and CEO FRANCISCO M. RAVECCA ARANA; Gen. Man. JOSÉ LUIS RUBIO.

**Banesto Banco Uruguay, SA:** Calle 25 de Mayo 401, esq. Zabala, Montevideo; tel. (2) 961444; telex 23754; fax (2) 960838; f. 1968; formerly Unión de Bancos del Uruguay (UBUR); cap. 45,000m., res 43,016m., dep. 1,235,357m. (Dec. 1993); Pres. JOSÉ LUIS FOMINAYA CISNEROS; Dir and Gen. Man. JULIO GARDE TORRES; 9 brs.

**Centrobanco:** 25 de Mayo 528, Montevideo; tel. (2) 960423; telex 26626; Dir-Gen. FRANCISCO ANQUELA MORIANO; Gen. Man. JUAN MARTÍNEZ GUIRAO; 6 brs.

**Internationale Nederlanden Bank (Uruguay) SA:** Misiones 1352/1360, 11000 Montevideo; tel. (2) 960961; telex 26672; fax (2) 958955; f. 1983 as Banco NMB Sudamericano, name changed as above 1992; cap. and res 459m., dep. 11,460m. (Dec. 1984); Pres. ONNO VAN DEN BROEK; Vice-Pres. and Man. Dir GERARDO P. VAN TIENHOVEN; 11 brs.

#### Foreign Banks

**American Express Bank, SA** (USA): Edif. Presidente, Rincón 473, Montevideo; tel. (2) 962244; telex 22055; fax (2) 962245; Pres. SERGIO J. MASVIDAL; Gen. Man. THOMAS LINDNER; 1 br.

**Banco do Brasil:** 25 de Mayo 506, esq. Treinta y Tres, Casilla 745, Montevideo; tel. (2) 957355; telex 22602; fax (2) 960889; Gen. Man. OTTO WERNER NOLTE; 4 brs.

**Banco Holandés Unido** (Netherlands): 25 de Mayo 501, Montevideo; tel. (2) 960702; telex 26619; fax (2) 960121; Gen. Man. BORIS MARTÍNEZ GARCÍA; 6 brs.

**Banco de Italia** (Italy): Misiones 1472, Casilla 120, Montevideo; tel. (2) 960925; telex 6652; planned liquidation announced in 1989; Pres. FEDERICO SLINGER; Dir-Gen. ROBERTO J. COUCE; 5 brs.

**Banco de la Nación Argentina:** Juan C. Gómez 1372, Montevideo; tel. (2) 960078; telex 22489; fax (2) 960078; Gen. Man. JUAN JORGE BARCELONA; 2 brs.

**Banco Sudameris** (France): Rincón 500, Montevideo; tel. (2) 961050; telex 26655; fax (2) 964292; Pres. Dr SAGUNTO PÉREZ FONTANA; Gen. Man. PAUL PINELLI; 6 brs.

**Bank of America NT & SA** (USA): 25 de Mayo 552, Montevideo; tel. (2) 960938; telex 820; Vice-Pres. and Gen. Man. JOSÉ O. FERNÁNDEZ; 2 brs.

**Citibank NA** (USA): Cerrito 455, esq. Misiones, Montevideo; tel. (2) 950374; telex 23075; fax (2) 963665; Gen. Man. CARLOS M. FEDRIGOTTI; 3 brs.

**Discount Bank (Latin America), SA** (USA): Rincón 390 y Zabala, Montevideo; tel. (2) 959525; telex 22302; fax (2) 960890; f. 1958; cap. 6,015m., res 13,808m., dep. 429,940m. (Dec. 1991); Pres. ARON KAHANA; Gen. Man. BITOUSH MENAHEM; 4 brs.

**First National Bank of Boston** (USA): Zabala 1463, Montevideo; tel. (2) 960127; telex 22433; fax (2) 962209; took over Banco Internacional in 1978; cap. US $10.8m., dep. $179.9m. (May 1990); Gen. Man. HORACIO VILARÓ NIETO; 11 brs.

**Leumi Le-Israel (Latin America) Casa Bancaria:** 25 de Mayo 549, 11000 Montevideo; tel. (2) 960223; telex 26963; fax (2) 957385; f. 1980; cap. 775m., res 6,902m., dep. 74,942m. (Dec. 1991); Chair. Dr ZALMAN SEGAL; Gen. Man. MORDECHAI KESSOUS; 1 br.

**Lloyds Bank (BLSA) Ltd** (United Kingdom): Zabala 1500, Casilla 204, Montevideo; tel. (2) 960976; telex 26632; fax (2) 961262; f. 1862; fmrly Bank of London and South America; Man. ANGUS M. MENARY.

#### Bankers' Association

**Asociación de Bancos del Uruguay** (Bank Association of Uruguay): Rincón 468, 2°, Montevideo; tel. (2) 962342; fax (2) 962329; f. 1945; 21 mem. banks; Pres. MARIO SAN CRISTÓBAL.

### STOCK EXCHANGE

**Bolsa de Valores de Montevideo:** Edif. de la Bolsa de Comercio, Misiones 1400, 11000 Montevideo; tel. (2) 965051; telex 26996; fax (2) 961900; f. 1867; 75 mems; Pres. IGNACIO VILASECA.

URUGUAY                                                                                                          *Directory*

### INSURANCE

In late 1993 legislation was introduced providing for an end to the state monopoly of most types of insurance. With effect from mid-1994 the Banco de Seguros del Estado lost its monopoly on all insurance except life, sea transport and fire risks, which have been traditionally open to private underwriters.

**Banco de Seguros del Estado:** Avda Libertador Brig.-General Lavalleja 1465, 11000 Montevideo; tel. (2) 989303; telex 26938; fax (2) 921063; f. 1912; State Insurance Organization; all risks; has the monopoly of all types of insurance and no new companies are allowed to be set up; Pres. NELSON COSTANZO; Vice-Pres. JORGE LUIS FRANZINI.

**Real Uruguaya de Seguros SA:** Julio Herrera y Obes 1365, 2°, Montevideo; tel. (2) 925858; telex 6915; fax (2) 924515; f. 1900; life and property; Pres. JOSÉ LUIS TOMAZINI; Dir JORGE L. CHANES CERRO.

## Trade and Industry

### CHAMBERS OF COMMERCE

**Cámara de Industrias del Uruguay** (Chamber of Industries): Avda General Rondeau 1665, 11100 Montevideo; tel. (2) 927481; fax (2) 920995; f. 1898; Pres. JACINTO MUXI.

**Cámara Nacional de Comercio** (National Chamber of Commerce): Edif. de la Bolsa de Comercio, Misiones 1400, Casilla 1000, 11000 Montevideo; tel. (2) 961277; fax (2) 961243; f. 1867; 1,500 mems; Pres. ALFONSO PABLO VARELA FERNÁNDEZ ; Sec. GUSTAVO VILARÓ SANGUINETTI.

**Cámara Mercantil de Productos del País** (Chamber of Commerce for Local Products): Avda General Rondeau 1908, 11800 Montevideo; tel. (2) 940644; telex 26993; fax (2) 940673; f. 1891; 230 mems; Pres. SIMÓN P. BERKOWITZ; Dir-Gen. GONZALO GONZÁLEZ PIEDRAS.

### INTERNATIONAL TRADING ASSOCIATION

**Consejo Interamericano de Comercio y Producción** (Inter-American Council of Commerce and Production): Edif. de la Bolsa de Comercio, Misiones 1400, 11000 Montevideo; tel. (2) 961277; f. 1941; 510 mems; Pres. JOHN P. PHELPS, Jr; Sec.-Gen. CARLOS ONS COTELO.

### GOVERNMENT ORGANIZATIONS

**Administración Nacional de Combustibles Alcohol y Portland (ANCAP):** Paysandú y Avda Libertador Brig.-General Lavalleja, Casilla 1090, Montevideo; tel. (2) 921136; telex 23168; fax (2) 961493; f. 1931; deals with the transport, refining and sale of petroleum products, and the manufacture of alcohol, spirit and cement; owns research laboratory in Pando-Canelones and a sugar-cane and sugar-beet processing plant in Salto; resumed petroleum exploration in 1985; Pres. JOSÉ LUIS BATLLE; Vice-Pres. Dr RAÚL JUDE; 6,587 employees (1988).

**Administración Nacional de las Usinas y Transmisiones Eléctricas del Estado (ANUTE):** Paraguay 2431, Montevideo; tel. (2) 215; telex 326627; f. 1912; autonomous state body; sole purveyor of electricity; Pres. RUPERTO LONG; 11,618 employees (1988).

**Corporación Nacional para el Desarrollo:** Rincón 528, 7°, Casilla 977, 11000 Montevideo; tel. (2) 962680; telex 6652; fax (2) 962683; f. 1985; national development corporation; mixed-capital organization; obtains 60% of funding from state; Pres. MILKA BARBATO; Dirs. CARLOS GONZÁLEZ ALVAREZ, IGNACIO OTEGUÍ, ROBERTO HORTA.

**Dirección Nacional de Costos, Precios e Ingresos (DINACOPRIN):** Montevideo; tel. (2) 981025; national prices and wages board; Dir CARLOS ARANCET ROMANELLI.

**Instituto Nacional de Pesca (INAPE):** Calle Constituyente 1497, 11200 Montevideo; tel. (2) 404689; telex 6503; fax (2) 413216; national fisheries institute; Dir-Gen. JUAN JOSÉ FERNÁNDEZ PARÉS.

**Obras Sanitarias del Estado (OSE):** Soriano 1613, Montevideo; f. 1962; processing and distribution of drinking water, sinking wells, supplying industrial zones of the country; Pres. Dr JUAN CARLOS PAYSSEE.

**Oficina de Planeamiento y Presupuesto de la Presidencia de la República:** Casa de Gobierno, Edif. Libertad, 3°, Montevideo; tel. (2) 819525; telex 22280; f. 1976; responsible for the implementation of development plans; co-ordinates the policies of the various ministries; advises on the preparation of the budget of public enterprises; Dir JAVIER DE HAEDO.

### EMPLOYERS' ORGANIZATIONS

**Asociación de Importadores y Mayoristas de Almacén** (Importers' and Wholesalers' Association): Edif. de la Bolsa de Comercio, Esc. 317/319, Rincón 454, Montevideo; tel. (2) 956103; f. 1926; 65 mems; Pres. JOSÉ L. BRAGA REQUENA.

**Asociación Rural del Uruguay:** Avda Uruguay 864, Montevideo; tel. (2) 920484; f. 1871; 1,800 mems; Pres. GERARDO GARCÍA PINTOS.

**Comisión Patronal del Uruguay de Asuntos Relacionados con la OIT** (Commission of Uruguayan Employers for Affairs of the ILO): Edif. de la Bolsa de Comercio, Misiones 1400, Casilla 1000, 11000 Montevideo; tel. (2) 961277; fax (2) 961243; f. 1954; mems Cámara Nacional de Comercio, Asociación Comercial del Uruguay; Sec. and Man. GUSTAVO VILARÓ SANGUINETTI.

**Federación Rural del Uruguay:** 18 del Julio 965, 1°, Montevideo; tel. (2) 905583; fax (2) 904791; f. 1915; 2,000 mems; Pres. RAMÓN SIMONET FLETCHER.

**Unión de Exportadores del Uruguay** (Uruguayan Exporters' Association): Edif. Bolsa de Comercio, 2°, Rincón 454, Montevideo; tel. (2) 970105; fax (2) 961117; Pres. CARLOS LANGWAGEN; Exec. Sec. TERESA AISHEMBERG.

### TRADE UNIONS

All trade union activity was under strict control between 1973 and 1985. In June 1973 the central organization (Confederación Nacional de Trabajadores), which claimed some 400,000 members, was declared illegal. In December 1979 a new labour law was submitted to the Council of State allowing three levels of association and optional union membership. A further law, introduced in October 1981, allows for the holding of secret ballots to elect union officials, and the establishment of company unions (sindicatos por empresa) in firms with 15 or more employees. On taking office in March 1985, President Julio María Sanguinetti ordered the restoration of the legal status of the principal workers' and university students' federations.

**Plenario Intersindical de Trabajadores—Convención Nacional de Trabajadores (PIT—CNT):** 18 de Julio 2190, Montevideo; tel. (2) 492267; fax (2) 404160; f. 1966; organization comprising 83 trade unions, 17 labour federations; 320,000 mems; Pres. JOSÉ D'ELÍA; Exec.-Sec. VÍCTOR SEMPRONI.

## Transport

**Ministerio de Obras Públicas y Transporte:** Rincón 561, Montevideo; tel. (2) 957386; telex 22057; fax (2) 962883; exercises control over all state forms of transport: railways, airline, river and maritime fleets; also exercises some control over private transport companies; the Municipal Intendancies are responsible for urban and departmental transport.

**Dirección Nacional de Transporte:** Mercedes 1041, Montevideo; tel. (2) 904613; co-ordinates national and international transport services.

### RAILWAYS

**Administración de los Ferrocarriles del Estado (AFE):** La Paz 1095, Casilla 419, Montevideo; tel. (2) 905866; fax (2) 921530; f. 1952; state organization; 3,002 km of track connecting all parts of the country; there are connections with the Argentine and Brazilian networks; passenger services ceased in 1988; passenger service between Montevideo and Canelones was resumed in mid-1993; Pres. MICHAEL CASTLETON; Dir JULIO CÉSAR HERNÁNDEZ.

### ROADS

In 1989 Uruguay had 9,713 km of motorways (forming the most dense motorway network in South America), connecting Montevideo with the main towns of the interior and the Argentine and Brazilian frontiers. There was also a network of approximately 40,000 km of paved roads under departmental control. In 1989 Uruguay received loans of US $84m. from the Inter-American Development Bank and $81m. from the World Bank for the modernization of major international routes and for the construction of the new 'Ruta 1', which links Montevideo with Buenos Aires. The total cost of the project was estimated to be $257m.

### INLAND WATERWAYS

There are about 1,250 km of navigable waterways which provide an important means of transport.

**Nobleza Naviera, SA:** Avda General Rondeau 2257, Montevideo; tel. (2) 943222; telex 22356; fax (2) 943218; operates cargo services on the River Plate, and the Uruguay and Paraná rivers; Chair. AMÉRICO DEAMBROSI.

### SHIPPING

**Administración Nacional de Combustibles, Alcohol y Portland (ANCAP):** see under Government Organizations; tanker services, also river transport.

**Administración Nacional de Puertos (ANP):** Rambla 25 de Agosto de 1825 160, Montevideo; tel. (2) 950358; telex 22351;

# URUGUAY

fax (2) 958535; f. 1916; plans for transfer to private ownership announced in April 1990; Pres. EDUARDO ALVAREZ MAZZA.

**Prefectura Nacional Naval:** Edif. Comando General de la Armada, 5°, Rambla 25 de Agosto de 1825 s/n, esq. Maciel, Montevideo; tel. (2) 955500; telex 23929; fax (2) 963969; f. 1829; Commdr Rear-Adm. RICARDO MURIALDO.

**Navegación Atlántida, SA:** Plaza Independencia 822, Esc. 901, Montevideo; tel. (2) 983160; telex 6014; f. 1967; ferry services for passengers and vehicles between Argentina and Uruguay; Pres. H. C. PIETRANERA.

## CIVIL AVIATION

Civil aviation is controlled by the following: Dirección General de Aviación Civil; Dirección General de Infrastructura Aeronáutica; Comisión Nacional de Política Aeronáutica.

The main airport is at Carrasco, 21 km from Montevideo, and there are also airports at Paysandú, Rivera, Salto, Melo, Artígas, Punta del Este and Durazno.

**Aero Atlántico:** Montevideo; service to the Falkland Islands.

**Aero Uruguaya SA:** Florida 1280, Apdo 206, Montevideo; tel. (2) 987312; telex 747; cargo charter services to the USA, Europe, Africa and other destinations in South America; Chair. Col ATILIO BONELLI.

**Primeras Líneas Uruguayas de Navegación Aérea (PLUNA):** Colonia 1021, Casilla 1360, Montevideo; tel. (2) 930273; telex 23187; fax (2) 921478; f. 1936, nationalized 1951; transferred to private ownership in 1995, with the controlling stake (51%) acquired by consortium led by Varig, SA (Brazil); operates international services to Argentina, Brazil, Chile, Paraguay and Spain; Pres. ROSARIO MEREA; Gen. Man. JUAN ANDREZ VENZANO.

**TAMU:** Colonia 959, 11100 Montevideo; tel. (2) 900904; telex 22457; fax (2) 982446; f. 1970; branch of Uruguayan Air Force; operates domestic flights and charter flights; Dir Col EDUARDO D. GESTIDO.

# Tourism

The sandy beaches and tropical swamps on the coast and the forests of the interior, with their variety of wild life and vegetation, provide the main tourist attractions. About 80% of tourists come from Argentina, and 20% from Brazil, Paraguay and Chile. Uruguay received some 1,801,000 visitors in 1992. Revenue from the sector amounted to US $381.3m. in that year.

**Dirección Nacional de Turismo:** Agraciada 1409, 4°, 5° y 6°, Montevideo; tel. (2) 904148; supervises and executes national tourism policy.

**Asociación Uruguaya de Agencias de Viajes (AUDAVI):** San José 942, Of. 201, Montevideo; tel. (2) 912326; telex 22675; fax (2) 921972; f. 1951; 100 mems; Pres. FEDERICO GAMBARDELLA; Man. MÓNICA W. DE RAIJ.

# UZBEKISTAN

## Introductory Survey

**Location, Climate, Language, Religion, Flag, Capital**

The Republic of Uzbekistan (formerly the Uzbek Soviet Socialist Republic) is located in Central Asia. It is bordered by Kazakhstan to the north, Turkmenistan to the south, Kyrgyzstan to the east, Tajikistan to the south-east and Afghanistan to the south. The climate is marked by extreme temperatures and low levels of precipitation. Summers are long and hot with average temperatures in July of 32°C (90°F); daytime temperatures often exceed 40°C (104°F). During the short winter there are frequent severe frosts, and temperatures can fall as low as −38°C (−36°F). The official language is Uzbek, a member of the Eastern Turkic language group. Since 1940 it has been written in Cyrillic, although it was due to revert gradually to the Latin script during the 1990s. Islam is the predominant religion. Most Uzbeks are Sunni Muslims (Hanafi school), but there are small communities of Wahhabis, whose influence is reported to be growing; Sufism is relatively well established in southern Uzbekistan. There are also Orthodox Christians among the Slavic communities, and some 65,000 European Jews and 28,000 Central Asian Jews. The national flag (proportions 2 by 1) consists of five unequal horizontal stripes of (from top to bottom) light blue, red, white, red and light green, with a white crescent and 12 white stars near the hoist on the top stripe. The capital is Tashkent.

**Recent History**

The Uzbeks are descendants of nomadic Mongol tribes who mixed with the sedentary inhabitants of Central Asia in the 13th century AD. In the 18th and 19th centuries the most prominent political formations in the region were the khanates of Bukhara, Samarkand and Kokand. Russian control of the territory between the Syr-Dar'ya and Amu-Dar'ya rivers was completed when Russian forces conquered the Khanate of Kokand, in 1876.

Soviet power was first established in parts of Uzbekistan in November 1917. In April 1918 the Turkestan Autonomous Soviet Socialist Republic (ASSR), a vast region in Central Asia including Uzbekistan, was proclaimed, but Soviet forces then withdrew against opposition from the nationalist *basmachi* movement, the White Army and a British expeditionary force. Soviet power was re-established in September 1919, although armed opposition continued until the early 1920s. Bukhara and Khiva became nominally independent people's soviet republics in 1920, but were incorporated into the Turkestan ASSR by 1924. On 27 October 1924 the Uzbek Soviet Socialist Republic (SSR) was established (including, until 1929, the Tajik ASSR). In May 1925 the Uzbek SSR became a constituent republic of the Union of Soviet Socialist Republics (USSR, which had been established in December 1922). In 1936 Karakalpakstan was transferred from the Russian Federation to the Uzbek SSR, none the less retaining its autonomous status.

The National Delimitation of the Central Asian republics of 1924–25 established an Uzbek nation-state for the first time. Its formation was accompanied by the creation of corresponding national symbols, including the development of a new literary language (the ancient Uzbek literary language, Chatagai, was accessible only to a small minority of the population). Campaigns promoting literacy were an integral part of the establishment of the Soviet ideology in the region, and the level of literacy rose from 3.8%, at the 1926 census, to 52.5% in 1932. There was an increase in the provision of educational facilities, which formed an important part in the policy of secularization in the region. The campaign against religion, initially promoted by educational means, became a repressive policy against all who admitted their adherence to Islam. Muslim schools, courts and mosques were closed, and Muslim clergy were subject to persecution.

There had been little industrial development in Central Asia under the Tsarist regime, although the extraction of raw materials was developed. Under the first two Five-Year Plans (1928–33 and 1933–38), however, there was considerable economic growth, aided by the immigration of skilled workers from the Slavic republics of the USSR. Although economic growth continued at a significant rate after the Second World War (during which Uzbekistan's industrial base was enlarged by the transfer of industries from the war-zone), most Uzbeks continued to lead a traditional rural life style, affected only by the huge increase in the amount of cotton grown in the republic.

The policies of *glasnost* (openness) and *perestroika* (restructuring), introduced by the Soviet leader, Mikhail Gorbachev, in the 1980s, did not result in significant political changes in the short term. The traditional respect for authority and the relatively small size of the intelligentsia in Uzbekistan allowed the leadership to hinder, or actively oppose, attempts at political or economic reform. Nevertheless, there was a greater measure of freedom of the press in the late 1980s, allowing discussion of previously unexamined aspects of Uzbek history and contemporary ecological and economic problems. The poor condition of the environment was one major source of popular dissatisfaction. The over-irrigation of land to feed the vast cotton-fields had caused both salination of the soil and, most importantly, the desiccation of the Aral Sea, the southern part of which is in Karakalpakstan, and is a vital element in the ecology of the entire region. By the early 1980s it was evident that excessive drainage of the Amu-Dar'ya and Syr-Dar'ya rivers was resulting in dangerously low levels of water reaching the Aral Sea. The problem was not addressed, however, until the introduction of *glasnost* in the media.

Environmental problems and the status of the Uzbek language were among the issues on which Uzbekistan's first major non-communist political movement, Birlik (Unity), campaigned. It was formed in 1989 by a group of intellectuals in Tashkent, but quickly grew to be the main challenger to the ruling Communist Party of Uzbekistan (CPU). However, the movement was not granted official registration, and its attempts to nominate a candidate in the 1989 elections to the USSR's Congress of People's Deputies were unsuccessful. Nevertheless, its campaign for recognition of Uzbek (and not Russian) as the official language of the republic led to the adoption of legislation, in October of that year, which declared Uzbek to be the state language.

On 18 February 1990 elections were held to the 500-seat Uzbek Supreme Soviet (legislature). Members of Birlik were not permitted to stand as candidates, and many leading members of the CPU stood unopposed, as had been the tradition in old-style Soviet elections. In such constituencies there were isolated protests by opposition groups. The new Supreme Soviet convened in March and elected Islam Karimov, the First Secretary (leader) of the CPU, to the newly-created post of executive President. Shakurulla Mirsaidov was elected Chairman of the Council of Ministers (premier). In November there was a reorganization of government structures. The Council of Ministers was abolished and replaced by a Cabinet of Ministers, headed by the President of the Republic.

In April 1991 Uzbekistan agreed, together with eight other Soviet republics, to sign a new Union Treaty to redefine the state structure of the USSR. However, on 19 August, the day before the signing was to take place, a State Committee for the State of Emergency (SCSE) attempted to stage a *coup d'état* in Moscow. President Karimov did not initially oppose the coup, and some opposition leaders in Uzbekistan were temporarily detained. However, once it became clear that the coup had failed, Karimov declared that the orders of the SCSE were invalid. On 31 August, after the coup had collapsed, an extraordinary session of the Supreme Soviet voted to declare the republic independent and changed its name to the Republic of Uzbekistan. The CPU voted to dissociate itself from the Communist Party of the Soviet Union, and in November 1991 the party was restructured as the People's Democratic Party of Uzbekistan (PDPU), with Karimov remaining as its leader.

After its declaration of independence, Uzbekistan sought to develop relations with other former Soviet republics, in particular the four neighbouring Central Asian states. In October 1991 Uzbekistan signed, with seven other (former) Soviet republics, a treaty establishing an economic community, and in November it agreed to a draft of the proposed Union of Sovereign States. These agreements were nullified by the agreement between the three Slavic republics, in early December, to establish a Commonwealth of Independent States (CIS, see p. 126). On 13 December Uzbekistan (together with the other four Central Asian republics) agreed to join the CIS, providing it would be acknowledged as a co-founder of the Commonwealth. Uzbek membership was formalized at a ceremony in Almaty (Kazakhstan), on 21 December, when Karimov agreed, together with 10 other republican leaders, to dissolve the USSR and formally establish the CIS.

Uzbekistan's membership of the CIS was followed, on 29 December 1991, by direct presidential elections, which were won by Karimov with a reported 86% of the total votes. His only rival (winning 12% of the votes) was Muhammad Solikh, the leader of the Erk (Freedom) opposition party, which had been established as an offshoot of Birlik in 1990. Birlik itself was banned from contesting the election, as it had still not been granted official registration as a political party. A referendum was held simultaneously, in which 98.2% of participants endorsed Uzbekistan's independence.

During 1992 the PDPU remained dominant both in the Supreme Soviet and the Cabinet of Ministers, a position indistinguishable from that held by the CPU during the Soviet period. Under Karimov's increasingly authoritarian leadership, there was widespread repression of opposition and Islamic groups, which included brutal physical attacks on several of their leaders and the banning of all religious parties. In order to justify such oppressive measures, the Government used the example of neighbouring Tajikistan, where religious, ethnic and ideological conflicts had combined to provoke a violent civil war (see below). Uzbekistan's new Constitution, adopted on 8 December, firmly enshrined the concept of state secularism. It also guaranteed a democratic multi-party system, freedom of expression and the observance of human rights. However, on the same day as the adoption of the Constitution, three leading opposition members who were attending an international conference on human rights in the Kyrgyz capital, Bishkek, were seized by Uzbek security police on charges of sedition. (Although they were subsequently released, one of their number was put on trial.) On the following day Birlik was banned for its allegedly subversive activities. The Constitution also provided for a new, smaller legislature, the 250-member Oly Majlis (Supreme Assembly). However, until the election of the Majlis in late 1994, the Supreme Soviet was to be retained as the republican parliament.

The Government's repressive treatment of opposition and religious activists provoked strong criticism by international human rights organizations during 1992; however, there was no indication of a more liberal policy towards dissenters in the following year. According to an announcement by the Ministry of Justice in February 1993, some 166 members of Birlik had been arrested in 1991–93, and criminal proceedings had been initiated against 20. Throughout the year opposition activists disappeared, were abducted or attacked, both in Uzbekistan and abroad. Restriction of the media was also intensified: in mid-1993 the Government instructed all newspapers and periodicals to be re-registered with the State Committee for the Press; the process was completed in December, when only organs of state and government were permitted official registration.

There was no liberalization in the Government's attitude towards its opponents during 1994, and, despite a pledge, in May, by President Karimov that all political parties would be able to participate in the forthcoming election to the Oly Majlis, in the event, only the PDPU and its ally, Progress of the Fatherland (PF), were permitted to register and thus take part. At the election, which was held on 25 December (with a second round of voting in January 1995), the PDPU won 69 of the 250 seats, while the PF gained 14. The remaining 167 deputies elected had been nominated by local councils rather than by political parties; however, the overwhelming majority of these deputies (some 120) were members of the PDPU, and thus the party's domination of the Majlis was retained. Approximately 94% of the registered electorate was reported to have participated in the election. In January 1995 Karimov announced that the Government would welcome a diversification of opinions in the Oly Majlis and that it would not object to the formation of blocs within the assembly. In February a new political party, the Adolat (Justice) Social Democratic Party of Uzbekistan, was registered, and immediately declared its intention to establish such a parliamentary faction (it claimed to have the support of some 47 deputies within the Majlis). A referendum, held in March, produced a 99.6% vote in favour of extending Karimov's presidential term from 1997 to 2000, ostensibly to coincide with parliamentary elections. In April 1995 several members of Erk were imprisoned for allegedly attempting to provide military training overseas for Uzbek citizens in preparation for a *coup d'état*. In May two new political formations emerged: the Milli Tiklanish (National Revival) Democratic Party and the Khalk Birliki (People's Unity) Movement. Both were reported to be pro-Government, and were officially registered in early June.

Like several other Soviet republics in the years prior to, and immediately after, the dissolution of the USSR, Uzbekistan experienced outbreaks of inter-ethnic strife, beginning in June 1989, when conflict was reported between ethnic Uzbeks and the Meskhetian Turk minority. The origins of the conflict were unclear, but seemed to stem from high levels of unemployment and the shortage of housing in the Fergana region. During a two-week period in early June at least 100 people died during rioting, most of them Meskhetians. In February and March 1990 there was a resurgence of inter-ethnic conflict. On 3 March, in Parkent, near Tashkent, three people died after clashes between demonstrators and the police. In mid-1990 there was further inter-ethnic tension in connection with clashes in Osh, a region in Kyrgyzstan with an Uzbek majority (see chapter on Kyrgyzstan). Border crossings were sealed to prevent up to 15,000 armed Uzbek citizens crossing the Kyrgyz–Uzbek border to join the Uzbeks in Kyrgyzstan. Karimov declared a state of emergency in Andizhan region (which borders Kyrgyzstan's Osh region).

Although Uzbekistan has retained full membership of the CIS since that body's establishment in December 1991, its closest relations are with the four neighbouring Central Asian republics—Kazakhstan, Kyrgyzstan, Tajikistan and Turkmenistan—also CIS members. In early 1994 Uzbekistan formed an economic union with Kazakhstan and Kyrgyzstan, although it abandoned plans to introduce a common currency with the former. All five republics established, in January 1994, a joint fund and a permanent committee to examine and attempt to redress the ecological damage to the Aral Sea and also to improve the health of those living in the region. With the exception of Tajikistan, each republic pledged 1% of their respective budgets for 1994 to the fund. President Karimov was anxious to prevent the spread of Islamic extremism from other countries in the region, in particular Tajikistan. In late 1992 the Uzbek Government agreed to send troops to Tajikistan as part of a CIS peace-keeping contingent, and it also tightened border controls with Tajikistan in an attempt to prevent the civil conflict there from spreading into Uzbekistan. It was also reported that the Uzbek Government actively supported the communist regime in Tajikistan in its efforts to suppress opposition Islamic and democratic forces. This was attributed in part to Uzbek concerns for their co-nationals in Tajikistan (who form that republic's largest ethnic minority, numbering more than 1m. people). In April 1995 President Karimov urged the various parties in the Tajik conflict to form a national congress, which would include outlawed opposition parties. It was claimed that the Uzbek Government provided military and financial assistance to the Afghan militia leader, Gen. Rashid Dostam (an ethnic Uzbek), whose forces controlled parts of northern Afghanistan (which has a short border with southern Uzbekistan). In October 1994 the Uzbek Government denied that it had become militarily involved in Afghanistan; later in the same month, however, President Rabbani of Afghanistan reiterated his claim that Uzbekistan was supplying military equipment and ammunition to Gen. Dostam.

Relations with the Russian Federation, the most influential member state of the CIS, have been intermittently strained by the issue of Uzbekistan's large ethnic Russian population. Uzbekistan has repeatedly refused to grant dual citizenship to its ethnic Russian minority, and since independence many thousands of Russians have emigrated from the republic. This, in turn, has adversely affected Uzbekistan's economic and cultural life, as Russians are believed to form the best-educated and most highly-skilled social group.

### Government

Under the terms of the Constitution of 8 December 1992, Uzbekistan is a secular, democratic presidential republic. The

# UZBEKISTAN

directly-elected President is Head of State and also holds supreme executive power; he may serve for no more than two consecutive five-year terms. The Government (Cabinet of Ministers) is subordinate to the President, who appoints its Chairman (Prime Minister), Deputy Chairmen and Ministers (subject to the approval of the legislature). The highest legislative body is the 250-member Oly Majlis (Supreme Assembly), elected for a five-year term (the Oly Majlis replaced the 500-member Supreme Soviet following legislative elections in December 1994 and January 1995). The Majlis may be dissolved by the President (with the approval of the Constitutional Court). For administrative purposes, Uzbekistan is divided into 12 regions and one autonomous republic (Karakalpakstan).

## Defence

Prior to independence, Uzbekistan had no armed forces separate from those of the USSR. The establishment of Uzbek national armed forces was initiated in 1992, and, by June 1994, these comprised approximately 45,000, including an army of 35,000 and an air force of 4,000. There were also paramilitary forces numbering some 8,000 (including a 700-strong National Guard). Compulsory military service lasts for 18 months. Projected defence expenditure for 1994 was US $375m. In May 1992 Uzbekistan signed a collective security treaty with five other members of the Commonwealth of Independent States (CIS). In July 1994 Uzbekistan joined NATO's 'partnership for peace' programme of military co-operation (see p. 192).

## Economic Affairs

In 1993, according to preliminary estimates by the World Bank, Uzbekistan's gross national product (GNP), measured at average 1991–93 prices, was US $21,100m., equivalent to $960 per head. During 1985–93, it was estimated, GNP per head decreased, in real terms, at an average annual rate of 1.6%. The population increased by an annual average of 2.4% in 1985–93. Gross domestic product (GDP) decreased, in real terms, by 0.9% in 1991, and was estimated to have declined by a further 9.6% in 1992, by 2.4% in 1993 and by 3.5% in 1994.

In 1992 agriculture (including forestry) contributed 35.9% of GNP and employed 43.4% of the working population. Some 60% of the country's land is covered by desert and steppe, while the remainder comprises fertile valleys watered by two major river systems. The massive irrigation of arid areas has greatly increased production of the major crop, cotton, but has caused devastating environmental problems (most urgently the desiccation of the Aral Sea). Uzbekistan is among the five largest producers of cotton in the world, and the crop accounts for more than 40% of the value of total agricultural production. Other major crops include grain, vegetables and fruit. Silkworm breeding is also important, as is the production of astrakhan wool. Since independence the Government has striven to reduce the area under cultivation of cotton in order to produce more grain. Private farming was legalized in 1992; by February 1995 the process of transforming Uzbekistan's 715 state farms into co-operative and private farms, joint-stock companies and other forms of ownership was nearing completion. In 1992 agricultural output declined by about 7%, compared with the previous year.

In 1992 industry (including mining, manufacturing, construction and power) contributed 41.6% of GNP and provided 21.3% of employment. Industrial activity focuses largely on the processing of agricultural and mineral raw materials as well as the manufacturing of agricultural machinery, chemical products and metallurgy. Industrial production declined by an estimated 8% in 1993, compared with the previous year.

Uzbekistan is well endowed with mineral deposits, in particular natural gas, petroleum and coal. Natural gas is an important export commodity and is also used domestically for industrial purposes and power generation. There are also large reserves of gold, silver, uranium, copper, lead, zinc and tungsten. Uzbekistan is the eighth largest producer of gold in the world, and the Murantau mine, in the Kyzylkum desert, is reportedly the world's largest single open-cast gold mine, producing some 70% of Uzbekistan's average annual output of 70 metric tons. In 1991 89.2% of electricity was generated by thermal power stations, while the remaining 10.8% came from hydroelectric sources.

In 1992 Uzbekistan recorded a visible trade deficit of US $259m., while there was a deficit of $369m. on the current account of the balance of payments. In 1990 about 83% of Uzbekistan's trade was conducted with other republics of the USSR, and in 1992 the proportion remained unchanged, despite attempts to expand economic links with non-traditional trading partners. The principal imports are machinery, light industrial goods, food and raw materials. The principal exports are cotton, textiles, machinery, chemicals, food and energy products.

The 1992 budget registered a deficit of 54,100m. roubles (12% of GDP). At the end of 1993 Uzbekistan's total external debt was US $739.3m., of which $735.9m. was long-term public debt. The annual rate of inflation was 1,312% in 1993, declining to 460% in 1994. In December 1993 some 13,300 people were officially registered as unemployed, although the true level was believed to be considerably higher.

In 1992 Uzbekistan became a member of the IMF and the World Bank, also joining, as a 'Country of Operations', the European Bank for Reconstruction and Development (EBRD, see p. 140). In the same year Uzbekistan was admitted, with five other former republics of the USSR, to the Economic Co-operation Organization (ECO, see p. 238). In 1993 Uzbekistan became a member of the Asian Development Bank (ADB, see p. 107), and in mid-1994 the republic formalized an agreement on a common economic area with neighbouring Kazakhstan and Kyrgyzstan.

The collapse of the USSR in December 1991 and the manifold economic problems that ensued—most particularly the widespread disruptions in the former Soviet trading system—did not initially affect Uzbekistan as adversely as many other republics. This was largely due to the country's near self-sufficiency in energy sources and agricultural products, as well as continued demand for its exports of raw materials. However, the comparatively limited economic decline in 1991 was followed by a far sharper decline in 1992 (when GDP decreased, in real terms, by an estimated 9.6%), as shortages of primary products and the breakdown in inter-republican trade became more acute. Moreover, the fact that Uzbekistan initially retained the rouble as its currency meant that the country was inevitably affected by developments in other republics remaining in the rouble area, in particular a rapid increase in the rate of inflation. Nevertheless, in 1992 the Government announced measures designed to lead to a gradual transition to a market-economic system (including the extensive liberalization of prices and privatization of state assets, as well as financial and fiscal reforms). The need for greater economic diversity—particularly the wider exploitation of Uzbekistan's mineral and energy resources, as opposed to the traditional reliance on the production and export of cotton—was also emphasized. In this connection the Government encouraged the establishment of joint ventures with foreign enterprises; more than 1,400 had been created by May 1995.

The economy performed slightly better in 1993 and 1994; none the less, GDP declined, in real terms, by an estimated 2.4% and 3.5%, respectively. Although the annual rate of inflation was alarmingly high in 1993, it declined significantly in 1994. The Government's economic programme for 1995 aimed to reduce the monthly rate of inflation to 2% by the end of that year and to stabilize the new national currency, the sum, the value of which declined rapidly in late 1994 after entering circulation on 1 July. The privatization programme achieved considerable success during 1992–94, and in February 1995 it was reported that more than 50% of the labour force were working in the private sector. In late 1994 and early 1995 international donor institutions granted Uzbekistan a series of loans designed to assist the privatization programme and support the sum.

## Social Welfare

A comprehensive social welfare system was introduced in Uzbekistan during the Soviet period. This was modified following the disintegration of the USSR in December 1991, with certain provisions being made to protect those social groups most affected by the country's transition to a market-economic system. Foremost among these reforms was the establishment, in 1991–92, of three extrabudgetary funds, the Pension Fund, the Social Insurance Fund and the Employment Fund. In 1994 the Pension Fund and the Social Insurance Fund were re-organized into a larger Social Insurance Fund.

In 1990 there were 124 hospital beds and 36 physicians per 10,000 inhabitants. The rate of infant mortality was 35.5 per 1,000 live births in 1992. In 1993 budgetary expenditure on social and cultural services (including education) was estimated to be 693,700m. roubles (or 38% of total expenditure).

# UZBEKISTAN

## Education

Until the early 1990s education was based on the Soviet model, but some changes were subsequently introduced, including a greater emphasis on Uzbek history and literature, and study of the Arabic script. In 1988/89 76.8% of pupils at day schools were educated in Uzbek. Other languages used included Russian (15.0%), Kazakh (2.9%), Karakalpak (2.4%), Tajik (2.3%), Turkmen (0.4%) and Kyrgyz (0.2%). Primary and secondary education (Grades one to 11) is provided at general schools for children between six and 16 years of age. However, general education is compulsory only until the age of 14 (Grades one to nine). In the 1992/93 academic year 4.9m. pupils were enrolled in general schools (84% of the relevant age group). In that year 5,300 of the total 8,500 general schools in Uzbekistan operated in two shifts, affecting 25% of students. In 1992/93 there were 220,000 students in 440 vocational schools. Higher education was provided in 53 institutes, with a total enrolment of 321,682 students. In 1992–93 a number of religious schools (madrasahs) of the Wahhabi branch of Islam were established with Saudi Arabian financial assistance, providing education free of charge. In 1993 the construction of a Saudi-financed university at Margilan was under way; when completed it was to offer places for 5,000 students. However, legislation adopted in May 1993 banned private educational establishments in Uzbekistan; those already in existence were reportedly to be transferred to state control. In 1993 budgetary expenditure on education was estimated to be 442,700m. roubles (some 25% of total expenditure).

## Weights and Measures

The metric system is in force.

# Statistical Survey

Principal sources (unless otherwise indicated): IMF, *Uzbekistan, Economic Review*; World Bank, *Statistical Handbook: States of the Former USSR*; World Bank, *Uzbekistan: An Agenda for Economic Reform*.

## Area and Population

### AREA, POPULATION AND DENSITY

| | |
|---|---|
| Area (sq km) | 447,400* |
| Population (census result) 12 January 1989 | 19,905,158 |
| Population (official estimates at 1 January) | |
| 1991 | 20,739,000 |
| 1993 | 21,700,000† |
| Density (per sq km) at 1 January 1993 | 48.5 |

* 172,740 sq miles.
† Provisional.

### POPULATION BY NATIONALITY
(census of 12 January 1989)

| | % |
|---|---|
| Uzbek | 71.4 |
| Russian | 8.3 |
| Tajik | 4.7 |
| Kazakh | 4.1 |
| Tatar | 2.4 |
| Others* | 9.1 |
| **Total** | **100.0** |

* Including Karakalpaks, Crimean Tatars, Koreans, Kyrgyz, Ukrainians, Turkmen and Turks.

### PRINCIPAL TOWNS
(estimated population at 1 January 1990)

| | | | |
|---|---|---|---|
| Tashkent (capital) | 2,094,000 | Karshi | 163,000 |
| Samarkand | 370,000 | Chirchik | 159,000 |
| Namangan | 312,000 | Angren | 133,000 |
| Andizhan | 297,000 | Urgench | 129,000 |
| Bukhara | 228,000 | Margilan | 125,000 |
| Fergana | 198,000 | Almalyk | 116,000 |
| Kokand | 176,000 | Navoi | 110,000 |
| Nukus | 175,000 | Jizak | 108,000 |

Source: UN, *Demographic Yearbook*.

### BIRTHS AND DEATHS (per 1,000)

| | 1987 | 1988 | 1989 |
|---|---|---|---|
| Birth rate | 37.0 | 35.2 | 33.3 |
| Death rate | 6.9 | 6.8 | 6.3 |

### EMPLOYMENT (annual averages, '000 persons)

| | 1990 | 1991 | 1992 |
|---|---|---|---|
| Agriculture and forestry | 3,120 | 3,456 | 3,577 |
| Industry | 1,201 | 1,179 | 1,135 |
| Construction | 710 | 676 | 622 |
| Transport and communications | 250 | 250 | 222 |
| Trade and catering | 459 | 464 | 462 |
| Other activities of the material sphere | 144 | 149 | 123 |
| Government | 119 | 103 | 96 |
| Other non-material services | 1,938 | 1,977 | 1,998 |
| **Total** | **7,941** | **8,255** | **8,234** |

## Agriculture

### PRINCIPAL CROPS ('000 metric tons)

| | 1991 | 1992 | 1993 |
|---|---|---|---|
| Wheat | 610 | 964 | 950* |
| Rice (paddy) | 515 | 539 | 500* |
| Barley | 324 | 361 | 300* |
| Maize | 431 | 367 | 341* |
| Potatoes | 351 | 365 | 425 |
| Sunflower seed | 5* | 5 | 5† |
| Cottonseed | 2,644* | 2,452 | 2,537* |
| Vegetables‡ | 3,858 | 4,244 | 3,500 |
| Grapes | 481 | 439 | 480† |
| Other fruit | 517 | 701 | 520† |
| Tobacco (leaves) | 21 | 19* | 20† |
| Cotton (lint) | 1,443 | 1,306 | 1,376 |

* Unofficial figure.   † FAO estimate.
‡ Including watermelons, melons, pumpkins and squash.

Source: FAO, *Production Yearbook*.

### LIVESTOCK ('000 head at 1 January)

| | 1991 | 1992 | 1993 |
|---|---|---|---|
| Horses | 105 | 113 | 123 |
| Cattle | 4,600 | 5,113 | 5,275 |
| Pigs | 700 | 654 | 529 |
| Sheep | 8,370 | 8,275 | 8,407 |
| Goats | 830 | 918 | 961 |
| Chickens | 35,000* | 34,000* | 33,000† |

* Unofficial figure.   † FAO estimate.

Source: FAO, *Production Yearbook*.

# UZBEKISTAN

## LIVESTOCK PRODUCTS ('000 metric tons)

|  | 1991 | 1992 | 1993 |
|---|---|---|---|
| Beef and veal | 323 | 323 | 265* |
| Mutton and lamb | 62 | 68 | 55† |
| Pig meat | 44 | 36 | 46* |
| Poultry meat | 60 | 39 | 58† |
| Cows' milk | 3,207 | 3,679 | 2,800* |
| Sheep's milk† | 34 | 40 | 40 |
| Goats' milk† | 90 | 80 | 95 |
| Butter | 14.6 | 17.3 | 12.0* |
| Hen eggs | 130.0* | 90.0* | 88.0† |
| Wool: |  |  |  |
| greasy | 25.3 | 27.4 | 26.0† |
| scoured | 15.2 | 16.4 | 15.6† |

\* Unofficial figure    † FAO estimate(s)

Source: FAO, *Production Yearbook*.

## Fishing

('000 metric tons, live weight)

|  | 1991 | 1992 |
|---|---|---|
| Common carp | 1.7 | 1.6 |
| Roach | 1.3 | 0.9 |
| Silver carp | 11.7 | 14.5 |
| Hoven's carp | 10.9 | 8.3 |
| Other fishes | 1.8 | 2.9 |
| **Total catch** | **27.4** | **28.1** |

Source: FAO, *Yearbook of Fishery Statistics*.

## Mining

('000 metric tons, unless otherwise indicated)

|  | 1992 | 1993 | 1994 |
|---|---|---|---|
| Coal | 4,680 | 3,800 | 3,800 |
| Crude petroleum (incl. gas condensate) | 3,293 | 3,943 | 5,517 |
| Natural gas (million cu m) | 42,800 | 45,800 | 47,200 |

## Industry

### SELECTED PRODUCTS

('000 metric tons, unless otherwise indicated)

|  | 1990 | 1991 | 1992 |
|---|---|---|---|
| Woven cotton fabrics | 469.1 | 391.7 | 482.0 |
| Paper | 25.8 | 20.2 | 15.8 |
| Mineral fertilizers | 1,762.3 | 1,660.1 | 1,361.0 |
| Insecticides | 40.7 | 34.6 | 28.3 |
| Plastics | 154.9 | 142.1 | 94.0 |
| Cement | 6,388.6 | 6,190.5 | 5,934.5 |
| Rolled metal products | 955.7 | 749.3 | 604.0 |
| Footwear (million pairs) | 46.7 | 45.4 | 39.2 |
| Refrigerators and freezers ('000 units) | 201.0 | 211.9 | 84.2 |
| Tractors ('000 units) | 23.2 | 21.1 | 16.9 |
| Electric energy (million kWh) | 56,300 | 54,200 | 50,900 |

**Mineral fertilizers** ('000 metric tons): 1,273.4 in 1993; 809.0 in 1994.
**Electric energy** (million kWh): 49,100 in 1993; 47,700 in 1994.

## Finance

### CURRENCY AND EXCHANGE RATES

**Monetary Units**
100 teen = 1 sum.

**Sterling and Dollar Equivalents** (31 December 1994)
£1 sterling = 39.11 sum;
US $1 = 25.00 sum;
1,000 sum = £25.57 = $40.00.

Note: Prior to the introduction of the sum (see below), Uzbekistan used a transitional currency, the sum-coupon. This had been introduced in November 1993 to circulate alongside (and initially at par with) the Russian (formerly Soviet) rouble. Based on the official rate of exchange, the average value of the Soviet currency (roubles per US dollar) was: 0.6274 in 1989; 0.5856 in 1990; 0.5819 in 1991. However, a multiple exchange rate system was in operation, with separate non-commercial and tourist rates. A commercial exchange rate was introduced on 1 November 1990, replacing the official rate for most transactions. The commercial rate (roubles per US dollar) was: 1.692 at 31 December 1990; 1.671 at 31 December 1991. Between November 1989 and April 1991 the tourist exchange rate valued the rouble at one-tenth of the official rate. In April 1991 this rate, renamed the 'special rate', was set at $1 = 27.6 roubles. It was subsequently adjusted. Following the dissolution of the USSR in December 1991, Russia and several other former Soviet republics retained the rouble as their monetary unit. The average interbank market rate in 1992 was $1 = 222.1 Russian roubles. The Russian rouble ceased to be legal tender in Uzbekistan from 15 April 1994, but some of the figures in this Survey are still in terms of roubles.

On 1 July 1994 a permanent currency, the sum, was introduced to replace the sum-coupon at 1 sum per 1,000 coupons. The initial exchange rate was set at US $1 = 7.00 sum. Sum-coupons continued to circulate, but from 15 October 1994 the sum became the sole legal tender.

### BUDGET (million roubles)*

| Revenue† | 1991 | 1992 | 1993‡ |
|---|---|---|---|
| Corporate income tax | 3,800 | 23,900 | 330,900 |
| Individual income tax | 1,800 | 11,400 | 139,100 |
| Social security contributions | — | — | 69,100 |
| Taxes on domestic goods and services | 6,100 | 51,200 | 534,900 |
| Value-added tax | — | 38,400 | 491,200 |
| Excises | — | 9,500 | 40,400 |
| Taxes on inter-republican and international trade | 200 | 4,700 | 75,600 |
| Other receipts | 6,900 | 48,600 | 454,200 |
| Revenue from cotton marketing | — | 29,300 | 241,800 |
| 6% resource payment | — | — | 107,200 |
| **Total** | **18,800** | **139,800** | **1,603,800** |

| Expenditure§ | 1991 | 1992 | 1993‡ |
|---|---|---|---|
| National economy | 5,900 | 20,900 | 232,800 |
| Social and cultural services | 9,200 | 70,800 | 693,700 |
| Education | 5,300 | 45,300 | 442,700 |
| Health and sports | 2,700 | 20,900 | 196,600 |
| Food subsidies for consumers | 3,300 | 26,000 | 196,400 |
| Other subsidies and transfers to population | 5,400 | 22,400 | 163,900 |
| Services | 100 | 8,700 | 96,300 |
| Defence, public order and safety | 200 | 11,700 | 207,400 |
| State authorities and administration | 300 | 2,800 | 46,300 |
| Other purposes | 8,100 | 39,300 | 264,500 |
| Compensation to mining enterprises | n.a. | n.a. | 86,200 |
| **Total** | **32,400** | **193,900** | **1,805,000** |

\* Excluding the accounts of extrabudgetary funds.
† Excluding grants received (million roubles): 11,400 in 1991.
‡ Including estimates for the fourth quarter of the year.
§ Excluding net lending (million roubles): 525,000 in 1993.

### COST OF LIVING
(Index of retail prices; base: previous year = 100)

|  | 1991 | 1992 | 1993 |
|---|---|---|---|
| All items | 205.0 | 627.7 | 951.1 |

## UZBEKISTAN

**NATIONAL ACCOUNTS** (million roubles at current prices)

**Gross National Product by Economic Activity**

|  | 1991 | 1992 |
|---|---|---|
| Agriculture (incl. forestry) | 22,900 | 149,500 |
| Industry (incl. mining) | 15,600 | 119,000 |
| Construction | 6,400 | 54,400 |
| Trade | 2,400 | 10,300 |
| Transport and communications | 2,600 | 20,200 |
| Other services | 11,600 | 63,500 |
| **Total** | 61,500 | 416,900 |

**BALANCE OF PAYMENTS** (US $ million)

|  | 1992 |
|---|---|
| Merchandise exports (excl. former USSR) | 869 |
| Merchandise imports (excl. former USSR) | −929 |
| Inter-republican trade balance | −199 |
| **Trade balance** | −259 |
| Services (net) | −110 |
| **Current balance** | −369 |
| Capital investment (net) | 165 |
| Net errors and omissions | 97 |
| **Overall balance** | −107 |

## External Trade

**PRINCIPAL COMMODITIES** (million roubles)

| Imports | 1989 | 1990 |
|---|---|---|
| Petroleum and gas | 1,032 | 888 |
| Iron and steel | 676 | 661 |
| Non-ferrous metals | 424 | 409 |
| Chemicals and products | 1,111 | 1,147 |
| Machine-building | 3,553 | 3,625 |
| Wood and paper products | 725 | 560 |
| Construction materials | 228 | 205 |
| Light industry | 2,761 | 2,963 |
| Food industry | 2,156 | 1,983 |
| Agricultural products (unprocessed) | 661 | 1,309 |
| **Total** (incl. others) | 14,158 | 14,662 |
| Foreign | 2,112 | 2,798 |
| Inter-republican (USSR) | 12,046 | 11,864 |

| Exports | 1989 | 1990 |
|---|---|---|
| Petroleum and gas | 646 | 598 |
| Electric energy | 214 | 207 |
| Non-ferrous metals | 468 | 447 |
| Chemicals and products | 894 | 853 |
| Machine-building | 1,190 | 1,231 |
| Light industry | 4,659 | 4,242 |
| Food industry | 795 | 824 |
| Agricultural products (unprocessed) | 757 | 447 |
| **Total** (incl. others) | 10,169 | 9,351 |
| Foreign | 1,628 | 1,182 |
| Inter-republican (USSR) | 8,542 | 8,169 |

**1991** (million roubles): Imports 21,475 (Foreign 3,709, Inter-republican 17,766); Exports 19,535 (Foreign 2,196, Inter-republican 17,339).
**1992** (preliminary figures, million roubles): Imports 191,885 (Former USSR 162,246, Other countries 29,639); Exports 150,518 (Former USSR 123,136, Other countries 27,382).
**1994** (US $ million): Imports 2,475 (Commonwealth of Independent States 1,325, Other countries 1,150); Exports 2,223 (Commonwealth of Independent States 1,279, Other countries 944).

**PRINCIPAL TRADING PARTNERS (FORMER USSR)** (million roubles)

| Imports | 1992 |
|---|---|
| Belarus | 9,347 |
| Kazakhstan | 19,822 |
| Kyrgyzstan | 5,462 |
| Russia | 85,818 |
| Tajikistan | 5,126 |
| Turkmenistan | 11,395 |
| Ukraine | 22,137 |
| **Total** (incl. others) | 162,249 |

| Exports | 1992 |
|---|---|
| Belarus | 4,259 |
| Kazakhstan | 13,786 |
| Kyrgyzstan | 4,527 |
| Moldova | 2,474 |
| Russia | 65,387 |
| Tajikistan | 3,708 |
| Turkmenistan | 6,561 |
| Ukraine | 17,291 |
| **Total** (incl. others) | 123,157 |

## Communications Media

|  | 1992 |
|---|---|
| Daily newspapers: |  |
|   Titles | 12 |
|   Average circulation ('000) | 452 |
| Non-daily newspapers: |  |
|   Titles | 43 |
|   Average circulation ('000) | 1,279 |
| Other periodicals: |  |
|   Titles | 61 |
|   Average circulation ('000) | 1,598 |

Source: UNESCO, *Statistical Yearbook*.

**Telephones** ('000 main lines in use): 1,350 in 1989; 1,420 in 1990; 1,478 in 1991. (Source: UN, *Statistical Yearbook*.)

## Education

(1992/93)

|  | Institutions | Students |
|---|---|---|
| General schools (primary and secondary) | 8,500 | 4,900,000 |
| Vocational schools | 440 | 220,000 |
| Higher schools (incl. universities) | 53 | 321,682 |

# Directory

## The Constitution

A new Constitution was adopted by the Supreme Soviet on 8 December 1992. It declares Uzbekistan to be a secular, democratic and presidential republic. Basic human rights are guaranteed.

The highest legislative body is the Oly Majlis (Supreme Assembly), comprising 250 deputies. It is elected for a term of five years. Parliament may be dissolved by the President (by agreement with the Constitutional Court). The Oly Majlis enacts normal legislation and constitutional legislation, elects its own officials, the judges of the higher courts and the Chairman of the State Committee for Environmental Protection. It confirms the President's appointments to ministerial office, the procuracy-general and the governorship of the Central Bank. It must ratify international treaties, changes to borders and presidential decrees on emergency situations. Legislation may be initiated by the deputies, by the President, by the higher courts, by the Procurator-General and by the Autonomous Republic of Karakalpakstan.

The President of the Republic, who is directly elected by the people for a five-year term, is Head of State and holds supreme executive power. An individual may be elected President for a maximum of two consecutive terms. The President is required to form and supervise the Cabinet of Ministers, appointing the Chairman (Prime Minister) and Ministers, subject to confirmation by the Oly Majlis. The President also nominates the candidates for appointment to the higher courts and certain offices of state, subject to confirmation by the Oly Majlis. The President appoints the judges of the lower courts and the khokims (governors) of the regions. Legislation may be initiated, reviewed and returned to the Oly Majlis by the President, who must promulgate all laws. The President may dissolve the Oly Majlis. The President is also Commander-in-Chief of the Armed Forces and may declare a state of emergency or a state of war (subject to confirmation by the Oly Majlis within three days).

The Cabinet of Ministers is the Government of the country; it is subordinate to the President, who appoints its Chairman, Deputy Chairmen and Ministers, subject to the approval of the legislature. Local government is carried out by elected councils and appointed khokims, the latter having significant personal authority and responsibility.

The exercise of judicial power is independent of government. The higher courts, of which the judges are nominated by the President and confirmed by the Oly Majlis, consist of the Constitutional Court, the Supreme Court and the High Economic Court. There is also a Supreme Court of the Autonomous Republic of Karakalpakstan. Lower courts, including economic courts, are based in the regions, districts and towns. The Procurator-General's office is responsible for supervising the observance of the law.

## The Government

### HEAD OF STATE

**President of the Republic:** ISLAM A. KARIMOV (elected 24 March 1990; re-elected, by direct popular vote, 29 December 1991; term of office extended to 2000, by popular referendum, 27 March 1995).

### CABINET OF MINISTERS
(June 1995)

**Chairman (Prime Minister):** ABDULKHASHIM M. MUTALOV.
**First Deputy Chairman:** ISMAIL KH. JURABEKOV.
**Deputy Chairmen:** YURY F. PAYGIN, SAIDMUKHTAR S. SAIDKAZYMOV, MIRABROR Z. USMONOV, RUSTAM R. YUNUSOV, KAYIM ZH. KHAKKULOV, DILBAR M. GHULOMOVA.
**Deputy Chairman and Minister of Foreign Economic Relations:** UKTUR S. SULTANOV.
**Deputy Chairman and Minister of Finance:** BAKHTIYAR S. KHAMIDOV.
**Deputy Chairman and Chairman of the State Committee for the Management of State Property and for Privatization:** VIKTOR A. CHZHEN.
**Minister of Foreign Affairs:** ABDULAZIZ H. KOMILOV.
**Minister of Defence:** Maj.-Gen. RUSTAM U. AKHMEDOV.
**Chairman of the National Security Service:** GULYAM A. ALIYEV.
**Minister of Higher and Specialized Secondary Education:** AKIL U. SALIMOV.
**Minister of the Interior:** ZOKIRJON A. ALMATOV.
**Minister of Health:** SHAVKAT I. KARIMOV.
**Minister of Culture:** ERKIN K. KHAITBAYEV.
**Minister of Land Improvement and Water Resources:** RIM A. GINIYATULLIN.
**Minister of Education:** JURA G. YULDASHEV.
**Minister of Agriculture:** RASULMAT KHUSANOV.
**Minister of Communications:** KAMILJAN R. RAKHIMOV.
**Minister of Social Security:** BAKHODYR K. UMURZAKOV.
**Minister of Labour:** AKILJON ABIDOV.
**Minister of Power and Electrification:** VALERY Y. ATAYEV.
**Minister of Justice:** ALISHER M. MARDIYEV.
**Minister of Municipal Economy:** VIKTOR K. MIKHAILOV.

### MINISTRIES

**Office of the President:** 700163 Tashkent, ul. Uzbekistanskaya 43; tel. (3712) 39-57-46; fax (3712) 39-55-25.
**Office of the Cabinet of Ministers:** 700008 Tashkent, Government House; tel. (3712) 39-82-95; fax (3712) 39-86-01.
**Ministry of Agriculture:** Tashkent; tel. (3712) 41-00-20.
**Ministry of Communications:** Tashkent, ul. A. Tolstogo 1; tel. (3712) 33-65-03; telex 116108; fax (3712) 39-87-82.
**Ministry of Culture:** Tashkent; tel. (3712) 44-18-30.
**Ministry of Defence:** Tashkent; tel. (3712) 39-46-69.
**Ministry of Education:** Tashkent, alleya Paradov 5; tel. (3712) 39-47-38.
**Ministry of Finance:** 700078 Tashkent, alleya Paradov 6; tel. (3712) 39-15-69; fax (3712) 44-56-43.
**Ministry of Foreign Affairs:** 700047 Tashkent, ul. Gogolya 87; tel. (3712) 33-64-75; telex 116116; fax (3712) 39-43-48.
**Ministry of Foreign Economic Relations:** 700077 Tashkent, ul. Bujuk Ipak Yuli 75; tel. (3712) 68-92-56; telex 116294; fax (3712) 68-72-31.
**Ministry of Health:** Tashkent, ul. Navoi 12; tel. (3712) 44-12-02.
**Ministry of Higher and Specialized Secondary Education:** Tashkent, Mustaqillik maidony 6; tel. (3712) 39-48-08; fax (3712) 39-43-29.
**Ministry of the Interior:** Tashkent, ul. Germana Lopatina 1; tel. (3712) 33-95-32.
**Ministry of Justice:** Tashkent, ul. A. Kadiry 1; tel. (3712) 41-42-33.
**Ministry of Labour:** 700195 Tashkent, ul. Abai 4; tel. (3712) 41-77-06; telex 116358; fax (3712) 41-77-21.
**Ministry of Land Improvement and Water Resources:** Tashkent, ul. A. Kadiry 5A; tel. (3712) 41-18-04; telex 116180; fax (3712) 41-49-24.
**Ministry of Municipal Economy:** Tashkent.
**Ministry of Power and Electrification:** Tashkent.
**Ministry of Social Security:** Tashkent, ul. Babura 20A; tel. (3712) 53-53-71.

### Principal State Committees

**National Information Agency:** 700000 Tashkent, ul. Khamza 28; tel. (3712) 33-16-22; fax (3712) 33-24-45; Dir MAMATSKUL KHAZRATSKULOV.
**National Security Service:** Tashkent; tel. (3712) 33-56-48; Chair. GULYAM A. ALIYEV.
**State Committee for Environmental Protection:** Tashkent, ul. A. Kadiry 5A; tel. (3712) 41-04-42; fax (3712) 41-39-90; Chair. ASKHAT SH. KHABIBULLAYEV.
**State Committee for Forecasting and Statistics:** 700003 Tashkent, ul. Uzbekistanskaya 45A; tel. (3712) 39-82-16; fax (3712) 39-86-39; Chair. MURAT SHARIFKHOJAYEV.
**State Committee for the Management of State Property and for Privatization:** 700008 Tashkent, pl. Mustakilik 6; tel. (3712) 39-82-03; fax (3712) 39-46-66; Chair. VIKTOR A. CHZHEN.
**State Committee for Precious Metals:** 700019 Tashkent, proyezd Turakorgan 26; tel. (3712) 48-07-20; fax (3712) 44-26-03; Chair. SH. NAZHIMOV.
**State Committee for Science and Technology:** 700017 Tashkent, Hadicha Suleymonova 29; tel. (3712) 39-18-43; fax (3712) 39-12-43; Chair. POLAT K. HABIBULLAYEV.
**State Tax Directorate:** 700195 Tashkent, ul. Abai 4; tel. (3712) 41-78-70; telex 116054; Chair. SHAMIL K. GATAULIN.

# UZBEKISTAN

## Legislature

**OLY MAJLIS**
(Supreme Assembly)

**General Election, 25 December 1994 and 8 and 22 January 1995\***

| Parties, etc. | Seats |
| --- | --- |
| People's Democratic Party of Uzbekistan (PDPU) | 69 |
| Progress of the Fatherland | 14 |
| Local council nominees† | 167 |
| **Total** | **250** |

\* The PDPU and Progress of the Fatherland were the only two political organizations permitted to contest the election.
† The overwhelming majority (some 120) of local council nominees were members of the PDPU.

**Supreme Assembly:** 700008 Tashkent, Government House; tel. (3712) 39-87-40; fax (3712) 39-87-49.

**Chairman:** ERKIN KHALILOV.

**Deputy Chairmen:** UBBINIYAZ ASHIRBEKOV, BORIS BUGROV, BORITOSH SHODIYEVA, AKMOLZHON KHOSIMOV.

## Political Organizations

Following Uzbekistan's independence (achieved in August 1991), the ruling People's Democratic Party of Uzbekistan (PDPU) took increasingly repressive measures against opposition and Islamic parties; all religious political parties were banned in 1991, and in the following year the leading opposition group, Birlik, was likewise outlawed. In June 1995 the only registered political parties were the PDPU, Progress of the Fatherland, the Adolat (Justice) Social Democratic Party of Uzbekistan, the Milli Tiklanish (National Revival) Democratic Party and the Khalk Birliki (People's Unity) Movement. Since independence a number of opposition elements have been based in the Russian Federation, in particular in Moscow.

**Adolat (Justice) Social Democratic Party of Uzbekistan:** Tashkent; f. 1995; advocates respect of human rights, improvement of social justice and consolidation of democratic reform; First Sec. ANWAR JURABAYEV; 6,000 mems.

**Birlik** (Unity): c/o Union of Writers of Uzbekistan, 700000 Tashkent, ul. Pushkina 1; tel. (3712) 33-79-21; f. 1989; leading opposition group, banned in 1992; registered as a social movement; Chair. Prof. ABDURAKHIM PULATOV.

**Erk** (Freedom): Tashkent; f. 1990; banned; Chair. MUHAMMAD SOLIKH; Sec. DIKH EGITALIYEV; 5,000 mems (1991).

**Ishtiqlal Yoli** (Independence Path): Tashkent; f. 1994; Leader SHADI KARIMOV.

**Islamic Renaissance Party:** Tashkent; banned in 1991; advocates introduction of a political system based on the tenets of Islam; Leader ABDULLAH UTAYEV.

**Khalk Birliki (People's Unity) Movement:** Tashkent; f. 1995; pro-Government.

**Milli Tiklanish (National Revival) Democratic Party:** Tashkent; f. 1995; Chair. AZIZ KAYUMOV.

**People's Democratic Party of Uzbekistan:** 700163 Tashkent, ul. Uzbekistanskaya 43; f. 1991; successor of Communist Party of Uzbekistan; Chair. ISLAM A. KARIMOV; 352,662 mems (April 1994).

**Watan Taraqqioti** (Progress of the Fatherland): Tashkent; f. 1992; supports privatization and the development of the market economy; registered; Chair. ANWAR Z. YOLDASHEV; Sec.-Gen. SHAVQITDIN JURAYEV; 35,000 mems.

## Diplomatic Representation

### EMBASSIES IN UZBEKISTAN

**Afghanistan:** Tashkent, ul. Gogolya 73; tel. (3712) 33-91-76.
**Belarus:** Tashkent, alleya Paradov 5; tel. (3712) 39-10-26; Ambassador: ALEKSANDR KOSSOV.
**China, People's Republic:** Tashkent, ul. Gogolya 79; tel. (3712) 64-26-39; Ambassador: GUAN HENGGUANG.
**France:** Tashkent, Hotel Uzbekistan, Rm 701; tel. (3712) 33-15-36.
**Germany:** 700067 Tashkent, pr. Sharaf-Rashidov 15; tel. (3712) 34-66-96; Ambassador: Dr KARL HEINZ KUHNA.
**India:** Tashkent, ul. A. Tolstogo 5; tel. (3712) 33-82-67; fax (3712) 33-56-65; Ambassador: VEENA SEKRI.
**Iran:** Tashkent, ul. Timiryazova 16–18; tel. (3712) 35-07-77.
**Israel:** Tashkent, ul. Lakuti 16A; tel. (3712) 32-14-26; fax (3712) 56-57-79; Ambassador: ISRAEL MEY-AMI.
**Italy:** Tashkent, ul. Amir Temur 95, tel. (3712) 35-20-09; Ambassador: CARLO UNGARO.
**Japan:** 700031 Tashkent, ul. G. Lopatina 64, Hotel Turkiston, Rm 4; tel. (3712) 56-46-43; fax (3712) 89-11-55; Ambassador: MAGOSAKI UKURU.
**Kazakhstan:** Tashkent.
**Malaysia:** Tashkent; Ambassador: MOHAMAD REDZUAN MOHAMAD.
**Pakistan:** 700115 Tashkent, ul. Chilanzarskaya 25; tel. (3712) 77-10-03; telex 116431; fax (3712) 77-14-42; Ambassador: SHAFQAT ALI SHEIKH.
**Russia:** 700015 Tashkent, ul. Nukusskaya 83; tel. (3712) 39-17-63; fax (3712) 55-87-74; Ambassador: FILIP SIDORSKY.
**Switzerland:** Tashkent, ul. Murtazayeva 6, kv. 10–12; tel. (3712) 44-27-88; Ambassador: PAUL WIPFLI.
**Turkey:** Tashkent, ul. Gogolya 87; tel. (3712) 33-21-07; telex 116167; fax (3712) 33-13-58.
**United Kingdom:** 700084 Tashkent, ul. Murtazayeva 6, kv. 84–85; tel. (3712) 34-56-52; fax (3712) 34-04-65; Ambassador: BARBARA HAY.
**USA:** 700115 Tashkent, ul. Chilanzarskaya 55; tel. (3712) 77-14-07; fax (3712) 77-10-81; Ambassador: HENRY LEE CLARK.
**Viet Nam:** Tashkent, ul. Rashidova 100; tel. (3712) 34-45-36; Ambassador: NGUYEN VAN DAC.

## Judicial System

**Chairman of the Supreme Court:** M. IBRAGIMOV.
**Procurator-General:** BURITOSH MUSTAFAYEV.

## Religion

The Constitution of 8 December 1992 stipulates that, while there is freedom of worship and expression, there may be no state religion or ideology. The most widespread religion in the country is Islam; the majority of ethnic Uzbeks are Sunni Muslims (Hanafi school), but the number of Wahhabi communities is increasing. Most ethnic Slavs in Uzbekistan are adherents of Orthodox Christianity. In the early 1990s there were reported to be some 65,000 European Jews and 28,000 Central Asian Jews.

**State Committee for Religious Affairs:** 700000 Tashkent, ul. Ulyanova, 1-ogo proyezd 14; tel. (3712) 33-41-50; Chair. Sheikh ABDULGANY ABDULLAYEV.

### ISLAM

**Muslim Board of Central Asia:** Tashkent 2, Zarkainar 103; tel. (3712) 40-39-33; fax (3712) 40-08-31; f. 1943; has spiritual jurisdiction over the Muslims in the Central Asian republics of the former USSR; Chair. MUKHTORJON KHOJA IBN ABDULO AL-BUKHARI, Chief Mufti of Mowarounnahr (Central Asia).

## The Press

In 1990, according to official statistics, there were 279 newspapers published in Uzbekistan, including 185 published in Uzbek. The average daily circulation was 5,158,400 copies (4,120,500 in Uzbek). There were 93 periodicals published, including 33 in Uzbek. Newspapers were also published in Russian, Greek, Tajik, Crimean Tatar and Karakalpak. In the early 1990s many newspapers and periodicals were forced to reduce their circulation and frequency of publication, owing to the shortages and rising prices of paper. As a consequence, the prices of many publications increased substantially. In 1992, according to UNESCO figures, there were 12 daily newspapers, with a total circulation of 452,000 copies, 43 non-daily newspapers, with a total circulation of 1,279,000 copies, and 61 periodicals, with a total circulation of 1,598,000 copies. In mid-1993 the Government ordered all publications to be re-registered with the State Committee for the Press, but in December, when the registration process was completed, the Committee did not license any of the independent publications.

The publications listed below are in Uzbek, unless otherwise stated.

**State Committee for the Press:** Tashkent, ul. Navoi 30; tel. (3712) 44-32-87; telex 116108; fax (3712) 44-26-03; Chair. RUSTAM SH. SHAGULYAMOV.

### PRINCIPAL NEWSPAPERS

**Khaik Suzi** (The People's World): Tashkent; f. 1991; 5 a week; organ of the Supreme Assembly; Editor N. MUKHTAROV.

# UZBEKISTAN

**Molodets Uzbekistana** (Young Person of Uzbekistan): 700083 Tashkent, ul. Matbuochilar 32; tel. (3712) 32-56-51; f. 1926; 5 a week; in Russian; Editor A. Pukemov; circ. 30,000.

**Narodnoye Slovo** (People's Word): 700163 Tashkent, ul. Uzbekistanskaya 43; Government newspaper; in Russian; Editor Anwar Jurabayev.

**Pravda Vostoka** (Eastern Truth): 700008 Tashkent, Government House; f. 1917; 5 a week; organ of the Supreme Assembly and Cabinet of Ministers; in Russian; Editor R. Safarov.

**Tashkentskaya Pravda** (Tashkent Truth): 700008 Tashkent, Government House; 5 a week; in Russian.

**Turkiston** (Turkestan): 700083 Tashkent, ul. Matbuochilar 32; tel. (3712) 33-89-61; f. 1925 as *Yash Leninchy* (Young Leninist), renamed as above 1992; 3 a week; Editor Zhabbar Razzakov; circ. 70,000.

**Uzbekiston Adabiyoti va San'ati** (Literature and Art of Uzbekistan): 700000 Tashkent, ul. Matbuochilar 32; tel. (3712) 32-52-91; f. 1956; weekly; organ of the Union of Writers of Uzbekistan; Editor A. Meliboyev.

### PRINCIPAL PERIODICALS

Monthly, unless otherwise indicated.

**Chelovek i Politika** (Man and Politics): Tashkent; f. 1920; political; in Uzbek and Russian.

**Fan va Turmush** (Science and Life): 700000 Tashkent, ul. Gogolya 70; tel. (3712) 33-69-61; f. 1933; publ. by the Fan (Science) Publishing House; journal of the Academy of Sciences of Uzbekistan; popular scientific.

**Gulistan** (Flourishing Area): Tashkent; f. 1925; fiction.

**Gulkhan** (Bonfire): 700083 Tashkent; tel. (3712) 32-78-85; f. 1929; illustrated juvenile fiction.

**Guncha** (Small Bud): Tashkent, ul. Buyuk Turon 41; tel. (3712) 32-78-80; f. 1958; illustrated; literary, for pre-school-age children; Editor-in-Chief Y. U. Sagdullayeva; circ. 111,000.

**Mushtum** (Fist): Tashkent; f. 1923; fortnightly; satirical.

**Obshchestvennye Nauki v Uzbekistane** (Social Sciences in Uzbekistan): 700000 Tashkent, ul. Gogolya 70; tel. (3712) 33-69-61; f. 1957; publ. by the Fan (Science) Publishing House of the Academy of Sciences of Uzbekistan; history, oriental studies, archaeology, economics, ethnology, etc.; in Russian.

**Saodat** (Happiness): Tashkent; f. 1925; women's popular.

**Sharq Yulduzi** (Star of the East): 700000 Tashkent, ul. Buyuk Turon 41; tel. (3712) 33-21-81; f. 1932; journal of the Union of Writers of Uzbekistan; fiction.

**Uzbekistan-Contact:** 700083 Tashkent, ul. Matbuochilar 32; tel. (3712) 33-02-15; f. 1984; publ. by National Asscn for International Cultural-Educational Relations; history, culture, general interest; in Uzbek and English; Editor-in-Chief Kakhar F. Rashidov; circ. 15,000.

**Uzbek Tili va Adabiyoti** (Uzbek Language and Literature): 700047 Tashkent, ul. Gogolya 70; f. 1958; bimonthly; publ. by the Fan (Science) Publishing House; journal of the Academy of Sciences of Uzbekistan; history and modern development of the Uzbek language, folklore, etc.

**Uzbekiston Kishlok Khuzhaligi** (Agriculture of Uzbekistan): Tashkent; f. 1925; journal of the Ministry of Agriculture; cotton-growing, cattle-breeding, forestry.

**Zvezda Vostoka** (Star of the East): 700000 Tashkent, ul. Buyuk Turon 41; tel. (3712) 33-42-68; f. 1932; publ. by Gafur Gulyam Publishers; journal of the Union of Writers of Uzbekistan; fiction; translations into Russian from Arabic, English, Hindi, Turkish, Japanese, etc.; Editor-in-Chief Sabit Madaliyev; circ. 82,678.

### NEWS AGENCY

**UzTAG** (Uzbek Telegraph Agency): Tashkent, ul. Khamza 2; tel. (3712) 39-49-82; Dir Erkin K. Khaitbayev.

## Publishers

In 1989 there were 2,336 book titles (including pamphlets and brochures) published in Uzbekistan, in a total of 48m. copies, including 929 (28.6m. copies) in Uzbek.

**Chulpon** (Little Star): Tashkent, ul. Buyuk Turon; Dir N. Norbutayev.

**Esh Gvardiya** (Young Guard Publishing House): Tashkent, ul. Navoi 30; juvenile books and journals; Dir Kh. E. Pirmukhamedov.

**Fan** (Science Publishing House): 700047 Tashkent, ul. Gogolya 70, k. 102; tel. (3712) 33-69-61; scientific books and journals; Dir N. T. Khatamov.

**Gafur Gulyam Publishers:** 700129 Tashkent, ul. Navoi 30; tel. (3712) 44-22-53; fax (3712) 44-11-68; f. 1957; fiction, the arts; books in Uzbek, Russian and English; Dir B. S. Sharipov.

**Meditsina** (Medicine Publishing House): Tashkent, ul. Navoi 30; tel. (3712) 44-51-72; f. 1958; medical sciences; Editor-in-Chief Penat P. Pirshiyev.

**Sharq Publishing House:** 700000 Tashkent, ul. Buyuk Turon 41; tel. (3712) 33-47-86; fax (3712) 33-18-58; largest publishing house; govt-owned.

**Ukituvchi** (Teacher): Tashkent, ul. Navoi 30; tel. (3712) 44-23-86; fax (3712) 44-23-86; f. 1936; literary textbooks, education manuals, scientific literature, juvenile; Dir A. I. Mirzayev.

**Uzbekistan Publishing House:** 700129 Tashkent, ul. Navoi 30; tel. (3712) 44-38-10; fax (3712) 44-11-35; f. 1924; socio-political, economic, illustrated; Dir I. A. Akhzarov.

**Uzbekskoy Entsiklopedii** (Uzbekistan Encyclopaedia): Tashkent, ul. Zhukovskogo 52; tel. (3712) 33-50-17; f. 1968; encyclopaedias, dictionaries and reference books; Editor-in-Chief N. Tuchliyev.

### WRITERS' UNION

**Union of Writers of Uzbekistan:** 700000 Tashkent, ul. Pushkina 1; tel. (3712) 33-79-21; Pres. Jamal Kemal.

## Radio and Television

**State Television and Radio Broadcasting Company:** 700047 Tashkent, ul. Khorezmskaya 49; tel. (3712) 41-05-51; Dir-Gen. Shavqat G. Yakhyayev.

**Uzbek Radio:** 700047 Tashkent, ul. Khorezmskaya 49; tel. (3712) 44-12-10; telex 116062; fax (3712) 44-00-21; f. 1947; broadcasts in Uzbek, Russian, English, Urdu, Hindi, Farsi, Dari, Pushtu, Turkish, Tajik, Kazakh, Crimean Tatar, Karakalpak, Arabic, Chinese and Uighur.

**Uzbek Television:** 700011 Tashkent, ul. Navoi 69; tel. (3712) 49-52-14; two local programmes as well as relays from Russia, Kazakhstan, Kyrgyzstan, Tajikistan and Turkey.

**Kamalak Television:** Tashkent; f. 1992; joint venture between State Television and Radio Broadcasting Company and a US company; satellite broadcasts; relays from Russia, the United Kingdom, the USA and India.

## Finance

(cap. = capital; res = reserves; dep. = deposits; m. = million; amounts in Russian roubles, unless otherwise stated; brs = branches)

### BANKING

In 1991 Uzagroprombank and Uzpromstroibank were the largest banks, providing 96% of total credit to enterprises.

#### State Banks

**Central Bank of the Republic of Uzbekistan:** 700001 Tashkent, ul. Uzbekistanskaya 6; tel. (3712) 33-68-29; telex 116396; fax (3712) 33-35-09; Chair. of Bd Faizulla M. Mullajanov; Vice-Chair. Mahmudion Askarov.

**Uzbek National Bank for Foreign Economic Relations:** 700001 Tashkent, ul. Akhunbabayeva 23; tel. (3712) 33-84-25; f. 1991; Chair. Rustam Azimov.

#### Other Banks

**ANDIZHANBANK:** 700011 Andizhan, ul. Babura 85; tel. (37422) 4-34-89; fax (37422) 4-36-88; Chair. Ikrom Ibragimov.

**GALLA Bank—Republican Specialized Joint-Stock Commercial Bank:** 700015 Tashkent, ul. Lakhuti 38; tel. (3712) 56-05-26; Chair. Yuldashbai Ergashev.

**Ipak Yuli Bank—Joint-Stock Innovation Commercial Bank:** 700000 Tashkent, ul. Alimjanova 5; tel. (3712) 33-48-86; fax (3712) 33-82-05; Chair. Khamza Ikramov.

**NAMANGANBANK:** 716030 Namangan, ul. Tereshkova 2; tel. (36922) 2-05-21; Chair. Mamasoli Ubaidullayev.

**Privatbank—Uzbek Joint Bank:** Tashkent, ul. Amir Temur 24; tel. (3712) 39-82-03; Chair. Ulrich Dagg.

**Rustambank:** 700000 Tashkent, ul. Frunze 27; tel. (3712) 33-21-18; telex 116547; fax (3712) 33-77-49; f. 1992; private commercial bank; cap. 1,311m. sums, res 315m. sums, dep. 7,817m. sums. (Dec. 1993); Pres. Rustam T. Usmanov; Gen. Man. Liliya B. Kantzerova.

**Stroikommerbank—Joint-Stock Commercial Bank:** 700011 Tashkent, ul. Abai 6; tel. (3712) 41-47-71; fax (3712) 44-00-47; Chair. Mikhail Mukhortov.

# UZBEKISTAN

**Utbank—Uzbek-Turkish Bank:** 700096 Tashkent, ul. Mukimi 43; tel. (3712) 78-29-44; fax (3712) 78-19-11; Dir-Gen. Ahmed Yurdasiper.

**Uzagroprombank—Agroindustrial Bank of Uzbekistan:** 700096 Tashkent, ul. Mukimi 43; tel. (3712) 78-21-77; telex 116412; fax (3712) 78-12-96; f. 1991 (fmrly part of USSR Agroprombank); joint-stock commercial bank; cap. and res 48,918m., dep. 423,094m. (Jan. 1994); Chair. Rafik Akhadov; 188 brs.

**Uzaviabank:** 700015 Tashkent, ul. Nukusskaya 73B; tel. (3712) 54-79-51; joint-stock commercial bank.

**Uzavtodorbank Commercial Bank:** 700031 Tashkent, Pedagogicheskaya ul. 14; tel. (3712) 56-66-05; Chair. Talat Gayubov.

**Uzinbank—Uzbek Joint-Stock Innovation Bank:** 700015 Tashkent, ul. Pavla Rzhevskogo 3; tel. (3712) 55-82-59; telex 116152; fax (3712) 55-76-16; f. 1988; cap. 1,700m., dep. 531.4m.; Man. Dir Yury P. Gordeyev; 5 brs.

**Uzpromstroibank—Uzbek Joint-Stock Commercial Industrial Construction Bank:** 700000 Tashkent, ul. A. Tukai 3; tel. (3712) 33-34-26; telex 116342; fax (3712) 33-63-54; f. 1922; cap. 3,054m., res 760m., dep. 471,097m. (Jan. 1993); Chair. Akhmat I. Ibotov; Gen. Man. Maria V. Bondarevskaya.

**Uzsavdogarbank Joint-Stock Commercial Bank:** 700015 Tashkent, ul. Tsotkina 78; tel. (3712) 54-19-91; Chair. Ubaidulla Alimullayev.

**Uzsberbank—Savings Bank of Uzbekistan:** 700017 Tashkent, Druzhba Narodov 6; tel. (3712) 45-35-35; fax (3712) 45-35-52; f. 1991; fmrly a br. of the USSR Savings Bank; holds almost all household deposits; state-controlled; Chair. Nuritdin Mukhitdinov.

**Uztadbirkorbank Joint-Stock Commercial Bank:** 700047 Tashkent, ul. Zhukovskogo 52; tel. (3712) 33-18-75; fax (3712) 32-28-29; Chair. Alijon Yusupov.

### COMMODITY EXCHANGE

**Tashkent Commodity Exchange:** 700003 Tashkent, ul. Uzbekistanskaya 45; tel. (3712) 45-71-41; fax (3712) 45-62-79; Chair. Exchange Cttee Kabul Usmanov.

### STOCK EXCHANGE

**Tashkent Stock Exchange:** Tashkent; f. 1992; Chair. Igor Butikov.

## Trade and Industry

### STATE PRIVATIZATION AGENCY

**State Committee for the Management of State Property and for Privatization:** 700008 Tashkent, pl. Mustakilik 6; tel. (3712) 39-82-03; fax (3712) 39-46-66; Chair. V. Chzhen.

### CHAMBER OF COMMERCE

**Chamber of Commerce and Industry:** 700017 Tashkent, pr. Timura 16A; tel. (3712) 33-62-82; Chair. Delbart Yu. Mirsiaadova.

### EMPLOYERS' ORGANIZATIONS

**Employers' Association of Uzbekistan:** 700017 Tashkent, ul. A. Kadiry 2; tel. (3712) 34-06-71; fax (3712) 34-13-39.

**Union of Entrepreneurs of Uzbekistan:** Uzbek Expo Information Centre, 700000 Tashkent, alleya Paradov 6; tel. (3712) 33-67-00; fax (3712) 33-32-00.

### SELECTED STATE-OWNED INDUSTRIAL COMPANIES AND ENTERPRISES

**Amantaytau Goldfields:** 700077 Tashkent, ul. Bujuk Ipak Yuli 75; f. 1993; joint venture between two state-owned Uzbek cos and British co Lonhro; gold mining near Zerafshan; scheduled to start production in 1995.

**Usselchosmash:** Tashkent; produces variety of motor vehicles; largest industrial concern in the country; operates joint venture to produce heavy trucks with Mercedes-Benz of Germany; 36,000 employees (1993).

**Uzbeklegprom:** Tashkent; state asscn for production of light industrial goods.

**Uzbekneftgaz** (State Petroleum and Natural Gas Co): Tashkent; f. 1991; responsible for the operation of the hydrocarbons industry; participates in joint ventures with foreign investors; Chair. Kayim Zh. Khakkulov.

**Uzbektelekom** (Telecommunications of Uzbekistan): Tashkent, ul. A. Tolstogo 1; f. 1992; consists of 14 regional enterprises; controls local telecommunications, with subsidiary controlling international and regional links; dept of Ministry of Communications; Chair. K. R. Rakhimov.

### TRADE UNIONS

**Federation of Trade Unions of Uzbekistan:** Tashkent; Chair. of Council Alla Murodov.

## Transport

### RAILWAYS

Uzbekistan's railway network is connected to those of the neighbouring republics of Kazakhstan, Kyrgyzstan, Tajikistan and Turkmenistan. In 1994 the Uzbekistan State Railway Company was established on the basis of the existing facilities of its predecessor, the Central Asian Railway. All track is standard gauge. The Tashkent Metro was inaugurated in 1977; in 1991 two new stations were opened, giving a total of 23, with 31 km of track.

**Uzbekiston Temir Yollari** (Uzbekistan State Railway Company): Tashkent; f. 1994, to replace the Central Asian Railway's operations in Uzbekistan; state-owned joint-stock company; Dir V. M. Zheltukhov.

### INLAND WATERWAYS

The extensive use of the waters of the Amu-Dar'ya and Syr-Dar'ya for irrigation lessened the flow of these rivers and caused the desiccation of the Aral Sea. This reduced a valuable transport asset. However, the Amu-Dar'ya Steamship Co still operated important river traffic and was able to add two vessels to its fleet in mid-1993.

### CIVIL AVIATION

Proposals to construct a new airport, 45 km from Tashkent, first discussed in 1991, were reportedly rejected in 1995 in favour of modernizing the capital's existing airport. In 1994 it was announced that the airport at Namangan would be upgraded to receive international flights.

**Uzbekistan Airways** (Uzbekistan Havo Yollari): 700061 Tashkent, ul. Proletarskaya 41; tel. (3712) 33-73-57; telex 116169; fax (3712) 33-18-85; f. 1992; operates flights to Central Asia, South-East Asia, the USA and other destinations; Dir-Gen. Gani Rafikov; Gen. Man. T. M. Rafikov.

## Tourism

Since independence Uzbekistan has sought to promote tourism as an important source of revenue. The republic has more than 4,000 historical monuments, many of which are associated with the ancient 'Silk Route', particularly the cities of Samarkand (Tamerlane's capital), Khiva and Bukhara, as well as other historical sites.

**Uzbektourism:** 700047 Tashkent, ul. Khorezmskaya 47; tel. (3712) 33-54-14; fax (3712) 32-79-48; Chair. Bakhtiyor M. Husanbayev.

# VANUATU

## Introductory Survey

### Location, Climate, Language, Religion, Flag, Capital

The Republic of Vanuatu comprises an irregular archipelago of about 80 islands in the south-west Pacific Ocean, lying about 1,000 km (600 miles) west of Fiji and 400 km (250 miles) north-east of New Caledonia. The group extends over a distance of about 900 km (560 miles) from north to south. The islands have an oceanic tropical climate, with a season of south-east trade winds between May and October. Winds are variable, with occasional cyclones for the rest of the year, and annual rainfall varies between 2,300 mm (90 ins) in the south and 3,900 mm (154 ins) in the north. In Port Vila, in the centre of the group, mean temperatures vary between 22°C (72°F) and 27°C (81°F). The national language is Bislama, ni-Vanuatu pidgin. There are many Melanesian languages and dialects. English, French and Bislama are the official languages. Most of the inhabitants (about 80%) profess Christianity, of which a number of denominations are represented. The national flag (proportions 5 by 3) consists of two equal horizontal stripes, red above green, on which are superimposed a black-edged yellow horizontal 'Y' (with its base in the fly) and, at the hoist, a black triangle containing two crossed yellow mele leaves encircled by a curled yellow boar's tusk. The capital is Port Vila, on the island of Efate.

### Recent History

During the 19th century the New Hebrides (now Vanuatu) were settled by British and French missionaries, planters and traders. The United Kingdom and France established a Joint Naval Commission for the islands in 1887. The two countries later agreed on a joint civil administration, and in 1906 the territory became the Anglo-French Condominium of the New Hebrides (Nouvelles-Hébrides). Under this arrangement, there were three elements in the structure of administration: the British National Service, the French National Service and the Condominium (Joint) Departments. Each power was responsible for its own citizens and other non-New Hebrideans who chose to be '*ressortissants*' of either power. Indigenous New Hebrideans were not permitted to claim either British or French citizenship. The result of this was two official languages, two police forces, three public services, three courts of law, three currencies, three national budgets, two resident commissioners in Port Vila (the capital) and two district commissioners in each of the four Districts.

Local political initiatives began after the Second World War, originating in New Hebridean concern over the alienation of native land. More than 36% of the New Hebrides was owned by foreigners. Na-Griamel, one of the first political groups to emerge, had its source in cult-like activities. In 1971 the leaders of Na-Griamel petitioned the UN to prevent further sales of land at a time when areas were being sold to US interests for development as tropical tourist resorts. In 1972 the New Hebrides National Party was formed, with support from Protestant missions and covert support from British interests. In response, French interests formed the Union des Communautés Néo-Hébridaises in 1974. Discussions in the United Kingdom in 1974 resulted in the replacement of the Advisory Council, established in 1957, by a Representative Assembly of 42 members, of whom 29 were directly elected in November 1975. The Assembly did not hold its first full working session until November 1976, and it was dissolved in early 1977, following a boycott by the National Party, which had changed its name to the Vanuaaku Pati (VP) in 1976. However, the VP reached an agreement with the Condominium powers on new elections for the Representative Assembly, based on universal suffrage for all seats.

In July 1977 it was announced, at a conference in France between British, French and New Hebrides representatives, that the islands would become independent in 1980, following a referendum and elections. The VP boycotted this conference, as it demanded immediate independence. The VP also boycotted the elections in November 1977, and declared a 'People's Provisional Government'. Nevertheless, a reduced Assembly of 39 members was elected, and a measure of self-government was introduced in early 1978. A Council of Ministers and the office of Chief Minister (occupied by Georges Kalsakau) were created, and the French, British and Condominium Services began to be replaced by a single New Hebrides Public Service. The VP initially declined to participate in the new Government, but in December a Government of National Unity was formed, with Fr Gérard Leymang (hitherto Minister of Social Services, Health and Works) as Chief Minister, while the President of the VP, Fr Walter Lini, became Deputy Chief Minister.

In September 1979 a conference was held to adopt a constitution, and independence was finally scheduled for July 1980. At elections in November 1979 the VP won 26 of the 39 seats in the Assembly. The outcome of the election led to rioting by supporters of Na-Griamel on the island of Espiritu Santo, who threatened non-Santo 'foreigners'. However, the new Assembly elected Lini to be Chief Minister.

In June 1980 Jimmy Stevens, the leader of Na-Griamel, declared Espiritu Santo independent of the rest of the New Hebrides, styling it the 'Independent State of Vemarana'. Members of his movement, armed with bows and arrows and allegedly assisted by French *colons* and supported by private US business interests, moved to the coast and imprisoned government officers and police, who were later released and allowed to leave the island, together with other European and indigenous public servants. About 200 British Royal Marines were deployed as a peace-keeping force, prompting strong criticism by the French, who would not permit Britain's unilateral use of force on Espiritu Santo.

In mid-July 1980, however, agreement was reached between the two Condominium powers and Lini, and the New Hebrides became independent within the Commonwealth, under the name of Vanuatu, as planned, on 30 July. The first President was the former Deputy Chief Minister, George Kalkoa, who adopted the surname Sokomanu ('leader of thousands'), although the post is a largely ceremonial one. Lini became Prime Minister. The Republic of Vanuatu signed a defence pact with Papua New Guinea, and in August units of the Papua New Guinea Defence Force replaced the British and French troops on Espiritu Santo and arrested the Na-Griamel rebels.

At a general election in November 1983 the VP retained a comfortable, though reduced, majority in Parliament, taking 24 of the 39 seats. Sokomanu resigned as President in February 1984, after pleading guilty in court to the late payment of road taxes, but was re-elected in March. Parliament was expanded to 46 seats for the general election held in December 1987. Of these, the VP won 26 seats, the Union of Moderate Parties (UMP) 19, and the Fren Melanesia one. In the aftermath of the election Barak Sope, Secretary-General of the VP, unsuccessfully challenged Lini for the party presidency, but later accepted a portfolio in the Council of Ministers.

In May 1988 a government decision to abolish a local land corporation, which had been a principal source of patronage for Sope, prompted a demonstration in Port Vila by Sope's supporters. Serious rioting ensued, in which one person was killed and several others injured. Lini accused Sope of being instrumental in provoking the riots, and subsequently dismissed him from the Council of Ministers. In July Sope and four colleagues resigned from the VP, and were subsequently dismissed from Parliament at Lini's behest. In addition, 18 members of the UMP were dismissed after they had boycotted successive parliamentary sittings in protest at the expulsions. In September Sope and his colleagues announced the formation of a new political party, the Melanesian Progressive Pati (MPP), and in October the VP expelled 128 of its own members for allegedly supporting the new party. In October the Court of Appeal ruled as unconstitutional the dismissal from Parliament of Sope and his colleagues, and reinstated them, but upheld the expulsion of the 18 members of the UMP. In November Sope resigned from Parliament, citing loss of confidence in its Speaker. At by-elections for the vacated parliamentary seats, which took place in December, the VP increased its majority, but there was a low level of electoral participation; President Sokomanu dissolved Parliament and announced that Sope would act as interim Prime Minister, pending a general election scheduled to be held in February 1989. Lini immediately denounced Sokomanu's actions, and the Governments of Australia, New Zealand and Papua New Guinea refused to recognize the interim Government. The islands' police force remained loyal to Lini, and later in December Sokomanu, Sope and other members of the interim Government were arrested and charged with treason. In order to ensure impartiality, a judge from Solomon Islands presided over the trials in March 1989, at which Sokomanu was sentenced to six years' imprisonment, and Sope and the then leader of the parliamentary opposition, Maxime Carlot Korman, were jailed for five-year terms, for seditious conspiracy and incitement to mutiny. However, representatives of the International Commission of Jurists, who had been present at the trials, criticized the rulings, and in April the Court of Appeal overturned the original judgment, citing insufficient evidence for the convictions. Fred Timakata, the former Minister of Health, replaced Sokomanu as President in January 1989.

In November 1990 Lini assumed the functions of several ministries. However, there was diminishing support for his leadership within the Council of Ministers, and in August 1991 a motion of 'no confidence' in Lini as party leader was approved at the VP's congress. Donald Kalpokas, the Secretary-General of the VP, was unanimously elected to replace Lini as President of the party. In September a motion of 'no confidence' in the premiership of Lini was narrowly approved in Parliament, and Kalpokas was elected Prime Minister. Subsequently, Lini, with the support of a substantial number of defectors from the VP, formed the National United Party (NUP). At a general election in December the UMP secured 19 seats, while the VP and NUP each won 10 seats, the MPP four and Tan Union, Fren Melanesia and Na-Griamel one each. The leader of the UMP, Maxime Carlot Korman, was appointed Prime Minister, and, unexpectedly, a coalition Government was formed between the UMP and Lini's NUP.

The NUP-UMP coalition was beset by internal problems during 1993. Serious conflict arose between the parties when Carlot refused to dismiss two NUP members of the Council of Ministers, whose expulsion had been sought by the party since October 1992 for alleged misconduct. In response to the controversy, the Prime Minister announced a reallocation of government portfolios in August 1993. However, the reorganization failed to meet Lini's demands, and, as a result, he declared the coalition invalid, causing several NUP members to resign from government office and several others to express support for Carlot. During the following 30 days (the period required formally to dissolve the coalition), and while Carlot was overseas, the UMP President, Serge Vohor, negotiated an agreement with Lini that would re-establish the two parties in government. Upon his return, however, Carlot rejected the agreement, deciding instead to form an alliance with the 'breakaway' members of the NUP who had remained in their ministerial posts.

In late November 1993 an estimated 2,000 public servants began a strike over low wage increases, relative to inflation. In December the Government announced that it was to prohibit all trade union action in 1994, and in January of that year began to dismiss striking employees. The dispute persisted, however, and by April the Public Service Commission announced that all remaining participants in the strike (who numbered 400, according to government estimates, and 1,300, according to union estimates) would be dismissed.

An attempt to select a new President in February 1994 failed when 26 opposition members (claiming that they had not been formally notified of the vote) boycotted the election. At a further vote, held two days later, neither the UMP's candidate, Fr Luc Dini, nor Fr John Bani, who was supported by the opposition, attained the requisite two-thirds of total votes cast. The election was rescheduled for early March, and in the intervening period an atmosphere of political uncertainty prevailed, as parties sought to form alliances and several members changed party allegiances. Lini reportedly rejected a proposed agreement between the anglophone parties, which would have been able to defeat the Government with a vote of 'no confidence', amid rumours that he was negotiating with Carlot to rejoin the Government. However, the VP agreed to vote with the ruling UMP, in return for a guaranteed role in a future coalition government. As a result of this agreement, the UMP's candidate, Jean-Marie Leye, was elected to the presidency with 41 votes, while Bani won only five. The VP subsequently withdrew its support for the UMP when Carlot refused to offer the party more than one ministerial post; the VP had requested three. By the end of March the UMP-led coalition was thought to control a total of 25 legislative seats.

In May 1994 the 'breakaway' members of the NUP who had remained in their ministerial posts, Sethy Regenvanu, Edward Tabisari and Cecil Sinker, were expelled from the party. They subsequently formed a new grouping, the People's Democratic Party (PDP), and on 25 May signed an agreement with the UMP to form a new coalition Government, the third since the election of December 1991. The UMP-PDP coalition held a total of 26 legislative seats.

In August 1994 Parliament approved legislation providing for the introduction of a new system of local government, and in mid-September 11 local councils were dissolved and replaced by six provincial governments. Elections to the newly-formed provincial authorities took place in the following month, at which the Unity Front (an opposition coalition comprising the VP, the MPP, Tan Union and Na-Griamel), the NUP and the UMP each won control of two councils.

Widespread controversy concerning a series of decisions taken by Leye led, in October 1994, to the granting to the Government by the Supreme Court of a restraining order against further actions by the President. Members of the Government and judiciary had become increasingly alarmed by Leye's exercise of his presidential powers, which had included orders to free 26 criminals (many of whom had been convicted on extremely serious offences), to appoint a convicted criminal to the position of Police Commissioner (on the recommendation of the Prime Minister) and to release a Taiwanese fishing vessel confiscated for fishing illegally in Vanuatu's waters. The Government was granted a restraining order pending the hearing of its application to the Supreme Court to overrule several of the President's recent decisions. A former Chief Justice of the Australian High Court was to hear the case, which began in April 1995.

The issue of press freedom was prominent in late 1994, following allegations concerning the censorship of several news reports at the government-controlled Vanuatu Broadcasting and Television Corporation. Further revelations of a similar nature were denied by the Government in early 1995. In April of that year Carlot attracted severe criticism from the Vanuatu-based regional news agency, Pacnews, when he dismissed two senior government officials for making comments critical of the Government; moreover, the journalists who reported the comments were threatened with dismissal. Carlot defended his actions by stating that, as the Government employs public servants, their censure of its authority cannot be permitted. Meanwhile, the Prime Minister's increasing reputation for intolerance of criticism was compounded by allegations that, as part of his Government's policy of reducing the number of employees in the public service, civil servants believed to be opposition sympathizers were among the first to lose their jobs.

Vanuatu has had an uneasy relationship with France. In February 1981 the French Ambassador to Vanuatu was expelled, following the deportation from New Caledonia of the VP Secretary-General, who had been due to attend an assembly of the New Caledonian Independence Front. France immediately withdrew aid to Vanuatu but, after relations between the countries improved in March, a US $A6.9m. aid agreement was signed and a new Ambassador appointed. However, the French Ambassador was expelled again in October 1987, for allegedly providing 'substantial financial assistance' to Vanuatu's opposition parties. In response to the expulsion, the French Government announced that it would greatly reduce its economic aid to Vanuatu. A re-examination of the allegations that had precipitated the expulsion resulted in an improvement in Vanuatu's relations with France in early 1990. Carlot, Vanuatu's first francophone Prime Minister, made an official visit to France in May 1992, and the two countries fully restored diplomatic relations in October. However, the Carlot Government reaffirmed its support for the Kanak independence movement on the French territory of New Caledonia, in July, following threats by Lini to withdraw from the Government unless Carlot's pro-French policies were modified. Improved relations with France were confirmed in July 1993, when Carlot, during an official visit to France, signed a bilateral Treaty of Friendship and Co-operation. A similar agreement relating to development co-operation was signed with New Caledonia in April 1994.

In March 1988 Vanuatu signed an agreement with Papua New Guinea and Solomon Islands to form the 'Spearhead Group', which aimed to preserve Melanesian cultural traditions and to lobby for independence for New Caledonia. In mid-1994 the group concluded an agreement regarded as the first step towards the establishment of a free-trade area between the three countries.

## Government

Vanuatu is a republic. Legislative power is vested in the unicameral Parliament, with 46 members who are elected by universal adult suffrage for four years. The Head of State is the President, elected for a five-year term by an electoral college consisting of Parliament and the Presidents of the Regional Councils. Executive power is vested in the Council of Ministers, appointed by the Prime Minister and responsible to Parliament. The Prime Minister is elected by and from members of Parliament. Legislation enacted in 1994 resulted in the replacement of the 11 local government councils by six provincial bodies, with greater executive powers. The six provincial authorities are Malampa, Penama, Sanma, Shefa, Tafea and Torba.

## Economic Affairs

In 1993, according to estimates by the World Bank, Vanuatu's gross national product (GNP), measured at average 1991–93 prices, was US $198m., equivalent to US $1,230 per head. During 1985–93, it was estimated, GNP per head increased, in real terms, at an average annual rate of 0.2%. Gross domestic product (GDP) increased, in real terms, by 5.2% in 1990 and 3.4% in 1991. GDP remained constant in 1992, but increased by some 4% in 1993. The population increased by 2.8% per year in 1985–93.

The agricultural sector contributed 20.0% of GDP in 1990, compared with some 40% in the early 1980s. About 61.4% of the employed labour force were engaged in agricultural activities at the time of the 1989 census. Coconuts, cocoa and coffee are grown largely for export, while yams, taro, cassava, breadfruit and vegetables are important in subsistence cultivation. Squash was introduced in the early 1990s as an additional export crop. Cattle, pigs, goats and poultry are the country's principal livestock, and beef is an important export commodity (earning $A5.7m. in 1994, equivalent to 27% of total export earnings). The Vanuatu Government has encouraged the development of a forestry industry, and several hardwood plantations have been established. However, the Government caused considerable controversy in mid-1993, when it granted a Malaysian consortium a licence to log 70,000 cu m of timber annually; previous licences for all operators had permitted total logging of only 5,000 cu m per year. In response to international pressure, a complete ban on the export of round logs was introduced in June 1994 and logged wood was restricted to an annual total of 25,000 cu m. However, these regulations were modified in late 1994, arousing fears that logging would again reach unsustainable levels. Fishing is one of the mainstays of Vanuatu's economy, providing income partly through the sale of fishing rights to foreign companies.

The industrial sector contributed about 13.5% of GDP in 1990, although only 3.5% of the employed labour force were engaged in the sector in 1989. Manufacturing, which contributed about 5.9% of GDP in 1990, is mainly concerned with the processing of agricultural products. Growth in the industrial sector during the late 1980s was largely attributable to an increase in construction activity (which contributed 5.8% of GDP in 1990). Vanuatu's first plywood mill was opened on Espiritu Santo in late 1991. In early 1992 an Australian mining company announced plans to mine 60,000 metric tons of manganese per year on the island of Efate for export to Japan and China (the deposits had not been exploited since 1979). In addition, an aerial geophysical survey of the islands, conducted in late 1994 (with Australian aid), identified several possibilities for gold- and copper-mining. Electricity generation is largely thermal. However, plans to construct a hydroelectric power station (with Japanese aid) on Espiritu Santo were announced in late 1993, while funding for a similar project on Malekula was secured from the People's Republic of China in late 1994.

The economy depends heavily on the services sector, which accounted for more than 66% of GDP in 1990. Tourism, 'offshore' banking facilities and a shipping registry, providing a 'flag of convenience' to foreign-owned vessels, make a significant contribution to the country's income.

In 1993 Vanuatu recorded a visible trade deficit of US $47.28m., and a deficit of US $0.98m. on the current account of the balance of payments. In 1990 the principal sources of imports were Australia (37%), Japan (12%) and New Zealand (10%), while the principal markets for exports were the Netherlands (26%), Japan (18%) and Australia (12%). Taiwan was also expected to become an important trading partner, following the signing of a trade agreement by the two countries in late 1992. The principal imports in 1992 were machinery and transport equipment, food and live animals, basic manufactures, miscellaneous manufactured goods, mineral fuels and chemicals. Copra, beef and cocoa were the main export commodities.

In 1989, according to provisional figures, there was an overall budget deficit of 1,323.6m. vatu. Vanuatu's total external debt was US $143.5m. at the end of 1993, of which US $39.4m. was long-term public debt. In that year the total cost of debt-servicing was equivalent to 4.7% of revenue from exports of goods and services. The annual rate of inflation averaged 6.9% in 1985–93; inflation was 5.4% in 1993, and stood at 3.3% in mid-1994.

Vanuatu is a member of the South Pacific Commission (see p. 215) and the South Pacific Forum (see p. 217), both of which promote economic co-operation and development in the region.

During the mid-1980s the economy was adversely affected by a reduction in the international price of Vanuatu's principal export commodity, copra (the dried coconut 'meat' that is the source of coconut oil). Exports of copra accounted for 37.2% of the value of domestic exports in 1990, compared with 70.7% in 1985. Copra prices continued to decline in the early 1990s, and in 1993 there were demonstrations by growers on Espiritu Santo who had not been paid for their crops. Moreover, economic development has been impeded by Vanuatu's vulnerability to adverse climatic conditions: in 1985, 1987 and 1992 cyclones struck Vanuatu, causing extensive damage. As a result, the Carlot Government began to encourage agricultural diversification. Various measures were undertaken in the early 1990s, with the aim of enhancing the performance of the tourism sector, such as the construction of new hotels and improvements in air transport facilities. A trade mission to Australia in early 1995 sought to secure investment for projects in Vanuatu, particularly in the mining and tourism sectors. In an attempt to increase government revenue, a 4% business sales tax was introduced in January of that year. Economic development, however, remained inhibited by a shortage of skilled indigenous labour, a weak infrastructure and frequent foreign exploitation.

## Social Welfare

Medical care is provided through a network of hospitals, health centres, clinics and dispensaries. The Government does not provide a free medical service, and patients still pay a nominal fee. In 1990 the islands had five hospitals (with a total of 364 beds). In that year there were 20 physicians and 321 registered nurses. The 1989 budget, according to provisional figures, allocated 478.8m. vatu to health (6.6% of total expenditure by the central Government).

## Education

The abolition of nominal fees for primary education following independence, resulted in a significant increase in enrolment at that level. Thus, at the beginning of the 1990s it was estimated that about 85% of children between the ages of six and 11 were enrolled at state-controlled primary institutions (which numbered 272 in 1992). Secondary education begins at 12 years of age, and comprises a preliminary cycle of four years and a second cycle of three years. In 1992 4,269 pupils attended the country's secondary schools (which numbered 21 in 1986). Vocational education and teacher-training are also available. The relatively low level of secondary enrolment is a cause of some concern to the Government, and a major programme for the expansion of the education system, costing US $17.8m., was inaugurated in 1989. The programme aimed to double secondary enrolment by 1996.

# VANUATU

*Introductory Survey, Statistical Survey*

An extension centre of the University of the South Pacific was opened in Port Vila in May 1989. The University was to establish its law school at the Port Vila centre in 1993. Students from Vanuatu can also receive higher education at the principal faculties of that university (in Suva, Fiji), in Papua New Guinea or in France.

The 1991 budget, according to provisional figures, allocated 929m. vatu to education (18.8% of total recurrent expenditure by the central Government).

**Public Holidays**

**1995:** 1 January (New Year's Day), 14–17 April (Easter), 1 May (Labour Day), 25 May (Ascension Day), 30 July (Independence Day), 15 August (Assumption), 5 October (Constitution Day), 29 November (Unity Day), 25 December (Christmas Day).

**1996:** 1 January (New Year's Day), 5–8 April (Easter), 6 May (Labour Day), 16 May (Ascension Day), 30 July (Independence Day), 15 August (Assumption), 5 October (Constitution Day), 29 November (Unity Day), 25 December (Christmas Day).

# Statistical Survey

Source (unless otherwise indicated): Statistics Office, NPSO, Port Vila; tel. 22110; telex 1040; fax 24583.

### AREA AND POPULATION

**Area:** 12,190 sq km (4,707 sq miles).

**Population:** 142,944 (males 73,674, females 69,270) at census of 16 May 1989; 156,000 (official estimate) at mid-1993. *Principal islands* (1989): Efate 30,868; Santo 25,581; Malekula 19,298; Tanna 19,825.

**Density** (mid-1993): 12.8 per sq km.

**Capital:** Port Vila (population 19,311 at census of 1989).

**Other town:** Luganville (population 6,983 at census of 1989).

**Expectation of Life** (World Bank estimate, years at birth, 1992): 63.

**Economically Active Population** (census of May 1989): Agriculture, forestry, hunting and fishing 40,889; Mining and quarrying 1; Manufacturing 891; Electricity, gas and water 109; Construction 1,302; Trade, restaurants and hotels 2,712; Transport, storage and communications 1,030; Financing, insurance, real estate and business services 646; Community, social and personal services 7,891; Activities not adequately defined 11,126; Total labour force 66,597 (males 35,692; females 30,905).

### AGRICULTURE, ETC.

**Principal Crops** (FAO estimates, '000 metric tons, 1993): Coconuts 259; Copra 35*; Roots and tubers 50; Vegetables and melons 8; Fruit 13; Groundnuts (in shell) 2; Maize 1; Cocoa beans 3*. Source: FAO, *Production Yearbook*.
* Unofficial figure.

**Livestock** (FAO estimates, year ending September 1993): Cattle 128,000; Pigs 59,000; Goats 11,000; Horses 3,000; Poultry 158,000 (1982). Source: FAO, *Production Yearbook*.

**Livestock Products** (FAO estimates, metric tons, 1993): Beef and veal 3,000; Pig meat 3,000; Cows' milk 3,000; Poultry eggs 280. Source: FAO, *Production Yearbook*.

**Forestry** (FAO estimates, 1992): Roundwood removals ('000 cu m): Sawlogs and veneer logs 39; Fuel wood 24; Total 63. Source: FAO, *Yearbook of Forest Products*.

**Fishing** (metric tons, live weight): Total catch 5,635 (FAO estimate) in 1990; 3,508 in 1991; 2,726 in 1992. Source: FAO, *Yearbook of Fishery Statistics*.

### FINANCE

**Currency and Exchange Rates:** Currency is the vatu. *Sterling and Dollar Equivalents* (31 December 1994): £1 sterling = 175.35 vatu; US $1 = 112.08 vatu; 1,000 vatu = £5.703 = $8.922. *Average Exchange Rate* (vatu per US $): 113.39 in 1992; 121.58 in 1993; 116.41 in 1994.

**Budget** (provisional, million vatu, 1989): *Revenue:* Tax revenue 3,379.9 (Taxes on goods and services 943.9, Import duties 2,436.0); Other current revenue 699.5; Capital revenue 75.3; Total 4,154.7, excluding grants from abroad (1,798.0). *Expenditure:* General public services 999.3; Public order and safety 331.5; Education 919.7; Health 478.8; Housing and community services 2.5; Recreational, cultural and religious affairs 9.8; Economic affairs and services 4,253.9 (Agriculture, forestry, fishing and hunting 489.7, Mining, manufacturing and construction 1,557.7, Transport and communications 762.1); Other purposes 291.8; Total 7,287.2, excluding net lending (-10.9). Source: IMF, *Government Finance Statistics Yearbook*.

**International Reserves** (US $ million at 31 December 1994): IMF special drawing rights 0.31; Reserve position in IMF 3.63; Foreign exchange 39.63; Total 43.58. Source: IMF, *International Financial Statistics*.

**Money Supply** (million vatu at 31 December 1993): Currency outside banks 1,224; Demand deposits at banks 4,448; Total money 5,679. Source: IMF, *International Financial Statistics*.

**Cost of Living** (Consumer Price Index for low-income households in urban areas; base: 1990 = 100): 106.5 in 1991; 108.8 in 1992; 114.7 in 1993. Source: IMF, *International Financial Statistics*.

**Expenditure on the Gross Domestic Product** (million vatu at current prices, 1990): Government final consumption expenditure 5,054; Private final consumption expenditure 11,267; Increase in stocks 488; Gross fixed capital formation 7,311; Total domestic expenditure 24,120; Exports of goods and services 8,301; *Less* Imports of goods and services 13,714; Sub-total 18,707; Statistical discrepancy -808; GDP at producers' prices 17,899.

**Gross National Product** (million vatu at current prices, 1993): GDP at producers' prices 21,959; Net income from abroad -1,970; GNP 19,989. Source: IMF, *International Financial Statistics*.

**Gross Domestic Product by Economic Activity** (million vatu at current prices, 1990, provisional): Agriculture, forestry and fishing 3,582; Manufacturing 1,050; Electricity, gas and water 339; Construction 1,033; Wholesale and retail trade, restaurants and hotels 5,771; Transport, storage and communications 1,517; Finance, insurance, real estate and business services 1,743; Community, social and personal services 2,863; GDP 17,899.

**Balance of Payments** (US $ million, 1993): Merchandise exports f.o.b. 17.43; Merchandise imports f.o.b. -64.71; *Trade balance* -47.28; Exports of services 61.01; Imports of services -39.43; Other income received 17.62; Other income paid -35.72; Private unrequited transfers (net) 10.76; Official unrequited transfers (net) 32.06; *Current balance* -0.98; Direct investment (net) 26.65; Other capital (net) -10.55; Net errors and omissions -11.67; *Overall balance* 3.45. Source: IMF, *International Financial Statistics*.

### EXTERNAL TRADE*

**Principal Commodities** (million vatu, 1992): *Imports:* Food and live animals 1,608; Beverages and tobacco 376; Mineral fuels 834; Chemicals 608; Basic manufactures 1,377; Machinery and transport equipment 2,540; Miscellaneous manufactured goods 975; Total (incl. others) 9,228. *Exports:* Copra 834; Cocoa 165; Beef and veal 338; Timber 90; Coffee 9; Total (incl. others) 2,539. Source: UN, *Statistical Yearbook for Asia and the Pacific*.

**Principal Trading Partners** (million vatu, 1990): *Imports:* Australia 3,996; Japan 1,310; New Zealand 1,107; Fiji 993; France 816; Total (incl. others) 10,768. *Exports:* Netherlands 413; Japan 289; Australia 197; New Caledonia 125; France 108; Total (incl. others) 1,606.

* Figures refer to domestic imports and exports only. In 1990 goods imported mainly for re-export were valued at 520m. vatu, while re-exports were valued at 596m. vatu.

### TRANSPORT

**Road Traffic** (1990): 3,961 vehicles in use.

**International Shipping** (estimated freight traffic, '000 metric tons, 1990): Goods loaded 80; Goods unloaded 55. Source: UN, *Monthly Bulletin of Statistics*. *Merchant Fleet* (vessels registered, '000 grt at 30 June 1992): 2,064. Source: UN, *Statistical Yearbook*.

**Civil Aviation** (traffic on scheduled services, 1992): Passengers carried 59,000; Passenger-kilometres 129 million; Total ton-kilometres 13 million. Source: UN, *Statistical Yearbook*.

### TOURISM

**Number of Visitors** (1992): 42,673.

**Hotel Beds** (1991): 1,150.

## COMMUNICATIONS MEDIA

**Radio Receivers** (1992): 45,000 in use*.

**Television Receivers** (1992): 2,000 in use*.

**Telephones** (1991): 3,000 main lines in use†.

**Non-daily Newspapers** (1990): 1 (estimated circulation 2,000)*.

* Source: UNESCO, *Statistical Yearbook*.
† Source: UN, *Statistical Yearbook*.

## EDUCATION

**Pre-primary** (1992): 252 schools; 49 teachers (1980); 5,178 pupils.
**Primary** (1992): 272 schools; 852 teachers; 26,267 pupils.
**Secondary** (1992): 21 schools (1986); 220 teachers; 4,269 pupils; including:
**Vocational:** 50 teachers (1981); 444 students (1992).
**Teacher-training:** 1 college (1989); 13 teachers (1983); 124 students (1991).
Source: mainly UNESCO, *Statistical Yearbook*.

# Directory

## The Constitution

A new Constitution came into effect at independence on 30 July 1980. The main provisions are as follows:

The Republic of Vanuatu is a sovereign democratic state, of which the Constitution is the supreme law. Bislama is the national language and the official languages are Bislama, English and French. The Constitution guarantees protection of all fundamental rights and freedoms and provides for the determination of citizenship.

The President, as head of the Republic, symbolizes the unity of the Republic and is elected for a five-year term of office by secret ballot by an electoral college consisting of Parliament and the Presidents of the Regional Councils.

Legislative power resides in the single-chamber Parliament, consisting of 39 members (amended to 46 members in 1987) elected for four years on the basis of universal franchise through an electoral system that includes an element of proportional representation to ensure fair representation of different political groups and opinions. Parliament is presided over by the Speaker elected by the members. Executive power is vested in the Council of Ministers which consists of the Prime Minister (elected by Parliament from among its members) and other ministers (appointed by the Prime Minister from among the members of Parliament). The number of ministers, including the Prime Minister, may not exceed a quarter of the number of members of Parliament.

Special attention is paid to custom law and to decentralization. The Constitution states that all land in the Republic belongs to the indigenous custom owners and their descendants. There is a National Council of Chiefs, composed of custom chiefs elected by their peers sitting in District Councils of Chiefs. It may discuss all matters relating to custom and tradition and may make recommendations to Parliament for the preservation and promotion of the culture and languages of Vanuatu. The Council may be consulted on any question in connection with any bill before Parliament. Each region may elect a regional council and the Constitution lays particular emphasis on the representation of custom chiefs within each one. (A reorganization of local government was initiated in May 1994, and resulted in September of that year in the replacement of 11 local councils with six principal governments.)

The Constitution also makes provision for public finance, the Public Service, the Ombudsman, a leadership code and the judiciary (see Judicial System).

## The Government

### HEAD OF STATE

**President:** JEAN-MARIE LEYE (took office 2 March 1994).

### COUNCIL OF MINISTERS
(June 1995)

A coalition of the Union of Moderate Parties (UMP) and the People's Democratic Party (PDP).

**Prime Minister, Minister of Foreign Affairs, Public Service, Planning and Statistics, Media and Language Services:** MAXIME CARLOT KORMAN (UMP).

**Deputy Prime Minister and Minister of Justice, Culture and Women's Affairs:** SETHY REGENVANU (PDP).

**Minister of Home Affairs:** CHARLES NAKO (UMP).

**Minister of Finance:** WILLIE JIMMY (UMP).

**Minister of Economic Affairs** (with responsibility for Tourism, External Trade, Commerce and Industry): SERGE VOHOR (UMP).

**Minister of Agriculture, Livestock, Forestry and Fisheries:** (vacant).

**Minister of Transport, Public Works, Ports and Marine and Urban Water Supply:** AMBAE AMOS BANGABITI (UMP).

**Minister of Natural Resources:** PAUL BARTHELEMY TELUKLUK (UMP).

**Minister of Education:** ROMAIN BATIK (UMP).

**Minister of Health and Rural Water Supply:** EDWARD TABISARI (PDP).

**Minister of Postal Services, Telecommunications and Meteorology:** CECIL SINKER (PDP).

### DEPARTMENTS

**Prime Minister's Office:** POB 110, Port Vila; tel. 22413; telex 1040.

**Department of Agriculture, Livestock, Forestry and Fisheries:** POB 129, Port Vila; tel. 23406; telex 1040.

**Department of Economic Affairs:** PMB 051, Port Vila; tel. 22913; telex 1040; fax 23142.

**Department of Education:** PMB 028, Port Vila; tel. 22309; telex 1040.

**Department of Finance:** PMB 058, Port Vila; tel. 23032; telex 1040; fax 23142.

**Department of Foreign Affairs:** PMB 51, Port Vila; tel. 22913; telex 1040; fax 23142.

**Department of Health and Rural Water Supply:** Port Vila.

**Department of Home Affairs:** PMB 036, Port Vila; tel. 22252; telex 1040.

**Department of Justice, Culture and Women's Affairs:** PMB 093, Port Vila; tel. 25290; fax 23142.

**Department of Natural Resources:** POB 151, Port Vila; tel. 23105; telex 1040.

**Department of Postal Services, Telecommunications and Meteorology:** PMB 011, Port Vila; tel. 25059; fax 25628.

**Department of Public Service, Planning and Statistics, Media and Language Services:** Port Vila.

**Department of Transport, Public Works, Ports and Marine and Urban Water Supply:** Port Vila.

## Legislature

### PARLIAMENT

**Speaker:** ALFRED MASENGNALO.

**General Election, 2 December 1991**

|  | Seats |
|---|---|
| Union of Moderate Parties | 19 |
| Vanuaaku Pati | 10 |
| National United Party | 10 |
| Melanesian Progressive Pati | 4 |
| Tan Union | 1 |
| Fren Melanesia | 1 |
| Na-Griamel | 1 |
| **Total** | **46** |

## Political Organizations

**Efate Laketu Party:** Port Vila; f. 1982; regional party, based on the island of Efate.

**Melanesian Progressive Pati (MPP):** POB 39, Port Vila; tel. 23485; fax 23315; f. 1988, by breakaway group from the VP; Chair. BARAK SOPE; Sec.-Gen. GEORGES CALO.

# VANUATU

*Directory*

**National Democratic Party (NDP):** Port Vila; f. 1986; advocates strengthening of links with France and the UK; Leader JOHN NAUPA.

**National United Party (NUP):** Port Vila; f. 1991 by supporters of Walter Lini, following his removal as leader of the VP; Pres. Fr WALTER HADYE LINI.

**New People's Party (NPP):** Port Vila; f. 1986; Leader FRASER SINE.

**People's Democratic Party (PDP):** Port Vila; f. 1994 by breakaway faction of the NUP.

**Union of Moderate Parties (UMP):** POB 698, Port Vila; f. 1980; Pres. SERGE VOHOR; Parl. Leader MAXIME CARLOT KORMAN.

**Vanuaaku Pati (VP)** (Our Land Party): Port Vila; f. 1971 as the New Hebrides National Party; advocates 'Melanesian socialism'; Pres. DONALD KALPOKAS; First Vice-Pres. IOLU ABBIL; Sec.-Gen. SELA MOLISA.

**Vanuatu Independent Alliance Party (VIAP):** Port Vila; f. 1982; supports free enterprise; Leaders THOMAS SERU, GEORGE WOREK, KALMER VOCOR.

**Vanuatu Labour Party:** Port Vila; f. 1986; trade-union based; Leader KENNETH SATUNGIA.

The **Na-Griamel** (Leader FRANKEY STEVENS), **Namaki Aute, Tan Union** (Leader VINCENT BOULEKONE) and **Fren Melanesia** represent rural interests on the islands of Espiritu Santo and Malakula.

## Diplomatic Representation

### EMBASSIES AND HIGH COMMISSIONS IN VANUATU

**Australia:** KPMG House, POB 111, Port Vila; tel. 22777; fax 23948; High Commissioner: PETER SHANNON.

**China, People's Republic:** Port Vila; Ambassador: ZHAN DAODE.

**France:** Kumul Highway, POB 60, Port Vila; tel. 22353; fax 22695; Ambassador: JEAN MAZÉO.

**New Zealand:** POB 161, Port Vila; tel. 22933; fax 22518; High Commissioner: BRIAN SMYTHE.

**United Kingdom:** KPMG House, rue Pasteur, POB 567, Port Vila; tel. 23100; telex 1027; fax 23651; High Commissioner: JAMES DALY.

## Judicial System

The Supreme Court has unlimited jurisdiction to hear and determine any civil or criminal proceedings. It consists of the Chief Justice, appointed by the President of the Republic after consultation with the Prime Minister and the leader of the opposition, and three other judges, who are appointed by the President of the Republic on the advice of the Judicial Service Commission.

The Court of Appeal is constituted by two or more judges of the Supreme Court sitting together. The Supreme Court is the court of first instance in constitutional matters and is composed of a single judge.

Magistrates' Courts have limited jurisdiction to hear and determine any civil or criminal proceedings. Island Courts have been established in several Local Government Regions, and are constituted when three justices are sitting together to exercise civil or criminal jurisdiction, as defined in the warrant establishing the court. A magistrate nominated by the Chief Justice acts as Chairman. The Island Courts are competent to rule on land disputes.

In 1986 Papua New Guinea and Vanuatu signed a memorandum of understanding, under which Papua New Guinea Supreme Court judges were to conduct court hearings in Vanuatu, chiefly in the Court of Appeal.

**Supreme Court of Vanuatu:** PMB 041, rue Querios, Port Vila; tel. 22420; fax 22692.

**Attorney-General:** PATRICK ELLUM.

**Chief Justice:** CHARLES VAUDIN D'IMECOURT.

**Chief Prosecutor:** JOHN BAXTER-WRIGHT.

## Religion

Most of Vanuatu's inhabitants profess Christianity. Presbyterians form the largest Christian group (with about one-third of the population being adherents), followed by Anglicans and Roman Catholics.

### CHRISTIANITY

**Vanuatu Christian Council:** POB 13, Luganville, Santo; tel. 03232; f. 1967 as New Hebrides Christian Council; five mem. churches, two observers; Chair. (vacant); Sec. Rev. JOHN LIU.

### The Roman Catholic Church

Vanuatu forms the single diocese of Port Vila, suffragan to the archdiocese of Nouméa (New Caledonia). At 31 December 1993 there were an estimated 23,700 adherents in the country. The Bishop participates in the Catholic Bishops' Conference of the Pacific, based in Fiji.

**Bishop of Port Vila:** Rt Rev. FRANCIS ROLAND LAMBERT, Evêché, POB 59, Port Vila; tel. 22640; fax 25342.

### The Anglican Communion

Anglicans in Vanuatu are adherents of the Church of the Province of Melanesia, comprising five dioceses: Vanuatu (which also includes New Caledonia) and four dioceses in Solomon Islands. The Archbishop of the Province is the Bishop of Central Melanesia, resident in Honiara, Solomon Islands. In 1985 the Church had an estimated 16,000 adherents in Vanuatu.

**Bishop of Vanuatu:** Rt Rev. MICHAEL TAVOA, Bishop's House, POB 238, Luganville, Santo.

### Protestant Churches

**Presbyterian Church of Vanuatu (Presbitirin Jyos long Vanuatu):** POB 150, Port Vila; tel. 22722; f. 1948; 46,000 mems (1985); Moderator Pastor TOM TALI; Assembly Clerk Pastor FIAMA RAKAU.

Other denominations active in the country include the Apostolic Church, the Assemblies of God, the Churches of Christ in Vanuatu and the Seventh-day Adventist Church.

### BAHÁ'Í FAITH

**National Spiritual Assembly of the Bahá'ís of Vanuatu:** POB 1017, Port Vila; tel. 22419; f. 1953; Sec. CHARLES PIERCE; mems resident in 93 localities.

## The Press

**Hapi Tumas Long Vanuatu:** POB 1292, Port Vila; tel. 23642; fax 23343; quarterly tourist information; in English; Publr MARC NEIL-JONES; circ. 12,000.

**Logging News:** Port Vila; environment and logging industry.

**Pacific Island Profile:** Port Vila; f. 1990; monthly; general interest; English and French; Editor HILDA LINI.

**The Trading Post:** POB 1292, Port Vila; weekly; English; Publr MARC NEIL-JONES; circ. 2,000.

**Vanuatu Weekly:** PMB 049, Port Vila; tel. 22999; telex 1046; f. 1980; weekly; govt-owned; Bislama, English and French; circ. 1,700.

**Viewpoints:** Port Vila; weekly; newsletter of Vanuaaku Pati; Editor PETER TAURAKOTO.

### NEWS AGENCY

**Pacnews:** Port Vila; tel. 26300; fax 26301; f. 1987; expelled from Fiji in 1990, relocated from Solomon Islands to Vanuatu in 1994; regional news agency; parent body is the Pacific Islands Broadcasting Assen; produces two bulletins of South Pacific news daily.

## Radio and Television

In 1992 there were an estimated 45,000 radio receivers and 2,000 television receivers in use.

**Vanuatu Broadcasting and Television Corporation (VBTC):** PMB 049, Port Vila; tel. 22999; telex 1046; fax 22026; fmrly Government Media Services, name changed in 1992; Dir KALTAU AYONG; Chair. PHIL RICHARDS; Dir of Programmes A. THOMPSON.

**Radio Vanuatu:** PMB 049, Port Vila; tel. 22999; telex 1046; fax 22026; f. 1966; govt-owned; broadcasts in English, French and Bislama; Dir GODWIN LIGO.

**Television Blong Vanuatu:** Port Vila; f. 1993; govt-owned; French-funded; broadcasts for four hours daily in French and English; Gen. Man. CLAUDE CASTELLY.

### Regional Broadcasting Association

**Pacific Islands Broadcasting Association (PIBA):** POB 116, Port Vila; tel. 24250; fax 24252; f. 1987; regional association, fmrly based in Fiji; parent body of training organization, Pacbroad, and news agency Pacnews; promotes development of broadcasting in the region, trains staff of broadcasting organizations in all aspects of broadcasting, provides a system of news and programme exchange and technical co-operation; Chair. HIMA DOUGLAS.

# VANUATU

## Finance

(cap. = capital; res = reserves; amounts in vatu)

Vanuatu has no personal income tax nor tax on company profits and is therefore attractive as a financial centre and 'tax haven'.

### BANKING

#### Central Bank

**Reserve Bank of Vanuatu:** PMB 062, Port Vila; tel. 23333; telex 1049; fax 24231; f. 1981 as Central Bank of Vanuatu; name changed as above in 1989; cap. 100m., res 933.4m., total resources 4,786.7m. (Dec. 1990); Gov. SAMPSON NGWELE.

#### Commercial Bank

**Vanuatu Commercial and Trading Bank:** Port Vila; f. 1991.

#### Development Banks

**Development Bank of Vanuatu:** rue de Paris, POB 241, Port Vila; tel. 22181; telex 1049; f. 1979; govt-owned; cap. 315m. (Nov. 1988); Man. Dir AUGUSTINE GARAE.

**Caisse Française de Développement:** POB 296, Port Vila; tel. 22171; telex 1085; fax 24021; fmrly Caisse Centrale de Coopération Economique, name changed 1992; provides finance for various development projects.

#### National Bank

**National Bank of Vanuatu:** POB 249, Port Vila; tel. 22201; telex 1017; fax 22671; f. 1991, when it assumed control of Vanuatu Co-operative Savings Bank; govt-owned; Chair. NICHOLSON WOREK; Gen. Man. KERRY JOWETT; 23 brs.

#### Foreign Banks

**ANZ Bank (Vanuatu) Ltd** (Australia): Kumul Highway, PMB 003, Port Vila; tel. 22536; telex 1012; fax 22814; Man. Dir J. G. LANGHORN; brs in Port Vila and Santo.

**Bank of Hawaii International** (USA): Port Vila; Gen. Man. MARK JOSEPH.

**Banque d'Hawaii (Vanuatu) Ltd** (France): Kumul Highway, POB 29, Port Vila; tel. 22412; telex 1100; fax 23579.

**Westpac Banking Corporation** (Australia): Kumul Highway, Port Vila; tel. 22084; telex 1018; fax 22357; Man. R. B. WRIGHT.

#### Financial Institution

**The Finance Centre Association:** POB 1128, Port Vila; tel. 22084; fax 22357; f. 1971; group of banking, legal, accounting and trust companies administering offshore banking and investment.

### INSURANCE

**QBE Insurance (Vanuatu) Ltd:** Oceania Bldg, Suite 19, rue de Paris, POB 186, Port Vila; tel. 22299; fax 23298; Gen. Man. GEOFFREY R. CUTTING.

## Trade and Industry

### CHAMBER OF COMMERCE

**Vanuatu Chamber of Commerce:** POB 189, Port Vila; tel. 23255; fax 23255.

### MARKETING BOARD

**Vanuatu Commodities Marketing Board:** POB 81, Port Vila; tel. 23123; telex 1036; fax 23993; f. 1982; sole exporter of major commodities, including copra, kava and cocoa; Gen. Man. FRANKLYN KERE.

### CO-OPERATIVES

During the early 1980s there were some 180 co-operative primary societies in Vanuatu and at least 85% of goods in the islands were distributed by co-operative organizations. Almost all rural ni-Vanuatu were members of a co-operative society, as were many urban dwellers. By the end of that decade, however, membership of co-operatives had declined, and the organizations' supervisory body, the Vanuatu Co-operative Federation, had been dissolved, after having accumulated debts totalling some $A1m.

### TRADE UNIONS

**Vanuatu Trade Union Congress (VTUC):** Sec.-Gen. EPHRAIM KALSAKAU.

**National Union of Labour:** Port Vila.

The principal trade unions include:

**Oil and Gas Workers' Union:** Port Vila; f. 1984.

**Vanuatu Airline Workers' Union:** Port Vila; f. 1984.

**Vanuatu Public Service Association:** Port Vila.

**Vanuatu Teachers' Union:** Port Vila; Gen. Sec. CHARLES KALO; Pres. OBED MASSING.

**Vanuatu Waterside, Maritime and Allied Workers' Union:** Port Vila.

## Transport

### ROADS

There are about 1,130 km of roads, of which 54 km, mostly on Efate Island, are sealed.

### SHIPPING

The principal ports are Port Vila and Luganville.

**Ifira Shipping Agencies Ltd:** POB 68, Port Vila; tel. 22929; telex 1111; fax 22052; f. 1986; Man. Dir CLAUDE BOUDIER.

**Vanua Navigation Ltd:** POB 44, Port Vila; tel. 22027; telex 1033; f. 1977 by the Co-operative Federation and Sofrana Unilines; Chief Exec. GEOFFREY J. CLARKE.

The following services call regularly at Vanuatu: Compagnie Générale Maritime, Kyowa Shipping Co, Pacific Forum Line, Papua New Guinea Shipping Corpn, Sofrana-Unilines, Bank Line, Columbus Line and Bali Hai Shipping. Royal Viking Line, Sitmar and P & O cruises also call at Vanuatu.

### CIVIL AVIATION

The principal airports are Bauerfield (Efate, for Port Vila) and Pekoa (Espiritu Santo). There are airstrips on all Vanuatu's principal islands. Plans to expand and upgrade the two principal airports were announced in September 1994, and work was due to be completed by late 1995. A new airport was to be constructed on Tanna, beginning in 1995, with French funding.

**Air Vanuatu Ltd:** POB 148, Port Vila; tel. 23838; fax 23250; f. 1981; govt-owned national carrier since 1987; regular services between Port Vila and Sydney, Brisbane and Melbourne (Australia), Nadi (Fiji), Nouméa (New Caledonia) and Auckland (New Zealand); Chair. K. KALSAKAU; Man. Dir and CEO JEAN-PAUL VIRELALA.

**Dovair:** Port Vila; privately-owned; operates domestic services.

**Vanair:** Port Vila; tel. 22643; telex 1112; fax 23910; f. 1989, following acquisition by the Government of Vanuatu of Air Melanesia; govt-owned; operates scheduled services to 28 destinations within the archipelago; Gen. Man. WILLIE WILSON.

## Tourism

Tourism is an important source of revenue for the Government of Vanuatu. Visitors are attracted by the islands' unspoilt landscape and rich local customs. The establishment of regular air services from Australia and New Zealand in the late 1980s precipitated a significant increase in the number of visitors to Vanuatu. In 1992 there were 42,673 foreign visitor arrivals in Vanuatu (of whom 31,008 were tourists). In 1990 passengers on cruise ships visiting the islands numbered 41,867. In 1991 more than 50% of visitors were Australian. There was a total of 1,150 hotel beds at the end of 1991. The development of the tourist industry has hitherto been restricted to the islands of Efate, Espiritu Santo and Tanna; however, the promotion of other islands as tourist centres is envisaged.

**National Tourism Office of Vanuatu:** Kumul Highway, POB 209, Port Vila; tel. 22685; fax 23889; Gen. Man. WAIMINI PEREI.

# THE VATICAN CITY

## (THE HOLY SEE)

## Introductory Survey

### Location, Climate, Language, Religion, Flag

The State of the Vatican City is situated entirely within the city of Rome, Italy, occupying 0.44 sq km (0.17 sq mile). The climate is Mediterranean (see Italy). Italian and Latin are the official languages. Roman Catholicism is the official religion. The state flag, which is square, consists of two vertical stripes of yellow and white, with the papal coat of arms superimposed on the white stripe.

### History

For a period of nearly 1,000 years, dating roughly from the time of Charlemagne to the year 1870, the Popes ruled much of the central Italian peninsula, including the city of Rome. During the process of unification, the Kingdom of Italy gradually absorbed these States of the Church, the process being completed by the entry into Rome of King Victor Emmanuel's troops in September 1870. From 1860 to 1870 many attempts had been made to induce the Pope, Pius IX, to surrender his temporal possessions. Since, however, he regarded them as a sacred trust from a higher Power, to be guarded on behalf of the Church, he refused to do so. After the entry of the Royal Army into Rome, he retired to the Vatican from where no Pope emerged again until the ratification of the Lateran Treaty of 11 February 1929. By the Law of Guarantees of May 1871, Italy attempted to stabilize the position of the Papacy by recognizing the Pope's claim to use of the Palaces of the Lateran and the Vatican, the Papal villa of Castelgandolfo, and their gardens and annexes, and to certain privileges customary to sovereignty. This unilateral arrangement was not accepted by Pius IX, and his protest against it was repeated constantly by his successors.

In 1929 two agreements were made with the Italian Government—the Lateran Treaty and the Concordat. By the terms of the Lateran Treaty, the Holy See was given exclusive power and sovereign jurisdiction over the State of the Vatican City, which was declared neutral and inviolable territory. Financial compensation was also given for the earlier losses. Under the Concordat, Roman Catholicism became the state religion of Italy, with special privileges defined by law. The new Italian Constitution of 1947 reaffirmed adherence to the Lateran Treaty, but in 1967 negotiations began for a revision of the Concordat. In December 1978 the two sides agreed on a draft plan for a new Concordat, under which Catholicism would cease to be the official Italian state religion and most of the Catholic Church's special privileges in Italy would be removed. The revised version, finally agreed, was signed in February 1984. The Lateran Treaty and the status of the Vatican City were not affected.

In 1917 the first legal code (Codex Iuris Canonici), the Code of Canon Law, was devised for the Catholic Church. In 1963 a pontifical commission was inaugurated to investigate possible reforms to the law and in 1981 the Pope received more than 70 cardinals and bishops who had prepared the new code's 1,752 rules. Revisions included a reduction in the number of cases meriting excommunication and a general relaxing of penalties, with increased emphasis on the importance of the laity within the church. The code was ratified by the Pope in January 1983, and came into force in November.

In October 1978 Cardinal Karol Wojtyła (then Archbishop of Kraków in Poland) became the first non-Italian Pope since the 16th century, taking the name John Paul II. Security surrounding the Pontiff was considerably tightened after an attempt on the Pope's life in May 1981 and another in May 1982.

In April 1984 Pope John Paul II announced a major reshuffle of offices in the Roman Curia, which included the delegation of most of his responsibility for the routine administration of the Vatican to the Secretary of State. Cardinal Gantin, from Benin, was appointed Prefect of the Congregation for the Bishops, responsible for the selection of bishops, under the Pope's authority. In November 1985 a meeting of the College of Cardinals, called to discuss proposals for reforms in the structure of the Curia, failed to reach agreement, and the implementation of the proposed changes was postponed. In July 1988, however, some reforms of the Curia were introduced. These consolidated the power of the Secretariat of State, as well as reorganizing some of the Congregations and Pontifical Commissions.

In February 1987 Italian judges issued a warrant for the arrest of Archbishop Paul Marcinkus, the Chairman of the Istituto per le Opere di Religione ('Vatican Bank'), and two other bank officials for alleged involvement in the fraudulent bankruptcy of the Banco Ambrosiano in Milan, which collapsed in 1982. In July, however, the Italian Supreme Court cancelled the warrants for the arrest of Archbishop Marcinkus and the two lay bank officials, stating that the Vatican stood outside Italian jurisdiction and that, according to the Lateran Treaty of 1929, Italy did not have the right to interfere in the affairs of the central organs of the Roman Catholic Church. In May 1988, after an appeal, the Archbishop's immunity was endorsed by the Constitutional Court. In March 1989 the Vatican announced a wide-ranging reorganization of the Istituto per le Opere di Religione, by abolishing the post of Chairman, held by Marcinkus, and appointing a commission of five cardinals, nominated by the Pope, to preside over the bank, assisted by a committee of financial experts. Archbishop Marcinkus retired from papal service in October 1990.

In November 1992 the Roman Catholic Church issued the first new, revised catechism since 1566.

The Vatican was prominent in international affairs in the first half of the 1990s. In July 1989 diplomatic relations with Poland, severed in 1945, were restored. The Vatican had hitherto maintained no diplomatic relations with eastern European governments under communist rule, except for Yugoslavia. In the same month diplomatic links with the USSR were upgraded and the Pope appointed the first bishop to a Soviet republic, Belarus (also known as Belarussia or Byelorussia), for 60 years. In November Mikhail Gorbachev became the first Soviet leader to be received by the Pope, during a state visit to the Vatican. In February 1990 diplomatic relations between the Vatican and Hungary were restored. In the following month permanent official contacts with the USSR were established and a Soviet ambassador to the Vatican was appointed. In April diplomatic relations between the Vatican and Czechoslovakia were restored. In the same month Pope John Paul II visited Czechoslovakia, his first visit to an eastern European country outside his native Poland. By mid-1992, following the collapse of communism in many parts of the world (particularly in eastern Europe) and the disintegration of the USSR in December 1991, the Vatican had established diplomatic relations with the former communist states of Mongolia, Romania, Bulgaria, and with Ukraine and the newly-independent Baltic states of Estonia, Latvia and Lithuania. In July 1992 the Vatican and Israel agreed to form a joint commission intended to further the establishment of full diplomatic relations between the two states, and in September full diplomatic relations were restored, after more than 120 years of discord, between the Vatican and Mexico. In December 1993 the Vatican and Israel signed a mutual-recognition agreement, which led to the establishment of full diplomatic ties and the exchange of ambassadors in September 1994. Meanwhile, in February 1994 the Vatican established diplomatic relations with Jordan, in an apparent move to strengthen links with the Arab world to counterbalance its recent recognition of Israel. Similarly, in October of that year the Vatican instituted 'official relations' with the Palestine Liberation Organization.

In September 1994 the Vatican conducted a vociferous, but ultimately unsuccessful, campaign to prevent the UN-sponsored International Conference on Population and Development, held in Cairo, Egypt, from sanctioning artificial birth control. Despite widespread concern about his deteriorating health, the Pope carried out an ambitious tour of Asia and Australia in January 1995. The extent of his popularity was manifested in the crowd of 4m. people who attended an open-air mass in Manila, the Philippines.

The population of the Vatican City was 766 at mid-1988.

## Finance

The Vatican has three main sources of income: the Istituto per le Opere di Religione (see Directory), 'Peter's pence' (voluntary contributions) and interest on investments, managed by the Administration of the Patrimony of the Holy See. Italian currency is used. The Vatican first revealed budget figures for the Holy See in 1979, when it disclosed a deficit of US $20.1m. This was incurred through the normal operating expenses of the Vatican bureaucracy, including the newspaper and radio services and overseas diplomatic missions. The alleged mismanagement of investments, banking scandals and the decline in the value of the US dollar contributed to a deficit of $56.7m. in 1986, when annual income reached $57m. The deficit was met by the receipt of $32m. from the 'Peter's pence' levy, and by the withdrawal of $24.7m. from the 'Peter's pence' reserve fund. A 'freeze' on spending was ordered for 1987; however, a deficit of $59.3m. was projected for the year. In 1987 the Vatican Radio incurred losses of about $17m., while *L'Osservatore Romano,* the Vatican daily newspaper, had a deficit of about $5m. In March 1988 the Vatican published an independently-audited annual balance sheet, thereby, for the first time in its history, revealing the church's financial affairs to public scrutiny. In 1988, despite attempts to expand revenue by increasing rents, the budget deficit reached $66m. It was estimated that in 1989 Vatican expenditure was $134m., while income totalled only $56m. Of the expenses incurred, $65m. was to pay for 2,366 employees and 889 retired staff of the Vatican. In 1989 'Peter's pence' contributions totalled $46.6m. An estimated budgetary deficit of $86m. was recorded in 1990, when 'Peter's pence' amounted to $58m. In April 1991 more than 100 representatives of bishops' conferences from around the world attended an unprecedented meeting held in the Vatican City, at which they discussed ways of making local dioceses systematically share the burden of the Vatican's annual budgetary deficit. In that year, however, the budgetary deficit reached a peak of $87.5m. In 1992 the deficit fell substantially and in 1993, after 23 years of budgetary deficits, a modest surplus, of $1.5m., was recorded (expenditure $167.5m.; income $169m., including $59.9m. in 'Peter's pence' contributions). An even smaller surplus, of $412,000, was registered in 1994; expectations of decreasing returns on the Vatican's market investments, however, led to a projected budgetary deficit of $22.3m. for 1995.

# Directory

## Government

The State of the Vatican City came into existence with the Lateran Treaty of 1929. The Holy See (a term designating the papacy, i.e. the office of the Pope, and thus the central governing body of the Roman Catholic Church) is a distinct, pre-existing entity. Both entities are subjects of international law. Ambassadors and Ministers are accredited to the Holy See, which sends diplomatic representatives (Nuncios and Pro-Nuncios) to more than 120 states, as well as having Delegates or Observers at the United Nations and other international organizations. The Vatican City is also a member of certain international organizations (see p. 60).

Both entities are indissolubly united in the person of the Pope, the Bishop of Rome, who is simultaneously ruler of the State and visible head of the Roman Catholic Church.

### THE GOVERNMENT OF THE VATICAN CITY STATE

The Vatican City State is under the temporal jurisdiction of the Pope, the Supreme Pontiff elected for life by a conclave comprising members of the Sacred College of Cardinals. He appoints a Pontifical Commission, headed by a President, to conduct the administrative affairs of the the Vatican City State.

#### Head of State

His Holiness Pope JOHN PAUL II (elected 16 October 1978).

#### Pontifical Commission for the Vatican City State

Cardinal ROSALIO JOSÉ CASTILLO LARA (President)
Cardinal ANTONIO INNOCENTI
Cardinal JOZEF TOMKO
Cardinal ANDRZEJ MARIA DESKUR
Cardinal ALFONSO LÓPEZ TRUJILLO
Mgr GIANNI DANZI (Secretary)
Marchese GIULIO SACCHETTI (Special Delegate)

### THE CENTRAL GOVERNMENT OF THE HOLY SEE

The central government of the Roman Catholic Church is vested in the Pope, who is supreme, and in the Sacred College of Cardinals, whose members are created by the Pope. Cardinals who reside in Rome as the Pope's immediate advisers are styled Cardinals 'in Curia'. The Roman Curia acts as the Papal court and the principal administrative body of the Church. The College of Cardinals derives from the Church's earliest days. Until the reign of Pope John XXIII, the number of Cardinals was limited by custom to 70. At 31 December 1994 there were 165 Cardinals. An Apostolic Letter in November 1970 decreed that, from 1 January 1971, Cardinals reaching 80 years of age would lose the right to take part in the election of the Pope. In March 1973 the Pope announced that the number of Cardinals permitted to participate in the conclave would be limited to 120. There are usually six Cardinal Bishops who are in titular charge of suburban sees of Rome—Sabina-Poggio Mirteto and Ostia, Albano, Frascati, Palestrina, Porto and Santa Rufina, and Velletri and Segni. The order of Cardinal Bishops also includes one Cardinal of Patriarchal Sees of Oriental Rites. Cardinal Priests occupy titular churches in Rome, founded soon after Christianity originated. The administration of the Church's affairs is undertaken through the Secretariat of State and the Council for the Public Affairs of the Church, under the Cardinal Secretary of State, and through a number of Congregations, each under the direction of a Cardinal or senior member of the Church, as well as through Tribunals, Offices, Commissions and Secretariats for special purposes.

The 'Apostolic Constitution' (Regimini Ecclesiae Universae), published in August 1967 and effective from 1 March 1968, reformed the Roman Curia. Among the changes were the creation of new organs and the restructuring of the Secretariat of State. In 1969 the Congregation of Rites was divided into two Congregations—one for Divine Worship and the other for the Causes of Saints. The Congregation for the Discipline of the Sacraments and the Congregation for Divine Worship were amalgamated in 1975, but separated again in 1984.

In July 1988 further reforms of the Curia were introduced. The Secretariat of State was divided into two sections: the first section dealing with 'General Affairs' and the second 'Relations with States'. The Congregation of Divine Worship was again amalgamated with the Congregation of the Sacraments.

### THE SUPREME PONTIFF

His Holiness Pope JOHN PAUL II (KAROL WOJTYŁA), Bishop of Rome, Vicar of Christ, Successor of the Prince of the Apostles, Supreme Pontiff of the Universal Church, Patriarch of the West, Primate of Italy, Archbishop and Metropolitan of the Province of Rome, Sovereign of the Vatican City State, Servant of the Servants of God; acceded 16 October 1978, as the 264th Roman Pontiff.

### THE SACRED COLLEGE OF CARDINALS

The cardinals are divided into three orders: Bishops (including the Cardinal of Patriarchal Sees of Oriental Rites), Priests and Deacons. Under the decree of November 1970, *Ingravescentem Aetatem,* only Cardinals under 80 years of age have the right to enter the conclave for the election of the Pope.

(Members in order of precedence)

#### Cardinal Bishops

BERNARDIN GANTIN (Benin), Titular Bishop of Palestrina and of Ostia, Prefect of the Congregation for the Bishops, President of

# THE VATICAN CITY

the Pontifical Commission for Latin America, Dean of the College of Cardinals.

Agostino Casaroli (Italy), Titular Bishop of Porto and Santa Rufina, Subdean of the College of Cardinals.

Paolo Bertoli (Italy), Titular Bishop of Frascati.

Joseph Ratzinger (Germany), Titular Bishop of Velletri-Segni, Prefect of the Congregation for the Doctrine of the Faith and President of the International Theological Commission, and of the Pontifical Biblical Commission.

Angelo Sodano (Italy), Titular Bishop of Albano, Secretary of State.

### Cardinal of Patriarchal Sees of Oriental Rites

Nasrallah Pierre Sfeir (Lebanon), Maronite Patriarch of Antioch.

### Cardinal Priests

Franz König (Austria).
Laurean Rugambwa (Tanzania).
Juan Landázuri Ricketts (Peru).
Raúl Silva Henríquez (Chile).
Leo Jozef Suenens (Belgium).
Léon-Etienne Duval (France).
Paul Zoungrana (Burkina Faso), Archbishop of Ouagadougou.
John Krol (USA).
Corrado Ursi (Italy).
Alfredo Vicente Scherer (Brazil).
Silvio Oddi (Italy).
Paul Gouyon (France).
John Joseph Carberry (USA).
Stephen Sou Hwan Kim (Republic of Korea), Archbishop of Seoul, Apostolic Administrator of Pyongyang.
Eugênio de Araújo Sales (Brazil), Archbishop of São Sebastião do Rio de Janeiro.
Johannes Willebrands (Netherlands), Emeritus President of the Pontifical Council for the Promotion of Christian Unity and Chamberlain of the College of Cardinals.
António Ribeiro (Portugal), Patriarch of Lisbon.
Pietro Palazzini (Italy).
Luis Aponte Martínez (Puerto Rico), Archbishop of San Juan de Puerto Rico.
Raúl Francisco Primatesta (Argentina), Archbishop of Córdoba.
Salvatore Pappalardo (Italy), Archbishop of Palermo.
Marcelo González Martín (Spain).
Ugo Poletti (Italy), Archpriest of the Patriarchal Liberian Basilica of Santa Maria Maggiore.
Maurice Michael Otunga (Kenya), Archbishop of Nairobi.
Paulo Evaristo Arns (Brazil), Archbishop of São Paulo.
Narciso Jubany Arnau (Spain).
Pio Taofinu'u (Western Samoa), Archbishop of Samoa-Apia.
Opilio Rossi (Italy).
Giuseppe-Maria Sensi (Italy).
Juan Carlos Aramburu (Argentina).
Corrado Bafile (Italy).
Hyacinthe Thiandoum (Senegal), Archbishop of Dakar.
Jaime L. Sin (Philippines), Archbishop of Manila.
William Wakefield Baum (USA).
Aloísio Lorscheider (Brazil), Archbishop of Fortaleza.
Eduardo Francisco Pironio (Argentina), President of the Pontifical Council for the Laity.
George Basil Hume (United Kingdom), Archbishop of Westminster.
Dominic Ignatius Ekandem (Nigeria).
Mario Luigi Ciappi (Italy).
Giuseppe Caprio (Italy).
Marco Cé (Italy), Patriarch of Venice.
Egano Righi-Lambertini (Italy).
Ernesto Corripio Ahumada (Mexico).
Joseph Asajiro Satowaki (Japan).
Roger Etchegaray (France), President of the Pontifical Council for Justice and Peace, of the Pontifical Council 'Cor Unum', and of the Central Committee of the Jubilee for the Holy Year 2000.
Anastasio Alberto Ballestrero (Italy).
Gerald Emmett Carter (Canada).
Franciszek Macharski (Poland), Archbishop of Kraków.
Ignatius Gong Pin-mei (People's Republic of China), Bishop of Shanghai and Apostolic Administrator of Suzhou.
Bernard Yago (Côte d'Ivoire).
Aurelio Sabattani (Italy).
Franjo Kuharić (Croatia), Archbishop of Zagreb.
Giuseppe Casoria (Italy).
José Alí Lebrún Moratinos (Venezuela), Archbishop of Caracas.
Joseph Louis Bernardin (USA), Archbishop of Chicago.
Michael Michai Kitbunchu (Thailand), Archbishop of Bangkok.
Alexandre do Nascimento (Angola), Archbishop of Luanda.
Alfonso López Trujillo (Colombia), President of the Pontifical Council for the Family.
Godfried Danneels (Belgium), Archbishop of Mechelen-Brussels.
Thomas Stafford Williams (New Zealand), Archbishop of Wellington.
Carlo Maria Martini (Italy), Archbishop of Milan.
Jean-Marie Lustiger (France), Archbishop of Paris.
Józef Glemp (Poland), Archbishop of Warsaw.
Joachim Meisner (Germany), Archbishop of Cologne.
Juan Francisco Fresno Larraín (Chile).
Miguel Obando Bravo (Nicaragua), Archbishop of Managua.
Angel Suquía Goicoechea (Spain).
Ricardo J. Vidal (Philippines), Archbishop of Cebu.
Henryk Roman Gulbinowicz (Poland), Archbishop of Wrocław.
Paulos Tzadua (Ethiopia), Archbishop of Addis Ababa (Alexandrian-Ethiopian rite).
Myroslav Ivan Lubachivsky (Ukraine), Archbishop-Major of Lvov (Ukrainian rite).
Louis-Albert Vachon (Canada).
Friedrich Wetter (Germany), Archbishop of Munich and Freising.
Silvano Piovanelli (Italy), Archbishop of Florence.
Adrianus Johannes Simonis (Netherlands), Archbishop of Utrecht.
Bernard Francis Law (USA), Archbishop of Boston.
John Joseph O'Connor (USA), Archbishop of New York.
Giacomo Biffi (Italy), Archbishop of Bologna.
Anthony Padiyara (India), Archbishop-Major of Ernakulam (Syro-Malabarese rite).
José Freire Falcão (Brazil), Archbishop of Brasília.
Michele Giordano (Italy), Archbishop of Naples.
José Maria dos Santos Alexandre (Mozambique), Archbishop of Maputo.
Giovanni Canestri (Italy), Archbishop of Genoa.
Simon Ignatius Pimenta (India), Archbishop of Bombay.
Maria Revollo Bravo (Colombia).
Edward Bede Clancy (Australia), Archbishop of Sydney.
Lucas Moreira Neves (Brazil), Archbishop of São Salvador da Bahia.
James Aloysius Hickey (USA), Archbishop of Washington.
Edmund Casimir Szoka (USA), President of the Prefecture of the Economic Affairs of the Holy See.
László Paskai (Hungary), Archbishop of Esztergom.
Christian Wiyghan Tumi (Cameroon), Archbishop of Douala.
Hans Hermann Groër (Austria), Archbishop of Vienna.
Vincentas Sladkevičius (Lithuania), Archbishop of Kaunas.
Jean Margéot (Mauritius).
John Baptist Wu Cheng-Chung (Hong Kong), Bishop of Hong Kong.
Alexandru Todea (Romania).
Frédéric Etsou-Nzabi-Bamungwabi (Zaire), Archbishop of Kinshasa.
Nicolás de Jesús López Rodríguez (Dominican Republic), Archbishop of Santo Domingo.
Antonio Quarracino (Argentina), Archbishop of Buenos Aires.
Roger Michael Mahoney (USA), Archbishop of Los Angeles.
Anthony Joseph Bevilacqua (USA), Archbishop of Philadelphia.
Giovanni Saldarini (Italy), Archbishop of Turin.
Cahal Brendan Daly (Ireland), Archbishop of Armagh.
Camillo Ruini (Italy), Vicar-General of His Holiness for the diocese of Rome, Archpriest of the Lateran Patriarchal Arcibasilica, Grand Chancellor of the Lateran Pontifical University, President of the 'Pilgrimage to the Seat of Peter'.
Ján Chryzostom Korec (Slovakia), Bishop of Nitra.

# THE VATICAN CITY

*Directory*

Henri Schwéry (Switzerland), Bishop of Sion.
Georg Maximilian Sterzinsky (Germany), Archbishop of Berlin.
Miloslav Vlk (Czech Republic), Archbishop of Prague.
Peter Seiichi Shirayanagi (Japan), Archbishop of Tokyo.
Cavada Carlos Oviedo (Chile), Archbishop of Santiago.
Thomas Joseph Winning (United Kingdom), Archbishop of Glasgow.
Adolfo Antonio Suárez Rivera (Mexico), Archbishop of Monterrey and Apostolic Administrator of Ciudad Victoria.
Jaime Lucas Ortega y Alamino (Cuba), Archbishop of San Cristóbal de la Habana.
Julius Riyadi Darmaatmadja (Indonesia), Archbishop of Semarang.
Pierre Eyt (France), Archbishop of Bordeaux.
Emmanuel Wamala (Uganda), Archbishop of Kampala.
William Henry Keeler (USA), Archbishop of Baltimore.
Augusto Vargas Alzamora (Peru), Archbishop of Lima.
Jean-Claude Turcotte (Canada), Archbishop of Montreal.
Ricardo María Carles Gordó (Spain), Archbishop of Barcelona.
Adam Joseph Maida (USA), Archbishop of Detroit.
Vinko Puljić (Bosnia and Herzegovina), Archbishop of Vrhbosna.
Armand Gaétan Razafindratandra (Madagascar), Archbishop of Antananarivo and Apostolic Administrator of Miarinarivo.
Paul Joseph Pham Dình Tung (Viet Nam), Archbishop of Hanoi.
Juan Sandoval Iñiguez (Mexico), Archbishop of Guadalajara.
Bernardino Echeverría Ruiz (Ecuador), Apostolic Administrator of Ibarra.
Kazimierz Swiatek (Belarus), Archbishop of Minsk and Mogilev and Apostolic Administrator of Pinsk.
Ersilio Tonini (Italy).

### Cardinal Deacons

D. Simon Lourdusamy (India).
Francis A. Arinze (Nigeria), President of the Pontifical Council for Inter-Religious Dialogue.
Antonio Innocenti (Italy), President of the Pontifical Commission 'Ecclesia Dei'.
Paul Augustin Mayer (Germany).
Jean Jérôme Hamer (Belgium).
Jozef Tomko (Slovakia), Prefect of the Congregation for the Evangelization of Peoples and Grand Chancellor of the Pontifical Urban University.
Andrzej Maria Deskur (Poland), Emeritus President of the Pontifical Council for Social Communication.
Paul Poupard (France), President of the Pontifical Council for Culture.
Rosalio José Castillo Lara (Venezuela), President of the Administration of the Patrimony of the Holy See and of the Pontifical Commission for the Vatican City State.
Edouard Gagnon (Canada), President of the Pontifical Committee for International Eucharistic Congresses.
Alfons Maria Stickler (Austria).
Eduardo Martínez Somalo (Spain), Chamberlain of the Holy Roman Church, Prefect of the Congregation for Institutes of Consecrated Life and for Societies of Apostolic Life.
Achille Silvestrini (Italy), Prefect of the Congregation for the Eastern Churches and Grand Chancellor of the Pontifical Eastern Institute.
Angelo Felici (Italy), Prefect of the Congregation for the Causes of Saints.
Antonio María Javierre Ortas (Spain), Prefect of the Congregation for Divine Worship and the Discipline of the Sacraments.
Pio Laghi (Italy), Prefect of the Congregation for Catholic Education, Grand Chancellor of the Pontifical Gregorian University and Patron of the Supreme Military Order of Malta.
Edward Idris Cassidy (Australia), President of the Pontifical Council for the Promotion of Christian Unity.
José T. Sánchez (Philippines), Prefect of the Congregation for the Clergy.
Virgilio Noè (Italy), Archpriest of the Vatican Patriarchal Basilica, President of the Fabbrica di San Pietro and President of the Cardinals' Commission for the Pontifical Sanctuaries of Pompeii, Loreto and Bari.
Fiorenzo Angelini (Italy), President of the Pontifical Council for the Pastoral Care of Health Workers.
Paolo Dezza (Italy).
Luigi Poggi (Italy), Archivist and Librarian of the Holy Roman Church.
Vincenzo Fagiolo (Italy), President of the Disciplinary Commission of the Roman Curia.
Carlo Furno (Italy).
Jan Pieter Schotte (Belgium), Secretary-General of the Synod of Bishops and President of the Office of Work of the Apostolic See.
Gilberto Agustoni (Italy), Prefect of the Supreme Tribunal of the Apostolic Signature.
Mikel Koliqi (Albania).
Alois Grillmeier (Germany).

### THE ROMAN CURIA

**Secretariat of State:** Palazzo Apostolico Vaticano, 00120 Città del Vaticano; tel. (6) 69883913; fax (6) 69885255; Sec. of State Cardinal Angelo Sodano; divided into two sections:

**First Section—General Affairs:** Palazzo Apostolico Vaticano, 00120 Città del Vaticano; tel. (6) 69883438; telex 2015; fax (6) 69885088; Asst Sec. of State Most Rev. Giovanni Battista Re, Titular Archbishop of Vescovio.

**Second Section—Relations with States:** Palazzo Apostolico Vaticano, 00120 Città del Vaticano; tel. (6) 69883014; telex 2029; fax (6) 69885364; Sec. Most Rev. Jean-Louis Tauran, Titular Archbishop of Thelepte.

#### Congregations

**Congregation for the Doctrine of the Faith:** Palazo delle Congregazioni, Piazza del Sant'Uffizio II, 00193 Rome; tel. (6) 69883357; fax (6) 69883409; concerned with questions of doctrine and morals; examines doctrines and gives a judgement on them. Prefect Cardinal Joseph Ratzinger; Sec. Most Rev. Alberto Bovone, Titular Archbishop of Caesarea.

**Congregation for the Eastern Churches:** Palazzo del Bramante, Via della Conciliazione 34, 00193 Rome; tel. (6) 69884282; fax (6) 69884300; f. 1862; exercises jurisdiction over all persons and things pertaining to the Oriental Rites. Prefect Cardinal Achille Silvestrini; Sec. Most Rev. Miroslav Stefan Marusyn, Titular Archbishop of Cadi.

**Congregation for Divine Worship and the Discipline of the Sacraments:** Palazzo delle Congregazioni, Piazza Pio XII 10, 00193 Rome; tel. (6) 69884316; fax (6) 69883499; considers all questions relating to divine worship, liturgy and the sacraments. Prefect Cardinal Antonio María Javierre Ortas; Sec Most Rev. Geraldo Majella Agnelo.

**Congregation for the Causes of Saints:** Palazzo delle Congregazioni, Piazza Pio XII 10, 00193 Rome; tel. (6) 69884247; concerned with the proceedings relating to beatification and canonization. Prefect Cardinal Angelo Felici; Sec. Most Rev. Edward Nowak, Titular Archbishop of Luni.

**Congregation for the Bishops:** Palazzo delle Congregazioni, Piazza Pio XII 10, 00193 Rome; tel. (6) 69884217; fax (6) 69885303; designed for the preparation of matters for the erection and division of dioceses and the election of Bishops and for dealing with Apostolic Visitations. Prefect Cardinal Bernardin Gantin; Sec. Most Rev. Jorge María Mejía, Titular Archbishop of Apollonia.

**Pontifical Commission for Latin America:** Palazzo di San Paolo, Via della Conciliazione 1, 00193 Rome; tel. (6) 69883131; fax (6) 69884260; Pres. Cardinal Bernardin Gantin; Vice-Pres. Rt Rev. Cipriano Calderón Polo, Titular Bishop of Thagora.

**Congregation for the Evangelization of Peoples:** Palazzo di Propaganda Fide, Piazza di Spagna 48, 00187 Rome; tel. (6) 6796941; fax (6) 6793906; exercises ecclesiastical jurisdiction over missionary countries. Prefect Cardinal Jozef Tomko; Sec. Most Rev. Giuseppe Uhač, Titular Archbishop of Tharros.

**Congregation for the Clergy:** Palazzo delle Congregazioni, Piazza Pio XII 3, 00193 Rome; tel. (6) 69884151; fax (6) 69884845; controls the life and discipline of the clergy and its permanent formation; parishes, chapters, pastoral and presbyterial councils; promotes catechesis and the preaching of the Word of God; deals with economic questions related to the compensation of the clergy and the patrimony of parishes. Prefect Cardinal José T. Sánchez; Sec. Most Rev. Crescenzio Sepe, Titular Archbishop of Grado.

**Congregation for Institutes of Consecrated Life and for Societies of Apostolic Life:** Palazzo delle Congregazioni, Piazza Pio XII 3, 00193 Rome; tel. (6) 69884128; fax (6) 69884526; promotes and supervises practice of evangelical counsels, according to approved forms of consecrated life, and activities of societies of apostolic life. Prefect Cardinal Eduardo Martínez Somalo; Sec. Most Rev. Francisco Javier Errázuriz Ossa, Titular Archbishop of Hólar.

# THE VATICAN CITY

**Congregation for Catholic Education:** Palazzo delle Congregazioni, Piazza Pio XII 3, 00193 Rome; tel. (6) 69884167; fax (6) 69884172; concerned with the direction, temporal administration and studies of Catholic universities, seminaries, schools and colleges. Prefect Cardinal PIO LAGHI; Sec. Most Rev. JOSÉ SARAIVA MARTINS, Titular Archbishop of Thuburnica.

### Tribunals

**Apostolic Penitentiary:** Palazzo della Cancelleria, Piazza della Cancelleria 1, 00186 Rome; tel. (6) 69887526; Grand Penitentiary Cardinal WILLIAM WAKEFIELD BAUM; Regent Mgr LUIGI DE MAGISTRIS.

**Supreme Tribunal of the Apostolic Signature:** Palazzo della Cancelleria Apostolica, Piazza della Cancelleria 1, 00186 Rome; tel. (6) 69887520; fax (6) 69887553; Prefect Cardinal GILBERTO AGUSTONI; Sec. Most Rev. ZENON GROCHOLEWSKI, Titular Archbishop of Agropoli.

**Tribunal of the Roman Rota:** Palazzo della Cancelleria, Piazza della Cancelleria 1, 00186 Rome; tel. (6) 69887502; fax (6) 69887554; Dean Mgr MARIO FRANCESCO POMPEDDA.

### Pontifical Councils

**Pontifical Council for the Laity:** Piazza S. Calisto 16, 00153 Rome; tel. (6) 69887322; fax (6) 69887214; advises and conducts research, on lay apostolic initiatives; Pres. Cardinal EDUARDO FRANCISCO PIRONIO; Vice-Pres. Rt Rev. PAUL JOSEF CORDES, Titular Bishop of Naisso.

**Pontifical Council for the Promotion of Christian Unity:** Via dell'Erba 1, 00193 Rome; tel. (6) 69883071; telex 2024; fax (6) 69885365; f. 1964; Pres. Cardinal EDWARD IDRIS CASSIDY; Sec. Rt Rev. PIERRE DUPREY, Titular Bishop of Thibaris.

**Pontifical Council for the Family:** Piazza S. Calisto 16, 00153 Rome; tel. (6) 69887243; fax (6) 69887272; Pres. Cardinal ALFONSO LÓPEZ TRUJILLO; Sec. Rt Rev. ELIO SGRECCIA, Titular Bishop of Zama Minore.

**Pontifical Council for Justice and Peace:** Piazza S. Calisto 16, 00153 Rome; tel. (6) 69887191; fax (6) 69887205; to promote social justice, human rights, peace and development in needy areas; Pres. Cardinal ROGER ETCHEGARAY; Vice-Pres. Rt Rev. FRANÇOIS XAVIER NGUYÊN VAN THUÂN, Titular Archbishop of Vadesi.

**Pontifical Council 'Cor Unum':** Piazza S. Calisto 16, 00153 Rome; tel. (6) 69887331; telex 2030; fax (6) 69887301; f. 1971; Pres. Cardinal ROGER ETCHEGARAY; Sec. Mgr IVÁN MARÍN LOPEZ.

**Pontifical Council for the Pastoral Care of Migrants and Itinerant People:** Piazza S. Calisto 16, 00153 Rome; tel. (6) 69887193; telex 2028; fax (6) 69887111; f. 1970; Pres. Most Rev. GIOVANNI CHELI, Titular Archbishop of Santa Giusta; Sec. Fr SILVANO M. TOMASI.

**Pontifical Council for the Pastoral Care of Health Workers:** Via della Conciliazione 3, 00193 Rome; tel. (6) 69883138; telex 2031; fax (6) 69883139; Pres. Cardinal FIORENZO ANGELINI; Sec. Fr JOSÉ LUIS REDRADO MARCHITE.

**Pontifical Council for the Interpretation of Legislative Texts:** Palazzo delle Congregazioni, Piazza Pio XII 10, 00193 Rome; tel. (6) 69884008; fax (6) 69884710; f. 1984; Pres. Most Rev. JULIÁN HERRANZ, Titular Archbishop of Vertara; Sec. Rt Rev. BRUNO BERTAGNA, Titular Bishop of Drivasto.

**Pontifical Council for Inter-Religious Dialogue:** Via dell'Erba 1, 00193 Rome; tel. (6) 69884321; fax (6) 69884494; f. 1964; Pres. Cardinal FRANCIS A. ARINZE; Sec. Rt Rev. MICHAEL LOUIS FITZGERALD, Titular Bishop of Nepte.

**Pontifical Council for Culture:** Piazza S. Calisto 16, 00153 Rome; tel. (6) 69887321; fax (6) 69887368; merged with Pontifical Council for Dialogue with Non-Believers in 1993; promotes understanding and dialogue between the Church and the arts; Pres. Cardinal PAUL POUPARD; Sec. Mgr FRANC RODÉ.

**Pontifical Council for Social Communication:** Palazzo S. Carlo, 00120 Città del Vaticano; tel. (6) 69883197; telex 2019; fax (6) 69885373; f. 1948 to examine the relationship between the media and religious affairs; Pres. Most Rev. JOHN PATRICK FOLEY, Titular Archbishop of Neapolis; Sec. Rt Rev. PIERFRANCO PASTORE, Titular Bishop of Forontoniana.

### Pontifical Commissions and Committees

**Holy See Press Office:** Via della Conciliazione 54, 00193 Rome; tel. (6) 698921; fax (6) 69885178; Dir Dr JOAQUÍN NAVARRO-VALLS; Asst Fr CIRO BENEDETTINI.

**Central Statistical Office of the Church:** Palazzo Apostolico, 00120 Città del Vaticana; tel. (6) 69883064; Dir Mgr PIETRO SILVI.

**Pontifical Commission for the Cultural Heritage of the Church:** Palazzo della Cancelleria Apostolica, Piazza della Cancellaria 1, 00186 Rome; tel. (6) 69887517; fax (6) 69887567; f. 1988; Pres. Most Rev. FRANCESCO MARCHISANO, Titular Archbishop of Populonia; Sec. Rev. Mgr PAOLO RABITTI.

**Pontifical Biblical Commission:** Palazzo della Congregazione per la Dottrina della Fede, Piazza del S. Uffizio 11, 00193 Rome; tel. (6) 69884886; Pres. Cardinal JOSEPH RATZINGER; Sec. Rev. Fr ALBERT VANHOYE.

**International Theological Commission:** Palazzo della Congregazione per la Dottrina della Fede, Piazza del S. Uffizio 11, 00193 Rome; tel. (6) 69884638; Pres. Cardinal JOSEPH RATZINGER; Sec.-Gen. Rev. Fr GEORGES MARIE MARTIN COTTIER.

**Pontifical Commission for the Revision and Amendment of the Vulgate:** Via di Torre Rossa 21, 00165 Rome; tel. (6) 6638792; Dir Rev. Fr JEAN MALLET.

**Pontifical Committee for International Eucharistic Congresses:** Piazza S. Calisto 16, 00153 Rome; tel. and fax (6) 69887366; Pres. Cardinal EDOUARD GAGNON; Sec. Rev. Fr FERDINAND PRATZNER.

**Pontifical Commission of Sacred Archaeology:** Palazzo del Pontificio Istituto di Archeologia Cristiana, Via Napoleone 111 1, 00185 Rome; tel. (6) 4465610; fax (6) 4467625; Pres. Most Rev. FRANCESCO MARCHISANO, Titular Archbishop of Populonia; Sec. Prof. FABRIZIO BISCONTI.

**Pontifical Committee of Historical Sciences:** Palazzo delle Congregazioni, Piazza Pio XII 3, 00193 Rome; tel. and fax (6) 69884618; Pres. Mgr VICTOR SAXER; Sec. Rev. Fr VITTORINO GROSSI.

**Pontifical Commission 'Ecclesia Dei':** Palazzo del Sant' Uffizio, Piazza del Sant' Uffizio 11, 00193 Rome; tel. (6) 69885213; Pres. Cardinal ANTONIO INNOCENTI.

**Archives of the Second Vatican Council:** Palazzo delle Congregazioni, Piazza Pio XII 10, 00193 Rome; tel. (6) 69884236; Dir Mgr VINCENZO CARBONE.

**Cardinals' Commission for the Pontifical Sanctuaries of Pompeii, Loreto and Bari:** Congregazione per il Clero, Piazza Pio XII 3, 00193 Rome; Pres. Cardinal VIRGILIO NOÈ; Sec. Most Rev. CRESCENZIO SEPE, Titular Archbishop of Grado.

**Disciplinary Commission of the Roman Curia:** 00120 Città del Vaticano; Pres. Cardinal VINCENZO FAGIOLO.

**Council of Cardinals for the Study of Organizational and Economic Problems of the Holy See:** 00120 Città del Vaticano.

**Central Committee of the Jubilee for the Holy Year 2000:** Piazza della Città Leonina 9, 00193 Rome; tel. (6) 69882258; fax (6) 69881227; Pres. Cardinal ROGER ETCHEGARAY.

### Offices

**Apostolic Chamber:** Palazzo Apostolico, 00120 Città del Vaticano; tel. (6) 69883554; Chamberlain of the Holy Roman Church Cardinal EDUARDO MARTÍNEZ SOMALO; Vice-Chamberlain Most Rev. ETTORE CUNIAL, Titular Archbishop of Soteropolis.

**Administration of the Patrimony of the Holy See:** Palazzo Apostolico, 00120 Città del Vaticano; tel. (6) 69884306; fax (6) 69883141; f. 1967; Pres. Cardinal ROSALIO JOSÉ CASTILLO LARA; Sec. Most Rev. GIOVANNI LAJOLO, Titular Archbishop of Caesariana.

**Prefecture of the Economic Affairs of the Holy See:** Palazzo delle Congregazioni, Largo del Colonnato 3, 00193 Rome; tel. (6) 69884263; fax (6) 69885011; f. 1967; Pres. Cardinal EDMUND CASIMIR SZOKA; Sec. Rt Rev. LUIGI SPOSITO, Titular Bishop of Tagaria.

**Prefecture of the Papal Household:** Via Monte della Farina 64, 00186 Rome; tel. (6) 69883273; fax (6) 69885863; f. 1967; responsible for domestic administration and organization; Prefect Rt Rev. DINO MONDUZZI, Titular Bishop of Capri.

**Office of the Liturgical Celebrations of the Supreme Pontiff:** Palazzo Apostolico, 00120 Città del Vaticano; tel. (6) 69883253; fax (6) 69885412; Master of Pontifical Liturgical Celebrations PIERO MARINI.

**Office of Work of the Apostolic See:** Via della Conciliazione 1, 00193 Rome; tel. (6) 69884449; fax (6) 69883800; Pres. Cardinal JAN PIETER SCHOTTE.

# Diplomatic Representation

### DIPLOMATIC MISSIONS IN ROME ACCREDITED TO THE HOLY SEE

**Andorra:** Rome.

**Argentina:** Palazzo Patrizi, Piazza S. Luigi de' Francesi 37, 00186 Rome; tel. (6) 6865303; fax (6) 6879021; Ambassador: FRANCISCO EDUARDO TRUSSO.

**Australia:** Via Paola 24/10, 00186 Rome; tel. (6) 6877688; fax (6) 6896255; Ambassador: MICHAEL C. TATE.

**Austria:** Via Reno 9, 00198 Rome; tel. (6) 8417427; fax (6) 8543058; Ambassador: CHRISTOPH CORNARO.

# THE VATICAN CITY

**Belgium:** Via G. de Notaris 6A, 00197 Rome; tel. (6) 3224740; fax (6) 3226042; Ambassador: Juan Cassiers.
**Bolivia:** Via Archimede 129/7, 00197 Rome; tel. (6) 8072225; fax (6) 8076876; Ambassador: Armando Loaiza Mariaca.
**Brazil:** Via della Conciliazione 22, 00193 Rome; tel. (6) 6875252; fax (6) 6872540; Ambassador: Gilberto Coutinho Paranhos Velloso.
**Bulgaria:** Via F. Galiani 36, 00193 Rome; tel. (6) 36307712; fax (6) 3292987; Ambassador: Kiril Kirilov Maritchkov.
**Canada:** Via della Conciliazione 4D, 00193 Rome; tel. (6) 68307316; fax (6) 68806283; Ambassador: Léonard H. Legault.
**Chile:** Piazza Risorgimento 55/20, 00192 Rome; tel. (6) 6868925; telex 612032; fax (6) 6874992; Ambassador: Javier Luis Egaña Baraona.
**China (Taiwan):** Piazza delle Muse 7, 00197 Rome; tel. (6) 8083166; fax (6) 8085679; Ambassador: Edward Wu Tsu-yu.
**Colombia:** Via Cola di Rienzo 285/12B, 00192 Rome; tel. (6) 3211681; telex 622155; fax (6) 3211703; Ambassador: Julio César Turbay Ayala.
**Costa Rica:** Via Val Padana 118, 00141 Rome; tel. (6) 8102882; Ambassador: (vacant).
**Côte d'Ivoire:** Via Sforza Pallavicini 11, 00193 Rome; tel. (6) 6877503; fax (6) 6867925; Ambassador: Joseph Amichia.
**Croatia:** Via della Fonte di Fauno 20, 00153 Rome; tel. (6) 57300620; fax (6) 57300650; Ambassador: Ive Livjanić.
**Cuba:** Via Aurelia 137/12B, 00165 Rome; tel. and fax (6) 636685; Ambassador: Hermes Herrera Hernández.
**Czech Republic:** Via Crescenzio 91/1B, 00193 Rome; tel. and fax (6) 6879731; Ambassador: František X. Halas.
**Dominican Republic:** Lungotevere Marzio 3/6, 00186 Rome; tel. (6) 6864084; Ambassador: Ramón Arturo Cáceres Rodríguez.
**Ecuador:** Borgo Santo Spirito 16, 00193 Rome; tel. (6) 6897179; fax (6) 6872826; Chargé d'affaires a.i.: Galo Andrés Yepez Holguín.
**Egypt:** Piazza della Città Leonina 9, 00193 Rome; tel. (6) 6865878; fax (6) 6832335; Ambassador: Ismail Azmy el-Kattan.
**El Salvador:** Via Panama 22/2, 00198 Rome; tel. (6) 8450538; fax (6) 85301131; Ambasssador: Roberto José Siman Jacir.
**Finland:** Villa Lante, Passeggiata del Gianicolo 10, 00165 Rome; tel. (6) 68804604; Ambassador: Henry Söderholm (resident in Bern, Switzerland).
**France:** Villa Bonaparte, Via Piave 23, 00187 Rome; tel. (6) 4883842; fax (6) 4821507; Ambassador: Alain Pierret.
**Germany:** Via di Villa Sacchetti 4, 00197 Rome; tel. (6) 809511; fax (6) 80951227; Ambassador: Dr Philipp Jenninger.
**Greece:** Via Giuseppe Mercalli 6, 00197 Rome; tel. (6) 8070786; fax (6) 8079862; Ambassador: Georges Christoyannis.
**Guatemala:** Piazzale Gregorio VII 65/A, 00165 Rome; tel. (6) 6381632; fax (6) 39376981; Ambassador: Mario Alfonso de la Cerda Bustamente.
**Honduras:** Via Boezio 45, 00192 Rome; tel. and fax (6) 6876051; Ambassador: Alejandro Emilio Valladares Lanza.
**Hungary:** Piazza Girolamo Fabrizio 2, 00161 Rome; tel. (6) 4402167; fax (6) 4402312; Ambassador: József Bratinka.
**Indonesia:** Piazzale Roberto Ardigò 42/2A, 00142 Rome; tel. (6) 5940441; fax (6) 5417934; Ambassador: (vacant).
**Iran:** Via Bruxelles 57, 00198 Rome; tel. (6) 8552494; fax (6) 8547910; Ambassador: Mohammed Masjed Jame'i.
**Iraq:** Via della Camilluccia 355, 00135 Rome; tel. (6) 3011140; Ambassador: Wissam Chawkat al-Zahawi.
**Ireland:** Villa Spada al Gianicolo, Via Giacomo Medici 1, 00153 Rome; tel. (6) 5810777; telex 623872; fax (6) 5895709; Ambassador: Gearóid P. Ó Broin.
**Israel:** Via Taramelli 7, 00197 Rome; tel. (6) 3236711; fax (6) 3236715; Ambassador: Shmuel Hadas.
**Italy:** Palazzo Borromeo, Viale delle Belle Arti 2, 00196 Rome; tel. (6) 3200741; fax (6) 3201801; Ambassador: Bruno Bottai.
**Japan:** Via Virgilio 30, 00193 Rome; tel. (6) 6875828; telex 610602; fax (6) 68807543; Ambassador: Dr Tadao Johannes Araki.
**Korea, Republic:** Via della Mendola 109, 00135 Rome; tel. (6) 3314505; fax (6) 3314522; Ambassador: Noh-Young Park.
**Lebanon:** Via di Porta Angelica 15, 00193 Rome; tel. (6) 6833512; fax (6) 6833505; Ambassador: Youssef Arsanios.
**Lithuania:** Piazza Farnese 44/4c, 00186 Rome; tel. (6) 6867855; fax (6) 6865786; Ambassador: Kazys Lozoraitis.
**Luxembourg:** Via Casale di S. Pio V 20, 00165 Rome; tel. (6) 6638809; fax (6) 66000915; Ambassador: Jean Wagner (resident in Luxembourg).
**Mexico:** Via Ezio 49, 00192 Rome; tel. (6) 3230857; fax (6) 3230361; Ambassador: Guillermo Jiménez Morales.
**Monaco:** Largo Nicola Spinelli 5, 00198 Rome; tel. (6) 8414357; fax (6) 8414507; Ambassador: César Charles Solamito.
**Netherlands:** Piazza della Città Leonina 9, 00193 Rome; tel. (6) 6868044; fax (6) 6879593; Ambassador: Roland Hugo van Limburg Stirum.
**Nicaragua:** Via Luigi Luciani 42/1, 00197 Rome; tel. (6) 36000880; fax (6) 3223549; Ambassador: Filadelfo Chamorro Coronel.
**Panama:** Viale Parioli 190 int. 7A, 00197 Rome; tel. (6) 8078052; fax (6) 8078053; Chargé d'affaires a.i.: Porfirio Castillo Meléndez.
**Paraguay:** Piazzo Americo Capponi 16, 00193 Rome; tel. (6) 6878524; fax (6) 6876941; Ambassador: Luis Angel Casati Ferro.
**Peru:** Via del Mascherino 75, 00193 Rome; tel. (6) 68308535; fax (6) 6896059; Ambassador: Luis Solari Tudela.
**Philippines:** Via Paolo VI 29, 00193 Rome; tel. (6) 68308020; fax (6) 6834076; Ambassador: Oscar S. Villadolid.
**Poland:** Borgo Santo Spirito 16/4, 00193 Rome; tel. (6) 68802000; fax (6) 6874408; Chargé d'affaires a.i.: Wojciech Bilinski.
**Portugal:** Villa Lusa, Via S. Valentino 9, 00197 Rome; tel. (6) 8077012; telex 622293; fax (6) 8084634; Ambassador: António Augusto de Medeiros Patrício.
**Romania:** Via Panama 92, 00198 Rome; tel. (6) 8541802; fax (6) 8554067; Ambassador: Gheorghe Pancratiu Iuliu Gheorghiu.
**Russia:** Via della Cava Aurelia 199, 00165 Rome; tel. (6) 39379133; fax (6) 39379132; Ambassador: Yuri Yevgeniyevich Karlov.
**San Marino:** Piazza G. Winckelmann 12, 00162 Rome; tel. (6) 86210353; fax (6) 86320821; Ambassador: Prof. Giovanni Galassi.
**Senegal:** Via dei Monti Parioli 51, 00197 Rome; tel. (6) 3218892; Ambassador: Henri Antoine Turpin.
**Slovakia:** Via dei Colli della Farnesina 144/Lotto VI/B, 00194 Rome; tel. and fax (6) 3296507; Ambassador: Anton Neuwirth.
**Slovenia:** Via della Conciliazione 10, 00193 Rome; tel. (6) 6833009; fax (6) 68307942; Ambassador: Dr Štefan Falež.
**Spain:** Palazzo di Spagna, Piazza di Spagna 57, 00187 Rome; tel. (6) 6784351; telex 610186; fax 6784355; Ambassador: Pedro López Aguirrebengoa.
**Sweden:** Via Maurizio Bufalini 2, 00161 Rome; tel. (6) 44194500; fax (6) 44194763; Ambassador: Torsten Örn.
**Turkey:** Via Lovanio 24, 00198 Rome; tel. (6) 8550454; fax (6) 8543986; Ambassador: Ömer Engin Lütem.
**United Kingdom:** Via Condotti 91, 00187 Rome; tel. (6) 6789462; fax (6) 69940684; Ambassador: Maureen MacGlashan.
**USA:** Villa Domiziana, Via delle Terme Deciane 26, 00153 Rome; tel. (6) 46741; fax (6) 6380159; Ambassador: Raymond L. Flynn.
**Uruguay:** Via Antonio Gramsci 9, 00197 Rome; tel. (6) 3218904; fax (6) 3613249; Ambassador: Jorge Silva Cencio.
**Venezuela:** Via Antonio Gramsci 14, 00197 Rome; tel. (6) 3225868; fax (6) 36001505; Ambassador: Alberto Vollmer.
**Zaire:** Via del Cottolengo 1/3B, 00165 Rome; tel. (6) 631075; telex 2024; fax (6) 69885378; Ambassador: M'Atembina-te-Bombo.

## Ecclesiastical Organization

The organization of the Church consists of:
 (1) Patriarchs, Archbishops and Bishops in countries under the common law of the Church.
 (2) Abbots and Prelates 'nullius dioceseos'.
 (3) Vicars Apostolic and Prefects Apostolic in countries classified as Missionary and under Propaganda, the former having Episcopal dignity.

The population of the world adhering to the Roman Catholic faith was estimated in 1994 at 958m., about 17% of the total.

Among the Pope's titles is that of Patriarch of the West. There are five other Patriarchs of the Latin Rite—Jerusalem, the West Indies, the East Indies, Lisbon and Venice. The Eastern Catholic Churches each have Patriarchs: Alexandria for the Coptic Rite, Babylon for the Chaldean Rite, Cilicia for the Armenian Rite, and Antioch for the Syrian, Maronite and Melkite Rites.

At 31 December 1994 there were 2,571 residential sees—13 patriarchates, 489 metropolitan archbishoprics, 70 archbishoprics and 1,999 bishoprics. Of the 2,024 titular sees (91 metropolitan archbishoprics, 91 archbishoprics and 1,842 bishoprics), 1,037 are filled by bishops who have been given these titles, but exercise no territorial jurisdiction. Other territorial divisions of the Church include 55 prelacies, 16 territorial abbacies, 10 apostolic administrations, 20 exarchates of the Eastern Church, 73 apostolic vicariates, 43 apostolic prefectures and 8 missions 'sui iuris'.

## The Press

**Acta Apostolicae Sedis:** The Secretariat of State, Palazzo Apostolico, 00120 Città del Vaticano; tel. (6) 69883693; f. 1909; official

# THE VATICAN CITY

bulletin issued by the Holy See; monthly, with special editions on special occasions; the record of Encyclicals and other Papal pronouncements, Acts of the Sacred Congregations and Offices, nominations, etc.; circ. 6,000.

**Annuario Pontificio:** Palazzo Apostolico, 00120 Città del Vaticano; tel. (6) 69883064; official year book edited by Central Statistical Office.

**L'Osservatore Romano:** Via del Pellegrino, 00120 Città del Vaticano; tel. (6) 69883461; telex 2021; fax (6) 69883675; f. 1861; an authoritative daily newspaper; its special columns devoted to the affairs of the Holy See may be described as semi-official; the news service covers religious matters and, in a limited measure, general affairs; weekly editions in Italian, French, Spanish, Portuguese, German and English; monthly edition in Polish; Dir Prof. MARIO AGNES; Chief Editor ANTONIO CHILÀ.

**Statistical Yearbook of the Church:** Via della Tipografia, 00120 Città del Vaticano; tel. (6) 69884834; fax (6) 69884716.

### NEWS AGENCY

**Agenzia Internazionale Fides (AIF):** Palazzo di Propaganda Fide, Via di Propaganda 1C, 00187 Rome; tel. (6) 6792414; fax (6) 69942468; f. 1926; handles news of missions throughout the world; Dir Dr ANGELO SCELZO.

## Publishers

**Biblioteca Apostolica Vaticana:** 00120 Città del Vaticano; tel. (6) 69885051; fax (6) 69884795; philology, classics, history, catalogues; Librarian of the Holy Roman Church Cardinal LUIGI POGGI; Prefect Fr LEONARD E. BOYLE.

**Libreria Editrice Vaticana:** Via della Tipografia, 00120 Città del Vaticano; tel. (6) 69885003; telex 2024; fax 69884716; f. 1926; religion, philosophy, literature, art, Latin philology, history; Pres. Most Rev. GIOVANNI DE ANDREA, Titular Archbishop of Acquaviva; Dir Rev. NICOLÒ SUFFI.

**Tipografia Vaticana** (Vatican Press): 00120 Città del Vaticano; tel. (6) 69883011; fax (6) 69884570; f. 1587; education, juveniles, natural and social sciences; prints *Acta Apostolicae Sedis* and *L'Osservatore Romano*; Dir-Gen. Rev. ELIO TORRIGIANI; Admin. Dir GIACOMO BONASSOLI.

## Radio and Television

Radio Vaticana was founded in 1931 and situated within the Vatican City. A transmitting centre, inaugurated by Pius XII in 1957, is located at Santa Maria di Galeria, about 20 km north-west of the Vatican. Under a special treaty between the Holy See and Italy, the site of this centre, which covers 420 ha, enjoys the same extra-territorial privileges as are recognized by international law for the diplomatic headquarters of foreign states.

The station operates an all-day service, normally in 37 languages, but with facilities for broadcasting liturgical and other religious services in additional languages, including Latin.

The purpose of the Vatican Radio is to broadcast Papal teaching, to provide information on important events in the Catholic Church, to express the Catholic point of view on problems affecting religion and morality, but above all to form a continuous link between the Holy See and Catholics throughout the world.

**Radio Vaticana:** Palazzo Pio, Piazza Pia 3, 00193 Rome; tel. (6) 69883551; telex 2023; fax (6) 69883237; Pres. Rev. Fr ROBERTO TUCCI; Dir-Gen. Rev. Fr PASQUALE BORGOMEO, SJ; Tech. Dir Rev. Fr EUGENIO MATIS, SJ; Dir of Programmes Rev. Fr FEDERICO LOMBARDI, SJ.

**Centro Televisivo Vaticano** (Vatican Television Centre): 00120 Città del Vaticano; tel. (6) 69885467; fax (6) 69885192; f. 1983; produces and distributes religious programmes; Pres. Dott. EMILIO ROSSI; Sec.-Gen. Rev. Fr ANTONIO STEFANIZZI.

## Finance

**Istituto per le Opere di Religione (IOR):** 00120 Città del Vaticano; tel. (6) 69883354; telex 610030; fax (6) 69883809; f. 1887 and re-named in 1942; oversees the distribution of capital designated for religious works; its assets are believed to lie between US $3,000m. and $4,000m.; it takes deposits from Vatican residents, including the Pope; administrative changes, announced in 1989, involved the abolition of the post of chairman, and the appointment of a commission of five cardinals, assisted by a committee of financial experts; Pres. Prof. ANGELO CALOIA; Dir-Gen. Comm. LELIO SCALETTI; Commission mems: Cardinals ANGELO SODANO, CARLO FURNO, JOHN JOSEPH O'CONNOR, ROSALIO JOSÉ CASTILLO LARA, EDUARDO MARTÍNEZ SOMALO.

## Trade Union

In March 1989 the Pope agreed to establish a Labour Council to settle any disputes between the Holy See and its lay employees.

**Associazione Dipendenti Laici Vaticani** (Association of Vatican Lay Workers): Arco del Belvedere, 00120 Città del Vaticano; tel. (6) 69885343; fax (6) 69884400; f. 1979; aims to safeguard the professional, legal, economic and moral interests of its members; Sec.-Gen. VALERIO ARRINGOLI; mems 2,000.

## Transport

There is a small railway (862m) which runs from the Vatican into Italy. It began to operate in 1934 and now carries supplies and goods. There is also a heliport used by visiting heads of state and Vatican officials.

# VENEZUELA

## Introductory Survey

**Location, Climate, Language, Religion, Flag, Capital**

The Republic of Venezuela lies on the north coast of South America, bordered by Colombia to the west, Guyana to the east and Brazil to the south. The climate varies with altitude from tropical to temperate; the average temperature in Caracas is 21°C (69°F). The language is Spanish. There is no state religion, but more than 90% of the population is Roman Catholic. The national flag (proportions 3 by 2) has three horizontal stripes of yellow, blue and red, with seven five-pointed white stars, arranged in a semi-circle, in the centre of the blue stripe. The state flag has, in addition, the national coat of arms (a shield bearing a gold wheat sheaf, a panoply of swords, flags and a lance, and a white running horse in its three divisions, flanked by branches of laurel and palm and with two cornucopias at the crest) in the top left-hand corner. The capital is Caracas.

**Recent History**

Venezuela was a Spanish colony from 1499 until 1821 and, under the leadership of Simón Bolívar, achieved independence in 1830. The country was governed principally by dictators until 1945, when a military-civilian coup replaced Isaías Medina Angarita by Rómulo Betancourt as head of a revolutionary junta. Col (later Gen.) Marcos Pérez Jiménez seized power in December 1952 and took office as President in 1953. He remained in office until 1958, when he was overthrown by a military junta under Adm. Wolfgang Larrazábal. Betancourt was elected President in the same year.

The Constitution now in force was promulgated in 1961. Three years later President Betancourt became the first Venezuelan President to complete his term of office. Dr Raúl Leoni was elected President in December 1963. Supporters of the former President, Pérez, staged an abortive military uprising in 1966. Dr Rafael Caldera Rodríguez became Venezuela's first Christian Democratic President in March 1969. He succeeded in stabilizing the country politically and economically, although political assassinations and abductions committed by underground organizations continued into 1974. At elections in December 1973 Carlos Andrés Pérez Rodríguez, candidate of Acción Democrática (AD), the main opposition party, was chosen to succeed President Caldera. The Government's policy was to invest heavily in agriculture and industrial development to create a more balanced economy, and to nationalize important sectors. The presidential election of December 1978 was won by the leader of the Partido Social-Cristiano (Comité de Organización Política Electoral Independiente—COPEI), Dr Luis Herrera Campíns, who took office in March 1979. As his party did not obtain an overall majority in the Congreso Nacional (National Congress) at the simultaneous general elections, President Herrera Campíns sought an alliance with smaller parties, particularly the Unión Republicana Democrática, in order to secure sufficient legislative support for the government programme.

In 1981 the deteriorating economic situation provoked social unrest and a wave of guerrilla attacks. In 1982 the left-wing parties under the Nueva Alternativa joined forces in preparation for presidential elections in 1983, in which José Vicente Rangel was to be their candidate. Dr Caldera and Dr Jaime Lusinchi were announced as the candidates for the COPEI and the AD, respectively. Twenty political parties and 13 presidential candidates participated in the election campaign, which commenced in April 1983. At the presidential election in December, Dr Lusinchi was elected with 56.8% of the votes cast. The AD won the majority of seats in the Congreso Nacional. On assuming power in February 1984, the President announced that the Government would launch a 'national crusade' against corruption, and reaffirmed his administration's opposition to any foreign intervention in Central America. In May the ruling party's dominance of political life was emphasized by its decisive victory in the municipal elections. However, President Lusinchi's personal popularity was thought to be waning, principally as a result of his Government's stringent economic policies.

Throughout 1985 domestic events were dominated by the Government's attempts to maintain an informal social pact with the business sector and the trade unions. In 1986 President Lusinchi announced a 21-point programme of economic measures including exchange rate changes, fiscal reform and foreign investment incentives, in order to compensate for the loss of income from petroleum exports. In February 1986 the Government signed an accord with its creditor banks on the rescheduling of most of Venezuela's public-sector debt. Demonstrations were held in Caracas during February and March by the COPEI and other opponents of the Government, in protest at the debt accord.

In 1987 indications of social unrest became apparent in a teachers' strike, in support of demands for an increase in wages, and in an outbreak of student rioting, the worst that had been experienced since Dr Lusinchi came to power. Another increasing problem which the Government encountered was that of drugs-trafficking. Venezuela had become a major trade route for illicit drugs, encouraged by the economic stagnation of the country. In June nine Venezuelan soldiers were killed during a clash with Colombian drug-smugglers in the north-western border area. In September the decision by a High Court judge to release seven prisoners, detained on drugs-trafficking charges, prompted renewed allegations of judicial corruption and collusion with drugs-traffickers. In addition, in March 1988 the Minister of Justice, José Manzo González, resigned, following accusations implicating him in drugs-trafficking through the activities of his personal secret police force. In 1988 and 1989 Venezuela and Colombia agreed to increase their military presence along their common border, and to co-operate in a campaign to suppress guerrilla and drugs-trafficking activities in the region.

In October 1988 14 fishermen, suspected of being Colombian drugs-smugglers, were killed by units of the Venezuelan army at Guafitas, near the town of El Amparo. The massacre provoked protests and rioting erupted in several cities. In January 1989 20 soldiers were arrested for their involvement in the killings. However, in April a military court reversed this decision, and the soldiers were released.

At the presidential and legislative elections in December 1988, Carlos Andrés Pérez Rodríguez became the first former President to be re-elected to the presidency (having previously held office in 1974–79). However, his party, the AD, lost its overall majority in the Congreso Nacional. Following his inauguration in February 1989, President Pérez implemented a series of measures designed to halt Venezuela's economic decline. These measures, which included increases in the prices of petrol and public transport, provoked rioting throughout the country in late February. The Government introduced a curfew and suspended various constitutional rights in order to quell the disturbances, but official sources claimed that some 246 people had died during the protests. In early March the curfew was revoked, and all constitutional rights were restored, after wages had been increased and the prices of some basic goods 'frozen'.

In May 1989 public protest against the Government's austerity programme continued in a more co-ordinated form, with the largest trade union, the Confederación de Trabajadores de Venezuela (CTV), organizing a 24-hour general strike (the first for 31 years) in favour of the introduction of pro-labour reforms. In June demonstrations in a number of cities resulted in violent clashes between demonstrators and the security forces. In the same month several thousand protesters marched through Caracas to demonstrate against official corruption. In July, despite its growing dissatisfaction with the stabilization plan then in progress, the CTV signed an agreement with the Government and the business sector to promote national harmony and to support the continuation of economic adjustment policies that had been agreed with the IMF in June.

In August 1989 several corruption scandals were exposed. The most damaging, in political terms, involved Recadi, a former government agency (abolished in March 1989) which had been responsible for the implementation of differential exchange controls. Losses arising from fraudulent use of the agency were estimated to amount to US $8,000m. In October, following a government refusal to investigate the alleged involvement of Lusinchi in the scandal, members of the Senate held a protest strike. Public confidence in the judicial system was weakened when investigations were apparently confined to members of the business community, leaving state officials unscathed. However, in December a former minister, José Angel Ciliberto, was arrested in connection with the Recadi scandal, on charges of embezzlement and abuse of public funds.

In December 1989 the first-ever direct elections of State Governors were held. There was a high degree of abstention (estimated at around 70%), and significant gains were made by left-wing parties, which had campaigned energetically against the corruption allegedly rife in the main parties. (However, the AD candidate for Caracas was elected while he was awaiting trial in prison on corruption charges.)

The Government approved wage increases in December 1989, prior to implementing a rise in petrol prices in January 1990. It was hoped that a repeat of the violence of the preceding year could thus be avoided. However, the price rises, together with the release of several officials who had been due to answer corruption charges, provoked an outbreak of riots and looting across the country in February.

In May 1990 the AD national directorate committee reinstated 11 of 15 officials (including Ciliberto) who had been expelled from the party by the party's ethics tribunal (created in 1989 to investigate corruption in the Lusinchi Government). The subsequent rift in the party led to the resignation of the majority of the tribunal members, who claimed that the task of eradicating corruption within the AD had been made impossible. In November 1990 a controversial new labour law was adopted by the Congreso Nacional, provoking fears that the resulting additional costs for employers would lead to redundancies and an increase in inflation. The law, which came into effect in May 1991, included provision for a severance benefit scheme and a social security system.

A series of widespread demonstrations and strikes followed the introduction, in August 1991, of monthly increases in the price of petrol. Protests at the increases and other measures in the Government's economic programme escalated during October and November. On 7 November trade union organizations staged a 12-hour general strike in support of various demands, including wage increases, the reintroduction of price controls on basic goods, and the suspension of government plans to dismiss some 300,000 public-sector employees, and appealed for an end to the increases in petrol prices. Clashes between demonstrators and the security forces resulted in several fatalities, provoking further demonstrations which continued into December.

The appointment of Pedro Rosas Bravo, a recognized author of the economic austerity programme, to the post of Minister of Finance in January 1992 prompted further criticism from the COPEI, which accused Pérez of failing to confront the prevailing economic and social crisis.

On 4 February 1992 an attempt to overthrow the President by rebel army units was defeated by armed forces loyal to the Government. The rebels, identified as members of the 'Movimiento Revolucionario Bolivariano 200' (MRB-200), attempted to occupy the Miraflores Palace, the seat of government, and the presidential residence but were forced to capitulate. Simultaneous rebel action in the cities of Macay, Valencia and Maracaibo ended when coup leader Lt-Col Hugo Chávez Frías broadcast an appeal for their surrender. More than 1,000 soldiers were arrested, and a group of 33 officers were subsequently charged. A number of constitutional guarantees were immediately suspended, and press and television censorship was imposed to exclude coverage of Chávez, who had received considerable passive popular support. The rebels' stated reasons for staging the insurrection were the increasing social divisions and uneven distribution of wealth resulting from government economic policy, and widespread corruption in the country's official institutions. President Pérez's public recognition, in January, of Colombia's claims to territorial rights in the Gulf of Venezuela had also angered the rebels.

In what was widely perceived as an attempt to appease disaffected sectors of society, immediately following the attempted coup Pérez authorized a 50% increase in the minimum wage and a 30% increase in the pay of middle-ranking officers of the armed forces. He also announced plans to bring forward a US $4,000m. social project, aimed at improving health care, social welfare and education.

In late February 1992 Pérez established an eight-member consultative committee, including members of opposition parties and independent individuals, to advise the Government on political and economic reform. In early March Pérez announced a series of proposed reforms arising from the recommendations of the committee. The proposals included the introduction of legislation for immediate reform of the Constitution. In addition, the President announced the suspension of increases in the price of petrol and electricity, and the reintroduction of price controls on a number of basic foodstuffs and on medicine.

In early March 1992, in an effort to broaden the base of support for his Government, Pérez appointed two members of the COPEI to the Council of Ministers. The appointments of Umberto Calderón Berti, as Minister of Foreign Affairs, and José Ignacio Moreno León, as President of the Venezuelan Investment Fund, were part of a larger ministerial reshuffle. Social unrest, however, continued in March with a series of demonstrations supporting demands for the resignation of President Pérez. Full constitutional rights were finally restored in April. In mid-June, following the withdrawal of the COPEI members from the Council of Ministers, Pérez effected a minor reshuffle. The appointment of Gen. Fernando Ochoa Antich, hitherto the Minister of National Defence, as Minister of Foreign Affairs was widely regarded as a conciliatory gesture to appease continuing discontent within the armed forces.

In September 1992, against a background of increasing public and political pressure for Pérez to resign, the President avoided the possibility of a reduction of his term of office when the Senate endorsed a decision by the Chamber of Deputies not to hold a referendum on the issue. However, the climate of political instability intensified in September and October, with widespread protests against government austerity measures and alleged official corruption. A series of bomb attacks, attributed to the rebel movements, Los Justicieros de Venezuela and the Fuerzas Bolivarianos de Liberación (an organization claiming to have links with MRB-200), were directed at the residences of allegedly corrupt senior politicians. In October the Government denied that an attack on the presidential motorcade which took place in the state of Zulia was an attempt to assassinate Pérez.

On 27 November 1992 a further attempt by rebel members of the armed forces to overthrow the President was suppressed by forces loyal to the Government. The attempted coup, led by senior officers of the air force and navy, was reported to have been instigated by members of MRB-200. A videotaped statement by the imprisoned Lt-Col Chávez, transmitted from a captured government-owned television station, urged Venezuelans to stage public demonstrations in support of the rebels. Principal air force bases were seized, and rebel aircraft attacked the presidential palace and other strategically important installations. The Government introduced a state of emergency and suspended the Constitution. Sporadic fighting continued into the following day, but by 29 November order had been restored and some 1,300 rebel members of the armed forces had been arrested. A further 93 rebels escaped by aircraft to Peru, where they were later granted political asylum (of these 41 returned to Venezuela in December, having been promised an official pardon). President Pérez rejected demands from the press and opposition parties for his resignation. The curfew imposed during the coup was ended at the beginning of December, and further constitutional rights were restored later in the month.

Popular discontent with the Government was reflected further in regional and municipal elections, held on 6 December 1992, which resulted in significant gains for the COPEI as well as revealing increasing support for the left-wing Movimiento al Socialismo (MAS) and Causa Radical (Causa R), whose candidate, Aristóbulo Istúriz, was elected mayor of Caracas. However, he refused to be inaugurated as mayor on the scheduled date in January 1993, in protest against the refusal of the authorities to respond to allegations of electoral malpractice in the regional and municipal elections. In late January the Supreme Electoral Council announced that new elections for the governorship of the states of Barinas and Sucre were to be held in March. In mid-February, however, the Supreme Court postponed the polls, leaving the AD representatives who had held the governorships before the disputed elections in their posts. The decision provoked riots and demonstrations in both the states.

In January 1993 the Minister of the Interior, Luis Piñerúa Ordaz, resigned in order to compete for the nomination of the AD for the presidential election, which was scheduled to take place in December. Under the terms of the Constitution, Pérez was not permitted to contest the election for a second consecutive term.

In March 1993 the Supreme Court annulled the rulings of an extraordinary summary court martial, which had been established by presidential decree to try those implicated in the attempted coup of November 1992, on the grounds that the court was unconstitutional. Those sentenced by the court were to be retried by an ordinary court martial.

In May 1993 an extraordinary joint session of the Congreso Nacional voted to endorse a Supreme Court ruling that sufficient evidence existed for Pérez to be brought to trial on corruption charges. The charges concerned allegations that Pérez, and two former government ministers, had, in 1989, embezzled US $17m. from a secret government fund. Pérez was subsequently suspended from office and, in accordance with the terms of the Constitution, replaced by the President of the Senate, Octavio Lepage, pending the election by the Congreso Nacional of an interim President who would assume control until the expiry of the presidential term in February 1994, should Pérez not be acquitted. On the 5 June the Congreso Nacional elected Ramón José Velásquez, an independent senator, as interim President. By mid-June Velásquez had completed a broad-ranging reorganization of the Council of Ministers, replacing 14 ministers, creating a new portfolio with responsibility for decentralization, and upgrading the Instituto de Comercio Exterior (ICE—foreign trade institute) to the status of ministry. In the same month the founder of the COPEI, former President Dr Rafael Caldera Rodríguez, was expelled from the party. Caldera was accused of contravening the interests and bylaws of the party by announcing his independent candidacy, in opposition to the party's official candidate, for the forthcoming presidential elections (to be held in conjunction with legislative elections in December 1993).

In late July 1993 a series of bomb attacks in the capital was attributed by the Government to 'extremists' seeking to create political instability and prevent the holding of the forthcoming presidential and legislative elections. In that month several letter bombs were sent to members of the Supreme Court, resulting in one casualty. It was widely believed that the perpetrators were supporters of former Presidents Pérez and Lusinchi, both of whom were expected to be indicted on corruption charges, and that the attacks were intended to intimidate the Court into giving a favourable ruling in their cases.

In August 1993 the Government announced salary increases of up to 50% for the armed forces in an attempt to allay discontent, particularly among middle-ranking officers, and forestall the possibility of a further military uprising. The decision followed rumours, denied by the Government, that a rebellion had been suppressed at a barracks in the capital where participants in the coup attempts of February and November 1992 were being detained. In the same month the Congreso Nacional approved legislation enabling Velásquez to introduce urgent economic and financial measures by decree in order to address the growing economic crisis. In late August a special session of the Congreso Nacional voted in favour of the permanent suspension from office of Pérez, regardless of whether he was acquitted of the corruption charges laid against him. At the same session Velásquez was ratified as interim President.

In late September 1993 students from a number of universities staged demonstrations against reductions in budgetary expenditure on education and at the introduction of value-added tax. Clashes between the demonstrators and the security forces resulted in the death of a student, provoking further protest the following day. Fears of an escalation of the disturbances prompted renewed rumours of a military coup. In the months directly preceding the presidential and legislative elections such rumours circulated with increasing frequency. The climate of political instability was aggravated further in October by the mutual recriminations of the AD and Causa R, each party accusing the other of seeking to precipitate a military-led coup. In late 1993 the US Government, concerned at the threat to democracy in Venezuela, issued a warning of the political and economic consequences that a coup would have on relations between the two countries.

On 5 December 1993 the presidential and legislative elections proceeded peacefully. Dr Rafael Caldera Rodríguez, the candidate of a newly-formed party, the Convergencia Nacional (CN), was elected President (having previously held office in 1969–74), winning 30.46% of the votes cast. However, the CN and its electoral ally, the MAS, secured only minority representation in the Congreso Nacional, with 50 seats of a total of 199 in the Chamber of Deputies, and 10 of a total of 49 elective seats in the Senate. The AD obtained a total of 71 seats in both chambers, while the COPEI won 68 seats and Causa R secured 49 seats. In that month Velásquez granted pardons to 15 members of the armed forces and three civilians alleged to have been involved in the coup attempts of February and November 1992.

In January 1994 a riot in a prison in Maracaibo resulted in more than 100 deaths. The riot, which had been precipitated by racial tensions between prisoners, drew attention to the problem of extreme overcrowding in the nation's prisons. In that month violent disturbances occurred in three major cities, including the capital, following the introduction of a second stage of value-added tax. Also in January the collapse of the country's second-largest commercial bank, Banco Latino, resulted in a serious financial crisis with a general loss of confidence in the domestic banking system causing liquidity problems for a further eight major financial institutions.

On 2 February 1994 Caldera took office and installed a Council of Ministers, including new portfolios with responsibility for economic reform, youth affairs, and higher education, science and technology. In that month the AD and the COPEI established a legislative pact using their combined majority representation in the Congreso Nacional in order to gain control of the major legislative committees. In response, Caldera warned that he would dissolve the legislature and organize elections to a constituent assembly should the government programme encounter obstructions in the Congreso Nacional. Also in February, in an attempt to consolidate relations with the armed forces, Caldera initiated proceedings providing for the release and pardon of all those charged with involvement in the coup attempts of February and November 1992.

In May 1994 a series of student demonstrations led to violent confrontations with the security forces and resulted in the death of a student. In the same month Pérez was arrested and imprisoned pending trial by the Supreme Court on charges of corruption. In late May Caldera conducted a reorganization of the Council of Ministers and restyled the ICE as the Ministry of Industry and Commerce. At the end of the month Asdrúbal Baptista resigned as Minister of Economic Reform and the portfolio was discontinued.

In June 1994 the Government announced the closure of the eight financial institututions that had been most seriously affected by the financial crisis precipitated by the collapse of Banco Latino in January. Later in June disturbances in the state of Carabobo resulted in one death and considerable injury when the security forces intervened to quell rioting following a demonstration held in protest against price speculation and increases in rates for public services. On 27 June the Government announced that, in view of the deepening economic crisis and the general climate of instability, it was to assume extraordinary powers. Six articles of the Constitution were suspended concerning guarantees including freedom of movement and freedom from arbitrary arrest and the right to own property and to engage in legal economic activity. The Government also announced the introduction of price controls and a single fixed exchange rate in order to address the problems of a rapidly depreciating currency and depleted foreign exchange reserves. In the weeks following the partial suspension of the Constitution the security forces conducted a series of arrests of prominent critics of the Government, profiteers and anyone deemed to be undermining government efforts to stabilize the economy.

On 30 June 1994 Caldera issued a decree establishing an Emergency Board for Banking Supervision and placing the financial system under its control. The measure prompted criticism of the Government, which was accused of imposing a virtual nationalization of the banking sector. In August the Government assumed direct control of a further four commercial banks and, in December, it intervened at Grupo

Latinoamericano, a large conglomerate of financial institutions, which was experiencing serious liquidity problems. In January 1995 the Government intervened at a further three commercial banks. Of those banks affected by the crisis a total of 10 were closed permanently; the majority of those still operational in mid-1995 were to be reprivatized.

In July 1994 a confrontation between the legislature and the presidency ensued when the Congreso Nacional voted to restore five of the six constitutional guarantees suspended by the Government in June. Despite protest, the Government promptly reintroduced the suspensions. Later that month, however, the legislative opposition, with the exception of Causa R, which withdrew from the legislature in protest, endorsed emergency financial measures, including an extension of price controls and the strengthening of finance-sector regulation, which were presented by the Government as a precursor to the restoration of full constitutional guarantees. In the same month former President Lusinchi, who had been indicted on corruption charges in 1993, was acquitted.

In November 1994, in response to increasing concern at the rising level of crime in urban areas, the Government announced the deployment of the National Guard to patrol the major cities. In February 1995 the Minister of Finance, Julio Sosa Rodríguez, resigned and was appointed to a newly created post, that of Minister of State for Economic Issues, with particular responsibility for international economic affairs. Sosa was succeeded at the Ministry of Finance by Luis Raúl Matos Azócar. In the following month the arrest of some 500 alleged subversives (including activists of the MRB-200) by the security forces prompted demonstrations in the capital in support of demands for the release of those detained and in opposition to the militarization of Venezuela's cities. Protesters also demanded the restoration of the constitutional guarantees suspended in June 1994. Later in March 1995 Caldera conducted a reorganization of the Council of Ministers. In July, with the promulgation of legislation allowing for government intervention in the economy without recourse to further emergency measures, the constitutional guarantees were restored.

Growing evidence in 1991 that Venezuela was becoming a major centre for the transhipment of illegal drugs and for the 'money laundering' operations of drugs-traffickers prompted President Pérez to announce the creation of a joint command to co-ordinate the anti-drugs-trafficking efforts of the Ministries of the Interior, Defence and Justice and the National Commission Against the Illicit Use of Drugs (Conacuid).

In 1982 Venezuela refused to renew the 1970 Port of Spain Protocol, declaring a 12-year moratorium on the issue of Venezuela's claim to a large area of Guyana to the west of the Essequibo river, which expired in June. Venezuela's border garrisons were strengthened and border violations were reported. In March 1985 it was announced that Venezuela and Guyana had requested UN mediation in an attempt to resolve their dispute over the Essequibo region. It was announced in November 1989 that a UN mediator had been appointed.

Venezuela also has a claim to some islands in the Netherlands Antilles, and a territorial dispute with Colombia concerning maritime boundaries in the Gulf of Venezuela. Relations with Colombia became increasingly strained in 1987, following the alleged incursions, in August, by a Colombian naval patrol ship and aircraft into Venezuelan territorial waters and airspace. In September Venezuela was reported to have closed its border with Colombia for an indefinite period. In March 1989 an agreement was reached with Colombia on the establishment of a border commission, the principal function of which was to negotiate a settlement for the territorial dispute. In March 1990 President Virgilio Barco of Colombia and President Pérez signed the 'San Pedro Alejandrino' document by which they pledged to implement the commission's proposals. At a meeting of the Presidents of Colombia and Venezuela in Caracas in January 1992, Pérez publicly recognized that Colombia had a legitimate claim to territorial rights in the Gulf of Venezuela. In late 1993 a series of confrontations on the border with Colombia between units of the Venezuelan armed forces and Colombian guerrillas led to diplomatic tensions between the two countries. In December the interim President, Ramón José Velásquez, ordered a reinforcement of troops on the border to combat the increasing criminal activity of the guerrillas, which included the trafficking of drugs and arms. Reinforcements were also deployed along the country's border with Brazil following the massacre in August of a settlement of Yanomami Indians in Venezuelan territory by Brazilian gold prospectors. In late 1994 a series of incursions by Colombian guerrillas resulted in the deaths of several Venezuelan soldiers and prompted the Government to deploy reinforcements to secure the border with Colombia. Despite assurances of increased vigilance by the Colombian Government, attacks by the guerrillas in February and May 1995 resulted in the deaths of a further 16 Venezuelan soldiers. In March Venezuelan troops deported some 1,000-1,500 illegal Colombian immigrants. The measure, which was taken ostensibly to prevent border violations, was widely recognized as a reprisal for the activities of the Colombian guerrillas.

Venezuela has observer status in the Non-aligned Movement (see p. 249).

### Government

Venezuela is a federal republic comprising 22 states, a Federal District (containing the capital) and 72 Federal Dependencies. Under the 1961 Constitution, legislative power is held by the bicameral Congreso Nacional (National Congress), which comprises the Senate (including elected members plus former Presidents of the Republic) and the elected Chamber of Deputies. Executive authority rests with the President. Senators, Deputies and the President are all elected for five years by universal adult suffrage. The President has wide powers, and is assisted by a Council of Ministers. Each state has a directly-elected executive governor and an elected legislature.

### Defence

Military service is selective for two years and six months between 18 and 45 years of age. In June 1994 the armed forces numbered 79,000 men: an army of 34,000, a navy of 15,000 (including 5,000 marines), an air force of 7,000 and a National Guard of 23,000. Proposed defence expenditure for 1994 was 111,000m. bolívares.

### Economic Affairs

In 1993, according to estimates by the World Bank, Venezuela's gross national product (GNP), measured at average 1991–93 prices, was US $58,916m., equivalent to $2,840 per head. During 1985–93, it was estimated, GNP per head increased, in real terms, at an average annual rate of 1.0%. Over the same period, the population increased by an annual average of 2.5%. Venezuela's gross domestic product (GDP) increased, in real terms, by an annual average of 1.9% in 1980–92, but declined by 1.0% in 1993 and by an estimated 3.3% in 1994.

Agriculture (including hunting, forestry and fishing) contributed 5.5% of GDP in 1991, and employed 10.6% of the economically active population in 1993. The principal crops are sugar cane, bananas, maize, rice, sorghum, plantains, oranges and cassava. During 1980–92 agricultural GDP increased by an estimated annual average of 2.6%. Cattle are the principal livestock, but the practice of smuggling cattle across Venezuela's border into Colombia has had a severe effect on the livestock sector.

Industry (including mining, manufacturing, construction and power) contributed 46.1% of GDP in 1991, and employed 26.3% of the economically active population in 1993. During 1980–92 industrial GDP increased by an annual average of 2.1%.

Mining and quarrying contributed 18.6% of GDP in 1991, and employed 1% of the economically active population in 1993. Petroleum production is the most important industry in Venezuela, providing about 80% of export revenue in 1990. At the end of 1994 reserves were estimated at 63,300m. barrels. Aluminium and iron ore are also major sources of export revenue. Venezuela also has substantial deposits of natural gas, coal, diamonds, gold, zinc, copper, lead, silver, phosphates, manganese and titanium.

Manufacturing contributed 19.9% of GDP in 1991, and employed 15.3% of the economically active population in 1993. The most important sectors in 1990, measured by gross value of output, were refined petroleum products, metals (mainly aluminium, pig-iron and steel), food products and chemicals. During 1980–92 manufacturing GDP increased by an annual average of 1.6%.

Energy is derived principally from domestic supplies of petroleum and coal, and from hydroelectric power. Imports of fuel products comprised 1.0% of the value of merchandise imports in 1993.

In 1993 Venezuela recorded a visible trade surplus of US $2,902m. while there was a deficit of $2,223m. on the current account of the balance of payments. In 1993 the principal source of imports (47.4%) was the USA; other major suppliers were Japan, Germany, Italy, Colombia and Brazil. Colombia was an important market for exports (25.2% of exports excluding iron ore and petroleum) in that year; other major recipients were the USA, Mexico and Japan. The principal exports in 1993 were mineral products (mainly petroleum, aluminium, iron ore and natural gas), petrochemicals and basic manufactures. The principal imports were machinery and transport equipment, basic manufactures, chemicals, food and live animals and crude materials.

There was an estimated bugetary deficit of 231,353m. bolívares in 1993 (equivalent to 4.3% of GDP). Venezuela's total external debt was US $37,465m. at the end of 1993, of which $26,856m. was long-term public debt. In that year the cost of servicing the debt was equivalent to 22.8% of the value of exports of goods and services. The average annual rate of inflation was 36.0% in 1985–93. Consumer prices increased by an annual average of 60.8% in 1994. Some 6.3% of the labour force were unemployed in 1993.

Venezuela is a member of the Andean Group (see p. 104), the Inter-American Development Bank (IDB, see p. 170), the Latin American Integration Association (Asociación Latinoamericana de Integración—ALADI, see p. 181), the Organization of the Petroleum Exporting Countries (OPEC, see p. 210), the Latin American Economic System (Sistema Económico Latinoamericano—SELA, see p. 239) and the Group of Three (G3, see p. 239).

Venezuela's economy is largely dependent on the petroleum sector, which provides some 80% of government revenue, and is therefore particularly vulnerable to fluctuations in the world petroleum market. In 1994 a severe financial crisis, precipitated by the collapse of Banco Latino, led to a rapid depreciation of the currency and a serious depletion of foreign exchange reserves. Emergency measures introduced by the Government, including the imposition of price controls and a fixed exchange rate, were successful in restoring the level of reserves. However, the cost of government intervention in support of the ailing banking sector, which amounted to some US $7,000m. in 1994, contributed significantly to an estimated budget deficit equivalent to 7% of GDP in that year, and to escalating inflation. In September the Government announced a two-year Stabilization and Economic Recovery Plan aimed at eliminating the fiscal deficit and reducing inflation to below 30% by the end of 1995. The plan also proposed to encourage investment in areas traditionally the preserve of the State; notably, the petroleum sector was to be opened up to profit-share agreements with foreign multinational companies, with the ensuing increases in production and tax revenue expected to generate additional revenue for the State of US $500m. per annum. Other measures envisaged in the plan included efforts to expedite the privatization programme initiated in 1991. The level of non-traditional exports was particularly high in 1994, and their eventual replacement of the petroleum sector as the country's main source of export revenue represented one of the key aims of a long-term National Development Plan outlined in early 1995.

## Social Welfare

Labour legislation protects workers, and there are benefits for accidents, sickness and old age. A modified insurance scheme was introduced in 1967, entitling insured workers and their dependants to medical assistance, pensions, etc. In May 1985 the Government approved the extension of the social security system to include unemployment benefit. In 1978 Venezuela had 444 hospital establishments, with a total of 41,386 beds, and in 1984 there were 24,038 physicians (14.3 per 10,000 population) working in the country. Of total expenditure by the central Government (excluding transfers to regional and local governments) in 1986, 10,539m. bolívares (11.3%) was for health services, and a further 7,273m. bolívares (7.8%) for social security and welfare.

## Education

Education is officially compulsory for ten years, to be undertaken between five and 15 years of age. Primary education, which is available free of charge, begins at six years of age and lasts for nine years. Secondary education, beginning at the age of 15, lasts for a further two years. In 1991 the total enrolment at primary and secondary schools was equivalent to 88% of the school-age population (males 86%; females 90%). Of children in the relevant age-groups, primary enrolment in 1991 was 91% (males 90%; females 92%), while secondary enrolment in that year was 19% (males 15%; females 22%). In 1981 the average rate of adult illiteracy was 15.3% (males 13.5%; females 17%), but by 1990 the rate had declined to 10.0% (males 9.1%; females 10.8%). In 1994 there were 20 universities. Expenditure on education by the central Government was 211,659m. bolívares (23.5% of total expenditure) in 1992.

## Public Holidays

**1995:** 1 January (New Year's Day), 27–28 February (Carnival), 10 March (La Guaira only), 14–17 April (Easter), 19 April (Declaration of Independence), 1 May (Labour Day), 24 June (Battle of Carabobo), 5 July (Independence Day), 24 July (Birth of Simón Bolívar and Battle of Lago de Maracaibo), 4 September (Civil Servants' Day), 12 October (Discovery of America), 24 October (Maracaibo only), 24–25 December (Christmas), 31 December (New Year's Eve).

**1996:** 1 January (New Year's Day), 19–20 February (Carnival), 10 March (La Guaira only), 5–8 April (Easter), 19 April (Declaration of Independence), 1 May (Labour Day), 24 June (Battle of Carabobo), 5 July (Independence Day), 24 July (Birth of Simón Bolívar and Battle of Lago de Maracaibo), 4 September (Civil Servants' Day), 12 October (Discovery of America), 24 October (Maracaibo only), 24–25 December (Christmas), 31 December (New Year's Eve).

Banks and insurance companies also close on: 6 January (Epiphany), 19 March (St Joseph), Ascension Day (25 May in 1995, 16 May in 1996), 29 June (SS Peter and Paul), 15 August (Assumption), 1 November (All Saints' Day), and 8 December (Immaculate Conception).

## Weights and Measures

The metric system is in force.

# Statistical Survey

Source (unless otherwise stated): Oficina Central de Estadística e Informática (formerly Dirección General de Estadística y Censos Nacionales), Edif. Fundación La Salle, Avda Boyacá, Caracas 1050; tel. (2) 782-1133; telex 21241; fax (2) 782-2243.

## Area and Population

### AREA, POPULATION AND DENSITY

| | |
|---|---:|
| Area (sq km) | |
|   Land | 882,050 |
|   Inland waters | 30,000 |
|   Total | 912,050* |
| Population (census results)† | |
|   20 October 1981 | 14,516,735 |
|   20 October 1990 | |
|     Males | 9,004,717 |
|     Females | 9,100,548 |
|     Total | 18,105,265 |
| Population (official estimates at mid-year)† | |
|   1991 | 19,787,000 |
|   1992 | 20,248,826 |
|   1993 | 20,712,000‡ |
| Density (per sq km) at mid-1993 | 23.5 |

* 352,144 sq miles.
† Excluding Indian jungle inhabitants, estimated at 140,562 in 1982. Census results also exclude an adjustment for underenumeration.
‡ Preliminary.

### ADMINISTRATIVE DIVISIONS
(population at 1990 census)

| State | Population | Capital | Population of capital |
|---|---:|---|---:|
| Federal District | 2,103,661 | Caracas | 1,824,892 |
| Amazonas | 55,717 | Puerto Ayacucho | 35,865 |
| Anzoátegui | 859,758 | Barcelona | 109,061 |
| Apure | 285,412 | San Fernando | 72,733 |
| Aragua | 1,120,132 | Maracay | 354,428 |
| Barinas | 424,491 | Barinas | 152,853 |
| Bolívar | 900,310 | Ciudad Bolívar | 225,846 |
| Carabobo | 1,453,232 | Valencia | 903,076 |
| Cojedes | 182,066 | San Carlos | 50,339 |
| Delta Amacuro | 84,564 | Tucupita | 40,946 |
| Falcón | 599,185 | Coro | 124,616 |
| Guárico | 488,623 | San Juan de los Morros | 67,645 |
| Lara | 1,193,161 | Barquisimeto | 602,622 |
| Mérida | 570,215 | Mérida | 167,992 |
| Miranda | 1,871,093 | Los Teques | 143,519 |
| Monagas | 470,157 | Maturín | 207,382 |
| Nueva Esparta | 263,748 | La Asunción | 16,585 |
| Portuguesa | 576,435 | Guanare | 83,380 |
| Sucre | 679,595 | Cumaná | 212,492 |
| Táchira | 807,712 | San Cristóbal | 220,697 |
| Trujillo | 493,912 | Trujillo | 32,683 |
| Yaracuy | 384,536 | San Felipe | 65,793 |
| Zulia | 2,235,305 | Maracaibo | 1,207,513 |
| Federal Dependencies | 2,245 | — | |
| **Total** | 18,105,265 | | |

### PRINCIPAL TOWNS
(metropolitan areas, estimated population at 30 June 1990)

| | | | |
|---|---:|---|---:|
| Caracas (capital) | 3,435,795 | Mérida | 275,359 |
| Maracaibo | 1,400,643 | Cumaná | 269,588 |
| Valencia | 1,274,354 | Guarenas-Guatire | 256,909 |
| Maracay | 956,656 | Acarigua-Araure | 228,824 |
| Barquisimeto | 787,359 | Cabimas | 223,147 |
| Ciudad Guayana | 542,707 | La Victoria | 208,599 |
| Barcelona-Puerto la Cruz | 455,309 | Valera | 196,282 |
| | | Barinas | 186,568 |
| San Cristóbal | 364,726 | Los Teques | 176,790 |
| Municipio Vargas | 347,488 | Punto Fijo | 174,703 |
| Ciudad Bolívar | 285,978 | Lagunillas | 131,735 |
| Maturín | 276,747 | | |

### BIRTHS, MARRIAGES AND DEATHS*

| | Registered live births | | Registered marriages | | Registered deaths | |
|---|---:|---:|---:|---:|---:|---:|
| | Number | Rate (per 1,000) | Number | Rate (per 1,000) | Number | Rate (per 1,000) |
| 1984 | 503,973 | 29.9 | 92,137 | 5.5 | 78,091 | 4.6 |
| 1985 | 502,329 | 29.0 | 93,939 | 5.4 | 78,938 | 4.6 |
| 1986 | 504,278 | 28.8 | 100,002 | 5.7 | 77,647 | 4.4 |
| 1987 | 516,773 | 28.8 | 105,058 | 5.8 | 80,322 | 4.5 |
| 1988 | 522,392 | 28.4 | 113,125 | 6.1 | 81,442 | 4.4 |
| 1989 | 529,015 | 28.0 | 111,970 | 5.9 | 84,761 | 4.5 |
| 1990 | 577,976 | 29.9 | 106,303 | 5.5 | 89,830 | 4.6 |
| 1991† | 602,024 | 30.4 | 107,136 | 5.4 | 88,634 | 4.5 |

* Excluding Indian jungle population.
† Provisional.

**Expectation of life** (UN estimates, years at birth, 1985–90): 69.6 (males 66.7; females 72.8) (Source: UN, *World Population Prospects: The 1992 Revision*).

### ECONOMICALLY ACTIVE POPULATION (household surveys, '000 persons aged 15 years and over, July–December)*

| | 1991 | 1992 | 1993 |
|---|---:|---:|---:|
| Agriculture, hunting, forestry and fishing | 795.5 | 766.9 | 749.7 |
| Mining and quarrying | 69.1 | 76.2 | 69.6 |
| Manufacturing | 1,106.7 | 1,131.6 | 1,080.8 |
| Electricity, gas and water | 62.2 | 64.1 | 52.1 |
| Construction | 567.7 | 619.0 | 653.8 |
| Trade, restaurants and hotels | 1,445.7 | 1,531.0 | 1,596.6 |
| Transport, storage and communications | 385.9 | 434.2 | 452.3 |
| Financing, insurance, real estate and business services | 395.7 | 419.9 | 463.6 |
| Community, social and personal services | 1,938.8 | 1,957.3 | 1,944.0 |
| Activities not adequately defined | 2.1 | 3.6 | 5.8 |
| **Total employed** | 6,769.3 | 7,003.9 | 7,068.3 |
| Unemployed | 648.7 | 533.9 | 477.9 |
| **Total labour force** | 7,417.9 | 7,537.8 | 7,546.2 |
| Males | 5,028.6 | 5,135.6 | 5,191.2 |
| Females | 2,389.3 | 2,402.2 | 2,355.0 |

* Figures exclude members of the armed forces.
Source: ILO, *Year Book of Labour Statistics*.

VENEZUELA

*Statistical Survey*

## Agriculture

**PRINCIPAL CROPS** ('000 metric tons)

|  | 1991 | 1992 | 1993 |
|---|---|---|---|
| Maize* | 964 | 800 | 700 |
| Rice (paddy)* | 660 | 595 | 645 |
| Sorghum* | 577 | 528 | 250 |
| Potatoes | 215* | 215† | 215† |
| Sesame seed | 40* | 45* | 45† |
| Seed cotton | 72* | 65* | 70† |
| Cottonseed* | 42 | 39 | 41 |
| Cotton (lint)* | 26 | 24 | 22 |
| Coffee (green)* | 65 | 57 | 72 |
| Cocoa beans* | 14 | 14 | 15 |
| Tobacco* | 12 | 14 | 14 |
| Cassava (Manioc) | 381* | 382† | 382† |
| Oranges | 438* | 440† | 440† |
| Tomatoes | 199* | 200† | 200† |
| Coconuts† | 205 | 222 | 220 |
| Copra* | 20 | 22 | 21 |
| Avocados | 53* | 53† | 54† |
| Bananas | 1,215* | 1,215† | 1,215† |
| Plantains† | 510 | 510 | 510 |
| Sugar cane* | 6,519 | 7,031 | 6,900 |

\* Unofficial figure(s).   † FAO estimate(s).

Source: FAO, *Production Yearbook*.

**LIVESTOCK** ('000 head, year ending September)

|  | 1991 | 1992 | 1993 |
|---|---|---|---|
| Horses* | 495 | 495 | 495 |
| Asses* | 440 | 440 | 440 |
| Cattle† | 13,368 | 14,192 | 14,660 |
| Pigs* | 2,445 | 2,300 | 2,100 |
| Sheep* | 525 | 525 | 525 |
| Goats* | 1,620 | 1,650 | 1,650 |

Poultry (million)*: 70 in 1991; 73 in 1992; 74 in 1993.

\* FAO estimates.   † Unofficial figures.

Source: FAO, *Production Yearbook*.

**LIVESTOCK PRODUCTS** ('000 metric tons)

|  | 1991 | 1992 | 1993 |
|---|---|---|---|
| Beef and veal* | 351 | 365 | 377 |
| Pig meat* | 103 | 118 | 110 |
| Poultry meat† | 450 | 470 | 480 |
| Cows' milk* | 1,505 | 1,575 | 1,655 |
| Cheese* | 84.0 | 70.0 | 72.0 |
| Butter and ghee* | 3.0 | 3.0 | 3.0 |
| Hen eggs* | 106.0 | 129.4 | 123.9 |
| Cattle hides (fresh)† | 40.1 | 43.7 | 44.5 |

\* Unofficial figures.   † FAO estimates.

Source: FAO, *Production Yearbook*.

## Forestry

**ROUNDWOOD REMOVALS** ('000 cubic metres, excl. bark)

|  | 1990 | 1991 | 1992 |
|---|---|---|---|
| Sawlogs, veneer logs and logs for sleepers | 852 | 724 | 724* |
| Other industrial wood† | 26 | 26 | 26 |
| Fuel wood* | 743 | 760 | 776 |
| **Total** | 1,621 | 1,510 | 1,526* |

\* FAO estimate(s).

† FAO estimates, assumed to be unchanged since 1975.

Source: FAO, *Yearbook of Forest Products*.

**SAWNWOOD PRODUCTION**
('000 cubic metres, incl. railway sleepers)

|  | 1990 | 1991 | 1992 |
|---|---|---|---|
| **Total** | 180 | 200* | 200* |

\* FAO estimate.

Source: FAO, *Yearbook of Forest Products*.

## Fishing

('000 metric tons, live weight)

|  | 1990 | 1991 | 1992 |
|---|---|---|---|
| Inland waters | 18.0 | 21.3 | 20.6 |
| Atlantic Ocean | 253.2 | 279.2 | 244.9 |
| Pacific Ocean | 60.7 | 51.2 | 55.2 |
| **Total catch** | 331.9 | 351.7 | 320.6 |

Source: FAO, *Yearbook of Fishery Statistics*.

## Mining

**PRODUCTION** ('000 metric tons, unless otherwise indicated)

|  | 1991 | 1992 | 1993 |
|---|---|---|---|
| Iron ore (gross weight)* | 21,216 | 18,876 | 16,871 |
| Hard coal | 2,557 | 2,427 | 3,940 |
| Crude petroleum | 124,684 | 123,786 | 127,778 |
| Natural gas (petajoules) | 997.2† | 957.4† | n.a. |
| Gold (kg) | 5,727 | 7,253 | 8,033 |
| Diamonds ('000 carats) | 200 | 475 | 410 |

\* The estimated iron content is 64%.

† UN estimate.

Sources: as above; UN, *Industrial Statistics Yearbook* and *Monthly Bulletin of Statistics*.

## Industry

**PETROLEUM PRODUCTS** ('000 metric tons)

|  | 1989 | 1990 | 1991 |
|---|---|---|---|
| Motor spirit (petrol) | 14,138 | 14,403 | 13,341 |
| Kerosene | 274 | 259 | 159 |
| Jet fuel | 2,788 | 3,255 | 3,990 |
| Distillate fuel oils | 11,721 | 12,257 | 15,301 |
| Residual fuel oils | 14,715 | 13,875 | 15,869 |

Source: UN, *Industrial Statistics Yearbook*.

# VENEZUELA

## SELECTED OTHER PRODUCTS
('000 metric tons, unless otherwise indicated)

|  | 1989 | 1990 | 1991 |
|---|---|---|---|
| Raw sugar | 523 | 499 | 567 |
| Cigarettes (million)* | 20,599 | 23,560 | 24,236 |
| Rubber tyres ('000) | 4,177 | 3,951 | 4,664 |
| Nitrogenous fertilizers† | 370 | n.a. | n.a. |
| Cement | 5,259 | 5,996 | 6,350 |
| Pig-iron | 455 | 314 | n.a. |
| Crude steel | 3,404 | 3,140 | 2,933 |
| Aluminium (unwrought) | 565.6 | 598.8 | 600.0 |
| Passenger cars—assembly ('000) | 16 | 21 | 26 |
| Commercial motor vehicles—assembly ('000) | 12 | 22 | 21 |
| Electric energy (million kWh) | 59,328 | 55,750 | 57,150 |

* Data from the US Department of Agriculture.
† Provisional output in terms of nitrogen.

Source: UN, *Industrial Statistics Yearbook*.

**1992** ('000 metric tons, unless otherwise indicated): Cement 6,585; Crude steel 2,664; Aluminium (unwrought) 507.5; Passenger cars—assembly ('000) 42; Commercial motor vehicles—assembly ('000) 31.
**1993**: Aluminium (unwrought, '000 metric tons) 566.2; Passenger cars — assembly ('000) 37; Commercial motor vehicles — assembly ('000) 29.

# Finance

## CURRENCY AND EXCHANGE RATES

**Monetary Units**
100 céntimos = 1 bolívar.

**Sterling and Dollar Equivalents** (31 December 1994)
£1 sterling = 266.0 bolívares;
US $1 = 170.0 bolívares;
1,000 bolívares = £3.760 = $5.882.

**Average Exchange Rate** (bolívares per US dollar)
1992   68.376
1993   90.826
1994  148.503

Note: Between March 1989 and June 1994 a market-determined exchange rate was in operation. In July 1994 a fixed rate of US $1 = 170 bolívares was introduced.

## BUDGET (million bolívares)*

| Revenue | 1991 | 1992 | 1993† |
|---|---|---|---|
| Tax revenue | 583,977 | 596,914 | 765,875 |
| Taxes on corporate income | 415,080 | 339,931 | 368,272 |
| Petroleum enterprises | 415,080 | 339,931 | 368,272 |
| Social security contributions | 38,182 | 41,698 | 58,072 |
| Taxes on property | 3,848 | 5,564 | 5,308 |
| Excises | 22,415 | 51,353 | 67,738 |
| Import duties | 56,855 | 84,324 | 101,092 |
| Customs duties, etc. | 43,905 | 74,553 | 89,752 |
| Other current revenue | 150,038 | 184,325 | 195,620 |
| Property income | 143,194 | 146,157 | 184,490 |
| Central Bank | 142,565 | 145,348 | 183,681 |
| **Total** | 734,015 | 781,239 | 961,495 |

| Expenditure‡ | 1991 | 1992 | 1993† |
|---|---|---|---|
| Current expenditure | 526,242 | 694,224 | 899,560 |
| Expenditure on goods and services | 186,638 | 250,572 | 345,253 |
| Wages and salaries | 139,531 | 195,439 | 262,876 |
| Interest payments | 102,453 | 149,771 | 198,477 |
| Subsidies and other current transfers | 237,151 | 293,881 | 355,830 |
| Capital expenditure | 196,726 | 218,188 | 293,288 |
| Capital transfers | 158,684 | 169,615 | 209,852 |
| **Total** | 722,968 | 912,412 | 1,192,848 |

* Figures represent the consolidated accounts of the central Government, comprising the operations of the General Budget, government agencies and social security funds.
† Provisional figures.
‡ Excluding lending minus repayments (million bolívares): −123,055 in 1991; nil in 1992 and 1993.

Source: IMF, *Government Finance Statistics Yearbook*.

## CENTRAL BANK RESERVES (US $ million at 31 December)

|  | 1991 | 1992 | 1993 |
|---|---|---|---|
| Gold* | 3,439 | 3,439 | 3,440 |
| IMF special drawing rights | 269 | 75 | 486 |
| Reserve position in IMF | — | 199 | 199 |
| Foreign exchange | 10,397 | 9,288 | 8,531 |
| **Total** | 14,105 | 13,001 | 12,656 |

* Valued at $300 per troy ounce.

Source: IMF, *International Financial Statistics*.

## MONEY SUPPLY (million bolívares at 31 December)*

|  | 1991 | 1992 | 1993 |
|---|---|---|---|
| Currency outside banks | 76,460 | 108,630 | 136,550 |
| Demand deposits at commercial banks | 241,610 | 245,240 | 256,540 |
| **Total** (incl. others) | 347,590 | 375,450 | 416,850 |

* Figures rounded to the nearest 10m. bolívares.

Source: IMF, *International Financial Statistics*.

## COST OF LIVING
(Consumer Price Index for Caracas metropolitan area. Base: 1984 = 100)

|  | 1991 | 1992 | 1993 |
|---|---|---|---|
| Food | 1,321.9 | 1,725.4 | 2,300.3 |
| Clothing | 491.1 | 614.7 | 782.2 |
| Rent | 440.4 | 570.0 | 828.2 |
| **All items** (incl. others) | 717.7 | 943.3 | 1,302.9 |

# VENEZUELA

## NATIONAL ACCOUNTS

**National Income and Product** (million bolívares at current prices)

|  | 1989 | 1990 | 1991 |
|---|---|---|---|
| Compensation of employees | 518,295 | 699,402 | 1,011,412 |
| Operating surplus | 836,152 | 1,391,835 | 1,696,141 |
| **Domestic factor incomes** | 1,354,447 | 2,091,237 | 2,707,553 |
| Consumption of fixed capital | 107,345 | 154,230 | 220,222 |
| **Gross domestic product (GDP) at factor cost** | 1,461,792 | 2,245,467 | 2,927,775 |
| Indirect taxes | 77,483 | 69,487 | 125,459 |
| Less Subsidies | 28,914 | 35,693 | 16,959 |
| **GDP in purchasers' values** | 1,510,361 | 2,279,261 | 3,036,275 |
| Factor income received from abroad | 62,065 | 103,102 | 109,045 |
| Less Factor income paid abroad | 124,484 | 170,802 | 170,870 |
| **Gross national product** | 1,447,942 | 2,211,561 | 2,974,450 |
| Less Consumption of fixed capital | 107,345 | 154,230 | 220,222 |
| **National income in market prices** | 1,340,597 | 2,057,331 | 2,754,228 |
| Other current transfers from abroad | 7,629 | 20,483 | 20,084 |
| Less Other current transfers paid abroad | 14,872 | 33,866 | 39,666 |
| **National disposable income** | 1,333,354 | 2,043,948 | 2,734,646 |

Source: UN, *National Accounts Statistics*.

**Expenditure on the Gross Domestic Product**
('000 million bolívares at current prices)

|  | 1992 | 1993 | 1994 |
|---|---|---|---|
| Government final consumption expenditure | 379.4 | 472.6 | 609.7 |
| Private final consumption expenditure | 2,877.6 | 3,989.1 | 6,039.1 |
| Increase in stocks | 109.3 | −41.3 | −471.0 |
| Gross fixed capital formation | 870.7 | 1,062.7 | 1,316.0 |
| **Total domestic expenditure** | 4,237.0 | 5,483.1 | 7,493.8 |
| Exports of goods and services | 1,088.8 | 1,428.8 | 2,556.8 |
| Less Imports of goods and services | −1,194.4 | −1,462.8 | −1,739.9 |
| **GDP in purchasers' values** | 4,131.5 | 5,449.1 | 8,310.7 |
| **GDP at constant 1990 prices** | 2,652.6 | 2,641.9 | 2,555.5 |

Source: IMF, *International Financial Statistics*.

**Gross Domestic Product by Economic Activity**
(million bolívares at current prices)

|  | 1989 | 1990 | 1991 |
|---|---|---|---|
| Agriculture, hunting, forestry and fishing | 92,044 | 122,765 | 167,418 |
| Mining and quarrying* | 271,136 | 530,565 | 562,687 |
| Manufacturing† | 314,339 | 467,778 | 602,706 |
| Electricity and water | 22,622 | 43,218 | 64,223 |
| Construction | 71,060 | 102,896 | 166,763 |
| Trade, restaurants and hotels | 275,780 | 400,861 | 556,792 |
| Transport, storage and communication | 73,285 | 104,158 | 173,238 |
| Finance, insurance, real estate and business services | 180,768 | 256,069 | 357,382 |
| Government services | 107,824 | 140,382 | 207,300 |
| Other community, social and personal services | 63,518 | 94,901 | 136,389 |
| Other | 15,615 | 24,533 | 34,411 |
| **Sub-total** | 1,487,991 | 2,288,126 | 3,029,309 |
| Import duties | 24,165 | 33,313 | 60,238 |
| Less Imputed bank service charge | 26,619 | 42,178 | 53,272 |
| Other adjustments | 24,824 | — | — |
| **GDP in purchasers' values** | 1,510,361 | 2,279,261 | 3,036,275 |

* Includes crude petroleum and natural gas production.
† Includes petroleum refining.

Source: UN, *National Accounts Statistics*.

## BALANCE OF PAYMENTS (US $ million)

|  | 1991 | 1992 | 1993 |
|---|---|---|---|
| Merchandise exports f.o.b. | 14,968 | 13,988 | 14,019 |
| Merchandise imports f.o.b. | −10,131 | −12,714 | −11,117 |
| **Trade balance** | 4,837 | 1,274 | 2,902 |
| Exports of services | 1,437 | 1,542 | 1,585 |
| Imports of services | −3,591 | −4,466 | −4,783 |
| Other income received | 2,168 | 1,607 | 1,689 |
| Other income paid | −2,766 | −3,357 | −3,299 |
| Private unrequited transfers (net) | −316 | −347 | −310 |
| Official unrequited transfers (net) | −33 | −6 | −7 |
| **Current balance** | 1,736 | −3,753 | −2,223 |
| Direct investment (net) | 1,769 | 429 | −55 |
| Portfolio investment (net) | 192 | 61 | 731 |
| Other capital (net) | −420 | 1,841 | 532 |
| Net errors and omissions | −1,516 | −295 | 407 |
| **Overall balance** | 1,761 | −1,717 | −608 |

Source: IMF, *International Financial Statistics*.

# External Trade

**PRINCIPAL COMMODITIES** (US $ million)

| Imports f.o.b. | 1991 | 1992 | 1993 |
|---|---|---|---|
| Food and live animals | 590 | 729 | 742 |
| Beverages and tobacco | 103 | 142 | 175 |
| Crude materials (inedible) except fuels | 685 | 671 | 619 |
| Mineral fuels, lubricants, etc. | 225 | 146 | 112 |
| Animal and vegetable oils and fats | 159 | 168 | 155 |
| Chemicals | 1,518 | 1,543 | 1,398 |
| Basic manufactures | 1,692 | 1,779 | 1,463 |
| Machinery and transport equipment | 4,402 | 6,544 | 5,702 |
| Miscellaneous manufactured articles | 636 | 934 | 895 |
| **Total (incl. others)** | 10,042 | 12,672 | 11,271 |

| Exports f.o.b.* | 1991 | 1992 | 1993 |
|---|---|---|---|
| Food and live animals | 228 | 234 | 307 |
| Beverages and tobacco | 84 | 110 | 80 |
| Crude materials (inedible) except fuels | 83 | 89 | 123 |
| Mineral fuels, lubricants, etc. | 89 | 88 | 143 |
| Chemicals and related products | 376 | 418 | 481 |
| Basic manufactures | 1,497 | 1,472 | 1,576 |
| Machinery and transport equipment | 174 | 211 | 428 |
| Miscellaneous manufactured articles | 89 | 82 | 90 |
| **Total (incl. others)** | 2,633 | 2,719 | 3,422 |

* Excluding exports of iron ore and petroleum. The total value of exports (in US $ million) was: 15,155 in 1991; 14,185 in 1992; 14,066 in 1993 (Source: IMF, *International Financial Statistics*).

# VENEZUELA

## PRINCIPAL TRADING PARTNERS (US $ million)

| Imports f.o.b. | 1991 | 1992 | 1993 |
|---|---|---|---|
| Argentina | 216 | 226 | 215 |
| Belgium-Luxembourg | 159 | 228 | 172 |
| Brazil | 452 | 496 | 398 |
| Canada | 280 | 283 | 268 |
| Colombia | 290 | 487 | 470 |
| France | 226 | 241 | 311 |
| Germany | 699 | 820 | 650 |
| Italy | 475 | 606 | 533 |
| Japan | 499 | 944 | 819 |
| Mexico | 150 | 251 | 215 |
| Netherlands | 151 | 168 | 217 |
| Panama | 126 | 202 | 131 |
| Spain | 237 | 286 | 235 |
| United Kingdom | 269 | 294 | 268 |
| USA | 4,716 | 5,860 | 5,342 |
| **Total** (incl. others) | 10,042 | 12,672 | 11,271 |

| Exports f.o.b.* | 1991 | 1992 | 1993 |
|---|---|---|---|
| Belgium-Luxembourg | 42 | 22 | 29 |
| Brazil | 29 | 24 | 46 |
| Colombia | 278 | 467 | 863 |
| Dominican Republic | 38 | 50 | 62 |
| France | 21 | 37 | 31 |
| Italy | 55 | 53 | 37 |
| Japan | 324 | 285 | 182 |
| Mexico | 106 | 162 | 192 |
| Spain | 58 | 37 | 23 |
| USA | 580 | 585 | 802 |
| **Total** (incl. others) | 2,633 | 2,719 | 3,422 |

* Excluding exports of iron ore and petroleum.

## Transport

### RAILWAYS (traffic)

|  | 1991 | 1992 | 1993 |
|---|---|---|---|
| Passenger-kilometres (million) | 55 | 47 | 44 |
| Freight ton-kilometres (million) | 40 | 36 | 26 |

### ROAD TRAFFIC ('000 motor vehicles in use at 31 December)

|  | 1991 | 1992 | 1993 |
|---|---|---|---|
| Passenger cars | 1,540 | 1,566 | 1,579 |
| Buses and coaches | 18 | 20 | 20 |
| Goods vehicles | 431 | 436 | 440 |
| Motorcycles, scooters and mopeds | 295 | 298 | 301 |

### SHIPPING

**Merchant Fleet** (vessels registered at 30 June)

|  | 1990 | 1991 | 1992 |
|---|---|---|---|
| Total displacement ('000 grt) | 147 | 147 | 96 |

Source: UN, *Statistical Yearbook*.

**International Sea-borne Shipping**
(freight traffic, UN estimates, '000 metric tons)

|  | 1988 | 1989 | 1990 |
|---|---|---|---|
| Goods loaded | 82,082 | 88,920 | 101,435 |
| Goods unloaded | 17,566 | 18,160 | 17,932 |

Source: UN, *Monthly Bulletin of Statistics*.

### CIVIL AVIATION (traffic on scheduled services)

|  | 1990 | 1991 | 1992 |
|---|---|---|---|
| Kilometres flown (million) | 55 | 66 | 76 |
| Passengers carried ('000) | 6,847 | 6,795 | 7,149 |
| Passenger-km (million) | 5,534 | 6,010 | 6,753 |
| Total ton-km (million) | 664 | 733 | 779 |

Source: UN, *Statistical Yearbook*.

## Tourism

('000 arrivals)

|  | 1991 | 1992 | 1993 |
|---|---|---|---|
| Tourists | 598.3 | 445.6 | 396.1 |
| Excursionists | 126.3 | 135.1 | 124.0 |
| **Total** | 724.6 | 580.7 | 520.1 |

## Communications Media

|  | 1990 | 1991 | 1992 |
|---|---|---|---|
| Radio receivers ('000 in use)* | 8,600 | 8,820 | 9,040 |
| Television receivers ('000 in use)* | 3,300 | 3,200 | 3,300 |
| Telephones ('000 main lines in use) | 1,495 | 1,598 | n.a. |
| Daily newspapers |  |  |  |
|   Number | 54 | n.a. | 82 |
|   Average circulation ('000 copies)* | 2,800 | n.a. | 4,200 |
| Book production (titles)† | 3,175 | 3,461 | 3,879 |

* Estimates. † First editions only.

Sources: UNESCO, *Statistical Yearbook*; UN, *Statistical Yearbook*.

## Education

(1991)

|  | Institutions | Teachers | Students Males | Females | Total |
|---|---|---|---|---|---|
| Pre-primary | 7,917* | 27,792 | 340,746 | 333,898 | 674,644 |
| Primary | 15,800 | 183,298 | 2,108,942 | 2,081,105 | 4,190,047 |
| Secondary | 1,517* | 32,572 | 124,745 | 164,685 | 289,430 |
| Higher* | 99 | 46,137 | n.a. | n.a. | 550,030 |

* 1990 figure(s).

Source: mainly UNESCO, *Statistical Yearbook*.

# Directory

## The Constitution

The Constitution of Venezuela was promulgated in January 1961.

The Federal Republic of Venezuela is divided into 22 States, one Federal District and 72 Federal Dependencies. The States are autonomous but must comply with the laws and Constitution of the Republic.

### LEGISLATURE

Legislative Power is exercised by the Congreso Nacional (National Congress), divided into two Chambers: the Senate and the Chamber of Deputies.

Senators are elected by universal suffrage, two to represent each State, and two to represent the Federal District. There are in addition other Senators, their number being determined by law, who are selected on the principle of minority representation. Former Presidents of the Republic are life members of the Senate. Deputies are also elected by direct universal and secret suffrage, the number representing each State being at least two. A deputy must be of Venezuelan nationality and be over 21 years of age. Ordinary sessions of both Chambers begin on the second day of March of each year and continue until the sixth day of the following July; thereafter, sessions are renewed from the first day of October to the thirtieth day of November, both dates inclusive. The Chamber of Deputies is empowered to initiate legislation. The Congreso Nacional also elects a Controller-General to preside over the Audit Office (Contraloría de la Nación), which investigates Treasury income and expenditure, and the finances of the autonomous institutes.

### GOVERNMENT

Executive Power is vested in a President of the Republic elected by universal suffrage every five years, who may not serve two consecutive terms. The President is empowered to discharge the Constitution and the laws, to nominate or remove Ministers, to take supreme command of the Armed Forces, to direct foreign relations of the State, to declare a state of emergency and withdraw the civil guarantees laid down in the Constitution, to convene extraordinary sessions of the Congreso Nacional and to administer national finance. The President also appoints an Attorney-General to act as a legal arbiter for the state.

### JUDICIARY

Judicial Power is exercised by the Supreme Court of Justice and by the Tribunals. The Supreme Court forms the highest Tribunal of the Republic and the Magistrates of the Supreme Court are elected by both Chambers in joint sessions.

## The Government

### HEAD OF STATE

**President of the Republic:** Dr Rafael Caldera Rodríguez (took office 2 February 1994).

### COUNCIL OF MINISTERS
(June 1995)

**Minister of Foreign Affairs:** Miguel Angel Burelli Rivas.
**Minister of the Interior:** Ramón Escovar Salom.
**Minister of National Defence:** Gen. Moisés Orozco Graterol.
**Minister of the Presidential Secretariat:** Andrés Caldera Pietri.
**Minister of Finance:** Luis Raúl Matos Azócar.
**Minister of Development, and of Industry and Commerce:** Werner Corrales.
**Minister of Energy and Mines:** Erwin José Arrieta Valera.
**Minister of Justice:** Rubén Creixems Savignon.
**Minister of Health and Social Assistance:** Carlos Walter.
**Minister of Education:** Antonio Luis Cárdenas.
**Minister of Labour:** Juan Nepomuceno Garrido Mendoza.
**Minister of Agriculture and Livestock:** Raúl Alegrett.
**Minister of Transport and Communications:** Ciro Zaa Alvarez.
**Minister of the Environment and Natural Resources:** Roberto Pérez Lecuna.
**Minister of the Family:** Mercedes Pulido de Briceño.
**Minister for Urban Development:** Francisco González.
**Minister of Decentralization:** José Guillermo Andueza Acuna.
**Minister of Higher Education, Science and Technology:** Guido Hernán Arroyo.
**Minister of Youth Affairs:** María del Pilar Iribarren de Romero.
**Minister of Social Development:** Pompeyo Márquez.
**Minister of State and President of the Office of Central Planning and Co-ordination:** Edgar Paredes Pisani.
**Minister of State and President of the Presidential Commission for State Reform:** Ricardo Conveias.
**Minister of State and President of the Tourism Corporation (Corporación de Turismo de Venezuela—Corpoturismo):** Hernán Luis Soriano.
**Minister in the Central Information Office of the Presidency:** Guillermo Alvarez Bajares.
**Minister of State and President of the Venezuelan Investment Fund:** Carlos Bernárdez Losada.
**Minister of State for Economic Issues:** Julio Sosa Rodríguez.
**Governor General of the Federal District:** Asdrúbal Aguiar Aranguren.

### MINISTRIES

**Central Information Office of the Presidency:** Palacio de Miraflores, Avda Urdaneta, Caracas 1010; tel. (2) 81-0811; telex 21162; fax (2) 571-0563.
**Ministry of the Presidential Secretariat:** Palacio de Miraflores, Avda Urdaneta, Caracas 1010; tel. (2) 81-0811; telex 21161; fax (2) 571-3134.
**Ministry of Agriculture and Livestock:** Torre Norte, 16°, Centro Simón Bolívar, Caracas 1010; tel. (2) 509-0111; telex 21483.
**Ministry of Decentralization:** Caracas.
**Ministry of Development:** Edif. Sur, 5°, Centro Simón Bolívar, Caracas 1010; tel. (2) 41-9341; telex 22753; fax (2) 483-8552.
**Ministry of Education:** Salas a Caja de Agua, Edif. Ministerio de Educación, Caracas 1010; tel. (2) 562-5444; telex 21943.
**Ministry of Energy and Mines:** Torre Oeste, Parque Central, Caracas 1010; tel. (2) 507-5080; telex 21692; fax (2) 575-4386.
**Ministry of the Environment and Natural Resources:** Torre Sur, 18°, Centro Simón Bolívar, Caracas 1010; tel. (2) 408-1111; telex 24434.
**Ministry of the Family:** Torre Oeste, 41°, Avda Lecuna, Parque Central, Caracas 1010; tel. (2) 574-8111; telex 24434.
**Ministry of Finance:** Torre Norte, 3°, Centro Simón Bolívar, Caracas 1010; tel. (2) 41-9811; telex 24215; fax (2) 41-5771.
**Ministry of Foreign Affairs:** Casa Amarilla, Biblioteca Central, esq. Principal, Caracas 1010; tel. (2) 81-9151; telex 24104; fax (2) 861-1336.
**Ministry of Health and Social Assistance:** Torre Sur, 5°, Centro Simón Bolívar, Caracas 1010; tel. (2) 483-3533; telex 21654.
**Ministry of Higher Education, Science and Technology:** Caracas.
**Ministry of Industry and Commerce:** Centro Comercial Los Cedros, Apdo 51852, Caracas 1050; tel. (2) 531-0016; telex 21838; fax (2) 762-3885.
**Ministry of the Interior:** Esq. Carmelitas, Edif. MRI PB, Caracas 1010; tel. (2) 81-3851; telex 29694.
**Ministry of Justice:** Edif. Lincoln, Avda Lincoln, Sabana Grande, Caracas 1050; tel. (2) 72-5831; telex 21320.
**Ministry of Labour and Social Development:** Torre Sur, Centro Simón Bolívar, Caracas 1010; tel. (2) 483-1623; telex 29640; fax (2) 483-5940.
**Ministry of National Defence:** Fuerte Tiuna, Santa Mónica, Caracas 1040; tel. (2) 662-1253; telex 29657.
**Ministry of Transport and Communications:** Torre Este, Parque Central, Caracas 1010; tel. (2) 509-1000; telex 29692.
**Ministry of Urban Development:** Edif. Banco de Venezuela, 12°, Reducto a Miranda, Caracas 1010; tel. (2) 41-9711; telex 24135.
**Ministry of Youth Affairs:** Caracas.

### Government Agencies

**National Commission Against the Illicit Use of Drugs (Conacuid):** Caracas.
**Office of Central Planning and Co-ordination (Cordiplán):** Torre Oeste, 26°, Parque Central, Caracas 1010; tel. (2) 507-7611; fax (2) 573-6419.

VENEZUELA

**Office for Guayanan Development:** Edif. Maravén, 14°, Avda La Estancia, Chuao, Caracas 1060; telex 28171.

**Office of the Presidential Commission for State Reform:** Caracas.

**Office of the Tourism Corporation (Corporación de Turismo de Venezuela—Corpoturismo):** Torre Oueste, 35°-37°, Avda Lecuna, Parque Central, Caracas 1010; tel. (2) 507-2679; telex 27328; fax (2) 574-2679.

**Office of the Venezuelan Investment Fund:** Edif. Seguros Avila, 8°, Jesuitas a Tienda Honda, Caracas 1010; telex 26529; fax (2) 834-6897.

## President

**Presidential Election, 5 December 1993**

| Candidates | Votes | % of Votes |
|---|---|---|
| Rafael Caldera Rodríguez (CN) | 1,710,722 | 30.46 |
| Claudio Fermín (AD) | 1,325,287 | 23.60 |
| Oswaldo Alvarez Paz (COPEI) | 1,276,506 | 22.73 |
| Andrés Velásquez (Causa R) | 1,232,653 | 21.95 |
| Others | 71,531 | 1.27 |
| Total* | 5,829,216 | 100.00 |

* Including 212,517 spoilt votes.

## Legislature
### CONGRESO NACIONAL

Elections for both Chambers of Congress were held on 5 December 1993.

**Senate**
President: Eduardo Gómez Tamayo (CN).

| Party | Seats |
|---|---|
| Acción Democrática | 16 |
| Partido Social-Cristiano | 14 |
| Convergencia Nacional/Movimiento al Socialismo—Movimiento de Izquierda Revolucionaria | 10 |
| Causa Radical | 9 |
| Total | 49 |

Note: Four former Presidents hold life membership of the Senate.

**Chamber of Deputies**
President: Carmelo Lauría (AD).

| Party | Seats |
|---|---|
| Acción Democrática | 55 |
| Partido Social-Cristiano | 54 |
| Convergencia Nacional/Movimiento al Socialismo | 50 |
| Causa Radical | 40 |
| Total | 199 |

## State Governors
(June 1995)

| State | Governor |
|---|---|
| Amazonas | Edgar Sayago Murillo |
| Anzoátegui | E. Navas |
| Apure | Marcelo Oquendo |
| Aragua | Carlos Tablante |
| Barinas | Gerhard Cartay Ramírez |
| Bolívar | Andrés Velázquez |
| Carabobo | Henrique Salas Romer |
| Cojedes | José Felipe Machado |
| Delta Amacuro | Enrique Mata Millán |
| Falcón | Aldo Cermeño |
| Guárico | José Antonio Malavé Risso |
| Lara | José Mariano Navarro |
| Mérida | José Rondón Nucete |
| Miranda | Arnaldo Arocha |
| Monagas | Guillermo Call |
| Nueva Esparta | Morell Rodríguez |
| Portuguesa | Elías D'Onighia Colaprico |
| Sucre | Ramón Martínez |
| Táchira | José Francisco Ron Sandoval |
| Trujillo | José Méndez Quijada |
| Yaracuy | Nelson Suárez |
| Zulia | Lolita Aniyar de Castro |

## Political Organizations

**Acción Democrática (AD):** Casa Nacional Acción Democrática, Calle Los Cedros, La Florida, Caracas 1050; f. 1936 as Partido Democrático Nacional; adopted present name and obtained legal recognition in 1941; member of Socialist International; 1,450,000 mems; Pres. Pedro París Montesinos; Leader Humberto Celli; Sec.-Gen. Luis Alfaro Ucero.

**Convergencia Nacional (CN):** Edif. Tajamar, Mezzanina, Parque Central, Avda Lecuna, El Conde, Caracas 1010; tel. (2) 576-9879; fax (2) 576-8214; f. 1993; Leader Dr Rafael Caldera Rodríguez; Gen. Co-ordinator Juan José Caldera.

**Derecha Emergente de Venezuela (DEV):** Caracas; f. 1989; rightwing legislative coalition, comprising Nueva Generación Democrática, Fórmula Uno and Organización Renovadora Auténtica; Leaders Vladimir Gessen, Rhona Ottolina, Godofredo Marín.

**Causa Radical (Causa R):** Caracas; Leader Andrés Velásquez; Sec.-Gen. Pablo Medina.

**Movimiento Electoral del Pueblo (MEP):** Caracas; f. 1967 by left-wing AD dissidents; 100,000 mems; Pres. Dr Luis Beltrán Prieto Figueroa; Sec-Gen. Dr Jesús Ángel Paz Galarraga.

**Movimiento de Integración Nacional (MIN):** Edif. José María Vargas, 1°, esq. Pajarito, Caracas; tel. (2) 563-7504; fax (2) 563-7553; f. 1977; Sec.-Gen. Gonzalo Pérez Hernández.

**Movimiento de Izquierda Revolucionaria (MIR):** c/o Fracción Parlamentaria MIR, Edif. Tribunales, esq. Pajaritos, Caracas; f. 1960 by splinter group from AD; left-wing; Sec.-Gen. Moisés Moleiro.

**Movimiento al Socialismo (MAS):** Quinta Alemar, Avda Valencia, Las Palmas, Caracas; tel. (2) 782-4022; telex 29717; fax (2) 782-9720; f. 1971 by PCV dissidents; democratic-socialist party; 220,000 mems; Pres. Argelia Laya; Leader Teodoro Petkoff; Sec.-Gen. Freddy Muñoz.

**Nueva Alternativa (NA):** Edif. José María Vargas, esq. Pajaritos, Apdo 20193, San Martín, Caracas; tel. (2) 563-7675; telex 21252; f. 1982; Leaders Eduardo Machado, Clemente Castro, Antonio García Ponce, Pedro Troconis; Sec.-Gen. Guillermo García Ponce; alliance of democratic left comprising:

**Constancia Gremial.**

**MIR:** dissident faction of party listed above.

**Movimiento Patria Socialista (MPS):** Caracas; f. 1983; splinter group formed by MAS dissidents, and members of the extreme left-wing Vanguardia Unitaria, Causa R and the Grupo de Acción Revolucionaria.

**Movimiento Revolucionario Popular (MRP).**

**Vanguardia Unitaria:** Apdo 20193, San Martín, Caracas; f. 1974 by PCV dissidents; Pres. Eduardo Machado; Sec.-Gen. Guillermo García Ponce.

**Opinión Nacional (OPINA):** Pájaro a Curamichate 92, 2°, Caracas 101; f. 1961; 22,000 mems; Pres. Dr Pedro Luis Blanco Peñalver; Sec.-Gen. Prof. Amado Corneilles.

**Partido Comunista de Venezuela (PCV):** Edif. Cantaclaro, esq. San Pedro, San Juan, Caracas; tel. (2) 41-0061; fax (2) 481-9737; f. 1931; Sec.-Gen. Trino Meleán.

**Partido Social-Cristiano (Comité de Organización Política Electoral Independiente) (COPEI):** esq. San Miguel, Avda Panteón cruce con Fuerzas Armadas, San José, Caracas 1010; tel. (2) 51-6022; telex 24218; fax (2) 52-1876; f. 1946; Christian Democratic; more than 1,500,000 mems; Pres. Dr Luis Herrera Campíns; Sec.-Gen. Dr Donald Ramírez.

**Tradición, Familia y Propiedad (TFP)\*:** Caracas; f. 1960; rightwing ultramontane Roman Catholic group (also active in Brazil and Argentina); 200 mems.

**Unión Republicana Democrática (URD):** Caracas; f. 1946; moderate left; Leader Ismenia Villalba.

Other parties include: Fuerza Espiritual Venezolana Orientadora (Leader Rómulo Abreu Fuerte); Liga Socialista (f. 1974; Pres. Carmelo Laborit; Tercer Camino* (Third Way—Marxist; Leader Douglas Bravo), Bandera Roja* (Red Flag—f. 1968; Marxist-Leninist); Poder Independiente (right-wing; Leader Leopoldo Díaz Bruzual); Rescate Nacional (right-wing; Leader Gen. (retd) Luis Enrique Rangel Bourgoin); Fuerzas Bolivarianos de Liberación*; Los Justicieros de Venezuela*; Movimiento Revolucionario Bolivariano 200 (MRB-200)*.

* Illegal organizations.

# Diplomatic Representation

### EMBASSIES IN VENEZUELA

**Algeria:** Quinta Aures, Avda Los Mangos, Los Chorros, Caracas; tel. (2) 284-8074; telex 21814; Ambassador: ABDERRAHIM SETTOUTI.

**Argentina:** Edif. FEDECAMARAS, 3°, Calle El Empalme, El Bosque, Apdo 569, Caracas; tel. (2) 731-3311; telex 28053; fax (2) 731-2659; Ambassador: OMAR M. VAQUIR.

**Australia:** Quinta Yolanda, Avda Luis Roche entre 6a y 7a Transversales, Apdo 61123, Caracas 1060-A; tel. (2) 263-4033; telex 23101; fax (2) 261-3448; Ambassador: Dr DOMINIQUE DE STOOP.

**Austria:** Edif. Torre Las Mercedes, 4°, Of. 408, Avda La Estancia, Chuao, Apdo 61381, Caracas 1060-A; tel. (2) 91-3863; telex 23435; Ambassador: Dr JOHANNES SKRIWAN.

**Barbados:** Quinta Chapaleta, 9a Transversal, entre 2a y 3a Avdas, Apdo 68829, Altamira, Caracas; tel. (2) 262-1820; telex 27106; Ambassador: JOHN A. CONNELL.

**Belgium:** Quinta la Azulita, Avda 11, entre 6a y 7a Transversales, Apdo del Este 61550, Altamira, Caracas 1060; tel. (2) 262-0421; telex 21223; fax (2) 261-0309; Ambassador: RONALD A. DE LANGHE.

**Bolivia:** Avda Luis Roche con 6a Transversal, Altamira, Caracas; tel. (2) 261-4563; telex 27408; fax (2) 261-3386; Ambassador: LYDIA GUEILER TEJADA.

**Brazil:** Avda Mohedano con Calle Los Chaguaramos, Centro Gerencial Mohedano, 6°, La Castellana, Caracas; tel. (2) 261-4481; telex 25391; Ambassador: RENATO PRADO-GUIMARÃES.

**Canada:** Edif. Torre Europa, 7°, Avda Francisco de Miranda, Campo Alegre, Caracas; tel. (2) 951-6166; fax (2) 951-4950; Ambassador: RUSSELL H. DAVIDSON.

**Chile:** Edif. Torre La Noria, 10°, Calle Paseo Enrique Eraso, Las Mercedes, Caracas; tel. (2) 92-3378; telex 29603; fax (2) 92-0614; Ambassador: ANICETO RODRÍGUEZ A.

**China, People's Republic:** Prados del Este, Apdo 80665, Caracas 1080-A; tel. (2) 978-4424; telex 21734; Ambassador: HUANG ZHI-LIANG.

**Colombia:** Torre Credival, 11°, 2a Calle de Campo Alegre con Avda Francisco de Miranda, Apdo 60887, Caracas; tel. (2) 261-6592; telex 23360; fax (2) 261-1358; Ambassador: RODRIGO PARDO GARCÍA-PEÑA.

**Costa Rica:** Avda San Juan Bosco, entre 1ª y 2ª transveral, Edif. For You P.H., Altamira, Apdo 62239, Caracas; tel. (2) 267-1104; telex 23574; fax (2) 262-0038; Ambassador: CLARA MONTERO M.

**Cuba:** Quinta Affise, Avda El Cafetal, Chuao, Caracas 1060; tel. (2) 92-1124; Ambassador: NORBERTO HERNÁNDEZ CURBELO.

**Czech Republic:** Avda Luis Roche 41, 5a Transversal, Altamira, Caracas; tel. (2) 33-9866.

**Denmark:** Edif. Easo, 17°, Avda Francisco de Miranda, Chacaíto, Apdo 61169, Caracas 1060-A; tel. (2) 951-4618; telex 23371; fax (2) 951-5278; Ambassador: JOHN HARTMANN BERNHARD.

**Dominican Republic:** Edif. Humboldt, 6°, Of. 26, Avda Francisco de Miranda, Altamira, Caracas; tel. (2) 284-2443; telex 27432; Ambassador: BIENVENIDO HAZIM EGEL.

**Ecuador:** Centro Andrés Bello, Torre Oeste, 13°, Avda Andrés Bello, Maripérez, Apdo 62124, Caracas 1060; tel. (2) 781-3180; telex 21047; Ambassador: GALO PICO MANTILLA.

**Egypt:** Quinta Maribel, Calle Guaicaipuro, Las Mercedes, Caracas; tel. (2) 92-6259; Ambassador: WAHIB FAHMY EL-MINIAWY.

**El Salvador:** Quinta Cuzcatlán, Calle Amazonas, final Avda Principal de Prados del Este, Caracas; tel. (2) 39-1129; Ambassador: JORGE HASFURA.

**Finland:** Edif. Atrium, Calle Sorocaima, entre Avdas Venezuela y Tamanaco, El Rosal, Apdo 61118-A, Caracas 1060; tel. (2) 951-4111; telex 29138; fax (2) 952-7536; Ambassador: TEPPO TAKALA.

**France:** Edif. Los Frailes, Calle La Guairita, Chuao, Apdo 60386, Caracas 106; tel. (2) 91-0333; telex 23110; fax (2) 91-0143; Ambassador: ANDRÉ-JEAN LIBOUREL.

**Gabon:** 4 Avda Mohedano, Caracas; tel. (2) 283-8849; telex 25532; Ambassador: CONGA TROUS QUINTA MOGOALLA.

**Germany:** Edif. Panavén, 2°, Avda San Juan Bosco, esq. 3a Transversal, Altamira, Apdo 2078, Caracas; tel. (2) 261-0181; telex 23262; fax (2) 261-0641; Ambassador: WILFRIED RICHTER.

**Greece:** Quinta La Cañada, 1a Avda El Casquillo, esq. con Calle Unión, Alta Florida, Caracas; tel. (2) 74-0106; telex 29124; Ambassador: ANTOINE N. PROTONOTARIOS.

**Grenada:** Edif. Los Frailes, 3°, Of. 34, Calle La Guairita, Chuao, Caracas; tel. (2) 91-1237; telex 29606; fax (2) 91-8907; Ambassador: FABIAN A. REDHEAD.

**Guatemala:** Edif. Los Frailes, 6°, Calle La Guairita, Chuao, Apdo 80238, Caracas 1080-A; tel. (2) 91-8639; telex 29304; Ambassador: MIRIAM CABRERA PASARELLI.

**Guyana:** Quinta 'Roraima', Avda El Paseo, Prados del Este, Apdo 51054, Caracas; tel. (2) 978-2781; telex 29228; Ambassador: SATYADEOW SAWH.

**Haiti:** Quinta Macuro, Calle 12 entre 7a y 8a Transversales, Altamira, Caracas; tel. (2) 74-7220; telex 27226; Ambassador: PAUL D. ESTIME.

**Holy See:** Avda La Salle, Los Caobos, Apdo 29, Caracas 1010-A (Apostolic Nunciature); tel. (2) 781-8939; telex 24040; fax (2) 793-2403; Apostolic Nuncio: Most Rev. ORIANO QUILICI, Titular Archbishop of Tabla.

**Honduras:** 6a Transversal, 2a y 3a Avda Quinta, No 15, Los Palos Grandes, Apdo 68259, Caracas; tel. (2) 284-5593; telex 23152; Ambassador: LEÓN PAREDES L.

**Hungary:** Quinta Budapest, Calle Las Colinas, Lomas de San Rafael, La Florida, Apdo 50888, Caracas; tel. (2) 74-3167; telex 21403; Ambassador: ROBERT LEDERER.

**India:** Apdo 61585, Chacao, Caracas 1060-A, Caracas; tel. (2) 285-7887; telex 25438; Ambassador: V.P. SINGH.

**Indonesia:** Quinta La Trinidad, Avda El Paseo, Prados del Este, Apdo 80807, Caracas 1080; tel. (2) 978-0793; fax (2) 976-0550; Ambassador: EDWARD MARK RURU.

**Iran:** Quinta Lourdes, Calle El Retiro, El Rosal, Caracas; tel. (2) 92-1854; telex 23492; Chargé d'affaires a.i.: MORTEZA TAVASSOLI.

**Iraq:** Avda San Carlos 404, La Floresta, Caracas; tel. (2) 91-5112; telex 23525; Chargé d'affaires: DORAID A. SALIH.

**Israel:** Centro Empresarial Miranda, 4°, Avda Principal de los Ruices cruce con Francisco de Miranda, Apdo 70081, Los Ruices, Caracas; tel. (2) 239-4511; telex 25373; Ambassador: HERZL INBAR.

**Italy:** Edif. Atrium, Calle Sorocaima, entre Avdas Tamanaco y Venezuela, El Rosal, Apdo 3995, Caracas; tel. (2) 952-7311; telex 29985; fax (2) 952-7120; Ambassador: PAULO BRUNI.

**Jamaica:** Centro Plaza, Torre A, 11°, Avda Francisco de Miranda 205, Los Palos Grandes, Caracas; tel. (2) 283-6933; telex 25462; fax (2) 283-9445; Ambassador: MATTHEW A. C. BEAUBRUN.

**Japan:** Quinta Sakura, Avda San Juan Bosco, entre 8a y 9a Transversales, Altamira, Apdo 68790, Caracas 1062; tel. (2) 261-8333; telex 23363; fax (2) 261-6780; Ambassador: JUTARO SAKAMOTO.

**Korea, Democratic People's Republic:** Caracas; Ambassador: PAK JUNG GUK.

**Korea, Republic:** Edif. Atrium, 3°, Avda Sorocaima con Avda Venezuela, El Rosal, Apdo 80671, Caracas; tel. (2) 952-3456; telex 23493; Ambassador: CHO KWANG-JE.

**Lebanon:** Quinta el Cedro del Lebanon, Avda Primera, Colinas Bello Monte, Calle Motatán, Caracas 1050; tel. (2) 752-3215; telex 29413; Ambassador: SALIM TABET.

**Libya:** 3a Avda entre 9a y 10a Transversales, Quinta Los Leones, Altamira, Apdo 68946, Caracas 1060; Ambassador: AHMED TAHER TABIB.

**Mexico:** Edif. Centro Plaza, Torre A, 11°, Avda Francisco de Miranda y Andrés Bello, Los Palos Grandes, Caracas; tel. (2) 283-6622; Chargé d'affaires: JUAN MANUEL NUNGARAY.

**Netherlands:** Edif. San Juan Bosco, 9°, San Juan Bosco con 2a Transversal de Altamira, Caracas; tel. (2) 263-3622; telex 23177; fax (2) 263-0462; Ambassador: C. M. VAN HANSWŸCK DE JONGE.

**Nicaragua:** Quinta Teocal, Calle Codazzi, Prados del Este, Caracas; tel. (2) 77-2459; telex 24672; Ambassador: ROBERTO LEAL CAMPOS.

**Nigeria:** Segunda Avda, No 25, Campo Alegre, Caracas; tel. (2) 263-4816; telex 24506; fax (2) 263-4635; Ambassador: ANTHONY E. B. AYENI.

**Norway:** Edif. EXA, 9°, Of. 905, Avda Libertador, El Rosal, Apdo 60532, Chacao, Caracas 1060-A; tel. (2) 262-1506; telex 23310; fax (2) 262-0482; Ambassador: BJØRNAR S. UTHEIM.

**Panama:** Edif. Los Frailes, 6°, Calle La Guairita, Chuao, Apdo 1989, Caracas; tel. (2) 92-9093; telex 27588; Ambassador: DIOGENES DE LA ROSA.

**Paraguay:** Quinta Lily, 8a Avda de Altamira norte entre 7a y 8a Transversales, Apdo 80668, Caracas; tel. (2) 781-8213; Chargé d'affaires: ELADIO BUENO DE LOS RÍOS.

**Peru:** Edif. Centro Andrés Bello, Torre Oeste, 7°, Avda Andrés Bello, Maripérez, Caracas; tel. (2) 781-7180; telex 21278; fax (2) 781-3930; Ambassador: ALLAN WÁGNER TIZÓN.

**Philippines:** Quinta Taray, Avda Tropical, La Floresta, Caracas; tel. (2) 284-2006; Ambassador: PABLO A. ARAQUE.

**Poland:** Quinta Ambar, Final Avda Nicolás Copérnico, Sector Los Naranjos, Las Mercedes, Apdo 62293, Caracas; tel. (2) 91-1461; telex 23273; fax (2) 92-2164; Ambassador: ANDRZEJ KRZANOWSKI.

**Portugal:** Edif. FEDECAMARAS, 1°, Avda El Empalme, El Bosque, Caracas 1050; tel. (2) 731-0539; telex 21530; fax (2) 731-0543; Ambassador: JULIO MASCARENHAS.

VENEZUELA

**Romania:** Avda Principal 42, La Castellana, Caracas; tel. (2) 33-1770; telex 23176; Ambassador: Ioan Les.
**Russia:** Quinta Soyuz, Calle Las Lomas, Las Mercedes, Caracas; tel. (2) 92-1164; telex 23397; Ambassador: (vacant).
**Saudi Arabia:** Edif. Sucre, Of. 300, Avda Francisco de Miranda, La Floresta, Caracas; tel. (2) 284-2622; telex 29398; Ambassador: Bakr A. Khomais.
**Spain:** Avda Mohedano entre la y 2a Transversal, La Castellana, Caracas; tel. (2) 263-2855; telex 23487; Ambassador: Alberto de Armas García.
**Suriname:** 4a Avda entre 7a y 8a Quinta 41, Altamira, Caracas; Apdo 61140, Chacao, Caracas; tel. (2) 261-2724; fax (2) 261-2095; Ambassador: Dr Edwin J. Sedoc.
**Sweden:** Torre Europa, 8°, Of. A, Avda Francisco de Miranda, Chacaíto, Caracas; tel. (2) 952-2111; telex 23418; fax (2) 952-2057; Ambassador: Peter Landelius.
**Switzerland:** Torre Europa, 6°, Avda Francisco de Miranda, Campo Alegre, Apdo 62555, Caracas 1060-A; tel. (2) 951-4064; fax (2) 951-4816; Ambassador: Dr Ernst Iten.
**Syria:** Quinta Damasco, Avda Casiquare, Colinas de Bello Monte, Caracas; tel. (2) 752-6687; telex 21686; Ambassador: Raslan Alloush.
**Trinidad and Tobago:** Quinta Serrana, 4a Avda entre 7a y 8a Transversales, Altamira, Caracas; tel. (2) 261-4772; telex 23234; fax (2) 261-9801; Ambassador: Babooram Rambissoon.
**Turkey:** Quinta Turquesa 6, Calle Kemal Atatürk, Valle Arriba, Apdo 62078; Caracas 1060-A; tel. (2) 91-0075; telex 23286; fax (2) 92-0442; Ambassador: Nazim Belger.
**United Kingdom:** Torre Las Mercedes, 3°, Avda La Estancia, Chuao, Apdo 1246, Caracas 1060; tel. (2) 993-4111; telex 23468; fax (2) 993-9989; Ambassador: John G. Flynn.
**USA:** Avda Principal de La Floresta, esq. Francisco de Miranda, La Floresta, Caracas; tel. (2) 285-3111; telex 25501; fax (2) 285-0336; Ambassador: Jeffrey Davidow.
**Uruguay:** Torre Delta, 8°, Of. A y B, Avda Francisco de Miranda, Altamira Sur, Apdo 60366, Caracas 1060-A; tel. (2) 261-5352; telex 29778; fax (2) 266-9233; Ambassador: Dr Raúl J. Lago Finsterwald.
**Yugoslavia:** Quinta No 13, 4 Avda de Campo Alegre, Caracas; tel. (2) 266-7995; telex 25488; fax (2) 266-9957; Chargé d'affaires: Milivoj Sucević.

## Judicial System

The judicature is headed by the Supreme Court of Justice. The judges are divided into penal and civil and mercantile judges; there are military, juvenile, labour, administrative litigation, finance and agrarian tribunals. In each state there is a superior court and several secondary courts which act on civil and criminal cases.

### SUPREME COURT OF JUSTICE

The Supreme Court comprises 15 judges appointed by the Congreso Nacional in joint session for nine years, five of them to be appointed every three years. It is divided into three courts, each with five judges: political-administrative; civil, mercantile and labour cassation; penal cassation. When these three act together the court is in full session. It has the power to abrogate any laws, regulations or other acts of the executive or legislative branches conflicting with the Constitution. It hears accusations against members of the Government and high public officials, cases involving diplomatic representatives and certain civil actions arising between the State and individuals.

**Supreme Court:** Avda Universidad, esq. La Bolsa, Caracas 101; tel. (2) 483-1152.
**President:** Gonzalo Rodríguez Corró.
**Attorney-General:** Jesús Petit da Costa.

## Religion

Roman Catholicism is the religion of the majority of the population, but there is complete freedom of worship.

### CHRISTIANITY
#### The Roman Catholic Church

For ecclesiastical purposes, Venezuela comprises seven archdioceses, 21 dioceses and four Apostolic Vicariates. There is also an apostolic exarchite for the Melkite Rite. At 31 December 1993 there were some 19,640,000 adherents (about 93% of the total population), of whom 48,000 were of the Melkite rite.

*Latin Rite*
**Bishops' Conference:** Conferencia Episcopal de Venezuela, Torre a Madrices, Edif. Juan XXIII, Piso 4, Apdo 4897, Caracas; tel. (2) 563-1360; telex 26476; fax (2) 563-8147; f. 1985; Pres. Most Rev. Ramón Ovidio Pérez Morales, Archbishop of Maracaibo.
**Archbishop of Barquisimeto:** Most Rev. Tulio Manuel Chirivella Varela, Arzobispado, Calle 23, cruce con Carrera 16, Barquisimeto; tel. (51) 31-3446; telex 51316; fax (51) 51-0109.
**Archbishop of Caracas (Santiago de Venezuela):** Cardinal José Alí Lebrún Moratinos, Arzobispado, Plaza Bolívar, Apdo 954, Caracas 1010-A; tel. (2) 545-0212; telex 28537; fax (2) 545-0297.
**Archbishop of Ciudad Bolívar:** Most Rev. Medardo Luis Luzardo Romero, Arzobispado, Avda Andrés Eloy Blanco con Avda Naiguatá, Apdo 43, Ciudad Bolívar; tel. (85) 44960; fax (85) 40821.
**Archbishop of Cumaná:** Most Rev. Alfredo José Rodríguez Figueroa, Arzobispado, Calle Catedral 3, Apdo 134, Cumaná; tel. (93) 31-4131; telex 93222; fax (93) 66-3413.
**Archbishop of Maracaibo:** Most Rev. Ramón Ovidio Pérez Morales, Arzobispado, Calle 95, entre Avdas 2 y 3, Apdo 439, Maracaibo; tel. (61) 22-5351; telex 61186; fax (61) 21-0805.
**Archbishop of Mérida:** Most Rev. Baltazar Enrique Porras Cardozo, Arzobispado, Avda 4, Plaza Bolívar, Apdo 26, Mérida; tel. (74) 52-5786; telex 74287; fax (74) 52-1238.
**Archbishop of Valencia en Venezuela:** Most Rev. Jorge Liberato Urosa Savino, Arzobispado, Avda Urdaneta 100-54, Apdo 32, Valencia 2001-A; tel. (41) 58-5865; telex 41472; fax (41) 57-8061.

*Melkite Rite*
**Apostolic Exarch:** Boutros Raï, Iglesia San Jorge, Montalbán 2, Final 3a Avda, Apdo 29002, Caracas 1022-A; tel. (2) 443-3019; fax (2) 443-0131.

#### The Anglican Communion

Anglicans in Venezuela are adherents of the Episcopal Church in the USA, in which the country forms a single, extra-provincial diocese attached to Province IX.

**Bishop of Venezuela:** Rt Rev. Orlando Guerrero, Avda Caroní 100, Apdo 49-143, Caracas 1042-A; tel. and fax (2) 993-8170.

#### Protestant Churches

**Iglesia Evangélica Luterana en Venezuela:** Apdo 68738, Caracas 1062-A; tel. (2) 264-1868; telex 27920; fax (2) 264-1363; Pres. Walter A. Erdmann; 4,000 mems.
**The National Baptist Convention of Venezuela:** Apdo 61152, Chacao, Caracas 1061-A; tel. (2) 782-2533; Pres. Ing. Paúl Eustache; Exec. Sec. Jacobo García.

### BAHÁ'Í FAITH

**National Spiritual Assembly of the Bahá'ís:** Colinas de Bello Monte, Apdo 49133, Caracas; tel. and fax (2) 751-7669; f. 1961; mems resident in 954 localities.

## The Press

### DAILIES
#### Caracas

**The Daily Journal:** Avda Fuerzas Armadas, Crucecita a San Ramón, Apdo 1408, Caracas 1010-A; tel. (2) 562-1122; telex 26499; f. 1945; morning; in English; Chair. Hans Neumann; Editor Tony Bianchi; circ. 18,500.
**El Diario de Caracas:** Avda Principal de Boleíta Norte, Apdo 76478, Caracas 1070-A; tel. (2) 239-1722; telex 29193; f. 1979; centre-right; Dir-Gen. James Stone Reverón; circ. 70,000.
**Meridiano:** Edif. Bloque Dearmas, final Avda San Martín cruce con Avda La Paz, Caracas 1020; tel. (2) 443-1066; telex 22698; f. 1969; morning; sports; Dir Dr Andrés de Armas; circ. 300,000.
**El Mundo:** Torre de la Prensa, Puente Trinidad a Panteón, Apdo 1192, Caracas; tel. (2) 81-4931; telex 21173; fax (2) 83-8835; f. 1958; evening; independent; Pres. Miguel Angel Capriles; Dir Luis Oscar Pont; circ. 270,315.
**El Nacional:** Edif. El Nacional, Puente Nuevo a Puerto Escondido, Apdo 209, Caracas; tel. (2) 483-9133; telex 21196; fax (2) 41-2365; f. 1943; morning; independent; Editor Franklin E. Whaite; circ. 175,000.
**Ultimas Noticias:** Torre de la Prensa, Puente Trinidad a Panteón, Apdo 1192, Caracas; tel. (2) 81-4931; telex 21173; fax (2) 83-8835; f. 1941; morning; independent; Pres. Miguel Angel Capriles; Dir Nelson Luis Martínez; circ. 352,479.
**El Universal:** Edif. El Universal, Avda Urdaneta esq. de Animas, Apdo 1909, Caracas; tel. (2) 561-7511; telex 21263; f. 1909; morning; Dir and Editor Luis Teófilo Núñez; circ. 140,000.

VENEZUELA

**2001:** Edif. Bloque Dearmas, 2°, final Avda San Martín, cruce con final Avda La Paz, Apdo 575, Caracas; tel. (2) 443-1575; telex 22683; f. 1973; afternoon; independent; Dir PEDRO R. ROMERA; circ. 150,000.

### Barcelona
**Diario de Oriente:** Barcelona; tel. (81) 561-8613; f. 1973; Dir RAFAEL TOVAR; circ. 19,780.

### Barquisimeto
**El Impulso;** Edif. El Impulso, Carrera 23, 27-63, Apdo 602, Barquisimeto; tel. (51) 31-3011; f. 1904; morning; independent; Dir GUSTAVO A. CARMONA; circ. 40,000.

**El Informador:** Carrera 21, esq. Calle 23, Barquisimeto; tel. (51) 31-1811; f. 1968; morning; Dir ALEJANDRO GÓMEZ SIGALA; circ. 60,000.

### Ciudad Bolívar
**El Bolivarense:** Calle Igualdad 18, Apdo 91, Ciudad Bolívar; tel. (85) 22-5465; f. 1957; morning; independent; Dir ALFREDO NATERA; circ. 5,000.

**El Expreso:** Calle Vidal con Urbina, Apdo 208, Ciudad Bolívar; tel. (85) 23936; telex 85350; f. 1969; morning; independent; Dir M. A. GUZMÁN GÓMEZ; circ. 20,000.

**El Luchador:** Edif. Bolívar, Calle Cumaná cruce con 28 de Octubre, Apdo 65, Ciudad Bolívar; tel. (85) 20779; f. 1905; morning; liberal; Dir and Editor VÍCTOR BARRANCO; circ. 12,000.

### Maracaibo
**La Columna:** Calle 95 No 7-11, Apdo 420, Maracaibo; f. 1924; morning; Catholic; Dir GUSTAVO OCANTO YAMARTE; circ. 20,000.

**La Crítica:** Torre de la Prensa Zuliana, Calle 92 No 3-21, Maracaibo; tel. (61) 81-4931; telex 61212; f. 1966; morning; independent; Dir PEDRO J. AVILA; circ. 82,570.

**Panorama:** Avda 15 No 95-60, Apdo 425, Maracaibo; tel. (61) 21-1000; telex 61199; f. 1914; morning; independent; Pres. ESTEBAN PINEDA BELLOSA; circ. 130,000.

**El Vespertino de Occidente:** Torre de la Prensa Zuliana, Calle 92 No 3-21, Apdo 840, Maracaibo; f. 1974; evening; Dir GASTÓN GUISANDES; circ. 69,520.

### Maracay
**El Aragueño:** Calle Negro Primero 19, Maracay; tel. (43) 21608; morning; Dir OSCAR J. GUEVARA; circ. 10,000.

**El Siglo:** Edif. 'El Siglo', Avda Bolívar Oeste 244, La Romana, Maracay; tel. (43) 54-9265; telex 48331; morning; independent; Dir Ing. MANUEL CAPRILES; circ. 75,000.

### Puerto la Cruz
**El Tiempo:** Avda Constitución, Paseo Miranda 39, Apdo 4733, Puerto la Cruz; tel. (81) 66-5422; telex 81358; fax (81) 66-5092; f. 1958; independent; Dir Dr GIOCONDA DE MÁRQUEZ; circ. 50,000.

### San Cristóbal
**Diario Católico:** Carrera 4a No 3-41, San Cristóbal; tel. (76) 43-2819; fax (76) 43-4683; f. 1924; morning; Catholic; Man. Dir Mgr NELSON ARELLANO ROA; circ. 28,000.

**Diario de la Nación:** Calle 4 entre Carreras 6 y 7, Edif. La Nación, La Concordia, Apdo 651, San Cristóbal; tel. (76) 46-2367; telex 76443; fax (76) 46-5051; f. 1968; morning; independent; Editor JOSÉ RAFAEL CORTEZ; circ. 31,500.

### El Tigre
**Antorcha:** Edif. Anzoátegui, Avda Francisco de Miranda, Apdo 145, El Tigre; tel. (83) 35-2383; telex 83135; fax (83) 35-3923; f. 1954; morning; independent; Pres. ANTONIO BRICEÑO; circ. 30,000.

### Valencia
**El Carabobeño:** Edif. El Carabobeño, Avda Soublette 99-60, Valencia; tel. (41) 89951; telex 41196; f. 1933; morning; Dir EDUARDO ALEMÁN; circ. 75,000.

## PERIODICALS
### Caracas
**Agricultura Venezolana:** Apdo 8373, Caracas 101; every 2 months; agricultural; circ. 5,000.

**Alarma:** Torre de la Prensa, Plaza del Panteón, Apdo 2976, Caracas 101; f. 1977; fortnightly; politics; Dir JOSÉ CAMPOS SUÁREZ; circ. 65,150.

**Automóvil de Venezuela:** Avda Caunimare, Qta Expo, Colinas de Bello Monte, Caracas 1041; tel. (2) 751-1355; fax (2) 751-1122; f. 1961; monthly; automotive equipment trade; Editor ARMANDO ORTIZ P.; circ. 7,500.

**Bohemia Venezolana:** Edif. Bloque Dearmas, Final Avda San Martín cruce con Avda La Paz, Apdo 575, Caracas; tel. (2) 443-1066; telex 22683; f. 1966; weekly; general interest; Dir ROSANA ORDÓÑEZ; circ. 86,270.

**Business Venezuela:** Apdo 5181, Caracas 1010-A; tel. (2) 63-0833; telex 23627; fax (2) 32-0764; every 2 months; business and economics journal in English published by the Venezuelan-American Chamber of Commerce and Industry; Dir MICHAEL E. HEGGIE; circ. 6,000.

**Caza y Pesca, Náutica:** Apdo 60764, Caracas 1060-A; f. 1954; monthly; fishing, hunting and water sports; Dir HEINZ DOEBBEL; circ. 25,500.

**Deportes:** Torre de la Prensa, Plaza del Panteón, Apdo 2976, Caracas 101; f. 1978; fortnightly; sports review; Dir RAÚL HERNÁNDEZ; circ. 71,927.

**Dominical:** Torre de la Prensa, Puente Trinidad a Panteón, Apdo 1192, Caracas; tel. (2) 81-4931; telex 21173; fax (2) 83-8835; f. 1970; weekly; Pres. MIGUEL ANGEL CAPRILES; Dir NELSON LUIS MARTÍNEZ; circ. 352,479.

**Economía Venezolana:** Apdo 8373, Caracas; economics.

**Elite:** Torre de la Prensa, 6°, Plaza del Panteón Apdo 2976, Caracas 101; tel. (2) 81-4931; f. 1925; weekly; general interest; Dir ASDRÚBAL ZURITA; circ. 89,830.

**Ellas:** Edif. El Bucaré, Avda Federico Solano, Caracas 101; tel. (2) 71-2798; fortnightly; women's interest; Dir NERY RUSSO; circ. 30,000.

**Gaceta Hípica:** Apdo 2935, Caracas; weekly; horse racing; circ. 150,000.

**Hipodromo:** Torre de la Prensa, Puente Trinidad a Panteón, Apdo 1192, Caracas; tel. (2) 81-4931; telex 21173; fax (2) 83-8835; f. 1969; monthly; sports review; Pres. MIGUEL ANGEL CAPRILES; Dir EDUARDO HERNÁNDEZ LÓPEZ; circ. 101,548.

**Kena:** Edif. Humboldt, 2°, Avda Federico de Miranda, Apdo 2976, Caracas 101; tel. (2) 81-4931; f. 1964; fortnightly; women's interest; Dirs OTTO CASALE, HORTENSIA BRACAMONTE; Editor MARÍA ELENA MATHEUS; circ. 88,750.

**Momento:** Torre de la Prensa, Plaza del Panteón, Apdo 2976, Caracas 101; tel. (2) 572-0322; weekly; general interest; Editor ARMANDO DE ARMAS; circ. 78,520.

**Número:** Apdo 75570, El Marqués, Caracas 1070; tel. (2) 283-3393; fax (2) 283-9104; f. 1980; monthly; financial, business and marketing; Editor ARTURO OBADIA BERACASA; circ. 21,000.

**Páginas:** Torre de la Prensa, Apdo 2976, Caracas 101; tel. (2) 81-4931; f. 1948; women's weekly; Dir NELSON ZURITA; Editor MIGUEL ANGEL CAPRILES; circ. 80,025.

**El Periodista:** Casa del Periodista, Avda Andrés Bello, Caracas; every 2 months; journalism.

**Prensa Médica:** Edif. San José, 1°, Avda Principal Maripérez, Caracas; monthly; medicine; circ. 8,000.

**¿Qué Pasa?:** Edif. Nuevo Central, 7°, Avda Libertador, Chacao, Caracas; tel. (2) 32-8603; fortnightly; entertainment guide; Editor MARYSABEL PAREDES; circ. 50,000.

**La Semana:** Apdo 60411, Chacao, Caracas 106; weekly; general interest; Dir TIBOR KORODY; circ. 40,000.

**Sic:** Centro Gumilla, Avda Berrizbeitia 14, Apdo 29056, Caracas; monthly; Liberal Jesuit publication.

**Tribuna Médica:** Apdo 50164, Caracas; weekly; medicine; circ. 7,000.

**Variedades:** Edif. Bloque Dearmas, final Avda San Martín cruce con Avda La Paz, Caracas 1020; tel. (2) 572-0322; women's weekly; Dir GLORIA FUENTES; Editor ARMANDO DE ARMAS; circ. 58,230.

**Venezuela Gráfica:** Torre de la Prensa, Plaza del Panteón, Apdo 2976, Caracas 101; tel. (2) 81-4931; f. 1951; weekly; illustrated news magazine, especially entertainment; Dir DIEGO FORTUNATO; Editor MIGUEL ANGEL CAPRILES; circ. 95,870.

**Viernes:** Urb. los Palos Grandes 4a Avda, Residencias Unión, Planta Baja, Local No 4, Caracas; weekly; independent; Editor MANUEL FELIPE SIERRA.

**Zeta:** Pinto a Santa Rosalía 44, Apdo 14067, La Candelaria, Caracas; f. 1974; weekly; politics and current affairs; Dir RAFAEL POLEO.

**Zona Franca:** Conda esq. Carmelitas, Caracas; monthly; literary.

### Maracaibo
**El Balancín:** Cabimas, Maracaibo; weekly.

**Maracaibo:** Apdo 1308, Maracaibo; weekly.

## PRESS ASSOCIATIONS
**Asociación Venezolana de Periodistas:** Edif. AVP, Avda Andrés Bello, Caracas; tel. (2) 782-1301.

# VENEZUELA

**Bloque de Prensa:** Edif. El Universal, Avda Urdaneta, Caracas; Pres. Dr ANDRÉS DE ARMAS; Sec.-Gen. LUISA CHIOSSONE.

**Colegio Nacional de Periodistas:** Casa del Periodista, Avda Andrés Bello, Caracas; tel. (2) 782-1301; Pres. GILBERTO ALCALA; Sec.-Gen. RUBÉN CHAPARRO.

## PRESS AGENCIES

**Agence France-Presse (AFP):** Edif. Plaza, Of. 8–1, Avda Urdaneta, esq. La Pelota, Apdo 6254, Caracas 1010; tel. (2) 563-7212; telex 26546; Bureau Chief EDOUARD PONS.

**Agencia EFE** (Spain): Quinta 'Altas Cumbres', entre Calles Coro y San Cristóbal, Las Palmas, Caracas 1050; tel. (2) 793-7618; telex 29703; fax (2) 781-7691; Bureau Chief FRANCISCO R. FIGUEROA.

**Agenzia Nazionale Stampa Associata (ANSA)** (Italy): Torre de la Prensa, 13°, Plaza del Panteón, Caracas; tel. (2) 81-2330; telex 63921; fax (2) 81-3225; Correspondent GUILLERMO BECERRA.

**Associated Press (AP)** (USA): Edif. El Nacional, Apto 46, Puerto Escondido a Puente Nuevo, Apdo 1015, Caracas; tel. (2) 42-7223; telex 24464; Chief HAROLD OLMOS.

**Deutsche Presse-Agentur (dpa)** (Germany): Edif. Caroata, Of. 106, Parque Central, Apdo 17018, Caracas 1080-A; tel. (2) 575-1235; telex 23120; fax (2) 573-6331; Correspondent ESTEBAN ENGEL.

**Informatsionnoye Telegrafnoye Agentstvo Rossii—Telegrafnoye Agentstvo Suverennykh Stran (ITAR—TASS)** (Russia): Edif. Fondo Común, Torre Norte, 9°, Avda Urdaneta, Caracas; Chief YEVGENIY ALEKSEYEV.

**Inter Press Service (IPS)** (Italy): Edif. La Línea, Of. 154-B, Avda La Libertador, Caracas 1060; tel. (2) 782-3753; telex 29098; fax (2) 782-0991; Correspondent ESTRELLA GUTIÉRREZ.

**Prensa Latina** (Cuba): Edif. Fondo Común, Torre Sur, 20°, Avda de las Fuerzas Armadas y Urdaneta, Apdo 4400, Carmelitas, Caracas; tel. (2) 561-9733; telex 21620; fax (2) 561-8489; Correspondent JORGE LUIS LUNA MENDOZA.

**Reuters** (United Kingdom): Jesuitas a Tienda Honda, Edif. Seguros Avila, 2°, Apdo 5794, Carmelitas 1010-A, Caracas; tel. (2) 83-5033; telex 24567; fax (2) 83-8977; Man. ANTONIO PISTOYA.

**Rossiyskoye Informatsionnoye Agentstvo—Novosti (RIA—Novosti)** (Russia): Edif. Magdalena, 4°, San Francisco a Sociedad, 48, Caracas; Bureau Chief AUGUSTO FIGUEROA.

**United Press International (UPI)** (USA): Centro Financiero Latino, 9°, Of. 5, Avda Urdaneta, Apdo 667, Caracas; tel. (2) 561-6548; telex 26159; Bureau Man. LUIS AZUAJE.

**Xinhua (New China) News Agency** (People's Republic of China): Final Calle Maracaibo, Prados del Este, Apdo 80564, Caracas; tel. (2) 40966; telex 21618; Bureau Chief XU YAOMING.

## Publishers

**Alfadil Ediciones:** Edif. Alfa, Calle Los Mangos, Las Delicias de Sabana Grande, Apdo 50304, Caracas 1050-A; tel. (2) 762-3036; fax (2) 762-0210; general; Pres. LEONARDO MILLA A.

**Armitano Editores, CA:** Edif. Centro Industrial Boleíta, 4a Transversal de Boleíta, Sabana Grande, Apdo 50853, Caracas; tel. (2) 234-2565; telex 23115; fax (2) 234-1647; art, architecture, ecology, anthropology, history; Dir ERNESTO ARMITANO.

**Bienes Lacónica, CA:** Avda Orinoco, Quinta Praga, Las Mercedes, Apdo 69732, Caracas 1063-A; tel. (2) 752-2111; fax (2) 751-8363; f. 1977; philosophy; Gen. Man. DIEGO GIL VELUTINI.

**Colegial Bolivariana, CA:** Edif. COBO, 1°, Avda Diego Cisneros (Principal), Los Ruices, Apdo 70324, Caracas 1071-A; tel. (2) 239-1433; f. 1961; Dir ANTONIO JUZGADO ARIAS.

**Editorial El Ateneo, CA:** Edif. Ateneo Caracas, 5°, Plaza Morelos, Los Caobos, Apdo 662, Caracas; tel. (2) 573-4622; f. 1955; schoolbooks and reference; Pres. MARÍA TERESA CASTILLO; Dir ANTONIO POLO.

**Ediciones Ekaré:** Edif. Banco del Libro, Final Avda Luis Roche, Altamira Sur, Apdo 68284, Caracas 1062; tel. (2) 263-0091; fax (2) 263-3291; f. 1978; children's literature; Pres. CARMEN DIANA DEARDEN; Exec. Dir ELENA IRIBARREN.

**Editora Ferga, CA:** Avda Francisco de Miranda, Torre Bazar Bolivar, 5°, Of. 501, El Marqués, Apdo 16044, Caracas 1011-A; tel. (2) 239-1564; telex 21381; fax (2) 234-1008; f. 1971; Venezuelan Exporters Directory; Dir NELSON SÁNCHEZ MARTÍNEZ.

**Fondo Editorial Común:** Edif. Royal Palace, Of. 401, Avda El Bosque, Chacaíto, Apdo 50992, Caracas 1050; tel. (2) 72-3714; telex 21753; Pres. ALBA ILLARAMENDI; Dir PETER NEUMANN.

**Fundación Biblioteca Ayacucho:** Centro Financiero Latino, 12°, Of. 1, 2 y 3, Avda Urdaneta, Animas a Plaza España, Apdo 14413, Caracas 1010; tel. (2) 561-6691; telex 26217; fax (2) 564-5643; f. 1974; literature; Pres. JOSÉ RAMÓN MEDINA; Gen. Man. RAMÓN JOSÉ MEDINA.

*Directory*

**Fundarte:** Edif. Tajamar, P. H., Avda Lecuna, Parque Central, Apdo 17559, Caracas 1015-A; tel. (2) 573-1719; fax (2) 574-2794; f. 1975; literature, history; Pres. ALFREDO GOSEN; Dir ROBERTO LOVERA DE SOLA.

**Editorial González Porto:** Sociedad a Traposos 8, Avda Universidad, Apdo 502, Caracas; Pres. Dr PABLO PERALES.

**Ediciones IESA:** Edif. IESA, 3°, Final Avda IESA, San Bernardino, Apdo 1640, Caracas 1010-A; tel. (2) 52-1533; telex 28381; fax (2) 52-4247; f. 1984; economics, business; Pres. JANET KELLY DE ESCOBAR.

**Editorial Kapelusz Venezolana, SA:** Avda Cajigal, Quinta K No 29, entre Avdas Panteón y Roralma, San Bernardino, Apdo 14234, Caracas 1011-A; tel. (2) 51-7601; telex 24039; f. 1963; schoolbooks; Man. Dir (vacant).

**Ediciones La Casa Bello:** Mercedes a Luneta, Apdo 134, Caracas 1010; tel. (2) 562-7100; f. 1973; literature, history; Pres. OSCAR SAMBRANO URDANETA.

**Ediciones María Di Mase:** 1a Avda Altamira Sur 233, Caracas 1062; tel. (2) 31-5167; telex 24325; f. 1979; children's books; Pres. MARÍA DI MASE; Gen. Man. ANA RODRÍGUEZ.

**Monte Avila Editores Latinoamericana, CA:** Avda Principal La Castellana, Quinta Cristina, Apdo 70712, Caracas 1070; tel. (2) 265-6020; fax (2) 263-8783; f. 1968; general; Dir-Gen. Dr LEONARDO AZPARREN JIMÉNEZ.

**Ediciones Panamericanas EP, SRL:** Edif. Freites, 2°, Avda Libertador cruce con Santiago de Chile, Apdo 14054, Caracas; tel. (2) 782-9891; Man. JAIME SALGADO PALACIO.

**Editorial Salesiana, SA:** Paradero a Salesianos 6, Apdo 369, Caracas; f. 1960; education; Man. P. CLARENCIO GARCÍA S.

**Nueva Sociedad:** Edif. IASA, 6°, Of. 606, Plaza La Castellana, Apdo 61712, Chacao, Caracas 1060-A; tel. (2) 265-0593; fax (2) 267-3397; f. 1972; social sciences; Dir HEIDULF SCHMIDT.

**Oscar Todtmann Editores:** Avda Libertador, Centro Comercial El Bosque, Local 4, Caracas 1050; tel. (2) 71-0881; fax (2) 762-5244; science, literature, photography; Dir CARSTEN TODTMANN.

**Vadell Hermanos Editores, CA:** Edif. Tacarigua, 6°, Calle Montes de Oca, Valencia; tel. (41) 58-4510; fax (41) 57-4152; f. 1973; science, social science; Gen. Man. MANUEL VADELL GRATEROL.

**Ediciones Vega S.R.L.:** Edif. Odeon, Plaza Las Tres Gracias, Los Chaguaramos, Apdo 51662, Caracas 1050-A; tel. (2) 662-2092; fax (2) 662-1397; f. 1965; educational; Man. Dir FERNANDO VEGA ALONSO.

### ASSOCIATION

**Cámara Venezolana del Libro:** Centro Andrés Bello, Torre Oeste, 11°, Of. 112-0, Avda Andrés Bello, Apdo 51858, Caracas 1050-A; tel. (2) 782-2711; f. 1969; Pres. LEONARDO MILLA A.; Sec. ISIDORO DUARTE.

## Radio and Television

In 1992 there were an estimated 9,040,000 radio receivers and 3,300,000 television receivers in use.

**Dirección General Sectorial de Telecomunicaciones:** División de Radiodifusión, Ministerio de Transportes y Comunicaciones, Torre Este, 35°, Parque Central, Caracas; tel. (2) 509-1000; telex 22832; fax (2) 574-0753; controls all broadcasting, television and amateur productions; Dir LUIS E. GARCÍA.

### RADIO

**Radio Nacional de Venezuela:** Apdo 3979, Caracas 1010; f. 1946; state broadcasting organization; 13 stations; Dir JAIME ALSINA.

There are also five cultural and some 200 commercial stations.

### TELEVISION

#### Government Stations

**Televisora Nacional:** Apdo 3979, Caracas 1010-A; Dir-Gen. RICARDO TIRADO.

**Venezolana de Televisión—Canal 5 y 8:** Avda Montecristo, Los Ruices, Apdo 2739, Caracas; tel. (2) 239-9811; telex 25401; fax (2) 239-2675; 26 relay stations.

#### Private Stations

**Canal 10:** Centro Empresarial Miranda, Avda Francisco de Miranda con Principal de los Ruices, Caracas; tel. (2) 239-8679; fax (2) 239-7757.

**Canal 12—Omnivisión:** Edif. Omnivisión, Calle Milan, Los Ruices Sur, Caracas; tel. (2) 256-3586; telex 21024; fax (2) 256-4482.

**Radio Caracas Televisión (RCTV):** 2a Transversal Los Cortijos de Lourdes, Apdo 2057, Caracas; tel. (2) 256-3696; telex 21527; fax (2) 256-1812; f. 1953; commercial station; station in Caracas

# VENEZUELA

and 13 relay stations throughout the country; Pres. ELADIO LÁREZ; Gen. Man. CARLOS ABREU.

**NCTV:** Avdas 57 y Maracaibo, La Paz, Maracaibo; tel. (61) 51-2662; fax (61) 51-2729; commercial station; controls Channel 11; Dir GUSTAVO OCANDO YAMARTE.

**Televisora Andina de Mérida—TAM:** Calle 23, Entre Avdas 4 y 5, Apdo 5101, Mérida; tel. (74) 52-5758; telex 74287; fax (74) 52-0098; f. 1982; controls Channel 6; Dir HUGO ANZIL Z.

**Venevisión—Channel 4:** Avda La Salle, Colina de los Caobos, Caracas 1050; tel. (2) 782-4444; fax (2) 781-1635; f. 1961; commercial; 19 relay stations; Gen. Man. M. FRAIZ-GRIJALBA.

## BROADCASTING ASSOCIATIONS

**Cámara Venezolana de la Industria de Radiodifusión:** Apdo 3955, Caracas; tel. (2) 261-1651; telex 29281; fax (2) 261-4783; Pres. MARIETTA HERNÁNDEZ DE GÓMEZ.

**Cámara Venezolana de la Televisión:** Edif. Torre La Previsora, 7°, cruce Avda Abraham Lincoln con Las Acacias, Sabana Grande, Apdo 60423, Chacao, Caracas; tel. (2) 781-4608; telex 21144; Pres. Dr HÉCTOR PONSDOMENECH.

# Finance

(cap. = capital; res = reserves; dep. = deposits; m. = million; brs = branches; amounts in bolívares)

## BANKING

### Central Bank

**Banco Central de Venezuela:** Avda Urdaneta esq. de las Carmelitas, Caracas 1010; tel. (2) 801-5111; telex 28250; fax (2) 861-0048; f. 1940; bank of issue and clearing house for commercial banks; granted autonomy 1992; controls international reserves, interest rates and exchange rates; cap. 10.0m., res 67,665.7m., dep. 819,469.6m. (April 1994); Pres. ANTONIO CASAS GONZÁLEZ; Vice-Pres. Dr OMAR BELLO R.

### Commercial Banks
#### Caracas

**Banco Caracas, SACA:** Avda Urdaneta, de Veroes a Santa Capilla, No 4, Apdo 2045, Caracas; tel. (2) 505-1906; telex 21222; fax (2) 81-2038; f. 1890; cap. 700.0m., dep. 19,792.5m. (Dec. 1993); Pres. Dr BERNARDO VELUTINI; Gen. Mans CARLOS MONTOLIÚ F., CARLOS SAHMKOW; 4 brs, 60 agencies.

**Banco del Caribe, SACA:** Edif. Banco del Caribe, Dr Paúl a esq. Salvador de León, Apdo 6704, Carmelitas, Caracas 1010; tel. (2) 506-5511; telex 21880; fax (2) 564-2659; f. 1954; cap. 500.0m., res 559.1m., dep. 21,017.8m. (Dec. 1991); Pres. EDGAR A. DAO; Vice-Pres. and Gen. Man. Dr LUIS E. DE LLANO M.; 70 brs and agencies.

**Banco Consolidado, CA:** Torre Consolidada, Nivel E3, Calle Blandin, La Castellana, Apdo 61357,Caracas 1060; tel. (2) 206-3333; telex 28283; fax (2) 208-4950; f. 1969; cap. 400m., res 561.6m., dep. 20,858m. (Dec. 1987); placed under government control in 1994, reprivatization pending in 1995; Pres. JOSÉ ALVAREZ STELLING; Vice-Pres. and Gen. Man. LEOPOLDO RAMÍREZ PÉREZ.

**Banco de los Trabajadores de Venezuela (BTV) CA:** Avda Universidad, esq. Colón a esq. Dr Díaz, Apdo 888, Caracas; tel. (2) 541-7322; telex 22604; f. 1968 to channel workers' savings for the financing of artisans and small industrial firms; came under state control in 1982; cap. and res 167.9m., dep. 8,419.9m. (Dec. 1985); Pres. JOSÉ SÁNCHEZ PIÑA; Man. SILVERIO ANTONIO NARVÁEZ; 11 agencies.

**Banco de Venezuela, SAICA:** Torre Banco de Venezuela, Avda Universidad, esq. Sociedad a Traposos, Apdo 6268, Caracas 1010-A; tel. (2) 501-3333; telex 26375; fax (2) 501-3704; f. 1890; cap. 5,000.0m., res 5,731.3m., dep. 132,172.8m. (Dec. 1993); placed under government control in 1994, reprivatization pending in 1995; Pres. JOSÉ BOUZA IZQUIERDO; 7 brs.

**Banco Exterior, CA:** Edif. Banco Exterior, Avda Urdaneta, Urapal a Río, Apdo 14278, Caracas 1011-A; tel. (2) 501-0111; telex 24951; fax (2) 575-3798; f. 1958; cap. 500.0m., res 761.4m., dep. 19,841.1m. (June 1992); Pres. IGNACIO FIERRO VIÑA; Gen. Man. ANTONIO POLANCO GALDERÓN; 34 brs.

**Banco Exterior de los Andes y de España, SA (Extebandes):** Centro Banaven, Núcleo A, Piso 6, Avda la Estancia, Chuao, Apdo 60064, Caracas 1060; tel. (2) 751-7822; telex 24633; fax (2) 91-4048; f. 1980; Chair. ROSARIO ORELLANA YÉPEZ; CEO HERMINIO MORENO RAMÍREZ.

**Banco Industrial de Venezuela, CA:** Avda Universidad, esq. Traposos, Apdo 2054, Caracas 1010; tel. (2) 545-9222; telex 21354; f. 1937; state-owned; cap. 939.2m., res 709.4m., dep. 29,459m. (Dec. 1986); Pres. BERNARDO MARTÍNEZ A.; Exec. Vice-Pres. LUIS DELGADO; 60 brs.

**Banco Internacional, CA:** Edif. Banco Internacional, esq. de Animas, Avda Urdaneta, Carmelitas, Apdo 6688, Caracas 101; tel. (2) 506-2111; telex 29201; f. 1971 to take over brs. of Royal Bank of Canada, as Banco Royal Venezolano, CA; cap. 129.3m., res 422.9m. (Dec. 1986); Pres. JOSÉ LUIS RAVENGA; Exec. Dir JAIME SILVEIRA; 9 brs.

**Banco Latino, SACA:** Centro Financiero Latino, Mezzanina, Avda Urdaneta de Animas a Plaza España, Apdo 2026, Caracas 1010-A; tel. (2) 564-0460; telex 21153; fax (2) 502-5093; f. 1950; cap. 10,000m., dep. 82,123.9m. (June 1994); placed under government control following collapse in January 1994, reprivatization pending in 1995; 99 brs.

**Banco Mercantil, CA:** Edif. Mercantil, Avda Andrés Bello 1, San Bernardino, Apdo 789, Caracas 1010-A; tel. (2) 507-1111; telex 29997; fax (2) 507-1133; f. 1925; cap. 5,000.0m., res. 5,949.3m., dep. 162,175.4m. (Dec. 1993); Exec. Pres. and CEO Dr GUSTAVO A. MARTURET; Gen. Man. ALFREDO RODRÍGUEZ G.; 126 brs.

**Banco Metropolitano, CA:** Edif. Banco Hipotecario de Crédito Urbano, Piso 10, Avda Universidad esq. Traposos, Apdo 881, Caracas 1010-A; tel. (2) 545-6022; telex 21188; fax (2) 545-9574; f. 1953; cap. 118.9m., res 66.0m., dep. 3,379m. (Dec. 1986); Pres. J. DAVID BRILLEMBOURG; Vice-Pres. UMBERTO PETRICCA.

**Banco Provincial, SAICA:** Centro Financiero Provincial, Avda Vollmer con Avda Este O., San Bernadino, Apdo 1269, Caracas 1010-A; tel. (2) 574-6611; telex 21501; fax (2) 574-9408; f. 1952; cap. 9,000.0m., res 8,850.6m., dep. 228,896.2m. (Dec. 1993); Pres. JOSÉ MARÍA NOGUEROLES; Exec. Vice-Pres ARTURO GANTEAUME.

**Banco República, CA:** Edif. EDSAM, Madrices a Ibarras No. 6, Avda Urdaneta, Apdo 6688, Caracas 1010-A; tel. (2) 563-9511; telex 21333; f. 1958; cap. 1,565m., res 2,073m., dep. 56,604m. (Dec. 1988); placed under government control in 1994, reprivatization pending in 1995; Pres. JUAN CARLOS ESCOTET R.; Exec. Vice-Pres. JOSÉ LUIS LAGOA; 39 brs.

**Banco Unión, CA:** Torre Grupo Unión, Avda Universidad, esq. El Chorro, Apdo 2044, Caracas; tel. (2) 501-7111; telex 22864; fax (2) 501-7342; f. 1946; 50% owned by Banco Ganadero (Colombia); cap. 2,000.0m., res 2,845.4m., dep. 82,938.5m. (June 1992); Pres. Dr S. HENRY BENACERRAF; Vice-Pres. Dr IGNACIO SALVATIERRA P.; 13 brs, 157 agencies.

**Banco Venezolano de Crédito, SA:** Monjas a San Francisco, Sur 2, No 7, Caracas 1010; tel. (2) 806-6111; telex 21498; fax (2) 541-2757; f. 1925; cap. 1,350.0m., res 5,348.4m., dep. 13,578.1m. (Dec. 1993); Pres. Dr OSCAR GARCÍA MENDOZA; Vice-Pres. JOSÉ MANUEL VELUTINI; 42 brs.

#### Barquisimeto, Lara

**Banco de Lara:** Edif. Torre Lara, Avda 20, entre Calles 27 y 28, Apdo 545, Barquisimeto, Lara; tel. (51) 31-5211; telex 51131; fax (51) 31-6820; f. 1953; cap. 1,000m., dep. 32,041m. (Feb. 1994); Pres. Dr LUIS JOSÉ OROPEZA; Vice-Pres. HANS PETER GERSTEL.

**Banco Capital, CA:** Apdo 442, Barquisimeto, Lara; tel. (51) 31-4979; telex 51428; f. 1980; cap. 600m. dep. 13,193.3m. (Dec. 1994); Chair. and Pres. VICENTE FURIATI; Gen. Man. JUAN CARLOS FURIATI; 24 brs.

#### Ciudad Guayana, Bolívar

**Banco Guayana, CA:** Edif. Banguayana, Prolongación Paseo Orinoco, Apdo 156, Ciudad Bolívar, Bolívar; tel. (85) 25511; telex 85175; f. 1955; state-owned; cap. 80m., dep. 683.2m. (Feb. 1988); Pres. ANDRÉS E. BELLO BILANCIERI; Gen. Man. OMAIRA UNCEIN DE NATERA.

**Banco del Orinoco, SACA:** Edif. Seguros Orinoco, Avda Cuchivero con Calle Caruachí, Alta Vista, Apdo 020010, Ciudad Guayana, Bolívar; tel. (85) 285-0875; telex 23282; fax (85) 285-3872; f. 1980; cap. 1,200.0m., res 593.7m., dep. 20,903.0m (Dec. 1993); Pres. ALFONSO TREDINIK B.; Gen. Man. HUGO CHÁVEZ O.; 48 brs.

#### Coro, Falcón

**Banco Federal, CA:** Avda Manaure, cruce con Avda Ruiz Pineda, Coro, Falcón; tel. (68) 51-4011; telex 56217; f. 1982; cap. 50m., dep. 357m. (Dec. 1986); Pres. BERNARDO PAUL; Vice-Pres. JOSÉ TOMÁS CANIELO BATALLA.

**Banco de Fomento Regional Coro, CA:** Avda Manaure, entre Calles Falcón y Zamora, Coro, Falcón; tel. (68) 51-4421; telex 56168; f. 1950; transferred to private ownership in 1994; cap. 20m., res 5m., dep. 353.2m. (Dec. 1985); Pres. ABRAHAM NAÍN SENIOR URBINA; Gen. Man. DIMAS BUENO ARENAS.

#### Maracaibo, Zulia

**Banco Popular, CA:** Edif. Comercial de Maracaibo, Avda 5 de Julio, Apdo 46, Maracaibo, Zulia; tel. (61) 70622; telex 62558; f. 1916; state-owned; cap. 80m., dep. 883.7m. (Dec. 1985); Pres. ANTONIO QUINTERO PARRA; Gen. Man. CARLOS RODRÍGUEZ ROJAS.

**Banco Occidental de Descuento, CA:** Avda 5 de Julio esq. Avda 17, Apdo 695, Maracaibo 4001-A, Zulia; tel. (61) 59-3011; telex

64273; fax (61) 59-3611; f. 1957; transferred to private ownership in 1991; cap. 864.0m., res 744.7m., dep. 14,782.9m. (Dec. 1993); Pres. Dr José Manuel Egui M.; Exec. Dir Cándido Rodríguez; 17 brs, 9 agencies.

### San Cristóbal, Táchira

**Banco de Fomento Regional Los Andes, CA:** Carrera 6, esq. Calle 5, San Cristóbal, Táchira; tel. (76) 43-1269; telex 76113; f. 1951; cap. 20m., res 18.8m., dep. 796.2m. (Dec. 1985); Pres. Edgar Moreno Méndez; Exec. Vice-Pres. Pedro Roa Sánchez.

**Banco de Occidente, CA:** Avda 7, entre Calles 9 y 10, Apdo 360, San Cristóbal, Táchira; tel. (76) 43-0481; telex 76118; f. 1944; cap. 45m., res 55.8m., dep. 1,157.3m. (Dec. 1986); Pres. Luis Alfredo Jugo Rueda; Vice-Pres. Edgar A. Espejo; 8 brs, 13 agencies.

### Mortgage and Credit Institutions
### Caracas

**Banco Hipotecario de Crédito Urbano, CA:** Edif. Banco Hipotecario de Crédito Urbano, Avda Universidad, esq. de Traposas, Caracas; tel. (2) 545-6666; f. 1958; cap. 100m., res 58.3m., dep. 268.8m. (Dec. 1986); Pres. Carlos Obregón V.

**Banco Hipotecario de la Vivienda Popular, SA:** Intersección Avda Roosevelt y Avda Los Ilustres, frente a la Plaza Los Símbolos, Caracas; tel. (2) 62-9971; telex 21664; f. 1961; cap. 100m., res 68.2m., dep. 259.3m. (Dec. 1987); Pres. Hely Malaret M.; First Vice-Pres. Alfredo Esquivar.

**Banco Hipotecario Unido, SA:** Edif. Banco Hipotecario Unido, Avda Este 2, No 201, Los Caobos, Apdo 1896, Caracas 1010; tel. (2) 575-1111; telex 21526; fax (2) 571-1075; f. 1961; cap. 230m., res 143m., dep. 8,075m. (May 1990); Pres. Arturo J. Brillembourg; Gen. Man. Alfonso Espinosa M.

### Maracaibo, Zulia

**Banco Hipotecario del Zulia, CA:** Avda 2, El Milagro con Calle 84, Maracaibo, Zulia; tel. (61) 91-6055; f. 1963; cap. 120m., res 133.5m., dep. 671.5m. (Nov. 1986); Pres. Alberto López Bracho.

### Foreign Banks

**Banco Santander** (Spain): Edif. Centro Financiero Latino, 12°, Of. 9, Avda Urdaneta, Plaza España, Caracas 1010-A; tel. (2) 561-2815; telex 26300; Rep. Julio Arca.

**Banco Germánico de la América del Sud** (Deutsch Südamerikanische Bank and Dresdner Bank) (Germany—joint representation): Centro Gerencial Mohedano, 7°, Of. 7A, Calle Los Chuaguaramos, esq. Avda Mohedano, Apdo 61379, Caracas 1060; tel. (2) 261-4097; fax (2) 261-9456; Rep. José Luis Laguna.

**Citibank NA** (USA): Edif. Citibank, esq. de Carmelitas a esq. de Altagracia, Apdo 1289, Caracas; tel. (2) 81-9501; telex 22808; fax (2) 801-2367; cap. 40m., res 203.8m., dep. 677.6m. (Dec. 1986); Pres. Thomas J. Charters; Vice-Pres. José L. García M.; 4 brs.

**Morgan Guaranty Trust Co of New York** (USA): Avda Caracas, Ciudad Comercial, Tamanco, Caracas; tel. (2) 261-1894.

### Banking Association

**Asociación Bancaria de Venezuela:** Torre Financiera Banco Latino, Avda Urdaneta, esq. Fuerzas Armadas, Caracas; f. 1959; 66 mems; Pres. José María Nogueroles; Sec. Dr Félix Martínez-Espino O.

### STOCK EXCHANGES

**Bolsa de Valores de Caracas, CA:** Edif. Atrium, Calle Sorocaima entre Avdas Tamanaco y Venezuela, Nivel P., El Rosal, Caracas 1061; tel. (2) 905-5511; telex 26536; fax (2) 952-2640; f. 1947; 55 mems; Pres. Norys Aguirre Zambrano.

**Bolsa de Comercio del Estado Miranda:** Caracas.

**Bolsa de Comercio de Valencia:** Valencia.

### INSURANCE
### Supervisory Board

**Superintendencia de Seguros:** Torre Metálica, 1°–4°, Avda Francisco de Miranda, cruce con Avda Loyola, Chacao, Caracas 1061; tel. (2) 263-1344; telex 24684; Superintendent Dr Morelia Corredor Ochoa.

### Principal Insurance Companies

All companies must have at least 80% Venezuelan participation in their capital. In 1984 there were 57 insurance companies in Venezuela; the following list comprises the most important companies on the basis of revenue from premiums.

**Adriática, CA de Seguros:** Edif. Venadria, 1°, Avda Andrés Bello, Apdo 1928, Caracas; tel. (2) 571-5311; telex 21500; fax (2) 571-4654; f. 1952; cap. 27m.; Pres. Dr Francesco Di Venere Ladisa; Gen. Man. Corisanda de Aulis.

**Avila, CA de Seguros:** Edif. Seguros Avila, 9°–15°, Jesuítas a Tienda Honda, Apdo 1007, Caracas 1010; tel. (2) 83-8311; telex 26192; f. 1936; cap. 30m.; Pres. José Luis Velutini; Vice-Pres Dr Sergio Madinabeitia, Dr Henrique Romer, Henrique Castillo B.

**Carabobo, CA de Seguros:** Edif. Seguros Carabobo, Calle Rondón, cruce con Avda Díaz Moreno, Apdo 138, Valencia; tel. (41) 88601; telex 41183; f. 1955; cap. 75m.; Pres. Dr Luis Betancourt y Galíndez; Gen. Man. William Alvarez Y.

**Latinoamericana de Seguros, CA:** Centro Comercial Concresa, Avda Humboldt, Nivel TD, Prados del Este, Apdo 50148, Caracas 1080; tel. (2) 979-3511; telex 21881; f. 1974; cap. 25m.; Pres. Joaquín Silveira Ortiz; Exec. Pres. Lic. Luis Xavier Lujan.

**Pan American, CA de Seguros:** Edif. Panavén, 1° y 4°–9°, Avda San Juan Bosco, cruce con 3a Transversal, Urb. Altamira, Apdo 6166, Caracas; tel. (2) 261-9655; telex 23187; fax (2) 261-9655; f. 1966; cap. 55m.; Pres. Dr Alberto Quiros Corradi; Vice-Pres. Dr Victoria Gurudi.

**Seguros Caracas, CAV:** Edif. Seguros Caracas, 1°, Marrón a Cují, Apdo 981, Caracas 1010; tel. (2) 561-6122; telex 22614; f. 1943; cap. 600m.; Pres. Dr Moises Benacerraf; Exec. Vice-Pres. Dr Ricardo Echeverría.

**Seguros Catatumbo, CA:** Avda 4 (Bella Vista), No 77–55, Apdo 1083, Maracaibo; tel. (61) 921-733; telex 61188; fax (61) 921-778; f. 1957; cap. 700m.; Pres. Esteban R. Pineda B.; Gen. Man. Atenágoras Vergel Rivera.

**Seguros La Metropolitana, SA:** Centro Financiero Metropolitano, Avda Andrés Bello con Avda El Parque, San Bernardino, Apdo 2197, Caracas 1011; tel. (2) 575-0033; telex 21286; fax (2) 576-5884; f. 1949; cap. 38m.; Pres. Dr Imanol Valdés Cantolla; Vice-Pres. José Díaz Devesa.

**Seguros Nuevo Mundo, SA:** Edif. Seguros Nuevo Mundo, Avda Luis Roche con 3a Transversal, Altamira, Apdo 2062, Caracas; tel. (2) 263-0333; telex 23894; f. 1856; cap. 100m.; Pres. Luisa Elena Mendoza de Pulido; Exec. Vice-Pres. Adolfo Aldana Gutiérrez.

**Seguros Orinoco, CA:** Esq. de Socarrás, Avda Fuerzas Armadas, Apdo 6448, Caracas 1010; tel. (2) 564-3111; telex 26275; fax (2) 564-2065; f. 1957; cap. 300m.; Pres. Dr Otho Perret Gentil; Exec. Pres. Miguel Angel Els.

**Seguros La Seguridad, CA:** Esq. El Chorro, Avda Universidad, Apdo 473, Caracas 1010; tel. (2) 563-4633; telex 21276; fax (2) 563-7404; f. 1943; cap. 1,700m.; Pres. Andrés Boulton; Exec. Vice-Pres. Alberto Sosa Schlageter.

### Insurance Association

**Cámara de Aseguradores de Venezuela:** Torre Taeca, 2°, Avda Guaicaipuro, El Rosal, Apdo 3460, Caracas 1010; tel. (2) 952-4411; telex 23593; fax (2) 951-3268; f. 1942; 65 mems; Pres. William R. Phelan.

## Trade and Industry

### CHAMBERS OF COMMERCE AND INDUSTRY

**Federación Venezolana de Cámaras y Asociaciones de Comercio y Producción—FEDECAMARAS:** Edif. FEDECAMARAS, 5°, Avda El Empalme, El Bosque, Apdo 2568, Caracas; tel. (2) 731-1711; telex 29890; fax (2) 731-0220; f. 1944; 307 mems; Pres. Dr Edgard Romero Nava.

**Cámara de Comercio de Caracas:** Edif. Cámara de Comercio de Caracas, 8°, Avda Este 2, Los Caobos, Caracas; tel. (2) 571-3222; telex 24652; fax (2) 571-0050; f. 1893; 650 mems; Pres. Dr Francisco Aguerrevere.

**Cámara de Industriales de Caracas:** Edif. Cámara de Industriales, 3°, esq. Pte Anauco, La Candelaria, Apdo 14255, Caracas 1011; tel. (2) 571-4224; telex 24453; fax (2) 571-2009; f. 1939; Pres. Dr Luis Henrique Ball; Exec. Dir Marisol Fuentes Niño; 550 mems.

**Cámara Venezolano-Americana de Industria y Comercio:** Torre Credival, 10°, Of. 'A', 2a Avda Campo Alegre, Apdo 5181, Caracas 1010-A; tel. (2) 263-0833; telex 28399; fax (2) 32-0764; f. 1950; Pres. Stephen J. Fellows.

There are chambers of commerce and industry in all major provincial centres.

### STATE CORPORATIONS AND DEVELOPMENT ORGANIZATIONS

**Consejo de Economía Nacional:** Caracas; economic planning advisory board.

**Corporación de Desarrollo de la Pequeña y Mediana Industria (Corpoindustria):** Avda Páez, esq. Avda Las Delicias, Maracay, Aragua; tel. (43) 23459; telex 43472; promotes the development of small- and medium-size industries; Pres. Dr Carlos González-López.

VENEZUELA                                                                                                                                        *Directory*

**Corporación de Mercadeo Agrícola (Corpomercadeo):** Edif. Torre Industrial, Calle Vargas-Boleíta, Caracas; tel. (2) 35-8044; responsible for marketing agricultural products; Pres. Dr ALBERTO SILVA GUILLÉN.

**Corporación Venezolana de Guayana (CVG):** Avda La Estancia 10, 13°, Apdo 7000, Caracas; f. 1960 to organize development of Guayana area, particularly its iron ore and hydroelectric resources; Pres. ALFREDO GRUBER.

**CVG Bauxita Venezolana (Bauxivén):** Caracas; f. 1978 to develop the bauxite deposits at Los Pijiguaos; financed by the FIV and the CVG which has a majority holding; Pres. JOSÉ TOMÁS MILANO.

**Dirección General Sectorial de Hidrocarburos:** Torre Oeste, 12°, Parque Central, Caracas 1010; tel. (2) 507-6201; division of Ministry of Energy and Mines responsible for determining and implementing national policy for the exploration and exploitation of petroleum reserves and for the marketing of petroleum and its products; Dir-Gen. MANUEL ALAYETO E.

**Dirección General Sectorial de Minas y Geología:** Torre Oeste, 4°, Parque Central, Caracas; tel. (2) 507-5401; fax (2) 575-2497; division of Ministry of Energy and Mines responsible for formulating and implementing national policy on non-petroleum mineral reserves; Dir MIGUEL H. CANO DE LOS RÍOS.

**Ferrominera Orinoco, CA:** Apdo 76500, Caracas 107; f. 1976; responsible for production and processing of iron ore; assets 750m. bolívares (Dec. 1981); Pres. Ing. LEOPOLDO SUCRE FIGARELLA; Gen. Man. Ing. ANTONIO GILIBERTI.

**Instituto Agrario Nacional (IAN):** Quinta Barrancas, La Quebradita, Caracas; f. 1945 under Agrarian Law to assure ownership of the land to those who worked on it; now authorized to expropriate and redistribute idle or unproductive lands; Pres. Dr ANTONIO JOSÉ ALVAREZ FERNÁNDEZ.

**Instituto de Crédito Agrícola y Pecuario:** 40–44 Salvador de León a Socarras, Caracas; formerly the Banco Agrícola y Pecuario; administers the government crop credit scheme for small farmers; Dir-Gen. Dr ANTONIO JOSÉ ALVAREZ FERNÁNDEZ.

**Instituto Nacional de Obras Sanitarias (INOS):** Edif. La Paz, Caracas; autonomous government institution; administers water supply and sewerage projects; privatization plans announced in April 1990; Pres. Dr ALEXIS CARSTENS RAMOS.

**Instituto Nacional de la Vivienda:** Edif. Banco Obrero, esq. Cruz Verde, Caracas; f. 1975; administers government housing projects; Pres. Dr LEANDRO QUINTA.

**Petróleos de Venezuela, SA (PDVSA):** Edif. Petróleos de Venezuela, Torre Este, Avda Libertador, La Campiña, Apdo 169, Caracas 1010-A; tel. (2) 708-4111; telex 21890; fax (2) 708-4661; f. 1975; holding company for national petroleum industry; responsible for petrochemical sector since 1978 and for development of coal resources in western Venezuela since 1985; Pres. LUIS E. GIUSTI LÓPEZ; Vice-Pres CLAUS GRAF, LUIS URDANETA. The following are subsidiaries of PDVSA:

**Barivén, SA:** Edif. Centro Empresarial Parque del Este, Avda Francisco de Miranda, La Carlota, Apdo 893, Caracas 1010-A; tel. (2) 201-4611; telex 29543; fax (2) 201-4729; handles the petroleum, petrochemical and hydrocarbons industries' overseas purchases of equipment and materials; Pres. ALFREDO VISO.

**Bitúmenes Orinoco, SA (BITOR):** Edif. Bitúmenes Orinoco, SA, Calle Cali, Las Mercedes, Apdo 3470, Caracas 1010-A; tel. (2) 907-5111; telex 23111; fax (2) 908-3982; plans, develops and markets the bitumen resources of the Orinoco belt; Pres. JORGE ZEMELLA; Vice-Pres. CARLOS BORREGALES.

**Carbozulia, SA:** Edif. Lagovén Maracaibo, Calle 77 (5 de Julio) con Avda 11, Apdo 1200, Maracaibo 4001; tel. (61) 76-091; telex 62160; fax (61) 520-334; f. 1978; responsible for the commercial exploitation of the Guasare coalfields in Zulia; Pres. LUIS RIOS.

**Corpovén, SA:** Edif. Petróleos de Venezuela, Avda Libertador, La Campiña, Apdo 61373, Caracas 1060-A; tel. (2) 708-1111; telex 21363; fax (2) 708-1833; exploration, production, refining and marketing of crude petroleum products, and gas distribution; merged with Menevén in 1986; Pres. Dr ROBERTO MANDINI; Vice-Pres. JUAN CARLOS GÓMEZ.

**Intervén, SA:** Edif. Centro Empresarial Parque del Este, Avda Francisco de Miranda, La Carlota, Apdo 60564, Caracas 1060-A; tel. (2) 203-1300; telex 21854; fax (2) 203-1300; f. 1986 to manage PDVSA's joint ventures overseas; Pres. REMIGIO FERNÁNDEZ; Vice-Pres. ARNOLDO VOLKENBORN.

**INTEVEP, SA:** Edif. Sede Central-Santa Rosa, Los Teques, Apdo 76343, Caracas 1010-A; tel. (2) 908-6111; telex 37126; fax (2) 908-6447; f. 1979; research and development branch of PDVSA; undertakes applied research and development in new products and processes and provides specialized technical services for the petroleum and petrochemical industries; Pres. GUSTAVO INCIARTE; Vice-Pres. NÉSTOR BARROETA.

**Lagovén, SA:** Edif. Lagovén, Avda Leonardo da Vinci, Los Chaguaramos, Apdo 889, Caracas; tel. (2) 661-1011; telex 24139; fax (2) 606-3637; f. 1978; state petroleum company; Pres. JULIUS TRINKUNAS; Vice-Pres. VICENTE LLATAS.

**Maravén, SA:** Edif. Maravén, Avda La Estancia 10, Chuao, Apdo 829, Caracas 1010-A; tel. (2) 908-2111; telex 23227; fax (2) 908-2885; f. 1976; state petroleum company; petroleum exploration, production, transport, refining and both domestic and international marketing; Pres. EDUARDO LÓPEZ QUEVEDO; Vice-Pres. GUSTAVO GABALDÓN.

**Palmavén:** Edif. Palmavén, Avda Tamanaco, El Rosal, Apdo 3505, Caracas 1010-A; tel. (2) 951-4144; telex 27045; fax (2) 905-1324; promotes agricultural development, provides agricultural and environmental services and technical assistance to farmers; Pres. ALFREDO GRÜBER; Man. Dir EDDIE RAMÍREZ.

**Petroquímica de Venezuela, SA (Pequivén):** Torre Pequivén, Avda Francisco de Miranda, Cruce Avda Mis Encantos, Chacao, Caracas; tel. (2) 201-3111; telex 23206; fax (2) 201-3306; f. 1956 as Instituto Venezolano de Petroquímica; became Pequivén in 1977; involved in many joint ventures with foreign and private Venezuelan interests for expanding petrochemical industry; active in regional economic integration; since 1978 has been an affiliate of PDVSA; Pres. ARNOLD VOLKENBORN; Vice-Pres. HUMBERTO VIDAL.

**Refinería Isla (Curazao), SA:** POB 3843, Curaçao, Netherlands Antilles; tel. 66-2700; fax 66-2299; f. 1985; operates a 320,000 b/d refinery and a deep-water terminal on Curaçao (Netherlands Antilles), formerly owned by the Royal Dutch-Shell group.

**Siderúrgica del Orinoco, CA (Sidor):** Edif. La Estancia, Chuao, Caracas; steel producer; privatization pending in 1995; Pres. CÉSAR MENDOZA.

**Superintendencia de Inversiones Extranjeras (SIEX):** Edif. La Perla, Bolsa a Mercaderes, 3°, Apdo 213, Caracas 1010; tel. (2) 483-6666; telex 26133; fax (2) 41-4368; f. 1974; supervises foreign investment in Venezuela; Supt. Dr ANSELMO CHUECOS PÉREZ.

**Venezolana de Aluminio, CA (Venalum):** Caracas; 80% owned by Govt, 20% by Japanese consortium; further privatization pending in 1995; production of aluminium; Pres. ROBERTO ARREAZA.

## EMPLOYERS' ASSOCIATIONS
### Caracas

**Alimentos Margarita, CA:** Calle Los Laboratorios, Torre Beta, Piso 1, Of. 107, Los Ruices, Apdo 3673, Caracas; tel. (2) 238-1711; telex 25113; fax (2) 239-1107; f. 1938; canned fish industry; Pres. EDUARDO OROPEZA CASTILLO.

**Asociación Nacional de Comerciantes e Industriales:** Plaza Panteón Norte 1, Apdo 33, Caracas; f. 1936; traders and industrialists; Pres. Dr HORACIO GUILLERMO VILLALOBOS; Sec. R. H. OJEDA MAZZARELLI; 500 mems.

**Asociación Nacional de Industriales Metalúrgicos y de Minería de Venezuela:** Edif. Cámara de Industriales, 9°, Puente Anauco a Puente República, Apdo 14139, Caracas; metallurgy and mining; Pres. JOSÉ LUIS GÓMEZ; Exec. Dir LUIS CÓRDOVA BRITO.

**Asociación Textil Venezolana:** Edif. Karam, 5°, Of. 503, Avda Urdaneta, Ibarras a Pelota, Apdo 6469, Caracas; tel. (2) 561-6851; telex 26145; fax (2) 562-8197; f. 1957; textiles; Pres. ALFREDO BLOHM; Exec. Dir FREDDY TINEO; 68 mems.

**Consejo Venezolano de la Industria—Conindustria:** Caracas; association of industrialists; Pres. JORGE REDMOND; Dir GERARDO LUCAS.

**Confederación Nacional de Asociaciones de Productores Agropecuarios—Fedeagro:** Edif. Casa de Italia, Planta Baja, Avda La Industria, San Bernardino, Caracas 1010; tel. (2) 571-4035; fax (2) 573-4423; f. 1960; agricultural producers; 133 affiliated associations; Pres. FERNANDO CAMINO PEÑALVER; Exec. Sec. IVÁN LÓPEZ GONZÁLEZ.

**Consejo Venezolano de la Industria:** Edif. Cámara de Industriales, esq. de Puente Anauco, Caracas; industry council; Pres. GUSTAVO PÉREZ MIJARES; Co-ordinator Ing. ISRAEL DÍAZ VALLES.

**Federación Nacional de Ganaderos de Venezuela:** Edif. Casa de Italia, 7°, Avda La Industria, San Bernardino, Caracas; cattle owners; Dir ELÍAS CASTRO CORREAS; Sec. MIGUEL A. GRANADOS.

**Unión Patronal Venezolana del Comercio:** Edif. General Urdaneta, 2°, Marrón a Pelota, Apdo 6578, Caracas; trade; Sec. H. ESPINOZA BANDERS.

### Other Towns

**Asociación de Comerciantes e Industriales del Zulia–ACIZ:** Edif. Los Cerros, 3°, Calle 77 con Avda 3c, Apdo 91, Maracaibo; tel. (61) 91-7174; telex 62499; fax (61) 91-2570; f. 1941; traders and industrialists; Pres. JORGE AVILA.

VENEZUELA                                                                                                                      Directory

**Asociación Nacional de Cultivadores de Algodón** (National Cotton Growers' Association): Planta Desmotadora, Carretera Guanare, Zona Industrial Acarigua; Sec. LEOPOLD BAPTISTA.

**Asociación Nacional de Empresarios y Trabajadores de la Pesca:** Apdo 52, Cumaná; fishermen.

**Unión Nacional de Cultivadores de Tabaco:** Urb. Industrial La Hamaca, Avda Hustaf Dalen, Apdo 252, Maracay; tobacco growers.

### TRADE UNIONS

About one-quarter of the labour force in Venezuela belongs to unions, more than one-half of which are legally recognized.

**Central General de Trabajadores (CGT):** Communist-led.

**Central Unida de Trabajadores.**

**Central Unitaria de Trabajadores de Venezuela (CUTV):** Miseria a Vetasquez, Caracas; leftist union affiliated to WFTU; 80,000 mems.

**Confederación de Sindicatos Autónomos de Venezuela (CODESA):** affiliated to COPEI; Pres. WILLIAM FRANCO CASALINS; Leader LAURIANO ORTIZ.

**Confederación de Trabajadores de Venezuela (CTV)** (Confederation of Venezuelan Workers): Edif. José Vargas, 17°, Avda Este 2, Los Caobos, Caracas; tel. (2) 575-1105; telex 26211; f. 1936; affiliated to Acción Democrática; Pres. FEDERICO RAMÍREZ LEÓN; Sec.-Gen. CÉSAR OLARTE; 1,500,000 mems from 24 regional and 16 industrial federations.

**Fedenaca:** peasant union.

**Federación Campesina (FC):** peasant union; CTV affiliate; Leader RUBÉN LANZ.

**Fetrametal:** union of metal workers; CTV affiliate; Leader JOSÉ MOLLEGAS.

**Movimiento Nacional de Trabajadores para la Liberación (MONTRAL):** Edif. Don Miguel, 6°, esq. Cipreses, Caracas; f. 1974; affiliated to CLAT and WFTU; Pres. LAUREANO ORTIZ BRAEAMONTE; Sec.-Gen. DAGOBERTO GONZÁLEZ; co-ordinating body for the following trade unions:

**Central Nacional Campesina (CNC):** Pres. REINALDO VÁSQUEZ.

**Cooperativa Nacional de Trabajadores de Servicios Múltiples (CNTSM).**

**Federación Nacional de Sindicatos Autónomos de Trabajadores de la Educación de Venezuela (FENASATREV):** Pres. LUIS EFRAÍN ORTA.

**Federación de los Trabajadores de Hidrocarburos de Venezuela (FETRAHIDROCARBUROS).**

**Frente de Trabajadores Copeyanos (FTC):** Sec.-Gen. DAGOBERTO GONZÁLEZ.

**Movimiento Agrario Social-Cristiano (MASC):** Sec.-Gen. GUSTAVO MENDOZA.

**Movimiento Magisterial Social-Cristiano (MMSC):** Sec.-Gen. FELIPE MONTILLA.

**Movimiento Nacional de Trabajadores de Comunicaciones (MONTRAC).**

**Movimiento Nacional de Trabajadores Estatales de Venezuela (MONTREV).**

## Transport

### RAILWAYS

**Ferrocentro:** Caracas; f. 1987; state railway corporation.

**Instituto Autónomo de Ferrocarriles del Estado (FERROCAR):** Torre Este, 37°-45°, Avda Lecuna, Parque Central, Caracas 1010; tel. (2) 509-3500; telex 28522; fax (2) 574-7021; state company; 336 km; Pres. LUCIANO HILZINGER LARES; Vice-Pres. OSCAR RAMÍREZ OSIO.

The Government plans to construct a 1,400-km rail network by the year 2000 at a cost of US $2,500m.; in 1994 work was in progress on lines linking Acarigua and Turén (45 km) and Morón and Riecito (100 km). Construction of the first section (Caracas–Cúa) of a line linking the capital to the existing network at Puerto Cabello (219 km in total) had also begun.

**CA Metro de Caracas:** Multicentro Empresarial del Este, Edif. Miranda, Torre B, Avda Francisco de Miranda, Caracas; tel. (2) 208-2111; telex 24936; f. 1976 to supervise the construction and use of the underground railway system; Pres. Ing. JOSÉ GONZÁLEZ LANDER.

Services began in 1983 on a two-line system: east to west from Palos Verdes to Propatria; north to south from Capitolio/El Silencio to Zoológico. Further extensions to the lines were under way in 1995.

**CVG Ferrominera Orinoco, CA:** Vía Caracas, Puerto Ordaz, POB 399, Bolívar; tel. (86) 30-3111; fax (86) 30-3656; f. 1976; state company; operates two lines Cerro Bolívar–Puerto Ordaz (207 km) and El Pao–Palua (55 km) for transporting iron ore; Pres. Ing. LEOPOLDO SUCRE FIGARELLA.

**Ferrocarril de CVG Bauxita Venezolana, CA:** Apdo 65038, Caracas 1065-A; tel. (2) 92-2311; f. 1989; state company; operates line linking Los Pijiguaos with river Orinoco port of Gumilla (52 km) for transporting bauxite; Pres. F. LAYRISSE.

### ROADS

In 1993 there were 93,472 km of roads, of which 29,954 km were asphalted.

Of the three great highways, the first (960 km) runs from Caracas to Ciudad Bolívar. The second, the Pan-American Highway (1,290 km), runs from Caracas to the Colombian frontier and is continued as far as Cúcuta. A branch runs from Valencia to Puerto Cabello. The third highway runs southwards from Coro to La Ceiba, on Lake Maracaibo.

A new 'marginal highway' was under construction along the western fringe of the Amazon Basin in Venezuela, Colombia, Ecuador, Peru, Bolivia and Paraguay. The Venezuelan section now runs for over 440 km and is fully paved.

### INLAND WATERWAYS

**Instituto Nacional de Canalizaciones:** Edif. INC, Calle Caracas, Chuao, al lado de la Torre Diamen, Apdo E.61959, Caracas; f. 1952; semi-autonomous institution connected with the Ministry of Transport and Communications; Pres. Rear-Adm. AGUEDO FELIPE HERNÁNDEZ; Vice-Pres. FERNANDO MARTÍ O.

**Compañía Anónima La Translacustre:** Maracaibo; freight and passenger service serving Lake Maracaibo, principally from Maracaibo to the road terminal from Caracas at Palmarejo.

### SHIPPING

There are nine major ports, 34 petroleum and mineral ports and five fishing ports. The main port for imports is La Guaira, the port for Caracas; Puerto Cabello handles raw materials for the industrial region around Valencia. Maracaibo is the chief port for the petroleum industry. Puerto Ordaz, on the Orinoco River, was also developed to deal with the shipments of iron from Cerro Bolívar.

The Instituto Nacional de Puertos designed a programme aimed at satisfying port handling requirements up to 1995, to alleviate the long-standing problem of port congestion. A new port, Carenero, was to be built at an estimated cost of US $139.5m., capable of handling 2m. tons of general freight and 300,000 tons of grain a year. Improvements and expansion of other ports, including five new docks at La Guaira, completed in 1979, significantly raised overall capacity.

**Instituto Nacional de Puertos:** Edif. Instituto Nacional de Puertos, Calle Veracruz, cruce con Cali, Las Mercedes, Caracas; tel. (2) 92-2811; telex 23447; f. 1976 as the sole port authority; Pres. Vice-Adm. FREDDY J. MOTA CARPIO.

**Consolidada de Ferrys, CA:** Torre Banhorient, 3°, Avda Las Acacias y Avda Casanova, Caracas 1010-A; tel. (2) 793-2030; telex 21736; fax (2) 793-0739; Pres. RAFAEL TOVAR.

**Consorcio Naviero Venezolano (Conavén):** Edif. Torre Británica, 3°, Avda José Félix Sosa, Altamira Sur, Caracas 1010-A; tel. (2) 261-0363; telex 23944; fax (2) 26-1595.

**Corpovén, SA:** Edif. Petróleos de Venezuela, Avda Libertador, La Campiña, Apdo 61373, Caracas 1060-A; tel. (2) 708-1111; telex 21363; fax (2) 708-1833; Pres. Dr ROBERTO MANDINI; Vice-Pres. JUAN CARLOS GÓMEZ; 2 oil tankers.

**Lagovén, SA:** Edif. Lagovén, Avda Leonardo da Vinci, Los Chaguaramos, Apdo 889, Caracas; tel. (2) 661-1011; telex 24139; fax (2) 606-3637; f. 1978 as a result of the nationalization of the petroleum industry; (formerly known as the Creole Petroleum Group); transports crude petroleum and by-products between Maracaibo, Aniba and other ports in the area; Pres. JULIUS TRINKUNAS; Marine Man. P. D. CAREZIS; 10 tankers.

**Maravén, SA:** Edif. Maravén, Avda La Estancia 10, Chuao, Apdo 829, Caracas 1010-A; tel. (2) 908-211; telex 23227; fax (2) 908-2885; Pres. EDUARDO LÓPEZ QUEVEDO; Vice-Pres. GUSTAVO GABALDÓN.

**Marítima Aragua, SA:** Centro Plaza Torre A, 15°, Avda Francisco de Miranda, Apdo 68404, Caracas 1062-A; tel. (2) 283-8355; telex 21567; fax (2) 285-5162; Pres. Capt. S. JUAN HUERTA.

**Tacarigua Marina, CA:** Torre Lincoln 7A-B, Avda Lincoln, Apdo 51107, Sabana Grande, Caracas 1050-A; tel. (2) 781-1315; telex 21580; Pres. R. BELLIZZI.

**Transpapel, CA:** Edif. Centro, 11°, Of. 111, Centro Parque Boyaca, Avda Sucre, Los Dos Caminos, Apdo 61316, Caracas 1071; tel. (2) 283-8366; telex 23563; fax (2) 285-7749; Chair. GUILLERMO ESPINOSA F.; Man. Dir Capt. NELSON MALDONADO A.

# VENEZUELA

**Transporte Industrial, SA:** Carretera Guanta, Km 5 Planta Vencemos, Pertigalete-Edif. Anzoategui, Apdo 4356, Puerto la Cruz; tel. (81) 68-3481; telex 81390; fax (81) 68-3422; f. 1955; bulk handling and cement bulk carrier; Chair. CLEVELAND BALLARD; Man. Dir RAFAEL A. ANEZ.

**Venezolana de Buques, CA:** Of. 2, 19°, esq. Puente Victoria, Caracas; tel. (2) 283-9954; telex 21362.

**Venezolana de Navegación, CA:** Avda Rómulo Gallegos 8007, Sector El Samán, entre Calle El Carmen y 1a Transversal de Monte Cristo, Los Dos Caminos, Apdo 70135, Caracas 1071; tel. (2) 203-6511; telex 24294; fax (2) 35-7185; regular services to US ports and Germany, the Netherlands, France and Spain; associated services from Scandinavian, Baltic, Mediterranean and Japanese ports; Chair. Rear Adm. CARLOS HERNÁNDEZ F.; Man. Dir Capt. L. E. LUGO MARÍN.

## CIVIL AVIATION

There are two adjacent airports 13 km from Caracas; Maiquetía for domestic and Simón Bolívar for international services. There are 61 commercial airports, seven of which are international airports.

### National Airlines

**Aero-Ejecutivos:** Maiquetía, Charallave, Miranda; tel. (2) 92-2179; fax (2) 993-5493; operates on domestic routes only.

**Aerolíneas Latinas:** Centro Comercial Ciudad Tamanaco, 1a Etapa, 3°, Calle 315, Caracas; tel. (2) 261-5554; f. 1989; international flights to destinations in Europe, North, Central and South America and the Caribbean; Pres. MARÍA EUGENIA MARTÍNEZ CAPRILES.

**Aerovías Venezolanas, SA (AVENSA):** Edif. 29, 2°, Avda Universidad, esq. El Chorro, Apdo 943, Caracas 101; tel. (2) 562-3022; telex 22659; fax (2) 563-0225; f. 1943; provides extensive domestic services from Caracas and an international service to Panama and Mexico; government-owned; Chair. ANDRÉS BOULTON; Pres. HENRY LORD BOULTON.

**Aeronaves del Centro:** Edif. Carabobo, 'ZIM' Valencia; f. 1980; operates on domestic routes only.

**Aereotuy, CA:** Edif. Gran Sabana, 5°, Blvd de Sabana Grande, Apdo 2923, Carmelitas, Caracas 1010; tel. (2) 71-7375; fax (2) 762-5254; f. 1982; operates on domestic and international routes; Pres. PETER BOTTOME.

**Interamericana Cargo Venezuela:** Torre Bellas Artes, 9°, Avda México, Caracas; tel. (2) 572-6464; telex 27761; fax (2) 572-3842; f. 1982; cargo carrier.

**Venezolana Internacional de Aviación, SA (VIASA):** Calle Oscar Machado-Zuloaga, Plaza Morelos, Los Caobos, Apdo 6857, Caracas 105; tel. (2) 572-9522; telex 21125; fax (2) 571-3731; f. 1961; transferred to private ownership in Sept. 1991, with the controlling stake (51%) acquired by Spain's state airline, Iberia; international flights to destinations in Europe, USA, South and Central America and the Caribbean; Exec. Pres. JOSÉ CAMPINA.

# Tourism

In 1993 Venezuela received some 520,100 foreign visitors. In 1990 tourism generated an income of US $359m.

**Departamento de Turismo:** c/o Central Information Office of the Presidency, Palacio de Miraflores, Caracas; Dir Dr JESÚS FEDERICO RAVEL.

**Corporación de Turismo de Venezuela (Corpoturismo):** see section on The Government (Ministries—Government Agencies).

**Sociedad Financiera para el Fomento del Turismo y de Recreo Público (FOMTUR):** Caracas; f. 1962; government tourist development agency.

**Corporación Nacional de Hoteles y Turismo (CONAHOTU):** Apdo 6651, Caracas; f. 1969; government agency; Pres. ERASTO FERNÁNDEZ.

# VIET NAM

## Introductory Survey

**Location, Climate, Language, Religion, Flag, Capital**

The Socialist Republic of Viet Nam is situated in South-East Asia, bordered to the north by the People's Republic of China, to the west by Laos and Cambodia, and to the east by the South China Sea. The climate is humid during both the hot summer and the relatively cold winter, and there are monsoon rains in both seasons. Temperatures in Hanoi are generally between 13°C (55°F) and 33°C (91°F). The language is Vietnamese. The principal religion is Buddhism. There are also Daoist, Confucian, Hoa Hao, Caodaist and Christian (mainly Roman Catholic) minorities. The national flag (proportions 3 by 2) is red, with a large five-pointed yellow star in the centre. The capital is Hanoi.

**Recent History**

Cochin-China (the southernmost part of Viet Nam) became a French colony in 1867. Annam and Tonkin (central and northern Viet Nam) were proclaimed French protectorates in 1883. Later all three were merged with Cambodia and Laos to form French Indo-China. Throughout the French colonial period, but especially after 1920, nationalist and revolutionary groups operated in Viet Nam. The best organized of these was the Vietnamese Revolutionary Youth League, founded by Ho Chi Minh. The League was succeeded in February 1930 by the Communist Party of Indo-China, also led by Ho.

In September 1940 Japanese forces, with French co-operation, began to occupy Viet Nam, and in June 1941 the nationalists formed the Viet Nam Doc Lap Dong Minh Hoi (Revolutionary League for the Independence of Viet Nam), known as the Viet Minh. In March 1945 French control was ended by a Japanese coup. Following Japan's surrender in August 1945, Viet Minh forces entered Hanoi, and on 2 September the new regime proclaimed independence as the Democratic Republic of Viet Nam (DRV), with Ho Chi Minh as President. The Communist Party, formally dissolved in 1945, continued to be the dominant group within the Viet Minh Government. In March 1946, after French forces re-entered Viet Nam, an agreement between France and the DRV recognized Viet Nam as a 'free' state within the French Union. The DRV Government, however, continued to press for complete independence. Negotiations with France broke down and full-scale hostilities began in December 1946.

In March 1949 the French established the State of Viet Nam in the South. Meanwhile, in the North the Viet Minh was dissolved in 1951, and the Communists formed the Dang Lao Dong Viet Nam (Viet Nam Workers' Party), with Ho Chi Minh as Chairman of the Central Committee. After the defeat of French forces at Dien Bien Phu in May 1954, terms for a cease-fire were settled in Geneva, Switzerland. Agreements signed in July 1954 provided for the provisional partition of Viet Nam into two military zones, with French forces south of latitude 17°N and DRV forces in the north. Later in 1954 the French withdrew from South Viet Nam. Ngo Dinh Diem became Prime Minister of the State of Viet Nam and in 1955, following a referendum, proclaimed himself President of the Republic of Viet Nam. Diem refused to participate in the elections envisaged by the Geneva agreement. In the DRV Ho Chi Minh was succeeded as Prime Minister by Pham Van Dong in 1955 but remained Head of State and Party Chairman.

The anti-communist Diem regime in the South was opposed by former members of the Viet Minh who became known as the Viet Cong. Diem was overthrown by a coup in November 1963, and a series of short-lived military regimes held power until June 1965, when some stability was restored by the National Leadership Committee, with Lt-Gen. Nguyen Van Thieu as Chairman and Air Vice-Marshal Nguyen Cao Ky as Prime Minister. In 1967 Gen. Thieu was elected President, with Marshal Ky as Vice-President, and in 1971, after splitting with Ky, President Thieu was re-elected unopposed.

From 1959 the DRV actively assisted the insurgent movement in South Viet Nam and it supported the establishment there of the communist-dominated National Liberation Front (NLF) in December 1960. In 1961 the USA joined the war on the side of the anti-communist regime in the South, later bombing the North extensively from 1965 to 1968. In November 1968 peace talks between the four participants in the Viet Nam war began in Paris, France, but remained deadlocked as the fighting continued. In June 1969 the NLF formed the Provisional Revolutionary Government (PRG) in the South. Ho Chi Minh died in September 1969: he was succeeded as Head of State by Ton Duc Thang, while political leadership passed to Le Duan, First Secretary of the Party since 1960.

In 1972 PRG and North Vietnamese forces launched a major offensive in South Viet Nam and US bombing of the North was renewed with greater intensity. In January 1973 a peace agreement was finally signed. It provided for a cease-fire in the South, the withdrawal of US forces, the eventual peaceful reunification of the whole country, and US aid to the Government in the North to assist in reconstruction. US troops were withdrawn, but in December 1974 combined PRG and North Vietnamese forces launched a major offensive, and the capital, Saigon, fell in April 1975. By May the new regime was in complete control of South Viet Nam.

While South Viet Nam, under the PRG, remained technically separate from the DRV, effective control of the whole country passed to Hanoi. In July 1976 the country's reunification was proclaimed under the name of the Socialist Republic of Viet Nam, and Saigon was renamed Ho Chi Minh City. A new Government was appointed, dominated by members of the former Government of the DRV but including some members of the PRG. In December Le Duan was appointed General Secretary of the Communist Party of Viet Nam (formerly the Viet Nam Workers' Party). President Ton Duc Thang died in March 1980. A new Constitution was adopted in December of that year. Truong Chinh was appointed President of the Council of State (head of state) in July 1981, but real power remained with Le Duan. In March 1982 the fifth Communist Party Congress elected a new Politburo and Central Committee. Some prominent figures were removed from office, while younger members were promoted.

In June 1986 several government changes (involving posts connected with the economy) occurred. In July Le Duan died, and was succeeded as General Secretary of the Communist Party by Truong Chinh. At the sixth Party Congress, held in December, a number of important changes were made in the party's leadership: the country's three most senior leaders, Truong Chinh, Pham Van Dong and Le Duc Tho (a senior member of the party Politburo), announced their retirement from the Politburo, owing to their advanced age and failing health; however, they continued to attend politburo meetings in an advisory capacity, and Truong Chinh and Pham Van Dong retained their respective posts as President of the Council of State and Chairman of the Council of Ministers (Prime Minister), until 1987. Le Duc Tho continued to wield considerable political influence until his death in October 1990. The Congress appointed Nguyen Van Linh (a party official of long standing, who had, however, been excluded from the Politburo in 1982) as General Secretary of the Party.

In February 1987 an extensive government reshuffle took place, involving the dismissal of 12 ministers (including the Ministers of National Defence and of the Interior), and a number of ministries were combined or restructured, apparently with a view to the implementation of economic reforms. An election to the National Assembly took place in April. There were 829 candidates for the 496 seats (compared with 613 candidates at the previous election). At its first meeting, in June, the Assembly elected Vo Chi Cong and Pham Hung, both former Vice-Chairmen of the Council of Ministers, to the posts of President of the Council of State and Chairman of the Council of Ministers respectively. These appointments were seen as upholding the tradition of respect for seniority. However, despite being a veteran of the struggle with the South, and reputedly a strict conservative, Pham Hung gave his support to the programme of economic reform, referred to as *doi moi* (renovation), initiated by Nguyen Van Linh. The new liberalism of the regime was demonstrated by the release, in September, of 480 political prisoners from 're-education' camps, as part of an amnesty for more than 6,600 prisoners on the anniversary of Vietnamese independence from France in 1945. In February 1988, to commemorate the lunar new year, more than 1,000 political prisoners were released. In March Pham Hung died. The Council of State appointed Vo Van Kiet, a Vice-Chairman of the Council of Ministers and the Chairman of the State Commission for Planning, as acting Chairman of the Council of Ministers until the next meeting of the National Assembly.

Bureaucratic mishandling of a food shortage in early 1988 led to a famine in northern Viet Nam during April and May. In an unprecedentedly critical gesture, members of the National Assembly, supported by a newly-formed pressure group comprising veteran soldiers, demanded the resignation of the Minister of Agriculture, whom they considered to be responsible. At the meeting of the National Assembly in June, members from the south took the unprecedented step of nominating Vo Van Kiet (an advocate of reform), to oppose the Central Committee's more conservative candidate, Do Muoi (ranked third in the Politburo) in the election for the chairmanship of the Council of Ministers. Do Muoi was elected by a majority to the chairmanship but Vo Van Kiet received unexpectedly strong support (36% of the votes). Despite his reputation, Do Muoi declared his commitment to the advancement of reform. Widespread dissatisfaction with the condition of the economy and the slow progress of reform (often due to the refusal of officials to implement new policies) led to the removal of hundreds of cadres from government posts in a 'purification' of the party. In an attempt to improve international relations, owing to an urgent need for Western aid, Viet Nam amended its Constitution in December, removing derogatory references to the USA, China, France and Japan. In March 1989 a reshuffle of senior economic ministers took place, adjusting the balance further towards reform and strengthening the position of Nguyen Van Linh.

In August 1989 68 members of an opposition movement of exiles based in the USA, the National Front for the Liberation of Viet Nam, were arrested while crossing from Thailand into Laos. In September Viet Nam formally protested to Thailand for supporting the resistance movement, which had allegedly attempted to incite an insurgency in southern Viet Nam, although the Thai Government denied the accusations. Thirty-eight of the suspected rebels were extradited to Viet Nam in January 1990. They were later charged with attempting to overthrow the Government, and in October 1990 they were sentenced to long terms of imprisonment.

Municipal elections to provincial and district councils took place in November 1989. Under new legislation, adopted during a meeting of the National Assembly in June, candidates who were not members of the Communist Party were allowed to participate for the first time. In December the National Assembly approved legislation that imposed new restrictions on the press. The appointment of editors became subject to government approval, and journalists were required to reveal the source of their information on request. Open dissension towards the policy of the Communist Party also became a criminal offence. In late 1989 progress towards political reform under *doi moi* was adversely affected by government concern regarding the demise of socialism in Eastern Europe. At a meeting of the Central Committee in March 1990, tension over the issue of political pluralism resulted in the dismissal of a member of the Politburo, Tran Xuan Bach, who had openly advocated political reform. In April the Council of State announced an extensive ministerial reshuffle, in which four ministers were dismissed and several portfolios reorganized.

In the second half of 1990 the Government dismissed or brought charges against more than 18,000 officials, in an attempt to eradicate corruption. In December the Central Committee produced draft political and economic reports, reaffirming the party's commitment to socialism and to the process of economic liberalization, which were to be submitted to the next Party Congress. In the same month Bui Tin, the Deputy Editor of the official organ of the Communist Party, *Nhan Dan*, criticized government policy and demanded extensive political reform. He was subsequently expelled from the Politburo and dismissed as Deputy Editor. Following a request by the Central Committee for public comment on the reports, in early 1991 the party journal, *Tap Chi Cong San* (Communist Review), published articles by prominent intellectuals that severely criticized the reports and questioned the effectiveness of a socialist system in Viet Nam. The Communist Party subsequently increased surveillance of dissidents and ordered the press to publish retaliatory articles condemning party critics. In June the Communist Party Congress approved the reports. It elected Do Muoi to replace Nguyen Van Linh as General Secretary of the Party. Seven members of the Politburo were removed from their posts, including Nguyen Van Linh, although he, together with Pham Van Dong and the President of the Council of State, Vo Chi Cong, remained in the Central Committee in an advisory capacity. At a subsequent session of the National Assembly, held between late July and early August, the pro-reform Vo Van Kiet was elected to replace Do Muoi as Chairman of the Council of Ministers. The Ministers of Foreign Affairs and of the Interior (both formerly close associates of Le Duc Tho) were removed from their posts. In addition, the National Assembly studied amendments to the Constitution that had been proposed by a constitutional commission.

A new draft Constitution, was published in December 1991, and, after being reviewed in public discussions and debated in the National Assembly, it was adopted by the Assembly in April 1992. Like the previous (1980) Constitution, it emphasized the central role of the Communist Party; however, it stipulated that the party must be subject to the law. While affirming adherence to a state-regulated socialist economic system, the new Constitution guaranteed protection for foreign investment in Viet Nam, and permitted foreign travel and overseas investment for Vietnamese. Land was to remain the property of the State, although the right to long-term leases, which could be inherited or sold, was granted. The National Assembly was to be reduced in number, but was to have greater power. The Council of State was to be replaced by a single President as Head of State: he or she would be responsible for appointing (subject to the approval of the National Assembly) a Prime Minister and senior members of the judiciary, and would command the armed forces. The new Constitution entered into effect after the July 1992 general election (see below).

In July 1992 a total of 601 candidates contested 395 seats at a general election to the National Assembly. Almost 90% were members of the Communist Party, and although independent candidates (i.e. those not endorsed by the Viet Nam Fatherland Front—the grouping of mass organizations, such as trade unions, affiliated to the Communist Party) were, for the first time, permitted to present themselves, in the event only two were deemed to qualify, and neither was elected. Of the members of the outgoing National Assembly, only 118 were candidates: more than 100 of these were re-elected.

At the first session of the new National Assembly, in September 1992, the conservative Gen. Le Duc Anh (a member of the Politburo and a former Minister of Defence) was elected to the new post of President. Vo Van Kiet was appointed Prime Minister (the equivalent of his former post) by the Assembly in October. Only four ministers, all of whom had been implicated in corruption scandals, were not reappointed. Vo Van Kiet identified corruption and smuggling as being among the principal problems to be overcome by the new administration. During 1993 the Government repeatedly stressed its determination to continue progress towards a market-led economy and to encourage foreign investment. Despite the country's economic liberalization, however, there was no toleration of political dissent. In August 14 people were sentenced to terms of imprisonment, after having been convicted of conspiring to overthrow the Government, and in November several Buddhist monks were imprisoned for having, it was alleged, incited anti-Government demonstrations. In January 1994, at a mid-term conference of the Communist Party, Do Muoi praised the country's recent economic achievements and its expanding relations with foreign countries (see below), but emphasized the continuing prevalence of poverty, the increase in corruption and crime, and the inadequacy of the educational system; he also strongly criticized the party for disunity and poor organization. Immediately before the conference four new members were appointed to the Politburo, including the Minister of Foreign Affairs, Nguyen Manh Cam, and during the conference 20 new members (all under the age of 55) were elected to the party's Central Committee. In February a former Minister of Energy (who had been dismissed in 1992) was sentenced to three years' imprisonment for corruption. In

June 1994 the National Assembly approved new legislation, including a labour law that guaranteed the right of workers to strike (providing the 'social life of the community' was not adversely affected). Strikes subsequently occurred in some southern provinces, and in August the first incident of industrial action in Hanoi was reported. At a plenum of the Central Committee of the party, held in late July–early August, Do Muoi reasserted the need to strengthen Viet Nam's 'open-door' policy in order to attract wide foreign investment. At the fourth Congress of the Fatherland Front, in mid-August, a new, 200-member Central Committee was elected, the Presidium of which was headed by the 73-year-old Le Quang Dao, described as a 'veteran revolutionary'. Elections to provincial and district councils took place during December 1994.

In February 1995 the human rights organization, Amnesty International, protested to the Vietnamese Government about the arrest, in late 1994 and early 1995, and continuing detention of further allegedly dissident Buddhist monks.

By the end of 1976 Viet Nam had established diplomatic relations with many countries, including all of its South-East Asian neighbours. However, tension arose over the growing number of Vietnamese refugees (particularly ethnic Chinese) arriving in Thailand and other nearby countries. In 1979 more than 200,000 fled Viet Nam, and in July an international conference was convened in Geneva to discuss the situation. The Orderly Departure Programme, sponsored by the office of the UN High Commissioner for Refugees (UNHCR), whereby Viet Nam agreed to legal departures, was negotiated, and by the end of 1988 about 140,000 people had left the country in this way. Illegal departures continued, however (numbering an estimated 47,834 in 1988), and the increasing reluctance of Western countries to provide resettlement opportunities led to a meeting in Malaysia, in March 1989, at which representatives of 30 nations were present and a comprehensive programme of action was drafted. Members of the Association of South East Asian Nations (ASEAN—see p. 109) subsequently ceased to accept refugees for automatic resettlement and planned to institute a screening procedure to distinguish genuine refugees from economic migrants. A similar procedure had been in effect since June 1988 in Hong Kong, and an agreement had been signed in November, whereby Viet Nam agreed to accept voluntary repatriation of refugees from Hong Kong, funded by UNHCR and the United Kingdom, with UN supervision to protect the returning refugees from punitive measures by the Vietnamese Government.

In June 1989 a UN-sponsored conference adopted the so-called Comprehensive Action Plan that had been drafted in March, introducing screening procedures to distinguish political refugees from economic migrants (who might be forcibly repatriated if efforts to secure their voluntary return proved unsuccessful). In December the United Kingdom forcibly repatriated a group of 51 Vietnamese from Hong Kong, provoking international criticism; this policy was abandoned as a result both of opposition by the USA and of Viet Nam's refusal to accept further deportations. In July 1990, however, the USA accepted in principle the 'involuntary' repatriation of refugees classed as economic migrants who did not actively oppose deportation. In September the United Kingdom, Viet Nam and UNHCR reached an agreement whereby the Vietnamese Government would no longer refuse refugees who had been repatriated 'involuntarily'. In October 1991 an agreement was concluded by the British and Vietnamese Governments for the repatriation of about 300 Vietnamese who had already been voluntarily repatriated from Hong Kong, but had returned for a second time. Later in the same month the two Governments agreed upon the compulsory repatriation (after screening) of newly-arrived economic migrants. Fifty-nine Vietnamese belonging to the former category were repatriated in November, followed by smaller groups in December and in February 1992. The policy appeared to have deterred all but a few Vietnamese from fleeing to Hong Kong during 1992. In May the United Kingdom and Viet Nam signed an agreement providing for the compulsory repatriation of all economic migrants from Hong Kong. During 1992 and 1993 more than 22,000 Vietnamese returned from Hong Kong under the voluntary repatriation programme. In March 1995 a conference, convened under UN auspices to assess the progress of the 1989 Comprehensive Action Plan, agreed that all Vietnamese residing in south-east Asian camps (numbering about 18,000) should be repatriated by the end of 1995, while the process of returning those remaining in camps in Hong Kong (some 22,000) should be completed soon afterwards; in order to facilitate adherence to this time-scale, the Vietnamese authorities agreed to simplify repatriation procedures.

Relations with Kampuchea (known as Cambodia until 1976 and again from 1989) deteriorated during 1977, and in December Viet Nam launched a major offensive into eastern Kampuchea. Sporadic fighting continued, and in December 1978 Viet Nam invaded Kampuchea in support of elements opposed to the regime (see chapter on Cambodia). By January 1979 the Government of Pol Pot had been overthrown and a pro-Vietnamese regime was installed. The invasion prompted much international criticism, and in February 1979 Chinese forces launched a punitive attack across the border into Viet Nam. Peace talks began in April but made little progress, and in March 1980 they were suspended by the People's Republic of China. In March 1983 Viet Nam rejected a five-point peace plan, proposed by China, aimed at resolving the dispute over Kampuchea. In 1984 Chinese and Vietnamese troops engaged in the heaviest fighting since the 1979 invasion, and accused each other of persistent border incursions and shelling. China refused to normalize relations with Viet Nam until the withdrawal of Vietnamese troops from Kampuchea. Throughout 1986 and 1987 further armed clashes between Vietnamese and Chinese soldiers occurred on the Sino-Vietnamese border. Both sides denied responsibility for initiating the attacks. In early 1988 the tension between the two countries was exacerbated by the re-emergence of conflict over the Spratly Islands (situated between the Philippines, Viet Nam and Malaysia) when the Vietnamese Government alleged that China had dispatched warships to the islands. For many years the sovereignty of the islands had been contested, not only by Viet Nam and China, which engaged in military conflict concerning the islands in 1974, but also by the neighbouring states of Brunei, Malaysia, the Philippines and Taiwan.

After the Vietnamese invasion of Kampuchea, Viet Nam's relations with Thailand worsened, and from 1979 onwards Vietnamese forces were reported to have entered Thai territory in attempts to prevent members of the Kampuchean resistance forces from entering Kampuchea via Thailand; in mid-1987 serious military clashes took place between Vietnamese and Thai forces (see chapter on Thailand).

In March 1984 Viet Nam agreed in principle that it would eventually withdraw its troops from Kampuchea, and in August 1985 it was announced that all Vietnamese troops would be withdrawn by 1990. An eight-point peace plan, proposed by Kampuchean resistance leaders in March 1986 (involving the installation of a quadripartite government in Kampuchea, to be followed by UN-supervised elections), was rejected by Viet Nam. Viet Nam's urgent need of Western aid, together with increasing pressure from the USSR — for which Kampuchea remained an obstacle to closer Sino-Soviet relations — prompted an announcement in May 1988 that Viet Nam would withdraw 50,000 (of an estimated total of 100,000) troops from Kampuchea by the end of 1988. The Vietnamese military high command left Kampuchea in June, placing the remainder of the Vietnamese forces under Kampuchean control. Viet Nam announced that the withdrawal from Kampuchea would be complete by the end of 1989.

In April 1989 the Vietnamese Government and the Heng Samrin regime in Kampuchea declared that Vietnamese troops would withdraw by September even if a political settlement had not been reached, on condition that military assistance to the three other Kampuchean factions also ceased by that date. The People's Republic of China responded that it would halt military aid to the Khmer Rouge only after a complete withdrawal of Vietnamese troops had been verified. The Vietnamese Government claimed that the withdrawal of troops was completed by the end of September 1989. However, the absence of a UN commission to verify the troops' departure led to claims by the Government-in-exile of Democratic Kampuchea that a number of troops remained in the country, while China, the ASEAN countries and the USA initially refused to recognize the alleged withdrawal. In July 1990 the USA finally acknowledged that all troops had been withdrawn.

In September 1990 secret negotiations took place between Viet Nam and the People's Republic of China, during which the Vietnamese endorsed a new UN Security Council agreement to resolve the conflict in Cambodia (see chapter on Cambodia). It was widely believed that the Chinese had promised an improvement in Sino-Vietnamese relations in exchange for Vietnamese support for the UN plan. In October 1991 Viet

Nam was a signatory to a peace agreement whereby an interim Supreme National Council was established in Cambodia, representing all four factions there, as a prelude to the holding of UN-supervised elections. The agreement allowed immediate progress towards ending Viet Nam's diplomatic and economic isolation (see below). During 1992–93 there were several massacres of civilians of Vietnamese origin living in Cambodia, and the future of the Vietnamese residents there (estimated to number several hundreds of thousands) appeared precarious.

From the mid-1970s Viet Nam developed closer relations with the USSR, and became increasingly dependent on its support. In 1990–91 the USSR substantially reduced financial assistance to Viet Nam, following the decline of the Soviet economy. Following the disintegration of the USSR, the Russian Government declared in February 1992 that it would maintain close economic relations with Viet Nam, and in January 1993 the Vietnamese authorities agreed to allow Russian vessels to continue using the former Soviet naval base at Cam Ranh, in central Viet Nam. The collapse of communism in Eastern Europe prompted renewed efforts by Viet Nam to restore political and economic links with the People's Republic of China. Relations between Viet Nam and China improved significantly in the second half of 1990, owing to the co-operation of the Vietnamese Government concerning Cambodia. After the conclusion of the Cambodian peace agreement in October 1991, Vo Van Kiet and Do Muoi paid an official visit to China in November, during which normal diplomatic relations were restored and agreements were concluded on trade and on border affairs, while in March 1992 further agreements were signed on the resumption of transport and communications links (severed in 1979), and on the reopening of border posts. In May 1992 Viet Nam protested to the Chinese Government at China's unilaterally granting exploration rights to a US petroleum company in an area of the South China Sea 260 km from Viet Nam and regarded by Viet Nam as part of its continental shelf. Several more protests were lodged later in the year over the presence of Chinese vessels in disputed areas. In November the Chinese Premier, Li Peng, made an official visit to Viet Nam (the first visit by a Chinese head of government since 1971): new agreements on economic, scientific and cultural co-operation were signed, and the two Governments agreed to accelerate negotiations on disputed territory that had begun in the previous month. In October 1993 Viet Nam and China concluded an agreement to avoid the use of force when resolving territorial disputes. In November 1994 the two countries agreed to co-operate in seeking an early resolution to all border disputes and to establish a specialist body to assess continuing rival claims to sovereignty over the Spratly Islands (now believed to possess substantial deposits of petroleum and natural gas, as well as occupying a major fishing ground). Tension concerning the Spratly Islands mounted during 1994 and early 1995: in July 1994 it was reported that Chinese warships were blockading a Vietnamese oil-prospecting operation in the disputed area, and in February 1995 Viet Nam accused China of erecting permanent structures on some of the islands.

From 1984 Viet Nam indicated that it would welcome a return to normal diplomatic relations with the USA, but the latter rejected any re-establishment of relations until agreements were made concerning the return to the USA of the remains of US soldiers 'missing in action' (MIA) from Viet Nam, and the proposed resettlement in the USA of some 10,000 Vietnamese 'political prisoners'. A number of senior US officials visited Hanoi during 1985 and 1986 for discussions about missing soldiers (estimated to total 1,797), and Viet Nam arranged for the return of some of the remains. In September 1987 the Vietnamese Government agreed to investigate the fate of some 70 soldiers who were believed to have been captured alive, while the US Government, in turn, agreed to facilitate humanitarian aid for Viet Nam from US charities and private groups, which had hitherto been illegal. In July 1988 Viet Nam agreed in principle to the resettlement of former political detainees in the USA or elsewhere. Vietnamese and US specialists held a series of meetings throughout 1989 in order to review efforts to search for the remains of MIA. In early 1991 a US representative was stationed in Hanoi to supervise inquiries into MIA, the first official US presence in Viet Nam since 1975. In April 1991 the USA proposed a four-stage programme for the resumption of normal diplomatic relations with Viet Nam, conditional on Vietnamese co-operation in reaching a diplomatic settlement in Cambodia and in accounting for the remaining MIA. Following the conclusion of the peace agreement on Cambodia in October, Viet Nam made a plea for the removal of the US economic embargo, and in November discussions on the establishment of normal relations began. In February and March 1992 the US Government agreed to provide humanitarian aid for Viet Nam, but refused to end the economic embargo, reiterating that relations would not fully return to normal until after the UN-supervised elections in Cambodia, due to take place in early 1993. The embargo was renewed for another year in September 1992, although in December the US Government announced that US companies would now be allowed to open offices and sign contracts in Viet Nam, in anticipation of a future removal of the embargo. In September 1993 the administration of the new US President, Bill Clinton, permitted US companies to take part in projects in Viet Nam that were financed by international aid agencies. The trade embargo was finally removed in February 1994; President Clinton expressed the hope that this would encourage the Vietnamese to give further assistance in the MIA investigations. In January 1995 Viet Nam and the USA signed an agreement that permitted the two countries to establish liaison offices in each other's capitals (these were opened immediately), and which resolved a long-standing dispute concerning former US diplomatic properties seized by the Vietnamese authorities in 1975. The establishment of full diplomatic relations was announced in July 1995.

In October 1990 the European Community (now European Union, see p. 143) announced the restoration of diplomatic relations with Viet Nam. In October 1991 a group of industrialized countries, led by France, agreed to assist Viet Nam in paying its arrears to the IMF, thereby enabling it to qualify for future IMF loans (which were, however, still dependent on the approval of the USA, as the IMF's principal voteholder). In February 1993 President Mitterrand of France made an official visit to Viet Nam (the first Western Head of State to do so since the country's reunification). Several co-operation agreements were signed during the visit, and Mitterrand urged the USA to end its economic embargo. In January 1992 a Japanese government mission visited Viet Nam to negotiate the repayment of Vietnamese debts, and in November Japan (which—although Viet Nam's principal trading partner in 1992—had hitherto imposed a ban on official economic co-operation) began to provide financial assistance to Viet Nam. In July 1993 the US Government removed its veto on assistance from the IMF and the World Bank for Viet Nam. In October (having paid its arrears to the IMF with the help of donor countries) Viet Nam was granted US $223m. in credits by the IMF, and large loans from the Asian Development Bank (for irrigation) and the World Bank (for education and road repairs) followed. In December a conference of international aid organizations and governments agreed to provide $1,860m. in aid to Viet Nam over the ensuing year, and in the same month creditor nations agreed to reschedule part of Viet Nam's external debt. In November 1994 the international donor community promised assistance totalling $2,000m. for disbursement during 1995. The resumption of large-scale external aid was expected to give impetus to the improvement of the country's infrastructure, regarded as essential for its economic development.

The Cambodian peace agreement allowed Viet Nam to initiate closer relations with ASEAN member states: Vo Van Kiet visited Indonesia, Thailand and Singapore in October and November 1991 and Malaysia, Brunei and the Philippines in early 1992, and agreements on economic co-operation were concluded with these countries, including guarantees of protection for future investment by them in Viet Nam. In July 1992 Viet Nam signed the ASEAN agreement (of 1976) on regional amity and co-operation; Viet Nam attended the July 1994 ASEAN summit meeting in Bangkok, Thailand, as an observer, and was expected to become a full member of ASEAN in July 1995. In September 1992 Viet Nam reached agreement with Malaysia and Thailand on co-operation in the use of overlapping territorial waters. In the same month an agreement was signed with Singapore (Viet Nam's second-largest trading partner in that year) on the mutual provision of 'most-favoured nation' trading status. Diplomatic relations with the Republic of Korea (already an important trading partner and investor in Viet Nam) were established in December. In March 1995 Viet Nam and Laos signed an agreement concerning economic cultural, scientific and technological co-operation. In April, meeting in Chiang Rai, Thailand, representatives of

Viet Nam, Cambodia, Laos and Thailand signed an agreement on the joint exploitation and development of the lower Mekong river. The accord provided for the establishment of a Mekong Commission, membership of which would (it was envisaged) eventually be extended to the People's Republic of China and Myanmar.

### Government

The 1992 Constitution declares the supremacy of the Communist Party. Legislative power is vested in the National Assembly, which is elected for a five-year term by universal adult suffrage, and which has a maximum of 400 members. The President, elected by the National Assembly from among its members, is the Head of State and Commander-in-Chief of the armed forces. The President appoints a Prime Minister (from among the members of the National Assembly, and subject to their approval), who forms a government (again, subject to ratification by the National Assembly). The country is divided into provinces and municipalities, which are subordinate to the central government. Local government is entrusted to locally-elected People's Councils.

### Defence

In June 1994 the active ('Main Force') armed forces of Viet Nam had an estimated total strength of 572,000: 500,000 in the army, an estimated 42,000 in the navy, 15,000 in the air force and 15,000 in the air defence force. Military service is compulsory and usually lasts for two years. Paramilitary forces number 4m.–5m. and include the urban People's Self Defence Force and the rural People's Militia. The defence budget for 1994 was estimated at 4,700,000m. dông. The National Defence and Security Council was established in October 1992.

### Economic Affairs

In 1993, according to estimates by the World Bank, Viet Nam's gross national product (GNP), measured at average 1991–93 prices, was US $11,997m., equivalent to $170 per head. During 1985–93, it was estimated, GNP per head increased, in real terms, at an average annual rate of 4.8%. Over the same period the population increased by an average annual rate of 2.4%. According to official statistics, Viet Nam's gross domestic product (GDP) increased at an average annual rate of 4.7% in 1991, 8.6% in 1992 and 8.1% in 1993.

Agriculture (including forestry and fishing) contributed 29.3% of GDP in 1993 and engaged 73.0% of the labour force in that year. The staple crop is rice, which also provided 12.3% of export earnings in 1993. Other important cash crops include coffee, rubber, tea, cotton, and groundnuts. In 1992, in an attempt to preserve Viet Nam's remaining forests, a ban was imposed on the export of logs and sawn timber. (The total forest area declined from 13.5m. hectares in 1943 to 9.2m. hectares in 1994). Livestock-rearing and fishing are also important. In 1993 agricultural goods (including forestry and fishing) accounted for more than 50% of total export revenue, and in the same year sea food (principally shrimps, crabs and cuttlefish) accounted for some 13% of export revenues. Agricultural production increased by an annual average of 5% in 1989–93; agricultural GDP increased by 3.1% in 1993.

In 1993 industry (comprising manufacturing, mining and quarrying, construction and power) contributed 28.4% of GDP. The industrial sector engaged 13.4% of the labour force in that year. In 1992 the non-state economic sector accounted for 31% of industrial production and employed about three-quarters of the industrial labour force. Industrial output increased by an annual average of some 13% per year in 1991–93.

Viet Nam's principal mineral exports are petroleum and coal. Tin, zinc, iron, antimony, chromium, apatite, phosphate and bauxite are also mined. In 1994 it was announced that recoverable reserves of offshore natural gas, discovered in 1993, were sufficient to generate enough electricity for Ho Chi Minh City for 25 years (at current levels of consumption). In 1993 exports of crude petroleum accounted for 30% of total merchandise exports.

Manufacturing contributed about 21% of GDP and accounted for 11% of employment in 1993. The main manufacturing sectors in 1993, measured by gross value of output, included food-processing, chemicals, machinery and textiles.

Energy is derived principally from hydroelectric installations, petroleum and coal. Although production of petroleum increased in the late 1980s and early 1990s, exports were mainly in the form of crude petroleum, and Viet Nam still relied on the import of refined products. Nuclear power was also being developed in the early 1990s.

In 1992 Viet Nam recorded a visible trade deficit of US $60m., and in 1993 there was an estimated trade deficit of $655m. The deficit on the current account balance of payments in 1993 was estimated to be $869m. (compared with $8m. in 1992). In 1992 Singapore was Viet Nam's principal trading partner, accounting for 26.7% of imports and 33.7% of exports. Other major trading partners were Japan, Hong Kong, France and Germany. The principal exports in 1993 were petroleum, handicrafts and light industrial goods, marine products and rice. Principal imports included petroleum products (some 19.5% of the total), machinery and spare parts and steel. Illegal trade, which is widespread (and was exacerbated by legislation adopted in September 1992 banning the import of 17 commodities), was estimated to be equivalent to 50% of official trade in 1992.

In 1993 there was an estimated budgetary deficit of 9,473,000m. dông, equivalent to 6.9% of GDP; in 1994 the forecast budget deficit was 9,153,000m. dông. In 1993 Viet Nam's total external debt was US $24,224m., of which $21,554m. was long-term public debt. In that year the cost of debt-servicing was equivalent to 13.6% of the value of exports of goods and services. The annual rate of inflation averaged more than 300% in 1987–88; the rate declined to 36.4% in 1990, increased to 83.1% in 1991, and slowed to 37.8% in 1992. Annual inflation was only 8.3% in 1993, but was reputed to have accelerated during 1994 and early 1995. In early 1994 about 6% of the workforce were officially stated to be unemployed, while a further 16% were underemployed.

Viet Nam is a member of the Asian Development Bank (see p. 107). In July 1992 Viet Nam signed the agreement on regional amity and co-operation of the Association of South East Asian Nations (ASEAN, see p. 109), and was expected to become a full member in July 1995. Viet Nam has also agreed to join the ASEAN Free Trade Agreement (AFTA).

In 1986 the Vietnamese Government began to introduce reforms, the *doi moi* (renovation), aimed at transforming Viet Nam from a centralized economy to a market-orientated system. In 1987 liberal foreign investment laws were introduced allowing wholly foreign-owned companies to operate in Viet Nam. Agricultural production was stimulated by the removal of price controls in 1988, and by a new system of land tenure, introduced in 1988–89, which allowed farmers to hold land from the state on a long-term basis, and to keep the profits from surplus production. By 1992 Viet Nam, previously an importer of rice, had become the world's third-largest rice exporter. Increased petroleum production, from 1989 onwards, made a still greater contribution to a substantial increase in export revenue. These factors allowed Viet Nam to escape the effects of the disintegration of the Council for Mutual Economic Assistance (with which most of its trade was conducted until 1991, and which had been a principal provider of aid), and also to be relatively unhindered by the USA's trade embargo and by its veto on aid for Viet Nam from the IMF and other agencies. Reforms in taxation included the introduction of income tax in 1991; the money supply was subject to strict control, and subsidized credits for unprofitable state enterprises were ended. Restructuring of state enterprises (about one-third of which were loss-making in the late 1980s) took place from 1988 onwards, but progress towards their privatization was slow. The resumpton of financing agreements with the IMF, the World Bank and other lending agencies from 1993, the ending of the US trade embargo in February 1994, and debt-relief concessions by external creditors, enabled Viet Nam to benefit from an increase in overall foreign investment interest, particularly in infrastructural development. The impressive growth rates achieved in the early 1990s were maintained in 1994, reflecting an exceptionally good rice harvest and continued expansion of industrial production. However, there was little indication that the disparity in income between rural and urban Viet Nam was beginning to narrow. Inflation began to increase rapidly in late 1994, and by February 1995 had reached 18.5% (the Government's target for the year was 10%). The Government began to develop a capital market in 1995, and the establishment of a national securities commission was scheduled for mid-1995; the eventual establishment of a national stock exchange was envisaged. However, under-developed infrastructure and bureaucratic corruption and inefficiency in the remaining state sector industries were still believed to be major hindrances to development in the mid-1990s. The Government began to address the perceived problem of bureaucratic inertia and corruption in 1995, and announced plans to simplify licensing arrangements for new investment projects in that year.

### Social Welfare

The state operates a system of social security. In 1982 there were 12,500 hospitals with a total of 208,400 beds (one for every 270 inhabitants). In 1991 there was one practising physician for every 3,140 inhabitants. There are also mobile medical teams. In 1990 five private health clinics were established, and the Government introduced a system of fees for hospital care. Of total projected budgetary expenditure by the central Government in 1994, 1,883,000m. dông (4.0%) was allocated to health, and 5,074,000m. dông (10.8%) to pensions and social relief.

### Education

Primary education, which is compulsory, begins at six years of age and lasts for five years. Secondary education, beginning at the age of 11, lasts for seven years, comprising a first cycle of four years and a second cycle of three years. Total secondary enrolment in 1992 was equivalent to 33% of children in the relevant age-group. In 1993/94 there were 104 universities and colleges of higher education, with a total enrolment of 118,589 students. In 1990, according to UNESCO estimates, the average rate of adult illiteracy was 12.4% (males 8.0%; females 16.4%). In 1989 Viet Nam's first private college since 1954 was opened in Hanoi; Thang Long College was to cater for university students. Of total projected budgetary expenditure by the central Government in 1994, 3,739,000m. dông (8.0%) was allocated to education.

### Public Holidays

**1995:** 1 January (New Year's Day), 31 January* (Tet, lunar new year), 30 April (Liberation of Saigon), 1 May (May Day), 1–2 September (National Day).

**1996:** 1 January (New Year's Day), 19 February* (Tet, lunar new year), 30 April (Liberation of Saigon), 1 May (May Day), 1–2 September (National Day).

* Varies according to the lunar calendar.

### Weights and Measures

The metric system is in force.

# VIET NAM

# Statistical Survey

Sources (unless otherwise stated): General Statistical Office of the Socialist Republic of Viet Nam, 2 Hoang Van Thu, Hanoi; tel. 263544; fax 264345; Communist Party of Viet Nam.

## Area and Population

### AREA, POPULATION AND DENSITY

| | |
|---|---:|
| Area (sq km) | 331,114* |
| Population (census results) | |
| 1 October 1979 | 52,741,766 |
| 1 April 1989 | 64,375,762 |
| Population (official estimates at mid-year) | |
| 1991 | 67,774,000 |
| 1992 | 69,405,200 |
| 1993 | 70,982,500 |
| Density (per sq km) at mid-1993 | 214.4 |

* 127,844 sq miles.

### ADMINISTRATIVE DIVISIONS (mid-1993)

| Provinces and Cities | Area (sq km) | Population ('000) | Density (per sq km) |
|---|---:|---:|---:|
| **North Mountains and Midlands** | 102,964.6 | 12,109.3 | 118 |
| Ha Giang | 7,831.1 | 520.4 | 66 |
| Tuyen Quang | 5,800.9 | 628.5 | 108 |
| Cao Bang | 8,444.7 | 624.7 | 74 |
| Lang Son | 8,187.2 | 671.9 | 82 |
| Lai Chau | 17,130.6 | 501.2 | 29 |
| Lao Cai | 8,049.5 | 535.4 | 66 |
| Yen Bai | 6,808.1 | 638.2 | 94 |
| Bac Thai | 6,502.9 | 1,144.5 | 176 |
| Son La | 14,210.0 | 776.0 | 55 |
| Hoa Binh | 4,611.8 | 712.9 | 155 |
| Vinh Phu | 4,834.8 | 2,203.2 | 456 |
| Ha Bac | 4,614.4 | 2,262.8 | 490 |
| Quang Ninh | 5,938.6 | 889.6 | 150 |
| **Red River Delta** | 12,510.7 | 13,808.8 | 1,104 |
| Hanoi | 920.6 | 2,154.9 | 2,341 |
| Haiphong | 1,503.5 | 1,583.9 | 1,053 |
| Hai Hung | 2,551.4 | 2,658.0 | 1,042 |
| Ha Tay | 2,147.0 | 2,217.8 | 1,033 |
| Thai Binh | 1,508.7 | 1,768.4 | 1,172 |
| Nam Ha | 2,492.0 | 2,585.9 | 1,038 |
| Ninh Binh | 1,387.5 | 839.9 | 605 |
| **North Central Coast** | 15,187.6 | 9,516.9 | 186 |
| Thanh Hoa | 11,168.3 | 3,311.9 | 296 |
| Nghe An | 16,380.6 | 2,680.6 | 164 |
| Ha Tinh | 6,054.0 | 1,293.6 | 214 |
| Quang Binh | 7,983.5 | 736.7 | 92 |
| Quang Tri | 4,592.0 | 520.9 | 113 |
| Thua Thien–Hué | 5,009.2 | 973.2 | 194 |
| **South Central Coast** | 45,876.0 | 7,374.7 | 161 |
| Quang Nam–Da Nang | 11,985.4 | 1,911.7 | 159 |
| Quang Ngai | 5,856.3 | 1,149.5 | 196 |
| Binh Dinh | 6,075.9 | 1,373.1 | 226 |
| Phu Yen | 5,278.0 | 708.9 | 134 |
| Khanh Hoa | 5,258.0 | 923.7 | 176 |
| Ninh Thuan | 3,430.4 | 449.1 | 131 |
| Binh Thuan | 7,992.0 | 858.7 | 107 |
| **Central Highlands** | 55,568.9 | 2,903.5 | 52 |
| Gia Lai | 15,661.9 | 737.7 | 47 |
| Kon Tum | 9,934.4 | 249.6 | 25 |
| Dac Lac | 19,800.0 | 1,173.3 | 59 |
| Lam Dong | 10,172.6 | 742.9 | 73 |
| **North-East South** | 23,450.7 | 8,692.9 | 371 |
| Ho Chi Minh City | 2,090.4 | 4,322.3 | 2,068 |
| Song Be | 9,519.4 | 1,081.7 | 114 |
| Tay Ninh | 4,020.0 | 868.9 | 216 |
| Dong Nai | 5,864.4 | 1,762.9 | 301 |
| Ba Ria–Vung Tau | 1,956.6 | 657.1 | 336 |

| Provinces and Cities — continued | Area (sq km) | Population ('000) | Density (per sq km) |
|---|---:|---:|---:|
| **Mekong River Delta** | 39,555.1 | 15,531.6 | 393 |
| Long An | 4,338.3 | 1,224.8 | 282 |
| Dong Thap | 3,276.3 | 1,462.9 | 446 |
| An Giang | 3,423.5 | 1,933.8 | 565 |
| Tien Giang | 2,339.2 | 1,622.0 | 693 |
| Ben Tre | 2,247.0 | 1,309.4 | 583 |
| Vinh Long | 1,487.3 | 1,041.3 | 700 |
| Tra Vinh | 2,369.4 | 938.5 | 396 |
| Can Tho | 2,950.6 | 1,780.6 | 603 |
| Soc Trang | 3,191.0 | 1,172.6 | 367 |
| Kien Giang | 6,243.1 | 1,326.6 | 212 |
| Minh Hai | 7,689.4 | 1,719.1 | 224 |
| **Total** | 331,113.6 | 70,982.5 | 214 |

### PRINCIPAL TOWNS
(official census results at 1 April 1989)

| | | | |
|---|---:|---|---:|
| Hanoi (capital) | 3,056,146 | Nam Dinh | 219,615 |
| Ho Chi Minh City (formerly Saigon) | 3,924,435 | Long Xuyen | 214,037 |
| | | Qui Nhon | 201,912 |
| Haiphong | 1,447,523 | Thai Nguyen | 171,815 |
| Da Nang | 369,734 | Vung Tau | 133,558 |
| Can Tho | 284,306 | Hong Gai | 129,394 |
| Nha Trang | 263,093 | Cam Pha | 127,408 |
| Hué | 260,489 | Viet Tri | 116,084 |

### BIRTHS AND DEATHS (UN estimates, annual averages)

| | 1975–80 | 1980–85 | 1985–90 |
|---|---:|---:|---:|
| Birth rate (per 1,000) | 38.3 | 34.7 | 31.8 |
| Death rate (per 1,000) | 11.4 | 11.1 | 9.5 |

**Expectation of life** (UN estimates, years at birth, 1985–90): 62.6 (males 60.6; females 64.8).

Source: UN, *World Population Prospects: The 1992 Revision*.

### ECONOMICALLY ACTIVE POPULATION ('000 persons)

| | 1991 | 1992 | 1993 |
|---|---:|---:|---:|
| Material sphere | 28,972.6 | 29,782.8 | 30,622.4 |
| Agriculture | 22,275.6 | 22,998.3 | 23,683.8 |
| Forestry | 207.0 | 210.0 | 214.4 |
| Industry* | 3,394.0 | 3,450.0 | 3,521.8 |
| Construction | 820.0 | 825.0 | 848.3 |
| Trade and catering | 1,719.0 | 1,735.0 | 1,776.0 |
| Transport and communications | 526.7 | 534.3 | 547.5 |
| Other activities | 30.3 | 30.2 | 30.6 |
| Non-material sphere | 2,001.6 | 2,036.1 | 2,093.9 |
| Housing and municipal services | 295.8 | 301.2 | 322.0 |
| Health care, social security, physical culture and sports | 117.8 | 114.2 | 117.3 |
| Education, culture and art | 850.7 | 871.5 | 894.1 |
| Science, research and development | 48.6 | 48.3 | 48.1 |
| Finance, banking and insurance | 117.8 | 114.2 | 117.3 |
| State management | 240.0 | 240.0 | 240.0 |
| Other activities | 139.0 | 143.1 | 145.8 |
| **Total** | 30,974.2 | 31,818.9 | 32,716.3 |

* Comprising manufacturing, mining and quarrying, and power.

VIET NAM

*Statistical Survey*

## Agriculture

**PRINCIPAL CROPS** ('000 metric tons)

|  | 1991 | 1992 | 1993 |
|---|---|---|---|
| Rice (paddy) | 19,622 | 21,590 | 22,300 |
| Maize | 672 | 747 | 800 |
| Sorghum† | 5 | 5 | 5 |
| Sweet potatoes | 2,137 | 2,554 | 2,620 |
| Cassava (Manioc) | 2,455 | 2,568 | 2,631 |
| Dry beans† | 110 | 112 | 115 |
| Other pulses† | 191 | 192 | 191 |
| Soybeans | 80 | 79 | 81 |
| Groundnuts (in shell) | 235 | 223 | 240 |
| Cottonseed† | 6 | 11 | 11 |
| Cotton (lint)† | 3 | 5 | 6 |
| Coconuts | 1,053 | 1,160* | 1,207 |
| Vegetables (including melons) | 3,662 | 3,784† | 3,905† |
| Fruit (excluding melons) | 3,969 | 4,062† | 4,185† |
| Sugar cane | 6,131 | 6,199 | 6,656 |
| Coffee (green) | 119* | 120† | 135* |
| Tea (made) | 46 | 50 | 54 |
| Tobacco (leaves) | 36 | 30 | 30† |
| Jute and substitutes | 25 | 26 | 28 |
| Natural rubber | 65 | 74 | 76 |

* Unofficial figure.   † FAO estimate(s).

Source: FAO, *Production Yearbook*.

**LIVESTOCK** ('000 head, year ending September)

|  | 1991 | 1992 | 1993 |
|---|---|---|---|
| Horses | 141 | 134 | 133 |
| Cattle | 3,117 | 3,136 | 3,320 |
| Buffaloes | 2,854 | 2,887 | 2,956 |
| Pigs | 12,261 | 12,194 | 14,861 |
| Goats | 313 | 310* | 300* |

Chickens (million): 82† in 1991; 80† in 1992; 83* in 1993.
Ducks (million): 29† in 1991; 30† in 1992; 30* in 1993.

* FAO estimate.   † Unofficial figure.

Source: FAO, *Production Yearbook*.

**LIVESTOCK PRODUCTS** ('000 metric tons)

|  | 1991 | 1992 | 1993 |
|---|---|---|---|
| Beef and veal* | 84 | 85 | 86 |
| Buffalo meat* | 89 | 90 | 92 |
| Pig meat | 716 | 730 | 750 |
| Poultry meat* | 168 | 176 | 178 |
| Cows' milk* | 39 | 40 | 41 |
| Buffaloes' milk* | 26 | 27 | 28 |
| Hen eggs† | 102.9 | 112.9 | 115.0 |
| Other poultry eggs* | 76.0 | 77.0 | 78.0 |
| Cattle and buffalo hides* | 30.1 | 30.4 | 32.1 |

* FAO estimates.   † Unofficial figures.

Source: FAO, *Production Yearbook*.

## Forestry

**ROUNDWOOD REMOVALS** ('000 cubic metres, excluding bark)

|  | 1990 | 1991 | 1992 |
|---|---|---|---|
| Sawlogs, etc.: |  |  |  |
| Coniferous | 176 | 167 | 134 |
| Broadleaved | 2,680 | 2,826 | 2,437 |
| Other industrial wood (all broadleaved)* | 1,813 | 1,851 | 1,889 |
| Fuel wood (all broadleaved)* | 24,147 | 24,652 | 25,160 |
| **Total** | 28,816 | 29,496 | 29,620 |

* FAO estimates.

Source: FAO, *Yearbook of Forest Products*.

**SAWNWOOD PRODUCTION** ('000 cubic metres, including railway sleepers)

|  | 1990 | 1991 | 1992 |
|---|---|---|---|
| Coniferous | 105 | 113 | 102 |
| Broadleaved | 791 | 772 | 747 |
| **Total** | 896 | 885 | 849 |

Source: FAO, *Yearbook of Forest Products*.

## Fishing

('000 metric tons, live weight)

|  | 1990* | 1991* | 1992 |
|---|---|---|---|
| Inland waters: |  |  |  |
| Freshwater fishes | 253.0 | 257.0 | 258.6 |
| Freshwater crustaceans | 10.0 | 12.0 | 12.0 |
| Pacific Ocean: |  |  |  |
| Marine fishes | 427.0 | 442.0 | 463.6 |
| Marine crabs | 150.0 | 180.0 | 200.0 |
| Shrimps and prawns | 75.0 | 80.0 | 88.0 |
| Molluscs | 45.0 | 49.0 | 58.1 |
| **Total catch** | 960.0 | 1,020.0 | 1,080.3 |

* FAO estimates.

Source: FAO, *Yearbook of Fishery Statistics*.

## Mining

(estimated production, '000 metric tons)

|  | 1991 | 1992 | 1993 |
|---|---|---|---|
| Hard coal | 4,700 | 5,000 | 5,400 |
| Chromium ore | 6.0 | 3.6 | 3.5 |
| Phosphate rock | 319 | 290 | n.a. |
| Salt (unrefined) | 583 | 594 | 488 |
| Crude petroleum | 4,000 | 5,500 | 6,300 |

## Industry

**SELECTED PRODUCTS** ('000 metric tons, unless otherwise indicated)

|  | 1991 | 1992 | 1993 |
|---|---|---|---|
| Raw sugar | 372 | 365 | 341 |
| Beer ('000 hectolitres) | 1,310 | 1,690 | 2,170 |
| Cigarettes (million packets) | 1,298 | 1,541 | 1,604 |
| Textile yarn | 40 | 44 | 40 |
| Textile fabrics (million metres) | 280 | 272 | 225 |
| Garments (million) | 106 | 104 | 85 |
| Leather footwear ('000 pairs) | 6,188 | 5,672 | n.a. |
| Chemical fertilizers | 450 | 530 | 661 |
| Insecticides | 12 | 11 | 9 |
| Soap (metric tons) | 834 | 1,644 | 1,746 |
| Bricks (million) | 3,769 | 4,274 | 4,370 |
| Cement | 3,127 | 3,926 | 4,413 |
| Steel | 149 | 196 | 236 |
| Machine tools (number) | 1,235 | 844 | 1,288 |
| Television receivers ('000) | 186 | 365 | 412 |
| Clocks ('000) | 56 | 40 | n.a. |
| Bicycles ('000) | 46 | 158 | 130 |
| Tractors (number) | 2,279 | 770 | 2,500 |
| Threshing machines (number) | 39,461 | 30,153 | 30,250 |
| Electric energy (million kWh) | 9,307 | 9,818 | 10,928 |

# VIET NAM

## Finance

### CURRENCY AND EXCHANGE RATES

**Monetary Units**
100 xu = 1 new dông.

**Sterling and Dollar Equivalents** (31 October 1994)
£1 sterling = 17,920.3 dông;
US $1 = 10,990.0 dông;
100,000 new dông = £5.580 = $9.099.

**Average Exchange Rate** (dông per US $)
1991   7,979.2
1992   11,202.2
1993   10,641.0

Note: The new dông, equivalent to 10 former dông, was introduced in September 1985.

### BUDGET ('000 million dông)

| Revenue* | 1992 | 1993† | 1994‡ |
|---|---|---|---|
| Tax revenue. | 14,586 | 23,701 | 30,987 |
| State enterprises | 9,106 | 12,685 | 16,087 |
| Profits tax | 2,028 | 4,019 | 5,042 |
| Turnover tax | 2,158 | 3,333 | 4,492 |
| Special consumption tax (excise) | 1,317 | 1,908 | 2,700 |
| Natural resources tax | 1,874 | 1,809 | 2,084 |
| Non-agricultural private sector | 1,992 | 3,376 | 4,550 |
| Profits tax | 420 | 593 | 913 |
| Turnover tax | 582 | 863 | 1,361 |
| Agricultural tax | 1,294 | 1,351 | 900 |
| Taxes on trade. | 2,194 | 5,900 | 8,500 |
| Joint ventures. | n.a. | 389 | 950 |
| Other revenue | 5,589 | 5,801 | 6,713 |
| State enterprises | 2,807 | 3,400 | 4,213 |
| Depreciation allowance | 2,277 | 2,594 | 2,884 |
| Capital user fee | 530 | 806 | 1,329 |
| **Total** | 20,175 | 29,502 | 37,700 |

| Expenditure | 1992 | 1993† | 1994‡ |
|---|---|---|---|
| Current expenditure. | 18,671 | 29,375 | 34,853 |
| General administrative services | 2,404 | 3,245 | 3,435 |
| Economic services. | 1,495 | 2,997 | 3,229 |
| Social services. | 6,245 | 10,854 | 13,475 |
| Education | 1,495 | 2,910 | 3,739 |
| Health | 1,136 | 1,656 | 1,883 |
| Pensions and social relief. | 2,374 | 4,135 | 5,074 |
| Training | n.a. | 984 | 1,214 |
| Other services (incl. defence) | 5,314 | 8,604 | 11,331 |
| Interest on public debt. | 3,218 | 3,675 | 3,383 |
| Capital expenditure | 6,450 | 9,600 | 12,000 |
| **Total** | 25,121 | 38,975 | 46,853 |

* Excluding grants received ('000 million dông): 848 in 1992; 1,000† in 1993; 960‡ in 1994
† Preliminary.
‡ Forecast.

Source: IMF, *Economic Review–Viet Nam, 1994*.

### MONEY SUPPLY ('000 million dông at 31 December)

|  | 1991 | 1992 | 1993 |
|---|---|---|---|
| Currency outside banks | 6,419 | 10,579 | 14,218 |
| Demand deposits at banks | 2,707 | 4,232 | 4,870 |

Source: IMF, *Economic Review–Viet Nam, 1994*.

## NATIONAL ACCOUNTS
### Gross Domestic Product by Economic Activity
('000 million dông at current prices)

|  | 1991 | 1992 | 1993 |
|---|---|---|---|
| Agriculture and forestry | 30,314 | 36,468 | 39,998 |
| Industry* | 15,193 | 23,956 | 29,371 |
| Construction | 3,059 | 6,179 | 9,423 |
| Transport and communications | 2,860 | 4,662 | 6,036 |
| Trade and catering | 9,742 | 15,281 | 17,549 |
| Finance, banking and insurance | 1,108 | 1,567 | 2,318 |
| State management, science, education, health and sport | 6,807 | 9,718 | 14,402 |
| Housing and tourism | 6,880 | 11,659 | 15,998 |
| Other activities | 744 | 1,045 | 1,476 |
| **GDP in purchasers' values** | 76,707 | 110,535 | 136,571 |
| **GDP at constant 1989 prices** | 31,286 | 33,991 | 36,735 |

* Comprising manufacturing, mining and quarrying, and power.

### BALANCE OF PAYMENTS (US $ million)

|  | 1991 | 1992 | 1993* |
|---|---|---|---|
| Merchandise exports f.o.b. | 2,042 | 2,475 | 2,850 |
| Merchandise imports f.o.b. | -2,105 | -2,535 | -3,505 |
| **Trade balance** | -63 | -60 | -655 |
| Services (net) | 179 | 311 | 78 |
| Other income received | 42 | 43 | 31 |
| Other income paid | -381 | -425 | -587 |
| Private unrequited transfers (net) | 35 | 59 | 70 |
| Official unrequited transfers (net) | 55 | 64 | 194 |
| **Current account balance** | -133 | -8 | -869 |
| Direct investment (net) | 220 | 260 | 300 |
| Medium- and long-term loans (net) | -191 | 52 | -403 |
| Short-term capital (net) | -88 | -41 | -58 |
| Net errors and omissions | 142 | 4 | -76 |
| **Overall balance** | -50 | 268 | -1,106 |

* Preliminary.

Source: IMF, *Economic Review–Viet Nam, 1994*.

## External Trade

### SELECTED COMMODITIES (US $ million)

| Imports | 1991 | 1992 | 1993* |
|---|---|---|---|
| Fertilizers | 246 | 320 | 158 |
| Petroleum products | 485 | 615 | 684 |
| Steel | 42 | 104 | 189 |
| Machinery and spare parts | 240 | 297 | 549 |
| **Total** (incl. others) | 2,105 | 2,535 | 3,505 |

| Exports | 1991 | 1992 | 1993* |
|---|---|---|---|
| Petroleum | 581 | 756 | 844 |
| Rice | 225 | 300 | 350 |
| Coal | 48 | 48 | 59 |
| Rubber | 50 | 54 | 70 |
| Coffee | 74 | 86 | 85 |
| Marine products | 285 | 302 | 370 |
| Other agricultural and forestry products | 440 | 434 | 602 |
| Handicrafts and light industrial goods | 224 | 156 | 450 |
| **Total** (incl. others) | 2,042 | 2,475 | 2,850 |

* Preliminary.

Source: IMF, *Economic Review–Viet Nam, 1994*.

# VIET NAM

## SELECTED TRADING PARTNERS

| Imports | 1989 | 1990 | 1991 |
|---|---|---|---|
| Trade in convertible currencies | | | |
| (US $ million) | 839.9 | 1,304.2 | 2,049.1 |
| France | 52.5 | 123.0 | 147.9 |
| Germany, Federal Republic | 5.2 | 20.7 | 101.2 |
| Hong Kong | 102.6 | 196.9 | 194.8 |
| Korea, Republic | 15.6 | 53.1 | 152.1 |
| Japan | 105.6 | 169.0 | 157.7 |
| Singapore | 41.3 | 497.0 | 722.2 |
| Trade in unconvertible currencies | | | |
| (million roubles) | 1,725.9 | 1,448.2 | 289.0 |
| Czechoslovakia | 43.9 | 28.8 | 18.9 |
| Hungary | 32.8 | 54.3 | 13.7 |
| Poland | 20.8 | 20.6 | 8.4 |
| USSR | 1,532.9 | 1,210.6 | 358.1 |

| Exports | 1989 | 1990 | 1991 |
|---|---|---|---|
| Trade in convertible currencies | | | |
| (US $ million) | 1,138.2 | 1,292.5 | 2,009.8 |
| France | 79.7 | 115.7 | 83.1 |
| Hong Kong | 78.9 | 243.2 | 223.3 |
| Japan | 261.0 | 340.3 | 719.3 |
| Singapore | 70.7 | 194.5 | 425.0 |
| Trade in unconvertible currencies | | | |
| (million roubles) | 807.5 | 1,111.5 | 77.3 |
| Czechoslovakia | 43.8 | 48.8 | 4.2 |
| Hungary | 20.1 | 16.6 | 5.0 |
| Poland | 89.2 | 10.6 | 4.1 |
| USSR | 548.6 | 919.7 | 214.5 |

## Transport

**RAILWAYS** (traffic)

| | 1991 | 1992 | 1993* |
|---|---|---|---|
| Passengers carried (million) | 9.5 | 8.7 | 8.0 |
| Passenger-km (million) | 1,767.0 | 1,751.7 | 1,833.7 |
| Freight carried (million metric tons) | 2.6 | 2.8 | 3.1 |
| Freight ton-km (million) | 1,103.3 | 1,076.8 | 965.1 |

* Estimates.

**ROAD TRAFFIC**

| | 1991 | 1992 | 1993* |
|---|---|---|---|
| Passengers carried (million) | 332.9 | 388.7 | 431.4 |
| Passenger-km (million) | 9,438.1 | 10,620.8 | 11,049.0 |
| Freight carried (million metric tons) | 34.0 | 40.1 | 43.9 |
| Freight ton-km (million) | 1,815.0 | 2,075.0 | 2,134.0 |

* Estimates.

**INLAND WATERWAYS**

| | 1991 | 1992 | 1993* |
|---|---|---|---|
| Passengers carried (million) | 92.6 | 92.5 | 98.3 |
| Passenger-km (million) | 1,186.0 | 1,145.0 | 1,259.0 |
| Freight carried (million metric tons) | 15.6 | 16.9 | 18.3 |
| Freight ton-km (million) | 1,765.0 | 1,817.0 | 1,955.0 |

* Estimates.

**SHIPPING**
**Merchant Fleet** (gross registered tons)

| | 1989 | 1990 | 1991 |
|---|---|---|---|
| Oil tankers | 18,000 | 18,000 | 91,000 |
| Total | 358,000 | 470,000 | 574,000 |

Source: UN, *Statistical Yearbook*.

**International Sea-Borne Shipping**
(estimated freight traffic, '000 metric tons)

| | 1988 | 1989 | 1990 |
|---|---|---|---|
| Goods loaded | 305 | 310 | 303 |
| Goods unloaded | 1,486 | 1,510 | 1,510 |

Source: UN, *Monthly Bulletin of Statistics*.

**CIVIL AVIATION** (traffic)

| | 1981 | 1982 | 1983 |
|---|---|---|---|
| Passengers carried ('000) | 27 | 27 | 12 |
| Passenger-km (million) | 22 | 23 | 63 |
| Freight ton-km (million) | 3 | 2 | 7 |

**1990:** Passengers carried ('000) 89; Passenger-km (million) 87; Total ton-km (million) 8 (Source: UN, *Statistical Yearbook*).

## Tourism

| | 1990 | 1991 | 1992 |
|---|---|---|---|
| Tourist arrivals ('000) | 180 | 180 | 180 |
| Receipts from tourism (US $million) | 85 | 85 | 80 |

Source: UN, *Statistical Yearbook*.

## Communications Media

| | 1990 | 1991 | 1992 |
|---|---|---|---|
| Radio receivers ('000 in use)* | n.a. | 7,050 | 7,215 |
| Television receivers ('000 in use)* | 2,600 | 2,800 | 2,900 |
| Book production | | | |
| Number of titles | 2,892 | 3,043 | 3,971 |
| Number of copies ('000) | 38,123 | 62,432 | 69,759 |
| Newspapers and magazines ('000 copies) | 291,192 | 297,300 | 445,787 |

* Estimates.
Source: partly UNESCO, *Statistical Yearbook*.

## Education

(1993/94)

| | Schools | Teachers | Students |
|---|---|---|---|
| Pre-primary | 6,870 | 65,691 | 1,659,247 |
| General | 18,856 | 442,608 | 13,540,947 |
| Primary | 13,092* | 275,640 | 9,725,095 |
| Secondary: | | | |
| First cycle | 4,616† | 132,722 | 3,101,483 |
| Second cycle | 1,148† | 34,246 | 714,369 |
| Vocational training | 187 | 4,469 | 49,498 |
| Technical secondary | 264 | 7,728 | 87,909 |
| Higher education | 104 | 20,648 | 118,589 |

* Includes 2,955 institutions that provide primary and the first cycle of secondary education
† Includes 534 institutions that provide both the first and second cycle of secondary education.

# Directory

## The Constitution

On 15 April 1992 the National Assembly adopted a new Constitution, a revised version of that adopted in December 1980 (which in turn replaced the 1959 Constitution of the Democratic Republic of Viet Nam). The main provisions of the new Constitution (which entered into force after elections, which took place in July 1992) are summarized as follows:

### POLITICAL SYSTEM

All state power belongs to the people. The Communist Party of Viet Nam is a leading force of the state and society. All party organizations operate within the framework of the Constitution and the law. The people exercise power through the National Assembly and the People's Councils.

### ECONOMIC SYSTEM

The State develops a multi-sectoral economy, in accordance with a market mechanism based on state management and socialist orientations. All lands are under state management. The State allots land to organizations and individuals for use on a stabilized and long-term basis: they may transfer the right to the use of land allotted to them. Individuals may establish businesses, and the State shall encourage foreign investment. Legal property of individuals and organizations, and business enterprises with foreign invested capital, shall not be subjected to nationalization.

### THE NATIONAL ASSEMBLY

The National Assembly is the people's highest representative agency, and the highest organ of state power, exercising its supreme right of supervision over all operations of the State. It elects the President and Vice-President, the Prime Minister and senior judicial officers, and ratifies the Prime Minister's proposals for appointing members of the Government. It decides the country's socio-economic development plans, national financial and monetary policies, and foreign policy. The term of each legislature is five years. The National Assembly Standing Committee supervises the enforcement of laws and the activities of the Government. Amendments to the Constitution may only be made by a majority vote of at least two-thirds of the Assembly's members.

### THE PRESIDENT OF THE STATE

The President, as Head of State, represents Viet Nam in domestic and foreign affairs. The President is elected by the National Assembly from among its deputies, and is responsible to the National Assembly. The President's term of office is the same as that of the National Assembly. He or she is Commander-in-Chief of the people's armed forces, and chairs the National Defence and Security Council. The President asks the National Assembly to appoint or dismiss the Vice-President, the Prime Minister, the Chief Justice of the Supreme People's Court and the Chief Procurator of the Supreme People's Organ of Control. According to resolutions of the National Assembly or of its Standing Committee, the President appoints or dismisses members of the Government, and declares war or a state of emergency.

### THE GOVERNMENT

The Government comprises the Prime Minister, the Vice-Prime Ministers, ministers and other members. Apart from the Prime Minister, ministers do not have to be members of the National Assembly. The Prime Minister is responsible to the National Assembly, and the term of office of any Government is the same as that of the National Assembly, which ratifies the appointment or dismissal of members of the Government.

### LOCAL GOVERNMENT

The country is divided into provinces and municipalities, which are subordinate to the central Government; municipalities are divided into districts, precincts and cities, and districts are divided into villages and townships. People's Councils are elected by the local people.

### JUDICIAL SYSTEM

The judicial system comprises the Supreme People's Court, local People's Courts, military tribunals and other courts. The term of office of the presiding judge of the Supreme People's Court corresponds to the term of the National Assembly, and he or she is responsible to the National Assembly. The Supreme People's Organ of Control ensures the observance of the law and exercises the right of public prosecution. Its Chief Procurator is responsible to the National Assembly. There are local People's Organs of Control and Military Organs of Control.

## The Government

### HEAD OF STATE

**President:** Gen. LE DUC ANH (elected by the Ninth National Assembly on 23 September 1992).
**Vice-President:** NGUYEN THI BINH.

### CABINET
(June 1995)

**Prime Minister:** VO VAN KIET.
**Vice-Prime Ministers:** PHAN VAN KHAI, NGUYEN KHANH, TRAN DUC LUONG.
**Minister of National Defence:** Lt-Gen. DOAN KHUE.
**Minister of the Interior:** BUI THIEN NGO.
**Minister of Foreign Affairs:** NGUYEN MANH CAM.
**Minister of Justice:** NGUYEN DINH LOC.
**Minister of Finance:** HO TE.
**Minister of Science, Technology and Environment:** DANG HUU.
**Minister of Labour, War Invalids and Social Welfare:** TRAN DINH HOAN.
**Minister of Education and Training:** TRAN HONG QUAN.
**Minister of Public Health:** NGUYEN TRONG NHAN.
**Minister of Culture and Information:** TRAN HOAN.
**Minister of Construction:** NGO XUAN LOC.
**Minister of Water Conservancy:** NGUYEN CANH DINH.
**Minister of Communications and Transport:** BUI DANH LUU.
**Minister of Agriculture and Food Industry:** NGUYEN CONG TAN.
**Minister of Marine Products:** NGUYEN TAN TRINH.
**Minister of Heavy Industry:** TRAN LUM.
**Minister of Light Industry:** DANG VU CHU.
**Minister of Energy:** THAI PHUNG NE.
**Minister of Commerce:** LE VAN TRIET.
**Minister of Forestry:** NGUYEN QUANG HA.
**Minister, Chairman of the State Planning Commission:** DO QUOC SAM.
**General State Inspector:** NGUYEN KY CAM.
**Governor of the State Bank:** CAO SY KIEM.
**Minister, Chairman of the Ethnic Minorities and Mountain Region Commission:** HOANG DUC NGHI.
**Minister, Head of the State Commission for Co-operation and Investment:** DAU NGOC XUAN.
**Minister, Head of the Government's Organization and Personnel Commission:** PHAN NGOC TUONG.
**Minister, Head of the Government Office:** LE XUAN TRINH.
**Minister, Head of the National Committee of Population Activities and Family Planning:** MAI KY.
**Minister in charge of Child Protection and Childcare:** TRAN THI THANH THANH.
**Minister in charge of Youth Work and Minister in charge of Government Affairs:** HA QUANG DU.
**Minister without Portfolio with responsibility for Economic Affairs:** PHAN VAN TIEM.

### MINISTRIES AND COMMISSIONS

**Ministry of Agriculture and Food Industry:** 6 Ngoc Ha, Hanoi; tel. (4) 268161; fax (4) 25399.
**Ministry of Commerce:** 31 Trang Tien, Hanoi; tel. (4) 254915; telex 411251; fax (4) 264696.
**Ministry of Communications and Transport:** 80 Tran Hung Dao, Hanoi; tel. (4) 256687; telex 412242; fax (4) 267291.
**Ministry of Construction:** 37 Le Dai Hanh, Hanoi; tel. (4) 268271; fax (4) 258122.
**Ministry of Culture and Information:** 51 Ngo Quyen, Hanoi; tel. (4) 253231.

**Ministry of Education and Training:** 49 Dai Co Viet, Hanoi; tel. (4) 264085; fax (4) 694085.
**Ministry of Energy:** 18 Tran Nguyen Han, Hanoi; tel. (4) 263725; fax (4) 254865.
**Ministry of Finance:** 8 Phan Huy Chu, Hanoi; tel. (4) 262357; fax (4) 262266.
**Ministry of Foreign Affairs:** 1 Ton That Dam, Hanoi; tel. (4) 258201; telex 111516; fax (4) 259205.
**Ministry of Forestry:** 123 Lo Duc, Hanoi; tel. (4) 253236; fax (4) 252542.
**Ministry of Heavy Industry:** 54 Hai Ba Trung, Hanoi; tel. (4) 258311.
**Ministry of the Interior:** Tran Binh Trong, Hanoi; tel. (4) 258300.
**Ministry of Justice:** 25A Cat Linh, Hanoi; tel. (4) 254658.
**Ministry of Labour, War Invalids and Social Welfare:** 2 Dinh Le, Hanoi; tel. (4) 252236.
**Ministry of Light Industry:** 7 Trang Thi, Hanoi; tel. (4) 253831; fax (4) 265303.
**Ministry of Marine Products:** Bach Thao, Hanoi; tel. (4) 252696.
**Ministry of National Defence:** 1 Hoang Dieu, Hanoi; tel. (4) 258101.
**Ministry of Public Health:** 138A Giang Vo, Hanoi; tel. (4) 264416.
**Ministry of Science, Technology and Environment:** 39 Tran Hung Dao, Hanoi; tel. (4) 252731; telex 412287; fax (4) 251518.
**Ministry of Water Conservancy:** 164 Tran Quang Khai, Hanoi; tel. (4) 268141.
**National Committee of Population Activities and Family Planning:** 226 Van Mieu, Hanoi; tel. (4) 258261; fax (4) 258993.
**State Commission for Co-operation and Investment:** 56 Quoc Tu Giam, Hanoi; tel. (4) 253666; fax (4) 259271.
**State Planning Commission:** 2 Hoang Van Thu, Hanoi; tel. (4) 258261.
**State Inspectorate:** 28 Tang Bat Ho, Hanoi; tel. (4) 254497.

### NATIONAL DEFENCE AND SECURITY COUNCIL
**Chairman:** Gen. LE DUC ANH.
**Vice-Chairman:** VO VAN KIET.
**Members:** NONG DUC MANH, Lt-Gen. DOAN KHUE, BUI THIEN NGO, NGUYEN MANH CAM.

## Legislature

### QUOC HOI
(National Assembly)

Elections to the Ninth National Assembly were held on 19 July 1992. The Assembly has 395 members, elected from among 601 candidates.
**Chairman:** NONG DUC MANH.
**Vice-Chairmen:** NGUYEN HA PHAN, DANG QUAN THUY, PHUNG VAN TUU.

## Political Organizations

**Dang Cong san Viet Nam** (Communist Party of Viet Nam): 1 Hoang Van Thu, Hanoi; f. 1976; ruling party; fmrly the Viet Nam Workers' Party, f. 1951 as the successor to the Communist Party of Indo-China, f. 1930; c. 2.1m. mems (1994); Gen. Sec. of Cen. Cttee DO MUOI.

#### Politburo
17 full members:

| | |
|---|---|
| DO MUOI | BUI THIEN NGO |
| VO VAN KIET | NONG DUC MANH |
| Gen. LE DUC ANH | PHAM THE DUYET |
| NGUYEN DUC BINH | VO TRAN CHI |
| Lt-Gen. DOAN KHUE | NGUYEN MANH CAM |
| DAO DUY TUNG | NGUYEN HA PHAN |
| VU OANH | DO QUANG THANG |
| LE PHUOC THO | Lt-Gen. LE KHA PHIEU |
| PHAN VAN KHAI | |

#### Secretariat

| | |
|---|---|
| LE PHUOC THO | HONG HA |
| DO MUOI | NGUYEN DINH TU |
| Gen. LE DUC ANH | TRUONG MY HOA |
| DAO DUY TUNG | DO QUANG THANG |
| NGUYEN HA PHAN | |

**Ho Chi Minh Communist Youth Union:** 60 Ba Trieu, Hanoi; f. 1931; 4m. mems; First Sec. NGUYEN DUC VIET.
**Viet Nam Fatherland Front:** 46 Trang Thi, Hanoi; f. 1930; replaced the Lien Viet (Viet Nam National League), the successor to Viet Nam Doc Lap Dong Minh Hoi (Revolutionary League for the Independence of Viet Nam) or Viet Minh; in 1977 the original organization merged with the National Front for the Liberation of South Viet Nam and the Alliance of National, Democratic and Peace Forces in South Viet Nam to form a single front; 200-member Cen. Cttee; Pres. Presidium of Cen. Cttee LE QUANG DAO; Gen. Sec. TRAN VAN DANG.
**Vietnamese Women's Union:** 39 Hang Chuoi, Hanoi; tel. (4) 253439; f. 1930; 11.4m. mems; Pres. TRUONG MY HOA.

## Diplomatic Representation

### EMBASSIES IN VIET NAM

**Afghanistan:** Thang Loi Hotel, Hanoi; tel. (4) 258211; Ambassador: ISMAIL MHASHOOR.
**Algeria:** 13 Phan Chu Trinh, Hanoi; tel. (4) 253865; Ambassador: MAAR AHMED.
**Australia:** 66 Ly Thuong Kiet, Hanoi; tel. (4) 252763; telex 411410; fax (4) 259268; Ambassador: SUSAN BOYD.
**Bahrain:** Hanoi.
**Bangladesh:** 101-104, A1 Van Phuc Quarter, Hanoi; tel. (4) 231625; fax (4) 4231628; Ambassador: MOSTAFA FARUQUE MOHAMMED.
**Belgium:** D1 Van Phuc, Rooms 105-108, Hanoi; tel. (4) 252263; fax (4) 257165; Ambassador: BENOIT RYELANAT.
**Bulgaria:** Van Phuc, 358 St, Hanoi; tel. (4) 252908; Ambassador: BORIS FRIFANOV.
**Cambodia:** 71 Tran Hung Dao, Hanoi; tel. (4) 253788; Ambassador: UCH BORIT.
**Canada:** 39 Nguyen Dinh Chieu, Hanoi; tel. (4) 265840; fax (4) 265837; Chargé d'affaires a.i.: CHRISTOPHER BROWN.
**China, People's Republic:** 46 Hoang Dieu, Hanoi; tel. (4) 253736; Ambassador: HUA ZHANGQING.
**Cuba:** 65 Ly Thuong Kiet, Hanoi; tel. (4) 254775; fax (4) 252426; Ambassador: TANIA MACEIRA DELGADO.
**Czech Republic:** 13 Chu Van An, Hanoi; tel. (4) 254131; Chargé d'affaires a.i.: JIŘÍ VATAHA.
**Denmark:** BT6 Van Phuc 3, Hanoi; tel. (4) 231888; fax (4) 231999; Ambassador: NIELS JULIUS LASSEN.
**Egypt:** 85 Ly Thuong Kiet, Hanoi; tel. (4) 252944; Ambassador: MOUSTAFA AHMED ALI.
**Finland:** 1–2 B3b Giang Vo Quarter, Hanoi; tel. (4) 256754; telex 411443; fax (4) 232821; Ambassador: KAI GRANHOLM.
**France:** 57 Traen Hung Dao St, Hanoi; tel. (4) 252719; telex 4411; fax (4) 264236; Ambassador: GILLES D'HUMIÈRES.
**Germany:** 29 Tran Phu, Hanoi; tel. (4) 253836; telex 411428; fax (4) 253838; Ambassador: KLAUS CHRISTIAN KRAEMER.
**Hungary:** 47 Dien Bien Phu, Hanoi; tel. (4) 252748; Ambassador: OSZKAR SZUROVSZKY.
**India:** 58 Tran Hung Dao, Hanoi; tel. (4) 253409; telex 411313; fax (4) 265169; Ambassador: SURINDER LAL MALIK.
**Indonesia:** 50 Ngo Quyen, Hanoi; tel. (4) 253353; fax (4) 259274; Ambassador: DJAFAR HUSIN ASSEGAFF.
**Iran:** 54 Tran Phut, Hanoi; tel. (4) 232068; fax (4) 32120; Ambassador: REZA HOSSEIN.
**Iraq:** 66 Tran Hung Dao, Hanoi; tel. (4) 255111; telex 411408; Ambassador: Dr MAHDI S. HAMOUDI AL-SAMARRAE.
**Israel:** 68 Nguyen Thai Hoc St, Hanoi; tel. (4) 266919; Ambassador: DAVID MATNAI.
**Italy:** 9 Le Phung Hieu, Hanoi; tel. (4) 256246; telex 411416; fax (4) 267602; Ambassador: GIANLUIGI PASQUINELLI.
**Japan:** 61 Trung Chinh St, Hanoi; tel. (4) 692600; telex 411414; Ambassador: HIROYUKI YUSHITA.
**Korea, Democratic People's Republic:** 25 Cao Ba Quat, Hanoi; tel. (4) 253008; Ambassador: HAN MIN CHOL.
**Korea, Republic:** 29 Nguyen Dinh Chieu, Hanoi; tel. (4) 226677; Ambassador: PARK NOH-SU.
**Laos:** 22 Tran Binh Trong, Hanoi; tel. (4) 254576; Ambassador: KHAMPHET PHENGMEUANG.
**Libya:** Van Phuc Residential Quarter, Hanoi; tel. (4) 253379; Secretary: SALEH AL-HOSNI.
**Malaysia:** A3 Van Phuc Residential Quarter, Hanoi; tel. (4) 233520; telex 411311; fax (4) 232166; Ambassador: CHEAH SAM KIP.

VIET NAM                                                                                                                                                         Directory

**Mongolia:** 39 Tran Phu, Hanoi; tel. (4) 253009; Ambassador: GOTOVDORJIYN LUUZAN.
**Myanmar:** Van Phuc Residential Quarter, BP 62, Hanoi; tel. (4) 253369; telex 411427; fax (4) 252404; Ambassador: U AYE.
**Netherlands:** Danchu Hotel, 29 Trang Tien St, Hanoi; tel. (4) 254937; fax (4) 266786; Ambassador: D.A.V.E. ADER.
**Philippines:** E1 Trung Tu Diplomatic Quarter, Hanoi; tel. (4) 257948; fax (4) 257873; Ambassador: MARIANO L. BACCAY.
**Poland:** 3 Chua Mot Cot, Hanoi; tel. (4) 252027; fax (4) 236914; Chargé d'affaires a.i.: MIROSŁAW GAJEWSKI.
**Romania:** 5 Le Hong Phong, Hanoi; tel. (4) 252014; fax (4) 430922; Ambassador: VALERIU ARTENI.
**Russia:** 58 Tran Phu, Hanoi; tel. (4) 254631; Ambassador: RASHIT L. KHAMIDULIN.
**Singapore:** B4 Van Phuc Quarter, Rooms 301-303, Hanoi; tel. (4) 233965; fax (4) 233992; Ambassador: TOH HOCK GHIM.
**Slovakia:** 6 Le Hong Phong, Hanoi; tel. (4) 254334; telex 411436; fax (4) 254145; Ambassador: JÁN GONZOR.
**Sweden:** 2, 358 St, Khu Ba Dinh, Hanoi; tel. (4) 254824; telex 411420; fax (4) 232195; Ambassador: BÖRJE LJUNGGREN.
**Switzerland:** 77B Kim Ma St, Hanoi; tel. (4) 232019; fax (4) 232045; Ambassador: PIERRE FRIEDERICH.
**Thailand:** E1 Trung Tu Residential Quarter, Hanoi; tel. (4) 253092; fax 265444; Ambassador: SURAPONG JAYANAMA.
**United Kingdom:** 16 Pho Ly Thuong Kiet, Hanoi; tel. (4) 252349; telex 411405; fax (4) 265762; Ambassador: PETER K. WILLIAMS.
**Yugoslavia:** 47 Tran Phu, Hanoi; tel. (4) 252343; Chargé d'affaires a.i.: MILOŠ BOGICEVIĆ.

## Judicial System

The Supreme People's Court in Hanoi is the highest court and exercises civil and criminal jurisdiction over all lower courts. The Supreme Court may also conduct trials of the first instance in certain cases. There are People's Courts in each province and city which exercise jurisdiction in the first and second instance. Military courts hear cases involving members of the People's Army and cases involving national security. In 1993 legislation was adopted on the establishment of economic courts to consider business disputes. The observance of the law by ministries, government offices and all citizens is the concern of the People's Organs of Control, under a Supreme People's Organ of Control. The Chief Justice of the Supreme People's Court and the Chief Procurator of the Supreme People's Organ of Control are elected by the National Assembly, on the recommendation of the President.

**Chief Justice of the Supreme People's Court:** PHAM HUNG.
**Chief Procurator of the Supreme People's Organ of Control:** LE THANH DAO.

## Religion

Traditional Vietnamese religion included elements of Indian and all three Chinese religions: Mahayana Buddhism, Daoism and Confucianism. Its most widespread feature was the cult of ancestors, practised in individual households and clan temples. In addition, there were (and remain) a wide variety of Buddhist sects, the sects belonging to the 'new' religions of Caodaism and Hoa Hao, and the Protestant and Roman Catholic Churches. The Government has guaranteed complete freedom of religious belief.

### BUDDHISM

In the North a Buddhist organization, grouping Buddhists loyal to the Democratic Republic of Viet Nam, was formed in 1954. In the South the United Buddhist Church was formed in 1964, incorporating several disparate groups, including the 'militant' An-Quang group (mainly natives of central Viet Nam), the group of Thich Tam Chau (mainly northern emigrés in Saigon) and the southern Buddhists of the Xa Loi temple. In 1982 most of the Buddhist sects were amalgamated into the state-approved Viet Nam Buddhist Church.

**President of the Executive Council of the Viet Nam Buddhist Church:** Most Ven. THICH TRI TINH.
**Unified Buddhist Church of Viet Nam:** Patriarch THICH HUYEN QUANG.

### CAODAISM

Formally inaugurated in 1926, this is a syncretic religion based on spiritualist seances with a predominantly ethical content, but sometimes with political overtones. A number of different sects exist, of which the most politically involved (1940–75) was that of Tay Ninh. Another sect, the Tien Thien, was represented in the National Liberation Front from its inception. There are an estimated 2m. adherents, resident mainly in the South.

**Leader:** Cardinal THAI HUU THANH.

### CHRISTIANITY

In 1991 the number of Christian adherents represented an estimated 7% of the total population; in 1993 an estimated 5.3% of the total population were Roman Catholic.

#### The Roman Catholic Church

The Roman Catholic Church has been active in Viet Nam since the 17th century, and since 1933 has been led mainly by Vietnamese priests. Many Roman Catholics moved from North to South Viet Nam in 1954–55, but some remained in the North. The total number of adherents was estimated at 3.6m. in 1993. For ecclesiastical purposes, Viet Nam comprises three archdioceses and 22 dioceses.

**Committee for Solidarity of Patriotic Vietnamese Catholics:** 59 Trang Thi, Hanoi; Pres. Rev. VO THANH TRINH.
**Bishops' Conference:** Conférence Episcopal du Viet Nam, Toa Giam Muc, BP 11, 70 Hung Vuong, Xuan Loc, Dong Noi; f. 1980; Pres. Rt Rev. PAUL MARIE NGUYEN MINH NHAT, Bishop of Xuan Loc.
**Archbishop of Hanoi:** Cardinal PAUL JOSEPH PHAM DINH TUNG, Archevêché, 40 Pho Nha Chung, Hanoi; tel. (4) 254424.
**Archbishop of Ho Chi Minh City:** (vacant), Archevêché, 180 Nguyen Dinh Chieu, BP 2371, Ho Chi Minh City 3; tel. (4)(8) 92828.
**Archbishop of Hué:** (vacant), Archevêché, 6 Nguyen-Truong-To, Hué; tel. (4) 23100.

#### The Protestant Church

Introduced in 1920 with 500 adherents; the total number is now estimated at 180,000.

### HOA HAO

A new manifestation of an older religion called Buu Son Ky Huong, the Hoa Hao sect was founded by Nguyen Phu So in 1939, and at one time claimed 1.5m. adherents in southern Viet Nam.

### ISLAM

The number of Muslims was estimated at 50,000 in 1993.

## The Press

The Ministry of Culture and Information supervises the activities of newspapers, news agencies and periodicals.

### DAILIES

#### Hanoi

**Hanoi Moi** (New Hanoi): 44 Le Thai To, Hanoi; tel. (4) 253067; f. 1976; organ of Hanoi Cttee of the Communist Party of Viet Nam; Editor HO XUAN SON; circ. 35,000.
**Nhan Dan** (The People): 71 Hang Trong, Hanoi; tel. (4) 254231; f. 1946; official organ of the Communist Party of Viet Nam; Editor-in-Chief HUU THO; circ. 200,000.
**Quan Doi Nhan Dan** (People's Army): 7 Phan Dinh Phung, Hanoi; tel. (4) 254118; f. 1950; organ of the armed forces; Editor NGUYEN PHONG HAI; circ. 60,000.
**Viet Nam News:** 79 Ly Thuong Kiet, Hanoi; tel. (4) 260987; telex 412311; fax 267447; f. 1991; English; published by the Vietnam News Agency; Editor-in-Chief NGUYEN KHUYEN; circ. 10,000.

#### Ho Chi Minh City

**Saigon Giai Phong** (Liberated Saigon): 432 Xo Viet Nghe Tinh, Ho Chi Minh City; tel. (8) 295942; f. 1975; organ of Ho Chi Minh City Cttee of the Communist Party of Viet Nam; Editor NGUYEN TUAT VIET; circ. 85,000.

### PERIODICALS

**Dai Doan Ket** (Great Unity): 66 Ba Trieu, Hanoi; and 176 Vo Thi Sau St, Ho Chi Minh City; tel. (4) 262420; f. 1977; weekly; organ of the Viet Nam Fatherland Front; Editor NGUYEN NGOC THACH.
**Giao Thong-Van** (Communications and Transport): 1 Nha Tho, Hanoi; tel. (4) 255387; f. 1962; weekly; Thursday; organ of the Ministry of Communications and Transport; Editor NGO DUC NGUYEN; circ. 10,000.

**VIET NAM**

**Giao Vien Nhan Dan** (People's Teacher): Le Truc, Hanoi; tel. (4) 252849; f. 1959; weekly; organ of the Ministry of Education and Training; Editor (vacant).

**Khoa Hoc Ky Thuat Kinh Te The Gioi** (World Science, Technology and Economy): 5 Ly Thuong Kiet, Hanoi; tel. (4) 252931; f. 1982; weekly.

**Khoa Hoc va Doi Song** (Science and Life): 70 Tran Hung Dao, Hanoi; tel. (4) 253427; f. 1959; weekly; Editor-in-Chief Tran Cu; circ. 30,000.

**Lao Dong** (Labour): 51 Hang Bo, Hanoi; tel. (4) 252441; fax (4) 254441; 3 a week; organ of the General Confederation of Labour; Editor-in-Chief (vacant); circ. 80,000.

**Nghe Thuat Dien Anh** (Cinematography): 65 Tran Hung Dao, Hanoi; tel. (4) 262473; f. 1984; fortnightly; Editor Dang Nhat Minh.

**Nguoi Cong Giao Viet Nam** (Vietnamese Catholic): 59 Trang Thi, Hanoi; f. 1984; tel. (4) 256242; fortnightly; organ of the Cttee for Solidarity of Patriotic Vietnamese Catholics; Editor-in-Chief So Chi.

**Nguoi Dai Bieu Nhan Dan** (People's Deputy): 35 Ngo Quyen, Hanoi; tel. (4) 252861; f. 1988; bi-monthly; disseminates resolutions of the National Assembly and Council of State; Editor Nguyen Ngoc Tho.

**Nguoi Hanoi** (The Hanoian): 19 Hang Buom, Hanoi; tel. (4) 255662; f. 1984; Editor (vacant).

**Nha Bao Va Cong Luan** (The Journalist and Public Opinion): 59 Ly Thai To, Hanoi; tel. (4) 253609; f. 1985; monthly review; organ of the Viet Nam Journalists' Asscn; Editor-in-Chief (vacant); circ. 15,000.

**Nong Nghiep Viet Nam** (Viet Nam Agriculture): 14 Ngo Quyen, Hanoi; tel. (4) 256492; fax (4) 252923; f. 1987; weekly; Editor Le Nam Son.

**Phu Nu Hanoi** (Hanoi Women): 72 Quan Su, Hanoi; tel. (4) 254304; f. 1987; fortnightly; magazine of the Hanoi Women's Union.

**Phu Nu Viet Nam** (Vietnamese Women): 47 Hang Chuoi, Hanoi; tel. (4) 253500; weekly; magazine of the Vietnamese Women's Union; Editor-in-Chief Phuong Minh.

**San Khau** (Theatre): 51 Tran Hung Dao St, Hanoi; tel. (4) 264423; f. 1976; monthly; Editor (vacant).

**Suc Khoe** (Health): 138 A Giang Vo St, Hanoi; tel. (4) 243144; fortnightly; published by the Ministry of Public Health; Editor Phung Truc Phong (acting).

**Tap Chi Cong San** (Communist Review): 1 Nguyen Thuong Hien, Hanoi; tel. (4) 252061; f. 1955 as *Hoc Tap*; monthly; political and theoretical organ of the Communist Party of Viet Nam; Editor-in-Chief Nguyen Phu Trong; circ. 40,000.

**Tap Chi Tac Pham Van Hoc**: 65 Nguyen Du St, Hanoi; tel. (4) 252442; f. 1987; monthly; organ of the Viet Nam Writers' Asscn; Editor-in-Chief Nguyen Dinh Thi; circ. 15,000.

**Tap Chi Tu Tuong Van Hoa** (Ideology and Culture Review): Hanoi; f. 1990; organ of the Central Committee Department of Ideology and Culture.

**Tap Chi Van Hoc** (Literature Magazine): 20 Ly Thai To St, Hanoi; tel. (4) 252895; monthly; published by the Institute of Literature; Editor Phong Le.

**The Thao Viet Nam** (Viet Nam Sports): 5 Trinh Hoai Duc St, Hanoi; f. 1968; weekly; Editor Tran Can.

**The Thao Van Hoa** (Sports and Culture): 5 Ly Thuong Kiet, Hanoi; tel. (4) 267043; fax (4) 267447; f. 1982; weekly; Editor-in-Chief Nguyen Huu Vinh.

**Thieu Nien Tien Phong** (Young Pioneers): 5 Hoa Ma, Hanoi; tel. (4) 263335; weekly; Editor Nguyen Phone Doanh; circ. 140,000.

**Thoi Bao Kinh Te Viet Nam**: Hanoi; f. 1994.

**Thuong Mai** (Commerce): 100 Lo Duc St, Hanoi; tel. (4) 263150; f. 1990; weekly; organ of the Ministry of Commerce; Editor Duc Tuong.

**Tien Phong** (Vanguard): 15 Ho Xuan Huong, Hanoi; tel. (4) 264031; f. 1957; weekly; organ of the Ho Chi Minh Communist Youth Union; Editor Duong Xuan Nam; circ. 110,000.

**Tuan Tin Tuc** (News Weekly): 5 Ly Thuong Kiet, Hanoi; tel. (4) 252931; f. 1982; Vietnamese.

**Tuoi Tre** (Youth): Ho Chi Minh City; weekly.

**Van Hoa Nghe Thuat** (Culture and Arts): 26 Dien Bien Phu St, Hanoi; tel. (4) 257781; f. 1957; fortnightly; Editor Phi van Tuong.

**Van Nghe** (Arts and Letters): 17 Tran Quoc Toan, Hanoi; tel. (4) 264430; f. 1949; weekly; organ of the Vietnamese Writers' Union; Editor Huu Thinh; circ. 40,000.

**Van Nghe Quan Doi** (Army Literature and Arts): 4 Ly Nam De St, Hanoi; tel. (4) 254370; f. 1957; monthly; Editor (vacant); circ. 50,000.

**Viet Nam Business Opportunities**: 33 Ba Trieu, Hanoi; tel. (4) 266233; telex 411257; fax (4) 256446; monthly in English and Vietnamese; publ. by Chamber of Commerce and Industry of Viet Nam.

**Viet Nam Dan Tu Nuoc Ngoai**: 175 Nguyen Thai Hoc, Hanoi; tel. (4) 250537; fax (4) 257937; weekly business newspaper publ. in Vietnamese.

**Viet Nam Economic Times**: Hanoi; weekly; in Vietnamese (with monthly edn in English); circ. 37,000.

**Viet Nam Foreign Trade**: 33 Ba Trieu, Hanoi; tel. (4) 266233; telex 411257; fax 256446; quarterly in English; publ. by Chamber of Commerce and Industry of Viet Nam; Editor-in-Chief (vacant).

**Viet Nam Investment Review**: 175 Nguyen Thai Hoc, Hanoi; tel. (4) 250537; fax (4) 257937; f. 1990; weekly; publ. in English; economic and political news; Man. Dir Alex McKinnon; circ 20,000.

**Viet Nam News Sunday**: 79 Ly Thuong Kiet, Hanoi; tel. (4) 254693; telex 412311; fax (4) 267447; f. 1991; English; published by the Viet Nam News Agency; Editor-in-Chief Nguyen Khuyen.

**Viet Nam Pictorial**: 79 Ly Thuong Kiet, Hanoi; tel. (4) 253508; f. 1954; publ. monthly in Vietnamese, Lao, French, English and Chinese edns; publ. quarterly in Spanish; Dir Do Phuong; circ. 138,000.

**Viet Nam Renovation**: Hanoi; f. 1994; quarterly magazine on reform of the agricultural sector; in Vietnamese, Chinese and English.

**Viet Nam Social Science**: 27 Tran Xuan Soan, Hanoi; tel. (4) 1261578; f. 1984; quarterly; publ. in English; organ of National Centre for Social and Human Sciences; Editor Pham Xuan Nam.

**Vietnamese Studies**: 46 Tran Hung Dao, Hanoi; quarterly; English and French edns; Dir Mai Ly Quang.

**Vietnamese Trade Unions**: 82 Tran Hung Dao, Hanoi; tel.(4) 268181; telex 412270; fax (4) 253781; every 2 months in English and French; organ of Viet Nam General Confederation of Labour; Editor-in-Chief Nguyen van Hung.

### NEWS AGENCIES

**Viet Nam News Agency (VNA)**: 5 Ly Thuong Kiet, Hanoi; tel.(4) 252931; mem. Organization of Asian and Pacific News Agencies; Dir-Gen. Do Phuong.

**Vinapress**: 79 Ly Thuong Kiet, Hanoi; tel.(4) 253508; f. 1988; non-governmental press agency; Dir Do Phuong.

#### Foreign Bureaux

**Agence France-Presse (AFP)**: 76 Ngo Quyen, BP 40, Hanoi; tel.(4) 250150; fax (4) 266032; Bureau Chief Pascale Trouillaud; Correspondent Robert Templer.

**Bulgarska Telegrafna Agentsia (BTA)** (Bulgaria): A2, 401–402, POB 80, Van Phuc Residential Quarter, Hanoi; tel.(4) 254660; telex 411427; Chief Ivan Todorov.

**Informatsionnoye Telegrafnoye Agentstvo Rossii—Telegrafnoye Agentstvo Suverennykh Stran (ITAR—TASS)** (Russia): Trung Tam Da Nganh, Thanh Xuan Bac, Dong Da, Hanoi; tel. (4) 281381; fax (4) 256177; Correspondent Sergei A. Blagov.

**Kyodo News Service** (Japan): Room 304, 8 Tran Hung Dao, Hanoi; tel.(4) 259622; fax (4) 255848; Bureau Chief Shingo Kiniwa.

**Polska Agencja Prasowa (PAP)** (Poland): B5 Van Phuc Residential Quarter, Hanoi; tel.(4) 252601; Chief Tomasz Trzcinski.

**Prensa Latina** (Cuba): 66 Ngo Thi Nham, Hanoi; tel.(4) 254366; telex 4438; Correspondent Fausto Triana.

**Reuters** (UK): Room 401, 8 Tran Hung Dao, Hanoi; tel.(4) 259623; fax 268606.

**Rossiyskoye Informatsionnoye Agentstvo—Novosti (RIA—Novosti)** (Russia): Z10-A1, Van Phuc Diplomatic Quarter, POB 34, Hanoi; tel. (4) 431607; fax (4) 460033; Bureau Chief Andrei Petrovich Shamshin.

**Xinhua (New China) News Agency** (People's Republic of China): 6 Khuc Hao, Hanoi; tel. (4) 252913; Chief Correspondent Liang de Quan.

### PRESS ASSOCIATION

**Viet Nam Journalists' Association**: 59 Ly Thai To, Hanoi; tel. (4) 253608; fax (4) 250797; f. 1950; asscn of editors, reporters and photographers working in the press, radio, television and news agencies; 7,300 mems (1994); Pres. Phan Quang; Vice-Pres Tran Mai Hanh.

## Publishers

All publishing enterprises are controlled by the Ministry of Culture and Information.

**Am Nhac Dia Hat** (Music) **Publishing House**: 61 Ly Thai To St, Hanoi; tel. (4) 256208; f. 1986; produces records, cassettes, books and printed music; Dir Pham Duc Loc.

**Cong An Nhan Dan** (People's Public Security) **Publishing House**: 167 Mai Hac De, Hanoi; f. 1981; managed by the Ministry of the Interior; cultural and artistic information, public order and security; Dir Pham Van Tham.

**Giao Duc** (Education) **Publishing House:** 81 Tran Hung Dao, Hanoi; tel. (4) 262011; fax (4) 262010; f. 1957; managed by the Ministry of Education and Training; Dir Tran Tram Phuong; Editor-in-Chief Prof. Nguyen Khac Phi.

**Giao Thong Van Tai** (Communications and Transport) **Publishing House:** 80 Tran Hung Dao, Hanoi; tel. (4) 255620; f. 1983; managed by the Ministry of Communications and Transport; Dir To Khanh Tho.

**Khoa Hoc Va Ky Thuat** (Science and Technology) **Publishing House:** 70 Tran Hung Dao, Hanoi; tel. (4) 254786; f. 1960; scientific and technical works, guide books, dictionaries, popular and management books; Dir Prof. Dr To Dang Hai.

**Khoa Hoc Xa Hoi** (Social Sciences) **Publishing House:** 61 Phan Chu Trinh, Hanoi; tel. (4) 255428; f. 1967; managed by the Institute of Social Science; Dir Dr Nguyen Duc Zieu.

**Kim Dong Publishing House:** 64 Ba Trieu, Hanoi; tel. (4) 264730; f. 1957; children's; managed by the Ho Chi Minh Communist Youth Union; Dir Nguyen Thang Vu; Editor-in-Chief Bui Hong.

**Lao Dong** (Labour) **Publishing House:** c/o 65 Quan Su, POB 627, Hanoi; f. 1945; translations and political works; managed by the Viet Nam General Confederation of Labour; Dir Le Thanh Tyng; Editor-in-Chief Ma Van Khang.

**My Thuat** (Fine Arts) **Publishing House:** 44B Hamlong, Hanoi; tel. (4) 253036; f. 1987; managed by the Plastic Arts Workers' Association; Dir Truong Hanh.

**Ngoai Van** (Foreign Languages) **Publishing House:** 46 Tran Hung Dao, Hanoi; tel. (4) 62996; f. 1957; managed by the Ministry of Culture and Information; Dir Mai Ly Quang.

**Nha Xuat Ban Giao Duc** (Education) **Publishing House:** 81 Tran Hung Dao, Hanoi; tel. (4) 264632; fax 262010; f. 1957; managed by the Ministry of Education and Training; Dir Tran Tram Phuong; Editor-in-Chief Prof. Nguyen Khac Phi.

**Nha Xuat Ban Hoi Nha Van** (Writers' Association) **Publishing House:** 65 Nguyen Du, Hanoi; tel. (4) 253985; f. 1957; managed by the Vietnamese Writers' Association; Dir Nguyen Kien; Editor-in-Chief Ngo Van Phu.

**Nong Nghiep** (Agriculture) **Publishing House:** Kim Lien Residential Quarter, Hanoi; tel. (4) 263887; f. 1976; managed by the Ministry of Agriculture and Food Industry; Dir Duong Quang Dieu.

**Phu Nu** (Women) **Publishing House:** 39 Hang Chuoi, Hanoi; tel. (4) 256727; f. 1957; managed by the Vietnamese Women's Union; Dir Tran Thu Huong.

**Quan Doi Nhan Dan** (People's Army) **Publishing House:** 25 Ly Nam De, Hanoi; tel. (4) 255766; managed by the Ministry of National Defence; Dir Doan Chuong.

**San Khau** (Theatre) **Publishing House:** 51 Tran Hung Dao, Hanoi; tel. (4) 252141; f. 1986; managed by the Stage Artists' Association; Dir Xuan Trinh.

**Su That** (Truth) **Publishing House:** 24 Quang Trung, Hanoi; tel. (4) 252008; f. 1945; managed by the Communist Party of Viet Nam; Marxist-Leninist classics, politics and philosophy; Dir Hoang Tung.

**Thanh Nien** (Youth) **Publishing House:** 64 Ba Trieu, Hanoi; tel. (4) 254004; managed by the Ho Chi Minh Communist Youth Union; Dir Hoang Phong.

**The Duc The Thao** (Physical Education and Sports) **Publishing House:** 7 Trinh Hoai Duc, Hanoi; tel. (4) 256155; f. 1974; managed by the Ministry of Culture and Information; Dir Nguyen Hieu.

**Thong Ke** (Statistics) **Publishing House:** 96 Thuy Khe, Hanoi; tel. (4) 264167; f. 1980; managed by the Gen. Dept of Statistics; Dir Nguyen Dao.

**Van Hoa** (Culture) **Publishing House:** 43 Lo Duc, Hanoi; tel. (4) 253517; f. 1971; managed by the Ministry of Culture and Information; Dir Quang Huy.

**Van Hoc** (Literature) **Publishing House:** 49 Tran Hung Dao, Hanoi; tel. (4) 252100; f. 1948; managed by the Ministry of Culture and Information; Dir Lu Huy Nguyen.

**Xay Dung** (Building) **Publishing House:** 34 Hang Chuoi, Hanoi; tel. (4) 255420; f. 1976; managed by the Ministry of Construction; Dir Nguyen Luong Bich.

**Y Hoc** (Medicine) **Publishing House:** 138B Giang Vo, Hanoi; tel. (4) 243145; managed by the Ministry of Public Health; Dir Dinh Van Chi.

## Radio and Television

In 1992, according to UNESCO, there were approximately 2.9m. television receivers and 7.2m. radio receivers in use. The Ministry of Culture and Information is responsible for the management of radio and television services.

### RADIO

In 1991 there were 288 FM stations and 8,365 radio-relay stations in Viet Nam. Local radio programmes reached 70%–80% of the populated areas.

**Voice of Viet Nam:** 58 Quan Su, Hanoi; tel. (4) 255669; telex 412320; fax 261122; home service in Vietnamese; foreign service in English, Japanese, French, Khmer, Laotian, Spanish, Thai, Cantonese, Mandarin, Indonesian and Russian; Dir-Gen. and Editor-in-Chief Phan Quang.

### TELEVISION

At the end of 1994 there were 53 provincial television stations and 232 relay stations in Viet Nam.

**Viet Nam Television (VTV):** 59 Giang Vo Ave, Hanoi; tel. (4) 355933; telex 412279; fax 355332; television was introduced in South Viet Nam in 1966 and in North Viet Nam in 1970; broadcasts from Hanoi (via satellite) to the whole country and Asia region; Vietnamese, French, English; Dir-Gen. Ho Anh Dung.

## Finance

(cap. = capital; res = reserves; dep. = deposits; m. = million; brs = branches)

### BANKING

In early 1990 the Government established four independent commercial banks, and introduced legislation to permit the operation of foreign banks in Viet Nam. By 1993 there were some 30 foreign banks with representative or branch offices in Hanoi or Ho Chi Minh City. In January 1994 it was announced that private citizens were to be permitted to open current bank accounts.

#### Central Bank

**State Bank of Viet Nam:** 47–49 Ly Thai To, Hanoi; tel. (4) 252831; telex 411244; f. 1951; central bank of issue; provides a national network of banking services and supervises the operation of the state banking system; Gov. Cao Sy Kiem; Gen. Man. Nguyen Duy Gia; 532 brs and sub-brs.

#### State Banks

**Bank for Foreign Trade of Viet Nam:** 47-49 Ly Thai To, Hanoi; tel. (4) 259859; telex 411229; fax 269067; f. 1963; authorized to deal in foreign currencies and all other international banking business; cap. and res 615,792m. dông, dep. 12,257,630m. dông (Dec. 1993); Chair. and Dir.-Gen. Nguyen Van De; 17 brs.

**Savings Fund for Socialism:** 7 Le Lai, Hanoi; Dir Ngo Quat (acting); Dep. Dir Cao Van Dang.

**Viet Nam Agricultural Bank:** Hanoi; f. 1991; Gen. Dir Pham Van Thuc.

**Viet Nam Export-Import Commercial Joint-Stock Bank** (Viet Nam Export-Import Bank): 7 Le Thi Hong Gam, Ho Chi Minh City; tel. (8) 223294; telex 812690; fax (8) 296063; f. 1989; authorized to undertake banking transactions for the production and processing of export-import products and export-import operations; cap. US $12m.; Dir-Gen. Nguyen Nhut Hong; 2 brs.

**Viet Nam Industrial and Commercial Bank:** 79A Ham Nghi, 1st District, Ho Chi Minh City; tel. (8) 299248; telex 811266; fax (8) 295342; f. 1987; authorized to receive personal savings, extend loans, issue stocks and invest in export-orientated cos and jt ventures with foreigners; cap. and res 393,000m. dông, dep. 4,468,000m. dông (Dec. 1993); Gen. Man. Phan Tanh Chau; 87 brs and 74 sub-brs.

**Viet Nam Investment and Development Bank:** 10 Phan Huy Chu, Hanoi; Dir Pham Ngoc Lam.

#### Other Banks

**Australia and New Zealand Banking Group Ltd:** 14 Ly Thai To, Hanoi; tel. (4) 258190; telex 411319; fax 258188; Gen. Man. Richard Martin.

**Bangkok Bank Public Co. Ltd** (Thailand): 117 Nguyen Hue Blvd, Ben Nghe Ward, District 1, Ho Chi Minh City; tel. (8) 223416; fax (8) 223421; cap. US $15m.; Man. Suphot Wasusri.

**Bank of America** (USA): Hanoi.

**Banque Française du Commerce Extérieur (BFCE)** (France): 11 Me Linh Sq., Phuong Ben Nghe, Quan 1, Ho Chi Minh City; tel. (8) 222830; telex 811563; fax (8) 299126.

**Banque Indosuez** (France): 39 Nguyen Cong Tru, Ho Chi Minh City; tel. (8) 296061; telex 812688; fax (8) 296065; Man. Eric Maurin.

**Banque Nationale de Paris SA** (France): Ho Chi Minh City.

**Crédit Lyonnais SA** (France): 17 Ton Duc Thang, Quan 1, Ho Chi Minh City; tel. (8) 299226; telex 812742; Fax (8) 296465; f. 1993; also has br in Hanoi.

**Deutsche Bank** (Germany): Ho Chi Minh City.

**Indovina Bank Ltd:** 36 Ton That Dam, District 1, Ho Chi Minh City; tel. (8) 224995; telex 811515; fax (8) 230131; f. 1991; joint venture of the PT Bank Dagang Nasional Indonesia (BDNI) and the Viet Nam Industrial and Commercial Bank (ICBV); also has brs in Hanoi and Haiphong; cap. US $10m.

**Sinhan Bank** (Korea): Ho Chi Minh City.

**Thai Military Bank Ltd** (Thailand): 11 Ben Chuong Duong, District 1, Ho Chi Minh City; tel. (8) 222218; telex 811547; fax (8) 230045; Man. TOSSATIS RODPRASERT.

**VID Public Bank:** 194 Tran Quang Khai, Hanoi; tel. (4) 266953; telex 412241; fax (4) 266965; f. 1992; joint venture between the Viet Nam Investment and Development Bank and the Public Bank Berhad (Malaysia); investment and devt bank; cap. US $10m.; Chair. NGUYEN VAN DOAN; Gen. Man. CHAN KOK CHOY; 3 brs.

**Viet Hoa Bank** (Viet Nam-China Joint-Stock Commercial Bank): 203 Phung Hung, District 5, Ho Chi Minh City; tel. (8) 554231; fax (8) 554244; f. 1992; cap. 60,000m. dông; Chair. of Bd of Administration TRAN TUAN TAI; Gen. Dir VU NGOC NHUNG; 7 brs.

### STOCK EXCHANGE

In 1995 the Government announced plans to establish a national securities commission which would be responsible for developing the capital markets, including the establishment of a stock exchange.

### INSURANCE

In January 1994 it was announced that foreign insurance companies were to be permitted to operate in Viet Nam.

**Baoviet** (Viet Nam Insurance Co): 7 Ly Thuong Kiet, Hanoi; tel. (4) 254922; telex 411283; f. 1965; marine insurance, incl. offshore oil drilling and production; personal insurance, aviation, agriculture and fire insurance; reinsurance; Gen. Dir TRUONG MOC LAM.

## Trade and Industry

**State Committee for Co-operation and Investments** (SCCI): Hanoi; provides licences for foreign investors.

**VCCI (Vietcochamber)** (Chamber of Commerce and Industry of Viet Nam): 33 Ba Trieu, Hanoi; tel. (4) 252961; telex 411257; fax (4) 256446; f. 1963; br. offices in Ho Chi Minh City, Da Nang, Haiphong, Can Tho and Vung Tau; promotes business between foreign and Vietnamese cos; organizes exhbns and fairs in Viet Nam and abroad; provides information about Viet Nam's trade and industry; represents foreign applicants for patents and trade mark registration; issues certificates of origin and other documentation; in 1993 foreign businesses operating in Viet Nam were permitted to become assoc. mems; Pres. and Chair. DOAN DUY THANH; First Vice-Pres. DOAN NGOC BONG; Dir PHAM CHI LAN; associated organizations: Viet Nam International Arbitration Centre, Viet Nam General Average Adjustment Committee, Advisory Board.

**Viet Nam International Arbitration Centre:** 33 Ba Trieu, Hanoi; tel. (4) 266230; fax (4) 256446; adjudicates in disputes concerning international economic relations.

**Vinacontrol** (Viet Nam Superintendence and Inspection Co): 54 Tran Nhan Tong, Hanoi; tel. (4) 253840; telex 411242; fax (4) 253844; f. 1959; brs in all main Vietnamese ports; controls quality and volume of exports and imports and transit of goods, and conducts inspections of deliveries and production processes; Gen. Dir BUI HUY HUONG.

### National Foreign Trade Corporations

**Agrexport** (Viet Nam National Agricultural Produce Export-Import Corpn): 6 Trang Tien, Hanoi; tel. (4) 254234; telex 411510; fax (4) 259170; f. 1958; imports and exports agricultural produce and coffee, natural silk, insecticides and agrochemicals; Gen. Dir TONG TRAN DAO.

**Agrimex** (Viet Nam National Agricultural Products Corpn): 59 Ly Tu Trong, District 1, Ho Chi Minh City; tel. (8) 224710; telex 811230; fax (8) 291349; f. 1956; imports and exports agricultural products; Gen. Dir NGO TRI SAM.

**Airimex** (General Civil Aviation Import-Export and Forwarding Co): Gia Lam Airport, Hanoi; tel. (4) 271513; telex 411260; fax (4) 259222; f. 1989; imports and exports aircraft, spare parts and accessories for aircraft and air communications; Dir NGUYEN CHI CAN.

**Animex** (Viet Nam National Animal and Poultry Products Import-Export Corpn): 379 Minh Khai, Hanoi; tel. (4) 622339; telex 411553; fax (4) 623645; f. 1979; imports and exports live animals and animal products and other foodstuffs; Gen. Dir NGUYEN VAN KHAC.

**Artexport–Hanoi** (Viet Nam National Handicrafts and Art Articles Export-Import Corpn): 31–33 Ngo Quyen St, Hanoi; tel. (4) 252760; telex 411519; fax (4) 259275; f. 1964; deals in craft products and art articles; Gen. Dir MAI VAN NGHIEM.

**Barotex** (Viet Nam Export-Import Co.): E6 Thai Thinh, Dong Da, Hanoi; tel. (4) 536428; telex 411508; fax (4) 533036; f. 1971; specializes in art and handicrafts, ceramics, fibres, agricultural and forest products; Gen. Dir NGHIEM MINH LE.

**Centrimex** (South Central Export-Import Co): 48 Tran Phu Rd, Nha Trang City; tel. (58) 221239; telex 581503; fax (58) 221914; exports and imports goods for five provinces in the south-central region of Viet Nam; Gen. Dir LE VAN NGOC.

**Coalimex** (Viet Nam National Coal Export-Import and Material Supply Corpn): 47 Quang Trung, Hanoi; tel. (4) 255634; telex 411517; fax (4) 252350; f. 1982; exports coal, imports mining machinery and equipment; Gen. Dir (vacant).

**Cocenex** (Central Production Import-Export Corpn): 80 Hang Gai, Hanoi; tel. (4) 254535; telex 411284; fax (4) 294306; f. 1988; Dir NGUYEN DUC HOI.

**Cokyvina** (Viet Nam National Communication Technical Service Co): 18 Nguyen Du St, Hanoi; tel. (4) 57934; telex 411521; f. 1987; imports and exports telecom equipment, and provides technical advice on related subjects; Dir NGUYEN BA THUOC.

**Confectimex** (The Viet Nam Garments Manufacture and Import-Export Corpn): 2 Le Thang Tong St, Hanoi; tel. (4) 257585; telex 411549; fax (4) 257554; f. 1986; produces and exports garments; imports textiles, garment accessories, sewing machines and spare parts; Gen. Dir VU CONG TOAN.

**Constrexim** (Viet Nam National Construction Materials and Technique Export-Import Corpn): 39 Nguyen Dinh Chieu, Hanoi; tel. (4) 263448; telex 411263; fax (4) 262701; f. 1982; exports and imports building materials, equipment and machinery; undertakes construction projects in Viet Nam and abroad, and production of building materials with foreign partners; assists Vietnamese enterprises in forming joint-venture projects with foreign partners; Gen. Dir DOAN MONG HUNG.

**Cosevina** (Overseas Vietnamese Service and Export-Import Co): 102 Nguyen Hue, District 1, Ho Chi Minh City; tel. (8) 291506; telex 811255; fax (8) 291024; f. 1987; Dir DO YEN THAI.

**Culturimex** (State Enterprise for the Export and Import of Works of Art and other Cultural Commodities): 22B Hai Ba Trung, Hanoi; tel. (4) 252226; fax (4) 259224; f. 1988; exports cultural items and imports materials for the cultural industry; Dir NGUYEN MANH HAI.

**Fostecco** (Viet Nam National Co with Scientific and Technological Co-operation with Foreign Countries): 70 Tran Hung Dao, Hanoi; tel. (4) 252513; telex 411225; co-operation in scientific and technological research with other countries; Dir HAN DUC PHU.

**Genecofov** (General Co of Food of Viet Nam): 64 Ba Huyen Thanh Quan, District 3, Ho Chi Minh City; tel. (8) 293366; telex 811420; fax (8) 295428; f. 1956; import and export of food products; under the Ministry of Commerce; Dir TANG VAN HONG.

**Generalexim** (Viet Nam National General Export-Import Corpn): 46 Ngo Quyen, Hanoi; tel. (4) 264009; telex 411527; fax (4) 259894; f. 1981; export and import on behalf of production and trading organizations, also garment processing for export; Dir LUONG VAN TU.

**Generalimex** (Viet Nam National General Import-Export Corpn): 66 Pho Duc Chinh, Ho Chi Minh City; tel (8) 292990; telex 811237; fax (8) 292968; exports of agricultural products and spices, imports of machinery, vehicles, chemicals and fertilizers; Dir NGUYEN XUANG QUANG.

**Geruco** (Viet Nam General Rubber Corpn): 236 Nam Ky Khoi Nghia, District 3, Ho Chi Minh City; tel. (8) 225235; telex 812666; fax (8) 297341; manages and controls the Vietnamese rubber industry including the planting, processing and trading of natural rubber; also imports chemicals, machinery and spare parts for the industry; Dir.-Gen. TRUONG VAN CAO.

**Lipaco** (Viet Nam National Essential Oils, Aromatics and Cosmetic Complex Enterprises): 171–175 Ham Nghi, District 1, Ho Chi Minh City; tel. (8) 297336; telex 8483; fax (8) 297384; exports and imports materials used in the processing of cosmetics, pharmaceuticals and tropical farm products; Dir DUONG TAN PHUOC.

**Machinoimport** (Viet Nam National Machinery Export-Import Corpn): 8 Trang Thi, Hanoi; tel. (4) 253703; telex 411531; fax (4) 254050; f. 1956; imports and exports machinery, spare parts and tools; comprises nine cos; Gen. Dir TRAN VAN NHA.

**Marine Supply** (Marine Technical Materials Import-Export and Supplies): 276A Da Nang Rd, Haiphong; tel. (31) 246539; telex

311243; f. 1985; imports and exports technical materials for marine transportation industry; Dir LE QUOC HUNG.

**Mecanimex** (Viêt Nam National Mechanical Products Export-Import Co): 54 Hai Ba Trung, Hanoi; tel. (4) 257459; telex 412285; exports and imports mechanical products and hand tools; Gen. Dir TRAN BAO GIOC.

**Minexport** (Viet Nam National Minerals Export-Import Corpn): 35 Hai Ba Trung, Hanoi; tel. (4) 255264; telex 411515; fax (4) 253326; f. 1956; exports minerals and metals, quarry products, chemical products; imports metals, chemical products, industrial materials, fuels and oils, fertilizers; Gen. Dir VO TRONG CUONG.

**Nafobird** (Viet Nam Forest and Native Birds, Animals and Ornamental Plants Export-Import Enterprises): 64 Truong Dinh, District 3, Ho Chi Minh City; tel. (8) 290211; telex 811313; fax (8) 293735; f. 1987; exports native birds, animals and plants, and imports materials for forestry; Dir VO HA AN.

**Naforimex** (Viet Nam National Forest and Native Produce Export-Import Corpn): 19 Ba Trieu, Hanoi; tel. (4) 254034; telex 411503; fax (4) 259264; f. 1960; imports chemicals, machinery and spare parts for the forestry industry, linseed oil and essences; exports oils, forest products, gum benzoin and resin; Dir TRAN DINH THUC.

**Packexport** (Viet Nam National Packaging Technology and Import-Export Co): 31 Hang Thung, Hanoi; tel. (4) 262792; telex 411257; fax (4) 269227; f. 1976; manufactures packaging for domestic and export demand, and imports materials for the packaging industry; Gen. Dir TRINH LE KIEU.

**Petechim** (Viet Nam National Petroleum Import-Export Corpn): 194 Nam Ky Khoi Nghia, District 3, Ho Chi Minh City; tel. (8) 293633; telex 811241; fax (8) 299686; f. 1981; imports equipment and technology for oil drilling, exploration and oil production, exports crude petroleum, rice, coffee and agricultural products; Gen. Dir TRAN HUU LAC.

**Petrolimex** (Viet Nam National Petroleum Import-Export Corpn): 1 Kham Thien, Hanoi; tel. (4) 512603; telex 411241; fax (4) 519203; f. 1956; import, export and distribution of petroleum products and liquefied petroleum gas; Dir-Gen. NGUYEN MANH TIEN.

**Printimex** (Viet Nam National Printing Materials and Equipment Export-Import Corpn): 175 Nguyen Thai Hoc, Hanoi; tel. (4) 232581; telex 411230; fax (4) 259254; exports and imports printing materials; Dir PHAM VAN THIET.

**Rubexim** (Viet Nam National Rubber Export-Import Corpn): 64 Truong Dinh, District 3, Ho Chi Minh City; tel. (8) 297171; telex 811358; fax (8) 297341; f. 1984; exports rubber wood, agricultural products, rubber products, general merchandise; imports consumer goods for workers in rubber plantations; Gen. Dir DUONG KY TRUNG.

**Seaprodex** (Viet Nam National Sea Products Export-Import Corpn): 2-4-6 Dong Khoi, District 1, Ho Chi Minh City; tel. (8) 291333; telex 811280; fax (8) 294951; f. 1978; exports frozen and processed sea products; imports machinery and materials for fishing and processing; Gen. Dir NGUYEN HONG CAN.

**Hanoi Sea Products Export-Import Co:** 42 Lang Ha, Hanoi; tel. (4) 253511; telex 411529; fax (4) 254125.

**Technimex** (Viet Nam Technology Export-Import Corpn): 70 Tran Hung Dao, Hanoi; tel. (4) 256751; telex 412287; fax (4) 265209; f. 1982; exports and imports technology; Dir NGUYEN TRAM.

**Technoimport** (Viet Nam National Complete Equipment Import and Technical Import-Export Corpn): 16–18 Trang Thi, Hanoi; tel. (4) 54974; telex 411230; fax (4) 54059; f. 1959; imports industrial plants and secures technical service of foreign specialists; Gen. Dir TRAN TRI KINH.

**Terraprodex** (Corpn for Processing and Export-Import of Rare Earth and Other Specialities): 35 Dien Bien Phu St, Hanoi; tel. (4) 232010; telex 411257; fax (4) 256446; f. 1989; processing and export of rare earth products and other minerals; Dir TRAN DUC HIEP.

**Textimex** (Viet Nam National Textiles Export-Import Corpn): 25 Ba Trieu, Hanoi; tel. (4) 262269; telex 411507; fax (4) 262268; f. 1978; imports textile machinery and materials, spare parts; exports textile products, garments, jute fibres, woollen carpets; Gen. Dir NGUYEN HUU HUAN.

**Tocontap** (Viet Nam National Sundries Export-Import Corpn): 36 Ba Trieu, Hanoi; tel. (4) 254191; telex 411258; fax (4) 255917; f. 1956; imports and exports miscellaneous consumer goods; Gen. Dir NGUYEN TRINH KHAC.

**Ho Chi Minh Sundries Import-Export Co:** 18 Nguyen Hue, Ho Chi Minh City; tel. (8) 299513; telex 811293; fax (8) 290508; Gen. Dir BUI THI PHUONG.

**Vegetexco** (Viet Nam National Vegetables and Fruit Export-Import Corpn): 2 Trung Tu, Dong Da, Hanoi; tel. and fax (4) 523396; telex 411512; f. 1971; exports fresh and processed vegetables and fruit, spices and flowers, and other agricultural products; imports vegetable seeds and processing materials; Gen. Dir LE NGOC SAU.

**Vegoilimex** (Viet Nam National Union of Vegetable Oils Manufacturers): 58 Nguyen Binh Khiem, District 1, Ho Chi Minh City; tel. (8) 223016; telex 811389; fax (8) 290586; f. 1987; exports vegetable oils and imports essential materials for processing oils; Gen. Dir TRAN VAN.

**Viet Nam National Petroleum Corpn** (PETROVIETNAM): 80 Nguyen Du, Hanoi; tel. (4) 223016; fax (4) 265942; f. 1991; exploration and production of petroleum and gas; Pres. HO SI THOANG; Gen. Dir TRUONG THIEN.

**Vietrans** (Viet Nam National Foreign Trade Forwarding and Warehousing Corpn): 13 Ly Nam Dê, Hanoi; tel. (4) 257801; telex 411505; fax (4) 255829; f. 1970; agent for forwarding and transport of exports and imports, diplomatic cargoes and other goods, warehousing, shipping and insurance; Gen. Dir PHAM TRONG HOAI.

**Vietranscimex** (Viet Nam National Transport and Communication Export-Import Corpn): 22 Nguyen Van Troi, Phu Nhuan District, Ho Chi Minh City; tel. (8) 442993; telex 811210; fax (8) 445240; exports and imports specialized equipment and materials for transportation and communications.

**Viettronimex** (Viet Nam Electronics Import-Export Corpn): 74–76 Nguyen Hue, Ho Chi Minh City; tel. (8) 294873; telex 811252; fax (8) 294873; f. 1981; imports and exports electronic goods; Gen. Dir NGUYEN NGOC NGOAN.

**Vigecam** (Viet Nam General Corpn of Agricultural Materials): 16, St 226, Hanoi; tel. (4) 252360; telex 411534; exports and imports agricultural products; Dir HUYNH KY.

**Vimedimex** (Viet Nam Medical Products Export-Import Corpn): 246 Cong Quynh, Ho Chi Minh City; tel. (8) 398441; telex 811287; fax (8) 325953; f. 1984; exports and imports medicinal and pharmaceutical materials and products, medical instruments; Gen. Dir NGUYEN VAN EN.

**Vinacafe** (Viet Nam National Coffee Export-Import Corpn): 5 Ong Ich Khiem, Hanoi; tel. (4) 252818; telex 412288; fax (4) 256422; f. 1987; exports coffee, and imports equipment and chemicals for coffee production; Gen. Dir DOAN TRIEU NHAN.

**Vinachimex** (Viet Nam Chemicals Export-Import Corpn): 4 Pham Ngu Lao, Hanoi; tel. (4) 256377; fax (4) 257727; f. 1969; exports and imports chemical products, minerals, rubber, fertilizers, machinery and spare parts; Dir NGUYEN VAN SON.

**Vinacimex** (Viet Nam National Union of Cement Factories): 108 Le Duan, Hanoi; tel. (4) 263748; telex 411564; fax (4) 263748; f. 1980; manufactures and exports cement, clinker and asbestos sheets; Gen. Dir NGUYEN VAN THIEN.

**Vinafim** (Viet Nam Film Import, Export and Film Service Corpn): 73 Nguyen Trai, Dong Da, Hanoi; tel. (4) 244566; f. 1987; export and import of films and video tapes; film distribution; organization of film shows and participation of Vietnamese films in international film festivals; Gen. Man. NGÔ MANH LAN.

**Vinafood Hanoi** (Hanoi Food Export-Import Corpn): 4 Ngo Quyen, Hanoi; tel. (4) 256771; telex 411526; fax (4) 258528; f. 1988; exports rice, maize, tapioca, imports fertilizers, insecticides, wheat and wheat flour; Dir NGUYEN DUC HY.

**Vinalimex** (Viet Nam National Foodstuffs Import-Export Corpn): 58 Ly Thai To, Hanoi; tel. (4) 255768; telex 411533; fax (4) 255476; f. 1984; exports cashews, rice, tea, peanuts, confectionery, coffee, salt, sesame and other foodstuffs, spirits, and jute; imports urea, sugar, hops, malt, fertilizer, milk powder and butter oil; Gen. Dir NGUYEN VAN THACH; Deputy Gen. Dirs VU THI BICH LOC, TRUONG GIA THE.

**Vinatea** (Viet Nam National Tea Import-Export and Development Investment Co): 52 Tang Bat Ho, Hanoi; tel. (4) 211699; telex (4) 411559; fax 252756; exports tea, imports tea-processing materials.

**Xunhasaba** (Viet Nam State Corpn for Export and Import of Books, Periodicals and other Cultural Commodities): 32 Hai Ba Trung St, Hanoi; tel. (4) 262989; fax (4) 252860; f. 1957; exports and imports books, periodicals, postage stamps, greetings cards, calendars and paintings; Dir TRAN PHU SON.

## CO-OPERATIVE ORGANIZATIONS

**Central Union of Small Industry and Handicraft Co-operatives:** Hanoi; Pres. TRAN LUU VI.

**Viet Nam Co-operatives Alliance:** Hanoi; f. 1993 (fmrly Viet Nam Co-operatives Council); Chair. HOANG MINH THANG.

## TRADE UNIONS

**Tong Lien Doan Lao Dong Viet Nam** (Viet Nam General Confederation of Labour): 65 Quan Su, POB 627, Hanoi; f. 1946; merged in 1976 with the South Viet Nam Trade Union Fed. for Liberation;

# VIET NAM

3,800,000 mems; Pres. Nguyen Van Tu; Vice-Pres Cu Thi Hau, Hoang Minh Chuc, Nguyen An Luong, Hoang Thi Khanh.

**Cong Doan Nong Nghiep Cong Nghiep Thu Pham Viet Nam** (Viet Nam Agriculture and Food Industry Trade Union): Hanoi; f. 1987; 550,000 mems.

**National Union of Building Workers:** 12 Cua Dong, Hoan Kiem, Hanoi; tel. (4) 252977; f. 1957; Pres. Vu Tat Ban.

**National Union of Workers in Metallurgical and Engineering Industries:** 54 Hai Ba Trung, Hanoi; tel. (4) 260027; f. 1971; Pres. Vu Xuan Khoat.

## TRADE FAIRS

**VINEXAD** (Viet Nam National Trade Fair and Advertising Co): 9 Dinh Le, Hanoi; tel. (4) 255546; fax (4) 255556; f. 1975; organizes Viet Nam International Trade Fair (every April), and other trade exhbns in Viet Nam and abroad; Gen. Dir Le Trong.

# Transport

## RAILWAYS

**Duong Sat Viet Nam (DSVN)** (Viet Nam Railway Central Department): 118 Duong Le Duan, Hanoi; tel. (4) 258281; fax (4) 254998; controlled by the Viet Nam Gen. Dept of Railways; 2,605 track-km (1993); lines reported to be in operation are: Hanoi–Ho Chi Minh City (1,730 km), Hanoi–Haiphong (104 km), Hanoi–Dong Dang (163 km), Hanoi–Lao Cai (296 km), Hanoi–Quan Trieu (76 km); Dir-Gen. Doan Van Xe.

## ROADS

In 1993 there were an estimated 105,000 km of roads, of which about 10% were paved. In 1995 the Government announced plans to upgrade 430 km of the national highway which runs from Hanoi in the north to Ho Chi Minh City in the south.

**National Automobile Transport Undertaking:** Hanoi; f. 1951; operates municipal and long-distance bus services.

## SHIPPING

The principal port facilities are at Haiphong, Da Nang and Ho Chi Minh City. In 1991 the Vietnamese merchant fleet had a combined displacement totalling 574,000 grt. In 1994 there were 150 shipping companies with a combined capacity of 800,000 dwt.

**Cong Ty Van Tai Duong Bien Viet Nam (VOSCO)** (Viet Nam Ocean Shipping Co): 15 Cu Chinh Lan, Haiphong; tel. (31) 246942; telex 45251; controlled by the Viet Nam Gen. Dept of Marine Transport; Dir Le My; Dir-Gen. Tran Xuan Nhon.

**Dai Ly Hang Hai Viet Nam (VOSA)** (VOSA group of companies): 7 Nguyen Hue, District 1, Ho Chi Minh City; tel. (8) 297723; telex 811258; fax (8) 293626; f. 1957; formerly the Viet Nam Ocean Shipping Agency; controlled by the Viet Nam National Maritime Bureau (Vinamarine); in charge of merchant shipping; arranges ship repairs, salvage, recruitment and welfare of crews, passenger services, air and sea freight forwarding services; main br. office in Haiphong; brs in Da Nang, Hon Gay, Cam Pha, Ben Thuy, Quy Nhon, Nha Trang, Vung Tau and Can Tho; Dir-Gen. Tran Van Tien.

**Viet Nam Transport and Chartering Corpn:** 74 Nguyen Du, Hanoi; tel. (4) 256342; telex 412273; fax (4) 253679; f. 1963; ship broking, chartering, ship management, international freight forwarding; consultancy services; Gen. Dir Nguyen Van Truong.

**Viet Nam Sea Transport and Chartering Co (Vitranschart):** 428-432 Nguyen Tat Thanh, District 4, Ho Chi Minh City; tel. (8) 723271; telex 811319; fax (8) 721123; Dir Dang Quang Sanh.

## CIVIL AVIATION

Viet Nam's principal airports are Tan Son Nhat International Airport (Ho Chi Minh City) and Thu Do (Capital) International Airport at Noi Bai (Hanoi). They cater for domestic and foreign traffic. Airports at Da Nang, Hué, Nha Trang, Da Lat, Can Tho, Haiphong and Muong Thanh (near Dien Bien Phu) handle domestic traffic. In 1990 a programme to expand Tan Son Nhat, Thu Do and Da Nang airports was initiated. The Government aims to expand the capacity of Tan Son Nhat to 30m. passengers and 1m. tons of freight by 2010. By 1993 15 foreign airlines had begun regular services to Viet Nam.

**Viet Nam Airlines:** Thu Do Airport, Hanoi; tel. (4) 271643; telex 412260; fax 272291; fmrly the Gen. Civil Aviation Admin. of Viet Nam, then Hang Khong Viet Nam; operates domestic passenger services from Hanoi and from Ho Chi Minh City to the principal Vietnamese cities, and international services to 18 countries; Dir-Gen. Nguyen Hong Nhi.

**Pacific Airlines:** 27B Nguyen Din Chieu, District 1, Ho Chi Minh City; tel. (8) 450092; telex 812628; fax (8) 450085; f. 1991; operates charter cargo flights, also scheduled internal and international services; Man. Dir Duong Cao Thai Nguyen.

**Viet Air:** Hanoi; f. 1991; subsidiary of Viet Nam Airlines, established to circumvent bans on Viet Nam's national airline.

# Tourism

The Vietnamese Government is encouraging tourism as a source of much-needed foreign exchange. About 1,000,000 foreign tourists visited Viet Nam in 1994, compared with about 600,000 tourists in 1993. In 1994 revenue from tourism totalled more than US $363m.

**Viet Nam Tourism:** 30A Ly Thuong Kiet, Hanoi; tel. (4) 264154; telex 411272; fax (4) 257583; f. 1960; Gen. Dir Ngo Huy Phuong; Dep. Chair. Bui Xuan Nhat.

**Haiphong Tourist Co:** 15 Le Dai Hanh St, Haiphong; tel. (31) 42957; telex 311250; fax: (31) 426741; f. 1960; Dir Bui Chi Chanh.

**Hanoi Tourism Service Company (TOSERCO):** 8 To Hien Thanh St, Hanoi; tel. (4) 263541; telex 411535; fax (4) 2260255; f. 1988; manages the development of tourism, hotels and restaurants in the capital and other services including staff training; Dir Vo Van Dien.

**Saigon Tourist:** 39 Le Thanh Ton, Ho Chi Minh City; tel. (8) 225887; telex 812745; fax (8) 291026; f. 1975; tour operator; Man. Dir Duong Van Day.

**Unitour** (Union of Haiphong Tourist Co): 40 Tran Quang Khai, Haiphong; tel. (31) 247295; telex 45214.

# WESTERN SAMOA

## Introductory Survey

**Location, Climate, Language, Religion, Flag, Capital**

The Independent State of Western Samoa lies in the southern Pacific Ocean, about 2,400 km (1,500 miles) north of New Zealand. Its nearest neighbour is American Samoa, to the east. The country comprises two large and seven small islands, of which five are uninhabited. The climate is tropical, with temperatures generally between 23°C (73°F) and 30°C (86°F). The rainy season is from November to April. The languages spoken are Samoan (a Polynesian language) and English. Almost all of the inhabitants profess Christianity, and the major denominations are the Congregational, Roman Catholic and Methodist Churches. The national flag (proportions 2 by 1) is red, with a rectangular dark blue canton, containing five differently-sized white five-pointed stars in the form of the Southern Cross constellation, in the upper hoist. The capital is Apia.

**Recent History**

The islands became a German protectorate in 1899. During the First World War (1914–18) they were occupied by New Zealand forces, who overthrew the German administration. In 1919 New Zealand was granted a League of Nations mandate to govern the islands. In 1946 Western Samoa was made a UN Trust Territory, with New Zealand continuing as the administering power. From 1954 measures of internal self-government were gradually introduced, culminating in the adoption of an independence Constitution in October 1960. This was approved by a UN-supervised plebiscite in May 1961, and the islands became independent on 1 January 1962. The office of Head of State was held jointly by two traditional rulers but, upon the death of his colleague in April 1963, Malietoa Tanumafili II became sole Head of State for life, performing the duties of a constitutional monarch.

Fiame Mata'afa Mulinu'u, Prime Minister since 1959, lost the general election in 1970, and a new Cabinet, led by Tupua Tamasese Lealofi, was formed. Mata'afa regained power in 1973, following another general election, and remained in office until his death in May 1975. He was again succeeded by Tamasese, who, in turn, lost the general election in March 1976 to his cousin Tupuola Taisi Efi. The previously unorganized opposition members formed the Human Rights Protection Party (HRPP) in 1979, and won the elections in February 1982, with 24 of the 47 seats in the Fono (Legislative Assembly). Va'ai Kolone was appointed Prime Minister, but in September he was removed from office as a result of past electoral malpractice. His successor, Tupuola Efi, with much popular support, sought to nullify an earlier agreement between Kolone and the New Zealand Government which, in defiance of a ruling by the British Privy Council, denied automatic New Zealand citizenship to all Western Samoans except those already living in New Zealand. However, Tupuola Efi resigned in December 1982, after the Fono had rejected his budget, and was replaced by the new HRPP leader, Tofilau Eti Alesana. At elections in February 1985 the HRPP won 31 of the 47 seats, increasing its majority in the Fono from one to 15 seats; the newly-formed Christian Democratic Party (CDP), led by Tupuola Efi, obtained the remaining 16 seats. In December Tofilau Eti resigned, following the rejection of the proposed budget by the Fono and the Head of State's refusal to call another general election. Va'ai Kolone, with the support of a number of CDP members and HRPP defectors, was appointed Prime Minister of a coalition Government in January 1986.

At the February 1988 general election the HRPP and an alliance composed of independents and the CDP (later known as the Samoa National Development Party—SNDP) both initially gained 23 seats, with votes in the remaining constituency being tied. After two recounts proved inconclusive, a judge from New Zealand presided over a third and declared the CDP candidate the winner. However, before a new government could be formed, a newly-elected member of the Legislative Assembly defected from the SNDP alliance to the HRPP. In April Tofilau Eti was re-elected Prime Minister, and a new Government, composed of HRPP members, was appointed.

In January 1990 proposed legislation permitting local village councils to fine or to impose forced labour or exile on individuals accused of offending communal rules was condemned by Tupuola Efi as unconstitutional. The legislation was widely perceived as an attempt by the Government to ensure the support of the Matai (elected clan chiefs) at the next general election. Of the 47 seats in the Fono, 45 were traditionally elected by holders of Matai titles. However, the political importance of the Matai had been increasingly diminished by the procurement of Matai titles by people seeking to be elected to the Fono. This practice was believed to have undermined the system of chief leadership to such an extent that universal suffrage would have to be introduced to decide all of the seats in the Fono. A referendum was conducted in October 1990, at which voters narrowly accepted government proposals for the introduction of universal suffrage. A second proposal, to create an upper legislative chamber composed of the Matai, was rejected. A bill to implement universal adult suffrage (in accordance with the result of the referendum), which was supported by the Head of State, was approved by the Fono in December 1990, despite strong opposition from the SNDP.

A general election was held on 5 April 1991 (the election had been postponed from February, owing to the need to register an estimated 80,000 newly-enfranchised voters). Preliminary results indicated that the HRPP had won 26 seats, while the SNDP had secured 18 seats and independent candidates had taken the remaining three seats. By early May petitions had been filed with the Supreme Court against 11 newly-elected members of the Fono who were accused of corrupt or illegal electoral practices. In the weeks of political manoeuvring that followed the election (as provided for in the Constitution), the HRPP increased its parliamentary representation to 30 seats, while the SNDP ultimately secured only 16 seats in the Fono, and the remaining seat was retained by an independent. At the first meeting of the new Fono, convened in early May, Tofilau Eti was re-elected for what, he later announced, would be his final term of office as Prime Minister.

In November 1991 the Fono approved legislation to increase the parliamentary term from three to five years and to create an additional two seats in the Fono. These seats were contested in early 1992 and won by the HRPP.

In December 1991 the islands were struck by a devastating cyclone (Cyclone Val), which caused 12 deaths, destroyed many crops and buildings, killed large numbers of livestock and caused damage estimated at 662m. tala. This was the second major cyclone to hit Western Samoa in two years, the first being Cyclone Ofa in February 1990, which left an estimated 10,000 islanders homeless. The dramatic increase in the incidence of cyclones occurring in the region was widely attributed to climatic change caused by the 'greenhouse effect' (the heating of the earth's atmosphere).

In March 1993 the independent Fono member, Sir Tagiloa Peter, formed the Samoa Democratic Party (SDP) to contest a forthcoming by-election, and announced that he would resign upon completion of the Government's term in office, in protest at the extension of the parliamentary term.

In June 1993, during the presentation of the 1993/94 budget, the Prime Minister confirmed that three HRPP members of the Fono had been expelled from the party for recommending a reduction in budgetary expenditure, and for signing a paper that advocated a change of government. Tofilau Eti accused Tuiatua Tupua Tamasese, the leader of the opposition, of fomenting disunity within the HRPP, as reports of further defections to the opposition increased the instability of the Prime Minister's position.

The introduction of a value-added tax on goods and services in January 1994 (which greatly increased the price of food and fuel in the country) provoked a series of demonstrations and protest rallies, as well as demands for the resignation of the Prime Minister. As a result of overwhelming opposition to the new regulations, the Government agreed, in March, to amend the most controversial aspects of the tax. Meanwhile, four members of the Fono (including three recently-expelled HRPP members), who had opposed the financial reforms, established a new political organization, the Samoa Liberal Party, under the leadership of the former Speaker, Nonumalo Leulumoega Sofara.

In May 1994 treasury officials warned the Government that a financial crisis at the national air carrier, Polynesian Airlines, was threatening Western Samoa's economic stability. It was estimated that the company's debts totalled more than 45m. tala, much of which consisted of unrepaid loans, secured by government guarantees. Furthermore, in July a report by the Chief Auditor, Tom Overhoff, accused the Government of serious financial mismanagement relating to a series of decisions to commit public funds to the airline, and charged seven cabinet ministers with fraud and negligence in their handling of government resources. As a result, a commission of inquiry was appointed to investigate the allegations in late 1994, amid speculation that the Prime Minister would resign unless all the charges were disproved. The commission subsequently produced a report, which was approved by the Fono in December, clearing the ministers in question of all the charges. The findings were, however, harshly criticized by Overhoff, who claimed that the commission had been neither independent nor impartial.

Meanwhile, in November 1994 the Supreme Court ruled that a case, filed in 1991 by six Matai, against the introduction of universal suffrage may proceed. The suit was based on the claim that electoral changes were not approved by all the Matai and, as such, were unconstitutional..

Protests against the value-added tax on goods and services continued in early 1995, following the Government's decision to charge two prominent members of the Tumua ma Pule group of traditional leaders and former members of the Fono, Toalepaiali Toesulusulu Siueva and Fa'amatuainu Tala Mailei, with sedition, for organizing demonstrations against the tax during 1994. In March 1995 3,000 people delivered a petition to the Prime Minister, bearing the signatures of 120,000 people (some 75% of the population), that demanded that the tax be revoked.

Western Samoa's close ties with New Zealand were strained in April 1989 by a dispute over immigration, when the New Zealand Government announced that it was considering abolishing the special immigration quotas for Western Samoans. In July, however, the New Zealand Government agreed to maintain the quota and accepted a Western Samoan offer to send two immigration officials to New Zealand, who would attempt to resolve the problem of Western Samoans who had overstayed the duration of their working permits.

The country established diplomatic relations with South Africa in April 1995.

## Government

The Constitution provides for the Head of State to be elected by the Legislative Assembly for a term of five years. The present Head of State, however, holds the office for life. The Legislative Assembly is composed of 49 members, all of whom are elected by universal suffrage. A total of 47 members are elected from among holders of Matai titles (elected clan chiefs), and two are selected from non-Samoan candidates. Members hold office for five years. Executive power is held by the Cabinet, comprising the Prime Minister and eight other members of the Assembly. The Prime Minister is appointed by the Head of State with the necessary approval of the Assembly.

## Defence

In August 1962 Western Samoa and New Zealand signed a Treaty of Friendship, whereby the New Zealand Government, on request, acts as the sole agent of the Western Samoan Government in its dealings with other countries and international organizations.

## Economic Affairs

In 1993, according to estimates by the World Bank, Western Samoa's gross national product (GNP), measured at average 1991–93 prices, was US $159m., equivalent to US $980 per head. During 1985–93, it was estimated, GNP per head decreased, in real terms, by an annual average of 0.1%. During the same period the population increased by an annual average of 0.5%. Gross domestic product (GDP) declined, in real terms, by 4.5% in 1990, by 1.5% in 1991 and by 5.0% in the following year, owing largely to major cyclones, which struck the islands each year.

Agriculture (including hunting, forestry and fishing) accounted for 40% of GDP in 1992. The sector is mainly of a subsistence nature, but also provides about 90% of total export earnings. The principal cash crops are cocoa (which accounted for more than 16% of export earnings in 1983, but only 2.4% in 1990), coconuts (from which copra is produced), taro, taamu and bananas. Breadfruit, yams, maize, passion fruit and mangoes are also cultivated as food crops. Pigs, cattle, poultry and goats are raised, mainly for local consumption. A small quantity of timber is exported. Foodstuffs accounted for 25% of the total cost of imports in 1983.

Industry (including manufacturing, mining, construction and power) employed 5.5% of the labour force in 1986. Between 1980 and 1985 industrial GDP increased, in real terms, at an average annual rate of 0.2%.

Manufacturing (including mining) employed 3.5% of the labour force in 1986, and is confined to the small-scale production of coconut-based products, foods, garments, construction materials, light engineering and leather goods. The sector was expanded considerably in 1992 with the opening, by a US company, of a garment factory and, by a Japanese company, of a wire factory (the latter accounted for some 80% of total export earnings in that year). The resumption of coconut oil production in late 1994, following several years of inactivity (owing to cyclone damage to plantations), was expected to contribute significantly to export earnings in the following year. In February 1995 a Japanese company opened a factory manufacturing motor-car parts, which was to provide some 500 jobs.

Energy is derived principally from hydroelectric power and thermal power stations. Imports of mineral fuels comprised more than 25% of the value of total imports in 1983.

Tourism makes a significant contribution to the economy, and tourist receipts totalled 33m. tala in 1987. 'Offshore' banking was introduced to the islands in 1989, and by July of that year more than 30 companies had registered in Apia. A large proportion of the islands' revenue is provided by remittances from nationals working abroad (which totalled US $39.4m. in 1991) and by aid from New Zealand.

In 1993 Western Samoa recorded a visible trade deficit of US $80.94m., and a deficit of US $38.68m. on the current account of the balance of payments. New Zealand is Western Samoa's principal trading partner, accounting for 38.6% of total trade (imports plus exports) in 1991. Other important trading partners are Australia, Fiji, Japan, the USA and the United Kingdom. The principal exports (including re-exports) are food, timber and beverages, and the main imports are food and live animals, machinery and transport equipment, fuel, and other manufactured goods.

In 1989 there was an estimated budgetary deficit of 24.4m. tala. In 1992, however, there was a projected surplus of 60.6m. tala on the recurrent budget. At the end of 1993 Western Samoa's total external debt was US $192.6m., of which US $139.2m. was long-term public debt. The total cost of debt-servicing in 1992 was equivalent to 5.3% of revenue from exports of goods and services. In 1985–93 the annual rate of inflation averaged 6.1%. Consumer prices increased by 1.8% in 1993, but the inflation rate increased to 17.4% in 1994.

Western Samoa is a member of the South Pacific Forum (see p. 217) and the South Pacific Commission (see p. 215).

According to UN criteria, Western Samoa is one of the world's least developed nations. Economic development has been adversely affected by inclement weather, limited agricultural exports and inadequate transport facilities. At the same time, Western Samoa has been vulnerable to fluctuations in international prices for copra and cocoa. Two cyclones in early 1990 and late 1991 devastated not only the islands' infrastructure, but also their main export crop, taro. In addition, the resulting decrease in coconut production had a ruinous effect on the copra industry and forced two of the three plants processing coconut products (which accounted for 27% of export revenue in 1990) to cease operating in early 1992. The industry resumed operations in early 1995. A severe outbreak of leaf blight in mid-1993 devastated the taro crop, and had a serious impact both on the islands' food supply and on its export performance. Western Samoa receives aid from various sources, Japan being the most important donor. In 1992 the Government launched a programme to encourage

# WESTERN SAMOA

external investment in the islands, particularly in export-orientated manufacturing and tourism. A controversial new value-added tax on goods and services was introduced in January 1994.

### Social Welfare
In 1981 Western Samoa had 16 hospital establishments. In 1989 there was a total of 644 hospital beds and 40 physicians. Budgetary expenditure on health services by the central Government in 1987 was about 7.1m. tala. In 1990 the Government announced plans to introduce an old-age pension scheme for those aged 65 and over.

### Education
The education system is based on that of New Zealand. About 97% of the adult population are literate in Samoan. In 1988 a national university was established, with an initial intake of 328 students. In 1992 the Government decided to reintroduce bonds for students awarded government scholarships for overseas study. Budgetary expenditure on education by the central Government in 1990 was 15m. tala (10.7% of total government expenditure).

### Public Holidays
**1995:** 1 January (Independence Day), 2 January (for New Year), 14–17 April (Easter), 25 April (Anzac Day), 5 June (Whit Monday), 1–3 June (Independence Celebrations), 23 November (National Women's Day), 25 December (Christmas Day), 26 December (Boxing Day).

**1996:** 1 January (Independence Day), 2 January (for New Year), 5–8 April (Easter), 25 April (Anzac Day), 27 May (Whit Monday), 1–3 June (Independence Celebrations), 21 November (National Women's Day), 25 December (Christmas Day), 26 December (Boxing Day).

# Statistical Survey

Source (unless otherwise indicated): Western Samoa Department of Statistics, POB 1151, Apia; tel. 21371.

## AREA AND POPULATION

**Area:** Savai'i and adjacent small islands 1,708 sq km, Upolu and adjacent small islands 1,123 sq km; Total 2,831 sq km (1,093 sq miles).

**Population:** Savai'i 44,930, Upolu and adjacent small islands 112,228, Total 157,158 (males 83,247; females 73,911) at census of 3 November 1986; Savai'i 45,050, Upolu and adjacent small islands 116,248, Total 161,298 at census of 3 November 1991; 163,000 (official estimate) at mid-1993.

**Density** (1993): 57.6 per sq km.

**Principal Town:** Apia (capital), population 34,126 at census of 3 November 1991.

**Births and Deaths** (sample survey, 1982–83): Birth rate 31.0 per 1,000; Death rate 7.4 per 1,000.

**Expectation of Life** (years at birth, 1992): Males 63.8; Females 70.0. Source: UN, *Statistical Yearbook for Asia and the Pacific*.

**Economically Active Population** (census of 3 November 1986): Agriculture, hunting, forestry and fishing 29,023; Manufacturing and mining 1,587; Electricity, gas and water 855; Construction 62; Trade, restaurants and hotels 1,710; Transport, storage and communications 1,491; Financing, insurance, real estate and business services 842; Community, social and personal services 9,436; Activities not adequately defined 629; Total labour force 45,635 (males 37,054; females 8,581).

## AGRICULTURE, ETC.

**Principal Crops** (FAO estimates, '000 metric tons, 1993): Taro 37; Yams 1; Other roots and tubers 3; Coconuts 130; Copra 11*; Bananas 10; Cocoa beans 1* (1991). Source: FAO, *Production Yearbook*.

* Unofficial estimate.

**Livestock** (FAO estimates, '000 head, year ending September 1993): Pigs 178,000; Cattle 25,000; Horses 3,000; Chickens 1,000 (1992). Source: FAO, *Production Yearbook*.

**Livestock Products** (FAO estimates, '000 metric tons, 1993): Beef and veal 1; Pigmeat 4. Source: FAO, *Production Yearbook*.

**Forestry** (roundwood removals, '000 cubic metres): 116 in 1977; 123 in 1978; 131 in 1979. 1980–92: Annual production as in 1979 (FAO estimates). Source: FAO, *Yearbook of Forest Products*.

**Fishing** (metric tons, live weight): Total catch 595 in 1990; 565 in 1991; 1,298 in 1992. Source: FAO, *Yearbook of Fishery Statistics*.

## FINANCE

**Currency and Exchange Rates:** 100 sene (cents) = 1 tala (Western Samoan dollar or WS$). *Sterling and US Dollar Equivalents* (31 December 1994): £1 sterling = 3.835 tala; US $1 = 2.452 tala; 100 tala = £26.07 = US $40.79. *Average Exchange Rate* (US $ per tala): 0.4056 in 1992; 0.3894 in 1993; 0.3945 in 1994.

**Budget** (estimates, million tala, 1992): Total expenditure 238.8 (Recurrent expenditure 102.7); Recurrent revenue 163.3.

**International Reserves** (US $ million at 31 December 1994): IMF special drawing rights 2.91; Reserve position in IMF 0.97; Foreign exchange 46.92; Total 50.80. Source: IMF, *International Financial Statistics*.

**Money Supply** (million tala at 31 December 1994): Currency outside banks 16.82; Demand deposits at banks 30.38; Total money 47.20. Source: IMF, *International Financial Statistics*.

**Cost of Living** (Consumer Price Index, excluding rent; base: 1990 = 100): 107.0 in 1992; 108.9 in 1993; 128.9 in 1994. Source: IMF, *International Financial Statistics*.

**Gross Domestic Product by Economic Activity** (million tala in current prices, 1986): Agriculture, hunting, forestry and fishing (incl. mining and quarrying) 85.5; Manufacturing 32.2; Electricity, gas and water 5.8; Construction 5.8; Trade, restaurants and hotels 46.8; Transport, storage and communications 14.2; Finance, insurance, real estate and business services 22.5; Community, social and personal services 29.6; Total 242.6. Source: UN, *Statistical Yearbook for Asia and the Pacific*.

**Balance of Payments** (US $ million, 1993): Merchandise exports f.o.b. 6.43; Merchandise imports f.o.b. −87.37; *Trade balance* −80.94; Exports of services 35.61; Imports of services −38.22; Other income received 4.50; Other income paid −4.42; Private unrequited transfers (net) 28.38; *Current balance* −38.68; Other capital (net) 15.55; Net errors and omissions 13.82; *Overall balance* −9.31. Source: IMF, *International Financial Statistics*.

## EXTERNAL TRADE

**Principal Commodities** (provisional, distribution by SITC, '000 tala, 1983): *Imports c.i.f.*: Meat and meat preparations 3,304; Cereals and cereal preparations 4,238; Fish and fish preparations 1,525; Sugar, sugar preparations and honey 2,561; Beverages 415; Tobacco and tobacco manufactures 1,498; Petroleum and petroleum products 13,074; Rubber manufactures 1,307; Paper, paperboard and manufactures 2,685; Textile yarn, fabrics and manufactured articles 1,611; Iron and steel 1,667; Machinery 8,276; Transport equipment 6,692; Miscellaneous manufactured articles 5,279; Total (incl. others) 54,132. *Exports f.o.b.* (incl. re-exports): Copra 1,397.5; Cocoa 4,616.8; Bananas 407.0; Taro and taamu 2,371.3; Timber 540.6; Other food and beverages 15,589.5; Other non-food 2,487.3; Total 27,410.0.

**1989** ('000 tala): *Imports c.i.f.* 171,220; *Exports* Coconut oil 7,000, Cocoa beans 2,143; Total (incl. re-exports) 29,206.

**1990** ('000 tala): *Imports c.i.f.* 186,120; *Exports* Coconut oil 4,168, Cocoa beans 502; Total (incl. re-exports) 20,494.

**1991** ('000 tala): *Imports c.i.f.* 225,337; *Exports* (incl. re-exports) 15,515.

**1992** ('000 tala): *Imports c.i.f.* 271,325; *Exports* (incl. re-exports) 14,349.

**1993** ('000 tala): *Imports c.i.f.* 269,079; *Exports* (incl. re-exports) 16,522.

**1994** ('000 tala): *Imports c.i.f.* 206,347; *Exports* (incl. re-exports) 9,121. Source: IMF, *International Financial Statistics*.

**Principal Trading Partners** (provisional, US $ million, 1991): *Imports*: Australia 19.8; Fiji 6.4; Japan 9.4; New Zealand 37.8; USA 10.3; Western Europe 6.5; Total (incl. others) 99.0. *Exports*: Australia 2.1; New Zealand 3.4; USA 0.6; Total (incl. others) 7.6. Source: UN, *Statistical Yearbook for Asia and the Pacific*.

# WESTERN SAMOA

## TRANSPORT

**Road Traffic** (motor vehicles in use, 1990): Private cars 2,295; Commercial vehicles 3,252. Source: UN, *Statistical Yearbook for Asia and the Pacific.*

**International Shipping** (freight traffic, '000 metric tons, 1990): Goods loaded 28; Goods unloaded 68. Source: UN, *Monthly Bulletin of Statistics.*

## TOURISM

**Visitor Arrivals:** 49,891 in 1990; 39,414 in 1991.
**Revenue** (million tala): 20.1 in 1986; 33.0 in 1987.

## COMMUNICATIONS MEDIA

**Telephones** (1992): 2,700 in use.
**Radio Receivers** (1992): 76,000 in use.*
**Television Receivers** (1992): 6,000 in use.*
**Non-Daily Newspapers** (1988): 5 (estimated circulation 23,000).*

* Source: UNESCO, *Statistical Yearbook.*

## EDUCATION

**Primary** (1989): 1,511 teachers (incl. teachers in intermediate education); 37,833 pupils.
**Intermediate** (1983): 8,643 pupils.
**General Secondary** (1986): 513 teachers; 20,168 pupils.
**Vocational** (1986): 19 teachers; 156 pupils.
**Teacher Training** (1986): 34 teachers; 280 pupils.
**Tertiary** (1983): 37 teachers; 562 students.

Source: UNESCO, *Statistical Yearbook.*

# Directory

## The Constitution

A new Constitution was adopted by a constitutional convention on 28 October 1960. After being approved by a UN-supervised plebiscite in May 1961, the Constitution came into force on 1 January 1962, when Western Samoa became independent. Its main provisions are summarized below:

### HEAD OF STATE

The office of Head of State is held (since 5 April 1963, when his co-ruler died) by HH Malietoa Tanumafili II, who will hold this post for life. After that the Head of State will be elected by the Fono (Legislative Assembly) for a term of five years.

### EXECUTIVE

Executive power lies with the Cabinet, consisting of the Prime Minister, supported by the majority in the Fono, and eight ministers selected by the Prime Minister. Cabinet decisions are subject to review by the Executive Council, which is made up of the Head of State and the Cabinet.

### LEGISLATURE

The Fono consists of 49 members. It has a five-year term and the Speaker is elected from among the members. Beginning at the election of 5 April 1991, members are elected by universal adult suffrage: 47 members of the Assembly are elected from among the Matai (elected clan leaders) while the remaining two are selected from non-Samoan candidates.

## The Government

### HEAD OF STATE

**O le Ao o le Malo:** HH MALIETOA TANUMAFILI II (took office as joint Head of State 1 January 1962; became sole Head of State 5 April 1963).

### CABINET
(June 1995)

**Prime Minister and Minister of Foreign Affairs, Broadcasting, Police and Prisons:** TOFILAU ETI ALESANA.
**Deputy Prime Minister and Minister of Finance:** TUILAEPA SAILELE MALIELEGAOI.
**Minister of Agriculture, Forestry and Fisheries:** MISA TELEFONI.
**Minister of Justice:** FUIMAONO LOTOMAU.
**Minister of Health:** SALA VAIMILI.
**Minister of Education, Youth, Sport, Culture and Labour:** FIAME NAOMI.
**Minister of Transport and Civil Aviation:** JACK NETZLER.
**Minister of Post Office, Telecommunications and Women's Affairs:** TOI AUKUSO.
**Minister of Public Works:** LEAFA VITALE.
**Minister of Lands, Survey and Environment:** FAASOOTAULOA PATI.

### MINISTRIES AND MINISTERIAL DEPARTMENTS

**Prime Minister's Department:** POB L 1861, Apia; tel. 21500; telex 221; fax 21504.
**Agriculture Department:** POB 206, Apia; tel. 22561.
**Broadcasting Department:** POB 200, Apia; tel. 21420.
**Customs Department:** POB 44, Apia; tel. 21561.
**Economic Affairs Department:** POB 862, Apia; tel. 20471.
**Education Department:** POB 1869, Apia; tel. 21911; fax 21917.
**Ministry of Foreign Affairs:** POB L 1861, Apia; tel. 22200; telex 221; fax 21504.
**Health Department:** Private Bag, Apia; tel. 21212; telex 277.
**Inland Revenue Department:** POB 209, Apia; tel. 20411.
**Justice Department:** POB 49, Apia; tel. 22671; fax 21050.
**Lands, Survey and Environment Department:** Private Bag, Apia; tel. 22481; fax 23176.
**Post and Telecommunications Department:** Apia; tel. 23456; telex 998; fax 24000.
**Public Works Department:** Private Bag, Apia; tel. 21611; telex 256; fax 21927.
**Trade, Industry and Commerce Department:** POB 862, Apia; tel. 20471; fax 21646.
**Ministry of Transport:** POB 1607, Apia; tel. 23700; fax 21990.
**Treasury Department:** Private Bag, Apia; tel. 22822; telex 233; fax 21312.
**Ministry of Youth, Sport and Culture:** Apia; tel. 23315.

## Legislature

### FONO
(Legislative Assembly)

The Assembly has 47 Matai members, representing 41 territorial constituencies, and two individual members. Elections are held every five years. At a general election in April 1991, the Human Rights Protection Party (HRPP) won 30 of the 47 seats, and the Samoa National Development Party (SNDP) won 16 seats. An independent candidate secured the remaining seat. Elections for two newly-created seats in the Fono were won by the HRPP in early 1992.

**Speaker:** AFAMASAGA FATU VAILI.

## Political Organizations

**Human Rights Protection Party (HRPP):** POB 3898, Apia; f. 1979; Western Samoa's first formal political party; Leader TOFILAU ETI ALESANA; Gen. Sec. LAULU DAN STANLEY.

**Samoa Democratic Party (SDP):** Apia; f. 1993; Leader Sir TAGILOA PETER.

**Samoa Liberal Party:** Apia; f. 1994; Leader NONUMALO LEULUMOEGA SOFARA.

**Samoa National Development Party (SNDP):** Apia; f. 1988 following general election; coalition party comprising the Christian Democratic Party (CDP) and several independents; Leaders TUIATUA TUPUA TAMASESE, TUPUOLA TAISI EFI, VA'AI KOLONE.

WESTERN SAMOA
*Directory*

## Diplomatic Representation

### EMBASSIES AND HIGH COMMISSIONS IN WESTERN SAMOA

**Australia:** Beach Rd, POB 704, Apia; tel. 23411; fax 23159; High Commissioner: David W. Hegarty.

**China, People's Republic:** Vailima, Apia; tel. 22474; telex 232; fax 21115; Ambassador: Wang Nongsheng.

**New Zealand:** Beach Rd, Apia; tel. 21711; fax 20086; High Commissioner: Peter Heenan.

**USA:** POB 3430, Apia; tel. 21631; telex 275; fax 22030; Ambassador: Josiah H. Beeman.

## Judicial System

**Attorney-General:** Tupai Se Apa.

**The Supreme Court** is presided over by the Chief Justice. It has full jurisdiction for both criminal and civil cases. Appeals lie with the Court of Appeal.

**Chief Justice:** Tiavaasue Falefatu Maka Sapolu.

**Secretary for Justice:** Tuala Donald Charles Kerslake.

**The Court of Appeal** consists of the President (the Chief Justice of the Supreme Court), and of such persons possessing qualifications prescribed by statute as may be appointed by the Head of State. Any three judges of the Court of Appeal may exercise all the powers of the Court.

**The Magistrates' Court** consists of two magistrates and eight Samoan judges.

**Magistrates:** R. B. Lussick, Tagaloa Enoka Fereti Puni.

**The Land and Titles Court** has jurisdiction in respect of disputes over Samoan titles. It consists of the President (who is also a judge of the Supreme Court) and three Deputy Presidents, assisted by Samoan judges and Assessors.

**President of The Land and Titles Court:** Tiavaasue Falefatu Maka Sapolu.

## Religion

Almost all of Western Samoa's inhabitants profess Christianity.

### CHRISTIANITY

**Fono a Ekalesia i Samoa** (Samoa Council of Churches): POB 574, Apia; f. 1967; four mem. churches; Sec. Rev. Faatoese Auvaa.

#### The Anglican Communion

Western Samoa lies within the diocese of Polynesia, part of the Church of the Province of New Zealand. The Bishop of Polynesia is resident in Fiji, while the Archdeacon of Tonga and Samoa is resident in Tonga.

**Anglican Church:** POB 16, Apia; tel. 20500; fax 24663; Rev. Peter E. Bentley.

#### The Roman Catholic Church

The islands of Western Samoa constitute the archdiocese of Samoa-Apia. At 31 December 1993 there were an estimated 36,180 adherents in the country. The Archbishop participates in the Catholic Bishops' Conference of the Pacific, based in Fiji.

**Archbishop of Samoa–Apia:** HE Cardinal Pio Taofinu'u, Cardinal's Residence, Fetuolemoana, POB 532, Apia; tel. 20400; fax 20402.

#### Other Churches

**Church of Jesus Christ of Latter-day Saints (Mormon):** Pres. Lini Lyon To'o, Samoa Apia Mission, POB 1865, Apia; f. 1888; 58,491 mems.

**Congregational Christian Church in Samoa:** Tamaligi, POB 468, Apia; tel. 22279; f. 1830; 78,500 mems; Gen. Sec. Rev. Laau I. Tanielu.

**Congregational Church of Jesus in Samoa:** Rev. Naituli Malepeai, 505 Borie St, Honolulu, HI 96818, USA.

**Methodist Church in Samoa (Ekalesia Metotisi i Samoa):** POB 1867, Apia; tel. 22282; f. 1828; 36,000 mems; Pres. Rev. Siatua Leuluaialii; Sec. Rev. Faatoese Auvaa.

**Seventh-day Adventist Church:** POB 600, Apia; tel. 20451; f. 1895; covers American Samoa and Western Samoa; 5,000 mems; Pres. Pastor R. Rimoni.

### BAHÁ'Í FAITH

**National Spiritual Assembly:** POB 1117, Apia; tel. 23348; fax 21363.

## The Press

**Samoa News:** POB 1160, Apia; daily; merged with the weekly *Samoa Times* (f. 1967) in Sept. 1994; Publr Lewis Wolman.

**The Samoa Observer:** POB 1572, Apia; tel. 21099; fax 23078; f. 1979; five times a week; English and Samoan; Editor Savea Sano Malifa; circ. 4,500.

**Samoa Weekly:** Saleufi, Apia; f. 1977; weekly; independent; bilingual; Editor (vacant); circ. 4,000.

**Savali:** POB 193, Apia; publ. of Lands and Titles Court; monthly; Samoan edn f. 1904; Editor Faleseu L. Fua; circ. 6,000; English edn f. 1977; circ. 500; bilingual commercial edn f. 1993; circ. 1,500; Man. Editor Tunumafono A. Aiavao.

**South Seas Star:** POB 800, Apia; tel. 23684; weekly.

## Radio and Television

In 1992 there were an estimated 76,000 radio receivers in use. The American Samoan television channel is widely received in Western Samoa, linking in with US television networks. A government-owned television station, operated by Television New Zealand, began broadcasting in June 1993. In 1992 there were an estimated 6,000 television sets in use in Western Samoa.

**Western Samoa Broadcasting Service:** Broadcasting Department, POB 1868, Apia; tel. 21420; telex 208; fax 24000; f. 1948; govt-controlled with commercial sponsorship; broadcasts on two channels in English and Samoan for 24 hours daily; Dir J. K. Brown.

**Radio Polynesia:** POB 762, Apia; tel. 25149; fax 25147; f. 1989; privately-owned; Man. Corey Keil.

## Finance

(cap. = capital; res = reserves; dep. = deposits; amounts in tala)

### BANKING

#### Central Bank

**Central Bank of Samoa:** Private Bag, Apia; tel. 24100; telex 200; fax 20293; f. 1984; cap. 8.0m., res 14.4m. (Dec. 1990); Chair. Oloipola T. Betham; Gen. Man. Papali'i Tommy Scanlan.

#### Commercial Banks

**Bank of Western Samoa:** Beach Rd, POB L 1885, Apia; tel. 22422; telex 258; fax 24595; f. 1959; 75% owned by ANZ Banking Group Ltd, 25% owned by the Govt of Western Samoa; cap. 1.5m., res 13.9m., dep. 108.2m. (Sept. 1994); Chair. A. L. T. Maitland; Man. Dir Paul J. Rolton.

**Pacific Commercial Bank Ltd:** Beach Rd, POB 1860, Apia; tel. 20000; telex 231; fax 22848; f. 1977; first independent bank; 42.7% owned by Westpac Banking Corpn (Australia), 42.7% by Bank of Hawaii International Inc, 14.6% by private Western Samoan interests; cap. 1.2m., res 4.6m., dep. 33.0m. (Dec. 1994); Chair. Paul Friend; Gen. Man. Simon Millett; 4 brs.

#### Development Bank

**Development Bank of Western Samoa:** POB 1232, Apia; tel. 22861; telex 212; fax 23888; f. 1974 by Govt to foster economic and social development; cap. 12.9m. (1992); Gen. Man. Falefa Lima.

### INSURANCE

**Western Samoa Life Assurance Corporation:** POB 494, Apia; tel. 23360; telex 233; fax 23024; f. 1977; Gen. Man. A. S. Chan Ting.

## Trade and Industry

### CHAMBER OF COMMERCE

**Chamber of Commerce and Industry:** c/o Pacific Forum Line, Matautu-tai, POB 655, Apia; tel. 20345.

### TRADE UNIONS

**Journalists' Association of Western Samoa:** Apia; Pres. Apulu Lance Polu.

**Western Samoa Public Services Association (WSPSA):** POB 1515, Apia; tel. 24134; fax 20014; f. 1981; affiliate of ICFTU; Pres. Peseta Sinave Isara; Gen. Sec. Vaosa Elisaia; 5,000 mems.

**Western Samoan Registered Nurses' Association (WSRNA):** Apia; Pres. Faamanatu Nielsen; 252 mems.

## Transport

**Public Works Department:** Private Bag, Apia; tel. 21611; telex 256; fax 21927; Dir of Works Isikuki Punivalu.

### ROADS

In 1983 there were 396 km of main roads on the islands, of which 267 km were bitumen surfaced; 69 km of urban roads, of which 32 km were bitumen surfaced; 440 km of unsealed secondary roads and about 1,180 km of plantation roads. The upgrading and expansion of the road network was a priority of the Government during the late 1980s. In February 1990 and December 1991 cyclones caused serious damage to many roads.

### SHIPPING

There are deep-water wharves at Apia and Asau. A programme of improvements to port facilities at Apia funded by Japanese aid, was completed in 1991. Regular cargo services link Western Samoa with Australia, New Zealand, American Samoa, Fiji, New Caledonia, Solomon Islands, Tonga, US Pacific coast ports and various ports in Europe. Shipping companies operating regular cargo services to Western Samoa include the China Navigations New Guinea Pacific Line, Pacific Forum Line, Warner Pacific Line, Polynesia Shipping Line, Kyowa Line, Bali Hai Shipping Line, Blue Star Line and the Columbus Line.

### CIVIL AVIATION

There is an international airport at Faleolo, about 35 km from Apia and a grassed airstrip at Fagali'i, 4 km east of Apia Wharf, which receives light aircraft from American Samoa.

**Polynesian Airlines (Holdings) Ltd:** Beach Rd, POB 599, Apia; tel. 21261; telex 249; fax 20023; f. 1959; govt-owned and -operated; international services to American Samoa, Rarotonga (Cook Islands), Tonga, Nouméa (New Caledonia), Sydney and Melbourne (Australia), New Zealand and Hawaii and Los Angeles (USA); domestic services between islands of Upolu and Savai'i; Chair. JACK O. NETZLER; Gen. Man. RICHARD GATES.

## Tourism

Western Samoa has traditionally maintained a cautious attitude towards tourism, fearing that the Samoan way of life might be disrupted by an influx of foreign visitors. The importance of income from tourism has, however, led to some development, including the expansion of hotel facilities and improvements to the road network and airport. Some 39,414 foreign visitors arrived in 1991, and in 1990 revenue from the tourist industry totalled an estimated US $20m. About one-half of tourist arrivals are from American Samoa and New Zealand. The principal attractions are the scenery and the pleasant climate.

In 1991 the Tourism Council of the South Pacific put forward a draft US $57m. 10-year tourism development plan for Western Samoa. Plans to develop 'eco-tourism', based on the conservation and appreciation of the natural environment, were discussed with Australian experts in 1994.

**Western Samoa Visitors' Bureau:** POB 862, Apia; tel. 20878; telex 220; fax 22848.

# YEMEN

## Introductory Survey

### Location, Climate, Language, Religion, Flag, Capital

The Republic of Yemen is situated in the south of the Arabian peninsula, bounded to the north by Saudi Arabia, to the east by Oman, to the south by the Gulf of Aden, and to the west by the Red Sea. The islands of Perim and Kamaran at the southern end of the Red Sea, the island of Socotra, at the entrance to the Gulf of Aden, and the Kuria Muria islands, near the coast of Oman, are also part of the Republic. The climate in the semi-desert coastal strip is hot, with high humidity and temperatures rising to more than 38°C (100°F); inland, the climate is somewhat less hot, with cool winters and relatively heavy rainfall in the highlands. The eastern plateau slopes into desert. The language is Arabic. The population is almost entirely Muslim, and mainly of the Sunni Shafi'a sect. The national flag (proportions 3 by 2) has three equal horizontal stripes, of red, white and black. The capital is San'a.

### Recent History

The Republic of Yemen was formed in May 1990 by the amalgamation of the Yemen Arab Republic (YAR) and the People's Democratic Republic of Yemen (PDRY). The YAR (from 1967 also known as North Yemen) had formerly been a kingdom. When Turkey's Ottoman Empire was dissolved in 1918, the Imam Yahya, leader of the Zaidi community, was left in control. In 1948 Yahya was assassinated in a palace coup, when power was seized by forces opposed to his feudal rule. However, Yahya's son, Ahmad, defeated the rebel forces and succeeded his father as Imam. In 1958 Yemen and the United Arab Republic (Egypt and Syria) formed a federation called the United Arab States, though this was dissolved at the end of 1961. The Imam Ahmad died in September 1962 and was succeeded by his son, Muhammad. A week later, army officers, led by Col (later Marshal) Abdullah as-Sallal, staged a coup, declared the Imam deposed and proclaimed the YAR. Civil war ensued between royalist forces, supported by Saudi Arabia, and republicans, aided by Egyptian troops. The republicans gained the upper hand and Egyptian forces withdrew in 1967. In November President Sallal was deposed while abroad, and a Republican Council took power.

The People's Republic of Southern Yemen, comprising Aden and the former Protectorate of South Arabia, was formed on 30 November 1967. Aden had been under British rule since 1839 and the Protectorate was developed by a series of treaties between the United Kingdom and local leaders. Prior to British withdrawal, two rival factions, the National Liberation Front (NLF) and the Front for the Liberation of Occupied South Yemen (FLOSY), fought for control. The Marxist NLF eventually prevailed and assumed power as the National Front (NF). The country's first President, Qahtan ash-Sha'abi, was forced out of office in June 1969, when a Presidential Council, led by Salem Rubayi Ali, took power. Muhammad Ali Haitham became Prime Minister. In November 1970, on the third anniversary of independence, the country was renamed the PDRY. In May 1971 a provisional Supreme People's Council (SPC) was established as the national legislature. In August Haitham was replaced as Prime Minister by Ali Nasser Muhammad. Following the introduction of repressive measures against dissidents by the Government after independence, more than 300,000 Southern Yemenis fled to the YAR. Backed by Saudi Arabia and Libya, many of the refugees joined mercenary organizations, aimed at the overthrow of the Marxist regime in Southern Yemen, and conducted raids across the border.

Intermittent fighting, beginning in early 1971, flared into open warfare between the two Yemens in October 1972, with the YAR receiving aid from Saudi Arabia and the PDRY being supplied with Soviet arms. A cease-fire was arranged in the same month, under the auspices of the Arab League, and soon afterwards both sides agreed to the union of the two Yemens within 18 months. The union was not, however, implemented.

On 13 June 1974 a 10-member Military Command Council (subsequently reduced in numbers) seized power in the YAR, under the leadership of the pro-Saudi Lt-Col Ibrahim al-Hamadi. Col Hamadi appointed Mohsin al-Aini as Prime Minister, but replaced him by Abd al-Aziz Abd al-Ghani in January 1975. During 1975 the Military Command Council was further reduced in size, and there were reports of an unsuccessful pro-royalist coup in August. After 1975 Hamadi attempted to reduce the influence of the USSR, and endeavoured to re-equip the army with US weapons, making use of financial assistance from Saudi Arabia. In October 1977, however, Hamadi was killed by unknown assassins in San'a. Another member of the Military Command Council, Lt-Col Ahmad ibn Hussein al-Ghashmi, took over as Chairman, and martial law was imposed. In February 1978 the Command Council appointed a Constituent People's Assembly, and in April the Assembly elected al-Ghashmi President of the Republic. The Military Command Council was then dissolved.

In June 1978 the proposed union of the two Yemens received a severe set-back when President al-Ghashmi of the YAR was assassinated by a bomb carried in the suitcase of a PDRY envoy. In the following month the Constituent People's Assembly elected a senior military officer, Lt-Col (later Gen.) Ali Abdullah Saleh, as President of the YAR. During recriminations that followed the assassination, President Rubayi Ali of the PDRY was deposed and executed by opponents within the ruling party, which had been known as the United Political Organization—National Front (UPO—NF), since its merger with two smaller parties in October 1975. The Prime Minister, Ali Nasser Muhammad, became interim Head of State. Two days after the overthrow of Rubayi Ali, it was announced that the UPO—NF had agreed to form a Marxist-Leninist 'vanguard' party. At the constituent congress of this Yemen Socialist Party (YSP), held in October 1978, Abd al-Fattah Ismail, who favoured uncompromising Marxist policies, became Secretary-General. A new SPC was elected in December and appointed Ismail to be Head of State. In April 1980 Ali Nasser Muhammad replaced Ismail as Head of State, Chairman of the Presidium of the SPC and Secretary-General of the YSP, while retaining the post of Prime Minister. It was claimed that Ismail relinquished office as a result of poor health, but he subsequently left the country for exile in the USSR. Ali Nasser Muhammad's position was consolidated in October 1980, when his posts were confirmed at an extraordinary congress of the YSP.

Renewed fighting broke out between the YAR and the PDRY in February and March 1979, when the National Democratic Front (NDF), an alliance of disaffected YAR politicians, won the support of the PDRY and began a revolt. Later in the same month, however, at a meeting in Kuwait arranged by the Arab League between the North and South Yemeni Heads of State, an agreement was signed pledging unification of the two states. Meetings between representatives of the two countries were inconclusive until December 1981, when both sides signed a draft constitution for a unified state and established a joint YAR/PDRY Yemen Council to monitor progress towards unification. NDF forces rebelled again, however, in 1982, but they were defeated and forced over the border into the PDRY.

Abd al-Aziz Abd al-Ghani was replaced as Prime Minister of the YAR in October 1980, but was reappointed in November 1983. Meanwhile, in May 1983 President Saleh submitted his resignation at an extraordinary meeting of the Constituent People's Assembly, saying that he would nominate himself for a presidential election. His five-year term of office was due to end in July. However, he was nominated and unanimously re-elected by the Assembly for a further five-year term. Elections for the Assembly itself were scheduled for early 1983, but were postponed.

In the PDRY, President Muhammad relinquished the post of Prime Minister on 14 February 1985, nominating the Minister of Construction, Haidar Abu Bakr al-Attas, as his successor. Muhammad retained his other senior posts. The former President, Abd al-Fattah Ismail, returned from exile in Moscow in the same month, and was reappointed to the Secretariat of the YSP's Central Committee. At the third General Congress of the YSP, in October, President Muhammad was re-elected to the posts of Secretary-General of the YSP and of its Political Bureau for a further term of five years. However, his control over the party was weakened by the enlargement of the Political Bureau from 13 members to 16 (including his rival, Abd al-Fattah Ismail), and by an increase in the membership of the Central Committee from 47 to 77, to incorporate a number of his critics.

On 13 January 1986 President Muhammad attempted to eliminate his opponents in the Political Bureau: his personal guard opened fire on six members who had assembled for a meeting with the President. Three were killed, and three escaped, including Abd al-Fattah Ismail (who was, however, officially declared to have been killed in subsequent fighting). President Muhammad was reported to have left Aden for his tribal stronghold in Abyan province, 130 km east of the city. In Aden itself, rival elements of the armed forces fought for control, causing widespread destruction, and the conflict quickly spread to the rest of the country, despite attempts at mediation by the Government of the USSR. Apparently prompted by reports of massacres by President Muhammad's supporters, the army intervened decisively, turning back pro-Muhammad tribesmen from Abyan who were advancing on Aden. On 24 January Haidar Abu Bakr al-Attas, the Prime Minister, who had been in India when the troubles began and had flown to Moscow, was named by the YSP Central Committee as head of an interim administration in Aden, and Ali Nasser Muhammad was stripped of all his party and state posts. On the same day, the USSR formally recognized the new regime. Muhammad was reported to have fled to Ethiopia. Some 5,000 people were estimated to have died in the conflict. A new Government of the PDRY was formed in February. Al-Attas was confirmed as President, Chairman of the Presidium of the SPC and Secretary-General of the YSP Political Bureau. The former Deputy Prime Minister and Minister of Fisheries, Dr Yasin Said Numan, was named as Prime Minister. The new Council of Ministers contained only three members of the previous government. In March a general amnesty was proclaimed, inviting supporters of Muhammad to return from the YAR, where an estimated 10,000 of them had sought refuge. In October a general election took place for a 111-member SPC. Al-Attas was unanimously elected Chairman of the YSP. In December the Supreme Court sentenced Ali Nasser Muhammad to death, *in absentia*, for treason; 34 other men received the same sentence, although it was only carried out in five cases.

In July 1988 the first general election took place in the YAR for 128 seats in the new 159-member Consultative Council, which replaced the non-elected Constituent People's Assembly. The remaining 31 seats were filled shortly thereafter by presidential decree. Over one million people registered to vote and more than 1,200 candidates stood for election. Approximately one-quarter of the elective seats were won by candidates sympathetic to the Muslim Brotherhood, an Islamic fundamentalist organization. Later in the same month President Saleh was re-elected by the Consultative Council for a third five-year term, winning 96% of the votes, while the Vice-President, Abd al-Karim al-Arashi, was elected as Speaker of the Consultative Council. Abd al-Aziz Abd al-Ghani was subsequently reappointed to his position as Prime Minister by President Saleh, and a new Council of Ministers was announced.

The first session of the joint YAR/PDRY Yemen Council (which had been established in 1981) was held in San'a in August 1983 and discussed the state of progress towards unification. These sessions were scheduled to take place every six months and to alternate between San'a and Aden. A joint committee on foreign policy met for the first time in March 1984 in Aden. In 1986 the new government of the PDRY, under Haidar Abu Bakr al-Attas, reaffirmed its commitment to the process of unification. In July Presidents Saleh of the YAR and al-Attas of the PDRY met for the first time in Tripoli, Libya, at the invitation of Col Qaddafi, to discuss unification. In early 1987 Kuwait's Minister of State for Foreign Affairs acted as a mediator between the two Yemens in an effort to solve the problem of the thousands of refugees from the PDRY who had sought refuge in the north in the previous year. In July 1987 it was reported that more than one-half of these refugees had returned to the PDRY.

In May 1988 the Governments of the YAR and the PDRY agreed to withdraw troops from their mutual border and to create a demilitarized zone, covering an area of 2,200 sq km, between Marib and Shabwah, where they intended to carry out joint projects involving exploration for petroleum. The movement of citizens between the two states was also to be facilitated. In June 1989 direct telephone links between the YAR and the PDRY were established. In July a programme of wide-ranging political and economic reforms was introduced in the PDRY, which indicated the country's intention to create a free market economy. In November President Saleh and the Secretary-General of the Central Committee of the YSP, Ali Salim al-Baid, signed an agreement to unify the two states. On 1 December a 136-article draft constitution for the unified state was published: it was to be ratified by both countries within six months, and was subsequently to be approved by a referendum. The draft Constitution stated that the unified Yemen state was to be a pluralist state headed by a five-member Presidential Council. The capital was to be San'a. Deputies to the legislature in San'a were to be elected for a four-year term. Political organizations and trade unions were to be permitted to operate, within the bounds of the constitution. The draft electoral law guaranteed universal suffrage for adult men and women. At the end of December the Governments of the YAR and the PDRY agreed to release all political prisoners in their respective countries.

The first joint meeting of the two Councils of Ministers was held in San'a in January 1990. Following the meeting, restrictions on travel between the two countries were rescinded. In February President Saleh held talks with King Fahd of Saudi Arabia, who pledged his official support for the unification of the YAR and the PDRY. The growing atmosphere of democracy in the PDRY gave a large section of the work-force the confidence to stage an unprecedented series of strikes, which led to the granting by the Government of significant wage increases.

Opposition to unification developed in the YAR in early 1990. The Muslim Brotherhood, which believed that Shari'a (Islamic) law should be enshrined in the Constitution of the unified state (as in the YAR Constitution), condemned the draft Constitution, which was based principally, but not solely, on Shari'a law. The leader of the Muslim Brotherhood, Sheikh Abd al-Hamid Zaidani, advocated a boycott of the referendum on the Constitution that was to follow unification. In the PDRY there were demonstrations by women, who feared that the rise of Islamic fundamentalism might jeopardize their freedom, and demanded that their existing rights in the secular republic be guaranteed in the new Yemeni Constitution.

In April 1990 it was reported by the Western media that tribes in the north of the YAR, supported by Saudi Arabia, were rebelling, in an attempt to disrupt the unification process. These reports were denied by the YAR and by Saudi Arabia. In May the armed forces of the YAR and the PDRY were declared to be technically dissolved, prior to their unification, and it was announced that they were to be withdrawn from their respective capitals to designated military zones. In the same month a draft law embodying the freedom of the press was signed.

On 22 May 1990 the unification of the YAR and the PDRY was proclaimed, six months ahead of the deadline agreed by the two countries, apparently in order to counter the threat to the unification process posed by disruption in the north of the YAR. The unification agreement had been ratified on the previous day by the legislatures of the PDRY and the YAR. The new country was to be known as the Republic of Yemen, with San'a as its political capital and Aden its economic and commercial centre. President Saleh of the YAR became President of the new state, while Ali Salim al-Baid was elected Vice-President. The President of the PDRY, Haidar Abu Bakr al-Attas, became Prime Minister, leading a transitional coalition Council of Ministers with 39 members, of whom 20 were from the YAR (members of the General People's Congress—GPC—a broad grouping of supporters of President Saleh) and 19 from the PDRY (all members of the YSP, under the continued leadership of Ali Salim al-Baid). A five-member Presidential Council (chaired by Saleh) was formed, together with a 45-member advisory council. The two countries' legislatures were amalgamated to form the House of Representatives, pending elections to be held after a 30-month transitional period; an additional 31 members, including opponents of the YAR and PDRY governments, were nominated by President Saleh.

In September 1990 it was reported that more than 30 new political parties had been formed in Yemen since unification.

The Yemeni Islah Party (YIP), an Islamic party with considerable support in the House of Representatives, was regarded as the most influential of the new parties.

In mid-May 1991 the people of Yemen voted in a referendum on the Constitution for the unified state. A few days earlier, religious fundamentalists and sympathizers, among whom were members of the YIP, demonstrated about the role of Islam under the proposed Constitution, and urged a boycott of the referendum. Those who participated in the referendum approved the new Constitution by a large majority, although fewer than 50% of the electorate registered to vote. Members of the YIP and other opposition groups claimed that irregularities in the voting procedure had invalidated the result.

During late 1991 and early 1992 the deteriorating economic situation (characterized by large increases in unemployment and consumer prices as well as reductions in public spending by the Government) prompted domestic unrest. A shooting incident in San'a in October 1991 led to two days of rioting, in which nine people were believed to have been killed. In early March 1992 workers in some parts of the country held a one-day strike, in support of demands for salary increases and the establishment of a job-creation programme for the estimated 850,000 returnees from Saudi Arabia (see below). A three-day general strike, which was due to be held later in the month, was abandoned, following an understanding reached by trade union leaders and the Government.

A series of political killings and assassination attempts, principally directed against members of the YSP, was attributed by some observers to infighting between the two parties, while other commentators implicated Islamic groups supported by Saudi Arabia. In April 1992 an attempt was made to assassinate the Minister of Justice, Abd al-Wasi Ahmad Salam. In May the home of Salem Salih Muhammad, a YSP representative on the Presidential Council, was attacked, and a bomb exploded at the house of Prime Minister al-Attas. In the same month an amnesty was extended to the former PDRY President, Ali Nasser Muhammad, and five of his associates. In June, in the southern town of Shihr, the brother of the Prime Minister was murdered. In September it was reported that bomb attacks had been made against the homes of several GPC members. YSP officials claimed that at least 30 of their members had been murdered in 1992. Ambushes, violent demonstrations and attacks on leading figures continued to occur, despite the Government's decision, in May, to prohibit the carrying of firearms in cities.

In December 1992 riots in San'a, Taiz and Hodeida spread rapidly to Aden and other towns. The apparent cause of the unrest was a rise of approximately 80% in consumer prices in the course of several days. It was officially reported that 15 people had been killed in the disturbances, with 98 injured and 661 arrested. Opposition sources, however, estimated significantly higher figures. In January 1993 it was reported that 36 Yemenis, suspected of allegiance to the pro-Iranian Islamic Jihad group, had been arrested in connection with the bombing of two hotels in Aden. Concern arose that the general economic situation and social unrest would lead to an increase in support for Islamic fundamentalist associations in Yemen, which displayed a high degree of organization in the provision of education and other services to local communities.

In spite of the climate of unrest, voter registration for the legislative elections, scheduled for 27 April 1993, took place between 15 January and 16 February. A series of attacks on expatriate workers prompted a warning, in February, that the Government could not guarantee the safety of expatriate residents. In April it was reported that a rocket attack on the YSP office in Hajjah, north-west of San'a, had resulted in 25 deaths. It was estimated that 4,730 candidates would contest the 301 seats available in the Yemeni House of Representatives. An estimated 30% of the candidates were affiliated to political parties, while the remainder were standing as independents.

International observers expressed broad satisfaction with the conduct of the elections, although there were reports of disturbances in several towns, and complaints of irregularities in some quarters. The GPC secured 123 of the 300 seats in which results were announced. The YIP won 62 seats, and the YSP 56, with independents accounting for 47 of the remaining seats. In May 1993 it was announced that the two former ruling parties, the GPC and YSP, had agreed to a merger, which would result in a single political group with an overall majority in the new House of Representatives. The subsequent election of the YIP's leader, Sheikh Abdullah bin Hussain al-Ahmar, as speaker of the House of Representatives was regarded as a concession to his party, whose influence had been weakened by the merger. At the end of the month, however, a 31-member coalition Government was announced, including representatives of all the three leading parties. Al-Attas was reappointed Prime Minister in the coalition Government. In June a further two YIP members were appointed to the Government, increasing the representation of that party from four to six.

In August 1993 the YSP leader, Ali Salim al-Baid, ceased to participate in the political process and withdrew from San'a to Aden. This followed a visit that he made to Washington, DC, apparently without the approval of President Saleh, for talks with the US Vice-President, Albert Gore. Al-Baid claimed that Saleh had made no attempt to halt the numerous armed attacks by northern officials on southerners, and claimed that as many as 150 YSP members had been assassinated since unification. He also protested at what he perceived to be the increasing marginalization of the south, particularly with regard to the distribution of petroleum revenues. On 11 October the House of Representatives elected a new five-member Presidential Council, and on 16 October the Council, in the absence of al-Baid, re-elected Saleh as its chairman, and, accordingly, as President of the Republic of Yemen, for a further four-year term. Al-Baid was unanimously re-elected as Vice-President, but was not sworn in.

The political deadlock persisted into November 1993, in spite of attempts by French, Omani, Jordanian, Palestinian and US diplomats to mediate. It became clear that the armies of the former YAR and the PDRY had remained separate since unification, and it was reported that some units were being deployed along the former frontier. In December, as a result of Jordanian mediation, representatives of the GPC and the YSP commenced negotiations with the aim of resolving the political crisis. In September al-Baid, who remained in Aden, had submitted an 18-point programme of conditions for his return to San'a. President Saleh responded in December by accepting the programme, but there was no indication of any improvement in the political situation. On 18 January 1994 representatives of the main political parties signed a 'Document of Pledge and Agreement' designed to resolve the political crisis. The document met several of the conditions that al-Baid had set forth for his return to San'a. By the end of the month, however, no meeting had taken place between Saleh and al-Baid, and neither had signed the document.

On 20 February 1994 President Saleh and Vice-President al-Baid together signed the 'Document of Pledge and Agreement' in Amman, Jordan. The agreement contained certain security guarantees, as well as providing for a degree of decentralization, and for a review of the Constitution and of the country's economic policies. Nevertheless, both leaders remained active in mustering support for their positions throughout the region. Al-Baid, in particular, made a tour of neighbouring states, following the signing of the agreement, for high-level talks with Arab leaders. At the same time there were reports of clashes between rival army units.

In March 1994 a joint military committee composed of senior officers from the former YAR and PDRY, representatives from Oman and Jordan, and the US and French military attachés, was reported to have had some success in separating the army units and averting outright armed conflict. On 3 March Saleh and al-Baid held talks in Oman, but at the end of the month al-Baid, together with Salim Muhammad, refused to attend a meeting of the Presidential Council, which he had been boycotting since August 1993. In the last week of March two meetings of the Council of Ministers, the first to take place in 1994, were held in Aden in an attempt to agree preliminary measures to implement the conciliation agreement.

Diplomatic initiatives continued throughout April 1994, while skirmishes between rival army units persisted. On 27 April, however, a tank battle took place at Amran, near San'a, which left 79 soldiers dead. On 28 April the First Deputy Prime Minister, Hassan Muhammad Makki, was wounded as the result of an assassination attempt in San'a. A series of pitched battles followed between battalions stationed in the territory of their former neighbour. On 4 May hostilities erupted around Aden and at Dhamar, on the highway connecting San'a to Aden, about 100 km south of the capital. It was reported that the fighting at Dhamar had resulted in a serious defeat for the forces of the former PDRY. On 5 May

President Saleh declared a 30-day state of emergency, and dismissed al-Baid from his position as Vice-President, together with four other southern members of the Government, including Salim Muhammad. On the same day missile attacks took place against economic and military targets, including San'a, Aden and other main airports. A large number of expatriates residing in Yemen were evacuated during the second week of May. On 9 May Saleh announced that al-Attas had been replaced as Prime Minister by the Minister of Industry, Muhammad Said al-Attar, and that the Minister of Petroleum and Minerals had also been replaced. By this time fighting had become concentrated around Aden, and along the line of the former north–south frontier. Several thousand southern reservists were mobilized, as the forces of the former YAR pursued their objective of encircling and capturing Aden. Diplomatic efforts, through the agency of the Arab League, to mediate in the conflict had little effect. By 18 May, with the conflict entering its third week, the heaviest fighting was concentrated around the military base of al-Anad, 60 km to the north of Aden, where the forces of the former YAR were attempting to achieve a breakthrough. Meanwhile, President Saleh rejected appeals for a negotiated settlement to the civil war, and demanded that al-Baid surrender.

On 21 May 1994, the fourth anniversary of the unification of Yemen, al-Baid, in a televised address, declared the independence of the new Democratic Republic of Yemen (DRY), with Aden as its capital. He also announced the formation of a Presidential Council, with himself as President and Abd ar-Rahman al-Jifri, the leader of the League of the Sons of Yemen (LSY), as Vice-President. The composition of the Council reflected al-Baid's need to achieve a consensus of the different political and tribal groups of the former PDRY in opposition to the forces of President Saleh. Saleh himself immediately denounced the secession as illegitimate, and offered an amnesty to all in the PDRY who rejected it, with the exception of 16 YSP leaders, including al-Baid.

At the end of May 1994, with the northern army attacking Aden on three fronts to the north and east of the city, the UN Security Council met, at the instigation of Egypt and five of the Gulf states, to discuss the conflict. The result was a unanimous resolution (No. 924) demanding a cease-fire and the resumption of dialogue, and ordering the dispatch of a UN commission of inquiry (with Lakhdar Brahimi, a former Minister of Foreign Affairs in Algeria, as special envoy), to the region. Although welcomed by the authorities in Aden, the resolution was initially rejected by the Government in San'a, which urged the Arab League to support the unity of Yemen. Subsequently, however, the San'a Government also declared itself positively disposed towards the resolution.

On 1 June 1994 the House of Representatives voted to extend the state of emergency for a further 30 days. On the following day al-Baid announced the composition of a DRY government, in which al-Attas was to be Prime Minister and Minister of Finance. Although most of the ministers were members of the YSP, the Government contained a range of religious, political and tribal representatives. On 5 June the oil refinery in Aden was damaged by two bombing raids, and it was reported that northern forces, having captured the military base at al-Anad, were engaged in fierce fighting with southern forces along the front that formed a circular arc from east to west in places as close as 14 km to the centre of Aden. It was reported that al-Baid had transferred his centre of operations to Mukalla, 700 km east of Aden. At the same time the foreign ministers of the six members of the Gulf Co-operation Council (GCC, see p. 130), 'with the exception of Qatar, issued a statement that it was 'absolutely impossible' for the unity of Yemen to be imposed militarily, thereby appearing implicitly to recognize the secession of the DRY. On 7 June the authorities in San'a declared a cease-fire, the first since the outbreak of the conflict. It was, however, almost immediately disregarded. Northern forces maintained their pressure on Aden for the remainder of June, and on 7 July the town came under the control of Saleh's troops. Many of the southern secessionist leaders fled to neighbouring Arab states, and it was officially announced that the civil war had ended. Al-Baid was reported to have requested political asylum in Oman.

According to President Saleh, 931 civilians and soldiers were killed in the civil war and 5,000 wounded, although this was generally regarded as a conservative estimate. Immediately after defeating the secessionists Saleh undertook measures to consolidate his regime and bring stability to the country. The state of emergency was lifted and the general amnesty reiterated; by mid-August 1994, when the amnesty expired, more than 5,000 Yemenis had returned to the country. In the same month, in an attempt to diminish the power of units in the south still loyal to the YSP, President Saleh announced that party membership would no longer be permitted within the armed forces. In September, moreover, Saleh introduced amendments to the Constitution which strengthened his position: the Presidential Council was abolished, and in future the President would be elected by universal suffrage. The Islamic Shari'a would also serve as the basis of all legislation. On 1 October Saleh was re-elected President; he appointed Abd ar-Rabbur Mansur Hadi as his deputy, and Abd al-Aziz Abd al-Ghani (hitherto a member of the Presidential Council) as Prime Minister. In the new Council of Ministers, announced on 6 October, members of the GPC retained the key portfolios, the YSP was denied representation, and the YIP was rewarded for its allegiance during the civil war by the allocation of a total of nine ministerial posts. In a reorganization of the Council of Ministers in mid-June 1995, the GPC increased its share of portfolios at the expense of independents, with the result that the Council consisted entirely of members of the GPC and YIP.

In late July 1994 UN-sponsored negotiations between the Yemeni leadership and the secessionists proved inconclusive. President Saleh announced that any further discussions would have to be conducted in Yemen, effectively terminating dialogue as the YSP leaders remained in exile. In August a faction of the YSP in Yemen declared itself the new party leadership, and selected a new leader and politburo. In October, nevertheless, exiled leaders of the YSP announced the formation of an opposition coalition, the National Opposition Front, which included former Prime Minister Haidar Abu Bakr al-Attas and Abd ar-Rahman al-Jifri, leader of the LSY. The role of the YSP in Yemeni politics had diminished considerably since the civil war, however, as it was deprived of military power, experienced leadership in the country, and its role in government. In February 1995 another opposition grouping, the Democratic Coalition of Opposition, was formed, embracing 13 political parties and organizations—including a faction of the YSP, Nasserite parties and the LSY.

The economic repercussions of the civil war on the population were significant, particularly in the south, and gave rise to a number of popular protests. In September 1994 hundreds demonstrated in Abyan province in the south to protest at water and electricity shortages and the price of basic foodstuffs, which in some instances had increased five-fold. In February 1995 more than 150 wholesalers were arrested in San'a for their alleged role in inflating prices. In late March and early April, moreover, following the devaluation of the riyal and the doubling of the price of fuel, demonstrators clashed with police in Aden, San'a and Dhamar, resulting in more than 50 arrests and three deaths. The activities of Islamic militants, meanwhile, posed an additional threat to internal stability. In early September 1994 some 20 people were reported to have been killed in clashes with the security forces in Abyan province, following the destruction of three Muslim saints' shrines by Islamic militants who deemed them idolatrous. In April 1995 Islamic militants were involved in skirmishes in Hadramawt province, resulting in the deaths of two members of the Hussainain tribe, after they levelled similar accusations at the tribe for un-Islamic burial practices.

In November 1987 and February 1988, respectively, the YAR and the PDRY resumed diplomatic relations with Egypt, following a decision by the the Arab League to adopt a resolution which permitted member states to re-establish links with Egypt at their own discretion. (In common with other members of the Arab League, they had broken off relations with Egypt following the signing of the Camp David Agreement by Israel and Egypt in 1979.)

Clashes on the long-disputed PDRY–Omani border resulted in the deaths of 10 soldiers in October 1987. A year later, formal demarcation of a border between the two countries was agreed in principle during a visit to Muscat by President al-Attas, the first to be undertaken by a PDRY Head of State. Despite the apparent success of border negotiations between the Governments of Oman and the unified Yemen, which were resumed during 1991, it was not until October 1992 that an agreement was signed in San'a on border demarcation, which, it was hoped, would finally resolve the long-standing dispute.

In February 1989 the YAR became one of the founder members (in addition to Egypt, Iraq and Jordan) of the Amman-based Arab Co-operation Council (see p. 237), which was to provide a framework within which inter-Arab co-operation was to be promoted.

In August 1990 Iraq's invasion of Kuwait placed the Government of Yemen in a difficult position. The economy of Yemen was heavily dependent on trade with and aid from Iraq, and also on aid from Saudi Arabia, which was host to a considerable number of Yemeni expatriate workers. Moreover, there was evidence of widespread popular support in Yemen for the President of Iraq, Saddam Hussain. These factors determined the Government's equivocal response to the Iraqi invasion of Kuwait and to the subsequent developments in the Gulf region. The Government condemned the invasion, but also criticized the deployment of US and other Western military forces to defend Saudi Arabia; Yemen abstained in a vote by the UN Security Council on a resolution to impose economic sanctions on Iraq. By late August, however, the Government appeared to be committed to implementing the UN sanctions against Iraq, albeit reluctantly. In October the Yemeni Minister of Foreign Affairs, Abd al-Karim al-Iryani, announced that Yemen would support any measures taken to achieve a peaceful withdrawal of Iraqi troops from Kuwait, but that this should result in the withdrawal of all foreign forces from the area.

Yemen's relations with Saudi Arabia deteriorated as a result of Yemen's initial strong opposition to the presence of foreign armed forces in the Gulf and to the ambiguous stance it had subsequently adopted in this respect. In mid-September 1990, in what was regarded as a retaliatory action, Saudi Arabia announced that it had withdrawn the privileges which Yemeni workers had previously enjoyed. This resulted in an exodus from Saudi Arabia of an estimated 850,000 Yemeni workers during October and November, which caused widespread economic and social disruption. The expulsion and consequent return to Yemen of the workers not only caused a reduction in the country's income from remittances, but also led to a serious increase in unemployment.

In December 1990 Yemen assumed the chair of the UN Security Council (which rotates on a monthly basis), and the Government increased its efforts to mediate in the Gulf crisis. In January 1991 Yemen presented a peace plan in an attempt to prevent war in the Gulf; however, despite numerous diplomatic initiatives undertaken by the Yemeni Government, prior to the UN deadline of 15 January, the peace plan failed to prevent the outbreak of war in the Gulf on 16–17 January. Following the US-led military offensive against Iraq, Yemen issued a statement in which it condemned the action, and hundreds of thousands of Yemenis demonstrated in support of Iraq. Later in January it was confirmed that US aid to Yemen was to be suspended indefinitely, apparently as a result of Yemen's policy towards Iraq. Reduced US economic aid was resumed in August 1991.

In 1992 thousands of refugees from the conflict in Somalia sought refuge in Yemen. By November of that year it was estimated that 62,000 Somali nationals were resident in temporary accommodation in Yemen.

Yemen's relations with the Gulf states showed signs of improvement in 1993. In March a delegation from Yemen visited the UAE, and in October Sultan Qaboos of Oman made his first visit to San'a, where he agreed the financing of a 250-km highway connecting the two countries. In the same month President Mitterrand of France held talks with President Saleh in San'a, and it was agreed that French assistance to Yemen in 1994 would be worth a total of US $12.3m. In September 1994 President Saleh made an official visit to Oman in an attempt to improve relations with the Gulf States, which had deteriorated following the GCC's apparent support for the secessionists during the 1994 civil war. Later in the month the Omani authorities returned to Yemen all weapons brought into the country by southern army units. In early June 1995 the demarcation of the Yemeni–Omani border, initiated in 1992 (see above), was officially completed.

The Governments of Yemen and Saudi Arabia held negotiations on the subject of the demarcation of their common border in July 1992 in Geneva, Switzerland, and in May 1993 in Riyadh, Saudi Arabia. Negotiations continued into 1994; however, in December Yemen accused Saudi Arabia of trespassing on Yemeni territory and alleged that three Yemeni soldiers had been killed during clashes earlier in that month.

Further clashes were reported in January 1995 following the failure of the two countries to renew the 1934 Ta'if agreement (renewable every 20 years), which delineated their existing frontier. Intense mediation by Syria culminated in a joint statement in mid-January, in which Yemen and Saudi Arabia pledged to cease all military activity in the border area. It was subsequently announced that the demarcation of the disputed border would be undertaken by a joint committee, which was to be formed within 30 days. In late February the Yemeni and Saudi Governments signed a memorandum of understanding which reaffirmed their commitment to the Ta'if agreement and provided for the establishment of six joint committees to delineate the land and sea borders and develop economic and commercial ties. On 8 March the memorandum was approved by the Yemeni Council of Ministers. In early June President Saleh and a high-ranking delegation visited Saudi Arabia, constituting the first official visit to that country since February 1990. In a joint statement, issued at the end of the visit, the two Governments expressed their satisfaction with the memorandum of understanding and, in addition, pledged their commitment to strengthening economic, commercial and cultural co-operation.

## Government

Legislative power is vested in the House of Representatives, with 301 members, directly elected by universal adult suffrage. Under the revised Constitution, the President of the Republic (Head of State) is to be elected directly by the voters for a period of five years, renewable once. The President appoints a Council of Ministers, headed by a Prime Minister.

## Defence

In June 1994 the total armed forces of the Republic of Yemen were estimated to number 66,000 (of whom about 43,000 were conscripts): 61,000 were in the army, an estimated 1,500 in the navy and 3,500 in the air force. There was a paramilitary force of 25,000. Tribal levies numbered at least 20,000. The defence budget for 1993 was estimated at 6,200m. riyals (US $375m.). In 1991 it was announced that compulsory military service in Yemen would comprise a period of two years.

## Economic Affairs

In 1992, according to the World Bank, the unified Yemen's gross domestic product (GDP), in purchasers' values, was US $9,615m. During 1985–93 the combined population of the YAR and the PDRY increased by an annual average of 4.4%. In 1991, according to estimates by the World Bank, the unified Yemen's gross national product (GNP), measured at average 1989–91 prices, was US $6,746m., equivalent to $520 per head. During 1980–88, it was estimated, the YAR's GNP increased, in real terms, at an average annual rate of 5.5%, and GNP per head increased by 2.7% per year. Over the same period, the population increased by an annual average of 2.7%. The YAR's GDP increased, in real terms, by an annual average of 5.6% in 1980–87.

In 1988, according to estimates by the World Bank, the PDRY's GNP, measured at average 1986–88 prices, was US $1,000m., equivalent to $430 per head. During 1980–88, it was estimated, GNP declined, in real terms, at an average annual rate of 3.2%, and GNP per head declined by 5.9% per year. Over the same period, the population increased by an annual average of 2.9%.

In the unified Yemen agriculture (including hunting, forestry and fishing) contributed 21% of GDP in 1993, according to World Bank estimates, and employed 53.7% of the labour force. The country's principal crops are sorghum, potatoes, tomatoes, wheat, grapes and watermelons. Livestock and fishing are also important. In 1990 exports of food and live animals provided 3.4% of total export earnings.

In the YAR agriculture (including forestry and fishing) contributed 23% (at purchasers' values) of GDP in 1988, according to estimates by the World Bank. In 1989 63.4% of the labour force were employed in agriculture. During 1980–88 agricultural GDP increased by an annual average of 2.9%.

In the PDRY agriculture (including forestry and fishing) contributed 14.8% of GDP in 1986. An estimated 32.7% of the labour force were employed in agriculture and fishing in 1989.

Industry (including mining, manufacturing, construction and power) contributed 24% of the unified Yemen's GDP in 1992. In 1975 7.9% of the YAR's labour force were employed in the sector. During 1980–88 the YAR's industrial GDP increased by an annual average of 11.5%. Industry contributed

21.3% of the PDRY's GDP in 1988. In 1986 11.1% of the labour force were employed in industry (excluding construction).

The Government of the unified Yemen gave priority to the development of its considerable reserves of petroleum and natural gas. In 1990 mining and quarrying contributed 9.5% of GDP. Petroleum production averaged 220,000 barrels per day in 1993, and at the beginning of 1994 Yemen's proven published petroleum reserves totalled 4,000m. barrels.

Mining employed only 0.05% of the labour force of the YAR in 1975. However, petroleum was discovered in commercial quantities in 1984 and large reserves were subsequently discovered along the border with the PDRY. Exports of crude petroleum began in 1987. In 1990 exports of petroleum and petroleum products provided 91.1% of total export earnings. There are significant reserves of natural gas, estimated at 283,000m. cu m at January 1989, although actual reserves are reportedly much greater. Salt is also exploited on a large scale. In the PDRY mining and quarrying contributed only 0.2% of GDP in 1986. Petroleum was discovered in potentially commercial quantities in 1983. In addition, the region of the former PDRY has deposits of copper, gold, lead, zinc and molybdenum.

Manufacturing contributed 10% of the unified Yemen's GDP in 1992. The sector contributed an estimated 12% of the YAR's GDP in 1988, at purchasers' values, and employed 3.2% of the labour force in 1975. In the PDRY the sector contributed 7.9% of GDP in 1986. The most important branches of manufacturing in Yemen are petroleum refining, building materials, food products, beverages, tobacco, and chemical products.

Locally-produced petroleum provided one-third of the YAR's domestic energy requirements in 1986; the rest was provided by imports of petroleum, mainly from Saudi Arabia and Libya. Imports of mineral fuels comprised 6.7% of the value of the YAR's total imports in 1985, and 15.3% of the value of the PDRY's total imports in 1986.

In 1989 the YAR recorded a visible trade deficit of US $676.6m., and there was a deficit of $579m. on the current account of the balance of payments. In 1990 the principal source of imports (9.2%) was Saudi Arabia, while the principal market for exports (46.9%) was the USA. Other major trading partners were Italy, France and the United Kingdom. In 1990 EC countries accounted for 34.4% of imports and 41.3% of exports. The YAR's principal exports in 1990 were petroleum and petroleum products, crude materials (excluding fuels), food and live animals. The principal imports in that year were food and live animals, basic manufactures, machinery and transport equipment.

In 1989 the PDRY recorded a visible trade deficit of US $440.1m., and there was a deficit of $416.6m. on the current account of the balance of payments. In 1986 the principal source of imports (17.7%) was the USSR. Other major sources of imports in that year were the United Kingdom, Japan, the People's Republic of China, and Denmark. The principal market for exports in 1986 (27.8%) was Japan, while other important export markets included France, Saudi Arabia, the UAE and the YAR. The principal commodities exported in 1986 were petroleum products, cotton, hides and skins, fish, rice and coffee. The principal imports were petroleum, basic manufactures, clothing, foodstuffs and livestock.

The unified Yemen's budget for 1992 estimated a deficit of 12,336m. riyals. Total external debt at the end of 1993 was estimated to be US $5,923m., of which $5,341m. was long-term public debt. In that year the cost of debt-servicing was equivalent to 7.5% of the value of exports of goods and services. The annual rate of inflation averaged 100% in 1992, for the second consecutive year, but was estimated to have decreased to between 45% and 50% in 1993, before rising to 60% in 1994. In the same year, unemployment was estimated at 30% of the labour force. The Government was unable to agree on a budget for 1993 or 1994; however, a budget announced for 1995 estimated a deficit of $1,200m.

In 1990 there was an estimated budgetary deficit of 3,965m. riyals in the YAR. In 1989 the YAR's total external public debt was US $2,445m., and the cost of debt-servicing was equivalent to 11.5% of the value of exports of goods and services. The annual rate of inflation averaged 11.6% in 1980-88. An estimated 13% of the labour force were unemployed in 1986.

In the financial year ending 31 March 1986 there was a budgetary deficit of 32m. dinars in the PDRY. The 1990 budget forecast a deficit of 57m. dinars, equivalent to about 10% of estimated GDP. The annual rate of inflation averaged 4.5% in 1980-88.

Yemen is a member of the Arab Fund for Economic and Social Development (AFESD, see p. 237) and the Council of Arab Economic Unity (see p. 133).

The establishment of the Republic of Yemen in 1990 was expected to facilitate economic transformation, based on the development of the large petroleum reserves within the newly unified state, and on industrial investment around the port of Aden. By April 1991, however, it was estimated that Yemen would lose US $1,800m. in 1991, and a similar amount in 1992, owing to the crisis in the region of the Persian (Arabian) Gulf. This was mainly attributed to the loss of remittances from expatriate workers (see Recent History). Financial pressures arising from the Gulf crisis dictated a policy of temporary austerity, which included reductions in expenditure and subsidies on some staple foods, and provoked considerable social unrest in 1992. Political instability in 1993 and 1994 prevented the Government from publishing a budget for either year, and precipitated a harmful paralysis of the Yemeni economy. In mid-1994 it was reported that the Yemeni riyal was trading at unprecedented low levels on unofficial exchanges, and that the annual rate of inflation was more than 100%. The civil war of May-July 1994 resulted in damage estimated at $3,000m., particularly evident in the south of the country. Although the Government favoured the adoption of austerity measures (recommended by the IMF and the World Bank) to revive the ailing economy, it was initially reluctant to implement them, fearing an escalation of social unrest. Nevertheless, in January 1995 the Government doubled the price of electricity, and in March devalued the riyal after raising the price of certain basic goods and fuel. A 30%-50% increase in the salaries of low-paid government employees and military personnel failed to quell public discontent, however, and a series of protests ensued (see Recent History). Economic growth in Yemen in the late 1990s would depend on the Government's ability to satisfy international opinion as to the stability of the regime, thereby attracting foreign investment, while implementing austerity measures without precipitating further social unrest. In March 1995 the Government announced plans for a wide-ranging programme of privatization, and in the following month presented its first budget since 1992, with an anticipated deficit of $1,200m.

### Social Welfare

In 1982 the YAR had 30 hospital establishments, with a total of 3,803 beds, and there were 896 physicians working in official medical services. By 1986 the number of beds in hospitals and health centres had risen to nearly 6,000. Public expenditure on social security was provisionally estimated at 370m. riyals in 1990. In the PDRY the number of hospitals and health centres increased from 19 in 1970 to 54 (33 hospitals, 19 medical centres and two maternity centres) in 1986. In the same year there were 3,169 beds in government hospitals, and 631 physicians were working in the country. Public expenditure on health in the Republic of Yemen in 1992 was provisionally estimated at 2,540m. riyals, equivalent to 4.65% of total expenditure in that year.

### Education

In the former YAR, primary education began at six years of age and lasted for six years. Secondary education, beginning at the age of 12, lasted for a further six years, comprising two cycles of three years each. As a proportion of the school-age population, the total enrolment at primary and secondary schools (according to UNESCO estimates) was 56% (males 85%; females 25%) in 1990, compared with only 7% in 1970. Enrolment at primary schools in 1990 was equivalent to 76% of children in the relevant age-group, while the comparable ratio for secondary enrolment was 31%. In 1988 23,457 students were enrolled in higher education. There is a university in San'a. Public expenditure on education totalled 4,486.4m. riyals in 1990, according to provisional figures.

In the former PDRY, primary education began at seven years of age and lasted for eight years. Secondary education lasted for a further four years. As a proportion of the school-age population, the total enrolment at primary and secondary schools was 62% (males 81%; females 42%) in 1989, compared with 36% in 1970. Enrolment at primary schools in 1990 was equivalent to 88% of children in the relevant age-group (109% of boys; 67% of girls). The comparable ratio for secondary

# YEMEN

## *Statistical Survey*

enrolment in 1989 was 21% (boys 30%; girls 12%). There is a university in Aden. In 1987 there were also 20 technical and vocational institutes and nine teacher-training institutes. According to estimates by UNESCO, the average rate of adult illiteracy in the Republic of Yemen in 1990 was 62%. Public expenditure on education in the Republic of Yemen in 1992 was provisionally estimated at 11,615m. riyals.

## Public Holidays

**1995:** 1 January (New Year's Day), 1 February* (Ramadan begins), 3 March* (Id al-Fitr, end of Ramadan), 8 March (International Women's Day), 1 May (Labour Day), 10 May* (Id al-Adha, Feast of the Sacrifice), 31 May* (Muharram, Islamic New Year), 13 June (Corrective Movement Anniversary), 9 June* (Ashoura), 9 August* (Mouloud, Birth of the Prophet), 14 October (National Day), 20 December* (Leilat al-Meiraj, Ascension of the Prophet).

**1996:** 1 January (New Year's Day), 22 January* (Ramadan begins), 21 February* (Id al-Fitr, end of Ramadan), 8 March (International Women's Day), 29 April* (Id al-Adha, Feast of the Sacrifice), 1 May (Labour Day), 19 May* (Muharram, Islamic New Year), 28 May* (Ashoura), 13 June (Corrective Movement Anniversary), 28 July* (Mouloud, Birth of the Prophet), 14 October (National Day), 8 December* (Leilat al-Meiraj, Ascension of the Prophet).

* These holidays are dependent on the Islamic lunar calendar and may vary by one or two days from the dates given.

## Weights and Measures

Local weights and measures are used, and vary according to location.

# Statistical Survey

Source (unless otherwise indicated): Republic of Yemen Central Statistical Organization, POB 13434, San'a; tel. (1) 250619; telex 2266; fax (1) 250664.

## Area and Population

### AREA, POPULATION AND DENSITY

| | |
|---|---|
| Area (sq km) | 536,869* |
| Population (official estimates at mid-year) | |
| 1992 | 11,952,000 |
| 1993 | 12,302,000 |
| Density (per sq km) at mid-1993 | 22.9 |

* 207,286 sq miles.

**Capital:** San'a (capital of the former YAR), population 427,185 at 1 February 1986.

### ECONOMICALLY ACTIVE POPULATION

**Mid-1993** (estimates in '000): Agriculture 1,679; Total 3,124. Source: FAO, *Production Yearbook*.

## Agriculture

### PRINCIPAL CROPS ('000 metric tons)

| | 1991 | 1992 | 1993 |
|---|---|---|---|
| Wheat | 100 | 152 | 160 |
| Barley | 29 | 63 | 66 |
| Maize | 46 | 70 | 75 |
| Millet | 25 | 66 | 60 |
| Sorghum | 247 | 459 | 465 |
| Potatoes | 157 | 179 | 213 |
| Pulses | 44 | 76 | 76 |
| Sesame seed | 8 | 11 | 11 |
| Cottonseed | 5 | 8 | 9 |
| Cotton (lint) | 2 | 4 | 5 |
| Tomatoes | 172 | 185 | 204 |
| Onions (dry) | 59 | 61 | 61 |
| Other vegetables | 91 | 97 | 97 |
| Watermelons | 126 | 123 | 120 |
| Melons | 36 | 35 | 35 |
| Grapes | 139 | 145 | 144 |
| Dates | 21 | 21 | 22 |
| Bananas | 52 | 58 | 62 |
| Papayas | 53 | 55 | 56 |
| Other fruit | 51 | 57 | 62 |
| Coffee (green) | 5 | 8 | 9 |
| Tobacco (leaves) | 7 | 9 | 8 |

Source: FAO, *Production Yearbook*.

### LIVESTOCK ('000 head, year ending September)

| | 1991 | 1992 | 1993 |
|---|---|---|---|
| Horses* | 3 | 3 | 3 |
| Asses | 500 | 500 | 500 |
| Cattle | 1,117 | 1,139 | 1,163 |
| Camels | 166 | 169 | 173 |
| Sheep | 3,568 | 3,640 | 3,715 |
| Goats | 3,166 | 3,230 | 3,297 |

Poultry* (million): 16 in 1991; 19 in 1992; 21 in 1993.

* FAO estimates.

Source: FAO, *Production Yearbook*.

### LIVESTOCK PRODUCTS ('000 metric tons)

| | 1991 | 1992 | 1993 |
|---|---|---|---|
| Beef and veal* | 31 | 31 | 32 |
| Mutton and lamb† | 19 | 20 | 20 |
| Goat meat† | 17 | 17 | 17 |
| Poultry meat | 35 | 46 | 52 |
| Cows' milk | 149 | 152 | 155 |
| Sheep's milk† | 12 | 12 | 13 |
| Goats' milk† | 15 | 15 | 16 |
| Cheese† | 9.0 | 9.2 | 9.4 |
| Butter† | 3.9 | 4.0 | 4.1 |
| Hen eggs* | 18.4 | 20.6 | 19.1 |
| Wool: | | | |
| greasy | 3.1 | 4.0 | 4.1 |
| clean | 2.2 | 2.2 | 2.3 |
| Cattle hides† | 6.0 | 6.1 | 6.3 |

* Unofficial figures.   † FAO estimates.

Source: FAO, *Production Yearbook*.

## Fishing

('000 metric tons, live weight)

| | 1990 | 1991 | 1992 |
|---|---|---|---|
| Freshwater fishes | 0.4 | 0.9 | 0.8 |
| Marine fishes* | 71.9 | 78.4 | 76.1 |
| Other marine animals* | 5.5 | 4.1 | 3.8 |
| **Total catch** | 77.9 | 83.4 | 80.7 |

* FAO estimates.

Source: FAO, *Yearbook of Fishery Statistics*.

# YEMEN

## Mining

('000 metric tons)

|  | 1991 | 1992 |
|---|---|---|
| Crude petroleum | 9,431 | 8,143 |

Source: UN, *Industrial Commodity Statistics Yearbook*.

## Industry

**SELECTED PRODUCTS**
('000 metric tons, unless otherwise indicated)

|  | 1991 | 1992 |
|---|---|---|
| Motor spirit (petrol) | 510 | 800 |
| Kerosene | 172 | 220 |
| Jet fuels | 360 | 400 |
| Distillate fuel oils | 1,281 | 1,880 |
| Residual fuel oils | 1,946 | 2,300 |
| Liquefied petroleum gas* | 50 | 50 |
| Electricity (million kWh) | 1,750 | 1,810 |

* Provisional.

Source: UN, *Industrial Commodity Statistics Yearbook*.

## Finance

**CURRENCY AND EXCHANGE RATES**

**Monetary Units**
100 fils = 1 Yemeni riyal.

**Sterling and Dollar Equivalents** (31 December 1994)
£1 sterling = 18.790 Yemeni riyals;
US $1 = 12.010 Yemeni riyals;
1,000 Yemeni riyals = £53.22 = $83.26.

**Average Exchange Rate** (Yemeni riyals per US $)
1987  10.3417
1988   9.7717
1989   9.7600

Note: The exchange rate of US $1 = 9.76 Yemeni riyals, established in the YAR in 1988, remained in force until February 1990, when a new rate of $1 = 12.01 riyals was introduced. Following the merger of the two Yemens in May 1990, the YAR's currency was adopted as the currency of the unified country.

**BUDGET** (million riyals)

| Revenue* | 1990 | 1991 | 1992† |
|---|---|---|---|
| Taxation | 13,733 | 20,077 | 27,109 |
| Taxes on income, profits, etc. | 4,882 | 8,164 | 7,941 |
| Excises | 2,283 | 2,746 | 8,192 |
| Import duties | 4,012 | 6,013 | 7,900 |
| Other current revenue | 10,173 | 17,672 | n.a. |
| Property income | 8,367 | 15,489 | n.a. |
| Capital revenue | 35 | 233 | 338 |
| **Total** | 23,941 | 37,982 | n.a. |

| Expenditure‡ | 1990 | 1991 | 1992† |
|---|---|---|---|
| General public services | 4,913 | 4,644 | n.a. |
| Defence | 10,382 | 13,227 | 11,220 |
| Public order and safety | 3,248 | 4,110 | 4,431 |
| Education | 6,120 | 8,461 | 11,615 |
| Health | 1,439 | 1,954 | 2,540 |
| Housing and community amenities | 427 | 1,116 | n.a. |
| Recreational, cultural and religious affairs and services | 730 | 1,242 | 1,686 |
| Economic affairs and services | 3,643 | 2,579 | 8,061 |
| Other purposes | 2,957 | 4,279 | n.a. |
| Unallocable capital expenditure | 5,758 | 2,050 | — |
| Unallocable capital transfers | — | 390 | n.a. |
| **Total** | 39,617 | 44,052 | 54,545 |
| Current§ | 27,877 | 36,728 | 44,237 |
| Capital | 11,740 | 7,324 | 10,309 |

* Excluding grants received from abroad (million riyals): 1,397 in 1990; 300 in 1991.
† Projected figures.
‡ Excluding lending minus repayment (million riyals): 1,312 in 1990; 1,335 in 1991; 2,717 in 1992.
§ Including interest payments (million riyals): 2,956 in 1990; 4,279 in 1991; 5,182 in 1992.

Source: IMF, *Government Finance Statistics Yearbook*.

**1995** (Budget estimates, million riyals): Revenue 87,000; Expenditure 124,100.

Note: The Government did not publish budget proposals for 1993, when it continued to operate according to its 1992 proposals: budget proposals were not published for 1994 either.

**INTERNATIONAL RESERVES** (US $ million at 31 December)

|  | 1991 | 1992 | 1993 |
|---|---|---|---|
| Gold* | 2.5 | 2.4 | 2.4 |
| IMF special drawing rights | 16.8 | 4.0 | 0.6 |
| Foreign exchange | 662.5 | 316.5 | 144.6 |
| **Total** | 681.8 | 322.9 | 147.6 |

* Valued at market-related prices.

Source: IMF, *International Financial Statistics*.

**MONEY SUPPLY** (million riyals at 31 December)

|  | 1991 | 1992 | 1993 |
|---|---|---|---|
| Currency outside banks | 45,161 | 55,531 | 79,019 |
| Demand deposits at commercial banks | 14,097 | 18,237 | 21,489 |

Source: IMF, *International Financial Statistics*.

**NATIONAL ACCOUNTS** (million riyals at current prices)

**National Income and Product**

|  | 1989 | 1990 |
|---|---|---|
| Domestic factor incomes* | 52,098 | 66,010 |
| Consumption of fixed capital | 2,499 | 4,202 |
| **Gross domestic product (GDP) at factor cost** | 54,597 | 70,212 |
| Indirect taxes, *less* subsidies | 6,809 | 6,947 |
| **GDP in purchasers' values** | 61,406 | 77,159 |
| Net factor income from abroad | 1,454 | 1,658 |
| **Gross national product (GNP)** | 62,860 | 78,817 |
| *Less* Consumption of fixed capital | 2,499 | 4,202 |
| **National income in market prices** | 60,361 | 74,615 |
| Other current transfers from abroad (net) | 3,706 | 10,875 |
| **National disposable income** | 64,067 | 85,490 |

* Compensation of employees and the operating surplus of enterprises.

YEMEN

#### Expenditure on the Gross Domestic Product

|  | 1989 | 1990 |
|---|---|---|
| Government final consumption expenditure | 16,470 | 21,154 |
| Private final consumption expenditure | 48,322 | 58,030 |
| Increase in stocks | 134 | 700 |
| Gross fixed capital formation | 11,356 | 11,970 |
| **Total domestic expenditure** | 76,282 | 91,854 |
| Exports of goods and services | 10,205 | 10,471 |
| *Less* Imports of goods and services | 25,081 | 25,166 |
| **GDP in purchasers' values** | 61,406 | 77,159 |

#### Gross Domestic Product by Economic Activity

|  | 1989 | 1990 |
|---|---|---|
| Agriculture, hunting, forestry and fishing | 14,682 | 16,101 |
| Mining and quarrying | 3,912 | 7,030 |
| Manufacturing | 5,861 | 6,586 |
| Electricity, gas and water | 1,191 | 1,400 |
| Construction | 2,838 | 3,394 |
| Trade, restaurants and hotels | 7,784 | 9,590 |
| Transport, storage and communications | 5,202 | 6,015 |
| Finance, insurance, real estate and business services | 4,154 | 4,929 |
| Government services | 10,875 | 18,201 |
| Other community, social and personal services | 483 | 572 |
| Private non-profit services to households | 79 | 95 |
| **Sub-total** | 57,061 | 73,913 |
| Import duties | 5,000 | 3,996 |
| *Less* Imputed bank service charge | 655 | 750 |
| **GDP in purchasers' values** | 61,406 | 77,159 |

## Transport

**ROAD TRAFFIC** (vehicles in use at 31 December)

|  | 1990 | 1991 | 1992 |
|---|---|---|---|
| Passenger cars | 162,961 | 165,438 | 186,172 |
| Buses and coaches | 1,986 | 2,223 | 2,576 |
| Goods vehicles | 235,042 | 235,734 | 251,779 |

Source: IRF, *World Road Statistics*.

*Statistical Survey, Statistical Survey of the former YAR*

**INTERNATIONAL SEA-BORNE SHIPPING**
(freight traffic, '000 metric tons)

|  | 1988 | 1989 | 1990 |
|---|---|---|---|
| Goods loaded | 1,836 | 1,883 | 1,936 |
| Goods unloaded | 7,189 | 7,151 | 7,829 |

Source: UN, *Monthly Bulletin of Statistics*.

**CIVIL AVIATION** (traffic on scheduled services)

|  | 1990 | 1991 | 1992 |
|---|---|---|---|
| Kilometres flown (million) | 13 | 9 | 13 |
| Passengers carried ('000) | 671 | 541 | 800 |
| Passenger-km (million) | 929 | 762 | 1,124 |
| Total ton-km (million) | 99 | 77 | 114 |

Source: UN, *Statistical Yearbook*.

## Communications Media

|  | 1991 | 1992 |
|---|---|---|
| Radio receivers ('000 in use) | 325 | 350 |
| Television receivers ('000 in use) | 330 | 350 |

Source: UNESCO, *Statistical Yearbook*.

**Telephones** ('000 main lines in use): 136 in 1991 (Source: UN, *Statistical Yearbook*).

# Statistical Survey of the former Yemen Arab Republic

Source (except where otherwise stated): Yemen Arab Republic Central Planning Organization, Data Processing Centre, POB 175, San'a; tel. (1) 3506; telex 2266.

## Area and Population

**AREA, POPULATION AND DENSITY**

| | |
|---|---|
| Area (sq km) | 200,000* |
| Population (census results)† | |
| February 1981 | 8,556,974‡ |
| 1 February 1986§ | |
| Males | 4,647,310 |
| Females | 4,626,863 |
| Total | 9,274,173 |
| Density (per sq km) at February 1986 | 46.4 |

\* 77,220 sq miles.
† The totals include Yemeni nationals abroad, numbering 1,395,123 (males 1,177,562; females 217,561) in 1981.
‡ Including an adjustment for underenumeration, estimated at 705,662.
§ Provisional.

**PRINCIPAL PROVINCES** (population; census results)

|  | 1981 | 1986 |
|---|---|---|
| San'a* | 1,740,744 | 1,429,651 |
| Taiz | 1,053,520 | 1,643,901 |
| Hodeida | 1,085,376 | 1,294,359 |
| Hajja | 880,619 | 897,814 |
| Baida | 327,539 | 381,249 |

\* Excluding San'a City, population: 277,818 in 1981; 427,185 in 1986.

**PRINCIPAL TOWNS** (population, including suburbs, at 1986 census)
San'a (capital) 427,185; Taiz 178,043; Hodeida 155,110.

YEMEN

*Statistical Survey of the former YAR*

**BIRTHS AND DEATHS** (UN estimates, annual averages)

|  | 1975–80 | 1980–85 | 1985–90 |
|---|---|---|---|
| Birth rate (per 1,000) | 55.6 | 54.4 | 53.6 |
| Death rate (per 1,000) | 20.7 | 18.3 | 16.1 |

Source: UN, *World Population Prospects 1990*.

**ECONOMICALLY ACTIVE POPULATION** (persons aged 10 years and over at census of 1 February 1975, excluding underenumeration)

| | |
|---|---|
| Agriculture | 830,340 |
| Mining | 576 |
| Manufacturing | 33,920 |
| Electricity | 1,511 |
| Construction | 52,640 |
| Trade | 68,979 |
| Transport | 24,709 |
| Finance | 1,976 |
| Social services | 85,775 |
| Unstated activities | 27,326 |
| **Total labour force** | **1,127,572*** |

* Of whom 1,057,566 (males 932,440; females 125,126) were employed and 70,006 (males 63,120; females 6,886) were unemployed.

## Mining

('000 metric tons)

|  | 1988* | 1989 | 1990 |
|---|---|---|---|
| Crude petroleum* | 7,070 | 8,982 | 8,468 |
| Salt (unrefined) | 163 | 222 | 220 |
| Gypsum (crude) | 60 | 66 | 66 |

* Provisional.

Source: UN, *Industrial Statistics Yearbook*.

## Industry

**SELECTED PRODUCTS**
('000 metric tons, unless otherwise indicated)

|  | 1988 | 1989 | 1990 |
|---|---|---|---|
| Motor spirit (petrol) | 100 | 100 | 110 |
| Distillate fuel oils | 124 | 125 | 130 |
| Residual fuel oils | 130 | 135 | 136 |
| Cement* | 646 | 700 | 700 |
| Electricity (million kWh) | 820 | 830 | 830 |

* Provisional.

Source: UN, *Industrial Statistics Yearbook*.

## Finance

**CENTRAL BANK RESERVES** (US $ million at 31 December)

|  | 1987 | 1988 | 1989 |
|---|---|---|---|
| Gold* | 0.5 | 0.5 | 0.5 |
| IMF special drawing rights | 26.9 | 32.2 | 20.8 |
| Foreign exchange | 512.6 | 252.9 | 258.3 |
| **Total** | **540.0** | **285.6** | **279.6** |

* Valued at 35 SDRs per troy ounce.

Source: IMF, *International Financial Statistics*.

**MONEY SUPPLY** (million riyals at 31 December)

|  | 1987 | 1988 | 1989 |
|---|---|---|---|
| Currency outside banks | 20,159 | 20,166 | 21,206 |
| Demand deposits at commercial banks | 4,646 | 4,714 | 5,135 |

Source: IMF, *International Financial Statistics*.

**NATIONAL ACCOUNTS** (million riyals at current prices)
**Expenditure on the Gross Domestic Product**

|  | 1985 | 1986 | 1987 |
|---|---|---|---|
| Government final consumption expenditure | 5,520 | 6,086 | 7,778 |
| Private final consumption expenditure | 29,457 | 35,728 | 40,115 |
| Increase in stocks | −75 | 50 | 150 |
| Gross fixed capital formation | 4,547 | 4,938 | 6,200 |
| **Total domestic expenditure** | 39,449 | 46,802 | 54,243 |
| Exports of goods and services | 1,164 | 1,155 | 1,616 |
| *Less* Imports of goods and services | −9,644 | −9,568 | −12,300 |
| **GDP in purchasers' values** | 30,969 | 38,389 | 43,559 |
| **GDP at constant 1985 prices** | 30,969 | 33,880 | 35,507 |

Source: IMF, *International Financial Statistics*.

**BALANCE OF PAYMENTS** (US $ million)

|  | 1987 | 1988 | 1989 |
|---|---|---|---|
| Merchandise exports f.o.b. | 48.2 | 447.0 | 606.0 |
| Merchandise imports f.o.b. | −1,189.4 | −1,309.4 | −1,282.7 |
| **Trade balance** | −1,141.2 | −862.4 | −676.6 |
| Exports of services | 128.0 | 170.9 | 204.9 |
| Imports of services | −271.0 | −346.9 | −407.2 |
| Other income received | 44.1 | 29.4 | 42.7 |
| Other income paid | −61.0 | −89.2 | −81.4 |
| Private unrequited transfers (net) | 707.7 | 313.7 | 242.3 |
| Official unrequited transfers (net) | 141.2 | 90.4 | 96.2 |
| **Current balance** | −452.2 | −694.3 | −579.0 |
| Direct investment (net) | 1.1 | — | — |
| Portfolio investment (net) | 1.1 | — | — |
| Other capital (net) | 481.3 | 476.1 | 510.9 |
| Net errors and omissions | 36.6 | −58.8 | 57.9 |
| **Overall balance** | 67.7 | −277.0 | −10.3 |

Source: IMF, *International Financial Statistics*.

# External Trade

**PRINCIPAL COMMODITIES** (distribution by SITC, million riyals)

| Imports c.i.f. | 1988 | 1989 | 1990 |
|---|---|---|---|
| **Food and live animals** | 3,901.9 | 4,387.8 | 5,522.6 |
| Live animals chiefly for food | 414.9 | 456.2 | 700.1 |
| Dairy products and birds' eggs | 595.7 | 496.1 | 574.4 |
| Cereals and cereal preparations | 1,069.6 | 1,709.5 | 2,548.9 |
| Sugar, sugar preparations and honey | 704.7 | 746.6 | 1,034.0 |
| **Beverages and tobacco** | 308.0 | 242.6 | 290.6 |
| Tobacco and tobacco manufactures | 301.7 | 237.8 | 286.5 |
| **Crude materials (inedible) except fuels** | 343.0 | 389.5 | 388.5 |
| Cork and wood | 266.3 | 331.6 | 307.3 |
| **Mineral fuels, lubricants, etc.** | 1,927.9 | 2,172.6 | 796.9 |
| Petroleum, petroleum products, etc. | 1,777.6 | 1,957.4 | 720.5 |
| **Animal and vegetable oils, fats and waxes** | 189.5 | 257.9 | 303.6 |
| Fixed vegetable oils and fats | 187.4 | 254.6 | 303.6 |
| **Chemicals and related products** | 1,348.2 | 874.6 | 1,114.1 |
| Medicinal and pharmaceutical products | 623.5 | 438.2 | 386.6 |
| Artificial resins, plastic materials, etc. | 358.1 | 204.3 | 337.7 |
| **Basic manufactures** | 2,920.6 | 2,215.3 | 2,803.2 |
| Paper, paperboard and manufactures | 348.9 | 221.4 | 360.0 |
| Non-metallic mineral manufactures | 398.1 | 351.2 | 274.5 |
| Iron and steel | 809.7 | 639.0 | 961.2 |
| **Machinery and transport equipment** | 1,848.5 | 2,462.5 | 2,102.2 |
| Machinery specialized for particular industries | 346.6 | 459.5 | 356.1 |
| General industrial machinery, equipment and parts | 355.1 | 451.3 | 239.9 |
| Electrical machinery, apparatus, etc. | 397.3 | 520.2 | 701.0 |
| Road vehicles and parts (excl. tyres, engines and electrical parts) | 503.9 | 780.4 | 542.3 |
| **Miscellaneous manufactured articles** | 705.6 | 696.1 | 626.1 |
| **Total** (incl. others) | 13,523.6 | 13,669.8 | 13,954.0 |

| Exports f.o.b. | 1988 | 1989 | 1990 |
|---|---|---|---|
| **Food and live animals** | 485.9 | 519.4 | 215.3 |
| **Crude materials (inedible) except fuels** | 119.8 | 223.5 | 221.0 |
| Hides, skins and furskins (raw) | 73.9 | 135.0 | 169.7 |
| **Mineral fuels, lubricants, etc.** | 3,887.7 | 5,462.3 | 5,790.5 |
| Petroleum, petroleum products, etc. | 3,887.7 | 5,462.3 | 5,789.8 |
| **Total** (incl. others) | 4,607.3 | 6,345.2 | 6,352.9 |

**PRINCIPAL TRADING PARTNERS** (million riyals)

| Imports c.i.f. | 1988 | 1989 | 1990 |
|---|---|---|---|
| Australia | 479.9 | 459.0 | 853.3 |
| Belgium | 311.4 | 275.0 | 483.6 |
| China, People's Republic | 285.0 | 420.0 | 563.5 |
| Djibouti | 122.4 | 207.8 | 296.7 |
| France | 700.7 | 1,409.3 | 1,094.1 |
| Germany, Federal Republic | 872.4 | 580.1 | 869.5 |
| Italy | 522.1 | 453.5 | 390.8 |
| Japan | 847.5 | 1,135.4 | 589.5 |
| Jordan | 58.5 | 52.8 | 192.9 |
| Korea, Republic | 497.4 | 375.5 | 444.1 |
| Kuwait | 209.1 | 89.7 | 294.7 |
| Malaysia | 316.4 | 469.7 | 448.4 |
| Netherlands | 1,182.7 | 567.8 | 604.3 |
| Saudi Arabia | 2,294.9 | 2,329.7 | 1,280.4 |
| Singapore | 392.0 | 315.8 | 338.3 |
| Somalia | 185.4 | 221.0 | 391.4 |
| Sweden | 171.0 | 99.2 | 164.5 |
| Thailand | 123.8 | 178.9 | 318.4 |
| United Arab Emirates | 164.3 | 112.9 | 360.5 |
| United Kingdom | 1,079.5 | 781.6 | 896.6 |
| USA | 746.9 | 1,118.2 | 1,026.0 |
| **Total** (incl. others) | 13,523.6 | 13,669.8* | 13,954.0* |

* Including imports from unspecified EC countries (million riyals): 177.0 in 1989; 188.2 in 1990.

| Exports f.o.b. | 1988 | 1989 | 1990 |
|---|---|---|---|
| Cuba | — | — | 263.6 |
| Djibouti | 5.9 | 53.5 | 65.4 |
| Italy | 779.9 | 1,129.5 | 1,894.4 |
| Japan | 181.2 | 152.9 | 55.2 |
| Kenya | — | 91.6 | — |
| Saudi Arabia | 526.1 | 516.5 | 223.5 |
| Singapore | 165.9 | 17.7 | 45.9 |
| United Kingdom | 516.5 | 0.0 | 686.3 |
| USA | 1,330.1 | 1,320.6 | 2,979.1 |
| Yemen, People's Democratic Republic | 82.3 | 104.6 | — |
| **Total** (incl. others) | 4,607.3 | 6,345.2* | 6,352.9 |

* Including exports for which the destination was not stated (2,838.3 million riyals).

# Education

| | Teachers | | Pupils | |
|---|---|---|---|---|
| | 1988 | 1990* | 1988 | 1990* |
| Primary | 27,732 | 35,350 | 1,250,599 | 1,291,372 |
| Secondary: | | | | |
| General | 10,841 | 12,106 | 289,615 | 394,578 |
| Teacher training | 716‡ | 783 | 12,806‡ | 21,051 |
| Vocational | 279† | 464 | 3,269§ | 5,068 |

**Higher education:** 454 teachers, 17,417 students in 1987; 470 teachers, 23,457 students in 1988.

* Figures for 1989 are not available.
† 1985.   ‡ 1986.   § 1987.

Source: UNESCO, *Statistical Yearbook*.

# Statistical Survey of the former People's Democratic Republic of Yemen

Source (unless otherwise stated): Central Statistical Organization, Steamer Point, POB 1193, Aden; tel. (2) 22235.

## Area and Population

**AREA, POPULATION AND DENSITY**

| | |
|---|---:|
| Area (sq km) | 336,869* |
| Population (census results) | |
| 14 May 1973 | 1,590,275 |
| 29 March 1988† | |
| Males | 1,184,359 |
| Females | 1,160,907 |
| Total | 2,345,266 |
| Population (official estimates at mid-year) | |
| 1988 | 2,337,000 |
| 1989 | 2,398,000 |
| 1990 | 2,460,000 |
| Density (per sq km) at mid-1990 | 7.3 |

* 130,066 sq miles. † Preliminary figures.

**GOVERNORATES** (estimated population, mid-1986)

| | Area (sq km) | Population ('000) | Density |
|---|---:|---:|---:|
| Aden | 6,980 | 407 | 58.3 |
| Lahej | 12,766 | 382 | 29.9 |
| Abyan | 21,489 | 434 | 20.2 |
| Shabwah | 73,908 | 226 | 3.1 |
| Hadhramaut | 155,376 | 686 | 4.4 |
| Al-Mahra | 66,350 | 85 | 1.3 |
| **Total** | 336,869 | 2,220 | 6.6 |

**Capital:** Aden (estimated population 271,590 at mid-1977).

**BIRTHS AND DEATHS** (UN estimates, annual averages)

| | 1975–80 | 1980–85 | 1985–90 |
|---|---:|---:|---:|
| Birth rate (per 1,000) | 47.6 | 47.0 | 47.3 |
| Death rate (per 1,000) | 20.9 | 17.4 | 15.8 |

Source: UN, *World Population Prospects 1990*.

**EMPLOYMENT** (estimates, 1986)

| | |
|---|---:|
| Agriculture and fishing | 216,000 |
| Industry | 57,000 |
| Construction | 49,000 |
| Transport | 34,000 |
| Commerce | 52,000 |
| Services | 107,000 |
| **Total** | 515,000 |

## Forestry

**ROUNDWOOD REMOVALS**
(FAO estimates, '000 cubic metres, excl. bark)

| | 1987 | 1988 | 1989 |
|---|---:|---:|---:|
| **Total** (all fuel wood) | 306 | 312 | 324 |

**1990–91:** Annual output as in 1989 (FAO estimates).
Source: FAO, *Yearbook of Forest Products*.

## Mining

('000 metric tons)

| | 1986 | 1987 | 1988* |
|---|---:|---:|---:|
| Crude petroleum | n.a. | n.a. | 200 |
| Salt (unrefined) | 40 | 56 | 72 |

**1989** ('000 metric tons): Crude petroleum 750*.
**1990** ('000 metric tons): Crude petroleum 800*.
* Provisional.
Source: UN *Industrial Statistics Yearbook*.

## Industry

**SELECTED PRODUCTS**
('000 metric tons, unless otherwise indicated)

| | 1988 | 1989 | 1990 |
|---|---:|---:|---:|
| Frozen fish | 3.3 | 3.0* | n.a. |
| Salted, dried or smoked fish | 6.1 | 6.1* | 6.3* |
| Motor spirit (petrol) | 200 | 210 | 220 |
| Kerosene | 170 | 165 | 170 |
| Jet fuels | 260 | 260 | 260 |
| Distillate fuel oils | 1,130 | 1,140 | 1,150 |
| Residual fuel oils | 1,360 | 1,370 | 1,800 |
| Liquefied petroleum gas | 45† | 46† | 50† |
| Electric energy (million kWh) | 845 | 850 | 910 |

* FAO figure. † Estimate.
Source: UN, *Industrial Statistics Yearbook*.

## Finance

**CURRENCY AND EXCHANGE RATES**
**Monetary Units**
  1,000 fils = 1 Yemeni dinar (YD).

**Sterling and Dollar Equivalents** (31 May 1990)
  £1 sterling = 774.6 fils;
  US $1 = 461.9 fils;
  100 Yemeni dinars = £129.09 = $216.49.

**Exchange Rate**
  Between February 1973 and May 1990 the Yemeni dinar's value was fixed at US $2.8952 ($1 = 345.4 fils).

# YEMEN

## Statistical Survey of the former PDRY

### CENTRAL BANK RESERVES (US $ million at 31 December)

|  | 1987 | 1988 | 1989 |
|---|---|---|---|
| Gold* | 1.77 | 1.77 | 1.77 |
| IMF special drawing rights | 2.96 | 20.00 | 2.39 |
| Foreign exchange | 94.14 | 59.93 | 74.46 |
| **Total** | 98.87 | 81.70 | 78.62 |

* Valued at $42.22 per troy ounce.

Source: IMF, *International Financial Statistics*.

### MONEY SUPPLY (million dinars at 31 December)

|  | 1987 | 1988 | 1989 |
|---|---|---|---|
| Currency outside banks | 299.65 | 315.79 | 322.87 |
| Demand deposits at commercial banks | 152.60 | 156.12 | 268.38 |
| **Total money** | 452.25 | 471.91 | 591.25 |

Source: IMF, *International Financial Statistics*.

### COST OF LIVING
(Consumer Price Index for Aden; base: 1980 = 100)

|  | 1986 | 1987 | 1988 |
|---|---|---|---|
| Food | 121.2 | 125.5 | 125.1 |
| Fuel, light and water | 120.6 | 121.2 | 121.2 |
| Clothing | 127.4 | 127.4 | 127.4 |
| Rent | 100.0 | 100.0 | 100.0 |
| **All items** (incl. others) | 135.4 | 139.2 | 139.2 |

Source: ILO, *Year Book of Labour Statistics*.

### BALANCE OF PAYMENTS (US $ million)*

|  | 1987 | 1988 | 1989 |
|---|---|---|---|
| Merchandise exports f.o.b. | 70.9 | 82.2 | 113.8 |
| Merchandise imports f.o.b. | −456.9 | −596.1 | −553.9 |
| **Trade balance** | −385.9 | −513.9 | −440.1 |
| Exports of services | 102.8 | 135.2 | 134.9 |
| Imports of services | −203.2 | −313.3 | −339.3 |
| Other income received | 15.9 | 15.1 | 14.2 |
| Other income paid | −13.6 | −16.5 | −13.3 |
| Private unrequited transfers (net) | 302.6 | 252.8 | 171.7 |
| Official unrequited transfers (net) | 51.8 | 36.2 | 55.3 |
| **Current balance** | −129.7 | −404.5 | −416.6 |
| Capital (net) | −70.3 | 315.6 | 403.0 |
| Net errors and omissions | 11.4 | 62.9 | −2.3 |
| **Overall balance** | −48.0 | −26.0 | −15.9 |

* Imports and exports of petroleum by the Aden refinery are not included in merchandise trade. Such transactions are reflected in a processing fee appropriate to exports of services, on the assumption that no change of ownership has taken place.

Source: IMF, *International Financial Statistics*.

## External Trade

### PRINCIPAL COMMODITIES ('000 dinars)

| Imports c.i.f.* | 1980 | 1985 | 1986 |
|---|---|---|---|
| Food and live animals | 66,117 | 70,819 | 49,292 |
| Wheat and wheat flour | 18,907 | 19,238 | 10,471 |
| Rice | 4,043 | 8,316 | 4,982 |
| Refined sugar | 10,862 | 3,838 | 3,311 |
| Crude materials (inedible) except fuels | 9,537 | 5,771 | 2,648 |
| Petroleum products | 51,920 | 36,551 | 23,581 |
| Animal and vegetable oils and fats | 5,497 | 9,222 | 6,374 |
| Chemicals | 8,103 | 10,938 | 9,520 |
| Basic manufactures | 30,098 | 39,574 | 24,740 |
| Machinery and transport equipment | 50,847 | 52,948 | 31,591 |
| Miscellaneous manufactured articles | 8,802 | 12,341 | 5,388 |
| **Total** (incl. others) | 236,259 | 241,115 | 154,357 |

| Exports f.o.b.* | 1980 | 1985 | 1986 |
|---|---|---|---|
| Food and live animals | 7,645 | 6,695 | 7,033 |
| Fresh fish | 6,386 | 5,167 | 4,665 |
| Beverages and tobacco | 958 | 1,265 | 618 |
| Crude materials (inedible) except fuels | 4,321 | 1,625 | 853 |
| Petroleum products | 875 | 3,356 | 1,212 |
| Basic manufactures | 422 | 78 | 117 |
| Miscellaneous manufactured articles | 220 | 248 | 123 |
| **Total** (incl. others) | 14,547 | 13,852 | 10,021 |

* Excluding imports and exports of foreign-owned companies. In 1980 total imports were 527.4 million dinars, and total exports 268.5 million dinars.

Detailed trade figures for 1981–84 are not available. Total imports (in million dinars) were: 490.1 in 1981; 552.4 in 1982; 512.3 in 1983; 532.9 in 1984. Total exports (in million dinars) were: 209.8 in 1981; 274.6 in 1982; 232.7 in 1983; 222.9 in 1984.

**1987** (million dinars, excl. trade of foreign-owned companies): Imports c.i.f. 170; Exports f.o.b. 24.

**1988** (million dinars, excl. trade of foreign-owned companies): Imports c.i.f. 226; Exports f.o.b. 28.

### PRINCIPAL TRADING PARTNERS ('000 dinars)*

| Imports | 1980 | 1985 | 1986 |
|---|---|---|---|
| China, People's Republic | 7,927 | 11,422 | 8,547 |
| Denmark | 5,002 | 7,528 | 8,476 |
| France | 13,435 | 11,634 | 4,398 |
| Germany, Fed. Republic | 4,660 | 7,857 | 5,457 |
| Iran | n.a. | 2,358 | 4,546 |
| Japan | 24,075 | 15,678 | 8,637 |
| Netherlands | 9,561 | 13,168 | 7,432 |
| Saudi Arabia | 6,692 | 3,712 | 5,761 |
| Singapore | 3,329 | 9,991 | 7,605 |
| USSR | 18,103 | 34,327 | 25,247 |
| United Arab Emirates | 292 | 1,534 | 5,042 |
| United Kingdom | 18,713 | 17,070 | 11,349 |
| **Total** (incl. others) | 213,171 | 212,993 | 142,937 |

## YEMEN

| Exports | 1980 | 1985 | 1986 |
|---|---:|---:|---:|
| Djibouti | 169 | 196 | 126 |
| Ethiopia | 261 | 99 | 47 |
| France | 9 | 517 | 2,321 |
| Italy | 1,352 | 416 | 432 |
| Japan | 5,991 | 3,981 | 2,731 |
| Saudi Arabia | 736 | 739 | 1,293 |
| Singapore | 1,102 | 1,005 | 163 |
| USSR | n.a. | 583 | 102 |
| United Arab Emirates | 55 | 135 | 1,127 |
| Yemen Arab Republic | 1,741 | 2,639 | 1,022 |
| **Total** (incl. others) | 13,938 | 11,125 | 9,826 |

* Excluding imports and exports of foreign-owned companies. Also excluded is trade with North and South America.

Figures are not available for 1981–84.

## Education

|  | Teachers |  | Pupils/Students |  |
|---|---:|---:|---:|---:|
|  | 1989 | 1990 | 1989 | 1990 |
| Pre-primary | 475 | n.a. | 11,500 | n.a. |
| Primary* | 13,744 | 13,240 | 331,042 | 379,908 |
| Secondary |  |  |  |  |
| General | 1,915 | n.a. | 34,179 | n.a. |
| Teacher training | 128 | 126 | 2,410 | 2,752 |
| Vocational | n.a. | 532 | n.a. | 6,351 |
| Higher | 643† | n.a. | 3,999† | n.a. |

* Excluding schools for nomads.   † 1987.

Source: UNESCO, *Statistical Yearbook*.

# Directory

## The Constitution

A draft constitution for the united Republic of Yemen (based on that endorsed by the Yemen Arab Republic (YAR) and the People's Democratic Republic of Yemen (PDRY) in December 1981) was published in December 1989, and was approved by a popular referendum on 15–16 May 1991.

On 29 September 1994 52 articles were amended, 29 added and one cancelled, leaving a total of 159 articles in the Constitution.

As revised in 1994, the Constitution defines the Yemeni Republic as an independent and sovereign Arab and Islamic country. The document states that the Republic 'is an indivisible whole, and it is impermissible to concede any part of it. The Yemeni people are part of the Arab and Islamic nation.' The Islamic Shari'a is identified as the basis of all laws.

The revised Constitution provides for the election, by direct universal suffrage, of the President of the Republic; the President is elected for a five-year term, renewable only once.* The President is empowered to appoint a Vice-President. The President of the Republic is, *ex officio*, Commander-in-Chief of the Armed Forces.

Legislative authority is vested in the 301-member House of Representatives, which is elected, by universal suffrage, for a four-year term. The legislature is empowered to debate and approve legislation, to decide general state policy, to supervise public spending, and to ratify international treaties and agreements. The Constitution states that 'the President can dissolve the House of Representatives only when necessary'.

The President of the Republic appoints the Prime Minister and other members of the Government on the advice of the Prime Minister. The Constitution empowers both the President and the legislature to impeach the Prime Minister and other government members 'for crimes committed in the performance of their duties'.

The Constitution delineates the separation of the powers of the organs of State, and guarantees the independence of the judiciary. The existence of a multi-party political system is confirmed, although serving members of the police and armed forces are banned from political activity.

* The amendments to the Constitution enacted in September 1994 provided for the abolition of the Presidential Council, which had previously been empowered to elect the President of the Republic. On 1 October the House of Representatives, meeting as an electoral college, confirmed Ali Abdullah Saleh as President for a five-year term; following the expiry of this mandate, subsequent elections to the presidency would be as defined above.

### HEAD OF STATE

**President:** Lt-Gen. ALI ABDULLAH SALEH (took office 24 May 1990, re-elected 1 October 1994).
**Vice-President:** Maj.-Gen. ABD AR-RABBUH MANSUR HADI (GPC).

### COUNCIL OF MINISTERS
(June 1995)

A coalition of the General People's Congress (GPC) and the Yemeni Islah Party (YIP).

**Prime Minister:** ABD AL-AZIZ ABD AL-GHANI (GPC).
**Deputy Prime Minister and Minister of Industry, Petroleum and Mineral Resources:** Dr MUHAMMAD SAID AL-ATTAR (GPC).
**Deputy Prime Minister and Minister of Foreign Affairs:** Dr ABD AL-KARIM AL-IRYANI (GPC).
**Deputy Prime Minister:** ABD AL-WAHAB ALI AL-ANISI (YIP).
**Deputy Prime Minister and Minister of Planning and Development:** ABD AL-QADIR BAJAMMAL (GPC).
**Minister of Supply and Trade:** MUHAMMAD AHMAD AFANDI (YIP).
**Minister of Local Administration:** MUHAMMAD HASSAN DAMMAJ (YIP).
**Minister of the Interior:** Col HUSSAIN MUHAMMAD ARAB (GPC).
**Minister of Finance:** Eng. MUHAMMAD AHMAD AL-JUNAYD (GPC).
**Minister of Justice:** Dr ABD AL-WAHAB LUTFI AL-DAYLAMI (YIP).
**Minister of Religious Endowments and Guidance:** Dr GHALIB ABD AL-KAFI AL-QURSHI (YIP).
**Minister of Information:** ABD AR-RAHMAN MUHAMMAD AL-AKWA (GPC).
**Minister of Culture and Tourism:** YAHYA HUSSAIN AL-ARASHI (GPC).
**Minister of Transport:** AHMAD MUSAID HUSSAIN (GPC).
**Minister of Construction, Housing and Urban Planning:** ALI HAMID SHARAF (GPC).
**Minister of Health:** Dr NAJIB GHANIM (YIP).
**Minister of Agriculture and Water Resources:** AHMAD SALIM AL-JABALI (GPC).
**Minister of Fisheries:** Dr ABD AR-RAHMAN BAFADL (YIP).
**Minister of Defence:** Brig. ABD AL-MALIK ALI AS-SAYYANI (GPC).
**Minister of Social Security and Labour:** MUHAMMAD ABDULLAH AL-BATTANI (GPC).
**Minister of Electricity and Water:** ABDULLAH MUHSIN AL-AKWA (YIP).
**Minister for Parliamentary and Legal Affairs:** ABDULLAH AHMAD GHANIM (GPC).
**Minister for the Civil Service and Administrative Reform:** SADIQ AMIN ABU RAS (GPC).
**Minister of Communications:** Eng. AHMAD MUHAMMAD AL-ANISI (GPC).
**Minister of Youth and Sport:** Dr ABD AL-WAHAB RAWIH (GPC).
**Minister of Education:** ABD ALI AL-QUBATI (YIP).

### MINISTRIES

All ministries are in San'a.

## Legislature

### THE HOUSE OF REPRESENTATIVES

The House of Representatives has 301 members, elected for a four-year term. It originally comprised the 159 members of the Consultative Council (*Majlis ash-Shura*) of the former YAR; the

# YEMEN

111 members of the Supreme People's Council of the former PDRY; and 31 new members nominated by President Saleh. A general election for a new House of Representatives was held on 27 April 1993.

**Speaker:** Sheikh ABDULLAH BIN HUSSAIN AL-AHMAR.

### General Election, 27 April 1993

| Party | Seats |
|---|---|
| General People's Congress (GPC) | 123 |
| Yemeni Islah Party (YIP) | 62 |
| Yemen Socialist Party (YSP) | 56 |
| Independents | 47 |
| Baathist parties | 7 |
| Nasserite parties | 3 |
| Al-Haq | 2 |
| Void | 1 |
| **Total** | 301 |

## Political Organizations

In the PDRY the YSP was the only legal political party until December 1989, when the formation of opposition parties was legalized. There were no political parties in the former YAR. The two leading parties that emerged in the unified Yemen were the GPC and the YSP. During 1990 an estimated 30 to 40 further political parties were reported to have been formed, and in 1995 43 were known to be in existence. Following the civil war from May to July 1994, President Saleh declared that the YSP would be excluded from the new government formed in October 1994.

**Al-Haq:** San'a; conservative Islamic party; Sec.-Gen. Sheikh AHMAD ASH-SHAMI.

**Democratic Coalition of Opposition:** San'a; f. 1995 as a coalition of 13 political parties and organizations, including a splinter faction of the YSP and the LSY.

**General People's Congress (GPC):** San'a; a broad grouping of supporters of President Saleh; Chair. Lt-Gen. ALI ABDULLAH SALEH; Vice-Chair. Maj.-Gen. ABD AR-RABBUH MANSUR HADI; Sec.-Gen. Dr ABD AL-KARIM AL-IRYANI.

**League of the Sons of Yemen (LSY):** Aden; represents interests of southern tribes; Leader ABD AR-RAHMAN AL-JIFRI; Sec.-Gen. MOHSEN FARID.

**Nasserite Unionist Popular Organization:** Aden; f. 1989 as a legal party.

**Yemen Socialist Party (YSP):** San'a; f. 1978 as successor to United Political Organization—National Front (UPO—NF); fmrly Marxist-Leninist 'vanguard' party based on 'scientific socialism'; has Political Bureau, Central Committee; Sec.-Gen. ALI SALEH OBAD.

**Yemeni Islah Party (YIP):** POB 23090, San'a; tel. (1) 213281; fax (1) 213311; f. 1990 by members of the legislature and other political figures, and tribal leaders; seeks constitutional reform based on Islamic law; Leader Sheikh ABDULLAH BIN HUSSAIN AL-AHMAR; Sec.-Gen. Sheikh MUHAMMAD ALI AL-YADOUMI.

**Yemeni Unionist Rally Party:** Aden; f. 1990 by intellectuals and politicians from the former YAR and PDRY to protect human rights; Leader OMAR AL-JAWI.

## Diplomatic Representation

### EMBASSIES IN YEMEN

**Algeria:** POB 509, 67 Amman St, San'a; tel. (1) 209689; fax (1) 209688; Ambassador: BEN HADID CHADLY.

**Bulgaria:** POB 1518, St No. 22, San'a; tel. (1) 207924; telex 3114; Chargé d'affaires: ALEXI ALAXIEV.

**China, People's Republic:** Az-Zubairy St, San'a; tel. (1) 275337; Ambassador: LI LIUGEN.

**Cuba:** POB 15256, St No. 6B, San'a; tel. (1) 217304; fax (1) 217305; Ambassador: HÉCTOR ARGILES PÉREZ.

**Czech Republic:** POB 2501, Safiya Janoobia, San'a; tel. (1) 247946; fax (1) 244418; Chargé d'affaires: KAROL FISHER.

**Egypt:** POB 1134, Gamal Abd al-Nasser St, San'a; tel. (1) 275948; fax (1) 274196; Ambassador: ATA'A M. HARDUN.

**Eritrea:** POB 11040, Western Safia Bldg, San'a; tel. (1) 209422; fax (1) 214088; Ambassador: MAHMOUD ALI JABRA.

**Ethiopia:** POB 234, Hadda Rd, San'a; tel. (1) 208833; Ambassador: YOUSUF H. NASSER.

**France:** POB 1286, al-Baonia, San'a; tel. (1) 275996; telex 2248; fax (1) 275996; Ambassador: MARCEL LAUGEL.

**Germany:** POB 41, Hadda Area, opposite Jamaa ar-Rahman, San'a; tel. (1) 413174; telex 2245; fax (1) 413179; Ambassador: Dr HELGA STRACHWITZ.

**Hungary:** POB 11558, As-Safiya Al-Gharbiyya, St No. 6B, San'a; tel. (1) 216250; fax (1) 216251; Ambassador: (vacant).

**India:** POB 1154, San'a; tel. (1) 241980; fax (1) 263062; Ambassador: M. VENKATARAMAN.

**Indonesia:** POB 19873, No. 1, St No. 16, Sixty Rd, San'a; tel. (1) 217388; fax (1) 414383; Ambassador: AHMAD NOOR.

**Iran:** POB 1437, Hadda St, San'a; tel. (1) 206945; telex 2241; Chargé d'affaires: ALI A. NASSERY.

**Iraq:** POB 498, South Airport Rd, San'a; tel. (1) 244153; telex 2237; Ambassador: MUHSIN KHALIL.

**Italy:** POB 1152, No. 5 Bldg, St No. 29, San'a; tel. (1) 265616; telex 2560; fax (1) 266137; Ambassador: Dr VITALIANO NAPOLEONE.

**Japan:** POB 817, San'a; tel. (1) 207356; telex 2345; fax (1) 209531; Ambassador: SUSUMU AKIYAMA.

**Jordan:** POB 2152, San'a; tel. (1) 413279; telex 2703; Ambassador: Dr FAIZ AR-RABI.

**Korea, Democratic People's Republic:** POB 1209, al-Hasaba, Mazda Rd, San'a; tel. (1) 232340; telex 2603; Ambassador: CHU WANG CHOL.

**Korea, Republic:** POB 1234, No. 15, Abu Bakr al-Saddik St, San'a; tel. (1) 245959; Ambassador: KYN TAE CHO.

**Kuwait:** POB 17036, near Ring Rd 60, San'a; tel. (1) 216317; telex 2481; Ambassador: MANSOUR AL-AWADI.

**Lebanon:** POB 2283, Haddah St, San'a; tel. (1) 203459; telex 2438; Chargé d'affaires: RIZKALLAH MACARON.

**Libya:** POB 1506, Ring Rd, St No. 8, House No. 145, San'a; telex 2219; Secretary of Libyan Brotherhood Office: A. U. HEFIANA.

**Mauritania:** POB 19383, No. 6, Algeria St, San'a; tel. (1) 216770; fax (1) 215926; Ambassador: AHMED OULD SIDY.

**Morocco:** POB 10236, West Safiya, San'a; tel. (1) 247964; telex 2299; Ambassador: AHMED DRISSI.

**Netherlands:** POB 463, Hadda Rd, San'a; tel. (1) 215626; telex 2429; Ambassador: A. PIJPERS.

**Oman:** POB 105, Aser area, Az-Zubairy St, San'a; tel. (1) 208933; telex 2253; Ambassador: AWAD M. BAKTHEER.

**Pakistan:** POB 2848, Ring Rd, San'a; tel. (1) 248812; Ambassador: FAIZUR ARIF.

**Poland:** POB 16168, No. 19, St No. 14B, San'a; tel. (1) 248362; fax (1) 265835; Ambassador: MIECZYSŁAW JACEK STEPIŃSKI.

**Romania:** POB 2169, Hadda Rd, San'a; tel. (1) 215579; telex 2361; Chargé d'affaires: TACHE PANAIT.

**Russia:** POB 1087, 26 September St, San'a; tel. (1) 278719; telex 2952; fax (1) 283142; Ambassador: IGOR G. IVASHENKO.

**Saudi Arabia:** POB 1184, Zuhara House, Hadda Rd, San'a; tel. (1) 240429; telex 2420; Ambassador: ALI AL-QUFAIDI.

**Somalia:** POB 12277, Hadda Rd, San'a; tel. (1) 208864; telex 2610; Ambassador: ABD AS-SALLAM MU'ALLIM ADAM.

**Sudan:** POB 2561, 82 Abou al-Hassan al-Hamadani St, San'a; tel. (1) 265231; fax (1) 265234; Ambassador: OMAR AS-SAID TAHA.

**Syria:** POB 494, Hadda Rd, St No. 1, San'a; tel. (1) 413153; telex 2335; Ambassador: YOUSUF GMAOTRA.

**Tunisia:** POB 2561, Diplomatic area, St No. 22, San'a; tel. (1) 240458; telex 2751; Ambassador: ABBÈS MOHSEN.

**Turkey:** POB 12450, As-Safiya, San'a; tel. and fax (1) 241395; telex 3159; Ambassador: VOLKAN COTUR.

**United Arab Emirates:** POB 2250, Ring Rd, San'a; tel. (1) 248777; telex 2225; Ambassador: SAIF BIN MAKTOOM AL-MANSOORY.

**United Kingdom:** POB 1287, 129 Hadda Rd, San'a; tel. (1) 215630; fax (1) 263059; Ambassador: DOUGLAS SCRAFTON.

**USA:** POB 1088, Sa'awan St, San'a; tel. (1) 238842; telex 2697; fax (1) 251563; Ambassador: DAVID G. NEWTON.

**Viet Nam:** POB 15267, St No. 66, San'a; tel. (1) 215985; Ambassador: DO CONG MINH.

## Religion

### ISLAM

The majority of the population are Muslims. Most are Sunni Muslims of the Shafi'a sect, except in the north-west of the country, where Zaidism (a moderate sect of the Shi'a order) is the dominant persuasion.

### CHRISTIANITY

#### The Roman Catholic Church

**Apostolic Vicariate of Arabia:** POB 54, Abu Dhabi, United Arab Emirates; tel. (2) 461895; fax (2) 465177; responsible for a terri-

YEMEN                                                                                                                    *Directory*

tory comprising most of the Arabian peninsula (including Saudi Arabia, the UAE, Oman, Qatar, Bahrain and Yemen), containing an estimated 750,000 Catholics (31 December 1993); Vicar Apostolic GIOVANNI BERNARDO GREMOLI, Titular Bishop of Masuccaba (resident in the UAE); Vicar Delegate for Yemen Rev. MATHEW VADACHERRY.

### The Anglican Communion

Within the Episcopal Church in Jerusalem and the Middle East, Yemen forms part of the diocese of Cyprus and the Gulf. The Anglican congregations in San'a and Aden are entirely expatriate; Bishop in Cyprus and the Gulf: Rt Rev. JOHN BROWN (resident in Cyprus); Archdeacon in the Gulf: Ven. MICHAEL MANSBRIDGE (resident in the UAE).

### HINDUISM

There is a small Hindu community.

## Judicial System*

In the former YAR:

**President of the State Security Court:** GHALEB MUTAHIR AL-QANISH.

**Public Prosecutor:** ABD AR-RIZAQ AR-ROQAIHI.

**Attorney General:** MUHAMMAD AL-BADRI.

**Shari'a Court:** San'a; deals with cases related to Islamic law.

**Central Organization for Supervision and Accountancy:** replaces old Disciplinary Court; presides over cases of misappropriation of public funds; Chair. IZZ AD-DIN AL-MOAZEN.

In the former PDRY:

The administration of justice in the PDRY was entrusted to the Supreme Court and Magistrates' Courts. In the former Protectorate states, Islamic (Shari'a) law and local common law (Urfi) were also applied.

**President of the Supreme Court:** Dr MUSTAFA ABD AL-KHALIQ.

* In 1994 amendments to the Constitution of the unified Republic of Yemen identified Islamic (Shari'a) law as the basis of all laws.

## The Press

Legislation embodying the freedom of the press in the unified Republic of Yemen was enacted in May 1990. The lists below include publications which appeared in the YAR and the PDRY prior to their unification in May 1990.

### DAILIES

**Ar-Rabi' 'Ashar Min Uktubar** (14 October): POB 4227, Crater, Aden; f. 1968; not published on Saturdays; Arabic; Editorial Dir FAROUQ MUSTAFA RIFAT; Chief Editor ABDULLAH SHARIF SAID; circ. 20,000.

**Ash-Sharara** (The Spark): 14 October Corporation for Printing, Publishing, Distribution and Advertising, POB 4227, Crater, Aden; Arabic; circ. 6,000.

**Ath-Thawra** (The Revolution): Ministry of Information, San'a; Arabic; government-owned.

### WEEKLIES AND OTHERS

**Attijarah** (Trade): POB 3370, Hodeida; telex 5610; monthly, Arabic; commercial.

**Al-Bilad** (The Country): POB 1438, San'a; weekly; Arabic; inclined to right.

**Al-Fanoon:** POB 1187, Tawahi 102, Aden; tel. (2) 23831; f. 1980; Arabic; monthly arts review; Editor FAISAL SOFY; circ. 15,500.

**Al-Gundi** (The Soldier): Ministry of Defence, Madinat ash-Sha'ab; fortnightly; Arabic; circ. 8,500.

**Al-Hikma** (Wisdom): POB 4227, Crater, Aden; monthly; Arabic; publ. by the Writers' Union; circ. 5,000.

**Al-Hares:** Aden; fortnightly; Arabic; circ. 8,000.

**Al-Ma'in** (Spring): Ministry of Information, San'a; monthly; general interest.

**Majallat al-Jaish** (Army Magazine): POB 17, San'a; monthly; publ. by Ministry of Defence.

**Al-Maseerah** (Journey): Ministry of Information, San'a; monthly; general interest.

**Al-Mithaq** (The Charter): San'a; weekly; organ of the General People's Congress.

**Qadiyat al-Asr** (Issues of the Age): Aden; f. 1981; weekly; Arabic; publ. by Central Committee of Yemen Socialist Party.

**Ar-Ra'i al-'Am** (Public Opinion): San'a; weekly; independent; Editor ALI MUHAMMAD AL-OLAFI.

**Ar-Risalah** (The Message): 26 September St, San'a; weekly; Arabic.

**As-Sahwa** (Awakening): San'a; weekly; Islamic fundamentalist; Editor MUHAMMAD AL-YADDOUMI.

**As-Salam** (Peace): POB 181, San'a; f. 1948; weekly; Arabic; political, economic and general essays; circ. 7,000; Editor ABDULLAH ASSAKAL.

**San'a:** POB 193, San'a; monthly; Arabic; inclined to left.

**Sawt al-'Ummal** (The Workers' Voice): POB 4227, Crater, Aden; weekly; Arabic.

**Sawt al-Yemen** (Voice of Yemen): POB 302, San'a; weekly; Arabic.

**At-Ta'awun** (Co-operation): At-Ta'awun Bldg, Az-Zubairy St, San'a; weekly; Arabic; supports co-operative societies.

**Ath-Thaqafat al-Jadida** (New Culture): POB 1187, Tawahi 102, Aden; tel. (2) 23831; f. 1970; a cultural monthly review; Arabic; circ. 3,000.

**Ath-Thawri** (The Revolutionary): POB 4227, Crater, Aden; weekly; published on Saturday; Arabic; organ of Central Committee of the Yemen Socialist Party; Editor Dr AHMAD ABDULLAH SALIH.

**26 September:** POB 17, San'a; tel. (1) 274240; telex 2557; armed forces weekly; circ. 25,000.

**Al-Wahda al-Watani** (National Unity): Al-Baath Printing House, POB 193, San'a; tel. (1) 77511; f. 1982; fmrly *Al-Omal*; weekly; Editor MUHAMMAD SALEM ALI; circ. 40,000.

**Al-Yemen:** POB 1081, San'a; tel. (1) 72376; f. 1971; fortnightly; Arabic; inclined to right; Editor MUHAMMAD AHMAD AS-SABAGH.

**The Yemen Times:** San'a; independent weekly; Editor ABDULAZIZ AL-SAQQAF.

**Yemeni Women:** POB 4227, Crater, Aden; monthly; circ. 5,000.

### NEWS AGENCIES

**Aden News Agency (ANA):** Ministry of Culture and Information, POB 1187, Tawahi 102, Aden; tel. (2) 24874; telex 2286; f. 1970; government-owned; Dir-Gen. AHMAD MUHAMMAD IBRAHIM.

**Saba News Agency:** POB 1475, San'a; tel. (1) 233228; telex 2568; f. 1970; Dir HASSAN AL-ULUFI.

#### Foreign Bureaux

In the former YAR:

**Informatsionnoye Telegrafnoye Agentstvo Rossii—Telegrafnoye Agentstvo Suverennykh Stran (ITAR—TASS)** (Russia): San'a; Correspondent VIKTOR LYSSECHKO.

**Xinhua (New China) News Agency** (People's Republic of China): POB 482, Az-Zubairy St, San'a; tel. (1) 72073; Correspondent CHEN WENRU.

In the former PDRY:

**Informatsionnoye Telegrafnoye Agentstvo Rossii—Telegrafnoye Agentstvo Suverennykh Stran (ITAR—TASS)** (Russia): POB 1087, Aden; Correspondent VLADIMIR GAVRILOV.

**Xinhua (New China) News Agency** (People's Republic of China): POB 5213, Aden; tel. (2) 42710; Correspondent FENG ZHERU.

## Publishers

**Armed Forces Printing Press:** POB 17, San'a; tel. (1) 274240; telex 2557.

**14 October Corporation for Printing, Publishing, Distribution and Advertising:** POB 4227, Crater, Aden; under control of the Ministry of Information; Chair. and Gen. Man. SALIH AHMAD SALAH.

**Ath-Thawrah Corpn:** POB 2195, San'a; fax (1) 251505; Chair. M. R. AZ-ZURKAH.

**Yemen Printing and Publishing Co:** POB 1081, San'a; telex 2363; Chair. AHMAD MUHAMMAD HADI.

## Radio and Television

In 1992 there were an estimated 350,000 radio receivers and 350,000 television receivers in use in the unified Republic of Yemen. The radio and television stations of the YAR were merged with their PDRY counterparts following unification to form the Yemen Radio and Television General Corporation.

# Finance

(cap. = capital; dep. = deposits;
res = reserves; m. = million; brs = branches;
amounts in Yemeni riyals, unless otherwise indicated)

## BANKING

### Central Bank

**Central Bank of Yemen:** POB 59, Ali Abd al-Mughni St, San'a; tel. (1) 274371; telex 2280; fax (1) 274131; f. 1971; united with Bank of Yemen in May 1990; Gov. ALAWI SALIH AS-SALAMI; Dep. Gov. SALEM AL-ASHWALI; 7 brs.

### Principal Banks

**Arab Bank PLC** (Jordan): POB 475, Az-Zubairy St, San'a; tel. (1) 276584; telex 2239; fax (1) 263187; f. 1972; Man. A. KARIM AZ-ZOURAIQI; brs in Aden, Hodeida and Taiz.

**Banque Indosuez** (France): POB 651, Al-Qasr al-Jumhuriya St, San'a; tel. (1) 272801; telex 2412; fax (1) 274161; Gen. Man. MANUEL GARCIA-LIGERO; brs in Hodeida, Aden, and Taiz.

**Co-operative and Agricultural Credit Bank:** POB 2015, Banks Complex, Az-Zubairy St, San'a; tel. (1) 207327; telex 2544; fax (1) 203714; f. 1976; cap. p.u. 280m., dep. 470m.; Chair. ABDALLAH AL-BARAKANI; Dir-Gen. HUSSAIN QASSIM AMER; 27 brs.

**Industrial Bank of Yemen:** POB 323, Banks Complex, Az-Zubairy St, San'a; tel. (1) 207381; telex 2580; f. 1976; industrial investment; cap. 100m., total assets 269.8m. (1987); Chair. and Man. Dir ABBAS ABDU MUHAMMAD AL-KIRSHY; Gen. Man. ABD AL-KARIM ISMAIL AL-ARHABI.

**International Bank of Yemen YSC:** POB 2847, 106 Az-Zubairy St, San'a; tel. (1) 272920; telex 2523; fax (1) 274127; f. 1980; commercial bank; cap. 96.3m., res 123.1m., dep. 2,698.5m., total assets 3,092.0m. (1992); Chair. ALI LUTF ATH-THOUR; Gen. Man. AHMAD THABIT; 3 brs.

**National Bank of Yemen:** POB 5, Arwa Rd, Crater, Aden; tel. (2) 253484; telex 2224; fax (2) 255004; f. 1970 as National Bank of Southern Yemen; adopted current name 1971; cap. 5m., res 8.1m., dep. 541.3m., total assets 554.4m. (1991); Chair. SALEM AL-ASHWALI; Gen. Man. ABDUL QAWI AS-SAYEGH; 30 brs.

**United Bank Ltd** (Pakistan): POB 1295, Ali Abd al-Mughni St, San'a; tel. (1) 272424; telex 2228; fax (1) 274168; Vice-Pres. and Gen. Man. INAYATULLAH BUTT; br. in Hodeida.

**Yemen Bank for Reconstruction and Development (YBRD):** POB 541, 26 September St, San'a; tel. (1) 271621; telex 2291; fax (1) 271684; f. 1962; consolidated bank; cap. 100m., dep. 17,663.2m., total assets 17,950m. (1990); Chair. A. A. AL-MOHANI; Gen. Man. HUSSAIN FADHLE; 38 brs.

**Yemen Commercial Bank:** POB 19845, Az-Zubairy St, San'a; tel. (1) 213662; telex 3373; fax (1) 209566; f. 1993; Chair. Sheikh MUHAMMAD BIN YAHYA AR-ROWAISHAN; Gen. Man. MEHDI NAQVI; brs in Hodeida and Mukalla.

**Yemen-Kuwait Bank for Trade and Investment YSC:** POB 987, Az-Zubairy St, San'a; tel. (1) 240783; telex 2478; f. 1977; total assets 549m. (1988); Chair. and Man. Dir BADER N. AL-BISHER.

## INSURANCE

**Marib Yemen Insurance Co:** POB 2284, Az-Zubairy St, San'a; tel. (1) 206114; telex 2279; fax (1) 206118; f. 1974; all classes of insurance; cap. 40m.; Gen. Man. KASSIM M. AL-SABRI; Deputy Gen. Man. ABD AL-LATIF AL-QUBATI.

**National Insurance and Re-insurance Co:** POB 456, Aden; tel. (2) 51464; telex 2245; f. 1970; Lloyd's Agents; cap. 5m. Yemeni dinars; Gen. Man. ABUBAKR S. AL-QOTI.

**United Insurance Co (YSC):** POB 1983, Al-Qasr al-Jumhuriya St, San'a; tel. (1) 272891; telex 2366; fax (1) 272080; f. 1981; all classes of general insurance and life; cap. 20m.; brs in Taiz and Hodeida; Gen. Man. SARGON D. LAZAR.

**Yemen General Insurance Co (SYC):** POB 2709, YGI Bldg, 25 Al Giers St, San'a; tel. (1) 265191; telex 2451; fax (1) 263109; f. 1977; all classes of insurance; cap. 20m.; brs in Aden, Taiz and Hodeida; Chair. ABD AL-GABBAR THABET; Gen. Man. WAMIDH AL-JARRAH.

# Trade and Industry

## CHAMBERS OF COMMERCE

**Aden Chamber of Commerce and Industry:** POB 473, Queen Arwa St, Crater 101, Aden; tel. (2) 51104; telex 2233; fax (2) 221176; f. 1886; 4,000 mems; Pres. MOHAMED OMER BAMASHMUS; Gen. Man. SALEM TAHER AL-ARDHI.

**Federation of Chambers of Commerce:** POB 16992, San'a; tel. (1) 211765; telex 2229; Dir JAMAL SHARHAN.

**Hodeidah Chamber of Commerce:** POB 3370, Az-Zubairy St, Hodeida; tel. (3) 217401; telex 5610; fax (3) 211528; f. 1960; over 1,000 mems; cap. 1m. riyals; Dir NABIL AL-WAJIH.

**San'a Chamber of Commerce and Industry:** Airport Rd, Al-Hasabah St, POB 195, San'a; tel. (1) 232361; telex 2629; fax (1) 232412; f. 1963; Pres. Al-Haj HUSSAIN AL-WATARI; Gen. Man. ABDULLAH H. AR-RUBAIDI.

**Taiz Chamber of Commerce:** POB 5029, 26 September St, Taiz; tel. (4) 210580; telex 8960; fax (4) 212335; Dir MOFID A. SAIF.

Ibb also has a Chamber of Commerce.

## PRINCIPAL PUBLIC CORPORATIONS

**Public Corporation for Maritime Affairs (PCMA):** POB 19395, San'a; tel. (1) 414412; telex 4025; fax (1) 414645; f. 1990; Chair. SAEED YAFAI.

**Public Electricity Corporation (PEC):** San'a; telex 2850; fax (1) 263115; Man. Dir AHMAD AL-AINI.

**Yemen Free Zone Public Authority:** Aden; tel. (2) 241210; fax (2) 221237; f. 1990; supervises creation of a free zone for industrial investment; Chair. ABD AL-QADIR BA-JAMMAL.

In the former YAR:

**General Corporation for Foreign Trade and Grain:** POB 710, San'a; tel. (1) 207571; telex 2349; formerly Yemen General Grain Corporation; present name adopted 1987; cap. and dep. 270m. riyals; Chair. ABDULLAH AL-BARAKANI; Gen. Man. Dr YAHYA SALIH AL-ANSI.

**General Corporation for Manufacturing and Marketing of Cement:** POB 1920, San'a; tel. (1) 215691; fax (1) 263168; Chair. AMIN ABD AL-WAHID AHMAD.

**General Corporation for Oil and Mineral Resources:** San'a; f. 1990; state petroleum company; Pres. AHMAD BARAKAT.

**General Corporation for Tourism:** San'a; tel (1) 226623; telex 2592; fax (1) 252316.

**General Corporation for Transport:** POB 1827, San'a; tel. (1) 77711; telex 2400.

**Government Consumption Assembly for Public and Semi-Public Sector Employees:** POB 833, San'a.

**Yemen Company for Industry and Commerce Ltd:** POB 5302, Taiz; tel. (4) 218058; telex 8804; fax (4) 218054; Chair. ALI MUHAMMAD SAID.

**Yemen Company for Investment and Finance Ltd:** POB 2789, San'a; tel. (1) 276372; telex 2564; fax (1) 274178; f. 1981; cap. 100m.; Chair. ABDULLAH ISHAQ; Chair. and Gen. Man. ABDULLAH ISHAQ.

**Yemen Drug Company for Industry and Commerce:** POB 40, San'a; tel. (1) 234250; telex 2289; fax (1) 251595; Chair. ALI AL-DOWAH; Gen. Man. Dr ALI SALEH AL-HAMDANI.

**Yemen Economical Corporation:** POB 1207, San'a; tel. (1) 262501; telex 2244; fax (1) 262508; Commercial Man. A. KARIM SAY-AGHI.

**Yemen Land Transport Corporation:** POB 279, Taiz St, San'a; tel. (1) 262108; telex 2400; f. 1961; Chair. Col ALI AHMAD AL-WASI; Gen. Man. HAMID MUKRID.

**Yemen Petroleum Company:** POB 81, San'a; tel. (1) 70432; telex 2257; Chair. HUSSAIN ABDULLAH AL-MAKDANI; Gen. Man. FATHI SALEM.

**Yemen Telecommunication Corporation:** POB 17045, San'a; tel. (1) 251140; telex 2617; fax (1) 251150; f. 1981; operates public telecommunication network.

**Yemen Textile and Weaving Corporation:** POB 214, San'a; tel. (1) 202460; telex 2249.

**Yemen Trading and Construction Company:** San'a; f. 1979; initial cap. 100m. riyals.

State organizations in the former PDRY:

**Cottonseed Oil Factory:** Main Pass Roundabout, Maalla, Aden; manufacture and export of cottonseed oil.

**Ministry of Oil and Mineral Resources, Aden branch:** POB 5176, Maalla, Aden; tel. (2) 24542; telex 2215; f. 1969; responsible for the refining and marketing of petroleum products, and for prospecting and exploitation of indigenous hydrocarbons and other minerals; subsidiaries include:

> **Aden Refinery Company:** POB 3003, Aden 110; tel. (2) 76234; telex 2213; fax (2) 76600; f. 1952; operates petroleum refinery; capacity 8.6m. tons per year; output 4.2m. tons (1990); operates 1 oil tanker; Exec. Dir. MUHAMMAD HUSSEIN AL-HAJ; Refinery Man. AHMAD HASSAN AL-GIFRI.

> **Yemen National Oil Company:** POB 5050, Maalla, Aden; sole petroleum concessionaire, importer and distributor of petroleum products; Gen. Man. MUHAMMAD ABD HUSSEIN.

**National Corporation for Bottling Soft Drinks:** POB 352, Crater, Aden; tel. (2) 82237; telex 2500; f. 1972; manufacturer and dis-

YEMEN                                                                                                    *Directory*

tributor of soft drinks, distilled water, ice and carbon dioxide; Gen. Man. ABD AL-HAFEZ MUQBIL.

**National Company for Foreign Trade:** POB 90, Crater, Aden; tel. (2) 42793; telex 2211; fax (2) 42631; f. 1969; incorporates main foreign trading businesses (nationalized in 1970) and arranges their supply to the National Co for Home Trade; Gen. Man. AHMAD MUHAMMAD SALEH (acting).

**National Company for Home Trade:** POB 90, Crater, Aden; tel. (2) 41483; telex 2211; fax (2) 41226; f. 1969; marketing of general consumer goods, building materials, electrical goods, motor cars and spare parts, agricultural machinery etc.; Man. Dir ABD AR-RAHMAN AS-SAILANI.

**National Dockyards Company:** POB 1244, Tawahi, Aden; tel. (2) 23837; telex 2217; Man. Dir SALEH AL-MUNTASIR MEHDI.

**National Drug Corporation:** POB 192, Crater, Aden; tel. (2) 04912; telex 2293; fax (2) 21242; f. 1972; import of pharmaceutical products, chemicals, medical supplies, baby foods and scientific instruments; Chair. and Gen. Man. Dr AWADH SALAM ISSA BAMATRAF.

**National Tanning Factory:** POB 4073, Sheikh Othman, Aden; tel. (2) 81449; f. 1972; Gen. Man. MANSOUR A. MANSOOR.

**National Yemeni Petroleum Co:** f. 1988 to exploit and market petroleum produced in the PDRY.

**Public Building Corporation:** POB 7022, al-Mansoura, Aden; tel. (2) 342296; telex 2373; fax (2) 345726; f. 1973; government contractors and contractors of private housing projects; Dir-Gen. HUSSAIN MOHAMMED ALWALI.

**Public Corporation for Fish Wealth:** POB 2242, Pier Rd, Tawahi, Aden; telex 2244; operates 1 fishing vessel.

**Public Organization for Carpentry:** POB 5034, Maalla, Aden; tel. (2) 23619; telex 2273.

**Public Organization for Dairy Products:** POB 1416, Crater, Aden; tel. (2) 31257; telex 2273.

**Public Organization for Salt:** POB 1169, Tawahi, Aden; tel. (2) 202048; telex 2250; f. 1970.

**Public Trading Corporation for Textiles and Electrical Goods:** POB 4490, Crater, Aden; tel. (2) 42242; telex 2223; marketing of all kinds of textiles, ready-made garments and electrical goods; Man. Dir SALEM ABD AS-SALEM.

### TRADE UNIONS

**General Confederation of Workers:** POB 1162, Maalla, Aden; f. 1956; affiliated to WFTU and ICFTU; 35,000 mems; Pres. RAJEH SALEH NAJI; Gen. Sec. ABD AR-RAZAK SHAIF.

**Trade Union Federation:** San'a; Pres. ALI SAIF MUQBIL.

# Transport

### RAILWAYS

There are no railways in Yemen.

### ROADS

At 31 December 1991 the Republic of Yemen had 51,467 km (31,980 miles) of roads, including 4,754 km of main roads, 2,384 km of secondary roads and 44,329 km of other roads.

**Yemen Land Transport Co:** Aden; telex 2307; f. 1980; incorporates former Yemen Bus Company and all other public transport of the former PDRY; Chair. ABD AL-JALIL TAHIR BADR; Gen. Man. SALIH AWAD AL-AMUDI.

### SHIPPING

Aden is the main port. In 1986 the port handled vessels with a combined displacement of 8.3m. net registered tons. Aden Main Harbour has 28 first-class berths. In addition there is ample room to accommodate vessels of light draught at anchor in the 18-foot dredged area. There is also 800 feet of cargo wharf accommodating vessels of 300 feet length and 18 feet draught. Aden Oil Harbour accommodates four tankers of 57,000 tons and up to 40 feet draught. A new port at Nishtun was opened in 1984 to assist in the exploitation of the rich fishing grounds nearby. A multi-purpose terminal at Maalla, part of a programme to expand facilities at Aden port, was opened in September 1993.

There were three ports in the former YAR: Hodeida, Mocha and Salif. Hodeida is a Red Sea port of some importance, which has been considerably extended with Soviet aid. The Yemen Navigation Line, which is based in Aden, operates passenger and cargo services to many parts of the Middle East and Africa.

**Aden Refinery Co:** POB 3003, Aden 110; tel. (2) 76234; telex 2213; Exec.-Dir M. H. AL-HAJ.

**Elkirshi Shipping and Stevedoring Co:** POB 3813, Al-Hamdi St, Hodeida; tel. (3) 224263; telex 5569; operates at ports of Hodeida, Mocha and Salif.

**Hodeida Shipping and Transport Co Ltd:** POB 3337, Hodeida; tel. (3) 238130; telex 5510; fax (3) 211533; cargo, container and ro-ro handling.

**Middle East Shipping Co Ltd:** POB 3700, Hodeida; tel. (3) 217276; telex 5505; fax (3) 211529; f. 1962; Chair. ABD AL-WASA HAYEL SAEED; Gen. Man. AHMAD GAZIM; Dep. Gen. Man. ABD AR-RAHIM ABD AL-GHAFUR; brs in Mocha, Aden, Taiz and Salif.

**National Shipping Co:** POB 1228, Steamer Point, Aden; tel. (2) 24861; telex 2216; fax (2) 22664; shipping, bunkering, clearing and forwarding, and travel agents; Gen. Man. MUHAMMAD BIN MUHAMMAD SHAKER.

**Yemen Navigation Line:** POB 4190, Aden; tel. (2) 24861; telex 295; fleet of 3 general cargo vessels.

**Yemen Ports Authority:** POB 1316, Steamer Point, Aden; tel. (2) 202666; telex 6278; fax (2) 213805; f. 1888; state administrative body; Dir-Gen. MUHAMMAD AHMED ALI.

**Yemen Shipping Development Co Ltd:** POB 3686, Hodeida; tel. (3) 239252; telex 5530; fleet of 4 general cargo vessels.

### CIVIL AVIATION

There are six international airports—San'a International (13 km from the city), Aden Civil Airport (at Khormaksar, 11 km from the port of Aden), al-Ganad (at Taiz), Mukalla (Riyan), Seyoun and Hodeida Airport. In 1989 a total of 426,000 passengers travelled on scheduled services in the former YAR.

It was announced in June 1990 that the former national carriers of the YAR and the PDRY (see below) would begin to operate as one airline (Yemen Airways) from 28 October 1990. The merger of the airlines was delayed by a disagreement between the Governments of Saudi Arabia (a 49% shareholder in Yemenia) and Yemen, caused by the Gulf War. Despite the Saudi Arabian Government's decision, in March 1992, to relinquish its shareholding in Yemenia, the merger of the two airlines had not been accomplished by mid-1995.

**Yemen Airways (Yemenia):** POB 1183, Airport Rd, San'a; tel. (1) 232389; telex 2204; originally formed in 1963 as Yemen Airlines; reorganized as Yemen Airways Corpn 1972 following nationalization; present name adopted 1978, following establishment of new airline, owned 51% by Government of former YAR and 49% by Government of Saudi Arabia; internal services and external services (all carriers) to destinations in the Middle East, Asia, Africa and Europe; supervised by a ministerial committee headed by the Minister of Communications; Chair. AHMED KAID BARAKAT; Man. Dir AMIN ABD AL-MAJEED.

**Yemen Air:** POB 6006, Alyemda Bldg, Khormaksar, Aden; tel. (2) 52267; telex 2269; f. 1961 as wholly owned corporation by the Government of the former PDRY; internal flights and passenger and cargo services to destinations in the Middle East, Asia, Africa and Europe; Chair. and Gen. Man. MUHAMMAD ASH-SHAIBAH.

# YUGOSLAVIA

## Introductory Survey

**Location, Climate, Language, Religion, Flag, Capital**

The Federal Republic of Yugoslavia (FRY), comprising the Republics of Serbia and Montenegro, lies in south-eastern Europe. The FRY is bordered to the north by Hungary, to the east by Romania and Bulgaria, and by the former Yugoslav republic of Macedonia and Albania to the south; Montenegro, in the south-west, has a coastline on the Adriatic Sea, and the FRY's inland western border is with Bosnia and Herzegovina and with Croatia. The climate is continental in the hilly interior and Mediterranean on the coast, with steady rainfall throughout the year. The average summer temperature in Belgrade is 22°C (71°F), the winter average being 0°C (32°F). The principal language is Serbo-Croat in its Serbian form (written in Cyrillic script). Orthodox Christianity is predominant, the Serbian Orthodox Church being the largest denomination. There is a significant Muslim population, principally in the south of the country, and Roman Catholicism is especially strong in the Vojvodina province of Serbia. There is a small Jewish community. The national flag (proportions 2 by 1) has three equal horizontal stripes, of blue, white and red. The capital is Belgrade (Beograd).

**Recent History**

A movement for the union of the South Slav peoples, despite long-standing ethnic rivalries and cultural diversity, began in the early 19th century. However, it was not until the end of the First World War, and the collapse of the Austro-Hungarian empire (which ruled Croatia, Slovenia and Bosnia and Herzegovina), that the project for a Yugoslav ('south Slav') state could be realized. A pact between Serbia (which was under Ottoman Turkish rule until the 19th century) and the other South Slavs was signed in July 1917, declaring the intention to merge all the territories in a unitary state under the Serbian monarchy. Accordingly, when the First World War ended and Austria-Hungary was dissolved, the Kingdom of Serbs, Croats and Slovenes was proclaimed on 4 December 1918.

Prince Alexander, Regent of Serbia since 1914, accepted the regency of the new state, becoming King in August 1921. Following bitter disputes between Serbs and Croats, King Alexander assumed dictatorial powers in January 1929. He formally changed the country's name to Yugoslavia in October 1929. Alexander's regime was Serb-dominated, and in October 1934 he was assassinated in France by Croatian extremists. His brother, Prince Paul, assumed power as Regent on behalf of King Peter II. Paul's regime maintained itself in power with the support of the armed forces, despite internal unrest, particularly in Croatia (which was granted internal autonomy in 1939). Among the anti-Government groups was the Communist Party of Yugoslavia (CPY), which had been officially banned in 1921 but continued to operate clandestinely. In 1937 the CPY appointed a new general secretary, Josip Broz (Tito).

In March 1941 the increasingly pro-German regime of Prince Paul was overthrown in a coup, and a pro-Allied Government was installed, with King Peter as Head of State. In April, however, German and Italian forces invaded, quickly overrunning the country and forcing the royal family and Government into exile. Resistance to the occupation forces was initially divided between two rival groups. The royalist Yugoslav Army of the Fatherland (chetniks), led by Gen. Draža Mihailović, operated mainly in Serbia and represented the exiled Government, while the National Liberation Army (partisans), led by the CPY, under Gen. (later Marshal) Tito, recruited followers mainly from Bosnia, Croatia, Montenegro and Slovenia. Rivalry between the two groups led to civil war, eventually won by the communist partisans. On 29 November 1943 the partisans proclaimed their own government in liberated areas. Attempts to reconcile the Tito regime with the exiled Government proved unsuccessful, and King Peter II was deposed in 1944.

After the war elections were held, under communist supervision, for a Provisional Assembly, which proclaimed the Federal Republic of Yugoslavia on 29 November 1945, with Tito as Prime Minister. A Soviet-type Constitution, establishing a federation of six republics (Serbia, Montenegro, Croatia, Slovenia, Macedonia, and Bosnia and Herzegovina), was adopted in January 1946.

The independent socialist policies of Tito led to tension in relations with the USSR, and in 1948 Yugoslavia was expelled from the Soviet-dominated Cominform. Nevertheless, agricultural collectivization and industrialization were continued on the Soviet model, although somewhat modified in 1950 by the introduction of a system of self-management in state-owned enterprises. The CPY was renamed the League of Communists of Yugoslavia (LCY) in November 1952, by which time it had established exclusive political control in the country. A new Constitution was adopted in January 1953, with Tito becoming President of the Republic, a post which he held until his death in 1980. Another Constitution, promulgated in April 1963, changed the country's name to the Socialist Federal Republic of Yugoslavia (SFRY).

In foreign relations, links with the USSR were resumed in 1955, but Yugoslavia largely pursued a policy of non-alignment, the first conference of the Non-aligned Movement (see p. 249) being held in the Serbian and federal capital, Belgrade, in 1961. Tito condemned the Soviet intervention in Hungary in 1956 and the Warsaw Pact invasion of Czechoslovakia in 1968, and attempted to improve relations with Western powers and developing countries. Close ties were developed with the People's Republic of China.

In July 1971 President Tito introduced a system of collective leadership and regular rotation of personnel between posts, in an attempt to unify the various nationalities. A collective State Presidency was established, which was led by Tito until his death. A new Constitution, introduced in February 1974, granted Tito the presidency for an unlimited term of office, and in May 1974 he became Life President of the LCY. Tito died in 1980, and his responsibilities were transferred to the collective State Presidency and to the Presidium of the LCY. In May 1984 a new state presidency was elected for five-year term.

During the late 1980s the economic situation in Yugoslavia deteriorated sharply, and in March 1987 the Government imposed a 'freeze' on wage increases, in an attempt to curb the high level of inflation. The decision provoked strike action on an unprecedented scale, with 1,570 strikes recorded in 1987. Minor modifications were made to the plan, and stringent price controls were implemented, but industrial unrest continued throughout the year, despite a government warning that all means, including the armed forces, would be used to halt the unrest.

Following the death of Tito, inter-ethnic tensions, largely suppressed during his period in power, became evident once more. In early 1981 there were widespread demonstrations in Kosovo (an autonomous province in Serbia, where ethnic Albanians account for about 90% of the population) by Albanian nationalists, demanding that the province be upgraded to full republican status. A state of emergency was declared, and the riots resulted in several deaths and many injuries. Further demonstrations took place in March 1982, and hundreds of Albanian nationalists were convicted and imprisoned. Following the 1981 riots, thousands of Serbs and Montenegrins emigrated from Kosovo, the number of departures totalling 22,000 by 1987. Measures to halt the emigration from Kosovo were announced in mid-1986, but they were largely ineffective. In late June of that year some 3,000 Serbs and Montenegrins attempted to march to Belgrade from Kosovo to protest against the Federal Government's failure to deal effectively with the threat of Albanian nationalism, but the march was stopped by the authorities.

Tension was renewed in April 1987 when thousands of Serbs and Montenegrins gathered at Kosovo Polje (site of a famous battle between the Serbs and the Ottoman Turks in 1389) for a meeting with the League of Communists of Serbia (LCS—the Serbian branch of the LCY) to discuss alleged harassment by the Albanian majority and other problems. Violent clashes erupted between the crowds and the police. In June 1987 thousands of Serbs and Montenegrins travelled from Kosovo to Belgrade, where they staged a protest march, and demonstrations continued in Kosovo itself, a large rally being held at Kosovo Polje in August. The perceived failure of the Serbian and Federal leadership to curb Albanian nationalism led to the dismissal, in September, of the First Secretary of the LCS, Ivan Stambolić, and his replacement by Slobodan Milošević. Milošević had denounced the Serbian leadership's policy on Kosovo and promised to reverse the emigration of Serbs from the area and halt the activities of Albanian nationalists.

During 1988 and 1989 ethnic unrest grew in Serbia, particularly in the autonomous provinces of Kosovo and Vojvodina. (The latter, in north-east Serbia, has a large Hungarian minority.) Proposals to amend the Serbian Constitution to reduce the level of autonomy of the two regions (providing Serbia with more direct control over security, financial and social policy in the two provinces) were supported by regular demonstrations by Serbs, especially those from Kosovo.

Demonstrations, organized by Milošević and his supporters, were also held in Vojvodina, directed against the local party leadership. In October 1988 protests by some 100,000 demonstrators in Novy Sad, the administrative centre of Vojvodina, forced the resignation of the Presidium of the League of Communists of Vojvodina, which had opposed some of the proposed constitutional amendments. Tension between the respective party leaderships of Kosovo and Serbia increased, and in November, following the resignation of several members of the Kosovo leadership (under pressure from the LCS), some 100,000 ethnic Albanians took part in a protest march in Priština (the administrative capital of Kosovo) to demand the reinstatement of the leaders. In Belgrade a rally by Serbs protesting against alleged discrimination by the Albanians in Kosovo attracted almost 1m. people. Albanians continued to stage demonstrations in Kosovo until such protests were banned in late November. In Montenegro continuing unrest resulted in the resignations of the members of the Montenegrin Presidency and of the republican party leadership in January 1989, and their replacement by leaders more sympathetic to Milošević.

In February 1989 the dismissal from the LCY Central Committee of Azem Vlasi, a popular Albanian from Kosovo, and the adoption by the Assembly of the Serbian Republic of the constitutional amendments limiting provincial autonomy, led to renewed unrest in Kosovo. A hunger strike by some 13,000 miners, supported by a general strike in the province, was ended when federal troops intervened. Rioting continued, however, after Vlasi was arrested in early March, and was renewed later in the month, when the Kosovo Provincial Assembly approved the new constitutional arrangements. Some 25 people were reported to have been killed during clashes with the security forces. Unrest persisted throughout the year, and protests escalated again in the first few weeks of 1990. The situation was further exacerbated when Milošević (who had become President of the Presidency of Serbia in May 1989) urged the Serbs to begin a campaign of mass settlement in Kosovo (some 50,000 Serbs and Montenegrins were reported to have left the province since 1981). A curfew was imposed in Priština, and units of the federal army were deployed to quell the disturbances. In April 1990 the state of emergency was ended, and Vlasi and other defendants were acquitted and released, but any expectations that Serbian control was weakening were ended in May, when the Serbian leadership announced new proposals for constitutional amendments that would remove Kosovo's autonomy entirely.

In May 1988 an emergency conference of the LCY took place. Radical economic and political reforms, including the separation of the powers of the LCY and the State, and greater democracy within the LCY itself, were proposed. Meanwhile, the Government initiated economic reforms, which resulted in increased prices for many goods. In June there were widespread strikes and demonstrations by workers to protest against the reforms. On two occasions, in July and October, thousands of demonstrators forced their way into the Federal Assembly building in Belgrade. At the end of December, having been defeated in a vote of 'no confidence' (based on the Government's economic policy), Branko Mikulić, the President of the Federal Executive Council (Prime Minister), and his Government, were obliged to resign. In January 1989 Ante Marković, a member of the Croatian Presidency and reputed to be a liberal politician, was appointed to head a new Government.

In September 1989 the Slovene Assembly voted to adopt radical amendments to the Constitution of Slovenia, affirming the sovereignty of Slovenia and its right to secede from Yugoslavia. The right to form political parties (the Slovene League of Communists being hitherto the sole legal party) was also introduced, and free, multi-party elections were envisaged. Relations between the leadership of Slovenia and that of Serbia and the other constituent republics deteriorated sharply. In Serbia and Montenegro there were demonstrations against the perceived threat to the unity of Yugoslavia. In early December Serbia imposed economic sanctions on Slovenia.

The LCY held its Extraordinary 14th Congress in January 1990, when the reforms proposed in May 1988 were due to be formalized. The Congress approved the abolition of the LCY's constitutional monopoly of power and the introduction of a multi-party system, but a proposal by Slovenia to give greater autonomy to the republican branches of the LCY was overwhelmingly defeated. As a result, the Slovene delegation left the Congress, which was then adjourned. It resumed its work in May, but was not attended by delegations from Croatia, Slovenia or Macedonia, where the local communist parties had effectively seceded from the LCY. The LCY was reorganized in November as the League of Communists—Movement for Yugoslavia.

Multi-party elections took place in Slovenia and Croatia in April and May 1990. In Slovenia the Democratic Opposition of Slovenia (DEMOS), a new coalition of conservative parties, won the greatest number of seats in the Assembly, while Milan Kučan, the candidate of the Party of Democratic Reform (the former Slovene League of Communists) but an outspoken opponent of President Milošević, won the presidential election. In Croatia the nationalist Croatian Democratic Union won almost two-thirds of the seats in the Assembly, while its leader, Franjo Tudjman, was elected President of the Republic.

In May 1990, under the system of rotating leadership, Dr Borisav Jović of Serbia replaced Janez Drnovšek of Slovenia as President of the Federal Presidency. On taking office, Jović promised to uphold national integrity and advocated the introduction of a stronger federal constitution. In early July a referendum in Serbia resulted in approval for proposed amendments to the republic's Constitution, effectively removing the autonomous status of the provinces of Kosovo and Vojvodina. The Kosovo Provincial Assembly and Government were dissolved by the Serbian authorities. In response, a group of 114 ethnic Albanian deputies to the Assembly attempted to declare Kosovo's independence from Serbia. Unrest continued, and in September a general strike was organized to protest against the mass dismissals of ethnic Albanian officials by the Serbian authorities. Criminal charges were brought against more than 100 members of the Provincial Assembly who attempted to re-establish the body, and several former ministers in the Government of Kosovo were charged with establishing an illegal separatist organization.

During November and December 1990 multi-party elections were held in four republics, the results confirming the increasing differences between the regions. In Bosnia and Herzegovina (where tension between Muslims and Serbs had led to clashes) and in Macedonia the nationalist parties were successful. In Montenegro the League of Communists was able to retain the Presidency and secure a majority of seats in the Assembly. In Serbia, amid allegations of widespread irregularities, Milošević was re-elected President, overcoming a challenge by Vuk Drašković of the nationalist and anti-communist Serbian Renewal Movement (SRM). In the Serbian Assembly 194 of the 250 seats were won by the Socialist Party of Serbia (SPS—formed in July 1990 by a merger of the Serbian Socialist Alliance of Working People and the LCS, and led by Milošević).

In October 1990 Croatia and Slovenia had proposed the transformation of the Yugoslav federation into a looser confederation, in which constituent republics would have the right to maintain armed forces and enter into diplomatic relations with other states. Serbia and Montenegro, however, advocated a centralized federal system, while Macedonia and Bosnia and Herzegovina supported the concept of a federation of sovereign states, based on the model of the European Community (EC, known as the European Union—EU—from November 1993). Tension was raised in December, when Croatia adopted a new Constitution, which gave it the right to secede from Yugoslavia, while in Slovenia, in a referendum on the question of secession, an overwhelming majority voted in favour. In January 1991 Macedonia declared its sovereignty and right to secede from the SFRY.

A serious crisis arose in March 1991, when Jović resigned as President of the Federal Presidency, following his failure to secure approval from other members of the Presidency for emergency measures to give greater powers to the armed forces. The emergency measures were requested by the Serbian authorities, in response to demonstrations, led by Drašković's SRM, demanding the resignation of Milošević. Earlier in the month two people were killed and hundreds injured when Serbian forces dispersed an anti-Government demonstration. Following an appeal from the Serbian Assembly, Jović withdrew his resignation.

In late March 1991 the six republican Presidents renewed their negotiations (begun in January, under the auspices of the Federal Presidency) on the future of the Federation. Both Slovenia and Croatia confirmed their intention to secede if an agreement could not be reached by mid-1991. The result of a referendum, held in Croatia in May, demonstrated huge support for Croatian independence. The poll was boycotted by the Serbian minority in Croatia, and armed clashes between Serbs and Croats in the republic intensified. One of the main areas of ethnic Serbian settlement in Croatia, Knin region, had voted to declare itself an autonomous region in February, in contravention of Croatian law, and in March the leadership of the Krajina region, also an area where the population largely comprised ethnic Serbs, voted to secede from Croatia.

Relations between Serbia and Croatia deteriorated further in May 1991, when Serbian representatives in the Federal Presidency refused to sanction the routine transfer of the Presidency to Stipe Mesić of Croatia. Mesić, however, asserted that he was the rightful Federal President. In early June the leaders of the six republics met to consider a compromise plan, which would transform the country into an alliance of sovereign states. However, later in the month, following the failure of the talks, Slovenia and Croatia declared full independence from Yugoslavia. In response, federal troops (largely Serb-dominated) took retaliatory actions, Ljubljana airport in Slovenia being among the targets that were bombed. A cease-fire agreement, sponsored by the EC, resulted in Serbia's acceptance of Mesić as President of the Federal Presidency. However, fighting continued in Slovenia and in eastern Croatia in early July.

In July 1991, following negotiations on the Adriatic island of Brioni, agreement was reached on the immediate cessation of hostilities and on the suspension, for three months, of the declarations of independence by Croatia and Slovenia. The withdrawal of federal troops from Slovenia began almost immediately, but fighting intensified in Croatia, where federal troops increasingly identified openly with local Serb nationalist forces. By September Serb forces had control of almost one-third of Croatia's territory, and successive cease-fire agreements failed to end the conflict. In the same month, at a referendum held in Macedonia, voters approved the establishment of an independent and sovereign republic.

In late September 1991 the UN Security Council adopted a resolution to impose an armaments embargo on Yugoslavia, urging that all hostilities end immediately. However, sporadic fighting continued in Croatia, and the presidential palace was bombed in the Croatian capital, Zagreb. In October Croatia and Slovenia formally ended their association with Yugoslavia, the moratoriums on independence (agreed in July) having expired. In the same month the Assembly of Bosnia and Herzegovina declared the republic's sovereignty, despite the objections of ethnic Serb deputies. The EC continued its negotiation efforts, and the UN also become directly involved, but several proposed cease-fires failed to bring about an end to hostilities. In Belgrade the Federal Prime Minister, Ante Marković, resigned, having been defeated in a vote of 'no confidence' in the Federal Assembly. In December, declaring that Yugoslavia had ceased to exist, Stipe Mesić resigned as President of the Federal Presidency. In late December Germany recognized Slovenia and Croatia as independent states; other EC states did likewise in January 1992, and recognition by numerous other countries followed.

By early 1992 thousands of citizens had been killed in the civil war, and an estimated 1m. people had lost or abandoned their homes. The deployment of an advance UN contingent of 50 peace-keeping troops (agreed by the Federal Presidency in December 1991) proceeded as scheduled, but the dispatch to Croatia of the main 14,000-member UN force was delayed by the objections of the President of the 'Republic of Serbian Krajina' (RSK, as the Serb-held enclaves within Croatia had termed themselves). The commander of the UN Protection Force (UNPROFOR—see p. 52) arrived in Zagreb in March 1992.

Following the recognition of the independence of Croatia and Slovenia by the international community, Serbia and Montenegro agreed to uphold the Yugoslav state, the Montenegrin commitment being overwhelmingly endorsed in a referendum held in March 1992 (although boycotted by the ethnic Albanian and Muslim minorities). Macedonia's representative to the Federal Presidency had resigned in January, but EC recognition of Macedonian independence was delayed, owing to opposition from Greece, which was concerned for the territorial integrity of its northern territory of the same name. In March Bosnia and Herzegovina also declared its independence from the Yugoslav Federation, the decision having been approved by the electorate in a referendum. The declaration of independence exacerbated Serb–Muslim tension in Bosnia, leading to clashes in the capital, Sarajevo, and elsewhere. In late March a 'Serbian Republic of Bosnia and Herzegovina' was proclaimed by Serbs within Bosnia and Herzegovina. There was serious escalation in the conflict in April, when fighting between Serb forces (including federal troops) and Bosnian government forces intensified. By the end of that month the Office of the UN High Commissioner for Refugees estimated that more than 400,000 citizens of the republic had been displaced.

In April 1992 in Belgrade the Federal Assembly adopted a Constitution for the newly-established Federal Republic of Yugoslavia (FRY), which comprised Serbia (including the provinces of Kosovo, now officially known as Kosovo and Metohija, and Vojvodina) and Montenegro. In late May elections for representatives of the Federal Assembly were held in Serbia and Montenegro, the SPS enjoying considerable success as a result of an opposition boycott of the elections. In June Dobrica Ćosić became President of the FRY, and the collective Federal Presidency ceased to exist.

In late May 1992 some 20,000 people attended anti-war demonstrations in Belgrade, organized by opponents of the Government, prominent among them being Drašković. In earlier protests Drašković had called for a campaign of civil disobedience to force the resignation of Milošević, whom he blamed for the war with Croatia and the collapse of the economy. In late May the Serbian Orthodox Church disassociated itself from the Milošević regime, criticizing the new federal Constitution and the conduct of the elections. Also in late May an alliance of opposition parties and movements formed the Democratic Movement of Serbia (Depos), led by Drašković. Students at the University of Belgrade boycotted classes in mid-June and further anti-Milošević demonstrations by as many as 100,000 people took place at the end of the month. Internal disagreements threatened to split the Serbian Government in June, but the administration survived a vote of 'no confidence' brought by the opposition parties. However, increasing public pressure forced Milošević to distance himself from the war in Bosnia and Herzegovina, claiming that he had no influence over the Bosnian Serbs.

In Kosovo, meanwhile, elections (declared illegal by the Serbian Assembly) were held in May 1992. The Democratic Alliance of Kosovo (DAK) secured most seats in the 130-member Assembly, and their leader, Dr Ibrahim Rugova, was elected 'President' of the self-proclaimed 'Republic of Kosovo'. However, Serbian security forces prevented the Assembly from holding its inaugural session. In mid-July a proposal by Lord Carrington (Chairman of the EC negotiating committee on the former Yugoslavia) for a conference on Kosovo was rejected by the FRY.

In July 1992 Milan Panić was elected Federal Prime Minister by a joint session of the Federal Assembly. He began a series of foreign visits in an attempt to improve Yugoslavia's reputation abroad. Following a visit to Albania in August (the first by a Yugoslav leader since 1948), Panić revoked the state of emergency in Kosovo, which had been in effect since the unrest of 1989–90. In October 1992 Panić attended talks in Priština with Cyrus Vance and Lord Owen (co-Chairmen of the joint UN-EC negotiating initiative on the former Yugoslavia) to discuss the situation in Kosovo. However, the arrest of two deputies of the Albanian Assembly and the banning of the Albanian newspaper, *Bujku*, exacerbated tensions, and there were further disturbances in the province in October and

November. There was also ethnic unrest in Sandžak (an area on the Serbian-Montenegrin border) in October, with several attacks on Muslims reported. Muslim leaders claimed that 70,000 Muslims (of a community of some 200,000) had left the area as a result.

At the Conference on the former Yugoslavia, which took place in London (United Kingdom) in August 1992, Panić condemned the policy of 'ethnic cleansing', following the discovery of Serb concentration camps in Bosnia and Herzegovina, and reiterated the claim that there was no federal military involvement in the republic. Tension between the strongly nationalist Milošević, whose policies were denounced by his opponents as repressive, and the more moderate Panić was evident at the Conference. In early September Panić survived a vote of 'no confidence', proposed in the Federal Assembly by supporters of Milošević. In an attempt to force Milošević's removal from office, presidential and legislative elections were called for December 1992, and Ćosić and Panić urged Milošević to resign. In October Milošević retaliated by using Serbian police forces to seize control of the federal police headquarters in Belgrade, blockading the building for several weeks. In November Panić survived a further vote in the Federal Assembly, expressing 'no confidence' in his premiership, by one vote. The Federal Minister of Foreign Affairs resigned in September, claiming that Panić's policies were 'against the interests of Serbia'; in November three more federal ministers resigned.

Presidential and parliamentary elections, held at both federal and republican levels, took place on 20 December 1992. Ćosić was re-elected as Federal President by some 85% of the votes cast, and Milošević was re-elected President of Serbia, receiving 57.5% of the votes cast. Panić, who stood against Milošević, won some 35% of the votes and subsequently demanded new elections, alleging widespread electoral malpractice. However, he was himself removed from the office of Federal Prime Minister on 29 December, after losing a vote of 'no confidence' in the Federal Assembly. Drašković, leader of the Depos alliance, also claimed that the election had been fraudulent. In February 1993 the Depos deputies (who had won 49 seats at the December elections) began a boycott of the Serbian Assembly. The SPS won 101 seats at the election to the Serbian Assembly, and the extreme nationalist Serbian Radical Party (SRP) 73. In February the SPS formed a new Serbian Government, headed by Nikola Šainović.

In Montenegro Momir Bulatović, of the ruling Democratic Party of Montenegrin Socialists (DPMS—the former League of Communists of Montenegro), failed to win an overall majority in the first round of the presidential election. He was re-elected President in a second round of voting on 10 January 1993, defeating his nationalist rival, Branko Kostić, by a substantial margin. Milo Djukanović formed a new multi-party coalition Government in Montenegro in March. In the same month a new federal Government, comprising the SPS and the DPMS, was formed, with Radoje Kontić as Federal Prime Minister.

On 1 June 1993 Ćosić (who was accused of conspiring with army generals to overthrow Milošević) was removed from office by a vote of 'no confidence' at an emergency debate of the Federal Assembly: the motion had been initiated by deputies of the SPS and the SRP, in what was widely regarded as an attempt by Milošević to consolidate his power. Ćosić's dismissal was followed by a large anti-Government demonstration in Belgrade, at which Drašković and his wife were arrested. Evidence that they had been tortured by the police prompted international protests; both were released in July.

In late June 1993 the Federal Assembly appointed Zoran Lilić of the SPS (recently the Chairman of the Serbian Assembly) as Federal President. Lilić was generally regarded as sympathetic to Milošević. A reorganization of the Serbian Government in July was believed to have further strengthened Milošević's position. A new Commander-in-Chief of the Yugoslav Army was appointed in late August; at the same time more than 40 senior members of the armed forces were replaced by younger (apparently pro-Milošević) officers. It was also announced that the Supreme Defence Council was to assume responsibility for all military and defence duties, and that the republican defence ministries were to be abolished (a plan that was opposed by the Montenegrin Government—see below).

By the second half of 1993 it appeared that the co-operation between Milošević and the SRP had ended: in October an attempt by the SRP to force a parliamentary vote expressing 'no confidence' in the Šainović Government prompted Milošević to dissolve the Serbian Assembly, scheduling new elections for December. In response to SRP allegations that the Serbian leadership was betraying national interests by its involvement in attempts to end the conflict in Bosnia and Herzegovina, as well as of economic mismanagement, racketeering and war crimes by the SPS, a campaign of denigration (believed to have been orchestrated by Milošević) against the SRP began. The party's leader, Dr Vojislav Seselj, and his associates were accused of involvement in atrocities committed in the former Yugoslavia, and prominent members of the party associated with its paramilitary wing (styled 'chetniks') were arrested. (In April 1994 it was reported that the SRP had abolished the 'chetnik' movement.)

In the elections to the 250-member Serbian National Assembly, which took place on 19 December 1993, the SPS increased its representation to 123 deputies, winning 36.7% of the votes cast. Depos secured 45 seats (with 16.6% of the votes), and the SRP took 39 (with 13.9%). Despite its increased level of representation, the SPS failed to achieve an outright majority in the legislature, and was therefore forced to seek the support of one of the other parties in order to form a government. Prolonged negotiations between the SPS and the opposition parties ensued, and in late February 1994 a new Serbian Government was formed, with the support of the six members of the New Democracy (ND) party, which had campaigned in the elections as a member of the Depos coalition. Mirko Marjanović, a pro-Milošević business executive, who had not previously held a political post, was appointed Prime Minister, replacing Šainović, who became a Deputy Prime Minister in the Federal Government. The new Government was approved by the Serbian Assembly in mid-March. In September a new Federal Government was appointed, with six new ministers entering a smaller, 14-member administration. Radoje Kontić retained the post of Federal Prime Minister.

The results of the December 1993 elections in Serbia and the defection of the ND to the Government permitted Milošević to further distance himself from his erstwhile allies in the nationalist opposition, notably Seselj's SRP, and to consolidate his political control in Yugoslavia. The campaign of denigration by the Government-controlled media against Seselj and the SRP continued in 1994, and Seselj's personal position was discredited when he was sentenced to 30 days' imprisonment in late September for assaulting the parliamentary speaker. (His sentence was subsequently extended by three months for his role in a brawl in the Federal Assembly in May.) Milošević also extended his control over the media during 1994. Several western news organizations were banned from working in Yugoslavia in April, and in December the editorial board of the independent daily Borba was replaced by pro-Milošević appointees.

The decision by the Serbian leadership to impose a blockade on the Bosnian Serbs in September 1994 (see below) was strongly opposed by the SRP (which retained close links with the leadership of the Bosnian Serbs) and other opposition movements. In late August, in a controversial vote that was boycotted by the opposition, the Serbian Assembly endorsed the international peace plan that the Bosnian Serbs had rejected earlier in the month. The SRP, the Democratic Party (DP) and the Democratic Party of Serbia (DPS) continued to condemn the peace proposals, the SRP, in particular, advocating the retention of all territories captured by the Bosnian Serbs and their absorption into a 'Greater Serbia'. Vuk Drašković's SRM supported the peace plan, although it also advocated the creation of a 'Greater Serbia', encompassing the RSK (in Croatia) and much of Bosnia and Herzegovina, but only by peaceful means. It condemned the SRP's support for military action in Bosnia and Herzegovina, and refused to join a loose alliance of opposition parties, formed in February 1995 by the SRP, the DP and the DPS.

There was increasing evidence during 1993 of concern within Montenegro regarding the extent of Serbian domination of the federation, and of dissatisfaction at the adverse consequences of the international economic sanctions against the FRY (which many Montenegrins viewed as having been incurred by Serbia). In mid-1993 the Montenegrin Government protested against what it alleged to be the harassment by radical Serbian nationalists of the Muslim community in Montenegro. The republican Government incurred Serbia's displeasure by advocating the deployment of UN monitors along

Montenegro's border with Bosnia and Herzegovina (where most of the Muslims were settled). Montenegro had also begun to pursue a foreign policy that was increasingly independent from that of Serbia, and had defied Serbia by concluding trade agreements with countries such as Italy and Albania. The republic also opposed (unlike Serbia) plans for the transfer of responsibility for defence, foreign affairs and foreign economic relations to a federal level. In late October 1993 Montenegro effectively dissociated itself from the Serbian Orthodox Church, electing an independent Montenegrin spiritual leader and proclaiming an autonomous Montenegrin Church for the first time since 1922. In March 1995 Patriarch Pavle, head of the Serbian Orthodox Church, announced the excommunication of Antonije Abramović, head of the Montenegrin Orthodox Church.

In November 1993 a report by the International Helsinki Federation for Human Rights condemned what it termed the policy of demographic restructuring, or 'Serbianization', in Kosovo, and cited incidents of the harassment and torture of ethnic Albanians. The elections to the Serbian Assembly, in December, were boycotted by ethnic Albanians in Kosovo and also in the Sandžak region. There were further reports of police harassment of ethnic Albanians and arrests of Albanian activists in Kosovo in 1994 and early 1995. In September 1994 Mihajlo Marković, a senior member of the SPS, met with Fehmi Agami, deputy leader of the DAK, in an attempt to initiate a dialogue between the Serbian authorities and the illegal structures established by ethnic Albanians in Kosovo. However, little progress appeared to have been made in the talks, and in December some 170 ethnic Albanian former police officers were arrested, charged with attempting to establish an illegal 'Ministry of the Interior' in Kosovo. Nine were subsequently sentenced to terms of imprisonment. During 1994 there were reports of criticism among radical Albanian leaders of the more moderate stance of the 'President' of Kosovo, Ibrahim Rugova, and several ministers were reported to have resigned from the Kosovo 'Government-in-Exile' (based in Croatia), dissatisfied with the policies of the head of the 'Government', Bujar Bukoshi. During the second half of 1993 there were reports of the detention of members of the ethnic-Muslim Party of Democratic Action of Sandžak (PDA—S), mostly in connection with the possession of firearms, and in September 1994 21 PDA—S members were convicted of plotting the armed secession of the region, and sentenced to terms of imprisonment.

In October 1992 Serb leaders of the self-proclaimed RSK (in Croatia) and the 'Serbian Republic' (in Bosnia and Herzegovina) declared themselves in favour of union with Serbia, following the eventual withdrawal of UN troops from their territories. Their aspirations were supported by most political forces within Serbia, including Milošević. However, there was frequent disagreement between Milošević and the leaderships of the RSK and the 'Serbian Republic'. The refusal of the Bosnian Serbs to agree to the so-called Vance-Owen peace proposals in May 1993 (see chapter on Bosnia and Herzegovina) prompted Milošević to order the temporary closure of the Bosnian–Yugoslav border. In early August 1994 the Serbian Government informed the leadership of the 'Serbian Republic' that continued opposition by the Bosnian Serbs to a peace plan proposed by the 'Contact Group' (Russia, the USA, France, Germany and the UK), which offered the Bosnian Serbs 49% of the territory of Bosnia and Herzegovina, would result in an embargo of the 'Serbian Republic' by Yugoslavia. When the Bosnian Serbs rejected the plan, Yugoslavia announced that it had closed its border with Bosnia and Herzegovina for the transport of all commercial goods, except for humanitarian aid. In mid-September the Yugoslav authorities announced their willingness to permit international observers to monitor the border and to report to the UN on Yugoslav observance of the embargo. In late September, after a report by the international monitors, the UN issued a resolution, announcing that certain sanctions (mainly relating to travel, sport and culture) against the FRY would be suspended for a trial 100-day period. However, the resolution allowed for the immediate reimposition of sanctions should it be discovered that the blockade of the Bosnian Serbs was being breached. In early October international flights to Belgrade recommenced, as did ferry services between Italy and Montenegro. The suspension of sanctions was extended for a further 100 days in January 1995, and for 75 days in April.

With the imposition by the UN, from May 1992, of economic sanctions against the FRY (reinforced in April 1993), in an attempt to force Serbia to exert its influence to bring about an end to the conflict in Bosnia and Herzegovina, and the FRY's exclusion from the UN and other major multilateral organizations, Yugoslavia was largely isolated from the international community. The country's international isolation was slightly lessened in 1994–95, after the imposition of an embargo of the Bosnian Serbs by Yugoslavia, and the subsequent partial suspension of UN sanctions. Relations with Croatia improved somewhat during 1992, with the withdrawal in October of that year of FRY troops from the Prevlaka Peninsula (a part of Croatia claimed by Montenegro). In January 1994 Yugoslavia and Croatia signed an agreement on the 'normalization' of relations, and a Croat representative office was opened in Belgrade in March. However, relations were strained in May 1995 by Croatian military intervention in the RSK. Meanwhile, there were indications that other countries of the region, principally Greece, Bulgaria, Hungary and Romania, the economies of which had been adversely affected by the international sanctions, were seeking to lessen the FRY's economic and diplomatic isolation.

## Government

Under the 1992 Constitution, federal legislative power in Yugoslavia is vested in the bicameral Federal Assembly, comprising the 138-member Chamber of Citizens, members of which are directly elected, by universal suffrage, and the 40-member Chamber of Republics, composed of 20 representatives from both Serbia and Montenegro. Executive power is held by the Federal President, who is directly elected and who is responsible for proposing the Federal Prime Minister (head of the Federal Government). Republican legislative power is vested in the respective (directly-elected) republican assemblies of Serbia and Montenegro, and each republic has its own elected President as well as its own Government.

The Serbian province of Vojvodina has an elected assembly. The assembly of the province of Kosovo and Metohija was dissolved by the Serbian Government in 1990.

## Defence

Military service is compulsory for men, and lasts for 12 months. Voluntary military service for women was introduced in 1983. In June 1994 the estimated total strength of the armed forces was 126,500 (including 60,000 conscripts), comprising an army of 90,000, a navy of 7,500 and an air force of 29,000. Projected budgetary expenditure on defence by the Federal Government in 1995 was 1,611m. dinars (76.2% of total federal expenditure).

## Economic Affairs

In 1989, according to official estimates, the level of social (material) product per inhabitant, measured in Yugoslav dinars, in the territory of the present Federal Republic of Yugoslavia (FRY—comprising the two republics of Serbia and Montenegro) was 87% of the average for the Socialist Federal Republic of Yugoslavia (SFRY—comprising six republics). On this basis, it has been calculated that the gross national product (GNP) of the present FRY in 1989, using World Bank criteria, was US $2,540 per head (at average 1987–89 prices). In subsequent years the territory experienced accelerating economic decline. Yugoslav sources estimated the FRY's GNP in 1993 to be $9,520m., equivalent to no more than $900 per head. Overall GNP was estimated to have declined, in real terms, by 11% in 1991, by 26% in 1992 and by 30% in 1993. However, in 1994 GNP was estimated to have increased by 4.7%. Gross domestic product (GDP), measured in constant dinars, fell by 8.4% in 1990, by 11.1% in 1991, and by an estimated 27% in 1992. In terms of international purchasing power, it has been estimated that real GDP per head in Serbia increased by 3.4% per year during 1985–89, but declined by 4.4% in 1990 and by 6.7% in 1991. On the same basis, Montenegro's GDP per head rose by 1.8% per year in 1985–89, but fell by 6.6% in 1990 and by 8.0% in 1991. In 1993 the FRY Government estimated that GDP had declined by some two-thirds from the level in 1989. The population of the present FRY, which accounted for 44.2% of the SFRY's total in 1991, increased at an average rate of 0.8% per year in 1985–93.

Agriculture, forestry and fishing engaged 37.7% of the employed labour force in the present FRY in 1981. In 1991 agriculture and fishing contributed 17.2% of the present FRY's net material product: a higher level than in any of the four other republics in the SFRY. The FRY's principal crops are maize, wheat, sugar beet and potatoes. The cultivation of fruit and vegetables is also important. Agricultural output in the present FRY declined by 9.7% in 1991, by an estimated 22% in 1992 and by 3.3% in 1993. However, in 1994 output increased by 4.0%, with crop production rising by 10%, although livestock production declined by 2%. Wheat production rose by 6.7%, maize by 21.3% and sugar beet by 78% in 1994, after very low levels of output in 1992 and 1993. Agricultural production continued to be adversely affected by shortages of fuel, fertilizers and imported machinery.

Industry (comprising mining, manufacturing, construction and utilities) engaged 28.9% of the employed labour force in the present FRY in 1981. In 1991 industrial activity provided 38.8% of net material product in the present FRY. The volume of industrial output (excluding construction) in the present FRY fell by 17.6% in 1991, and by about 23% in 1992 and by 37.7% in 1993. In 1994, however, industrial production increased by 1.2% in the FRY, although production in Montenegro declined by 8.5%.

Mining contributed 2.4% of GDP in the SFRY in 1989. The principal minerals extracted in the FRY are coal (mainly brown coal), copper ore and bauxite. Iron ore, crude petroleum, lead and zinc ore and natural gas are also produced. In 1990 the present FRY accounted for 60% of coal production, and 34% of petroleum output, in the SFRY. Mining has been less severely affected in recent years than other sectors. In 1994 production of coal increased by 1.7%, but output of petroleum and natural gas declined, by 9.2% and 14%, respectively.

The manufacturing sector provided 41.4% of GDP in the SFRY in 1989. Of total production in the SFRY in 1990, the present FRY accounted for 34% of cement, 28% of crude steel, 48% of machines and 62% of passenger cars. Efforts to promote import-substitution in the manufacturing sector were being encouraged in 1993–94, in response to the UN embargo on imports. All branches of manufacturing in the FRY suffered declines in output in 1991–93, the greatest reductions being in the manufacture of transport equipment and non-ferrous metals. A small increase in the production of some goods was recorded in 1994.

Energy in the FRY is derived principally from thermal power stations (providing about 68% of total electricity generated in 1994) and hydroelectric power (32%). The present FRY produced 49% of the SFRY's electric power in 1990. In the 1980s the SFRY depended heavily on imports of petroleum and natural gas. From 1990, however, imports of mineral fuels were restricted by difficulties relating to supply, which worsened for the FRY with the imposition of a UN embargo from May 1992. However, domestic energy requirements were generally fulfilled by the coal and hydroelectric industries, while the FRY's reserves of petroleum supplied basic industries. Production of electricity increased by 3.5% in 1994.

Services engaged 33.4% of the employed labour force in the present FRY in 1981. These activities accounted for 36.8% of GDP in the SFRY in 1989. In the present FRY the physical volume of retail trade fell by about 2% in 1991 and by an estimated 52% in 1992. There was a further decline in 1993, but in 1994 it was reported that the volume of retail trade rose by 53%. Receipts from tourism and remittances from Yugoslav workers abroad were important sources of foreign exchange for the former SFRY. As a result of the disintegration of the SFRY, the FRY has lost access to most tourist areas (particularly the long Adriatic coastline). The number of tourist nights spent in the present FRY by visitors from outside the former SFRY declined by 79% in 1992–93, but increased by 18% in 1994.

In 1992 the FRY recorded a trade deficit of $1,500m. The FRY's principal trading partners outside the SFRY were Germany (providing 20% of imports and taking 30% of exports in 1991) and the USSR (13% of imports and 18% of exports). The main exports from the present FRY in 1991 were basic manufactures (accounting for 27% of the total), machinery and transport equipment (20%) and clothing (14%). The principal imports were machinery and transport equipment (23%), mineral fuels and lubricants (19%), basic manufactures (14%) and chemicals (14%). The present FRY's exports declined, in volume terms, by 17% in 1991 and by 46% in 1992, while imports fell by 24% and 30%, respectively. Between March 1992 and March 1993 exports decreased by 69%, largely as a result of the UN economic sanctions against Yugoslavia, imposed in May 1992, while a new ban (from April 1993) on transit trade through the FRY further undermined trade prospects. Despite the embargo, according to unofficial figures, the total value of foreign trade in 1993 was some US $1,000m., approximately 20% of the pre-1991 level.

In 1993 the FRY's budgetary expenditure was about US $5,500m., while revenue was only $2,700m. (resulting in a deficit of some $2,800m.). At the end of 1993 the total external debt of the former Yugoslavia was US $11,314m., of which $8,199m. was long-term public debt. Under the terms of an agreement reached in 1992, the FRY was responsible for the repayment of $5,561m. of the SFRY's debt, the remainder being allocated to other former republics of the SFRY. The annual rate of inflation in the present FRY averaged 120% in 1991, but rose alarmingly in 1993 to 116,540,000m.%. Prior to the introduction of the new currency, in late January 1994, the monthly rate of inflation was 313.6m.%. The new monetary policy introduced at the beginning of 1994 sharply reduced inflation in 1994, the annual rate for the year being 3.3%. According to official data, the average number of registered unemployed persons in the FRY decreased from 738,700 in 1993 to 726,000 in 1994. However, about 700,000 workers (30% of the total labour force) were reported to be on compulsory leave in mid-1993, as most enterprises were forced to operate at considerably below full capacity.

Owing to continued armed conflict in parts of the former SFRY and the imposition by the UN of sanctions on the FRY, the country's membership of numerous international organizations has been suspended. The FRY was excluded from the General Agreement on Tariffs and Trade in June 1992, and from the International Monetary Fund in December of that year.

Following a slowing of economic growth in the early 1980s and a decline in real GDP in the late 1980s, the economy of the present FRY entered a severe crisis in the early 1990s, with a sharp fall in almost all sectors of activity. In the late 1980s there was a relaxation of central planning in the SFRY, as the transition to a more market-orientated economy took place. Support for this process has been reiterated by leaders of the FRY. The recent severe adverse trend is attributable mainly to non-economic factors, particularly the civil war in parts of the former SFRY and the imposition on the FRY (in May 1992, and extended in April 1993) of UN sanctions, including an embargo on supplies of petroleum. The combined impact of international isolation, sanctions, high inflation, unemployment, the loss of productive capacity and the reduction in investment has devastated the FRY's economy. By mid-1995 the Yugoslav authorities estimated that the cost to the FRY's economy of the UN sanctions hitherto amounted to some US $45,000m. Other observers, none the less, cited the continued high level of government expenditure on the public sector and on unprofitable industries, as well as on defence (some 75% of federal budgetary expenditure in both 1994 and 1995 being allocated to the military), as representing a considerable strain on the economy. In January 1994 the Federal Government introduced a new currency, the 'super dinar' (linked to the Deutsche Mark), and signifying a more austere monetary policy, in an attempt to curb the rate of inflation, which had risen to unprecedented levels during 1993. Inflation was almost halted by March 1994, and retail prices remained largely unchanged until October, when a monthly inflation figure of 1.2% was recorded. Prices rose further in November and December, and by January 1995 inflation had risen to a monthly rate of 12.4%, threatening to reverse the modest economic recovery experienced in 1994. It was evident that significant economic recovery could only begin following the complete ending of economic sanctions against the FRY, which was almost certainly dependent on the restoration of peace in the former Yugoslavia.

## Social Welfare

All employed persons and their families are covered by obligatory social insurance schemes, providing for health insurance, money and grants in kind in case of sickness, accidents, disablement, old age and death. Insured persons are entitled to medical care, including compensation for an unlimited period during sick leave, rehabilitation and preventive care. The retirement pension is usually equivalent to 85%–87% of average monthly income during the last five years of employment. Women and young children enjoy special protection under the health insurance scheme. Employed women are entitled to at least 270 days' paid leave before and after childbirth. Confinements in hospital and maternity care are

# YUGOSLAVIA

*Introductory Survey, Statistical Survey*

free of charge. Women are entitled to shorter working hours on account of their children's illness. All workers are entitled to annual leave which varies from 18 to 36 days. Social welfare programmes in the FRY were, however, severely disrupted by the economic crisis from 1992 onwards.

### Education

The educational system of Yugoslavia is organized at republican level. Elementary education is free and compulsory for all children between the ages of seven and 15, when children attend the 'eight-year school'. Various types of secondary education are available to all who qualify, but the vocational and technical schools are the most popular. Alternatively, children may attend a general secondary school (gymnasium) where they follow a four-year course which will take them up to university entrance. At the secondary level there are also a number of art schools, apprentice schools and teacher-training schools. In 1991/92 there were 4,424 primary schools, 2,284 secondary schools and 145 institutes of higher education (including six universities) in the FRY. In 1990/91 the total enrolment at elementary and secondary schools was equivalent to 96.13% and 86.99%, respectively, of the school-age population. Those who have attended the technical schools may pursue their education further at one of the two-year post-secondary schools, created in response to the needs of industry and the social services. There are facilities for adult education at evening schools and in part-time studies.

Since 1990 ethnic Albanian schools in the province of Kosovo and Metohija have been closed. In 1994 about 350,000 ethnic Albanian children did not attend state schools. Instead, most attended unofficial classes organized by the illegal 'Republic of Kosovo' authorities.

### Public Holidays

**1995:** 1–2 January (New Year), 1–2 May (Labour Days), 4 July (Fighters' Day), 29–30 November (Republic Days).
**1996:** 1–2 January (New Year), 1–2 May (Labour Days), 4 July (Fighters' Day), 29–30 November (Republic Days).

In addition, Montenegro observes a holiday on 13 July, and Serbia observes 7 July as a public holiday.

### Weights and Measures

The metric system is in force.

# Statistical Survey

Source: *Statistički godišnjak Jugoslavije* (Statistical Yearbook of Yugoslavia), published by Savezni zavod za statistiku (Federal Statistical Office), 11000 Belgrade, Kneza Miloša 20; tel. (11) 681999; telex 11317; fax (11) 642368.

Note: Unless otherwise indicated, figures in this Survey refer to the territory of the Federal Republic of Yugoslavia (FRY), comprising the two republics of Serbia and Montenegro. Where data for the FRY are not available, the Survey has retained tables relating to the former Socialist Federal Republic of Yugoslavia (SFRY), which comprised six republics. Such tables are indicated by the phrase 'former SFRY' after the heading.

## Area and Population

### AREA, POPULATION AND DENSITY

| | |
|---|---:|
| Area (sq km) | 102,173* |
| Population (census results) | |
| 31 March 1981 | |
| Males | 4,919,066 |
| Females | 4,978,920 |
| Total | 9,897,986 |
| 31 March 1991 | 10,406,742 |
| Population (official estimates at mid-year) | |
| 1992 | 10,630,000 |
| 1993 | 10,482,000 |
| Density (per sq km) at mid-1993 | 102.6 |

* 39,449 sq miles.

### REPUBLICS (Census of 31 March 1991)

| Republic | Area (sq km) | Population | Density (per sq km) | Capital (with population) |
|---|---:|---:|---:|---|
| Serbia | 88,361 | 9,791,475 | 111 | Belgrade (1,087,915) |
| Vojvodina* | 21,506 | 2,012,517 | 94 | Novi Sad (170,029) |
| Kosovo and Metohija* | 10,887 | 1,954,747 | 179 | Priština (108,020) |
| Montenegro | 13,812 | 615,267 | 45 | Podgorica† (96,074) |
| **Total** | 102,173 | 10,406,742 | 102 | — |

* Provinces within Serbia.   † Formerly Titograd.

### PRINCIPAL TOWNS (population at 1991 census)

| | | | |
|---|---:|---|---:|
| Beograd (Belgrade, the capital) | 1,087,915 | Subotica | 100,219 |
| Novi Sad | 170,029 | Podgorica* | 96,074 |
| Niš | 161,376 | Zrenjanin | 81,328 |
| Kragujevać | 146,607 | Pančevo | 72,717 |
| Priština | 108,020 | Čačak | 72,092 |

* Formerly Titograd.

### POPULATION BY ETHNIC GROUP
(1991 census, preliminary results)

| Ethnic Group | Population ('000) | % |
|---|---:|---:|
| Serbs | 6,486 | 62.3 |
| Albanians | 1,728 | 16.6 |
| Montenegrins | 521 | 5.0 |
| Hungarians | 345 | 3.3 |
| Yugoslavs | 344 | 3.3 |
| Muslims | 327 | 3.1 |
| **Total** (incl. others) | 10,407 | 100.0 |

### BIRTHS, MARRIAGES AND DEATHS

| | Registered live births | | Registered marriages | | Registered deaths | |
|---|---:|---:|---:|---:|---:|---:|
| | Number | Rate (per 1,000) | Number | Rate (per 1,000) | Number | Rate (per 1,000) |
| 1984 | 172,800 | 17.0 | 72,421 | 7.1 | 97,230 | 9.6 |
| 1985 | 166,587 | 16.3 | 70,140 | 6.9 | 97,588 | 9.6 |
| 1986 | 164,393 | 16.0 | 68,497 | 6.7 | 98,345 | 9.6 |
| 1987 | 165,067 | 16.0 | 70,502 | 6.8 | 97,723 | 9.4 |
| 1988 | 163,944 | 15.7 | 70,403 | 6.8 | 97,534 | 9.4 |
| 1989 | 154,560 | 14.8 | 69,438 | 6.6 | 99,270 | 9.5 |
| 1990 | 155,022 | 14.7 | 64,856 | 6.2 | 97,665 | 9.3 |
| 1991* | 149,221 | 14.1 | 55,326 | 5.6 | 97,645 | 9.2 |

* Provisional.

# YUGOSLAVIA

*Statistical Survey*

## ECONOMICALLY ACTIVE POPULATION
(persons aged 10 years and over, 1981 census)

|  | Males | Females | Total |
|---|---|---|---|
| Agriculture, hunting, forestry and fishing | 807,196 | 681,594 | 1,488,790 |
| Mining and quarrying | } 598,354 | 267,919 | 866,273 |
| Manufacturing |  |  |  |
| Electricity, gas and water |  |  |  |
| Construction | 250,883 | 23,799 | 274,682 |
| Trade, restaurants and hotels | 175,723 | 153,501 | 329,224 |
| Transport, storage and communications | 151,273 | 23,819 | 175,092 |
| Financing, insurance, real estate and business services | 40,489 | 38,963 | 79,452 |
| Community, social and personal services | 389,002 | 284,945 | 673,947 |
| Activities not adequately defined | 46,054 | 16,203 | 62,257 |
| **Total employed** | 2,458,974 | 1,490,743 | 3,949,717 |
| Unemployed | 288,447 | 190,064 | 478,511 |
| **Total labour force** | 2,717,421 | 1,680,807 | 4,428,228 |

## EMPLOYMENT IN THE 'SOCIALIZED' SECTOR
('000 employees, average of March and September each year)

|  | 1992 | 1993 | 1994 |
|---|---|---|---|
| Agriculture, forestry and fishing | 122 | 119 | 116 |
| Mining and industry | 940 | 916 | 892 |
| Electricity, gas and water | 57 | 55 | 53 |
| Construction | 171 | 158 | 148 |
| Trade, restaurants and hotels | 299 | 284 | 265 |
| Transport and communications | 158 | 151 | 146 |
| Arts and crafts | 43 | 40 | 38 |
| Financial and other services | 86 | 86 | 81 |
| Community, social and personal services | 452 | 439 | 432 |
| **Total** | 2,328 | 2,243 | 2,170 |
| Males | 1,398* | n.a. | n.a. |
| Females | 930* | n.a. | n.a. |

* Estimate.

# Agriculture

## PRINCIPAL CROPS ('000 metric tons)

|  | 1991 | 1992 | 1993 |
|---|---|---|---|
| Wheat | 4,109 | 2,137* | 3,027† |
| Barley | 299 | 250 | 253† |
| Maize | 7,818 | 4,311 | 4,237† |
| Oats | 128 | 130 | 124† |
| Other cereals | 27 | 23 | 22 |
| Potatoes | 867 | 711 | 592† |
| Dry beans | 85* | 61 | 35† |
| Other pulses | 33 | 25 | 18 |
| Soybeans | 115 | 91 | 83† |
| Sunflower seed | 380 | 362 | 394† |
| Cabbages | 344 | 226 | 160† |
| Tomatoes | 230 | 186* | 133† |
| Cucumbers and gherkins | 68 | 63* | 52* |
| Green peppers | 161 | 103* | 64* |
| Dry onions | 168 | 153* | 104† |
| Garlic | 34 | 28† | 19† |
| Carrots | 74 | 47* | 33* |
| Other vegetables | 28 | 21 | 16 |
| Watermelons and melons | 198† | 160† | n.a. |
| Grapes | 497† | 384 | 404† |
| Sugar beets | 4,713 | 2,730 | 1,304† |
| Apples | 210 | 209 | 182† |
| Pears | 83 | 91 | 77† |
| Peaches | 58 | 49† | 38* |
| Plums | 365 | 379 | 493† |
| Apricots | 17 | 31† | 20† |
| Strawberries | 31 | 27 | 20† |
| Raspberries | 42 | 44 | 38† |
| Other fruits | 134 | 125 | 135 |
| Walnuts | 20.9 | 15.6* | 12.5* |
| Tobacco (leaves) | 15 | 13 | 13* |

* FAO estimate.   † Unofficial figure.

Source: FAO, *Production Yearbook*.

## LIVESTOCK ('000 head, year ending 30 September)

|  | 1991 | 1992 | 1993 |
|---|---|---|---|
| Horses | 94 | 89 | 68† |
| Cattle | 2,102 | 1,975* | 1,991* |
| Buffaloes | 35 | 19 | n.a. |
| Pigs | 4,374 | 3,844 | 4,092* |
| Sheep | 3,043 | 2,715 | 2,752* |
| Poultry | 30,213 | 26,000 | 22,000* |

* Unofficial figure.   † FAO estimate.

Source: mainly FAO, *Production Yearbook*.

## LIVESTOCK PRODUCTS ( metric tons)

|  | 1991 | 1992 | 1993 |
|---|---|---|---|
| Beef and veal | 163,000* | 117,000† | 105,000* |
| Mutton and lamb | 29,000 | 26,000† | 23,000† |
| Pig meat | 378,000 | 373,000* | 365,000* |
| Poultry meat | 73,000 | 71,000* | 58,000* |
| Cows' milk | 1,829,000 | 1,815,000† | 1,778,000† |
| Sheep's milk | 54,000 | 50,000 | 44,000 |
| Cheese | 87,000 | 77,537† | 63,100* |
| Butter | 4,112 | 2,500* | 2,100* |
| Hen eggs | 84,600 | 80,000 | 68,100* |
| Honey | 1,934 | 1,800* | 1,380* |
| Wool: |  |  |  |
| greasy | 3,990 | 3,600* | 3,190* |
| scoured | 2,394 | 2,160* | 1,900* |
| Cattle and buffaloes hides* | 21,483 | 16,200 | 14,652 |
| Sheep skins* | 1,900 | 1,700 | 1,700 |

* FAO estimate(s).   † Unofficial figure.

Source: FAO, *Production Yearbook*.

# YUGOSLAVIA

## Forestry

**ROUNDWOOD REMOVALS** ('000 cubic metres)*

|  | 1989 | 1990 | 1991 |
|---|---|---|---|
| Sawlogs and veneer logs | 1,304 | 1,177 | 1,113 |
| Pitprops (mine timber) | 56 | 59 | 59 |
| Pulpwood | 472 | 344 | 277 |
| Other industrial wood | 128 | 102 | 104 |
| Fuel wood | 730 | 687 | 703 |
| **Total** (incl. others) | 2,704 | 2,385 | 2,267 |

* From socially-owned forests only.

**SAWNWOOD PRODUCTION** ('000 cubic metres)

|  | 1989 | 1990 | 1991 |
|---|---|---|---|
| Coniferous (softwood) | 758 | 643 | 555 |
| Non-coniferous (hardwood) | 4,225 | 3,708 | 3,599 |
| **Total** | 4,983 | 4,351 | 4,154 |

## Fishing

(metric tons, live weight)

|  | 1989 | 1990 | 1991* |
|---|---|---|---|
| Freshwater fishes | 9,263 | 7,658 | 1,983 |
| Marine fishes | 482 | 460 | 170 |
| Crustaceans and molluscs | 26 | 29 | 15 |
| **Total catch** | 9,771 | 8,147 | 2,168 |

* Preliminary figures.

## Mining

('000 metric tons, unless otherwise indicated)

|  | 1992 | 1993 | 1994 |
|---|---|---|---|
| Coal | 40,105 | 37,437 | 38,358 |
| Crude petroleum | 1,165 | 1,148 | 1,078 |
| Lead and zinc ore* | 804 | 337 | 270 |
| Bauxite | 792 | 102 | n.a. |
| Natural gas ('000 cu m) | 846 | 962 | 824 |

* Figures refer to gross weight of ores extracted. In the former Socialist Federal Republic of Yugoslavia lead and zinc ore contained 2.7% lead and 2.3% zinc in 1989 and 1990.

## Industry

**SELECTED PRODUCTS**
('000 metric tons, unless otherwise indicated)

|  | 1992 | 1993 | 1994 |
|---|---|---|---|
| Electric energy (million kWh) | 36,488 | 34,156 | 35,353 |
| Motor spirit (petrol) | 599 | 273 | 121 |
| Residual fuel oil | 862 | 465 | 285 |
| Pig iron | 512 | 62 | 17 |
| Crude steel | 665 | 183 | 137 |
| Electrolytic copper | 115 | 51 | 72 |
| Refined lead | 23 | 6 | 4 |
| Electrolytic zinc | 14 | 7 | 4 |
| Aluminium ingots | 67 | 26 | 7 |
| Tractors (number) | 14,423 | 5,369 | 4,508 |
| Lorries (number) | 4,252 | 278 | 696 |
| Motor cars (number)* | 26,386 | 7,713 | 8,360 |
| Bicycles (number) | 64,590 | 11,284 | 30,654 |
| Sulphuric acid | 293 | 75 | 23 |
| Soda ash | 23 | 4 | 5 |
| Cement | 2,036 | 1,992 | 1,493 |

| — continued | 1992 | 1993 | 1994 |
|---|---|---|---|
| Cotton yarn (metric tons)† | 18,035 | 10,225 | 10,303 |
| Woollen yarn (metric tons)† | 8,350 | 6,201 | 6,428 |
| Woven cotton fabrics ('000 sq metres)† | 38,370 | 26,345 | 26,821 |
| Footwear (excl. rubber) ('000 pairs) | 16,043 | 10,435 | 8,796 |
| Radio receivers ('000) | 689 | 642 | 301 |
| Television receivers ('000) | 51,351 | 23,769 | 39,746 |
| Edible vegetable oils | 95 | 99 | 78 |

* Including cars assembled from imported parts.
† Including yarn and fabrics produced from cellulosic fibres.

## Finance

**CURRENCY AND EXCHANGE RATES**

**Monetary Unit**
100 para = 1 Yugoslav dinar.

**Sterling and Dollar Equivalents** (31 December 1994)
£1 sterling = 8.81 dinars;
US $1 = 5.63 dinars;
100 Yugoslav dinars = £11.355 = $17.765.

**Average Exchange Rate** (new dinars per US $)
1989  2.876
1990  11.318
1991  19.638

Note: On 1 January 1990 the new dinar, equivalent to 10,000 old dinars, was introduced in the Socialist Federal Republic of Yugoslavia (SFRY). After the disintegration of the SFRY, the Federal Republic of Yugoslavia (FRY) continued to use the Yugoslav dinar as its currency. Meanwhile, the other republics of the former SFRY introduced their own currencies to replace (initially at par) the Yugoslav dinar. As a result of rapid inflation in the FRY, the value of the Yugoslav dinar depreciated sharply. By the end of May 1993 the exchange rate was about 89,000 dinars per US dollar. After further devaluations, the currency was redenominated from 1 October, with the introduction of another new dinar, worth 1,000,000 of the former units. However, the depreciation of the currency continued, and on 30 December the new dinar was replaced by a further dinar, worth 1,000 million of its predecessors. In January 1994 there was another currency reform, with the establishment of a dinar officially valued at 1 Deutsche Mark (equivalent to 13 million former dinars).

**BUDGETS** (million new dinars)*

| Revenue | Federal budget 1989 | Federal budget 1990 | Other budgets† 1989 | Other budgets† 1990 |
|---|---|---|---|---|
| Total receipts | 11,376.5 | 92,082.5 | 8,782.3 | 109,826.3 |

| Expenditure | Federal budget 1989 | Federal budget 1990 | Other budgets† 1989 | Other budgets† 1990 |
|---|---|---|---|---|
| Schools | — | — | 155.2 | 9,682.0 |
| Science and culture | — | — | 39.3 | 4,457.2 |
| Public health and social welfare | 1,105.7 | 8,269.0 | 308.9 | 1,758.0 |
| National defence | 6,112.4 | 4,693.1 | 37.2 | 487.0 |
| Non-economic investment | 44.1 | 195.0 | 154.8 | 1,480.6 |
| Government | 1,163.4 | 7,838.9 | 5,140.4 | 41,107.3 |
| Investment and interventions in the economy | 1,579.1 | 24,713.3 | 351.9 | 16,606.8 |
| Other | 822.1 | 8,522.6 | 2,487.9 | 33,622.5 |
| **Total** | 10,826.9 | 96,451.9 | 8,675.6 | 109,201.4 |

* Figures refer to the former Socialist Federal Republic of Yugoslavia.
† Republican, Provincial (Vojvodina and Kosovo) and Communal Budgets.

# YUGOSLAVIA

**INTERNATIONAL RESERVES** (former SFRY, US $ million at 31 December)

|  | 1989 | 1990 | 1991 |
|---|---|---|---|
| Gold* | 80 | 81 | 81 |
| IMF special drawing rights | — | 13 | — |
| Foreign exchange | 4,136 | 5,461 | 2,682 |
| Total | 4,216 | 5,555 | 2,763 |

* Valued at US $42.22 per troy ounce.

Source: IMF, *International Financial Statistics*.

**MONEY SUPPLY** (former SFRY, million new dinars at 31 December)

|  | 1988 | 1989 | 1990 |
|---|---|---|---|
| Notes in circulation | 585 | 12,375 | 52,517 |
| Private-sector deposits at national banks | 24 | 896 | 175 |
| Deposit money at basic and associated banks | 1,798 | 37,759 | 73,591 |
| Total money | 2,407 | 51,030 | 126,283 |

Source: IMF, *International Financial Statistics*.

**NATIONAL ACCOUNTS** (million new dinars* at current prices)
**Net Material Product by Economic Activity**

|  | 1989 | 1990 | 1991 |
|---|---|---|---|
| Agriculture and forestry | 1,228 | 5,276 | 12,121 |
| Industrial activity | 3,837 | 12,472 | 27,332 |
| Construction | 466 | 2,694 | 5,229 |
| Trade, restaurants, etc. | 1,337 | 7,282 | 17,458 |
| Transport and communications | 391 | 2,135 | 4,339 |
| Other activities of the material sphere | 291 | 1,770 | 3,937 |
| Total | 7,550 | 31,629 | 70,416 |

* Denominated in accordance with regulations in changes of dinar value that came into force in January 1992.

Source: UN, *National Accounts Statistics*.

**BALANCE OF PAYMENTS** (former SFRY, US $ million)

|  | 1989 | 1990 | 1991 |
|---|---|---|---|
| Merchandise exports f.o.b. | 13,560 | 14,308 | 13,799 |
| Merchandise imports f.o.b. | −13,502 | −16,984 | −13,287 |
| **Trade balance** | 58 | −2,676 | 512 |
| Exports of services | 5,441 | 6,374 | 2,465 |
| Imports of services | −8,245 | −15,012 | −5,586 |
| Other income received | 403 | 789 | 470 |
| Other income paid | −1,872 | −1,667 | −1,154 |
| Private unrequited transfers (net) | 6,645 | 9,830 | 2,134 |
| Official unrequited transfers (net) | −3 | −2 | −2 |
| **Current balance** | 2,427 | −2,364 | −1,161 |
| Capital (net) | −697 | 3,504 | −2,133 |
| Net errors and omissions | 201 | 228 | 497 |
| **Overall balance** | 1,931 | 1,368 | −2,797 |

Source: IMF, *International Financial Statistics*.

# External Trade

Note: Figures exclude trade with other former republics of the Socialist Federal Republic of Yugoslavia.

**PRINCIPAL COMMODITIES**
(distribution by SITC, million new dinars)

| Imports c.i.f. | 1989 | 1990 | 1991 |
|---|---|---|---|
| **Food and live animals** | 129 | 800 | 796 |
| Fruit and vegetables | n.a. | 135 | 143 |
| Coffee, tea, cocoa and spices | n.a. | 131 | 202 |
| **Beverages and tobacco** | 3 | 40 | 84 |
| **Crude materials (inedible) except fuels** | 154 | 547 | 525 |
| Textile fibres and waste | n.a. | 146 | 125 |
| **Mineral fuels, lubricants, etc.** | 263 | 1,331 | 1,985 |
| **Animal and vegetable oils and fats** | 9 | 25 | 23 |
| **Chemicals** | 233 | 955 | 1,429 |
| Chemical elements and compounds | n.a. | 119 | 160 |
| Medicinal and pharmaceutical products | n.a. | 140 | 222 |
| **Basic manufactures** | 317 | 1,256 | 1,502 |
| Textile yarn, fabrics, etc. | n.a. | 281 | 339 |
| Non-metallic mineral manufactures | n.a. | 110 | 143 |
| Iron and steel | n.a. | 326 | 297 |
| Non-ferrous metals | n.a. | 151 | 167 |
| Other metal manufactures | n.a. | 118 | 192 |
| **Machinery and transport equipment** | 464 | 2,066 | 2,374 |
| **Miscellaneous manufactured articles** | 89 | 846 | 1,087 |
| **Other commodities and transactions** | 1 | 492 | 652 |
| **Total** | 1,661 | 8,363 | 10,459 |

| Exports f.o.b. | 1989 | 1990 | 1991 |
|---|---|---|---|
| **Food and live animals** | 119 | 473 | 1,056 |
| Meat and meat preparations | n.a. | 126 | 126 |
| Cereals and cereal preparations | n.a. | 90 | 270 |
| Fruit and vegetables | n.a. | 120 | 330 |
| **Beverages and tobacco** | 56 | 44 | 120 |
| **Crude materials (inedible) except fuels** | 79 | 302 | 293 |
| **Mineral fuels, lubricants, etc.** | 21 | 220 | 397 |
| **Animal and vegetable oils and fats** | 2 | 6 | 11 |
| **Chemicals** | 197 | 640 | 819 |
| **Basic manufactures** | 381 | 1,794 | 2,435 |
| Textile yarn, fabrics, etc. | n.a. | 215 | 382 |
| Non-metallic mineral manufactures | n.a. | 106 | 162 |
| Iron and steel | n.a. | 342 | 483 |
| Non-ferrous metals | n.a. | 706 | 810 |
| **Machinery and transport equipment** | 413 | 1,615 | 1,760 |
| **Miscellaneous manufactured articles** | 215 | 1,409 | 2,046 |
| Furniture | n.a. | 112 | 149 |
| Clothing (excl. footwear) | n.a. | 808 | 1,278 |
| Footwear | n.a. | 270 | 349 |
| **Other commodities and transactions** | 5 | 36 | 34 |
| **Total** | 1,450 | 6,539 | 8,971 |

YUGOSLAVIA

**PRINCIPAL TRADING PARTNERS** (million new dinars)

| Imports c.i.f. | 1989 | 1990 | 1991 |
|---|---|---|---|
| Austria | 59 | 339 | 409 |
| Czechoslovakia | 48 | 220 | 292 |
| France | 55 | 329 | 397 |
| Germany | 338 | 1,680 | 2,109 |
| Hungary | 62 | 277 | 347 |
| Iran | 8 | 160 | 180 |
| Iraq | 78 | 72 | n.a. |
| Italy | 159 | 932 | 1,109 |
| Japan | 22 | 125 | 240 |
| Libya | 7 | 21 | 516 |
| Netherlands | 30 | 135 | 186 |
| Poland | 72 | 231 | 183 |
| Romania | 32 | 87 | 214 |
| Sweden | 17 | 82 | 100 |
| Switzerland | 32 | 190 | 207 |
| USSR | 264 | 1,223 | 1,319 |
| United Kingdom | n.a. | 198 | 306 |
| USA | 74 | 381 | 423 |
| **Total** (incl. others) | 1,661 | 8,363 | 10,459 |

| Exports f.o.b. | 1989 | 1990 | 1991 |
|---|---|---|---|
| Austria | 43 | 240 | 253 |
| Bulgaria | 19 | 80 | 191 |
| Czechoslovakia | 65 | 250 | 113 |
| Egypt | 20 | 110 | 144 |
| France | 33 | 228 | 259 |
| Germany | 160 | 1,254 | 2,704 |
| Greece | 30 | 131 | 276 |
| Hungary | 43 | 121 | 141 |
| Iran | 10 | 64 | 85 |
| Iraq | 35 | 45 | 310 |
| Italy | 121 | 875 | 1,253 |
| Netherlands | 19 | 70 | 110 |
| Poland | 69 | 114 | 156 |
| Romania | 24 | 141 | 383 |
| Switzerland | 17 | 94 | 682 |
| USSR | 382 | 1,334 | 1,598 |
| United Kingdom | 46 | 221 | 212 |
| USA | 60 | 259 | 398 |
| **Total** (incl. others) | 1,450 | 6,539 | 8,971 |

## Transport

**RAILWAYS** (traffic)

| | 1990 | 1991 | 1992* |
|---|---|---|---|
| Passenger journeys (million) | n.a. | 31 | 29.7 |
| Passenger-kilometres (million) | 4,794 | 2,926 | 2,642 |
| Freight carried (million metric tons) | n.a. | 25 | 20.1 |
| Freight ton-kilometres (million) | 7,744 | 5,348 | 4,676 |

* Source: *Railway Directory*.

**ROAD TRAFFIC** (registered motor vehicles at 31 December)

| | 1988 | 1989 | 1990 |
|---|---|---|---|
| Motor cycles (up to 50 cc) | 40,821 | 42,261 | 43,414 |
| Passenger cars | 1,225,043 | 1,309,681 | 1,405,455 |
| Buses | 12,390 | 12,693 | 13,133 |
| Lorries | 34,558 | 88,700 | 92,874 |
| Special vehicles | 24,486 | 25,789 | 26,475 |
| Tractors | 289,834 | 306,610 | 318,312 |

**INLAND WATERWAYS**
**Fleet** (number of vessels)

| | 1991 |
|---|---|
| Tugs | 188 |
| Motor barges | 73 |
| Barges | 424 |
| Tankers | 93 |
| Passenger vessels | 8 |

**Traffic** ('000 metric tons)

| | 1989 | 1990 | 1991 |
|---|---|---|---|
| Goods unloaded | 14,111 | 12,946 | 11,638 |

**SEA-BORNE SHIPPING** (international freight traffic)

| | 1989 | 1990 | 1991 |
|---|---|---|---|
| Vessels entered ('000 net reg. tons) | 6,939 | 5,469 | 2,394 |
| Goods loaded ('000 metric tons) | 636 | 727 | 705 |
| Goods unloaded ('000 metric tons) | 1,744 | 1,321 | 847 |
| Goods in transit ('000 metric tons) | 27 | 4.2 | 6.8 |

**CIVIL AVIATION** (traffic)

| | 1989 | 1990 | 1991 |
|---|---|---|---|
| Passengers carried ('000) | 5,189 | 5,304 | 5,146 |
| Passenger-kilometres (million) | 6,693 | 7,102 | 3,443 |
| Cargo carried (tons) | 47,840 | 37,141 | 16,122 |
| Ton-kilometres ('000) | 153,337 | 134,745 | 61,885 |
| Kilometres flown ('000) | 60,076 | 59,232 | 34,257 |

## Tourism

**FOREIGN TOURIST ARRIVALS** (by country of origin)

| | 1989 | 1990 | 1991 |
|---|---|---|---|
| Austria | 64,700 | 50,500 | 9,100 |
| Czechoslovakia | 34,300 | 35,100 | 12,200 |
| France | 44,300 | 43,000 | 15,200 |
| Germany, Federal Republic | 260,000 | 236,000 | 81,400* |
| Hungary | 57,900 | 28,600 | 9,000 |
| Italy | 91,500 | 91,800 | 22,800 |
| Netherlands | 39,600 | 37,300 | 6,500 |
| USSR | 217,000 | 188,000 | 30,400 |
| United Kingdom | 81,900 | 86,400 | 21,700 |
| USA | 34,300 | 33,500 | 9,700 |
| **Total** (incl. others)† | 5,350,000 | 5,062,000 | 3,508,000 |

* Including arrivals from the former German Democratic Republic.
† Including internal tourism.

# YUGOSLAVIA

## Communications Media

|  | 1989 | 1990 | 1991 |
|---|---|---|---|
| Telephones ('000 in use) | 1,948 | 1,839 | 1,782 |
| Radio licences ('000) | 1,907 | 1,877 | 1,877 |
| Television licences ('000) | 1,704 | 1,690 | 1,699 |
| Books (titles published) | 5,190 | 4,180 | 4,049 |
| Daily newspapers | 12 | 15 | n.a. |
| Average circulation ('000) | 956 | 1,084 | n.a. |
| Newspapers (all frequencies) | 1,046 | 962 | 801 |
| Average circulation ('000) | 12,554 | 11,275 | n.a. |
| Periodicals | 645 | 569 | 505 |
| Average circulation ('000) | 1,388 | 1,659 | n.a. |

## Education

(1991/92)

|  | Institutions | Teachers | Students |
|---|---|---|---|
| First level | 4,424 | 21,399 | 470,669 |
| Second level (first stage) | 1,746 | 29,994 | 465,800 |
| Second level (second stage) | 538 | 14,977 | 347,916 |
| General secondary (public general) | n.a. | n.a. | 74,626 |
| Teacher training | n.a. | n.a. | 3,568 |
| Technical and vocational | n.a. | n.a. | 269,722 |
| Religion and theology (private) | 2 | 194 | 2,427 |
| Institutions for higher education | 145 | 9,599 | 132,814 |

# Directory

## The Constitution

The Constitution of the Federal Republic of Yugoslavia, comprising Serbia and Montenegro, was adopted on 27 April 1992. Its main provisions are summarized below:

The Federal Republic of Yugoslavia (FRY) is a sovereign federal state, based on the principle of equality of its citizens and its member republics. The FRY comprises the Republic of Serbia and the Republic of Montenegro, and there are constitutional provisions for it to be joined by other republics. The FRY covers a unified territory consisting of the territories of the member republics. The FRY borders are inviolable.

Each member republic will have sovereignty over issues which, under the Federal Constitution, do not come within the competence of the FRY. In the FRY, power is in the hands of citizens, who exercise it either directly or through their freely-elected representatives. The FRY is based on the rule of law. The FRY recognizes and guarantees human liberties and citizens' rights as recognized by international law. The FRY recognizes and guarantees the rights of national minorities to preserve, develop and express their ethnic, cultural, linguistic and other characteristics, and their right to use their own national symbols in accordance with international law.

Authority in the FRY is shared between legislative, executive and judicial organs of state. Under the Constitution, the FRY is a single economic space with a single market. Political pluralism is a condition for, and a guarantee of, a democratic political system in the FRY.

In the FRY all citizens are equal before the law, regardless of their national affiliation, race, sex, language, religion, political or other convictions, education, social origin, property status and any other personal characteristic. Each citizen has a duty to respect the freedoms and rights of others and will be accountable for it.

The freedom of work and enterprise is guaranteed in the FRY. The right to private ownership is guaranteed. Nobody can be deprived of property, nor can it be limited (except when general interests require, as envisaged by the law and provided that compensation not lower than the market value of the property is paid to the owner). A foreigner assumes the right to private ownership and the right to enterprise under the conditions of reciprocity.

The FRY establishes policies, adopts and implements federal laws, other regulations and general documents, and secures constitutional and judicial protection in the following areas: human liberties, citizens' rights and duties as laid down in the Federal Constitution, the single market, the development of the FRY, communications and technical and technological systems, safety in all types of transport, the health service, international relations, and the defence and security of the FRY.

Bodies of the FRY are: the Federal Assembly, the President of the Republic, the Federal Government, the Federal Court, the Federal Public Prosecutor and the National Bank of Yugoslavia. Provision is made for the power and composition of the Federal Constitutional Court.

The FRY has an army which protects its sovereignty, territory, independence and constitutional system. The Yugoslav Army has both active and reserve staff. The active staff comprises professional soldiers and conscripts engaged in national service. The President of the Republic commands the Army both in time of peace and in time of war, in accordance with decisions of the Supreme Defence Council. The Supreme Defence Council consists of the President of the Republic and presidents of member republics. The FRY President is the president of the Supreme Defence Council. National service in the FRY is compulsory. A citizen who does not wish to perform regular military service on account of religious or other conscientious objections can participate in national service in the Yugoslav Army without weapons or in civilian service.

## The Federal Government

### HEAD OF STATE

**President of the Republic:** ZORAN LILIĆ (appointed 25 June 1993).

### FEDERAL GOVERNMENT
(June 1995)

**Prime Minister:** RADOJE KONTIĆ.

**Deputy Prime Minister and Federal Minister of Finance:** JOVAN ZEBIĆ.

**Deputy Prime Minister and Federal Minister of the Economy:** NIKOLA ŠAINOVIĆ.

**Deputy Prime Minister and Federal Minister of Justice:** UROS KLIKOVAĆ.

**Federal Minister of Foreign Affairs:** VLADISLAV JOVANOVIĆ.

**Federal Minister of National Defence:** PAVLE BULATOVIĆ.

**Federal Minister of Internal Affairs:** VUKASIN JOVANOVIĆ.

**Federal Minister of Trade:** DJORDJE SIRADOVIĆ.

**Federal Minister of Transport and Communications:** ZORAN VUJOVIĆ.

**Federal Minister of Employment, Health and Social Affairs:** MIROSLAV IVANESEVIĆ.

**Federal Minister of Development, Science and the Environment:** JANKO RADULOVIĆ.

**Federal Minister without Portfolio** (responsible for Human Rights and National Minority Affairs): MARGIT SAVOVIĆ.

**Federal Minister without Portfolio** (responsible for Sports): ZORAN BINGULAĆ.

**Federal Ministers without Portfolio:** TOMICA RAICEVIĆ, VUK OGNJANOVIĆ.

**Federal Secretary for Information:** DRAGUTIN BRCIN.

**Secretary-General of the Federal Government:** MLADEN VUKCEVIĆ.

### FEDERAL MINISTRIES

**Office of the Federal Government:** 11070 Belgrade, Lenjina 2; tel. (11) 334281.

**Federal Ministry of Development, Science and the Environment:** 11000 Belgrade, Lenjina 2; tel. (11) 635910; fax (11) 2223492.

YUGOSLAVIA                                                                                                                      *Directory*

**Federal Ministry of the Economy:** 11070 Belgrade, Omladinskih brigada 1; tel. (11) 2223550; telex 11062; fax (11) 195244.

**Federal Ministry of Employment, Health and Social Affairs:** 11070 Belgrade, AVNOJ-a 104, SIV-II; tel. (11) 602555; telex 11062; fax (11) 195244.

**Federal Ministry of Finance:** Belgrade.

**Federal Ministry of Foreign Affairs:** 11000 Belgrade, Kneza Miloša 24; tel. (11) 682555; telex 11173; fax (11) 682668.

**Federal Ministry of Internal Affairs:** 11000 Belgrade, Kneza Miloša 92; tel. (11) 685555; telex 11185; fax (11) 2351005.

**Federal Ministry of Justice:** 11070 Belgrade, bul. Lenjina 1; tel. (11) 2223765; telex 11062; fax (11) 636775.

**Federal Ministry of National Defence:** 11000 Belgrade, Kneza Miloša 29; tel. (11) 656122; telex 12216.

**Federal Ministry of Trade:** 11070 Belgrade, Omladinskih brigada 1; tel. (11) 2223550; telex 11062; fax (11) 195244.

**Federal Ministry of Transport and Communications:** 11070 Belgrade, AVNOJ-a 104; tel. (11) 602555; telex 12062; fax (11) 2223946.

## The Republican Governments

### MONTENEGRO
### STATE PRESIDENT

**President of the Republic:** MOMIR BULATOVIĆ (elected by popular vote 23 December 1990; re-elected 10 January 1993).

### MINISTERS
(June 1995)

**Prime Minister:** MILO DJUKANOVIĆ.
**Deputy Prime Ministers:** KRUNISLAV VUKCEVIĆ, RADE PEROVIĆ, ZORAN ŽIŽIĆ.
**Minister of Internal Affairs:** FILIP VUJANOVIĆ.
**Minister of Finance:** BOŽIDAR GAZIVODA.
**Minister of Foreign Affairs:** JANKO JEKNIĆ.
**Minister of National Defence:** (vacant).
**Minister of Justice:** MIODRAG LATKOVIĆ.
**Minister of Labour, Social Welfare and the Protection of Veterans and Disabled Persons:** MILIVOJE JAUKOVIĆ.
**Minister of Agriculture, Forestry and Water Resources Management:** BRANKO ABRAMOVIĆ.
**Minister of Culture:** GOJKO CELEBIĆ.
**Minister of Health and the Environment:** MIOMIR MUGOŠA.
**Minister of Education and Science:** Dr PREDRAG OBRADOVIĆ.
**Minister of Religious Affairs:** SLOBODAN TOMOVIĆ.
**Minister of Maritime Industry and Transport:** JUSUF KALAMPEROVIĆ.
**Minister of Energy, Mining and Industry:** MIODRAG GOMILANOVIĆ.
**Minister of Tourism:** DRAGAN MILIĆ.
**Minister of Trade:** DUSKO LAUĆEVIĆ.
**Ministers without Portfolio:** MILADIN VUKOTIĆ, MEVLUDIN NUHODŽIĆ.

### MINISTRIES

**Office of the President:** Podgorica; fax (81) 42329.
**Office of the Prime Minister:** Podgorica, Jovana Tomaševića bb; tel. (81) 52833; fax (81) 52246.
**Ministry of Agriculture, Forestry and Water Resources Management:** Podgorica, Omladinskih brig. 2; tel. (81) 31287; fax (81) 52935.
**Ministry of Culture:** Podgorica, Vuka Karadžića 3; tel. (81) 51355; fax (81) 42028.
**Ministry of the Economy:** Podgorica, Stanka Dragojevića 2; tel. (81) 42104; fax (81) 42028.
**Ministry of Education and Science:** Podgorica, Ulica slobode bb; fax (81) 612780.
**Ministry of Energy, Mining and Industry:** Podgorica.
**Ministry of Finance:** Podgorica, Blaža Jovanovića 2; tel. (81) 42835; fax (81) 42028.
**Ministry of Foreign Affairs:** Podgorica, Stanka Dragojevića 2; tel. (81) 52821; fax (81) 45752.
**Ministry of Health and the Environment:** Podgorica, Stanka Dragojevića 2; fax (81) 42028.
**Ministry of Internal Affairs:** Podgorica, Lenjina 6; tel. (81) 5223; fax (81) 52919.

**Ministry of Justice:** Podgorica, Vuka Karadžića 3; tel. (81) 51355; fax (81) 612780.
**Ministry of Labour, Social Welfare and Protection of Veterans and Disabled Persons:** Podgorica, Vuka Karadžića 3; tel. (81) 51255; fax (81) 612912.
**Ministry of Maritime Industry and Transport:** Podgorica, Pete proleterske brig. 36; tel. (81) 2142; fax (81) 52246.
**Ministry of National Defence:** Podgorica, Blaža Jovanovića 4; tel. (81) 42396; fax (81) 45431.
**Ministry of Religious Affairs:** Podgorica.
**Ministry of Tourism and Trade:** Podgorica; fax (81) 42028.

### SERBIA
### STATE PRESIDENT

**President of the Republic:** SLOBODAN MILOŠEVIĆ (took office as President of the collective Presidency May 1989 and re-elected, by direct ballot, November 1989; elected as sole President 9 December 1990, re-elected 20 December 1992).

### MINISTERS
(June 1995)

**Prime Minister:** MIRKO MARJANOVIĆ.
**Deputy Prime Ministers:** SLOBODAN RADULOVIĆ, RATKO MARKOVIĆ, SLOBODAN UNKOVIĆ, SVETOZAR KRSTIĆ.
**Minister of Internal Affairs:** ZORAN SOKOLOVIĆ.
**Minister of Finance:** DUSAN VLATKOVIĆ.
**Minister of Justice:** ARANDJEL MARKICEVIĆ.
**Minister of Agriculture, Forestry and Water Resources Management:** IVKO DJONOVIĆ.
**Minister of Industry:** OSKAR FODOR.
**Minister of Mining and Energy:** DRAGAN KOSIĆ.
**Minister of Transport and Communications:** ALEKSA JOKIĆ.
**Minister of Urban Planning and Construction:** BRANISLAV IVKOVIĆ.
**Minister of Trade and Tourism:** SRDJAN NIKOLIĆ.
**Minister of Labour, Veterans' and Social Affairs:** JOVAN RADIĆ.
**Minister of Education:** DRAGOSLAV MLADENOVIĆ.
**Minister of Culture:** NADA POPOVIĆ-PERIŠIĆ.
**Minister of Health:** LEPOSAVA MILICEVIĆ.
**Minister of Environmental Protection:** JORDAN ALEKSIĆ.
**Minister of Youth Affairs and Sport:** VLADIMIR CVETKOVIĆ.
**Minister of Religious Affairs:** DRAGAN DRAGOJLOVIĆ.
**Minister responsible for Liaison with Serbs outside Serbia:** RADOVAN PANKOV.
**Minister of Information:** RATOMIR VITO.
**Minister of Private Enterprise:** RADOJE DJUKIĆ.
**Government Co-ordinator for Local Self-Management:** ANDO MILOŠAVLJEVIĆ.
**Government Co-ordinator for Economic Affairs in Kosovo and Metohija:** VEKOSLAV SEŠEVIĆ.
**Government Co-ordinator responsible for the technological development of the Serbian economy:** MILAN BABIĆ.

### MINISTRIES

**Office of the President:** 11000 Belgrade, Andrićev venac 1.
**Office of the Prime Minister:** 11000 Belgrade, Nemanjina 11; tel. (11) 685872; fax (11) 659682.
**Ministry of Agriculture, Forestry and Water Resources Management:** 11000 Belgrade, Nemanjina 26; tel. (11) 642276; fax (11) 659146.
**Ministry of Culture:** 11000 Belgrade, Nemanjina 11; tel. (11) 657347; fax (11) 683854.
**Ministry of Education:** 11000 Belgrade, Nemanjina 22–26; tel. (11) 659595; fax (11) 683724.
**Ministry of Environmental Protection:** 11000 Belgrade, Nemanjina 22–26; (11) 657143; fax (11) 642242.
**Ministry of Finance:** 11000 Belgrade, Nemanjina 22–26; tel. (11) 658883; fax (11) 646436.
**Ministry of Health:** 11000 Belgrade, Nemanjina 22–26; tel. (11) 642291; fax (11) 642684.
**Ministry of Industry:** 11000 Belgrade, Nemanjina 22–26; (11) 659247; fax (11) 642681.
**Ministry of Information:** 11000 Belgrade, Nemanjina 11; tel. (11) 657056; fax (11) 685937.
**Ministry of Internal Affairs:** 11000 Belgrade, Kneza Miloša 103; tel. (11) 685157; fax (11) 641867.

YUGOSLAVIA

**Ministry of Justice:** 11000 Belgrade, Nemanjina 26; tel. (11) 657866; fax (11) 659147.

**Ministry of Labour, Veterans' and Social Affairs:** 11000 Belgrade, Nemanjina 22–26; tel. (11) 659547; fax (11) 682758.

**Ministry responsible for Liaison with Serbs outside Serbia:** 11000 Belgrade, Nemanjina 11; tel. (11) 684148; fax (11) 659798.

**Ministry of Mining and Energy:** 11000 Belgrade, Nemanjina 22–26; tel. (11) 658755.

**Ministry of Private Enterprise:** Belgrade.

**Ministry of Religious Affairs:** 11000 Belgrade, Nemanjina 11; tel. (11) 682185; fax (11) 688841.

**Ministry of Trade and Tourism:** 11000 Belgrade, Nemanjina 22–26; tel. (11) 658855; fax (11) 642148.

**Ministry of Transport and Communications:** 11000 Belgrade, Nemanjina 22–26; tel. (11) 661666; fax (11) 659379.

**Ministry of Urban Planning and Construction:** 11000 Belgrade, Nemanjina 22–26; tel. (11) 659078; fax (11) 659055.

**Ministry of Youth Affairs and Sport:** 11000 Belgrade, Nemanjina 11; tel. (11) 685353; fax (11) 682167.

# Federal President and Legislature

### FEDERAL PRESIDENT

The elected Federal President, DOBRICA ĆOSIĆ, was removed from office by the Federal Assembly on 1 June 1993; he was succeeded by ZORAN LILIĆ, who was appointed by the Federal Assembly on 25 June.

### SAVEZNA SKUPŠTINA
(Federal Assembly)

The Federal Assembly is composed of two chambers: the Chamber of Republics and the Chamber of Citizens, both comprising representatives of Serbia and Montenegro.

#### Chamber of Citizens

**Speaker:** Dr RADOMAN BOZOVIĆ.

**Election, 20 December 1992**

| Party | Votes | % of votes | Seats |
|---|---|---|---|
| Socialist Party of Serbia | 1,478,918 | 31.40 | 47 |
| Serbian Radical Party | 1,056,539 | 22.43 | 34 |
| Democratic Movement of Serbia | 809,731 | 17.19 | 20 |
| Democratic Party of Montenegrin Socialists | 130,431 | 2.77 | 17 |
| Democratic Party | 280,183 | 5.94 | 5 |
| Socialist Party of Montenegro | 36,390 | 0.77 | 5 |
| People's Party of Montenegro | 34,436 | 0.73 | 4 |
| Democratic Community of Vojvodina Hungarians | 106,036 | 2.25 | 3 |
| Coalition of Democratic Party and Reform Democratic Party of Vojvodina | 101,234 | 2.15 | 2 |
| Coalition of Democratic Party, Reform Democratic Party of Vojvodina and Bourgeois Party | 58,505 | 1.24 | 1 |
| Others | 617,519 | 13.11 | — |
| **Total** | **4,709,922** | **100.00** | **138** |

#### Chamber of Republics

**Speaker:** Dr MILOŠ RADULOVIĆ.

The Chamber of Republics comprises 40 members (20 each for Montenegro and Serbia), selected on a proportional basis to reflect the composition of the republican legislatures.

# Republican Presidents and Legislatures

## MONTENEGRO

### REPUBLICAN PRESIDENT

**Presidential Election, First Ballot, 20 December 1992**

| Candidate | Votes | % of votes |
|---|---|---|
| MOMIR BULATOVIĆ | 123,183 | 42.82 |
| BRANKO KOSTIĆ | 68,296 | 23.74 |
| SLAVKO PEROVIĆ | 52,736 | 18.33 |
| NOVAK KILIBARDA | 25,979 | 9.03 |
| DRAGAN HAJDUKOVIĆ | 10,270 | 3.57 |
| SLOBODAN VUJOŠEVIĆ | 2,770 | 0.96 |
| VESELIN KALUDEROVIĆ | 1,606 | 0.56 |
| PREDRAG POPOVIĆ | 1,419 | 0.49 |
| ŽIVOJIN-KIRO RADOVIĆ | 1,399 | 0.49 |
| **Total** | **287,658** | **100.00** |

**Second Ballot, 10 January 1993**

| Candidate | Votes | % of votes |
|---|---|---|
| MOMIR BULATOVIĆ | 158,722 | 63.29 |
| BRANKO KOSTIĆ | 92,045 | 36.71 |
| **Total** | **250,767** | **100.00** |

### REPUBLICAN ASSEMBLY

**Chairman:** SVETOZAR MAROVIĆ.

**Election, 20 December 1992**

| Party | Votes | % of votes | Seats |
|---|---|---|---|
| Democratic Party of Montenegrin Socialists | 126,083 | 43.97 | 46 |
| People's Party of Montenegro | 37,629 | 13.12 | 14 |
| Liberal Alliance of Montenegro | 35,596 | 12.41 | 13 |
| Serbian Radical Party | 22,329 | 7.79 | 8 |
| Social Democratic Reformist Party | 13,022 | 4.54 | 4 |
| Others | 52,063 | 18.16 | — |
| **Total** | **286,722** | **100.00** | **85** |

## SERBIA

### REPUBLICAN PRESIDENT

**Presidential Election, 20 December 1992**

| Candidate | Votes | % of votes |
|---|---|---|
| SLOBODAN MILOŠEVIĆ | 2,515,047 | 57.46 |
| MILAN PANIĆ | 1,516,693 | 34.65 |
| MILAN PAROŠKI | 147,693 | 2.37 |
| DRAGAN VASILJKOVIĆ | 87,847 | 2.01 |
| JEZDIMIR VASILJEVIĆ | 61,729 | 1.41 |
| MIROSLAV MILANOVIĆ | 28,010 | 0.64 |
| BLAŽO PEROVIĆ | 20,326 | 0.46 |
| **Total** | **4,377,345** | **100.00** |

### NATIONAL ASSEMBLY

**Chairman:** DRAGAN TOMIĆ.

**Elections, 19 December 1993**

| Party | Votes | % of votes | Seats |
|---|---|---|---|
| Socialist Party of Serbia | 1,576,287 | 36.65 | 123 |
| Democratic Movement of Serbia | 715,564 | 16.64 | 45 |
| Serbian Radical Party | 595,467 | 13.85 | 39 |
| Democratic Party | 497,582 | 11.57 | 29 |
| Democratic Party of Serbia | 218,056 | 5.07 | 7 |
| Democratic Community of Vojvodina Hungarians | 112,456 | 2.61 | 5 |
| Coalition of the Party of Democratic Action and the Democratic Party of Albanians | 29,342 | 0.68 | 2 |
| Others | 555,686 | 12.92 | — |
| **Total** | **4,300,440** | **100.00** | **250** |

## Provinces of Serbia

### Kosovo and Metohija

Until 1990 Kosovo (now Kosovo and Metohija) was an autonomous province within Serbia, with its own provincial assembly and government. In that year, following the adoption of amendments to the Yugoslav Constitution, the province's autonomous status was removed, and the provincial assembly and government were dissolved. Most ethnic Albanian deputies in the assembly were opposed to its dissolution, and formed a 'Kosovo Assembly-in-Exile', which proclaimed Kosovo a 'Republic'. They also established an interim 'government', based in Zagreb (Croatia). This body organized a referendum among the ethnic Albanian population in the province, at the end of September 1991, the result of which was overwhelmingly in favour of Kosovo's becoming a sovereign republic. The Assembly-in-Exile also arranged elections to a new 130-seat provincial assembly on 24 May 1992 (the Democratic Alliance of Kosovo won the most seats and its leader, Dr IBRAHIM RUGOVA, was declared the 'President of Kosovo'). Both the referendum and the elections were declared illegal by the Serbian and federal authorities.

### Vojvodina

The Province of Vojvodina has an elected Provincial Assembly, based at Novi Sad. The President of the Provincial Assembly is Dr MILUTIN STOJKOVIĆ. The President of the Provincial Government is BOŠKO PEROŠEVIĆ. The Prime Minister is KOVILJKO LOVRE.

## Political Organizations

**Alliance of Peasants of Serbia Party:** 11000 Belgrade, Srpskih Vladara 81; tel. (11) 789235; f. 1990 as Peasants' Party of Serbia; Pres. MILOMIR BABIĆ.

**Bourgeois Party:** Belgrade.

**Democratic Alliance of Kosovo (DAK)** (Demokratski Savez Kosovo—DSK): 38000 Priština; f. 1990 by dissidents taking over provincial brs of the Socialist Alliance of Working People; ethnic Albanian grouping; Chair. Dr IBRAHIM RUGOVA.

**Democratic Community of Vojvodina Hungarians** (Demokratska zajednica vojvodjanskih Madjara—DZVM): Ada, trg Oslobodjenja 11; tel. (24) 852248; f. 1990; supports interests of ethnic Hungarian minority in Vojvodina; c. 20,000 mems; Pres. ANDRAŠ AGOŠTON.

**Democratic Party** (Demokratska stranka): 11000 Belgrade, Terazije 3/IV; tel. (11) 338078; fax (11) 623686; regd 1990; nationalist; Leader ZORAN DJINDJIĆ.

**Democratic Party of Albanians** (Demokratska partija Albanaca): Preševo, Selami Halaci bb; f. 1990; Pres. ALI AHMETI.

**Democratic Party of Montenegrin Socialists (DPMS)** (Demokratska Partija Socijalista): Podgorica; name changed from League of Communists of Montenegro in 1991; supports continued federation; Chair. MOMIR BULATOVIĆ; Gen. Sec. SVETOZAR MAROVIĆ.

**Democratic Party of Serbia** (Demokratska stranka Srbije—DSS): Belgrade, Smiljanićeva 33; tel. (11) 459179; fax (11) 4446240; f. 1992 following split from Democratic Party; Leader VOJISLAV KOSTUNICA.

**Democratic Party of Vojvodina:** Novi Sad.

**Democratic Reform Party of Muslims** (Demokratska reformska stranka Muslimana): 38400 Prizren, Koritnik 3; tel. (29) 22322; party of ethnic Muslims; left-wing; Pres. AZAR ZULJI.

**Liberal Alliance of Montenegro:** Podgorica; pro-independence; Leader SLAVKO PEROVIĆ.

**Liberal Party** (Liberalna Stranka): Valjevo, POB 148; tel. (14) 22627; favours a free-market economy; Leader NIKOLA MILOŠEVIĆ.

**New Democracy:** Belgrade, Ho Ši Minova 27; tel. (11) 135804; f. 1990 as New Democracy—Movement for Serbia; Leader DUŠAN MIHAILOVIĆ.

**Nikola Pašić Serbian Radical Party:** Belgrade; f. 1995 following a split in the Serbian Radical Party; Pres. JOVAN GLAMOCANIN.

**Party of Democratic Action:** Preševo, 15 novembra 74; f. 1990; party of ethnic Albanians; Leader RIZA HALILI.

**Party of Democratic Action of Kosovo and Metohija (PDA-KM):** Vitomirića; party of ethnic Muslims; affiliated to the PDA of Bosnia and Herzegovina; Chair. NUMAN BALIĆ.

**Party of Democratic Action—Montenegro:** Rozaj; Slav Muslim party, affiliated to PDA of Bosnia and Herzegovina; support mainly in Sandžak region; Leader HARUN HADŽIĆ.

**Party of Democratic Action of Sandžak (PDA-S):** 36300 Novi Pazar, trg Maršala Tita 2; tel. (20) 25667; f. 1990; party of ethnic Muslims of Sandžak; affiliated to the PDA of Bosnia and Herzegovina; advocates autonomy for the Sandžak region; Chair. Dr SULEJMAN UGLJANIN.

**People's Assembly Party** (Narodna saborna stranka): 11040 Belgrade, Masarikova 5/VIII; tel. (11) 685490; fax (11) 656818; f. 1992 as Democratic Movement of Serbia (Depos), a coalition of four parties and a party faction; reconstituted as a political party and renamed in 1995; Pres. SLOBODAN RAKITIĆ.

**People's Party of Montenegro** (Narodna Stranka Crne Gore): 11000 Belgrade, Srpskih Vladara 14; Chair. KILIBARDA NOVAK.

**Reform Democratic Party of Vojvodina** (Reformska Demokratska Stranka Vojvodine): Novi Sad, Ilije Ognjanović 7/I; tel. and fax (21) 27774; f. 1992; Pres. Dr DRAGOSLAV PETROVIĆ.

**Serbian Radical Party (SRP)** (Srpska Radikalna Stranka—SRS): 11000 Belgrade, Ohridska 1; tel. (11) 457745; f. 1991; extreme nationalist; advocates a 'Greater Serbian' state; Leader Dr VOJISLAV SESELJ.

**Serbian Renewal Movement (SRM)** (Srpski pokret obnove—SPO): 11000 Belgrade, Nušićeva 8/3; tel. (11) 342918; f. 1990; right-wing; nationalist; Pres. VUK DRAŠKOVIĆ.

**Serbian Unity Party:** Belgrade; f. 1993; extreme nationalist; Leader ZELJKO RAZNJATIVIĆ (ARKAN).

**Social Democratic Reformist Party:** Podgorica.

**Socialist Party of Montenegro:** Podgorica.

**Socialist Party of Serbia (SPS)** (Socijalistička partija Srbije): 11000 Belgrade, bul. Lenjina 6; tel. (11) 634921; fax (11) 628642; f. 1990 by merger of League of Communists of Serbia and Socialist Alliance of Working People (SAWP) of Serbia; Pres. SLOBODAN MILOŠEVIĆ; Gen. Sec. MILOMAR MINIĆ.

**Yugoslav Green Party:** Belgrade, Mutapova 12; tel. (11) 4447030; f. 1990; open to all citizens regardless of national, religious or racial affiliation; Pres. DRAGAN JOVANOVIĆ.

## Diplomatic Representation

### EMBASSIES IN YUGOSLAVIA

Many countries withdrew their ambassadors from Belgrade in 1992–93; where known, the date of withdrawal is indicated below.

**Afghanistan:** 11000 Belgrade, Njegoševa 56/1; tel. (11) 4448716; Ambassador: SARWAR MANGAL (withdrawn 1992).

**Albania:** 11000 Belgrade, Kneza Miloša 56; tel. (11) 646864; telex 12294; Chargé d'affaires: VILI MINAROLI.

**Algeria:** 11000 Belgrade, Maglajska 26B; tel. (11) 668211; telex 12343; Ambassador: AHMED ATTAF (withdrawn May 1992).

**Angola:** 11000 Belgrade, Tolstojeva 51; tel. (11) 663199; telex 11841; fax (11) 662916; Ambassador: EVARISTO DOMINGOS.

**Argentina:** 11000 Belgrade, Knez Mihajlova 24/I; tel. (11) 621550; telex 12182; Ambassador: FEDERICO CARLOS BARTTFELD.

**Australia:** 11000 Belgrade, Čika Ljubina 13; tel. (11) 624655; telex 11206; fax (11) 624029; Ambassador: (vacant).

**Austria:** 11000 Belgrade, Kneza Sime Markovića 2; tel. (11) 635955; telex 11456; fax (11) 638215; Ambassador: Dr WALTER SIEGL (withdrawn May 1992).

**Belgium:** 11000 Belgrade, Proleterskih brigada 18; tel. (11) 330016; telex 11747; fax (11) 330016; Ambassador: Baron ALAIN GUILLAUME (withdrawn May 1992).

**Brazil:** 11000 Belgrade, Proleterskih brigada 14; tel. (11) 339781; telex 11100; Ambassador: ANTÔNIO AMARAL DE SAMPAIO.

**Bulgaria:** 11000 Belgrade, Birčaninova 26; tel. (11) 646222; telex 11665; Ambassador: MARKO MARKOV.

**Cambodia:** 11000 Belgrade, Gospodar Jovanova 67; tel. (11) 631151; Ambassador: RENE VANHON.

**Canada:** 11000 Belgrade, Kneza Miloša 75; tel. (11) 644666; telex 11137; fax (11) 641480; Ambassador: JAMES B. BISSETT.

**Chile:** 11000 Belgrade, Vasilija Gaćeše 9A; tel. (11) 648340; Ambassador: LUIS JEREZ RAMÍREZ.

**China, People's Republic:** 11000 Belgrade, Kralja Milutina 6; tel. (11) 331484; telex 11146; Ambassador: ZHU ANKANG.

**Colombia:** 11000 Belgrade, Njegoševa 54/II-5; tel. (11) 457246; telex 12530; fax (11) 457120; Ambassador: (vacant).

**Cuba:** 11000 Belgrade, Kneza Miloša 14; tel. (11) 657694; Chargé d'affaires: MANUEL ALVAREZ AGUIRRE.

**Cyprus:** 11040 Belgrade, Diplomatska Kolonija 9; tel. (11) 663725; telex 12729; fax (11) 665348; Chargé d'affaires: PAVLOS HADJITOFIS.

**Czech Republic:** 11000 Belgrade, bul. Revolucije 22; tel. (11) 330134; fax (11) 336448.

**Denmark:** 11040 Belgrade, Neznanog Junaka 9A; tel. (11) 667826; telex 11219; fax (11) 660759; Ambassador: HANS JESPERSEN (withdrawn May 1992).

# YUGOSLAVIA

**Ecuador:** 11000 Belgrade, Kneza Miloša 16; tel. (11) 684876; telex 12751; fax (11) 684876; Ambassador: Francisco Proaño Arandi.

**Egypt:** 11000 Belgrade, Andre Nikolića 12; tel. (11) 651225; telex 12074; Ambassador: Dr Hussein Hassouna.

**Ethiopia:** 11000 Belgrade, Knez Mihajlova 6/IV; tel. (11) 628666; telex 11818; Ambassador: (vacant).

**Finland:** 11000 Belgrade, Birčaninova 29; tel. (11) 646322; telex 11707; fax (11) 683365; Ambassador: Mauno Castrén.

**France:** 11000 Belgrade, Pariska 11; tel. (11) 636555; telex 11496; Ambassador: Michel Chatelais (withdrawn May 1992).

**Gabon:** 11000 Belgrade, Dragorska 3; tel. (11) 669683; telex 12019; Ambassador: Emmanuel Mendoume-Nze.

**Germany:** 11000 Belgrade, Kneza Miloša 74–76; tel. (11) 645755; telex 11107; fax (11) 656989; Ambassador: Dr Hansjörg Eiff (withdrawn May 1992).

**Ghana:** 11000 Belgrade, Ognjena Price 50; tel. (11) 4442445; telex 11720; fax (11) 436314; Chargé d'affaires: Kobina Sekyi.

**Greece:** 11000 Belgrade, Francuska 33; tel. (11) 621443; telex 11361; Ambassador: Eleftherios Karayannis (withdrawn May 1992).

**Guinea:** 11000 Belgrade, Ohridska 4; tel. (11) 431830; telex 11963; Ambassador: Morou Balde.

**Holy See:** 11000 Belgrade, Svetog Save 24; tel. (11) 432822; fax (11) 434631; Apostolic Pro-Nuncio: Most Rev. Gabriel Montalvo, Titular Archbishop of Celene.

**Hungary:** 11000 Belgrade, Proleterskih brigada 72; tel. (11) 4440472; Ambassador: István Oszi.

**India:** 11070 Belgrade, B-06/07 Genex International Centre, Vladimira Popovića 6; tel. (11) 2223325; telex 71127; fax (11) 2223357; Ambassador: (vacant).

**Indonesia:** 11000 Belgrade, bul. Mira 18; tel. (11) 662122; telex 11129; fax (11) 665995; Ambassador: (vacant).

**Iran:** 11000 Belgrade, Proleterskih brigada 9; tel. (11) 338782; telex 11726; fax (11) 338784; Ambassador: Nasrollah Kazemi Kamyab.

**Iraq:** 11000 Belgrade, Proleterskih brigada 69; tel. (11) 434688; telex 12325; Ambassador: Dr Wahbi al-Qaraguli.

**Italy:** 11000 Belgrade, Birčaninova 11; tel. (11) 659722; telex 12082; Ambassador: Sergio Vento (withdrawn May 1992).

**Japan:** 11000 Belgrade, Ilirska 5; tel. (11) 768255; telex 11263; fax (11) 762934; Ambassador: Taizo Nakamura (withdrawn June 1992).

**Jordan:** 11000 Belgrade, Kablarska 28; tel. (11) 651642; telex 12904; Ambassador: Hani B. Tabbara (withdrawn May 1992).

**Korea, Democratic People's Republic:** 11000 Belgrade, Dr Milutina Ivkovića 9; tel. (11) 668739; telex 11577; Ambassador: Chi Jae Ryong.

**Korea, Republic:** 11070 Belgrade, Genex International Centre, Vladimira Popovića 6; tel. (11) 2223531; telex 71054; fax (11) 2223903; Ambassador: (vacant).

**Kuwait:** 11000 Belgrade, Čakorska 2; tel. (11) 664961; telex 12774; Ambassador: Issa Ahmad al-Hammad.

**Lebanon:** 11000 Belgrade, Vase Pelagića 38; tel. (11) 651290; telex 11049; Ambassador: (vacant).

**Libya:** 11000 Belgrade, Generala Ždanova 42; tel. (11) 644782; telex 11787; Secretary of People's Committee: Assur Muhamed Karkum.

**Mali:** 11000 Belgrade, Generala Hanrisa 1; tel. (11) 493774; telex 11052; Ambassador: N'Tji Laico Traoré.

**Mexico:** 11102 Belgrade, trg Republike 5/IV; tel. (11) 638111; telex 12141; fax (11) 629566; Chargé d'affaires: Carlos Félix Corona.

**Mongolia:** 11000 Belgrade, Generala Vasića 5; tel. (11) 668536; telex 12253; Ambassador: Ludevdorjyn Khashbat.

**Morocco:** 11000 Belgrade, Sanje Živanović 4; tel. (11) 651775; Ambassador: Hassan Fassi Fihri.

**Myanmar:** 11000 Belgrade, Kneza Miloša 72; tel. (11) 645420; telex 72769; Ambassador: U Hla Maung.

**Netherlands:** 11000 Belgrade, Simina 29; tel. (11) 626699; telex 11556; fax (11) 628986; Ambassador: J. H. W. Fietelaars (withdrawn May 1992).

**Nigeria:** 11000 Belgrade, Geršićeva 14A; tel. (11) 413411; telex 12875; fax (11) 418562; Ambassador: Ezekiel Gotom Dimka.

**Norway:** 11000 Belgrade, Kablarska 30; tel. (11) 651626; telex 11668; fax (11) 651754; Ambassador: Georg Krane.

**Pakistan:** 11000 Belgrade, bul. Oktobarske Revolucije 62; tel. (11) 661676; fax (11) 660219; Ambassador: Adm. Tariq K. Khan (withdrawn October 1993).

**Panama:** 11000 Belgrade, Strahinjića Baua 51/II-5; tel. (11) 620374; telex 11451; Ambassador: Ricardo T. Pezet H.

**Peru:** 11000 Belgrade, Baba Višnjina 26/II-10; tel. (11) 454943; telex 12272; Ambassador: Eduardo Llosa.

**Poland:** 11000 Belgrade, Kneza Miloša 38; tel. (11) 644866; telex 72006; fax (11) 646275; Ambassador: Jerzy Chmielewski.

**Portugal:** 11110 Belgrade, Stojana Novakovića 19; tel. (11) 750358; telex 11648; fax (11) 754421; Chargé d'affaires: Hugo Solano Cabral de Moncada.

**Romania:** 11000 Belgrade, Kneza Miloša 70; tel. (11) 646071; telex 11318; fax (11) 646071; Chargé d'affaires a.i.: Constantin Ghirdă.

**Russia:** 11000 Belgrade, Deligradska 32; tel. (11) 657533; Ambassador: Gennady Shikin.

**Slovakia:** 11070 Belgrade, bul. Umetvosti 18; tel. (11) 2223293; telex 6272790; fax (11) 134520; Ambassador: (vacant).

**Spain:** 11000 Belgrade, Moravska 5; tel. (11) 454777; telex 12864; fax (11) 4440614; Ambassador: José Manuel Allendesalazar (withdrawn May 1992).

**Sri Lanka:** 11000 Belgrade, Sanje Zivanovic 15A; tel. (11) 648160; telex 12475; fax (11) 647060; Ambassador: Ajwad Cassim.

**Sudan:** 11000 Belgrade, Maglajska 5; tel. (11) 667762; telex 12479; Ambassador: Ibrahim A. Hamra (withdrawn May 1992).

**Sweden:** 11000 Belgrade, Pariska 7; tel. (11) 626422; telex 11595; fax (11) 626492; Chargé d'affaires: Göran Jacobsson.

**Switzerland:** 11000 Belgrade, Birčaninova 27; tel. (11) 646899; telex 11383; fax (11) 657253; Ambassador: (vacant).

**Syria:** 11000 Belgrade, Mlade Bosne 31; tel. (11) 4449985; telex 11889; fax (11) 453367; Ambassador: Ismail al-Kadi.

**Thailand:** 11000 Belgrade, Molerova 11/V; tel. (11) 454053; telex 12657; Ambassador: (vacant—withdrawn September 1992).

**Tunisia:** 11000 Belgrade, Vase Pelagića 19; tel. (11) 652966; telex 11461; fax (11) 647656; Ambassador: (vacant).

**Turkey:** 11000 Belgrade, Proleterskih brigada 1; tel. (11) 335431; telex 12081; Ambassador: Berhan Ekinci.

**United Kingdom:** 11000 Belgrade, Generala Ždanova 46; tel. (11) 645055; telex 11468; fax (11) 659651; First Sec.: David Austin.

**USA:** 11000 Belgrade, Kneza Miloša 50; tel. (11) 645655; telex 11529; fax (11) 645221; Ambassador: Warren Zimmermann (withdrawn May 1992).

**Uruguay:** 11000 Belgrade, Vasina 14; tel. (11) 620994; telex 12650; Ambassador: Dr Fernando Gómez Fyns.

**Venezuela:** 11000 Terazije 45/II; tel. (11) 331604; telex 12856; Ambassador: Freddy Christians.

**Viet Nam:** 11000 Belgrade, Lackovićeva 6; tel. (11) 663527; telex 11292; Ambassador: Vo Anh Tuan.

**Yemen:** 11000 Belgrade, Vasilija Gaćeše 9C; tel. (11) 653932; Ambassador: Mohamed Mahmood Hassan al-Baihi.

**Zaire:** 11000 Belgrade, Oktobarske revolucije 47; tel. (11) 668931; telex 11491; Ambassador: Lundunge Kadahi Chiri-Mwami.

**Zimbabwe:** 11000 Belgrade, Perside Milenković 9; tel. (11) 647047; Ambassador: Chimbidzayi E. C. Sanyangare.

# Judicial System

Judicial functions are to be discharged within a uniform system, and the jurisdiction of the courts shall be established and altered only by law. In general, court proceedings are conducted in public (exceptionally the public may be excluded to preserve professional secrets, public order or morals) in the national language of the region in which the court is situated. Citizens who do not know the language in which the proceedings are being conducted may use their own language.

The judicial system comprises courts of general jurisdiction, i.e. communal courts, county courts, republican supreme courts and the Federal Court. The courts of general jurisdiction are organized in accordance with individual republican legislation. In general, the courts are entitled to proceed in criminal, civil and administrative matters. Military courts, headed by the Supreme Military Court, proceed in criminal and administrative matters connected with military service or national defence. Economic or trade matters are under the jurisdiction of economic courts. They proceed also in penal-economic matters.

Judges are elected or relieved by the republican assemblies or the Federal Assembly.

### THE FEDERAL JUDICIARY
#### Constitutional Court

This court decides on the conformity of the Constitutions of the member republics with the federal Constitution, whether or not a republican regulation is contrary to federal statute and on the conformity of enactments of federal agencies with the Constitution

# YUGOSLAVIA

and federal statute. The court has seven judges, who elect the president of the Court from among themselves.

**President of the Constitutional Court:** MILOVAN BUZADZIĆ.

### Federal Court

This is the highest organ of justice. In the final instance, it decides on appeals in cases when the death sentence has been passed for criminal offences defined by federal statutes. It decides on extraordinary legal remedies against decisions of republican courts and military courts in cases involving federal statutes. The Court also decides disputes between the republics and between the Federation and its member republics, as well as disputes related to the protection of property rights of Yugoslavia, in the case of non-implementation or violation of federal statute. The Federal Court assesses the legality of irrevocable administrative decisions of federal authorities adopted in the implementation of federal laws. The Federal Court consists of 11 judges who are elected and relieved by the Federal Assembly. The judges of the Federal Court elect the president of the Court from among themselves.

**President of the Federal Court of Yugoslavia:** Dr RAFAEL CIJAN, 11000 Belgrade, Svetozara Markovića 21; tel. (11) 333911.

### Office of the Public Prosecutor

The Federal Public Prosecutor is elected or dismissed by the Federal Assembly.

**Federal Public Prosecutor:** LJUBO PRLJETA.

### Office of the Public Attorney

Represents proprietary rights and interests of the federation, republics, autonomous provinces, towns and communes. The Federal Attorney-General is appointed by the Federal Assembly.

**Federal Attorney-General:** SAŠO IVANOVSKI.

**Federal Social Attorney of Self-Management:** carries out his or her function within the framework of federal rights and duties.

**Social Attorney of Self-Management:** IVICA ČAĆIĆ.

## THE REPUBLICAN JUDICIARIES

### Montenegro

The courts in Montenegro are supervised by the republican Ministry of Justice. The highest courts in the republican judicial system are the Supreme Court and the Constitutional Court. Final appeal lies to the Yugoslav Federal Court and, in constitutional matters, to the federal Constitutional Court.

**Constitutional Court of the Republic of Montenegro:** 81000 Podgorica, Lenjina 3; tel. (81) 41846; Pres. LJUBOMIR SPASOJEVIĆ.

**Supreme Court:** 81000 Podgorica, Njegoševa 6; tel. (81) 43070; Pres. MARKO MARKOVIĆ.

**Office of the Public Prosecutor:** 81000 Podgorica, Njegoševa 6; tel. (81) 43053; Public Prosecutor VLADIMIR ŠUŠOVIĆ.

### Serbia

All courts in Serbia are within the jurisdiction of the republican Ministry of Justice. The Federal Court and the federal Constitutional Court are the final courts of appeal.

**Constitutional Court of the Republic of Serbia:** 11000 Belgrade, Nemanjina 22–26; tel. (11) 658755; Pres. Dr BALŠA SPADIJER.

**Supreme Court of Serbia:** 11000 Belgrade, Nemanjina 22–26; tel. (11) 658755; Pres. CASLAV IGNJATOVIĆ.

**Office of the Public Prosecutor of the Republic of Serbia:** 11000 Belgrade, Nemanjina 22–26; tel. (11) 658755; Public Prosecutor MILOMIR JAKOVLJEVIĆ.

**Provincial Secretariat of Justice for the Province of Kosovo and Metohija:** 38000 Priština, Zejnel Salihu br. 4; fax (38) 31929.

**Provincial Secretariat of Justice for the Province of Vojvodina:** 21000 Novi Sad, Srpskih Vladara; fax (21) 56672.

# Religion

Most of the inhabitants of the FRY are, at least nominally, Christian, but there is a significant Muslim minority. The main Christian denomination is Eastern Orthodox, but there is a strong Roman Catholic presence. There are also small minorities of Old Catholics, Protestants and Jews.

## CHRISTIANITY

### The Eastern Orthodox Church

**Serbian Orthodox Church:** Headquarters: 11001 Belgrade, Kralja Petra 5, POB 182; tel. (11) 638161; fax (11) 182780; 11m. adherents (mainly in Yugoslavia); Patriarch of Serbia: His Holiness PAVLE, Archbishop of Peć and Metropolitan of Belgrade-Karlovci; Sec. Archdeacon MOMIR LEČIĆ.

**Montenegrin Orthodox Church:** Cetinje; outlawed 1992, restored 1993; its jurisdiction is denied by the Serbian Church and not acknowledged by the Ecumenical Patriarch; its leadership was excommunicated by the Serbian Church in 1995; Patriarch of Montenegro: His Holiness ANTONIJE ABRAMOVIĆ.

### The Roman Catholic Church

The Federal Republic of Yugoslavia and the former Yugoslav republic of Macedonia together comprise two archdioceses (including one, Bar, directly responsible to the Holy See) and four dioceses. At 31 December 1993 these areas of jurisdiction contained an estimated 537,173 adherents, of whom the majority were in the Serbian province of Vojvodina.

**Archbishop of Bar:** Most Rev. PETAR PERKOLIĆ, Nadbiskupski Ordinarijat, 85000 Bar, Popovići 98; tel. (85) 21705.

**Archbishop of Belgrade:** Most Rev. Dr FRANC PERKO, Nadbiskupski Ordinarijat, 11000 Belgrade, Svetozara Markovića 20; tel. and fax (11) 334846.

### Old Catholic Church

**Old Catholic Church in Serbia and Vojvodina:** 11000 Belgrade; Dir of Bishop's Diocese JOVAN AJHINGER.

### Protestant Churches

**Christian Assemblies—Church of Christ's Brethren:** 21470 Bački Petrovac, Janka Kralja 4; tel. (21) 780153; Pres. of Elders SAMUEL RYBAR.

**Christian Church Jehovah's Witnesses:** 11000 Belgrade, Milorada Mitrovića 4; tel. (11) 450383.

**Christian Nazarene Community:** Hrišćanska nazarenska zajednica, 21000 Novi Sad, Vodnikova br. 12; tel. (21) 390577; Pres. KAROL HRUBIK VLADIMIR.

**Christian Reformed Church:** 24323 Feketic, Bratsva 26; tel. (11) 738570; f. 1919; 22,000 mems; Bishop IMRE HODOSY.

**Evangelical Church of Republic of Croatia, Republic of Bosnia and Herzegovina and Vojvodina:** 41000 Zagreb, Gundulićeva 28; tel. (41) 420685; 4,950 mems; Pres. Dr VLADO L. DEUTSCH.

**Evangelical Hungarian Church:** Subotica, Brace Radiča 17; Pastor DANNY NOVÁK.

**Seventh-Day Adventist Church:** Hrišćanska adventistička crkva, 11000 Belgrade, Božidara Adzije 4; tel. (11) 453842; telex 72645; fax (11) 458604; Pres. JOVAN LORENCIN; Sec. NEDELJKO KAČAVENDA.

**Slovak Evangelical Church of the Augsburg Confession:** 21000 Novi Sad, Karadžićeva 2; tel. (21) 611882; Lutheran; 51,500 mems (1990); Bishop Dr ANDREJ BEREDI.

**Union of Baptist Churches in Serbia:** 11000 Belgrade, Slobodanke D. Savic 33; tel. and fax (11) 410964; f. 1992; Gen. Sec. Rev. AVRAM DEGA.

**United Methodist Church:** 21000 Novi Sad, L. Mušičkoga 7; tel. (21) 610377; f. 1898; 3,000 mems; Superintendent MARTIN HOVAN.

## ISLAM

Almost 20% of the Montenegrin population profess Islam as their faith, many being ethnic Muslims of the Sandžak region (which was partitioned between Montenegro and Serbia in 1913). Most Muslims in Serbia are ethnic Albanians, mainly resident in the Province of Kosovo and Metohija, but there are also ethnic Slav Muslims in the part of Sandžak located in south-west Serbia. Serbian Islam is predominantly Sunni, although a Dervish sect, introduced in 1974, is popular among the Albanians (some 50,000 adherents, mainly in Kosovo and Metohija).

**Islamic Community in the Republic of Serbia:** 38000 Priština; Pres. of the Mesihat Dr REDZEP BOJE.

## JUDAISM

**Federation of Jewish Communities in Yugoslavia:** Belgrade, Kralja Petra 71A/III, POB 841; tel. (11) 624359; fax (11) 626674; f. 1919, revived 1944; Pres. DAVID ALBAHARI.

# The Press

In 1991 a total of 801 national and local newspapers were published in Serbia and Montenegro. Most were printed in Serbo-Croat, but there were also publications in Albanian, Hungarian, Romanian, Czech, Turkish and Bulgarian. In the same year a total of 505 periodicals were published. Important daily newspapers include *Borba* and *Politika* (Belgrade), and *Pobjeda* (Podgorica). Evening papers are also popular, notably *Večernje novosti* (Belgrade).

# YUGOSLAVIA

## PRINCIPAL DAILIES
(In Serbo-Croat, except where otherwise stated)

### Belgrade

**Borba:** Belgrade, trg Nikole Pašića 7; tel. (11) 334531; telex 11104; fax (11) 344913; f. 1922; morning; taken under govt control in 1994; Editor-in-Chief ZIVORAD DJORDJEVIĆ; circ. 46,000.

**Naša Borba:** Belgrade; f. 1995 by journalists from *Borba* who rejected imposition of govt control; independent; Editor-in-Chief GORDANA LOGAR.

**Newsday:** 11001 Belgrade, Obiličev Venac 2, POB 439; f. 1983; Mon.–Fri; published in English by Tanjug and *Privredni Pregled*.

**Politika:** 11000 Belgrade, Makedonska 29; tel. (11) 3221836; telex 11416; fax (11) 3249395; f. 1904; morning; non-party; Pres. ŽIVORAD MINOVIĆ; Dir-Gen. HADŽI DRAGAN ANTIĆ; Editor-in-Chief BOŠKO JAKŠIĆ; circ. 200,000.

**Politika Ekspres:** 11000 Belgrade, Makedonska 29; tel. (11) 325630; telex 11852; evening; Editor-in-Chief MILE KORDIĆ; circ. 76,000.

**Privredni Pregled:** 11000 Belgrade, M. Birjuzova 3; tel. (11) 182888; telex 11509; fax (11) 627591; f. 1950; business and economics; Dir and Chief Editor DUŠAN DJORDJEVIĆ; circ. 14,000.

**Sport:** 11000 Belgrade, trg Nikole Pašića 7; tel. (11) 333429; telex 12022; fax (11) 455862; f. 1945; Editor SLAVOLJUB VUKOVIĆ; circ. 100,000.

**Večernje novosti:** 11000 Belgrade, trg Nikole Pašića 7; tel. (11) 334531; telex 12200; fax (11) 344913; f. 1953; evening; Chief and Executive Editor RADISAV BRAJOVIĆ; circ. 169,000.

### Niš

**Narodne Novine:** 18000 Niš, Vojvode Gojka 14; morning; Chief Editor LJUBIŠA SOKOLOVIĆ (acting); circ. 7,210.

### Novi Sad

**Dnevnik:** 21000 Novi Sad, 23; f. 1942 as *Slobodna Vojvodina*; morning; Editor-in-Chief DRAGAN RADEVIĆ; circ. 61,000. (In December 1993 publication of this newspaper was suspended owing to lack of production materials.)

**Magyar Szó:** 21000 Novi Sad, V. Mišića 1; f. 1944; morning; in Hungarian; Editor-in-Chief (vacant); circ. 25,590.

### Podgorica

**Pobjeda:** Podgorica, Marka Milanova 7; daily; morning; Editor-in-Chief VIDOJE KONTAR (acting); circ. 17,959.

### Priština

**Bukju:** Priština; in Albanian; banned by Serbian authorities October 1992; Editor-in-Chief AVNI SPAHU.

**Jedinstvo:** 38000 Priština, Srpskih Vladara 41; morning; Editor-in-Chief DRAGAN MALOVIĆ; circ. 2,465.

## PERIODICALS

### Belgrade

**4. Jul.:** Belgrade, trg Bratstva i Jedinstva 9/III–IV; weekly; organ of Federation of Veterans of the People's Liberation War of Yugoslavia; Dir and Editor-in-Chief RAJKO PAVIĆEVIĆ; circ. 10,000.

**Duga:** Belgrade; news magazine; Editor-in-Chief ILIJA REPAIĆ.

**Ekonomist:** Belgrade, Nušićeva 6/III; f. 1948; quarterly; journal of the Yugoslav Association of Economists; Editor Dr HASAN HADŽI-OMEROVIĆ.

**Ekonomska Politika:** 11000 Belgrade, trg Nikole Pašića 7; tel. (11) 335355; telex 11410; f. 1952; weekly; Editor-in-Chief MILOŠ MARKOVIĆ.

**Finansije:** Belgrade, Jovana Ristića 1; f. 1945; 6 a year; organ of the Federal Ministry of Finance; Editor BOGOLJUB LAZAREVIĆ.

**Front:** Belgrade, Proleterskih brigada 13; f. 1945; fortnightly; illustrated review; Editor-in-Chief STEVAN KORDA; circ. 263,000.

**Ilustrovana Politika:** Belgrade, Makedonska 29; tel. (11) 326938; telex 11099; f. 1958; weekly illustrated review; Editor-in-Chief RADE ŠOŠKIĆ; circ. 100,000.

**Jež:** Belgrade, Nušićeva 6/IV; f. 1935; humorous weekly; Editor RADIVOJE IVANOVIĆ; circ. 50,000.

**Književne Novine:** Belgrade, Francuska 7; f. 1948; fortnightly; review of literature, arts and social studies; Editor-in-Chief (vacant); circ. 7,500.

**Književnost:** Belgrade, Čika Ljubina 1; tel. (11) 620130; fax (11) 182581; f. 1946; monthly; literary review; Editor VUK KRNJEVIĆ; circ. 1,800.

**Medjunarodna Politika** (Review of International Affairs): Belgrade, Nemanjina 34, POB 413; f. 1950 by the Federation of Yugoslav Journalists; monthly; published in English and Serbian; Dir and Editor-in-Chief Dr RANKO PETKOVIĆ.

**Medjunarodni Problemi:** Belgrade, Makedonska 25; tel. (11) 321433; fax (11) 324013; f. 1949; quarterly; review of the Institute of International Politics and Economics; Editor B. MARKOVIĆ; circ. 1,000.

**NIN (Nedeljne informativne novine):** Belgrade, Cetinjska 1, POB 208; tel. (11) 324410; telex 12000; fax (11) 633368; f. 1935; weekly; Editor-in-Chief MILO GLIGORIJEVIĆ; circ. 35,000.

**Novi Glasnik:** Belgrade; f. 1993; 6 a year; military magazine; Editor-in-Chief Col MILE SUSNJAR.

**Official Gazette of the Federal Republic of Yugoslavia:** 11000 Belgrade, Jovana Ristića 1; f. 1945; editions in Serbo-Croat, Slovene, Albanian, Hungarian and Macedonian; Dir VELJKO TADIĆ; circ. 73,000.

**Politikin Zabavnik:** Belgrade, Makedonska 29; f. 1939; weekly; comic; Editor RADOMIR ŠOŠKIĆ; circ. 41,000.

**Pravoslavlje:** 11000 Belgrade, 7 Jula 5; tel. (11) 635699; fax (11) 630865; fortnightly; religious; published by the Serbian Orthodox Church; Editor Dr SLOBODAN MILEUSNIĆ; circ. 22,500.

**Rad:** Belgrade, trg Nikole Pašića 5; tel. (11) 330927; telex 11121; weekly; organ of the Confederation of Trade Unions; Dir RADOSLAV ROSO; Editor-in-Chief STANISLAV MARINKOVIĆ; circ. 70,000.

**Tehničke novine:** 11000 Belgrade, Vojvode Stepe 89; tel. (11) 468596; fax (11) 473442; monthly; technical; Chief Editor SAŠA IMPERL; circ. 70,000.

**Vojska:** Belgrade, Proleterskih brig. 13; f. 1945; weekly; Yugoslav Army organ; Dir MILAN KAVGIĆ; Editor-in-Chief Col MILORAD PANTELIĆ.

**Yugoslav Law (1975–):** Belgrade, Terazije 41; tel. (11) 333213; 3 a year in English and French; publ. by the Institute of Comparative Law and the Union of Jurists' Asscn; Editor Dr VLADIMIR JOVANOVIĆ.

**Yugoslav Survey:** Belgrade, Moše Pijade 8/1, POB 677; tel. (11) 333610; fax (11) 332295; f. 1960; quarterly; general reference publication of basic documentary information about Yugoslavia in English; Dir ILE KOVAČEVIĆ; Editor-in-Chief TOMO KOSOVIĆ (acting); circ. 3,000.

### Niš

**Bratstvo:** Niš; Bulgarian-language magazine; Dir VENKO DIMITROV.

### Novi Sad

**Letopis Matice Srpske:** Novi Sad, Matice srpske 1; f. 1824; monthly; literary review; Editor Dr SLAVKO GORDIĆ.

### Podgorica

**Koha** (Time): Podgorica; f. 1978; Albanian-language magazine; circ. 2,000 (estimated).

**Stvaranje:** Podgorica, Revolucije 11; f. 1946; monthly; literary review; publ. by the Literary Asscn of Montenegro; Man. SRETEN ASANOVIĆ.

### Priština

**Koha** (Time): Priština; f. 1994; Albanian-language magazine; Editor-in-Chief VETON SUROI.

**Zeri:** Priština; political weekly; in Albanian; Editor-in-Chief BLERIM SHALA.

## NEWS AGENCY

**Novinska Agencija Tanjug:** 11001 Belgrade, Obilićev Venac 2, POB 439; tel. (11) 332230; telex 11220; f. 1943; 90 correspondents in Yugoslavia and 30 offices abroad; press and information agency governed by self-management; news service for Yugoslavia press, radio and television; news and features service for abroad in English, French and Spanish; photo and telephoto service; economic and financial services for home and abroad; publishes EITI, service for trade, industry and banking in Serbo-Croat, English and French; computerized commodity service for Yugoslav businesses and banks; Dir SLOBODAN JOVANOVIĆ; Editor-in-Chief DUŠAN ZUPAN.

### Foreign Bureaux

**Agence France-Presse (AFP)** (France): 11000 Belgrade, trg Marksa i Engelsa 2; tel. (11) 332622; telex 11262; fax (11) 620638; Correspondent NICOLAS MILETITCH (accreditation withdrawn by the Yugoslav authorities April 1994).

**Agenzia Nazionale Stampa Associata (ANSA)** (Italy): 11000 Belgrade, Braće Jugovića 5; tel. (11) 620221; telex 11680; fax (11) 628225; Bureau Chief LUCIANO CAUSA.

**Allgemeiner Deutscher Nachrichtendienst (ADN)** (Germany): 11000 Belgrade, Šiva Stena 1A; tel. (11) 461752; telex 11338; Correspondent Dr WILLFRIED MUCH.

**Associated Press (AP)** (USA): 11000 Belgrade, Dositejeva 12; tel. (11) 631553; telex 11264; Correspondent IVAN STEFANOVIĆ.

YUGOSLAVIA　　　　　　　　　　　　　　　　　　　　　　　　　　　　　　　　　　　　　　　　　　　　　　　　　　　　　　　*Directory*

**Bulgarska Telegrafna Agentsia (BTA)** (Bulgaria): Belgrade, Gospodar Jevremova 41; tel. (11) 636361; telex 11114; fax (11) 636361; Correspondent NIKOLA KITSEVSKI.

**Česká tisková kancelář (ČTK)** (Czech Republic): 11070 Belgrade, 190/Stan. 6/III, Blok 37; tel. (11) 134892; telex 11657; Correspondent MIROSLAV JILEK.

**Informatsionnoye Telegrafnoye Agentstvo Rossii—Telegrafnoye Agentstvo Suverennykh Stran (ITAR—TASS)** (Russia): 11000 Belgrade, Ognjena Price 17; tel. (11) 4446928; Correspondent MIKHAIL ABELEV.

**Korean Central News Agency (KCNA)** (Democratic People's Republic of Korea): Belgrade, Dr Milutina Ivkovića 9; tel. (11) 668426; telex 11577; Bureau Chief KIM JONG SE.

**Magyar Távirati Iroda (MTI)** (Hungary): 11030 Belgrade, Vladimira Rolovica 176; tel. (11) 506508; telex 11783; Correspondent GYÖRGY WALKO.

**Rossiyskoye Informatsionnoye Agentstvo—Novosti (RIA—Novosti)** (Russia): Belgrade, Strahinjića Bana 50; tel. (11) 629419; Bureau Chief SERGEY GRIZUNOV.

**United Press International (UPI)** (USA): 11000 Belgrade, Generala Zdanova 19; tel. (11) 342490; telex 11250; Correspondent NESHO DJURIĆ.

**Xinhua (New China) News Agency** (People's Republic of China): Belgrade, Bože Jankovica 23; tel. (11) 493789; telex 11375; Correspondent YANG DAZHOU.

### PRESS ASSOCIATIONS

**Federation of Yugoslav Journalists** (Savez Novinara Jugoslavije): Belgrade, trg Republike 5/III; tel. (11) 624993; f. 1945; 11,500 mems; Pres. MILISAV MILIĆ.

**Independent Association of Journalists of Serbia:** Belgrade; f. 1994; Pres. DRAGAN NIKITOVIĆ.

**Yugoslav Newspaper Publishers' Association:** Belgrade; Dir RASTKO GUZINA.

There is also an **Association of Professional Journalists of Montenegro.**

## Publishers

**BIGZ—Beogradski izdavačko-grafički zavod:** 11000 Belgrade, vojvode Mišića 17; tel. (11) 651666; telex 11855; fax (11) 651841; f. 1831; literature and criticism, children's books, pocket books, popular science, philosophy, politics; Gen. Dir. ILIJA RAPAIĆ.

**Dečje novine:** 32300 Gornji Milanovac, T. Matijevića 4; tel. (32) 711195; telex 13731; fax (32) 711248; general literature, children's books, science, science fiction, textbooks; Gen. Dir. MIROSLAV PETROVIĆ.

**Forum:** Novinsko-izdavačka i štamparska radna organizacija, 21000 Novi Sad, Vojvode Mišića 1, POB 200; tel. (21) 611300; telex 14199; f. 1957; newspapers, periodicals and books in Hungarian; Dir. GYULA GOBBY.

**Gradjevinska Knjiga:** 11000 Belgrade, trg Nikole Pašića 8/II; tel. (11) 333565; fax (11) 333565; f. 1948; technical, scientific and educational textbooks; Dir. MILAN VIŠNJIĆ.

**IP Matice srpske:** 21000 Novi Sad, trg Heroja Toze Markovića 2; tel. (21) 615599; Yugoslav and foreign fiction and humanities; Dir. DRAGOLJUB GAVARIĆ.

**Jedinstvo:** 38000 Priština, Dom štampe bb, POB 81; tel. (38) 27549; telex 18285; fax (38) 29809; poetry, novels, general literature, science, children's books; Dir. JORDAN RISTIĆ.

**Jugoslovenska knjiga:** 11000 Belgrade, trg Republike 5/VIII, POB 36; tel. (11) 621992; telex 12466; fax (11) 625970; art and culture; Dir. ŽIVORAD JAKOVLJEVIĆ.

**Medicinska knjiga:** 11001 Belgrade, Mata Vidakovića 24–26; tel. (11) 458165; f. 1947; medicine, pharmacology, stomatology, veterinary; Dir. MILE MEDIĆ.

**Minerva:** Izdavačko-štamparsko preduzeće, 24000 Subotica, trg 29 novembra 3; tel. (24) 25712; fax (24) 23208; novels and general; Dir. LADISLAV ŠEBEK.

**Narodna knjiga:** 11000 Belgrade, Šafarikova 11; tel. (11) 328610; f. 1950; economics, scientific and popular literature, reference books, dictionaries; Dir. NEDELJKO DRČELIĆ.

**Naučna knjiga:** 11000 Belgrade, Uzun Mirkova 5; tel. (11) 637220; f. 1947; school, college and university textbooks, publications of scientific bodies; Dir. Dr BLAŽO PEROVIĆ.

**Nolit:** 11000 Belgrade, Terazije 27/II; tel. (11) 345017; fax (11) 627285; f. 1929; Yugoslav and other belles-lettres, philosophy and fine art; scientific and popular literature; Dir-Gen. RADIVOJE NEŠIĆ; Editor-in-Chief MILOŠ STAMBOLIĆ.

**Obod:** 81250 Cetinje, Njegoševa 3; tel. (86) 21331; fax (86) 21953; general literature; Dir. VLADIMIR MIRKOVIĆ.

**Panorama:** Priština; f. 1994; publishes newspapers and journals in Serbian, Albanian and Turkish; Dir. JORDAN RISTIĆ.

**Pobjeda:** 81000 Podgorica, Južni bul. bb; tel. (81) 44433; f. 1974; poetry, fiction, lexicography and scientific works.

**Proex:** 11000 Belgrade, Terazije 16; tel. (11) 688563; fax (11) 641052; editorial and typographic co-productions; export and import of books and periodicals.

**Prosveta:** 11000 Belgrade, Čika Ljubina 1/I; tel. (11) 629843; fax (11) 182581; f. 1944; general literature, art books, dictionaries, encyclopaedias, science, music; Dir. BUDIMIR RUDOVIĆ.

**Rad:** 11000 Belgrade, M. Pijade 12; tel. (11) 339998; f. 1949; labour and labour relations, politics and economics, sociology, psychology, literature, biographies, science fiction; Man. Dir. VESNA ALEKSIĆ; Editor-in-Chief DRAGAN LAKIĆEVIĆ.

**Rilindja:** 38000 Priština, Dom štampe; tel. (38) 23868; telex 18163; popular science, literature, children's fiction and travel books, textbooks in Albanian; Dir. NAZMI RRAHMANI.

**Savremena administracija:** 11000 Belgrade, Crnotravska 7–9; tel. (11) 667633; fax (11) 667277; f. 1954; economy, law, science university textbooks; Dir. TOMISLAV JOVIĆ.

**Sportska knjiga:** 11000 Belgrade, Makedonska 19; tel. (11) 320226; f. 1949; sport, chess, hobbies; Dir. BORISLAV PETROVIĆ.

**Srpska književna zadruga:** 11000 Belgrade, Srpskih Vladara 19/I; tel. (11) 330305; fax (11) 626224; f. 1892; works of classical and modern Yugoslav writers, and translations of works of foreign writers; Pres. RADOVAN SAMARDŽIĆ; Editor RADOMIR RADOVANAĆ.

**Svetovi:** 21000 Novi Sad, Arse Teodorovića 11; tel. (21) 28036; general; Dir. JOVAN ZIVLAK.

**Tehnička Knjiga:** 11000 Belgrade, Vojvode Stepe 89; tel. (11) 468762; fax (11) 473442; f. 1948; technical works, popular science, reference books, 'how to' books, hobbies; Dir. RADIVOJE GRBOVIĆ.

**Vuk Karadžič:** 11000 Belgrade, Kraljevića Marka 9, POB 762; tel. (11) 628066; fax (11) 623150; scientific literature, popular science, children's books, general; Gen. Man. VOJIN ANČIĆ.

**Zavod za udžbenike i nastavna sredstva:** 11000 Belgrade, Obilićev Venac 5; tel. (11) 638463; fax (11) 630014; f. 1958; textbooks and teaching aids; Dir. DOBROSLAV BJELETIĆ.

### PUBLISHERS' ASSOCIATION

**Udruženje izdavača i knjižara Jugoslavije** (Association of Yugoslav Publishers and Booksellers): 11000 Belgrade, Kneza Miloša 25, POB 883; tel. (11) 642533; fax (11) 646339; f. 1954; organizes Belgrade International Book Fair; Dir. OGNJEN LAKIĆEVIĆ; 97 mem. organizations.

## Radio and Television

**Jugoslovenska Radiotelevizija (JRT)** (Association of Yugoslav Radio and Television Organizations): 11000 Belgrade, Generala Ždanova 28; tel. (11) 330194; telex 12158; fax (11) 334380; f. 1952; Exec. Dir. SLOBODAN DUMIĆ.

**Radio Jugoslavija:** 11000 Belgrade, Hilandarska 2/IV, POB 200; tel. (11) 346884; telex 12432; fax (11) 332014; f. 1951; foreign service; broadcasts in Serbo-Croat, Arabic, English, French, German, Russian and Spanish; Dir. Dr DRAGAN MARKOVIĆ.

**Radiotelevizija Crne Gore:** 81000 Podgorica, Cetinjski put bb; tel. (81) 41800; telex 61133; fax (81) 43640; f. 1944 (Radio), 1971 (Television); 2 radio and 2 television programmes; broadcasts in Serbo-Croat; Dir-Gen. ZORAN JOCOVIĆ; Dir. of Radio (vacant); Dir. of Television MILUTIN RADULOVIĆ (acting).

**Radiotelevizija Srbije (RTS):** 11000 Belgrade, Takovska 10; tel. (11) 342001; telex 11884; fax (11) 543178; f. 1992; Dir-Gen. MILORAD VUČELIĆ; comprises:

　**Radiotelevizija Beograd:** 11000 Belgrade, Hilandarska 2; tel. (11) 346801; telex 11727; fax (11) 326768 (Radio); 11000 Belgrade, Takovska 10; tel. (11) 342001; telex 11884; fax (11) 543178 (Television); f. 1929 (Radio), 1958 (Television); 5 radio programmes, plus 1 experimental, and 3 television programmes in Serbo-Croat; Dir-Gen. DOBROSAV BJELETIĆ; Dir. of Radio DRAGOSLAV NIKITOVIĆ (acting); Dir. of Television SLOBODAN IGNJATOVIĆ.

　**Radiotelevizija Novi Sad:** 21000 Novi Sad, Žarka Zrenjanina 3; tel. (21) 611588; telex 14127; fax (21) 26624 (Radio); 21000 Novi Sad, Kamenički put 45; tel. (21) 56855; telex 14303; fax (21) 52079 (Television); f. 1949 (Radio), 1975 (Television); 7 radio and 2 television programmes; broadcasts in Serbo-Croat, Slovak, Romanian, Hungarian and Ruthenian; Dir-Gen. MILAN TODOROV; Dir. of Radio MIROSLAV BONDŽIĆ; Dir. of Television PETAR LJUBOJEV.

# YUGOSLAVIA

**Radiotelevizija Priština:** 38000 Priština, Srpskih Vladara bb; tel. (38) 26255; telex 18134; fax (38) 25355 (Radio); 38000 Priština, Zejnel Ajdini 12; tel. (38) 31211; telex 18186; fax (38) 32073 (Television); f. 1944 (Radio), 1975 (Television); 3 radio and 1 television programme; broadcasts in Albanian, Serbo-Croat, Romany and Turkish; Dir-Gen. PETAR JAKŠIĆ; Dir of Radio MILORAD VUJOVIĆ; Dir of Television NIKOLA SARIĆ.

**B92:** Belgrade, Makedonska 22; tel. (11) 3248577; fax (11) 3248075; f. 1989; independent radio station; Editor-in-Chief VERAN MATIĆ.

## Finance

(cap. = capital; res = reserves; dep. = deposits; m. = million; amounts in convertible Yugoslav dinars unless otherwise stated; br. = branch)

### BANKING

#### Central Banking System

The National Bank of Yugoslavia is the country's central bank, its powers and obligations being determined by law. Its functions include the issue of money, provision of credit to banks and government authorities, control of credits and bank activities, recommendation of legislation relating to the activities, recommendation of legislation relating to the foreign exchange system and its implementation, management of gold and foreign exchange reserves, control of foreign exchange operations and other special activities.

**Narodna banka Jugoslavije** (National Bank of Yugoslavia): 11000 Belgrade, revolucije 15, POB 1010; tel. (11) 3248841; telex 72000; f. 1883, present name since 1963; Gov. Prof. Dr DRAGOSLAV AVRAMOVIĆ.

**National Bank of Montenegro:** 81000 Podgorica, Blaža Jovanovića 7; tel. (81) 43381; Gov. KRUNISLAV VUKČEVIĆ.

**National Bank of Serbia:** 11000 Belgrade, 7 jula 12; tel. (11) 625555; Gov. BORISLAV ATANACKOVIĆ.

#### Bank for International Economic Co-operation

**Jugoslovenska Banka Za Medjunarodnu Ekonomsku Saradnju—JUBMES** (Yugoslav Bank for International Economic Co-operation): Head Office: 11070 Belgrade, AVNOJ-a 121, POB 219; tel. (11) 143004; telex 11710; fax (11) 131457; f. 1979; replaced the Export Credit and Insurance Fund and assumed the assets and liabilities of the Fund; established by a special Law; grants export credits; underwrites insurance of exports against non-commercial risks, etc.; total assets US $209.9m. (1992); Pres. IVAN STAMBOLIĆ; Exec. Dir BRANKA MIJANOVIĆ.

#### Other Banks

**Beogradska Banka d.d., Beograd:** 11001 Belgrade, POB 955, Knez Mihajlova 2–4; tel. (11) 624455; telex 11712; fax (11) 633128; f. 1978; cap. 28,077m., res 5,249m., dep. 206,168m. (Dec. 1991); Pres. LJUBIŠA IGIĆ.

**Beogradska Banka Beobanka d.d., Beograd:** 11000 Belgrade, Zeleni Venac 16; tel. (11) 629696; telex 11802; fax (11) 632829; f. 1978; total assets US $1.152m. (Dec. 1993); Man. Dir and Chief Exec. ZLATAN PERUČIĆ (acting).

**Glavna filijala Investbanka, Beograd:** 11000 Belgrade, Terazije 7–9; tel. (11) 335201; telex 11147; f. 1862; main br. within Beogradska Banka d.d., Belgrade; total assets 83,499,532 (Sept. 1989); Man. Dir and Chief Exec. Dr STOJAN DABIĆ (acting).

**Investiciona Banka Podgorica:** 81000 Podgorica, Revolucije 1; tel. (81) 42922; telex 61118; f. 1966; total assets 1,606,826m. old dinars (Dec. 1987); in process of reorganization.

**Jugobanka d.d., Beograd:** 11000 Belgrade, 7 Jula 19–21; tel. (11) 630022; telex 71004; fax (11) 637264; f. 1955 as Yugoslav Bank for Foreign Trade; name changed 1971; cap. 115,520m., res 52,131m., dep. 1,218,535m. (Dec. 1992); Chair. MILOŠ MILOSAVLJEVIĆ.

**Jugobanka d.d., Beograd, Jugobanka Beograd:** 11000 Belgrade, Srpskih Vladara 11; tel. (11) 334931; telex 11280; f. 1956; total assets 4,019,740m. old dinars (Dec. 1988); Gen. Man. LJUBOMIR POTKONJAK.

**Jugobanka d.d., Beograd, Jugobanka k.b. Beograd:** 11000 Belgrade, Radivoja Koraća 6; tel. (11) 455666; telex 12133; fax (11) 458396; f. 1970 as br. of Sremska banka, joined Jugobanka 1977; total assets 3,500m. (March 1991); Gen. Man. LJUBOMIR POTKONJAK.

**Jugoslovenska izvozna i kreditna banka d.d.** (Yugoslav Export & Credit Bank Inc.): 11000 Belgrade, Knez Mihailova 42, POB 234; tel. (11) 632822; telex 12906; fax (11) 183198; f. 1946; cap. and res 16,151m., dep. 182,580m. (Dec. 1992); Pres. MIODRAG PRICA.

**Montex Bank:** 11000 Belgrade, Kneza Miloša 61; tel. (11) 646797; telex 72080; fax (11) 659995; f. 1991; cap. 176,414.1m., res 1,213.8m., dep. 807,591.7m. (Dec. 1991); Pres. ILIJA ČULJKOVIĆ.

##### Kosovo and Metohija

**Udružena Kosovska Banka** (Kosovo Associated Bank): 38000 Priština, Srpskih Vladara 4; tel. (38) 34111; telex 18149; cap. 316,474.8m., res 112,184.5m., dep. 6,300,309.9m. old dinars (Dec. 1988); Pres. MUHAREM ISMAILJI.

##### Vojvodina

**Privredna Banka d.d., Novi Sad:** 21001 Novi Sad, Grčkoškolska 2; tel. (21) 412277; telex 15457; fax (21) 623025; f. 1956; cap. 17,867m., res 1,079m., dep. 292,270m. (Dec. 1993); Gen. Man. GOJKO BJELICA; 27 brs.

**Vojvodjanska Banka, d.d.:** 21001 Novi Sad, POB 391, M. Tita 14; tel. (21) 57222; telex 14129; fax (21) 624940; f. 1978; res 195,473m., dep. 522,700m. (Dec. 1991); Gen. Dir ŽIVOTA MIHAJLOVIĆ; 117 brs.

#### Banking Association

**Udruženje banaka Jugoslavije** (Association of Yugoslav Banks): 11001 Belgrade, Masarikova 5/IX; tel. (11) 684797; telex 11767; fax (11) 684947; f. 1955; association of Yugoslav business banks; works on improving inter-bank co-operation, organizes agreements of mutual interest for banks, gives expert assistance, establishes co-operation with foreign banks, other financial institutions and their associations, represents banks in relations with the Yugoslav Government and the National Bank of Yugoslavia; Pres. ŽIVOTA MIHAJLOVIĆ; Sec.-Gen. MILOVAN MILUTINOVIĆ.

### STOCK EXCHANGE

**Belgrade Stock Exchange:** 11070 Belgrade, Vladimira Popovića 6 BO2; tel. (11) 2224049; fax (11) 2224355; f. 1886, ceased operation 1941, reopened 1990.

### INSURANCE

**'DUNAV' Deoničko Društvo za Osiguranje** (Dunav Insurance Company): 11001 Belgrade, Makedonska 4, POB 624; tel. (11) 324001; telex 11359; fax (11) 624652; f. 1974; all types of insurance.

## Trade and Industry

### CHAMBERS OF ECONOMY

**Privredna Komora Jugoslavije** (Yugoslav Chamber of Economy): 11000 Belgrade, Terazije 23, POB 1003; tel. (11) 339461; telex 11638; fax (11) 631928; independent organization affiliating all Yugoslav economic organizations; promotes economic and commercial relations with foreign countries; Pres. MIHAJLO MILOJEVIĆ.

**Chamber of Economy of Montenegro:** 81000 Podgorica, Novaka Miloševa 29/II; tel. (81) 31071; fax (81) 34926; Pres. VOJIN DJUKANOVIĆ.

**Chamber of Economy of Serbia:** 11000 Belgrade, Gen. Zdanova 13–15; tel. (11) 340611; fax (11) 330949; Pres. Dr VLAJKO STOJILJOVIĆ.

### FOREIGN TRADE INSTITUTE

**Institut za Spoljnu Trgovinu:** 11000 Belgrade, Moše Pijade 8; tel. (11) 339041; telex 12214; Dir Dr SLOBODAN MRKŠA.

### TRADE UNIONS

**Confederation of Autonomous Trade Unions of Yugoslavia** (Savez Samostalnih Sindikata Jugoslavije): 11000 Belgrade, Nikola Pašić 5; tel. (11) 332931; fax (11) 341911; 1,900,000 mems.

Trade unions forming the Confederation of Autonomous Trade Unions of Yugoslavia (address, telephone and telex number as above unless otherwise stated):

**Agricultural, Food and Tobacco Industry Workers' Union** (Sindikat radnika poljprivrede, prehrambene i duvanske industrije): Pres. Federal Cttee ERNE KIĆI.

**Building Workers' Union** (Sindikat radnika gradjevinarstva): Pres. Federal Cttee MILOŠ ŽORIĆ.

**Catering and Tourism Workers' Union** (Sindikat radnika u ugostiteljstvu i turizmu): Pres. Federal Cttee MILAN FRKOVIĆ.

**Chemistry and Non-Metallic Industry Workers' Union** (Sindikat radnika hemije i nemetala): Pres. Federal Cttee STOJMIR DOMAZETOVSKI.

**Commerce Workers' Union** (Sindikat radnika u trgovini): Pres. Federal Cttee LJUBICA BRAČKO.

# YUGOSLAVIA

**Education, Science and Culture Workers' Union** (Sindikat radnika delatnosti vaspitanja, obrazovanja, nauke i kulture): Pres. Federal Cttee BORIS LIPUŽIĆ.

**Energy Workers' Union** (Sindikat radnika energetike): Pres. Federal Cttee VASKRSIJE SAVIČIĆ.

**Forestry and Wood Industry Workers' Union** (Sindikat radnika šumarstva i prerade drveta): Pres. Federal Cttee DRAGOLJUB OBRADOVIĆ.

**Health and Social Care Workers' Union** (Sindikat radnika delatnosti zdravstva i socijalne zaštite): Pres. Federal Cttee LJILJANA MILOŠEVIĆ.

**Metal Production and Manufacturing Workers' Union** (Sindikat radnika proizvodnje i prerade metala): Pres. Federal Cttee SLAVKO URŠIĆ.

**Public Utilities and Handicrafts Workers' Union** (Sindikat radnika u komunalnoj privredi i zanatstvu): Pres. Federal Cttee JOSIP KOLAR.

**Printing, Newspaper, Publishing and Information Workers' Union** (Sindikat radnika grafičke, novinsko-izdavačke i informativne delatnosti): Pres. Federal Cttee BORIS BIŠĆAN.

**State Administration and Finance Workers' Union** (Sindikat radnika državne uprave i finansijskih organa): Pres. Federal Cttee RAM BUĆAJ.

**Textile, Leather, and Footwear Workers' Union** (Sindikat radnika industrije tekstila, kože i obuće): Pres. Federal Cttee JOZEFINA MUSA.

**Transport and Communications Workers' Union** (Sindikat radnika saobraćaja i veza): 11000 Belgrade, Miloša Pocerca 10; tel. (11) 646321; Pres. Federal Cttee HASAN HRNJIĆ.

**Federation of Independent Trade Unions of Yugoslavia:** Pres. MOMO COLAKOVIĆ.

### TRADE FAIRS

**Belgrade Fair:** Belgrade, Vojvode Mišića 14, POB 408; tel. (11) 655555; telex 11306; fax (11) 688173; Internat. Technical Fair, annually in May; Internat. Motor Show, annually in April; Internat. Chemical Fair, annually in May; Internat. Clothing Fair 'Fashions in the World', annually in October; Internat. Book Fair, annually in October; Internat. Furniture Fair, annually in November; and other fairs; Pres. SINIŠA ZARIĆ.

**Novi Sad:** Novosadski Sajam, Novi Sad, Hajduk Veljkova 11; tel. (21) 25155; telex 14180; fax (21) 616121; Novi Sad Internat. Agricultural Fair, annually in May; Internat. Fair of Hunting, Fishing, Sports and Tourism, annually in October; Internat. Autumn Fair, annually in October; and other fairs; Dir-Gen. JOVAN NEŠIN.

## Transport

Much international transport activity to or from Yugoslavia was halted in 1992–94 as a result of UN sanctions. In October 1994 sanctions affecting international travel to and from Yugoslavia were partially suspended, permitting the resumption of international flights to and from Belgrade and the ferry service between Bar (Montenegro) and Bari (Italy).

### RAILWAYS

In 1991 there were 3,947 km of railway track in use, of which 1,339 km were electrified. In 1992–95 some rail services were suspended, owing to shortages of fuel.

**Zajednica Jugoslovenskih Železnica** (Yugoslav Railways): 11000 Belgrade, Nemanjina 6, POB 563; tel. (11) 688722; telex 12495; fax (11) 641352; Gen. Man. S. KOSTADINOVIĆ.

### ROADS

The road network is the responsibility of the Federal Ministry of Transport and Communications. In 1991 there were some 47,500 km of roads, of which 9,200 km were unpaved.

### INLAND WATERWAYS

Inland waterways are supervised by the Federal Ministry of Transport and Communications.

### SHIPPING

With the dissolution of the SFRY, Yugoslavia lost much of its access to the sea; the principal coastal outlet is the Montenegrin port of Bar, which is linked to Bari (Italy) by a regular ferry service.

**Jugoslovenska Oceanska Plovidba** (Yugoslav Ocean Lines): 85330 Kotor; tel. 25011; telex 61116; Pres. ANTON MOŠKOV.

**Jugoslovenska Pomorska Agencija** (Yugoslav Shipping Agency): Belgrade, bul. Lenjina 165A, POB 210; tel. (11) 130004; telex 11140; f. 1947; charter services, liner and container transport, port agency, passenger service, air cargo service; Gen. Man. STEVAN OBRADOVIĆ.

### CIVIL AVIATION

There are international airports at Belgrade and Podgorica, as well as several domestic airports.

**Jugoslovenski Aerotransport (JAT)** (Yugoslav Airlines): 11070 Belgrade, Umetnosti 16; tel. (11) 2224222; fax (11) 2222853; f. 1947; 51% owned by Govt of Serbia; international operations curtailed by imposition of sanctions in mid-1992, services partially restored in 1994–95; operates two domestic routes; Pres. and Dir-Gen. ZIKA PETROVIĆ.

Smaller operators, the international operations of which were also suspended, included:

**Air Jugoslavia:** 11000 Belgrade, Moše Pijade 1/III; tel. (11) 338812; telex 12125; fax (11) 327832; f. 1969; wholly-owned subsidiary of JAT; Gen. Man. A. SKEPANOVIĆ.

**Air Montenegro:** Podgorica; tel. (81) 43020; telex 61425; fax (81) 41939.

**Aviogenex:** 11070 Belgrade, Milentija Popovića 9; tel. (11) 149729; telex 11711; fax (11) 2222439; f. 1968; passenger and cargo flights within Europe, the Mediterranean and the Middle East; Gen. Man. MIROSLAV SPASIĆ.

## Tourism

Prior to the disintegration of the SFRY, tourism was a major source of foreign exchange (receipts were estimated at US $2,700m. in 1990); most foreign tourists were, however, attracted to Croatia and Slovenia. The great lake of Scutari, in Montenegro, is a notable tourist attraction, as is Montenegro's Adriatic coastline. The Yugoslav tourist industry was adversely affected by the imposition of UN sanctions, in May 1992. As well as the suspension of foreign visits, most domestic tourists were unable to travel, owing to reduced incomes. In 1994, however, some recovery in the tourism industry was achieved, with an increase of 16.6% in the number of tourist nights spent in the FRY, the first such increase for seven years.

**Turistički savez Jugoslavije** (Tourist Association of Yugoslavia): 11001 Belgrade, Moše Pijade 8/IV, Poštanski fah 595; tel. (11) 339041; telex 11863; fax (11) 634677; f. 1953; produces tourist information in foreign languages; Pres. (vacant); Sec.-Gen. GEORGI GOŠEV.

**Yugotours:** 11000 Belgrade, Kneza Mihaila 50; tel. (11) 187822; telex 11000; fax (11) 180745; f. 1957; organizes travel and accommodation arrangements for foreign and domestic tourists; 3 branch offices, 2 European; Man. Dir LJUBIŠA RADOVANOVIĆ.

# ZAIRE

## Introductory Survey

### Location, Climate, Language, Religion, Flag, Capital

The Republic of Zaire lies in central Africa, bordered by the Republic of the Congo to the north-west, by the Central African Republic and Sudan to the north, by Uganda, Rwanda, Burundi and Tanzania to the east and by Zambia and Angola to the south. There is a short coastline at the outlet of the River Zaire (Congo). The climate is tropical, with an average temperature of 27°C (80°F) and an annual rainfall of 150 to 200 cm. French is the official language. Over 400 Sudanese and Bantu dialects are spoken; Kiswahili, Kiluba, Kikongo and Lingala being the most widespread. An estimated 52% of the population is Roman Catholic, and there is a smaller Protestant community. Many inhabitants follow traditional Zairean (mostly animist) beliefs. The national flag (proportions 3 by 2) is green with a central yellow disc in which a brown arm bears a brown torch with a red flame. The capital is Kinshasa (formerly Léopoldville).

### Recent History

Zaire, formerly called the Belgian Congo, became independent from Belgium as the Republic of the Congo on 30 June 1960. Five days later the armed forces mutinied. Belgium's actions during the ensuing unrest and its support for the secession of Katanga (now Shaba) province were condemned by the UN, which dispatched troops to the Congo to maintain order. In September the Head of State, Joseph Kasavubu, dismissed the Prime Minister, Patrice Lumumba. Later in that month the Government was taken over temporarily by Col (later Gen. and, from December 1982, Marshal) Joseph-Désiré Mobutu. Mobutu returned power to President Kasavubu in February 1961. Shortly afterwards Lumumba, who had been imprisoned in December 1960, was murdered. In August 1961 a new Government was formed, with Cyrille Adoula as Prime Minister. In July 1964 Kasavubu appointed Moïse Tschombe, the former leader of the Katangan secessionists, as interim Prime Minister, pending elections, and in August the country was renamed the Democratic Republic of the Congo. Following elections in March and April 1965, a power struggle developed between Tshombe and Kasavubu; in November 1965 Mobutu intervened, seizing power and proclaiming himself head of the 'Second Republic'. In June 1967 a new Constitution was adopted. In October–November 1970 Gen. Mobutu was elected President, unopposed, and took office for a seven-year term. (From January 1972 he became known as Mobutu Sese Seko.) In November 1970 elections took place to a new national assembly (subsequently renamed the National Legislative Council). In October 1971 the Democratic Republic of the Congo became the Republic of Zaire, and a year later the Government of Zaire and the Executive Committee of the Mouvement populaire de la révolution (MPR), Zaire's sole legal political party, merged into the National Executive Council.

In March 1977 and May 1978 the Front national pour la libération congolaise (FNLC), established in 1963 by Katangan separatists, invaded Zaire from Angola, taking much of Shaba (formerly Katanga) province; however, the FNLC were repulsed on both occasions by the Zairean army, with armed support from a number of Western Governments. In October 1978 the Governments of Zaire and Angola agreed that neither country would allow its territory to be used for guerrilla attacks against the other.

The invasion of 1977 had prompted Mobutu to introduce a number of political reforms, including the introduction of a new electoral code. Legislative elections took place in October and, at a presidential election held in December, Mobutu (the sole candidate) was re-elected for a further seven-year term. In March 1979 the President appointed a new Government, with Bo-Boliko Lokonga, former head of the National Legislative Council, as First State Commissioner (equivalent to Prime Minister). In January 1980, as part of a large-scale campaign against corruption, Mobutu reorganized the National Executive Council, dismissing 13 of the 22 Commissioners.

In a series of political reforms in August 1980, the new post of Chairman of the MPR, to be held by the President in his position as leader of the MPR, became the central organ of decision-making and control of the Party's activities. In the same month Nguza Karl-I-Bond was appointed First State Commissioner; in April 1981, however, he went into self-imposed exile in Belgium and was replaced by N'Singa Udjuu Ongwakebi Untube, who also became Executive Secretary of the MPR when the posts were merged in October 1981. In early 1982 opponents of Zaire's one-party system of government formed the Union pour la démocratie et le progrès social (UDPS). This was followed by the formation, later in that year, of the Front congolais pour le rétablissement de la démocratie (FCD), a coalition of opposition parties, for which Nguza Karl-I-Bond was the spokesman. Léon Kengo Wa Dondo was appointed First State Commissioner in a ministerial reshuffle in November.

In May 1983, following the publication of a highly critical report on Zaire by the human rights organization, Amnesty International, Mobutu offered an amnesty to all political exiles who returned to Zaire by the end of June. A number of exiles accepted the offer, but a substantial opposition movement remained in Belgium. Violent opposition to Mobutu's regime continued to manifest itself in Zaire during 1984. However, Mobutu was re-elected President without hindrance in July of that year, and was inaugurated in December. In July 1985 restrictions were lifted on seven members of the outlawed UDPS under the terms of another amnesty for political opponents, and Karl-I-Bond returned from exile (he was appointed Ambassador to the USA in July 1986).

In March 1986 Amnesty International published another unfavourable report on Zaire, citing the alleged illegal arrest, torture or killing of UDPS supporters in November and December 1985. In October 1986 Mobutu admitted that some of the allegations in the report were justified, and announced the appointment of a State Commissioner for Citizens' Rights. Elections to the 210-member National Legislative Council (reduced from 310 members) were held in September 1987. In November 1988, in the fourth ministerial reshuffle of the year, Mobutu replaced about one-third of the members of the National Executive Council and reappointed Kengo Wa Dondo to the post of First State Commissioner, from which he had been removed in October 1986. Further government reshuffles took place in May 1989 and January 1990.

The organization of opposition demonstrations (violently suppressed by the security forces) during 1989 and early 1990, prompted Mobutu's announcement, in late April 1990, that a multi-party political system, initially comprising three parties (including the MPR), would be introduced after a transitional period of one year; the UDPS was immediately legalized. At the same time Mobutu declared the inauguration of the 'Third Republic' and announced his resignation from both the post of Chairman of the MPR and from the post of State Commissioner for National Defence in the National Executive Council. However, he remained as the country's Head of State. N'Singa Udjuu Ongwakebi Untube, formerly First State Commissioner and Executive Secretary of the MPR, was subsequently appointed the new Chairman of the MPR. The National Executive Council was dissolved and Kengo Wa Dondo was replaced as First State Commissioner by Prof. Lunda Bululu. In early May a new, and smaller, transitional National Executive Council was formed. Furthermore, Mobutu announced the imminent 'depoliticization' of the armed forces, the Gendarmerie, the Civil Guard, the security services and the administration in general'.

In late June 1990, as part of the ongoing political reform process, Mobutu relinquished presidential control over the National Executive Council and over foreign policy. At the same time, the establishment of independent trade unions was authorized. In early October Mobutu announced that a full multi-party political system would be established, thereby reversing his former decision to permit the existence initially of only three parties. In November legislation to this effect was introduced. In the same month, the USA announced its decision to end all military and economic aid to Zaire. This development followed renewed allegations of abuses of human rights by the Mobutu regime, and also reflected speculation that for many years Mobutu had misappropriated large amounts of foreign economic aid for his personal enrichment. Popular unrest re-emerged in late 1990: in November an anti-Government rally in Kinshasa, organized by the UDPS, was violently suppressed, and in the following month several people were reported to have been killed by government troops during demonstrations in Kinshasa and Matadi in protest against recent increases in consumer prices.

By February 1991 a large number of new parties had been established. Prominent among these was the Union des fédéralistes et républicains indépendants (UFERI), led by Karl-I-Bond. In early February it was reported that several hundred thousand civil servants and public-service employees joined a three-day general strike that had been organized by the Union Nationale des Travailleurs du Zaïre to demand both improved living and working conditions and the resignation of the Government. Later in the same month some 20,000 people attended an anti-Government rally, organized by the UDPS, in Kinshasa.

An enlarged transitional Government, which was appointed in late March 1991 and reshuffled in the following month, was reported to include members of minor opposition groups. None of the larger opposition parties, including the UDPS and the UFERI, agreed to join the new Government. Lunda Bululu was replaced as First State Commissioner by Prof. Mulumba Lukoji, a prominent economist who had served in previous administrations. The reorganization followed minor government changes that had been effected in June and November of the previous year.

In early April 1991 Mobutu announced that a national conference would be convened at the end of that month, at which members of the Government and of opposition organizations would draft a new constitution. However, the Conference was postponed, owing to widespread disturbances and anti-Government demonstrations in several parts of the country. In mid-April 42 people were reported to have been killed, and many others wounded, when security forces opened fire on demonstrators in the town of Mbuji-Mayi, in central Zaire. In late April Mobutu resumed the chairmanship of the MPR. In July some 130 opposition movements formed a united front, known as the Union sacrée. Later in July Mulumba Lukoji resigned as First State Commissioner, and Mobutu appointed Etienne Tshisekedi Wa Mulumba, leader of the UDPS, in his place. Following threats to his life, however, Tshisekedi refused the post, and Mulumba Lukoji was reappointed as First State Commissioner. The National Conference was convened at the beginning of August, but was subsequently repeatedly suspended, initially owing to the dissatisfaction of the Union sacrée with the composition of its participants, and eventually by the Government, prompting renewed civil unrest, and the dispatch of French and Belgian troops to Zaire to evacuate nationals of those countries. (All foreign troops were withdrawn by early November.) In late September Tshisekedi finally accepted the post of First State Commissioner. In mid-October, however, Tshisekedi refused to swear allegiance to the President and the Constitution; shortly afterwards he was replaced as First State Commissioner by Bernardin Mungul Diaka, also a member of the opposition. At the end of October the Cabinet was reshuffled. In late November Mobutu dismissed Mungul from the premiership, and appointed Karl-I-Bond as the new First State Commissioner. The Union sacrée denounced the appointment, and expelled the UFERI (Karl-I-Bond's party) from its ranks. A new Cabinet was announced at the end of November (and was subsequently reorganized in February and March 1992). Despite the expiry of his mandate as President in early December, Mobutu remained in office. In mid-December the Roman Catholic Archbishop of Kisangani, Most Rev. Laurent Monsengwo Pasinya, was elected President of the National Conference.

In mid-January 1992 further demonstrations took place in Kinshasa in protest against the continued suspensions of the National Conference. Shortly afterwards an alleged attempted military coup was suppressed (17 soldiers were subsequently sentenced to death in connection with this), and rioting by members of the armed forces was reported in the capital. In mid-February government troops were reported to have killed at least 30 people who were attending a pro-democracy demonstration in Kinshasa. In early April the National Conference reopened, and in mid-April it declared its status to be sovereign and its decisions to be binding. Mobutu reacted with cautious opposition to the erosion of his powers, anxious to secure confirmation of his position as Head of State.

In mid-August 1992 the National Conference employed its new sovereign powers by electing Tshisekedi as the First State Commissioner, following the resignation of Karl-I-Bond, who had not stood for re-election. A 'transition act', adopted by the Conference in early August, afforded Tshisekedi a mandate to govern for 24 months, pending the promulgation of a new constitution which would curtail the powers of the President. On 30 August Tshisekedi, whose election was widely applauded as a victory for pro-democratic forces within Zaire, appointed a transitional Government of 'national union', which included opponents of Mobutu. The election of the State Commissioner was also welcomed by the international community, particularly the USA, France, Belgium and the EU, and it was hoped that renewed financial commitments from these sources would be promptly negotiated.

The political interests of Tshisekedi and Mobutu clashed almost immediately when the President declared his intention to promote the adoption of a 'semi-presidential constitution', in opposition to the parliamentary system favoured by the Conference. In October 1992 attacks on opposition leaders and the offices of newspapers critical of the President became increasingly frequent in Kinshasa, while Shaba was beset by ethnic violence. Meanwhile, rumours persisted of an imminent coup, organized by generals loyal to the President. On 14 November the National Conference (without the participation of Mobutu's supporters) adopted a draft Constitution providing for the establishment of a 'Federal Republic of the Congo', the introduction of a bicameral parliament and the election of the President, by universal suffrage, to fulfil a largely ceremonial function. (Executive and military power was to be exercised by the Prime Minister.) The draft document was vigorously opposed by Mobutu who, having failed to persuade Tshisekedi to broaden his Government in order to accommodate the President's own supporters, unsuccessfully attempted in early December to declare the Tshisekedi Government dissolved. On 6 December the National Conference dissolved itself and was succeeded by a 453-member High Council of the Republic, headed by Monsengwo, which, as the supreme interim executive and legislative authority, was empowered to amend and adopt the new Constitution and to organize legislative and presidential elections. At the same time, Monsengwo declared that the report of a special commission, established by the Conference in order to examine allegations of corruption brought against the President and his associates, would be considered by the High Council. In response to this effective expropriation of his powers, Mobutu ordered the suspension of the High Council and the Government, and decreed that civil servants should usurp ministers in the supervision of government ministries (a demand which they refused). Attempts by the presidential guard to obstruct the convening of the High Council ended following the organization of a parade through the streets of Kinshasa, undertaken by Monsengwo and other members of the High Council, in protest at the actions of the armed forces. Bolstered by support from the USA, Belgium and France, Monsengwo reiterated the High Council's recognition of Tshisekedi as head of Zaire's Government.

In mid-January 1993 the High Council declared Mobutu to be guilty of treason, on account of his mismanagement of state affairs, and threatened impeachement proceedings unless he recognize the legitimacy of the transitional Government headed by Tshisekedi. A short-lived general strike and campaign of civil disobedience, organized by the Union sacrée, failed in their stated aims of forcing the resignation of the President and liberating the national radio and television stations from Mobutu's control. Five people were killed and many were injured in disturbances which ensued. At the end of the month several units of the army rioted in protest at an attempt by the President to pay them with discredited 5m.-zaire banknotes. Order was eventually restored, but not before the deaths of some 65 individuals (including the French Ambassador to Zaire) and the intervention of military contingents from France and Belgium.

In early March 1993, in an attempt to reassert his political authority, Mobutu convened a special 'conclave' of political forces to debate the country's future. The High Council and the Union sacrée declined an invitation to attend. In mid-March the 'conclave' appointed Faustin Birindwa, a former

UDPS member and adviser to Tshisekedi, as Prime Minister, charged with the formation of a 'government of national salvation'. The somewhat perfunctory National Assembly was also revived to rival the High Council, and was reconvened to operate within the terms of reference of the old Mobutu-inspired Constitution. In early April Birindwa appointed a Cabinet which included Karl-I-Bond (as First Deputy Prime Minister in charge of Defence) and three members of the Union sacrée, who were immediately expelled from that organization. While the Birindwa administration was denied official recognition by Belgium, France, the USA and the EU, Tshisekedi became increasingly frustrated at the impotence of his own Government (the armed forces recommenced blocking access to the High Council), and the deteriorating stability of the country (during April the army embarked upon a campaign of intimidation of opposition members, while tribal warfare re-emerged in Shaba and also erupted in the north-eastern province of Kivu), and urged the intervention of the UN. In July the Secretary-General of the UN appointed Lakhdar Brahimi, a former Minister of Foreign Affairs in Algeria, as his Special Envoy to Zaire, charged with a humanitarian mission of mediation. Meanwhile, in late June, six of Birindwa's ministers, all former activists in the Union sacrée, had announced the formation of the Union sacrée rénovée (USR), claiming that the Union sacrée had abandoned its political objectives in the pursuit of extremist policies. A series of pre-negotiations, conducted during August between representatives of the 'conclave', the Union sacrée and the High Council, failed to conclude a significant initiative for future consensus.

At the end of September 1993, following some 20 days of negotiations, an agreement was concluded between representatives of President Mobutu and of the principal opposition groups, providing for the adoption of a single constitutional text for the transitional period, which would be subject to approval by a national referendum. Under the provisions of the agreement, national transitional institutions would include the President of the Republic, a reorganized transitional parliament (a unicameral legislature to be composed of more than 500 representatives, including all existing members of the High Council and the National Legislative Council—with the exception of 44 National Legislative Council 'substitutes' who were appointed following the expulsion of opposition representatives—and independent legislators, to be co-opted in order to ensure full national representation), the transitional Government and the national judiciary. As previously agreed, the organization of presidential and legislative elections would provide for the establishment of a new Republic in January 1995. During October 1993, however, attempts to finalize the terms of the agreement were complicated by the insistence of Tshisekedi's supporters that he should continue in the office of Prime Minister, despite the objections of Mobutu's representatives that Tshisekedi's mandate, proceeding from the National Conference, had been superseded by the September agreement. The opposing positions of the principal political parties (largely polarized as the pro-Tshisekedi Union sacrée de l'opposition radicale—USOR and the pro-Mobutu Forces politiques du conclave—FPC) became more firmly entrenched during November and December.

An ultimatum, issued to all political parties by President Mobutu in early January 1994, in an attempt to end the political impasse, resulted in the conclusion of an agreement to form a government of national reconciliation, signed by all major constituent parties of the FPC and the USOR (with the notable exception of Tshisekedi's own UDPS). Encouraged by the unexpected level of political support for the initiative, on 14 January Mobutu announced the dissolution of the High Council and the National Legislative Council, the dismissal of the Government of National Salvation, headed by Birindwa, and the candidacy for the premiership of two contestants, Tshisekedi and Mulumba Lukoji, to be decided by the transitional legislature (to be known as the Haut Conseil de la République-Parlement de Transition—HCR-PT) within 15 days of its inauguration, provisionally scheduled for 17 January. Despite widespread opposition condemnation of Mobutu's procedural circumvention of the High Council's authority, and a well-supported 24-hour general strike, organized in Kinshasa on 19 January in protest at Mobutu's unilateral declarations, the HCR-PT convened for the first time on 23 January (following a preliminary meeting on 19 January at which the former President of the High Council, the Most Rev. Laurent Monsengwo Pasinya, was confirmed as the new President of the HCR-PT). The HCR-PT promptly rejected Mobutu's procedure for the selection of a new Prime Minister. Subsequent attempts by the legislature to formulate a new procedure were frustrated by the increasingly divergent interests of the member parties of the USOR, and by Tshisekedi's insistence of his legitimate claim to the office.

On 8 April 1994 the HCR-PT endorsed a new Transitional Constitution Act, reiterating the provisions of previous accords for the organization of a constitutional referendum and presidential and legislative elections, and defining the functions of and relationship between the President of the Republic, the transitional Government and the HCR-PT, during a 15-month transitional period. The Government, to be accountable to the HCR-PT, was to assume some former powers of the President, including the control of the Central Bank and the security forces and the nomination of candidates for important civil service posts. A new Prime Minister was to be appointed from opposition candidates, to be nominated within 10 days of the President's promulgation of the Act (on 9 April). Despite the initial indignation of Tshisekedi's supporters at the Act's identification of a prime-ministerial vacancy that they did not recognize, by the end of April Tshisekedi was reported to have agreed to be considered for the post. Widening divisions within the USOR frustrated attempts to unite the opposition behind Tshisekedi as sole candidate, prompting the expulsion, in May, of 10 dissident parties from the USOR (including the Union pour la république et la démocratie—URD, whose members occupied several ministerial posts in the transitional Government).

In June 1994 the HCR-PT ratified the candidature of seven opposition representatives for the premiership, rejecting that of Tshisekedi for having failed to attend a parliamentary commission in order to explain the promotion of his position as 'Prime Minister awaiting rehabilitation', rather than candidate for the office. On 14 June it was reported that Léon Kengo Wa Dondo, described as a moderate opposition leader, had been elected Prime Minister by 322 votes to 133 in the HCR-PT. However, Kengo Wa Dondo's election was immediately denounced as illegitimate, under the terms of the April Constitution Act, by opposition spokesmen and by the President of the HCR-PT (who refused to endorse the actions of the legislature). A new transitional Government, announced on 6 July, was similarly rejected by the radical opposition, despite the offer of two cabinet posts to the UDPS. On 11 July, during a motion of confidence, the government received overwhelming support from the HCR-PT. The new Prime Minister swiftly sought to restore the confidence of the international donor community in the commitment of the new administration to the implementation of political change (general elections were to be conducted before the end of July 1995) and economic adjustment (more financial control was to be exerted over the armed forces, and the central bank was to be awarded greater autonomy). In early October an expanded radical opposition grouping (the Union sacrée de l'opposition radicale et ses alliés–USORAL) resumed its participation in the HCR-PT, having boycottted proceedings since the election of Kengo Wa Dondo in June. By early November a reformist wing of the UDPS, led by Joseph Ruhana Mirindi, had agreed to participate in the Government, and a reallocation of portfolios, effected in mid-November, included the appointment of two ministers and two deputy ministers who were (or had previously been) members of the UDPS.

Despite the successful adoption, in May 1995, of the electoral law establishing the National Electoral Commission, a lack of government funds and the logistical problems presented by the presence in Zaire of as many as 2.5m. refugees seemed likely to force the extension of the 15-month period of transitional government beyond the 9 July deadline. In late June political consensus was achieved between the FPC and the USORAL, resulting in the HCR-PT's adoption of a constitutional amendment whereby the period of national transition was to be extended by two years. On 1 July deputies from both groups voted to remove Monsengwo Pasinya from the post of President of the transitional legislature, prompting concern that the concerted political strength of the FPC and the USORAL would be sufficient to oust the Prime Minister. Meanwhile, Monsengwo's protest at the unconstitutional nature of the parliamentary procedure undertaken to effect his dismissal received cautious support from the French and Belgian Governments.

Economic difficulties were compounded in September 1994 by the circulation throughout the country of some 30 tons of counterfeit Zairean banknotes. Government initiatives to address the economic crisis included the announcement, in the same month, of the closure of more than half of its 64 diplomatic missions abroad and the President's statement of intent to privatize the state mining corporation, GÉCAMINES. By the end of December it was reported that national financial reserves had dwindled to just US $2,000. In early December the Prime Minister had announced an economic austerity plan for 1995 which aimed to reduce inflation massively, to just 20%. In March it was reported that some 300,000 civil servants (around one-half of the total number) were to be dismissed as part of a programme to rationalize the public sector and reduce public expenditure. Later in the month, widespread industrial action was organized by public sector workers in protest at this decision and in support of demands for the payment of substantial amounts of salary arrears.

Mounting concern that the political frustration of the opposition would be translated into an armed struggle increased, in March 1994, following the declaration of intent of the newly-proclaimed Congolese National Army (an armed wing of the Zairean radical opposition) to 'restore legitimacy and democracy' to the country.

In December 1993, at a rally in Kolwezi attended by the Mobutu-sponsored Government's Deputy Prime Minister, Karl-I-Bond, the Governor of Shaba (Gabriel Kyungu Wa Kumwanza) declared the autonomy of the province (reverting to the name of Katanga). While Karl-I-Bond denied that his presence had in any way endorsed the declaration, his own (separatist) UFERI welcomed the development and encouraged provincial political committees to pursue the establishment of greater regional autonomy. President Mobutu's subdued response to the Shaba declaration was attributed to his reluctance to engender further political opposition during negotiations that might dictate his political future (see above). In March 1995 Kumwanza was arrested and transported to Kinshasa following the discovery, at his home, of an arms cache, believed to be intended for use in an armed struggle to secure the secession of Shaba. Considerable tension mounted in the province after clashes between security forces and demonstrating UFERI members who were demanding Kumwanza's release. However, the situation was temporarily defused, on 20 April, by the Government's lenient decision merely to suspend Kumwanza from the post of Governor for a three-month period.

Reports published by Amnesty International in September 1993 and February 1994 accused security forces of the Mobutu administration of having perpetrated numerous violations of human rights against civilians and political opponents during the previous four years.

In January 1995 considerable international concern was aroused by an outbreak, in the south-western town of Kikwit, of the highly contagious and often fatal Ebola virus. By late May the World Health Organization (WHO) estimated that 108 of the town's 144 reported cases of the virus had resulted in death. By mid-1995 medical sources in Kinshasa claimed that the spread of the virus was being effectively contained.

From the late 1980s relations between Zaire and Belgium deteriorated. In November 1988 a serious dispute arose between the two countries, following reports in the Belgian press criticizing the degree of corruption in Zaire, and alleging that funds granted annually by Belgium for development purposes in Zaire had been misappropriated by Mobutu. Mobutu responded by ordering all Zairean nationals living in Belgium to return to Zaire, and to sell their assets or move them from Belgium; it was announced in January 1989 that the Belgian-based operations of Zairean state companies had relocated elsewhere. In that month Mobutu announced the abrogation of the two treaties of friendship and co-operation upon which post-colonial relations between the two countries had been based. Nevertheless, in early February Mobutu and the Belgian Prime Minister, Wilfried Martens, met in France to discuss the dispute. In the same month King Hassan II of Morocco offered to mediate a reconciliation, and, accordingly, further talks were held in May and July between Mobutu and Martens. In late July an agreement was signed in Rabat, Morocco, restoring 'full and amicable relations' between Zaire and Belgium, and in March 1990 a new treaty of co-operation was signed. In early May, however, Belgian sources reported that members of the security forces, acting on Mobutu's orders, had killed between 50 and 150 Lubumbashi University students who were attending an anti-Government demonstration. Strong condemnation was voiced by many humanitarian organizations, and the Belgian Government announced the immediate suspension of all official bilateral assistance to Zaire. In June the Government of Zaire, which had initially denied the reports, published the findings of an official parliamentary inquiry into the affair; in accordance with the recommendations of the inquiry, a provincial governor and other senior local government officials, who were accused of having organized the killing of one student and the injury of 13 others, were arrested. However, in response to demands by the Belgian Government that an international inquiry be established to investigate the case further, Mobutu expelled some 700 Belgian technical assistants from Zaire, recalled the Zairean Ambassador to Belgium and closed all but one of Belgium's consular offices in Zaire. (In January 1992 Mobutu finally agreed to permit an international investigation into the alleged massacre.)

Zaire's relations with its neighbours have been complicated by the presence of refugees in the border areas, and the activities of anti-Government rebels. In 1984 Tanzania denied Zairean allegations that it was harbouring rebels from Zaire. In 1985 the Angolan President visited Zaire, and an agreement was signed on border security and on trade and cultural matters. Zaire is a member of the OAU, but differs from most of its fellow-members in supporting the annexation of Western Sahara by Morocco (q.v.). In 1984 Zaire suspended its participation in OAU meetings over this issue, but in 1986 it resumed active membership. A frontier dispute with Zambia was resolved by an agreement signed in April 1986. In the following month, however, Zaire's relations with Zambia and other southern African countries deteriorated, owing to allegations that the USA was covertly supplying weapons, through Zaire, to the South African-backed União Nacional para a Independência Total de Angola (UNITA), which was in conflict with the Angolan Government. Although the Zairean Government denied these allegations and, in July, President Mobutu visited Angola and declared his support for the Angolan Government, reports that military equipment was reaching UNITA through Zaire nevertheless continued. In April 1987 the Presidents of Zaire, Mozambique and Angola signed a declaration of intent to reopen the Benguela Railway, which runs between the port of Lobito in Angola and the copper-producing areas of Zaire and Zambia. (The railway had been closed since 1975 because of sabotage by UNITA guerrillas.) Relations with the Congo deteriorated during 1992, following the forced repatriation, by the Congo, of some 30,000 Zaireans (many of them refugees) in late 1991.

Zaire's relations with Belgium, France, the USA and the EU improved considerably following the election of Tshisekedi as First State Commissioner in August 1992. Tshisekedi's efforts to harness African support, however, suffered a reversal in May 1993, when the African, Caribbean and Pacific group of states (see p. 165) accepted the participation of a delegation from Mobutu's appointed Prime Minister, Faustin Birindwa, at a meeting with the EU in Brussels. Birindwa's representatives were also afforded formal recognition by the International Labour Organisation and by the UN's Food and Agriculture Organization. In October the Minister of External Affairs in the Birindwa Government was recognized as the head of Zaire's official delegation to the UN General Assembly. In mid-1994, the credibility of the new Government was further enhanced by its support for French and US initiatives to address the humanitarian crisis presented by the flight to Zaire of more than 1m. Rwandan refugees hoping to escape the violent aftermath of the death of President Habyarimana.

## Government

Under the Constitution promulgated in February 1978 (and subsequently amended), legislative power is held by the 210-member unicameral National Legislative Council, which is elected for five years by universal adult suffrage, and executive power is vested in the President, directly elected for seven years. Between 1970 and 1990 the only authorized political party was the ruling Mouvement populaire de la révolution (MPR). In November 1990 legislation was adopted that provided for a multi-party political system. From August 1991–December 1992 a National Conference was convened, at which delegates drafted a new Constitution. In April 1992 the National Conference declared itself to have sovereign status, and in August it installed a new Government. In December a

453-member High Council of the Republic was established as the supreme interim executive and legislative authority, empowered to amend and adopt the new Constitution and to organize legislative and presidential elections. The legitimacy of the High Council of the Republic was recognized by several foreign states. President Mobutu, however, refused to recognize either the sovereign status of the National Conference or the authority of the High Council of the Republic. In September 1993 and April 1994 the adoption of Transitional Constitution Acts provided a constitutional framework for government, for a 15-month period of transition, leading to the proclamation of a new Republic, scheduled for July 1995. In June 1995, however, a constitutional amendment was approved by the transitional legislature whereby the period of national transition was to be extended for a further two years (see Recent History).

### Defence

Military service is compulsory. In June 1994 the armed forces totalled 28,100, of whom 25,000 were in the army, 1,800 in the air force and 1,300 in the navy. There is also a paramilitary gendarmerie of about 21,000. A civil guard, numbering 10,000, is responsible for security and anti-terrorist operations. Defence expenditure for 1993 was expected to total 590m. new zaires.

### Economic Affairs

In 1990, according to estimates by the World Bank, Zaire's gross national product (GNP), measured at average 1988–90 prices, was US $8,123m., equivalent to $220 per head. During 1985–93, it was estimated, GNP per head decreased, in real terms, at an average annual rate of 0.8%. Over the same period the population increased by an annual average of 3.3%. Zaire's gross domestic product (GDP) increased, in real terms, by an annual average of 1.2% in 1980–90 but decreased by 6.8% per year in 1988–92.

Agriculture (including forestry and fishing) contributed about 45% of GDP in 1993. About 64% of the working population were employed in agriculture at mid-1993. The principal cash crops are coffee (which accounted for 4.2% of export earnings in 1990), palm oil and palm kernels, sugar, tea, cocoa, rubber and cotton. In recent years the Government has sought to revitalize the forestry industry (an estimated 6% of the world's woodlands are located in Zaire). During 1985–93 agricultural production increased by an annual average of 3.1%.

Industry (including mining, manufacturing, power and construction) contributed 30% of GDP in 1988. Some 15.9% of the working population were employed in industry in 1991. During 1980–90 industrial production increased by an annual average of 2.3%.

Mining and metallurgy contributed about 19% of GDP in 1990. Mineral products accounted for about 92% of export earnings in 1993. The most important minerals are copper and cobalt (of which Zaire has 65% of the world's reserves). Manganese, zinc, uranium, tin and gold are also mined. There are rich diamond deposits, and in the late 1980s Zaire was the world's second largest producer of industrial diamonds. (Diamonds became Zaire's principal source of foreign exchange—US$ 532m.—in 1993.) There are also extensive offshore reserves of petroleum (revenue from petroleum accounts for about 20% of total government income). In 1993, however, it was reported that production of copper, cobalt and diamonds had decreased dramatically.

Apart from the smelting and refining of copper and other metals, manufacturing contributed 1.7% of GDP in 1988. The most important sectors are textiles, cement, engineering and agro-industries producing consumer goods. During 1980–90 manufacturing production increased by an annual average of 2.3%. However, the sector was thought to have suffered a considerable reversal in 1993, with production of cement alone declining by some 28% compared with 1992.

Energy is derived principally from hydroelectric power. In the mid-1980s an estimated 98% of electric energy was generated by hydroelectric plants. In 1991 imports of fuels comprised 7.5% of the value of merchandise imports.

In 1990 Zaire recorded a visible trade surplus of US $600m., but there was a deficit of $643m. on the current account of the balance of payments. In 1993 the deficit on the current account of the balance of payments was estimated at US $400m. As the former colonial power, Belgium (which received 40% of Zaire's exports and provided 20% of imports in 1993) is Zaire's principal trading partner. Other important trading partners include the USA, France and the United Kingdom. In the late 1980s the principal exports were mineral products (mainly copper and petroleum) and agricultural products (primarily coffee). The principal imports were manufactured goods, food and raw materials.

In 1993 there was an estimated budgetary deficit of 3,584.6m. new zaires. At the end of 1993 Zaire's external debt totalled US $11,280m., of which $8,769m. was long-term public debt. In 1990, when the external debt totalled $10,270m., the cost of debt-servicing was equivalent to 15.1% of the value of exports of goods and services. Annual inflation averaged 401.2% in 1985–93. Consumer prices increased by an average of 1,987% in 1993.

Zaire maintains economic co-operation agreements with its neighbours, Burundi and Rwanda, through the Economic Community of the Great Lakes Countries (see p. 238). Zaire is also a member of the International Coffee Organization (see p. 235).

Potentially one of Africa's richest states, Zaire has extensive agricultural, mineral and energy resources. However, the country has experienced severe economic decline in recent years, with the result that, in the late 1980s, Zaire's GNP per head was among the lowest in the world. Traditionally, the mainstay of the economy has been the mining sector. However, attempts by the Government to diversify the economy, in particular by developing agricultural exports, have been hampered by the country's poor infrastructure. In the late 1980s and early 1990s Zaire's economic difficulties were exacerbated by burgeoning inflation, which, in turn, precipitated widespread public unrest and industrial action, and by the suspension of financial assistance by the IMF, Belgium, France and the USA (see Recent History). During the early 1990s most foreign investment in Zaire was withdrawn. In February 1994 the World Bank closed its office in the capital, Kinshasa, having declared Zaire 'insolvent'. In October 1993 a new currency, the new zaire, was introduced as part of a programme of monetary reforms aimed at stabilizing the exchange rate and controlling inflation. The changes, however, failed to address Zaire's major economic problems, provoking violent demonstrations throughout the country, and in June 1994 Zaire was suspended from the IMF.

### Social Welfare

There is an Institut National de la Sécurité Sociale, guaranteeing insurance coverage for sickness, pensions and family allowances under an obligatory scheme of national insurance. In the budget for 1989, 5,427.2m. zaires (1.5% of total expenditure by the central Government) was allocated to public health. In 1979 Zaire had 942 hospitals, with a total of 79,244 beds, and there were 1,900 physicians working in the country. In 1984–89, it was estimated, there were, on average, 13,540 Zaireans for every doctor and 1,880 Zaireans for every nurse in the country.

### Education

Primary education, beginning at six years of age and lasting for six years, is officially compulsory. Secondary education, which is not compulsory, begins at 12 years of age and lasts for up to six years, comprising a first cycle of two years and a second of four years. In 1985 the total enrolment at primary and secondary schools was equivalent to 59% of the school-age population (males 73%; females 44%). In 1991 primary enrolment was equivalent to 72% of the school-age population (boys 81%; girls 62%). The comparable ratio for secondary enrolment in 1985 was 23% (boys 32%; girls 13%). There are four universities in Zaire, situated at Kinshasa, Kinshasa/Limete, Kisangani and Lubumbashi. According to estimates by UNESCO, the average rate of adult illiteracy in 1990 was 28.2% (males 16.4%; females 39.3%). In the budget for 1989 a total of 24,291.5m. zaires (6.7% of total expenditure by the central Government) was allocated to education.

### Public Holidays

**1995:** 1 January (New Year's Day), 4 January (Commemoration of the Martyrs of Independence), 1 May (Labour Day), 20 May (Anniversary of the Mouvement populaire de la révolution), 24 June (Anniversary of Zaire currency, Promulgation of the 1967 Constitution and Day of the Fishermen), 30 June (Independence Day), 1 August (Parents' Day), 14 October (Youth Day, birthday of President Mobutu), 27 October (Anniversary of the country's change of name to Zaire), 17 November (Army Day), 24 November (Anniversary of the Second Republic), 25 December (Christmas Day).

ZAIRE

**1996:** 1 January (New Year's Day), 4 January (Commemoration of the Martyrs of Independence), 1 May (Labour Day), 20 May (Anniversary of the Mouvement populaire de la révolution), 24 June (Anniversary of Zaire currency, Promulgation of the 1967 Constitution and Day of the Fishermen), 30 June (Independence Day), 1 August (Parents' Day), 14 October (Youth Day, birthday of President Mobutu), 27 October (Anniversary of the country's change of name to Zaire), 17 November (Army Day), 24 November (Anniversary of the Second Republic), 25 December (Christmas Day).

**Weights and Measures**

The metric system is in force.

# Statistical Survey

Sources (unless otherwise stated): Département de l'Economie Nationale, Kinshasa; Institut National de la Statistique, Office Nationale de la Recherche et du Développement, BP 20, Kinshasa; tel. (12) 31401.

## Area and Population

### AREA, POPULATION AND DENSITY

| | |
|---|---:|
| Area (sq km) | 2,344,885* |
| Population (census result) | |
| 1 July 1984 | |
| Males | 14,593,370 |
| Females | 15,078,037 |
| Total | 29,671,407 |
| Population (official estimates at mid-year) | |
| 1989 | 34,491,000 |
| 1990 | 35,562,000 |
| 1991 | 36,672,000 |
| Density (per sq km) at mid-1991 | 15.6 |

* 905,365 sq miles.

### REGIONS

| | Area (sq km) | Population (31 Dec. 1985)* |
|---|---:|---:|
| Bandundu | 295,658 | 4,644,758 |
| Bas-Zaïre | 53,920 | 2,158,595 |
| Equateur | 403,293 | 3,960,187 |
| Haut-Zaïre | 503,239 | 5,119,750 |
| Kasaï Occidental | 156,967 | 3,465,756 |
| Kasaï Oriental | 168,216 | 2,859,220 |
| Kivu | 256,662 | 5,232,442 |
| Shaba (formerly Katanga) | 496,965 | 4,452,618 |
| Kinshasa (city)† | 9,965 | 2,778,281 |
| **Total** | **2,344,885** | **34,671,607** |

* Provisional.  † Including the commune of Maluku.

Source: Département de l'Administration du Territoire.

### PRINCIPAL TOWNS (population at census of July 1984)

| | |
|---|---:|
| Kinshasa | 2,653,558 |
| Lubumbashi | 543,268 |
| Mbuji-Mayi | 423,363 |
| Kananga | 290,898 |
| Kisangani | 282,650 |
| Kolwezi | 201,382 |
| Likasi | 194,465 |
| Bukavu | 171,064 |
| Matadi | 144,742 |
| Mbandaka | 125,263 |

Source: UN, *Demographic Yearbook*.

### BIRTHS AND DEATHS (UN estimates, annual averages)

| | 1975–80 | 1980–85 | 1985–90 |
|---|---:|---:|---:|
| Birth rate (per 1,000) | 47.8 | 48.3 | 47.8 |
| Death rate (per 1,000) | 17.5 | 16.4 | 15.0 |

**Expectation of life** (UN estimates, years at birth, 1985–90): 51.6 (males 49.8; females 53.3).

Source: UN, *World Population Prospects: The 1992 Revision*.

### ECONOMICALLY ACTIVE POPULATION
(UN estimates, '000 persons, 1991)

| | Males | Females | Total |
|---|---:|---:|---:|
| Agriculture, etc. | 4,484 | 4,537 | 9,021 |
| Industry | 2,121 | 79 | 2,200 |
| Services | 2,371 | 256 | 2,627 |
| **Total** | **8,976** | **4,872** | **13,848** |

Source: UN Economic Commission for Africa, *African Statistical Yearbook*.

**Mid-1993** (estimates in '000): Agriculture, etc. 9,312; Total 14,510 (Source: FAO, *Production Yearbook*).

## Agriculture

### PRINCIPAL CROPS ('000 metric tons)

| | 1991 | 1992 | 1993 |
|---|---:|---:|---:|
| Rice (paddy) | 418 | 440 | 458 |
| Maize | 1,030 | 1,052 | 1,201* |
| Millet | 32 | 32 | 32† |
| Sorghum | 51 | 53 | 53† |
| Potatoes | 34 | 34† | 35† |
| Sweet potatoes | 381 | 382† | 385† |
| Cassava (Manioc) | 19,500 | 20,210 | 20,835 |
| Yams† | 300 | 310 | 315 |
| Taro (Coco yam) | 39 | 40 | 41 |
| Dry beans | 122 | 123† | 123† |
| Dry peas† | 62 | 63 | 64 |
| Groundnuts (in shell) | 550 | 575 | 604 |
| Cottonseed† | 50 | 50 | 50 |
| Palm kernels† | 72 | 72 | 72 |
| Cabbages† | 28 | 29 | 30 |
| Tomatoes | 41 | 41† | 41† |
| Onions (dry)† | 31 | 31 | 32 |
| Pumpkins† | 42 | 43 | 44 |
| Sugar cane | 1,699 | 1,400† | 1,400† |
| Oranges† | 155 | 156 | 156 |
| Grapefruit† | 14 | 14 | 14 |
| Avocados† | 46 | 47 | 47 |
| Mangoes† | 210 | 212 | 212 |
| Pineapples† | 145 | 145 | 145 |
| Bananas | 406 | 406† | 406† |
| Plantains | 2,160 | 2,224 | 2,291 |
| Papayas† | 208 | 210 | 210 |
| Coffee (green)* | 102 | 98 | 78 |
| Cocoa beans | 7 | 7† | 7† |
| Tea (made) | 3 | 3† | 3† |
| Tobacco (leaves) | 3 | 3† | 3† |
| Cotton (lint)† | 26 | 26 | 26 |
| Natural rubber (dry weight) | 11 | 8* | 5* |

* Unofficial figure(s).  † FAO estimate(s).

Source: FAO, *Production Yearbook*.

ZAIRE

**LIVESTOCK** ('000 head, year ending September)

|  | 1991 | 1992* | 1993* |
|---|---|---|---|
| Cattle | 1,586 | 1,600 | 1,650 |
| Sheep | 974 | 980 | 985 |
| Goats | 4,109 | 4,110 | 4,120 |
| Pigs | 1,118 | 1,120 | 1,130 |

Poultry (million): 34 in 1991; 34* in 1992; 34* in 1993.

* FAO estimate(s).

Source: FAO, *Production Yearbook*.

**LIVESTOCK PRODUCTS** (FAO estimates, '000 metric tons)

|  | 1991 | 1992 | 1993 |
|---|---|---|---|
| Cows' milk | 8 | 8 | 8 |
| Beef and veal | 28 | 29 | 30 |
| Mutton and lamb | 3 | 3 | 3 |
| Goat meat | 10 | 10 | 10 |
| Pig meat | 40 | 40 | 40 |
| Poultry meat | 29 | 30 | 30 |
| Other meat | 122 | 123 | 126 |
| Hen eggs | 8.2 | 8.3 | 8.4 |

Source: FAO, *Production Yearbook*.

## Forestry

**ROUNDWOOD REMOVALS** ('000 cubic metres)

|  | 1990 | 1991 | 1992 |
|---|---|---|---|
| Sawlogs, veneer logs and logs for sleepers | 465 | 391 | 391* |
| Other industrial wood* | 2,587 | 2,672 | 2,759 |
| Fuel wood* | 37,766 | 38,918 | 40,093 |
| **Total** | 40,818 | 41,981 | 43,243* |

**Sawnwood production** ('000 cubic metres, incl. railway sleepers): 117 in 1990; 105 in 1991; 105* in 1992.

* FAO estimate(s).

Source: FAO, *Yearbook of Forest Products*.

## Fishing

(FAO estimates, '000 metric tons, live weight)

|  | 1990 | 1991 | 1992 |
|---|---|---|---|
| Inland waters | 160.0 | 158.0 | 148.0 |
| Atlantic Ocean | 2.0 | 2.0 | 2.0 |
| **Total catch** | 162.0 | 160.0 | 150.0 |

Source: FAO, *Yearbook of Fishery Statistics*.

## Mining

(metric tons, unless otherwise indicated)

|  | 1990 | 1991 | 1992 |
|---|---|---|---|
| Copper ore* | 355,500 | 250,000 | 144,000 |
| Tin concentrates*† | 1,600 | 1,800 | n.a. |
| Coal‡ | 126,000 | 128,000 | 128,000 |
| Zinc concentrates*§ | 61,800 | 42,400 | 36,000‡ |
| Cobalt ore*‖ | 19,000 | 9,900 | n.a. |
| Tungsten ore*‖ | 14 | 13 | 15‡ |
| Industrial diamonds ('000 carats)‖ | 16,513 | 14,814 | 12,000 |
| Gem diamonds ('000 carats)‖ | 2,914 | 3,000 | 3,000 |
| Silver*§ | 84 | 50 | 35 |
| Gold (kilograms)*‖ | 4,236 | 4,500 | 7,000 |
| Crude petroleum ('000 metric tons)‡ | 1,410 | 1,372 | 1,375 |

* Figures relate to metal content.
† Data from UNCTAD, *International Tin Statistics* (Geneva).
‡ Provisional or estimated figure(s).
§ Data from Metallgesellschaft Aktiengesellschaft (Frankfurt).
‖ Data from the US Bureau of Mines.

Source: UN, *Industrial Statistics Yearbook*.

## Industry

**SELECTED PRODUCTS**
('000 metric tons, unless otherwise indicated)

|  | 1990 | 1991 | 1992 |
|---|---|---|---|
| Raw sugar* | 85 | 94 | 78 |
| Cigarettes (million)† | 5,200 | 5,200 | 5,200 |
| Jet fuels | 15 | 17 | 15 |
| Motor spirit (petrol) | 39 | 40 | 42 |
| Kerosene | 37 | 38 | 40 |
| Distillate fuel oils | 75 | 72 | 73 |
| Residual fuel oils | 168 | 172 | 175 |
| Quicklime‡ | 100 | 83 | 64 |
| Cement‡ | 460 | 449 | n.a. |
| Copper—unwrought: | | | |
|   Smelter‡ | 355.8 | 237.5§ | n.a. |
|   Refined‡ | 140.9 | 104.0 | 57.0§ |
| Zinc—unwrought† | 38.2 | n.a. | n.a. |
| Electric energy (million kWh) | 6,155 | 6,168 | 6,180 |

* Data from the FAO.
† Estimates from US Department of Agriculture.
‡ Data from the US Bureau of Mines.
§ Provisional or estimated figure.

Source: UN, *Industrial Statistics Yearbook*.

## Finance

**CURRENCY AND EXCHANGE RATES**

**Monetary Units**
    100 new makuta (singular: likuta) = 1 new zaire (NZ).

**Sterling and Dollar Equivalents** (31 December 1994)
    £1 sterling = 5,084.6 new zaires;
    US $1 = 3,250.0 new zaires;
    10,000 new zaires = £1.967 = $3,077.

**Average Exchange Rate** (old zaires per US $)
    1990    719
    1991   15,587
    1992  645,549

Note: The new zaire (NZ), equivalent to 3m. old zaires, was introduced in October 1993. The average exchange rate (new zaires per US $) was: 2.51 in 1993; 1,194.1 in 1994.

## ZAIRE

### BUDGET ('000 million old zaires)

| Revenue* | 1989 | 1990 | 1991 |
|---|---|---|---|
| Taxation | 374 | 632 | 6,268 |
| Taxes on income, profits, etc. | 113 | 180 | 2,105 |
| Domestic taxes on goods and services | 65 | 124 | 1,071 |
| Import duties | 112 | 285 | 1,877 |
| Export duties | 73 | 26 | 293 |
| Other taxes | 11 | 17 | 922 |
| Non-tax revenue | 20 | 46 | 786 |
| **Total** | 394 | 678 | 7,054 |

* Excluding grants from abroad ('000 million old zaires): 74 in 1989; 145 in 1990; 1,586 in 1991.

| Expenditure | 1989 | 1990 | 1991 |
|---|---|---|---|
| Current expenditure | 351 | 1,054 | 25,368 |
| Expenditure on goods and services | 282 | 915 | 23,240 |
| Interest payments | 46 | 83 | 589 |
| Subsidies and other current transfers | 23 | 56 | 1,539 |
| Capital expenditure | 118 | 206 | 3,617 |
| **Total** | 469 | 1,260 | 28,985 |

Source: IMF, *Government Finance Statistics Yearbook*.

**Revenue** (revised figures, million new zaires, excluding grants): 2.4 in 1991; 55.8 in 1992; 1,104.3 in 1993.

**Expenditure** (revised figures, million new zaires): 9.7 in 1991; 269.0 in 1992; 4,688.9 in 1993.

(Source: IMF, *International Financial Statistics*.)

### BANK OF ZAIRE RESERVES (US $ million at 31 December)

| | 1992 | 1993 | 1994 |
|---|---|---|---|
| Gold | 9.32 | 8.59 | 10.71 |
| Foreign exchange | 156.73 | 46.20 | 120.69 |
| **Total** | 166.05 | 54.79 | 131.40 |

Source: IMF, *International Financial Statistics*.

### MONEY SUPPLY (million new zaires at 31 December)

| | 1991 | 1992 | 1993 |
|---|---|---|---|
| Currency outside banks | 3.6 | 121 | 4,693 |
| Demand deposits at deposit money banks | 2.0 | 126 | 1,618 |
| **Total money** (incl. others) | 6.0 | 254 | 6,495 |

**1994:** Demand deposits at deposit money banks 92,000m. new zaires.
Source: IMF, *International Financial Statistics*.

### CONSUMER PRICE INDEX (base: 1990 = 0.01)

| | 1992 | 1993 | 1994 |
|---|---|---|---|
| All items | 10 | 199 | 47,501 |

Source: IMF, *International Financial Statistics*.

### NATIONAL ACCOUNTS

**Expenditure on the Gross Domestic Product**
('000 new zaires at current prices)

| | 1990 | 1991 | 1992 |
|---|---|---|---|
| Government final consumption expenditure | 258 | 6,282 | 383,801 |
| Private final consumption expenditure | 1,600 | 37,688 | 1,214,393 |
| Increase in stocks | −85 | −245 | −3,666 |
| Gross fixed capital formation | 288 | 2,878 | 125,484 |
| **Total domestic expenditure** | 2,248* | 47,323* | 1,720,012 |
| Exports of goods and services | 621 | 10,323 | 381,128 |
| *Less* Imports of goods and services | 630 | 10,438 | 335,683 |
| **GDP in purchasers' values** | 2,239 | 47,208 | 1,765,457 |

* Including adjustment.
Source: IMF, *International Financial Statistics*.

**Gross Domestic Product by Economic Activity**
(million old zaires at current prices)

| | 1986 | 1987 | 1988 |
|---|---|---|---|
| Monetary sector: | | | |
| Agriculture | 25,566.6 | 43,852.8 | 59,348.9 |
| Mining and metallurgy | 66,404.5 | 78,792.8 | 131,413.9 |
| Manufacturing | 3,452.7 | 4,409.7 | 9,977.0 |
| Electricity and water | 110.6 | 179.4 | 24,166.2 |
| Building and public works | 6,432.1 | 12,041.0 | 475.2 |
| Transport and telecommunications | 1,504.8 | 2,528.9 | 3,378.0 |
| Commerce | 33,309.5 | 58,076.2 | 108,300.1 |
| Services | 27,795.6 | 53,460.0 | 139,478.2 |
| Imputed bank service charge | −591.2 | −672.1 | −739.1 |
| **Sub-total** (goods and services) | 163,958.2 | 252,668.7 | 475,798.4 |
| Import taxes and duties | 4,506.2 | 9,665.4 | 31,616.5 |
| **Total monetary product** (at market prices) | 168,464.4 | 262,334.1 | 507,414.9 |
| Non-monetary sector: | | | |
| Agriculture | 31,837.8 | 58,591.7 | 103,323.5 |
| Construction | 3,113.9 | 6,020.5 | 12,083.1 |
| **Gross domestic product** | 203,416.1 | 326,946.3 | 622,821.5 |

Source: Banque du Zaïre, *Rapport Annuel*.

**National Income**
(million old zaires at current prices, monetary sector only)

| | 1986 | 1987 | 1988 |
|---|---|---|---|
| Gross domestic product | 168,464.4 | 262,334.1 | 507,414.9 |
| *Less:* Net transfers abroad of interest and investment income | 30,797.6 | 36,269.7 | 50,775.3 |
| Net transfers abroad of private income | 5,410.1 | 6,382.5 | 18,648.6 |
| Gross national product | 132,256.7 | 219,681.9 | 437,991.0 |
| *Less:* Indirect taxation, net of subsidies | 22,993.8 | 39,763.8 | 86,831.5 |
| Consumption of fixed capital | 8,573.7 | 12,392.4 | 17,797.1 |
| National income at factor cost | 100,689.2 | 167,525.7 | 333,362.4 |

Source: Banque du Zaïre, *Rapport Annuel*.

ZAIRE
Statistical Survey

## BALANCE OF PAYMENTS (US $ million)

|  | 1988 | 1989 | 1990 |
|---|---|---|---|
| Merchandise exports f.o.b. | 2,178 | 2,201 | 2,138 |
| Merchandise imports f.o.b. | -1,645 | -1,683 | -1,539 |
| **Trade balance** | 534 | 518 | 600 |
| Exports of services | 149 | 137 | 157 |
| Imports of services | -895 | -922 | -908 |
| Other income received | 36 | 28 | 14 |
| Other income paid | -563 | -540 | -642 |
| Private unrequited transfers (net) | -67 | -109 | -81 |
| Official unrequited transfers (net) | 226 | 276 | 217 |
| **Current balance** | -581 | -611 | -643 |
| Capital (net) | -8 | -60 | -222 |
| Net errors and omissions | -134 | 113 | 105 |
| **Overall balance** | -723 | -558 | -761 |

Source: IMF, *International Financial Statistics*.

## External Trade

### PRINCIPAL COMMODITIES (UN estimates, million old zaires)

| Imports c.i.f. | 1989 | 1990 | 1991 |
|---|---|---|---|
| Food and live animals | 63,380 | 121,824 | 2,172,956 |
| Beverages and tobacco | 3,436 | 6,605 | 117,812 |
| Crude materials (inedible) except fuels | 9,545 | 18,347 | 327,252 |
| Mineral fuels, lubricants, etc. | 24,436 | 46,968 | 837,761 |
| Chemicals | 33,217 | 63,848 | 1,138,847 |
| Basic manufactures | 68,343 | 131,365 | 2,343,137 |
| Machinery and transport equipment | 102,706 | 197,414 | 3,521,243 |
| Miscellaneous manufactured articles | 16,418 | 31,557 | 562,877 |
| Other commodities and transactions | 2,673 | 5,137 | 91,628 |
| **Total** | 324,154 | 623,066 | 11,113,531 |

| Exports f.o.b. | 1989 | 1990 | 1991 |
|---|---|---|---|
| Food and live animals | 93,541 | 148,201 | 2,535,635 |
| Beverages and tobacco | 5,071 | 8,035 | 137,474 |
| Crude materials (inedible) except fuels | 14,087 | 22,319 | 381,865 |
| Mineral fuels, lubricants, etc. | 36,064 | 57,138 | 977,599 |
| Chemicals | 49,024 | 77,672 | 1,328,924 |
| Basic manufactures | 100,866 | 159,807 | 2,734,207 |
| Machinery and transport equipment | 151,581 | 240,157 | 4,108,950 |
| Miscellaneous manufactured articles | 24,230 | 38,389 | 656,814 |
| Other commodities and transactions | 3,944 | 6,249 | 106,917 |
| **Total** | 478,409 | 757,967 | 12,968,384 |

Source: UN Economic Commission for Africa, *African Statistical Yearbook*.

**Total imports c.i.f.** (million new zaires): 4 in 1991; 90 in 1992; 936 in 1993.
**Total exports** (million new zaires): 4 in 1991; 92 in 1992; 927 in 1993.
(Source: IMF, *International Financial Statistics*.)

### SELECTED TRADING PARTNERS (US $'000)

| Imports c.i.f. | 1982 | 1984* | 1985 |
|---|---|---|---|
| Belgium/Luxembourg | 156,600 | 116,994 | 176,920 |
| Brazil | n.a. | 87,031 | 150,514 |
| France | 53,400 | 52,293 | 88,590 |
| Japan | 7,400 | 20,704 | 39,431 |
| Netherlands | 7,700 | 31,152 | 41,791 |
| United Kingdom | 29,500 | 24,339 | 44,259 |
| USA | 60,800 | 73,600 | 71,302 |
| **Total** (incl. others) | 475,600 | 658,741 | 997,067 |

* Figures for 1983 are not available.

| Exports f.o.b. | 1981 | 1982 | 1985* |
|---|---|---|---|
| Belgium/Luxembourg | 521,300 | 385,100 | 165,784 |
| France | 25,500 | 68,100 | 42,018 |
| Italy | 400 | 200 | 57,676 |
| Netherlands | 2,100 | 1,500 | 44,579 |
| Switzerland | 71,500 | 60,500 | 32,971 |
| United Kingdom | 13,700 | 10,700 | 21,444 |
| USA | 10,900 | 20,100 | 228,391 |
| **Total** (incl. others) | 685,200 | 585,700 | 796,905 |

* Figures for 1983 and 1984 are not available.
Source: UN, *International Trade Statistics Yearbook*.

## Transport

### RAILWAYS (Total traffic, million)*

|  | 1986 | 1988† | 1990† |
|---|---|---|---|
| Passenger-km | 330 | 200 | 260 |
| Freight (net ton-km) | 1,785 | 1,901 | 1,732 |

* Figures are for services operated by the Société Nationale des Chemins de Fer Zaïrois (SNCZ), which controls 4,772 km of railway line out of the country's total facility of 5,252 km.
† Figures for 1987 and 1989 are not available.
Source: *Railway Directory and Year Book*.

### ROAD TRAFFIC (motor vehicles in use at 31 December)

|  | 1991 | 1992 | 1993 |
|---|---|---|---|
| Passenger cars | 569,285 | 665,853 | 693,974 |
| **Total vehicles** | 965,475 | 1,109,432 | 1,156,624 |

Source: IRF, *World Road Statistics*.

### INTERNATIONAL SEA-BORNE SHIPPING
(estimated freight traffic, '000 metric tons)

|  | 1988 | 1989 | 1990 |
|---|---|---|---|
| Goods loaded | 2,500 | 2,440 | 2,395 |
| Goods unloaded | 1,400 | 1,483 | 1,453 |

Source: UN, *Monthly Bulletin of Statistics*.

### CIVIL AVIATION (traffic on scheduled services)

|  | 1990 | 1991 | 1992 |
|---|---|---|---|
| Kilometres flown (million) | 7 | 5 | 4 |
| Passengers carried ('000) | 207 | 150 | 116 |
| Passenger-km (million) | 500 | 384 | 295 |
| Total ton-km (million) | 102 | 68 | 56 |

Source: UN, *Statistical Yearbook*.

## Tourism

|  | 1990 | 1991 | 1992 |
|---|---|---|---|
| Tourist arrivals ('000) | 55 | 33 | 22 |
| Tourist receipts (US $ million) | 7 | 7 | 7 |

Source: UN, *Statistical Yearbook*.

## Communications Media

|  | 1990 | 1991 | 1992 |
|---|---|---|---|
| Radio receivers ('000 in use) | 3,650 | 3,740 | 3,870 |
| Television receivers ('000 in use) | 40 | 41 | 55 |
| Telephones ('000 in use) | 33 | 34 | n.a. |
| Daily newspapers | 5 | n.a. | 9 |

Sources: UNESCO, *Statistical Yearbook*; UN Economic Commission for Africa, *African Statistical Yearbook*.

## Education

|  | Teachers 1986 | Teachers 1987 | Pupils 1986 | Pupils 1987 |
|---|---|---|---|---|
| Primary* | 113,468 | n.a. | 4,156,029 | 4,356,516 |
| Secondary† | 49,153 | n.a. | 983,334 | 1,066,351 |
| Higher | 3,280 | 3,506 | 45,731 | 52,800 |

* The number of primary schools was 10,757 in 1986 and 10,819 in 1987.
† In 1987 there were 507,944 pupils enrolled in general secondary schools, 266,664 pupils enrolled at teacher training institutions and 291,743 pupils attending vocational secondary schools.

**1988:** Higher education teachers 3,873; Higher education pupils 61,422.
**1992:** Primary school pupils 4,870,933. (Primary schools 12,658.)

Source: UNESCO, *Statistical Yearbook*.

# Directory

## The Constitution

From August 1991–December 1992 a National Conference was convened, at which delegates drafted a new Constitution (to be approved by a national referendum). In April 1992 the National Conference declared itself to have sovereign status, and in August 1992 it installed a new Government. In December 1992 a 453-member High Council of the Republic was established as the supreme interim executive and legislative authority, empowered to amend and adopt the new Constitution and to organize legislative and presidential elections. The legitimacy of the High Council of the Republic was recognized by several foreign states. Nevertheless, President Mobutu, who retained control of the armed forces, refused to recognize either the sovereign status of the National Conference or the authority of the High Council of the Republic. In October 1992 Mobutu, abiding by the 1978 Constitution (see below), reconvened the National Legislative Council (which the National Conference had dissolved) and entrusted it to draft a rival new constitution. In September 1993 and April 1994 the adoption of Transitional Constitution Acts provided a constitutional framework for a 15-month transitional period (subject to approval by constitutional referendum) leading to the proclamation of a new Republic in 1995. National transitional institutions would include the President of the Republic, the unicameral High Council of the Republic-Parliament of Transition (HCR-PT—inaugurated in January 1994) and the transitional Government, to be accountable to the HCR-PT. Presidential and legislative elections were to be conducted during 1995. In June 1995, however, a constitutional amendment was approved by the HCR-PT whereby the period of national transition was to be extended for a further two years.

The provisions below relate to the Constitution promulgated on 15 February 1978 (and subsequently amended):

### HEAD OF STATE

The President of the Republic is elected for a seven-year term, renewable once only. Candidates must be natives of Zaire and more than 40 years of age.

### EXECUTIVE POWER

The programme and decisions of the National Executive Council are carried out by the State Commissioners who are heads of their departments. The National Executive Council is dissolved at the end of each presidential term, though it continues to function until a new National Executive Council is formed. The members of the National Executive Council are appointed or dismissed by the President, on the recommendation of the First State Commissioner (Prime Minister).

### LEGISLATURE

The legislature consists of a single chamber, the National Legislative Council; its members are designated People's Commissioners, and are elected for five years by direct, universal suffrage with a secret ballot. Candidates must be natives of Zaire and aged over 25. The Bureau of the National Legislative Council is elected for the duration of the legislature, and consists of the President, two Vice-Presidents and two Secretaries. The members of the National Executive Council have the right and, if required, the obligation to attend the meetings of the National Legislative Council. It meets twice yearly, from April to July and from October to January.

### POLITICAL PARTIES

In November 1990 legislation was adopted to provide for the existence of a multi-party political system.

### REGIONAL GOVERNMENTS

Local government in each region is administered by a regional commissioner and six councillors. Regional commissioners are appointed and dismissed by the President.

## The Government

### HEAD OF STATE

**President:** Marshal MOBUTU SESE SEKO KUKU NGBENDU WA ZA BANGA (assumed power 24 November 1965; elected by popular vote 31 October–1 November 1970, re-elected 28–29 July 1984).

The following Transitional Government was announced by the Office of the President on 6 July 1994. (Léon Kengo Wa Dondo was elected as Prime Minister by the High Council of the Republic-Parliament of Transition in June 1994.)

### TRANSITIONAL GOVERNMENT
(June 1995)

**Prime Minister:** LÉON KENGO WA DONDO.

**Deputy Prime Minister with responsibility for Institutional Reforms, Minister of Justice and Keeper of the Seals:** GÉRARD KAMANDA WA KAMANDA.

**Deputy Prime Minister and Minister of the Interior:** GUSTAVE MALUMBA M'BANGULA.

**Deputy Prime Minister and Minister of International Co-operation:** MOZAGBA MBOKA.

**Deputy Prime Minister and Minister of National Defence:** Adm. MAVUA MUDIMA.

**Minister of Agriculture:** WIVINE N'GUZ NDLANDU.

**Minister of Arts and Culture:** FAUTIN LUKONZOLA MUGNUNGWA.

**Minister of Budget:** BAHATI LUKUEBO.

**Minister of the Civil Service:** BOLEONGUE MEKESOMBO.

**Minister of Energy:** KISANGA KABONGELO.

**Minister of the Environment, Nature Conservation and Tourism:** JOSEPH RUHANA MIRINDI

**Minister of External Trade:** JIBI N'GOY.

ZAIRE                                                                                                                    Directory

**Minister of Finance:** PAY-PAY WA KASIGE.
**Minister of Foreign Affairs:** LUNDA BULULU.
**Minister of Health and the Family:** MBUMB MUSSONG.
**Minister of Higher and University Education and Scientific Research:** KISSIMBA N'GOY.
**Minister of Labour and Social Security:** OMBA PENE DJUNGA.
**Minister of Land Affairs:** MANGUADA GIFUDI.
**Minister of Mines:** MUTOMBO BAKAFWA N'SENDA.
**Minister of National Economy, Industry and Small Businesses:** KATANGA MUKMADIYA MUTUMBA.
**Minister of Planning:** KIAKWAMA KIA KIZIKI.
**Minister of Posts, Telephones and Telecommunications:** PIERRE LUMBI OKONGO.
**Minister of Press and Information:** MASSEGABIO ZANZU.
**Minister of Primary, Secondary and Vocational Education:** SEKIUMOYO WA MANGANGU.
**Minister of Public Works, Territorial Development, Town Planning and Housing:** MUANDO SIMBA.
**Minister of Social Affairs:** FLORENTINE SOKI FUANI EYENGA.
**Minister of Transport and Communications:** JOSEPH N'SINGA UDJU.
**Minister of Youth, Sports and Leisure:** BOFASSA NJEMA.
**Minister without Portfolio:** ASEYA MINDRE.

### MINISTRIES

**Office of the President:** Mont Ngaliema, Kinshasa; tel. (12) 31312; telex 21368.
**Office of the Prime Minister:** Hôtel du Conseil Exécutif, ave des 3Z, Kinshasa-Gombe; tel. (12) 30892.
**Ministry of Agriculture:** BP 8722, Kinshasa-Gombe; tel. (12) 31821.
**Ministry of Arts and Culture:** BP 8541, Kinshasa 1; tel. (12) 31005.
**Ministry of the Environment, Nature Conservation and Tourism:** 15 ave de la Clinique, BP 1248, Kinshasa; tel. (12) 31252.
**Ministry of Finance:** blvd du 30 juin, BP 12997, Kinshasa-Gombe; tel. (12) 31197; telex 21161.
**Ministry of Foreign Affairs and International Co-operation:** BP 7100, Kinshasa-Gombe; tel. (12) 32450; telex 21364.
**Ministry of Health and the Family:** BP 3088, Kinshasa-Gombe; tel. (12) 31750.
**Ministry of Higher and University Education and Scientific Research:** ave Colonel Tshatshi, Kinshasa-Gombe; tel. (12) 32074; telex 21394.
**Ministry of Justice:** BP 3137, Kinshasa-Gombe; tel. (12) 32432.
**Ministry of Labour and Social Security:** blvd du 30 juin, Kinshasa-Gombe; tel. (12) 26727.
**Ministry of National Economy, Industry and Small Businesses:** Immeuble ONATRA, BP 8500, Kinshasa-Gombe; tel. (12) 22945; telex 21232.
**Ministry of Planning:** BP 9378, Kinshasa 1; tel. (12) 31346; telex 21781.
**Ministry of Posts, Telephones and Telecommunications:** BP 800, Kinshasa-Gombe; tel. (12) 24854; telex 21403.
**Ministry of Press and Information:** BP 3171, Kinshasa; tel. (12) 23171.
**Ministry of Primary, Secondary and Vocational Education:** ave des Ambassadeurs, BP 32, Kinshasa-Gombe; tel. (12) 30098; telex 21460.
**Ministry of Public Works, Territorial Development, Town Planning and Housing:** BP 26, Kinshasa-Gombe; tel. (12) 30578.
**Ministry of Transport and Communications:** Immeuble ONATRA, BP 3304, Kinshasa-Gombe; tel. (12) 23660; telex 21404.

### NATIONAL SECURITY COUNCIL

The National Security Council (NSC) comprises the First State Commissioner, the State Commissioners for Foreign Affairs, Defence, Justice, the Administrators-General of the National Research and Investigations Centre (CNRI) and the National Intelligence Service (SNI), the President's special adviser on security matters, and the Chiefs of Staff of the Zairean armed forces and the national Gendarmerie. A Security Committee and a Secretariat were established within the NSC in May 1982.

## President

At the presidential election which took place on 28 and 29 July 1984, President Mobutu Sese Seko, the sole candidate, obtained 14,885,977 (99.16%) of the total of 15,012,078 votes cast. President Mobutu remained in office beyond the expiry of his presidential mandate in December 1991.

## Legislature

### HIGH COUNCIL OF THE REPUBLIC-PARLIAMENT OF TRANSITION

A National Conference, convened from August 1991–December 1992, legislated to abolish the former National Legislative Council and replace it with a 453-member High Council of the Republic (HCR), an action which President Mobutu refused to sanction. In September 1993, adoption of a constitutional text for transition provided for the installation of the High Council of the Republic-Parliament of Transition (HCR-PT), a unicameral transitional parliament formed by the merger of the former National Legislative Council and the HCR, and inaugurated in January 1994 for a 15-month period. A constitutional amendment, adopted by the legislature in June 1995, extended the mandate of the HCR-PT for a further two years (see Recent History).

**President of the High Council of the Republic-Parliament of Transition:** ANZULINI BEMBE (acting).

## Regional Governments

Local government in each region is administered by a regional commissioner and six councillors. In October 1982 the first of a number of regional assemblies, with limited powers, was installed in Kinshasa.

**Governor of Kinshasa:** BERNADIN MUNGUL DIAKA.

| Region | Commissioners |
|---|---|
| Bandundu | Brig.-Gen. AMELA LOTI BAGATI |
| Bas-Zaïre | THSALA MWANA |
| Equateur | SAMPASSA KAWETA MILOMBE, KISANGA KABONGELO |
| Haut-Zaïre | NOMBEYA BOSONGO (suspended Oct. 1993) |
| Kasaï Occidental | TSHIBUABUA KAPIA KALUBI |
| Kasaï Oriental | BACHALA KAMTUA MILANDU |
| Kivu* | NDALA KASHALA, KAKULE MBAKE |
| Shaba | GABRIEL KYUNGU WA KUMWANZA (suspended in May 1995 for three-month period) |

* Divided into three regions in May 1988.

## Political Organizations

A multi-party political system was introduced in November 1990; previously the Mouvement populaire de la révolution had been the sole legal political organization. Prominent organizations include the following:

**Alliance des nationalistes africains (ANA):** Kinshasa; f. 1994; agricultural manifesto; Chair. THÉOPHANE KINGOMBO MULULA.
**Alliance des republicains pour le développement et le progrès (ARDP):** Kinshasa; f. 1994; Chair. JOHN MILALA MBONO-MBUE; Sec.-Gen. MATAMO KUAKA.
**Fédération des libéraux du Zaire (FLZ):** Kinshasa; f. 1994; association of 10 liberal political groups.
**Forces politiques du conclave (FPC):** Kinshasa; f. 1993; alliance of pro-Mobutu groups, including the UFERI, led by MPR.
**Front Lumumba pour l'unité et la paix en afrique (FLUPA):** Kinshasa; f. 1963, recognized 1994; supports aims of former Prime Minister, Patrice Lumumba.
**Katanga Gendarmes:** based in Angola; guerrilla group which aims to win independence for the province of Shaba (formerly Katanga).
**Mouvement national du Congo-Lumumba (MNC-Lumumba):** Kinshasa; f. 1994; coalition of seven parties, including the Parti lumumbiste unifié (PALU), supporting the aims of the fmr Prime Minister, Patrice Lumumba; Co-ordinating Cttee PASCAL TABU, MBALO MEKA, OTOKO OKITASOMBO.
**Mouvement populaire de la révolution (MPR):** Palais du Peuple, angle ave des Huileries et ave Kasa-Vubu, Kinshasa; tel. (12) 22541; f. 1967; sole legal political party until Nov. 1990; advocates national unity and African socialism; opposes tribalism; Chair. Marshal MOBUTU SESE SEKO; Sec.-Gen. KITHIMA BIN RAMAZANI.
**Parti démocrate et social chrétien (PDSC):** f. 1990; moderate; Pres. JOSEPH ILÉO NSONGO AMBA.
**Parti démocrate et social chrétien national (PDSCN):** Kinshasa; f. 1994; moderate.

**Parti des nationalistes pour le développement integral (PANADI):** Kinshasa; f. 1994; Leader BALTAZAR HOUNGANGERA.

**Parti de la révolution populaire (PRP):** Brussels, Belgium; maintains guerrilla presence in southern Kivu region; Leader LAURENT KABILA.

**Parti ouvrier et paysan du Congo (POP):** f. 1986; Marxist-Leninist.

**Rassemblement des démocrates libéraux:** Kinshasa; Leader MWAMBA MULANDA.

**Sacré alliance pour le dialogue (SAD):** Kinshasa; f. 1993; alliance of 10 political groups; Leader Gen. NATHANIEL MBUMBA.

**Union des fédéralistes et républicains indépendants (UFERI):** Kinshasa; f. 1990; separatist; Pres. NGUZA KARL-I-BOND.

**Union pour la démocratie et le progrès social (UDPS):** Kinshasa; f. 1982; Leader ETIENNE TSHISEKEDI WA MULUMBA.

**Union pour la démocratie et le progrès social national:** Kinshasa; f. 1994; Chair. CHARLES DEOUNKIN ANDEL.

**Union pour la république et la démocratie (URD):** Kinshasa; moderate party expelled from USOR in May 1994; Chair. GÉRARD KAMANDA WA KAMANDA.

**Union sacrée de l'opposition radicale (USOR):** Kinshasa; f. July 1991; comprises c. 130 movements and factions opposed to Pres. Mobutu; led by the UDPS. The existence, within the transitional legislature of an umbrella radical opposition grouping, known as the **Union sacrée de l'opposition radicale et ses alliés (USORAL),** was announced in late 1994.

**Union sacrée rénovée:** Kinshasa; f. 1993 by several ministers in Govt of Nat. Salvation; Leader KIRO KIMATE.

## Diplomatic Representation

### EMBASSIES IN ZAIRE

**Algeria:** 50/52 ave Colonel Ebeya, BP 12798, Kinshasa; tel. (12) 22470; Chargé d'affaires a.i.: HOCINE MEGHLAOUI.

**Angola:** 4413–4429 blvd du 30 juin, BP 8625, Kinshasa; tel. (12) 32415; Ambassador: MIGUEL GASPARD NETO.

**Argentina:** 181 blvd du 30 juin, BP 16798, Kinshasa; tel. (12) 25485; Ambassador: WERNER ROBERTO JUSTO BURGHARDT.

**Austria:** 39 ave Lubefu, BP 16399, Kinshasa-Gombe; tel. (12) 22150; telex 21310; Ambassador: Dr HANS KOGLER.

**Belgium:** Immeuble Le Cinquantenaire, place du 27 octobre, BP 899, Kinshasa; tel. (12) 20110; telex 21114; fax 22120; Ambassador: JOHAN VAN DESSEL.

**Benin:** 3990 ave des Cliniques, BP 3265, Kinshasa-Gombe; tel. (12) 33156; Ambassador: PIERRE DÉSIRÉ SADELER.

**Brazil:** 190 ave Basoko, BP 13296, Kinshasa; tel. (12) 21781; telex 21515; Ambassador: AYRTON G. DIEGUEZ.

**Burundi:** 17 ave de la Gombe, BP 1483, Kinshasa; tel. (12) 31588; telex 21655; Ambassador: LONGIN KANUMA.

**Cameroon:** 171 blvd du 30 juin, BP 10998, Kinshasa; tel. (12) 34787; Chargé d'affaires a.i.: DOMINIQUE AWONO ESSAMA.

**Canada:** BP 8341, Kinshasa I; tel. (12) 21801; telex 21303; Ambassador: CLAUDE LAVERDURE.

**Central African Republic:** 11 ave Pumbu, BP 7769, Kinshasa; tel. (12) 30417; Ambassador: J.-G. MAMADOU.

**Chad:** 67–69 ave du Cercle, BP 9097, Kinshasa; tel. (12) 22358; Ambassador: MAITINE DJOUMBE.

**China, People's Republic:** 49 ave du Commerce, BP 9098, Kinshasa; tel. 23972; Ambassador: AN GUOZHENG.

**Congo:** 179 blvd du 30 juin, BP 9516, Kinshasa; tel. (12) 30220; Ambassador: ALEXIS OKIO.

**Côte d'Ivoire:** 68 ave de la Justice, BP 9197, Kinshasa; tel. (12) 30440; telex 21214; Ambassador: GASTON ALLOUKO FIANKAN.

**Cuba:** 4660 ave Cateam, BP 10699, Kinshasa; telex 21158; Ambassador: ENRIQUE MONTERO.

**Czech Republic:** 54 ave Colonel Tshatshi, BP 8242, Kinshasa-Gombe; tel. (12) 34610; telex 21183.

**Egypt:** 519 ave de l'Ouganda, BP 8838, Kinshasa; tel. (12) 30296; Ambassador: AZIZ ABDEL HAMID HAMZA.

**Ethiopia:** BP 8435, Kinshasa; tel. (12) 23327; Ambassador: Col LEGESSE WOLDE-MARIAM.

**France:** 97 ave de la République du Tchad, BP 3093, Kinshasa; tel. (12) 30513; telex 21074; Ambassador: JACQUES DEPAIGNE.

**Gabon:** ave du 24 novembre, BP 9592, Kinshasa; tel. (12) 68325; telex 21455; Ambassador: JOSEPH KOUMBA MOUNGUENGUI.

**Germany:** 82 ave des 3Z, BP 8400, Kinshasa-Gombe; tel. (12) 21529; telex 21110; fax (12) 21527; Ambassador: KLAUS BÖNNEMANN.

**Ghana:** 206 ave du 24 novembre, BP 8446, Kinshasa; tel. (12) 31766; Ambassador: KWAKU ADU BEDIAKO.

**Greece:** 72 ave des 3Z, BP 478, Kinshasa; tel. (12) 33169; Ambassador: STELIO VALSAMAS-RHALLIS.

**Guinea:** 7–9 ave Lubefu, BP 9899, Kinshasa; tel. (12) 30864; Ambassador: FÉLIX FABER.

**Holy See:** 81 ave Goma, BP 3091, Kinshasa; tel. (12) 33128; telex 21527; Apostolic Nuncio: Mgr FAUSTINO SAINZ MUÑOZ, Titular Archbishop of Novaliciana.

**India:** 188 ave des Batétéla, BP 1026, Kinshasa; tel. (12) 33368; telex 21179; Ambassador: ARUN KUMAR.

**Iran:** 76 blvd du 30 juin, BP 16599, Kinshasa; tel. (12) 31052; telex 21429.

**Israel:** 12 ave des Aviateurs, BP 8343, Kinshasa; tel. (12) 21955; Ambassador: SHLOMO AVITAL.

**Italy:** 8 ave de la Mongala, BP 1000, Kinshasa; tel. (12) 23416; telex 21560; Ambassador: VITTORIO AMEDEO FARINELLI.

**Japan:** Immeuble Marsavco, 2e étage, ave Col Lusaka, BP 1810, Kinshasa; tel. (12) 22118; telex 21227; Ambassador: KYOICHI OMURA.

**Kenya:** 5002 ave de l'Ouganda, BP 9667, Kinshasa; tel. (12) 30117; telex 21359; Ambassador: MWABILI KISAKA.

**Korea, Democratic People's Republic:** 168 ave de l'Ouganda, BP 16597, Kinshasa; tel. (12) 31566; Ambassador: YI HYON SIK.

**Korea, Republic:** 2A ave des Orangers, BP 628, Kinshasa; tel. (12) 31022; Ambassador: CHUN SOON-KYU.

**Kuwait:** Suite 232, Intercontinental Hotel, Kinshasa.

**Lebanon:** 3 ave de l'Ouganda, Kinshasa; tel. (12) 32682; telex 21423; Ambassador: MUSTAFA HOREIBE.

**Liberia:** 3 ave de l'Okapi, BP 8940, Kinshasa; tel. (12) 82289; telex 21205; Ambassador: JALLA D. LANSANAH.

**Libya:** BP 9198, Kinshasa.

**Mauritania:** BP 16397, Kinshasa; tel. (12) 59575; telex 21380; Ambassador: Lt-Col M'BARECK OULD BOUNA MOKHTAR.

**Morocco:** 4497 ave Lubefu, BP 912, Kinshasa; tel. (12) 30255; Ambassador: ABOUBKEUR CHERKAOUI.

**Netherlands:** 11 ave Zongo Ntolo, BP 10299, Kinshasa; tel. (12) 30733; Chargé d'affaires: J. G. WILBRENNINCK.

**Nigeria:** 141 blvd du 30 juin, BP 1700, Kinshasa; tel. (12) 43272; Ambassador: DAG S. CLAUDE-WILCOX.

**Pakistan:** Kinshasa; Chargé d'affaires: SHAFQAT ALI SHAIKH.

**Poland:** 63 ave de la Justice, BP 8553, Kinshasa; tel. (12) 33349; telex 21057; Ambassador: ANDRZEJ M. LUPINA.

**Portugal:** 270 ave des Aviateurs, BP 7775, Kinshasa; tel. (12) 24010; telex 221328; Ambassador: LUÍS DE VASCONCELOS PIMENTEL QUARTIN BASTOS.

**Romania:** 5 ave de l'Ouganda, BP 2242, Kinshasa; tel. (12) 33127; telex 21316; Ambassador: EMINESCU DRAGOMIR.

**Russia:** 80 ave de la Justice, BP 1143, Kinshasa I; tel. (12) 33157; telex 21690; Ambassador: YURI SPIRINE.

**Rwanda:** 50 ave de la Justice, BP 967, Kinshasa; tel. (12) 30327; telex 21612; Ambassador: ANTOINE NYILINKINDI.

**Spain:** Immeuble de la Communauté Hellénique, 4e étage, blvd du 30 juin, BP 8036, Kinshasa; tel. (12) 21881; telex 21401; Ambassador: ANTONIO LÓPEZ MARTÍNEZ.

**Sudan:** 83 ave des Treis, BP 7347, Kinshasa; Ambassador: MUBARAK ADAM HADI.

**Sweden:** 89 ave des 3Z, BP 11096, Kinshasa; tel. (12) 33201; Chargé d'affaires a.i.: L. EKSTRÖM.

**Switzerland:** 654 ave Colonel Tshatshi, BP 8724, Kinshasa I; tel. (12) 34243; fax (12) 34246; Ambassador: WILHELM SCHMID.

**Togo:** 3 ave de la Vallée, BP 10197, Kinshasa; tel. (12) 30666; telex 21388; Ambassador: MAMA GNOFAM.

**Tunisia:** ave du Cercle, BP 1498, Kinshasa; tel. (12) 31632; telex 21171; Ambassador: ABDEL KRIM MOUSSA.

**Turkey:** 18 ave Pumbu, BP 7817, Kinshasa; tel. (12) 33774; Ambassador: HIKMET SENGENÇ.

**Uganda:** 177 ave Tombalbaye, BP 1086, Kinshasa; tel. (12) 22740; telex 21618; Ambassador: Dr AJEAN.

**United Kingdom:** ave des 3Z, BP 8049, Kinshasa; tel. (12) 34775; Ambassador: (vacant).

**USA:** 310 ave des Aviateurs, BP 697, Kinshasa; tel. (12) 21532; telex 21405; fax 21232; Chargé d'affaires: JOHN YATES.

**Yugoslavia:** 112 quai de l'Etoile, BP 619, Kinshasa; tel. (12) 32325; Ambassador: (vacant).

**Zambia:** 54–58 ave de l'Ecole, BP 1144, Kinshasa; tel. (12) 23038; telex 21209; Ambassador: C. K. C. KAMWANA.

ZAIRE

## Judicial System

A Justice Department, under the control of the State Commissioner for Justice, is responsible for the organization and definition of competence of the judiciary; civil, penal and commercial law and civil and penal procedures; the status of persons and property; the system of obligations and questions pertaining to Zairean nationality; international private law; status of magistrates; organization of the lawyers' profession, counsels for the defence, notaries and of judicial auxiliaries; supervision of cemeteries, non-profit-making organizations, cults and institutions working in the public interest; the operation of penitentiaries; confiscated property.

There is a Supreme Court in Kinshasa, and there are also nine Courts of Appeal and 36 County Courts.

**President of the Supreme Court:** GÉRARD KAMANDA WA KAMANDA.
**Procurator-General of the Republic:** MONGULU T'APANGANE.

**Courts of Appeal**
**Bandundu:** Pres. MUNONA NTAMBAMBILANJI.
**Bukavu:** Pres. TINKAMANYIRE BIN NDIGEBA.
**Kananga:** Pres. MATONDO BWENTA.
**Kinshasa:** Pres. KALONDA KELE OMA.
**Kisangani:** Pres. MBANGAMA KABUNDI.
**Lubumbashi:** Pres. BOKONGA W'ANZANDE.
**Matadi:** Pres. TSHIOVO LUMAMBI.
**Mbandaka:** Pres. MAKUNZA WA MAKUNZA.
**Mbuji-Mayi:** Pres. LUAMBA BINDU.

## Religion

Many of Zaire's inhabitants follow traditional Zairean beliefs, which are mostly animistic. A large proportion of the population is Christian, predominantly Roman Catholic.

In 1971 new national laws officially recognized the Roman Catholic Church, the Protestant (ECZ) Church and the Kimbanguist Church. The Muslim and Jewish faiths and the Greek Orthodox Church were granted official recognition in 1972.

### CHRISTIANITY
#### The Roman Catholic Church

Zaire comprises six archdioceses and 41 dioceses. At 31 December 1993 there were an estimated 21,308,860 adherents in the country.

**Bishops' Conference:** Conférence Episcopale du Zaïre, BP 3258, Kinshasa-Gombe; tel. (12) 30082; telex 21571; f. 1981; Pres. Rt Rev. FAUSTIN NGABU, Bishop of Goma.
**Archbishop of Bukavu:** Most Rev. CHRISTOPHE MUNZIHIRWA MWENE NGABO, Archevêché, BP 3324, Bukavu; tel. 2707.
**Archbishop of Kananga:** Most Rev. MARTIN-LÉONARD BAKOLE WA ILUNGA, Archevêché, BP 70, Kananga; tel. 2477.
**Archbishop of Kinshasa:** Cardinal FRÉDÉRIC ETSOU-NZABI-BAMUNGWABI, Archevêché, ave de l'Université, BP 8431, Kinshasa 1; tel. (12) 71762.
**Archbishop of Kisangani:** Most Rev. LAURENT MONSENGWO PASINYA, Archevêché, ave Mpolo 10B, BP 505, Kisangani; tel. 211404.
**Archbishop of Lubumbashi:** Most Rev. EUGÈNE KABANGA SONGA-SONGA, Archevêché, BP 72, Lubumbashi; tel. (2) 21442.
**Archbishop of Mbandaka-Bikoro:** JOSEPH KUMUONDALA MBIMBA, Archevêché, BP 1064, Mbandaka; tel. 2234.

#### The Anglican Communion

The Church of the Province of Zaire comprises five dioceses.

**Archbishop of the Province of Zaire and Bishop of Boga-Zaïre:** Most Rev. BYANKYA NJOJO, c/o POB 21285, Nairobi, Kenya.
**Bishop of Bukavu:** Rt Rev. FIDÈLE BALUFUGA DIROKPA, BP 2876, Bukavu.
**Bishop of Kisangani:** Rt Rev. SYLVESTRE TIBAFA MUGERA, BP 861, Kisangani.
**Bishop of Nord Kivu:** Rt Rev. METHUSELA MUNZENDA MUSUBAHO, BP 322, Butembo.
**Bishop of Shaba:** Rt Rev. EMMANUEL KOLINI MBONA, c/o United Methodist Church, POB 22037, Kitwe, Zambia.

#### Kimbanguist

**Eglise de Jésus Christ sur la Terre par le Prophète Simon Kimbangu:** BP 7069, Kinshasa; tel. (12) 68944; telex 21315; f. 1921 (officially established 1959); c. 5m. mems (1985); Spiritual Head HE DIANGIENDA KUNTIMA; Sec.-Gen. Rev. LUNTADILLA.

#### Protestant Churches

**Eglise du Christ au Zaïre (ECZ):** ave de la Justice (face no. 75), BP 4938, Kinshasa-Gombe; f. 1902 (as Zaire Protestant Council); a co-ordinating org. for all the Protestant churches, with the exception of the Kimbanguist Church; 62 mem. communities and a regional org. in each of Zaire's admin. regions; c. 10m. mems (1982); Pres. Bishop BOKELEALE ITOFO; includes:

**Communauté Baptiste du Zaire-Ouest:** BP 4728, Kinshasa 2; f. 1970 (as Eglise Baptiste du Congo-Ouest); 450 parishes; 170,000 mems (1985); Gen. Sec. Rev. LUSAKWENO-VANGU.
**Communauté des Disciples du Christ:** BP 178, Mbandaka; tel. 31062; telex 21742; f. 1964; 250 parishes; 650,000 mems (1985); Gen. Sec. Rev. Dr ELONDA EFEFE.
**Communauté Episcopale Baptiste en Afrique:** 2 ave Jason Sendwe, BP 3866, Lubumbashi 1; tel. (2) 24724; f. 1956; 1,300 episcopal communions and parishes; 150,000 mems (1993); Pres. Bishop KITOBO KABWEKA-LEZA.
**Communauté Evangélique:** BP 36, Luozi; f. 1961; 50 parishes; 33,750 mems (1985); Pres. Rev. K. LUKOMBO NTONTOLO.
**Communauté Lumière:** BP 10498, Kinshasa I; f. 1931; 150 parishes; 220,000 mems (1985); Patriarch KAYUWA TSHIBUMBU WA KAHINGA.
**Communauté Mennonite:** BP 18, Tshikapa; f. 1960; 40,000 mems (1985); Gen. Sec. Rev. KABANGY DJEKE SHAPASA.
**Communauté Presbytérienne:** BP 117, Kananga; f. 1959; 150,000 mems (1985); Gen. Sec. Dr M. L. TSHIHAMBA.
**Eglise Missionaire Apostolique:** BP 15859, Kinshasa 1, f. 1986; 3 parishes; 1,000 mems.; Apostle for Africa L. A. NANANDANA.

## The Press

### DAILIES

**L'Analyste:** 129 ave du Bas-Zaïre, BP 91, Kinshasa-Gombe; tel. (12) 80987; Dir and Editor-in-Chief BONGOMA KONI BOTAHE.
**Boyoma:** 31 blvd Mobutu, BP 982, Kisangani, Haut-Zaïre; Dir and Editor BADRIYO ROVA ROVATU.
**Elima:** 1 ave de la Révolution, BP 11498, Kinshasa; tel. (12) 77332; f. 1928; evening; operations suspended by Govt in Nov. 1993; Dir and Editor-in-Chief ESSOLOMWA NKOY EA LINGANGA.
**Mjumbe:** BP 2474, Lubumbashi, Shaba; tel. (2) 25348; f. 1963; Dir and Editor TSHIMANGA KOYA KAKONA.
**Salongo:** 143 10e rue Limete, BP 601, Kinshasa/Limete; tel. (12) 77367; morning; operations suspended by Govt in Nov. 1993; Dir and Editor BONDO-NSAMA; circ. 10,000.

### PERIODICALS

**Allo Kinshasa:** 3 rue Kayange, BP 20271, Kinshasa-Lemba; monthly; Editor MBUYU WA KABILA.
**BEA Magazine de la Femme:** 2 ave Masimanimba, BP 113380, Kinshasa I; every 2 weeks; Editor MUTINGA MUTWISHAYI.
**Beto na Beto:** 75 ave Tatamena, BP 757, Matadi; weekly; Dir-Gen. and Editor BIA ZANDA NE NANGA.
**Bibi:** 33 ave Victoria, Kinshasa; f. 1972; French; general interest; monthly.
**Bingwa:** ave du 30 juin, zone Lubumbashi no 4334, Shaba; weekly; sport; Dir and Editor MATEKE WA MULAMBA.
**Cahiers Economiques et Sociaux:** BP 257, Kinshasa XI, (National University of Zaire); sociological, political and economic review; quarterly; Dir Prof. NDONGALA TADI LEWA; circ. 2,000.
**Cahiers des Religions Africaines:** Faculté de Théologie Catholique de Kinshasa, BP 712, Kinshasa/Limete; tel. (12) 78476; f. 1967; English and French; religion; 2 a year; circ. 1,000.
**Le Canard Libre:** Kinshasa; f. 1991; Editor JOSEPH CASTRO MULEBE.
**Champion du Zaïre:** Cité de la Voix du Zaïre, BP 9365, Kinshasa I; weekly; sport; Dir and Editor-in-Chief KASONGA TSHILUNDE BOYA YAWUMWE.
**Circulaire d'Information:** Association Nationale des Entreprises du Zaïre, 10 ave des Aviateurs, BP 7247, Kinshasa; f. 1959; French; business news; monthly; circ. 1,000.
**Conseiller Comptable:** Immeuble SNCZ, 17 ave du Port, BP 308, Kinshasa; f. 1974; French; public finance and taxation; quarterly; circ. 1,000.
**Le Courrier du Zaïre:** aut. no 04/DIMOPAP 0018/84, 101 Lukolela, Kinshasa; weekly; Editor NZONZILA NDONZUAU.
**Cultures au Zaïre et en Afrique:** BP 16706, Kinshasa; f. 1973; French and English; quarterly.
**Dionga:** Immeuble Amassio, 2 rue Dirna, BP 8031, Kinshasa; monthly.

**Documentation et Informations Africaines (DIA):** BP 2598, Kinshasa I; tel. (12) 33197; fax (12) 33196; Roman Catholic news agency reports; 3 a week; Dir Rev. Père VATA DIAMBANZA.

**Documentation et Informations Protestantes (DIP):** Eglise du Christ au Zaïre, BP 4938, Kinshasa-Gombe; French and English; religion.

**L'Entrepreneur:** Association Nationale des Entreprises du Zaire, 10 ave des Aviateurs, BP 7247, Kinshasa; tel. (12) 22286; f. 1978; French; business news; quarterly.

**Etudes d'Histoire Africaine:** National University of Zaire, BP 1825, Lubumbashi; f. 1970; French and English; history; annually; circ. 1,000.

**Etudes Zaïroises:** c/o Institut National d'Etudes Politiques, BP 2307, Kinshasa I; f. 1961; quarterly.

**Horizons 80:** Société Zaïroise d'Edition et d'Information, BP 9839, Kinshasa; economy; weekly.

**JUA:** BP 1613, Bukavu, Kivu; weekly; Dir and Editor MUTIRI WA BASHARA.

**Les Kasaï:** 161 9e rue, BP 575, Kinshasa/Limete; weekly; Editor NSENGA NDOMBA.

**Kin-Média:** BP 15808, Kinshasa I; monthly; Editor ILUNGA KASAMBAY.

**KYA:** 24 ave de l'Equateur, BP 7853, Kinshasa-Gombe; tel. (12) 27502; f. 1984; weekly for Bas-Zaïre; Editor SASSA KASSA YI KIBOBA.

**Maadini:** Generale des Carrières et des Mines, BP 450, Lubumbashi; quarterly.

**Mambenga 2000:** BP 477, Mbandaka; Editor BOSANGE YEMA BOF.

**Ngabu:** Société Nationale d'Assurances, Immeuble Sonas Sankuru, blvd du 30 juin, BP 3443, Kinshasa-Gombe; tel. (12) 23051; f. 1973; insurance news; quarterly.

**Njanja:** Société Nationale des Chemins de Fer Zaïrois, place de la Gare, BP 297, Lubumbashi; tel. (2) 23430; telex 41056; railways and transportation; monthly.

**NUKTA:** 14 chaussée de Kasenga, BP 3805, Lubumbashi; weekly; agriculture; Editor NGOY BUNDUKI.

**L'Opinion:** BP 15394, Kinshasa; weekly; Editor SABLE FWAMBA KIEPENDA.

**Presse et Information Kimbanguiste (PIK):** ave Bongolo, Kinshasa-Kalamu.

**Problèmes Sociaux Zaïrois:** Centre d'Exécution de Programmes Sociaux et Economiques, Université de Lubumbashi, 208 ave Kasavubu , BP 1873, Lubumbashi; f. 1946; quarterly; Editor N'KASHAMA KADIMA.

**Promoteur Zaïrois:** Centre du Commerce International du Zaïre, 119 ave Col Tshatshi, BP 13, Kinshasa; f. 1979; French; international trade news; six a year.

**La Revue Juridique du Zaïre:** Société d'Etudes Juridiques du Zaïre, Université de Lubumbashi, BP 510, Lubumbashi; f. 1924; 3 a year.

**Sciences, Techniques, Informations:** Centre de Recherches Industrielles en Afrique Centrale (CRIAC), BP 54, Lubumbashi.

**Le Sport Africain:** 13è niveau Tour adm., Cité de la Voix du Zaïre, BP 3356, Kinshasa-Gombe; monthly; Pres. TSHIMPUMPU WA TSHIMPUMPU.

**Taifa:** 536 ave Lubumba, BP 884, Lubumbashi; weekly; Editor LWAMBWA MILAMBU.

**Telema:** 7–9 ave Père Boka, BP 3277, Kinshasa-Gombe; f. 1974; religious; quarterly; Editor BOKA DI MPASI LONDI; circ. 3,000.

**Umoja:** Kinshasa; weekly.

**Zaïre-Afrique:** Centre d'Etudes pour l'Action Sociale, 9 ave Père Boka, BP 3375, Kinshasa-Gombe; tel. (12) 30066; f. 1961; economic, social and cultural; monthly; Editors KIKASSA MWANALESSA, RENE BEECKMANS; circ. 5,500.

**Zaïre Agricole:** 5 rue Bonga-Equateur, Matonge, Zone de Kalamu; monthly; Editor DIAYIKWA KIMPAKALA.

**Zaire Business:** Immeuble Amasco, 3986 rue ex-Belgika, BP 9839, Kinshasa; f. 1973; French; weekly.

**Zaïre Informatique:** Conseil Permanent de l'Informatique au Zaïre, BP 9699, Kinshasa I; f. 1978; French; quarterly.

**Zaïre Ya Sita:** Direction Generale et Administration, 1 rue Luozi Kasavubu, BP 8246, Kinshasa; f. 1968; Lingala; political science; six a year.

### NEWS AGENCIES

**Agence Zaïre-Presse (AZAP):** 44–48 ave Tombalbaye, BP 1595, Kinshasa I; tel. (12) 22035; telex 21096; f. 1957; state-controlled; Del.-Gen. LANDU LUSALA KHASA.

**Documentation et Informations Africaines (DIA):** BP 2598, Kinshasa I; tel. (12) 34528; telex 2108; f. 1957; Roman Catholic news agency; Dir Rev. Père VATA DIAMBANZA.

### Foreign Bureaux

**Agence France-Presse (AFP):** Immeuble Wenge 3227, ave Wenge, Zone de la Gombe, BP 726, Kinshasa I; tel. (12) 27009; telex 21648; Bureau Chief JEAN-PIERRE REJETTE.

**Agencia EFE** (Spain): BP 2653, Lubumbashi; Correspondent KANKU SANGA.

**Agência Lusa de Informação** (Portugal): BP 4941, Kinshasa; tel. (12) 24437; telex 21605.

**Agenzia Nazionale Stampa Associata (ANSA)** (Italy): BP 2790, Kinshasa 15; tel. (12) 30315; Bureau Chief (vacant).

**Pan-African News Agency (PANA)** (Senegal): BP 1400, Kinshasa; tel. (12) 23290; telex 21475; f. 1983; Bureau Chief ADRIEN HONORÉ MBEYET.

**Xinhua (New China) News Agency** (People's Republic of China): 293 ave Mfumu Lutunu, BP 8939, Kinshasa; tel. (12) 25647; telex 21259; Correspondent CHEN WEIBIN.

### PRESS ASSOCIATION

**Union de la Presse du Zaïre (UPZA):** BP 4941, Kinshasa I; tel. (12) 24437; telex 21605.

## Publishers

**Centre Protestant d'Editions et de Diffusion (CEDI):** 209 ave Kalémie, BP 11398, Kinshasa I; tel. (12) 22202; fax (12) 26730; f. 1935; fiction, poetry, biography, religious, juvenile; Christian tracts, works in French, Lingala, Kikongo and other languages of Zaire; Dir-Gen. HENRY DIRKS.

**Maison d'Editions 'Jeunes pour Jeunes':** BP 9624, Kinshasa I; youth interest.

**MEDIASPAUL:** BP 127 Limete, Kinshasa; tel. (12) 70726; religion, education, literature; Dir LUIGI BOFFELLI.

**Les Presses Africaines:** place du 27 Octobre, BP 12924, Kinshasa I; general non-fiction, poetry; Man. Dir MWAMBA-DI-MBUYI.

**Presses Universitaires du Zaïre (PUZ):** 290 rue d'Aketi, BP 1682, Kinshasa I; tel. (12) 30652; telex 21394; f. 1972; scientific publications; Dir Prof. MUMBANZA MWA BAWELE.

## Radio and Television

According to estimates by UNESCO, there were 3,870,000 radio receivers and 55,000 television receivers in use in 1992.

**Radio Candip:** Centre d'Animation et de Diffusion Pédagogique, BP 373, Bunia; educational broadcasts in French, Lingala, Swahili and six local dialects.

**La Voix du Zaïre:** Station Nationale, BP 3164, Kinshasa-Gombe; tel. (12) 23175; telex 21583; state-controlled; home service broadcasts in French, Swahili, Lingala, Tshiluba, Kikongo; regional stations at Kisangani, Lubumbashi, Bukavu, Bandundu, Kananga, Mbuji-Mayi, Matadi, Mbandaka and Bunia; Pres. DONGO BADJANGA.

**Zaïre Télévision:** BP 3171, Kinshasa-Gombe; tel. (12) 23171; telex 21583; govt commercial station; broadcasts for 5 hours daily on weekdays and 10 hours daily at weekends; Dir-Gen. DONGO BADJANGA.

## Finance

(cap. = capital; res = reserves; dep. = deposits; m. = million; brs = branches; amounts in old zaires unless otherwise indicated)

### BANKING

#### Central Bank

**Banque du Zaïre:** blvd Colonel Tshatshi au nord, BP 2697, Kinshasa; tel. (12) 20701; telex 21365; f. 1964; cap. and res 50,088.4m. (Dec. 1988); Gov. PATRICE DJAMBOLEKA; Vice-Gov. MATOMINA KYALA 8 brs, 34 agencies.

#### Commercial Banks

**Banque Commerciale Zaïroise SARL:** blvd du 30 juin, BP 2798, Kinshasa; tel. (12) 23772; telex 21127; f. 1909 as Banque du Congo Belge, name changed 1971; cap. and res NZ 722.1m., dep. NZ 1,666.1m. (Dec. 1993); Chair. (vacant); Vice-Chair. MICHEL ISRALSON; 29 brs.

**Banque Continentale Africaine (Zaïre) SZARL:** 4 ave de la Justice, BP 7613, Kinshasa-Gombe; tel. (12) 28006; telex 21508; fax (12) 25243; f. 1983; cap. 90m. (Dec. 1991); Chair. PAUL LENOIR.

**Banque de Crédit Agricole:** angle ave Kasa-Vubu et ave M'Polo, BP 8837, Kinshasa I; tel. (12) 21800; telex 21383; fax (12) 27221; f. 1982 to expand and modernize enterprises in agriculture, livestock

ZAIRE                                                                                                      Directory

and fishing, and generally to improve the quality of rural life; state-owned; cap. 5m. (Dec. 1991); Pres. a.i. Bazin Lukubika Dimbu.

**Banque Internationale pour l'Afrique au Zaïre SARL:** Immeuble Nioki, ave de la Douane, BP 8725, Kinshasa 1; tel. (12) 26910; telex 21355; fax (12) 24774; f. 1971; cap. 60m. (Dec. 1992); Pres. J. C. Kapotwe; Vice-Pres. T. C. Ingram; 3 brs.

**Banque Paribas Zaïre:** Immeuble Unibra, ave Colonel Ebeya, BP 1600, Kinshasa 1; tel. (12) 24747; telex 21020; f. 1954; cap. and res 1.4m. (Dec. 1980).

**Banque Zaïroise du Commerce Extérieur SARL (BZCE):** blvd du 30 juin, BP 400, Kinshasa 1; tel. (12) 20393; telex 21108; fax (12) 24947; f. 1947, reorg. 1987; state-owned; cap. NZ 133.0m., res NZ 19,170.1m., dep. NZ 27,419.9m. (Dec. 1994); Chair. and Gen. Man. Gbendo Ndewa Tete; Dirs Makuma Ndeseke, Zikondolo Biwabeki; 31 brs.

**Caisse Générale d'Epargne du Zaïre (CADEZA):** 38 ave de la Caisse d'Epargne, BP 8147, Kinshasa-Gombe; tel. (12) 33701; telex 21384; f. 1950; state-owned; Chair. and Man. Dir Nsimba M'Vuedi; 45 brs.

**Caisse Nationale d'Epargne et de Crédit Immobilier:** BP 11196, Kinshasa; f. 1971; state-owned; cap. 2m. (Dec. 1983); Dir-Gen. Biangala Elonga Mbaü.

**Citibank (Zaïre) SARL:** Immeuble Citibank Zaïre, angle aves Col Lukusa et Ngongo Lutete, BP 9999, Kinshasa 1; tel. (12) 20554; telex 21622; fax (12) 21064; f. 1971; cap. and res 152,120.0m., dep. 1,613,301.9m. (Dec. 1991); Chair. Shaukat Aziz; Man. Dir Michel Accad; 1 br.

**Compagnie Immobilière du Zaïre (IMMOZAIRE):** BP 332, Kinshasa; f. 1962; cap. 150m. (Dec. 1983); Chair. A. S. Gerard; Man. Dir M. Heraly.

**Crédit Foncier de l'Afrique Centrale:** BP 1198, Kinshasa; f. 1961; cap. 40,000 (Dec. 1983).

**Fransabank (Zaïre) SARL:** Immeuble Zaïre-Shell 14/16, ave du Port, Kinshasa 1; tel. (12) 20119; telex 21430; fax (12) 27864; cap. 300m. (1993); Pres. Adnan Wafic Kassar.

**Nouvelle Banque de Kinshasa:** 1 place du Marché, BP 8033, Kinshasa 1; tel. (12) 26361; telex 21304; f. 1969 as Banque de Kinshasa; nationalized 1975; state-owned; control transferred to National Union of Zairean Workers (UNTZA) in 1988; cap. 6,000,000m. (Dec. 1992); Pres. Diang Kabul; 16 brs.

**Société de Crédit aux Classes Moyennes et à l'Industrie:** BP 3165, Kinshasa-Kauna; f. 1947; cap. 500,000 (Dec. 1983).

**Société Financière de Développement SZARL (SOFIDE):** Immeuble SOFIDE, 9–11 angle aves Ngabu et Kisangani, BP 1148, Kinshasa 1; tel. (12) 20676; telex 21476; fax (12) 20788; f. 1970; partly state-owned; provides technical and financial aid, primarily for agricultural development; cap. 260m. (Dec. 1992); Pres. and Dir-Gen. Kiyanga Ki-N'Lombi; 4 brs.

**Stanbic Bank (Zaïre) SZARL:** 12 ave de Mongala, BP 16297, Kinshasa 1; tel. (12) 20074; telex 21413; fax (12) 41644; f. 1973 as Grindlays Bank; acquired by Standard Bank Investment Corpn (South Africa) in 1992; adopted current name in 1993; cap. 4.0m. (Dec. 1992); Chair. A. D. B. Wright; Man. Dir J. Murray Miller; 1 br.

**Union Zaïroise de Banques SARL:** angle ave de la Nation et ave des Aviateurs 19, BP 197, Kinshasa 1; tel. (12) 25801; telex 21026; fax (12) 25527; f. 1929, renamed in 1972; cap. 240m. (Dec. 1992); Pres. Isungu Ky-Maka; 12 brs.

### INSURANCE

**Société Nationale d'Assurances (SONAS):** 3473 blvd du 30 juin, Kinshasa-Gombe; tel. (12) 23051; telex 21653; f. 1966; state-owned; cap. 23m.; 9 brs.

## Trade and Industry

### DEVELOPMENT ORGANIZATIONS

**Caisse de Stabilisation Cotonnière (CSCo):** BP 3058, Kinshasa-Gombe; tel. (12) 31206; telex 21174; f. 1978 to replace Office National des Fibres Textiles; acts as an intermediary between the Govt, cotton ginners and textile factories, and co-ordinates international financing of cotton sector; Exec. Chair. A. Kibangula.

**La Générale des Carrières et des Mines (GÉCAMINES):** BP 450, Lubumbashi; tel. (2) 13039; telex 41034; f. 1967 as state holding co to acquire assets in Zaire (then the Congo) of Union Minière du Haut-Katanga; privatization announced in 1994; Chair. and CEO Atundu Liongo; operates the following enterprises:

  **GÉCAMINES—Exploitation:** mining operations; Chair. Umba Kyamitala.

  **GÉCAMINES—Commercial:** marketing of mineral products; Chair. Djamboleka Loma Okitongono; Man. Dir Atundu Liongo.

  **GÉCAMINES—Développement:** operates agricultural and stockfarming ventures in Shaba region; Chair. Kanobana Kigesa.

**Institut National pour l'Etude et la Recherche Agronomiques:** BP 1513, Kisangani, Haut-Zaïre; f. 1933; agricultural research; Dir-Gen. Dr Botula Manyala.

**Office Zaïrois du Café (OZACAF):** ave Général Bobozo, BP 8931, Kinshasa 1; tel. (12) 77144; telex 20062; f. 1979; state agency for coffee and also cocoa, tea, quinquina and pyrethrum; Chief Rep. Munga Wa Mbasa; Commercial Dir Feruzi Wa Ngenda.

**Pêcherie Maritime Zaïroise (PEMARZA):** Kinshasa; the sole sea-fishing enterprise.

**PetroZaïre:** 1513 blvd du 30 juin, BP 7617, Kinshasa 1; tel. (12) 25356; telex 21066; f. 1974; state-owned; petroleum refining, processing, stocking and transporting; Dir-Gen. Ndondi Mbungu Kiyaka.

### TRADE ASSOCIATIONS

**Association Nationale des Entreprises du Zaïre (ANEZA):** 10 ave des Aviateurs, BP 7247, Kinshasa; tel. (12) 24623; telex 21071; f. 1972; represents business interests in Zaire for both domestic and foreign institutions; Pres. Bemba Saolona; Man. Dir Luboya Diyoka; Gen. Sec. Masudi Mungilima.

**Chambre de Commerce, d'Industrie et d'Agriculture du Zaïre:** 10 ave des Aviateurs, BP 7247, Kinshasa 1; tel. (12) 22286; telex 21071.

### TRADE FAIR

**FIKIN—Foire Internationale de Kinshasa** (Kinshasa International Trade Fair): BP 1397, Kinshasa; tel. (12) 77506; telex 20145; f. 1968; state-sponsored; held annually in July; Pres. Togba Mata Boboy.

### TRADE UNIONS

The Union Nationale des Travailleurs du Zaïre was founded in 1967 as the sole trade union organization. In mid-1990 the establishment of independent trade unions was legalized, and in early 1991 there were 12 officially recognized trade union organizations.

**Union Nationale des Travailleurs du Zaïre (UNTZA):** BP 8814, Kinshasa; f. 1967; embraces 16 unions; Pres. Katalay Moleli Sangol.

## Transport

**Office National des Transports au Zaïre (ONATRA):** BP 98, Kinshasa 1; tel. (12) 24761; operates 12,174 km of waterways, 366 km of railways and road transport; administers ports of Kinshasa, Matadi, Boma and Banana; Pres. K. Wa Ndayi Muledi.

### RAILWAYS

The main line runs from Lubumbashi to Ilebo. International connections run to Dar es Salaam (Tanzania) and Lobito (Angola), and also connect with the Zambian, Zimbabwean, Mozambican and South African systems. In March 1994 an agreement was concluded with the South African Government for the provision of locomotives, rolling stock and fuel, to help rehabilitate the Zairean rail system.

**Kinshasa–Matadi Railway:** BP 98, Kinshasa 1; 366 km operated by ONATRA; Dir M. Kitanda Wetu.

**Société Nationale des Chemins de Fer Zaïrois (SNCZ):** place de la Gare, BP 297, Lubumbashi; tel. (2) 23430; telex 41056; f. 1974; 4,772 km (including 858 km electrified); administers all internal railway sections as well as river transport and transport on Lakes Tanganyika and Kivu; Pres. B. Mbatshi.

### ROADS

In 1993 there were approximately 145,000 km of roads, of which some 68,000 km were main roads. In general road conditions are poor, owing to inadequate maintenance.

### INLAND WATERWAYS

For over 1,600 km the River Zaire is navigable. Above the Stanley Falls the Zaire becomes the Lualaba, and is navigable along a 965-km stretch from Bubundu to Kindu and Kongolo to Bukama. The River Kasai, a tributary of the River Zaire, is navigable by shipping as far as Ilebo, at which the line from Lubumbashi terminates. The total length of inland waterways is 13,700 km.

**East African Railways and Harbours:** operates services on Lake Mobutu Sese Seko.

# ZAIRE

**Régie des voies fluviales:** 109 ave Lumpungu, Kinshasa-Gombe, BP 11697, Kinshasa I; administers river navigation; Gen. Man. MONDOMBO SISA EBAMBE.

**Société Zaïroise des Chemins de Fer des Grands Lacs:** River Lualaba services: Bubundu–Kindu and Kongolo–Malemba N'kula; Lake Tanganyika services: Kamina–Kigoma–Kalundu–Moba–Mpulungu.

**Zaire Network:** services on the Luapula and Lake Mweru.

## SHIPPING

The principal seaports are Matadi, Boma and Banana on the lower Zaire. The port of Matadi has more than 1.6 km of quays and can accommodate up to 10 deep-water vessels. Matadi is linked by rail with Kinshasa.

**Compagnie Maritime Zaïroise SARL:** Immeuble CMZ (AMIZA), place de la Poste, BP 9496, Kinshasa; tel. (12) 25816; telex 21626; fax (12) 26234; f. 1946; services: North Africa, Europe, North America and Asia to West Africa, East Africa to North Africa; Chair. MAYILUKILA LUSIASIA.

## CIVIL AVIATION

There are international airports at Ndjili (for Kinshasa), Luano (for Lubumbashi), Bukavu, Goma and Kisangani. There is also an internal air service.

**Air Charter Service:** Place Salongo, BP 5371, Kinshasa 10; tel. (12) 27891; telex 21573; passenger and cargo charter services; Dir TSHIMBOMBO MAKUNA; Gen. Man. N. MCKANDOLO.

**Air Zaïre:** BP 10120, Kinshasa; tel. (12) 20939; telex 21156; fax (12) 20940; f. 1961 as Air Congo, name changed 1971; 80% state-owned; domestic and international services to Africa and Europe; Dir-Gen. HUBERT ANDRADE; Pres. YUMA MORISHO LUSAMBIA.

**Scibe Airlift of Zaire:** BP 614, Kinshasa; tel. (12) 26237; fax (12) 24386; f. 1979; domestic and international passenger and cargo charter services between Kinshasa, Lubumbashi, Bujumbura (Burundi) and Brussels; Pres. BEMBA SAOLONA; Dir-Gen. BEMBA GOMBO.

**Shabair:** Aeroport de la Luano, BP 1060, Lubumbashi; tel. (2) 25686; telex 550020; fax (2) 24597; f. 1989; domestic and international passenger and cargo services; Man. Dir Capt. S. PAPAIOANNOU.

**Zairean Airlines:** BP 2111, blvd du 30 juin, Kinshasa; tel. (12) 24624; telex 21525; f. 1981; passenger and freight services and charter flights throughout Africa; Dir-Gen. Capt. ALFRED SOMMERAUER.

# Tourism

Zaire has extensive lake and mountain scenery. Tourist arrivals totalled about 22,000 in 1992, generating some US $7m. in revenue.

**Office National du Tourisme:** 2A/2B ave des Orangers, BP 9502, Kinshasa-Gombe; tel. (12) 30070; f. 1959; Man. Dir BOTOLO MAGOZA.

**Société Zaïroise de l'Hôtellerie:** Immeuble Memling, BP 1076, Kinshasa; tel. (12) 23260; Man. N'JOLI BALANGA.

# ZAMBIA

## Introductory Survey

**Location, Climate, Language, Religion, Flag, Capital**

The Republic of Zambia is a land-locked state in southern central Africa, bordered to the north by Tanzania and Zaire, to the east by Malawi and Mozambique, to the south by Zimbabwe, Botswana and Namibia, and to the west by Angola. The climate is tropical, modified by altitude, with average temperatures from 18°C to 24°C (65°F–75°F). The official language is English. The principal African languages are Nyanja, Bemba, Tonga, Lozi, Lunda and Luvale. Christians comprise an estimated 20% of the population and are roughly divided between Protestants and Roman Catholics. An estimated 70% of the population follow traditional animist beliefs. Most Asians are Muslims, although some are Hindus. The national flag (proportions 3 by 2) is green, with equal red, black and orange vertical stripes in the lower fly corner, and an orange eagle in flight in the upper fly corner. The capital is Lusaka.

**Recent History**

In 1924 control of Northern Rhodesia was transferred from the British South Africa Company to the Government of the United Kingdom. In 1953 the protectorate united with Southern Rhodesia (now Zimbabwe) and Nyasaland (now Malawi) to form the Federation of Rhodesia and Nyasaland (also known as the Central African Federation). In 1962, following a campaign of civil disobedience, organized by the United National Independence Party (UNIP), in support of demands that Northern Rhodesia be granted independence, the British Government introduced a new Constitution, which provided for a limited African franchise. In December 1963 the Federation was formally dissolved. Following elections in January 1964, the leader of UNIP, Dr Kenneth Kaunda, formed a Government, which comprised members of UNIP. Northern Rhodesia, which was henceforth known as Zambia, became an independent republic within the Commonwealth on 24 October 1964, with Kaunda as the country's first President.

Following its accession to power, the Kaunda administration supported African liberation groups operating in Southern Rhodesia (then known as Rhodesia) and Mozambique; repeated clashes along the border with both countries were reported, while incidents of internal political violence, particularly in the Copperbelt region, also occurred. In December 1972 Zambia was declared a one-party state. In January 1973 the Rhodesian administration closed the border with Zambia.

In October 1978 Kaunda was nominated by UNIP as sole presidential candidate, after the party had approved constitutional changes that effectively eliminated all opposition. The presidential and legislative elections took place in December 1978, and Kaunda was returned for a fourth term as President.

In October 1980 an attempted coup, allegedly involving several prominent business executives, government officials and UNIP members, was staged against the Government. Kaunda accused South Africa and other foreign powers of supporting the coup attempt.

Despite the implementation of unpopular economic austerity measures in 1982 and 1983, Kaunda was re-elected President in October 1983, with 93% of the votes cast. A campaign was subsequently inaugurated against corruption and inefficiency within the Government and in industry. In March 1985 Kaunda adopted emergency powers to prohibit industrial action in essential services, following a series of strikes by public-sector employees and bank staff in support of demands for higher wages. In April several cabinet members and senior party officials were replaced, apparently as part of the campaign against corruption. During 1985, 1986 and early 1987 the Government introduced further austerity measures in response to the increasing economic decline, which precipitated sporadic civil unrest. In December 1986 the removal of the government subsidy on refined maize meal, the staple food, resulted in an increase of 120% in the price of that commodity. Following violent rioting in the towns of Kitwe and Ndola in the Copperbelt region, in which at least 15 people died and 450 people were arrested, the Government reintroduced the subsidy. Although peace in the region was restored by the end of December, strikes for higher pay occurred in early 1987, and in April of that year the Government was forced to cancel a 70% increase in the price of fuel, following protests in Lusaka. In the same month Kaunda alleged that the South African Government, in collusion with Zambian business executives and military personnel, had conspired to overthrow his administration.

In August 1988 the Central Committee of UNIP was expanded from 25 to 68 members. In October nine people, six of whom were military officers, were arrested and accused of plotting to overthrow the Government. One of the civilians was subsequently released; four of the military officers were convicted of treason in August 1989 (but were released under the terms of a general amnesty in July 1990). Presidential and legislative elections took place later in October 1988. Kaunda, the only candidate, received 95.5% of the votes in the presidential election; however, only 54% of the electorate voted. At the legislative election four cabinet ministers lost their seats in the National Assembly. In March Kebby Musokotwane, who had been widely considered to be a potential rival to Kaunda, was replaced as Prime Minister by Gen. Malimba Masheke, hitherto Minister of Home Affairs.

During 1989 unrest was reported among workers and students, and in July the introduction of increases in the prices of essential goods provoked rioting in the Copperbelt region. In late 1989 the Governor of the Bank of Zambia was dismissed and arrested on corruption charges. In June 1990 Frederick Hapunda (who was widely believed to be a supporter of multi-party politics) was dismissed as Minister of Defence, and several other prominent state officials were similarly removed from office. Later in the month the introduction of economic austerity measures provoked violent rioting in the capital. On 30 June a junior army officer, Lt Mwamba Luchembe, announced on the state radio that the Government had been overthrown by the armed forces. On the same day, however, the revolt was suppressed by troops loyal to Kaunda. Luchembe and his associates were arrested, but were pardoned in July.

In May 1990 Kaunda announced that a popular referendum on the subject of multi-party politics would take place in October of that year, and that supporters of such a system (which Kaunda and UNIP opposed) would be permitted to campaign and hold public meetings. Accordingly, in July the Movement for Multi-party Democracy (MMD), an unofficial alliance of political opponents of the Government, was formed. The MMD, which was led by a former government minister, Arthur Wina, and the Chairman of the Zambian Congress of Trade Unions, Frederick Chiluba, swiftly gained widespread public support. Later in July Kaunda announced that the referendum on multi-party politics was to be postponed until August 1991, to facilitate the registration of a large section of the electorate. Although he welcomed the registration procedure, Wina criticized the referendum's postponement, and requested that it take place before December 1990. In August the National Assembly proposed the introduction of a multi-party system, to which Kaunda again expressed his opposition. In the following month, however, at a session of the National Council of UNIP, Kaunda recommended the reintroduction of a multi-party political system. In addition, he proposed that multi-party elections be organized by October 1991, that the national referendum be abandoned, and that a commission be appointed to revise the Constitution. On 27 September 1990 the National Council endorsed the proposals for multi-party legislative and presidential elections, and accepted recommendations that had been presented by a parliamentary committee regarding the restructuring of the party.

A reorganization of ministerial portfolios in November 1990 included the dismissal of the Minister of State for Decentralization, Michael Chilufya Sata, owing to his alleged criticism of government policy. In December the Minister of Defence and the editors of Zambia's two official daily newspapers were also replaced. On 17 December Kaunda formally adopted constitutional amendments (which had been approved by the National Assembly earlier in the same month), that permitted the formation of other political associations to contest the forthcoming elections. The MMD was subsequently granted official recognition as a political organization. In early 1991 several prominent members of UNIP resigned from the party and declared their support for the MMD, while the Zambian Congress of Trade Unions officially transferred allegiance to the MMD. Several other opposition movements were also established. In February violent clashes between supporters of the MMD and members of UNIP were suppressed by the security forces.

In June 1991 the constitutional commission presented a series of recommendations, including the creation of the post of Vice-President, the expansion of the National Assembly from 135 to 150 members and the establishment of a constitutional court. Kaunda accepted the majority of the proposed constitutional amendments, which were subsequently submitted for approval by the National Assembly. The MMD, however, rejected the draft Constitution, and announced that it would boycott the forthcoming elections if the National Assembly accepted the proposals. In July, following discussions between Kaunda, Chiluba and delegates from seven other political associations, Kaunda agreed to suspend the review of the draft Constitution in the National Assembly, pending further negotiations. It was also announced that state subsidies would be granted to all registered political parties. Subsequent discussions between the MMD and UNIP resulted in the establishment of a joint commission to revise the draft Constitution. In late July, following a meeting of the two parties under the aegis of the constitutional commission, Kaunda conceded to opposition demands that ministers be appointed only from the National Assembly, and that the proposed creation of the constitutional court be abandoned. A constitutional provision granting the President the power to impose martial law was also rescinded. On 2 August the National Assembly formally adopted the new Constitution, which had been revised accordingly.

In August 1991, at the UNIP party congress, Kaunda was unanimously re-elected as President of the party. (A recent challenge for the party presidency by another member of the Central Committee, Enoch Kavindele, had been withdrawn.) However, several prominent party officials, including the incumbent Secretary-General, refused to contest the election to a new Central Committee. Later in August Kaunda agreed to permit international observers to monitor the electoral process, in an attempt to counter opposition allegations that the elections would not be conducted fairly. Kaunda also announced the disassociation of the armed forces from UNIP; senior officers in the armed forces were subsequently obliged to retire from the Central Committee of UNIP.

In September 1991 Kaunda announced the dissolution of the National Assembly, in preparation for the presidential and legislative elections, which were scheduled for 31 October. In addition, he officially disassociated UNIP from the State; workers in the public sector were henceforth prohibited from engaging in political activity.

On 31 October 1991 Chiluba, with 75.79% of votes cast, defeated Kaunda in the presidential election. In the concurrent legislative elections, contested by 330 candidates representing six political parties, the MMD secured 125 seats in the National Assembly, while UNIP won the remaining 25 seats; only four members of the previous Government were returned to the National Assembly. Although there had been numerous reports of violence in the pre-election period, and despite fears of electoral malpractice, international observers reported that the elections had been conducted fairly. Kaunda's failure to secure re-election to the presidency was attributed to widespread perceptions of economic mismanagement by his administration. On 2 November Chiluba was inaugurated as President. He subsequently initiated a major restructuring of the civil service and of parastatal organizations, as part of efforts to reverse the country's significant economic decline. Chiluba appointed Levy Mwanawasa, a constitutional lawyer, as Vice-President and Leader of the National Assembly, and formed a new 22-member Cabinet. In addition, a minister was appointed to each of the country's nine provinces, which had hitherto been administered by governors. Later in November Chiluba dismissed senior executives in a number of parastatal organizations, in an attempt to eradicate widespread corruption among officials.

In December 1991, following a road accident in which Mwanawasa was severely injured, the Minister without Portfolio, Brig.-Gen. Godfrey Miyanda, was accused of attempting to bring about his death. A commission of inquiry was later informed that Miyanda had conspired with members of the former Government to kill Mwanawasa, and subsequently to assume the vice-presidency. In March 1992, however, following an investigation of the incident by detectives from the United Kingdom, the circumstances of the accident were pronounced to be normal, and Miyanda was exonerated of involvement.

In mid-1992 widespread opposition to government policies was reported. In May a dissident faction of academics within the MMD, the Caucus for National Unity (CNU), emerged. The CNU, which claimed support from several members of the Government, demanded that Chiluba review procedures for the appointment of cabinet ministers and heads of parastatal organizations, to ensure that all ethnic groups were represented. The CNU, together with other pressure groups, also advocated the establishment of a constitutional commission to curtail the executive power vested in the President and the Cabinet. However, Chiluba refused to initiate a review of the Constitution, on the grounds that it would prove too expensive. The Government was also criticized for its rigid enforcement of the structural adjustment programme supported by the IMF and World Bank, which had resulted in an increase in economic hardship.

In June 1992 Kavindele resigned from UNIP and formed the United Democratic Party (UDP); a large number of members of UNIP subsequently transferred their allegiance to the UDP. In July two cabinet ministers (who reportedly supported the CNU) resigned in protest at what they alleged was the Government's failure to suppress corruption and to institute democratic measures, following the refusal of the National Assembly to accept a report that implicated several government members in alleged financial malpractice. Later that month the CNU registered as an independent political party. In late September, Kaunda formally resigned from active participation in UNIP; Musokotwane, of late the party's Secretary-General, was subsequently elected as its President. At local government elections in November the MMD won the majority of seats; the high rate of abstention (more than 90% of the registered electorate) was, however, widely attributed to disillusionment with the Chiluba administration.

In March 1993 Chiluba declared a state of emergency, following the discovery of UNIP documents that revealed details of an alleged conspiracy to destabilize the Government by inciting unrest and civil disobedience. Several prominent members of UNIP, including Kaunda's three sons, were subsequently arrested. Musokotwane conceded the existence of the documents, but denied that UNIP officials were involved in the conspiracy, which he attributed to extreme factions within the party. Kaunda, however, claimed that the conspiracy had been fabricated by Zambian security forces, with the assistance of US intelligence services, in an attempt to undermine the opposition. Later that month diplomatic relations with Iran and Iraq were suspended, following allegations by the Zambian Government that the two countries had funded subversive elements within UNIP. Shortly afterwards (in accordance with constitutional requirements) the National Assembly approved the state of emergency, which was to remain in force for a further three months. As a result of pressure from Western Governments, however, Chiluba reduced the maximum period of detention without trial from 28 to seven days.

In April 1993, in an apparent attempt to eradicate government corruption, Chiluba effected an extensive reorganization of the Cabinet, in which four ministers were dismissed; however, he failed to remove a number of ministers who were implicated in allegations of malpractice. Divisions within the MMD became apparent in August, when 15 prominent members (11 of whom held seats in the National Assembly) resigned from the party. The rebels accused the Government of protecting corrupt cabinet ministers and of failing to respond to numerous reports linking senior party officials with the illegal drugs trade. Their opposition to the Government was consolidated later in the month by the formation of a new political group, the National Party (NP).

In January 1994 two senior cabinet ministers announced their resignation, following persistent allegations of their involvement in drugs-trafficking activities. One of the ministers, Vernon Mwaanga, a founder member of the MMD, who had held the foreign affairs portfolio, had been implicated in the drugs trade by a tribunal in 1985, although he had not been convicted of the alleged offences. The resignations prompted Chiluba to announce an extensive government reorganization, in which a further two ministers were dismissed. Opposition groups remained critical of the Government, however, claiming that the changes effected were merely designed to appease public opinion. At partial elections for 10 of the 11 vacated seats in the National Assembly, which took place in November 1993 and April 1994, the MMD regained five seats, while the NP secured four and UNIP one. In June seven opposition parties, including UNIP, established an informal alliance, the Zambia Opposition Front, which was to present joint candidates to contest future elections.

In early July 1994 Mwanawasa announced his resignation from the office of Vice-President, as a result of long-standing differences with Chiluba, and was subsequently replaced by Miyanda. In the same month Chiluba dismissed the Minister of Legal Affairs, who had accused him of receiving payments from drugs-traffickers. In mid-July Kaunda denounced MMD leaders for corrupt practices, and stated that he intended to contest the presidential election in 1996. However, UNIP officials indicated that he would only be allowed to resume the leadership of the party if he were officially elected by members. (Kaunda's decision to return to active politics subsequently resulted in factional division within UNIP.) In August Kaunda was apparently warned against inciting revolt, after he conducted a number of rallies in the Northern Province (where the MMD traditionally attracted considerable support). Later that month the Government announced that Kaunda had been replaced under surveillance in the interests of national security, following reports that he had received support from foreign diplomatic missions in Zambia.

In October 1994 two deputy government ministers were dismissed, after criticizing the modalities of government plans to privatize the country's principal industrial enterprise, Zambia Consolidated Copper Mines. At a partial election in December UNIP secured the remaining vacant seat in the National Assembly. In January 1995 Chiluba dismissed the Minister of Lands, Dr Chuulu Kalima, on grounds of misconduct; Kalima had apparently accused the President of involvement in a transaction in which a deputy minister had acquired land formerly owned by the University of Zambia. In early February Chiluba ordered members of the Government to declare their financial assets and liabilities within a period of two days. In the same month Kaunda was charged with convening an illegal political gathering, after he had addressed a public rally. Later in February the Governor of the Bank of Zambia was replaced, following a sharp depreciation in the value of the national currency. In March increasing divisions became evident within the MMD between the Bemba ethnic group (to which Chiluba belonged) and the traditionalist Nsenga; it was reported that MMD factions had circulated tracts criticizing Chiluba and Mwanawasa (who continued to hold the position of MMD Vice-President). In April a former cabinet minister, Dean Mung'omba, announced that he intended to contest Chiluba's leadership of the MMD. In the same month a pro-Kaunda faction of UNIP indicated that it would challenge the leadership of the incumbent party President, Musokotwane, at a forthcoming party congress. Later in April the MMD retained two parliamentary seats contested in further partial elections. In July Chiluba reorganized the Cabinet.

Kaunda undertook a major role in peace initiatives in the region and supported the African National Congress (ANC) of South Africa in its opposition to the Government there. In September 1985 he succeeded President Nyerere of Tanzania as Chairman of the 'front-line' states. In May 1986 South African troops launched several attacks on alleged ANC bases in Zambia, Zimbabwe and Botswana, and following this a number of foreigners and Zambian citizens were arrested in Zambia on suspicion of spying for South Africa. In August Zambia and Zimbabwe undertook to impose economic sanctions against South Africa, and in the same month the South African Government retaliated by temporarily enforcing trade restrictions on Zambia and Zimbabwe. Further attacks on ANC targets took place during 1987, 1988 and 1989: South African involvement was suspected. During the 1980s President Kaunda's support for the Governments of Angola and Mozambique resulted in attacks on Zambian civilians by Angolan rebels (with assistance from the Governments of South Africa and the USA) and by Mozambican rebels (also allegedly supported by South Africa). In September 1992 the Governments of Zambia and Angola signed a security agreement that provided for common border controls. In January 1993 Zambia contributed some 950 troops to the UN peace-keeping force in Mozambique (see chapter on Mozambique), and in September of that year Zambia signed a border co-operation agreement with Malawi.

## Government

Under the provisions of the Constitution that was approved by the National Assembly in August 1991, Zambia is a multi-party state. Executive power is vested in the President, who is the constitutional Head of State. Legislative power is vested in a National Assembly, which comprises 150 members. The President and the National Assembly are elected simultaneously by universal adult suffrage for a five-year term. The maximum duration of the President's tenure of office is limited to two five-year terms. The President governs with the assistance of a Vice-President and a Cabinet, whom he appoints from members of the National Assembly. The Constitution also provides for a 27-member House of Chiefs, which represents traditional tribal authorities. Each of Zambia's nine provinces has a minister, who is appointed by the President.

## Defence

The total strength of armed forces in June 1994 was 21,600, with 20,000 in the army and 1,600 in the air force. Paramilitary forces numbered 1,400. Military service is voluntary. There is also a National Defence Force responsible to the Government. The 1994/95 budget allocated K26,200m. to defence.

## Economic Affairs

In 1993, according to estimates by the World Bank, Zambia's gross national product (GNP), measured at average 1991–93 prices, was US $3,152m., equivalent to US $370 per head. During 1985–93, it was estimated, GNP per head increased, in real terms, at an average annual rate of 1.8%. During 1985–93, the population increased by an annual average of 3.1%. Zambia's gross domestic product (GDP) increased, in real terms, by an annual average of 0.7% in 1989–93.

Agriculture (including hunting, forestry and fishing) contributed 29% of GDP in 1993, and employed 68.5% of the labour force in 1991. The principal crops are maize, cassava, millet, sorghum and beans. Wheat, rice, cotton, tobacco, sunflower seeds, groundnuts, sugar cane and horticultural produce are also cultivated. Cattle-rearing is important. During 1989–93 agricultural GDP declined by an annual average of 0.7%.

Industry (including mining, manufacturing, construction and power) contributed 48.3% of GDP in 1990, and engaged 37.4% of all wage-earning employees in 1989. During 1989–93 industrial production declined increased by an annual average of 1.4%.

In 1990 mining and quarrying contributed 9.6% of GDP, and in 1989 engaged 15.1% of wage-earning employees. Copper is the main mineral export, accounting for 93% of foreign exchange earnings in 1991. Cobalt, zinc and lead are also important exports, while coal, gold, emeralds, amethyst, limestone and selenium are also mined. In addition, Zambia has reserves of phosphates, fluorspar and iron ore. During 1989–93 mining GDP declined by an annual average of 3.1%.

Manufacturing contributed 34.0% of GDP in 1990, and engaged 14.2% of all wage-earning employees in 1989. The principal manufacturing activities are the smelting and refining of copper and other metals, vehicle assembly, petroleum-refining, food-canning and the production of fertilizers, explosives, textiles, bottles, batteries, bricks and copper wire. During 1989–93 manufacturing GDP increased by an annual average of 4.8%.

Energy is derived principally from hydroelectric power, in which Zambia is self-sufficient. Imports of fuel comprised about 18% of the value of merchandise imports in 1992.

In 1991 Zambia recorded a visible trade surplus of US $420m., while there was a deficit of US $307m. on the current account of the balance of payments. In 1990 the principal source of imports (18.1%) was the South African Customs Union; other major suppliers were the United Kingdom, the USA, Germany and Japan. The principal market for exports in 1990 was Japan (accounting for 31.0% of the total); other significant purchasers were France, Thailand and India. The principal exports in 1993 were copper, cobalt and zinc. The principal imports in 1982 were machinery and transport equipment, mineral fuels, lubricants and electricity, basic manufactures and chemicals.

In 1993 there was an estimated budgetary surplus of K19,000m. Zambia's external public debt totalled US $6,788m. at the end of 1993, of which US $4,666m. was long-term public debt. In 1993 the cost of debt-servicing was equivalent to 32.8% of the value of exports of goods and services. In 1985–93 the average annual rate of inflation was 101.8%. Consumer prices increased by an average of 189.0% in 1993; in early 1995, however, the average rate of inflation was only 31.5%.

Zambia is a member of the Southern African Development Community (see p. 219). In November 1993 Zambia was among members of the Preferential Trade Area for Eastern and Southern African States (see p. 240) to sign a treaty establishing the Common Market for Eastern and Southern Africa.

During the 1980s Zambia's economic performance was adversely affected by fluctuations in world prices for copper, while the agricultural sector remained underdeveloped and vulnerable to unfavourable weather conditions. The mismanagement of the Kaunda administration resulted in a further deterioration in the economy, which included severe food shortages, and a dramatic increase in inflation and unemployment. Following the elections in October 1991, however, the new administration initiated an economic programme that involved further devaluations of the kwacha, as well as measures that aimed to reduce public spending and to attract private investment. In March 1992 the Government formally adopted a three-year structural adjustment programme, in agreement with the IMF and World Bank, which emphasized the decentralization of social services, the reorganization of the civil service and the transfer of parastatal organizations to the private sector. By late 1994 austerity measures had achieved some success, resulting in a reduction in the budgetary deficit and in the rate of inflation. Funds that had been pledged by external creditors in support of the economic reform programme were principally used to service debt arrears owed to the IMF. Owing to increasing social and economic hardship, however, the reforms proved widely unpopular, particularly the privatization programme, which contributed to rising unemployment; government plans to privatize Zambia Consolidated Copper Mines (the principal source of foreign exchange) prompted considerable controversy. In April 1995 the IMF announced that Zambia had not fulfilled the pre-conditions to qualification for concessionary debt relief under an Enhanced Structural Adjustment Facility.

### Social Welfare

The Department of Labour and Social Services is responsible for relief of distress, care of the aged, protection of children, adoption and probation services. It gives grants for group welfare services including voluntary schemes. A form of pension is granted to the indigent aged. In October 1990 free medical care in hospitals was abolished. In 1990 Zambia had 82 hospitals, with a total of 13,906 beds; the Government operated about 2,000 health centres in 1995. In 1985 there were an estimated 986 physicians working in the country. Of total budgetary expenditure by the central Government in 1988, health was allocated K635.6m. (7.4%), and social security and welfare K129.9m. (1.5%).

### Education

Between 1964 and 1979 enrolment in schools increased by more than 260%. Primary education, which is compulsory, begins at seven years of age and lasts for seven years. Secondary education, beginning at the age of 14, lasts for a further five years, comprising a first cycle of two years and a second of three years. In 1988 an estimated 81% of children (83% of boys; 80% of girls) in the relevant age-group attended primary schools, while the comparable ratio at secondary schools was 16% of children (19% of boys; 12% of girls). Some 1,461,206 pupils were enrolled at primary schools in 1990, while about 161,349 pupils were enrolled at secondary schools in 1988. There are two universities: the University of Zambia at Lusaka, and the Copperbelt University at Kitwe (which is to be transferred to Ndola). There are 14 teacher training colleges. In 1990, according to estimates by UNESCO, the average rate of adult illiteracy was 27.2% (males 19.2%; females 34.7%). Education was allocated K2,737m., or 8.7% of total expenditure, by the central Government in 1990.

### Public Holidays

**1995:** 1 January (New Year's Day), 11 March (Youth Day), 14–17 April (Easter), 1 May (Labour Day), 24 May (African Freedom Day, anniversary of OAU's foundation), 5 July (Heroes' Day), 8 July (Unity Day), 5 August (Farmers' Day), 24 October (Independence Day), 25 December (Christmas Day).

**1996:** 1 January (New Year's Day), 11 March (Youth Day), 5–8 April (Easter), 1 May (Labour Day), 24 May (African Freedom Day, anniversary of OAU's foundation), 5 July (Heroes' Day), 8 July (Unity Day), 5 August (Farmers' Day), 24 October (Independence Day), 25 December (Christmas Day).

### Weights and Measures

The metric system is in use.

# Statistical Survey

Source (unless otherwise indicated): Central Statistical Office, POB 31908, Lusaka; tel. (1) 211231; telex 40430.

## Area and Population

### AREA, POPULATION AND DENSITY

| | |
|---|---:|
| Area (sq km) | 752,614* |
| Population (census results) | |
| 1 September 1980 | 5,661,801 |
| 20 August 1990 | |
|   Males | 3,975,083 |
|   Females | 3,843,364 |
|   Total | 7,818,447 |
| Population (official estimate at 20 August) | |
| 1991 | 8,023,000 |
| Density (per sq km) at August 1991 | 10.7 |

* 290,586 sq miles.

**PRINCIPAL TOWNS** (estimated population at mid-1988)

| | | | |
|---|---:|---|---:|
| Lusaka (capital) | 870,030 | Chingola | 194,347 |
| Kitwe | 472,255 | Luanshya | 165,853 |
| Ndola | 442,666 | Livingstone | 98,480 |
| Kabwe (Broken Hill) | 200,287 | Kalulushi | 94,376 |
| Mufulira | 199,368 | Chililabombwe | 81,803 |

**BIRTHS AND DEATHS** (UN estimates, annual averages)

| | 1975–80 | 1980–85 | 1985–90 |
|---|---:|---:|---:|
| Birth rate (per 1,000) | 51.6 | 49.3 | 48.6 |
| Death rate (per 1,000) | 16.5 | 15.1 | 15.9 |

**Expectation of life** (UN estimates, years at birth, 1985–90): 48.6 (males 47.7; females 49.5).

Source: UN, *World Population Prospects: The 1992 Revision*.

ZAMBIA

## ECONOMICALLY ACTIVE POPULATION
(ILO estimates, '000 persons at mid-1980)

|  | Males | Females | Total |
|---|---|---|---|
| Agriculture, etc. | 959 | 438 | 1,398 |
| Industry | 174 | 14 | 188 |
| Services | 257 | 69 | 326 |
| **Total labour force** | 1,390 | 522 | 1,912 |

Source: ILO, *Labour Force Estimates and Projections, 1950–2025*.

**1980 census:** Total labour force 1,302,944 (males 908,606; females 394,338).
**Mid-1984** (official estimates): Total labour force 2,032,300 (males 1,464,800; females 567,500).
**Mid-1993** (estimates in '000): Agriculture, etc. 1,972; Total 2,918 (Source: FAO, *Production Yearbook*).

## EMPLOYMENT ('000 employees at June)

|  | 1987 | 1988 | 1989 |
|---|---|---|---|
| Agriculture, forestry and fishing | 36.4 | 36.8 | 37.2 |
| Mining and quarrying | 55.8 | 55.0 | 54.2 |
| Manufacturing | 50.0 | 50.4 | 50.9 |
| Electricity, gas and water | 8.5 | 8.6 | 8.7 |
| Construction | 25.4 | 23.1 | 20.8 |
| Trade, restaurants and hotels | 27.9 | 27.2 | 26.6 |
| Transport, storage and communications | 25.4 | 25.8 | 26.1 |
| Financing, insurance, real estate and business services | 23.9 | 24.3 | 24.7 |
| Community, social and personal services* | 108.7 | 109.5 | 110.2 |
| **Total** | 361.8 | 360.7 | 359.6 |

* Excluding domestic services.

Source: ILO, *Year Book of Labour Statistics*.

## Agriculture

### PRINCIPAL CROPS ('000 metric tons)

|  | 1991 | 1992 | 1993 |
|---|---|---|---|
| Wheat | 65 | 58 | 71 |
| Rice (paddy) | 15 | 9 | 14 |
| Maize | 1,096 | 483 | 1,598 |
| Millet | 26 | 48 | 37 |
| Sorghum | 21 | 13 | 35 |
| Sugar cane* | 1,150 | 1,300 | 1,300 |
| Potatoes* | 10 | 8 | 10 |
| Sweet potatoes* | 56 | 52 | 56 |
| Cassava (Manioc)* | 530 | 560 | 570 |
| Pulses | 14 | 20 | 24 |
| Onions (dry)* | 30 | 25 | 26 |
| Tomatoes* | 30 | 25 | 26 |
| Soybeans | 28 | 7 | 28 |
| Sunflower seed | 11 | 1 | 21 |
| Groundnuts (in shell) | 28 | 21 | 42 |
| Cottonseed† | 31 | 16 | 37 |
| Cotton (lint)† | 18 | 9 | 21 |
| Tobacco (leaves) | 6 | 2 | 7 |

* FAO estimates.   † Unofficial figures.

Source: FAO, *Production Yearbook*.

### LIVESTOCK ('000 head, year ending September)

|  | 1991 | 1992 | 1993 |
|---|---|---|---|
| Cattle* | 2,984 | 3,095 | 3,204 |
| Sheep* | 62 | 63 | 67 |
| Goats* | 556 | 560 | 600 |
| Pigs† | 296 | 290 | 293 |

* Unofficial figures.   † FAO estimates.

Poultry (FAO estimates, million): 17 in 1991; 19 in 1992; 21 in 1993.

Source: FAO, *Production Yearbook*.

## LIVESTOCK PRODUCTS (FAO estimates, '000 metric tons)

|  | 1991 | 1992 | 1993 |
|---|---|---|---|
| Beef and veal | 37 | 41 | 41 |
| Pig meat | 10 | 9 | 9 |
| Poultry meat | 21 | 23 | 25 |
| Other meat | 31 | 32 | 33 |
| Cows' milk | 81 | 84 | 87 |
| Hen eggs | 27.8 | 30.4 | 33.4 |
| Cattle hides | 4.9 | 5.3 | 5.4 |

Source: FAO, *Production Yearbook*.

## Forestry

### ROUNDWOOD REMOVALS ('000 cubic metres)

|  | 1990 | 1991 | 1992 |
|---|---|---|---|
| Sawlogs, veneer logs and logs for sleepers | 262 | 307 | 343 |
| Other industrial wood* | 467 | 481 | 495 |
| Fuel wood* | 12,466 | 12,952 | 12,952 |
| **Total** | 13,195 | 13,740 | 13,790 |

* FAO estimates.

Source: FAO, *Yearbook of Forest Products*.

### SAWNWOOD PRODUCTION
('000 cubic metres, incl. railway sleepers)

|  | 1990 | 1991 | 1992 |
|---|---|---|---|
| Coniferous (soft wood) | 53 | 62 | 78 |
| Broadleaved (hard wood) | 28 | 32 | 34 |
| **Total** | 81 | 94 | 112 |

Source: FAO, *Yearbook of Forest Products*.

## Fishing

('000 metric tons, live weight)

|  | 1990 | 1991 | 1992 |
|---|---|---|---|
| Freshwater fishes | 51.6 | 53.2 | 54.9 |
| Dagaas | 12.8 | 12.8 | 12.6 |
| **Total catch** (inland waters) | 64.5 | 65.9 | 67.5 |

Source: FAO, *Yearbook of Fishery Statistics*.

## Mining

(metric tons)

|  | 1989 | 1990 | 1991 |
|---|---|---|---|
| Hard coal | 397,000 | 377,000 | 380,000 |
| Cobalt ore*† | 7,255 | 7,086 | 7,000 |
| Copper ore* | 496,000 | 621,600 | 400,000 |
| Lead ore* | 8,900 | 4,100 | 9,000 |
| Zinc ore* | 20,700 | 10,900 | n.a. |
| Gold (kg)* | 225‡ | 129 | 120 |

* Figures relate to the metal content of ores and concentrates (or, for cobalt, the metal recovered).
† Data from the US Bureau of Mines.
‡ Estimate.

Source: UN, *Industrial Statistics Yearbook*.

ZAMBIA

## Industry

**SELECTED PRODUCTS** (metric tons, unless otherwise indicated)

|  | 1989 | 1990 | 1991 |
|---|---|---|---|
| Raw sugar* | 132,000 | 147,000 | n.a. |
| Cigarettes (million) | 1,500† | 1,500 | 1,500 |
| Nitrogenous fertilizers | 2,000 | n.a. | n.a. |
| Cement | 385,000 | 432,000 | 376,000 |
| Copper (unwrought)† | | | |
|   Smelter‡ | 485,200 | 461,400 | 409,000 |
|   Refined | 450,800 | 424,800 | 430,000 |
| Lead (primary) | 3,800 | 4,800 | n.a. |
| Zinc (primary) | 12,800 | 10,400 | n.a. |
| Electric energy (million kWh) | 6,742 | 7,771 | 7,775 |

* Data from the International Sugar Organization, London.
† Estimate(s).
‡ Including some production at the refined stage.

Source: UN, *Industrial Statistics Yearbook*.

## Finance

**CURRENCY AND EXCHANGE RATES**

**Monetary Units**
100 ngwee = 1 Zambian kwacha (K).

**Sterling and Dollar Equivalents** (31 July 1994)
£1 sterling = 1,536.6 kwacha;
US $1 = 1,000.0 kwacha;
10,000 Zambian kwacha = £6.508 = $10.000.

**Average Exchange Rate** (US $ per Zambian kwacha)
1991    0.0162
1992    0.0064
1993    0.0023

**BUDGET** (K million)*

| Revenue† | 1986 | 1987 | 1988 |
|---|---|---|---|
| Taxation | 2,879.1 | 3,981.8 | 4,699.7 |
|   Taxes on income, profits, etc. | 806.0 | 1,118.1 | 1,957.6 |
|   Taxes on property | 14.1 | 6.4 | 9.5 |
|   Domestic taxes on goods and services | 1,023.5 | 1,559.1 | 1,901.8 |
|     Sales taxes | 598.7 | 1,048.1 | 1,208.0 |
|     Excises | 409.4 | 487.4 | 667.8 |
|   Taxes on international trade | 1,019.8 | 1,282.9 | 811.6 |
|     Import duties | 505.7 | 811.0 | 800.5 |
| Other current revenue | 142.9 | 282.1 | 441.2 |
|   Property income | 66.7 | 186.8 | 90.7 |
| Capital revenue | 0.8 | 3.0 | 1.1 |
| **Total** | 3,022.8 | 4,266.9 | 5,142.0 |

| Expenditure‡ | 1986 | 1987 | 1988 |
|---|---|---|---|
| General public services | 1,778.6 | 3,231.7 | 3,049.5 |
| Public order and safety | 156.6 | 207.1 | 278.5 |
| Education | 406.5 | 594.6 | 737.5 |
| Health | 222.4 | 349.3 | 635.6 |
| Social security and welfare | 55.0 | 87.6 | 129.9 |
| Housing and community amenities | 36.0 | 29.6 | 40.6 |
| Other community and social services | 56.2 | 99.5 | 134.7 |
| Economic services | 1,126.0 | 562.8 | 2,122.4 |
|   Agriculture, forestry and fishing | 778.8 | 283.0 | 1,665.6 |
|   Mining, manufacturing and construction | 33.3 | 56.9 | 59.7 |
|   Transport and communications | 248.7 | 187.5 | 171.5 |
| **Total** | 5,406.8 | 6,819.8 | 8,558.5 |
| Current | 4,140.6 | 4,739.5 | 6,693.1 |
| Capital | 1,266.2 | 2,080.3 | 1,865.4 |

* Figures refer to the consolidated accounts of the central Government, including administrative agencies and social security funds.
† Excluding grants from abroad (K million): 173.2 in 1986; 91.4 in 1987; 494.7 in 1988.
‡ Excluding net lending (K million): 593.5 in 1986; 87.3 in 1987; 544.5 in 1988.

**1989** (provisional figures, K million): Revenue 6,553.1 (current 6,551.8, capital 1.3), excl. grants from abroad (1,331.5); Expenditure 11,984.8 (current 7,481.3, capital 4,503.5), excl. net lending (−1,343.2).

Source: IMF, *Government Finance Statistics Yearbook*.

**INTERNATIONAL RESERVES**
(US $ million at 31 December)

|  | 1986 | 1987 | 1988 |
|---|---|---|---|
| Gold* | 1.0 | 1.8 | 4.1 |
| Foreign exchange† | 70.3 | 108.8 | 134.0 |
| **Total** | 71.3 | 110.6 | 138.1 |

* Valued at market-related prices.
† Foreign exchange (US $ million at 31 December): 116.2 in 1989; 193.1 in 1990; 184.6 in 1991; n.a. in 1992; 192.3 in 1993.

Source: IMF, *International Financial Statistics*.

**MONEY SUPPLY** (K million at 31 December)

|  | 1989 | 1990 | 1991 |
|---|---|---|---|
| Currency outside banks | 2,250 | 4,610 | 9,188 |
| Demand deposits at commercial banks* | 5,695 | 7,927 | 13,166 |

* Demand deposits at commercial banks (K million at 31 December): 32,403 in 1992; 55,821 in 1993.

Source: IMF, *International Financial Statistics*.

**COST OF LIVING** (Consumer Price Index, average of monthly figures for low-income group; base: 1980 = 100)

|  | 1990 | 1991 | 1992 |
|---|---|---|---|
| Food | 4,261.6 | 8,138.9 | 25,916 |
| Clothing | 3,921.1 | 6,564.6 | n.a. |
| Rent, fuel and light | 1,720.2 | 5,704.5 | n.a. |
| **All items** (incl. others) | 4,239.0 | 8,163.3 | 24,283 |

Source: ILO, *Year Book of Labour Statistics*.

ZAMBIA

## NATIONAL ACCOUNTS
(K million at current prices)

### Expenditure on the Gross Domestic Product

|  | 1991 | 1992 | 1993 |
|---|---|---|---|
| Government final consumption expenditure | 35,758 | 83,497 | 130,659 |
| Private final consumption expenditure | 114,334 | 421,998 | 1,173,588 |
| Increase in stocks | 7,201 | 19,805 | 60,846 |
| Gross fixed capital formation | 24,973 | 60,187 | 93,170 |
| **Total domestic expenditure** | 182,266 | 585,487 | 1,458,263 |
| Exports of goods and services | 74,967 | 180,291 | 579,036 |
| *Less* imports of goods and services | 37,879 | 197,048 | 596,636 |
| **GDP in purchasers' values** | 219,353 | 568,730 | 1,440,663 |

Source: IMF, *International Financial Statistics*.

### Gross Domestic Product by Economic Activity

|  | 1989 | 1990 | 1991 |
|---|---|---|---|
| Agriculture, hunting, forestry and fishing | 6,390 | 14,175 | 28,132 |
| Mining and quarrying | 10,042 | 25,272 | 33,755 |
| Manufacturing | 13,027 | 25,510 | 61,725 |
| Electricity, gas and water | 308 | 635 | 1,909 |
| Construction | 3,019 | 6,300 | 10,911 |
| Wholesale and retail trade, restaurants and hotels | 8,963 | 13,148 | 24,021 |
| Transport and communications | 3,116 | 6,861 | 15,812 |
| Finance, insurance, real estate and business services | 6,837 | 13,290 | 24,832 |
| Community, social and personal services | 4,148 | 9,484 | 19,254 |
| **Sub-total** | 55,850 | 114,675 | 220,351 |
| *Less* imputed bank service charge | 768 | 1,471 | 2,726 |
| GDP at factor cost | 55,082 | 113,204 | 217,625 |
| Indirect taxes, *less* subsidies | 3,624 | 10,283 | 16,879 |
| **GDP in purchasers' values** | 58,706 | 123,487 | 234,504 |

Source: UN, *National Accounts Statistics*.

### BALANCE OF PAYMENTS (US $ million)

|  | 1989 | 1990 | 1991 |
|---|---|---|---|
| Merchandise exports f.o.b. | 1,340 | 1,254 | 1,172 |
| Merchandise imports f.o.b. | −774 | −1,511 | −752 |
| **Trade balance** | 566 | −257 | 420 |
| Exports of services | 85 | 107 | 83 |
| Imports of services | −444 | −386 | −363 |
| Other income received | 1 | 2 | 10 |
| Other income paid | −509 | −439 | −696 |
| Private unrequited transfers (net) | −30 | −18 | −22 |
| Official unrequited transfers (net) | 109 | 395 | 261 |
| **Current balance** | −222 | −597 | −307 |
| Direct investment (net) | 164 | 203 | 34 |
| Other capital (net) | 1,664 | 285 | −24 |
| Net errors and omissions | 1,712 | 322 | 110 |
| **Overall balance** | −105 | 213 | −187 |

Source: IMF, *International Financial Statistics*.

# External Trade

### PRINCIPAL COMMODITIES (K'000)

| Imports f.o.b. | 1980 | 1981 | 1982* |
|---|---|---|---|
| Food and live animals | 38,850 | 50,799 | 49,402 |
| Beverages and tobacco | 775 | 1,175 | 1,007 |
| Crude materials (inedible) except fuels | 12,108 | 13,570 | 11,047 |
| Mineral fuels, lubricants, etc. (incl. electricity) | 198,284 | 202,439 | 193,106 |
| Animal and vegetable oils and fats | 7,386 | 10,673 | 11,820 |
| Chemicals | 108,296 | 126,302 | 148,947 |
| Basic manufactures | 178,556 | 173,480 | 165,774 |
| Machinery and transport equipment | 302,340 | 314,443 | 320,996 |
| Miscellaneous manufactured articles | 29,319 | 29,608 | 29,960 |
| **Total** (incl. others) | 876,688 | 924,444 | 929,997 |

* Provisional.

**Total imports** (K million, f.o.b.): 6,898.1 in 1988; 12,600.5 in 1989; 36,553.7 in 1990; 51,772.8 in 1991; 144,108.5 in 1992. Source: UN, *International Trade Statistics Yearbook*.

| Exports f.o.b. | 1985* | 1986* | 1987* |
|---|---|---|---|
| Copper | 1,960,600† | 4,428,600 | 6,845,200 |
| Zinc | 53,189 | 99,154 | 130,944 |
| Lead | 7,400 | 15,537 | 19,765 |
| Cobalt | 23,867 | 385,151 | 466,221 |
| Tobacco | 2,233 | 4,254 | 16,612 |
| **Total** (incl. others) | 2,451,400† | 5,366,584 | 8,058,653 |

* Provisional.

**Total exports** (K million, f.o.b.): 9,786.2 in 1988; 18,434.0 in 1989; 39,143.3 in 1990; 69,607.4 in 1991; 129,475.4 in 1992. Source: UN, *International Trade Statistics Yearbook*.

### PRINCIPAL TRADING PARTNERS (US $'000)

| Imports f.o.b. | 1988 | 1989 | 1990 |
|---|---|---|---|
| France | 31,574 | 15,937 | 12,471 |
| Germany | 53,058 | 184,038 | 144,015 |
| India | 34,931 | 29,302 | 22,930 |
| Italy | 39,368 | 38,706 | 30,289 |
| Japan | 84,440 | 105,590 | 82,627 |
| South African Customs Union | 169,801 | 286,500 | 224,177 |
| United Kingdom | 19,596 | 256,049 | 200,365 |
| USA | 213,075 | 67,071 | 125,522 |
| **Total** (incl. others) | 886,054 | 1,258,321 | 1,237,717 |

| Exports f.o.b. | 1988 | 1989 | 1990 |
|---|---|---|---|
| Belgium-Luxembourg | 31,776 | 48,619 | 34,405 |
| France | 50,310 | 98,121 | 81,008 |
| Greece | 36,144 | 19,648 | 16,221 |
| India | 55,785 | 44,141 | 36,443 |
| Italy | 46,822 | 32,243 | 26,620 |
| Japan | 193,150 | 223,194 | 184,268 |
| Saudi Arabia | 47,595 | 38,732 | 31,977 |
| Thailand | 27,814 | — | 40,673 |
| United Kingdom | 29,652 | 14,712 | 12,147 |
| USA | 206,158 | 13,781 | 9,752 |
| **Total** (incl. others) | 866,711 | 667,811 | 594,765 |

Source: UN, *International Trade Statistics Yearbook*.

ZAMBIA                                                                                              Statistical Survey, Directory

## Transport

**ROAD TRAFFIC**
(UN estimates, '000 motor vehicles in use)

|  | 1989 | 1990 | 1991 |
|---|---|---|---|
| Passenger cars | 74 | 74 | 75 |
| Commercial vehicles | 47 | 47 | 48 |

Source: UN Economic Commission for Africa, *African Statistical Yearbook*.

**CIVIL AVIATION** (scheduled services: Passengers carried—thousands; others—millions)

|  | 1990 | 1991 | 1992 |
|---|---|---|---|
| Kilometres flown | 10 | 7 | 5 |
| Passengers carried | 407 | 293 | 246 |
| Passenger-km | 985 | 655 | 509 |
| Total ton-km | 122 | 82 | 63 |

Source: UN, *Statistical Yearbook*.

## Tourism

|  | 1990 | 1991 | 1992 |
|---|---|---|---|
| Tourist arrivals ('000) | 141 | 171 | 159 |
| Tourist receipts (US $ million) | 41 | 35 | 5 |

Source: UN, *Statistical Yearbook*.

## Communications Media

|  | 1990 | 1991 | 1992 |
|---|---|---|---|
| Radio receivers ('000 in use)* | 650 | 680 | 705 |
| Television receivers ('000 in use)* | 250 | 217 | 225 |
| Telephones ('000 main lines in use) | 65 | 69 | n.a. |
| Daily newspapers: |  |  |  |
| Number | 2 | n.a. | 2 |
| Circulation ('000 copies) | 99 | n.a. | 70 |

* Estimate(s).

Sources: UNESCO, *Statistical Yearbook*; UN, *Statistical Yearbook*.

## Education

(1989)

|  | Institutions | Pupils | Teachers |
|---|---|---|---|
| Primary | 3,587* | 1,461,206* | 3,584 |
| Secondary | 480 | 161,349† | 5,786† |
| Trades and technical | 12 | 3,313* | 438 |
| Teacher training | 14 | 4,669* | 408 |
| University | 2 | 7,361‡ | 320§ |

* 1990 figures.
† 1988 figures.
‡ Excluding part-time and correspondence students.
§ Excluding part-time lecturers and teaching assistants.

Sources: the former Ministry of Higher Education and the former Ministry of General Education, Lusaka; University of Zambia; UNESCO, *Statistical Yearbook*.

# Directory

## The Constitution

The Constitution for the Republic of Zambia, which was approved by the National Assembly on 2 August 1991, provides for a multi-party form of government. The Head of State is the President of the Republic, who is elected by popular vote at the same time as elections to the National Assembly. The President's tenure of office is limited to two five-year terms. The legislature comprises a National Assembly of 150 members, who are elected by universal adult suffrage. The President appoints a Vice-President and a Cabinet from members of the National Assembly.

The Constitution also provides for a House of Chiefs numbering 27: four from each of the Northern, Western, Southern and Eastern Provinces, three each from the North-Western, Luapula and Central Provinces and two from the Copperbelt Province. It may submit resolutions to be debated by the Assembly and consider those matters referred to it by the President.

The Supreme Court of Zambia is the final Court of Appeal. The Chief Justice and other judges are appointed by the President. Subsidiary to the Supreme Court is the High Court, which has unlimited jurisdiction to hear and determine any civil or criminal proceedings under any Zambian law.

## The Government

### HEAD OF STATE

**President:** Frederick J. T. Chiluba (took office 2 November 1991).

### THE CABINET
(July 1995)

**Vice-President:** Brig.-Gen. Godfrey Miyanda.
**Minister of Defence:** Benjamin Yoram Mwila.
**Minister of Foreign Affairs:** Gen. Christon Tembo.
**Minister of Finance:** Ronald Penza.
**Minister of Home Affairs:** Chitalu M. Sampa.
**Minister of Agriculture, Food and Fisheries:** Suresh Desai.
**Minister of Health:** Michael Sata.
**Minister of Education:** Alfeyo Hambayi.
**Minister of Local Government and Housing:** Bennie Mwiinga.
**Minister of Labour and Social Security:** Newstead Zimba.
**Minister of Legal Affairs:** Dr Remmy Mushota.
**Minister of Community Development and Social Services:** Paul Kaping'a.
**Minister of Mines and Mineral Development:** Keli Walubita.
**Minister of Tourism:** Gabriel Maka.
**Minister of Commerce, Trade and Industry:** Dipak Patel.
**Minister of Communications and Transport:** Dawson Lupunga.
**Minister of Energy and Water Development:** Edith Nawakwi.
**Minister of Lands:** Luminzu Shimaponda.
**Minister of Information and Broadcasting Services:** Amusa Mwanamwambwa.
**Minister of Works and Supply:** Simon Zukas.
**Minister of Science, Technology and Vocational Training:** Dr K. Kayongo.
**Minister of Sport, Youth and Child Development:** Lt-Col Patrick Kafumukache.

### MINISTRIES

**Office of the President:** POB 30208, Lusaka; tel. (1) 218282; telex 42240.

**Ministry of Agriculture, Food and Fisheries:** Mulungushi House, Independence Ave, Nationalist Rd, POB RW50291, Lusaka; tel. (1) 213551; telex 43950.

**Ministry of Commerce, Trade and Industry:** Kwacha Annex, Cairo Rd, POB 31968, Lusaka; tel. (1) 213767; telex 45630.

ZAMBIA

**Ministry of Communications and Transport:** Fairley Rd, POB 50065, Lusaka; tel. (1) 251444; telex 41680; fax (1) 253260.
**Ministry of Community Development and Social Services:** Lusaka.
**Ministry of Defence:** POB 31931, Lusaka; tel. (1) 252366.
**Ministry of Education:** 15102 Ridgeway, POB RW50093, Lusaka; tel. (1) 227636; telex 42621; fax (1) 222396.
**Ministry of Energy and Water Development:** Mulungushi House, Independence Ave, Nationalist Rd, POB 36079, Lusaka; tel. (1) 252589; telex 40373; fax (1) 252589.
**Ministry of Finance:** Finance Bldg, POB RW50062, Lusaka; tel. (1) 213822; telex 42221.
**Ministry of Foreign Affairs:** POB RW50069, Lusaka; tel. (1) 252640; telex 41290.
**Ministry of Health:** Woodgate House, 1st–2nd Floors, Cairo Rd, POB 30205, Lusaka; tel. (1) 227745; fax (1) 228385.
**Ministry of Home Affairs:** POB 32862, Lusaka; tel. (1) 213505.
**Ministry of Information and Broadcasting Services:** Independence Ave, POB 51025, Lusaka; tel. (1) 228202; telex 40113.
**Ministry of Labour and Social Security:** Lechwe House, Freedom Way, POB 32186, Lusaka; tel. (1) 212020.
**Ministry of Lands:** POB 50694, Lusaka; tel. (1) 252288; telex 40681; fax (1) 250120.
**Ministry of Legal Affairs:** Fairley Rd, POB 50106, 15101 Ridgeway, Lusaka; tel. (1) 228522; telex 40564.
**Ministry of Local Government and Housing:** Lusaka.
**Ministry of Mines and Mineral Development:** Chilufya Mulenga Rd, POB 31969, Lusaka; tel. (1) 251402; telex 40539.
**Ministry of Science, Technology and Vocational Training:** POB 50464, Lusaka; tel. (1) 229673; telex 40406; fax (1) 252951.
**Ministry of Sport, Youth and Child Development:** Lusaka.
**Ministry of Tourism:** Electra House, Cairo Rd, POB 30575, Lusaka; tel. (1) 227645; telex 45510.
**Ministry of Works and Supply:** POB 50003, Lusaka; tel. (1) 253088; fax (1) 253404.

## President and Legislature

### PRESIDENT
**Presidential election, 31 October 1991**

|  | % of votes |
|---|---|
| Frederick Chiluba | 75.79 |
| Dr Kenneth Kaunda | 24.21 |
| **Total** | **100.00** |

### NATIONAL ASSEMBLY
**General election, 31 October 1991**

|  | Seats |
|---|---|
| Movement for Multi-party Democracy (MMD) | 125 |
| United National Independence Party (UNIP) | 25 |
| **Total** | **150** |

## House of Chiefs

The House of Chiefs is an advisory body which may submit resolutions for debate by the National Assembly. There are 27 Chiefs, four each from the Northern, Western, Southern and Eastern Provinces, three each from the North Western, Luapula and Central Provinces, and two from the Copperbelt Province.

## Political Organizations

The United National Independence Party was the sole authorized political party in 1972–90, when constitutional amendments permitted the formation of other political associations. Among the most prominent political organizations in mid-1995 were:

**Democratic Party (DP):** Lusaka; f. 1991; Pres. Emmanuel Mwamba.
**Independent Democratic Front:** Lusaka; Pres. Mike Kaira.
**Labour Party (LP):** Lusaka; Leader Chibeza Mufune.
**Movement for Democratic Process (MPD):** Lusaka; f. 1991; Pres. Chama Chakomboka.
**Movement for Multi-party Democracy (MMD):** POB 365, 10101 Lusaka; f. 1990; ruling party since Nov. 1991; Pres. Frederick Chiluba; Sec. Brig.-Gen. Godfrey Miyanda.
**Multi-Racial Party (MRP):** Lusaka; Leader Aaron Mulenga.
**National Democratic Alliance (NADA):** Lusaka; f. 1991; Pres. Yonam Phiri.
**National Party (NP):** Lusaka; f. 1993 by former mems of MMD; Chair. Arthur Wina.
**National People's Salvation Party (NPSP):** Lusaka; Pres. Lumbwe Lambanya.
**United Democratic Congress Party:** Lusaka; f. 1992; Leader Daniel Lisulo.
**United National Independence Party (UNIP):** POB 30302, Lusaka; tel. (1) 221197; telex 43640; fax (1) 221327; f. 1958; sole legal party 1972–90; Pres. Kebby Musokotwane; Sec.-Gen. Benjamin Mibenge.
**Zambia Opposition Front (ZOFRO):** Lusaka; f. 1994 by seven opposition parties; Chair. Mike Kaira.

## Diplomatic Representation

### EMBASSIES AND HIGH COMMISSIONS IN ZAMBIA

**Angola:** Plot 5548, Lukanga Rd, Kalundu, POB 31595, Lusaka; tel. (1) 254346; telex 41940; Ambassador: Pedro Fernando Mavunza.
**Austria:** 30A Mutende Rd, Woodlands, POB 31094, Lusaka; tel. (1) 260407; telex 43790; Ambassador: Dr H. Schurz.
**Belgium:** Anglo-American Bldg, 74 Independence Ave, POB 31204, Lusaka; tel. (1) 252512; telex 40000; fax (1) 250075; Ambassador: Luc Willemarck.
**Botswana:** 2647 Haile Selassie Ave, POB 31910, Lusaka; tel. (1) 250804; telex 41710; High Commissioner: Soblem Mayane (acting).
**Brazil:** 74 Anglo-American Bldg, Independence Ave, POB 34470; tel. (1) 252749; telex 40102; fax (1) 251652; Chargé d'affaires a.i.: Cecilia de Brase Bidant.
**Bulgaria:** 4045 Lukulu Rd, POB 31996, Lusaka; tel. and fax (1) 263295; telex 40215; Chargé d'affaires a.i.: Yuli Minchev.
**Canada:** Plot 5199, United Nations Ave, POB 31313, Lusaka; tel. (1) 250833; telex 42480; fax (1) 254176; High Commissioner: Aubrey L. Morantz.
**China, People's Republic:** Plot 7430, Haile Selassie Ave, POB 31975, Lusaka; tel. (1) 253770; telex 41360; Ambassador: Yang Zengye.
**Cuba:** Plot 5509, Lusiwasi Rd, Kalundu, POB 33132, Lusaka; tel. (1) 251380; telex 40309; Ambassador: Juan Carretero.
**Czech Republic:** 2278 Independence Ave, POB 30059, Lusaka; tel. (1) 250908.
**Denmark:** 352 Independence Ave, POB 50299, Lusaka; tel. (1) 251634; telex 43580; Ambassador: Jorn Krogbeck.
**Egypt:** Plot 5206, United Nations Ave, POB 32428, Lusaka; tel. R.i.(1) 253762; telex 40021; Ambassador: Khaled M. Aly Osman.
**Finland:** Anglo-American Bldg, 6th Floor, POB 50819, 15101 Ridgeway, Lusaka; tel. (1) 228492; telex 43460; fax (1) 261472; Chargé d'affaires a.i.: Hannu Ikonen.
**France:** Anglo-American Bldg, 4th Floor, 74 Independence Ave, POB 30062, Lusaka; tel. (1) 251322; telex 41430; fax (1) 254475; Ambassador: Jean Brouste.
**Germany:** United Nations Ave, POB 50120, Lusaka; tel. (1) 229068; telex 41410; Ambassador: Dr Peter Schmidt.
**Holy See:** Hussein Saddam Blvd, POB 31445, Lusaka; tel. (1) 251033; telex 40403; fax (1) 250601; Apostolic Pro-Nuncio: Most Rev. Giuseppe Leanza, Titular Archbishop of Lilibeo.
**India:** 5220 Haile Selassie Ave, POB 32111, Lusaka; tel. (1) 253152; telex 41420; fax (1) 254118; High Commissioner: (vacant).
**Ireland:** Katima Mulilo Rd, Olympia Park, POB 34923, Lusaka; tel. (1) 290650; telex 43110; Chargé d'affaires a.i.: Brendan Rogers.
**Israel:** Lusaka; Ambassador: Dr Arye Oded.
**Italy:** Embassy Park, Diplomatic Triangle, POB 31046, Lusaka; tel. (1) 260382; telex 43380; fax (1) 260329; Ambassador: Dr G. Mingazzini.
**Japan:** Plot 5218, Haile Selassie Ave, POB 34190, Lusaka; tel. (1) 251555; telex 41470; fax (1) 253488; Ambassador: Tadashi Masui.
**Kenya:** Harambee House, Plot 5207, United Nations Ave, POB 50298, Lusaka; tel. (1) 227938; telex 42470; High Commissioner: Jackson Tumwa.
**Malawi:** Woodgate House, Cairo Rd, POB 50425, Lusaka; tel. (1) 228296; telex 41840; High Commissioner: B. H. Kawonga.

ZAMBIA                                                                                                   *Directory*

**Mozambique:** Mulungushi Village, Villa 46, POB 34877, Lusaka; tel. (1) 250436; telex 45900; Ambassador: ALBERTO CUVELO.
**Netherlands:** 5028 United Nations Ave, POB 31905, Lusaka; tel. (1) 250468; telex 42690; Ambassador: S. VAN HEEMSTRA.
**Nigeria:** 5203 Haile Selassie Ave, Longacres, POB 32598, Lusaka; tel. (1) 253177; telex 41280; High Commissioner: Chief L. O. C. AGUBUZU.
**Portugal:** Plot 25, Yotom Muteya Rd, POB 33871, Lusaka; tel. (1) 252996; telex 40010; Ambassador: A. LOPES DA FONSECA.
**Romania:** 2 Leopard's Hill Rd, POB 31944, Lusaka; tel. (1) 262182; Ambassador: L. FLORESCU.
**Russia:** Plot 6407, Diplomatic Triangle, POB 32355, Lusaka; tel. (1) 252183; Ambassador: MIKHAIL N. BATCHARNIKOV.
**Saudi Arabia:** Premium House, 5th Floor, POB 34411, Lusaka; tel. (1) 227829; telex 45550; Ambassador: (vacant).
**Somalia:** G3/377A Kabulonga Rd, POB 34051, Lusaka; tel. (1) 262119; telex 40270; Ambassador: Dr OMAN UMAL.
**Spain:** Lusaka; Ambassador: JESÚS CARLOS RIOSALIDO.
**Sweden:** POB 30788, Lusaka; tel. (1) 251249; telex 41820; fax (1) 223338; Ambassador: PER TAXELL.
**Tanzania:** Ujamaa House, Plot 5200, United Nations Ave, POB 31219, Lusaka; tel. (1) 227698; telex 40118; fax (1) 254861; High Commissioner: NIMROD LUGOE.
**Uganda:** Kulima Tower, 11th Floor, Katunjila Rd, Lusaka; tel. (1) 214413; telex 40990; High Commissioner: VALERIANO KARAKUZA-BAGUMA.
**United Kingdom:** Plot 5201, Independence Ave, POB 50050, 15101 Ridgeway, Lusaka; tel. (1) 228955; telex 41150; fax (1) 262215; High Commissioner: PATRICK NIXON.
**USA:** cnr Independence and United Nations Aves, POB 31617, Lusaka; tel. (1) 250955; telex 41970; fax (1) 252225; Ambassador: ROLAND KUCHEL.
**Yugoslavia:** Plot 5216, Diplomatic Triangle, POB 31180, Lusaka; tel. (1) 250247; Chargé d'affaires a.i.: STANIMIR JOVANOVIĆ.
**Zaire:** Plot 1124, Parirenyatwa Rd, POB 31287, Lusaka; tel. (1) 213343; Ambassador: Dr ATENDE OMWARGO.
**Zimbabwe:** Memaco House, 4th Floor, Cairo Rd, POB 33491, Lusaka; tel. (1) 229382; telex 45800; fax (1) 227474; High Commissioner: (vacant).

## Judicial System

**Supreme Court of Zambia:** Independence Ave, POB 50067, Ridgeway, Lusaka; tel. (1) 251330; telex 40396; fax (1) 251743; the final Court of Appeal. Judges of the Supreme Court include the Chief Justice and the Deputy Chief Justice. The High Court consists of the Chief Justice and 20 Judges. Senior Resident and Resident Magistrates' Courts also sit at various centres. The Local Courts deal mainly with customary law, although, they have certain limited statutory powers.
**Chief Justice:** MATHEW M. S. W. NGULUBE.
**Deputy Chief Justice:** B. K. BWEUPE.
**Supreme Court Judges:** B. T. GARDNER, E. L. SAKALA, M. S. CHAILA, E. K. CHIRWA, W. M. MUZYAMBA.

## Religion

### CHRISTIANITY

**Christian Council of Zambia:** Church House, Cairo Rd, POB 30315, Lusaka; tel. (1) 224308; telex 45160; f. 1945; 17 mem. churches and 18 other Christian orgs; Chair. Rt Rev. CLEMENT SHABA; Gen. Sec. VIOLET SAMPA-BREDT.

#### The Anglican Communion

Anglicans are adherents of the Church of the Province of Central Africa, covering Botswana, Malawi, Zambia and Zimbabwe. The Church comprises 10 dioceses, including three in Zambia. The Archbishop of the Province is the Bishop of Botswana. There are an estimated 40,000 adherents in Zambia.
**Bishop of Central Zambia:** Rt Rev. CLEMENT SHABA, POB 70172, Ndola; fax (2) 615954.
**Bishop of Lusaka:** Rt Rev. STEPHEN MUMBA, Bishop's Lodge, POB 30183, Lusaka.
**Bishop of Northern Zambia:** Rt Rev. BERNARD MALANGO, POB 20173, Kitwe; fax (2) 214778.

#### Protestant Churches

**African Methodist Episcopal Church:** POB 31478, Lusaka; tel. (1) 264013; 400 congregations, 80,000 mems; Presiding Elder Rev. D. K. SIMFUKWE.

**Baptist Church:** Lubu Rd, POB 30636, Lusaka; tel. (1) 253620.
**Baptist Mission of Zambia:** 3061/62 cnr Makishi and Great East Rds, POB 50599, 15101 Ridgeway, Lusaka; tel. (1) 222492; fax (1) 227520.
**Brethren in Christ Church:** POB 115, Choma; tel. (3) 20278; f. 1906; Bishop Rev. SHAMAPANI; 116 congregations, 7,699 mems.
**Reformed Church of Zambia:** POB 510013, Chipata; tel. (62) 21559; f. 1899; African successor to the Dutch Reformed Church mission; 170 congregations, 200,000 mems.
**Seventh-day Adventists:** POB 31309, Lusaka; tel. (1) 219775; telex 43760; 66,408 active mems.
**United Church of Zambia:** Synod Headquarters, Nationalist Rd at Burma Rd, POB 50122, Lusaka; tel. (1) 250641; f. 1967; c. 1m. mems; Synod Moderator Rev. GODFREY SIKAZWE; Gen. Sec. Rev. BENSON CHONGO.

Other denominations active in Zambia include the Assemblies of God, the Church of Christ, the Church of the Nazarene, the Evangelical Fellowship of Zambia, the Kimbanguist Church, the Presbyterian Church of Southern Africa, the Religious Society of Friends (Quakers) and the United Pentecostal Church.

#### The Roman Catholic Church

Zambia comprises two archdioceses and seven dioceses. At 31 December 1993 there were an estimated 2,541,543 adherents in the country, equivalent to 26.5% of the total population.
**Bishops' Conference:** Zambia Episcopal Conference, Catholic Secretariat, Unity House, cnr Freedom Way and Katunjila Rd, POB 31965, Lusaka; tel. (1) 227854; telex 43560; fax (1) 220996; f. 1984; Pres. Rt Rev. TELESPHORE GEORGE MPUNDU, Bishop of Mbala-Mpika; Sec.-Gen. Rev. IGNATIUS MWEBE.
**Archbishop of Kasama:** Most Rev. JAMES SPAITA, Archbishop's House, POB 410143, Kasama; tel. (4) 221248; fax (4) 222202.
**Archbishop of Lusaka:** Most Rev. ADRIAN MUNG'ANDU, 41 Wamulwa Rd, POB 32754, Lusaka; tel. (1) 213188; fax (1) 290631.

### ISLAM

There are about 10,000 members of the Muslim Association in Zambia.

### BAHÁ'Í FAITH

**National Spiritual Assembly:** POB 227, Ridgeway, Lusaka; tel. and fax (1) 254505; mems resident in 1,456 localities.

## The Press

### DAILIES

**The Times of Zambia:** POB 30394, Lusaka; tel. (1) 229076; telex 41860; fax (1) 222880; f. 1943; govt-owned; English; Man. Editor CYRUS SIKAZWE; circ. 65,000.
**Zambia Daily Mail:** POB 31421, Lusaka; tel. (1) 211722; telex 44621; f. 1968; govt-owned; English; Man. Editor EMMANUEL NYIRENDA; circ. 40,000.

### PERIODICALS

**African Social Research:** Institute for African Studies, University of Zambia, POB 32379, Lusaka; tel. (1) 292462; fax (1) 253952; f. 1944; 2 a year; Editor Dr L. J. CHINGAMBO; circ. 1,000.
**Chipembele Magazine:** POB 30255, Lusaka; tel. (1) 254226; 6 a year; publ. by Wildlife Conservation Soc. of Zambia; circ. 20,000.
**Farming in Zambia:** POB 50197, Lusaka; tel. (1) 213551; telex 43950; f. 1965; quarterly; publ. by Ministry of Agriculture, Food and Fisheries; Editor L. P. CHIRWA; circ. 3,000.
**Icengelo:** Chifubu Rd, POB 71581, Ndola; tel. (2) 680456; telex 30054; fax (2) 680484; f. 1970; monthly; Bemba; social, educational and religious; Roman Catholic; Editors Fr U. DAVOLI, A. CHAMBALA; circ. 40,000.
**Imbila:** POB RW20, Lusaka; tel. (1) 217254; f. 1953; monthly; publ. by Zambia Information Services; Bemba; Editor D. MUKAKA; circ. 20,000.
**Intanda:** POB RW20, Lusaka; tel. (1) 219675; f. 1958; monthly; general; publ. by Zambia Information Services; Tonga; Editor J. SIKAULU; circ. 6,000.
**Journal of Adult Education:** University of Zambia, POB 50516, Lusaka; tel. (1) 216767; telex 44370; f. 1982; Exec. Editor FRANCIS KASOMA.
**Leisure Magazine:** Farmers House, Cairo Rd, POB 8138, Woodlands, Lusaka; general interest.
**Liseli:** POB RW20, Lusaka; tel. (1) 219675; monthly; publ. by Zambia Information Services; Lozi; Editor F. AMNSAA; circ. 7,700.

# ZAMBIA

**Lukanga News:** POB 919, Kabwe; tel. (5) 217254; publ. by Zambia Information Services; Lenje; Editor J. H. N. NKOMANGA; circ. 5,500.

**Mining Mirror:** POB 71605, Ndola; tel. (2) 640133; f. 1973; monthly; English; Editor-in-Chief G. S. MUKUWA; circ. 50,000.

**National Mirror:** Bishops Rd, Kabulonga, POB 320199, Lusaka; tel. (1) 261193; telex 40630; fax (1) 263050; f. 1972; weekly; publ. by Multimedia Zambia; Editor FANWELL CHEMBO; circ. 40,000.

**Ngoma:** POB RW20, Lusaka; tel. (1) 219675; monthly; Lunda, Kaonde and Luvale; publ. by Zambia Information Services; Editor B. A. LUHILA; circ. 3,000.

**Orbit:** POB RW18X, Lusaka; tel. (1) 254915; f. 1971; publ. by Ministry of Education; children's educational magazine; Editor ELIDAH CHISHA; circ. 65,000.

**The Post:** POB 352, Lusaka; tel. (1) 225455; fax (1) 224250; f. 1991; independent; Editor-in-Chief and Man. Dir FRED M'MEMBE; circ. 22,000.

**Speak Out:** POB 70244, Ndola; tel. (2) 612241; fax (2)610556; f. 1984; bi-monthly; Christian; circ. 40,000.

**The Sportsman:** POB 31762, Lusaka; tel. (1) 224250; telex 40151; f. 1980; monthly; Man. Editor SAM SIKAZWE; circ. 18,200.

**Sunday Express:** Lusaka; f. 1991; weekly; Man. Editor JOHN MUKELA.

**Sunday Times of Zambia:** POB 30394, Lusaka; tel. (1) 229076; telex 41860; fax (1) 222880; f. 1965; owned by UNIP; English; Man. Editor ARTHUR SIMUCHOBA; circ. 78,000.

**Tsopano:** POB RW20, Lusaka; tel. (1) 217254; f. 1958; monthly; publ. by Zambia Information Services; Nyanja; Editor S. S. BANDA; circ. 9,000.

**VOW** (Voice of Women): POB 31791, Lusaka; tel. (1) 261263; telex 45390; bi-monthly; publ. by the women's section of the African National Congress of South Africa; circ. 8,000.

**Workers' Challenge:** POB 270035, Kitwe; tel. and fax (2) 220904; f. 1981; 2 a month; publ. by the Workers' Pastoral Centre; English and Bemba; Co-Editors Fr MISHECK KAUNDA, JUSTIN CHILUFYA; circ. 16,000.

**Workers' Voice:** POB 652, Kitwe; tel. (2) 211999; f. 1972; fortnightly; publ. by Zambia Congress of Trade Unions.

**Youth:** POB 30302, Lusaka; tel. (1) 211411; f. 1974; quarterly; publ. by UNIP Youth League; Editor-in-Chief N. ANAMELA; circ. 20,000.

**Zambia Government Gazette:** POB 30136, Lusaka; tel. (1) 228724; telex 40347; fax (1) 224486; f. 1911; weekly; English; official notices.

### NEWS AGENCY

**Zambia News Agency (ZANA):** Mass Media Complex, POB 30007, Lusaka; tel. (1) 219673; telex 42120; Editor-in-Chief DAVID KASHWEKA.

### Foreign Bureaux

**Agence France-Presse:** POB 33805, Lusaka; tel. (1) 212959; telex 45960; Bureau Chief ABBE MAINE.

**Informatsionnoye Telegrafnoye Agentstvo Rossii–Telegrafnoye Agentstvo Suverennykh Stran (ITAR–TASS)** (Russia): POB 33394, Lusaka; tel. (1) 254201; telex 45270; Correspondent ANDREY K. POLYAKOV.

**Inter Press Service (IPS)** (Italy): POB 30765, Lusaka; tel. (1) 217857; telex 40151; Stringer SAM SIKAZWE.

**Reuters** (UK): POB 31685, Lusaka; tel. (1) 253430; telex 41160.

**Rossiyskoye Informatsionnoye Agentstvo—Novosti (RIA—Novosti)** (Russia): POB 31383, Lusaka; tel. (1) 252849; telex 45190; Rep. VIKTOR LAPTUKHIN.

**Xinhua (New China) News Agency** (People's Republic of China): United Nations Ave, POB 31859, Lusaka; tel. (1) 252227; fax (1) 252227; telex 40455; Chief Correspondent QIU XIAOYI.

### PRESS ASSOCIATION

**Press Association of Zambia (PAZA):** c/o The Times of Zambia, POB 30394, Lusaka; tel. (1) 229076; f. 1983; Chair. ROBINSON MAKAYI.

## Publishers

**Africa:** Literature Centre, POB 1319, Kitwe; tel. (2) 84712; general, educational, religious; Man. Dir E. C. MAKUNIKE.

**African Social Research:** Publications Office, Institute of African Studies, University of Zambia, POB 32379, Lusaka; tel. (1) 292462; telex 44370; social research in Africa; Editor L. J. CHINGAMBO.

**Daystar Publications Ltd:** POB 32211, Lusaka; f. 1966; religious; Man. Dir S. E. M. PHEKO.

**Directory Publishers of Zambia Ltd:** POB 30963, Lusaka; tel. (1) 292845; f. 1958; trade directories; Gen. Man. W. D. WRATTEN.

**Multimedia Zambia:** Woodlands, POB 320199, Lusaka; tel. (1) 261193; telex 40630; fax (1) 263050; f. 1971; religious and educational books, audio-visual materials; Exec. Dir JUMBE NGOMA.

**Temco Publishing Co:** 10 Kabelenga Rd, POB 30886, Lusaka; tel. (1) 211883; telex 45250; f. 1977; educational and general; Man. Dir S. V. TEMBO.

**University of Zambia:** Publications Office, POB 32379, Lusaka; tel. (1) 292884; telex 44370; fax (1) 253952; f. 1938; academic books, papers and journals.

**Zambia Educational Publishing House:** Chishango Rd, POB 32664, Lusaka; tel. (1) 229211; telex 40056; f. 1967; educational and general; Dir H. LOMBE.

**Zambia Printing Co Ltd:** POB 34798, 10101 Lusaka; tel. (1) 227673; telex 40068; fax (1) 225026; Gen. Man. BERNARD LUBUMBASHI.

### Government Publishing Houses

**Government Printer:** POB 30136, Lusaka; tel. (1) 228724; telex 40347; fax (1) 224486; publr of all official documents and statistical bulletins.

**Zambia Information Services:** POB 50020, Lusaka; tel. (1) 219673; telex 41350; state-controlled; Dir BENSON SIANGA; Dep. Dir MUNDIA NALISHEBO (acting).

### PUBLISHERS' ASSOCIATION

**Booksellers' and Publishers' Association of Zambia:** POB 31838, Lusaka; tel. (1) 222647; fax (1) 225195; Chair. RAY MUNAMWIMBU; Sec. BASIL MBEWE.

## Radio and Television

In 1992, according to UNESCO, there were an estimated 705,000 radio receivers and 225,000 television receivers in use.

**Zambia National Broadcasting Corporation:** Broadcasting House, POB 50015, Lusaka; tel. (1) 220864; telex 41221; fax (1) 254317; f. 1961; state-controlled; radio services in English and seven Zambian languages; television services in English; Dir-Gen. DUNCAN H. MBAZIMA.

**Educational Broadcasting Services:** Headquarters: POB 50231, Lusaka; tel. (1) 251724; radio broadcasts from Lusaka; television for schools from POB 21106, Kitwe; audio-visual aids service from POB 50295, Lusaka; Controller MICHAEL MULOMBE.

## Finance

(cap. = capital; res = reserves; dep. = deposits; m. = million; br. = branch; amounts in kwacha)

### BANKING

Capitalization of banks must total at least K500,000 in the case of any commercial bank wholly or partially owned by the Government, and not less than K2m. in the case of any other commercial bank. At least one-half of the directors of these latter banks must be established residents in Zambia. All foreign-owned banks are required to incorporate in Zambia.

### Central Bank

**Bank of Zambia:** POB 30080, Lusaka; tel. (1) 216529; telex 41560; fax (1) 42999; f. 1964; bank of issue; cap. and res 35.3m., dep. 783.2m. (Oct. 1985); Gov. JACOB MWANZA; Gen. Man. GODFREY MBULO; br. in Ndola.

### Commercial Banks

**African Commercial Bank Ltd:** Superannuation House, Ben Bella Rd, POB 30097, Lusaka; tel. (1) 229482; telex 40092; fax (1) 227495; f. 1984; cap. 91.4m., res 281.7m., dep. 2,728.5m. (March 1993); Chair. JOHN MWANAKATWE; Man. Dir W. FEARON; 4 brs.

**Commerce Bank Ltd:** 627 South End Cairo Rd, POB 32393, Lusaka; tel. (1) 229948; telex 40715; fax (1) 223769; f. 1992; cap. 225m.; Chair. MUSALILWA SIAME.

**Co-operative Bank of Zambia (Co-operative Society) Ltd:** Co-operative House, Chachacha Rd, North End, POB 33666, Lusaka; tel. (1) 223849; fax (1) 225505; f. 1991; cap. 27.9m. (March 1992); Chair. M. D. NCHIMUNYA; Man. Dir H. N. MUFALO.

ZAMBIA

**Finance Bank Zambia Ltd:** 2101 Chanik House, POB 37102, Lusaka; tel. (1) 229736; telex 40338; fax (1) 227290; cap. 490m., res 190.2m., dep. 6,461.1m. (Dec. 1992); Chair. Dr R.L. MAHTANI.

**Manifold Investment Bank Ltd:** Cusa House, Cairo Rd, POB 36595, Lusaka; tel. (1) 224109; telex 40368; fax (1) 224071; f. 1988; cap. 6.5m., res 61.0m., dep. 463.7m. (June 1993); Chair. HELLINS CHABI; Man. Dir VINCENT N. CHALWE.

**National Savings and Credit Bank of Zambia:** Plot 248, Cairo Rd, POB 30067; Lusaka; tel. (1) 227534; telex 40089; fax (1) 223296; f. 1973; dep. 2,405m. (Dec. 1994); Man. Dir G. J. M. CHEMBE.

**Union Bank Zambia Ltd:** Zimco House, Cairo Rd, POB 34940, Lusaka; tel. (1) 221093; telex 40112; fax (1) 221866; cap. 246.1m. (Dec. 1991); Chair. O. J. IRWIN; Man. Dir S. A. J. RIZVI.

**Zambia National Commercial Bank Ltd:** Plot 2118, Cairo Rd, POB 33611, Lusaka; tel. (1) 228979; telex 42360; fax (1) 223082; f. 1969; govt-controlled; cap. 1,050m., res 7,749.6m., dep. 81,902.0m. (March 1993); Chair. R. L. BWALYA; Man. Dir J.Y. NG'OMA; 40 brs.

### Foreign Banks

**Barclays Bank of Zambia Ltd** (UK): Kafue House, Cairo Rd, POB 31936, Lusaka; tel. (1) 228858; telex 41570; fax (1) 222519; f. 1971; cap. 477.0m., res 2,146.2m., dep. 10,065.9m. (Dec. 1991); Chair. A. B. MUNYAMA; Man. Dir M. M. MCNIE; 35 brs.

**Citibank Zambia Ltd** (USA): Kulima Tower, Katunjila Rd, POB 30037, Lusaka; tel. (1) 229025; telex 45610; fax (1) 226264; f. 1979; cap. res 1,481.4m., dep. 4,146.3m. (Dec. 1993); Man. Dir KANDOLO KASONGO.

**Indo-Zambia Bank (IZB):** Indeco House, 686 Cairo Rd, POB 35411, Lusaka; tel. (1) 224653; telex 40178; fax (1) 225090; f. 1984; cap. 100m., res 476.8m., dep. 5,977.2m. (March 1993); Chair. R. L. BWALYA; Man. Dir M. R. MALLYA; 4 brs.

**Meridien BIAO Bank Zambia Ltd:** Meridien BIAO House, Chachacha Rd, POB 37763, 10101 Lusaka; tel. (1) 229464; telex 41270; fax (1) 223997; f. 1984; cap. 450.0m., res 3,517.8m., dep. 51,877.4m. (Sept. 1993); parent co in liquidation 1995; Chair. JOHN CRUICKSHANK (acting); Man. Dir S. J. ANZSAR; 11 brs.

**Stanbic Bank Zambia Ltd:** Woodgate House, Nairobi Place, Cairo Rd, POB 31955, Lusaka; tel. (1) 229285; telex 42461; fax (1) 221152; f. 1971 as Grindlays Bank International (Zambia) Ltd; cap. 160m. (Sept. 1992), dep. 281.3m. (Sept. 1986); Chair. D. A. R. PHIRI; Gen. Man. I. F. PETERKIN; 7 brs and 1 sub-br.

**Standard Chartered Bank Zambia Ltd** (UK): Standard House, Cairo Rd, POB 32238, Lusaka; tel. (1) 229242; telex 41660; fax (1) 222092; f. 1971; cap. 1,950.0m., res 2,306.7m., dep. 20,200.1m. (Dec. 1992); Chair. A. K. MAZOKA; Man. Dir B. R. KNIGHT; 26 brs and 5 agencies.

### Development Banks

**Development Bank of Zambia:** cnr Katondo and Chachacha Rds, POB 33955, Lusaka; tel. (1) 228580; telex 45040; fax (1) 222426; f. 1972; 60% state-owned; provides medium- and long-term loans and offers business consultancy and research services; cap. 403.1m. (Feb. 1993); Chair. Dr J. M. MTONGA; Man. Dir G. M. B. MUMBA; 2 brs.

**Lima Bank:** Kulima House, Chachacha Rd, POB 32607, Lusaka; tel. (1) 228073; telex 40126; fax (1) 228074; cap. 57m. (March 1986); Chair. N. MUKUTU; Man. Dir K. V. KASAPATU.

**Zambia Agricultural Development Bank:** Society House, Cairo Rd, POB 30847, Lusaka; tel. (1) 219251; telex 40126; f. 1982; loan finance for development of agriculture and fishing; auth. cap. 75m.; Chair. K. MAKASA; Man. Dir AMON CHIBIYA.

**Zambia Export and Import Bank Ltd:** Society House, Cairo Rd, POB 33046, Lusaka; tel. (1) 229486; telex 40098; fax (1) 222313; f. 1987; cap. 50m. (March 1992), dep. 50.9m. (March 1990); Chair. J. M. MTONGA.

### STOCK EXCHANGE

**Zambia Stock Exchange:** Lusaka; f. 1994; Sec. of Securities and Exchange Comm. MUMBA KAPUMPA.

### INSURANCE

**Zambia State Insurance Corporation Ltd:** Premium House, Independence Ave, POB 30894, Lusaka; tel. (1) 218888; telex 42521; f. 1968; took over all insurance business in Zambia in 1971; Chair. E. WILLIMA; Man. Dir MWENE MWINGA.

## Trade and Industry

### CHAMBER OF COMMERCE

**Lusaka Chamber of Commerce and Industry:** POB 30844, Lusaka; tel. (1) 252369; telex 40124; f. 1933; Chair. R. D. PENZA; Sec. Dr E. BBENKELE; 400 mems.

### INDUSTRIAL AND COMMERCIAL ASSOCIATIONS

**Copper Industry Service Bureau Ltd:** POB 22100, Kitwe; tel. (2) 214122; telex 52620; f. 1941 as Chamber of Mines.

**Zambia Association of Manufacturers:** POB 30844, Lusaka; tel. (1) 252369; telex 40124; f. 1985; Chair. DEV BABBAR; Sec. N. NAMUSHI; 250 mems.

**Zambia Confederation of Industries and Chambers of Commerce:** POB 30844, Lusaka; tel. (1) 252369; telex 40124; fax (1) 252483; f. 1938; Chair. R. D. FROST; CEO THEO BULL; 2,000 mems.

**Zambia Farm Employers' Association:** V.T.A. House, Chachacha Rd, POB 30395, Lusaka; tel. (1) 213222; telex 40164; Chair. D. FLYNN; Vice-Chair. M. J. H. BECKETT; 300 mems.

**Zambia Seed Producers' Association:** POB 30013, Lusaka; tel. (1) 223249; telex 40164; fax (1) 223249; f. 1964; Chair. BARRY COXE; 300 mems.

### STATUTORY ORGANIZATIONS
#### Industry

**Industrial Development Corporation of Zambia Ltd (INDECO):** Indeco House, Buteko Place, POB 31935, Lusaka; tel. (1) 228463; telex 41821; fax (1) 228868; f. 1960; auth. cap. K300m.; c. 47 subsidiaries and assoc. cos in brewing, chemicals, property, manufacturing, agriculture and vehicle assembly; Chair. R. L. BWALYA; Man. Dir S. K. TAMELÉ.

**Metal Marketing Corporation (Zambia) Ltd (MEMACO):** Memaco House, Sapele Rd, POB 35570, Lusaka; tel. (1) 228131; telex 40070; fax (1) 223671; f. 1973; sole sales agents for all metal and mineral production; Chair. R. L. BWALYA; Man. Dir U. M. MUTATI.

**National Import and Export Corporation (NIEC):** National Housing Authority Bldg, POB 30283, Lusaka; tel. (1) 2288018; telex 44490; fax (1) 252771; f. 1974.

**Posts and Telecommunications Corporation:** POB 71630, Ndola; tel. (2) 2281; telex 33430.

**Small Industries Development Organization (SIDO):** Sido House, Cairo Rd, POB 35373, Lusaka; tel. (1) 219801; telex 40169; f. 1981 to promote development of small and village industries.

**Zambia Electricity Supply Corporation (ZESCO):** Lusaka; Man. Dir ROBINSON MWANSA.

**Zambia Industrial and Mining Corporation Ltd (ZIMCO):** Zimco House, Cairo Rd, POB 30090, Lusaka; tel. (1) 212487; telex 40790; f. 1970 as holding co for govt interests in mining, industrial, commercial transport and energy, communications, hotels and land, financial and agrarian enterprises; c. 135 subsidiaries and assoc. cos; fixed assets K25,898m. (March 1987); Exec. Dir JAMES NGOMA.

#### Agriculture

**The Dairy Produce Board of Zambia:** Kwacha House, Cairo Rd, POB 30124, Lusaka; tel. (1) 214770; telex 41520; f. 1964; purchase and supply of dairy products to retailers, manufacture and marketing of milk products.

**Department of Marketing and Co-operatives:** POB 50595, Lusaka; tel. (1) 214933; a dept of Ministry of Agriculture, Food and Fisheries; Dir S. B. CHIWALA.

**Tobacco Board of Zambia:** POB 31963, Lusaka; tel. (1) 288995; telex 40370; Sec. L. C. SIMUMBA.

**Zambia Co-operative Federation Ltd:** Kwacha House, Cairo Rd, POB 33579, Lusaka; tel. (1) 228538; telex 43210; fax (1) 222516; agricultural marketing; supply of agricultural chemicals and implements; cargo haulage; insurance; agricultural credit; auditing and accounting; property and co-operative development; Chair. C. CHILALA; Man. Dir G. Z. SIBALE.

### TRADE UNIONS

**Zambia Congress of Trade Unions:** POB 20652, Kitwe; tel. (2) 211999; telex 52630; f. 1965; 18 affiliated unions; c. 400,000 mems; Pres. JACKSON SHAMENDA; Sec.-Gen. ALEC CHIORMA.

#### Affiliated Unions

**Airways and Allied Workers' Union of Zambia:** POB 30272, Lusaka; Pres. F. MULENGA; Gen. Sec. B. CHINYANTA.

**Guards Union of Zambia:** POB 21882, Kitwe; tel. (2) 216189; f. 1972; 13,500 mems; Chair. D. N. S. SILUNGWE; Gen. Sec. MICHAEL S. SIMFUKWE.

**Hotel Catering Workers' Union of Zambia:** POB 35693, Lusaka; 9,000 mems; Chair. IAN MKANDAWIRE; Gen. Sec. STOIC KAPUTU.

**Mineworkers' Union of Zambia:** POB 20448, Kitwe; tel. (2) 214022; telex 52650; 50,000 mems; Chair. (vacant); Gen. Sec. K. G. SHENG'AMO.

**National Union of Building, Engineering and General Workers:** POB 21515, Kitwe; tel. (2) 213931; 18,000 mems; Chair. LUCIANO MUTALE (acting); Gen. Sec. P. N. NZIMA.

ZAMBIA

*Directory*

**National Union of Commercial and Industrial Workers:** 87 Gambia Ave, POB 21735, Kitwe; tel. (2) 217456; f. 1982; 16,000 mems; Chair. P. L. Nkhoma; Gen. Sec. I. M. Kasumbu.

**National Union of Plantation and Agricultural Workers:** POB 80529, Kabwe; tel. (5) 224548; 15,155 mems; Chair. L. B. Ikowa; Gen. Sec. S. C. Silwimba.

**National Union of Postal and Telecommunications Workers:** POB 70751, Ndola; tel. (2) 611345; 6,000 mems; Chair. G. C. Mwape; Gen. Sec. F. U. Shamenda.

**National Union of Public Services' Workers:** POB 32523, Lusaka; tel. (1) 215167; Chair. W. Chipasha; Gen. Sec. Willie Mbewe.

**National Union of Transport and Allied Workers:** POB 32431, Lusaka; tel. (1) 214756; Chair. B. Mulwe; Gen. Sec. L. K. Mabuluki.

**Railway Workers' Union of Zambia:** POB 80302, Kabwe; tel. (5) 224006; 10,228 mems; Chair. H. K. Ndamana; Gen. Sec. Calvin J. Mukabaila.

**University of Zambia and Allied Workers' Union:** POB 32379, Lusaka; tel. (1) 213221; telex 44370; f. 1968; Chair. Beriate Sunkutu; Gen. Sec. Saini Phiri.

**Zambia Electricity Workers' Union:** POB 70859, Ndola; f. 1972; 3,000 mems; Chair. Cosmas Mpampi; Gen. Sec. Adam Kaluba.

**Zambia National Farmers' Union:** TAZ House, Chiparamba Rd, POB 30395, Lusaka; tel. (1) 222797; telex 40164; fax (1) 222736; Gen. Sec. G. R. Gray.

**Zambia National Union of Teachers:** POB 31914, Lusaka; tel. (1) 216670; 2,120 mems; Chair. Jackson Mulenga; Gen. Sec. A. W. Chibale.

**Zambia Typographical Workers' Union:** POB 71439, Ndola; Chair. R. Shikwata; Gen. Sec. D. Nawa.

**Zambia Union of Financial Institutions and Allied Workers:** POB 31174, Lusaka; tel. (1) 219401; Chair. B. Chikoti; Gen. Sec. Geoffrey Alikipo.

**Zambia United Local Authorities Workers' Union:** POB 70575, Ndola; tel. (2) 615022; Chair. A. M. Mutakila; Gen. Sec. A. H. Mudenda.

### Principal Non-Affiliated Unions

**Civil Servants' Union of Zambia:** POB 50160, Lusaka; tel. (1) 221332; f. 1975; 26,000 mems; Chair. W. D. Phiri; Gen. Sec. J. C. Moonde.

**Zambian African Mining Union:** Kitwe; f. 1967; 40,000 mems.

## Transport

### RAILWAYS

Total length of railways in Zambia was 2,164 km (including 891 km of the Tanzania–Zambia railway) in 1988. There are two major railway lines: the Zambia Railways network, which traverses the country from the Copperbelt in northern Zambia and links with the National Railways of Zimbabwe to provide access to South African ports, and the Tanzania–Zambia Railway (Tazara) system, linking New Kapiri-Mposhi in Zambia with Dar es Salaam in Tanzania. The Tazara railway line increased its capacity from 1986, in order to reduce the dependence of southern African countries on trade routes through South Africa. In April 1987 the Governments of Zambia, Angola and Zaire declared their intention to reopen the Benguela railway, linking Zambian copper-mines with the Angolan port of Lobito, following its closure to international traffic in 1975 as a result of the guerrilla insurgency in Angola.

**Tanzania–Zambia Railway Authority (Tazara):** POB 98, Mpika; Head Office: POB 2834, Dar es Salaam, Tanzania; tel. 62191; telex 41059; f. 1975; operates passenger and freight services linking New Kapiri-Mposhi, north of Lusaka, with Dar es Salaam in Tanzania, a distance of 1,860 km of which 891 km is in Zambia; jtly owned and administered by the Tanzanian and Zambian Govts; a 10-year rehabilitation programme, assisted by the USA and EC countries, began in 1985; it was announced in 1990 that a line linking the railway with the Zambian port of Mpulungu was to be constructed; Chair. Richard Mariki; Gen. Man. A. S. Mweemba.

**Zambia Railways:** cnr Buntungwa St and Ghana Ave, POB 80935, Kabwe; tel. (5) 222201; telex 81000; fax (5) 224411; f. 1967; controlled by ZIMCO; a 10-year rehabilitation programme, estimated to cost US $200m., was initiated in 1990; Chair. J. Y. Ng'oma; Man. Dir Oswell Simumba.

### ROADS

At December 1994 there was a total road network of 37,359 km, of which 6,577 km were tarred. The main arterial roads run from Beit Bridge (Zimbabwe) to Tunduma (the Great North Road), through the copper-mining area to Chingola and Chililabombwe (the Zaire Border Road), from Livingstone to the junction of the Kafue river and the Great North Road, and from Lusaka to the Malawi border (the Great East Road). In 1984 the 300-km BotZam highway linking Kazungula with Nata, in Botswana, was formally opened. A 1,930-km main road (the TanZam highway) links Zambia and Tanzania.

**Department of Roads:** POB 50003, Lusaka; tel. (1) 253088; fax (1) 253404; Dir of Roads T. Ngoma.

### SHIPPING

**Zambia National Shipping Line:** Lusaka; f. 1989; state-owned; cargo and passenger services from Dar es Salaam in Tanzania to northern Europe; Gen. Man. Martin Phiri.

### CIVIL AVIATION

In 1984 there were 127 airports, aerodromes and air strips. An international airport, 22.5 km from Lusaka, was opened in 1967. Following the liquidation of the state-owned Zambia Airways in December 1994, there were plans to establish a new national airline, Zambia Express Airways, in which the Government would hold 10% of the shares.

**National Air Charters (Z) Ltd (NAC):** POB 33650, Lusaka; tel. (1) 229774; telex 43840; fax (1) 229778; f. 1973; air cargo services; Gen. Man. Stafford Mudiyo.

## Tourism

Zambia's main tourist attractions are its wildlife and unspoilt scenery; there were 19 national parks in 1990. In 1994 an estimated 174,570 tourists visited Zambia. In 1992 tourist receipts totalled an estimated US $5m.

**Zambia National Tourist Board:** Century House, Cairo Rd, POB 30017, Lusaka; tel. (1) 229087; telex 41780.

# ZIMBABWE

## Introductory Survey

### Location, Climate, Language, Religion, Flag, Capital

The Republic of Zimbabwe is a land-locked state in southern Africa, with Mozambique to the east, Zambia to the north-west, Botswana to the south-west and South Africa to the south. The climate is tropical, modified considerably by altitude. Average monthly temperatures range from 13°C (55°F) to 22°C (72°F) on the highveld, and from 20°C (68°F) to 30°C (86°F) in the low-lying valley of the Zambezi river. The rainy season is from November to March. The official language is English, while the principal African languages are Chishona and Sindebele. About 55% of the population are Christians. Many Africans follow traditional beliefs. The Asian minority comprises both Muslims and Hindus. The national flag (proportions 2 by 1) has seven equal horizontal stripes, of green, gold, red, black, red, gold and green, with a white triangle, bearing a red five-pointed star on which a gold 'Great Zimbabwe bird' is superimposed, at the hoist. The capital is Harare (formerly known as Salisbury).

### Recent History

In 1923 responsibility for Southern Rhodesia (now Zimbabwe) was transferred from the British South Africa Company to the United Kingdom Government, and the territory became a British colony. It had full self-government (except for African interests and some other matters) under an administration controlled by European settlers. African voting rights were restricted.

In 1953 the colony united with two British protectorates, Northern Rhodesia (now Zambia) and Nyasaland (now Malawi), to form the Federation of Rhodesia and Nyasaland, also known as the Central African Federation. Sir Godfrey Huggins (later the 1st Viscount Malvern), the Prime Minister of Southern Rhodesia from 1933 to 1953, became the first Prime Minister of the Federation, being succeeded by Sir Roy Welensky in 1956. In Southern Rhodesia itself, Garfield Todd was Prime Minister from 1953 until 1958, when Sir Edgar Whitehead came to power. A new Constitution, which ended most of the United Kingdom's legal controls and provided for a limited African franchise, came into effect in November 1962. At elections in December Sir Edgar Whitehead lost power to the Rhodesian Front (RF), a coalition of white opposition groups committed to maintaining racial segregation. The RF's leader, Winston Field, became Prime Minister.

As a result of pressure from African nationalist movements in Northern Rhodesia and Nyasaland, the Federation was dissolved in December 1963. African nationalists were also active in Southern Rhodesia. The African National Congress, founded in 1934, was revived in 1957, with Joshua Nkomo as President. Following the banning of the Congress in February 1959, some of its members formed the National Democratic Party (NDP) in January 1960. Nkomo, although in exile, was elected President of the NDP in October. When the NDP was banned in December 1961, Nkomo formed the Zimbabwe African People's Union (ZAPU). This was declared an unlawful organization in September 1962. ZAPU split in July 1963 and a breakaway group, led by the Rev. Ndabaningi Sithole, formed the Zimbabwe African National Union (ZANU) in August. Robert Mugabe became Secretary-General of ZANU.

In April 1964 Field was succeeded as Prime Minister of Southern Rhodesia by his deputy, Ian Smith. The new regime rejected British conditions for independence, including acceptance by the whole Rhodesian population and unimpeded progress to majority rule. In August ZANU was banned. After Northern Rhodesia became independent as Zambia in October 1964, Southern Rhodesia became generally (although not officially) known as Rhodesia. At elections in May 1965 the RF won all 50 European seats in the legislature. On 5 November a state of emergency (to be renewed annually) was declared, and on 11 November Smith made a unilateral declaration of independence (UDI) and proclaimed a new Constitution, naming the country Rhodesia. The British Government regarded Rhodesia's independence as unconstitutional and illegal, and no other country formally recognized it. The United Kingdom terminated all trading and other relations with Rhodesia, while the UN applied economic sanctions against the regime (although it was subsequently revealed that many international companies had circumvented the restrictions). Both ZAPU and ZANU took up arms against the RF regime, and African guerrilla groups were frequently involved in clashes with Rhodesian security forces. Armed South African police were called in to assist the regime in 1967.

Following a referendum in June 1969, Rhodesia was declared a republic in March 1970. The 1969 Constitution provided for a bicameral Legislative Assembly, comprising a 23-member Senate and a 66-member House of Assembly (50 Europeans and 16 Africans). The President had only formal powers and Smith remained Prime Minister. The RF won all 50 European seats in the House of Assembly in 1970, 1974 and 1977.

In November 1971 the British and Rhodesian Governments agreed on draft proposals for a constitutional settlement, subject to their acceptability to the Rhodesian people 'as a whole'. In December the African National Council (ANC), led by Bishop Abel Muzorewa, was formed to co-ordinate opposition to the plan. A British commission which visited Rhodesia in 1972 reported that the proposals were unacceptable to the majority of Africans. In December 1974, however, the Rhodesian Government and leaders of four nationalist organizations (including ZAPU, ZANU and the ANC) agreed the terms of a cease-fire, conditional on the release of African political detainees and on the convening of a constitutional conference in 1975. The African organizations agreed to unite within the ANC, with Muzorewa as President. (Mugabe, hitherto Secretary-General of ZANU, was not in favour of the incorporation of ZANU into the ANC. In mid-1975 Mugabe left Rhodesia for neighbouring Mozambique, where he took control of ZANU's external wing, and challenged Sithole with a rival claim to the leadership of ZANU.) In August 1975 the expanded ANC held unsuccessful constitutional talks with the Rhodesian Government. In September the ANC split into rival factions, led by Muzorewa and Nkomo. Constitutional talks between the Government and the Nkomo faction began in December 1975 but were abandoned in March 1976. In April the US Secretary of State entered into negotiations with the British Government, the Rhodesian Government and the leaders of several African states, including South Africa. In September, under pressure from South Africa, Smith announced his Government's acceptance of proposals leading to majority rule within two years. In late 1976 representatives of the RF, the African nationalists and the British Government met to discuss the transition to majority rule. The nationalists were led by Muzorewa, Sithole, Nkomo and Mugabe (by then the recognized leader of ZANU). Nkomo and Mugabe adopted a joint position as the Patriotic Front (PF). Although an independence date not later than 31 March 1978 was provisionally agreed, the talks were adjourned in December, owing to failure to agree on the composition of the proposed interim government.

In January 1977 negotiations were resumed, and Angola, Botswana, Mozambique, Tanzania and Zambia (the 'front-line' states) declared their support for the PF. Smith rejected British proposals for an interim administration and received a mandate from the RF to repeal racially discriminatory laws and to seek agreement with such African factions as he chose. In July the PF demanded that power be handed directly to them by the Rhodesian Government. In November Smith accepted the principle of universal adult suffrage, and talks on an internal settlement were initiated with Muzorewa's United African National Council (UANC), the Rev. Sithole's faction of the ANC and the Zimbabwe United People's Organization, led by Chief Jeremiah Chirau. These talks led to the signing of an internal settlement on 3 March 1978, providing for an interim power-sharing administration to prepare for independence on 31 December 1978. The proposals were rejected by the PF and by the UN Security Council. In May 1978 the newly-created Executive Council, consisting of

Smith, Sithole, Muzorewa and Chirau, ordered the release of all political detainees in an attempt to bring about a cease-fire. Frequent clashes between Rhodesian security forces and PF guerrillas resulted in the introduction of selective martial law in September.

In January 1979 a 'majority rule' Constitution, containing entrenched safeguards for the white minority, was approved by the House of Assembly and endorsed by a referendum of European voters. In April elections to the new House of Assembly (the country's first by universal adult suffrage) were held in two stages: first for 20 directly-elected European members (chosen by non-African voters only) and then for 72 African members (chosen by the whole electorate). The elections were boycotted by the PF. The UANC emerged as the majority party, with 51 seats in the new House, while the RF won all 20 seats for whites. In May the new Parliament elected Josiah Gumede as President. Muzorewa became Prime Minister of the country (renamed Zimbabwe Rhodesia) in June. In accordance with the Constitution, Muzorewa formed a government of 'national unity', a coalition of parties in the new House, including European members (Smith became Minister without Portfolio). However, international recognition was not forthcoming, and UN sanctions remained in force.

New impetus for a lasting and internationally-recognized settlement came following the Commonwealth Conference in Zambia in August 1979. In September a Rhodesian Constitutional Conference was convened at Lancaster House, in London, under the chairmanship of the British Secretary of State for Foreign and Commonwealth Affairs, and attended by delegations under Muzorewa and the joint leaders of the PF. The PF reluctantly agreed to special representation for the whites under the proposed new Constitution, which was eventually accepted by both parties; complete agreement was reached on transitional arrangements in November, and the details of a cease-fire between the guerrillas of the PF and the Rhodesian security forces were finalized in the following month. On 11 December the Zimbabwe Rhodesia Parliament voted to renounce independence and to revert to the status of a British colony, as Southern Rhodesia. Illegal rule ended on the following day, when Parliament was dissolved, the President, Prime Minister and Cabinet resigned, and the British-appointed Governor, Lord Soames, was vested with full executive and legislative authority for the duration of the transition to legal independence. The United Kingdom immediately lifted economic sanctions.

Lord Soames paved the way for fresh elections to a new House of Assembly by lifting the ban on the two wings of the PF (PF—ZAPU and ZANU—PF) and by ordering the release of most of the detainees who were held under the 'emergency powers' laws. The election campaign was marred by factional violence and intimidation, and the cease-fire (which was being supervised by a Commonwealth Monitoring Force) was briefly threatened by the anger of the PF and the 'front-line' states over the presence of South African troops in Rhodesia. However, elections were held in February 1980 (again in two stages) under the supervision of a British Electoral Commissioner. Mugabe's ZANU—PF emerged as the largest single party, winning 57 of the 80 African seats. Nkomo's PF—ZAPU won 20 seats and the UANC only three. In a separate poll of white voters, Smith's RF won all 20 reserved seats. The new state of Zimbabwe became legally independent, within the Commonwealth, on 18 April, with Rev. Canaan Banana as President and Mugabe as Prime Minister, at the head of a coalition Government including ZANU—PF and PF—ZAPU members.

Following the war of independence, in which 27,000 people had been killed, factional differences between former guerrillas continued. Relations between Mugabe and Nkomo remained uneasy, particularly concerning the former's intention of eventually introducing a one-party state. Nkomo was 'demoted' in a cabinet reshuffle in January 1981, and removed from the Cabinet altogether, with two PF colleagues, in February 1982, under suspicion of plotting to overthrow Mugabe. In March 1982 several MPs of the Republican Front (RF) (formerly the Rhodesian Front) resigned from the party over its unwillingness to co-operate with the Government, and sat as Independents.

Many of the unpopular practices of the Smith regime, including 'emergency powers' and the detention of political opponents, continued after independence. (The state of emergency continued to be renewed at intervals of six months until August 1990.) In early 1983 government troops were sent to Matabeleland to quell serious unrest, caused by pro-Nkomo dissidents. In September of that year laws were introduced which provided for increased press censorship and granted the security forces greater powers under the state of emergency. In November Bishop Muzorewa was arrested on suspicion of having subversive links with South Africa. He remained in detention, without trial, until his release in September 1984. In February 1984, in a renewed anti-insurgency campaign, an estimated 10,000 troops were again sent into Matabeleland. It was estimated that up to 2,000 civilians died during the two army campaigns of 1983 and 1984.

By May 1984 the RF retained only seven of the 20 seats reserved for whites, the remaining 13 being held by Independents. In July the RF was renamed the Conservative Alliance of Zimbabwe (CAZ), and opened its membership to all races. During 1984 the political strength of ZAPU was undermined by the defection to ZANU of one of the three ZAPU members of the Cabinet in April, and the dismissal of the two remaining ZAPU cabinet Ministers in November, following the murder of a senior ZANU party official by dissidents whom ZANU alleged to be supported by ZAPU. A ZANU party Congress, held in August 1984, unanimously approved a new party constitution, committing the party to the establishment of a Marxist-Leninist one-party state. Other resolutions passed by the Congress called for the creation of an executive presidency (combining the functions of the head of state and the head of government), for all civil servants to be members of ZANU, and for increased efforts to 'socialize' the economy.

A general election took place in June and July 1985. Several outbreaks of violence occurred during the course of the election campaign. ZANU—PF was returned to power with an increased majority, winning 63 of the 79 'common roll' seats in the House of Assembly (and an additional seat at a by-election in August). ZAPU won 15 seats, retaining its traditional hold over Matabeleland, and ZANU—Sithole won a single seat. The UANC failed to gain representation. Of the 20 seats reserved for whites, 15 were won by Smith's CAZ. However, CAZ was not represented in the new Cabinet.

During mid-1985 a large number of ZAPU officials were detained, and reportedly tortured while undergoing questioning about dissident activity in Matabeleland. In late 1985, however, ZANU and ZAPU reached broad agreement on the terms of a merger of the two parties, in the interests of national unity. Negotiations between ZANU and ZAPU continued during 1986, but were suspended in April 1987. In the two months following the failure of the talks, there was a resurgence of violence in Matabeleland. In June ZAPU, which was accused of fomenting the unrest, was banned from holding public meetings. ZAPU denied all responsibility for the violence, and in July its representatives in the House of Assembly voted, contrary to expectations, in favour of a six-month renewal of the state of emergency. The failure, in August, of further talks aimed at uniting ZANU and ZAPU led to a renewed outburst of rebel activity, whereupon the Government took steps to prevent ZAPU from functioning effectively: in September all offices of the party were closed, six district councils in Matabeleland, controlled by ZAPU, were dissolved, and a number of prominent ZAPU officers were detained. Furthermore, ZANU declined to endorse seven ZAPU members nominated by ZAPU to be candidates for the parliamentary seats made vacant in September by the abolition of seats reserved for whites (see below). However, the possibility of a unity agreement was renewed in November, when the ban on public meetings by ZAPU was lifted, and the party was permitted to reopen its offices in Harare and Bulawayo. In December Mugabe and Nkomo finally signed an agreement of unity, which was ratified by both parties in April 1988 and implemented in December 1989 (see below). In January 1988 Nkomo was appointed as one of the Senior Ministers in the President's Office, and two other ZAPU officials were given government posts. Following the unity agreement there was a significant improvement in the security situation in Matabeleland. However, the state of emergency remained in force, owing to incursions into eastern Zimbabwe by the Mozambican rebel movement, the Resistência Nacional Moçambicana (Renamo) (see below).

Two major constitutional reforms were adopted during 1987. In September the reservation for whites of 20 seats in the House of Assembly and 10 seats in the Senate was abolished, as permitted by the Constitution, subject to a majority vote in the House. (In anticipation of this reform, several white MPs joined ZANU. In May Smith resigned as President of CAZ.) In October the 80 remaining members of the House of Assembly elected 20 candidates, who were nominated by ZANU, including 11 whites, to fill the vacant seats in the House of Assembly until the next general election. In the same month Parliament approved the replacement of the ceremonial presidency by an executive presidency. The post of Prime Minister was to be incorporated into the presidency. President Banana (who, as the only candidate, had been sworn in for a second term of office as President in April 1986) retired in December 1986, and at the end of that month Mugabe (the sole candidate) was inaugurated as Zimbabwe's first executive President.

Late 1988 and early 1989 were dominated by accusations of corruption against members of the Government. In October 1988 Edgar Tekere, a former Secretary-General of ZANU, was expelled from the party, having persistently made such accusations, in addition to criticizing the Government's plans to introduce a one-party state. Nevertheless, in January 1989 President Mugabe appointed a joint commission to investigate reports of illegal financial transactions involving several senior ZANU officials; as a result of the commission's findings, five cabinet Ministers and one provincial Governor resigned from their posts in March and April. During April Tekere founded the Zimbabwe Unity Movement (ZUM), intending to challenge ZANU at the next general election. In November the Government was accused by the Supreme Court of failing to respect judicial decisions. In mid-December ZANU and ZAPU merged to form a single party, known as the Zimbabwe African National Union—Patriotic Front (ZANU—PF). The united party aimed to establish a one-party state with a Marxist-Leninist doctrine. Mugabe was appointed President of ZANU—PF, while Nkomo became one of its two Vice-Presidents.

Presidential and parliamentary elections were held concurrently in March 1990; at these elections, legislation passed in late 1989 came into effect, which abolished the Senate and increased the number of seats in the House of Assembly from 100 to 150 (of which 120 were to be directly elected, 12 were to be allocated to presidential nominees, 10 were to be allocated to traditional Chiefs and eight were to be allocated to provincial Governors). Mugabe won nearly 80% of all votes cast at the presidential election, thereby defeating Tekere, his sole opponent. At the parliamentary election ZANU—PF secured 116 of the 120 elective seats in the House of Assembly; the ZUM (which had entered into an informal electoral alliance with CAZ) won only two seats and the UANC took one seat. (The election for the remaining seat in the House was postponed; it was subsequently secured by ZANU—PF.) Although ZANU—PF won an outright victory, only 54% of the electorate voted, and representatives of the ruling party were accused of employing intimidatory tactics towards voters. Following the elections Nkomo was appointed as one of two Vice-Presidents (the other being Simon Muzenda, also a Vice-President of ZANU—PF), and remained one of the Senior Ministers in the President's Office.

In August 1990, at a meeting of the Political Bureau of ZANU—PF, a majority of the members announced their opposition to a proposal by President Mugabe for the reintroduction of a one-party political system. Later in that month the state of emergency, which had been in force since independence, was revoked. In January 1991 President Mugabe announced that he had abandoned his earlier plan to establish a one-party state. In October, while Commonwealth heads of government were attending a conference in Harare, riots were organized in the capital by university students, who claimed to be drawing attention to alleged violations by the Government of academic freedom and human rights.

In March 1992 the House of Assembly approved legislation (the Land Acquisition Act) that permitted the compulsory acquisition of land by the Government; this was expected to facilitate the redistribution of land ownership from Europeans (who owned about one-third of farming land in early 1992) to Africans.

In May 1992 opponents of the Government formed a pressure group, the Forum for Democratic Reform. In early July Mugabe reorganized the Cabinet, reducing the number of ministries in accordance with a policy to restrain public expenditure. Later in July several opposition organizations, including CAZ, the UANC and the ZUM, formed an informal alliance, known as the United Front, which aimed to remove Mugabe from power. In August several ZANU—PF members of the House of Assembly denounced the creation (in the July reorganization) of the new Ministry of National Affairs, Employment Creation and Co-operatives, claiming that it was superfluous to the country's needs. In the following month the House of Assembly approved legislation which granted government funding to any party with at least 15 seats in the Assembly (in effect only ZANU—PF); the opposition strongly contested this measure, accusing the Government of misappropriating public money during a period of national economic hardship. In October the Forum for Democratic Reform was constituted as a political party, with Enoch Dumbutshena (a former Chief Justice) as its leader, and in March 1993 it merged with a small opposition organization to form the Forum Party of Zimbabwe, again under the leadership of Dumbutshena. In April the ruling ZANU—PF won three legislative by-elections.

In an apparent attempt to improve the Government's standing with the public, a list of 70 commercial farms, covering some 190,000 ha, was published in May 1993, detailing those properties allotted for acquisition by the State under the Land Acquisition Act. Publication of the list provoked a strong protest from the white-dominated Commercial Farmers' Union. The High Court subsequently ruled against three white farmers who had attempted to prove that the confiscation of their land was unconstitutional.

In January 1994 the UANC was incorporated into Tekere's ZUM; later in that year Bishop Muzorewa, the former UANC leader, founded a new opposition grouping, the United Parties (UP). In February, in anticipation of a possible exodus of whites from South Africa following that country's first democratic general election in April 1994, the Zimbabwean Government drafted a bill which would make immigration laws significantly more stringent and would lengthen—to 10 years—the qualifying period for resident status. The bill was also designed to deprive former residents of their automatic right to return and settle in Zimbabwe.

In February 1994 the Supreme Court ruled that the 34-year-old section of the Law and Order Maintenance Act that prevented opposition members from holding peaceful public demonstrations without prior permission from the authorities was in conflict with the Zimbabwean Bill of Rights and should therefore be repealed.

ZANU—PF won an overwhelming victory at legislative elections which took place on 8–9 April 1995. The ruling party received more than 82% of the votes cast and secured 118 of the 120 elective seats in the House of Assembly (55 of which were uncontested). The remaining two elective seats were taken by ZANU–Ndonga. Following the allocation of nominated and reserved seats, ZANU-PF held 148 of the total 150 seats. The elections were, however, contested by only six parties and boycotted by eight opposition groups, including the ZUM and the UP. In mid-April Mugabe appointed a reorganized cabinet; Nkomo and Muzenda remained as Vice-Presidents. Presidential elections were scheduled to take place in early 1996.

Zimbabwe severed diplomatic relations with South Africa in September 1980 and, as one of the 'front-line' states, subsequently played an important role in international attempts to stabilize southern Africa and to end apartheid in South Africa. In July 1987 the Cabinet rejected a proposal by Mugabe to impose sanctions against South Africa, and the Government opted instead for less stringent economic measures. South Africa is believed to have been responsible for intermittent attacks during the 1980s against African National Congress of South Africa (ANC) targets in Zimbabwe (the ANC was then a banned South African opposition group). A meeting between President Mugabe and a South African government official in April 1991 (following the implementation of a programme of political reforms by President F. W. de Klerk of South Africa in February 1990) constituted the first direct contact between the Zimbabwean and South African Governments since 1980. In December 1993 the South African and Zimbabwean Ministers of Foreign Affairs met in Messina, South Africa—the highest-level meeting between the two countries for 13 years—after which the Zimbabwean Minister of Foreign Affairs stated that it would be both 'desirable and possible' for South Africa to join the Southern African Development Community (SADC) and the Preferential Trade Area for Eastern and Southern African States (PTA) following the holding of the first South African democratic elections

# ZIMBABWE

*Introductory Survey*

(leading to the formation of a government of national unity) in April 1994. Zimbabwe subsequently re-established full diplomatic relations with South Africa after the victory of Nelson Mandela and the ANC in the South African general election.

During the 1980s and early 1990s Zimbabwe provided support to the Mozambican Government against Renamo rebels; in late 1992–early 1993, under the terms of a cease-fire between the two sides, Zimbabwean troops, who had been stationed in Mozambique since 1982, were withdrawn. In 1992 there were an estimated 250,000 Mozambican refugees in Zimbabwe. Plans for the repatriation of some 145,000 Mozambican refugees were announced in March 1993; this scheme, under the auspices of UNHCR, was not expected to be completed before April 1996.

President Mugabe made his first official visit to the United Kingdom in May 1994.

## Government

Under the terms of the 1980 Constitution (as subsequently amended), legislative power is vested in a unicameral Parliament, consisting of a House of Assembly, which comprises 150 members, of whom 120 are directly elected by universal adult suffrage, 20 are nominated by the President, 10 are traditional Chiefs and eight are Provincial Governors. Members of the House of Assembly serve for six years. Executive authority is vested in the President, elected by Parliament for six years. The President appoints, and acts on the advice of, a Cabinet, which comprises two Vice-Presidents and other Ministers and Deputy Ministers. The Cabinet must have the confidence of Parliament, to which it is responsible.

## Defence

Total armed forces numbered about 46,900 in June 1994: 42,900 in the army and 4,000 in the air force. Zimbabwe receives military aid and training from the United Kingdom and the Democratic People's Republic of Korea. There is a police force of 19,500, a police support unit of 2,300 and a national militia of 1,000. In February 1993 Zimbabwe and the USA commenced joint military training manoeuvres. By mid-1996 the size of the armed forces is scheduled to be reduced to about 35,000 troops, and the army and the air force are to be merged. The defence sector was allocated 9.5% of total budgetary expenditure by the central Government in 1994/95.

## Economic Affairs

In 1993, according to estimates by the World Bank, Zimbabwe's gross national product (GNP), measured at average 1991–93 prices, was US $5,756m., equivalent to $540 per head. During 1985–93, it was estimated, GNP per head decreased, in real terms, at an average annual rate of 1.1%. Over the same period, the population increased by an annual average of 3.1%. Zimbabwe's gross domestic product (GDP) increased, in real terms, by an annual average of 2.8% in 1980–92. GDP declined by 8% in 1992/93, owing to the effects of drought on the country's agricultural production; however, GDP growth of 4% was reported in 1994.

Agriculture (including forestry and fishing) contributed 22% of GDP in 1992 and employed about 67% of the labour force in 1993. The principal cash crops are tobacco (which accounted for 34.3% of export earnings in 1991), maize, cotton, coffee and sugar. Wheat, soybeans, groundnuts and horticultural products are also cultivated. Beef production is an important activity. During 1980–92 agricultural GDP increased by an annual average of 1.1%.

Industry (including mining, manufacturing, construction and power) engaged 8.2% of the employed labour force in 1986–87 and provided 35% of GDP in 1992. During 1980–92 industrial production increased by an annual average of 1.9%.

Mining contributed 6.1% of GDP in 1991, and employed less than 1% of the labour force in 1987. Gold, nickel and asbestos are the major mineral exports. Chromium ore, copper, silver, emeralds, lithium, tin, iron ore, cobalt, coal and diamonds are also mined. In addition, Zimbabwe has large reserves of kyanite and platinum, and smaller reserves of zinc and lead.

Manufacturing contributed 30% of GDP in 1992, and employed about 5.5% of the labour force in 1987. The most important sectors, measured by gross value of output, are food-processing, metals (mainly ferrochrome and steel), chemicals and textiles.

Energy is derived principally from hydroelectric power and coal. Imports of mineral fuels comprised 15% of the value of total imports in 1992.

In 1993 Zimbabwe recorded a visible trade surplus of US $122.1m., while there was a deficit of $116.1m. on the current account of the balance of payments. In 1991 the principal source of both imports (28.9%) and exports (17.1%) was the Southern African Customs Union. Other major trading partners were the United Kingdom, the Federal Republic of Germany, Japan and the USA. The principal exports in 1991 were tobacco, metals and metal alloys. The main imports were machinery and transport equipment, basic manufactures, chemicals and mineral fuels.

In the financial year ending 30 June 1994 there was a budgetary deficit equivalent to 7.9% of GDP. At the end of 1993 Zimbabwe's external debt totalled US $4,168m., of which $3,021m. was long-term public debt. In that year the cost of debt-servicing was equivalent to 32.3% of the value of exports of goods and services. The rate of inflation averaged 18.7% annually in 1985–92. Consumer prices increased by an annual average of 42.1% in 1992, by 27.6% in 1993 and by 22.3% in 1994. About 44% of the labour force were reported to be unemployed in mid-1993.

Zimbabwe is a member of the Southern African Development Community (see p. 219), which aims to reduce the economic dependence of the region on South Africa and to promote closer economic integration among its members, and also belongs to the Preferential Trade Area for Eastern and Southern African States (PTA, see p. 240); in November 1993 Zimbabwe announced that it would adhere to a treaty, agreeing to establish the Common Market for Eastern and Southern Africa, signed by other PTA members earlier in the month.

Zimbabwe's agricultural development has been adversely affected by frequent drought, while lack of foreign exchange has hindered the import of goods essential for industrial expansion. However, the country has benefited from a well-developed infrastructure, mineral wealth and a highly diversified manufacturing sector. A five-year development plan (1991–95), including a three-year structural adjustment programme supported by the IMF, sought to restrict government expenditure by reducing the number of public-sector employees, and to relax government controls on prices, imports and investment. In early 1994 the Government announced a series of reforms, which included the flotation of the Zimbabwean dollar and the devaluation of the currency by 17%, the introduction of a two-tier exchange rate system and the easing of controls on the availability of foreign exchange.

## Social Welfare

A national social security scheme providing pensions and other benefits was introduced in 1994. However, under the 1991–95 development plan, public expenditure on health was reduced and fees charged to patients were raised. In 1981 there were about 672 hospitals and clinics, and 1,200 physicians. Health received 4.9% of total budgetary expenditure by the central Government in 1991/92.

## Education

Primary education, which begins at seven years of age and lasts for seven years, is free, and has been compulsory since 1987. Secondary education begins at the age of 14 and lasts for six years. Between 1980 and 1993 the numbers of primary school pupils increased from 1,235,036 to 2,436,671. There were 635,502 pupils at secondary schools in 1993, compared with 74,746 in 1980. In 1992 the number of pupils attending primary and secondary schools was equivalent to 89% of children in the relevant age group (boys 92%; girls 86%). The number of primary schools rose from 2,411 at independence to 4,567 in 1992, and the number of secondary schools increased from 177 at independence to 1,512 in 1990; there is at least one rural secondary school in each of the country's 55 districts. In 1992 some 61,553 students were attending institutions of higher education. There are two universities, the University of Zimbabwe, which is located in Harare, and the University of Science and Technology, at Bulawayo. The estimated rate of adult literacy in 1990 was 66.9% (males 73.7%; females 60.3%). Education received about 20% of total expenditure by the central Government in the budget for 1994/95.

## ZIMBABWE

### Public Holidays

**1995:** 2 January (for New Year's Day), 14–17 April (Easter), 18 April (Independence Day), 1 May (Workers' Day), 25 May (Africa Day, anniversary of OAU's foundation), 11–12 August (Heroes' Day), 25–26 December (Christmas).

**1996:** 1 January (New Year's Day), 5–8 April (Easter), 18 April (Independence Day), 1 May (Workers' Day), 25 May (Africa Day, anniversary of OAU's foundation), 11–12 August (Heroes' Day), 25–26 December (Christmas).

### Weights and Measures

The metric system is in use.

# Statistical Survey

Source (unless otherwise stated): Central Statistical Office, Kaguvi Bldg, Fourth St, POB 8063, Causeway, Harare; tel. (4) 706681.

## Area and Population

### AREA, POPULATION AND DENSITY

| | |
|---|---:|
| Area (sq km) | 390,759* |
| Population (census results) | |
| March–May 1969 | 5,107,330 |
| 18 August 1982 | 7,608,432 |
| 18 August 1992 (provisional) | 10,401,767 |
| Density (per sq km) at August 1992 | 26.6 |

* 150,873 sq miles.

### PRINCIPAL TOWNS (population at census of August 1982)

| | | | |
|---|---:|---|---:|
| Harare (Salisbury) | 656,000 | Masvingo (Fort Victoria) | 30,600 |
| Bulawayo | 413,800 | Zvishavane (Shabani) | 26,800 |
| Chitungwiza | 172,600 | Chinhoyi (Sinoia) | 24,300 |
| Gweru (Gwelo) | 78,900 | Redcliff | 22,000 |
| Mutare (Umtali) | 69,600 | Marondera (Marandellas) | 20,300 |
| Kwekwe (Que Que) | 47,600 | | |
| Kadoma (Gatooma) | 44,600 | | |
| Hwange (Wankie) | 39,200 | | |

**Mid-1983** (estimated population): Harare 681,000; Bulawayo 429,000; Chitungwiza 202,000.

### BIRTHS AND DEATHS (UN estimates, annual averages)

| | 1975–80 | 1980–85 | 1985–90 |
|---|---:|---:|---:|
| Birth rate (per 1,000) | 44.2 | 42.7 | 42.5 |
| Death rate (per 1,000) | 13.1 | 11.7 | 11.0 |

**Expectation of life** (UN estimates, years at birth, 1985–90): 56.8 (males 55.1; females 56.8).

Source: UN, *World Population Prospects: The 1992 Revision*.

### ECONOMICALLY ACTIVE POPULATION
(sample survey, '000 persons aged 15 years and over, 1986–87)

| | Males | Females | Total |
|---|---:|---:|---:|
| Agriculture, hunting, forestry and fishing | 937 | 1,172 | 2,109 |
| Mining and quarrying | 16 | 1 | 17 |
| Manufacturing | 141 | 26 | 167 |
| Electricity, gas and water | 11 | 1 | 12 |
| Construction | 46 | 5 | 51 |
| Trade, restaurants and hotels | 76 | 53 | 129 |
| Transport, storage and communications | 70 | 6 | 76 |
| Financing, insurance, real estate and business services | 17 | 7 | 17 |
| Community, social and personal services | 251 | 146 | 397 |
| Activities not adequately defined | 25 | 19 | 44 |
| **Total in employment** | **1,591** | **1,436** | **3,027** |
| Unemployed | 110 | 123 | 233 |
| **Total labour force** | **1,701** | **1,559** | **3,260** |

Source: International Labour Office, *Year Book of Labour Statistics*.

**Mid-1993** (estimates in '000): Agriculture, etc. 2,818; Total labour force 4,228 (Source: FAO, *Production Yearbook*).

### EMPLOYMENT ('000 persons)*

| | 1991 | 1992 | 1993† |
|---|---:|---:|---:|
| Agriculture, forestry and fishing | 304.2 | 300.4 | 317.4 |
| Mining and quarrying | 50.9 | 50.2 | 47.7 |
| Manufacturing | 205.4 | 197.2 | 185.4 |
| Construction | 81.0 | 89.5 | 90.7 |
| Electricity and water | 8.9 | 8.2 | 7.8 |
| Transport and communications | 56.4 | 99.3 | 94.8 |
| Trade | 100.7 | 52.6 | 50.0 |
| Finance, insurance and real estate | 18.2 | 66.3 | 65.9 |
| Community, social and personal services | 418.3 | 372.5 | 367.3 |
| **Total** | **1,244.0** | **1,236.2** | **1,227.0** |

* Excluding small establishments in rural areas.
† At September.

ZIMBABWE

## Agriculture

**PRINCIPAL CROPS** ('000 metric tons)

|  | 1991 | 1992 | 1993 |
|---|---|---|---|
| Wheat | 259 | 58 | 300* |
| Barley | 24 | 4 | 24 |
| Maize | 1,586 | 362 | 2,562* |
| Millet | 122 | 27 | 95 |
| Sorghum | 68 | 29 | 90 |
| Sugar cane | 3,236 | 300† | 700† |
| Potatoes† | 31 | 25 | 30 |
| Cassava (Manioc)† | 100 | 110 | 130 |
| Dry beans† | 48 | 40 | 45 |
| Soybeans | 111 | 51 | 65 |
| Vegetables† | 153 | 132 | 140 |
| Oranges† | 63 | 55 | 60 |
| Bananas† | 76 | 60 | 65 |
| Groundnuts (in shell) | 107 | 34 | 64 |
| Sunflower seed | 68 | 31 | 74 |
| Cottonseed | 125 | 39 | 119 |
| Cotton lint | 72 | 21* | 67 |
| Tobacco (leaves) | 179 | 211* | 205 |
| Tea (made) | 14 | 9 | 14* |
| Coffee (green) | 12 | 5 | 4 |

* Unofficial figure.   † FAO estimate(s).

Source: FAO, *Production Yearbook*.

**LIVESTOCK** ('000 head, year ending September)

|  | 1991 | 1992* | 1993* |
|---|---|---|---|
| Horses* | 24 | 24 | 23 |
| Asses* | 104 | 104 | 103 |
| Cattle | 6,374 | 4,700 | 4,000 |
| Sheep | 584 | 550 | 530 |
| Pigs | 305 | 285 | 270 |
| Goats | 2,539 | 2,539 | 2,500 |

* FAO estimates.

Poultry (FAO estimates, million): 13 in 1991; 12 in 1992; 12 in 1993.

**LIVESTOCK PRODUCTS** (FAO estimates, '000 metric tons)

|  | 1991 | 1992 | 1993 |
|---|---|---|---|
| Beef and veal | 80 | 90 | 74 |
| Goats' meat | 9 | 9 | 9 |
| Pig meat | 11 | 11 | 8 |
| Poultry meat | 18 | 17 | 17 |
| Other meat | 20 | 17 | 20 |
| Cows' milk | 610 | 435 | 400 |
| Butter | 4.8 | 3.4 | 3.2 |
| Cheese | 6.4 | 4.6 | 4.2 |
| Poultry eggs | 16.8 | 15.3 | 15.3 |
| Cattle hides | 8.4 | 10.5 | 8.0 |

Source: FAO, *Production Yearbook*.

## Forestry

**ROUNDWOOD REMOVALS**
('000 cubic metres, excl. bark)

|  | 1990 | 1991 | 1992 |
|---|---|---|---|
| Sawlogs, veneer logs and logs for sleepers | 512† | 525 | 525† |
| Pulpwood | 119† | 157 | 157† |
| Other industrial wood | 1,017 | 1,050 | 1,082† |
| Fuel wood* | 6,269† | 6,269† | 6,269† |
| **Total** | 7,917 | 8,001 | 8,033 |

* Assumed to be unchanged since 1988.
† FAO estimate.

Source: FAO, *Yearbook of Forest Products*.

**SAWNWOOD PRODUCTION**
('000 cubic metres, incl. railway sleepers)

|  | 1990* | 1991 | 1992* |
|---|---|---|---|
| Coniferous (soft wood) | 168 | 221 | 221 |
| Broadleaved (hard wood) | 22 | 29* | 29 |
| **Total** | 190 | 250 | 250 |

* FAO estimate(s).

Source: FAO, *Yearbook of Forest Products*.

## Fishing

('000 metric tons)

|  | 1990 | 1991 | 1992* |
|---|---|---|---|
| Dagaas | 21.8 | 19.3 | 19.5 |
| Other fishes | 4.0 | 2.8 | 3.0 |
| **Total catch** | 25.8 | 22.2 | 22.5 |

* FAO estimates.

Source: FAO, *Yearbook of Fishery Statistics*

## Mining

|  | 1988 | 1989 | 1990 |
|---|---|---|---|
| Antimony ore (metric tons)* | 150 | 210 | 101 |
| Asbestos ('000 metric tons) | 186.6 | 187.0 | 160.5 |
| Chromium ore ('000 metric tons)† | 561.6 | 627.5 | 562.6 |
| Clay ('000 metric tons) | 113 | 124 | 100 |
| Coal ('000 metric tons)‡ | 5,065 | 5,112 | 5,504 |
| Cobalt ore (metric tons)* | 122 | 111 | 121 |
| Copper ore ('000 metric tons)* | 16.1 | 15.8 | 14.8 |
| Gold ('000 troy oz)* | 481 | 515 | 544 |
| Graphite (metric tons) | 10,468 | 18,147 | 16,384 |
| Iron ore ('000 metric tons)† | 1,020 | 1,143 | 1,260 |
| Magnesite ('000 metric tons) | 28.3 | 33.4 | 32.6 |
| Nickel ore (metric tons)* | 11,489 | 11,634 | 11,442 |
| Phosphate rock ('000 metric tons) | 124 | 134 | 148 |
| Silver ('000 troy oz)* | 704 | 718 | 680 |
| Tin ore (metric tons)* | 885 | 849 | 839 |

* Figures refer to the metal content of ores and concentrates.
† Figures refer to gross weight. The estimated metal content is: Chromium 33%; Iron 64%.
‡ Figures refer to sales of coal.

**1991** ('000 metric tons, unless otherwise indicated): Antimony ore (metric tons) 160; Asbestos 142; Chromium ore 290 (estimated metal content); Clay 124; Coal 5,600 (estimated production); Cobalt ore (metric tons) 12,903; Iron ore 728 (metal content); Magnesite 23.3; Nickel ore (metric tons) 11,312; Phosphate rock 117; Silver (metric tons) 19; Tin ore (metric tons) 797 (Source: UN, *Industrial Statistics Yearbook*).

**1992** ('000 metric tons, unless otherwise indicated): Coal 6,000 (estimated production); Copper ore 10.6; Tin ore (metric tons) 716 (Sources: UN, *Monthly Bulletin of Statistics*, and UNCTAD, *International Tin Statistics*).

**1993**: Copper ore ('000 metric tons) 8.0; Tin ore (metric tons) 600 (estimate) (Source: UN, *Monthly Bulletin of Statistics*).

ZIMBABWE

## Industry

**SELECTED PRODUCTS**
('000 metric tons, unless otherwise indicated)

|  | 1989 | 1990 | 1991 |
|---|---|---|---|
| Raw sugar* | 502 | 464 | 329 |
| Cigarettes (million)† | 2,623 | 2,500 | 2,600 |
| Coke | 300† | 566 | 560† |
| Cement | 910 | 996 | 698 |
| Pig-iron | 520 | 521 | 525† |
| Ferro-chromium‡ | 198 | 242 | 217 |
| Crude steel‡ | 592 | 580 | 600 |
| Refined copper—unwrought‡ | 24.0† | 22.5 | 22.2 |
| Nickel—unwrought (metric tons) | 12,823 | 12,700† | 11,313 |
| Tin—unwrought (metric tons)§ | 848 | 839 | 796 |
| Electric energy (million kWh) | 8,040 | 9,559 | 9,565 |

* Data from the FAO.
† Estimate(s).
‡ Data from the US Bureau of Mines.
§ Primary metal only.

Source: UN, *Industrial Statistics Yearbook*.

**1992:** Cement ('000 metric tons) 828; Tin—unwrought (metric tons) 720 (provisional); Electric energy (million kWh) 9,000 (Sources: UN, *Monthly Bulletin of Statistics*, and UNCTAD, *International Tin Statistics*).

## Finance

**CURRENCY AND EXCHANGE RATES**

**Monetary Units**
100 cents = 1 Zimbabwe dollar (Z.$).

**Sterling and US Dollar Equivalents** (31 December 1994)
£1 sterling = Z.$ 13.122;
US $1 = Z.$ 8.387;
Z.$ 1,000 = £76.21 = US $119.23.

**Average Exchange Rate** (US $ per Zimbabwe dollar)
1992   0.1963
1993   0.1545
1994   0.1227

**BUDGET** (Z.$'000, year ending 30 June)

| Revenue | 1990/91 | 1991/92* |
|---|---|---|
| Taxes on income and profits: | | |
| Income tax | 3,035,135 | 3,620,000 |
| Non-resident shareholders' tax | 34,823 | 40,000 |
| Non-residents' tax on interest | 2,922 | 5,000 |
| Resident shareholders' tax | 24,442 | 28,000 |
| Branch profits tax | 1,492 | 2,150 |
| Capital gains tax | 22,517 | 28,000 |
| Non-residents' tax on fees | 11,558 | 13,850 |
| Total | 3,132,890 | 3,737,000 |
| Taxes on goods and services: | | |
| Sales tax | 1,052,702 | 1,298,000 |
| Customs duties | 1,122,291 | 1,320,000 |
| Excise duties | 476,780 | 610,000 |
| Betting tax | 14,907 | 23,000 |
| Other | 1,936 | 2,495 |
| Total | 2,668,616 | 3,253,495 |
| Miscellaneous taxes: | | |
| Stamp duties and fees | 64,273 | 75,000 |
| Estate duty | 16,670 | 21,500 |
| Other | 31,084 | 35,000 |
| Total | 112,027 | 131,500 |
| Revenue from investments and property: | | |
| Interest, dividends and profits | 182,734 | 242,500 |
| Rents | 13,592 | 24,713 |
| Water supplies | 4,507 | 6,000 |
| Royalties | 10 | 5 |
| Total | 200,842 | 273,218 |

| Revenue — *continued* | 1990/91 | 1991/92* |
|---|---|---|
| Fees: Departmental facilities and services: | | |
| Agriculture | 1,471 | 1,500 |
| Civil aviation | 6,682 | 8,000 |
| Companies, trade marks and patents | 4,370 | 5,200 |
| Education | 53,217 | 72,735 |
| Health | 7,379 | 8,000 |
| National parks | 8,709 | 10,500 |
| Roads and road traffic | 4,738 | 5,932 |
| Water development | 6,085 | — |
| Other | 7,504 | 15,500 |
| Total | 100,155 | 127,367 |
| Recoveries of development expenditure | 1,367 | 3,100 |
| Foreign reserves adjustment surplus | — | 45,000 |
| Other: | | |
| Pension contributions | 191,779 | 235,000 |
| Judicial fines | 18,232 | 23,030 |
| Sale of state property | 14,896 | 16,332 |
| Refunds of miscellaneous payments from votes | 43,264 | 39,900 |
| Miscellaneous | 42,889 | 40,450 |
| Total | 311,060 | 354,712 |
| **Grand Total** | 6,526,956 | 7,925,392 |

* Provisional figures.

| Expenditure | 1990/91 | 1991/92* |
|---|---|---|
| Recurrent expenditure: | | |
| Goods and services: | | |
| Salaries, wages and allowances | 2,940,483 | 3,179,951 |
| Subsistence and transport | 191,372 | 187,780 |
| Incidental expenses | 176,699 | 133,445 |
| Other recurrent expenditure | 926,327 | 1,496,268 |
| Total | 4,234,881 | 4,997,444 |
| Transfers: | | |
| Interest | 1,140,250 | 1,514,961 |
| Subsidies | 529,471 | 453,700 |
| Pensions | 213,875 | 250,055 |
| Grants and transfers | 739,212 | 767,331 |
| Total | 2,622,808 | 2,986,047 |
| Capital expenditure: | | |
| Land purchase | 8,060 | 16,663 |
| Buildings | 411,271 | 463,104 |
| Land development | 107,705 | 132,274 |
| Civil engineering | 273,171 | 289,046 |
| Plant, machinery and equipment | 31,332 | 41,577 |
| Office equipment and furniture | 10,775 | 11,450 |
| Other capital expenditure | 1,199 | 7,112 |
| Total | 843,513 | 961,226 |
| **Grand Total*** | 7,701,202 | 8,944,717 |

* Provisional figures.

**INTERNATIONAL RESERVES** (US $ million at 31 December)

|  | 1992 | 1993 | 1994 |
|---|---|---|---|
| Gold* | 88.1 | 79.1 | 89.7 |
| IMF special drawing rights | 0.4 | 0.9 | 0.1 |
| Reserve position in IMF | 0.1 | 0.1 | 0.1 |
| Foreign exchange | 221.7 | 431.1 | 405.1 |
| Total | 310.3 | 511.2 | 495.0 |

* Valued at a market-related price which is determined each month.

Source: IMF, *International Financial Statistics*.

**MONEY SUPPLY** (Z.$ million at 31 December)

|  | 1992 | 1993 | 1994 |
|---|---|---|---|
| Notes and coins in circulation | 861.3 | 1,191.4 | 1,467.1 |
| Demand deposits at deposit money banks | 2,285.0 | 4,079.9 | 5,146.4 |

Source: IMF, *International Financial Statistics*.

# ZIMBABWE

## COST OF LIVING
(Consumer Price Index; base: 1990 = 100)

|  | 1991 | 1992 | 1993 |
|---|---|---|---|
| Food | 112.6 | 192.7 | 267.4 |
| Clothing and footwear | 122.7 | 161.5 | 185.6 |
| Rent, fuel and light | 117.9 | 150.2 | 204.4 |
| **All items** (incl. others) | 123.3 | 175.2 | 223.6 |

Source: ILO, *Year Book of Labour Statistics*.

**1994**: All items 273.3 (Source: IMF, *International Financial Statistics*).

## NATIONAL ACCOUNTS (Z.$ million at current prices)
### Expenditure on the Gross National Product

|  | 1987 | 1988 | 1989* |
|---|---|---|---|
| Private household consumption | 4,416 | 5,251 | 6,915 |
| Private non-profit-making bodies | 87 | 97 | |
| Net government current expenditure | 2,531 | 3,004 | 3,250 |
| Gross fixed capital formation | 1,673 | 2,031 | 2,402 |
| Increase in stocks | −134 | 459 | 210 |
| **Total domestic expenditure** | 8,573 | 10,842 | 12,777 |
| Net exports of goods and services | 366 | 599 | 411 |
| Net investment income from abroad | −355 | −478 | −538 |
| **GNP at market prices** | 8,584 | 10,963 | 12,650 |

* Source: IMF, *International Financial Statistics*.

### Composition of the Gross National Product

|  | 1986 | 1987 | 1988 |
|---|---|---|---|
| Compensation of employees | 4,351 | 4,859 | 5,611 |
| Operating surplus | 3,058 | 3,160 | 4,573 |
| Consumption of fixed capital | | | |
| **GDP at factor cost** | 7,409 | 8,019 | 10,184 |
| Indirect taxes | 1,251 | 1,346 | 1,645 |
| *Less* Subsidies | 370 | 426 | 388 |
| **GDP at market prices** | 8,290 | 8,939 | 11,441 |
| Net factor income from abroad | −384 | −355 | −478 |
| **GNP at market prices** | 7,906 | 8,584 | 10,963 |

Source: UN, *National Accounts Statistics*.

### Gross Domestic Product by Economic Activity
(Z.$ million at current factor cost)

|  | 1989 | 1990 | 1991 |
|---|---|---|---|
| Agriculture, hunting, forestry and fishing | 1,753 | 2,391 | 3,709 |
| Mining and quarrying | 827 | 923 | 1,175 |
| Manufacturing | 3,162 | 3,691 | 4,849 |
| Electricity and water | 391 | 417 | 567 |
| Construction | 284 | 323 | 368 |
| Trade, restaurants and hotels | 1,258 | 1,569 | 1,898 |
| Transport, storage and communications | 930 | 1,067 | 1,243 |
| Finance, insurance and real estate | 863 | 977 | 1,133 |
| Government services | 895 | 1,057 | 1,230 |
| Other services | 1,878 | 2,423 | 3,197 |
| **Sub-total** | 12,241 | 14,838 | 19,369 |
| *Less* Imputed bank service charges | 338 | 344 | 366 |
| **Total** | 11,903 | 14,494 | 19,003 |

Source: UN, *National Accounts Statistics*.

## BALANCE OF PAYMENTS (US $ million)

|  | 1991 | 1992 | 1993 |
|---|---|---|---|
| Merchandise exports f.o.b. | 1,693.8 | 1,527.6 | 1,609.1 |
| Merchandise imports f.o.b. | −1,645.7 | −1,782.1 | −1,487.0 |
| **Trade balance** | 48.1 | −254.5 | 122.1 |
| Exports of services | 271.9 | 304.1 | 371.3 |
| Imports of services | −587.4 | −655.1 | −558.5 |
| Other income received | 27.7 | 27.0 | 35.9 |
| Other income paid | −318.0 | −308.1 | −292.4 |
| Private unrequited transfers (net) | 3.4 | 39.7 | 26.5 |
| Official unrequited transfers (net) | 94.6 | 241.8 | 179.0 |
| **Current balance** | −459.8 | −605.1 | −116.1 |
| Direct investment (net) | 2.8 | 15.0 | 28.0 |
| Portfolio investment (net) | 7.3 | −9.5 | −5.1 |
| Other capital (net) | 526.4 | 367.9 | 304.3 |
| Net errors and omissions | −31.4 | 37.2 | 14.9 |
| **Overall balance** | 45.2 | −194.6 | 225.9 |

Source: IMF, *International Financial Statistics*.

# External Trade

**PRINCIPAL COMMODITIES** (distribution by SITC, US $'000, excl. stores and bunkers for aircraft)

| Imports f.o.b.* | 1988 | 1990 | 1991 |
|---|---|---|---|
| **Food and live animals** | n.a. | 42,042 | 18,380 |
| **Crude materials (inedible) except fuels** | n.a. | 69,271 | 90,178 |
| **Mineral fuels, lubricants, etc. (incl. electricity)** | n.a. | 289,259 | 252,115 |
| Petroleum, petroleum products, etc. | n.a. | 271,541 | 243,624 |
| Refined petroleum products | n.a. | 262,085 | 235,567 |
| Motor spirit (gasoline) and other light oils | 26,944 | 67,037 | 61,121 |
| Motor and aviation spirit | 26,944 | 65,413 | 59,800 |
| Gas oils | 71,988 | 133,880 | 111,805 |
| **Chemicals and related products** | n.a. | 284,584 | 323,919 |
| Inorganic chemicals | n.a. | 62,997 | 60,293 |
| Artificial resins, plastic materials, etc. | 55,188 | 58,895 | 71,696 |
| Products of polymerization, etc. | n.a. | 45,998 | 58,221 |
| **Basic manufactures** | n.a. | 308,570 | 341,849 |
| Textile yarn, fabrics, etc. | n.a. | 84,386 | 90,382 |
| Non-metallic mineral manufactures | n.a. | 43,068 | 46,019 |
| Iron and steel | n.a. | 69,708 | 74,419 |
| Universals, plates and sheets | 29,043 | 46,503 | 45,714 |
| **Machinery and transport equipment** | n.a. | 692,196 | 822,310 |
| Power-generating machinery and equipment | n.a. | 44,091 | 38,621 |
| Machinery specialized for particular industries | n.a. | 160,705 | 192,089 |
| Civil engineering and contractors' plant and equipment | n.a. | 51,672 | 31,312 |
| Construction and mining machinery | 14,552 | 44,269 | 26,995 |
| Textile and leather machinery | 17,183 | 36,862 | 52,645 |
| General industrial machinery, equipment, etc. | n.a. | 110,420 | 124,852 |
| Telecommunications and sound equipment | 31,154 | 28,842 | 44,198 |
| Other electrical machinery, apparatus, etc. | n.a. | 62,017 | 75,939 |

# ZIMBABWE

| Imports f.o.b.* — continued | 1988 | 1990 | 1991 |
|---|---|---|---|
| Road vehicles and parts† | n.a. | 125,865 | 278,597 |
|   Passenger motor cars (excl. buses) | 20,212 | 21,351 | 48,627 |
|   Motor vehicles for goods transport, etc. | n.a. | 62,605 | 147,779 |
|   Goods vehicles | n.a. | 57,794 | 120,772 |
|   Other road motor vehicles (excl. motorcycles, etc.) | n.a. | 11,585 | 40,156 |
| Other transport equipment† | n.a. | 113,382 | 16,842 |
|   Aircraft, associated equipment and parts† | 12,356 | 105,919 | 10,972 |
| **Miscellaneous manufactured articles** | n.a. | 85,164 | 68,001 |
| **Total** (incl. others) | 1,129,455 | 1,852,008 | 2,007,142 |

\* The distribution by commodities is not available for 1989 (total imports US $1,627 million).

† Excluding tyres, engines and electrical parts.

| Exports f.o.b.* | 1988 | 1990 | 1991 |
|---|---|---|---|
| **Food and live animals** | n.a. | 285,572 | 162,877 |
| Meat and meat preparations | n.a. | 7,491 | 10,015 |
|   Fresh, chilled or frozen meat | 39,689 | 4,162 | 3,575 |
| Cereals and cereal preparations | n.a. | 117,460 | 63,499 |
|   Maize (unmilled) | 62,269 | 108,600 | 48,644 |
| Sugar, sugar preparations and honey | n.a. | 66,590 | 37,838 |
|   Sugar and honey | 43,936 | 61,344 | 34,515 |
|   Raw sugars | 43,138 | 49,876 | 17,870 |
| Coffee, tea, cocoa and spices | n.a. | 73,202 | 33,624 |
|   Coffee and coffee substitutes | 22,287 | 60,033 | 21,538 |
|     Green coffee (incl. husks and skins) | 22,287 | 60,012 | 21,527 |
| **Beverages and tobacco** | n.a. | 345,875 | 431,278 |
| Tobacco and tobacco manufactures | n.a. | 345,726 | 429,714 |
|   Unmanufactured tobacco | 274,922 | 339,710 | 424,234 |
| **Crude materials (inedible) except fuels** | n.a. | 217,559 | 153,927 |
| Textile, fibres and waste | n.a. | 86,699 | 58,551 |
|   Cotton | 82,109 | 86,292 | 58,278 |
| Crude fertilizers and crude minerals | n.a. | 86,928 | 63,373 |
|   Asbestos | 57,450 | 59,289 | 46,064 |
| **Basic manufactures** | n.a. | 446,403 | 366,993 |
| Textile yarn, fabrics, etc. | n.a. | 44,116 | 44,683 |
| Iron and steel | n.a. | 213,393 | 166,443 |
|   Pig-iron, etc. | n.a. | 154,415 | 112,007 |
|   Ferro-alloys | 189,659 | 154,404 | 111,864 |
|   Ingots and other primary forms | 45,834 | 46,776 | 42,274 |
|   Blooms, billets, slabs, etc. | 45,834 | 43,515 | 38,284 |
| Non-ferrous metals | n.a. | 134,283 | 110,243 |
|   Copper and copper alloys | 36,691 | 28,008 | 15,319 |
|   Nickel and nickel alloys | 170,196 | 100,246 | 85,538 |
| **Machinery and transport equipment** | n.a. | 54,048 | 26,501 |
| **Miscellaneous manufactured articles** | n.a. | 62,596 | 63,423 |
| Clothing and accessories (excl. footwear) | n.a. | 37,925 | 37,972 |
| **Non-monetary gold (excl. gold ores and concentrates)** | 209,430 | 2,864 | 2,623 |
| **Total** (incl. others) | 1,630,741 | 1,470,432 | 1,250,990 |

\* The distribution by commodities is not available for 1989.

Source: UN, *International Trade Statistics Yearbook*.

## PRINCIPAL TRADING PARTNERS (US $'000)*

| Imports f.o.b.† | 1988 | 1990 | 1991 |
|---|---|---|---|
| Australia | 6,086 | 50,516 | 20,837 |
| Belgium-Luxembourg | 13,684 | 20,184 | 23,299 |
| Canada | 19,658 | 20,853 | 17,903 |
| China, People's Repub. | n.a. | 36,280 | 15,605 |
| France | 35,549 | 38,338 | 60,746 |
| Germany | 107,265 | 135,988 | 189,470 |
| Italy | 18,975 | 40,719 | 47,609 |
| Japan | 45,537 | 84,489 | 120,043 |
| Netherlands | 30,251 | 36,116 | 34,113 |
| South Africa‡ | 315,353 | 445,841 | 578,626 |
| Sweden | 17,398 | 25,062 | 24,795 |
| Switzerland | 15,002 | 37,149 | 43,332 |
| United Kingdom | 121,688 | 212,757 | 306,445 |
| USA | 66,334 | 211,201 | 109,655 |
| **Total** (incl. others) | 1,129,455 | 1,851,440 | 2,003,917 |

| Exports f.o.b. | 1988 | 1990 | 1991 |
|---|---|---|---|
| Belgium-Luxembourg | 30,204 | 37,285 | 52,563 |
| China, People's Repub. | 16,599 | 24,253 | 37,178 |
| France | 15,896 | 23,909 | 18,764 |
| Germany | 129,525 | 173,363 | 132,210 |
| Hong Kong | 9,242 | 23,495 | 14,163 |
| Italy | 92,638 | 67,714 | 44,747 |
| Japan | 95,966 | 80,752 | 90,344 |
| Kenya | 16,197 | 18,053 | 12,921 |
| Malawi | 41,157 | 70,785 | 41,404 |
| Mozambique | 41,563 | 54,009 | 34,317 |
| Netherlands | 103,160 | 63,045 | 37,450 |
| Portugal | 20,835 | 39,405 | 13,585 |
| South Africa‡ | 207,151 | 222,264 | 213,208 |
| Spain | 12,337 | 22,592 | 22,086 |
| Sweden | 15,292 | 9,034 | 8,042 |
| Switzerland | 6,926 | 24,318 | 26,883 |
| United Kingdom | 159,269 | 157,806 | 169,912 |
| USA | 102,345 | 95,977 | 73,007 |
| Zambia | 61,115 | 51,364 | 44,557 |
| **Total** (incl. others) | 1,630,741 | 1,467,569 | 1,248,367 |

\* Imports by country of production; exports by country of last consignment.

† Data for 1989 are not available.

‡ Including Botswana, Lesotho, Namibia and Swaziland.

Source: UN, *International Trade Statistics Yearbook*.

# Transport

## RAIL TRAFFIC
(National Railways of Zimbabwe, including operations in Botswana)

| | 1991 | 1992 | 1993 |
|---|---|---|---|
| Total number of passengers ('000) | 1,975 | 2,355 | 2,220 |
| Revenue-earning metric tons hauled ('000) | 17,928 | 13,038 | 10,464 |
| Gross metric ton-km (million) | 10,930 | 11,913 | 9,649 |
| Net metric ton-km (million) | 5,413 | 5,887 | 4,581 |

## ROAD TRAFFIC (motor vehicles in use)

| | 1989 | 1990 | 1991* |
|---|---|---|---|
| Passenger cars | 285,000 | 290,000* | 300,000 |
| Commercial vehicles | 82,000 | 83,000 | 85,000 |

\* Estimate(s).

Source: UN, *Statistical Yearbook*.

# ZIMBABWE

**CIVIL AVIATION** (traffic on scheduled services)

|  | 1990 | 1991 | 1992 |
|---|---|---|---|
| Kilometres flown ('000) | 12,000 | 12,000 | 12,000 |
| Passengers carried ('000) | 601 | 606 | 595 |
| Passenger-km (million) | 797 | 817 | 772 |
| Freight ton-km ('000) | 65,000 | 64,000 | n.a. |

Source: UN, *Statistical Yearbook*.

## Tourism

|  | 1990 | 1991 | 1992 |
|---|---|---|---|
| Number of tourist arrivals | 606,000 | 664,000 | 737,533 |
| Tourist receipts (US $ million) | 64 | 75 | 105 |

Source: UN, *Statistical Yearbook*.

## Communications Media

|  | 1990 | 1991 | 1992 |
|---|---|---|---|
| Radio receivers ('000 in use) | 830 | 860 | 890 |
| Television receivers ('000 in use) | 300 | 270 | 280 |
| Telephones ('000 in use) | 301 | n.a. | n.a. |
| Book production: | | | |
|   Titles | 349 | n.a. | 232 |
| Daily newspapers: | | | |
|   Number | 2 | n.a. | 2 |
|   Circulation ('000 copies) | 206 | n.a. | 195 |

Sources: UNESCO, *Statistical Yearbook*; UN, *Statistical Yearbook*.

## Education
(1992)

|  | Schools | Teachers | Students |
|---|---|---|---|
| Primary | 4,567 | 60,834 | 2,301,642 |
| Secondary | 1,512* | 25,225† | 710,619† |
| Higher | n.a. | 3,076 | 61,553 |

* Figure for 1990. Source: Ministry of Education and Culture, Causeway, Harare.
† Figures for 1991.

Source: UNESCO, *Statistical Yearbook*.

**1993:** Primary students 2,436,671; Secondary students 635,502. Source: Ministry of Education and Culture, Causeway, Harare.

# Directory

## The Constitution

The Constitution of the Republic of Zimbabwe took effect at independence on 18 April 1980. Amendments to the Constitution must have the approval of two-thirds of the members of the House of Assembly (see below). The provisions of the 1980 Constitution (with subsequent amendments) are summarized below:

### THE REPUBLIC

Zimbabwe is a sovereign republic and the Constitution is the supreme law.

### DECLARATION OF RIGHTS

The declaration of rights guarantees the fundamental rights and freedoms of the individual, regardless of race, tribe, place of origin, political opinions, colour, creed or sex.

### THE PRESIDENT

Executive power is vested in the President, who acts on the advice of the Cabinet. The President is Head of State and Commander-in-Chief of the Defence Forces. The President appoints two Vice-Presidents and other Ministers and Deputy Ministers, to be members of the Cabinet. The President holds office for six years and is eligible for re-election. Each candidate for the Presidency shall be nominated by not fewer than 10 members of the House of Assembly; if only one candidate is nominated, that candidate shall be declared to be elected without the necessity of a ballot. Otherwise, a ballot shall be held within an electoral college consisting of the members of the House of Assembly.

### PARLIAMENT

Legislative power is vested in a unicameral Parliament, consisting of a House of Assembly. The House of Assembly comprises 150 members, of whom 120 are directly elected by universal adult suffrage, 12 are nominated by the President, 10 are traditional Chiefs and eight are Provincial Governors. The life of the House of Assembly is ordinarily to be six years.

### OTHER PROVISIONS

An Ombudsman shall be appointed by the President, acting on the advice of the Judicial Service Commission, to investigate complaints against actions taken by employees of the government or of a local authority.

Chiefs shall be appointed by the President, and shall form a Council of Chiefs from their number in accordance with customary principles of succession.

Other provisions relate to the Judicature, Defence and Police Forces, public service and finance.

## The Government

### HEAD OF STATE

**President:** ROBERT GABRIEL MUGABE (took office 31 December 1987; re-elected March 1990).

### THE CABINET
(June 1995)

**Vice-Presidents:** SIMON VENGAYI MUZENDA, JOSHUA MQABUKO NKOMO.
**Minister of Defence:** MOVEN ENOCK MAHACHI.
**Minister of Home Affairs:** DUMISO DABENGWA.
**Minister of Justice, Legal and Parliamentary Affairs:** EMMERSON DAMBUDZO MNANGAGWA.
**Minister of Finance:** ARISTON CHAMBATI.
**Minister of National Affairs, Employment Creation and Co-operatives:** FLORENCE CHITAURO.
**Minister of Public Service, Labour and Social Welfare:** NATHAN MARWIRAKUWA SHAMUYARIRA.
**Minister of Local Government, Rural and Urban Development:** JOHN LANDA NKOMO.

ZIMBABWE

**Minister of Agriculture:** DENIS NORMAN.
**Minister of Lands and Water Resources:** KUMBIRAI MANYIKA KANGAI.
**Minister of Industry and Commerce:** HERBERT MURERWA.
**Minister of Mines:** EDDISON MUDADIRWA ZVOGBO.
**Minister of the Environment and Tourism:** CHEN CHIMUTINGWENDE.
**Minister of Public Construction and National Housing:** ENOS CHAMUNORWA CHIKOWORE.
**Minister of Information, Posts and Telecommunications:** DAVID ISHEMUNYORO KARIMANZIRA.
**Minister of Foreign Affairs:** STANISLAUS MUDENGE.
**Minister of Higher Education:** Dr IGNATIUS MORGAN CHIMINYA CHOMBO.
**Minister of Education:** THENJIWE VIRGINIA LESABE.
**Minister of Sports, Recreation and Culture:** WITNESS MANGWENDE.
**Minister of Health and Child Welfare:** Dr TIMOTHY STAMPS.
**Minister of Transport and Energy:** SIMON K. MOYO.

### MINISTRIES

**Office of the President:** Munhumutapa Bldg, Samora Machel Ave, Private Bag 7700, Causeway, Harare; tel. (4) 707091; telex 24478.
**Office of the Vice-President:** Munhumutapa Bldg, Samora Machel Ave, Private Bag 7700, Causeway, Harare; tel. (4) 707091; telex 24478.
**Ministry of Defence:** Munhumutapa Bldg, Samora Machel Ave, Private Bag 7713, Causeway, Harare; tel. (4) 700155; telex 22141.
**Ministry of Education:** Ambassador House, Union Ave, POB 8022, Causeway, Harare; tel. (4) 734050; telex 26430.
**Ministry of the Environment and Tourism:** Karigamombe Centre, Private Bag 7753, Causeway, Harare; tel. (4) 794455.
**Ministry of Finance:** Munhumutapa Bldg, Ground Floor, Samora Machel Ave, Private Bag 7705, Causeway, Harare; tel. (4) 794571; telex 22141; fax (4) 706293.
**Ministry of Foreign Affairs:** Munhumutapa Bldg, Samora Machel Ave, POB 4240, Causeway, Harare; tel. (4) 727005.
**Ministry of Health and Child Welfare:** Kaguvi Bldg, Fourth St, POB 1122, Causeway, Harare; tel. (4) 730011; telex 22141; fax (4) 729154.
**Ministry of Higher Education:** Union Ave, POB 275, Harare; tel. (4) 795991; fax (4) 728730.
**Ministry of Home Affairs:** Mukwati Bldg, Samora Machel Ave, Private Bag 505D, Harare; tel. (4) 703641; telex 22141.
**Ministry of Industry and Commerce:** Mukwati Bldg, Fourth St, Private Bag 7708, Causeway, Harare; tel. (4) 702731; telex 24472.
**Ministry of Information, Posts and Telecommunications:** Linquenda House, Baker Ave, POB 1276, Causeway, Harare; tel. (4) 703894; telex 24142; fax (4) 707213.
**Ministry of Justice, Legal and Parliamentary Affairs:** Mapondera Bldg, Samora Machel Ave, Private Bag 7704, Causeway, Harare; tel. (4) 790905; telex 22141; fax (4) 790901.
**Ministry of Lands and Water Resources:** Makombe Complex, Block 3, Harare St, Private Bag 7712, Causeway, Harare; tel. (4) 707861; telex 22141.
**Ministry of Local Government, Rural and Urban Development:** Mukwati Bldg, Private Bag 7706, Causeway, Harare; tel. (4) 790601; telex 22179.
**Ministry of Mines:** ZIMRE Centre, cnr Leopold Takawira St and Union Ave, Private Bag 7709, Causeway, Harare; tel. (4) 703781; telex 22416.
**Ministry of National Affairs, Employment Creation and Co-operatives:** Private Bag 8158, Causeway, Harare; tel. (4) 734691.
**Ministry of Public Construction and National Housing:** cnr Leopold Takawira St and Herbert Chitepo Ave, POB 8081, Causeway, Harare; tel. (4) 704561.
**Ministry of Public Service, Labour and Social Welfare:** Compensation House, cnr Central Ave and Fourth St, Private Bag 7707, Causeway, Harare; tel. (4) 790871; telex 22141.
**Ministry of Sports, Recreation and Culture:** Harare.
**Ministry of Transport and Energy:** Kaguvi Bldg, POB 8109, Causeway, Harare; tel. (4) 707121; telex 22141; fax (4) 708225.

### PROVINCIAL GOVERNORS

**Manicaland:** KENNETH VHUNDUKAYI MANYONDA.
**Mashonaland Central:** JOYCE MAJURE.
**Mashonaland East:** EDMUND GARWE.
**Mashonaland West:** Dr IGNATIUS MORGAN CHIMINYA CHOMBO.
**Masvingo:** JOSAYA DUNIRA HUNGWE.
**Matabeleland North:** WELSHMAN MABHENA.
**Matabeleland South:** STEPHEN JEQE NYONGOLO NKOMO.
**Midlands:** Lt-Col HERBERT MAHLABA.

## President and Legislature

### PRESIDENT

Election, 28–30 March 1990

| Candidate | Percentage of total votes cast |
|---|---|
| ROBERT GABRIEL MUGABE | 78 |
| EDGAR TEKERE | 16 |

### HOUSE OF ASSEMBLY

**Speaker:** CYRIL NDEBELE.

Election, 8–9 April 1995

| | Seats* |
|---|---|
| Zimbabwe African National Union—Patriotic Front | 118 |
| Zimbabwe African National Union—Ndonga | 2 |
| **Total** | 120 |

* In addition to the 120 directly elective seats, 12 are held by nominees of the President, 10 by traditional Chiefs and eight by Provincial Governors.

## Political Organizations

**Committee for a Democratic Society (CODESO):** f. 1993; Kalanga-supported grouping, based in Matebeleland; Leader SOUL NDLOVU.
**Conservative Alliance of Zimbabwe (CAZ):** POB 242, Harare; f. 1962, known as Rhodesian Front until June 1981, and subsequently as Republican Front; supported by sections of the white community; Pres. GERALD SMITH; Chair. MIKE MORONEY.
**Democratic Party:** f. 1991 by a breakaway faction from the ZUM; Nat. Chair. GILES MUTSEKWA; Pres. DAVIDSON GOMO.
**Federal Party:** Nketa, Bulawayo; f. 1994; aims to create national federation of five provinces; Leader TWOBOY JUBANE.
**Forum Party of Zimbabwe (FPZ):** Harare; f. 1993; conservative; Pres. Dr ENOCH DUMBUTSHENA.
**Front for Popular Democracy:** f. 1994; Chair. Prof. AUSTIN CHAKAWODZA.
**Independent Zimbabwe Group:** f. 1983 by a breakaway faction from the fmr Republican Front; Leader BILL IRVINE.
**National Democratic Union:** f. 1979; conservative grouping with minority Zezeru support; Leader HENRY CHIHOTA.
**National Progressive Alliance:** f. 1991; Chair. CANCIWELL NZIRAMASANGA.
**United National Federal Party (UNFP):** Harare; f. 1978; conservative; seeks a federation of Mashonaland and Matabeleland; Leader Chief KAYISA NDIWENI.
**United Parties (UP):** f. 1994; Leader Bishop (retd) ABEL MUZOREWA.
**Zimbabwe Active People's Unity Party:** Bulawayo; f. 1989; Leader NEWMAN MATUTU NDELA.
**Zimbabwe African National Union—Patriotic Front (ZANU—PF):** 88 Manica Rd, Harare; f. 1989 following the merger of PF ZAPU (f. 1961) and ZANU—PF (f. 1963); Pres. ROBERT GABRIEL MUGABE; Vice-Pres SIMON VENGAYI MUZENDA, JOSHUA MQABUKO NKOMO.
**Zimbabwe African National Union—Ndonga (ZANU—Ndonga):** POB UA525, Union Ave, Harare; tel. and fax (4) 614177; f. 1977; breakaway faction from ZANU, also includes fmr mems of UANC; centrist, promotes free market economy; Pres. Rev. NDABANINGI SITHOLE; Sec.-Gen. GODFRY MUMBAMARWO.
**Zimbabwe Congress Party:** Harare; f. 1994.
**Zimbabwe Democratic Party:** Harare; f. 1979; traditionalist; Leader JAMES CHIKEREMA.
**Zimbabwe National Front:** f. 1979; Leader PETER MANDAZA.
**Zimbabwe Peoples' Democratic Party:** f. 1989; Chair. ISABEL PASALK.
**Zimbabwe Unity Movement (ZUM):** f. 1989 by a breakaway faction from ZANU—PF; merged with United African National Council (UANC, f. 1971) in 1994; Leader EDGAR TEKERE.

ZIMBABWE                                                                                    *Directory*

## Diplomatic Representation

**EMBASSIES AND HIGH COMMISSIONS IN ZIMBABWE**

**Afghanistan:** 26 East Rd, POB 1227, Harare; tel. (4) 720083; telex 22276; Chargé d'affaires a.i.: ABD AL-SATAR FROTAN.

**Angola:** Doncaster House, 26 Speke Ave/Ongwa St, POB 3590, Harare; tel. (4) 790070; telex 24195; Ambassador: ARISTIDES VAN-DÚNEN.

**Argentina:** Club Chambers Bldg, cnr Baker Ave and Third St, POB 2770, Harare; tel. (4) 730075; telex 22284; fax (4) 730076; Ambassador: VALENTIN LUCO ORIGONE.

**Australia:** Karigamombe Centre, 4th Floor, 53 Samora Machel Ave, POB 4541, Harare; tel. (4) 794591; telex 24159; fax (4) 704644; High Commissioner: JOHN THWAITES.

**Austria:** 216 New Shell House, 30 Samora Machel Ave, POB 4120, Harare; tel. (4) 702921; telex 22546; Ambassador: Dr FELIX MIKL.

**Bangladesh:** 9 Birchenough Rd, POB 3040, Harare; tel. (4) 727004; telex 24806; High Commissioner: HARUN AHMED CHOWDHURY.

**Belgium:** Tanganyika House, 5th Floor, 23 Third St, POB 2522, Harare; tel. (4) 793306; telex 24788; fax (4) 703960; Ambassador: BERNARD R. PIERRE.

**Botswana:** 22 Phillips Ave, Belgravia, POB 563, Harare; tel. (4) 729551; telex 22663; High Commissioner: PHENEAS M. MAKEPE.

**Brazil:** Old Mutual Centre, 9th Floor, Jason Moyo Ave, POB 2530, Harare; tel. (4) 730775; telex 22205; fax (4) 737782; Chargé d'affaires a.i.: ANA MARIA PINTO MORALES.

**Bulgaria:** 15 Maasdorp Ave, Alexandra Park, POB 1809, Harare; tel. (4) 730509; telex 24567; Ambassador: CHRISTO TEPAVITCHAROV.

**Canada:** 45 Baines Ave, POB 1430, Harare; tel. (4) 733881; telex 24465; High Commissioner: CHARLES BASSET.

**China, People's Republic:** 30 Baines Ave, POB 4749, Harare; tel. (4) 724572; telex 22569; fax (4) 794959; Ambassador: GU XINER.

**Cuba:** 5 Phillips Ave, Belgravia, POB 4139, Harare; tel. (4) 720256; telex 24783; Ambassador: EUMELIO CABALLERO RODRÍGUEZ.

**Czech Republic:** 11 Walmer Drive, Highlands, POB 4474, Harare; tel. (4) 700636; telex 22413; fax (4) 737270.

**Denmark:** UDC Centre, 1st Floor, cnr 59 Union Ave and First St, POB 4711, Harare; tel. (4) 758185; telex 24677; fax (4) 758189; Ambassador: BIRTE POULSEN.

**Egypt:** 7 Aberdeen Rd, Avondale, POB A433, Harare; tel. (4) 303445; telex 24653; Ambassador: Dr IBRAHIM ALY BADAWI EL-SHEIK.

**Ethiopia:** 14 Lanark Rd, Belgravia, POB 2745, Harare; tel. (4) 725822; telex 22743; fax (4) 720259; Ambassador: FANTAHUN H. MICHAEL.

**Finland:** Karigamombe Centre, 3rd Floor, 53 Samora Machel Ave, POB 5300, Harare; tel. (4) 751654; telex 24813; fax (4) 757743; Ambassador: ILARI RANTAKARI (resident in Dar es Salaam, Tanzania).

**France:** Ranelagh Rd, Highlands, POB 1378, Harare; tel. (4) 48096; telex 24779; fax (4) 45657; Ambassador: JACQUES MIGOZZI.

**Germany:** 14 Samora Machel Ave, POB 2168, Harare; tel. (4) 731955; telex 24609; fax (4) 790680; Ambassador: Dr NORWIN Graf LEUTRUM VON ERTINGEN.

**Ghana:** 11 Downie Ave, Belgravia, POB 4445, Harare; tel. (4) 738652; telex 24631; fax 738654; High Commissioner: Prof. P. A. TWUMASI.

**Greece:** 8 Deary Ave, Belgravia, POB 4809, Harare; tel. (4) 793208; telex 24790; Ambassador: ALEXANDROS SANDS.

**Holy See:** 5 St Kilda Rd, Mount Pleasant, POB MP191, Harare (Apostolic Nunciature); tel. (4) 744547; fax (4) 744412; Apostolic Nuncio: Most Rev. PETER PAUL PRABHU, Titular Archbishop of Tituli in Numidia.

**Hungary:** 20 Lanark Rd, Belgravia, POB 3594, Harare; tel. (4) 733528; telex 24237; fax (4) 730512; Ambassador: TAMÁS GÁSPÁR GÁL.

**India:** 12 Nathal Rd, Belgravia, POB 4620, Harare; tel. (4) 795955; telex 24630; fax (4) 722324; High Commissioner: SIDDHARTH SINGH.

**Indonesia:** 3 Duthie Ave, Belgravia, POB 3594, Harare; tel. (4) 732561; telex 24237; Ambassador: SAMSI ABDULLAH.

**Iran:** 8 Allan Wilson Ave, Avondale, POB A293, Harare; tel. (4) 726942; telex 24793; Chargé d'affaires a.i.: ALIREZA GAKARANI.

**Iraq:** 21 Lawson Ave, Milton Park, POB 3453, Harare; tel. (4) 725727; telex 24595; fax (4) 724204; Ambassador: ISSAM MAHBOUB.

**Italy:** 7 Bartholomew Close, Greendale North, POB 1062, Harare; tel. (4) 498190; telex 24380; fax (4) 498199; Ambassador: Dr RICCARDO LEONINI.

**Japan:** Karigamombe Centre, 18th Floor, 53 Samora Machel Ave, POB 2710, Harare; tel. (4) 790108; telex 24566; fax (4) 727769; Ambassador: MITSUO IIJIMA.

**Kenya:** 95 Park Lane, POB 4069, Harare; tel. (4) 790847; telex 24266; High Commissioner: CRISPUS MWEMA.

**Korea, Democratic People's Republic:** 102 Josiah Chinamano Ave, Greenwood, POB 4754, Harare; tel. (4) 724052; telex 24231; Ambassador: RI MYONG CHOL.

**Kuwait:** 1 Bath Rd, Avondale, POB A485, Harare; Ambassador: NABILA AL-MULLA.

**Libya:** 124 Harare St, POB 4310, Harare; tel. (4) 728381; telex 24585; Ambassador: M. M. IBN KOURAH.

**Malawi:** Malawi House, Harare St, POB 321, Harare; tel. (4) 705611; telex 24467; High Commissioner: ANSLEY D. KHAUYEZA.

**Malaysia:** 12 Lawson Ave, Milton Park, POB 5570, Harare; tel. (4) 796209; fax (4) 796200 High Commissioner: GHAZZALI S. A. KHALID.

**Mexico:** 26 Connaught Rd, Avondale, POB 3812, Harare; tel. (4) 35724; telex 26124; fax (4) 308115; Ambassador: VÍCTOR M. SOLANO MONTANO.

**Mozambique:** 152 Herbert Chitepo Ave, cnr Leopold Takawira St, POB 4608, Harare; tel. (4) 790837; telex 24466; Ambassador: LOPES NDELANA.

**Netherlands:** 47 Enterprise Rd, Highlands, POB HG601, Harare; tel. (4) 731428; telex 24357; fax (4) 790520; Ambassador: WIM WESSELS.

**New Zealand:** 57 Jason Moyo Ave, Batanai Gardens, POB 5448, Harare; tel. (4) 759221; telex 22747; fax (4) 759228; High Commissioner: BRIAN ABSOLUM.

**Nigeria:** 36 Samora Machel Ave, POB 4742, Harare; tel. (4) 790765; telex 24473; High Commissioner: MUHAMMED METTEDEN.

**Norway:** 5 Lanark Rd, Belgravia, POB A510, Avondale, Harare; tel. (4) 792419; telex 26576; Ambassador: JOHAN H. DAHL.

**Pakistan:** 11 Van Praagh Ave, Milton Park, POB 3050, Harare; tel. (4) 720293; fax (4) 722446; High Commissioner: TARIQ FATEMI.

**Poland:** 16 Cork Road, Belgravia, POB 3932, Harare; tel. (4) 732159; telex 22745; fax (4) 732159; Chargé d'affaires a.i.: ANDRZEJ KASPRZYK.

**Portugal:** 10 Samora Machel Ave, POB 406, Harare; tel. (4) 725107; telex 24714; Ambassador: Dr EDUARDO NUNEZ DE CARVALHO.

**Romania:** 105 Fourth St, POB 4797, Harare; tel. (4) 700853; telex 24797; Ambassador: Dr GHEORGHE POPESCU.

**Russia:** 70 Fife Ave, POB 4250, Harare; tel. (4) 720358; telex 22616; fax (4) 700534; Ambassador: YOURI A. YOUKALOV.

**Senegal:** 17 Beveridge Rd, Avondale, POB 6904, Harare; tel. (4) 303147; telex 26314; fax (4) 35087; Ambassador: OUSMANE CAMARA.

**Slovakia:** 32 Aberdeen Rd, Avondale, POB HG72, Harare; tel. (4) 302636; telex 22460; fax (4) 302236; Ambassador: Dr JÁN VODERADSKÝ.

**Spain:** 16 Phillips Ave, Belgravia, POB 3300, Harare; tel. (4) 738681; telex 24173; fax (4) 795440; Ambassador: JOSÉ MANUEL PAZ AGUERAS.

**Sudan:** 4 Pascoe Ave, Harare; tel. (4) 725240; telex 26308; Ambassador: ANGELO V. MORGAN.

**Sweden:** Pegasus House, 52 Samora Machel Ave, POB 4110, Harare; tel. (4) 790651; telex 24695; fax (4) 702003; Ambassador: NILS DAAG.

**Switzerland:** 9 Lanark Rd, POB 3440, Harare; tel. (4) 703997; telex 24669; Ambassador: PETER HOLLENWEGER.

**Tunisia:** 5 Ashton Rd, Alexandra Park, POB 4308, Harare; tel. (4) 791570; telex 24801; fax (4) 727224; Ambassador: HAMID ZAOUCHE.

**United Kingdom:** Stanley House, Jason Moyo Ave, POB 4490, Harare; tel. (4) 793781; telex 24607; fax (4) 728380; High Commissioner: RICHARD DALES.

**USA:** 172 Herbert Chitepo Ave, POB 3340, Harare; tel. (4) 794521; telex 24591; fax (4) 796480; Ambassador: E. GIBSON LANPHER.

**Viet Nam:** 14 Carlisle Drive, Alexandra Park, POB 5458, Harare; tel. (4) 701118; telex 22047; Chargé d'affaires a.i.: TRAN NHUAN.

**Yugoslavia:** 1 Lanark Rd, Belgravia, POB 3420, Harare; tel. (4) 738668; fax (4) 738660; Ambassador: LJUBISA KORAC.

**Zaire:** 24 Van Praagh Ave, Milton Park, POB 2446, Harare; tel. (4) 724494; telex 22265; Ambassador: BEMBOY BABA.

**Zambia:** Zambia House, cnr Union and Julius Nyerere Aves, POB 4698, Harare; tel. (4) 790851; telex 24698; fax (4) 790856; High Commissioner: NCHIMUNYA SIKAULU.

## Judicial System

The legal system is Roman-Dutch, based on the system which was in force in the Cape of Good Hope on 10 June 1891, as modified by subsequent legislation.

ZIMBABWE                                                                                                          Directory

The Supreme Court has original jurisdiction in matters in which an infringement of Chapter III of the Constitution defining fundamental rights is alleged. In all other matters it has appellate jurisdiction only. It consists of the Chief Justice and four Judges of Appeal. A normal bench consists of any three of these.

The High Court consists of the Chief Justice, the Judge President, and 11 other judges. Below the High Court are Regional Courts and Magistrates' Courts with both civil and criminal jurisdiction presided over by full-time professional magistrates.

The Customary Law and Local Courts Act, adopted in 1990, abolished the village and community courts and replaced them with customary law and local courts, presided over by chiefs and headmen; in the case of chiefs, jurisdiction to try customary law cases is limited to those where the monetary values concerned do not exceed Z.$1,000 and in the case of a headman's court Z.$500. Appeals from the Chiefs' Courts are heard in Magistrates' Courts and, ultimately, the Supreme Court. All magistrates now have jurisdiction to try cases determinable by customary law.

**Attorney-General:** PATRICK ANTHONY CHINAMASA.
**Chief Justice:** ANTHONY R. GUBBAY.
**Judges of Appeal:** A. M. EBRAHIM, N. J. MCNALLY, K. R. A. KORSAH, S. C. G. MUCHECHETERE.
**Judge President:** WILSON R. SANDURA.

## Religion

### AFRICAN RELIGIONS
Many Africans follow traditional beliefs.

### CHRISTIANITY
About 55% of the population are Christians.

**Zimbabwe Council of Churches:** 128 Mbuya Nehanda St, POB 3566, Harare; tel. (4) 791208; telex 26243; f. 1964; 20 mem. churches, nine assoc. mems; Pres. Rt Rev. JONATHAN SIYACHITEMA (Anglican Bishop of the Lundi); Gen. Sec. MUROMBEDZI KUCHERA.

#### The Anglican Communion
The Church of the Province of Central Africa includes four dioceses in Zimbabwe. The Archbishop of the Province is the Bishop of Botswana.

**Bishop of Harare:** Rt Rev. RALPH HATENDI, Bishop's Mount, Bishopsmount Close, POB UA7, Harare; tel. (4) 487413; fax (4) 700419.
**Bishop of the Lundi:** Rt Rev. JONATHAN SIYACHITEMA, POB 25, Gweru; tel. (54) 51030; fax (54) 3658.
**Bishop of Manicaland:** Rt Rev. ELIJAH MUSEKIWA PETER MASUKO, 115 Herbert Chitepo St, Mutare; tel. (20) 64194; fax (20) 63076.
**Bishop of Matabeleland:** Rt Rev. THEOPHILUS T. NALEDI, POB 2422, Bulawayo; tel. (9) 61370; fax (9) 68353.

#### The Roman Catholic Church
For ecclesiastical purposes, Zimbabwe comprises two archdioceses and five dioceses. At 1 January 1994 there were an estimated 890,537 adherents.

**Zimbabwe Catholic Bishops' Conference:** General Secretariat, 29 Selous Ave, POB 738, Causeway, Harare; tel. (4) 705368; telex 2390; fax (4) 704001; f. 1969; Pres. Mgr FRANCIS MUGADZI, Bishop of Gweru.
**Archbishop of Bulawayo:** Most Rev. HENRY KARLEN, POB 837, Bulawayo; tel. (9) 63590; fax (9) 60359.
**Archbishop of Harare:** Most Rev. PATRICK FANI CHAKAIPA, POB 330, Causeway, Harare; tel. (4) 727386; fax (4) 721598.

#### Other Christian Churches
**City Presbyterian Church:** POB 50, Harare; tel. (4) 790366; f. 1904; Minister (vacant); Session Clerk H. JACK; 240 mems.
**Dutch Reformed Church** (Nederduitse Gereformeerde Kerk): 35 Samora Machel Ave, POB 967, Harare; tel. (4) 722436; fax (4) 727030; f. 1895; 16 parishes; Moderator Rev. A. S. VAN DYK; Gen. Sec. Rev. F. MARITZ; 2,500 mems.
**Evangelical Lutheran Church:** POB 2175, Bulawayo; tel. (9) 62686; f. 1903; Sec. Rt Rev. D. D. E. SIPHUMA; 57,000 mems.
**Greek Orthodox Church:** POB 808, Harare; tel. (4) 791616; Archbishop (vacant).
**Methodist Church in Zimbabwe:** POB 71, Causeway, Harare; tel. (4) 724069; f. 1891; Pres. Rev. Dr CRISPIN C. G. MAZOBERE; Sec. of Conference Rev. ENOS M. CHIBI; 111,374 mems.
**United Congregational Church of Southern Africa:** POB 2451, Bulawayo; Synod Sec. for Zimbabwe Rev. J. R. DANISA.
**United Methodist Church:** POB 3408, Harare; tel. (4) 704127; f. 1890; Bishop of Zimbabwe ABEL TENDEKAYI MUZOREWA; 45,000 mems.

Among other denominations active in Zimbabwe are the African Methodist Church, the African Methodist Episcopal Church, the African Reformed Church, the Christian Marching Church, the Church of Christ in Zimbabwe, the Independent African Church, the Presbyterian Church, the United Church of Christ, the Zimbabwe Assemblies of God and the Ziwezano Church.

### JUDAISM
There were 968 members of the Jewish community in 1994.

**Jewish Board of Deputies of Zimbabwe:** POB 342, Harare; tel. (4) 723647; Pres. S. C. HARRIS; Gen. Sec. Miss J. R. GRUBER.

### BAHÁ'Í FAITH
**National Spiritual Assembly:** POB GD380, Harare; tel. (4) 45945; fax (4) 744244; mems resident in more than 3,000 localities.

## The Press

### DAILIES
**The Chronicle:** POB 585, Bulawayo; tel. (9) 65471; telex 3059; f. 1894; circulates throughout south-west Zimbabwe; English; Editor STEPHEN A. MPOFU; circ. 74,032.
**The Herald:** POB 396, Harare; tel. (4) 795771; telex 26196; fax (4) 791311; f. 1891; English; Editor TOMMY SITHOLE; circ. 134,000.

### PERIODICALS
**Africa Calls Worldwide:** POB 2677, Harare; tel. (4) 704715; telex 26334; fax (4) 752162; f. 1960; travel; 6 a year; Editor MIKE HAMILTON; circ. 14,000.
**Business Herald:** Harare; weekly; Editor ANDREW RUSINGA.
**Central African Journal of Medicine:** POB A195, Avondale, Harare; tel. (4) 791631; f. 1955; monthly; Editor-in-Chief Dr J. A. MATENGA.
**Chaminuka News:** POB 251, Marondera; f. 1988; fortnightly; English and Chishona; Editor M. MUGABE; circ. 10,000.
**City Observer:** POB 990, Harare; tel. (4) 706536; telex 26189; fax (4) 708544; monthly.
**Commerce:** POB 1683, Harare; tel. (4) 736835; journal of Zimbabwe National Chambers of Commerce; monthly; Editor PENELOPE PARKER; circ. 5,000.
**Computer and Telecom News:** Thomson House, cnr Speke Ave and Harare St, POB 1683, Harare; tel. (4) 736835; telex 24705; fax (4) 752390; publ. by Thomson Publs Zimbabwe; monthly.
**Economic Review:** c/o Zimbabwe Financial Holdings, POB 3198, Harare; tel. (4) 751168; telex 24163; fax (4) 757497; 4 a year; circ. 3,000.
**Executive:** POB 2677, Harare; bi-monthly.
**The Farmer:** POB 1622, Harare; tel. (4) 753278; telex 22084; fax (4) 750754; f. 1928; commercial farming; weekly; English; Editor FELICITY WOOD; circ. 6,000.
**Farming World with Kurima Ukulima:** POB 909, Harare; tel. (4) 722322; f. 1975; monthly; English; Editors S. DICKIN, D. H. B. DICKIN; circ. 7,000.
**The Financial Gazette:** POB 66070, Kopje, Harare; tel. (4) 738722; weekly; Editor TREVOR NCUSE; circ. 27,500.
**Gweru Times:** POB 66, Gweru; weekly; Editor R. SPROAT; circ. 5,000.
**Horizon Magazine:** POB UA196, Union Ave, Harare; tel. (4) 704645; monthly; circ. 35,000.
**Hotel and Catering Gazette:** POB 2677, Kopje, Harare; tel. (4) 738722; telex 26334; fax (4) 707130; monthly; Editor PAULA CHARLES; circ. 1,800.
**Indonsakusa:** POB 150, Hwange; f. 1988; monthly; English and Sindebele; Editor D. NTABENI; circ. 10,000.
**Industrial Review:** POB 1683, Harare; tel. (4) 736835; fax (4) 752390.
**Insurance Review:** POB 1683, Harare; tel. (4) 36; telex 24705; fax (4) 752390; monthly; Editor M. CHAVUNDUKA.
**Journal on Social Change and Development:** POB 4405, Harare; tel. (4) 700047; telex 22055; fax (4) 725565; f. 1981; quarterly; Chair. JOYCE KAZEMBE; circ. 4,500.
**Just for Me:** POB 66070, Kopje, Harare; tel (4) 704715; f. 1990; English-language family and women's interest; Editor BEVERLEY TILLEY.
**Karoi News:** POB 441, Karoi; tel. 6216; fortnightly.
**Kwayedza-Umthunywa:** POB 396, Harare; tel. (4) 795771; weekly; Editor G. M. CHITEWE; circ. 84,696.

## ZIMBABWE

**Look and Listen:** POB UA589, Harare; tel. (4) 705619; fax (4) 705411; English-language radio and TV programmes; fortnightly; Editor AULORA SUERGA; circ. 23,000.

**Mahogany:** POB UA589, Harare; tel. (4) 705412; telex 24748; fax (4) 705411; f. 1980; English; women's interest; 6 a year; Editor G. BEACH; circ. 33,000.

**Makonde Star:** POB 533, Kwekwe; tel. (55) 2248; f. 1989; weekly; English; Editor FELIX MOYO; circ. 21,000.

**Makoni Clarion:** POB 17, Rusape; monthly.

**Management Zimbabwe:** POB 2677, Harare; fortnightly.

**Manica Post:** POB 960, Mutare; tel. (20) 61212; telex 81237; fax (20) 61149; 2274; f. 1893; weekly; Editor J. GAMBANGA; circ. 20,000.

**Masiye Pambili** (Let Us Go Forward): POB 591, Bulawayo; tel. (9) 75011; telex 50563; fax (9) 69701; f. 1964; English; 2 a year; Editor M. M. NDUBIWA; circ. 21,000.

**Masvingo Mirror:** POB 798, Masvingo; tel. (39) 62469; fax (39) 64484; weekly.

**Midlands Observer:** POB 533, Kwekwe; tel. (55) 2248; f. 1953; weekly; English; Editor FELIX MOYO; circ. 4,500.

**Moto:** POB 890, Gweru; tel. (54) 4886; fax (54) 51991; Roman Catholic; Editor DONATUS BONDE; circ. 30,000.

**Nehanda Guardian:** POB 150, Hwange; f. 1988; monthly; English and Chishona; Editor K. MWANAKA; circ. 10,000.

**Nhau Dzekumakomo:** POB 910, Mutare; f. 1984; publ. by Mutare City Council; monthly.

**North Midlands Gazette:** POB 222, Kadoma; tel. (68) 2021; fax (68) 2841; f. 1912; weekly; Editor MARY READ.

**On Guard:** National Social Security Authority, POB 1387, Causeway, Harare; tel. (4) 728931; Editor E. D. MAPONDERA.

**The Outpost:** POB HG106, Highlands; tel. (4) 724571; f. 1911; English; 6 a year; Editor WAYNE BVUDZIJENA; circ. 18,500.

**Parade Magazine:** POB 3798, Harare; tel. (4) 736835; telex 24705; fax (4) 752390; f. 1953; monthly; English; Editor MARK CHAVANDUKA; circ. 85,540.

**Prize Africa:** POB UA460, Harare; tel. (4) 705411; telex 24748; f. 1973; monthly; English; Editor STEPHAN DZIVANE; circ. 15,300.

**Quarterly Economic and Statistical Review:** POB 1283, Harare; publ. by the Reserve Bank of Zimbabwe; quarterly.

**Quarterly Guide to the Economy:** First Merchant Bank of Zimbabwe Ltd, FMB House, 67 Samora Machel Ave, POB 2786, Harare; tel. (4) 703071; telex 26025; fax (4) 738810; quarterly.

**RailRoader:** POB 596, Bulawayo; f. 1952; tel. (9) 363526; telex 33173; fax (9) 363502; monthly; Editor M. GUMEDE; circ. 10,000.

**The Record:** POB 179, Harare; tel. (4) 708911; journal of the Public Service Asscn; 6 a year; Editor GAMALIEL RUNGANI; circ. 30,000.

**Southern African Economist:** POB 6290, Harare; tel. (4) 738891; monthly; circ. 16,000.

**Southern African Political and Economic Monthly:** POB MP111, Harare; tel. (4) 727875; fax (4) 732735; monthly; Editor-in-Chief IBBO MANDAZA.

**Sunday Mail:** POB 396, Harare; tel. (4) 795771; telex 26196; fax (4) 791311; f. 1935; weekly; English; Editor CHARLES CHIKEREMA; circ. 154,000.

**Sunday News:** POB 585, Bulawayo; tel. (9) 65471; telex 33481; fax (9) 75522; f. 1930; weekly; English; Editor LAWRENCE CHIKUWIRA; circ. 66,171.

**Teacher in Zimbabwe:** POB 396; monthly; circ. 47,000.

**The Times:** 73 Seventh St, POB 66, Gweru; tel. (54) 2459; weekly; English.

**Tobacco News:** POB 1683, Harare; tel. (4) 736836; telex 24705; fax (4) 752390; circ. 2,700.

**Vanguard:** POB 66102, Kopje; tel. 751193; every 2 months.

**Voice:** POB 8323, Causeway, Harare; monthly.

**The Worker:** POB 8323, Causeway, Harare; tel. 700466.

**World Vision News:** POB 2420, Harare; tel. 703794; quarterly.

**Zambezia:** POB MP203, Harare; tel. (4) 303211; telex 26580; fax (4) 333407; journal of the Univ. of Zimbabwe; 2 a year; Editor Prof. M. C. M. BOURDILLON.

**Zimbabwe Agricultural Journal:** POB CY 594, Causeway, Harare; tel. (4) 704531; telex 22455; fax (4) 728317; f. 1903; 6 a year; Editor R. J. FENNER; circ. 1,600.

**Zimbabwe Defence Forces Magazine:** POB 7720, Harare; tel. (4) 722481; f. 1982; 6 a year; circ. 5,000.

**The Zimbabwe Engineer:** POB 1683, Harare; Man. Dir A. THOMSON.

**Zimbabwe News:** POB 5988, Harare; tel. (4) 68428; telex 22102; monthly.

**Zimbabwean Government Gazette:** POB 8062, Causeway, Harare; official govt journal; weekly; Editor L. TAKAWIRA.

### NEWS AGENCIES

**Zimbabwe Inter-Africa News Agency (ZIANA):** POB 511, Causeway, Harare; tel. (4) 730151; telex 26127; fax (4) 794336; f. 1981; owned and controlled by Zimbabwe Mass Media Trust; Editor-in-Chief HENRY E. MURADZIKWA.

#### Foreign Bureaux

**Agence France-Presse (AFP):** Robinson House, Union Ave, POB 1166, Harare; tel. (4) 758017; telex 26161; fax (4) 753291; Rep. FRANÇOIS-BERNARD CASTÉRAN.

**ANGOP** (Angola): Mass Media House, 3rd Floor, 19 Selous Ave, POB 6354, Harare; tel. (4) 736849; telex 22204.

**Agenzia Nazionale Stampa Associata (ANSA)** (Italy): Harare; tel. (4) 723881; telex 74177; Rep. IAN MILLS.

**Associated Press (AP)** (USA): POB 785, Harare; tel. (4) 706622; telex 24676; fax (4) 703994; Rep. JOHN EDLIN.

**Deutsche Presse-Agentur (dpa)** (Germany): Harare; tel. (4) 700875; telex 24339; Correspondent JAN RAATH.

**Informatsionnoye Telegrafnoye Agentstvo Rossii—Telegrafnoye Agentstvo Suverennykh Stran (ITAR—TASS)** (Russia): Mass Media House, 19 Selous Ave, POB 4012, Harare; tel. (4) 790521; telex 26022; Correspondent YURI PITCHUGIN.

**Inter Press Service (IPS)** (Italy): 127 Union Ave, POB 6050, Harare; tel. (4) 790104; telex 26129; fax (4) 728415; Rep. PETER DA COSTA.

**News Agency of Nigeria (NAN):** Harare; tel. (4) 703041; telex 24674.

**Pan-African News Agency (PANA)** (Senegal): 19 Selous Ave, POB 8364, Harare; tel. (4) 730971; telex 26403; Bureau Chief PETER MWAURA.

**Prensa Latina** (Cuba): Mass Media House, 3rd Floor, 19 Selous Ave, Harare; tel. (4) 731993; telex 22461; Correspondent HUGO RIUS.

**Press Trust of India (PTI):** Mass Media House, 3rd Floor, 19 Selous Ave, Harare; tel. (4) 795006; telex 22038; Rep. N. V. R. SWAMI.

**Reuters** (United Kingdom): 901 Tanganyika House, Union Ave, Harare, POB 2987; tel. (4) 724299; telex 24291; Bureau Chief DAVID BLOOM.

**Rossiyskoye Informatsionnoye Agentstvo—Novosti (RIA—Novosti)** (Russia): 503 Robinson House, cnr Union Ave and Angwa St, POB 3908, Harare; tel. (4) 707232; telex 22293; fax (4) 707233; Correspondent A. TIMONOVICH.

**SADC Press Trust:** Mass Media House, 19 Selous Ave, POB 6290, Harare; tel. (4) 738891; telex 26367; fax (4) 795412; Editor-in-Chief LEONARD MAVENEKA.

**Tanjug** (Yugoslavia): Mass Media House, 19 Selous Ave, Harare; tel. (4) 479018; Correspondent DEJAN DRAKULIĆ.

**United Press International (UPI)** (USA): Harare; tel. (4) 25265; telex 24177; Rep. IAN MILLS.

**Xinhua (New China) News Agency** (People's Republic of China): 4 Earls Rd, Alexander Park, POB 4746, Harare; tel. (4) 731467; telex 22310; fax (4) 731467; Chief Correspondent LU JIANXIN.

## Publishers

**Academic Books (Pvt) Ltd:** POB 567, Harare; tel. (4) 706729; fax (4) 702071; educational.

**Amalgamated Publications (Pvt) Ltd:** POB 1683, Harare; tel. (4) 736835; telex 24705; fax (4) 752390; f. 1949; trade journals; Man. Dir A. THOMSON.

**Anvil Press:** POB 4209, Harare; tel. (4) 751202; f. 1988; general; Dirs PAUL BRICKHILL, PAT BRICKHILL, STEVE KHOZA.

**The Argosy Press:** POB 2677, Harare; tel. (4) 755084; magazine publishers; Gen. Man. A. W. HARVEY.

**Baobab Books (Pvt) Ltd:** POB 1559, Harare; tel. (4) 706729; fax (4) 702071; general, literature, children's.

**Books of Zimbabwe Publishing Co (Pvt) Ltd:** POB 1994, Bulawayo; tel. (9) 61135; f. 1968; Man. Dir LOUIS W. BOLZE.

**College Press Publishers (Pvt) Ltd:** POB 3041, Harare; tel. (4) 754145; telex 22558; fax (4) 754256; f. 1968; educational and general; Man. Dir B. B. MUGABE.

**Directory Publishers Ltd:** POB 1595, Bulawayo; tel. (9) 78831; telex 33333; fax (9) 78835; directories; Man. BRUCE BEALE.

**Graham Publishing Co (Pvt) Ltd:** POB 2931, Harare; tel. (4) 752437; f. 1967; general; Dir GORDON M. GRAHAM.

ZIMBABWE — *Directory*

**Harare Publishing House:** Chiremba Rd, Hatfield, POB 4735, Harare; tel. (4) 570613; f. 1984; Dir Dr T. M. SAMKANGE.

**HarperCollins Publishers (Zimbabwe) Pvt) Ltd:** Union Ave, POB 201, Harare; tel. (4) 721413; fax (4) 721413; Man. S. D. MCMILLAN.

**Longman Zimbabwe (Pvt) Ltd:** Tourle Rd, Harare Drive, Adbennie, Harare; tel. (4) 62711; telex 22566; f. 1964; general and educational; Man. Dir S. CONNOLLY.

**Mambo Press:** Senga Rd, POB 779, Gweru; tel. (54) 4016; fax (54) 51991; f. 1958; religious, educational and fiction in English and African languages; Gen. Man. LEONZ FISCHER.

**Modus Publications (Pvt) Ltd:** Modus House, 27-29 Charter Rd, POB 66070, Kopje, Harare; tel. (4) 738722; Man. Dir ELIAS RUSIKE.

**Munn Publishing (Pvt) Ltd:** POB UA460, Harare; tel. (4) 752144; telex 24748; fax (4) 752062; Man. Dir A. F. MUNN.

**Standard Publications (Pvt) Ltd:** POB 3745, Harare; Dir G. F. BOOT.

**Thomson Publications Zimbabwe (Pvt) Ltd:** Thomson House, cnr Speke Ave and Harare St, POB 1683, Harare; tel. (4) 736835; telex 24705; fax (4) 752390; trade journals; Man. Dir A. THOMSON.

**University of Zimbabwe Publications:** POB MP203, Mount Pleasant, Harare; tel. (4) 303211; telex 26580; fax (4) 333407; f. 1969; Dir SAMUEL MATSANGAISE.

**Zimbabwe Newspapers (1980) Ltd:** POB 396, Harare; tel. (4) 795771; telex 26196; fax (4) 791311; f. 1981; state-owned; controls largest newspaper group; Chair. Dr DAVIDSON M. SADZA.

**Zimbabwe Publishing House:** POB 350, Harare; tel. (4) 497548; telex 26035; fax (4) 497554; f. 1982; Chair. DAVID MARTIN.

### Government Publishing House

**The Literature Bureau:** POB 749, Causeway, Harare; tel. (4) 726929; f. 1954; controlled by Ministry of Education and Culture; Dir B. C. CHITSIKE.

## Radio and Television

In 1992, according to UNESCO estimates, there were 890,000 radio receivers and 280,000 television receivers in use.

### RADIO

Broadcasts in English, Chishona, Sindebele, Kalanga, Venda, Tonga and Chewa; four programme services comprise a general service (predominantly in English), vernacular languages service, light entertainment, educational programmes.

### TELEVISION

The main broadcasting centre is in Harare, with a second studio in Bulawayo; broadcasts on two channels (one of which serves the Harare area only) for about 190 hours per week.

**Zimbabwe Broadcasting Corporation:** POB HG444, Highlands, Harare; tel. (4) 707222; telex 24175; fax (4) 795698; f. 1957; Chair. HOSEA MAPONDERA; Dir-Gen. ONIAS GUMBO (acting).

## Finance

(cap. = capital; dep. = deposits; res = reserves; m. = million; br. = branch; amounts in Zimbabwe dollars)

### BANKING

#### Central Bank

**Reserve Bank of Zimbabwe:** 76 Samora Machel Ave, POB 1283, Harare; tel. (4) 790731; telex 26075; fax (4) 708976; f. 1964; bank of issue; cap. 2m., res 6m., dep. 6,682m. (April 1995); Gov. Dr LEONARD TSUMBA.

#### Commercial Banks

**Barclays Bank of Zimbabwe Ltd:** Barclay House, First St and Jason Moyo Ave, POB 1279, Harare; tel. (4) 729811; telex 24185; fax (4) 707293; cap. and res 285.8m., dep. 2,940m. (Dec. 1993); Chair. JOHN D. CARTER; Man. Dir I. G. TAKAWIRA.

**Stanbic Bank Zimbabwe Ltd:** Ottoman House, 1st Floor, 59 Samora Machel Ave, POB 300, Harare; tel. (4) 705481; telex 26103; fax (4) 751324; f. 1990 as ANZ Grindlays Bank PLC, name changed 1993; Chair. L. H. COOK; Man. Dir H. F. J. FERGUSON; 10 brs.

**Standard Chartered Bank Zimbabwe Ltd:** John Boyne House, 38 Speke Ave, POB 373, Harare; tel. (4) 753212; telex 22115; fax (4) 725769; f. 1983; cap. and res 401m., dep. 2,659m. (Dec. 1993); Chair. P. T. ELLIS;CEO A. CLEARY, W. J. DENT; 42 brs and sub-brs; 14 agencies.

**Zimbabwe Banking Corporation Ltd:** Zimbank House, 46 Speke Ave, POB 3198, Harare; tel. (4) 735011; telex 24163; fax (4) 735600; f. 1951; wholly-owned subsidiary of Zimbabwe Financial Holdings Ltd, which is 59% govt-owned; cap. and res 123.0m., dep. 2,577.2m. (Sept. 1993); Group CEO. E. N. MUSHAYAKARARA; 47 brs, sub-brs and agencies.

#### Development Bank

**Zimbabwe Development Bank (ZDB):** POB 1720, Harare; tel. (4) 721008; telex 26279; fax (4) 720723; f. 1985; cap. 49m. (June 1993); Chair. E. D. CHIURA; Man. Dir R. JARAVAZA; 3 brs.

#### Merchant Banks

**First Merchant Bank of Zimbabwe Ltd:** FMB House, 67 Samora Machel Ave, POB 2786, Harare; tel. (4) 703071; telex 26025; fax (4) 738810; f. 1956 as Rhodesian Acceptances Limited; cap. and res 110.4m., dep. 1.119.0m. (Dec. 1993); Chair. R. P. LANDER; Man. Dir R. FELTOE; br. in Bulawayo.

**Merchant Bank of Central Africa Ltd:** Old Mutual Centre, 14th Floor, cnr Third St and Jason Moyo Ave, POB 3200, Harare; tel. (4) 738081; telex 26568; fax (4) 708005; f. 1956; cap. and res 51m., dep. 509m. (March 1993); Chair. A. M. CHAMBATI; Man. Dir F. R. G. READ.

**National Merchant Bank of Zimbabwe Ltd:** Fanum House, 6th Floor, 57 Samora Machel Ave, POB 2564, Harare; tel. (4) 735752; telex 26392; fax (4) 735619; f. 1993; cap. 25m. (June 1993); Chair. C. G. MSIPA; Gen. Man. T. WILLIAM NYEMBA.

**Standard Chartered Merchant Bank Zimbabwe Ltd:** Standard Chartered Bank Bldg, Second St, POB 60, Harare; tel. (4) 708585; telex 22208; fax (4) 725667; f. 1971; cap. and res 123m., dep. 1,076m. (Dec. 1993); Chair. J. M. MCKENNA; Man. Dir W. MATSAIRA.

**Syfrets Merchant Bank Ltd:** Zimbank House, 46 Speke Ave, POB 2540, Harare; tel. (4) 757535; telex 26292; fax (4) 751741; subsidiary of Finhold Group; cap. and res 62.1m., dep. 710.7m. (Sept. 1994); Chair. A. NHAU; Man. Dir A. D. HENCHIE.

#### Discount Houses

**Bard Discount House Ltd:** POB 3321, Harare; tel. (4) 752756; fax (4) 750192; cap. 4.1m. (Aug. 1993); Chair R. P. LANDER; Man. Dir C. J. GURNEY.

**The Discount Co of Zimbabwe (DCZ):** POB 3424, Harare; tel. (4) 705414; fax (4) 731670; cap. 2.5m. (Feb. 1993); Chair. S. J. CHIHAMBAKWE.

**Intermarket Discount House:** UDC Centre, 3rd Floor, cnr Union and First Sts, Harare.

#### Banking Organization

**Institute of Bankers of Zimbabwe:** POB UA521, Harare; tel. (4) 752474; fax (4) 737499; f. 1973; Pres. I. E. H. HELBY FIBZ; Gen. Sec. S. A. H. BROWN.

### STOCK EXCHANGE

**Zimbabwe Stock Exchange:** Southampton House, 8th Floor, Union Ave, POB UA234, Harare; tel. (4) 736861; telex 24196; fax (4) 791045; f. 1946; Chair. M. J. S. TUNMER.

### INSURANCE

**CU Fire, Marine and General Insurance Co Ltd:** Harare; tel. (4) 796171; telex 24194; fax (4) 790214; mem. of Commercial Union group; Chair. J. M. MAGOWAN.

**Fidelity Life Assurance of Zimbabwe (Pvt) Ltd:** 66 Julius Nyerere Way, POB 435, Harare; tel. (4) 750927; telex 24189; fax (4) 704705; Chair. M. SIFELANI; Gen. Man. J. P. WEEKS.

**National Insurance Co of Zimbabwe (Pvt) Ltd:** cnr Baker Ave and First St, POB 1256, Harare; tel. (4) 704911; telex 24605; fax (4) 704914.

**Old Mutual:** POB 70, Harare; tel. (4) 308400; telex 22118; fax (4) 308468; f. 1845; life assurance; Chair. D. C. SMITH; Gen. Man. B. R. BRADFORD.

**RM Insurance Co (Pvt) Ltd:** Royal Mutual House, 45 Baker Ave, POB 3599, Harare; tel. (4) 731011; telex 24683; fax (4) 731028; f. 1982; cap. p.u. 2m.; Chair. C. WRIGHT; Gen. Man. D. K. BEACH.

**Zimnat Life Assurance Co Ltd:** Zimnat House, cnr Baker Ave and Third St, POB 2417, Harare; tel. (4) 737611; telex 22003; fax (4) 791782; Gen. Man. B. MCCURDY.

## Trade and Industry

### CHAMBER OF COMMERCE

**Zimbabwe National Chambers of Commerce (ZNCC):** Equity House, Rezende St, POB 1934, Harare; tel. (4) 753444; telex 22531; fax (4) 753450; f. 1983; Pres. E. S. MAKONI; Dep. Pres. D. MEYER.

# ZIMBABWE

## INDUSTRIAL AND EMPLOYERS' ASSOCIATIONS

**Bulawayo Agricultural Society:** PO Famona, Bulawayo; tel. (9) 77668; telex 33273; f. 1907; sponsors an agricultural show; Pres. W. R. WHALEY; Vice-President C. P. D. GOODWIN.

**Bulawayo Landowners' and Farmers' Association:** Bulawayo.

**Cattle Producers' Association:** Harare; Pres. G. FRANCEYS.

**Chamber of Mines of Zimbabwe:** 4 Central Ave, POB 712, Harare; tel. (4) 702843; telex 26271; fax (4) 707983; f. 1939; CEO C. D. C. BAIN.

**Coffee Growers' Association:** Agriculture House, Leopold Takawira St, POB 4382, Harare; tel. (4) 750238; telex 22084; fax (4) 702481; Chair. ROBIN J. FENNELL.

**Commercial Cotton Growers' Association:** Agriculture House, 113 Leopold Takawira St, POB 592, Harare; tel. (4) 791881; fax (4) 791891; Pres. M. G. MENAGE.

**Commercial Farmers' Union:** POB 1241, Harare; tel. (4) 791881; telex 22084; f. 1942; Pres. PETER MACSPORRAN; Dir D. W. HASLUCK; 4,200 mems.

**Confederation of Zimbabwe Industries:** Fidelity Life Tower, cnr Luck and Raleigh Sts, Harare; tel. (4) 739833; telex 2073; fax (4) 750953; f. 1957; Pres. J. WAKATAMA; Chief Exec. J. FORDMA (acting); 1,000 mems.

**Construction Industry Federation of Zimbabwe:** POB 1502, Harare; tel. (4) 746661; fax (4) 746937; Pres. R. A. C. MAASDORP; CEO M. B. NAROTAM.

**Employers' Confederation of Zimbabwe:** POB 158, Harare; tel. (4) 705156; Pres. S. O. SHONHIWA; Exec. Dir Dr DAVID CHANAIWA.

**Employment Council for the Motor Industry:** POB 1084, Bulawayo; tel. (9) 78161.

**Industrial Development Corporation of Zimbabwe Ltd:** POB CY 1431, Causeway, Harare; tel. (4) 706971; telex 24409; fax (4) 796028; f. 1963; Chair. J. B. WAKATAMA; Gen. Man. M. N. NDUDZO.

**Kadoma Farmers' and Stockowners' Association:** Kadoma; tel. (68) 3658; Chair. A. REED; Sec. P. M. REED; 66 mems.

**Kwekwe Farmers' Association:** POB 72, Kwekwe; tel. (55) 247721; f. 1928; Chair. D. EDWARDS; Sec. J. TAPSON; 87 mems.

**Manicaland Chamber of Industries:** POB 92, Mutare; tel. (20) 62300; f. 1945; Pres. L. BAXTER; 60 mems.

**Mashonaland Chamber of Industries:** POB 3794, Harare; tel. (4) 739833; telex 22073; fax (4) 750953; f. 1922; Pres. A. I. S. FERGUSON; Sec. M. MUBATARIPI; 729 mems.

**Matabeleland Chamber of Industries:** POB 2317, Bulawayo; tel. (9) 60642; fax (9) 60814; f. 1931; Pres. E. V. MATIKITI; Sec. N. McKAY; about 300 mems.

**Matabeleland Region of The Construction Industry Federation of Zimbabwe:** POB 1970, Bulawayo; tel. (9) 65787; f. 1919; Sec. M. BARRON; 124 mems.

**Midlands Chamber of Industries:** POB 213, Gweru; tel. (54) 2812; Pres. J. W. PRINGLE; 50 mems.

**Minerals Marketing Corporation of Zimbabwe:** 90 Mutare Rd, Msasa, POB 2628, Harare; tel. (4) 486945; fax (4) 487261; f. 1982; sole authority for marketing of mineral production; Chair. E. MUTOWO; Gen. Man. LIZ CHITIGA.

**Mutare District Farmers' Association:** POB 29, Mutare; tel. (20) 64233; Chair. R. C. TRUSCOTT; Sec. Mrs J. FROGGATT; 45 mems.

**National Association of Dairy Farmers:** Agriculture House, 113 Leopold Takawira St, POB 1241, Harare; tel. (4) 791881; telex 22084; fax (4) 752614; Chair. I. M. WEBSTER; CEO D. R. PASCOE.

**National Employment Council for the Construction Industry of Zimbabwe:** St Barbara House, Moffat St, POB 2995, Harare; tel. (4) 726740; Gen. Sec. F. CHITSVA.

**National Employment Council for the Engineering and Iron and Steel Industry:** Chancellor House, 5th Floor, Samora Machel Ave, POB 1922, Harare; tel. (4) 705607; fax (4) 791221; f. 1943; Chair. H. S. CLEMENTS.

**Tobacco Marketing Board:** POB UA214, Harare; tel. (4) 66311; telex 24656.

**Zimbabwe Farmers' Union:** POB 3755, Harare; tel. (4) 704763; telex 26217; fax (4) 700829; Chair. GARY MAGADZIRE.

**Zimbabwe Tobacco Association:** POB 1781, Harare; tel. (4) 727441; telex 22090; fax (4) 724523; Pres. PETER RICHARDS; CEO CHRIS R. L. MOLAM; 3,627 mems.

**Zimtrade:** POB 2738, Harare; tel. (4) 732974; telex 26677; fax (4) 706930; f. 1991; national export promotion org.; Chair. C. MSIPA; CEO M. SIFELANI.

## TRADE UNIONS

All trade unions in Zimbabwe became affiliated to the ZCTU in 1981. The ZCTU is encouraging a policy of union amalgamations.

**Zimbabwe Congress of Trade Unions (ZCTU):** Chester House, 10th Floor, Speke Ave, 3rd St, POB 3549, Harare; tel. (4) 793093; fax (4) 751604; f. 1981; co-ordinating org. for trade unions; Pres. GIBSON SIBANDA; Sec.-Gen. MORGAN TSVANGIRAI.

### Principal Unions

**Air Transport Union:** POB AP40, Harare Airport, Harare; tel. (4) 52601; f. 1956; Pres. J. B. DEAS; Gen. Sec. C. J. GOTORA; 580 mems.

**Associated Mineworkers' Union of Zimbabwe:** POB 384, Harare; tel. (4) 700287; Pres. J. S. MUTANDARE; 25,000 mems.

**Building Workers' Trade Union:** St Barbara House, POB 1291, Harare; tel. (4) 720942; Gen. Sec. E. NJEKESA.

**Commercial Workers' Union of Zimbabwe:** Nestle House, Samora Machel Ave, POB 3922, Harare; tel. (4) 707845; Gen. Sec. S. CHIFAMBA; 6,000 mems.

**Federation of Municipal Workers' Union:** Bulawayo; tel. (9) 60506; Gen. Sec. F. V. NCUBE.

**Furniture and Cabinet Workers' Union:** POB 1291, Harare; Gen. Sec. C. KASEKE.

**General Agricultural and Plantation Workers' Union:** Harare; tel. (4) 792860; Gen. Sec. M. MAWERE.

**Graphical Association:** POB 27, Bulawayo; tel. (4) 62477; POB 494, Harare; Gen. Sec. A. NGWENYA; 3,015 mems.

**Harare Municipal Workers' Union:** Office No 12, Harare Community, Harare; tel. (4) 62343; Gen. Sec. T. G. T. MAPFUMO.

**National Airways Workers' Union:** POB AP1, Harare; tel. (4) 737011; telex 40008; fax (4) 231444; Gen. Sec. B. SPENCER.

**National Engineering Workers' Union:** POB 4968, Harare; tel. (4) 702963; Pres. I. MATONGO; Gen. Sec. O. KABASA.

**National Union of Clothing Industry Workers' Union:** POB RY28, Raylton; tel. 64432; Gen. Sec. C. M. PASIPANODYA.

**Railways Associated Workers' Union:** Bulawayo; tel. (9) 70041; f. 1982; Pres. SAMSON MABEKA; Gen. Sec. A. J. MHUNGU.

**Technical & Salaried Staff Association:** POB 33, Redcliff; tel. (55) 68798; Gen. Sec. J. DANCAN.

**Transport and General Workers' Union:** Dublin House, POB 4769, Harare; tel. (4) 793508; Gen. Sec. F. MAKANDA.

**United Food and Allied Workers' Union of Zimbabwe:** Harare; tel. (4) 74150; f. 1962; Gen. Sec. I. M. NEDZIWE.

**Zimbabwe Amalgamated Railwaymen's Union:** Unity House, 13th Ave, Herbert Chitepo St, Bulawayo; tel. (9) 60948; Gen. Sec. T. L. SHANA.

**Zimbabwe Bank and Allied Workers' Union:** Pres. SHINGEREI MUNGATE.

**Zimbabwe Catering and Hotel Workers' Union:** Nialis Bldg, POB 3913, Harare; tel. (4) 708359; Gen. Sec. A. P. KUPFUMA.

**Zimbabwe Chemical & Allied Workers' Union:** POB 4810, Harare; Gen. Sec. R. MAKUVAZA.

**Zimbabwe Domestic & Allied Workers' Union:** Harare; tel. (4) 795405; Gen. Sec. G. SHOKO.

**Zimbabwe Educational, Welfare & Mission Workers' Union:** St Andrews House, Samora Machel Ave, Harare; Pres. I. O. SAMAKOMVA.

**Zimbabwe Leather Shoe & Allied Workers' Union:** Harare; tel. (4) 793173; Gen. Sec. I. ZINDOGA.

**Zimbabwe Motor Industry Workers' Union:** POB RY00, Bulawayo; tel. (9) 74150; Gen. Sec. M. M. DERAH.

**Zimbabwe Posts and Telecommunications Workers' Union:** POB 739, Harare; tel. (4) 721141; Gen. Sec. GIFT CHIMANIKIRE.

**Zimbabwe Society of Bank Officials:** POB 966, Harare; tel. (4) 23104; Gen. Sec. A. CHITEHWE.

**Zimbabwe Textile Workers' Union:** POB UA245, Harare; tel. (4) 705329; Sec. F. C. BHAIKWA.

**Zimbabwe Tobacco Industry Workers' Union:** St Andrews House, Samora Machel Ave, Harare; Gen. Sec. S. MHEMBERE.

**Zimbabwe Union of Musicians:** POB 232, Harare; tel. (4) 708678; Gen. Sec. C. MATEMA.

# Transport

In 1986 a Zimbabwe-registered company, the Beira Corridor Group (BCG), was formed to develop the transport system in the Beira corridor as an alternative transport link to those running through South Africa. The transport sector received 4.1% of total expenditure in the government budget for 1991/92. In 1991 National Railways of Zimbabwe (NRZ) announced a Z.$700m. development programme which included plans to electrify and extend some railway lines to previously uncovered areas.

## RAILWAYS

In 1992 the rail network totalled 2,759 km. Trunk lines run from Bulawayo south to the border with Botswana, connecting with the Botswana railways system, which, in turn, connects with the South African railways system; north-west to the Victoria Falls, where there is a connection with Zambia Railways; and north-east to Harare and Mutare connecting with the Mozambique Railways' line from Beira. From a point near Gweru, a line runs to the south-east, making a connection with the Mozambique Railways' Limpopo line and with the port of Maputo. A connection runs from Rutenga to the South African Railways system at Beitbridge.

**National Railways of Zimbabwe (NRZ):** cnr Fife St and 10th Ave, POB 596, Bulawayo; tel. (9) 363111; telex 33173; f. 1899 as Rhodesia Railways; reorg. 1967 when Rhodesia and Zambia each became responsible for its own system; in 1993 NRZ began a 10-year programme of improvements; Chair. MIKE NDUDZO; Gen. Man. ALVORD MABENA.

## ROADS

In 1992 the road system in Zimbabwe totalled 91,078 km, of which 11,778 km were designated primary and secondary roads; some 16% of the total network was paved.

## CIVIL AVIATION

International and domestic air services connect most of the larger towns.

**Air Zimbabwe Corporation (AirZim):** POB AP1, Harare Airport, Harare; tel. (4) 575111; telex 40008; fax (4) 575053; f. 1967; scheduled domestic and international passenger and cargo services to Africa, Australia and Europe; Chair. M. J. THOMPSON; Man. Dir and CEO HUTTUSH R. MURINGI.

**Affretair:** POB AP13, Harare; tel. (4) 731781; telex 40005; fax (4) 731706; f. 1965 as Air Trans Africa; state-owned; freight carrier; scheduled services to Europe, and charter services worldwide; Chair. M. J. THOMPSON; Man. Dir G. T. MANHAMBARA.

**Zimbabwe Express Airlines:** Harare; f. 1995; domestic services.

# Tourism

In 1992 an estimated 737,533 tourists visited Zimbabwe. Revenue from tourism in that year totalled about US $105m. The principal tourist attractions are the Victoria Falls, the Kariba Dam and the Hwange Game Reserve and National Park. Zimbabwe Ruins, near Fort Victoria, and World's View, in the Matapos Hills, are of special interest. In the Eastern Districts, around Umtali, there is trout fishing and climbing.

**Zimbabwe Tourist Development Corporation (ZTDC):** POB 286, Causeway, Harare; tel. (4) 793666; telex 26082; fax (4) 793669; f. 1984; promotes tourism domestically and abroad; Dir-Gen. N. T. C. SAMKANGE (acting).

# INDEX OF TERRITORIES IN VOLUMES I AND II

| | Page | | Page |
|---|---|---|---|
| Abu Dhabi | 3110 | Cayman Islands | 3212 |
| Afghanistan | 293 | Central African Republic | 759 |
| Ajman | 3110 | Ceuta | 2825 |
| Åland Islands | 1167 | Chad | 769 |
| Albania | 310 | Chafarinas Islands | 2830 |
| Alderney | 3197 | Channel Islands | 3192 |
| Algeria | 326 | Chile | 782 |
| American Samoa | 3333 | China, People's Republic | 801 |
| Andorra | 346 | China (Taiwan) | 833 |
| Angola | 350 | Christmas Island | 432 |
| Anguilla | 3198 | Cocos Islands | 433 |
| Antarctic Territory, Australian | 436 | Colombia | 851 |
| Antarctic Territory, British | 3207 | Comoros | 872 |
| Antarctica | 366 | Congo | 880 |
| Antigua and Barbuda | 368 | Cook Islands | 2260 |
| Argentina | 374 | Coral Sea Islands Territory | 436 |
| Armenia | 397 | Costa Rica | 892 |
| Aruba | 2225 | Côte d'Ivoire | 905 |
| Ascension | 3251 | Croatia | 920 |
| Ashmore Islands | 436 | Cuba | 935 |
| Australia | 407 | Cyprus | 953 |
| Australian Antarctic Territory | 436 | Czech Republic | 972 |
| Austria | 437 | | |
| Azad Kashmir | 2385 | Denmark | 988 |
| Azerbaijan | 456 | Djibouti | 1015 |
| | | Dominica | 1022 |
| Bahamas | 468 | Dominican Republic | 1028 |
| Bahrain | 476 | Dronning Maud Land | 2346 |
| Baker Island | 3344 | Dubai | 3110 |
| Bangladesh | 485 | | |
| Barbados | 504 | Ecuador | 1042 |
| Barbuda | 368 | Egypt | 1058 |
| Belarus | 511 | El Salvador | 1081 |
| Belau (see Palau) | | Equatorial Guinea | 1096 |
| Belgium | 524 | Eritrea | 1103 |
| Belize | 547 | Estonia | 1110 |
| Benin | 555 | Ethiopia | 1123 |
| Bermuda | 3202 | | |
| Bhutan | 567 | Falkland Islands | 3217 |
| Bolivia | 577 | Faroe Islands | 1008 |
| Bosnia and Herzegovina | 593 | Federated States of Micronesia | 2089 |
| Botswana | 603 | Fiji | 1138 |
| Bouvetøya | 2346 | Finland | 1148 |
| Brazil | 614 | Former Yugoslav republic of Macedonia | 1941 |
| Brechou | 3197 | France | 1169 |
| British Antarctic Territory | 3207 | French Guiana | 1211 |
| British Indian Ocean Territory | 3207 | French Polynesia | 1236 |
| British Virgin Islands | 3208 | French Southern and Antarctic Territories | 1242 |
| Brunei | 640 | Fujairah | 3110 |
| Bulgaria | 647 | Futuna Islands | 1248 |
| Burkina Faso | 668 | | |
| Burma (see Myanmar) | | Gabon | 1252 |
| Burundi | 681 | Gambia | 1265 |
| | | Georgia | 1275 |
| Caicos Islands | 3254 | Germany | 1287 |
| Cambodia | 693 | Ghana | 1328 |
| Cameroon | 707 | Gibraltar | 3221 |
| Canada | 723 | Great Britain | 3125 |
| Cape Verde | 752 | Greece | 1343 |
| Cartier Island | 436 | | |

3514

# INDEX OF TERRITORIES IN VOLUMES I AND II

| | Page | | Page |
|---|---|---|---|
| Greenland | 1011 | Macau | 2525 |
| Grenada | 1362 | Macedonia, former Yugoslav republic | 1941 |
| Grenadines | 2618 | Madagascar | 1951 |
| Guadeloupe | 1215 | Malawi | 1966 |
| Guam | 3337 | Malaysia | 1977 |
| Guatemala | 1369 | Maldives | 2003 |
| Guernsey | 3194 | Mali | 2010 |
| Guinea | 1386 | Malta | 2023 |
| Guinea-Bissau | 1397 | Malvinas | 3217 |
| Guyana | 1407 | Man, Isle of | 3188 |
| | | Marshall Islands | 2032 |
| Haiti | 1416 | Martinique | 1220 |
| Heard Island | 436 | Mauritania | 2037 |
| Herm | 3197 | Mauritius | 2049 |
| Herzegovina | 593 | Mayotte | 1230 |
| Holy See | 3377 | McDonald Islands | 436 |
| Honduras | 1430 | Melilla | 2825 |
| Hong Kong | 3227 | Mexico | 2062 |
| Howland Island | 3344 | Micronesia, Federated States | 2089 |
| Hungary | 1443 | Midway Island | 3344 |
| | | Miquelon | 1233 |
| | | Moldova | 2093 |
| Iceland | 1462 | Monaco | 2105 |
| India | 1470 | Mongolia | 2109 |
| Indian Ocean Territory, British | 3207 | Montenegro | 3447 |
| Indonesia | 1513 | Montserrat | 3244 |
| Iran | 1538 | Morocco | 2123 |
| Iraq | 1556 | Mozambique | 2141 |
| Ireland | 1574 | Myanmar | 2158 |
| Ireland, Northern | 3176 | | |
| Islas Malvinas | 3217 | Namibia | 2174 |
| Isle of Man | 3188 | Nauru | 2187 |
| Israel | 1593 | Nepal | 2191 |
| Israeli-occupied Territories and Emerging Palestinian Autonomous Areas | 1618 | Netherlands | 2205 |
| | | Netherlands Antilles | 2230 |
| Italy | 1623 | Nevis | 2604 |
| Ivory Coast (see Côte d'Ivoire) | | New Caledonia | 1242 |
| | | New Zealand | 2239 |
| Jamaica | 1656 | Nicaragua | 2268 |
| Jan Mayen | 2345 | Niger | 2285 |
| Japan | 1669 | Nigeria | 2300 |
| Jarvis Island | 3344 | Niue | 2265 |
| Jersey | 3192 | Norfolk Island | 434 |
| Jethou | 3197 | Northern Areas (Pakistan) | 2385 |
| Johnston Atoll | 3344 | Northern Ireland | 3176 |
| Jordan | 1702 | Northern Mariana Islands | 3319 |
| | | Norway | 2325 |
| Kampuchea (see Cambodia) | | Oman | 2347 |
| Kazakhstan | 1731 | | |
| Keeling Islands | 433 | Pakistan | 2358 |
| Kenya | 1744 | Palau | 2386 |
| Kingman Reef | 3344 | Palestinian Autonomous Areas, Emerging | 1618 |
| Kiribati | 1760 | Palmyra | 3344 |
| Korea, Democratic People's Republic (North Korea) | 1766 | Panama | 2390 |
| Korea, Republic (South Korea) | 1780 | Papua New Guinea | 2407 |
| Kuwait | 1802 | Paraguay | 2421 |
| Kyrgyzstan | 1819 | Peñón de Alhucemas | 2830 |
| | | Peñón de Vélez de la Gomera | 2830 |
| Laos | 1830 | Peru | 2435 |
| Latvia | 1841 | Peter I Øy | 2346 |
| Lebanon | 1855 | Philippines | 2454 |
| Lesotho | 1875 | Pitcairn Islands | 3248 |
| Liberia | 1886 | Poland | 2480 |
| Libya | 1900 | Portugal | 2502 |
| Liechtenstein | 1914 | Príncipe | 2628 |
| Lihou | 3197 | Puerto Rico | 3323 |
| Lithuania | 1918 | | |
| Luxembourg | 1932 | Qatar | 2533 |

3515

# INDEX OF TERRITORIES IN VOLUMES I AND II

| Territory | Page |
|---|---|
| Ras al-Khaimah | 3110 |
| Réunion | 1225 |
| Romania | 2540 |
| Ross Dependency | 2257 |
| Russian Federation | 2562 |
| Rwanda | 2591 |
| Saint Christopher and Nevis | 2604 |
| St Helena | 3250 |
| St Kitts (Saint Christopher) | 2604 |
| Saint Lucia | 2611 |
| St Pierre and Miquelon | 1233 |
| Saint Vincent and the Grenadines | 2618 |
| San Marino | 2624 |
| São Tomé and Príncipe | 2628 |
| Sark | 3197 |
| Saudi Arabia | 2634 |
| Senegal | 2651 |
| Serbia | 3447 |
| Seychelles | 2669 |
| Sharjah | 3110 |
| Sierra Leone | 2676 |
| Singapore | 2690 |
| Slovakia | 2709 |
| Slovenia | 2722 |
| Solomon Islands | 2737 |
| Somalia | 2745 |
| South Africa | 2760 |
| South Georgia | 3253 |
| South Sandwich Islands | 3253 |
| Spain | 2791 |
| Spanish North Africa | 2825 |
| Sri Lanka | 2831 |
| Sudan | 2851 |
| Suriname | 2867 |
| Svalbard | 2344 |
| Swaziland | 2877 |
| Sweden | 2886 |
| Switzerland | 2908 |
| Syria | 2929 |
| Taiwan | 833 |
| Tajikistan | 2945 |
| Tanzania | 2957 |
| Thailand | 2972 |
| Tobago | 3014 |
| Togo | 2993 |
| Tokelau | 2257 |
| Tonga | 3008 |
| Trinidad and Tobago | 3014 |
| Tristan da Cunha | 3152 |
| Tunisia | 3027 |
| Turkey | 3043 |
| Turkmenistan | 3066 |
| Turks and Caicos Islands | 3254 |
| Tuvalu | 3076 |
| Uganda | 3081 |
| Ukraine | 3094 |
| Umm al-Qaiwain | 3110 |
| United Arab Emirates | 3110 |
| United Kingdom | 3125 |
| United States of America | 3258 |
| US Virgin Islands | 3341 |
| Uruguay | 3345 |
| Uzbekistan | 3360 |
| Vanuatu | 3370 |
| Vatican City | 3377 |
| Venezuela | 3384 |
| Viet Nam | 3405 |
| Virgin Islands, British | 3208 |
| Virgin Islands, US | 3341 |
| Wake Island | 3344 |
| Wallis and Futuna Islands | 1248 |
| Western Samoa | 3423 |
| Yemen | 3429 |
| Yugoslavia | 3447 |
| Zaire | 3468 |
| Zambia | 3484 |
| Zimbabwe | 3497 |